S0-AGF-861

CONGRESSIONAL QUARTERLY

Almanac

99th CONGRESS
1st SESSION....1985

VOLUME XLI

Congressional Quarterly Inc.

1414 22nd St. N.W.
Washington, D.C. 20037

Congressional Quarterly Inc.

Congressional Quarterly Inc., an editorial research service and publishing company, serves clients in the fields of news, education, business and government. It combines Congressional Quarterly's specific coverage of Congress, government and politics with the more general subject range of an affiliated service, Editorial Research Reports.

Congressional Quarterly publishes the *Congressional Quarterly Weekly Report* and a variety of books, including college political science textbooks under the CQ Press imprint and public affairs paperbacks designed as timely reports to keep journalists, scholars and the public abreast of developing issues and events. CQ also publishes information directories and reference books on the federal government, national elections and politics, including the *Guide to Congress*, the *Guide to the U.S. Supreme Court*, the *Guide to U.S. Elections* and *Politics in America*. The *CQ Almanac*, a compendium of legislation for one session of Congress, is published each year. *Congress and the Nation*, a record of government for a presidential term, is published every four years.

CQ publishes *The Congressional Monitor*, a daily report on current and future activities of congressional committees, and several newsletters including *Congressional Insight*, a weekly analysis of congressional action, and *Campaign Practices Reports*, a semimonthly update on campaign laws.

An electronic online information system, the Washington Alert Service, provides immediate access to CQ's databases of legislative action, votes, schedules, profiles and analyses.

Printed in the United States of America

Library of Congress Catalog Number 47-41081
ISBN: 0-87187-388-5

1985 Almanac

Editor: Mary W. Cohn
Editorial Coordinator: Renee Amrine
Assistant Editors: Martha Angle, Marsha Canfield, Barbara J. Coleman, John R. Cranford, Harrison Donnelly, Philip D. Duncan, Robin D. Meszoly, Peg O'Hara, Elder Witt
Indexer: Jan Danis

Editorial Department

Director, Editorial Operations: Michael Glennon

Managing Editor: Kathryn Waters Gest

Assistant Managing Editors: Martha Angle, Peg O'Hara

Political Editor: Alan Ehrenhalt

News Editors: Marsha Canfield, Barbara J. Coleman, John R. Cranford, Robin D. Meszoly

Assistant Political Editor: Philip D. Duncan

Reporters: Bob Benenson, Steve Blakely, Jacqueline Calmes, Nadine Cohodas, Rhodes Cook, Joseph A. Davis, Harrison Donnelly, John Felton, Pamela Fessler, Stephen Gettinger, Diane Granat, Rob Gurwitt, Janet Hook, Steven Pressman, David Rapp, Robert Rothman, Pat Towell, Tom Watson, Elizabeth Wehr, Elder Witt

Production Editor: Guy Lamolinara

Editorial Coordinator: Dave Kaplan

Proofreaders: Eugene J. Gabler, Gabriel Shapiro, Charles Southwell

Editorial Assistants: Peter Bragdon, Shari Cohen, Rowena Olegario, Hugh Swarts

Research

Michael L. Koempel *(Director)*, Barbara L. Miracle *(Assistant Director)*, Martha Bomgardner Alito *(Library Director)*, David Cantalupo, Ralph Dumain, Bena A. Fein, Lyle Fowlkes, Jane S. Gilligan, Diane Huffman, Nancy Kervin, Julie A. Lopes, Lauren Macdonald, Michael V. Maloney Jr., Lori McGrogan, Charles Potter, Neal Santelmann, Stephen F. Stine, Lenore Webb, David L. Wilson

Production

Production Manager: I. D. Fuller
Assistant Production Manager: Maceo Mayo

"By providing a link between the local newspaper and Capitol Hill we hope Congressional Quarterly can help to make public opinion the only effective pressure group in the country. Since many citizens other than editors are also interested in Congress, we hope that they too will find Congressional Quarterly an aid to a better understanding of their government.

"Congressional Quarterly presents the facts in as complete, concise and unbiased form as we know how. The editorial comment on the acts and votes of Congress, we leave to our subscribers." Foreword, Congressional Quarterly, Vol. I, 1945.

Henrietta Poynter, 1901-1968
Nelson Poynter, 1903-1978

CQ

SUMMARY TABLE OF CONTENTS

TABLE OF CONTENTS

Chapter 1 — 99th Congress

Chapter 2 — Foreign Policy

Chapter 3 — Defense

Chapter 4 — Environment/Energy

Chapter 5 — Law/Judiciary

Chapter 6 — Trade Policy

Chapter 7 — Transportation/Commerce/Consumers

Chapter 8 — Health/Education/Welfare

Chapter 9 — Appropriations

Chapter 10 — General Government

Chapter 11 — Economic Policy

Chapter 12 — Agriculture

APPENDIXES

Supreme Court

Political Report

Voting Studies

Presidential Messages

Lobby Registrations

Public Laws

Congress and Its Members

Roll-Call Charts

Errata

1982 Almanac, p. 265, col. 1, 4th paragraph under Senate Floor Action: The Bumpers amendment would have deleted $2.13 million (not $2.3 million) for the coal leasing program; **p. 311**, col. 1, 2nd paragraph: President Reagan signed the bill Jan. 4 (not Jan. 3); **p. 365**, col. 1, 1st paragraph of commodity futures story: Reagan signed the bill Jan. 11 (not Jan. 10); **p. 436**, col. 2, 1st paragraph of barrier islands bill provisions: The measure that cleared was S 1018 (not HR 3252).

1983 Almanac, p. 581, box: The list should have included 1978 House censure proceedings against Rep. Edward R. Roybal, D-Calif. The House declined to censure Roybal, who was charged with making false statements to a House committee. Instead, the House voted its mildest form of punishment, a reprimand.

1984 Almanac, p. 202, col. 2, 6th paragraph: The bill cleared later Oct. 10 when the House accepted the Senate amendments; **p. 277**, col. 2, 4th paragraph, provision should read: Required that all joint agreements be filed with the FMC (deleting remainder of sentence); **p. 282**, col. 1, 8th paragraph of telephone access fee story: The access charge would be capped at $4 a month until 1990 (not 1980); **p. 368**, chart: Labor, Health and Human Services, and Education funding was provided by PL 98-139, signed Oct. 31, 1984 (not by PL 98-473).

Session Summary boxes: 1984 Almanac, p. 10, 4th paragraph of Session Summary box and corresponding paragraphs of previous volumes: The number given for public bills signed into law includes measures that were enacted over the president's veto or permitted to become law without his signature (not just bills signed by the president).

99th CONGRESS

CQ

Major Leadership Changes as 99th Convenes

Major leadership changes in both chambers and a bitter election dispute in the House marked the opening of the 99th Congress in January 1985.

In the Republican-controlled Senate, a new team of GOP leaders was installed, headed by Robert Dole, Kan.

In the House, the Democratic majority dumped Melvin Price, Ill., from the chairmanship of the Armed Services Committee and replaced him with Les Aspin, Wis., the panel's seventh-ranking Democrat. The choice of Aspin to succeed Price, who at 80 was considered too frail to lead the important panel, gave an unprecedented jolt to the House seniority system.

In other House action, Democrats set off a months-long controversy by refusing to seat the Republican candidate in a hotly contested Indiana race.

Although Congress convened Jan. 3, as provided by the Constitution, neither chamber conducted any legislative business until after President Reagan was formally inaugurated for his second term Jan. 21. *(Reagan inauguration, p. 7; session summary, p. 10; House, Senate membership, p. 8)*

Senate

At the opening session Jan. 3, 32 of the 33 senators elected in November 1984 took the oath of office in groups of four, after being escorted to the front of the chamber by their state's other senator.

Four Democrats and two Republicans were sworn in as senators for the first time on the opening day. The seventh freshman, Democrat John D. "Jay" Rockefeller IV of West Virginia, was not sworn in until Jan. 15, after he ended his term as governor of West Virginia.

Rockefeller's swearing-in brought the Senate to its full strength of 53 Republicans and 47 Democrats.

The transition to a new group of GOP leaders went smoothly in the Senate. Dole and five other Republicans had been elected as the party's leaders in a November 1984 caucus. Dole had prevailed over four other contenders for the post of majority leader, finally defeating Alaska's Ted Stevens on a 28-25 vote. He succeeded Howard H. Baker Jr., R-Tenn., who retired from the Senate at the end of the 98th Congress.

The other new GOP leaders were Alan K. Simpson, Wyo., assistant majority leader; John H. Chafee, R.I., chairman of the Republican Conference; Thad Cochran, Miss., conference secretary; William L. Armstrong, Colo., Policy Committee chairman; and John Heinz, Pa., chairman of the National Republican Senatorial Committee, the Republican Party's campaign support organization for the Senate.

Senate Democrats retained their 98th Congress leadership team. During December 1984 caucus meetings, Minority Leader Robert C. Byrd, W. Va., had headed off a last-minute challenge by Lawton Chiles, Fla. *(Leadership box, this page; 1984 organizational action for 99th Congress, 1984 Almanac p. 3)*

House

Opening-day ceremonies in the House were marred by wrangling over contested elections in Indiana's 8th District and Idaho's 2nd District.

Indiana Republican Richard D. McIntyre and Idaho Democrat Richard Stallings, who had been certified the winners of their elections, were asked to stand aside when Speaker Thomas P. O'Neill Jr., D-Mass., administered the oath of office to representatives. About a dozen members were absent, and took their oath of office later. Stallings also took the oath later after the House agreed to seat him.

Following a bitterly partisan debate, the House voted 238-177 to leave the Indiana seat vacant, pending an inquiry by the Committee on House Administration. The seat ultimately was awarded to Democrat Frank McCloskey, who had held it in the previous Congress. *(Vote 2, p. 2-H; election dispute details, p. 28)*

Excluding the Indiana seat, the House lineup consisted of 252 Democrats and 182 Republicans, including 43 freshmen — 12 Democrats and 31 Republicans.

99th Congress Leadership

SENATE

President Pro Tempore — Strom Thurmond, R-S.C.
Majority Leader — Robert Dole, R-Kan.
Assistant Majority Leader — Alan K. Simpson, R-Wyo.
Republican Conference Chairman — John H. Chafee, R-R.I.
Republican Conference Secretary — Thad Cochran, R-Miss.

Minority Leader — Robert C. Byrd, D-W.Va.
Minority Whip — Alan Cranston, D-Calif.
Democratic Conference Secretary — Daniel K. Inouye, D-Hawaii

HOUSE

Speaker — Thomas P. O'Neill Jr., D-Mass.
Majority Leader — Jim Wright, D-Texas
Majority Whip — Thomas S. Foley, D-Wash.
Chairman of the Caucus — Richard A. Gephardt, D-Mo.

Minority Leader — Robert H. Michel, R-Ill.
Minority Whip — Trent Lott, R-Miss.
Chairman of the Conference — Jack F. Kemp, R-N.Y.
Republican Policy Committee Chairman — Dick Cheney, R-Wyo.

Public Laws

A total of 240 bills cleared by Congress in 1985 became public laws. Following is a list of the number of public laws enacted since 1968:

Year	Public Laws	Year	Public Laws
1985	240	1976	383
1984	408	1975	205
1983	215	1974	404
1982	328	1973	247
1981	145	1972	383
1980	426	1971	224
1979	187	1970	505
1978	410	1969	190
1977	223	1968	391

Both parties retained their existing leaders. For the fifth and final time, the House chose O'Neill as Speaker. In a straight party-line vote, O'Neill received 247 Democratic votes for the job. The 175 Republicans in the chamber cast their votes for Minority Leader Robert H. Michel, R-Ill. *(Vote 1, p. 2-H)*

O'Neill and Michel each voted present, as did Texan Ralph M. Hall, a conservative Democrat who had participated in a threatened revolt against O'Neill's leadership in December 1984.

O'Neill, 72, planned to retire at the end of the 99th Congress, after a decade as the top House leader.

In a move with implications for future leadership selections, the Democratic Caucus Jan. 29 voted 133-36 to elect the party whip in the future. Traditionally, the whip had been appointed by the Speaker and majority leader. The new rule was not to take effect until the next time the job became vacant, which was expected when the Democrats reshuffled their leadership after O'Neill's retirement. The change was pushed by the liberal Democratic Study Group, and Majority Leader Jim Wright, Texas — a likely successor to O'Neill — did not oppose it in the caucus.

Rules Changes

One of the first items of House business Jan. 3 was a package of internal rule revisions.

The changes, adopted by the House Democratic Caucus in December 1984, were approved as H Res 7 by the full House on a 235-174 party-line vote after Republicans tried to substitute their own proposals to alter House procedures. Although Republicans complained about the Democratic package, it was not hotly contested. *(Vote 6, p. 2-H)*

The new rules adopted Jan. 3:

- Allowed the Speaker, with House approval, to designate a member to act as Speaker pro tempore to sign enrolled bills in his absence.
- Removed the 30-member limit on the size of the Budget Committee. Budget was the only existing committee whose size was specified in House rules; the change permitted Democratic leaders to expand the panel.
- Made motions to dispense with the first reading of a bill in committee a "non-debatable motion of high privilege" if copies of the bill were available.
- Granted committee and subcommittee chairmen authority to determine the number of television and still cameras allowed in committee meetings and hearings. Before the change, there were specified limits on the number of cameras permitted in meetings.
- Automatically provided interim committee funding from January through March at the start of each Congress.
- Allotted one-third of the debate time on a conference report to a member who was opposed to the conference report, but only when both the Democratic and Republican floor managers of the bill supported the report. The same procedure would apply to debate on Senate amendments that conferees were unable to agree upon.
- Provided one hour of debate on motions to recommit a bill with instructions to a committee, if so demanded by the majority floor manager. Previously, the rules provided only 10 minutes of debate on motions to recommit with instructions. This rule change was opposed by Republicans, who complained that only Democrats would be able to acquire the extra time to debate a motion to recommit a bill with instructions.

In lieu of the Democratic package, Republican leaders offered their own set of rules changes, which had been adopted by Republicans in December 1984.

Among other things, the GOP revisions would have required party ratios on committees to reflect party ratios in the entire House, abolished proxy voting, cut the size of committee staffs and created a bipartisan advisory board to control the House broadcast system. Republicans were particularly incensed over an existing imbalance in party ratios on committees, which the Democrats had engineered in the 98th Congress.

No direct vote was taken on the GOP rules changes because Republicans failed by a vote of 238-176 to defeat a

Membership Changes, 99th Congress

House

Party	Member	Died	Resigned	Successor	Party	Elected	Sworn In
D	Gillis W. Long, La.	1/20/85		Cathy (Mrs. Gillis) Long	D	3/30/85	4/4/85
	Vacancy *			Frank McCloskey	D	11/6/85	5/1/85
D	Sam B. Hall Jr., Texas		5/27/85	Jim Chapman	D	8/3/85	9/4/85

* *The results of the election in the Indiana 8th District were contested. The House voted May 1, 1985 to seat McCloskey.*

motion to cut off debate. *(Vote 4, p. 2-H)*

Before voting on the Democratic rules package, Trent Lott, R-Miss., offered a motion to recommit the resolution with instructions for the Rules Committee to study three separate issues: creating a joint House-Senate Budget Committee, reducing the number of House committee assignments, and giving control of the House broadcast system to a bipartisan group. The motion was defeated 176-237. *(Vote 5, p. 2-H)*

Committee Changes

In the Senate, Dole's election as majority leader set off a chain reaction that produced three new standing committee chairmen. Two standing committees changed hands in the House.

In addition, new ethics committee chairmen were appointed in both chambers. Dole appointed Warren B. Rudman, R-N.H., to head the Senate Select Ethics Committee. Rudman succeeded Ted Stevens, R-Alaska. Speaker O'Neill named Julian C. Dixon, D-Calif., to replace Louis Stokes, D-Ohio, as chairman of the House Committee on Standards of Official Conduct.

Senate

Dole's elevation to the leadership post required him to yield his chairmanship of the tax-writing Finance Committee to Bob Packwood, Ore., the panel's next ranking Republican. Packwood in turn yielded the Commerce Committee chair to John C. Danforth, R-Mo.

Richard G. Lugar, R-Ind., who had unsuccessfully challenged Dole for the leadership position, took over the Foreign Relations Committee after the previous chairman, Charles H. Percy, Ill., was defeated for re-election in 1984. Jesse Helms, N. C., the ranking Republican on Foreign Relations, was already chairman of the Agriculture Committee and decided not to give up that post. Lugar was next in line on Foreign Relations.

Under Republican Party rules, Simpson also was required to give up his chairmanship of the Veterans' Affairs Committee when he was elected assistant majority leader. Frank H. Murkowski, R-Alaska, succeeded him.

House

The Democratic Caucus elected chairmen of all House standing committees during its Jan. 4 meeting.

Armed Services. In a secret ballot behind closed doors, the Democratic Caucus voted to remove Price as chairman of the Armed Services panel; 118 members voted to retain him as chairman, while 121 voted to replace him.

Then, in a startling break with the House's seniority tradition, Democrats passed over the member next in line behind Price — Florida Democrat Charles E. Bennett — and by a 125-103 vote chose the seventh-ranking Aspin to head Armed Services.

The selection of Aspin, 46, was a show of strength by the House's junior Democrats and a setback to Speaker O'Neill, who offered an emotional appeal to save Price's chairmanship.

Price had chaired Armed Services for 10 years, first winning the job in 1975, when reform-minded Democrats challenged the House seniority system and unseated three aging committee chairmen. Price, who was then second-ranking on Armed Services, replaced F. Edward Hebert, D-La. (1941-77). The 1975 revolt was the last time Democrats had toppled a committee chairman. *(1975 Almanac p. 32)*

Blacks Gain in House

Reflecting their growing numbers and seniority in the House, black members — for the first time in the history of the Congress — chaired five standing committees and two select committees in the 99th Congress.

Blacks also chaired 16 subcommittees, including one on Armed Services and two on Ways and Means.

The latest black member to attain the chairmanship of a major committee was William H. Gray III, D-Pa., elected by his Democratic colleagues in January 1985 to chair the Budget Committee.

Other black committee chairmen were Augustus F. Hawkins, D-Calif., of Education and Labor; Ronald V. Dellums, District of Columbia; Parren J. Mitchell, D-Md., Small Business; Julian C. Dixon, D-Calif., Standards of Official Conduct; Mickey Leland, D-Texas, Select Committee on Hunger, and Charles B. Rangel, D-N.Y., Select Narcotics Abuse and Control.

Rangel also was one of seven deputy whips, making him the highest-ranking black in the House Democratic leadership. He was one of six declared candidates for whip in the 100th Congress.

Black Caucus' Growth

Gray's selection to head the Budget Committee, engineered by skillful coalition building, brought attention to the Congressional Black Caucus, which had grown from nine members in 1969, when it was formed, to 20 — all the black members of the House — in 1985.

The caucus, funded by dues from members, operated in a House annex with a staff of three full-time employees. Leland was chairman in 1985.

Already influential because of its size and cohesiveness on issues, the caucus was beginning to ally with such groups as the Hispanic and Women's Caucuses to increase its clout on matters of mutual interest. And with more of its members moving into positions of power within the establishment, it was increasingly able to work within the power structure to achieve its goals.

There were no blacks in the Senate in 1985. The last black to serve in that body was Edward W. Brooke, R-Mass. (1967-79).

Since 1870, when the first black was seated, there had been 57 blacks in Congress. Three of them, all Republicans, served in the Senate. The first 21 House members were Republicans; all since the 1930s were Democrats. Franklin D. Roosevelt's "New Deal" led blacks to shift their loyalty from the GOP, the party of Abraham Lincoln, to the Democrats.

Despite the unusual action Jan. 4, Majority Leader Wright claimed it was not a repudiation of the seniority tradition. Instead, Wright said, it reflected concerns about Price's failing health.

Budget. William H. Gray III, D-Pa., was chosen chairman of the Budget Committee in a unanimous vote. Gray, a black Baptist minister from an inner-city Philadelphia district, succeeded James R. Jones, D-Okla., whose six-year term on Budget expired at the end of the 98th

Vetoes Cast by President Reagan

President Reagan vetoed six bills cleared by Congress in 1985, bringing his total vetoes to 45.

Congress overrode one 1985 veto, the only one on which an override attempt was made. That bill was HR 2409, which reauthorized selected biomedical research activities at the National Institutes of Health and set up a new arthritis research institute and nursing research center.

Two 1985 bills were vetoed in January 1986, between the first and second sessions of the 99th Congress. While asserting his right to "pocket-veto" bills between sessions, Reagan returned both measures to Congress for possible override action. The administration was challenging before the Supreme Court a 1984 federal appeals court ruling that pocket vetoes could not be used between sessions of the same Congress. *(Background, 1984 Almanac p. 204)*

The Constitution stipulates that when Congress is in session, a bill becomes law without the president's signature if he does not act upon it within 10 days, excluding Sundays, from the time he receives it. But if Congress adjourns within that 10-day period, preventing return of the bill, the president can kill — or pocket-veto — the bill by withholding his signature.

1981

1. H J Res 357 (Continuing Appropriations)
   Vetoed: Nov. 23, 1981; no override attempt
2. HR 4353 (Bankruptcy Fees on Lifetime Communities Inc.)
   Pocket-vetoed: Dec. 29, 1981†

1982

3. S 1503 (Standby Petroleum Allocation)
   Vetoed: March 20, 1982
   Senate sustained March 24: 58-36 *
4. HR 5118 (Southern Arizona Water Rights Settlement Act)
   Vetoed: June 1, 1982; no override attempt
5. HR 5922 (Urgent Supplemental Appropriations, Fiscal 1982)
   Vetoed: June 24, 1982
   House sustained June 24: 253-151 *
6. HR 6682 (Urgent Supplemental Appropriations, Fiscal 1982)
   Vetoed: June 25, 1982
   House sustained July 13: 242-169 *
7. HR 6198 (Manufacturers Copyright Bill)
   Vetoed: July 8, 1982
   Veto overridden July 13 *
   House: 324-86, July 13
   Senate: 84-9, July 13
8. HR 6863 (Supplemental Appropriations, Fiscal 1982)
   Vetoed: Aug. 28, 1982
   Veto overridden Sept. 10 *
   House: 301-117, Sept. 9
   Senate: 60-30, Sept. 10
9. HR 1371 (Contract Disputes)
   Vetoed: Oct. 15, 1982; no override attempt
10. S 2577 (Environmental Research and Development)
    Vetoed: Oct. 22, 1982; no override attempt
11. S 2623 (Indian Controlled Community Colleges)
    Pocket-vetoed: Jan. 3, 1983†
12. HR 5858 (Private Bill)
    Pocket-vetoed: Jan. 4, 1983†
13. HR 7336 (Education Consolidation and Improvement Act Amendments)
    Pocket-vetoed: Jan. 12, 1983†
14. HR 9 (Florida Wilderness Act)
    Pocket-vetoed: Jan. 14, 1983†
15. HR 3963 (Anti-Crime Bill)
    Pocket-vetoed: Jan. 14, 1983†

1983

16. S 366 (Indian Claims Bill)
    Vetoed: April 5, 1983; no override attempt
17. S 973 (Tax Leasing Plan)
    Vetoed: June 17, 1983; no override attempt
18. HR 3564 (Feed Grains Bill)
    Vetoed: Aug. 12, 1983; no override attempt
19. H J Res 338 (Chicago School Desegregation)
    Vetoed: Aug. 13, 1983; no override attempt
20. S J Res 149 (Dairy Assessment Delay Bill)
    Vetoed: Aug. 23, 1983; no override attempt
21. HR 1062 (Oregon Land Transfer Bill)
    Vetoed: Oct. 19, 1983
    Veto overridden Oct. 25 *
    Senate: 95-0, Oct. 25
    House: 297-125, Oct. 25
22. HR 4042 (El Salvador Certification)
    Pocket-vetoed: Nov. 30, 1983

1984

23. S 684 (Water Resources Research)
    Vetoed: Feb. 21, 1984
    Veto overridden March 22 *
    Senate: 86-12, March 21
    House: 309-81, March 22
24. S 2436 (Corporation for Public Broadcasting)
    Vetoed: Aug. 29, 1984
25. HR 1362 (Private Bill)
    Vetoed: Oct. 8, 1984; no override attempt
26. S 1967 (Indian Affairs)
    Pocket-vetoed: Oct. 17, 1984†
27. HR 2859 (Private Bill)
    Pocket-vetoed: Oct. 17, 1984
28. S 1097 (NOAA Research and Services Act)
    Pocket-vetoed: Oct. 19, 1984†
29. S 607 (Corporation for Public Broadcasting)
    Pocket-vetoed: Oct. 19, 1984†
30. S 2166 (Indian Health Care Improvement Act)
    Pocket-vetoed: Oct. 19, 1984†
31. HR 6248 (Armed Career Criminal Act of 1984)
    Pocket-vetoed: Oct. 19, 1984†
32. HR 5172 (National Bureau of Standards Authorizations)
    Pocket-vetoed: Oct. 30, 1984†
33. S 540 (Health Research Extension Act of 1984)
    Pocket-vetoed: Oct. 30, 1984†
34. S 2574 (Public Health Service Act Amendments of 1984)
    Pocket-vetoed: Oct. 30, 1984†
35. HR 999 (American Conservation Corps Act of 1984)
    Pocket-vetoed: Oct. 30, 1984†
36. HR 5760 (Indian Affairs)
    Pocket-vetoed: Oct. 30, 1984†
37. HR 723 (Private Bill)
    Pocket-vetoed: Oct. 31, 1984
38. HR 452 (Private Bill)
    Pocket-vetoed: Oct. 31, 1984
39. HR 5479 (Civil Actions and Procedures)
    Pocket-vetoed: Nov. 8, 1984†

1985

40. HR 1096 (Farm Credit/African Famine Relief)
    Vetoed: March 6, 1985; no override attempt
41. HR 2409 (National Institutes of Health Research)
    Vetoed: Nov. 8, 1985
    Veto overridden Nov. 20*
    House: 380-32, Nov. 12
    Senate: 89-7, Nov. 20
42. HR 3036 (Treasury/Postal Service Appropriations)
    Vetoed: Nov. 15, 1985; no override attempt
43. HR 1562 (Textile Import Restrictions)
    Vetoed: Dec. 17, 1985; override attempt scheduled Aug. 6, 1986
44. HR 1404 (Virginia Wildlife Refuge)
    Vetoed: Jan. 14, 1986; no override attempt
45. HR 3384 (Federal Employees' Health Benefits)
    Vetoed: Jan. 17, 1986; no override attempt

** Veto overrides require a two-thirds majority vote of both houses.*
† President's memorandum of disapproval issued on this date.

Congress. *(Black committee chairmen, box, p. 5)*

Gray's ascension to the Budget Committee chairmanship was a routine matter because he was unopposed for the job. His only formal challenger, Martin Frost, D-Texas, withdrew from the race.

The chairmanship became vacant because House rules required Jones to leave the Budget panel at the end of the 98th Congress, after having served three consecutive two-year terms. Jones wanted a rules change that would allow him to remain on the committee for more than three terms, a change also sought by Leon E. Panetta, D-Calif., whose Budget term was about to expire and who wanted to run for chairman. But the House Democratic Caucus refused to alter the rules.

Other Chairmen. There were no challenges to committee chairmen other than Price, but more than a dozen negative votes were cast against each of five other chairmen: E. "Kika" de la Garza, Texas, of Agriculture; Jamie L. Whitten, Miss., of Appropriations; Fernand J. St Germain, R.I., of Banking, Finance and Urban Affairs; Walter B. Jones, N.C., of Merchant Marine and Fisheries; and Dan Rostenkowski, Ill., of Ways and Means.

Committee Assignments

Members' committee assignments provoked controversy in both chambers in 1985.

House. In the House, Democratic leaders agreed to give Republicans more seats on most major committees. The Democratic decision to adjust party ratios followed angry protests by Republicans who claimed that in recent years committees had been stacked in favor of Democrats.

Republicans were granted 30 more seats on standing committees than they had in the 98th Congress, even though they gained only 14 seats in the 1984 elections. Democrats gave up 21 standing committee seats.

The House voted March 7 to re-establish three select committees, despite complaints by some members that the panels duplicated work handled by regular standing committees and were a needless expense. By votes of 286-124 and 310-94, the House continued the Select Committees on Hunger and on Narcotics Abuse and Control. The Children, Youth and Families panel was reauthorized by voice vote. *(Votes 28, 29, p. 10-II)*

Senate. In the Senate, committee appointments were delayed while Senate leaders sought to reduce the size of committees by asking some senators with three major committee assignments to give up one of those seats. While the total number of major committee slots shrank from 231 to 214, 14 senators kept three major committees each.

Of the 12 major committees, seven were reduced in size. Armed Services added one seat.

Republicans got 115 major committee assignments, 12 fewer than in the 98th Congress. Democrats got 99 slots, a loss of only five, reflecting the two-seat Senate gain their party achieved in the 1984 elections. *(Details, committee and subcommittee membership list, p. 16-G)* ▮

Reagan Inauguration

Ronald Reagan opened his second term as the nation's 40th president Jan. 21 by declaring that the United States was "poised for greatness," and by restating the conservative philosophical tenets that marked his first administration and his hugely successful re-election campaign.

In a 20-minute speech delivered inside the Capitol Rotunda on a shivery day in Washington, Reagan stressed the broad themes that dominated his first term: scaling back the size of the federal government and strengthening the country's defensive forces. *(Text of speech, p. 3-D)*

Reagan began his second term by taking the 35-word oath of office twice in 24 hours. The first — and official — ceremony was held at the White House Jan. 20, the date prescribed in the Constitution since 1933. (Prior presidents were sworn in on March 4). Fewer than 100 guests attended the nationally televised White House ceremony, at which the oath of office also was administered to Vice President George Bush.

Reagan followed a tradition set by earlier presidents who did not schedule public oath-taking ceremonies when Inauguration Day fell on a Sunday. Reagan was the sixth president to observe that tradition.

Reagan and Bush repeated their oaths shortly before noon on Jan. 21 at the Capitol. Sub-freezing temperatures in Washington forced inauguration officials to cancel the outdoor ceremony scheduled for the steps of the Capitol's West Front before 140,000 invited guests. Instead, Reagan and Bush took their oaths inside the cavernous Capitol Rotunda, before an audience limited to members of Congress, Supreme Court justices, diplomats, Reagan and Bush family members and other dignitaries.

The ceremony marked the first time that a president took the oath of office in the Rotunda and the first time since 1909 that the Capitol's interior provided an inaugural's setting. That year, cold and windy weather forced William Howard Taft to take his oath in the Senate chamber.

The bone-chilling conditions also forced cancellation of the traditional inaugural parade between the Capitol and the White House.

Reagan began his second term with a high level of public confidence in his handling of the presidency, according to a *New York Times*/CBS News poll conducted a week before the inauguration. According to the survey of 1,534 adults, 62 percent approved of Reagan's performance while 29 percent disapproved. That compared with a 67 percent approval rating registered immediately after the attempt on Reagan's life in March 1981, two months after he entered office.

Members of the 99th Congress, First Session . . .

As of Jan. 3, 1985

Representatives

D 252; R 182

1 Vacancy *

A

Ackerman, Gary L., D-N.Y. (7)
Addabbo, Joseph P., D-N.Y. (6)
Akaka, Daniel K., D-Hawaii (2)
Alexander, Bill, D-Ark. (1)
Anderson, Glenn M., D-Calif. (32)
Andrews, Michael A., D-Texas (25)
Annunzio, Frank, D-Ill. (11)
Anthony, Beryl Jr., D-Ark. (4)
Applegate, Douglas, D-Ohio (18)
Archer, Bill, R-Texas (7)
Armey, Dick, R-Texas (26)
Aspin, Les, D-Wis. (1)
Atkins, Chester G., D-Mass. (5)
AuCoin, Les, D-Ore. (1)

B

Badham, Robert E., R-Calif. (40)
Barnard, Doug Jr., D-Ga. (10)
Barnes, Michael D., D-Md. (8)
Bartlett, Steve, R-Texas (3)
Barton, Joe L., R-Texas (6)
Bateman, Herbert H., R-Va. (1)
Bates, Jim, D-Calif. (44)
Bedell, Berkley, D-Iowa (6)
Beilenson, Anthony C., D-Calif. (23)
Bennett, Charles E., D-Fla. (3)
Bentley, Helen Delich, R-Md. (2)
Bereuter, Doug, R-Neb. (1)
Berman, Howard L., D-Calif. (26)
Bevill, Tom, D-Ala. (4)
Biaggi, Mario, D-N.Y. (19)
Bilirakis, Michael, R-Fla. (9)
Bliley, Thomas J. Jr., R-Va. (3)
Boehlert, Sherwood, R-N.Y. (25)
Boggs, Lindy (Mrs. Hale), D-La. (2)
Boland, Edward P., D-Mass. (2)
Boner, Bill, D-Tenn. (5)
Bonior, David E., D-Mich. (12)
Bonker, Don, D-Wash. (3)
Borski, Robert A., D-Pa. (3)
Bosco, Douglas H., D-Calif. (1)
Boucher, Frederick C., D-Va. (9)
Boulter, Beau, R-Texas (13)
Boxer, Barbara, D-Calif. (6)
Breaux, John B., D-La. (7)
Brooks, Jack, D-Texas (9)
Broomfield, William S., R-Mich. (18)
Brown, George E. Jr., D-Calif. (36)
Brown, Hank, R-Colo. (4)
Broyhill, James T., R-N.C. (10)
Bruce, Terry L., D-Ill. (19)
Bryant, John, D-Texas (5)
Burton, Dan, R-Ind. (6)
Burton, Sala, D-Calif. (5)
Bustamante, Albert G., D-Texas (23)
Byron, Beverly B., D-Md. (6)

C

Callahan, Sonny, R-Ala. (1)
Campbell, Carroll A. Jr., R-S.C. (4)
Carney, William, R-N.Y. (1)
Carper, Thomas R., D-Del. (AL)
Carr, Bob, D-Mich. (6)
Chandler, Rod, R-Wash. (8)
Chappell, Bill Jr., D-Fla. (4)
Chappie, Gene, R-Calif. (2)
Cheney, Dick, R-Wyo. (AL)
Clay, William L., D-Mo. (1)
Clinger, William F. Jr., R-Pa. (23)
Coats, Dan, R-Ind. (4)
Cobey, Bill, R-N.C. (4)
Coble, Howard, R-N.C. (6)
Coelho, Tony, D-Calif. (15)
Coleman, E. Thomas, R-Mo. (6)
Coleman, Ronald D., D-Texas (16)
Collins, Cardiss, D-Ill. (7)
Combest, Larry, R-Texas (19)
Conte, Silvio O., R-Mass. (1)
Conyers, John Jr., D-Mich. (1)
Cooper, Jim, D-Tenn. (4)
Coughlin, Lawrence, R-Pa. (13)
Courter, Jim, R-N.J. (12)
Coyne, William J., D-Pa. (14)
Craig, Larry E., R-Idaho (1)
Crane, Philip M., R-Ill. (12)
Crockett, George W. Jr., D-Mich. (13)

D

Daniel, Dan, D-Va. (5)
Dannemeyer, William E., R-Calif. (39)
Darden, George "Buddy", D-Ga. (7)
Daschle, Thomas A., D-S.D. (AL)
Daub, Hal, R-Neb. (2)
Davis, Robert W., R-Mich. (11)
de la Garza, E. "Kika", D-Texas (15)
DeLay, Thomas D., R-Texas (22)
Dellums, Ronald V., D-Calif. (8)
Derrick, Butler, D-S.C. (3)
DeWine, Michael, R-Ohio (7)
Dickinson, William L., R-Ala. (2)
Dicks, Norman D., D-Wash. (6)
Dingell, John D., D-Mich. (16)
DioGuardi, Joseph J., R-N.Y. (20)
Dixon, Julian C., D-Calif. (28)
Donnelly, Brian J., D-Mass. (11)
Dorgan, Byron L., D-N.D. (AL)
Dornan, Bob, R-Calif. (38)
Dowdy, Wayne, D-Miss. (4)
Downey, Thomas J., D-N.Y. (2)
Dreier, David, R-Calif. (33)
Duncan, John J., R-Tenn. (2)
Durbin, Richard J., D-Ill. (20)
Dwyer, Bernard J., D-N.J. (6)
Dymally, Mervyn M., D-Calif. (31)
Dyson, Roy, D-Md. (1)

E

Early, Joseph D., D-Mass. (3)
Eckart, Dennis E., D-Ohio (11)
Eckert, Fred J., R-N.Y. (30)
Edgar, Bob, D-Pa. (7)
Edwards, Don, D-Calif. (10)
Edwards, Mickey, R-Okla. (5)
Emerson, Bill, R-Mo. (8)
English, Glenn, D-Okla. (6)
Erdreich, Ben, D-Ala. (6)
Evans, Cooper, R-Iowa (3)
Evans, Lane, D-Ill. (17)

F

Fascell, Dante B., D-Fla. (19)
Fawell, Harris W., R-Ill. (13)
Fazio, Vic, D-Calif. (4)
Feighan, Edward F., D-Ohio (19)
Fiedler, Bobbi, R-Calif. (21)
Fields, Jack, R-Texas (8)
Fish, Hamilton Jr., R-N.Y. (21)
Flippo, Ronnie G., D-Ala. (5)
Florio, James J., D-N.J. (1)
Foglietta, Thomas M., D-Pa. (1)
Foley, Thomas S., D-Wash. (5)
Ford, Harold E., D-Tenn. (9)
Ford, William D., D-Mich. (15)
Fowler, Wyche Jr., D-Ga. (5)
Frank, Barney, D-Mass. (4)
Franklin, Webb, R-Miss. (2)
Frenzel, Bill, R-Minn. (3)
Frost, Martin, D-Texas (24)
Fuqua, Don, D-Fla. (2)

G

Gallo, Dean A., R-N.J. (11)
Garcia, Robert, D-N.Y. (18)
Gaydos, Joseph M., D-Pa. (20)
Gejdenson, Sam, D-Conn. (2)
Gekas, George W., R-Pa. (17)
Gephardt, Richard A., D-Mo. (3)
Gibbons, Sam, D-Fla. (7)
Gilman, Benjamin A., R-N.Y. (22)
Gingrich, Newt, R-Ga. (6)
Glickman, Dan, D-Kan. (4)
Gonzalez, Henry B., D-Texas (20)
Goodling, Bill, R-Pa. (19)
Gordon, Bart, D-Tenn. (6)
Gradison, Bill, R-Ohio (2)
Gray, Kenneth J., D-Ill. (22)
Gray, William H. III, D-Pa. (2)
Green, Bill, R-N.Y. (15)
Gregg, Judd, R-N.H. (2)
Grotberg, John E., R-Ill. (14)
Guarini, Frank J., D-N.J. (14)
Gunderson, Steve, R-Wis. (3)

H

Hall, Ralph M., D-Texas (4)
Hall, Sam B. Jr., D-Texas (1)
Hall, Tony P., D-Ohio (3)
Hamilton, Lee H., D-Ind. (9)
Hammerschmidt, John Paul, R-Ark. (3)
Hansen, James V., R-Utah (1)
Hartnett, Thomas F., R-S.C. (1)
Hatcher, Charles, D-Ga. (2)
Hawkins, Augustus F., D-Calif. (29)
Hayes, Charles A., D-Ill. (1)
Hefner, W. G. "Bill", D-N.C. (8)
Heftel, Cecil, D-Hawaii (1)
Hendon, Bill, R-N.C. (11)
Henry, Paul B., R-Mich. (5)
Hertel, Dennis M., D-Mich. (14)
Hiler, John, R-Ind. (3)
Hillis, Elwood, R-Ind. (5)
Holt, Marjorie S., R-Md. (4)
Hopkins, Larry J., R-Ky. (6)
Horton, Frank, R-N.Y. (29)
Howard, James J., D-N.J. (3)
Hoyer, Steny H., D-Md. (5)
Hubbard, Carroll Jr., D-Ky. (1)
Huckaby, Jerry, D-La. (5)
Hughes, William J., D-N.J. (2)
Hunter, Duncan L., R-Calif. (45)
Hutto, Earl, D-Fla. (1)
Hyde, Henry J., R-Ill. (6)

I, J

Ireland, Andy, R-Fla. (10)
Jacobs, Andrew Jr., D-Ind. (10)
Jeffords, James M., R-Vt. (AL)
Jenkins, Ed, D-Ga. (9)
Johnson, Nancy L., R-Conn. (6)
Jones, Ed, D-Tenn. (8)
Jones, James R., D-Okla. (1)
Jones, Walter B., D-N.C. (1)

K

Kanjorski, Paul E., D-Pa. (11)
Kaptur, Marcy, D-Ohio (9)
Kasich, John R., R-Ohio (12)
Kastenmeier, Robert W., D-Wis. (2)
Kemp, Jack F., R-N.Y. (31)
Kennelly, Barbara B., D-Conn. (1)
Kildee, Dale E., D-Mich. (7)
Kindness, Thomas N., R-Ohio (8)
Kleczka, Gerald D., D-Wis. (4)
Kolbe, Jim, R-Ariz. (5)
Kolter, Joe, D-Pa. (4)
Kostmayer, Peter H., D-Pa. (8)
Kramer, Ken, R-Colo. (5)

L

LaFalce, John J., D-N.Y. (32)
Lagomarsino, Robert J., R-Calif. (19)
Lantos, Tom, D-Calif. (11)
Latta, Delbert L., R-Ohio (5)
Leach, Jim, R-Iowa (1)
Leath, Marvin, D-Texas (11)
Lehman, Richard H., D-Calif. (18)
Lehman, William, D-Fla. (17)
Leland, Mickey, D-Texas (18)
Lent, Norman F., R-N.Y. (4)
Levin, Sander M., D-Mich. (17)
Levine, Mel, D-Calif. (27)
Lewis, Jerry, R-Calif. (35)
Lewis, Tom, R-Fla. (12)
Lightfoot, Jim, R-Iowa (5)
Lipinski, William O., D-Ill. (5)
Livingston, Bob, R-La. (1)
Lloyd, Marilyn, D-Tenn. (3)
Loeffler, Tom, R-Texas (21)
Long, Gillis W., D-La. (8)
Lott, Trent, R-Miss. (5)
Lowery, Bill, R-Calif. (41)
Lowry, Mike, D-Wash. (7)
Lujan, Manuel Jr., R-N.M. (1)
Luken, Thomas A., D-Ohio (1)
Lundine, Stan, D-N.Y. (34)
Lungren, Dan, R-Calif. (42)

M

Mack, Connie, R-Fla. (13)
MacKay, Buddy, D-Fla. (6)
Madigan, Edward R., R-Ill. (15)
Manton, Thomas J., D-N.Y. (9)
Markey, Edward J., D-Mass. (7)
Marlenee, Ron, R-Mont. (2)
Martin, David O'B., R-N.Y. (26)
Martin, Lynn, R-Ill. (16)
Martinez, Matthew G., D-Calif. (30)
Matsui, Robert T., D-Calif. (3)
Mavroules, Nicholas, D-Mass. (6)
Mazzoli, Romano L., D-Ky. (3)
McCain, John, R-Ariz. (1)
McCandless, Al, R-Calif. (37)
McCollum, Bill, R-Fla. (5)
McCurdy, Dave, D-Okla. (4)
McDade, Joseph M., R-Pa. (10)
McEwen, Bob, R-Ohio (6)
McGrath, Raymond J., R-N.Y. (5)
McHugh, Matthew F., D-N.Y. (28)
McKernan, John R. Jr., R-Maine (1)
McKinney, Stewart B., R-Conn. (4)
McMillan, J. Alex, R-N.C. (9)
Meyers, Jan, R-Kan. (3)
Mica, Daniel A., D-Fla. (14)
Michel, Robert H., R-Ill. (18)
Mikulski, Barbara A., D-Md. (3)
Miller, Clarence E., R-Ohio (10)
Miller, George, D-Calif. (7)
Miller, John R., R-Wash. (1)
Mineta, Norman Y., D-Calif. (13)
Mitchell, Parren J., D-Md. (7)
Moakley, Joe, D-Mass. (9)
Molinari, Guy V., R-N.Y. (14)
Mollohan, Alan B., D-W.Va. (1)
Monson, David S., R-Utah (2)
Montgomery, G. V. "Sonny", D-Miss. (3)
Moody, Jim, D-Wis. (5)
Moore, W. Henson, R-La. (6)
Moorhead, Carlos J., R-Calif. (22)
Morrison, Bruce A., D-Conn. (3)
Morrison, Sid, R-Wash. (4)
Mrazek, Robert J., D-N.Y. (3)
Murphy, Austin J., D-Pa. (22)
Murtha, John P., D-Pa. (12)
Myers, John T., R-Ind. (7)

N

Natcher, William H., D-Ky. (2)
Neal, Stephen L., D-N.C. (5)
Nelson, Bill, D-Fla. (11)
Nichols, Bill, D-Ala. (3)
Nielson, Howard C., R-Utah (3)
Nowak, Henry J., D-N.Y. (33)

O

Oakar, Mary Rose, D-Ohio (20)
Oberstar, James L., D-Minn. (8)
Obey, David R., D-Wis. (7)
O'Brien, George M., R-Ill. (4)
Olin, James R., D-Va. (6)
O'Neill, Thomas P. Jr., D-Mass. (8)
Ortiz, Solomon P., D-Texas (27)
Owens, Major R., D-N.Y. (12)
Oxley, Michael G., R-Ohio (4)

P

Packard, Ron, R-Calif. (43)
Panetta, Leon E., D-Calif. (16)
Parris, Stan, R-Va. (8)
Pashayan, Charles Jr., R-Calif. (17)
Pease, Don J., D-Ohio (13)
Penny, Timothy J., D-Minn. (1)
Pepper, Claude, D-Fla. (18)
Perkins, Carl C., D-Ky. (7)
Petri, Thomas E., R-Wis. (6)
Pickle, J. J., D-Texas (10)

. . . Governors, Supreme Court, Cabinet-rank Officers

Porter, John Edward, R-Ill. (10)
Price, Melvin, D-Ill. (21)
Pursell, Carl D., R-Mich. (2)

Q, R

Quillen, James H., R-Tenn. (1)
Rahall, Nick J. II, D-W.Va. (4)
Rangel, Charles B., D-N.Y. (16)
Ray, Richard, D-Ga. (3)
Regula, Ralph, R-Ohio (16)
Reid, Harry, D-Nev. (1)
Richardson, Bill, D-N.M. (3)
Ridge, Tom, R-Pa. (21)
Rinaldo, Matthew J., R-N.J. (7)
Ritter, Don, R-Pa. (15)
Roberts, Pat, R-Kan. (1)
Robinson, Tommy F., D-Ark. (2)
Rodino, Peter W. Jr., D-N.J. (10)
Roe, Robert A., D-N.J. (8)
Roemer, Buddy, D-La. (4)
Rogers, Harold, R-Ky. (5)
Rose, Charlie, D-N.C. (7)
Rostenkowski, Dan, D-Ill. (8)
Roth, Toby, R-Wis. (8)
Roukema, Marge, R-N.J. (5)
Rowland, J. Roy, D-Ga. (8)
Rowland, John G., R-Conn. (5)
Roybal, Edward R., D-Calif. (25)
Rudd, Eldon, R-Ariz. (4)
Russo, Marty, D-Ill. (3)

S

Sabo, Martin Olav, D-Minn. (5)
St Germain, Fernand J., D-R.I. (1)
Savage, Gus, D-Ill. (2)
Saxton, H. James, R-N.J. (13)
Schaefer, Dan L., R-Colo. (6)
Scheuer, James H., D-N.Y. (8)
Schneider, Claudine, R-R.I. (2)
Schroeder, Patricia, D-Colo. (1)
Schuette, Bill, R-Mich. (10)
Schulze, Richard T., R-Pa. (5)
Schumer, Charles E., D-N.Y. (10)
Seiberling, John F., D-Ohio (14)
Sensenbrenner, F. James Jr., R-Wis. (9)
Sharp, Philip R., D-Ind. (2)
Shaw, E. Clay Jr., R-Fla. (15)
Shelby, Richard C., D-Ala. (7)
Shumway, Norman D., R-Calif. (14)
Shuster, Bud, R-Pa. (9)
Sikorski, Gerry, D-Minn. (6)
Siljander, Mark D., R-Mich. (4)
Sisisky, Norman, D-Va. (4)
Skeen, Joe, R-N.M. (2)
Skelton, Ike, D-Mo. (4)
Slattery, Jim, D-Kan. (2)
Slaughter, D. French Jr., R-Va. (7)
Smith, Christopher H., R-N.J. (4)
Smith, Denny, R-Ore. (5)
Smith, Larry, D-Fla. (16)
Smith, Neal, D-Iowa (4)
Smith, Robert C., R-N.H. (1)
Smith, Robert F., R-Ore. (2)
Smith, Virginia, R-Neb. (3)
Snowe, Olympia J., R-Maine (2)
Snyder, Gene, R-Ky. (4)
Solarz, Stephen J., D-N.Y. (13)
Solomon, Gerald B. H., R-N.Y. (24)
Spence, Floyd, R-S.C. (2)
Spratt, John M. Jr., D-S.C. (5)
Staggers, Harley O. Jr., D-W.Va. (2)
Stallings, Richard H., D-Idaho (2)
Stangeland, Arlan, R-Minn. (7)
Stark, Fortney H. "Pete", D-Calif. (9)
Stenholm, Charles W., D-Texas (17)
Stokes, Louis, D-Ohio (21)
Strang, Mike, R-Colo. (3)
Stratton, Samuel S., D-N.Y. (23)
Studds, Gerry E., D-Mass. (10)
Stump, Bob, R-Ariz. (3)
Sundquist, Don, R-Tenn. (7)
Sweeney, Mac, R-Texas (14)
Swift, Al, D-Wash. (2)
Swindall, Pat, R-Ga. (4)
Synar, Mike, D-Okla. (2)

T

Tallon, Robin, D-S.C. (6)
Tauke, Tom, R-Iowa (2)
Tauzin, W. J. "Billy", D-La. (3)
Taylor, Gene, R-Mo. (7)
Thomas, Robert Lindsay, D-Ga. (1)
Thomas, William M., R-Calif. (20)
Torres, Esteban Edward, D-Calif. (34)
Torricelli, Robert G., D-N.J. (9)
Towns, Edolphus, D-N.Y. (11)
Traficant, James A. Jr., D-Ohio (17)
Traxler, Bob, D-Mich. (8)

U, V

Udall, Morris K., D-Ariz. (2)
Valentine, Tim, D-N.C. (2)
Vander Jagt, Guy, R-Mich. (9)
Vento, Bruce F., D-Minn. (4)
Visclosky, Peter J., D-Ind. (1)
Volkmer, Harold L., D-Mo. (9)
Vucanovich, Barbara F., R-Nev. (2)

W

Walgren, Doug, D-Pa. (18)
Walker, Robert S., R-Pa. (16)
Watkins, Wes, D-Okla. (3)
Waxman, Henry A., D-Calif. (24)
Weaver, James, D-Ore. (4)
Weber, Vin, R-Minn. (2)
Weiss, Ted, D-N.Y. (17)
Wheat, Alan, D-Mo. (5)
Whitehurst, G. William, R-Va. (2)
Whitley, Charles, D-N.C. (3)
Whittaker, Bob, R-Kan. (5)
Whitten, Jamie L., D-Miss. (1)
Williams, Pat, D-Mont. (1)
Wilson, Charles, D-Texas (2)
Wirth, Timothy E., D-Colo. (2)
Wise, Bob, D-W.Va. (3)
Wolf, Frank R., R-Va. (10)
Wolpe, Howard, D-Mich. (3)
Wortley, George C., R-N.Y. (27)
Wright, Jim, D-Texas (12)
Wyden, Ron, D-Ore. (3)
Wylie, Chalmers P., R-Ohio (15)

X, Y, Z

Yates, Sidney R., D-Ill. (9)
Yatron, Gus, D-Pa. (6)
Young, C. W. Bill, R-Fla. (8)
Young, Don, R-Alaska (AL)
Young, Robert A., D-Mo. (2)
Zschau, Ed, R-Calif. (12)

Delegates

Blaz, Ben, R-Guam
de Lugo, Ron, D-Virgin Islands
Fauntroy, Walter E., D-D.C.
Sunia, Fofō I. F., D-American Samoa

Resident Commissioner

Fuster, Jaime B., Pop. Dem.-Puerto Rico

Senators

R 53; D 47

Abdnor, James, R-S.D.
Andrews, Mark, R-N.D.
Armstrong, William L., R-Colo.
Baucus, Max, D-Mont.
Bentsen, Lloyd, D-Texas
Biden, Joseph R. Jr., D-Del.
Bingaman, Jeff, D-N.M.
Boren, David L., D-Okla.
Boschwitz, Rudy, R-Minn.
Bradley, Bill, D-N.J.
Bumpers, Dale, D-Ark.
Burdick, Quentin N., D-N.D.
Byrd, Robert C., D-W.Va.
Chafee, John H., R-R.I.
Chiles, Lawton, D-Fla.
Cochran, Thad, R-Miss.
Cohen, William S., R-Maine
Cranston, Alan, D-Calif.
D'Amato, Alfonse M., R-N.Y.
Danforth, John C., R-Mo.
DeConcini, Dennis, D-Ariz.
Denton, Jeremiah, R-Ala.
Dixon, Alan J., D-Ill.
Dodd, Christopher J., D-Conn.
Dole, Robert, R-Kan.
Domenici, Pete V., R-N.M.
Durenberger, Dave, R-Minn.
Eagleton, Thomas F., D-Mo.
East, John P., R-N.C.
Evans, Daniel J., R-Wash.
Exon, J. James, D-Neb.
Ford, Wendell H., D-Ky.
Garn, Jake, R-Utah
Glenn, John, D-Ohio
Goldwater, Barry, R-Ariz.
Gore, Albert Jr., D-Tenn.
Gorton, Slade, R-Wash.
Gramm, Phil, R-Texas
Grassley, Charles E., R-Iowa
Harkin, Tom, D-Iowa
Hart, Gary, D-Colo.
Hatch, Orrin G., R-Utah
Hatfield, Mark O., R-Ore.
Hawkins, Paula, R-Fla.
Hecht, Chic, R-Nev.
Heflin, Howell, D-Ala.
Heinz, John, R-Pa.
Helms, Jesse, R-N.C.
Hollings, Ernest F., D-S.C.
Humphrey, Gordon J., R-N.H.
Inouye, Daniel K., D-Hawaii
Johnston, J. Bennett, D-La.
Kassebaum, Nancy Landon, R-Kan.
Kasten, Bob, R-Wis.
Kennedy, Edward M., D-Mass.
Kerry, John, D-Mass.
Lautenberg, Frank R., D-N.J.
Laxalt, Paul, R-Nev.
Leahy, Patrick J., D-Vt.
Levin, Carl, D-Mich.
Long, Russell B., D-La.
Lugar, Richard G., R-Ind.
Mathias, Charles McC. Jr., R-Md.
Matsunaga, Spark M., D-Hawaii
Mattingly, Mack, R-Ga.
McClure, James A., R-Idaho
McConnell, Mitch, R-Ky.
Melcher, John, D-Mont.
Metzenbaum, Howard M., D-Ohio
Mitchell, George J., D-Maine
Moynihan, Daniel Patrick, D-N.Y.
Murkowski, Frank H., R-Alaska
Nickles, Don, R-Okla.
Nunn, Sam, D-Ga.
Packwood, Bob, R-Ore.
Pell, Claiborne, D-R.I.
Pressler, Larry, R-S.D.
Proxmire, William, D-Wis.
Pryor, David, D-Ark.
Quayle, Dan, R-Ind.
Riegle, Donald W. Jr., D-Mich.
Rockefeller, John D. IV, D-W.Va.
Roth, William V. Jr., R-Del.
Rudman, Warren B., R-N.H.
Sarbanes, Paul S., D-Md.
Sasser, Jim, D-Tenn.
Simon, Paul, D-Ill.
Simpson, Alan K., R-Wyo.
Specter, Arlen, R-Pa.
Stafford, Robert T., R-Vt.
Stennis, John C., D-Miss.
Stevens, Ted, R-Alaska
Symms, Steven D., R-Idaho
Thurmond, Strom, R-S.C.
Trible, Paul S. Jr., R-Va.
Wallop, Malcolm, R-Wyo.
Warner, John W., R-Va.
Weicker, Lowell P. Jr., R-Conn.
Wilson, Pete, R-Calif.
Zorinsky, Edward, D-Neb.

Governors

D 34; R 16

Ala.—George C. Wallace, D
Alaska—Bill Sheffield, D
Ariz.—Bruce Babbitt, D
Ark.—Bill Clinton, D
Calif.—George Deukmejian, R
Colo.—Richard D. Lamm, D
Conn.—William A. O'Neill, D
Del.—Michael N. Castle, R
Fla.—Bob Graham, D
Ga.—Joe Frank Harris, D
Hawaii—George R. Ariyoshi, D
Idaho—John V. Evans, D
Ill.—James R. Thompson, R
Ind.—Robert D. Orr, R
Iowa—Terry E. Branstad, R
Kan.—John Carlin, D
Ky.—Martha Layne Collins, D
La.—Edwin W. Edwards, D
Maine—Joseph E. Brennan, D
Md.—Harry Hughes, D
Mass.—Michael S. Dukakis, D
Mich.—James J. Blanchard, D
Minn.—Rudy Perpich, D
Miss.—Bill Allain, D
Mo.—John Ashcroft, R
Mont.—Ted Schwinden, D
Neb.—Robert Kerrey, D
Nev.—Richard H. Bryan, D
N.H.—John H. Sununu, R
N.J.—Thomas H. Kean, R
N.M.—Toney Anaya, D
N.Y.—Mario M. Cuomo, D
N.C.—James G. Martin, R
N.D.—George Sinner, D
Ohio—Richard F. Celeste, D
Okla.—George Nigh, D
Ore.—Victor G. Atiyeh, R
Pa.—Dick Thornburgh, R
R.I.—Edward DiPrete, R
S.C.—Richard W. Riley, D
S.D.—William J. Janklow, R
Tenn.—Lamar Alexander, R
Texas—Mark White, D
Utah—Norman H. Bangerter, R
Vt.—Madeleine M. Kunin, D
Va.—Charles S. Robb, D
Wash.—Booth Gardner, D
W.Va.—Arch A. Moore Jr., R
Wis.—Anthony S. Earl, D
Wyo.—Ed Herschler, D

Supreme Court

Burger, Warren E. — Minn., Chief Justice
Blackmun, Harry A. — Minn.
Brennan, William J. Jr. — N.J.
Marshall, Thurgood — N.Y.
O'Connor, Sandra Day — Ariz.
Powell, Lewis F. Jr.— Va.
Rehnquist, William H. — Ariz.
Stevens, John Paul — Ill.
White, Byron R. — Colo.

As of Feb. 23, 1985

Cabinet

Baker, James A. III — Treasury
Baldridge, Malcolm — Commerce
Bennett, William J. — Education
Block, John R. — Agriculture
Dole, Elizabeth Hanford — Transportation
Donovan, Raymond J. — Labor
Heckler, Margaret M.— HHS
Herrington, John S. — Energy
Hodel, Donald P. — Interior
Meese, Edwin III — Attorney General
Pierce, Samuel R. Jr. — HUD
Shultz, George P. — State
Weinberger, Caspar W. — Defense

Other Officers With Cabinet Rank

Brock, William E. III — U.S. Trade Representative
Bush, George — Vice President
Casey, William J. — CIA Director
Kirkpatrick, Jeane J. — U.N. Representative
Regan, Donald T. — Chief of Staff
Stockman, David A. — OMB Director

* *Indiana 8th District.*

On Balance, a Year of Taking the Initiative

Congress seized the legislative initiative from the White House in 1985 and dominated the Capitol Hill agenda to a degree unmatched since President Reagan took office in 1981.

Although Reagan was able to rescue his top domestic priority, tax-overhaul legislation, with a last-minute personal lobbying campaign, the close call was a testament to the altered relationship between the White House and Capitol Hill.

On other issues ranging from deficit reduction to federal farm spending, from South Africa sanctions to Middle East arms sales, Congress called the shots — in stark contrast to the opening year of Reagan's first term, when he clearly ran the show.

"This year came as close to congressional government as we've had in a long time. The whole agenda was set by Congress," observed political scientist Norman Ornstein of the American Enterprise Institute, a Washington think tank.

Several factors helped shift the relationship between Congress and Reagan:

- In starting his last term of office, Reagan automatically became a lame duck to many members of Congress. He no longer had to worry about reelection, but congressional Republicans did, which meant occasionally bucking the president.

In addition, Ornstein said, "the president had exhausted most of his ideas by the time he got to his second term, so he was left with a set of congressional ideas."

The exception was Reagan's tax-overhaul proposal, the major new item on his wish list. Reagan and his supporters claimed that his ability to turn around a Republican rebellion on the tax bill was evidence that he was not functioning as a lame duck.

But others pointed out that relatively few votes were changed on the second tax vote Dec. 17. And some agreed with New York Democratic Rep. Charles B. Rangel, who said, "Our president was forced to come down here, embarrass himself and ask for the support of our [Republican] colleagues."

- Reagan lost ground on several important issues because of rocky relations between Congress and a new White House advisory team led by Chief of Staff Donald T. Regan. Many members accused Regan of insensitivity to Congress, and his strategic mistakes were blamed for setbacks such as the president's first-round loss on the tax bill.

"We don't need the heavy hand of a board room dictator," said Rep. Tom Loeffler, R-Texas, alluding to Regan's background as a Wall Street executive.

The late-January job swap between Regan and new Treasury Secretary James A. Baker III also was ill-timed, Ornstein said. "They couldn't have had a worse time to turn things upside down. It was at a crucial transition time [starting Reagan's second term] and no one was in charge."

- The new Senate majority leader, Kansas Republican Robert Dole, was more willing to fight the White House than his predecessor, Sen. Howard H. Baker Jr., R-Tenn.

Although Dole helped the administration on several foreign policy and defense matters, he disagreed with Reagan on key economic issues, such as the eventual need for a tax increase to shrink the federal deficit. And while Reagan made tax reform his top priority, Dole insisted that deficit reduction come first.

Well aware that 22 GOP Senate

First Session Summary

The first session of the 99th Congress ended Dec. 20 when the House adjourned sine die at 6:40 p.m. The Senate had adjourned at 6:28 p.m.

Convened on Jan. 3, the session lasted 352 days. It ranked as the 11th longest in history. The third session of the 76th Congress, which ran from Jan. 3, 1940, to Jan. 3, 1941, was the longest on record. *(CQ Guide to Congress Third Edition, p. 410)*

The Senate met for 170 days in 1985, the House for 152 days. A total of 7,777 bills and resolutions were introduced during the session, compared with 3,764 in 1984 and 8,434 in 1983.

A total of 240 bills cleared by Congress in 1985 became public laws, 168 fewer than in 1984 and 25 more than in 1983. President Reagan vetoed six bills; one veto was overridden and the bill enacted into law without his signature.

During 1985, the House took 439 recorded votes, 31 more than in 1984. The Senate took 381 recorded votes, 106 more than in 1984.

Following are the recorded congressional vote totals between 1973 and 1985:

Year	House	Senate	Total
1985	439	381	820
1984	408	275	683
1983	498	371	869
1982	459	465	924
1981	353	483	836
1980	604	531	1,135
1979	672	497	1,169
1978	834	516	1,350
1977	706	635	1,341
1976	661	688	1,349
1975	612	602	1,214
1974	537	544	1,081
1973	541	594	1,135

seats — including his own — would be at stake in the 1986 elections, Dole was willing to break with the White House in order to protect the political flanks of Senate Republicans.

Iowa GOP Sen. Charles E. Grassley, one of those up for re-election in 1986, attributed some of the new assertiveness to "an evolution of 16 freshman Republicans [first elected in 1980] finally feeling their oats and feeling secure to cut their own swath."

Deficit Obsession

Despite the take-charge mentality on Capitol Hill, lawmakers made a historic year-end decision that could result in the abdication of some congressional power.

That decision was passage of the Gramm-Rudman-Hollings legislation, which mandated steady paring of the federal deficit over the following five years until the budget was balanced in fiscal 1991. Congress could lose much of its "power of the purse" through the bill's provision for automatic across-the-board spending cuts if the required deficit targets were not met.

What was ironic about the enactment of this program was that while it promised great strides in erasing the deficit, Congress could not take even a modest step in that direction in 1985.

On the session's last day Dec. 20, lawmakers failed to agree on a budget reconciliation package that would slice $74 billion out of the deficit over the next three years. This foreshadowed the problems they were expected to face in 1986 in achieving the new deficit targets.

Although Congress embraced the budget plan — offered by Republican Sens. Phil Gramm of Texas and Warren B. Rudman of New Hampshire and Democratic Sen. Ernest F. Hollings of South Carolina — as the best hope for future deficit control, many who shaped the measure were skeptical about its chances for working.

Referring to Howard Baker's description of Reagan's 1981 economic policies as a "riverboat gamble," Rep. Leon E. Panetta, D-Calif., said the new plan was "Las Vegas and Reno put together."

Because of Congress' yearlong obsession with the deficit, other key issues — such as renewal of the "superfund" toxic-waste cleanup program and changes in the nation's immigration laws — were pushed to the sidelines. Some members were disappointed by that development.

"No one is saying that $200 billion deficits aren't important. But there are other things that are important, and we're ignoring them," protested Rep. Mike Lowry, D-Wash.

Other Domestic Issues

Congress did spend considerable time worrying about two sectors of the economy that were still hurting in the midst of general prosperity: the nation's farmers and import-threatened industries.

Eager to give farmers a clear sense of direction, Congress at the end of the session finished an omnibus, five-year farm bill dealing with commodity price supports, soil conservation, nutrition, farm exports and farm credit.

And for workers hard hit by the trade deficit, Congress earlier in the fall passed legislation curbing textile, shoe and copper imports. But Reagan vetoed the bill, which ran counter to his free-trade philosophy.

One notable trend in 1985 was a burst of regionalism on Capitol Hill. This was evident in debates on farm and trade issues, as well as the tax reform package, where members from states producing oil, steel and timber were among the bill's leading opponents because they thought it harmed local interests.

On several domestic issues, one chamber passed legislation that was ignored or made slow progress in the other chamber.

The Senate, for example, passed bills revising immigration laws and relaxing federal gun controls. The House Judiciary Committee planned to produce an immigration reform bill in 1986, but the gun control legislation was likely to be buried there.

Likewise, the House passed legislation reauthorizing federal subsidies for low-income housing, but the Senate refused to accept the measure.

Defense, Foreign Affairs

Congress made several significant decisions in 1985 in the foreign policy and defense arena.

For the first time since 1981, it passed a full-scale authorization bill for foreign aid programs. The House reversed itself and agreed to aid rebels fighting the government in Nicaragua.

Congress also resolved a three-year battle over production of the MX missile, voting to fund the missile but limit to 50 the number of MXs that could be deployed in existing silos.

The votes on Nicaraguan "contra" aid and the MX were victories for Reagan, as were congressional decisions to resume production of chemical weapons and preserve Reagan's "strategic defense initiative," or "star wars" program.

But Reagan lost a round when arms control advocates successfully blocked for a year additional testing of the anti-satellite (ASAT) missile.

And on two key foreign policy matters, Reagan was forced to bow to congressional pressures. One was a demand for sanctions against the Pretoria government as a way to steer South Africa away from its apartheid policies. Another was a congressional move to block until 1986 Reagan's proposed sale of advanced weapons to Jordan.

Even while congressional leaders enjoyed their resurgence in 1985, some said they would be better served if Reagan took more of a lead on issues such as curbing the budget deficit.

"The system functions best when there is strong, positive presidential leadership. He is an essential actor on the legislative stage," said House Majority Whip Thomas S. Foley, D-Wash.

Following is a summary of the major legislative actions taken by Congress in 1985:

Agriculture

Omnibus Farm Bill. The president signed a bill (HR 2100 — PL 99-198) Dec. 23 reauthorizing federal farm programs for fiscal 1986-90. The measure replaced the 1981 farm bill (PL 97-98).

Both the House and Senate Dec. 18 approved a conference report calling for reduced outlays for government loans that effectively propped up prices paid for major farm crops, such as wheat, corn, cotton and rice.

At the same time, the bill maintained for at least two years existing levels of direct income subsidies to farmers, allowing only gradual reductions in the final three years.

The total estimated price tag for the five-year authorization was $169.2 billion. That included about $69.4 billion for price and income supports and $68.6 billion for food stamps.

The bill amended and added to — but did not repeal — permanent enabling legislation of 1938 and 1949, authorizing programs for commodity price supports, agricultural exports, soil conservation, farm credit, agricultural research and food assistance to low-income persons.

The House passed its version of the bill Oct. 8, and the Senate followed suit with a significantly different version on Nov. 23. In the final days of Senate debate on the measure it appeared there might be a perpetual impasse over the level of income support for farmers. Majority Leader Robert Dole, R-Kan., finally won enough votes for passage by offering a compromise that appealed to most commodity interests.

Included in the omnibus bill was a provision that exempted certain Agriculture Department export financing programs from so-called "cargo-preference" requirements that half of specified cargoes be shipped on U.S.-flag vessels.

Also included in the farm bill were the basic components of a Senate measure requiring the Agriculture Department to give away $2 billion worth of government-owned surpluses as bonuses to foreign buyers.

Farm Credit System. A bill (S 1884 — PL 99-205) to reorganize and rescue the struggling Farm Credit System rolled through Congress on a "fast track" and was signed by the president Dec. 23. The credit system was a loosely federated network of agriculture lending institutions that held $70 billion in farm debts.

After informal negotiations between leaders of the two chambers, the Senate passed the bill by voice vote Dec. 17 and the House followed suit the next day.

The bill created a new institution in the federally chartered system called the Farm Credit System Capital Corporation. The capital corporation was given the power to take over and restructure bad loans from the diffuse network of 37 banks and 800-plus farmer-owned lending cooperatives, and redistribute surplus funds among them.

In addition, the bill gave the secretary of the Treasury power to infuse federal funds into the system to shore up losses that system officials believed would total as much as $10 billion over the next two years.

A third provision restructured the Farm Credit Administration (FCA), an independent federal agency with oversight and management responsibility for the entire system. The FCA was to become an "arms-length" regulator on the model of the Federal Deposit Insurance Corporation, which regulated commercial banks. A new three-member board of directors, including a chairman/chief executive officer, would be appointed by the president and confirmed by the Senate. The existing board appointed by the banks would become an advisory panel only.

Appropriations

By Oct. 1, the start of fiscal 1986, Congress had not cleared any of the 13 regular appropriations bills. Several, however, were nearing House-Senate agreements, and six were signed into law before enactment of an omnibus spending bill (H J Res 465 — PL 99-190) to pay for most government spending through fiscal 1986.

Congress needed four short-term bills (PL 99-103, PL 99-154, PL 99-179, PL 99-184) to keep the government running while it haggled over the regular spending bills.

Not since 1975, according to Appropriations Committee aides, had Congress cleared all the appropriations bills before the start of the fiscal year. Instead, stopgap continuing resolutions were used to keep funds flowing in the new fiscal year to government agencies and departments for which Congress had not enacted separate appropriations measures.

The House passed 12 of the 13 bills; only the foreign aid bill did not come to the floor. The Senate passed 10 of the bills, failing to complete action on spending for the Defense and Interior departments and foreign operations.

By the time the omnibus spending bill was enacted Dec. 19, Congress had made considerable progress. The six bills signed into law were those for energy and water projects (HR 2959 — PL 99-141), legislative branch (HR 2942 — PL 99-151), the Department of Housing and Urban Development (HR 3038 — PL 99-160), military construction (HR 3327 — PL 99-173), the Departments of Labor, Health and Human Services and Education (HR 3424 — PL 99-178), and the Departments of Commerce, Justice, State and the judiciary (HR 2965 — PL 99-180).

Reagan vetoed one bill, for the Treasury Department and the Postal Service, and it was folded into PL 99-190. The other bills in the stopgap measure were for the Agriculture, Defense, Interior and Transportation departments, foreign aid programs, and the District of Columbia.

In addition, Congress cleared three supplemental appropriations measures for fiscal 1985. The first (HR 1239 — PL 99-10) provided famine relief aid for Africa. The second (H J Res 342 — PL 99-71) provided $1 billion in urgent aid for the Commodity Credit Corporation, which made crop loans to farmers. The third (HR 2577 — PL 99-88) included $13.02 billion for a variety of programs, including nearly $2.3 billion for aid to Middle Eastern nations and $27 million for anti-government rebels in Nicaragua.

Banking/Commerce

Banking. Six months after committee approval, legislation to allow nationwide interstate banking languished in the House Rules Committee, blocked from floor consideration by Rules Chairman Claude Pepper, D-Fla.

One bill (HR 2707) would introduce coast-to-coast branch banking July 1, 1990. On that date, states that allowed banks from their regions to open branches also would have to open their borders to banks from any other state with a regional-banking law. Pepper, whose home state of Florida had a regional-banking law, did not want his state to be forced to welcome banks from states outside the Southeast.

A related bill (HR 20) would close a loophole through which banks and other companies had circumvented the longstanding federal ban on interstate banking. The House Banking, Finance and Urban Affairs Committee approved both HR 2707 and HR 20 in June.

Banking Consumer Issues. The House Banking Committee Nov. 20 approved a bill (HR 2443) limiting the amount of time that financial institutions could hold a customer's check before giving the depositor use of the funds. (The House passed the bill Jan. 23, 1986.)

Similar proposals were introduced in the Senate, but no action was taken. The measures were aimed at what critics called "the float game," which allowed banks to withhold funds from customers for up to two weeks, on grounds that the checks might bounce, while the banks earned interest by lending the money.

The House bill would limit check holds from one day (for certain local or government checks) to no more than six days. After three years, maximum delays would be halved to three days.

Another consumer-related question before Congress was whether to cap the interest rates that financial firms charged for credit card purchases. Though interest rates had dropped to single digits in recent years, the average credit card interest was more than 18 percent, still reflecting 1970s conditions. Several bills (HR 3408, HR 1197, S 1603) to cap the rates were introduced, but they generally were considered as prods for institutions to drop their rates voluntarily; Congress usually left usury issues to the state governments.

Corporate Takeovers. The steam had gone out of most efforts to restrict hostile takeovers of businesses, in which outsiders obtained control of a company by buying a majority of its stock.

Many members of Congress were alarmed at the tactics of both raiders and their targets, such as the use of highly speculative "junk bonds" to finance takeovers. But, despite numerous committee hearings, no legislation was marked up.

The takeover fever subsided partly because corporate managers invented new defensive tactics to thwart raiders. Also, legislative proposals aimed at curbing abuses proved extremely complex.

In December, the first federal action against takeovers was taken by the Federal Reserve Board, which proposed new rules to rein in the use of junk bonds.

Also in December, Sen. Alfonse M. D'Amato, R-N.Y., chairman of the Banking, Housing and Urban Affairs Subcommittee on Securities, introduced a long-promised bill (S 1907) to tighten federal rules governing takeovers. But the bill proposed only relatively minor changes, such as requiring disclosure of a takeover bid within 24 hours, rather than 10 days required by existing law.

Daylight-Saving Time. The House voted Oct. 22 to extend daylight-saving time by at least four weeks every year, but the proposal was stalled in the Senate Commerce Committee by opposition from Midwestern senators.

The measure (HR 2095) would begin daylight-saving time on the first Sunday in April, rather than the last Sunday of the month. Clocks would return to standard time on the first Sunday in November, rather than on the last Sunday in October.

Advocates of the bill said it was a compromise, since they had pushed previously to make the change on the first Sunday in March. But opponents argued that any extension would endanger children traveling to school early in the morning.

Product Liability. Manufacturers and insurance companies, frustrated at their inability in the first session to move legislation (S 100) setting federal standards for lawsuits on defective products, hoped a new approach and a mounting insurance crisis would shake loose a bill in 1986.

S 100, which would tighten many rules for product liability suits, was sidetracked by an 8-8 tie vote May 16 in the Senate Commerce, Science and Transportation Committee.

After that, proponents tried to satisfy consumer critics by proposing a new system to enable victims to recover damages without going to court.

John C. Danforth, R-Mo., chairman of the Senate panel, Dec. 20 introduced a bill (S 1999) combining such a system with most provisions of S 100, and said he would try to move it early in the second session.

In the latter part of 1985, many small businesses had insurance policies canceled or their rates raised. While those changes were due partly to the cyclical nature of the insurance business and to the drop in interest rates on insurance companies' investments, they were expected to revive interest in the product liability bill.

Trial lawyers said they would continue to fight the bill as an infringement on states' and victims' rights.

Congress

Contested Elections. Three 1984 House races were so close that the losers contested the results.

The most contentious, in Indiana's 8th District, led to an acrimonious four-month partisan struggle. Charging election irregularities, the Democratic-controlled House Jan. 3 refused to seat Republican Richard D. McIntyre, who had been certified by the Indiana secretary of state as the winner by 34 votes over incumbent Democrat Frank McCloskey.

A House Administration Committee task force conducted a recount and, on a 2-to-1 partisan split, found McCloskey the winner by four votes. When the House settled the issue, voting 236-190 on May 1 to seat McCloskey, GOP lawmakers walked out in protest, accusing Democrats of stealing the election.

On July 24, the House dismissed a challenge by Antonio Borja Won Pat, the former non-voting Democratic delegate from Guam, against Republican Ben Blaz.

On Oct. 2, the House threw out a challenge by former GOP Rep. George Hansen against Democrat Richard H. Stallings of Idaho's 2nd District.

Senate TV. The Senate Oct. 29 moved a step closer to broadcasting its proceedings, when the Rules and Administration Committee approved S Res 28. The resolution would begin gavel-to-gavel radio broadcasts of Senate proceedings as soon as technically possible, but would delay general television coverage until after a trial period of closed-circuit TV broadcasts.

Although bills authorizing Senate broadcasts had been reported in past years, they failed on the floor. But in 1985, a majority of the Senate was said to favor moving into the television age. However, many members wanted to make changes in Senate rules — always a controversial issue — as part of the broadcasting agreement.

Honoraria. The limit on the amount members of Congress could earn from honoraria was raised from 30 percent of their annual salaries to 40 percent, a jump from $22,500 to $30,000 a year. Members' salaries were $75,100 in 1985.

The provision was included in the fiscal 1986 continuing resolution (PL 99-190) passed by Congress Dec. 19.

The new cap on the amount members could collect from speeches and articles did not affect House members because they were bound by a House rule adopted in 1981 setting the honoraria limit at 30 percent. To raise the cap, House members would have to vote to alter that rule.

Campaign Finance. The Senate Dec. 3 sidestepped a controversial proposal to limit contributions from political action committees (PACs) to congressional candidates. Instead, it agreed to revisit the issue in 1986, along with other campaign finance measures.

The proposal by David L. Boren, D-Okla., would set ceilings on total PAC contributions to House and Senate candidates and lower individual PAC gift limits to $3,000, from $5,000.

Technically, the Senate voted to keep the issue alive by agreeing not to table Boren's proposal, which he offered as an amendment to an unrelated bill dealing with low-level radioactive waste (S 655). But the effect of the vote was to remove the issue from the Senate's agenda, with assurances only that hearings would be held in 1986.

On another campaign finance issue, the House included in its massive tax-overhaul bill (HR 3838) a provision to provide up to a $100 tax credit ($200 for joint returns) for contributions to congressional candidates in a taxpayer's state. The provision would replace the existing $50 tax credit that applied to any kind of political contribution.

Defense

Defense Budget. Congress approved a total defense budget of $297.6 billion, a reduction of $24.4 billion from President Reagan's fiscal 1986 request of $322 billion.

This was $5.1 billion more than the $292.5 billion appropriated for defense in fiscal 1985, but that increase was less than the cost of inflation, so there was a real decline in the Pentagon's purchasing power for the first time since fiscal 1975.

Reagan's budget request would have provided a real defense increase of 5.9 percent. But by April popular domestic programs were facing severe budgetary constraints and looming deficits, and it was clear that Congress would approve no boost for the Pentagon above the cost of inflation. Even the inflation allowance was in doubt.

On all three of the annual measures governing the defense budget — the first concurrent budget resolution, the defense authorization bill and the defense appropriations bill (S Con Res 32, S 1160, HJ Res 465) — the Senate backed the inflation allowance, bringing the total budget up to $302 billion.

In each instance, the House approved a $292 billion total.

Conference agreements at the Senate-passed level were accepted for the budget resolution and the authorization bill, over the vigorous objections of many House Democrats. On the appropriations measure, they dug in, insisting on a figure that nearly split the difference between the totals approved by the Senate and House.

MX Missile. A three-year battle might finally have been resolved by a provision in the fiscal 1986 defense authorization bill (S 1160 — PL 99-145) limiting to 50 the number of MX missiles that could be deployed in existing missile silos.

Additional MXs would be purchased for the next several years, but only for test launches.

The new missile was designed to carry 10 nuclear warheads, each with enough accuracy and explosive power to destroy an underground Soviet missile launcher. And beginning in 1983 it became the symbolic focus of congressional debate over Reagan's nuclear weapons policy.

Arms control advocates charged that it would only escalate the nuclear-arms race. But the administration contended that the new missile was needed to offset Soviet missiles able to attack U.S. missile launchers.

A grass-roots lobbying campaign and strong efforts by the House Democratic leadership came close to blocking MX production several times. In 1983 and in 1984 they dueled Reagan to a stalemate on the issue: A decision on actually spending fiscal 1985 money for MX production was deferred until early 1985.

The administration's case was severely handicapped by Reagan's abandonment of earlier efforts to base the new missile in a way intended to protect it from a Soviet attack. But the program survived the critics' assault because of a small but influential group of predominantly Democratic defense specialists who supported production of a limited number of MXs in return for changes in the administration arms control policy.

The final showdown of that battle came in March, when both houses approved the procurement of 21 MXs in the fiscal 1985 budget — the decision that had been deferred from the previous year. With that matter settled, the moderates moved immediately to end the MX fight by "capping" the MX deployment at 50 missiles — half the number Reagan planned.

Weapons in Space. Arms control advocates failed in repeated efforts to impose substantial restraints on Reagan's anti-missile research program, the so-called "strategic defense initiative" (SDI) or "star wars." But on a closely related issue, they won a partial but significant victory: They blocked for a year additional testing of a related weapon, the anti-satellite (ASAT) missile.

Reagan requested $3.7 billion for SDI research in fiscal 1986. But, faced with budgetary constraints that would allow a defense budget no larger than had been appropriated in fiscal 1985, the fundamentally pro-Pentagon defense funding panels on Capitol Hill trimmed $1 billion from Reagan's request.

Arms control advocates, who saw SDI as a mortal threat to weapons reduction prospects, tried repeatedly in the Senate and the House to reduce SDI funding further and to impose specific limits on parts of the program that they claimed would violate existing arms control treaties.

But during debate on the defense authorization bill (S 1160) in late spring, both bodies rejected several SDI reduction amendments as well as other amendments intended to speed up the program.

The Senate and House had been deadlocked over ASAT testing since the summer of 1984. The House voted several times to bar tests against a target in space — so long as the Russians continued their ASAT test moratorium. The Senate repeatedly enacted only insignificant limits on U.S. testing.

In 1984, the two bodies compromised to allow three tests after a five-month moratorium.

In 1985, conferees on the defense authorization bill agreed in July to allow three tests through the end of fiscal 1986, and the Air Force conducted the first test shortly after that bill was signed into law. But conferees on the defense appropriations measure — a part of the omnibus continuing appropriations resolution (HJ Res 465 — PL 99-190) passed in the closing days of the session — agreed to an unqualified test moratorium.

Chemical Weapons. Offsetting their victory on ASAT testing, arms control advocates lost a battle in which they had prevailed since 1982: Congress approved production of lethal chemical weapons for the first time since 1969.

The Reagan administration and

the armed services insisted that the new weapons — called binary munitions — were needed to replace existing arms that they called militarily ineffective and unsafe to handle.

But in 1982, 1983 and 1984, the House voted against binary production. In 1982 and 1983, the Senate approved it only by narrow margins; a pair of Senate votes in 1983 required Vice President George Bush to cast a tie-breaking vote in favor of chemical weapons production. In each of those years, the House position prevailed.

In 1985, the Pentagon made a concerted effort to beat down the congressional opposition to binary production. During debate on the defense authorization bill (S 1160), the House approved binary production with conditions, including a formal request by NATO that the new weapons be produced. The House-passed strings on binary production were first weakened in the defense authorization conference and then slightly re-tightened in the conference report on the defense appropriations bill (H J Res 465 — PL 99-190).

Procurement Policy. Congress added several provisions to the defense authorization and appropriations bills (S 1160, H J Res 465) to change the way the Pentagon bought goods and services. They were a response to public unhappiness over reports of high prices, delayed schedules and potential conflicts of interest in several weapons programs.

In general, the provisions attached by the House to the defense authorization bill were more stringent than the corresponding Senate provisions and the authorization conference report reflected a compromise on the various provisions. Among the new legal requirements:

- Any presidential appointee in the Pentagon who acted as the government's principal negotiator in any dealing with a contractor would be barred for two years after leaving the government from going to work for that firm.
- Contractors were barred from billing the Pentagon for certain costs, including entertainment and lobbying and legal fees resulting from charges of contract fraud.
- The Pentagon would have to plan for the use of more than one firm to develop and produce major weapons systems.

Pentagon Reorganization. The House passed a bill (HR 3622) that would reorganize the top military hierarchy and, by all indications, the Senate Armed Services Committee was planning to push similar legislation early in 1986.

Proponents of reorganization wanted to increase the bureaucratic clout of the chairman of the Joint Chiefs of Staff and of other officials charged with coordinating the separate armed services. Under existing arrangements, the critics charged, the services' parochial interests impeded the Pentagon's ability to prepare for and conduct combat operations.

Secretary of Defense Caspar W. Weinberger and some military officers, particularly in the Navy and Marine Corps, warned that the proposed changes would narrow the range of professional military advice available to the president — thus, in effect, eroding civilian control of the military.

The House bill would designate the Joint Chiefs' chairman as principal military adviser to the president and would give him control of the Joint Staff, which served the Joint Chiefs as a body under the existing system. The measure was approved by very large margins both in the House Armed Services Committee and on the House floor.

Economic Affairs

Budget Resolution. On Aug. 1 Congress adopted the fiscal 1986 budget resolution (S Con Res 32), a nonbinding plan specifying how much money should be spent in the 1986 fiscal year in some 21 broad "functional" categories ranging from agriculture to national security to government services.

The plan called for the largest volume of program spending cuts ever, a major part of which was to be achieved through separate "reconciliation" legislation, in which laws authorizing programs were to be changed to reduce spending.

But the resolution caused much frustration among budget-minded members of Congress because the cuts did not appear to forestall the continuation of very large federal deficits.

Congress failed to enact the reconciliation changes in 1985, but some projected savings of S Con Res 32 were achieved through appropriations.

In what it did not do, the resolution negatively reflected the year's bitter budget battles, which pitted Congress against the White House, with Senate and House Republicans alternately occupying the uncomfortable middle ground.

The resolution, which projected a $171.9 billion deficit for fiscal 1986, called for neither tax increases nor reductions in the sizable Social Security program. Yet influential members of both parties in Congress thought these two options were essential ingredients of any solution, and the Republican-controlled Senate had included in its budget resolution some spending restraints on the retirement program for the elderly.

After reluctantly supporting that plan, President Reagan abruptly made common cause with House Democratic and Republican leaders against Social Security cuts, and continued to come down hard on increasing taxes.

In one significant congressional victory for members who sought to curb the defense buildup, the resolution assumed no growth — beyond allowances for inflation — in military spending for fiscal 1986. Reagan had wanted a defense growth rate of nearly 6 percent above inflation.

Debt Limit/Gramm-Rudman-Hollings. For decades, legislation raising the ceiling on the federal debt had attracted controversy, as members sought to establish their budgetary *bona fides* by objecting to what was essentially retrospective legislation, providing borrowing authority for spending decisions already made.

In 1985, the debt measure (H J Res 372 — PL 99-177) raised the ceiling to an extraordinary $2.079 trillion, from $1.824 trillion. The new level was more than double the debt when Reagan took office.

In the Senate, the debt measure also became the vehicle for a radical overhaul of budgeting procedures, designed to eliminate the federal deficit by the beginning of fiscal 1991, through a program of forced spending reductions.

Dubbed Gramm-Rudman-Hollings for its three original Senate sponsors — Republicans Phil Gramm of Texas and Warren B. Rudman of New Hampshire, and Democrat Ernest F. Hollings of South Carolina — it cleared Congress Dec. 11 and was signed into law Dec. 12.

Lengthy negotiations on the measure had delayed the debt increase and the signing prevented an immediate default for the federal government

— the first in its history.

Hours after Reagan signed the measure, Rep. Mike Synar, D-Okla., filed a suit challenging the constitutionality of a pivotal feature of the legislation. The feature drawing the suit was a procedure for automatic and uniform spending cuts, affecting about half the federal budget, if conventional budget and appropriations legislation failed to bring deficits down to levels specified in the statute.

A three-judge federal panel Feb. 7, 1986, found that section unconstitutional; the ruling was immediately appealed to the Supreme Court.

Reconciliation. Although Congress extended its 1985 session, the House and Senate still could not break a stalemate that prevented enactment in 1985 of a three-year $74 billion deficit-reduction package (HR 3128).

After a two-day standoff in which each side twice rejected the other's position, on Dec. 20 the Senate finally called it quits and voted by voice vote to send the measure, known as a reconciliation bill, back to a conference committee.

The dispute centered on a provision passed in the Republican-controlled Senate that would require manufacturers to pay a new excise tax to help pay for the "superfund" toxic-waste cleanup program.

Democrats who controlled the House, joined by Republicans reflecting President Reagan's aversion to the business tax, blocked the conference report.

The House earlier had passed a separate bill (HR 2817) that would finance superfund through increased taxes on the petrochemical industry, supplemented by general revenues.

The House did not respond to the Senate's call for a new conference before it adjourned. However, in February 1986 the superfund provisions were split off and a separate conference committee appointed to deal with that issue, freeing the other deficit-reduction provisions of the bill for further action.

Ironically, Congress' failure to enact the immediate savings in the deficit-reduction package in 1985 was due in part to its months-long preoccupation with passing the budget-balancing Gramm-Rudman-Hollings law (PL 99-177), which promised unspecified cuts in the future. A less important factor was the president's threat to veto the bill because of opposition to a number of provisions.

Tax Overhaul. As one of its last acts of the session, the House passed legislation (HR 3838) to revise the federal income tax system and to lower individual and corporate tax rates. The measure, modeled after a sweeping tax-overhaul plan proposed by Reagan in May, was sent to the Senate, where it faced an uncertain future.

The bill's voyage through the House was bumpy and unpredictable. The legislation, opposed by a wide range of interest groups, was thought to be near death several times during a two-month markup in the Ways and Means Committee. But Chairman Dan Rostenkowski, D-Ill., managed to negotiate enough changes to Reagan's original plan to keep the effort alive.

A bigger threat awaited on the House floor, however. In an unexpected defeat for the president, House Republicans banded together in opposition to the legislation, and a rule to bring the measure to the floor was defeated by a vote of 202-223. Only 14 Republicans voted "aye." Many in the party said they were annoyed they had not been consulted by the administration, which had worked closely with Rostenkowski on the bill. They also charged that the final product did not live up to Reagan's initial goals of simplicity, fairness and economic growth.

But the White House stepped up its lobbying efforts — which included a rare trip by Reagan to Capitol Hill to stump for his No. 1 domestic priority — and the vote was turned around. The second time, 70 Republicans joined 188 Democrats to pass the rule 258-168.

The legislation was passed subsequently by voice vote.

Imputed Interest. After a lengthy and convoluted debate, Congress cleared legislation (HR 2475 — PL 99-121) to revise a little-noticed provision in the 1984 Deficit Reduction Act (PL 98-369) dealing with the taxation of low-rate, seller-financed real estate transactions.

The original provision was intended to prevent tax avoidance through the use of such transactions, but critics claimed the limits were too severe and hurt honest taxpayers as well. Most of the opposition came from the real estate industry, farmers and others who often resorted to seller financing.

In response, Congress agreed to reduce the amount of interest the Internal Revenue Service would "impute" for tax purposes on such transactions, especially those involving seller financing of $2.8 million or less.

To pay for the cost of the change, the measure also extended from 18 to 19 years the depreciation period for real estate investments.

Auto Record Keeping. Responding to angry constituents, Congress repealed a 1984 law requiring taxpayers to keep daily logs when claiming tax breaks for business use of automobiles, home computers or other equipment.

Members said they never envisioned the tough record-keeping rules issued by the Internal Revenue Service when they passed the provision as part of the Deficit Reduction Act of 1984 (PL 98-369).

Under the repeal legislation (HR 1869 — PL 99-44), cleared May 16, taxpayers still were required to show some proof to back up their tax-deduction claims. But the Treasury Department said more than $885 million in tax cheating likely would result by 1990 from the record-keeping repeal. To help pay for the loss, Congress agreed in the bill to limit tax breaks for the business use of high-priced automobiles.

Line-Item Veto. After failing three times to stop a filibuster in July, Senate leaders set aside plans to bring to the floor a bill (S 43) giving Reagan authority to veto spending for individual programs in appropriations bills.

The measure was opposed by most Democrats and several moderate Republicans who charged it would mean an unconstitutional and unnecessary shift of power from Congress to the president. Led by Senate Appropriations Committee Chairman Mark O. Hatfield, R-Ore., opponents refused to let the Senate vote on a motion to bring the bill to the floor.

Sponsor Mack Mattingly, R-Ga., said the veto power, sought by Reagan, was needed to bring government spending under control.

Education

Student Loans. Congress refused to go along with Reagan administration proposals to limit sharply the eligibility of middle-class students for federal loans and grants to help pay tuition. However, more modest restrictions were proposed for college student aid under legislation reauthorizing programs under the Higher Education Act through fiscal 1991.

The bills (HR 3700, S 1965) were approved by the House and by a Senate subcommittee.

Both bills would require all applicants for low-interest Guaranteed Student Loans to pass a financial needs test in order to qualify. Under existing law, only students with more than $30,000 annual family income were subject to a needs test.

The House version would authorize about $10.5 billion in fiscal 1987, including increased Pell Grants for low-income students.

S 1965, approved by the Labor and Human Resources Subcommittee on Education, also increased Pell Grants but would bar students from receiving the grants if their family income was more than $30,000 a year.

Handicapped Education. Congress failed to finish work on legislation (S 415) that would force many school districts to pay the legal fees of parents who won court disputes to enforce the education rights of the handicapped.

Both the House and Senate approved versions of the bill, which would overturn a 1984 Supreme Court decision that parents who prevailed in court could not be awarded attorneys' fees under the Education for All Handicapped Children Act (PL 94-142). *(1984 Almanac p. 9-A)*

However, House and Senate negotiators failed to iron out differences between the two versions before Congress adjourned. House negotiators in particular opposed a Senate provision that would impose new limits on fee awards to attorneys who worked for publicly funded legal aid groups.

Energy

Low-Level Radioactive Waste. Congress Dec. 19 cleared and sent to the president a bill (HR 1083 — PL 99-240) imposing strict deadlines for states to set up their own disposal facilities for low-level nuclear waste. The action averted a looming crisis that could have left hospitals, universities, industries and nuclear electric utilities with no place to dispose of the large volumes of slightly radioactive wastes they produced.

The three states that provided disposal facilities for all the other states had threatened to stop accepting out-of-state waste unless other states took action to develop individual or regional disposal sites.

Approved as part of the legislation were seven interstate agreements among 37 states for developing regional disposal sites.

HR 1083 set a Jan. 1, 1993, deadline for the states to open their own sites, as well as a series of intermediate deadlines for developing the sites. States missing those deadlines faced rapidly escalating surcharges, and could be denied access altogether to the three existing sites.

Synfuels Rescission. Congress dismantled the U.S. Synthetic Fuels Corporation, ending the program to commercialize technologies for making abundant resources such as coal and shale into other fuels.

Language rescinding most of the synfuels corporation's $7.3 billion in remaining funds was part of the fiscal 1986 continuing appropriations bill, signed by the president Dec. 19 (H J Res 465 — PL 99-190).

The administration Dec. 12 abandoned its stance of formal neutrality on the issue and came out in favor of the rescission. The House had voted to kill the corporation entirely, but the Senate Dec. 6 had narrowly voted to keep it alive with only $3.6 billion. Conferees on H J Res 465 Dec. 16 decided to abolish the corporation.

The conferees also agreed to appropriate $400 million over three years for a program to be administered by the Energy Department for research and development on ways to burn coal with less pollution.

Offshore Oil. Congress debated several issues related to offshore oil and gas drilling, but scarcely settled any of them by the end of the year.

Offshore leasing bans for California and other states had been included in the annual Interior Department appropriations bill for the past four years. Some members of the California delegation sought a leasing ban again in 1985 when negotiations with Interior Secretary Donald P. Hodel broke down. But no such ban was put in H J Res 465, the fiscal 1986 continuing appropriations measure, although the bill did include language encouraging the parties to continue talks.

Two provisions that would bring windfall revenues to coastal oil states were included in the fiscal 1986 budget reconciliation bill (HR 3128), which did not clear in 1985. One provided for disposition of some $5.8 billion in leasing revenues that had piled up in escrow during a seven-year dispute between federal and state governments over how to split the money. Another divided up $50 million a year of undisputed federal revenues among coastal and Great Lakes states.

Environment

Superfund Reauthorization. The "superfund" hazardous-waste cleanup program began sputtering to a halt during the fall as Congress failed to enact reauthorization legislation (HR 2005) including the taxes to finance the program.

Both the House and Senate passed superfund bills, but no conference to reconcile their differences was held. Instead, the issue of who should pay for superfund was fought out in the context of the deficit-reduction bill (HR 3128). The Senate wanted to impose a new general tax on manufacturers, and added its tax provisions to HR 3128. But the House wanted to continue to keep the major burden on oil and chemical companies, and it repeatedly rejected the Senate bill.

Taxes to pay for the cleanup of abandoned toxic-chemical dumps expired Sept. 30, 1985. The Environmental Protection Agency (EPA), which administered the program, stopped signing new cleanup contracts in late summer to preserve the remaining funds for emergency work.

The House passed its $10 billion superfund bill Dec. 10, after committee leaders accepted changes that environmental groups had unsuccessfully sought in the House Energy and Commerce Committee. The Senate passed its $7.5 billion measure Sept. 26. Both bills would fund the program for 1986-90.

Safe Drinking Water. Although both the House and Senate passed bills to strengthen federal controls over the purity of drinking water, no conference was held to resolve differences between them.

One of the disputes holding up agreement on a bill was over regulation of the groundwater that fed the wells from which many people's water supply was drawn.

The House bill (HR 1650), passed by voice vote June 17, required states within three years to give the EPA plans for protection of underground sources of drinking water. The Senate bill (S 124), passed May 16, included no such requirement.

Both bills would force EPA to set health standards for scores of toxic chemicals in drinking water. EPA had had authority to do so since 1974 under the Safe Drinking Water Act (PL 93-523), but had set limits for only 22 chemicals. The Reagan administration opposed both House and Senate bills, saying regulation of drinking water should be left to the states.

Water Pollution Control. Congress adjourned without a House-Senate conference agreement on reauthorization of the Clean Water Act (PL 92-500).

Two conflicts remained unsettled. One was a dispute among states over how to allocate money for construction of sewage treatment plants; the other pitted Congress against the White House over the level of funding for the program. Congress wanted to continue a $2.4 billion annual spending level; the White House proposed phasing out the program.

The House passed its bill (HR 8) July 23, authorizing $21 billion in grants and loans for the sewer program through 1994 and keeping the existing formula for dividing funds among the states.

The Senate bill (S 1128), passed June 13, authorized $18 billion for the sewer program through 1994. It changed the existing formula in favor of Southern and Western states, which claimed that rapid growth over the previous decade entitled them to an increased share.

Water Projects. A landmark agreement in June between Senate leaders and Reagan administration budget officials held out promise that construction could start on new federal water projects in 1985 after a nine-year hiatus. But with an omnibus authorizing bill not enacted by year's end, Congress still had to settle the key issue of how the federal government and local beneficiaries should share costs.

The maneuvering took place on two interlocked pieces of legislation: an omnibus authorizing bill (HR 6, S 1567), which passed the House but not the Senate, and a fiscal 1985 supplemental appropriations bill, which cleared Congress Aug. 1 and was signed into law (HR 2577 — PL 99-88).

Congress appropriated funds in the supplemental appropriation for some projects that had not yet been authorized but added language that kept the money from being spent until enactment of authorizing legislation with cost-sharing formulas or the signing of federal-local cost-sharing agreements. Spending on authorized projects was allowed.

The administration opposed new water spending unless local beneficiaries paid a greater share of costs. The supplemental only passed the Senate after the administration and Senate leaders agreed on a general cost-sharing formula. But that formula had to be made part of the authorizing bill.

The Senate Environment and Public Works Committee put the formula into the $12 billion authorizing measure it approved July 18. But the measure was not approved until Dec. 11 by the Senate Finance Committee, which had jurisdiction over new port user fees and increased barge fuel taxes that were part of the agreement.

The House passed its $20 billion water projects authorizing bill (HR 6) on Nov. 13, but without the barge fuel tax increase the administration demanded. The administration also objected to the higher funding level in the House bill.

Foreign Policy

Foreign Aid. Congress in 1985 took a big step toward restoring its process for considering foreign assistance programs. For the first time since 1981, Congress passed a full-scale authorizations bill for foreign aid. That measure (S 960 — PL 99-83) included overall policy guidance and a total of $12.8 billion annually in authorizations for military, economic and development aid programs in fiscal 1986-87.

Passage of the bill was made possible by the skillful legislative maneuvering of Senate Foreign Relations Committee Chairman Richard G. Lugar, R-Ind., and House Foreign Affairs Committee Chairman Dante B. Fascell, D-Fla. In previous years, both committees had produced aid bills, but only the House panel had been able to get its measure passed on the floor.

In contrast to that success, Congress once again failed to produce a separate appropriations bill for foreign aid programs. Instead, those appropriations were included in an omnibus continuing resolution (H J Res 465 — PL 99-190) for fiscal 1986. The main practical effect of the lack of a regular bill was that neither chamber of Congress had to vote directly on foreign aid spending. House leaders had said foreign aid would suffer major cuts if there was an up-or-down vote on a bill.

The continuing resolution appropriated $15 billion for foreign aid; the total amount nearly matched Reagan's request, but the bill made substantial cuts from the president's military aid programs. The appropriations bill included several programs (particularly U.S. contributions to international development banks) that were not part of the authorizations legislation.

Nicaraguan 'Contras.' A badly timed trip to Moscow by Nicaraguan President Daniel Ortega changed the political climate in Washington on the issue of U.S. support for guerrilla forces seeking to overthrow Ortega's government. The House in late April rejected a Reagan appeal for resumed aid to the Nicaraguan contras. A few days later, Ortega flew to Moscow seeking financing for his regime, angering House Democrats who had opposed aid for the contras.

On June 12, the House reversed itself and agreed to supply $27 million for the guerrillas. Although called "humanitarian" aid, most of the money was set aside for uniforms and other logistical support for the "contras." The money was included in a fiscal 1985 supplemental appropriations bill (HR 2577 — PL 99-88). A related provision established a procedure for rapid congressional consideration of Reagan's expected request for follow-up aid to the contras in 1986.

Congress in November expanded U.S. backing of the contras by approving an intelligence authorizations bill (HR 2419 — PL 99-169) that allowed the CIA to give them advice and intelligence information.

South Africa Sanctions. Spurred by demonstrations at the South African Embassy in Washington and by growing racial violence in South Africa, Congress in 1985 forced Reagan to impose limited economic and political sanctions against Pretoria's white-minority government.

Both chambers passed legislation (HR 1460) that would have imposed sanctions and, implicitly, rejected Reagan's policy of "constructive engagement" with South Africa. Yielding to the political pressure created by that legislation, Reagan on Sept. 9 signed an executive order imposing his own set of sanctions, such as banning sales in the United States of South African gold coins and barring new bank loans to the government of South Africa.

Israel, Egypt Aid. Responding to a growing economic crisis in Israel, and to a belated Israeli government plan to deal with it, Congress in 1985 approved an extraordinary $1.5 billion economic aid supplemental for Israel. For political "balance," Congress also approved $500 million in extra economic aid for Egypt. Both amounts were included in a supplemental funding bill (HR 2577 — PL 99-88), and were to be spent over fiscal 1985-86.

The supplemental aid was in addition to $3 billion in regular economic and military aid the United States provided Israel each year; the Egypt aid topped a regular $2.3 billion annual program.

At year's end, some Senate supporters tried to get another $500 million military aid bonus for Israel. That move failed because of the overall budget crunch and because of strong opposition by the administration.

Jordan Arms. Faced with an all-but-certain defeat in Congress, Reagan in October agreed to legislation (S J Res 228 — PL 99-162) that postponed a major arms sale to Jordan at least until early 1986. Reagan had notified Congress of his intent to sell Jordan advanced warplanes, missiles and other weapons — in spite of congressional warnings against such a sale until there was more progress in Middle East peace talks.

When about two-thirds of all members of Congress endorsed bills rejecting the sale, Reagan agreed to a compromise that delayed the sale at least until March 1, 1986, unless "direct and meaningful" peace talks between Jordan and Israel were under way. In theory, he was free to pursue the sale after March 1; however, congressional leaders warned that he would face a major battle if he did so in the absence of progress on peace.

The fiscal 1986 continuing resolution (H J Res 465 — PL 99-190) established a procedure for averting a Senate filibuster of any resolution to block the arms sale.

Police Training. Reagan failed to win congressional approval for a new program of aid to police forces in Central America. He labeled the program a "counter-terrorism" effort, in response to the June 20 killing in El Salvador of four U.S. Marines and several others. But critics said Reagan wanted to give aid to police and security forces that for years had been responsible for serious human rights violations, especially in El Salvador and Guatemala.

Reagan in September requested $54 million for police aid and supplemental military aid to five Central American countries. The proposal never advanced anywhere in the House. After long debate, the Senate Foreign Relations Committee on Dec. 5 approved a stripped-down version (S 1915) allowing only $22 million in police aid for the region but under conditions designed to guard against U.S. association with repressive security forces. That measure never reached the floor for procedural reasons and because of opposition by Sen. Tom Harkin, D-Iowa.

Genocide Treaty. Backers had viewed 1985 as the best chance ever to secure Senate approval of a United Nations treaty declaring genocide to be a crime. Sen. Jesse Helms, R-N.C., long the treaty's staunchest opponent, supported it in April when the Foreign Relations Committee attached several conditions that he and other conservatives said would protect the U.S. Constitution. But when leaders tried on Dec. 5 to take the treaty to the Senate floor, Helms objected and threatened a filibuster — thus killing it for another year.

The treaty (Exec O, 81st Cong, 1st Sess) had been before the Senate since 1949, and every president since Harry S Truman sought its approval.

State Department Funds. Congress effectively froze spending by the State Department and related agencies in legislation passed during 1985. An authorizations bill (HR 2068 — PL 99-93), cleared on Aug. 1, allowed $7.6 billion over fiscal 1986-87 for the State Department's operations and for the United States Information Agency, the Arms Control and Disarmament Agency and the Board for International Broadcasting.

A follow-up appropriations bill for fiscal 1986 (HR 2965 — PL 99-180) contained $3.5 billion for those agencies.

Embassy Security. The Reagan administration failed to follow through on its pledge to seek several billion dollars from Congress to rebuild 126 U.S. diplomatic posts overseas that were vulnerable to terrorist attacks. A State Department commission headed by former CIA Deputy Director Adm. Bobby R. Inman in June recommended the huge building program as one of several steps to reduce U.S. vulnerability to terrorism. Secretary of State George P. Shultz on July 24 endorsed the recommendation, but the Office of Management and Budget held up submission of a presidential request for months, apparently for budget reasons. (The request was included in the fiscal 1987 budget, released Feb. 7, 1986.)

Angolan Rebels. Opposition by the State Department headed off congressional approval of "humanitarian" aid to a rebel group called UNITA that was battling the leftist government of Angola. However, President Reagan reportedly was ready at year's end to initiate his own aid program for the rebels, to be run by the CIA.

Congress did agree, in the foreign aid authorizations bill (S 960 — PL 99-83) to repeal a 1976 law, called the "Clark amendment," that barred U.S. intervention in Angola. That law was one of the principal legislative restraints on presidential action that resulted from the Vietnam War.

China Nuclear Accord. Congress approved a 30-year agreement providing for sales of nuclear equipment and supplies to China, in spite of widespread concern on Capitol Hill that the agreement did not contain tough enough provisions to ensure Chinese cooperation in halting the spread of nuclear weapons. A bill (S J Res 238 — PL 99-183) approving the agreement but imposing conditions on nuclear exports to China was cleared on Dec. 11.

One attempt to impose tougher conditions on nuclear exports to China failed on Dec. 16, when conferees deleted a Senate-passed amendment to the fiscal 1986 continuing appropriations resolution (H J Res 465). That amendment, sponsored by John Glenn, D-Ohio, would have required China to accept international standards for ensuring the peaceful use of all its nuclear power facilities.

Intelligence Authorizations. For the first time since 1981, Congress made substantial cuts in President Reagan's request for spending by the

CIA and other intelligence agencies. The secret budgets for those agencies were included in a fiscal 1986 intelligence authorizations bill (HR 2419 — PL 99-169) and in the defense appropriations section of the fiscal 1986 continuing resolution (H J Res 465 — PL 99-190). Members said those bills allowed only modest spending boosts for the intelligence agencies, compared with Reagan's request for increases averaging about 10 percent.

Micronesia Compact. Shortly before it adjourned, Congress passed the Compact of Free Association with Micronesia (H J Res 187 — PL 99-239), a measure that bestowed limited autonomy on much of that Pacific island region while retaining U.S. military interests. The compact still had to be reviewed by the island governments and endorsed by the United Nations before it took effect.

Passage of the compact came more than two months after the Oct. 1 expiration of the U.S. lease on the Kwajalein missile range in the Marshall Islands, the Pentagon's main testing ground for the MX missile and certain parts of President Reagan's space-based defense plan. The compact included a 30-year renewal on Kwajalein.

The House gave final approval to the measure Dec. 11, and the Senate passed it Dec. 13.

Both chambers made numerous changes in the compact to tighten up trade and tariff concessions negotiated by the administration. Lawmakers feared original terms of the compact would have created a new tax haven for wealthy Americans and a major trade loophole for Asian imports.

Philippines. Congress and the Reagan administration worked together in 1985 to pressure Philippine President Ferdinand E. Marcos to make reforms. Congress took the lead, voting in two separate bills to reduce Reagan's request for military aid to the Marcos regime in fiscal 1986. First, in a foreign aid authorizations bill (S 960 — PL 99-83), Congress set a $70 million ceiling on that aid, $30 million less than Reagan wanted. At the end of the session, in the continuing appropriations resolution (H J Res 465 — PL 99-190), Congress reduced the aid further, to $55 million.

The administration exerted its own pressure with a series of tough statements warning that a rapidly growing communist insurgency could overwhelm Marcos if he did not reform his country's economic, political and military systems. Reagan also sent Sen. Paul Laxalt, R-Nev., one of his closest advisers, to Manila with a similar warning. Possibly in response to those urgings, Marcos called presidential elections for Feb. 7, 1986.

African Famine Relief. Early in 1985, pictures of starving children in feeding camps in Ethiopia, the Sudan and other African countries helped lead Congress to approve an emergency relief bill. Cleared on April 2, the bill (HR 1239 — PL 99-10), appropriated $784 million for food, seeds, clothing and shelter. That was about three times what President Reagan had requested.

By year's end, there were reports that the emergency food shipments, better-than-usual rainfalls and unexpectedly good harvests had sharply curtailed starvation in Africa — eliminating the need for yet another emergency relief bill.

Government Operations

Small Business Administration. Despite President Reagan's attempts to kill the Small Business Administration (SBA), Congress voted to preserve the agency, although at sharply reduced funding levels.

The budget reconciliation bill (HR 3128), which did not clear in 1985, would reauthorize the SBA for three years, while saving a total of $2.5 billion. The savings would come primarily from eliminating most direct loans to businesses and barring farmers from receiving SBA disaster loans.

Reagan had proposed abolishing the agency and transferring some functions to the Commerce Department. But the Senate voted 94-3 for a bill (S 408) reauthorizing the agency, and the House added the version (HR 2540) of a reauthorization reported by the Small Business Committee to the budget reconciliation package.

Federal Pensions. Members gave themselves a new deadline to enact a new retirement system for federal employees hired after Jan. 1, 1984, who, unlike their predecessors, paid Social Security taxes.

The fiscal 1986 continuing appropriations bill (H J Res 465 — PL 99-190) moved the deadline from Dec. 31, 1985, to April 30, 1986. Failure to meet it would mean that the newer workers would be forced to pay 7 percent of their salaries toward the existing retirement plan, on top of the 5.7 percent they paid for Social Security.

The Senate passed a bill (HR 2672) to set up a new system, and the House Post Office and Civil Service Committee approved a similar measure. House leaders agreed to bypass floor action and go directly to conference with the Senate, but conferees were unable to meet because of the crush of end-of-session business.

Both bills would give the newer workers benefits from three sources: Social Security, a basic pension in which benefits were based on salary and years of service, and a new thrift plan that would enable workers to set aside before taxation a portion of their wages toward retirement, matched with a government contribution.

But the Senate bill would cut the government's cost of pensions from 25 percent of payroll to 21.9 percent, primarily by raising the retirement age and reducing cost-of-living allowances for some retirees. The House bill would boost costs to 25.4 percent.

Veterans' Disability COLA. After weeks of disagreement, Congress eventually approved a 3.1 percent fiscal 1986 cost-of-living allowance (COLA) for disabled veterans (HR 1538 — PL 99-238).

The Senate passed a bill (S 1887) authorizing the COLA at 3.1 percent, the same level as Social Security recipients'. But the House argued that disabled veterans should receive a higher COLA, since they received less than Social Security recipients in fiscal 1985. House members also said it was too late in the session to consider the other issues in the Senate bill. The House passed HR 1538, authorizing a 3.4 percent COLA.

Senators insisted on the lower figure and amended the House bill to provide 3.1 percent, and to include a one-year authorization of a job training program for Vietnam-era veterans. The House accepted the amendment.

Veterans' Health Care. For the first time, Congress agreed to place a means test on veterans using Veterans Administration (VA) health care facilities and to require the VA to bill private insurers for care provided to veterans who carried insurance.

But the measures, expected to

save $1.2 billion over three years, were included in a budget reconciliation bill (HR 3128) that did not clear in 1985.

The Reagan administration proposed restricting access to VA facilities for veterans without service-connected injuries to those with incomes below $15,000. HR 3128 would require the VA to admit those patients, as well as veterans with service-connected disabilities, former prisoners of war and veterans from World War I and before.

But the legislation also would allow the VA to admit patients with incomes above $20,000, if space and resources were available, provided they paid an amount equal to the co-payment required by Medicare ($492 in fiscal 1986) for three months of treatment.

Pay Equity. The House, for the second year in a row, voted to require a study of the federal work force to determine if differences in pay arose because of sex discrimination. But as in 1984, the Senate took no action after the Governmental Affairs Subcommittee on Civil Service held hearings.

The House passed the so-called "pay-equity" bill (HR 3008) Oct. 9 by a 259-162 vote, far short of the 413-6 vote for the 1984 measure. Sponsors attributed the larger negative vote to an aggressive lobbying campaign against the bill by business groups and the Reagan administration, which called the measure an intrusion into the labor market.

But sponsors said the study was necessary to determine if wages were influenced by sex, race or national origin, and noted that the federal work force had not been studied since 1923.

Devine Nomination. The Senate Aug. 1 confirmed Constance Horner as director of the Office of Personnel Management, after her predecessor, Donald J. Devine, withdrew his name from consideration for a second four-year term.

Devine, whose relations with federal employee groups and Congress were often stormy, faced three days of angry questioning from Democrats on the Senate Governmental Affairs Committee, who charged him with trying to politicize the civil service agency.

But Republicans as well as Democrats objected to a memorandum Devine signed on his last day in office, delegating to himself authority to run the agency while he served as executive assistant to the acting director, Loretta Cornelius. Cornelius testified that Devine had asked her to say that she knew about the memo when in fact she did not. Devine withdrew his name the next day.

By contrast, the nomination of Horner, formerly associate director of the Office of Management and Budget, sailed through the committee and the full Senate. In her first months in office, she reached an agreement with members of Congress on an issue that was one of Devine's priorities for years: a pay-for-performance system for federal workers.

Health

Medicare, Medicaid. A major element of the budget reconciliation measure (HR 3128) Congress failed to enact before the end of the session was a proposal to reduce by $11.2 billion in fiscal 1986-88 projected outlays under Medicare, the federal health insurance program for the elderly.

Although the Medicare provisions had bipartisan support, the compromise bill stalled short of enactment amid controversy over provisions for financing the "superfund" toxic-waste removal program.

Most of the bill's Medicare savings would be made through limits on reimbursements to doctors and hospitals.

Having failed to pass the budget package, Congress cleared another measure (HR 4006 — PL 99-201) extending through March 15 the existing freeze on Medicare reimbursements to hospitals and physicians.

The budget measure also included proposals affecting Medicaid, the federal-state health care program for the poor. Among other things, the bill would liberalize eligibility for low-income pregnant women.

Family Planning. Legislation renewing federal aid to family planning clinics stalled amid controversy over funding of abortion counseling, but the program was kept alive through stopgap appropriations measures.

The focus of controversy was a plan by Sen. Orrin G. Hatch, R-Utah, and Rep. Jack F. Kemp, R-N.Y., to cut off aid to family planning clinics that made referrals for abortions.

Kemp was prevented from offering the amendment when the House considered a bill (HR 2369) to reauthorize Title X of the Public Health Service Act. Sponsors brought HR 2369 to the floor June 18 under special rules that barred amendments. However, the bill failed to garner the two-thirds majority needed to pass under the special procedures.

In the Senate, the Labor and Human Resources Committee Dec. 11 approved a compromise bill (S 881) to extend family planning aid through fiscal 1989. Hatch, chairman of the committee, agreed to back down from his anti-abortion amendment in order to win inclusion of special funding for Utah's family planning program.

Biomedical Research. Congress rebuffed the White House by overriding President Reagan's veto of legislation (HR 2409 — PL 99-158) reauthorizing the National Institutes of Health.

The measure extended through fiscal 1988 selected programs within the biomedical research agency and established a new institute for the study of arthritis. It also included guidelines for research involving human fetuses and laboratory animals.

In his Nov. 8 veto message, Reagan said the bill's mandates represented an effort to exert "undue political control" on decisions that he believed should be left to scientists.

But the legislation, which was the culmination of at least five years of debate over the NIH authorization, enjoyed broad support in Congress. The votes to override Reagan's veto were taken Nov. 12 by the House and Nov. 20 by the Senate.

Drug Exports. Legislation (S 1848) was sent to the Senate floor, but was not taken up, that would lift a ban on the export of U.S.-made drugs that had not been approved for use in the United States by the Food and Drug Administration (FDA).

Advocates of the measure argued that the export ban had not kept the drugs from reaching foreign markets since they could be sold overseas if U.S. firms manufactured them abroad.

The bill, approved Nov. 19 by the Senate Labor and Human Resources Committee, specified when such drugs could be exported, such as when they had been approved by another country with a stringent drug regulatory system. It also included provisions to prevent the illicit shipment of drugs to underdeveloped countries that lacked the ability to ensure their safe use.

Those safeguards were included to win the endorsement of the com-

mittee's ranking Democrat, Edward M. Kennedy of Massachusetts. But the changes did not satisfy consumer groups, which argued that manufacturers should not sell abroad drugs that had not been certified as safe and effective by the FDA.

Vaccine Compensation. Legislation (S 827) to compensate people who suffered adverse reactions to vaccines stalled without action in the Senate Labor and Human Resources Committee, despite pressure from parents seeking compensation for their children's injuries.

Concern focused primarily on the victims of the rare but severe side effects of DPT (diphtheria, pertussis and tetanus) vaccine.

Lawmakers also faced pressure from pharmaceutical companies to limit their liability in vaccine-injury cases — a thorny issue that critics feared would set a precedent for victim compensation policy in other areas such as exposure to asbestos.

The Senate Labor and Human Resources Committee held a hearing on the bill. Despite several attempts to schedule markup sessions, no further action was taken.

S 827 would allow victims of vaccine injuries to choose between seeking compensation through a no-fault system or pursuing their claims in court. Sen. Robert T. Stafford, R-Vt., a member of the Labor Committee, strongly objected to requiring victims to give up their right to sue to receive compensation from the government.

Housing/Community Development

Housing Programs. Pervasive divisions between the House and Senate stymied an attempt to enact a housing authorization bill to expand existing programs or start new ones.

The House included in its budget reconciliation package (HR 3128) a housing authorization providing $14.3 billion for housing, including new programs such as aid for construction of new owner-occupied housing and for the homeless. But the Senate refused to accept the housing provisions.

In his fiscal 1986 budget, President Reagan had proposed no new units of assisted housing. But the fiscal 1986 appropriations bill (HR 3038 — PL 99-160), signed by the president on Nov. 25, provided 97,000 new units.

Community Development. Congress rejected President Reagan's proposals to abolish several community development programs, but it cut funding sharply.

In appropriations bills for fiscal 1986, Congress approved $201 million for the Economic Development Administration (EDA), which provided grants for public works improvements; $330 million for Urban Development Action Grants (UDAG), which aided development projects in distressed urban areas; and $120 million for the Appalachian Regional Commission (ARC), which supported public works and highway developments in the 13-state Appalachian region.

The House also passed a bill (HR 10) reauthorizing EDA and ARC. The measure would tighten eligibility for EDA funds, phase out the ARC development program over five years, and end the highway program after seven years.

There was no comparable Senate bill.

Congress postponed until fiscal 1987 Reagan's plan to kill general revenue sharing, which funneled money to 39,000 local governments with no strings attached. Reagan had proposed abolishing it in 1985, arguing that a federal government with a deficit could not afford to support local governments. But Congress agreed to maintain it, after cutting it by 8.36 percent, and to eliminate it when its authorization expired Sept. 30, 1986.

Reagan's proposal to offer tax incentives to businesses that located in designated "enterprise zones" in distressed urban or rural areas was not enacted. But the housing authorization bill, approved by the House as part of the budget reconciliation package (HR 3128), would authorize the secretary of housing and urban development to designate 100 zones, in which businesses would be eligible for regulatory relief.

Human Services

Nutrition. Responding to reports of an increase in hunger in America, Congress voted to expand food stamp eligibility and benefits, but was unable to complete action on a bill to expand child nutrition programs.

The omnibus farm bill (HR 2100 — PL 99-198) added $523 million over five years above what would have been spent on the food stamp program if existing levels were extended. Most of the additional funds were required by a boost in the amount of deductions from income that families receiving food stamps could claim, which increased their benefits, and from raising the level of assets a household could have in order to qualify for food stamps.

The bill also required states to set up employment and training programs for eligible food stamp recipients, and called for computerization of the program in order to reduce the number of erroneous payments.

The House and Senate passed separate versions of a bill (HR 7) reauthorizing expiring child nutrition programs. The House bill would boost spending for child nutrition by increasing the federal contribution to school breakfasts by 7 cents per meal and by increasing the authorization for the special supplemental feeding program for needy pregnant women, infants and children (WIC) by $60 million. The Senate version did not add funding. Conferees were unable to meet at the end of the session.

AFDC Changes. Congress agreed to expand welfare benefits for the unemployed. But the budget reconciliation bill (HR 3128), which would require all states to provide Aid to Families with Dependent Children (AFDC) benefits to two-parent families in which the principal wage-earner was unemployed, failed to clear. In 1985, half the states provided benefits to those families; most AFDC recipients were in one-parent families.

The House version of HR 3128 required the remaining states to provide benefits to unemployed parents. The Senate version contained no similar provision. Conferees agreed to delay the provision until 1988.

Labor

Conservation Corps. For the third year in a row, the House passed legislation to create a new program to put unemployed teenagers to work on conservation projects — primarily rehabilitating public and Indian lands.

The measure (HR 99) passed July 11 by only a two-vote margin. It was not considered by the Senate. President Reagan pocket-vetoed a similar bill passed in 1984.

Overtime Pay. Congress cleared a bill Nov. 7 to ease the impact of a February Supreme Court decision requiring overtime pay for state and local government workers.

Reagan signed the measure (S 1570 — PL 99-150) Nov. 13. Instead of requiring pay for overtime, the new law allowed public employers to provide time-and-a-half compensatory time off for workers who put in overtime. Such compensation must be given to all employees, except police and firefighters, who would have to work a longer period of time to be eligible for overtime compensation.

In the case of *Garcia v. San Antonio Metropolitan Transit Authority*, the Supreme Court ruled that the Fair Labor Standards Act (FLSA) applied to state and local government workers, reversing a 1976 decision that had exempted those workers from coverage. The FLSA set minimum pay and overtime requirements for workers. The law enacted Nov. 13 continued coverage of state and local employees under the FLSA, but it made clear that compensatory time was allowed for overtime work instead of pay.

The bill set a cap of 480 hours of compensatory time earned for public safety and seasonal employees. Overtime hours worked after this cap would have to be compensated in cash. Other employees, such as clerical workers, would get cash after working 240 hours of overtime.

Unemployment Compensation. Legislation to phase out special assistance for the long-term unemployed was signed by Reagan April 4 (HR 1866 — PL 99-15).

Congress decided not to press for continuation of the program because of Reagan's repeated veto threats, although some House Democrats were angry about the bill; they wanted to challenge Senate Republicans and Reagan by pushing for an extension of the program.

Under HR 1866, no new beneficiaries could qualify for the supplemental compensation program, which provided up to 14 weeks of additional aid for jobless people who had exhausted regular unemployment benefits. To cushion the effects of ending the program, the bill allowed people already on the rolls to draw their remaining benefits.

Plant Closing. A strong business lobby was critical Nov. 21 in derailing House legislation (HR 1616) designed to cushion the impact of plant closings.

By 203-208, the House rejected a watered-down version of the bill that had been rewritten in an effort to pick up business support. The measure would have required employers to give employees advance notice when they intended to close a plant or lay off a large number of workers.

The bill failed to garner a majority even though the substitute had removed a requirement that employers consult with workers before a shutdown and had stripped out a provision giving employees the right to get a court order halting a shutdown.

A spokesman for the U.S. Chamber of Commerce, which led the fight against the bill, claimed the measure was a "union bill" that would give organized labor a back door into plants in order to organize.

Members from financially pressed districts claimed that even the notice provision could hurt businesses near collapse that were trying to find creditors to help them keep going.

Pension Benefit Guaranty Corporation. Legislation to shore up the Pension Benefit Guaranty Corporation (PBGC) was put on hold until 1986, when the House and Senate Dec. 20 shelved a major budget-cutting bill (HR 3128).

The PBGC was a federal corporation that insured workers' retirement benefits in case companies terminated their pension plans. Separate funds were maintained for single-employer plans, which covered individual firms, and for multi-employer plans, which covered many firms within a single industry. The corporation had a growing deficit because of the large number of businesses that had terminated their plans but remained in business.

The House Education and Labor Committee, Senate Labor and Human Resources Committee and House Ways and Means Committee each came up with their own plans for rescuing the PBGC, and while there were differences in the proposals, they were similar in important respects.

The plans would require companies to prove financial distress before they could dump their pension liabilities on the government. If a firm remained in business after a plan termination, the PBGC could recover any losses by taking a share of the firm's pretax profits for up to a decade, in addition to its immediate claim under existing law to 30 percent of a company's net worth. A healthy firm could terminate its plan only if the plan had sufficient assets to pay all promised benefits, not just those that were federally guaranteed.

All three proposals would raise the annual premiums that employers paid for single-employer pension plans. The Senate version raised the fee from $2.60 per employee to $8.10, the House Education and Labor plan raised it to $8.50 and the Ways and Means plan raised it to $8.

Law/Judiciary

Immigration. The Senate passed but the House did not complete action on a major overhaul of U.S. immigration law (S 1200). It was the third time since 1982 the Senate had passed an immigration reform bill.

The House Judiciary Subcommittee on Immigration, Refugees and International Law completed action on its version of the bill (HR 3080) Nov. 19, but the full committee did not act.

The panel postponed consideration to give a group of Democratic House members, led by Judiciary member Charles E. Schumer, N.Y., more time to iron out what had become a pivotal issue in the immigration debate: temporary foreign farm workers.

Both bills would create a new system of penalties against employers who knowingly hired illegal aliens. And they would create a program for granting legal status to illegal aliens already in the country who met certain requirements. The Senate program would start three years after enactment; the House program would begin upon enactment.

Western growers, who relied heavily on illegal workers, lobbied all year for a new program to allow thousands of foreigners into the country for farm work. They succeeded in getting the program attached to the Senate bill, but faced stiff opposition in the House.

Schumer worked through the fall trying to come up with a compromise program that would provide some type of foreign worker program that also included new protections for the agricultural laborers.

Meese, Reynolds Nominations. The Senate Feb. 23 confirmed Edwin Meese III as attorney general, 13 months after he was first nominated to the post. The vote was 63-31. But one of Meese's associates, William Bradford Reynolds, did not fare as well.

Reynolds had been nominated to be associate attorney general, the No. 3 post at Justice and a step up from his position as head of the department's civil rights division. But the Senate Judiciary Committee June 27 decisively rejected Reynolds' promotion.

When Meese was nominated in the 98th Congress, his appointment was put on hold after Judiciary Committee hearings raised questions about his ethical conduct. Senators probed some of his financial transactions and whether Meese, while counselor to President Reagan, had acted improperly in approving for federal jobs people who had helped him out of financial difficulties.

At Meese's request, an independent counsel was appointed to investigate the allegations. On Sept. 20, 1984, the counsel, Washington lawyer Jacob A. Stein, issued his report, saying he had "no basis" for prosecuting Meese for violating any criminal statute. Stein made no comment on Meese's ethics or the propriety of his conduct. As soon as the 99th Congress began Jan. 3, Reagan renominated Meese.

In Reynolds' case, it was the decisions he made as head of the civil rights division and the manner in which he defended his record before the committee that led to the negative vote.

The panel June 27 voted three times on the nomination: it refused 8-10 to send Reynolds' name to the Senate with a favorable recommendation, then tied 9-9 on motions to report the nomination without recommendation or unfavorably. Although some administration officials toyed briefly with trying to force a Senate floor vote on Reynolds, the White House backed off on that move.

Balanced Budget Amendment. The Senate did not act on either of two versions of a constitutional amendment requiring a balanced federal budget (S J Res 13, S J Res 225). The Senate Judiciary Committee reported them Oct. 23.

Sponsors of a strict version (S J Res 13) that would make it hard to increase taxes to achieve a balanced budget agreed to support the second, more flexible proposal as well, recognizing the political problems facing their own plan.

President Reagan had long supported a balanced-budget amendment like S J Res 13 that would restrict Congress' authority to raise taxes to avoid deficit spending. But chief sponsors Strom Thurmond, R-S.C., and Orrin G. Hatch, R-Utah, conceded in mid-July that they did not have the two-thirds vote necessary to win passage of S J Res 13 on the Senate floor.

The committee also reported a bill (S 40) establishing procedures for holding a constitutional convention. By the end of 1985, 32 states (of 34 needed) had called for a convention on a balanced-budget amendment, and some in Congress worried that a convention might have to be called in the next several years to deal with that. Without procedures spelled out to govern it, they feared the session could turn into a "runaway" meeting, opening up the entire Constitution to change.

'Grove City' Legislation. A dispute over abortion stalled progress on a major civil rights bill (HR 700) to overturn a 1984 Supreme Court decision that had restricted enforcement of four civil rights laws.

Meetings between members of Congress, their staffs and the U.S. Catholic Conference — the chief opponent of the bill — failed to yield a compromise version in 1985.

Two House committees — Judiciary, and Education and Labor — approved differing versions of the bill in May. But sponsors did not push for floor action because of the abortion dispute. It centered on assertions by the Catholic Conference that provisions of the bill could broaden abortion rights, forcing Catholic hospitals that received federal aid, for example, to perform abortions.

Supporters of HR 700 rejected this claim; they said the bill would simply restore to their previous scope of coverage the four civil rights laws: Title IX of the 1972 Education Act Amendments, Title VI of the 1964 Civil Rights Act, Section 504 of the Rehabilitation Act of 1973 and the Age Discrimination Act of 1975.

The Supreme Court, in *Grove City College v. Bell*, ruled that Title IX barred sex discrimination only in a "program or activity" that received federal aid. Civil rights lawyers said an entire institution should be barred from discriminating if any part of it got aid. The other three laws were affected because they contained the same "program or activity" language.

Two bills dealing with the issue (S 431, S 272) were pending in the Senate Labor and Human Resources Committee.

Gun Control. By a lopsided 79-15 vote July 9, the Senate passed a bill (S 49) relaxing federal gun control laws to allow interstate sales of rifles and handguns.

The bill was not considered in the House, however, where it faced strong opposition among key members of the Judiciary Committee. Sponsors of a companion House bill (HR 945), led by Harold L. Volkmer, D-Mo., were trying to force the legislation out of the committee through a "discharge petition." Once 218 members — a majority of the House — signed the petition, the full House must act on the issue. When Congress adjourned Dec. 20, Volkmer had secured about 150 signatures.

The Senate-passed bill eased many restrictions of the 1968 Gun Control Act, including those that barred interstate sales of guns. It had the strong backing of the National Rifle Association (NRA), which had been seeking relaxation of the 1968 law almost since its enactment.

By better than 2-to-1 margins, the Senate defeated two amendments designed to strengthen gun controls. One would have kept the ban on interstate sales of small handguns; the other required a 14-day waiting period between the purchase of a handgun and its delivery.

In a related development, the House Dec. 17 by voice vote passed a bill (HR 3132) barring the manufacture, importation and sale of armor-piercing bullets that could penetrate protective vests worn by police officers. The Senate Judiciary Committee reported a similar bill (S 104) July 29, but it was not considered by the full chamber because of opposition by some senators who claimed the measure was unnecessary.

School Prayer. The Senate Sept. 10 decisively rejected legislation designed to allow organized, recited prayer in public schools. The vote to table, and thus kill the bill, was 62-36. The Senate had voted on similar legislation 10 times in the past seven years, and the Sept. 10 tally was the lowest level of support for the measure since 1979, when it passed the Senate.

The bill (S 47) would have barred the federal courts, including the Supreme Court, from hearing any case involving prayer in public schools.

Thus, if a state or local government chose to adopt a policy allowing public school prayer, opponents would have no means of challenging it in the federal courts.

A proposed constitutional amendment to allow silent prayer in public schools (S J Res 2) was reported by the Senate Judiciary Committee, on Oct. 29.

Trade

Textiles. The nation's estimated $150 billion trade deficit led to a dramatic surge in congressional concern over trade issues in 1985. The cutting edge of the tide of support for tough measures against foreign competition was legislation (HR 1562) to curb imports of textiles and apparel.

Heavy lobbying by domestic textile manufacturers and unions helped round up strong support for the bill, which called for sharp reductions in imports from a number of countries in Asia and the rest of the Third World. Although the measure faced determined opposition in the Senate, it passed both chambers by comfortable margins.

But the bill never overcame vocal opposition from President Reagan. Even though sponsors modified the bill in the Senate to make its textile cutbacks less severe — and added trade curbs for the shoe and copper industries to expand their support — the bill never mobilized the two-thirds majority needed to surmount Reagan's widely anticipated veto.

When the veto came Dec. 17, sponsors did not even attempt to override in the House. Instead, they put off an override vote until August 1986, in hope of keeping pressure on the administration to pursue a tough stance in international textile negotiations.

Export Controls. Legislation (S 883 — PL 99-64) to renew the main trade law regulating exports of U.S. goods and technology cleared Congress June 27.

The bill extended the Export Administration Act through fiscal 1989. In order to aid U.S. exporters, S 883 revised the act by easing a variety of licensing and procedural restrictions on the sale of products to other countries, and by limiting presidential authority to impose trade embargoes.

The bill also tightened controls aimed at preventing advanced equipment from falling into the hands of unfriendly nations, and stiffened penalties for firms that evaded export controls. In addition, the legislation strengthened congressional oversight of nuclear cooperation pacts.

Final action on S 883 marked the end of a long congressional struggle over the export act. Similar legislation almost cleared the 98th Congress in 1984, only to die at the last moment because of disputes over sanctions on South Africa and Pentagon review of export licenses. In 1985, sponsors dropped the two issues, and the bill went through in short order.

Telecommunications. House and Senate committees approved legislation aimed at forcing foreign countries to open their markets for telecommunications products to U.S. manufacturers.

The bills (S 942, HR 3131) were in response to the growing influx of foreign-made telephones and related products into the United States since the 1984 breakup of the American Telephone & Telegraph Co. telephone monopoly. Foreign telecommunications markets, by contrast, frequently were closed to U.S. products.

The bills would use the possibility of trade sanctions to persuade other countries to open their telecommunications markets. While the two bills differed in a number of respects, both threatened restrictions on imports of telecommunications equipment from countries that did not agree to let in similar U.S.-made products.

Export Aid. Concern over the soaring trade deficit added to congressional interest in programs to help U.S. businesses increase their sales abroad. But Reagan's proposal for a new export-promotion program went no further than a House committee, and an existing credit program of export aid received deep funding cuts.

In his Sept. 23 trade policy speech, Reagan called for a $300 million "war chest" providing direct grants and low-interest loans to the foreign purchasers of U.S. goods. The fund was aimed at countering other countries' increasing reliance on such "tied-aid" programs to gain a foothold in foreign markets.

Although the concept enjoyed broad congressional support, legislation to authorize the new program ran into serious problems among House Banking Committee Democrats, who worried that the new funds would be obtained by cutting existing housing and other programs. The panel approved authorization legislation (HR 3667) Dec. 12, but only after forcing a delay in the program until fiscal 1987, instead of 1986 as the administration initially had requested.

Congress rejected Reagan's proposal for a fundamental change in the operations of another export-aid program, the subsidized loans to foreign purchasers provided by the Export-Import Bank. The final stopgap funding bill (PL 99-190) approved at the end of the session included only $1.1 billion for the program in fiscal 1986, compared with $3.9 billion in 1985.

Comprehensive Trade Bills. Congress began work on a major overhaul of the standards and procedures that underlie U.S. trade policy.

The wide variety of comprehensive trade bills that began circulating in the fall were in marked contrast to legislation, such as the ill-fated textile-import bill (HR 1562), that sought to ease the trade problems of specific industries. Instead, the wide-ranging "generic" bills would revise the way the United States conducted international trade negotiations, attacked unfair trade practices of other countries and protected domestic industries against serious import competition.

Although support waned for an import-surcharge bill introduced by prominent Democrats in July (HR 3035), party task forces in the House released comprehensive trade plans. A bipartisan group in the Senate outlined a massive package of changes (S 1860) aimed at reasserting the congressional role in trade policy. And the House Energy and Commerce Committee Nov. 21 approved a related omnibus trade measure (HR 3777).

Transportation

Conrail. Congress did not approve the sale of Conrail to the Norfolk Southern Corp. by the Dec. 31 deadline set by the corporation.

But Norfolk Southern said it would extend its offer, and legislation to allow the corporation to buy the railroad for $1.2 billion (S 638) passed the Senate Feb. 4, 1986, by a vote of 54-39. The sale still was expected to face serious difficulty in the House.

The legislation had been blocked in the Senate in the closing days of the first session by filibuster threats. Opponents said the $1.2 billion sale price was too low, and that a merger of Conrail with Norfolk Southern's lines would raise antitrust problems that would hurt shippers, employees and competing railroads.

In the House, multiple hearings were held on the Norfolk Southern bid and a rival offer from the investment firm Morgan Stanley and Co., but no attempts were made to mark up bills favoring either offer.

Shortly before Congress adjourned, a new bid was submitted by two investment firms, which offered more cash but less in other areas.

Interstate Highway Funds. For the first time in years, Congress released federal highway funds to the states on time Oct. 1.

The action was made possible Sept. 19 when the House cleared a measure (S 1514 — PL 99-104) approving the 1986 cost estimate of federal highway work, which was necessary to trigger release of the funds. The Senate passed the bill July 30.

Disputes over matters such as local highway projects, mass-transit funding and gasoline-tax distribution to the states, which held up action in previous years, were deferred. Most highway program authorizations expired Sept. 30, 1986, and key members of Congress agreed to settle problems in a major reauthorization bill.

Federal funds that were supposed to go to the states Oct. 1, 1983, were held up until March 5, 1985, because of conflicts over the issues. That was the date Congress cleared a cost-estimate bill (HR 1251 — PL 99-4) that was stripped of controversies that delayed action in the 98th Congress.

One recurring highway controversy was settled in September when New York officials agreed to abandon the Westway highway and development project. The New York City project was opposed by environmentalists and critics who said it could cost up to $10 billion. The major blow against the project was struck Sept. 11 when the House voted to bar funding for it in the transportation appropriations bill (HR 3244).

Amtrak, Mass Transit. Despite administration opposition, both Amtrak and federal mass transit programs survived with minor budget cuts.

The continuing resolution that funded the Department of Transportation and other federal agencies (PL 99-190) set subsidies for Amtrak at $616 million, compared with $684 million in fiscal 1985. President Reagan had argued for elimination of federal aid. Reagan also proposed cutting mass transit aid by two-thirds, including the elimination of all operating aid for local transit systems. But the continuing resolution provided $3.7 billion in federal spending, about 10 percent less than in fiscal 1985. This included $875 million for operating assistance, the same level as 1985. ∎

Reagan Undergoes Operation for Cancer

President Reagan had a cancerous polyp removed from his large intestine and two small malignant growths removed from his nose in separate surgical procedures in 1985.

In a two-hour and 53-minute operation at the Bethesda (Md.) Naval Medical Center July 13, surgeons removed a malignant tumor about two inches in diameter, along with a two-foot section of Reagan's lower intestine. Doctors later diagnosed the tumor as a malignant villous adenoma, a type of cancerous growth classified as Dukes-B, meaning that it had invaded but not breached the intestinal wall.

After his recovery, doctors said Reagan's prospects of living a normal lifespan and completing his term as president were excellent. Dr. Steven Rosenberg, chief of surgery at the National Cancer Institute and a member of the surgical team that removed the tumor, said there was "a greater than 50 percent chance" that the 74-year-old president "has no cancer whatsoever, that there are no cancer cells in his body, and he is completely cured."

The tumor was discovered during treatment July 12 for a separate benign polyp discovered in March. An earlier polyp was found and removed in May 1984.

In addition to the colon cancer, two small skin cancers were removed from Reagan's nose in 1985. And on Jan. 17, 1986, three more small intestinal polyps and a tiny growth on Reagan's face were removed; none of them was cancerous, the White House announced.

Reagan's July 13 abdominal surgery gave Vice President George Bush an eight-hour term as chief executive of the United States, and marked the first time the 25th Amendment to the Constitution had been applied to a temporarily incapacitated president.

Reagan transferred his powers to Bush just before receiving anesthesia, and signed papers reclaiming them almost as soon as he awoke, seven hours and 54 minutes later. During that time, Bush served as acting president.

The 25th Amendment, ratified in 1967, spelled out in Section 3 the procedure for a temporary transfer of power to the vice president. It called for the chief executive to notify the president pro tempore of the Senate and the Speaker of the House "that he is unable to discharge the powers and duties of his office." A second letter was required when he was able to resume his duties. *(CQ Guide to Congress Third Edition, p. 284; text of Reagan letters, p. 42-D)*

Because of the deliberate wording of Reagan's official letter of notification, it remained unclear whether the 25th Amendment was actually "invoked." Reagan stated, "I am mindful of the provisions" of the 25th Amendment. But he added, "I do not believe that the drafters of this amendment intended its application" to situations such as his, and added that he took the action "not intending to set a precedent. . . ."

But although Reagan avoided designating Bush as "Acting President" — the phrase used in the 25th Amendment — White House officials acknowledged that Bush played that role while Reagan was in the operating room. And various officials contended that Reagan did, in fact, set a precedent, whether he wanted to or not. "Now it's been done," said former Sen. Birch Bayh, D-Ind. (1963-1981), the principal author of the 25th Amendment. "It seems to me they should emphasize the fact this is a good precedent. . . . It's only the normal thing to do, to have an insurance policy so that somebody is always watching the store."

Senate Cloture Votes, 1977-85

Following is a list of all cloture votes taken by the Senate during 1977-85. Motions to limit debate by invoking cloture required a three-fifths majority of the total Senate (60 if there were no vacancies), under a revised version of the Senate filibuster rule (Rule 22) adopted in 1975. That revision applied to any matter except proposed rules changes, for which the previous requirement of a two-thirds majority of senators present and voting still applied.

The nine cloture votes taken in 1985 brought to 215 the total number of cloture votes taken since 1917, when Rule 22 was adopted; 71 of the votes were successful. Successful 1977-85 cloture votes are indicated in **boldface type.** *(Previous votes, 1977 Almanac p. 813)*

Issue	Date	Vote	Yeas Needed
Draft Resisters Pardons	Jan. 24, 1977	53-43	60
Campaign Financing	July 29, 1977	49-45	60
Campaign Financing	Aug. 1, 1977	47-46	60
Campaign Financing	Aug. 2, 1977	52-46	60
Natural Gas Pricing	Sept. 26, 1977	77-17	60
Labor Law Revision	June 7, 1978	42-47	60
Labor Law Revision	June 8, 1978	49-41	60
Labor Law Revision	June 13, 1978	54-43	60
Labor Law Revision	June 14, 1978	58-41	60
Labor Law Revision	June 15, 1978	58-39	60
Labor Law Revision	June 22, 1978	53-45	60
Revenue Act of 1978	Oct. 9, 1978	62-28	60
Energy Taxes	Oct. 14, 1978	71-13	60
Windfall Profits Tax	Dec. 12, 1979	53-46	60
Windfall Profits Tax	Dec. 13, 1979	56-40	60
Windfall Profits Tax	Dec. 14, 1979	56-39	60
Windfall Profits Tax	Dec. 17, 1979	84-14	60
Lubbers Nomination	April 21, 1980	46-60	60
Lubbers Nomination	April 22, 1980	62-34	60
Rights of Institutionalized	April 28, 1980	44-39	60
Rights of Institutionalized	April 29, 1980	56-34	60
Rights of Institutionalized	April 30, 1980	53-35	60
Rights of Institutionalized	May 1, 1980	60-34	60
Bottlers' Antitrust Immunity	May 15, 1980	86-6	60
Draft Registration Funding	June 10, 1980	62-32	60
Zimmerman Nomination	Aug. 1, 1980	51-35	60
Zimmerman Nomination	Aug. 4, 1980	45-31	60
Zimmerman Nomination	Aug. 5, 1980	63-31	60
Alaska Lands	Aug. 18, 1980	63-25	60
Vessel Tonnage/Strip Mining	Aug. 21, 1980	61-32	60
Fair HousingAmendments	Dec. 3, 1980	51-39	60
Fair Housing Amendments	Dec. 4, 1980	62-32	60
Fair Housing Amendments	Dec. 9, 1980	54-43	60
Breyer Nomination	Dec. 9, 1980	68-28	60
Justice Department Authorization	July 10, 1981	38-48	60
Justice Department Authorization	July 13, 1981	54-32	60
Justice Department Authorization	July 29, 1981	59-37	60
Justice Department Authorization	Sept. 10, 1981	57-33	60
Justice Department Authorization	Sept. 16, 1981	61-36	60
Justice Department Authorization	Dec. 10, 1981	64-35	60
State, Justice, Commerce, Judiciary Appropriations	Dec. 11, 1981	59-35	60
Broadcast Senate Proceedings	April 20, 1982	47-51	60
Criminal Code Reform Act	April 27, 1982	45-46	60
Urgent Supplemental Appropriations, Fiscal 1982	May 27, 1982	95-2	60
Voting Rights Act	June 15, 1982	86-8	60
Debt Limit Increase	Sept. 9, 1982	41-47	60
Debt Limit Increase	Sept. 13, 1982	45-35	60
Debt Limit Increase	Sept. 15, 1982	50-44	60
Debt Limit Increase	Sept. 20, 1982	50-39	60
Debt Limit Increase	Sept. 21, 1982	53-47	60
Debt Limit Increase	Sept. 22, 1982	54-46	60
Debt Limit Increase	Sept. 23, 1982	53-45	60
Antitrust Equal Enforcement Act	Dec. 2, 1982	38-58	60
Antitrust Equal Enforcement Act	Dec. 2, 1982	44-51	60
Transportation Assistance Act	Dec. 13, 1982	75-13	60
Transportation Assistance Act	Dec. 16, 1982	48-50	60
Transportation Assistance Act	Dec. 16, 1982	5-93	60
Transportation Assistance Act	Dec. 19, 1982	89-5	60
Transportation Assistance Act	Dec. 20, 1982	87-8	60
Transportation Assistance Act	Dec. 23, 1982	81-5	60
Emergency Jobs Appropriations/Interest Withholding	March 16, 1983	50-48	60
Emergency Jobs Appropriations/Interest Withholding	March 16, 1983	59-39	60
International Trade and Investment/Interest Withholding	April 19, 1983	34-53	60
International Trade and Investment/Interest Withholding	April 19, 1983	39-59	60
Defense Authorizations, 1984	July 21, 1983	55-41	60
Radio Broadcasting to Cuba	Aug. 3, 1983	62-33	60
Natural Gas Policy Act	Nov. 3, 1983	86-7	60
Capital Punishment	Feb. 9, 1984	65-26	60
Hydroelectric Power Plants	July 30, 1984	60-28	60
Wilkinson Nomination	July 31, 1984	57-39	60
Agriculture Appropriations, Fiscal 1985	Aug. 6, 1984	54-31	60
Agriculture Appropriations, Fiscal 1985	Aug. 8, 1984	68-30	60
Wilkinson Nomination	Aug. 9, 1984	65-32	60
Financial Services Competitive Equity Act	Sept. 10, 1984	89-3	60
Financial Services Competitive Equity Act	Sept. 13, 1984	92-6	60
Broadcasting of Senate Procedures	Sept. 18, 1984	73-26	60
Broadcasting of Senate Procedures	Sept. 21, 1984	37-44	60
Surface Transportation and Uniform Relocation Assistance Act	Sept. 24, 1984	70-12	60
Continuing Appropriations	Sept. 29, 1984	92-4	60
Anti-Apartheid	**July 10, 1985**	**88-8**	**60**
Line-item Veto	July 18, 1985	57-42	60
Line-item Veto	July 23, 1985	57-41	60
Line-item Veto	July 24, 1985	58-40	60
Anti-Apartheid	Sept. 9, 1985	53-34	60
Anti-Apartheid	Sept. 11, 1985	57-41	60
Anti-Apartheid	Sept. 12, 1985	11-88	60
Debt Limit/Balanced Budget	Oct. 6, 1985	57-38	64†
Debt Limit/Balanced Budget	Oct. 9, 1985*	53-39	62†

** Vote was taken after midnight in the session that began Oct. 8.*
† Senate rules change; two-thirds majority required.

House Battles Over Contested Indiana Seat

After four months of partisan wrangling, the House May 1 finally settled an issue that had plagued it since the first day of the session, voting 236-190 along party lines to seat Democrat Frank McCloskey as the representative of the 8th District of Indiana.

GOP members, who claimed Republican Richard D. McIntyre had won the contested seat, marched out of the House chamber to protest the decision. They also blocked much of the week's scheduled legislative business and threatened to use parliamentary guerrilla tactics in the future. *(Box, p. 29)*

The seat had been vacant since the beginning of the 99th Congress, when the House voted to leave it unfilled pending an investigation by the House Administration Committee of alleged irregularities in the Nov. 6, 1984, election.

Three times after that — in February, March and April — Republicans pushed the seating of McIntyre to a vote, losing each time while picking up no more than a handful of votes from Democrats. Debate on the contest took up far more time than almost any other issue the House considered in 1985.

After the House Administration Committee concluded April 23 that McCloskey had won by four votes, Republicans tried to get a new election by declaring the seat vacant. The vote on their attempt (H Res 148) came April 30. Although 19 Democrats voted with them, they lost 200-229. *(Vote 74, p. 26-H)*

The next day, before the committee's recommendation to seat McCloskey (H Res 146 — H Rept 99-58) came to a vote, Republicans moved to send the issue back to the panel with orders to count 32 controversial absentee ballots that had not been counted. That motion was rejected, 183-246. *(Vote 82, p. 28-H)*

The House then approved the resolution, 236-190, with 10 Democrats joining the Republicans in voting against it. *(Vote 83, p. 28-H)*

While the seat was empty, the clerk of the House maintained an office to represent the district. Both McCloskey and McIntyre were paid full salaries.

The Contested Election

The McCloskey-McIntyre race was the closest House contest of the 20th century, according to the three-member House Administration Committee task force that investigated it.

McCloskey was the apparent winner by 72 votes — out of more than 234,000 cast — right after the Nov. 6 election. But in two precincts in one of the district's 15 counties, ballots had been counted twice. Correction of that arithmetical error gave McIntyre an apparent 34-vote victory. On that basis, Indiana Secretary of State Edwin J. Simcox, a Republican, on Dec. 14 certified McIntyre as the winner.

But when Congress convened Jan. 3, House Democrats refused to seat McIntyre, voting instead to declare the seat vacant.

A full recount was completed Jan. 22. It showed McIntyre's lead had increased to 418 votes after more than 4,800 ballots were thrown out for technical reasons.

The House Administration Committee Feb. 6 created a task force consisting of Leon E. Panetta, D-Calif., chairman; William L. Clay, D-Mo.; and William M. Thomas, R-Calif., to investigate the election. Under the Constitution, each chamber of Congress has the power to decide its own contested elections.

The task force hired auditors from the General Accounting Office to do the actual counting of ballots. It also decided to count many of the ballots that had been thrown out in the official recount, arguing that if the intent of the voter was clear, a ballot should not be rejected for lack of a poll-worker's initials or a missing precinct number.

The most controversial issue that arose was the question of how certain absentee ballots were treated. Indiana law required absentee ballots to be both notarized and signed. But the task force found 62 absentee ballots that either had not been signed or had not been notarized, which county clerks mistakenly had sent to precincts for counting. Fifty-two of those had been opened at the precincts, counted and kept with the rest of the ballots; 10 were returned uncounted to the county clerks.

The task force decided to count all 62 on the grounds that the 52 were then inseparable from other ballots and the 10 were of an identical class but had not been counted.

Thirty-two other absentee ballots lacking either signatures or notarization had been retained and secured by the county clerks and never sent to the precincts. On April 18, the task force, on a partisan 2-1 vote, decided not to count the additional ballots. Republican Thomas called the process "nothing short of a rape."

House Republicans went on the warpath the next week, keeping the House in session all night April 22 and blocking legislative business on April 25. They claimed that Democrats had insisted on counting all the ballots only until their man was ahead, and then quit counting.

House Votes

Jan. 3. When the 99th Congress convened Jan. 3, Democratic leaders decided not to seat either McIntyre or McCloskey.

The House voted 238-177 along party lines for a resolution (H Res 1) declaring the Indiana 8th District seat vacant pending an investigation by the House Administration Committee. At the same time it voted unanimously to seat Democrat Richard Stallings of Idaho, whose election also was challenged. *(Votes 2, 3, p. 2-H; Stallings contest, box, p. 30)*

McIntyre spoke on his own behalf, the first challenged member-elect to speak on the floor since Adam Clayton Powell Jr., D-N.Y. (1945-67, 1969-71), did in 1967. McCloskey was on the floor during the debate but did not speak.

Republicans charged that Democrats, who outnumbered them 182-253, were using their numerical superiority to deny McIntyre his seat.

"A great injustice is being done here today," said Minority Leader Robert H. Michel, R-Ill. "To do anything short of seating McIntyre in effect disenfranchises 500,000 citizens of Indiana."

But Majority Leader Jim Wright, D-Texas, said he was recommending "the only fair and honorable procedure available to us," noting that if Democrats really wanted to use "raw power," they would have seated McCloskey.

Wright said the House was following a precedent set in a 1961 Indiana election, when the secretary of state certified Republican George O. Chambers the winner but later sent a message indicating he was in error. When the House convened, it voted not to seat Chambers; an investigation

House GOP Wages 'Guerrilla Warfare'

The May 1 walkout of House Republicans to protest the seating of Indiana Democrat Frank McCloskey climaxed several months of "guerrilla warfare" by the GOP. *(Contested election, p. 28)*

The Republicans, outnumbered 182-253, had been angry for years at what they viewed as the arrogance of the Democratic majority. They complained that partisan committee ratios stacked the deck for Democrats and that other rules unfairly favored the majority. But more than any other issue, the Indiana election contest galvanized them.

GOP bitterness over the failure to seat Indiana Republican Richard D. McIntyre grew all year, reaching a peak in late April, when angry members kept the House in session all night April 22 and blocked later floor action with parliamentary guerrilla tactics.

In what they called "sample Thursday" on April 25, Republicans brought the House to a halt with a display of parliamentary procedures and votes. They forced roll-call votes on minor procedural questions and then delayed those by switching their votes, finally forcing the House to adjourn without completing its business.

They showed more of the same the week of April 29 with motions to adjourn and votes on procedures or bills that normally would not receive time-consuming roll-call votes. For example, on April 29, during consideration of a resolution (S Con Res 37) to accept a statue of former Rep. Jeannette Rankin, R-Mont. (1917-19, 1941-43), in the Capitol, Frenzel demanded a second for the motion to suspend the rules and pass the resolution.

Then F. James Sensenbrenner Jr., R-Wis., requested a "teller vote," which required members to walk between other members designated to count. When Sensenbrenner "lost" by a vote of 21-10, he demanded a roll call. That ordered a second by a vote of 318-0 but took at least 20 minutes, dragging members to the floor from committee meetings and luncheons. *(Vote 71, p. 26-H)*

The day after the GOP walkout, however, Republicans returned to the House and it returned to business, debating a State Department authorization bill (HR 2068), which was favored by the Reagan administration. Republicans did force a roll-call vote on an unrelated item to delay the proceedings. *(Vote 85, p. 30-H)*

Just the Beginning?

Although Minority Leader Robert H. Michel, R-Ill., said the May 1 walkout was "just the beginning" of GOP efforts to create public awareness of "the autocratic, tyrannical rule of the Democratic majority," the "war" appeared to wind down after the seating of McCloskey.

(The walkout, incidentally, was not without precedent. On Sept. 23, 1890, Democrats, then in the minority, left the chamber during debate on another contested election. In that case, Republicans decided to seat Republican Thomas E. Miller to represent the 7th District of South Carolina.)

The Republicans, while unified over the contested election issue, were divided on how confrontational they should be. Although Michel insisted future parliamentary disruptions would be done selectively at the call of the GOP leadership, others suggested they might act independently.

Newt Gingrich, R-Ga., leader of a group of about a dozen Republicans called the Conservative Opportunity Society who were far more strident and confrontational than Michel, said the GOP would continue to use "guerrilla warfare" on occasion. If the disruptions caused a problem for President Reagan's bills, Gingrich said, Reagan could solve that by going directly to the American people for support.

Some members also wanted to disrupt the committee process with boycotts and parliamentary delaying tactics. But Michel said most Republicans opposed that tactic, and except for several walkouts early in the year to protest party ratios on subcommittees, there was no evidence of its happening.

---

by House Administration found that Democrat J. Edward Roush was the winner, and he eventually was seated.

Republicans said the McIntyre case was significantly different, and the House's action would set a new and dangerous precedent. "If he [McIntyre] is denied his seat," said Thomas, "then any certified candidate ... is open to political attack."

But Democrat Lee H. Hamilton, dean of the Indiana delegation, said the secretary of state's certification was "an invalid document that the House should not recognize." He added, "It would be a disservice to the residents of the 8th Congressional District to seat the wrong man today only to have him unseated tomorrow."

Feb. 7. House Democrats Feb. 7 again thwarted Republican efforts to seat McIntyre.

Following completion of a recount, which put McIntyre ahead of McCloskey by 418 votes, Michel moved to seat McIntyre until the House Administration Committee reported. But the House voted 221-180 to refer Michel's resolution to the committee. Five Democrats — Texans Sam B. Hall Jr., Ralph M. Hall and Charles W. Stenholm; Romano L. Mazzoli, Ky.; and Douglas Applegate, Ohio — jumped ship and voted to seat McIntyre. *(Vote 8, p. 4-H)*

The setback was the second in a week for the Republicans. At the House Administration Committee's first organizational meeting Feb. 6, Bill Frenzel, R-Minn., moved to seat McIntyre, but the committee on a party-line 12-7 vote refused to consider the motion. The task force to investigate the election was named the same day.

March 4. In a surprise move March 4, House Republicans again tried to seat McIntyre, but failed by one vote. By 168-167, the House referred the proposal to the House Administration Committee. *(Vote 23, p. 10-H)*

The GOP motion was designed to catch Democrats off guard during a pro forma session in which no legislative business was to be conducted; 79 Democrats and 19 Republicans were absent.

In a bitter exchange, O'Neill accused Michel of bringing up the matter without giving Democrats adequate notice. But Michel said the issue had been handled "in a very shoddy, shoot-from-the-hip, partisan manner" and that Republicans "simply cannot stand by and wait for the majority in this House to find a way to seat someone else other than one duly elected under Indiana law."

Only four Democrats voted with the Republicans this time. Applegate, whose vote would have made the difference, voted with the Democratic leadership. He said his vote was based not on the merits but the fact that "the Republicans had tried to sneak one through."

April 2. For the fourth time in three months, after another heated, partisan debate, House Democrats April 2 again refused to seat McIntyre.

The vote was 241-183 to send a resolution (H Res 121) to seat him to the House Administration Committee. All Republicans voted against the referral; all but a handful of Democrats voted for it. Voting with the GOP minority were the same five Democrats who joined them Feb. 7, with Applegate switching back. *(Vote 38, p. 16-H)*

While Frenzel contended that not seating McIntyre made the House look like "the partisan playpen of an arrogant majority...," Philip R. Sharp, D-Ind., said Indiana's election laws and recount procedures "did not give us a clear, timely result in which the people of the 8th District could have confidence."

April 30, May 1. The sometimes rancorous debate April 30 on whether to call for a special election and May 1 on seating McCloskey focused primarily on the 32 uncounted absentee ballots and on the damage the fight was doing to civility in the House.

The Republicans' basic claim was that there was a cloud of uncertainty over a four-vote victory when there were still at least 32 uncounted ballots "on the table." But Panetta said the 32 ballots were illegal under Indiana law and should not be counted. He said they were substantially different from the 62 other absentee ballots the task force did count because they were never sent to the precincts for counting. He said the decisions of the task force were fair and reasonable.

The key decision was the April 30 vote against having a special election. Although 19 Democrats voted with the Republicans, only one Democrat took the floor on their behalf. Mazzoli, who had voted with the GOP on seating McIntyre since February, said the election appeared "to have a cloud hanging over it, which can only be dispelled if there were a special election." Other Democrats who voted with the GOP were a mixture of Northern liberals and Southern conservatives.

Court Cases

The Supreme Court May 28 refused to get involved in the dispute. Without a dissenting vote, it denied Indiana permission to sue the House in the Supreme Court.

Indiana Attorney General Linley E. Pearson had asked the justices in early March to invoke the court's "original jurisdiction" to hear the suit. Although the justices did not explain their action, the high court rarely exercised its original jurisdiction, under which it could hear cases between states or between states and the federal government, before any other court decided them.

Earlier in the year, a U.S. district court judge in Washington, D.C., dismissed a suit brought by McIntyre against House Democrats and House officers. Judge June L. Green ruled March 1 that the House had the constitutional right to judge its own membership.

McIntyre had filed the suit Feb. 11, charging the Democrats had denied him constitutional due process in refusing to seat him. The mayor of Oakland City, Ind., joined in the suit, charging that the House's Jan. 3 decision to leave the seat open deprived him and other residents of the 8th District of their constitutional right to representation.

On Feb. 7, a federal district court in Indiana dismissed a separate suit filed by McIntyre challenging recount procedures in two of the district's counties. Judge Gene Brooks of the Southern District of Indiana ruled that the House alone was responsible for determining the validity of contested ballots. ∎

Other Contested Elections

In addition to the long, bitter contest over who should represent Indiana's 8th Congressional District, two other 1984 House elections were so close that the losers contested the results. *(Indiana race, p. 28)*

Unlike the Indiana case, where the candidate who was certified the winner ultimately lost the seat, challenges in Idaho and Guam were unsuccessful.

On July 24 the House dismissed a challenge by Democrat Antonio Borja Won Pat, the former non-voting delegate from Guam, against Republican Ben Blaz. And on Oct. 2 it threw out a challenge by former Rep. George Hansen, R-Idaho (1965-69, 1975-85), against Democrat Richard H. Stallings.

While the Indiana seat remained unfilled until May 1, when the House voted to seat Democrat Frank McCloskey, both Stallings and Blaz were sworn in on the opening day of the session and served while House Administration Committee task forces investigated the challenges against them.

Guam. The committee July 10 unanimously recommended that the House dismiss Won Pat's challenge to Blaz, and the House did so on July 24, agreeing to H Res 229 (H Rept 99-220) by voice vote.

Won Pat had represented Guam in Congress since 1973. He said Blaz, who won the November 1984 election by about 350 votes, failed to win an absolute majority of the votes cast, as required by law; Won Pat said blank ballots and overvotes should have been included in the total number of "votes cast." He also said absentee ballots were mailed out too late.

A three-member committee task force disagreed with these and other issues raised and said there was not sufficient reason to hold a runoff election.

Idaho. Hansen, who was convicted in 1984 of filing false financial disclosure forms, charged vote fraud in his 170-vote loss to Stallings. He also contended there should have been a full, rather than a partial, election recount. *(1984 Almanac, p. 210)*

A House Administration task force split 2-1 along party lines July 18 as it recommended dismissal of the challenge. The committee by a 12-1 vote July 24 reported H Res 272 (H Rept 99-290), dismissing the challenge, and the House approved the resolution Oct. 2 by a 247-4 vote, with 169 members, mostly Republicans, voting "present." *(Vote 296, p. 94-H)*

Senate Procedural Changes

Members of the Senate Dec. 5 informally agreed to several procedural moves designed to improve the "quality of life" in that chamber.

The changes came out of an extraordinary private meeting attended by about 70 senators of both parties. The hourlong session, held off the Senate floor with no staff or press present, was called to discuss senators' frustrations about legislative delays, their unpredictable schedules and what Missouri Democrat Thomas F. Eagleton called "the state of incipient anarchy" in the Senate.

Four changes, which took effect immediately, were accepted:

- Roll-call votes were restricted to 15 minutes.

The Senate customarily agreed to a 15-minute limit by unanimous consent at the beginning of each Congress, but the time often was extended to allow stragglers to cast their votes. David Pryor, D-Ark., said the average length of each vote in 1985 was 22.8 minutes, and he said the Senate lost nearly 45 hours by stretching roll calls beyond 15 minutes.

- The Senate was to adhere to the constitutional requirement (Article I, Section 5) that one-fifth of the members present must second a roll-call request. The presiding officer must assume a quorum of at least 51 senators was present, which meant that at least 11 senators must endorse a roll call. This change was aimed at cutting down the number of roll-call votes.
- The practice by which a senator privately could place a "hold" on a bill to keep it from the floor was changed so that other senators could learn who was blocking the bill's consideration. Previously, only party leaders were aware who placed the hold. This change would make it easier for a bill's sponsor to negotiate with the measure's opponents. Assistant Majority Leader Alan K. Simpson, R-Wyo., said the change would prevent a hold from being used, in effect, as a veto by one senator.
- No recorded votes were to be taken after 6 p.m. on Mondays. This would permit senators to plan other activities on Monday evenings, such as campaign fund-raising events, but they would not be protected from roll calls on other nights. Several times in 1985 the Senate suspended work because one member was busy with a fund-raiser.

The new procedures did not require formal rules changes by the Senate.

The recommendations were offered by an unofficial group of eight senators led by Pryor and John C. Danforth, R-Mo., that had met to discuss the Senate's procedural problems. The idea for the unusual bipartisan meeting, to which all 100 senators were invited, came earlier in the year from Majority Leader Robert Dole, R-Kan.

One outcome of the meeting was that senators decided to hold a similar session in late January 1986 to discuss major procedural issues, such as limiting filibusters or beginning television broadcasts of the Senate.

The Senate had received several reports in recent years recommending rules changes to help it work better. But except for slight reductions in the number of committee assignments in 1985, as recommended in 1984 by a panel headed by Dan Quayle, R-Ind., the suggestions were ignored. *(Committee slots, p. 16-G; 1983 Almanac p. 598)* ∎

Senate Radio, TV Coverage

Live broadcasts of Senate debate would reach the nation's radio listeners before its television viewers under a proposal approved Oct. 29 by the Senate Rules and Administration Committee.

By an 8-1 vote, the committee approved S Res 28, which would begin gavel-to-gavel radio broadcasts of Senate proceedings as soon as technically possible, but would delay general television coverage until after a trial period of closed-circuit TV broadcasts.

The committee filed its report Nov. 19 (S Rept 99-190), and Majority Leader Robert Dole, R-Kan. — the one committee member who voted against the resolution — said it would be among the first items on the Senate's agenda in 1986.

The resolution's sponsor, Minority Leader Robert C. Byrd, D-W.Va., said the committee's decision confirmed that Senate broadcasting "is an idea whose time has come." But Dole, who never was enthusiastic about the idea of televising Senate proceedings, said he thought the Senate should test TV and radio simultaneously, rather than have a lengthy TV tryout.

House proceedings had been televised since 1979, and the broadcast industry had pushed for years for coverage of the Senate.

Rules Changes Dropped

As approved by the committee, S Res 28 was stripped of a series of rules changes Byrd had suggested to help the Senate "shape up and clean up its act" before opening its doors to TV cameras.

His proposals included replacing verbal roll calls with electronic voting, ending protracted debate after a cloture vote to shut off a filibuster, limiting dilatory debate on motions to take up an issue, and instituting a "germaneness" rule, as in the House. To avoid the possibility of members abandoning their committee work to get before the cameras, Byrd also proposed that floor sessions be held only on Mondays, Tuesdays and Thursdays, with committee meetings on Wednesdays and Fridays.

"The Senate now is at its lowest point in the view of the public. If we go to television and radio with this post-cloture situation being what it is, we'll do harm to the Senate," Byrd said, in urging committee members to keep his package intact.

But after several senators warned that controversy over the rules changes could sink the entire radio-TV proposal, the committee agreed to an amendment by Albert Gore Jr., D-Tenn., to detach the proposals. "It gives the Senate more time to reflect on rules changes while movement begins on broadcasting," Gore said.

Although Byrd wanted to start radio and TV coverage together, Gore's amendment stipulated that radio coverage would begin soon after passage of S Res 28. TV coverage would go only to congressional offices during a test period of unspecified duration. During that period, the Rules Committee would consider rules changes necessitated by TV coverage, and then decide whether to distribute the TV signal to the public and continue the radio broadcasts.

The resolution authorized up to $3.5 million for equipment and associated costs. It also required that the Senate control TV cameras, which would focus on the senator speaking rather than pan the chamber.

Changing Times

In the 98th Congress, a bill to allow Senate broadcasts was reported under prodding from then-Majority Leader Howard H. Baker Jr., R-Tenn. The measure failed on the floor in September 1984, however. *(1984 Almanac p. 209)*

Baker's retirement at the end of the 98th Congress robbed the proposal of its leading proponent. But Byrd, who once opposed the idea, stepped in as its advocate when he concluded that the Senate had faded in the public eye compared with the House. Up to 21 million Americans a month watched House proceedings on C-SPAN, the Cable Satellite Public Affairs Network, according to surveys.

Another factor working in favor of Senate TV was the pending retirement of Russell B. Long, D-La., the idea's prime opponent. Long, who planned to step down at the end of the 99th Congress, had filibustered the 1984 Senate TV measure as well as earlier versions. But he said, "I'm not going to be able to oppose this change forever."

Long argued that the Senate's often arcane, confusing and murky legislative procedures gave members the protection they needed to take politically dangerous but necessary stands on controversial issues. "It's very important that we preserve the potential of the Senate ... to say the unpopular things," he said. "Some of those things you can't do before television."

Long also predicted the Senate would be in session 50 percent longer" if TV were allowed, because members would "grandstand" for the cameras.

Although Byrd claimed the committee's Oct. 29 vote was a boost for the proposal, he warned against starting radio broadcasts while still testing television. "I'm concerned about going down the road with radio only. I'm afraid television wouldn't catch up for a while," he said.

But radio supporters argued that broadcasts could begin "with the flick of a switch," as Gore put it, by having networks hook up to the existing public address system that transmitted floor debate to Senate offices.

Byrd's original proposal was for radio and TV coverage of floor debate only when party leaders wanted it. But after hearings Sept. 17-18, he changed his mind in favor of gavel-to-gavel broadcasts because he decided selective coverage would confuse viewers.

At least one Senate procedure would need to be changed to accommodate broadcasts, committee members generally agreed. That was the frequent use of quorum calls as a stalling tactic while senators worked out differences off the floor. ■

Congressional Mailing Costs

The Senate Dec. 9 revealed for the first time how much individual members spent on mass mailings, after last-minute efforts to postpone the disclosure failed.

According to a report by the secretary of the Senate, 79 senators spent a total of $10.95 million on mass mailings during the three-month period covered by the report (July-September 1985). The cost was paid by the taxpayers.

Twenty-one senators sent out no mass mailings.

Alan Cranston, D-Calif., ran up the single biggest postage bill — $1.63 million — during the three-month reporting period. Next on the list were Arlen Specter, R-Pa.; John Heinz, R-Pa.; Christopher J. Dodd, D-Conn.; Charles E. Grassley, R-Iowa; and Donald W. Riegle Jr., D-Mich.

With the exception of Heinz and Riegle, whose seats were up in 1988, all of the top mailers faced re-election in 1986. The top two spenders, Cranston and Specter, were both considered vulnerable.

The spending disclosures were required under a rule pushed through the Rules and Administration Committee in May by Chairman Charles McC. Mathias Jr., R-Md.

Mathias had criticized the growing cost of congressional mail as "an embarrassing example of the waste of the taxpayers' money," and "the congressional equivalent of the Pentagon's $500 hammer." He said disclosure would remind senators that "mailings are not cost-free and that the real control of this rests with the voters."

The House declined to disclose mailing information on its members.

Members of Congress were expected to send out more than a billion pieces of mail in fiscal 1986 at a cost of $144 million ($56 million in the Senate, $88 million in the House), although those estimates were cut — arbitrarily, according to some members — when funding for official mail was included in the fiscal 1986 legislative branch appropriations bill (HR 2942). *(Story, p. 326)*

Fighting Disclosure

The "franking privilege," which allowed members of Congress to mail out virtually unlimited amounts of correspondence to voters back home, had become an increasingly sensitive political issue as mail costs soared.

Incumbents said it was an essential means of letting constituents know about special town meetings and important congressional action — for some, the only way around hostile or indifferent local news media. But critics, such as the self-styled citizens' lobby Common Cause, called it a weapon of protection for incumbents. They pointed to the tendency of incumbents to boost their mailings during campaign years and slack off during non-election years.

Senate wrangling over the mass-mail issue reached a peak the week of Nov. 18, when Ted Stevens, R-Alaska, twice tried to persuade the Rules Committee to postpone the disclosure rule.

On Nov. 20 he convinced the panel to draft legislation that would apply the rule to the House as well as the Senate. The committee met again Nov. 21 and by voice vote approved S Con Res 91, requiring disclosure by both the House and Senate.

But when Stevens sought to amend the resolution to suspend the Senate's disclosure rule, he was outnumbered 4-6 and withdrew the amendment. He accused the Democrats of trying to help Democratic House members planning to run against GOP senators in 1986, by shielding them from mail-cost disclosure while embarrassing the incumbent senators.

Republican leaders tried to bring up S Con Res 91 for a floor vote before the Thanksgiving recess, but Minority Leader Robert C. Byrd, D-W.Va., blocked the move. Floor consideration would have given Stevens another chance to block the disclosure rule.

Stevens made one last attempt to stop the rule administratively. He sent a letter to Secretary of the Senate Jo-Anne L. Coe, challenging her legal authority to publish the mass-mail costs and demanding that she delete the information from her quarterly report on Senate spending.

Coe sought a legal opinion from the Senate counsel, who ruled against Stevens.

New Controversy

One day after Coe's report was released, the Rules Committee deadlocked on a proposed requirement that Senate committees and leaders also disclose their mass-mailing costs.

Albert Gore Jr., D-Tenn., charged that three GOP senators — Majority Leader Robert Dole, Kan., Jeremiah Denton, Ala., and Rudy Boschwitz, Minn. — avoided full disclosure of their mass-mailing costs by sending out 48,000 "individualized newsletters" in August through the Senate Republican Conference, a partisan organization for the GOP majority. By using the party organization to send the mail, Gore said, they legally escaped Senate restrictions on paper allotments and mailing cost disclosure.

Gore said the way to close this "gigantic loophole" was to require all Senate committees and leadership offices to report their mailing costs. But Stevens challenged the committee's authority to extend the mail disclosure rule beyond individual senators.

Mathias agreed to study the question, and postponed further action on the issue until 1986. ∎

PAC Spending Limits

The Senate Dec. 3 sidestepped a definitive vote on legislation to curb the role of political action committees (PACs) in congressional campaigns, effectively agreeing instead to postpone the issue until 1986.

A much-anticipated showdown on the proposal by David L. Boren, D-Okla., dissipated when supporters and critics joined together in calling for hearings by the Senate Rules and Administration Committee on Boren's plan and other campaign finance measures.

That paved the way for an overwhelming 7-84 vote against tabling (killing) the PAC proposal, which was offered as an amendment to a bill (S 655) dealing with low-level radioactive waste. Under a previous agreement, the waste bill then was pulled from further consideration. *(Vote 344, p. 59-S; nuclear waste, p. 214)*

Touchy Issue

Although the Senate did not reject the amendment, Boren failed to pin down Majority Leader Robert Dole, R-Kan., on when his plan would return to the Senate floor. Dole said it might be wise to appoint a commission to study campaign finance changes — a suggestion that, if followed, could further delay congressional action on the subject.

The Senate's disposition of the PAC issue largely reflected a lack of desire on the part of many members to declare themselves one way or the other on the touchy political issue of "special interest" campaign contributions. It would have been Congress' first vote in six years on a measure to limit PAC spending.

Nonetheless, Boren said he was "elated" by the result. "This is an issue that is not going to go away," he declared. "We're much more likely to get back to it with a positive vote than with a negative vote."

Under Boren's proposal, originally introduced as a bill (S 1806), House candidates could accept a maximum of $100,000 in PAC contributions, with another $25,000 permitted if they faced opposition in both primary and general elections.

A Senate candidate could collect $175,000 to $750,000, depending on the size of the state.

The ceiling on individual PAC contributions would be lowered to $3,000 per election, from $5,000, while the limit on maximum individual gifts would be raised to $1,500, from $1,000.

Another provision would require television and radio broadcasters to provide free response time to candidates opposed by groups operating "independent expenditure" campaigns.

Senate Debate

During Senate debate Dec. 2 and 3, Boren and his allies charged that PAC money in politics had led to excessive special-interest influence over Congress.

"We cannot expect members of Congress to act in the national interest when their election campaigns are being financed more and more by special interests," said Boren, one of a handful of lawmakers who did not accept PAC contributions.

During the 1983-84 election cycle, 3,006 PACs gave a record $105.3 million to House and Senate candidates, with 72 percent of the total funneled to incumbents, according to a Dec. 1 report by the Federal Election Commission. Ten years earlier, PAC contributions to congressional candidates totaled $12.5 million. In the 1984 elections, one-third of the House's members received more than half their campaign contributions from PACs.

Opponents of Boren's package claimed it would boost the role of political "fat cats" by increasing individual contributions and would favor wealthy and well-organized PACs that could shower candidates with donations early in the campaign season before running up against overall PAC ceilings.

Some foes also disputed the notion that PACs were a threat to the legislative process.

"I don't worry about being bought, because I'm not for sale," said Phil Gramm, R-Texas, one of the seven senators who voted to table Boren's amendment. "The truth is I am proud of the PACs and the people who support me," Gramm said.

During his 1984 Senate campaign, Gramm received $1.3 million in PAC gifts. That amounted to about 14 percent of the $9.8 million he raised from all sources, including individuals.

Gramm said he did not understand why an individual who gave $1,000 was not considered a special interest while 100 individuals who gave $10 apiece to a PAC, which then gave $1,000 to a candidate, were considered a special interest.

The decision to stave off conclusive Senate action on the PAC-limiting amendment came after both sides admitted they were uncertain how the vote would go. Neither Boren nor John Heinz, R-Pa., chairman of the National Republican Senatorial Committee, who led the fight against the amendment, claimed a majority.

With the vote a tossup, Boren's opponents found themselves in a difficult position — against his plan but unenthusiastic about being on the losing side in a close roll call and being accused of caving in to special interests.

Shortly before the vote, Dole suggested to GOP senators that they oppose a tabling amendment because that would postpone any further consideration of the issue.

Heinz offered his tabling motion but said he would vote against it and urged others to do the same. The tactic essentially allowed almost everyone to come away from the debate able to claim a victory.

Boren did just that, seizing on the vote as evidence of the Senate's desire to act on campaign finance reform, while Heinz and other critics succeeded in temporarily derailing the anti-PAC measure without appearing to be against campaign reform and without forcing anyone into a potentially embarrassing vote.

One unhappy group was Common Cause, the self-styled citizens' lobby, which lobbied for the Boren proposal and had planned to use the Senate vote as the centerpiece of a major anti-PAC campaign.

The last time either chamber of Congress voted on PAC-related legislation was 1979, when the House passed a bill to limit PAC spending but Senate opponents filibustered it to death. *(1979 Almanac p. 556)* ∎

Ethics Investigations

The House Committee on Standards of Official Conduct announced Sept. 19 it would conduct an inquiry into charges that Rep. Dan Daniel, D-Va., accepted numerous free rides between Washington, D.C., and his district on a corporate airplane owned by a defense contractor.

House rules prohibited the acceptance of gifts of $100 or more, including transportation, from persons with a direct interest in legislation before Congress.

Daniel, a senior member of the Armed Services Committee, already had announced he would repay the company for the value of the rides and would amend his financial disclosure forms.

The ethics panel by a vote of 11-0 on Feb. 5, 1986, approved a 343-page report concluding that Daniel wrongly accepted the free plane rides and billed the government as though he had made the trips by car. But the committee said he had misunderstood federal laws and House rules and should not be punished.

(The committee also voted to expand informal staff probes involving three other House Democrats into official investigations. The three were Banking Committee Chairman Fernand J. St Germain, R.I.; James Weaver, Ore., and Bill Boner, Tenn. All had been accused in newspaper reports of using their office to build personal wealth.)

Common Cause, the self-styled "citizens' lobby," had asked the ethics committee Sept. 13 to investigate both Daniel and St Germain.

Senate. The Senate Ethics Committee issued a final report Jan. 10 on a 1984 staff review of Sen. Mark O. Hatfield's dealings with Greek businessman Basil A. Tsakos, which cleared the Oregon Republican of any wrongdoing.

The committee said there was no evidence of "corrupt behavior" by Hatfield, who had helped Tsakos promote a trans-Africa pipeline at the same time the senator's wife, Antoinette, was collecting $55,000 from Tsakos. The report said Mrs. Hatfield received the money for real estate services she performed for Tsakos. *(1984 Almanac p. 211)* ∎

Members in Space

Sen. Jake Garn, R-Utah, became the first sitting member of Congress to participate in a space flight.

Garn, chairman of the Appropriations Subcommittee on HUD-Independent Agencies, which had jurisdiction over the budget of the National Aeronautics and Space Administration (NASA), flew with six other astronauts on the space shuttle *Discovery*. The shuttle lifted off April 12, 1985, from Cape Canaveral, Fla., and landed there a week later. The mission had been delayed five times.

Garn was aboard primarily as an observer, but he also was strapped with sensors to record his responses to weightlessness and motion sickness. Garn, a colonel in the Air Force Reserve with 10,000 hours of flight time, had been asking NASA to let him fly since 1981. He underwent more than 100 hours of training for the space flight.

In early 1986, Rep. Bill Nelson, D-Fla., became the second member of Congress to go into space. He flew on the space shuttle *Columbia,* which took off from Cape Canaveral Jan. 12 and landed at Edwards Air Force Base, Calif., Jan. 18. Both its takeoff and landing also were delayed.

Nelson, chairman of the House Science and Technology Space Subcommittee, also served as an experimental subject for tests of space sickness and operated a protein crystal growth experiment. Cape Canaveral was in his congressional district.

Several ex-astronauts subsequently became members of Congress, including Sen. John Glenn, D-Ohio, and former Sen. Harrison H. Schmitt, R-N.M. (1977-83). ∎

'Abscam' Prison Terms

The last two of the seven members of Congress convicted in the 1980 "Abscam" scandal began serving prison terms in 1985 after exhausting all legal appeals. Both were convicted of bribery and conspiracy.

Former Rep. John W. Jenrette Jr., D-S.C. (1975-80), convicted Oct. 7, 1980, began serving a two-year prison term April 4 at a federal prison camp in Atlanta, Ga.

Former Rep. Richard Kelly, R-Fla. (1975-81), convicted Jan. 26, 1981, began serving a 6- to 18-month sentence Nov. 4 at the minimum security prison at Eglin Air Force Base, Fla.

Abscam was an undercover FBI investigation in which agents posing as Arab sheiks and businessmen offered bribes to lawmakers in exchange for favors. The members of Congress were videotaped accepting the money and promising illegal favors. *(Background, previous convictions, 1983 Almanac p. 585)* ∎

Congressional Pay

Members of Congress, their staffs and white-collar federal employees received a 3.5 percent pay raise effective Jan. 1, 1985. The raise boosted congressional salaries to $75,100 a year, from $72,600.

In addition, starting in 1986, members of the Senate were allowed to keep an extra $7,500 a year in honoraria for speeches or articles. The limit on honoraria was raised to 40 percent of members' annual salary, or $30,000 a year, from 30 percent of salary, or $22,500, by a provision of the fiscal 1986 continuing appropriations resolution (HJ Res 465 — PL 99-190), passed Dec. 19. *(Story, p. 360)*

While the provision covered House members, too, it would not affect them unless they voted to alter a 1981 House rule limiting members' honoraria to 30 percent.

The Jan. 1 pay raise, which also applied to Vice President George Bush, Cabinet officers and the White House staff, was proposed Aug. 30, 1984, by President Reagan. It took effect automatically because the 98th Congress failed to block it before adjourning Oct. 12. The raise came on top of a 4 percent raise that federal white-collar employees and members of Congress received in 1984.

Since 1971, under the Federal Pay Comparability Act (PL 91-656), federal white-collar workers received automatic raises set by the president. In 1975 Congress tied its own raises to those, but kept them subject to an annual vote. In 1981, however, Congress included a provision in the fiscal 1982 continuing appropriations resolution (PL 97-51) that made the annual cost-of-living pay raise automatic beginning in fiscal 1983. *(1984 Almanac p. 203)*

The Senate May 3 on a 49-49 tie vote rejected a move to recommit the first congressional budget resolution (S Con Res 32) to the Budget Committee with instructions to lower the salaries of members of Congress by 10 percent and use the resulting savings to lower the federal budget deficit. *(Vote 41, p. 13-S; story, p. 441)* ∎

FOREIGN POLICY

CQ

Foreign Policy

After four years of bickering and feuding on foreign policy issues, Congress and President Reagan reached an accommodation in 1985: Congress adopted Reagan's aggressive posture toward communist regimes in the Third World, and the president allowed Congress to set the agenda on a handful of issues that were tangential to his preoccupation with the East-West struggle.

Because it emerged from intense struggles that were likely to continue, this informal accommodation did not appear to signal the beginning of the "bipartisan consensus" that Reagan wanted for his policies. Rather, it appeared to be the means by which an assertive Congress and an activist administration settled their differences.

Ending a decade of reluctance to intervene in foreign conflicts, Congress in 1985 supported or removed obstacles to U.S. aid for guerrilla movements in Afghanistan, Angola, Cambodia and Nicaragua. Gaining that backing was a major achievement for Reagan, who charged that Congress had almost an isolationist tendency to shrink from combating the Soviet Union and its proxies.

But moderates and liberals in Congress also demonstrated their independence from Reagan on a range of issues that did not directly involve confrontation with the Soviets. Congress forced Reagan to modify, if not abandon, his policy of "constructive engagement" with the white minority government of South Africa, and it induced the administration to take a tougher stand against the authoritarian regime of Philippine President Ferdinand E. Marcos. Congress also rejected outright Reagan's proposal to sell advanced weapons to Jordan before King Hussein sat down at the peace table with Israel.

Reagan's ability to deal with Congress on foreign issues was hampered by divisions among his own advisers and by an open rebellion against his administration led by Sen. Jesse Helms, R-N.C.

Secretary of State George P. Shultz and Defense Secretary Caspar W. Weinberger clearly disagreed over arms control, responding to terrorism and several other issues — creating confusion in Congress and among the public about where the administration stood. And the Helms wing of the Republican Party used every opportunity to undermine Shultz, with the apparent goal of getting him fired. Helms and his allies delayed Senate approval of key State Department nominations, sought to block administration compromises with Congress on controversial matters and launched whispering campaigns highlighting Shultz' alleged failures and predicting his impending departure.

The GOP warfare helped lead in December to the resignation of Robert C. McFarlane, Reagan's national security adviser and an important Shultz ally. McFarlane abruptly quit two weeks after Reagan's summit meeting with Soviet leader Mikhail Gorbachev in Geneva; the apparent reason was because McFarlane was losing bureaucratic battles with Donald T. Regan, the White House chief of staff who was exercising a firm grip on the reins of power. McFarlane was succeeded by his deputy, Adm. John M. Poindexter, who became Reagan's fourth national security adviser in five years.

Avoiding Defeat

By 1985, Reagan had perfected the technique of shifting his own policies or tactics just enough to avoid defeat at the hands of Congress. Repeatedly, upon encountering congressional opposition to his foreign policies, Reagan maneuvered abruptly and deftly, managing to gain more political credit for acknowledging reality than blame for having made mistakes in the first place.

In some cases, he simply surrendered to his political adversaries and adopted their position. That happened in 1983 when he withdrew U.S. Marines from Lebanon and again in 1985 when he imposed sanctions on the white minority government of South Africa.

On other occasions, the president's nose for compromise rescued him from what could have been humiliating defeats. In 1985, facing overwhelming congressional opposition to his proposal to sell advanced weapons to Jordan, Reagan readily agreed to postpone the sale.

In most of these cases, Reagan merely ratified recommendations made to him by administration officials. But members of Congress generally applauded the president himself for establishing a cooperative atmosphere that made compromises and rapid policy turnarounds possible.

Middle East

Terrorism and talk of peace dominated the Middle East in 1985. A connection between the two was certain but not always easy to define in specific terms.

At the outset, the region's "moderate" Arab leaders pronounced the year to be the last chance for real progress toward peace with Israel, and they sought U.S. leadership for a renewal of talks that had been dormant since 1980.

King Fahd of Saudi Arabia, President Hosni Mubarak of Egypt and King Hussein of Jordan all traveled to Washington early in the year and asked Reagan to give urgent attention to the Middle East peace process.

Hussein was particularly vocal in saying that 1985 could be the last opportunity for peace — presumably because it was to be the last full year for Labor Party control of Israel's shaky coalition government. Prime Minister Shimon Peres, the Labor Party leader who seemed willing to deal with Hussein, was scheduled to give up his post in October 1986 to Yitzhak Shamir, the Likud coalition leader who long had opposed any concessions to Arabs.

Hussein on Feb. 11 signed an accord with Yasir Arafat, chairman of the Palestine Liberation Organization, pledging to work toward peace talks. But the agreement did not address directly the main condition Israel and the United States had placed on a PLO role in any talks: PLO acceptance of two U.N. resolutions that imply Israel's right to exist.

Reagan responded by giving his administration's, if not his own, attention to the peace process. Richard W. Murphy, assistant secretary of state for Near Eastern and South Asian affairs, spent much of the year jetting around Middle East capitals and trying to develop a consensus on how to get negotiations under way among Israelis, Jordanians and Palestinians.

Murphy failed to overcome procedural obstacles that each side had erected to disguise unreadiness to get down to serious negotiating. Jordan demanded that any talks be held under the auspices of an "international conference" and that the PLO be present as the official representative of Palestinians in Israeli-occupied territories. Israel rejected both demands unless certain conditions were met, such as exclusion of both the PLO and the Soviet Union.

By year's end, U.S. officials insisted that key actors in the region had committed themselves to negotiate and that only a handful of troublesome technical issues stood in the way. However, there seemed to be little evidence that the year of opportunity for peace had substantially improved the chances for peace talks to get under way.

The lack of progress did not deter Reagan from following through on his promise to Hussein in May that the United States would help meet Jordan's economic and security needs. Reagan in September announced plans for a major arms sale to Jordan, including advanced warplanes, missiles and other items. The price tag was to be in the $1.5 billion-$2 billion range, depending on whether the Air Force decided to sell the new Northrop Corp. F-20 plane or a stripped-down version of General Dynamics' F-16.

As expected, Reagan's proposal encountered a storm of opposition on Capitol Hill, where pro-Israel members argued that Hussein had an aversion to the peace table. The administration did little to overcome such opposition, and so by early October nearly three-fourths of all senators had cosponsored a resolution to block any arms sale to Jordan until peace talks were under way.

To avert an outright defeat of the president, Richard G. Lugar, R-Ind., chairman of the Senate Foreign Relations Committee, engineered a resolution deferring the Jordan arms sale until March 1, 1986, unless Jordan and Israel had begun "direct and meaningful" negotiations. The Senate passed that measure 97-1 on Oct. 24, and the House followed suit on Nov. 12.

Although a major setback for Reagan, the administration's reluctant acceptance of that resolution demonstrated its ability to make the best of a bad political situation.

Hussein viewed delay of the sale as more than a temporary political problem. From his perspective, the congressional action was the latest in a series of American knee-jerk concessions to Israeli pressure. In response, he turned to Syria — the country that U.S. officials had said was most likely to attack Jordan. Hussein and Syrian President Hafez al-Assad met in December, for the first time in six years; while that session produced no firm agreements, it demonstrated the limits of U.S. influence.

Hijackings, Terrorism

Throughout the year, the modest steps toward peace in the Middle East were overshadowed by kidnappings, hijackings, bombings, shootings and other terrorist deeds that killed or wounded hundreds of people throughout the world. The United States and Israel were among the most frequent targets, lending credence to charges that Middle East radicals would go to any lengths to derail a peace process affirming Israel's existence.

In June, when radical Shiite Lebanese Moslems hijacked a Trans World Airlines jet, killed a Navy seaman and held 39 other passengers captive in Beirut, Americans feared a rerun of the Iran hostage nightmare. Reagan vowed never to negotiate with the hijackers and threatened to retaliate. But as the days passed and the threats produced no response, he negotiated with Syria for the peaceful release of the hostages. The hostages left Lebanon on June 30 after 17 days, and a grateful Reagan restrained his urge for revenge.

Four months later, in October, the hijacking in the Mediterranean of the Italian cruise liner *Achille Lauro* offered Reagan a better chance to gain satisfaction against terrorists. The Palestinian hijackers killed a handicapped passenger from New York City named Leon Klinghoffer and held the ship for two days before surrendering to authorities in Egypt. Egypt put the hijackers on a plane bound for Tunisia, but U.S. Navy warplanes intercepted the escape aircraft and forced it to land in Italy. Italian authorities put the hijackers on trial but allowed the alleged mastermind — renegade Palestinian leader Abu Abbas — to escape, causing a momentary rift in U.S.-Italian relations that led to the collapse of the government in Rome.

Americans were again victimized by terrorism in December, when members of a Palestinian faction staged simultaneous attacks on Israeli airline counters at the Rome and Vienna airports. Nineteen persons, including five Americans, died. Reagan accused Libya of giving training and support to the terrorists, and in January he ordered a complete U.S. trade embargo against that country.

Central America

For the first time since taking office, Reagan managed in 1985 to win a broad measure of congressional support for his policies toward Central America. But on several counts that support was given grudgingly and only after Congress attached conditions that demonstrated a fundamental mistrust of what the president was doing.

In the early Reagan years, El Salvador was the focal point of contention between the administration and Congress. Reagan demanded hundreds of millions of dollars in military and economic aid to shore up a succession of Salvadoran governments against a rapidly spreading leftist insurgency. Congress voted most of the aid but threatened a cutoff unless the security forces stopped killing civilians. That controversy came to an end in 1984, when moderate José Napoleón Duarte won the presidency and appeared to gain some control over far-right elements of the military.

As the political debate over El Salvador cooled, Washington's attention shifted to Nicaragua, where U.S.-backed guerrillas were battling the leftist Sandinista regime. Reagan called the rebels "freedom fighters" and insisted they were fighting for democracy against a government that was exporting communist revolution to the rest of Central America. But critics said the rebels — called "contras" for counter-revolutionaries — were mercenaries hired to overthrow a government that Washington found distasteful.

Congress in 1984 suspended the U.S. supply of money and arms to the contras in the wake of revelations about the CIA's bungling of a campaign to mine Nicaraguan harbors. Reagan sought early in 1985 to renew the aid, and in a compromise agreed that any U.S. funds would be used only for "humanitarian" purposes such as food and clothing for the contras and stipulated that the United States was not trying to overthrow the Nicaraguan government. The House rebuffed that request in April, with Democrats remarkably united in opposition to the president.

Shortly after the House acted, Nicaraguan President Daniel Ortega flew to Moscow, seeking financial support for his regime. The trip itself was not unusual; Ortega and other Sandinista leaders frequently went to Moscow for handouts. But the timing offended many Democrats who were nervous that Reagan would portray them as having done a favor for the Sandinistas and their Soviet backers by voting against aid to the contras.

Six weeks later, on June 12, the House reversed itself and approved $27 million in non-military aid to the contras. On the key vote, 58 Democrats joined all but a handful of Republicans in supporting Reagan's position. Perhaps most startling, the House voted to dismantle a 1984 absolute prohibition against CIA military backing for the contras.

By August, Reagan was able to sign into law a supplemental spending bill containing the $27 million. The bill also established a procedure for rapid congressional consideration of a presidential request to replenish those funds when they ran out early in 1986, thus ensuring renewed debate on the issue.

Adding political fuel to the administratrion's case was the gradual collapse of a regional peace-making effort led by Colombia, Mexico, Panama and Venezuela. Many Democrats had demanded aggressive U.S. backing of the "Contadora" negotiations as an alternative to aiding the contras, arguing that a regional peace treaty offered the only hope for ending the multiple wars in Central America. But the Reagan administration was cool to the Contadora talks, and the unwavering hostility between the United States and Nicaragua sharply reduced any prospects for success.

Testing the new-found backing for his policies, Reagan in September asked Congress for authority to give aid and equipment to Central America's police forces, as well as another round of money to the region's military units.

Ostensibly, the request was geared to improving the counter-terrorism capabilities of friendly countries in the wake of a June 19 guerrilla attack in El Salvador that killed 13 persons, including four U.S. Marines. But the administration's broader purpose was to re-establish ties between the United States and Latin police forces. Congress in the early 1970s had barred foreign police aid, in response to allegations that police in some South American countries had engaged in torture and other human rights abuses.

Reagan's request stalled in the House, but the Senate Foreign Relations Committee in December gave bipartisan approval to a limited police aid program. In the waning days of the session, liberal Democrats blocked Senate consideration of the committee proposal.

The Philippines

After years on Washington's back burner, the Philippines suddenly emerged as a major foreign policy issue in 1985. But it was an unusual case because the administration and its staunchest Democratic critics differed only on a relatively minor question of tactics and not on overall goals.

All sides in Congress and the administration agreed that the Philippine islands were of enormous importance to the United States. The reasons were historic (the Philippines was the only former U.S. colony) and strategic (two of the largest and most important U.S. military bases in the world were located there).

There also was broad agreement in Washington that Ferdinand E. Marcos, the Philippine president since 1965, was fumbling the battle against a growing communist insurgency. The U.S. prescription was for military and economic reforms, topped with a heavy dose of free elections.

The debate in Washington was over the extent to which the United States could use its foreign aid and public statements to encourage Marcos to make those reforms. Rep. Stephen J. Solarz, D-N.Y., and other liberals argued that Marcos would not heed the call for reform unless the United States took a tougher public stance against his intransigence and reduced its aid for the corrupt Philippine military. The administration defended its approach of "quiet diplomacy" — while gradually escalating its public criticism of Marcos — and insisted that arms aid boosts were needed to implement the agreement providing for the two U.S. bases in the Philippines.

The administration lost the debate, at least for the time being, when Congress cut Reagan's $100 million request for military aid to $55 million. That decision came in December, shortly after Marcos announced plans to hold "snap" presidential elections in February 1986. There was general agreement that Marcos called the elections, in large part, to quell the U.S. criticism of him. In the end, however, Marcos was forced out of office.

South Africa

Like the Philippines, South Africa emerged as a major political issue in Washington in 1985, and for some of the same reasons.

American civil rights leaders focused new attention on the white minority government of South Africa, starting in December 1984 with a series of daily protests at the South African embassy in Washington. Those protests coincided with a sudden explosion of racial violence in South Africa, resulting in part from a decision by black opposition groups to take a more confrontational approach to their anti-government activities.

Those events helped create a consensus in Congress against the Reagan administration's policy of "constructive engagement" with South Africa.

As conceived by Chester A. Crocker, the assistant secretary of state for African affairs, constructive engagement was intended to persuade the South African government, in a friendly way, to give blacks more political rights and economic opportunities. Crocker's policy also was aimed at getting South African cooperation in easing a border dispute with Mozambique and in resolving thorny questions about Namibia and Angola.

But by 1985 American political leaders across a broad spectrum came to believe that constructive engagement had failed to achieve its goals and had created the impression that the United States actually supported the white government of South Africa. Key among those leaders were several conservative Republicans, especially in the House, who feared that Reagan's policy could undermine efforts to attract blacks to their party.

To symbolize a sharp break with constructive engagement, administration critics promoted the idea of imposing economic sanctions against South Africa, such as banning sales of nuclear equipment and computers to the government and ending the importation into the United States of South African gold coins called Krugerrands. Over administration opposition, legislation to impose sanctions steadily picked up support during the first half of the year, especially as the South African government increasingly used force to suppress black protests.

The House in June passed a bill imposing several

sanctions and threatening a future cutoff of U.S. investment in South Africa. Under the guiding hand of Foreign Relations Chairman Lugar, the Senate followed in July with its own bill to impose much milder sanctions.

Just before the August recess, House-Senate conferees agreed on a compromise set of sanctions, including a Krugerrand ban. But several conservatives, including Helms and Malcolm Wallop, R-Wyo., prevented final Senate action on the compromise before the recess. That gave the administration time to reassess its policy in light of the growing congressional opposition.

On Sept. 9, just as the Senate was about to take up the compromise bill, Reagan announced his own economic sanctions against South Africa, including the Krugerrand ban. The president's about-face undercut support in the Senate for the compromise bill, and the Republican leadership went to extraordinary lengths to block a vote on adopting it — including removing the official copy of the bill from the Senate chamber so it could not be considered.

U.S.-Soviet Relations

The first U.S.-Soviet summit meeting in six years failed to produce any real movement toward an arms control agreement but did spawn new hope that the two countries could negotiate their many differences.

Reagan and Soviet General Secretary Gorbachev met in Geneva on Nov. 19-20 and agreed on the broad principle of a 50-percent cut in nuclear weapons, on accelerating a new round of arms talks and on holding follow-up summits in 1986 and 1987. More importantly, the two men brushed aside a prearranged schedule and spent hours in direct, private meetings — a development that optimists said gave each leader a personal stake in improving relations between their countries.

A grim reminder of the underlying conflict between the two countries was the steady flow of arrests of current and former U.S. government employees on espionage charges. A year full of spy stories began in May with the arrest of John Anthony Walker, a retired Navy communications specialist who allegedly recruited his son and brother to spy for the Soviet Union. Others were arrested for selling secrets to the Soviet Union, Ghana, China and even Israel.

The most spectacular espionage case broke on Nov. 2, when Vitaly Yurchenko "re-defected" to the Soviet Embassy in Washington. A KGB official, Yurchenko supposedly had defected to the United States in August and had provided valuable information about Soviet intelligence capabilities. Months later, U.S. officials were still debating whether he had been a genuine defector who changed his mind or had been planted to confuse and embarrass the United States.

Foreign Aid

Skillful and determined politicking by the chairmen of the House and Senate foreign policy committees helped give new life to the process by which Congress considered foreign aid programs.

Under the leadership of Foreign Relations Chairman Lugar and House Foreign Affairs Chairman Dante B. Fascell, D-Fla., Congress in 1985 passed a foreign aid authorization bill for the first time since 1981. That action greatly enhanced the credibility of the two committees, which had suffered politically because of their inability to get aid bills enacted in 1982-84. Authorization legislation was the main tool those two committees — and Congress as a whole — used to influence U.S. foreign policy.

The bill authorized nearly $13 billion for foreign aid annually in fiscal years 1986-87. The passage of a two-year bill meant that Congress would not have to deal with the always unpopular measure in 1986, an election year.

The most important feature of the bill was its general acceptance of the administration's proposition that the United States should support a broad range of guerrilla forces that were battling established communist regimes. The bill authorized aid, directly or indirectly, to guerrilla groups in Afghanistan, Cambodia and Nicaragua and lifted a mid-1970s ban on U.S. aid to a similar group in Angola.

In spite of the successful completion of an authorizations bill, Congress failed once again to pass a separate appropriations bill for foreign aid. As it had done annually since 1982, Congress tucked foreign aid appropriations into an omnibus continuing resolution; the primary effect was to shield foreign aid spending from floor votes and public scrutiny since it was hidden in the larger bill.

The foreign aid portion of the continuing resolution represented a major achievement for Rep. David R. Obey, D-Wis., the new chairman of the House Appropriations Subcommittee on Foreign Operations. Largely at Obey's behest, the bill halted the Reagan administration buildup of military aid to friendly countries.

During the first Reagan term, military aid had been one of the fastest growing parts of the federal budget, growing at an annual rate of nearly 20 percent. Reagan portrayed military aid, and a related program of economic aid, as an adjunct of the defense budget because it bolstered Israel, Egypt, South Korea, Turkey and scores of pro-Western countries. But Obey and other liberals in Congress argued that the administration put too much emphasis on security concerns and failed to heed the need for economic development in Third World countries.

At Obey's insistence, the fiscal 1986 continuing resolution cut foreign aid across the board, both from the Reagan request and from the previous year's levels. But the main weight of the budget ax fell on military aid, helping reverse the priorities that Reagan previously had pushed through Congress.

Congress' new-found ability to resist presidential demands for increased foreign aid did not transfer to the one politically sacred item in the aid budget: Israel. With little debate and no open dissent, Congress in mid-1985 approved $1.5 billion in emergency aid to prop up Israel's ailing economy. Authorized over fiscal years 1985-86, that money was on top of Israel's regular annual allotment of $3 billion in U.S. economic and foreign aid.

To maintain the appearance of balance in the U.S. posture toward the Middle East, Congress also approved a special $500 million dose of economic aid for Egypt — Israel's partner in the 1978-79 Camp David accords and peace treaty. That aid was on top of about $2.2 billion in regular military and economic aid for Egypt.

Capitol Hill enthusiasm for the Israel aid was so great that congressional committees began approving it even before the administration had requested it. Shultz had asked Congress to withhold the aid until the Israeli government implemented a series of economic reforms aimed at lowering inflation and cutting government spending. But Congress, responding to pleas by Israel and its influential lobbying organizations, voted the aid and directed the administration to spend it before all the reforms Shultz wanted were in place.

—By John Felton

Congress Clears Foreign Aid Authorization Bill

For the first time in four years, Congress cleared for the president a foreign aid authorization bill (S 960 — PL 99-83).

The bill gave President Reagan most of the economic, military and development aid he had requested and lifted several major foreign policy restrictions Congress had imposed in recent years. It authorized $12.77 billion in each of fiscal years 1986 and 1987, nearly $500 million below Reagan's request. In addition, it authorized $2 billion in emergency economic aid to Israel and Egypt in fiscal 1985-86.

The conference report on the bill (H Rept 99-237) was adopted by the Senate on July 30 by a voice vote. The next day, the House cleared the bill on a 262-161 vote, an unusually wide margin for a foreign aid bill. *(Vote 249, p. 80-H)*

Congress is supposed to enact a separate aid measure annually, or at least every other year, but both chambers had not done so since 1981. Instead, the politically unpopular foreign aid authorizations had been incorporated into omnibus continuing appropriations resolutions. *(1984 Almanac p. 390)*

In passing S 960, Congress signaled a renewed willingness to intervene in foreign wars by giving help to anticommunist insurgencies in Nicaragua, Cambodia and Afghanistan.

The measure also moderated, but did not entirely lift, controversial House-passed provisions that had limited Reagan's flexibility in dealing with Jordan and the Philippines. And it implemented the heart of the once-controversial recommendations by the Kissinger commission on Central America. *(1984 Almanac p. 93)*

Administration Objections

Reagan signed the bill into law on Aug. 8, although the administration had opposed from the outset some of its provisions — notably curbs on sales of weapons to Jordan and on his Central America policies.

The administration also had complained that House- and Senate-passed cutbacks in military and economic aid would force the United States to eliminate or reduce substantially programs in nearly 20 countries.

House Foreign Affairs Chairman Dante B. Fascell, D-Fla., said the administration position amounted to "this question of Congress being an impediment to the execution and implementation" of executive branch policy. "But since we're here and we intend to stay here, we're going to continue to express our opinion, and we did it in the bill."

The Jordan issue was settled by conferees, who approved compromise language requiring that the president could not sell advanced arms to Jordan unless he certified that Jordan had publicly agreed to recognize and negotiate with Israel.

And Richard G. Lugar, R-Ind., chairman of the Senate Foreign Relations Committee, said he narrowly averted a potential veto over a provision barring the United States from making an agreement with another country to provide aid to the anti-government "contra" guerrillas in Nicaragua. *(Contra aid, p. 61)*

Lugar and the provision's sponsor, Claiborne Pell, D-R.I., on July 29 agreed to a modification that merely barred the United States from forcing foreign aid recipients to give help to the contras.

Aid Amounts

House conferees had set a goal of freezing aid programs in fiscal 1986 at the 1985 level, and they succeeded. Overall authorizations in the bill were about $1 million below the $12.775 billion appropriated for 1985 as of July 31. *(Final provisions, p. 54; chart, p. 43)*

The final bill represented a compromise between the two chambers on priorities.

The House had boosted funding for development aid programs above Reagan's request while cutting back sharply on military programs. The Senate trimmed both categories, but voted to give Reagan substantially more military aid than had the House.

In the conference committee, the Senate agreed to the higher development aid figures while the House accepted the higher military aid figures.

House Committee Action

Foreign Affairs subcommittees laid much of the groundwork on the foreign aid bill the week of March 18, and most of these provisions were accepted when the full committee drafted HR 1555 on April 2-3. The committee bill (H Rept 99-39), reported April 11, authorized $14.5 billion for foreign aid programs.

Even as the committee was taking its final vote, a senior State Department official pronounced the bill "unacceptable." The administration objected most to a provision banning sales of warplanes and other advanced weapons to Jordan unless that country recognized and agreed to negotiate with Israel. The administration also opposed the panel's restrictions on policy options in Central America.

In pursuit of a freeze on aid spending, committee Chairman Fascell instructed all subcommittees to hold their recommendations to the level approved by Congress for fiscal 1985 in the continuing appropriations resolution (PL 98-473). Most of the panels complied with Fascell's directive by reducing Reagan's requests for boosts in military aid.

Fascell's Subcommittee on International Security on March 20 mandated nearly $400 million in arms aid cuts from Reagan's $6.7 billion request. But it exempted Israel and Egypt, the two biggest aid recipients.

Cambodian Rebel Aid

Triggering debate on whether the United States should get involved in trying to force Vietnam to end its occupation of Cambodia, the Subcommittee on Asian and Pacific Affairs on March 20 voted, 6-3, to provide $5 million to help arm and equip non-communist Cambodian guerrillas. *(Details, p. 56)*

The aid, not requested by the administration, was to be the first U.S. support for the rebels.

Subcommittee Chairman Stephen J. Solarz, D-N.Y., proposed the aid, saying he was responding to a Feb. 11 plea from Thailand and other U.S. allies in the region for international support of the Cambodian resistance.

Under his plan, Congress would give the special economic aid to Thailand, with the understanding that Thailand would use it to provide "appropriate assistance" to the non-communist guerrillas in Cambodia.

Solarz said the aid would be used to strengthen the

resistance. He did not reject a characterization of it as military aid by other members of the subcommittee. No U.S. military personnel would be involved in aiding the guerrillas, Solarz said.

The administration previously had rejected all requests for military support, insisting that U.S. involvement in the war could complicate negotiations aimed at convincing Vietnam to leave Cambodia.

The proposal split the subcommittee's liberal members. Ranking Republican Jim Leach of Iowa and Democrats Michael D. Barnes of Maryland and Sam Gejdenson of Connecticut opposed it.

Joining Solarz in backing it were Democrats Robert G. Torricelli of New Jersey and Mervyn M. Dymally of California, and three Republicans, Gerald B. H. Solomon of New York, Toby Roth of Wisconsin and Doug Bereuter of Nebraska.

On April 3, the full committee took up the issue and beat back Leach's effort to kill the Cambodia arms aid. The Leach amendment, rejected 9-24, instead would have authorized humanitarian aid, such as food and medicine.

While the administration neither supported nor actively opposed the aid, William Schneider Jr., under secretary of state for security assistance, appeared to undermine opposition to the Solarz proposal by refusing to give unqualified support to Leach.

Israel, Egypt

In its March 20 working session, the strongly pro-Israel Subcommittee on Europe and the Middle East resisted the temptation to approve $1.5 billion in emergency economic aid for Israel that the administration had not yet requested. *(Israel aid, p. 90)*

But on April 3, the full committee approved the supplemental aid, aimed at easing Israel's severe economic crisis, over fiscal 1985-86.

The money, all to be authorized and appropriated in fiscal 1985, was to be spent over 1985-86. It came on top of $1.2 billion in regular annual economic aid to Israel and military aid of $1.4 billion in 1985 and $1.8 billion in 1986.

The aid bill also included Reagan's 1986 requests for Egypt: $815 million in economic aid, $213 million in food aid and $1.3 billion in military aid.

Secretary of State George P. Shultz had sought to delay the extra $1.5 billion, saying that it would do little good unless Israel continued long-term economic and budget reforms.

Shultz sent two aides to Capitol Hill on April 2 to ask the panel not to vote the money for at least six weeks. But members of the House committee were unmoved.

The amendment approving the $1.5 billion was drafted by committee leaders on March 29 — four days before the administration aides made their pitch. Its sponsors were senior members: Rep. Lee H. Hamilton, D-Ind.; Chairman Fascell; ranking Republican William S. Broomfield, R-Mich.; and Benjamin A. Gilman, R-N.Y.

Hamilton, who had been among the Hill leaders most willing to accept arguments for delay, defended the panel's action, noting that it was only "a preliminary step" and that Congress likely would not give final approval to the aid for several months. He insisted that the $1.5 billion was a one-time-only injection of emergency aid.

Gerry E. Studds, D-Mass., noted that with the $1.5 billion amendment, Israel and Egypt would receive $6.6 billion of the $14.5 billion authorized in the bill for all foreign aid recipients.

The committee approved the $1.5 billion amendment by voice vote; the only member clearly voting "no" was Ed Zschau, R-Calif., who had supported a delay.

The bill also included language complaining about the "less than normal relations between Egypt and Israel" and calling on Egypt to return an ambassador to Israel. Egyptian President Hosni Mubarak withdrew his ambassador from Tel Aviv in 1982, in reaction to the Israeli invasion of Lebanon, and had refused to send one back.

The bill also:

- Contained $400 million in U.S. aid to finance Israel's development of its new warplane, the Lavi. Of that amount, up to $150 million could be spent in the United States and not less than $250 million would be spent in Israel. Congress had been providing funds for the Lavi since 1983.
- Made permanent a legal ban on the administration conducting negotiations with the Palestine Liberation Organization. U.S. policy had barred such talks since 1975, but Congress voted in 1984 (in PL 98-473) to put that prohibition in law for fiscal 1985.

Jordan Arms

On March 20, for the second year in a row, the Europe and Middle East subcommittee voted to ban any sales to Jordan of advanced weapons, such as F-16 jet fighters or mobile HAWK anti-aircraft missiles, unless that country was publicly committed to recognizing and negotiating directly with Israel.

But the panel coupled that proposed ban with two bouquets to Jordan: a $5 million increase in economic aid (to $25 million) and a statement praising Jordan for making progress "in the search for a just and lasting peace in the Middle East." *(Jordan arms, p. 93)*

Larry Smith, D-Fla., sponsor of the arms sales ban, insisted that he and other subcommittee members were offering a balanced approach to Jordan and were not attacking the country or its leader, King Hussein.

But subcommittee Chairman Hamilton attacked the arms ban, saying it would be "detrimental to the peace process" by rebuffing Hussein even as he was seeking a way to negotiate with Israel.

Fiscal 1985 foreign aid law (PL 98-473) included a sense-of-Congress statement opposing advanced arms sales to Jordan. The subcommittee sought to toughen that by imposing a flat prohibition unless Jordan moved to negotiate with Israel. *(1984 Almanac p. 396)*

Philippines, Other Asian Issues

With little debate, the Asia subcommittee approved a proposal by Solarz to reduce military aid to the Philippines as a symbol of congressional unhappiness with the authoritarian rule of President Ferdinand E. Marcos. *(Philippines, p. 113)*

The panel took two actions on Philippine aid used as rent for two major U.S. bases there. First, it reduced that overall aid amount to $180 million, from Reagan's $195 million request. Then it cut the portion of military aid to $25 million, from Reagan's $100 million request, and boosted economic aid to $155 million, from Reagan's $95 million request.

The shift from military to economic aid paralleled a move that Congress made in 1984 to demonstrate unhappiness with Marcos.

The panel also adopted a sense-of-the-Congress statement calling on Marcos to respect human rights, hold free

Foreign Aid Authorizations, 1986-1987

Following are the authorizations made in PL 99-83 for foreign aid programs in fiscal 1986. Identical amounts were authorized for fiscal 1987. Not included in these figures are supplemental authorizations in fiscal 1985-86 for Economic Support Fund aid to Israel ($1.5 billion), Egypt ($500 million) and Middle East regional programs ($8 million).

(Figures in thousands of dollars)

Program	Reagan Request	House Amount	Senate Amount	Final Amount
Foreign Military Sales forgiven loans	$ 3,100,000	$ 3,100,000.0	$ 3,100,000.0	$ 3,100,000
Foreign Military Sales concessional and market-rate loans	2,555,000	2,128,384.4	2,364,500.0	2,271,000
Military Assistance Program grants	949,350	761,648.0	805,100.0	805,100
Military Education and Training	65,650	54,421.9	56,221.0	56,221
Peacekeeping	37,000	35,816.0	37,000.0	37,000
Subtotal, Military Aid	**$ 6,707,000**	**$ 6,080,270.3**	**$ 6,362,821.0**	**$ 6,269,321**
Economic Support Fund	**$ 4,024,000**	**$ 3,775,587.2**	**$ 3,841,000.0**	**$ 3,800,000**
Agriculture aid	792,352	766,996.7	755,551.0	760,000
Population aid	250,017	309,760.0	270,017.0	290,000
Health aid	146,427	215,997.6	186,427.0	205,000
Child Survival Fund	0	48,400.0	25,000.0	25,000
Education aid	183,533	182,790.3	177,100.0	180,000
Selected development programs	223,071	215,932.7	200,000.0	207,000
Sahel Development	80,500	91,476.0	80,500.0	87,750
Africa Development Foundation	1,000	3,872.0	1,000.0	3,872
Subtotal, Development Aid	**$ 1,676,900**	**$ 1,835,225.4**	**$ 1,695,595.0**	**$ 1,758,622**
Anti-terrorism	5,000	9,840.0	5,000.0	9,840
American Schools and Hospitals Abroad	10,000	38,720.0	30,000.0	35,000
International organizations	196,211	275,787.1	267,675.5	270,000
Narcotics control	57,529	55,688.1	50,217.0	57,529
Disaster aid	25,000	24,200.0	25,000.0	25,000
Trade and development	20,000	20,328.0	20,000.0	20,000
AID operating expenses	387,000	379,004.1	387,000.0	387,000
Peace Corps	124,400	131,744.8	128,600.0	130,000
Inter-American Foundation	8,699	11,616.0	11,969.0	11,969
Subtotal, Other Programs	**$ 833,839**	**$ 946,928.1**	**$ 925,461.5**	**$ 946,338**
TOTAL	**$ 13,241,739**	**$ 12,638,011.0**	**$ 12,824,877.5**	**$ 12,774,281**

elections, and implement a wide range of economic and military reforms. The statement also required the president to report to Congress every six months, beginning Oct. 1, on the status of Philippine reforms.

On other regional issues, the House bill:

- Reduced overall aid to countries under its jurisdiction to $1.52 billion, $31.9 million below Reagan's request. Most of the cuts were in military aid to such countries as the Philippines.
- Approved an amendment that would bar U.S. foreign aid to any country that attempted illegally to obtain materials, equipment or technology from the United States to help construct a nuclear weapon. The amendment potentially could have an impact on Pakistan, one of the largest recipients of U.S. aid, which had been accused by some critics of using illegal means to obtain nuclear supplies from the United States.
- Approved a statement that U.S. arms aid to South Korea was given "in the expectation" that the government there would move toward democracy.

Greece, Turkey

Greek Prime Minister Andreas Papandreou, who for years had made harsh attacks on the United States, came in for unusually tough criticism March 20 from subcommittee members. They backed up their anger by trimming $1.75 million from Reagan's request for $500 million in military loans to Greece.

Torricelli led the attack on Papandreou, citing particularly the prime minister's statements casting doubt on whether the Soviet Union posed a threat to Western Europe. If Papandreou continued to make such statements, Torricelli said, "it will be increasingly difficult to ask the American people to make financial sacrifices" to aid Greece.

The panel also expressed its unhappiness with Papandreou by recommending an unusually small trim in aid to Turkey, Greece's traditional rival and the frequent target of foreign aid-cutting by Congress. But the bill included an approximation of the usual balance in U.S. aid to Greece and Turkey.

The bill included $890 million for Turkey, including $740 million in arms aid, $45 million less than Reagan had requested.

Committee members agreed that about 60 percent of arms loans to each country would carry below-market interest rates. Members used the concessional loan provision to denounce Papandreou for attacking the United States and attempting to gain favor with the Soviets.

Olympia J. Snowe, R-Maine, complained that Papandreou's "objectionable statements" and "erratic actions" made it difficult to defend that country. But cutting the traditional level of aid to Greece would boost anti-U.S. elements there, she said.

The bill did not impose strict conditions on Turkey's aid. In the past, the committee often tried to restrict the aid unless Turkey was taking steps to end its occupation of Cyprus.

Western Hemisphere

In its most harmonious markup session in years, the Western Hemisphere Affairs Subcommittee on March 19 imposed conditions on Central America aid, but several of these were watered down by the full committee on April 2. In some cases, subcommittee Chairman Barnes and other Democrats openly sought to placate the administration.

The bill included $1.4 billion for economic, development, military and other programs for Latin American and Caribbean countries in fiscal 1986, the identical amount that Congress approved for fiscal 1985 and about $250 million below Reagan's request. Subcommittee Republicans made no effort to restore the president's requests, and liberal Democrats did not move to slash further the figures that Barnes suggested.

Most of the cuts — $152 million — were made in aid to four Central American countries for which Reagan had sought major increases: El Salvador (a $54.5 million cut to $378 million), Guatemala (a $22.5 million cut to $46 million), Honduras (a $43.1 million cut to $170 million) and Panama (a $31 million cut to $51 million). The subcommittee trimmed only $500,000 from Reagan's $167 million request for Costa Rica.

Of the amount approved for El Salvador, $113 million was for military aid, about $20 million below Reagan's request. *(El Salvador police aid, supplemental military assistance to Central America, p. 80)*

The bill imposed human rights and other conditions on El Salvador's aid similar to requirements that had been in effect at various times since 1981. Reagan had proposed eliminating all strings on aid to El Salvador.

But in a sign of continued congressional backing for President José Napoleón Duarte, the subcommittee watered down an attempt by liberals to add a condition aimed at restraining the Salvadoran army's bombing campaign against leftist guerrillas. Several human rights groups had charged that the military had killed civilians through indiscriminate bombings, and Peter H. Kostmayer, D-Pa., offered an amendment that would have barred the United States from providing additional planes that could be used for bombings. But on the suggestion of Barnes, the subcommittee adopted an alternative requiring the administration to report to Congress on the types of weapons provided El Salvador.

In another sign of support for Duarte, the full committee weakened a subcommittee provision that the president could provide assistance only if he certified to Congress that the Salvadoran government was willing to "pursue a dialogue" with its leftist opposition, had made "demonstrated progress" in curtailing death squads and establishing an effective judicial system.

Robert J. Lagomarsino, R-Calif., said that requirement implied a "lack of confidence" in Duarte and proposed that the president would be required to submit reports, rather than certifications, to Congress on El Salvador.

Barnes' willingness to make the change, in a "bipartisan spirit," brought protests from some Democrats. Torricelli said it was "merely a partisan retreat" on human rights.

Democrats also accepted a push by Republicans to scale back a requirement for the president to report to Congress 30 days before each U.S. military exercise in Central America. John McCain, R-Ariz., said the requirement would be "shackling the ability of the military commanders in the field to carry out the exercises."

Barnes professed puzzlement at why the required reports would have that effect. Nevertheless, he and the committee accepted a GOP move to limit the formal requirement of how much information had to be given Congress.

On other issues, the bill:

- Barred any foreign aid funds from being used to support the Nicaraguan contras. Barnes drafted the provision in response to press reports that El Salvador, Honduras and possibly other countries had used some of their U.S. aid to back the contras.

- Prohibited the president from sending U.S. troops into combat in El Salvador or Nicaragua unless Congress had declared war or otherwise given its approval. When the full committee met April 2, Republicans did not try to eliminate this provision, even though the administration opposed it most strongly.

The House had approved an identical provision in May 1984; it later was watered down in a House-Senate conference committee. *(1984 Almanac p. 59)*

- Allowed $5 million in each of fiscal years 1986-87 that could be used for military training aid and to help the Guatemalan military build such civil works as schools, bridges and medical clinics. However, at Democrats' insistence, the aid would not be provided until the president certified to Congress that an elected civilian government was in power in Guatemala and had demonstrated progress in improving human rights.
- Eliminated Reagan's request for a multi-year authorization of non-military aid to Central American countries, as recommended in 1984 by a presidential commission headed by former Secretary of State Henry A. Kissinger. Reagan had requested $1.2 billion per year for the region in fiscal years 1987-89. The subcommittee approved about $1 billion for 1987, but rejected the funds for the later years.

Bolivia

By a 14-9 vote, the committee softened a provision in the bill barring aid to Bolivia until it moved to eliminate cocaine production.

As drafted by committee leaders, the bill would have withheld all of Bolivia's $21 million in economic development aid until it met several conditions for reducing production of coca, from which cocaine is made.

Barnes, expressing concern that such a tough provision would undermine the civilian leadership of Bolivia, proposed instead conditioning only $10 million. The panel approved that milder condition after heated debate during which members said the United States should suspend all aid to Bolivia as a symbol of its determination to crack down on drug-producing countries.

Africa Assistance

Meeting on March 19, the Africa subcommittee joined its fellow Foreign Affairs panels in using the overall budget freeze as a reason to impose arms aid cuts. Like the others, the Africa panel had complained that the Reagan administration was loading up foreign countries with arms and skirting long-term development needs.

The Africa panel sliced $113 million in military and military-related aid from Reagan's $950 million request for aid to the region. But, in doing so, it acknowledged that the administration "has made some progress in moving toward" greater emphasis on development aid to Africa.

As in the past, Zaire was a major issue. The panel voted a $4 million limit on military aid to the authoritarian regime of President Mobutu Sese Seko; Reagan had requested $10.4 million. The bill also included Reagan's request for $56 million in economic, development and other assistance, but the subcommittee insisted that $15 million in economic aid be used for development projects, and be administered "as far as practicable" by private groups so that it was "insulated from corruption."

When the full committee met, members rejected by voice vote an administration-backed move to lift the $4 million limit.

Committee Democrats argued that Mobutu's government had misused past U.S. aid and done little to reduce corruption. Howard Wolpe, D-Mich., the Africa Subcommittee chairman, said that Zaire had misused aid and failed to maintain equipment supplied in the past by the United States, especially C-130 transport planes.

But Republicans and a State Department official, Pierre Shostal, insisted that Mobutu had made reforms and that Zaire was an important ally in Central Africa. Mark D. Siljander, R-Mich., who offered the amendment to restore Reagan's request, said Zaire had offered amnesty to its political prisoners, had recognized Israel and "stands up to Libya."

The bill also included $14.3 million in arms aid to Liberia "in the expectation" that elections were to be held in October and that the military would allow a return to full civilian rule.

Population Planning

The committee on April 2 rejected efforts by conservatives to put language in the bill that would enforce a cutoff of U.S. funds to two international family planning agencies: the International Planned Parenthood Federation and the U.N. Fund for Population Activities.

And, over administration objections, the panel boosted U.S. funding for family planning overseas to $320 million, a $70 million increase over Reagan's request and $30 million above the fiscal 1985 level.

Population programs in foreign countries, especially those that might be involved with abortions, were the focus of growing controversy.

The administration raised the political stakes in 1984 when it suspended U.S. funding for International Planned Parenthood and the U.N. agency. The administration on March 30 released $36 million for the U.N. agency, but withheld $10 million; that is the amount the U.N. fund was spending in China, which was alleged to practice forced abortions and permit female infanticide.

As drafted by Foreign Affairs subcommittees, the bill would have prohibited the administration from denying funds to agencies that supported voluntary family planning programs.

However, committee members accepted an amendment by Snowe to bar any U.S. money from being used for any population programs in China — even indirectly through the U.N. agency.

The amendment also instructed U.S. representatives at international organizations to vote against funding population programs in China, as long as the president determined that there were "valid reports" of infanticide and coerced abortion there.

The committee adopted Snowe's amendment, along with the increase in population funding, on a 24-11 vote that was largely along party lines.

By a 12-23 vote, the committee also rejected an attempt by Christopher H. Smith, R-N.J., to undermine the Snowe amendment. Smith offered the same amendment that had been accepted the previous week by the Senate Foreign Relations Committee. It would have barred U.S. funds to agencies that supported family planning programs in countries that practiced or permitted infanticide and forced abortion.

Snowe, offering her amendment to make explicit the bar on U.S. money going to China, attacked Smith and anti-abortion groups that were pressuring the committee on the issue. "This anti-abortion crusade has become an anti-family planning crusade," she said.

Peace Corps

The committee approved, by voice vote, two amendments by Leach mandating an expansion of the Peace Corps. One amendment set a goal of 10,000 corps volunteers, compared with the current limit of 5,800; the other boosted funding for the agency to $136 million, $11.6 million above Reagan's request.

Leach's amendments caused some discomfort for the Peace Corps official at the meeting, Jan Nichols-Hinkley, who told the committee that her agency had no comment. But a higher-ranking State Department official, Edward Fox, acting assistant secretary of state for legislative affairs, flatly opposed the amendments, saying: "If they [the Peace Corps] have no position, I will give them one."

Senate Committee Action

Working with extraordinary speed and harmony, the Senate Foreign Relations Committee on March 26-27 approved a $12.8 billion foreign aid authorization bill for fiscal 1986. The bill (S Rept 99-34) was reported April 19.

The panel's new chairman, Richard G. Lugar, R-Ind., was determined to keep out of the bill controversial amendments that could spark administration opposition; he wielded a firm gavel and made effective use of his paper-thin 9-8 Republican majority.

Democrats, also anxious to see a foreign aid bill enacted, offered to compromise on most of the politically sensitive issues they raised.

The committee's markup was also smoothed by a relative lack of controversy over support for El Salvador; in 1984, the panel was so torn over El Salvador that it was unable to muster a majority for any Central America provisions.

The panel approved the bill 15-1, with Jesse Helms, R-N.C., dissenting.

An example of the panel's ability to skirt sensitive issues was its handling of proposals for U.S. sanctions against the white minority government in South Africa. Responding to killings of blacks in South Africa, most committee members clearly wanted to take some action condemning the government's racial policies.

But Lugar argued that attaching administration-opposed provisions on South Africa would have placed too heavy a burden on the foreign aid bill. The panel drafted a separate measure threatening sanctions unless progress was made in two years. *(South Africa, p. 83)*

In another example of bipartisan agreement, the committee gave speedy approval to funding levels drafted by Lugar and Chistopher J. Dodd, D-Conn., that would have substantially frozen foreign aid spending in fiscal 1986 at the 1985 amounts. That resulted in a savings of $417 million from President Reagan's request. The panel pared $344 million from Reagan's $6.7 billion request for military aid and $73 million from his $6.4 billion request for economic and development aid.

Although committee members were anxious to give extra aid to Israel, they agreed to delay at the behest of Secretary of State Shultz.

Israel had requested $1.5 billion in emergency economic aid during fiscal years 1985-86, on top of its $1.2 billion regular amount.

Central America

In its only action that directly contradicted the administration on a major issue, the committee voted 9-8 on March 27 to restrict aid to the anti-government "contras" in Nicaragua.

But panel members immediately disputed what they had done.

Lugar said the panel had voted only to bar the use of U.S. foreign aid to support the contras.

However, the sponsor of the Nicaragua provision, Pell, insisted that the committee also had voted to bar the administration from conspiring with foreign aid recipients to channel money to the guerrillas.

Lugar insisted he never saw the amendment, and he noted that a transcript of the meeting showed that the latter part of Pell's amendment was never discussed.

After discussing the matter March 28, Lugar and Pell still could not agree on what language the committee had adopted. But they agreed to put Pell's language into the committee report, with Lugar reserving the right to move to delete it on the Senate floor.

The lone Republican voting for the Pell amendment was Charles McC. Mathias Jr. of Maryland.

Earlier, the committee had rejected, on an 8-8 tie, a Dodd amendment that also would have barred foreign aid to any country that provided funding or material support to the contras. Opponents said that could mean a cutoff of U.S. aid to Israel, which reportedly had given some aid to the contras.

The panel also rejected several other Dodd amendments that would have restricted Reagan's policies in Central America:

- By a 6-10 vote, a sweeping amendment that would have barred the foreign aid to the contras, imposed conditions on aid to El Salvador and Guatemala and reduced U.S. aid for Costa Rica, El Salvador, Guatemala and Honduras to $750 million, from Reagan's $908 million request.
- By a 7-10 vote, the conditions on military aid to El Salvador.
- By an 8-9 vote, the conditions on military aid to Guatemala.

Also, on an 8-8 vote, the panel rejected an amendment by Nancy Landon Kassebaum, R-Kan., that would have deleted from the bill a $1.2 billion annual authorization for economic and development aid to Central America in fiscal years 1987-89. The administration had said the advance authorization was necessary to assure the region of long-term U.S. support.

Greece-Turkey

For years one of the strongholds of pro-Greek, and anti-Turkish, sentiment in Congress, the Foreign Relations Committee on March 27 broke with the past and directed most of its fire at Greece, particularly that country's outspoken socialist prime minister, Andreas Papandreou.

Panel members said they were distressed by Papandreou's repeated political attacks on the United States, by his attempts to curry favor with the Soviets and by his refusal to take part in routine NATO military exercises.

As in the past, the committee voted, 9-4, to impose a 7-10 ratio on U.S. military aid to the two countries: $500 million for Greece and $715 million for Turkey. But the committee did not couple that action with its usual harsh attacks on Turkey or with a threatened aid cutoff unless Turkey began withdrawing its 20,000-some troops from the island of Cyprus.

In perhaps the most startling reversal from the past, several members expressed a reluctance to give Greece the same concessional terms on its military aid loans that Turkey received. Rudy Boschwitz, R-Minn., said: "I see little in what the Greeks are doing and saying that would justify" the special low-interest loans.

Boschwitz cited as "very disturbing" Papandreou's surprise decision in March to oust the head of state, conservative President Constantine Caramanlis, and to abolish the little authority that the president had over the government.

Greece's supporters on the panel offered little defense for Papandreou. Paul S. Sarbanes, D-Md., the only committee member of direct Greek descent, said, "this is a testing time for Greek democracy."

Other Issues

On other issues, the committee:

- Included in the bill a requirement that the president certify to Congress that Saudi Arabia had met all the conditions that Reagan imposed in 1981 for the sale of five AWACS radar planes. Among the conditions was that Middle East peace negotiations be completed or that "significant progress toward that goal has been accomplished with the substantial assistance of Saudi Arabia."

Alan Cranston, D-Calif., sponsor of the amendment, said he was "somewhat skeptical that the Saudis have complied" with Reagan's conditions.

William Schneider Jr., under secretary of state for security assistance, said it was "a bad practice to codify" such presidential conditions. *(Background, 1981 Almanac p. 129)*

- Adopted two seemingly contradictory amendments on U.S. funding for private and international organizations involved in family planning programs. The purpose of both actions was to bar any chance that U.S. aid would go for abortion or forced family planning programs in China. But it was unclear what impact the amendments were to have on organizations that ran voluntary family planning programs in China.

By a 9-7 vote, the committee adopted an amendment by Kassebaum aimed at overturning a Reagan administration policy that had resulted in the suspension of U.S. funding for the International Planned Parenthood Federation and the U.N. Fund for Population Activities. The administration stopped supporting International Planned Parenthood because some of its affiliates provided advice on abortions, and the U.N. agency because it funded family planning efforts in China.

But by a 13-3 vote, the committee also adopted a Helms amendment to bar further funding of the U.N. agency. That amendment would have prohibited any U.S. family planning aid to a country "which permits, officially or in practice, infanticide or coerced abortion" or to "any organization which provides funds, directly or indirectly, with respect to such a country."

- Rejected, 8-9, an amendment by John Kerry, D-Mass., reducing arms aid to the Philippines and imposing conditions on that aid. The amendment would have cut the aid to $40 million, from Reagan's $100 million request, and allowed the Philippines to get the money only if the president reported to Congress that the government there had made progress on human rights and other issues and was prepared to hold free elections.

Kerry said that unless the United States actively pressured President Ferdinand E. Marcos to reform his government, "there is an inevitability to a communist takeover" of the Philippines. But Lugar said the Reagan administration had been "reasonably adept" at encouraging reform in the Philippines, and it was uncertain whether congressional intervention would help.

- Took two steps to criticize Pakistan for its alleged efforts to build a nuclear bomb. The panel adopted an amendment by Larry Pressler, R-S.D., denying foreign aid to any country that attempted illegally to obtain U.S. material or technology to build a nuclear weapon. Second, the panel voted to require the president to suspend all aid if he determined that Pakistan had obtained a nuclear weapon.

Senate Floor Action

Breaking a four-year dry spell, the Senate on May 15 approved a foreign aid authorization bill that gave Reagan nearly everything he wanted and placed few restraints on his foreign policies.

S 960 authorized $12.8 billion for foreign aid programs in each of fiscal years 1986-87, plus $2 billion for emergency economic aid to Israel and Egypt. The Senate passed the measure 75-19 after only two days of debate and amendments. *(Vote 82, p. 18-S)*

Lugar steered the always-unpopular bill through the Senate with remarkable ease, prevailing upon his colleagues not to offer controversial amendments. To advocates of tough economic sanctions against the white minority government in South Africa, Lugar gave assurances of a June 4 committee vote on sanctions legislation — if they would keep the issue off the aid bill.

Lugar shared in the Senatewide exercise in self-restraint. He had wanted to offer an amendment that would have repealed a committee-passed provision barring the administration from giving any U.S. foreign aid to anti-government guerrillas in Nicaragua. But to pacify Democrats who wanted that aid ban, Lugar withheld his amendment.

Totals

The $12.8 billion in the Senate bill for regular aid programs in 1986-87 was about $400 million less each year than Reagan had sought. The bulk of the cut — $344 million — was made by the Foreign Relations Committee in Reagan's $6.7 billion request for military aid programs. State and Defense Department officials fought to have some of that money restored, but Senate leaders prevailed upon their colleagues and the administration to forgo any increases over the committee-approved amounts.

In spite of administration complaints about the cuts, Secretary of State Shultz endorsed the bill just before final passage.

The bill was more than twice as costly as the last aid bill passed by the Senate. That 1981 measure (S 1196) authorized only $5.8 billion. About half of the difference was due to a bookkeeping change; starting in 1983, Congress and the administration had put "on-budget" several billion dollars' worth of military aid programs that previously did not count as part of the budget.

But the bloating of the aid bill also was a result of huge increases in military and arms-related aid that Reagan had won from Congress. Under the Senate-passed measure, U.S. loans and grants to help foreign countries buy weapons and military services were to be 45 percent higher than the 1981-approved amount. Military-related economic aid for countries such as Israel were to be 52 percent higher. *(1981 Almanac p. 161)*

Cambodia

The Senate accelerated the move in Congress to provide open aid to non-communist guerrillas battling the Vietnamese occupation of Cambodia.

Acting on May 15, it approved $5 million for military and economic aid to the rebels. The aid was included in two separate amendments, both adopted by voice vote. One, by Frank H. Murkowski, R-Alaska, made the assistance contingent on a finding by the secretary of state that the Association of Southeast Asian Nations (ASEAN) also was publicly providing such aid.

The other amendment, offered by Lugar and Majority Leader Robert Dole, R-Kan., authorized the aid without conditions.

Although House liberals had warned that the Cambodia aid could lead to renewed U.S. intervention in Southeast Asia, no such qualms were expressed on the Senate floor. No senator spoke against it or raised questions about it. And the administration dropped its earlier opposition to the aid.

Murkowski said his amendent tying U.S. aid to ASEAN's efforts was needed to demonstrate that the United States was playing a "secondary role" in the matter. ASEAN included Thailand, the Philippines, Singapore, Indonesia, Malaysia and Brunei. In February, ASEAN appealed for outside countries to aid the guerrillas in ousting the Vietnamese.

Before voting the $5 million, the Senate on May 14 adopted an amendment by William Proxmire, D-Wis., prohibiting any U.S. aid from supporting "directly or indirectly" the Khmer Rouge, the communist faction that governed Cambodia from 1975 until the Vietnamese invasion.

Israel, Egypt Aid

By voice vote and with little debate, the Senate on May 14 approved a Lugar amendment adding emergency economic aid of $1.5 billion for Israel and $500 million for Egypt. The amendment also included $8 million for economic development programs to aid residents of the Israeli-occupied West Bank and Gaza Strip areas. The president could provide the aid any time during fiscal years 1985 and 1986.

The aid already had started moving through Congress, in the form of a fiscal 1985 supplemental appropriations bill. *(Supplemental, p. 350)*

At first, Shultz asked Congress not to act on the emergency aid for Israel until the United States and Israel had agreed on the terms under which it would be provided. But in mid-April there was growing pressure in Congress to provide the aid anyway, and Israeli Prime Minister Shimon Peres wrote Shultz promising action on 10 economic and budgetary reforms that had been recommended by the United States.

Shultz on April 29 told congressional leaders that the administration was ready to request the aid for Israel, along with the additional aid for Egypt and the occupied territories.

After the Senate acted, the administration formally sent Congress its request for the aid.

Lugar said the president would have authority to provide the aid to Israel "at such times as he finds helpful to the stability and growth of the Israeli economy."

The Senate's action came after the administration, in an effort to hold down the size of the overall foreign aid budget, had delayed its formal request for $1.2 billion in regular economic aid for Israel in fiscal 1986.

Afghanistan

The Senate on May 14 approved $15 million in aid, under the Economic Support Fund, for "the Afghan people." The money was included in an amendment, sponsored by Gordon J. Humphrey, R-N.H., specifying that it was to be used for "food, medicine or other humanitarian assistance." Noting that the aid would be administered by private, voluntary organizations, Humphrey said he hoped it "will serve to stem the flow of refugees out of Afghanistan."

The United States for several years secretly had provided military aid to Afghan guerrillas battling the Soviet occupation of their country, and the Reagan administration revealed that it also had provided non-military aid to the guerrillas. The United States also had shipped food, medicine and other supplies to Afghan refugees living in Pakistan. *(1984 Almanac p. 118)*

Central America

The Senate on May 14 rejected two efforts to dismantle major portions of the Reagan administration's economic and development aid programs in Central America.

The most important action was the rejection, on a 41-52 vote, of a Kassebaum amendment to delete a multi-year authorization of non-military aid to Central America. *(Vote 76, p. 18-S)*

As reported by Foreign Relations, the bill authorized $1.2 billion in economic and development aid to the region in each of fiscal years 1986-89 — a sharp break from the standard procedure of authorizing funds for one or two years, at most. Kassebaum's amendment would have deleted the authorizations for fiscal years 1987-89.

The multi-year authorization was a major recommendation of the Kissinger commission on Central America.

Kassebaum objected to the precedent established by the multi-year authorization, and said it reduced the ability of Congress to review aid funding annually.

But Mathias, a member of the Kissinger commission, argued that the multi-year funding "represents a commitment by the United States to the well-being of the people in Central America, and it gives them hope for the future."

By a 33-60 vote, the Senate also rejected a Helms amendment to bar the use of U.S. foreign aid to reimburse property owners in Central America whose land was confiscated for land reform. The main effect of the amendment would have been in El Salvador, where the government wanted to use U.S. aid to reimburse farmers who lost property in the land reform program. *(Vote 77, p. 18-S)*

Military Aid

By a 56-39 vote, the Senate tabled on May 15 an amendment by Jeff Bingaman, D-N.M., to cut $100 million from the bill for loans to enable foreign countries to buy U.S. weapons, under the Foreign Military Sales program. *(Vote 80, p. 18-S)*

Bingaman originally proposed a two-part amendment that cut the $100 million and shifted it to Food for Peace programs. But at the request of Senate leaders he agreed to allow a vote only on the $100 million cut.

The amendment would have excluded from the cut aid to Israel, Egypt, Greece and Turkey.

Bingaman said he was attacking the Reagan administration's "shortsighted" policy of boosting military programs overseas while reducing or freezing spending on many economic development programs. "We cannot continue to increase security assistance while droughts in Africa continue and 40,000 children die each day," he said.

In arguing against the amendment, Lugar noted that, under Senate rules, Food for Peace programs were to be authorized in an agriculture bill, not the foreign aid bill. More fundamentally, he warned that the administration might decide to oppose the bill if the Senate made further cuts in military aid. The bill, as reported by the Foreign Relations Committee, already was $190 million below the president's request for military loans.

"There is not any latitude left in this bill" for further cuts, he said.

Murkowski failed in two attempts to curtail military loan programs that he insisted had encouraged foreign countries to build up huge debts to the United States.

First, the Senate rejected, 27-70, a Murkowski amendment ending a program that gave selected countries 30 years to repay their Foreign Military Sales loans from the United States. Normally, such loans had to be repaid in 12 years. The administration had argued that the longer term made it easier for countries to pay back their loans; Murkowski argued that it lured them into a "horrendous and very burdensome potential debt" to the United States. *(Vote 81, p. 18-S)*

Facing opposition by Senate leaders, Murkowski withdrew another amendment that would have ended a program of low-interest-rate loans to some foreign countries that bought U.S. weapons. He would have replaced the program with a combination of grants and market-rate loans. Offering loans at 5 percent, when the market rate should be 12 percent, disguised the grant nature of the program, Murkowski said.

Anti-Narcotics Moves

In a sign of growing congressional anger about narcotics abuse, the Senate adopted, by voice votes, amendments restricting foreign aid to countries that were major sources of illegal drugs in the United States, especially Bolivia and Peru.

The toughest amendment, by Paula Hawkins, R-Fla., was directed at Bolivia, a major producer of coca, from which cocaine was made. The amendment barred aid to Bolivia beginning in fiscal 1986 unless the president certified to Congress that Bolivia had reduced coca production by 10 percent. It also required U.S. representatives at international development banks, such as the World Bank, to vote against loans to Bolivia under the same condition.

Another provision suspended $5 million of Jamaica's aid until the president certified to Congress that the Jamaican government had committed itself to controlling and reducing marijuana production and distribution.

Reagan had requested $28 million in military and economic aid to Bolivia in fiscal 1986, all of which was to be affected by the Hawkins amendment. Another $29 million in food aid to Bolivia was not to be affected by the amendment. "It is time that this government stopped funding our own destruction," Hawkins said, in describing U.S. aid to Bolivia. "Bolivia must be forced to accept its responsibility in this situation, and I am convinced the only way to make them understand is in economic terms and they must be strong economic terms."

A similar amendment, sponsored by Mack Mattingly, R-Ga., barred aid to Peru unless the government there produced a plan to establish limits on coca production and eliminate production above those limits. Reagan had requested $93 million in military and non-military aid to Peru in fiscal 1986.

Mattingly said Peru accounted for about 45 percent of the cocaine entering the United States, and he charged that Peru had failed to implement a 1961 international treaty limiting coca production. The amendment, he said, "says to the government of Peru that the United States is serious about seeing the influx of illegal drugs into this nation curbed."

Lawton Chiles, D-Fla., offered, and the Senate adopted, a broad amendment aimed at narcotics production in several Latin American countries. Its major provisions:

- Required the secretary of state to negotiate with Brazil, with the goal of reducing illegal coca production there by 10 percent in 1986.
- Established a schedule for allocation of U.S. aid to Bolivia, with 25 percent of the fiscal 1986 aid to be provided if Bolivia enacted legislation limiting coca production to two hectares per family, and the remaining 75 percent to be provided if the Bolivian government had achieved its 1985 targets for eradicating coca production. A schedule with stricter requirements would be required for Bolivia to receive aid in fiscal 1987.
- Allowed the Agency for International Development to carry out a drug control project in the Upper Huallaga Valley of Peru only if the project would effectively eliminate coca production there.
- Allowed U.S. narcotics control aid only to foreign countries that agreed to pay at least 26 percent of the cost of all narcotics control efforts.
- Barred the use of U.S. foreign aid to reimburse persons whose illegal drug crops were eradicated.

A related amendment, offered by Dennis DeConcini, D-Ariz., allowing U.S. narcotics officials to participate in drug-related arrests in foreign countries, also was adopted by voice vote. It would effectively repeal a 1975 prohibition on U.S. involvement in such arrests.

The Senate also adopted an amendment by Hawkins and Pell establishing an International Narcotics Control Commission. Composed of 23 representatives from Congress and the executive branch, it was to monitor compliance with international narcotics control treaties. The commission was modeled on the Helsinki Commission monitoring the 1975 Helsinki accords on human rights.

Mozambique

In an effort by conservatives to impose the same style of conditions on aid to leftist governments as Congress imposed on rightist regimes, Helms offered, and the Senate adopted, an amendment restricting aid to Mozambique.

The amendment would bar arms aid unless the president certified to Congress that Mozambique's Marxist government was taking steps to comply with international human rights standards, was undertaking political and economic reforms such as restoring private property rights, had implemented a plan by Sept. 30, 1986, to reduce the number of foreign military advisers to 55, and was committed to holding free elections by that date.

The conditions were similar to those Congress had imposed at various times on aid to El Salvador. Reagan had requested $18.2 million in economic and military aid to Mozambique in 1986, along with $12 million in development and food aid.

"It is inconceivable, at least to this senator, that the United States is allocating $18,150,000 for the communist regime of Mozambique in this year's foreign aid bill," Helms said.

The Reagan administration had been trying to improve relations with Mozambique. The administration began providing military aid in 1985, for the first time in years, and also made Mozambique eligible to buy U.S. weapons.

The main impetus for the U.S. overtures was a 1984 agreement between South Africa and Mozambique, in which those two countries pledged not to intervene in each other's affairs.

As originally proposed, the Helms amendment would have ended aid unless Mozambique had cut back foreign military advisers to 55 by Sept. 30, 1986. But at Lugar's urging, Helms modified his proposal to require only that Mozambique implement a plan by then to cut the number of advisers.

Other Amendments

Other major amendments approved by the Senate were:

- By Dole, deleting Syria from the list of countries prohibited from receiving U.S. aid. The Foreign Relations Committee had added Syria to the list, which included such countries as Cuba and Libya. By voice vote.

Dole noted that Syria was not getting U.S. aid, but he argued that Congress should not bar such aid "at a particularly delicate time" during efforts to revive Middle East peace negotiations. "Whether we approve of its policies or not, we have to acknowledge and act on the fact that Syria has a key role to play in the Middle East, especially in Lebanon and in the search for a secure peace for Israel," Dole said.

The administration had opposed the Syrian aid prohibition.

- By Bill Bradley, D-N.J., urging the Federal Reserve Board and the Treasury to take steps to reduce the value of the dollar in comparison with foreign currencies — if necessary by intervening in foreign exchange markets. The amendment said such action "must be strong enough to achieve the Congress' intent of lowering the dollar's value but sufficiently moderate to prevent a sudden drop in its value." The administration generally opposed government intervention in exchange markets. The Senate at first rejected, 39-56, a Lugar motion to table the Bradley amendment.

The Senate then passed the Bradley amendment by voice vote. *(Vote 79, p. 18-S)*

- By John F. Kerry, D-Mass., stating the sense of the Senate that Congress should give aid to the Philippines only if the government there had made "sufficient progress" in implementing reforms.

Included among them: guaranteeing free elections by 1985 or 1987, ensuring full prosecution of those responsible for killing opposition leader Benigno S. Aquino Jr., ensuring freedom of speech and press, establishing habeas corpus, releasing political prisoners and stopping illegal killings by police and security forces. Adopted 89-8. *(Vote 78, p. 18-S)*

- By Arlen Specter, R-Pa., authorizing the president to bar trade with Libya or "any other country determined [by Congress] to be engaged in terrorism." By voice vote.
- By Bob Kasten, R-Wis., and Edward M. Kennedy, D-Mass., establishing an Africa Famine Recovery and Development Fund. The amendment authorized $100 million, taken from amounts already in the bill, for long-term economic development and agricultural recovery in sub-Saharan Africa. By voice vote.

House Floor Action

The House passed its version of the bill (HR 1555) on July 11, authorizing $12.6 billion annually in foreign aid for fiscal 1986-87. Passage came on a highly unusual voice vote, and over the opposition of the administration, which objected to several items in the bill.

The House attached more than 60 amendments to the bill during three days of debate, July 9-11; ironically, adoption of controversial amendments backed by conservatives seemed to have helped the bill gain passage.

Within the space of several hours on July 10, the House dismantled several foreign policy pillars that had been erected over the years by liberals. First, the House endorsed a Reagan administration policy of withdrawing or restricting U.S. support for the two largest international family planning agencies because of charges that they were linked to abortions overseas. Then, in a stunning reversal, the House voted to repeal a 1976 ban on U.S. military or paramilitary aid to anti-government rebels in Angola.

The House also approved aid to anti-communist rebels in Cambodia, Afghanistan and Nicaragua, leading one liberal Democrat, Sam Gejdenson of Connecticut, to remark: "We're starting three wars, or is it four?"

But while many liberals opposed those amendments, they found enough other items in the bill to their liking, such as its huge doses of aid for Israel, to justify backing it.

The anti-communist amendments gave conservatives, many of whom normally oppose foreign aid, a stake in the bill. Henry J. Hyde, R-Ill., a leading conservative on the Foreign Affairs Committee, told his colleagues he had developed a "sentimental attachment" to the bill.

Aid 'Freeze'

Prospects for passage also were eased by the Foreign Affairs panel's decision to trim the overall level of aid authorizations by 3.2 percent, effectively freezing the bill at 1985 appropriations levels. Reagan had requested $13.24 billion for aid programs, and the committee had approved $13.05 billion. A "freeze" amendment adopted by the House July 9 on a 386-2 vote cut the bill to $12.64 billion. Those figures did not include $1.5 billion in the bill for emergency economic aid to Israel in fiscal 1985-86. *(Vote 191, p. 64-H)*

Although it satisfied many House members who were opposed to boosting foreign aid in a year of cuts in domestic programs, the freeze amendment stiffened the administration's opposition to the bill. The net result was that military aid, the administration's prime concern, was cut to $6.04 billion, nearly 10 percent below the original request.

Under Secretary of State Schneider said the cuts were so deep that the bill "requires us to defund entirely a large number of countries."

The cuts were made "particularly acute" by the House's practice of exempting from cutbacks Israel, Egypt and several other countries that received large chunks of aid, Schneider said. That meant that any reductions had to be focused on countries that already were scheduled to receive small amounts of aid.

The administration also opposed a committee-drafted provision barring sales of advanced weapons to Jordan until that country had agreed to recognize and negotiate with Israel.

Administration objections led William S. Broomfield, R-Mich., ranking Republican on the Foreign Affairs Committee, to draft an omnibus substitute without some of the policy restrictions. Broomfield also trimmed several other major items in the bill, hoping to attract support from House members who were reluctant to back foreign aid at a time of deep domestic budget cuts. But he pared so much that the administration refused to support his substitute. When the House took up the bill, Broomfield did not bring up his substitute because the House made enough changes to satisfy him.

A Surprise Vote

A side consequence of the House action was to rescue the Foreign Affairs panel from a political graveyard. That committee had lost much of its stature and influence because Congress had not approved an aid bill.

Chairman Fascell attributed the bill's success to "a very strong effort by members of the committee from both parties."

The passage of the bill by voice vote startled nearly everyone in the chamber. House leaders had expected that someone would demand a roll-call vote on the bill, and few were willing to bet on the outcome. After the voice vote, when it was time for a roll call to be requested, Democrats looked across the aisle at Republicans, and Republicans stared back at Democrats.

"There was a momentary gasp on everybody's part," House Minority Whip Trent Lott, R-Miss., said later.

But no one moved to demand a vote, and so Speaker Thomas P. O'Neill Jr., D-Mass., declared the bill passed.

Striding out of the chamber a few moments later, O'Neill said: "That was a surprise, wasn't it?"

Setbacks for Liberals

Liberals and conservatives said the House was in a new mood on foreign policy and defense issues.

Hyde said the House was sending a message "that the United States is no longer paralyzed, that we can help create events around the world and not just respond." He traced the beginnings of the changed attitude to the October 1983 invasion of Grenada.

Peter H. Kostmayer, D-Pa., a liberal who opposed many of the initiatives in the bill, charged that the House was overreacting to recent events, including a highly publicized Soviet espionage case and the hijacking of Americans aboard a TWA airliner after it left Athens, Greece.

"There is some anger in the country, and the House, as a representative institution, is reflecting that anger," Kostmayer said.

The most visible manifestation of the new mood was the House's willingness to intervene around the world on behalf of forces opposed to communism. But the House also reversed course on several secondary matters.

For example, in one little-noticed action, the House adopted an amendment exempting El Salvador and Honduras from a longstanding ban on U.S. aid for police forces overseas. Until recently that amendment would have provoked an outcry from liberals because of the long history of U.S. collusion with repressive security forces in Latin America. But there was no dissent because proponents said the police aid was needed in the wake of a June 19 guerrilla killing of six Americans, including four Marines, in El Salvador. *(Police aid, p. 80)*

Fascell insisted some elements of the aid bill contradicted the new trend. He noted that the House backed the Foreign Affairs panel's decision to pare back some military aid programs, which generally were favored by conservatives, and to increase economic and development aid programs, which many liberals supported.

But overall, Stephen J. Solarz, D-N.Y., told reporters only half-jokingly: "The message is, we are ready to march on Moscow."

Angolan Guerrillas

The crowning touch on the House's turnaround was the adoption on July 10 of a provision repealing the "Clark amendment" on Angola, named after its sponsor, former Sen. Dick Clark, D-Iowa (1973-79).

Enacted into law in 1976, the amendment originally barred any U.S. support for military or paramilitary operations in Angola. The amendment effectively stopped CIA aid to a pro-Western guerrilla group that was battling for control in Angola. Congress in 1980 modified the amendment to allow such aid only if the president openly requested it and Congress approved. *(1980 Almanac p. 326)*

The Clark amendment long had stood as a major symbol of congressional reaction to the Vietnam War. To liberals, it signaled that the United States would not intervene recklessly in regional wars where its own security was not at stake. To conservatives, the amendment was a demonstration that the United States had lost its nerve to oppose communism wherever it reared its head.

Following the House's reversal of opposition to the even more controversial guerrilla war in Nicaragua, conservatives saw the aid bill as the ideal opportunity to overturn the Clark amendment. They bolstered their cause by obtaining support from several moderate and Southern Democrats.

Samuel S. Stratton, D-N.Y., offered the repealing amendment, but the key speech on its behalf was delivered by Claude Pepper, D-Fla., the chairman of the Rules Committee, who rarely engaged in foreign policy debates.

Pepper portrayed the issue as a symbolic one: whether the United States would be seen as favoring freedom or communism for Africans. "All we are saying is, those people in Africa, they have a right to be free," Pepper told the House in an emotional speech. "We may not be able to help everybody to the same degree, but do we need to write anybody off?"

Noting administration assurances that there were no immediate plans to aid the Angolan guerrillas, Pepper said: "We are not advocating that we give money to anybody for anything. We are simply saying, let us remove the perception that the Clark amendment gives the world that we washed our hands of Angola. . . ."

Opponents argued that repealing the Clark amendment would align the United States with the white minority government of South Africa, which reportedly subsidized the main anti-government guerrilla group in Angola.

"We get all the negatives as a result of an association with South Africa," Solarz said.

And Howard Wolpe, D-Mich., said it was ironic that Jonas Savimbi, leader of the Angolan rebel group UNITA, "is a Marxist" and not the anti-communist that conservatives portrayed him to be.

The House adopted Stratton's repealing amendment 236-185; 60 Democrats joined all but six Republicans in backing the measure. *(Vote 199, p. 66-H)*

The next day, Lee H. Hamilton, D-Ind., chairman of the Intelligence Committee, tried to assure fellow liberals that repeal of the Clark amendment "should not be construed as approval by the Congress" of aid to the rebels. Any administration request for covert CIA aid to the guerrillas would be subject to the "normal legislative procedures," under which the administration would have to justify a program to the two Intelligence committees, which could raise objections but not block it.

Cambodian Guerrillas

Rejecting warnings that the United States was on the verge of re-entering the wars of Southeast Asia, the House on July 9 approved a symbolic authorization of $5 million for economic or military aid to non-communist guerrillas battling the Vietnamese occupiers in Cambodia.

The wide margin by which the House approved the money (288-122), and the small amount involved, masked the deep political controversy on the issue, especially among liberal Democrats. *(Vote 193, p. 64-H; story, p. 56)*

The Foreign Affairs panel had approved a Solarz-sponsored provision setting aside $5 million in economic aid for Thailand, which could be used for aid, including military supplies, for the non-communist elements of the Cambodian insurgency.

When the aid bill reached the House floor, Jim Leach, R-Iowa, and other opponents of the Cambodian aid offered an amendment stipulating that the money could be used only for "humanitarian" purposes.

Solarz countered with a substitute, which had been adopted by the Senate in May, allowing either economic or military aid but that deleted the committee's provision for channeling the money through Thailand.

The Senate language also included an explicit prohibition on any of the money going to the communist Khmer Rouge faction, which ruled Cambodia from 1975-1979 and had been accused of killing thousands of its citizens.

Nicaragua

In spite of the past dispute over Nicaragua, the House on July 10, with no debate, added to the bill a provision authorizing $27 million in "humanitarian" or non-military aid to the guerrillas who were battling the Nicaraguan government. Sponsored by Dave McCurdy, D-Okla., the provision was identical to one the House had approved in June in a fiscal 1985 supplemental appropriations bill (HR 2577). *(Story, p. 350)*

The aid was to remain available for expenditure until March 31, 1986. The McCurdy provisions were approved by voice vote.

The House also adopted, by voice vote, a companion amendment by Bill Richardson, D-N.M., that required the president to establish procedures to ensure that aid given to the Nicaraguan rebels would be used only for the intended purpose and would not be diverted to purchase weapons, ammunition or other military supplies. The amendment also required the president to suspend such aid if he determined that the guerrillas were engaging consistently in human rights violations. In addition, it stated concern about Nicaragua's domestic and foreign policies.

Population Programs

The House on July 10 endorsed administration attacks on two international family planning agencies. The effect of the House action was to give the administration a free hand to curtail U.S. contributions to the two largest agencies conducting family planning programs overseas: the United Nations Fund for Population Activities (UNFPA) and the International Planned Parenthood Federation.

House action was a key test of strength in Congress of anti-abortion groups, which had lobbied hard to retain the administration position. One group, the National Right to Life Committee, hailed the House votes on the issue as "major legislative victories."

Although no U.S. foreign aid dollars were used for abortions overseas, the anti-abortion groups had insisted that the administration stance was necessary to distance the United States from any possible involvement with abortions.

The House acted first on the United Nations program, for which the Foreign Affairs Committee had earmarked $38 million in U.S. contributions.

Anti-abortion organizations charged that UNFPA, in its family planning programs in China, had not done enough to set itself apart from that country's practice of forcing women who already had one child to undergo abortions.

Responding to such concerns, the Reagan administration withheld $10 million of the U.S. contribution to UNFPA. However, the Foreign Affairs Committee drafted a provision to the aid bill specifying a minimum contribution, or "earmark" for the agency.

Christopher H. Smith, R-N.J., offered an amendment attacking China's population programs, eliminating the committee's earmark for UNFPA and authorizing the president to withhold funds for that agency if he determined there were valid reports of coerced abortion, coerced sterilization and infanticide in China.

Fascell and other committee leaders attempted to weaken Smith's amendment by offering a substitute that modified the attacks on China and that restored the funding earmark for UNFPA.

But in its key vote on the issue, the House rejected the Fascell substitute 198-221; it then adopted the underlying Smith amendment 289-130. *(Votes 195, 196, p. 64-H)*

Action on the Planned Parenthood issue was more complicated. The administration suspended U.S. aid to that agency because some of its overseas affiliates conducted abortion-related programs, such as counseling women on whether to have abortions. Planned Parenthood officials insisted that no U.S. money ever had been used for those services.

First, Smith offered an amendment deleting a Foreign Affairs Committee provision that would have barred the president from denying funds to any governmental or non-governmental organization because of the types of family planning programs it conducted with non-U.S. money.

Olympia J. Snowe, R-Maine, attempted to amend Smith's amendment with a substitute reaffirming existing law that barred use of U.S. money for abortions.

Smith countered with yet another amendment that allowed the president to deny funds to any organization because of the types of family planning programs it conducted, regardless of whether U.S. funds were involved. The House approved that Smith amendment 234-189. *(Vote 197, p. 64-H)*

Smith insisted that his amendments were narrow efforts to ensure that the United States had nothing to do with the use of abortion as a method of family planning overseas.

The amendment eliminating the earmark for the United Nations program, Smith said, was necessary "if we are to get their attention" in demanding an end to U.N. support for family planning in China.

But opponents insisted that Smith and his colleagues were attempting to undermine U.S. support for population control programs in developing countries. "This anti-abortion crusade has now become an anti-family planning crusade," Snowe charged.

Philippines

By a 2-1 margin, the House on July 9 rejected a Republican-backed effort to restore $60 million in military aid for the Philippines.

An amendment sponsored by Gerald B. H. Solomon, R-N.Y., would have put back in the budget most of the $100 million in military aid that Reagan had requested for the Philippines. Pentagon officials said all military aid to that country would be used for "non-lethal" purposes, such as buying communications equipment. Solomon's amendment was rejected 125-279. *(Vote 192, p. 64-H; related story, p. 113)*

The Foreign Affairs Committee had deleted all but $25 million of Reagan's military aid request, and made a comparable increase in economic aid, as a signal of dissatisfaction with the authoritarian regime of President Ferdinand E. Marcos.

Solomon argued that cutting aid to the Philippines was a "purely vindictive" attack on Marcos that undercut U.S. backing for a key Asian ally.

Noting that the Philippines housed two key U.S. bases, Subic Bay Naval Station and Clark Air Base, Solomon said such an action would damage "our own strategic interests."

Solarz, who had initiated a similar shift from military to economic aid in 1984, said a communist-backed insurgency was gaining strength because of the country's economic problems.

The United States also needed to encourage Marcos to make reforms in the country's military, economic and political structures, Solarz said. But if the United States boosted military aid even before Marcos made those reforms, Solarz asked, "then what incentive will the Philippine government have?"

On July 11, the House adopted an amendment by Tony P. Hall, D-Ohio, stating that Congress might defer future military aid to the Philippines if that country had not made significant progress on political, economic and military reforms. That amendment was adopted 254-169. *(Vote 204, p. 66-H)*

Later that day, the House adopted by voice vote an amendment by Charles E. Schumer, D-N.Y., requiring that one-fourth of the Philippines development and food aid be distributed through private organizations, to take it out of government hands.

Airport Security

On July 10 the House adopted an amendment incorporating several pieces of legislation aimed at encouraging a U.S. boycott of foreign airports with lax security standards. The legislation was prompted by the June 14 hijacking of a TWA airliner shortly after it left Athens, Greece, airport.

Offered by Norman Y. Mineta, D-Calif., the amendment: directed the Transportation Department to publish a list of foreign airports that failed to meet minimum international security standards; authorized a boycott of those airports; directed a ban on foreign aid to countries where those airports were located (with the president having the right to waive the ban); doubled, to $10 million, the annual budget for the U.S. anti-terrorism program; and authorized $5 million for research into devices to detect explosives.

Mozambique

In a series of votes on amendments offered by Mark D. Siljander, R-Mich., the House did a turnaround on aid to Mozambique, ultimately deciding to cut aid to that country.

Members at first on July 9 rejected by voice vote an amendment that would delete from the bill $3 million in military aid for Mozambique. Siljander said its government is a "Marxist-Leninist dictatorship." But others noted that the administration requested the aid in the wake of a 1984 non-aggression pact between Mozambique and neighboring South Africa.

Two days later, with no debate and by voice vote, the House decided to end all arms aid to Mozambique. Members also voted, 247-177, to cut off non-food economic aid. *(Vote 202, p. 66-H)*

Other Amendments

In other action, the House:

- Approved, by voice vote, an amendment by William S. Broomfield, R-Mich., setting a limit of $711.4 million on military aid for Turkey. Although a cut from Reagan's $785 million request, that would be an increase over the $700 million approved by Congress for fiscal 1985. The Foreign Affairs Committee had approved $740 million. Broomfield said the limit would keep the "proper balance" between military aid to Turkey and Greece, for which the House

Poindexter Succeeds McFarlane

President Reagan on Dec. 4 announced the resignation of his national security adviser, Robert C. McFarlane, and appointed Vice Adm. John M. Poindexter to the post.

McFarlane rejected as "nonsense" widespread press reports that he resigned because of long-running conflicts with White House Chief of Staff Donald T. Regan. There also were reports that McFarlane had tired of mediating conflicts among senior administration officials, especially Secretary of State George P. Shultz and Secretary of Defense Caspar W. Weinberger.

McFarlane, a 30-year veteran of government service, said he had no firm future plans other than spending time with his family.

Poindexter joined the National Security Council staff in June 1981 and had been McFarlane's deputy since October 1983. He was the fourth person to hold the post of Reagan's national security adviser — known formally as the president's assistant for national security affairs. McFarlane's predecessors were Richard V. Allen and William P. Clark.

Reagan said Poindexter would report directly to him. Regan reportedly had wanted McFarlane to report through him to the president.

In a joint appearance with Reagan and Poindexter before reporters at the White House, McFarlane credited the president with a "national renewal" during his presidency. When Reagan took office, McFarlane said, many observers were predicting the decline of the Western democracies. Now, he said, the United States had a recovering economy and was "once more leading and deterring."

voted $498 million. For years, Congress had insisted on a ratio under which Greece received $7 in military aid for every $10 for Turkey.

- Rejected, 47-375, an amendment by John Conyers Jr., D-Mich., that effectively would have barred U.S. military aid to El Salvador. The amendment would have allowed the aid only if the president certified to Congress that the Salvadoran government had made "sufficient progress" in prosecuting those responsible for more than 45,000 murders since 1980 and in carrying out its land reform program, and had agreed to pursue a negotiated settlement with leftist guerrillas. *(Vote 198, p. 64-H)*

The House also adopted, by voice vote, an amendment by Brian J. Donnelly, D-Mass., providing $79.6 million in development aid to El Salvador in each of fiscal years 1986-87. That was a $10 million boost over the amount voted by Foreign Affairs.

- Adopted, by voice vote, an amendment by Larry Smith, D-Fla., that tightened restrictions already in the bill on aid to Bolivia and Peru — countries that were major sources of illegal narcotics. Bolivia could get one-fourth of its economic and military aid from the United States in fiscal 1986 if the president certified to Congress that it had enacted legislation setting legal requirements for production of coca, which was used to make cocaine. The rest of Bolivia's aid would be freed if the president certified that the Bolivian government had made "substantial progress" toward achieving coca eradication targets in a 1983 agreement with the United States. Even tighter restrictions would be placed on Bolivia's aid in fiscal 1987. The amendment also permitted aid to Peru in 1986 if the president certified to Congress that it had "demonstrated substantial progress" in developing a plan to limit coca production; for fiscal 1987, Peru could receive aid only if it was implementing that plan.
- Adopted, by voice vote, an amendment by Bill Lowery, R-Calif., that reduced U.S. contributions to United Nations organizations in proportion to their spending on programs in communist countries. The president could waive this reduction if he determined that it was in the national interest to do so.
- Adopted, by voice vote, an amendment barring U.S. aid to any country determined by the president to have supported international terrorism or to have granted sanctuary to terrorists. As offered by John R. Miller, R-Wash., and modified by Benjamin A. Gilman, R-N.Y., the amendment also called for an international civil aviation boycott of Iran and Libya and directed the president to bar imports from and exports to Libya.
- Adopted, by voice vote, an amendment by Jim Kolbe, R-Ariz., prohibiting aid to Lebanon unless all U.S. citizens held hostage in that country had been released before the aid bill was enacted into law. The ban would apply to $2.5 million in economic aid approved in the bill by the Foreign Affairs Committee; Reagan had requested $10 million. Congress already was moving to suspend $18 million in aid to Lebanon left over from a 1983 appropriation.

Conference Action, Provisions

With House Foreign Affairs Chairman Fascell firmly wielding the gavel and pressing for action on some 200 items in disagreement, House-Senate conferees worked on S 960 for nearly nine hours, finishing shortly before 1 a.m. on July 26.

The final issue to be resolved was the most contentious: whether the CIA could be involved in the new program of non-military aid to anti-government guerrillas in Nicaragua.

Foreign Relations Chairman Lugar staunchly held out for the Senate's position that the president should be given the freedom to decide which U.S. agency would administer aid to the contras.

But House conferees of both parties said the House would reject the entire bill rather than allow renewed CIA involvement in Nicaragua.

Lugar nodded grimly as the House members argued for a provision barring the CIA or the Defense Department from aiding the contras. As senior House members were readying to declare the conference at an impasse, Lugar backed down, saying: "We hear you loud and clear."

The agreement on the aid bill also helped break an impasse on a fiscal 1985 supplemental spending bill (HR 2577 — PL 99-88) that had a similar conflict on Nicaragua. *(Supplemental, p. 350)*

Hours after the foreign aid conference finished, administration officials sought to reopen the bill to delete a provision barring Reagan from making a deal with a foreign country to aid the contras. Lugar and Fascell rejected that appeal.

With the administration threatening a veto, however, Lugar and provision sponsor Claiborne Pell, D-R.I., on July 29 agreed to a modification that merely barred the United States from forcing foreign aid recipients to help the contras.

The next day, the Senate adopted the conference report (H Rept 99-237) by voice vote. On July 31, the House cleared the bill for the president on a 262-161 vote, an unusually wide margin for a foreign aid bill. *(Vote 249, p. 80-H)*

Aid Amounts

Total foreign aid in the bill was pegged at $12.77 billion for each of fiscal years 1986-87, $500 million less than Reagan's request. Not included in that figure was an additional $2 billion in emergency aid to Israel and Egypt in 1985-86.

Most of the bill's overall reduction from Reagan's request came from military assistance, always the most controversial section of the bill.

Reagan had requested $6.7 billion for military aid programs in fiscal 1986, a 13 percent increase over the $5.9 billion appropriated for fiscal 1985. The House had voted only a slight increase, while the Senate had granted most of Reagan's request. Conferees approved slightly under $6.3 billion, a 5 percent increase.

The bulk of the cuts came in the Foreign Military Sales loan program, which subsidized arms purchases by foreign countries. But the bill also froze spending at 1985 levels for the grant Military Assistance Program, used by the administration to provide weapons and military services to economically hard-pressed countries.

Other military aid provisions:

- Retained the traditional 7-10 ratio of military aid between Greece and Turkey. The bill earmarked $500 million in military loans for Greece and $714.28 million in military aid for Turkey (of which $215 million was in grants and the rest in loans). It also required comparable interest rates on the loans for the two countries. Reagan had requested $500 million for Greece and $785 million for Turkey.
- Established a 5 percent minimum on interest rates charged for "concessional" loans under the Foreign Mili-

tary Sales program. The standard rate for military loans was about 10 percent.

- Gave the administration the discretion to determine what portion of military loans would be made at concessional rates; the Senate bill had set a $2.4 billion limit on such loans.
- Allowed military aid to Paraguay only if the president certified to Congress that the government had ended the torture and abuse of prisoners and had instituted procedures to ensure prompt trials. Military training aid was exempted from this prohibition.
- Authorized on a permanent basis 30-year arms loans for Greece, South Korea, Portugal, Spain, Thailand, the Philippines and Turkey. Those countries had been receiving the special loans on a year-to-year basis. Standard loans must be repaid in 12 years.
- Earmarked $15 million in Military Assistance Program grants for Tunisia. Conferees recommended, but did not require, providing another $25 million, for a total of $40 million.
- Made several changes in the president's special authority (under section 614 of the foreign aid law) to waive congressionally imposed restrictions on foreign aid and arms sales. Using that authority, the president could waive such limits as prohibitions on aid to specific countries or requirements that all aid recipients meet minimum human rights standards.

The bill allowed the president to waive restrictions on up to $750 million a year in foreign arms sales and up to $250 million a year in foreign aid. Using his waiver authority, the president could provide no more than $50 million in aid and arms sales annually to any country.

However, in the case of a country that was the victim of "active communist or communist-supported aggression," the annual limit was $500 million. This provision was prompted by reports in 1981 that Reagan would use his special authority to sidestep congressional objections to the sale of AWACS radar planes to Saudi Arabia; Congress approved that sale, making the issue moot. The provision would prevent him from avoiding congressional controls in the future.

- Authorized the president to use Foreign Military Sales loans to replenish the Guaranty Reserve Fund, which paid for loan defaults by foreign countries. It also required the president to make recommendations to Congress on how the Foreign Military Sales loan program could be protected against future defaults.
- Required the president to return to Congress for approval of any decision to upgrade the level of technology to be included in a foreign arms sale after Congress had approved the original sale. This provision was spawned by the Reagan administration's decision to add sensitive radar equipment to F-16 warplanes sold to Pakistan.

Philippines Assistance

The bill included a compromise $70 million figure for arms aid to the Philippines in each fiscal year. Reagan had requested $100 million, and the House had voted to impose a $25 million limit. Of the $70 million, $50 million was earmarked in Military Assistance Program grants and $20 million in Foreign Military Sales loans.

In a concession to House conferees who opposed the $70 million figure, the bill specified that all military aid was to buy only "non-lethal" equipment, such as trucks, communications gear and uniforms. The administration had said it was planning to provide only non-lethal military aid to the Philippines, but the conferees put that requirement in law and included in their report the administration's proposed equipment list.

The Philippines also was to receive $100 million in economic aid.

Conferees adopted the bulk of a statement in the Senate bill calling for reforms in the Philippines. It said that in determining future aid, Congress would consider whether the Philippine government had permitted free and honest elections, had guaranteed a full trial in the case of those accused of murdering opposition leader Benigno S. Aquino Jr., had ensured freedom of the press, had released political prisoners and had made substantial progress in curbing illegal killings by the security forces.

Sen. John Kerry, D-Mass., prime sponsor of the language, called it "a very important statement by the Congress about our expectations."

Middle East

As in the past, Israel and Egypt were to receive the bulk of aid authorized in the bill. For each fiscal year, Israel was to receive $1.8 billion in military aid and $1.2 billion in economic aid, and Egypt was to receive $1.3 billion in military aid and $815 million in economic aid. All aid to the two countries was to be in the form of grants. Israel was to receive all of its economic aid as a direct cash transfer, meaning that the money did not have to be linked to specific programs. Up to $115 million of Egypt's economic aid was to be a cash transfer.

Of Israel's military aid, $400 million a year was set aside for development of that country's new warplane, the Lavi. At least $250 million of that had to be spent in Israel.

The bill also authorized supplemental economic aid of $1.5 billion to Israel, $500 million to Egypt and $8 million for Mideast regional programs.

One of the most important compromises worked out quietly by House and Senate negotiators was on the issue of arms sales to Jordan. The House bill would have made it almost impossible under current circumstances for the president to sell advanced weapons to Jordan, as he had planned to do later in 1985.

The conference version stated congressional opposition to such sales and required that any notification to Congress "with respect to a proposed sale to Jordan of U.S. advanced aircraft, new air defense systems or other new advanced military weapons, must be accompanied by a presidential certification of Jordan's public commitment to the recognition of Israel and to negotiate promptly and directly with Israel under the basic tenets of United Nations Security Council resolutions 242 and 338."

The bill also included a provision, originally adopted by both houses, that put into law several promises that Reagan made in 1981 when he was seeking congressional approval of the sale of AWACS radar planes to Saudi Arabia. *(1981 Almanac p. 129)*

Under that provision, the United States could transfer the planes, as scheduled in 1986, only if the president certified to Congress that Saudi Arabia had signed agreements protecting their technology and allowing U.S. access to information obtained by the planes. The president also was required to certify, before sending the planes, that Middle East peace initiatives "either have been successfully completed or that significant progress toward that goal has been accomplished with the substantial assistance of Saudi Arabia." Opponents of the AWACS sale insisted that, under current conditions, the president would not be

Vietnam Colors Congressional Debate . . .

Touching off debate over whether the United States should get involved in trying to force Vietnam to end its occupation of Cambodia, Congress voted in 1985 to provide $5 million in economic or military aid to non-communist Cambodian guerrillas.

The $5 million was earmarked annually in the fiscal 1986-87 foreign aid authorization bill (S 960 — PL 99-83). The companion appropriation, contained in a fiscal 1986 continuing resolution (H J Res 465 — PL 99-190), directed the president to provide at least $1.5 million, but no more than $5 million, in economic or military aid for the non-communist rebels. *(Appropriations, p. 367)*

Although the money represented only a tiny part of the foreign aid budget, the issue was fraught with political and diplomatic significance, as it raised the specter of an active U.S. role in Indochina for the first time in 10 years.

The Reagan administration, which had preferred to give any aid to the Cambodian rebels secretly rather than publicly, had not announced as of January 1986 how much assistance would be given. For several years, the United States had provided food, medicine and other humanitarian supplies for Cambodian refugees in neighboring Thailand.

Vietnam occupied Cambodia beginning in January 1979, when it ousted the communist Khmer Rouge government, led by Pol Pot, which had ruled since 1975. The Khmer Rouge was waging guerrilla war against the Vietnamese, as were two non-communist groups: the Khmer People's National Liberation Front, headed by former Prime Minister Son Sann, and a band led by Prince Norodom Sihanouk, Cambodia's leader in the 1950s-1960s.

China backed the Khmer Rouge, and pro-Western countries provided aid to the non-communist forces. But there were reports that the non-communist guerrillas were poorly equipped and trained and unable to coordinate their military operations against Vietnam.

In early 1984, Vietnam launched massive assaults against the rebels. Thailand and other non-communist governments in the region sought international aid, expressing fear that militarily aggressive Vietnam could wipe out the internal resistance.

Liberals Divided

The new aid was initiated by the House Foreign Affairs Committee. Proposed by Chairman Stephen J. Solarz, D-N.Y., at the Subcommittee on Asian and Pacific Affairs' March 20 markup of the foreign aid authorization bill, it called for $5 million to be given to Thailand, to be used to buy arms and equipment for the Cambodian rebels.

The proposal split the panel's liberal members. Ranking Republican Jim Leach of Iowa, one of the most liberal members of his party in the House, attacked the aid plan. Joining him in opposition were Democrats Michael D. Barnes of Maryland and Sam Gejdenson of Connecticut.

Joining Solarz in backing it were two other Democrats, Robert G. Torricelli of New Jersey and Mervyn M. Dymally of California, and three Republicans, Gerald B. H. Solomon of New York, Doug Bereuter of Nebraska and Toby Roth of Wisconsin.

The Vietnam War, as well as the Vietnamese occupation of Cambodia, dominated the debate. Leach said that the United States should have discovered "the liabilities of involvement in land wars in Asia," and he warned that the guerrilla aid, while small, would risk transforming the Cambodian resistance "into a U.S. military operation."

Leach also objected to what he called congressional "interventionism without executive sanction." Noting that Foreign Affairs Committee Democrats and the Reagan administration had been at odds on a wide range of similar foreign policy issues, he added: "I have a sense that this committee is trying to make a mark on this town that we're going to be more anti-communist than Ronald Reagan. That is tough competition."

Solarz, one of the committee's most experienced and

How Members Voted on Aid

Following is the 9-24 vote by which the House Foreign Affairs Committee on April 3 rejected an amendment by Jim Leach, R-Iowa, that would have had the effect of killing a proposed $5 million program of military and other aid to non-communist guerrilla forces in Cambodia.

For the Leach amendment:

Democrats Sam Gejdenson, Conn.; Michael D. Barnes, Md.; Howard Wolpe, Mich.; Gerry E. Studds, Mass.; Ted Weiss, N.Y.; Lee H. Hamilton, Ind.; Mervyn M. Dymally, Calif.

Republicans Ed Zschau, Calif.; Leach.

Against the Leach amendment:

Democrats Dante B. Fascell, Fla.; Daniel A. Mica, Fla.; Gary L. Ackerman, N.Y.; Edward F. Feighan, Ohio; Don Bonker, Wash.; Stephen J. Solarz, N.Y.; Gus Yatron, Pa.; Howard L. Berman, Calif.; Larry Smith, Fla.; Peter H. Kostmayer, Pa.; Tom Lantos, Calif.

Republicans Benjamin A. Gilman, N.Y.; Robert J. Lagomarsino, Calif.; Olympia J. Snowe, Maine; Henry J. Hyde, Ill.; Gerald B. H. Solomon, N.Y.; Doug Bereuter, Neb.; Mark D. Siljander, Mich.; Toby Roth, Wis.; Michael DeWine, Ohio; Connie Mack, Fla.; Christopher H. Smith, N.J.; Dan Burton, Ind.; John McCain, Ariz.

. . . Over Assistance to Cambodian Rebels

articulate liberals, defended his proposal as "the very least we can do" to respond to the pleas by Thailand and other countries for support of the guerrillas.

Aiding the Cambodians "is not the beginning of a new American military involvement in Indochina," he said.

"We need to learn the lessons of Vietnam, but it would be a tragic mistake if we were to be paralyzed by them," Solarz added.

The subcommittee approved the aid by a 6-3 vote.

On April 3, the full committee beat back an effort, led by Leach, to kill the Cambodian military aid. Instead, Leach would have authorized humanitarian aid, such as food and medicine.

In emotional debate, several members and aides said they viewed the action as a historic step — an attitude borne out by the air of tension in the committee chamber.

While small in dollars, Solarz said in defense of his proposal, the U.S. support would be "a real boost in morale" for the Cambodians and would encourage the U.S. allies to continue their efforts against the Vietnamese.

Gejdenson objected to aid that would "put the American flag in the midst of a conflict" in Indochina.

Referring to Chinese backing of the communist resistance in Cambodia, and to Soviet backing of Vietnam, Gejdenson said: "Clearly, America's reinvolvement in the area will create reactions by other forces that will be far more significant than the $5 million commitment."

Leach worried that, if the aid eventually led to a broader U.S. role in Cambodia, the Republican Party and the Reagan administration would bear the blame even though it was first proposed by Democrats.

"I personally believe that there is no stomach in this country for a renewed military involvement in Indochina, and what we may have here is a Democratically propelled resort to force," Leach said.

One conservative Republican who backed the $5 million, Dan Burton of Indiana, warned colleagues to expect further requests from the Cambodians. "Make no mistake about it," he said, "this is not going to be the end of it."

Some conservative Republicans implied, but never directly argued, that Solarz and other liberals were offering the proposal as "guilt money" in compensation for their refusal to support U.S. aid to another set of anticommunist guerrillas, in Nicaragua.

While the administration neither supported nor actively opposed the aid, William Schneider Jr., under secretary of state for security assistance, appeared to undermine opposition to the Solarz proposal by refusing to give unqualified support to several of Leach's arguments.

The Leach amendment was rejected 9-24. *(Box, p. 56)*

Senate Action

By the time the Senate took up its foreign aid bill in May, the administration had dropped its opposition to the Cambodia aid. And the Senate accelerated the move to provide it.

Voting May 15, senators approved the $5 million in military and economic aid. The aid was included in two separate amendments, both of which were adopted by voice vote.

One, by Frank H. Murkowski, R-Alaska, made the assistance contingent on a finding by the secretary of state that the Association of Southeast Asian Nations (ASEAN) also was publicly providing such aid.

The other amendment, offered by Lugar and Majority Leader Robert Dole, R-Kan., authorized the aid without conditions.

Despite the objections the aid proposal produced among House members, no such qualms were expressed on the Senate floor. No senator spoke against it or even raised questions about it.

Dole, in a prepared statement, said "This is not the first installment of anything, or an open-ended commitment to do anything."

Murkowski said his amendment tying U.S. aid to ASEAN's efforts was needed to demonstrate that the United States was playing a "secondary role." ASEAN included Thailand, the Philippines, Singapore, Indonesia, Malaysia and Brunei. In February, ASEAN appealed for outside countries to aid the guerrillas in ousting Vietnam.

Before voting the $5 million, the Senate on May 14 adopted an amendment by William Proxmire, D-Wis., prohibiting any U.S. aid from supporting "directly or indirectly" the Khmer Rouge.

House Floor Action

When the foreign aid bill reached the House floor in July, Leach and other opponents tried again to weaken the Solarz proposal, offering an amendment stipulating that the money could be used only for "humanitarian" purposes.

Solarz, however, countered with a substitute that restated the committee-passed plan, deleting the provision for channeling the money through Thailand.

The House voted July 9 for the Solarz proposal. The deep political controversy on the issue was masked by the vote, 288-122. *(Vote 193, p. 64-H)*

In the House debate, Solarz acknowledged that "there is no way, under any circumstances, that the Cambodians can militarily drive the Vietnamese out of Cambodia." But he said the rebels, with U.S. support, can increase the cost to the Vietnamese of occupying Cambodia, thus encouraging them to reach a political settlement.

Several other liberals reiterated their objections that Cambodian aid raised the specter of another U.S. conflict with Vietnam. Gejdenson said that the U.S. involvement, rather than encouraging Vietnam to seek a settlement, might "stiffen the Vietnamese resolve" to stay.

The Vietnamese, Gejdenson said, "will see it as the beginning of reintroduction of American influence in Southeast Asia that they want to stop."

able to certify that the latter condition had been met.

The bill also barred the administration from conducting any negotiations with the Palestine Liberation Organization (PLO). It had been U.S. policy since 1975 not to negotiate with or recognize the PLO; this provision put the policy into law, with an exemption for talks for emergency or humanitarian reasons.

'Contra' Aid

The bill authorized $27 million for "humanitarian" or non-military aid through March 31, 1986, for the anti-government guerrillas in Nicaragua. But in a major rebuke to the administration, the conferees agreed to bar the CIA or the Defense Department from administering the aid. Reagan had wanted to funnel the aid through the CIA, which had administered the original military aid program to the rebels.

Fascell said the administration never adequately explained why it wanted freedom for the CIA and the Pentagon to administer the aid. "There's no magic in this," he said. "You don't have to have a bunch of four-star generals and guys with flying cloaks and stuff like that to administer $27 million for humanitarian reasons."

Conferees said in their report that the ban on CIA and Defense Department involvement did not prevent those agencies from giving the contras advice or intelligence information.

Actual appropriations for the contra aid were included in HR 2577, the fiscal 1985 supplemental appropriations bill that was worked out in conference committee shortly after the foreign aid conferees finished.

Other contra aid provisions:

- Barred the administration from entering into an agreement that forced a country receiving U.S. foreign aid or weapons to provide aid to the Nicaraguan contras. The provision stated: "The United States shall not enter into any agreement conditioning, expressly or impliedly, the provision of assistance under this act, or the purchase of defense articles and services under the Arms Export and Control Act, on the provision of assistance by a recipient country to persons or groups engaged in an insurgency or other act of rebellion against the government of Nicaragua."

In their report, the conferees said that provision was not intended to prohibit administration officials from discussing U.S. policy in Central America with foreign aid recipients, or to prohibit those recipients from giving aid to the contras on their own volition from their own resources.

This was the modified version of a provision, originally passed by the Senate, that barred the United States from making an agreement or understanding that provided for another country to aid the contras. The original provision, strongly opposed by the administration, was aimed at preventing the administration from asking El Salvador or other Central American countries to use their U.S. foreign aid on behalf of the contras.

- Divided the $27 million into three parts, to be provided every 90 days upon the president's submission to Congress of reports on Nicaragua and peace-making efforts in Central America.
- Allowed the provision to the contras of food, clothing, medicine or other humanitarian aid, but expressly barred weapons, weapons systems, ammunition, vehicles or "material which can be used to inflict serious bodily harm or death."
- Required the president to establish procedures to prevent the humanitarian aid from being diverted to military purposes.
- Required the president to suspend aid to the contras if he determined that they were engaged in a consistent pattern of human rights abuses.
- Authorized $2 million in fiscal 1986 to help implement a regional peace accord resulting from talks led by the "Contadora" countries: Colombia, Mexico, Panama and Venezuela.
- Established a procedure for expedited congressional consideration of any future request by the president for additional aid to the contras. Among other things, that procedure was aimed at guaranteeing a House vote early in 1986 on Reagan's request.

Other Insurgencies

Also ratified, but unmentioned during the conference, were three other guerrilla-aid issues on which the House and Senate were in agreement:

- Repeal of a 1976 law that barred U.S. aid to South African-backed guerrillas who were fighting the Marxist government of Angola. The administration had sought the repeal of the Angola provision, while saying it had no plans to aid the guerrillas there.
- A new $5 million-a-year program of military or economic aid to non-communist guerrillas in Cambodia. Rep. Solarz, a New York Democrat, had led the campaign for aiding the Cambodians.
- A new $15 million-a-year relief program for "the Afghan people." Although not stated publicly by members, the purpose of that money was to support the Moslem rebels who were battling the Soviet occupation of Afghanistan. The United States also had provided hundreds of millions of dollars in military aid to the rebels through the CIA.

Kissinger Commission Plan

One little-noticed section of the aid bill implemented the heart of the once-controversial recommendations by the Kissinger commission on Central America. The panel, headed by former Secretary of State Henry A. Kissinger, issued a report in January, 1984, recommending long-term economic, development and military aid to the region. *(1984 Almanac p. 93)*

The most important commission recommendation included in the bill was for a long-term authorization of economic and development aid to Central America. The bill authorized regular aid programs totaling nearly $1 billion annually for the region in fiscal 1986-87, and $1.2 billion annually in fiscal 1988-89. That four-year authorization was highly unusual for foreign aid programs, normally authorized one or two years at a time.

House conferees had opposed the multi-year authorization. But when Senate conferees insisted on it, Rep. Lee H. Hamilton, D-Ind., suggested a compromise: The House would accept the four-year aid program for Central America if the Senate would accept the House proposal for a two-year, rather than a one-year, authorization for the entire foreign aid bill. The senators immediately accepted that deal.

Another Kissinger commission recommendation included in the aid bill authorized the president to negotiate with other countries for the creation of a Central American Development Organization. That agency would make recommendations for U.S. and other aid programs. The organization would not have a veto over U.S. aid, but one-fourth of U.S. aid to Central America in any fiscal year would be held up pending the organization's recommendations.

Other Central America Issues

In a major departure from longstanding congressional policy, the bill exempted El Salvador and Honduras from a prohibition against U.S. aid to foreign police forces. The only conditions were that the president must notify Congress 30 days before providing such aid, giving a description of the aid and stating that each country had made significant progress in curbing human rights violations.

Also exempted were countries that were longtime democracies, that had no standing armed forces and that did not violate human rights. That provision was intended to allow police aid to Costa Rica.

Reagan had requested a blanket exemption from the police aid ban for all Central American countries. Congress had imposed the ban in 1974 in response to reports that U.S. aid was being used by repressive police forces in several Latin American nations.

In a related provision, the aid bill authorized the president to provide up to $20 million each year in aid to strengthen the administration of justice in Latin American and Caribbean countries. Included under the authorization were seminars, training and other programs aimed at improving "prosecutorial and judicial capabilities" and to protect participants in court cases.

The aid bill dropped a requirement, in effect under various guises since 1981, that the president could aid El Salvador only if he certified to Congress that various conditions had been met. Instead, the bill stated that the United States was providing aid to El Salvador "in the expectation that" several conditions would be met, including a willingness by the government to conduct a dialogue with the opposition, and demonstration of progress by the government in curtailing death squads, reforming the judicial system and implementing land reform programs.

Conferees made it clear that their willingness to loosen specific conditions on El Salvador's aid stemmed from their support of President José Napoleón Duarte, who was elected in 1984 with U.S. backing. As evidence of that support, they kept in the bill a fiscal 1985 appropriations provision barring any U.S. aid to El Salvador in the event of a military coup.

In discussing the issue, Rep. Solarz said the rights conditions "would send a very powerful signal to elements on the right in El Salvador that this is still a matter of grave concern in Congress."

But Henry J. Hyde, R-Ill., made a case for eliminating all conditions: "I give President Duarte some little micrometer of sovereignty."

The bill retained a House-passed provision requiring the president to notify Congress 15 days before providing El Salvador with any helicopters or other aircraft. That provision was a response to reports that the Salvadoran military had conducted indiscriminate bombing that killed civilians as well as leftist guerrillas; the government had denied those reports.

In another departure from past practice, the bill did not specify the amount of aid for El Salvador. Reagan had requested $350 million in economic and development aid and $132.6 million in military aid for El Salvador in fiscal 1986. The House bill had set aside $195 million in economic aid, but the conference report eliminated that provision.

The bill barred military aid to Guatemala until an elected civilian government was in power and had made demonstrated progress in controlling the military and eliminating kidnappings and other human rights abuses, particularly against Indians.

Once those conditions had been met, Guatemala could receive up to $10 million per year in military aid, to be used only for construction equipment and mobile medical facilities. No U.S. aid could be used to buy weapons or ammunition, and all aid would have to be suspended in the event of a military coup.

Military training aid to Guatemala was exempted from the pre-elections ban.

Conferees also adopted a House provision requiring U.S. economic and development aid to Guatemala to be channeled through private organizations to the maximum extent possible, and barring that aid from being used for the government's rural resettlement program there.

Conferees eliminated from the bill a requirement that the Pentagon report to Congress 30 days before beginning any military exercises in Central America. However, the conferees stated in their report that they expected such reports anyway.

Anti-Narcotics Aid

The bill contained the toughest provisions ever voted by Congress against countries that failed to curtail illicit narcotics production. Bolivia and Peru were the prime targets, but the bill also included a direct warning to Jamaica and an implied warning to other countries.

For fiscal 1986, the provision allowed the president to provide half of the intended economic and military aid to Bolivia after he certified to Congress that the government there had enacted legislation to limit production of coca, which was used to make cocaine. The president could provide the rest of the aid after he certified to Congress that Bolivia had achieved its calendar year 1985 targets for eradication of illegal coca production.

For fiscal 1987, the president could provide half of Bolivia's aid after he certified that half of its coca eradication targets for calendar year 1986 had been met. The remaining half could be provided once the president certified that Bolivia had achieved all of its eradication targets.

The bill conditioned all economic, development and military aid to Peru for 1986 on a presidential report to Congress that Peru had made "substantial progress" in developing a plan to establish legal limits on coca production. For 1987, the aid was conditioned on a presidential certification that Peru was implementing its plan to limit coca production.

Peru also was barred from getting aid for its project to reduce coca production in the Upper Huallaga Valley unless the administration certified that the project would be effective.

The bill also stated that any aid withheld from Bolivia or Peru would be reallocated to other countries that had taken steps to curb narcotics production.

For Jamaica, the bill required the president to take into consideration, in allocating economic aid, whether that country was developing a plan to curtail marijuana production.

A broader provision in the bill prohibited aid to any country found by the president to have failed to take "adequate steps" to prevent production of or trafficking in narcotics.

Another important provision repealed, on a case-by-case basis, the so-called "Mansfield amendment," which barred U.S. government officials from participating in drug-related arrests overseas. Under the new provision, U.S. officials could be present at such arrests if the U.S. ambassador and the country involved agreed, and if the incident was reported to Congress.

Foreign Airport Security

The foreign aid bill included a series of provisions expanding the administration's authority to prohibit service between the United States and foreign airports found to have inadequate security against hijacking and other terrorist acts. The provisions were prompted by the June 14 hijacking of a TWA airliner outside Athens, Greece, which resulted in 39 Americans being held hostage for 17 days.

The airport provisions:

- Required the secretary of transportation to assess security at foreign airports to determine whether they met international standards, and to report the results to Congress and to nations where those airports were located.

In a case where the security was found to be inadequate, the country involved was to be given 90 days to correct any deficiencies. If the security was not improved within 90 days, the secretary of transportation, after consulting with the secretary of state, was to issue a public notice stating that the airport did not meet security standards; the notice was to be posted at U.S. airports and to be included on airline tickets. The secretary could waive the 90-day waiting period if he determined that conditions threatened the safety of passengers or airline crew members. The secretary of state also was authorized to issue a travel advisory concerning any airport that failed to meet the security standards.

- Authorized the president to invoke a U.S. boycott of any foreign airport that did not meet international standards and did not correct deficiencies within the 90 days.
- Required the president to suspend U.S. aid to any country that had refused to correct security problems at any of its airports within the 90 days. However, the president could waive this requirement if doing so was in the U.S. "national security interest."
- Required the secretary of state to seek international agreements on ways to improve compliance with minimum safety standards at airports.
- Authorized a Transportation Department study of an expanded program to put air marshals aboard U.S. flights.

Anti-Terrorism

The bill included provisions intended to combat international terrorism. The major provisions:

- Authorized $9.84 million in each fiscal year for the State Department's anti-terrorism program, which provided training to help other countries. The bill also repealed a "sunset provision" in previous law that would have terminated the anti-terrorism program at the end of fiscal 1985, and authorized the United States to provide up to $325,000 per year worth of small arms and munitions to foreign countries under that program.
- Authorized the president to prohibit trade with Libya and to prohibit imports of goods and services from countries found by the State Department to be supporting terrorism.
- Prohibited aid to countries that harbored terrorists or that otherwise supported international terrorism. The president could waive this ban if he reported to Congress that doing so was justified by national security or humanitarian reasons.
- Called for an international civil aviation boycott of countries that harbored terrorists or that otherwise supported international terrorism.

Mozambique

Both houses had adopted amendments by conservatives barring or restricting aid to the Marxist government of Mozambique, and conferees approved a blend of those provisions.

The administration, which had moved to improve ties with Mozambique, opposed the restrictions.

The final bill included a Senate provision that barred any arms aid to Mozambique (Reagan had requested $3 million) unless the president certified to Congress that the government was making a concerted effort to comply with international human rights standards, was making progress in implementing economic and political reforms, had implemented a plan by Sept. 30, 1986, to reduce the number of foreign military personnel to 55, and was committed to holding free elections by Sept. 30, 1986.

The bill also allowed economic and development aid for Mozambique solely to help the private sector "to the maximum extent practicable." The aid also had to be provided through non-governmental agencies.

Development Aid

Major development aid provisions:

- Set aside $50 million in development aid funds for the U.S. contribution to the International Fund for Agricultural Development. Reagan had requested no money for that agency, pending action by Saudi Arabia and other oil-producing countries to follow through on their promises of increased contributions.
- Required that "a substantial percentage" of development aid go to improve the lives of the poor, especially those living in "absolute poverty."
- Required that at least 13.5 percent of all economic and development aid be channeled through private, voluntary organizations.
- Required the administration to reduce U.S. contributions to international organizations by the proportionate U.S. share of their spending on programs aiding the PLO, the South West Africa Peoples' Organization, Libya, Iran and Cuba.

Population Programs

After an hour's heated debate over a flurry of amendments, the conferees took the easy route to settling the emotional issue of U.S. support for family planning programs overseas: They deleted from the bill all references to the issue.

The House and Senate bills had contained conflicting and complicated provisions restricting U.S. contributions to international agencies that conducted family planning programs. The House-passed language endorsed the Reagan administration's policy of barring aid to agencies that had any involvement with abortions. The Senate's provisions were somewhat less supportive of administration policy.

When it became clear that the issue was too complex and politically sticky to be resolved, the conferees agreed to kill all provisions that endorsed or restricted administration actions.

The result was an authorization of $290 million for family planning programs, with no clear congressional direction on how to spend the money.

Other Provisions

Other provisions of the bill:

- Set a limit of $7 million annually on military grants to Zaire, and barred military loans to that country. The House had voted a $4 million limit on grants. The bill also required that economic aid to Zaire be used for development and be channeled through private agencies, rather than through the government, to the maximum extent practicable.
- Declared that U.S. policy was to support a "negotiated settlement" of the war in the Western Sahara between Morocco and a local guerrilla organization called the Polisario. However, conferees deleted House-passed language that called for U.S. "direct contacts" with all parties to the war and that barred U.S. military advisers from operating in the Western Sahara during the war.
- Barred use of Economic Support Fund aid by foreign countries to build or operate nuclear power facilities, except for countries that had signed the Nuclear Non-Proliferation Treaty or had taken other non-proliferation steps consistent with U.S. policy.
- Earmarked $15 million in Economic Support Fund aid for Cyprus and stated congressional support for a special $250 million reconstruction fund for that country if the Greek and Turkish communities made substantial progress toward resolving their disputes. However, the $250 million would have to be authorized in future legislation.
- Authorized economic, development and military training aid for Haiti on the condition that the president certify to Congress annually that Haiti was attempting to stop illegal immigration into the United States, was implementing U.S. conditions on its aid program and was making progress on human rights. The bill also allowed training of Haitian police to stop illegal immigration into the United States, and military aid for that purpose and to control narcotics production.
- Barred economic aid to Ethiopia except for disaster relief or aid that directly benefited needy people. The bill also required the president to report to Congress on whether the Ethiopian government was conducting a policy of deliberately starving people in areas controlled by rebel forces; if the president found that the government was conducting such a policy, and Congress agreed by passing a joint resolution, all U.S. trade with that country would be suspended.
- Avoided the issue of economic aid to Lebanon. Reagan had requested $10 million in fiscal 1986, and the House had approved $2.5 million on the condition that all seven remaining U.S. hostages in that country were released. Conferees deleted the House condition, but called on the administration to give a "higher priority" to obtaining release of hostages. Conferees also expressed their "regret" at the administration's decision to divert economic aid, originally appropriated for Lebanon in 1983, to other countries.
- Established new minimum levels for regular, non-emergency shipments of free food under Title II of the PL 480 Food for Peace Program. In fiscal 1986, the government would be required to ship at least 1.8 million metric tons, of which 1.3 million must be distributed through private agencies and the World Food Program. In fiscal 1987, the comparable figures would be 1.9 million tons, with 1.425 million to be distributed through private agencies. The bill also encouraged the president to enter into multi-year agreements to provide food through private agencies, and authorized private agencies to sell or barter PL 480 food so they could provide other services.
- Authorized military and economic aid to Pakistan only if the president certified to Congress that Pakistan did not possess a nuclear weapon and that the aid would "reduce significantly" the risk that Pakistan would acquire such weapons.
- Stated the sense of Congress in favor of increasing the number of Peace Corps volunteers to 10,000 by 1989; in 1985 the figure was about 5,000. The bill also allowed a limited number of Peace Corps staff members to serve for 7½ years, rather than the previous limit of five years. ▮

Congress Votes to Resume Nicaragua Rebel Aid

After two years of sustained battles, President Reagan won in 1985 congressional approval — if not full-hearted support — for U.S. involvement in the war against the leftist government of Nicaragua.

Congress authorized and appropriated $27 million for non-military aid to some 15,000 "contras" in 1985. That action represented a dramatic turnaround from a previous-year cutoff of assistance to the rebels in their fight against the Sandinista regime in Managua. *(Box, p. 76)*

But with the aid to the anti-government rebels to expire on March 31, 1986, the stage was set for a renewed confrontation over the issue. President Reagan returned to Congress early in 1986 to ask for additional support for the Nicaraguan guerrillas.

The contra funding was included in supplemental appropriations legislation (PL 99-88) for fiscal 1985. Voting in April, the House rejected a joint resolution (H J Res 239) that would have granted Reagan's request to resume aid to the contras. A trip to Moscow by Nicaraguan President Daniel Ortega helped shift the political climate in favor of the rebels and the House reversed itself when it took up the appropriations bill in June.

It was a major victory for Reagan, who had thrown the weight of his presidency behind the contras' battle against the Sandinistas. Reagan had called the issue "one of the greatest moral challenges" to the United States and described the contras as "freedom fighters." *(Policy background, box, p. 70)*

However, Reagan's temporary abandonment of arms aid to the contras deflated some of the symbolic meaning in the high-pressure struggle between the president and congressional Democrats over the direction of Central America policy.

The shift by the House had many causes, the most important of which appeared to be a new receptiveness by many Democrats to Reagan's argument that Nicaragua was a test of American will to fight communism. Rep. Bill Richardson, D-N.M., long a Reagan critic, said: "I am willing to give the president of the United States a chance and the benefit of the doubt. I hope and pray he does not let us down."

To gain victory, Reagan compromised on two technical matters of enormous political importance.

The first was the insistence by most congressional

leaders that U.S. tax dollars be spent for food, clothing and other "humanitarian" purposes, not for guns, bullets and other military items. Reagan accepted that condition, but retained the right to ask for direct military aid later.

And members rejected an administration request that either the CIA or the Defense Department be allowed to administer the aid. The CIA had administered the original military aid program to the rebels.

Authorization for the $27 million in aid was contained in the fiscal 1986-87 foreign aid bill (PL 99-83), which also prohibited the CIA or Pentagon from administering the assistance.

In November, however, Congress loosened some of its restrictions. Adopting the fiscal 1986 authorizations bill for the CIA and other intelligence agencies (PL 99-169), members allowed the CIA to give the contras advice and intelligence information. The measure also broadened previous congressional definitions of "humanitarian" aid.

Those provisions were reaffirmed in defense-related provisions of the fiscal 1986 continuing appropriations resolution (PL 99-190). And the defense authorization bill (PL 99-145), cleared in October, contained a sense-of-Congress declaration that no combat forces should be sent into Nicaragua. *(Stories, pp. 377, 138)*

Final Provisions

As authorized in the foreign aid bill (S 960 — PL 99-83) and appropriated in the supplemental (HR 2577 — PL 99-88), the United States could give the contras $27 million for "humanitarian" or non-military aid through March 31, 1986. *(Authorization, p. 41; supplemental, p. 350)*

But in a major rebuke to the administration, both measures barred the CIA or the Defense Department from administering the aid. Dante B. Fascell, D-Fla., chairman of the House Foreign Affairs Committee, said the administration never adequately explained why it wanted freedom for the CIA and the Pentagon to administer the aid. "There's no magic in this," he said. "You don't have to have a bunch of four-star generals and guys with flying cloaks and stuff like that to administer $27 million for humanitarian reasons."

Conferees on the foreign aid bill said in their report (H Rept 99-237) that the ban on CIA and Defense Department involvement did not prevent those agencies from giving the contras advice or intelligence information.

Other contra provisions in the foreign aid bill:

- Barred the administration from entering into an agreement that forced a country receiving U.S. foreign aid or weapons to help the contras. The provision stated: "The United States shall not enter into any agreement conditioning, expressly or impliedly, the provision of assistance under this act, or the purchase of defense articles and services under the Arms Export and Control Act, on the provision of assistance by a recipient country to persons or groups engaged in an insurgency or other act of rebellion against the government of Nicaragua."

Conferees said that provision was not intended to prohibit administration officials from discussing U.S. policy in Central America with foreign aid recipients, or to prohibit those recipients from giving aid to the contras on their own volition from their own resources.

This was the modified version of a provision, originally passed by the Senate, that barred the United States from making an agreement or understanding that provided for another country to aid the contras. The original provision, strongly opposed by the administration, was aimed at preventing the administration from asking El Salvador or other Central American countries to use their U.S. foreign aid on behalf of the contras.

- Divided the $27 million into three parts, to be provided every 90 days upon the president's submission to Congress of reports on Nicaragua.
- Allowed the provision to the contras of food, clothing, medicine or other humanitarian aid, but expressly barred weapons, arms systems, ammunition, vehicles or "material which can be used to inflict serious bodily harm or death."
- Required the president to establish procedures to prevent the humanitarian aid from being diverted to military purposes.
- Required the president to suspend aid to the contras if he determined that they were engaged in a consistent pattern of human rights abuses.
- Authorized $2 million in fiscal 1986 to help implement a regional peace accord resulting from talks led by the "Contadora" countries: Colombia, Mexico, Panama and Venezuela.
- Established a procedure for expedited congressional consideration of any future request by the president for additional aid to the contras.

Intelligence Bill

The fiscal 1986 intelligence bill (HR 2419 — PL 99-169) expanded the U.S. backing of the contras. It allowed the administration to provide radios, trucks and other gear that could be used to help the guerrillas wage war on the Sandinista government. *(Intelligence bill, p. 96)*

The conference report filed Nov. 14 (H Rept 99-373) on the intelligence bill contained two features on the issue: It barred the CIA from using its contingency fund to resume "covert" military aid to the contras, and it broadened previous congressional statements of what "humanitarian aid" meant.

The State Department, which administered the aid, reported to Congress on Nov. 15 that it had provided $5.5 million worth of clothing, food, medicine and other items to the United Nicaraguan Opposition, a political umbrella group for the guerrillas.

Contingency Fund. Both chambers expressly denied Reagan's request for renewed CIA funding of the contras in fiscal 1986; the conferees said that meant the agency could not dip into its multimillion-dollar contingency reserve to provide aid to the guerrillas. To resume aiding the contras, the conferees said, the CIA would have to return to the Intelligence committees for explicit approval of a "reprogramming" or transfer of funds from a lower priority account.

Congress authorized only one role for the CIA in the Nicaraguan war: the provision of intelligence information and advice to the contras. There was no clear definition of what that meant; however, conferees said the CIA could not provide training or advice that would "amount to participation in the planning or execution of military or paramilitary operations" or participation in "logistics activities integral to such operations."

Radios, Trucks. The conferees consented to an administration request for a broadened definition of humanitarian aid — thus increasing the scope of U.S. involvement in the contras' war against Managua.

First, the conferees authorized a secret amount to buy radios to allow contra leaders at their base camps along the Nicaraguan-Honduran border to receive intelligence information from the United States and to pass that information along to units stationed deep within Nicaragua. Conferees cautioned that the CIA should exchange information "without compromising U.S. intelligence sources and methods."

However, the conferees avoided the question of whether the CIA could provide only "defensive" information aimed at helping the contras ward off government attacks or could also provide a broader range of information that would allow them to mount offensive operations against the government. The effect of skirting that question was to allow the CIA to make its own determination of what kinds of information it could provide.

Second, the conferees accepted the administration's contention that the $27 million aid law allowed the provision of "transportation equipment" to the contras.

The administration had said it should be allowed to give the contras trucks and possibly helicopters to transport food, clothing and other supplies to their camps in the Nicaraguan interior. Some members of Congress, however, noted that trucks and helicopters could be armed and used for military purposes — something expressly prohibited by the July contra aid law.

The Intelligence conferees took a middle ground, saying the United States could give transportation gear to the contras "so long as no modifications are made to the equipment designed to be used to inflict serious bodily harm or death."

Third, the conferees said the State Department was allowed to solicit other sources, including other countries, for humanitarian aid to the contras. The only restrictions were that any aid provided by another country as a result of U.S. solicitations had to come from its own resources, and that the United States could not condition its foreign aid on another country's willingness to back the contras. The CIA, the Defense Department and other intelligence agencies also were excluded from asking other countries to aid the contras.

Background

Officially, the United States halted its involvement in the Nicaraguan war in mid-1984, when leaders of the House Intelligence Committee successfully maneuvered Congress into cutting off aid to the contras.

In October 1984, Congress set aside $14 million for the rebels for fiscal 1985. But to get use of the money, Reagan was required to submit a report to Congress, after Feb. 28, 1985, and convince both houses to approve the aid by joint resolution.

At the beginning of the year, that prospect looked extremely unlikely. The Democratic-controlled House already had voted four times since 1983 against U.S. aid to the contras. Support for the contras dwindled in the Senate in 1984 after the administration committed a series of political blunders, such as failing to inform the Intelligence Committee about CIA involvement in the mining of Nicaraguan harbors.

A bellwether for the Senate on the Nicaragua issue was Dave Durenberger, R-Minn., a moderate and the incoming chairman of the Intelligence Committee, who had supported the contra aid program.

In 1984, Durenberger decried Reagan's emphasis on military action in Central America and said the administration had bungled its role in Nicaragua's war. But he continued to vote for the contra aid.

But at the end of the year, he announced he would support open aid "to support the democratic revolution" but no more "covert" assistance funneled through the CIA. "I want the CIA out of running an open covert action to implement a policy that everybody's confused about," he said.

Meanwhile, the Republican-controlled Senate Intelligence Committee — long the main source of congressional support for contra aid — joined its House counterpart in condemning the CIA for its handling of the aid. *(1984 Almanac p. 86)*

Aid Diversions?

Early in 1985, the intelligence panels launched probes into reports that several countries had used U.S. foreign aid to support the contras.

The New York Times and other publications had reported that the Nicaraguan rebels were getting weapons, ammunition and logistical support from El Salvador, Honduras, Israel and possibly other countries that, in turn, were major recipients of U.S. foreign aid. Those countries' support for the contras reportedly had escalated since CIA funding of the contras ran out in May 1984.

Direct diversion of U.S. foreign aid to the contras from a recipient country would have violated several provisions of aid laws. It also potentially would have violated the fiscal 1985 continuing appropriations resolution (PL 98-473), which barred the United States from aiding the contras "directly or indirectly" without explicit congressional approval.

Secretary of State George P. Shultz said U.S. foreign aid was being used "for the purposes it was given for." But he said foreign aid recipients were sovereign countries, "and if they have things they want to do with their own funds, that's up to them."

In addition to the Intelligence panels, the House Defense Appropriations Subcommittee and the House Foreign Affairs Subcommittee on Western Hemisphere Affairs also looked into the aid diversion reports.

One bit of circumstantial evidence cited by a House aide was that U.S. arms aid to Honduras exceeded that country's military spending. The Honduran military budget averaged about $50 million, the aide said, while U.S. military aid was $77 million in fiscal 1984 and $61 million in fiscal 1985.

By year's end, however, the probes had stalled for lack of evidence.

Reagan Campaigns for Support

In the weeks before renewing his request for military aid to the contras, Reagan mounted what administration officials called a "public education" campaign.

In a weekly radio broadcast on Feb. 16 and at a nationally televised news conference Feb. 21, Reagan made some of his harshest attacks ever on the policies of the Sandinistas and acknowledged publicly for the first time that he was seeking to overthrow the Managua regime.

Reagan and his aides for three years had given several purposes for aiding the anti-government guerrillas, but the ousting of the Sandinistas had not been among Washington's official aims.

In the radio broadcast on Feb. 16, Reagan called the Nicaraguan guerrillas "our brothers." Leaders of several guerrilla organizations had stated repeatedly that they wanted to overthrow the Sandinista regime.

And, asked at the news conference if U.S. policy was to

remove the Sandinista leaders in Nicaragua, Reagan responded: "Well, removed in the sense of its present structure in which it is a communist, totalitarian state." The United States, he added, had "an obligation to be of help where we can to freedom fighters" in such places as Nicaragua and Afghanistan.

In his Feb. 16 radio broadcast, Reagan compared the contras with Americans who fought the British during the American Revolution. The United States should aid the contras now, he said, just as the French aided the Americans then.

The president insisted that the Sandinistas were bent on spreading communism throughout the Western Hemisphere. "We must remember that if the Sandinistas are not stopped now, they will, as they have sworn, attempt to spread communism to El Salvador, Costa Rica, Honduras and elsewhere."

The Sandinistas repeatedly had denied that claim.

At his Feb. 21 news conference, the president repeated his longstanding contention that the Sandinistas violated pledges they made to the OAS in 1979, when they and other groups overthrew Nicaraguan dictator Somoza. Among those pledges was the holding of free elections.

Instead, he said, the Sandinistas established a totalitarian government that was "brutal, cruel."

Reagan said the United States would ease its pressure on the Sandinistas "if they'd say: 'Uncle. All right and come on back into the revolutionary government and let's straighten this out and institute the goals' " of the 1979 revolution.

Shultz, Nicaraguans Lobby

Secretary of State Shultz hammered at the same theme in public appearances on Capitol Hill Feb. 19. He told the House Foreign Affairs and Senate Budget committees that the Nicaraguan regime was "bad news" not only for its own people but also for "its neighbors in Central America and for our own security interests here in the United States."

At the Foreign Affairs Committee, Shultz skirted a question by Michael D. Barnes, D-Md., about why the United States had not gone to the Organization of American States with a complaint about Nicaragua's behavior.

"If Nicaragua poses a potential threat, there are legitimate mechanisms in place that can be used," Barnes said, referring to the OAS and to the Rio Treaty, under which most countries in the Western Hemisphere had pledged to come to each other's aid to thwart aggression.

Shultz insisted that the United States was "looking at all alternatives," but he declined to discuss the OAS and the Rio Treaty.

Rep. Gerry E. Studds, D-Mass., attacked Reagan's reference to the contras as "our brothers." Noting charges by the Sandinistas and some human rights groups that the contras had killed civilians and plundered the Nicaraguan countryside, Studds asked Shultz: "Can't we do better than this ... than to provide aid to a mixed group of mercenaries, thugs — and democrats? ... Surely, a struggle for freedom should be something other than one between their terrorists and our terrorists."

Shultz rejected Studds' characterization of the contras.

The administration's campaign prompted some lobbying by the Sandinista government. Nicaragua's deputy foreign minister, Victor Tinoco, visited Capitol Hill the week of Feb. 25 to lobby against the contra aid. And Nicaraguan President Ortega on Feb. 27 invited members of Congress to travel to his country to inspect the military bases that Reagan said threatened other countries in the region.

Ortega also offered to send home 100 Cuban military advisers and impose a moratorium on Nicaragua's acquisition of new weapons systems.

Reagan Makes a Peace Proposal

Reagan in early April asked Congress for $14 million in renewed U.S. military aid to the contras. But in a shift of tactics, he coupled his request with a proposal for a 60-day cease-fire and an offer of church-mediated negotiations.

The request seemed to put Reagan's Capitol Hill critics on the defensive. Democrats who had opposed his Central America policies were forced to quibble with the vague details of his plan and to scramble to come up with their own alternative, while Reagan declared that he was promoting peace.

House Speaker Thomas P. O'Neill Jr., D-Mass., called Reagan's plan a "dirty trick" to win over wavering members of Congress.

But Robert C. McFarlane, Reagan's national security adviser, said "the climate is changing" in Congress. And Richard G. Lugar, R-Ind., Senate Foreign Relations Committee chairman, described the plan as a potential "breakthrough" for Reagan on one of the most contentious disputes with Congress.

McFarlane conceded that the Reagan plan was put together to overcome Hill opposition to aiding the guerrillas. Asked by reporters if Reagan would have advanced such a plan if he already had the votes in Congress, McFarlane said: "I don't have a good answer for you on that."

Reagan sent his request in a secret report on April 3 and publicly announced his "Central American Peace Proposal" the next day. He portrayed his plan as an Eastertime peace offering that would give the Sandinistas and opposition forces a chance to negotiate.

Reagan pegged his plan to a declaration in Costa Rica on March 1 by key Nicaraguan opposition leaders, all of whom had gone into exile and some of whom had taken up arms against the Sandinistas. The declaration demanded that the Sandinistas agree to negotiations, in return for a cease-fire. The cease-fire offer was to expire on April 20.

Under Reagan's plan, the contras were to extend their offer of a cease-fire to June 1. In the meantime, Congress would be asked to free up the $14 million, with Reagan's pledge that the money would be spent for food, clothing, medicine and "other support for survival" of the contras — but not for arms or munitions.

If the Sandinistas did not accept the cease-fire by June 1, Reagan would use what was left of the $14 million to resume contra arms aid.

If the Sandinistas agreed to negotiations, Reagan would retain his pledge of non-military use of the $14 million. But he said he would not allow the talks to "become a cover for deception or delay"; if there was no agreement between the Sandinistas and the contras within 60 days after talks started, he would resume the arms aid unless both sides asked him not to do so.

Reagan and his aides insisted that the plan required concessions by both sides. But, by the very nature of the situation, the Sandinistas were to make the greater sacrifice by conceding a share of their sovereignty. The Sandinistas also would be under severe time pressure to conclude an agreement within 60 days or face resumption of the war.

The major contra group, the Nicaraguan Democratic Force, immediately accepted Reagan's request for an extension of the cease-fire negotiations.

But Nicaragua's government rejected the plan. Carlos Tunnermann, ambassador to Washington, said the contras would have an incentive to drag out negotiations past 60 days so they could receive more U.S. military aid.

Reagan also repeated several longstanding demands of the Sandinistas: that they reduce their armed forces and expel Soviet bloc military advisers, that they stop supporting leftist guerrillas in El Salvador, and that they respect their 1979 promise of establishing a free democracy in Nicaragua.

Congressional Reaction

Members of Congress on both sides of the Nicaragua issue praised Reagan for talking about peace in Central America after emphasizing military actions for several years. But while Reagan's supporters hailed the plan as a major step toward peace, critics voiced suspicion about his motives and quarreled with the specifics.

One of the most enthusiastic reactions came from Lugar, who said the plan would have given the Sandinistas at least a two-month respite from the devastating guerrilla war and improved the contras' negotiating position. "If there is a disposition on the part of anybody to negotiate, this provides a face-saving way to do it," he said.

But Reagan's critics unleashed a barrage of complaints about key elements of the plan. House Democratic Whip Thomas S. Foley, D-Wash., said Reagan was demanding that the Sandinistas negotiate "with a gun to their head," and others said Reagan was asking the Nicaraguans to forfeit their sovereignty.

Bill Alexander, D-Ark., called the plan "a new face on an old horror" — U.S. aid to guerrillas who were battling a government with which the United States had diplomatic relations.

Sen. Durenberger, while calling the plan "a positive step," said it fell short of the "comprehensive policy" for Central America. He said the plan offered no clear route for reducing the Sandinistas' military potency or their support for Salvadoran rebels.

And Patrick J. Leahy, D-Vt., vice chairman of the Senate Intelligence Committee, charged that Reagan was asking for a "Central American Tonkin Gulf" resolution.

Several critics also noted that giving the contras humanitarian aid, such as food and clothing, would allow them to buy arms and ammunition with the money they reportedly received from private sources and foreign governments. Reagan's definition of humanitarian aid also was broad enough to include trucks and other equipment that could sustain military operations.

White House officials acknowledged the possible diversion of U.S.-supplied funds, but insisted that the contras would not pose a serious military threat to the Nicaraguan regime.

House Democrats began working on an alternative to Reagan's request. O'Neill asked Lee H. Hamilton, D-Ind., chairman of the Intelligence Committee, and Western Hemisphere Subcommittee Chairman Barnes to draw up a plan that could give members something to vote for other than the $14 million.

Another group of House members, led by Larry J. Hopkins, R-Ky., on April 2 canceled a planned trip to Nicaragua because the Sandinistas refused to allow unlimited inspection of military facilities there.

Joint Resolution

Two weeks later, confronted by opposition in both houses of Congress, Reagan backed down from the $14 million military aid request.

On April 18, Reagan agreed tentatively to a compromise, advocated by Republicans and conservative Democratic senators, restricting contra aid to non-military purposes — at least through the end of the 1985 fiscal year, Sept. 30. A White House spokesman said Reagan would pursue his request for fiscal 1986 military aid to the rebels.

Reagan had begun the week of April 15 hoping for a narrow victory in both houses on his request for $14 million to aid the guerrillas, coupled with his Nicaragua peace plan.

But the option in his peace plan to resume military aid generated deep opposition on Capitol Hill.

The Democratic-controlled House blunted the administration's lobbying efforts by pushing up the planned House Nicaragua vote to April 23, the same day as the Senate vote.

On April 16, Republican leaders told Reagan that his plan could not pass the House and was in danger of failing in the Senate. Two days later, after Sen. Sam Nunn, D-Ga., added his voice to that appeal and Secretary of State Shultz privately met with 54 restive senators, Reagan agreed reluctantly to a compromise.

A White House official said Reagan coupled his agreement with a demand that Congress generally endorse his call for Nicaraguan peace talks, and that Congress not take any action that could be interpreted as abandoning the contras.

House Democrats' Proposal

In the House, leaders agreed on at least three Nicaragua votes for April 23. The first was to occur on Reagan's request (H J Res 239), which was expected to be defeated by a narrow margin. Next, the House would vote on a substitute crafted by Hamilton and Michael D. Barnes, D-Md., barring further military aid to the contras and instead providing $4 million to foster peace talks and $10 million for humanitarian aid to Nicaraguan refugees. The White House rejected this plan as "totally unacceptable." The House also would vote on a GOP alternative. The Rules Committee on April 18 approved the three-vote arrangement.

The Hamilton-Barnes plan, to be offered as a joint resolution, would have taken $14 million that Reagan wanted for military aid and diverted it to two other uses: $4 million to be set aside to implement a possible peace treaty in Central America, including border patrols or verification of agreements to reduce military forces; and $10 million to go to the International Committee of the Red Cross or the United Nations High Commissioner for Refugees for humanitarian aid to the Nicaraguan refugees outside that country, regardless of whether they had been involved in the fighting.

The Hamilton-Barnes proposal also continued the ban on direct or indirect U.S. aid to military or paramilitary forces in Nicaragua. Congress could repeal that ban by passing a joint resolution.

The plan also:

- Required the president to report to Congress every three months on progress toward peace in Central America and how the money was being spent. After Oct. 1, 1985, the president could request further action from Congress, with the assurance of action under expedited procedures.

- Stated congressional support for regional peacekeeping efforts, including those of the Contadora countries.
- Condemned "disturbing trends" in Nicaragua's foreign and domestic policies, such as press censorship, dominance of the ruling Sandinista party and the regime's ties to the Soviet Union and Cuba.
- Stated that Congress would monitor the situation in Nicaragua and would base its future decisions, in part, on how much progress had been made in curtailing the trends disapproved by the United States.

Senate Options

In the Senate, negotiations were under way among the White House, Republicans and conservative Democrats on a plan that would provide non-military aid to the Nicaraguan guerrillas and invite Reagan to return to Congress for military aid should peace talks fail.

The Senate Appropriations Committee on April 18 approved Reagan's original (S J Res 106) request 15-13, although several of the 15 said they opposed it as written and preferred to vote on non-military aid.

The outlines of the Senate version of the compromise included: providing $14 million in food, medicine and other humanitarian aid to the contras, using funds appropriated in PL 98-473 to the CIA; calling on the Sandinistas to accept their foes' offer of a cease-fire and direct talks within a set time, such as 90 or 120 days; and asking the president to seek further aid if warranted.

The main difference between the approaches was that House Democratic leaders adamantly opposed giving any aid directly to the contras, and Reagan and the Republicans were insisting on symbolic support for them.

The Democrats complained that the contras were the tool of Reagan's determination to overthrow the leftist government of Nicaragua, by direct U.S. intervention if necessary.

"I don't think the president of the United States will be happy until troops are in there, and I'm going to do everything in my power to stop that," House Speaker Thomas P. O'Neill Jr., D-Mass., said on April 17.

Reagan said backing for the contras was a key test of U.S. resolve to resist communism in the hemisphere. And while retreating from his request for direct military aid to the contras, Reagan insisted that House Democrats were doing the country a disservice. Their insistence on voting on April 23 — a week earlier than White House officials had expected — was "immoral," he said.

Negative Feedback

Reagan conceded on the military aid after Senate leaders told him their chamber would approve his original request only if he personally undertook a full-scale lobbying campaign. White House officials reportedly were split over the wisdom of having the president commit himself to such an effort at the same time his persuasion would be needed for Senate action on the 1986 budget resolution, a concern shared by Majority Leader Robert Dole, R-Kan. *(Story, p. 441)*

House Democrats on April 17 completed a poll of members that seemed to show that Reagan's contra request would be defeated by 10-20 votes. Although narrow, that margin appeared to be firm.

Democrats had counted 48 solid votes in the Senate against Reagan's request, with another 2-3 negative votes possible.

One development that helped convince the administration of the trouble for Reagan's plan was the April 17 speech against it by Nunn, widely respected among senators on foreign and military policy.

Nunn suggested giving the contras humanitarian, not military, aid. As a reward for an agreement by the Sandinistas to negotiate, Nunn said the United States should suspend its major military maneuvers in Honduras and off the Nicaraguan coast.

Nunn said he was offering his proposal because U.S. policy toward Nicaragua "does not command the support of the American people and the Congress, and until it does it is unlikely to succeed."

That view appeared to be widely held on Capitol Hill, and it helped explain why Reagan's April 4 "Central American peace plan" fell flat.

Members were particularly suspicious of Reagan's April 4 promise not to use the $14 million for military aid as long as the Sandinistas were negotiating with their opponents. After years of appearing to push for military solutions to conflicts in Central America, the president's sudden eagerness for peace talks struck many in Congress as having been contrived merely to win votes in Congress.

First Round: a Reagan Defeat

Handing Reagan one of the most serious defeats of his presidency, the House on April 23-24 rejected the resumption of U.S. aid to the contras. But Reagan vowed to demand "again and again" that Congress aid the rebels and ordered a review of options for sustained pressure on the Sandinistas.

Both the House and Senate acted on the Nicaragua issue in a highly partisan, pressure-cooker atmosphere.

The Senate on April 23 narrowly approved S J Res 106, which would have provided $14 million in aid to the contras. That 53-46 vote came only after Reagan had promised not to use the money for military purposes, had agreed to resume negotiations with the Sandinistas and had given a nod to building sentiment in Congress for economic rather than military pressure on Nicaragua. *(Vote 31, p. 11-S)*

An hour later, the House overwhelmingly rejected that same request (H J Res 239). The House ratified its action on April 24 with a series of votes on H J Res 247.

The two-vote margin by which the House rejected a GOP plan for non-military aid foreshadowed future battles on the issue on the 1985 supplemental appropriations bill and the fiscal 1986-87 foreign aid authorizations bill.

Many members seemed to have tired of repeated debates and votes that had had little demonstrable effect on U.S. policy or on the course of events in Nicaragua.

"We find ourselves in a quagmire, with every six months coming back to vote on aid to the contras and no movement," said Sen. Christopher J. Dodd, D-Conn., one of Reagan's most persistent critics. "When does it end, where do we go, what's happening? There's no movement at all anywhere to resolve the issues."

The votes, and public statements, put strong majorities in both houses on record as opposing military aid. The 180-248 vote by which the House on April 23 rejected military aid was the widest margin in that chamber. The Senate's 53-46 vote approving the $14 million in aid was the closest — and it was made possible only by Reagan's promise that the money would be used for food, clothing and other assistance for "survival and well-being" of the contras — not for arms.

The promise did not satisfy many Democrats, who argued that giving the contras money for food and clothing would enable them to continue fighting by using money they were getting from private sources. Democrats also noted that the administration's definition of humanitarian aid was broad enough to include trucks, radios and other supplies that would help the contras keep fighting.

But Reagan succeeded in shifting the terms of the congressional debate. Many long-term opponents of contra aid, while denouncing the president's policies, adopted his basic attitude that the Nicaraguan government must make internal changes or face increased U.S. pressure.

Rep. Bill Richardson, D-N.M., warned the Nicaraguans to "clean up their act" in coming months or face a congressional endorsement of Reagan's policies. And Rep. Edward P. Boland, D-Mass., former Intelligence Committee chairman, said that if the Sandinistas did not ease internal repression "they will find the Congress much less reluctant [to aid the contras] the next time."

Nicaraguan President Ortega had promised to drop press censorship, enter into a cease-fire with the contras and oust some Cuban military advisers if Congress refused further aid to the contras.

Rhetoric and Politics

Reagan's newfound willingness to negotiate with the Sandinistas and with Senate Democrats stood in sharp contrast to his increasingly harsh attacks on House Democrats. Reagan antagonized many Democrats in both chambers in an April 20 radio address, in which he labeled as "shameful surrender" a Democratic alternative to his $14 million request.

"A lot of Democrats, even if they like the president's proposal, will vote against it just because of his radio address," Sen. Dodd said.

But some Republicans eagerly joined Reagan in using harsh words to describe the Democrats. During a party caucus on April 24, House Minority Whip Trent Lott, Miss., complained about Democratic "goons." Others, including Sen. Jesse Helms, N.C., and Foreign Relations Committee Chairman Richard G. Lugar, Ind., threatened to use contra aid votes against Democrats in future campaigns.

SENATE ACTION

In the Senate, administration officials started with the proposition that they would be defeated on a straight up-or-down vote on Reagan's request, and that the only way of gaining a victory was to offer concessions responding to widely held concerns.

The administration tried to work with a broad spectrum of Democrats, in hopes of fashioning a compromise that would give the president an overwhelming Senate victory and put pressure on the House. But when the White House concluded that it could not swallow putting into law a plan offered by the Democrats, it returned to its traditional tactic of negotiating with individual Democrats.

The Democrats had a source of leverage: For parliamentary reasons, the Senate could not consider anything other than Reagan's original request unless the rules were suspended by a two-thirds vote, and Democrats had enough votes to block that move.

The Democrats hammered out their compromise proposal the weekend of April 20-21 and presented it to the administration on April 22.

J. Bennett Johnston, D-La., called the Democrats' ability to craft a unified proposal a "minor miracle" because the key actors ranged from David L. Boren, D-Okla., and himself on the right to John Kerry, D-Mass., and Tom Harkin, D-Iowa, on the left. In the previous four years of debates on Central American issues, Senate Democrats never had been able to agree on a single plan of action. Patrick J. Leahy, D Vt., said the Democrats' agreement offered the administration "a golden opportunity for bipartisan support" on the Nicaragua issue.

But the party unity merely masked the deep divisions among the Democrats; it did not cure them. Even while asking Reagan to accept the Democrats' plan, Boren, Johnston, Nunn and others said they would support the president if that was their only choice. And several Democrats pointedly refused to back the party compromise, saying it gave Reagan too much of what he wanted.

Senate Republicans also were divided, and the administration devoted substantial efforts to wooing back the 10 to 12 moderate and liberal Republicans who had threatened to oppose the request. But that effort was less successful than the lobbying of conservative Democrats. When the Senate approved the request 53-46, nine Republicans voted "no," one more than had opposed aid to the contras on the last vote of 1984. *(Vote 31, p. 11-S)*

Negotiations

Negotiations began April 22 in the Cabinet Room between senators, Reagan, and White House aides. Republicans and Democrats each offered a proposal for providing $14 million in humanitarian aid to the contras and calling for a mutual cease-fire in Nicaragua. Neither side proposed giving outright military aid for the foreseeable future.

The primary differences between the two proposals were over what conditions would be attached to the money. The Republicans proposed to put pressure on the Sandinistas by demanding that they negotiate with the contras and that they not engage in a further military buildup. The Democrats sought to use release of the $14 million as a lever to force Reagan to resume direct U.S. talks with the Sandinistas.

A secondary disagreement was over the method of disbursing the $14 million to the contras.

Administration officials insisted the CIA was the best organization to channel the money — in part because the $14 million on which Congress was voting already was authorized to that agency. Intelligence Committee Chairman Durenberger admitted that "there is a trust problem" with the CIA but insisted that requiring public accountability would eliminate any chance that the money would be used for military rather than humanitarian purposes.

While not spelling out which agency should provide the money, the Democrats opposed using the CIA because it had been the conduit for military aid to the contras.

At the conclusion of the White House talks April 22, a senior official told reporters that the administration was insisting on Congress' including in its resolution a call for direct talks between the Sandinistas and the contras.

The official said Reagan had already "gone quite far" in meeting the Democrats' demands. To make more concessions, he said, "would lead to a less stable situation in Nicaragua."

But Democrats said they, too, had made all the concessions that were possible while maintaining a unified position. Dodd said he had "gone a thousand miles" to accommodate a compromise.

Reagan Imposes Trade Embargo on Nicaragua

Acting on advice from many members of Congress, President Reagan on May 1 imposed a trade embargo and other economic sanctions against the leftist government of Nicaragua. *(Text, p. 16-D)*

Administration officials acknowledged that the action was largely symbolic, because Nicaragua's trade with the United States had dropped sharply and because other nations could make up for whatever trade was lost.

Reagan did not bar U.S. citizens from traveling to Nicaragua, as was the case for many years with Cuba, nor did he freeze Nicaraguan government assets in the United States, as President Carter did with Iranian assets during the hostage crisis.

But the sanctions filled in what many in Congress saw as an inconsistent gap in the Reagan administration's policy toward Nicaragua. The United States was maintaining full economic and diplomatic relations with Nicaragua, while waging rhetorical and military warfare against the Sandinista government.

Conservative Democratic senators had led the call for Reagan to impose sanctions as an alternative to military support of anti-Sandinista "contras."

Reagan on April 23 told Congress he was considering a trade embargo in conjunction with his request for $14 million in renewed U.S. aid to the contras. In open letters to the House and Senate, Reagan also promised to resume direct talks between the United States and the Nicaraguan government. *(Text, p. 14-D)*

But when the House on April 23-24 rejected the $14 million request, Reagan officials said that nullified the statements the president made in his letters, particularly the promise to resume talks. Reagan had said he would press Congress "again and again" on contra aid.

Reagan on April 26 ordered a review of U.S. policy toward Nicaragua. The major recommendation from that review by State Department and other agencies apparently was the sanctions.

On May 1 Reagan sent Congress notice of his decision on the sanctions, and White House spokesman Larry Speakes announced the decision in Bonn, West Germany, where Reagan was attending the summit of industrialized nations.

Economic Sanctions

Reagan's economic sanctions, which took effect on May 7, included:

- A U.S. embargo on all exports to or imports from Nicaragua. The administration allowed Nicaraguan imports to continue for up to six months if payment on them had been made prior to May 1. And exports were allowed to Nicaragua if they were in transit on May 1, if no buyer outside Nicaragua could be found or if the exporter had an obligation under a performance bond.
- A ban on flights to and from the United States by the Nicaraguan airline Aeronica.
- A ban on ships of Nicaraguan registry from entering U.S. ports.
- Unilateral abrogation of a Treaty of Friendship, Commerce and Navigation between the two countries.

Nicaraguan officials said the sanctions would damage their country's distressed economy by halting exports to the United States of beef, coffee, bananas and other products, which totaled $57 million in 1984. The embargo also threatened to worsen acute shortages of many consumer goods in Nicaragua, which bought $112 million worth of U.S. items and services in 1984.

To impose sanctions, Reagan was required to declare a national emergency and file follow-up reports to Congress every six months.

He told Congress that the "policies and actions of the government of Nicaragua constitute an unusual and extraordinary threat to the national security and foreign policy of the United States."

Reagan cited several actions by Managua, including its "aggressive activities" in the region; its "rapid and destabilizing military buildup"; its refusal to negotiate with the contras; and Ortega's visit to Moscow.

Congressional Reaction

Most Hill reaction to the sanctions was favorable. Sen. Lloyd Bentsen, D-Texas, a leading advocate of sanctions, said Reagan's action could "help persuade those in power in Managua to send home the 2,500 to 3,500 Cuban and Soviet military advisers . . . and to stop supporting armed insurgents against their neighbors."

But some critics of Reagan's Central American policies charged that the embargo would be counterproductive. Sen. Mark O. Hatfield, R-Ore., said the United States was "slamming the door on the possibility of peace" with the Nicaraguans. "We're driving them into the permanent embrace of the Russian bear."

But Rep. Michael D. Barnes, D-Md., chairman of the Foreign Affairs subcommittee on the Western Hemisphere, said the declaration of a national emergency because of a threat from Nicaragua was "ludicrous."

Criticism also came from Rep. Don Bonker, chairman of the Foreign Affairs subcommittee on International Economic Policy and Trade. In a May 7 hearing of the two panels that sparked heated partisan bickering, Bonker said: "We will see, as we have so often in the past, that these economic sanctions are not effective."

In response, Republicans gleefully quoted earlier statements by Democrats in both the House and Senate endorsing the use of sanctions against Nicaragua or encouraging Reagan to consider them.

Langhorne A. Motley, assistant secretary of state for inter-American affairs, acknowledged that sanctions, by themselves, would not force the Sandinistas to make the changes Reagan had demanded. But sanctions were "an additional element of pressure," especially if Congress would resume funding for the contras, he said.

Under questioning, Motley at first said the sanctions would have little effect on private business in Nicaragua because "the private sector today is virtually non-existent." When Motley acknowledged that about 55 percent of Nicaragua's production was in private hands, Peter H. Kostmayer, D-Pa., said the sanctions "are going to be penalizing the very people" who the United States hoped would take power from the Sandinistas.

Negotiating resumed April 23 on Capitol Hill. Early in the day, the administration abandoned negotiations with the full Democratic Caucus and shifted strategy to building support for the president's position based on a Reagan letter accepting some, but not all, of what the Democrats had proposed. One administration lobbyist called that strategy "picking off Democrats one by one."

The administration made changes in the letter to win converts. For example, a threat to use economic sanctions against Nicaragua was toughened at the request of Lloyd Bentsen, D-Texas, and others.

As the administration expected, some conservative Democrats quickly grabbed the opportunity to support the president. Boren's public statements demonstrated the success of the White House approach. At mid-afternoon on April 23, Boren told reporters he was disappointed by the administration's refusal to accept the Democratic proposal and bemoaned the prospect of a close Senate vote. Five hours later, as the final version of the letter was on its way to the Capitol, Boren took the Senate floor to announce his "enthusiastic support" for it.

The president's firm promise not to use any of the $14 million for military purposes — and to limit all his spending on the contras to $14 million — brought support from several senators who had agonized over the issue. One of them was Alfonse M. D'Amato, R-N.Y.; another was Warren B. Rudman, R-N.H., who a week before had voted for Reagan's request in the Appropriations Committee but had said he could not support it on the floor.

Senate Debate

The climactic portion of the Senate's 10-hour debate on the issue April 23 focused on Reagan's letter and the question of whether it signaled a shift in his strategies for dealing with Nicaragua.

Nunn said the letter demonstrated that Reagan "has taken at least three steps backward" on his Nicaragua policy: Reagan had reduced the emphasis on military action against the Sandinistas by accepting humanitarian aid for the contras, examined the possibility of imposing economic sanctions and pressed the contras to end human rights abuses.

The president's letter, he said, "represents the beginning of a possible approach in Nicaragua that can enjoy a centrist-type bipartisan following." Nunn voted for the contra aid.

John Glenn, D-Ohio, was among those attacking passage of a resolution calling for military aid.

"We are not voting on letters. We are not voting on stated intentions. We are not voting on negotiations at the White House," Glenn said. "We are voting on whether we send money down there that can be used for food and so on, and release of other money that can be used for arms."

But Boren said the Senate should accept Reagan's stated intentions. "I would only say as one senator, one American senator, I hope I never see the day when any of us stand up and say we cannot accept the word of the president of the United States, no matter what party we belong to."

The agony of senators torn on the Nicaragua issue was demonstrated by William S. Cohen, R-Maine, a former Intelligence Committee member who first opposed aid to the contras in October 1984 but voted for the contra money on April 23.

Cohen had argued that Reagan had failed to outline clearly U.S. objectives and strategy in Nicaragua. He said April 23 that he wanted neither to endorse the contras' goal of overthrowing the Sandinista government nor to "hand Mr. Ortega a victory" by rejecting Reagan's request.

Approving non-military aid for the contras would give the United States "breathing space" to try diplomatic and economic pressures on the Sandinistas, Cohen said. But unless the administration fashioned a policy "that is very clear in its objectives, that has full responsibility and accountability, then I think we are only deferring disaster."

John C. Danforth, R-Mo., attacked the underlying premise of what Congress was doing on the issue: that it had a legitimate role in helping fashion foreign policy.

"We have gone so far in taking foreign policy from the hands of the president that we have nearly immobilized the president," he said. Congressional activity in foreign affairs was reminiscent of the "Pink Panther" movies, he said: "We are the Inspector Clouseaus of foreign policy."

HOUSE ACTION

Taking up H J Res 239 the same day, the House was resuming what had become an institutional battle: House Democrats vs. Ronald Reagan.

Starting in early 1983, Speaker O'Neill and many of his followers had staked out a clear position opposing Reagan on the Nicaraguan war, a record of defiance to Reagan's legendary control of Congress.

As the House entered its concluding debate on Nicaragua April 24, Reagan called O'Neill to complain that the speaker was pressuring Democrats into opposing any aid to the contras.

O'Neill reportedly offered to postpone a final vote, but Reagan rebuffed the move. "I said to the president, 'I sincerely believe you're not going to be happy until you're in Nicaragua,' " O'Neill said later. "I told him, 'Your policy is wrong.' "

Democrats for weeks were confident that they had enough votes to defeat arms aid to the contras, even if the president mounted a high-pressure lobbying campaign. But Reagan's April 4 and 18 concessions on using the aid for humanitarian purposes gave new impetus to the effort to draft a Democratic alternative.

Barnes and Hamilton intended their alternative to emphasize diplomatic, rather than military, pressure on Nicaragua. It split Reagan's $14 million request into two parts: $10 million for aid to Nicaraguan refugees, including contras outside Nicaragua, and $4 million to help implement any regional peace treaty. The proposal also threatened unspecified action against Nicaragua if the Sandinistas failed to make internal reforms, and it retained indefinitely the legal ban on military aid to the contras.

House Republicans also drafted an alternative to Reagan's original request, which, for procedural reasons, was worded as providing military or paramilitary aid to the contras. Offered by Minority Leader Robert H. Michel, R-Ill., the plan would have funneled $14 million in humanitarian aid to the contras through the Agency for International Development.

The two-day debate in the House was highly partisan and frequently bitter. The harshest rhetoric came from Republicans, some of whom came close to accusing the House Democratic leadership of treason.

There was sharp disagreement about whether the Sandinistas posed an active threat to other countries in the region, and over the appropriate U.S. response. Democrats said Reagan's backing of the contras had failed and that it

Reagan Escalated Anti-Sandinista Talk . . .

Although the Reagan administration outlined specific goals in pressing for continued aid to the anti-government "contras," it did not make clear its long-term policies toward Nicaragua.

Officials from President Reagan on down gave conflicting answers to such basic questions as whether the United States would accept a communist government in Central America or whether the ultimate aim was the ouster of the Sandinista leaders.

While the administration imposed a trade embargo on Nicaragua May 1, that action was largely symbolic, because trade between the two countries had dropped sharply. *(Box, p. 68)*

The administration declined to take more serious steps, such as severing diplomatic relations, that might have had a major impact on the Sandinistas. The driving policy force appeared to be military actions.

At the beginning of the "covert war" in 1981, Reagan officials privately told Congress they wanted to stop the flow of arms from Nicaragua to leftist guerrillas in El Salvador. Some members of the Senate and House Intelligence committees later said they never understood whether the administration meant to do that by blocking arms shipments or by applying military pressure to convince the Sandinistas to stop the shipments.

In 1982 and 1983, according to members of the Intelligence panels, it became clear that the CIA-organized guerrillas had no interest in blocking arms shipments to El Salvador. The contras told reporters that they were fighting to oust the Sandinistas, or at least to pressure the Nicaraguan government into holding free elections.

After Congress, in late 1982, barred the CIA from trying to overthrow the Nicaraguan government, administration officials said that U.S. policy was still directed at stopping the arms flow to El Salvador and that the contras' stated goal was irrelevant.

In an April 27, 1983, address to Congress, Reagan insisted that the United States did not seek to overthrow Nicaragua's government but "to prevent the flow of arms to El Salvador, Honduras, Guatemala and Costa Rica."

But later in 1983 U.S. officials instead began talking about pressuring the Sandinistas to allow free elections, as they had promised in 1979. In March 1984, Reagan said contra aid would stop when the Sandinistas "keep their promises and restore the democratic rule and have elections." Reagan went on to say that any elections held in Nicaragua would be merely a Sandinista "rubber stamp."

Several senators said that statement, by saying that any elections the Sandinistas held would be unacceptable, implied that the United States was seeking to overthrow the Sandinistas. Reagan denied that was the case.

But later in 1984 and into 1985, Reagan escalated his attacks on the Sandinistas, calling them a "Marxist-Leninist clique" with no legitimate claim to government.

At a press conference on Feb. 21, 1985, Reagan said he sought to have the Nicaraguan government "removed, in the sense of its present structure, in which it is a communist totalitarian state . . ."

On Feb. 6, Secretary of State George P. Shultz sent Lee H. Hamilton, D-Ind., chairman of the House Intelligence Committee, a letter stating what the administration sought: an end to Nicaraguan support for guerrilla groups operating in other countries; severance of Nicaraguan military and security ties to Cuba and the Soviet bloc; reduction of Nicaragua's military strength to levels that would restore "military equilibrium" in the region; and fulfillment of the Sandinistas' promises "to support democratic pluralism within Nicaragua."

Reagan cited the same four goals on April 4, when he proposed a cease-fire and church-mediated peace talks.

Military Pressure

Support for the rebels was the most direct form of military pressure Reagan had applied to the Sandinistas.

The contras inflicted heavy damage on Nicaragua's economy and tapped a deep well of dissatisfaction with the Sandinista rule. But they failed to control large amounts of territory.

The main contra group organized by the CIA in 1981-82, the Nicaraguan Democratic Force (FDN, in the Spanish acronym) operating out of Honduras, attracted up to 15,000 fighters and made inroads in northern Nicaragua. Some top military leaders of the FDN had held posts in the regime of Nicaragua's deposed dictator Anastasio Somoza — a fact that had dogged the organization.

The other major group, led by former Sandinista military hero Eden Pastora, operated from Costa Rica. Called the Revolutionary Democratic Alliance (ARDE), Pastora's group suffered from internal rivalries.

When Congress approved $27 million in "humanitarian" aid in mid-1985, key opposition leaders formed the United Nicaraguan Opposition (UNO) to receive it.

But as of January 1986, only one planeload of the aid, mostly medicine and clothing, had reached the rebels. A second shipment was blocked by Honduras. The rebels were making purchases in Central America and the State Department was paying the bills.

U.S. officials also reportedly played a role in helping the contras buy SAM-7 anti-aircraft missiles from foreign dealers. One missile downed a Soviet-made helicopter on Dec. 2, 1985, killing Nicaraguan soldiers aboard. Money for the SAM-7s came from foreign donors or from overseas accounts where Americans had deposited money, a private contra fund raiser, retired Army Maj. Gen. John K. Singlaub, told the *Miami Herald* in January 1986.

Private groups also supported the contras indirectly by donating medicine, clothing and supplies to Nicaraguan refugees in Honduras. The Defense Department on April 6 shipped some 20,000 tons of supplies to the refugees, using a "humanitarian aid" provision of fiscal 1985 defense appropriations (PL 98-473).

War Games

Another form of military pressure was massive military exercises. Although the stated goal was to train U.S. and friendly countries' armed forces, the timing and location of most of the maneuvers left little doubt that frightening Nicaragua was another, if not the major, purpose.

Most closely tied to diplomatic goals were naval maneuvers in 1983 off Nicaragua and a series of mock land

. . . While Long-Term Policy Was Murky

battles in Honduras, some within a few miles of the Nicaraguan border. Two war games in Honduras in early April 1985 — Universal Trek '85 and Big Pine III — involved nearly 10,000 U.S. combat-ready troops. House Majority Leader Jim Wright, D-Texas, wrote Reagan to express concern that the Big Pine III exercise could provoke a U.S.-Nicaragua military conflict.

The administration built or expanded more than a dozen military facilities in Honduras, two of which the contras used as bases. The United States also stationed about 1,300 military personnel in Honduras regularly since 1983, about 100 of whom manned intelligence-gathering flights over El Salvador and Nicaragua.

The administration also boosted the armed forces of all of Nicaragua's neighbors, citing two purposes: helping them fight their own leftist insurgencies and bolstering them against an unspecified threat from Nicaragua.

Diplomatic Efforts

The United States endorsed regional peacemaking; beginning in 1983, diplomacy focused on talks directed by Colombia, Mexico, Panama and Venezuela, the "Contadora" countries. The administration repeatedly endorsed these efforts, but critics on Capitol Hill and in some of the Contadora countries said that support was lukewarm.

The Contadora countries and the five Central American nations (Costa Rica, El Salvador, Guatemala, Honduras and Nicaragua) on Sept. 9, 1983, agreed to a "Document of Objectives," calling on each country to take military, political and economic steps to reduce tension. A year later, on Sept. 7, 1984, the Contadora countries produced a draft agreement to implement the 21 objectives. But the United States objected to several major provisions, arguing that they would have given Nicaragua a built-in military advantage over its neighbors by allowing it to retain most of its Cuban advisers and by forcing an end to U.S. military exercises in the region.

Representatives of Costa Rica, El Salvador and Honduras on Oct. 20 wrote a counter-draft that satisfied the U.S. objections but Guatemala and Nicaragua opposed it.

The talks were resumed in the spring of 1985, but collapsed again in June, when disagreements prompted the Nicaraguans to walk out. U.S. and Honduran officials were trying in January 1986 to revive the Contadora process.

The United States conducted direct talks with the Sandinistas in mid-1985, when Shultz made a surprise visit to Managua after attending the inauguration of Salvadoran President José Napoleón Duarte. Harry W. Shlaudeman, Reagan's special envoy for Central America, held talks with a Nicaraguan Foreign Ministry official.

But the United States suspended the talks on Jan. 17, 1985, saying that Nicaragua was not serious about making progress. Nicaragua denied that charge and said it was willing to resume the talks any time.

Reagan pegged his April 4 peace plan to yet another diplomatic effort: a declaration in San José, Costa Rica, on March 2 by several prominent Nicaraguan exile leaders calling for a "national dialogue" to be mediated by the Roman Catholic Church. But several other key Nicaraguan exiles refused to sign it, and the Sandinistas rejected it.

Cuban-Soviet Connection

The heart of the administration's case was that Nicaragua was a communist outpost promoting leftist subversion in Central America. The Sandinistas, Reagan said, had become "Cuba's Cubans."

Administration officials claimed that the Sandinistas took power with the intention of turning Nicaragua into a Marxist-Leninist state.

The revolution that overthrew Somoza had broad support, within Nicaragua and from other countries, largely because the Sandinistas were joined by businessmen and moderate political leaders. But within months, the Sandinistas consolidated their power and the two non-Sandinistas resigned from the governing junta.

Many U.S. conservatives said that the Sandinistas used the moderates to win Carter administration economic aid, including a total of $116 million in 1979 and 1980.

Reagan stepped up rhetoric against the Sandinistas. On March 25, 1985, for example, he read a bill of particulars against the Managua regime: "It has moved to crush personal freedoms, attack the church, nearly wipe out an entire culture — the Miskito Indians — summarily execute suspected dissidents, drive leading democrats into exile, and force young boys to defend the revolution while Soviet-bloc advisers sit in Managua living off the people."

Some members of Congress, reporters, human rights groups and other observers backed many of Reagan's specific complaints, while rejecting as exaggerated his broader allegations that the Sandinistas had created a Marxist-Leninist totalitarian state.

The other half of Reagan's brief against the Sandinistas was that they were threatening their neighbors.

The administration insisted that the Sandinistas supported leftist insurgencies from the beginning of their days in power. The Sandinistas trained Salvadoran rebels starting in 1979 and provided the bulk of their weapons, the administration said.

Nicaragua also built the region's largest military force and it relied heavily on Cuban advisers, Reagan said. The Sandinistas had "over 100,000" trained armed forces, he claimed, compared with 10,000 in 1979. Reagan said that some 10,000 Cuban advisers were in Nicaragua, implying that all were engaged in the arms buildup. Most were teachers and doctors, the Sandinistas said.

Critics faulted the administration for a lack of substantial evidence to bolster some charges. The administration released photographs of Nicaraguan and guerrilla installations and claimed that huge amounts of weaponry were flowing from Nicaragua to El Salvador — but it produced only a few captured weapons. The administration did not acknowledge that Salvadoran rebels captured or bought weapons from the army they were battling.

As evidence of Nicaragua's hostile intentions, Reagan cited the Sandinistas' possession of some 110 Soviet-made T-55 tanks, of early 1960s vintage. But in a March 22, 1985, report, the administration acknowledged that a Nicaraguan attack on Honduras "could prove difficult."

The Sandinistas said their military buildup was needed to help ward off a potential U.S. invasion.

was time to try another course. Republicans said only the use of military muscle would force the Sandinistas to ease repression and stop supporting leftist insurgencies elsewhere.

"We would not be here today debating this resolution if military pressure on the Sandinistas had worked," Boland said.

The House took four votes on the issue. First, by a 180-248 vote April 23, it rejected Reagan's request (H J Res 239) for $14 million in direct aid to the contras. That vote effectively killed the request because approval by both houses of Congress was needed. *(Vote 58, p. 22-H)*

On April 24, the House voted three times on a separate resolution (H J Res 247) on the Nicaragua issue.

By a 219-206 vote, the House tentatively adopted the Barnes-Hamilton proposal, with 15 Republicans joining 204 Democrats in support. *(Vote 60, p. 22-H)*

Then came the key vote on the Michel alternative; if adopted, it would have overturned the earlier action on the Barnes-Hamilton plan and given Reagan a watered-down victory.

Just before the vote, Michel made a dramatic plea. Staring straight at the Democrats and throwing his arms wide open, he said: "I would say for this occasion, damn the politics, let's do what is right for the country."

As with most high-stakes votes in the House, the tally was close throughout the allotted 15 minutes. When the time expired, the vote was tied 205-205, and O'Neill, who rarely voted, plucked a "no" card from a table in the well of the House in case it was needed. But the vote was held open for nearly a minute longer while 16 more members cast their ballots, half on each side. Finally, two Democratic loyalists, Edward R. Roybal, D-Calif., and Henry B. Gonzalez, D-Texas, arrived to cast the deciding votes. The final tally was 213-215. *(Vote 61, p. 22-H)*

O'Neill took the chair and rushed the House into a final vote on the underlying bill. After a few minutes, it was clear the bill would go down to defeat, and a stampede against it ensued. The final vote was 123-303, with a majority in both parties voting no. *(Vote 62, p. 24-H)*

House leaders offered several explanations for the final vote — nearly all with partisan overtones.

Majority leader Jim Wright (D-Texas) said the overwhelming opposition among Republicans was a result of earlier partisan skirmishes. "They are in a fit of pique," he said.

Bill Alexander, D-Ark., a deputy majority whip, said some Democrats voted against the bill because they opposed any aid to the contras and feared that sending a bill to the Senate would run the risk of a House-Senate agreement "which gives license to continued military aid."

And Lott said Democrats opposed the president at every turn because they were "more interested in scoring points" than in passing legislation.

Round Two: 'Humanitarian' Aid

Within weeks of the votes to reject contra aid, many critics of the program were having doubts, second thoughts that ultimately led to the congressional turnaround in favor of $27 million in nonlethal assistance for the contras.

A major reason for the change in Capitol Hill climate was Nicaraguan President Ortega's aid-seeking trip to Moscow, less than a week after the congressional votes against the contra aid.

Several moderate and conservative House Democrats, many of whom voted against the $14 million in contra aid in April, soon began trying to revive proposals for humanitarian aid to the rebels.

And Reagan, acting on advice from many in Congress, on May 1 imposed a trade embargo and other economic sanctions on Nicaragua. *(Box, p. 68)*

"We should not be tying our own hands while Daniel Ortega is shaking those in the Kremlin," said Rep. Dave McCurdy, D-Okla. He was the chief sponsor of a resolution (H J Res 283) introduced May 8 that sought to provide $14 million in non-military aid to the contras.

McCurdy proposed funneling U.S. aid through the Agency for International Development (AID). Funds would be used only for food, clothing, medicine and similar purposes.

The resolution left intact the Boland amendment, which barred the use of U.S. funds for military purposes in Nicaragua.

The resolution also called on the Organization of American States to impose a trade boycott and embargo against Nicaragua, along with a request that other nations also suspend trading with that country.

Speaker O'Neill, reiterating his opposition to direct aid to the contras, acknowledged on May 6 that Ortega's mission had put pressure on some Democrats to reverse themselves and support some kind of aid to the contras.

House Minority Leader Michel and other GOP legislators drafted their own Nicaraguan proposal to provide $14 million in humanitarian aid to the contras in 1985 and an additional $28 million in 1986. The $28 million matched the administration's fiscal 1986 request for aid to the contras. The aid was not to be provided through the CIA.

Meanwhile, several Nicaragua-related proposals were prepared in the Senate:

- By Nunn, Lugar and other leaders, providing $32 million in non-military aid to the contras in fiscal 1985-86.
- By Dodd, providing $14 million to resettle outside of Nicaragua the roughly 15,000 contras, plus $10 million to help implement a potential regional peace treaty. This plan would have retained in law a bar on arms aid to the contras. Dodd's proposal, introduced as S 1161, also declared that Congress would approve the use of military force if needed to counter the establishment of a foreign military base or the introduction of advanced offensive weapons into any "communist country" in Central America.
- By Edward M. Kennedy, D-Mass., barring the introduction of U.S. combat troops into Central America without explicit authorization by Congress.

Senators wanted to consider Nicaragua-related amendments during action on the 1986 defense authorization bill (S 1160). But on May 22, Tom Harkin, D-Iowa, a staunch opponent of contra aid, threatened a filibuster. Senate leaders, anxious to finish work on the defense bill, delayed the Nicaragua debate.

SENATE ACTION

The Nicaragua issue returned to the Senate floor June 6-7, as amendments to a routine bill (S 1003) making authorizations for the State Department and related agencies. The Senate, which consistently supported the contra aid, reaffirmed that position by approving $38 million for food, clothing and other non-military aid in fiscal years 1985-86. *(State Department authorization, p. 104)*

While Nicaraguan President Ortega's ill-timed trip to Moscow made many in Congress reconsider the House's rejection of the contra aid in April, the administration revved up its rhetorical engines. Reagan on June 5 called Ortega "the little dictator" and demanded that Congress back his policy.

The Republican-controlled Senate was the first to respond, approving the $38 million in non-military aid by a 55-42 vote on June 6. *(Vote 112, p. 23-S)*

That vote was similar to the Senate's 53-46 pro-contra-aid vote on April 23.

The aid proposal approved by the Senate was offered by Nunn, ranking Democrat on the Armed Services Committee, and by Lugar, chairman of the Foreign Relations Committee.

It provided $14 million in fiscal 1985 and $24 million in 1986 for "food, clothing, medicine or other humanitarian assistance" for the contras. The aid was to be monitored by the National Security Council, and sponsors said they expected the CIA would administer the aid.

The Senate plan also repealed a bar on military or paramilitary aid and specifically authorized the CIA to provide intelligence information to the contras.

The Senate also rejected several Democratic-sponsored proposals to restrict the nature of the contra aid and to limit Reagan's freedom to send U.S. troops to Central America. The wide margins against those proposals were similar to ones by which the Senate had rejected Democratic challenges to Reagan's policies during the past year.

As the Senate neared completion of its action on Nicaragua on June 7, it got entangled in a dispute over an amendment by John Kerry, D-Mass. Kerry proposed to prohibit U.S. funding of activities in Nicaragua that would violate international law or U.S. obligations to the United Nations or Organization of American States.

Lugar offered to accept the amendment on behalf of the GOP leadership, even though the administration opposed it as a slap at Reagan policies. But Kerry demanded a roll-call vote — angering Majority Leader Dole, who was trying to speed action on the bill.

Nevertheless, the Senate backed the amendment 47-42, with most Republicans voting "no." Dole then forced through, 48-42, a move to reconsider the approval of the amendment. Armed with that vote, Dole persuaded Kerry to compromise. After a lengthy delay, Kerry proposed and the Senate accepted an amendment that weakened his ban by allowing activities authorized under U.S. law, even if they violated international law.

Amendments Rejected

The Senate defeated several Democratic-sponsored amendments that sought to narrow the use of the contra aid or to restrict Reagan's policy options in Central America. They were:

- By Kennedy, D-Mass., urging the United States to resume bilateral negotiations with Nicaragua. Reagan suspended such talks in January, claiming that Nicaragua was refusing serious discussions. The amendment was rejected on a 48-48 tie, surprising even some administration supporters who thought it would pass. *(Vote 108, p. 23-S)*
- By Kennedy, barring the president from introducing U.S. combat troops into Nicaragua without explicit approval of Congress or under certain other conditions. Rejected 31-64. *(Vote 109, p. 23-S)*
- By Gary Hart, D-Colo., barring the president from introducing U.S. combat troops anywhere in Central America without congressional approval, except to rescue U.S. citizens or to meet a direct attack on the United States. Rejected 15-81. *(Vote 110, p. 23-S)*
- By Dodd, authorizing $10 million to implement a regional peace agreement in Central America and $14 million to help the contras withdraw from Nicaragua. His amendment also retained the Boland amendment prohibition on military aid to the contras. Rejected 17-79. *(Vote 107, p. 23-S)*
- By Harkin, to bar the administration from using the CIA or the Defense Department to administer aid to the contras. Rejected 35-57. *(Vote 113, p. 24-S)*
- By Harkin, to reimpose the Boland amendment prohibiting military or paramilitary aid to the contras, but giving the president the right to seek congressional approval of such aid. Rejected 30-62. *(Vote 114, p. 24-S)*
- By Alan J. Dixon, D-Ill., stating the sense of Congress that the president should lift the economic sanctions he imposed against Nicaragua in May. Rejected 22-68. *(Vote 117, p. 24-S)*
- By Joseph R. Biden Jr., D-Del., authorizing $14 million in non-lethal assistance to the contras in fiscal 1985, provided the aid was independently monitored and peace talks resumed. The amendment also would have ended the trade embargo Reagan imposed on Nicaragua May 1. Rejected 22-75. *(Vote 111, p. 23-S)*

Under pressure from the Senate leadership, Pete Wilson, R-Calif., withdrew an amendment that called on the president to provide direct military and non-military aid to the contras. It would have authorized $14 million for non-military aid in fiscal 1985 and $24 million in unrestricted aid in 1986.

Humanitarian vs. Military

Although the money voted by the Senate was called "humanitarian aid" and was defined to include food, clothing and other non-military items, there was little doubt among most senators that the actual effect of the funding was to resume U.S. support for a paramilitary operation.

Democrats insisted that the contras simply would use the money they would get from the U.S. government to replace private funding they had been getting in the past. The private money, along with aid given covertly by other countries, could then be diverted to buying weapons.

"This assistance is nothing more than logistical support for the contras" and calling it humanitarian aid "is totally misleading," said Kennedy. "This is more money for more war."

Nunn himself gave a broad definition of what could be included in humanitarian aid: military uniforms, combat boots and even a radar, if it were used for "defensive purposes."

The administration would have to decide exactly what to include under humanitarian aid, and would have to justify its decision to the congressional Intelligence committees "behind closed doors," Nunn told reporters after the Senate vote. "I don't think we can set the definition in concrete."

But he added that if the administration used the money to supply military equipment, "the consensus will fall apart" on Capitol Hill.

Sending Troops?

Much of the Senate debate centered on the question of whether resumed support for the contras would increase the prospect of U.S. military intervention in Nicaragua.

Dodd argued that Reagan was bent on pursuing a "military solution" for removing Nicaragua's Sandinista government and that aiding the contras would lead inevitably to a commitment of U.S. troops.

The administration was insisting that the Sandinistas change, but they were Marxists who would change only if they were overthrown, Dodd said. And since the contras could not overthrow the regime, U.S. intervention "is the only option," he said. "We are getting closer and closer to it."

But Lugar and Nunn argued that supporting the contras would reduce, rather than increase, the chance that the United States would be forced to send troops into Nicaragua.

"The best way to make it more likely is to do nothing," Nunn said, insisting that without U.S. backing of the contras the Sandinistas would consolidate their power and would feel free to attack their neighbors.

On June 13, the Senate Appropriations Committee attached the Nicaragua provisions to its version of a fiscal 1985 supplemental appropriations bill (HR 2577). The aid was adopted by the panel, 11-8, as an amendment sponsored by Ted Stevens, R-Alaska.

HOUSE FLOOR ACTION

The House's stunning turnaround on contra aid came June 12, when members voted to attach $27 million in nonmilitary contra aid to HR 2577, the supplemental appropriations bill. *(Supplemental, p. 350)*

Reagan's victory came after he yielded to congressional insistence that the aid be spent for food, clothing and other "humanitarian" purposes, not for military items. Hill leaders also warned him not to put the operation under the control of the CIA.

On a broader level, Reagan also gave assurances that he was not seeking to overthrow the Nicaraguan government. In a letter to Rep. McCurdy, the president said: "We do not seek the military overthrow of the Sandinista government" in Managua.

Nevertheless, many of the president's supporters in Congress said they were voting for the aid to help remove a communist government that could threaten all of Central America.

"Where and when do you finally draw the line on our southern border?" Michel, the House minority leader, asked the Democrats in an emotional, arm-waving speech. "You tell us we should talk. Well, the communists never listen to talk unless it's backed up by force."

Faced with a big loss to Reagan, House Democratic leaders resorted to warning their colleagues about the long-term consequences of their action. The most likely result, they said, would be the eventual commitment of U.S. troops to complete the war that the contras could not win by themselves. Intelligence Committee Chairman Hamilton told the House: "Funding the contras is not an alternative to intervention, it is an avenue to intervention."

Hours before the vote, Speaker O'Neill derided the president for seeking a "complete victory" against Nicaragua. "He can see himself leading a contingent down Broadway, with a big smile on his face, kind of like a grade-B motion picture actor, coming home the conquering hero," O'Neill said.

House Votes

The House voted directly on the contra issue four times on June 12 and supported the president by comfortable margins each time.

The first, closest and most important vote came on the issue of whether to extend indefinitely a legal ban on any U.S. aid for "military or paramilitary operations in Nicaragua." That prohibition, which the House had supported consistently since 1983, had been U.S. law since October, 1984, and was to expire on Oct. 1, 1985; it was called the "Boland amendment," after Edward P. Boland, D-Mass., former chairman of the Intelligence Committee.

Boland on June 12 offered his provision as an amendment to an underlying amendment by Michel that provided the aid for the contras. The House rejected Boland's amendment 196-232, with 58 Democrats joining all but seven Republicans in opposition to it. *(Vote 140, p. 46-H)*

Republicans charged that Boland was a "killer" amendment because it would have barred the United States from helping the contras in any fashion, even by providing non-military aid or intelligence information. But some Democrats said that interpretation was too broad. The amendment might permit giving "defensive intelligence" data to the contras and might be construed as allowing non-military aid provided by agencies other than U.S. intelligence services, they said.

Without the Boland amendment, the CIA would be free to use its contingency reserve fund to aid the contras. Congress could block such an action only by passing a law over Reagan's likely veto.

About an hour after rejecting the Boland amendment, the House turned back the Democrats' second attempt to thwart aid to the contras. By a 172-259 vote, it rejected an amendment by Richard A. Gephardt, D-Mo., that would have postponed implementation of the aid for six months — with the money available then only if Reagan made a new request and both houses approved. *(Vote 141, p. 46-H)*

Gephardt said his amendment would give the president time to pursue negotiations with Nicaragua, directly through bilateral meetings and indirectly through the Contadora negotiations.

But Republicans decried the amendment as a rebuff to the contras when they needed U.S. backing. "It says, 'Hang in there, boys, for six more months,' " said Henry J. Hyde, R-Ill.

By a 248-184 vote, the House then approved the basic Michel amendment, offered by Joseph M. McDade, R-Pa., providing the $27 million in aid to the contras. *(Vote 142, p. 46-H)*

And after two more hours of debate, the House rejected a broad alternative offered by the Democratic leadership, 174-254. *(Vote 143, p. 48-H)*

Sponsored by Hamilton, the Democrats' plan would have provided $14 million in aid, through international agencies such as the Red Cross, to Nicaraguan refugees outside of their country. It also would have authorized an unspecified amount of economic aid to help implement a regional peace treaty, and would have extended indefinitely the Boland ban on aid to Nicaraguan military operations.

Finally, by a 271-156 vote, the House passed the supplemental. The no votes came from liberals who could not accept the contra aid and from conservatives who opposed other spending items. *(Vote 144, p. 48-H)*

The Turnaround

Leaders of both parties had a multitude of explanations for the turnabout on the issue. Among the most important appeared to be:

- Reaction to Ortega's trip to Moscow immediately after

the House on April 24 rejected Reagan's earlier contra aid request. Wright said Ortega's "maladroit behavior" embarrassed some Democrats because it seemed to confirm Reagan's contention that the Sandinistas were Soviet pawns.

- The House's April 24 action gave the impression that Congress, and Democrats in particular, were opposed to doing anything about the situation in Nicaragua. That impression was inaccurate, the Democrats said, because Republicans provided the bulk of the votes to defeat the bill (H J Res 247) containing the Nicaragua provisions.
- Many Democrats had been cowed by sustained attacks in which Reagan and his supporters had accused them of lacking the will to resist communism. As if on cue, Dan Burton, R-Ind., opposed a Democratic amendment by saying: "My friends, don't be soft on communism."

Reagan portrayed the decision on contra aid as a stark choice between freedom and communism, putting members who opposed his policies in the position of appearing to choose communism. Boland said he had never seen "such frenetic rhetoric" from a president.

- It was difficult for members to oppose something labeled "humanitarian" aid for the contras, even though everyone understood that the money would be used to keep a military force fighting in the field.

Hamilton said the term humanitarian aid "rings less harshly in the ear" than military aid. But he said Reagan could use the humanitarian aid just as he would have used military aid: to double the number of contras to 35,000 and to "destabilize the Nicaraguan government."

- The administration targeted those members most vulnerable to Reagan's persuasion on the issue: moderate Republicans who might be worried about opposing him too frequently, and conservative, southern Democrats whose constituents were worried that a communist victory in Central America could lead to a tidal wave of refugees. Michel said the latter concern was especially potent because "the streets are filling up" with refugees in the South.

The lobbying efforts, including telephone calls from the president and a mass meeting at the White House the day before the vote, paid off. Only seven Republicans deserted Reagan on the Boland amendment vote, half as many as had opposed him on a key vote April 24.

Particularly damaging to the Democratic cause were defections by several members who in the past had opposed aiding the contras. Key among them were McCurdy, a member of the Armed Services and Intelligence committees, and Richardson, long a harsh critic of Reagan's policies in Central America.

- The Michel amendment was designed to have the broadest possible appeal. In addition to providing nonmilitary aid, it excluded CIA or Defense Department involvement and appeared to rule out the resumption of military aid. Boland called the Michel plan "a well-crafted amendment for catching votes."

HOUSE, SENATE PROVISIONS

The Senate's State Department authorizations bill and the House's supplemental appropriations bill contained contra provisions that differed in several respects.

Amounts, Timing. The House included $27 million for "humanitarian" aid to the contras, available until March 31, 1986. The money was to be divided into thirds: $9 million to be available upon enactment of the supplemental; $9 million to be available 90 days later, when the president submitted a report to Congress; and the final third in another 90 days, when the president submitted a second report to Congress.

The Senate bill included a total of $38 million: $14 million for the remainder of fiscal 1985 and $24 million for fiscal 1986. There was no timetable for release of the money; however, Senate sponsors said any part of the $14 million unspent by the end of fiscal 1985 would have to be returned to the Treasury.

The House bill also included $2 million to help implement a regional peace agreement in Central America, while the Senate measure contained no such funds.

Reports. Both bills required the president to report to Congress every 90 days on the use of the aid and the progress made toward peace in Central America.

Definitions. Both bills defined humanitarian aid as "food, clothing, medicine, and other humanitarian assistance." The Senate bill added "transportation associated with the delivery of such assistance."

In slightly different language, the two measures excluded arms, weapon systems, ammunition or other equipment or material that could inflict serious bodily harm or death. The House also excluded vehicles.

Although the definitions appeared to be loose enough to permit military-related items such as radars, sponsors in both chambers of Congress warned the administration not to stray too far from congressional intent.

CIA Role. The major difference between the House and Senate versions appeared at first glance to be bureaucratic: The Senate plan would have allowed the National Security Council — an arm of the White House — to designate what agency would administer the aid, while the House bill was to allow the president to use any agency except the CIA or the Defense Department.

Boland Amendment. A major difference was treatment of the Boland amendment, which from October 1984-October 1985 barred U.S. aid for military operations in Nicaragua.

The House amendment exempted the $27 million in humanitarian aid from the Boland restrictions but did not change the amendment itself.

The Senate bill sought to repeal the Boland amendment as of the date of enactment. However, that bill also stated that "no other material assistance" — other than the $38 million in humanitarian aid — could be given to the contras by any U.S. agency unless the president requested such aid and Congress approved.

Sharing Intelligence. Both bills allowed the United States to exchange intelligence information with the contras. The Senate bill also specifically permitted U.S. collection of intelligence information in Nicaragua.

Policy Provisions. Using almost identical language, the two bills urged the president to take several steps. Among them: using "diplomatic and economic measures" to resolve the Nicaraguan conflict, including negotiations to implement a regional agreement under the auspices of the Contadora and working with other countries to develop measures to complement the economic sanctions Reagan imposed on Nicaragua on May 1; suspending those sanctions and halting U.S. military exercises in Honduras if Nicaragua agreed to a cease-fire, opened a dialogue with all elements of its opposition and suspended the state of emergency; calling upon the contras to remove from their ranks individuals "who have engaged in human rights abuses"; and resuming direct U.S. talks with Nicaragua to encourage a church-mediated internal dialogue and a regional Contadora settlement.

Congress Sought to Place Limits Early . . .

Almost from the beginning of U.S. aid to anti-government guerrillas in Nicaragua, Congress sought to set limits on both the tactics and goals of that aid.

Administration officials first told the House and Senate Intelligence committees in December 1981 about President Reagan's secret decision to channel money and arms through the CIA to Nicaraguan exiles.

Members of both committees said they expressed concern at the time about the covert program. In a letter to CIA Director William J. Casey from Chairman Edward P. Boland, D-Mass., the House committee said it was worried about such things as the number of guerrillas to be supported and whether the United States would have any control over their actions.

Casey early in 1982 assured the committees that the CIA would support no more than a few thousand guerrillas and would monitor their actions closely. However, the number of the Honduran-based guerrillas, formally called the Nicaraguan Democratic Force and informally called "contras" or counterrevolutionaries, expanded rapidly to more than 10,000 by 1983.

1982: Boland's Curbs

In April 1982, the House committee secretly rejected a move by some Democratic members to kill the covert aid. Instead, the committee voted to impose two restrictions. One required that the aid be used solely to interdict arms shipments from Nicaragua to leftist guerrillas in El Salvador. The second stipulated that it was not to be used to overthrow the Nicaraguan government or to provoke a military exchange between Nicaragua and Honduras, where most of the Nicaraguan guerrillas were based.

Language establishing those two restrictions was included in the classified portion of the fiscal 1983 authorization bill (PL 97-269) for the CIA and other intelligence agencies that was cleared by Congress in September 1982. *(1982 Almanac p. 134)*

On Dec. 8, several Democrats attempted to amend the fiscal 1983 defense appropriations bill to bar U.S. aid to the Nicaraguan contras. Boland headed off that move by offering the language that had been incorporated into the intelligence authorization bill. The House approved the so-called "Boland amendment" 411-0, and the full Congress eventually included it in the defense portion of the fiscal 1983 continuing appropriations resolution (PL 97-377). *(1982 Almanac p. 286)*

The Boland amendment said: "None of the funds provided in this act may be used by the Central Intelligence Agency or the Department of Defense to furnish military equipment, military training or advice, or other support for military activities, to any group or individual, not part of a country's armed forces, for the purpose of overthrowing the government of Nicaragua or provoking a military exchange between Nicaragua and Honduras."

The Boland amendment expired on Sept. 30, the end of fiscal 1983.

During fiscal years 1982 and 1983, the CIA provided $45 million-$55 million to the contras, according to intelligence sources.

1983: The Boland Cap

Early in 1983, publicity about the supposedly covert operation mushroomed, with the media carrying detailed reports on the war in Nicaragua. The contras and some officials in the Reagan administration sought the publicity, which, ironically, helped undermine public and congressional support for the war. *(1983 Almanac p. 123)*

Boland declared in April that the publicity showed that the amendment carrying his name was being violated because the Reagan administration appeared to be seeking to overthrow the government of Nicaragua. He later told the House that "one with any sense, any legal sense, would have to come to the conclusion that the operation is illegal, that the purpose and mission of the operation was to overthrow the government in Nicaragua."

On May 3, 1983, the House Intelligence Committee approved a bill (HR 2760) that barred further U.S. aid to the contras, after a secret date. It also substituted for the covert aid an open $80 million program to help friendly Central American countries interdict cross-border arms shipments to guerrilla movements. The House Foreign Affairs Committee endorsed the latter provision June 7.

After heated partisan debate, the House approved HR 2760 on July 28, by a 228-195 vote. The Senate Intelligence Committee refused to consider HR 2760, and that bill died. *(Vote 270, 1983 Almanac p. 82-H)*

The House ratified its July vote on Oct. 20, when it voted 227-194 to include a similar Nicaraguan provision in the fiscal 1984 intelligence authorization bill (HR 2968). But the Senate took a contrary position Nov. 3 by passing by voice vote a version of the intelligence authorization that approved at least $28 million for the contras. *(Vote 377, 1983 Almanac p. 112-H)*

Before final action on the intelligence authorization was completed, the contra issue was decided by House-Senate conferees on the fiscal 1984 defense appropriations bill (PL 98-212). At Boland's insistence, the conferees set a $24 million cap on funding for the contras in fiscal 1984.

The language said: "During fiscal year 1984, not more

Later Aid Request. Both bills made provision for expedited congressional consideration of a later request by the president for Central America funds.

The House provided for such a request if the president reported to Congress that a regional peace accord had been reached or was near, or if "other trade and economic measures will assist in a resolution of the conflict" in the region. Adopting a more pessimistic approach, the Senate bill provided for a presidential request if regional peace talks failed or if economic or trade measures "failed to resolve the conflict in Central America."

CONFERENCE ACTION

The two chambers' contra aid differences contributed to a delay in appointment of House-Senate conferees on the supplemental appropriations bill. The question of who would handle the funding was the most serious sticking

. . . On U.S. Covert Assistance to 'Contras'

than $24 million of the funds available to the Central Intelligence Agency, the Department of Defense or any other agency or entity of the United States involved in intelligence activities may be obligated or expended for the purpose, or which would have the effect, of supporting, directly or indirectly, military or paramilitary operations in Nicaragua by any nation, group, organization, movement or individual." *(1983 Almanac p. 123)*

There were reports in 1984 that the CIA had used accounting devices to exceed the $24 million limit. The Senate Intelligence Committee said its investigation found no evidence to support the charge, but the House committee said it found "several possible departures from the CIA's own guidelines" for complying with the limit.

1984: The Boland Cutoff

In March 1984, Reagan asked Congress to approve $21 million for the contras, in addition to the $24 million limit then in the law.

As Congress was considering that request in early April, Reagan's Nicaraguan policy was shaken by the revelation that the CIA had provided the logistics and supervision for the mining of several Nicaraguan harbors.

The mines had little explosive power, but they damaged several ships and caused a furor in Congress. Barry Goldwater, R-Ariz., chairman of the Senate Intelligence Committee, was particularly infuriated by the CIA's failure to give his committee advance notice of the mining. Both chambers overwhelmingly condemned the mining.

Nevertheless, the Senate approved the $21 million request in a fiscal 1984 supplemental appropriations bill (H J Res 492). To help gain approval of the money, Reagan on April 4 sent the Senate a letter saying that the United States "does not seek to destabilize or overthrow the government of Nicaragua; nor to impose or compel any particular form of government there."

But House leaders refused to include the $21 million request in the supplemental, and on May 24 the House decisively voted against it, 241-177. *(Vote 162, 1984 Almanac p. 54-H)*

The Senate supported the contra aid again on June 18 by a 58-38 vote on a defense authorization bill (S 2723). But on that vote, several key Democrats on the Intelligence Committee publicly dropped their support for the contras. *(Vote 141, 1984 Almanac p. 26-S)*

The dispute held up congressional approval of several items in the 1984 supplemental appropriations bill that were wanted both by Congress and the administration, including money for summer jobs for youths. On June 25 the Senate backed down and deleted the $21 million from the supplemental bill. In the meantime, the $24 million that Congress had voted in 1983 ran out in the spring.

Reagan made no further effort to get the $21 million for fiscal 1984, but he did press Congress to approve $28 million in renewed aid to the contras for fiscal year 1985.

The House rejected Reagan's request on Aug. 2, when it approved, by a 294-118 vote, a 1985 intelligence authorization bill (HR 5399) that barred any further aid to the contras. *(Vote 306, 1984 Almanac p. 94-H)*

As it had the previous year, Congress resolved the issue in an omnibus continuing resolution (PL 98-473) that included funding for the Defense Department and the CIA. The House had rejected Reagan's $28 million request when it passed its version of the funding bill. The Senate had approved the request by turning aside, 42-57, an effort by Democrats to provide only $6 million to end the contras' war. *(Vote 252, 1984 Almanac p. 44-S)*

Under enormous administration pressure, conferees on the continuing resolution Oct. 10 adopted a complicated provision that rejected Reagan's request but gave him the opportunity to return to Congress in 1985. Its major elements:

- Barred any U.S. agency from spending money "for the purpose of or which would have the effect of supporting, directly or indirectly, military or paramilitary operations in Nicaragua by any nation, group, organization or individual."
- Stated that the ban would cease to apply if, after Feb. 28, 1985, the president submitted a report to Congress asking for aid for military or paramilitary operations in Nicaragua, and Congress approved it by passing a joint resolution. The president's report was to state that the Nicaraguan government was supporting guerrillas in El Salvador or other Central American countries and analyze the military significance of that support; justify the amount and type of aid sought for operations in Nicaragua; and explain the goals of U.S. policy for Central America and how the aid would further those goals.
- Expedited procedures for consideration of the joint resolution approving the president's request. In each house the resolution was to be referred to the Appropriations Committee, which could report it no sooner than eight days after receiving it but no later than 15 days. Debate was limited to 10 hours in each chamber, and motions to delay or amend the resolution were barred.
- Set a $14 million limit in fiscal 1985 on funds for military or paramilitary operations in Nicaragua, if approved by joint resolution.

point, with the House strongly opposed to a CIA role.

Agreement on HR 2577 eventually was reached after several hours of sporadic negotiations July 26, and Congress cleared the measure Aug. 1.

Senate conferees accepted both the House amount — $27 million — for the contras and its method of distributing the funds.

Sen. Stevens, chairman of the Appropriations Subcommittee on Defense, argued that certain regulations, from which the CIA and Defense Department were exempt, would prevent aid from being distributed promptly to the contras by other agencies. He cited, for example, restrictions on the employment of foreign nationals and regulations requiring competitive bidding.

Stevens proposed allowing the president to exempt other government agencies, such as the State Department, from those regulations for purposes of distributing aid.

But House leaders said such a proposal was too vague.

"The CIA wants to get their fingers in this any way it can," said Joseph P. Addabbo, D-N.Y., chairman of the House Appropriations Subcommittee on Defense.

Stevens said the Senate backed down because the president could already have the authority to make the exemptions and because fighting the issue out on the House and Senate floors, a tactic that House conferees suggested, would have left the measure open to a variety of controversial amendments.

"I think the president won on the vote in the House, and there's no reason to endanger that victory," Stevens said.

The conference agreement (H Rept 99-236) exempted the $27 million from the Boland amendment bar against aiding military operations in Nicaragua, but did not repeal the amendment, as the Senate had wanted.

Conferees also accepted House conditions on timing of the aid, and defined it as "food, clothing, medicine and other humanitarian assistance," not to include "weapons, weapons systems, ammunition or other equipment, vehicles or material which can be used to inflict serious bodily harm or death."

The conference report also included $2 million in the House bill to help implement a Contadora regional peace treaty.

Foreign Aid Bill

Authorization of the $27 million in non-lethal aid for the contras was contained in the fiscal 1986-87 foreign assistance authorization act (S 960 — PL 99-83), which cleared Congress July 31. *(Foreign aid authorization, p. 41)*

Earlier action on the legislation, however, produced ironies. The Senate, usually more supportive of contra aid, did not include money for the rebels as part of leadership efforts to keep controversial issues off the bill. And the Democratic-controlled House, in spite of its past disputes over the program, followed up its June pro-contra vote by adding the provisions to the foreign aid bill.

House, Senate Committee Action

Marking up the House version of the foreign aid bill, the Foreign Affairs Subcommittee on Western Hemisphere Affairs on March 19 agreed to bar any foreign aid funds from being used to support the contras. Subcommittee Chairman Barnes drafted the provision in response to press reports that El Salvador, Honduras and possibly other countries had used some of their U.S. aid to back the contras.

Another provision in the bill prohibited the president from sending U.S. troops into combat in Nicaragua or El Salvador unless Congress had declared war or otherwise given its approval. The House had approved an identical provision in May 1984; it later was watered down in a House-Senate conference committee.

The Senate Foreign Relations Committee also adopted an amendment restricting U.S. support for the rebels when it drafted companion foreign aid legislation on March 27. The 9-8 vote for the amendment represented the panel's only direct contradiction of the president on a major issue.

But the next day, Chairman Lugar and ranking Democrat, Claiborne Pell, R.I., immediately disputed what the committee had done.

Pell, sponsor of the Nicaragua provision, insisted that the committee had voted to bar the administration from using any foreign aid to support the contras and from conspiring with foreign aid recipients to channel money to the guerrillas.

Lugar insisted he never saw that amendment, and he noted that a transcript of the meeting showed that the latter part of Pell's amendment was never discussed. Lugar said he understood that the committee was debating and voting on only the first part of the amendment: barring direct or indirect funding of the guerrillas with foreign aid. That provision was also in another amendment, offered by Dodd, that the committee rejected earlier on an 8-8 tie.

After discussing the matter March 28, Lugar and Pell still could not agree on which amendment the committee had passed. They agreed to put Pell's language in the committee-passed bill, with Lugar reserving the right to move to delete it when the bill reached the floor.

Floor Action

Nicaragua did not provoke floor fights when the full Senate and House acted on the foreign aid bill.

When the full Senate took up S 960 May 14-15, Lugar successfully got his colleagues to refrain from offering controversial amendments that would have burdened the bill. One of the casualties was his own planned amendment to repeal the committee-passed ban on contra aid.

And the House on July 10 voted to authorize the $27 million in non-military aid to the contras appropriated in the supplemental.

The House also adopted, by voice vote, a companion amendment by Bill Richardson, D-N.M., that required the president to establish procedures to ensure that aid given to the contras would be used only for the intended purpose and would not be diverted to purchase weapons, ammunition or other military supplies. The amendment also required the president to suspend such aid if he determined that the guerrillas were engaging consistently in human rights violations, and it stated concern about Nicaragua's domestic and foreign policies.

Conference

House-Senate conferees on S 960, meeting July 25-26, authorized the $27 million in non-military contra aid (H Rept 99-237). But even in agreeing to allow Reagan to resume U.S. involvement in Nicaragua, the conferees kept some restrictions on the president. Most important was the bar on CIA or Defense Department involvement in distributing the aid. The bill also strictly defined humanitarian aid to exclude trucks and other items that could be used for military purposes, and it barred the administration from entering into agreements encouraging other countries (such as El Salvador or Honduras) to aid the contras.

Conferees deleted a House-passed provision extending into fiscal 1986 the Boland amendment, which barred U.S. aid to military or paramilitary operations in Nicaragua; that issue was to be resolved in the fiscal 1986 intelligence authorizations bill.

Defense Bill

An effort to bar the introduction of U.S. combat troops into Nicaragua produced debate and amendments to the fiscal 1986 defense authorization bill (S 1160) in the House in late June. The previous month, the threat of a filibuster by Tom Harkin, D-Iowa, had kept the Nicaragua issue off the counterpart Senate bill. *(Defense authorization, p. 138)*

In a series of votes June 27, the House adopted a combat-troops ban, but with larger loopholes than had been included in a similar amendment to the fiscal 1985 defense bill. *(1984 Almanac p. 43)*

As introduced by Majority Whip Foley, the amendment barring the introduction of U.S. combat troops into Nicaragua without express congressional authorization allowed four exceptions. Troops could be sent:

- To meet a clear and present danger of hostile attack on the United States.
- To protect the U.S. Embassy.
- To evacuate U.S. citizens.
- To meet U.S. obligations to its Latin American allies under the Rio Treaty, the basic document of the Organization of American States. The OAS treaty committed member states to treat an attack on one as an attack on all.

The Foley amendment also included a declaration that it would not affect the War Powers Act.

Liberal critics of Reagan's Central America policy had worried before the Foley debate that they were losing ground. They were particularly concerned in light of the House's decision June 12 to reverse itself and give $27 million in non-military aid to the contras.

In addition, Reagan critics feared members would adopt a get-tough stance in the wake of the detention of U.S. airline crew and passengers by terrorists in Beirut and a June 19 guerrilla attack in El Salvador that killed four off-duty U.S. Marines.

Duncan L. Hunter, R-Calif., was one of many Foley opponents who cited those factors. "They're trampling the American flag in Beirut; They're killing American Marines in El Salvador and what do we say to our president? We say, 'We don't trust you,'" Hunter told the House.

Foley did not contest two amendments that added further exemptions to the original list.

One, offered by Hunter and adopted 377-45, waived the troop ban if Nicaragua acquired Soviet-built MiG jet fighters or similarly modern combat planes. *(Vote 183, p. 60-H)*

Another Hunter amendment, adopted by voice vote, added to the circumstances that would waive the ban:

- Acquisition by Nicaragua of nuclear weapons.
- A need "to respond to hijacking, kidnapping, or other acts of terrorism involving citizens of the United States or ... of any ally."

But Foley strongly opposed an amendment by Dan Burton, R-Ind., that would have waived the troop ban if the president found that Nicaragua was supporting "directly or indirectly" any military or terrorist operations in El Salvador, Honduras or Costa Rica. Reagan repeatedly had made such charges.

Foley insisted that his amendment simply would codify the president's denial of any intention to invade Nicaragua. But more fundamentally, Foley's supporters argued that the amendment prevented usurpation of Congress' power to declare war.

"You people don't have the guts, you don't have the nerve to take the responsibility for what the Constitution gave you," charged David E. Bonior, D-Mich.

When the Burton amendment was rejected 186-235, Foley supporters seized on it as a token of victory. The House then adopted the much-amended Foley amendment 312-111. *(Votes 184, 185, p. 60-H)*

Foley later insisted that the modifications had not subverted the intent of his original amendment which was, he said: "to involve Congress in any decision to use American troops against Nicaragua, except in certain stated emergencies."

But Minority Whip Lott claimed that the modifications had "defanged, completely denuded," the Foley measure. Hunter later said that the original amendment "was sending an invitation to Managua that they could get away with certain acts. We changed that invitation to a warning."

The House also rejected an amendment designed to limit the actions of U.S. troops in Honduras near that country's border with Nicaragua. Edward J. Markey, D-Mass., proposed an amendment to bar U.S. troops from within 20 miles of the border. A much less restrictive substitute by Dan Daniel, D-Va., was adopted 320-69. *(Vote 188, p. 60-H)*

But conservatives led by Thomas F. Hartnett, R-S.C., defeated the modified version, 172-217. *(Vote 189, p. 62-H)*

The House adopted two related amendments by voice vote:

- By Bill Richardson, D-N.M., barring the use of the Defense Department or the CIA to supply contra guerrillas, restating the House position on that issue.
- By Robert S. Walker, R-Pa., authorizing the president to take any anti-terrorist action necessary to protect U.S. military personnel and to take counter-terrorist action against persons responsible for the death of U.S. military personnel. Some Reagan critics warned against so open-ended a warrant for military action.

Conference Action. In conference, the Foley provision was transformed into a sense-of-Congress declaration that no combat forces should be sent into Nicaragua, as had been done in the fiscal 1985 defense authorization conference report.

Intelligence Bill

The fiscal 1986 authorizations bill for the CIA and other intelligence agencies (HR 2419 — PL 99-169) addressed two aspects of the Nicaragua controversy: It barred the CIA from using its contingency fund to resume "covert" military aid to the contras, and it broadened previous congressional definitions of "humanitarian aid." *(Intelligence authorization, p. 96)*

House Bill

In approving the House version of the intelligence bill (HR 2419 — H Rept 99-106, Part 1), the House Intelligence Committee on May 14 adopted a provision narrowing its previous opposition to any U.S. involvement with the contras.

It was the first time in three years that the House panel had voted to allow the CIA to provide information and advice to the rebels.

The provision was voted in a closed session by the committee's six Republican members and three Democrats over the opposition of seven other Democrats.

The panel's action was one sign of the shifting attitude among members of Congress in the wake of Nicaraguan President Ortega's trip to Moscow. The amendment had the effect of allowing the administration to give the contras intelligence information and advice. The administration had complained that the existing ban on aid was so broad that it precluded the CIA from giving the rebels any information it had collected, such as details of Nicaraguan government troop movements.

The provision stated: "During fiscal year 1986, no

funds available to the Central Intelligence Agency, the Department of Defense or any other agency or entity of the United States involved in intelligence activities may be obligated or expended, directly or indirectly, for material assistance to the Nicaraguan democratic resistance including arms, ammunition or other equipment or material which could be used to inflict serious bodily harm or death, or which would have the effect of providing arms, ammunition or other weapons of war for military or paramilitary operations in Nicaragua by any group, organization, movement or individual."

That provision was adopted by a 9-7 vote, with Democrats McCurdy, Dan Daniel, Va., and Robert A. Roe, N.J., joining the six Republicans in favor. All of the committee's remaining seven Democrats opposed the provision.

The full committee, in its report, offered only a limited explanation of the provision.

It said the prohibition on U.S. aid "applies only to the provision of funds, goods, equipment, civilian or military supplies, or any materiel, but does not include the provision of intelligence information or advice to the contras."

One committee source acknowledged that the administration could interpret that provision broadly as an authorization for the CIA to resume active participation in the contras' war against the Nicaraguan government. But the source said the committee did not include in its report an explicit definition of what it meant by intelligence information and advice because that would be "micro-managing" the CIA by Congress.

In their minority statement, the Republicans complained that the provision was an "unreasonably rigid encumbrance on the president's ability to conduct foreign policy." But they said it was "more reasonable" than the blanket prohibition that Democrats previously had imposed.

Before adopting its new provision, the committee on May 8 took three votes on the issue:

- By a party-line 6-10 vote, it rejected a GOP-sponsored amendment approving Reagan's request for at least $28 million in direct arms aid to the contras in 1986. In addition to authorizing the $28 million, the amendment would have allowed the CIA to use money from its contingency fund to support the contras — thus giving the administration nearly an open-ended authority to provide the aid.
- By a 7-9 vote, it rejected another Republican-backed amendment providing $28 million for "food, clothing, medical and other humanitarian assistance" to the contras. Daniel was the lone Democrat joining the six Republicans in supporting the amendment. Under the amendment, the money was to be funneled through the State Department's Bureau of Intelligence and Research. The amendment also would have established a procedure for expedited congressional consideration of future requests for contra arms aid.
- By a party-line 6-10 vote, it rejected a GOP-backed amendment eliminating the current ban on military aid to the contras. The amendment would not have specifically authorized funds for the contras, but it would have allowed the CIA to use its contingency fund for that purpose.

Senate Bill

Echoing the position of the full Senate, the Intelligence Committee in June attached non-military contra aid to its measure (S 1271 — S Rept 99-79) authorizing funds in fiscal 1986 for the CIA and other intelligence agencies. However, the committee put the Nicaragua aid provision in the secret part of its bill.

A major goal of the committee's provision was to allow the CIA to collect intelligence in Nicaragua and to share that information with the contras.

Floor Action, Conference

The intelligence bills passed both chambers by voice votes. The House approved HR 2419 on July 18, with little debate. And the Senate approved its version on Sept. 26. Senate Intelligence Committee leaders said the bill had the same provisions on $27 million in humanitarian contra aid that were in the supplemental appropriations (HR 2577 — PL 99-88).

Conferees on the legislation, which cleared Congress in late November, said the CIA could not provide training or advice that would "amount to participation in the planning or execution of military or paramilitary operations" or participation in "logistics activities integral to such operations."

But they expanded congressional definitions of "humanitarian" aid, thus increasing the scope of U.S. involvement in the Nicaraguan war.

The intelligence bill allowed the administration to provide radios, trucks and other gear to help the guerrillas.

Both proponents and opponents of aid to the contras expressed disappointment with the intelligence bill. Dick Cheney (R-Wyo.) complained that the bill "continues to contain counterproductive restrictions" on the aid. And Rep. Ted Weiss, D-N.Y., said the bill, by easing some restrictions, "has taken us closer and closer to direct military involvement" in Nicaragua. ∎

Congress Balks at Salvador Police Aid Proposal

Reviving a controversy more than a decade old, President Reagan tried in vain to win congressional approval in 1985 for police aid and supplemental military assistance for El Salvador and four other Central American countries.

Reagan called the program a "counter-terrorism" effort, in response to the June 19 killing in El Salvador of four U.S. Marines and several others.

But Democrats feared the plan risked getting the United States back into the business of supporting brutal Latin American police forces. And some Republican leaders said the administration could overload the tiny countries of Central America with military aid.

The police aid request produced debate in a Congress that had come to terms with the Reagan administration's determination to give massive military and economic aid to the Salvadoran government, which was fighting leftist guerrillas. While Congress had approved most of the aid, it had threatened to halt it unless Salvadoran security forces stopped killing civilians. After moderate José Napoleón Duarte was elected president in 1984, the issue faded. *(El Salvador aid authorizations, p. 59; appropriations, p. 367; earlier funding, 1984 Almanac pp. 73, 439; 1983 Almanac p. 154)*

In September 1985, Reagan requested $54 million for

the police and supplemental military aid package. It would have been the first such assistance since Congress barred U.S. involvement with foreign police in 1974.

After long debate, the Senate Foreign Relations Committee on Dec. 5 approved a stripped-down version (S 1915 — S Rept 99-213), allowing only $22 million in police aid for the region but under conditions designed to guard against U.S. association with repressive security forces. The measure never reached the floor for procedural reasons and because of opposition by Sen. Tom Harkin, D-Iowa.

The measure (HR 3643) got nowhere in the House. The House and Senate Appropriations committees, which would have initiated legislation actually funding the aid, also delayed taking any action.

Meantime, the administration took steps to provide some of the aid requested for El Salvador. The State Department on Oct. 29 notified Congress that the United States would take money from other foreign aid accounts to provide $9 million worth of training and equipment — including weapons — to help the Salvadoran police combat terrorism.

The issue also was expected to resurface in 1986, as a Reagan-requested item in an omnibus supplemental appropriations bill.

Reagan's Proposal

Reagan formally requested the $54 million for Central America on Sept. 27. He justified the program as a response to the June 19 killing of the four Marines and others in El Salvador by leftist guerrillas.

The $54 million included: $27 million in military aid, $26 million to assist police forces, and a special $1 million fund to protect witnesses in court cases involving terrorism in Central America.

Reagan wanted to give El Salvador the biggest chunk of aid in his proposal: $12 million for police units and $10 million for the military services. The latter figure was in addition to $132.6 million in regular military aid Reagan previously asked for El Salvador in fiscal 1986.

One critic of Reagan's proposal, Sen. Nancy Landon Kassebaum, R-Kan., suggested congressional approval of an experimental aid program limited to El Salvador.

For other countries, the president requested: $5 million for the military and $6 million for the police in Honduras; $6 million for civilian guard forces and $3 million for the police in Costa Rica (which had no uniformed military); $4 million for the military and $2 million for the police in Panama; $2 million for the military and $3 million for the police in Guatemala.

The U.S. and the Police

For many in Congress, especially Democrats leery of Reagan's emphasis on military solutions to Central America's problems, the anti-terrorism program raised the specter of a discredited "public safety" program the United States conducted in Latin America in the 1960s and early 1970s.

Aimed at making Latin police and security forces more professional, that program instead created a widespread impression in the region that the United States was contributing to police torture and brutality in such countries as Brazil. Congress in 1973 and 1974 barred further aid to any foreign police forces, law enforcement agencies or prisons. *(1974 Almanac p. 537)*

In July, responding to the killing of the Marines in San Salvador, the House voted, with little debate, to exempt El Salvador and Honduras from the police aid ban. That marked the first significant change in the ban since 1974. That exemption was enacted into law in the fiscal 1986 foreign aid authorization bill (PL 99-83), along with a similar exception for Costa Rica. *(Story, p. 41)*

Reagan's request sought to take advantage of the new exception, and add Guatemala and Panama to the list of countries exempted from the police aid ban.

The request met objections:

- Democrats and some Republicans in both chambers said it revived the prospect of U.S. involvement with unsavory police forces.

"We would be held responsible in the region for abuses," Sen. Larry Pressler, R-S.D., said. Nevertheless, Pressler said he likely would support much of Reagan's request.

At a hearing Nov. 19, Pat Holt, former Foreign Relations Committee staff director whose probes helped prompt the ban on police aid, warned that Reagan's proposed program bore a strong resemblance to the old public safety program. "I have a very strong sense of déjà vu," he said.

And Robert K. Goldman of America's Watch, a human rights monitoring group, said: "It was U.S. aid that helped create the monsters that we are now trying to cope with."

- Guatemala was of particular concern because its military governments had developed an unmatched reputation in the region for human rights abuses.

Under U.S. pressure, Guatemala was holding presidential elections at the end of 1985, with Marco Vincicio Cerezo, a longtime opponent of military regimes, the leading candidate. The administration wanted to begin aiding the Guatemalan police and military after the Dec. 8 runoff but before the Jan. 14 inauguration. Capitol Hill critics and human rights groups wanted the United States to wait until after the inauguration, to avoid any appearance of collaboration with the outgoing military regime.

- Reagan seemed to be targeting terrorism by leftist rebels and ignoring similar human rights abuses by right-wing groups in Central America, some of which were known to have ties to police and security forces. "This program has an unfortunate single-sided bent," Sen. John Kerry, D-Mass., said.

Kerry charged that the Salvadoran government — cited by the administration as a model of democratic development — still had not eliminated from its security forces 14 officers implicated in rightist "death squad" activities.

- Reagan's request had the appearance of a backdoor attempt to get Congress to restore some military aid it had cut during past deliberations on foreign aid. Senate staff aides noted that Reagan officials first discussed the proposal on Capitol Hill the day after Congress completed work on the fiscal 1986 foreign aid authorization bill. That measure forced Reagan to cut military aid to most countries, including those in Central America. If enacted in full, the anti-terrorism proposal would have restored some of the aid.

- Reagan wanted broad exemptions for Central America from existing restrictions on U.S. foreign aid, when more limited exemptions might have sufficed. Among other things, Reagan's proposal would have voided for Central America limits on the amount and types of equipment the United States could give foreign security forces for anti-terrorism purposes. Charging that Reagan wanted "sweeping exceptions" from existing law, Sen. Paul S. Sarbanes, D-Md., suggested Congress should impose narrow restric-

Salvador Aid Curb Waived

President Reagan on March 14, 1985, used his executive authority to waive a limit on military aid to El Salvador that Congress had imposed in 1984.

Reagan notified Congress that he was sending El Salvador an additional $10 million in fiscal 1984 funds for training of military officers and troops. The money was on top of a $70 million 1984 supplemental appropriation for El Salvador that Congress voted in August 1984. *(1984 Almanac p. 439)*

Although Congress appropriated the money in 1984, it gave Reagan until the end of March 1985, to spend it.

Reagan avoided the $70 million limit that Congress imposed on that supplemental aid (in PL 98-396) by invoking a little-used power enabling a president to waive nearly any restriction on the use of foreign aid funds by stating that it was "important to the security interests of the United States" to do so. That power was in section 614(a) of the general foreign aid laws.

Reagan got the $10 million — along with an additional $5 million for Honduras and $2 million for Costa Rica — by abandoning plans to spend $18.5 million expanding a regional military training center in Honduras. Honduras in 1984 decided not to allow continued training of Salvadoran troops at the center; rather than spend all the $18.5 million to train only Hondurans, the Pentagon divided up the money for training of armed forces in each of the three countries. The remaining $1.5 million would go to close the center.

tions on how the money was spent in each country.

- Under questioning, administration aides said Central American security forces could use the aid to buy such items as electric-shock-producing devices that could be used for crowd control or to inflict torture. Sen. Claiborne Pell, R.I., ranking Democrat on the Foreign Relations panel, was particularly critical of the administration on that issue. At his insistence, James Michel, deputy assistant secretary of state for inter-American affairs, promised on Nov. 19 to bar the supply of cattle prods or "other equipment that could be used for torture."

Administration Response

Administration officials tried to allay congressional fears in hearings and briefings on Capitol Hill.

Michel said the program responded to a "serious, urgent and growing threat of terrorism" in Central America. While terrorists had struck most prominently in El Salvador, they also had carried out attacks in Honduras and could strike elsewhere, he said.

Michel also insisted that U.S.-backed countries in the region had mustered the "political will" to end police abuses, right-wing death squads and other vestiges of their traditional military regimes. The overall political situation in the region had changed markedly since Congress cut off police training, Michel said. In 1974, "we were seeking a transition away from democratic governments" in Central America, he said. "Now, we're seeing a transition to democratic governments."

Foreign Relations Chairman Richard G. Lugar, R-Ind., echoed that sentiment, noting that some of the region's new leaders had "suffered in the past" at the hands of police. The prime example, he said, was Salvadoran President Duarte, detained and beaten by security forces in 1972.

Michel insisted that the aid would be "carefully monitored" to prevent abuses of U.S.-supplied equipment and training. He noted that Congress also would be able to supervise the program because existing law required the administration to report 30 days in advance the details of aid to each country.

Senate Bill

The Senate Foreign Relations Committee on Dec. 5 approved the police aid bill as S 1915, but watered it down and loaded it with conditions. The bill authorized $22 million for an "anti-terrorism" program in Central America. It funded aid to police and security forces in Costa Rica, El Salvador, Guatemala and Honduras.

The $22 million approved by Foreign Relations was less than half of the $54 million anti-terrorism program that Reagan had requested in September. Most of the difference was accounted for by the committee's rejection of $27 million in supplemental military aid to Central American countries. The panel also spurned a request for police aid to Panama, where the military in September forced an elected president to resign.

Foreign Relations approved the $22 million bill on a 15-1 vote, with the support of several liberal Democrats who had been reluctant to resume aid to Latin police forces. Christopher J. Dodd, D-Conn., said the aid was a "risk" for the United States. But he argued that if there was to be reform in Central America, "it is essential that the security forces be part of it."

Kerry was the lone dissenter.

To prevent the aid from going to repressive police units, the committee put a long string of conditions in the bill. Most of the curbs were demanded by Dodd and other panel Democrats. Lugar, who also expressed hesitations about resuming aid to Latin police forces, said he agreed to the conditions as a means of getting a committee consensus on the bill.

State Department officials insisted the conditions were unnecessary but raised no serious objections.

The major conditions in the bill:

- Barred aid to security forces in each of the four countries until the president reported to Congress that those forces were not engaged in systematic human rights violations, that the governments were making progress in creating law enforcement agencies and judicial systems that investigated and prosecuted criminal acts, and that the aid would achieve the purpose of professionalizing independent police agencies. The president would have to make a follow-up report if he wanted to continue giving aid after July 1, 1986.
- Barred any involvement by the CIA or other intelligence agencies except for training directly involved with anti-terrorism programs.
- Allowed only 10 percent of equipment provided to police forces to be "lethal" items such as guns and ammunition. Cattle prods and similar devices were barred.
- Required the General Accounting Office to give Congress three quarterly reports in 1986 stating whether recipient countries had improved human rights practices and had tortured or abused prisoners.

At Dodd's insistence, the panel also put special restrictions on aid to security forces in Guatemala. Before helping Guatemalan forces, the president would certify to Congress that an elected civilian government was in power and had requested the aid, and that the new government had made progress toward controlling the military and ending human rights abuses by security forces.

Subsequently, moderate candidate Cerezo was elected president of Guatemala and pledged a humanitarian government and "active neutrality" in the region's conflicts. In a December visit to Washington, he met with senators and said if U.S. police aid were offered, he would ask that it be delayed. Cerezo was inaugurated Jan. 14, 1986.

In considering the bill, the committee rejected two proposals by Jesse Helms, R-N.C. One, rejected 1-14, would have approved Reagan's original $54 million request; another, rejected 2-13, would have added Panama to the list of recipient countries but under several conditions.

Floor Action Thwarted

Foreign Relations Chairman Lugar tried to get the $22 million measure to the full Senate Dec. 9 as an amendment to an omnibus continuing appropriations resolution for fiscal 1986 (H J Res 465). But he failed in two attempts. *(Continuing resolution, p. 360)*

Senate leaders, fearing that allowing the police aid amendment would open the floodgates for other senators to attach pet projects, blocked Lugar's effort to attach the aid to the spending bill.

And Tom Harkin, D-Iowa, blocked Lugar's subsequent attempts to bring the police aid bill to the floor on its own. Senate sources said Harkin threatened a filibuster, so Lugar did not move to offer the bill. ∎

Hill Pressure Leads to South Africa Sanctions

Spurred by demonstrations at the South African Embassy in Washington, D.C., and by growing racial violence in South Africa, Congress in 1985 forced President Reagan to impose limited economic and political sanctions against Pretoria's white-minority government.

Both the House and Senate passed versions of a bill (HR 1460) to impose sanctions and, implicitly, reject Reagan's policy of "constructive engagement" of South Africa. Yielding to the political pressure created by that legislation, Reagan Sept. 9 signed an executive order imposing his own set of sanctions and headed off final congressional action on the anti-apartheid bill.

The legislation and the administration's sanctions were intended to signal U.S. rejection of apartheid, South Africa's official policy of racial segregation. Previous efforts to prod South Africa to eliminate apartheid had failed to win enactment.

The House in 1983 approved sanctions as part of legislation renewing the Export Administration Act. The Senate rejected the sanctions that year, and, in late 1984, the issue helped kill export renewal legislation. In 1985, however, members were under pressure to act because of escalating violence in South Africa and widening anti-apartheid demonstrations around the United States. *(Export Administration Act, p. 259; background, 1984 Almanac p. 169)*

The House Foreign Affairs Committee approved HR 1460 (H Rept 99-76, Part I) on a 29-6 vote May 2. The House passed the bill June 5 on a 295-127 vote. *(Vote 130, p. 44-H)*

The Senate Foreign Relations Committee reported its version of the anti-apartheid bill (S 995 — S Rept 99-99) June 27. The Senate approved it, 80-12, on July 11. *(Vote 149, p. 30-S)*

The House Aug. 1 adopted the conference report (H Rept 99-242) on a 380-48 vote *(Vote 262, p. 84-H)*.

The Senate had been expected to vote on HR 1460 Aug. 1, but a threat from opponents to filibuster the conference report delayed action until after Congress' August recess. The Senate returned to the bill Sept. 9, and the president, facing near certain approval of the final bill, announced his package of sanctions.

The Senate Republican leadership Sept. 12 prevented further consideration of the bill by taking the extraordinary step of removing the official copy of HR 1460 from the Senate chamber. Under the rules, the Senate cannot consider a bill that is not physically present.

Backers of the curbs in HR 1460 pledged to continue pressing for a sanctions bill during the first session of the 99th Congress, threatening to attach anti-apartheid amendments to such must-pass legislation as appropriations bills or an extension of the debt limit. But the session ended without further action on the issue.

Reagan Sanctions and HR 1460

Reagan's Sept. 9 executive order on South Africa included several, but not all, of the economic sanctions and other measures that were contained in the final version of HR 1460 pending in Congress.

Reagan copied the exact language of the bill on some sanctions, but on other sanctions he made major changes that weakened the legislation.

Following is a comparison of the provisions in the conference report and Reagan's executive order, No. 12532, issued under the authority of the International Emergency Economic Powers Act (PL 95-223). *(Executive order text, p. 28-D)*

Krugerrands

Reagan's executive order directed the secretary of state and the U.S. trade representative to consult with other parties to the General Agreement on Tariffs and Trade "with a view toward adopting a prohibition on the import of Krugerrands," the South African gold coins sold worldwide.

The conference bill imposed an immediate ban on the importation into the United States of Krugerrands. However, the president could have waived the ban for an initial one-year period, and for subsequent six-month periods, if he had determined that the South African government had made at least one of eight reforms, such as releasing all political prisoners or negotiating in good faith with representative black leaders. Before the president's waiver of the ban could take effect, Congress would have had to pass a joint resolution approving his report.

HR 1460 would have no effect on Krugerrands already in the United States; nor did Reagan's order. U.S. sales of Krugerrands fell sharply in mid-1985 as the violence in South Africa escalated.

The president Oct. 1 ordered the ban on importing Krugerrands into the United States. It took effect Oct. 11. Reagan acted a few hours after Sen. Richard G. Lugar, R-Ind., the chairman of the Foreign Relations Committee, threatened to revive action on HR 1460 in the Senate. White House officials had told Lugar Sept. 25 that Reagan was ready to issue the ban. But when Reagan stalled for several days, Lugar threatened to bring up the bill.

Gold Coin

The conference bill authorized the minting of new U.S. gold coins to replace the Krugerrand.

Reagan directed the secretary of the Treasury to conduct a study within 60 days of the feasibility of minting such a coin, with a view toward "expeditiously" seeking authorization by Congress for it. *(Story, p. 270)*

Bank Loans

The bill banned new loans by U.S. banks or other agencies to the South African government, with certain exceptions, as did Reagan's order.

The conference bill exempted loans to educational, housing or health facilities that were freely open to persons of all races.

Reagan's order made a similar exemption, and also exempted any loans to improve the welfare or expand the economic opportunities of disadvantaged persons in South Africa. However, no loans could be made under the exemptions to "any apartheid-enforcing agency." The Treasury secretary, after consulting with the secretary of state, would determine what loans would qualify under the exemptions.

Computer Sales

The president's order barred all exports of computers, computer software and related equipment and technology to the South African police, military, prison system, national security agencies, weapons manufacturers or agencies that enforced apartheid. HR 1460 would have mandated identical limits.

Reagan directed the secretary of commerce to issue regulations for enforcement of the ban.

Nuclear Supplies

Reagan's order and the conference bill barred the export to South Africa of goods or technology that were intended for, or could be used for, nuclear production facilities.

The conference bill would have repealed that ban if the president reported to Congress that South Africa had become a party to the 1968 international nuclear non-proliferation treaty.

The president's order exempted from the ban assistance to South Africa that would be used to implement international safeguards against the diversion of nuclear material into weapons production. The order also exempted exports determined by the secretary of state to be necessary "for humanitarian reasons to protect the public health and safety."

Future Sanctions

The conference bill directed the president, within 12 months of enactment of the bill, to impose at least one additional sanction on South Africa if he determined that the government had not made "significant progress" toward eliminating apartheid.

The bill listed three possible sanctions: a ban on new commercial investment, a denial of most-favored-nation trading status and a prohibition against the importation of South African coal or uranium. The bill also said the president could instead choose any other economic or political sanction he found appropriate.

The measure required the president to impose additional sanctions at the end of subsequent 12-month periods if he again found no significant progress toward ending apartheid.

Reagan's order directed the secretary of state to establish an Advisory Committee on South Africa to recommend, within 12 months, measures "to encourage peaceful change" in South Africa. The president made no suggestion about what those measures might be.

Sullivan Principles

The conference bill would have required all U.S. firms employing more than 25 persons in South Africa to adhere to the Sullivan principles of non-discriminatory employment and living conditions developed by Philadelphia minister Leon Sullivan. The bill would require the secretary of state to publish annual reports on compliance, but it would not have established penalties for failure to adhere to the principles.

Reagan's executive order encouraged, but did not require, U.S. firms to adhere to the Sullivan principles.

As an incentive for compliance, however, the president adopted a provision in the bill that barred the U.S. government from giving export marketing assistance to U.S. companies doing business in South Africa unless they adhered to the principles.

The bill also would require U.S. agencies with offices in South Africa to adhere to the principles. Reagan's order mandated identical treatment of U.S. agencies.

South African Arms

Reagan imposed one sanction not included in HR 1460: a ban on importation into the United States of arms, ammunition or military vehicles produced in South Africa.

Black Scholarships

Reagan's order, in a provision also contained in HR 1460, provided for scholarships for South African blacks and other non-whites to attend secondary and post-secondary institutions. The conference bill authorized $8 million in fiscal 1986, $11 million in fiscal 1987 and $15 million in each subsequent year. Reagan set aside $8 million for fiscal 1986 and said he would consider appropriate amounts in future years.

Anti-Apartheid Aid

Reagan's order, as HR 1460 would have done, set aside $1.5 million for aid to anti-apartheid groups in South Africa.

The conference bill would authorize aid to groups that worked for improved human rights conditions and that provided legal and other assistance to persons prosecuted for political reasons. Reagan's order set aside $1.5 million for a Human Rights Fund in South Africa, of which a third was to be used for "legal assistance for South Africans."

Loans to Black Businesses

Conferees on HR 1460 directed the Export-Import Bank to take "active steps" to lend to firms owned by non-white South Africans to buy U.S. exports. Reagan directed all U.S. agencies to buy goods and services, to the maximum extent practical, from minority-owned South African businesses.

Penalties

HR 1460 established penalties for sanction violations, ranging from a $50,000 fine or five years in prison for individuals to a $1 million fine for businesses. Reagan's order set no penalties.

Background

Members of Congress were among the first protesters arrested when demonstrations against apartheid began at the South African Embassy in November 1984. As peaceful protests in the United States and violent disturbances in South Africa continued into 1985, the Pretoria government and its racial separation policies became the focus of an emotional debate in Congress.

Members were united in their abhorrence of the institutionalized racism of South African society and the often brutal repression used to maintain it. But they were sharply divided on what the United States could and should do to convince the white government in South Africa to allow full citizenship for the black majority.

Constructive Engagement

Until the very end of his first term, President Reagan had been conspicuously silent about apartheid, relying instead on a policy of "constructive engagement," or maintaining good relations with South Africa while quietly pressing for reform. Critics, including some Republican allies in Congress, said that policy smacked of U.S. collaboration with or acquiescence in discrimination against blacks. With Reagan's 1984 re-election an apparent indication that constructive engagement would continue as administration policy, sentiment grew in Congress for taking the lead in putting the United States on record against apartheid.

Support in the Democratic-controlled House for sanctions was strong. The GOP-led Senate had opposed such sanctions in the past, but some members felt in early 1985 that it was time the Senate made a symbolic gesture, such as mandating that U.S. firms doing business in South Africa adhere to the Sullivan fair-employment guidelines.

Conservatives' Involvement

Adding spice was the involvement of House conservatives. Led by Robert S. Walker, R-Pa., 35 conservatives in December 1984 wrote a letter to South African Ambassador Bernardus G. Fourie threatening to support limits on U.S. investment and other economic sanctions "unless certain economic and civil rights guarantees for all persons are in place."

Early in 1985, Walker and his colleagues negotiated with liberal House members, led by William H. Gray III, D-Pa., and Howard Wolpe, D-Mich., in hopes of producing compromise legislation.

Those efforts failed in late February. Liberals rejected the conservatives' demand: strictly limited South Africa sanctions coupled with tough measures against the Soviet Union and other communist countries. The liberals wanted more far-reaching sanctions than the conservatives were willing to accept.

The South African government made it clear it would reject any congressional demands. "South Africa is bent on reform. South Africa wants to reform for its own sake," said Fourie. "But if anybody, anybody comes and says to us that 'if you don't do this we do that,' our answer is: 'We didn't hear you.' "

The Reagan administration firmly opposed actions that would amount to punishing South Africa. Chester A. Crocker, assistant secretary of state for African affairs, told the Conservative Political Action Conference Feb. 28 that imposing sanctions was "a path of madness." The U.S. role in pushing for change was "modest, finite," he said.

U.S. Policy

The United States traditionally had followed a two-pronged approach to South Africa: expressing concern about apartheid while recognizing the strategic value of having a pro-Western, anti-communist government in place.

The goal of every administration since President Truman had been to encourage gradual change in South Africa as a way of avoiding a civil war that could lead to a takeover by a pro-Soviet regime. The United States had never supported or encouraged groups that took up arms against the government.

The Kennedy administration took the first step toward a clear repudiation of apartheid, voting for the first time for United Nations resolutions condemning it and supporting the United Nations voluntary arms embargo against South Africa in 1963.

The Carter administration, as part of its human rights campaign, escalated U.S. criticism of apartheid and, in 1978, imposed an embargo on sales of U.S. goods to South African military and police forces.

Within months of taking office, the Reagan administration substantially relaxed U.S. pressure on the South African government. In 1981 and 1982, the Commerce Department eased the embargo on sales to South African security forces of non-military industrial equipment, computers and other items.

Under Crocker's leadership, the administration implemented the overall policy of constructive engagement with South Africa. In addition to relaxing Carter's arms embargo restrictions, that policy resulted in a lowered tone of criticism of apartheid and in U.S. mediation of negotiations between South Africa and its neighbors, especially Mozambique and Angola.

Reagan maintained near silence on apartheid until December 1984, when the demonstrations in Washington, New York and other cities heightened public concern about the issue.

On Dec. 10, 1984, in his annual speech commemorating International Human Rights Day, Reagan said he felt a "moral responsibility" to speak out, "to emphasize our concerns and our grief over the human and spiritual cost of apartheid in South Africa."

Resolution

The Senate April 3 approved by an overwhelming 89-4 vote a resolution (S J Res 96) condemning apartheid. The measure, offered by Sen. Edward M. Kennedy, D-Mass., also requested that the State Department report by June 15 on a March 21 incident in South Africa's Eastern Cape area in which police apparently opened fire on an unarmed crowd, killing at least 19 people. *(Vote 29, p. 9-S)*

The House Foreign Affairs Committee May 2 approved S J Res 96 by voice vote. It did not reach the House floor.

House Committee Action

The House Foreign Affairs Committee approved HR 1460 May 2. The vote approving immediate sanctions followed a call by some Republicans on the committee for possible economic reprisals in three years. That proposal was voted down 4-19.

But the defeated alternative (HR 2288), introduced by Mark D. Siljander, R-Mich., as a substitute to HR 1460, was the strongest legislative stand some of the Republicans on the committee had taken as a group to date against apartheid.

The Banking Committee, which technically shared jurisdiction over the bill, did not hold separate hearings or markup.

Committee Provisions

The sanctions bill approved by the House committee would have imposed two reprisals immediately:

- A ban on new bank loans to the Pretoria government.
- A prohibition of sales to South African government agencies of U.S. computers that might help those agencies track political dissidents and enforce race laws.

The measure, sponsored by Rep. Gray, also would have forbidden new investment by U.S. firms doing business in South Africa and barred U.S. purchases of Krugerrands unless Pretoria made more progress toward ending racial segregation.

The latter two sanctions could be waived for an initial period of one year and for successive periods of six months if the president and Congress agreed that the South African government had taken at least one of eight steps:

- Freed all political prisoners.
- Given full South African citizenship to the more than eight million blacks currently considered citizens of tribal "homelands."
- Eliminated all restrictions on where South African residents could live because of their race or ethnic origin.
- Ended its policy of forcibly moving blacks from areas designated for whites.
- Let blacks seek work without restriction and live near their jobs in any part of South Africa.
- Enabled black workers' families to live near workers' jobs.
- Begun "meaningful negotiations" with black leaders for a fully representative political system and an end to racial and ethnic discrimination.
- Agreed to an internationally recognized settlement for Namibia, formerly South West Africa, which South Africa occupied in violation of U.N. resolutions.

The bill also directed the president to urge other nations to adopt similar sanctions.

The four Republicans who joined all Democrats on the committee in voting for the bill were: Benjamin A. Gilman, N.Y.; Jim Leach, Iowa; Olympia J. Snowe, Maine; and Christopher H. Smith, N.J.

Alternatives

Opponents made two attempts to soften the impact of the bill.

One amendment, by Toby Roth, R-Wis., would have deleted the ban on the purchase of Krugerrands. The amendment was rejected 4-21.

The broader Siljander alternative was rejected 4-19. It would have:

- Established penalties for U.S. firms doing business in South Africa that failed to comply with the Sullivan code. Violators would be barred from U.S. government contracts, loans and other aid.
- Created a U.S. Commission on South Africa to submit semiannual reports to Congress on progress Pretoria had made in curbing apartheid.
- Required a final commission report in three years recommending what — if any — sanctions should be imposed.
- Offered several incentives to South African blacks, including $15 million in scholarships for black students studying in South Africa and aid to black business.

Subcommittee Markup

The Siljander alternative originally was proposed as an amendment to the Gray bill during joint markup April 30 by the Africa and International Economic Policy and Trade subcommittees. It was defeated by voice vote by the Africa Subcommittee and was not offered in the Trade subcommittee sitting at the same dais.

Republicans on the subcommittees walked out of the meeting in an unsuccessful effort to prevent a final vote on the Gray bill. But the effort to deny a quorum failed, and both subcommittees approved the bill by voice votes.

House Floor Action

The House June 5 voted overwhelmingly to impose immediate economic sanctions on South Africa.

Fifty-six Republicans supported the measure, along with all but six Democrats.

Among the Republicans opposing the bill were the conservatives led by Rep. Walker who had threatened to back sanctions if the South African government failed to make immediate reforms. They said the House measure was too strong for them to support.

Floor Votes

The House began work on the sanctions bill May 21, and completed it on June 4-5. It defeated, by margins of at least 2-to-1, seven attempts by Republicans to water down or postpone implementation of the sanctions. The House also turned back two attempts to toughen the sanctions, including one to withdraw all U.S. business investment from South Africa immediately.

Considering the political sensitivity of the sanctions, House debate was restrained and free of partisan rhetoric. Only a handful of members took an active part in the debate.

Leaders on both sides of the issue said they agreed on the major proposition: that the United States should take a stronger stand against apartheid in South Africa. The disagreement was about means to that end.

Proponents of immediate sanctions said the South African government would only heed tough action by the United States. Just as important, even if the sanctions did not produce changes, at least they would distance the United States from apartheid.

But Siljander, who was leading the opposition to the bill, said the black majority in South Africa would suffer the most from economic attacks on their country.

The administration made only feeble efforts against the bill on the House floor. One State Department official said the outcome in the House was "preordained," and so it was futile for the administration to launch a major lobbying campaign.

On the final day of House action, three members of the Cabinet — Secretary of State George P. Shultz, Treasury Secretary James A. Baker III and Commerce Secretary Malcolm Baldrige — sent letters to House members affirming U.S. distaste for apartheid but opposing the bill.

However, the letters appeared to soften the administration's previous stand opposing congressional actions against the South African government. All three officials concentrated their criticisms on the future ban on new U.S. investments, virtually ignoring other provisions of the bill.

Amendments Adopted

On June 4, the House accepted three amendments to the sanctions bill as reported by the Foreign Affairs Committee.

The most important, by John Conyers Jr., D-Mich., barred "any kind" of sales to or cooperation with South Africa on nuclear power. Adopted by voice vote, it would prohibit the U.S. government and private companies from selling, to South Africa, directly or indirectly, nuclear equipment, supplies, materials and technology.

The House also adopted, by voice vote, two amendments by Ed Zschau, R-Calif. One urged the president to consult with other countries to encourage "multilateral, rather than unilateral" sanctions against South Africa.

The other amendment directed the president to report annually to Congress on the status of apartheid in South Africa. It also stated the sense of Congress that the United States should impose additional sanctions unless the South African government "makes substantial progress" toward eliminating apartheid.

Amendments Rejected

During its May 21 action, the House rejected, 148-256, a major amendment by Zschau that would have allowed U.S. businesses to continue investing in South Africa if they adhered to the Sullivan principles. *(Vote 110, p. 38-H)*

By overwhelming votes on June 4-5, the House rejected six additional amendments or substitutes offered by Republicans to weaken or delay the sanctions. The amendments were:

- By Zschau, to make the ban on importation of Krugerrands effective only if it did not violate the General Agreement on Tariffs and Trade, the international system governing trade among most countries. Rejected 127-292. *(Vote 123, p. 42-H)*
- By Dan Burton, R-Ind., to allow the secretary of state to waive the ban on future U.S. business investments in South Africa if he determined, through a poll, that most non-whites in that country opposed such a step. Rejected 40-379. *(Vote 124, p. 42-H)*
- By Burton, to waive the ban on future business investments in South Africa if a majority of non-whites there, in an internationally supervised election, opposed the ban. Rejected 30-384. *(Vote 125, p. 42-H)*
- By Siljander, to establish a commission to study apartheid and to recommend in three years what actions the United States should take against the South African government. The substitute bill also would have required U.S. firms doing business in South Africa to comply with the Sullivan fair-labor principles, and would have authorized $18.5 million for scholarships and other benefits for non-whites in that country. Rejected 108-310. *(Vote 126, p. 42-H)*
- By Steve Gunderson, R-Wis., to impose sanctions against South Africa in two years, unless the president and Congress determined they were not needed. It also would have required U.S. business to adhere to the Sullivan principles and would have authorized funds for benefits for non-whites in South Africa. Rejected 112-313. *(Vote 127, p. 42-H)*
- By Philip M. Crane, R-Ill., to delay imposition of the sanctions for one year, and to allow the president to waive the sanctions if he determined that the African National Congress, an anti-apartheid guerrilla group, had not renounced violence. Rejected 139-282. *(Vote 129, p. 44-H)*

The House also rejected two attempts to toughen the sanctions.

One, by Bill Richardson, D-N.M., would have barred the importation of uranium and coal from South Africa and Namibia. It was rejected by voice vote when Howard Wolpe, D-Mich., the floor manager of the bill, said he feared additional sanctions might jeopardize chances for the measure once it reached the Senate.

By a 77-345 vote, the House on June 5 rejected a substitute by Ronald V. Dellums, D-Calif., that ordered the withdrawal of all U.S. business investments from South Africa and barred all trade with that country. *(Vote 128, p. 42-H)*

Senate Committee Action

The Senate Foreign Relations Committee approved two anti-apartheid bills. First, on March 27, it approved a bill (S 998 — S Rept 99-37) calling for economic sanctions against South Africa if "significant progress" toward ending apartheid had not been made in two years. The panel passed the bill 16-1 after rejecting another to ban loans to South Africa's government. Jesse Helms, R-N.C., voted no.

The committee then, on June 4, approved S 995, which incorporated much of the substance of S 998, but made the imposition of some of the sanctions immediate and contained additional provisions aimed at improving the lot of blacks in South Africa. It also was approved by a 16-1 vote. The lone dissenting vote again was cast by Helms, who did not attend the session and who voted by proxy.

The Reagan administration, which had not expected the committee to vote for such strong sanctions, was surprised. One State Department official said the administration was caught "flat-footed."

House, Senate Bills Compared

The Foreign Relations Committee bill and the House bill contained three similar sanctions. Both measures immediately would:

- Ban new U.S. bank loans to the South African government.
- Curb sales of U.S. computer goods and technology that the South African military, police and other government agencies could use to track people and enforce race laws.
- Halt exports of U.S. nuclear technology to the Pretoria government.

The main difference between the two bills was in the timetable for imposing even tougher sanctions, most notably on investment. The House would have immediately barred new investment by U.S. firms doing business in South Africa. However, the ban could have been waived if the president and Congress agreed that Pretoria was making progress toward ending apartheid.

The Senate legislation recommended the ban as one of several possible future sanctions. During its markup, the Foreign Relations panel unanimously agreed to trim the time limit for imposing tougher sanctions such as the investment ban from two years to 18 months.

Foreign Relations Chairman Lugar opposed an immediate investment ban, saying that as a "first cut," sanctions should be directed at the South African government, not U.S. businesses.

The bills also differed in schedules for barring the purchase in the United States of Krugerrands. The House bill would have imposed the ban immediately but would have lifted it if apartheid were curbed. The Senate bill suggested the cutoff as a possible reprisal in 18 months.

Committee Compromise

The bill was a compromise between S 995 as originally offered by Republicans Lugar, Charles McC. Mathias Jr., Md., and Majority Leader Robert Dole, Kan., and a stronger alternative (S 1228) proposed by Christopher J. Dodd, D-Conn., and two Republicans who were not on the committee, Mitch McConnell, Ky., and William V. Roth Jr., Del.

The winning combination drew the support of Democrats who wanted tougher sanctions and Republicans. It blended aid to blacks with conditional and immediate sanctions aimed at South Africa's government.

The panel first defeated by a 7-9 party-line vote an attempt by Alan Cranston, D-Calif., to substitute even stronger sanctions, nearly identical to the House-passed bill.

These sanctions, in a bill (S 635) sponsored by Kennedy and Lowell P. Weicker Jr., R-Conn., banned new investment by U.S. firms, prohibited U.S. citizens from buying Krugerrands, barred new bank loans to the South African government and halted sales to the Pretoria government of U.S. computer goods and technology.

Next, the panel adopted three sanctions from the Roth-McConnell-Dodd bill: the immediate ban on bank loans and curbs on nuclear and computer technology.

Dodd withdrew two other sanctions: a ban on U.S. landing rights for South African planes and a requirement that South Africa close one consulate in the United States.

Then the panel adopted the Roth-McConnell-Dodd bill by 12-5, with five Republicans — Lugar, Helms, Rudy Boschwitz, Minn., Larry Pressler, S.D., and Frank H. Murkowski, Alaska — voting against it. That measure was attached as an amendment to the Lugar-Mathias-Dole bill (S 995).

Provisions

The bill would immediately:

- Ban new bank loans to the Pretoria government.
- Prohibit the sale of U.S. nuclear technology to South Africa.
- Block U.S. computer goods and technology to some South African government agencies.
- Require most U.S. firms doing business in South Africa to comply with the Sullivan code. U.S. businesses that failed to follow the Sullivan principles were barred from getting some U.S. government export aid.

The bill also required additional sanctions, such as a ban on purchase of gold coins in the United States, within 18 months if the president had determined and Congress agreed that Pretoria had not made enough progress toward ending apartheid.

The panel also strengthened a provision in the Lugar-Mathias-Dole bill requiring the United States to press other nations to adopt sanctions against South Africa.

The measure provided $15 million in scholarships for black South Africans studying in South Africa and $1.5 million for a human rights fund, 20 percent of which would be earmarked for legal aid to South African political prisoners.

Senate Floor Action

The Senate passed S 995 July 11 by an 80-12 vote. *(Vote 149, p. 30-S)*

Given the overwhelming support for the measure in the Senate, administration officials did not mount a major effort to block the bill.

The Senate acted as the racial violence in South Africa that had claimed the lives of some 400 blacks since the summer of 1984 continued to escalate. The day debate on the measure began in the Senate, Desmond Tutu, the South African Anglican bishop who had been awarded the Nobel Peace Prize in 1984, intervened to save a black alleged informer from an angry mob in a black settlement.

The only vocal opposition to S 995 on the floor came from a group of GOP conservatives led by Jesse Helms. But while Helms and his allies were able to delay action on the bill for much of the week of July 8, they were unable to change it, and a last-minute flurry of amendments seeking to extend the South Africa sanctions to the Soviet Union and other communist countries was turned back easily.

However, Helms said he was satisfied that he was able to block toughening amendments pushed by liberals, particularly a proposal by Kennedy to follow the House's lead in banning importation of Krugerrands. The only significant floor change was the inclusion of an authorization for production of a U.S. gold coin to compete with Krugerrands.

Backers of S 995 conceded that it would have little immediate impact on apartheid. But they argued that it would demonstrate firm U.S. opposition to the system and begin to raise its economic costs.

In an attempt to force the House to accept the Senate bill, the Senate inserted its provisions into HR 1460 and returned it to the House. That meant the House would have had to decide whether to demand a conference committee. A key issue was the timetable for blocking new investment and Krugerrands; the House would have done so immediately unless South Africa undertook major reforms. The Senate called for similar sanctions 18 months from enactment, but would have implemented them only after further congressional action. Senate Republicans opposed tougher sanctions as probably leading to a presidential veto.

Floor Action

To get S 995 to final approval, Lugar, the Senate floor manager of the bill, had to steer around two sharply different pitfalls: conservative efforts to delay action on the measure and Democratic attempts to expand its sanctions.

At first, Helms and his allies were able to block consideration of the bill when it came to the floor July 8, raising the specter of a filibuster. Majority Leader Dole filed a cloture petition to cut off debate on the motion to proceed to consideration of the bill. That cloture motion was approved easily July 10, by an 88-8 vote. *(Vote 143, p. 29-S)*

The motion to begin work on the bill itself was approved by voice vote the following day. Kennedy and his allies then marshaled their forces for an amendment to force an immediate ban on Krugerrand imports. They agreed to drop that effort, however, in exchange for a GOP leadership pledge to oppose other amendments, especially a proposal by Sen. Roth to make clear that the federal legislation would pre-empt state and local actions against apartheid.

While there was some question about the legal necessity or validity of such an amendment, apartheid foes strongly opposed it as undermining efforts for sanctions by localities.

However, both sides agreed to an amendment, adopted by voice vote, to authorize minting of U.S. gold coins.

GOP conservatives mounted one last attack on the bill. With both parties' leaderships opposed to the proposals, the Senate rejected a series of amendments offered by:

- Gordon J. Humphrey, R-N.H., to impose sanctions on signatories of the 1975 Helsinki accords, such as the Soviet Union, if they did not comply with the Helsinki human rights standards; tabled by a 67-29 vote. *(Vote 144, p. 30-S)*
- Steven D. Symms, R-Idaho, to bar economic sanctions if the president or Congress determined that they would lead to increased unemployment among South African blacks; tabled 78-17. *(Vote 145, p. 30-S)*
- Malcolm Wallop, R-Wyo., to extend economic sanctions to the Soviet Union and other countries with serious human rights violations, as well as nations that encouraged terrorist attacks on Americans; rejected 37-57. *(Vote 146, p. 30-S)*
- Jeremiah Denton, R-Ala., to declare that the black African National Congress organization of South Africa was a terrorist group, and impose a series of restrictions on ANC members and activities; tabled 72-21. *(Vote 147, p. 30-S)*

The last amendment was a bit of parliamentary strategy by Helms and Wallop aimed at strengthening resistance among Senate conferees to the House bill's provisions. They offered the whole House bill as an amendment, and then moved immediately to table it; the amendment was killed by a 90-2 vote. *(Vote 148, p. 30-S)*

Conference

Before the conference on HR 1460 began, Senate Foreign Relations Chairman Lugar tried without success to get leaders of the House Foreign Affairs Committee to accept the Senate version of HR 1460, warning them that the administration could pre-empt their campaign if they did not accept the milder sanctions bill passed by the Senate.

Attempting to muscle the House into accepting the Senate bill, Lugar at first refused to appoint Senate conferees, and had warned that Jesse Helms would filibuster South Africa legislation stronger than the Senate bill. Even if Congress passed a tougher bill, the president would likely veto it, Lugar said. Lugar made those arguments during a July 25 House-Senate conference committee meeting on the foreign aid authorization bill (S 960).

When House-Senate conferees met July 31, it was evident that a majority wanted to reach agreement on a bill that could clear Congress rapidly. Lugar said he could not guarantee that Reagan would sign anything stronger than the original Senate bill, but House conferees said they were willing to run the risk of a veto.

In spite of their general agreement in favor of doing something, the two sides approached the issue from opposite perspectives.

Lugar said his concept, and that of the Senate bill, was that "the United States ought to be more involved in South Africa" by using its influence to encourage change. The Senate bill, he said, had several "positive elements" such as a scholarship program for blacks and a requirement that U.S. firms in South Africa adhere to fair-employment principles.

House members responded that direct action against the South African government was long overdue and that the Senate bill merely reflected a failed administration policy.

The major issue facing the conferees was whether the Senate would accept either or both of two sanctions that the House bill would have imposed immediately: the ban on Krugerrands and a ban on new U.S. business investments in South Africa.

At a private meeting July 30, Senate Democrats had told their House counterparts that it would be impossible to get a bill through the Senate with both sanctions, especially the ban on new investments. As a result, the Democrats agreed to press for the Krugerrand ban and to sacrifice the new investments prohibition.

Lugar at first resisted accepting the Krugerrand ban. He again warned the House members that the only way of ensuring that a bill would be passed before the recess was for them to accept the Senate-passed measure, with no changes.

Lugar found himself facing a personal appeal from one of the few black members of the conference committee, Rep. Parren J. Mitchell, D-Md.

Calling himself a "very, very proud man" who rarely wanted favors, Mitchell directly asked Lugar to give way on the Krugerrand issue: "I'm pleading with you today, you and your Senate conferees, I'm pleading with you to take that one quantum step so that this nation can hold its head high in the international community. Let's go ahead and vote for the ban on Krugerrands."

After more bargaining, Lugar formally offered to accept the Krugerrand ban in exchange for an agreement by House members to withdraw their immediate ban on new investments. House conferees accepted the deal after a brief caucus.

Final Floor Action

The House Aug. 1 overwhelmingly approved the conference report on HR 1460. Thirty conservatives, led by Robert S. Walker, R-Pa., immediately sent the president a letter warning against a veto.

In the Senate the same day, a handful of conservatives led by Helms and Wallop blocked action by threatening a filibuster that would have delayed the Senate's long-scheduled recess. Helms had said that attempting to clear the bill before the recess would be "a waste of time."

The conservatives also thwarted a last-minute effort by liberals to put the Senate on record in favor of the final bill. In a procedural step, Weicker moved to table the bill, but asked senators to vote against the motion to signal support for the measure. But the bill's opponents joined to defeat the motion, thus making the 0-97 vote meaningless. *(Vote 168, p. 34-S)*

Majority Leader Dole then filed a petition to cut off a filibuster and set a vote for Sept. 9.

Conservatives at Odds

The debate over the sanctions issue revealed, even more clearly than before, the deep split among conservatives on South Africa.

Sens. Helms and Wallop and Reps. Siljander and Dan Burton were among the few members of Congress to speak out against the compromise legislation. They said sanctions would harm South Africa's black workers and would undermine a strongly anti-communist government.

Wallop also charged that Congress was worsening, rather than helping, the situation in South Africa. Noting a spate of violence that prompted the government to impose a sweeping state of emergency, he said: "It is no coincidence that the violence in South Africa escalated after the House and the Senate separately acted" on HR 1460 in June and July.

One House member, Mickey Edwards, R-Okla., challenged his fellow conservatives, saying: "Some of my friends seem to have a strange attachment to South Africa. South Africa for some reason in their minds rises to the status of special friend. Mr. Speaker, no nation which represses its citizens and denies basic human freedoms is a friend of mine or of the principles on which this country was founded."

During the August recess, Lugar urged Secretary of State Shultz to head off a presidential veto of HR 1460. Lugar also reiterated an earlier recommendation that Reagan implement the provisions of the bill without waiting for final congressional action on the measure.

At an Aug. 5 press conference, Reagan refused to say whether he would veto HR 1460. He repeated his objections to economic sanctions, arguing they would hurt South African blacks and neighboring African countries. But he praised other features of the bill — apparently referring to provisions that would fund scholarships for South African blacks and encourage exports by black-owned firms.

Botha Speech

Congressional ire at South Africa was heightened, rather than eased, by a long-awaited speech Aug. 15 by that country's state president, P. W. Botha. Addressing a meeting in Durban of the ruling National Party, Botha rejected all calls for quick changes in apartheid, especially reforms that would lead to black control.

Botha's major concession was an agreement to negotiate with black leaders for the citizenship and other "legitimate rights" of blacks living outside tribal homelands that the government had created. But he refused to say how far the government was willing to go in granting political rights to the 23 million blacks, which black leaders would be permitted in the negotiations, or when the talks would begin.

Senate Floor Finale

In a series of votes on Sept. 9, 11 and 12, the Republican-controlled Senate accepted Reagan's executive order imposing sanctions by refusing to consider HR 1460. A majority of the Senate supported the bill — the high-water mark was 57 votes on Sept. 11 — but 60 senators were required to kill a threatened filibuster that was blocking action. *(Votes 171, 173-175, p. 35-S)*

In the climactic Senate confrontation on Sept. 11, supporters of the sanctions bill had their best shot at passage. As a result, the Senate votes on ending the filibuster became a major test of congressional support for Reagan and his revised South Africa policy. Reagan telephoned Republicans asking for support; 11 House members of the Congressional Black Caucus entered the Senate chamber to lobby on behalf of breaking the filibuster.

When the key vote came, several wavering Republicans hovered over tally sheets until it was clear that the effort to shut off debate had failed. Republicans Robert T. Stafford, Vt., and Mack Mattingly, Ga., both of whom had voted on Sept. 9 to end the filibuster, switched at the last minute, enabling two others, Charles E. Grassley, Iowa, and Alfonse M. D'Amato, N.Y., to vote in opposition to Reagan.

Only one Democrat, Minority Leader Robert C. Byrd, W.Va., voted against ending the filibuster, but he did so as a procedural move so he could ask for reconsideration of the vote. That request was tabled 50-48. *(Vote 174, p. 35-S)*

After another vote on Sept. 12, Republican Leader Dole took the official copy of the bill and gave it to Lugar, who locked it in the Foreign Relations Committee's safe.

The move infuriated Democrats, but Lugar defended it as necessary to assert GOP control of the Senate.

Lugar insisted that the purloined bill was "still a living, vital being" that could be resurrected if Reagan failed to carry out his executive order.

Dole and Lugar returned the bill to the Senate Sept. 25 after they discovered that Byrd and other Democrats were planning a belated protest and were threatening to hold up Senate action on other legislation until the bill was returned. Byrd and nine colleagues staged their protest on Sept. 26, in a three-hour series of speeches denouncing Dole and Lugar for removing the bill.

Reagan's Maneuver

During the first week of September Lugar and Dole had pressed key White House officials to accept the sanctions bill or at least adopt most of its provisions. Both leaders had supported the bill, over White House opposition, but they clearly were uncomfortable about their prospective role in an all-out confrontation with the president.

Lugar's and Dole's arguments finally swayed the White House on Sept. 5-6, as Reagan's aides agreed to draw up the executive order implementing many of the sanctions. But the White House insisted on major modifications to make it clear the president was not surrendering entirely to Capitol Hill.

Reagan Sept. 9 signed his executive order during a nationally televised speech just five hours before the Senate was scheduled to vote on ending debate on the sanctions bill. Declaring that he would be forced to veto the sanctions legislation, Reagan said: "I want to work with the Congress to advance bipartisan support for America's policy toward South Africa. That is why I have put forward this executive order today." *(Text, p. 28-D)* ▮

Israel Gets an Aid Boost

Responding to a severe economic crisis in Israel, and to a belated Israeli government plan to deal with it, Congress in 1985 approved an extraordinary \$1.5 billion economic aid supplemental for Israel. For political "balance," Congress also approved \$500 million in extra economic aid for Egypt.

Both amounts were included in a supplemental appropriation (HR 2577 — PL 99-88), and were to be spent over fiscal 1985-86. Authorizations also were contained in the fiscal 1986-87 foreign aid bill (S 960 — PL 99-83). *(Supplemental, p. 350; foreign aid bill, p. 41)*

Both bills also included \$8 million for development in the West Bank and Gaza Strip.

The supplemental aid was in addition to \$3 billion in

regular economic and military aid the United States provided each year for Israel, the biggest single recipient of U.S. aid. The assistance for Egypt — Israel's partner in the 1978-79 Camp David accords and peace treaty — topped a regular $2.3 billion annual program.

President Reagan's request and congressional approval of the politically popular aid increase were a foregone conclusion. But Secretary of State George P. Shultz asked Capitol Hill to wait until Israel had put in place economic reforms before boosting funding. Eager House members, however, began marking it up anyway, and in late April, Shultz informally told Congress he was ready to support the aid.

In voting for the emergency aid boost, Congress instructed the administration to spend it before all of Israel's reforms were in place.

But early in 1986, Israel agreed to return $51.6 million of the aid, to help the United States meet fiscal 1986 budget cuts mandated by the Gramm-Rudman-Hollings law (H J Res 372 — PL 99-177). *(Story, p. 459)*

Among Israel's economic problems were an inflation rate that exceeded 1,000 percent in 1984, rising unemployment and huge government budgets that absorbed nearly all the country's gross national product, the total of the nation's production of goods and services.

At the end of 1985, some Senate supporters tried to get another $500 million military aid bonus for Israel. That move failed because of the overall budget crunch and because of strong administration opposition. However, there were likely to be moves in 1986 to reduce the amount Israel would have to pay the United States on past military aid loans.

While members of Congress responded to the influential Israeli lobby on the aid issue, they also were pressured on an administration proposal to sell advanced weapons to one of Israel's Arab neighbors, Jordan.

Israel's friends on Capitol Hill argued that Jordanian King Hussein was not serious about peace talks, and, with opposition to the sale overwhelming, Reagan was forced to delay it. *(Story, p. 93)*

Foreign Aid Committees' Action

Senate Foreign Relations Committee members were eager to give Israel the extra $1.5 billion in economic aid, but at their March 27 markup of the foreign aid bill, they agreed to defer to Shultz and wait.

"As senators thought about that, they did not want to change the situation of the secretary of state," said committee Chairman Richard G. Lugar, R-Ind.

The strongly pro-Israel House Foreign Affairs Subcommittee on Europe and the Middle East also had resisted the temptation to back the aid in its March 20 working session.

But on April 3, the full House committee went ahead and approved the aid. The money, all to be authorized and appropriated in fiscal 1985, was to be spent over 1985-86. It came on top of $1.2 billion in regular annual economic aid to Israel and military aid of $1.4 billion in 1985 and $1.8 billion in 1986.

The House aid bill (HR 1555 — H Rept 99-39) also included Reagan's 1986 requests for Egypt: $815 million in economic assistance, $213 million in food aid and $1.3 billion in military aid.

Shultz sent two aides to Capitol Hill on April 2 to ask the panel not to vote the supplemental money for at least six weeks. Herbert Stein, a former chairman of the president's Council of Economic Advisers, and William Schneider Jr., under secretary of state for security, told members that the panel's approval of the aid would reduce Israel's incentive to make politically painful reforms.

A similar appeal had convinced members of the Senate Foreign Relations Committee not to add the Israel money to their aid bill. But members of the House committee were unmoved.

The amendment approving the $1.5 billion was drafted by committee leaders on March 29 — four days before Stein and Schneider made their pitch. Its sponsors were senior members: Lee H. Hamilton, D-Ind., chairman of the Middle East subcommittee; full committee Chairman Dante B. Fascell, D-Fla.; ranking Republican William S. Broomfield, R-Mich.; and Benjamin A. Gilman, R-N.Y.

Hamilton, who had been among the Hill leaders most willing to accept arguments for delay, defended the panel's action, noting that it was only "a preliminary step" and that Congress likely would not give final approval to the aid for several months. He insisted that the $1.5 billion was a one-time-only injection of emergency aid.

The introduction of the $1.5 billion amendment, at the very end of the committee's consideration of the aid bill, prompted a brief but highly unusual debate about the extent of U.S. aid for Israel and the overall balance of the foreign aid program. Gerry E. Studds, D-Mass., noted that, with the amendment, Israel and Egypt would receive $6.6 billion of the $14.5 billion authorized in the bill for all foreign aid recipients.

While saying he did not question support for those countries, Studds said his colleagues should "reflect upon the complexity and diversity of the globe and of all the challenges that confront United States foreign policy around it, and the extent to which we may limit our capacity to respond with any degree of effectiveness or wisdom or impact if we persist year after year after year in directing almost half of our aid to two countries."

Doug Bereuter, R-Neb., also had concerns: "As surely as we are funding 45 or 55 percent of our foreign aid to two countries, we are taking food out of the mouths of people in Africa."

Fascell responded that Congress had to set priorities "based on what we conceive to be the best interests of the United States."

The committee approved the $1.5 billion by voice vote; the only member clearly voting "no" was Ed Zschau, R-Calif., who had supported a delay.

The bill also included language complaining about the "less than normal relations between Egypt and Israel" and calling on Egypt to return an ambassador to Israel. Egyptian President Hosni Mubarak withdrew his ambassador from Tel Aviv in 1982, in reaction to the Israeli invasion of Lebanon, and had refused to send one back.

The full House passed the foreign aid bill on July 11.

Administration Request

With pressure growing in Congress to provide the emergency aid to Israel, Secretary of State Shultz on April 29 informally told Congress that he was ready to support it.

Administration and congressional sources said Shultz agreed to proceed with the aid request for two reasons: Leaders on Capitol Hill warned him that Congress would approve the aid anyway, and Shultz on April 22 received a letter from Israeli Prime Minister Shimon Peres offering a positive response to most economic reforms the United States had suggested.

Once Shultz agreed to the aid, budget director David A. Stockman resisted it, saying that such a large foreign aid request might jeopardize Reagan's demands for cuts in domestic programs. But sources said Stockman agreed to the request on April 30, at the urging of Shultz and White House Chief of Staff Donald T. Regan.

The $1.5 billion was to be authorized and appropriated in fiscal 1985, and about half of it was to be transferred to Israel during that fiscal year, which expired Sept. 30. The rest was to be held until fiscal 1986 and given to Israel in return for implementation of its reforms in banking, budgeting and other economic matters.

The administration's $500 million request for Egypt came as a surprise. Some State Department officials for months had predicted a $185 million supplemental, putting Egypt's 1985 economic aid at $1 billion. But the Egyptian government and the State Department's Near East Bureau won the larger amount, citing Egypt's pressing economic programs.

Egypt also was to receive military aid: $1.175 billion in fiscal 1985 and $1.3 billion in 1986.

Although there was no legal or official tie between U.S. aid to Israel and Egypt, both the Carter and Reagan administrations informally had linked the aid since the 1979 peace treaty between the two countries.

The administration also wanted $8 million for several programs to improve the "quality of life" for Palestinians living in the Israeli-occupied West Bank area.

Senate Floor Action

On May 14, the full Senate voted to add the $1.5 billion in emergency assistance for Israel and $500 million for Egypt to the foreign aid bill.

The amendment, offered by Lugar, was approved by voice vote after little debate. It also included $8 million for economic development programs to aid residents of the Israeli-occupied West Bank and Gaza Strip areas. The president could provide the aid any time during fiscal years 1985 and 1986.

After the Senate acted, the administration formally sent Congress its request for the aid.

Lugar said the president would have authority to provide the aid to Israel "at such times as he finds helpful to the stability and growth of the Israeli economy."

Thomas F. Eagleton, D-Mo., inserted in the *Congressional Record* a list of the 10 reforms that Peres promised in a letter to Shultz. An administration official confirmed that Eagleton's list was accurate.

Among the major reforms were: adoption by the Israeli government of an inflation target for fiscal years 1985-86, with the agreement of labor and business leaders; establishment of government budget targets for each quarter, expressed in Israeli shekels; passage of a bill requiring Cabinet departments to live within their budgets; and passage of a bill freeing the Bank of Israel from a requirement to print money to cover all budget deficits.

Senate action came as the administration, in an effort to hold down the size of the overall foreign aid budget, had delayed its formal request for $1.2 billion in regular economic aid for Israel in fiscal 1986.

Appropriations

The administration and many supporters of Israel had planned to push the Israeli and Egyptian aid through Congress as a special supplemental appropriations bill because of Israel's urgent need for cash to pay its bills. But House Appropriations Chairman Jamie L. Whitten, D-Miss., decreed that the money should be included in an omnibus fiscal 1985 supplemental spending bill (HR 2577 — H Rept 99-142) under consideration by his committee.

The administration go-ahead prompted quick action on the aid; the House Appropriations Foreign Operations Subcommittee included it in its May 1 markup of the supplemental. The full committee approved it May 21.

The subcommittee's 12-0 vote for the aid boosts came after a spirited debate about whether the United States should impose conditions on Israel's aid.

Jack F. Kemp, R-N.Y., charged that Shultz, in demanding reforms, was treating Israel "like some non-aligned Third World country."

But Subcommittee Chairman David R. Obey, D-Wis., said Shultz was "absolutely correct" in pressing Israel on reforms. "I don't happen to think that increasing dependence by Israel on the United States is in their interest or ours," he said. Obey said Peres had given him assurances in April that Israel was not requesting the $1.5 billion as a permanent increase in its regular aid from the United States.

At its May 1 meeting, the subcommittee left unresolved its report describing conditions on the aid. Kemp and several others said the subcommittee should attach no conditions; Obey wanted the panel to endorse Shultz' efforts. The full committee's report contained language commending those efforts.

The House approved the supplemental on June 12. When the bill reached the floor June 11, members rejected, 110-314, an amendment by Hank Brown, R-Colo., to drop the $500 million in aid for Egypt. *(Vote 136, p. 46-H)*

Brown argued that Egypt had not spent the $2.2 billion it was given in regular appropriations and that Egypt was failing to live up to the 1978 Camp David agreement by not maintaining an ambassador in Israel.

"It is inappropriate for us to provide a bonus for a country that has failed to live up to the Camp David accords," Brown said.

Other members — including some of the strongest supporters of aid to Israel — replied that striking the funds would be an insult that could cause Egypt to back away from negotiations with Israel.

"I think it is important, if you are pro-Israel, to recognize that it is incredibly important to Israel to have Egypt and other moderate Arab nations involved in the peace process, not outside of it," said Kemp. "Denying aid to this country would be a terrible message to send to friends of the peace process in the Middle East at this very criticial point."

The House passed the bill on June 12.

On the Senate side, the Appropriations Committee had also included the $1.5 billion for Israel, the $500 million for Egypt and the $8 million for Gaza Strip and West Bank development in its version of HR 2577 (S Rept 99-82) reported June 13. The full Senate approved the supplemental on June 20.

After weeks of dickering over other issues, conferees on the supplemental reached agreement July 26, and Congress cleared the bill Aug. 1.

Gramm-Rudman Giveback

The depth of Capitol Hill support for Israel was again demonstrated at the end of the year, when members of Congress gave Israel the chance for an exemption from the automatic budget cuts to be forced by the Gramm-Rudman act. The Israeli Embassy and pro-Israel lobbyists declined the exemption.

Rep. David R. Obey, D-Wis., chairman of the House Appropriations Subcommittee on Foreign Operations, said several members of Congress offered Israel an exemption from the Gramm-Rudman cuts.

"They didn't want it. It would have been counterproductive, politically," Obey said.

Congress directed the Treasury Department to send $1.2 billion in economic grants to Jerusalem within 30 days of enactment of the continuing appropriations resolution, well before the Gramm-Rudman procedures took effect.

Under that law, all non-defense programs faced cutbacks of 4.3 percent. Because Israel's $1.2 billion economic aid already had been sent, U.S. officials worried that aid to other countries would have to be cut by 6.4 percent to make up the difference.

In mid-January 1986, responding to U.S. pleas for help in the budget-cutting process, Israeli Prime Minister Shimon Peres agreed to return the $51.6 million that would have been cut under Gramm-Rudman. Israel's projected $1.8 billion in military aid also was to be pared by $77.4 million.

Sources said that Israel and its lobbyists in Washington rejected the prospect of an exemption because it might have caused resentment among advocates of domestic programs that would face sharp budget cuts under the Gramm-Rudman legislation. ▮

Reagan Accepts Hill Delay of Jordan Arms

Sidestepping a bruising battle with Congress, President Reagan in October agreed to legislation (S J Res 228 — PL 99-162) that postponed a major arms sale to Jordan at least until early 1986. Reagan had notified Congress of his intent to sell Jordan advanced warplanes, missiles and other weapons — in spite of congressional warnings against such a sale until there was more progress in Middle East peace talks.

When about two-thirds of all members of Congress endorsed bills rejecting the $1.5 billion-$2 billion sale, Reagan agreed to a compromise that delayed the package at least until March 1, 1986, unless "direct and meaningful" peace talks between Jordan and Israel were under way. In theory, Reagan was free to pursue the sale after March 1; however, congressional leaders warned that he faced a major battle if he did so in the absence of progress on peace.

Reagan signed the resolution Nov. 25.

The fiscal 1986 continuing appropriations resolution (H J Res 99-465 — PL 99-190) established a procedure for averting a Senate filibuster of any resolution to block the arms sale. *(Continuing resolution, p. 367)*

Both the continuing resolution and the foreign aid authorizations law (S 960 — PL 99-83) also contained language stating congressional opposition to a Jordan arms sale until Middle East peace talks were under way. *(Authorizations bill, p. 41)*

House Foreign Affairs Committee Chairman Dante B. Fascell, D-Fla., said Congress was looking for more than "some chitchat." Specifically, he said:

- "Direct, publicly acknowledged, ongoing peace negotiations between leaders of Jordan and Israel or their designated negotiating teams";
- "The establishment of a mechanism by the two parties to ensure the continuation of the substantive negotiating process and regular face-to-face talks between the two parties"; and
- "A process which would result in a clear public declaration to end the state of belligerency between Jordan and Israel."

Background

The Jordan arms proposal was a replay of a familiar scenario: an American president agrees to sell sophisticated weapons to an Arab country, stirring concerns in Congress about the security of Israel.

At the heart of the debate was whether selling weapons would promote the seemingly opposite goal of peace in the Middle East. The Reagan administration, like its predecessors, argued that military cooperation would encourage political cooperation by "moderate" Arab regimes. That position helped sway Congress to approve controversial sales to Jordan in 1975-76, to Saudi Arabia and Egypt in 1978, and to Saudi Arabia again in 1981. *(1975 Almanac p. 356; 1978 Almanac p. 405; 1981 Almanac p. 129)*

In 1983, however, Congress held up funding for a "rapid deployment force" of Jordanians, and in 1984, Capitol Hill opposition to a sale of Stinger anti-aircraft missiles mounted so rapidly that Reagan was forced to withdraw it. *(1983 Almanac p. 134; 1984 Almanac p. 116)*

In 1985, Reagan proposed selling advanced warplanes and missiles to Jordan, saying that King Hussein would feel more secure in negotiating peace with Israel if he had U.S. backing against potential threats by Syria and other nations that rejected any dealings with the Jewish state.

But that argument swayed few in Congress, in spite of Hussein's sustained effort to open peace talks with Israel.

Hussein traveled to Washington twice in 1985, asking for backing of a complicated Jordanian-Egyptian plan for talks. He said it might be "the last opportunity" for peace.

Israeli Prime Minister Shimon Peres touched on the same theme, also in a visit to Washington. "Time is running out" for peace talks, he said. "In the Middle East, time is arms. Arms are crowding the very narrow sky of peace in the Middle East."

Speaking to the U.N. General Assembly, Peres called on Hussein to negotiate directly with Israel. In a break with past policy, Peres also invited the U.N. to play a role "by ushering the parties to the conflict into a new diplomatic initiative."

Hussein responded by praising the "spirit" of Peres' speech but criticizing some of the details.

What prevented the two sides from getting together was a matter of procedure.

Hussein promoted a complicated formula for jump-starting the peace process; it featured a key mediating role for the United States; it asked for some form of participation by the Soviet Union, and it called for the Palestine Liberation Organization (PLO) to have a seat at the negotiating table.

The United States and Israel both rejected Hussein's proposals for Soviet and PLO involvement. Israel's supporters on Capitol Hill argued that Hussein was not ready for peace and that he had given veto power over his participation in negotiations to Yasir Arafat, chairman of the PLO. U.S. arms sales to Jordan, they argued, would reduce Hussein's incentives to enter peace talks.

An escalation of Middle East violence in October further clouded the climate for peace talks. Arab leaders were upset in early October when Reagan endorsed an Israeli aerial bombardment of a PLO headquarters in Tunisia. And U.S. ties with Egypt — the only Arab country openly backing Hussein's peace moves — were severely strained in the aftermath of the Palestinian hijacking of an Italian cruise ship, the *Achille Lauro,* in which an American was slain.

Reagan Proposal

Ignoring warnings of a battle with Congress, Reagan on Sept. 27 sent informal notice to Congress of his proposed arms sale to Jordan.

The package — valued at $1.5 billion-$2 billion — was the largest ever for Jordan and one of the largest for an Arab country. The centerpiece of the package was the sale of 40 warplanes to bolster Jordan's small aging fleet of 130 combat aircraft. Jordan was to get either the new F-20, made by Northrop Corp., or a stripped-down version of the general Dynamics Corp. F-16 fighter. The choice was to be made by the Air Force, which was seeking a cheaper alternative to the top-of-the-line F-16.

Also in the package were:

- 300 AIM-9P4 Sidewinder infrared air-to-air missiles.
- 12 mobile Improved Hawk anti-aircraft missile batteries.
- Conversion of Jordan's 14 Hawk batteries — immobilized in concrete — into mobile units.
- 72 portable Stinger anti-aircraft missiles, with 36 spares.
- 32 Bradley infantry combat vehicles.

If the package included F-20s, its total cost would have been about $1.55 billion; with F-16s, the total cost would be about $2 billion. Administration officials said Jordan would need financial help from other Arab countries and the United States to pay for the arms. There were no official estimates of the U.S. share, but Capitol Hill sources said they were told to expect requests for about $1 billion over several years.

In a 14-page statement justifying the sale, the State and Defense Departments said Jordan needed to modernize its armed forces, especially its air defense capability, in the face of a potential threat from Syria. The statement said the Jordanian air force would quickly succumb to an attack by Syria's "overwhelming force of more advanced Soviet fighters."

Administration officials acknowledged that, aside from demonstrating U.S. backing, the sale would do little to help Jordan's armed forces in the immediate future. The first planes would not be delivered until 1988, at the earliest.

Congressional Reaction

Shortly after Reagan announced his proposal, two senators cried foul. Bob Kasten, R-Wis., and Daniel K. Inouye, D-Hawaii, chairman and ranking minority member, respectively, of the Appropriations Subcommittee on Foreign Operations, claimed Secretary of State George P. Shultz had broken his word to them. They said Shultz had promised in June to consult with Senate leaders before a decision was made on the arms sale. Shultz made that offer to help win Senate approval of $250 million in economic aid to Jordan, free of restrictions on arms sales.

In a restrained but firm letter to Shultz on Sept. 27, Inouye noted that in June he had lobbied fellow senators to vote for the aid to Jordan, based on the secretary's pledge of future consultations on arms sales. Now, with those consultations having failed to materialize, Inouye said: "I regret having relied on [the promises] in my discussions with my fellow senators."

Kasten on Sept. 30 wrote Shultz: "Frankly, Mr. Secretary, I believe you have broken your word to us." He added that the State Department's failure to consult signaled "a significant deterioration of relations between you and your department and the Appropriations Committee."

Shultz responded to Kasten's letter by sending Deputy Secretary John C. Whitehead to visit the senator on Oct. 1. A Senate source said Whitehead "apologized" to Kasten, and a senior State Department official said Whitehead "offered an explanation."

At the same time, Hussein visited Washington and tried to convince members of Congress of his sincerity in wanting to negotiate a peace treaty with Israel. But members said Hussein would have to do more to get talks under way before they would approve the sale of arms.

On the Hill, Hussein edged closer to formal recognition of Israel — a key congressional demand of Jordan. Members quoted him as saying that "Jordan recognizes Israel's right to exist."

One staunch friend of Israel on the House Foreign Affairs Committee, Robert G. Torricelli, D-N.J., said Hussein was "unequivocal on Israel's right to exist. He was impressive." Nevertheless, Torricelli said: "We're still dealing with a situation where a state of war exists between the two countries."

Another Foreign Affairs member, Mel Levine, D-Calif., said he found Hussein's statements throughout the U.S. trip disappointing: "While I think there remains good will on his part, there was really nothing new that would be encouraging, that shows that we were making progress."

There was broad agreement in Congress that Hussein still had not met its terms for advanced arms sales to Jordan, as written into the foreign aid bill, prohibiting the president from making a sale unless he certified that Jordan was "publicly committed to the recognition of Israel."

Two weeks later, Prime Minister Peres visited Capitol Hill and delivered his country's view: that Israel saw a security threat from U.S. sales of advanced weapons to any Arab country, including Jordan. Peres met with members of the Foreign Affairs and Foreign Relations committees, and lunched separately with Jewish members of Congress. He also huddled with officials of the American Israel Public Affairs Committee, the major private pro-Israel lobby.

Secretary of State Shultz made the administration's case to the foreign aid committees on Oct. 10 and Oct. 17. But his appeals were received with skepticism by members, who demanded evidence that Hussein was ready to negotiate peace with Israel and not just talk about it.

Senate and House members were rounding up backers for joint resolutions to bar the sale "prior to the commencement of direct bilateral negotiations between Jordan and Israel." That condition was substantially tougher than previous congressional restrictions on Jordan arms sales.

Senate Action

Reagan officially proposed the Jordan arms sale on Oct. 21, and three days later the Senate overwhelmingly rejected it before March 1, 1986 — unless Jordan and Israel had begun "direct and meaningful" peace talks.

The vote on S J Res 228 was 97-1. *(Vote 250, p. 46-S)*

The Senate's action was the sharpest rebuke the Republican-led chamber had administered to Reagan on a major foreign policy issue since June 1984, when it denied funds for anti-government "contras" in Nicaragua.

Told by leading Republicans that the only alternative was outright rejection of the sale, Reagan on Oct. 23 agreed reluctantly to sign the resolution if it reached him unchanged. Seventy-four senators had signed another resolution (S J Res 223) that would have blocked the sale indefinitely unless peace talks were under way.

Backers called the Senate-passed resolution a victory for everyone. Foreign Relations Chairman Lugar said Hussein should be "pleased" because the Senate did not take more drastic action that "would have been adverse to the king, adverse to our president, adverse to the peace process."

But Hussein clearly was not pleased. Shortly before the Senate acted, he said in Amman, Jordan: "One wouldn't like to use the word blackmail, but it's totally unacceptable. Obviously, it's not a way to deal with problems among friends."

Several senators bristled at Hussein's comments. Majority Leader Robert Dole, R-Kan., said: "We're not trying to blackmail anyone."

Reagan officials appeared to accept a congressional rebuke as inevitable. Shultz had told Lugar on Oct. 18 that other matters, especially preparations for Reagan's Nov. 19-20 summit with Soviet leader Mikhail S. Gorbachev, precluded active lobbying on behalf of the Jordan sale. Lugar then set out to negotiate a compromise, and the result was the delay until March 1.

As passed by the Senate, S J Res 228 stated that a contract for the Jordan sale would not be valid prior to March 1, 1986, "unless direct and meaningful peace negotiations between Israel and Jordan are under way."

Under usual procedures, Congress had 30 days to review arms sales. Critics of the Jordan sale said that was not enough time to determine whether there was a realistic chance for the start of Jordan-Israel peace talks.

To meet that objection, the Foreign Relations Committee decided on Oct. 23 to demand at least 120 days. The March 1 date was chosen as an approximation of 120 days after the Oct. 21 notice to Congress.

The resolution's call for "direct and meaningful" negotiations was crafted to set a high standard. Lugar said senators who advocated that term "wanted to make sure that it did not mean a chance meeting or a casual meeting on procedures."

Christopher J. Dodd, D-Conn., cast the sole vote against the resolution. Lugar had denied his request for an amendment mandating quick Senate action on any future resolution blocking the sale.

House Action

Facing a lack of practical alternatives, the House Foreign Affairs Committee on Nov. 7 approved the Senate's compromise legislation (S J Res 228) delaying the Jordan arms sale.

On Nov. 12, after little debate, the full House approved the resolution, clearing it for the president.

The resolution barred Reagan from selling Jordan advanced warplanes, missiles and other equipment before March 1, 1986, unless Jordan and Israel had begun "direct and meaningful" peace negotiations.

The Foreign Affairs panel had approved the measure by voice vote, even though a majority of its members, and more than 280 House members, had supported a much tougher House measure (H J Res 428) that would have blocked the sale indefinitely.

But the panel settled for the Senate resolution, with no changes, because it was the only legislation with a chance of being enacted into law by Nov. 20, when a 30-day period for congressional review of the sale was to expire. If Congress had not acted by then, Reagan would have been free to carry out the sale. Administration officials warned that Reagan might go ahead with the sale, if he had the choice, to assert his executive authority.

Senate Foreign Relations Chairman Lugar told the House members that if anything stronger than S J Res 228 had reached the Senate, it likely would have been filibustered past Nov. 20. And White House officials said Reagan would sign the Senate measure only in its original version. Reagan had agreed to the Senate resolution as a way of averting outright defeat on the issue.

Foreign Affairs members said the Senate resolution was the best available course for another reason: It postponed a decision on the arms sale at a potentially critical moment in the Middle East peace process.

Reagan had said the arms sale was a sign of U.S. support for Jordan's efforts for peace. Hussein and Israeli Prime Minister Shimon Peres had edged closer to talks than ever before.

While committee members rejected Reagan's arms-before-peace argument, they were leery of taking any action that could antagonize Hussein and give him a reason to shy away from the peace table.

Committee members also were concerned because they were legislating in uncharted territory and because any action on Jordan could set a precedent for future congressional consideration of arms sales.

Those concerns arose because of a 1983 Supreme Court decision overturning Congress' right to veto an arms sale unilaterally. Congress thus could block a sale only by passing a bill or a joint resolution — either of which would be subject to presidential veto. The ruling had a side effect of wiping out a process requiring rapid congressional action on legislation to block an arms sale. *(1983 Almanac p. 565)*

Committee members were looking for a way to approve the Senate resolution and to preserve their option of acting against the Jordan sale in 1986 if peace talks failed to materialize. They wanted the latter option because the Senate resolution, in effect, approved the sale as of March 1. The committee found a two-part solution:

- Foreign Affairs Chairman Dante B. Fascell, D-Fla., asked for and got a letter from Lugar pledging action by Foreign Relations on legislation to block the sale if peace talks were not under way by early 1986. Lugar also assured Fascell, "I would oppose parliamentary maneuvering that would allow the sale to go forward [after March 1] against the wishes of the majority of the Senate."
- Fascell decided to move quickly on separate legislation that would mandate rapid action on future joint resolutions to block an arms sale. A bill to do that, introduced by Alan Cranston, D-Calif., and nine others, was passed by the Senate Dec. 19 and the House on Feb. 3, 1986. Reagan signed it Feb. 12 (PL 99-247). It would thwart a possible Senate filibuster against legislation to veto the Jordan sale.

Subsequently, acting on the continuing resolution, Congress established a procedure for a guaranteed reconsideration of the issue early in 1986. An amendment offered by Dodd in the Senate and included in the continuing resolution was to take effect Feb. 1, 1986; it would force Senate floor action as early as 10 days after any legislation was introduced to prohibit Reagan from carrying out the Jordan arms sale.

Economic Aid Flap

Earlier in the year, the administration won congressional approval of $250 million in economic aid for Jordan, but not without controversy.

Many on Capitol Hill were skeptical about whether the money was necessary and was the appropriate reward for Hussein's peacemaking efforts.

Reagan requested the money on June 13. The Senate on June 20 added the aid to the omnibus fiscal 1985 supplemental appropriations bill (HR 2577) and it survived in the final measure (PL 99-88).

However, the Senate tied strings to the aid as a sign of its displeasure with Jordan's past reluctance to negotiate with Israel. The Senate also said it would consider an arms sales request for Jordan only when those negotiations were under way. *(Supplemental, p. 350)*

Secretary of State Shultz had told the Senate Foreign Relations Committee on June 19 that Jordan was "a small but vital country" in need of help from the United States.

Reagan had wanted the aid for the last four months of fiscal 1985 and all of fiscal 1986. The Senate required him to spread the aid over three fiscal years: 1985-86-87.

In a provision drafted by the Foreign Relations Committee, the Senate also rejected Reagan's request for $100 million of the aid to be a cash grant for general support of the Jordanian economy. Instead, the Senate said $160 million would have to be spent for specific projects, such as water and agricultural development, with the remaining $90 million available to finance imports of raw goods from the United States.

The committee took its action on a 14-2 vote on June 20, with Jesse Helms, R-N.C., and Edward Zorinsky, D-Neb., dissenting.

Joseph R. Biden Jr., D-Del, said Foreign Relations had vetoed the cash transfer because there were no strings attached. "How do we know if it would go to the Soviets to pay off weapons?" he asked. ▮

Intelligence Authorization

Congress Nov. 21 cleared the fiscal 1986 authorization bill for the CIA and other intelligence agencies. Nearly all the major funding items in the bill were classified secret, as in previous years. However, sources said the bill authorized at least $10 billion for the intelligence agencies, which included the Defense Intelligence Agency, National Security Agency and others. Less than $2 billion of the total was for the CIA.

The House Nov. 19 approved the conference report on the bill (HR 2419 — H Rept 99-373) by a 387-21 vote. The Senate adopted the conference report by voice vote Nov. 21. *(Vote 376, p. 118-H)*

President Reagan signed the bill (PL 99-169) Dec. 4.

A key provision of the bill eased some, but not all, of the conditions Congress earlier in 1985 had placed on resumed U.S. aid to the insurgents, called "contras," battling the leftist government of Nicaragua. Under the terms of HR 2419, previously approved congressional definitions of "humanitarian" aid for the rebels were broadened to include radios, trucks and other gear. Congress had voted $27 million for the Nicaraguan rebels in July, but the bill expressly had prohibited expenditures for military items. *(Story, p. 61)*

House members said the bill made major cuts from Reagan's budget, which had called for increases in nearly all areas of intelligence agency spending. Congress had boosted the intelligence budgets every year since 1978. And while spending was slated to rise again in fiscal 1986, the intelligence agencies would be forced to live under a "regime of fiscal restraint" along with all other government agencies, said House Intelligence Committee Chairman Lee H. Hamilton, D-Ind.

Provisions

In provisions that were made public, conferees on the fiscal 1986 intelligence bill:

- Accepted an administration request to enlarge the definition of humanitarian aid to contras to include radios and transportation equipment.
- Barred the CIA from using its contingency fund to resume "covert" military aid to the rebels.
- Permitted the State Department to solicit other sources, incuding other countries, for humanitarian aid to the contras. The only restrictions were that any aid provided by another country as a result of U.S. solicitations had to come from its own resources, and that the United States could not condition its foreign aid on another country's willingness to back the rebels.
- Authorized $50.6 million for the FBI's domestic and international counter-terrorism programs, including $500,000 to reimburse state and local law enforcement agencies for their cooperation. The House had voted $15.2 million to fight terrorism within the United States, with an unspecified amount for those efforts overseas. The Senate had voted $59 million for both domestic and foreign programs, on a floor amendment sponsored by Lloyd Bentsen, D-Texas.
- Authorized $75 million over three years for design and construction of a new research and engineering building for the National Security Agency, monitor of electronic communications around the world. The authorization for the agency, headquartered at Fort Meade, Md., was $21.4 million in fiscal 1986, with the rest for fiscal 1987-88.
- Authorized $22.1 million for operations of the 233-member intelligence community staff, which served the CIA director in his role as coordinator of all the intelligence agencies. That was an increase of $1.1 million and 26 employees over fiscal 1985.
- Authorized $101.4 million for the CIA's retirement and disability system.
- Required the president to report to Congress within 120 days after enactment of the bill on U.S. counter-intelligence capabilities and policies, along with recommendations for improvements. Also required an interim report within 60 days to help the Senate Intelligence Committee prepare its own report to the Senate on that subject. Counter-intelligence was the term for operations designed to combat espionage by countries hostile to the United States. Among other things, it included FBI monitoring of Soviet agents stationed in the United States.
- Authorized Defense Department, Office of Personnel Management and CIA access to state and local criminal history records for information used in determining

Casey-Senate Panel Feud

A long-simmering feud between CIA Director William J. Casey and some members of the Senate Intelligence Committee broke into the open Nov. 13 when Committee Chairman Dave Durenberger, R-Minn., publicly expressed disappointment with the CIA's handling of several issues. Durenberger said the agency lacked a "sense of direction" and failed to understand the Soviet Union. He added, however, that he retained confidence in Casey as "a darn good guy in that job."

The remarks, featured the next day in an article in *The Washington Post,* prompted an extraordinarily tough response from Casey. In a letter dated Nov. 14, which the CIA made public, Casey wrote: "When congressional oversight of the intelligence community is conducted off-the-cuff through the news media and involves the repeated compromise of sensitive intelligence sources and methods, not to mention unsubstantiated appraisals of performance, it is time to acknowledge that the process has gone seriously awry."

Casey accused Durenberger of praising the CIA in private while attacking it in public and of failing to read intelligence studies the agency had provided to the committee.

Durenberger responded that he supported Casey and the intelligence agencies "both privately and publicly." Committee Vice Chairman Patrick J. Leahy, D-Vt., said Casey was trying to undermine congressional review of the CIA.

Durenberger was the second GOP chairman of the Senate panel to cross swords with Casey. In February 1984, Casey and then-chairman Barry Goldwater, R-Ariz., battled over the CIA's failure to notify the committee of its role in the mining of Nicaraguan harbors. *(1984 Almanac p. 88)*

whether federal employees and contractors should have access to classified information or should be assigned to sensitive national security duties. Most states and localities already provided such access. Conferees said juvenile records, investigatory files or records that had been sealed by law or court action were exempt from the requirement.

- Required the president to notify Congress whenever an intelligence agency gave weapons or other military items valued at $1 million or more to a foreign government, group or individual. This would not apply if the arms transfer was authorized under the foreign aid laws or was not connected to an intelligence activity.
- Put into permanent law a series of provisions aimed at ensuring that the intelligence agencies spent money only on activities approved by Congress, and that they notified Congress at least 15 days in advance whenever they shifted money between accounts.
- Established special procedures for granting U.S. citizenship to as many as five foreigners per year who had made an "extraordinary contribution" to U.S. national security or intelligence programs. Applicants for the special citizenship had to reside in the United States for at least a year.
- Allowed the Defense Department, on a one-year experimental basis, to spend profits it made on counterintelligence operations. In the past the Pentagon was required to turn profits over to the U.S. Treasury.
- Authorized special retirement credits for CIA personnel stationed in "unhealthful" posts overseas. State Department personnel already received these credits, which allow earlier-than-normal retirement.

House Action

The House Intelligence Committee reported HR 2419 (H Rept 99-106, Part I) May 15. The action marked the first time in three years that the panel voted to allow the CIA to provide information and advice to the anti-government rebels in Nicaragua. But the committee remained opposed to outright U.S. aid for the contras.

Most of the amounts approved by the committee were placed in the portion of the bill classified secret.

The only amounts publicly revealed by the committee were $21.9 million for the Intelligence Community Staff and $101.4 million for the 1986 contribution to the CIA's retirement and disability system.

Some members of the committee had expressed concern that, under the Reagan administration, the intelligence agencies were pouring millions of dollars into sophisticated data collection techniques, such as spy satellites, and were not doing enough to improve the analysis of the information they collected. The committee made an oblique reference to that concern in its report, saying that it "finds certain shortcomings in the management and conduct of certain of the nation's intelligence activities."

Covert Arms Transfers

In a change of law with potential significance for future covert actions, such as the CIA's early support for the contras, the committee demanded that Congress be notified any time the agency transferred $1 million or more in weapons or defense services to a foreign government or group.

That was aimed at closing a major legal loophole that had enabled the administration to avoid notifying Congress of overseas arms shipments connected to ongoing intelligence operations. The committee bill closed the loophole by defining foreign arms transfers of $1 million or more by an intelligence agency as a "significant anticipated intelligence activity" — and therefore subject to a notification to Congress.

Also in the public portion of the bill, the panel voted to put into permanent law several provisions from previous annual authorizations that were aimed at keeping Congress informed about intelligence operations. Major oversight provisions included:

- A requirement that all intelligence and intelligence-related activities be authorized by Congress, either explicitly through the annual intelligence authorization bill or implicitly through congressional approval of the administration's annual budgets.
- A requirement that any shifting of funds by the administration after Congress had authorized the intelligence budget be for higher priority programs, be for unforeseen requirements, and be reported to Congress.
- A prohibition against spending funds for intelligence activities that were specifically denied by Congress.

The bill was reported May 23 (H Rept 99-106, Part II) by the House Armed Services Committee, which shared jurisdiction with the Intelligence Committee and reviewed spending for most intelligence programs.

House Floor

With little debate, the House July 18 passed HR 2419.

Before approving the bill by voice vote, the House adopted, also by voice vote, two Intelligence Committee-sponsored amendments. They:

- Barred fiscal 1986 appropriations for any intelligence agency at a level higher than that authorized by Congress. If Congress failed to enact an intelligence authorizations bill for 1986, the appropriations level for each agency would be limited to the 1985 authorization.
- Reduced by $900,000 the amount in the bill for the staff that helped the director of central intelligence coordinate the various intelligence agencies. The new amount was $21 million.

Senate Action

The Senate Intelligence Committee reported its version of the bill June 11 (S 1271 — S Rept 99-79).

In the part of the bill dealing with the Nicaraguan rebels, the committee allowed the CIA to collect intelligence in Nicaragua and to share that information with the contras. Under existing law that barred U.S. aid for paramilitary operations in Nicaragua, the CIA could not provide the contras with intelligence data.

Parts of the bill were sequentially referred to the Foreign Relations, Armed Services, Judiciary and Governmental Affairs panels, which shared jurisdiction. The Judiciary and Foreign Relations panels were discharged Sept. 11. The bill was reported jointly from Governmental Affairs and Armed Services (S Rept 99-136) on Sept. 11.

In its report, the Intelligence Committee gave no hint of how it dealt with the president's specific requests for intelligence programs. As in the past, virtually all of the multi-billion-dollar budget for the intelligence agencies was put in a secret appendix of the authorizations bill.

However, a source said the panel made few significant cuts from the president's request, and the report justified spending increases by saying that "the enhancement of U.S. intelligence capabilities must remain among the nation's highest priorities." The report also said the budget continued "major investments" in improving such areas as technical and human collection of intelligence, analysis of intelligence information, counter-intelligence and counter-terrorism.

Soviet Spies

The Senate panel adopted two amendments aimed at reducing U.S. vulnerability to Soviet spying.

One, sponsored by William V. Roth Jr., R-Del., required the State Department to impose restrictions on travel and other activities by Russians assigned to temporary duty at the United Nations.

The Senate June 10 attached a broader version of the Roth amendment to the State Department authorization. That version applied to all Soviet and Soviet bloc U.N. employees, on temporary or permanent assignment. *(Story, p. 108)*

Another anti-spying amendment, attached to both the intelligence and State Department bills, stated as U.S. policy that the number of Russian diplomats in the United States could not exceed the number of U.S. diplomats in the Soviet Union.

The committee noted that Congress in 1984 urged the administration to reduce the number of Russian diplomats in the United States. But the administration had not responded, the panel said, so Congress should put the requirement in law.

Other Provisions

Other amendments in the public portion of the intelligence bill:

- Exempted foreigners who had made "extraordinary" contributions to U.S. intelligence efforts from three requirements to obtain U.S. citizenship: the minimum period for residency in the United States; a 10-year waiting period for individuals who had belonged to communist parties or other communist-dominated organizations; and a stipulation that anyone seeking citizenship must file a naturalization petition in the federal district court that had jurisdiction over his local residence.
- Authorized $21.4 million in fiscal 1986 for the first phase of construction on a new research and engineering facility for the National Security Agency headquarters.
- Allowed counter-intelligence units of the Defense Department to spend money they received through "double agents" — U.S. intelligence agents who pretended they were providing secret information to the Soviet Union. The committee cited the case of an Army sergeant who had received nearly $25,000 from the Soviet Union during a 10-year period while, in fact, he was loyal to the United States and was turning the money over to the Army. Under current law, the Army was required to hand the money over to the U.S. Treasury.

Senate Floor

The Senate Sept. 26 passed its version of HR 2419 by voice vote.

Before passing the bill, the Senate approved Bentsen's amendment increasing to $59.5 million, from $40 million, the amount for the FBI's counter-terrorism program. The increase would have allowed the FBI to hire more agents and buy more equipment to combat potential terrorist attacks in the United States. ■

Genocide Treaty

Senate conservatives in 1985 again thwarted action on the genocide treaty, the 1949 accord that declared genocide an international crime. But on Feb. 19, 1986, the Senate overcame that opposition and approved the treaty, 83-11.

Jesse Helms, R-N.C., leading Senate foe of the treaty, on Dec. 5 blocked 1985 action on it by objecting to a unanimous consent request for the Senate to consider it on Dec. 10.

Helms and several other conservatives had blocked approval of the treaty (Exec O, 81st Cong, 1st Sess) under similar circumstances in late 1984. Then, the Senate passed a resolution promising to act "expeditiously" on the treaty in 1985. *(1984 Almanac p. 123)*

The treaty, the Convention on the Prevention and Punishment of the Crime of Genocide, was first submitted to the Senate in 1949 by President Truman. Every president since had asked for its approval.

The unanimous consent request to which Helms objected would have given him an enormous parliamentary advantage over the treaty's proponents. Among other things, the request made by Majority Leader Robert Dole, R-Kan., would have allowed only 41 primary amendments to the treaty, all to be sponsored by Helms and 11 other conservatives who opposed it.

Helms' action on the treaty reversed his stand taken earlier in 1985. On May 21, Helms joined nine other members of the Senate Foreign Relations Committee in voting to approve the treaty (Exec Rept 99-2). That vote came after the panel adopted several reservations that Helms and Chairman Richard G. Lugar, R-Ind., had proposed.

At that time, Helms reportedly told fellow committee members that he would support the treaty when it reached the Senate floor if the reservations remained attached to it.

The reservations, Helms said, were necessary to protect the United States against misuse of the treaty by communist countries.

The reservations, however, angered many treaty supporters who said those measures were unnecessary and possibly damaging to the treaty itself. They promised to move to delete or modify the two most controversial qualifiers when the Senate considered the treaty.

Of the eight qualifiers approved, four were non-controversial provisions the committee had approved in past years. The other four were drafted in the spring of 1985 by Helms and Lugar and approved by the committee May 21 on a 9-8 vote.

Disputed Reservations

Two of the four new provisions, legally referred to as reservations, had sparked sharp controversy among treaty supporters and opponents. A reservation would not have amended the treaty itself, but its adoption by the United States would have had to be acknowledged by all other countries that had ratified the treaty.

Most of the controversy surrounded a reservation giving the United States the right to exempt itself from jurisdiction over genocide cases by the World Court, formally known as the International Court of Justice.

The administration, which in 1984 opposed such a reservation, reversed course in 1985 and supported it. The apparent reason was the World Court's assertion of jurisdiction in a suit filed by Nicaragua against the United States because of the CIA's mining of Nicaraguan harbors. In that case, Washington refused to recognize the court's jurisdiction. *(Nicaragua, p. 61)*

In its report, the committee said the reservation would enable the United States to protect itself if World Court jurisdiction in a genocide treaty case was "contrary to the national interest." As an example, the committee said the United States could withdraw from any case "brought solely for the propaganda value that might result."

But in a dissent, the eight committee opponents of the reservation said its adoption would undermine the United States' ability to take another country to the World Court on a genocide charge. Under the legal doctrine of "reciprocity," if the United States were to charge another country with genocide, that country could avoid the court's jurisdiction by noting that the United States had protected itself from the court.

The dissenters also noted that communist countries predominated among the 19 nations that had exempted themselves from World Court jurisdiction. The United States, the eight dissenters said, should not be "defensively embracing a shield that to date has largely been adopted only by countries that may well have reason to fear charges of genocide."

The other controversial reservation stated that nothing in the treaty required the United States to take any action that might be prohibited by the U.S. Constitution.

The committee majority said the purpose of that reservation was to "avoid placing the United States in a position of having to choose between its obligations under the Constitution and those under the convention [treaty]."

Opponents said that reservation was unnecessary because the genocide treaty did not conflict with the Constitution. And William Proxmire, D-Wis., the Senate's major booster of the treaty, said the reservation would set a damaging precedent. The Soviet Union, he said, could ward off legal action brought under the treaty by declaring that its constitution was paramount.

Helms' Opposition

As the year progressed, Senate sources said, Helms came under pressure from conservative groups that opposed the treaty as a threat to the U.S. Constitution.

On Nov. 21, Helms told a conservative audience in Washington, D.C., that Dole "may as well forget about it [the treaty] because if he doesn't forget about it, he's got a filibuster on his hands." Helms later told the Raleigh, N.C., *News and Observer* that he was "totally opposed" to the treaty and did not remember voting for it in committee.

In blocking the treaty, Helms said "many, many Jewish citizens" had told him that they opposed it because "Israel will most likely be the first victim of it." Helms did not elaborate, but some treaty critics had said Palestinians might accuse Israel of committing genocide against them.

Israel was one of the first countries to ratify the treaty, and leading Jewish groups in the United States long had lobbied for approval of it. Helms' comments brought a sharp retort from Sen. Howard M. Metzenbaum, D-Ohio, who said the "American Jewish community" favored the treaty. ∎

Micronesia Compact

The Compact of Free Association with Micronesia, a measure to bestow limited autonomy on the sole remaining U.S. trust territory in the Pacific, cleared Congress Dec. 13.

By voice vote Dec. 11, the House approved the compact (H J Res 187 — PL 99-239), which provided about $2.4 billion over 15 years in aid and tax and trade benefits in return for exclusive and permanent U.S. military rights to the island region. The Senate followed suit two days later.

President Reagan signed PL 99-239 Jan. 14, 1986. Before the compact could go into effect, it had to win United Nations approval, which was expected in March 1986.

Congress' action came after an Oct. 1 deadline to approve the compact; that was the expiration date for the U.S. lease on the Kwajalein missile range in the Marshall Islands. Kwajalein was the Pentagon's single most important facility for testing the MX missile and parts of the administration's proposed anti-missile defense program. As a result of the delay in Congress, some missile tests at Kwajalein were delayed. *(MX, p. 119; anti-missile defense, p. 162)*

Of larger significance was the islands' strategic importance in the region. Pentagon officials wanted to maintain good U.S.-Micronesia relations in light of a growing communist insurgency in the Philippines, the site of two huge U.S. military bases serving the Pacific. *(Philippines, p. 113)*

Approval of H J Res 187 came after an internal policy

dispute over the measure that had led some members of Congress to describe the administration as being "at war with itself." The Pentagon had backed the compact because of the military rights and the renewal of the lease on the Kwajalein range.

But the Treasury Department had opposed the economic aid provisions as too expensive and harmful to U.S. trade. Disputes also centered on how the compact was to be administered and which federal aid programs would be continued. Congress mandated that the Interior Department would administer the bill; the White House had preferred the State Department.

The House passed a version of the compact July 25, after voting sharp reductions in the tax and trade benefits for the islands. The Senate approved a similar version Nov. 14, after making more tax and trade changes.

Provisions

As cleared, H J Res 187:

- Granted sovereign status as "freely associated states" (FAS) to the Federated States of Micronesia and the Marshall Islands, with self-government under their own constitutions and authority to conduct their own foreign policy in consultation with the United States.
- Committed the United States to defend the FAS for at least 15 years.
- Required the United States to provide $2.39 billion in aid, primarily economic assistance, to the FAS over the 15 years.
- Gave the United States a 30-year lease on the Kwajalein missile range.
- Granted the United States the right in perpetuity to deny other nations a military presence in the region.
- Established a $150 million trust fund to settle all claims against the United States resulting from nuclear weapons tests in the region in the 1940s and '50s. About $5 billion worth of lawsuits were pending, filed by 1,525 islanders whose health or property was damaged by the radiation. The fund would generate an estimated $18 million in interest annually, for a $270 million total over 15 years.
- Permitted citizens of the Marshall Islands and the Federated States of Micronesia to live and work in the United States. The Immigration and Naturalization Service was directed to deny entry to individuals who became naturalized Micronesians in order to move to the United States.
- Allowed Micronesia to receive economic aid from other nations and international organizations.
- Provided duty-free treatment for goods from Micronesia, except watches, clocks, certain timing devices, buttons, textile and apparel articles, footwear, handbags, luggage, work gloves and leather apparel.
- Exempted from tariff Micronesian canned, water-packed tuna, up to 10 percent of total U.S. consumption, or about 80 million pounds a year. Tuna was the region's chief export.
- Established a $30 million aid package to compensate for other tax and trade benefits cut by Congress.
- Included the government of Palau on a contingency basis, to expedite congressional approval if Palau's residents endorsed the compact.

Background

Largely undeveloped, Micronesia encompassed about 130,000 residents and 2,000 islands spread over three million square miles. The nearest islands were about 2,000 miles from Hawaii. The territory consisted of four governments: Northern Mariana Islands, the Federated States of Micronesia, the Marshall Islands and Palau.

During World War II, Micronesia was the site of bloody "island hopping" campaigns against the Japanese in which thousands of Americans died. And it was from a U.S. air base at Tinian that two B-29s took off for atomic bombing runs against Hiroshima and Nagasaki in 1945.

In 1947, the United States became the administrator of the Micronesian islands under a trusteeship arranged by the United Nations. Bikini and Enewetok atolls subsequently were used by the Pentagon as nuclear target ranges.

In 1970, the United States began talks to end its trusteeship of Micronesia, the last of 11 U.S. trust territories in the Pacific. A 1976 accord granted commonwealth status to the Northern Mariana Islands. *(PL 94-241, 1976 Almanac p. 264)*

In 1982-83, the United States agreed, after negotiations with each of the other three units, to set up a new relationship that was detailed in the Compact of Free Association.

The compact was approved by the voters of all three units, but the 67 percent majority it received in Palau did not reach the 75 percent approval needed to override the Palau Constitution's prohibition on the storage or testing of nuclear weapons.

House Action

The House July 25 approved the Compact of Free Association by a vote of 360-12. *(Vote 237, p. 76-H)*

Six House panels reviewed the legislation. It was reported from the House Foreign Affairs Committee July 1 (H Rept 99-188, Part I), from the Interior and Insular Affairs Committee July 15 (Part II) and from the Merchant Marine and Fisheries Committee July 19 (Part III). The bill was discharged from the House Judiciary and Armed Services committees July 19. The House Ways and Means Committee, the only panel among the six that had major objections to the compact, reported its version of the bill (Part IV) July 22.

The House, after about two hours of debate, adopted an amendment by that panel's chairman, Dan Rostenkowski, D-Ill., tightening tax and trade provisions.

Tax Controversy

Rostenkowski and his supporters, including Bill Frenzel, R-Minn., argued the initial version of the compact gave the FAS unduly generous benefits. Rostenkowski's amendment removed a provision giving FAS citizens exemptions from certain U.S. taxes and instead applied existing rules, which permitted the United States to tax any U.S.-source passive income and to impose a transfer tax on worldwide assets of U.S. citizens who moved to the islands.

The amendment also removed a provision that exempted FAS residents (defined as an individual who lived in the islands at least 183 days in a year) from U.S. taxes on income taxed by the FAS. Rostenkowski argued this would create a generous tax haven.

Rostenkowski deleted liberal investment incentives for the FAS, substituting basically the same tax incentives available to U.S. territories. The FAS would have been entitled to extra aid if U.S. tax and tariff laws changed.

Provisions granting duty-free status to FAS products

were replaced by trade-privilege language that combined elements of the 1983 Caribbean Basin Initiative that offered aid to Central American and Caribbean nations and the duty-free treatment accorded certain imports from developing nations under the Generalized System of Preferences (GSP). *(Caribbean Basin, 1983 Almanac p. 252; GSP, 1984 Almanac p. 171)*

House Provisions

As approved by the House, the compact also would:

- Place a tariff on all Micronesian tuna.
- Set up a $150 million trust fund to settle all claims against the United States resulting from U.S. nuclear weapons tests.
- Require the United States to provide $2.4 billion in aid, primarily economic assistance, to the FAS over the 15 years.
- Allow the FAS to receive aid from other nations and international organizations.
- Permit FAS citizens to live and work in the United States, but directed the Immigration and Naturalization Service to deny entry to individuals who became naturalized FAS citizens for the purpose of moving to this country.

Senate Action

The Senate version of the compact (S J Res 77) was reported by the Energy and Natural Resources Committee (S Rept 99-16) on March 22 and by the Finance Committee July 29. The Finance panel did not issue a written report on the measure.

Senate floor consideration was stalled for several weeks after senators threatened to offer unrelated trade amendments to the resolution.

In an effort to meet the Sept. 30 deadline, House sponsors of the measure tried Sept. 19 and 20 to pass what they called a "pre-conferenced" compromise bill (H J Res 392) that had been developed by House, Senate and administration representatives. But Rep. Robert S. Walker, R-Pa., acting on objections from the White House Office of Management and Budget, blocked consideration of the measure.

When the resolution reached the Senate floor Oct. 2 it was derailed by a trade amendment offered by South Carolinians Strom Thurmond, R, and Ernest F. Hollings, D, to limit textile and shoe imports. After Thurmond and Hollings defeated an effort to table (kill) their amendment, by a 42-53 vote, the bill was pulled off the floor by Majority Leader Robert Dole, R-Kan. *(Vote 201, p. 39-S; trade story, p. 255)*

Floor Approval

The deadlock was broken Nov. 14, and the Senate approved H J Res 187 by voice vote after amending it to conform to the text of S J Res 77.

During its debate, the Senate accepted amendments modifying the compact's tax and trade provisions. While the House amendments generally followed the guidelines of the GSP, which restricted some imports, Finance Committee Chairman Bob Packwood, R-Ore., offered an amendment, agreed to by voice vote, that produced a "blend" of provisions under GSP and other, more liberal trade pacts.

Packwood's amendment provided duty-free treatment for goods from Micronesia, except watches, clocks, certain timing devices, buttons, textile and apparel articles, footwear, handbags, luggage, work gloves and leather apparel — all items more likely to come from Asia. Most significantly, it allowed duty-free treatment of tuna.

Packwood's amendment was estimated to save the United States — and cost the Micronesians — as much as $135 million in benefits.

The Senate also added an amendment by James A. McClure, R-Idaho, Energy and Natural Resources chairman, expanding Micronesia's eligibility for federal aid programs, and creating a $30 million development loan fund for each government in the compact. It also set up a procedure to make sure the governments received an equivalent amount of U.S. financial aid if any benefits originally negotiated were later reduced by Congress.

The Senate debated an amendment by David L. Boren, D-Okla., that would have made major changes in federal campaign finance laws.

Late on Nov. 14, however, Boren agreed to withdraw his proposal with the understanding it would be debated by the Senate at a later date.

Nuclear Tests, Oil Imports

Two controversial amendments to the compact were rejected:

- By 53-42, the Senate voted to table (kill) an amendment by Orrin G. Hatch, R-Utah, to create a $150 million trust fund to compensate American victims of nuclear tests. *(Vote 315, p. 54-S)*
- By 78-18, the Senate voted to table an amendment by Gary Hart, D-Colo., to impose a $10-a-barrel fee on imported oil. *(Vote 316, p. 54-S)*

Hatch's amendment was designed to parallel the compact's provisions providing compensation to islanders harmed by nuclear tests by offering similar aid to residents of Nevada, Utah and Arizona exposed to large doses of radiation from nuclear bomb tests at the Nevada Test Site between 1951 and 1962. Opponents argued that it would upset federal rulings on the issue. And the president, in a letter, threatened to veto the measure if Hatch's amendment was adopted.

Final Action

The measure then returned to the House. When it took up the compact again Dec. 11, the House amended it with a substitute text that incorporated numerous changes agreed to by the administration; the Senate accepted the changes Dec. 13. Among them were:

- Adoption of the less-restrictive Senate provisions on taxes and trade. The differences between the two bills' treatment of tuna exports was resolved by exempting from taxes Micronesian tuna up to 10 percent of total U.S. consumption, or about 80 million pounds a year.
- Inclusion of a $30 million aid package to compensate for other tax and trade benefits cut by Congress.
- Inclusion of the government of Palau on a contingency basis, to expedite congressional approval if Palau's residents endorsed the compact. ▮

Export-Import Bank

Efforts by the Reagan administration to terminate the direct loan program of the Export-Import (Ex-Im) Bank found little congressional support in 1985. However, by the end of the year Congress had voted to cut the program's funding sharply from its previous level.

Helsinki Commission

Congress in 1985 passed legislation (S 592 — PL 99-7)) revising the membership and chairmanship of the Helsinki Commission, thus putting to an end a two-year dispute between Senate Majority Leader Robert Dole, R-Kan., and House Foreign Affairs Committee Chairman Dante B. Fascell, D-Fla.

The Senate passed the bill by voice vote March 6; the House followed suit on March 19. President Reagan signed the measure into law March 27.

The next day, Sen. Alfonse M. D'Amato, R-N.Y., was named the new chairman of the commission.

The commission, formally called the Commission on Security and Cooperation in Europe, monitored the 1975 Helsinki accords on human rights and other issues.

Fascell had been chairman of the commission since its inception in 1976; Dole, until he became majority leader in 1985, had wanted the chairmanship for himself, or at least for a member of the Senate.

The two men settled the issue early in the year by agreeing to rotate the chairmanship between the two chambers. Starting in 1985, a senator was chairman; a House member was expected to take over in 1987, the beginning of the 100th Congress. A House member was to be co-chairman when a senator was chairman, and vice versa.

The bill also added four members of Congress to the commission, bringing its membership to 21: nine senators, nine House members and three executive branch representatives.

It also resolved a dispute between Dole and Fascell over the staffing of the commission by allowing the chairman and co-chairman each to designate five staff members.

The Ex-Im direct loan program made long-term low-interest loans to induce foreigners to buy costly U.S. exports, such as Boeing aircraft. The program was funded at $3.8 billion in fiscal 1985.

In its fiscal 1986 budget, the administration proposed to eliminate the existing program and replace it with a new program to encourage U.S. exporters to use private banks to arrange loans for foreign buyers of their goods. To give incentives to private banks, the administration proposed boosting federal loan guarantees and insurance and creation of a new subsidy pool to lower commercial interest rates on export loans.

The administration's plan would have radically restructured the bank. The change was needed, officials said, to get the federal government out of the business of subsidizing businesses and save the Treasury money in a time of budgetary constraints.

The administration plan would :

- Eliminate the $3.8 billion direct loan program.
- Earmark $1.8 billion for financing at fixed rates.
- Boost loan guarantees and insurance by $2 billion, to $12 billion.
- Establish a subsidy pool to lower interest rates on commercial loans to finance U.S. exports.
- Charge borrowers a new fee for the proposed subsidy.
- Tap an existing private banking consortium, called the Private Export Funding Corp., for funds. The purpose was to make certain that commercial export loans would be available.

Opposition on Capitol Hill

The proposal immediately met strong opposition on Capitol Hill, however. The existing Ex-Im loan program had strong lobbying support from a number of major corporations, who argued that it was a vital tool in helping U.S. businesses survive against foreign competition. "If this isn't unilateral surrender to Japanese trading companies and others, what is?" asked Sen. John Heinz, R-Pa.

A key battle in the fight over the Reagan proposal came in the Senate Budget Committee. Initially, the committee voted to go along with the administration and kill the direct-loan program. Under pressure from business supporters of the current program, however, the committee reversed itself on March 14 and decided to retain the existing program at reduced funding of $1.25 billion.

The panel's stand was subsequently changed again on the Senate floor, leaving the Senate-backed version of the fiscal 1986 budget resolution (S Con Res 32) calling for a modified version of the administration's interest subsidy program, with $175 million set aside for subsidies supporting up to $3 billion in loans.

But House opposition to the administration proposal was overwhelming. The Banking Committee in May approved a bill (HR 1787 — H Rept 99-89) barring implementation of the plan. And the budget resolution approved by the House called for $2.8 billion for the existing program.

In conference, House-Senate budget negotiators eventually agreed (H Rept 99-249) to $1.8 billion for the existing direct loan program. *(Budget resolution, p. 441)*

Another problem for backers of the existing program arose in the House Appropriations Committee, however. Working under strict budgetary limits and engaged in a struggle with Reagan over levels of foreign military assistance, the Democratic majority on the Foreign Operations Subcommittee voted July 16 to provide $784 million for the loan program — a quarter of its 1985 level.

Final settlement of the funding issue came when Congress in December cleared the final fiscal 1986 continuing resolution (H J Res 465 — PL 99-190). The resolution provided $1.1 billion for the direct loan program. *(Foreign aid appropriations, p. 367)* ∎

Sub-Saharan Africa Aid

After resolving disputes that held up final action for a month past the schedule requested by the Reagan administration, Congress on April 2 cleared a bill (HR 1239 — PL 99-10) appropriating a total of $784 million for emergency African relief.

The money, which included both food and non-food aid, was in response to continuing famine caused by drought and civil strife in Ethiopia, the Sudan and some 20 other countries in sub-Saharan Africa. *(1984 Almanac p. 121)*

Congress March 21 had cleared a separate bill (S 689 — PL 99-8) authorizing $175 million for non-food aid to Africa. The other funds contained in HR 1239, for food assistance, did not require an authorization bill in 1985.

Although HR 1239 had more than three times as much money as he had requested, President Reagan signed the bill April 4. Reagan on Jan. 3 had asked Congress to appropriate $235 million for Africa by early March.

There were two main reasons for the funding delay, which occurred despite broad bipartisan support for the idea that the United States should supply half of Africa's emergency food needs. One obstacle was a dispute between the administration and some members of Congress over how much food would be needed to meet that goal. The administration was consistently more optimistic than its critics in estimating food supplies in Africa, and consequently favored a lower funding level for food assistance.

Another problem was that the authorization bill for non-food aid got entangled with an unrelated controversy over emergency credit assistance to American farmers. Reagan vetoed an earlier version of S 689 (HR 1096) because it contained provisions adding to the cost of farm loan guarantee programs. *(Farm credit bill, p. 542)*

Authorization Bill

Action on both the authorization and appropriation bills proceeded at the same time but on separate tracks during the first three months of the 99th Congress.

The first step for the authorization bill came when the House Foreign Affairs Committee Feb. 19 approved HR 1096 (H Rept 99-3), authorizing $175 million for non-food aid. On Feb. 21, the Senate Foreign Relations Committee approved its version (S 457 — S Rept 99-4), also providing $175 million.

Additional authorizations were required for the non-food aid because the administration already had used up the amounts provided in existing law for those programs. There was sufficient authorization for the food aid, however, under the PL 480 "Food for Peace" program.

The House passed HR 1096 by a 391-25 vote Feb. 26. There was little debate on the measure, although a few members said the bill contained too much aid at a time when the United States had a huge budget deficit. *(Vote 13, p. 6-H)*

The Senate approved the bill with slightly different Africa provisions by a 62-35 vote Feb. 27. But the Senate also added three amendments providing emergency credit aid to American farmers. *(Vote 17, p. 5-S)*

The House then cleared HR 1096 by voting March 5 to accept the Senate amendments to the bill. The vote was 255-168. *(Vote 25, p. 10-H)*

Reagan quickly vetoed the measure, however, claiming March 6 that its farm-loan provisions were "a massive new bailout that would add billions to the deficit." *(Veto message, p. 11-D)*

There was no attempt to override the veto. Senate leaders moved to bring a new non-food aid authorization bill to the floor, but their efforts were blocked by farm-state senators. Meanwhile, the administration moved to use presidential emergency powers to continue the flow of aid to the stricken continent.

Two weeks later, a new non-food authorization (S 689) that had been stripped of the farm-credit provisions bill did clear. Both chambers passed the measure by voice vote with little debate, the Senate on March 20 and the House March 21. The president signed the bill April 2.

Provisions. As cleared by Congress, S 689:

- Authorized $135 million in fiscal year 1985 for grants to private, voluntary and international organizations to provide aid to African countries affected by famine. The relief was to include seeds and other agricultural supplies, blankets, clothing, shelter, health care, small-scale agricultural projects and water projects such as well-digging.
- Authorized $2.5 million in 1985 for the Agency for International Development to supervise and monitor U.S. aid to Africa.
- Authorized $37.5 million in fiscal 1985 for emergency relief to refugees in Africa. Up to 54 percent of that amount was to be channeled through the United Nations Office of Emergency Operations in Africa, with the remainder to be spent by the State Department.
- Authorized reimbursement of the Defense Department for any extraordinary costs it might incur in providing assistance to Africa.
- Exempted African countries receiving the special famine aid from the requirements of the "Hickenlooper amendment," a 1962 law that barred aid to any country that expropriated, without prompt reimbursement, property owned by U.S. companies or citizens.
- Required the president to report to Congress by June 30, 1985, on U.S. aid to famine-stricken countries in Africa. The president also was required to report to Congress by Sept. 30, 1985, on the use of funds authorized in S 689. The latter report also was to assess the need for additional aid.

Appropriations Bill

The House Appropriations Committee Feb. 21 approved HR 1239 (H Rept 99-2) appropriating $880 million for emergency Africa relief.

The bill included $705 million to buy food, ship it to Africa and transport it inland. The money was in addition to about $490 million in emergency food aid the administration already had provided in fiscal 1985. Also in the bill was $175 million for non-food aid.

Of the $705 million for food aid, the bill provided $480 million in immediate funds, as well as $225 million for a food aid reserve to be spent if the president determined it was needed.

Action on the bill came despite growing concern on Capitol Hill about whether the food provided in the past by the United States and other countries was reaching the starving people for whom it was intended. Members were most worried about the actions of the Marxist government of Ethiopia, which reportedly had blocked food shipments to two northern provinces that were controlled by rebel guerrilla groups.

The House passed HR 1239 by voice vote Feb. 28.

The Senate Appropriations Committee reported its version of HR 1239 March 6 (S Rept 99-8). It contained $669 million in food and non-food aid. However, prompt action on the bill on the Senate floor was blocked by farm-state senators anxious to offer farm-credit amendments.

The Senate then passed HR 1239 by a 98-1 vote March 20. The bill as passed by the Senate was reluctantly supported by the administration. *(Vote 21, p. 7-S)*

Before passing HR 1239, the Senate adopted, by voice vote, an amendment by John Melcher, D-Mont., directing the Agriculture Department to donate at least 200,000 metric tons of food to private organizations for aid to Africa. Also by voice vote, the Senate adopted a requirement that the Agriculture Department certify to Congress that none of the aid provided under the Melcher amendment would pass through the hands of the Ethiopian government.

House-Senate conferees on HR 1239 March 27 approved a compromise bill (H Rept 99-29) providing $784 million. The two versions had differed on two key issues: the amount of money to be appropriated and how much time the president would be given to spend the money. The House bill included $480 million for immediate food aid, all to be spent by the end of fiscal 1985. The Senate bill included $269 million and did not set a time limit for the money to be spent. Conferees approved $384 million and allowed the president until Dec. 31, 1985, to spend it.

The House adopted the conference report by a 400-19 vote April 2. The Senate approved it by voice vote the same day. *(Vote 39, p. 16-H)*

Provisions. As cleared by Congress, HR 1239 included $609 million for food aid, and gave the administration authority to use another $16 million carried over from fiscal year 1984. It also included $175 million for non-food aid.

Of the $609 million for food aid, the bill provided $384 million under Title II of the Food for Peace program. The bill also provided $225 million for an emergency reserve the president could use if he certified to Congress it was needed.

Another provision authorized the Agriculture Department to give African countries up to 200,000 tons of surplus food owned by the Commodity Credit Corp. Of that amount, half was to be provided in wheat and wheat products. Before providing any of the food, the secretary of agriculture was required to certify to Congress that none of it would be given to the Ethiopian government. ∎

Congress Enacts State Department Authorization

Congress Aug. 1 cleared legislation (HR 2068 — PL 99-93) authorizing funds for the State Department and related agencies in fiscal years 1986 and 1987.

Final action on HR 2068, which authorized a total of $7.6 billion over two years, came when the House approved the conference report (H Rept 96-240) by a 350-74 vote. The Senate had accepted the agreement by voice vote July 31. *(Vote 260, p. 82-H)*

In addition to funding State Department operations, the bill authorized spending for the United States Information Agency (USIA), the Arms Control and Disarmament Agency and the Board for International Broadcasting (BIB), overseer of Radio Free Europe and Radio Liberty.

As approved by Congress, HR 2068 had the potential of leading to a major change in American policy towards the United Nations. The bill provided for a limitation on U.S. contributions to the world body unless it agreed to shift to a system under which voting strength on budget matters was proportional to each member state's financial contributions.

Critics of the U.N. charged that the United States was supplying a substantial share of funding for the organization while allowing a large number of poor countries with very small contributions to determine how the money was spent.

That system encouraged the U.N. budget to triple in the preceding decade, critics said. Passage of the U.N. amendment also reflected congressional frustration with the anti-American stance frequently taken by the world forum's communist and radical Third World majority.

The amendment was opposed by the State Department, which argued that the United Nations already was making progress in controlling the growth of its spending. President Reagan criticized the contribution limit, saying it could cause "serious problems" for the United States. Nevertheless, he signed the bill Aug. 17, citing the importance of the other programs authorized by the legislation.

HR 2068 also contained provisions on two national security issues that attracted considerable attention during the year. The bill set aside $311 million in State Department administrative funds for improvements in embassy security. Those funds were just the precursor, however, to a major new embassy security program requested by the administration during the year but not acted upon by Congress. *(Embassy security, p. 105)*

In addition, the bill called for limits on the number of Soviet nationals who could serve as diplomats in the United States, or be employed in U.S. diplomatic or consular missions in the Soviet Union. The provisions were in response to a number of reports of Soviet spy activities that surfaced during the year. *(Spies, p. 108)*

During the course of its passage through Congress, the bill also picked up a number of provisions relating to hotly debated foreign policy issues. As approved by the Senate, it contained provisions repealing a 1976 law against aid to anti-government rebels in Angola, and authorizing $38 million in non-military aid for "contra" forces battling the leftist government of Nicaragua. The House version did not contain either provision.

However, both the Angola and Nicaragua provisions were also contained in the foreign aid authorization bill (S 960) that cleared Congress July 31. So they were dropped from the conference version of the State Department bill without opposition. *(Foreign aid, p. 41)*

With those contentious issues out of the measure, conferees were able to settle their differences informally, without a conference meeting. One action by conferees was to drop a House provision concerning the Paris-based Coordinating Committee for Export Controls (COCOM), a multinational group that worked to prevent the Soviet bloc from obtaining Western military technology. The House had sought to bar Defense Department officials from the U.S. delegations to COCOM, limiting the delegation to State Department officials.

Overall, funding levels in the bill adhered to a spending "freeze" approved by the House. The conference version's total authorization for fiscal 1986 was $72 million less than the 1985 authorization, and $131 million less than the amount sought by the Reagan administration.

Major Provisions

As cleared by Congress, HR 2068:

- Authorized $3,765,796,000 in fiscal 1986 and $3,808,818,000 in fiscal 1987 for operations of the State Department, the USIA and the BIB. Included in those totals were the following authorizations for major programs: $1.8 billion in 1986 and $1.9 billion in 1987 for basic State Department operations; $534 million annually for aid to international organizations; $345 million annually for refugee assistance; $888 million annually for USIA; and $125 million annually for the BIB.

Included in the fiscal 1986-87 authorization total was $90.5 million for educational and exchange programs in Latin America and the Caribbean. The legislation also

$4 Billion Sought to Boost Embassy Security

Frustrated and angered by a wave of terrorist attacks that hit Americans in the Middle East and elsewhere during 1985, members of Congress joined the Reagan administration in pushing for a variety of tough measures to curb and punish terrorism.

One of the most significant was the recommendation of a high-level State Department commission for funding of a new $4 billion program to improve security at U.S. embassies and other diplomatic buildings.

Chaired by retired Adm. Bobby R. Inman, former deputy director of the CIA, the secretary of state's Advisory Panel on Overseas Security issued a report June 25 calling for the United States to replace or renovate many of its overseas facilities because they were vulnerable to terrorist attacks and other security threats.

The panel also recommended a reshuffling of the State Department bureaucracy to streamline security programs and an expansion of the department's security force.

Secretary of State George P. Shultz formed the commission in the wake of 1983 and 1984 bombing attacks on U.S. Embassy buildings and Marine headquarters in Lebanon. *(1984 Almanac p. 114; 1983 Almanac p. 113)*

In February 1986, the administration transmitted a formal request to Congress for the new program, funded at $4.4 billion, as part of its fiscal 1987 budget request.

A Growing Threat

The Inman commission warned that diplomats and other Americans serving overseas in official capacities would face increasing threats from "calculated terror campaigns." It cited a consensus among U.S. officials that "terrorism will be with us for a long time," with the threat greatest in the Middle East, Europe and Latin America. But it also said attacks would increase in the United States, especially against senior government officials and public buildings.

The prospects for preventing terrorist attacks "are not good," the commission said, adding that "no amount of money can guarantee complete protection against terrorism." But the commission recommended what it called "prudent steps" to thwart attacks and minimize damage when attacks occurred.

The most expensive recommendation of the panel was for replacement or renovation of 126 of the State Department's 262 embassies and other buildings overseas, along with at least 210 buildings operated by other agencies. The report argued that 75 State Department buildings should be replaced because they did not meet existing security standards.

The report said that the location of the buildings was the most common problem. Many of the buildings were located on main streets in capital cities, and were vulnerable to car bombings such as those that hit the Beirut posts.

The panel also called for a "major effort" to restructure security responsibilities within the State Department, as well as increases in departmental training programs combating security threats.

Among the changes the panel recommended were:

- Creation of a new Bureau of Diplomatic Security, headed by an assistant secretary of state. The bureau would take over several existing offices, including the Emergency Planning Program and the Anti-Terrorism Program.
- Creation of a Diplomatic Security Service to coordinate protection of posts at home and abroad. The panel estimated a need for 1,156 State Department security officers, a net increase of 375 over the then-estimated number.
- Establishment of boards of inquiry to investigate security failures involving future attacks on U.S. facilities overseas.

Hostage Compensation

Diplomats and other U.S. employees who were the targets of terrorism would get special aid under a bill (HR 2851) approved in 1985 by the House Post Office and Civil Service and Foreign Affairs committees. The legislation would grant benefits to government employees held hostage at home or abroad. *(Details, p. 416)*

called for establishment of a new college scholarship program for students from developing nations.

- Earmarked $311 million in State Department administration funds for capital spending and salaries to improve security at U.S. embassies.
- Repealed the permanent authorization, enacted in 1975 (PL 94-37), for the U.S. contribution to the U.N. peacekeeping force in the Mideast.
- Provided that travel restrictions imposed by existing law on foreign diplomats in the United States also apply to foreign employees of the United Nations; authorized the president to waive the restriction.
- Limited the U.S. contribution to U.N. organizations to 20 percent of their budgets, unless the United Nations moved toward a system under which voting strength in each organization was proportionate to each member state's financial contribution; also prohibited U.S. contributions to certain U.N. organizations.
- Required that, to the extent practicable, Soviet nationals not be employed in U.S. diplomatic or consular missions in the Soviet Union after Sept. 30, 1986; established a policy that the number of Soviet nationals serving in diplomatic or consular posts in the United States be roughly equivalent to the number of U.S. nationals serving in similar positions in the Soviet Union; and called for expulsion of at least one senior Soviet military attaché from the United States in retaliation for the March 1985 killing of U.S. Army Major Arthur D. Nicholson Jr. by Soviet forces in East Germany.
- Directed the United States to support a flexible pricing policy for some routes of the International Telecommunications Satellite Organization (INTELSAT), instead of the uniform rate currently required.
- Established an independent Office of Inspector General at the State Department.
- Made the National Endowment for Democracy, which

Walters Succeeds Kirkpatrick

The Senate by voice vote May 16 confirmed President Reagan's nomination of Vernon A. Walters as U.S. representative to the United Nations.

Walters, a retired Army lieutenant general who was a former deputy director of the CIA, had served the Reagan administration as a trouble-shooting ambassador-at-large. In that post, he made hundreds of trips, most of them secret, to smooth U.S. relations with foreign countries.

Walters replaced Jeane J. Kirkpatrick, who had resigned the post she had held since 1981. Kirkpatrick's conservative supporters had sought to find her another major foreign-policy job in the Reagan administration, but in the end she decided to return to her teaching position at Georgetown University in Washington, D.C.

made grants to private organizations abroad that promoted democracy, subject to the provisions of the Freedom of Information Act; required that the quasi-governmental agency submit to audits conducted by USIA; and barred use of endowment funds for partisan activities by the Republican or Democratic national committees.

- Required the president to submit an annual report on the compliance of other nations with arms control agreements.
- Established a new "Radio Free Afghanistan" to broadcast to that country as long as it was occupied by Soviet forces.
- Set up an International Narcotics Control Commission to monitor compliance with narcotics control treaties.
- Expressed the sense of Congress that Japan should undertake efforts to expand its defense capabilities.
- Called on the Treasury Department and Federal Reserve Board to take steps to lower the value of the dollar relative to other currencies.
- Expressed the sense of Congress that the United States should continue seeking an accord with the Soviet Union to ban chemical weapons.

House Action

The House passed HR 2068 by voice vote May 9. Before passing the bill, however, the House voted for a spending "freeze" and acted on amendments relating to a variety of sensitive foreign-policy issues.

The major change made by the House in the bill reported by the Foreign Affairs Committee (H Rept 99-40) came on an amendment offered by bill manager Daniel A. Mica, D-Fla. Approved 398-1, the amendment fixed fiscal 1986 spending authority under the bill at the fiscal 1985 level of $3.84 billion. For fiscal 1987, the amendment provided $3.97 billion. *(Vote 98, p. 34-H)*

The House-passed authorizations were $59 million lower than the amount requested by the Reagan administration for fiscal 1986, and $193 million less than the administration request for 1987.

During debate on HR 2068, the House took the following actions on amendments:

- Adopted, on a 322-93 vote, a William S. Broomfield, R-Mich., amendment recommending the expulsion of the top Soviet diplomat in the United States by June 1 unless the Soviets formally apologized for killing a U.S. Army major in East Germany. *(Vote 96, p. 34-H)*
- Adopted, on a 224-189 vote, a Dan Burton, R-Ind., amendment to delete $50,000 that would have been used to teach U.S. foreign service officers about the religious beliefs of the nations where they served. *Vote 97, p. 34-H)*
- Rejected, on a 196-222 vote, an Earl Hutto, D-Fla., amendment to allow Defense Department and other U.S. officials to join State Department diplomats on the permanent U.S. delegation to COCOM. *(Vote 95, p. 32-H)*
- Adopted by voice vote an amendment, offered by Mark D. Siljander, R-Mich., to require U.S. missions in South Africa to comply with a code of worker rights.
- Adopted by voice vote a Jim Courter, R-N.J., amendment prohibiting Soviet citizens from working in U.S. missions in the Soviet Union.
- Adopted by voice vote a Gerald B. H. Solomon, R-N.Y., amendment to cut the fiscal 1987 contribution to the U.N. by 15 percent. The amendment was limited to personnel and administrative costs.
- Adopted by voice vote a Thomas E. Petri, R-Wis., amendment to bar the State Department from accepting a gift of a house to be the official residence of the secretary of state, unless Congress approved it.
- Adopted by voice vote a Don Bonker, D-Wash., amendment relating to INTELSAT, the global satellite consortium. The amendment directed the United States to support a flexible pricing policy for some routes, instead of the uniform rate required under existing procedures.

Senate Action

The Senate approved its version of HR 2068 by an 80-17 vote June 11. There was lengthy debate on the Senate bill (S 1003 — S Rept 99-39), as senators argued over aid to anti-communist rebels in Nicaragua and Angola, as well as amendments restricting contributions to the U.N. and international family-planning agencies. *(Vote 122, p. 25-S)*

Nicaragua

The Senate approved an amendment to provide $38 million in non-military aid to the contra guerrillas by a 55-42 vote June 6. *(Vote 112, p. 23-S)*

The aid proposal approved by the Senate was offered by Sam Nunn, Ga., ranking Democrat on the Armed Services Committee, and by Richard G. Lugar, R-Ind., chairman of the Foreign Relations Committee.

It provided $14 million in fiscal 1985 and $24 million in 1986 for "food, clothing, medicine or other humanitarian assistance" for the contras. The aid was to be monitored by the National Security Council, and sponsors said they expected the CIA would administer the aid. *(Nicaragua, p. 61)*

The Senate plan also repealed an existing bar on military or paramilitary aid and specifically authorized the CIA to provide intelligence information to the contras.

The Senate also rejected several Democratic-sponsored proposals to restrict the nature of the contra aid and to limit Reagan's freedom to send U.S. troops to Central America. The wide margins against those proposals were similar to ones by which the Senate had rejected Democratic challenges to Reagan's policies during the past year.

As the Senate neared completion of its action on Nicaragua on June 7, it got entangled in a dispute over an amendment by John Kerry, D-Mass. Kerry proposed to prohibit U.S. funding of activities in Nicaragua that would violate international law or U.S. obligations to the United Nations or Organization of American States.

Lugar offered to accept the amendment on behalf of the GOP leadership, even though the administration opposed it as a slap at Reagan policies. But Kerry demanded a roll-call vote — angering Majority Leader Robert Dole, R-Kan., who was trying to speed action on the bill.

Nevertheless, the Senate backed the amendment 47-42, with most Republicans voting "no." Dole then forced through, 48-42, a move to reconsider the approval of the amendment. Armed with that vote, Dole persuaded Kerry to compromise. After a lengthy delay, Kerry proposed and the Senate accepted an amendment that weakened his ban by allowing activities authorized under U.S. law, even if they violated international law. *(Votes 115, 116, p. 24-S)*

Amendments Rejected

The Senate rejected several Democratic-sponsored amendments that sought to narrow the use of the contra aid or to restrict Reagan's policy options in Central America. They were:

- By Edward M. Kennedy, D-Mass., urging the United States to resume bilateral negotiations with Nicaragua. Reagan suspended such talks in January, claiming that Nicaragua was refusing serious discussions. The amendment was rejected on a 48-48 tie, surprising even some administration supporters who thought it would pass. *(Vote 108, p. 24-S)*
- By Kennedy, barring the president from introducing U.S. combat troops into Nicaragua without explicit approval of Congress or under certain other conditions. Rejected 31-64. *(Vote 109, p. 23-S)*
- By Gary Hart, D-Colo., barring the president from introducing U.S. combat troops anywhere in Central America without congressional approval, except to rescue U.S. citizens or to meet a direct attack on the United States. Rejected 15-81. *(Vote 110, p. 23-S)*
- By Christopher J. Dodd, D-Conn., authorizing $10 million to implement a regional peace agreement in Central America and $14 million to help the contras withdraw from Nicaragua. His amendment also retained the "Boland amendment" prohibition on military aid to the contras. Rejected 17-79. *(Vote 107, p. 23-S; Boland amendment, p. 76)*
- By Tom Harkin, D-Iowa, to bar the administration from using the CIA or the Defense Department to administer aid to the contras. Rejected 35-57. *(Vote 113, p. 24-S)*
- By Harkin, to reimpose the Boland amendment prohibiting military or paramilitary aid to the contras, but giving the president the right to seek congressional approval of such aid. Rejected 30-62. *(Vote 114, p. 24-S)*
- By Alan J. Dixon, D-Ill., stating the sense of Congress that the president should lift the economic sanctions he imposed against Nicaragua in May. Rejected 22-68. *(Vote 117, p. 24-S)*
- By Joseph R. Biden Jr., D-Del., authorizing $14 million in non-lethal assistance to the contras in fiscal 1985, provided the aid was independently monitored and peace talks resumed. The amendment also would have ended the trade embargo Reagan imposed on Nicaragua May 1. Rejected 22-75. *(Vote 111, p. 23-S)*

Under pressure from the Senate leadership, Pete Wilson, R-Calif., withdrew an amendment that called on the president to provide direct military and non-military aid to the contras. It would have authorized $14 million for non-military aid in fiscal 1985 and $24 million in unrestricted aid in 1986.

Angola

The Senate took a major policy step June 11, when it voted overwhelmingly to repeal a 1976 law that had thwarted U.S. support for anti-government rebels in Angola. Although not taken at the official request of Reagan, the Senate's action was welcomed by the administration, which had chafed at the legal curb on Reagan's authority.

By a 63-34 vote, the Senate voted to repeal the "Clark amendment" on Angola. *(Vote 119, p. 24-S)*

Originally passed by Congress in 1976 under the sponsorship of Sen. Dick Clark, D-Iowa (1973-79), the amendment banned any U.S. "covert" aid to factions then fighting in Angola.

The effect of the amendment was to stop CIA aid to a rightist guerrilla group called UNITA and headed by Jonas Savimbi. Another faction, the Marxist MPLA, later gained control of the government and since had been aided by thousands of Cuban troops. But UNITA was continuing its guerrilla struggle and had gained control of large chunks of Angolan territory.

Congress in 1980 modified the Clark amendment to allow the president to aid the Angolan rebels if he publicly justified the operation to Congress, and Congress approved by passing a joint resolution. That provision effectively barred the resumption of a typical CIA covert operation. *(1980 Almanac p. 326)*

Reagan in 1981 sought the total repeal of the Clark amendment. The Senate approved his request 66-29, but the House refused, ending the matter. *(1981 Almanac p. 165)*

Only four senators discussed the Angola issue — and briefly at that — on June 10. The Senate postponed the vote until the next day.

Steven D. Symms, R-Idaho, who had long championed the cause of the Angolan rebels and referred to Savimbi as "one of the world's greatest leaders," offered the provision repealing the Clark amendment. His amendment did not authorize funding for the Angolan rebels, but its effect would be to free the CIA to aid them through its contingency fund, over which Congress had little direct control.

"This is a place where we can achieve a victory, not only an actual victory on the field but a moral victory, a psychological victory, which will give strength to free men all over the world," Symms said.

Repeal of the Clark amendment also might encourage other countries to aid the UNITA forces, he said.

Richard G. Lugar, R-Ind., chairman of the Foreign Relations Committee, supported Symms, arguing that the Senate already had spoken in 1981 in opposition to such a "country-specific" bar on CIA activities.

But Claiborne Pell, D-R.I., ranking Democrat on Foreign Relations, said repeal of the Clark amendment would not help the Reagan administration's stated goals for the region: a long-term peace accord between South Africa and Angola. The two countries had fought cross-border battles ever since the leftist government took over in Angola, and South Africa had been the major source of money and arms for the UNITA rebels.

The United States tried to broker pacts for removal of the Cubans from Angola and a South African pledge to respect Angolan sovereignty, and full independence for Namibia (South West Africa). South Africa was controlling Namibia in violation of U.N. resolutions.

Unilateral U.S. action "would undermine, rather than promote," peacemaking efforts, Pell said. It would lead Angola to conclude that the United States was readying to support UNITA, thus increasing Angola's dependence on the Soviet Union and Cuba.

Family Planning

Other than Nicaragua, the most controversial issue dealt with by the Senate on the State Department bill was family planning overseas. By 53-45, the Senate on June 11 tabled a Jesse Helms, R-N.C., amendment that sought to give the president a free hand in determining what agencies could get U.S. family planning funds. *(Vote 121, p. 25-S)*

The core issue was whether Congress would intervene in Reagan's decision to withhold some or all U.S. funds from the U.N. Fund for Population Activities and the International Planned Parenthood Federation. The U.N. agency was supporting some family planning programs in China, which was alleged to practice forced abortion, and the Planned Parenthood programs in some countries provided counseling and other services for abortions. In neither case were U.S. funds used for abortions, the administration said. *(Story, p. 112)*

Helms portrayed his amendment as a "human rights" initiative that would attack forced abortion, infanticide, involuntary sterilization "and racial or ethnic discrimination" overseas. He said it would "maintain in an explicit way the president's current authority to curb human rights abuses in population control" programs.

The amendment would have overridden a provision approved by the Senate three weeks earlier as part of the fiscal 1986-87 foreign aid authorization bill (S 960). The foreign aid provision prevented the president from applying stricter standards to U.S. funding of international agencies than he applied to governments. *(Foreign aid, p. 41)*

Helms called the foreign aid provision "an unjustified tying of the president's hands."

But Nancy Landon Kassebaum, R-Kan., argued that the foreign aid provision, which she authored, merely restored the traditional treatment of U.S. funding for family planning agencies. Providing funds for the U.N. and Planned Parenthood agencies was necessary to ensure "the viability of our population planning efforts overseas," she said.

And in an emotional speech, Bill Bradley, D-N.J., said the issue was "whether the United States should help provide family planning services to developing countries." The Helms amendment "will do a great deal to suppress family planning — the most effective way to prevent abortions."

Recalling a visit to a Calcutta orphanage sponsored by Mother Teresa, Bradley said: "One cannot experience the horror of street life in Calcutta and support this kind of amendment."

Other Amendments

Other amendments adopted were:

- By Kassebaum, limiting U.S. contributions to all U.N. organizations to 20 percent of their budgets, a cut from the 25 percent share the United States currently provided to most agencies. The cap would not apply to any agency that adopted a plan of proportionate voting on budget matters — based on each country's contributions — and had adopted a plan to reduce salaries and pensions to the level of the U.S. civil service. In the case of one agency, the United Nations Children's Fund (UNICEF), the amendment specified that U.S. funds would be set aside for grants to private voluntary organizations if UNICEF could not comply with the conditions. Adopted 71-13 on June 7. *(Vote 118, p. 24-S)*

Kassebaum said she offered the amendment because "the United Nations can no longer be a sacred cow."

- By William V. Roth Jr., R-Del., imposing the same travel restrictions on foreigners employed by the United Nations as were imposed on other foreign diplomats in the United States. The amendment would allow the State Department to restrict travel by some 800 Russians at the United Nations. By voice vote.
- By Lowell P. Weicker Jr., R-Conn., to subject the National Endowment for Democracy to the Freedom of Information Act and to subject that quasi-governmental agency to auditing by the USIA. The endowment made grants to several private organizations that attempted to promote democracy overseas. By voice vote.
- By Pete V. Domenici, R-N.M., to authorize $45.4 million in fiscal 1986 and $45.1 million in fiscal 1987 for educational and exchange programs for Latin American and Caribbean countries. A major purpose of the funding would be to provide college scholarships. By voice vote on June 10. ▮

Spies and Soviet Restrictions

A series of revelations about spying activity on behalf of the Soviet Union spurred Congress to take steps in 1985 to place new restrictions on Soviet diplomats.

Early in 1985, the administration discovered that some typewriters at the U.S. Embassy in Moscow had been fitted in 1982 with electronic devices that enabled Soviet officials to monitor what was being typed. Later in 1985, a storm of diplomatic protest arose after it was revealed that Soviet agents had exposed U.S. Embassy workers to a potentially dangerous chemical.

In May, the FBI arrested three Virginians — John Anthony Walker Jr., his son, Michael Lance Walker, and John Walker's brother, Arthur James Walker — on charges of selling secrets to the Soviets. A fourth man, Jerry Alfred Whitworth of California, was arrested on a conspiracy charge June 3. Michael Walker was a Navy seaman; the other three were retired Navy personnel. John and Michael Walker pleaded guilty to charges Oct. 28; Arthur Walker was found guilty and sentenced to life in prison Nov. 12.

The incidents gave new impetus to congressional efforts to reduce the number of Soviet spies, both at the U.S. Embassy in Moscow and at the Soviet Embassy in Washington.

The United States employed more than 200 Russians at its embassy in Moscow and consulate in Leningrad, nearly all in service positions such as janitors. At the same time, the Soviet Union refused to hire U.S. citizens for its diplomatic offices in the United States. As a result, there were about 200 more Russian diplomatic personnel in the United States than there were U.S. diplomats in the Soviet Union. Intelligence officials told congressional committees that many Soviet diplomats and embassy employees were active espionage agents.

The State Department authorization bill (HR 2068 — PL 99-93) contained a number of provisions aimed at reversing the imbalance. The final version of the bill contained a provision based on a House-passed amendment to bar Soviet citizens from working at U.S. missions.

Rep. Jim Courter, R-N.J., sponsored the amendment, arguing that the employment of Russians "poses a totally unacceptable security risk." The State Department opposed the amendment as an infringement on its administrative flexibility, and the final version of the bill applied the prohibition only to the extent practicable.

The Senate attacked the issue from a different angle. It approved an amendment to declare that the number of Soviet diplomatic and consular personnel in the United States could not exceed the corresponding number of U.S. representatives in the Soviet Union.

That amendment was sponsored by Patrick Leahy, D-Vt., and William S. Cohen, R-Maine, who had tried to get a similar provision through Congress in 1984 but were stymied by opposition from the State Department and Senate Foreign Relations Committee. The final version of HR 2068 established a policy that the numbers of diplomatic personnel should be roughly equivalent.

United Nations

Concern over spying also was directed towards the large number of Soviet citizens employed by the United Nations. A report released June 5 by the Senate Intelligence Committee found that about one-fourth of the 800 Russians working for the United Nations were intelligence agents.

All the Russians reported directly to the Soviet government and used their positions to promote Soviet policy, even though they were supposed to be international civil servants responsible only to the United Nations, the report said. The same was true for U.N. employees from most Soviet-bloc countries, it added.

"The Soviet Union is effectively using the U.N. Secretariat for the conduct of its foreign relations, and the West is paying for most of it," the report said. The Russians "have gained significant advantage over the West" by assigning personnel to the United Nations "to achieve Soviet foreign policy and intelligence objectives."

After release of the report, the Intelligence Committee moved to close a legal loophole under which Russians working for the United Nations had total freedom to travel in the United States. All other Russian diplomats were required to get permission from the State Department before they could travel away from their assigned posts — thus making it easier for the FBI to keep track of them. Such permission was rarely granted, because of the Soviets' tight curbs on travel by U.S. diplomats.

The final version of the State Department authorization bill contained a provision applying existing travel restrictions on foreign diplomats to foreign employees of the United Nations. ▮

Reagan, Gorbachev Meet in 'Fireside Summit'

President Reagan held a "summit" meeting with Soviet leader Mikhail S. Gorbachev in Geneva, Switzerland, on Nov. 19-21. It was the first such encounter of Reagan's presidency.

The meeting did not produce any accords on arms control or other major issues between the two superpowers. However, it was viewed by many in Congress as helping to put U.S.-Soviet relations back on a businesslike basis, stripped of the confrontational rhetoric so evident in the preceding five years.

Addressing a joint session of Congress the evening of Nov. 21, Reagan said that the 15 hours of discussions — five of them involving the two leaders accompanied only by translators — marked a "fresh start" for the two countries. *(Text, p. 38-D)*

Reagan's speech, which was devoid of harsh denunciations of Soviet policy, received a warm reception on Capitol Hill. Many members held out further hopes for the future summits that the two leaders agreed to have — a Gorbachev visit to Washington planned for 1986 and a Reagan trip to Moscow for a third meeting in 1987.

At their summit, Reagan and Gorbachev reached agreement on cultural exchanges and other routine issues. However, the meeting apparently did little to settle one of the biggest arms-control issues — Reagan's "strategic defense initiative" (SDI) for a space-based anti-missile defense system. The Soviets had insisted that SDI be stringently limited as part of any far-reaching arms reduction agreement. *(SDI, p. 130; arms control, p. 175)*

Laying the Groundwork

The first step to the summit came March 13, when Reagan reversed his longstanding opposition to a get-acquainted summit meeting and offered to meet with Gorbachev. Vice President George Bush delivered the offer in a meeting with Gorbachev, following funeral services in Moscow for Soviet leader Konstantin U. Chernenko, who died March 10. Gorbachev was named general secretary of the Soviet Communist Party on March 11.

Gorbachev responded to Reagan's proposal by announcing April 7 that he was ready to meet the U.S. president. At the same time, Gorbachev revealed that the Soviet Union was unilaterally freezing until November its deployment of SS-20 medium-range missiles in Europe. He urged the United States to reciprocate by stopping deployment of Pershing II and cruise missiles in Western Europe. White House officials dismissed Gorbachev's missile moratorium as a propaganda gesture, while cautiously welcoming his comments on a meeting.

The two countries formally announced the Reagan-Gorbachev meeting on July 3. However, the announcement did not refer to the November encounter as a "summit," and U.S. officials said they did not expect any important agreements to be reached. Throughout his first term, Reagan had been reluctant to hold such a meeting unless there was a likelihood of agreement on major issues.

Pre-Summit Maneuvering

As November drew nearer, leaders of both countries maneuvered to gain tactical advantages going into the meeting. Two main themes emerged in the Reagan administration's attitude to the approaching encounter.

On the one hand, administration officials hoped to use the prospect of agreement on arms control to spur congressional support for SDI and the continuing arms buildup. The resumption of full-dress arms-control talks in March had helped Reagan deflect congressional criticism of his defense strategy, on the grounds that the programs were needed as bargaining chips.

However, administration officials and conservative defense specialists worried that too great an emphasis on arms control would put the United States at a political disadvantage. So they sought to shift the focus of the talks to other issues, such as regional conflicts and human rights, as well.

One step in that effort was a United Nations speech by Reagan. Addressing the world body on its 40th anniversary Oct. 24, Reagan called on the Soviet Union to move to resolve conflicts in five countries with pro-Soviet regimes. In his speech, Reagan said battles in Afghanistan, Angola, Cambodia, Ethiopia and Nicaragua should be settled through negotiations. But the Soviet Union quickly rejected Reagan's proposal.

In addition, some administration officials worked to dampen public pressure for arms control by stressing alleged Soviet violations of existing treaties.

Moscow sought to pre-empt those efforts, however, by announcing Sept. 30 a new arms negotiating proposal that seemed to offer stark reductions: a 50 percent cut in strategic nuclear weapons. The Soviet offer promised particularly steep reductions in the Soviet force of land-based missiles. The Soviet offer also called for tight restrictions on SDI research

A month later, the Reagan administration responded with a counteroffer that was similar in some respects to Gorbachev's plan — notably, the idea of a "50 percent reduction." But the seeming convergence of the U.S. and Soviet positions on some issues only underscored the deep disagreements over SDI.

But while public attention focused on arms control issues, administration officials worked to ensure that the summit agenda would also touch on bilateral issues and human rights, as well as the regional conflicts addressed by Reagan. While the bilateral issues seemed to hold some promise of progress, the question of human rights in the Soviet Union was an extremely touchy one.

Several dozen members of Congress had written to Reagan asking him to raise human rights issues at the summit. Even without congressional urging, Reagan was seen as likely to bring up two kinds of issues: Moscow's treatment of political dissidents, and the sharp decline in the number of Jews allowed to emigrate from the Soviet Union. However, in an Oct. 30 interview, Reagan said the human rights issue should not be "a kind of public discussion and accusing fingers being pointed at each other."

Reagan's final public step before going to Geneva was to give a Nov. 14 television speech to the nation, in which he mapped out goals that were more sweeping — but also less immediate — than the nuclear arms issues that had dominated public expectations for the summit.

Reagan said that the summit would provide "an historic opportunity to set a steady, more constructive course for the 21st century." As a road to a more lasting peace, Reagan called for an expanded program of U.S.-Soviet people-to-people exchanges. But Reagan made only a brief reference to SDI, and administration officials continued to insist that there was no chance the two leaders could negotiate an arms-control agreement, given the remaining differences between the two sides.

The day before the speech, Reagan had received united congressional backing for his efforts. The Senate by a 99-0 vote adopted a resolution (S Res 257) voicing its "full support and best wishes for success" for the summit. And House Democratic leaders held a press conference promising their full backing for the president. *(Vote 304, p. 53-S)*

Summit Outcome

Reagan left Washington for Geneva on Nov. 16. That same day, a minor tempest arose when *The New York Times* published a letter to Reagan from Defense Secretary Caspar W. Weinberger, who was not going to the summit. The letter repeated Weinberger's often-stated skepticism about the value of past arms control agreements, and urged Reagan to resist pressures to accept limits on SDI research in return for reductions in Soviet missiles.

From its outset on Nov. 19, the summit meeting departed from its announced schedule. Although only two days of talks originally were scheduled, a third day was quickly added. In addition, Reagan and Gorbachev ended up spending much more time in private talks than the 15 minutes initially allocated. At one point, the two men walked to a garden pavilion where they held an extended private conversation sitting by a roaring fire.

In a joint communiqué released Nov. 21, Reagan and Gorbachev called their discussions "frank and useful," while acknowledging that "serious differences remain on a number of critical issues." *(Text, p. 36-D)*

Specifically, the communiqué provided for:

More Meetings. In addition to scheduling two more summit meetings, the two leaders announced plans for "regular meetings" between the U.S. secretary of state and the Soviet foreign minister, as well as regular "exchanges of views on regional issues."

Focused Arms Talks. The communiqué called for "early progress" on arms reduction, "particularly in areas where there is common ground." Two areas were singled out: agreement on a 50 percent reduction in nuclear weapons of the two sides, and a separate agreement on medium-range nuclear missiles in Europe. The communiqué made no reference to Moscow's demands that an agreement to ban SDI and other space weapons accompany limits on intercontinental and medium-range missiles. But, in a post-summit news conference, Gorbachev seemed to reaffirm the Soviet position that SDI limits be part of any arms deal.

Formal Agreements. Accords were reached on: renewal of academic and cultural exchanges; authorization of a Soviet consulate in New York City and a U.S. consulate in Kiev, contingent on restoration of civil air service between the two countries; and a pact arranging communications between the United States, the Soviet Union and Japan to avoid civil airliner incidents in the northwest Pacific.

New Efforts. Three new bilateral initiatives were announced: a study of "nuclear risk reduction centers" to monitor nuclear weapons activity by third parties, including terrorists; discussions of ways to prevent the spread of chemical weapons; and advocacy of international cooperation to develop controlled nuclear fusion as an energy source.

Continuing Agenda. The leaders promised to continue efforts to: reduce conventional forces in Europe; ban chemical and biological weapons; and institute measures to reduce the fear of a surprise attack in Europe. ∎

Chinese Nuclear Accord

Congress on Dec. 11 cleared a resolution (S J Res 238 — PL 99-183) approving a nuclear cooperation agreement between the United States and China.

The resolution ratified an agreement reached between

the Reagan administration and the Chinese government on the sale to China of nuclear fuel, equipment or technology for nuclear power plants for the next 30 years.

The agreement was the first nuclear agreement between the United States and a communist country, and the first bilateral nuclear accord with another country that acknowledged possessing nuclear weapons.

Although Congress accepted the agreement, passage of the resolution was an implicit rebuke to the administration. There were widespread doubts on Capitol Hill about whether the accord contained adequate safeguards to ensure that the Chinese did not contribute to the spread of nuclear weapons. The resolution as cleared contained some mild non-proliferation provisions.

But the provisions failed to satisfy the agreement's congressional critics, who sought unsuccessfully to push through additional safeguards requiring China to accept international standards for guaranteeing the peaceful use of all its nuclear power facilities.

Congressional approval of the nuclear accord was sought by President Reagan, who had accepted an informal agreement on the issue during a 1984 trip to China. It was also backed by the U.S. nuclear industry, which hoped to recoup its sagging economic prospects in the United States by selling billions of dollars of nuclear equipment to the Chinese. China sought U.S. techology as part of a plan to build 10 new nuclear power plants by the year 2000.

Agreement Signed

The formal agreement between the United States and China was signed July 23. Final approval of the accord followed months of negotiations between officials of the two countries, as the United States sought to allay concerns about China's role in providing nuclear materials and technology to countries seeking to develop their own nuclear weapons. According to press reports, China had provided Pakistan with plans for construction of a nuclear bomb. It also was a major supplier of nuclear-power equipment to other countries, such as Argentina and Brazil.

The 1978 nuclear non-proliferation act (PL 95-242) barred the United States from selling nuclear supplies to any country that had "assisted, encouraged or induced" any other country to obtain nuclear weapons and that had failed to make "sufficient progress" toward ending such a relationship. Eventually, U.S. officials proclaimed themselves satisfied with public and private assurances from the Chinese that they would not help other countries acquire nuclear weapons capabilities.

U.S. officials said the agreement prohibited China from using American-supplied equipment or technology for building weapons. In addition, the agreement allowed the United States to inspect facilities where any U.S.-supplied equipment was located.

Under non-proliferation and export control laws (PL 95-242, PL 99-64), the agreement was to go into effect in 90 legislative days unless Congress passed, and the president signed, a joint resolution blocking it. Although there was little chance that that would occur, there was a considerable amount of vocal objection to the agreement. Critics such as Sen. William Proxmire, D-Wis., charged that the agreement was "riddled with loopholes."

Another prominent non-proliferation advocate, Sen. Alan Cranston, D-Calif., initially indicated his support for the agreement. In an Oct. 21 floor speech, however, he attacked the accord, charging that China had "in the recent past engaged in the most egregious effort in history to export nuclear bomb-making know-how." He said China already was providing, or was about to provide, nuclear equipment or technology that could help five nations build bombs: Pakistan, Brazil, Argentina, South Africa and Iran.

Legislation

The House Foreign Affairs and Senate Foreign Relations Committees Nov. 13 approved legislation (H J Res 404, S J Res 238) setting conditions on the nuclear agreement.

While endorsing the agreement, however, the resolution demanded more information about China's intentions than either Peking or the administration had been willing to provide.

The Senate panel approved the measure by a 12-3 vote, with Republicans Jesse Helms, N.C., Nancy Landon Kassebaum, Kan., and Larry Pressler, S.C., voting against. The House panel approved it by voice vote.

The resolution barred licensing or approval of nuclear transfers until 30 days of congressional session after the president sent Congress a certification indicating that China had provided "additional information concerning its nuclear non-proliferation policies." The president was also required to state that China was not helping other countries acquire nuclear weapons.

In its report on the resolution (H Rept 99-382), the House committee sharply criticized the agreement. The committee said it was concerned that the "vague and unorthodox language" in the agreement "might lead to future misunderstandings in the implementation of the provisions of the agreement." Because of those concerns, the panel said the provisions of the China agreement should not be considered precedents for future agreements. In the future, the panel added, nuclear agreements must contain "clear and unequivocal provisions" to ensure that U.S. materials were used for peaceful purposes.

The Senate approved S J Res 238 by voice vote without debate Nov. 21. In the House, however, sponsors were blocked in their first attempt to bring the resolution to the floor. The measure did not reach the floor until Dec. 11.

There was considerable opposition to the resolution from both liberals and conservatives. However, the measure cleared because members realized the agreement would go into effect without any conditions if Congress failed to act. The conditions in the resolution were "better than nothing," said Edward J. Markey, D-Mass., who had been strongly critical of the agreement.

The closest vote on the resolution was the 252-158 vote for approving the rule providing for floor consideration of the measure. *(Vote 412, p. 130-H)*

Provisions

As cleared by Congress, S J Res 238 stated that Congress favored the agreement. It also stated that no transfer to China of nuclear materials, facilities or components could take place until 30 days of continuous congressional session after the president had certified to Congress:

- That the United States and China had made arrangements that were "designed to be effective" in ensuring that any nuclear supplies provided China would be used solely for "intended peaceful purposes." Such arrangements normally included exchanges of information, inspections of nuclear plants by the supplying country or by the International Atomic Energy Agency (IAEA), and standards for keeping track of nuclear materials. However, neither the agreement nor the resolution specifically required IAEA inspections or adherence to other IAEA arrangements, as some critics had wanted.

• That the Chinese government had provided "additional information" about its nuclear non-proliferation policies and that, based on this and all other information available to the U.S. government, China was not in violation of provisions in the 1978 non-proliferation law that would require termination of the nuclear supply agreement. That law barred nuclear exports to any nation that had materially violated a supply agreement with the United States, that had helped or encouraged a non-nuclear-weapons nation to develop or acquire such weapons, or that had agreed to give a non-nuclear weapons nation equipment or technology to reprocess spent nuclear fuel.

Critics had charged that the Reagan administration relied on oral assurances that China would not help other countries acquire nuclear weapons. This provision was designed to force the president to obtain additional assurances on that score from the Chinese.

• That a clause in the agreement obligating the United States to "consider favorably" a Chinese request for permission to enrich or reprocess U.S.-supplied nuclear fuel would not prejudice the U.S. decision on whether to approve or deny such a request. The agreement required China to get permission from the United States before it could enrich U.S.-supplied uranium or reprocess spent U.S.-supplied reactor fuel. Enriching uranium and reprocessing fuel were two ways of obtaining the necessary ingredients for nuclear weapons.

The resolution further barred nuclear licenses or transfers to China until the president sent Congress a report detailing the history and current developments of China's nuclear non-proliferation policies. That report was to be submitted in both classified and unclassified form.

The resolution also stated that each nuclear export to China should be subject to U.S. laws and regulations in effect at the time of the export. The purpose of that provision was to affirm that the U.S.-China agreement would be subject to any future U.S. laws or regulations, in spite of a clause in the agreement stating that domestic law did not provide justification for failure to carry out a treaty.

Finally, the resolution stated that nothing in the pact or in the resolution itself might be construed as setting a precedent for negotiations on future nuclear cooperation agreements.

Appropriations Action

Another round of struggle over the nuclear agreement came during congressional action on the fiscal 1986 continuing appropriations resolution (H J Res 465 — PL 99-190). *(Appropriations measure, p. 360)*

Despite opposition from the administration, the Chinese government and the nuclear industry, the Senate on Dec. 9 approved an amendment by John Glenn, D-Ohio, to bar exports of nuclear power supplies to China unless the president certified that Peking had agreed to accept international standards ensuring they would be used only for peaceful purposes.

The amendment was attached to the spending bill after the Senate rejected, 28-59, an effort to kill it. *(Vote 356, p. 61-S)*

Glenn said his amendment would not put "an onerous burden on the Chinese" because they already had accepted similar conditions on nuclear imports from Japan and other countries. The amendment required China to accept standards equivalent to those enforced by the IAEA.

Administration and Chinese officials said the amendment would kill the accord. By Dec. 13, the provision had become the focus of an intense struggle within a House-Senate conference committee on H J Res 465, as the State Department charged it would "do serious damage to U.S.-China relations."

Conferees agreed to drop the amendment Dec. 16. ∎

Population Control Programs

The Reagan administration in 1985 continued its efforts to change longstanding U.S. policies towards family planning programs overseas.

Under pressure from anti-abortion groups, the administration sought to shift U.S. aid away from population control programs that included abortion and contraceptive techniques, and towards programs that advocated only "natural" birth control methods.

The most controversial population control issue involved U.S. support for United Nations programs in China. Anti-abortion groups charged that the United Nations Fund for Population Activities (UNFPA) had helped the Chinese government carry out forced abortions and sterilizations and other involuntary family planning activities, and sought to reduce funding for the agency.

The fiscal 1985 foreign aid appropriations bill (PL 98-473) had directed the administration to provide not less than $46 million to UNFPA. However, on March 30 M. Peter McPherson, director of the Agency for International Development (AID), said that the administration would provide only $36 million to the agency, pending a review of its activities in China. The $10 million was equal to the agency's annual program in China.

McPherson found support for his stance in an amendment included in the fiscal 1985 supplemental appropriations bill (HR 2577 — PL 99-88). The provision, sponsored by Rep. Jack F. Kemp, R-N.Y., said that no U.S. funds could be given to any organization that "supports or participates in the management of a program of coercive abortion or involuntary sterilization." The provision also stated that the decision on the issue had to be made by the president or secretary of state. *(Supplemental appropriations, p. 350)*

McPherson reaffirmed his decision in a Sept. 25 statement, pointing to the Kemp amendment as justification for overriding Congress' original mandate for a $46 million grant. McPherson pointed to a statement by Kemp during debate that the administration should define "coercive" programs in China as including such government activities as collecting information on women's menstrual cycles and publicizing the need for birth control. If the U.N. agency aided such activities, Kemp said, the United States should not support it.

In his Sept. 25 statement, McPherson warned that the United States would continue withholding aid until it had evidence that China was "punishing abuses" such as forced abortions or that the UNFPA "radically changes" its activities in China by, for example, providing only contraceptives.

The decision was sharply criticized by Rep. Peter Kostmayer, D-Pa., who noted that on March 30 McPherson had said that the United States had no evidence of U.N. involvement with coercive family planning programs in China.

Natural Birth Control

The administration also continued to change U.S. policies towards other population control programs. In 1984, the administration had cut off U.S. contributions to the International Planned Parenthood Federation, the largest private family planning agency.

In July 1985, the administration announced that for the first time the United States would provide funds to agencies that advocated only "natural" or non-contraceptive methods of family planning, such as abstinence. McPherson announced that he was setting aside $40 million over five years for grants to groups that advocated such methods exclusively.

That new policy was modified in Congress, however. The fiscal 1986 continuing appropriations resolution (H J Res 465 — PL 99-190) included a Senate amendment, sponsored by Dennis DeConcini, D-Ariz., to ensure that funds be given only to agencies that offered access to a broad range of family planning methods. The change was seen as requiring AID either to ban aid to groups that supported only natural methods, or pressuring them to provide at least some information on other birth control methods.

PL 99-190 also included the Kemp amendment on coercive control methods.

The resolution provided $250 million for family planning programs overseas, the same amount as was requested by the administration. In fiscal 1985, Congress had increased the administration's request for $250 million to $290 million. *(Fiscal 1986 appropriations, p. 367)*

Crisis in the Philippines

The Philippine government of President Ferdinand E. Marcos came under increasing pressure in 1985 from both Congress and the Reagan administration to undertake reforms aimed at heading off a growing communist-led insurgency.

In late February 1986, that pressure helped force Marcos from office and into exile.

Deeply worried by the potential loss of two crucial military bases located in the Philippines, U.S. policy makers in 1985 pushed Marcos to accept a variety of economic, political and military changes in his 20-year-old regime in order to respond to grievances exploited by the leftist guerrillas.

The broad consensus on the outlines of the U.S. stance towards the Philippines was in marked contrast to the sharp battles between the legislative and executive branches on foreign policy issues raging from Central America to the Middle East. However, Congress and the administration emphasized different methods for achieving the agreed-upon goals.

Congress focused its efforts on using continuing U.S. aid to the Philippines as a tool to bring about changes. It voted in two separate bills to reduce President Reagan's request for military aid to the Marcos regime.

Administration officials concentrated on using dire warnings about the dangers ahead to secure altered policies. By the end of the year, a visit from one of Reagan's closest advisers and other forms of pressure had pushed Marcos into ordering a presidential election in February 1986.

But allegations that Marcos and his supporters stole the election from challenger Corazon Aquino provoked further congressional debate over the U.S. role in the Philippines. Fueling members' concerns was a spate of killings of Aquino supporters.

Sam Nunn, D-Ga., ranking Democrat on the Senate Armed Services Committee, told Reagan in a letter that "Marcos or forces allied with him are in the process of making an all-out effort to steal the election by massive fraud, intimidation and murder."

Nunn asked that U.S. aid be halted if the will of the Filipino voters was thwarted through fraud.

Congress moved to distance itself from the Marcos regime; the Senate on Feb. 19, 1986, passed a resolution (S Res 345) declaring that the elections were marked by fraud and the House Foreign Affairs Subcommittee on Asian and Pacific Affairs adopted a bill (HR 4198) suspending arms aid to the Philippines.

But the next week, after key Philippine military officials defected to the Aquino camp and the Reagan administration issued a series of statements associating the United States with the mutiny, Marcos stepped down. An important congressional player in Marcos' Feb. 25 ouster was Sen. Paul Laxalt, R-Nev., a close friend of President Reagan. In his final hours as president, Marcos telephoned Laxalt for advice; the Nevadan said he suggested that Marcos "cut and cut cleanly."

U.S. Policy

Because of its strategic and political importance — along with memories of its status as the only former U.S. colony — the Philippines long had been a major concern for the United States. In the 1980s that concern grew in direct proportion to the rising success of the communist insurgency.

At the heart of U.S. interest in the archipelago were Clark Air Base and Subic Bay Naval Station, the two largest U.S. military installations outside the United States.

Situated on Luzon, the largest Philippine island, the bases were uniquely capable of giving the United States control of vital Pacific Ocean sea lanes through which passed much of the world's commerce, including about half of all Persian Gulf oil.

Subic Bay was the main supply base for the U.S. Seventh Fleet, and it included a major naval air station and ship repair center. Clark was headquarters for the 13th U.S. Air Force; from its runways, American planes could patrol the skies west of Hawaii and east of the Persian Gulf.

In 1947, a year after the Philippines gained independence from the United States, it agreed to allow this country to retain the two bases. Under the accord, the United States kept sovereignty over the bases and was to have use of them until 2046.

The expiration date was later changed to 1991 and the Philippines assumed sovereignty; modifications were agreed to in 1979 and 1983. The 1983 agreement called for $900 million in aid during fiscal years 1985-89, with $475 million of that in economic aid and $425 million in military aid.

All of that would change, however, if the guerrilla New Peoples Army and the Philippine Communist Party were to come to power. By 1985, the guerrilla force was expanding rapidly and was active in all 73 provinces.

According to U.S. intelligence estimates, the guerrillas

had some 15,000 armed, full-time troops, aided by an equal number of part-time irregulars.

A Nov. 1 report by the Senate Intelligence Committee estimated that Marcos had only three years to implement major reforms to save his government. The committee report painted a bleak picture of the prospects for effective reform, however.

"We believe such a change of course is very unlikely," it said. The report also said the Philippine military was inept, poorly led and ill-equipped.

That assessment was only slightly more pessimistic than the official Reagan administration position. Richard L. Armitage, assistant secretary of defense for international security affairs, repeatedly told congressional committees that the guerrillas could force a "strategic stalemate" in three to five years.

Aid Shifts

Led by Stephen J. Solarz, D-N.Y., chairman of the House Foreign Affairs Subcommittee on Asian and Pacific Affairs, congressional critics of Marcos forced cutbacks in military aid and wrote strongly worded resolutions demanding rapid reform in the Philippines.

Under the 1983 pact providing for U.S. use of the two bases, the Philippines received $180 million annually in economic and military aid.

On the theory that Marcos was more interested in military than economic aid, Solarz for several years led a campaign to reduce the military aid and increase the economic aid.

In 1984, Congress approved $40 million in military aid — a $45 million cut from Reagan's request. The $45 million was shifted to economic aid instead. *(1984 Almanac p. 398)*

In 1985, the foreign aid authorization bill (PL 99-473) allowed $70 million in military aid, a $30 million cut from the president's request. Again, the saving was shifted to economic aid. *(Foreign aid, p. 41)*

At the end of the 1985 session, Congress reduced the military aid further to $55 million, as part of the continuing appropriations resolution (PL 99-190). *(Story, p. 367)*

Elections, Marcos' Downfall

While Congress was cutting military aid, the Reagan administration was intensifying its efforts to bring about changes. In October, Reagan sent Sen. Laxalt to Manila with a three-page letter urging reforms.

That letter might have been a key factor in convincing Marcos suddenly to call speeded-up presidential elections. On Nov. 3 Marcos announced the elections, which were held Feb. 7.

Philippine opposition forces quickly united behind Corazon Aquino, the widow of opposition leader Benigno S. Aquino Jr.

The assassination of Aquino in 1983, in which the Philippine military had been implicated, set off protests that helped convince the administration to drop its uncritical support for Marcos.

Philippine army chief of staff Gen. Fabian Ver and 25 other military personnel were charged with conspiring to kill Benigno Aquino. They were acquitted Dec. 2, however, and Marcos announced his intention to reinstate Ver in his former post.

Once the elections were announced, Congress and the administration united in insisting that the balloting be free and fair. On Nov. 14, both House and Senate approved a resolution (H Con Res 232) calling on Marcos to honor his pledge for honest elections. The Senate approved the measure by voice vote; the House by 407-0. *(Vote 371, p. 116-H)*

The resolution said that at least five steps had to be taken if the elections were to be "deemed credible" by the Philippine people. The steps were:

- Determination of the timing and arrangements for the election in accordance with the Philippine Constitution.
- The appointment of an impartial elections commission.
- The timely accreditation of an independent citizens' election monitoring organization, with free access to all polling places.
- Provision of adequate access by opposition candidates to radio, television and newspapers during the campaign.
- Neutral conduct during the election by the Philippine military.

The resolution said that Congress, in considering future foreign aid allocations, would "take into account the degree to which democratic reforms are taking place" in the Philippines.

The Reagan administration also exerted pressure on Marcos to guarantee honest voting procedures. The rigging of the elections would be "a disaster of large and undefinable proportions," Paul D. Wolfowitz, assistant secretary of state for East Asian and Pacific affairs told the House Asian and Pacific Affairs Subcommittee.

But in the weeks before and after the Feb. 7, 1986, elections, members of Congress watched with growing anger as Marcos rigged the voting, the counting of the ballots and then the proclamation of his victory by the Philippine National Assembly.

The final series of actions that led to Marcos' downfall began early on Feb. 22 (Manila time) when Defense Minister Juan Ponce Enrile, a close Marcos associate, and Lt. Gen. Fidel Ramos, the armed forces deputy chief of staff, abruptly resigned, demanded that Marcos give up power, and took up positions in military installations in Manila. The two men reportedly acted because of rumors that Marcos was about to have them arrested. Responding to a call by Roman Catholic Archbishop Cardinal Jaime Sin, thousands of civilians surrounded the military camps to protect Enrile and Ramos against an expected attack by forces loyal to Marcos. The civilians, with scores of flower-carrying nuns in the forefront, blocked the advance of Marcos forces on Feb. 23.

Marcos remained defiant, declaring on government television stations that he would never resign.

In Washington, the White House issued its statements associating the United States with the rebellion against Marcos.

By Feb. 24, totally isolated in his ornate presidential palace, Marcos sought desperately to cling to power, offering to serve as "honory president" and calling Sen. Laxalt for confirmation that Reagan really wanted him to resign. In a last pretense that he retained control, Marcos staged a truncated inaugural ceremony in the courtyard of the presidential palace — shortly after Aquino and joyous supporters held their own swearing-in ceremony across town.

Under cover of darkness, Marcos flew to Clark Air Base on Feb. 25 and left the country the next day for Guam and then Hawaii.

Aquino immediately took power, proclaiming that she had won the disputed Feb. 7 election. In a speech Feb. 26, she promised reconciliation, saying it was "time to heal the wounds, to forget the past." ∎

DEFENSE

CQ

Defense

President Reagan managed to win some battles over individual weapons in his arms buildup, but congressional actions in 1985 may have signaled an end to his extraordinary success in boosting the overall defense budget.

His fortunes on Capitol Hill were heavily influenced by outside events. With a summit in the works between Reagan and the new Soviet leader, Mikhail S. Gorbachev, the administration persuaded members not to undercut the president's negotiating position by denying him the MX missile or making deep cuts in his program to develop anti-missile defenses.

Reagan's only defeat in the arms control area came on the one issue which he refused to negotiate with Moscow: development of anti-satellite (ASAT) weapons. Despite vigorous White House objections, Congress barred any U.S. ASAT tests against target satellites unless the Soviet Union ended its ASAT test moratorium.

And with overall budget deficits mounting and Draconian cuts looming in domestic programs, members were hesitant to approve big boosts in defense spending.

For fiscal 1986, Congress approved an overall defense budget of $297.6 billion — only about $3 billion more than it had appropriated for fiscal 1985.

In addition to funds for the Department of Defense, the national defense budget included about $8 billion for other agencies, the bulk of it for the Energy Department, which developed and manufactured all nuclear weapons.

Because of inflation, it would have taken $302.5 billion in fiscal 1986 to equal the purchasing power of the fiscal 1985 budget. So in "real" terms, the congressionally approved budget represented a decline of nearly 2 percent.

That amount was further reduced in March 1986 by automatic reductions imposed by the Gramm-Rudman-Hollings deficit reduction law. The actual fiscal 1986 defense budget totaled $286.7 billion, a real decrease of more than 5 percent from the fiscal 1985 level.

The Budget Fight

During the congressional defense debates in 1983 and 1984, a widespread consensus among participants and knowledgeable observers had emerged early each year: It was taken for granted that the final defense appropriation in each year would allow a "real" increase over the cost of inflation of about 5 percent.

Both years, Reagan requested far larger hikes — a real increase of 10 percent in 1983 (for the fiscal 1984 budget) and 13.3 percent in 1984 (for fiscal 1985).

And in both years, Defense Secretary Caspar W. Weinberger adamantly rejected pleas from some of the Pentagon's longtime friends in Congress that he tell them where to make the reductions that the Hill consensus demanded.

Weinberger's position was that any compromise on his part would only have prompted Congress to insist on even deeper reductions in the defense request.

But many members — including some Republicans — disagreed. They pointed out that agreement on the overall defense total had been reached very early each year, and argued that Weinberger's rigid insistence on a much higher level merely diminished his own credibility.

In any case, Congress approved in both 1983 and 1984 exactly the increase in the defense budget that the congressional consensus had agreed on from the start: about 5 percent, in addition to the cost of inflation.

At the start of the 1985 debate over the fiscal 1986 defense budget, the same general pattern seemed to be in prospect, with one difference. The early consensus was that the defense budget would increase by 3 percent above inflation. The lower growth rate reflected both the prospect of $200 billion deficits for years to come and the political difficulty of making further reductions in domestic discretionary programs.

By comparison with previous years, the administration request was relatively moderate: a real increase of 5.9 percent to $322.2 billion. Once again, Weinberger refused to brook any talk of compromise on a lower increase.

But by mid-March, the political climate had become even more disadvantageous from Weinberger's standpoint: According to the new conventional wisdom, the defense budget would increase by no more than enough to keep pace with inflation (zero real growth or $302 billion) and it might not be increased at all (zero nominal growth or $292.5 billion).

By the end of May, the Democratic-controlled House had set the lower figure — with no allowance for inflation — as the defense target in its version of the first concurrent budget resolution for fiscal 1986.

The Senate agreed to the higher figure — an increase to cover inflation — in its version of the measure.

Both houses agreed to 3 percent real defense increases in the following two years (fiscal 1987-88).

In early August, the two houses agreed on a compromise budget resolution that incorporated the higher, Senate-passed defense figure: $302.5 billion. But House liberals bitterly opposed the move and blocked for several weeks final action on a defense authorization bill that was drafted to meet the $302.5 billion ceiling.

The House passed the defense bill only after House Democratic leaders assured the insurgents that they could try again to reduce the defense total to $292.5 billion on the companion defense appropriations measure.

The two houses took positions on the defense appropriations bill that mirrored their initial stands on defense appropriations, the House assuming an overall defense total of $292.5 billion, the Senate assuming $302.5 billion.

Ultimately, the defense funding measure was absorbed in an omnibus continuing appropriations bill, which essentially split the difference between the Senate and House-passed defense ceilings. Counting defense funds appropriated in other bills, the continuing resolution brought the overall defense total for fiscal 1986 to $297.6 billion.

Procurement and Organizational 'Reform'

In addition to discounting Weinberger's case for continuing defense budget increases, Congress also took aim at Weinberger's management of the Pentagon.

In the wake of widely reported instances of inefficiency, impropriety, and outright fraud in defense contracting, Congress imposed several changes in the Pentagon's purchasing system. Among other things, the new laws barred contractors from billing the government for certain types of expenses, such as entertainment and political lobbying.

Some leaders in the so-called "procurement reform" effort were longtime critics of Reagan's defense buildup.

But Weinberger was challenged on another front by some of the Pentagon's staunchest congressional allies. Over the secretary's strong objections, senior members of the Senate and House Armed Services committees pressed for reorganization of the nation's top military command.

According to these critics, the parochial views of the separate armed services wasted money in peacetime and might impair combat efficiency in case of war.

Strategic Arms and Arms Control

On the face of it, Reagan easily bested his critics in the liberal arms control community during 1985:

The long political wrangle over the MX missile, since 1983 the focus of congressional debate over Reagan's nuclear arms policy, lurched to an end late in March with Reagan beating the arms controllers' final effort to slash production of the missile.

Both houses approved production of 21 MXs in fiscal 1985 after the administration made a very forceful pitch that it needed to win the vote to preserve its bargaining leverage in the Geneva arms negotiations — which had resumed only days before the votes on MX. In the House, Reagan's narrow victory came after chief arms control negotiator Max M. Kampelman flew back to Washington from Geneva to make the case to wavering members.

Even before the dust had settled on that round of the MX fight, centrist defense experts on Capitol Hill, led by Sen. Sam Nunn, D-Ga., unveiled a plan to end the MX fight once and for all: Their proposal was for a cap of 40-50 on the number of MXs that would be deployed in existing missile silos, where they were vulnerable to Soviet attack.

Reagan and Weinberger held out against the Nunn proposal until the final days of Senate action on the annual defense authorization bill, when they agreed to a cap on 50 missiles — half the number Reagan had planned to deploy in existing silos. But it was clear from the moment Nunn and his allies unveiled the proposal that it would carry.

On other arms control fronts, Reagan:

- Quashed by margins that were respectable, if not always safe, several efforts in the Senate and House to cut back his program to develop a nationwide anti-missile defense and to impose special limits on specific parts of the program that the critics deemed particularly threatening to existing arms control agreements.

Officially, the project was called the "strategic defense initiative" (SDI) but it was more widely referred to as "star wars." Congress trimmed $1 billion from Reagan's $3.7 billion budget request for SDI. However, the congressional defense funding panels that made the cut explained it purely as a response to budgetary stringency — not a challenge to SDI's underlying rationale such as those the arms controllers mounted unsucessfully.

- Brushed aside a concerted effort by Common Cause and several other arms control lobby groups to "raise expectations" before his November summit meeting with Gorbachev. The lobby groups had hoped to generate strong political pressure for Reagan to reach some sort of arms control agreement, however limited, in Geneva. But the meeting produced no tangible arms control progress and still Reagan's popularity soared to record heights.
- Sidetracked House action on a non-binding resolution urging him to resume negotiations with Moscow leading to a complete ban on nuclear weapons testing. Reagan invoked the imminence of the summit, then six weeks away.
- Finally won conditional assent by Congress to producing lethal chemical weapons — "binary munitions" — for the first time since 1969. The House had thwarted three earlier efforts.

Against those defeats, the arms controllers chalked up only two victories:

- The continuing appropriations resolution enacted in December included a permanent bar on full-scale testing of the anti-satellite missile, contingent on Soviet abstention from ASAT tests.
- And in June, against the public recommendation of Weinberger and other administration hard-liners, Reagan decided to dismantle a missile-firing submarine to remain within a limitation of the unratified SALT II U.S.-Soviet arms control treaty.

Before Reagan announced his decision, the Senate had voted 90-5 to recommend that he continue the policy of informal adherence to the SALT limits. A more influential factor could have been intense demands by allied governments that the SALT limits be respected.

However, Reagan's winning scorecard at the end of the 1985 congressional duels might obscure a more fundamental point. Reagan's political fortunes on arms control looked very different in 1985 than in 1982 — when nationwide pressure for a nuclear arms freeze had the White House on the ropes.

But the magnitude of that change was equaled by — and in large part resulted from — the symbolic changes in the administration's treatment of arms control issues and of U.S.-Soviet relations more generally.

By the time of Reagan's 1984 re-election campaign, confrontational, anti-Soviet rhetoric was far less common than in his early years in office. When Congress took up the defense debate in 1985, Reagan had embraced the arms control process (in general terms), "gone the extra mile" to continue the informal observance of existing treaties and scheduled a meeting with his Soviet counterpart — all things that flew in the face of his pre-1983 rhetoric.

Hard-line Reagan backers were dismayed that he no longer was challenging the public belief that talking with the Russians would make things better.

Meanwhile, liberal arms control activists fumed in frustration that he had deflected their campaigns with mere symbolic actions. But some of them took comfort in their ability to sidetrack the ASAT program, and they saw in that a hopeful sign: If it became clear that Reagan was blocking a sweeping arms reduction agreement with Moscow by refusing to rein in SDI, the critics hoped that perception would give them an instrument to mobilize public and congressional pressure against the anti-missile program.

—*By Pat Towell*

Reagan, Congress Compromise on MX Missile

The politically bruising, three-year-long battle over the MX missile — the centerpiece of President Reagan's nuclear arms program — moved toward resolution in 1985. Congress took two major legislative actions:

- It freed up funding for 21 more MXs in fiscal 1985. After intense administration lobbying, Congress in March approved resolutions (S J Res 71 — PL 99-17, H J Res 181 — PL 99-18), giving the go-ahead for procurement of the 21 MXs, a decision that had been deferred from the previous year. *(1984 Almanac p. 59)*

Reagan prevailed largely because U.S.-Soviet arms control negotiations had resumed in Geneva only days before the showdown.

- It limited to 50 the number of MXs that could be deployed in existing missile silos, while funding 12 additional missiles in fiscal 1986. The cap, a compromise reached with the administration, was contained in the fiscal 1986 defense authorization bill (S 1160 — PL 99-145) and companion appropriations bill (H J Res 465 — PL 99-190). The legislation also included $1.7 billion to fund the 12 MXs. Reagan had requested $3 billion for 40 missiles. *(Authorization bill, p. 138; defense appropriations, p. 377)*

Under the deal, additional MXs were to be purchased in future years, but only for test launches.

The idea of a cap had been advanced by congressional moderates who earlier had played key roles in the battle to save the MX.

During consideration of the defense authorization bill, the Senate approved a 50-missile cap; the House voted a cap of 40. House conferees on the measure concurred in return for making the limit "permanent" instead of a one-year pause.

Background

Called "Peacekeeper" by Reagan, the MX was designed to carry 10 nuclear warheads, each with enough accuracy and explosive power to destroy an underground Soviet missile launcher. Beginning in 1983 it became the symbolic focus of congressional debate over Reagan's nuclear weapons policy.

Arms control advocates charged that it would only escalate the nuclear arms race. But the administration contended that the new missile was needed to offset Soviet missiles able to attack U.S. missile launchers.

A grass-roots lobbying campaign and strong efforts by the House Democratic leadership came tantalizingly close to blocking MX production several times.

But the program survived because of a small but influential group of predominantly Democratic defense specialists who supported production of a limited number of MXs in return for changes in the administration's negotiating stance in the strategic arms reduction talks (START). *(Background, 1983 Almanac p. 195; 1982 Almanac p. 120)*

Leading this group were Democratic House members Les Aspin, Wis.; Albert Gore Jr., Tenn.; and Norman D. Dicks, Wash.; and Sens. William S. Cohen, R-Maine; Sam Nunn, D-Ga.; and Charles H. Percy, R-Ill. — the so-called "Gang of Six."

In that year's action on MX, Congress agreed to fiscal 1984 funding of the first batch of 21 missiles. Reagan's support on Capitol Hill was helped in the spring by his softened stance on arms talks with the Soviets and in the fall by the Soviets' downing of a Korean airliner. But at the end of 1983, the Soviets broke off arms talks.

Questions of Vulnerability

By spring of 1984, the MX critics had persuaded the House Democratic leadership to oppose the $25 billion missile program as a symbol of Reagan's large defense buildup.

Also by that time, opposition to MX spread in the Senate, largely because Reagan planned to put the new missile in existing launchers believed to be vulnerable to attack. During June 1984 debate on the 1985 defense authorization bill (PL 98-515), an effort to kill MX production outright failed 55-41.

But the missile's opponents found an ally in Sen. Lawton Chiles, D-Fla., an influential moderate with a staunchly pro-defense record, who wanted to halt production of MX because of its vulnerability.

Chiles proposed an amendment that would have provided enough money to preserve the option of future MX production without buying 21 additional missiles in fiscal 1985. It attracted more support: five Democrats from Southern or border states and three Republicans. Only Vice President Bush's tie-breaking vote killed Chiles' amendment.

By late 1984, the anti-MX coalition had fought the administration to a draw over the missile: Efforts to kill the program had failed, but Congress decided — over the administration's objections — to put off until the spring of 1985 the question of continued production.

Elections and Arms Talks

The procedure for the deferred decision was contained in a continuing appropriations resolution (PL 98-473) for fiscal 1985. Before the Pentagon could buy the second batch of 21 missiles, each chamber of Congress would have to pass two joint resolutions, one authorizing the missiles, the other appropriating the missiles.

The arms controllers thus needed to muster enough strength in only one house to block the missile. The two sets of votes would come no more than a day apart, but the timing would be in the hands of the administration.

At the beginning of 1985, two major factors figured in the MX's fortunes: the results of the November 1984 elections, and the Reagan administration's agreement to resume nuclear arms control negotiations with the Soviets.

MX opponents had a narrow House majority in 1984, and by the estimate of Common Cause, the November election still left the missile foes with a slim advantage.

In the Senate, the liberal arms controllers picked up some strength in November. However, MX opponents would again need the support of budget-motivated conservatives, such as Chiles.

The administration argued that Reagan's re-election in November vindicated a fundamental premise of his policy: that Moscow would negotiate away its existing advantage in nuclear weaponry only if it faced a U.S. arms buildup.

At the same time, Reagan had toned down his anti-Soviet rhetoric, and in early January he agreed to resume arms control talks.

Early Pressure

In a press conference Jan. 9, Reagan pledged to be "flexible, patient and determined" in keeping the new talks alive. The next day, his secretary of state, George P. Shultz, briefed 45 House members and 21 senators in two meetings, telling them that the U.S. negotiating position would be undermined if Congress scrapped the controversial MX or cut back on other defense efforts "necessary to the security of the nation."

Reagan and top administration officials stressed that theme into March, with the arms talks to start on March 12 and the MX votes to come later in that month.

Many Democratic opponents of the missile tried in vain to get Aspin, the new Armed Services Committee chairman, to change his mind and oppose the MX.

And MX opponents also faced two other disadvantages:

- House Speaker Thomas P. O'Neill Jr., D-Mass., whose zest for battling Reagan on MX was a key to the opponents' partial win in the House in 1984, had warned that an anti-MX crusade could contribute to an image that Democrats were "soft" on defense.
- Neither house ever had approved killing MX production outright; earlier votes had involved slowing down the program. The procedures governing the March MX votes would complicate any effort to introduce nuance into the votes.

The Fiscal 1985 Fight

The MX issue gave Reagan his first legislative showdown on defense in 1985, and he won congressional approval for 21 more of the controversial missiles.

The Senate's approval came in a pair of 55-45 votes on March 19 and 20. The March 19 vote on S J Res 71 authorized use of $1.5 billion in the fiscal 1985 defense budget to buy the 21 missiles. The identical vote on March 20 on S J Res 75 approved appropriation of the MX funds. *(Votes 19, 20, p. 7-S)*

Ten Democrats joined 45 Republicans voting "aye," while the 45 "nay" votes included eight Republicans. Most senators whose positions had not been previously announced sided with Reagan and voted for the missiles.

The House approved S J Res 71 on a 219-213 vote; two days later, members approved H J Res 181, appropriating the funds, by a 217-210 vote. A few absentees accounted for the changes. *(Votes 34, 36, p. 14-H)*

SENATE FLOOR ACTION

Most observers agreed that timing was a critical element in Reagan's Senate victory. The president and his allies insisted that U.S. negotiators at the arms talks with the Soviets in Geneva would be handicapped if Congress blocked production of MX.

That was the theme of several presidential speeches and White House meetings with members of Congress, individually and in groups of up to 30 at a time.

The Geneva negotiations began on March 12. By the time of the vote a week later, some senators had received the same message in phone calls from chief U.S. arms negotiator Max M. Kampelman, in Geneva.

What MX critic Chiles called "the Geneva card" was widely cited as the explanation for Reagan's 55-45 Senate advantage. "There are not 30 people out there that think you ought to build MX," Chiles fumed to reporters. "A lot of them say, 'If anything happens at Geneva, we'd be blamed.' "

During two days of Senate debate March 18-19, several senators who voted for the president's position said they did so with reluctance and that they would insist on substantial reductions in the administration's future MX plans, which included appropriation of $3.2 billion for 48 additional missiles in the fiscal 1986 budget.

Anatomy of a Vote

The November elections gave MX foes a net gain of one Senate vote. Democratic MX critics Tom Harkin and Paul Simon replaced GOP missile backers Roger Jepsen and Charles H. Percy, in Iowa and Illinois, respectively, while Republican Mitch McConnell succeeded anti-MX Democrat Walter D. Huddleston in Kentucky.

Since Minority Leader Robert C. Byrd, D-W.Va., had criticized Reagan's MX plan, the opponents hoped they could win his support and that he would bring along one or two other conservative Democrats.

So while the MX opponents conceded that the Geneva talks would give Reagan powerful political leverage, they insisted down to the last day that they had a shot at blocking the 21 missiles in the Senate. To counter widespread speculation that Reagan would win these votes with ease, the critics emphasized that none of the senators who had supported the Chiles amendment the previous June had announced a change of position.

But when it counted on March 19, the MX opponents:

- Did not convert Byrd and they lost two of the Southern Democrats who had been won over to Chiles' 1984 amendment, Lloyd Bensten, Texas, and Russell B. Long, La. *(Box, p. 121)*
- Lost moderate Democrat David L. Boren, Okla., who had voted not only for Chiles, but also for the earlier 1984 amendment that would have killed production outright.
- Lost one Republican who had supported Chiles, Arlen Specter, Pa.
- Lost three other Republicans, who had voted against fiscal 1985 MX production: Charles McC. Mathias Jr., Md., Bob Packwood, Ore., and Gordon J. Humphrey, N.H.

Opponents persuaded only one MX supporter to switch and vote against the MX on March 19: Nancy Landon Kassebaum, R-Kan.

Anti-MX Lobbyists' Efforts

As the MX contest heated up in mid-March, the first task confronting anti-MX lobbyists was erasing the widespread impression that Reagan had insuperable momentum on his side. The wave of bipartisan support for U.S. negotiators at Geneva was at the root of the image.

The opponents were greatly upset when Senate Minority Whip Alan Cranston, D-Calif., a longtime MX opponent widely regarded as a good Senate head-counter, told reporters that Reagan would win the fight easily.

The lobby organizations tried to orchestrate grassroots pressure from the states of targeted senators. By the end of the debate, the offices of some undecided senators such as Mathias and Daniel J. Evans, R-Wash., received hundreds of calls a day on the issue, the vast bulk of them urging opposition to MX.

The lobbyists also arranged interviews with targeted senators for former national security officials who would lend their authority to the case against the MX. Three of the most active of these expert-lobbyists were Gerard

Senate 'Undecideds': Path to an 'Aye' Vote

Eight senators, whose intentions were unknown up until March 19, the day the Senate voted on MX, all voted to give President Reagan money for the missiles.

Their reasons were largely variations on the theme of arms control talks. The heavily lobbied Arlen Specter, R-Pa., provided the most unlikely twist: Paul C. Warnke, President Carter's arms control chief, who argued against MX. On Feb. 27, Warnke inadvertently convinced Specter of the role of MX as a "bargaining chip."

Warnke recalled his unhappiness — and that of the Soviet negotiator across the table from him in 1977 — when Warnke was suddenly told of Carter's decision to cancel production of the B-1 bomber.

Warnke would have liked to get something from the Russians in return for giving up the plane, according to Specter, and the Soviet diplomat would have liked credit back in Moscow for driving such a tough bargain.

The lesson Specter drew from that tale, he said before voting for MX, was "that an important weapons system should not be abandoned without some concession from the other side."

Gordon J. Humphrey, R-N.H., had been the only Senate conservative to vote against Reagan's plan to base MX in existing silos. He reasoned that the missiles would be vulnerable to attack. But in the week before the vote, Humphrey got two secret briefings that persuaded him otherwise.

On the day of the vote, former Sen. John Tower, R-Texas (1961-85), phoned Humphrey from Geneva, where Tower was in charge of U.S.-Soviet talks on long-range nuclear weapons like MX. Humphrey said he already was on board for the vote and then quipped to the hard-line Tower: "Make sure they don't take you for a ride over there."

"Who do you think you're talking to?" Tower shot back.

Charles McC. Mathias Jr., R-Md., an ardent arms control supporter, in the end was one of the few senators who argued for MX on its military merits. The issue was what the Pentagon called "prompt, hard-target kill capability" — ballistic missiles that could destroy armored military targets. MX was the quickest way to redress the Soviets' advantage in such missiles, Mathias argued.

Bob Packwood, R-Ore., like Specter and Mathias, was the target of heavy grass-roots lobbying by anti-MX constituents. But to at least one Packwood aide, the MX foes were just one more vocal minority.

Packwood interviewed specialists and agonized. But chief arms control negotiator Max M. Kampelman was pivotal in Packwood's "aye" vote. Kampelman had several conversations with Packwood, calling from Geneva on the day of the vote. Packwood later cited "the humanity, decency and judgment of Max Kampelman."

Daniel J. Evans, R-Wash., mentioned the Geneva connection, but also U.S. ties with European allies. He cited their willingness to deploy U.S. Pershing and cruise missiles despite domestic opposition. "They would be dismayed if we now shrank from our share of our joint defense," said Evans.

Backing up the allies also loomed large in the argument Minority Leader Robert C. Byrd, D-W.Va., made for approving the 21 missiles. But Byrd also charged that Reagan had "put political priorities over our basic national security," abandoning an earlier plan to scatter MX launchers to avoid a Soviet attack. Reagan's alternative of putting the MXs in potentially vulnerable existing missile silos was "the easy way out for a tough-talking administration," Byrd said.

The other two "undecideds" — Russell B. Long, D-La., and Lloyd Bentsen, D-Texas — explained their support for MX this time in terms of the Geneva talks. "I don't want to see any action taken by the Senate that would show a lack of resolve," Bentsen put it.

Smith, who had negotiated the 1972 U.S.-Soviet arms agreements (SALT I) for President Nixon, Paul C. Warnke, who had been President Carter's chief arms control negotiator, and former CIA chief William Colby.

When the opponents spotted a wavering senator, they tried to assign what Cranston called "designated hitters" on a senator-to-senator basis.

For example, at about the time the Geneva talks began, rumor spread that Wendell H. Ford, D-Ky., an MX foe, was reconsidering his position. Moderate Democrat John Glenn, Ohio, and the two Arkansas Democrats, Dale Bumpers and David Pryor, were assigned to talk to Ford.

On March 15, the opponents got their first big boost in Kassebaum's announcement that she would oppose release of the MX funds.

That was offset later the same day when Boren announced that he would support the president this time, citing Geneva. The loss of Boren was particularly disappointing to the critics; it suggested they would be unable to capitalize on farm-state resentment of Reagan's veto of farm credit legislation. *(Farm credit veto, p. 542)*

MX opponent John Melcher, D-Mont., had tried to form a "silo coalition" of members who would oppose the missile unless Reagan relented on the farm issue.

The White House Push

The administration turned to the most successful lobbyist at its disposal — the president himself.

Using phone calls and cozy fireside chats at the White House, Reagan sought to win over undecided or wavering members. And even before the Senate voted, the president had turned his lobbying attention to the House.

Other senior administration officials also lobbied in person and by phone. Gen. John W. Vessey Jr., chairman of the Joint Chiefs of Staff, and Air Force Chief of Staff Gen. Charles A. Gabriel also made some phone calls. And Brig. Gen. Gordon Fornell, the Air Force's chief MX salesman, was a frequent visitor to Capitol Hill.

A few days after the Geneva talks opened, unnamed White House aides ruffled some senatorial feathers with tough talk to *The New York Times*. Reagan would weigh senators' support on MX and other important issues in

The Committees and How They Voted

SENATE ARMED SERVICES: Voted 11-6 on March 18 to report S J Res 71, authorizing the expenditure of $1.5 billion to procure 21 MX missiles.

For MX (11): Republicans Goldwater, Ariz.; Thurmond, S.C.; Warner, Va.; Cohen, Maine; Quayle, Ind.; East, N.C.; Wilson, Calif.; Denton, Ala.; Gramm, Texas. Democrats Nunn, Ga., and Stennis, Miss.

Against MX (6): Democrats Hart, Colo.; Exon, Neb.; Levin, Mich.; Kennedy, Mass.; Bingaman, N.M.; Glenn, Ohio.

Not voting (2): Republican Humphrey, N.H.; Democrat Dixon, Ill.

SENATE APPROPRIATIONS: Voted 15-14 on March 20 to report S J Res 75 (S Rept 99-14), releasing $1.5 billion to procure 21 MX missiles.

For MX (15): Republicans Stevens, Alaska; McClure, Idaho; Laxalt, Nev.; Garn, Utah; Cochran, Miss.; Abdnor, S.D.; Kasten, Wis.; D'Amato, N.Y.; Mattingly, Ga.; Rudman, N.H.; Specter, Pa.; Domenici, N.M. Democrats Stennis, Miss.; Byrd, W.Va.; DeConcini, Ariz.

Against MX (14): Republicans Hatfield, Ore.; Weicker, Conn.; Andrews, N.D. Democrats Proxmire, Wis.; Inouye, Hawaii; Hollings, S.C.; Chiles, Fla.; Johnston, La.; Burdick, N.D.; Leahy, Vt.; Sasser, Tenn.; Bumpers, Ark.; Lautenberg, N.J.; Harkin, Iowa.

HOUSE APPROPRIATIONS: Voted by 28-26 on March 20 to oppose H J Res 181 (H Rept 99-22), releasing $1.5 billion to procure 21 MX missiles.

Opposing MX (28): Democrats Whitten, Miss.; Boland, Mass.; Natcher, Ky.; Smith, Iowa; Addabbo, N.Y.; Yates, Ill.; Obey, Wis.; Roybal, Calif.; Alexander, Ark.; Traxler, Mich.; Early, Mass.; Boggs, La.; McHugh, N.Y.; Lehman, Fla.; Sabo, Minn.; Dixon, Calif.; AuCoin, Ore.; Akaka, Hawaii; Gray, Pa.; Dwyer, N.J.; Carr, Mich.; Mrazek, N.Y.; Durbin, Ill.; and Coleman, Texas. Republicans Conte, Mass.; Coughlin, Pa.; Smith, Neb.; and Green, N.Y.

Supporting MX (26): Democrats Bevill, Ala.; Chappell, Fla.; Murtha, Pa.; Wilson, Texas; Dicks, Wash.; Fazio, Calif.; Hefner, N.C.; Watkins, Okla.; Boner, Tenn.; and Hoyer, Md. Republicans McDade, Pa.; Myers, Ind.; Miller, Ohio; Young, Fla.; Kemp, N.Y.; Regula, Ohio; O'Brien, Ill.; Rudd, Ariz.; Edwards, Okla.; Livingston, La.; Loeffler, Texas; Lewis, Calif.; Porter, Ill.; Skeen, N.M.; Wolf, Va.; and Lowery, Calif.

Not voting (3): Democrat Stokes, Ohio; Republicans Pursell, Mich., and Rogers, Ky.

HOUSE ARMED SERVICES: Voted 37-8 on March 20 to report H J Res 180 (H Rept 99-23), authorizing expenditure of $1.5 billion for 21 MX missiles.

For MX (37): Democrats Aspin, Wis.; Price, Ill.; Stratton, N.Y.; Nichols, Ala.; Daniel, Va.; Montgomery, Miss.; Byron, Md.; Hutto, Fla.; Skelton, Mo.; Leath, Texas; McCurdy, Okla.; Dyson, Md.; Ray, Ga.; Ortiz, Texas; Darden, Ga.; Robinson, Ark.; Bustamante, Texas. Republicans Dickinson, Ala.; Whitehurst, Va.; Spence, S.C.; Holt, Md.; Hillis, Ind.; Badham, Calif.; Stump, Ariz.; Courter, N.J.; Hopkins, Ky.; Davis, Mich.; Kramer, Colo.; Hunter, Calif.; Hartnett, S.C.; Martin, N.Y.; Kasich, Ohio; Carney, N.Y.; Martin, Ill.; Bateman, Va.; Sweeney, Texas; Blaz, Guam.

Against MX (8): Democrats Bennett, Fla.; Dellums, Calif.; Schroeder, Colo.; Mavroules, Mass.; Foglietta, Pa.; Hertel, Mich.; Sisisky, Va.; Spratt, S.C.

Not voting: Democrat Lloyd, Tenn.

deciding how much help to give in campaign fund raising, the aides said.

Mark Andrews, R-N.D., one of the GOP caucus' mavericks, denounced this as a "thug" tactic.

Rounding Up the Undecideds

On the morning of March 18, James Abdnor, S.D., a GOP conservative who had kept his own counsel, announced he would back Reagan and the missile. This seemed to mark the end of any hopes the MX opponents had for the "silo-coalition" tactic.

Also throwing in with Reagan was GOP moderate John H. Chafee, R.I., who, like Abdnor, cited Geneva. "I am saying to the president and his negotiators, 'I don't want any excuses,'" Chafee explained. "'I expect you to come back with an agreement. I don't want anybody saying you would have succeeded but for the lack of MX.'"

Late in the morning, the Senate Armed Services Committee reported S J Res 71 by a vote of 11-6. Humphrey, the only committee member believed to be still undecided, did not attend the meeting. *(Committee vote, this page)*

At about 2:30 p.m., the opponents scored their second clear win of the campaign, when Larry Pressler, R-S.D., announced he would continue to oppose MX. "In its current [basing] mode, the MX is almost an invitation to attack," he said. "There are too many eggs in one basket when you put 10 warheads in one vulnerable silo."

The administration's blitz continued during the day, with Reagan calling at least one senator from Air Force One on his way back from a summit meeting in Canada with Prime Minister Brian Mulroney.

Meanwhile, a desultory floor debate on the resolution had begun.

Sen. Sam Nunn, D-Ga., drew the most attention with a speech that focused as much on his frustration with the administration as on his reluctant support for producing 21 more missiles. Nunn was one of the influential group of moderates whose compromise proposals had saved MX from political oblivion repeatedly since 1983.

He would vote to continue MX production, he said, to prevent the Russians from retaining their current monopoly on MX-type missiles. Otherwise, he said, they would have no incentive to accept reductions.

But he complained that the administration showed no urgency about redressing the vulnerability of the old missile silos into which it planned to put MX. And Nunn emphasized that he would not support the planned deployment of 100 missiles in that way.

Warming Up for the Vote

The Senate came to work at 9:30 a.m. on March 19 with a general impression afoot that the MX fight was a horse race.

Majority Whip Alan K. Simpson, Wyo., reinforced that belief before the Senate convened, saying: "I think it could possibly even take the vice president to break the tie. No fooling."

Debate on the MX resolution resumed at about 10:30 a.m. Goldwater linked a "yea" vote to the U.S. position in Geneva — not because of the missile's credibility as bargaining leverage but because Reagan had gone out on a limb to demand it. It was "a decision we may quarrel with," Goldwater said, "but he is the commander in chief and the only man in this country charged with the responsibility for these decisions."

Chiles repeated his argument that, contrary to White

House claims, the vote on the fiscal 1985 money was not a live-or-die vote for the MX program. There was enough money in the appropriations pipeline to keep the MX production line "warm," and ready to start up in case a survivable basing method was devised or in case it proved impossible to develop a small ICBM, dubbed Midgetman.

"It is far more sensible to keep our options open while we monitor the arms control talks and make any further [MX] procurement decisions when we address the 1986 authorization and appropriation bills," Chiles said.

The opponents then got some good news: Freshman Sen. Jay Rockefeller, D-W.Va., said he would vote "no."

During the Senate's customary Tuesday recess from noon to 2 p.m., Reagan made a rare visit to Capitol Hill to press for votes. In remarks to waiting reporters before a closed meeting with senators, he warned that the MX vote would "bear directly on the outcome of the arms talks in Geneva." Rejection of the missile would "show the Soviets that . . . at a moment of historic importance, a majority in the Congress of the United States still lacks resolve."

Arlen Specter, R-Pa., said after the meeting that he had protested vigorously against the threat of political strong-arm tactics by the anonymous White House aides in *The New York Times* story of March 14. Specter had been named by the aides as a senator who could "raise the money himself" if he did not back Reagan. Specter said Reagan assured him that he would back all GOP candidates.

Meanwhile, the Democrats were huddling about 30 yards away. A committee that Byrd had appointed under Nunn's chairmanship to study the issue on the caucus' behalf was returning a split decision.

Glenn argued against MX, insisting that a smaller missile in a mobile launcher would solve the vulnerability problem.

Sen. Albert Gore Jr., D-Tenn., argued his and Nunn's case that these 21 missiles should be approved, but that significant limits should be put on the administration's request for 48 more MXs in the fiscal 1986 budget.

At about 1:45 p.m., senators began drifting out of the Democratic meeting. It became known that Byrd had announced that he would support production of the 21 missiles, though he said it was a close call.

Finale

As the afternoon wore on, time was parceled out in four-minute bites. Evans, who still had not announced his position when he rose to speak, ran out of time while enumerating the pros and cons and sat down leaving listeners baffled as to his decision.

But there could be no doubt about Mathias. His speech, late in the afternoon, was an unqualified endorsement of the administration's fundamental argument for MX, regardless of whether arms talks were under way or not. Large ICBMs were a special kind of weapon because of their ability to destroy armored targets quickly, he said. Moscow thus could not be permitted its current monopoly on such weapons.

The vote began a few minutes before 5 p.m. with Bush in the chair, just in case. But any suspense quickly evaporated as the "undecideds" broke for Reagan.

After the vote, Common Cause President Fred Wertheimer waited for Chiles off the Senate floor to thank him for leading the fight against the missile. "It shows us a bad thing," Chiles told him: "It shows us they've got the votes in the Appropriations Committee," which would meet the following morning to report out the companion resolution approving appropriation of the MX funds.

As Chiles predicted, the Appropriations panel approved the second resolution (S Rept 99-14) March 20 by a 15-14 vote. And after a few hours of speeches, the Senate adopted the resolution by the same vote as on S J Res 71.

HOUSE FLOOR ACTION

Reagan got final approval for the MX in fiscal 1985 when the House voted on March 26 and 28 to spend the $1.5 billion for 12 more missiles.

But while the president won his case for those missiles, congressional moderates, led by House Armed Services Chairman Aspin, served notice that they would try to reduce sharply MX production in the future.

Reagan's House victory March 26 came on S J Res 71, in effect authorizing the missiles; the vote was 219-213. *(Vote 34, p. 14-H)*

Two days later, the House passed H J Res 181, which in effect appropriated funds for the missiles, by a 217-210 vote. *(Vote 36, p. 14-H)*

To underscore his claim that he needed the missile to demonstrate resolve in the arms control talks with the Soviets, Reagan brought chief arms control negotiator Max M. Kampelman back from Geneva on March 25 for a day of lobbying on behalf of MX.

As in past MX struggles, the House Democratic leadership and a group of mostly liberal pressure groups mounted a unified lobbying campaign against the missile. Although the opponents did not succeed in killing the missile, they held Reagan to a much narrower edge than the Senate's 10-vote margin.

Speaker O'Neill and his allies convinced a handful of members to abandon their support for the MX. But those conversions were offset by GOP House gains in the November elections. *(Box, p. 124)*

A Symbolic Victory in Committee

In preliminary sparring March 20, the House Armed Services Committee — which typically supported major defense programs — recommended approval of the missiles by a 37-8 vote (H J Res 180 — H Rept 99-23).

But then the MX foes won a round. Opposing the missile for the first time, the House Appropriations Committee voted 26-28 against procurement (H J Res 181 — H Rept 99-22). *(Box, p. 122)*

However, under the special procedures governing the MX votes, the House had to act on the resolution despite the Appropriations panel's disapproval.

The panels' votes had followed strong lobbying by the White House and by the House's Democratic leadership.

Continuing their two-year pattern, members and lobbyists who comprised the core leadership of the opposition had been meeting regularly, chaired by Rep. Downey. The official House Democratic leadership once again was enlisted under a steering committee chaired by Majority Whip Thomas S. Foley, Wash., and Caucus Chairman Richard A. Gephardt, D-Mo.

Between those two committees, at least 20 members were involved in lobbying their Democratic colleagues to oppose release of the $1.5 billion.

Among those working other members one-on-one were O'Neill and Majority Leader Jim Wright, Texas, both of whom had disappointed MX foes in some earlier stages of the fight for a seeming lack of commitment.

Switches and New Faces: Advantage, Reagan

In winning House approval of continued MX production March 26, the Reagan administration picked up enough support from freshman members to offset growing opposition among incumbents, chiefly Democrats. MX backers won by six votes, 219-213. *(Vote 34, p. 14-H)*

One useful comparison is with a vote on May 16, 1984, in which MX supporters also won by six votes: 212-218 to table (and thus kill) an anti-MX amendment to the fiscal 1985 defense authorization bill (PL 98-525). In another vote on May 31, 1984, four Democrats who voted for MX on May 16 swung to anti-MX positions. *(May 16, May 31 votes, 1984 Almanac p. 60; 1984 votes 133, 178, pp. 44-H, 58-H)*

The four Democrats stayed there on the March 26 vote: Charlie Rose, N.C.; Robin Tallon, S.C.; J. J. Pickle, Texas; and Ronald D. Coleman, Texas. Republican Bill Goodling, Pa., followed the same pattern.

Incumbents Who Switched

The Democrats' chief deputy whip, Bill Alexander, Ark., voted for MX May 16 and did not vote May 31. On March 26 he voted against MX, rounding out the solid front of opposition among House Democratic leaders.

Pat Roberts, R-Kan., supported MX in both 1984 votes, but voted "no" on the most recent vote.

William J. Hughes, D-N.J., and Christopher H. Smith, R-N.J., had opposed the missile until 1984, when they cast pro-MX votes. In 1985 they reverted to earlier form and voted "no." Nancy L. Johnson, R-Conn., an MX opponent who did not vote May 16, also voted against the missile in 1985.

Democrats Stephen L. Neal, N.C., and Roy Dyson, Md., voted against MX in 1984 but supported the president in the 1985 vote. Wayne Dowdy, D-Miss., voted against MX May 16, did not vote May 31 and supported production on March 26.

The anti-MX vote also was diminished by vacancies in two seats formerly held by MX opponents: the late Gillis W. Long, D-La., and Frank McCloskey, D-Ind., whose seat was vacant because of a contested election.

How the Freshmen Voted

Of the 43 members first elected in November 1984, 25 voted the same way on MX their predecessors had on May 16, 1984. This group included 16 Republicans who voted for MX: Dick Armey, Texas; Joe L. Barton, Texas; Beau Boulter, Texas; Sonny Callahan, Ala.; Bill Cobey, N.C.; Howard Coble, N.C.; Bob Dornan, Calif.; Fred J. Eckert, N.Y.; Harris W. Fawell, Ill.; John E. Grotberg, Ill.; J. Alex McMillan, N.C.; Jan Meyers, Kan.; David S. Monson, Utah; D. French Slaughter Jr., Va.; Mac Sweeney, Texas; and Pat Swindall, Ga. Democrats Tommy F. Robinson, Ark., and Albert G. Bustamante, Texas, also voted for MX and had pro-MX predecessors.

On the other hand, seven freshmen who voted against MX March 26 had succeeded anti-MX members: They were Joseph J. DioGuardi, R-N.Y., and Democrats Chester G. Atkins, Mass.; Kenneth J. Gray, Ill.; Paul E. Kanjorski, Pa.; Thomas J. Manton, N.Y.; Carl C. Perkins, Ky.; and Peter J. Visclosky, Ind.

Five freshmen who voted against MX replaced MX supporters: Terry L. Bruce, D-Ill.; Bart Gordon, D-Tenn.; Paul B. Henry, R-Mich.; John R. Miller, R-Wash.; and James A. Traficant Jr., D-Ohio.

But MX supporters picked up 10 GOP freshmen whose predecessors voted against MX: Helen Delich Bentley, Md.; Thomas D. DeLay, Texas; Dean A. Gallo, N.J.; Bill Hendon, N.C.; Jim Kolbe, Ariz.; Jim Lightfoot, Iowa; John G. Rowland, Conn.; Bill Schuette, Mich.; Robert C. Smith, N.H.; and Mike Strang, Colo.

Three other freshmen replaced members who did not vote on May 16, 1984: Republicans Larry Combest, Texas, and H. James Saxton, N.J., voted for MX while Democrat Richard H. Stallings, Idaho, voted against it.

In hopes of winning an early psychological edge, they concentrated much of their initial effort on wavering members of the Armed Services and Appropriations panels.

So did the White House.

When former CIA chief Colby and some other MX opponents showed up for an appointment with Appropriations Committee member Lindy (Mrs. Hale) Boggs, D-La., on the afternoon of March 19, their meeting was delayed some 20 minutes while she took a Reagan phone call.

The same day, Reagan met with a group of three Democratic "swing" votes: Appropriations member Steny H. Hoyer, Md., and Armed Services members Norman Sisisky, Va., and Roy Dyson, Md.

When the Appropriations Committee took up the MX issue on March 20, Defense Subcommittee Chairman Joseph P. Addabbo, D-N.Y., led off with an emotional attack on the missile: "Last year we were told we had to build the MX because the Russians had broken off talks. Now we're told we have to build the MX because the Russians have returned to Geneva."

Joseph M. McDade, Pa., the Defense Subcommittee's senior Republican, rebutted: "There is no getting away from one central fact in the world today, and that is that our negotiators are in Geneva, finally sitting across the table from the Russians. . . . The Russians are intransigent. They usually understand us only when we show resolve."

Majority Whip Bill Alexander, D-Ark., then announced that he would oppose the missiles, for the first time. As the last member of the Democratic leadership to abandon Reagan on the issue, Alexander had come under intense pressure to fall in line and had "taken a walk" on the House vote May 31, 1984.

When the roll was called on Addabbo's motion that the resolution be reported unfavorably, Hoyer supported the president but Boggs voted "aye" — against MX.

GOP moderate Lawrence Coughlin, Pa., who had been lobbied by Bush the day before, also voted against MX. The final tally was 28-26 against Reagan.

When House Armed Services refought the battle a few hours later, Reagan again batted .500. Of his two guests the day before, Dyson changed his previous position and voted for MX, while Sisisky stood pat, against the 21 missiles.

Presidential Lobbying

The administration and anti-MX lobbyists next stepped up their attention to undecided members.

Reagan already had telephoned Rep. Frank Horton, N.Y., a liberal Republican who had voted for MX in 1984, from Air Force One as the president was returning March 18 from a summit meeting in Canada.

On March 22, Horton got a follow-up phone call — this time from former President Gerald R. Ford.

Another presidential phone call that day went to Democrat Carroll Hubbard Jr. in Lexington, Ky. Hubbard had broken a string of pro-MX votes on May 31, 1984, to vote against the missile.

Some members sought to turn the lobbying to their advantage. Tobacco farming was an economic mainstay of Harold Rogers' district in eastern Kentucky, and the third-term Republican was very unhappy with Reagan plans to try phasing out parts of the tobacco price support system. On March 19, the day before the Appropriations vote, Rogers got an appointment on the issue with White House Chief of Staff Donald T. Regan on March 21.

But on March 20, Rogers fired a shot across the administration's bow. Although he supported MX, he "took a walk" when the Appropriations panel voted.

When Rogers returned to his office after that vote, Minority Whip Trent Lott, R-Miss., was waiting for him and the Kentuckian explained his position. The next day, Rogers had a 30-minute discussion of future tobacco policy with Regan. He voted with Reagan on March 26.

Stephen L. Neal, D-N.C., who had opposed MX earlier, took advantage of an MX meeting with Reagan to complain of plans by the House GOP campaign committee to spend $6 million on an advertising campaign to "soften" up Neal and 24 other House Democrats prior to the 1986 elections. White House political operative Edward Rollins later phoned Neal to say the campaign would be called off.

Warming Up the House

With Foley and Gephardt leading the charge, the House Democratic leadership worked hard to beat Reagan on the MX. Also joining them in 1985 was chief deputy whip Alexander.

During the House debate in March, Alexander emphasized the budgetary case against MX. But many observers speculated that his conversion also was related to his hope of succeeding Foley as whip in the 100th Congress.

In January, the caucus had made the position of whip an elective one, and several members firmly against the missile talked as though opposition to MX were a litmus test for future leadership candidates.

Meanwhile, anti-MX lobbyists were keeping up a barrage of grass-roots pressure. Washington volunteers working for Common Cause and SANE over the weekend of March 23-24 got about 1,000 people to promise to phone members' offices and call for a "nay" vote.

On March 25, the first of two days of House debate on the first of the two resolutions (S J Res 71), 28 anti-MX lobbyists gathered at 7:45 a.m. before one more round of personal contacts with undecided members.

Common Cause President Fred Wertheimer worried that the MX opponents' job might have been complicated by anti-Soviet sentiment. The day before, a Soviet soldier had killed a U.S. Army liaison officer in East Germany.

The Kampelman Factor

On March 21, at his customary press conference before the House convened, O'Neill drove home the Democratic leadership's budgetary theme. The missile would be as economically disastrous for the country as the Vietnam War had been, O'Neill argued: "$41 billion is a mighty expenditure for a sitting duck."

Meanwhile, the administration had loosed on Capitol Hill what one White House lobbyist called "the big Max attack." This was chief arms control negotiator Kampelman, who had returned from Geneva so that he could argue to members in person that prospects for arms control progress would be harmed if Congress voted against MX.

Kampelman, a lifelong Democrat who had been a close confidant of the late Hubert H. Humphrey, spent the morning meeting with O'Neill, then with Minority Leader Robert H. Michel, R-Ill., and then with the two groups of members whom the Senate and House had designated as official observers of the Geneva talks.

At about 2 p.m., he met privately with Aspin, White House lobbyist Dennis Thomas and a small group of other members, some of whom were undecided or not firmly committed, including John M. Spratt Jr., D-S.C., and Ronald D. Coleman, D-Texas.

Kampelman cited examples from his past experience negotiating with the Russians in Madrid on the Helsinki human rights accords. And he warned, one participant said, that canceling MX would delay meaningful negotiations while Moscow stalled awaiting further windfalls.

On the House floor, Edward J. Markey, D-Mass., a leading opponent of Reagan's nuclear arms policies, complained: "Our chief arms control negotiator may miss talks in Geneva in order to lobby for more nuclear missiles. That says it all about this administration's attitude about new nuclear weapons."

But there seemed to be no widespread backlash against Reagan's use of his Democratic chief negotiator to help sell the missile.

Meanwhile, the scheduled 10 hours of debate on S J Res 71 began, with MX supporters leaning heavily on the Geneva connection.

"If this Congress serves notice on the Soviets that we are not going to build and deploy this system anyway," argued William L. Dickinson, Ala., the Armed Services Committee's senior Republican, "there is very little for them to negotiate about."

But Nicholas Mavroules, D-Mass., insisted that Congress' general support of Reagan's across-the-board military buildup displayed enough determination to make the Russians bargain seriously, without the additional $1.5 billion in the MX vote.

At about 4:30 p.m., more than 100 members boarded military buses outside the Capitol to attend a White House briefing by Kampelman.

Shortly after 5, Reagan opened the meeting in the ornate East Room. Rehearsing the litany of bipartisan support for MX deployment, and stressing the Democratic element, Reagan warned the group that a "nay" vote "could very well spell the difference between success and defeat in our arms control efforts."

Kampelman essentially repeated his argument that cancellation of MX inevitably would delay the negotiations while the Russians would "ask themselves, 'What else might we obtain that we will not have to pay for?' "

On the morning of the vote, March 26, O'Neill told reporters that, by his count, the vote on MX was "still close; half a dozen either way."

But he and other Democratic leaders conveyed the impression that they felt bested in the battle — particularly by Kampelman's efforts.

The previous afternoon — before Kampelman's White House briefing — O'Neill had counted 216 votes against the MX, he said. But since then, six Democrats had changed their positions.

"The office of the president has enormous prestige," Majority Whip Foley commented, "especially in the area of foreign affairs."

The Democratic chiefs lamented that Reagan also had the advantage of a president's inherent power to reward and punish members by the apportionment of federal grants and projects.

In the view of many observers, those natural presidential advantages were compounded by another factor in the MX political equation: some Democrats' fear that the party would seem "soft" on defense if the Democratic-controlled House killed off the MX.

According to several sources, O'Neill had insisted that the GOP-controlled Senate vote first on the MX funds, in hope that it would kill the program and spare the House the need to vote on it at all.

On the day of the vote, rumors were rampant among the anti-MX lobbyists that some Democrats would vote against MX only if they were confident that the missile would be approved. GOP leader Michel said as much to reporters: "I just can't imagine that Tip O'Neill wants this thing to go down and give us the opportunity to lay it on the Democratic Party."

When debate resumed in the early afternoon, Patricia Schroeder, D-Colo., grappled the "softness" argument head-on: "We have all become afraid of being called a wimp," she said. "Our constituents are going to think we are the weak ones if we cannot possibly stand on our own two legs and talk back."

But Charles Wilson, D-Texas, voiced the opposite thesis: "If the perception persists in this country that the Democratic Party is the party of isolation and . . . weakness on defense, we are flat through in the South and West, and we can forget about winning presidential elections."

Down to the Wire

As the afternoon wore on, the "unannounceds" began declaring their positions. The White House seemed to be doing well.

New York Republican Horton had received yet another phone call in the morning, this one from Kampelman who, by then, had returned to Geneva and conducted a negotiating session with the Russians. Horton had been unable to attend the White House briefing and had requested the call. He would cast what he called "the most difficult vote in my 23 years in the House," for MX.

Democrat Hubbard, back from Kentucky, credited his decision not to long-distance phone calls but face-to-face conversations: "In my heavily Democratic Party area, my constituents were saying to me yesterday, 'We trusted President Reagan on Nov. 6 and we trust him on March 26.' "

Jim Lightfoot, R-Iowa, also announced that he would back the president. Opponents had thought they had a shot at his support, partly because the other seven members of the Iowa congressional delegation opposed MX. Moreover, Reagan's veto of a farm credit bill was presumed unpopular in Lightfoot's heavily agricultural southern Iowa district.

But Lightfoot devoted much of the press release on his pro-MX vote to an explanation of why the $1.5 billion at stake for MX production could not have been diverted to fund farm programs.

The anti-MX lobby groups were throwing their every resource into the lineup, including Esther Peterson, the 78-year-old veteran of labor and consumer causes who was on the governing board of Common Cause.

Peterson intercepted Claude Pepper, D-Fla., as he left the House floor. But several minutes of earnest conversation, during which she kept a hand on each of Pepper's arms, was unavailing. Though a crusading liberal since his election to the Senate in 1936, the 84-year-old Pepper had, for the most part, gone along with Aspin on MX.

At the end of the day, only minutes before the vote, the MX foes unlimbered one of their biggest guns — former CIA Director William Colby — for one last mission: a 10-minute conversation just outside the House chamber with freshman Harris W. Fawell, R-Ill.

A moderate who represented a wealthy district in the southwest suburbs of Chicago, Fawell had shown up on some opponents' target lists. But Colby had no luck persuading him.

Out on the floor, as the debate wound up, Democratic leaders hammered away at the budgetary impact of MX.

That factor, according to Gephardt, was one reason why the vote would be so close despite all the political resources Reagan had thrown into the battle. "Members are starting to focus on the fact that in a few weeks we're going to have to vote on a budget," he said.

J. J. Pickle, D-Texas, was one. The moderately conservative Pickle had supported MX until May 31, 1984, when he followed the Democratic leadership to vote "nay." Now he said he would do the same, for budgetary reasons. However, he added that he could support the missile if the administration proposed reasonable defense budget cuts.

Aspin — who had sat out the floor debate on a major defense measure for the first time in years — closed the debate with one more pitch for the Geneva connection: "To remove these missiles by a 'no' vote would in effect be giving some help to the Soviet Union," he said, drawing hisses from the Democratic side.

As the tally of "aye" and "nay" votes mounted on the electronic scoreboards in the House chamber, the opponents ran slightly ahead for the first several minutes.

With about six minutes to go in the voting period, the two sides tied at 185 each and a few Republicans raised a brief cheer.

For most of the next six minutes the pro-MX votes edged ahead.

Just as the allotted 15 minutes expired, the "yea" vote hit 217 — an absolute majority of the 433 members who were present — and a cheer went up on the GOP side of the House.

A few more votes trickled in and the final tally was 219-213. As is customary, O'Neill did not vote.

The MX opponents were surprised by only one vote: Wayne Dowdy, D-Miss., whom they had counted in their column, voted for the missile.

Wertheimer professed delight that the opponents had held on to all 23 GOP votes on which they had counted, and they had gotten Pat Roberts, R-Kan., whom they had listed as a possible vote against MX.

Though the Democratic leaders had decided immediately that they would contest the second vote on MX, they seemed less hopeful than the lobbyists.

Before the night was over, the anti-MX lobbyists had unleashed their telephone banks to drum up indignant phone calls to Dowdy, Fawell, Lightfoot and Vic Fazio, D-Calif. Fazio had been one of Aspin's original allies on the MX issue, and they saw no prospect of switching his vote. But in the words of SANE's Mike Mawby, "We're going to be sure he suffers for it back home."

But a subdued Foley seemed to be concentrating on the future battle over the fiscal 1986 MX request, which, he predicted, was clearly in trouble. "Sure, we'll make the effort," to win the second vote, he said. But he conceded that it "would be difficult to turn around."

The Second Time Around

The next morning, O'Neill put a new face on the anti-MX drive: By voting to approve authorization of the missile, the House had shown "resolve" in arms control negotiations. Now, it could show resolve in reducing the deficit by voting not to approve appropriation of the funds.

Sen. John Glenn, D-Ohio, had called House Majority Leader Jim Wright, D-Texas, that morning, offering to brief Democratic members on the cost of MX.

For years, Glenn had championed a "truly mobile" small missile as an alternative to the silo-based MX, which he dismissed as too vulnerable. If missile launchers were indistinguishable from long-haul trucks, he argued, they could blend into traffic on Interstate highways, making a Soviet first strike practically impossible.

Since joining the Senate Armed Services Committee in January, Glenn had begun to stress a cost argument against the MX.

Administration officials were increasingly emphasizing the possibility of "superhardening" MX silos with extra steel and concrete, to give the silos a better chance of protecting the missiles from a Soviet attack.

Citing an Air Force estimate that this might cost $18 billion, Glenn said protecting the missile would boost the total cost of the MX program to more than $40 billion.

Deputy Majority Whip Alexander rounded up several Democratic members to hear the former astronaut and Marine test pilot criticize the missile at a meeting in O'Neill's office shortly after noon.

"Glenn can't be accused of being soft on communism," Alexander told reporters, "and he's not exactly a wimp."

But evidently no minds were changed by the meeting, nor by a letter Glenn circulated to all House Democrats the next day, before the vote.

On the afternoon of March 27, the Democratic whips met to review the prospects for finding members who had voted for MX on March 26 and would either switch to "nay" or take a walk on March 28.

"What you're really doing," one whip, who demanded anonymity, later said, "is looking for the three dumbest political people in the [Democratic] caucus."

By the time the House convened March 28, for one last hour of debate before the vote on H J Res 181, there was a matter-of-fact quality to the battle. Advocates on both sides of the issue had contacted their supporters, to be sure they would be present and voting "right" on the second vote. But there seemed to be little real expectation of any change in the outcome.

The vote, shortly after noon, itself held no surprises. The five members who did not vote included two Republicans who had voted for MX on March 26: Philip M. Crane, Ill., and Bill Archer, Texas.

Also not voting were three members who had voted against MX on March 26 — Mervyn M. Dymally, D-Calif.; John Conyers Jr., D-Mich.; and Tom Ridge, R-Pa.

The Fiscal 1986 Cap

Even before the House finished action on the resolutions to allow fiscal 1985 MX production to proceed, influential moderates were proposing to put an end to the debate. Their solution: a congressionally mandated limit on the overall size of Reagan's MX program.

The proposal, advanced by Sen. Nunn in March, called for a cap of 40 or 50 on the number of MXs deployed in existing silos. Nunn's backing lent the position credibility among moderate and conservative Democrats.

Reagan struck a deal with Nunn in late May: the president endorsed an amendment to the Senate's fiscal 1986 defense authorization bill (S 1160) that seemed to halve his initial request for 100 MXs, making the position respectable for Republicans. That chamber approved 12 MXs and a temporary MX deployment cap of 50.

The next month, with Aspin and other Democratic moderates' support, the House approved no new MXs and a somewhat more restrictive version of Nunn's cap. The scenario was to give House members a vote to kill the missile, with the expectation that House members would settle for a small annual production run in House-Senate conference on the defense bill.

In the July conference, House members agreed to authorize 12 more MXs, and Senate conferees accepted the House's demand that the cap of 50 be "permanent."

Opponents of the missile made a brief run at dropping the $1.7 billion for the 12 MXs when the House took up a fiscal 1986 defense appropriations bill (HR 3629) in November. But the White House beat back that effort and the defense appropriations portion of the continuing resolution (PL 99-190) contained the compromise.

Looking for a Cap

The Senate proposal for a cap was announced March 28 by Nunn and Minority Leader Robert C. Byrd, W.Va.; Albert Gore Jr., Tenn.; and David L. Boren, Okla. They proposed limiting the total number of MXs deployed in launch silos to 40.

All four had voted to build 21 MXs in fiscal 1985; added to the 21 approved in 1984, Congress had funded production of 42 MXs.

The senators proposed continuing MX production at the rate of about 12 per year, to provide spares for testing and training and to keep the production line ready if arms control talks failed.

Reagan wanted to deploy 100 missiles and buy 123 more for tests and training. He had requested 48 new MXs in fiscal 1986.

The four senators did not commit themselves to a specific total of missiles. But Gore suggested a total of 140: a deployment of 40 and 100 backup missiles. Nunn talked of halving the administration's request for backups and deploying 40 MXs — for a total of just over 100 missiles.

Byrd and the others justified their proposal for holding down MX deployment partly in terms of the widespread congressional sentiment to rein in Reagan's planned defense budget increases.

If MX production proceeded at the planned rate, they warned, development of other strategic weapons — which the four deemed far more promising than MX — might have to be cut back. These included the "stealth" bomber, designed to evade enemy detection, a small, single-warhead ICBM dubbed "Midgetman" and the Trident II (or D-5) submarine-launched missile.

The four senators warned that too many MXs — in conjunction with Midgetman and Trident II — could destabilize the U.S.-Soviet military balance.

Senate, House Committee Action

The missile cap got its first boost April 4, when the Senate Armed Services Committee approved its version of the defense authorization bill (S 1160).

During the Republican-controlled committee's deliberations, the MX program escaped by a one-vote margin (9-10) Nunn's proposal to slash the fiscal 1986 number from the 48 missiles Reagan had requested to 12.

Instead, the panel cut the number to 21 — the amount approved in the previous two fiscal years. That was a reduction of $820 million, to $1.1 billion.

But the panel insisted that no more than 50 MXs be deployed in existing Minuteman missile silos.

The counterpart House Armed Services Committee, in its defense bill (HR 1872 — H Rept 99-81), reported May 10, also authorized 21 more MXs.

Two Democrats — longtime MX foe Nicholas Mavroules, Mass., and Dave McCurdy, Okla., who had backed Aspin's efforts to save the missile in the past — offered a cap amendment. It would have imposed a permanent limit of 40 on MXs deployed and provided no new funds for additional missiles in fiscal 1986.

Their amendment was rejected by a vote of 13-32 in the pro-Pentagon committee, but it was expected to command considerable support on the House floor.

The "zero MXs" position in the McCurdy-Mavroules package was widely acknowledged to be a political tactic, aimed at setting the stage for a compromise in conference.

SENATE FLOOR ACTION

To avert a near-certain defeat in the Senate on the MX missile, Reagan May 23 endorsed the Nunn amendment halving the number of MXs the president had planned to deploy in existing silos.

The amendment, sponsored by Nunn, was approved 78-20 in the fifth day of debate on the fiscal 1986 defense authorization bill. *(Vote 93, p. 20-S)*

It reflected Senate weariness with Reagan's basing plan. But with arms talks resuming within days, Nunn and his allies gave Reagan room to claim a partial victory.

The Nunn amendment:

- Expressed the sense of the Senate that after 50 MXs had been bought for deployment, additional missiles would be bought only as spares, unless the president proposed and Congress approved a different basing method.
- Reduced the number of MXs authorized in fiscal 1986 to 12, compared with Reagan's request for 48 and the Armed Services Committee's recommendation of 21. Under the amendment, all 12 would be used as spares and test missiles.
- Expressed the sense of the Senate that 12 to 21 MXs should be funded in fiscal 1987.

Squaring Off

Though contemptuous of Reagan's decision to put MXs in vulnerable launch sites, Nunn had supported deployment of a small number as a military and symbolic offset to the Soviet force of powerful and accurate land-based nuclear missiles. And he wanted to keep the MX production line open as a hedge against a Soviet buildup.

That position had won the support of MX opponents with whom Nunn had dueled for two years. Though opposed to further production of any missiles, this group was anxious to wind up the MX debate so they could focus on the battle against "star wars." *(Story, p. 130)*

The administration apparently made no effort to cut a deal with Nunn until the morning of May 21, the day Nunn planned to offer his amendment on the Senate floor.

Conceding that Nunn had the votes to win some sort of limit on MX deployment in silos far below Reagan's plans, administration officials began scrambling to find a way to mute the political impact.

Over the next three days, in negotiation with Nunn and his principal cosponsors — Byrd, Gore and Boren — Reagan aides tried to modify the deployment limit to something that sounded less permanent than a "cap." At various times, "pause" and "moratorium" were suggested.

They also tried to increase the numerical limits to:

- A limit of 50 MXs deployed in existing silos, rather than 40. Air Force missile squadrons were organized in increments of 50 silos, they argued, and it would be difficult to have 40 MXs and 10 of the existing Minuteman missiles in the same unit.
- Authorization of 21 missiles in fiscal 1986, rather than the 12 Nunn approved. The cost-per-copy would be very high at a rate of only one missile per month, they argued.

The Reagan team also hammered away at the argument that any congressional action that appeared to kill the program would undermine the U.S. position in the Geneva arms control talks with Moscow.

Whether to Deal?

While senators and Reagan aides negotiated privately, the longtime MX foes said there was no reason to deal.

It was one thing, they argued, for them grudgingly to hold off their opposition to a small annual MX production run that clearly was earmarked not to be deployed. But if the limit were raised to 50, MX opponents would be asked to tolerate the funding in fiscal 1987 of at least eight additional MXs intended for deployment.

More fundamentally, the lobbyists for Common Cause, SANE and Council for a Livable World simply wanted a clear-cut political win over Reagan.

But on the other hand, one Senate aide associated with the Nunn coalition warned against underestimating Reagan's ability to peel away Republicans from Nunn's amendment, particularly if he could claim that Nunn had refused to consider a compromise that seemed reasonable.

Moreover, the fear of being charged with damaging prospects for an agreement in Geneva was a real factor for some of the Democrats. Nunn's ally Chiles said the Georgian had the votes to win but he "didn't necessarily want to crush the president on this."

Setting the 'Spin'

An agreement was reached at about 6 p.m. on May 23. But the contestants continued to jockey to impose their interpretation on the event.

Administration officials, anxious that the move not be seen as a permanent lid on the number of missiles deployed, called the limit a "pause" or "moratorium," stressing the implication that it could be lifted. National security adviser Robert C. McFarlane told reporters that the limit of 50 could be seen as "50 on the way to 100" — the number Reagan had planned to deploy in existing silos.

In a statement read to reporters by McFarlane, Reagan said, "The Senate has acknowledged the importance of this program for the Geneva negotiations as well as the requirement to deter an ever expanding Soviet buildup."

Nunn and his allies insisted on calling the limit a "cap," which — they argued — did not carry any connotation that the limit would lapse.

Nunn had designed the amendment to give Reagan an incentive to improve the method of basing the new missiles.

Minority Leader Byrd put it this way: "There is a cap and the only missiles beyond that can be used for testing," unless Reagan were to come up with a better basing method.

Leading anti-MX lobbyists also declared they were satisfied with the outcome.

HOUSE FLOOR ACTION

The House took up the MX issue June 18, as it debated the fiscal 1986 defense authorization bill, HR 1872. The House handed Reagan a clear loss, voting by a comfortable margin to limit the number of MXs that would be deployed to 40. But although the House authorized no new funds for missile production in fiscal 1986, it expressly anticipated that some additional MXs eventually would be purchased for testing.

For all the energy and political ingenuity that had gone into the three-year-long MX battle, there seemed a perfunctory quality to the June 18 debate.

In part, this reflected a widespread sense among the protagonists that the outcome was a foregone conclusion: All signs pointed to House approval of a cap of 40 or 50 on the number of missiles to be deployed.

Samuel S. Stratton, D-N.Y., one of the Pentagon's most combative House allies, objected to the whole tenor of the debate, with its implicit assumption that Reagan's initial request for 48 MXs in fiscal 1986 would be cut back lower than Armed Services' recommendation of 21 missiles.

"On what kind of honeydew have these individuals who want to shut down the MX system been feeding?" he demanded. "Have they gotten a new message from the negotiators in Geneva that MX no longer is needed?"

But the missile had been handicapped by the general belief that it would be vulnerable to Soviet attack if based in existing missile silos. And political momentum behind the cap idea had been building for nearly three months.

Leading MX opponents in the House wanted a somewhat more restrictive version of Nunn's cap; in coalition with them were several of the self-styled Democratic moderates — led by Aspin — whose support had kept MX alive during the last three years.

Sheer fatigue also seemed to have drained much of the earlier passion from the MX debate: "Let us make a final decision today," William L. Dickinson, R-Ala., urged his colleagues. "We have rehashed this thing so many times."

The compromise was embodied in an amendment offered by Mavroules, who had led earlier efforts that came close to killing off the program entirely. Mavroules, collaborating with McCurdy, offered an amendment that:

- Imposed a permanent limit of 40 on the number of MXs that would be deployed.
- Allowed no additional production of MXs in fiscal 1986, but approved $921 million for equipment to base already approved MXs in existing missile silos and to keep the missile production line "warm" and ready to crank out additional missiles that would be used for testing while MXs were in service.

Dickinson offered an amendment that would have approved production of an additional 12 missiles in fiscal 1986 and set the cap at 50 missiles deployed.

But the cutting issue between Dickinson and Mavroules was the degree of permanence of the MX production cap. Dickinson's was a sense of Congress statement, rather than binding law, and Dickinson described it as a pause that would be re-evaluated in a few years.

Mavroules and McCurdy demanded a permanent limit on the number deployed. Any such legislative provision could be repealed subsequently, but the two insisted on putting the onus on Reagan to request positive congressional action in order to remove the limit.

The House was offered a third option by Charles E. Bennett, D-Fla., who had cosponsored previous anti-MX amendments with Mavroules. Bennett's amendment would have denied any MX procurement money in fiscal 1986 and diverted unspent MX money from earlier years to be used for conventional weapons.

"Now we are playing numbers games with the missile," Bennett complained, referring to the relatively minor differences between the Dickinson and Mavroules amendments. "I see no reason to vote for even one more missile."

Bennett's amendment was rejected 185-230. *(Vote 151, p. 50-H)*

Complex procedural jockeying ensued, with Dickinson and Mavroules each angling for his amendment to be voted on first.

Mavroules prevailed in this minuet, and the first vote came, in effect, on his position — specifically on an amendment by McCurdy to Dickinson's amendment. The McCurdy measure was approved 233-184. *(Vote 152, p. 50-H)*

The House then cast a nearly identical vote (182-234) against a substitute for the Mavroules amendment, offered by Jim Courter, R-N.J. The Courter amendment restated Dickinson's. *(Vote 153, p. 50-H)*

The Mavroules original amendment then was passed by voice vote.

When the House approved the production of 21 MXs for fiscal 1985 in March, the margin was six votes. Of the members who voted "aye" then, 30 supported the Mavroules-McCurdy cap. Among the 19 Democrats in that group were Aspin, McCurdy, Dicks and two other members of the group of self-styled MX moderates: Steny Hoyer, Md., and Vic Fazio, Calif. Also switching were 11 Democrats from Southern or border states.

CONFERENCE AGREEMENT

The conference agreement on the defense authorization bill (S 1160 — H Rept 99-235), reached July 25, incorporated both chambers' positions on the missile.

It accepted the Senate number — 50 — for the cap on missiles to be deployed in existing silos. And it authorized funding of 12 more missiles in fiscal 1986, as the Senate had voted.

But the cap was to be permanent, not the temporary one adopted by the Senate.

"There's no way we're ever going to build more than 50 MXs," for deployment, said Aspin. "It's over, it's done."

Aspin estimated that in addition to the 50 missiles to be deployed, an additional 75 to 125 MXs would be produced for test launches. Reagan's plan had included 132 test missiles in addition to the 100 to be deployed.

Some of the lobbyists who had battled against MX since 1982 complained that the House conferees had agreed too quickly to the Senate position of 50 deployed missiles instead of the House-passed limit of 40.

But leading MX foe Mavroules dismissed the complaints. The key issue, he insisted, was the Senate's acceptance of the House demand for a "permanent" MX cap.

APPROPRIATIONS

The fiscal 1986 MX compromise was ratified by the House and Senate Appropriations Committees, when they approved their defense spending bills in October and November, respectively.

But a brief skirmish over MX broke out on the House floor Oct. 30, when members were considering HR 3629, the defense appropriations bill. Contributing to the political climate were Reagan's impending Nov. 19 summit with Soviet Leader Mikhail Gorbachev; congressional deficit-cutting efforts; and the unhappiness of some Capitol Hill Republicans with Reagan's approach to farm money problems.

For upwards of two hours, the laboriously negotiated compromise over the missile agreed to in the summer seemed to have come apart, with the House voting 211-208 to drop from the appropriations bill $1.7 billion earmarked to buy 12 MXs in fiscal 1986. *(Vote 341, p. 106-H)*

But after the White House and the House GOP leadership rounded up their troops, the House reversed itself, rejecting the amendment 210-214. *(Vote 342, p. 106-H)*

The amendment to cut MX funds was offered by Barney Frank, D-Mass., a fervent opponent of MX. Frank offered the amendment without prior publicity, later telling reporters that he wanted to give members a chance to vote on MX without being lobbied by the administration.

But a more fundamental part of Frank's strategy was his exploitation of the strong pressure for deficit reductions that had been generated by the so-called Gramm-Rudman amendment to the bill raising the national debt limit. That measure would force automatic reductions in federal spending unless the budget was balanced by fiscal 1991. *(Story, p. 459)*

Frank insisted that the 40 MXs that could be deployed from funds already appropriated would be just as significant militarily as the 50 that would be deployed if additional missiles were built in fiscal 1986.

"You can kill the $1.7 billion and no one is going to tell you that you have damaged our national security," he said.

At least one Republican who previously had backed MX, Toby Roth, Wis., later said he backed the amendment because he agreed with Frank that 10 more deployed missiles would make no significant difference.

House Armed Services Committee Chairman Aspin was one of several senior Democrats who later described the vote to kill MX as a political response to White House rhetoric on the deficit: "They can't play politics on deficits and not have it come back and bite them," he said.

But Minority Whip Trent Lott, R-Miss., a Gramm-Rudman backer, dismissed that explanation, pointing out that MX votes always had been close in the House.

"All it says to me is that we have a large group of very liberal members" who want to cut defense budgets, Lott told reporters.

But he conceded that there was at least one group of members who voted "aye" on Frank to twist the administration's tail on another issue: This was a small number of farm-state Republicans who wanted to signal to the White House their frustration with administration farm policy. *(Farm bill, p. 517)*

"Sometimes one vote is adequate to send a message," said Rod Chandler, R-Wash., one of Frank's farm-state supporters.

Also contributing to Frank's surprising win were a few pro-MX Republicans who did not make it to the floor in time to vote "nay."

Immediately after the amendment was adopted, the White House and MX backers scrambled to round up enough votes to defeat the amendment on a second try. Bill Chappell Jr., the hawkish Florida Democrat who was managing the bill, urged Claude Pepper, D-Fla., who had supported MX in most earlier votes, to reconsider his vote for Frank.

Pepper later said he found Chappell's case persuasive: "We're on the eve of the summit . . . and the administration was pleading not to be interfered with."

After the second vote overturned his amendment, Frank said that the House was not willing to follow through with the kind of cuts Gramm-Rudman backers claimed to favor. "It shows we have a couple of hundred fakers when it comes to cutting the deficit," he said. ▮

Reagan Fends Off Major Cuts in SDI Program

Arms control advocates failed in repeated efforts in 1985 to impose substantial restraints on President Reagan's anti-missile research program, the "strategic defense initiative" (SDI), which critics called "star wars."

Reagan requested $3.7 billion for SDI research in fiscal 1986. Faced with constraints that would allow a defense budget no larger than had been appropriated in fiscal 1986, Congress trimmed the request to $2.75 billion. But that amount was almost double the $1.4 billion Congress approved for SDI in fiscal 1985. *(1984 Almanac p. 403)*

Congress split the difference between the Senate's $3 billion authorization and the House's $2.5 billion. The $2.75 billion was included in the fiscal 1986 defense authorization bill (S 1160 — PL 99-145) and in an omnibus continuing resolution (H J Res 465 — PL 99-190). *(Authorization bill, p. 138, appropriations measure, p. 377)*

SDI encompassed research on several possible kinds of anti-missile defenses, including laser-armed space satellites and atomic-particle beams. Reagan inaugurated the program in 1983, calling for an effort to find out whether a nationwide anti-missile defense could make nuclear weapons "impotent and obsolete."

The arms controllers depicted SDI as a mortal threat to future weapons reduction prospects; they argued that an effective anti-missile defense was technologically impossible, and the effort to develop one nevertheless would spur new Soviet arms efforts that would carry the weapons race into new dimensions. In addition to wanting cuts in the funding request for the program, the SDI critics sought to impose specific limits on parts of it that, they claimed, would violate existing arms control treaties.

But during debate on the defense authorization bill, both bodies rejected several SDI reduction amendments as well as amendments intended to speed up the program.

During the year, the White House used ongoing arms talks with the Soviets in Geneva and a November summit meeting between Reagan and Soviet leader Mikhail Gorbachev in fighting for the SDI program on Capitol Hill.

The Soviets had insisted that SDI be stringently limited as part of any far-reaching arms reduction deal, but the summit evidently produced no agreement on the program's future. *(Arms control, p. 175; summit, p. 109)*

Final Provisions

In addition to authorizing $2.75 billion for SDI, conferees on the defense bill pressed the Pentagon to focus more on near-term projects that would defend armored military targets with relatively straightforward weapons, rather than concentrating on an "astrodome" defense of the entire country, using more exotic weapons, like space-based lasers.

They approved a Senate-passed provision requiring the president to certify, before deployment of any SDI system, that it would work despite Soviet efforts to attack it, and that it could be deployed more cheaply than the Soviets could expand their missile forces to overwhelm it.

The conference report also included a provision barring the use of any SDI funds "in a manner inconsistent with" various treaties, including the 1972 ABM treaty and the 1967 treaty barring nuclear weapons in space. The House bill had included a provision explicitly barring any SDI test that used nuclear explosions.

Reagan and Defense Secretary Caspar W. Weinberger had emphasized that SDI offered a non-nuclear defense against nuclear weapons. But one of the most technically promising weapons under study was a space-borne X-ray laser that would be powered by a nuclear explosion.

The continuing appropriations resolution conference report retained a Senate provision prohibiting the Pentagon from setting aside some SDI contracts to be awarded only to firms from other countries. Some critics had suspected that the administration might do this to win other countries' political support for the project.

Administration Report

In a report to Congress in March, the administration insisted that planned SDI tests would be consistent with the 1972 U.S.-Soviet treaty limiting anti-ballistic (ABM) defenses.

Deployment of an anti-missile defense would require revision — or abrogation — of the pact, the administration acknowledged. But that choice did not need to be faced until the early 1990s, it contended.

The treaty allowed small ABM deployments to defend either some nuclear missiles or the national capital, but was designed expressly to rule out the kind of nationwide population shield Reagan had been seeking.

"The ABM treaty prohibits the development, testing and deployment of ABM systems and components that are space-based, air-based, sea-based or mobile land-based," according to the administration's report. "However, that agreement does permit research short of field testing of a prototype ABM system or component."

Tests of weapons and detection devices were allowed, the report insisted, so long as the test equipment was not technically capable of being used in an anti-missile system and was not tested against a ballistic missile.

For example:

- The so-called "airborne optical adjunct" would be a telescope mounted in a converted jetliner to be used to track missile warheads as they re-entered the atmosphere. The test would be permissible, according to the report, because the device tested would not be usable as part of an ABM system because of unspecified "limitations" in the telescope and the airplane.
- A satellite designed to detect missiles and determine their courses in the first few minutes of flight would not be an "ABM component," according to the treaty, since it would not be designed to relay the information on to other parts of an ABM system, the administration argued.
- A guided missile, to be launched from a satellite against missile warheads in mid-course, would be tested against another satellite, instead of against a missile warhead, thus skirting the treaty's ban on space-based ABM components.
- A so-called "railgun," designed to use a powerful electrical charge to shoot a "bullet" from a U.S. satellite at Soviet warheads in mid-course, would be tested within treaty limits in ways yet to be determined, the report said.

Later in the year, the treaty's limits on SDI was the focus of disputes between the program's critics and the administration. *(Box, p. 132)*

Senate Committee Action

The Senate Armed Services Committee, citing budget restraints, shaved $300 million from Reagan's $3.7 billion SDI request in marking up the fiscal 1986 defense authorization bill (S 1029 — S Rept 99-41) reported April 29.

A proposal that would further reduce SDI funding to $2.5 billion if the overall defense budget were held to no-growth was rejected 6-12 with only Democrats voting "aye."

The panel said that the SDI program should place more emphasis on developing anti-missile techniques that could be deployed within the next 10 years, as a hedge against the possibility that the 1972 ABM treaty might break down.

The effect of the committee's injunction likely would be to de-emphasize the kind of exotic systems — such as laser-armed space satellites — that would be needed to provide a nationwide shield against missile attack. The committee's approach would have stressed designs that would protect only heavily armored military sites, such as missile silos and command posts.

Before the bill reached the Senate floor in June, Armed Services pared SDI back to $3 billion in a second round of cuts made to keep the overall bill within the ceiling set in the Senate's first concurrent budget resolution (S Con Res 32). *(Budget, p. 441)*

House Committee Action

The House Armed Services Committee trimmed funding for SDI to $2.5 billion, a $1.2 billion cut. The program was included in the panel's version of the fiscal 1986 defense authorization bill (HR 1872 — H Rept 99-81), reported May 10.

According to panel member Jim Courter, R-N.J., the reductions fell most heavily on parts of SDI that would be

Legal Fine Points of the ABM Treaty . . .

President Reagan's anti-missile research plan provoked skirmishing in the fall of 1985 over whether the program would violate the 1972 treaty limiting anti-ballistic missile (ABM) defenses.

The three-week war over the treaty turned on arcane points of law. Essentially, the administration's critics — led by some of the men who had negotiated the treaty with the Soviets in 1972 — argued that it ruled out many of the exotic anti-missile weapons envisioned in Reagan's "strategic defense initiative" (SDI), or "star wars."

That view had been virtually uncontested until Oct. 6, when Robert C. McFarlane, White House national security adviser, announced a new interpretation: The pact did not ban development and testing — short of deployment — of space-based and air-based anti-missile weapons using lasers and other technologies not available in 1972.

After a firestorm of protest from U.S. allies and members of Congress, Secretary of State George P. Shultz announced Oct. 14 that SDI would continue to be governed by the more restrictive interpretation.

However, Shultz insisted that the new, more lenient reading of the treaty was legally correct.

Even under the restrictive interpretration, experts differed over the treaty's impact on SDI. The administration had argued that it could test airborne sensors and space-based weapons through the early 1990s while steering clear of the treaty's prohibitions by testing devices that could not be used as weapons or testing weapons against satellites rather than against target ballistic missiles. Traditional arms control supporters insisted that the planned tests would make a mockery of the treaty. *(SDI, p. 130; ABM treaty, 1972 Almanac p. 589)*

The Treaty Language

At the core of the lawyers' debate over the meaning of the ABM treaty were five pieces of text:

- **Article I**, which provided that the two parties undertake "not to deploy ABM systems for a defense of the territory of its country and not to provide a base for such a defense and not to deploy ABM systems for defense of an individual region except as provided for in Article III."
- **Article II**, which defined an ABM system as one "to counter strategic ballistic missiles or their elements in flight trajectory, currently consisting of" radars, interceptor missiles and launchers for the interceptors. In the second paragraph of Article II, those three types of equipment were referred to as "ABM system components."
- **Article III**, limiting each country to no more than two ABM sites, each with no more than 100 launchers. In 1974, the two nations agreed that each would deploy ABMs at only one of the two sites allowed by the treaty.
- **Article V**, which said: "Each party undertakes not to develop, test or deploy ABM systems or components which are sea-based, air-based, space-based or mobile land-based."
- **Agreed Statement D**, one of a series of explanatory statements appended to the treaty, which read:

"In order to insure fulfillment of the obligation not to deploy ABM systems and their components except as provided in Article III of the treaty, the parties agree that in the event ABM systems based on other physical principles and including components capable of substituting for ABM interceptor missiles, ABM launchers or ABM radars are created in the future, specific limitations on such systems and their components would be subject to discussion," according to the provisions of the treaty that provided for amendment by mutual agreement.

The Brief for a Less Restrictive Treaty . . .

From a legal standpoint, the issue was whether Articles III and V applied to all conceivable ABM systems, or just the 1972 versions made up of radars, missiles and launchers.

Fundamental to that question was the definition of an ABM system contained in Article II.

Arms control advocates critical of the new reading insisted that the definition — and thus the treaty's restrictions — was intended to be all-inclusive. The reference to radars, interceptor missiles and launchers in Article II was merely illustrative; they were the 1972 version of the type of weapon the treaty was intended to ban.

But on Oct. 22, Abraham D. Sofaer, the State Department's legal adviser, told the House panel that the treaty, and the record of talks that produced it, were ambiguous.

Speaking to a hearing of the House Foreign Affairs Subcommittee on Arms Control, he argued that the treaty consistently used the phrases "ABM system" and "components" in contexts that made it clear that they referred only to the 1972-style technology. Accordingly, he main-

needed to deploy a defense within a decade. These were the programs to develop "kinetic energy" weapons — missiles and guns that destroyed enemy warheads by running into them — and detection devices that would be needed to control any defense.

Kinetic energy programs were cut 41 percent (to $510 million) while sensor development was cut 36 percent (to $174 million). The program for "directed-energy" weapons — lasers and other devices designed to destroy a target with a beam of energy — was cut by 25 percent (to $725 million).

The committee's recommendations appeared to have a different emphasis from those of the Senate Armed Services Committee. The Senate panel urged the Pentagon to concentrate SDI research on approaches that could be deployed soonest. Some Senate arms control advocates who had called for allowing only $1.8 billion for SDI in 1986 agreed with that approach.

Senate Floor Action

By comfortable margins, the Senate on June 4 turned back amendments to the defense authorization bill that would have cut the Armed Services Committee's $3 billion in funds for research on anti-missile defenses.

The most drastic of the reductions, an amendment

. . . Spur New Wrangling Over 'Star Wars'

tained, the limits on ground-based deployment in Article III and the ban on mobile or space-based deployment in Article V applied only to that type of ABM system.

If Article III covered future ABM types as well as the 1970s' version, he insisted, Agreed Statement D would have been superfluous.

Moreover, Sofaer denied that the new reading marked a radical break with the past. "We do not accept the premise that the administration is departing from a consistent record of 13 years of the restrictive view," he said.

"Although the U.S. delegates initially sought to ban development and testing of non-land-based systems or components based on future technology, the Soviets refused to go along and no such agreement was reached," Sofaer said. "The record reflects that they failed to obtain the ban they sought and that we could never have enforced such a ban against the Soviets."

Paul Nitze, a senior Reagan administration arms control adviser who had been a member of the 1972 negotiating team, concurred in Sofaer's interpretation. However, Nitze acknowledged that the new interpretation "differs somewhat from what my opinion was at one time."

. . . And the Case for Tough Controls

Leading the charge against the administration position was Gerard C. Smith, who had led the U.S. negotiating team that produced the ABM treaty and the contemporaneous strategic arms limitation treaty (SALT I), limiting offensive nuclear weapons.

Smith disputed Sofaer's contention that the Soviets had rejected any ban on futuristic, space-based ABMs.

He also played down the claim that the negotiating record was ambiguous, insisting that international negotiations always contained some ambiguities. "But be that as it may," he continued, "the 13-year record for the parties holding to the original version should carry far greater weight than some statements reportedly inconsistent with the final language of the treaty."

Backing up Smith was John B. Rhinelander, who had been legal adviser to Smith's negotiating team in 1971-72.

It was clear on its face, he insisted, that Article V's ban on development and testing of mobile and space-based ABMs had been intended to cover future types of weapons, such as those encompassed in SDI. "Any other result is patently absurd and would frustrate the stated premise of this treaty of indefinite duration: to prohibit the deployment of a nationwide ABM system or a 'base' for such a system," Rhinelander said.

The United States had proposed the "currently consisting of" language in Article II precisely to emphasize that the treaty's limits were to apply not only to those types of ABMs but future types as well, he said.

Moreover, in the negotiations over how to limit future ABM types, Rhinelander said, U.S. delegates were under instructions to preserve the option of development and testing — but not deployment — of ground-based, anti-missile lasers.

In 1972, the Joint Chiefs of Staff were very interested in such weapons. Ironically, 13 years later the SDI program emphasized instead space-based lasers and similar weapons that the treaty was intended to ban. Meanwhile, the Soviets were pursuing intensive development of precisely the kind of fixed, ground-based anti-missile lasers for which the treaty allowed testing (but not deployment), according to Rhinelander.

Rhinelander added that the pact had been interpreted from the outset as banning development and testing of space-based "exotic" systems. During Senate Armed Services Committee hearings in 1972, this interpretation had been offered by then-Secretary of Defense Melvin R. Laird and other Pentagon officials, Rhinelander said.

Second-Guessing the Strategy

Barely submerged beneath the lawyers' argument was the fundamental split between liberals and conservatives over the wisdom of the arms control policies of the 1970s — of which the ABM treaty was the crown jewel.

Stephen J. Solarz, D-N.Y., was one of several committee Democrats who flayed the administration's approach for creating "the worst of all possible worlds." By declaring a less restrictive interpretation, the administration had removed treaty-imposed limits on Soviet ABM programs while announcing that the counterpart U.S. programs would continue to be limited by a more restrictive interpretation.

But Henry J. Hyde, R-Ill., cited various Soviet programs that were widely viewed as violations of the ABM pact and other arms control treaties. "They've never felt constrained," Hyde said. "They ignore the damn treaty."

---

offered by freshman John Kerry, D-Mass., would have held the fiscal 1986 authorization to the level appropriated in fiscal 1985: $1.4 billion.

It would have denied all funds for 11 projects within the program, on the ground they were aimed at hardware demonstrations that would violate the ABM treaty. Among these were an airborne telescope for spotting incoming missile warheads and two kinds of satellite-mounted weapons to shoot at them: a so-called "railgun" powered by electricity and a small guided missile.

However, Kerry would have increased by 23 percent the funds for basic research not directly linked to field testing, to hedge against any Soviet breakthroughs.

Like most of the other liberal SDI critics, Kerry insisted that such a defense never would work. But he also argued that finding out whether defense was possible was not worth sacrificing the ABM treaty.

He rejected administration arguments that SDI tests would not violate the 1972 treaty and he warned that a breakdown in that pact would undermine future arms control prospects.

"What would we say if the Soviet Union did any one of those things?" he demanded. "As long as we continue to ride into the gray area . . . then how can we expect to ever try to gain control over this technology or to reassert the notion that arms control takes precedence?"

Armed Services Chairman Barry Goldwater, R-Ariz., suggested that Kerry should spend his time attacking existing Soviet violations rather than prospective U.S. actions.

John W. Warner, R-Va., echoed the administration claim that "the present program ... is in full compliance" with the treaty. Moreover, he warned, Kerry's amendment would "gut" SDI and "jerk the chairs from beneath our negotiators" in Geneva.

Kerry's amendment was rejected 21-78. Liberals with strong records of support for 1970s-style arms control accounted for all the "yea" votes, including only two Republicans: Mark O. Hatfield, Ore., and Lowell P. Weicker Jr., Conn. *(Vote 99, p. 22-S)*

Bumpers-Proxmire

Early in the maneuvering leading up to the Senate's SDI debate on the authorization bill, many arms control advocates who opposed Reagan's program saw the Kerry freeze amendment as an effort to stake out the left end of the spectrum of legislative options, rather than as something they expected to prevail.

Though they publicly supported Kerry, their real hope for racking up a strong Senate vote against Reagan's plan lay with an amendment cosponsored by Bumpers; William Proxmire, D-Wis.; John H. Chafee, R-R.I.; and Charles McC. Mathias Jr., R-Md. This would have trimmed the SDI authorization to $1.9 billion by allowing an increase of only 4 percent — enough to cover inflation — in several demonstration projects the sponsors warned would violate the ABM treaty.

Funds for most other SDI projects would have been increased by 30 percent, though some would have risen by larger proportions.

Some of the larger increases were to go to projects the sponsors said would be essential to deploy a "traditional" ABM system early in the 1990s, in case ongoing arms controls broke down. The SDI program had "seriously downgraded research into conventional ABM systems and in its place is pursuing research into far-out technologies," Proxmire claimed.

The amendment also increased the bureaucratic clout of the SDI program's so-called "red team," which was supposed to try to think of ways the Soviet Union could stymie an anti-missile system. And it expressed the sense of Congress that the United States should continue to observe the ABM treaty.

The $1.1 billion to be trimmed from SDI by the amendment was to be reallocated to boost funding for projects that Proxmire and his allies said would improve morale and conventional force readiness.

As he did in each debate over an SDI reduction amendment, Warner cautioned that a funding cut would weaken the U.S. negotiating position in Geneva. By that logic, Chafee responded, Senate Armed Services already had undermined the U.S. team by cutting Reagan's SDI request from $3.8 billion to $2.9 billion.

The committee's reduction had been driven by budgetary necessity, Warner replied. "The negotiators understood the problem."

Mathias retorted that Warner was claiming that, "It's not the cut, but the cutter that matters."

The four sponsors cited preservation of the ABM treaty as one reason for slowing down the pace of the demonstration projects.

But they also warned that an emphasis on early demonstrations could lead the program down technological blind alleys. "All the research effort ends up going into getting the hardware into the air rather than developing further the technology," Proxmire said.

Nunn countered that blocking demonstration programs would turn SDI into "a massive research program that will never have a conclusion or a judgment point.... How can you ever know what you have if you do not ever have a demonstration project?" he asked.

Some leading anti-SDI lobbyists had set 40 votes as their goal for the Proxmire-Bumpers amendment, and many supporters believed the measure would draw 40-42 votes. But it failed 38-57, with the vote following the usual pattern on arms control controversies: six Republicans joined 32 Democrats, most of them relatively liberal, to support the measure. *(Vote 100, p. 22-S)*

Gore Amendment

If the Proxmire-Bumpers amendment was the club with which the SDI opponents expected to bruise the administration, the actual cut many observers expected the Senate to make was one offered by Gore, trimming SDI to $2.5 billion.

At the outset of debate, Gore conceded that the figure was his estimate of the lowest authorization the Senate might agree to.

Like the Kerry and Proxmire-Bumpers amendments, Gore's tried to avert demonstrations that would violate the ABM treaty, but Gore's tactic was milder.

It would put what Gore called "a temporary hold" on the three tests he said might pose the most immediate threat to the treaty: the airborne telescope, the railgun and the satellite-launched guided missiles.

The amendment would have authorized the amounts requested for those three projects. But the projects were to be held to their fiscal 1984 or 1985 levels until the administration provided Congress with additional technical justification for their necessity and with a report on the demonstrations' consistency with the ABM treaty.

The treaty compliance report was to be submitted by a committee comprising the general counsels of the Defense and State departments and the Arms Control and Disarmament Agency.

Following receipt of those reports, Congress would vote whether or not to release the additional authorization for the projects.

"This thing has grown up so rapidly that we really haven't looked very closely at whether these projects are going to violate the treaty," Gore said. "The political climate in the country is such that a great deal of money is going to be authorized" for SDI. "With that as a given, let us exercise caution," he said.

Contrary to the expectation of SDI opponents, Gore's smaller reduction drew fewer votes than the Proxmire-Bumpers effort. The amendment was rejected 36-59. It was a more partisan vote than the vote on Proxmire-Bumpers: three Democrats who had opposed Proxmire's deeper cut supported Gore, while four Republicans — including Chafee — who supported Proxmire opposed Gore. Mathias, the other GOP cosponsor of Proxmire-Bumpers, did not vote on the Gore amendment. *(Vote 101, p. 22-S)*

Glenn Amendment

The most modest of the SDI reduction amendments — Ohio Democrat John Glenn's reduction of $172 million (to $2.8 billion) — was rejected after brief debate by 36-59, the same margin as the Gore proposal.

The Glenn proposal would have increased SDI funding by 100 percent over the fiscal 1985 level. The amendment would have imposed no limitations on the details of the program.

Seizing on Glenn's repeated statements that the program needed $2.8 billion in fiscal 1986, Warner contended that the Senate needed to approve more than that to bargain in conference with the House, which was expected to approve a lower amount.

Glenn picked up the support of several senators who had opposed the deeper SDI reductions. But seven liberal Democrats who had voted for all three of the deeper cuts voted against Glenn's modest trim. *(Vote 102, p. 22-S)*

Near-Term Emphasis

The Senate also rejected an effort to refocus the committee's recommended SDI budget to emphasize development of anti-missile defenses that could be deployed relatively quickly. This amendment, by Malcolm Wallop, R-Wyo., would have ordered that $800 million of the $2.9 billion authorization be allocated to speed up work on weapons which could be deployed within 5-7 years.

Starting in the late 1970s, Wallop waged a lonely crusade for a crash program to develop crude but effective anti-missile defenses similar to those which, he insisted, Moscow had been producing.

As SDI took shape in 1983, Wallop charged that it was warped by conventional Pentagon thinking that downgraded approaches that could be deployed soon in favor of exotic equipment designed for the turn of the century.

With the support of a small group of scientists and engineers, Wallop argued that upgraded anti-aircraft missiles, the anti-satellite (ASAT) missile and certain kinds of satellite-borne lasers could provide a useful, if less than perfect, defense against the expanding Soviet-missiles fleet.

"The Soviet Union will not give us the time and the Treasury Department and the two houses of Congress will not give us the money to accommodate the [currently planned] way of doing things," Wallop told the Senate.

Wallop's amendment was rejected 33-62. *(Vote 103, p. 22-S)*

Anti-Missile Advice

With nearly every voting Republican casting a "nay" vote, the Senate rejected 38-49 a Bumpers amendment to establish a 10-member Strategic Defense Advisory Panel, appointed by the chairmen and senior Democrats on the Armed Services and Foreign Relations committees and by the majority and minority leaders of the Senate. *(Vote 104, p. 22-S)*

The panel would advise the Senate on technical aspects of SDI, including questions of its compatibility with arms control agreements.

Bumpers argued that the panel would provide information to senators who were not members of the Armed Services panel.

The move drew sharp opposition from Armed Services Committee Republicans Pete Wilson, Calif., who emerged as the most fervent SDI backer on the committee, and Phil Gramm, Texas.

Wilson argued that senators had myriad sources of technical advice on SDI, naming the General Accounting Office, the Office of Technology Assessment and the committees on Armed Services and Foreign Relations.

Gramm objected to granting the Senate's imprimatur to a group of advisers who would have become a permanent part of the SDI political arena.

A move to reconsider the vote rejecting Bumpers' amendment was dropped when Goldwater and Nunn promised to name a panel of expert advisers on the issue.

House Floor Action

The House's June 20 action on the fiscal 1986 defense authorization bill (HR 1872) marked that chamber's first full-scale debate on the Reagan anti-missile defense plan.

Members rejected several amendments that would have trimmed varying amounts from Reagan's $3.7 billion SDI request before settling on an Armed Services Committee proposal to cut it to $2.5 billion.

Though the $2.5 billion was a hefty, one-third reduction, it was substantially above the level favored by most arms control activists. Moreover, the Armed Services panel, dominated by conservatives, had emphasized that it supported the program and was making its trims purely because of the need to cut the nation's overall budget deficit.

Pros and Cons

In the seven hours of SDI debate on June 20, the arguments fell into roughly four categories.

Conservative Republicans endorsed Reagan's goal of a defense that could make nuclear weapons "impotent and obsolete." They touted SDI as a way out of the existing system of nuclear deterrence, in which U.S. and Soviet nuclear forces were keeping each other at bay by threat of retaliation.

At the other pole, liberal arms control advocates dismissed "star wars" as a dangerous fantasy that would not work and would extend the arms race.

Many moderate and conservative members supported research on missile defenses, if only to ensure that Moscow would not steal a technological march. But they argued that the Pentagon could not efficiently absorb in one year an SDI budget that jumped from the $1.4 billion Congress approved in fiscal 1985 to $3.7 billion.

Finally, a group of arms controllers — among them Norman D. Dicks, D-Wash., and Nicholas Mavroules, D-Mass. — seemed to be trying political judo on Reagan: citing his own rhetoric to hem in SDI, rather than making a frontal assault on Reagan's goals for the program. In trying to block some SDI projects, Dicks, Mavroules and others cited Reagan's pledge that the program would be kept within the limits of the 1972 ABM treaty.

They opposed several experiments designed to test lasers, guns, guided missiles and missile detection devices aboard airplanes and space satellites.

The administration said none of these experiments would violate the 1972 treaty's ban on tests of anti-ballistic missile systems or components that were space-borne or airborne. The claim was that the devices were designed to be effective enough to test basic concepts that would have to work as part of an anti-missile defense, but not to count as a "prototype" of an actual system.

The treaty banned only prototypes, the administration stressed.

Amendments

The House voted on six different SDI funding level amendments.

First came an effort by Ronald V. Dellums, D-Calif., to

reduce the committee's $2.5 billion amount to $960 million. This would have denied all funds for certain projects Dellums said would violate the ABM treaty. This was rejected 102-320, with only three Republicans voting "aye." *(Vote 159, p. 52-H)*

Then came Mavroules' amendment, which would have approved a $1.4 billion authorization — the amount Congress appropriated in fiscal 1985. The amendment also would have barred violations of the ABM treaty and provided no funds for certain projects that Mavroules warned would violate the pact. The amendment was rejected 155-268 with nearly solid opposition by Republicans — only four voted in favor — and conservative Democrats. *(Vote 160, p. 52-H)*

An effort by Jim Courter, R-N.J., to restore the authorization to Reagan's full $3.7 billion request then was rejected by about the same margin as Dellums' effort: 104-315. Democrats lined up solidly against this effort — only seven supported it. But even among Republicans, Reagan's request won by only a slight majority (97-83). *(Vote 161, p. 52-H)*

Dicks offered an amendment that would have authorized $2.1 billion and sharply reduced funds for four tests, which Dicks regarded as potential treaty violations. Aspin had been involved for weeks in the drafting of the amendment, which had been adjusted several times in search of a funding level that would be high enough to win moderate support without being so high it would alienate liberal SDI opponents.

The Dicks amendment was rejected 195-221. Still, the Republican line held firm. Democrats backed the move 183-54 with a solid core of conservative Democrats casting the "nays." *(Vote 162, p. 52-H)*

An effort by Marjorie S. Holt, R-Md., to increase the committee's recommendation by the same amount Dicks would have cut it — by $400 million, to $2.9 billion — then was rejected 169-242. *(Vote 163, p. 54-H)*

An amendment by Melvin Price, D-Ill., which essentially repeated the position in the bill as reported by Armed Services, then was approved 256-150. *(Vote 164, p. 54-H)*

Aspin attributed the SDI outcome to members' unfamiliarity with the issue: "People are cautious," he said. "A committee position is something to hang your hat on."

Arms control advocates planned to continue battle with an amendment to ensure that SDI would not violate existing arms control agreements, particularly the ABM treaty.

But that move was called off in return for Courter's agreement not to call up amendments challenging U.S. compliance with other arms agreements.

The House adopted by voice vote on June 26 an amendment by Thomas M. Foglietta, D-Pa., prohibiting SDI development that would use nuclear explosions in space.

Conference, Final Action

House-Senate conferees agreed to authorize $2.75 billion for SDI, halfway between the Senate-approved $2.96 billion and the $2.5 billion approved by the House.

The defense authorization conference agreement (S 1160 — H Rept 99-235) was reached July 25. But final passage of the bill was delayed until Oct. 29 because of disputes in the House over budget levels, procurement reform and nerve gas.

Appropriations

Critics of SDI were hoping for deeper cuts in the program in appropriations legislation, but their efforts were complicated in the fall by Reagan's November summit with Soviet leader Mikhail Gorbachev. *(Summit, p. 109)*

The SDI critics wanted to encourage Reagan to trade the planned anti-missile research program for deep cuts in the Soviet fleet of long-range nuclear missiles. But the timing of the summit meeting — less than four weeks away — put the critics in a tight spot Oct. 24 when the House Appropriations Committee marked up its fiscal 1986 defense spending bill (HR 3629).

Members of Congress traditionally had been reluctant to seem to undercut a president engaged in negotiations with Moscow, and the Reagan administration had exploited that reluctance very successfully.

In the Oct. 24 markup, the House panel rejected a move to trim SDI back to $2.1 billion.

Before the panel's 23-31 vote, the White House had strenuously lobbied Appropriations members to close ranks behind Reagan before the Nov. 19-20 summit and the campaign evidently paid off. The SDI reduction amendment was opposed by seven Democrats — including four of the committee's most senior members — and a moderate Republican, all of whom had voted for a $2.1 billion SDI amendment on the House floor in June.

Looking for a Victory

After they failed to achieve deep cuts in SDI in the defense authorization round, critics of the program tried to get the House Appropriations panel to make a more modest reduction.

In September, an Appropriations panel member, Robert J. Mrazek, D-N.Y., organized a working group of SDI skeptics among committee members. Consulting with defense experts, the group tried to develop a case on technical and managerial grounds — steering clear of strategic issues — for a funding level lower than the authorization bill's $2.75 billion.

From the outset, there was strong pressure from anti-SDI lobbyists to cut the program to less than $2 billion in order to make a symbolic rebuff to Reagan's program. Whatever figure was settled on, the opponents' amendment would be offered by Vic Fazio, D-Calif., an influential member with solid, mainstream credentials and a knack for both private dealing and public debate.

Addabbo's Absence

Meanwhile, the opponents had suffered a major tactical loss: Joseph P. Addabbo, D-N.Y., chairman of the Appropriations Subcommittee on Defense, was ill and absent from this round of the debate.

A master of the "inside game" on the Appropriations panel who was skeptical of Pentagon spending requests, Addabbo was undergoing hospital treatment of an unspecified kidney ailment. Leadership of the Defense panel passed for the time from one of the military's most powerful critics to one of its most powerful allies: Bill Chappell Jr., Fla., the second-ranking Democrat.

When the Defense Subcommittee drafted the appropriations measure in late September, Chappell made sure that the total fell within the $292 billion overall defense ceiling on which House Democrats were insisting.

The generally pro-Pentagon subcommittee increased SDI funds from the $1.75 billion recommended by Addabbo to $2.5 billion, the amount the House had supported during the authorization debate.

So as full committee action on the measure neared, Chappell and John P. Murtha, D-Pa., another senior hawk on the subcommittee, argued that the subcommittee proposal deserved the full committee's support. SDI foes feared the argument was reaching senior committee Democrats who had voted for a $2.1 billion SDI amendment on the House floor in June. "People feel that since the subcommittee met its overall [budget] goal, they should give some leeway" to Chappell on SDI, Fazio said the day before the committee met.

A Pitch From the President

On Oct. 22, the Appropriations Committee journeyed to the White House for a personal SDI pitch by Reagan and his senior national security aides, among them Secretary of State George P. Shultz and Defense Secretary Caspar W. Weinberger.

Fazio, Dicks, and other leaders of the SDI-skeptics had hoped for a sign that, despite his public stance to the contrary, Reagan would accept some limitations on the program in return for hefty reductions in the Soviet land-based nuclear missile force. Moscow had offered to reduce its total nuclear arsenal by 50 percent, as one part of an arms offer.

But Reagan restated his dream of a nationwide shield against nuclear weapons, and insisted that SDI was not up for trading at Geneva.

He urged the panel not to make any cuts in SDI as he prepared to negotiate with "the glamour boy," Gorbachev.

After the meeting, Fazio complained to reporters that Reagan was trying to have it both ways. If SDI was not going to be negotiated at the summit, Fazio said, then reductions on grounds of managerial efficiency could not possibly undermine the president's negotiating position.

But Fazio and his allies were worried enough about the impact of Reagan's pitch that they abandoned their goal of cutting SDI to $1.9 billion: They would try for a reduction to $2.1 billion. During the House authorization debate, 33 of the Appropriations panel's 57 members had voted for that level or a lower one.

The next morning, the cadre of the anti-SDI working group — including Fazio, Dicks, Mrazek and Richard J. Durbin, D-Ill., began canvassing committee members to assess the prospects for a $2.1 billion amendment. The outlook was not promising.

The summit argument had convinced Edward P. Boland, D-Mass., the committee's liberal, second-ranking Democrat. "I don't think we ought to be tying the president's hands when he's got such an important meeting coming up with Gorbachev," Boland told a reporter that afternoon.

Ronald D. Coleman, D-Texas, who had voted — with Boland — for $2.1 billion in June and who had attended meetings of Mrazek's study group, shared Boland's view. "The reality is that we're heading for a summit," he said. "The timing couldn't be worse" for trying to cut SDI.

Meeting the evening of Oct. 23, the opponents decided to go ahead with the amendment even though they knew it would fail. According to one source, some members felt they owed the effort to the still-hospitalized Addabbo, who had written each member of the committee, and had called some of them, urging support for Fazio's amendment. Addabbo netted at least one vote for the SDI opponents, the source said.

Budgets vs. Summitry

When the Appropriations panel took up the defense bill the next morning, Fazio insisted that SDI funding was increasing far too rapidly for sound management. He cited the contention of former Defense Secretary James R. Schlesinger that a research program could not efficiently absorb an annual budget increase larger than 30-35 percent. "We're not ready to absorb this kind of increase," he said. "We need to bring 'star wars' down to earth."

Joseph M. McDade, Pa., the Defense panel's senior Republican, countered that some massive national research projects had been given far more rapid budget increases than SDI, including Project Apollo — to put a man on the moon — and the Manhattan Project, which developed the atomic bomb during World War II.

But the SDI backer's main emphasis was on the approaching summit. "The driving force that brought the Soviets to the table was that SDI program," McDade insisted. "There is no good logic for us to cut the legs off of that driving force."

Eight members who had voted for $2.1 billion in June opposed Fazio's amendment. This included four of the committee's senior Democrats: Chairman Jamie L. Whitten, Miss., and three subcommittee chairman: Boland, William H. Natcher, Ky., and Neal Smith, Iowa. The other Democrats who switched to oppose $2.1 billion were Coleman, Bill Boner, Tenn., and Wes Watkins, Okla. Moderate Republican Carl D. Pursell, Mich., followed the same pattern.

Senate Committee Action

The Senate Appropriations Committee on Nov. 5 approved $2.96 billion for SDI, an amount higher than the $2.75 billion for the program in the final authorization bill.

The money was included in a fiscal 1986 defense appropriations bill (HR 3629 — S Rept 99-176).

Ted Stevens, R-Alaska, chairman of the Appropriations Subcommittee on Defense, said he wanted the higher figure as bargaining leverage with the House, which had appropriated $2.5 billion for SDI. Stevens hoped that the appropriations conference thus would approve the entire $2.75 billion authorized.

Before approving the appropriations bill by voice vote, the panel rejected 13-15 an amendment by J. Bennett Johnston, D-La., that would have established a blue-ribbon commission to analyze the cost and technical feasibility of SDI.

Johnston had prepared another amendment that would have trimmed funding for the program to $2.1 billion.

But after the committee rejected the SDI study panel, Johnston dropped the funding amendment.

"If we can't pass a commission, I don't think we can deal with the funding level," Johnston said.

As had been the case during House action on the defense bill, SDI critics were handicapped by the imminence of the Reagan-Gorbachev summit.

The vote on Johnston's SDI study proposal split basically along party lines.

Republicans opposed the amendment, except Appropriations Chairman Mark O. Hatfield, Ore., and Lowell P. Weicker Jr., Conn., who voted "aye."

Democrats supported it except John C. Stennis, Miss., and Ernest F. Hollings, S.C., who voted "nay," and Lawton Chiles, Fla., who favored the amendment but did not cast a vote.

Continuing Resolution

With time running short before the end of the session, the defense appropriations bills were folded into H J Res 465, the fiscal 1986 continuing resolution.

That measure was passed by the House Dec. 4 and the Senate on Dec. 10. Neither chamber changed its SDI provisions.

House-Senate conferees on the measure accepted the authorization ceiling for SDI — $2.75 billion — and the measure was cleared Dec. 19.

Congress Authorizes $302.5 Billion for Defense

Congress approved a $302.5 billion defense authorization bill for fiscal 1986 that gave President Reagan his major weapons programs — the MX missile, the antisatellite (ASAT) missile, and his anti-missile defense research — with conditions.

The Senate approved the conference report on the bill (S 1160 — H Rept 99-235) by a 94-5 vote on July 30. *(Vote 167, p. 33-S)*

But final House passage was delayed nearly three months by a Democratic revolt over some of the compromises made by House-Senate conferees on the bill. House liberals objected that House Armed Services Committee Chairman Les Aspin, D-Wis., had too readily given in to Senate conferees on the defense budget total, accepting the Senate-passed figure of $302.5 billion instead of insisting on the House's $292.5 billion.

The lower figure was the amount appropriated for defense in fiscal 1985. The higher figure included a $10 billion inflation allowance. *(1984 Almanac p. 37)*

House Democrats were also unhappy over two other conference issues: procurement "reforms" and nerve gas.

Proponents of House-passed provisions that would change the way the Pentagon purchased goods and services complained that those provisions had been unacceptably watered down in the conference. *(Procurement reform issues, p. 164)*

And conditions that were attached to the production of new types of lethal chemical weapons — binary munitions — also had been eased in the conference.

After prolonged negotiations in early September, agreement in principle was reached on resolving the main disputes: The procurement changes would be incorporated into the companion defense appropriations bill (HR 3629) and the appropriations measure would be held to a level producing an overall defense budget of $292 billion. *(Appropriations, p. 377)*

The House eventually passed S 1160 by voice vote on Oct. 29, and President Reagan signed it into law Nov. 8 (PL 99-145).

Final Provisions

The conference report on S 1160 (H Rept 99-235) was filed July 29.

The annual authorization bill covered the major parts of the defense budget: procurement, research and operating costs, including civilian pay. Since the authorization bill did not cover military personnel or construction costs, the amount actually authorized was less than the total defense budget. *(Charts, pp. 139, 183)*

It authorized $215.3 billion for Defense Department programs and $7.7 billion for military programs of the Energy Department.

Strategic Warfare

The conferees' agreement provided a total of $2.6 billion for the MX missile program. This included $1.75 billion to buy 12 additional missiles and the equipment needed to bring to 50 the total number of MXs deployed in missile silos, ready for firing. *(MX, p. 119)*

An additional $105 million was authorized for MX spare parts and $734 million to continue development of the missile.

Reagan had requested $3.8 billion for MX, including funds for 48 missiles.

The bill provided that no more than 50 MXs could be deployed as Reagan planned, in existing Minuteman missile silos. A Reagan proposal to deploy additional MXs in any other basing method would require congressional approval.

The conferees did not settle on the total number of additional MXs that would need to be built for test purposes. Aspin estimated it would be between 75 and 125. But the conferees said that 12 to 21 MXs would be needed for that purpose in the fiscal 1987 budget.

The bill also authorized $724 million — $100 million more than requested — to develop a small, single-warhead missile and a mobile launcher. The conferees emphasized their support for such a "Midgetman" missile, on grounds that its mobility would make it less vulnerable to Soviet attack than the much larger MX.

But the conferees also told the Pentagon to report to the Armed Services panels by Oct. 1 on whether the congressionally mandated weight limit of 30,000 pounds would undermine the Midgetman's military effectiveness. Critics had charged that the missile would be unable to carry decoy warheads needed to penetrate anti-missile defenses.

Conferees also approved $70 million to develop other specially armored or "hard" launch silos for the small missile — less than half the amount requested — and $20 million to develop alternative missile-launcher designs. They complained that Air Force plans for a hard silo were too expensive.

Bomber Weapons. Both houses had approved Reagan's request for $5.5 billion for 48 B-1 bombers. But the House had cut an amount — by one indication, perhaps $250 million — from the secret amount requested for the "stealth" bomber, designed to evade enemy detection.

The Senate had insisted on approving the full amounts requested in the fiscal 1986 budget to develop both the stealth bomber and an advanced cruise missile (ACM), also designed to be "stealthy." The conferees approved full funding of both programs and authorized $100 million of the $123 million requested to equip B-1s and existing B-52 bombers to carry the ACM.

Citing overall budgetary limits, the conferees trimmed the amount for modernizing B-52s by $35 million, to $429 million.

To develop a short-range bomber-launched missile (SRAM II), the conferees approved $35 million of the $79 million requested. They ordered the Air Force to reconsider whether SRAM II had to fly at supersonic speeds, as

Defense Authorizations for Fiscal 1986

The conference report on the fiscal 1986 defense authorization bill (S 1160 — H Rept 99-235) authorized $223 billion for defense programs, out of an overall defense budget of $302.5 billion. The bill included Defense Department programs as well as nuclear weapons programs conducted by the Energy Department.

Totals may not add because of rounding *(in millions of dollars).*

	Reagan Request	House Amount	Senate Amount	Conference Agreement
Procurement				
Army	$ 21,366.1	$ 19,310.3	$ 19,756.3	$ 20,032.3
Navy, Marine Corps	37,430.1	32,722.4	33,635.2	35,024.4
Air Force	46,566.2	37,931.4	42,246.4	42,015.0
NATO programs	0.0	117.9	0.0	75.0
National Guard, Reserve equipment	0.0	0.0	332.0	658.4
Defense agencies	1,391.9	1,290.1	1,318.1	1,342.3
Subtotal	$106,754.3	$ 91,372.1	$ 97,288.0	$ 99,147.4
Research and Development				
Army	$ 5,279.9	$ 4,793.7	$ 4,782.8	$ 4,848.7
Navy, Marine Corps	11,264.3	9,637.6	10,468.6	10,106.4
Air Force	15,578.5	13,051.2	14,294.7	13,719.7
Defense agencies	7,157.4	6,285.3	6,126.3	6,814.0
Subtotal	$ 39,280.1	$ 33,767.8	$ 35,672.3	$ 35,488.8
Operation and Maintenance				
Army	$ 20,190.6	$ 19,172.8	$ 19,230.3	$ 19,177.4
Navy	25,797.7	24,423.4	24,732.9	24,608.8
Marine Corps	1,667.4	1,623.4	1,628.0	1,626.7
Air Force	20,924.4	20,034.0	20,100.7	20,096.1
Defense agencies	7,568.9	7,606.5	7,503.3	7,553.3
Reserves, National Guard	6,138.7	6,065.7	6,018.6	6,072.0
Other	162.4	993.4	147.4	157.4
Subtotal	$ 82,450.2	$ 79,919.2	$ 79,361.1	$ 79,291.7
Working Capital Funds	$ 1,859.6	$ 1,759.6	$ 1,659.6	$ 1,659.6
Civil Defense	$ 119.1	$ 141.4	$ 119.1	$ 130.0
Other	$ 2.1	$ 9.6	$ 451.6*	$ —409.2*
Total, Pentagon	$230,465.4	$206,969.7	$214,551.8	$215,308.3
Energy Department Security Programs	$ 7,958.7	$ 7,718.1	$ 7,637.7	$ 7,684.3
TOTAL	**$238,424.1**	**$214,687.8**	**$222,189.5**	**$222,992.6**

**The Senate bill and conference agreement repealed the Walsh-Healey Act, which required federal contractors to pay overtime to employees who worked more than eight hours a day. The Senate bill assumed repeal would save $555 million; the conference report estimated the savings at $416.3 million.*

the existing SRAM did and as SRAM II was planned to do.

Missile Submarines. For the 13th Trident missile-launching submarine, the conferees approved $1.2 billion, $50 million less than requested.

They also approved $2.1 billion for development of the Trident II missile, $35 million less than requested. The $582 million requested to gear up for Trident II production had been approved by both houses.

The conferees approved $297 million for the first two of a projected fleet of 15 E-6A radio planes — modified Boeing jetliners equipped to communicate with submerged missile subs through five-mile-long radio antennas. The House had refused to fund the new planes. However, the Senate conferees argued that because of their greater speed, the new planes could cover Trident submarine patrol zones in the Pacific better than existing propeller-driven radio planes.

But the Senate Armed Services panel had worried that the Navy might not earmark enough money to buy the planned E-6A fleet in the wake of slower-than-anticipated defense budget increases. So the conferees ordered the secretary of defense to provide a funding plan with the fiscal 1987 budget.

Strategic Defense

For Reagan's plan to develop an anti-missile defense — the strategic defense initiative (SDI), unofficially called "star wars," — the conferees split the difference between the amounts approved by the two houses. The Senate had trimmed Reagan's $3.7 billion request to $2.96 billion; the House to $2.5 billion. The conferees authorized $2.75 billion. *(SDI, p. 130)*

They pressed the Pentagon to focus more on near-term projects that could defend armored military targets with relatively straightforward weapons, rather than concentrating on an "astrodome" defense of the entire country, using more exotic weapons, like space-based lasers.

They approved a Senate-passed provision requiring the president to certify, before deployment of any SDI system, that it would work despite Soviet efforts to attack it, and that it could be deployed more cheaply than the Soviets could expand their missile forces to overwhelm it.

The conference report also included a provision barring the use of any SDI funds "in a manner inconsistent with" various treaties, including the 1972 U.S.-Soviet treaty limiting anti-ballistic missile defenses and the 1967 treaty barring nuclear weapons in space. The House bill had included a provision explicitly barring any SDI test that used nuclear explosions.

Reagan and Defense Secretary Caspar W. Weinberger emphasized that SDI offered a non-nuclear defense against nuclear weapons. But one of the most technically promising weapons being studied was a space-borne X-ray laser that would be powered by a nuclear explosion.

Both houses had approved the $83 million request for procurement of the anti-satellite (ASAT) missile. But the conferees noted that continuing technical problems had delayed for well over a year the first test of the missile against a target satellite. They approved only $33 million for ASAT procurement, but the entire $150 million requested for ASAT development. *(ASAT, p. 162)*

Though anti-missile defenses had drawn much more public attention, the Reagan team also boosted funding to defend North America against bomber attack. Because of budgetary limits, the conferees authorized only $180 million of the $254 million requested for so-called "over-the-horizon" radar, designed to detect planes at more than 1,000 miles, much farther than would be possible with conventional radar.

Ground Forces

Both houses approved the Army's major weapons requests, though with modest funding reductions and with strings attached.

The conferees authorized 840 M-1 tanks ($1.6 billion) and 716 Bradley armored troop carriers ($982 million), but ordered the Pentagon to report to Congress by Jan. 1, 1986, on the feasibility of inducing a second firm to compete with the manufacturer of each vehicle. This was one of numerous provisions reflecting congressional insistence that the Pentagon rely more on competition to hold down weapons costs.

They also accepted a House provision requiring the Pentagon to report on tests in which captured Soviet anti-tank missiles were fired at Bradleys loaded with fuel and ammunition. Critics had complained that the Army was unduly reluctant to conduct realistic tests of the Bradley.

Both houses had approved the request for 144 missile-armed Apache anti-tank helicopters ($1.2 billion). But the conferees accepted a provision that had originated in the staunchly pro-defense House Armed Services panel barring any additional Apache purchases until the manufacturer, Hughes Helicopter Inc., made certain accounting changes demanded by Pentagon auditors.

The conferees made relatively small reductions in the request to develop a new type of weapon: missiles that would spew out anti-tank warheads over concentrations of Soviet vehicles a hundred miles behind the front lines. For the missile (called J-TACMS), $130 million was authorized of $155 million requested. For an airborne radar (JSTARS) to find enemy tank columns and guide the missiles to them, $284 million was authorized of $304 million requested.

But the House Armed Services panel had objected strongly to the Air Force's plan to mount JSTARS in a converted jetliner, arguing that so unwieldy a plane would not last long during a war. The conferees transferred management of the Air Force's share of JSTARS to a Pentagonwide research agency.

DIVAD Gun. The conferees approved $210 million for 72 DIVAD mobile anti-aircraft guns (of the $406 million requested for 117 of the guns). DIVAD had a record of dubious test performances and the conferees barred use of the newly authorized funds until the Pentagon certified that the weapon had passed a series of tests. Subsequently, Weinberger canceled the weapon. *(Box, p. 154)*

The conferees also authorized $75 million, which was not in the budget request, to buy anti-aircraft missiles for U.S. bases in Europe that would be manned by host-nation forces. The House had added $118 million for such cooperative projects.

Chemical Weapons

The conferees authorized $148 million of the $164 million Reagan requested to set up chemical-weapon production lines and begin assembling components of a 155mm artillery shell and an air-dropped bomb called Bigeye.

These "binary munitions" were to contain two liquids in separate compartments; they would combine to form the highly toxic gas only after the shell was fired or the bomb dropped. Proponents claimed this would make them much safer to store and transport in peacetime.

The provision also required that:

- None of the funds be spent to build binary parts until the president certified to Congress that he had a plan for getting the new weapons from wherever they would be stored to Europe in case of a crisis, and that NATO allies had been consulted on the plan.
- Assembly of binary weapons in the form in which they would be stored would not occur before December 1987. However, components could be built as soon as the president's certification was made to Congress. The House-passed bill would have placed a two-year hold on even the production of binary components.
- The Pentagon would draw up a plan to replace all existing U.S. chemical munitions with binary weapons and to destroy the older weapons by Sept. 30, 1994.
- The two parts of each binary weapon would be stored in separate states and transported separately.

Tactical Air Combat

The Senate and House had disagreed over how many to purchase of each of five kinds of jet fighters and ground-attack planes being bought by the Navy and Air Force. In each case, the conferees authorized purchase of the larger of the two numbers:

- $293 million for 11 A-6E Navy bombers, as approved by the House. The Senate had approved only the six planes requested.
- $554 million for 18 F-14 Navy fighters, as requested and approved by the House. The Senate had approved 15.
- $848 million for 46 AV-8B vertical takeoff bombers used by the Marine Corps, which was the package approved by the House. The budget requested $45 million more for the same number of planes. The Senate authorized 43 planes for $848 million.
- $1.8 billion for 48 Air Force F-15 fighters, $72 million less than the budget requested and $42 million less than the Senate approved for that many planes. The House had trimmed the purchase to 42 planes for $1.6 billion.
- $2.6 billion for 180 smaller F-16 fighters. This was $211 million less than the budget requested for 180 planes and $159 million less than the Senate had authorized. The House approved 150 planes for $2.3 billion.

The conference report ordered the Air Force to conduct during fiscal 1986 a competition among "all suitable aircraft" for future fighter purchases. But unlike the House-passed bill, it did not single out the Northrop Corp.'s F-20 as a competitor to General Dynamics' F-16, nor did it guarantee that a minimum purchase would be made of some F-16 competitor.

AMRAAM Missile. The Pentagon had requested $118 million for development and $366 million for initial production of a new air-to-air missile, AMRAAM. Production funds were cut back by the Senate. The House denied all money for the program and the conferees considered following suit largely because of the missile's growing cost.

Built around a radar system only seven inches in diameter, the missile had proven extremely difficult to develop. The missiles would cost about $400,000 apiece, nearly three times the original estimate. The program was at least two years behind schedule.

Were it to work, it would give the F-16 (and the F-20, should any be bought) a missile that could be used at long range, at night and when visibility was poor. The F-16 was carrying only the shorter-range, heat-seeking Sidewinder missile, which could not be used at night or in bad weather.

The conferees approved $106 million for AMRAAM development, but only about half that money could be spent before the secretary of defense certified in writing to Congress that the missile met its performance specifications and that the production of 17,000 missiles would not cost more than $5.2 billion. If the certification was not made by March 1, 1986, the program would be canceled.

The conferees approved $150 million in procurement funds, to be used to equip a second firm to compete with Hughes Aircraft for AMRAAM production contracts.

The conferees added to the bill $25 million to develop a modified version of the existing Sparrow missile to replace the AMRAAM should the project fail.

Both houses had agreed with the budget request for 2,297 of the current model Sparrows ($442 million). But they increased the number of shorter-range Sidewinder air-to-air missiles from the 2,020 requested ($129 million) to 3,352 ($212 million).

Naval Warfare

Both houses had approved all major warship projects in the budget request:

- Four ship-hunting submarines ($2.1 billion).
- Three cruisers carrying the Aegis anti-cruise missile defense system ($2.8 billion).
- Components to be used in large-scale modernizations of an aircraft carrier ($133 million) and a battleship ($54 million).

The only ships not funded were two of four minesweepers, a $167 million cut from the budget request.

As had been the case for several years, both houses had made up several hundred million dollars of the shipbuilding request — $860 million in fiscal 1986 — from unspent funds appropriated in earlier budgets.

Anti-Sub Warfare. For three kinds of submarine-hunting aircraft, the conferees authorized the number requested by the Navy: 18 LAMPS III helicopters, carried by most modern surface warships ($316 million); six smaller LAMPS I helicopters, carried by older warships ($65 million); and nine P-3C, long-range land-based patrol planes ($323 million).

However, they warned that the Navy would have to squeeze more anti-submarine capability out of aircraft budgets that would increase only very slowly. They said that $120 million of the P-3C funds could be used either to buy new planes or to modernize sub-hunting gear on older ones. And they told the service to consider cheaper versions of the LAMPS III, which was linked to expensive detection gear on its mother ship.

They also told the Navy to consider putting more helicopter support equipment on a new class of destroyers, which had been designed without hangars and other equipment to save money. Lower-than-expected bids on the first of the new ships now might make helicopter equipment affordable, the committee said.

Airlift and Sealift

Both houses had approved $239 million (the amount requested) for 12 DC-10 jetliners equipped to refuel other planes in midair. Both also had authorized 16 C-5B cargo planes for $1.8 billion, $100 million less than the budget had requested for that number.

Conferees followed the House's lead in trimming $70 million from the $454 million request for development of a new cargo plane, the C-17. The conferees insisted that the reduction would not slow the program down.

A large helicopter carrier, called an LHD, able to haul 2,000 Marines and their combat gear, had been approved by both houses ($1.1 billion) as had two, smaller amphibious landing ships (called LSDs) built to carry tanks and other vehicles and small landing barges to haul them to the beach ($414 million).

A $604 million request to develop a hybrid airplane/helicopter, called JVX, intended to replace the current generation of Marine Corps troop helicopters, was trimmed to $584 million.

The conferees also adopted a House provision authorizing $5 million to begin buying the Arapaho kit, which would equip commercial cargo ships so that Army helicopter units could fly off them.

Reserve and National Guard

Congress traditionally used defense bills to boost funding for the politically powerful National Guard and reserve forces. This time-honored pattern recently had become more respectable, as burgeoning arms costs and expanding military commitments forced policy makers to look at reserve forces as a cheaper way to perform some missions.

The conferees added to the bill $658 million, which had not been requested, for aircraft and other equipment for Guard and reserves. But in addition, they earmarked some of the most sophisticated weapons being purchased by the Army for assignment to National Guard units:

- Of the 144 Apache anti-tank helicopters authorized, 12 were to go to the Guard, provided funds were appropriated for all 144.
- Of the 72 DIVAD anti-aircraft guns in the bill, 12 were to go to Guard units, though not until after all the active-duty units in Europe received their allotment of guns.

Another sign of the greater attention given to the Guard and reserve role was the conferees' acceptance of a House-passed requirement of a nationwide test of the Pentagon's ability to muster the several hundred thousand members of the individual ready reserves. These were recently discharged service personnel who were not members of reserve units, but who could replace casualties in wartime.

Procurement 'Reforms'

Both chambers passed a package of changes in the way the Pentagon did business; in most cases, the House-passed changes were more sweeping than the Senate's. *(Details, p. 168)*

Predictably, the conferees eased the House provisions. Major compromises:

- **'Revolving Door.'** Pentagon officials were required to excuse themselves from dealing with contractors with whom they had begun discussing prospective employment. Presidential appointees who acted as the government's principal negotiator in dealing with a contractor were barred for two years from going to work for that contractor.
- **Allowable Costs.** Contractors were barred by law from receiving Pentagon reimbursement for such costs as entertainment, lobbying and contract-related legal fees.
- **Multiple-Sourcing.** The secretary of defense was required to plan for the use of multiple sources in both the development and production of major weapons systems. The rule could be waived on grounds of national security.

Compensation Issues

Both houses had approved a 3 percent military pay raise. The conferees agreed that it would take effect Oct. 1, 1985, as passed by the Senate. The House had delayed it until Jan. 1, 1986.

Pension Costs. Both houses also had chopped the $18.7 billion request for retirement pay, ordering the Pentagon to propose changes in the system that would save money without affecting current retirees or active-duty personnel. The conferees cut the retirement request by $2.9 billion, the midpoint between the $4 billion cut by the House and the $1.8 billion cut by the Senate.

As the two Armed Services panels had done earlier in recommending reductions, the conferees emphasized that no one then in the service or on a military pension would take a cut in benefits.

To accommodate the $2.9 billion reduction, the conferees told the Pentagon to recommend two alternative revisions of the existing system, one of which would change only the system for paying cost-of-living increases (COLAs).

The conferees also rejected several Senate-passed amendments to the system of educational fringe benefits. This G.I. Bill was re-enacted in 1984 over the objections of the Senate Armed Services Committee. *(1984 Almanac p. 56)*

The conference report extended the existing hospitalization plan for military dependents (CHAMPUS) to cover dental care.

Family Issues. It established an office of family policy in the office of the secretary of defense and contained provisions intended to ease the needs of military families. One of these would allow the president to establish a hiring preference for the spouses of active-duty personnel on Pentagon installations overseas.

But the conferees rejected another provision that would have directed the Pentagon to establish 24-hour-a-day child-care facilities on military bases "if necessary to meet mission requirements." Instead, the conference report required a study of the need for such centers.

Labor Rules

Conferees dropped a Senate provision that would have sharply narrowed the application to military construction projects of the Davis-Bacon Act. That law required that contractors on federal projects pay the prevailing wage. Conservatives long had argued that the way the act was being administered forced contractors in largely non-union areas to pay higher, union wage rates.

But Senate conferees won partial victories, watering down two other pieces of labor legislation:

- The Monroney amendment basing Pentagon blue-collar wage rates on surveys that covered broad geographic areas, thus sometimes bringing urban wage rates to rural localities. The Senate bill narrowed the geographic scope of the surveys and the conferees accepted that, with the proviso that current employees continued to be covered under the old system.
- The Walsh-Healey Act requiring overtime payment for any time over eight hours worked in one day. The Senate had exempted defense contractors from the measure; the conference report repealed it entirely.

Treason and Drugs

A House provision was retained, allowing imposition of the death penalty on military personnel for peacetime espionage. But another anti-spy provision, which the House also passed in the wake of press reports of the alleged Walker family spy ring, was substantially watered down.

The conference report continued for one year a pilot program allowing random polygraph examination of up to 3,500 persons holding high-level security clearances. Then the pilot program was to be expanded for one year to screen 7,000 persons. The House had passed a provision requiring random screening of everyone holding security clearances.

The conferees also dropped a House provision that would have given civil police power to military personnel to arrest drug smugglers on the high seas. The conferees warned against tampering with the traditional insulation of the military from civilian law enforcement. Instead, they added to the bill $15 million for 500 additional Coast Guard personnel — who already had civilian police power — to be assigned to Navy ships in drug-trafficking areas.

Arms Control Issues

Apart from the major weapons funding issues, the conferees approved several other provisions related to arms control policy. Among these were provisions:

- Urging the president to continue the current policy of "not undercutting" existing U.S.-Soviet arms control agreements, as long as the Soviets did likewise. The president would be required to report by Feb. 1, 1986, on the projected state of the U.S.-Soviet nuclear balance through the rest of the decade, with and without a U.S.-Soviet continuation of the "not undercut" policy. *(Story, p. 175)*

- Requiring administration reports on Soviet compliance with existing arms control agreements, on the military implications of Soviet violations and on U.S. capability to monitor treaty compliance.
- Authorizing the use of up to $100,000 for exchange visits of senior U.S. and Soviet defense officials.
- Limiting the number of nuclear warheads to be built for the MX missile to the number that would be needed since Congress had limited the number of deployed missiles to 50 instead of the 100 planned.

Other Provisions

Base Closings. The conferees greatly simplified the political hurdles the Pentagon had to go through to close a major installation. The new procedure required notification of Congress only when a decision had been made to close a facility, after which no irrevocable action could be taken for at least two months.

Under previous law, Congress had to be notified when a facility became a "candidate" for closure, ensuring time for local interests to mobilize their political muscle against the move.

The provision also repealed a requirement that any major base closure be accompanied by a full-scale environmental impact statement.

Nicaragua. A House-passed provision barring the introduction of U.S. combat forces into Nicaragua, with certain exceptions, was transformed by the conferees into a sense-of-Congress declaration that no combat forces should be sent into Nicaragua, as had been done in the previous year's defense authorization conference report. *(Nicaragua, p. 61)*

The conference report also included:

- A moratorium, at least through May 1, 1986, on the construction of any new commercial franchise businesses on military bases. The provision originated in the Senate, where restaurateurs feared that on-base fast-food stands would cut into business in neighboring towns.
- A sense-of-Congress declaration that the bands of the armed services should use domestically produced instruments and equipment when available.

Senate Committee Action

The Senate Armed Services Committee on April 29 reported a fiscal 1986 defense authorization bill (S 1029 — S Rept 99-41) that would have allowed military spending to grow by 3 percent beyond the cost of inflation.

The bill, trimming $10.6 billion from Reagan's $322 billion budget request, was approved April 4 by a 13-6 vote. The minority — all Democrats — had held out for a bill that would allow no real growth in the defense budget.

On May 10, however, the Senate approved a first concurrent budget resolution (S Con Res 32) allowing "zero real growth" in the defense budget. *(Story, p. 441)*

On May 16, the Armed Services Committee reported a revised version of the bill (S 1160) that would fit into an overall defense budget of $302 billion — the defense ceiling in the Senate's budget resolution.

Finding Reductions

In making its first round of budget cuts in April, the Armed Services panel pared dozens of programs, but few of them very deeply. The committee's most dramatic reduction in a single weapons program was a sharp cut in funds for the MX missile; the panel voted to authorize 21 new missiles, not the 48 Reagan wanted.

The Senate panel's bill also included legislative provisions governing military personnel costs and other items aimed at trimming an additional $1.85 billion from the Reagan budget. For instance, it would have saved $1.2 billion by delaying from July 1, 1985, to Jan. 1, 1986, a 3 percent military pay raise.

In an extraordinary procedure, the committee had marked up three versions of the authorization bill, assuming real growth rates of 4, 3 and zero percent, respectively. Only the 3 percent version was reported.

In views appended to S Rept 99-41, committee member Jeff Bingaman, D-N.M., contended that the panel demonstrated the relative ease with which the defense budget could be cut to zero real growth.

For example, Bingaman said, compared with Reagan's request, the committee's zero-growth budget included:

- 791 combat and support aircraft, 42 more than Congress funded in fiscal 1985 and 16 fewer than the budget request.
- All of the combat ships and all but four of the support vessels requested by the Navy. Two minesweepers, a tanker and modification of a cargo ship would be deferred a year.
- 720 M-1 tanks instead of the 840 requested, over the objection of committee Democrats. The panel's 3 percent growth bill had approved 840 tanks in fiscal 1986 but scaled back the proposed production for fiscal 1987 to 720 because of budgetary limits.

According to other sources, the committee's no-growth bill froze military personnel levels at 2.17 million, instead of allowing a 14,900-man increase. But it still included the Jan. 1, 1986, pay raise of 3 percent.

In the second round of trims in May, the committee again made no substantial changes in funding for major weapons programs. Some $4 billion of the panel's second cutback reflected a May 14 announcement by Defense Secretary Weinberger that a corresponding amount had been "found" in Pentagon accounts that had been appropriated in earlier years but not spent.

Procurement 'Reform'

The committee's original bill, S 1029, contained several provisions intended to tighten up Pentagon management. One would have required each new weapons program to have a production plan that included at least two manufacturers — thus, presumably, reducing weapons prices through competition. Dual sources would be required in cases in which the projected price reduction would offset the cost of setting up a second production line, and in which production would not be delayed "unacceptably."

Other provisions would have set minimum training standards for officers involved in managing weapons procurement and would tighten up existing restrictions on dealings with the Pentagon by retired military personnel who worked for contractors.

But when Sen. David Pryor, D-Ark., and other members of Congress came up with a package of tougher provisions, to be offered as a floor amendment, the Armed Services panel removed its own package from the new defense bill, S 1160. The committee later offered its proposals as a floor amendment. This was a tactical move to allow senators to vote against Pryor's amendment with the assurance that they then could vote for an alternative "reform" package. *(Details, p. 164)*

Nuclear Offensive Forces

In its April 29 report, the committee recommended production of 21 MX missiles in fiscal 1986 — the same number as in the two prior years — instead of the 48 Reagan had requested. It also approved enough support equipment to deploy a total of 50 MXs in existing missile silos. The administration had planned to deploy 100 MXs in existing silos.

However, the committee decided against placing a legal cap of 50 on the number of silo-based MXs. During the markup, a proposal to cap deployment at 40 missiles was rejected 8-11 with J. James Exon, D-Neb., joining all 10 Republicans to vote "nay"; all the other Democrats voted in favor.

The Senate panel's changes in the program amounted to an overall reduction of $981 million in the $3.2 billion MX procurement request.

Approved without change was $799 million requested to continue MX development, $515 million requested to develop the single-warhead Midgetman missile and $157 million to develop a heavily armored, mobile launcher for it.

The committee ordered the Air Force to study ways to cut Midgetman costs, including use of a simpler guidance system and a less heavily protected version of the mobile launcher.

Because of budgetary pressures, the panel trimmed $15 million from the $157 million requested to develop future missile-basing techniques. These included "superhard" silos that would be designed to have a better chance of surviving a nuclear blast.

The panel approved $174 million requested to develop decoys and maneuvering warheads for MX, Midgetman and the existing Minuteman missile. The devices were intended to thwart any future Soviet anti-missile defense. The panel argued that a controversial new Soviet radar and other developments suggested that Moscow was "creeping out" from under the limitations of the 1972 treaty limiting anti-missile systems and it told the Air Force to emphasize development of equipment that could be added to U.S. missiles soon.

The panel trimmed $75 million from the $1.3 billion requested for the 13th Trident missile-launching submarine. Lower-than-anticipated bids on earlier subs suggested that at least that much could be saved.

The committee approved the request for $2.17 billion to continue development of the Trident II; the program would produce the first submarine-launched missile accurate enough to destroy Soviet missiles in their armored silos. Also approved was $582 million requested to gear up for Trident II production, scheduled to begin in fiscal 1987.

For two E-6A airplanes, built to relay radio messages to submerged missile subs, the committee approved the $297 million requested. The Navy planned to buy 15 of these planes, Boeing 707 jetliners modified to tow five-mile-long radio antennas. They were to replace older Hercules transport planes performing this mission, which the Navy called TACAMO — "Take Charge And Move Out."

For the last 48 B-1 bombers (of the 100 aircraft planned), the committee approved the $5.5 billion request. The committee did not report its action on the secret amount requested to continue development of the "stealth" bomber, intended to evade enemy radar. In the past, the panel had strongly supported stealth development.

Some B-1 proponents suggested that some production of the bomber be continued, if only for potential competition that would keep down the stealth's price. But the committee accepted administration arguments that the Pentagon's own cost-control techniques would serve that purpose.

Citing pressure to reduce the budget, the committee trimmed $75 million from the $464 million requested for modifications of the existing fleet of B-52 bombers. Among the changes were equipment the older planes would need to carry nuclear-tipped cruise missiles designed to be launched at enemy targets more than 1,500 miles distant — hopefully beyond the reach of Soviet air defenses.

The secret amount requested to continue development of a new stealth cruise missile was approved. But to cut the budget, the committee pared $15 million from the $79 million requested to develop an improved version of the short-range attack missile (SRAM) for U.S. bombers to carry in addition to long-range cruise missiles.

The panel asked the Air Force for a comparison of the planned version of a new SRAM with a less expensive version.

Approved without change was $698 million to continue putting new, more powerful engines on the fleet of tanker planes used to refuel bombers and fighters in midair.

Strategic Defense

Citing budgetary restraints, the committee cut $300 million from the $3.7 billion requested for Pentagon research on anti-ballistic missiles defenses — the president's "strategic defense initiative" (SDI).

A proposal to reduce SDI funding to $2.5 billion if the overall defense budget were held to no-growth was rejected 6-12 with only Democrats voting "aye."

The panel said that the SDI program should emphasize developing anti-missile techniques that could be deployed within 10 years, as a hedge against the possibility that the 1972 anti-missile treaty might break down.

The committee did not elaborate, but the effect of its injunction appeared to de-emphasize the kind of exotic systems — such as laser-armed space satellites — that would be needed to provide a nationwide shield against missile attack. The committee's approach would stress designs that would protect only heavily armored military sites, such as missile silos and command posts.

To buy three additional anti-satellite (ASAT) guided missiles, the committee approved the $83 million requested. Moscow's existing ASAT was regarded by most analysts as inferior to the newer U.S. version.

Arms control advocates sought to limit ASAT tests, arguing that successful tests would foreclose the possibility of a U.S.-Soviet agreement to ban the weapons.

ASATs were among the arms under discussion in U.S.-Soviet talks in Geneva. The Senate panel warned: "While these negotiations are under way . . . it would be ill-advised and counterproductive to our negotiating efforts for Congress to impose any unilateral limitations."

Ground Combat Forces

The committee approved the request for 840 M-1 tanks in fiscal 1986 ($1.75 billion). But because of budgetary limits, it approved only $318 million of the $359 million requested for components that would be used in M-1s funded in fiscal 1987. That was to have the effect of cutting tank production back to 720 M-1s in fiscal 1987.

However, the panel approved the request for 716 Bradley armored troop carriers ($1 billion) and enough components to build 870 Bradleys in fiscal 1987 ($28 million).

The request for 78 Blackhawk troop-carrying helicopters ($267 million) was approved as was $199 million requested for components to continue that production rate in fiscal 1987.

Similarly, the committee accepted the proposal to buy 144 Apache missile-armed anti-tank helicopters in fiscal 1986 ($1.2 billion) and $55 million worth of components for 144 more that would be funded in fiscal 1987.

But the panel sharply reined in Army plans to develop new helicopter types. It dropped from the bill $14 million requested to resume construction of a very large cargo helicopter (the XCH-62) designed to lift cargoes weighing several tens of tons. The partially completed plane had been in mothballs since Congress stopped work on it in 1975. The committee's rationale was the same used by Congress before: The Army had no funds earmarked to begin production of the large helicopter once it was tested.

Senate Armed Services also cut $20 million from the $76 million request to develop a new, small helicopter called LHX. The Army planned to buy some 4,800 LHXs to replace 7,000 small helicopters used for troop-carrying, anti-tank missile-launching, and reconnaissance. According to the Army, development of one new type for several missions would save money in the long run. But the committee pointed out that under existing projections, it would cost $4 billion to develop LHX and $40 billion — spent over many years, through the late 1990s — to buy the planned fleet.

"It is unfortunate but true that in times of severe budgetary pressure significant long-term economies are often sacrificed to achieve relatively minor near-term savings," the panel said.

It told the Army to study the possibility of using simplified versions of its current helicopter models or modified commercial helicopters to perform the LHX missions.

To preserve the option of continuing production of the technically troubled DIVAD anti-aircraft gun, the committee approved $150 million of the $407 million requested to purchase more of the weapons. *(Story, p. 154)*

A miniature remote-control airplane called Aquila, designed to find artillery targets behind enemy lines, was too complex and expensive, the panel said. It approved $105 million of the $135 million requested to begin production of the planes and told the Army to use $3 million to buy less sophisticated, cheaper drones for some missions.

The request for $163 million to begin producing a new generation of lethal chemical weapons was strongly approved by the committee, which noted ruefully that "this is an emotional and politically unpopular issue." The committee insisted that the new binary munitions would be safer than existing U.S. nerve gas weapons and that they would be militarily more effective. U.S. chemical weapons were not adequate militarily to deter a Soviet attack, the committee argued. This "undermines the United States' ability to conduct a successful conventional defense of Europe and thus lowers the nuclear threshold," it declared.

The committee approved $63 million requested to develop modifications to existing anti-aircraft missiles that would let them shoot down short-range ballistic missiles. It emphasized that this so-called "anti-tactical missile" program was not designed to attack strategic ballistic missiles and was consistent with the 1972 anti-missile treaty. But many arms control advocates argued that the effort to develop anti-tactical missiles might undermine the treaty.

To continue development of the JTACMS missile, designed to spew conventional warheads over enemy tank columns more than a hundred miles away, the committee approved $115 million of the $155 million requested. The other $40 million could be made up from funds appropriated for the project in fiscal 1985 but not spent.

Citing budgetary stringency, the committee cut $50 million from the $260 million requested to develop the airborne radar JSTARS, intended to locate targets for JTACMS.

Tactical Air Combat

An increase in production of the F-15 fighter from 42 in fiscal 1985 to 48 in fiscal 1986 ($2.0 billion) was approved by the committee as was production of 180 smaller F-16s ($3.2 billion). Those represented cuts of $80 million and $75 million, respectively, in those two budget requests.

The panel cut $100 million from the $326 million requested to buy radar jammers to equip those fighters, arguing that technical problems had slowed the production rate.

The request for $396 million to begin production of the AMRAAM air-to-air missile was cut by $125 million. Because the missile's price had been increasing, the Pentagon had delayed production while one group studied cheaper ways to build the AMRAAM and another analyzed alternatives that might be built instead. The committee ordered the Air Force to spend none of the fiscal 1986 money until 30 days after the two Armed Services panels had received the conclusions of those studies.

AMRAAM was critical to Air Force war plans since it would be a radar-guided missile — and thus could be used at night or in bad weather — but was small enough to be carried by the F-16. At the time, the F-16 carried only the shorter-range, heat-seeking Sidewinder missile, which could not be used at night or in bad weather.

As a hedge against a final decision to cancel AMRAAM — or to pare back the planned purchase because of cost — the committee ordered the Air Force to report on whether the F-16 could be modified to carry an existing — and much heavier — radar-guided missile, the Sparrow.

The panel approved $436 million to begin production of a combination of radar and night-viewing equipment, called LANTIRN, designed to let pilots fly at very low altitude and find ground targets in the dark.

For development of a new fighter plane that would enter production in the 1990s, the committee approved $203 million of the $243 million requested. In hopes of reducing costs, the panel told the Air Force and Navy — which also was beginning work on a new fighter — to report on how at least 90 percent of the electronic gear on each plane might be made identical with the gear on the other.

The request for six more A-6Es — the Navy's medium-weight, carrier-based bomber — was approved ($203 million) as was the request for $238 million to develop an improved version of the plane, scheduled to begin production later in the decade. But the committee warned the Navy that it would support development of the new model only if enough money was budgeted to modernize Navy air squadrons more rapidly than previously planned.

As an example of the committee's support for increased production rates of Navy planes, the committee lauded the request for 12 EA-6B radar jamming planes, compared with the six that had been requested in previous years. Doubling the EA-6B production rate reduced the unit price by one-third — to $39 million a copy — the committee said. The request for $446 million was agreed to.

But the committee made some production cutbacks of its own, because of budgetary pressures:

- It approved 15 F-14 fighters ($554 million), compared with the 18 requested (and the 24 that had been purchased in each of the last few years), a $100 million reduction.
- It authorized 43 Harriers ($848 million), instead of the 46 requested, a $45 million cut. The Harrier, a small jet bomber used by the Marine Corps, could take off and land vertically.
- It approved the request for 84 F-18 combination fighter-bombers ($2.5 billion). But it authorized the purchase of only enough additional components to build 96 planes in fiscal 1987 instead of the 102 planned, a reduction of $53 million.

Also agreed to was $348 million requested to develop an improved model of the F-14.

Naval Forces

For equipment to modernize and reactivate the *Wisconsin* — the last of four World War II battleships due to be equipped with modern cruise missiles — the committee approved the $53.5 million requested. The fiscal 1987 budget was to include some $436 million for the project.

For components to be used in rebuilding the aircraft carrier *Kitty Hawk*, the panel approved $133 million, as requested. This "service life extension program" (SLEP) was intended to add 15 years to the normal 30-year service life of the big carriers built in the 1950s and 1960s by replacing worn out engines and electrical and mechanical gear. Some $522 million — less than a quarter of the cost of a new carrier — was to be requested in fiscal 1987 for the *Kitty Hawk.*

Only $86 million of the fiscal 1986 money could be spent until 90 days after the Navy reaffirmed to the committee its decision to rebuild the ship at the Philadelphia Navy Yard. The three other scheduled carrier SLEPs had gone to Philadelphia. Some members of Congress from the West Coast had agitated to have some of the work done in Pacific shipyards.

The panel approved $2.8 billion as requested for three more cruisers equipped with the Aegis anti-aircraft system. Aegis, a powerful, computer-controlled radar and missile battery, was designed to protect a fleet against swarms of attacking cruise missiles. The panel lauded the Navy's use of competition between two shipyards to drive down the cost of the ship. But it urged the service to accelerate the selection of a second firm to compete with RCA to build the Aegis system, accounting for about half the cost of each ship. A second source for Aegis was planned in fiscal 1989.

The committee approved $164 million for components to be used in two *Burke*-class destroyers — scaled-down Aegis ships — to be requested in the fiscal 1987 budget. And it told the Navy to consider including a helicopter hangar in the first ship of the class, which was funded in fiscal 1985. For more than a decade, all the Navy's ships designed to hunt submarines had carried sonobuoys — small helicopters with disposable listening devices — with homing torpedoes to be dropped near enemy subs.

Since the *Burke*-class ships were designed to concentrate on fending off missile attacks — and under strict cost limits — they were given a landing pad, on which other ships' helicopters could refuel, but no way to repair or rearm the aircraft.

To signal its displeasure with Navy foot-dragging over reports on a variety of issues raised by previous authorization bills, the Senate panel made several reductions in Navy research requests. One example was the denial of all $54 million requested to develop improvements in existing shipboard anti-aircraft missiles.

For four *Los Angeles*-class submarines, designed chiefly to hunt other subs, the committee authorized $2.1 billion, a reduction of $60 million from the request.

Around $350 million was requested for research projects associated with designing a new submarine, the SSN-21. The first of these was expected to be included in the fiscal 1989 budget. The panel approved the requests, but warned that the new sub's cost might make it impossible to build as many as were needed to deal with the Soviets' larger submarine force. Once the first few ships of the new class had been built, the Navy projected that SSN-21s would cost about $1 billion each in fiscal 1985 dollars, compared with the $665 million price of a *Los Angeles*-class sub.

The committee trimmed $11 million from the $75 million requested for development of a "stand-off weapon" — a missile with which a submarine could launch a torpedo or a nuclear depth charge at an enemy sub some 60 miles away. The panel complained that the Navy's submarine hierarchy did not place a high enough priority on the weapon, and threatened to try to kill it during the authorization bill conference unless the Navy secretary were to set a firm timetable to begin building the missile.

The committee added a provision barring expenditure of any shipbuilding funds authorized by the bill until the Navy had submitted a six-months-overdue report on procedures under which foreign countries could contract with U.S. shipyards to build non-nuclear-powered submarines. According to some critics who long had argued for complementing the U.S. nuclear sub fleet with a large number of cheaper conventional subs, the Navy was resisting the project for fear it would lend credibility to the call for some non-nuclear U.S. subs.

For 24 LAMPS III anti-submarine helicopters, carried by most new surface warships, the panel approved $357 million, a boost of six aircraft and $41 million over the request.

The committee approved only two of four deep-sea minesweepers (MCMs) for $167 million — almost exactly half the amount requested. But it approved all four of the smaller coastal minesweepers (MSHs) that were requested, for $184 million.

Airlift and Sealift

The committee approved requests for 16 C-5 cargo planes ($1.9 billion) and 12 KC-10 tanker planes, designed to refuel cargo planes and fighters in midair ($239 million). But it also cut the Air Force's aircraft procurement request across the board by a total of $189 million, leaving the service to make the cuts at its discretion in several cargo and transport programs, including the C-5 and KC-10.

The $454 million requested to develop a new, wide-body cargo plane — the C-17 — was reduced by $40 million. The panel blamed overall budget limits and said the reduction should not slow the program's timetable.

In general, the committee treated seaborne transportation systems with a lighter hand.

Three ships designed to support amphibious landings by the Marine Corps were approved: a large helicopter carrier or LHD ($1.15 billion) and two so-called LSDs to carry tanks and other heavy items as well as barges to haul them ashore ($414 million).

Also approved with no reduction were several programs to beef up the Navy's fleet of cargo ships that could be used to haul combat equipment:

- $203 million to buy up commercial ships for inclusion in the "ready reserve force," supposedly capable of going to sea on 10 days' notice.
- $82 million to equip three container ships with heavy cranes so they could unload other container ships at sites without elaborate shore-based equipment.
- $27 million to convert another container ship to carry the maintenance equipment needed to set up a Marine air base.

Operations and Maintenance

The committee approved $81.3 billion for operations and maintenance costs, $1.1 billion less than the request.

About 90 percent of the cut came from a handful of changes. According to the committee, most of these reflected fact-of-life economic changes and would have no impact on Pentagon programs. Reductions included:

- $350 million, based on revised estimates of fuel prices.
- $668 million, reflecting the continued decline of many foreign currencies against the dollar. The effect of this was to reduce the dollars needed to pay the operating costs of U.S. forces stationed abroad.
- $260 million that would be saved by the committee's recommendation of a freeze on the size of the Pentagon's civilian payroll. An additional $73.4 million was cut from the research and development request for the same reason. The budget assumed that the Pentagon's civilian work force would increase by 19,000 to 1,106,800.
- $700 million based on the expectation that items used up in day-to-day operations — everything from spark plugs to clothing — would cost less than had been allowed for when the budget was drawn up.
- $75 million from the total request for day-to-day "housekeeping" chores on military bases. The panel said it wanted to encourage greater efficiency in base operations.

About half those trims were used to increase civilian pay, which the budget assumed would be cut 5 percent. There was general agreement on Capitol Hill that no such cut would be imposed on federal workers, so the committee added to the defense bill $1.1 billion to make up the difference.

Personnel Issues

The committee approved a ceiling on active duty military manpower of 2,167,370. This was 14,900 more than the fiscal 1985 ceiling but 10,730 less than the budget requested.

The ceiling on military reserve strength also was increased by less than the administration requested. The panel approved reserve strength of 1,096,134, a reduction of 12,866 from the request.

The committee also approved several requested policy changes intended to pay a larger share of the costs when military personnel were transferred between bases.

The committee rejected a proposal, originally sponsored by Appropriations Committee member Warren B. Rudman, R-N.H., to cut the Pentagon's payroll over a two-year period by 75,000 military personnel in non-combat positions and about 100,000 civilians.

Senate Floor Action

The Senate June 5 passed by 91-4 its $232 billion version of the defense authorization bill (S 1160). *(Vote 106, p. 23-S)*

The bill authorized a total of $231.6 billion for defense programs in fiscal 1986 — the entire defense budget except for military personnel costs. It would fit into an overall defense budget of $302 billion, amounting to an increase over the fiscal 1985 defense budget only enough to cover the cost of inflation.

As passed, S 1160 included authorization for parts of the defense program that subsequently were passed as separate bills: S 1042, authorizing $8.8 billion for military construction projects; and S 1043, authorizing $7.6 billion for nuclear-power programs — including all nuclear-weapons programs — conducted for the Pentagon by the Energy Department. *(Military construction, p. 182; nuclear weapons, energy-water appropriations, p. 323)*

On balance, Reagan fared well during the Senate debate on nuclear weapons and arms control issues.

His Senate allies beat back efforts to cancel or severely restrict several controversial weapons, including anti-missile defenses, lethal nerve gas and the anti-satellite missile.

But to avoid a near-certain defeat, he was forced to accept a reduction in the total number of MX missiles Congress would agree to fund. Under a deal brokered by Sam Nunn, Ga., the Armed Services panel's senior Democrat, the controversial missile would be limited to 50 deployed in existing launchers. The number of MXs to be authorized in fiscal 1986 would be 12, not 21 as the committee had recommended. That $310 million cut in funds was the only substantial modification the Senate made in the committee's authorizations.

On another arms control question — whether to continue observing existing arms control agreements — the Senate adopted a compromise that endorsed selective U.S. departures from the existing limits in response to alleged Soviet violations.

But although Reagan's allies fended off explicit attacks on his arms control policy, Senate action on the bill foreshadowed political difficulty for his defense program.

The Senate adopted a Nunn amendment ordering the Pentagon to prepare long-range plans that assumed its future budgets would rise by no more than the cost of inflation and by inflation plus 3 percent. Nunn argued that long-term Pentagon planning was warped by the assumption that budgets would increase faster than seemed politically likely.

The MX Deal

Nunn's MX amendment was approved 78-20 on May 23. It reflected Senate weariness with Reagan's basing plan. But with arms control negotiations due to resume within days, Nunn and his allies gave Reagan room to claim a partial victory. *(Vote 93, p. 20-S)*

The Nunn amendment:

- Expressed the sense of the Senate that after 50 MXs had been bought for deployment, additional missiles would be bought only as spares, unless the president proposed and Congress approved a different basing method.
- Reduced the number of MXs authorized in fiscal 1986 to 12, compared with Reagan's request for 48 and the Armed Services Committee's recommendation of 21. All 12 would be used as spares and test missiles.
- Expressed the sense of the Senate that 12-21 MXs should be funded in fiscal 1987.

Anti-Satellite Missile

On May 24, the Senate moved to give the president new flexibility to conduct tests of anti-satellite (ASAT) weapons. First, it rejected, 35-51, an amendment to bar tests of an ASAT weapon to be fired from F-15 warplanes. *(Vote 95, p. 21-S)*

Then it adopted, 74-9, an alternative allowing the president to conduct more than three tests in fiscal 1986 if he certified to Congress that the United States was negotiating seriously with the Soviet Union toward an eventual limit on such weapons. That would lift a provision in existing defense appropriations law barring more than three ASAT tests in 1985. *(Vote 96, p. 21-S)*

The rejected amendment was sponsored by John Kerry, D-Mass., who argued that conducting the tests would encourage the Soviets to speed up work on a new anti-satellite system of their own.

Opposing the amendment, John W. Warner, R-Va., said U.S. arms control negotiators Max M. Kampelman and former Sen. John Tower, R-Texas, had told him that congressional action barring the ASAT tests would be "a unilateral concession that would undercut our negotiating position" at arms control talks in Geneva.

Kerry disagreed, saying his amendment "doesn't give up anything, it gains something ... the opportunity to negotiate with the current, perceived threat level."

The amendment accepted by the Senate, offered by Warner, restated language in existing defense authorization law requiring the president to submit a certification to Congress before conducting any ASAT tests. It applied the same requirement to any tests beyond the three tests that Congress allowed in the companion defense appropriations law.

Pentagon Management, 'Found' Money

The Senate adopted a raft of amendments reflecting unhappiness with reports of exorbitant weapons prices. *(Details, p. 164)*

Congressional complaints over the way the Pentagon was doing business had been exacerbated by reports that large sums left over from earlier budgets suddenly were being discovered in Pentagon accounts.

Defense Secretary Weinberger's May 14 announcement that $4 billion had been "found" that could be used to trim from the fiscal 1986 defense request further undercut his credibility in arguing for higher defense budgets.

During Senate debate May 21, John Glenn, D-Ohio, blasted the timing of the Pentagon's announcement as "self-serving.... They think we in Congress are dupes or idiots or both."

Three days after Weinberger's disclosure, House Armed Services Committee Chairman Les Aspin, D-Wis., claimed that erroneously high inflation estimates in the fiscal 1982-85 defense budgets had given the Pentagon a windfall of $18 billion to $50 billion.

Procurement 'Reform' Amendments

The main debate over procurement "reform" on May 20 pitted Pryor and Charles E. Grassley, R-Iowa, against the Armed Services panel represented on this issue chiefly by Dan Quayle, R-Ind., and Carl Levin, D-Mich. Quayle was chairman and Levin the senior Democrat on the Subcommittee on Defense Acquisition Policy.

Senators faced a choice between two amendments, one by Pryor and one by the committee. Each amendment covered a wide range of weapons procurement policy issues.

One was the so-called "revolving door" between the Pentagon and major defense contractors.

The Armed Services Committee's amendment required an official to recuse himself from handling any contract with a firm with which the official was discussing post-retirement employment. It also required more extensive reporting by retired senior Pentagon officials about their post-retirement employment.

Pryor's proposal would have banned any Pentagon official (for three years after his retirement) from accepting employment or consulting work with a firm over whose contracts the official exercised "significant" responsibility in the last three years of his Pentagon employment.

The committee's amendment and Pryor's also differed in their approach to discouraging "sole-source" contracts for major weapons — contracts bid for by only one firm.

Both groups favored more reliance on competitive bids to award Pentagon contracts.

The committee measure required the Pentagon to draw up a purchasing plan for each major weapon that would keep two manufacturers competing for each year's production contract. The requirement for two sources could be waived on grounds of cost, delay or "national security."

Pryor's version was intended to make recourse to sole-source contracting onerous. One of these provisions would require explicit legislative authorization of any major sole-source contract.

Ultimately, Pryor's amendment was rejected, 22-67. *(Vote 83, p. 19-S)*

With Pryor's effort disposed of, the Senate approved the Armed Services amendment 89-0. *(Vote 84, p. 19-S)*

The Senate also agreed by voice vote to several other amendments aimed at tightening up the Defense Department's procurement system, including amendments:

- By Bingaman, to require the Pentagon to provide additional information in its quarterly reports to Congress on the cost of major weapons programs.
- By William V. Roth Jr., R-Del., to establish a blue-ribbon panel, composed of members of the Senate and House and presidential appointees, to review studies of the Pentagon's purchasing system and recommend specific changes.
- By Alan J. Dixon, D-Ill., requiring the Pentagon to report to Congress quarterly on appropriated funds that the department deemed excess because of revised estimates of inflation, currency exchange rates or other economic facts of life. Dixon said his amendment, which Goldwater co-sponsored, was intended "to put an end to midnight surprises" such as Weinberger's last-minute announcement of $4 billion in surplus funds from prior years.
- By Thomas F. Eagleton, D-Mo., requiring the Pentagon to study excluding inflation allowances from the budget request. Under this plan, the cost of inflation would be absorbed by an "inflation adjustment fund" as it occurred, rather than on the basis of prior estimates. At the end of a fiscal year, the fund would be replenished by a supplemental appropriation.

Base Closings

Some provisions of S 1160 that Armed Services panel Republicans billed as cost-cutting met strong floor opposition. The committee bill would have allowed the secretary of defense to close any military base after giving Congress 60 days' notice, whenever the federal government was running a deficit.

This was to let the Pentagon bypass more extensive reporting, including environmental impact statements. Congress established the requirements in the late 1970s so it could keep a hand in the politically volatile base-closing issue. *(1977 Almanac p. 342; 1976 Almanac p. 311)*

S 1160 also included $1 billion, not requested in the budget, to pay for the initial costs associated with any base closings or consolidations. But this amount was not included in the construction section of the bill.

Goldwater placed great stock in closing under-utilized military bases as a cost-cutting measure. On March 25, Weinberger submitted to Goldwater an "illustrative" list of 22 bases that would be considered as candidates for closing. One was McConnell Air Force Base, a bomber base in the home state of Majority Leader Robert Dole, R-Kan.

In its report on the first version of its bill, the Senate panel insisted that it did not intend for its action to be taken as a sign of support for any base closure. However, of $211 million requested for facilities to house the new B-1 bomber at four bases, the committee approved all but the $71.5 million earmarked for McConnell.

When the committee produced its revised bill, it included $71.5 million for B-1 basing at an undecided location. Republicans indignantly denied Democratic innuendoes that Dole had anything to do with the restoration of the $71.5 million.

During debate on S 1160 May 24, the Senate rejected two amendments that would have changed the base-closing provison:

- By Dale Bumpers, D-Ark., deleting the provision entirely, and restoring existing reporting requirements. It was rejected 41-58. *(Vote 91, p. 20-S)*
- By Bingaman, restoring some of the existing controls, with limits. It was rejected 48-48. *(Vote 92, p. 20-S)*

Chemical Weapons

For the third time in four years, the Senate in effect approved Reagan's plan to end a 16-year moratorium and begin manufacturing a new type of nerve gas weapons — binary munitions.

By a 46-50 vote, it rejected an amendment by Pryor that would have deleted $163 million earmarked to begin production of two kinds of weapons: a 155mm artillery shell and the aerial bomb Bigeye. *(Vote 90, p. 19-S)*

Vice President George Bush took his chair as president of the Senate during the vote on Pryor's amendment, ready if needed to break a tie. In 1983, Bush's vote was needed twice, to break tie-votes to save the binary program from Senate defeat on both the defense authorization and defense appropriations bills. *(1983 Almanac pp. 186, 489)*

At that time, it became known that Bush's mother strongly opposed his support for chemical weapons. This time, as he left the Senate chamber without having to vote on the issue, Bush was overheard quipping to administration officials that his mother would "rest easy."

Binary weapons were to contain two liquids, which were not to be mixed until the bomb was dropped or the shell fired. Though each fluid would be toxic, a lethal cloud of vapor could not form until the two were mixed. By contrast, existing "unitary" chemical weapons contained the lethal agent in liquid form and could devastate an area in case of an accidental spill. One of the Pentagon's chief arguments for building the new weapons was the allegation that they would be safer to move and store.

"This is a repackaging effort," in search of improved safety for U.S. troops, Glenn argued in behalf of the new program.

The opponents countered that the new weapons were unnecessary, since existing nerve gas weapons were adequate to deter the Soviets from using their chemical arsenal. Therefore, they insisted, the $2.3 billion Reagan planned to spend on binary munitions over the next years should go instead for more critical defense improvements.

"There is no way that we can justify this expenditure economically or militarily," Pryor declared.

But the underlying reason for the widespread opposition to binary production was that the notion of "nerve gas" evoked a special revulsion among members willing enough to vote for other kinds of weapons.

John C. Danforth, R-Mo., a Pryor ally, expressed that view, arguing against the new weapons precisely because they would be easier for the Pentagon to handle. "So it is a step in the direction of chemical warfare," he argued, "a step we should not take." What made chemical weapons so awful, Danforth argued, was that they could not be aimed strictly at combatants, but could kill large numbers of innocent civilians. "The whole concept is abhorrent ... to what Western values have stood for since Thomas Aquinas," Danforth said.

Binary opponents had gained votes as a result of the 1984 elections, but they lost the battle of the converts to the Pentagon. Five senators who had voted against binary production in 1983, opposed Pryor's amendment this time: Bingaman, Chiles, and Republicans Thad Cochran, Miss.; Slade Gorton, Wash.; and Larry Pressler, S.D.

Only Kentucky Democrat Wendell H. Ford switched from support to opposition of the new weapons.

An administration official credited a blue-ribbon commission chaired by former Under Secretary of State Walter J. Stoessel Jr. with the turnaround. That panel, chartered by Congress in 1984, had issued a report that endorsed the binary plan.

But critics had charged the Stoessel panel with bias, since it included no announced opponent of the binary program.

After the vote, binary opponents dismissed the Stoessel commission as a factor.

John Isaacs of Council for a Liveable World, a leading anti-binary lobbyist, cited instead strong lobbying by the Army — including the politically powerful National Guard — and by committee members Nunn and Glenn.

Arms Control Compliance

The Senate on June 5 adopted a compromise amendment on arms control policy. The amendment, adopted 90-5, called for continued U.S. observance of existing arms limits through 1986 — but with a large loophole. It expressly endorsed a policy of "proportionate" U.S. responses to Soviet violations of existing arms control agreements. *(Vote 105, p. 23-S)*

Because the amendment did not define the central concept of a "proportionate response," it did not tie Reagan's hands on the question of whether to break up older nuclear missile launchers when a new Trident missile-launching submarine, the *Alaska*, went to sea.

Most arms control specialists agreed that various Soviet activities at the very least pressed at the margins of three existing arms agreements: the 1972 and 1979 agreements on offensive strategic arms (SALT I and II) and the 1972 treaty limiting anti-ballistic missile (ABM) systems.

SALT I expired in 1977. SALT II, a treaty, never was ratified and would have expired at the end of 1985. But so far, the U.S. and Soviet governments had agreed, in effect, to observe most of the SALT provisions.

The *Alaska*'s 24 launchers for multi-warhead missiles would bring the U.S. arsenal 14 over the SALT II limit of

1,200 multi-warhead missile launchers.

Foreign policy hard-liners — led in the Senate by Republicans James A. McClure, Idaho; Malcolm Wallop, Wyo.; and Steven D. Symms, Idaho — long had criticized the SALT and ABM pacts. They called on Reagan to signal that Soviet violations would not be tolerated by announcing that the United States would not destroy existing missiles to remain under the SALT II limits.

Supporters of the existing agreements, led in the Senate by Bumpers and Patrick J. Leahy, D-Vt., contended that the core of the SALT agreements — the limits on various classes of nuclear weapons — had been observed by both sides. To violate one of those ceilings would unravel the web of restraints and evoke powerful anti-U.S. sentiment in Western Europe, they argued. Moreover, they warned, the Soviet Union would get off to a much faster start than the United States in an untrammeled race to build more nuclear missiles.

Bumpers and Leahy drafted an amendment to the defense bill that would call on Reagan to continue through 1986 the current policy of "not undercutting" the arms accords.

The GOP leadership originally planned to block action on the Bumpers amendment until Reagan reported to Congress on his plans for dealing with the *Alaska*.

But in three hours of closed-door talks on June 5, Nunn broke the impasse by suggesting that Bumpers include in his amendment a provision recognizing the right in international law of "proportionate response" to treaty violations, but without trying to apply the principle in specific terms to the *Alaska* case.

McClure and Bumpers accepted the deal and the compromise was agreed to 90-5. Wallop, Symms and three other conservatives opposed what Wallop called "an exercise in self-deception."

Edward M. Kennedy, D-Mass., a SALT backer, called the amendment "a major victory ... for the forces of arms control."

On the other hand, McClure stressed to reporters that the amendment endorsed the notion of "shades of violation" of the agreements by Moscow and gave Reagan flexibility to tailor a U.S. response, including dry-docking, not breaking up, a missile submarine.

'Star Wars' Battles

By comfortable margins, the Senate turned back amendments that would have cut back funds for research on anti-missile defenses.

Reagan's $3.7 billion request for Pentagon funding of the "strategic defense initiative" (SDI) had been trimmed to $3 billion by the Armed Services panel. SDI critics argued that the program would not work and would step up the arms race; proponents of the program warned against undercutting U.S. arms negotiators in Geneva.

Kerry Amendment. The most drastic of the SDI funding cuts, an amendment offered by Kerry, would have held the fiscal 1986 authorization to the level appropriated in fiscal 1985: $1.4 billion.

It would have denied all funds for 11 projects within the program, on the ground they were aimed at hardware demonstrations that would violate the ABM treaty. But it would have increased by 23 percent the funds for basic research not directly linked to field testing, to hedge against any Soviet technical breakthroughs. Kerry's amendment was rejected 21-78. *(Vote 99, p. 22-S)*

Bumpers-Proxmire. The real hope of many arms control advocates for racking up a strong Senate vote against SDI lay with an amendment cosponsored by Bumpers; William Proxmire, D-Wis.; John H. Chafee, R-R.I.; and Charles McC. Mathias Jr., R-Md. It would have trimmed the SDI authorization to $1.9 billion by allowing an increase of only 4 percent — enough to cover inflation — in several demonstration projects the sponsors warned would violate the ABM treaty.

Funds for most other SDI projects would have been increased by 30 percent, though some would be increased by larger proportions.

Some of the larger increases would go to projects the sponsors said would be essential to deploy a "traditional" ABM system early in the 1990s, in case current arms controls broke down.

The amendment also increased the bureaucratic clout of the SDI program's so-called "red team," which was supposed to try to think of ways the Soviet Union could stymie an anti-missile system. And it expressed the sense of Congress that the United States should continue to observe the ABM treaty.

The $1.1 billion trimmed from SDI by the amendment would be reallocated to boost funding for projects that Proxmire and his allies said would improve morale and conventional force readiness.

Some leading anti-SDI lobbyists had set 40 votes as their goal for the Proxmire-Bumpers amendment, but it failed 38-57. *(Vote 100, p. 22-S)*

Gore Proposal. The next amendment, offered by Gore, would have trimmed SDI to $2.5 billion. Like the Kerry and Proxmire-Bumpers amendments, Gore's tried to avert demonstrations that would violate the ABM treaty, but Gore's tactic was milder.

It would have put what Gore called "a temporary hold" on the three tests he said might have posed the most immediate threat to the treaty: the airborne telescope, the railgun and the satellite-launched guided missiles.

The amendment would have authorized the amounts requested for those three projects. But the projects were to be held to their fiscal 1984 or 1985 levels until the administration provided Congress with additional technical justification and with a report on the demonstrations' consistency with the ABM treaty.

The treaty compliance report would be submitted by a committee comprising the general counsels of the Defense and State departments and the Arms Control and Disarmament Agency. Following receipt of those reports, Congress would vote whether or not to release the additional authorization for the projects.

Gore's smaller reduction drew fewer votes than the Proxmire-Bumpers effort. The amendment was rejected 36-59. *(Vote 101, p. 22-S)*

Glenn Amendment. The most modest of the SDI cuts — Ohio Democrat Glenn's reduction of $172 million (to $2.8 billion) — was rejected after brief debate by 36-59, the same margin as the Gore proposal. *(Vote 102, p. 22-S)*

The Glenn proposal would have increased SDI funding by 100 percent over the fiscal 1985 level. The amendment imposed no limitations on the details of the program.

Wallop Proposal. The Senate also rejected an effort to refocus the SDI budget to emphasize development of anti-missile defenses that could be deployed relatively quickly. This amendment, by Wallop, would have ordered that $800 million of the $2.9 billion authorization be allocated to speed up work on weapons that could be deployed within 5-7 years. It failed 33-62. *(Vote 103, p. 22-S)*

Advisory Panel. With nearly every voting Republican casting a "nay," the Senate rejected 38-49 a Bumpers amendment to establish a 10-member Strategic Defense Advisory Panel, appointed by the chairmen and senior Democrats on the Armed Services and Foreign Relations committees and by the Senate majority and minority leaders. *(Vote 104, p. 22-S)*

The panel would have advised the Senate on technical aspects of SDI, including questions of its compatibility with arms control agreements.

Bumpers argued that the panel would provide information to senators who were not members of the Armed Services panel. It drew sharp opposition from Armed Services Committee Republicans Pete Wilson, Calif., and Phil Gramm, Texas.

A move to reconsider the vote rejecting Bumpers' amendment was dropped when Goldwater and Nunn promised to name a panel of expert advisers on the issue.

Retirement Pay

The Senate easily turned back a Glenn amendment that would have restored $1.8 billion the committee cut from the $18 billion requested for the fiscal 1986 contribution to the military retirement trust fund. The amendment also would have required the Pentagon to recommend possible changes that would reduce the pension budget by 10, 20 and 30 percent.

The committee had ordered the Pentagon to propose changes in the retirement system that would reduce future pensions — for persons who had not yet joined the services — by that amount. The House Armed Services Committee had proposed a $4 billion cut in the pension trust fund contribution, under similar terms.

Glenn, a retired Marine colonel, warned that changes in the retirement system should be made very carefully, lest they damage military morale and harm recruiting. His amendment was tabled 85-9. *(Vote 88, p. 19-S)*

The Senate then approved by voice vote a Glenn amendment simply calling for the Pentagon studies of alternative reductions in the pension budget.

Battleships and Bombers

Nebraska Democrat J. James Exon's effort to delete funds to modernize a battleship fared no better than similar efforts in earlier years. The Exon amendment was rejected 30-68. *(Vote 89, p. 19-S)*

At stake was $53.5 million for components that would be used to renovate the USS *Wisconsin.* This was to be the fourth — and last — of the World War II-era leviathans to be pulled out of mothballs by Reagan and equipped with long-range cruise missiles. The bulk of funds for the project — an estimated $436 million — was planned for inclusion in the fiscal 1987 defense budget.

Even more popular than the battlewagon, it seemed, were the so-called "stealth" bomber and "stealth" cruise missile, both of which were designed to evade detection by enemy radars. The Armed Services Committee had approved in full the secret amounts requested for these two programs — evidently well over $1 billion.

In what had become an annual event, the Senate agreed by voice vote to two amendments by Robert C. Byrd, D-W.Va., intended to block the Pentagon from diverting funds from those programs.

The bill included the $5.5 billion requested for the last 48 (of 100) B-1 bombers, which stealth was intended to complement.

Davis-Bacon Labor Rules

In a blow to organized labor, the Senate June 4 backed a plan to exempt most military construction projects from wage standards set in a 54-year-old labor law.

The Senate rejected, 49-49, an amendment that would have restored the full force of the Davis-Bacon Act, which required that construction workers on federal projects be paid the prevailing local wage. *(Vote 97, p. 22-S)*

The act, a basic labor law fiercely defended by organized labor, applied to all federal construction contracts of more than $2,000. The Senate tie vote preserved a provision of S 1160 authored by Gramm that would have raised the threshold to $1 million for military construction work.

That increase, which was later dropped in conference, would have exempted from Davis-Bacon requirements more than 90 percent of all Pentagon construction projects, which accounted for about 40 percent of the dollars awarded for defense construction.

The Gramm proposal also included a revised formula for determining how wage rates and job classifications would be set for projects covered by Davis-Bacon.

The changes, largely reflecting revised regulations put in place by the Reagan administration, were intended to respond to complaints that Davis-Bacon in the past had artificially inflated wage standards and forced payment of union wages in places that were not heavily unionized.

Edward M. Kennedy, D-Mass., sponsor of the amendment to strike the proposed Davis-Bacon changes, contended that waiving prevailing wage standards would undermine the quality of military construction.

Other Amendments

The Senate also agreed by voice vote to the following amendments:

- By Nunn, earmarking $200 million of the amount already in the bill for research and development to be used in joint projects with other NATO governments.
- By Dennis DeConcini, D-Ariz., to authorize creation of Air Force Reserve units equipped with surveillance planes that could cooperate with civilian law enforcement agencies to interdict drug smugglers.
- By Strom Thurmond, R-S.C. barring civil service employment of any person who was required to register for the military draft and had not done so.

House Committee Action

The House Armed Services Committee cut $19.6 billion from the president's $322.2 billion fiscal 1986 defense budget in its defense authorization bill (HR 1872).

But like its Senate counterpart, the panel found that its trims were not enough to meet the ceiling in its chamber's version of the concurrent budget resolution (S Con Res 32).

The bill (H Rept 99-81), reported May 10, would have allowed the defense budget to increase only enough to meet inflation.

But the House on May 23 approved a first concurrent budget resolution freezing the defense budget at its fiscal 1985 level — $292.6 billion — allowing no inflation increase.

Technically, the Armed Services Committee was not required to make further cuts in its bill, since the budget resolution limited bills that appropriated money rather than authorization bills. However, in past years both houses had held defense authorization bills to budget resolution ceilings.

Krings Takes Testing Post

The Senate April 16 confirmed the nomination of career test pilot John E. Krings as the Pentagon's first chief of so-called "operational" testing. The vote was 73-18. *(Vote 30, p. 10-S)*

Congress mandated creation of the new testing job in 1983 out of concern that too many new weapons were entering production without having been tested for their ability to function in battlefield-like conditions.

Critics led by David Pryor, D-Ark., complained that Krings was inexperienced in the conduct of weapons tests that simulated battlefield conditions. They also warned that his 29 years of employment by McDonnell Douglas, a major supplier of airplanes to the Pentagon, suggested he would lack the independence needed to oppose production of a weapon that performed inadequately in operational tests.

But Senate Armed Services Committee Chairman Barry Goldwater, R-Ariz., and senior committee Democrat Sam Nunn, Ga., insisted that Krings was qualified for the testing job. Nunn argued that Pryor exaggerated the distinction between operational testing and the kind of development tests Krings had overseen as McDonnell Douglas' chief test pilot.

The Pentagon's disclosure that $4 billion in unspent prior-year money had been "found" went part of the way to reducing the $10 billion gap between the committee's bill and the budget ceiling.

Trimming Back Procurement

For the most part, the specific reductions the House panel made in its report on the bill represented the sort of marginal trimming typical of congressional action on the defense budget. Only two major weapons programs — the AMRAAM air-to-air missile and the E 6-A communications plane — were killed outright. Production starts for several others were delayed.

The committee warned the Pentagon it would have to rethink long-term weapons purchases "to reflect the changing budget climate." The panel did not challenge the desirability of the administration's basic planning, but it argued, "the question of affordability cannot be ignored."

The panel singled out one facet in each of the services' plans for potential revision to slow down the rate of budget growth over the long run:

- In addition to modernizing its "heavy" divisions, designed to block a Soviet invasion of Western Europe, the Army was hoping to equip several "light" divisions. These would lack the huge tanks and artillery pieces earmarked for Europe but would have equipment light enough that the entire division could be flown abroad in about 500 flights of large cargo planes.

The light division would have enough firepower to deal with regional forces in Third World countries, according to the theory; and since the equipment could arrive on the scene so quickly, its presence would deter Moscow from sending its more heavily armed forces to the scene.

The House panel had been unenthusiastic for years about light equipment. This time it cited affordability as an argument against buying relatively small numbers of items that could be used only in some parts of the world by a few Army units.

Accordingly, the committee denied $3.1 million requested for 88 dune buggies armed with anti-tank guided missiles and $15 million requested to begin mounting Stinger anti-aircraft missiles on jeeps.

- The Navy was modernizing its air squadrons, and increasing the proportion of more sophisticated and more expensive planes in them. At the same time, it was organizing new squadrons to equip an enlarged carrier fleet. An expansion from 12 to 15 active-duty carriers was at the heart of the Reagan administration's "600-ship Navy."

According to the committee, even if the Pentagon carried out its planned purchases of Navy aircraft for the next several years, the Navy would wind up with too few of the more sophisticated planes that planners wanted for squadron modernization. Though the panel took no dramatic action, it warned that the Navy might have to give up its plan to change the composition of carrier squadrons or its goal of having 15 carriers on duty.

- The House panel had previously dismissed as too ambitious Air Force plans to expand from 36 wings of fighter planes to 40 wings by 1990. In past years, the panel had reshaped the service's procurement budget to buy proportionally fewer F-15s and more F-16s. The F-15 was the more sophisticated plane, while the F-16 was the less expensive.

This time, it tried to boost the total number of planes the Air Force could buy for the amount it planned to spend on fighters by creating a bidding war between the F-16 and another fighter competitive in certain respects: the F-20.

The committee ordered the Air Force to sign contracts with both General Dynamics, builder of the F-16, and Northrop Corp., builder of the F-20, that would guarantee each firm the sale of a minimum number of planes for each year from fiscal 1986 to fiscal 1990. For fiscal 1986, this would give each firm about 20 percent of the $2.8 billion the panel approved for F-16s. The firms would compete for the remaining 60 percent in fiscal 1986.

Northrop, which developed the F-20 with private funds, had offered the Air Force in April a fixed-price contract over the next four years for 396 of its planes, which it claimed were substantially cheaper than the same number of F-16s.

The House committee also added to the budget $30 million to begin modernizing Vietnam War-era Phantom jets so they could be kept in the Air Force inventory. Air Force plans to replace older planes with new F-15s and F-16s were understandable, the committee said, but impractical.

Operating Costs

The administration's $84 billion request for operations and maintenance costs and for related supply funds was cut by $1.9 billion. But, as had been the case for years, the overwhelming preponderance of the cuts reflected bookkeeping adjustments that would have no effect on Pentagon operations. These cuts included:

- $568 million, based on greater-than-anticipated strength of the dollar abroad. Favorable exchange rates reduced the operating cost of U.S. units stationed overseas.
- $500 million, based on inflation rates that were lower than expected and unanticipated savings in the purchasing contracts.
- $235 million, reflecting dropping fuel prices.

• $530 million, shifted from the operations and maintenance account to the procurement account.

An additional $290 million was cut in hopes of enforcing compliance with cost-cutting recommendations by auditors from the Pentagon and the General Accounting Office.

Less than $500 million of the committee's reduction in the operations budget was driven by budgetary limits. This included a $100 million cut (to $1 billion) in the request for building up the inventory of day-to-day supplies in the so-called stock funds. An additional total of $382 million was cut from some 50 programs the committee said had requested too rapid an increase in funds.

The non-budgetary reductions in operating costs were partly offset by some hefty committee additions:

• $214 million to reduce a projected backlog of equipment and facilities overdue for major overhauls.

• $96 million to improve combat-readiness of National Guard and reserve forces.

• $315 million for medical care that the administration had assumed would not be necessary because of proposed legislation that would trim the cost of CHAMPUS, the Pentagon's hospitalization plan for military dependents. The committee said that the savings could not be assumed, since the proposals were controversial.

The committee warned that relatively painless reductions in operating costs were possible in the current year, as in prior years, only because of budgetary windfalls — dropping prices at home and a strengthening dollar overseas — which could not go on indefinitely.

If the windfalls stopped and future defense budgets increased more slowly than the Pentagon planned, the committee said, future budgets for operations and maintenance would face an especially tight squeeze.

Strategic Offensive Weapons

The panel approved 21 of the 48 MX missiles requested, a reduction of $820 million (to $1.1 billion). Counting committee reductions in the request for spare parts and support equipment associated with the MX, the panel cut a total of $1.1 billion from the overall procurement request.

A move to cap the number of MXs deployed at 40 was rejected by a vote of 13-32, but proponents rounded up considerable support for an amendment on the House floor.

Approved without change was the request for funds to develop a small, single-warhead missile, informally dubbed Midgetman ($515 million), and an armored mobile launcher for it ($109 million). But the committee denied the $172 million requested to continue development of other possible launching sites for Midgetman, including "super-hard" silos designed to better withstand a nuclear blast.

The $5.5 billion request for 48 B-1 bombers — the last of a planned 100 planes — was approved. So was $123 million to equip B-1s to carry a new, long-range cruise missile with a "stealth" design, intended to make the missile hard for enemy radars to find.

The committee did not announce its action on the secret amount requested to continue development of a stealth bomber.

A request for $79 million to develop a new, short-range attack missile for bombers (SRAM II) was rejected. The project was expected to cost $1 billion and the committee argued that other weapons to perform the same mission were nearing production.

The 13th of a fleet of Trident missile-launching submarines (expected eventually to number at least 20 ships) was agreed to ($1.3 billion) as was the request for components that would be used in future Trident subs ($248 million).

The Trident II submarine-launched missile, due to start production in fiscal 1987, was designed to be much more accurate than the existing Trident I — accurate enough to destroy armored, underground missile silos, just like MX. The committee approved without change the $582 million requested to gear up for Trident II production. It trimmed the Trident II development request by $66 million (to $2.1 billion).

The panel refused to begin production of new radio planes called E-6As; these were Boeing 707 jetliners modified to tow five-mile-long radio antennas for relaying messages to submerged missile submarines.

The committee noted that the Navy's own support for the new plane was contingent on continuing budget increases that seemed unlikely. In all, it dropped from the bill the administration's total request of $486 million for the first two E-6As, spare parts, components for future planes and continued development of the plane. It said modified C-130 transport planes used for radio relay could continue to do the job if they were equipped to be refueled in midair.

Strategic Defense

Funding for the effort to develop anti-ballistic missile defenses — the strategic defense initiative (SDI) — was trimmed to $2.5 billion, a $1.2 billion cut.

According to panel member Jim Courter, R-N.J., the cuts fell most heavily on parts that would be needed to deploy a defense within a decade. These were the programs to develop "kinetic energy" weapons — missiles and guns that destroyed enemy warheads by running into them — and detection devices needed to control any defense.

Kinetic energy programs were cut 41 percent (to $510 million) while sensor development was cut 36 percent (to $174 million). The program for "directed-energy" weapons — lasers and other devices designed to destroy a target with a beam of energy — was cut by 25 percent (to $725 million).

The House panel approved $98 million requested to continue production of the anti-satellite (ASAT) missile. *(Details, p. 162)*

Ground Combat

The committee criticized as "nebulous" the Army's plan to develop a small helicopter (called LHX) to be built in the 1990s to replace several different copters built in the 1960s. The panel approved $54 million of the $76 million requested for LHX.

Lower-than-anticipated bids let the panel reduce by $24 million (to $229 million) the amount to continue modernizing the Army's medium-sized cargo helicopter, the CH-47.

For 78 of the smaller Blackhawk troop-carrying copters, the panel approved the $267 million request. The committee added to the bill $20 million to gear up to equip Blackhawks with Hellfire anti-tank missiles.

To buy 144 of the Apache anti-tank helicopters — for which Hellfire was designed — the committee approved the $1.2 billion requested. It also reiterated its position of the previous year that 18 of the new Apaches should be earmarked for reserve units.

Contracts to modernize the smaller Cobra anti-tank copter had come in below budget. So the panel shifted $20 million from the fiscal 1985 budget to pay for Cobra modifications in fiscal 1986. Accordingly, it reduced the new appropriation for Cobra changes from $124 million to $104 million.

Pointing out that the budget would increase production of the TOW anti-tank guided missile by 70 percent in one year, the panel trimmed $35 million from the request, authorizing 15,000 TOWs instead of 20,100 ($192 million).

The panel approved $1.7 billion to buy 840 M-1 tanks — the amount requested except for a $78 million reduction to be made up by surplus funds from earlier budgets and the proceeds of selling old tanks to other countries.

The panel also added to the bill $15 million to develop ways to give the tank's turbine engine better mileage.

As requested, the panel approved $1 billion for 716 Bradley armored troop carriers, equipped to fire TOW missiles. To give National Guard units more anti-tank firepower, the committee added $30 million to buy 138 of the older M-113 troop carriers equipped to fire TOWs.

The $287 million Reagan requested for Copperhead laser-guided artillery shells — designed partly to let cannons hit tanks miles away — was approved. But the committee halved the request to buy little remote control airplanes equipped with a laser to guide Copperheads to their targets. The panel approved $66 million of the $135 million requested for Aquila, as the robot plane was called.

Like its Senate counterpart, the House panel told the Army to come up with a cheaper plan for buying the robot planes, arguing that Aquila's sophisticated gear would not be needed for many missions.

The House panel added to the budget $40 million to buy two cheaper kinds of robot planes.

The committee denied the $260 million requested for development of the JSTARS airborne radar, intended to locate tanks up to 100 miles behind enemy lines. For more than a year, the panel had been unhappy with Air Force plans to put the radar in a converted jetliner, warning that so bulky a plane could easily be attacked. Now, the panel complained that the Air Force was not looking for an alternative plane to carry JSTARS, and it insisted that other detection equipment could fill the bill.

As it had done in each of the last three years, the committee warmly endorsed Reagan's request to resume production of lethal chemical weapons. To begin work on a new type of nerve gas — binary munitions — the budget included $164 million. The panel approved all but $39 million, which, it said, was covered in the military construction authorization bill (HR 1409). *(Story, p. 182)*

The House had rejected binary weapons production in the previous three years.

Aerial Combat

The committee trimmed the $2.8 billion requested for 180 F-16 fighters to $2.3 billion. This was to buy 150 F-16s under projected prices, but the committee also told the Air Force to use the money to buy a mix of F-16s and F-20s, which might produce a larger total number of planes.

It also approved 42 of the larger F-15 fighters ($1.6 billion) instead of the 48 requested, a $271 million cut.

The Air Force was moving too fast with its plan for a new fighter (the advanced tactical fighter — ATF) to be built in the mid-1990s, the committee complained. It approved $150 million of the $243 million requested. The panel hoped to slow the program down so that new technologies for ATF would be perfected and so that the Air Force could be sure that the new plane would be a worthwhile improvement over updated F-15s and F-16s.

The committee approved 18 Navy F-14 fighters ($554 million) and 46 of the Harrier vertical-takeoff bombers used by the Marines ($848 million). Those amounts were lower than the request by $100 million and $45 million, respectively, in anticipation of low bids.

DIVAD Gun Is Canceled

Defense Secretary Caspar W. Weinberger Aug. 27 canceled further purchases of the Sgt. York DIVAD mobile anti-aircraft gun, saying it did not perform well enough to justify its cost.

It was one of the few times a major weapons system had been canceled in mid-production. DIVAD, a two-barrelled, radar-aimed gun mounted on a tank chassis, was designed to protect Army columns from air attacks. But critics said it was too complex and could not withstand Soviet attacks.

The Defense Department already had spent $1.8 billion on the weapon, which was expected to cost a total of $4.5 billion. The gun was named for World War I hero Sgt. Alvin York and made by Ford Aerospace and Communications Corp.

Congress had authorized 146 of the guns; about 60 had been delivered. The Pentagon planned to buy a total of 648; it requested an additional 117 in 1985. In the fiscal 1986 defense authorization bill (S 1160 — PL 99-145), Congress included $210 million for 72 DIVADs, but withheld the funds until the gun passed performance tests. Weinberger concluded that it failed.

The companion defense appropriations, contained in a fiscal 1986 continuing resolution (H J Res 465 — PL 99-190), included an earmark of funds for the Pentagon to select and begin buying some other anti-aircraft weapon "off the shelf."

The conferees approved $191 million for the DIVAD replacement.

At the end of 1985, DIVAD again drew public scrutiny in connection with alleged cost overruns by one of the two firms developing the weapon. James M. Beggs, head of the National Aeronautics and Space Administration, was indicted Dec. 2 on charges of trying to defraud the Pentagon on the DIVAD contract while he worked at General Dynamics Corp. Two days later, he began an indefinite leave of absence from NASA.

Beggs denied any wrongdoing.

The federal grand jury in Los Angeles also named three other General Dynamics officials, along with the firm itself. The indictment charged that Beggs and the others improperly charged the Pentagon for cost overruns associated with the DIVAD.

General Dynamics, the country's third largest defense contractor, denied the allegations.

Beggs was an executive vice president at General Dynamics during the time of the alleged cost overruns, which took place between 1978 and 1981, according to the indictment.

The committee also approved 84 F-18 fighters, but denied $40 million requested for a reconnaissance version of the plane. Citing budgetary limits, it also approved only enough components to build 84 more F-18s in fiscal 1987 instead of the 102 planes planned, a $63 million reduction.

Production of the A-6E, the Navy's largest carrier-based bomber, would be boosted from six planes annually to 11 by the committee's bill, a $100 million addition to the budget. The committee approved $293 million for 11 of the planes in fiscal 1986 and $21 million for components to be used in 11 more in fiscal 1987.

Potentially as significant as the committee's endorsement of the F-20 fighter, in terms of its impact on long-range Air Force planning, was the panel's decision to kill the new AMRAAM air-to-air missile, which had proven costly and extremely difficult to develop.

The House committee said it would not authorize procurement of AMRAAM until Pentagon reviews of the missile had been completed.

Naval Forces

The committee trimmed the Navy's shipbuilding budget by $672 million — to $10.7 billion — but funded every one of the 23 new ships and five major ship modernizations the Navy requested.

In light of the overall budget situation, this was possible only because $438 million appropriated for ships in fiscal 1983 and 1984 turned out to be unnecessary, and thus could be used for fiscal 1986 projects. The committee credited "a very competitive shipbuilding industry, prudent Navy management and lower than anticipated inflation" for the savings.

But at the same time, the committee warned that awarding shipbuilding contracts strictly on the basis of the lowest bids could drive out business shipyards that would be needed in wartime. A provision directed the Navy to study the effect of adding one shipyard — either a commercial yard on the West Coast or a Navy yard — to the ones building major Navy vessels. West Coast yards were at a competitive disadvantage to yards on the Atlantic or Gulf coasts, because of their higher wage rates.

In 1984 and early 1985, Todd Shipyards Corp. of San Diego, the only West Coast yard currently building major warships, had conducted an aggressive public relations campaign for the contract to build a new destroyer. Todd argued in newspaper and television ads that, with half its ships deployed in the Pacific, the Navy needed to keep at least one West Coast yard in the warship-building business. But Navy Secretary John F. Lehman Jr. disagreed and the contract was awarded to the lower-bidding Bath Iron Works in Maine.

The committee also approved $133.4 million for components that would be used to modernize the 25-year-old carrier *Kitty Hawk* at the Philadelphia Navy Yard, a project expected to be included in the fiscal 1987 budget. But the committee asked the Navy to comment on a proposal to modernize the ship, assigned to the Pacific Fleet, on the West Coast.

Among the new ships authorized were four *Los Angeles*-class submarines, designed to hunt other subs ($2.1 billion), and three Aegis cruisers, designed to protect fleets against anti-ship cruise missiles ($2.8 billion). The panel also authorized $54 million for components to be used to modernize the battleship *Wisconsin*, a project to be included in the fiscal 1987 budget.

The panel denied $205 million requested for a project called SUBACS, aimed at developing a new target detection computer for the existing *Los Angeles*-class and for a new class of hunter subs (called SSN-21). The panel cited rising costs for SUBACS and added to the bill $190 million for the Navy to start over on a target detection system for the SSN-21.

The committee also ordered the Navy not to interfere with commercial U.S. shipyards that wanted to build non-nuclear powered submarines for U.S. allies. The Navy had opposed overtures by Israel and South Korea to U.S. yards. Reportedly, it feared such contracts would feed congressional pressure on the Navy to build some non-nuclear subs instead of the more expensive nuclear-powered ships.

The panel approved purchase of 18 LAMPS III anti-submarine helicopters ($282 million), which were carried by most new classes of surface warships. This marked a reduction from the budget of $34 million, based on anticipated favorable bids.

The panel also approved $65 million for six of the smaller LAMPS I helicopters, which were carried by some older ships. This was $4.5 million less than the budget, an amount the committee earmarked to keep the production line open in fiscal 1987. The planned end of LAMPS I production with the fiscal 1986 purchase would leave some sub hunters short of helicopters, the committee said.

The committee refused funds for production of nine P-3C anti-submarine planes, a shore-based plane developed from the 1950s-vintage Electra airliner. The panel complained that the costs were rising too fast for a plane that had been in production for years. Of a total of $496 million requested for P-3C procurement, the committee allowed $82 million for parts that could be used to resume production in fiscal 1987, if the price came down.

Airlift and Sealift

The panel approved construction of a helicopter carrier (or LHD) able to carry 2,000 Marines. The committee authorized $1.3 billion for that ship and preparations to build two more later. This was $193 million less than the request.

Two ships called LSDs, built to carry Marines, their combat vehicles and the landing barges to haul them ashore, were approved without change ($414 million).

For 14 more CH-53Es — the Marines' largest cargo helicopters, able to lift 16 tons of equipment — the committee authorized $235 million. The panel assumed a contract could be signed for $25 million less than had been budgeted.

The committee also trimmed $50 million from $604 million Reagan requested for development of a hybrid airplane/helicopter called Osprey (formerly JVX). Starting in the 1990s, this was intended to carry Marines ashore much farther and faster than current helicopters.

Major programs for long-range cargo planes were approved:

- $1.8 billion for 16 jumbo C-5s. This was $102 million less than the request, but the committee said that amount could be made up from funds appropriated in earlier years.
- $239 million for 12 KC-10 combination tanker/cargo planes, able to refuel other cargo planes in midair.
- $436 million to continue the development of the C-17 transport, a wide-body plane designed to haul tanks and other heavy equipment to primitive airstrips.

Personnel Issues

As did the Senate Armed Services Committee, the

House panel delayed until Jan. 1, 1986, a 3 percent military pay raise. The administration had proposed to make the increase effective July 1, 1985.

But the House committee's most sweeping effort to change personnel policy was its reduction of $4 billion in the $18.2 billion earmarked for the fiscal 1986 contribution to the military retirement trust fund.

Since pensions were paid out of the fund, the action was not to reduce existing pensions, but force the Pentagon to change the system for future retirees to reduce overall pension costs.

Though the administration opposed the committee move, reportedly it was reconciled to the political inevitability of some retirement cutbacks in order to reduce the deficit. Senate Armed Services proposed a retirement cut of $1.8 billion.

In hopes of making the retirement reduction more palatable to the services, the House panel earmarked some of the savings to pay for new fringe benefits that would reimburse military personnel for more of the costs of moving between assignments.

These "permanent change of station" (or PCS) costs ranked high on the list of military members' complaints. Under existing law, service members were reimbursed for a much lower proportion of their moving costs than were civilian federal workers, even though military were moved more often.

House Floor Action

After two weeks of debate on issues ranging from space weapons to spies, the House on June 27 passed its defense authorization bill for fiscal 1986.

As passed by a vote of 278-106, HR 1872 authorized $206 million for weapons procurement, military research and operating costs of the Pentagon. This would have fit into an overall defense budget of $292.5 billion, the same size as the fiscal 1985 budget. *(Vote 190, p. 62-H)*

Despite adopting 165 amendments, the House made few significant changes in the Armed Services Committee's version of the bill. It accepted the Armed Services panel's recommendation of how to trim $10 billion from the bill as reported, in order to meet the defense ceiling in the House-passed budget resolution.

The committee position on controversial weapons was overruled by the House only in its denial of funds to produce additional MX missiles in fiscal 1986 and in its vote to bar tests of the anti-satellite (ASAT) missile.

But the committee finally prevailed in its four-year-long fight to win House approval for producing a new generation of lethal chemical weapons.

Following passage of HR 1872, the House substituted its text for that of the Senate-passed bill, clearing the way for a conference on the measure.

Anti-Missile Research

The House conducted its first full-scale debate on Reagan's strategic defense initiative on June 20. The House Armed Services Committee had trimmed Reagan's request for the program from $3.7 billion to $2.5 billion.

In seven hours of floor debate on SDI, members rejected several amendments that would have cut the program further.

First came an effort by Ronald V. Dellums, D-Calif., to reduce the SDI funding level to $960 million. This would have denied all funds for certain projects Dellums said would violate the ABM treaty. This was rejected 102-320. *(Vote 159, p. 52-H)*

Then came an amendment by Nicholas Mavroules, D-Mass., which would have approved a $1.4 billion authorization — the amount Congress appropriated in fiscal 1985. The amendment also would have barred violations of the ABM treaty and provided no funds for certain projects that Mavroules warned would violate the pact. The amendment was rejected 155-268. *(Vote 160, p. 52-H)*

An effort by Jim Courter, R-N.J., to restore the authorization to Reagan's full $3.7 billion request then was rejected by about the same margin as Dellums' effort: 104-315. *(Vote 161, p. 52-H)*

Norman D. Dicks, D-Wash., offered an amendment that would have authorized $2.1 billion and sharply reduced funds for four tests, which Dicks regarded as potential treaty violations. Aspin had been involved for weeks in the drafting of the amendment, which had been adjusted several times in search of a funding level that would be high enough to win moderate support without being so high it would alienate liberal SDI opponents.

The Dicks amendment was rejected 195-221. Still, the Republican line held firm. Democrats backed the move 183-54 with a solid core of conservative Democrats casting the "nays." *(Vote 162, p. 52-H)*

An effort by Marjorie S. Holt, R-Md., to increase the committee's recommendation by the same amount Dicks would have cut it — by $400 million, to $2.9 billion — then was rejected 169-242. *(Vote 163, p. 54-H)*

An amendment by Melvin Price, D-Ill., which essentially repeated the position in the bill as reported by Armed Services, then was approved 256-150. *(Vote 164, p. 52-H)*

Arms control advocates held out the prospect of a further battle over ensuring that SDI research would not violate existing arms control agreements, particularly the ABM treaty. But that was called off in return for Courter's agreement not to call up amendments challenging continued U.S. compliance with other arms agreements.

The House adopted by voice vote June 26 an amendment by Thomas M. Foglietta, D-Pa., prohibiting SDI development that would use nuclear explosions in space.

MX Missile

Without killing off the program entirely, the House on June 28 voted by a comfortable margin to limit the number of MXs that would be deployed in existing silos to 40, compared with Reagan's initial request for 100.

The cap was embodied in an amendment offered by Mavroules, a longtime opponent of the missile. This time Mavroules collaborated with Dave McCurdy, D-Okla., one of the Aspin allies who had backed MX in the past. Their amendment:

- Imposed a permanent limit of 40 on the number of MXs that would be deployed.
- Allowed no additional production of MXs in fiscal 1986, but approved $921 million for equipment to base already approved MXs in existing missile silos and to keep the missile production line ready to crank out additional missiles for testing while MXs were in service.

William L. Dickinson, Ala., Armed Services' senior Republican, offered an amendment that would have approved production of an additional 12 missiles in fiscal 1986 and set the cap at 50 missiles deployed. MX backers argued that the Air Force's communication and control system was geared to handle missiles in squadrons of 50 and that it would be expensive and inefficient to combine 10 existing Minuteman missiles with 40 MXs to fill a squadron.

But the cutting issue between Dickinson and Mavroules was the degree of permanence of the MX production cap. Dickinson's was a sense of Congress statement, rather than binding law.

Mavroules and McCurdy demanded a permanent limit on the number deployed. Any such legislative provision could be repealed subsequently, but the two insisted on putting the onus on Reagan to request positive congressional action in order to remove the limit.

The House was offered a third option by Charles E. Bennett, D-Fla., who had cosponsored previous anti-MX amendments with Mavroules. Bennett's amendment would have denied any MX procurement money in fiscal 1986 and diverted unspent MX money from earlier years to be used for conventional weapons.

Bennett's amendment was rejected 185-230. *(Vote 151, p. 50-H)*

Complex procedural jockeying ensued, with Dickinson and Mavroules each angling for his amendment to be voted on first.

Mavroules prevailed and the first vote came, in effect, on his position — specifically on an amendment by McCurdy to Dickinson's amendment. The McCurdy measure was approved 233-184. *(Vote 152, p. 50-H)*

The House then cast a nearly identical vote (182-234) against a substitute for the Mavroules amendment, offered by Courter. The Courter amendment restated Dickinson's. *(Vote 153, p. 50-H)*

Mavroules' original amendment then was passed by voice vote.

On June 20, two days after the House voted to cap MX deployment, members rejected by voice vote an amendment by Ken Kramer, R-Colo., that would have canceled development of a small, single-warhead intercontinental missile, informally dubbed Midgetman. The Kramer amendment would have dropped all $624 million earmarked for Midgetman but would have used $524 million of that amount to increase the authorization for SDI, boosting it to $3 billion.

The House then agreed by voice vote to a McCurdy amendment increasing by $150 million (to $774 million) the Midgetman authorization.

Trident II

An amendment by Ted Weiss, D-N.Y., that would have blocked production of the Trident II submarine-launched missile, was rejected 79-342. *(Vote 155, p. 52-H)*

This was the weakest showing yet by liberal arms control advocates, who warned that the new missile — also called D-5 — would destabilize the U.S.-Soviet nuclear balance. In 1984, a Weiss amendment to deny D-5 funds was rejected 93-319. A similar amendment by Thomas J. Downey, D-N.Y., in 1982 was rejected 89-312. *(1984 Almanac p. 43; 1982 Almanac p. 99)*

Trident II opponents argued that the missile would be too accurate — roughly as accurate as the MX, and thus able to destroy Soviet missiles in their armored, underground silos. Weiss and his allies argued that D-5 warheads could strike their targets in about half the time it would take MX — 15 minutes rather then 30. Accordingly, the Soviet Union would have to put its nuclear missiles on a hair-trigger.

But supporters of the new missile maintained that its great accuracy was needed to make the U.S. deterrent threat credible to Soviet leaders by being able to threaten the armored command posts from which Soviet leaders would try to conduct a war. The existing Trident I missile was not accurate enough to destroy military targets, they argued: It would threaten "women, children, old men and cities," Armed Services member Duncan L. Hunter, R-Calif., said. "The requirement we have is to put the Soviet leadership at risk.... You don't see a great concern for their civilian population."

D-5 supporters also argued that the missile's potentially longer range, compared with that of the Trident I, would give U.S. missile subs more ocean to hide in while still being within range of their targets.

Nerve Gas

On its fourth try in as many years, the administration on June 19 finally won House approval for lethal chemical weapons. Opponents credited administration lobbying that emphasized the argument that the new weapons would be safer for U.S. troops to handle than existing chemical arms.

The new "binary" munitions were to be artillery shells and aerial bombs containing two relatively harmless chemicals that would combine to form nerve gas only after the bomb was dropped or the shell fired. The United States had not produced lethal chemical weapons in 16 years.

By a vote of 229-196, the House adopted an amendment by Ike Skelton, D-Mo., which retained in the bill $124 million for binary production. *(Vote 156, p. 52-H)*

The weapons could not start coming off the assembly line before October 1987. The production line could begin then only if certain conditions were met. Among the requirements:

- Both types of weapons met current performance specifications.
- NATO officially requested production of the new weapons to replace chemical weapons currently in Europe.
- The NATO nations in whose territory the new weapons would be stored agreed to accept them.
- If any of the weapons were stored in the United States, their two components would have to be kept in separate states to eliminate the possibility that they could combine in case of an accident.

John Edward Porter, R-Ill., who led an unsuccessful effort to delete binary funds from the bill, dismissed the Skelton conditions as "smoke," which, he predicted, "will be changed or put in the hands of conferees and lost."

Reagan apparently was especially effective among first-term Republicans. Of 30 who voted on the issue, 28 voted for the Skelton amendment; Dick Armey, Texas, and Paul B. Henry, Mich., voted "nay."

After Skelton's amendment to Porter's amendment was agreed to, Porter ally Dante B. Fascell, D-Fla., Foreign Affairs Committee chairman, offered an amendment that would have deleted the $124 million authorization. The Skelton language was reaffirmed by a nearly identical second vote, 223-196. *(Vote 157, p. 52-H)*

ASAT Test Curb

For the second year in a row, the House adopted an amendment to the defense bill by George E. Brown Jr., D-Calif., and Lawrence Coughlin, R-Pa., that barred anti-satellite missile tests against targets in space, so long as Moscow continued its current moratorium on ASAT testing.

The moratorium was to cover not only fiscal 1986 but

also the three tests that were permitted in fiscal 1985.

The Brown amendment was adopted June 26 by a vote of 229-193. *(Vote 178, p. 58-H)*

An identical amendment to the fiscal 1985 defense authorization bill was adopted in 1984 in a series of votes, by slightly larger margins. *(1984 Almanac p. 62)*

In the June 26 debate, Brown and his allies warned that once the U.S. missile's guidance system had been successfully tested in a shot against a target, it would be impossible to negotiate a mutual ban on deployment.

Before adopting the Brown amendment, the House adopted by voice vote an amendment by Steny H. Hoyer, D-Md., adding to the bill $20 million to speed efforts to protect U.S. satellites against attack.

Other Arms Control Efforts

An amendment by Edward J. Markey, D-Mass., to bar work on a new nuclear artillery shell was rejected by voice vote June 27; so was a substitute by Vic Fazio, D-Calif., that would have blocked the project for a year.

Markey offered four other amendments intended to stop or slow down nuclear weapons projects, but he had negotiated with the House Armed Services Committee on watered-down versions. Offered by Samuel S. Stratton, D-N.Y., all of these were agreed to by voice vote:

- Limit MX missile warheads to the number needed for the MX force size to be agreed upon by conferees.
- Restrict development of a nuclear warhead for the Navy's Standard anti-aircraft missile.
- Limit development on a small, nuclear demolition device designed to obstruct transportation routes.
- Require a report on long-term requirements for the nuclear "fuel" used in nuclear weapons.

Budget Ceiling

On June 18, the House voted 301-115 to trim $10 billion from the amount recommended by the committee. *(Vote 150, p. 50-H)*

The amendment, offered by Aspin, was intended to bring the authorization in line with the overall defense ceiling embodied in the House-passed version of the first concurrent budget resolution, which would hold the fiscal 1986 defense budget at the fiscal 1985 level.

As reported by the committee, HR 1872 allowed the fiscal 1986 budget to increase by $10 billion to cover the estimated cost of inflation.

The $10 billion trimmed by Aspin's amendment came from two sources:

- $4.4 billion Defense Secretary Weinberger had told the Senate in May could be trimmed from the budget because of surplus funds left over from prior years' budgets.
- $5.6 billion scattered across hundreds of procurement requests to cover the cost of estimated future inflation.

With a few exceptions, Congress insisted on "full funding" for weapons appropriations; it wanted the Pentagon to request in one year the entire cost of a ship or a certain number of planes, even though construction of the weapons would take several years. The rule was designed to give Congress a view of a system's full cost, only a small fraction of which, typically, would be spent in the first year.

For multi-year projects, full funding included the estimated cost of inflation for future years. In the late 1970s, those estimates routinely proved to be too low but in recent years, they had tended to run higher than the inflation actually experienced. These overestimates accounted for a large part of Weinberger's $4.4 billion windfall.

By cutting the $5.5 billion in estimated inflation, Aspin wanted to force a discussion in the Senate-House conference on the authorization bill of whether weapons programs should simply be funded at their current cost. Congress then could add funds later on to meet the cost of inflation as it occurred, he argued.

Central American Involvement

The House voted to bar the introduction of U.S. combat troops into Nicaragua, but with larger loopholes than had been included in a similar amendment to the fiscal 1985 defense bill. *(1984 Almanac p. 43)*

As introduced by Thomas S. Foley, D-Wash., the amendment barring the introduction of U.S. combat troops into Nicaragua without express congressional authorization allowed four exceptions. Troops could be sent:

- To meet a clear and present danger of hostile attack on the United States.
- To protect the U.S. Embassy.
- To evacuate U.S. citizens.
- To meet U.S. obligations to its Latin American allies under the Rio Treaty.

The Foley amendment also included a declaration that it would not affect the War Powers Act.

Liberal critics of Reagan's Central America policy had worried for several days before the Foley debate that they were losing ground. They were particularly concerned in light of the House's decision June 12 to reverse itself and give $27 million in non-military aid to "contras" fighting the leftist government in Managua. *(Nicaragua, p. 61)*

In addition, Reagan critics feared members would adopt a get-tough stance in the wake of terrorist attacks in Beirut and El Salvador.

Foley did not contest two amendments that added further exemptions to the original list.

One, offered by Hunter and adopted 377-45, waived the troop ban if Nicaragua acquired Soviet-built MiG jet fighters or similarly modern combat planes. *(Vote 183, p. 60-H)*

Another Hunter amendment, adopted by voice vote, added to the circumstances that would waive the ban:

- Acquisition by Nicaragua of nuclear weapons.
- A need "to respond to hijacking, kidnapping, or other acts of terrorism involving citizens of the United States or . . . of any ally."

But Foley strongly opposed an amendment by Dan Burton, R-Ind., that would have waived the troop ban if the president found that Nicaragua was supporting "directly or indirectly" any military or terrorist operations in El Salvador, Honduras or Costa Rica. Reagan repeatedly had made such charges.

When the Burton amendment was rejected 186-235, Foley supporters seized on it as a token of victory. The House then adopted the much-amended Foley amendment 312-111. *(Votes 184, 185, p. 60-H)*

The House also rejected an amendment designed to limit the actions of U.S. troops in Honduras near that country's border with Nicaragua. Edward J. Markey, D-Mass., proposed an amendment to bar U.S. troops from within 20 miles of the border. A much less restrictive substitute by Dan Daniel, D-Va., was adopted 320-69. *(Vote 188, p. 60-H)*

But conservatives led by Thomas F. Hartnett, R-S.C., defeated the modified version, 172-217. *(Vote 189, p. 62-H)*

The House adopted two related amendments by voice vote:

• By Bill Richardson, D-N.M., barring the use of the Defense Department or the CIA to supply contra guerrillas, restating the House position on that issue.

• By Robert S. Walker, R-Pa., authorizing the president to take any anti-terrorist action necessary to protect U.S. military personnel and to take counter-terrorist action against persons responsible for the death of U.S. military personnel. Some Reagan critics warned against so open-ended a warrant for military action.

Espionage Death Penalty

Bill McCollum, R-Fla., offered an amendment making espionage during peacetime a capital offense under the Uniform Code of Military Justice. Espionage had been punishable under the military code only in wartime.

The maximum penalty for peacetime espionage was 10 years in prison.

The amendment was agreed to by voice vote after only a brief debate. McCollum requested a roll-call vote, but the request was not supported by the requisite number of members.

Immediately before the House voted on final passage of the bill, conservative GOP activist Walker demanded another vote on the McCollum amendment. It was adopted by a standing vote of 104-34.

Walker then asked for a roll-call vote. Aspin later speculated that Walker hoped to force Democrats who opposed capital punishment to cast a vote that could be used against them in future campaigns.

But under the parliamentary situation at the time, Walker's request would have needed the support of 44 members. Majority Leader Jim Wright, D-Texas, acting as Speaker, announced that only 43 members — an insufficient number — had stood to support Walker's request.

Walker declared Wright's head-count "absolutely incredible."

Pay Comparability

By a 122-281 vote, the House rejected an amendment by Bruce A. Morrison, D-Conn., that would have required an increase in civil service pay to match any increase in military pay during fiscal 1986. *(Vote 187, p. 60-H)*

The House and Senate versions of the defense bill both authorized 3 percent military pay hikes, taking effect at different times, and assumed a freeze in federal civilian pay.

Waste, Fraud and Abuse Issues

By a vote of 411-4, the House on June 25 adopted an amendment by Bill Nichols, D-Ala., which barred government reimbursement of contractors' costs for entertainment, lobbying, advertising, club memberships and promotional souvenirs. *(Vote 167, p. 56-H)*

The amendment would not affect contractors' rights to claim such costs as business expenses for the purpose of income tax deductions.

Nichols' amendment also:

• Limited costs charged to the government for the use of a corporate airplane. Contractors could be reimbursed for only the commercial coach fare for the same trip.

• Required that Pentagon contract supervisors not be assigned to the same defense plant for more than five years.

• Empowered the secretary of defense to subpoena contractors' records to verify cost claims.

• Required that a contractor formally certify that all indirect costs claimed were allowable under law and Pentagon purchasing regulations.

In so-called "cost-plus" contracts, a manufacturer was reimbursed for the cost of producing a weapon and also paid a fee. In addition to direct costs — the labor and materials used to build the item — reimbursement also could be claimed for indirect costs. These were the contract's "share" of the overhead cost of running the firm.

Before adopting Nichols' amendment, the House adopted by voice vote the following amendments to it:

• By Dennis M. Hertel, D-Mich., providing criminal penalties of up to a year in jail and a fine of $250,000 for individuals and up to $500,000 for corporations that submitted claims for prohibited expenses. Nichols' original amendment provided civil penalties for repeat offenders of up to twice the cost of the claim or $10,000 — whichever was higher.

• By John Bryant, D-Texas, extending the ban on disallowed costs to subcontractors of prime defense contractors and adding to the list of prohibited costs claims for legal expenses or fines incurred as a result of fraud.

• By Gerry Sikorski, D-Minn., requiring that contractors certify that all their cost claims were allowable at the time they first were submitted, rather than at a "final" stage, after preliminary negotiations.

Also adopted by voice vote was a "pay-as-you-go" amendment by Ron Wyden, D-Ore. This required that so-called progress payments to contractors be made only as certain stages of production actually were completed. Under existing law, the payments were made at the time the various stages were scheduled for completion.

The House rejected 176-240 an amendment by Hertel that would have allowed the Pentagon's inspector general to stop payments to firms that Pentagon auditors charged with waste, fraud, abuse or excessive charges to the government. *(Vote 171, p. 56-H)*

The amendment also would have allowed the inspector general to debar firms from receiving new Pentagon contracts.

The secretary of defense could overrule such actions, but would have to justify his decision to Congress.

In addition to the Armed Services Committee leadership, which largely opposed the amendment, the battle engaged leaders of two other powerful House committees. The Energy and Commerce Committee, chaired by John D. Dingell, D-Mich., supported Hertel. Meanwhile, Jack Brooks, D-Texas, chairman of the Government Operations Committee, and Frank Horton, N.Y., the panel's senior Republican, opposed the amendment.

The House also adopted by voice vote an amendment by Byron L. Dorgan, D-N.D., that barred from supervising any defense contract a contractor employee who was convicted of fraud or other contract-related felony. The ban would last at least five years. Contractor officials indicted for fraud or contract felonies would be suspended from supervision of defense projects.

Such a bar or suspension would not cover others in the same firm.

The amendment would authorize the Pentagon's inspector general to appoint an officer to oversee existing contracts by firms that the secretary of defense barred from receiving new contracts.

Increased Competition

The House adopted 342-52 an amendment by Mel Levine, D-Calif., and Denny Smith, R-Ore., designed to encourage the Pentagon to use more than one producer in contracting for equipment. The goal was to reduce prices through competitive pressure. *(Vote 172, p. 56-H)*

The amendment would require the secretary of defense to plan for the use of at least two competing contractors in the development and production of any major weapon bought in the future.

It exempted weapons which by the end of fiscal 1986 were already in production or in the stage of "advanced development," the point at which prototypes were built.

The defense secretary could waive the two-source requirement for up to half of its total new procurement and development contracts.

Levine and Smith had negotiated the version of the amendment adopted with Aspin who told the House that it had "the right kind of tilt toward dual-sourcing, with enough loopholes to provide exceptions."

The House also adopted a modified version of a Courter amendment designed to force an annual increase in the proportion of procurement contracts awarded competitively. Originally, the amendment would have required competition in 40 percent of the contracts awarded in fiscal 1986 with that floor rising by 5 percent in each succeeding year until 1992, when 70 percent would be needed.

But by voice vote, the House adopted a Nichols amendment to the Courter measure that made the 40 percent competitive contracts (and the subsequent annual boosts) goals rather than absolute requirements.

The Pentagon would have to report to Congress on shortfalls from those targets. The amended Courter amendment was adopted 416-0. *(Vote 168, p. 56-H)*

'Revolving Door' Amendments

An amendment was adopted June 25 prohibiting any former Pentagon procurement official, for two years after leaving the Defense Department, from accepting compensation from a firm over whose work the official exercised "significant" responsibility while at the Pentagon. The measure would cover payment as a consultant as well as employment by the firm.

Sponsored by Charles E. Bennett, D-Fla., and Barbara Boxer, D-Calif., the amendment was adopted 397-19 after the House rejected a substitute by John M. Spratt Jr., D-S.C. *(Vote 170, p. 56-H; details, p. 164)*

Because of procedural jockeying, the Spratt language was voted on in a slightly modified form offered by Beverly B. Byron, D-Md. The Spratt-Byron language, rejected 140-272, would have imposed the two-year ban only on officials holding positions specifically designated by the secretary of defense. *(Vote 169, p. 56-H)*

Spratt's measure also would have let the defense secretary, with the concurrence of the Office of Government Ethics, waive the ban in cases in which it would hamper his ability to hire or keep qualified people.

The Spratt amendment also incorporated a provision of the Senate-passed defense authorization bill requiring that Pentagon procurement officials recuse themselves from overseeing contracts with any firms with which the officials had begun to discuss employment prospects.

Contractors' Cost Records

By a vote of 384-31, the House on June 26 adopted a Boxer amendment requiring the Pentagon to keep records of contractors' costs in carrying out defense contracts. It would require separate listing of costs for material, labor and overhead and of profits. *(Vote 177, p. 58-H)*

The House first rejected 189-232 a Courter amendment that would instead have called for a study by the General Accounting Office of the impact on the defense industry of requiring such record-keeping. *(Vote 175, p. 58-H)*

It then adopted 276-147 an amendment by Hank Brown, R-Colo., exempting firms with only relatively small amounts of defense contracts. *(Vote 176, p. 58-H)*

Fighting Spies

By a vote of 333-71, the House adopted an amendment by Dickinson and C. W. Bill Young, D-Fla., requiring the Pentagon to use random polygraph examinations to screen some four million Defense and contractor employees with access to classified information. *(Vote 182, p. 60-H)*

Screening tests would be restricted to questions about technical matters involving unauthorized contacts with foreign agents and unauthorized release of classified data.

Once the program got under way, Young said, it would cost about $2.5 million annually.

Before approving the amendment, the House first rejected 121-281 a substitute by Brooks that would merely have authorized the continuation of a pilot program authorized in fiscal 1985 of 3,500 such screening exams. *(Vote 181, p. 60-H)*

Brooks denounced the polygraph — popularly referred to as the "lie detector" — as "a false bellwether" and warned against a "hysteria to do something" in the wake of the Walker spy case revelations.

"There is no scientific basis for relying on the polygraph as a valid indicator of veracity," he declared, citing several studies revealing polygraph success rates well below 100 percent.

U.S. intelligence agencies had reported that there was a Soviet spy school that trained agents in spoofing the lie detector, Brooks said. "The good criminals will survive and the [Soviet] moles will go deeper."

But Dickinson and Young insisted that Brooks was setting too high a standard of perfection: "If you're only 10 percent effective" in catching spies, Dickinson said, "it's worth it."

Dick Cheney, R-Wyo., quoted several senior U.S. intelligence officials who favored the use of random polygraph examinations, if only as a deterrent to espionage.

Drug Enforcement

An amendment allowing military forces to arrest suspected drug smugglers other than on U.S. soil was approved 364-51. *(Vote 180, p. 58-H)*

The amendment by Bennett — whose son died as the result of a drug overdose — would authorize the use of military forces in a drug enforcement operation, under the control of federal drug enforcement officials, if:

- The attorney general found that the operation might not succeed without the military participation; and
- The secretary of defense found that military readiness would not suffer as a result.

In general, the so-called "posse comitatus" act, dating from the post-Civil War period, barred the use of military forces for law enforcement. In 1981, that was amended to let the military share information and provide equipment and training to civilian drug enforcement agencies.

As a practical matter, the Bennett amendment likely would apply chiefly to Navy ships, which could participate directly in drug enforcement operations only when carrying teams of Coast Guard personnel to perform the actual arrests.

Before adopting Bennett's proposal, the House first rejected a substitute by Glenn English, D-Okla., that would have required the Pentagon to study the relative effectiveness of allowing military personnel to participate in arrests compared with increasing the number of Coast Guard and civilian law enforcement teams assigned to Navy ships. The English amendment was rejected 81-328. *(Vote 179, p. 58-H)*

The Bennett amendment drew impassioned support from members as politically disparate as Harlem Democrat Charles B. Rangel and conservative Florida Republican E. Clay Shaw Jr.

Another Bennett supporter was Stewart B. McKinney, R-Conn., whose daughter, a former cocaine user, had crusaded across Connecticut against drug abuse.

Dan Daniel, D-Va., and other opponents warned that Bennett's proposal would result in ships' crews being tied up ashore for months while drug cases crawled through the courts.

By voice vote, the House rejected an amendment to Bennett's language by Tommy F. Robinson, D-Ark., that would have directed the attorney general to establish training standards for military personnel who would be involved in such anti-drug operations.

Other Amendments

The House approved by voice vote several non-controversial amendments.

One by Bennett increased the procurement authorization by $1 billion, most of it earmarked for the Army, to beef up conventional military forces.

Another, by Larry J. Hopkins, R-Ky., required the Pentagon to destroy existing chemical weapons stockpiles as the new "binary" chemical weapons authorized by the bill enter the U.S. inventory.

To save time, Aspin offered 20 other non-controversial amendments en bloc, constituting what one member called "the most popular amendment in the history of Congress." The macro-amendment, approved by voice vote, incorporated among others, amendments:

- By Patricia Schroeder, D-Colo., providing certain benefits to military personnel and their families who were victims of terrorism.
- By Joseph P. Addabbo, D-N.Y., authorizing coverage of home health care under certain circumstances by the Pentagon's health insurance program for military dependents (called CHAMPUS).
- By Wyden, ordering a report on alternative methods of budgeting for inflation.
- By Bill McCollum, R-Fla., authorizing transportation of non-lethal aid to Afghan rebels and refugees.
- By John E. Grotberg, R-Ill., expressing the sense of Congress that U.S. military bands should use domestically manufactured equipment.

Other amendments approved by voice vote were:

- By Mel Levine, D-Calif., requiring the Army to submit to the Senate and House Armed Services committees the results of tests scheduled for the summer of 1985 in which Soviet anti-tank rockets would be fired at one of the Army's new Bradley armored troop carriers loaded with fuel and ammunition.

Critics had speculated that troops riding in a Bradley would be more vulnerable than those in the earlier, and much cheaper, M-113 troop carrier.

Under strong pressure, the Army agreed early in 1985 to test anti-tank weapons against a loaded Bradley.

- By Denny Smith, R-Ore., requiring "rigorous and realistic" field testing of any types of combat vehicles before they were bought by the Army.

This would have to include the kind of "live fire" tests against potential enemy weapons that the Levine amendment specified for the Bradley.

- By Smith, earmarking $11 million already in the bill to buy portable anti-tank cannons that could be strapped onto Marine Corps Reserve planes.
- By Stratton, barring payments to Hughes Helicopter Industries for production of the Army's Apache anti-tank helicopter, until the company modified its accounting system.

According to Stratton, Armed Services Committee investigators had found Hughes' cost records incomplete.

- By Mike Synar, D-Okla., requiring the Pentagon to report to Congress, not later than Feb. 1, 1986, on the cost of the program to develop and produce a new bomber, with so-called "stealth" features: that is, designed to evade enemy detection.

Conference/Final Action

Senate-House conferees agreed July 25 on S 1160 after two weeks of negotiations in which procurement reform and nerve gas loomed as the most contentious issues.

The Senate approved the report 94-5 on July 30. *(Vote 167, p. 33-S)*

But in the House, the conference report (H Rept 99-235) encountered a buzz saw of opposition, much of it from liberal Democrats. Critics objected to several facets of the compromise:

- The bill authorized $223 billion, covering most Pentagon programs and the Energy Department's nuclear weapons development and production program. But that amount fit into an overall defense budget of $302 billion, the budget ceiling initially voted by the Senate and agreed to, with reluctance, by the House.

The prevailing sentiment in the House was for a defense total of $292.6 billion, the amount appropriated for fiscal 1985.

- Proponents of House-passed procurement reforms complained that those provisions had been unacceptably watered down in the conference.
- Conditions that were attached to the production of the new types of lethal chemical arms — "binary munitions" — also were eased in the conference.

After prolonged negotiations between the disaffected Democrats and House Democratic leaders, agreement was reached on resolving the disputes.

The Pentagon procurement changes would be incorporated into the companion defense appropriations bill (HR 3629) and the appropriations measure would be held to a level producing an overall defense budget of $292 billion.

Through late September and October, final House action on the conference report awaited agreement on one of the disputed procurement provisions, requiring the Pentagon to keep records of contractor efficiency.

That obstacle was breached Oct. 29 when the House adopted by a vote of 397-18, a bill (HR 3606) revising the conference report's version of the provision. *(Vote 337, p. 106-H)*

It then went on to clear the conference report on S 1160 by voice vote.

The Senate did not act on HR 3606 in 1985. ▮

Arms Controllers Win a Ban on ASAT Tests

Arms control advocates in 1985 won a partial but significant victory: They blocked for a year additional testing of the anti-satellite (ASAT) missile against a target in space.

Earlier in the year, conferees on the defense authorization bill (S 1160 — PL 99-145) had agreed to allow three tests through the end of fiscal 1986. The Air Force conducted the first test in September, shortly after that bill was signed into law. *(Authorization bill, p. 138)*

But conferees on the defense appropriations measure — a part of the omnibus continuing appropriations resolution (H J Res 465 — PL 99-190) passed in the closing days of the session — agreed to a moratorium on further tests. *(Appropriations, pp. 377, 360)*

The testing ban capped a two-year effort by a coalition of arms control lobbyists and members of Congress — the bulk of them liberals — to slow down the ASAT program. Their ultimate goal was a U.S.-Soviet agreement banning the weapon.

The Soviets had their own version of ASAT deployed for more than a decade, but some analysts questioned its value. More recently, Moscow had refrained from testing its ASAT.

Critics argued that the smaller U.S.-built ASAT, designed to be fired from an F-15 fighter plane, would escalate the arms race. They said that once the 19-foot-long missile's heat-seeking guidance device was demonstrated, it would become much more difficult to negotiate a U.S.-Soviet pact limiting ASATs.

"Because of its small size, the U.S. ASAT would be a verification nightmare," said Rep. Joe Moakley, D-Mass. "Every F-15 would be a potential ASAT platform."

The Senate and House had been deadlocked over ASAT testing since the summer of 1984. The House voted several times to bar tests against a target in space — so long as the Soviets continued their moratorium. The Senate repeatedly enacted only insignificant limits on U.S. testing.

In 1984, the two bodies compromised to allow three tests after a five-month moratorium. *(1984 Almanac p. 62)*

After the defense authorization conferees gave the go-ahead for three tests through the end of fiscal 1986, the Air Force conducted the ASAT test Sept. 13. The missile destroyed a scientific satellite that the Air Force said had outlived its usefulness.

But even though the test crossed what the ASAT opponents had said was a critical threshold, they continued to press for a congressionally imposed test moratorium.

Authorization Bill

For fiscal 1986, Reagan requested a total of $263 million for development, procurement and construction of facilities.

The Senate Armed Services Committee, in its report filed April 29 on the defense authorization bill (S Rept 99-41), approved Reagan's request for purchase of three more ASAT missiles.

ASATs were among the weapons under discussion in the wide-ranging arms control talks begun in March in Geneva. The Senate panel warned that negotiations to limit ASATs likely would be difficult. "While these negotiations are under way ... it would be ill-advised and counterproductive to our negotiating efforts for Congress to impose any unilateral limitations," the panel argued. *(Arms control, p. 175)*

When senators considered the bill on the floor May 24, they rejected, 35-51, an amendment to bar ASAT tests. *(Vote 95, p. 21-S)*

Then they adopted, 74-9, an alternative allowing the president to conduct more than three tests in fiscal year 1986 if he certified to Congress that the United States was negotiating seriously with the Soviet Union toward an eventual limit on such weapons. That amendment amounted to a lifting of a provision in existing defense appropriations law barring more than three ASAT tests in 1985. *(Vote 96, p. 21-S)*

The rejected amendment was sponsored by John Kerry, D-Mass. He insisted that many of the tests of the Soviets' existing ASAT missile had failed. Therefore, that weapon posed little threat to most U.S. military satellites, he argued.

Conducting tests of the U.S. version would encourage the Soviets to speed up work on a new anti-satellite system of their own and "would jeopardize the chances for a treaty that prevents either side from threatening the other's satellites," Kerry said.

Opposing Kerry's amendment, John W. Warner, R-Va., said Geneva arms control negotiators Max M. Kampelman and former Sen. John Tower, R-Texas, had told him that congressional action barring the ASAT tests would be "a unilateral concession that would undercut our negotiating position."

Kerry disagreed, saying his amendment "doesn't give up anything, it gains something ... the opportunity to negotiate with the current, perceived threat level."

The amendment accepted by the Senate, offered by Warner, restated language in the fiscal 1985 defense authorization law requiring the president to submit a certification to Congress before conducting any ASAT tests. It applied the same requirement to any tests beyond the three tests that Congress allowed in the companion defense appropriations law.

House Action

Like its Senate counterpart, the House Armed Services Committee included $98 million for ASAT production in its version of the defense bill (HR 1872 — H Rept 99-81), reported May 10.

But the full House, voting June 26, handed Reagan a defeat on the issue for the second year in a row.

Members adopted an amendment offered by George E. Brown Jr., D-Calif., and Lawrence Coughlin, R-Pa., that barred ASAT tests against targets in space, so long as Moscow continued its moratorium.

The ban was to cover not only fiscal 1986 but also the three tests permitted in fiscal 1985.

The Brown amendment was adopted June 26 by a vote of 229-193. *(Vote 178, p. 58-H)*

Brown and his allies restated the warning that once the U.S. missile's guidance system had been successfully tested in a shot against a target, it would be impossible to negotiate a mutual ban on deployment.

A flat ASAT ban should be the U.S. goal, the critics

argued, because the Soviet ASAT was militarily insignificant. U.S. missile-detecting satellites orbited at more than 20,000 miles, too high for the Russian weapon to reach.

"We have no need for an ASAT," insisted Les AuCoin, D-Ore. "Our need is to keep the Russians from getting one which works for them." Eventually they would, AuCoin warned, if ASAT development were not stopped in its tracks.

ASAT backers said that the existing Soviet weapon could reach U.S. reconnaissance satellites at heights of several hundred miles. "The Soviets have a way of taking away our eyes and ears," warned Ken Kramer, R-Colo.

At a minimum, according to the ASAT supporters, development of a similar U.S. weapon was needed to deter use of the existing Soviet weapon. "They will be less inclined to deploy and to utilize an ASAT weapon if we could respond in kind," said Jim Courter, R-N.J.

But Brown's opponents also maintained that development of the U.S. weapon was needed to give Moscow an incentive to negotiate an ASAT ban.

"If you give up all your marbles before you get to the marble game, there isn't much hope of winning," Kramer reasoned.

Before adopting the Brown amendment, the House adopted by voice vote an amendment by Steny H. Hoyer, D-Md., adding to the bill $20 million to speed efforts to protect U.S. satellites against attack.

Conference Agreement

Conferees on the defense bill agreed July 19 to allow three ASAT tests against a target in space. Leading ASAT opponents had hoped the conferees would limit the tests to two, and only in the second half of the fiscal year.

The conferees approved only $33 million for ASAT procurement, but the entire $150 million requested for ASAT development.

The conferees' decision angered critics of the missile in part because they believed the Air Force was allowed to do as much as possible, in light of technical difficulties with the missile.

"They couldn't do more than three tests," declared Charles Monfort of the Union of Concerned Scientists. "It's no restriction at all."

Several lobbyists who focused on ASAT limits said that the House position on the missile had suffered because the arms control lobbies collectively had not treated it as a priority.

In part, this judgment reflected the longstanding complaint of the space-oriented lobby groups that their priorities had for too long been taking a back seat to the anti-MX campaign.

But lobbyists for some of the space-oriented groups also complained specifically that during a July 12 meeting with Les Aspin, D-Wis., chairman of the House Armed Services Committee, representatives of six arms control lobbies had refused to tell him their conference priorities.

"The longer we maintain the strongest position, the better we do," argued Laurie Duker of SANE, supporting the position taken in the meeting. "You don't want to become irrelevant to the process of horse-trading in the conference, but you don't want to let them make those tradeoffs easily."

At the meeting, Aspin warned the lobbyists that the tempo of wheeling and dealing would be too rapid for them to wait for the Senate to show its hand before declaring their position on a compromise.

Court Challenge, ASAT Test

At summer's end, the Pentagon was planning the ASAT's first test against a target in space. But a congressional notification requirement forced a postponement.

Among the restrictions in the fiscal 1985 defense authorization and appropriations bills (PL 98-525, PL 98-473) was a provision barring ASAT tests until 15 days after the president had certified that the test was needed for national security and would not impair chances for an arms control agreement with the Soviets. Reagan made that certification Aug. 20.

The first test was scheduled for Sept. 4. At the last minute, however, Pentagon officials decided the date fell within the 15-day waiting period. So the test was rescheduled for Sept. 13, on a target different from the one originally planned.

Meanwhile, the Soviet Union announced Sept. 4 that it would resume its own anti-satellite weapon tests, in abeyance since 1983, if the United States proceeded with the ASAT test.

The following week, four House members and the Union of Concerned Scientists filed suit in federal district court, seeking a temporary restraining order to block the test. Following oral arguments Sept. 12, the suit was dismissed on grounds that it turned on political issues that should not be resolved in courts.

That same day, ASAT opponents backed down from an effort to add a rider to the fiscal 1986 continuing appropriations resolution that would have barred an ASAT target test so long as the Soviets did likewise.

A clear majority of the House Appropriations Committee, marking up the measure, had voted for an ASAT test moratorium in June. But Chairman Jamie L. Whitten, D-Miss., wanted an uncluttered temporary funding measure. Other senior panel members — many of whom had previously voted to stop ASAT testing — concurred on procedural grounds, so ASAT opponents decided not to risk a vote.

Later on Sept. 12, Sen. John Kerry, D-Mass., tried — over the objections of some leading anti-ASAT lobbyists — to add an ASAT moratorium amendment to an immigration bill then before the Senate. It was tabled 62-34. *(Vote 177, p. 35-S)*

The Sept. 13 test, in which an ASAT's infrared homing device guided the missile into a collision with the target satellite, was pronounced a success by the Pentagon.

Appropriations

The House included the ASAT target test ban in its version of the defense appropriations bill (HR 3629 — H Rept 99-332), passed Oct. 30. The Senate Appropriations Committee's version of the bill (S Rept 99-176), reported Nov. 6, deleted the ban, setting the stage for a repeat of the 1984 standoff over ASAT testing.

But in 1985, timing offered a tactical boost to arms control advocates as they focused on the ASAT missile.

A busy floor schedule delayed Senate consideration of the defense spending bill until after Reagan's Nov. 19-21 summit with Soviet leader Mikhail S. Gorbachev. This mooted one of the administration's arguments for protecting the ASAT program: bolstering the president's summit bargaining position.

And the delay ultimately meant that, with Congress rushing to adjourn, the defense bill would not be enacted separately; instead, it was shoehorned into an omnibus continuing appropriations resolution (H J Res 465 — PL 99-190).

Had the defense bill been passed by the Senate and become the subject of a separate conference committee with the House, the House conferees by tradition would have consisted of the members of the Appropriations Subcommittee on Defense, a predominantly pro-Pentagon group unenthusiastic about certain House-passed provisions that challenged administration policy.

But with the defense appropriations measure folded into a continuing resolution, the House conferees were the chairmen and senior Republican members of all the House Appropriations subcommittees. They were a much more liberal group of Democrats, more likely to drive a harder bargain with their Senate counterparts. And the conference also included a number of junior members of the Appropriations panel, led by Norman D. Dicks, D-Wash., who insisted on taking part.

Making their tradeoffs in mid-December, House conferees on the spending measure yielded or compromised on such sticky defense issues as procurement reform, antimissile defenses, nerve gas and budget.

But they managed to win Senate agreement to ban ASAT tests for a year. ∎

Hill Enacts Pentagon Procurement 'Reforms'

Driven by widespread public unhappiness over reports of overpricing and other abuses in Pentagon purchasing, Congress in 1985 enacted changes in the way the Pentagon bought goods and services.

A central theme was increased reliance on competition to keep weapons prices down and quality up.

The changes were contained in the fiscal 1986 defense authorization bill (S 1160 — PL 99-145). In general, the House-passed provisions were more stringent than the corresponding Senate provisions and the authorization conference report reflected compromises. *(Authorization bill, p. 138)*

Among the new legal requirements:

- Any presidential appointee in the Pentagon who acted as the government's principal negotiator in any dealing with a contractor would be barred for two years after leaving the government from going to work for that firm.
- Contractors were barred from billing the Pentagon for certain costs including entertainment and lobbying and legal fees resulting from charges of contract fraud.
- The Pentagon would have to plan for the use of more than one firm to develop and produce major weapons systems.

The conferees' compromises on the procurement "reforms" were one of the issues that contributed to a revolt by House members that stalled final passage of the authorization bill for three months. After prolonged negotiations, members agreed in principle to revisit the procurement change provisions in the companion defense appropriations bill, and the authorization bill was cleared on Oct. 29.

Despite a House effort to attach new restrictions, the defense portion of the fiscal 1986 continuing appropriations resolution (H J Res 465 — PL 99-190) did not contain the broader changes procurement reform proponents had wanted. *(Continuing resolution, pp. 360, 377)*

Background

While popular domestic programs faced budget cuts in 1985, congressional and public opinion was aroused by reports that contractors had charged the Pentagon $400 for hammers and $600 for toilet seat covers. Several instances of indirect cost claims also had been highly publicized; among them was a claim for the kennel cost for boarding the dog of a General Dynamics Corp. executive. *(Box, p. 166)*

Some demands for procurement "reform" came from Capitol Hill liberals who opposed the pace of Reagan's defense buildup. But some of the defense establishment's senior congressional backers also had embraced the call for changes, partly in hopes of restoring the Pentagon's political credibility.

Conservative Democrat Bill Nichols, D-Ala., chairman of the House Armed Services Subcommittee on Investigations, was an example. "Every time I go home, people grab me by the shoulder and say, 'Hey, I'm for defense, but . . . .' " Nichols told reporters.

Nichols and Seapower Subcommittee Chairman Charles E. Bennett, D-Fla., had ordered investigators to probe the cost claims of seven major defense firms. Nichols acknowledged that he hoped to find that General Dynamics was unusual in the large number of questionable cost claims it had submitted.

In May, an outraged Nichols announced that the investigators had found questionable cost claims by all of the firms.

Early Proposals

Nichols and Bennett announced on May 8 two procurement reform bills. The same day, a more far-reaching package was announced by a bipartisan group including Sens. David Pryor, D-Ark., and Charles E. Grassley, R-Iowa; and Reps. Mel Levine, D-Calif.; Denny Smith, R-Ore.; and Barbara Boxer, D-Calif.

The Pryor bill was intended to be offered in the Senate as an amendment to the defense authorization bill, as a substitute for procurement reforms included in the bill by the Senate Armed Services Committee. These were largely the fruit of a newly created subcommittee on procurement policy, chaired by Dan Quayle, R-Ind.

Dual Sourcing. The Senate Armed Services bill (S 1029 — S Rept 99-41), reported April 29, required the secretary of defense to prepare for any major weapon a procurement plan that would establish two production sources for the weapon.

The requirement for two competing contractors could be waived if it would cost more to set up a second source than would be saved by lower prices, or if it would create "unacceptable delays" in production or if otherwise required for national security.

In its report, the Armed Services panel commented that formal cost analyses would not be necessary in cases in which it was obvious that two contractors should not be used.

Competitive Bidding. The Pryor group took a much more intransigent stand in favor of formally advertised, sealed-bid competition. The lowest bidder was to be awarded the largest share of the production run at issue, but the second-lowest bidder was to be given enough business to be able to continue competing for subsequent contracts.

Pryor wanted to require at least two bidders on every major contract. Under current law governing federal contracting, a contract for which only one firm bid could be technically labeled a "competitive" contract.

The requirement for dual production lines could be waived only on grounds of unacceptable cost or delay — not on unspecified grounds of "national security." But even then, two sealed bids would be needed, unless the Pentagon went through an elaborate process of justifying a sole-source contract.

A Pentagon statement commenting on the Pryor amendment said that competition based strictly on formally advertised sealed bids "is not suitable for buying state-of-the-art or advanced equipment [that is] not easily described with detailed design specifications."

In a letter circulated to all senators on May 16, Sens. William S. Cohen, R-Maine, and Carl Levin, D-Mich., argued that sealed bidding was appropriate only for relatively simple items for which all relevant criteria could be detailed in design specifications.

Later in the month, Pryor yielded to Cohen's and Levin's opposition and agreed to drop this proposal.

Allowable Costs. Both the Senate Armed Services Committee and the Nichols and Bennett package aimed to block contractors from charging certain kinds of overhead expenses — such as entertainment, lobbying and advertising costs and fines — against Pentagon contracts.

Nichols and Bennett introduced a bill (HR 2397) banning contractors from charging certain types of costs and would impose stiff penalties for trying to do so. Ultimately, the House adopted HR 2397 as an amendment to the defense authorization bill.

The Senate bill directed the secretary of defense to ban the costs by regulation.

The situation arose only with so-called "cost-plus" contracts, in which the Pentagon negotiated with a firm to perform some work for the cost of the work plus a fee. Early in May, after Nichols and Bennett had seven major defense firms audited, they concluded that firms routinely loaded up cost claims with dubious charges.

Revolving Door. The Senate Armed Services bill also included a provision barring any high-level Defense Department employee from working on a contract while negotiating for a job with the contractor.

The provision, sponsored by Levin, was aimed at slowing the "revolving door" through which government employees left to work for the contractors they once oversaw. Levin and others said the practice drove up procurement costs, because workers might be lax in enforcing quality control and auditing in order to land high-paying jobs with contractors.

Under Levin's proposal, an employee who was discussing the possibility of a job with a contractor had to recuse himself from contract negotiations with the future employer.

If the employee did not, he could not take a job with that contractor for two years. The bill also would allow the Defense Department to fine violators $10,000.

To enforce the provision, the bill required employees to report contacts with prospective employers to their supervisors and to agency ethics officers. Failure to report would also be grounds for a $10,000 fine.

Bennett and Nichols joined the Pryor group in taking a tougher line on the revolving door.

Bennett's other bill (HR 2356) and Pryor's measure both would have barred Pentagon officials from going to work for firms with which they had substantial contracting dealings for a certain period after the official left the government. Bennett's limit was to run for two years, Pryor's for three years.

Senate Floor Action

Procurement reform prompted lively debate May 20 during the Senate's consideration of S 1160, the fiscal 1986 defense authorization bill, and senators ultimately chose the Armed Services panel's approach.

Committee Chairman Barry Goldwater, R-Ariz., cited one of the more highly publicized examples of exorbitant prices — a $640 toilet seat for a Navy patrol plane — to explain hostility toward Reagan's defense budget. "When you go home and your wife asks, 'What is a $600 toilet seat?' and you cannot explain it to her, you are in bad shape," Goldwater complained.

Congressional unhappiness was exacerbated in the days leading up to the Senate debate by reports that large sums left over from earlier budgets suddenly were being discovered in Pentagon accounts.

Defense Secretary Caspar W. Weinberger had announced May 14 that $4 billion — mostly the result of lower-than-anticipated inflation in earlier years — had been found that could be trimmed from the fiscal 1986 defense request.

This came four days after the Senate adopted a first concurrent budget resolution (S Con Res 32) holding the Pentagon to "zero real growth" in fiscal 1986.

Three days after Weinberger's disclosure, House Armed Services Committee Chairman Les Aspin, D-Wis., claimed that erroneously high inflation estimates in the fiscal 1982-85 defense budgets had given the Pentagon a windfall of $18 billion to $50 billion.

Locking the Door

The main debate over procurement "reform" pitted Pryor and Grassley against the Armed Services panel represented on this issue chiefly by Quayle and Levin. Quayle was chairman and Levin the senior Democrat on the Subcommittee on Defense Acquisition Policy.

Senators faced a choice between two amendments, one by Pryor and one by the committee. Each amendment covered a wide range of weapons procurement policy issues.

One was the "revolving door," through which Pentagon personnel left to take jobs with contractors whose work they had just supervised.

Both sides in the Senate debate agreed that the practice created at least the suspicion that employees, while still in federal service, might have been dealing too gently with their prospective civilian employers.

"Have these employees been watching after the interests of the taxpayers or have they been watching after their own interests?" Levin demanded.

The Armed Services Committee's amendment required an official to recuse himself from handling any contract with a firm with which the official was discussing post-retirement employment. It also required more extensive reporting by retired senior Pentagon officials about their post-retirement employment.

Overpricing, Billing Fraud and Abuses . . .

Congressional demands for reform in the way the Pentagon had been buying weapons and parts were fueled by reports of seemingly outlandish prices for simple items, faulty products and fraudulent billing of the Pentagon. Some of the more widely publicized accounts involved:

Overpriced Items

$7,622 Coffeepot. The Air Force in March 1984 paid Lockheed Corp. $7,622 for a coffee machine to be used aboard its C-5A cargo planes, according to September 1984 congressional testimony by two Air Force maintenance technicians. The Air Force did an analysis of the price for the coffee machine and concluded that the price was reasonable.

$748 Pliers. Boeing Military Airplane Co. in 1984 charged the Air Force $748 for a pair of duckbill pliers. After the price was publicized, Boeing cut the tab to $90.

$640 Toilet Seat. The Navy paid Lockheed-California Co. $640 apiece for 54 toilet seats for P-3 Orion anti-submarine planes. After a price review, Lockheed reduced the bill to $554.78 per toilet seat and agreed to refund the difference to the Navy. When the publicity continued, Lockheed slashed the price to $100 and repaid the Defense Department.

$44 Light Bulb. According to June 1983 testimony by John W. Melchner, assistant Pentagon inspector general, the Navy paid Sperry Corp. $44 for a light bulb.

Faulty Microchips

National Semiconductor Corp. on March 6, 1984, pleaded guilty in federal court in San Francisco to charges that it failed to test adequately computer microchips it had sold the Pentagon for use in jet fighters, battleships, jeeps and walkie-talkies. The company agreed to pay $1.75 million in fines and fees, and the government agreed not to press further charges.

The Defense Logistics Agency proposed on May 29, 1984, that the company be barred as a military supplier. National Semiconductor was given 30 days to reply. The company filed suit against the government, but on June 29, 1984, a federal judge in San Jose, Calif., upheld the contracting ban, which could last up to three years. Under a Pentagon regulation, National Semiconductor still could do some business with the government if it were the only source of a product.

National Semiconductor previously was decertified as a defense supplier for two months in 1982. The company was recertified after testing procedures were changed and the government retested its chips and found them to meet specifications.

Texas Instruments Inc. did not test its semiconductors adequately, according to the Pentagon. In September 1984, the Pentagon ordered its procurement officers not to accept delivery of weapons containing Texas Instruments chips. The Pentagon also ordered all contractors to return unused Texas Instruments chips to the manufacturer for retesting. International Business Machines (IBM), after discovering the testing problems, alerted the Defense Logistics Agency.

Signetics Corp. semiconductors also were tested improperly, according to the Defense Department. The Pentagon in October 1984 suspended deliveries from military contractors who used Signetics Corp. semiconductors. As with Texas Instruments, IBM alerted the Pentagon to the testing problem.

Poor Workmanship

Missile Quality. The Air Force and Navy in 1984 halted deliveries from the Hughes Aircraft Co. because of concern over the workmanship on missiles the company had manufactured.

On July 22, 1984, the Navy informed Hughes that it would not accept delivery of the AIM-54C Phoenix because of poor workmanship on the missiles. The Air Force on Aug. 9 stopped deliveries of the AGM-65D Maverick.

On Aug. 22, 1984, the Air Force announced that it had suspended progress payments on missiles manufactured by Hughes. These were periodic payments to a contractor before the final delivery of a product.

A day later, Hughes halted deliveries of advanced radar systems for the F-14, F-15 and F-18 jets; the Navy had discovered poor workmanship in the radar systems used in the F-14 fighter. According to the Pentagon, the decision to halt delivery was made voluntarily by Hughes.

The Defense Department on Nov. 19 announced that the "corrective action plan" submitted by Hughes had been approved by the Air Force Contract Management Division. Hughes agreed to fix all faulty missiles at its own expense, and to reimburse the government for all costs resulting from the time involved in approving the corrective action plan. But problems persisted, and the Air Force refused delivery of 22 Mavericks.

Hughes continued to receive government contracts, but was also being monitored by the Air Force.

Overhead, Fraudulent Billing

New Rules. After press accounts of fraudulent billings, Defense Secretary Caspar W. Weinberger on March 5, 1985, ordered a Pentagon review of defense contractors' billing procedures. On March 12, he approved new guidelines allowing contractors to bill the

Pryor insisted that this would be circumvented by a contractor clever enough "to do everything but offer the government worker a job" while hinting at the prospect.

His proposal would have banned any Pentagon official (for three years after his retirement) from accepting employment or consulting work with a company over whose contracts the official had exercised "significant" responsibility in the last three years of his Defense Department employment.

The committee had rejected an outright ban, for fear that it would deter experienced defense industry officials from accepting high-level Pentagon appointments.

. . . Prompt Calls for Procurement Reform

Pentagon for only those overhead expenses that were within the limits of federal regulations and were "demonstratively related to or necessary for the performance" of the contract. Contractors would have to sign a certificate swearing that they would not charge for expenses that were not permitted by the Federal Acquisition Regulations.

General Electric Co. Indictment. GE was indicted March 26, 1985, in Philadelphia, for criminal fraud in billing the government. According to the indictment, GE from 1980 to 1983 billed the government for more than $800,000 in fraudulent labor costs on the Air Force's Mark 12A warhead for the Minuteman missile. The warheads were manufactured in GE's Space Systems Division in Philadelphia and King of Prussia, Pa. On May 14, GE pleaded guilty to fraud, and agreed to pay $1.04 million in fines. GE also agreed to reimburse the government the $800,000.

The Pentagon on March 28 barred GE from any new defense contracts unless there was a "compelling reason" to deal with the company. GE also was asked to return voluntarily some $168 million in profits that Air Force Secretary Verne Orr described as "significantly greater than negotiated." By year's end, the money had not been returned.

The second week in April, because of "national security reasons," GE's Space Systems Division was awarded a $4.36 million contract with the Air Force for "the planning and support of launch operations" for two defense communications satellites.

By the end of April, the Defense Department lifted its general ban on GE after the company agreed to some organizational changes the Air Force demanded. The ban still applied to the Space Systems Division, however, unless there were "compelling reasons," as in the award of the communications satellite contract for "national security reasons."

In July, the Air Force resumed awarding contracts with the Space Systems division, but it was not until September that the part of the division making missile reentry systems was taken off the restricted list.

Repayments by General Dynamics Corp. On March 5, 1985, the same day he ordered an investigation into all defense contractors' billing procedures, Weinberger ordered a freeze for at least 30 days on all overhead payments to General Dynamics Corp. The freeze was to last until the company changed accounting and management practices to prevent charges to the government for expenses unrelated to the production of weapons. In July the monthly overhead payments were resumed.

On March 25, General Dynamics announced that it would withdraw $23 million in overhead charges for the years 1979-82. The Defense Contract Audit Agency had challenged $63.6 million of $170 million the company had charged for overhead expenses for those years.

Pentagon auditors concluded on April 4 that General Dynamics had charged the government $244 million more than it should have over the past 12 years. On April 30, the Defense Department announced that it had recovered the entire $244 million.

Secretary of the Navy John F. Lehman announced on May 21 that two of General Dynamics' divisions would be suspended from receiving new contracts with the Pentagon. The two were the Electric Boat division in Groton, Conn., and the Pomona, Calif., division. Lehman also canceled two contracts worth $22.5 million and opened them up for competitive bidding. The ban on these two divisions was lifted in August.

Lehman also fined the company $676,283 for its gifts over the years to Adm. Hyman G. Rickover. Rickover, currently retired, directed the Navy's nuclear submarine program.

Lehman rejected the recommendation of Pentagon Inspector General Joseph H. Sherick that three top General Dynamics officers be banned from doing business with the Pentagon. Nonetheless, the company's chairman and chief executive officer, David S. Lewis, announced his retirement May 22.

On Dec. 2, General Dynamics and four of its officials, including James M. Beggs, head of the National Aeronautics and Space Administration, were indicted on fraud conspiracy charges by a federal grand jury in Los Angeles.

The grand jury's seven-count indictment charged Beggs and the others with improperly charging the Pentagon for cost overruns associated with the Sgt. York DIVAD anti-aircraft gun. Beggs denied any wrongdoing. *(DIVAD, p. 154)*

The Navy announced on Dec. 3 that the company would be suspended from receiving any new government contracts for at least 30 days.

Pratt & Whitney Refund Request. In late March 1985, Air Force Secretary Orr announced that Pratt & Whitney had been asked to refund $38 million in defense contract billings for what the government had found to be improper overhead expenses. The money had not been refunded by year's end.

House Committee Probe. The House Armed Services Committee in the spring of 1985 investigated overhead charges by seven major defense contractors. Panel members led by Charles E. Bennett, D-Fla., and Bill Nichols, D-Ala., questioned $109.7 million of the $3.66 billion that was submitted for payment.

The seven companies investigated were General Dynamics, Sperry Corp., Newport News Shipbuilding, Bell Helicopter, McDonnell Douglas, Rockwell International and Boeing.

Promoting Competition

The committee's amendment and Pryor's also differed in their approach to discouraging "sole-source" contracts for major weapons — contracts bid for by only one firm.

Both groups favored more reliance on competitive bids to award Pentagon contracts.

The committee measure required the Pentagon to draw up a purchasing plan for each major weapon that would keep two manufacturers competing for each year's production contract. The requirement for two sources could be waived on grounds of cost, delay or "national security."

Pryor ridiculed the national security waiver as "a loophole large enough to drive a Mack truck through." Though he had watered down the competition provisions of an earlier version of the amendment, Pryor retained several provisions intended to make recourse to sole-source contracting onerous: "cumbersome, time-consuming procedures," in the words of Gary Hart, D-Colo., who supported Pryor's measure. "We should make it difficult, obvious and somewhat embarrassing," Hart added.

One of these provisions required explicit legislative authorization of any major sole-source contract: "It is time for Congress to deal itself back into this game," Pryor said.

But that position drew fire from former Secretary of the Navy John H. Chafee, R-R.I. "What is Congress going to do?" Chafee demanded. "Everyone who is from a state that does not get the sole-source [contract] is going to demand that they get a piece of the action. That is the last you will see of our sole sourcing," Chaffee concluded. A sole-source contract might be necessary, he argued, in the case of very expensive items built in small numbers.

Tougher Than Thou

The powerful political appeal of being opposed to $600 toilet seats was evident in the rhetorical dueling over whether Pryor's or the committee's procurement amendment was the "tougher."

Pryor described his as "hardball" and the committee's as "softball." He dismissed the committee package as "weak provisions, filled with loopholes, going into effect years from now."

The proof of Pryor's charge, according to Hart, was that the Pentagon had said it could live with the committee approach. "Anything the Pentagon can live with will not bring real reform," Hart declared.

Pryor announced at the outset of debate on the issue that his amendment was opposed by the Pentagon and the defense industry. "Were it otherwise, I might worry that our proposal was not strong enough," he added.

The only reason the committee offered its own approach as a floor amendment was so that senators could cast a "pro-reform" vote after voting against Pryor's measure. The committee procurement provisions had been incorporated in the version of the defense bill reported initially. They were removed when the bill was redrafted to meet a congressionally mandated lower defense budget ceiling.

During the debate, Quayle played down the differences between the two amendments as "technicalities." But he charged that opponents were using "false statements" to characterize the committee's position.

For his part, Levin insisted that both amendments played "hardball," though of different styles. On the revolving door problem, Levin insisted, the committee took the tougher position since it could bar an official from joining a contractor for 10 years, compared with a three-year bar in Pryor's amendment.

The 10-year ban occurred only if an official were found guilty of violating the committee amendment's requirement to recuse himself from dealing officially with a firm with which he was discussing prospective employment.

Ultimately, the committee's approach prevailed easily and Pryor's amendment was rejected, 22-67.

Grassley was the only Republican to vote for the Pryor amendment, though Mark O. Hatfield, Ore., who did not vote, had announced support. Democrats supported Pryor narrowly (21-19) with liberals typically critical of the Pentagon, accounting for most of the "yea" votes. *(Vote 83, p. 19-S)*

With Pryor's effort disposed of, the Senate approved the Armed Services amendment 89-0. *(Vote 84, p. 19-S)*

The Senate also agreed by voice vote to several other amendments aimed at tightening up the Defense Department's procurement system, including amendments:

- By Jeff Bingaman, D-N.M., to require the Pentagon to provide additional information in its quarterly reports to Congress on the cost of major weapons programs.
- By William V. Roth Jr., R-Del., to establish a blue-ribbon panel, composed of members of the Senate and House and presidential appointees, to review studies of the Pentagon's purchasing system and recommend specific changes.
- By Alan J. Dixon, D-Ill., requiring the Pentagon to report to Congress quarterly on appropriated funds that the department deemed excess because of revised estimates of inflation, currency exchange rates or other economic facts of life. Dixon said his amendment, which Goldwater co-sponsored, was intended "to put an end to midnight surprises" such as Weinberger's last-minute announcement of $4 billion in surplus funds from prior years.

House Floor Action

The House, acting on a companion defense authorization bill (HR 1872 — H Rept 99-81) June 25-26, adopted a series of procurement-reform amendments.

The first was Nichols' proposal to ban certain kinds of Pentagon cost claims, approved 411-4. *(Vote 167, p. 56-H)*

Nichols' amendment was the text of HR 2397, the bill he and Bennett had introduced in May; it barred government reimbursement of contractors' costs for entertainment, lobbying, advertising, club memberships and promotional souvenirs, such as the model planes bedecking some congressional offices.

The amendment did not affect contractors' rights to claim such costs as business expenses for the purpose of income tax deductions.

Nichols' amendment also:

- Limited costs that could be charged to the government for the use of a corporate airplane. Contractors could be reimbursed for only the commercial coach fare for the same trip.
- Required that Pentagon contract supervisors not be assigned to the same defense plant for more than five years.
- Empowered the secretary of defense to subpoena contractors' records to verify cost claims.
- Required that a contractor formally certify that all indirect costs claimed were allowable under law and Pentagon purchasing regulations.

In "cost-plus" contracts, a manufacturer was reimbursed for the cost of producing a weapon and also paid a fee. In addition to direct costs — the labor and materials used to build the item — reimbursement also could be claimed for indirect costs. These were the contract's "share" of the overhead cost of running the firm.

Thomas N. Kindness, R-Ohio, said the amendment merely codified in law the changes Weinberger already had made by regulation, and he argued against making the system too rigid: "If there's one jot or title that's wrong in here — and there is — how are you going to change it?" he demanded. "You're going to regret not having the flexibility that currently is in the law."

Before adopting Nichols' amendment, the House

adopted by voice votes the following amendments to it:

- By Dennis M. Hertel, D-Mich., providing criminal penalties of up to a year in jail and a fine of $250,000 for individuals and up to $500,000 for corporations that submitted claims for prohibited expenses. Nichols' original amendment provided civil penalties for repeat offenders of up to twice the cost of the claim or $10,000 — whichever was higher.
- By John Bryant, D-Texas, extending the ban on disallowed costs to subcontractors of prime defense contractors and adding to the list of prohibited costs claims for legal expenses or fines incurred as a result of fraud.
- By Gerry Sikorski, D-Minn., requiring that contractors certify that all their cost claims were allowable at the time they first were submitted, rather than at a "final" stage, after preliminary negotiations.

Also adopted by voice vote was a "pay-as-you-go" amendment by Ron Wyden, D-Ore. This required that so-called progress payments to contractors be made only as certain stages of production were completed. Under existing rules, the payments were made at the time the various stages were scheduled for completion, even if the actual progress of construction was behind schedule.

Boosting the Penalties

The House rejected 176-240 an amendment by Hertel that would have allowed the Pentagon's inspector general to stop payments to firms that Pentagon auditors charged with waste, fraud, abuse or excessive charges to the government. *(Vote 171, p. 56-H)*

The amendment also would have allowed the inspector general to debar firms from receiving new Pentagon contracts.

The secretary of defense would have been able to overrule such actions, but would have had to justify his decision to Congress.

In addition to the Armed Services Committee leadership, which largely opposed the amendment, the battle engaged leaders of two other powerful House committees:

- The Energy and Commerce Committee, chaired by John D. Dingell, D-Mich., supported Hertel. Dingell's panel had held hearings in which Pentagon Inspector General Joseph Sherick had complained that his Pentagon chiefs and the Justice Department had not taken aggressive action on the basis of auditors' findings.

"The amendment only becomes operative after the audit system has failed," Dingell said. "It simply lets [the inspector general] stop rascality, indifference, slothfulness, laziness and disregard of public responsibility" by the Pentagon.

- Jack Brooks, D-Texas, chairman of the Government Operations Committee, and Frank Horton, N.Y., the panel's senior Republican, opposed the amendment. Both men played key roles in the establishment of independent inspectors general in federal agencies. In 1982, they wrestled with House Armed Services to make the Pentagon's inspector general more independent.

But both men warned that Hertel's amendment would compromise the inspector general's independence by, in effect, requiring him to make decisions on the management of contracts. "You're going to take away the principal agent for pulling out waste, fraud and abuse," Horton said.

The House also adopted by voice vote an amendment by Byron L. Dorgan, D-N.D., that barred from supervising any defense contract a contractor employee who had been convicted of fraud or other contract-related felony. The ban was to last at least five years. Contractor officials indicted for fraud or contract felonies were to be suspended from supervision of defense projects.

Such a bar or suspension would not cover others in the same firm.

The amendment adopted would authorize the Pentagon's inspector general to appoint an officer to oversee existing contracts by firms that the secretary of defense barred from receiving new contracts.

Dorgan had drafted, but did not offer, another amendment that would have barred for a minimum of five years the award of any new defense contracts to firms convicted of fraud or contract felony.

The dropping of that amendment reflected Dorgan's negotiation with Aspin and other committee leaders. "There are some companies we just can't afford to debar from doing work," Nichols warned. "We want to get their attention."

Increased Competition

The House adopted 342-52 an amendment by Mel Levine, D-Calif., and Denny Smith, R-Ore., designed to encourage the Pentagon to use more than one producer in contracting for equipment. The goal was to reduce prices through competitive pressure. *(Vote 172, p. 56-H)*

The amendment would require the secretary of defense to plan for the use of at least two competing contractors in the development and production of any major weapon bought in the future.

It would exempt weapons which, by the end of fiscal 1986 already were in production or in the stage of "advanced development," the point at which prototypes were built.

The defense secretary could waive the two-source requirement for up to half of its total new procurement and development contracts.

Levine and Smith had negotiated the version of the amendment adopted with Aspin who told the House that it had "the right kind of tilt toward dual-sourcing, with enough loopholes to provide exceptions."

The House also adopted a modified version of a Courter amendment designed to force an annual increase in the proportion of procurement contracts awarded competitively. Originally, the amendment would have required competition in 40 percent of the contracts awarded in fiscal 1986 with that floor rising by 5 percent in each succeeding year until 1992, when 70 percent would be needed.

But by voice vote, the House adopted a Nichols amendment to the Courter measure that made the 40-percent competitive contracts (and the subsequent annual boosts) goals rather than absolute requirements.

The Pentagon would have to report to Congress on shortfalls from those targets. The amended Courter amendment was adopted 416-0. *(Vote 168, p. 56-H)*

'Revolving Door' Amendments

An amendment was adopted June 25 prohibiting any former Pentagon procurement official, for two years after leaving the Defense Department, from accepting compensation from a firm over whose work the official exercised "significant" responsibility while at the Pentagon. The measure would cover payment as a consultant as well as employment by the firm.

Sponsored by Bennett and Boxer, the amendment was adopted 397-19 after the House rejected a substitute by John M. Spratt Jr., D-S.C. *(Vote 170, p. 56-H)*

Because of procedural jockeying, the Spratt language was voted on in a slightly modified form offered by Beverly B. Byron, D-Md. The Spratt-Byron language, rejected 140-272, would have imposed the two-year ban only on officials holding positions specifically designated by the secretary of defense. *(Vote 169, p. 56-H)*

Spratt's measure also would have let the defense secretary, with the concurrence of the Office of Government Ethics, waive the ban in cases in which it would hamper his ability to hire or keep qualified people.

The Spratt amendment also incorporated a provision of the Senate-passed defense authorization bill, requiring that Pentagon procurement officials recuse themselves from overseeing contracts with any firms with which the officials had begun to discuss employment prospects.

Several Armed Services members warned that the Bennett version would make it difficult to fill top Pentagon positions with experienced managers from the defense industry. This also had been the position of the Senate Armed Services Committee.

"People from industry virtually contribute their time," Robert E. Badham, R-Calif., said, "taking leave from jobs paying $100,000 or $200,000 . . . to teach [Pentagon careerists] something."

Spratt warned that Bennett might be unconstitutionally vague, since it made each official responsible for deciding whether he or she had "significant responsibility" for procurement.

But Bennett's supporters hammered at several widely publicized cases in which military or civilian officials managing controversial weapons programs had retired and taken jobs with the firms whose work they previously had been overseeing.

"We can no longer afford to have our Defense Department employees . . . tempted to go easy on a contractor by the possibility of a job," said Boxer.

Frank dismissed the warning that Bennett-Boxer's broad scope might have a chilling effect on officials who technically would not be covered. "I think that's a good thing. We're not talking about freedom of speech or freedom of religion," Frank said. "I don't think there ought to be an expectation that you will work for the Army or the Navy or the Marine Corps and then go to work for a defense contractor."

Frank argued that Weinberger could not be trusted with the waiver power in the Spratt version. Spratt's measure "has a lot of tough teeth in it, and then it makes the secretary of defense the dentist-in-chief and he will pull all the teeth," Frank said. "The bill will be gumming everybody over at the Pentagon."

Before adopting the Bennett language, the House adopted by voice vote an amendment by Hartnett, extending its ban to cover ex-members of Congress — "we, ourselves, who probably do more influence-peddling than anyone else," Hartnett said.

Contractors' Cost Records

By a vote of 384-31, the House on June 26 adopted a Boxer amendment requiring the Pentagon to keep records of contractors' costs in carrying out defense contracts. It would require separate listing of costs for material, labor and overhead, and of profits. *(Vote 177, p. 58-H)*

The House first rejected 189-232 a Courter amendment that would instead have called for a General Accounting Office study of the impact on the defense industry of requiring such record-keeping. *(Vote 175, p. 58-H)*

It then adopted 276-147 an amendment by Hank Brown, R-Colo., exempting firms with only relatively small amounts of defense contracts. *(Vote 176, p. 58-H)*

"We're not setting onerous requirements," Boxer argued. "We just want information."

Courter and his allies warned that the reporting requirements would drive small businesses out of defense contracting.

Carl D. Pursell, R-Mich., who said he was seeking defense contracts for his district, declared: "Businesses aren't interested in more red tape and more complications and more procurement amendments. . . . We're going to be basically telling small businesses, 'We don't want your business.' "

But that was rejected as a "desperation argument" by Boxer ally Bryant, who charged the Armed Services Committee was trying to stifle other members' amendments. "What you're saying today is, 'We don't want any outsiders to be a part of the process,' " Bryant said.

House-Senate Differences

In acting on the defense authorization bill, both chambers adopted a series of amendments with the general intent of making the Pentagon's relationship with contractors more adversarial. In general, the House-passed provisions were more stringent.

Defense industry lobbyists objected strongly to several of the stiffer House-passed positions. But two provisions, to which some industry sources were particularly opposed, had been agreed to by both houses and so were not open to revision in conference. These were provisions:

- Authorizing the Pentagon to subpoena books and records of defense contractors.
- Requiring contractors to compare their projected labor costs with standard time allowances for comparable work in commercial manufacturing. In the past, Pentagon critics had used such comparisons to argue that worker productivity on major weapons programs had been lower than was typical of commercial manufacturing projects. Defense contractors maintained that such comparisons ignored the special requirements of producing complex weapons in relatively small numbers. The only difference between the two houses over the "should-cost" study provision was that the House exempted contracts of less than $100,000.

'Revolving Door'

The most intractable issue facing conferees on the defense bill was how to limit a Pentagon official's right to leave the government and immediately take a job with the very defense contractor whose performance the official previously was supposed to be monitoring.

Senate position:

- Any Pentagon contracting official would have to remove himself from oversight of a contractor's work as soon as the official began to discuss with that firm the prospect of employment after the official left government service. In such a case, the official would have to report his discussions with the contractor to Pentagon ethics officials.
- Existing law would be made more stringent, defining the information that former defense officials would have to report to the Pentagon regarding the work they performed for defense contractors.

House position:

- Any former Pentagon official or former member of Congress who had "significant responsibilities" for procurement within two years before his departure from government service would be barred, for two years after leaving the government, from accepting compensation from a defense contractor over whose work the person had authority.

• No waivers were provided for and the ban covered payment as a consultant as well as outright employment.

• An official discussing post-retirement employment with a contractor would have to remove himself from oversight of that firm's work.

Competitive Bidding

Both houses adopted provisions requiring that the Pentagon draw up a plan for acquiring each of its major items of equipment competitively. But the Senate version offered more leeway in applying that general rule.

Senate position:

• The defense secretary would have to draw up a plan for purchasing any major type of equipment that involved the use of competitive procedures. In addition, the plan would have to provide for maintenance of at least two production sources for each type of equipment.

• The Pentagon could waive the requirement for at least two production sources on grounds of cost, delay or "national security interest of the United States."

House position:

• The secretary of defense would have to draw up a plan for competitive procedures in both the development and production of any major item of equipment and any major subsystem of a major item.

• If the secretary determined that competitive, alternative sources of development or production would not otherwise be available, he would plan to award contracts so as to provide and maintain at least two such sources. This provision could be waived if the second-best bid for a contract was "not within a competitive range" of the best bid.

• The requirement for maintaining at least two sources of development and production could be waived on grounds of cost or delay, but not on grounds of "national security requirements." But the total cost of programs for which a waiver was granted could not exceed 50 percent of the total cost of major development or production programs begun after fiscal 1986.

Allowable Costs

Both versions of the bill moved to bar government reimbursement of certain kinds of contractor costs. But here, too, the House approach was more restrictive.

Senate position:

• The secretary of defense would have to issue regulations defining in detail administrative costs for which contractors could not request reimbursement by the government. Among the costs to be "generally unallowable" were: advertising, club dues, entertainment and lobbying costs, fines and legal fees associated with defense against federal fraud charges (unless the firm was found innocent).

• Submission of a cost claim that was unallowable under those regulations would be punishable by a penalty equal to the amount of the claim plus interest. Repeated submission of such disallowed claims by a contractor would be punishable by a penalty equal to twice the amount of any such claim.

House position:

• Most of the costs cited in the Senate version were declared unallowable, but by law, rather than by federal regulation. Each disputed cost claim would be resolved individually, unless the contractor agreed never again to claim any of the disputed costs, in which case a lump-sum settlement could be made.

• Any claim for a cost that was expressly disallowed by law or regulation was to be punishable by a fine of up to twice the amount of the claim plus interest. Anyone submitting a claim for an expressly prohibited cost "knowing that such cost is unallowable" would be imprisoned not more than five years and/or fined not more than $250,000 (if an individual) or $500,000 (if a corporation).

Conference

The disputes over procurement "reform" accounted for only about 10 percent of the 350 non-monetary items of disagreement before the July Senate-House conference on the fiscal 1986 defense authorization bill.

But by many accounts, they accounted for the most divisive battles in the conference, pitting House against Senate rather than liberal against conservative.

The two houses had addressed most of the same issues. In most cases, the House imposed more sweeping changes, and allowed less discretion in carrying them out, than did the Senate.

Predictably, the conference compromises, contained in the report (H Rept 99-235), for the most part relaxed the stringency of the House versions.

'Revolving Door.' The conferees kept the Senate provision requiring any Pentagon official to excuse himself from dealing with any contractor with whom the official had begun discussing prospective employment. They dropped the House provision that barred a procurement official, for two years, from going to work for the contractor whose work the official had supervised.

Instead, the conference report applied the two-year ban to "presidential appointees" who acted as the government's principal negotiator in any dealing with a contractor. Proponents of the House version complained that this would apply only to a handful of senior officials, exempting thousands of oversight officers.

Allowable Costs. Both houses had moved to disallow contractors from receiving Pentagon reimbursement for certain costs, including entertainment and lobbying, and contract-related legal fees.

The conferees barred those claims by law, as the House had done, rather than ordering the Pentagon to draw up regulations to that effect, which was the Senate course. But, bowing to the Senate's desire to allow some discretion, the conferees included a provision allowing the Pentagon to define exemptions from those bans.

The conferees dropped the House provision banning reimbursement for the use of corporate airplanes and for the premium cost of first-class commercial air travel. But they insisted in the conference report that they envisaged only very limited exceptions to the general bar on reimbursement for such travel costs.

Multiple-Sourcing. The conference report required the secretary of defense to plan for the use of multiple sources in both the development and production of major weapons systems.

A House provision was dropped that would have stipulated in law how production contracts were to be shared between the two best bidders so that a second source would maintain market pressure on the costs and performance of the primary source. But the conferees said they expected the Pentagon to follow the House-passed procedures for splitting contracts to keep competition alive through the production run of a weapon.

The conferees also included a Senate provision letting the defense secretary waive the dual-source rule on grounds of national security. Both houses had agreed that it could be waived on grounds of cost or delay.

The conferees dropped a House provision that would have allowed waiver of the dual-source requirement for any reason only as long as the total cost of programs for which the requirement was waived did not exceed 50 percent of the total value of development or production programs begun after fiscal 1986.

The 50 percent limit was too rigid to write into law, the conferees said, but they warned they would reconsider if the Pentagon appeared to be using the waiver authority to subvert the provision's intent of increasing the use of multiple sources in defense contracting.

Progress Payments. The conferees accepted the basic idea of a House provision that required that progress payments to contractors be made only as work actually was completed, rather than on a predetermined schedule. But the conferees emphasized that "work" on a contract included ordering materials, training workers and other activity that would produce no tangible evidence in the form of assembled products.

How Much Is Enough?

As the Senate took up the conference report on S 1160 July 30, senior Armed Services Committee Democrat Sam Nunn, Ga., sounded a lonely note of caution about the depth of congressional involvement in the Pentagon's purchasing system.

"Today's problems were perhaps yesterday's solutions" to perceived procurement abuses, Nunn said. "I hope tomorrow's problems are not today's solutions."

The cumulative effect of congressional legislation on procurement, Nunn complained, was to restrict the flexibility of Pentagon managers. "I would like to find a few pilot projects," he said, "where we could waive most if not all procurement regulations and see how our managers can do if we simply tell them to use good management and common sense."

Sources said Nunn's idea — which he had been exploring for more than a year — was to waive for the pilot projects most of the current Pentagon rules. Labor laws on worker safety and non-discrimination in hiring would remain in force, as would requirements that the contracts be awarded competitively.

The Senate approved the conference report 94-5 on July 30. *(Vote 167, p. 33-S)*

Final Approval

In the House, however, procurement reform contributed to a Democratic rebellion that stalled final approval of the defense bill until Oct. 29.

In early August, Charles E. Schumer, N.Y.; George Miller, Calif.; Boxer and other House Democrats objected that the House authorization conferees, led by Armed Services Chairman Aspin, had yielded too much to their generally more pro-Pentagon Senate counterparts.

The dissident House members were most unhappy with the budget number in the bill; they felt House conferees had failed to fight for the lower, House-passed amount. And they opposed funding for nerve gas.

But the procurement-reform compromises also accounted for complaints. Some lawmakers, such as Boxer, who had fought hardest for the House-passed provisions, reported strong criticism of the conference report by some constituents and local editorials.

In September, Aspin, his House critics and Speaker Thomas P. O'Neill, Jr., Mass., met and agreed to allow a vote on the authorization conference report, while giving the critics some procedural and political chips for the appropriations battle.

The agreement also called for the Senate and House to adopt a concurrent resolution that would change the interpretation that the authorization conferees had placed on another procurement provision. This was the so-called "should-cost" provision requiring the Pentagon to record certain cost and pricing data on weapons contracts. According to Boxer and others, the statement weakened the provision.

That obstacle was breached Oct. 29, when the House adopted 397-18 a bill (HR 3606) revising the conference report's version of the should-cost provision. *(Vote 337, p. 106-H)*

Joint Chiefs Reorganization

Brushing aside Pentagon opposition, the House in 1985 passed legislation that would reorganize the top military hierarchy and increase the bureaucratic clout of the chairman of the Joint Chiefs of Staff.

Proponents said the bill (HR 3622) would give civilian decision makers a better chance to hear professional military advice that was not dominated by the parochial interests of the four armed services.

The Nov. 20 vote was 383-27. *(Vote 379, p. 118-H)*

The bill would make the chairman of the Joint Chiefs the principal military adviser to the president and the secretary of defense — a role assigned under existing law to the Joint Chiefs as a corporate body.

Secretary of Defense Caspar W. Weinberger said the changes were not needed because the existing organization yielded a full range of advice.

Two weeks after the House acted, however, Weinberger softened his stance. In a Dec. 2 letter to Senate Armed Services Committee Chairman Barry Goldwater, R-Ariz., he agreed in general terms to several of the changes, including the chairman's designation as a principal adviser to the president and secretary of defense.

On the House floor, opposition to Joint Chiefs reorganization was led by Charles E. Bennett, Fla., the third-ranking Democrat on the House Armed Services Committee. He warned that the proposal would reduce civilian control by limiting the president's ability to choose among competing military recommendations. "What secretary of defense or even president would find it possible to repeatedly overrule the single-voice recommendation of the entire military establishment?" Bennett asked.

But most other members of the Armed Services Committee favored the bill, which was sponsored by Chairman Les Aspin, D-Wis.; Bill Nichols, D-Ala.; and Ike Skelton, D-Mo.

On the Senate side, Goldwater and Sam Nunn, Ga., the Armed Services panel's senior Democrat, were planning to push similar legislation in 1986.

The Senate panel in late 1985 held a series of hearings based on a staff study of Pentagon organization that carried the House bill's approach further. The staff study suggested abolishing the Joint Chiefs and creating a "joint" advisory council — made up of a senior officer from each service other than the service chief.

Organizing the Brass

Under existing law, the Joint Chiefs chairman was the nation's highest ranking military officer, but he merely presided over the Joint Chiefs — a committee consisting of the uniformed chiefs of the Army, Navy, Air Force and Marine Corps.

Critics said that each service chief was trapped in an inherent conflict of interest: To retain the loyalty of his subordinates, he had to advocate his service's traditional way of preparing to fight. But as a member of the Joint Chiefs, he was expected to take a "cross-service" viewpoint, taking account of the strengths and weaknesses of each service.

According to this argument, joint advice rendered to civilian leaders was watered down to accommodate the special interests of each service. For instance, some critics contended that the 1980 effort to rescue hostages from the U.S. Embassy in Tehran was made unduly complex because each service wanted a piece of the action.

Hard choices among the different service approaches — such as deciding where to cut back the defense budget under pressure of the deficit — simply were not being made, the critics said.

Many senior officers — active duty and retired — objected to the suggestion that senior officers could not subordinate their bureaucratic loyalties to the national interest. But the criticism was echoed by some senior officers and by former Pentagon officials from both Democratic and GOP administrations. Among them were six of the seven former secretaries of defense since 1960 — all but Donald H. Rumsfeld, who served for 15 months of President Ford's term.

Early Moves

The round of public pressure for changes in the Joint Chiefs system was launched in 1982 by Air Force Gen. David C. Jones, the outgoing chairman of the Joint Chiefs.

After the House Armed Services Subcommittee on Investigations, chaired by Richard C. White, D-Texas (1965-83), looked into the issue, the committee reported a bill on Aug. 12, 1982. The measure (HR 6954) passed the House four days later, but died when the 97th Congress ended without the Senate having acted. *(1982 Almanac p. 110)*

According to some proponents of change, the Senate Armed Services Committee's inaction on the bill — and its relatively slow action on the overall issue — reflected the opposition of Chairman John Tower, R-Texas (1961-85).

In 1983, the House passed a modified version of the earlier bill (HR 3718). The Senate committee still did not act on it, and a year later, when Congress took up the fiscal 1985 defense authorization bill, the House Armed Services Committee incorporated the House-passed Joint Chiefs bill into its version of the authorization measure.

During the conference committee on that bill (HR 5167 — PL 98-525), the Senate conferees refused to accept House provisions that would have given the chairman a seat on the National Security Council and allowed him to give military advice in his own right. But they accepted some House provisions, including one allowing the chairman to select the officers from each service who would serve on the Joint Staff. *(1984 Almanac p. 59; 1983 Almanac p. 215)*

New Joint Chiefs Chairman

Adm. William J. Crowe Jr. succeeded Army Gen. John W. Vessey Jr. as chairman of the Joint Chiefs of Staff.

The Senate confirmed Crowe's nomination by voice vote July 31.

A submariner with a Princeton doctorate in political science, Crowe was highly regarded as a strategic thinker. His extensive experience in "joint" jobs — positions involving command of personnel from several armed services — suggested he might be a strong voice for "unified" military judgment, at the expense of the parochial viewpoints of the armed services.

Before his nomination to the chairmanship, Crowe capped a long string of joint positions with two years as commander in chief of all U.S. forces in the Pacific: CINCPAC.

In his confirmation hearing before the Senate Armed Services Committee July 30, Crowe demurred from commenting on specific proposals to reorganize the Joint Chiefs, asking for time to review the situation from his new vantage point. But he did not foreclose the possibility of supporting some changes.

However, in response to questions from the Senate and House Armed Services committees in March 1985, he had called for strengthening the joint side of the bureaucracy one level down: giving the CINCs of the unified combat commands more power over their service components in peacetime.

The 1985 Push

When the 99th Congress convened, the proponents of stronger "joint" institutions hit the ground running.

In the House, Nichols and Skelton were determined to renew the battle for a stronger Joint Chiefs chairman.

With Aspin's election in January to chair Armed Services, the "pro-joint" movement got another important boost. And two other factors contributed to the political momentum behind the reorganization effort:

- Tower having retired, the Senate Armed Services chair passed to Goldwater, a firm advocate of reorganization. With Nunn the senior committee Democrat, this meant that two of the most influential "hawks" in the Senate were demanding changes and were in a position to do something.
- Looming deficits, high defense budgets and "horror stories" about $400 hammers and $600 toilet seats evidently put many members of Congress in a mood to back relatively substantial changes in Pentagon organization and procedure. Weinberger's influence on Capitol Hill had reached such a low ebb that his opposition to certain proposals may have increased the margin of congressional support for change. *(Procurement "reform," p. 164)*

After yet another series of hearings, Nichols, Skelton and Aspin melded their slightly differing approaches into a compromise bill.

Committee Report

The compromise bill (HR 3622) was reported by House Armed Services Nov. 14 (H Rept 99-375) by a vote of 38-2. On the strongly pro-Pentagon committee, the only two negative votes were cast by Samuel S. Stratton, D-

N.Y., and Ronald V. Dellums, D-Calif.

Chairman's Role. The House Armed Services bill retained the Joint Chiefs. But it designated the chairman as principal military adviser to the president and secretary of defense. It also extended the chairman's term from two years to four.

In its report, the committee recommended that the chairman concentrate particularly on "those issues that the corporate JCS has been unable to address effectively" such as the allocation among services of budgets and missions.

The panel also said that the chairman should "assume sole responsibility for handling second-order joint military issues," leaving only the most important matters for the Joint Chiefs as a body. Under the existing system, the committee said, the Joint Chiefs took up about 3,000 issues annually, of which no more than 100 to 200 involved major issues.

Bureaucratic Tools. To assist the chairman in developing his recommendations, the bill also gave him control of the Joint Staff. It removed the ceiling of 400 on the number of officers assigned to the Joint Staff and provided that the secretary of defense could waive the four-year limit on any officer's tour of duty with the Joint Staff.

To provide continuity of a "joint" perspective at the top of the military hierarchy, the bill would give the chairman a deputy.

To discourage undue service parochialism, the bill would require the chairman to evaluate each nominee for promotion to the top two military ranks — general (or admiral) and lieutenant general (or vice admiral) — in terms of the nominee's previous performance in joint assignments.

The bill also required that the chairman or his deputy attend all meetings of the National Security Council and "participate fully" in the deliberations.

It would allow the secretary of defense — at his discretion — to route the military chain of command from the president to the secretary through the chairman to the major commanders. Weinberger had indicated that he would exercise this option.

Under the existing system, the chain went from the secretary through the Joint Chiefs as a corporate body. In either case, the chairman or the Joint Chiefs would act purely as a conduit for the secretary's orders, with no independent authority to command.

Ties to the CINCs. The bill also built on the provision of 1984 law making the chairman "spokesman" for the 10 commanders in chief (or CINCs) actually in charge of all U.S. combat units. The bill would give the CINCs — through the chairman — a larger role as military advisers to the top civilian leadership.

During Weinberger's tenure at the Pentagon, the commanders were given a formal role in the department's budgetary deliberations. The bill would go beyond the current practice to require the commanders to submit budget proposals to the Joint Chiefs chairman.

Based on those submissions and the defense secretary's guidance, the chairman then would submit his own budget proposals to the secretary. The committee said it intended for the chairman to "integrate the recommendations" of the CINCs, "establish priorities and provide civilian authorities with a coherent, fiscally constrained set of combat command proposals."

Floor Action

During six hours of debate Nov. 20, supporters of HR 3622 accepted by voice vote several amendments to the bill:

- By Bennett, as amended by Aspin, to require that the chairman submit to the secretary of defense any dissenting views given him by another member of the Joint Chiefs.
- By Bennett, to retain the current legislative ceiling of 400 on the number of officers in the Joint Staff.

Through various bureaucratic arrangements, some 1,400 officers actually worked for the Joint Chiefs of Staff, though only 400 were officially part of the Joint Staff.

- By Dellums, making the chairman's attendance at and participation in meetings of the National Security Council subject to the president's discretion.
- By Dave McCurdy, D-Okla., establishing within the Joint Staff an office to provide the chairman with "net assessments" of how U.S. forces would stack up against enemies.

By a vote of 47-366, the House rejected a Bennett amendment that would have allowed the chairman to assign undivided authority for any operation to a single officer. *(Vote 378, p. 118-H)*

Senate Study

On Oct. 16, the Senate Armed Services Committee received its staff study calling for sweeping changes in the organization of the Pentagon's top military and civilian hierarchy.

Of the 91 recommendations made in the study, the most dramatic would displace the chiefs of the four armed services — the Joint Chiefs of Staff — from their role as senior military advisers to the president and secretary of defense.

Under the proposal, the service chiefs would run their respective organizations — the Army, Navy, Air Force and Marine Corps — while another group of senior officers would play the advisory role. The new group would consist of an officer from each service in his last assignment before retirement — thus, the report argued, freeing the advisers from pressure to support their services' turf interests.

The study also recommended giving to the 10 commanders in chief (or CINCs) who would command U.S. forces in case of war more authority over units of the various armed services that were assigned to their command. And it would give the CINCs a larger role in Pentagon budgeting.

Under the existing system, the report said, the requirements of coordinated, multi-service war-planning took second place to those missions that each service saw as its specialty. Missions that involved supporting other services' missions — for example, Air Force ground attack missions to support Army troops — routinely were shortchanged, it contended.

Moreover, according to the study, the services closed ranks behind each other's parochial viewpoints to such an extent that civilian leaders were denied the professional military advice they would need to choose among competing budget priorities. The result, the study warned, was "critical gaps in war-fighting capabilities, wasted resources through unwarranted duplication, inter-operability problems, unrealistic plans, inconsistent doctrine, inadequate joint training and ineffective fighting forces."

"There will be those who say the system 'ain't broke, so don't fix it,'" Goldwater said Oct. 16. "However, it is broke and we need to fix it."

But a day earlier, Pentagon spokesman Robert B. Sims said the existing command system worked. He cited the Navy's Oct. 10 interception of an Egyptian airliner carrying four Palestinian hijackers of the cruise ship *Achille Lauro* as evidence.

"These levels that have been described as being in disrepair ... were operating well during the course of that day," Sims declared. "The chain of command from the White House to the Joint Chiefs, through the secretary of defense to the European command and to the operating forces in the field — it seemed to work."

Arms Control: Negotiations but No Accords

After more than a year's hiatus, the Reagan administration and the Soviet Union in 1985 resumed talking about nuclear arms limitations.

But while the series of negotiating sessions, conducted in Geneva, presented at least the potential for eventual agreements to control nuclear arms, they also provided the administration with a strong rhetorical weapon in its Capitol Hill battles for President Reagan's military buildup.

Time and again, in congressional actions on major weapons programs, members were exhorted not to cast a vote that would undercut the administration's negotiating position in Geneva. That argument gained more punch with the decision of Reagan and the Soviets' new leader, Mikhail S. Gorbachev, to hold a summit meeting in November. *(Summit, p. 109)*

The bargaining-chip argument contributed to Reagan victories in skirmishes over the MX missile and the "strategic defense initiative" (SDI) for anti-missile research. The imminence of the summit also helped sideline congressional action on a non-binding resolution urging Reagan to resume negotiations with Moscow leading to a complete ban on nuclear testing. *(MX, p. 119; SDI, p. 130)*

Although the summit produced no agreements to limit weapons, it and the resumption of the Geneva talks reflected a symbolic change in Reagan's treatment of arms control issues and of U.S.-Soviet relations in general.

That shift was illustrated in June, when Reagan ignored the advice of his administration hard-liners and decided to dismantle a missile-firing submarine in order to remain within a limitation of the unratified SALT II U.S.-Soviet arms control treaty.

The Senate earlier had voted 90-5 to recommend that the president continue the policy of informal adherence to SALT II. A more influential incentive, however, apparently was the demand by allied governments that the treaty's limits be respected.

Resuming the Talks

After discussions Jan. 7-8 in Geneva, Secretary of State George P. Shultz and Soviet Foreign Minister Andrei A. Gromyko announced the two countries would negotiate over three kinds of weapons: strategic nuclear missiles and bombers, intermediate-range nuclear forces (INF) located in Europe and space weaponry.

In a press conference Jan. 9 — his first in seven months — Reagan said he hoped the agreement to resume talks was "the beginning of a new dialogue between the United States and the Soviet Union." He pledged to be "flexible, patient and determined" in keeping that dialogue alive.

The resumption of talks — broken off by Moscow in late 1983 — complemented Reagan's increasingly conciliatory tone toward Moscow.

In 1981-82, the president's confrontational approach toward the Soviets had fueled unprecedented domestic opposition to his nuclear arms programs.

By the time Reagan squared off against Democratic presidential rival Walter F. Mondale in 1984, the softening of rhetoric evidently had neutralized the "war-peace" issue as a Reagan liability.

But the administration argued that the resumption of talks vindicated a fundamental premise of Reagan policy: that Moscow would negotiate away its advantage in nuclear weaponry only if it faced a U.S. arms buildup.

Liberal arms control activists denied that the Soviet Union had any advantage in the strategic balance. The U.S.-Soviet nuclear balance would become even more dangerously unstable, they argued, unless a new arms limitation agreement headed off more sophisticated weapons.

To reach an agreement, they argued, Reagan would have to accommodate certain Soviet demands at which he was likely to balk because of his belief that Moscow had an advantage in nuclear forces.

The Geneva Team

Reagan named three men as chief negotiators in Geneva. The nominations were approved by the Senate Foreign Relations Committee on Feb. 28 and by the full Senate by voice vote on March 5, seven days before the talks formally opened.

The negotiators were:

- **Max M. Kampelman**, led the U.S. delegation and conducted the negotiations on anti-missile defenses, including Reagan's SDI effort to develop space-based, anti-missile weapons.

Kampelman, a longtime associate of the late Sen. Hubert H. Humphrey, D-Minn. (1949-64, 1971-78), was a leader of Democratic foreign policy hard-liners. Kampelman co-authored an article in the Jan. 27 *New York Times Magazine* that supported SDI research.

- **John Tower**, a Republican senator from Texas who served from 1961-85, conducted negotiations to reduce long-range weapons, including intercontinental missiles and bombers, and missiles launched from submarines. Before leaving the Senate, Tower had been chairman of the Armed Services Committee.

- **Maynard Glitman**, a career diplomat, negotiated for limitations on intermediate-range nuclear weapons — principally missiles based on the Eurasian landmass.

A 12-member Senate observer group — including Majority Leader Robert Dole, R-Kan., and Minority Leader Robert C. Byrd, D-W.Va. — also was formed to monitor the negotiations, on a rotating basis.

Though they did not attend the negotiating sessions, the senators received briefings by the U.S. team and met informally with Soviet negotiators.

Other Republicans in the Senate group were Ted Stevens, Alaska; John W. Warner, Va.; Richard G. Lugar, Ind.; Don Nickles, Okla.; and Malcolm Wallop, Wyo. Other Democrats were Sam Nunn, Ga.; Claiborne Pell, R.I.; Albert Gore Jr., Tenn.; Edward M. Kennedy, Mass.; and Daniel Patrick Moynihan, N.Y.

Summit Plans

The March 12 opening of the Geneva talks coincided with a change at the top in the Kremlin. On March 10, Soviet leader Konstantin U. Chernenko died; Gorbachev was named general secretary of the Soviet Communist Party the next day.

On March 13, Reagan reversed his longstanding opposition to a get-acquainted summit meeting and offered to meet with Gorbachev. Vice President George Bush delivered the offer in a meeting with Gorbachev, following funeral services in Moscow for Chernenko.

Gorbachev responded to Reagan's proposal by announcing April 7 that he was ready to meet the U.S. president. At the same time, Gorbachev said the Soviet Union was unilaterally freezing until November its deployment of SS-20 medium-range missiles in Europe. He urged the United States to reciprocate by stopping deployment of Pershing II and cruise missiles in Western Europe. White House officials dismissed Gorbachev's missile moratorium as a propaganda gesture, while cautiously welcoming his comments on a meeting.

The two countries formally announced the Reagan-Gorbachev meeting on July 3. However, U.S. officials said they did not expect any important agreements to be reached at the November event.

Throughout his first term, Reagan had been reluctant to hold such a meeting unless there was a likelihood of agreement on major issues.

SALT Compliance

While U.S. and Soviet officials were moving to firm up the summit plans and arms control negotiations had been renewed, Reagan decided to "go the extra mile" to maintain an interim arrangement of nuclear arms restraint. *(Text, p. 22-D)*

He announced on June 10 that he would dismantle a Poseidon missile-launching submarine. That action would continue the U.S. policy of informally abiding by most terms of the 1979 U.S.-Soviet strategic arms limitation agreement (SALT II). The treaty, never ratified, expired at the end of 1985.

The dismantling of the Poseidon's missile launchers was prompted by the imminence of the launch of the seventh Trident missile-launching submarine, the USS *Alaska*. Its 24 missile-launch tubes would have brought to 1,214 the total number of U.S. launchers for multiple warhead missiles on land and sea. This would have been 14 above the limit set by SALT II.

Reagan's announcement delighted liberals and confounded some of Reagan's staunchest conservative allies.

For months, conservatives in the Senate and in the administration, including Defense Secretary Caspar W. Weinberger, had urged Reagan to keep the Poseidon sub in service and to end the administration's policy of "not undercutting" SALT II.

The hard-liners argued that denouncing the treaty would highlight alleged Soviet violations of this and other arms control agreements as well as signal a new firmness in dealing with Moscow.

Administration officials and congressional sources on both sides of the issue emphasized NATO politics as a factor in Reagan's decision.

Secretary of State George P. Shultz had warned that repudiation of the SALT limits would provoke a surge of anti-American opinion in allied countries.

Senate Action

Domestic politics also played a role. On June 5, the Senate voted, 90-5, to retain the SALT II limits in general terms through 1986 — but with a large loophole. The amendment expressly endorsed a policy of "proportionate responses" by the United States to Soviet violations.

The vote came on the fiscal 1986 defense authorization bill (S 1160). *(Authorization bill, p. 138)*

The Senate's amendment represented a compromise that allowed Reagan's conservative supporters as well as his liberal critics to claim victory.

Because it did not define the central concept of a "proportionate response," it would not force the president to decide to break up existing nuclear missile launchers when the *Alaska* went to sea. Strict compliance with the agreements would have required destroying the launchers.

Most arms control specialists agreed that various Soviet activities at the very least pressed at the margins of three existing arms agreements: the 1972 and 1979 agreements on offensive strategic arms (SALT I and II) and the 1972 treaty limiting anti-ballistic missile (ABM) systems. *(ABM treaty, p. 132)*

SALT I expired in 1977, and although SALT II was soon to expire, the U.S.and Soviet governments had agreed, in effect, to observe most of the SALT provisions.

Foreign policy hard-liners — led in the Senate by Republicans James A. McClure, Idaho; Malcolm Wallop, Wyo.; and Steven D. Symms, Idaho — long had criticized the SALT and ABM pacts. They called on Reagan to signal that Soviet violations would not be tolerated by not destroying the existing submarine missiles.

Supporters of the existing agreements, led in the Senate by Dale Bumpers, D-Ark., and Patrick J. Leahy, D-Vt., contended that the core of the SALT agreements — the limits on various classes of nuclear weapons — had been observed by both sides. To violate one of those ceilings would unravel the web of restraints and evoke powerful anti-U.S. sentiment in Western Europe, they argued. Moreover, they warned, the Soviet Union would get off to a much faster start than the United States in an untrammeled race to build more nuclear missiles.

"The United States and the president would be d-u-m-b, dumb, to respond to any one of the [Soviet] violations by breaking out of the 1,200 [launcher] limit," Bumpers told the Senate.

Within the administration, some officials had promoted a third option for dealing with the *Alaska* deployment: an existing missile submarine could be put in drydock — and thus its missiles removed from service — but not broken up, as required by SALT II.

Bumpers and Leahy drafted an amendment to the defense bill that would call on Reagan to continue through 1986 the policy of "not undercutting" the arms accords.

The GOP leadership originally planned to block action on the Bumpers amendment until Reagan reported to Congress on his plans for dealing with the *Alaska* case — the report scheduled for June 10.

But in three hours of closed-door talks on June 5, Nunn broke the impasse by suggesting that Bumpers include in his amendment a provision recognizing the right in international law of "proportionate response" to treaty violations, but without trying to apply the principle in specific terms to the *Alaska* case. Nunn had publicly called for strict compliance with the SALT II limits in that instance, opposing the dry-docking option.

McClure and Bumpers accepted the deal and the compromise was agreed to 90-5. Wallop, Symms and three other conservatives opposed what Wallop called "an exercise in self-deception." *(Vote 105, p. 23-S)*

Edward M. Kennedy, D-Mass., a SALT backer, called the amendment "a major victory . . . for the forces of arms control."

On the other hand, McClure stressed to reporters that the amendment endorsed the notion of "shades of violation" of the agreements by Moscow and gave Reagan flexibility to tailor a U.S. response, including the dry-docking option.

Albert Gore Jr., D-Tenn., contended that the amendment "clearly" urged the administration not to merely dry-dock a submarine, but to destroy it as SALT II required. Gore cited Wallop's opposition as evidence that the compromise had not stripped the amendment of meaning.

'Missilectomy'

Reagan's June 10 announcement brought the Navy's ballistic missile submarine full circle. Under his plan, the USS *Sam Rayburn*, a 21-year-old missile-launching sub was sliced like a sausage into three parts. The middle-third of the ship, containing 16 launch tubes for Poseidon missiles, was removed and dismantled in a manner designed to allow confirmation by Soviet spy satellites.

After this "missilectomy,' the front section, holding the ship's controls and torpedo tubes, was welded onto the back section, holding its nuclear power plant. The reconstructed ship then likely would be used by the Navy as a training submarine.

The process was nearly a mirror image of the start of the Navy's crash program to build ballistic-missile launching subs, in 1958. Then, a torpedo-armed sub on which construction had just begun, the USS *Scorpion*, was lengthened by 130 feet to carry 16 launch tubes for Polaris missiles. The *Scorpion* thus became the USS *George Washington*, first of the "boomers," as the Navy called big missile subs.

Charges of Soviet Violations

In his June 10 statement, Reagan reiterated earlier administration charges that the Soviets were violating SALT II and other arms control agreements and called for "appropriate and proportional responses." Among the alleged Soviet violations:

- Testing a new, small intercontinental ballistic missile — the SS-25 — that would not be permitted by SALT II. The treaty allowed each country only one new-type ICBM, the Soviet SS-24 and the similar U.S. MX.
- Coding most of the flight data radioed to Earth from Soviet missile tests, impairing U.S. efforts to ensure Soviet compliance with SALT limits.

Reagan ordered the Joint Chiefs of Staff to advise him by Nov. 15 of the military implications of Soviet arms control violations and of U.S. options to respond. As an example, he said that the United States reserved the right to deploy a small single-warhead missile, called Midgetman, as a reponse to Soviet deployment of the SS-25.

"This is not an open-ended commitment in perpetuity," to observe SALT II, Reagan's national security adviser, Robert C. McFarlane, told reporters.

The administration said that it would approach the issue of SALT observance each time new deployments brought the U.S. arsenal up against one of the SALT limits. The next such hurdle was expected in early summer of 1986 when an eighth Trident submarine, USS *Nevada*, was due to enter service. At about the same time, the Air Force program to equip B-52 bombers with cruise missiles was expected to have reached the point at which SALT limits would require that a multiple-warhead missile launcher be retired for each additional bomber conversion.

From Members, Pros and Cons

Reagan's announcement was lauded by three Senate leaders of the campaign for SALT compliance: Bumpers, Leahy and John H. Chafee, R-R.I.

Chafee told reporters after Reagan's announcement that the United States had "seized the high ground." Senate Minority Leader Byrd concurred, calling the decision to remain in compliance with the treaty "pre-eminently correct," though Byrd had favored meeting the treaty requirement by dismantling land-based missile launchers, rather than the submarine.

By contrast, the decision drew a sharp attack from Symms. "I think the Soviets are popping their vodka bottles," he said of the move. Symms also likened the decision to "the time Neville Chamberlain knuckled under to Hitler."

McClure also opposed the decision, though in less harsh terms. "I would have preferred a decision that would have been more clearly reversible," he said on June 11. This referred to the widely discussed option of dry-docking the missile submarine and removing its missiles, but without permanently disabling its missile launchers.

But McClure also claimed to be winning the long-term war in drawing attention to Soviet treaty violations, even if he had lost the battle over the Poseidon ship.

"We're immensely ahead of where we were a year ago," he said June 11. "Nobody argues that there are no [Soviet] violations."

Test-Ban Treaty

If the administration was willing to "go the extra mile" for the SALT II agreement, it stood its ground later in the year, when the House was poised to take up a non-binding resolution (H J Res 3) urging the president to renew U.S.-Soviet negotiation of a nuclear test ban treaty.

Citing ongoing U.S.-Soviet arms negotiations in Geneva and the scheduled November summit meeting between Reagan and Gorbachev, Secretary of State George P. Shultz asked House Speaker Thomas P. O'Neill Jr., D-Mass., to defer floor action. The debate could show "an image of internal discord on arms control matters," Shultz noted in a letter.

Early on the evening of Oct. 1, the Democratic leadership told backers of the resolution that it would not be called up the following day, as had been planned. Sponsored by Iowa Reps. Berkley Bedell, a Democrat, and Jim Leach, a Republican, H J Res 3 had 205 other cosponsors.

Administration Lobbying

In addition to seeking resumption of comprehensive test-ban talks, H J Res 3 called on Reagan to ask Senate approval of two treaties signed in the mid-1970s but never ratified. The treaties would limit underground nuclear explosions to an explosive power of 150 kilotons — that is, 150,000 tons of TNT.

Only underground tests were permitted under a 1963 treaty to which the United States and Soviet Union were party.

The Republican-controlled Senate, despite Reagan administration opposition, had adopted the resolution in 1984 as an amendment to the fiscal 1985 defense authorization bill on a 77-22 vote. *(1984 Almanac p. 51)*

But in 1985, administration lobbyists strongly emphasized to House members, including some of the resolution's cosponsors, the imminence of the summit as a reason to put the measure aside.

Shultz' letter to O'Neill struck a similar tone: "During this delicate period, it is especially important that Congress and the administration show unity to the maximum extent possible and that we give the Soviets no opportunities for exploiting domestic political debate and thereby delaying progress in arms control and the positive development of relations between our two countries."

By Oct. 1, test-ban proponents were finding signs that many of their supporters were losing interest in the fight — at least just then. "A lot of members felt they did not want to be put on the spot," said one lobbyist.

Most of the resolution's backers thought they could win a straight yea-or-nay vote on the resolution. But they feared losing support to a substitute sponsored by Henry J. Hyde, R-Ill. The substitute would have put Congress on record in support of an administration position that:

- Improved methods of verifying a 150-kiloton limit should be negotiated with the Soviets before the two threshold treaties were ratified.
- A comprehensive test ban should be sought following deep reductions in the existing nuclear arsenals.

With the schedule complicated by the farm bill and other measures and Shultz invoking the need to support the president as he dealt with Moscow, O'Neill made his decision to put the resolution off.

Pre-Summitry

Meanwhile, the administration and the Soviets were jockeying for advantage in pre-summit politics.

The Reagan team insisted that the November summit agenda would be far-reaching, touching on many subjects. Among those were some which — from the administration's standpoint — would put the Russians on the defensive: human rights in the Soviet Union and Soviet military intervention in Afghanistan.

That broad agenda was set out in an Oct. 24 speech by Reagan to the U.N. General Assembly. *(Text, p. 32-D)*

And with the help of Senate conservatives, some administration officials tried to dampen public ardor for new deals with Moscow by reminders of alleged Soviet treaty violations.

For two years, the centerpiece of the Soviet non-compliance brief had been a large radar at Krasnoyarsk in Siberia; U.S. officials said it was a violation of the ABM treaty.

On Oct. 22, Defense Secretary Weinberger said the Russians had begun to deploy the so-called SS-25 intercontinental ballistic missile (ICBM). According to the administration and most U.S. observers, this also violated SALT II.

Soviet Initiative, U.S. Response

But Reagan's effort to focus summit attention on other issues and Weinberger's new charge of Soviet cheating were pre-empted by Moscow.

On Sept. 30, the Soviets made a new negotiating offer that, at least on its face, seemed to offer stark reductions: a 50 percent cut in strategic nuclear weapons.

The Soviet offer promised particularly steep reductions in the Soviet force of land-based missiles (ICBMs).

The attractiveness of that offer highlighted the quid pro quo — tight restrictions on research into anti-missile defenses envisioned in Reagan's "strategic defense initiative." At least as a public opening position, the Soviet Union demanded a ban on SDI-related testing outside the laboratory.

Within days, allied governments led by British Prime Minister Margaret Thatcher and West German Chancellor Helmut Kohl pressed Reagan to match Gorbachev with an equally dramatic proposal.

A month later, the Reagan team presented a counter-offer that picked up some politically catchy elements of Gorbachev's proposal — notably, the idea of a "50 percent reduction."

At the same time, the U.S. offer redefined the scope of the reduction — what it was that would be cut by 50 percent — in line with the traditional U.S. position: Only long-range ballistic missiles and intercontinental bombers would be counted against the limit. *(Balance of weapons, box, p. 179)*

The seeming convergence of the U.S. and Soviet positions on certain points underscored the stark disagreement on SDI.

The Soviets insisted on a virtual halt in the testing of space-based and air-based anti-missile systems, which accounted for much of the SDI program, a tradeoff that Reagan rejected.

When Reagan announced the new American proposal Oct. 31, he declined to comment on the specifics of the offer.

But the president gave reporters a thumbnail sketch of his goal: "deep cuts, no first-strike advantage, defensive research — because defense is safer than offense — and no cheating."

Comparison of Proposals

Even at half their existing size, the U.S. and Soviet strategic arsenals would number more than 5,000 weapons each, enough to destroy both countries in an all-out war.

Moreover, some experts made the case that if the two nuclear arsenals were slashed by even more than 50 percent, the situation would become more dangerous rather than less. Each side might be more confident of disarming the other with a surprise attack if only a few hundred missiles and bombers had to be wiped out rather than thousands.

But regardless of the analytical paradoxes, Reagan said he was firmly committed to including substantial reductions in any future arms treaty. One of his arguments against the earlier SALT I and SALT II treaties was that they did not even prevent future increases in U.S. and Soviet forces, let alone make reductions.

The U.S. and Soviet offers both were labeled as 50 percent reductions in nuclear forces. But that seeming accord masked two fundamental disagreements over what forces were being cut.

- The Soviet position long had been that a "strategic" nuclear weapon was one that could strike either U.S. or Soviet territory. By this definition, the category included not only medium-range U.S. missiles in Europe but also 380 medium-range airplanes in Europe and Asia and 560 bombers aboard aircraft carriers. All those planes were

Lineup of U.S., Soviet Nuclear Weapons

Following is a breakdown of the strategic force balance between the United States and the Soviet Union as of November 1985. The chart was compiled from figures assembled by the Arms Control Association, a private group that frequently had criticized Reagan administration policy, and other official and private sources.

The numbers do not include several hundred shorter-range planes and missiles in each force that could strike the other side's territory under certain circumstances. The chart also omits British and French planes and missiles that the Soviets said must be counted. Dates in parentheses indicate when initial deployment was expected.

	UNITED STATES			SOVIET UNION		
	Number	**Type**	**Number of Warheads**	**Number**	**Type**	**Number of Warheads**
'Prompt Hard-Target Killers' [1]						
Heavy land-based missiles (ICBMs)[2]	0	—	—	308	SS-18	1-10
Other ICBMs	550	Minuteman III[4]	3	360	SS-19[4]	6
		MX *(1986)*	10	18	SS-25[3]	1
		"Midgetman" *(1990s)*	1		SS-24 *(1986)*	*10*
Submarine-launched missiles		Trident II *(1989)*	8			
Other ICBMs						
	450	Minuteman II	1	150	SS-17	4
	24	Titan II[5]	1	502	SS-11[6]	1
				60	SS-13	1
Other Submarine-Launched Missiles						
	360	Trident I[3]	8	16	SSN-23[3]	7
	288	Poseidon[7]	10	60	SSN-20[3]	7-9
				224	SSN-18	1-7
					SSN-6[8]	
				634	SSN-8	1
				12	SSN-17	
Bombers Carrying Long-Range, Air-Launched Cruise Missiles						
		B-1 *(1986)*	24	30	Bear H[3]	8
	15	B-52H	20		Blackjack *(1987-89)*	1
	98	B-52G	12			
Other Long-Range Bombers						
Heavy Bombers		"Stealth" *(1990s)*	?	100	Bear	4
	81	B-52H	12-20	45	Bison[9]	4
	69	B-52G	12-20			
	270-307	B-52 hulks[10]	0			
Medium Bombers	63	FB-111	4	260	Backfire	2-3
Homeland Defenses						
Anti-Ballistic Missile Launchers	0			100[11]		
Anti-Aircraft Missile Launchers	0			12,000 at 1,200 sites		
Anti-Bomber Fighter Planes	270			1,200		

[1] Missiles with the accuracy and explosive power needed to destroy armored underground targets within minutes of launch.
[2] U.S. officials say these missiles need special limits because they have such powerful engines they could be modified to carry 30-40 warheads.
[3] New system still being deployed.
[4] U.S. officials now say that the Minuteman III and SS-19 cannot destroy modernized missile silos.
[5] Titan IIs are being scrapped at a rate of about 1 per month.
[6] SS-11s are being scrapped as SS-25s are deployed.
[7] Poseidons can carry 14 warheads apiece, but according to most sources they carry only 10.
[8] SSN-6s are being scrapped as newer missiles are deployed.
[9] Bisons are being scrapped as newer bombers are deployed.
[10] These are old planes that have been stripped of parts — including engines in some cases — but still count as bombers under the rules agreed to in U.S.-Soviet negotiations over SALT II.
[11] Reagan administration officials say that several hundred of the newer types of Soviet anti-aircraft missiles can be used against some missile warheads.

equipped to carry nuclear weapons and could reach Soviet territory — at least in a one-way mission.

The consistent U.S. position had been that those planes were intended primarily to carry conventional weapons and could not be limited by a nuclear arms treaty. There seemed to be no significant congressional opposition to that view.

In the Vladivostok agreement of 1974 between President Ford and then-Soviet leader Leonid I. Brezhnev, the Russians dropped their insistence on counting what they called "forward-based systems" (FBS) on the U.S. side in return for U.S. acceptance of very large Soviet ICBMs, which the Pentagon called SS-18s.

- Both the U.S. and Soviet offers counted under the 6,000-weapon ceiling long-range air-launched cruise missiles (ALCMs) able to strike targets up to 1,500 miles away from the point where they were launched from a bomber. But the Soviet proposal also counted each bomb and short-range missile carried by heavy bombers. U.S. bombers carried several so-called SRAM nuclear missiles with a range of up to 100 miles, partly to blast a way through the dense network of Soviet anti-aircraft defenses.

Following is a comparison of the two sides' major arms control proposals:

Overall Limits on Nuclear Weapons

U.S. offer:

- Warheads on long-range ballistic missiles and air-launched cruise missiles (ALCMs) would be limited to a total of 6,000. The limit would not cover intermediate-range missiles in Europe.
- The number of long-range ballistic-missile launchers and bombers would be limited to 1,800, of which not more than 1,450 could be missile launchers. The Soviet Union had more than 2,300 missile launchers that would be covered and a long-range bomber force of between 170 and 420 planes (depending on whether or not 250 Backfire medium bombers were counted). The missile launchers alone would be cut by more than one-third. The U.S. force included 1,666 missile launchers and either 263 or 533 heavy bombers (depending on whether mothballed B-52s, many of them missing key parts, would be counted). The U.S. missile force would be cut by about one-eighth.
- The total number of long-range weapons allowed would depend on the number of bombs and short-range missiles — which were not covered by the limit — that would be carried by non-ALCM-carrying bombers. If the average load was eight per plane, as one outside expert had suggested, this would amount to 2,200 weapons, bringing the total allowed under the U.S. proposal to 8,200 long-range nuclear weapons.

Soviet offer:

- A limit would be set of 6,000 on ballistic missile warheads, ALCMs, short-range bomber weapons and bombs in either arsenal that could strike the territory of the other country. The limit would not include medium- and short-range Soviet missiles and bombers able to strike Western Europe.
- The number of missiles and planes on each side able to strike the other country's home territory would be cut by 50 percent. In addition to long-range missiles and intercontinental bombers, the Soviet Union insisted that the U.S. force to be cut include short-range missiles and planes based in Europe and Asia and planes aboard aircraft carriers that could strike Soviet territory. By this accounting, the U.S. force would number 3,360 "delivery vehicles" and a reduction of 50 percent would bring the force to 1,680. Since strategic arms reduction talks (START) began in 1969, the United States had refused to include its short-range planes in any limit of intercontinental weapons. In its own force, the Soviet limit would apply only to long-range missiles and heavy bombers, of which they claimed 2,504. The 50 percent cut would bring them to 1,250, well below the level allowed by the U.S. proposal.

Ballistic Missile Warheads

U.S. offer:

- Sublimits would be set: 4,500 warheads on land-based missiles (ICBMs) and submarine-launched missiles, of which no more than 3,000 would be allowed on ICBMs. This would require a reduction of more than 50 percent in the existing Soviet ICBM force (6,420 warheads) and a reduction of more than 40 percent in the current Soviet submarine missile force (2,700 warheads).
- The existing U.S. ICBM force stood at 2,126 warheads, so the 500 MX warheads approved by Congress (50 missiles with 10 warheads apiece) could be added without hitting the ICBM limit. But the U.S. submarine missile force had more than 5,700 warheads, bringing the missile warhead total to 7,854, so a reduction of more than 40 percent would have to be made somewhere.

Soviet offer:

- No more than 3,600 warheads could be carried by any one type of weapon (ICBMs, submarine missiles or bombers). That would require a 44 percent cut in the number of Soviet ICBM warheads.
- The U.S. submarine missile force would lose more than one-third of its current warhead total.

Bans on Types of Strategic Weapons

U.S. offer:

- Mobile ICBMs and the modernization of heavy ICBMs would be prohibited. The ban on mobiles would kill mobile deployment of the Soviet SS-25 then under way and would limit the SS-24 to deployment in missile silos, ruling out a projected future deployment in large freight trains. It also would rule out mobile deployment of a projected small U.S. missile — dubbed "Midgetman" — for which congressional sponsors favored mobile deployment.
- The ban on modernization of heavy missiles would prevent replacement or expansion of the Soviet force of 308 SS-18s.

Soviet offer:

- Cruise missiles with a range greater than 600 kilometers would be banned, thus killing off the U.S. ALCM. Apparently, an exception to the ban would be made for some U.S. long-range, ground-launched cruise missiles-(GLCMs) in Europe.
- "New types" of missiles also would be banned. Depending on the definition, this could be read to allow deployment of the Soviet SS-24 and SS-25 ICBMs and the SSN-20 and SSN-23 submarine missiles, which were at or near the deployment stage, while barring testing and deployment of the U.S. Midgetman ICBMs, Trident II submarine missile and "stealth bomber."

Throwweight

U.S. offer:

- The total throwweight of ballistic missiles and ALCMs would be approximately 3 million kilograms. The existing U.S. level was about 1.9 million kilograms. But Soviet throwweight — estimated at 5.7 million kilograms — would be sharply cut, thus, according to Pentagon officials, reducing the risk that the Soviets could "break out" of a treaty by suddenly adding more warheads.

Soviet offer:

• No explicit total throwweight limits would be set, but according to Soviet sources, the practical effect of the Soviet proposal likely would be to trim total throwweight for ballistic missiles alone to 2.5 million to 3 million kilograms.

Bombers, Bomber Weapons

U.S. offer:

• Heavy bombers would be limited to 350 planes. There might be a sublimit of 120 ALCM-carrying bombers.

• Only 1,500 ALCMs could be deployed. Most U.S. planes were equipped to carry 20 ALCMs each, which would allow deployment of only 75 ALCM carriers.

• The Soviet Union was just beginning to deploy long-range ALCMs similar to the U.S. type and was far short of the 1,500 limit. The Soviet bomber fleet exceeded the 350-plane limit if the Backfire was counted as an intercontinental bomber, a point on which the two sides disagreed.

Soviet offer:

• No long-range ALCMs would be allowed. No special sublimits on bombers or their weapons would apply under the overall limit of 6,000. Weapons carried by the Backfire would not count against the 6,000 limit.

• The U.S. bomber force would be hard hit by any limit that covered bombs and short-range (100-mile) attack missiles (SRAMs). The U.S. position was that SRAMs were needed to offset the very heavy Soviet anti-aircraft defenses, which had no U.S. counterpart. B-52s not carrying ALCMs typically carried up to eight SRAMs and four bombs each.

Intermediate-Range Nuclear Forces

U.S. offer:

• The number of intermediate-range missile launchers in Europe would be limited to 140 for each country. This was about the number of Pershing II missile launchers (with one missile each) and GLCM launchers (with four missiles each) due to be deployed by the end of 1985.

• The number of Soviet SS-20 launchers in Asia would be reduced (reportedly from 170 to 100).

• The U.S. offer would not cover British and French forces, both of which were due to replace existing single-warhead missiles with multiple-warhead missiles in the late 1980s and 1990s.

Soviet offer:

• The official Soviet offer would ban the U.S. Pershing II and GLCM while reducing the number of SS-20 launchers (one missile per launcher) from 270 to 243, the number deployed in June 1984.

• Soviet officials proposed an interim deal freezing the number of Soviet, U.S., British and French intermediate-range missile launchers. Implicitly, this conceded the U.S. right to deploy about 140 such missiles, the number due in the field by year's end. The number of Soviet and NATO missiles in Europe was roughly equal, but there were more Soviet warheads, since each SS-20 carried three.

Space and Anti-missile Weapons

U.S. offer:

• The United States took no position except to discuss with Soviets the wisdom of greater reliance on strategic defenses. The Reagan administration claimed its planned tests of anti-missile weapons and sensors would be consistent with the 1972 ABM treaty, at least through 1990.

Soviet offer:

• Testing of space-based or air-based anti-missile weapons and sensors would be banned.

• Ongoing Soviet experiments with anti-missile lasers at fixed locations were consistent with the 1972 treaty limiting anti-missile weapons.

Treaty Compliance Disputes

U.S. position:

• Though it was not formally part of the U.S. negotiating offer, Washington was unlikely to accept a major agreement that was not accompanied by Soviet action on the huge radar under construction near Krasnoyarsk in central Siberia. U.S. officials said that it was a violation of the 1972 U.S.-Soviet ABM treaty which required that such radars be located only at the periphery of each country.

• The administration also contended that deployment of the SS-25 ICBM violated the provision of the unratified 1979 U.S.-Soviet SALT II treaty that allowed deployment of only one new type of ICBM for each country. The Soviet Union claimed the larger SS-24 as its allowed "new type." The administration saw this Soviet violation as a warrant for deploying two new U.S. types: the large MX and the proposed single-warhead Midgetman.

Soviet position:

• The Soviet Union insisted that the Krasnoyarsk radar was designed to track space satellites, and thus was permitted by the ABM treaty. But in late October, Soviet negotiators offered to stop work at Krasnoyarsk if the United States abandoned plans to modernize large ballistic-missile detection radars at Thule, Greenland, and at Fylingdales Moor, England. At those two sites, existing missile radars, "grandfathered" under the ABM treaty, were being replaced with much more powerful radars and computers to estimate the likely targets of attacking missiles. The Reagan administration refused to equate a Soviet radar it said was clearly in violation of the treaty with U.S. programs seen as clearly consistent with the pact.

• The Soviet Union insisted that the SS-25 was an improved version of the older SS-13, permitted under SALT II. But it accused the United States of violating the limit of "one new type" with the Midgetman.

Summit Outcome

Before heading for Geneva, Reagan gave a Nov. 14 television speech to the nation in which he mapped out goals that were more sweeping — but also less immediate — than the nuclear arms issues that had dominated public interest in the event.

Reagan said that the summit would provide "an historic opportunity to set a steady, more constructive course for the 21st century." He made only a brief reference to SDI, and administration officials continued to insist that there was no chance the two leaders could negotiate an arms-control agreement, given the remaining differences between the two sides.

The day before the speech, Reagan had received united congressional backing for his efforts. The Senate by a 99-0 vote adopted a resolution (S Res 257) voicing its "full support and best wishes for success" for the summit. And House Democratic leaders held a press conference promising their full backing for the president. *(Vote 304, p. 53-S)*

Reagan left Washington for Geneva on Nov. 16. That same day, a minor tempest arose when *The New York Times* published a letter to Reagan from Defense Secretary Weinberger, who was not going to the summit. The letter repeated Weinberger's often-stated skepticism about the value of past arms control agreements, and urged Reagan to resist pressures to accept limits on SDI research in return for reductions in Soviet missiles.

From its outset on Nov. 19, the summit departed from its announced schedule. Although only two days of talks originally were scheduled, a third day was added. In addition, Reagan and Gorbachev ended up spending much more time in private talks than the 15 minutes initially allocated.

But the summit did not produce any surprise announcement of arms agreements.

In a joint communiqué released Nov. 21, Reagan and Gorbachev called their discussions "frank and useful," while acknowledging that "serious differences remain on a number of critical issues." *(Text, p. 36-D)*

On arms control issues, the communiqué called for "early progress" on weapons reduction, "particularly in areas where there is common ground." Two areas were singled out: agreement on a 50 percent reduction in nuclear weapons of the two sides, and a separate agreement on medium-range nuclear missiles in Europe.

The communiqué made no reference to Moscow's demands that an agreement to ban SDI and other space weapons accompany limits on intercontinental and medium-range missiles.

But, in a post-summit news conference, Gorbachev seemed to reaffirm the Soviet position that SDI limits be part of any arms deal.

And three new bilateral initiatives were announced: a study of "nuclear risk reduction centers" to monitor nuclear weapons activity by third parties, including terrorists; discussions of ways to prevent the spread of chemical weapons; and advocacy of international cooperation to develop controlled nuclear fusion as an energy source.

The leaders also promised to continue efforts to: reduce conventional forces in Europe; ban chemical and biological weapons; and institute measures to reduce the fear of a surprise attack in Europe. ∎

Military Construction

Congress trimmed the Pentagon's $10.3 billion budget for construction of military facilities in fiscal 1986 by $1.1 billion.

On Nov. 19, it cleared the military construction authorization bill (S 1042 — PL 99-167); President Reagan signed it on Dec. 3.

Like the House-passed version, the compromise military construction authorization measure approved spending for hundreds of projects, totaling $9.56 billion.

But the House bill had contained a provision that no more than $9.2 billion would be appropriated for the projects authorized by the bill. The conference report made the reduction formal by cutting $360 million across the board. *(Appropriations bill, p. 392)*

In each case, cuts were made on the assumption that construction bids likely would be lower than had been estimated in the Pentagon's facilities budget.

The Senate approved the compromise version of S 1042 by voice vote on Nov. 12. The House followed suit Nov. 19.

Final Provisions

The conference report on the construction authorization measure (H Rept 99-366) was filed Nov. 12.

The bill authorized facilities for deployment of the MX missile ($44.8 million) and B-1 bomber ($206 million). *(MX, p. 119)*

It also included $178 million for facilities in Europe at which ground-launched cruise missiles (GLCMs) were to be deployed and for dependents of the Air Force personnel assigned to that mission. This included $15.9 million for a site in the Netherlands which the House had refused to authorize on grounds that the Dutch had not yet formally agreed to the deployment.

House conferees agreed to authorize the program after the Dutch government approved deployment.

The conferees approved $101 million to improve security around deployment sites in West Germany for the Pershing II missile. But they approved no new budget authority for the project. Of the total, $56 million could be drawn from funds authorized in prior years but not spent. The remaining $45 million could be drawn from funds authorized in the bill that turned out not to be needed for their original purpose, they said.

The conferees authorized $8 million for a plant in Indiana to produce components of a new type of lethal chemical weapon — called a binary munition. *(Nerve gas, p. 140)*

New Navy Bases

The conferees approved funds to begin work on the first two of a network of 15 new Navy bases in the United States.

So far, the Navy had announced plans to base a battleship and several escorts at Staten Island, just north of the Verrazano-Narrows Bridge at the mouth of New York harbor, and an aircraft carrier and its escorts at Everett, Wash., in Puget Sound.

Another battleship group was earmarked for San Francisco, while a third battleship was to be based at Corpus Christi, Texas, with its escorts at several other Gulf Coast ports. But no funds for those projects were requested in fiscal 1986.

The bill included $17.6 million to begin buying land at Everett and $21.5 million to begin work on facilities at Staten Island. An additional $11.7 million was authorized but only if it could be funded with unspent funds otherwise appropriated. The conferees dropped an additional $49.8 million added to the request by the House bill.

However, the companion appropriations measure, HR 3327, appropriated a total of $79 million to begin work on the Staten Island and Everett ports.

The authorization conferees barred use of the money authorized for Everett and Staten Island until 90 days after the Navy had sent Congress a report justifying on military grounds the increase in the number of so-called "home ports."

The panel said it had "serious concerns that at a time when the defense budget is under serious constraints, the Navy is starting a billion dollar construction program."

The provision was added at the behest of Republican Senate conferees John W. Warner, Va., and Strom Thurmond, S.C., whose states were home to two of the largest existing home ports: Norfolk, Va., serving 120 ships, and Charleston, S.C., where 70 were based.

The 90-day waiting period was to expire sometime in February 1986. On Nov. 21, Pentagon spokesman Robert B. Sims said that unless Congress moved to block the New York battleship project before February, the Navy would begin work on it.

The Navy justified the new ports on grounds that its present bases were overcrowded, and would become more so with the Reagan administration's planned expansion of the fleet. In addition to the ships based at the large bases at Norfolk and Charleston, another 120 ships were based in San Diego.

Moreover, the Navy cited military advantages in having battle groups stationed closer to potential trouble spots in the northern Atlantic and Pacific.

Opponents charged that the Navy was spreading its ships around to develop new pork-barrel constituencies for its expanded fleet. And some critics of the administration's nuclear weapons program saw a more subtle political motive in the plan to deploy in New York and San Francisco ships that were equipped to carry nuclear weapons.

The renovated battleships were to carry long-range Tomahawk cruise missiles that could carry either nuclear or conventional warheads. Some of the escorts assigned to the two ships might be able to carry nuclear-tipped anti-submarine rockets. It long had been U.S. government policy neither to confirm nor deny whether nuclear weapons were located at any base — or on any ship.

Anti-nuclear groups, objecting to the location of ships carrying nuclear arms in metropolitan areas, were trying to block the deployments.

Overseas Bases

For the most part, the conferees agreed with the House position to defer funding for selected projects in three foreign countries.

They approved $98 million of $117 million requested for projects in the Philippines, denying funds for an aircraft maintenance hangar. *(Philippines, p. 113)*

Also rejected was a $21 million project to expand the airplane parking ramp at Howard Air Force Base in Panama.

Of $19.2 million requested for projects at three sites in Spain, the committee approved only $2.9 million for one project: an emergency hospital. The conferees noted that the Spanish government was pressing for a reduction in the 12,500 U.S. military personnel stationed in that country.

Incremental Funding

Contrary to their usual practice, the conferees agreed to authorize funds for three large projects piece by piece. They authorized the projects in sections, thus reducing their budgetary impact in any one year.

As a rule, Congress insisted on "full funding" of construction projects and weapons purchases: authorizing and appropriating in a single year the entire cost of a construction project or a ship or a group of fighter planes.

The three facilities funded incrementally were:

- An Army hospital at Fort Lewis, near Tacoma, Wash. The conferees approved $26 million of the $338 million total that had been authorized in the fiscal 1986 construction bill.
- An Army depot at New Cumberland, Pa. Of the $88 million authorized overall, the conferees said $15 million could be appropriated in fiscal 1986.

Military Construction

Following are the amounts requested by the administration and authorized by S 1042 for military construction projects in fiscal 1986. *(Dollar amounts are in thousands.)*

	Administration Request	Final Authorization
Army	$3,649,674	$3,312,803
Navy	2,886,249	2,408,184
Air Force	2,917,048	2,700,991
Defense Agencies	329,900	258,598
NATO Infrastructure	98,000	38,000
Reserves and National Guard	428,600	481,251
TOTAL	**$ 10,309,471**	**$ 9,199,827**

- A research facility for the National Security Agency — the Pentagon's super-secret code-breaking arm — at Fort Meade, Md., south of Baltimore. The panel authorized a total of $75,064,000 of which $21,364,000 could be appropriated in fiscal 1986.

Committee Reports

The Senate and House Armed Services committees were nearly $750 million apart in their recommendations for the Pentagon's construction budget.

The House Armed Services Committee approved an authorization of $9.55 billion in its military construction measure (HR 1409) reported May 15 (H Rept 99 128).

As in the past, the Senate Armed Services Committee incorporated its version of the construction authorization into the overall military authorization bill (S 1160) reported May 16.

The Senate bill included $8.81 billion in new construction authorization. An earlier version of the bill (S 1029 — S Rept 99-41), reported April 29, recommended $9.16 billion for military construction.

The committee's two-step drafting process stemmed from a May 10 Senate vote to allow a defense increase only large enough to cover inflation. *(Budget, p. 441; authorization bill, p. 138)*

In finding $10 billion more in cuts to meet that target, the panel pared an additional $346 million from military construction, and the overall bill was redrafted as S 1160.

Senate Budget Assumptions

Both panels assumed that hundreds of millions of dollars could be trimmed from the budget without hindering construction. But the Senate panel claimed a far larger amount could be found in such "free" cuts.

Of the $1.5 billion trimmed by the Senate Armed Services Committee in its final version of the bill, some $700 million came from what the panel treated as bookkeeping adjustments that would not slow down any construction projects. The largest component of this amount — $433 million — was money the Senate panel insisted had become superfluous because of economic factors:

- $106 million left over from Army construction projects funded earlier that had cost less than anticipated.
- $237 million that could safely be trimmed on the as-

sumption that bidding for construction would run below budgeted amounts, as in recent years.

- $90 million cut from projects overseas on grounds that the dollar's increasing strength against foreign currencies would reduce the U.S. cost of construction abroad.

The Senate committee pared an additional $139 million because of a provision in its bill exempting Pentagon construction projects from the Davis-Bacon Act. Davis-Bacon required construction workers on federal projects to be paid the "locally prevailing wage" for their skills.

Conservatives complained that the Davis-Bacon rule was being interpreted in a way that sometimes mandated urban pay scales on distant rural sites.

The committee provision directed the Pentagon to use a different formula, tying wages on federal projects to the wages paid to similar types of workers on similar types of projects in the same local jurisdiction.

But the committee's provision drew intense criticism from organized labor.

An additional $139.6 million was cut from two projects when the Senate panel decided to fund them incrementally. As a general rule, Congress required that major Pentagon construction projects, like major weapons, be "fully funded" in the first fiscal year in which money would be spent.

The Senate panel exempted the two projects from that norm, approving in each fiscal year only amounts to cover work to be completed in that year. The two projects were:

- A $125.6 million drydock for 560-foot-long Trident missile-launching submarines in Kings Bay, Ga. The committee authorized $40 million for the project in fiscal 1986; $278.5 million more requested for other Trident projects at Kings Bay was approved.
- A $75 million engineering building at Fort Meade, Md., for the super-secret National Security Agency, which monitored electronic communications. For fiscal 1986, the committee approved $21.4 million.

These kinds of seemingly painless adjustments accounted for all but a small amount of the trims made by the Senate committee in military construction the second time around.

New reductions included $210 million for past and anticipated contract savings and currency fluctuations, the $139 million in savings associated with the Davis-Bacon waiver and the $85.6 million trimmed from the Kings Bay drydock.

The committee found enough bookkeeping reductions to claim more than a third of a billion dollars in additional construction savings in its second bill. At the same time, it restored $71.5 million for B-1 bomber facilities that had been requested but dropped from the first bill.

House Budget Assumptions

By contrast with its Senate counterpart, House Armed Services cut only $80 million from the construction request on grounds of anticipated savings and currency revaluation.

The panel claimed that $82.5 million more in unspent funds was available from earlier Army construction budgets, but it earmarked that money for a project that had not been requested: purchase of land near Fort Drum in northern New York, to house a newly organized Army division.

The House committee cut $158.6 million from two projects that it said could be funded incrementally:

- The Trident drydock at Kings Bay, from which $85.6 million was trimmed for fiscal 1986, a cut identical to that in the Senate bill.
- A supply facility at the New Cumberland, Pa., Army depot. For fiscal 1986, the committee approved $15 million of the $88 million requested.

The House committee denied all funds for the NSA building at Fort Meade, citing budgetary limits.

Base Closings

A centerpiece of the Senate bill was a provision that would allow the secretary of defense to close any military base after giving Congress 60 days' notice, whenever the federal government was running a deficit.

This would let the Pentagon bypass more extensive reporting requirements, including environmental impact statements. Congress established the requirements in the late 1970s so it could keep a hand in the politically volatile issue of base closings. *(1977 Almanac p. 342; 1976 Almanac p. 311)*

S 1160 also included $1 billion, not requested in the budget, to pay for the initial costs associated with any base closings or consolidations. But this amount was not included in the construction section of the bill.

Senate committee Chairman Barry Goldwater, R-Ariz., placed great stock in closing under-utilized military bases as a way to trim Pentagon operating costs. On March 25, Defense Secretary Caspar W. Weinberger submitted to Goldwater an "illustrative" list of 22 bases that would be considered as candidates for closing because of relatively light use or other reasons. One was McConnell Air Force Base, a bomber base in the home state of Majority Leader Robert Dole, R-Kan.

In its report on the first version of its bill, the Senate panel insisted that it did not intend for its action to be taken as a sign of support for any base closure. However, of $211 million requested for facilities to house the new B-1 bomber at four bases, the committee approved all but the $71.5 million earmarked for McConnell.

When the committee produced its revised bill, it included $71.5 million for B-1 basing at an undecided location. Republicans indignantly denied Democratic innuendoes that Dole had anything to do with the restoration of the $71.5 million.

On the other hand, the House committee complained that Weinberger's "illustrative" list had taken on a political life of its own and ordered the secretary to continue abiding by existing base closing procedures.

New Facilities

The two committees differed over proposals to expand existing posts and open new ones.

To house a newly formed infantry division, the Army planned extensive construction over several years at Fort Drum. Located at the northern tip of New York, Fort Drum had been used principally as a training site.

The only funding request for the post in the budget — $67.5 million for 800 family housing units — was approved by the House panel, which also earmarked $82.5 million saved from earlier budgets to enlarge the base.

The Senate panel rejected the housing request, citing only budgetary limits.

The House Armed Services panel also seemed more supportive of Navy plans for two new home ports for combat fleets, which it said eventually would cost a total of $750 million. One of the new sites was at Everett, Wash., at the north end of Puget Sound, for an aircraft carrier and its escorts; the other was at Staten Island, in New York Bay, for a battleship and supporting vessels.

Both committees approved the $17.6 million requested to buy land at Everett, and the Senate panel approved $18.6 million for dredging and initial work at the Staten Island site.

The House committee increased the authorization for Staten Island to $86.3 million, arguing that more rapid construction was needed to meet the scheduled docking of the battleship at the site by 1988. This did not include $15 million for work the committee said would be performed by the New York/New Jersey Port Authority.

The Senate panel barred expenditure of the Everett and Staten Island funds until 90 days after the Pentagon had justified the projects to Congress on military and economic grounds.

Dealing With Allies

The House committee cut $62.4 million from the request for three overseas construction projects because of political complications with host governments. The cuts included:

- $22.7 million for facilities at a Netherlands air base for ground-launched cruise missiles.

Despite strong domestic opposition to the long-range nuclear missiles, the Dutch government had decided tentatively to accept their deployment, with a final decision in November 1985. The House panel wanted to hold up the authorization until the decision was final. The Senate committee authorized $16 million with no strings attached and another $4 million contingent on final Dutch approval.

- $19.2 million earmarked for air and naval bases in Spain. The House committee noted that the existing treaty governing U.S. base rights would expire in 1988 and the Spanish government had called for reducing the number of U.S. forces in the country. The Senate approved the Spanish base requests.
- $20.5 million for airplane parking ramps and roads at an airport terminal in Keflavik, Iceland. The terminal was funded by the United States and Iceland. The committee insisted that these facilities, too, be jointly funded. The Senate approved the request.

California Water Project

Both panels also dropped from the bill $148 million for the Pentagon's share of the Santa Margarita water project, near the Marine Corps base at Camp Pendleton, Calif.

The Senate committee reiterated the stand taken by the congressional defense committees in 1984: It endorsed the project but refused to authorize funds because the Pentagon and the local water district had not agreed on its scope and because the congressional Public Works committees had not yet authorized its construction.

Floor Action

The Senate's version of the military construction measure was debated as part of S 1160, the defense authorization bill, which was passed June 5.

In a blow to organized labor, the Senate June 4 backed exemption of most military construction projects from wage standards set in the 54-year-old Davis-Bacon Act.

The Senate rejected, 49-49, an amendment to restore the full force of Davis-Bacon, which required that construction workers on federal projects be paid the prevailing local wage. *(Vote 97, p. 22-S)*

Davis-Bacon applied to all federal construction contracts of more than $2,000. The Senate tie vote preserved a provision authored by Phil Gramm, R-Texas, that would have raised the threshold to $1 million for military construction work.

That increase would exempt from Davis-Bacon requirements more than 90 percent of all Pentagon construction projects, which accounted for about 40 percent of the dollars awarded for defense construction.

The Gramm proposal also included a revised formula for determining how wage rates and job classifications would be set for projects covered by Davis-Bacon.

The changes, largely reflecting revised regulations put in place by the Reagan administration, were intended to respond to complaints that the Davis-Bacon rules in the past had artificially inflated wage standards and forced payment of union wages in localities that were not heavily unionized.

Gramm described the vote as a sign of support for "economy and efficiency" in federal contracting.

Edward M. Kennedy, D-Mass., sponsor of the amendment to strike the proposed Davis-Bacon changes, contended that waiving prevailing wage standards would undermine the quality of military construction. Work would suffer, he argued, because the wage change would invite contractors to hire workers at substandard wages.

Base closings. Earlier, during debate May 24, the Senate rejected two amendments that would have changed the Armed Services Committee's provision on base closings.

The panel's bill would have allowed the secretary of defense to close any military base after giving Congress 60 days' notice, whenever the federal government was running a deficit.

This was to allow the Pentagon to bypass more extensive reporting, including environmental impact statements.

The amendments rejected were:

- By Dale Bumpers, D-Ark., deleting the provision entirely, and restoring the current reporting requirements. Rejected 41-58. *(Vote 91, p. 20-S)*
- By Jeff Bingaman, D-N.M., restoring some of existing controls, with limits. Rejected 48-48. *(Vote 92, p. 20-S)*

House Passage

On Oct. 16, the House passed HR 1409, its version of the construction bill, setting a ceiling of $9.2 billion on military construction funding for fiscal 1986. The vote was 354-38. *(Vote 325, p. 102-H)*

By voice vote, the House adopted an amendment by Ronald V. Dellums, D-Calif., that provided that not more than $9.2 billion would be appropriated even though the amount authorized by the bill was $9.55 billion. The floor amendment made no reductions in the amounts authorized for specific programs.

The lower figure had been agreed to informally by members of the Senate and House Armed Services committees during the July conference on S 1160, the main defense bill.

Conferees' Agreements

House-Senate conferees on S 1160 also settled some other military construction-related issues:

- They dropped a Senate provision that would have sharply narrowed the application to military construction projects of the Davis-Bacon Act.

- And they greatly simplified the political hurdles the Pentagon had to go through to close a major installation. The new procedure required notification of Congress only when a decision had been made to close a facility, after which no irrevocable action could be taken for at least two months. Under previous law, Congress had to be notified when a facility became a "candidate" for closure, ensuring time for local interests to fight the move.

The provision also repealed a requirement that any major base closure be accompanied by a full-scale environmental impact statement.

After the House passed its separate military construction bill in October, the House asked for a conference Oct. 16. The Senate agreed to a conference Nov. 1. The conference report (H Rept 99-366) was filed Nov. 12 and agreed to by the Senate on that date. The House agreed on Nov. 19. The report authorized $9.2 billion of Reagan's $10.3 billion request for military construction authorizations. ∎

ENVIRONMENT/ENERGY

CQ

Environment/Energy

The year 1985 was one of measured progress but few final results in energy and environmental legislation.

Fiscal issues pushed aside or dominated energy and environmental legislation. Because legislation begun in 1985 would not "die" with congressional inaction until 1986, and because few bills needed to reach final enactment, few bills did.

Long-smoldering debates over fundamental policy choices — such as resource development vs. environmental protection — continued without much resolution.

Still, Congress advanced legislation aimed at resolving a number of those policy disputes further than in years previously.

Synfuels Program Abolished

One of the few major energy decisions to be made by Congress in 1985 — the abolition of the U.S. Synthetic Fuels Corporation (SFC) — represented the climate on Capitol Hill in several ways.

For one thing, the rescission of some $7.3 billion in unspent funds from the agency reflected the deficit-reduction pressures that preoccupied Congress all year — sometimes pushing energy and environmental legislation aside and sometimes providing a vehicle for it.

For another, the SFC's abolition reflected the easing of concerns over an "energy crisis" that dominated the public agenda through much of the 1970s. Established in 1980 to produce substitutes for oil and gas from abundant natural resources such as coal and shale, the synfuels program was undercut by rising supplies of oil and gas and the resulting falling prices. Diehard supporters of the program, such as James A. McClure, R-Idaho, chairman of the Senate Energy and Natural Resources Committee, warned that the apparent brightening of the energy outlook was only temporary, and that the nation was leaving itself unprepared for future shortages.

Another reflection of easing congressional concerns over the energy crisis, and rising concerns over the budget, was the fact that Congress appropriated no fiscal 1986 funds to buy oil for the Strategic Petroleum Reserve. Carry-over funds from 1985, sufficient to fill the reserve to 500 million barrels, were deemed enough.

It was the large budget-related bills, such as the budget resolution, the budget reconciliation bill and the final fiscal 1986 continuing appropriations resolution, that became the vehicles for the energy policy issues Congress was trying to settle in 1985.

Both the synfuels rescission and the zero funding for the Strategic Petroleum Reserve were enacted as part of the continuing resolution, for example.

Partly as a result of these forces, the year in Congress largely lacked the bitter quarreling over how fast to develop energy resources that had been common since President Reagan took office.

Low-Level Radioactive Wastes

Perhaps the only other major piece of energy legislation to be enacted was a bill forcing states to take responsibility for their own low-level radioactive wastes.

The legislation cleared Congress in response to a perceived near-term crisis. The governors of the three states currently accepting all of the nation's low-level waste — South Carolina, Washington and Nevada — had threatened to bar outside wastes unless Congress acted by the end of the year.

Offshore Leasing: Pursuit of Consensus

Congress in 1985 confirmed Donald P. Hodel as interior secretary and John S. Herrington as energy secretary, and with those appointments Reagan continued the courtship of consensus on energy policy he began after the 1983 downfall of former Interior Secretary James G. Watt.

One of the major projects Hodel set himself as interior secretary was to build a consensus on offshore oil and gas leasing that had eluded the contentious Watt. Congress for the previous four years had banned federal offshore leasing in some areas as a way of showing its unhappiness with the rapid energy development sought by Watt and the administration.

By 1985, however, with changes in oil and gas markets, and with prospects for offshore reserves looking much less promising than a few years earlier, the offshore drilling debate was losing steam. The main bone of contention left was the fate of areas off the coast of California, where petroleum prospects looked good, and where environmental sensitivities were especially high.

Hodel ambitiously tried to bring the large, diverse and argumentative California congressional delegation together around an offshore drilling compromise — and almost succeeded. But a tentative agreement that was dramatically announced during the summer eventually fell apart. No California leasing ban was included in the 1986 interior appropriations bill — but the Interior Department had no lease sales scheduled during the period anyway. Congress did urge the parties to keep talking.

It was an inconclusive and anticlimactic end to a year that lacked much of a crisis.

'Superfund' Bill Snags; Others Proceed Smoothly

Congress made significant strides toward enacting bills renewing several of the nation's key environmental laws, but did not complete final action in 1985.

Reauthorizations of the Clean Water Act (which controls pollution of lakes and streams) and the Safe Drinking Water Act (which regulates the purity of water at the tap) passed both chambers of Congress. No conference committee on either bill was convened before adjournment, however.

A renewal of the Endangered Species Act passed the

House and was reported out of committee in the Senate.

In most cases, delay of enactment threatened no crisis.

The one exception, where the ticking of the legislative clock threatened serious consequences, was legislation to renew and expand the "superfund" hazardous-waste cleanup program. Funding for that program, totaling $1.6 billion during 1981-85, started drying up Sept. 30.

There was little argument in Congress over whether the cleanup program should be renewed for another five years; in fact, there was consensus that it should be expanded. Superfund legislation passed both houses, but disagreement over who should pay the increased costs of the program kept it from being enacted during the year.

It was in some ways the very intensity of congressional interest in superfund issues that delayed the legislation. All told, eight committees in the House and three in the Senate were formally or informally involved in trying to shape the bill during the year. That meant not only a procedural morass, but jurisdictional wrangling — most notably between the leaders of the House Energy and Commerce Committtee and those of the Public Works and Transportation Committee.

When the tax on petroleum and raw chemicals that fed the superfund expired Sept. 30, some funds were still left in the program's accounts. Although a freeze on new funding commitments was in effect during the fall, ongoing cleanups continued to eat away at what was left. And by the end of the year, the prospect of a halt to ongoing cleanups had begun to loom.

The hottest and most divisive superfund debates came over who would pay the extra taxes needed to boost program levels as high as $10 billion for 1986-90. The House approach, favored by Ways and Means Committee Chairman Dan Rostenkowski, D-Ill., would have taken the money from oil and chemical companies. The Senate alternative, defended by Finance Committee Chairman Bob Packwood, R-Ore., would have spread the burden over a broad base of U.S. businesses through a small new tax that critics denounced as a "value-added tax."

That issue tied Congress in knots when Packwood insisted on attaching his broad-based superfund tax to the budget reconciliation bill during the final weeks of the session. The Senate's repeated insistence on the broad tax, and the House's repeated rejection of it, was enough to derail the reconciliation bill for the year.

Water Pollution and Purity

The conflicts that stalled the pollution-control and drinking-water bills were less intense than those over superfund. In fact, preoccupation with superfund was a major reason why committee leaders did not push to finish those other bills.

Although the Senate passed a Clean Water Act reauthorization in June and the House passed one in July, no conference was held to resolve differences. One major conflict was over how to divide about $20 billion in sewage-plant construction funding among the various states — with the House backing the existing system and the Senate supporting a revised formula that advocates called fairer to Southern and Western states.

Discharges of inadequately treated municipal sewage into lakes and rivers had for decades been a significant source of pollution. But budget-cutters in the Reagan administration saw the sewage plant construction program as wasteful largess, and even environmentalists warned that some of the funds had been used to promote new residential growth in local areas.

Both chambers, by the bills they passed, declared their intention to keep spending significant amounts of federal money through 1994 to help local government build sewers and sewage treatment plants. Both, in effect, rejected the Reagan administration's call, in its 1986 budget, for a quick end to the program.

The administration said it would veto a clean water bill with unacceptably high sewer spending, pointing specifically to the $21 billion in the House bill. But Congress never tested that threat by sending the president a bill.

Congress poised itself for another showdown with the Reagan administration over the Safe Drinking Water Act — which authorized the Environmental Protection Agency (EPA) to set health-based standards for the purity of drinking water delivered to homes by utilities. The standards were enforced by the states.

For years after the act was first passed in 1974, environmentalists had criticized EPA for moving too slowly and for setting standards for too few contaminants. The Reagan administration slowed standard-setting even further. Reagan gave policy control of environmental regulation to his Office of Management and Budget (OMB), and former OMB Director David A. Stockman had let it be known that he did not think the federal government should be regulating drinking water at all.

But the Senate in May and the House in June passed bills that would force EPA to set standards for scores of new contaminants within a certain time. EPA officials who helped draft the legislation said OMB had overruled them — and OMB had indeed made its own feelings clear by threatening a presidential veto.

Both bills also contained new initiatives for the protection of the underground water, tapped by wells, which supplied drinking water for about half of the nation's population. The House bill contained stronger groundwater provisions, notably a requirement that states draw up plans for protecting underground drinking water sources from contamination. EPA would have to approve the plans.

Any expansion of federal authority over groundwater, however, met with objections from the Western states as well as Reagan's deregulatory team. Those arid states, where water is so important to economic survival, jealously guarded their existing legal authorities to determine water rights. The Senate, where Western states held greater sway than in the House, left the mandatory state groundwater planning provision out of its bill.

No conference met on the drinking water bill in 1985, however, and the issue was not settled.

—*By Joseph A. Davis*

House, Senate Pass Superfund Authorization

Both the House and the Senate approved legislation (HR 2005) in 1985 to extend and expand the "superfund" program for the cleanup of abandoned hazardous-waste dumps, but they ran out of time to reconcile the two measures as the year ended.

Despite passage by both chambers, the legislation still faced stiff challenges to final enactment in the second session. The Senate had authorized a five-year, $7.5 billion program financed in large part by a new broad-based business tax, while the House version provided more than $10 billion over the same time period, mostly through higher taxes on oil and chemical companies.

The two versions also differed significantly in their provisions for cleanup standards and schedules.

The business tax in the Senate bill became the focus of an end-of-the-session effort by Senate supporters to push for its enactment through a package of spending cuts and tax increases (HR 3128) intended to reduce the deficit by $74 billion over three years.

But stiff House opposition to the tax proposal — which opponents were denouncing as a "value-added tax" — prevented its passage. Disagreement on the issue also stymied the efforts of Congress to enact the deficit-reduction bill itself. *(Deficit-reduction bill, p. 498)*

President Reagan had proposed a smaller superfund program of $4.5 billion-$5.3 billion over fiscal 1986-90. The president also was opposed to the proposed financing in both the Senate and House bills.

The taxing authority for the existing program expired Sept. 30, 1985, causing the Environmental Protection Agency (EPA) to slow action on cleanups to conserve $130 million remaining in the fund at that time. The House Oct. 1 by voice vote approved a bill (HR 3453) providing a 45-day extension of the taxing authority, but the Senate refused to act on a temporary renewal.

The Senate Sept. 26 by an 86-13 vote passed its five-year, $7.5 billion reauthorization. Because all revenue bills must originate in the House, the Senate attached its reauthorization measure to a minor House-passed bill (HR 2005) dealing with Social Security. *(Vote 196, p. 38-S)*

The House version (HR 2817), authorizing $10 billion over the same five-year period, was passed Dec. 10 on a 391-33 vote. *(Vote 409, p. 128-H)*

Debate during House and Senate consideration of the legislation was marked by controversy and close votes. Environmentalists, oil and chemical companies and business in general had strong interests at stake in the outcome of battles over the taxing provisions to finance the expanded program and other issues such as community "right-to-know" about chemical emissions that could cause cancer or birth defects and the right of citizens to sue dumpers for damages and injuries they believed were caused by hazardous substances.

Background

A $1.6 billion superfund was created in 1980 with the passage of the Comprehensive Environmental Response, Compensation and Liability Act (PL 96-510). The bulk of the revenues for the program, $1.14 billion, came from a tax on sales of petroleum and chemical raw materials (feedstocks). *(Congress and the Nation Vol. V, p. 583)*

The superfund was created to deal with abandoned dump sites where no one was willing to take responsibility for cleanups. The law allowed EPA to go after whoever caused the problem — generators or transporters of waste, owners or operators of dumps. If owners and dumpers did not cooperate, EPA could do the cleanup itself, and then sue them later for up to three times the actual costs. If EPA could not recover the cleanup costs, it paid them directly out of the superfund.

The House passed a $10.2 billion superfund program in August 1984. The Senate Environment and Public Works Committee approved its own $7.5 billion measure, but that bill was referred to the Finance Committee, which did not act on it that year.

Although Reagan had initially opposed reauthorization of the superfund program, he changed his position in 1984 and voiced support for an extension in his State of the Union address that year. *(1984 Almanac p. 309)*

The administration proposal was not unveiled, however, until February 1985 when Reagan sent Congress a $5.3 billion reauthorization proposal.

While EPA estimated that there were about 2,000 dangerous waste sites that required cleanup, a May 1985 report by the Office of Technology Assessment put the number closer to 10,000 sites.

Senate Committee Action

Environment and Public Works Committee

The Senate Environment and Public Works Committee March 1 approved its superfund measure on a 14-1 vote. The bill was reported March 7 (S 51 — S Rept 99-11).

The committee adopted by voice vote an amendment setting up a small experimental program of medical aid to victims of toxic incidents. The demonstration program, proposed by George J. Mitchell, D-Maine, set aside $30 million annually for a five-year program in five to 10 geographic areas chosen by EPA.

The committee adopted two amendments offered by Frank R. Lautenberg, D-N.J., in response to the 1984 Bhopal, India, disaster in which some 2,000 people were killed by toxic releases. One required firms to notify a federal hotline of toxic spills immediately and imposed penalties for failure to do so. The other required EPA to set up a national inventory, available to the public, of facilities using, storing or releasing substances deemed hazardous under the superfund law, if they stored more than 6,000 kilograms of even diluted forms of substances that could escape.

Another amendment, offered by Gary Hart, D-Colo., and adopted by the committee, brought the Defense Department and other federal agencies explicitly under the superfund law for the first time. Military toxic-waste dumps made up a major share of the nation's worst sites.

A proposal by Max Baucus, D-Mont., adopted 9-3, allowed affected citizens to sue EPA to force it to perform non-discretionary duties under the law. A similar provision survived efforts in 1984 to remove it from the House bill.

Finance Committee

The Senate Finance Committee May 23, by a 19-1 vote, reported a package of nearly $7.5 billion in revenues to pay for superfund cleanups (S Rept 99-73). Steven D. Symms, R-Idaho, cast the only "nay."

To raise the funds, the committee relied mainly on a new broad-based business tax. A tax of .08 percent was to be levied on the sales price of manufactured and raw goods. The tax was to apply to import sales, but not exports and unprocessed agricultural, food and timber products. Manufacturers but not producers would also receive a credit of .08 percent of their direct costs in producing such goods, so that the tax would actually be imposed on the difference between the cost of producing and selling a product.

The measure that emerged from Finance was based on a bill (S 957) introduced by Malcolm Wallop, R-Wyo., and Lloyd Bentsen, D-Texas. As introduced, that version contained only the new broad-based business tax. The committee by a 17-2 vote adopted as a working text a more comprehensive package that also included current funding levels from general revenues and a tax on feedstocks. Sens. William L. Armstrong, R-Colo., and Robert Dole, R-Kan., dissented.

The Environment Committee had authorized $1.03 billion in general revenues for the superfund over five years. Finance struck that funding because it was seeking to block the proposed demonstration program of compensation for victims of toxic-waste poisoning.

That demonstration program had been authorized by the Environment Committee with the proviso that all $150 million earmarked for it over five years come from general revenues.

William V. Roth Jr., R-Del., moved to delete the general revenue funding, and his motion was adopted 11-9 by the Finance Committee.

Judiciary Committee

S 51 was referred on May 24 to the Judiciary Committee, which had until June 14 to act on it. Although Judiciary did not complete work by the deadline, Chairman Strom Thurmond, R-S.C., Environment Committee Chairman Robert T. Stafford, R-Vt., EPA and the Justice Department later agreed on two amendments to be brought to the floor. One blocked legal challenges to EPA cleanup plans until after they were carried out. A second allowed the courts to decide when the suit would be heard.

Senate Floor Action

After five days of debate, the Senate Sept. 26 overwhelmingly passed HR 2005.

The 86-13 vote on final passage masked several deep divisions among senators over specific provisions of the bill — particularly the new broad-based business tax to provide the bulk of the funds for the program. *(Vote 196, p. 38-S)*

The Reagan administration objected to the tax and officials from the Office of Management and Budget in a Sept. 17 letter threatened a presidential veto.

The bill's managers defused a fight over the tax by accepting an unusual "sense of the Senate" amendment, offered by Jesse Helms, R-N.C., opposing the use of the business tax, which opponents were calling a value-added tax.

While it left intact the tax language in the bill, the Helms amendment called for a future House-Senate conference on the program "to report legislation containing a reliable financing mechanism for the superfund program which does not contain the value-added tax."

The Senate rejected, by a 46-48 vote, an amendment by James Abdnor, R-S.D., to exempt fertilizer, animal feed and raw material used to produce them from the superfund excise tax. *(Vote 194, p. 38-S)*

Efforts to lower the bill's funding level failed when the Senate by a 15-79 vote rejected an amendment by Steven D. Symms, R-Idaho, to reduce funding for the program to $5.7 billion. *(Vote 192, p. 38-S)*

Other Amendments

The Senate Sept. 23 adopted by voice vote an amendment offered by Pete V. Domenici, R-N.M., that:

- Authorized EPA, at hazardous-waste sites for which multiple dumpers were responsible, to use superfund money to pay for that portion of cleanup costs attributable to parties it formally determined to be unknown, insolvent or unavailable.
- Authorized EPA and the Justice Department to accept or reject good-faith settlement offers for small amounts of cleanup costs from parties potentially liable for such costs.
- Authorized the federal government to provide releases from future liability to parties who were in full compliance with an administrative cleanup order or consent decree.
- Established a detailed set of procedures for promoting voluntary settlements before the government sued a private party for cleanup.

On Sept. 24, the Senate struck from the bill, on a 49-45 vote, the victim assistance demonstration program that had been adopted by the Environment Committee. The amendment to strike was offered by William V. Roth Jr., R-Del. *(Vote 193, p. 38-S)*

Roth and his allies objected that individual victims would not have to prove that their ailments were specifically caused by a certain toxic release.

In other actions, the Senate:

- Adopted by voice vote an amendment sponsored by Stafford and Lloyd Bentsen, D-Texas, exempting state and local governments from cleanup liability in cases where title or control of a polluting facility had shifted to them because of abandonment, bankruptcy, tax delinquency or similar causes.
- Adopted by voice vote an amendment sponsored by Stafford and Bentsen allowing companies that handled hazardous wastes to form "risk retention groups" or "purchasing groups" to insure themselves against liability for environmental harm. The amendment allowed them to share liability for potential environmental damages when commercial insurance was not available to them individually for such risks.
- Adopted by voice vote an amendment sponsored by Frank R. Lautenberg, D-N.J., strengthening provisions already in the bill giving communities a "right-to-know" about hazardous chemicals handled in nearby plants and mandating new mechanisms for emergency response to hazardous chemical spills and leaks. The amendment required EPA to develop a list of facilities that handled such substances in potentially dangerous amounts. Governors were required to establish emergency response districts and to appoint emergency response committees formed around such facilities. If accidents occurred, facilities were to notify state and local authorities immediately of the substances released and their health hazards.
- Approved an amendment sponsored by Lautenberg and Mitchell, authorizing EPA explicitly for the first time to conduct research on hazardous indoor air pollution and to report to Congress its findings. EPA had to report within

a year on the extent of indoor pollution from radon, a radioactive gas. It authorized $3 million annually for fiscal 1986-87.

- Adopted by voice vote an amendment sponsored by Stafford and Bentsen to ease the requirements imposed, especially on small businesses, under a hazardous substances inventory provision in the bill.

The committee bill required manufacturers and users of hazardous substances to report on the nature and hazards of those chemicals to federal, state and local officials, health facilities and the public. The amendment limited the requirement to businesses in the manufacturing sector only, and only those manufacturing or processing more than 200,000 pounds per year or using more than 2,000 pounds per year.

Major Senate Provisions

As amended and passed by the Senate, HR 2005:

- Required EPA to update within 12 months of enactment of the bill the National Contingency Plan, the main regulatory mechanism by which EPA conducted the cleanup program. EPA was required to revise the Hazard Ranking System (by which it selected sites eligible for permanent cleanup funds) to assure that the system reflected the relative risk to human health and the environment presented by candidate sites.
- Gave EPA leeway to choose "appropriate" and "cost-effective" cleanup methods, rather than listing detailed legislative cleanup standards. However, the bill directed EPA to consider both short-term and long-term costs and to assure protection of human health and the environment. It instructed EPA to choose permanent solutions, such as waste treatment, over such temporary measures as transferring waste from one site to another.

Taxes

- Extended for fiscal 1986-90 the taxes on petroleum and basic chemicals in current law, imposing them on the same substances at the same rates. The taxes would be suspended if the unobligated balance in the superfund exceeded $2.25 billion at the end of fiscal 1988 or $3 billion at the end of fiscal 1989. The taxes would yield an estimated $1.5 billion.
- Levied a new "superfund excise tax" of .08 percent on the sales price of many manufactured and raw goods expected to raise $5.4 billion. Manufacturers would get a credit of .08 percent of their direct costs in producing such goods. Exempted manufacturers with sales of less than $5 million annually.

Public Safety

- Authorized EPA to use the fund for permanent relocation of residents, businesses and community facilities in contaminated areas when that was the most cost-effective way to protect public health. Also authorized payment of debt service for businesses in such areas during temporary relocation, and unemployment compensation to individuals put out of work by relocation.
- Required EPA to provide household water for purposes such as washing when health concerns required the agency to provide alternative drinking water supplies.

Notification

- Required handlers of hazardous substances to notify state and local emergency officials as soon as they discovered a release of toxic substances. Stiffened penalties for failure to comply with these notification requirements to a maximum criminal penalty of a $50,000 fine and five years' imprisonment, and added a new civil penalty with a maximum of $75,000 for repeat offenders.
- Required facilities handling hazardous substances to prepare an inventory of all toxic substances they handled, to be distributed to federal, state, and local officials, area medical services and area libraries. The inventories had to be updated every two years.
- Required EPA and the states to provide public notice and opportunity for public comment before selecting a particular remedial action at a site or entering into any settlement agreement in action against a private party for cleanup.

State Actions

- Gave states three years to come up with in-state disposal sites or plans guaranteeing enough disposal capacity elsewhere — on pain of losing most superfund cleanup money.
- Extended to five years, instead of one year as in current law, the time during which the pumping and treating of contaminated water was eligible for a 90 percent federal cost share as part of a remedial action. Under current law, states were responsible for 100 percent of long-term operation and maintenance costs.
- Allowed EPA to assess the states for 50 percent or more of cleanup costs only when a state or local government operated a hazardous-waste facility causing contamination. States normally paid 10 percent of cleanup costs, but current law allowed EPA to assess them 50 percent or more if they owned or operated the site.

Liability

- Limited the liability of state and local governments that took non-negligent, "good Samaritan" actions as an emergency response to a toxic spill or leak. Authorized EPA to limit, at its own discretion, the liability of a contractor hired to perform cleanup work.
- Codified current case law affirming the right of dumpers found liable for cleanup costs to seek contribution of a fair share of costs from other responsible parties. Affirmed that liable parties who reached judicially approved settlement agreements with the government were not liable for the contribution claims of other parties.
- Prohibited court challenges to EPA's choice of a cleanup method before EPA went to court to recover cleanup costs from responsible parties.

Federal Agencies

- Stiffened current legal requirements that federal agencies clean up their own hazardous dump sites by setting a partial timetable. Required a preliminary assessment of hazardous federal sites within 18 months of enactment. Required a cleanup study to begin within one year of a site being included on the National Priorities List.
- Required the Interior Department to issue regulations for assessing claims against the superfund for damages to natural resources.

Court Actions

- Provided citizens with a right to sue in federal court to enforce requirements under the act and to seek performance of non-discretionary duties under the act by EPA and other federal agencies. Citizens had to give 90 days' notice to state and federal governments and any alleged violators before bringing a suit. No action could be brought if the state or federal government was diligently prosecuting for the same violation.

- Required the federal government, if it wished to recover the costs of a cleanup, to file court actions within six years after the completion of the cleanup.

Miscellaneous

- Spelled out, more strongly than current law, the authority of EPA or other federal agents to request information on the handling of hazardous substances and to enter premises where they were handled.
- Authorized EPA to allow those potentially responsible for a dump site to conduct the studies on which EPA based its choice of a remedy.
- Set up a detailed, mandatory work schedule for studies of the health effects of exposure to hazardous substances, to be conducted by the Agency for Toxic Substances and Disease Registry of the Department of Health and Human Services. Required the agency to finish health assessments for sites currently on the National Priority List within two years of enactment and for other sites within a year of the time they were added to the list.

House Committee Action

Energy and Commerce Committee

The House Energy and Commerce Committee July 25 approved a $10 billion superfund bill (HR 2817) after six days of bitter debate over whether its provisions strengthened or weakened the program.

HR 2817 was reported Aug. 1 (H Rept 99-253, Part I).

In the 31-10 vote to order the bill reported, all 10 dissenters were Democrats, who thought the bill was too weak. Fourteen Democrats and all 17 committee Republicans voted for the bill.

Opposing the bill was James J. Florio, D-N.J., a principal architect of the existing superfund law, who said the cleanup schedule in the bill would not require any actual cleanup action to begin for six years. He also criticized the committee's rejection of an amendment allowing citizens to sue polluters for cleanup when the government had not acted to abate imminent hazards.

As approved by the subcommittee, the bill set a mandatory schedule for EPA to start pre-cleanup studies, and set a mandatory deadline for most cleanups to begin after those studies were finished. But Florio and Henry A. Waxman, D-Calif., argued that EPA could delay the start of cleanups by delaying the completion of studies — leaving no effective deadline for actual cleanup.

Amendments were offered to set deadlines for study completions. The committee first rejected a schedule requiring 600 actual cleanup starts in five years and then accepted a schedule requiring 540 cleanup starts within six years.

The bitterest disputes were among Democrats on the committee, rather than between Democrats and Republicans. The markup was adjourned abruptly July 17 after a testy confrontation between Energy Chairman John D. Dingell, D-Mich., and Waxman, who chaired the Subcommittee on Health and the Environment.

Dingell headed a coalition of Republicans and oil-state Democrats who pushed their preferred superfund bill through the Subcommittee on Commerce, Transportation and Tourism, chaired by Florio.

Dingell drew support from 16 of the committee's 17 Republicans — and only nine of the panel's 25 Democrats — when he defeated an amendment to put mandatory cleanup deadlines into the bill. When Waxman, one of the losers, asked permission to try again with a compromise amendment, he and Dingell got into a parliamentary confrontation that stopped the meeting for the day.

On July 18, however, a compromise offered by Ron Wyden, D-Ore., prevailed by voice vote.

Merchant Marine and Fisheries

The Merchant Marine Committee Oct. 1 voted 38-1 to approve its package of amendments to HR 2817. The package was reported Oct. 31 (Part IV). A major action by the committee was the adoption of the entire text of HR 1232 (H Rept 99-247, Part I), a comprehensive oil spill liability and cleanup bill reported Aug. 1.

The oil spill legislation set limits on the liability of owners and operators of ships, barges and offshore oil rigs and pipelines. If the parties responsible for a pollution incident could not be found, or the damage exceeded the liability limit, compensation came from a new $200 million Marine Oil Pollution Insurance Fund. The fund was financed with a 1.3-cents-per-barrel premium on oil brought to or refined in the United States.

Similar bills passed by the House in previous years died in the Senate, and committee members said attaching the language to superfund could improve prospects for Senate passage of the oil spill provisions. The House attached a similar bill to superfund legislation in 1984. *(1984 Almanac p. 309)*

The single dissenting vote on the motion to report the bill came from Barbara A. Mikulski, D-Md., who explained that her vote was against the underlying text of HR 2817 as reported by the Energy Committee, which she said lacked adequate cleanup standards and schedules.

Judiciary Committee

The House Judiciary Committee approved its amendments to the superfund bill by voice vote on Oct. 8. The Judiciary amendments were reported Oct. 31 (Part III).

The committee broadened the right of various parties to challenge in court EPA's choice of a cleanup remedy.

The Energy Committee's version had precluded such "pre-enforcement review" of cleanup methods. The Judiciary subcommittee allowed a challenge only in limited circumstances, such as when a company had already agreed to pay cleanup costs. The full committee bill allowed any potentially liable company or local citizens' group to go to court if they alleged that EPA was violating the superfund law.

The Judiciary Committee amendments also gave companies that were liable or potentially liable for cleanup costs the right to sue other dumpers for "contribution" of a share of those costs. Judges would be allowed to decide, under the same rules that governed other civil cases, whether to hear a contribution suit before the main suit. The provision limited, in effect, the ability of original dumpers to use contribution suits to delay action on their own cases.

Another amendment gave federal courts the power to apportion cleanup costs among liable parties. Companies that entered into judicially approved settlements with the federal government would be released from liability for contribution claims from other companies, although the release would apply only to matters addressed in the settlement.

Public Works and Transportation

The House Public Works and Transportation Committee Oct. 10 approved a version of HR 2817 that environmentalists hailed as toughening standards and schedules for hazardous-waste cleanups.

The Public Works bill forced EPA to increase the number of sites on its priorities list and complete work within five years on currently identified sites.

The bill was reported Nov. 12 (Part V).

The absence of public debate or dissent by committee members during the bill's swift passage through the Water Resources Subcommittee Oct. 9 and the full Public Works Committee the next day contrasted with the bitter two-week struggle during the Energy markup.

The Public Works bill was personally assembled by Water Resources Chairman Robert A. Roe, D-N.J., during weeks of private meetings and closed-door caucuses, and offered as a substitute to HR 2817. Committee Republican leaders also supported it.

The bill required EPA to expand the current National Priorities List of 541 sites, to include 1,600 by Jan. 1, 1989. Cleanups would have to be started at no fewer than 150 sites per year beginning Oct. 1, 1987, and finished at all currently listed sites within five years.

The Energy Committee's bill did not specify when cleanups were to be completed. The Energy bill also lacked any requirement as to how many sites should be on the priorities list.

Environmentalists argued that a legally enforceable schedule was needed to prevent a repeat of alleged foot-dragging by the EPA in carrying out the program during 1981-83. The Reagan administration and EPA, however, opposed mandatory schedules, saying that without flexibility the agency might be forced into hasty actions.

Ways and Means Committee

Defying its chairman and President Reagan, the House Ways and Means Committee Oct. 17 approved a new business tax similar to the one adopted by the Senate in its version of the superfund legislation.

The committee ratified the decision by voice vote on Oct. 23 and formally reported the package Oct. 28 (H Rept 99-253, Part II). But committee members also voted to seek a rule allowing two floor challenges — one by Thomas J. Downey, D-N.Y., which provided the bulk of the program funds through increased taxes on oil and chemical companies, and another by John J. Duncan, R-Tenn., ranking member of the committee. The Duncan proposal provided for doubling the tax on oil and chemical companies, increasing general revenues and levying a surcharge on a broad range of companies if the program needed additional revenues to reach the $10 billion level.

Earlier in the Ways and Means markup, Chairman Dan Rostenkowski, D-Ill., had commanded barely enough votes to block the broad-based tax. But no alternatives commanded greater support in the committee. Facing pressures to move a bill and avoid delays in the cleanup program, Democrats in caucus agreed to report the version with the broad-based tax and allow opponents to challenge it on the floor.

As ordered reported by voice vote, the Ways and Means package included $4.5 billion from the broad-based tax, $1.5 billion from an increase in the current tax on chemical raw materials, $1 billion from an increase in the current tax on raw petroleum, $1.5 billion from a new tax on hazardous waste going to disposal facilities, $180 million from general revenues, and $500 million from interest and government suits against dumpers to recover cleanup costs — all cumulatively over the five years.

Also included in the total was $850 million from a new tax on gasoline to be used for a separate fund to clean up leaks from underground storage tanks, such as those at gasoline stations. The tax would translate into one-fifth of 1 cent per gallon at the pump.

The bulk of the approved funding package was contained in an amendment offered by Wyche Fowler Jr., D-Ga., approved on an 18-17 vote. But when it came time to report the product of the markup session, Rostenkowski pulled out of his pocket the proxies he needed to defeat by a vote of 16-20 a motion to report the bill. Only after some two hours of party caucusing did the committee reconvene and order the bill reported with no further changes.

The House bill exempted businesses with sales under $10 million annually, while the Senate put the cutoff at $5 million a year.

Like the Senate bill, the House bill exempted food products, unprocessed agricultural or fishery products and unprocessed timber. Unlike the Senate bill, it also exempted fertilizer products.

House Floor Action

The House Dec. 10 by a vote of 391-33 passed HR 2817 after voting to collect much of the added cost of the $10 billion program from increasing taxes on oil and chemical companies. *(Vote 409, p. 128-H)*

The measure had been stalled for almost two months because of disagreements between the chairmen of the Energy and Public Works committees over the versions of the bills reported by their respective committees.

A compromise was reached Dec. 3 and embodied in a new bill (HR 3852), introduced Dec. 4 by Majority Leader Jim Wright, D-Texas, with Minority Leader Robert H. Michel, R-Ill., as cosponsor. The text of the compromise bill was substituted for the text of HR 2817 as floor action began. After passing HR 2817, the House substituted the text for that of the Senate-passed bill, HR 2005.

The compromise bill was viewed as a victory for environmentalists since it contained stiffer requirements for cleanup schedules and standards than under existing law and community "right-to-know" provisions requiring companies to notify local officials about hazardous chemicals in the area. The compromise also included new comprehensive programs for cleanup of hazardous-waste dumps at federal facilities, leaking underground storage tanks and offshore oil spills. Each of these programs would have its own smaller fund similar to the larger superfund program.

Tax Decision

The key vote on the tax issue was on Downey's proposal, which was adopted by the House on a 220-206 vote. The vote was a victory for general manufacturers and service industries who opposed a broad-based tax. *(Vote 406, p. 128-H)*

The first vote was on the proposal by Duncan, which would have provided $1.1 billion from petroleum, $1.5 billion from chemicals, at least $1.1 billion from a tax on hazardous-waste disposal, $2.3 billion from general revenues and about $1.5 billion from miscellaneous sources. The amendment also would have imposed a different kind of broad-based tax on businesses, styled as a "surcharge," yielding up to $2.3 billion, if the Treasury secretary found the program required additional funds.

Duncan's proposal failed 74-349. *(Vote 405, p. 128-H)*

It drew no support from the Reagan administration or the oil and chemical industries, although scattered members from petrochemical states supported it. Fiscal conservatives, mostly Republicans, provided much of its support. The next vote was on the Downey amendment, which proposed financing the superfund program by raising $5.2 billion from increased taxes on petroleum and chemicals, $2 billion from a tax on hazardous-waste disposal, $1.6 billion from general revenues and the rest from other sources.

If both the Downey and Duncan amendments had failed, the Ways and Means alternative would have won by default — in effect allowing House members to pass a broad-based business tax without an identifiable vote for it.

Downey's victory came from his ability to assemble a majority coalition out of very different interest groups — all opposed to the broad-based business tax, but for different reasons: fiscal conservatives, environmentalists and non-petrochemical businesses. He gained regional support from the Northeast-Midwest Congressional Coalition, representing areas where general manufacturing firms were plentiful and petrochemical interests less dominant than in the Southwest.

Environmental Issues

Environmentalists said the stiffer Public Works provisions, which they preferred, prevailed on major points in the compromise bill, which finally went to the House floor.

Environmentalists won a key test of their voting strength late in the night of Dec. 5 when members approved an amendment requiring companies to disclose routine venting or discharge of chemicals that caused cancer, birth defects and other chronic health problems.

The amendment, offered by Bob Edgar, D-Pa., was adopted on a 183-166 vote. *(Vote 396, p. 126-H)*

The Energy bill had no such requirement. The Public Works bill required disclosure only of chemicals that could cause "acute" or immediate poisoning. Thus, Edgar's amendment went beyond both versions.

But Dingell and other opponents of the amendment said it would impose massive paperwork requirements on small businesses, and was too open-ended in terms of the number of chemicals it could include.

Opponents of the Edgar amendment forced a second vote on the issue Dec. 10. With 85 members absent during the first vote, which came at 11 p.m., the opponents believed that there was a chance they could reverse the outcome. On the second vote, the Edgar amendment won a narrow 212-211 victory. *(Vote 408, p. 128-H)*

Right-to-Sue

Another key issue the House addressed was whether citizens should have a right to sue dumpers in federal court for damages and injuries they thought were caused by hazardous substances.

Members defeated, 162-261, an amendment by Barney Frank, D-Mass., that would for the first time have established such a right. *(Vote 407, p. 128-H)*

Many states allowed such suits, but federal courts had no jurisdiction to hear them. One of Frank's supporters, John F. Seiberling, D-Ohio, argued that "toxic tort victims ... face difficult obstacles in the state courts in their attempts to secure adequate compensation for their injuries."

Seiberling offered an amendment, adopted by voice vote, that prohibited federal suits from being brought for injuries incurred and discovered before enactment of the bill.

Environmental groups supported Frank's amendment, and insurance-industry and other business groups opposed it, as did the Reagan administration.

Other Action

In other action, the House:

- Rejected by voice vote an amendment by Bruce F. Vento, D-Minn., that would have authorized federal reimbursement for alternative water supplies when towns installed them in cases of federal pollution.
- Approved by voice vote an amendment by Frank relieving landowners of liability for toxic sites if they could prove that they had nothing to do with the dumping and did not know of the pollution when they bought the property.
- Rejected, 62-330, an amendment by Hal Daub, R-Neb., to relieve from liability for a hazardous-waste site any parties who could prove that wastes they deposited at the site had not caused a hazardous release from the site. *(Vote 395, p. 126-H)*
- Rejected, 142-256, an amendment by John R. McKernan Jr., R-Maine, allowing states that had existing state oil spill funds to continue their operation. The bill phased them out and substituted a federal program. *(Vote 398, p. 126-H)*

Following passage, the House substituted the amended text of HR 2817 for the Senate-passed version of HR 2005, clearing the way for a conference on the superfund measure.

Provisions

As passed by the House, HR 2005:

Schedules

- Required EPA to list at least 1,600 sites on its National Priority List by Jan. 1, 1988, and to complete by Jan. 1, 1987, preliminary assessments on all the sites on the priority list as of the date of enactment.
- Stipulated that EPA begin 925 cleanup studies within five years: 150 sites during the first 12 months, 175 during the second 12 months and 200 during each year thereafter.
- Required EPA to begin long-term ("remedial") cleanups at 600 sites over four years; 125 during fiscal 1987, 140 in 1988, 160 in 1989 and 175 in 1990.
- Provided that EPA complete long-term cleanups within five years at all sites on the priority list as of the date of enactment or to publish an explanation of why this could not be accomplished.

Standards

- Required EPA to select appropriate cost-effective cleanup methods that protect human health and the environment.
- Provided that EPA select a permanent cleanup method when it was feasible and achievable.
- Required EPA to maintain a separate list of sites for which it had chosen non-permanent remedies, to review them every five years and to carry out a permanent remedy when one was available and practical.
- Required EPA, for on-site cleanups, to choose a remedy achieving standards equivalent to relevant and appro-

priate standards under the Toxic Substances Control Act, the Safe Drinking Water Act, the Clean Air Act, the Clean Water Act (including water quality criteria) or the Resource Conservation and Recovery Act, and to consider tolerance levels established under the Federal Food and Drug Act.

- Allowed EPA to waive standards based on other laws if (1) different action would provide equivalent protection of health and the environment, (2) compliance with the standard would cause greater risk to health and the environment, (3) compliance was technically impractical, (4) compliance would consume a disproportionate share of the superfund, or (5) compliance would require a private party to pay more than EPA would have spent for a federal cleanup action.
- Required, for off-site cleanups, that waste be moved only to a facility operating in compliance with the Resource Conservation and Recovery Act, and only to a unit of such a facility not releasing wastes into surface water or groundwater.

Funding

- Increased the current tax of .79 cents per barrel on the first sale of raw petroleum to 11.9 cents per barrel, estimated to yield $3.1 billion over fiscal 1986-90.
- Increased tax rates on the currently taxed list of 12 organic and 32 inorganic raw chemicals ("feedstocks") to yield $2 billion over five years. Imports would be taxed and exports would not.
- Levied a new tax on the receipt of hazardous waste at a qualified hazardous-waste management facility, or for ocean disposal or transport from the United States. Land disposal would be taxed on a scale increasing from $37 per ton in 1986 to $47 per ton in 1990. Other treatment or disposal methods would be taxed at $4.15 per ton. Certain exemptions would apply to wastewater treatment, incineration and recycling operations. The new tax was estimated to yield $2 billion.
- Authorized appropriations from the general fund of the Treasury of $316 million annually during fiscal 1986-90, to yield $1.6 billion.
- Levied a new tax on imports of substances derived from chemicals taxable under the bill, with rates set by the Treasury secretary equivalent to the tax that would have been imposed on their constituent raw materials had they been manufactured in the United States. The tax would yield about $70 million.
- Authorized the above amounts, together with an estimated $320 million to be recovered from dumpers, to be deposited in the superfund.
- Raised the rate of the existing federal tax on gasoline, diesel and certain other fuels by one-fifth of a cent per gallon, with the revenues to go to the Leaking Underground Storage Tank Trust Fund. Revenues were estimated at $850 million over five years.
- Raised an existing federal tax on raw petroleum by an additional 1.3 cents per barrel (beyond the superfund tax), with revenues to go to the Oil Spill Liability Trust Fund.

Emergency Response

- Required state and local governments to establish a system of emergency plans for response to emergencies involving releases of hazardous substances. Within six months, each state had to appoint an emergency response commission, and within another six months, those commissions had to establish emergency response planning districts and appoint for each a local committee consisting of local elected and public safety officials, health professionals, media, plant operators, community groups and other groups. Within an additional year, those local committees had to draw up plans for dealing with such emergencies, including evacuation plans.
- Kept the requirement in current law that facilities report releases of hazardous substances to a National Response Center.
- Added a new requirement that facilities notify state and local emergency officials of a spill immediately, with a written bulletin as soon as possible.
- Required operators of plants or facilities handling hazardous substances to furnish to local and state officials Material Safety Data Sheets giving basic information on the chemicals they handle.
- Established a system of requirements for more detailed reporting by facilities that handled especially hazardous materials, with the specific substances and threshold amounts to be set by EPA.
- Allowed state and local governments to set "right-to-know" requirements more stringent than federal ones.

Citizen Suits

- Authorized citizens to sue EPA or other federal agencies to compel them to perform any non-discretionary duty under the superfund law, such as meeting deadlines mandated in the act.
- Authorized citizens to sue any party alleged to be in violation of the superfund law, including local, state and federal agencies, to compel compliance with the law.
- Authorized citizens to sue private parties to compel cleanup when they contributed to a release, or threatened release, that could present an imminent and substantial danger to public health or the environment.

Liability and Settlements

- Generally maintained the court-set principle that liability under the superfund law should be "strict, joint and several" (meaning that dumpers were liable regardless of negligence and that one dumper was responsible for harm done by all).
- Authorized parties held liable for superfund cleanups to seek in court a contribution of costs from other responsible parties.
- Left to the courts to determine whether to hear contribution cases before or after the government's original suit to recover its cleanup costs was completed.
- Barred legal challenges to EPA's choice of a cleanup remedy until after a government cleanup was completed or until EPA ordered a private party to conduct the cleanup.
- Exempted contractors conducting cleanups for EPA from liability except for negligent, reckless or willful misconduct.

Miscellaneous

- Incorporated legislation (HR 1232) consolidating the current systems for oil pollution cleanup and damage compensation. The bill set various limits on the liability of owners and operators of ships, offshore drilling rigs and pipelines. If damages exceeded those limits or responsible parties could not be found, compensation was to come from a $300 million Marine Oil Pollution Compensation Fund.
- Established a new program especially for cleanup of pollution from leaking underground storage tanks for petroleum and petroleum products. EPA could order tank

owners or operators to clean up pollution, but EPA could conduct cleanups if the tank owners were not willing or available to do so. EPA could then sue to recover its costs. The bill established a Leaking Underground Storage Tank Trust Fund ($850 million over five years) to pay the costs of government cleanups.

- Required federal agencies to comply with provisions of the law to the same extent as private parties.
- Set a schedule for agencies and EPA to move toward cleanup of federal hazardous waste sites and required each agency to request adequate funding for cleanup in the president's budget. Established a separate account for cleanup of military sites.
- Authorized businesses to form "risk retention groups" and insurance purchasing groups to insure themselves against pollution liability.
- Authorized a program of studies of human health effects of exposure to hazardous substances by the Agency for Toxic Substances and Disease Registry within the U.S. Public Health Service. Citizens would be able to petition the agency to perform health assessments at individual hazardous-waste sites.

House-Senate Differences

A number of major differences existed between the House and Senate versions of the superfund legislation.

One was the Senate funding level of $7.5 billion compared with the House $10 billion figure and the different ways the two chambers proposed to raise those amounts — whether through the Senate's reliance on a broad business tax or the House's reliance on oil and chemical taxes.

The House bill also contained a one-fifth of 1 cent per gallon tax on gasoline and diesel fuel to pay for cleanups of leaking underground storage tanks. The Senate bill contained no similar tax or program.

The House bill had a mandatory schedule requiring EPA to meet specific deadlines on cleanups, while the Senate bill had no mandatory schedule for similar sites.

Both House and Senate bills required EPA to set cleanup standards to achieve the general goals of cost-effectiveness, permanence and protection of public health and the environment. But the Senate bill contained few further specific requirements, leaving EPA broad discretion — while the House bill required EPA to clean sites up to standards in other environmental laws such as the Clean Water Act and the Safe Drinking Water Act.

The House bill incorporated legislation (originally HR 1232) combining previously established federal and state oil-spill cleanup and liability funds into a single federal program. The Senate bill did not include an oil-spill cleanup program.

The House bill included a right for citizens to sue companies to force them to clean up sites presenting an imminent and substantial danger to public health. The Senate bill contained no similar provision.

The Senate bill gave EPA more leeway than did the House bill to grant releases from liability to companies that had deposited wastes in superfund sites in exchange for voluntary cleanup agreements. ▮

House Passes Omnibus Water Resources Bill

For the second year in a row, Congress came close to passing an omnibus water resources authorization, only to run out of time to complete action by the end of the year.

The last comprehensive water projects bill was enacted in 1976 (PL 94-587). *(Congress and the Nation Vol. IV, p. 316)*

The House Nov. 13 passed a $20 billion omnibus bill (HR 6) authorizing construction of about 360 specific projects for port deepening, lock and dam construction, flood control, shoreline protection and other purposes. HR 6 also significantly increased the share of project construction costs paid by local beneficiaries.

A $12 billion Senate water projects bill (S 1567) was reported Aug. 1 by the Senate Environment and Public Works Committee and approved by the Senate Finance Committee on Dec. 11.

Background

Water projects had for years stirred intense debate and controversy on Capitol Hill.

At stake were billions of dollars in funding, economic boosts for whole regions of the country, basic decisions about the federal role in water development, the fate of thousands of acres of fish and wildlife habitat and the political fortunes of dozens of members of Congress.

Although no omnibus water projects bill had been passed since 1976, funding continued for projects already authorized and under construction and for operation of projects already built.

In 1984, the House passed an $18 billion water projects bill (HR 3678) and the Senate Environment and Public Works Committee approved an $11 billion version (S 1739). *(1984 Almanac p. 320)*

A fiscal 1985 supplemental appropriations bill (HR 2577), cleared by Congress Aug. 1, 1985, appropriated $48.8 million for 41 water projects by the Army Corps of Engineers and $14.3 million for four projects by the Bureau of Reclamation. *(Supplemental appropriations bill, p. 350)*

One of several issues that held up final passage of the supplemental was the lack of authorization for 21 of the 41 projects in the bill and the absence of local cost-sharing requirements for the projects, a key provision demanded by the Reagan administration. Administration officials threatened a presidential veto if the cost-sharing proposal was not included in the legislation.

A compromise was reached in mid-June when administration officials and key Senate leaders agreed on specific formulas for cost-sharing to be spelled out in authorizing legislation.

As cleared, HR 2577 prohibited any federal money from being spent on unauthorized projects until May 15, 1986, a delay meant to give Congress time to act on authorizing legislation. If that legislation was not enacted, the projects could start, but only if cost-sharing agreements were worked out between local governments and federal officials by June 30, 1986, and sent to Congress for ratification. The conditions applied to authorized and unauthorized projects alike.

For fiscal 1986, Congress Oct. 17 cleared an energy and water appropriations bill (HR 2959 — PL 99-141) that gave $3.6 billion for water projects under the Corps of Engineers and the Interior Department's Bureau of Reclamation. *(Energy and water appropriations bill, p. 323)*

House Committee Action

Public Works Committee

HR 6 was reported Aug. 1 by the Public Works and Transportation Committee (H Rept 99-251, Part I). The committee had approved the measure on June 26 by voice vote after amending it to incorporate some key provisions of the cost-sharing compromise agreed to by the Reagan administration and Senate Republican leaders. Those provisions dramatically increased the share of costs paid by local beneficiaries of water projects.

The compromise formula was linked to the Senate version of HR 2577, the fiscal 1985 supplemental appropriations bill.

Leaders of the Senate Environment and Public Works Committee and the Senate Appropriations Committee agreed to the formula, promising in advance that it would be embodied in omnibus authorizing legislation that had not yet moved in the Senate.

But the House Public Works Committee did not accept all elements of the compromise cost-sharing formula that the Reagan administration was demanding as a condition for signing legislation funding new water projects.

The cost-sharing language was put into HR 6 before the Water Resources Subcommittee approved the bill June 25. The panel adopted by voice vote a package of amendments offered by Gene Snyder, R-Ky., aimed at bringing the bill closer to the administration-Senate formula.

The amendments tracked the provisions of the Senate agreement in requiring port authorities to pay a share of construction costs for deepening channels and in imposing a .04 percent tax on commercial cargo going through ports.

The House committee bill did not, however, include another 10 percent amortized local contribution that was in the Senate agreement. Instead, the Public Works version required local interests to pay an additional contribution of up to 5 percent of total project costs in the form of lands, easements and rights of way.

On lock and dam projects for the inland waterways that carry barge traffic in grain, coal and other bulk commodities, the Public Works bill required that non-federal parties pay one-third of construction costs and none of operating and maintenance costs. The non-federal share came from a trust fund containing the proceeds from an existing 10-cents-per-gallon tax on barge fuel.

The Senate formula, by contrast, required half of inland waterway construction costs to come from the trust fund and doubled the fuel tax to 20 cents over a 10-year period to provide the extra money.

Interior Committee

The House Interior and Insular Affairs Committee Sept. 11 approved by voice vote a package of amendments to HR 6 and reported the measure Sept. 16 (H Rept 99-251, Part II).

The committee deleted language in the Public Works bill establishing a new Cabinet-level federal Water Policy Board. Sponsors George Miller, D-Calif., and Dick Cheney, R-Wyo., argued that authority already existed for such a body. Miller and Cheney also sponsored a successful amendment requiring local beneficiaries of proposed Bureau of Reclamation water projects to pay 50 percent of the costs of feasibility studies. Public Works included such a requirement for Army Corps of Engineers projects.

Ways and Means

The House Ways and Means Committee Sept. 18 approved by voice vote an amended version of the port-user fee adopted by the Public Works Committee. The Ways and Means version was reported Sept. 23 (Part III).

The Ways and Means Committee exempted from the tax the initial landing of U.S.-harvested fish and seafood, as well as cargoes to or from Hawaii and U.S. island territories. It also waived the tax for cargoes when a toll had been imposed in the Great Lakes-St.Lawrence Seaway.

The Ways and Means bill made the tax effective Jan. 1, 1986, while the Public Works version set an effective date of Oct. 1, 1985.

Merchant Marine and Fisheries

The House Merchant Marine and Fisheries Committee in its Sept. 23 report on HR 6 (Part IV) supported the port-user fee formula in the Public Works bill.

The panel also approved an amendment allowing local ports to charge their own user fees to recover the local share of project construction costs, regardless of port depth.

House Floor Action

The House Nov. 13 overwhelmingly passed HR 6 authorizing some $20 billion in new water projects, after House Public Works Committee leaders fended off all major challenges to the bill as they had written it.

The 358-60 vote on passage reflected support from both parties and all regions of the country. *(Vote 370, p. 114-H)*

A major feature of HR 6 was a requirement for greatly increased local cost-sharing.

Final action on HR 6 was temporarily derailed Nov. 6 by a surprise move to cut back spending levels in the massive package.

Connie Mack, R-Fla., caught backers of the bill off guard when he offered an amendment to trim the fiscal 1986 funding levels in the measure by 8.2 percent.

Mack said the 8.2 percent cut reflected the amount of deficit reduction that the Congressional Budget Office said would be required in fiscal 1986 for Congress to meet the deficit-reduction targets in the Gramm-Rudman-Hollings budget-balancing measure (H J Res 372). *(Budget plan, p. 459)*

Mack said that the reduction would be applied to the fiscal 1986 $1.5 billion authorization cap already in HR 6. But committee leaders expressed fears that a reference to H J Res 372 in Mack's amendment could subject the water bill to an 8.2 percent cut even if H J Res 372 were further modified to require a smaller cut. Then Robert A. Roe, D-N.J., offered an amendment to Mack's amendment to delete any reference to H J Res 372.

When the House resumed work on the bill Nov. 13, Mack withdrew his amendment saying he had received a new and different estimate from CBO of how big a spending cut would be needed to meet the deficit-reduction goals in H J Res 372. He said the cut would need to be 3.8 percent, not 8.2 percent. Instead of trying to hit what he called a "moving target," he said he would offer similar amendments on other bills once the figures had been clarified.

The House did not make any of the changes sought by the Reagan administration — most of which were aimed at easing the drain on the Treasury. A Nov. 4 White House statement said the president's advisers would recommend a veto if the bill were enacted unchanged.

Managing the bill were Roe, chairman of the Public Works Subcommittee on Water Resources, and ranking subcommittee Republican Arlan Stangeland, Minn. All of the amendments they opposed were rejected or withdrawn, and all of the amendments they supported were adopted. Roe and Stangeland were in agreement on virtually every amendment.

Cost-Sharing

HR 6 significantly increased the share of project costs paid by local beneficiaries, compared with previous authorization bills. For example, local governments had to pay 25 to 30 percent of costs for flood control projects under HR 6, compared with as little as 5 percent under previous authorizations.

Another major change was the new port tax to pay for port development.

But HR 6 did not include provisions the administration sought to raise the diesel fuel tax for inland waterways to pay for lock and dam improvements.

Amendments

An amendment offered Nov. 6 by Bob Edgar, D-Pa., would have canceled a provision favored by Appropriations Committee Chairman Jamie L. Whitten, D-Miss. The Appropriations Committee had to approve the appropriations for actual construction of the water projects authorized in HR 6.

The bill left new flood control projects on the Mississippi River system exempt from local cost-sharing requirements applied to other new flood control projects in the bill. Edgar wanted the Mississippi River system projects to pay the same share.

The Edgar amendment Nov. 6 was defeated on a 124-296 vote. *(Vote 358, p. 110-H)*

Another amendment, offered by James Weaver, D-Ore., would have deauthorized the Elk Creek Lake project on a tributary of the Rogue River in Oregon. The $120 million project was authorized in 1962 but never built. The amendment was rejected 200-220. *(Vote 359, p. 112-H)*

The Elk Creek Dam was originally authorized as part of a three-dam flood control project, and the other two dams had already been built. Weaver said those two dams were adequate to control floods, and that the Army Corps of Engineers no longer recommended building the third.

Robert F. Smith, R-Ore., in whose district the third dam was to be built, supported its construction and opposed Weaver's amendment. Opponents of the dam said it could harm fishing and tourism elsewhere on the Rogue River system, including Weaver's district. The state's delegation was divided on the issue.

Committee leaders had modified the bill after it was reported. One set of changes was embodied in a new bill (HR 3670). Under the rule by which HR 6 was considered, the text of HR 3670 was ruled in order as a committee substitute to be considered as an original bill for purposes of amendment. It was adopted by voice vote.

Provisions

As passed by the House, HR 6:

- Authorized appropriations that could result in outlays of $20 billion through 1998, according to Congressional Budget Office (CBO) estimates on the bill as reported.
- Authorized by specific reference as many as 362 water resource projects for various purposes, including approximately 35 port projects, 7 inland navigation projects, 110 flood control projects, 28 shoreline protection projects, 81 modifications of existing projects and 101 miscellaneous water resources development and conservation projects. (Estimates of the number of projects in the bill vary because several distinct project components are often counted as parts of a single project.)
- Authorized seven new inland waterway projects: Oliver Lock and Dam, Black Warrior-Tombigbee River, Ala.; Gallipolis Lock and Dam Replacement, Ohio River, Ohio and W.Va.; Winfield Locks and Dam, Kanawha River, W.Va.; Lock and Dam No. 7 Replacement, Monongahela River, Pa.; Lock and Dam No. 8 Replacement, Monongahela River, Pa.; Second Lock, Lock and Dam No. 26, Mississippi River, Ill. and Mo.; and Bonneville Lock and Dam, Ore. and Wash.
- Established a new federal loan program to help cities to rehabilitate aging and leaking drinking-water supply systems, or to expand and improve existing systems. The Army Corps of Engineers was authorized to make such loans to state and local governments or private utilities for up to 80 percent of project costs. Loans were capped at $40 million per operator and $80 million per state. The bill authorized appropriations of $800 million for fiscal 1986, $800 million for 1987 and such sums as may be necessary after that.
- Deauthorized more than 300 water resource projects previously authorized by Congress that had never received appropriations to start up construction. CBO estimated the cost of building those projects would have been some $18 billion.
- Required the Corps of Engineers to consider benefits of environmental enhancement features to be at least equal to costs and authorized $35 million for a program to help offset any environmental damages.
- Established a National Board on Water Resources Policy, consisting of seven members: the interior secretary, the agriculture secretary, the secretary of the Army, the administrator of the Environmental Protection Agency, two members appointed by the president (one nominated by the Speaker of the House and one by the president pro tempore of the Senate) and a chairman appointed by the president. The three presidential appointees would have to be confirmed by the Senate. The board would establish principles and standards for evaluating federal water projects and would make grants to the states to aid them in water planning. The bill authorized $20 million a year for fiscal 1986-90 for the grants.

Port Provisions

- Authorized six new deep-draft port projects: Norfolk Harbor and channels, Va.; Mobile Harbor, Ala.; Mississippi River Ship Channel, Gulf of Mexico to Baton Rouge, La.; Texas City Channel, Texas; New York Harbor and adjacent channels, N.Y. and N.J.; and Los Angeles and Long Beach harbors, San Pedro Bay, Calif.
- Required non-federal interests to pay a share of new port project construction costs amounting to zero for ports with depths of 14 feet or less, 10 percent for the increment between 14 and 20 feet, 25 percent for the increment between 20 and 45 feet, and 50 percent for the increment deeper than 45 feet.

• Authorized the federal government to guarantee as much as 90 percent of the revenue bonds issued by local port authorities to finance their share of project costs, with a $1 billion annual cap on such guarantees.

• Authorized federal payment of the full costs of operation and maintenance for most ports. Local authorities, however, were required to pay 50 percent of the incremental costs of maintaining port depths greater than 45 feet.

• Imposed a new tax of .04 percent on the value of commercial cargo loaded or unloaded at U.S. ports. Exempted from the tax were ports in Hawaii or U.S. territories, and cargo loaded at a mainland port for shipment to Hawaii or U.S. possessions. Also exempted were the initial landings of U.S.-harvested fish or seafood. A credit for payment of tolls on the Great Lakes-St. Lawrence Seaway would be deducted from the amount of tax due.

• Authorized local port or harbor authorities to levy tonnage duties to finance their share of project construction costs. Such fees could be imposed only on vessels that actually benefited from the project.

• Authorized the federal government to reimburse local authorities for costs of projects built at their own initiative. Such reimbursement was subject to appropriations by Congress and would only apply to that portion of the costs of planning, design or construction normally a federal responsibility.

Senate Committee Action

Environment and Public Works

The Senate Environment and Public Works Committee July 18 approved by voice vote S 1567 authorizing almost $12 billion in water projects and programs. The bill was reported Aug. 1 (S Rept 99-126).

The Environment Committee bill authorized six major new lock and dam projects for inland navigation and 32 harbor projects. The total cost of major projects in the bill was about $11.1 billion, including federal and non-federal costs. The bill also authorized some $200 million for minor projects and about $600 million for programs conducted by the Army Corps of Engineers. Only projects under the jurisdiction of the corps, largely in the East, were authorized in the bill.

For navigation on inland canals, rivers and lakes, the bill doubled the existing tax on barge fuel from 10 cents per gallon, its level in 1986, to 20 cents per gallon by 1995. The increase would not take effect until 1988 and the tax would increase gradually.

The bill also imposed a fee of .04 percent on the value of all commercial cargo loaded onto or unloaded from vessels using U.S. harbors, including those on the Great Lakes. The fee was intended to raise 40 percent of port maintenance costs, with proceeds to be used only for that purpose.

The committee adopted an amendment by Sen. George J. Mitchell, D-Maine, exempting freshly caught fish from the cargo fee.

Before approving the bill, the Environment Committee approved by voice vote an amendment deleting an exemption for the Tennessee-Tombigbee Waterway from the barge fuel tax. That massive federal project ran through Mississippi, home state of Appropriations Chairman Whitten, and Alabama, home state of Tom Bevill, Democratic chairman of the House Appropriations Subcommittee on Energy and Water Development.

The Environment Committee also added an amendment to deauthorize the Cross-Florida Barge Canal, using a compromise formula similar to one in HR 6 that had drawn support from the Florida delegation.

Major inland navigation projects authorized in the Senate bill included the Oliver Lock Replacement, Black Warrior and Tombigbee rivers, Ala. (total federal and non-federal cost: $147 million); Gallipolis Lock and Dam Replacement, Ohio River, Ohio and W. Va. ($256 million); Bonneville Lock and Dam, Columbia River, Ore. and Wash. ($191 million); Lock and Dam 7 Replacement, Monongahela River, Pa.; and a second lock at Lock and Dam 26, Mississippi River, Ill. and Mo. ($220 million).

Major harbor projects included Mobile Harbor, Ala. ($69 million); Mississippi River Ship Channel, Gulf of Mexico to Baton Rouge, La. ($456 million); Kill Van Kull and Newark Bay channels, N.Y. and N.J. ($248 million); and Norfolk Harbor and channels, Va. ($538 million).

Finance Committee

The Senate Finance Committee Dec. 11 approved by voice vote new harbor and waterway taxes to be part of S 1567. The proposed new taxes embodied the agreement Senate Republicans had made earlier in the year with the administration.

The existing tax of 8 cents per gallon on barge fuel was to be raised to 20 cents per gallon by 1997. Port users were to pay a fee of .04 percent on the value of cargo loaded or unloaded from commercial vessels at U.S. ports. Exempt from the tax were to be cargo shipped from Hawaii or U.S. possessions, freshly caught fish and ports that got no federal funds. ▮

Endangered Species Act

The House July 29 passed a bill (HR 1027) to renew the Endangered Species Act for three years without major changes. A companion Senate measure (S 725) was awaiting action in the Environment and Public Works Committee at year's end.

The 1973 Endangered Species Act (PL 93-205) was aimed at protecting species threatened with extinction from hunting, trading and federal actions that could destroy their habitat. The law banned the sale, purchase, possession or killing of species listed as endangered or threatened. *(Congress and the Nation Vol. IV, p. 289)*

The Merchant Marine and Fisheries Committee reported the bill May 15 (H Rept 99-124). No amendments to the committee bill were made on the House floor.

As passed, the bill authorized $39.25 million for fiscal 1986 (the same level as the 1985 authorization), $46.75 million for 1987 and $54.2 million for 1988.

The Reagan administration had asked for a four-year reauthorization at levels near 1985 appropriations. *(Previous authorization, 1982 Almanac p. 435)*

The bill included a compromise aimed at settling a dispute over California sea otters, which lived in a single colony along the central California coast. Conservationists had been urging the government to move some of the animals and establish a second colony in order to increase the species' chance of surviving a major offshore oil spill. But oil companies were worried such an action might put more of the coast off-limits to drilling, and commercial fishermen were concerned that otters could consume a major portion of the shellfish they currently harvested.

The bill set up a procedure for the federal government

to establish a second colony of the otters, probably on San Nicolas Island off Southern California. But it required the colony to be surrounded by a special management zone aimed at keeping the otters from moving further. Animals found outside the zone would be picked up and returned to the colony.

Another change to existing law required increased monitoring of "candidate species," those awaiting a decision on whether they would be added to the endangered or threatened lists. It also required the Commerce Department to use its emergency listing authority to protect such species when the monitoring found them to be threatened.

The bill did not address concerns of Western water developers, who feared the act's protections for endangered fish species in the Colorado River could block construction of new hydroelectric and irrigation projects.

The bill also left intact protection of bald eagles. Indian tribes claimed treaty rights allowed them to take bald eagles for religious purposes.

The Senate Environment and Public Works Subcommittee on Environmental Pollution had scheduled a markup Nov. 13 but failed to get a quorum. Subcommittee Chairman John H. Chafee, R-R.I., decided to send the bill to full committee for markup but no further action took place during 1985. ∎

Coastal Zone Management

The House July 30 by voice vote approved a bill (HR 2121) reauthorizing the Coastal Zone Management Act, after agreeing by voice vote to an amendment freezing the bill's fiscal 1986 authorization at the $36 million fiscal 1985 appropriation level.

As reported May 15 by the House Merchant Marine and Fisheries Committee (H Rept 99-103), HR 2121 authorized $40 million for fiscal 1986, with a gradual shrinking of authorizations to $35 million for fiscal years 1989 through 1991.

The freeze amendment was offered by Merchant Marine and Fisheries Committee Chairman Walter B. Jones, D-N.C., who said it would save $193 million in five years over fiscal 1985 authorized levels.

The 1972 coastal zone act (PL 92-583) authorized federal grants to help states develop and implement comprehensive plans to manage and conserve coastal areas. *(Congress and the Nation Vol. III, p. 799; 1980 Almanac p. 613)*

HR 2121 lowered the federal share of costs for state coastal zone management plans from 80 percent to 50 percent in fiscal 1989-90.

The Senate Commerce, Science and Transportation Committee May 9 approved a five-year reauthorization (S 959 — S Rept 99-71) of the coastal zone program. S 959 authorized $43.2 million for fiscal 1986, $45.1 million for 1987, $47.2 million for 1988, $49.3 million for 1989 and $51.5 million for 1990.

The Reagan administration budget proposed that grants to coastal states be ended. ∎

Ocean Dumping of Wastes

For the fourth year in a row the House passed a bill to overhaul the program regulating the dumping of wastes in the ocean, but there was no Senate action on the measure.

The bill (HR 1957), passed Dec. 10 by voice vote, reauthorized and amended Title I of the Marine Protection, Research and Sanctuaries Act (PL 92-532). Title I, known as the Ocean Dumping Act, gave the Environmental Protection Agency (EPA) authority to regulate ocean dumping of wastes and prohibited the dumping of any wastes EPA considered harmful. *(Congress and the Nation Vol. III, p. 798; 1984 Almanac p. 333)*

HR 1957 also attempted to settle a longstanding dispute between New York and New Jersey over the dumping of sewage sludge at an ocean site 12 miles off the New York-New Jersey coast, in an area known as the New York Bight Apex. New Jersey complained that the sludge, which came primarily from New York City, was polluting its shores and sought to move the dump site to deeper waters 106 miles offshore.

EPA Ruling

On April 1, 1985, EPA issued a final rule closing the 12-mile dump site and requiring municipalities using it to switch to the 106-mile site. HR 1957 legally barred the door to a reversal of the EPA decision and set a mandatory 18-month schedule for phasing out all use of the 12-mile site.

As passed, HR 1957 (H Rept 99-107, Parts I and II) authorized $8.9 million annually to carry out the program in fiscal 1986-87 and an additional $5 million over fiscal 1986-88 for EPA to develop a New York Bight Apex Restoration Plan. ∎

Fish Conservation Bill

The House March 19 passed one fisheries bill opposed by the Reagan administration, but a second measure failed to win the two-thirds majority needed under suspension of the rules.

Passed by a 268-133 vote was the Anadromous Fish Conservation Act (HR 1025), which reauthorized a state-federal program for conservation of fish such as salmon that migrate upstream to spawn. *(Vote 31, p. 12-H)*

HR 1025 authorized $7.5 million annually for fiscal 1986-88, the same level of funding as in 1985.

A second bill (HR 1028), to revise programs under the Commercial Fisheries Research and Development Act, failed 252-149, 16 votes short of the margin needed. *(Vote 32, p. 12-H)*

HR 1028 would have authorized $7.85 million yearly for fiscal 1986-88 and focused program activities on fish that moved across jurisdictional boundaries. The administration argued that states should pay for the programs because they benefited from them.

The Merchant Marine and Fisheries Committee March 13 approved both bills by voice vote. The reports were filed March 19 (HR 1025 — H Rept 99-19 and HR 1028 — H Rept 99-20). ∎

Call for EPA/Justice Probe

The House Judiciary Committee Dec. 5 approved, 22-13, a report calling for an independent counsel to investigate charges that Justice Department officials acted improperly, and perhaps criminally, in 1982-83 when they resisted congressional probes into the Environmental Protection Agency (EPA).

The 1,300-page report on the committee's long investigation into Justice Department actions was endorsed by 20 Democrats and two Republicans.

The report stated that the department misrepresented key facts of the case to President Reagan when it advised him to withhold EPA documents from Congress and claim executive privilege.

It stated that Justice Department officials certified that the withheld documents contained no evidence of wrongdoing while they were aware the documents contained political references.

Congressional committees at the time were looking into charges that EPA had manipulated "superfund" hazardous-waste cleanups for political purposes.

The dispute forced the resignation of EPA Administrator Anne McGill Burford and more than 20 other political appointees.

A Justice Department spokesman did not immediately say whether it would appoint an independent counsel. *(1983 Almanac p. 332)*

Offshore Drilling Revenues

Congress came close in 1985 to resolving a long-running dispute between coastal states and the federal government over how to divide offshore drilling revenues. But the plan, included in a budget reconciliation bill (HR 3128), got caught in an end-of-the-session dispute between the House and the Senate over final provisions. *(Budget reconciliation story, p. 498)*

The offshore oil revenues in HR 3128 included $5.8 billion that had piled up in escrow over seven years while the Interior Department and the coastal states quarreled about how much each should get from the disputed drilling revenues. *(1984 Almanac p. 334)*

The bill gave seven coastal states 27 percent of the money, with 73 percent going to the Treasury, and it called for splitting future revenues in the same fashion. The administration objected to the formula, which it said could cost the Treasury up to $12 billion over the next 30 years.

Background

The states involved were Louisiana, Texas, California, Alabama, Alaska, Mississippi and Florida.

The Submerged Lands Act (PL 83-31) and the Outer Continental Shelf (OCS) Lands Act (PL 83-212) granted the states title to underwater lands and natural resources that extended three miles off their coastlines. (The boundary is about 10 miles for Texas and parts of Florida because of previous agreements with the federal government.) Beyond the limit, ownership and jurisdiction were entirely federal. *(Congress and the Nation Vol. I, p. 1401)*

One area of continuing dispute, however, was whether to split revenues from so-called "common pool" formations underground that straddled the state-federal boundary. Amendments to the OCS Lands Act (PL 95-372), passed in 1978, sought to settle the issue. Section 8(g) of the act provided for another three-mile zone to be set up beyond the state three-mile boundary and decreed that revenues from drilling in that zone should be split on a "fair and equitable" basis with the states. *(Congress and the Nation Vol. V, p.485)*

The 1978 amendments left to the states and the Interior Department the question of what a fair split actually was. While they debated the issue, $5.8 billion accumulated in an escrow fund from rents, bonuses and interest and another $1 billion in royalties. (A one-time "bonus" is bid by each company seeking an offshore lease for drilling. The high bidder gets the lease.)

Legislative Action

The fiscal 1986 budget resolution (S Con Res 32) adopted by Congress in August called for the oil states to get 27 percent of the escrow fund, with the remaining 73 percent going to the federal government. Three congressional committees — House Interior and Insular Affairs, House Merchant Marine and Fisheries and Senate Energy and Natural Resources — took the formula a step further. They proposed that the oil states get 27 percent of the entire escrow fund, including the $1 billion in past royalties, and 27 percent of all future revenues, including royalties.

Although the Interior Committee had approved the formula, its chairman, Morris K. Udall, D-Ariz., objected to the inclusion of royalties in the states' share, a position shared by the Reagan administration.

But the House Rules Committee Oct. 17, by a 6-7 vote, rejected a motion by Butler Derrick, D-S.C., to allow Udall to challenge the provision on the House floor.

Another effort to delete the plan was made in the Senate, where Howard M. Metzenbaum, D-Ohio, and Daniel J. Evans, R-Wash., proposed during Senate debate on the budget reconciliation bill that most royalties be dropped from the agreement. Their amendment also would have required that lease and bonus revenues to states be prorated according to the portion of an oil field tract that lay in the three-mile zone. Their amendment was tabled, 54-45, on Nov. 14. *(Vote 308, p. 53-S)*

But when House-Senate conferees on HR 3128 agreed to include in the measure a broad-based business tax the Senate had approved to finance the "superfund" hazardous-waste cleanup program, the House would not accept the final version of the bill.

Alaska Mining Road Bill

President Reagan Sept. 25 signed into law a bill (S 444 — PL 99-96) granting a right-of-way across the Cape Krusenstern National Monument in Alaska to allow construction of a major mining road.

The monument is a 659,000-acre area above the Arctic Circle that was brought under federal protection from development under the Alaska Lands Act of 1980 (PL 96-487). A largely treeless tract of mountains and tundra, it contained mineral deposits described as "world class," as well as habitat for grizzly bear, caribou, Dall sheep, musk oxen and peregrine falcons. *(1980 Almanac p. 575)*

The NANA Regional Corporation, a native landholding body in that high-unemployment area, wanted to build a road through the monument area to carry lead, zinc and silver from deposits it owned in the Red Dog mineral area to a NANA-owned port site on the Chuchki Sea.

The bill also ratified a land-exchange proposal by which NANA would consolidate its holdings within the monument boundaries.

S 444 was passed by the Senate July 18 (S Rept 99-97) and by the House July 29. The Senate agreed to a compromise Aug. 1 and the House cleared the bill Sept. 12.

Final Action Stalls on Clean Water Act Revision

Despite the budget-cutting fervor in Congress in 1985, both the House and Senate passed legislation authorizing billions of dollars to clean up lakes and streams. But the two chambers failed to meet in conference to resolve differences between their versions of the legislation.

The measures (HR 8, S 1128) reauthorized and strengthened the Clean Water Act, the nation's principal means of controlling water pollution and funding local sewage treatment works. The act had been awaiting reauthorization since 1982.

The Senate June 13 passed an $18 billion authorization and the House July 23 approved a $21 billion version.

Background

The 1972 Clean Water Act (PL 92-500) consisted of two main parts: a federal-state regulatory program to control water pollution and a program of grants to aid local governments in building sewage treatment plants. *(Congress and the Nation Vol. III, p. 792)*

In 1981 Congress passed a four-year reauthorization of the program (PL 97-117). The legislation limited potential federal funding obligations to about $23 billion by restricting grant eligibility to work needed to meet water quality standards, rather than funding future growth in the form of extra treatment capacity and collector sewers for new subdivisions. In addition, the share of costs the federal government would pay was reduced from 75 percent to 55 percent after fiscal 1984. Congress then extended authorization for the construction grants through fiscal 1985. *(1981 Almanac p. 515; 1984 Almanac p. 329)*

While it was not written into the law, members from both parties in both chambers believed they had an agreement with the administration to fund the remaining $23 billion at $2.4 billion annually over the next 10 years.

But the administration in its fiscal 1986 budget requests proposed that construction grants be funded at $2.4 billion in fiscal 1986, $1.8 billion in 1987, $1.2 billion in 1988, $600 million in 1989 and zero in 1990. Beginning in fiscal 1986, no new projects could be started with federal funds under the administration proposal.

Senate Committee

The Senate Environment and Public Works Committee May 14 reported S 1128 (S Rept 99-50) by a 13-2 vote.

S 1128 authorized $18 billion through 1994 in grant and loan funds for sewage treatment plant construction. The bill also adjusted the law's regulatory provisions.

Senators from Great Lakes states slowed and nearly stopped the markup with protests over how the sewer funds would be divided among the states. They claimed the allocation formula adopted by the committee benefited the South and West at the expense of the North and East.

Toxic Variance

The committee approved a provision that partially reversed a Feb. 27 Supreme Court decision involving requirements for treatment of toxic pollutants. *(Chemical Manufacturers Association v. Natural Resources Defense Council (NRDC), EPA v. NRDC, p. 15-A)*

Under the Clean Water Act, the Environmental Protection Agency (EPA) set general pollution-control technology requirements, called "effluent limitation guidelines," for each type of industry. The effluent limitation was a rule specifying how dirty the wastewater from a company in a particular industry could be.

EPA set similar limits on how much pollution could be in the wastewater companies discharged to local sewage treatment plants. "Categorical pre-treatment standards," as these were called, also were based on unique circumstances in each industry.

In 1978 EPA set up a variance for companies that could show that their circumstances were fundamentally different from those EPA considered in setting effluent limits or pre-treatment standards.

Environmentalists went to court, claiming that the law did not authorize such waivers and actually prohibited waivers for toxic discharges. The Supreme Court ruled against the environmentalists in a 5-4 decision. The majority said the waivers were legal because the law did not clearly forbid them, while the minority said Congress had not intended to allow them.

The Reagan administration supported the waivers and proposed specific authorizing language.

The Senate committee authorized the variances, but it imposed strict limits on when they could be granted and put the burden of proof on companies applying for the variance.

Senate Floor

The Senate June 13 approved S 1128 on a 94-0 vote. *(Vote 126, p. 25-S)*

The bill authorized $18 billion over 1986-94 in federal grants and loan funds.

The question of how that money should be split up among the states prompted filibuster threats and acrimonious debate before a bargain was finally struck. A coalition of senators from Great Lakes states, some Northern and Eastern states and California protested that the bill as reported from committee unfairly reduced the shares their states would receive.

Led by Daniel Patrick Moynihan, D-N.Y., and Dave Durenberger, R-Minn., the dissidents threatened to block consideration of the bill until their concerns were met. Thirty-five senators, representing 18 states losing funds under the committee bill, signed on as cosponsors to an amendment Durenberger planned to offer.

The final agreement, worked out with floor managers John H. Chafee, R-R.I., and George J. Mitchell, D-Maine, gave them more than the committee bill did, but still less than current law.

The committee bill had divided the states into three groups, or tiers, according to population. Tier I included the 30 largest states, Tier II included seven mid-sized states and the District of Columbia, and Tier III included the 13 smallest states. The net effect of the committee formula was to take funds from larger states and give them to smaller states, and to average out somewhat the variations within each tier.

To moderate the changes, the committee added a "hold harmless" proviso guaranteeing each Tier I state no less than 80 percent of the allotment it had under current law. The money to bring each up to the floor came from the other Tier I states.

The compromise, embodied in an amendment offered by Chafee and adopted by voice vote June 13, raised the hold harmless floor for Tier I to 85 percent. A ceiling was imposed of 20 percent on how much any state in Tiers II and III could increase its share over current law. That amounted to a shift of $65 million, between the committee bill and the Senate compromise, from the smaller states in Tiers II and III to the larger states in Tier I.

Other Amendments

In other major action before final passage, the Senate:

- Agreed 70-26 to table (kill) an amendment by Malcolm Wallop, R-Wyo., that would have prevented EPA from taking civil enforcement actions against certain violators of the act while state enforcement action was still pending. *(Vote 125, p. 25-S)*
- Agreed by voice vote to an amendment by Alan K. Simpson, R-Wyo., giving the Army Corps of Engineers, rather than EPA, authority to enforce certain new civil penalties in the bill for violations of dredge-and-fill permits under Section 404.
- Adopted by voice vote an amendment by Mack Mattingly, R-Ga., limiting a requirement for EPA stormwater discharge permits to industrial facilities, municipal storm sewers and other dischargers actually found to be polluting waterways. Commercial and residential facilities would not have to apply for individual permits.

Senate Provisions

As passed by the Senate, S 1128:

- Authorized appropriations totaling $18 billion in fiscal 1986-94 for grant and loan programs. Within that total, authorized $2.4 billion annually in fiscal 1986-88 and $1.2 billion annually in fiscal 1989-90 for grants to aid the construction of local sewage treatment works.
- Authorized establishment of new state revolving funds to help finance sewage works through loans and other mechanisms. To help the states capitalize the funds, the bill authorized federal grants amounting to $1.2 billion annually for fiscal 1989-90, $2.4 billion for 1991, $1.8 billion for 1992, $1.2 billion for 1993 and $600 million for 1994. States had to match 15 percent of the federal grant.
- Extended deadlines for compliance with "best available technology" (BAT) to control toxic pollutants and with "best conventional treatment" for conventional pollutants. The new deadline would be three years after EPA issued effluent limitations, but not later than July 1, 1988.
- Restricted the availability of waivers of "secondary" treatment requirements for municipal sewage discharged into oceans or estuaries. For a waiver, a municipality had to be complying with requirements for pre-treatment of industrial wastes going into its sewers and had to be using "primary" treatment and disinfection where appropriate.
- Imposed new restrictions on EPA's power to grant variances from pollution control requirements for industrial facilities claiming to be subject to "fundamentally different factors" than EPA considered in setting the original requirements.
- Established a procedure for EPA to set pollution control requirements more stringent than BAT in waters where BAT was insufficient to achieve health standards for toxic pollutants. Within two years of enactment, states had to identify such waters, and within another two years, set toxic effluent limits. Industries had three years to comply.
- Increased maximum civil penalties for violations of the law from $10,000 to $25,000 per violation per day.
- Established a new type of enforcement authority that could be used by EPA against violators without going to court. The agency could assess administrative civil penalties of up to $10,000 per violation per day, up to a total of $125,000, for any individual enforcement action.
- Increased penalties for criminal violations of the law to not less than $5,000 nor more than $50,000 per violation per day and up to three years' imprisonment. In cases involving knowing endangerment of human life, the maximum fine was $250,000 for individuals and $1 million for corporations, plus up to 15 years in prison.
- Established a mandatory, state-run program to control pollution from "non-point," or diffuse, sources. States had to submit plans to EPA within 18 months for approval and were required to identify "best management practices" for controlling such pollution.
- Authorized $70 million in fiscal 1985, $100 million in 1986 and $130 million in 1987 for grants to states for up to 75 percent of the costs of carrying out non-point source control programs.
- Exempted from permit requirements unpolluted discharges of stormwater from oil and gas operations.
- Left unchanged the current five-year term for wastewater discharge permits.
- Prohibited "backsliding" by wastewater discharge permit holders. Once a discharger had achieved a certain level of pollution control under preliminary permit limits and effluent guidelines, a permit could not be made less stringent.
- Set a new timetable for EPA rulemaking on use and disposal of sewage sludge containing toxic contaminants. For contaminants about which EPA had enough information to act, EPA had to issue criteria for use and disposal of sludge by March 1, 1987. For others, it had to issue criteria by Dec. 15, 1987. Disposers or users of sludge had to comply within 12 months of issuance, or two years if new pollution control equipment had to be constructed.

House Committee

The House Public Works and Transportation Committee May 22 approved HR 8. The bill was reported July 2 (H Rept 99-189).

The committee stuck with the existing law's formula for dividing sewage treatment funds among the states. The panel also retained a provision in existing law that set aside 20 percent of each state's funding allotment for governors to use on otherwise ineligible projects — including collector sewers.

A regulatory issue left unresolved in the House markups was whether permits should be required for discharges of storm water runoff — especially for oil, gas and mining operations. The committee bill prohibited EPA from requiring a permit when such discharges were not contaminated "above natural background levels." It required companies to test for pollution and report the results to EPA.

House Floor

The House July 23 passed HR 8 by a vote of 340-83, after rejecting an effort to freeze fiscal 1986 spending at 1985 levels. *(Vote 226, p. 72-H)*

Defeat of the freeze amendment on a 207-219 vote marked the first time in 1985 that the House refused in a direct floor vote to hold a fiscal 1986 authorization to fiscal 1985 spending levels. The amendment had been offered by Carl D. Pursell, R-Mich. *(Vote 225, p. 72-H)*

During debate, Pursell read a letter to the House from Lee M. Thomas, EPA administrator, who said "excessive" authorization levels in HR 8 would "reverse four years of fiscal restraint at a time when control of the deficit continues to be one of the nation's gravest problems."

As passed, HR 8 authorized $21 billion in grants and loans over fiscal 1986-94 for construction of local sewage treatment works. HR 8 also authorized new or increased spending for programs to control pollution from farmland and city streets, pollution in lakes and estuaries and pollution of underground drinking water supplies.

Industry won extensions of pollution control deadlines, limits on requirements for stormwater control, and authority for some waivers of pollution control requirements. Environmentalists won "anti-backsliding" restrictions against relaxation of some permit requirements when a permit was reissued, renewed or modified.

Other Amendments

Another major issue during House consideration of the bill was pre-treatment of industrial wastewater going into municipal sewers.

The House rejected, by a vote of 167-257, an amendment by Arlan Stangeland, R-Minn., authorizing EPA to allow up to 40 municipal sewage treatment programs to use their own pre-treatment programs if they could show results at least equal to those achieved through the national pre-treatment standards. *(Vote 224, p. 72-H)*

The House by voice vote adopted an amendment by Walter B. Jones, D-N.C., modified by a substitute by Robert A. Roe, D-N.J., that set up a federal-state program under the direction of EPA to identify and manage pollution threats to important estuaries around the nation.

Also adopted by voice vote were two amendments by James L. Oberstar, D-Minn., dealing with water pollution attributable to acid rain. The first required EPA to set up and carry out a $10 million demonstration program aimed at cleaning up lakes that had been damaged by acid rain.

The second amendment authorized $25 million per year for fiscal years 1986-90 in grants to states to help them identify waters harmed by acid rain and to devise methods of mitigating such damage.

Major Provisions

As passed by the House, HR 8 included the following major provisions:

- Authorized $12 billion ($2.4 billion annually) during fiscal 1986-90 for federal grants to pay 55 percent of costs for construction of local sewage treatment works. Retained the current formula for dividing sewage treatment funds among the states.
- Authorized $9 billion in federal grants over fiscal 1986-94 for state revolving loan funds to finance municipal sewage treatment works.
- Established a procedure for EPA to set technology requirements more stringent than "best available technology" for so-called "toxic hot spots," where water quality failed to meet standards because of discharges of toxic pollutants.

EPA and the states had to list such waters within one year and issue cleanup plans and regulations within another year.

Industries had three years to comply.

- Required states to submit within nine months a program to control pollution from diffuse or "non-point sources," such as runoff from large areas of farm or forest land. EPA had six months to approve the plans. Authorized $150 million annually during fiscal 1986-90 for federal grants for up to 50 percent of the cost of carrying out the plans. Governors could add to this amount from the 20 percent of each state's discretionary sewer grant allocation.
- Authorized $50 million annually during fiscal 1986-90 for federal grants to the states for up to 70 percent of the costs of controlling non-point sources polluting lakes.
- Authorized $22.8 million annually during fiscal 1986-90 for research on water pollution, $75 million annually for grants to states to help them run their water pollution control programs, $50 million annually in grants to local and state governments for developing and carrying out areawide water quality management plans, $50 million annually to aid farmers and ranchers in controlling pollution from land runoff, $50 million annually to implement interagency agreements for pollution control under other federal laws and $30 million annually for the Clean Lakes Program to restore water quality in degraded lakes.
- Required industry compliance with "best available technology" and "best conventional technology" effluent limits no later than three-and-a-half years after EPA issued those requirements.
- Allowed industries discharging wastewater into municipal sewage systems a two-year extension of the deadline for pre-treatment of their wastewater if they used innovative pre-treatment methods and if the wastewater did not cause a violation of the municipal system's permit.
- Extended to 10 years the current five-year term for wastewater discharge permits given to industries and municipalities for non-toxic discharges. Required EPA to re-examine 10-year permits if effluent limits or water quality standards changed during the 10-year period. Discharges of toxic and "non-conventional" pollutants remained under five-year permits.
- Established a procedure for regulating discharges of stormwater runoff. Prohibited EPA from requiring a permit for a stormwater discharge before 1990 unless EPA found the discharge could or did cause pollution. Municipal storm sewers required permits.
- Increased maximum court-ordered civil penalties under the act from $10,000 per day to $25,000 per day. Increased certain criminal penalties to a maximum fine of $50,000 per day and two years in prison. Granted EPA new authority to impose administrative penalties of $10,000 per day up to a maximum of $125,000 for effluent limit and permit violations.
- Allowed companies to receive variances, under strictly limited circumstances, from pollution control requirements when they could demonstrate that they were subject to "fundamentally different factors" from EPA industrywide requirements.
- Imposed "anti-backsliding" requirements on permit holders — prohibiting renewed or revised permits from specifying controls less stringent than those a company had already achieved.
- Established a new grant program at $150 million annually during fiscal 1986-88 to aid publicly and privately owned drinking water supply systems whose water had been rendered unfit for human consumption because of groundwater contamination. Provided up to 50 percent of the costs for temporary water supplies or permanent remedies.

Safe Drinking Water

Both the House and Senate in 1985 passed bills (HR 1650, S 124) to beef up federal protections for drinking water. Further action was stalled, however, by the failure of conferees to meet to reconcile differences between the two bills.

The legislation directed the Environmental Protection Agency (EPA) to regulate health-threatening contaminants by certain deadlines. The bills amended and reauthorized the 1974 Safe Drinking Water Act.

One major issue in dispute was a provision in the House bill requiring states to write EPA-approved plans for protecting underground sources of drinking water. The Senate bill contained no groundwater planning requirement.

The groundwater provisions had drawn fire from the Reagan administration and from some Western states, which claimed they had the exclusive right to regulate groundwater under state law.

The Senate passed its bill (S 124) on May 16; the House approved its version (HR 1650) on June 17.

Background

The 1974 Safe Drinking Water Act (PL 93-523) gave EPA authority to set standards limiting chemical and bacteriological contaminants in drinking water systems serving more than 25 people. EPA delegated most enforcement authority to the states. *(1974 act, Congress and the Nation Vol. IV, p. 293)*

Funding authorization had expired at the end of fiscal 1982, but the program had been kept alive through yearly appropriations. The fiscal 1985 appropriation was $62.7 million. The administration had requested $59.6 million for fiscal 1986.

HR 1650, as introduced, was identical to a bill that passed the House in 1984 by a 366-27 margin, despite opposition from the Reagan administration. *(1984 Almanac p. 331)*

Senate Action

The Senate Environment and Public Works Committee May 2 approved S 124 by voice vote after scarcely half an hour of deliberation. The bill was reported May 15 (S Rept 99-56).

The committee bill gave EPA some leeway to choose which contaminants (beyond those on EPA published lists) to regulate, but also set a Jan. 1, 1991, deadline for final action on 25 contaminants not currently listed.

S 124 authorized $131.3 million annually for EPA and the states to run the regulatory program during fiscal 1986-89. The total compared with an existing $98 million authorization and a fiscal 1985 appropriation of $62.7 million.

The Senate passed S 124 by voice vote on May 16.

The only suggestion of controversy accompanying the bill came over the issue of expanding federal programs to protect groundwater. Daniel Patrick Moynihan, D-N.Y., called the absence in the Senate bill of such provisions a "major omission." But Alan K. Simpson, R-Wyo., called it "prudent and reasonable to leave a full and comprehensive approach to groundwater regulation for another day."

Senate Provisions

Major provisions of S 124 as passed by the Senate:

- Authorized $131.3 million annually for existing regulatory programs under the act for fiscal 1986-90.
- Authorized $10 million annually for 1987-90 for technical assistance to small public water systems and $20 million annually for sole source aquifers.
- Established a mandatory monitoring program for unregulated contaminants and authorized $30 million for the program.
- Simplified existing law to do away with the distinction between interim and revised drinking water standards. EPA had not issued any revised standards, but retained authority to do so.
- Required EPA to publish maximum contaminant-level goals and legally enforceable maximum contaminant levels for two lists of contaminants (about 62 in all) it had published in the *Federal Register*. EPA had to act on nine of the substances within 12 months, 40 of them within 24 months and the remainder within 36 months.
- Required EPA to publish a separate "priority" list of additional contaminants which, in the judgment of the administrator, might have an adverse effect on the health of persons and were known to occur in public water systems. This list was to be published by Jan. 1, 1988, and at three-year intervals after that.
- Required EPA to propose maximum contaminant levels for at least 25 of the contaminants on the priority list within 24 months and to make them final within 36 months.
- Required EPA within 18 months to issue regulations specifying when filtration was required for public water systems supplied by surface sources. States had to adopt implementing regulations within 18 months after that, and had to decide which systems needed filtration within another 12 months.
- Required EPA to begin enforcement action for violations of standards if a state had not acted within 30 days of notification.
- Set maximum civil penalties of $25,000 per day of violation for persons failing to comply with EPA administrative orders.
- Gave EPA more flexibility in setting requirements that customers of a drinking water system be notified when the system violated EPA rules. Notice of serious violations had to be given as promptly as possible, or within 14 days.
- Required EPA to issue regulations within 18 months requiring public water systems to test their water for unregulated contaminants.
- Set a maximum penalty of a $50,000 fine or five years' imprisonment, or both, for tampering with a public water system with the intention of harming people.

House Action

The House Energy and Commerce Committee approved HR 1650 (H Rept 99-168) by voice vote on May 15.

As introduced, HR 1650 contained the same $131.3 million funding level for existing regulatory programs as in S 124. But the Energy Subcommittee on Health and the Environment dropped the authorization ceiling to $74 million annually for 1986-87, and $82.8 million annually for 1988-89.

Like the Senate bill, HR 1650 generally made the law more protective of public health, by tightening requirements on EPA to set standards, adding requirements that utilities check their water for unregulated contaminants, giving EPA tougher enforcement powers, streamlining requirements that utilities notify their customers when the utilities violated federal rules, adding penalties for tampering with public water systems, authorizing EPA technical assistance to small utilities, banning injection of hazardous wastes above underground drinking water sources and setting up new planning and grant programs for groundwater protection.

Bill sponsors wanted to push EPA to set maximum contaminant levels on the contaminants allowed in tap water supplied by public utilities or private companies.

One of the most controversial parts of the standard-setting language in HR 1650 was the so-called "rational basis" requirement. It required EPA to set standards for contaminants if there was a rational basis to believe there might be any adverse effect on the health of persons.

Current law left the decision on whether health risks necessitated regulations to the "judgment" of the EPA administrator. Advocates of the "rational basis" language believed it would give EPA much less discretion.

Opponents, however, feared it could force EPA to regulate when a single scientific study found a health threat, even if a host of other studies found no threat.

To address such concerns, the Energy Committee amended the "rational basis" language to require EPA to make its decisions "based on a weighing of all available health evidence."

The committee defeated a series of amendments offered by Howard C. Nielson, R-Utah, that would have deleted or weakened provisions aimed at protecting groundwater.

The House June 17 by voice vote passed HR 1650.

After approving its bill, the House substituted its language for S 124.

House Provisions

As passed by the House, HR 1650:

- Authorized $74 million for fiscal 1986-87 and $82.8 million in fiscal 1988-89 for existing regulatory programs.
- Authorized $10 million annually over fiscal 1986-89 for technical assistance for small systems.
- Authorized $20 million annually in fiscal 1986-87 and $35 million annually in fiscal 1988-89 for grants to states to pay 50 percent of the cost of carrying out the state groundwater protection plans once they were approved by EPA and $10 million in fiscal 1986-87 and $15 million in fiscal 1988-89 for sole source aquifers.
- Required EPA within 12 months of enactment to set standards for 14 organic chemicals it listed in March 1982 — and within 36 months for more than 50 other contaminants it listed in October 1983 — unless it determined from all available evidence that there was no "rational basis" to believe they might adversely affect health.
- Required EPA to list substances that might pose health threats and set standards for them within three years.
- Ordered EPA within 18 months to issue rules to determine which surface waters should be treated by processes such as coagulation, sedimentation or filtration before disinfection. States had to adopt implementing regulations within 18 months of EPA action and apply them to specific water systems within 12 months after that.
- Directed EPA to issue regulations requiring disinfection as a treatment technique for all public water systems.
- Ordered EPA to issue regulations requiring every public water system to test for unregulated contaminants once every five years, unless EPA determined it should be done more often. Customers of each system had to be notified of test results.
- Gave EPA new authority to fine violators up to $5,000 through administrative orders.
- Set civil penalties for violations of up to $25,000 per violation per day.
- Made tampering with a public water system a federal crime with a maximum fine of $50,000, five years in prison or both.
- Required EPA within 12 months to amend its rules requiring systems to notify customers when in violation of the act. EPA would have to vary the notice requirements according to the frequency and seriousness of the violations.
- Barred the disposal of hazardous wastes by underground injection above or into geological formations that contained a drinking water source within one-quarter mile of the injection well. Required EPA and the states to conduct a nationwide inventory of hazardous-waste injection wells.
- Required states within three years to give EPA a comprehensive plan to protect underground sources of drinking water. If states failed to meet the requirement, they became ineligible for U.S. aid to run their underground injection control programs. ▮

California Offshore Leasing

For the first time in five years, Congress did not impose a moratorium on federal oil and gas leasing off the California coast as part of an Interior Department appropriations bill.

During the summer, members of the California delegation who opposed offshore leasing negotiated an agreement with Interior Secretary Donald P. Hodel that would have barred leasing off most of that state's coast in return for drilling in a few areas.

But the "preliminary agreement," as it was called, unraveled in September and an effort began again to attach a moratorium to the Interior appropriations bill (HR 3011).

When Congress failed to complete action on HR 3011, the issue came up again during consideration of the fiscal 1986 continuing appropriations bill (H J Res 465 — PL 99-450). A compromise amendment, adopted during House consideration of H J Res 465 and accepted by the Senate, required Hodel to meet with a congressional negotiating team every 60 days for the rest of fiscal 1986 to work out an agreement for drilling off the California coast. The amendment established a 19-member committee, including senators and representatives from California and from the committees with jurisdiction over the oil drilling issue. *(Details, Interior appropriations, p. 337; continuing resolution, p. 360; previous action 1984 Almanac p. 335)*

Background

Before companies could drill for oil on the federally owned Outer Continental Shelf, they had to lease tracts. If they found oil, they paid royalties to the Treasury and sold the oil for profit.

Congress had included offshore leasing bans in the fiscal 1982-85 Interior funding bills or continuing appropriations bills, to block the Reagan administration's accelerated energy development policies. An aggressive offshore leasing program had been initiated by former Interior Secretary James G. Watt, despite the protests of environmentalists and objections from several coastal states.

The last moratorium, a rider to the fiscal 1985 appropriation, expired Sept. 30. *(1984 Almanac p. 378)*

Interior Appropriations Bill

The administration and members of the California delegation announced agreement on the offshore drilling issue just as the House Appropriations Committee July 16 began its markup of HR 3011. Nine members of the 45-member House delegation and the two senators announced support in principle for the agreement at a July 16 press conference. Rep. Leon E. Panetta, D-Calif., who had been a leading supporter of the moratorium effort, played a key role in negotiating the agreement.

A new moratorium had been approved June 20 by the Appropriations Subcommittee on Interior as part of HR 3011. But when the administration-delegation agreement was announced, the Appropriations Committee deleted the moratorium language and approved report language incorporating the principles in the agreement.

The terms of the accord called for only 150 of the 6,460 California tracts protected under the existing moratorium to be offered for leasing, but they were tracts that were supposedly highly prized by oil companies.

The remaining tracts were to be off-limits for federal leasing until the year 2000, except under a national energy emergency declared by the president under the Energy Policy and Conservation Act (PL 94-163). Three test wells, however, could be drilled in these areas, no closer than 18 miles from the shoreline.

California members praised Hodel for his efforts to settle the issue by consensus, rather than by the confrontational approach of James Watt. But they admitted they chose compromise rather than test their shaky voting strength. During the June 28, 1984, markup of the fiscal 1985 Interior bill, a motion to remove all offshore leasing moratoriums had been rejected by a 20-21 vote.

When the House July 31 passed HR 3011, there was no challenge to the endorsement of the offshore leasing agreement, although oil companies and some California members had denounced it.

A dispute developed, however, on Sept. 10 when Hodel told the Californians that he could not support the July 16 proposal unless it were changed to include a different set of 150 tracts. Panetta denounced Hodel for taking that position, saying he had broken the earlier agreement.

But Hodel, in a Sept. 11 hearing before a House Merchant Marine and Fisheries subcommittee, said both sides had understood that the earlier plan was "preliminary," and subject to change after further consultation with affected parties.

During the August recess while Hodel toured California to gather views, Panetta had mustered 29 signatures (including those of the two senators and his own) for a telegram urging Hodel to stick with the July 16 plan.

Panetta said Interior officials had, during the original negotiations, presented the Californians with maps showing tracts whose petroleum potential made them most interesting to the oil and gas companies. The 150 tracts specified in the July 16 plan were taken from those shown on the maps.

But Hodel told the Merchant Marine Subcommittee on the Panama Canal and Outer Continental Shelf that the Interior maps contained out-of-date, unreliable information, and that he had voiced reservations about the resource potential of the 150 tracts.

Representatives of the oil and gas industry, who had little direct role in forming the July 16 plan, said the 150 tracts did not have high potential.

Hodel told Congress he was willing to work out a different list of 150 tracts and to consider banning leasing on the other tracts for longer than 15 years.

The version of HR 3011 approved by the Senate Appropriations Committee Sept. 24 did not contain any moratorium on federal oil and gas leasing off the California coast.

Continuing Appropriations Resolution

When the House Appropriations Committee Nov. 21 reported the fiscal 1986 continuing appropriations bill (H J Res 465 — H Rept 99-403), the most extended debate was over an amendment by Sidney R. Yates, D-Ill., that sought to extend the offshore leasing moratorium included in a previous continuing resolution that expired Dec 12. The amendment was rejected, 26-27.

Yates, chairman of the Interior Appropriations Subcommittee, said his amendment was necessary to "keep faith with members of the California delegation." But Ralph Regula, R-Ohio, and members from Louisiana and Texas, where there already was offshore drilling, vigorously opposed it.

Regula, ranking member of the subcommittee, said the moratorium was a bad policy decision that could hurt the country's long-range interests. Even if it were lifted, he said, no drilling probably would begin for another eight years.

Charles Wilson, D-Texas, said California should be willing to help supply the nation with oil as other states had. But Bill Lowery, R-Calif., said the Californians wanted to keep negotiating and needed the moratorium "to get Interior to the table." Vic Fazio, D-Calif., warned that if the moratorium did not continue, the issue would be tied up in the courts for years.

When H J Res 465 went to the House floor Dec. 4, the Rules Committee made in order only one proposal, a compromise worked out between Regula and Panetta on the offshore leasing issue.

The House adopted the Regula-Panetta amendment by voice vote.

The amendment required Hodel to work out an agreement with a congressional negotiating team for drilling off the California coast. The congressional team was to consist of 19 members, including senators and representatives from California and from the committees with jurisdiction over the oil drilling issue.

Panetta said that the amendment was better than nothing. He said he and his supporters were not sure they had support in the Rules Committee and in the full House to continue the moratorium.

The Senate Appropriations Committee accepted the compromise Dec. 5. ∎

Hazardous-Waste Liability

The House Dec. 16 swiftly passed a bill to keep open hazardous-waste disposal facilities that had to close because they could not meet a Nov. 8 deadline for obtaining mandatory insurance coverage.

The bill (HR 3917), passed by voice vote under suspension of the rules, had bipartisan support from House leaders. It had been whisked through a House Energy and

Commerce subcommittee Dec. 11.

Despite the speedy House action, the Senate failed to take up the measure before adjournment.

HR 3917 extended for up to a year deadlines for disposal facilities to comply with the Resource Conservation and Recovery Act of 1976 (PL 94-580), under which they were licensed to operate. The 1976 law authorized the Environmental Protection Agency (EPA) to set requirements for safe disposal of hazardous wastes. Companies already operating hazardous-waste disposal facilities (such as landfills) in 1976 could continue to operate under interim permits — without meeting all safety requirements — until EPA decided whether they should receive final permits. *(Congress and the Nation Vol. IV, p. 309)*

Background

In 1980, EPA issued a rule requiring facilities with interim permits to monitor the groundwater beneath the facilities for pollution and to carry liability insurance to cover any cleanup costs.

Faced with slow progress by EPA in carrying out the 1976 law, Congress set deadlines for compliance in a 1984 reauthorization (PL 98-616). It included a Nov. 8, 1985, deadline for facilities with interim permits to have groundwater monitoring and pollution liability insurance. *(1984 Almanac p. 305)*

Many companies facing the deadline were unable to buy pollution liability insurance because commercial availability of such insurance had diminished dramatically. EPA in December announced that only about 500 of the 1,600 facilities required to meet that deadline did so. Under the law, the rest were required to close.

House Action

Only the insurance requirement was waived in HR 3917. To be eligible for the extension, companies had to show they were complying with groundwater requirements and trying to get insurance.

While the House was considering the "superfund" hazardous-waste cleanup bill (HR 2817) Dec. 5, James T. Broyhill, R-N.C., had offered and then withdrawn an amendment that would have allowed EPA to extend the deadline for complying with the liability insurance requirement for up to two years. Broyhill had introduced an earlier version of his proposal in bill form as HR 3692.

The threat that the RCRA issue could stall passage of the superfund bill was defused by an agreement that yielded prompt action the next day by the Commerce, Transportation and Tourism Subcommittee, chaired by James J. Florio, D-N.J.

The subcommittee bill was more restrictive than the Broyhill amendment in the requirements facilities had to meet to get an extension and the length of the extension.

Broyhill would have required facilities to meet the groundwater monitoring requirements, but the subcommittee imposed the additional requirement that they must not be contaminating groundwater or must be undertaking a cleanup of any contamination. The subcommittee allowed an initial 45-day extension once facilities certified that they had complied with those requirements and another extension until June 30, 1986, if EPA certified that they were in fact complying. An additional extension until Nov. 8, 1986, could be granted at EPA's discretion.

To get the final extension, facilities had to certify that they were trying in good faith to get insurance, and EPA had to find that the insurance market was still constrained.

The bill also required EPA, by March 1, 1986, to revise its rules to provide methods other than commercial insurance (for example, indemnity contracts, surety bonds and corporate guarantees) by which facilities could cover themselves against liability.

Dennis E. Eckart, D-Ohio, expressed misgivings about the RCRA extension and the retroactive restoration of interim permits for facilities that had already missed the Nov. 8 deadline.

"This means that any facility covered by this bill that continued to accept waste after Nov. 8, in criminal violation of the law, would be safe from prosecution," Eckart said. "I frankly do not feel that we should be going forward with this bill at all."

Eckart also expressed concern over setting a precedent by legislatively waiving the first of many stringent deadlines written into the 1984 RCRA amendments, asking: "Will we now be expected to blink every time a new, supposedly onerous deadline approaches?"

But Florio assured Eckart and other members that the action was taken to deal specifically with the insurance problem and should not be taken as a sign that Congress was willing to waive other RCRA deadlines.

Florio said the bill was drafted to apply only to a "narrow class" of facilities and cited an EPA estimate that it would apply only to between 50 and 90 facilities.

Many facilities that had to close Nov. 8, according to committee staff, were operated by companies solely for disposal of their own wastes. Many of the larger facilities accepting waste from other companies had begun the process of getting a final permit.

Nancy L. Johnson, R-Conn., said the bill could ease the predicament of several small metal-plating companies in her district. She pointed to a similar drying up of the insurance market for day-care providers, truckers and ski lift operators, and said those plating companies "are among the first victims of what is certain to be an epidemic of insurance-related problems in the business sector in coming years." ▮

Dawson Appointment

The Senate by a vote of 60-34 approved the nomination Dec. 4 of Robert K. Dawson as assistant secretary of the Army for civil works — the civilian chief of the Army Corps of Engineers. *(Vote 352, p. 60-S)*

Opponents argued that Dawson, who has been acting assistant secretary since May 1984, had failed to enforce laws protecting the nation's wetlands from development under Section 404 of the Clean Water Act (PL 95-217).

A leader in the effort to block the confirmation, John H. Chafee, R-R.I., quoted Dawson as having told the Environment and Public Works Subcommittee on Environmental Pollution earlier in 1985 that "Congress did not design Section 404 to be a wetland protection mechanism." Chafee charged Dawson with frustrating the goals of the Clean Water Act and provoking "unprecedented levels of confrontation" with the state and federal agencies that shared a role in the 404 program.

Robert T. Stafford, R-Vt., chairman of the Environment and Public Works Committee, said Dawson had done a "sound job" running the corps' water resources development programs but had failed to operate the wetlands protection program in a manner that came "even within whistling distance" of the standards and criteria in the Clean Water Act.

Environmental groups, including the National Wildlife Federation, the Sierra Club and the National Audubon Society, also opposed the nomination.

Dawson was a legislative assistant to Rep. Jack Edwards, R-Ala. (1965-85), from 1972 to 1974, and staff director of the House Public Works Committee from 1974-81. He was deputy assistant secretary of the Army for civil works from 1981 to 1984.

Preserving Olmsted Legacy

The House June 3 suspended the rules and passed a bill (HR 37) to preserve the legacy of Frederick Law Olmsted Sr., the "father of landscape architecture in the United States."

The landscape designs of Olmsted, his sons and followers were found on the U.S. Capitol grounds, New York City's Central Park, dozens of national, state and local parks, college campuses, parkways and private estates.

The bill authorized an inventory of Olmsted heritage landscapes by the National Park Service, which was to issue standards for preservation of such landscapes, provide technical assistance to public and private entities in preserving them and conduct in-depth five-year studies of which landscapes might qualify as national historic landmarks. No new funding was authorized for these programs, estimated to cost $2 million to $3 million over 10 years.

HR 37 was approved by the House Interior and Insular Affairs Subcommittee on Public Lands on April 3 and reported by the full committee May 24 (H Rept 99-148).

Petroleum Reserve, IEA

Congress June 27 completed action on legislation (HR 1699 — PL 99-58) extending two programs intended to protect against a future energy crisis. The bill cleared when the House accepted a compromise version approved by the Senate earlier in the day.

HR 1699 reauthorized for four years the Strategic Petroleum Reserve, an oil stockpile that could be used in times of severe energy shortages, and reauthorized for three years U.S. participation in the International Energy Agency (IEA) through which oil-importing nations planned for a coordinated response to an international oil shortage.

Both programs were authorized by the 1975 Energy Policy and Conservation Act (PL 94-163) and expired June 30. *(Congress and the Nation Vol. IV, p. 235; 1984 Almanac pp. 349, 356)*

The bill included a House provision requiring a test sale of 1.1 million barrels of oil from the 470-million-barrel reserve, and a Senate provision requiring the Department of Energy to study coal imports.

HR 1699 repealed provisions in the law that allowed one chamber to block changes proposed by the president to the plan for distribution of oil from the reserve, requiring instead a 60-day waiting period.

Legislative Action

The House and Senate Energy committees both approved measures May 22 to extend authority for the Strategic Petroleum Reserve and for U.S. participation in the International Energy Agency.

By 11-2 the Senate Energy and Natural Resources Committee approved S 979 (S Rept 99-74), extending the authority for the oil reserve for four years and the authority for the international agency for two years. The IEA authorization was cut from four years by voice vote because of concerns about agency activities expressed by Sens. Don Nickles, R-Okla., and Howard M. Metzenbaum, D-Ohio.

The committee rejected, 6-11, an amendment by Bill Bradley, D-N.J., to set up a standby program for assistance to low-income citizens in the event of a petroleum shortage.

The House Energy and Commerce Committee approved by voice vote HR 1699 (H Rept 99-152), extending authority for both the petroleum reserve and IEA activities for four years.

The committee incorporated the provisions of HR 1698 which directed the Energy Department to conduct a test sale of oil from the petroleum reserve.

The House June 4 passed HR 1699 by voice vote.

The Senate June 18 passed an amended version of HR 1699 by a vote of 98-1. *(Vote 128, p. 26-S)*

The lone vote against the measure was cast by Bradley. Not voting was Sen. David L. Boren, D-Okla.

The Senate rejected, 44-55, an amendment by Bradley to set up a standby program of block grants to states to assist low-income citizens in the event of a petroleum shortage. *(Vote 127, p. 26-S)*

During debate on the measure June 17, the Senate accepted by voice vote an amendment by Metzenbaum to give Congress 60 days to examine and reject by joint resolution any expansion of antitrust exemptions given to oil companies by the Departments of Energy and Justice.

Metzenbaum, a longtime opponent of the IEA and antitrust immunity given to oil companies to participate in it, contended that new regulations under consideration by the administration would give oil companies a chance to manipulate prices.

Energy Committee Chairman James A. McClure, R-Idaho, defended the administration's actions but agreed to the provision allowing congressional review.

The Senate also approved by voice vote an amendment by Minority Leader Robert C. Byrd, D-W.Va., requiring the Energy Department to study coal imports, which alarmed coal producers although they equaled less than 0.2 percent of domestic production.

Residential Energy Efficiency

The Senate July 29 approved a bill on residential energy conservation after killing an unrelated amendment calling for retention of automobile fuel economy standards that the Reagan administration had decided to relax. The House took no action on the measure.

As passed by voice vote, the bill (S 410) was essentially the same as the version reported June 27 by the Senate Energy and Natural Resources Committee (S Rept 99-94). It revived for three years the Residential Conservation Service (RCS), established in 1978 as part of a larger energy conservation package (PL 95-619). Under RCS, which expired in 1984, utilities inspected homes for energy efficiency. *(1978 Almanac p. 645, 1984 Almanac p. 355)*

The bill as introduced merely would have killed another program, the Commercial and Apartment Conservation Service (CACS), established in 1980. But James A. McClure, R-Idaho, chairman of the Energy Committee, offered an amendment during the markup of S 410 to extend the RCS until 1988. It was adopted by voice vote.

S 410 also permitted utilities or states that could show they had energy conservation programs at least as effective as the Residential Conservation Service to seek a waiver from that program's requirement that utilities inform their customers about various energy-saving techniques and offer them home energy audits.

Daniel J. Evans, R-Wash., offered the unsuccessful amendment urging the National Highway Traffic Safety Administration (NHTSA) to drop its announced plan to roll back from an average of 27.5 miles per gallon (mpg) to 26 mpg the fuel efficiency standard that passenger cars had to meet for the 1986 and subsequent model years.

General Motors Corp. and the Ford Motor Co. had lobbied hard for the rollback, arguing that they could not meet the 27.5 mpg standard without sharply curtailing production of big, high-performance cars that were selling well. Such production cutbacks would mean major job losses, they said.

Chrysler Corp., which invested billions of dollars in production of cars that met the fuel economy standard, had vigorously protested the July 18 decision by NHTSA, saying it would allow GM and Ford to "reap a windfall for scoffing at that law."

Evans argued that the auto companies had had 10 years to meet the standard set by Congress. He said GM and Ford could have met the standard, just as Chrysler did, by replacing their gas-guzzling models with newer, more efficient ones.

After considerable debate, the Evans amendment was tabled (killed) by 52-39. *(Vote 166, p. 33-S)* ▮

Congress Dismantles Synthetic Fuels Program

Congress dismantled the U. S. Synthetic Fuels Corporation in the last days of the 1985 session, thus ending the controversial program to commercialize technologies for making abundant resources like coal and shale into other fuels.

Language rescinding most of the synfuels corporation's $7.3 billion in remaining funds was included in the fiscal 1986 continuing appropriations resolution (H J Res 465 — PL 99-190) signed by President Reagan on Dec. 19. *(Continuing resolution, p. 360)*

Earlier in the year, opponents tried to kill the program through various legislative vehicles: a separate bill (HR 935) approved by the House Energy Committee, a House-passed deficit-reduction bill (HR 3500) and the fiscal 1986 appropriations bill for the Interior Department and related agencies (HR 3011). *(Deficit reduction, p. 498; Interior appropriations, p. 337)*

Background

Interest in synthetic fuels developed in the 1970s when oil imports from the Mideast were cut and the price of oil rose. President Ford proposed government support for a synthetic fuels industry in 1975. Legislation to establish a program passed the Senate in 1975, but was killed in the House. A similar House bill was killed in 1976 by one vote. *(Congress and the Nation Vol. IV, p. 267)*

In 1979, after a second round of gasoline shortages revived public concern, President Jimmy Carter pushed synthetic fuels development as his major initiative to increase energy independence. The Energy Security Act of 1980 (PL 96-294) authorized $20 billion for the new federally chartered Synthetic Fuels Corporation and other projects. Congress earmarked $17.5 billion for the synfuels program out of $19 billion it appropriated to the Energy Security Reserve in 1980. *(1980 Almanac p. 477)*

The corporation was supposed to offer price supports and loan guarantees to private industries that would turn substances such as oil shale and coal into fuels that could replace petroleum products. The corporation was given ambitious goals: to produce fuels equivalent to 500,000 barrels of oil per day by 1987, and two million barrels per day by 1992, compared with 7.5 million barrels per day of oil imported in 1980.

But the program fell far short of its production goals and the corporation was plagued by serious management troubles.

Congressional criticism of the synfuels corporation focused on conflicts of interest among board members, high salaries for staff, lack of interest on the part of private industry, lack of production and the possibility of huge subsidies going to profitable oil companies.

The effort to get rid of the corporation was joined by several environmental organizations, including the Sierra Club, the Natural Resources Defense Council, the Environmental Policy Institute and Friends of the Earth. Environmental groups were suspicious of synthetic fuels projects because of pollutants and waste produced by plants, and because they feared strip mining and water usage by large projects in the West.

In May 1984, when the corporation could not conduct business because its board of directors was down to two of seven members, the Reagan administration demanded that $9 billion be taken away from it and refused to appoint new directors.

Congress rescinded $2 billion from the corporation in the deficit-reduction act passed in July (PL 98-369). Opponents were not satisfied, and another $5.375 billion was rescinded in the Interior appropriation that was included in the fiscal 1985 continuing resolution (PL 98-473). The corporation was left with $7.9 billion. Congress scaled down its mission and President Reagan appointed a new majority to the corporation's board of directors. *(1984 Almanac p. 347)*

Legislative Action

House opponents of the synthetic fuels program lost their first battle to take back nearly $8 billion the corporation had not obligated when the House Budget Committee May 16 did not factor savings from the synfuels program into the fiscal 1986 budget it approved.

The Budget panel's action was forecast when the Democrats on the committee caucused May 14 and narrowly defeated a proposal to help reduce the deficit by rescinding the corporation's appropriation.

House Energy Committee Bill

The next move came June 19 when the House Energy and Commerce Subcommittee on Fossil Fuels approved legislation to eliminate the corporation and replace it with a much smaller program within the Department of Energy (DOE). The bill (HR 935) was approved by voice vote, with only Dan L. Schaefer, R-Colo., dissenting.

As originally introduced, HR 935 would have abolished the synfuels program entirely. The panel accepted a substitute, offered by Mike Synar, D Okla., that authorized a $500 million DOE program to encourage development of substitute fuels for traditional petroleum products.

The bill required a separate appropriation for the DOE program. Federal support was limited to 60 percent of a project's cost, and price supports were held to a maximum of 125 percent of market prices. HR 935 also gave Congress an opportunity to review any awards made by the synfuels corporation after Feb. 5, 1985.

The full committee June 25 approved HR 935 and reported the bill July 11 (H Rept 99-196, Part I).

The committee rejected, by voice vote, an amendment offered by Timothy E. Wirth, D-Colo., to increase the substitute DOE program from $500 million to $2.25 billion.

Wirth, whose state had several synfuels projects and large oil shale reserves awaiting commercial development, argued that the DOE program was too small to help an industry that would be vital in the event of a future energy shortage.

The committee also defeated, by voice vote, an amendment by Richard C. Shelby, D-Ala., to increase the DOE program to $750 million.

Tom Tauke, R-Iowa, offered an amendment to require congressional approval of any contract signed by the synfuels corporation since Feb. 5, 1985, the day after HR 935 was introduced. The bill provided that Congress could disapprove any such contract by joint resolution. The amendment was defeated by voice vote.

Interior Appropriations Bill

House. The strategy of synfuels opponents was to have HR 935 attached to the fiscal 1986 Interior appropriations bill to force the Senate, where support for the corporation was strong, to deal with the issue.

The opportunity to do so came when the House July 24 voted 179-251 to reject the rule setting terms for debate on the Interior bill, HR 3011. The rule would have prevented synfuels opponents from proposing amendments to the appropriations bill to kill the synfuels funding. *(Vote 228, p. 72-H)*

The rule had been approved by the Rules Committee July 18, after the committee had defeated on a 5-7 vote a motion to allow a synfuels amendment on the floor.

Although unusual, the vote against the rule paralleled a 1984 vote, when the House also defeated a rule on the Interior appropriations bill that blocked amendments having to do with the synfuels question. The 1984 vote defeating the rule was 148-261. *(1984 Almanac p. 381)*

Before passing HR 3011 on July 31, the House adopted an amendment to kill the synfuels corporation.

House supporters of the corporation, in the face of the heavy voting strength demonstrated on the vote against the rule, agreed to save time by not debating the issue again. The amendment to rescind previously appropriated funds for the corporation, except for $500 million, was approved by a 312-111 margin. *(Vote 255, p. 82-H)*

After rescinding the synfuels funds, which had been appropriated in 1980 but not spent, the House approved an amendment to appropriate $500 million for research and development on technologies for burning coal more cleanly in industrial and utility boilers.

That money was appropriated out of the "Clean Coal Technology Reserve," a $750 million special fund set up late in 1984 with money taken from an earlier synfuels rescission. No money had been spent from the fund and the Reagan administration had requested that no funds be appropriated for fiscal 1986. As passed, the fiscal 1986 bill appropriated $100 million for fiscal 1986 and $200 million for each of the fiscal years 1987 and 1988. *(1984 Almanac p. 378)*

The committee bill would have appropriated all $750 million in the Clean Coal Technology Reserve over 1986-88. But when Silvio O. Conte, R-Mass., offered an amendment to strike the advance funding for 1987 and 1988, leaving just $100 million for fiscal 1986, Ralph Regula, R-Ohio, offered a substitute to give the program $500 million over three years. Regula's amendment was adopted by voice vote, and the amended Conte proposal was then adopted 238-184. *(Vote 256, p. 82-H)*

Senate. During Senate Appropriations Committee consideration of HR 3011, the synfuels corporation was not an issue. But before reporting the bill Sept. 24, the committee took care to protect from Reagan administration budget-cutters the $750 million fund for clean coal technology (S Rept 99-141).

The fund was the focus of a major dispute during subcommittee markup of the bill Sept. 19 when Minority Leader Robert C. Byrd, D-W. Va., proposed appropriating the entire amount in advance over 1986-89, to give industry enough confidence to invest in the public-private cost-sharing program.

But the subcommittee delayed action on Byrd's proposal after Chairman James A. McClure, R-Idaho, expressed concern that appropriating the entire amount in fiscal 1986 would put the subcommittee over its fiscal 1986 budget ceiling.

The full committee approved a Byrd amendment providing appropriations of $100 million in fiscal 1986 and advance appropriations of $175 million in 1987, $300 million in 1988 and $175 million in 1989 from the coal fund.

When HR 3011 went to the Senate floor Oct. 31, a controversy immediately developed over the synfuels program. The Senate defeated, 41-58, an amendment that would have blocked a move to kill the program. Synfuels opponents said their margin of support was greater than they had expected. *(Vote 270, p. 48-S)*

The Senate vote was on a motion by McClure to table (kill) an amendment by Howard M. Metzenbaum, D-Ohio, that would have rescinded most of the corporation's remaining funds.

But Metzenbaum and his allies had not achieved a final victory; the Senate turned to other business without actually adopting Metzenbaum's amendment or completing action on the appropriations bill itself.

Deficit-Reduction Bill

House opponents of the synfuels program were taking no chances on the Senate accepting their provisions in HR 3011 abolishing the synthetic fuels corporation. The Energy and Commerce Committee Sept. 18 voted to kill the program during actions to bring spending in line with the fiscal 1986 budget resolution (S Con Res 32).

The budget resolution, which required congressional committees to reconcile spending for programs under their jurisdiction with savings targets, had not addressed the future of the synfuels agency. But members of the committee said quick action was needed to prevent the corporation from spending millions of dollars before Congress finally decided its fate. The committee also included a provision to void contracts the corporation signed after July 31.

The Energy Committee's recommendations went into the deficit-reduction bill (HR 3500) passed by the House Oct. 31. HR 3500 was later combined with another deficit-reduction measure (HR 3128) by a rule that sent the bills to conference between the House and Senate. But in the final days of the session, the deficit-reduction measure got caught in a controversy between House and Senate over a taxing proposal for the "superfund" hazardous-waste cleanup program and did not clear. *(Deficit-reduction bill, p. 498)*

Continuing Resolution

Congress finally administered the coup de grâce to the Synthetic Fuels Corporation in H J Res 465, the fiscal 1986 continuing appropriations resolution, which incorporated the Interior appropriations measure.

The final bill slammed the door on further spending by the synfuels corporation as of the moment it was signed, and ordered that the agency be virtually dismantled within 60 days of the bill's enactment.

Congress rescinded all of the corporation's estimated $7.3 billion in remaining funds — except for almost $400 million that went to a clean coal technology program and $10 million to pay costs of closing down the agency. Congress prohibited the corporation's board of directors from making any further commitments of aid to synfuels projects.

The $400 million went to a program, to be administered by the energy secretary, for research and development of technologies for burning coal with less pollution. That program in effect superseded the one Congress authorized in 1984 that had not been carried out. Of the funds rescinded in 1984, $750 million had been put into a Clean Coal Technology Reserve for such research. Those funds, however, could not be spent unless appropriated by Congress.

Congress kept the $400 million in the Energy Security Reserve but appropriated it to the clean coal program; then it reduced the amount in the Clean Coal Technology Reserve to $350 million. Thus, the $400 million set aside for clean coal was merely used to replace some of the $750 million set aside the previous year. ∎

Low-Level Nuclear-Waste Bill Clears Congress

The Senate Dec. 19 cleared and sent to the president a bill (HR 1083 — PL 99-240) imposing strict deadlines for states or regions to set up disposal facilities for low-level radioactive wastes. The measure made states legally liable for damages incurred by businesses that had to shut down because their states had not provided for disposal of wastes with low levels of radioactivity.

As cleared, the bill included provisions of separate legislation approving seven regional compacts involving 37 states that had agreed to join together for the disposal of such wastes.

Congress speeded up its work in December to complete action on the legislation because of an end-of-year deadline set by three states that had been taking in all of the civilian low-level nuclear waste generated in the nation: South Carolina, Washington and Nevada. Those three states had threatened to stop accepting out-of-state waste unless other states took action to develop individual or regional disposal sites.

Low-level wastes included such items as soiled protective garments used by workers at nuclear electric utilities, medical laboratories and hospitals. South Carolina and Washington state had each been getting about 45 percent of the waste and Nevada the other 10 percent.

Provisions

As cleared by Congress, HR 1083:

- Reaffirmed as national policy that each state would be responsible, alone or in cooperation with other states, for disposal of non-federal low-level radioactive wastes generated within its borders.
- Amended the Low Level Radioactive Waste Policy Act of 1980 (PL 96-573) to provide that South Carolina, Washington and Nevada would continue to accept waste from other states during a seven-year transition period.
- Authorized the three sited states to impose a surcharge, in addition to their normal fees, for disposal of low-level wastes from states not belonging to their compacts. The surcharge per cubic foot would be up to $10 in 1986-87, up to $20 in 1988-89, and $40 in 1990-92.
- Set a deadline of July 1, 1986, by which states either had to join a compact or indicate their intent to develop a facility for disposal of low-level waste.
- Authorized the three sited states to charge double the normal surcharge to states not meeting that deadline until Dec. 31, 1986. As of Jan. 1, 1987, the sited states could deny disposal access to states still not meeting the requirement.
- Set a deadline of Jan. 1, 1988, by which each compact commission had to have identified a "host state" for its disposal facility, and each host state had to have a plan for establishing the location for a facility. States that were not members of a compact also had to develop plans for choosing facility sites within their own borders by then.

States failing to meet that deadline could be charged double the normal surcharge until June 30, 1988, after which they could be charged four times the normal surcharge. States still not complying as of Jan. 1, 1989, could be denied access.

- Set a deadline of Jan. 1, 1990, by which compacts had to file complete applications to the Nuclear Regulatory Commission (NRC) for licenses to operate disposal facilities.
- Required non-compact states, by the same deadline, either to file such applications or to certify to the NRC that they would provide for low-level waste storage and disposal within their borders after Dec. 31, 1992.
- States not meeting the Jan. 1, 1990, deadline could be denied access by the three states with disposal sites.
- Required sited states to set aside in a federal escrow account 25 percent of the funds collected in surcharges, and to rebate them under a certain schedule to the states and compact commissions from which they were collected if they met the deadlines.
- Set an overall limit of 19.6 million cubic feet on how much waste the three sites had to accept and provided the

following allocations: 8.4 million cubic feet for the facility in Barnwell, S.C.; 9.8 million cubic feet for the facility in Richland, Wash.; and 1.4 million cubic feet for the facility in Beatty, Nev.

- Allocated, out of the same total capacity, 11.9 million cubic feet to commercial nuclear power reactors and 7.7 million cubic feet to other waste sources.
- Made non-complying states liable after Dec. 31, 1992, for damages incurred by the generator unless the state agreed to take legal possession of the waste. States would have three years in which to take possession.
- Provided that states that did not immediately take responsibility for the waste had to forgo certain rebates on surcharges to which they would otherwise have been entitled.
- Gave the NRC authority to provide waste-generating states with emergency access to disposal sites if the NRC found it necessary "to eliminate an immediate and serious threat to public health and safety or the common defense and security."
- Prohibited sited states that denied disposal access to non-complying states from discriminating among the wastes of the non-complying state according to their type or source.
- Gave Congress' approval to seven interstate compacts (states that currently belonged to each are shown in parentheses): Southeast (Alabama, Florida, Georgia, Mississippi, North Carolina, South Carolina, Tennessee and Virginia); Northwest (Alaska, Hawaii, Idaho, Montana, Oregon, Utah and Washington); Rocky Mountain (Colorado, Nevada, New Mexico and Wyoming); Central (Arkansas, Kansas, Louisiana, Nebraska and Oklahoma); Central Midwest (Illinois and Kentucky); Midwest (Indiana, Iowa, Michigan, Minnesota, Missouri, Ohio and Wisconsin); Northeast (Connecticut, New Jersey, Delaware and Maryland).

Background

Under PL 96-573, states were encouraged to form regional compacts for joint disposal of wastes with low levels of radioactivity. During the next five years, however, the states made little concrete progress toward opening disposal sites. *(1980 Almanac p. 494)*

South Carolina, Washington and Nevada had the only disposal sites. Under PL 96-573, the regional compacts to which those states belonged (Southeast, Northwest and Rocky Mountain) had the right to exclude waste from other states after Jan. 1, 1986.

Congressional ratification of the interstate compacts was held up because some waste-producing states feared waste-receiving states would cut off their access to disposal sites once the compacts were in effect. That right was contingent on congressional approval of the compacts, and states outside those regions blocked approval because they found it difficult to open their own sites.

The three states with sites stepped up pressure on Congress to break the impasse. In mid-1985, Govs. Richard W. Riley, D-S.C., Booth Gardner, D-Wash., and Richard H. Bryan, D-Nev., agreed on conditions under which they would temporarily continue to accept the waste. Their proposal included requiring other states to move in steps toward establishing regional or state disposal sites. Each step would have a deadline and states missing those deadlines could be denied access to disposal sites until they complied. The governors also insisted that their three states should not have to accept more low-level waste than they did in 1983, except for a small increase for Nevada.

House Action

Committee

Interior Committee. The House Interior and Insular Affairs Committee July 31 by voice vote approved legislation ratifying six regional agreements for disposal of low-level radioactive waste from some 34 states.

The package included separate bills giving congressional consent to six interstate compacts (HR 862, HR 1046, HR 1267, HR 2062, HR 2635, HR 2702) and another "umbrella" bill (HR 1083) specifying rules under which the compacts were to operate. Reports were filed Oct. 22 on both HR 1083 (H Rept 99-314, Part I) and the separate bills (H Repts 99-315 through 99-320, Part I).

The seventh compact, for the Northeast, was reported Nov. 13 (HR 3372 — H Rept 99-371).

As approved by the committee, HR 1083 gave states until Dec. 31, 1992, to comply with PL 96-573 as long as they were meeting a timetable for developing new sites within their own compacts. HR 1083 set a series of "milestones" or interim deadlines, toward the goal of having a disposal site. The three states currently receiving wastes could cut off access to any state not meeting the milestones.

A key amendment offered by committee Chairman Morris K. Udall, D-Ariz., adjusted the milestones as set in subcommittee. It also in some cases provided non-complying states with a grace period before they would be cut off — but progressively raised the disposal fees their industries would have to pay in the meantime. Even for complying states, the bill allowed receiving states to impose specified surcharges beyond normal fees after 1985.

Udall's amendment, accepted by voice vote, also provided for emergency access to current sites to be granted by the NRC "if necessary to eliminate an immediate and serious threat to the public health and safety."

The committee also adopted by voice vote an amendment by Peter H. Kostmayer, D-Pa., that left further definition of which wastes would be included in the low-level facilities to the NRC.

Energy and Commerce Committee. The House Energy and Commerce Committee Oct. 29 approved the package of bills, after overturning several subcommittee changes and restoring language reported by the Interior and Insular Affairs Committee.

The legislation was reported Dec. 4 (H Repts 99-314 through 99-320, Part II).

One change adopted by the subcommittee would have allowed individual states choosing to operate their own disposal sites instead of joining compacts to exclude waste from other states. The language drew fire from committee opponents, who argued it would encourage states to drop out of existing compacts and run counter to the goal of discouraging proliferation of disposal sites. It was dropped by voice vote in full committee.

Another controversial subcommittee change allowed states with disposal sites to grant selective exemptions when they cut off access to states failing to meet the milestones. An effort by ranking subcommittee Republican Carlos J. Moorhead, Calif., to nullify it in subcommittee was defeated on an 8-8 vote. In full committee, however, he prevailed on a 16-9 show of hands.

Energy Subcommittee Chairman Edward J. Markey,

D-Mass., had sought to keep the exemption to ease the effect of a cutoff on hospitals, which he said could "threaten the quality of health care." But Moorhead said the sanctions were "designed to foster political pressure on state officials" to develop waste sites, and that easing them for one group would weaken that pressure.

Another dispute in the markup came over "mixed wastes" that were both radioactive and otherwise hazardous and therefore subject to radioactive-waste laws administered by the NRC and hazardous-waste disposal laws under the Environmental Protection Agency (EPA). Critics of the agencies said their rules on mixed wastes sometimes conflicted.

The committee adopted by voice vote an amendment by Al Swift, D-Wash., requiring the two agencies jointly to revise regulations in conflict. They would also have to come up with a consolidated application process for their respective permits — what Swift called "one-stop shopping."

Swift's amendment was opposed by Moorhead, who offered a substitute requiring EPA to write the regulations with NRC concurrence, and NRC to enforce them. The Moorhead substitute was rejected 20-22, largely along party lines.

Floor

The House Dec. 9 by a vote of 378-0 passed HR 1083, which set policies and deadlines for carrying out the seven interstate compacts. *(Vote 400, p. 126-H)*

It then passed by voice vote a bill (HR 3878) granting the constitutionally required consent of Congress to the seven compacts. That bill replaced seven separate bills giving consent, which were tabled.

The version of HR 1083 that passed reconciled largely similar versions approved by the two committees. Committee leaders had announced agreement Dec. 4.

The Interior bill had allowed the three states to agree annually on how to allocate capacity among themselves, while the Energy bill had not. The compromise allowed states to refuse to take more waste if they were accepting their annual limit. If all three states had reached their annual limits, the limit was increased in 10 percent increments for each state. The three states could give priority access to states within their compact region.

The final bill relied largely on Energy Committee language on emergency access to disposal sites. When access was cut off to a non-complying state, the two bills allowed the NRC to grant access to generators if it found a serious threat to public health and safety. The final bill kept an Interior provision that none of the three sites would have to give emergency access for more than 20 percent of the waste it accepted in the previous year.

The bill combined committee efforts to resolve a deadlock between NRC and EPA on regulation of "mixed" wastes that were both radioactive and hazardous for other reasons such as toxicity. The two agencies had to develop joint regulations to be approved by Congress, and consolidate their license and permit procedures.

Senate Action

Committee

Judiciary. The Senate Judiciary Commiteee Sept. 19 approved by voice vote six interstate agreements for regional dispoal of wastes with low levels of radioactivity. The bills (S 44, S 356, S 442, S 655, S 802 and S 899) ratified compacts involving 34 states. The committee reported the seventh compact, S 1978, on Nov. 21.

Energy and Natural Resources. The Senate Energy and Natural Resources Committee Nov. 13 approved by a vote of 16-2 a bill (S 1517) setting up a system under which the states in the regional compacts would operate.

The two dissenting votes on the Nov. 13 motion to report the bill were by Bill Bradley, D-N.J., and Howard M. Metzenbaum, D-Ohio. The bill was reported Nov. 22 (S Rept 99-199).

Before approving S 1517, the committee adopted an amendment providing for the possibility of emergency access to disposal facilities by states when denial of access threatened public health or safety. The governor of a generator state could simply declare such an emergency. It would be up to the governor of the state having the disposal site, however, to grant access, subject to whatever conditions he decided to impose.

In its general structure and most of its provisions, S 1517 as approved was similar to the versions of HR 1083 drafted by the House committees. Both House and Senate versions allowed the three states to cut off all access to states outside their compacts as of Jan. 1, 1993.

Environment and Public Works. The Senate Environment and Public Works Committee Dec. 4 by a vote of 14-1 approved a different bill (S 1578) to set out ground rules for low-level waste disposal.

While the Senate Energy bill allowed the three states with disposal sites to cut off disposal privileges altogether for waste-generating states not meeting the milestones, the Environment bill allowed grace periods to non-complying states before disposal access was cut off. During those grace periods, states would pay rapidly escalating surcharges until they met the milestone.

Pete V. Domenici, R-N.M., cast the sole dissenting vote because the committee failed to adopt an amendment requiring study of the issue of so-called "orphan wastes," which did not fit into the legal definition of either low-level or high-level wastes.

Floor

With time running out on the 1985 session and Congress facing the end-of-the year deadline set by South Carolina, Washington and Nevada, marathon negotiations took place in the Senate to get a bill through.

As late as Dec. 18, the legislation seemed to be stalled because of objections from Daniel J. Evans, R-Wash., who thought the proposed legislation was not tough enough. Leaders of the Senate Energy, Environment and Judiciary committees negotiated a compromise version of HR 1083 incorporating provisions of both House bills.

The Senate passed HR 1083 Dec. 19 after approving by voice vote a substitute amendment offered by Strom Thurmond, R-S.C. The principal change made by the Senate involved language imposing liability on non-complying states after Dec. 31, 1992. At that time, any waste generator within a delinquent state could ask the state to take legal possession of the waste. If the state refused, it became liable for all damages incurred by the generator. If the states did not immediately take responsibility for the waste, they also had to forgo certain rebates on surcharges to which they would otherwise have been entitled.

Final Action

When the bill returned to the House, that body stripped from it certain provisions on "mixed wastes" —

those wastes that are both radioactive and hazardous for other reasons, such as toxicity. The language had been meant to solve a jurisdictional dispute between the NRC and the Environmental Protection Agency. Bill managers said they would hold hearings on the subject in 1986.

The House made a few minor amendments of its own, in which the Senate concurred, clearing the bill late Dec. 19.

NRC Reauthorization Stalls

Congress failed to complete action on a two-year reauthorization for the Nuclear Regulatory Commission (NRC), but funding for the agency was not in jeopardy. The fiscal 1986 energy and water development appropriations bill (HR 2959 — PL 99-141) included $418 million for the NRC. *(Energy and water development appropriations bill, p. 323)*

The Senate June 13 approved a reauthorization measure (S 895) by voice vote, authorizing $437 million annually for the NRC for fiscal 1986-87.

The Senate accepted, without objection, an amendment to require the NRC to report annually on its licensing and regulatory objectives. In floor debate, Gary Hart, D-Colo., criticized the NRC for decisions in 1985 to close some meetings to the public and to restart an undamaged reactor at the Three Mile Island power plant.

The Senate Environment and Public Works Committee approved S 895 (S Rept 99-54) on May 2.

A bill (HR 1711 — H Rept 99-93, Parts I and II) authorizing $429 million for fiscal 1986 and $460 million for 1987 was reported June 25 by the House Energy and Commerce Committee and May 14 by the House Interior and Insular Affairs Committee.

Biomass Fuels

President Reagan April 16 signed a measure (S 781 — PL 99-24) allowing four projects to remain eligible for federal funds to make alcohol fuel from crops.

The bill was cleared by the House April 2 by voice vote; it passed the Senate March 28 by voice vote.

The projects, located in Louisiana, Maine, Minnesota and Nebraska, had applied for federal support available under a Department of Energy (DOE) program to foster biomass fuels. Established in 1980 under the Energy Security Act (PL 96-294) the program was scheduled to begin phasing out in 1984. *(1980 Almanac p. 477)*

The Department of Energy interpreted the law to mean that projects that were under consideration but had not received final approval by Sept. 30, 1984 (or, in the case of the Louisiana project, April 30, 1985) would be ineligible.

PL 99-24 extended eligibility of the four projects for $250 million in federal loan guarantees until Sept. 30, 1985, but it did not require DOE to approve the projects.

In signing the bill, Reagan directed the energy secretary to make sure that the projects could produce fuel at competitive prices, since the loan guarantees could make the government liable for as much as $250 million.

The House had not originally voted on a separate bill for a one-year eligibility extension but on Feb. 27 had inserted a similar provision in HR 1035, an emergency farm credit authorization bill that passed the House the same day. *(Vote 17, p. 8-H)*

Wildlife Refuge Veto

Citing budget pressures, President Reagan Jan. 14, 1986, vetoed and returned to Congress a bill (HR 1404) authorizing land acquisition for a wildlife refuge at Cape Charles on the Eastern Shore of Virginia.

The area, which was threatened by development, offered the last food and rest to waterfowl before they crossed the Chesapeake Bay going south for the winter. It provided habitat for the endangered peregrine falcon, bald eagle and brown pelican.

"This is the first response to Gramm-Rudman," said one official of the U.S. Fish and Wildlife Service, referring to a new law (PL 99-177) requiring deficit reductions to reach a balanced budget by fiscal 1991. "It's money that we don't have." *(Gramm-Rudman, p. 459)*

The bill not only gave legal sanction to an already established wildlife refuge in Virginia but also authorized development of a training center there for wildlife managers. In his veto message, Reagan said he opposed only the training center, not the refuge itself. *(Text of message, p. 41-D; Reagan vetoes, box, p. 6)*

HR 1404 had been passed by voice vote in the House Dec. 2, 1985, and in the Senate Dec. 19, one day before adjournment of the 99th Congress' first session. Reagan's veto, his fifth of a public bill during the Congress, came a week before the second session convened.

While returning the bill to Capitol Hill for possible override action, the president asserted his authority, during Congress' adjournment, to prevent it from becoming law simply by withholding his approval. The administration was challenging before the Supreme Court a 1984 federal appeals court ruling that such "pocket vetoes" may not be used between sessions of the same Congress. *(Background, 1984 Almanac p. 204)*

Lawmakers made no immediate attempt to override the president's veto. Staff members suggested that no authorizing legislation was really needed either to continue acquiring land for the refuge or to build a training center. The existing 174-acre refuge was created administratively on surplus federal land formerly used by the Cape Charles Air Force Station. There already were buildings from the air station on the site.

The fiscal 1986 continuing appropriations resolution (H J Res 465 — PL 99-190) included $2.64 million to acquire additional land for the refuge — 396 of the 1,400 acres ultimately planned for inclusion in the refuge. It also included $600,000 for rehabilitation and construction of buildings there. *(Continuing resolution, p. 360)*

LAW/JUDICIARY

CQ

Law/Judiciary

Congress and the Reagan administration were at loggerheads over a host of legal issues during much of 1985, and in marked contrast to the previous year, there was little legislative action in this area.

In 1984, a major anti-crime bill was enacted, along with legislation that restructured the federal bankruptcy courts. The year ended with the Justice Department in a state of flux over the Senate's delay in the confirmation of Edwin Meese III, then counselor to the president, to be attorney general.

1985 started where 1984 left off — with the Meese nomination — and the Senate's continued debate over it signaled what was generally to be a year of tension between the executive and legislative branches of government.

Meese, Reynolds Fights

Although Meese finally was confirmed by the Senate, 63-31, members never got a chance to vote on the elevation of one of his subordinates. Meese and President Reagan wanted to promote William Bradford Reynolds, head of the Justice Department's civil rights division, to associate attorney general, the No. 3 position at Justice. But the Senate Judiciary Committee refused to send the nomination to the Senate floor.

A majority of the committee was critical of the decisions Reynolds made in a variety of areas, including voting rights enforcement, school prayer and affirmative action, and the way he defended his actions before the panel. Key members said they were troubled by conflicts between Reynolds' testimony and information provided by other witnesses and documents from his own division.

Like the Meese fight, the dispute over Reynolds reflected the continuing disagreement between Congress and the administration over legal issues. At the core were persistent differences in philosophies over civil rights enforcement and the role of the federal government in this area.

Affirmative Action Disputes

Meese and Reynolds continued their opposition to affirmative action programs, contending that the programs ended up requiring quotas for women and ethnic minorities.

Reynolds angered some members of Congress by his interpretation of a 1984 Supreme Court decision, *Firefighters Union No. 1784 v. Stotts*, which held that federal judges could not override a valid seniority system to preserve the jobs of black workers hired under a court-approved affirmative action plan. The court overturned a federal court order directing the Memphis, Tenn., fire department to ignore its usual rule of "last hired, first fired" in carrying out budget-dictated layoffs.

Reynolds contended that the decision meant federal courts could not support affirmative action programs as a remedy for discrimination. But three separate federal appeals courts disagreed with him. Nonetheless, Reynolds in 1985 sent letters to 50 jurisdictions asking them to modify consent decrees that included quotas as remedies for affirmative action.

This move angered civil rights advocates in the House and Senate as well as the civil rights community. The House Judiciary Committee even included language in a Justice Department authorization restricting Reynolds' authority to challenge consent decrees. However, the bill was never enacted.

Reynolds was closely questioned about his affirmative action policies during his confirmation hearings, and while he refused to promise that the department would stop bringing lawsuits, Reynolds said the division was "not going to pick fights" with cities and counties in this area.

Meese and Reynolds attempted a more sweeping change in affirmative action policy when they tried to convince the president to rewrite a 1965 executive order that served as the foundation of federal efforts to achieve equal employment opportunity.

Their effort met with strong opposition in the civil rights community and in Congress. By year's end, 69 senators and 175 House members had written the president urging him to leave the executive order alone.

The executive order, issued by President Lyndon B. Johnson in 1965 and supported by every president since then, required all businesses with government contracts to take "affirmative action" to ensure that workers were employed without regard to race, creed or color. Failure to comply could make a contractor ineligible for federal work.

Labor Department regulations put into effect to implement the order required companies doing business with the government to submit plans with goals and timetables for hiring minorities. The regulations specifically prohibited quotas, stating that "goals must not be rigid and inflexible quotas which must be met, but must be targets reasonably attainable by means of applying every good-faith effort to make all aspects of the entire affirmative action program work."

While Meese and Reynolds had support within the administration, they faced persistent opposition from Labor Secretary William E. Brock III, who resisted efforts to weaken the order in ways he thought would make it ineffective.

Voting Rights

Congress and the administration also battled over voting rights enforcement, although the battlefield was the Supreme Court, not the House or Senate floors.

In 1982 Congress passed a bill to renew and strengthen the 1965 Voting Rights Act. Reagan signed the bill, but the administration, led by Reynolds, fought Congress every step of the way.

The first lawsuit filed under the 1982 amendments reached the Supreme Court in 1985. The Justice Department backed North Carolina Attorney General Lacy

Thornburg in contending that a federal court misinterpreted the 1982 law when it struck down seven of the state's multi-member legislative districts on the grounds that the use of such districts illegally diluted the black vote.

The department's position angered the principal authors of the bill, who filed a vigorous "friend-of-the-court" brief arguing that the lower court properly followed the intent of Congress in reaching its decision.

'Grove City' Legislation

The administration, along with the U.S. Catholic Conference, was also in the forefront of another civil rights fight with Congress. This one, which began a year earlier, focused on a 1984 Supreme Court decision, *Grove City College v. Bell*, that narrowed the coverage of four civil rights laws.

The court ruled 6-3 that Title IX of the 1972 Education Act Amendments banned sex discrimination only in a "program or activity" receiving federal aid, not in the entire institution.

Civil rights lawyers and their allies in Congress contended the court misread the law. They said Congress always intended an entire educational institution to be barred from discriminating if any of its components received federal aid.

The ruling also restricted enforcement of three other laws — Title VI of the 1964 Civil Rights Act, Section 504 of the Rehabilitation Act of 1973 and the Age Discrimination Act of 1975 — because they contained the same "program or activity" language as Title IX.

The House Judiciary and Education and Labor committees approved bills to overturn the *Grove City* decision by making clear that an entire institution was covered by the discrimination ban when federal aid went to any of its components. However, only the division or department receiving federal aid would be subject to a cutoff of federal funds if it continued to discriminate.

The administration, again led by Reynolds, contended that the language was too broad and would give the federal government too much authority over the private sector. The Catholic Conference argued tenaciously that the Title IX changes would amount to an expansion of abortion rights and could force Catholic hospitals affiliated with schools receiving aid to perform abortions.

Civil rights lawyers disagreed with this analysis, but the combined opposition of the administration and the Catholic church hierarchy was enough to stall progress on the bill.

Federal Judgeships

Federal judgeships were another source of strain between the administration and Senate Judiciary Committee Democrats, and disputes in this area also took on a partisan tinge within the committee.

By the end of the year, Reagan had named 248 judges to the district and regional appeals courts, approaching the record 258 appointments President Jimmy Carter made.

At the start of Reagan's second term, conservative lobbying groups such as the Washington Legal Foundation and the Center for Judicial Studies made clear that they would push the administration to name conservatives to the federal bench. They wanted to reverse what they claimed was a trend toward liberal "judicial activism" on the bench as a result of Carter's appointments.

Senate Judiciary Committee Democrats expressed concern about conservatives' emphasis on ideology in judicial appointments, but an equally serious concern was the pace of nomination hearings. The Democrats claimed that Chairman Strom Thurmond, R-S.C., under pressure from the administration, was pushing judgeships through the committee too fast. The Democrats said they did not have enough time to investigate the nominees.

By November, the panel, made up of 10 Republicans and eight Democrats, was a step away from open warfare over judicial appointments. But within a month members had worked out a new agreement giving Democrats more time to look into nominations and limiting to six the number of nominations that could be considered at any hearing.

—By Nadine Cohodas

Senate Votes to Revamp Immigration Laws

The Senate Sept. 19 passed legislation (S 1200) revamping the nation's immigration laws, after voting to create a controversial "guest worker" program that would allow up to 350,000 foreign workers into the United States temporarily to do agricultural work.

However, markup of similar legislation by the House Judiciary Committee was put off until 1986 to give a group of Democratic members time to try to work out a compromise on the seasonal worker issue. The panel's Immigration, Refugees and International Law Subcommittee finished all other work on the bill Nov. 19.

Both the House and Senate bills were aimed at curbing the flow of illegal aliens into the United States by penalizing employers who knowingly hired them.

The legislation also would establish a program to grant legal status to millions of illegal aliens already in the country who met certain requirements.

S 1200 would begin the "legalization" program three years after enactment, or sooner if a commission created by the bill determined that the employer sanctions plus increased enforcement at U.S. borders had succeeded in cutting the number of illegal aliens entering the country. Illegal aliens in the United States prior to Jan. 1, 1980, would be eligible to apply for legal status.

The House bill, sponsored by Judiciary Chairman Peter W. Rodino Jr., D-N.J., and Immigration Subcommittee Chairman Romano L. Mazzoli, D-Ky., would begin the legalization program upon enactment, although it would take about a year for it to be fully operational. Aliens in the country before Jan. 1, 1982, would be eligible to apply for legal status.

Both bills would expand and streamline an existing program, known as "H-2," that allowed foreign workers into the country for a variety of agricultural and other jobs. S 1200 would give growers three years to phase out their use of illegal workers; the House bill would make them subject to the same sanctions as other employers immediately.

Some 20,000 foreign agricultural workers a year came into the United States through the H-2 program, mostly to work in the Florida sugar-cane industry and to pick apples in the Northeastern United States. But many Western growers contended the program was inadequate to provide the large volume of workers needed to harvest perishable crops in the West.

It was these growers who successfully lobbied for the Senate amendment creating a new guest worker program. The amendment was adopted 51-44 over the objections of the bill's chief sponsor, Alan K. Simpson, R-Wyo.

Background

With hundreds of thousands of aliens entering the United States illegally every year, in addition to the growing number of legal immigrants, immigration was widely regarded as "out of control." Some estimates put the net inflow of illegal entrants at 500,000 a year, with millions permanently settled in the country, according to the Senate Judiciary Committee.

The committee said this influx had adverse job impacts, especially on low-income, low-skilled Americans. Since it was the lure of jobs that attracted many illegal aliens, Congress for several years had sought to create a program of sanctions to discourage employers from hiring them, while at the same time "legalizing" aliens who had already established themselves in the United States.

An immigration reform bill passed the Senate in 1982 but died on the House floor in the last days of a lame-duck session. *(1982 Almanac p. 405)*

The Senate passed another bill in 1983, by a 76-18 vote, but the House did not pass its version — by a close 216-211 vote — until June 1984. With Congress in recess much of the summer for the national political conventions, conferees did not begin meeting on the bill until September, and time ran out before they could reach agreement on the complicated and politically sensitive issues involved. *(1984 Almanac p. 229)*

Senate Committee Action

The Senate Judiciary Committee approved S 1200 July 30 by a vote of 12-5, and filed its report Aug. 28 (S Rept 99-132).

Only two of the committee's eight Democrats — Howard M. Metzenbaum, Ohio, and Patrick J. Leahy, Vt. — joined the panel's 10 Republicans in voting for the bill. Robert C. Byrd, D-W.Va., did not vote.

The most controversial issue during committee markups July 18, 23, 25 and 30 was the legalization program.

Amnesty for illegal aliens who met specified conditions had been a feature of previous Senate bills. But as introduced, S 1200 would have delayed any legalization program until a commission determined that employer sanctions and increased border enforcement by the Immigration and Naturalization Service (INS) had curtailed the flow of illegal aliens into the country. There was no guarantee a legalization program ever would go into effect.

Simpson said he believed it was necessary politically to put off an amnesty program until there was evidence the nation had regained control of its borders. But the provision was controversial from the day he introduced the bill May 23. Hispanic and civil rights groups contended that an immediate and generous legalization program was necessary to end the exploitation faced by illegal aliens, many of whom were longtime U.S. residents with few legal protections. ***(Laws affecting agricultural workers, box, p. 226)***

Kennedy Amendment. On a party-line 6-8 vote, the committee rejected an amendment by Edward M. Kennedy, D-Mass., to create a legalization program upon enactment of the bill.

The amendment, which was identical to provisions agreed to by conferees in 1984, would have given permanent resident status to aliens who could prove they entered the United States prior to Jan. 1, 1977, and lived there continuously ever since. Those in the country before Jan. 1, 1981, could apply for temporary resident status; within two years they could seek to change their status to permanent resident. They would have to show a "minimal understanding" of English and knowledge of U.S. history and government, or be pursuing a course to gain such knowledge.

Kennedy said S 1200 was "backtracking in a very significant" way by providing that legalization be triggered only upon the commission's findings that the number of illegal aliens entering the country had been reduced.

Metzenbaum also opposed the idea, saying, "I'm tired of creating commissions to do the work we ought to do."

But Simpson maintained that his approach was the most feasible, given the political climate.

Voting for Kennedy's amendment were Democrats Metzenbaum; Joseph R. Biden Jr., Del.; Dennis DeConcini, Ariz.; Paul Simon, Ill.; Leahy and Kennedy. Voting no were Republicans Simpson; Strom Thurmond, S.C.; Paul Laxalt, Nev.; Orrin G. Hatch, Utah; John P. East, N.C.; Charles E. Grassley, Iowa; Jeremiah Denton, Ala.; and Mitch McConnell, Ky. Charles McC. Mathias Jr., R-Md.; Arlen Specter, R-Pa.; Howell Heflin, D-Ala., and Byrd did not vote.

Simpson Compromise. The committee approved S 1200 July 30 after Simpson made two accommodations to win the support of Metzenbaum:

- He accepted a Metzenbaum amendment adding criminal penalties for employers who repeatedly hired illegal aliens after having paid civil fines for doing so. The amendment called for imprisonment of up to six months and a fine of up to $3,000 per alien for a person convicted a second time of a "pattern or practice" of hiring illegal aliens.
- He accepted a Metzenbaum amendment, adopted 10-4, to guarantee that within three years after enactment, a legalization program would go into effect.

Metzenbaum said he preferred that the program start quickly but that three years after enactment was better than no time limit at all. Two other committee Democrats disagreed, however. Simon and DeConcini said the waiting period would leave too many illegal aliens vulnerable to arrest and deportation as the INS started to implement the sanctions program.

Metzenbaum negotiated his amendment directly with Simpson, committee aides said, irritating some fellow Democrats. Several of them, particularly DeConcini, Simon, Biden and Kennedy, wanted an immediate legalization program and had been trying to negotiate with Simpson to get more generous amnesty provisions.

Hispanic and civil rights lobbyists also were angered by Metzenbaum's move. Richard Fajardo of the Mexican American Legal Defense and Educational Fund called the amendment "a cruel joke." He said that while it appeared to be a step forward on legalization, it really was no gain at all for those favoring an amnesty program.

Other Amendments Rejected

The committee also rejected two other Kennedy amendments:

- To terminate the employer sanctions program at the end of three years if the General Accounting Office determined that sanctions had resulted in a "widespread pattern of discrimination" against U.S. citizens or those non-citizens eligible to work. Rejected 7-9.
- To remove provisions making it easier for growers to get temporary foreign labor for harvesting crops. Kennedy wanted to retain instead the existing "H-2" program, which allowed employers to get temporary workers by petitioning the secretary of labor. Rejected 4-13.

Kennedy called S 1200 "a significant retreat" in protections for workers. And Metzenbaum said the Senate should not pass a bill that would make it easier for foreigners to get work when there was high unemployment in the United States. But Leahy said he thought Simpson's approach was "in the long-range best interests of agriculture in this country." He said the H-2 program had been used successfully in Vermont. He also said growers there "had never been able to get U.S. citizens" to do the work the foreign employees did.

The committee also rejected, 4-10, a Metzenbaum amendment to cap the number of foreign workers allowed in the country each year at 100,000.

Senate Floor Action

The Senate passed S 1200 Sept. 19, after voting to create the controversial foreign farm worker program. The vote on final passage was 69-30. *(Vote 191, p. 37-S)*

It was the third time the Senate had passed an overhaul of immigration law since 1982, but the margin of passage, while comfortable, was considerably smaller than in previous years. In 1982, an immigration bill passed 80-19, and the 1983 vote was 76-18.

Debate on S 1200 stretched over a week (Sept. 11-13, 16-19), and final action was delayed for nearly two days because of attempts by John Heinz, R-Pa., to attach an unrelated amendment on Social Security to the bill. The amendment eventually was removed through complicated procedural maneuvers, clearing the way for passage of the bill.

Farm Worker Fight

The major controversy was over the proposal by Pete Wilson, R-Calif., to add a new foreign "guest worker" program to the bill. The amendment would allow foreign workers to stay in the country for up to nine months and travel around to different growers within "agricultural regions" defined by the attorney general. To ensure that the workers would return home after nine months, 20 percent of their wages would be held in escrow and could be collected only when the workers left the United States.

A similar program was added to the House immigration bill in 1984 but was stripped off by conferees.

First Proposal Tabled. When Wilson originally proposed the amendment Sept. 12, it was tabled by a vote of 50-48 after a three-hour debate. *(Vote 176, p. 35-S)*

Simpson called the program "an open-ended guest worker program" that would "repeat the most serious errors we have ever made in immigration policy. It would legalize the status quo of illegal labor in agriculture, and in my mind, that is not immigration reform."

Wilson insisted his amendment was "not a killer amendment [but] a saving amendment. It will save an industry."

The AFL-CIO and a number of church and civil rights groups opposed the amendment. The Reagan administration also opposed it initially, saying it was too broad. However, after lengthy negotiations among the Labor, Agriculture and Justice departments, the administration agreed to endorse a "self-financed, limited seasonal worker program." It proposed that two years after the program went into effect, a special commission set a cap on the number of foreign workers to be admitted the following year; that number would be reduced annually for 20 years or so until the program was phased out.

Revised Amendment. Wilson huddled with the growers and on Sept. 17 offered a revised version of his amendment, including a cap on the number of temporary foreign workers. The amendment was basically the same as the original proposal, but it provided that no more than 350,000 foreign workers could be in the country at any one time. It was adopted 51-44. *(Vote 186, p. 37-S)*

The difference in the vote was made by five senators who opposed the program Sept. 12 but supported the revised version Sept. 17: Republicans Specter; Richard G.

Lugar, Ind.; Dan Quayle, Ind.; and Warren B. Rudman, N.H.; and Democrat Donald W. Riegle Jr., Mich.

Wilson said his modification answered critics who claimed the guest worker program was "open-ended." But Simpson said it still would allow more than 350,000 foreign workers to come into the country each year because any time some left, more could come in to take their place.

Lugar and Quayle said Wilson and other colleagues from Western states lobbied hard between Sept. 12 and 17. "They explained to me their predicament and I had a great deal of sympathy for them," Quayle said.

'Sunset' Provision. The second Wilson amendment was not the end of the issue, however. On Sept. 18, Simon offered an amendment to end the seasonal worker program after three years unless Congress voted to extend it.

Wilson moved to table the proposal, but his motion lost, 40-56. *(Vote 188, p. 37-S)*

Simon's amendment then was adopted by voice vote.

Leahy, who voted for both the Wilson program and Simon's "sunset" provision, echoed the views of several senators when he said the two amendments together were "a good package."

"I thought the idea was worth trying," he said of the guest worker program. "But I feel a lot more comfortable knowing we have to revisit it."

Hispanic groups and representatives of organized labor claimed the program would hurt domestic farm workers. Farm unemployment was running at 13 percent, they said.

Other Amendments Adopted

Open-Field Searches. The growers won a clear victory Sept. 13 when members adopted, 51-39, an amendment by James A. McClure, R-Idaho, requiring government agents to have warrants before conducting "open-field" searches for illegal aliens. The Senate had adopted a similar amendment in 1983. *(Vote 180, p. 36-S)*

Financial Assistance. The Senate also adopted several amendments aimed at helping states and localities meet costs associated with illegal and newly legalized aliens. The Congressional Budget Office had said Sept. 11 that about 1.4 million of the estimated 5.6 million illegal aliens in the country could qualify for legal status under S 1200, costing about $1.8 billion over the next four years for social services.

- By voice vote, the Senate adopted an amendment by Wilson, authorizing $300 million in each of the first two years after enactment, and $600 million in each of the following four years, to help states pay for social services for newly legalized aliens.
- By a 74-22 vote Sept. 17, it adopted an amendment by Alfonse M. D'Amato, R-N.Y., requiring the federal government to reimburse states for the costs of incarcerating in state prisons illegal aliens and Cubans who entered the country from the port of Mariel and committed felonies. *(Vote 185, p. 36-S)*
- By voice vote Sept. 12, the Senate adopted an amendment by Paula Hawkins, R-Fla., and Kennedy, authorizing a $35 million contingency fund for border patrols or aid to localities in an immigration "emergency."

Other Amendments. Other amendments adopted by the Senate included:

- By Hawkins, to make mandatory nationwide a demonstration program requiring states to verify whether applicants for specified federal welfare benefits were legal U.S. residents. Benefits, including Medicaid, unemployment compensation, food stamps and Aid to Families with Dependent Children, would be prohibited for illegal aliens. After rejecting, 31-59, a Kennedy motion to table the amendment, the Senate adopted it by voice vote. *(Vote 178, p. 36-S)*
- By Kennedy, requiring Congress to vote on ending employer sanctions within three years if a study by the General Accounting Office (GAO) showed that a widespread pattern of discrimination had resulted. Voice vote.
- By Metzenbaum, to terminate after 3½ years a provision that allowed employers of temporary foreign farm workers to provide workers with a housing allowance instead of actual housing. Voice vote.
- By Max Baucus, D-Mont., to delete provisions that would have allowed the INS to impose a fee on aliens entering the United States. Voice vote.
- By McClure, declaring the sense of the Senate that English was the official language of the country. Voice vote.
- By J. James Exon, D-Neb., a non-germane amendment expressing the sense of the Senate that a 60-cent-per-gallon tariff on imported ethanol should be implemented immediately. Adopted 82-15. *(Vote 182, p. 36-S)*

The Treasury Department had announced it would not implement the tariff, enacted in 1980 (PL 96-499), until Nov. 1. Exon said the delay would harm the U.S. agriculture and ethanol industries.

Amendments Rejected

Kennedy tried again to have the legalization program begin immediately upon enactment of the bill. He moved to delete the commission whose recommendations would trigger a legalization program and to allow illegal aliens in the United States prior to Jan. 1, 1981, to apply for legal status.

The amendment was rejected Sept. 13 by a vote of 26-65. *(Vote 179, p. 36-S)*

The Senate tabled the following amendments:

- By Alan Cranston, D-Calif., to allow documents such as a rent receipt, bank book, utility bill or affidavit from a "credible witness" such as a parish priest to be used as documentation to establish residence and physical presence in the United States. (S 1200 called for employment records as the preferable proof of residence.) Tabled 82-6 Sept. 13. *(Vote 181, p. 36-S)*
- By Simon, to revise a provision in existing immigration law that denied temporary visas to past or present members of the Communist Party, anarchists or persons who advocated the overthrow of the U.S. government by force.

Simon's amendment provided that "notwithstanding any other provision of [the law], no one shall be denied a non-immigrant visa because of his or her lawful political beliefs, activities or associations." It also added terrorist activities to the list of reasons why persons could be denied entry to the United States.

The amendment was tabled 66-30 Sept. 17 after Simpson promised hearings on the issue. *(Vote 184, p. 36-S)*

- By Carl Levin, D-Mich., to protect from deportation illegal aliens who would qualify for legalization between the date of enactment of the bill and the time the legalization program took effect three years later. Tabled 54-41 Sept. 17. *(Vote 187, p. 37-S)*

The Senate also voted to table several non-germane amendments:

- By John Kerry, D-Mass., to delay a scheduled Sept. 13 test of the U.S. anti-satellite weapon until after the Nov. 19 U.S.-Soviet summit meeting in Geneva. Tabled 62-34 Sept. 12. *(Vote 177, p. 35-S; related stories, pp. 109, 162)*
- By Symms, to provide that no agency of the United

Laws Affecting U.S. Agricultural Workers

The major labor laws affecting agricultural workers in the United States included:

National Labor Relations Act. This law, enacted in 1935, guaranteed all workers except those in government, agriculture and those subject to the Railway Labor Act the right to organize and join labor unions, bargain collectively through representatives of their own choosing and to strike.

While federal employees subsequently were granted some collective bargaining rights (though not the right to strike), federal law never extended such rights to farmworkers. Farmworkers did have collective bargaining agreements in three states: California, the only state with a law giving them the right to organize; Florida and Hawaii, where agreements had been worked out with certain employers.

Fair Labor Standards Act. Enacted in 1938, this law set basic minimum wage and overtime pay standards and regulated employment for minors. Agricultural workers were exempt from the act until 1966. Minimum-wage requirements for these workers were phased in, and did not equal those for other jobs until 1978. The law applied only to workers on farms with at least seven full-time employees.

Unlike other workers, farm laborers did not get time-and-a-half for overtime. The law also had lower age requirements for employees doing farm work. In non-agricultural jobs, workers must be at least 18 to perform full-time hazardous work; on farms such work could be done at age 16. The minimum age for non-hazardous work was 16 in non-farm jobs; in agriculture it was 14.

Federal Unemployment Tax Act of 1939 (PL 76-379). Farmworkers were covered by this law starting in 1978. The federal unemployment tax applied only to agricultural employers who had at least 10 workers over a 20-week period or who paid at least $20,000 a quarter in wages. States also had unemployment compensation laws, but only a handful covered smaller farms than the federal law. Farmworkers could not collect unemployment benefits unless they met state eligibility requirements.

Occupational Safety and Health Act (PL 91-596). This law, enacted in 1970, required employers to maintain certain health and safety standards for the protection of their employees. The only farmworker regulations issued under it covered migrant labor camps. While there were regulations covering the use of certain machinery, such as tractors, there were no federal health and sanitation regulations covering field workers.

Workers' Compensation. There was no federal workers' compensation law. States were free to develop their own programs. The Farmworker Justice Fund, a farmworker rights group, said farm laborers only began to get coverage for injuries on the job in the late 1970s.

Migrant and Seasonal Agricultural Worker Protection Act (PL 97-470). This law, signed by President Reagan Jan. 14, 1983, replaced the Farm Labor Contractor Registration Act. It required farm labor contractors, who recruited, hired and transported workers, to register with the Labor Department, and to ensure, among other things, that housing for migrant workers met federal and state health and safety standards; that vehicles used to transport them met federal and state safety regulations; that migrant workers were informed in writing at the time of recruitment about their wages, hours and working conditions and that they then be paid what they were promised. *(1982 Almanac p. 66)*

H-2 Program. This program, part of U.S. immigration law for 30 years, regulated the employment of legal foreign workers. The law set standards covering wage rates, working conditions and types of jobs available to foreign workers.

States should extend loans or credits to any country in North America that allowed access to its ports to Soviet vessels capable of delivering nuclear weapons. The amendment was aimed at Mexico, which reportedly had agreed to let several Soviet warships dock in Veracruz in October. Tabled 66-30 Sept. 17. *(Vote 183, p. 36-S)*

Social Security Amendment

By a 22-77 vote Sept. 19, the Senate refused to table a Heinz amendment declaring it to be the sense of the Senate that the Social Security program should be removed from the unified federal budget at "the earliest possible date." *(Vote 189, p. 37-S)*

Congress in 1983 had voted to make that change, effective in fiscal 1993, but Heinz wanted action sooner to separate the Social Security trust funds covering old-age and survivors' benefits, disability insurance and Medicare from the federal budget in order to insulate the programs from budget-cutting pressures. *(1983 Almanac p. 219)*

After several days of delay on his amendment, Heinz finally moved to table it himself and urged his colleagues to join him in voting "no."

After the tabling motion failed, the Senate in a series of complicated maneuvers agreed to commit the bill to the Budget and Finance committees with instructions to report legislation by Nov. 3, 1985, to prevent the use of Social Security benefit reductions to help reduce the federal deficit. The purpose of the motion to commit was to remove the Social Security issue from the debate on S 1200. *(Vote 190, p. 37-S; Social Security, p. 465)*

Major Provisions

As passed by the Senate, S 1200:

Employer Sanctions

- Barred any person from knowingly hiring, recruiting or referring for a fee any illegal alien.
- Provided a civil fine of $100 to $2,000 per illegal alien for a first offense. A second offense would bring a fine of $2,000 to $5,000 per alien, and the employer could be subject to a court order to stop hiring illegal aliens. On a third violation, the fine per alien would be $3,000 to $10,000.

- Provided a fine of up to $3,000 per alien and six months' imprisonment for an employer convicted a second time of a "pattern and practice" of hiring illegal aliens.
- Delayed the start of the sanctions for one year after enactment. The first six months would be an "education" period. In the second six months, an employer violating the law would get a warning; if a second violation occurred in that period, he would be fined.
- Gave an employer the option to keep records verifying that he had checked specified documents of his employees, such as a U.S. passport, citizenship certificate or driver's license, to determine their eligibility to work. Employers of four or more persons would be presumed to know that they had hired an illegal alien if such a person was found on their payrolls; however, they would have an affirmative defense to charges of violating the law if they kept the specified records.
- Required the GAO to monitor the implementation of employer sanctions to determine whether they resulted in discrimination; directed the attorney general, in conjunction with the U.S. Civil Rights Commission and Equal Employment Opportunity Commission, to review the reports and recommend remedial legislation if necessary.
- Required Congress to vote on terminating employer sanctions within three years if the GAO found that a widespread pattern of discrimination resulted from the new penalty system.
- Authorized $840 million in fiscal 1987 and $830 million in 1988 for the Justice Department and the INS to enforce immigration laws.

Agricultural Workers

- Expanded and streamlined the H-2 program for temporary agricultural workers to make it easier for growers to get such laborers. Growers would not have to apply for foreign workers more than 65 days in advance of need. (Existing law required them to request workers at least 80 days in advance of need.)
- Authorized a 72-hour emergency procedure for getting workers if U.S. workers referred to a grower were not qualified for the particular work or failed to show up, or if a grower was faced with a critical labor need because of unforeseen harvest conditions.
- Authorized $10 million to enforce and monitor the revised H-2 program.
- Gave agricultural employers three years to phase out their use of illegal aliens. By the fourth year, the employer sanctions provisions would apply to these employers, requiring them to get workers through legal channels.
- Established a new "seasonal worker" program for perishable-crop growers that would allow up to 350,000 foreign workers in the country at any one time. The attorney general would determine how many workers would be allowed in each of 10 "agricultural regions" designated by the attorney general. Growers could petition for more workers in "extraordinary and unusual circumstances."
- Allowed the foreign workers to remain in the United States for up to nine months and to travel around to different growers within specified agricultural regions; limited their activities to field work, such as planting and harvesting perishable crops; provided that 20 percent of their wages be held in escrow until they returned home.
- **Required the attorney general, in consultation with the Labor and Agriculture departments, to determine appropriate wages and working conditions to avoid adversely affecting the wages and working conditions of U.S. workers.**
- Required the attorney general after three years to establish a limit on the total number of seasonal workers who could be admitted under the new program.
- Terminated the program after three years unless Congress voted to continue it.
- Required INS officers to obtain warrants before searching "open fields" for illegal aliens.

Legalization

- Required that a program to grant legal status to certain illegal aliens already in the United States begin no later than three years after enactment.
- Established a nine-member commission to study whether employer sanctions and increased border enforcement curtailed the flow of illegal aliens into the country, and allowed the legalization program to take effect sooner than three years after enactment if the commission so recommended.
- Made illegal aliens eligible for temporary resident status if they could prove they arrived in the United States prior to Jan. 1, 1980, and had lived in the country continuously since then. They could seek to become permanent residents after three years if they met certain conditions, including a minimal understanding of English.
- Barred newly legalized aliens from most public assistance during temporary residency and the first three years of permanent residency.
- Authorized $300 million in each of the first two years after enactment for social services and administrative costs associated with legalization, and $600 million in each of the following four years.

House Subcommittee Action

The House Judiciary Subcommittee on Immigration, Refugees and International Law Nov. 19 approved its immigration bill, after broadening its coverage and adding protections for foreigners who came into the country for temporary work.

However, the panel had only perfunctory discussion on whether to create a new temporary foreign farm worker program. It decided to bypass consideration of the matter to give a group of Democrats headed by Charles E. Schumer of New York a chance to continue compromise talks on the so-called "guest worker" program.

The subcommittee worked on Rodino's bill (HR 3080), but a new bill incorporating changes made during markup was to be introduced before the full Judiciary Committee took it up. The panel took nearly eight hours over two days (Nov. 18-19) to work through some 35 amendments.

The House bill was similar in structure to S 1200 but did not include a guest worker program. Dan Lungren, R-Calif., made a symbolic offering of the guest worker program in the subcommittee, but after a brief debate, the panel rejected the proposal by voice vote.

The House bill also did not contain the three-year transition period for agricultural employers to phase out their use of illegal aliens. HR 3080 as introduced included the transition period, but Howard L. Berman, D-Calif., moved to delete it from the bill, and his amendment was adopted 6-4.

Employer Requirements. John Bryant, D-Texas, an advocate of a strong immigration reform bill, offered amendments to extend its coverage. One, adopted 5-4, would require all employers to keep records showing that they checked documents, such as a U.S. passport, birth certificate or Social Security card, to determine whether an employee was eligible to work in the United States.

The original bill required only employers of four or more persons to check workers' credentials and keep records. Bryant said it "basically exempted upper-income people," referring to households that employed South American and Central American domestic help. "Having this exemption is a chance for obfuscation and muddling of the issue," he said.

Lungren, who opposed the amendment, said he doubted the INS would enforce the law against those who hired a nanny or gardener who was an illegal alien.

S 1200 made record-keeping optional, but employers of four or more persons would be presumed to know they had hired an illegal alien if such a person was found on the payroll. Keeping records would be an affirmative defense to the charge of violating the law.

Another Bryant amendment, adopted by voice vote, closed what he said was a loophole involving the use of contractors and subcontractors. The amendment would apply the sanctions' provisions to persons who routinely used subcontractors in their business and would make the chief contractor liable if a subcontractor hired illegals. The provision would apply only when the work being done by a subcontractor was a normal part of a larger job.

Anti-Discrimination. Hispanic and civil rights groups had claimed that employer sanctions would exacerbate employment discrimination because employers, fearing penalties, would balk at hiring anyone who looked and sounded foreign. To help ease these concerns, the House bill would create a new office of special counsel in the Justice Department to investigate and prosecute charges of discrimination stemming from the sanctions.

It also barred discrimination based on citizenship or alien status when the person was a newly legalized alien who intended to become a U.S. citizen.

The Senate bill did not include this anti-discrimination section, and F. James Sensenbrenner Jr., R-Wis., tried to knock it out of HR 3080. Barney Frank, D-Mass., who wrote the provisions, opposed the move, arguing that they were necessary to help remedy problems that could occur because of the sanctions.

Sensenbrenner's amendment was rejected 4-5.

The subcommittee did accept a Sensenbrenner amendment making clear that an employer could require a knowledge of English as a condition of employment.

Welfare Benefits. By voice vote, the panel adopted a Lungren amendment to make mandatory a demonstration program requiring states to verify whether applicants for specified federal benefits were legal U.S. residents. The programs involved were Aid to Families with Dependent Children, Medicaid, unemployment compensation, food stamps and housing assistance.

The amendment was similar to a provision in S 1200.

Legalization Program. The subcommittee rejected, 3-7, an amendment by Bill McCollum, R-Fla., to kill the legalization program. It also rejected two amendments that would have altered the program.

The bill provided temporary resident status for aliens who had continuously resided in the United States since Jan. 1, 1982. (S 1200's eligibility date was Jan. 1, 1980.)

A Schumer amendment to move the date to Jan. 1, 1985, was rejected 4-6. His amendment would have enabled thousands more aliens to qualify for legal status.

Lungren then offered an amendment that would have restricted the program considerably. It would have created a two-tiered program, providing permanent resident status for those in the country since Jan. 1, 1977, and temporary resident status for those who came before Jan. 1, 1980.

The amendment was rejected 4-5.

Aid to States. By voice vote, the panel accepted a Bryant amendment to provide states 100 percent reimbursement for costs associated with legalization. It first rejected, 3-7, a Lungren amendment to put a $1 billion yearly cap on the amount paid to all states for administrative, social services and other program costs.

The original bill included a formula grant program for reimbursing state legalization costs.

H-2 Amendments. Berman, who strongly opposed foreign worker programs, sought to strike the entire section of the bill revising the H-2 program, but his amendment was rejected on a 5-5 tie.

Like S 1200, the House bill would spell out the operation of the program in law rather than leave it to Labor Department regulation, and would revise existing regulations so that agricultural employers could use the program more easily to get laborers during harvest time.

Berman did win approval of two amendments to strengthen protections for foreign workers who came into the country through the program. One, adopted 6-4, would make the workers eligible for free legal assistance through the Legal Services Corporation, the federal program that provided legal aid to the poor. The second would require employers to provide H-2 workers with housing, not just a housing allowance. It also required employers to give the same travel advances to domestic workers that they provided for foreign H-2 workers, and barred the use of foreign laborers to break a strike. ∎

Federal Gun Law

The Senate July 9 handily passed legislation relaxing federal gun control laws to allow interstate sales of rifles, shotguns and handguns.

The bill (S 49), passed by a vote of 79-15, would ease many restrictions of the 1968 Gun Control Act, including those barring such interstate sales. *(Vote 142, p. 29-S)*

Westerners in Congress, encouraged by the National Rifle Association (NRA), had sought relaxation of the 1968 law almost from the day it was enacted. They contended the law did not prevent violent firearms abuse and put an onerous if not unconstitutional burden on legitimate gun owners and dealers.

Advocates of strong gun controls, led by Edward M. Kennedy, D-Mass., sought to retain the ban on interstate sales of handguns. But a Kennedy amendment to preserve the ban was tabled (killed) by a 69-26 vote.

The Senate also rejected an amendment to require a 14-day waiting period for anyone seeking to purchase a handgun — again by better than a 2-to-1 margin. A number of police organizations had endorsed both amendments.

Passage of the bill was a major victory for the NRA, which had worked relentlessly for years to get a bill to the floor. Meanwhile, advocates of strict handgun laws, led by Handgun Control, a Washington, D.C.-based organization, worked hard to strengthen the bill. They marshaled the support of five national police organizations to lobby for amendments to retain the ban on interstate handgun sales and to require a waiting period for handgun purchases.

But their efforts were no match for the three-million-strong NRA and its allies, including the Gun Owners of America and Citizens Committee for the Right to Keep and Bear Arms. In the two weeks before S 49 was considered, the NRA orchestrated a massive grass-roots lobbying campaign for it.

James A. McClure, R-Idaho, said the large margin of victory was in part a reaction to "abusive enforcement" of the 1968 law over the past 17 years. But others said the vote was a tribute to the gun lobby. "This place is marching in lock step with the NRA," said a disgruntled Senate aide.

S 49 was the first gun legislation to be considered by the full Senate in 13 years. In 1972, the Senate passed a measure that would have strengthened the 1968 law, but the bill died in the House. *(1972 Almanac p. 520)*

In 1985, a companion bill to S 49 (HR 945) remained buried in the House Judiciary Committee, which consistently had opposed any moves to weaken existing gun controls.

Sponsors, led by Harold L. Volkmer, D-Mo., were circulating a discharge petition that would permit the bill to come to the House floor without action by the committee. When Congress adjourned Dec. 20, they had about 150 of the 218 signatures needed.

Background

The 1968 gun control law was enacted following the assassinations that year of the Rev. Dr. Martin Luther King Jr. and Sen. Robert F. Kennedy, D-N.Y. *(1968 Almanac p. 549)*

It had long been a thorn in the side of many gun owners and dealers, who contended it put too many restrictions on their activities and subjected them to harassment by overzealous federal authorities.

The law barred mail-order or interstate shipment of firearms and ammunition, and established detailed licensing procedures for those who manufactured, imported, sold or collected guns and ammunition. It required licensed dealers to keep records of all firearms transactions and authorized federal authorities to inspect a licensee's firearms inventory and records at all "reasonable" times. The authorities were not required to give a licensee notice of these inspections.

Legislation to relax the law's requirements was approved by the Senate Judiciary Committee in 1982 and 1984, but went no further. The 1984 bill was offered as a floor amendment to unrelated legislation but was withdrawn when it became snarled in a procedural imbroglio. *(1984 Almanac pp. 226, 242; 1982 Almanac p. 415)*

In 1985, chief sponsors McClure and Orrin G. Hatch, R-Utah, bypassed the Judiciary Committee and had S 49 placed directly on the Senate calendar.

Provisions

As passed, S 49 relaxed many of the requirements of the 1968 law. For example, it required federal agents to give notice to gun dealers before conducting routine inspections aimed at determining their compliance with the law's record-keeping requirements. Such inspections in most cases would be limited to one a year.

The bill allowed surprise inspections when government officials obtained a warrant based on a "reasonable cause to believe that a violation of the law has occurred." Such inspections also would be allowed during a criminal investigation of someone other than the gun dealer or when authorities were tracing a firearm.

Gun collectors no longer would have to get dealers' licenses to sell weapons from their private collections. And those who sold ammunition would be exempt from record-keeping requirements.

Another provision would bar prosecution under the act unless the alleged violator knew he violated the law or acted "willfully" to violate the law. Under existing law, federal authorities could prosecute any time they found a violation, regardless of the state of mind of the defendant.

While S 49 removed the ban on interstate sales of guns, sponsors said it retained adequate controls on such transactions. It allowed interstate sales face-to-face, over-the-counter, only if the sale did not violate the laws of either the seller's or the buyer's state. The seller would be presumed to know the law in the buyer's state and could be penalized for a sale that violated the law in either state.

The bill also included a mandatory five-year sentence for use of a firearm during commission of a federal crime of violence, and made it illegal for anyone, not just a licensed gun dealer, to sell a firearm to persons prohibited by law from owning one, such as convicted felons, drug addicts or persons committed to mental institutions. The bill kept the same penalty as existing law for selling a firearm to a person prohibited from owning one — a fine of up to $5,000 and imprisonment for up to five years.

It also banned the importation of barrels, frames and receivers for so-called "Saturday night specials" — small handguns not suitable for sporting purposes but frequently used in the commission of crimes. The 1968 law banned the importation of most firearms, but not of gun parts.

Floor Action

Handgun Ban. In offering his amendment to retain the ban on interstate sales of handguns, Kennedy argued that Congress should treat handguns differently from long guns. "There are no sporting purposes whatsoever — no hunting purposes whatsoever — for a Saturday night special," he said. "You cannot hit anything accurately beyond a few feet."

The FBI's "Crime in the United States" report for 1983, the last year for which complete figures were available, showed that handguns were used in 44 percent of all murders that year, with other types of firearms accounting for an additional 14 percent of murders.

Kennedy noted that the 1984 Judiciary Committee bill retained the ban on interstate sales of guns with barrels of three inches or less.

But Hatch and McClure opposed the amendment, contending that the existing ban was "more restrictive than necessary" to ensure adequate regulation of guns. The amendment was tabled, 69-26. *(Vote 139, p. 29-S)*

Notice of Inspections. An amendment by Charles McC. Mathias Jr., R-Md., to delete the provision requiring notice before routine inspections also was tabled, 76-18. *(Vote 140, p. 29-S)*

Mathias contended the provision would "cripple federal enforcement of the law. Only the dishonest dealer will benefit from such pre-inspection notification," he said. "But all of the American people will suffer because of a reduction in enforcement effectiveness."

Hatch said the provision was needed to stop federal authorities from conducting "fishing expeditions for inadvertent record-keeping violations."

Waiting Period. By 71-23, the Senate tabled an amendment by Daniel K. Inouye, D-Hawaii, to require a 14-day waiting period between the purchase of a handgun and its delivery. Exceptions would have been permitted if the purchaser's local police chief certified that immediate delivery of the handgun was necessary to "protect against a threat of immediate danger to the physical safety of the buyer." *(Vote 141, p. 29-S)*

Inouye said the waiting period would allow local authorities to verify information the buyer gave about himself, although the amendment did not require either the gun dealer or police to conduct a records check.

The Judiciary Committee's 1982 gun bill included a similar waiting period, and a number of law enforcement officials and organizations had urged adoption of a waiting period for handgun purchases.

Inouye said 15 states and a number of localities had waiting periods ranging from three to 15 days. He said Congress should establish a federal minimum "to ensure national uniformity and reinforce the government's commitment to the enforcement of the law."

But McClure said the amendment would inconvenience people and would not be effective because it did not require background or criminal record checks.

Guns in Transit. In action on the bill June 24, the Senate by voice vote adopted an amendment that would bar prosecution under state laws regulating transportation of guns when the gun in question was unloaded and inaccessible — for example, a gun packed in the trunk of a car.

As introduced, S 49 would have nullified all state and local gun laws regulating interstate transportation of firearms, but gun control advocates said that was far too broad. Proponents of the bill argued that some state laws interfered with the legitimate movement of guns by hunters or collectors traveling interstate.

Another amendment agreed to after negotiations among supporters and foes of S 49 would ban the importation of barrels, frames and receivers for "Saturday night specials."

A third amendment adopted June 24 tightened a provision designed to allow gun dealers to operate at temporary locations outside of their shops. The amendment made clear that gun sales could take place only at gun shows or other events sponsored by legitimate gun organizations. ■

'Grove City' Civil Rights Measure Stalled

By wide margins, two House committees in May approved legislation to restore the full reach of four major civil rights laws curtailed by the Supreme Court in 1984. However, further action on the bill (HR 700) was stalled because of a dispute over abortion.

HR 700 would overturn the court's decision in *Grove City College v. Bell*, which narrowed the coverage of Title IX of the 1972 Education Act Amendments and three other civil rights laws. The ruling had resulted in a sharp retrenchment in the enforcement of the laws.

A 1984 bill to reverse the decision passed the House 375-32, but died in the Senate. *(1984 Almanac p. 239)*

The House Judiciary and Education and Labor committees approved differing versions of HR 700 on May 21 and 22, but chief sponsors Don Edwards, D-Calif., and Augustus F. Hawkins, D-Calif., did not push for floor action until the abortion problem was resolved.

Proponents of HR 700 blamed the U.S. Catholic Conference, the policy-making arm of the nation's Roman Catholic bishops, for blocking the bill. The conference claimed the measure would expand abortion rights — for example, possibly forcing Catholic hospitals to perform abortions and forcing schools to fund student abortions.

Supporters of the bill rejected that claim. They said the measure would simply restore the four civil rights laws to their previous scope of coverage.

The Education and Labor Committee adopted language designed to meet the bishops' concerns by narrowing abortion regulations in force under Title IX of the 1972 Education Act Amendments. But Edwards, Hawkins and civil rights groups backing the bill opposed the provision. They said it was unnecessary and in fact would restrict already available abortion rights.

Background

In *Grove City College v. Bell*, the Supreme Court ruled 6-3 that Title IX of the 1972 Education Amendments banned sex discrimination only in a particular education "program or activity" receiving federal aid, not in the entire institution.

Civil rights lawyers and their allies in Congress said the court misread Title IX, and that Congress always intended an entire educational institution to be barred from discriminating if any of its components got federal aid.

But the National Women's Law Center said the Department of Education's Office of Civil Rights had ended or restricted the focus of dozens of anti-discrimination lawsuits in the wake of the court ruling. The center filed a lawsuit against the department.

The ruling also had restricted enforcement of three other laws — Title VI of the 1964 Civil Rights Act, Section 504 of the Rehabilitation Act of 1973, and the Age Discrimination Act of 1975 — because they contained the same "program or activity" language as Title IX.

The 1984 bill to overturn the ruling specified that any "recipient" of federal aid was covered by the anti-discrimination laws. Opponents argued that the legislation was too broad and worded too vaguely, so in 1985 sponsors redrafted it in an effort to make clear that the bill would merely restore the scope of the four laws to what it was before the *Grove City* ruling.

Instead of referring to "recipients" of federal aid, HR 700 defined "program or activity" in each of the four statutes to clarify that entire institutions were covered by the ban on discrimination when federal aid went to any one component of the institution. However, only the component receiving aid would be subject to a cutoff of federal funds if it continued to discriminate.

The abortion issue arose solely in the context of Title IX, the law barring sex discrimination in educational institutions.

Neither Title IX nor HR 700 as introduced mentioned abortion. However, 1975 regulations promulgated under Title IX specified that educational institutions receiving federal aid "shall treat pregnancy, childbirth, false pregnancy, termination of pregnancy and recovery therefrom in the same manner and under the same policies as any other temporary disability" where leave, health services or insurance for students or employees were concerned. The regulations also barred an aid recipient from discriminating against any student because she had an abortion.

Anti-abortion forces led by the Catholic Conference and the National Right to Life Committee Inc. mounted an aggressive campaign to narrow the regulations and their application. On Feb. 26, the conference issued a legal analysis arguing that HR 700 would extend application of Title IX regulations beyond the scope of existing law.

Catholic bishops from around the country decided at a March 21 meeting in Washington, D.C., that they would lobby for an amendment to restrict abortion coverage. The Catholic Conference had not actively participated in debate on the 1984 House bill.

Planned Parenthood Federation of America, Inc. and the American Civil Liberties Union worked to counter the bishops' lobbying, as did Edwards, Hawkins and other members of Congress.

Edwards contended that anti-abortion forces saw HR 700 as a way to make the ban on federal funding for abortion permanent, rather than having it attached each year to appropriations bills. *(1984 Almanac p. 465)*

House Committee Action

The Education and Labor Committee approved HR 700 by a vote of 29-2 on May 21. The Judiciary Committee ordered the bill reported a day later, 21-12. *(Committee votes, box, this page)*

The committees shared jurisdiction over the legislation because it would amend civil rights laws in the purview of both panels.

Abortion Amendments

In Education and Labor, Tom Tauke, R-Iowa, offered an amendment designed to prevent any expansion of abortion rights. It stated that nothing in the legislation "shall be construed to grant or secure or deny any right relating to abortion or the funding thereof, or to require or prohibit any person, or public or private entity or organization, to provide any benefit or service relating to abortion."

"I want this legislation to be abortion-neutral," Tauke said. "I don't want to give anything. I don't want to take anything away." Tauke insisted the amendment was simply "trying to make certain" that no one could be forced to perform an abortion and that there could be "no discrimination against anyone who has had an abortion or participated in an abortion."

James M. Jeffords, R-Vt., and Pat Williams, D-Mont., argued that the amendment was unnecessary because the bill would not expand abortion rights. However, the committee adopted Tauke's amendment, 18-14.

Ralph G. Neas, executive director of the Leadership Conference on Civil Rights, contended that the amendment in effect repealed the 1975 Title IX regulations, removing the legal underpinnings for the regulations requiring that abortion be treated in the same manner as pregnancy where leave policies and insurance benefits were concerned.

Judiciary. At the Judiciary markup, F. James Sensenbrenner Jr., R-Wis., offered the same amendment, also claiming it was "abortion-neutral."

Barney Frank, D-Mass., disputed that, asserting that opponents were trying to change substantive abortion law.

In a move to short-circuit the argument, Edwards offered a substitute amendment that had been part of the committee's report on the 1984 *Grove City* bill. It stated that nothing in the bill was "intended to convey either the approval or disapproval of Congress concerning the validity or appropriateness" of Title IX regulations on abortion.

Edwards' proposal was adopted 20-14. Hamilton Fish Jr., R-N.Y., was the only Republican to vote with the Democrats; Kentucky Democrat Romano L. Mazzoli joined the panel's other 13 Republicans in opposing the measure.

With little debate, both panels rejected amendments guaranteeing "the right to life of the unborn from the moment of conception, except to save the life of the mother." That proposal was offered in Education and Labor by Dick Armey, R-Texas, and rejected 8-23. The Judiciary version, offered by William E. Dannemeyer, R-Calif., was defeated 14-20.

Religious Institutions

The committees also dealt with a controversy over religious institutions.

Under existing law, educational institutions "controlled" by a religious organization were exempted from the sex discrimination ban if the application of Title IX would be inconsistent with the organization's religious tenets. Some members of both committees contended that the provision, which was included in HR 700, was too narrow.

At the Education and Labor markup, Jeffords offered an amendment to widen the religious exemption. His proposal, adopted 18-12, exempted from the ban on sex discrimination any institution controlled by or "affiliated with" a religious organization "when the religious tenets of that organization are an integral part of such organization."

Neas called the amendment "dangerous," saying it

Committee Votes

Following were the votes by which the House Education and Labor Committee and the House Judiciary Committee approved HR 700:

Education and Labor

For (29): Democrats Atkins, Mass.; Biaggi, N.Y.; Boucher, Va.; Bruce, Ill.; Clay, Mo.; Dymally, Calif.; Eckart, Ohio; Ford, Mich.; Gaydos, Pa.; Hawkins, Calif.; Hayes, Ill.; Kildee, Mich.; Martinez, Calif.; Owens, N.Y.; Penny, Minn.; Perkins, Ky.; Solarz, N.Y.; Williams, Mont.; Republicans Chandler, Wash.; Coleman, Mo.; Fawell, Ill.; Goodling, Pa.; Gunderson, Wis.; Henry, Mich.; Jeffords, Vt.; McKernan, Maine; Petri, Wis.; Roukema, N.J.; Tauke, Iowa.

Against (2): Republicans Armey, Texas; Bartlett, Texas.

Judiciary

For (21): Democrats Berman, Calif.; Brooks, Texas; Boucher, Va.; Conyers, Mich.; Crockett, Mich.; Edwards, Calif.; Feighan, Ohio; Frank, Mass.; Glickman, Kan.; Hughes, N.J.; Kastenmeier, Wis.; Morrison, Conn.; Rodino, N.J.; Schroeder, Colo.; Schumer, N.Y.; Seiberling, Ohio; Smith, Fla.; Staggers, W.Va.; Synar, Okla.; Republicans Brown, Colo.; Fish, N.Y.

Against (12): Democrat Mazzoli, Ky.; Republicans Coble, N.C.; Dannemeyer, Calif.; DeWine, Ohio; Gekas, Pa.; Hyde, Ill.; Lungren, Calif.; McCollum, Fla.; Moorhead, Calif.; Sensenbrenner, Wis.; Shaw, Fla.; Swindall, Ga.

could allow hundreds of schools to claim the religious exemption as "a license to discriminate."

Sensenbrenner offered the same amendment at the Judiciary markup.

Arguing in support, Dan Lungren, R-Calif., said some universities, such as Notre Dame, could find themselves subject to the non-discrimination ban — including the abortion regulations — unless the law was changed because, while they were clearly religious universities, they were no longer "controlled" by the church but were governed by laymen. But Charles E. Schumer, D-N.Y., contended the religious exemption was applied liberally. He said no school that had applied for it had been turned down by the Education Department.

Frank said the Sensenbrenner proposal would get the government involved in "thought control" trying to decide which religious tenets were "integral" and which were not.

The amendment was rejected 13-21, but several members said they would try to work on compromise language.

Other Amendments

Both panels rejected amendments that would have changed language covering private-sector entities, such as corporations, partnerships and other "private organizations." The Education and Labor proposal, offered by Steve Bartlett, R-Texas, was rejected 12-20. The Judiciary proposal, offered by Fish, was turned down 14-19.

The bill provided that private entities were covered "as a whole" if federal aid was extended to the entire entity. Sponsors used as an example the 1979 federal bailout of the Chrysler Corp. *(1979 Almanac p. 285)*

Entire entities also would be covered if they were "principally engaged in the business of providing education, health care, housing, social services or parks and recreation." Sponsors said these were quasi-governmental services that were performed increasingly by private firms.

The U.S. Chamber of Commerce opposed this section, contending it would prove too burdensome on businesses.

The rejected amendments would have limited coverage to the particular plant or facility of a private entity that "directly conducts" the operation receiving federal aid.

The committees also rejected amendments to bring Congress within coverage of the civil rights laws. Several members said Congress should be covered but that this bill was not the appropriate way to do it. A similar amendment was adopted in 1984 when the *Grove City* bill was considered by the full House.

Barlett's amendment in Education and Labor was rejected 11-21; the proposal offered by Michael DeWine, R-Ohio, in Judiciary was rejected on a 17-17 tie.

The Judiciary Committee also rejected 13-20 an amendment by Carlos J. Moorhead, R-Calif., stating that a school or college would not be covered by Title IX if the only federal aid it received came indirectly, through students who had received federal grants to attend school. In the *Grove City* decision, the court had ruled 9-0 that receipt of indirect aid through students was sufficient to bring a school within Title IX coverage.

Negotiations

Negotiations continued through the summer and fall to resolve the abortion dispute. Members of the Congressional Black Caucus met with officials of the Catholic Conference, and some suggested a representative go to Rome to urge Pope John Paul II to support the legislation.

Mickey Leland, D-Texas, chairman of the Black Caucus and a Catholic, wrote several bishops in August criticizing the conference position. He said the group's actions "seriously jeopardize the supportive relationship which it and the civil rights community have enjoyed over the years as well as the fragile social gains which we have jointly struggled to achieve for minorities, women and disabled and elderly people."

The letter prompted at least a dozen replies. The Rev. J. Bryan Hehir, conference spokesman, said the bishops generally wanted Leland to know they backed the organization's position on HR 700 but felt secure that their record on civil rights was "pretty solid."

There also were heated meetings among the bill's sponsors, other members of Congress and lobbyists over whether new compromise language should be drafted to address the abortion issue. Sponsors resisted such a move, saying abortion was not a part of the civil rights legislation and was being used as a scare tactic by those opposed to broad enforcement of civil rights laws.

Two bills dealing with the *Grove City* ruling (S 431, S 272) were pending in the Senate Labor and Human Resources Committee, but no action was taken on them. ∎

Armor-Piercing Bullets

The House Dec. 17 passed a bill (HR 3132) to ban the manufacture, importation and sale of bullets that could pierce police officers' protective vests.

The measure, which was actively sought by national law enforcement organizations, passed by a vote of 400-21 under suspension of the rules, a procedure that bars amendments and requires a two-thirds majority to pass. *(Vote 424, p. 134-H)*

The Judiciary Committee had reported the so-called "cop-killer bullet" bill — the product of four years' work — Nov. 6 (H Rept 99-360). Earlier versions were opposed by the National Rifle Association (NRA), which claimed the bill amounted to a foot in the door for gun control. The NRA did not actively oppose HR 3132. *(Background, earlier action, 1984 Almanac p. 226)*

The Senate Judiciary Committee approved a similar bill (S 104) July 24 by a 17-0 vote, and sponsors sought to bring it to the Senate floor the week of Dec. 16. But they were blocked by Steven D. Symms, R-Idaho. Symms believed the legislation was unnecessary and amounted to an intrusion on citizens' rights under the Second Amendment to the Constitution to "keep and bear arms," according to a spokesman. (The Senate passed the bill on March 6, 1986.)

Both bills would require manufacturers and importers to mark ammunition and label packages of armor-piercing bullets. The bullets could be produced only for use by federal and state government agencies, for export, or for testing or experimentation authorized by the secretary of the Treasury.

The penalty for unlawful manufacture or importation of the bullets would be up to five years in prison and a fine of up to $250,000. Ammunition dealers who "willfully" violated the law could have their licenses revoked. The bill also provided a prison sentence of five to 10 years for anyone convicted of a crime of violence with a firearm who had in his possession armor-piercing bullets "capable of being fired" from the gun used in the crime.

The Senate bill would apply only to bullets manufactured after the date of enactment. Sponsors said it would be unfair to punish dealers for accidentally selling armor-piercing bullets already packaged with other bullets on their shelves.

William J. Hughes, D-N.J., chairman of the House Judiciary Subcommittee on Crime, called the measure a "balanced, workable bill" that would "in no way" interfere with the legitimate pursuits of sportsmen. He said the prohibited ammunition was carefully defined and involved only bullets that had "no sporting purpose."

But Larry E. Craig, R-Idaho, one of the 21 members who voted against the bill, said it attempted to control criminal behavior "by controlling little pieces of metal. That approach is what gun control is all about," he contended, "and this bill, like all other forms of gun control, will fail to achieve its stated objective." ∎

Balanced-Budget Plans

The Senate Judiciary Committee July 11 approved two separate versions of a constitutional amendment to require a balanced federal budget.

Sponsors of a strict version (S J Res 13) that would make it difficult to use tax increases to achieve a balanced budget agreed to support a second, more flexible, measure (S J Res 225) as well in recognition of the political problems facing their own plan. Reports on both measures were filed Oct. 23 (S Rept 99-162, S Rept 99-163).

Helping to prompt committee action was a drive by balanced-budget proponents to get the states to call for a constitutional convention to approve a balanced-budget amendment. Thirty-two states (of 34 needed) had done so.

However, interest in any balanced-budget constitutional amendment waned as the deficit reduction-balanced budget plan known as "Gramm-Rudman-Hollings" roared through Congress. *(Story, p. 459)*

President Reagan had long championed a balanced-budget constitutional amendment that would restrict Congress' ability to raise taxes to avoid deficit spending. An amendment of this type was approved by the Senate in 1982 but was rejected by the House. *(1982 Almanac p. 391)*

S J Res 13, approved 11-7 by the committee, was nearly identical to the 1982 measure. It would require Congress to adopt a budget prior to each fiscal year in which outlays were not greater than receipts. It would allow deficit spending during a declared war or upon a three-fifths vote of each house of Congress. Any taxes that would increase receipts by more than the rate of increase in the "national income" the previous year would have to be approved by a majority vote of the entire membership of each chamber (not just those present and voting).

S J Res 225, approved 14-4, also called for a balanced budget except in time of war or when three-fifths of the Congress voted to suspend the requirement. However, it did not contain the provisions relating to tax receipts.

Judiciary Chairman Strom Thurmond, R-S.C., and Orrin G. Hatch, R-Utah, chief sponsors of S J Res 13, conceded they could not achieve the two-thirds majority vote required to push the proposal through the Senate. They and Paul Laxalt, R-Nev., made this clear in a meeting with President Reagan July 11, and subsequently said they were willing to support an alternative proposal that eliminated the restriction on tax increases. They said Reagan still supported S J Res 13, however.

There was no action in the House in 1985 on a balanced-budget constitutional amendment.

Opposition

Lobbyists on both sides of the balanced-budget issue were not entirely happy with the Senate Judiciary Committee's action. Representatives of the National Tax Limitation Committee and the National Taxpayers Union, which supported S J Res 13, said the alternative amendment would be ineffective because it failed to prevent tax increases and would not slow the growth of government, although a spokesman said the taxpayers' union could support the alternative as a step in the right direction.

Lobbyists opposed to any balanced-budget amendment also were disgruntled, but for different reasons. They had been confident they could block S J Res 13, but were uncertain what appeal the alternative might have. S J Res 225 had the support of Paul Simon, D-Ill., as well as of more conservative senators, and opponents feared he could attract support for the plan from moderates and liberals.

Simon said he supported the concept of a balanced-budget amendment but that S J Res 13, with its limitation on tax increases, would unduly restrict the ability of government to deal with the problems of society.

Two Judiciary members filed minority views to the committee reports opposing both the proposed amendments. Charles McC. Mathias Jr., R-Md., and Howard M. Metzenbaum, D-Ohio, said the amendments were unworkable, unenforceable and would "open the door to unprecedented judicial involvement in the budget process." ∎

Constitutional Convention

The Senate Judiciary Committee July 23 approved legislation (S 40) establishing procedures for holding a constitutional convention to debate proposed amendments to the Constitution.

The bill, approved 17-0, was similar, though not identical, to one reported by the committee in 1984. That bill was not brought to the Senate floor. *(1984 Almanac p. 262)*

Enacting such legislation took on increasing importance in 1985 to some members of Congress worried that the states would force a constitutional convention to consider an amendment requiring a balanced federal budget. By year's end, 32 states (of 34 needed) had passed resolutions calling for such a convention. *(Story, this page)*

Although all 26 amendments to the Constitution were passed by Congress and then ratified by three-fourths of the states, Article V of the Constitution also provided an alternative method. If two-thirds of the states (34) called for a constitutional convention, Congress must convene one. Any amendment adopted by the convention would have to be ratified by three-fourths of the states.

While the Constitution provided this method of adopting amendments, no procedures existed for running a convention. As a result, there was no guidance on what a convention could debate, who would be delegates, how many there would be, and who would preside. Unless procedures were established, some members feared, a convention could become a "runaway" session that would open up the entire Constitution for amendment.

Provisions

As reported Sept. 10 (S Rept 99-135), S 40 provided that each state and the District of Columbia would have two delegates to a constitutional convention, elected on an at-large basis, plus one elected from each congressional district. No member of Congress or any person "holding an office of trust or profit under the United States" could be a delegate.

The bill specified that, in general, a call for a convention would be valid for seven years after the date it was received by Congress. However, applications that were less than 12 years old when the bill was enacted would be considered effective for another two years. Thus, some resolutions could be valid for a 14-year period.

An amendment by Patrick J. Leahy, D-Vt., to restrict this time limit to seven years was rejected 6-10.

The bill required the states, in asking Congress to convene a convention, to specify the subject matter of the constitutional amendments the convention was to consider. No amendment could be proposed that differed from the subject matter stated in the resolution Congress adopted in calling the convention.

S 40 specified that the president pro tempore of the Senate and the Speaker of the House would convene the convention and preside until the delegates elected a presiding officer. Delegates would adopt their own rules by a three-fifths majority.

The bill authorized "such sums as may be necessary" for the expenses of the convention, including paying each delegate an amount equal to the salary of members of Congress, prorated for the term of the convention. Travel expenses also would be included.

A convention would be limited to six months unless an extension were agreed to by the House and Senate.

Criticisms of Bill

The bill's delegate-selection provisions drew criticism from the American Civil Liberties Union (ACLU) and from Citizens to Protect the Constitution, a private, non-partisan organization formed around the convention issue.

Morton H. Halperin, head of ACLU's Washington office, said the number of delegates violated the one-person, one-vote rule the Supreme Court said was mandated by the Constitution. He said delegates should be chosen by congressional district only and that at-large state delegates were unnecessary. The states already would participate in any process because they would have passed resolutions calling for a convention and would ratify anything the convention produced, Halperin said.

Halperin also contended there was great uncertainty about whether Congress had the authority to limit the scope of a convention.

Stephen J. Markman, an aide who helped draft S 40 for chief sponsor Orrin G. Hatch, R-Utah, defended the delegate scheme. He said it was intended to make the convention analogous to Congress, which had one chamber with equal state representation and the other with members elected by population.

Linda Rogers-Kingsbury, executive director of the citizens' group, contended the criteria for selecting delegates would bar government employees from serving, which she said was unfair. Markman said the language in the bill was drawn directly from the Constitution's description of eligibility for serving in the Electoral College. He said it was not clear it would bar government employees from serving, but if that turned out to be so, the bill might be amended to make clear that they could be delegates. ▮

Sentencing Commission

Congress Dec. 18 cleared legislation (HR 3837 — PL 99-217) extending for one year the deadline by which a newly created sentencing commission must set guidelines for punishment of federal crimes.

The House passed the bill by voice vote Dec. 16, and the Senate followed suit Dec. 18.

The commission was established under 1984 legislation (PL 98-473) that made sweeping changes in federal criminal laws. Sentencing reform was a key objective of the law, which also included tougher bail and drug laws and restrictions on the insanity defense. *(1984 Almanac p. 215)*

The commission was charged with writing guidelines that judges must follow in sentencing. The aim was to reduce the disparity in penalties for similar crimes.

The 1984 law required that the guidelines be written within 18 months of enactment. But the commission was slow getting started, and at its request, Congress extended the deadline until mid-April 1987.

Earlier in the year, Congress cleared HR 1847 (PL 99-22), making two minor changes affecting the commission.

The 1984 law required that the seven-member commission include three federal judges. HR 1847 amended the law to allow judges in "senior" status to serve on the panel. Such judges handled a variety of cases but were not in regular active service. Chief Justice Warren E. Burger and the U.S. Judicial Conference, the policy-making arm of the federal judiciary, had voiced concern about the effect on the courts' dockets if three active judges were taken out of service and put on the commission.

HR 1847 also authorized the Administrative Office of the U.S. Courts, which operated the federal judiciary, to seek an initial appropriation to get the commission going.

The House passed the bill April 2, the Senate April 3.

The Senate Oct. 16 confirmed the commission members: Stephen G. Breyer of Massachusetts, Paul H. Robinson of New Jersey, Michael K. Block of Arizona, Helen G. Corrothers of Arkansas, George E. MacKinnon of Maryland, Ilene H. Nagel of Indiana and William W. Wilkins Jr. of South Carolina, as chairman. ▮

Senate Rejects Bill to Permit School Prayer

The Senate Sept. 10 decisively rejected legislation designed to allow organized, recited prayer in public schools. The bill was tabled by a 62-36 vote. *(Vote 172, p. 35-S)*

The bill (S 47) would have prohibited the federal courts, including the Supreme Court, from hearing any case involving prayer in public schools. Thus, if a state or local government chose to adopt a policy allowing public school prayer, opponents would have no means of challenging it in the federal courts.

The Senate had voted on similar legislation 10 times in the past seven years. The Sept. 10 vote marked the lowest level of support for the measure since 1979, when it passed the Senate.

Opponents labeled S 47 a "court-stripping" measure and contended it represented an unconstitutional exercise of congressional authority. But despite the bill's defeat, chief sponsor Jesse Helms, R-N.C., said he and his supporters would continue their drive to restore school prayer.

The Supreme Court since 1962 had barred virtually all forms of public school prayer as violating the First Amendment to the Constitution, which said government "shall make no law respecting an establishment of religion." On June 4, the court struck down an Alabama law authorizing a one-minute period of silence in schools for "meditation or voluntary prayer." *(Wallace v. Jaffree, p. 11-A)*

That decision stepped up pressure on Congress to approve a constitutional amendment permitting prayer in the public schools. After the defeat of S 47, the Senate Judiciary Committee reported out such an amendment (S J Res 2). However, unlike Helms' bill, which needed only a majority vote to pass, a constitutional amendment would require a two-thirds majority of both houses and must be ratified by three-fourths of the states. *(S J Res 2, box, this page)*

In 1984 the Senate rejected proposed constitutional amendments that would have allowed vocal or silent school prayers. *(Background, 1984 Almanac p. 245)*

Past Prayer Votes

Helms first offered his prayer bill in 1979, as an amendment to a bill establishing the Education Department. His move caught the Democratic-controlled Senate by surprise, and the proposal was adopted. Fearing the amendment would kill the bill, the Senate, through a series of parliamentary maneuvers, added it instead to a bill involving Supreme Court procedures. That measure was adopted 61-30 but subsequently died in the House. *(1979 Almanac pp. 396, 465)*

In 1982, Helms sought to attach the prayer bill to a measure raising the national debt ceiling. He tried four times to cut off a filibuster on the measure but failed on each vote. The most support he garnered was 54 votes, six shy of the 60 needed to invoke cloture. Helms' legislation finally was tabled, 51-48. *(1982 Almanac p. 403)*

In 1985, Helms bypassed Judiciary Committee action on S 47 by having it placed directly on the Senate calendar when the 99th Congress convened.

Floor Debate

In contrast to consideration of past bills, debate on S 47 was short and desultory. Both Helms and Lowell P. Weicker Jr., R-Conn., who led the opposition to the bill, said the subject had been discussed so much in the past that there was no need for extended debate.

Barry Goldwater, R-Ariz., who had moved twice in 1982 to kill Helms' prayer bill, chided Helms for bringing up the issue again, saying he was "surprised that the senator from North Carolina decided to outlaw the Supreme Court from our life.... [and] that he would write this bill. If I wrote it, I would have been ashamed of it."

"I am certainly not ashamed of it," Helms retorted. He defended the bill as an appropriate exercise of congressional authority over the jurisdiction of the federal courts.

Leaders on both sides said the vote tally reflected changed political circumstances.

"This is really a liberal Senate. It is under control of Republicans but it's not a conservative Senate," said Helms. He cited in particular the loss of pro-prayer advocates Jennings Randolph, D-W.Va. (House, 1933-47; Senate, 1958-85), who retired; and Roger W. Jepsen, R-Iowa (1979-85), who was defeated in 1984. Their successors opposed S 47.

"There's no question there has been a change in sentiment," said Weicker. He maintained the public was "becoming more sensitive" to the issues involved in the prayer fight. "The more times the television preachers go ahead and talk about what Congress ought to do, the more people realize it is these people who are bringing government into religion, and they don't want it," he said. ▮

School Prayer Amendment

The Senate Judiciary Committee by a 12-6 vote Oct. 3 approved a proposed constitutional amendment to allow individual or group silent prayer in public schools (S J Res 2).

The committee report (S Rept 99-165) was filed Oct. 29, but the measure was not brought to the floor.

The amendment stated: "Nothing in this Constitution shall be construed to prohibit individual or group silent prayer or reflection in public schools. Neither the United States nor any state shall require any person to participate in such prayer or reflection nor shall they encourage any particular form of prayer or reflection."

The committee action came in response to a June 4 Supreme Court decision that struck down an Alabama law allowing a minute of silence in schools for "meditation or voluntary prayer," and to the defeat of a bill (S 47) that would have allowed organized, recited prayer in schools. *(Story, this page)*

Although S J Res 2 had considerable support in the Judiciary Committee, it did not go far enough for fundamentalist religious groups such as the Moral Majority. They were pushing for an amendment that would allow organized, recited prayer in public schools — the approach also favored by President Reagan.

However, Orrin G. Hatch, R-Utah, chief sponsor of S J Res 2, said there was not enough support to pass such an amendment. Constitutional amendments must be approved by a two-thirds vote of each chamber of Congress and be ratified by three-fourths of the states.

In 1984 the Senate rejected several school prayer amendments. *(1984 Almanac p. 245)*

There was only brief debate in the Judiciary Committee about S J Res 2. Hatch said it was "a good constitutional amendment that deserves to come to the floor." But Paul Simon, D-Ill., a leading opponent of the amendment, said it was designed "to promote religion and I don't think that is something the federal government ought to be a part of."

Voting for S J Res 2 were Republicans Strom Thurmond, S.C., the committee chairman; Paul Laxalt, Nev.; Hatch; Alan K. Simpson, Wyo.; Charles E. Grassley, Iowa; John P. East, N.C.; Jeremiah Denton, Ala., and Mitch McConnell, Ky.; and Democrats Joseph R. Biden Jr., Del.; Robert C. Byrd, W.Va.; Dennis DeConcini, Ariz.; and Howell Heflin, Ala.

Voting against it were Republicans Charles McC. Mathias Jr., Md., and Arlen Specter, Pa.; and Democrats Edward M. Kennedy, Mass.; Howard M. Metzenbaum, Ohio; Patrick J. Leahy, Vt., and Simon.

In the House, several school prayer constitutional amendments were pending in the Judiciary Committee, which consistently had opposed such measures. The House defeated a prayer amendment in 1971, the last time it considered the issue.

Meese Confirmed After Delay of 13 Months

After a 13-month wait — longer than any other Cabinet nominee in recent history — Edwin Meese III was confirmed by the Senate as attorney general Feb. 23.

The vote was 63-31. All the negative votes were cast by Democrats, who raised questions about Meese's ethical conduct and his fitness for office. *(Vote 9, p. 4-S)*

Meese, who was counselor to the president, drew more "nay" votes than any other attorney general since 1925, when Charles B. Warren was rejected 39-46 as attorney general under President Calvin Coolidge.

The Judiciary Committee had approved Meese's nomination Feb. 5 by a 12-6 vote. Majority Leader Robert Dole, R-Kan., hoped to get a vote on the nomination Feb. 19 but ran into opposition from farm-state senators who refused to allow a vote until they had worked out a program they said would help financially beleaguered farmers. After five days of negotiations, Senate leaders and farm-state Democrats resolved their differences over a farm credit package, clearing the way for a vote on Meese during an unusual Saturday session.

The 53-year-old Meese, a close friend of President Reagan, was sworn in Feb. 25. He succeeded William French Smith, who returned to private law practice in California. Smith had been Reagan's personal lawyer before becoming attorney general.

Background

Meese was first nominated by President Reagan Jan. 23, 1984, but his confirmation ran into trouble when questions arose about some of his personal financial transactions. The controversy centered on whether Meese helped get federal jobs for people who provided him financial assistance. *(Details, 1984 Almanac p. 248)*

At Meese's request, an independent counsel was appointed to investigate the allegations. In September 1984, the counsel, Washington, D.C., lawyer Jacob A. Stein, issued his report, finding "no basis" for prosecuting Meese for violation of a criminal statute. Because his mandate was very specific, Stein said the report made "no comment on Mr. Meese's ethics and the propriety of his conduct for office."

Meese and his supporters contended that the Stein report cleared him of any wrongdoing and that he should be quickly confirmed as attorney general.

But Howard M. Metzenbaum, D-Ohio, a leader of the Senate opposition to Meese, and Common Cause, the public affairs lobby, argued that Meese was unfit for the post. They contended the Stein report was only the starting point for asking questions about Meese's ethical conduct, particularly his failure to disclose financial relationships with people he later approved for federal jobs.

Meese was renominated Jan. 3, 1985, at the start of the 99th Congress. In hearings, he maintained that he had always acted ethically, but conceded that as a result of the Stein probe, "I have a much higher level of sensitivity to matters now than I did when I arrived in Washington.... I would take pains to avoid the appearance" of impropriety.

Such statements were not enough for his opponents. A speech by George J. Mitchell, D-Maine, on the floor Feb. 20 was typical. "The degree of ethical insensitivity Mr. Meese has demonstrated reveals a disregard for the appearance of probity that I cannot endorse in the attorney general of the United States," said the former federal judge.

William Proxmire, D-Wis., said there were more than 1,000 lawyers in the country of both political parties better qualified than Meese to be attorney general. To prove his point, Proxmire prepared a list of these lawyers and unrolled it down the center aisle of the Senate chamber.

Opponents also cited some 160 editorials from papers across the country urging opposition to the nomination.

But Dole contended "the record shows Ed Meese is an ethical man, a man of character and integrity.... In retrospect, there were some things Ed Meese should have done differently. But then he was a newcomer to Washington and had not yet been indoctrinated into our hypersensitivity over the appearance of potential conflict."

Another supporter, John P. East, R-N.C., accused Meese's opponents of trying to "undercut his personal integrity." East added: "I doubt if Mother Teresa could get approved by this group to be head of the Department of Health and Human Services."

Committee Action

The Judiciary Committee approved Meese's nomination Feb. 5 on a largely party-line vote of 12-6.

Two Democrats — Howell Heflin, Ala., and Dennis DeConcini, Ariz. — voted to report Meese's nomination to the Senate, along with all 10 committee Republicans: Chairman Strom Thurmond, S.C.; Charles McC. Mathias Jr., Md.; Paul Laxalt, Nev.; Orrin G. Hatch, Utah; Dole; Alan K. Simpson, Wyo.; East; Charles E. Grassley, Iowa; Jeremiah Denton, Ala.; and Arlen Specter, Pa.

Voting against Meese were Democrats Joseph R. Biden Jr., Del.; Edward M. Kennedy, Mass.; Robert C. Byrd, W.Va.; Metzenbaum; Patrick J. Leahy, Vt.; and Max Baucus, Mont.

DeConcini and Heflin had been considered swing votes, and they attended most of the Judiciary Committee's hearings Jan. 29-31 on the Meese nomination. Both kept their own counsel until the Feb. 5 meeting. In remarks before the tally, each said that while he had concerns about Meese's ethical fitness for the post, he was giving him the benefit of the doubt.

Heflin said his vote was not really a vote for Meese but a vote to send the nomination to the Senate for all members' consideration. Mathias also made clear that his vote was cast largely to give the Senate a chance to debate the nomination. Both voted for Meese on the floor, as did DeConcini.

"I just don't believe Mr. Meese understands the importance of public trust," Baucus said before the vote. "Many of Mr. Meese's actions appear to be improper. And Mr. Meese doesn't seem to care," he said.

But Thurmond, Meese's chief supporter, said the Stein investigation plus the committee's hearings had "firmly established and indeed underscored that not only is Mr. Meese qualified to be attorney general but that he is also a man of honesty, dedication and integrity."

At the hearings, a number of law enforcement officials testified in support of Meese, praising his dedication to law enforcement. Archibald Cox, chairman of Common Cause, and Joseph L. Rauh Jr., counsel for the Leadership Conference on Civil Rights, an umbrella group of 165 organizations, testified in opposition.

Cox blasted as "unbelievable" the conclusion of the Office of Government Ethics, which routinely looked into the fitness of presidential nominees, that while there was "an appearance" of impropriety in some of Meese's dealings, there in fact was no impropriety.

Rauh said civil rights groups believed Meese would not vigorously and objectively enforce civil rights laws and would not exhibit the ethical standards required of the nation's chief law enforcement officer. ■

Reynolds Nomination

The Senate Judiciary Committee June 27 decisively rejected the nomination of William Bradford Reynolds to be associate attorney general, the third-ranking post in the Justice Department.

Reynolds was head of the department's civil rights division and remained in that job. It was the decisions he had made there, and the way he defended them at his confirmation hearings, that led to his rejection for the higher position. As associate attorney general, Reynolds would have been in charge of all civil law matters.

In three dramatic votes, the Judiciary Committee first refused, 8-10, to report the nomination favorably. It then tied 9-9 on motions to report it without a recommendation or with an unfavorable recommendation.

On the first motion, the committee's eight Democrats were joined by Republicans Charles McC. Mathias Jr., Md., and Arlen Specter, Pa., in opposing Reynolds. On the tie votes, Specter voted for the motions, while Mathias sided with the Democrats.

The vote had been postponed once because Chairman Strom Thurmond, R-S.C., knew he lacked the votes to win. Even on June 27, the outcome was in doubt until Howell Heflin, D-Ala., the only uncommitted member, cast his first vote — "nay." Heflin, a former state Supreme Court chief justice, said he had concluded there were many legal experts better qualified than Reynolds for the post and was concerned about Reynolds' "credibility."

The votes appeared to mark the first time in four years that a committee had actively barred a major presidential nomination from reaching the Senate. In 1981, the Labor and Human Resources Committee refused to report the nomination of John R. Van de Water to be chairman of the National Labor Relations Board. A move to bring it directly to the floor also failed. *(1981 Almanac p. 20-A)*

After Reynolds' rejection by the Judiciary Committee, the administration considered seeking a rarely used "discharge" procedure to bring the nomination to the floor, or appointing him during a congressional recess. But Senate Republican leaders said Reynolds lacked the votes to be confirmed, and the White House dropped its efforts.

President Reagan said he was "deeply disappointed" by the committee's action. "That some members of the committee chose to use the confirmation process to conduct an ideological assault on so superbly qualified a candidate was unjust and deeply wrong," he said. Adding that Reynolds "retains my full faith and confidence," Reagan said his "civil rights views reflect my own. The policies he pursued are the policies of this administration. . . ."

The defeat of Reynolds was a major triumph for civil rights activists, who charged he had failed to enforce civil rights laws and had misapplied federal court decisions to suit his own policy ends. He was particularly criticized for his decisions on enforcement of voting rights laws and his opposition to affirmative action and school busing as remedies for discrimination.

But what ultimately swung key committee members against him were conflicts between his testimony and information provided by other witnesses and by documents from his own department regarding certain decisions he had made.

In hearings June 4-5, Reynolds defended his record and claimed that in several controversial voting rights cases he had talked with civil rights lawyers before making the decisions they disliked — decisions that in some cases overrode the recommendations of his own staff.

However, civil rights lawyers challenged his assertions. Reynolds was called back for a third session June 18, but his testimony failed to satisfy some committee members.

At the hearings, Edward M. Kennedy, D-Mass., said Reynolds had "done enough damage to civil rights at his current level in the Department of Justice and does not deserve to be promoted," while Howard M. Metzenbaum, D-Ohio, accused him of "coming down on the side of the bigots" in civil rights cases. But Orrin G. Hatch, R-Utah, Reynolds' chief defender at the hearings, said he had "sincere" interpretations of the law and had "sincerely enforced civil rights laws" as he saw them.

A number of civil rights groups, as well as the heads of the Congressional Black Caucus and the Congressional Caucus on Women's Issues, testified against Reynolds. He was supported by several lawyers in private practice and by spokesmen for the U.S. Chamber of Commerce and the Washington Legal Foundation, a public-interest law center with a conservative bent. ■

Cooper Nomination

By voice vote Nov. 12, the Senate confirmed the nomination of Charles J. Cooper to head the Office of Legal Counsel in the Justice Department — the top legal adviser to Attorney General Edwin Meese III.

Cooper had been a top aide to William Bradford Reynolds, assistant attorney general for civil rights. Civil rights advocates criticized his elevation to the legal counsel post largely because of their unhappiness with Reynolds' stewardship of the civil rights division. Reynolds was an outspoken opponent of the use of affirmative action and school busing to remedy past racial and sex discrimination, and civil rights lawyers said Cooper was a principal architect of these policies.

Civil rights groups did not mount a full-scale attack on Cooper, however, and the Judiciary Committee, which in June had blocked Reynolds' nomination to the post of associate attorney general, approved Cooper's nomination Oct. 31 by an 11-5 vote. *(Reynolds nomination, this page)* ■

Nuclear Plant Security

The Senate by voice vote Oct. 3 passed a bill (S 274) that would allow companies that own nuclear power plants to use FBI criminal history files to conduct background checks on persons with access to critical areas of the plants.

The Judiciary Committee had reported the bill Sept. 26 (S Rept 99-143).

Chief sponsor Jeremiah Denton, R-Ala., said that under existing law, plant owners could conduct background checks on employees only through state and local police files, and those files did not include information about a person's criminal record, if any, in other parts of the country. Allowing plant operators to have access to FBI files would permit them to obtain more complete criminal histories before deciding whether employees should have access to all areas of a plant, Denton said.

According to the Nuclear Regulatory Commission (NRC), there were 85 operating nuclear plants in the United States, with construction permits granted for 37 more. The NRC had investigated more than a dozen incidents of suspected sabotage by plant employees, and a commission report said that between 1974 and 1982 there were 32 possibly deliberate acts of damage at 24 reactors and reactor construction sites. The NRC said the major threat of sabotage to nuclear plants was from "insiders." ▮

Military Malpractice Suits

The House Oct. 7 handily passed legislation (HR 3174) to allow active-duty military personnel to sue the federal government for medical or dental malpractice in government facilities.

The bill passed by a vote of 317-90 under suspension of the rules, a procedure that bars amendments and requires a two-thirds majority for passage. *(Vote 309, p. 98-H)*

The legislation was prompted by increasing concern in Congress about incidents of medical malpractice at military hospitals. The Judiciary Subcommittee on Administrative Law and Governmental Relations held hearings on the issue July 8-9, and the bill grew out of those sessions. The full Judiciary Committee reported the measure Sept. 26 (H Rept 99-288).

Because of a 1950 Supreme Court decision, *Feres v. United States*, members of the armed services were barred from suing for injuries suffered while on active duty. Yet civilians with access to government medical facilities, including dependents of active-duty service members and retired military personnel, were allowed to do so.

HR 3174 would not change substantive personal injury law, but would give service members the right to seek damages for certain types of injuries not related to combat. The law of the state in which the injury occurred would govern.

To prevent personnel from being paid twice for the same injury, the bill provided that any judgment awarded to a service member would be reduced by the value of government benefits available to him.

Administration Opposed

The administration opposed the bill, contending that the *Feres* decision was correct in barring active-duty personnel from filing malpractice suits and that to overturn it would disrupt military operations.

But chief sponsor Barney Frank, D-Mass., said the measure was a limited one. "What we say is that members of the armed services now have the same right as civilians. I do not think that that is a radical step. It excludes combat-type operations. No one is going to be suing Hawkeye under this bill," Frank said, referring to the Korean War combat doctor in the television series "M*A*S*H."

Opponents of HR 3174 said it could add thousands of lawsuits to an already overburdened civil court system while doing nothing to improve the quality of medical care in the military health system.

A bill addressing the same issue (S 489) was pending in the Senate Judiciary Subcommittee on Administrative Practice and Procedure. ▮

Patent Fee Curb

By voice vote, the House June 24 passed a three-year reauthorization bill (HR 2434) for the U.S. Patent and Trademark Office that barred any increase in patent fees beyond those needed to compensate for inflation.

The measure, reported May 15 by the Judiciary Committee (H Rept 99-104), also prohibited the imposition of user fees for public search rooms. It authorized $101.6 million for fiscal 1986, $110.4 million for 1987 and $111.9 million for 1988.

The Senate Judiciary Subcommittee on Patents, Copyrights and Trademarks held hearings on HR 2434 July 23, but took no further action.

Background. In 1980 and 1982, Congress revised the patent commissioner's authority to set fees to cover the cost of processing patent and trademark applications. The 1982 law set up a two-tiered system, requiring large firms to pay at a level that recouped 100 percent of patent application and maintenance costs, while individual inventors, small firms and non-profit organizations paid at a rate designed to recoup 50 percent of costs. *(1980 Almanac p. 405; 1982 Almanac p. 384)*

The Reagan administration in 1985 sought to rely more heavily on fees to operate the office, while cutting the annual appropriation to $84.7 million for fiscal 1986. Patent officials estimated they needed $101 million; the Office of Management and Budget said the $16 million shortfall should be made up with increased fees.

Congress appropriated $84.7 million, the amount requested, for the Patent and Trademark Office in 1986.

House Committee Action. The House Judiciary Committee approved HR 2434 by voice vote after putting restrictions on the amount and use of fees collected for patent examinations.

The bill also prohibited the office from using fees to buy equipment to automate its operations, requiring it to seek appropriations for such purchases instead. This provision, proposed by Jack Brooks, D-Texas, was in response to a General Accounting Office (GAO) report criticizing the office for being deficient in automating operations.

Another Brooks provision barred the office for three years from making "exchange agreements" with private companies to get automatic data processing equipment. Agreements with foreign governments were exempted.

The GAO said that while the office received benefits from its existing exchange agreements, the benefits were less than those the companies got in return. The office gave companies special access to trademark data and agreed to restrict the public's access to its trademark data base. ▮

'Designer Drug' Ban

The Senate by voice vote Dec. 18 passed legislation (S 1437) to make it a federal crime to manufacture, distribute or possess "designer drugs."

The Judiciary Committee had reported the bill Nov. 21 (S Rept 99-196).

"Designer drugs" were drugs that had a chemical structure and effect "substantially similar" to controlled substances, such as heroin, but had a molecular structure that was slightly altered. Under existing law, which defined controlled substances according to their precise chemical makeup, these drugs were not illegal.

Sponsors said legislation was needed because of the growth of the designer drug market and the serious physical damage the drugs could cause. Some 100 deaths in the United States had been attributed to designer drugs.

S 1437 provided a fine of up to $250,000 and imprisonment of up to 15 years for anyone who intentionally manufactured, distributed or possessed with an intent to distribute a designer drug. Simple possession would be a misdemeanor punishable by imprisonment of up to one year, a fine of up to $25,000 or both.

Judiciary Chairman Strom Thurmond, R-S.C., said designer drugs often were more potent than previously available drugs and that users thus were more subject to overdoses that could cause death or serious injury.

"Whether generated by individual back-alley chemists or by those associated with organized crime, these easily manufactured and unregulated chemical compounds present us with a truly frightening problem: designer drugs dealing designer death," Thurmond said.

Joseph R. Biden Jr., D-Del., who cosponsored S 1437 with Thurmond, said the "underground" chemists who produced the drugs had been "able to create new drug analogs faster than the federal government can identify and define them."

There was no action on designer drugs in the House Judiciary Committee in 1985. ▮

Justice Dept. Authorization

For the fifth year in a row, Congress failed to complete action on legislation authorizing Justice Department programs. However, department activities continued under the fiscal 1986 appropriations bill for the Commerce, Justice and State departments (PL 99-180). ***(Story, p. 346)***

In theory, no money could be appropriated for programs that had not been formally authorized by Congress, but this rule frequently was waived.

The House Judiciary Committee May 15 reported a $3.72 billion fiscal 1986 authorization bill (HR 2348 — H Rept 99-113) that included new restrictions on department activities. Committee Democrats were angry at the department's refusal to enforce a "competition in contracting" law and its attempts to scale back affirmative action remedies for past discrimination against women and minorities.

However, HR 2348 was not brought to the floor in 1985.

The Senate Judiciary Committee May 9 debated but did not complete action on its $3.78 billion version of the bill (S 1065). That measure also got tangled up in a dispute over administration efforts to relax affirmative action plans. Howard M. Metzenbaum, D-Ohio, proposed curtailing the Justice Department's authority to open up consent decrees in civil rights cases, but his amendment to S 1065 was never fully debated.

House Committee Action

In action on HR 2348, the House Judiciary Committee May 8-9 voted new restrictions on Justice Department activities. The curbs, pressed by the Democratic majority, were aimed at forcing compliance with a 1984 statute intended to promote competition in federal procurement, and at discouraging department efforts to relax affirmative action plans.

Competition in Contracting

By a 21-12 vote largely along party lines, the committee adopted an amendment barring any expenditures by the attorney general's office in fiscal 1986 unless the attorney general directed federal agencies to enforce the 1984 Competition in Contracting Act. That law allowed an unsuccessful bidder for a federal contract to file a protest with the General Accounting Office (GAO), and the GAO was authorized to suspend the awarding of the contract until the challenge was resolved. *(1984 Almanac p. 197)*

Administration officials contended the law unconstitutionally breached the separation of powers between the branches of government. They said GAO was a legislative office that had no constitutional authority to compel an executive branch agency to act in a particular way. Congressional legal experts insisted the GAO was not a legislative agency, even though it performed studies for Congress, because its head was appointed by the president and confirmed by the Senate, like any executive agency chief.

Attorney General Edwin Meese III told Judiciary members during an oversight hearing in April the department would not enforce the law even though its constitutionality was upheld March 27 by a federal district court in New Jersey. Meese said the court was "not competent" to rule on the law's validity.

Jack Brooks, D-Texas, sponsored the provision intended to force adherence to the contracting act. Brooks was chairman of the Government Operations Committee, which wrote the 1984 law. He said the administration's actions "strike at the very heart of our constitutional form of government. In effect, the president has decreed that he has the 'obligation' to revise or rescind any law which is inconsistent with his interpretation of the Constitution."

Brooks also was critical of Meese, declaring, "I can hardly believe an attorney general who practiced law would do this."

Brooks and several other Democrats said that if the administration opposed the law, Reagan should have vetoed it, not refused to enforce it. But Republicans noted that the law was enacted as part of the much broader Deficit Reduction Act (PL 98-369). Absent line-item veto power, which the president had sought unsuccessfully, he had no choice but to accept the bad with the good on wide-ranging bills, GOP members said.

Hamilton Fish Jr., R-N.Y., called the fund cutoff a "draconian, punitive overreaction." And Henry J. Hyde, R-Ill., called it "a cure for dandruff by decapitation."

George W. Gekas, R-Pa., offered an amendment to suspend enforcement of the law until a federal appeals court determined that the act was constitutional. His amendment was rejected by voice vote.

Only one Republican, Hank Brown of Colorado, voted with the panel's Democrats to block funding for Meese's office until the contracting law was enforced.

Civil Rights

The other restriction in HR 2348 barred the department from reopening any litigation that had resulted in a court order establishing numerical goals and quotas "to remedy illegal discrimination." The section also established new procedures the department must follow to open up any "consent decree" reached among parties in a civil rights suit.

William Bradford Reynolds, head of the department's Civil Rights Division, was an outspoken opponent of numerical goals and quotas and had moved aggressively to curtail the use of such remedies. *(Reynolds nomination rejected, p. 237)*

The Supreme Court had ruled 6-3 in June 1984 that federal judges could not override a valid seniority system in making layoffs, even to preserve the jobs of black workers hired under a court-approved affirmative action plan.

That decision, in *Firefighters Local Union No. 1784 v. Stotts*, left considerable confusion in legal circles about the permissible boundaries of affirmative action plans, but Reynolds interpreted the ruling broadly. He asserted that the decision meant federal courts "may not require or permit race- or gender-conscious hiring, promotion or layoff quotas" as a remedy for discrimination. *(Court ruling, 1984 Almanac p. 8-A)*

After the *Stotts* decision, the department sent letters to 50 jurisdictions asking them to modify substantially consent decrees that included numerical goals and quotas as a remedy for past discrimination.

The Justice Department also took three cities to court in an effort to remove hiring goals from consent decrees requiring the jurisdictions to bring more women, blacks and Hispanics into municipal jobs.

In response, Don Edwards, D-Calif., drafted provisions in HR 2348 to restrict any future attempts to modify affirmative action agreements.

One of the provisions inserted by Edwards barred the Justice Department from reopening any affirmative action decree unless the appeals court governing the district court had previously endorsed the department's claim that goals or quotas to remedy employment discrimination were improper.

A second section barred the attorney general from seeking to modify a consent decree in civil rights cases unless two conditions were met:

- He must provide reasonable notice of any proposed modification and notice of a court hearing for all persons likely to be affected by the modification.
- There must be a court hearing in which all affected persons had an opportunity to participate.

F. James Sensenbrenner Jr., R-Wis., offered an amendment to delete the provisions, contending they "would seriously hamper" the department's ability to implement the *Stotts* decision. But the committee rejected the amendment 8-21; Fish and Brown were the only Republicans to vote with the Democrats.

Other Provisions

The House and Senate bills were fairly close in the authorization levels for various entities within the Justice Department, such as the Immigration and Naturalization Service and the FBI. However, they were far apart on funding for U.S. attorneys, who handled the federal government's civil litigation and criminal prosecutions.

The Justice Department had asked for 560 new positions for U.S. attorneys' offices, arguing that 398 of these were necessary to handle the work created by the addition of 85 new judges to the federal bench in 1984.

The House committee flatly rejected that assertion. Chairman Peter W. Rodino Jr., D-N.J., said the new judgeships were created expressly to relieve overloaded courts. Adding new prosecutors would lead to expanded caseloads, counteracting any benefit from the added judges, he said.

The committee voted $312 million, just enough funding to support the existing number of U.S. attorneys.

The Senate bill authorized $487.4 million, enough for the 560 positions the department wanted. ∎

Refugee Assistance

The House June 13 passed a two-year reauthorization for refugee resettlement programs (HR 1452), after refusing to kill a $50 million impact aid program for states with large refugee populations.

Members did vote to freeze authorized spending for refugee social services and medical screening at the fiscal 1985 appropriations level, adjusted for inflation. It was the fifth time during 1985 the House had adopted such a freeze amendment to a fiscal 1986 reauthorization bill.

The same day, the Senate Judiciary Committee approved a similar measure (S 1262) that did not include the impact aid, or "targeted assistance," money, which was opposed by the Reagan administration. The committee filed its report (S Rept 99-154) June 13, but the measure was not brought to the Senate floor.

Both bills reauthorized programs established in a 1980 law (PL 96-212) that overhauled the process for admitting refugees into the United States. The law defined refugees as people who fled their homelands because of persecution. *(1980 Almanac p. 378)*

Some 32,918 refugees were admitted to the United States between January and March 1985, according to the House Judiciary Committee. President Reagan, after consulting with Congress, said 70,000 refugees a year could be admitted to the country in 1985 and 1986. *(Box, p. 241)*

Provisions

HR 1452 (H Rept 99-132), approved by the Judiciary Committee 30-3 May 9, was similar to a measure that was passed by the House in 1983 but died in the Senate. *(1984 Almanac p. 238)*

The bill did not set an overall funding ceiling, but it did set specific funding levels for social services, health screening and targeted assistance to areas with a heavy refugee influx.

For social services, the bill authorized $74.8 million in fiscal 1986 and $77.9 million in 1987; for health screening, $8.7 million in 1986 and $9.1 million in 1987, and for targeted assistance, $50 million each year.

HR 1452 did not contain specific authorizations for other items, such as cash and medical assistance to refugees, special educational aid and administrative costs for running the resettlement program; instead, it authorized such sums as were necessary.

The bill modified existing law by providing that social service funding to states be based on the total number of refugees in a state, including children. Existing law used a formula based on the number of adult refugees in a state and how long they had been in the United States.

HR 1452 required greater accountability from the voluntary agencies that helped find homes and jobs for refugees; the agencies received federal money for their efforts. Agencies would have to submit detailed reports on the number of refugees placed, how much money was spent to settle them, and how their progress was being monitored.

The measure also sought to reduce welfare dependency among refugees, barring them from receiving cash assistance if they refused to take a job or go to a job interview arranged by their sponsor.

The bill would make all refugees presumptively eligible for Medicaid, the federal-state medical program for the poor, for the first year they were in the country. This provision, which was opposed by the administration and

Refugee Admissions

The Reagan administration and Congress agreed to hold the line on the number of refugees allowed to enter the United States in fiscal 1986.

Secretary of State George P. Shultz and other officials told the Senate and House Judiciary committees Sept. 17 and 19 that the administration planned to admit 70,000 refugees in 1986 — the same limit as in fiscal 1985.

Of the total, 48,500 would be from Southeast Asia. Other refugee admission ceilings for 1986 would be: Soviet Union/Eastern Europe, 9,500; Near East, 6,000; Africa, 3,000; and Latin America/Caribbean, 3,000.

Under U.S. immigration law, refugees were defined as people fleeing persecution in their own countries. They were screened by U.S. personnel abroad, who determined whether they met the criteria for refugees before they were approved for admission.

The ceilings were announced during the annual consultation with Congress, a feature of refugee policy since enactment of a 1980 law (PL 96-212) that revised the refugee admissions process. The Judiciary committees had until Sept. 30 to make their own recommendations on refugee admissions, but did not do so. *(1980 Almanac p. 378)*

In fiscal 1985, 68,045 refugees were admitted to the United States — about 3,000 fewer than the 71,113 admitted in fiscal 1984, according to the State Department. The drop resulted from lower-than-expected admissions from Cuba and Africa. *(1984 Almanac p. 238)*

The number of refugees admitted each year had dropped considerably since President Reagan took office in 1981, when 159,252 refugees were admitted. The number declined to a low of 61,681 in fiscal 1983 before rising to 71,113 in fiscal 1984.

Most of the refugees who entered the country came from Southeast Asia. In the past decade, about 755,000 refugees came to the United States from that part of the world, Shultz said.

As in fiscal 1985, the 48,500 refugees from Southeast Asia in 1986 were to be in two categories:

- One category, with a ceiling of 8,500, was for the "orderly departure program," for political prisoners, Amerasian children fathered by U.S. servicemen, and immediate family members of refugees already in the United States.
- The other category, with a ceiling of 40,000, was for Southeast Asian refugees in resettlement camps.

was not in the Senate bill, was intended to encourage refugees to take jobs that carried no health benefits rather than trying to qualify for welfare programs that entitled them to Medicaid.

In 1980, 70 to 80 percent of all refugees in the United States were dependent on welfare, but that number had dropped to about 50-54 percent, according to the Judiciary Committee.

However, in California, the state with the largest concentration of refugees, about 85 percent of the refugees who had arrived since 1982 received some type of public assistance.

House Floor Action

The House passed the bill by voice vote after floor fights over several controversial amendments.

Targeted Assistance. F. James Sensenbrenner Jr., R-Wis., offered an amendment to delete the $50 million authorization for targeted assistance. The amendment had been rejected in the Judiciary Committee by voice vote.

Sensenbrenner said the need for the program had diminished because the refugee flow into the country had slowed over the past four years. He said the targeted aid amounted to a special bailout for California and Florida, which had received 71 percent of the funding.

But Rep. Romano L. Mazzoli, D-Ky., chairman of the Subcommittee on Immigration, Refugees and International Law, said 21 states had gotten money from the program in the past two years.

After more than an hour's debate — much of it by Californians and Floridians defending the program — the amendment was rejected, 104-307. *(Vote 145, p. 48-H)*

Freeze Amendment. As part of a continuing effort to shrink the budget deficit, Carl D. Pursell, R-Mich., supported by Bruce A. Morrison, D-Conn., moved to reduce the $100 million the Judiciary Committee had authorized for social services and the $14 million it had allotted for health screening.

Pursell's amendment authorized $74.8 million in fiscal 1986 and $77.9 million in 1987 for social services, and $8.7 million in 1986 and $9.1 million in 1987 for health screening. Morrison said these figures represented the existing appropriation plus an inflation adjustment.

Mazzoli charged that the amendment was "irredeemably ungenerous" and "lacking in the magnanimity" that had characterized U.S. treatment of refugees.

Dan Lungren, Calif., ranking Republican on the Immigration Subcommittee, also opposed the freeze. He said the refugee assistance program needed to do more, not less.

Despite such pleas, the amendment was adopted 278-112. *(Vote 146, p. 48-H)*

Attorneys' Fees

President Reagan Aug. 5 signed into law a bill (HR 2378 — PL 99-80) allowing individuals, small businesses and certain local governments to collect attorneys' fees when they prevailed in legal disputes with federal agencies.

The government could avoid paying the fees if it proved its position in a particular case was "substantially justified."

The House passed the bill June 24, and the Senate accepted it without amendment July 24, clearing it for the president.

The measure was a compromise that had the support of the administration, various business groups and the House and Senate Judiciary committees. It was similar to a 1984 bill pocket-vetoed by President Reagan because of language he said would have required the government to justify every step of the process in bringing a lawsuit or administrative proceeding in order to avoid paying a fee award. *(1984 Almanac p. 259)*

That provision was changed in the new bill so that the government must justify an agency's position only at the administrative level or in court.

The bill reinstated a 1980 law, the Equal Access to Justice Act (PL 96-481), which expired in 1984. *(1980 Almanac p. 550)*

Meese Claim Spotlights Attorneys' Fees

Edwin Meese III, President Reagan's nominee for attorney general, raised some congressional eyebrows with his request that the government pay $720,924 in legal fees he incurred while under investigation by an independent counsel, or special prosecutor. *(Story, p. 236)*

But Congress itself authorized such claims for attorneys' fees in 1982 amendments (PL 97-409) to the 1978 Ethics in Government Act (PL 95-521), the law providing for appointment of independent counsels to investigate alleged wrongdoing by high government officials. *(1982 Almanac p. 386; 1978 Almanac p. 835)*

In fact, the ethics law was only one of about 130 statutes that permitted the award of attorneys' fees to litigants who prevailed in battles with the government. It authorized reimbursement of legal fees to anyone investigated under the ethics law but not indicted, provided the person would not have been subject to investigation as a private citizen in similar circumstances. Meese was the first person to invoke this fee provision.

Fee Statutes

Historically in U.S. jurisprudence, each party in litigation bore its own legal expenses. But as early as 1875, when the first fee-award provision was approved as part of a civil rights law, Congress recognized that citizens should not have to pay often sizable legal fees to enforce rights they were guaranteed by law.

While fee provisions helped citizens combat the government on an equal legal footing, they also were a boon to lawyers. Some fee awards totaled millions of dollars, and they regularly ran into thousands of dollars, Justice Department figures showed.

A century after the first attorneys' fee provision became law, a 1975 Supreme Court decision prompted a spate of new ones. In *Aleyska Pipeline Service Co. v. Wilderness Society*, the court ruled that without specific authorization from Congress, courts could not award attorneys' fees. Prior to that, lawyers believed courts could award fees when they determined that prevailing litigants were enforcing important rights.

But the Supreme Court rejected that theory, stating in part that "it would be difficult, indeed, for the courts, without legislative guidance, to consider some statutes important and others unimportant and to allow attorneys' fees only in connection with the former."

Within a year of the ruling, Congress passed one of the more important fee laws, the Civil Rights Attorneys' Fees Awards Act of 1976 (PL 94-559), which allowed fees to prevailing parties in suits to enforce all civil rights laws passed since 1866. *(1976 Almanac p. 411)*

In 1980 Congress passed the Equal Access to Justice Act (PL 96-481), which allowed individuals and small businesses to collect attorneys' fees when they prevailed in legal disputes with the government. The law was renewed in 1985. *(Story, p. 241)*

Attorneys' fees awards were permitted under a host of other laws as well, covering areas from black-lung compensation to antitrust challenges, from consumer product safety to environmental protection.

Virtually all the laws gave judges great discretion in making awards, specifying only that lawyers' fees be "reasonable." That prompted a multitude of lawsuits; in 1980, for example, the Supreme Court issued nine rulings involving attorneys' fees, six of them in one month, according to a 1984 article for the *John Marshall Law Review* in Chicago.

Justice William J. Brennan Jr. lamented in one case that shifting judicial interpretations of fee-award laws created "a Frankenstein's monster [that] meanders its well-intentioned way through the legal landscape leaving waste and confusion ... in its wake."

Meese's principal lawyers billed him at $250 per hour for their own time, and at lower rates for work performed by their associates, paralegals and clerks. Their charges were far above the level the Reagan administration advocated for parties prevailing against the government in civil cases, and more than 10 times the rates permitted for attorneys appointed by the courts to represent indigent defendants in federal criminal cases. Congress in 1984 set those rates at $40 per hour for out-of-court work and $60 per hour for in-court work.

The administration since 1982 had pressed for a $75 per hour cap on legal fees under civil rights and other laws. In 1984, it sought to write such a cap into law, but the legislation was not approved by Congress.

Deputy Attorney General Carol E. Dinkins called the $75 per hour limit "necessary and appropriate to forestall skyrocketing legal fee awards" and contended it was "adequate to ensure quality representation."

Noting that government attorneys made far less than many of their counterparts in private practice, Dinkins added, "A reasonable limitation on attorneys' fees awards would greatly reduce the anomaly that currently exists: Taxpayers presently compensate attorneys who sue the government at vastly higher rates than they pay attorneys who represent the government."

Although the Justice Department enforced a $75 per hour cap on fees it paid when it hired outside lawyers, other government agencies did not.

A Feb. 4 *National Law Journal* article revealed that private attorneys hired by more than 20 government agencies were paid at least $50 million in 1983-84, at rates as high as $285 per hour.

Senate sponsor Charles E. Grassley, R-Iowa, said enactment of the measure meant "the legal playing field had been leveled. Now those with modest means have an equal access to justice."

Robert W. Kastenmeier, D-Wis., chief House sponsor, said the bill was a particularly "high priority for the small-business community."

Provisions

As signed into law, HR 2378 included the following provisions:

- Made permanent the authorization for awarding attorneys' fees to individuals, small businesses and certain local governments that prevailed in legal disputes with the government.

• Required fees to be paid by the agency that lost the case, from any funds available to it.

• Exempted the government from paying attorneys' fees when its position was "substantially justified."

• Defined "position of the government" to mean the government's action or non-action in an administrative or court proceeding. The determination of the government's position would be based on the record made at the adversary proceeding or at the proceeding to award attorneys' fees.

• Made eligible for fee awards individuals with a net worth of $2 million or less at the time the adversary adjudication was initiated, and small businesses or local governments with a net worth of $7 million or less and no more than 500 employees.

Under the 1980 law, the limits had been $1 million for individuals and $5 million for small businesses and local governments.

• Allowed private litigants to appeal a decision on attorneys' fees to a federal court within 30 days of the fee determination.

• Required an attorney who collected a fee under this law in a Social Security case to use that amount to offset any fee he was awarded under the Social Security Act for handling the same case.

This provision was designed to prevent "double dipping" by lawyers.

Legislative History

The House Judiciary Committee reported HR 2378 May 15 (H Rept 99-120), and the House passed it by voice vote June 24 under suspension of the rules, a procedure that barred amendments and required a two-thirds vote for passage.

HR 2378 was placed directly on the Senate calendar instead of being referred to the Judiciary Committee. The Senate July 24 first passed Grassley's identical bill (S 1487) by a vote of 95-2, then cleared HR 2378 by voice vote. *(Vote 159, p. 32-S)*

President Reagan signed HR 2378 Aug. 5.

The Congressional Budget Office estimated the cost of the bill would be $7 million by 1990.

Under the 1980 law, which expired Sept. 30, 1984, a total of $3.9 million was paid in fee awards, according to the Administrative Office of the U.S. Courts.

During the House committee markup, Bruce A. Morrison, D-Conn., offered an amendment to expand coverage for Social Security recipients.

The original law exempted the Social Security Administration from being sued for attorneys' fees in administrative proceedings but allowed fee recovery in Social Security cases that went into federal court.

Few Social Security cases were decided by federal judges, however. Most were "remanded," or sent back, to the agency for administrative disposition. Recipients frequently won their claims at that point, but they could not recoup their attorneys' fees.

Morrison's amendment would have allowed fee recoveries for recipients who prevailed after their cases were remanded to the agency. The amendment was rejected 12-19.

Kastenmeier said both the administration and key senators opposed it, and that it could derail the legislation entirely if adopted.

Morrison said colleagues opposed the amendment "not because it's wrong but because it is inconvenient." ▮

Drunken Driving

The Senate by voice vote Nov. 21 passed a bill (S 850) making it a federal crime for anyone to operate a train, plane, bus or ship while under the influence of drugs or alcohol.

The penalty for violating the law would be a fine of up to $10,000, imprisonment of up to five years, or both.

While there were state laws on drunken driving and operating a vehicle while under the influence of drugs, there was no specific federal law covering this area, according to Judiciary Committee Chairman Strom Thurmond, R-S.C., chief sponsor of the bill. The Judiciary Committee reported the legislation Nov. 14. There was no written report.

Thurmond said Transportation Department figures showed that since 1975 there had been 48 alcohol- or drug-related train accidents, resulting in at least 41 deaths and more than $34 million in property damage. ▮

Bank Bribery

The House Oct. 29 passed a bill (HR 3511) to narrow the coverage of a 1984 law aimed at curbing bribery in the banking industry.

The measure, reported by the Judiciary Committee Oct. 28 (H Rept 99-335), passed by voice vote under suspension of the rules, a procedure that barred amendments and required a two-thirds vote for passage.

Banking officials had complained that the 1984 law, passed as part of an omnibus anti-crime bill (PL 98-473), made a crime out of conduct that was appropriate within the banking industry.

The 1984 law barred, except in specific circumstances, employees, officers, directors, agents and attorneys in a variety of financial institutions from accepting anything of value connected with transactions or the business of the financial institution. *(1984 Almanac p. 215)*

John Conyers Jr., D-Mich., chairman of the Judiciary Subcommittee on Criminal Justice, said that because the law did not require showing intent to commit a crime, a person could violate it if he paid for a bank official's lunch while the two discussed bank business.

HR 3511 made clear that the law was violated only if a person "corruptly" gave, offered or promised anything of value to a bank official, or if that official "corruptly" solicited or demanded a benefit in exchange for doing work for the person.

The bill specifically exempted wages, fees, and compensation and expenses paid "in the usual course of business."

If the item given was worth at least $100, a violation would be punishable by a fine of up to $5,000 or three times the value of the item, whichever was greater, and imprisonment of up to five years.

The Justice Department strongly opposed the legislation, saying existing law was adequate and that its guidelines to federal prosecutors were sufficient to curb any abuses that might occur under the 1984 law. A spokesman said the department would attempt to derail the legislation in the Republican-controlled Senate.

The Senate Judiciary Committee reported the measure Dec. 13 (no written report), but it was not brought to the floor. ▮

Beer Industry Antitrust Bill

The Senate Judiciary Committee Oct. 31 by voice vote approved legislation (S 412) that would make it easier for beer distributors to have exclusive markets for their products.

The bill, known as the Malt Beverage Interbrand Competition Act, would protect from antitrust challenge a distributor's arrangement with a brewery for an exclusive market as long as there was competition for beer sales in the market in question. The bill would modify the "rule of reason," which required a judge to determine on a case-by-case basis whether a particular arrangement was anti-competitive.

The bill also made clear that it would not legalize any existing anti-competitive practices, such as price-fixing agreements and group boycotts.

The measure was similar to a 1980 law protecting exclusive marketing arrangements in the soft drink industry. The beer industry had sought similar protection since then. *(1980 Almanac p. 381)*

Exclusive marketing agreements already were the rule rather than the exception in the beer industry, so wholesalers said they were not seeking anything new, only to preserve an existing marketing system that had worked well.

The legality of such agreements was in question, however, because of a 1977 Supreme Court decision, *Continental TV Inc. v. GTE Sylvania Inc.* The court said that while such contracts did not violate antitrust laws per se, a judge must evaluate each case by the "rule of reason," based on an assessment of why the agreement was undertaken and its consequences on the market. An agreement could violate antitrust laws if it was found to have anti-competitive effects.

S 412 prompted intense opposition from consumer advocates, who said it would mean higher beer prices, as well as from the Federal Trade Commission. Howard M. Metzenbaum, D-Ohio, and Paul Simon, D-Ill., sought to strengthen the bill in committee to make sure it did not weaken antitrust laws, but their efforts were rebuffed. Judiciary Chairman Strom Thurmond, R-S.C., also opposed the bill as "anti-consumer."

Dennis DeConcini, D-Ariz., a chief sponsor of S 412, said the beer industry was a logical one for exclusive territorial agreements because it was very competitive. He also denied the bill would result in beer price increases.

A companion bill (HR 1108) was pending in the House Judiciary Committee, where Chairman Peter W. Rodino Jr., D-N.J., and other key Democrats had little enthusiasm for it.

Intercircuit Tribunal

A Senate Judiciary subcommittee Oct. 30 approved legislation to create a temporary new U.S. court of appeals to help ease the Supreme Court's workload.

The bill (S 704) had the support of six justices, led by Chief Justice Warren E. Burger. But it prompted sharp criticism from some federal appeals judges, who worried that their authority would be diluted and their own workload problems exacerbated by creation of the new court. The new court's members would be taken from the ranks of the appellate judges.

Burger had campaigned for years for ways to lighten the Supreme Court's workload, which reached a high of 5,311 cases in the 1981-82 term and leveled off subsequently at about 5,100 cases a year. However, three justices, John Paul Stevens, William J. Brennan Jr. and Thurgood Marshall, said the new court — known as the "intercircuit tribunal" — was not necessary.

Robert W. Kastenmeier, D-Wis., chairman of the House Judiciary Subcommittee on Courts, Civil Liberties and Administration of Justice, said he would hold hearings on the issue early in 1986.

Both the Senate and House subcommittees approved similar legislation in the 98th Congress, but the bills went no further. *(1983 Almanac p. 311; 1984 Almanac p. 260)*

Provisions. S 704 would establish a nine-member tribunal, with four alternates, composed of sitting appeals court judges. The judges would be selected by the Supreme Court. The chief justice would select the presiding judge from the members of the panel.

The new court was designed as a judicial experiment and would terminate after five years. It would have jurisdiction over cases referred to it by the Supreme Court. The high court could refer any case to the tribunal before or after granting or denying *certiorari* — the term used to describe petitions sent to the justices asking them to hear a case. The justices took such cases at their own discretion.

The Supreme Court also could refer to the new panel other types of cases that it was required to consider on appeal from the lower courts.

The new tribunal could deny review in any case stemming from a petition for *certiorari*. However, the high court could direct the panel to decide the case.

Decisions of the new court could be appealed to the Supreme Court. But the rulings would be final and binding on the 12 regional courts of appeals unless the high court modified them or overruled the tribunal.

Amendments Rejected. The Senate Judiciary Subcommittee on Courts approved S 704 by a 5-1 vote. Chairman John P. East, R-N.C., cast the only "nay" vote.

East said he doubted the legislation would help reduce the high court's workload, and expressed concern that it would give new powers to the court, which would name the judges to the intercircuit panel.

East offered two amendments, but both were rejected. One would have made clear that the new court could handle only cases that would resolve differing rulings on the same point of law among the 12 circuits. The other would have allowed the president to appoint the judges who would serve on the new tribunal.

Legal Services Corporation

For the first time since President Reagan took office, the Legal Services Corporation (LSC) in 1985 had a board of directors confirmed by the Senate.

The corporation, which provided legal help to the nation's poor, had remained in operation despite the administration's continuing effort to abolish it. However, by appointments to the board and to top positions within the corporation, the administration was able to shift the direction of some programs.

The LSC stayed in business because Congress had continued to appropriate money for its programs, although at a reduced rate. Fiscal 1986 funding was set at $305.5

million. In fiscal 1981, the last year of the Carter administration, the agency received $321 million in appropriations. Funding dropped to $241 million in fiscal 1982, stayed there in 1983, climbed to $275 million in fiscal 1984 and reached $305 million in 1985.

The LSC had not had an authorization, or formal approval of its programs by Congress, since 1979, although the House Judiciary Committee reported a three-year reauthorization bill Dec. 18 (HR 2468 — H Rept 99-448). The committee had actually approved the bill June 18.

The Senate Labor and Human Resources Committee did not report a bill. Chairman Orrin G. Hatch, R-Utah, was an ardent critic of the LSC, although he had abandoned his effort to abolish it.

Board of Directors

The Senate June 12 confirmed 11 members of the LSC board of directors.

Nine nominees were considered en bloc and confirmed by voice vote. The Labor and Human Resources Committee May 8 had approved their nominations 16-0.

Two more controversial nominees were confirmed by roll-call votes. Michael B. Wallace, a former aide to House Minority Whip Trent Lott, R-Miss., was confirmed 62-34, and LeaAnne Bernstein was confirmed 58-38. She had been an aide to former LSC President Donald P. Bogard, who resigned in January after a stormy 27-month tenure. *(Votes 123, 124, p. 25-S)*

Wallace and Bernstein had been approved by the Labor and Human Resources Committee 10-6. Wallace drew opposition because, while working for Lott in 1981-83, he opposed a bill to strengthen enforcement sections of the 1965 Voting Rights Act. Congressional sources said he and Lott also encouraged the administration to change a long-standing Internal Revenue Service policy of denying tax exemptions to private schools that discriminated against blacks.

Bernstein's opponents said she helped Bogard develop a strategy to hold national LSC board meetings in far-off places that discouraged public participation, and supported cuts in LSC programs.

All 11 nominees had been serving on the board under recess appointments made by Reagan Nov. 23, 1984, after the 98th Congress adjourned. Recess appointments were made to avoid Senate confirmation. *(1984 Almanac p. 262)*

Five members were to serve until July 13, 1986, and six until July 13, 1987.

In addition to Wallace and Bernstein, those confirmed June 12 were: William Clark Durant III, acting board chairman and a Detroit lawyer active in Republican Party politics; Hortencia Benavidez of El Paso; Paul Eaglin, a Fayetteville, N.C., lawyer who once worked as a legal aid attorney; Pepe J. Mendez, a Denver lawyer who worked in Reagan's 1980 campaign; Lorain Miller of Detroit; Thomas F. Smegal Jr., a San Francisco lawyer with ties to the Republican Party; Claude G. Swafford, a South Pittsburg, Tenn., lawyer and GOP activist; Basile J. Uddo, a law professor at New Orleans' Loyola Law School and an anti-abortion activist; and Robert A. Valois, a Raleigh, N.C., lawyer whose nomination stirred some controversy because of charges that he helped companies develop "union-busting" strategies. He denied those allegations.

New President

The other major personnel change at LSC was a new president. Bogard, who had been president since October 1982, resigned effective Jan. 31. His appointment had been controversial among poverty lawyers who contended he had no background to run an organization designed to help the poor with their legal problems. Bogard had been on the staff of the Indiana attorney general and later served as head of litigation for Stokely Van Camp, Inc., where he defended the company against suits by LSC lawyers on behalf of migrant farm workers. *(1982 Almanac p. 413)*

James H. Wentzel, assistant director for litigation at the Federal Trade Commission's Bureau of Competition, was named to succeed Bogard. He previously was a legislative adviser in the Justice Department and an assistant district attorney in Denver. Legal services advocates were unhappy about this appointment as well, noting that Wentzel had no legal aid experience.

House Committee Action

The House Judiciary Committee's consideration of HR 2468 June 11 and June 18 was extremely partisan. In past years, some Republicans joined Democrats to support the program, but in 1985, key votes were along party lines.

The bill, which authorized $319 million in fiscal 1986 and "such sums as were necessary" in 1987-88, was approved 21-14, with all the "nay" votes coming from Republicans.

Before approving the bill, the committee voted 21-14 to raise the authorization level to $319 million, from $305 million recommended May 14 by the Subcommittee on Courts, Civil Liberties and Administration of Justice. The amendment was offered by Barney Frank, D-Mass., who said the House budget resolution (H Con Res 152) allowed the higher amount.

On a party-line vote June 11, the committee rejected 14-21 a substitute by Carlos J. Moorhead, R-Calif., to strengthen existing restrictions on LSC lawyers and give the agency's national board more authority.

Moorhead charged that HR 2468, drafted by subcommittee Chairman Robert W. Kastenmeier, D-Wis., "subtly destroys the corporation here in Washington, D.C., by dismantling control over local organizations." Moorhead also contended that provisions in the bill aimed at preventing lobbying by LSC attorneys were too weak and would turn local legal aid programs into "political action centers."

But Kastenmeier, and Bruce A. Morrison, R-Conn., said HR 2468 made few changes in existing law and was, in many respects, identical to a bill approved by the committee in 1983. *(1983 Almanac p. 322)*

Moorhead had offered the same amendment in subcommittee, and lost there on a 6-9 party-line vote.

The committee rejected, 15-20, an amendment by F. James Sensenbrenner Jr., R-Wis., to sharply restrict involvement of LSC officers and employees in political activities. Kastenmeier said existing law already included such prohibitions and the amendment went too far.

While HR 2468 was similar to the 1983 legislation, the 1985 bill established more detailed procedures and standards the corporation was to follow in regulating local programs that received LSC money. Sponsors said the provisions were intended to ensure that local programs had the opportunity to be heard by the national office when problems arose that could lead to a termination of funding.

To prevent arbitrary funding cutoffs, the bill spelled out specific circumstances that would justify a termination, such as failure to comply with restrictions Congress imposed on the activities of program lawyers.

"With the new confirmed board, I think Congress

needs to be a little more explicit about what it expects from the corporation in pursuing the purposes of the agency," Kastenmeier said. "We didn't really want to give [the board] an opportunity, if it were of a mind to do so, to undercut the program."

Republicans and Democrats also clashed over provisions designed to restrict lobbying by legal services lawyers. Provisions in HR 2468 would bar virtually all lobbying activities at the federal, state and local level except on behalf of an "eligible client" or in connection with the funding or legislative oversight of the corporation or a local legal aid program. Any "communications" with federal, state or local officials would have to be approved by the director of the LSC project involved to make sure they were in accord with guidelines established by the project.

These constraints were almost identical to those in the 1983 authorization bill reported by the committee. They also were similar to lobbying restrictions in the fiscal 1985 appropriations law covering the corporation.

The lobbying provisions of the rejected Moorhead substitute were more restrictive, requiring, for example, exhaustion of judicial and administrative relief for a client before a Legal Services Corporation lawyer could seek a legislative solution. ▮

Reagan Nears Carter Record in Naming Judges

President Reagan in 1985 appointed 21 new judges to the 12 regional federal appeals courts and 62 new federal district court judges, accelerating the shift from a predominantly Democratic to a conservative Republican bench.

By year's end, Reagan had named a total of 248 persons to federal district and appeals courts and one to the Supreme Court, according to the Administrative Office of the U.S. Courts, which operated the federal judiciary. Dozens of other openings were likely in the final three years of his term, many of them the result of a 1984 law (PL 98-353) that created 85 new judgeships. *(Previous appointments, 1984 Almanac p. 243; PL 98-353, 1984 Almanac p. 263)*

President Jimmy Carter made 258 appointments during his term, the most of any president in history.

Reagan had named 192 of the 573 authorized district court judges and 52 of the 156 judges authorized to hear cases on the 12 regional appeals courts.

Reagan's appointees were likely to have a long-lasting impact on the judiciary. The average age of judges appointed to the appeals courts in his first term was 51.5 years, with several in their 30s and 40s, according to a study by Sheldon Goldman, a political science professor at the University of Massachusetts at Amherst. Carter appointees averaged 51.9 years of age.

Conservative Pressure

Conservative groups continued to press Reagan to appoint more federal judges who shared their ideology. They wanted him to recast the judiciary from one dominated by liberal "judicial activists" appointed by Carter to one with a majority committed to "judicial restraint."

Conservatives defined that term as adherence to a strict view of the Constitution that gave judges limited authority in interpreting laws. It would preclude such landmark Supreme Court decisions as *Roe v. Wade*, which made abortion legal, and rulings that sanctioned court-ordered busing and prohibited virtually all forms of prayer in public schools.

Many conservatives, including some administration officials, believed former GOP Presidents Richard M. Nixon and Gerald R. Ford were not sufficiently concerned with ideology. "They had the idea that if you were a Republican, automatically you would have the right approach," said one official.

To provide a formal structure for conservative views, Daniel J. Popeo, general counsel and founder of the Washington Legal Foundation, established a judicial evaluation project to rate candidates according to conservative principles. Popeo said he hoped the project eventually would

Committee Review Process

Democrats and Republicans on the Senate Judiciary Committee worked out an agreement late in 1985 for handling judicial nominations — a subject that had caused bitter controversy among members.

The agreement was reached by Chairman Strom Thurmond, R-S.C.; ranking Democrat Joseph R. Biden Jr., Del.; Majority Leader Robert Dole, R-Kan.; and Minority Leader Robert C. Byrd, D-W.Va. It was ratified by the full committee Dec. 5.

Democrats had complained that Republicans were trying to move too many judgeships through the committee too fast — "ramrodding" them through, Biden charged. The Democrats said their staffs did not have enough time to investigate nominees for the lifetime appointments. Before Congress' Thanksgiving recess, Biden threatened to hold up all nominations unless the two sides could work out a new process.

Thurmond denied any intent to ramrod nominations through, but agreed to slow the process down somewhat. According to the Congressional Research Service, Thurmond had moved judicial nominees through the hearing process faster than any committee chairman in the past 20 years, with an average of 18.5 days elapsing between the time the panel received a nomination and the hearing on the nominee.

By contrast, when more than 200 nominees of President Carter moved through the committee in 1978-79 under then-Chairman Edward M. Kennedy, D-Mass., the average time was 57.8 days. In 1977-78, when 66 judges went through the committee, the average time lag was 22.7 days.

The new agreement provided that there would be at least three weeks between the time a nomination reached the committee and the hearing on that nomination. The nomination would not go on the agenda for a vote for at least one week after the hearing. Republicans could schedule up to six nominations at any one hearing, but "the efficacy" of this would be evaluated in five months.

Democrats had wanted only three judges considered at each hearing.

The two sides also agreed to revise the questionnaire sent to candidates to get more financial information and more detail on their writings and speeches.

compete with the American Bar Association (ABA), which had rated judicial candidates for more than 30 years.

In light of the conservatives' press on judicial appointments, some organizations were concerned about the future of the judiciary. In 1985, groups including the Leadership Conference on Civil Rights, a coalition of some 175 organizations, and People for the American Way, which lobbied on constitutional liberties, formed the Judicial Selection Project to monitor Reagan's court appointments.

Ralph G. Neas, executive director of the Leadership Conference, warned that conservatives, unable to implement their agenda legislatively and aware that policy changes administratively could be undone by the next president, were out to pack the judiciary with "like-minded ideologues."

The Justice Department, which was at the center of the judicial selection process, contended it played no favorites, but listened to the concerns of conservatives and liberals alike.

Nevertheless, efforts by conservatives to influence judicial selection appeared to be paying off. Since 1982 at least three potential nominees had been dropped, despite strong legal credentials, because groups such as the Free Congress Research and Education Foundation Inc., the Center for Judicial Studies and the Washington Legal Foundation convinced the administration the candidates were too liberal.

By contrast, the administration, with these organizations' blessing, sought out and appointed a number of conservatives to seats on the appeals courts. Unlike district court appointments, where senators by tradition had considerable influence in selecting nominees, the president had a relatively free hand in picking appellate judges. Furthermore, most of the decisions these judges made were final. Appellate courts reviewed the decisions of federal district judges, and only a fraction of their rulings were considered by the Supreme Court.

The Reagan administration was taking pains to select judges it believed would follow the Reagan line. Bruce E. Fein, who worked on judicial selection in Reagan's first term, said the administration was "more meticulous in its concern about judicial philosophy than other presidents." Fein said it was imperative that Reagan find judges who adhered "to the intent of the Founding Fathers in constitutional interpretation" and did not "smuggle their personal conceptions of ethics, morality, justice or enlightened public policy into the process of constitutional interpretation."

Civil rights and civil liberties activists conceded that judicial appointments were among the fruits of a president's electoral victory, but contended the administration's concern with ideology went beyond the bounds of appropriate judicial selection criteria. "What is now being proposed is judges committed to undoing vast bodies of law, to throwing out legal precedent, to prejudging cases not on their merits — the traditional, time-honored way — but on ideological grounds," said Anthony T. Podesta, president of People for the American Way.

Judiciary Committee Role

While most jockeying over federal judges took place before the nominations were ever made, the Senate Judiciary Committee also played a key role in reviewing them.

Historically, the committee approved most nominees, despite ideological differences, on the theory a president had the right to appoint people of his own political persuasion if they were qualified for the job. Just as committee Republicans did not stop Carter when he put record numbers of women, blacks and Hispanics on the bench, committee Democrats had not put up roadblocks to many Reagan nominees.

However, Judiciary Democrats had become increasingly concerned about the quality of judges named by Reagan. In his first term, many candidates were white men from established law practices, and while they were conservative, they were considered well-qualified lawyers, a Democratic committee staffer said. But more nominees were being picked for ideological reasons, and some of them were not rated as "qualified" by the ABA, the aide said.

Anticipating dozens more nominees in the final three years of Reagan's term, Judiciary Democrats beefed up their investigative capacity, hiring a new staffer to focus on judicial selections and developing their own questionnaire for candidates. In addition, Joseph R. Biden Jr., Del., the panel's ranking Democrat, designated Paul Simon, D-Ill., to monitor judgeship selections and alert his colleagues to any controversial candidates.

The Democrats developed their own questionnaire after three GOP senators — Orrin G. Hatch, Utah; Jeremiah Denton, Ala.; and John P. East, N.C. — sent several nominees an eight-page questionnaire asking their views on

Kozinski Nomination

The Senate by a 54-43 vote Nov. 7 approved the controversial nomination of Alex Kozinski to be a judge on the 9th U.S. Circuit Court of Appeals, which was headquartered in California. *(Vote 288, p. 51-S)*

At 35, Kozinski became the youngest federal appellate judge. He had been chief judge of the U.S. Claims Court since 1982. Previously, he was a law clerk for Chief Justice Warren E. Burger and in private practice. He worked in President Reagan's 1980 campaign, in the White House Office of Legal Counsel, and as director of the Office of Special Counsel at the Merit Systems Protection Board.

His nomination was held up for almost two months because of allegations that he was not suited for the federal bench. Chief opponents Carl Levin, D-Mich., and Howard M. Metzenbaum, D-Ohio, said they were particularly concerned with his actions at the merit board, where his job was to represent federal workers in disputes with their supervisors.

Levin's opposition was enough to force an unusual second confirmation hearing Nov. 1, six weeks after the Judiciary Committee had approved the nomination. Most of it focused on allegations that Kozinski treated some employees harshly and did not accurately represent a settlement with a 21-year employee whom he fired. Metzenbaum also charged Kozinski with "red-baiting" for condoning a radio editorial that accused opponents of his nomination of having ties to anti-Semitic Palestinian terrorists.

Kozinski denied the allegations, and Judiciary Chairman Strom Thurmond, R-S.C., said they were "some of the puniest, most nit-picking charges that have ever been brought before any hearing I have held." But Levin said Kozinski lacked the "fairness, decency and forthrightness" necessary to be a judge.

abortion, the Equal Rights Amendment, the right to bear arms, affirmative action and whether legislation could be upheld if it was based on a moral belief "in the existence of a supreme being." The questionnaire also asked for a list of political contributions of $15 or more made in the past 10 years.

The senators said they had the right to ask nominees whatever they believed would be helpful in reviewing their credentials, but angry committee Democrats saw the questionnaire as symptomatic of the conservatives' demand for ideological purity on the federal bench.

Toward the end of the year, the Democrats were angered again by what they called GOP attempts to "ramrod" judicial nominations through the committee without sufficient time for investigation. Before Congress' Thanksgiving recess, Biden threatened to hold up all nominations unless the two sides could work out a new process.

On Dec. 5 the committee ratified an agreement reached by Chairman Strom Thurmond, R-S.C.; Biden; Majority Leader Robert Dole, R-Kan.; and Minority Leader Robert C. Byrd, D-W.Va. *(Box, p. 246)* ▮

Sanctuary for Salvadorans

The Senate Judiciary Subcommittee on Immigration and Refugee Policy Sept. 30 approved a bill (S 377) to grant temporary legal status to Salvadorans who had made their way illegally into the United States.

The bill would grant "extended voluntary departure" to some 570,000 Salvadorans believed to be in the country. In effect, this would be a suspension of deportation for Salvadorans who entered the country illegally. They would have to return home when conditions there improved.

Subcommittee Chairman Alan K. Simpson, R-Wyo., said he believed the bill was unwise, but he agreed to allow it to be sent to the full Judiciary Committee without recommendation. The committee took no action in 1985.

Generally, subcommittees sent bills to committee with a positive recommendation. The panel's refusal to endorse S 377 indicated the bill would have tough going.

Dennis DeConcini, D-Ariz., chief sponsor of S 377, and his supporters both in and out of Congress contended that Salvadorans who were sent back to their country faced violence, and in some cases, death, upon their return. DeConcini said Americas Watch, an organization that monitored human rights in Latin America, had found "a resurgence of death squad activity" and that 173 people had disappeared since January.

Opponents of S 377, including Simpson and the Reagan administration, said there was no clear evidence that returned Salvadorans were persecuted when they returned home. Simpson maintained that most of those entering the United States were "economic migrants" seeking better jobs, not fleeing for their safety. He noted that those who entered the United States passed through two countries — Honduras and Mexico — where they could find refuge.

Simpson also said the number of civilian deaths in El Salvador had dropped from 9,000 in 1981 to 218 in 1985 (as of July 30).

Some opponents said S 377 and a House companion bill (HR 822) were attempts to criticize the administration's Central American policies. President Reagan strongly supported the government of El Salvador, and legitimizing the flow of Salvadorans into the United States suggested to some that the government there could not ensure public safety.

Jeremiah Denton, R-Ala., called the bill "an effort to throw a great deal of money at a problem in order to appease a movement in our country which is dedicated to undermining our policies in Central America." But DeConcini insisted he was not out to embarrass the administration, and said he generally backed Reagan's policies.

The government had given "extended voluntary departure" status to aliens from Afghanistan, Ethiopia, Uganda and Poland, all of which, like El Salvador, had experienced civil wars and unrest. But unlike El Salvador, none of them was regarded as an ally.

In addition to suspending deportations of Salvadorans, S 377 would require the General Accounting Office to study and report back to Congress on: the number of displaced Salvadorans and their location; the living, safety, medical, housing and nutritional conditions of Salvadorans who had fled to other countries in Central America; efforts to improve these conditions; and the circumstances of those returned by the United States to El Salvador.

Sanctuary Movement

Concern about the plight of Salvadorans prompted a number of U.S. churches and communities to offer them sanctuary. The government began a crackdown on such groups, resulting in the trials of 12 persons in Phoenix, Ariz., and three in Texas, for illegally aiding Salvadorans.

Civil rights and church groups protested government tactics during its investigation of the Phoenix case, charging that the Immigration and Naturalization Service used undercover agents to infiltrate legitimate religious activities, including Bible classes and prayer services.

The administration's policy of incarcerating illegal aliens who refused to return home voluntarily after they were caught also prompted controversy. By fiscal 1985, 2,200 to 2,300 aliens were in detention centers on any given day. The government's seven detention facilities were filled beyond capacity, and funds were being sought for more.

Illegal aliens apprehended in the United States had the option of returning voluntarily to their home countries, but in recent years many of them, particularly from war-torn El Salvador, had refused to leave and instead applied for asylum. However, in 1984 asylum was granted in only 328 cases and denied in 13,045. ▮

Abortion Amendments

Advocates on both sides of the abortion issue essentially were at a stalemate in Congress during 1985.

The anti-abortion movement sought to add further restrictions on the use of public money for abortions but failed in its effort. However, its members did succeed in convincing the administration to withhold $10 million in aid to the United Nations Fund for Population Activities, which right-to-life groups claimed helped the Chinese government carry out forced abortions, sterilizations and other involuntary family planning measures.

Anti-abortion advocates, led by the U.S. Catholic Conference, also were able to stymie progress on a civil rights bill because of concerns that the measure would expand abortion rights. *(Story, p. 230)*

Those favoring legalized abortion were able to hold the line on existing restrictions but made no headway in easing the ban on federal funding for abortions.

Although there were no efforts in Congress to enact legislation or a constitutional amendment to bar abortion, there were skirmishes on three appropriations bills.

District of Columbia Funds

Anti-abortion advocates led by Rep. Christopher H. Smith, R-N.J., and Sen. Gordon J. Humphrey, R-N.H., sought to block the District of Columbia from using locally raised revenue to pay for abortions.

Since 1980, Congress had barred the use of federal funds for abortions in the District, except where the mother's life was in danger or in cases of rape.

The House July 30 adopted a Smith amendment barring D.C. revenues from being used for abortions, but the Senate refused to go along. Conferees dropped the House language, and the final D.C. funding measure, which was wrapped into an omnibus fiscal 1986 appropriations bill (PL 99-190), did not include the new funding ban. *(Story, p. 360)*

Abortions in Federal Prisons

Jesse Helms, R-N.C., the Senate's leading abortion foe, sought to bar federal prisons from providing abortions to pregnant inmates unless the woman's life was in danger.

He attempted Oct. 24 to add such an amendment to the fiscal 1986 Commerce, Justice, State appropriations bill (HR 2965). Federal prison funding was included in the Justice Department appropriation, and Helms said that during fiscal 1985, at least 37 elective abortions had been performed on women in federal prisons.

Warren B. Rudman, R-N.H., sought to table (kill) Helms' amendment, but his effort failed on a 46-46 tie vote.

When the Senate debated the bill again Nov. 1, members by voice vote decided that Helms' amendment was unconstitutional, after rejecting, 47-48, a motion to table a point of order challenging the proposal. *(Story, p. 346; vote 274, p. 49-S)*

Family Planning Restrictions

During House Appropriations Committee debate on the fiscal 1986 continuing appropriations resolution, Jack F. Kemp, R-N.Y., sought to add a new abortion restriction to the principal federal family planning program.

Under Title X of the 1970 Public Health Service Act (PL 91-572), more than 5,000 clinics that dispensed family planning information and contraceptive services received federal aid. The law specifically barred the use of money for performing abortions, but counseling and referrals for abortion were permitted.

Kemp sought to bar referrals, but by a 37-16 vote, the committee instead adopted a substitute by Richard J. Durbin, D-Ill., that barred the use of Title X money only for providing abortions or for advocating abortion. Durbin said that language was consistent with existing Title X regulations, which allowed "non-directive" counseling on abortion. *(Related stories, pp. 300, 333)*

When the House Rules Committee took up the bill, the Durbin amendment was deleted. Henry J. Hyde, R-Ill., sponsor of the longstanding law that barred federal money for most abortions, said that because of the way Durbin's amendment was worded, it could open the way for allowing federal funding of abortions. Durbin agreed to withdraw his amendment as long as Kemp was barred from offering his more restrictive language on the floor. Hyde supported that, and the Rules Committee concurred.

The Senate left the Title X provisions alone, and the funding bill was signed into law with no new abortion language in the family planning law.

Friend-of-the-Court Briefs

In addition to voting on abortion issues in 1985, more than 160 members of Congress participated in friend-of-the court briefs filed in two Supreme Court cases involving abortion.

In its fall term, the court heard two cases concerning Pennsylvania and Illinois laws that regulated and restricted the right to abortion *(Thornburgh v. American College of Obstetricians and Gynecologists, Diamond v. Charles)*. The state statutes were invalidated by federal appeals courts for the 3rd and 7th circuits.

Led by Sens. Humphrey and Orrin G. Hatch, R-Utah, and Reps. Smith and Alan B. Mollohan, D-W.Va., 82 members urged the court in a July brief to use these cases to reverse the 1973 *Roe v. Wade* decision that made abortion legal. In August, 81 other legislators filed a brief written by Harvard University law professor Laurence Tribe urging the court to reaffirm the 1973 ruling. ▮

TRADE POLICY

CQ

Trade Policy

Pushed by the United States' deepening difficulties in international trade, Congress in 1985 displayed an enthusiasm for trade legislation not seen on Capitol Hill for decades.

The burst of interest in trade issues did not lead to enactment of many major bills on the subject during the year. Congress did clear a bill limiting imports of textile products, but President Reagan successfully vetoed the measure.

For a few weeks in early fall, however, trade concerns pushed aside fights over budget and defense to rise to the top of the congressional agenda. Normally the preserve of a few specialists, trade issues suddenly became a headline topic and the apparent linchpin of the 1986 elections.

Sensing possible partisan political gain from the issue, members of Congress, even those with little previous interest in the subject, began scrambling to show that they had the "toughest" response to trade problems.

The trade fervor subsided almost as quickly as it arose. But the rise and fall of the topic provided a good case study of the way Congress responds to issues.

Moreover, the problems that were behind the heightened interest in trade remained. Throughout the year, government statistics showed the U.S. trade deficit with other countries growing at a record rate, headed toward a total shortfall estimated at $150 billion. Increasingly, many of the nation's basic industries — steel, mining, textiles and machine tools, among others — were seen as in danger of succumbing to foreign competition.

Experts pointed to a variety of reasons for the swelling flood of imports. The rise of the dollar against other currencies since 1980 made imports cheaper to U.S. consumers, and at the same time made it harder for U.S. companies to sell their goods abroad.

The trade policies of other nations also were seen as contributing to U.S. trade problems. Many specialists argued that Japan and other leading trading partners were pursuing a protectionist course that worked to exclude U.S. goods from their markets. In addition, some countries were accused of seeking an unfair advantage in world markets by providing various subsidies to their domestic producers.

Reagan Stance

To Democrats and a substantial number of Republicans, however, a chief cause of the outbreak of trade fever was President Reagan's seemingly passive approach to trade issues throughout much of the year.

An ardent supporter of the free-trade philosophy, Reagan strenuously opposed efforts to limit imports as threats to the world trading system. But his belief in the merits of unfettered trade struck some members of Congress as plain indifference to the needs of those of their constituents whose jobs were jeopardized by foreign competition.

Critics saw that alleged lack of concern in a temporary leadership vacuum on trade issues in the administration. William E. Brock III, who had won widespread praise on Capitol Hill for his four years as U.S. trade representative, was appointed in March to be secretary of labor. The Senate did not confirm Brock's replacement, Clayton K. Yeutter, until late June, leaving the administration without a strong voice on trade issues for three months.

Reagan also angered many members by refusing to back import protections for hard-pressed industries. In March, Reagan announced that he would not ask Japan to extend its voluntary four-year program of restraints on auto exports to the United States. Combined with a perceived lack of progress in negotiations with Japan on trade barriers, Reagan's stance fostered action on retaliatory legislation against the Asian economic giant.

Reagan received even more criticism in Congress for his August decision not to grant import relief to the domestic shoe industry. His refusal to accept a recommendation of the U.S. International Trade Commission to curb the growth of shoe imports infuriated many members and led to much of the surge in support for restrictive trade legislation in the months that followed.

Although his administration eventually shifted to a more assertive trade stance, Reagan continued his rhetorical assault on protectionist legislation throughout the year. "A mindless stampede towards protectionism would be a one-way trip to economic disaster," he said at a September news conference.

Political Maneuvering

Partisan political maneuvering was another factor behind the explosion of interest in trade legislation.

Many Democrats, eager to gain political advantage for the 1986 elections, seized on a tough stance on trade as a way to allow them to appear strong on national security. Rep. Tony Coelho, Calif., chairman of the Democratic Congressional Campaign Committee, called trade "a Democratic macho issue. We're for American strength."

Republicans, on the other hand, were worried about the political costs of being associated with Reagan's free-trade stance. Polls showed that many Americans favored import restraints to bring down the trade deficit, and Republicans were eager to prove that trade was not just a Democratic issue.

The political aspects of trade had become increasingly clear during the summer, when leading Democrats proposed strong retaliation against some of the nation's toughest trading partners. Led by House Ways and Means Committee Chairman Dan Rostenkowski, Ill., Democratic leaders put forth a bill to impose a 25 percent surcharge on products from Japan, Taiwan, South Korea and Brazil.

The interest generated by that measure paled, however, compared with the excitement stirred up by the results of a special House election held in Texas in August. Democratic candidate Jim Chapman made trade problems a major issue in his campaign, blaming administration policy for the closing of a local steel plant.

Chapman's Republican opponent, Edd Hargett, added to his problems by telling a local newspaper that "I don't know what trade policies have to do with bringing jobs to East Texas." Despite Hargett's heavy campaign funding from national Republicans, Chapman won narrowly.

That victory greatly reinforced the view that trade could become a major issue in the 1986 elections. By the time members finished their August recess — when many heard from local businesses that were increasingly burdened by foreign competition — they were exceptionally eager to move on tough trade legislation.

"I'm beginning to think that the trade deficit is surpassing the national deficit" as a concern among members, said House Speaker Thomas P. O'Neill Jr., D-Mass., and the intense maneuvering over trade issues during September seemed to bear him out.

Still, there were a number of Democrats who were concerned that their party might go too far on trade and risk being branded as protectionist. Memories of Sen. Reed Smoot (R-Utah, 1909-33) and Rep. Willis C. Hawley (R-Ore., 1907-33) — authors of the 1930 high-tariff bill that helped bring on the Depression that pushed Republicans into minority party status for decades — seemed to lurk in the back of many members' minds.

When the House Democratic Caucus Sept. 19 adopted a statement of principles on trade, for example, the declaration steered away from explicit support of import protections for textiles and other industries. Caucus Chairman Richard A. Gephardt of Missouri and others made clear that they were more interested in pressuring the administration to take a tougher line in international negotiations than in enacting legislation. "I don't think you can say that the textile bill is the capstone of the Democratic Party's position on trade," he said.

Administration Countermoves

Timely countermoves by the Reagan administration also helped slow the rush to adopt restrictive trade legislation.

After waging a vocal battle against import-limiting legislation for weeks, Reagan Sept. 23 unveiled a package of administrative and legislative trade proposals aimed at pressuring other nations to drop a variety of "unfair" trading practices in world markets.

Reagan's package followed a Sept. 22 announcement that the United States and four key economic allies would work together to reduce the value of the dollar against other currencies. The move was a sharp turn in policy for the Reagan administration, which had resisted similar efforts in the past.

Reagan officials hoped that a stepped-up "fair trade" campaign, targeting foreign import barriers and counterfeiting of U.S. products, would defuse some of the support in Congress for limiting imports into this country.

Included in the Reagan proposal was a call for Congress to create a $300 million "war chest" to combat other nations' export-credit subsidies.

The Reagan plan also urged streamlining of trade procedures and enhanced presidential authority in international trade negotiations.

Although the actions of Reagan and the finance ministers received a mixed reaction in Congress, they fostered a subtle but significant change in mood. If many members agreed with Missouri Republican Sen. John C. Danforth — "I await results" — they also seemed less eager to push restrictive legislation.

"The president's speech should help cool the protectionist fires on Capitol Hill," said Senate Majority Leader Robert Dole, R-Kan.

Omnibus Proposals

The shift in congressional sentiment caused by the administration moves helped slow the momentum for import-restrictive bills such as the textile measure. But members continued to propose a variety of overall trade packages in hopes of influencing a future "generic" trade bill that would change basic U.S. trade policies and procedures instead of offering help for specific industries.

The first such bill to come out was a House GOP plan, released Oct. 8. That package included proposals to:

- Make it easier for hard-hit industries to gain protection against imports. The plan would take the dominant decision-making authority away from the president, who is subject to advice from agencies less concerned about trade than with foreign policy or national security, and give it to the U.S. trade representative.
- Step up government support for exporters.
- Provide quicker, stronger action against unfair trading practices of other countries.
- Set goals for U.S. negotiators in a new round of global trade talks.
- Establish mutual free-trade policies with Canada and other important trading partners.
- Authorize talks with Japan aimed at securing trade concessions from that country in exchange for access to petroleum and natural gas from Alaska.

A task force of House Democrats followed Oct. 17 with a related trade package.

"We are trying to propose a responsible course between the Reagan policy of free trade at any cost and outright protectionism," said task force member Don J. Pease of Ohio.

The package called for a reduction in the value of the dollar against other currencies, stepped-up promotion of exports, a crackdown on other countries' unfair trading practices and new help for businesses and workers undermined by foreign competition.

In the Senate, a bipartisan group introduced another comprehensive bill in November.

The plan's major goals were to step up the campaign against unfair trading practices by other countries, expand help for industries hard hit by import competition, provide new authority to the Reagan administration to engage in worldwide trade talks and stress increased coordination with other industrialized countries in setting international monetary policy.

Backers emphasized that they were seeking a historic shift in authority over trade policy, which Congress controls under the Constitution but has delegated almost totally to the executive branch. "It is time for Congress to reassert its constitutional role in foreign trade," said chief Democratic sponsor Daniel Patrick Moynihan, N.Y.

The House Energy and Commerce Committee approved yet another comprehensive trade bill on Nov. 21.

—By Harrison Donnelly

Textile-Import Bill Draws a Presidential Veto

Textile-import legislation — the major trade bill of 1985 — cleared Congress on Dec. 3. But President Reagan vetoed the measure Dec. 17, and there was no attempt during the year to override the veto. *(Veto message, p. 40-D)*

The vanguard of the surge of "protectionist" sentiment that swept through Congress in the fall of 1985, the bill (HR 1562) would force cutbacks of about 30 percent in textile imports from Taiwan, South Korea and Hong Kong, as well as limit growth of imports from many other Third World countries.

In addition, the measure would cut shoe imports and press for reductions in world copper production to help those hard-pressed domestic industries survive their foreign competition. *(Previous action, 1984 Almanac p. 171)*

Conceding that they did not have the two-thirds majority needed to surmount Reagan's veto, congressional textile allies decided not to seek an override vote in 1985. The bill passed both House and Senate by substantially less than the required margins.

Instead, bill backers won House approval Dec. 17 of a motion to push back an override attempt until Aug. 6, 1986. They hoped with the delay to pressure the administration into taking a tough line in upcoming international negotiations renewing the Multifiber Arrangement (MFA), which provided the structure for the world trade in textiles.

Veto Message

Although he rejected HR 1562, Reagan sought to reassure members of Congress that he was concerned about the plight of import-threatened industries and their workers.

"I am well aware of the difficulties of the apparel, textile, copper and shoe industries," he said, "and deeply sympathetic about the job layoffs and plant closings that have affected many workers in these industries."

Reagan outlined three steps his administration would take to assist textile producers. They were:

- A new study of textile and apparel imports. Reagan directed Treasury Secretary James A. Baker III to determine within 60 days whether import levels were exceeding limits set by previous negotiations.
- A promise not to weaken existing import restraints under the MFA. Reagan made clear that a new agreement would have to be at least as restrictive toward imports as the current one.
- An additional $100 million for retraining of workers who lost their jobs due to import competition.

Reagan did not formally reject HR 1562 until late in the evening of Dec. 17, just an hour before expiration of the constitutional deadline for a veto. The delay was due at least in part to the desire of administration officials not to offend the many House Republicans from the South who backed HR 1562, but whose support was needed for the tax-revision bill (HR 3838) that passed at about the same time. *(Tax action, p. 480)*

Final Provisions

As cleared by Congress, HR 1562:

- Established a new system of country-by-country quotas regulating the importation of textiles, apparel and related products.
- Stated that the purpose of the legislation was to enforce the Multifiber Arrangement (MFA), the international agreement set up in 1974 to regulate the world trade in textiles and apparel.
- Set the strictest import limits on countries — Hong Kong, Taiwan and South Korea — that each provided more than 10 percent of total U.S. textile and apparel imports in 1984.

Individual categories of textile products (for example, women's blouses or men's suits) from those countries would be subject to numerical limits in 1985, according to the following formula: 1 percent above a hypothetical 1984 level that would have been in effect if actual 1980 import levels had been increased by a rate of 6 percent a year.

In general, imports of most categories of products from those countries increased at a level well above 6 percent a year; therefore, the provision would force major cutbacks in import levels of many products.

However, the bill would ease reductions in individual categories if the cuts in total imports from each country amounted to more than 30 percent.

- Established a second tier of countries — China, Japan, Pakistan, Indonesia, India, the Philippines, Thailand, Brazil and Singapore — that each provided between 1.25 percent and 10 percent of total U.S. textile and apparel imports in 1984.

Individual categories of textiles from those countries would be held in 1985 to their actual 1984 import levels.

- Permitted limits on textile imports from the two preceding groups of countries to grow at a rate of 1 percent a year after 1985.
- Allowed other countries to increase textile and apparel exports to the United States in 1985 by 15 percent over actual 1984 levels.

Limits on textile imports from those countries would in most cases be allowed to grow at a rate of 6 percent a year after 1985. However, certain categories of products — those made from wool, or in which foreign producers already controlled a significant share of the U.S. market — would be limited to 1 percent annual growth.

- Exempted products from Canada and the European Economic Community from the import limits in the bill.
- Exempted textile and apparel products of the insular possessions of the United States from the import limits in the bill.
- Extended coverage of the bill to all types of natural and man-made fibers, except apparel containing at least 70 percent silk by weight.
- Established a new licensing system governing textile and apparel imports, and authorized the Commerce Department to charge fees on importers to cover the costs of the new system.
- Limited imports of non-rubber footwear to no more than 60 percent of the domestic shoe market, for an eight-year period beginning with enactment of the bill.
- Required the president within nine months to undertake negotiations with other copper-producing nations to establish a voluntary five-year agreement limiting copper production.
- Called for the U.S. International Trade Commission to conduct studies of the labor practices of countries with which the United States had a trade deficit of more than $4 billion in 1984.

Background

The deepening economic problems of the U.S. textile industry were responsible for much of the political impetus behind the import-limiting legislation.

In the five years preceding congressional action, a surge of foreign-made clothes had threatened to push the "Made in the U.S.A." label off store shelves. Textile producers claimed that some 250 factories had been forced out of business by import competition, leading to the loss of more than a quarter-million jobs.

The volume of textile imports had grown substantially during the five-year period, rising from 4.9 million square yards in 1980 to 10.2 million square yards in 1984. Moreover, import growth was accelerating. From 1980 to 1982, the average annual increase was 10.2 percent; from 1982 to 1984, increases averaged 30.9 percent a year.

Textile forces argued that the rapid growth in imports was due in part to the Reagan administration's failure to enforce adequately the Multifiber Arrangement (MFA), the international agreement first established in 1974 to provide a structure for world trade in textiles. The original goal of the MFA was to give developing countries a chance to sell textiles in Europe and North America, while still providing some protection for domestic producers in those countries.

Backers of HR 1562 claimed that the goal of the MFA was to limit textile import growth in the developed countries to 6 percent a year. Arguing that the administration's policies had not met that goal, they wanted to write into law import limits that reflected 6 percent annual growth since 1980. Since textile imports from many countries had grown considerably more than 6 percent a year since 1980, the effect of the legislation was to mandate deep cuts in import levels.

Opponents of the bill argued that the proposed textile quotas would not save many jobs in the United States, since any jobs saved in the textile industry would be balanced by job losses in the retail and transportation industries. In addition, critics said, the effect of the bill would be to hurt consumers by raising the average prices of clothes and other textiles by more than 10 percent, adding $14 billion a year to consumer costs.

House Committee Action

The House Ways and Means Trade Subcommittee approved HR 1562 Sept. 19.

The bill approved by the subcommittee was significantly more restrictive than the version that ultimately cleared Congress. It applied the most severe reductions in import limits to products from the dozen largest exporting countries: Brazil, China, Hong Kong, India, Indonesia, Japan, South Korea, Pakistan, the Philippines, Singapore, Taiwan and Thailand.

The broad popularity of the textile bill was shown by the ease with which it brushed aside what might have been a formidable obstacle for any other measure — opposition from the relevant House committee and subcommittee chairmen.

Both Ways and Means Committee Chairman Dan Rostenkowski, D-Ill., and Trade Subcommittee Chairman Sam Gibbons, D-Fla., had strongly expressed their distaste for textile import restrictions. Gibbons, a longtime opponent of import curbs, attacked the legislation as a "white man's bill" for imposing limits on Asian textiles while leaving European and Canadian products untouched.

The strongest support for the bill came from members whose districts had been hit by the loss of jobs in apparel firms weakened by foreign competition. The key supporter of HR 1562 on the trade panel was Democrat Ed Jenkins, from a textile-producing district in northern Georgia.

Faced with a bill backed by nearly 300 cosponsors, Rostenkowski and Gibbons elected not to fight. For one thing, failure to act on the bill in committee probably would have resulted in a discharge petition or other move designed to force full House action.

So HR 1562 sped through the subcommittee in short order, approved by voice vote without any changes. No amendments were formally considered, although critics made clear that they hoped to offer amendments in the future.

The subcommittee met in closed session after voting 8-5 to exclude reporters and lobbyists from its deliberations.

Full Committee. The Ways and Means Committee approved HR 1562 by voice vote Sept. 26. However, committee action on the measure did not represent a ringing endorsement of the bill, since the panel defeated by only a one-vote margin a key amendment sharply limiting the bill's effects.

The attack on the bill's toughest provisions was led by Missouri Democrat Richard A. Gephardt, chairman of the House Democratic Caucus. Gephardt's amendment, which was rejected by a 17-18 vote, would have made the measure significantly less stringent, at least in the short run.

The key provision of Gephardt's amendment would have been to exempt from the deep import reductions required by HR 1562 products from the 32 countries with which the United States already had bilateral textile trade pacts. But textile producers that had not already agreed with the United States to curb imports would still face the restrictions in HR 1562.

The Gephardt amendment also sought to use the threat of tough import restrictions to win more favorable provisions in the upcoming rewriting of the MFA. The MFA, which provided the structure for world trade in textiles, was to expire July 31, 1986.

Under the amendment, U.S. negotiators at the MFA talks would be required to seek expansion of the agreement to cover all fibers, including currently unrestricted silk and linen products. In addition, negotiators were to push for recognition of the right of textile-importing countries to limit growth of imports to the rate of growth of their domestic textile markets.

If negotiators could not reach agreement on a new MFA, the amendment would have imposed stringent import restraints on all exporting countries — including the Canadian and European producers exempted by HR 1562. The amendment also exempted Israeli textiles.

The only other amendment formally considered by the panel was an effort by Richard T. Schulze, R-Pa., to exempt textiles used in toys and stuffed animals from import limits. The amendment was defeated on a division vote.

Another key decision made by the committee was to seek a closed rule prohibiting amendments on the House floor. Bill backers worried that it could be delayed on the floor if it was open to a variety of other import restrictions.

The committee formally reported the bill Sept. 30 (H Rept 99-293).

House Floor Action

House passage of HR 1562 signaled that textile forces did not have the strength to overcome Reagan's expected veto.

The bill passed the House by a 262-159 vote Oct. 10. *(Vote 320, p. 100-H)*

The bill was handicapped by bad timing. It was originally scheduled to come to the floor on Oct. 9, immediately after a speech to the House by Singapore Prime Minister Lee Kuan Yew, whose country would be hurt by the bill's import limits. House Speaker Thomas P. O'Neill Jr., D-Mass., postponed action on HR 1562 one day, but the memory of Lee's fervent attack on world protectionism seemed to linger in many members' minds.

Debate on HR 1562 evoked an emotional response from House members, who trooped to the well in great numbers either to bemoan the plight of unemployed textile workers or warn of the dangers of a world trade war. At times, the House chamber almost seemed like a department store, as members waved towels, shirts, a baseball bat and a stuffed toy bear to make points for or against the measure.

HR 1562 backers stressed both the special problems of the textile industry and the need for the House to provide a clear signal of its support for a more assertive trade stance in general. Frustration with the administration's overall trade policy was a key factor in mobilizing support for the bill among members without significant textile interests in their districts.

"This is probably the only trade bill that you will get an opportunity to vote on in the session," Jenkins told his colleagues. "If there is any message to go to the American people and the White House, it will have to come from this floor today."

But Jenkins faced a serious obstacle in his efforts to mobilize support for the bill. In order to get the measure out of the Ways and Means Committee, where it was opposed by both Gibbons and Rostenkowski, Jenkins had to agree not to offer any amendments that would make it more acceptable to wavering members.

The rule providing for floor consideration of the bill (H Res 286) barred any changes other than minor technical amendments. The rule was adopted on a 277-139 vote. *(Vote 319, p. 100-H)*

The Rules Committee had approved H Res 286 on Oct. 3.

Action on HR 1562 clearly illustrated the regional nature of the fight over import restraints.

Although Democrats had hoped for potential political gain from the emergence of trade issues, they were far from unanimous in backing the textile bill; 187 Democrats voted for the measure, while 62 opposed it. On the Republican side, the split was 75-97 against.

A clear pattern emerged, however, when the vote was broken down by states. Members from Southern states, where textile interests were particularly important, were overwhelmingly in support of the bill, regardless of party. Delegations from 15 states voted unanimously for the measure.

Similarly, members from states that were heavily dependent on international trade, particularly in the Pacific Northwest, were solidly against the bill. There were 12 state delegations that did not give the bill a single vote.

Senate Floor Action

In the Senate, textile forces were unable to get action on their companion bill to HR 1562 (S 680), because of opposition from a majority of members on the Finance Committee. So sponsors, led by Strom Thurmond, R-S.C., and Ernest F. Hollings, D-S.C., sought to attach their proposal as an amendment to a number of unrelated bills.

The first maneuvers centered around a resolution (S J Res 77) granting limited autonomy to Micronesia. *(Story, p. 99)*

Recognizing that the tough House bill stood little chance in the Senate, Thurmond and Hollings first moved to change their bill. They sought to shore up their strength by making their bill less restrictive against clothing imports from some countries, while adding new import protections for the domestic shoe industry.

The proposed changes spared China from the deep cutbacks in textile imports ordered by the original version of the bill — thus avoiding possible trade retaliation by that country, with its huge potential market for U.S. products.

The practical effect of the Thurmond-Hollings substitute amendment was to target the most severe import restrictions on South Korea, Taiwan and Hong Kong.

The original bill had called for tough new quota limits on the 12 countries that each provided more than 1.25 percent of total U.S. textile imports. The amendment would raise that cutoff point to 10 percent, leaving only the three Asian producers subject to deep reductions.

But China and the eight other nations that provided between 1.25 percent and 10 percent of textile imports would continue to face limits on future import growth. The amendment would freeze those countries' 1985 quotas at 1984 levels and allow subsequent annual growth of only 1 percent.

The footwear provisions of the amendment sought to limit imports to no more than 60 percent of the domestic shoe market. Imports currently made up about three-quarters of the shoes sold in this country. The new shoe quotas would be in effect for eight years.

The new strategy survived its first test Oct. 2, when the Senate refused by an 11-vote margin to kill the Thurmond-Hollings amendment, offered as an amendment to S J Res 77. The motion to table the Thurmond-Hollings amendment was made by Energy Committee Chairman James A. McClure, R-Idaho, who expressed concern that S J Res 77 would be fatally weighted down by the textile amendment and other unrelated issues. His motion was rejected 42-53. *(Vote 201, p. 39-S)*

In other action Oct. 2, the Senate rejected an amendment, offered by New Jersey Democrat Bill Bradley, that called for speedy action by the U.S. International Trade Commission on textile protections. Bradley's amendment, which also imposed a 6 percent annual growth limit on textile imports until approval of a new worldwide treaty on textiles, was tabled on an 87-9 vote. *(Vote 200, p. 39-S)*

Next Round — Reconciliation

The Senate put aside S J Res 77 and the textile issue after the first votes on the Thurmond-Hollings amendment, turning instead to consideration of legislation to require a balanced federal budget.

With further delays anticipated in action on S J Res 77, the two South Carolinians looked to the budget reconciliation bill (S 1730) as the new vehicle for their amendment.

The textile proposal soon met its first test as an amendment to S 1730. On a 54-42 vote Oct. 24, the Senate gave tentative backing to the Thurmond-Hollings package, although senators did not formally attach the amendment to the bill itself. *(Vote 253, p. 46-S)*

Debate on the textile amendment focused on the merits of using the reconciliation bill as a vehicle for unrelated legislation as well as on the need for import limits.

Hollings and Thurmond turned to S 1730 because it offered them an opportunity to avoid a filibuster threatened by the most outspoken opponents of their proposal, Republicans Daniel J. Evans of Washington and Phil Gramm of Texas. Debate on reconciliation was limited under Senate rules.

Hollings argued that his move was justified because of the frustration felt by him and his allies in finding a vehicle for a proposal backed by a majority of the Senate. "When we go to Micronesia they will suggest the continuing resolution. You go to the continuing resolution and they say, 'No, go to reconciliation.' You go to reconciliation and they say, 'Just go. Just go.' "

But opponents of the strategy warned that it would undermine the Senate's tradition of unlimited debate by encouraging members to use future reconciliation bills for a variety of controversial proposals. "We will be setting a precedent . . . that really means the end of free debate in the Senate as we have known it," warned Russell B. Long, D-La.

The first hurdle for the textile amendment was to overcome objections that it was not germane to the reconciliation bill. A motion by Hollings to waive the Budget Act rule requiring amendments to be germane was adopted by the Senate 57-39, after a Pete V. Domenici, R-N.M., motion to table Hollings' motion was rejected 38-55. *(Votes 252, 251, p. 46-S)*

After the votes on the textile amendment, Majority Leader Robert Dole, R-Kan., moved to lay aside S 1730 and move to other legislation.

Procedural Knot Unsnarled

The effort to attach the textile amendment forced the Senate into a procedural snarl that slowed action for two weeks. The deadlock finally resolved by a unanimous-consent agreement unveiled by Dole Nov. 7.

The breakthrough came after Senate leaders secured enough support to assure backers of the textile limits that their proposal could be voted on as a separate bill without danger of filibuster.

What made the reconciliation bill a magnet for unrelated and contentious amendments was its uncommon protection from filibusters. Senate rules limited debate on reconciliation to 20 hours, barring bill-killing filibusters.

The only way to avoid a filibuster, textile supporters saw, was to have their bill piggyback on reconciliation.

For two weeks after Dole shelved the budget bill Oct. 24, he and other Senate leaders worked to persuade the textile bill's sponsors to leave reconciliation alone. To succeed, the leaders had to identify at least 60 members who would agree to vote for cloture, which ended a filibuster.

By Nov. 7, Senate aides had counted 68 members who would vote for cloture. The 60-plus tally cleared the way for Dole to seek unanimous consent for the Senate to proceed with reconciliation and consider the import bill separately. The agreement called for the Senate to take up HR 1562 on Nov. 13, beginning with a cloture vote.

Final Passage

After weeks of intermittent maneuvering, the Senate passed HR 1562 by a 60-39 vote Nov. 13. *(Vote 305, p. 53-S)*

The first step toward fulfillment of the unanimous-consent agreement approved Nov. 7, which cleared the way for action on the bill, was a vote on limiting debate on HR 1562. The Senate agreed to restrain debate by a 91-6 vote, with most opponents of the bill voting for a limitation in order to resolve the parliamentary impasse and settle the issue without further delays. *(Vote 298, p. 52-S)*

The remainder of action on HR 1562 showed textile forces in firm control. Only two amendments to the Thurmond-Hollings plan were approved, and both were accepted without opposition.

The more important amendment, offered by Pete V. Domenici, R-N.M., aimed at limiting world copper production. U.S. copper companies were suffering seriously from the low prices caused by a world copper glut. Domenici's amendment required the administration to begin negotiations with other copper-producing nations in pursuit of an agreement voluntarily cutting production back to 1982 levels. The amendment was accepted by bill sponsors in hopes of winning support from Western states, where the hard-pressed copper industry was a major economic force.

The other amendment, offered by bill critic Max Baucus, D-Mont., provided for a study by the International Trade Commission of the effects of the low wage rates prevalent in many of the United States' economic competitors.

Other changes in the House bill were made by the two South Carolinians during Nov. 13 debate on HR 1562. They agreed to exempt U.S. insular possessions such as Guam and the Virgin Islands from the House measure's import limits, for example, and exempted garments made largely of silk from new restrictions. The House bill had extended import quotas for the first time to garments made of silk, linen and other natural fibers.

Amendments Rejected

The Senate rejected several amendments offered by opponents of HR 1562. These would have:

- Ensured that the bill did not indirectly harm U.S. farmers. Many agricultural groups warned that the textile import restraints would lead to retaliation by other countries against U.S. agricultural products.

A Baucus amendment, tabled by a 60-39 vote, would have exempted from the bill countries that purchased at least $400 million worth of U.S. agricultural products a year. Baucus said the amendment would have protected China, South Korea, Taiwan, Hong Kong, Japan, Indonesia and Brazil. *(Vote 300, p. 52-S)*

A related amendment, offered by Rudy Boschwitz, R-Minn., would have barred implementation of the bill unless the president determined it would not lead to a reduction in U.S. agricultural exports. The amendment was tabled 62-37. *(Vote 299, p. 52-S)*

- Exempted from the bill countries whose import policies were less restrictive than those of the United States. Sponsored by Phil Gramm, R-Texas, the amendment would most clearly have applied to Hong Kong, which had no import tariffs or quotas. The amendment was tabled 68-30. *(Vote 301, p. 53-S)*

Another Gramm amendment would have exempted Taiwan if the bill was found to harm its interests more than the bill harmed the interests of China. The amendment was tabled 68-31. *(Vote 302, p. 53-S)*

- Extended coverage of the bill to all exporting countries. HR 1562 specifically excluded products from the European Community and Canada from the new import restraints.

Arguing that the bill unfairly discriminated against

Asian nations, Spark M. Matsunaga, D-Hawaii, offered an amendment providing for worldwide coverage. His proposal was tabled by a 67-32 vote. *(Vote 303, p. 53-S)*

- Provided help for the textile and shoe industries under a section of existing law protecting industries severely harmed by import competition.

John C. Danforth, R Mo., argued that the problems of the two industries were better handled through section 201 of the 1974 Trade Act than through separate legislation. The law allowed temporary import restraints if the U.S. International Trade Commission and the president agreed an industry was in serious trouble. *(1974 Almanac p. 553)*

Danforth's amendment would have implemented HR 1562 only if the Reagan administration declined to provide section 201 protections for textiles and shoes. The amendment was tabled by voice vote.

- Exempted Hawaii and Alaska from the bill's import limits. Matsunaga, who offered the amendment, argued that the bill would cripple Hawaii's apparel industry by restricting imports of the printed cloth used in the state's distinctive tropical garments. The amendment was tabled by voice vote.

A related amendment, offered by Daniel K. Inouye, D-Hawaii, would have limited the bill's import limits to finished apparel, exempting textiles that had not been made into garments. It also was tabled by voice vote.

- Eliminated the new import licensing system established by the bill. Offered by Evans, the amendment was tabled by voice vote.

Final House Action

Although there were major differences between the House- and Senate-passed versions of HR 1562, House sponsors decided to accept the Senate version entirely, avoiding a conference on the bill.

The House Rules Committee Nov. 21 approved a rule (H Res 325) providing for floor consideration of the Senate version.

The House then approved the Senate amendments to the bill by a 255-161 vote Dec. 3, clearing the bill for the president. *(Vote 386, p. 122-H)*

House action on the final version of HR 1562 was relatively brief and routine, with most members simply reaffirming stands on the bill they had staked out long before.

Although the bill as approved by the Senate in November was significantly less stringent in its textile import limits than the House-passed measure, there was little discussion of the changes on the floor. Nor was there any substantial increase in House support for the bill produced by the Senate's inclusion of provisions on shoe imports and copper production.

The first step in floor action was adoption of the rule (H Res 325) providing for action on the Senate-passed version of HR 1562. The resolution was adopted by a 298-109 vote. *(Vote 385, p. 122-H)* ▮

Congress Renews Export Administration Act

After two and a half years of negotiations, Congress June 27 cleared legislation (S 883) renewing the main trade law that regulated exports of U.S. goods, technology and technical data.

The House and Senate adopted by voice vote the conference report (H Rept 99-180) to renew the Export Administration Act (PL 96-72) through Sept. 30, 1989. House and Senate negotiators approved the report on June 25.

President Reagan signed the bill July 12 (PL 99-64).

The export act gave the president power to block exports of potential military value. It also authorized curbs on trade to protest other nations' foreign policies or to safeguard domestic supplies. The Reagan administration had controlled exports under emergency powers since the act expired in 1984.

Legislative History

Congress tried to renew the complex act in 1983 and 1984. But although the House and Senate passed renewal bills, conference negotiations to settle differences in both versions broke down after more than six months of talks. A last-ditch effort to package the conference agreements into bills and pass them failed in the closing hours of the 98th Congress. *(1984 Almanac p. 169)*

In 1985, sponsors Rep. Don Bonker, D-Wash., and Sen. John Heinz, R-Pa., sought to put renewal legislation on a "fast track." They included in the new bills the 1984 conference agreements, but they kept off the measures two issues that helped kill the legislation the previous year: controversial new sanctions against South Africa and Pentagon review of some export licenses.

On April 3, the Senate passed S 883, to extend the act through mid-June. The same day, the House Foreign Affairs Committee approved its version of renewal legislation (HR 1786). The House passed HR 1786 on April 16, attaching it to S 883. The House version extended the act through Sept. 30, 1989.

Although the two chambers were not far apart on most substantive issues, the 1985 conference required two months of informal negotiation. Both sides were afraid of opening up the bill to new areas of dispute and wanted to ensure that issues they had settled were clearly defined.

When conferees met June 25, it appeared the agreement might break down when Judiciary Committee Chairman Peter W. Rodino Jr., D-N.J., insisted on giving the attorney general power to review other agencies' activities to block illegal exports.

In particular, Rodino urged conferees to grant the Justice Department authority to regulate Commerce Department and Customs Service actions in carrying firearms, issuing warrants and making arrests while tracking illegal exports. Senate negotiators objected, claiming that such review would complicate enforcement.

Conferees finally reached a compromise that would let the attorney general issue guidelines for Commerce, although not for Customs.

Members also dropped a requirement that the State Department certify whether Iraq was supporting terrorism. The State Department urged the deletion, arguing that the rule would harm U.S.-Iraqi ties. Secretary of State George P. Shultz promised that the administration would curb some exports to Iraq if it found that any group based in or backed by Iraq was promoting terrorism.

Conferees reworded a provision that would establish a

90-day period for Congress to review pacts that the United States negotiated with other nations to ship them nuclear materials and technology. The new language made it clear that recesses within any particular Congress would not count as part of the 90 days.

Provisions

As cleared by Congress, S 883:

- Renewed the act through Sept. 30, 1989.
- Limited the president's authority to impose export controls for foreign-policy purposes; required the president to consult with Congress before instituting such controls.
- Prohibited the president from ordering termination of existing contracts in international trade unless the action was in response to a serious threat to peace, and he determined that the action would contribute directly to reducing that threat to peace.
- Specifically limited the president's authority to order export controls on agricultural products, by requiring affirmative action by Congress to approve controls lasting more than 60 days, and limiting the total period of controls to no more than one year. Under existing law, embargoes remained in effect unless Congress acted within 30 days to end them.
- Exempted from existing requirements for export licensing sales of products with a relatively low level of technological sophistication, such as personal computers, to most NATO countries and Japan.
- Reimposed, for one year from date of enactment, certain restrictions on exports to South Africa of computers and products for police and military units. President Reagan lifted the previous restrictions in 1982 and 1983.
- Streamlined the process of granting export licenses for high-level technology products. Most licenses for sales of products to allied nations would be granted in 15 days. Commerce could ask for more time, and take 15 more days to do its review. At the end of that period, unless it rejected the application, the license would be approved automatically.
- Tightened controls on exports of the most militarily sensitive products, and provided stricter penalties for violations of export rules.
- Strengthened and clarified enforcement responsibilities of the Customs Service and the Commerce Department.
- Strengthened congressional oversight of nuclear cooperation pacts.
- Boosted export promotion. The Commerce Department was authorized to spend $113.3 million in each of fiscal 1985 and 1986 to spur sales of U.S. goods abroad.
- Extended the existing ban on export of Alaskan North Slope oil through Sept. 30, 1990.
- Extended through Sept. 30, 1989, provisions that prohibited U.S. businesses from complying with an Arab boycott of Israel. *(1977 Almanac p. 353)*

Israel Free Trade Pact

President Reagan June 11 signed legislation (HR 2268 — PL 99-47) to drop all duties and other restraints on U.S.-Israel trade by 1995.

The bill implemented the first free trade pact that the United States had signed with another nation to end all barriers on trade between them. The two countries signed the agreement April 22.

The accord with politically popular Israel passed with ease through Congress. The House approved it (H Rept 99-64) by a 422-0 vote May 7. *(Vote 89, p. 32-H)*

The Senate passed the bill by voice vote May 23.

Israel had sought the agreement to shore up its troubled economy. It especially hoped to boost civilian exports of its extensive military technology, such as night radar that could be used in security systems.

The United States wanted the pact for two reasons: supplementing military aid to Israel and providing a model for future trade accords.

Under the pact, Israel would immediately drop restraints on more than half of its imports from the United States. Remaining barriers would be phased out by 1995.

The United States immediately would lift barriers on 80 percent of imports from Israel currently affected by U.S. tariffs, quotas and other restraints. The rest would be phased out in a complex schedule by 1995.

Congress had granted the president authority to negotiate the pact in the Tariff and Trade Act of 1984 (PL 98-573), and paved the way for swift approval of implementing legislation. *(1984 Almanac p. 171)*

The 1984 law gave the House Ways and Means and Senate Finance committees the chance to review the pact at every stage of its negotiation and approval. After the United States and Israel settled on an agreement, but before it was signed, the panels suggested changes to protect U.S. industries most vulnerable to competition from Israeli products, such as gold jewelry. These changes were incorporated in the final agreement and the implementing bill.

Although administration officials hoped that the pact would provide a model for future free-trade agreements, the Senate report on the measure (S 1114 — S Rept 99-55) carefully stated that future accords should not exactly mirror the pact with Israel. It said that goods and services to be covered and the schedule for lifting curbs should be negotiated nation-by-nation.

The Senate provision in part reflected concerns raised by Max Baucus, D-Mont., about granting full trade concessions to Canada. The United States and its northern neighbor began moving in 1985 toward a similar free-trade pact.

In addition to lifting barriers on some 80 percent of now-restricted imports from Israel, the pact:

- Ended U.S. duties on another 5.5 percent of imports from Israel in three stages by Jan. 1, 1989.
- Lifted U.S. duties on about 1 percent of Israeli goods in eight steps by Jan. 1, 1995.
- Froze U.S. duties on the remaining roughly 13 percent of imports from Israel for five years. All duties would end by Jan. 1, 1995. The schedule will be set after consultations with Israel.

Under existing law, about 90 percent of Israeli products entered the United States duty-free, through current trade concessions or a congressionally approved system to spur imports from developing nations. But Congress tightened eligibility requirements for that program in 1984. Israel wanted the free-trade pact to guarantee and extend the benefits of that system.

Retaliation Against Japan

Frustrated by slow progress in trade negotiations with Japan, members of Congress pushed in 1985 for retaliation against that country's continuing barriers to U.S. goods.

But legislation (S 1404) to implement that goal got no further than approval by the Senate Finance Committee.

Several factors helped focus congressional concern over trade problems with Japan. One was the sheer size of the U.S. trade deficit with the Asian economic giant — $37 billion in 1984.

Another issue was the March 31 expiration of a four-year-old agreement under which Japan voluntarily restrained its auto exports to the United States. President Reagan announced March 1 that he would not ask Japan to extend the agreement, angering members such as Sen. John C. Danforth, R-Mo., chairman of the Finance Subcommittee on International Trade. Japan in turn announced March 28 that it would allow auto exports to the United States to grow by 25 percent.

Members of Congress also were frustrated by Japan's seeming reluctance to lower trade barriers against U.S. goods. They pointed to a variety of studies showing that Japan blocked imports through "non-tariff" barriers, such as elaborate testing requirements and lengthy inspections of foreign-made goods. The Reagan administration had undertaken negotiations with Japan to lower those barriers, but critics were dissatisfied with their progress. Japan also acted during the year on an array of measures to open its markets to imports, but the efforts also met with congressional skepticism.

Non-binding Resolutions

The first move in the Senate was a non-binding resolution. By a 92-0 vote, the Senate March 28 approved a resolution (S Con Res 15) calling on the president to retaliate against Japan if that country refused to step up its purchases of U.S. exports. *(Vote 22, p. 8-S)*

The resolution urged the president to strike back with duties, quotas or other barriers against Japanese imports unless Japan bought enough U.S. goods to offset its increases in auto shipments.

The House then passed a related non-binding resolution (H Con Res 107) by a 394-19 vote April 2. *(Vote 42, p. 16-H)*

The House resolution urged the president to take "all appropriate action" to get Japan to end unfair trade practices. It asked the president to "develop a concrete plan for reducing the deficit by attacking its causes, including the high dollar." Unlike the Senate resolution, however, the House measure did not suggest that the United States offset the expected jump in auto imports with curbs on other Japanese goods.

Senate Committee Action

The Senate Finance Committee quickly acted to convert the overwhelming displays of sentiment expressed in the non-binding resolutions into legislation. On April 2, the committee approved by a 12-4 vote a bill (S 1404) to force the president to impose tariffs, quotas or other restraints on Japanese imports if Japan did not end what many members saw as unfair trade practices, such as making some U.S. firms in Japan advertise in English.

The Finance bill, formally reported by the panel July 9 (S Rept 99-102), would give the president 90 days to get Japan to curb unfair trade barriers.

If his approach failed, he would have to use quotas, tariffs or other restraints to redress "the cumulative impact" of unfair trade practices.

In particular, the president would have to block enough Japanese imports to offset Japan's decision to increase the number of cars it sent to the United States each year.

Before approving the bill, the committee rejected an effort by John H. Chafee, R-R.I., to narrow retaliation to telecommunications equipment. Chafee pushed an approach similar to his bill (S 728), which would bar sales of Japanese telecommunications equipment in the United States until Japan bought more U.S. gear. But his effort to substitute that language for the committee's entire bill was defeated, 5-11.

Later, John Heinz, R-Pa., tried to add the Chafee bill to the Finance Committee's measure; that amendment failed on an 8-8 tie. However, the Finance Committee later in the year reported a related telecommunications measure (S 942). *(Story, p. 262)*

Floor Action Postponed

But S 1404 did not reach the Senate floor in 1985. It was tentatively scheduled for floor action in late July, but ran into problems because it was a tempting vehicle for other restrictive trade proposals. Senators from textile- and shoe-producing states, for example, were eager to attach amendments limiting imports of those products.

Unwilling to allow the bill to face a flurry of amendments, Senate leaders sought to secure a unanimous-consent agreement to limit floor amendments to issues relating directly to Japan. That proved impossible, so floor action was postponed. ■

'Natural Resources' Subsidies

Two House panels in 1985 approved legislation to combat subsidized trade competition from other countries by boosting tariffs on products made with raw materials that were provided by foreign governments to producers at below-market rates.

The House Ways and Means Subcommittee on Trade Oct. 24 approved a bill (HR 2451) to counter "natural resource" subsidies of other countries. And a similar provision was included in an omnibus trade bill (HR 3777) approved by the House Energy and Commerce Committee. However, neither bill became law by the end of the year.

HR 2451 enjoyed particularly strong support from the U.S. timber industry, which was hit hard by competition from Canadian lumber. The bill classified as export subsidies the low "stumpage" fees paid by companies to harvest trees from government land in Canada. The effect of the provision was to impose a tariff estimated at up to 60 percent of value on lumber imports from that country.

The bill was opposed by the Canadian government; the U.S. housing industry, which feared that it would lead to higher lumber prices; and the Reagan administration, which warned that the measure could violate international trade agreements.

The proposal was pushed by Trade Subcommittee Chairman Sam Gibbons, D-Fla., who had won House approval in 1984 of similar legislation as part of an omnibus trade bill. The provision was rejected in conference that year, however. *(1984 Almanac p. 171)*

Subcommittee markup of HR 2451 centered on the provisions relating to "removal rights" of Canadian trees and other products. An amendment by subcommittee ranking Republican Philip M. Crane, Ill., to delete the provisions was rejected 4-5.

Opponents of the bill's provisions argued that the reduced Canadian fees for tree harvesting were not in themselves proof that the Canadian government was subsidizing production. Companies operating in Canada had to cope with higher costs for harvesting and transportation that offset the low fees, they said.

Supporters of the removal right provisions emphasized that they were not directed just against the Canadian timber industry, but could be applied against a variety of subsidized products from around the world.

Provisions

As approved by the subcommittee, HR 2451:

- Determined that an export subsidy, subject to countervailing U.S. duties, existed if a foreign government provided a raw material to its domestic producers at a price that was below the material's fair market value. An export subsidy would be found only if the low-cost raw material was not available, by government regulation, to U.S. companies, and constituted a significant portion of the cost of the final exported product.
- Also permitted a finding of export subsidies in cases in which governments provided removal rights — access to trees or minerals on government-owned land — at rates that were below those rights' fair market value.
- Provided that, in general, the "fair market value" of a raw material or removal right be the price that a willing buyer would pay a willing seller in the absence of government regulation.
- Provided that countervailing duties under the bill be imposed only if the industry affected by subsidized exports were found to have suffered substantial economic injury as a result of import competition. ▮

Telecommunications Bills

Legislation aimed at helping U.S. manufacturers of telephones and other telecommunications equipment compete in world markets was approved by full committees in the House and Senate in 1985. But neither measure reached the floor during the year.

The bills (S 942, HR 3131) both sought to persuade other countries to make their markets for telecommunications equipment more open to U.S. suppliers. Countries that refused to do so would be subject to a variety of U.S. trade sanctions.

The two measures were the indirect products of the 1984 breakup of the American Telephone & Telegraph Co. (AT&T) telephone monopoly. Before 1984, AT&T's Western Electric subsidiary had almost total control of domestic telephone sales.

After the breakup, however, imports into the United States grew dramatically. In 1984, sales of foreign-made telecommunications products grew 44 percent; imports from Japan alone amounted to $2 billion.

In addition, U.S. telecommunications producers argued that they did not have equivalent opportunities in foreign markets. Most countries had state-controlled telephone systems that were explicitly closed to foreign suppliers.

So, while imports into the United States of telephones, switching equipment and related products rose sharply, exports from this country remained low. That left the United States with a deepening trade deficit in telecommunications products — $608 million worth in 1984.

Japan Target

Although a prime target of the legislation was Japan, that country had one of the more open telecommunications markets. In 1980, the United States and Japan approved a pact committing the state-owned Nippon Telegraph and Telephone Public Corp. (NTT) to a willingness to buy foreign equipment. In 1985, the Japanese market was made more competitive by the conversion of NTT into a private corporation.

Still, U.S. companies saw little progress. Telecommunications exports to Japan grew between 1980 and 1985, but at some $200 million in 1984 they were a small fraction of equivalent Japanese sales in this country. U.S. firms said various Japanese reporting and testing requirements kept out their products almost as effectively as a flat ban.

Senate Bill

The Senate Finance Committee Sept. 17 approved S 942, which required retaliation against Japanese imports unless that country acted within four months to open more fully its vast telecommunications market to U.S. producers.

Other countries, particularly Canada and European Common Market nations, also faced sanctions under the bill. But they had up to 18 months to agree to allow U.S. companies a chance to sell telephones and other communications equipment.

Sanctions in most cases would be applied against telephone imports. But countries that did not export those products would still face restrictions on other kinds of goods sold in the United States.

The panel approved S 942 by voice vote.

S 942 Goal

The goal of S 942 was to give the president the negotiating clout, through the threat of retaliation, needed to convince Japan and other countries to make their telecommunications policies less restrictive.

The first step under the bill as approved by the Finance panel would be a four-month study of the world telecommunications market by the U.S. trade representative.

The bill would pursue two different strategies after the study period. If Japan — the only country with an existing agreement with the United States to open its telecommunications market — was found to have retained its restrictive policies, sanctions would be applied immediately. The administration would have to act within 15 days to curb imports of Japanese telecommunications products.

Other countries would have an additional 14-month period for negotiations. Countries willing to open their telecommunications markets would escape sanctions. Congress would have the right to reject market-opening agreements between the United States and other countries. At the end of the negotiating period, countries that did not agree to lower import barriers would face U.S. retaliation.

The committee issued its report on S 942 Nov. 26 (S Rept 99-204).

House Measure

The House Energy and Commerce Committee approved HR 3131 by a 33-0 vote Nov. 21.

Although it shared a common goal with S 942, HR 3131 would follow somewhat different tactics. For example, the bill would not single out Japan by making a distinction between countries with which the United States already had an existing agreement and those with which it did not.

The House bill would go into effect in July 1986. Before that, the president was assumed to have engaged in negotiations aimed at removing foreign barriers to U.S. products.

The first step under the bill would be for the Commerce Department to make a study of foreign telecommunications trade barriers. The president would then be required to take steps against countries which were found to have retained such barriers.

The bill directed the president to order the Federal Communications Commission (FCC) to take steps to limit or deny access to U.S. telecommunications markets to products from countries whose own markets were restricted. Instead of acting through the FCC, however, the president could also take equivalent action to restrict imports under sections of the 1974 Trade Act. ∎

Exchange Rates

The House Banking Committee Dec. 12 approved a bill (HR 3498 — H Rept 99-456) encouraging efforts to lower the value of the dollar against other currencies in order to help U.S. businesses compete in world markets.

The bill essentially was a congressional endorsement of moves by the Reagan administration and other leading industrialized countries to reduce the relative value of the dollar.

The high value of the dollar had been widely seen during the year as an important factor in causing the record U.S. trade deficit, by making American-made goods more expensive abroad and reducing the cost to consumers of imports into this country.

For most of his time in office, President Reagan had argued along with other administration officials that the high dollar was a sign of the good health of the U.S. economy. But, on Sept. 22, Treasury Secretary James A. Baker III and other finance ministers announced that they would work together to depress the price of the dollar on world money markets.

HR 3498 would not require major changes in U.S. monetary policy. Rather, sponsors portrayed it as an effort to put political pressure on the administration not to go back on its efforts to lower the dollar.

The key provision of HR 3498 would be to establish as a goal of U.S. economic policy the achievement of a currency exchange rate that would give domestic producers a good chance to compete in world markets. "We are not mandating policy," said John J. LaFalce, D-N.Y. "We are mandating that the competitiveness of the exchange rate always be a consideration in the formulation of our economic policies."

LaFalce offered the substitute amendment that scaled back the scope of HR 3498 as introduced by Stan Lundine, D-N.Y. The original version had called for mandatory currency intervention whenever trade deficits reached high levels.

Other provisions of HR 3498 called for international negotiations on exchange rates, authorized a strategic currency reserve in the Treasury Department to fund intervention in currency markets and required increased reporting to Congress on efforts to adjust the level of the dollar.

Before approving the bill, the committee agreed to drop a provision establishing a new commission to study U.S. policy on exchange rates. ∎

Tied Aid 'War Chest'

Congress began work in 1985 on President Reagan's request for establishment of a new $300 million "war chest" to help U.S. exporters compete in world markets. But budget concerns slowed action on the proposal.

Reagan asked for the new program on Sept. 23, as part of his administration's new trade policy. The new funds were intended to counter other nations' use of "tied aid" programs combining low-interest loans with outright grants to encourage foreign purchasers of their exports.

Administration officials hoped that they could persuade other nations, particularly France, to drop their tied aid programs by brandishing the threat of a competing U.S. program.

Two House panels — the full Banking Committee and a Foreign Affairs subcommittee — approved differing versions of legislation (HR 3667, HR 3296) to authorize the war chest. Neither bill reached the House floor, however, and there was no action on related legislation in the Senate in 1985.

House Banking Committee Action

The Banking Subcommittee on International Finance, Trade and Monetary Policy approved HR 3667 by a 19-0 vote Nov. 7. The bill as approved was similar in all but a few points to the proposal (HR 3515) put forward by the administration.

Supporters of HR 3667 described it as following an "offensive" strategy. In contrast to the Foreign Affairs Committee bill, the measure aimed to use grants to open up new markets for U.S. exports, even when other governments were not already providing tied aid.

In keeping with its emphasis on an offensive strategy against foreign competitors, HR 3667 placed responsibility for the new program with the Treasury Department. Since that agency was to be responsible for pressuring other governments to drop their tied aid programs, backers said, it should have control in order to use the grant funds as a negotiating tool.

Under the bill, the tied aid program would be operated by Treasury, in coordination with the Export-Import Bank's existing program of loans financing purchases of U.S. products by foreigners.

HR 3667 as approved by the subcommittee authorized $300 million in fiscal 1986.

The full committee approved HR 3667 (H Rept 99-457), authorizing $300 million in fiscal 1987, by voice vote Dec. 12.

However, the bill had encountered serious problems before gaining full committee approval. Since the new program as reported by the subcommittee was to be funded in fiscal 1986, the current fiscal year, Democratic members in particular were worried that it would lead to offsetting cuts in housing or other programs.

Because of those concerns, the committee twice voted to delay the bill. Finally, it was recommitted to the International Finance Subcommittee, where an administration-backed amendment was approved to delay funding until fiscal 1987.

But while the funding delay calmed members' budget fears, it also seemed to undermine the administration's negotiating strategy. Administration officials hoped that they would be able to use the threat of a new tied aid program to persuade other countries to drop their own similar programs — a bargaining threat that could have been seriously weakened by the delay in funding.

To allay that concern, International Finance Subcommittee Chairman Stephen L. Neal, D-N.C., proposed an amendment to encourage the Export-Import Bank to make aggressive use of existing authority to offer assistance to foreign purchasers. The amendment, approved by voice vote, also promised the bank that its efforts would be repaid from the new appropriation.

Foreign Affairs Action

The Foreign Affairs Subcommittee on International Economic Policy and Trade approved HR 3296 by voice vote Nov. 5. The bill authorized a total of $500 million in fiscal 1986 for a tied aid program.

HR 3296 differed from HR 3667 in that sponsors saw it as pursuing a primarily "defensive" strategy. The bill would restrict the new tied aid program to responses to specific cases in which other governments were providing subsidies to foreign purchasers.

With its emphasis on helping businesses respond to individual cases of foreign competition, HR 3296 would operate partially through the Export-Import Bank, the agency that already was providing low-interest loans to foreign buyers. The bill authorized $250 million for a bank-operated tied aid program.

In addition, HR 3296 authorized a further $250 million to be used by the Agency for International Development (AID) for the same purpose.

Before approving the bill, the subcommittee rejected a Toby Roth, R-Wis., amendment to authorize $300 million for the Treasury Department, on top of the $500 million already in the bill. Roth argued that the extra funds were needed to step up pressure on other countries to negotiate.

Roth's amendment also provided for punitive actions against countries that refused to drop their tied aid programs. Countries that did not agree within two years would be subject to retaliation for engaging in unfair trade practices. Although the amendment was modified at the last minute to reduce the total cost of the bill to $500 million — $250 million for Treasury, $150 million for the Export-Import Bank and $100 million for AID — it was rejected by voice vote. ∎

Congress Reauthorizes OPIC

Congress Dec. 12 cleared legislation (S 947 — PL 99-204) extending for three years the authorization for the Overseas Private Investment Corporation (OPIC). The bill was signed Dec. 23.

The bill to authorize activities of the government-owned corporation through fiscal year 1988 cleared when the Senate adopted by voice vote the conference report (H Rept 99-428). The House had accepted the report Dec. 11.

Established by Congress in 1969, OPIC insured U.S. businesses operating in lesser-developed nations of the Third World against the risks of war and political upheaval.

S 947 went through Congress without strong opposition, and did not make any major changes in the way the corporation operated. But the limited debate on the measure showed that the longstanding doubts among union allies about OPIC's effects on U.S. employment had not gone away. Critics argued that OPIC provided support for companies that wanted to operate in poor countries, where wages were low, instead of in the United States.

In 1977, fears about possible job losses forced sponsors of the OPIC reauthorization to withdraw their bill, delaying final action until 1978. But the 1981 reauthorization bill cleared easily. *(1978 Almanac p. 267; 1981 Almanac p. 109)*

In 1985, the OPIC bill (HR 3166), with a four-year authorization, sailed through the House. It was reported by the Foreign Affairs Committee Sept. 23 (H Rept 99-285), and passed the House by voice vote the same day.

In the Senate, however, S 947 was the target of some pointed criticism from Democrats, including Foreign Relations ranking member Claiborne Pell (D) of Rhode Island. The Foreign Relations panel had reported the bill (S Rept 99-156) on Oct. 10.

Citing an AFL-CIO study estimating that OPIC activities had contributed to the loss of 500,000 American jobs in the preceding four years, Howard M. Metzenbaum, D-Ohio, offered an amendment to extend the authorization only through July 1, 1987. Adopted by voice vote, the amendment also required a General Accounting Office (GAO) study of the corporation's employment effects.

The Senate then passed S 947 by voice vote Nov. 14.

Senate critics of the bill also cited a House Government Operations Committee study of OPIC, which was released Nov. 5 (H Rept 99-359).

The panel argued that the corporation's efforts to operate like a "private-sector firm concerned with profits" had caused it to neglect important goals intended by Congress. The report said that OPIC had shifted its operations away from the very poorest countries, in favor of countries where considerable development had already taken place.

Final Provisions

As cleared by Congress, S 947:

- Extended the authorization for OPIC activities through Sept. 30, 1988.
- Required OPIC-backed projects to observe certain environmental, health and safety standards.
- Limited OPIC operations to countries that observed certain "internationally recognized" rights of workers, such as collective bargaining or child-labor laws. However, the president could waive the limitation if he determined that OPIC operations in a particular country would be in the U.S. national interest.
- Required a study by the GAO of the effects of OPIC activities on employment in the United States.
- Authorized OPIC to provide insurance on new investments by businesses that suffered losses because their operations were interrupted by war or other political problems.
- Authorized OPIC to establish a pilot program of reinsurance, under which the corporation would assume some of the risks taken on by private political risk insurance companies.
- Increased to 15 percent from 10 percent the share of total OPIC investment guarantee coverage that could be issued to a single investor.
- Adjusted for inflation the per capita income limits on countries eligible for OPIC operations. ∎

TRANSPORTATION COMMERCE CONSUMERS

CQ

Transportation/Commerce/Consumers

An unprecedented wave of corporate mergers dominated financial news and helped send the stock market to record highs in 1985.

But some experts feared that the feverish activity was not healthy for the economy.

Mergers, acquisitions and takeovers began to accelerate in 1984, but the pace escalated in 1985. The value of firms changing hands rose from $122 billion in 1984 to an estimated $180 billion in 1985. Many were friendly takeovers, but others were forced by speculators who wanted to take control of companies against the will of current management.

Highly publicized battles for control engulfed some of the nation's largest companies, including Trans World Airlines (TWA), Phillips Petroleum Co. and CBS Inc. Phillips and CBS managed to outmaneuver unfriendly raiders, but TWA was taken over by financier Carl C. Icahn.

Many members of Congress were alarmed by the market focus on takeovers, rather than on normal economic expansion by building new factories and introducing new products. "I believe the rising tide of takeovers threatens the very foundations of our American business system," said William Proxmire, D-Wis., ranking Democrat on the Senate Banking, Housing and Urban Affairs Committee.

Critics of the merger fever said that the acquisitions led companies to increase their debt to unhealthy levels, hurt communities by closing plants and stampeded current managers into making shortsighted decisions to protect their jobs.

Both raiders and their targets turned to Congress to stop what they saw as dirty tactics by their adversaries.

Raiders wanted Congress to prohibit defensive moves by corporate managers, such as the "poison pill" — a provision in a company's charter that would make a takeover unattractive by increasing the cost of stock if a purchase was not approved by the board of directors.

Management, on the other hand, sought a ban on some of the raiders' favorite tactics that made it possible for a small company to buy out a much larger one, such as the use of "junk bonds" — high-risk securities with little financial backing. But the administration opposed intervention on the grounds that mergers allowed economies of scale and made American industry more competitive in worldwide markets.

Despite congressional interest and a spate of hearings, members found the issues too complex for quick legislation. No major bills were moved.

On the regulatory level, the Federal Reserve Board ignored pressure from the administration and adopted a new rule to restrict the use of junk bonds to finance takeovers. The rule would apply the Fed's margin regulations, which required a minimum amount of financial backing, to securities issued by "shell" companies formed to assist in a takeover.

The year ended with the Dow Jones industrial average of 30 blue-chip stocks at 1553, up 28 percent over the year before. The market had a shock Jan. 8, 1986, when the average fell a record 39 points, even more than in the 1929 stock market crash. But the fall involved a much smaller percentage of the total market, and was viewed as normal adjustment to a steady surge in stock prices that preceded it.

Liability Insurance Problems

Skyrocketing premiums for liability insurance sent businesses to Capitol Hill to plead for relief. Among property-casualty insurance companies, which provide liability insurance, premiums rose 21 percent in 1985, compared with 9 percent in 1984. Another 20 percent increase was forecast for 1986.

The squeeze was particularly hard for certain fields: municipal government, manufacturers, doctors, hazardous-waste disposers, restaurant owners, pharmaceutical companies and day-care centers. They often faced increases of 300 to 1,000 percent in their premiums, or found no insurance available at any price.

"Complaints are coming in to the members of Congress at a level that is unprecedented," said James L. Oberstar, D-Minn., chairman of the House Public Works and Transportation Subcommittee on Investigations and Oversight.

Insurance companies said the increases were required because interest rates had fallen, cutting into investment income, and because excessive litigation had driven up the cost of settling claims. They appealed for changes in tort laws that concerned damage claims, such as establishing a federal law to govern state suits for damages caused by unsafe products.

Consumer groups replied that the settlements had not risen disproportionately; the problem, they said, was that insurance companies had cut premiums too deeply in their quest for investment dollars.

But despite a spate of hearings near the end of the year, Congress was slow to intervene. Insurance had long been exempted from federal regulation and from antitrust laws, and members of Congress were only beginning to understand how it worked.

Air Safety

Concern over air safety ran high in 1985. It was the worst year in history for commercial aviation, with more than 2,000 people killed around the world. The worst disasters involved large jetliners, such as an August crash of a Japan Air Lines jet that killed 520, and the explosion of an Air-India flight over the sea near Ireland in June that killed 329.

While the accidents caused widespread concern in the United States, experts rushed to reassure the traveling public that it was still safe to fly. U.S. fatalities did not reach record proportions: The 197 killed on scheduled flights and 329 on unscheduled commercial flights were fewer than the fatality total for 1977. And on a per-mile basis, flying was safer in 1985 than it had been a decade before — and far safer than driving.

Nevertheless, members of Congress lambasted the Reagan administration and the Federal Aviation Administration (FAA) for not giving safety enough priority. And some voiced concern that deregulation of the airline industry, approved by Congress in 1978, had diminished the margin of safety.

The August crash of a Delta flight at Dallas-Fort Worth Regional Airport, which killed 136 people, focused attention on federal efforts to detect wind shear. A sudden shift of winds was suspected as the cause of the Delta crash. Federal agencies had been working on new radar systems to warn pilots of its presence, but critics charged that the administration had slowed down development to save money. They also accused the administration of not hiring enough air traffic controllers and inspectors.

Congress increased funding for FAA operations, at the administration's request, to provide 500 new air traffic controllers and 300 safety inspectors.

Highways

Congress sent to the states approximately $12 billion in federal highway funds in 1985 but only by deferring the controversies associated with the funds until 1986.

Most of the money came from the Highway Trust Fund, which was supported by federal gasoline taxes, truck taxes and other road-related fees.

Congress failed in 1983 and 1984 to release to the states $7.2 billion for federal highway programs because of differences between the House and Senate over mass-transit funding, special "demonstration" projects that appealed to members' constituencies and formulas under which funds were distributed to the states.

Congress cleared legislation to release the $7.2 billion for fiscal 1984 and 1985 in March, and added another $4.8 billion to cover fiscal 1986 in September.

House and Senate committee leaders decided to skirt the controversies because many state highway departments were running out of funds and because most federal highway programs had to be reauthorized by Sept. 30, 1986. The controversies could be settled then, members said.

One of the problems deferred was the question of how to pay for the highway program. Federal tax funds supported the construction of the Interstate Highway System; a larger network of state highways; repair and replacement of federal-aid roads; bridge replacement; and highway beautification.

A study by the Congressional Budget Office (CBO) in July showed that at the current rate of spending, the Highway Trust Fund would run out of cash in 1990. The CBO study said that a 2-cents-per-gallon increase in the federal gasoline tax, currently 9 cents per gallon, would fund the program for the next decade.

The only significant highway controversy settled by Congress in 1985 was the abandonment of federal funding for a major highway and land-development project in New York City called Westway. The project was opposed by environmentalists. New York officials dropped the project, which could have cost $4 billion to $10 billion, eight days after the House voted 237-132 Sept. 11 to block federal funding for the project in the fiscal 1986 transportation appropriations bill.

Mass Transit, Railroads

The administration made a strong push to slash federal aid for commuters but made only a small dent in it.

The president's budget proposed cutting mass transit aid by two-thirds, including elimination of federal aid to start new transit systems. But the final continuing resolution cut it by only 10 percent.

Budget director David A. Stockman also argued for elimination of federal subsidies for Amtrak, even if that killed the national passenger railroad. But the continuing resolution cut Amtrak by only 10 percent from fiscal 1985 levels.

The administration proposed to sell the government's 85 percent share of Conrail to the Norfolk Southern Corp. for $1.2 billion cash, with several covenants to protect the railroad. But legislation to implement the sale was blocked in the Senate in the closing days of the session and remained stalled in the House. Concern focused on the competitive impact of the sale and its consequences for government revenues.

—By Stephen Gettinger

Impasse Over States' Interstate Funds Broken

Congress in 1985 broke an impasse that for two years had blocked billions of dollars owed to the states for Interstate highway construction and other work.

At issue were normally routine bills that Congress was supposed to approve biennially by Oct. 1. The legislation in effect would release each state's share of the Highway Trust Fund for Interstate highway construction, and for highway and transit projects that states substituted for previously planned Interstate projects.

However, the scheduled Oct. 1, 1983, release of funds was blocked when the required legislation became mired in controversies over such matters as special highway demonstration projects, mass transit funding authorizations and distribution formulas. Because of the impasse, the 98th Congress approved a temporary measure giving states only six-months' worth of funds for fiscal 1984. *(1983 Almanac p. 559; 1984 Almanac p. 290)*

By February 1985, states were nearly 18 months behind in receiving their full highway fund allocations. Federal highway officials said that at least 45 states were "virtually bankrupt" and could not continue work on the Interstate system.

With that impetus, Congress agreed to drop the divisive issues and cleared two bills making available funds covering the last half of fiscal 1985 and all of 1986.

The Senate March 5 cleared a bill (HR 1251 — PL 99-4) that had been stripped of the disputed provisions. It released $7.2 billion from the Highway Trust Fund for the second half of 1984 and all of 1985. Included was $5.3 billion for Interstate construction, $979 million for substitute projects and about $960 million to ensure that states received 85 percent of the gasoline and other road-related taxes they contributed to the trust fund.

Then, Sept. 19, the House cleared another streamlined bill (S 1514 — PL 99-104) that released $4.8 billion for all of fiscal 1986, including $3.6 billion for Interstate construction, $538 million for substitute projects and $649 million to assure that states receive at least 85 percent of their contribution to the trust fund.

The key in both cases was acknowledgement by members that the prior disagreements had created chaos in their home states, delaying highway construction and costing jobs. House and Senate leaders promised that the more divisive issues could be debated during the consideration of legislation authorizing major highway programs, which would expire Oct. 1, 1986.

Background

In passing the bills, Congress technically approved estimates of the cost of the construction, called an Interstate Cost Estimate (ICE) and an Interstate Substitute Cost Estimate (ISCE).

The approval was supposed to be routine, but the ICE and ISCE bills had become vehicles for members to attach "special demonstration" highway projects.

Members especially liked the demonstration projects because they were financed completely with federal funds, compared with the 90 percent federal share for regular Interstate work. However, the demonstration projects were criticized for being unauthorized add-ons to the construction programs proposed by state highway departments and for straining the trust fund.

Ray A. Barnhart, administrator of the Federal Highway Administration (FHWA), said three demonstration projects were added to ICE/ISCE legislation in 1973-74, six in 1978, 12 in 1982 and 77 in 1984.

"I don't call all of them boondoggles because many are desirable projects, but in toto, they are such a heavy drain that the trust fund cannot support it," Barnhart said. The trust fund was designed to meet the needs of state highway departments, and the extra projects depleted the fund faster than otherwise would occur, he said.

In 1985, the issue of the special projects continued to cause disagreement. One especially disputed proposal was a House-backed $2.5 billion highway and tunnel project in Boston that touched the district of House Speaker Thomas P. O'Neill Jr., D-Mass.

Another issue that returned to block the 1985 bill was the insistence of House Public Works and Transportation Chairman James J. Howard, D-N.J., that the House bill include an increase in funding authorizations for mass transit capital projects. One cent of the 5-cent 1982 gasoline-tax increase was earmarked for mass transit, and Howard contended more money was available than was anticipated originally.

The Senate Banking, Housing and Urban Affairs Committee, with jurisdiction over mass transit, did not want transit authorizations included in the highway bill.

First Highway Bill

Senate Action. Before ordering an ICE/ISCE bill reported Jan. 29, the Senate Environment and Public Works Committee voted to limit overall highway spending and to drop all special demonstration projects.

The spending cuts involved rolling back the fiscal 1986 trust fund obligation ceiling by $1.7 billion, from $14.45 billion to $12.75 billion. The special projects deleted would have cost another $153.6 million. The total would be $500 million less than the fiscal 1985 level.

Members noted that the reductions would not provide money for non-highway programs to cut the federal deficit because unspent money by law remained in the trust fund to be obligated for highway work in future years. But the moves were hailed by senators as a symbol of their resolve that no program should escape budget cuts in an effort to control the deficit.

"This is bitter medicine for all of us," said John H. Chafee, R-R.I., sponsor of the amendment to cut the 1986 ceiling on trust fund spending. "But if we don't reduce the deficit, it is going to require major surgery later, not just medicine."

His amendment was approved 15-0.

The bill contained 14 demonstration projects, all carried over from the 1984 Senate bill. James Abdnor, R-S.D., moved to delete the projects on the grounds that if the states were to get less money because of the reduced obligation ceiling, it was not fair to earmark funds for projects not sought by state highway departments.

The motion passed by voice vote.

The panel approved two measures: S J Res 8, a simple release of the funds with no other provisions, and S 178, a more complex measure that contained some programmatic changes.

Both bills released funds not only for the overdue 18-month period but provided for the administrative release of funds in the future to avoid entanglement in the legislative process. They would free Interstate funds for fiscal 1986-87 and funds for projects substituted for Interstate work through 1986.

S 178 also included a controversial provision proposed by Lloyd Bentsen, D-Texas, that would change the way some funds were distributed.

Under existing law, states were guaranteed a return of 85 percent of their tax contributions to the trust fund, but the computations excluded several major programs. Bentsen's change would include all highway money, with the result that Texas would receive more than $64 million extra in fiscal 1985.

S 178 also preserved a provision that would keep Illinois from losing a large amount of funds for one year. That provision was added in 1984 after the two Illinois senators mounted a filibuster on the Senate floor.

The bill also would make several minor changes in highway programs, such as requiring that a small proportion of landscaping funds be spent on planting wildflowers, and ending federal oversight of tolls charged at certain bridges.

The more complex S 178 was re-introduced as S 391 and the report (S Rept 99-2) filed Feb. 5.

Floor debate took place in an unusual Saturday session Feb. 23; an impasse over farm aid had tied the chamber in knots the week of Feb. 18 and delayed bringing the highway bill to the floor. When the highway bill did come up, it whisked through without amendment by a vote of 94-0. *(Vote 10, p. 4-S)*

House, Final Action. On Feb. 27, the Public Works and Transportation Committee decided to excise all the extraneous provisions from its bill (HR 1251 — H Rept 99-11). The House passed the bill Feb. 28 by a vote of 392-4 and demanded that the Senate accept it without change. Members complained that insisting on some provisions in the Senate bill, such as reducing the trust fund obligation ceiling, could lead to months-long delays. Although some senators bristled at the ultimatum, they agreed not to amend it and cleared the measure by voice vote. *(Vote 21, p. 8-H)*

The final legislation did include a cost estimate for Interstate work in Speaker O'Neill's state of Massachusetts that some senators suspected might be an attempt to fund the controversial highway and tunnel project. The project involved building a third tunnel under Boston Harbor, from Logan International Airport into Boston on Interstate 90; the reconstruction of the Central Artery (Interstate 93) as a widened, below-ground highway through downtown Boston; and an interchange to connect the tunnel and artery.

Howard said the Massachusetts estimate merely preserved the status quo in a controversy between the state and the Department of Transportation (DOT) over what portion of the project was eligible for federal financing.

Second Highway Bill

As reported by the Senate Environment and Public Works Committee July 29, S 1514 contained none of the demonstration projects or extraneous provisions of prior years. It was passed by the Senate by voice vote July 30.

Bypassing committee, the House cleared the measure by voice vote Sept. 19. ▮

Statue of Liberty Coin

Congress June 24 cleared a bill (HR 47 — PL 99-61) authorizing the minting in 1986 of commemorative coins to raise an estimated $137 million toward the renovation of the Statue of Liberty and Ellis Island.

Final action came when the House accepted by voice vote an amendment adopted by the Senate June 21. The amendment, sponsored by Sen. James A. McClure, R-Idaho, provided for minting, in addition to the commemorative coins, a silver bullion Liberty dollar, with the silver to be purchased from the national stockpile.

The House, bypassing committee action, originally passed the bill March 5 by voice vote under suspension of the rules. The Senate Banking, Housing and Urban Affairs Committee reported the bill May 7 (no written report). The president signed it into law July 9.

Under the bill, three coins made of gold or silver and alloy were to be minted. There were to be a half-million $5 gold coins commemorating the centennial of the Statue of Liberty, 10 million silver dollars commemorating Ellis Island and 25 million half dollars depicting the contributions of immigrants to America. All were to be sold at face value, plus a surcharge: $35 for the $5 coin, $7 for the silver dollar and $2 for the half dollar.

Proceeds from the sale were to be used for renovation of the statue and island. The rest of the estimated $230 million restoration cost was being raised by a private foundation.

The Liberty dollar, made of pure silver, was to be minted in unlimited quantities and sold at a price equal to the market price of silver, plus production and distribution costs. ▮

Gold Coins Authorized

Legislation giving Americans the chance to buy new non-commemorative U.S. gold coins for the first time in more than 50 years was cleared Dec. 2 by Congress.

The bill (S 1639 — PL 99-185), signed by the president Dec. 17, authorized the minting of four gold coins in denominations of $5, $10, $25 and $50 to be sold after Oct. 1, 1986. They would depict the American eagle.

The new coins would be the first domestic gold currency since President Franklin D. Roosevelt effectively took the United States off the gold standard in 1933, forbidding Americans to hold gold or convert paper currency into gold.

While other gold coins had been issued, all had been limited-edition commemoratives. In June, for example, Congress authorized the minting of 500,000 gold Statue of Liberty coins (HR 47 — PL 99-61). *(Story, above)*

The coins would give investors an alternative to the South African Krugerrand, which was banned from U.S. importation by President Reagan and which the South African government Nov. 13 announced would no longer be produced, sponsors said.

The selling price of the coins would be the market price of gold plus the government's costs of minting, marketing and distribution. Excess revenues could be used to reduce the national debt, William Proxmire, D-Wis., added. Although the coins would be legal tender, it was not likely they would be used as such because the actual value would be much higher than the face value of the coins.

Legislative Action

The Senate passed the bill Nov. 14 by voice vote. "... We need an American alternative which will keep investment in the United States and give the world coin collectors and investors an opportunity to purchase American gold coins," Sen. J. James Exon, D-Neb., chief backer of the bill, said.

Before bringing the measure to the Senate floor, sponsors made two adjustments intended to ease passage.

To assuage gold-state senators, led by Chic Hecht, R-Nev., the Treasury was required to buy recently mined domestic gold for the coins first, before using gold from the U.S. reserve.

Vietnam Coin Linkage. To prevent the original bill from bogging down in the Democratic-controlled House, a section introduced by Charles McC. Mathias Jr., R-Md., to award commemorative gold medals to Jan Scruggs, Robert Doubek and Jack Wheeler in recognition of their efforts to build the Vietnam Veterans Memorial, was split off as separate legislation. Scruggs was considering running as a Republican for the seat of Mathias, who planned to retire.

Legislation (S 1752) containing both the legal-tender and Vietnam memorial commemorative coin provisions had been reported Oct. 9 by the Banking, Housing and Urban Affairs Committee. Panel members approved two separate bills by poll Nov. 13: S 1639, authorizing the legal-tender coin, and S 865, authorizing the commemorative coins.

Following Senate passage Nov. 14, the House, bypassing committee, cleared S 1639 by voice vote Dec. 2.

The House took no action on S 865, which the Senate also had passed by voice vote Nov. 14.

Anti-Apartheid Roots

Momentum for the legislation stemmed from anti-apartheid sentiment in the country. The South African government had been garnering considerable revenues from sales of its gold Krugerrand coins. U.S. sales alone were estimated at up to $600 million annually, with some two million Americans owning the coins. An estimated five million Americans owned gold coins as investments.

President Reagan Sept. 9 had banned the importation of Kruggerands into the United States, effective Oct. 12, as part of a program of limited economic sanctions against South Africa. Reagan ordered the sanctions to forestall congressional approval of a harsher anti-apartheid measure (HR 1460). *(Story, p. 83)*

Sports Team Bill

The Senate Commerce, Science and Transportation Committee approved a bill to make it harder for professional sports teams to abandon one city in search of greater profits in another, but there was no further action.

The bill (S 259), which would have given professional sports leagues the authority to control franchise shifts, was approved April 2 by a vote of 10-6 after two amendments to limit the power of the National Football League (NFL) to control television rights were defeated. The report (S Rept 99-69) was filed May 21.

The measure, backed by chairman John C. Danforth, R-Mo., was sought by the NFL. The league had been forbidden to block owners from relocating teams by a 1982 court decision that allowed the Oakland Raiders to move to Los Angeles despite opposition from the city of Oakland and other NFL owners.

Supporters said S 259 would protect communities from losing teams that were valuable sources of civic pride. Foes, including the United States Football League, argued that it would give too much power to the dominant NFL.

Until Raiders owner Al Davis successfully challenged the NFL in court, league rules had required the approval of other owners before a team could move to another city.

The Raiders' move was followed by the 1984 shift of the Baltimore Colts to Indianapolis, in which equipment was trucked out of Baltimore under cover of night to avoid the wrath of city officials and fans.

Legislation to allow communities to block such moves was approved by the Senate Commerce Committee in June 1984 by 9-8, but it never reached the floor. *(1984 Almanac p. 284)*

At the time, Danforth — who was not chairman — said the legislation was unnecessary. But subsequently, two Missouri teams, the St. Louis Cardinals football team and the Kansas City Kings basketball team, were wooed by other cities. Danforth cosponsored S 259 with Thomas F. Eagleton, D-Mo.

Daylight-Saving Time

A bill that would provide at least four more weeks of daylight-saving time was passed by the House Oct. 22 but was not acted on by the Senate in 1985.

Under existing law, the daylight-saving time change began on the last Sunday in April and ended on the last Sunday in October. The bill (HR 2095 — H Rept 99-185), approved by a vote of 240-157, would extend it from the first Sunday in April to the first Sunday in November, adding an extra week of daylight-saving time in the fall to make sunset occur later on Halloween. *(Vote 330, p. 104-H)*

The measure represented a compromise between rural legislators, whose constituents disliked the later sunrises under daylight-saving time, and urban and suburban legislators, whose voters wanted more light in the evening.

A more extensive measure that would have begun the time shift on the first Sunday in March, rather than the first Sunday in April, was defeated by the House in 1983, 199-211. *(1983 Almanac p. 551)*

HR 2095 was approved by the Energy and Commerce Committee June 25 and the report was filed June 27.

The administration supported the measure, although it opposed continuing provisions in existing law that allowed a state or territory to keep standard time all year. Arizona, Hawaii, Puerto Rico, the Virgin Islands, American Samoa and the part of Indiana in the Eastern time zone all refused to set their clocks forward.

Congress experimented with year-round daylight-saving time in 1974 in order to save electricity during the energy crisis, but complaints about schoolchildren traveling in the dark led to trimming back the time change.

Odometer Fraud

The Senate in 1985 for the second year in a row passed a bill aimed at assuring used-car buyers that the odomenter reading of the vehicle was accurate, but the House again did not act on the legislation before adjournment.

The bill (S 475), approved by voice vote Dec. 13, would provide greater uniformity of state motor vehicle registration and titling procedures to establish a more easily followed "paper trail" of odometer readings. A similar measure (S 1407) was passed by the Senate in 1984 but was not considered by the House. *(1984 Almanac p. 295)*

The new legislation would increase the civil penalty for turning back an odometer from $1,000 to $2,000 and make the crime a felony, with violators subject to a maximum penalty of $50,000 and/or three years imprisonment. Under existing law, violators were subject to one year in jail.

Another major provision would grant new authority to the Secretary of Transportation to issue rules and regulations to address problems of false and misleading odometer disclosure or unauthorized alteration of disclosure documents.

Sponsors said that the National Highway Traffic Safety Administration estimated that about 3 million used cars sold each year had had their odometers rolled back, reducing the mileage an average of 30,000 miles per car. Turning back the odometer took only seconds, they said, and disclosure forms currently were easy to alter to mask the fraud.

The measure was reported May 14 by the Commerce, Science and Transportation Committee (S Rept 99-47). ∎

Senate Foes Block Reagan Plan to Sell Conrail

The Reagan administration's controversial plan to sell Conrail won the endorsement of a key Senate committee in 1985, but critics kept the bill (S 638 — S Rept 99-98) from the floor and skeptical House members took no action.

Advocates of the sale — the Department of Transportation (DOT) and the buyer it selected, the Norfolk Southern Corp. — pledged a major push in the second session to carry out the sale. Congressional action was needed to remove obstacles to the private operation of the railroad, such as laws dictating the makeup of the board of directors.

The Reagan administration wanted to sell the railroad to the private sector for financial and philosophical reasons. Norfolk Southern was among the three finalists selected by DOT in 1984 to buy the government's 85 percent share of the freight railroad. *(1984 Almanac p. 298)*

Transportation Secretary Elizabeth Hanford Dole announced Feb. 8 that because of its railroad experience, she recommended Norfolk Southern over the other two prime bidders, Alleghany Corp. and a group of investors led by J. Willard Marriott Jr.

Norfolk Southern offered $1.2 billion in cash for the government's share of Conrail, plus any cash in excess of the $800 million Conrail had on hand. Norfolk Southern agreed to forgo almost $2.4 billion in potential tax advantages, and agreed to a series of covenants designed to keep Conrail intact. It offered Conrail employees, who owned the other 15 percent, a package it valued at $375 million.

If approved, the sale would create the nation's largest rail network, stretching from New Orleans and Jacksonville, Fla., to Boston, Montreal and Kansas City. Norfolk Southern operated two railroads, the Southern, and the Norfolk and Western, covering 18,000 miles in 20 states. Conrail's service area included 13,500 miles in 14 states and Canada.

But opposition surfaced almost immediately from members from the Northeast and the Midwest, the areas Conrail served; from shippers, who feared higher prices and loss of service; from labor, which feared the loss of jobs; and from Conrail management, which wanted a public stock offering that would retain the railroad's independence.

Two weeks after the Senate Commerce, Science and Transportation Committee April 30 approved S 638 to implement DOT's recommendation, the investment firm of Morgan Stanley and Co. announced that a group of investors would pay the same amount as Norfolk Southern but keep Conrail as an independent railroad. That offer won the endorsement of labor, Conrail management and some members.

Senators backing Norfolk Southern were unable to bring the bill to the floor partly because of the crush of major legislation that had to be completed by the end of the year. An 11th-hour effort in the waning days of the session was frustrated by opponents, including Howard M. Metzenbaum, D-Ohio, who preferred continued government ownership of the railroad, and Arlen Specter, R-Pa., who had introduced legislation (S 1361) to implement the Morgan Stanley offer.

Support in the Senate was relatively shallow, with the principal backers being John C. Danforth, R-Mo., chairman of the Commerce, Science and Transportation Committee, and Majority Leader Robert Dole, R-Kan., who was married to Secretary Dole. Although Danforth and Dole had taken a personal interest in the sale, neither would be seriously hurt in his home state if the proposal failed.

In the House, John D. Dingell, D-Mich., chairman of the Energy and Commerce Committee, and James J. Florio, D-N.J., chairman of the Subcommittee on Commerce, Transportation and Tourism, did not endorse either proposal. Florio's panel, along with the Judiciary and Ways and Means committees, held numerous hearings on the issue, but no markups were held.

At a Ways and Means Committee hearing May 1, Florio summed up his dissatisfaction. "We don't know what the competitive results of a merger will be," he testified. "No one has analyzed the effect this will have on shippers.... No one has looked at the effect on employment.... Perhaps most importantly, no one has been able to tell us what the effect is on the U.S. Treasury, on the taxpayer."

Bankruptcy to Profit

The Consolidated Rail Corporation, or Conrail, was created by Congress in 1975 from the bankrupt Penn Central and six other failing railroads. The Reagan administration first proposed selling it in 1981. The system had lost $244 million in 1980; over the years, the government had poured more than $7 billion into the railroad to buy equipment, upgrade facilities and provide operating subsidies.

Congress rejected the 1981 suggestion because it would have broken up the railroad and sold it piecemeal. Members instead passed legislation giving management greater flexibility to improve efficiency (PL 97-35) and to allow the railroad to be sold intact if it was profitable. *(1981 Almanac p. 561)*

New management, led by chairman L. Stanley Crane, who took over in 1981, used those reforms to revive the railroad. Since 1981 it cut its labor force in half and reduced route mileage by 25 percent. Conrail took its last federal subsidy in June 1981 and began showing a profit. In 1984, it made a $500 million profit, and in 1985, it made $440 million despite restoring wages to industry standards.

DOT set a June 18, 1984, deadline for offers to purchase Conrail and received 15 bids. It narrowed the list to three, but it became clear that a sale to any of the three finalists would be controversial.

Opposition to Dole's choice of Norfolk Southern centered on the fact that Norfolk Southern and Conrail competed in some areas. DOT asked the Justice Department to study the antitrust implications of the sale. Its report identified more than 100 markets in 21 states where a merger "could have a significant anti-competitive effect." The Justice Department required that Norfolk Southern sell or lease track rights to smaller railroads in affected areas. Norfolk Southern agreed to do so.

Dole said that the Justice Department's conditions should protect shippers by guaranteeing that they would have as many routes to choose from as they did before the sale. But that did not satisfy critics, who claimed that the Justice Department study represented only the tip of the iceberg with regard to potential antitrust problems.

In late November, the Justice Department announced that it found a revised purchase plan "quite different and vastly improved" from earlier versions and gave its tentative approval. But the preliminary approval turned out to be based on Norfolk Southern's data. At year's end, the Justice Department was conducting a full-scale review.

Some members also charged that DOT's proposal would not recover enough of the more than $7 billion the government had sunk into Conrail. DOT countered that the bidding showed that no one would pay more than $1.2 billion, and that Conrail's 1984 profits were artificially high because its workers were paid 12 percent less than the industry standard and because it paid no state taxes.

Studies of the Merger

In addition to hearings, Congress also examined a barrage of studies on the effects of a merger between Norfolk Southern and Conrail. Some of their conclusions challenged the rationale put forward by DOT and Norfolk Southern for the sale. Members were particularly interested in reports by the U.S. Railway Association (USRA), an agency set up by Congress to oversee Conrail.

Among the topics examined were these:

• **Conrail's Viability.** A USRA study released in July concluded that Conrail would continue to make a profit for the foreseeable future and could stand alone as an independent company. That undercut DOT's basic rationale for selling Conrail, which was that Conrail would need a parent company to support it in bad times.

The Federal Railroad Administration (FRA) challenged the USRA analysis. "The [USRA] proposal to sell off Conrail's assets and increase its debts to pay dividends is reminiscent of the Penn Central in its last years before bankruptcy," FRA said.

• **Financial Aspects.** A Congressional Budget Office (CBO) study released in June estimated that selling Conrail to Norfolk Southern would bring $1.4 billion in revenues in 1986 and would save the government another $10 million per year in payments to compensate laid-off workers. But it estimated that the government would lose a potential $400 million in tax revenues and $800 million in interest and dividend payments over the next five years, almost as much as the sale price. Critics of the sale said that despite Norfolk Southern's offer to forgo some tax benefits, it would retain others that could save the corporation more than the purchase price.

• **Traffic Diversions.** USRA and the staff of the Interstate Commerce Commission (ICC) both produced studies showing that a combined Norfolk Southern-Conrail system would divert a significant amount of traffic away from other railroads, particularly in the Midwest. Critics of the sale said such a development would weaken those railroads.

The FRA responded that "diversions are a normal consequence of rail mergers and a desirable consequence as they represent efficiencies that translate into lower rates and improved service to shippers."

• **Competition.** In line with the Justice Department's recommendation that Norfolk Southern sell some track and routes to smaller railroads, Norfolk Southern reached agreements with Guilford, and Pittsburgh & Lake Erie (P&LE). But critics questioned whether the railroads were strong enough to provide true competition.

A study by the staff of the ICC and Florio's panel, released in September, concluded that neither the Guilford nor P&LE plans would be financially sound, because of the financial weakness of the firms or because of the poor outlook for the lines they proposed to acquire.

Senate Committee Action

S 638 to implement the sale to Norfolk Southern Corp. was approved by the Senate Commerce, Science and Transportation Committee by a 12-5 vote April 30.

Chairman Danforth had attempted a markup April 18, but Larry Pressler, R-S.D., forced a delay so that he could study agreements to give Midwestern railroads access to Conrail routes after a merger.

On April 30, Pressler offered an amendment that would protect other railroads against loss of traffic by freezing current arrangements those railroads had with Conrail and Norfolk Southern. That would prevent the merged railroad from offering lower rates for shipments on its own tracks than for shipments that moved over two railroads.

Danforth said Pressler's amendment could hurt shippers and might cause Norfolk Southern to withdraw its offer. The plan was defeated, 3-14.

In the final vote ordering the bill reported, Pressler was joined in opposing S 638 by four Democrats: Wendell H. Ford, Ky.; Donald W. Riegle Jr., Mich.; J. James Exon, Neb., and John D. Rockefeller IV, W.Va.

Among the 12 voting for it was Paul S. Trible Jr., R-Va. Both Norfolk Southern and its chief opponent, CSX Corporation, were based in Virginia.

As reported, S 638 allowed the transportation secretary to sell Conrail to Norfolk Southern according to the terms of a "memorandum of intent" signed by DOT and Norfolk Southern officials Feb. 8.

The legislation would forgive approximately $3.2 billion that Conrail owed in return for government aid. It also removed other statutory conditions that would prevent a private owner from operating the railroad and gave antitrust protection to Norfolk Southern for merging Conrail with the Norfolk Southern's two railroads.

The committee adopted by voice vote a series of amendments by Danforth to tighten the terms of the sale. One amendment provided that the sale would not become final until the Justice Department approved arrangements by Norfolk Southern to give smaller railroads sections of track to ensure competition.

Others required the transportation secretary to notify Congress of any waiver of covenants that DOT negotiated to protect Conrail's operations, and establish a complaint procedure for shippers or other railroads.

The committee also adopted by voice vote two amendments by Ford to give employees of any railroad who lost their jobs as a result of the sale first rights to be hired when a vacancy occurred.

Late Flurry of Activity

The last weeks of the session saw a flurry of activity, as sale backers tried to meet Norfolk Southern's requirement for "substantial progress" by Dec. 31 toward approving its offer. The week of Dec. 2, the bill was listed on the Senate schedule as a priority item for several days, and Capitol Hill swarmed with lobbyists ready for battle.

But opponents, led by Metzenbaum and Specter, used a variety of parliamentary tools to block action. Metzenbaum warned that he would fight the bill with every available method, including an all-out filibuster, a tactic of which he was a master. He had the support of Specter; Larry Pressler, R-S.D.; John Heinz, R-Pa.; and several other senators.

Norfolk Southern officials said they would keep their offer open after Majority Leader Dole announced Dec. 20, the last day of the session, that S 638 would be the Senate's first order of business in 1986.

Morgan Stanley and Co. extended its $1.2 billion offer to June 30.

A third bid was made Dec. 17 by Allen & Co. Inc. and First Boston Corp. They offered $1.4 billion, plus $250 million from Conrail's cash reserves if they exceeded $900 million. All the bids would deal with the 15 percent owned by rail labor separately.

DOT officials noted that the Allen offer did not include restrictive covenants negotiated with Norfolk Southern designed to preserve Conrail's viability, nor did Allen propose to give up $300 million in potential investment tax credits, as both other offers did. The buyer would still receive some tax advantages from buying Conrail. ∎

Debt Collection

The House passed a bill intended to protect the public from harassment by some attorneys in the debt collection business, but there was no further action before adjournment.

The legislation (HR 237 — H Rept 99-405), passed by voice vote Dec. 2, would repeal an exemption for lawyers that was contained in the 1977 Fair Debt Collection Practices Act (PL 95-109). *(1977 Almanac p. 761)*

That law did not apply to lawyers because even though they collected funds for third parties, they were not thought to be "debt collectors," explained Frank Annunzio, D-Ill., chairman of the Banking, Finance and Urban Affairs Subcommittee on Consumer Affairs.

However, some lawyers had formed collection agencies, advertised their exemption from the law and acted in an unethical manner, he charged.

"Complaints to bar associations have brought little or no action against lawyers who use questionable tactics in debt collection," Annunzio said.

John Hiler, R-Ind., opposed the bill, arguing that it was not needed and that the Federal Trade Commission already had authority to police lawyers engaged in abusive or unfair practices. He said that attorneys who collected debts on behalf of clients should continue to be exempt from the debt collection act but that the exemption should be clarified to "eliminate its abuse by misguided lawyers." ∎

Banking Bills Fail to Reach House Floor

Legislation to allow nationwide interstate banking languished in the House Rules Committee as the 1985 session ended, blocked from floor consideration by Rules Committee Chairman Claude Pepper, D-Fla.

One bill (HR 2707 — H Rept 99-174) would introduce coast-to-coast branch banking July 1, 1990. On that date, states that allowed banks from their regions to open branches also would have to open their borders to banks from any other state with a regional banking law.

Pepper, whose home state of Florida had a regional banking law, did not want his state to be forced to welcome states outside the Southeast.

A related bill (HR 20 — H Rept 99-175) would close a loophole through which banks and other companies had circumvented the longstanding federal ban on interstate banking and established limited-service banks. The so-called "non-bank bank" bill became entangled in the nationwide banking stalemate and did not emerge from the Rules Committee either.

However, a Jan. 22, 1986, decision by the U.S. Supreme Court that the Federal Reserve Board and state bank regulators did not have the authority to restrain the proliferation of limited service non-bank banks might boost the stalled legislation in the second session.

Like Pepper, Senate Banking Committee Chairman Jake Garn, R-Utah, also was from a regional banking state and opposed any legislation that would force states to phase in nationwide banking in 1990. In addition, Garn contended that Congress need not take up the interstate banking issue because the U.S. Supreme Court June 10 upheld the constitutionality of states' regional banking laws.

Further, Garn said that he would not accept a bill that simply closed loopholes; he wanted a broad deregulation bill that would grant new powers to financial institutions, including allowing them to deal in certain securities. However, despite vows to do so, Garn did not introduce a deregulation bill in the first session.

In 1984, the Senate approved his proposal 89-5, but it died in the House because of the opposition of Fernand J. St Germain, D-R.I., chairman of the House Banking, Finance and Urban Affairs Committee. *(1984 Almanac p. 271)*

Nationwide Banking

The House Banking Committee, by a surprisingly wide margin, approved HR 2707 June 12. The bill, ordered reported by a vote of 31-18, was similar to one endorsed by an 18-12 vote June 5 by the Banking Subcommittee on Financial Institutions Supervision, Regulation and Insurance.

The bill would lift a longtime federal ban against banks opening branches in other states. Its passage could portend a revolution in the U.S. banking structure, a system built on the fear of big banks and belief in states' rights. The existing system of more than 14,000 mostly small and locally controlled banks could give way to a spate of mergers and acquisitions, leaving larger firms controlling branches coast-to-coast.

The legislation would sanction state laws that limited interstate banking to firms within a region. Such laws, enacted by at least 16 states since 1982, were largely intended to bar big banks from New York and California.

However, the bill would require any state with a regional law to permit entry to banks from any state with interstate banking laws after July 1, 1990, or two years after the state passed its regional law, whichever was later.

Until the markup, the so-called "trigger" in HR 2707 requiring states to move from regional to nationwide banking had been thought so controversial that, in April, St Germain had said only New Yorkers and Californians would vote for it.

The issue of interstate banking had split the financial industry sharply. Big banks, eager to reach new customers in an expanded market, said nationwide banking would promote competition and provide consumers with more choices for credit and investments. Smaller banks countered that concentration, not competition, would result, with large firms swallowing local institutions, replacing hometown bankers sensitive to the credit needs of local residents.

Federal banking regulators supported nationwide banking, but state officials were opposed, arguing that federal law gave them the right to determine whether to welcome out-of-state banks.

But the subcommittee's endorsement June 5 after a 10-hour session signaled growing support. Even so, St Germain said, the 13-vote margin of victory "was more substantial than we had anticipated."

Court Decision on Regional Banking

The panel apparently was little influenced by the Supreme Court's 8-0 ruling June 10 upholding the constitutionality of regional banking laws. The case, *Northeast Bancorp Inc. et.al. v. Board of Governors of the Federal Reserve System,* involved a challenge by several large banks to Massachusetts and Connecticut laws that barred the acquisition of their banks by banks from states outside New England. *(Court, p. 13-A)*

The challenges were led by Citicorp, the nation's largest bank, and Northeast Bancorp, a Connecticut bank barred by Connecticut law from merging with the Bank of New York. They argued that regional banking networks were illegal under the 1956 Bank Holding Company Act, which generally prohibited interstate banking. They also contended that the regional laws were an unconstitutional barrier to interstate commerce.

Initially, observers had expected the decision to bolster the arguments of regional banking proponents who opposed a trigger to nationwide banking.

But in the end, Charles E. Schumer, D-N.Y., a supporter of nationwide banking, said the ruling "did not enter very strongly into [members'] calculations."

Contrary to earlier expectations, if the ruling had an effect at all, it may have been to the advantage of those who supported nationwide banking.

A lobbyist for the Independent Bankers Association of America, which opposed interstate banking on behalf of 7,400 small banks, said some members may have grown concerned that the court ruling would spark regional warfare and a "Balkanized" banking system of the sort Federal Reserve Board Chairman Paul A. Volcker had warned about.

Volcker's April 24 proposal for a transition from regional to nationwide banking was considered a major reason for the committee's approval of a trigger bill.

Attacks Rebuffed

The committee easily rebuffed critics' attacks. First, by a 17-32 vote, members rejected a motion by Doug Barnard Jr., D-Ga., to postpone the bill indefinitely.

Barnard argued that the Supreme Court had upheld the right of states to enact regional laws, making Congress' blessing unnecessary. He urged the panel not to go beyond the ruling by endorsing a transition to nationwide banking.

Barnard, whose state of Georgia was part of a Southeastern banking region, objected that a trigger "is just a sly way to enact full nationwide banking — with or without the individual state's approval."

John J. LaFalce, D-N.Y., countered that regional banking would lead to a "hodgepodge of conflicting state laws for many years to come."

After his postponement motion failed, Barnard offered a substitute bill authorizing regional banking without a trigger. To win support, he added antitrust safeguards and consumer-protection provisions. He lost, 19-30.

By a 10-31 vote, the panel then defeated an amendment by Bruce F. Vento, D-Minn., that would allow a state to implement a regional banking law until July 1, 1990, after which regional banking would end and the state would not have to participate in nationwide banking.

The bill, as approved, would allow a state to avoid nationwide banking by not enacting a regional banking law; those that had regional laws already could escape the trigger by not allowing any regional acquisitions to occur.

That escape provision answered some members' concerns about states' rights, supporters said.

Antitrust Protections

Other major provisions addressed longstanding fears that interstate banking would lead to monopolistic growth, with big banks siphoning money from communities and leaving local businesses and residents without credit funds or affordable services.

The panel voted to strengthen the subcommittee's antitrust safeguards. That version would have prevented the Fed from approving mergers among the 25 biggest banks and savings and loans (S&Ls); any deals giving a bank holding company control of 2.5 percent of all U.S. deposits (unless the acquired bank was new or had less than $100 million in assets); or acquisitions violating antitrust law of a state where a bank to be acquired was located.

No U.S. banking institution held 2.5 percent of domestic deposits as of mid-1984, according to committee data; San Francisco-based BankAmerica Corp. had 2.46 percent. Therefore, several members complained the antitrust cap in the subcommittee bill was too high.

Schumer proposed tightening the antitrust provision, and Vento offered an even stricter alternative.

But the committee, by a 39-10 vote, settled for a compromise proposed by Jim Leach, R-Iowa.

The bill, as amended, would bar interstate deals giving any company control of 1 percent of U.S. deposits. Based on the 1984 data, three bank giants exceeded that cap — BankAmerica, Citicorp of New York and First Interstate Bancorp of Los Angeles.

Under the bill, such big companies could expand interstate only by buying failing banks and S&Ls, opening new banks or buying small ones with less than $100 million in assets.

Unchanged by Leach's amendment were the bill's antitrust bans of mergers among the top 25 institutions and deals violating state law.

Investing in the Community

The panel by voice vote accepted twin amendments imposing consumer safeguards on interstate deals.

One amendment would require the Fed, before approving a bank holding company's planned acquisition, to determine that it would improve credit and deposit services, especially for low- to moderate-income customers and small businesses.

Regulators also would have to review the holding company's record of community investment. Public hearings could be held on a proposal. If it was approved, the firm would have to file periodic reports of its activity in the new area, which regulators would evaluate and make public.

A related amendment would require the Federal Home Loan Bank Board, which regulated S&Ls, to apply the same tests to S&L holding companies that applied to move interstate.

The subcommittee had rejected the proposals because members had not studied them. Afterwards, their cosponsors, Schumer and Mary Rose Oakar, D-Ohio, had lobbied colleagues and made some changes.

Non-Bank Banks

Before agreeing to open the door to nationwide banking, the committee voted to close a loophole through which banks and non-banks alike had evaded the ban on interstate banking.

However, the bill it approved (HR 20) protected 109 interstate firms approved by federal regulators before May 9, 1984.

Since 1983, companies had filed more than 400 applications with federal regulators to open limited-service branches, known as "non-bank banks." By not offering both demand deposits, such as checking accounts, and commercial loans, the offices were not "banks" as defined by U.S. law and thus were free of key restrictions.

Banks could open offices unrestricted by the ban on interstate banking. And non-banking firms, such as Sears, Roebuck and Co. and J. C. Penney Co., could skirt a federal law banning commercial firms from banking.

Both banks and other businesses rushed to open the limited-purpose banks since 1983, when Comptroller of the Currency C. Todd Conover, the primary regulator of national banks and a proponent of nationwide banking, encouraged them to seek charters from his office.

In Congress, non-bank banks were widely opposed as blatant circumventions of the law's intent. But proposals to close the loophole foundered in a stalemate between St Germain and Garn over broader legislation to deregulate banking.

The anti-deregulation House Banking Committee chairman in introducing HR 20 said: "While there is wide divergence of opinion about what the future of the financial community should be, I sense an overwhelming concern about these non-bank banks and a desire to end this backdoor silliness forthwith."

Panel's Approval Expected

The easy voice-vote approval of HR 20, which redefined "bank" to close the loophole, was expected. The major argument was over whether any of the non-bank banks should be divested by their parent companies.

St Germain's bill originally would have let any limited-purpose banks formed before July 1, 1983, escape divestiture. But he changed the date to May 9, 1984, to win support in his committee and the Rules Committee. That protected 21 more firms than the earlier date, including such firms as E. F. Hutton Group Inc. and Merrill Lynch & Co.

During full committee markup, Bill McCollum, R-Fla., proposed to protect 88 non-bank banks formed before July 1, 1983. He lost, 15-30.

Marcy Kaptur, D-Ohio, attempted to make the date Oct. 15, 1982, which would have protected only about 35 banks. She lost by voice vote.

A proposal by Buddy Roemer, D-La., that all loophole banks be divested lost by a close vote, 23-26, indicating broad dissatisfaction with allowing such major firms as E. F. Hutton Group Inc. and Merrill Lynch & Co. Inc. to avoid giving up their non-bank banks.

But St Germain argued that the bill could not pass the Rules Committee or the floor without the provision protecting 109 firms.

The committee also relaxed a provision in the subcommittee bill requiring an S&L holding company with one S&L subsidiary to have at least 65 percent of its assets in mortgage-related investments. If the company did not meet the test, it would be subject to the same restrictions applied to S&L holding companies with multiple S&L subsidiaries.

Because of its traditional role in housing, the S&L industry was largely free of federal restrictions on geographic expansion and ownership by non-banking firms.

Volcker had urged Congress to boost the asset test for S&Ls, complaining that many were neglecting their role in housing because recent laws gave them some powers of commercial banks.

Frank Annunzio, D-Ill., backed by the S&L industry, won voice-vote acceptance of his amendment making two changes in the subcommittee provision that Volcker supported.

As approved, HR 20 would allow an S&L to count more of its holdings in government obligations, such as housing bonds issued by the Federal Home Loan Mortgage Corp. (Freddie Mac), in meeting the asset test. Also, an S&L could count mortgage loans that it had made and then sold to investors within 90 days.

The Fed version had limited the allowance for government obligations and precluded consideration of mortgage resales in meeting the 65 percent asset test.

The 'Wendy's Amendment'

In return for the relaxed test, Annunzio included in his amendment a provision sought by Edwin J. Gray, chairman of the Federal Home Loan Bank Board, the S&L regulator who lobbied members moments before the markup began.

The provision, dubbed the "Wendy's amendment," would allow the bank board to draw a list of non-financial activities — such as ownership of hamburger franchises — that would be off-limits to S&Ls that were state-chartered but federally insured. Federally chartered S&Ls already were subject to such regulations.

Gray was less successful in lobbying against the interstate trigger in HR 2707. He said the promise of nationwide banking would dissuade banks from acquiring failing S&Ls. Many out-of-state banks had become rescuers of financially threatened S&Ls as a way to cross state lines.

"Why take a failing thrift (S&L) to get into another state when you know there is a certainty that in five years, you will have nationwide banking?" Gray asked.

Non-Bank Bank Court Decision

In its decision Jan. 22, 1986, the Supreme Court made it clear that Congress must amend the nation's banking laws if it intended to bring non-bank banks within the reach of federal regulation.

By a vote of 8-0, the court ruled that the Federal Reserve Board of Governors exceeded its authority to administer the Bank Holding Company Act of 1956 when it redefined key terms in that law in an effort to bring the new types of banks within its jurisdiction.

"Without doubt there is much to be said for regulating" the limited-service banks, wrote Chief Justice Warren E. Burger. But "if the Bank Holding Company Act falls short of providing safeguards desirable or necessary to protect the public interest, that is a problem for Congress, and not the board or the courts, to address," he said.

After the ruling, St Germain said that the court's decision might make it possible to pry HR 20 out of Rules.

In 1984 the Fed changed its definition of a bank, defining demand deposits to include NOW accounts — which did not give a depositor a legal right to withdraw his money on demand but were as a matter of practice payable on demand. In addition, the Fed redefined "commercial loan" to include any loan other than a loan to an individual for personal, family, household or charitable purposes, including certificates of deposit.

The Reagan administration opposed the Fed's move, telling the Supreme Court in September that the Fed was attempting to "usurp congressional power over fundamental questions of banking policy."

Deciding the case of *Board of Governors, Federal Reserve System v. Dimension Financial Corp.*, the court agreed with the administration. Justice Byron R. White did not take part. ∎

Government Securities Firms

Scandals within the government-securities industry gave impetus to legislation imposing new rules on the industry, but no bill was enacted in the first session.

The House by voice vote Sept. 17 suspended the rules and passed a bill to police unregulated government securities firms in an effort to prevent costly failures that could undermine confidence in the U.S. economy. There was no action on a similar measure (S 1416) pending in the Senate Banking, Housing and Urban Affairs Committee.

The House, in approving the bill (HR 2032 — H Rept 99-258), rejected a late bid by the Treasury Department to block the legislation. Secretary James A. Baker III in a letter to House Speaker Thomas P. O'Neill Jr., D-Mass., said he opposed the bill and wanted time to develop his own proposal.

John D. Dingell, D-Mich., chairman of the Energy and Commerce Committee, which approved the bill July 31, complained that the Treasury Department had been "naysaying" the legislation during the two years it had been under consideration. Meanwhile, he said, the worldwide economy had been jarred by the collapse of several government securities firms, which buy and sell Treasury bills, notes and bonds to finance the federal debt.

"Failures of government securities dealers have been going on under Treasury's nose since 1977 and have cost investors approximately $1 billion in losses," Dingell said.

"Treasury . . . says that we should stop the train and wait for them to develop their own legislation. My response is: 'Where have they been?' " he added.

Key Republicans also urged quick passage, including James T. Broyhill of North Carolina, the ranking minority member on Energy and Commerce, and Matthew J. Rinaldo of New Jersey, ranking member of the Subcommittee on Telecommunications, Consumer Protection and Finance.

Self-Regulatory Board

There were 36 "primary" government securities dealers, including the nation's top banks and investment firms, that bought about $4 billion in securities directly from the Federal Reserve Board each day.

There were about 500 "secondary dealers" that bought Treasury securities from primary dealers and sold them to investors, typically cities and financial institutions. Secondary dealers included banks, which were regulated by federal agencies; broker-dealers supervised by the Securities and Exchange Commission (SEC); and about 100 unregulated dealers.

The bill, intended to reach the unregulated dealers, was a compromise reached by panel members, the industry and regulators, including Paul A. Volcker, chairman of the Fed.

It called for the Fed to create a nine-member Government Securities Regulatory Board with members from industry, investors and the public. The board, with Fed oversight, would make rules for registration and recordkeeping, and establish financial requirements for dealers.

The SEC would enforce the law, with power to censure dealers or revoke their registration. U.S. banking regulators would retain authority over financial institutions that were dealers.

The lack of supervision led to the failure of unregulated government securities companies, which had international consequences, according to Telecommunications Subcommittee Chairman Timothy E. Wirth, D-Colo.

He cited the March collapse of ESM Government Securities, which resulted in the loss of more than $300 million to investors, including Ohio's Home State Savings Bank. A run on that Ohio bank led to a statewide crisis that closed 71 privately insured savings and loan institutions and undermined confidence in the dollar abroad, he said.

Administration Objections

Baker said the regulatory system would disrupt the market for U.S. Treasury obligations, leading to higher financing costs and larger budget deficits. He said the Treasury, not the Fed, should manage the federal debt and urged that the Treasury secretary's authority be expanded to assure that securities dealers met standards.

Wirth, calling the department "a Johnny-come-lately to the facts," said the charge that costs would increase had been countered by testimony before his subcommittee. ∎

Product Liability Stalled

The Senate Commerce, Science and Transportation Committee May 16 failed to approve a bill (S 100) that had been pushed for years to change the nation's product liability laws.

The measure, which would set federal standards for lawsuits brought by victims charging they were injured by unsafe products, was blocked by an 8-8 tie vote that caught its backers by surprise. Similar legislation (S 44) was approved by the committee in 1984 by a vote of 11-5, but it never reached the Senate floor. *(1984 Almanac p. 296)*

"We missed it," said John C. Danforth, R-Mo., chairman of the committee, after the May 16 meeting. "I had assumed the vote would be 9-7."

Bob Kasten, R-Wis., the bill's sponsor, said that he had been counting on the vote of J. James Exon, D-Neb. Exon, who backed the legislation in 1984, voted "no" by proxy. He was in the hospital, recovering from gall bladder surgery.

Danforth and Kasten said they hoped to bring the bill back to the committee after hearings on a subject in which several senators expressed interest: setting up an alternative to the courts for recovering damages in product liability cases.

However, HR 100 was not brought before the committee again.

Background

Product liability laws were the focus of fierce struggles in both the 97th and 98th Congresses between manufacturers, who sought a federal law, and trial lawyers, unions, consumer groups, state judges and attorneys general, who opposed most changes. *(1984 Almanac p. 296; 1982 Almanac p. 330)*

Proponents said federal action was needed because conflicting laws and excessive judgments in some states threatened interstate commerce. S 100 would have preempted state laws to provide uniform standards to be applied in state courts.

The key provision in S 100 would have required plaintiffs suing a manufacturer for injuries caused by a product to prove negligence by the manufacturer. Most state laws, to one degree or another, did not require such proof.

Kasten dropped a controversial 1984 provision that would have allowed only one victim to receive punitive damages even if hundreds were injured by a defective product.

Opponents claimed that S 100 would confuse, rather than simplify, the legal situation, would violate states' rights and would result in denying victims compensation for injuries. They contended that the fear of large damage claims was necessary to pressure manufacturers to be sure their products were safe. ∎

Improving Air First Aid

After years of prodding by congressional and consumer critics, the federal government in 1985 began addressing complaints that the medical supplies on commercial flights were inadequate.

The Federal Aviation Administration (FAA) began drafting rules to require planes to carry more extensive supplies, including diagnostic equipment and certain drugs. The Senate July 31 approved legislation (S 63 — S Rept 99-93) that would give the agency six months after enactment to write final rules.

The airline industry fought the proposal, saying that additional medical supplies were unnecessary and potentially dangerous. But faced with the likelihood that the requirement would be imposed, the industry urged Congress to provide protection against lawsuits arising from the improper use of the equipment.

The FAA currently required planes to carry only limited first-aid supplies, such as bandages and burn ointment. Critics such as Sen. Barry Goldwater, R-Ariz., said such supplies were useless in dealing with conditions requiring immediate treatment such as heart attacks.

The FAA estimated that about 21 people a year died as a result of in-flight medical emergencies, although other estimates ran as high as 100 deaths annually.

Airline spokesmen warned that medications and other supplies could be misused if they fell into unqualified hands. They maintained that the best way to handle medical emergencies in flight was to land quickly and get the passenger appropriate medical care.

The regulations proposed by the FAA would require commercial planes to carry such items as a stethoscope, scalpel and drugs for such conditions as severe allergic reactions.

The FAA in 1982 had denied a petition from two consumer groups to draft such rules. But in 1983 the FAA was ordered by a federal appeals court to reconsider the issue. The proposed rules were published in the March 14 *Federal Register*.

The FAA did not have the authority to propose rules to relieve individuals of liability if they used the kit to assist others. Airline officials argued that without such protections against lawsuits, people would not take the risk of using the medical kits.

As reported June 27 by the Senate Commerce Committee, S 63 granted immunity to physicians, crew members and the airlines, unless medical supplies were used recklessly or with gross negligence. But the Senate adopted an amendment by Goldwater that dropped the "good Samaritan" protections for airlines.

As approved, S 63 provided protections against lawsuits only to nurses, paramedics and crew members. Physicians were not exempted from liability because it was expected that they would be protected by malpractice insurance, aides said. ∎

Check 'Holds' Limited

Members of the House took steps in 1985 to limit the length of time that banks could hold checks before letting customers use the money.

Their target was what critics called the "float game," referring to the practice of banks holding up access to a deposit until the check had cleared. Banks said the practice was to be sure the checks did not bounce. But consumer advocates said banks "flotated" checks, not to see if they were bad, since only about 1 percent were returned, but to earn millions by loaning the money and earning interest.

A bill (HR 2443 — H Rept 99-404) to limit holds to one to six days, depending on the type of check, and halve maximum delays to three days within three years of enactment was reported Nov. 26 by the House Banking, Finance and Urban Affairs Committee. The House passed the bill in early 1986.

Related bills pending in the Senate generally would give banks and federal regulators more flexibility than the House bill.

Under the committee bill, customers immediately would have next-day access to checks of $100 or less, checks drawn on in-state branches of the same institution, cashier's and certified checks, and government checks.

In the first year, banks would have up to two business days after deposit to clear all other local checks. In the next two years, they would have no more than one business day.

"Local" was defined broadly to include checks from institutions within the same state or check-clearing region of the Federal Reserve System. The Fed, which acted as a clearinghouse for payments between U.S. banks, had 48 such districts.

In the first three years, delays of up to six days would be permitted for checks drawn on accounts in institutions from other states or Fed check-clearing regions. Within three years, the Fed would have to establish a permanent check-clearing process giving customers access to funds in one to three days.

While banking industry groups generally opposed the measure, the most notable opposition came from the Fed board, which called instead for technological improvements in the clearing system and for voluntary disclosure by banks of their check-hold policies.

Changes in Committee

The committee adopted several amendments.

One, approved by voice vote, would allow the Fed to suspend the act if it caused banks to suffer "unacceptable" losses from fraud. The suspension would be limited to 45 days to allow congressional review.

The panel also voted, 28-21, to cap the amount of a check available for early withdrawal to $5,000 a day, rather than $5,000 *a check*. The idea was to prevent con artists from breaking large, fraudulent deposits into $5,000 chunks.

Another change approved by voice vote would set a $5,000 limit on the amount available one day after a customer opened a new account with a large bank-issued check, such as a cashier's check. The bill initially had no cap on next-day access to such deposits.

By a 28-21 vote, the committee agreed to require banks to pay customers interest on their checks from the time the banks received provisional credit from the Fed and began earning interest on the amount themselves. The bill initially had required that banks pay interest from the time of deposit. Members said the change would not reduce customers' interest much since banks got same-day credit for most checks.

All Banks Covered

The bill would apply to all financial institutions, whether chartered by the states or the federal government. States or banking institutions still could impose their own check-hold limits if those were more generous to consumers than the federal version.

Several states had passed anti-float laws and, according to the Banking Committee, more than a dozen others would consider measures in 1986.

The legislation was a priority of the Consumer Federation of America and other consumer groups that mobilized in 1985 to seek consumer-oriented changes in banking. Their targets included high credit card rates and banking service charges. ∎

FTC Bill Stalled

The House and Senate were unable to settle their differences in 1985 on legislation (S 1078) reauthorizing the Federal Trade Commission (FTC).

The bills set similar funding levels. The House would authorize $63.9 million for fiscal 1986, $64.2 million for 1987 and $64.3 million for 1988; the Senate would authorize $65.8 million in 1986, with $1 million increases for each of the following two years.

And both versions were silent on FTC regulation of such professionals as doctors and lawyers, an issue that had helped block reauthorization since 1982.

But there were substantial differences on other issues that staff was unable to resolve in preparation for a conference. Conferees did not meet.

The Senate version would extend a 1980 law barring the FTC from initiating rules on an industrywide basis that would regulate advertising on the grounds that it was an unfair act or practice. The House-passed measure did not address the ban, and members objected to the Senate proposal. *(1980 Almanac p. 233)*

The chambers also disagreed on how Congress should veto agency rules. The Senate bill would permit Congress to veto rules of both the FTC and Consumer Product Safety Commission (CPSC) by passing a joint resolution signed by the president. The House measure applied only to the FTC.

In addition, the Senate set up procedures to speed up a veto, while the House provided no expedited procedures. House members also disapproved of the Senate's allowing Congress to hold up appropriations to implement rules vetoed by Congress.

Legislative History

Senate. S 1078 was passed by the Senate July 26 by a vote of 84-5. *(Vote 165, p. 33-S)*

It had been reported (S Rept 99-81) June 11 by the Commerce, Science and Transportation Committee.

The veto provision, a compromise proposed by Bob Kasten, R-Wis., would allow FTC and CPSC regulations to be overturned if a resolution of disapproval were passed by Congress and signed by the president. If Congress did not act, rules would take effect 90 days after being submitted to Congress.

Kasten said the procedure was constitutional because it required White House approval, unlike past legislative-veto mechanisms struck down by the Supreme Court in 1983.

After approving the Kasten amendment 67-22, the Senate accepted a proposal by Charles E. Grassley, R-Iowa, setting up procedures for amending appropriations bills to deny funds to implement FTC and CPSC rules vetoed by Congress, in the event the president vetoed the disapproval resolution. It was adopted by voice vote after a motion to table it failed, 34-56. *(Votes 163, 164, p. 33-S)*

The Senate killed, 71-26, an amendment by James A.

Amtrak, Highways and Public TV Supported

Funding for Amtrak, highways and public television would have been reauthorized by the budget reconciliation bill (HR 3128) that stalled as the first session of the 99th Congress came to a close.

However, agreements reached on those programs were not in dispute when Congress refused to take final action on the conference report (H Rept 99-453) before adjourning Dec. 20. Appropriations for Amtrak and highways were provided by the continuing resolution (PL 99-190) funding government agencies. *(Reconciliation, p. 498; continuing resolution, p. 360)*

Highlights of the authorizations included:

- **Amtrak.** Members rejected President Reagan's plan to cut off funding for the national passenger railroad, which got $684 million in fiscal 1985. Reagan argued that if the service was needed, it should be supported by state or local funds or by fare increases.

Members, particularly from the Northeast, charged that ending subsidies would wipe out a rail system that each year carried 20 million persons through 44 states. They said that while Amtrak had improved its performance, it was still losing money and no one other than the federal government could take it over.

The House Sept. 19 passed a one-year authorization (HR 2266 — H Rept 99-149) setting fiscal 1986 funding at $603.5 million. The Senate, which did not pass a separate bill, in its reconciliation measure proposed $582 million in fiscal 1986; $606.1 million in 1987; and $630.3 million in 1988.

The reconciliation agreement called for $600 million, $606.1 million and $603.5 million, respectively.

The fiscal 1986 appropriation included in the continuing resolution was $616 million.

- **Highways.** The fiscal 1985 ceiling on spending from the Highway Trust Fund, which financed major highway programs, was $13.25 billion and was to rise to $14.45 billion in 1986 under a 1982 law (PL 97-424). *(1982 Almanac p. 317)*

The reconciliation conference report would set the ceiling at $13.125 billion in fiscal 1986; $13.525 billion in 1987; and $14.1 billion for 1988. Those levels were slightly lower than proposed by the House and slightly higher than the Senate level.

The fiscal 1986 stopgap funding bill established a ceiling of $12.75 million.

- **Corporation for Public Broadcasting.** Members continued to support federal funding for CPB, the private, non-profit trustee for appropriations for public broadcasting. Reagan had consistently called for sharp funding cuts and twice in 1984 vetoed legislation that authorized spending far above his request. *(1984 Almanac p. 288)*

The reconciliation conferees wanted to retain "strong support" for the public broadcast system and recommended $200 million for fiscal 1987, $214 million for 1988, $238 million for 1989 and $254 million for 1990. The fiscal 1987 and 1988 appropriations, enacted two years in advance, was for $200 million and $214 million, respectively.

Conferees also rejected the administration plan to stop funding the Public Telecommunications Facilities Program, which provided grants for planning and constructing non-commercial TV and radio stations. The conference agreement would set funding levels at $24 million in fiscal 1986, $28 million in 1987 and $32 million in 1988.

McClure, R-Idaho, curbing the FTC's authority to regulate professionals. It would have limited the FTC's ability to pre-empt state laws regulating the qualifications and licensing of professions, such as medicine and law. As approved, S 1078 was silent on the issue. *(Vote 161, p. 32-S)*

House Action. The House Sept. 17 by voice vote passed HR 2385, which had been reported June 6 (H Rept 99-162) by the Energy and Commerce Committee. It then amended its text to S 1078, and sent the measure back to that chamber. ∎

CPSC Bill Fails

Efforts to enact the first authorization for the Consumer Product Safety Commission (CPSC) since 1981 failed when the bill became embroiled in controversy over amusement park rides.

The Senate July 24 passed an authorization (S 1077 — S Rept 99-60) after watering down a proposal that would have restored CPSC authority to inspect amusement park rides. But the House version failed Nov. 19 to win the two-thirds majority required to suspend the House rules and pass. The vote on the measure (HR 3456 — H Rept 99-377) was 264-146; 274 votes were needed. *(Vote 375, p. 118-H)*

Opposition to the bills centered on a provision restoring partial CPSC authority to regulate some fixed-site amusement-park rides. In 1981, Congress rescinded the CPSC authority over rides at permanent sites, leaving the commission only able to inspect rides or order repairs for traveling carnivals. However, members whose districts included amusement parks that had had serious accidents wanted to beef up inspection requirements. *(1984 Almanac p. 294)*

Legislative Action

The Senate July 24 by voice vote approved S 1077, a two-year CPSC authorization setting funding at $35 million annually, which would have been about $1 million less than the current appropriation.

Paul Simon, D-Ill., noting a rash of amusement park accidents, proposed an amendment allowing the CPSC to inspect rides.

John C. Danforth, R-Mo., chairman of the Commerce, Science and Transportation Committee, offered a substitute amendment to establish a commission to study amusement park safety. He argued that the CPSC did not use its existing inspection authority and that Simon's plan would infringe on state powers. Danforth's substitute was adopted, 52-41. *(Vote 160, p. 32-S)*

In the House, CPSC advocates noted that changes had been made in a 1984 version of the bill, which had passed the House but died in the Senate, partly because of industry opposition.

HR 3456, the 1985 bill, narrowed the CPSC inspection authority in an effort to compromise with the industry; for example, the new bill would not permit CPSC to issue industrywide rules.

Critics, however, contended that the issue was complex and should be thoroughly studied before the authority was bestowed.

HR 3456 would have reauthorized the CPSC for fiscal 1986-88 at a total of $114 million. It was reported by the Energy and Commerce Committee Nov. 18 after an earlier version (HR 2630) was dropped when it became enmeshed with a proposal to revise the CPSC board.

In that controversy, Henry A. Waxman, D-Calif., chairman of the Subcommittee on Health, wanted to cut the number of CPSC commissioners from five to three, and eliminate staff that would have been assigned to the two. Backers said the change would mean savings, but critics said it was an attempt to curtail presidential appointments. ∎

CPSC Chairman Blocked

The nomination of Terrence M. Scanlon to be chairman of the Consumer Product Safety Commission (CPSC) was stalled just before the close of the session.

Confronted Dec. 19 by critics trying to block the nomination, Majority Leader Robert Dole, R-Kan., agreed to put off a vote on Scanlon until Congress returned in 1986.

Sens. Paul Simon, D-Ill., and William Proxmire, D-Wis., objected to the nomination. Simon contended that Scanlon "absolutely has no business" being CPSC chairman and cited Scanlon's objection as a commissioner to reinstating some CPSC authority to inspect amusement park rides.

Simon had been pushing legislation to broaden CPSC amusement park inspections. *(Story, p. 280)*

Consumer Opposition

Consumer groups opposed the nomination. At his confirmation hearings, Joan Claybrook, president of Public Citizen, charged that Scanlon had used his staff to further anti-abortion and real estate activities.

Scanlon denied the charges, but after a CPSC employee said she had performed such work many times, Scanlon acknowledged he had requested her to perform some tasks.

John C. Danforth, R-Mo., chairman of the Commerce, Science and Transportation Committee, said an investigation by the General Accounting Office showed that while CPSC staff had run errands and typed letters relating to Scanlon's personal interests, the incidents had been infrequent and minor. Senators voting against confirmation said Scanlon had not been forthright in replying to the charges.

Scanlon, interim chairman since January 1985, was approved by a narrow 9-7 vote of the Commerce, Science and Transportation Committee.

Bob Packwood, R-Ore., and Nancy Landon Kassebaum, R-Kan., joined five Democrats in voting against Scanlon. Democrats Daniel K. Inouye of Hawaii and Donald W. Riegle Jr. of Michigan voted with the Republican majority. ∎

Titanic Memorial

The House approved a bill Dec. 2 encouraging efforts to designate the shipwreck of the luxury liner *Titanic* as an international maritime memorial and to fend off unwarranted salvage.

The measure (HR 3272 — H Rept 99-393) would direct the secretary of state to negotiate with other nations to develop an agreement providing for the designation of the shipwreck as a memorial and for guidelines governing research, exploration and salvage. It was reported by the Merchant Marine and Fisheries Committee Nov. 21.

The *Titanic* was discovered Sept. 1 by a U.S.-French research team in the North Atlantic at a depth of nearly 2.5 miles. The liner sank on its maiden voyage in 1912. ∎

Rail Safety

Both chambers passed legislation in 1985 aimed at strengthening U.S. rail safety programs, but members did not resolve differences over the measure before adjourning for the year.

The bill (S 1080 — S Rept 99-76), reported May 30 by the Senate Commerce, Science and Transportation Committee, was passed by the Senate by voice vote June 6. It authorized funding of $32.2 million in each of fiscal 1986 and 1987.

The version approved by the House Sept. 5 had been reported May 23 by the House Energy and Commerce Committee (HR 2372 — H Rept 99-147). The House amended its text to S 1080 before passing the Senate bill.

The House bill contained several provisions not passed by the Senate and opposed by the Reagan administration, including one that would allow railroad employees or their union to sue the Transportation Department to enforce safety laws.

The House bill authorized $40.9 million in fiscal 1986 and $42.9 million in 1987. The House rejected, 106-254, an amendment by Robert S. Walker, R-Pa., to cut $6.3 million over fiscal 1986-87 for reimbursements to states that conducted their own safety programs. The administration had not requested the funds. *(Vote 269, p. 86-H)* ∎

Airport Security

In response to the hijacking of a Trans World Airlines (TWA) jet with 40 Americans on board and other terrorist acts, the House and Senate passed legislation clarifying federal authority to assist foreign governments in improving airport security.

The measure (HR 2796), however, was not enacted, in deference to the anti-terrorist provisions contained in the foreign aid authorization (S 960) cleared by Congress July 31, according to an aide for the House Public Works and Transportation Subcommittee on Aviation. *(Story, p. 41)*

The House passed HR 2796 by voice vote June 19, five days after TWA flight 847 was hijacked following takeoff from the Athens airport. The bill required the Department of Transportation to study an airport's security and notify the public within 120 days if security risks had not been improved.

The Senate July 25 by a vote of 96-0 approved a broader version (S Rept 99-113) that allowed the Transportation secretary to bar U.S. carriers from using an airport identified as a security risk. *(Vote 162, p. 32-S)*

The foreign aid bill was more stringent, authorizing a boycott of foreign airports that failed to meet security standards and a cutoff of foreign aid to countries where such airports were located. ∎

Corporate Mergers

Throughout much of 1985 Congress struggled with complicated issues unleashed by a wave of corporate takeovers that sent buyers and their targets scrambling to Capitol Hill for legislative protection.

Although several committees held hearings on potential legislation involving tax, banking, antitrust and securities laws, only two panels advanced bills.

A House Judiciary subcommittee June 13 approved legislation (HR 2735) designed to strengthen the federal government's role in regulating corporate mergers under antitrust laws. On the same date, the Senate Commerce, Science and Transportation Committee approved a measure (S 1218 — S Rept 99-90) to inhibit the takeover of Trans World Airlines (TWA). There was no further action on either measure.

Two subcommittees made major attempts to craft broad legislation to rein in merger activity without favoring either raiders or management: the House Energy and Commerce Subcommittee on Telecommunications, Consumer Protection and Finance, under Chairman Timothy E. Wirth, D-Colo., and the Senate Banking, Housing and Urban Affairs Subcommittee on Securities, under Chairman Alfonse M. D'Amato, R-N.Y. But after numerous hearings, they did not try to mark up bills.

One reason for the lack of action was that the acquisition or defense of each proposed takeover was accomplished before Congress could act. Another was caution because the area was extraordinarily complex; many proposed solutions would have changed the rules of the game under which the stock market operated and threatened its stability, members said.

Ever since the stock market crash of 1929, stock trading had been governed by a growing web of federal laws and regulations. The Securities and Exchange Commission supervised stock transactions, the Justice Department kept an eye on mergers for antitrust implications, and other federal agencies such as the Federal Communications Commission and the Department of Transportation regulated specific industries.

Another major obstacle to legislation was the Reagan administration, which opposed virtually all proposals to regulate mergers as an inhibition of the free market.

Judiciary Bill

HR 2735 was approved by the Monopolies and Commercial Law Subcommittee by a 9-6 vote. However, the full committee did not act on the bill.

The legislation, sponsored by Committee Chairman Peter W. Rodino Jr., D-N.J., would establish a 30-day review period for all corporate acquisitions, twice the time allowed under existing law for most takeovers.

If the acquiring company had assets or annual sales in the United States of at least $1 billion, the waiting period would be 60 days. The period could be extended by the Federal Trade Commission or the Antitrust Division of the Justice Department, which had authority over mergers, if either agency determined more information to assess the acquisition was required.

The panel agreed to an amendment by John F. Seiberling, D-Ohio, prescribing a set of factors a federal court would have to consider in ruling whether a challenged merger would have anti-competitive effects.

Those factors included whether sources of supply and distribution outlets for goods and services involved in the merger would be diminished; whether plants or corporate headquarters would be closed down or relocated, and the impact of such actions; and whether the acquiring company would have to borrow so much money for the acquisition that it would have to sell off large parts of the acquired company to satisfy the debt.

Senate Commerce Bill

Carl C. Icahn's attempt to acquire TWA inspired Sen. John C. Danforth, R-Mo., who had 10,000 TWA employees in his state, to sponsor a bill to restrict the takeover. The bill whisked through the Commerce, Science and Transportation Committee, which he chaired, by a 15-1 vote on June 13, only three weeks after it was introduced (S Rept 99-90).

The impetus behind the bill faded when TWA announced, on the same day that Danforth's committee approved his bill, that it would merge with Texas Air Corp. That merger was stalled by labor opposition, however, and Icahn's bid was later accepted by TWA.

Sen. D'Amato in December introduced his long-promised bill (S 1907) regarding takeovers. But the bill proposed only relatively minor changes, such as requiring disclosure of a takeover bid within 24 hours rather than 10 days as under existing law. No action was taken on it. ∎

HEALTH
EDUCATION
WELFARE

CQ

Health/Education/Welfare

Medical inflation continued to slow in 1985, as hospitals and other health care providers responded to ongoing pressure from business and the federal government to keep costs down. But health policy makers increasingly questioned whether the quality and availability of medical care were being undermined by cost-containment efforts.

The Department of Health and Human Services (HHS) announced at midyear that health spending nationwide grew 9.1 percent in 1984, the most recent year for which figures were available. It was the first time since 1965 that the rate of increase in health spending dipped below double digits. The $387 million spent in 1984 represented 10.6 percent of the gross national product (GNP), a slight drop from 1983 and the first time since 1978 that health spending as a share of GNP declined.

HHS analysts attributed the slowdown in health spending increases in large part to the drop in general inflation. But they also cited important changes in the way health services were being delivered and financed.

The most prominent change at the federal level was the implementation of a new method of paying hospitals under Medicare, the federal health care program for the elderly and disabled. Approved by Congress in 1983, the new "prospective payment system" gave hospitals powerful new incentives to economize and operate more efficiently. Instead of reimbursing hospitals after the fact for their costs in treating Medicare patients, the new system set fixed fees for treating specific categories of illnesses, known as "diagnosis-related groups" (DRGs).

The program in 1985 was in the middle of a three-year phase-in period during which an increasing portion of hospital costs were being paid under the new system.

Another factor slowing health care inflation was increased use of lower-cost forms of treatment, such as free-standing surgical centers or outpatient services, as an alternative to costly inpatient hospital care. The American Hospital Association reported that 1.5 million fewer patients were admitted to hospitals in 1984 than in 1983, while the number of outpatient visits increased one million.

HHS said the average length of a hospital stay for Medicare patients had dropped from 9.3 days in fiscal 1983 to 7.7 days for the first two-thirds of fiscal 1985.

While these developments were widely hailed as signs that fat was being trimmed from the health care system, some experts worried that cost-containment pressures were eroding the quality and availability of medical care. Congressional concern focused particularly on the effects of Medicare's prospective payment system. Critics said it provided incentives for hospitals to cut costs not simply by operating more efficiently, but by scrimping on services.

The debate was fueled by reports that some hospitals were responding to cost-containment pressures by discharging elderly patients "quicker and sicker," saving money by cutting stays short. A four-month staff investigation by the Senate Special Committee on Aging found evidence that "seriously ill Medicare patients are inappropriately and prematurely discharged from hospitals."

However, the administration, hospital officials and others said there was no solid data to document charges of a widespread decline in the quality of care for the elderly. They said critics had cited only anecdotal evidence, not signs of systematic problems.

Members of Congress also raised questions about whether people without either public or private health insurance coverage were falling through the cracks of an increasingly cost-conscious health care system. Estimates of the number of people not covered by any type of health insurance ranged from 15 million to 32.5 million. They included people too young for Medicare; low-income people not poor enough to qualify for Medicaid, the federal-state health care program limited primarily to people receiving public assistance; part-time, seasonal and other workers who had no job-related insurance, and the unemployed.

In the past, hospitals found it easier to absorb the cost of providing free care to the indigent by jacking up prices charged paying patients. That in effect shifted the cost to Medicare, private insurers and patients who paid their own bills. That "cost-shifting" became more difficult as hospitals came under increasing pressure from private insurers, Medicare and Medicaid to control costs.

In the face of those pressures, hospitals were showing signs of increased reluctance to provide charity care for those lacking insurance or the resources to pay their own medical bills. Policy makers and the public reacted with alarm to reports of hospitals imposing new limits on charity care; particularly worrisome were reports of emergency rooms turning away patients, including pregnant women in labor, because they had no insurance and could not pay. Private hospitals were accused of "dumping" patients onto public hospitals by transferring them inappropriately.

Education

States and localities continued to promote efforts to improve schools and colleges in 1985, but relatively little initiative came from federal officials. While proposals to boost education funding were weighed in legislatures around the country, Congress' appetite for expanding federal school aid was dulled by demands to curb the deficit.

A prominent "reform" issue at the state and local level was efforts to make teaching a more attractive and respected profession. Hoping to attract higher-quality people into the field, many legislatures voted to raise teacher salaries. According to the National Education Association, the average classroom teacher's salary for 1984-85 rose 7.3 percent over the previous year, to $23,546.

The administration continued to advocate a hands-off federal education policy, leaving the primary responsibility for overseeing and financing education to states and localities. But President Reagan, who in the past called for abolition of the Education Department, in 1985 installed an outspoken new secretary of education who became one of the most visible members of the Cabinet. William J. Bennett, who had been chairman of the National Endowment for the Humanities, in January succeeded T. H. Bell as education secretary.

Bennett cut a controversial figure from the outset, aggressively defending the administration's education policies and openly criticizing the education establishment. At his first press conference, he ruffled feathers by saying that some college students could cope with cuts in federal financial aid by simply forgoing such luxuries as cars, stereos and vacations. College lobbyists and their allies in Congress said such charges of student-aid abuse had been put to rest by eligibility curbs imposed on student loans in 1981.

Bennett's rhetoric mellowed as the year progressed, but he continued to be a high-profile spokesman on such subjects as the relationship between religion and education and the failings of bilingual education. He also launched a renewed administration drive to transform federal education aid to disadvantaged schoolchildren into a program of vouchers that families could use at public or private schools. But Congress showed little interest in the idea.

Attention on Capitol Hill focused primarily on college programs, as the Higher Education Act came up for renewal. In the five years since Congress had last reauthorized aid to colleges and needy students, the landscape of the nation's college campuses had shifted significantly. A steady increase in the number of older students attending college part time radically reshaped the profile of the "typical" undergraduate. Although the stereotypical college student was someone fresh out of high school, more than 40 percent of all college students in 1985 were over 25.

The cost of attending college had increased about 60 percent since 1980, and the gap widened between tuition at public and private colleges. The College Board, a nonprofit higher-education group, said that in the 1985-86 school year, the average four-year public college cost $5,314, while four-year private colleges averaged $9,659.

It was the fifth year in a row that college tuition hikes, on average, outpaced the general rate of inflation. Many college officials said the increases were needed for overdue building repairs and faculty salary increases. But Bennett questioned whether students were getting their money's worth, citing reports critical of undergraduate education.

Education groups in Washington, accustomed to focusing attention on the Education Department budget, found themselves on relatively unfamiliar lobbying ground during Congress' 1985 debate on overhauling the federal tax code. The groups vigorously fought a proposal to eliminate the federal deduction for state and local taxes — a plan, ultimately rejected by the House, that critics said would have a profound effect on school financing.

School groups and teachers' unions said ending the deduction would make it harder for states and localities to raise revenues needed to pay for education and other public services. They said it was an especially inopportune time to undercut state financing of education because interest in promoting school improvement was starting to bear fruit.

Welfare

Amid reports that hunger and poverty among children were increasing — partly because of federal budget cuts — Congress moved to increase spending modestly on anti-poverty programs and to protect them from further cuts.

Official poverty figures released by the Census Bureau in August showed an improvement in the poverty rate. In 1984, 14.4 percent of the nation — 33.7 million Americans — were living below the poverty line, compared with 15.3 percent, or 35.5 million persons, the year before. The poverty line in 1984 was $10,609 for an urban family of four.

Reagan hailed the figures as a tribute to the success of his economic policies. But critics noted the rate did not fall as sharply as the drop in unemployment, and that there was little improvement for certain groups, particularly children. They also noted that the poverty rate was higher than when Reagan took office; it was 14 percent in 1981. About 22 percent of U.S. children lived below the poverty line in 1984, an increase of 29 percent over the 1979 level.

A separate study by the Physician Task Force on Hunger in America, at the Harvard University School of Public Health, found that up to 20 million Americans were hungry at least sometime each month. The group said the problem was getting worse, and blamed federal cutbacks in food and nutrition programs.

In response to such reports, Congress acted to restore federal funding, and, despite a general mood to reduce spending, protected most programs for the poor from further cuts. At the urging of House Democrats, several anti-poverty programs — child nutrition, food stamps, Aid to Families with Dependent Children (AFDC), a supplemental feeding program for needy pregnant women, infants and children (WIC), Supplemental Security Income and Medicaid — were exempted from automatic cuts mandated by the Gramm-Rudman-Hollings plan to eliminate the federal deficit over five years.

At the same time, the omnibus farm bill signed by Reagan broadened eligibility for food stamps and increased benefits. And House-Senate conferees agreed on a bill, which did not clear in 1985, requiring all states to provide AFDC benefits for two-parent families in which the principal wage-earner was unemployed. Only half the states were providing such benefits.

The House also passed a bill boosting spending on child nutrition programs by $121 million. While a companion Senate measure did not contain the spending increases, it did not contain any cuts sought by Reagan.

Despite widespread attention to the plight of the homeless, legislation authorizing spending on housing or shelter programs did not clear. The House, as part of its budget reconciliation package, approved a major reauthorization of federal housing programs; it would have preserved several construction programs the administration opposed, and created new programs, including aid to the homeless. But at the insistence of Jake Garn, R-Utah, chairman of the Senate Banking, Housing and Urban Affairs Committee, the provisions were stripped from the bill.

The administration's oversight of health and welfare programs changed hands in late 1985, when former Indiana Gov. Otis R. Bowen became Reagan's third secretary of health and human services. Widely respected as a politician and medical professional, Bowen succeeded Margaret M. Heckler, who agreed Oct. 1 to step down from the top HHS post to become ambassador to Ireland.

Heckler's job shift came after persistent reports that senior White House officials were pressing for her ouster because they considered her a poor administrator and insufficiently committed to conservative social causes. But Reagan denied he was forcing her out because of dissatisfaction with her performance.

—By Janet Hook and Robert Rothman

Congress Overrides Reagan Veto of NIH Bill

Congress Nov. 20 overrode President Reagan's veto of a bill (HR 2409) reauthorizing selected research activities of the National Institutes of Health (NIH) and creating a new institute for research on arthritis.

The House acted first, on Nov. 12 voting 380-32 to override. The bill became law (PL 99-158) Nov. 20 when the Senate also voted to override, 89-7. *(Vote 364, p. 114-H; vote 321, p. 55-S)*

In his Nov. 8 veto message, Reagan said he took the action because the legislation would have imposed "undue political control" over research decisions. He said HR 2409 was "overloaded with objectionable provisions that seriously undermine and threaten the ability of NIH to manage itself." *(Veto message, p. 35-D)*

It was the fifth time since Reagan took office in 1981 that Congress had overturned a presidential veto. The NIH bill was the 41st bill to be vetoed by Reagan since 1981, the second in 1985.

Reagan in 1984 killed a similar NIH bill, but Congress did not have a chance to override the veto because the president pocket-vetoed the measure after the end of the 1984 congressional session. *(1984 Almanac pp. 474, 26-E)*

Background

The National Institutes of Health, created under the open-ended authority of the secretary of health and human services, financed almost two-thirds of all health-related research in U.S. universities and medical schools. NIH had a fiscal 1985 budget of $5.1 billion.

Nine of the 11 institutes that comprised the NIH did not require periodic reauthorization by Congress, and their budgets were not constrained by authorized spending ceilings. The exceptions were the National Cancer Institute and the National Heart, Lung and Blood Institute, the two largest institutes.

Authorizations for the two institutes expired in fiscal 1982. Congress continued their funding, however, through annual continuing appropriations resolutions.

Provisions

As enacted over President Reagan's veto, HR 2409:

- Provided explicit statutory authority for each of the institutes, not just the cancer and heart institutes. However, the bill did not require regular reauthorization for these institutes, and it retained the authority of HHS to reorganize the institutes.
- Established a National Institute of Arthritis and Musculoskeletal and Skin Diseases.
- Established a National Center for Nursing Research within NIH to promote research on patient care and nursing.
- Authorized $1.26 billion in fiscal 1986, $1.34 billion in 1987 and $1.42 billion in 1988 for the National Cancer Institute.
- Authorized $891 million in 1986, $961 million in 1987 and $1 billion in 1988 for the Heart, Lung and Blood Institute.
- Authorized $779 million in fiscal 1986-88 for National Research Service Awards, an NIH research training program, and $39 million over three years for aid to medical libraries.
- Limited NIH's administrative expenses to no more than 5.5 percent of its annual appropriation.
- Tightened restrictions on research on human fetuses by barring the secretary of HHS for three years from waiving those restrictions in certain circumstances.
- Allowed NIH to support research involving living, nonviable human fetuses outside the womb if that research improved their well-being or chances of survival. Such research also was permitted if needed to obtain information otherwise unavailable, so long as it posed no added risk of injury to the fetus. Fetuses intended for abortion could be exposed to no greater risk in research than those expected to be carried to term.
- Required each institution receiving NIH funds to set up a committee to monitor the treatment and use of animals in research. NIH was directed to explore alternatives to the use of animals in research.
- Increased emphasis on health maintenance by requiring the appointment of an NIH associate director for disease prevention. Similar posts were created in the National Institute on Child Health and Human Development and the National Cancer Institute.
- Established a new commission to study ethical questions raised by fetal research and other controversial issues in biomedical research. The bill authorized $2 million in fiscal 1986, $2.5 million in 1987 and $3 million in 1988 for the program.
- Required NIH to strengthen procedures for investigating scientific misconduct and to set up a peer review system for its in-house research.
- Required NIH to support research on Alzheimer's disease, spinal cord injury and mental retardation.

Legislative History

The House Energy and Commerce Committee June 4 reported a bill (HR 2409 — H Rept 99-158) only slightly changed from the 1984 bill vetoed by Reagan. HR 2409 contained provisions for the creation of new institutes devoted to nursing and arthritis research. The measure, however, did not include previous proposals requiring line-item authorizations for all 11 institutes.

The House June 17 by voice vote passed HR 2409 after brief debate, without changing the committee version. Administration officials warned of another presidential veto.

The Senate Labor and Human Resources Committee July 8 reported S 1309 (S Rept 99-108), including provision for an arthritis research institute but not one for nursing research. The Senate July 19 by voice vote passed the bill. After passage of S 1309, the Senate substituted the text of its bill for HR 2409.

The Senate Oct. 18 by voice vote approved the conference report on HR 2409 (H Rept 99-309). The House Oct. 23 by a vote of 395-10 cleared the bill for the president's signature. *(Vote 333, p. 104-H)*

The Override

President Reagan Nov. 8 vetoed HR 2409, saying the bill included directives that would tie the hands of NIH officials and "exert undue political control" over scientific decisions.

The veto angered Republican backers of the NIH bill

who said they had believed the final compromise bill accommodated administration objections to the 1984 version.

Although the measure originally approved by the House in June departed little from the 1984 bill, the Senate tried to address some of the administration's concerns before passing its version in July.

In drafting the final conference report, sponsors thought they had addressed other administration objections by setting authorization levels within the fiscal 1986 congressional budget and by dropping the proposal to set up a new institute on nursing within NIH. The final version of HR 2409 called for a smaller-scale nursing center.

Reagan's veto message nonetheless objected to the nursing center, saying its focus was incompatible with NIH's biomedical research mission.

"Frankly, I was really shocked to find they vetoed the bill," said Sen. Orrin G. Hatch, R-Utah, chairman of the Labor and Human Resources Committee.

"I believe the president received bad advice on this and he underestimated its vast support on Capitol Hill," he said. "I felt we had commitments on this matter." ∎

NSF Authorization Cleared

President Reagan Nov. 22 signed a $1.52 billion fiscal 1986 authorization bill (HR 1210 — PL 99-159) for the National Science Foundation (NSF).

Senate action on Nov. 1 clearing the bill for the president marked the first time since 1980 that an NSF authorization had passed Congress. *(1984 Almanac p. 454)*

The House by voice vote had approved the compromise measure on Oct. 24.

Authorizing legislation for NSF had stalled in the past because of a jurisdictional dispute between two Senate committees: Labor and Human Resources and Commerce, Science and Transportation. Funds were provided each year, however, through appropriation measures, with fiscal 1985 funding totaling $1.5 billion.

Early in 1985, the committees agreed to share jurisdiction over NSF, removing the roadblock to passage of an NSF authorizing bill.

Provisions

As cleared, HR 1210 authorized $1,518,156,00, which was $16 million more than the House bill authorized and $51 million less than the administration request.

The largest single category of funding was about $400 million for mathematics and physical science research programs, followed by about $360 million for research in astronomical, earth and ocean sciences.

HR 1210 also extended through fiscal 1988 a $75 million-per-year program of grants to "magnet" schools that offered special curricula to attract minority students. The final bill retained language from the Senate version specifying that magnet school funds be used directly for the improvement of core academic courses, a provision intended to bar the use of any grant money for the teaching of "secular humanism."

A 1984 law (PL 98-377) setting up the magnet school program barred use of any grant money for the teaching of "secular humanism," as some conservatives labeled subjects they saw as anti-religious, but the term was not defined in the law. *(1984 Almanac p. 491)*

HR 1210 also:

- Defined the obligations of NSF in education activities to include promoting public understanding of mathematics, science and engineering, awarding graduate fellowships and conducting teacher institutes.
- Elevated fundamental engineering research to the same level as basic scientific research in the foundation's priorities.
- Authorized $50 million for each of fiscal years 1986 through 1988 for a "Partnership in Education" program that encouraged schools, colleges and businesses to share resources to enhance math and science education. Transferred the program from NSF to the Department of Education.
- Authorized for three years through fiscal 1988 a block grant program that helped state and local education agencies develop teacher training programs in math and science education.
- Required that at least $1 million of total authorized funds be used for a program on ethics and values in science and technology.

Legislative Action

The House Science and Technology Committee April 16 reported HR 1210 (H Rept 99-44), authorizing $1.57 billion for NSF.

Although the total recommended by the committee was almost 7 percent more than the fiscal 1985 appropriation, it was in line with President Reagan's request for fiscal 1986.

But the House April 17 voted overwhelmingly to hold the NSF budget at the fiscal 1985 level of $1.5 billion. By a 407-4 vote, the House adopted an amendment to pare $100 million from the bill. *(Vote 50, p. 20-H)*

The action was billed as a bipartisan show of support for a spending freeze in fiscal 1986.

The House accepted modifications proposed by the Science Committee that provided for some parts of the foundation's budget, such as support for advanced computers, to exceed fiscal 1985 levels. But to keep overall spending within the 1985 total of $1.5 billion, other programs, including international affairs, were cut.

The Senate Labor and Human Resources Committee Aug. 28 reported S 801 (S Rept 99-131). During committee debate July 17, the committee adopted an amendment to extend grants through fiscal 1988 for the mathematics and science education authorized by PL 98-377.

But the panel decided to let the full Senate debate whether to lift the prohibition in PL 98-377 on use of federal funds by magnet schools for courses teaching "secular humanism." S 801 as reported by the committee did not include the term, which critics complained was so vague that it was used by conservatives to attack anything they did not like in school curricula. "You can't prohibit the teaching of secular humanism when no one knows what it is," said Howard M. Metzenbaum, D-Ohio. "I think what we're talking about is anything that doesn't have an emphasis on the Bible is [considered] questionable."

Robert T. Stafford, R-Vt., chairman of the education subcommittee, agreed to offer a floor amendment to S 801 reauthorizing the magnet-school program without the secular humanism provision.

The Senate Sept. 26 by voice vote passed HR 1210 after incorporating the provisions of S 801. Before passing the bill, the Senate by voice vote added $16 million for research.

The Senate also adopted by voice vote an amendment

to extend through fiscal 1988 the magnet-school program. To address concerns of Orrin G. Hatch, R-Utah, author of the secular humanism language in PL 98-377, HR 1210 specified that magnet school funds had to be used directly for the improvement of core academic courses. ▮

Nursing Education Funds

After opposing the legislation, President Reagan Aug. 16 signed a bill (HR 2370 — PL 99-92) renewing federal aid for nursing education for three years through fiscal 1988.

Reagan argued that the program had outlived its original purpose of alleviating nurse shortages. The number of nursing school graduates had doubled since federal nurse training programs had begun in 1964. But supporters of the legislation said shortages still existed in advanced fields and special practices, such as nurse administrators and nurse midwives.

In 1984 Reagan vetoed an omnibus health bill that included a three-year reauthorization of nurse training assistance at somewhat higher spending ceilings than in the 1985 legislation. *(1984 Almanac p. 475)*

HR 2370 authorized $54.1 million in fiscal 1986, $55.4 million in 1987 and $56.6 million in 1988 for grants to nursing schools and their students. The bill focused federal aid on advanced, specialized nurse training in fields where there was still a shortage.

The bill also included a provision on cigarette labeling that had been added by the Senate.

A 1984 law (PL 98-474) required four different health warning labels to appear on cigarette packs, with the text rotating quarterly. The Senate added an amendment to the nursing bill to allow small companies that produce cigarette brands selling in limited volumes to print all four labels simultaneously, with each of the four labels appearing on roughly one-quarter of the cigarette packs distributed. *(1984 Almanac p. 478)*

Legislative History

The House Energy and Commerce Committee June 5 reported HR 2370 (H Rept 99-161), rejecting a subcommittee recommendation to allow a 17 percent increase in fiscal 1986 spending over 1985 levels.

As reported, HR 2370 froze fiscal 1986 spending for aid to nursing schools and their students to the fiscal 1985 level of $50.3 million, with 5 percent increases in fiscal 1987 and 1988.

The freeze amendment, offered by Edward R. Madigan, R-Ill., was approved 22-20. Henry A. Waxman, D-Calif., chairman of the Health and Environment Subcommittee, had succeeded in defeating the Madigan freeze proposal during subcommittee markup. But in the full committee the amendment drew support from six Democrats, reflecting bipartisan sentiment in the House for a budget freeze to promote deficit reduction.

An administration proposal to abolish nursing education aid was rejected by the committee by voice vote.

The Senate Labor and Human Resources Committee July 8 reported S 1284 (S Rept 99-106). S 1284 increased support for nurse training to $54.1 million in fiscal 1986, $55.4 million in fiscal 1987 and $56.6 million in fiscal 1988.

The House July 15 by voice vote approved HR 2370 as reported by the House Energy and Commerce Committee. The Senate July 22 by voice vote approved HR 2370, after incorporating the text of S 1284 and adding the cigarette labeling amendment. The amendment, introduced by Thomas F. Eagleton, D-Mo., was a response to complaints from small cigarette companies about the cost of changing packaging and labels four times a year.

The House July 31 by voice vote cleared the bill for the president by accepting the Senate-passed version, including the cigarette labeling amendment. ▮

Saccharin Ban Extended

President Reagan May 24 signed into law a bill (S 484 — PL 99-46) extending for two years a prohibition against a government ban on the marketing and sale of saccharin, the controversial artificial sweetener linked to bladder cancer in laboratory animals.

Passage of the bill marked the fourth extension of the prohibition since Congress in 1977 first blocked the Food and Drug Administration (FDA) from banning saccharin. The most recent ban approved in 1983 expired April 22, 1985.

Under S 484, the moratorium was extended through May 1, 1987.

The moratorium did not entirely prevent FDA from taking action against saccharin but only barred the agency from actions based on research findings from before 1978. If new evidence of health risks was discovered, FDA had authority to ban use of the sweetner.

Background

The ban FDA proposed in 1977 was strongly opposed by the soft drink industry, dieters and other critics who said the research on which the federal agency based its recommendation failed to prove that saccharin caused cancer in humans. Proponents of keeping saccharin on the market argued that there was no alternative sweetener for diabetics, dieters and other consumers who needed or wanted to avoid sugar.

The ban was put on hold for eight years by a series of congressionally imposed moratoriums. *(Previous extension, 1983 Almanac p. 401)*

Congressional Action

The Senate Labor and Human Resources Committee April 22 by voice vote reported S 484 (S Rept 99-36). The committee approved the bill after rejecting an amendment by Howard M. Metzenbaum, D-Ohio, to require special labeling of aspartame, another popular artificial sweetener.

Labor Committee Chairman Orrin G. Hatch, R-Utah, opposed the labeling amendment, arguing that there was no evidence that aspartame posed a significant health risk. The amendment was rejected on a 7-9 party-line vote.

The Senate May 7 by a 94-1 vote approved S 484. William Proxmire, D-Wis., cast the lone "nay" vote. *(Vote 48, p. 14-S)*

The Senate sent the measure to the House May 7 after rejecting, 27-68, an amendment that would have required special labeling of soft drinks that contained aspartame. *(Vote 47, p. 14-S)*

However, the report accompanying the bill required FDA to expedite clinical studies of possible adverse side effects of aspartame.

The House by voice vote approved S 484 on May 14, clearing the bill for the president. ▮

Health Professions Training

Despite earlier opposition, President Reagan Oct. 22 signed a bill (HR 2410 — PL 99-129) reauthorizing aid to medical schools and their students.

In 1984, Reagan vetoed similar legislation, arguing that the bill was too costly and the program unnecessary in light of projected surpluses of doctors. *(1984 Almanac p. 475)*

As cleared, HR 2410 authorized about $50 million less over three years than the 1984 bill. The new bill held the fiscal 1986 authorization to the 1985 appropriation level of $141 million and increased authorization levels by 2.7 percent in 1987 and 2.3 percent in fiscal 1988. The bill also included an additional $6.3 million for low-interest Health Professions Student Loans over the three-year period, earmarking half of the money for disadvantaged students.

HR 2410 extended an array of relatively small health training programs, including grants to support family medicine programs and to help disadvantaged students pay medical school tuition.

The measure also sought to improve collections of the loans, which were administered by schools.

Background

Most of the programs covered in HR 2410 had been established in the 1960s to remedy a shortage of doctors and other medical professionals. In 1984, the administration said that the doctor shortage had been alleviated and Congress should reauthorize only certain loans to health professional students, supported by a revolving fund of repaid loans. Backers of the program said that practitioners were still in short supply in certain parts of the country and in fields such as geriatric medicine, public health and primary care.

Legislative History

The House Energy and Commerce Committee May 23 reported HR 2410 (H Rept 99-145). The committee May 15 by a 17-6 vote had approved an authorization of $141 million for fiscal 1986 and allowed adjustments for inflation in fiscal 1987 and 1988.

The Senate Labor and Human Resources Committee unanimously approved a similar bill on June 27, reporting it July 8 (S 1283 — S Rept 99-105). S 1283 capped both fiscal 1986 and 1987 spending at $141 million and authorized $135.4 million for fiscal 1988.

The House by voice vote July 15 passed HR 2410 as reported by the Energy and Commerce Committee. The Senate July 19 passed HR 2410 after incorporating the text of S 1283 with the authorization levels approved by the Labor and Human Resources Committee.

The House Oct. 3 and the Senate Oct. 4 by voice vote approved the compromise worked out between the House Subcommittee on Health and the Environment and the Senate Committee on Labor and Human Resources. ∎

'Orphan' Drug Bill

Congress completed action July 31 on a bill (S 1147) reauthorizing a federal program to promote the development of drugs to treat rare diseases.

President Reagan signed the measure Aug. 15 (PL 99-91).

The bill authorized $4 million in grants for fiscal years 1986-88 for the development of "orphan" drugs, which are needed by so few people that drug companies have no marketplace incentive to produce them.

The grants were set up in 1982 under a law (PL 97-414) that also authorized tax credits for the development of rare-disease drugs. *(1982 Almanac p. 490)*

S 1147 authorized the Food and Drug Administration (FDA) to grant seven years of exclusive marketing rights for all orphan drugs. Under current law, such protection was granted only to those orphan drugs that could not be patented. *(1984 Almanac p. 473)*

S 1147 also established a commission to assess the status of federal and non-governmental research on rare diseases.

The final version included a provision amending an unrelated program for people with developmental disabilities (PL 98-527). The amendment imposed new limits on the circumstances in which states could apply for a waiver of certain requirements for how they used money under the programs.

The Senate May 23 passed S 1147 by voice vote.

The House June 18 passed its version (HR 2290 — H Rept 99-153) on a 413-0 vote and then substituted the text of its bill for S 1147. HR 2290 had been reported by the House Energy and Commerce Committee June 3. *(Vote 149, p. 50-H)*

S 1147 was cleared for the White House July 31 when the House approved a compromise version of the measure by voice vote. The Senate had approved the compromise July 25. ∎

Community Health Centers

The Senate July 19 approved a bill (S 1282) extending through fiscal 1988 funding for community and migrant health centers. A House committee reported a similar bill (HR 2418), but the measure was not acted on by the House in 1985.

As passed by voice vote, S 1282 authorized, over three years, $1.3 billion for community health and $167 million for migrant health. The bill also created a modest new program of grants to help states improve primary health care for underserved groups.

In 1984, President Reagan vetoed an omnibus health bill (S 2574) that reauthorized community and migrant health centers at $1.7 billion and $213 million respectively for fiscal 1985-88. S 2574 also authorized for the three-year period $76 million for a new primary-care block grant to states and a new technical assistance program. *(1984 Almanac p. 475)*

Legislative Action

The House Energy and Commerce Committee May 15 by voice vote approved HR 2418. The report was filed June 4 (H Rept 99-157).

HR 2418 eliminated a block grant program created in 1981 to give states the option of taking responsibility for community health centers. No state exercised the option, but the Reagan administration wanted to keep the grant on the books. *(1981 Almanac p. 463)*

The block grant proposal, offered as an amendment by William E. Dannemeyer, R-Calif., was rejected by a vote of 17-25.

As approved by the committee, HR 2418 authorized $406 million for community health centers in fiscal 1986, rising to $472 million in fiscal 1988. Migrant centers were authorized at $50 million in 1986, rising to $61 million in 1988.

The Senate Labor and Human Resources Committee June 27 by voice vote approved S 1282 at the same funding levels as the House bill. The Senate bill also authorized $17.5 million in fiscal 1986 for a new program of aid to states for research and demonstration projects in primary health care. The report was filed July 8 (S Rept 99-104).

The Senate passed the bill unamended on July 19. ∎

National Health Service Corps

The Senate July 19 approved a bill (S 1285) providing National Health Service Corps scholarships to health professions students who agreed to work in medically underserved areas after they finished their education.

A similar House bill (HR 2237), was reported May 23 by the Energy and Commerce Committee.

S 1285 imposed a cap of $15,000 on the scholarships in the 1986-87 academic year and authorized the secretary of health and human services to adjust the cap in subsequent years. No cap was included in HR 2237.

The Senate bill authorized 450 new scholarships over three years — less than half the number of awards in the House bill. S 1285 also authorized $70 million in fiscal 1986, $65 million in 1987 and $60 million in 1988 to pay for placement and salaries of corps members in the field.

Congress appropriated $75 million for the corps in fiscal 1985. However, the Department of Health and Human Services spent only $60 million, using the remaining $15 million to support community health centers. *(Background, 1984 Almanac p. 475, 1981 Almanac p. 475)*

Legislative History

The House Energy and Commerce Committee May 9 approved HR 2237 authorizing $75 million annually over three years for the National Health Service Corps. The report was filed May 23 (H Rept 99-144).

The measure was approved by voice vote after committee Democrats warded off two attempts to lower the spending ceiling.

William E. Dannemeyer, R-Calif., proposed an amendment to cut program funding to the $50 million level requested by President Reagan for fiscal 1986, with small increases in 1987 and 1988. His amendment was rejected 7-11.

The committee also rejected, 10-12, another Dannemeyer amendment to authorize $60 million a year, a level he described as a spending "freeze."

The Senate Labor and Human Resources Committee June 27 unanimously approved S 1285 and reported the bill July 8 (S Rept 99-107).

The Senate July 19 passed S 1285 by voice vote. ∎

Protections for Mentally Ill

The Senate July 31 approved legislation (S 974) to bolster protections against abuse and neglect of the mentally ill, but a similar measure (HR 3492) never got to the House floor in 1985.

Passed by voice vote, S 974 authorized new grants to support advocacy programs and protective services for residents of mental institutions.

The Senate bill authorized $10 million in fiscal 1986, $10.5 million in 1987 and $11.75 million in 1988 to set up advocacy agencies independent of state mental-health systems. The agencies could investigate reports of abuse and pursue legal and administrative remedies to protect the rights of the mentally ill.

Background

S 974 was introduced in response to a six-month staff investigation into the treatment of residents of state mental institutions.

The probe, which culminated in a series of hearings April 1-3, uncovered cases of violence, neglect and substandard living conditions in state mental institutions. Many victims of such mistreatment had not been able to obtain legal representation to enforce their rights, said Lowell P. Weicker Jr. (R-Conn.) when he introduced S 974.

Similar protection and advocacy programs already existed for the mentally retarded and others with developmental disabilities. In 1984 Congress reauthorized aid for those agencies under the Developmental Disabilities Act of 1984 (PL 98-527). *(1984 Almanac p. 481)*

Senate Committee Action

S 974 was unchanged from the version reported July 25 by the Labor and Human Resources Committee (S Rept 99-109).

The committee July 10 had unanimously approved a compromise designed to address some of the objections raised by conservatives to the version approved June 6 by the Subcommittee on the Handicapped.

The compromise bill added a new provision requiring advocacy agencies, in most cases, to exhaust administrative remedies before going to court. It also added provisions designed to protect the confidentiality of patient records obtained by the agencies.

John Kerry, D-Mass., tried but failed to remove a limit on awards of attorneys' fees in cases involving the rights of the mentally ill. Most awards of attorneys' fees are based on market rates, but the bill allowed advocacy lawyers who prevail in court to receive only their actual litigation costs. By a 7-9 party-line vote, the committee refused to delete that cap.

House Committee Action

The House Energy and Commerce Committee Oct. 29, by a vote of 17-7, approved HR 3492. The bill authorized $33.03 million over fiscal 1986-88 to establish programs of protection and advocacy for the institutionalized mentally ill. The bill was reported Nov. 21 (H Rept 99-401). But no further action was taken in the House in 1985. ∎

HMO Authorization

The House June 18 passed a bill (HR 2417) phasing out federal grant-and-loan aid to health maintenance organizations (HMOs), but the Senate failed to act on a similar bill (S 1762) approved Nov. 19 by the Senate Labor and Human Resources Committee.

Under HR 2417, funds were authorized only to pay defaults and other costs related to loans already made.

At issue was a 1973 law (PL 93-222) designed to promote the establishment of HMOs, which provide comprehensive health care to members for a fixed prepaid fee. No aid had been disbursed since 1981 under the federal program, which provided grants, loans and loan guarantees for planning and initial operating costs of HMOs. *(Congress and the Nation Vol. IV, p. 327)*

HMOs had been credited with cutting health care costs. Prepaid, fixed fees were believed to be incentives for the HMOs to practice more efficient medicine than fee-for-service medicine.

The Reagan administration proposed repealing the act, arguing that the law had accomplished its purpose and was no longer needed, in light of the wide availability and growth of HMOs.

In 1984 President Reagan vetoed an omnibus health bill (S 2574) that included $400,000 annually for fiscal 1985-88 for HMO training and technical aid, plus funds as needed through fiscal 1988 for the program's loan default fund. S 2574 phased out or canceled other HMO grant, loan and loan guarantee programs. *(1984 Almanac p. 475)*

Legislative History

The House Energy and Commerce Committee May 15 approved HR 2417. A report was filed June 3 (H Rept 99-154). The House June 18 passed the bill by a vote of 411-2. *(Vote 148, p. 50-H)*

The Senate Labor and Human Resources Committee Nov. 19 by voice vote approved S 1762. However, the panel refused to repeal other provisions of federal law that gave HMOs a competitive edge in the health care marketplace.

During committee debate on S 1762, Malcom Wallop, R-Wyo., offered the administration's proposal to repeal the act, but it was rejected, 3-13.

As approved by the committee, S 1762 included a provision calling on the secretary of health and human services to conduct a study of key provisions of the HMO act, including the requirement that companies with 25 or more employees offer workers the option of enrolling in an HMO, if one meeting federal standards was available in the area. ∎

Curbing Medicare Abuses

By voice vote, the House June 4 approved legislation designed to close loopholes in the government's authority to exclude unscrupulous and incompetent doctors from Medicare and Medicaid.

The bill (HR 1868 — H Rept 99-80, Parts I and II) gave the Department of Health and Human Services (HHS) authority to bar doctors from participating in Medicare if they had lost their licenses in any state or been found guilty of drug trafficking or other crimes related to health care delivery. Such practitioners also would be barred from Medicaid and from federally funded, state-run health programs.

HR 1868 also allowed the U.S. attorney general to strip doctors of their authority to prescribe drugs if they had been excluded from Medicare for crimes related to the program.

A similar bill (S 837) was introduced in the Senate, but no action was taken on it in 1985.

Background

Under current law, doctors and other health care professionals could be barred from Medicaid and Medicare only for offenses directly related to the programs. In addition, doctors who lost their licenses in one state could relocate to another where they were licensed and still participate in government health programs.

The gaps in federal authority to exclude physicians from the programs were highlighted by a 1984 report by the General Accounting Office (GAO).

The GAO investigated 328 medical practitioners whose licenses in their home states were revoked or suspended for offenses including drug trafficking, insurance fraud and medical malpractice. The study found that 122 of the practitioners held licenses in at least one other state, and that 39 or more of them had relocated and continued participating in Medicare or Medicaid.

Committee Action

Identical versions of HR 1868 were reported by the Ways and Means Committee May 10, and by the Energy and Commerce Committee May 23.

In approving HR 1868, both House committees included the provisions of another bill (HR 1369) that authorized the U.S. attorney general to revoke physicians' authority to prescribe drugs if they had been excluded from Medicare. ∎

Curran Rejected for NEH

The Senate Labor and Human Resources Committee Nov. 19 effectively killed the nomination of Edward A. Curran to be chairman of the National Endowment for the Humanities (NEH).

The committee refused, on an 8-8 vote, to report the nomination favorably to the Senate floor. The panel then defeated, on another 8-8 tie, a motion to report the nomination without recommendation.

On both tallies, the decisive vote was cast by Robert T. Stafford, R-Vt., who joined the panel's seven Democrats in opposing Curran as lacking the qualifications for the job.

Curran was deputy director of the Peace Corps, a position he had held since 1982. He was expected to remain in that post.

The confirmation votes marked the second time in 1985 that a committee had barred a major nomination by President Reagan from reaching the Senate floor. The Judiciary Committee June 27 rejected the nomination of William Bradford Reynolds to be associate attorney general. *(Story, p. 237)*

Before going to the Peace Corps, Curran served under Reagan as director of the National Institute of Education (NIE), the Education Department's research arm. In 1982 he was forced to resign that post by then-Education Secretary T. H. Bell after urging the president to abolish the institute. He argued the agency wasted taxpayers' money and had become a tool of liberal ideology.

Before his government service, Curran was headmaster of the National Cathedral School, a private school in Washington, D. C.

Opposition from Scholars

The top NEH post became vacant after Reagan's first endowment chairman, William J. Bennett, became secretary of education. President Reagan announced his intention to nominate Curran April 4.

Critics argued that Curran lacked the credentials and academic experience to oversee NEH, one of the largest and most prestigious sources of support for scholarly research. Curran had a bachelor's degree from Yale University and a master's degree from Duke University, but he had no Ph.D. and never held a college post.

Curran's defenders said that he, like all NEH chairmen, would rely on the agency's peer review system of asking experts in the relevant fields to evaluate grant applications.

Arts, Humanities Funding

Congress Dec. 4 cleared legislation (S 1264 — PL 99-194) that reauthorized three cultural support agencies for five years, through fiscal 1990.

S 1264 reauthorized the National Endowment for the Arts (NEA), the National Endowment for the Humanities (NEH) and the Institute of Museum Services, a tiny agency that provided grants to museums. The three agencies were the most prominent sources of federal support for humanities scholars, artists and museums. The Reagan administration had sought to cut the endowments' budgets and to abolish the museum institute. *(1984 Almanac p. 454)*

The 1985 bill stirred controversy in the House where critics of NEA succeeded in limiting the extension to two years. Although the final version adopted Senate provisions for a five-year extension, it also included House language to strengthen protections against conflict of interest in grant application processing and to increase oversight of projects.

Provisions. As cleared by Congress, S 1264:

- Authorized for NEA $167.1 million in fiscal 1986, $170.2 million in 1987 and $177 million in 1988.
- Authorized for NEH $139.9 million in fiscal 1986, $145.1 million in 1987 and $150.9 million in 1988.
- Authorized for the museum institute $21.6 million in fiscal 1986, $22.5 million in 1987 and $23.4 million in 1988.
- Authorized for all three agencies such sums as Congress considered necessary in fiscal 1989-90.
- Barred service on an NEA grant panel by anyone who had an application pending before that panel.
- Gave NEH new authority to support construction projects.
- Expanded a program of federal insurance against damage for foreign art exhibits brought to the United States or exhibits sent abroad from American museums.
- Authorized $5 million annually through fiscal 1991 for an educational program for the commemoration of the bicentennial of the U.S. Constitution in 1987.
- Designated a post within the Library of Congress for a "poet laureate" to serve as an official poetry consultant.

Legislative History. The Senate Labor and Human Resources Committee July 31 unanimously approved a five-year extension of the three agencies through fiscal 1990 (S 1264 — S Rept 99-125). The Senate Oct. 3 passed S 1264 by voice vote, after adding the Constitution bicentennial and poet laureate provisions.

The version reported by the House Education and Labor Committee Sept. 18 (HR 3248 — H Rept 99-274) provided a four-year renewal of the three agencies through fiscal 1989. The House Oct. 10 passed HR 3248 by a 349-57 vote, after reducing the authorization to two years, through fiscal 1987, and adopting other amendments to blunt charges of cronyism and lack of public accountability at NEA. *(Vote 321, p. 100-H)*

The Senate Dec. 3 by voice vote approved a compromise version of S 1264 that had been agreed to by floor leaders of the bill. The House gave its approval Dec. 4 by voice vote, completing congressional action.

Senate Confirms Bennett as Education Secretary

The Senate Feb. 6 unanimously confirmed the nomination of William J. Bennett to be secretary of education. The vote was 93-0. *(Vote 2, p. 3-S)*

Bennett, who had served as chairman of the National Endowment for the Humanities (NEH) since 1982, replaced T. H. Bell, who left the Education Department Dec. 31, 1985. Bennett was nominated for the post by President Reagan on Jan. 10.

Senators from both sides of the aisle praised Bennett's qualifications, which included a record of strong support for liberal arts education and an academic background in philosophy and law.

Bennett was the third person to occupy the secretary's post since the Department of Education was created in 1980. Bell's predecessor was Shirley M. Hufstedler, who was named by President Carter.

Confirmation Hearing

The Senate Labor and Human Resources Committee Feb. 1 unanimously recommended confirmation of Bennett, after President Reagan assured skeptical committee members in a Jan. 29 letter that he had shelved past proposals to abolish the Department of Education.

In his letter to Orrin G. Hatch, R-Utah, chairman of the committee, Reagan said he still believed that a Cabinet-level department was not needed to administer federal education aid effectively. But he acknowledged that his proposal to replace the Education Department with a stripped-down education foundation had "very little support in Congress."

The letter was sent after committee members, during a Jan. 28 hearing on Bennett's nomination, insisted on an explicit White House commitment to the department's existence — despite Reagan's 1980 campaign pledge to abolish it.

At Bell's recommendation, Reagan in 1982 had proposed downgrading the Education Department into a federal education foundation, but the idea was ignored by Congress. *(1982 Almanac p. 501)*

Bennett had won public note for his promotion of liberal arts education and returning to the classics in humanities study. Questions during the confirmation hearing focused largely on Bennett's views on civil rights and on administration proposals to curb federal aid to middle-class college students.

In his opening statement, Bennett committed himself to "full enforcement" of civil rights and other laws administered by the Education Department.

"At the same time, I will make every effort to prevent the department from being needlessly meddlesome or intrusive," Bennett added.

He restated his much-publicized opposition to the use

of hiring quotas and preferential treatment to advance women and minorities. In 1984 he refused to submit a report on NEH hiring goals required of all federal agencies by the Equal Employment Opportunity Commission.

"I do not think we should count by race," Bennett said. "We should move to a colorblind society."

On administration proposals to curb college aid to middle-income students, Bennett said he had not been involved in developing the recommendations and was not familiar with all the details. But he agreed with the principle, he said, that at a time of federal budget constraints, the poorest students should be helped before the middle class.

Bennett Background

Prior to becoming chairman of the NEH in 1982, Bennett, 41, was president of the National Humanities Center in North Carolina. He earlier taught philosophy and law at a number of universities.

A graduate of Williams College in Massachusetts, Bennett received a law degree from Harvard Law School and a Ph.D. in philosophy from the University of Texas at Austin.

At the NEH, he emphasized the traditional core of humanities study in literature, history, the classics and philosophy.

In November 1984, Bennett issued a report on the liberal arts that aired his deep disenchantment with college humanities teaching, which he said left too many students "lacking even the most rudimentary knowledge about the history, literature, art and philosophical foundations of their nation and civilization." ∎

House Passes Higher Education Authorization

The House Dec. 4 approved a $10.5 billion, five-year higher education reauthorization bill that largely ignored Reagan administration efforts to curb college student-aid programs.

The bill (HR 3700), passed on a 350-67 vote, authorized roughly $10.5 billion in fiscal 1987 and more in subsequent years for student loan and grant assistance and various college aid programs under the Higher Education Act (PL 89-329). *(Vote 391, p. 122-H)*

The House approved HR 3700 after rejecting, 127-289, an amendment to freeze spending for several of the programs at fiscal 1985 levels. *(Vote 390, p. 122-H)*

In his fiscal 1986 budget recommendations, President Reagan had proposed $4 billion in student-aid cuts over fiscal 1986-88. The cuts were to be accomplished by setting an annual cap on the amount of federal aid a student could receive and by tightening income eligibility for subsidized loans.

Although HR 3700 imposed new restrictions on who could get student loans and required borrowers to pay higher interest rates after they joined the workforce, the bill also liberalized grants to low-income students and increased aid in other areas.

One of the most important changes in the bill was the requirement that all students demonstrate financial need to qualify for a loan. Under existing law, only students whose annual family income was more than $30,000 a year had to pass a financial needs test.

HR 3700 also reduced the projected cost of the Guaranteed Student Loan program by about $750 million over five years. That program, the largest single source of student aid and the only Education Department entitlement program, cost some $3.8 billion in fiscal 1985. Entitlement programs guarantee a certain level of benefits to all who meet the requirements set by law.

The focus of House debate was on the cost of the bill, with proponents pointing to a fiscal 1987 authorization in HR 3700 that was $1 billion less than fiscal 1986 authorization levels. Critics charged, however, that the bill was still too costly because the fiscal 1987 total was higher than the $9.2 billion fiscal 1986 appropriation.

The Senate Labor and Human Resources Subcommittee on Education Dec. 12 approved by voice vote a five-year extension of higher education programs. According to preliminary estimates, the total authorization in the Senate bill came to about $9.4 billion for the programs in fiscal 1987. The bill barred Pell Grants to students with family incomes of more than $30,000 per year.

Background

The Higher Education Act of 1965 was an eight-title, $840 million bill. Included in the act were guaranteed loans to college students, grants for library books and materials and for university extension programs and funds to help small colleges.

In amending the act over the years, Congress began to channel most higher education aid to needy students rather than to colleges. By 1985, roughly half of all students were receiving some form of federal financial aid for their college costs. Student aid totaled about $9 billion in fiscal 1985.

The largest programs were Pell Grants for low-income students and low-interest Guaranteed Student Loans, which helped low- and middle-income students pay college bills.

But as the student aid programs grew, they became part of the focus of Reagan administration efforts to reduce federal spending. At first Congress went along with the administration in trimming the programs. For instance, federal aid to college students was cut sharply by the 1981 budget reconciliation bill (PL 97-35). The legislation established a "needs test" limiting Guaranteed Student Loans for individual students to the amounts needed to cover their educational costs. The bill also required students when they got a loan to pay an "origination fee" of 5 percent of the value of the loan. *(1981 Almanac p. 493)*

However, by 1982 Congress was taking actions to head off administration moves to cut back on student aid. The Education Department had issued proposed regulations during the summer that could have resulted in a $1.2 billion reduction in student aid funding, but the legislation cleared by Congress (PL 97-301) barred the department, in effect, from increasing the share of college costs that a student's family was expected to provide.

The bill also set the maximum Pell Grant at $1,800, or 50 percent of the cost of attendance, for the 1983-84 school year. *(1982 Almanac p. 483)*

In 1983 and 1984 Congress also moved to block administration efforts to rewrite eligibility standards for college student aid that would have had the effect of lowering the number of students who could be eligible for the programs. *(1983 Almanac p. 400, 1984 Almanac p. 493)*

In his fiscal 1986 budget recommendations, President Reagan recommended imposing a cap of $4,000 on the total federal aid a student could receive. The president also proposed limiting subsidized loans to those students whose family income was $32,500 or less.

The proposal that all students demonstrate financial need to qualify for a loan and other cost-cutting changes in HR 3700 also were included in the budget reconciliation bill (HR 3500) approved Oct. 24 by the House. The Senate reconcilation bill (S 1730) also called for student loan cuts, but did not include a financial needs test. *(Reconciliation, p. 498)*

House Committee Action

The House Education and Labor Committee Nov. 12 by 28-2 approved HR 3700, although some Republicans warned that it faced budget-cutting challenges on the House floor.

HR 3700 was reported Nov. 20 (H Rept 99-383).

The committee paid little heed to the administration's budget proposals to sharply curb middle-income students' eligibility for college loans and grants.

But committee members did approve an administration-backed proposal to require all student loan recipients to demonstrate their financial need for the loans. The bill also made it harder for student aid applicants to claim they were financially independent of their parents simply to improve their chances of getting aid.

The legislation liberalized spending in other areas — for example, by allowing increases in Pell Grants to the lowest-income students. HR 3700 allowed a gradual increase in the ceiling on Pell Grants from $2,100 to $3,100 in fiscal 1991. However, student grants would continue to be limited to no more than 60 percent of college costs.

Holding Down Costs

William D. Ford, D-Mich., chairman of the Education and Labor Subcommittee on Postsecondary Education and a leading student aid advocate, said he had reluctantly tried to hold down overall costs of HR 3700. With an eye to convincing budget-minded lawmakers to support the bill, Ford emphasized that the measure approved Oct. 29 by the subcommittee was more than $1 billion under the $11.9 billion authorized under current law for fiscal 1986.

Steve Bartlett, R-Texas, complained after the committee session that the bill was "a substantial budget buster." He cited in particular the cost of proposals to eliminate gradually a 5 percent "origination fee" students paid when they took out federally backed loans and to increase the amount students could borrow. Bartlett and Dick Armey, R-Texas, were the only panel members to vote against the bill.

One of the most important changes in the bill was the requirement that all students demonstrate financial need to qualify for a loan. Under current law, only students whose annual family income was more than $30,000 a year had to pass a financial needs test.

E. Thomas Coleman of Missouri, ranking Republican on the Postsecondary Subcommittee, warned that House floor debate was likely to bring demands for further reductions in the price tag of HR 3700. But he failed to win committee approval of proposals designed to make additional cuts in the loan program.

Coleman proposed retaining the 5 percent loan origination fee, which would be phased out under HR 3700 at a cost of more than $700 million over five years. To ease the effect of retaining the fee, which was deducted from the amount students received in their loans, Coleman proposed raising borrowing limits by 5 percent. His amendment was rejected, 12-18.

As approved by the committee, HR 3700 retained the current $2,500 annual loan limit for freshmen and sophomores. However, third- and fourth-year students were to be allowed to borrow $5,000 a year. Ford had originally proposed a $3,500 limit in the draft bill considered by his subcommittee, but that panel raised it to $5,000. The aggregate limit on undergraduate borrowing was raised by the committee from $12,500 to $14,500.

Defining 'Financial Independence'

A point of controversy during committee debate on HR 3700 was a subcommittee proposal to tighten the requirements governing who could claim financial independence when applying for student aid.

Critics of the existing rules, including the Reagan administration and many college officials, said it was too easy for students to claim they were financially independent of their parents simply to qualify for more federal aid. Parents' income was not counted in determining eligibility of independent students. Applicants could claim to be self-supporting if for two years they had received less than $750 a year from their parents, had not lived with them for more than six weeks a year and were not claimed as dependents

Student Aid Programs

Following are the Education Department's major college student aid programs as of 1985. Figures in parentheses are fiscal 1985 appropriations for each program.

Pell Grants: Awards to low-income students, limited in 1985-86 to $2,100 per student and to no more than 60 percent of college costs. ($3.9 billion)

Guaranteed Student Loans: Made by commercial banks with federal insurance against default. Banks receive a "special allowance" to supplement up to market rate the 8 percent interest paid by borrowers; the government pays all interest while students are in school. Another category of guaranteed loans, known as "PLUS" loans, allows higher-income parents and self-supporting students to borrow at 12 percent interest. ($3.8 billion)

Supplemental Educational Opportunity Grants: For up to $2,000 per student, distributed through campus financial aid offices. ($412.5 million)

College Work-Study: Helps colleges subsidize part-time jobs for students. ($592.5 million)

National Direct Student Loans: Financed by federal appropriations and distributed by college officials. Students pay 5 percent interest. Money repaid is recycled by colleges to make additional loans. ($217.5 million)

State Student Incentive Grants: Provides matching grants to states for their own scholarship programs. ($76 million)

on their parents' tax returns.

The draft bill considered by the subcommittee recommended barring students under the age of 22 from claiming financial independence, unless they were orphans, married, in graduate school or in other special circumstances. In an effort to achieve additional cost savings, the subcommittee raised the age cutoff to 24.

During committee debate, Steve Gunderson, R-Wis., complained that the provision was too strict and would disqualify many students who were legitimately self-supporting.

The committee approved, by voice vote, a Gunderson amendment to lower the age cutoff to 23 and to allow younger students to qualify as independent if they could document that they had supported themselves for two years.

Supplemental Grants

Reflecting some members' concern that campus-based aid should be more carefully targeted on the neediest students, Ford proposed in his original draft of HR 3700 to require colleges to use two-thirds of their supplemental grant funds for first-generation college students. Current law had no such requirement.

Coleman argued that the new requirement was not a relevant criterion for distributing money intended for needy students. But his effort to strike the provision failed in subcommittee.

In full committee, Ford agreed to a compromise that he said would focus supplemental funds on the lowest-income students. The committee adopted the compromise, which required three-quarters of all supplemental grant recipients at a school to be students receiving Pell Grants.

House Floor Action

During House debate on HR 3700, backers of the measure from both sides of the aisle emphasized that the Education and Labor Committee, despite its reputation as a bastion of liberals, had brought to the floor a bill that was not a "budget-buster."

Proponents praised the committee bill for having a lower price tag than current authorizations. Bill Goodling, R-Pa., a member of the committee, said the bill "more than meets the test of fiscal responsibility."

"It represents a reasonable balance between the need to control spending and the need to provide student assistance for post-secondary education," he said.

But the bill was still too costly for some Republicans' taste.

"Send this bill back to committee and let them come back with a bill that has some budgetary constraints," said Bartlett, sponsor of an amendment to freeze spending at fiscal 1985 levels for all but the student aid programs in the bill.

An official of the Office of Management and Budget said the bill was opposed by the Reagan administration because of its cost.

Broad Bipartisan Support

Some members said the broad bipartisan support garnered for HR 3700 was a tribute not only to the popularity of college aid programs, but also to the skill of Ford in resolving major controversies in committee or in behind-the-scenes negotiations.

During the first day of floor debate Dec. 3, Ford quietly resolved his major disagreements with Coleman.

With little debate on the floor, Ford accepted a Coleman amendment to retain the existing 5 percent fee students currently paid when they took out a guaranteed loan.

Although Ford fought in committee to eliminate the fee, he gave his blessing on the floor to Coleman's amendment, which was then adopted by voice vote. In exchange, Coleman agreed not to offer another cost-cutting amendment.

By reinstating the loan fee, the House trimmed $560 million from the bill's price tag over five years.

Bartlett Amendments

In subsequent action, the House blocked additional cuts in student loan spending by rejecting a Bartlett amendment to continue requiring students to begin repaying their loans six months after they left school. HR 3700 stretched that period to nine months. The amendment was rejected 177-221, largely along party lines. *(Vote 387, p. 122-H)*

But several of Bartlett's fellow Republicans took the lead in opposing his second amendment to freeze college aid programs.

The amendment would not have applied to student aid but would have capped spending only for other portions of the bill. The amendment would have authorized $310 million for those college aid programs in 1987 and allowed increases to reflect inflation in later years.

Bartlett said the freeze would trim spending authorized in the bill by $743 million in fiscal 1987 and by $4 billion over five years.

Critics, including several committee Republicans, disputed Bartlett's characterization of HR 3700 as a "budget-buster," emphasizing that the bill did not mandate increases but only set spending guidelines.

Others argued that the five-year freeze proposed by Bartlett would limit Congress' ability to set spending priorities in the future, when federal money might be flowing more freely.

Other Amendments

During floor debate, the House took the following actions by voice vote:

- Adopted an amendment by James M. Jeffords, R-Vt., to scale back the bill's provisions allowing borrowers to defer repaying student loans for up to five years if they became schoolteachers. The amendment limited the deferment to three years. The repayment break was one of several provisions included in HR 3700 that reflected members' interest in providing new incentives for people to enter teaching and stem a projected teacher shortage.
- Adopted an amendment by Marge Roukema, R-N.J., to bar students from declaring themselves financially independent when they applied for aid if they were claimed as a dependent on their parents' tax returns the year before. Even before the amendment was adopted, HR 3700 included provisions that would make it harder for students to declare themselves financially independent simply to improve their chances of getting financial aid. Parents' income was not counted in determining eligibility of independent students.
- Rejected an amendment by Gunderson to drop provisions earmarking funding for projects at specific colleges. He termed the provisions "pork-barrel" projects, and said that the funds should be distributed on a competitive basis.
- Rejected an amendment by Gary L. Ackerman, D-

N.Y., to strengthen provisions of the bill requiring universities to disclose certain information about large donations received from foreign countries.

As approved, the bill required colleges to file reports with the Education Department on foreign donations of more than $250,000 — a threshold Ackerman wanted to drop to $100,000.

The disclosure requirements were backed by members disturbed by cases in which universities had accepted money from foreign sources with restrictions on how the money could be used and what could be taught. Some members and college officials opposed the disclosure requirements, saying they feared the requirements would have a "chilling effect" on donors who wanted to give money anonymously.

Provisions

For most programs, HR 3700 authorized specific amounts for fiscal 1987, but provided open-ended authorizations for fiscal 1988-91.

As passed by the House, HR 3700:

Guaranteed Student Loans

- Required all students to pass a financial needs test to qualify for loans and allowed applicants to borrow no more than they demonstrated they needed. The bill required family assets to be taken into account, not just income as under current law.
- Increased the interest rate charged on guaranteed loans from 8 percent to 10 percent beginning in the fifth year of repayment.
- Continued to limit the amount freshmen and sophomores could borrow to no more than $2,500 a year, while raising the annual limit for juniors and seniors to $5,000. The aggregate limit on undergraduate borrowing would be raised to $14,500, an increase of $2,000.
- Required banks to disburse loans in installments during the school year rather than in one lump sum.
- Allowed undergraduates of all income levels to borrow under a program of higher interest loans, similar to auxiliary loans currently available to graduate students, self-supporting undergraduates and parents of undergraduates. The interest rate would be 12 percent or higher, depending on market rates. Unlike regular guaranteed student loans, these supplemental loans would not be interest-free during the years the borrower was in school.
- Allowed borrowers with more than $7,500 in college loans to consolidate their debts and take longer to repay them.

Other Student Aid

- Authorized Pell Grants of up to $2,300 in the 1987-88 academic year, up from the current maximum of $2,100. The limit on awards would rise annually in $200 increments. Awards would continue to be limited to no more than 60 percent of a student's college costs.
- Barred student aid applicants under the age of 23 from claiming they were financially independent of their parents, unless they were married, in graduate school or able to document that they had supported themselves for two years. Applicants generally could not be considered independent if they had been claimed as a dependent on their parents' tax returns the previous year.
- Renewed three "campus-based" financial aid programs, which were administered by college officials, authorizing $500 million for Supplemental Educational Opportunity Grants, $700 million for College Work-Study and $300 million for National Direct Student Loans in fiscal 1987.
- Revised the formula for distributing campus-based aid by eliminating current provisions that guaranteed each college's annual allotment would be at least as much as in 1979. The funding guarantees would be phased out over 20 years, and be replaced by a formula basing allocations on the financial need of each college's students.
- Raised the limit on supplemental grants from $2,000 to $4,000 a year.
- Targeted supplemental grants on low-income students by specifying that 75 percent of the recipients be students already receiving Pell Grants.
- Established a single system for analyzing students' financial need for aid under most federal programs run by the Education Department. Three different needs-analysis methods were being used for student loans, Pell Grants and campus-based aid.
- Allowed students enrolled less than half time to receive aid under the principal federal programs, except guaranteed loans.
- Allowed college graduates to defer repayment of their student loans for up to five years if they became elementary or secondary school teachers.

Institutional Aid

- Authorized $175 million in 1987 to help financially struggling colleges improve their management and academic quality. At least 30 percent of appropriations would be earmarked for grants to community colleges. In addition, $45.7 million a year would be set aside for colleges with large minority enrollments.
- Authorized $110 million in 1987 for a new program for historically black colleges to improve their academic programs and facilities and aid for black graduate and professional schools.
- Renewed existing "challenge grants" to help build the endowments of struggling colleges, which were required to put up matching funds.

Other Programs

- Overhauled federal aid for continuing education, authorizing $35 million in 1987 for improving programs and services for non-traditional students.
- Set up a new corporation to increase the availability of private capital for campus construction and renovation projects. The private corporation would insure commercial loans obtained by colleges.
- Provided $112 million in 1987 for a range of new and revised programs to train and recruit schoolteachers. ▮

Handicapped Legal Fees

The House and Senate in 1985 both passed a measure allowing parents to recoup the legal costs of defending a handicapped child's educational rights, but the two chambers failed to compromise their differences by the end of the year.

The bill (S 415), approved by the Senate July 30 and the House Nov. 12, overturned a 1984 Supreme Court ruling, *Smith v. Robinson*, that barred courts from awarding attorneys' fees to parents who prevailed in cases brought under the Education for All Handicapped Children Act (PL 94-142). *(1984 Almanac p. 9-A)*

Background

PL 94-142 guaranteed disabled children a public education tailored to their needs and abilities. It set up administrative procedures for settling disputes between parents and school districts over the appropriate education program for individual children. *(1975 Almanac p. 651)*

Unlike most federal civil rights statutes, however, PL 94-142 did not authorize courts to award attorneys' fees to parents who prevailed in legal disputes. Some courts had allowed parents to recover legal expenses under other laws, including Section 504 of the Rehabilitation Act (PL 93-112), which barred discrimination against the handicapped in federally funded programs and activities.

But in *Smith v. Robinson*, the court said parents who won cases under PL 94-142 could not recover legal fees under other laws because Congress meant the act to be the exclusive legal avenue for securing educational rights for the handicapped.

Sen. Lowell P. Weicker Jr., R-Conn., the leading sponsor of S 415, argued that, unless it was possible for parents to be able to recover their legal expenses, the handicapped-education law would become "a mere hollow pronouncement which the financially strapped parents and legal representatives of handicapped children cannot enforce."

School administrators warned that the availability of attorneys' fees would fuel litigation and make relations between parents and schools unnecessarily adversarial.

Legislative History

Senate. The Senate Labor and Human Resources Committee July 10 unanimously approved S 415. As reported July 25 (S Rept 99-112), S 415 embodied a compromise reached by Weicker and Committee Chairman Orrin G. Hatch, R-Utah, who sought to accommodate criticisms by the Reagan administration.

As approved June 6 by the Senate Subcommittee on the Handicapped, S 415 had allowed parents to recover attorneys' fees, including those arising from administrative proceedings. The Education Department objected, saying attorneys' fees should be awarded only for costs incurred in court.

The compromise reached by the full committee provided that if the school district brought in a lawyer, it had to pay for the parents' attorney as well. If parents initiated the use of legal counsel, they had to pay. If the school district did have to foot the bill, it had to pay even if the parents did not prevail.

In another change from the subcommittee version, the committee limited awards to the actual costs of litigation if the lawyer involved was from a legal advocacy group receiving federal funds. The subcommittee version would have allowed courts to award legal fees based on the standard generally applied, the prevailing market rate.

The Senate July 30 by voice vote approved S 415 after adopting a substitute amendment that rewrote the committee bill. The Senate dropped the committee provisions requiring a school district to pay for parents to hire a lawyer if school officials initiated the use of lawyers in administrative proceedings.

As passed by the Senate, S 415 allowed courts to award attorneys' fees only to parents who prevailed in disputes under the handicapped-education act. Parents could be compensated for expenses incurred in administrative proceedings as well as in court.

The Senate retained the committee provision imposing stricter limits on fee awards to attorneys who worked for publicly funded legal aid groups.

S 415 also included a requirement that parents exhaust administrative remedies before going to court. The bill applied to all cases initiated after July 3, 1984, and to cases pending on July 4, 1984 — the day before the *Smith* decision.

House. By voice vote, the House Education and Labor Committee Sept. 19 approved HR 1523.

As approved by the Select Education Subcommittee, HR 1523 had allowed recovery of attorneys' fees at the court level, but had limited the circumstances in which parents could recover expenses incurred in pre-court administrative proceedings. The full House committee dropped the limits on fee awards at the administrative level.

The House Nov. 12 by voice vote passed HR 1523 (H Rept 99-296) after sponsors agreed to changes that blunted opposition from the Reagan administration and Republican critics.

After approving HR 1523, the House substituted its text for that of S 415.

Pat Williams, D-Mont., chairman of the Education and Labor Subcommittee on Select Education, brought to the House floor an amended version of the bill approved by the Education and Labor Committee.

The amended bill provided that the authority for courts to award attorneys' fees incurred at the administrative level would "sunset" after four years. It called for a General Accounting Office study of the effects of the legislation in the interim. No such provisions were included in the Senate version of S 415.

In another change that won qualified support for the bill from the Reagan administration, Williams agreed to drop a provision that would have written into law current regulations for enforcing Section 504 of the Rehabilitation Act of 1973 (PL 93-112). That section barred discrimination against the handicapped in federally funded programs and activities. *(1973 Almanac p. 557)*

Advocates for the disabled had supported codification of the rules to prevent the anti-bias standards from being weakened by the Reagan administration. Mario Biaggi, D-N.Y., called the provision "critical to permanently protect the rights of the handicapped children."

The administration assailed the provision as an inappropriate limit on its ability to enforce and revise the civil rights rules. But administration officials told key lawmakers that they could support the attorneys' fees bill if codification of the rules was dropped. Williams said he would accept the change because "the administration is expressing no current desire to modify these regulations anyway."

Other provisions of the House bill not included in the Senate version:

- Prohibited school districts from taking retaliatory action against people who filed complaints, testified or otherwise participated in disputes — a protection intended primarily to protect teachers who got involved in disputes between parents and schools.
- Required school districts to allow school officials and parents to meet informally to resolve a complaint before a formal hearing. ∎

Health Planning Program

House and Senate committees completed work on measures to revamp and extend the federal health planning system, but neither bill saw floor action in 1985.

The House Energy and Commerce Committee Nov. 5 voted 22-2 to report HR 3010, extending the health planning system for one year. HR 3010 also provided that the program would be abolished automatically on Oct. 1, 1986 if Congress did not renew it.

The Senate Labor and Human Resources Committee Nov. 19 approved S 1855, providing for a three-year renewal of the planning program.

Background

Created in 1974 (PL 93-641), the federal health planning program had been kept alive through the annual appropriations process since 1981, when the Reagan administration recommended phasing it out. *(1981 Almanac p. 476; 1983 Almanac p. 420)*

The planning program was created to combat inflation in health care costs by curbing excessive hospital investments in medical equipment, services and construction.

State and local planning agencies, supported by federal funds, surveyed medical resources and decided what additions would be appropriate. Hospitals and other health care institutions had to receive official approval from state review agencies through a "certificate of need" process before starting major projects.

Critics argued that the regulatory scheme had become unnecessary as changes in the health care industry including changes in the Medicare payment system — had increased pressures on hospitals to hold down costs.

Congress faced an Oct. 1, 1986, deadline for deciding how Medicare, the federal health care program for the elderly, should pay hospitals for capital expenses, which had been reimbursed on a cost basis.

Congress appropriated $65 million in fiscal 1985 for the health planning program.

House Committee

Before approving HR 3010, the House Energy and Commerce Committee by a vote of 22-19 endorsed an amendment by Edward R. Madigan, R-Ill., to end the program at the beginning of fiscal 1987 unless Congress enacted another extension by that date. Madigan's amendment to "sunset" the health planning program succeeded despite strong opposition from Henry A. Waxman, D-Calif., Health Subcommittee chairman.

An amendment by Cardiss Collins, D-Ill., to prohibit the termination of federal funding for any local health planning agency in fiscal 1986 was defeated on a tie vote of 21-21.

HR 3010 relaxed some federal requirements in the health planning system, but did not turn the program into a block grant, as some in Congress proposed.

Other provisions of HR 3010 provided that state participation in the federal health planning program be made optional instead of mandatory, as in existing law. The bill also raised the dollar thresholds for projects that had to go through certificate of need review. The threshold for capital expenditures was increased from $600,000 to $1 million; for the annual operating costs of health services, from $250,000 to $500,000; for major medical equipment, from $400,000 to $500,000.

Senate Committee

The Senate bill, S 1855, approved by voice vote, represented a compromise between two sharply different views of what to do with the health planning program.

The compromise bill dropped many current federal requirements but did not go as far as Dan Quayle, R-Ind., had proposed in legislation (S 1560) to turn the health planning program into state block grants with few strings attached.

Opposition to the block grant approach came from Lowell P. Weicker Jr., R-Conn., who had sponsored a competing bill (S 1104) to maintain key elements of the existing health planning program for three years.

Both Quayle and Weicker sponsored S 1855 as an acceptable compromise of their opposing positions.

S 1855 authorized $65.1 million in fiscal 1986, $69.2 million in fiscal 1987 and $73.8 million in 1988.

Under S 1855, states were no longer required to have certificate of need programs. But for those states that chose to, the review programs had to meet specifications set out in the bill.

S 1855 required such programs to review all proposed capital expenditures over $1 million, equipment purchases over $400,000 and health services with annual operating costs of over $310,000.

States that did not choose to have a certificate of need program could use their federal grants for other health planning activities, including studies of health care financing and of the availability of services to people lacking health insurance. ▮

Medical Training

The Senate Labor and Human Resources Committee July 26 reported a bill (S 1210 — S Rept 99-117) intended to encourage teaching hospitals to train fewer doctors in narrow subspecialties and more in primary health care.

S 1210 established a council of medical professionals to make recommendations about how many doctors should be trained in primary-care fields such as family medicine, pediatrics and internal medicine.

The medical council would recommend national medical training goals to the Department of Health and Human Services, including proposed minimum percentages of primary-care doctors that should be trained by different kinds of hospitals. The bill also recommended that graduates of foreign medical schools be allowed to hold no more than 25 percent of the slots in any graduate medical program.

S 1210 was approved unanimously by the committee on July 10, despite complaints from some members that it would inject the government into decisions about the allocation of medical professionals.

Hospitals' compliance with the recommendations of the council would be voluntary. However, after the committee ordered S 1210 to be reported, the panel approved an amendment to be offered separately on the Senate floor that provided financial incentives for hospitals to comply.

The amendment, approved 13-3, boosted Medicare payments for medical training by up to 10 percent for hospitals that did comply.

Because the amendment affected Medicare reimbursements, it did not fall within the Labor Committee's jurisdictional purview and thus could not be incorporated into the committee bill.

HHS had projected that by 1990, there would be 35,000 more doctors overall than the nation needed. However, some health experts and members of Congress said that those figures masked imbalances in specialties, and that too few practitioners were going into primary care.

The largest source of federal funding for graduate medical education was Medicare, which expected to pay some $1.3 billion in fiscal 1986 to reimburse hospitals for its share of residents' salaries and other direct training costs. (Medicare also provided supplemental payments to teaching hospitals to compensate for their generally higher patient care costs, which were attributed in part to the presence of training programs.)

The Senate proposed in its version of the budget reconciliation measure (HR 3128) to freeze payments to cover hospitals' direct costs for medical education, such as resident physicians' salaries and classroom costs. The House version prohibited HHS from imposing a one-year freeze on Medicare payments for the direct costs of medical education. But Congress failed to complete action on HR 3128 as reported from conference at the end of the 1985 session. *(Budget reconciliation, p. 498)*

Bowen Succeeds Heckler

The Senate Dec. 12 by a 93-2 vote confirmed the nomination of Otis R. Bowen to head the Department of Health and Human Services (HHS). *(Vote 373, p. 63-S)*

Bowen, a professor of family medicine at the Indiana University School of Medicine and a former governor of Indiana, succeeded Margaret M. Heckler, who Oct. 1 agreed to step down as HHS secretary to become ambassador to Ireland.

The move of Heckler from HHS secretary to ambassador was widely reported to be at the urging of senior White House officials, critical of her job performance and commitment to conservative social causes. Heckler, who served eight terms in the House, was named to the HHS position in 1983 after losing a reelection bid to Rep. Barney Frank, D-Mass. *(1983 Almanac p. 390)*

The Senate Finance Committee Dec. 11 unanimously recommended approval of Bowen's nomination.

In testimony a day earlier, Bowen told the committee he would give top priority to finding ways to help the elderly pay for long-term health care and for the cost of lengthy hospital stays for "catastrophic" illnesses.

Members said Bowen was particularly well suited for the HHS job because of his work in 1982-84 as chairman of a federal advisory council studying Medicare, the federal health insurance program for the elderly and disabled. That panel proposed a broad agenda for overhauling Medicare, including recommendations geared to rescuing the hospital insurance trust fund from impending insolvency.

Family Planning Program

Renewal of the government's major family planning program, known as Title X, was stymied in Congress in 1985.

The House June 18 blocked a move to put renewal of the Title X program on a fast track and shield it from amendments related to abortion and other sensitive issues. A bill (HR 2369) to extend family planning aid for three years was brought up in the House under suspension of the rules, which did not allow amendments to be offered.

HR 2369 drew a majority, 214-197, but fell 60 votes short of the two-thirds margin it needed to pass under suspension of the rules. *(Vote 147, p. 50-H)*

The Senate Labor and Human Resources Committee Dec. 11 approved a bill (S 881) to reauthorize aid for family planning, but no further action was taken in the Senate.

The program continued to receive funding, however, through the fiscal 1986 continuing appropriations resolution (H J 465 — PL 99-190), at the fiscal 1985 level of $142.5 million. *(Story, p. 360)*

Background

The family planning program, which was created as Title X of the Public Health Service Act of 1970 (PL 91-572), provided funds to more than 5,000 family planning clinics run by states, local health departments and private non-profit groups that disseminated information on family planning and contraceptives. While abortion counseling and referrals for abortion were permitted, no funds could be used to perform abortions. *(Congress and the Nation Vol. III, p. 557)*

The Reagan administration repeatedly sought to eliminate the Title X program, leaving states to support family planning under a proposed block grant for a range of primary health care activities. Congress refused to agree but cut Title X spending by almost one-quarter in fiscal 1982. While funding increased from that level for the next three fiscal years, it never regained the $161.7 million level appropriated in fiscal 1981.

Critics said that family planning clinics contributed to increased sexual promiscuity among teenagers. Some anti-abortion groups charged that federal family planning funds were improperly used to lobby Congress on abortion.

In 1984, a multi-year reauthorization of Title X stalled when House and Senate negotiators disagreed on whether to require federally funded clinics to notify parents when their teenagers sought contraceptives, as the Senate wanted. *(1984 Almanac p. 464)*

House Action

Opposition to HR 2369 in the House was spearheaded by conservative Republicans who wanted to propose amendments related to abortion and to "traditional family values," as one member put it. No amendments were permitted by the suspension procedure under which the bill was brought up for a vote.

Objecting to the procedure, William E. Dannemeyer, R-Calif., said the bill was too significant for members to be denied an opportunity to vote on amendments, such as a parental notification amendment he sponsored that had been rejected by voice vote during Energy and Commerce Committee consideration of HR 2369.

The Energy Committee had reported HR 2369 on June 4 (H Rept 99-159). The bill had been approved May 22 on a 18-4 vote.

The committee also rejected by voice vote an amendment by Rep. Thomas J. Bliley Jr., R-Va., that would have denied federal aid to family planning clinics located in or near facilities that performed abortions.

Senate Action

The Senate Labor and Human Resources Committee approved S 881 by voice vote, after committee Chairman Orrin G. Hatch, R-Utah, said he would drop his plan to offer an amendment to deny federal funds to family-planning clinics that made referrals for abortion.

As approved by the committee, S 881 embodied a compromise hammered out by Hatch, a leading foe of abortion, and Lowell P. Weicker Jr., R-Conn., who supported legalized abortion and opposed efforts to restrict family-planning clinics.

In a concession to Hatch, the bill allowed federal funding for Utah's state family-planning program, which had been denied federal aid because it required parental consent before minors could receive services. A federal court had ruled that the Utah requirement was inconsistent with congressional intent for the program.

Weicker opposed funding of the Utah program. But he said accepting the provision was a suitable compromise to break a longstanding logjam over reauthorization of family-planning aid.

The Reagan administration in 1983 tried through regulations to impose a requirement similar to the one used by the Utah program on all Title X clinics. But those rules, which would have required clinics to notify parents when teenagers sought contraceptives, also were ruled by federal courts to be inconsistent with Congress' intent.

Program guidelines barred clinics from disclosing information about clients without their consent.

S 881 channeled funds to the Utah program by authorizing $600,000 a year for four years to study the effects of its parental consent requirement.

In other action, the committee approved, 10-6, an amendment by Charles E. Grassley, R-Iowa, allowing clinics to use Title X funds for adoption services.

As approved by the committee, S 881 authorized $143.1 million in fiscal 1986, $150.2 million in 1987, $157.8 million in 1988 and $165.7 million in 1989 for family-planning services, training grants and public information programs.

The committee also approved by voice vote another bill (S 1566) to reauthorize demonstration projects to discourage sexual activity among teenagers. The bill authorized $48 million over fiscal 1986-88 for the program, known as Adolescent Family Life.

Labor-HHS Appropriations Fight

A related fight over family planning funds came up in the Senate during debate on the fiscal 1986 appropriations bill for the departments of Labor, Health and Human Services (HHS) and Education (HR 3424).

As reported from committee, HR 3424 had included $142.5 million for Title X programs, although authorizing legislation had not been enacted and funding for Title X had not been included in the House version of HR 3424. The Senate deleted the Title X money as part of a unanimous consent agreement. *(Appropriations story, p. 333)*

The removal of Title X money during Oct. 22 Senate debate on HR 3424 was part of a larger unanimous consent agreement between Weicker, chairman of the Labor/HHS Appropriations Subcommittee, Hatch and Jesse Helms, R-N.C., one of the Senate's leading abortion opponents. In exchange for deleting the Title X money, Hatch promised to hold hearings and move legislation reauthorizing the program.

Weicker also agreed to add language to HR 3424 barring any federal funds from being used to provide abortions for poor women unless the mother's life was endangered.

Helms agreed not to push for an amendment, included in the House bill, that would have authorized the U.S. surgeon general to shut down bathhouses and massage parlors if they were found to facilitate the transmission of AIDS.

Continuing Resolution

When the House Dec. 4 began debate on H J Res 465, the continuing appropriations measure, a potentially controversial debate on abortion had already been defused by an action by the Rules Committee. The committee, with the approval of key members, deleted Appropriations Committee language relating to abortion and federal family planning funds. The Senate panel concurred with this decision.

Jack F. Kemp, R-N.Y., had tried to add language in the Appropriations Committee Nov. 21 to bar the use of Title X money for referring pregnant women for abortions. Richard J. Durbin, D-Ill., offered a substitute that barred money for performing abortions and for "advocating" abortions unless the life of the pregnant woman might be endangered by carrying the fetus to term. Durbin's substitute was accepted 37-16.

During the Rules Commiteee meeting Dec. 3, Henry J. Hyde, R-Ill., sponsor of the longstanding law that barred most federal funding for abortions, said that because of the way Durbin's amendment was worded, it could open the way for allowing federal funding for abortions. Hyde said he would prefer no new restrictions on Title X money to the Durbin language.

Durbin said he would withdraw his language if Kemp was barred from offering his amendment on the floor, and Hyde said he would support the move. The Rules Committee accepted the deal, and drafted the rule to delete the Durbin language.

The final bill funded Title X programs at the fiscal 1985 level of $142.5 million. ▮

Health Warning Labels

The Senate Labor and Human Resources Committee on Nov. 19 approved legislation (S 1574 — S Rept 99-209) to require health warnings on product labels and in advertising for snuff and chewing tobacco. The bill, approved by voice vote, was reported Dec. 4. It required "smokeless" tobacco packages and advertisements to carry one of three labels, which warned that the product might cause cancer, mouth disease and tooth loss, and should not be considered "a safe alternative to cigarettes."

The House Energy and Commerce Subcommittee on Health Oct. 23 approved a bill requiring health warning labels on aspirin, chewing tobacco and snuff.

By a 9-7 vote, the subcommittee approved a substitute to a bill (HR 1381) that required a label on aspirin products warning that their use by children with chicken pox or flu might increase the risk of contracting Reyes Syndrome, a rare neurological disease.

The substitute (HR 3640), a compromise authored by

Edward R. Madigan, R-Ill., required the warning to appear in advertising and in retail stores where aspirin was sold.

By 16-2, the panel approved a separate bill (HR 3510) requiring warning labels on chewing tobacco and snuff, and banning TV and radio advertising for them. The bill was in response to studies that showed smokeless tobacco was addictive and might cause mouth cancer, gum disease and tooth loss.

Home Health Care Services

The Senate Labor and Human Resources Committee Nov. 19 by voice vote approved legislation (S 1181) authorizing $100 million a year beginning in fiscal 1987 for block grants to states for home health care services for elderly people who otherwise would have to be institutionalized. The bill was reported Dec. 4 (S Rept 99-208).

The move was unusual for the Republican-dominated committee at a time when most congressional efforts were directed at cutting programs to reduce the federal deficit. But Labor Committee Chairman Orrin G. Hatch, R-Utah, argued that the bill's expenditures would result in long-term savings because caring for the elderly at home was generally cheaper than care in an institution.

The measure was symptomatic of a broader congressional interest in developing alternatives to institutional long-term care for the elderly. Both House and Senate versions of a deficit-reduction measure (HR 3128) included provisions designed to increase Medicaid coverage for home health care. *(Deficit reduction bill, p. 498)*

As approved by the Labor Committee, S 1181 provided aid to states to provide and coordinate home and community health services and to increase public awareness of the availability of such services.

Drug Export Ban

The Senate Labor and Human Resources Committee Nov. 19 approved a bill (S 1848) lifting a ban on the export by pharmaceutical companies of drugs that had not been certified by the Food and Drug Administration (FDA).

The bill, ordered reported on a 13-2 vote, allowed such exports if the drugs had been approved by other countries with advanced drug regulatory processes. The committee's report on the bill was not filed by year's end.

Advocates of the measure, led by Labor Committee Chairman Orrin G. Hatch, R-Utah, argued that the export ban on medicines lacking FDA approval had not kept such drugs from reaching foreign markets. The drugs could legally be sold overseas if U.S. firms manufactured them abroad.

Only antibiotics were exempt from the law that since 1938 had banned the export of American-made drugs that the FDA had not certified as safe and effective enough to be sold in the United States.

Hatch introduced a drug export bill in 1984, but the measure died without action after House and Senate hearings. The measure stalled amid complaints that lifting the export ban would make it too easy for U.S. manufacturers to "dump" dubious drugs abroad — particularly on Third World countries lacking review procedures to ensure the safe and proper use of drugs. *(1984 Almanac p. 475)*

In what sponsors said was a significant departure from past versions of the legislation, S 1848 incorporated new safeguards against the unauthorized shipment of drugs to underdeveloped countries.

As approved by the committee, S 1848 continued to bar the export of drugs banned by the FDA. Drugs awaiting approval or otherwise lacking FDA certification could be exported if they had been approved by one of a specified group of industrialized countries with sophisticated drug-regulatory systems. Those countries would be designated by the secretary of health and human services (HHS), but S 1848 specified 15 countries that should be included.

Drugs approved by those designated countries could also be exported to other nations certified as having regulatory procedures adequate to ensure that the drugs were properly labeled and to detect and monitor adverse drug reactions.

Medicare Payment Freeze

Congress attempted to impose further cost-saving measures on Medicare in 1985, but the effort stalled when the budget reconciliation bill to which the Medicare provisions were attached failed to clear Congress in the last days of the session.

More than $11.2 billion in Medicare savings over fiscal 1986-88 were included in the budget reconciliation package (HR 3128). Most of the savings in Medicare, the nation's health program for the elderly, came from limits on reimbursements to physicians and hospitals.

In addition to its Medicare reimbursement limits, the stalled reconciliation bill included provisions requiring all employees of state and local governments to be enrolled in Medicare and thus subject, beginning July 1, 1987, to the payroll tax that financed the hospital insurance program. The bill also made changes in Medicaid, the federal health insurance program for the poor. *(Budget reconciliation story, p. 498)*

When HR 3128 got caught in a last-minute squabble between the House and the Senate over a proposed tax for the "superfund" hazardous-waste cleanup program, Congress cleared legislation Dec. 20 (HR 4006 — PL 99-201) extending through March 15, 1986, the existing freeze on Medicare reimbursements to hospitals and physicians.

Background

Congress in 1984 ordered a temporary halt to increases in Medicare payment rates for doctors. In a deficit reduction bill (PL 98-369) enacted in 1984, Congress imposed the fee freeze until October 1985 and also limited the rate of increase in Medicare payments to hospitals for fiscal 1985 and 1986. *(1984 Almanac p. 480)*

As it attempted to move HR 3128, the budget reconciliation bill, toward final passage in the fall of 1985, Congress passed a series of temporary extensions of the hospital and fee freezes. When it became apparent on Dec. 19 that the budget reconciliation bill would not pass in time to meet a Dec. 20 expiration date for several taxes and the Medicare freeze, the House and Senate acted to extend a cigarette tax and the Medicare provisions into mid-March.

Medicare was an inviting target for congressional deficit-cutters. If no changes were made, the program's cost was expected to reach $77.2 billion in fiscal 1986.

The president's fiscal 1986 budget called for cutting some $4 billion from Medicare — the largest chunk of money to be taken from any single program.

The fiscal 1986 budget resolution (S Con Res 32), which Congress approved Aug. 1, assumed $276 billion in spending cuts and revenue increases through fiscal 1988, of which $11 billion was to be achieved through freezing payments to doctors and hospitals. *(Fiscal 1986 budget resolution, p. 441)*

A June 10 Department of Health and Human Services (HHS) regulation froze fiscal 1986 Medicare payment rates for hospitals at the fiscal 1985 level. HHS said that rates for 1985 had been set too high — in part because medical inflation turned out to be lower than expected. Current law allowed increases of more than 5 percent to compensate for medical inflation. ■

Stalemate Dooms Rewrite of Housing Policy

Pervasive differences between House and Senate conferees stymied enactment of a fiscal 1986 housing authorization bill that would have expanded existing programs or started new ones.

Democrats on the House Banking, Finance and Urban Affairs Committee could not convince the Republican-controlled Senate Banking, Housing and Urban Affairs Committee to accept a $14.3 billion reauthorization the House had included in its budget reconciliation bill (HR 3128). *(Reconciliation, p. 498)*

And the Democrats refused to accept, either as part of reconciliation or as separate legislation, the relatively minor housing items that senators offered as a compromise.

The House-passed reconciliation bill included a revised version of HR 1 (H Rept 99-230), approved by the House Banking Committee, that made extensive changes in federal housing and community development programs operated by the U.S. Department of Housing and Urban Development (HUD) and the Department of Agriculture's Farmers Home Administration (FmHA).

Panel Democrats added HR 1 to the reconciliation measure because they were convinced the Senate committee would not act on a housing bill, and they wanted to force a conference on housing issues. That tactic succeeded in 1983 when the House attached a housing bill to unrelated legislation that the administration wanted badly. *(1983 Almanac p. 277)*

But Jake Garn, R-Utah, chairman of the Senate committee, insisted that reconciliation should be used only to make savings required by the budget resolution and that housing policy should be separate legislation. His committee had held hearings on housing but no legislation had been marked up.

Recognizing that Garn was unwilling to yield, and refusing themselves to accept the limited provisions the senators offered, the House Democrats agreed to strip the housing language from the reconciliation bill, leaving basically extensions of existing non-controversial programs. They said they would try to pass a housing authorization separately in early 1986, despite deficit-reduction pressures that might threaten domestic spending legislation.

"I may be overly optimistic," said Rep. Henry B. Gonzalez, D-Texas, chairman of the Subcommittee on Housing and Community Development, "but I think that we'll come out, before this [99th] Congress is over, with an authorization bill."

Gonzalez noted that an authorization was needed to make policy changes to improve existing programs and create better ones. But Congress had not passed a housing authorization through regular legislative channels since 1980.

When Congress failed to act on the reconciliation bill, members passed a temporary extension of several programs whose authority had expired, including the Federal Housing Administration's mortgage insurance programs, flood and crime insurance, Home Mortgage Disclosure Act and others. The measure (H J Res 495 — PL 99-219) extending them through March 17, 1986, was passed by the House Dec. 19 and cleared by the Senate Dec. 20.

Summary of Provisions

As passed by the House, HR 3128 authorized $20.5 billion, including $14.3 billion in new funds, for fiscal 1986 housing and community development programs. The bill included $8.2 billion in savings through fiscal 1988, as required by the budget resolution, primarily by reducing rural housing programs and changing the method of financing public housing.

In fiscal 1985, Congress provided $15.9 billion, covering 174,730 units. The 1986 authorizations included $9.2 billion for assisted housing, which would support an additional 91,509 dwellings.

The bill rejected the administration's call for a two-year moratorium on housing and for housing vouchers, which tenants could use like cash toward rent in housing they found on their own. If the rent was less than the value of the voucher, the tenant could pocket the difference; if it was more, the tenant would pay.

The administration contended that vouchers allowed "freedom of choice" for renters and would save money. But critics argued that a test of the program had just gotten under way and Congress should wait for the results. *(1983 Almanac p. 277)*

The bill continued the existing subsidy, generally a payment by the government to a landlord of privately owned housing to make up the difference between a percentage of the tenant's income and the market rent.

The change in public housing financing permitted annual capital grants from the government to build and modernize public housing; existing law allowed only long-term loans. The new alternative, requested by the administration, required less budget authority for each unit, allowing more units than under the previous system.

The administration objected to some other new proposals, including a $100 million authorization for grants to non-profit organizations for loans to moderate-income families to help them buy first homes. Known as the "Nehemiah plan," it was based on a New York City program and was expected to support 6,666 units. The organizations would provide interest-free loans up to $15,000 to be secured by a second mortgage held by the secretary.

In addition, $50 million was authorized for new grants to non-profit groups to acquire and rehabilitate structures for the homeless. Another $100 million was earmarked for new grants to state and local governments, to be matched with local contributions, to renovate shelters for the homeless and for basic services.

The measure also contained a fair housing initiative backed by the administration but opposed by the National Association of Realtors.

The bill reduced budget authority for Community Development Block Grants (CDBG) from the previously authorized level of $3.472 billion to $2.980 billion. It also reduced the authorization for Urban Development Action Grants (UDAG) from $440 million to $352 million. CDBGs were used by cities for a variety of development programs, while UDAGs were designed to stimulate private investment in deteriorated neighborhoods.

Also, the funding formula for UDAGs was revised to ensure that newer cities received more grants.

For rural housing, the bill authorized $2.266 billion for loans, including $1.328 billion for home ownership and $900 million for rental housing, supporting 63,000 units. FmHA initiatives included permitting the sale of home loans directly to the public to save off-budget outlays and authorizing guaranteed loans for moderate income persons unable to obtain credit elsewhere.

Subcommittee Cuts

As originally introduced by Gonzalez, HR 1 would have increased housing aid over the fiscal 1985 appropriation by about 50 percent, providing $22 billion in new budget authority and 283,605 new units of housing.

Democrats rejected Reagan's proposal for a two-year moratorium on most housing aid and the elimination of several programs, including rural housing and grants to build new rental housing. But they could not accept the increases sought by Gonzalez. At a caucus April 16, they agreed to freeze funding at the fiscal 1985 levels, which they calculated at $16.7 billion in new budget authority, for 222,962 additional units of subsidized housing.

But Democrats encountered GOP criticism during markups May 14 and May 21, and amid growing pressure for spending restraint, the subcommittee June 4 voted to further cut $437.36 million from the bill, bringing it to $16.3 billion. Before approving the bill June 20, the subcommittee considered 91 amendments over six days and adopted 58.

The panel June 4 defeated by voice vote an amendment by John Hiler, R-Ind., to delete a requirement that HUD notify Congress of proposed new regulations as they were submitted to the Office of Management and Budget (OMB) for review. Many members blamed the deregulation-minded OMB for killing or revising housing rules, and HR 1 would require "before and after" disclosure of rules that HUD wanted to promulgate. Hiler met bipartisan opposition.

By a vote of 14-20, the subcommittee defeated an amendment by Toby Roth, R-Wis., to make permanent a housing voucher demonstration program. Amendments adopted included those by Steve Bartlett, R-Texas, stating the importance to housing of lowering the federal deficit, 20-19; and by Chalmers P. Wylie, Ohio, ranking GOP member, earmarking $1.5 million to develop and assist resident management groups.

Fair Housing

On June 11, the subcommittee by voice vote rejected GOP efforts to cut still more from the bill, particularly in FmHA rural housing programs. By voice vote, it adopted an amendment by Stan Lundine, D-N.Y., which he said would save $1.3 billion by allowing FmHA to sell loans in the secondary mortgage market, which in turn would sell them to investors.

The panel rejected a proposal by Bill McCollum, R-Fla., to kill rental housing development grants, called HODAGs. McCollum said that the $76,000 it cost to build each new unit would be better spent on other programs, such as rent subsidies, which provided housing at less expense. His plan was rejected, 11-26.

The panel also adopted, 26-13, a Bartlett amendment distributing public housing modernization funds by formula, which would be drawn up by 1987, rather than requiring local public housing authorities to apply for funds as they currently did.

The subcommittee June 19 voted 25-13 to retain a program authorizing $4 million in grants to non-profit groups to investigate housing discrimination. However, Congress would review proposed regulations before HUD obligated any money.

The grants were strongly opposed by the National Association of Realtors and created an unusual alliance between Samuel R. Pierce Jr., HUD secretary, who proposed them, and many subcommittee Democrats.

Gerald D. Kleczka, D-Wis., offered an amendment to strike the provision. He objected to "testing," in which two people of different races attempted separately to rent or buy a dwelling to determine whether a seller discriminated by race. He described the practice as an "attempt to entrap."

But Steward B. McKinney, R-Conn., said that testing was not as nefarious as suggested. "You would think we were sending out the storm troopers," he said.

Together with Sander M. Levin, D-Mich., McKinney offered a substitute requiring congressional review of HUD regulations on the fair housing program, which the panel adopted.

Full Committee Action

As ordered reported July 10 by the House Banking Committee, HR 1 authorized $16.3 billion in new funds in fiscal 1986 and provided for more than 210,000 new subsidized dwellings. With the exception of amendments on enterprise zones and home mortgage disclosure, the bill essentially was the version approved by the subcommittee.

It included funding for the construction of new rental housing, which the Reagan administration strongly opposed, and rejected cuts Reagan had proposed in existing programs.

Democrats said HR 1 constituted a freeze: The $16.3 billion total included the fiscal 1985 level of funding plus an inflation adjustment allowed by the House budget resolution.

But Republicans still said the bill should not exceed the fiscal 1985 total. Wylie said that the Congressional Budget Office (CBO) and the OMB could not say how much actually would be spent in fiscal 1985. The committee by voice vote adopted an amendment by Wylie expressing the "policy of the Congress" that funding should not exceed the fiscal 1985 appropriation.

Enterprise Zones. The full committee voted 26-22 to authorize the HUD secretary to designate 75 "enterprise zones" and to allow the secretary to waive HUD regulations to entice businesses to locate in the zones. The subcommittee rejected a similar amendment.

The president strongly supported enterprise zones, and legislation providing tax incentives for businesses that located in enterprise zones had passed the Senate three times. However, it was stalled in the Ways and Means Committee, where Chairman Dan Rostenkowski, D-Ill., remained opposed. *(1984 Almanac p. 168)*

The amendment approved by the committee, sponsored by Bartlett, omitted the tax incentives. However, Bartlett said adopting the amendment might spur the Ways and Means Committee to act.

Mortgage Disclosure. The committee voted 26-19 to make the Home Mortgage Disclosure Act (HMDA) permanent (PL 94-200). The law required financial institutions to provide information on the number and type of mortgages they issued. The Housing Subcommittee June 20 voted 18-14 to authorize it for five years.

The full committee adopted an amendment by Parren J. Mitchell, D-Md., removing the expiration date.

The panel rejected, by a 21-25 vote, a Wylie plan to limit the number of institutions required to disclose mortgage information. *(Background, Congress and the Nation Vol. IV, p. 490)*

Reconciliation

The reconciliation legislation was required to make the savings mandated by the congressional budget resolution (S Con Res 32). The resolution required the Banking committees to find $8.2 billion in savings in housing programs and assumed that the savings could be achieved, in part, by cutting rural housing programs and operating assistance to local public housing authorities.

Both the House and Senate panels basically agreed on the savings, but the House committee went further and attached the entire text of HR 1 to its recommendations. Garn had reluctantly agreed to add a housing program to the Senate reconciliation package too, but after his committee was unable to agree on a housing program, he maintained that he would accept only a housing bill passed through regular channels.

House Republicans then switched and insisted that HR 1 proposals be stripped from their reconciliation bill. However, by a narrow 10-vote margin, the House voted Oct. 24 to leave the housing and other program authorizaions in the bill. The vote was 209-219 against an amendment by Delbert L. Latta, R-Ohio, to strike extraneous provisions. The House subsequently passed the reconciliation bill, 228-199. *(Votes 334, 336, p. 104-H)*

Before reaching the floor, the housing provisions were revised to bring them in line with the budget resolution, lowering the total from $16.3 billion to $14.3 billion.

In conference on the reconciliation measure, House and Senate staffs sought common ground, but they failed to agree on any of the major issues, such as dollar amounts, restrictions on HUD regulatory authority and tenant protection.

At one point, St Germain and other House members offerred a list of housing provisions, including many of the major programmatic changes backed by the House committee. But Garn and others refused to accept the proposals and instead suggested a much smaller list that included, for example, the changes in funding for UDAGs.

House Democrats said that without the big policy changes, they would refuse to accept the smaller matters that senators were suggesting.

"If we can't let all the cattle out of the barn, we'd rather not let a few out," said Charles E. Schumer, D-N.Y., a Banking Committee member. ▮

Food Stamp Benefits, Eligibility Expanded

Responding to reports of increased hunger in the United States, Congress voted to expand benefits and eligibility for the largest federal food aid program, food stamps.

The final version of the omnibus farm bill (HR 2100 — PL 99-198) cleared by Congress Dec. 18 authorized food stamp spending of up to $13.03 billion in fiscal 1986, rising to $15.97 billion in 1990. Over the five-year life of the law, $523 million more would be spent on food stamps than would have been spent by extending the existing level of funding, which was $13.93 million in fiscal 1985. The House had authorized $13.58 billion and the Senate, $12.98 billion. ***(Farm bill, p. 517; food stamp provisions, p. 525)***

Most of the additional spending was caused by increases in the allowances recipients could deduct from gross income, which raised benefit levels. Also, the bill relaxed limits on a family's assets — such as cash resources and certain automobiles — that were used to determine eligibility for the program. In addition, the measure prohibited states from charging sales tax on purchases made with food stamps, which increased the buying power of food stamp recipients.

For the first time, all states were required to set up employment and training programs for eligible food stamp recipients. Currently, about 40 states had some type of work requirement, but they varied in effectiveness.

The final bill permitted states to design their programs, subject to approval by the secretary of agriculture. They could provide job search, job training, "workfare" or other means to help recipients gain skills, training or experience to increase their ability to gain employment.

Rep. Leon E. Panetta, D-Calif., chairman of the House Agriculture Subcommittee on Domestic Marketing, Consumer Relations and Nutrition, praised the food program expansions.

"There is a crisis of hunger in our society," Panetta said. "There is a great deal of talk about the problem. This is a chance to do something about it."

Panetta, whose subcommittee held 16 hearings on the hunger issue, said, "Witness after witness in hearing after hearing confirms the fact that hunger is a problem that is on the increase in our society, doubling and tripling the services provided by soup kitchens and food pantries in recent years."

He noted that the food stamp program had been cut by about $2 billion a year since 1981.

Other members cited official poverty figures, released by the Census Bureau in August, showing that in 1984, 14.4 percent of the nation — 33.7 million Americans — were living below the poverty line of $10,609 for an urban family of four.

Also noted was a study, conducted by the Physician Task Force on Hunger in America at the Harvard University School of Public Health, that found that up to 20 million Americans were hungry at least sometime each month. The task force concluded that the problem was getting worse, and that it was the result of federal cutbacks in food and nutrition programs. *(Hunger, 1984 Almanac p. 470)*

The five-year farm bill was reported by the House Agriculture Committee Sept. 13 (H Rept 99-271) and was passed by the House Oct. 8.

A sharply divided Senate Agriculture, Nutrition and Forestry Committee by a 10-6 vote Sept. 19 ordered reported a four-year version (S 616). That bill was renumbered and reported Sept. 30 (S 1714 — S Rept 99-145). On Nov. 23, the Senate amended and passed HR 2100.

Both chambers adopted the conference report (H Rept 99-447) Dec. 18, with the Senate clearing it for the president.

House Action

By a one-vote margin, the House Agriculture Committee agreed July 11 to expand food stamp eligibility and benefit levels.

The panel by 21-22 rejected an amendment by Bill Emerson, R-Mo., that would have eliminated all the program expansions approved by the Subcommittee on Domestic Marketing, Consumer Relations and Nutrition.

The bill, which authorized the food stamp program for five years, set a cap on spending at $13.58 billion in fiscal 1986. That was $245 million more than would be spent in fiscal 1986 under existing law, primarily because the bill granted additional income deductions to persons receiving food stamps and based benefit levels on a more up-to-date estimate of food costs. In addition, beginning in 1987, asset limits used to determine eligibility for food stamps would be increased from $1,500 to $2,250 for most households.

Emerson said that his amendment, which had been defeated by the Subcommittee on Nutrition, was necessary to restrain federal spending. However, he added, "there's not a nickel's worth of cutting in my amendment. It is simply limiting the increase."

But Panetta argued that studies and his own travels around the country showed that hunger was increasing. "Are we just going to walk away from that or are we going to do something about it?" he asked.

Further, he noted that Emerson's amendment would eliminate $50 million in annual administrative reimbursements to states for the Temporary Emergency Food Assistance Program, under which states distributed surplus commodities to the needy. Panetta said that without those funds, states would drop the program.

Charles W. Stenholm, D-Texas, proposed retaining the administrative reimbursement, and the committee agreed, but Emerson's plan with Stenholm's change was defeated by one vote.

The committee also, by a 17-27 vote, rejected a proposal by Emerson to allow states the option of receiving food stamp funds in a block grant and designing their own program. A similar proposal was defeated in subcommittee.

The panel adopted an amendment by James M. Jeffords, R-Vt., raising the limit on assets for single elderly people to qualify for food stamps, so that an older woman could remain eligible after her husband died. The plan was expected to cost $62 million over five years.

The committee adopted an amendment by Berkley Bedell, D-Iowa, allowing self-employed farmers to deduct losses from their farm operations from income in order to qualify for food stamps.

The food stamp provisions of the bill were those of HR 2422, which the Subcommittee on Nutrition had approved June 13.

Floor Action

The full House Oct. 7 also refused to scale back the proposed increases in food stamp eligibility and benefits.

By a 171-238 vote, the House turned back Emerson's renewed efforts to eliminate program expansions. An amendment similar to one the Agriculture Committee rejected was defeated by one vote. *(Vote 306, p. 98-H)*

As passed Oct. 8, the bill's food stamp section over three years would cost $1 billion more than would have been spent under current law. The measure would grant additional deductions from income for medical expenses and child care for persons receiving food stamps, and would base benefits on a more up-to-date estimate of food costs.

Also, the bill would increase the limits on assets used to determine eligibility from $1,500 to $2,250 for most households, and from $3,000 to $3,500 for households with elderly members, which would make more people eligible for food stamps.

Another fight erupted over the provision in HR 2100 that would require all states to set up employment and training programs for food stamp recipients but allowed states to design them according to local needs.

Newt Gingrich, R-Ga., proposed a tougher requirement, based on a Reagan administration proposal. Under Gingrich's amendment, states would be required to enroll 75 percent of eligible recipients in some sort of work program over three years.

"This amendment provides that an increasing number of recipients will indeed be required to participate in a workfare program," said Gingrich.

But Panetta argued that requiring states to meet stringent quotas would place an administrative burden on state governments and would not necessarily help the recipients. "The problem," he said, "is that if we just mandate a certain program for all states, what this becomes is a full employment program for bureaucrats."

The House rejected the amendment, 183-227. *(Vote 307, p. 98-H)*

Members also adopted, by voice vote, two amendments by Jeffords that would expand benefits for certain recipients. One amendment eliminated language that in some cases would have required that food stamp benefits be cut for some persons because they received energy assistance payments. Jeffords said that counting the payments was unfair to families that depended on energy assistance.

His amendment would cost an additional $5 million in fiscal 1986 and $20 million over three years.

The other amendment would not count as income the first six months' worth of earnings by a youth in an on-the-job training program under the Job Training Partnership Act (PL 97-300). Jeffords said that would mean that families could become ineligible for food stamps because their child was enrolled in an on-the-job training program. *(1982 Almanac p. 39)*

That amendment would cost $8 million in fiscal 1986 and $24 million over three years.

Senate Action

The omnibus farm bill (S 616) approved Sept. 19 by the Senate Agriculture Committee would save more than $700 million in food stamp spending over three years.

However, Majority Leader Robert Dole, R-Kan., called most of the savings "phony," since about one-third came from not indexing the food aid grant for Puerto Rico for inflation.

Other savings came from counting recipients' earnings from the Job Training Partnership Act as income for determining benefit levels and not allowing them to deduct from income any low-income energy assistance payments. Those provisions would have the effect of reducing benefits for some recipients.

The panel had agreed Sept. 13 to a work program similar to that contained in the House bill, requiring that 45 percent of a state's recipients be enrolled in a job program by 1990, rejecting for the second time an administration proposal to require 75 percent to be enrolled in three years.

Another administration plan — to abolish the Temporary Emergency Food Assistance program — also was rejected. Senators agreed to a two-year extension of the program, which distributed surplus commodities to the poor, and authorized $50 million a year in matching grants for state administrative expenses.

In its Sept. 19 meeting, the committee also agreed, by a 9-7 vote, to set a ceiling on food stamp spending in the next four fiscal years of 2.5 percent more than projected costs. It authorized ceilings of $12.98 billion in fiscal 1986, $13.57 billion in fiscal 1987, $14.15 billion in 1988, and $14.69 billion in 1989.

Senators strengthened penalties for states that made a high number of erroneous food stamp payments, either by awarding benefits to ineligible persons or through overpayments. States would be required to pay the U.S. government 75 cents for each dollar in overpayments that were between 5 percent and 7 percent of the total paid; for errors above 7 percent, states would pay the federal government the full amount of the erroneous payment.

Under existing law, states with error rates of more than 5 percent were required to pay the government a percentage of administrative costs.

The panel also agreed to bar states from collecting sales taxes on food stamp purchases, a practice in effect in about 17 states. The provision would take effect at the beginning of the fiscal year following the first session of the state legislature to allow states to adjust for reduced revenues. HR 2100 contained a similar provision.

Senators agreed to allow states the option of deducting from recipients' income the first $50 they paid in child support. However, the committee provided that if states did so, they must bear the costs themselves. The provision would conform to a similar provision in the Aid to Families with Dependent Children program.

Floor Action

The Senate Nov. 21 rejected efforts to cut the food stamp program and approved some increases in benefits.

As approved by the Agriculture Committee, S 1714 would have saved $586 million in the food stamp program over three years. But the Senate added $180 million, by reaffirming votes taken during debate on the budget reconciliation bill (HR 3128). *(Reconciliation, p. 498)*

One of the proposals, offered by Robert T. Stafford, R-Vt., struck a provision that counted payments under the low-income energy assistance program as income when calculating food stamp benefits.

Not counting those payments as income would reduce recipients' net income and raise benefits.

Stafford argued that regarding the payments as income would harm poor families in Northern states during the winter, forcing them to choose between "heating and eating." He added that the 1984 reauthorization of the energy aid program prohibited the aid from counting against other benefits. *(1984 Almanac p. 485)*

But Rudy Boschwitz, R-Minn., responded that under Stafford's amendment, energy aid recipients could benefit from the payments twice: once as a direct payment, and then again as a deduction for food stamps. "The issue is, should there be a double deduction," said Boschwitz.

The Senate adopted Stafford's amendment by voice vote, after rejecting, 36-63, an attempt to table (kill) it. *(Vote 329, p. 56-S)*

The Senate then adopted by voice vote an amendment by Paul Simon, D-Ill., that would not count as income needs-based payments made under the Job Training Partnership Act.

Senators also rejected several attempts to cut spending. James A. McClure, R-Idaho, proposed cutting from $95 a month to $60 a month the standard deduction that food stamp recipients subtract from gross income to determine benefit levels.

McClure argued that his amendment, which would save $805 million, would be a start toward balancing the federal budget, which, he noted, the Senate had agreed to do by 1991.

"Do you really mean it?" he asked. "Are you ready to start now exercising that restraint? Or were you only kidding when you voted for [the deficit-reduction plan]?"

But Boschwitz argued that the amendment would cut benefits for food stamp recipients. "It really would be the most Draconian cut that I think has ever been attempted on food stamp provisions," he said, and the Senate rejected the proposal by voice vote.

The Senate rejected, 32-67, an amendment by Jeremiah Denton, R-Ala., that would have eliminated language prohibiting states from charging sales tax on purchases made with food stamps. *(Vote 328, p. 56-S)*

Denton said the prohibition would hurt the food stamp program because his state — one of 16 that charged sales tax on food stamp purchases — used the proceeds to administer the program. But Thomas F. Eagleton, D-Mo., whose state also taxed food stamp purchases, said the tax effectively cut benefits available for recipients.

McClure also unsuccessfully tried to improve the quality control of the program. The bill would increase penalties for states whose error rates, from overpayments or payments to ineligible recipients, exceeded 5 percent. McClure would have lowered the error rate standard to 3 percent, but the Senate killed his amendment, 77-21. Then the Senate agreed to suspend collection of fiscal sanctions on states for two years, while an independent commission studied the quality control program. *(Vote 330, p. 56-S)*

An amendment to give states the option of receiving their food stamp funds in a block grant and designing their own programs was killed 68-30. *(Vote 325, p. 56-S)*

Conference Agreement

The final version of the food stamp provisions was presented to conferees on the farm bill late Dec. 13 by Panetta and Boschwitz.

The conferees approved it the next day, overriding objections from Senate Agriculture Committee Chairman Jesse Helms, R-N.C., who sought cuts in the program.

Unlike other meetings on the farm bill in which conferees adopted packages put together by staffs and debated only major issues, Helms had been insisting on approving each item of the food stamp section separately.

"Obviously, we knew we had to compromise" to make progress, said Panetta.

The final version included several House provisions increasing benefits and eligibility but at levels lower than those passed by that chamber. And conferees postponed the date on which those provisions would go into effect to reduce costs.

The agreement increased from $139 a month to $147 a month the amount a recipient could deduct from his or her income for shelter costs, instead of the $155 a month set by the House bill. However, the final version followed the House bill in adding a separate deduction of up to $160 a month to cover child care costs. Currently, child care costs were included in the shelter deduction.

The bill raised the amount of earned income that could be deducted from 18 percent to 20 percent, as the House bill had provided.

In addition, the measure raised asset levels used to determine eligibility. Currently, households of two or more persons with at least one elderly member were allowed to own assets valued at up to $3,000 to qualify for food stamps; other households were allowed up to $1,500. The bill raised allowable assets to $2,000 for non-elderly households and $3,000 for all households that included an elderly member.

Both the House and Senate bills barred states from charging sales tax on food stamp purchases, which was retained in the final compromise.

The conference version dropped House provisions basing benefits on a more up-to-date estimate of food costs, and increasing medical deductions for the elderly.

The final measure, to improve state administration, required the federal government and states to develop a plan for computerizing the food stamp program. However, conferees dropped a Senate provision that would have increased penalties for states that made a large number of erroneous payments. States were required to forfeit a percentage of their administrative reimbursement if more than 5 percent of their payments went to the wrong people or were overpayments.

The bill retained that system but suspended penalties for six months, pending a study of the fiscal sanctions program. Collections of penalties would be speeded up when they resumed. ▮

AFDC Changes

Congress agreed to expand welfare benefits for the unemployed but did not complete action in 1985 on the conference report on the budget reconciliation bill (HR 3128 — H Rept 99-453) that contained the changes.

The bill would require all states to provide Aid to Families with Dependent Children (AFDC) benefits to two-parent families in which the principal wage earner was unemployed, which was defined as working fewer than 100 hours per month. Although such aid currently was optional, nearly half the states and the District of Columbia provided it. Most AFDC recipients were in one-parent families. *(Reconciliation, p. 498)*

The House version of HR 3128 would have required the other states to provide benefits to unemployed families. The Senate bill contained no similar provision. The conference report followed the House provision but changed the effective date from Oct. 1, 1986, to Jan. 1, 1988.

Conferees also accepted Senate language imposing a two-year moratorium on sanctions against states whose error rates in the AFDC and Medicaid programs were higher than allowed for administrative mistakes and overpayments. The provision would cost the Treasury $4 million in penalties that states otherwise would have to pay.

In the meantime, the secretary of health and human services and the National Academy of Sciences were to conduct separate studies of how best to operate a federal-state system to control errors. The conference agreement made the studies due one year after enactment, and within 18 months of enactment, HHS would be required to propose regulations and legislation to restructure the system.

The agreement also would follow the Senate version in extending through fiscal 1987 a ceiling on federal matching payments to states under the AFDC foster-care program. The measure would authorize $45 million each for fiscal 1987 and 1988 for a new program of grants to states that helped children 16 and older in federally funded foster care to live independently. Acceptable services would include enabling the child to complete high school or receive vocational training, or to receive budgeting and career planning counseling. Currently, payments generally ended when a child became 18. ▮

Child Abuse Bill Passed

The Senate Aug. 1 passed a bill (S 140 — S Rept 99-123) providing federal aid to states that enacted reforms to make it easier to prosecute and convict persons who sexually abused children, and to protect victims of child abuse.

However, there was no additional action in the first session of the 99th Congress.

The Senate measure, passed by voice vote, authorized $12 million in each of fiscal 1987 and 1988 for technical assistance grants to the states. To qualify for the funding, states would be required to establish task forces to recommend legal and administrative reforms for dealing with child abuse cases. States would be encouraged to act on those recommendations.

Sponsor Paula Hawkins, R-Fla., who revealed in April 1984 that she had been a victim of child sexual abuse, said that the public had become more aware of the problem in 1985.

But the administrative and judicial system for handling such cases remained "inadequate," she said.

"The administrative and legal system is not equipped to provide justice to these victims," she said.

Reps. Gerry Sikorski, D-Minn., and Joseph J. DioGuardi, R-N.Y., introduced identical legislation (HR 2999), but there was no further action.

Background

S 140 was an outgrowth of legislation (PL 98-457) enacted in 1984 that authorized grants to states for the prevention and treatment of child abuse. *(1984 Almanac p. 482)*

But as Hawkins, chairman of the Labor and Human Resources Subcommittee on Children, Family, Drugs and

Alcoholism, and Christopher J. Dodd, D-Conn., ranking minority member of the subcommittee, pointed out, the bill went beyond the previous law by focusing on the judicial system.

Hawkins noted that court cases were dismissed in California and Minnesota because of difficulties in trying sexual abuse cases.

The measure was approved by Hawkins' Labor and Human Resources subcommittee June 26 and reported by the full panel July 31.

Before ordering the bill reported, the committee agreed to alter some references to reforms, such as changes in rules involving hearsay evidence and videotaped testimony. Howard M. Metzenbaum, D-Ohio, had warned that some of the criminal justice reforms suggested by the bill might be unconstitutional.

Provisions

The bill would require states to establish a task force composed of law enforcement officers, judicial officers representing both the prosecution and defense, child protective services, advocates of children's interests, health and mental health professionals, and parents. The task forces would make recommendations to state governments on necessary reforms in state responses to child sexual abuse cases.

Specifically, the bill would require the task forces to address three areas and suggest — not mandate — possible changes.

First, they would be required to make recommendations on ways to proceed with child abuse cases to reduce trauma to the victim. For example, states could include child protective service workers, medical personnel, prosecutors and law enforcement officers on teams handling child abuse cases. They could also provide special training for law enforcement or judicial employees to deal with abuse victims.

Second, task forces must recommend reforms to improve the chances of successful prosecution of child molesters. States could, for example, strengthen the definition of sexual abuse, alter restrictions on admissible evidence or let victims testify by videotape.

Finally, states would be required to make reforms to protect children from abuse, such as giving courts authority to issue orders to protect children from accused offenders and providing treatment programs for child molesters and abused children.

The bill would authorize $12 million in each of fiscal 1987 and 1988 for grants to states. To qualify, states must show that they had made progress toward implementing reforms in the three areas, or explain to the Department of Health and Human Services why they had not. ∎

House, Senate Pass Child Food Aid Extension

Legislation to extend child nutrition programs passed both chambers in 1985, but conferees were unable to meet before adjournment and final action was put off until 1986.

The bill (HR 7) authorized funding for a supplemental feeding program for needy pregnant women, infants and children (WIC); a summer food program for children; nutrition education and training; a surplus commodity distribution program; and payments to states for administrative costs. The programs expired Sept. 30 but were continued under appropriations measures.

The House passed its three-year version of the bill Sept. 18, and the Senate passed a four-year extension Nov. 22. While the Senate did not increase spending above levels needed to maintain current services, the House allowed a $121 million increase in fiscal 1986. President Reagan had sought an $800 million cut.

In other action on nutrition programs, Congress voted to expand food stamp eligibility and benefits as part of the omnibus farm bill (HR 2100 — PL 99-198) cleared Dec. 18. *(Food stamps, p. 305)*

Background

Food program funding had been sharply curtailed under President Reagan's 1981 budget-cutting plan. The administration and its congressional allies had succeeded in blocking House attempts to restore funding in 1983 and 1984. *(Background, 1984 Almanac p. 469; 1983 Almanac p. 417)*

In 1985, the administration proposed an 11 percent cut in child nutrition programs, arguing that the reductions would stop upper-income families from using the program while keeping assistance focused on the poor. In its fiscal 1986 budget, the administration proposed cutting child nutrition programs by $700 million and WIC by $100 million.

But House Democrats revived their calls for more money for child nutrition and other food programs, citing a new report that 20 million Americans suffered from hunger and that their numbers were growing.

The report was released in February by the Physician Task Force on Hunger, a foundation-supported task force, which concluded: "Hunger is a public health epidemic. The fact that hunger is spreading so rapidly and afflicts so many citizens may well make it the most serious epidemic presently facing the nation."

The physicians' task force, a Harvard-based group of 22 physicians that undertook a 10-month study funded by private foundations, said that about 20 million Americans went without food at least two days a month. The report pointed out that the lack of proper nutrition was particularly damaging to children.

The task force said that hunger was worsening nationwide and was not restricted to one region. A Jackson, Miss., food bank, for example, reported a 900 percent increase in the number of pounds of food distributed in 1984 alone. In Peoria, Ill., food distribution went up 300 percent between 1983 and 1984.

Further, the report cited 15 national studies and 24 state-level studies corroborating its findings.

House Action

Committee

The House Education and Labor Committee reported HR 7 May 15 (H Rept 99-96). The panel May 7 approved the $6.4 billion bill, making small increases in child nutrition programs, after rejecting Republican-sponsored proposals to hold funding at fiscal 1985 levels.

The committee made only minor changes to HR 7 as approved by the Subcommittee on Elementary, Secondary and Vocational Education May 1.

HR 7 would freeze all programs except the school breakfast and WIC programs at fiscal 1985 levels. It would expand those two programs, costing $102 million more than the $6.2 billion needed to maintain the programs at current service levels in fiscal 1986. The bill would provide an extra $42 million for the school breakfast program and $60 million for WIC.

Also, the panel adopted amendments adding $18 million to restore milk programs for kindergartens, raise the tuition level required for private schools to qualify for lunch programs and provide funds for schools to buy or repair kitchen equipment.

Republicans argued that all food spending should be frozen to reduce the federal deficit. "Once we start opening that door [to increasing spending], as we're doing here, we'll never stop," said Harris W. Fawell, R-Ill.

But Pat Williams, D-Mont., said that Congress' job was to determine where to spend more money. "The notion of putting the budget on automatic pilot really does away with the need for legislators, for hearings, for markups," he said. "I think a freeze is bad government."

Floor

The House passed HR 7 Sept. 18, by a 367-59 vote, after turning back Republican attempts to reduce funding. *(Vote 283, p. 90-H)*

As passed by the House, the bill would raise the current authorization for WIC by $60 million, to $1.6 billion in fiscal 1986. In addition, it would add 6 cents per meal to the current subsidy for the school breakfast program, at a cost of $42 million, and allow certain kindergartens to participate in a special milk program, which would cost an additional $15 million.

HR 7 also would increase the tuition limit for private schools participating in school meal programs from $1,500 a year to $2,500, adding $3 million. And it would authorize $1 million for grants to school districts to purchase food service equipment.

Augustus F. Hawkins, D-Calif., chairman of the Education and Labor Committee, rejected GOP charges that the bill provided for excessive spending. "We have scaled down," he said, noting that a similar bill the House passed in 1984 provided for three times the increase in HR 7. Further, Hawkins said, the increases in HR 7 were allowed by the congressional budget resolution (S Con Res 32) cleared Aug. 1. *(Fiscal 1986 congressional budget resolution, p. 441)*

The House rebuffed a series of efforts by Steve Bartlett, R-Texas, to trim the increases in HR 7.

A heated debate erupted over Bartlett's attempt to eliminate the 12½-cents-per-meal cash subsidy paid to schools for lunches bought by children from families with incomes above 185 percent of the poverty line, currently $19,627 for an urban family of four.

Under the existing program, the federal government distributed the cash subsidy, as well as 11.7 cents' worth of commodities per meal, for those children. In addition, the Agriculture Department, using its discretionary authority, distributed an additional 10 cents' worth of commodities per meal for those children.

"This amendment," Bartlett said, "would eliminate the cash subsidy for children who are not low income and who would not otherwise go hungry." He added that it would save $287 million in fiscal 1986 and $922 million over three years.

But Bill Goodling, R-Pa., argued that the subsidy helped support the infrastructure of the meal program, and without it, schools would drop the program, harming poor children. "This would destroy the National School Lunch Program," he said. "That's how devastating it is."

Goodling said that after Congress voted to cut the subsidy for upper-income students by 5½ cents in 1981, three million fewer children received school lunches, including one million poor children.

Dick Armey, R-Texas, said it was unfair that his children receive subsidies from taxpayers, including lower-income families. He proposed, as an amendment to Bartlett's proposal, eliminating the cash and commodity subsidies for children from families with incomes above 250 percent of the poverty line, or $26,522 for an urban family of four. Armey would have retained the 10-cent bonus commodity subsidy for those families, however.

But Democrats said Armey's amendment would further complicate the program by asking more families to submit income statements in order for schools to receive subsidies. "This amendment is designed for one purpose and one purpose only — it is to gut the program," said George Miller, D-Calif., chairman of the Select Committee on Children, Youth and Families.

Thomas E. Petri, R-Wis., proposed what he said was a compromise between the Bartlett and Armey proposals. Petri's plan would have eliminated the cash subsidy for children from families above 250 percent of the poverty line.

Petri's amendment was rejected, 174-254, and Armey's, 146-279. Bartlett's amendment then failed by voice vote. *(Votes 281, 282, p. 90-H)*

The House also rejected Bartlett amendments to:

- Eliminate the $1 million authorized by the bill for grants for food service equipment; 157-235. *(Vote 278, p. 90-H)*
- Delay for one year the fiscal 1986 cost-of-living adjustment (COLA) for child nutrition programs; 143-284. *(Vote 280, p. 90-H)*

Senate Action

Bypassing consideration by its Agriculture, Nutrition and Forestry Committee, the Senate passed HR 7 by voice vote late Nov. 22. While rejecting the cuts sought by the president, the Senate-passed bill did not add funding as the House had proposed.

Paula Hawkins, R-Fla., and Tom Harkin, D-Iowa, brought up the issue during Senate consideration of omnibus farm legislation. Although they agreed the programs should be reauthorized, they differed over spending.

Harkin argued for more money. Noting that the authorizations for child nutrition programs were cut by one-third in 1981, Harkin said, "What we have before us doesn't even take the first step in repairing the damage of the last four years."

But Hawkins warned that increased spending might jeopardize passage of the bill. "This package, to the best of my knowledge, represents a consensus of what is doable with the time left in this body," she said. Congress adjourned for the year Dec. 20.

Major Provisions

As passed by the Senate, major provisions of HR 7:

- Extended through fiscal 1989 WIC, the summer food program for children, commodity distribution program, aid for state administrative expenses, and the Nutrition Education and Training program (NET).
- Authorized for WIC $1.57 billion in fiscal 1986, $1.64 billion in fiscal 1987, $1.71 billion in fiscal 1988 and $1.78 billion in fiscal 1989. These amounts were estimated by the Congressional Budget Office as necessary to maintain the current caseload of three million participants a month.
- **School Lunch, Breakfast.** Based the amount of commodities available to a state on the number of free and reduced-price meals served in the previous school year, rather than on an estimate by the Agriculture Department late the same year.
- Required schools to offer whole milk as part of the lunch program.
- Provided automatic eligibility for free meals for children of families receiving food stamps or Aid to Families with Dependent Children.
- Allowed school facilities, equipment and personnel to be used for non-profit food programs for the elderly.
- **WIC.** Barred states from charging sales tax on purchases made with WIC vouchers, effective the first day of the fiscal year after the state legislature convened.
- Established priorities for WIC participation: pregnant women first, then breast-feeding women, and then infants at nutritional risk.
- Extended from 20 to 30 days after the first visit to a WIC clinic the amount of time a state could take to notify applicants they could participate.
- Required that if a state determined that benefits had been over-issued to participants, the state must recover the cash value of the excess benefits, unless the state determined that recovery was not cost-effective. Existing law provided that participants could be disqualified or subject to criminal fines in the event of fraud.
- **NET.** Reduced from $75,000 to $50,000 a year the amount a state could receive in any fiscal year for conducting nutrition education and training. ▮

APPROPRIATIONS

CQ

Appropriations

Cost-cutting pressures hampered the appropriations process in 1985, as Congress chafed under White House calls for greater fiscal austerity while struggling with the uncomfortable demands of its own budget guidelines.

By year's end, only six of the 13 regular annual appropriations bills had been enacted into law. Programs covered by the other seven bills were funded under a $368.2 billion omnibus spending bill, known as a continuing resolution, cleared Dec. 19. The final appropriation was $18.4 billion under President Reagan's requests for agencies and programs covered by the measure.

The largest portion of the resolution provided $281.2 billion for the Defense Department. The total, which was $1.3 billion less than Senate-House conferees originally proposed, marked a significant reduction in the Pentagon's purchasing power for the first time in a decade. The White House nonetheless agreed to accept the defense cut in return for a $300 million reduction in domestic programs.

The continuing resolution also included $13 billion in funding for the Treasury Department, Postal Service and related agencies. On Nov. 15, the president had vetoed a separate funding bill on grounds that it contained $900 million more than he had requested, most of it for a postal subsidy he sought to end. Reagan noted that he had agreed to "accept appropriations bills, even if above my budget, that were within the limits set by Congress' own budget resolution." The vetoed bill, he said, did not meet that test. In approving the continuing resolution, Congress cut $117 million from the earlier measure — $72 million from the disputed postal subsidy and $45 million from the Internal Revenue Service.

Congress also rolled into the continuing resolution a $10.5 billion transportation appropriations measure that had been threatened with a veto. A $36.3 billion agriculture appropriations bill was added to the omnibus measure after Congress pared $200 million to meet spending limits set by the fiscal 1986 budget resolution, cleared Aug. 1.

For the fourth year in a row, foreign aid appropriations were included in the continuing measure, which provided $15 billion to maintain fiscal 1985 funding levels for most aid programs. Other appropriations that found their way into the continuing resolution were $8.1 billion for the Interior Department and related agencies and $546.8 million for the District of Columbia.

President Reagan signed several appropriations bills that substantially exceeded his budget requests. On Nov. 25, Reagan signed a $57.3 billion funding measure for the Department of Housing and Urban Development and various independent agencies, even though the bill was $7.1 billion over his request. On Dec. 12, he signed a $106.5 billion appropriations bill for the Departments of Labor, Health and Human Services, and Education that provided $5 billion more than he requested but exceeded congressional targets for discretionary social programs by less than $100 million. The following day, Reagan signed a bill appropriating $11.9 billion, $244 million more than he requested, for the Departments of Commerce, Justice, State and the judiciary; the bill continued funding for several agencies the administration wanted to abolish.

The $8.5 billion military construction funding bill, signed Dec. 10, was $1.8 billion below the budget request.

Budget vs. Appropriations

With some success, Senate Budget Committee Chairman Pete V. Domenici, R-N.M., and the panel's senior Democrat, Lawton Chiles, Fla., waged a bipartisan assault on appropriations bills that exceeded the limits assumed in the fiscal 1986 budget resolution. Both men also were members of the Appropriations Committee.

In an exercise that brought to the surface a long-simmering turf fight between the two Senate panels that directly control federal spending, Domenici and Chiles succeeded in forcing Appropriations to make cuts in several bills, including some already approved, under threat of across-the-board reductions on the Senate floor.

The issue surfaced Sept. 24, when Domenici and Chiles won Senate approval of an amendment paring 2 percent, about $139 million, from the Treasury funding bill so that it would comply with the budget resolution's outlay targets.

The bill already met budget authority targets, and Appropriations Chairman Mark O. Hatfield, R-Ore., complained that appropriations bills had never been measured in terms of outlays. But the Budget leaders insisted outlays should be considered, since deficits were calculated in those terms. The Senate backed Domenici and Chiles; an effort to derail the cuts failed by a 20-vote margin.

Subsequently, Domenici and Chiles also won Senate support for cuts to hold the transportation and housing bills to the budget level.

1986 Delays, 1985 Supplementals

The Senate dispute was one reason the appropriations process fell far behind schedule in 1985. Action had not been completed on even one of the 13 fiscal 1986 funding bills by the time the fiscal year began Oct. 1. The first bill, providing funds for energy and water programs, did not clear until Oct. 17, followed by the legislative branch measure Oct. 29. Delays in appropriations action forced Congress to rely on a series of short-term continuing resolutions to keep money flowing to agencies and avert a governmental shutdown.

During the year, Congress also approved three supplemental appropriations bills for fiscal 1985. The first, cleared April 2, provided $784 million for African famine victims. A second, cleared July 19, provided $1 billion in urgent aid for the Commodity Credit Corporation, which made crop loans to farmers. The final bill, cleared Aug. 1, provided $13.02 billion for a wide variety of government programs, including nearly $2.3 billion for aid to Middle Eastern nations and $27 million for anti-government rebels in Nicaragua.

Fiscal 1986
Status of Appropriations
99th Congress, First Session

Appropriation Bills	House	Senate	Final	Almanac Page
Agriculture and related agencies (HR 3037)	Passed 7/24/85	Passed 10/16/85	Included in PL 99-190	395
Commerce, Justice, State, Judiciary (HR 2965)	Passed 7/17/85	Passed 11/1/85	PL 99-180 signed 12/13/85	346
Defense (HR 3629)	Passed 10/30/85	Committee reported 11/6/85	Included in PL 99-190	377
District of Columbia (HR 3067)	Passed 7/30/85	Passed 11/7/85	Included in PL 99-190	359
Energy and Water Development (HR 2959)	Passed 7/16/85	Passed 8/1/85	PL 99-141 signed 11/1/85	323
Foreign Operations (HR 3228, S 1816)	Committee reported 8/1/85	Committee reported 10/31/85	Included in PL 99-190	367
Housing and Urban Development, Independent Agencies (HR 3038)	Passed 7/25/85	Passed 10/18/85	PL 99-160 signed 11/25/85	317
Interior and related agencies (HR 3011)	Passed 7/31/85	Floor debate began 10/31/85	Included in PL 99-190	337
Labor, Health and Human Services, Education (HR 3424)	Passed 10/2/85	Passed 10/22/85	PL 99-178 signed 12/12/85	333
Legislative Branch (HR 2942)	Passed 7/18/85	Passed 7/31/85	PL 99-151 signed 11/13/85	326
Military Construction (HR 3327)	Passed 10/17/85	Passed 11/7/85	PL 99-173 signed 12/10/85	392
Transportation and related agencies (HR 3244)	Passed 9/12/85	Passed 10/23/85	Included in PL 99-190	342
Treasury, Postal Service, General Government (HR 3036)	Passed 7/30/85	Passed 9/26/85	Included in PL 99-190	329
Interim Continuing Resolutions (H J Res 388) (H J Res 441) (H J Res 476) (H J Res 491)	Passed 9/18/85 Passed 11/12/85 Passed 12/12/85 Passed 12/17/85	Passed 9/25/85 Passed 11/13/85 Passed 12/12/85 Passed 12/17/85	PL 99-103 PL 99-154 PL 99-179 PL 99-184	361
Continuing Resolution (H J Res 465)	Passed 12/4/85	Passed 12/10/85	PL 99-190 signed 12/19/85	360

$57.3 Billion Approved for HUD/Agencies

Congress Nov. 13 cleared a $57.3 billion fiscal 1986 appropriations bill (HR 3038 — PL 99-160) for the Department of Housing and Urban Development (HUD) and various independent agencies.

Final action came when the Senate adopted the conference report on the bill (H Rept 99-363) by voice vote. The House had adopted the conference report earlier the same day by a 268-153 vote. *(Vote 368, p. 114-H)*

The measure provided $14.8 billion for HUD, $26.1 billion for the Veterans Administration (VA), $2.4 billion for the Environmental Protection Agency (EPA), $7.7 billion for the National Aeronautics and Space Administration (NASA), $1.5 billion for the National Science Foundation (NSF) and $4.2 billion for general revenue sharing grants to local governments.

Final figures reflected changes in economic assumptions and recalculations by congressional staff that altered some funding levels originally approved by the House and Senate. *(Revised figures, chart, next page)*

President Reagan signed the bill Nov. 25, even though it provided $7.1 billion more than he had requested.

Most of the difference between HR 3038 and Reagan's request was in subsidized housing. The administration sought a two-year moratorium on new assisted housing, but the bill provided $10 billion for 97,000 new units. The House had provided 95,000 new housing units; the Senate, 99,000. In fiscal 1985, Congress funded 100,000 new units.

The final bill also provided nearly $2 billion more than the versions passed by the House and Senate. Several House members questioned whether Congress should accept such an increase at a time when it was considering ways to cut federal spending.

"What we have here is a bill that clearly does not meet the obligation the House has to reduce the deficit," said Judd Gregg, R-N.H.

But Edward P. Boland, D-Mass., chairman of the Appropriations HUD Subcommittee, cited two reasons why the bill was $1.9 billion above the level passed by the House:

- The House initially had deferred action on the "superfund" hazardous-waste cleanup program, which had not been authorized; the final bill provided $900 million for superfund. *(Superfund, p. 191)*
- The final bill cut revenue sharing by 8.36 percent from fiscal 1985 funding of $4.6 billion, compared with a House-passed cut of 25 percent. Boland noted that the budget resolution (S Con Res 32) adopted by both the House and Senate assumed full funding for revenue sharing in fiscal 1986, although it would eliminate funding at the end of the year. *(Budget resolution, p. 441)*

Subsidized housing accounted for the difference from the Senate bill; conferees accepted the House funding level, which called for fewer but more expensive units than the Senate had approved.

The Senate originally passed its bill after a difficult floor fight over cuts required to meet outlay targets set by S Con Res 32. Conferees then cut the bill again to meet the budget's outlay targets.

Jake Garn, R-Utah, Boland's Senate counterpart, said he would not bring up the conference report if the leadership of the Budget Committee objected. But he won an assurance that the final version met the budget ceilings and that the bill would be signed by the president.

The housing program in the final bill included funding for 5,000 units of public housing and 2,000 units of Indian housing. Also, the bill provided funding for 12,000 units of housing for the elderly and handicapped, 36,000 vouchers for rental housing and 32,000 certificates for Section 8 rent subsidies, plus 10,000 Section 8 certificates for moderately rehabilitated housing.

The Senate bill had provided for no public housing but would have funded 40,000 vouchers and 40,000 Section 8 certificates.

The final version rejected a change proposed by the House that would have replaced long-term financing of public housing modernization with up-front grants. Grants required less budget authority.

As cleared, the bill included language barring the use of funds to carry out any regulation if a resolution of disapproval had been adopted by Congress opposing it. In signing the measure, Reagan noted that such a resolution of disapproval must be a joint resolution requiring the president's signature, in accordance with the Supreme Court's 1983 decision outlawing legislative vetoes. *(1983 Almanac p. 565)*

House Committee Action

As reported by the House Appropriations Committee July 18 (H Rept 99-212), the bill provided $57.8 billion in spending, $1 billion less than current funding.

The measure provided $10.3 billion more than requested by Reagan. Almost all of the increase was for additional subsidized housing, which the administration had slated for a two-year moratorium.

The committee also set aside $500 million for programs that had not yet been authorized, such as building homes for moderate-income families.

HUD Programs

The panel provided $16.4 billion for HUD, $456 million less than fiscal 1985. Major elements included:

- **Assisted Housing.** The committee agreed to fund 100,000 units of new assisted housing, increasing from 3.7 million to 3.8 million the number of families receiving assistance.

Included was $1.98 billion for 10,000 new units of public housing, which was owned by local housing authorities and built and operated with federal and local funds. In fiscal 1985, Congress provided 5,000 units of public housing. The committee also directed HUD to expedite the approval of new public housing construction to speed up building apartments for families and to convert empty smaller units to accommodate them.

In addition, it provided $164 million for 1,000 units of housing on Indian reservations and $735 million to modernize existing public housing units. The modernization funds would be in the form of one-time grants, rather than paid over a long period of time as in the past. The housing authorization (HR 1) approved July 10 by the House Banking Committee also made this change, which required less budget authority than the old method. *(Authorization, p. 303)*

A total of $1.6 billion was set aside for 12,000 new

Fiscal 1986 HUD/Agency Funds

Following is the new budget authority for fiscal 1986 for the Department of Housing and Urban Development and independent agencies requested by President Reagan, and included in HR 3038 as passed by the House July 25 and by the Senate Oct. 18, and as cleared by Congress Nov. 13.

Because of changes in economic assumptions and recalculations by congressional staff, some of the numbers in the table differ from those originally reported and used by Congress at various stages of action.

	President's Request	House-Passed	Senate-Passed	Final Amount
Department of Housing and Urban Development				
Housing Programs	$ 698,916,000	$ 10,188,722,781	$ 9,253,985,618	$ 10,952,859,581
Community Development	3,136,800,000	3,466,800,000	3,353,501,200	3,466,668,000
Policy Development and Research	18,900,000	16,900,000	18,692,100	16,900,000
Fair Housing Assistance	5,000,000	6,700,000	6,626,300	6,626,300
Management and Administration	324,027,000	341,427,000	318,774,480	336,427,000
Solar Energy Bank	--	20,000,000	--	--
TOTAL, HUD	$ 4,183,643,000	$ 14,040,549,781	$ 12,951,529,698	$ 14,779,480,881
Independent Agencies				
American Battle Monuments Commission	11,004,000	10,954,000	10,833,506	10,833,506
Consumer Product Safety Commission	34,575,000	37,000,000	34,516,100	36,000,000
Cemeterial Expenses, Army	14,932,000	7,759,000	14,615,442	14,615,442
Environmental Protection Agency	4,683,316,000	1,496,176,000	2,645,304,014	2,390,176,000
Council on Environmental Quality	732,000	700,000	723,948	700,000
Office of Science and Technology Policy	2,153,000	2,343,000	2,317,227	2,317,227
Federal Emergency Management Agency	545,393,000	631,656,000	571,821,998	533,656,000
GSA Consumer Information Center	1,249,000	1,249,000	1,235,261	1,235,261
HHS Office of Consumer Affairs	1,988,000	1,988,000	2,005,692	1,988,000
National Aeronautics and Space Administration	7,928,000,000	7,666,000,000	7,570,795,000	7,656,000,000
National Science Foundation	1,571,243,000	1,523,855,000	1,508,867,850	1,523,855,000
Neighborhood Reinvestment Corporation	14,669,000	17,669,000	16,485,641	17,669,000
Selective Service System	27,664,000	27,780,000	27,780,000	27,474,420
Treasury Department				
General Revenue Sharing	4,566,700,000	3,425,025,000	4,237,897,600	4,185,000,000
Salaries and Expenses	8,000,000	8,000,000	7,714,200	7,714,200
Veterans Administration	26,548,969,000	26,503,810,000	25,989,170,395	26,101,426,553
GRAND TOTAL	**$ 50,144,230,000**	**$ 55,402,513,781**	**$ 55,593,663,572**	**$ 57,290,141,490**

SOURCE: House Appropriations Committee

dwellings for the elderly and handicapped, the same as in fiscal 1985. The panel also agreed to $534 million for 30,000 housing vouchers, which families could use like cash toward rent in housing they found on their own. The Reagan administration had strongly supported the voucher program, which offered tenants an incentive to shop around for housing by allowing them to pocket the difference between the amount of the voucher and rent, if the rent was lower. Tenants also could pay more for rent.

Also, the committee provided $2.5 billion for 32,000 certificates in the Section 8 rent subsidy program, which paid the difference between 30 percent of a tenant's adjusted income and a HUD-determined fair market rent in existing private housing. Another $1.3 billion was approved for 15,000 Section 8 certificates for housing undergoing moderate rehabilitation.

The committee included a reserve fund of $500 million for programs that had not yet been authorized, such as a home-ownership program for moderate income families and aid to the homeless. In addition, it set aside $75 million for rental rehabilitation grants and $75 million for grants for the construction of new rental housing.

- **Elderly and Handicapped.** A limit of $631 million was put on loans to build 12,000 units for the elderly and handicapped.
- **Congregate Services.** The panel provided $2.7 million for grants to local housing agencies or non-profit sponsors to provide meals and other supportive services for eligible residents of public housing and housing for the elderly and handicapped, who might otherwise require nursing home or institutional care; in fiscal 1985, Congress provided $4.1 million.
- **Operating Subsidies.** The panel approved $1.2 billion for payments to local public housing authorities for operating assistance, $62 million more than in fiscal 1985 and $200 million more than Reagan had requested. It estimated that an additional $135 million would be carried over from the current fiscal year.
- **Counseling Assistance.** To support agencies providing assistance to 40,000 families to cope with housing problems, such as default and foreclosure, the panel provided $4 million, $500,000 more than in fiscal 1985.

- **Federal Housing Administration (FHA).** The committee allowed $240 million to repay FHA losses incurred in the liquidation of assigned mortgages and the sale of HUD-owned properties.
- **Solar Bank.** Another $20 million was provided for the Solar Energy and Energy Conservation Bank, $5 million above the current level. Reagan had been trying since 1981 to kill the bank, which, through grants to states, subsidized loans for energy-conserving home improvements.
- **Community Development Block Grants.** The program, which made grants to states for development programs, was cut 10 percent from its fiscal 1985 level, to $3.1 billion.
- **Urban Development Action Grants (UDAG).** For UDAG, which provided grants to stimulate economic development in distressed areas in inner cities, the committee provided $330 million, a 25 percent cut from the fiscal 1985 level. Reagan wanted to abolish the program.
- **Rehabilitation Loans.** As Reagan had requested, the panel allowed no new funds for Section 312 rehabilitation loans to finance the rehabilitation of single-family and multifamily housing and commercial properties. However, it included language to continue the program in fiscal 1986 using an estimated $86 million from loan repayments.
- **Urban Homesteading.** As requested, the committee provided $12 million to permit approximately 825 single-family properties to be conveyed to local governments and made available to the public under the urban homesteading program.
- **Policy Development and Research.** Reagan's request for research was cut from $18.9 million to $16.9 million. Also, the panel directed that no money be spent in a demonstration program of selling public housing units to tenants until HUD requested funds to build public housing to replace the 2,000 units being sold.
- **Fair Housing.** Members added $1.7 million to Reagan's request of $5 million for grants to state and local governments to enforce fair housing laws. But it deferred action on a request for another $10 million for a new "fair housing initiatives" program, which would provide grants to non-profit agencies to aid enforcement.
- **Management and Administration.** Because members rejected Reagan's proposals to eliminate or sharply curtail HUD programs, the committee exceeded his request for salaries and administrative costs and provided $341 million.

Other Agencies

- **Veterans Administration.** The bill included $26.5 billion for the Veterans Administration, $442 million more than fiscal 1985 and $183 million above the request. David A. Stockman, director of the Office of Management and Budget, objected in a letter to the panel, but Boland, the HUD subcommittee chairman, said the increase was necessary to maintain staffing of the health care system at current levels.

In addition, the bill provided $99 million more than Reagan requested for VA construction. Boland said the increase would allow full funding of a clinical addition to the VA hospital in Philadelphia and a replacement and modernization of a hospital in Houston. The administration requested partial funding for those projects.

- **Environmental Protection Agency.** Stockman also objected to a $175 million increase for the Environmental Protection Agency (EPA). The committee provided $1.5 billion for EPA, which Bill Green, R-N.Y., ranking minority member of the HUD subcommittee, said would "try to restore that agency to some semblance of its former glory."

The panel deferred action on two major elements of the EPA budget, the superfund program and construction grants. Those programs had not yet been authorized.

- **Revenue Sharing.** The committee agreed to a 25 percent cut in general revenue sharing, the $4.6 billion program that gave money to 39,000 local governments with no strings attached. The House budget resolution called for the reduction.
- **National Aeronautics and Space Administration.** For NASA, the committee approved $7.67 billion, a $175 million increase over fiscal 1985. During consideration of NASA authorization legislation, the House in April had voted to freeze the space agency's funding at the fiscal 1985 level. *(Vote 46, p. 18-H; authorization, p. 405)*
- **Federal Emergency Management Agency (FEMA).** For the Federal Emergency Management Agency, the panel approved $632 million, $89 million more than requested. Of the increase, $70 million was to fund an emergency food and shelter program for the homeless, which the administration had wanted to eliminate.

Boland chided FEMA's management, contending that its budget request could not support its current staff. The bill limited the funds that could be used for personnel and capped the number of full-time employees in management and administration.

- **Consumer Product Safety Commission (CPSC).** The committee agreed to add $3.3 million to Reagan's request of $33.7 million for the agency, whose purpose was to reduce unreasonable risk of injury associated with consumer products. It earmarked $1 million to study cigarette fire safety and $300,000 to study indoor air pollution.
- **Neighborhood Reinvestment Corporation.** The panel approved $17.7 million, a $3 million increase over Reagan's request for the agency, which sponsored programs to preserve and revitalize urban neighborhoods. In fiscal 1985, the agency received $15.5 million.

House Floor Action

Before passing the bill July 25, the House cut $1.5 billion from the committee's recommendation for subsidized housing but balked at reducing veterans', space and science programs. Approved by a vote of 340-73 after two days of debate, the bill provided $56.3 billion for HUD and the related agencies. *(Vote 236, p. 76-H)*

It included $14.9 billion for HUD, $7.7 billion for NASA, $26.5 billion for the Veterans Administration and $1.5 billion for EPA.

The bill was $8.9 billion over the Reagan administration's request. Almost all of the difference was in subsidized housing, which the administration wanted to halt for two years.

Steve Bartlett, R-Texas, offered a series of amendments to reduce housing aid to fiscal 1985 levels. Two of his proposals were adopted.

But similar attempts to bring down the funding levels for veterans' programs, NASA and NSF were defeated overwhelmingly.

Opponents of the funding reductions said that housing was an easy target for budget-cutters. Low-income housing, said Charles E. Schumer, D-N.Y., "has a small, limited, concentrated constituency. When it comes time to cut budgets, it's the first to go."

But Bartlett and his supporters said that his amendments succeeded because they were aimed at specific items, rather than overall funding levels. "We were able to demonstrate that specific programs were appropriated at higher levels this year than last year," said Timothy J. Penny, D-Minn.

Housing Cuts

Bartlett first proposed dropping the $500 million reserve fund the committee had set aside for new housing programs that were not yet authorized. The new programs included a home-ownership program for moderate-income families and aid for the homeless.

Bartlett noted that the House had voted to freeze spending on existing programs such as defense. "This is not the year, not the place, not the time, not the bill to create new programs," he said.

But Schumer, the author of the home-ownership program, said the amendment would "move housing backwards" by blocking more efficient ways to provide housing.

The House adopted Bartlett's amendment, 236-172. *(Vote 232, p. 76-H)*

His second amendment, adopted 213-204, cut the number of new public housing units funded in the bill from 10,000 to 5,000, the same amount as in fiscal 1985. The amendment pared $1 billion from the bill. *(Vote 233, p. 76-H)*

Bartlett said he was merely trying to reinforce the notion of a budget freeze by rejecting the committee's attempt to increase funding for one item by 100 percent.

But Bruce A. Morrison, D-Conn., who had sponsored several floor amendments calling for a budget freeze, said the bill's total was below current spending. He said trying to hold each item to the previous year's level was "making a fetish out of a freeze."

HUD subcommittee Chairman Boland said public housing was the only program aimed at the poorest of the poor and should be a priority item. He noted that in fiscal 1985, the House voted for 10,000 units, while the Senate voted for none; in conference, they agreed to 5,000.

Bartlett then tried to cut housing aid by an additional $231 million by reducing every item by 2.5 percent. He said that together with the other amendments, this change would bring funding to the same level as fiscal 1985.

But Boland said housing had suffered enough, having been cut from $30 billion in 1981 to the $11 billion left in the bill after the earlier reductions.

"How much of a pound of flesh do you want?" he asked.

Bartlett's amendment was rejected, 203-213. *(Vote 234, p. 76-H)*

Veterans, Space

Other attempts to cut funding were soundly defeated. Bill Frenzel, R-Minn., tried to cut discretionary spending for veterans' programs by $180 million, which he said would bring spending to the same level as the budget resolution.

Frenzel's amendment would not have affected veterans' disability compensation, pensions or readjustment benefits.

But John Paul Hammerschmidt, R-Ark., ranking minority member of the Veterans' Affairs Committee, said the amendment would cut deeply into health care. He noted that demand on the VA health care system would increase sharply as the number of older veterans skyrocketed in the next decade.

Frenzel's amendment was rejected by voice vote.

Paul B. Henry, R-Mich., then proposed freezing funding for NASA and NSF at fiscal 1985 levels.

Henry noted that the House had already voted to freeze funding for the agencies during action on their fiscal 1986 authorization bills. *(NSF authorization, p. 288)*

"Let's keep some degree of consistency here," said Carl D. Pursell, R-Mich. "If we don't, all bets are off, and we're right back in the soup."

But others argued that those votes occurred before the House had passed its budget resolution. Now, said Don Fuqua, D-Fla., chairman of the Science and Technology Committee, the House had an overall spending guideline and need not be bound by prior votes.

Henry's amendment was rejected, 112-300. *(Vote 235, p. 76-H)*

Other Amendments

By voice vote, the House adopted an amendment by Robert S. Walker, R-Pa., that deleted a provision setting a maximum price NASA could charge private companies and other countries that used the space shuttle. He said the issue would be settled in the authorization process.

Also by voice vote, the House adopted an amendment by Frank Horton, R-N.Y., changing the way revenue sharing funds would be distributed in fiscal 1986.

The bill would have called for a 25 percent cut from the fiscal 1985 level of $4.6 billion, with each quarterly payment reduced by that percentage. Under Horton's amendment, cities and counties would receive their full funding for the first three quarters of fiscal 1986.

Boland said that if the final version of the congressional budget resolution called for full funding for revenue sharing in fiscal 1986, he would support a supplemental appropriation to provide the difference.

Senate Committee Action

The Senate Appropriations Committee July 31 approved a $54.8 billion version of the bill that differed only in minor respects from the version the House passed July 25. The Senate committee did not file its report until Aug. 28 (S Rept 99-129).

Following were some of the major recommendations made by the Senate Appropriations Committee for fiscal 1986 funding:

HUD Programs

Major elements in the $12.6 billion for HUD included:

- **Assisted Housing.** The Senate panel provided $7.5 billion in new budget authority, assuming a carry-over of $909 million available from previous years and $859 million available from funds recaptured from approved projects that would not be completed.

The panel recommended no new construction of public housing, for which the House provided funding for 5,000 units. However, the committee agreed to $409 million for 2,500 units of housing on Indian reservations, compared with the 1,000 units allowed by the House.

The committee provided $735 million to modernize public housing. At first, committee members, like the House, endorsed one-time up-front grants, rather than the existing method of spreading payments over a long period. However, as brought to the floor, the bill retained the old long-term financing method.

The panel matched the House's total of $1.6 billion for 12,000 units for the elderly and handicapped. But senators provided $772 million for 40,000 housing vouchers, 10,000 more than the House.

The committee agreed to $2.1 billion for 40,000 certificates in the Section 8 rent subsidy program; to save $1 billion, members provided budget authority for the certificates for 10 years, rather than 15, as was done currently.

• **Operating Subsidies.** To help local public housing authorities meet expenses, the panel approved $1.26 billion in operating subsidies, compared with $1.2 billion in the House bill. The committee noted that insurance premiums had increased sharply.

• **Counseling Assistance.** The House increased from $3.5 million to $4 million the funding for local public and private agencies that provided assistance to homeowners and tenants experiencing housing problems, such as default and foreclosure, but the committee approved the lower figure.

• **Solar Bank.** Citing unused existing balances, the Senate committee recommended no funds for the Solar Energy and Energy Conservation Bank. The House allowed $20 million for the bank, which through grants to states, subsidized loans for energy conservation home improvements.

• **Urban Development Action Grants.** For grants to stimulate economic development in inner cities, the committee provided $352 million, a 20 percent cut from fiscal 1985 but $22 million more than the House provided.

• **Policy Development and Research.** The Senate panel agreed with the administration's request to boost funding for research from $16.9 million in fiscal 1985 to $18.9 million. The House froze the research budget.

Other Agencies

• **Veterans Administration.** For the VA, the panel allowed $26.2 billion, $282 million less than the House bill. The biggest difference was in readjustment benefits, which included education and training programs. Although both versions assumed a large drop in the number of veterans and dependents eligible for the programs, the Senate version assumed that the drop would require much less money to be spent.

• **EPA.** The $1.5 billion provided for EPA was slightly more than the House figure and $113 million more than the president requested. Like the House, the Senate panel deferred action on the superfund program and construction grants, which had not been authorized.

• **NASA.** Also like the House, the Senate refused to freeze funding for NASA at the fiscal 1985 level and gave the president less than he wanted. The panel recommended $7.7 billion, $200 million over fiscal 1985. The Senate version was $50 million over the House bill.

• **FEMA.** Committee members voted $33 million less than the House for the Federal Emergency Management Agency, for a total of $598 million. Senators agreed on $50 million for an emergency food and shelter program for the homeless; the House bill allowed $70 million.

• **CPSC.** The committee provided $34.9 million, $2.1 million less than the House, for the CPSC. Members agreed to spend up to $1 million on cigarette fire safety studies and increased by $200,000 the request for investigations into chain saw safety.

• **NSF.** For NSF, which supported basic and applied research in the sciences and engineering, $1.54 billion was provided, $16 million more than the House level and $32 million less than the president's request. The committee raised funding for travel associated with program reviews.

• **Neighborhood Reinvestment Corporation.** The Senate panel allocated $16.7 million, $2 million more than the request but $1 million less than the House, for the corporation.

Senate Floor Action

After two days of bitter debate, the Senate Oct. 18 passed HR 3038 by a 76-9 vote. *(Vote 234, p. 44-S)*

As passed, the bill provided $55.8 billion, less a 1.1 percent reduction in non-defense discretionary items.

The fiscal 1986 funding measure provoked unaccustomed controversy as senators struggled to reduce spending from the levels reported by the Appropriations Committee in order to bring the bill in line with targets set by the budget resolution that cleared Aug. 1.

The Senate first accepted by unanimous consent cuts recommended by Garn to meet the resolution, then turned around and restored some funding, which required still additional adjustments before passage to bring the bill into accord.

The First Cuts

Following passage of the budget resolution, Pete V. Domenici, R-N.M., Budget Committee chairman, and Lawton Chiles, D-Fla., the ranking minority member, said that while budget authority in the bill fell below the budget targets, fiscal 1986 outlays — what actually got spent — exceeded budget ceilings by $800 million.

Garn wanted to avoid an across-the-board cut, preferring to allow members to decide which agencies could best withstand reductions. When debate on the appropriations bill began Oct. 17, he offered a package of amendments to the bill as reported. He said the amendments had the approval of the Appropriations Committee that cut budget authority by $1.4 billion and fiscal 1986 outlays by $800 million.

Included were an $82 million reduction in Indian housing, a $100 million cut in the superfund program and a $45 million reduction for NASA.

But the largest cuts proved to be the hardest. Garn's proposal would have reduced revenue sharing by $570 million, or 12.5 percent, and cut the $9.4 billion VA medical care program by $296 million.

Garn said that while he did not like to recommend reducing funding for those programs, he was forced to choose them because cutting other programs in the bill would produce small savings in the first year. For example, cutting assisted housing by $300 million, Garn said, would save $9 million or $10 million in outlays.

But revenue sharing and veterans' care proved enormously popular. After agreeing by unanimous consent to accept Garn's proposed reductions, the Senate then twice voted to restore $100 million in cuts in VA medical care, and voted to restore half the reduction in revenue sharing.

Restoring Cut Funds

Frank H. Murkowski, R-Alaska, chairman of the Veterans' Affairs Committee, and Alan Cranston, D-Calif., the ranking minority member, argued that the cut made in VA health care would be too drastic. They and Garn quickly agreed to restore $100 million, and the Senate approved.

Then Dave Durenberger, R-Minn., proposed restoring the $570 million that Garn's package cut from revenue sharing. He argued that local governments had already drawn up budgets expecting the funds.

"The signal has already been sent," he said. "The budget resolution assured full funding for revenue sharing. That was in July. Now it's October, and we are talking about changing the game plan."

Garn argued that the cut was painful for him, because as mayor of Salt Lake City, he had lobbied to create the program. But he said that restoring the funds would require every other program in the bill to be reduced.

"I want my colleagues to recognize that what they are making a choice on here," he said, "is between revenue sharing and funds coming out of EPA, out of superfund . . ., out of veterans. . . ."

But the Senate voted 39-57 against Garn's motion to table Durenberger's amendment, and reaffirmed that decision, 57-39, by tabling Garn's motion to reconsider the vote. Durenberger's amendment then was adopted by voice vote. *(Votes 227, 228, p. 43-S)*

Adjusting the Figures

Later Oct. 17, to make up for the addition of the revenue sharing and veterans' health care funds, Domenici and Chiles offered an amendment, which the Senate adopted by voice vote, to cut revenue sharing by 6.1 percent, or $279 million, and everything else in the bill, including veterans' care, by 1.1 percent.

Several senators said the amendment was similar in approach to the then-pending Gramm-Hollings-Rudman amendment to force a balanced budget by 1991. *(Story, p. 459)*

However, Murkowski and Dennis DeConcini, D-Ariz., objected to the effect the Domenici-Chiles amendment would have on VA medical care. The next day, they offered an amendment restoring $166 million for veterans' health.

A visibly frustrated Garn admonished members against accepting cuts and then restoring funds. "Let's not vote for a budget resolution and say we are going to be for deficit reduction and then not vote for individual reductions," he said. "Let's stop having it both ways."

But the Senate voted 36-56 against tabling the Murkowski-DeConcini amendment, and it was adopted by voice vote. *(Vote 232, p. 44-S)*

Domenici then offered, instead, to restore $100 million for VA health care, and take $100 million from revenue sharing to pay for it. Wendell H. Ford, D-Ky., objected, arguing that the revenue-sharing program had suffered enough, since Congress agreed to kill it in 1986.

"We've already cut revenue sharing," he said. "We've cut it to the bone. We've cut it out. O. U. T."

After extended discussions behind closed doors, the Senate, 82-3, agreed to an amendment that would add $100 million for veterans' health, take $50 million from revenue sharing, and $63 million from administrative expenses in several agencies. That paved the way for passage of the bill. *(Vote 233, p. 44-S)*

Spending Cuts Rejected

The Senate rejected two other attempts to cut programs Oct. 17.

William Proxmire, D-Wis., proposed eliminating the 100,000 new units of subsidized housing provided by the bill. Reagan, in his fiscal 1986 budget, proposed a two-year moratorium on new assisted housing.

Proxmire said that his amendment, which would save $7.2 billion in budget authority, would reduce fiscal 1986 outlays by $135 million.

William L. Armstrong, R-Colo., argued that cutting out the housing units would save a great deal of money in the future. "This is an amendment that shoots with real bullets," he said.

Although no senator spoke against it, Proxmire's amendment was rejected, 44-52. *(Vote 229, p. 43-S)*

Later, the Senate rejected an amendment by Armstrong that would have eliminated funding for the Urban Development Action Grant program. After listing several expensive projects developed with UDAG grants, Armstrong said, "To suggest that we ought to tax people, the poor people of this country, the working people of this country, to pay for such extravagance, seems completely off the wall."

But Donald W. Riegle Jr., D-Mich., said that the program had spurred development in areas that needed revitalization. "This is one of the few federal programs which has been a genuine success," he said.

The Senate tabled Armstrong's amendment, 53-42. *(Vote 231, p. 44-S)*

Other Amendments

After a bitter two-hour fight, the Senate adopted, 70-26, an amendment by Slade Gorton, R-Wash., that deleted $7 million earmarked for a demonstration wastewater treatment project for the Alaska Pulp Corp. in Sitka, Alaska. Gorton said the Japanese-owned firm had avoided compliance with clean water laws for years and did not deserve a federal bailout. *(Vote 230, p. 43-S)*

Ted Stevens, R-Alaska, sought the money to enable the plant to meet federal clean water standards, arguing that if it failed to meet the standards, the plant would close, threatening 2,000 jobs.

But Gorton argued that Stevens was asking the Senate to bail out the mill for failing to abide by the law. "What we will be saying if we include this appropriation in this bill is that it pays to defy the law," he said.

Further, Gorton said that a competing mill in Washington would be placed at a disadvantage.

Other amendments were adopted by voice vote. Alan J. Dixon, D-Ill., and Gorton succeeded in adding $25 million to the $50 million in the bill for aid for the homeless. Their amendment provided $70 million for an emergency food and shelter program currently run by FEMA, with transfer of the program from FEMA to HUD by March.

Also, their amendment provided $5 million for a demonstration program to help the homeless in their transition to independent living.

The Senate also adopted an amendment by John Heinz, R-Pa., adding $2 million for a demonstration project providing funds for neighborhood development programs, and an amendment by Patrick J. Leahy, D-Vt., adding $3 million for 50 additional awards to encourage young scientists to stay in academic careers.

Conference Action

Conferees reached agreement Nov. 7 on a $56.5 billion version of the funding bill.

But Garn said he would not file a conference report until he won assurances that Budget Committee members would not block the bill and the president would sign it.

Senate Budget Committee Chairman Domenici had threatened to keep over-budget bills from the floor. While the conferees' proposals seemed to match budget targets, and Domenici — a conferee — did not object to them, Garn said he needed more assurance.

As approved by the conferees, the measure was $1 billion above the $55.5 billion versions passed by the Senate Oct. 18 and the House July 25. The conference bill included about $1 billion more than the Senate allowed for housing. It also provided $900 million for the superfund program. The House had deferred action on superfund, which had not yet been authorized, while the Senate approved $1.2 billion.

Domenici, who demanded the Senate trim its bill on the floor, argued that the House had exceeded budget outlay targets. Prior to the conference meeting, staffs of the House and Senate Appropriations HUD subcommittees agreed on reducing outlays to $100 million above the targets. Domenici objected, and the panels found $106 million more in savings, including a $53 million cut in revenue sharing.

In agreeing to those reductions, Leahy, ranking minority member of the Senate HUD Appropriations Subcommittee, said he backed Garn's strategy. "Everybody is voting on this thing to cut programs we like," he said. "It would be a shame to do that and have it vetoed."

Garn said the fiscal 1986 cuts were more difficult than those that would be required by the Gramm-Hollings-Rudman balanced-budget amendment.

"I don't think Gramm-Rudman can be any tougher than what these two subcommittees did this year," he said.

Energy/Water Spending Bill Is First to Clear

The first fiscal 1986 appropriations bill to be cleared by Congress was a $15.25 billion energy and water development package funding politically popular projects in most congressional districts.

President Reagan signed the bill into law (HR 2959 — PL 99-141) on Nov. 1. Congress had cleared HR 2959 on Oct. 17.

Final action came when the Senate approved the conference report on the bill after House approval earlier in the day. Both chambers passed the compromise by voice vote.

The appropriations bill funded construction and operation of hundreds of dams, harbors, canals and irrigation systems by the U.S. Army Corps of Engineers and the Interior Department's Bureau of Reclamation, plus high-technology energy research projects under the Department of Energy.

A major issue in passage of the legislation was the inclusion of $100 million for 62 new water projects that the House had approved in its version of the bill. The administration objected to funding of the proposed new starts because more than half the projects had not been authorized and because Congress had not yet enacted administration-proposed cost-sharing reforms that would apply to the projects.

Agreement was reached to drop the projects from HR 2959 after 45 of the projects were included in the fiscal 1985 supplemental appropriations bill (HR 2577 — PL 99-88), subject to cost-sharing agreements being worked out. *(Supplemental appropriations bill, p. 350)*

Passage of HR 2959 was also eased because omnibus water projects authorizing legislation (HR 6, S 1567) was moving through Congress at the same time that made major policy changes on the issue of cost-sharing by local project users. *(Omnibus water bill, p. 198)*

Final Provisions

As cleared, HR 2959 appropriated $15,251,718,000 in net new budget authority. The bill passed by the House July 16 provided $15.27 billion, while the Senate bill passed Aug. 1 totaled $15.21 billion. *(Fiscal 1986 funding, chart, p. 325)*

The total in the bill was $92 million less than the president had requested. HR 2959 included higher funding than Reagan had requested for water projects, but less than he wanted for nuclear weapons. Roughly half of the money in the bill ($7.6 billion) was for atomic energy defense activities such as the production of nuclear warheads. Both the House and Senate had cut the president's $8 billion request for a beefed-up nuclear weapons program.

The bill also included $778 million for water projects under the Bureau of Reclamation and $2.8 billion for those carried out by the Corps of Engineers. Reagan had sought only $2.4 billion for the corps, expecting to make up much of the difference with a package of new port and waterway user fees, contained in the omnibus water resources authorizing bill.

Funding in the bill for two controversial water projects, the Garrison Diversion in North Dakota ($41.3 million) and the Bonneville Unit of the Central Utah Project ($62.3 million), could not be spent until certain conditions were met.

For the Garrison Diversion, Congress had to pass authorizing legislation to redesign the project. But that legislation (HR 1116) never got out of the House Interior and Insular Affairs Subcommittee on Water and Power Resources in 1985.

For the Bonneville Unit, the Interior Department had to reach a new cost-sharing agreement with the local water district. The current repayment contract had been criticized for not recovering the full local share of costs.

House Committee Action

The House Appropriations Committee July 10 approved by voice vote its $15.27 billion version of the bill (H Rept 99-195). The measure had been approved by the Energy and Water Development Subcommittee on June 20.

Before approving the measure, the committee added $100 million to start construction on 62 new water projects. The panel earlier had put that funding into HR 2577, the fiscal 1985 supplemental appropriations bill, only to see the full House reduce the total. The Reagan administration had sought fewer new construction starts and more local cost-sharing for the projects.

The immediate effect of the House committee's action was to bolster its position when members went to conference with the Senate on the supplemental. Energy and Water Subcommittee Chairman Tom Bevill, D-Ala., recommended adding the $100 million for new starts "in order to have something to fall back on" if the water project dispute could not be settled in the supplemental funding measure.

Although the bill totaled less than the president's request, the administration signaled unhappiness with the bill's spending priorities in a July 10 letter from David A. Stockman, director of the Office of Management and Budget (OMB). He called the bill "unacceptable to the administration in its present form," saying water funds should be linked to reforms in project cost-sharing.

Garrison Diversion

The Garrison Diversion, a $1.1 billion system of aqueducts and irrigation canals, was to deliver water from the massive lake behind Garrison Dam in North Dakota, irrigating some 250,000 acres.

In voting $41 million for construction on the project, the committee prohibited actual expenditures of the money unless Congress enacted authorizing legislation by March 31, 1986.

The 1985 energy and water appropriations bill (PL 98-360) contained $53 million for Garrison, but blocked spending of the money until a commission appointed by the interior secretary recommended how to revamp the project. *(1984 Almanac p. 372)*

North Dakotans generally wanted to use the water already in the Garrison reservoir to irrigate farms and supply urban homes and factories. But conservationists said canals needed to deliver the water would destroy waterfowl habitat, and Canada feared drainage from the project would harm its fisheries.

The recommendations of the Garrison Diversion Unit Study Commission did not settle the long dispute. Although funding of renewed construction on the project was supposed to be automatic if two-thirds of the commissioners agreed on a plan, some features of the plan were thought to require new authorizing legislation.

Other Provisions

Spending increases made by the committee were offset by cuts in other areas, including several significant reductions in energy programs.

The committee included $134 million for highway and other economic development programs under the Appalachian Regional Commission, rebuffing Reagan's efforts to terminate those programs.

But the panel followed Reagan's lead in cutting solar and renewable energy programs to $147 million, down from $178 million in fiscal 1985.

For nuclear fission research and development, the committee cut funding to $608 million, instead of increasing it to $658 million as the president had requested.

Another cut from the president's budget came in the appropriation from the Nuclear Waste Disposal Fund for commercial high-level radioactive waste. Reagan had asked for $571 million, but the committee cut that to $521 million. The fund came from fees paid by nuclear electric utilities, so that spending was offset by revenues. Unused revenues stayed in the fund for future needs.

In a swipe at the Nuclear Regulatory Commission (NRC), the committee trimmed its budget to $404 million from the $448 million level of 1985. The panel's report called the commission's structure "a blueprint for regulatory paralysis" and said, "The NRC may be the single largest impediment facing the nuclear power industry in America today." The NRC, an independent agency, was responsible for licensing nuclear power plants.

The administration had requested $437.6 million for the NRC.

House Floor Action

HR 2959 passed the House with ease on July 16. The bill was approved by voice vote after debate that focused mainly on water resource issues.

One water policy reformer who had challenged such bills in the past, Rep. Bob Edgar, D-Pa., supported the 1985 measure. He noted that the Public Works Committee in June had approved a water projects authorizing bill (HR 6) that made major policy changes on the issue of cost-sharing by local project users. "I believe we are really on the road to a new direction in water policy," Edgar said.

The bill made several major concessions to critics who wanted a greater share of water project costs to be paid by local users and beneficiaries.

HR 2959 got caught up in a budget squabble when a rule (H Res 221) came before the House to allow consideration of HR 2959. That rule exempted the water bill and two other funding bills from Budget Act requirements that Congress adopt a budget resolution before spending money through appropriations.

Bevill, who was floor manager for the bill, said its total spending was less than the 1985 appropriation, less than Reagan's budget request, and consistent with the "freeze" levels of the House-passed budget resolution.

But Robert S. Walker, R-Pa., reflecting the views of the Reagan administration and OMB, challenged the accounting methods used by the committee, saying, "This bill costs considerably more money than what the committee claims."

Water Projects

Funds for 62 water projects, opposed by the administration, were put into the $952 million line-item for general construction by the Corps of Engineers. The bulk of the money was for continuing construction on projects already begun.

The $2.87 billion total for the corps' civil works budget also included $138 million for general investigations, $321 million for flood control on the Mississippi River system, $1.3 billion for operation and maintenance of projects already built, and other miscellaneous expenses.

The Reagan administration requested $2.4 billion for the corps and proposed that Congress make up most of the difference by imposing some $400 million in new fees on waterway users.

Also included in the bill was $541 million for the construction budget of the Bureau of Reclamation, for which the administration had requested $536 million. The fiscal 1985 amount had been $740 million.

Cost-Sharing

HR 2959 as passed by the House contained no general cost-sharing language, nor did the report accompanying it. Furthermore, it did not contain any "fencing" language prohibiting outlays of the new corps construction money until Congress had authorized the projects.

In a colloquy on the floor, Edgar elicited assurances from Bevill that the new project starts in HR 2959 would be subject to whatever cost-sharing requirements were contained in HR 6, the omnibus authorizing bill approved June 26 by the Public Works and Transportation Committee, when and if that bill became law.

On reclamation projects, the House bill showed other signs of restraint — restricting outlays of appropriated money until local sponsors of several large projects agreed

Fiscal 1986 Energy/Water Funds

Following are estimated net new budget authority totals in HR 2959, the fiscal 1986 appropriations bill for energy and water development. *(Figures in thousands of dollars)*

	Reagan Request *	House Bill	Senate Bill	Conference
Corps of Engineers				
Construction	$ 848,530	$ 952,438	$ 829,581	$ 919,345
Mississippi River System	271,440	321,685	285,735	314,760
Operation and Maintenance	976,560	1,325,195	1,302,800	1,319,973
Other	263,210	272,189	244,697	267,972
Subtotal	$ 2,359,740	$ 2,871,507	$ 2,662,813	$ 2,822,050
Bureau of Reclamation				
Construction	536,114	541,074	512,730	521,700
Operation and Maintenance	135,159	132,665	132,665	132,665
Other	125,353	126,800	121,665	123,550
Subtotal	$ 796,626	$ 800,539	$ 767,060	$ 777,915
Energy Department				
Energy Supply R&D	1,971,013	1,730,436	1,879,721	1,772,271
Uranium Supply and Enrichment	(1,612,700)	(1,612,700)	(1,612,700)	(1,612,700)
General Science and Research	685,479	685,400	679,400	685,400
Nuclear Waste Disposal Fund	571,460	521,460	552,460	521,460
Atomic Energy Defense	8,032,900	7,593,415	7,647,800	7,604,615
Administration	175,839	166,138	166,138	166,138
Power Marketing Administrations	241,159	229,391	229,391	229,391
Federal Energy Regulatory Commission	32,775	26,991	29,491	29,491
Geothermal Resources Fund	76	72	72	72
Subtotal	$ 11,710,701	$ 10,953,303	$ 11,184,473	$ 11,008,838
Independent Agencies				
Appalachian Regional Commission	0	134,000	71,800	120,000
Nuclear Regulatory Commission	437,600	403,671	429,000	418,000
Tennessee Valley Authority	38,605	109,000	90,861	104,000
Others	846	915	915	915
Subtotal	$ 477,051	$ 647,586	$ 592,576	$ 642,915
TOTAL	$ 15,344,118	$ 15,272,935	$ 15,206,922	$ 15,251,718

*As amended.

to cost-sharing or other reforms.

During floor consideration July 16, the House also adopted by voice vote fencing language on two other big Western projects.

One of the modifications pertained to the $2.1 billion Bonneville Unit of the Central Utah Project. A substitute amendment offered by George Miller, D-Calif., to an amendment by Gerald B. H. Solomon, R-N.Y., barred further funding on that project until local sponsors signed a new repayment agreement with the federal government and Congress had 100 days to examine it. The amendment was adopted by voice vote.

Another Miller amendment, also approved by voice vote, barred funding for the Animas-La Plata Project in Colorado and New Mexico until local sponsors had signed a cost-sharing agreement and Congress had 120 days to study it.

Miller chaired the House Interior and Insular Affairs Subcommittee on Water and Power Resources, which had authorizing jurisdiction over reclamation projects.

Senate Committee Action

The Senate Appropriations Committee July 25 approved a $15.18 billion version of HR 2959 (S Rept 99-110) that did not include any funding for construction of new water projects.

During the July 25 meeting, committee Chairman Mark O. Hatfield, R-Ore., persuaded Pete V. Domenici, R-N.M., to withdraw a $64.7 million amendment for safety and security improvements at nuclear weapons facilities around the country. Several minor amendments were added by other senators, mostly earmarking funds for specific water projects from money already in the bill.

The Senate committee bill restored a $25 million cut made by the House in the budget of the Nuclear Regulatory Commission and also restored $31 million of $50 million cut by the House from Reagan's request for the high-level nuclear-waste program, and $20 million of the House cut of $30 million in Reagan's request to clean up uranium mill tailings.

The Senate committee restored much of the funding the administration proposed to cut from solar energy research and development. Reagan recommended dropping the program from $178 million for 1985 to $148 million in 1986. The House reduced the funding further to $147 million, but the Senate raised the amount to $162 million.

Struck by the Senate committee was a House-passed requirement that only American-made electrical transmission equipment be bought by U.S. agencies.

Senate Floor Action

The Senate Aug. 1 passed HR 2959 by voice vote, after agreeing not to use the bill to block natural gas pricing rules.

The key controversy that threatened to stall floor action until after the August recess was prompted by a May 30 proposal by the Federal Energy Regulatory Commission (FERC) to overhaul rules governing natural gas pipelines.

The Appropriations Committee had included in its bill a ban on spending to carry out the proposed regulations because of opposition from senators from gas-producing states. They feared the rules would force price reductions for more expensive "new" gas, tapped since 1977.

Senators from gas-consuming states in the Northeast welcomed the rules as a way to lower gas prices paid by consumers.

At an Aug. 1 agency conference in Washington, FERC Chairman Raymond J. O'Connor assured both sides that the rule changes would take their concerns into consideration.

For that reason, J. Bennett Johnston, D-La., a sponsor of the committee proposal, asked that the ban be stricken from the bill. Bill Bradley, D-N.J., who had planned to lead a floor fight against the ban, agreed readily.

There was little debate or controversy during Senate consideration of the appropriations bill.

Left out of the Senate bill was $100 million to start or continue construction of 62 new water projects included in the House version. In its report, the Senate committee had said it wanted to wait until the issue was settled in negotiations over HR 2577, the fiscal 1985 supplemental appropriations bill.

The supplemental, cleared by the House the same day as Senate passage of the appropriations bill, included start-up funds for 45 new water projects, but no new water funds were added to HR 2959 on the Senate floor.

Amendments

Domenici was successful in getting Senate approval of a modified version of his amendment, rejected in committee, to add money for safety and security programs at nuclear weapons facilities. His floor amendment, adopted by voice vote, called for $17 million for the program, rather than the $64.7 million he had sought in committee. In supporting the amendment, Strom Thurmond, R-S.C., said the amendment would restore funding to the authorization level agreed to by the House and the Senate in the fiscal 1986 Department of Defense authorization bill.

The Senate also adopted by voice vote an amendment by Edward M. Kennedy, D-Mass., to increase funding by $7.5 million for Department of Energy research on verification and control technology of nuclear testing. Kennedy said such research had "high payoff," since improvements in verification could lead to new opportunities for arms control and "head off new escalation of the arms race."

Another amendment adopted by voice vote was offered by Daniel J. Evans, R-Wash., to earmark $2,750,000 of funds appropriated for the Federal Energy Regulatory Commission to enable the commission to evaluate environmental impact when reviewing multiple hydroelectric license applications for projects that could possibly be clustered together in limited geographical areas.

Conference/Final Action

House-Senate conferees reached agreement Oct. 9 on a $15.25 billion fiscal 1986 appropriations bill (H Rept 99-307) for energy and water development.

The conference recommended spending $45 million more than the Senate had provided, but $21 million less than the House appropriation.

The conferees appropriated no new funds to continue construction of the 45 "new start" water projects Congress had approved in the fiscal 1985 supplemental. They did, however, allow unobligated funds from other projects to be made available for the new starts.

A "Buy American" proviso for extra-high-voltage electrical transmission equipment was also included in the conference report. The five federal power-marketing authorities and the Tennessee Valley Authority would be required to buy U.S.-manufactured equipment if its price was not more than 25 percent greater than equivalent foreign equipment. ▮

Legislative Branch Funding

President Reagan Nov. 13 signed into law a $1.598 billion fiscal 1986 appropriations bill for the legislative branch of the federal government (HR 2942 — PL 99-151).

The measure cleared Congress Oct. 29, when the conference report (H Rept 99-321) was adopted by a vote of 251-164 in the House and by voice vote in the Senate. *(Vote 340, p. 106-H)*

The conference agreement effectively froze legislative branch spending at the fiscal 1985 level, falling short of that year's total by $1.7 million. *(Provisions, box, p. 327)*

However, some members warned that supplemental appropriations would be needed to cover soaring congressional mail costs unless something was done to restrain them. *(Congressional mail, p. 32)*

Legislative Branch Appropriations, Fiscal 1986

Following are the amounts contained in the House- and Senate-passed versions and in the final version of the fiscal 1986 legislative branch appropriations bill (HR 2942 — PL 99-151):

	House	Senate	Final Amount
Congressional Operations			
Senate	$ —	$ 290,453,800	$ 290,453,800
House	447,465,000	447,465,000	447,465,000
Joint Items	114,900,000	110,645,000	110,649,000
Office of Technology Assessment	15,300,000	15,300,000	15,300,000
Congressional Budget Office	16,609,000	17,541,000	16,886,000
Architect of the Capitol	65,681,000	84,115,000	84,653,000
Congressional Research Service	38,963,000	40,333,000	38,963,000
Government Printing Office (congressional printing)	69,405,000	69,405,000	69,405,000
Subtotal	$ 768,323,000	$ 1,075,257,800	$ 1,073,774,800
Related Agencies			
Botanic Garden	2,197,000	2,113,000	2,188,000
Library of Congress	178,634,000	181,340,000	180,112,000
Architect of the Capitol (Library buildings)	5,785,000	5,785,000	5,785,000
Copyright Royalty Tribunal	156,000	156,000	156,000
Government Printing Office (non-congressional printing)	37,636,000	34,536,000	34,536,000
General Accounting Office	300,992,000	299,726,000	300,992,000
Railroad Accounting Principles Board	750,000	750,000	750,000
Subtotal	$ 526,150,000	$ 524,406,000	$ 524,519,000
TOTAL	$ 1,294,473,000	$ 1,599,663,800	$ 1,598,293,800

As signed into law, HR 2942 was $185 million, or about 10 percent, below the $1.7 billion request in the president's budget. And the budget figure was 10 percent below the amount originally requested by the legislative branch; the White House, departing from the tradition of not tampering with the budget request submitted by Congress, had called for a 10 percent across-the-board cut.

The House Appropriations Legislative Branch Subcommittee, which originated HR 2942, initially proposed an .8 percent increase over 1985 funding, but Republican members threatened to attack the bill on the floor. Democrats on the full committee later agreed to a funding freeze, and the House and Senate went along with it to demonstrate their commitment to fiscal restraint.

Budget Request

By law, the legislative branch's funding requests are included in the president's budget without change. But in his fiscal 1986 budget, Reagan recommended a 10 percent cut that would lower budget authority for the legislative branch from $1.93 billion to $1.737 billion. The reduction was in line with Reagan's call for a similar cut at many federal agencies, administration officials said.

The $1.93 billion request by the legislative branch was $215 million, or 12.5 percent, above the fiscal 1985 spending level. *(Fiscal 1985 bill, 1984 Almanac p. 387)*

The president's action drew protests from lawmakers. Vic Fazio, D-Calif., chairman of the House Appropriations Legislative Branch Subcommittee, called it "an unprecedented break with comity between the branches. We usually get back whatever we send over."

Edwin L. Dale, spokesman for the Office of Management and Budget (OMB), said the request was simply "a suggestion." But an OMB document accompanying the budget said there was "ample ground for achieving staffing and operations economies in the far-flung operations of the legislative branch — without directly affecting key legislative support activities."

The 1986 legislative branch budget request included:

- $296 million for Senate operations, including $9 million for senators' pay and $228 million for staff salaries.
- $494 million to run the House, including $38 million for members' pay, $49 million for salaries for the staff of House officers, $91 million for committee employees' salaries and $170 million for members' personal staffs.
- $156 million for joint accounts, comprised primarily of $144 million for official mail costs. The mail expenses were nearly double the 1985 rate because members typically sent more mail during an election year.
- $18 million for the Congressional Budget Office (CBO), which provides economic analyses for congressional committees.
- $120 million for the Architect of the Capitol's office, to cover salaries, maintenance of buildings and the Capitol grounds, and the operation of House and Senate office buildings. The account for House office buildings jumped from $23 million to $41 million to allow the hiring of an exterminator other than the lowest bidder to rid House office buildings of cockroaches, mice and other pests. A spokesman for the architect said there had been occasional

dissatisfaction with the performance of some low bidders.

- $345 million for the Library of Congress, including $43 million for the Congressional Research Service.
- $122 million for the Government Printing Office, which prints the *Congressional Record*, bills and other documents for Congress.
- $340 million for the General Accounting Office (GAO), Congress' investigative arm. The budget called for 200 additional full-time employees.
- $17 million for the Office of Technology Assessment, which provided technical and scientific studies to Congress.

House Subcommittee Action

The Legislative Appropriations Subcommittee June 25 approved $1.3 billion for House expenses and related agencies — .8 percent above fiscal 1985 funding. But Republican members vowed to fight the bill on the floor unless it was cut by $10.9 million to eliminate the increase.

In an effort to defuse the opposition, Fazio reluctantly agreed to offer an amendment in full committee to achieve a funding freeze. "I realize the symbolism is important," he said, although he said the subcommittee bill already was 10 percent below the budget request and within the limits set by the House-passed budget resolution.

Fazio maintained that the bill, which met Reagan's 10 percent cut target, was "not in any way related to the administration's request." But he added, "there is a desire to show restraint in the legislative branch appropriations."

The subcommittee achieved its saving by eliminating dozens of positions that were vacant and by deferring maintenance projects, including restoration work on the Capitol Rotunda. That drew objections from Lindy (Mrs. Hale) Boggs, D-La., who argued for immediate repairs since, she said, the Capitol would sustain exceptionally heavy use during the bicentennial celebrations for Congress in 1987 and 1988.

As approved by the subcommittee, the bill contained no pay raise or cost-of-living increase for members of Congress or legislative employees.

During the markup, Democratic and GOP members engaged in highly partisan sniping at each other. Democrats complained that Republicans made the legislative appropriation process a political spectacle each year, while the GOP charged that Democrats allowed waste and improper patronage. Silvio O. Conte, R-Mass., said spending could easily be cut by eliminating the vast amount of "dead wood" he said existed among congressional staff, particularly the Capitol police and garage and gallery attendants.

House Committee Action

The House Appropriations Committee reported its $1.29 billion version of HR 2942 July 10 (H Rept 99-194), providing fiscal 1986 funding for the House and other legislative agencies at levels about the same as fiscal 1985. (The Senate later added funds to cover its operations.)

Before approving the bill by voice vote, the committee adopted an amendment by Fazio to cut $11.7 million from the version approved by the subcommittee. The amendment cut out additional funds the subcommittee had provided for congressional staff and printing, the GAO, Architect of the Capitol and three other accounts.

The committee also adopted by voice vote an amendment by Wes Watkins, D-Okla., to provide on-call chiropractic services to lawmakers through the House attending physician. "Probably the No. 1 injury our members have is strained backs," Watkins said.

Jerry Lewis, Calif., ranking Republican on the Legislative Branch Subcommittee, indicated he would support the bill on the floor because committee Democrats agreed to hold the line on legislative spending. But Conte said he would offer an amendment to cut Capitol police, doorkeepers and garage attendants.

Several members warned that supplemental funds would be needed if lawmakers failed to restrain their use of franked mail privileges. Official mail costs were estimated at $85.7 million for fiscal 1985 and were budgeted for an $18.5 million increase in 1986, to $104.2 million.

House Floor Action

The House passed HR 2942 July 18, 263-136, after several hours of what members called self-flagellation over congressional perquisites and waste. *(Vote 223, p. 72-H)*

Before passing the bill, the House voted to cut funds for the production of Braille editions of *Playboy* magazine. It also voted to start trimming the ranks of congressional garage attendants, but rejected a move to freeze the number of patronage workers who ran the automatic elevators on Capitol Hill. Amendments to cut legislative branch funding by 2.7 percent and chop $10 million from congressional mailing accounts also were defeated.

The first cost-cutting amendment to succeed was Conte's proposal to eliminate through attrition 10 of the 64 parking garage attendant jobs, for a saving of $230,000. It was adopted by voice vote.

The only other successful amendment was offered by Chalmers P. Wylie, R-Ohio. Adopted 216-193, it cut $103,000 from the Library of Congress for Braille reproductions of magazines for the blind. Wylie's target was *Playboy* because of articles he said promoted "wanton and illicit sex." Wylie brought copies of the Braille *Playboy* to the floor, amid hoots of laughter from other members, who rushed over to take a look. *(Vote 221, p. 72-H)*

Fazio defended the Braille edition, pointing out that it contained no photographs and many serious articles, including interviews with Sen. Barry Goldwater, R-Ariz., and columnist William F. Buckley.

The House rejected three cost-cutting amendments:

- By Clarence E. Miller, R-Ohio, to cut $10 million in official mail funds. Rejected 204-217. *(Vote 219, p. 70-H)*
- By Hank Brown, R-Colo., to eliminate a $106,000 increase for five new elevator operator positions. Rejected 191-221. *(Vote 220, p. 70-H)*

Brown's attempt to block the increase in the number of patronage employees who ran the automatic elevators on Capitol Hill was perhaps the most controversial amendment. Democrats defended the employees, some of whom were handicapped, saying they helped members rushing to the floor to vote and tourists visiting the Capitol. Republicans called them a prime example of wasteful spending.

- By Bill Cobey, R-N.C., to cut funding in the bill by 2.7 percent. Rejected 193-211. *(Vote 222, p. 72-H)*

In 1984, the House adopted a 2 percent across-the-board cut in legislative branch appropriations, although in the final fiscal 1985 bill, conferees settled on savings amounting to about 1 percent.

Senate Committee Action

The Senate Appropriations Committee reported HR 2942 on July 25 (S Rept 99-111) after adding $290.12 million for Senate operations. That brought spending in the bill to $1.599 billion, slightly less than the $1.6 billion appropriated for fiscal 1985.

The committee followed the lead set by the House, seeking to restrain legislative spending to set an example of fiscal restraint for other funding bills to follow. Its bill trimmed legislative branch funds by $728,338 below existing appropriations.

Funds added by the committee included $725,000 to install anti-terrorist barriers around the U.S. Capitol, to replace the trucks and buses that were being used to block vehicular access to the Capitol grounds. The steel hydraulic barricades would recess into the street during the day and be raised at night. The proposal was part of a plan by Architect of the Capitol George M. White to turn the East Front of the Capitol, which was used for parking, into a pedestrian mall.

The committee also voted to restore $593,000 cut by the House from funding for the Library of Congress.

It deferred a $7 million request for a new Senate telecommunications system, for which a final contract had not yet been negotiated.

Senate Floor Action

The Senate passed HR 2942 July 31 by voice vote, without the long and rancorous debate the measure had engendered in the House.

The only serious debate centered on two amendments — one successful, one withdrawn — to create new panels.

Dan Quayle, R-Ind., offered but later withdrew an amendment to form a Select Committee on the Two-Year Budget. A commission he headed had recommended in 1984 that Congress go to a two-year budget cycle, instead of the existing annual budget system.

Before withdrawing his amendment, Quayle won assurances from Pete V. Domenici, R-N.M., chairman of the Budget Committee, and William V. Roth Jr., R-Del., chairman of the Governmental Affairs Committee, that joint hearings would be held on the issue.

The other amendment, sponsored by Paula Hawkins, R-Fla., and adopted by voice vote, would create a U.S. International Narcotics Control Commission, to monitor and promote compliance with international drug control treaties. An appropriation of $325,000 was added to the bill for the new panel, which would be composed of seven senators and five experts from the private sector.

Wendell H. Ford, D-Ky., and Howard M. Metzenbaum, D-Ohio, questioned the worth of such a group. Metzenbaum said it would not solve the narcotics problem, and added, "I am sick and tired of creating new commissions." Ford suggested the money could be used more effectively in other ways to reduce drug abuse.

Alfonse M. D'Amato, R-N.Y., chairman of the Appropriations Subcommittee on the Legislative Branch, said the $325,000-a-year cost of the commission was "a minuscule amount of money," and rejected criticism by Ford that the panel would merely provide new opportunities for junkets.

D'Amato won adoption of two amendments extending the authority to spend funds already appropriated to demolish a Senate annex building and renovate the Senate TV studio.

Conference Action

Conferees Oct. 23 agreed on a total of $1.598 billion for the legislative branch — $1.7 million below the 1985 level and $185 million below the budget request. The conference report (H Rept 99-321) was filed the same day.

House conferees accepted the Senate's addition of $725,000 to install anti-terrorist devices around the U.S. Capitol. Conferees also decided to spend $290,000 to conserve the fresco canopy and frieze in the Capitol Rotunda — a compromise between the House's appropriation of $800,000 for the project and the Senate's vote to delete the money for the sake of fiscal restraint.

They also agreed to a House request that the U.S. International Narcotics Control Commission added by the Senate be renamed the U.S. Senate Caucus on International Narcotics Control because no House members were included on the panel.

Fazio warned that a supplemental appropriation could be needed for the CBO, whose workload would increase with the adoption of the Gramm-Rudman-Hollings balanced budget proposal. *(Story, p. 459)*

Vetoed Treasury/Postal Bill Included in 'CR'

Citing the nation's "chronic budgetary crisis," President Reagan Nov. 15 vetoed a $13.15 billion appropriations bill (HR 3036) for the Treasury Department, U.S. Postal Service, Executive Office of the President and various other agencies.

Congress had cleared the measure Nov. 7, the Senate adopting the conference report (H Rept 99-349) by voice vote several hours after the House approved it, 237-171. *(Vote 362, p. 112-H)*

Reagan said the bill contained some $900 million more than he had requested, most of it for a federal postal subsidy he had sought to end. While a presidential veto was "an instrument to be used with care," he said he would not hesitate to employ it "until the Congress comes to grips with the problem of the large budget deficit." *(Veto text, p. 35-D)*

Congress did not attempt to override the veto. The 237-171 House vote for the conference report indicated that there was not the necessary support for an override — two-thirds of both chambers.

Instead, Congress included fiscal 1986 funds for the affected agencies in the omnibus "continuing resolution" (PL 99-190), after cutting a total of $117 million — $45 million from the Internal Revenue Service (IRS) and $72 million from the postal subsidy — to meet the president's objections. *(Provisions, story, p. 360)*

Congress and the administration had been at odds all year over staffing levels for the IRS and the Customs Service and over the federal postal subsidy. The subsidy reimbursed the Postal Service for revenue forgone due to lower postage rates given to charitable and religious organizations, newspapers and other non-first-class categories of mail. The administration wanted to eliminate the subsidy, but it was politically popular in Congress because of the nature of the groups that could take advantage of less expensive postal rates.

There also was strong opposition in Congress to the administration's proposals to save money by cutting back on the number of IRS and Customs personnel, since these agencies produced revenue for the federal government.

Provisions

As signed into law, PL 99-190 provided the following amounts:

Agency	Budget Request	Final Amount
Treasury Department		
Office of the Secretary	$ 78,699,000	$ 54,274,000
International Affairs	—	22,442,000
Federal Law Enforcement Training Center	17,803,000	23,803,000
Financial Management Service	246,902,000	244,621,000
Bureau of Alcohol, Tobacco and Firearms	173,725,000	174,212,000
U.S. Customs Service	725,202,000	792,000,000
Bureau of the Mint	47,942,000	46,500,000
Bureau of the Public Debt	199,215,000	195,225,000
Internal Revenue Service	3,611,332,000	3,642,268,000
U.S. Secret Service	290,340,000	294,000,000
Subtotal	**$ 5,391,160,000**	**$ 5,489,345,000**
Payment to the U.S. Postal Service	**$ 39,128,000**	**$ 748,000,000**
Executive Office of the President		
President's compensation	250,000	250,000
Office of Administration	15,794,000	15,597,000
White House Office	25,499,000	24,906,000
Executive residence	4,719,000	4,577,000
Vice president's residence	204,000	204,000
Vice president's staff	1,694,000	1,794,000
Council of Economic Advisers	2,381,000	2,301,000
Office of Policy Development	2,828,000	2,726,000
National Security Council	4,748,000	4,627,000
National Critical Materials Council	—	500,000
Office of Management and Budget	39,420,000	37,299,000
Office of Federal Procurement Policy	1,656,000	1,611,000
Unanticipated needs	1,000,000	1,000,000
Subtotal	**$ 100,193,000**	**$ 97,392,000**
Independent Agencies		
Administrative Conference of the U.S.	$ 1,484,000	$ 1,430,000
Advisory Commission on Intergovernmental Relations	2,110,000	2,041,000
Advisory Committee on Federal Pay	222,000	210,000
Committee for Purchase from the Blind and Other Severely Handicapped	749,000	730,000
Federal Election Commission	12,756,000	12,433,000
General Services Administration	380,316,000	404,972,000
National Archives	99,549,000	101,363,000
Office of Personnel Management	6,115,880,000	6,113,245,000
Merit Systems Protection Board	25,631,000	24,594,000
Federal Labor Relations Authority	17,613,000	17,064,000
U.S. Tax Court	24,556,000	24,556,000
Subtotal	**$ 6,680,866,000**	**$ 6,702,638,000**
TOTAL	**$12,211,347,000**	**$13,037,375,000**

House Committee Action

The House Appropriations Committee reported HR 3036 on July 18 (H Rept 99-210).

As reported, the bill contained $13.3 billion — $5.5 billion for the Treasury Department, $961.1 million for the Postal Service, $97.7 million for the executive office of the president, and $6.7 billion for 12 independent agencies.

The largest item in the bill was $6.1 billion for the Office of Personnel Management (OPM). That sum included $4.4 billion for the government's share of federal employee retirement costs — $40.3 million above the fiscal 1985 level — and $1.6 billion for health insurance costs for federal employees and retirees, an increase of $264.6 million over 1985.

Although the bill called for total appropriations of $13.3 billion, the actual amount needed by the agencies covered by the bill amounted to more than $268 billion. However, much of that spending did not require an annual appropriation by Congress.

The largest item in that category was interest paid on the national debt. The committee said interest on the $1.8 trillion debt was expected to reach $170 billion in fiscal 1986, but noted that that amount might be understated.

Other non-appropriated items included interest on income tax refunds, payments on judgments against the government and disbursements under the presidential election campaign fund. In all, the committee said it expected payments for such non-appropriated items to increase by more than $20 billion in fiscal 1986.

Treasury Department

The bill contained $5.5 billion for the Treasury Department. The IRS received the bulk of that — $3.7 billion, $178 million above its fiscal 1985 appropriation.

Prompted by reports of severely backlogged IRS processing centers in Philadelphia and elsewhere, the committee provided funds to upgrade the IRS' computer system and to hire additional personnel to process tax returns more effectively. It said the increased funding would permit the agency to collect more than $400 million in additional revenue by examining more tax returns, and another $250 million by closing 6,600 tax shelter cases.

The committee included funds for 1,254 IRS positions the administration wanted to eliminate, and for 1,500 additional employees for the agency.

The committee also included a provision barring the IRS from collecting taxes on money paid by people over 65 to enter "continuing care facilities" that combined retirement communities and medical care. However, the provision subsequently was removed from the bill on a point of order on the House floor. *(Related story, p. 302)*

For the Customs Service, the committee provided $785.4 million, a $97.5 million increase over its 1985 level. The administration had requested $699.5 million.

The bill restored 887 Customs Service positions the administration wanted to eliminate, and added funds for 800 new ones. The committee said more customs agents were needed to stem the flow of drugs and other illegal products into the United States.

Postal Service

The committee approved $961.1 million for the Postal Service, compared with $39.1 million requested by the administration. President Reagan wanted the government to stop subsidizing the nearly $1 billion-a-year difference between postal costs and postal revenues lost because of lower rates for various categories of mail.

The committee sought to shave $13 million off the subsidy by closing a loophole used by large, national publications such as *Time, Newsweek* and *The Wall Street Journal*. These publications were eligible for lower postal rates when they mailed out large numbers of copies within heavily populated counties, although the lower rate was intended to benefit small, rural newspapers.

The committee bill would have excluded the large publications by restricting the lower in-county rate to publications with circulations of 10,000 or less or with more than 50 percent of their circulation within a particular county. However, this provision subsequently was deleted on a point of order on the House floor.

Carried over from previous appropriations bills were provisions requiring free mail for the blind and for overseas voting, and continuation of six-day and rural mail delivery.

Office of the President

The committee approved $97.6 million for the executive office of the president, which covered everything from Reagan's $250,000 salary and expenses to running the Office of Management and Budget (OMB).

OMB, the prime advocate of reduced government spending in the Reagan administration, took its own funding slice in the bill. The $37.7 million allowed was more than $800,000 below the 1985 level and $740,000 below the budget request. It would require the agency to reduce its 594-person staff by 19 positions.

The committee also included a provision that would prevent OMB from reviewing in advance testimony given by other federal agency officials to the Appropriations Committee. The panel said the provision was included "in order to prevent revision of testimony which had actually been presented and unacceptable delays in the preparation of printed hearings."

The committee included $1.2 million for pensions, office space and allowances for former presidents, $19,000 below the 1985 level.

Other Provisions

HR 3036 contained a number of general provisions affecting how funds in the bill were spent. For example, the committee directed the Customs Service to crack down on "forces now at work in America" that "pose threats to the basic liberties and freedoms of our society" in the areas of drug smuggling, child pornography and terrorism.

Taking notice of 39 Americans held hostage in Beirut, the committee directed the Customs Service to consider reviving the air marshal program as a deterrent to airplane hijackings. It also ordered Customs to recommend specific actions and request supplemental funding to strengthen anti-terrorist activities; to strengthen enforcement of U.S. import quotas, and to fight import fraud, particularly involving textile and apparel products. It said foreign goods being dumped in the United States with phony country-of-origin labels were hurting many domestic industries.

In other areas, the bill continued various restrictions placed on the use of funds in past years, including:

- A prohibition on the use of federal employee health benefits to pay for abortions, except in cases where the life of the woman was endangered.
- A prohibition on the use of funds by the Bureau of Alcohol, Tobacco and Firearms (BATF) to require labeling of ingredients in alcoholic beverages.
- A bar on the use of OMB funds to review agricultural marketing orders.
- A prohibition on the use of funds by OPM to implement regulations on merit pay and promotions for federal employees.

Criticism of Bill

The bill was criticized by some members because it was about $497 million above the fiscal 1985 level, and $1.2 billion above Reagan's budget request. *(Fiscal 1985 bill, 1984 Almanac p. 425)*

John Edward Porter, R-Ill., said the Treasury, Postal Service and General Government Subcommittee should have exercised more restraint and warned that the measure was likely to be "pared back with a meat ax on the floor."

But subcommittee Chairman Edward R. Roybal, D-Calif., contended that both the IRS and the Customs Service needed more money to overcome staffing shortages. "If you want to do something about the deficit, you can't continue to reduce money for agencies that produce revenues for the Treasury of the United States," he said.

The committee blamed the administration's budget policies for the problems the IRS was experiencing, and said the proposed personnel cutbacks also "would have a severe adverse impact on the government's ability to interdict the flow of illegal drugs and other contraband into the country" and to prevent the illegal exportation of high-technology items to unfriendly countries.

The only roll-call during committee markup was on an amendment by Bill Alexander, D-Ark., that would have the effect of requiring the White House to make its daily news summary available to House Democrats as well as Republicans. The amendment was adopted 17-13.

House Floor Action

The House, ignoring administration opposition, passed the bill July 30 by a 249-172 vote. *(Vote 245, p. 78-H)*

The House made only minor spending cuts, totaling $35.2 million, before passing the bill.

Bill Frenzel, R-Minn., offered an amendment to shave $192 million off the bill by reducing most spending in it by 2.65 percent. But the House agreed only to a $35 million cut, substituting a Ronald D. Coleman, D-Texas, amendment for Frenzel's proposal. Coleman's amendment, adopted 288-133, exempted the Postal Service, IRS, Customs and several law enforcement agencies from the across-the-board reduction. *(Vote 243, p. 78-H)*

Coleman and others said it made little sense to reduce spending for agencies that generate revenue for the federal government. They said every dollar spent on the Customs Service, for example, yielded $21 in revenue.

But Frenzel disputed that argument. "Last year we increased the number of IRS agents. It did not do a damn thing to reduce our budget deficit," he said.

In earlier action on the bill July 26, the House, in a largely symbolic effort to cut the federal deficit, voted to cut $219,400 from expense allowances for former presidents. However, it rejected a move to eliminate the allowances, which cover office, staff and travel expenses.

Under existing law, former Presidents Richard M. Nixon, Gerald R. Ford and Jimmy Carter each received a yearly allowance of nearly $300,000 in addition to their $86,200 presidential pensions.

On a 219-130 vote, the House agreed to a new formula offered by Bill Nelson, D-Fla., that would lower the allowance the longer a former president was out of office. *(Vote 241, p. 78-H)*

Under Nelson's amendment, an ex-president would receive $300,000 during each of his first four years out of office. The figure would drop to $250,000 during the fifth through eighth years and to $200,000 thereafter. Nixon and Ford thus would receive $200,000 and Carter would get $250,000 under the House-passed provision. The change would save $219,400 in fiscal 1986.

Before adopting the amendment, the House by a 199-162 vote substituted it for an amendment by Andrew Jacobs Jr., D-Ind., that would have eliminated all expense allowances for former presidents. *(Vote 240, p. 78-H)*

Members successfully raised points of order against two provisions of the bill as approved by the Appropriations Committee, thus dropping them from the bill.

William D. Ford, D-Mich., chairman of the Post Office and Civil Service Committee, objected to the provision that would have prevented publications such as *Time*, *Newsweek* and *The Wall Street Journal* from using lower postal rates designed to aid small, rural newspapers. Ford said he was sympathetic to the effort to close the loophole, which would save $13 million, but that the issue should be addressed by his committee rather than in an appropriations bill.

Byron L. Dorgan, D-N.D., raised a similar objection to the provision to bar the IRS from collecting taxes on entry fees paid by elderly people for "continuing care" facilities. Tax treatment of such payments was being considered by conferees on imputed interest legislation. *(Story, p. 476)*

An amendment dealing with the Federal Election Commission (FEC) also was ruled out of order. The amendment, by Thomas J. Bliley Jr., R-Va., would have required the FEC to enforce a 1984 decision by the U.S. Supreme Court, *Ellis v. Brotherhood of Railway, Airline and Steamship Clerks*. In that case, the court held that labor unions could not use compulsory union dues to finance political activities. Frenzel raised the point of order, calling the amendment "unauthorized and legislative earmarking."

A second attempt to offer the amendment was cut off July 30 by a parliamentary maneuver. The House, meeting as the Committee of the Whole, voted 233-186 to rise and report HR 3036 back to the House, thus precluding the amendment from being offered. *(Vote 244, p. 78-H)*

Senate Committee Action

The Senate Appropriations Committee approved a $13 billion version of HR 3036 July 31. It filed its report (S Rept 99-133) on Sept. 9.

For the IRS, the committee included $3.6 billion, about $135.2 million less than the House amount and $29.7 million below the agency's 1985 budget. The amount was $57.3 million less than the administration's request.

While acknowledging that the IRS had problems handling 1984 tax returns, the committee said it believed that "when the computer system's problems have been worked out, processing of tax returns should be greatly streamlined" without the need for additional employees.

For the Postal Service, the Subcommittee on Treasury, Postal Service and General Government had recommended $139 million to subsidize lower postal rates for various users. However, the committee voted 17-9 for an amendment by Quentin N. Burdick, D-N.D., to increase the subsidy by $662 million, bringing it to a total of $801 million.

By adding the extra money, the Senate panel threatened prospects for floor passage because the bill exceeded the figure allowed in the Senate-passed budget resolution (S Con Res 32) by about $660 million.

The Customs Service would receive $784 million in the Senate committee bill, $1.4 million less than the House version but $66.9 million above the administration request. The Senate panel approved an additional $8 million that could be used for Customs expenses if agents were able to sell that much worth of government-seized goods. The House version did not provide the additional money.

Senate Floor Action

The Senate Sept. 26 approved fiscal 1986 funding of $12.9 billion for the agencies in HR 3036. The bill passed by a vote of 88-6. *(Vote 198, p. 38-S)*

The bill contained about $387 million less than the House-passed version. Senators' concerns about the federal deficit led to passage of an amendment that sliced 2 percent — about $139 million — from all discretionary programs in the bill. Exempted from the cut were the mandatory spending portions of the bill that included the president's salary and federal contributions to civil service retirement plans and to federal employees' health benefits.

Budget Committee Chairman Pete V. Domenici, R-N.M., who offered the amendment, said the cuts were necessary to bring the bill in line with deficit-reduction targets set by the fiscal 1986 budget resolution adopted by Congress Aug. 1. Lawton Chiles of Florida, senior Democrat on the Budget panel, supported the move, calling on the Senate to adopt a "truth-in-budgeting" approach to appropriations bills.

The debate over the bill underscored the tension between congressional budget writers and those responsible for specific appropriations measures.

"Let us not try to impose upon the appropriations process all of the frustrations we have had in our failures in achieving what we wanted in the budget process, or in the revenue process, or in any other process," said Appropriations Committee Chairman Mark O. Hatfield, R-Ore.

James Abdnor, R-S.D., chairman of the Appropriations Subcommittee on Treasury, Postal Service and General Government, tried to derail the across-the-board cut by moving to table Domenici's amendment. But his motion failed, 38-58. *(Vote 197, p. 38-S)*

Domenici's amendment then passed easily by voice vote.

Abdnor and others criticized the amendment, charging it would end up costing the government much more than it would save. For example, Abdnor said a 2 percent, or $71 million, drop in the IRS budget would lead to more than $700 million in uncollected tax revenues. Similarly, he said, a $15.8 million cut at the Customs Service would mean a loss of $150 million in duty fees.

Despite the savings from the 2 percent cut, the Senate bill was about $639 million above the administration's budget request, mainly because of the postal subsidy. The Senate approved a postal subsidy payment of $785 million, compared with the House level of $961 million.

Other Amendments

The Senate rejected 24-72 an amendment by Abdnor to add 5 percent to the $36.9 million allotted for the OMB. *(Vote 195, p. 38-S)*

Abdnor had supported the reduced OMB budget when the bill was moving through the committee stage, but said he "possibly got a little heavy with the knife in doing it." OMB officials lobbied senators for the extra money, but the chamber was in no mood to spare the agency from overall budget cuts.

Abdnor did succeed in adding about $500,000 to the Office of Special Counsel, the office within the Merit Systems Protection Board that investigated improper activities by federal employees.

The Senate sidestepped a controversial amendment relating to potentially dangerous ingredients added to alcoholic beverages. The amendment, offered by Abdnor, was aimed at preventing the BATF from issuing regulations to require ingredient labeling of alcoholic beverages until pending litigation on the subject was completed.

Abdnor agreed to withdraw the amendment following critics' complaints that it was too broadly worded and might prevent BATF from issuing regulations requiring the labeling of sulfite preservatives in wine and other alcoholic beverages. Sulfites posed a serious health hazard to 800,000 Americans, according to the Center for Science in the Public Interest, and had been linked to some fatalities.

The House bill's alcohol-labeling provision was narrower than Abdnor's proposal.

The Senate by voice vote adopted an amendment by Jesse Helms, R-N.C., to bar the IRS from granting tax-exempt status to religious organizations that promoted "satanism" or "witchcraft."

Treasury Secretary James A. Baker III, in a July letter to Helms, said the IRS had denied tax exemptions to an organization espousing devil worship, black magic and other satanic rituals but had granted exemptions to several organizations "that espouse a system of beliefs, rituals and practices, derived in part from pre-Christian Celtic and Welsh traditions, which they label as witchcraft."

Conference Action

Despite warnings of a veto, House-Senate conferees Oct. 30 approved a $13.15 billion version of HR 3036 (H Rept 99-349).

OMB officials, while not directly threatening a veto, informed conferees it would be difficult for them to recommend that the president sign the bill because it included too much money for the postal subsidy, the IRS and the Customs Service. The administration also was upset over a House provision that would restrict its issuance of new regulations dealing with job reviews for federal employees.

In approving the bill, conferees also appeared to risk the wrath of budget-minded colleagues in the House and Senate. At the outset, they quickly agreed to drop the 2 percent across-the-board cut voted by the Senate and the more selective 2.65 percent cut adopted by the House. The action reflected the sponsors' views that the two chambers had cut too much from various programs.

For the IRS, conferees approved $3.69 billion, about $76 million more than the administration requested. In doing so, they rejected a White House proposal to cut the IRS by about 1,250 positions. Instead, they included enough money to add about 1,800.

Conferees allowed $792 million for the Customs Service, $67 million more than the administration requested. Here, too, they ignored Reagan's call to cut the Customs staff by 887 positions, instead including enough money to add 623 jobs.

The conferees voted $820 million for the postal subsidy, a compromise between the House and Senate figures.

Dennis DeConcini, D-Ariz., warned conferees they were "baiting for a veto" by approving a postal subsidy above the Senate's original figure. The conference total also exceeded the $749 million postal subsidy allowed by "reconciliation" legislation that was supposed to bring federal spending in line with the budget resolution.

The final bill was about $54 million above the $13.1 billion budget authority target in the budget resolution.

Conferees voted $37.3 million for the OMB, splitting the difference between House and Senate figures. They also approved $1.1 million to cover former presidents' expenses, restoring money the House had cut.

Conferees modified the House provision prohibiting the administration from issuing new regulations making civil service pay raises and job security more dependent on performance and less on seniority. OPM had been trying for years to write new regulations, but Congress had blocked them.

The House ban was defended by House conferees Steny H. Hoyer, D-Md., and Frank R. Wolf, R-Va., who represented thousands of federal employees. They said they feared new regulations could jeopardize the job security of older workers with lower performance ratings than younger ones, despite having more seniority. However, on hearing that a compromise on regulations was in the works, conferees altered the provision to allow the administration to revise existing rules. *(Related story, p. 415)*

Conferees also dropped the Senate provision barring the IRS from granting tax-exempt status to groups that promote "satanism" or "witchcraft." They said the provision came under the jurisdiction of the House Ways and Means Committee. ▮

$106.5 Billion Labor-HHS Funding Bill Clears

President Reagan Dec. 12 signed into law a fiscal 1986 appropriations bill (HR 3424 — PL 99-178) providing $106.5 billion for the Departments of Health and Human Services (HHS), Labor, Education and related agencies.

HR 3424 froze spending for many programs at fiscal 1985 levels, but provided increases in selected programs, including handicapped education and research on acquired immune deficiency syndrome (AIDS). However, the bill cut funding in other areas such as health planning and summer jobs for youths.

Congress had completed action on the bill Dec. 6 when the Senate adopted the conference report, which the House had approved a day earlier. The House originally passed the bill Oct. 2; the Senate, Oct. 22.

HR 3424 provided about $94.8 billion in fiscal 1986 funding and $11.7 billion in advance fiscal 1987-88 funding for several welfare programs, the Corporation for Public Broadcasting and other activities.

The fiscal 1986 total included $6.5 billion for the Labor Department, $69.2 billion for HHS, $18.3 billion for the Education Department and $765 million for related agencies, such as the National Labor Relations Board.

More than two-thirds of the bill was for mandatory spending for such entitlement programs as welfare benefits that must be paid to anyone who meets federal eligibility criteria. For discretionary programs, controlled by annual appropriations, HR 3424 included about $33 billion.

Although the bill provided about $5 billion more than the president requested, it exceeded congressional budget targets for discretionary social programs by less than $100 million.

As signed into law, HR 3424 contained the following funding for the Departments of Labor, HHS, Education and related agencies:

Provisions

	Budget Request	Final Amount
Labor Department		
Employment and Training Administration		
Program administration	$ 62,914,000	$ 68,155,000
Training and employment services	2,805,521,000	3,461,045,000
Community service employment for older Americans	326,000,000	326,000,000
Federal unemployment benefits	10,000,000	10,000,000
Grants to states for unemployment insurance and employment services	23,600,000	23,600,000
Advances to unemployment trust fund	465,000,000	465,000,000
Labor-Management Services Administration	57,505,000	57,505,000
Employment Standards Administration	1,428,259,000	1,438,996,000
Occupational Safety and Health Administration	217,208,000	218,045,000
Mine Safety and Health Administration	148,911,000	151,679,000
Bureau of Labor Statistics	151,853,000	158,640,000
Departmental Management	131,902,000	138,080,000
Total, Labor Department	$5,828,673,000	$6,516,745,000
Health and Human Services		
Health resources and services	1,012,957,000	1,355,434,000
Medical facilities guarantee and loan fund	25,000,000	25,000,000
Centers for Disease Control	420,434,000	471,861,000
National Institutes of Health		
Cancer	1,131,479,000	1,258,159,000
Heart, Lung and Blood	774,147,000	859,572,000
Dental Research	94,678,000	103,377,000
Arthritis, Diabetes, and Digestive and Kidney Diseases	521,616,000	569,597,000
Neurological and Communicative Disorders and Stroke	375,515,000	433,595,000
Allergy and Infectious Diseases	358,813,000	383,717,000
General Medical Sciences	458,854,000	514,814,000
Child Health and Human Development	294,282,000	321,972,000
Eye	161,669,000	195,168,000
Environmental Health Sciences	183,679,000	197,686,000
Aging	135,376,000	156,592,000
Research resources	263,224,000	305,696,000
John E. Fogarty Center	11,464,000	11,568,000
National Library of Medicine	54,124,000	57,956,000
Director	36,591,000	117,085,000
Buildings and facilities	5,000,000	14,900,000
(NIH administrative reductions)	——	(-3,000,000)
Alcohol, Drug Abuse and Mental Health Administration	888,585,000	968,860,000
St. Elizabeths Hospital	43,696,000	43,696,000
Assistant secretary for health	189,209,000	170,482,000
Health Care Financing Administration	37,453,727,000	36,861,533,000
(Fiscal 1987 advance)	(6,500,000,000)	(6,500,000,000)
Social Security Administration		
Payments to Social Security trust funds	497,008,000	497,008,000
Black lung payments	715,519,000	715,519,000
(Fiscal 1987 advance)	(270,000,000)	(270,000,000)
Supplemental Security Income	7,535,221,000	7,535,221,000
(Fiscal 1987 advance)	(2,339,250,000)	(2,339,250,000)
Assistance payments	6,059,262,000	6,239,262,000
(Fiscal 1987 advance)	(2,193,754,000)	(2,193,754,000)
Child support enforcement	432,601,000	432,601,000
(Fiscal 1987 advance)	(170,750,000)	(170,750,000)
Low-income energy assistance	2,100,075,000	2,100,000,000
Assistant secretary for human development	5,410,161,000	5,713,159,000
Community services	3,923,000	370,300,000
Departmental management	187,804,000	204,668,000
Total, HHS	$67,835,693,000	$69,203,058,000
(Fiscal 1987 advance)	(11,473,754,000)	(11,473,754,000)
Education Department		
Compensatory education	3,646,615,000	3,695,663,000
Special programs	647,909,000	705,109,000
Impact aid	543,000,000	692,500,000
Bilingual education	142,951,000	172,951,000
Handicapped education	1,306,100,000	1,411,000,000
Rehabilitation services	1,216,400,000	1,362,000,000
Vocational and adult education	831,314,000	940,777,000
College student assistance	3,569,000,000	4,887,000,000
Guaranteed student		

	Budget Request	Final Amount
loans	2,714,482,000	3,300,000,000
Higher and continuing education	247,078,000	450,238,000
Higher education facilities loans	17,996,000	17,996,000
Education research and statistics	59,978,000	59,978,000
Libraries	——	127,500,000
Special institutions	245,709,000	263,730,000
Departmental management	283,619,000	285,759,000
Total, Education Department	$15,472,151,000	$18,372,201,000
Related agencies		
ACTION	148,199,000	151,287,000
Corporation for Public Broadcasting (Fiscal 1988 advance)	(214,000,000)	(214,000,000)
Federal Mediation and Conciliation Service	23,394,000	23,394,000
Federal Mine Safety and Health Review Commission	3,815,000	3,815,000
National Commission on Libraries and Information Science	——	690,000
National Council on the Handicapped	704,000	765,000
National Labor Relations Board	134,854,000	134,854,000
National Mediation Board	6,432,000	6,358,000
Occupational Safety and Health Review Commission	5,901,000	5,901,000
Railroad Retirement Board	394,200,000	394,200,000
Soldiers' and Airmen's Home	37,506,000	48,391,000
National Center for the Study of Afro-American History and Culture	——	200,000
Total, related agencies	$755,005,000	$769,855,000
(Fiscal 1988 advance)	(214,000,000)	(214,000,000)
Total, Fiscal 1986	$89,891,522,000	$94,861,859,000
(Fiscal 1987 advance)	(11,473,754,000)	(11,473,754,000)
(Fiscal 1988 advance)	(214,000,000)	(214,000,000)
GRAND TOTAL	$101,579,276,000	$106,549,613,000

House Committee

As reported by the House Appropriations Committee Sept. 26 (H Rept 99-289), HR 3424 provided $105 billion for the Departments of Labor, HHS, Education and various independent agencies.

The bill, approved by voice vote, kept spending for those agencies below fiscal 1985 levels and financed no new programs. A substantial hike was provided, however, in funding for research on AIDS.

The bill included $6.7 billion for the Labor Department, $68.4 billion for HHS, $17.5 billion for the Education Department and $768 million for other agencies in fiscal 1986. It also provided $11.5 billion in advance fiscal 1987 funding for certain HHS programs.

For discretionary programs, the bill provided $31.8 billion in fiscal 1986.

The House panel deferred action on all unauthorized programs.

The committee refused by a one-vote margin to block a Supreme Court decision requiring overtime pay for state and local employees.

The decision was issued Feb. 19 in *Garcia v. San Antonio Metropolitan Transit Authority*. Reversing a previous decision, the court ruled that employees of state and local governments were covered by the Fair Labor Standards Act (FLSA), which required time-and-a-half pay for hours worked in excess of 40 hours a week. *(Supreme Court cases, p. 15-A)*

Many states and localities avoided paying overtime to their workers by allowing them to take compensatory time off. State and local officials claimed it would cost more than $1 billion to comply with the *Garcia* decision, which the Labor Department planned to begin enforcing Oct. 15.

Rep. John Edward Porter, R-Ill., proposed an amendment to postpone enforcement of the decision until March 31, saying the delay would give Congress time to consider legislation to reverse or adjust the ruling.

Tom Loeffler, R-Texas, offered a substitute that would have exempted state and local workers from the overtime provisions of the FLSA.

Loeffler's amendment was rejected on a 13-27 show of hands, largely along party lines.

Porter's amendment drew the support of five Democrats and 17 Republicans. It was rejected 22-23, only after Bill Chappell Jr., D-Fla., switched his vote from "yes" to "no."

House Floor

The House Oct. 2 approved HR 3424 on a 322-107 vote, after adopting an amendment to postpone for one month the enforcement of the *Garcia* decision. *(Vote 299, p. 94-H)*

The amendment was a compromise designed to give the Education and Labor Committee time to consider legislation to respond to the ruling.

The amendment to delay enforcement of the court decision until Nov. 14 was introduced by Porter and adopted by voice vote. Porter backed down from an earlier proposal to delay implementation until March 31, 1986.

The House approved the amounts in the committee bill.

During House floor debate on HR 3424, many lawmakers hailed the Appropriations Committee for keeping fiscal 1986 spending recommendations below 1985 levels.

However, Augustus F. Hawkins, D-Calif., chairman of the Education and Labor Committee, complained that the bill's funding freeze was more austere than he had been led to expect when the House passed the fiscal 1986 budget resolution (S Con Res 32). *(Budget resolution, p. 441)*

The budget assumed that spending for social programs would be increased to compensate for inflation.

A prominent theme of House debate on HR 3424 was growing concern about the spread of AIDS. One of the few substantial funding increases in the bill was the $190 mil-

Fiscal 1986 Labor-HHS-Education Funding

	Budget Request	House Bill	Senate Bill	Final Amount
Labor Department	$ 5,828,673,000	$ 6,676,633,000	$ 6,509,299,000	$ 6,516,745,000
Health and Human Services	67,835,693,000	68,440,788,000	69,739,318,000	69,203,058,000
(Fiscal 1987 advance)	(11,473,754,000)	(11,473,754,000)	(11,473,754,000)	(11,473,754,000)
Education Department	15,472,151,000	17,526,805,000	18,273,115,000	18,372,201,000
Related agencies	755,005,000	767,666,000	766,421,000	769,855,000
(Fiscal 1988 advance)	(214,000,000)	—	(214,000,000)	(214,000,000)
Total	**$ 89,891,522,000**	**$ 93,411,892,000**	**$ 95,288,153,000**	**$ 94,861,859,000**
(Fiscal 1987 advance)	(11,473,754,000)	(11,473,754,000)	(11,473,754,000)	(11,473,754,000)
(Fiscal 1988 advance)	(214,000,000)	—	(214,000,000)	(214,000,000)
***GRAND TOTAL**	**$101,579,276,000**	**$104,885,646,000**	**$106,975,907,000**	**$106,549,613,000**

**The House and Senate deferred consideration of funding for certain programs that had not been authorized. In the House bill $1,236,828,000 in requested funds for fiscal 1986 and $214,000,000 in advance funding for fiscal 1988 were not considered. In the Senate bill and the final bill, $478,991,000 in requested funds were not considered. The final 1986 continuing resolution (HJ Res 465) provided an additional $616.2 million for Health and Human Services programs.* (Story, p. 360)

lion provided for AIDS research.

The House also adopted an amendment by Bob Dornan, R-Calif., that authorized the U.S. surgeon general to shut down bathhouses and massage parlors if they were found to facilitate the transmission of AIDS.

Critics said the amendment was unnecessary, because the surgeon general already had the authority to take such actions, but the amendment was adopted 417-8. *(Vote 297, p. 94-H)*

In another action related to AIDS, William E. Dannemeyer, R-Calif., sought to introduce an amendment to discourage hospitals from preventing health care workers from wearing protective garments when treating AIDS patients.

Dannemeyer was blocked from offering the amendment on a procedural vote of 238-185. *(Vote 298, p. 94-H)*

Senate Committee

The Senate Appropriations Committee Oct. 3 approved a $107 billion version of HR 3424 (PL 99-178).

The bill, approved by a 16-5 vote, included about $1.3 billion more for discretionary programs than was provided by the House. However, the Senate committee included funding for a number of unauthorized programs not considered by the House.

The panel adopted, by voice vote, an amendment to provide an additional $73.5 million for research on AIDS. That brought the total in the bill to $203.5 million — double the amount spent for AIDS research in fiscal 1985 and slightly higher than the $190 million in the House version of the bill.

In other areas where the two versions of the bill differed, the Senate committee provided $1.4 billion for rehabilitation programs for the disabled — $128 million more than the House. Handicapped education was funded at $1.4 billion under the Senate bill, compared with $1.3 billion approved by the House.

Senate Floor

The Senate Oct. 22 approved HR 3424 by a vote of 83-15 after deleting funding for the government's major family planning program, known as Title X. *(Vote 238, p. 44-S)*

The move was intended to forestall what could have been a protracted fight over government funding of abortion and contraceptive services.

As passed by the Senate, HR 3424 provided $6.5 billion for Labor, $69.7 billion for HHS, $18.3 billion for Education, $766.4 million for related agencies and $11.5 billion in advance fiscal 1987 funding for certain HHS programs. The measure also included $221 million for research and treatment of AIDS.

Despite concerns about cutting government funding, the Senate refused, 29-69, to adopt an amendment by William Proxmire, D-Wis., cutting 5 percent across the board from discretionary programs. *(Vote 237, p. 44-S)*

The Senate also rejected 20-66 a Proxmire amendment to delete $266.8 million for the Work Incentive Program, which provided employment and training services for welfare recipients. *(Vote 236, p. 44-S)*

An effort by Alan J. Dixon, D-Ill., to add $122.5 million to the Job Training Partnership Act (PL 97-300) was killed by a 53-33 vote. The program helped retrain displaced workers. *(1982 Almanac p. 39)*

Dixon's amendment would have raised funding for the program from $100 million to the fiscal 1985 level of $222.5 million. *(Vote 235, p. 44-S)*

Family Planning Issue

The family planning program, which was created as Title X of the Public Health Service Act of 1970 (PL 91-572), provided funds to more than 5,000 family planning clinics run by states, local health departments and private non-profit groups that disseminated information on family planning and contraceptives. While abortion counseling and referrals for abortion were permitted, no funds could be used to perform abortions. *(Background, 1984 Almanac p. 465)*

But Orrin G. Hatch, R-Utah, chairman of the Labor and Human Resources Committee and a staunch abortion opponent, claimed the program had gotten out of control.

The Title X program had not been reauthorized for fiscal 1986, and funding for it was not included in the House version of HR 3424. However, the program was being funded through a series of continuing appropriations resolutions at the fiscal 1985 level of $142.5 million. This was the amount that was trimmed from the Senate bill.

The removal of Title X money was part of a larger unanimous consent agreement between Lowell P. Weicker Jr., R-Conn., chairman of the Labor/HHS Appropriations Subcommittee, Hatch and Jesse Helms, R-N.C., one of the Senate's leading abortion opponents.

In exchange for deleting the Title X money, Hatch promised to hold hearings and move legislation reauthorizing the program. *(Family planning story, p. 300)*

Weicker also agreed to add language to HR 3424 barring any federal funds from being used to provide abortions for poor women unless the mother's life was endangered.

Helms agreed not to push for an amendment, included in the House bill, that would have authorized the U.S. surgeon general to shut down bathhouses and massage parlors if they were found to facilitate the transmission of AIDS. Opponents said the surgeon general already had such authority.

Other Amendments. The Senate, by voice vote Oct. 21, adopted several amendments adding $51.54 million to the bill, including the following:

- By Lawton Chiles, D-Fla., providing an additional $30 million to restore 1,000 positions in the Social Security Administration.
- By Dixon, adding $2.5 million for development of an Alzheimer's disease registry.
- By Albert Gore Jr., D-Tenn., providing $3 million for implementing the 1984 National Organ Transplant Act (PL 98-507). *(1984 Almanac p. 476)*
- By Dale Bumpers, D-Ark., adding $2.5 million for the Childhood Immunization Program administered by the Centers for Disease Control.

Conference

Conferees Nov. 20 approved a compromise bill (H Rept 99-402) to provide $106.5 billion for the departments of Labor, HHS, Education and related agencies after managing to avoid confrontation over thorny social issues that so often had been raised during past debates on the spending bill.

The House and Senate versions of HR 3424 included identical language on abortion — a longstanding ban on the use of federal funds for abortions except when a pregnant woman's life would be endangered by carrying the fetus to term.

In another area where controversy had been quelled, conferees dropped House language postponing implementation of the *Garcia* decision. That language was superseded by separate legislation signed into law Nov. 13 (S 1570 — PL 99-150). *(Story, p. 471)*

The compromise bill included about $230 million for research and special projects related to AIDS. Senate negotiators reluctantly accepted the House provision authorizing the U.S. surgeon general to shut down bathhouses if they were found to facilitate the transmission of AIDS.

Major items of the compromise bill included:

Summer Jobs. House negotiators agreed to the Senate's proposal to provide $665 million for the 1987 summer jobs program — the amount requested by Reagan. The House had included $725 million for the summer of 1987 and an additional $100 million for 1986. Congress already had appropriated $725 million for 1986.

National Institutes of Health (NIH). Conferees agreed to provide a total of about $5.5 billion for NIH — up from $5.15 billion appropriated in fiscal 1985 and $4.86 billion requested by Reagan.

Social Security. Conferees dropped a provision in the Senate bill that would have barred the Social Security Administration from closing any of its regional offices. The ban, backed by lawmakers who feared such closings were in the offing, was strongly opposed by the administration.

Health Planning. The compromise bill cut funding for health planning to $28 million in fiscal 1986, down from $65 million in 1985. The Senate had proposed continuing 1985 funding levels, rejecting an administration proposal to eliminate the program. The House bill had included no money because fiscal 1986 funds had not been authorized.

Aid to the Disabled. The conference accepted the Senate's more generous funding for programs serving the handicapped. The conference agreed to provide $1.41 billion for education of the handicapped, $90 million over fiscal 1985 spending. Another $1.36 billion was provided for rehabilitation programs for the disabled, $126 million more than 1985 levels. Reagan requested $1.31 billion for handicapped education and $1.21 billion for rehabilitation.

Impact Aid. The Senate backed down from its provision to cut impact aid, which went to school districts that educated large numbers of children of federal employees, to $632 million from $695 million in fiscal 1985. The compromise bill continued funding at the 1985 level. Reagan had requested $543 million for impact aid. ■

Interior Funding Rolled Into Catchall Measure

Congress finally administered the coup de grâce to the U.S. Synthetic Fuels Corporation in its fiscal 1986 appropriations for the Interior Department and related agencies.

The $8.1 billion Interior funding bill was rolled into the yearlong fiscal 1986 continuing appropriations resolution (H J Res 465 — PL 99-190) signed Dec. 19 by President Reagan. *(Continuing resolution, p. 360)*

PL 99-190 slammed the door on further spending by the synfuels corporation as of the moment it was signed, and ordered that the agency be virtually dismantled within 60 days. The program's funds had remained largely unspent and charges of mismanagement at the corporation had encouraged critics to call for its elimination.

Funds in H J Res 465 covered the Interior and Energy departments, the U.S. Forest Service, Indian health programs, and various other cultural and natural resource agencies. After the conferees had agreed on spending levels, they still fell short of targets demanded by the administration. As a result, the conferees made a further cut of .6 percent across-the-board against each spending account, which reduced funding for Interior and related agencies by about $50 million.

The House passed a regular fiscal 1986 Interior spending bill (HR 3011) July 31, and the Senate briefly considered its own version of the measure on Oct. 31. But Senate passage of the bill got caught up both in a dispute over the fate of the synfuels program and end-of-the-session time pressures.

The final funding was slightly below the amount provided under both the House and Senate versions, but still about $730 million more than Reagan's $7.4 billion budget request. The total was about $20 million less than the fiscal 1985 appropriation. *(Chart, p. 341)*

Synthetic Fuels Corporation

The U.S. Synthetic Fuels Corporation was established by Congress in 1980 to encourage commercialization of technologies for turning abundant resources like coal and shale into fuels that could substitute for natural gas and petroleum. *(Background, 1980 Almanac p. 477; synfuels story p. 212)*

Congress in 1984 rescinded $7.4 billion of the agency's previously appropriated funds. *(1984 Almanac p. 347)*

In H J Res 465, Congress rescinded all remaining funds — estimated at $7.3 billion — except for almost $400 million that went to a clean coal technology program and $10 million to pay costs of closing down the agency. Congress prohibited the corporation's board of directors from making any further commitments of aid to synfuels projects.

The clean-coal technology program in effect superseded one Congress authorized in 1984 that had not yet been carried out. Of the synfuels funds rescinded in 1984, $750 million had been put into a Clean Coal Technology Reserve for such research. Those funds, however, could not be spent unless appropriated by Congress.

Congress kept the $400 million in the Energy Security Reserve but appropriated it to the clean coal program; then it reduced the amount in the Clean Coal Technology Reserve to $350 million. Thus, the $400 million set aside for clean coal in 1985 was merely used to replace some of the $750 million set aside in 1984.

Offshore Leasing Ban

For the first time in five years, Congress approved an Interior Department appropriations bill that did not include a ban on oil and gas leasing off the coast of California. But Congress kept the pressure on the Interior Department to work out a settlement of the controversial issue by requiring meetings every 60 days between the interior secretary and a congressional negotiating team until an agreement was reached. *(Offshore leasing, p. 203)*

In the fiscal 1982-85 Interior funding bills, Congress had expressed its objections to the administration's accelerated energy development policies by applying offshore leasing bans to several areas of California and to the Georges Bank fishing grounds off New England. *(1981 Almanac p. 369; 1982 Almanac p. 262; 1983 Almanac p. 462; 1984 Almanac p. 378)*

But members of the California congressional delegation opposed to leasing off the coast of their state thought in July that they had worked out an agreement with Interior Secretary Donald P. Hodel barring most leasing in return for drilling in a few areas. Hodel changed his position in September, however, causing the moratorium issue to be raised again. By the time the Interior appropriations bill got wrapped up into the continuing resolution, another agreement had been worked out.

The agreement was embodied in an amendment to H J 465 offered on the House floor by Ralph Regula, R-Ohio, and Leon E. Panetta, D-Calif. The amendment required Hodel to meet with a congressional negotiating team every 60 days for the remainder of fiscal 1986 to work out an agreement for drilling off the California coast. The amendment established a 19-member committee, including senators and representatives from California and from the committees with jurisdiction over the oil drilling issue. H J Res 465 also continued an existing moratorium on drilling of selected environmentally sensitive areas in Georges Bank off the New England coast.

Other Agencies

The final bill provided $188.2 million for forest roads construction, only a slight reduction from the administration request for $195.6 million (other funds come from amounts timber companies owe the government).

Bill managers said they expected the Forest Service to realize the difference between $195.6 million and the final figure by reducing the average construction cost per road-mile by 5 percent. But they also indicated that the Forest Service should reduce the actual number of miles built by concentrating sales on reofferings of tracts where previous contracts had been canceled.

The final bill also provided funding for a timber sales program of 11.4 billion board feet, which the bill's managers called a continuation of the actual sales in 1985.

No funds were appropriated to the Energy Department to buy oil for the Strategic Petroleum Reserve. But bill managers said carry-over funds from 1985 were sufficient to fill the reserve, meant to cushion the shock of a disruption of foreign oil imports, to 500 million barrels. The bill also authorized a so-called "Food for Crude" program, in which the government could barter surplus food from the Commodity Credit Corporation for foreign oil.

House Committee Action

The House Appropriations Committee July 16 reported HR 3011 (H Rept 99-205) by voice vote, providing a funding level of $8.26 billion for Interior and the other agencies.

As in previous years, the committee balked at President Reagan's request to slash funds for park land acquisition, research to make coal burn cleaner, weatherization of homes to conserve energy, reclamation of strip mines, and Indian health.

The committee also moved to slow the administration's program to cut and sell timber from the national forests by dramatically cutting the budget for forest roads needed to conduct logging operations.

HR 3011 also included language, adopted by voice vote July 16, blocking use of funds for a proposed land exchange between the Bureau of Land Management and the Forest Service until Congress approved.

The Reagan administration in January had proposed consolidating the scattered and intermingled holdings of the two agencies for more efficient and less expensive management. But many Western members feared that the proposal could cut the services currently provided by the two agencies.

Leasing Ban

The committee was completing its action on HR 3011 just as a tentative agreement was reached between the Interior Department and members of the California delegation on the offshore leasing ban issue.

Nine members of the 45-member House delegation and the two senators announced support in principle for the agreement at a July 16 press conference.

Under the agreement, only 150 of the 6,460 California tracts protected under an existing moratorium would be offered for leasing, but they were tracts that were supposedly highly prized by oil companies. Leasing was to proceed in accord with all environmental safeguards required under existing law.

The remaining tracts were to be off-limits for federal leasing until the year 2000, except under a national energy emergency declared by the president under the Energy Policy and Conservation Act (PL 94-163). Three test wells, however, could be drilled in these areas, no closer than 18 miles from the shoreline.

By voice vote, the Appropriations Committee deleted a new moratorium in the version of the 1986 appropriation approved June 20 by the Subcommittee on Interior. Then it approved report language incorporating the principles in the agreement.

House Floor Action

The House July 31 passed HR 3011 by 270-143, after adopting an amendment to kill the synthetic fuels program. *(Vote 258, p. 82-H)*

The synfuels issue came up July 24 when the House voted on a rule (H Res 227) setting terms for debate on HR 3011. The rule would have prevented synfuels opponents from proposing amendments to the bill to kill funding for the program. The House voted 179-251 to reject the rule. *(Vote 228, p. 72-H)*

Although unusual, the action paralleled a 1984 vote, when the House defeated the rule on the Interior appropriations bill also over the synfuels question. The 1984 margin was 148-261.

In the face of the heavy voting strength demonstrated on the rule question, House supporters of the synfuels program agreed on July 31 to save time by not debating the issue again. The amendment to rescind previously appropriated funds for the corporation, except for $500 million, was adopted by a 312-111 margin. *(Vote 255, p. 82-H)*

Spending Levels

As passed by the House, the bill provided a total of $8.24 billion. About $23 million was cut on the House floor from the version reported by the Appropriations Committee. Amendments were agreed to by voice vote cutting funds from the Smithsonian Institution and the National Endowment on the Arts, and freezing funds at fiscal 1985 levels for the National Endowment on the Humanities and the Institute of Museum Services.

Sidney R. Yates, D-Ill., chairman of the Appropriations Subcommittee on Interior, said spending in the bill was below 1985 levels once adjustments were made to count some funds from the fiscal 1984 supplemental as part of 1985 spending on the Strategic Petroleum Reserve. He discounted arguments by some Republicans that the bill was above 1985 levels, saying spending was within the allocation to his subcommittee under the House-passed budget resolution.

The House bill was about $1 billion above the Reagan administration budget request of $7.22 billion. The largest increases came in funding for the National Park Service, Energy Department civilian programs, such as conservation, and Indian health programs under HHS.

Clean Coal Fund

After rescinding the synfuels funds, which had been appropriated in 1980 but not yet spent, the House approved an amendment to appropriate $500 million for research and development on technologies for burning coal more cleanly in industrial and utility boilers.

That money was appropriated out of the "Clean Coal Technology Reserve," a $750 million special fund set up late in 1984 with money taken from an earlier synfuels rescission. No money had been spent from the fund. As passed, HR 3011 appropriated $100 million for fiscal 1986 and $200 million for each of the fiscal years 1987 and 1988.

Coal was one of the raw materials made into petroleum substitutes through synfuels technology. In addition to that spending, the Interior bill also contained some $317 million for fossil energy research and development, much of which went for clean coal technology.

The committee bill would have appropriated all $750 million in the Clean Coal Technology Reserve over 1986-88.

But when Silvio O. Conte, R-Mass., offered an amendment to strike the advance funding for 1987 and 1988, leaving just $100 million for fiscal 1986, Regula offered a substitute to give the program $500 million over three years. Regula's amendment was adopted by voice vote, and the amended Conte proposal was then adopted 238-184. *(Vote 256, p. 82-H))*

Policy Disputes

The House gave President Reagan more than he had requested for acquisition of recreation lands under the Land and Water Conservation Fund. Reagan had proposed a moratorium on new acquisition that would have cut funds from $257 million to $15 million. The House set the funding at $194 million. The money went to Interior's Park Service, Bureau of Land Management and Fish and Wildlife Service, and to Agriculture's Forest Service.

The bill contained no money to buy oil to fill the Strategic Petroleum Reserve — a $2 billion item in 1984, although it was not counted in budget totals. Carry-over funds would allow the reserve to continue being filled, but at slower rates. The Appropriations Committee's report had recommended that the reserve be filled at 100,000 barrels per day until it reached 500 million barrels, as required by existing law, in about 110 days. After that, carry-over funds would allow it to be filled at 50,000 barrels per day through fiscal 1986.

The Appropriations Committee did add $199 million the Reagan administration had not requested to continue construction of a strategic reserve storage facility at Big Hill, Texas. Although the committee bill included language barring any test sale of oil from the reserve, that language was struck from the bill on the House floor on a point of order raised by Philip R. Sharp, D-Ind., chairman of the Energy and Commerce Subcommittee on Fossil and Synthetic Fuels, which had authorizing jurisdiction.

Senate Committee Action

The Senate Appropriations Committee Sept. 24 approved by voice vote an $8.12 billion version of HR 3011 (S

Rept 99-141), which was $125 million less than the House bill provided.

The Clean Coal Technology fund was the focus of a major dispute during subcommittee markup of the bill Sept. 19 when Minority Leader Robert C. Byrd, D-W.Va., proposed appropriating the entire amount in advance over 1986-89, to give industry enough confidence to invest in the public-private cost-sharing program.

But the subcommittee delayed action on Byrd's proposal after Chairman James A. McClure, R-Idaho, expressed concern that appropriating the entire amount in fiscal 1986 would put the subcommittee over its fiscal 1986 budget ceiling.

The full committee approved a Byrd amendment providing appropriations of $100 million in fiscal 1986 and advance appropriations of $175 million in 1987, $300 million in 1988 and $175 million in 1989 from the coal fund. McClure said he had been assured that the advance appropriations would not be charged against the subcommittee's budget ceiling for fiscal 1986.

The bill did not contain any moratorium on federal oil and gas leasing off the California coast nor did it include the House rescission of the synfuels funds.

Forest Roads

The committee compromised on a controversial amendment offered by Dale Bumpers, D-Ark., that would have cut $25 million from the U.S. Forest Service road-building account in the Agriculture Department to discourage the sale of federal timber to private loggers.

Environmentalists had criticized the Forest Service for the sales. They charged that the agency often did not recover the costs of selling the timber.

The forest products industry and the administration said that the program was profitable to the Treasury and that many logging towns needed the sales to avoid severe unemployment.

The House cut the administration's $195.6 million request for the forest road-building program to $151.3 million. McClure recommended that the Senate committee give the administration the $195.6 million. Some $190 million more was expected to be spent on Forest Service roads in 1986 by private companies, which could deduct the cost from what they owed the government for the timber they bought.

Bumpers said the $25 million reduction he proposed amounted to savings of about 6 percent in all road-building expenditures. McClure said the administration request had already cut the program by almost $40 million from fiscal 1985 levels.

The compromise came in a substitute McClure amendment, which required the Forest Service to achieve 5 percent savings below the administration's recommended amounts. The committee added report language saying that the Forest Service could not put the money saved into building more roads than in current plans.

The substitute and the amendment were adopted by voice vote.

Continuing Resolution

The Senate began consideration of HR 3011 on Oct. 31 by rejecting, 41-58, an amendment that would have blocked a move to kill the synfuels program. *(Vote 270, p. 48-S)*

The Senate vote was on a motion by McClure to table (kill) an amendment by Howard M. Metzenbaum, D-Ohio, that would have rescinded most of the corporation's remaining funds.

But the Senate never returned to the measure, and funding for the Interior Department and related agencies became part of H J Res 465, the fiscal 1986 continuing appropriations bill.

The oil and gas leasing moratorium became an issue during House Appropriations Committee consideration of H J Res 465 on Nov. 21 when Yates offered an amendment to continue the moratorium on leasing off the California coast. The amendment was rejected, however, on a vote of 26-27.

House consideration of H J Res 465 Dec. 4 was brief and relatively smooth.

The quick House floor action was a result of decisions the Rules Committee had made the day before in order to make only one proposal, a compromise worked out between Regula and Panetta on the oil and gas leasing issue.

Regula and Panetta sought a compromise that they could get approved by the House. Their proposal, which the House adopted by voice vote, required Hodel to meet with a congressional negotiating team every 60 days for the rest of fiscal 1986 to work out an agreement for drilling off the California coast. The amendment established a 19-member committee, including senators and representatives from California and from the committees with jurisdiction over the oil drilling issue.

The Senate Appropriations Committee accepted the offshore leasing compromise, but the fate of the synfuels program remained an issue as H J Res 465 went to the Senate floor on Dec. 6.

The House had voted to kill the entire program in HR 3011, the regular Interior appropriations bill, but McClure, chairman of the Senate Interior Appropriations Subcommittee, was battling to save it. The Senate version of H J Res 465 included provisions to restructure the program, cutting it from $7.9 billion to about $3.6 billion.

On Dec. 6, the Senate rejected, 40-43, an amendment by Metzenbaum and Daniel J. Evans, R-Wash., to eliminate funding for the synfuels program. *(Vote 355, p. 61-S)*

When the conferees Dec. 12 met to work out differences between the House and Senate versions of H J Res 465, the fate of the program was one of the major issues to be resolved. That same day, the administration formally announced that it no longer supported the program.

Office of Management and Budget Director James C. Miller III and Energy Secretary John S. Herrington joined the deliberations of the conferees Dec. 13, but even their participation failed to yield a solution.

Another point of controversy in the conference was the level of timber sales to be allowed in fiscal 1986.

Interior conferees did agree on a controversial water issue in California. They decided to require congressional review of any agreement Interior Secretary Hodel made with farmers in the Westlands water district near Fresno, Calif. The House had wanted to require congressional authorization of any agreement.

Hodel had been close to a pact with farmers in the district giving them the right to purchase subsidized water. But critics contended that it reversed a longstanding government position that Westlands farmers had brought thousands of acres of land under irrigation illegally.

Interior conferees worked into the weekend Dec. 14-15 putting finishing touches on their section of H J Res 465 and presented their proposals to the full conference Dec. 16. Although he had fought determinedly to save the Syn-

Final Fiscal 1986 Interior Appropriations

Following are funding totals for the Interior Department and related agencies in the fiscal 1986 continuing appropriations bill (H J Res 465 — PL 99-190) as cleared by Congress. Not shown are offsetting revenues and the deficit-reduction effect of rescinding approximately $7.3 billion from the U.S. Synthetic Fuels Corporation. *(Amounts in thousands of dollars, net new budget authority.)*

	Reagan Request*	House Bill	Senate Committee Bill	Final
Department of the Interior				
Bureau of Land Management	$ 495,301	$ 567,026	$ 579,014	$ 574,149
Fish and Wildlife Service	362,087	397,026	376,770	381,530
National Park Service	684,186	896,628	822,526	876,160
U.S. Geological Survey	415,348	428,098	437,655	429,369
Minerals Management Service	161,918	165,118	171,067	167,010
Bureau of Mines	107,060	122,298	131,445	133,449
Office of Surface Mining	331,606	319,123	276,333	290,783
Bureau of Indian Affairs	950,889	909,493	1,039,121	1,006,403
Territorial Affairs	83,567	182,724	158,538	159,784
Departmental Offices	76,229	164,129	83,619	81,293
Subtotal	$ 3,668,191	$ 4,151,663	$ 4,076,088	$ 4,099,930
Related Agencies				
Forest Service	1,495,215	1,444,698	1,493,869	1,486,970
Energy Department	633,509	1,069,939	1,047,585	974,444
Clean Coal**				
(Fiscal 1986)	(0)	(100,000)	(100,000)	(99,400)
(1987 advance)	(0)	(200,000)	(175,000)	(149,100)
(1988 advance)	(0)	(200,000)	(300,000)	(149,100)
(1989 advance)	(0)	(0)	(175,000)	(0)
Indian Health	766,583	897,966	838,572	864,859
Smithsonian	211,816	205,025	200,644	199,983
National Endowment for the Arts	144,800	166,660	162,900	165,661
National Endowment for Humanities	126,330	139,478	139,478	138,641
Other Agencies	318,877	162,668	159,998	166,633
Subtotal	$ 3,697,130	$ 4,086,434	$ 4,043,046	$ 3,997,191
Grand Total	$ 7,365,321	$ 8,238,097	$ 8,119,134	$ 8,097,121

*As amended.
**Energy Security Reserve or Clean Coal Technology Reserve.

thetic Fuels Corporation, McClure bowed to opposition from House colleagues and the White House and agreed to the agency's termination.

In exchange, conferees agreed to put $400 million into the clean-coal program. Only $100 million of the money was to be spent in fiscal 1986, with $150 million available in each of the next two years.

The House and Senate both approved the conference report (H Rept 99-450) on Dec. 19. President Reagan signed the measure (PL 99-190) later the same day. ▮

$10.5 Billion Approved for Transportation

The $10.5 billion appropriated for fiscal 1986 for transportation programs included the air-safety and Coast Guard funds President Reagan wanted, but Congress turned down many of his other policy proposals.

Funds for the Department of Transportation (DOT) and related agencies were included in the continuing appropriations resolution (H J Res 465 — PL 99-190) signed by the president Dec. 19. The resolution rejected the major cuts sought by the president for mass transit, Amtrak and air service to small cities. *(Story, p. 360)*

The total fiscal 1986 funding was 33 percent above the president's request but 10 percent below fiscal 1985 funding. *(Chart, p. 345)*

In addition to the $10.5 billion in new budget authority, the bill set a ceiling of $15 billion on the funds that could be obligated over a number of years from highway and airport trust funds, which were supported by taxes on gasoline, tires and air tickets. Trust fund spending was not included in the bill's total, which was based on spending from the Treasury, but was counted against the deficit.

The original transportation appropriations bill (HR 3244) was passed by the House Sept. 12 at a level of $10.9 billion (H Rept 99-256) and by the Senate Oct. 23 at a level of $9.9 billion (S Rept 99-152).

A conference committee resolved some issues Nov. 13, but never met again, largely because of a veto threat.

When revised provisions were rolled into the continuing resolution, the administration reiterated its objections to mass transit funding, which it wanted reduced by two-thirds. But even though mass transit funding in the final bill was only 10 percent below the 1985 level, that issue itself did not provoke a veto.

Both the administration and the House objected strongly to the Senate's proposal to cut $300 million from the Federal Aviation Administration (FAA) and $200 million from the Coast Guard. They contended that such cuts would cripple the agencies' efforts to upgrade air safety and drug enforcement efforts.

Senators contended the cuts were necessary because the administration had made late requests for extra funds that would exceed the levels in the fiscal 1986 budget resolution (S Con Res 32). *(Story, p. 441)*

Senators agreed to restore the FAA and Coast Guard funds when marking up the continuing resolution, raising the total from $9.9 billion to $10.4 billion. In conference, senators also backed off from a 1.6 percent across-the-board cut imposed in Senate floor action.

Funding for Major Programs

Highlights of final funding in H J Res 465 included:

- **Office of the Secretary.** The bill provided $82.8 million, including $51.3 million for salaries and expenses and $28 million for subsidies to air carriers providing service to small towns. The administration wanted to drop the subsidies.
- **Coast Guard.** Of the $2.35 billion provided, $1.65 billion was for operations, such as search and rescue missions. The funds were in addition to $100 million included in the defense section of the continuing resolution. The defense section also contained $235 million for new boats, aircraft and radar equipment for the Coast Guard. *(Story, p. 377)*
- **Aviation.** The measure provided slightly less than $4 billion for the FAA, including $2.7 billion in new budget authority for FAA operations and $1.1 billion from the Airport and Airways Trust Fund for facilities, equipment, research and development.

In response to concern about air crashes, the conference report directed the FAA to hire 500 new air traffic controllers and 300 safety inspectors. The administration had proposed to hire 1,000 controllers and 500 inspectors in the next two years.

- **Mass Transit.** Reagan had proposed eliminating federal aid to start new transit systems and subsidies for operating expenses of existing systems, contending that the services were purely local and should be funded by local taxes.

Congress rejected those proposals.

For bus and rail construction, it set spending from the Highway Trust Fund at $1.045 billion. Of that, $385 million was earmarked for new transit systems that the administration had argued would eventually cost $4 billion. *(Box, p. 343)*

The House bill required that the administration guarantee funding to complete new transit projects in Miami, Los Angeles and Seattle, which were receiving funds on a year-to-year basis. But conferees required only that the administration begin negotiations on full-funding contracts.

Conferees accepted a Senate provision rejecting the administration's proposed deferral of $234 million previously appropriated for work on new mass transit projects in five cities.

For subsidies for the operation and improvement of existing local transit systems, which were distributed by formulas, the bill provided $2.15 billion, 12 percent less than the fiscal 1985 level.

Of that amount, $875 million would go for operating assistance, the same amount as in fiscal 1985.

- **Highways, Auto Safety.** Spending from the Highway Trust Fund, financed by gasoline taxes and other road-related fees, was capped at $12.75 billion. The ceiling for fiscal 1985 was $13.25 billion, and it had been scheduled to rise to $14.45 billion in fiscal 1986 under the 1982 law (PL 97-424) authorizing the gasoline tax. *(1982 Almanac p. 317)*

The bill contained $7 million of the $16 million sought on the Senate floor by Budget Committee Chairman Pete V. Domenici, R-N.M., for a highway project in New Mexico. It also provided $9 million for a project in the district

Mass Transit Projects

These are the new mass transit projects that Congress decided to fund in fiscal 1986. President Reagan, contending that national taxes should not be used for local transit projects, requested no money for new systems.

Los Angeles	$ 101,000,000
Atlanta	69,000,000
Santa Clara, Calif.	65,000,000
Houston	54,750,000
Miami	38,000,000
Seattle	24,650,000
St. Louis	13,500,000
San Diego	9,300,000
Portland, Ore.	8,950,000
Buffalo, N.Y.	850,000
TOTAL	**$ 385,000,000**

of Rep. Vic Fazio, D-Calif., and $16 million to improve rail crossings in Arkansas, Georgia, Illinois, Indiana, Nebraska and Texas.

The measure provided $89 million for the National Highway Traffic Safety Administration, plus $127 million for grants for state and community safety programs.

It dropped a provision, added by the Senate Appropriations Committee during its markup of the continuing resolution, that would have toughened penalties for states that did not raise their minimum drinking age to 21.

Another controversial provision that was dropped would have denied automakers credits for meeting automobile fuel-efficiency standards that were lowered Oct. 1 by the Department of Transportation.

• **Railroads.** The bill provided $616 million for Amtrak, the national passenger railroad. In remarks Dec. 18, Reagan again cited taxpayer funding for Amtrak as a prime example of wasteful government spending. *(Text, p. 41-D)*

Two other rail programs the administration sought to eliminate were continued. The Northeast Corridor Improvement Program, to upgrade facilities in the most heavily traveled region of the country, received $12.5 million. The U.S. Railway Association, which monitored Conrail, the government-owned freight railroad that was slated to be sold, was continued at $2.4 million. *(Conrail, p. 272)*

House Committee

The House Appropriations Committee Sept. 5 voted to provide $11.1 billion for fiscal 1986 transportation programs — 42 percent more than the administration requested and about $500 million more than the level set by the fiscal 1986 budget resolution (S Con Res 32).

Committee leaders warned that they might have to trim the amount on the floor to make the total conform to the resolution. Transportation Subcommittee members said that when they marked up the bill on July 18, they had pegged spending to the House version of the budget resolution, which allowed higher funding.

Joseph R. Wright Jr., acting director of the Office of Management and Budget (OMB), threatened a presidential veto of the bill because of its spending for Amtrak, mass transit and highway projects.

The bill (HR 3244 — H Rept 99-256) recommended $616 million for Amtrak subsidies, which the administration had fought to eliminate.

The committee also established a cap of $13.8 billion on spending from the Highway Trust Fund, $550 million over the president's request and the budget resolution.

The administration wanted to slash aid for mass transit by two-thirds, from $4.2 billion to $1.4 billion. But the committee recommended a cut of only $43 million and included operating aid, which the administration wanted to eliminate.

Also, the panel earmarked funds for new construction of mass transit systems. The administration had proposed no funding for new starts.

In 1984, the Appropriations Committee's decision to designate the new projects to be funded had aroused the ire of the authorizing committee, Public Works and Transportation, and DOT, both of which felt they should be making those decisions. The turf fight between the committees kept the fiscal 1985 funding bill from the floor. During the markup of HR 3244, Appropriations panel members said Public Works leaders had agreed on key provisions. *(1984 Almanac p. 410)*

Confronting Controversies

Before approving the measure by voice vote, the committee rejected, 15-21, an amendment by Lawrence Coughlin, R-Pa., to prevent federal funding for Westway, a major highway and land development project in New York City.

Westway was opposed by many environmentalists and advocates of mass transit, and by New Jersey officials who feared that it would depress growth in their state.

Coughlin argued that the project would cost $4 billion to $6 billion, draining money from other states' shares of the Highway Trust Fund.

He was opposed by Bill Green, R-N.Y., who said that selecting projects to fund was a decision that belonged to the states.

In an attempt to defuse another controversy, Julian C. Dixon, D-Calif., proposed requiring a safety study of a Los Angeles rail project, which was in the early stages of construction.

The project was opposed by some Los Angeles officials, and the opposition picked up steam in August when Rep. Henry A. Waxman, D-Calif., announced that he would try to block construction because of the possibility of methane gas explosions along the route. Such an explosion occurred in March 1985, raising public concern.

Dixon, who supported the project, said he hoped his amendment would prevent a floor fight. It was adopted by voice vote.

Major Agencies

The committee included the following funding for the Department of Transportation and related agencies:

• **Coast Guard.** The bill would allocate $2.5 billion, including $1.8 billion for operations.

• **Federal Aviation Administration.** The FAA would receive $4 billion, $260 million less than fiscal 1985 spending and $166 milllion less than requested.

The total included $1.1 billion from the Airport and Airway Trust Fund for air traffic control facilities and other airport equipment and $2.7 billion for operations, a $50 million cut, despite an OMB warning that the reduced funding would hamper air traffic control efforts.

The bill included $36 million in new budget authority, plus $12 million in leftover 1985 funds, for a program that made payments to air carriers for providing service to small communities. The president had proposed eliminating the program, which received $52 million in 1985.

- **U.S. Railway Association.** The agency that monitored Conrail was given $2.1 million.

House Floor Action

The House Sept. 12 approved a $10.85 billion transportation appropriations bill by a vote of 307-102, preserving the funding for Amtrak, subsidies for air service to small communities, and operating assistance and start-up money for mass transit systems, all of which Reagan wanted to kill. *(Vote 277, p. 88-H)*

However, there was little debate on those provisions of HR 3244. Most of the discussion focused on local issues, with the major controversy centering on an amendment to bar fiscal 1986 funds from being used to build Westway. The amendment was adopted 287-132. *(Vote 270, p. 88-H)*

In addition to the $10.85 billion in new spending authority, the bill permitted $15.46 billion to be spent from trust funds and other accounts previously authorized.

Some Programs Cut on Floor

OMB continued to threaten a presidential veto of the bill, but Appropriations Committee members defended their actions, saying the bill was $822 million — 7 percent — under the fiscal 1985 spending level.

The Appropriations Subcommittee on Transportation offered an amendment, adopted by voice vote, that cut several programs to bring spending in line with the levels in the budget resolution.

The amendment, by subcommittee Chairman William Lehman, D-Fla., cut $285 million in new budget authority and $715 million from annual ceilings on spending from the highway and airport trust funds from the levels approved by the Appropriations Committee Sept. 5.

Specific reductions included:

- $12.5 million from Amtrak subsidies, bringing them from $616 million to $603.5 million. That was an 11.4 percent cut from the fiscal 1985 level of $684 million.
- $239.5 million from mass transit grants distributed to states and cities by formula, reducing the program from $2.45 billion to $2.21 billion.
- $12.5 million, a 5 percent cut, from a program under which states could substitute mass transit projects for planned Interstate highway segments.
- $12.5 million, a 5 percent cut, in aid for the Washington, D.C., area subway system.
- $550 million from the ceiling on spending from the Highway Trust Fund, which froze the obligation ceiling at $13.25 billion, the same level as fiscal 1985.
- $90 million from the ceiling on spending from the mass transit account of the Highway Trust Fund.
- $75 million from the cap on spending for airport development and planning from the Airport and Airway Trust Fund.

The Amtrak cut was not deep enough for some members, who saw the program as a test of Congress' will to cut spending. Bill Richardson, D-N.M., offered an amendment to cut an additional $22.1 million from the national passenger railroad. Richardson, an Amtrak supporter, argued that the House should stick to the totals used by the Budget Committee in calculating the budget resolution.

But the amendment was rejected, 173-245. *(Vote 271, p. 88-H)*

Air subsidies and mass transit aid were continued at levels slightly under those for fiscal 1985.

Subway, Bridge Issues Surface

The House by voice vote approved an amendment by Dixon to prevent a new subway in Los Angeles from tunneling through an area filled with pockets of methane gas. Dixon's amendment came as a substitute for a Waxman amendment that would have put further restrictions on the subway. The two Californians agreed to set up a commission to examine the problem.

Bobbi Fiedler, R-Calif., an opponent of the Los Angeles subway, tried to put tougher restrictions on the subway project, but her amendment was rejected, 172-242. *(Vote 272, p. 88-H)*

The House accepted by voice vote an amendment by Norman Y. Mineta, D-Calif., to shift $15 million in funds for the FAA in order to add 200 federal aircraft inspectors. Mineta, chairman of the Public Works and Transportation Subcommittee on Aviation, said the move was needed in light of recent air crashes.

Senate Committee Action

After reluctantly cutting several programs to meet deficit-reduction targets, the Senate Appropriations Committee Oct. 3 voted, 16-2, to provide $10 billion for fiscal 1986 transportation activities.

The bill, which was reported the next day (HR 3244 — S Rept 99-152), did not differ markedly in most respects from the $10.85 billion measure passed by the House Sept. 12. The big differences came from cuts in funding for the FAA and Coast Guard proposed by Mark Andrews, R-N.D., chairman of the Subcommittee on Transportation.

Andrews offered amendments to reduce spending from the $10.5 billion bill his subcommittee approved Sept. 26. He said he had little choice but to propose cuts, since the Appropriations Committee was under pressure from the Budget Committee to readjust spending to match the budget resolution.

Andrews' proposals were:

- To reduce the cap on spending from the Highway Trust Fund from $13.25 billion to $12.75 billion. Similar action was recommended Sept. 24 by the Environment and Public Works Committee.

The proposal was approved, 16-4.

- To cut $300 million from the FAA, bringing the level for operations down from $2.7 billion to $2.4 billion.
- To trim $200 million from the Coast Guard, reducing operating expenses from $1.8 billion to $1.6 billion.

Andrews said the FAA and Coast Guard accounts were the areas that had pushed the bill over the budget resolution's level. He said that the higher funding was due to administration requests — made after passage of the budget resolution — for more money for the FAA and Coast Guard to increase air safety programs and combat drug smuggling. The twin cuts were approved, 16-2.

The Senate panel also deleted a House provision barring 1986 funds for Westway, the major land-development and highway project in New York City. The issue had become moot since New York officials dropped the project Sept. 19.

The bill included $616 million for Amtrak — $588 million in new funds and $28 million in transfers. The

House approved $603.5 million and the budget resolution counted $582 million for Amtrak.

Senate Floor Action

The Senate, after bickering over how to bring spending in line with budget goals, voted Oct. 23 to provide $9.9 billion for fiscal 1986 transportation activities.

HR 3244 was approved by 84-13, after senators accepted by voice vote an across-the-board cut of 1.6 percent offered by Budget Committee Chairman Domenici. *(Vote 247, p. 46-S)*

Spending under the Senate bill would be 15 percent below fiscal 1985 levels.

The administration opposed the measure because of cuts of $300 million for the FAA and $200 million for the Coast Guard approved Oct. 3 by the Appropriations Committee in response to pressure from the Budget Committee.

Transportation Secretary Elizabeth Hanford Dole said the reductions would undercut efforts to reduce drug smuggling and to improve aviation safety.

The Senate rejected an attempt to restore funding for the FAA and Coast Guard by voting, 59-38, to table (kill) an amendment by Nancy Landon Kassebaum, R-Kan. The amendment would have shifted money to those programs and reduced overall spending by further cutting Amtrak and mass transit and by a 6 percent cutback for other agencies. *(Vote 246, p. 45-S)*

Acrimony Over Budget Process

Floor debate was marked by sporadic skirmishes between floor manager Andrews and leaders of the Budget Committee, Domenici and Lawton Chiles, D-Fla. Chiles was the ranking Democrat on both Domenici's and Andrews' panels.

Domenici accused Andrews of making unrealistic cuts in FAA and Coast Guard programs, rather than spreading reductions among other agencies, because Andrews knew the House would not accept them in conference.

The reductions would have forced cuts in two activities

Fiscal 1986 Transportation Funds

Following are the amounts of fiscal 1986 budget authority for the Transportation Department and related agencies requested by President Reagan, approved by the House and Senate in passing their versions of the continuing resolution (H J Res 465) and appropriated in the final version of the resolution signed by the president:

	Budget Request	House-Passed Bill	Senate-Passed Bill	Final Amount
Department of Transportation				
Office of the Secretary	$ 57,553,000	$ 89,500,000	$ 83,300,000	$ 82,800,000
Coast Guard	2,548,793,000	2,503,622,000	2,459,802,000	2,300,802,000
Federal Aviation Administration	4,210,048,000	4,040,400,000	4,004,900,000	3,983,100,000
Federal Highway Administration	36,493,000	105,100,000	68,662,000	79,400,000
National Highway Traffic Safety Administration	81,101,000	89,365,000	78,851,000	83,851,000
Federal Railroad Administration	54,715,000	702,520,000	684,988,000	702,184,000
Urban Mass Transportation Administration	277,405,000	2,744,103,000	2,534,900,000	2,624,400,000
Research and Special Programs Administration	19,353,000	19,400,000	19,200,000	19,300,000
Office of the Inspector General	27,692,000	27,950,000	27,250,000	27,600,000
Subtotal	7,313,153,000	10,321,960,000	9,961,853,000	9,903,437,000
Related Agencies				
Architectural and Transportation Barriers Compliance Board	1,975,000	2,000,000	1,975,000	1,975,000
National Transportation Safety Board	22,087,000	22,400,000	22,200,000	22,300,000
Civil Aeronautics Board	0	0	0	0
Interstate Commerce Commission	52,557,000	48,180,000	47,000,000	48,180,000
Panama Canal Commission	446,784,000	427,784,000	425,784,000	425,784,000
U.S. Railway Association	0	2,100,000	2,400,000	2,400,000
Washington Metropolitan Area Transit Authority	51,663,569	51,663,569	51,663,569	51,663,569
Subtotal	575,066,569	554,127,569	551,022,569	552,302,569
General reduction			-147,606,281	
GRAND TOTAL	**$7,888,219,569**	**$10,876,087,569**	**$10,365,269,288**	**$10,455,739,569**

with political momentum behind them: adding air traffic controllers and inspectors, and increasing Coast Guard efforts to stop drug smugglers.

Domenici and Chiles favored Kassebaum's amendment, which included several reductions recommended by Secretary Dole to Appropriations Committee Chairman Mark O. Hatfield, R-Ore.

But Kassebaum's amendment was strongly opposed by Andrews and by backers of federal aid for mass transit, highways and Amtrak. It would have cut operating assistance for mass transit by 10 percent, Amtrak by 5 percent, and reduced federal spending from the Highway Trust Fund from $12.75 billion to about $12 billion.

After the defeat of Kassebaum's amendment, Andrews accepted Domenici's smaller across-the-board cut without discussion. It exempted the Panama Canal Commission, which was self-supporting.

Domenici Adds Road Project

Andrews and other Appropriations Committee members retaliated against Domenici's pressure on spending cuts by making him squirm when he tried to add money for a parochial project.

Domenici moved to add $16.3 million for improvements to roads leading to a nuclear-waste storage site in New Mexico. Such projects usually were accepted by consensus, but Andrews and Lowell P. Weicker Jr., R-Conn., another Appropriations subcommittee chairman who had crossed swords with Domenici, demanded a recorded vote and argued against the provision.

Domenici's amendment was accepted, 56-40, although most of the Appropriations panel voted against it. It was the only amendment adopted that added spending to the bill. *(Vote 245, p. 45-S)*

Automakers Lose Credits

The Senate accepted an amendment that would deny to auto manufacturers the ability to earn credits for meeting automobile fuel efficiency standards that they had succeeded in getting lowered.

DOT Oct. 1 announced that new car fleets for the 1986 model year must average 26 miles per gallon (mpg), rather than the 27.5 mpg set in 1975. Credits for exceeding the standards could be applied against performance in future years.

The amendment was offered by Daniel J. Evans, R-Wash., who argued that having failed to meet the 27.5 mpg standard, manufacturers should not be rewarded for exceeding the lower goal.

Other members reiterated arguments by General Motors Corp. and DOT that failure to give the credits would mean lost jobs in America and increased sales of imported cars.

The amendment was adopted by voice vote after it survived two attempts to kill it.

One was a 56-39 vote holding that the amendment was germane to the bill. The other came on a motion by Andrews to table the amendment; it was rejected, 46-48. *(Votes 243, 244, p. 45-S)*

The Senate voted 71-25 to table an amendment by William L. Armstrong, R-Colo., to drop all subsidies for Amtrak. *(Vote 242, p. 45-S)*

Another Reagan administration effort to cut programs was thwarted when the Senate by voice vote adopted an amendment that rejected a proposed deferral that would have prevented $234 million in previously appropriated funds from being spent to begin work on new mass transit projects in Los Angeles, Miami, San Diego, St. Louis and Jacksonville, Fla. ∎

Commerce/Justice/State Funding Bill Cleared

Congress Dec. 6 cleared an $11.92 billion fiscal 1986 appropriations bill (HR 2965) for the Commerce, State and Justice departments, the federal judiciary and a number of related agencies. President Reagan signed the measure into law Dec. 13 (PL 99-180).

The bill contained $244 million more than the administration had requested and provided funds for a number of agencies, such as the Economic Development Administration, Small Business Administration and Legal Services Corporation, that Reagan had sought to abolish. It provided about $2.1 billion for the Commerce Department, $4 billion for Justice, $2.5 billion for State, $1.1 billion for the judiciary and $2.3 billion for related agencies.

The spending levels approved July 17 by the House and Nov. 1 by the Senate were only $6 million apart, leaving conferees with few major decisions. The conferees reached agreement Dec. 4 on all the differences except for the issue of whether the political parties should continue to be eligible for grants from the National Endowment for Democracy (NED). They left it up to the Senate and House to resolve that question.

The House approved the conference report on the bill (H Rept 99-414) by voice vote Dec. 5, and the Senate followed suit Dec. 6, after narrowly acquiescing to the House position of continuing the political parties' NED grants but with new restrictions.

The endowment, created in 1983, provided grants to private organizations such as the AFL-CIO, the U.S. Chamber of Commerce and the Democratic and Republican parties to establish programs in foreign countries to teach people about the U.S. political system and to promote democracy. *(1983 Almanac p. 148)*

Provisions

HR 2965 appropriated the following amounts in fiscal 1986 budget authority:

	Final Budget Request	Final Appropriation
	(in thousands of dollars)	
Commerce Department		
General Administration	$ 36,227	$ 32,300
Bureau of the Census	199,162	196,000
Economic and Statistical Analysis	30,331	30,500
Economic Development Administration	15,467	201,000
International Trade Administration	175,824	192,000
Minority Business Development Agency	45,163	45,000

	Final Budget Request	Final Appropriation
	(in thousands of dollars)	
U.S. Travel and Tourism Administration	4,011	12,000
National Oceanic and Atmospheric Administration	999,955	1,169,949
Patent and Trademark Office	89,484	84,700
National Bureau of Standards	122,415	123,985
National Telecommunitions and Information Administration	13,527	37,400
Subtotal	**$ 1,731,566**	**$ 2,124,834**
Related Agencies		
Federal Communications Commission	94,904	94,400
Federal Maritime Commission	11,940	11,870
Federal Trade Commission	65,626	65,500
International Trade Commission	28,901	28,600
Marine Mammal Commission	800	900
Maritime Administration	70,367	79,600
Office of the U.S. Trade Representative	11,510	13,158
Securities and Exchange Commission	110,974	111,100
Small Business Administration	300,900	385,500
Subtotal	**$ 695,922**	**$ 790,628**
Justice Department		
General Administration	72,364	70,800
U.S. Parole Commission	9,609	9,800
Legal Activities	902,086	876,500
Interagency Law Enforcement	1,000	1,000
Federal Bureau of Investigation	1,207,182	1,209,000
Drug Enforcement Administration	351,349	380,000
Immigration and Naturalization Service	591,540	593,800
Federal Prison System	615,283	613,963
Office of Justice Programs	140,015	203,982
Subtotal	**$ 3,890,428**	**$ 3,958,845**
Related Agencies		
Christopher Columbus Quincentenary Jubilee Commission	220	——
Civil Rights Commission	12,386	12,300
Commission on the Bicentennial of the Constitution	775	775
Equal Employment Opportunity Commission	163,094	165,000
Legal Services Corporation	305,000[1]	305,500
U.S. Sentencing Commission	——	1,100
State Justice Institute	8,883	8,000
Subtotal	**$ 490,358**	**$ 492,675**
State Department		
Adm. of Foreign Affairs	1,976,134	1,940,274
International Organizations and Conferences	553,574	498,400
International Commissions	28,233	28,612
U.S. Bilateral Science and Technology Agreements	2,000	2,000
The Asia Foundation	9,785	10,000
Soviet-East European Research and Training	5,000	4,800
Subtotal	**$ 2,574,726**	**$ 2,484,086**
Related Agencies		
Arms Control and Disarmament Agency	26,243	25,850
Board for International Broadcasting	142,149	102,700
Commission on Security and Cooperation in Europe	550	550
Commission on the Ukraine Famine	——	400
Japan-United States Friendship Commission	1,550	775
U.S. Information Agency	982,762	872,450
Subtotal	**$ 1,153,254**	**$ 1,002,725**
The Judiciary		
Supreme Court	17,602	17,275
U.S. Court of Appeals for the Federal Circuit	5,720	5,500
U.S. Court of International Trade	6,538	6,400
Court of Appeals, District Courts, other judicial services	1,067,051	997,850
Administrative Office of the U.S. Courts	32,217	29,200
Federal Judicial Center	9,923	9,600
Subtotal	**$ 1,139,051**	**$ 1,065,825**
Grand Total	**$11,675,305**	**$11,919,618**

[1] *Submitted to Congress directly.*

House Committee Action

The House Appropriations Committee July 11 reported a $12.04 billion version of HR 2965 (H Rept 99-197).

The committee approved the measure by voice vote. Like similar bills for the previous four years, HR 2965 was a repository of funding for programs that President Reagan sought to eliminate or drastically reduce. Among those were the Legal Services Corporation (LSC), funded at $305 million; the Economic Development Administration (EDA), at $206 million; a program to help states combat juvenile delinquency, $70 million; and grants for public radio and television facilities, $24 million.

The bill was $265.5 million above the administration's request of $11.8 billion but about $18 million less than the fiscal 1985 appropriation. *(1984 Almanac p. 373)*

The committee voted $1.19 billion for the FBI, an increase of $8.47 million above Reagan's request. All the added money was earmarked for counterterrorism programs. The committee report noted that the FBI had been allocating resources from other areas to supplement antiterrorism funding provided in the fiscal 1985 appropriations law.

Legal Services Cutback. The Subcommittee on Commerce, Justice, State and the Judiciary had recommended $312 million for the LSC, which financed legal aid for the poor in civil cases. But the full committee cut that to $305 million, the fiscal 1985 level. An LSC reauthorization bill (HR 2468 — H Rept 99-448) approved by the House Judiciary Committee June 18 allowed $319 million, the same as the House-passed budget resolution. *(Authorization bill, p. 244; budget resolution, p. 441)*

The Appropriations subcommittee also picked up provisions in HR 2468 restricting certain activities of the LSC's board of directors. Robert W. Kastenmeier, D-Wis., sponsor of HR 2468, said these strings were intended to force the board to comply with the law creating and governing the LSC.

In 1984, the LSC was directed by a board appointed by Reagan during a congressional recess and never confirmed by the Senate. However, the Senate June 12 confirmed a full board of LSC directors, the first since 1981. Some Republicans complained that the provisions in HR 2468 were an attempt to prevent the new board from running the corporation.

On a motion by Neal Smith, D-Iowa, chairman of the subcommittee handling the bill, the Appropriations Committee deleted the restrictions — with a proviso that if HR 2468 were passed by the House, its provisions would take precedence over the language in HR 2965. (HR 2468 did not pass the House in 1985.)

House Floor Action

The House July 17 approved $11.92 billion for the Commerce, Justice and State departments and the federal judiciary, after trimming $118 million from HR 2965. The bill passed 273-136. *(Vote 218, p. 70-H)*

The biggest cut was a $95 million reduction in SBA direct loan authority. An amendment by John Hiler, R-Ind., to cut loan authority from $216 million to $121 million was adopted 257-158 although SBA backers said the move would "massacre" the program. *(Vote 214, p. 70-H)*

Despite its cost-cutting mood, the House refused, 98-315, to delete $206 million for the EDA, which provided grants to local governments to stimulate development projects. *(Vote 211, p. 68-H)*

The House also rejected, 149-266, an amendment by Bill Frenzel, R-Minn., and James R. Jones, D-Okla., to cut 4 percent from all discretionary funding in the bill. *(Vote 215, p. 70-H)*

As passed, the bill was $148 million above the administration's request of $11.7 billion and $136 million less than the fiscal 1985 appropriation of $12.06 billion.

Before taking up HR 2965, the House adopted two rules to facilitate action. H Res 221, adopted July 16 by a vote of 239-181, waived a provision of the Congressional Budget and Impoundment Control Act of 1974 requiring adoption of a first budget resolution, which set spending targets, before appropriations bills could be considered. H Res 221 applied to three funding bills. *(Vote 208, p. 68-H)*

H Res 225, adopted 234-188 on July 17, allowed funding of some 32 agencies and programs in the Commerce-Justice-State bill that had not yet been authorized for fiscal 1986. *(Vote 210, p. 68-H)*

Authorizations set general policy guidelines for federal agencies and programs, and under House rules they had to be in place before appropriations bills were passed. However, that rule frequently was waived.

Domestic Program Cuts

Although HR 2965 had breezed through the Appropriations Committee, it took a full day to get the bill through the House.

The amendment by Robert S. Walker, R-Pa., to delete funding for EDA prompted an hour of heated debate. Walker called the program a waste of taxpayers' money, contending that since its creation in 1967, EDA had been "spending money all over the place for things having nothing to do with economic development."

James L. Oberstar, D-Minn., countered that EDA "pays its own way," and Bill Alexander, D-Ark., said he knew of "no government program that has received such universal approval." Alexander said more than 70,000 private-sector jobs had been created in his state because of EDA seed money to local communities.

Hiler's amendment to trim SBA loan authority also provoked intense debate. Hiler said the cut would make the agency "leaner and meaner" and more efficient. Bob Carr, D-Mich., agreed, saying, "Some of us come from districts where we don't think [the SBA] has done very well."

Subcommittee Chairman Smith argued for retaining the money. He said the recommended funding was $215 million less than fiscal 1985 funding for the loan program. "The SBA has already taken a shellacking," Smith said. "Why try to massacre it?"

International Programs

By voice vote, the House adopted an amendment by Tom Tauke, R-Iowa, to trim $2.7 million in funding for Radio Marti, a Voice of America program that broadcast to Cuba. The controversial Radio Marti, created in 1983, began broadcasting May 20, 1985. *(1983 Almanac p. 21)*

The amendment, which provoked the most heated debate of the day, set funding at $8.5 million, the existing level. Tauke said that was more than adequate to fund a radio station that broadcast only 14 hours a day. Several members agreed. "If I've ever seen a gold-plated radio station in my life, it's Radio Marti," said Al Swift, D-Wash.

The program's supporters, led by Matthew J. Rinaldo, R-N.J., defended the station as an important tool in combating Cuban propaganda. "This is not a normal radio station," Rinaldo said. "You're cutting it without giving Radio Marti a chance."

Rinaldo made a move to get a recorded vote on the amendment, but was admonished by colleagues not to. Larry Smith, D-Fla., a Radio Marti supporter, shouted across the aisle, "Matt, sit down. Sit down."

By 302-116, the House adopted an amendment by Eldon Rudd, R-Ariz., to cut $20 million from the U.S. contribution to international organizations. He said that represented the amount the Soviet Union got in "salary kickbacks" from its employees who worked for the United Nations. *(Vote 213, p. 70-H)*

Neal Smith and George M. O'Brien, Ill., ranking Republican on Smith's subcommittee, opposed the amendment as "misguided."

Legal Fees, Abortion

By 244-177, the House adopted an amendment by Sidney R. Yates, D-Ill., to strike $500,000 from the Justice Department budget that would be used to pay the legal fees of non-Indian defendants in water rights suits under way in New Mexico. *(Vote 212, p. 68-H)*

The money subsequently was added to the budget for the LSC. The government thus would fund attorneys' fees only for persons in financial need.

By voice vote, the House adopted an amendment by Michael DeWine, R-Ohio, barring the use of any LSC funds for litigation related to abortion.

Senate Committee Action

The Senate Appropriations Committee reported HR 2965 Oct. 4 (S Rept 99-150), after cutting $68.2 million from the version approved by the Subcommittee on Commerce, Justice, State on Sept. 26.

The cuts were made so that projections of actual spending during fiscal 1986 for the agencies covered by the bill would comply with outlay limits in the fiscal 1986 budget resolution. With the cuts, the bill was slightly below the $11.92 billion version passed by the House July 17. It also was below the administration's revised request of $11.94 billion.

The cuts were spread over all three departments and the judiciary, but the biggest share of the savings — about $26.2 million — came from State Department-related programs. The largest cut was $11 million trimmed from the U.S. contribution to the peacekeeping force in Lebanon, reducing the amount from $47.4 million to $36.4 million.

Another $8.4 million — the second-largest cut — came in funds for the NED, reducing its appropriation from $18.5 million to $10.1 million. Ernest F. Hollings, D-S.C., had tried to eliminate all the NED funding in subcommittee, but his motion was rejected 3-4.

Senate Floor Action

The Senate passed HR 2965 by a vote of 84-10 on Nov. 1, after threats of a filibuster over an anti-abortion amendment delayed consideration for a week. *(Vote 275, p. 49-S)*

Despite the cost-cutting mood in Congress, the bill grew by $28 million on the floor. As passed, it contained $11.93 billion, slightly more than the Appropriations Committee version, $6.14 million more than the House bill and $268.9 million more than the administration request.

Abortions for Prisoners

The Senate began debating HR 2965 Oct. 24, but Majority Leader Robert Dole, R-Kan., abruptly pulled the bill off the floor after Howard M. Metzenbaum, D-Ohio, indicated he would filibuster it because of an anti-abortion amendment.

The amendment, by Jesse Helms, R-N.C., would bar federal women's prisons from providing abortions to inmates, except to save the life of the pregnant woman. The bill included $612 million for the federal prison system.

Helms said the prison system had provided elective abortions for women inmates — 37 in fiscal 1985, by preliminary check, Helms said — without any restrictions, and should be brought into conformity with federal law. By law, no federal funds could be used for abortions except to save the life of the mother. *(1984 Almanac p. 465)*

Metzenbaum and Warren B. Rudman, R-N.H., opposed Helms' amendment. Rudman said the issue was not abortion but "minimum standards . . . for the medical care of prisoners." Metzenbaum said the Senate had considered 431 abortion proposals in the last nine years. "It just seems to me enough is enough," he said.

Rudman moved to table (kill) Helms' amendment but his motion failed on a 46-46 tie. *(Vote 255, p. 47-S)*

Metzenbaum, unfurling a computer printout from Legis, the congressional bill-tracking service, then announced he wanted to discuss past abortion proposals. Sensing a filibuster, Dole pulled the bill.

When the bill was brought back up Nov. 1, Rudman raised a point of order challenging the amendment's constitutionality on grounds it would deny women prisoners medical care. Helms moved to table the point of order, but his motion was rejected, 47-48. *(Vote 274, p. 49-S)*

The Senate then decided by voice vote that the amendment was unconstitutional, and it was dropped.

EDA Funding

The most vigorous debate Nov. 1 was over an amendment by John H. Chafee, R-R.I., to delete $160 million for the EDA. Chafee said the program, which had not been reauthorized by Congress since 1982, was a waste of money. But several senators, led by George J. Mitchell, D-Maine, and Dale Bumpers, D-Ark., defended the program and said critics should work to improve it, not kill it.

The amendment lost, 39-57. *(Vote 272, p. 49-S)*

The largest addition of funds to the bill on the Senate floor also involved the EDA. On an amendment by Alfonse M. D'Amato, R-N.Y., the Senate by voice vote agreed to add $32.1 million to EDA funding for four projects to build facilities to train more microelectronic engineers.

Of the total, $11.1 million was earmarked for the Rochester Institute of Technology in D'Amato's home state; $4 million for Lexington County, in South Carolina, home state of Hollings, the ranking Democrat on the Commerce, Justice, State Appropriations Subcommittee; $13.5 million for Northeastern University in Boston, Mass.; and $3.5 million for the school of engineering at the University of Nevada at Las Vegas. Paul Laxalt, R-Nev., was the subcommittee chairman.

To help offset the increase, the Senate adopted a Hollings amendment trimming $7 million from U.S. contributions to United Nations peacekeeping forces.

Other Amendments

In action on the bill Oct. 24, the Senate adopted an amendment by Richard G. Lugar, R-Ind., restoring $4.8 million for a program of Soviet-East European research and training. To offset the addition, the amendment struck $4.8 million from funds allocated for maintenance of State Department buildings abroad.

The Senate rejected, 21-74, an amendment by Mark O. Hatfield, R-Ore., designed to reverse an Oct. 7 Reagan administration decision to withdraw the United States from the compulsory jurisdiction of the International Court of Justice, known as the World Court. The amendment would have barred U.S. contributions to all international organizations unless the United States rejoined the court. *(Vote 249, p. 46-S)*

The Senate adopted an amendment by Strom Thurmond, R-S.C., adding $1.1 million for a new U.S. Sentencing Commission to establish guidelines for punishment in federal crimes. The commission was created in 1984. *(1984 Almanac p. 215)*

To offset the addition, the amendment trimmed a like amount from the Justice Department's Community Relations Service.

Conference Action

The principal controversy in the conference was funding for the National Endowment for Democracy, and whether the nation's two major political parties should be able to continue receiving grants from it. The Senate had voted to bar such grants; the House said they should continue, but added several new restrictions on the use of the money.

Hollings and Sen. Lowell P. Weicker Jr., R-Conn., argued that NED funding should be eliminated entirely. They said the money had been misspent on such activities as support for right-wing groups opposing the government of French President François Mitterrand and on many unproductive conferences.

But the Senate conferees voted 5-3 to reject Hollings' motion. The conferees then approved $18 million for NED, compared with $10 million in the Senate bill and $19.3 million in the House measure, and left it to the two chambers to decide whether the grants to the political parties should be allowed.

The House restrictions did not satisfy the Senate managers of the bill, Rudman and Hollings. Rudman asked the Senate to insist on its ban, and Hollings offered an amendment to eliminate all NED funds. The Senate rejected Rudman's motion, 43-44, and then defeated the Hollings amendment, 32-57, before clearing the funding bill by voice vote. *(Votes 353, 354, p. 61-S)*

Conferees also deleted the $32 million added by the Senate for the EDA, for projects in Massachusetts, Nevada, New York and South Carolina.

The final bill contained $175 million for EDA, compared with $160 million in the Senate bill and $180 million in the House version. ∎

$13.02 Billion Fiscal '85 Supplemental Cleared

Overcoming sharp controversies over new water projects and foreign aid, Congress Aug. 1 cleared a bill providing $13.02 billion in fiscal 1985 supplemental appropriations for a variety of government programs.

The $13.02 billion appropriated by the final measure (HR 2577 — H Rept 99-236) was $405 million under the House-passed amount; $920 million under the Senate version; and $139 million over the administration's request. The president signed it into law (PL 99-88) Aug. 15.

The major items, such as $2.9 billion for farm price support programs and $3.5 billion for Social Security, were not in dispute. But there were strong disagreements over non-military aid for the anti-government "contra" rebels in Nicaragua and over funding for new water projects, such as dams, waterways and harbor dredging. *(Nicaragua story, p. 61; water projects, p. 198)*

The House for two years had been the center of resistance to aiding the contras, while the Senate consistently had supported it. The Reagan administration achieved a stunning breakthrough when the House, before passing the bill June 12, voted to supply $27 million in non-military aid to the rebels. However, the House rejected the administration request that either the CIA or the Defense Department be allowed to administer the assistance.

The Senate version of HR 2577, approved June 20, provided $38 million and would have allowed the CIA to administer it. The Senate wanted to allow the CIA to collect intelligence in Nicaragua and share it with the contras. Under current law barring U.S. aid for paramilitary operations in that country, the CIA could not provide the contras with intelligence data.

After weeks of contention, a conference committee began meeting July 22. The deadlock over the contra aid was broken July 26 when senators agreed to accept both the House dollar amount and its method of distributing funds.

Water Financing Controversy

The disagreement over water projects involved differences between the chambers, between the administration and Congress over financing, and between chairmen of powerful appropriations and authorizing committees.

A key issue was increasing the share of water projects paid by state and local governments. Generally the federal government paid the bulk of the costs of new dams, locks, irrigation projects, waterways and harbors.

New cost-sharing formulas were included in pending omnibus water project authorizations (HR 6, S 1567). Authorizations normally precede appropriations, but Congress had not passed a comprehensive authorization for water projects since 1976. *(Authorizations, p. 198)*

The House Appropriations Committee's bill contained $171 million for 62 new projects — 31 not authorized. Members of the authorizing Public Works and Transportation Committee succeeded in slashing funding on the floor to $71.85 million for 35 starts.

The Senate bill provided $63.1 million for 25 new projects, but under administration pressure, it barred funding unless a cost-sharing agreement was reached by June 30, 1986, after which funding would lapse. House Appropriations Committee Chairman Jamie L. Whitten, D-Miss., balked at the provision.

Conferees eventually agreed July 26 on $48.8 million for 41 projects by the U.S. Army Corps of Engineers and $14.3 million for four projects by the Interior Department's Bureau of Reclamation. But none could start unless a cost-sharing formula was reached by June 30, 1986, or unless an omnibus authorization was enacted. The compromise exempted major flood-control projects in the Mississippi River basin from the cost-sharing requirement, which won Whitten's endorsement. *(Water projects, box, p. 351)*

However, on July 31 Public Works Chairman James J. Howard, D-N.J., prodded the House into rejecting that conference plan and voting to put the projects on indefinite hold until the authorizing legislation was enacted.

The Senate, after adopting the conference report by voice vote Aug. 1, voted to suspend funding for new projects until May 15, 1986, to give Congress time to enact the comprehensive legislation. That condition provided a way around the fact that 21 of the 41 projects on the final conference list had not yet been authorized.

House appropriations committee leaders assured authorizing panel leaders that they would work to pass an authorization bill, and that they had a commitment from their Senate counterparts as well. The House cleared the measure later Aug. 1.

Separate Farm Supplemental Enacted

During the conference impasse, some U.S. agencies began to run out of money, and Congress was forced to move separate legislation to prevent programs from shutting down.

Agriculture Secretary John R. Block announced July 17 that the Commodity Credit Corporation (CCC) immediately would suspend price support payments to farmers because of a lack of funds. He said the federal crop insurance program also had run out of money and would be suspended.

The Senate July 19 by voice vote cleared a bill (H J Res 342) to rescue the CCC from bankruptcy by providing $1 billion. The House had passed the measure by voice vote the previous day. It was signed into law July 24 (PL 99-71).

Provisions

As signed into law, HR 2577 included the following appropriations and provisions for fiscal 1985:

Agriculture, Rural Development

- $2.9 billion for the Commodity Credit Corporation for farm price supports. Another $1 billion was provided in a separate supplemental bill (H J Res 342 — PL 99-71).
- $318.9 million to fully fund the food stamp program through 1985.
- $113 million for emergency borrowing authority for the Federal Crop Insurance Corporation.
- $17 million for the Farmers Home Administration. The final bill dropped a House requirement that the agency suspend payments for some borrowers.
- $7 million for transporting surplus commodities for distribution to low-income people.

Commerce, State and Judiciary

- $126 million for the National Oceanic and Atmospheric Administration to begin commercialization of land-remote sensing satellites.
- Allowed DOT to implement a rule allowing shipowners to repay federal subsidies in return for being allowed to engage in domestic trade. The House had barred implementation.
- $12 million in new funds and $3 million in transfers to hire additional U.S. marshals and attorneys.
- $1.5 million for additional Federal Bureau of Investigation personnel.
- $4.1 million for the Arms Control and Disarmament Agency for the Geneva arms reduction talks.
- $26 million to restructure the bankruptcy courts.
- $241 million to improve security at U.S. embassies.
- Set guidelines for the Federal Communications Commission for use in granting licenses for competitors to INTELSAT, the international communications satellite system.
- Removed certain curbs on fees and travel expenses paid to board members of the Legal Services Corporation, imposed in 1982.

Defense, Foreign Affairs

- $27 million for non-military aid for contra rebels fighting the Nicaraguan government, to be distributed by any U.S. agency except the Defense Department or the CIA. The funds were to be available through March 1986.
- $236.7 million for multilateral development banks.
- $1.5 billion in economic aid for Israel.
- $500 million in economic aid for Egypt.
- $250 million in economic aid for Jordan, spread out over fiscal 1985-87, in commodity credits and aid for public works projects, not cash.
- $8 million for West Bank and Gaza Strip development.

New Water Projects

The urgent fiscal 1985 supplemental appropriations bill (HR 2577 — PL 99-88) included $48.8 million to begin construction on 41 water resource development projects by the Army Corps of Engineers and $14.3 million for four projects by the Bureau of Reclamation.

Following are the projects listed in the bill signed by the president Aug. 15, 1985. The projects that had not been authorized by Congress in separate legislation are in italics:

Army Corps of Engineers

Alabama: *Mobile Harbor; and William Bacon Oliver Lock and Dam*
Arkansas: *Eight Mile Creek*
California: Merced County streams; *Richmond Harbor; Sacramento River deepwater ship channel;* and Fairfield vicinity streams
Florida: Tampa Harbor branch channels, including East Bay channel maintenance; *Dade County, north of Haulover Beach Park*
Georgia: *Savannah Harbor widening*
Hawaii: Kahoma Stream
Illinois-Missouri: *Lock and Dam No. 26, with a second lock, including environmental management, Alton, Ill.*
Iowa: *Des Moines recreational river and Greenbelt*
Louisiana: *Mississippi River ship channel, Gulf to Baton Rouge; Pearl River, Slidell, St. Tammany Parish; and Atchafalaya Basin*
Maine: Jonesport Harbor
Maryland-Virginia: Baltimore Harbor and channels
Minnesota: Bassett Creek
Mississippi: *Gulfport Harbor*
Nebraska-South Dakota: Missouri National Recreational River
New Jersey: Barnegat Inlet; and Liberty State Park levee and seawall
New Jersey-New York: *Kill Van Kull, Newark Bay Channel*
New York: Ardsley; Ellicott Creek; Moriches Inlet; and Port Ontario Harbor
Ohio: Geneva-on-the-Lake; and *Cleveland Harbor*
Ohio-West Virginia: *Gallipolis locks and dam*
Oklahoma: *Parker Lake*
Oregon-Washington: *Bonneville navigation lock*
Pennsylvania: Cowanesque Lake modification
Texas: Clear Creek; Freeport Harbor, including relocation of north jetty; and *Colorado River and tributaries, Boggy Creek at Austin*
Utah: Little Dell Lake
Virginia: *Richmond local protection project;* Virginia Beach streams, Canal No. 2; and *Norfolk Harbor*

Bureau of Reclamation

Arizona-Nevada: Boulder Canyon
Arizona: Headgate Rock
Colorado-New Mexico: Animas-La Plata
Wyoming: Buffalo Bill Dam

SOURCE: House-Senate conference committee report (H Rept 99-236)

- $35 million for the CIA to combat spying at U.S. embassies.
- Denied U.S. funds to any group that supported, even indirectly, a family planning program that involved forced abortions or involuntary sterilizations, and ordered the president to determine if a program did so.

Energy and Water Development

- $48.8 million for 41 new water projects of the U.S. Army Corps of Engineers. Funds could not be spent before May 15, 1986, unless an authorization bill containing new cost-sharing formulas was enacted. If no bill was enacted by that date, funds would be available to start construction if a cost-sharing agreement between local sponsors and the administration was sent to Congress before June 30, 1986.

- Exempted multi-state flood control projects, such as those that were part of the Mississippi River and tributaries program, from future increases in local cost-sharing.
- $14.3 million for four new water projects of the Bureau of Reclamation.
- $5 million for the Tennessee Valley Authority for a water transmission line in Bristol, Tenn.
- Dropped Senate restrictions on Federal Energy Regulatory Commission fees on hydroelectric plants.

HUD-Independent Agencies

- Dropped a House provision rescinding $75 million for public housing operating subsidies.
- $24 million for the Environmental Protection Agency to begin hazardous-waste control programs.
- Allowed the Federal Emergency Management Agency (FEMA) to transfer $1.1 million from other accounts to pay salaries.
- $20 million for a FEMA emergency food and shelter program.
- $40 million for the National Aeronautics and Space Administration for cost overruns in the Centaur program.
- $152.5 million for pay increases for medical personnel in the Veterans Administration (VA).
- $175 million for compensation payments to veterans and dropped $44 million the House had included for readjustment benefits since the VA had withdrawn its request.

Interior

- Deferred $537 million to buy oil for the Strategic Petroleum Reserve, but directed the administration to spend another $290 million in 1985 funds to bring the reserve to 500 million barrels in fiscal 1986.
- Rejected a proposed $271 million deferral for construction of additional capacity for the petroleum reserve.
- Approved $9.2 million of the administration's request for deferral of $48.4 million for fossil energy research programs of the Energy Department.
- Barred the Bureau of Land Management and the Forest Service from swapping land to consolidate holdings.

Labor-HHS-Education

- $3.5 billion for the Social Security Trust Fund to offset military service credit, for which contributions to the fund were not made before 1957.
- $11 million for child-abuse and family violence programs and shelters.
- $102 million for new vocational education programs.
- $287 million for Pell grants to low-income college students, to fully fund the program.
- $720 million for guaranteed student loans.
- $79.5 million for foster care and adoption assistance.

Miscellaneous

- $47.5 million for Congress for increased mail costs and salaries.
- Rejected the proposed deferral of $30 million for rehabilitation of a rail line between Philadelphia, Pa., and Atlantic City, N.J.
- $3.1 million for the Interstate Commerce Commission to end staff furloughs and reduce case backlogs.
- Authorized the Customs Service to set user fees to support customs operations at small airports.
- $168.6 million for the Postal Service to help support non-profit, educational and library mailing rates.
- Dropped a House provision barring the Office of Personnel Management from implementing new rules for determining layoffs.
- $65.2 million to avert Internal Revenue Service layoffs.

House Committee Action

The House Appropriations Committee by voice vote May 21 approved $13.49 billion in supplemental appropriations, despite the objections of budget director David A. Stockman. The panel filed its report (H Rept 99-142) May 22.

Stockman, while stopping short of a veto threat, called HR 2577 "unacceptable," largely because it would fund new dams and water projects similar to those that had endangered enactment of the fiscal 1985 continuing appropriations resolution. That measure (PL 98-473) was passed after conferees agreed to drop the controversial projects. *(1984 Almanac p. 444)*

The new bill was about $69 million below the administration request, but the panel raised spending in many areas and rejected some reductions proposed by the Office of Management and Budget (OMB).

"We, as Congress, can't let the budget director run everything," committee Chairman Whitten said. "We need to balance the budget at a high enough level to take care of things urgently needed."

Silvio O. Conte, Mass., ranking GOP member, said the bill contained more than $2 billion in questionable spending. He was particularly critical of including water projects in the supplemental appropriations bill.

"We are not going to win a game of political chicken where we simply roll this pork barrel down Capitol Hill toward the White House," he said.

Bill Highlights

In addition to $3.9 billion for price support programs administered by the CCC and $3.5 billion for payments to the Social Security Administration for military retirees' benefits, the bill included more than $2 billion the administration requested in economic aid for the Middle East.

The panel provided full funding for several programs the administration had wanted to cut, including student aid and a program to feed needy women, infants and children (WIC). It also rejected the request to stop filling the Strategic Petroleum Reserve.

It provided $1.73 billion for mandatory federal pay increases to support a 3.5 percent raise that became effective Jan. 1. That was $723 million less than the presidential request. The committee directed most agencies to absorb much of the cost from existing funding.

Water Projects Resurface

The committee recommended $150 million for the U.S. Army Corps of Engineers to start 62 new water projects and $20.85 million for the Department of the Interior's Bureau of Reclamation to start four.

Only about half of the projects in HR 2577 were authorized, but the bill specified that work could not start without the enactment of authorizing legislation and made the projects subject to cost-sharing agreements.

Stockman, in a letter to Whitten and Conte, objected strongly to including the projects in the bill. The administration had requested 32 projects in its fiscal 1986 budget, but Stockman complained that the additional projects would add $4.8 billion by the time they were finished. He also opposed providing funds before new cost-sharing rules were established.

Committee aides said that his estimate was exaggerated and that the total of all 66 initiatives would be approximately $4.2 billion. Funding was not broken down for each proposal, which aides said was necessary to give the agencies flexibility.

"We can't just sit back and wait," said Tom Bevill, D-Ala., chairman of the Subcommittee on Energy and Water Development. "We're running out of authorized projects, and we have a lot of critical needs. We're picking up where we left off [last year]."

The committee deleted, without objection, two projects the Subcommittee on Energy and Water Development had approved April 24. One in Oregon, at Strube Lake and Cougar Dam, was called unnecessary by James Weaver, D-Ore., in whose district it was located. The other, the Narrows Unit in northeastern Colorado, had been criticized by environmentalists.

The panel also adopted without objection an amendment by Bevill blocking work on the Animas-La Plata irrigation project in Colorado and New Mexico until a cost-sharing agreement had been submitted to Congress.

Foreign Aid

As ordered reported, the bill contained no Nicaragua aid because members had not decided what legislative vehicle to use in response to the administration request.

It did include $1.5 billion in emergency economic aid for Israel, $500 million in emergency economic aid for Egypt and $8 million for development projects for Palestinians in the West Bank and Gaza areas.

The administration had filed an official request for the Middle East funds shortly before the committee meeting. But Stockman objected to a committee decision to make the funds available only through Sept. 30, 1986.

The panel accepted, 42-4, a proposal by Conte to add $236.7 million for multilateral development banks but only after the administration had lined up reluctant Republican support. Democrats said they were tired of backing the administration's international aid requests only to be criticized by the GOP.

It deleted, over some protests, a provision to punish foreign air carriers whose planes were used for drug smuggling. The administration had objected that the provision violated international air agreements.

Strategic Petroleum Reserve

In denying two OMB proposals to defer spending already approved for the Strategic Petroleum Reserve, the committee rejected the administration's plan to quit filling the emergency oil reserve at the end of fiscal 1985.

OMB had requested deferral of $827 million for oil purchases and $271 million for construction of additional storage capacity at Big Hill, Texas.

The bill directed the Department of Energy to continue filling the reserve but at a rate of 50,000 barrels per day, instead of the current 159,000 barrels per day mandated by the fiscal 1985 continuing resolution.

At the lower rate, there would be enough funds to buy oil for the reserve throughout fiscal 1986. However, that meant that no new budget authority would be needed in fiscal 1986.

Abortions

A fight erupted during the markup when Jack F. Kemp, R-N.Y., proposed denying U.S. funds to "any organization or program which supports or participates in the management of a program of coercive abortion."

Kemp said the United Nations Fund for Population Activities was, at least indirectly, supporting a program in China that was alleged to force women to have abortions. Conservatives had made an issue of abortions in foreign population-planning programs on several fronts, including the foreign aid authorization (HR 1555). *(Story, p. 41)*

The Kemp amendment was opposed by David R. Obey, D-Wis., chairman of the Subcommittee on Foreign Operations, who said the U.N. program was not funding the Chinese policy in any way, and was in fact providing an alternative to it.

Obey offered a substitute that restated current law, which already barred U.S. aid for programs that included forced abortions. But the substitute was defeated, 20-24, on a roll call vote, and the Kemp amendment was adopted, 20-15, by a show of hands.

Student Aid Supported

The committee by voice vote adopted an amendment by William H. Natcher, D-Ky., chairman of the Subcommittee on Labor-Health and Human Services-Education, to increase from $75 million to $287 million the supplemental appropriation for Pell grants for needy college students.

That would allow students to continue to receive grants for 60 percent of college costs, up to a maximum of $2,100 a year. The administration had requested no additional funds for Pell grants, suggesting instead that grants be reduced. Natcher's subcommittee had originally proposed a compromise at $75 million.

Other key amendments adopted by voice vote included those by:

- Whitten, providing $113 million for the crop insurance program.
- Conte, adding $6 million to fund a previously authorized program of state grants to prevent child abuse and family violence (PL 98-473). *(1984 Almanac p. 484)*
- Conte, to increase $3.15 million for the Interstate Commerce Commission by $500,000.
- Norman D. Dicks, D-Wash., to allow the transfer of $240 million from Navy shipbuilding accounts to pay for installing new wings on A-6E bombers, which had worn out more quickly than expected.

House Floor Action

The House considered the bill June 6, June 11 and June 12, taking sharply dramatic votes on the two key controversies: water projects and contra aid.

On June 6, the House voted 203-202 to slash funds for new water projects. The vote came on an amendment by Bob Edgar, D-Pa., to cut the $150 million for projects of the U.S. Army Corps of Engineers to $51 million. *(Vote 133, p. 44-H)*

On June 12, in a stunning turnaround, the House agreed to supply $27 million in non-military aid to the contras. It was the first time since July 1983 that a majority of House members agreed to Reagan's request for U.S. backing for the rebels. It was a major victory for the president.

After rejecting a proposal by the Democratic leadership to aid Nicaraguan refugees and adopting a GOP plan to give the contras $27 million in non-military aid, the House approved the bill by a vote of 271-156. *(Vote 144, p. 48-H)*

Pruning Water Projects

The groundwork for pruning the water projects had been laid June 5 by the Rules Committee, which issued rules governing floor consideration of a bill.

The Appropriations Committee had requested a waiver from a House regulation that prevented funding of unauthorized projects. The waiver would have prohibited opponents of the water projects from raising a point of order that would automatically eliminate the projects. Such waivers were given frequently.

Edgar told the committee that he had no hope that it would reject the request for a waiver, and he asked merely that he be allowed to offer an amendment to cut the projects.

But Chairman Claude Pepper, D-Fla., rebuked Edgar, saying he should not presume to know what the committee would do. The next day committee Democrats unexpectedly proposed a rule that allowed the projects to be struck if anyone raised a point of order.

The decision was apparently the product of several factors: the desire of several members for reform of water-project financing; maneuvering by members of the authorizing committee, Public Works and Transportation; and remembrances of the close of the 98th Congress.

In September 1984, the Rules panel had been dealt an embarrassing defeat when the House voted against a rule that would have kept a stopgap continuing resolution (PL 98-473) free of water projects. The House added scores of projects, which soon became the focus of a White House veto threat that helped keep Congress in session beyond its scheduled adjournment date. Pepper said that the committee remembered that snarl. *(1984 Almanac p. 444)*

Jurisdictional Clash

Also important, he said, was the stance taken by Public Works Chairman Howard and Robert A. Roe, D-N.J., chairman of the Subcommittee on Water Resources.

The two had been the foremost proponents of federal aid for water projects, but they told the Rules Committee that they wanted the supplemental measure to incorporate *all* of HR 6, their omnibus bill that would authorize as many as 300 new projects.

"[Howard] wanted everything or nothing," Pepper said. "It was grossly too much. If we put all those big projects in, the president would have vetoed the bill."

Howard said his motive was to ensure that all projects were treated equally and to include procedural reforms from HR 6 that would increase the share of the cost of construction to be borne by local governments and users.

Language in the supplemental bill made the water project funding subject to authorization, but Howard charged that the Appropriations panel would drop the language in conference with the Senate.

The rule was debated for an hour by members unhappy with the water projects provision, by those opposed to the extra spending throughout the bill and by Republicans critical of the rules for considering Nicaragua aid.

GOP Whip Trent Lott of Mississippi complained of "shabby treatment" by the Rules Committee. The rule allowed Democrats to weaken a GOP proposal for aid to the contras with two amendments, but it gave Republicans no chance to amend the Democratic alternative to aid refugees.

The rule was approved by a vote of 267-149. *(Vote 132, p. 44-H)*

Whitten Defends Water Projects

On the floor, Whitten defended the water projects, many of which were desperately sought by members for flood control or economic development. He said that no new Army Corps of Engineers projects had been authorized since 1976, and the administration was unlikely to approve a bill this Congress.

"I know they call it pork barrel, but it's not true," he said. "I say the time has come for Congress to speak up and take up its obligation. We'd better start looking after our own country."

Howard, however, made a successful motion to delete all the projects on a point of order that unauthorized projects were included in the spending bill.

Whitten then was expected to offer an amendment to reinstate only the authorized projects. But instead, he proposed restoring the full funding for the Corps, $150 million, without specifying which projects would get the money.

Edgar, in an amendment to Whitten's proposal, proposed instead cutting funding to $51 million.

Edgar was supported by Howard and Roe, who again contended that with the full funding, the Appropriations Committee would restore the unauthorized projects in conference with the Senate.

Howard told reporters that if powerful members were able to win funding for projects in their districts in the appropriations bill, there would be little pressure to pass the comprehensive authorization.

It was especially necessary to keep pressure on the Senate, Howard said, pointing out that in 1984, the House passed a water project authorization bill, but the Senate did not. *(1984 Almanac p. 320)*

"If we keep giving the heavyweights in the Senate their projects through appropriations, it takes the pressure off them," Howard said.

After Edgar's amendment was approved 203-202, the House voted 325-74 for the altered Whitten amendment, restoring $51 million to the supplemental bill. *(Vote 134, p. 44-H)*

Edgar said the success of his amendment represented a combination of forces: the drive for fiscal austerity at a time of budget deficits, desire to reform the public works financing, jealousy of authorizing committees over the appropriations panel's encroachment on their turf, administration pressure and opposition from members whose projects were not included in the committee's original list of 62.

Despite his victory, Edgar said he expected the unauthorized projects to be funded eventually.

"Whitten *never* loses," he told reporters. "He may lose on the merits; he may lose on procedure.... But his committee will stay up all night to figure out how to get those projects funded."

Nevertheless, Edgar said, the vote highlighted the need for comprehensive reform of U.S. aid to water projects, including new cost-sharing agreements and a method of determining which projects were most needed.

Some additional spending for water projects remained in the bill. It included $20.85 million for four projects of the Department of the Interior's Bureau of Reclamation. Those had been authorized.

The bill also allowed the Army Corps of Engineers to use previously appropriated money for design and land acquisition for seven major inland waterway projects that had not been authorized.

Other Funding Changes

By voice vote, the House June 6 also approved amendments by:

- Byron L. Dorgan, D-N.D., adding $4.27 million to provide for transportation of surplus commodities for distribution to low-income people.
- John B. Breaux, D-La., providing $4 million to establish a Gillis W. Long Poverty Law Center at Loyola University School of Law in New Orleans, in memory of the late Democrat who served in the House from 1963-65 and from 1973-85.
- Norman D. Dicks, D-Wash., adding language that made the transfer of funds to pay for replacing wings on the Navy's A-6E aircraft subject to enactment of authorizing legislation.

Chairmen of several authorizing committees complained that the measure contained money for programs that were not authorized, and they were able to delete some funds on the grounds that they constituted legislation on an appropriations bill, which was forbidden by House rules.

Provisions deleted included:

- Authority for the Federal Communications Commission to relocate a monitoring station in Fort Lauderdale, Fla.
- $11 million for 434 more positions for U.S. attorneys and marshals, and for relocation of the U.S. attorney's office for the District of Columbia.
- $2.9 million for 339 additional positions for the Federal Bureau of Investigation (FBI).
- Authority for the FBI to relocate its Washington, D.C., field office.

June 11 Action

The House completed action June 11 on all of HR 2577, except the Nicaragua aid.

By a vote of 110-314, members rejected an amendment by Hank Brown, R-Colo., to eliminate $500 million in aid for Egypt. *(Vote 136, p. 46-H)*

Brown argued that Egypt had not spent the $2.2 billion it had been given in regular appropriations and that Egypt was failing to live up to the 1978 Camp David agreement by not maintaining an ambassador in Israel.

"It is inappropriate for us to provide a bonus for a country that has failed to live up to the Camp David accords," Brown said.

Other members — including some of the strongest supporters of aid to Israel — replied that striking the funds would be an insult that could cause Egypt to back away from negotiations with Israel.

"I think it is important, if you are pro-Israel, to recognize that it is incredibly important to Israel to have Egypt and other moderate Arab nations involved in the peace process, not outside of it," said Kemp. "Denying aid to this country would be a terrible message to send to friends of the peace process in the Middle East at this very critical point."

Spending Cuts Rejected

The House June 11 also rejected three amendments that sought to cut spending to reflect concern with deficits.

Robert S. Walker, R-Pa., lost a 202-217 vote on his plan to eliminate about $30 million for the House and the executive office of the president. *(Vote 137, p. 46-H)*

"One of the places that we ought to begin to get serious is with our own legislative shop," Walker argued.

Other members replied that the funds were necessary for the large volume of mail and for pay raises for staff members.

After losing on that amendment, Walker moved to cut $11.9 million to pay for additional congressional mail costs, which he said could be reduced if every member would send one fewer newsletter. The amendment was defeated by voice vote.

An amendment by Ed Zschau, R-Calif., to reduce all funding for discretionary programs covered by the bill by 5 percent was rejected by a vote of 190-226. *(Vote 138, p. 46-H)*

Other Amendments

Amendments accepted by voice vote included those by:

- Glenn English, D-Okla., to require the secretary of the Army to approve work on a chloride control project on the Arkansas River Basin, and to separate it from the Red River Basin project.

English contended that the Arkansas River project would destroy 60,000 acres of land in western Oklahoma for a project with a negative cost-benefit ratio. The Red River and Arkansas River projects were lumped together in the original authorization.

- Vic Fazio, D-Calif., to require the Federal Energy Regulatory Commission to rule within two years on an application to build a high-power transmission line to bring electricity from the Pacific Northwest to California.

The amendment replaced a provision that would have approved the line and given it antitrust exemptions. Objections were raised by the Judiciary Committee and the Energy and Commerce Committee that the action invaded their jurisdictions.

- Gerry E. Studds, D-Mass., to transfer $15 million from a boat safety account supported by gasoline taxes on motorboat fuel to the Coast Guard. Studds said the money was needed to keep open 13 search and rescue stations on the Great Lakes and to keep the Coast Guard at full personnel strength.

June 12: Contra Aid

The House voted directly on the contra issue four times on June 12 and supported the president by comfortable margins each time.

The first, closest and most important vote came on the issue of whether to extend indefinitely a legal ban on any U.S. aid for "military or paramilitary operations in Nicaragua." That prohibition, which the House had supported consistently since 1983 and which had been U.S. law since October 1984 (PL 98-473), was called the "Boland amendment," after Edward P. Boland, D-Mass., former chairman of the Intelligence Committee. *(1984 Almanac p. 86)*

Boland on June 12 proposed extending the ban indefinitely and offered an amendment to an underlying amendment sponsored by Joseph M. McDade, R-Pa., on behalf of Minority Leader Robert H. Michel of Illinois, that provided $27 million in aid for the contras. The House rejected Boland's amendment 196-232, with 58 Democrats joining all but seven Republicans in opposition to it. *(Vote 140, p. 46-H)*

Republicans charged that Boland's plan was a "killer" amendment because it would have barred the United States from helping the contras in any fashion, even by providing non-military aid or intelligence information. But some Democrats said that interpretation was too broad. The amendment might permit giving "defensive intelligence" data to the contras and might be construed as allowing non-military aid provided by agencies other than U.S. intelligence services, they said.

About an hour after rejecting the Boland amendment, the House turned back the Democrats' second attempt to thwart aid to the contras. By a 172-259 vote, it rejected an amendment by Richard A. Gephardt, D-Mo., to Michel's amendment that would have postponed implementation of the aid for six months — with the money available then only if Reagan made a new request and both houses approved. *(Vote 141, p. 46-H)*

Gephardt said his amendment would give the president time to pursue negotiations with Nicaragua, directly through bilateral meetings and indirectly through the "Contadora" negotiations sponsored by Colombia, Mexico, Panama and Venezuela. The amendment, he said, was an "opportunity to support, in clear and decisive terms, a diplomatic solution."

But Republicans decried the amendment as a rebuff to the contras when they needed U.S. backing. "It says, 'Hang in there, boys, for six more months,' " said Henry J. Hyde, R-Ill., adding sarcastically that the threat of another congressional vote ought to bring the Sandinistas "to their knees."

By a 248-184 vote, the House then approved the basic Michel amendment providing the $27 million in aid to the contras. *(Vote 142, p. 46-H)*

And after two more hours of debate, the House by 174-254 rejected a broad alternative offered by the Democratic leadership. *(Vote 143, p. 48-H)*

The leadership plan would have provided $14 million in aid, through international agencies such as the Red Cross, to Nicaraguan refugees outside of their country. It also would have authorized an unspecified amount of economic aid to help implement a regional peace treaty, and would have extended indefinitely the Boland ban on aid to Nicaragua military operations.

Senate Committee Action

The Senate Appropriations Committee June 13 by voice vote approved as its version of HR 2577 (S Rept 99-82), a $13.47 billion measure that included $38 million for the contras.

The committee provided $63.1 million for new water projects, compared with $71.85 million in the House bill.

The bills agreed on the largest items, such as farm price support programs, Social Security and economic aid for Israel and Egypt.

The committee's Nicaraguan aid provision, identical to what the Senate had added June 6 to the State Department authorization (S 1003 — S Rept 99-39), was adopted by the panel, 11-8, as an amendment sponsored by Ted Stevens, R-Alaska. *(Story p. 61)*

The bill provided $14 million in fiscal 1985 and $24 million in fiscal 1986 for non-military aid to the contras.

The panel's 25 water projects were the same ones that had been approved by the Senate in 1984 as part of the continuing appropriations bill (H J Res 648 — PL 98-473) but removed prior to enactment because of a veto threat.

All were among the 66 projects originally included in HR 2577 that were deleted on the House floor. Eleven of the Senate projects had not been authorized; 10 were requested by the administration.

The Senate panel, led by Chairman Mark O. Hatfield, R-Ore., had been negotiating with the OMB on cost-sharing by states and other procedural reforms in the construction of large water projects.

The bill provided that money could not be spent until cost-sharing agreements had been reached and submitted to Congress. But the administration did not agree to support the projects, Hatfield said, and he vowed to fight to retain the projects.

House, Senate Panel Differences

Major differences in the House and Senate committee bills were:

- The Senate panel allowed the deferral of $827 million for oil purchases for the Strategic Petroleum Reserve.
- The committee added $148 million for vocational education to implement changes made in 1984 (PL 98-524). *(1984 Almanac p. 455)*
- It added $126 million for the National Oceanic and Atmospheric Administration to begin commercialization of land-remote sensing satellites, as mandated in 1984 (PL 98-365). *(1984 Almanac p. 195)*
- Senators increased by $71.8 million the $40 million the House included to combat drug trafficking.
- The committee objected to a House provision that would prevent shipowners from repaying construction subsidies in order to serve domestic routes.
- Panel members required the Defense Department to fund $307 million more than the House from existing appropriations for pay increases.
- The House bill included $44 million for veterans' readjustment benefits, while the committee bill did not.
- The Senate committee approved a $40 million deferral for fossil energy research programs; the House approved only $9 million in deferrals.
- The panel included $10 million for additional U.S. attorneys and marshals; the House did not.
- Senators provided $14 million for the District of Columbia; HR 2577 included no funds. The money was for criminal justice activities.

Senate Floor Action

After agreeing by voice vote to add $250 million in economic aid for Jordan that the administration had requested June 13, the Senate June 20 by voice vote passed the bill providing $13.93 billion in supplemental appropriations for fiscal 1985. The Senate began consideration June 19.

Despite including items that the administration eagerly sought, such as the aid to Nicaraguan rebels, the Senate proceeded under a veto threat, delivered June 17 to Majority Leader Robert Dole, R-Kan., by OMB Director Stockman.

The administration continued to object to the funds for water projects, and negotiations between Stockman and Senate leaders went on in the Capitol while the bill was debated June 19-20.

The matter was not resolved until June 21, after the bill was passed, when a colloquy on the floor set out agreements reached by the administration and key senators on the federal share of water project costs.

Major differences between the House and Senate bills included whether aid for anti-government contras in Nicaragua should be handled by the CIA; the Senate's addition of aid for Jordan, which faced significant House opposition; and $827 million for the Strategic Petroleum Reserve, which the Senate deferred but the House did not.

Jordan Aid Approved

The Jordan aid provoked little controversy after senators watered down the administration's proposal. *(Story, p. 93)*

Instead of providing $100 million in cash and spreading the total over 15 months as requested, the Senate provided no cash and spread the payments over 27 months. Also, it required periodic reports from the administration on the progress of peace in the Middle East before the next installment could be released.

The aid would be in the form of credits to buy commodities ($50 million each in fiscal 1985 and 1986, $60 million in 1987) and in assistance for specific public works projects ($30 million each year). Senators were leery of providing cash because they said it might be used to purchase arms for use against Israel.

The bill also stated that Congress would consider major military aid for Jordan only after that country resumed direct negotiations with Israel.

The assistance was added by voice vote on amendments by Richard G. Lugar, R-Ind., to authorize the funds and Bob Kasten, R-Wis., to appropriate them.

The only debate came on an amendment by Dennis DeConcini, D-Ariz., declaring that it was the sense of the Senate that Jordan would receive new military aid only after signing a peace treaty with Israel. It was killed by a vote of 84-9. *(Vote 132, p. 27-S)*

DeConcini said he feared the administration's request would commit the nation to billions in future aid without assurances from Jordan that it would make peace with Israel.

Opponents said the provision would show too much mistrust in the moves of King Hussein toward negotiations with Israel. "I don't think we want to humiliate the king — I would wish we would encourage him," said John H. Chafee, R-R.I.

Water Projects

The controversy with the administration over the water projects took place entirely behind the scenes, with no floor debate on the subject.

In an attempt to mollify administration concerns, the bill prohibited any federal money from being spent until a cost-sharing agreement had been reached between the administration and state officals. OMB feared, however, that the requirement could be lifted in the future, congressional aides said. An even greater concern, they said, was to keep the pressure on the authorizing committees to include cost-sharing and user fees in the larger omnibus authorization (S 366) that was pending.

An amendment by Appropriations Committee Chairman Hatfield to restrict the funding was adopted June 19 by voice vote. It required cost-sharing agreements to be submitted to Congress by June 30, 1986, or the funding would lapse. That was thought to exert additional pressure on state and local sponsors to reach agreements quickly.

That satisfied OMB on HR 2577, but Stockman refused to lift the veto threat until key Senate Republicans agreed to include specific reforms on cost-sharing in the pending water-project authorizations.

That group included Robert T. Stafford, R-Vt., chairman of the Environment and Public Works Committee; James Abdnor, R-S.D., chairman of its Water Resources Subcommittee; Hatfield; John C. Danforth, R-Mo., chairman of the Commerce, Science and Transportation Committee; Bob Packwood, R-Ore., chairman of the Finance Committee; and senators with major projects in their states.

Danforth, the last holdout, opposed fee increases for the use of inland waterways. But after accepting an increase, he said, "There's a great feeling of relief that an agreement will be made after years of stalemate."

Compromise With Administration

The following plan was agreed to by OMB and key senators that was to be included in future authorizations, according to OMB. The figures were a substantial increase in the costs borne by local and state governments or financed by fees paid by users:

- **Ports:** For operations and maintenance, a new tax of .04 percent on the value of exports and imports, to pay for 30 to 40 percent of a project.

For dredging depths up to 20 feet, local governments would pay 10 percent in advance and 10 percent over a period of years. For depths from 20 to 45 feet, the local share would be 25 percent up front and 10 percent amortized. For depths over 45 feet, the local share would be 50 percent in advance, 10 percent amortized.

- **Inland Waterways:** The diesel fuel tax would go from the current 8 cents per gallon to 10 cents in 1986, with an additional 1-cent-per-year increase for the next 10 years. That would fund 50 percent of the cost.
- **Dams:** The local share would be allocated as follows: hydropower, municipal and industrial water, 100 percent; irrigation (Army Corps of Engineers projects), 35 percent; recreation, 50 percent; beach erosion control, 35 50 percent; flood control, 25-35 percent; new project feasibility studies, 50 percent.

Concern With Spies, Hijackings

Controversies over an alleged spy ring within the Navy and the hijacking of Trans World Airlines flight 847 in the Middle East triggered a flurry of amendments dealing with national security.

The most controversial was by Minority Leader Robert C. Byrd, D-W.Va., to establish a high-level commission on espionage and security. The amendment, identical to legislation (S J Res 148) introduced June 17, would have included a former defense secretary, director of the CIA and national security adviser on a panel to examine classification procedures and security clearances.

The administration said the commission was unnecessary. Also, members of the Select Intelligence Committee contended that it would infringe on their responsibility.

It was rejected June 20, 48-50, on a vote that broke mostly along party lines. *(Vote 130, p. 27-S)*

With little discussion, the Senate later accepted by voice vote an amendment by Dave Durenberger, R-Minn., to add $50 million for the CIA to take countermeasures against spying at overseas embassies.

Also accepted by voice vote June 19 was an amendment by Thad Cochran, R-Miss., to provide $2 million to the Federal Aviation Administration for aviation security.

Other Amendments

Other amendments accepted by voice vote included those by:

- James A. McClure, R-Idaho, to require the Bureau of

Land Management of the Department of the Interior and the Agriculture Department's Forest Service to submit a request to Congress to implement a proposed exchange of about 34 million acres. It would prohibit any exchange in Arizona, New Mexico, Montana, Wyoming, Oregon or North Dakota.

The administration had proposed that the agencies swap isolated tracts to consolidate holdings, but some Westerners feared that they might lose services in the exchange.

- Lawton Chiles, D-Fla., to bar the Soviet Union from using its new embassy in Washington until it reimbursed the United States for delays it allegedly caused in the construction of a new U.S. embassy in Moscow.
- Daniel J. Evans, R-Wash., to bar the Federal Energy Regulatory Commission from imposing fees on hydroelectric plants that had contracts allowing the utility to keep all revenues.

The provision was similar to legislation (S 1132 — S Rept 98-363) that passed the Senate in 1984 but never made it to the House floor.

- Albert Gore Jr., D-Tenn., to set up an organ transplant network that Congress created in 1984 (PL 98-507). *(1984 Almanac p. 476)*
- Alan J. Dixon, D-Ill., to add $110 million for an emergency food and shelter program to be run by the Federal Emergency Management Agency.
- Jesse Helms, R-N.C., to expand a ban on U.S. aid to population assistance programs that supported forced abortion to include involuntary sterilization.

Skirting Controversies

Several potentially divisive amendments were disposed of quickly in the debate.

Helms offered an amendment to bar the president from dismantling missiles or submarines to comply with the unratified SALT II treaty. But it was killed June 19, by 79-17, after senators argued that such decisions should rest with the president. *(Vote 129, p. 26-S)*

Another Helms amendment permitting states to carry some funds for the feeding program for women, infants and children (WIC) over to the next fiscal year was rejected June 20, 40-58. Critics argued that states should not be encouraged to withhold benefits from needy people. *(Vote 131, p. 27-S)*

Conference Action

While the Senate named conferees immediately after passing the bill, the House, wary of Senate positions on contra aid, economic assistance to Jordan and water project financing, balked.

Congress recessed for the Fourth of July with no further action on the supplemental funding bill.

Hatfield said the major stumbling block to agreement appeared to be whether aid for the contras would be handled by the CIA, as the Senate proposed, or by other agencies, as the House required.

But staff aides said that Whitten also was not happy with the Senate's prohibiting any federal money from being spent on water projects until a cost-sharing agreement had been reached between the administration and state sponsors.

Also, as a condition to removing a presidential veto threat, Senate leaders agreed to specific cost-sharing requirements for future projects.

Nicaraguan Aid

After several hours of sporadic negotiations July 26, senators agreed to accept both the House dollar amount of $27 million for the contras and its method of distributing the funds through any agency, other than the CIA or Defense Department.

Sen. Stevens, chairman of the Appropriations Subcommittee on Defense, argued that certain regulations, from which the CIA and Defense Department were exempt, would prevent aid from being distributed promptly to the contras by other agencies. He cited, for example, restrictions on the employment of foreign nationals and regulations requiring competitive bidding.

Stevens proposed allowing the president to exempt other government agencies, such as the State Department, from those regulations for purposes of distributing aid.

But House leaders said such a proposal was too vague.

"The CIA wants to get their fingers in this any way it can," said Joseph P. Addabbo, D-N.Y., chairman of the House Appropriations Subcommittee on Defense.

"That's what this [the Senate's] language is trying to do, get them indirectly involved," he said.

Stevens said the Senate backed down because the president might already have the authority to make the exemptions and because fighting the issue out on the House and Senate floors, a tactic that House conferees suggested, would have left the measure open to a variety of controversial amendments.

"I think the president won on the vote in the House, and there's no reason to endanger that victory," Stevens said.

Conferees July 26 also agreed that funding would be available for water projects only if a cost-sharing agreement was worked out by June 30, 1986, unless an omnibus authorization bill containing cost-sharing agreements was enacted in the meantime.

They provided $48.8 million for 41 projects of the Army Corps of Engineers and $14.3 million for four projects of the Interior Department's Bureau of Reclamation.

Other Issues

The conference agreement called for oil purchases to continue filling the Strategic Petroleum Reserve at a reduced rate. The Senate had proposed cutting off all purchases and deferring $827 million in fiscal 1985 funds, as the administration had requested. The House had rejected the deferral.

But conferees decided that $290 million of the funds should be spent, which would buy enough oil to raise the reserve from approximately 486 million barrels to 500 million barrels.

The administration's request for $250 million in economic aid for Jordan was approved by the conference, with the condition that it be made available over three years. The Senate had spread the money over 27 months. The House passed its bill before the administration made its request.

Conferees also reached agreement on bitterly contested regulations of the Office of Personnel Management (OPM). The rule would make the pay raises and job security of 1.4 million federal workers more dependent on their performance and downgrade the importance of seniority.

The regulations, first proposed in 1983, were delayed for several years by provisions in various appropriations bills, but they went into effect July 3.

The House bill contained language blocking the regulations from taking effect, while the Senate did not include the ban. Conferees agreed to include language in the report specifying that the OPM director had promised to review and modify the regulations.

Final Action

Continued controversy over the water projects threatened the agreement. Although the House July 31 by a vote of 320-106 adopted the conference report, it rejected the water project recommendations and voted to put them on indefinite hold until authorizing legislation was enacted that would increase the share of the costs borne by users and local governments. *(Vote 251, p. 80-H)*

The Senate, after adopting the conference report by voice vote Aug. 1, added a time limitation. Its compromise put funding for the new projects on hold only until May 15, 1986, to give Congress time to enact comprehensive authorizing legislation including new cost-sharing formulas.

It sent the matter back to the House, where it was accepted by voice vote, clearing the measure for the president.

Conferees had recommended $48.8 million for 41 Army Corps of Engineers projects but stipulated that none could start unless a cost-sharing agreement between local sponsors and the administration was reached by June 30, 1986, or unless an omnibus authorization bill was enacted in the meantime.

Howard and Roe charged that if the 21 unauthorized projects included in the bill were started, the Senate would lose interest in passing a comprehensive authorization bill.

"All of you who do not have a project in this bill (HR 2577) are orphans of the storm," Roe said, warning his colleagues that members of the Appropriations committees had taken care of their own projects in the appropriations bill.

At Howard's urging, the House defeated Whitten's motion to accept the conferees' proposal, 170-258. It then approved, by a standing vote of 97-5, Howard's substitute that contained the conference agreement but added that no project could begin until a comprehensive cost-sharing law was passed. *(Vote 252, p. 80-H)*

When the amendment went back to the Senate, Hatfield objected that it would hold both authorized and unauthorized projects hostage to legislation so controversial that none had been enacted in more than a decade. He offered an amendment to suspend funding for the projects only until May 15, 1986. He said that would give the authorizing committees time to enact their measures. It was approved by voice vote.

If the legislation was not enacted, the projects could start — but only if cost-sharing agreements were worked out by June 30 and sent to Congress. Committee aides said that even if the funds lapsed because no agreement was reached, the projects would still be considered as authorized and could start if other funds were appropriated.

Senators accepted Hatfield's proposal by voice vote, and after House leaders said key senators had promised to push to pass an authorizing bill, the House agreed.

In the only other conflict, the Senate agreed to rescind $7.5 million from a seat-belt education program of the Department of Transportation (DOT). That replaced a provision that would have required DOT to rule on whether state mandatory seat-belt usage laws met criteria that would allow automakers to avoid installing either air bags or automatic seat belts if enough states passed such laws, under DOT regulations adopted in 1984. *(1984 Almanac p. 295)* ▮

District Funding

Fiscal 1986 federal funding for the District of Columbia was included in the omnibus continuing appropriations resolution (H J Res 465 — PL 99-190). *(Story, p. 360)*

The regular District appropriations bill (HR 3067) had passed both chambers, and House and Senate negotiators worked out details in conference. The provisions in the conference report (H Rept 99-419) were incorporated into the continuing resolution.

The measure provided $546.8 million in federal funds for the District of Columbia, slightly less than the $550 million approved by the Senate Nov. 7, but almost $15 million more than voted by the House July 30 and sought by the Reagan administration. The measure also called for the expenditure of $2.7 billion in District funds.

Before reaching agreement Dec. 5, conferees, with little debate, decided to drop a House-passed abortion restriction.

The House had voted 221-199 to bar the District from using any funds provided in the bill — either federal or local — to pay for abortions. The Senate twice refused to accept that restriction, leaving in place existing law, which prohibited the use of federal funds to pay for abortions, except when the life of the mother was in danger or in cases of rape or incest. *(Vote 247, p. 78-H)*

When the abortion issue came up in conference, Rep. Julian C. Dixon, D-Calif., chairman of the Appropriations Subcommittee on the District, noted that the House vote had been close and added that he personally supported the Senate position.

The federal appropriation included $425 million to compensate the District for expenses caused by the presence of the U.S. government, such as lost tax revenue. Also, the bill provided $52 million for police, firefighters', teachers' and judges' retirement funds, $30.1 million for water and sewer services to federal facilities and $25 million for St. Elizabeths Hospital.

Conferees accepted $10 million the Senate had added to help pay for a new D.C. prison but required local officials to notify Congress of construction plans before the funds would be available.

Also accepted was a Senate provision for $500,000 for a job training program, but conferees approved only half of the $6.7 million the Senate had added for criminal justice initiatives.

Legislative History

House. The House Appropriations Committee reported HR 3067 July 24 (H Rept 99-223). The House passed the measure July 30 after voting to expand restrictions on taxpayer-funded abortions in the District of Columbia.

House members adopted, by a 221-199 vote, an amendment by Christopher H. Smith, R-N.J., barring the District from using local or U.S. funds to pay for any abortions. The bill was passed, 242-173. *(Vote 248, p. 80-H)*

The bill provided $532.2 million in federal funds and called for $2.7 billion in District funds for fiscal 1986.

Since 1980, Congress had barred the use of federal funds for abortions in the District, except where the life of the mother was in danger or in cases of rape or incest. Smith extended the ban to all abortions and included District funds as well. He said that in fiscal 1983, the last year for which he had statistics, the District paid for 4,393 abortions.

But Dixon, chairman of the Appropriations Subcommittee on the District, said the amendment undermined the District's authority to govern itself.

Senate. The next day, July 31, the Senate Appropriations Committee rejected the House abortion language and voted to continue the existing ban. The panel then approved the spending bill, which was officially reported Sept. 9 (S Rept 99-134).

On Nov. 7, after rejecting two attempts to restrict abortions, the Senate passed HR 3067 by a vote of 80-14. The measure provided $550 million in federal funds. *(Vote 292, p. 51-S)*

Jesse Helms, R-N.C., moved to table (kill) the Appropriations Committee's abortion amendment, which would have had the effect of reinstating the language contained in the House-passed version.

Howard M. Metzenbaum, D-Ohio, threatened to filibuster the bill if Helms' motion carried. However, it failed, 35-60. *(Vote 290, p. 51-S)*

Then an amendment by Gordon J. Humphrey, R-N.H., prohibiting the use of federal and local funds for abortions, except to save the life of the mother, was tabled, 54-41. *(Vote 291, p. 51-S)*

$368.2 Billion Omnibus Spending Bill Cleared

Overcoming a brief House rebellion and fights over defense spending and senators' honoraria, Congress Dec. 19 cleared a $368.2 billion fiscal 1986 appropriations bill (H J Res 465 — PL 99-190) to keep the government running until Sept. 30, 1986, the end of the fiscal year.

The House approved the conference report on the continuing resolution (H Rept 99-450) by a vote of 261-137; the Senate, by voice vote. *(Vote 433, p. 136-H)*

President Reagan signed the measure the evening of Dec. 19. A short-term catchall funding bill (H J Res 491 — PL 99-184) — the fourth since the start of fiscal 1986 — expired at midnight that day. Congress adjourned Dec. 20. *(Short-term continuing resolutions, box, p. 361)*

H J Res 465 was reported by the House Appropriations Committee Nov. 21. It passed the House Dec. 4 and was reported by the Senate Appropriations Committee the next day. It passed the Senate Dec. 10, and conferees reached agreement Dec. 16.

However, House members, angry about defense and other provisions and about the way the measure was handled, rejected the conference report in a night session, and conferees had to go back to the drawing board.

In its final form, H J Res 465 contained funding for programs covered by seven regular fiscal 1986 appropriations that were not enacted in 1985: Agriculture, Defense, Interior, Transportation, Treasury-Postal Service, foreign aid, and the District of Columbia. It also included some supplemental funding for all the other appropriations bills except military construction. *(Status of appropriations chart, p. 316)*

The largest portion of the bill was $281.2 billion in new spending authority for the Defense Department — $1.3 billion less than the conferees originally agreed to. The bill barred anti-satellite (ASAT) testing for a year as long as the Soviet Union did not test such a weapon; allowed $27.1 million for production of chemical weapons and $2.75 billion for Reagan's "strategic defense initiative" (SDI), and included some reform of Pentagon procurement procedures. *(Defense appropriations, p. 377)*

The measure also shut down the five-year-old Synthetic Fuels Corporation and funded a "clean coal" technology program instead.

It allowed senators to accept an extra $7,500 in honoraria for speeches and articles — 40 percent of their $75,100 salaries instead of the existing 30 percent, and extended until April 30, 1986, the deadline for enacting a new retirement system for federal workers. *(Story, p. 34)*

The final bill contained $5.9 billion less than spending for comparable programs in fiscal 1985, and $18.4 billion less than the president had requested.

Although the administration had said both the House and Senate versions of H J Res 465 were unacceptably expensive, Reagan's approval of the conference report was assured before it went to the House and Senate floors.

The administration, principally through the Office of Management and Budget (OMB), was an unseen partner during negotiations over the bill. Senate Appropriations Committee Chairman Mark O. Hatfield, R-Ore., was in constant contact with OMB Director James C. Miller III or White House Chief of Staff Donald T. Regan about where the administration stood each step of the way.

In fact, it was Regan who telephoned final instructions to Hatfield the afternoon of Dec. 18, telling him the White House would accept a $1.3 billion trim in defense spending if conferees would cut $300 million from domestic programs.

Those reductions came from a $50 million trim in the Coast Guard's capital account and .6 percent across-the-board cuts in discretionary funding in the Agriculture Department, saving $200 million, and in the Interior Department, saving $50 million.

Gone from the final version of H J Res 465 was controversial language that would have restricted exports of nuclear material to China; a provision requiring the Agriculture Department to help financially pressed farmers; and a section to beef up penalties against states that refused to raise their drinking age to 21. *(China, p. 110)*

The bill also contained no new abortion restrictions, although it once had been targeted for a fight over abortion and family-planning services.

Provisions

Following were the fiscal 1986 funding levels and highlights of H J Res 465:

Agriculture — $36.34 billion.

- Provided $9.1 billion for the Commodity Credit Corporation, which made crop loans and income-support payments to farmers; also made another $400 million available if the administration requested it.
- Provided $11.8 billion for food stamps, about the fiscal 1985 level. *(Story, p. 395)*

Defense — $281.16 billion.

- Provided $2.75 billion for the "strategic defense initia-

Four Short-Term Stopgap Funding Bills Needed

Four temporary continuing appropriations resolutions were needed in 1985, to continue government funding until the long-term "omnibus" spending bill (H J Res 465 — PL 99-190) or regular fiscal 1986 spending bills could be enacted. *(Omnibus bill, p. 360)*

H J Res 388 (PL 99-103) extended spending authority for 45 days, from Sept. 30, the end of fiscal 1985, to Nov. 14. None of the 13 fiscal 1986 appropriations bills had been enacted by the beginning of the new fiscal year. *(Status of appropriations, p. 316)*

The House Appropriations Committee reported H J Res 388 Sept. 17 (S Rept 99-272). Members had approved it by voice vote Sept. 12 after agreeing not to load it down with costly or controversial amendments.

The resolution continued funding for federal agencies as follows: If by Oct. 1 both the House and Senate had passed an appropriations bill, a program's funding would be the lower of the two levels. If only the House had passed a bill, funding would be as provided in that bill or the 1985 spending level, whichever was lower. If no bill had passed, funding would be at the 1985 level.

The measure continued all existing limitations on the use of appropriated funds, such as limits on abortion and school prayer. It barred the start of any new weapons production lines and set a 50-missile cap on MX missile production, as agreed to in the conference version of the defense authorization bill (S 1160). Norman D. Dicks, D-Wash., withdrew his amendment for a moratorium on testing of anti-satellite (ASAT) missiles.

The House passed H J Res 388 Sept. 18 by a vote of 272-156. *(Vote 279, p. 90-H)*

The Senate Appropriations Committee reported H J Res 388 Sept. 24 (S Rept 99-142), and the Senate passed it Sept. 25 by voice vote, with only a handful of members present. President Reagan signed it Sept. 30.

H J Res 441 (PL 99-154) continued government spending authority for another month, until midnight Dec. 12, at the same levels and conditions as H J Res 388. The House passed it, 259-151, Nov. 12, and the Senate followed suit by voice vote Nov. 13. Reagan signed it Nov. 14. Only two regular fiscal 1986 funding bills had been enacted by then. *(Vote 365, p. 114-H)*

What had been billed as a cost-cutting fight between Republicans and Democrats evaporated into harmony instead. Members of both parties attributed the measure's smooth sailing to the forthcoming Nov. 19-20 Geneva summit meeting between President Reagan and Soviet leader Mikhail S. Gorbachev. Neither Congress nor the White House, they said, wanted Reagan to go to Geneva in the midst of a domestic fiscal crisis.

House members had expected H J Res 441 to be the vehicle for a rough-and-tumble debate about trimming federal spending. But just as discussion got under way, House leaders received a letter from the White House urging them to pass a simple extension of H J Res 388. The White House said it opposed any amendments to the new bill beyond extending its date from Dec. 5, which was in an early draft, to Dec. 12.

Democratic Whip Thomas S. Foley, Wash., had planned to offer an amendment cutting spending levels across the board by 3.8 percent, which the Congressional Budget Office (CBO) said would reduce the projected fiscal 1986 deficit to $161 billion. Disputing CBO's figure, Minority Leader Robert H. Michel, R-Ill., planned to push for an 8.2 percent cut. But after Majority Leader Jim Wright, D-Texas, read the White House letter on the floor, Foley and Michel dropped their plans.

The $161 billion figure was the fiscal 1986 deficit target set in the House version of the so-called "Gramm-Rudman-Hollings" bill requiring a balanced federal budget by October 1990 (H J Res 372). *(Story, p. 459)*

The White House letter appeared to catch members off guard, and some Republicans were unhappy at the turn of events. "People were just surprised," said Dan Lungren, R-Calif. "We were ready for a big fight."

Wright said the Democrats were willing to back off after the White House, in effect, cried a brief "uncle" in the spending fight. The letter, he said, should temporarily protect Democrats from criticism of their fiscal program "if this is a universe of mutual trust."

H J Res 476 (PL 99-179) extended government funding authority for four more days, until 6 p.m. Dec. 16. It was hastily cleared by Congress to give itself temporary relief from a fiscal crisis while conferees continued work on the long-term continuing resolution, H J Res 465. H J Res 476 passed both the House and Senate by voice vote Dec. 12 and was signed into law Dec. 13.

H J Res 491 (PL 99-184) was passed Dec. 17, the day after H J Res 476 expired. It continued federal funding authority until midnight Dec. 19. By that time, the omnibus spending bill had been signed into law.

After the House rejected the first conference report on the omnibus bill, Appropriations Committee Chairman Jamie L. Whitten, D-Miss., tried to get unanimous consent to extend H J Res 476, but he was unable to do so. So the Rules Committee met at 12:45 a.m. Dec. 17 and adopted a rule for another temporary bill to last until Dec. 19.

That bill (H J Res 491) was passed by the House the morning of Dec. 17, 334-74, and by the Senate later in the day by voice vote. President Reagan signed it the same day. *(Vote 423, p. 134-H)*

tive" and $21.7 million for production of a new type of nerve gas artillery shell.

- Banned further tests of anti-satellite missiles as long as the Soviet Union did not test any.
- Barred defense contractors from billing the Pentagon for entertainment, lobbying and legal fees.
- Earmarked $6.3 billion in fiscal 1985 carry-over funds largely for military pay and retirement. *(Story, p. 377)*

Foreign Aid — $15.03 billion.

- Cut or held to fiscal 1985 levels funding for most economic, military and development aid programs.
- Set a $55 million limit on aid to the Philippines. *(Story, p. 367)*

Interior — $8.1 billion.

- Deleted funding for the Synthetic Fuels Corporation, except for $10 million in shut-down costs.

• Added $400 million for a "clean coal" technology program. *(Story, p. 337)*

Transportation — $10.46 billion.

• Continued funding for mass transit and Amtrak at close to 1985 levels.

• Restored funds for air safety and the Coast Guard. *(Story, p. 342)*

District of Columbia — $546.8 million. *(Story, p. 359)*

Treasury/Postal Service — $13.037 billion.

• Cut $45 million from funding for the Internal Revenue Service and $72 million from the federal postal subsidy to overcome objections that had led to a veto of the regular funding bill. *(Story, p. 329)*

Although regular fiscal 1986 spending bills had been enacted for the other departments of the government, some provisions affecting them were included in H J Res 465:

Commerce/Justice/State: Added $42.9 million, including $12 million for the Bicentennial of the Constitution Commission, $24 million for Economic Development Administration projects and $2.5 million for the U.S. Information Agency. *(Regular funding bill, p. 346)*

Housing and Urban Development and Independent Agencies: Added $2.4 billion for Environmental Protection Agency sewer construction grants. *(Regular funding bill, p. 317)*

Labor/Health and Human Services/Education: Added $616.2 million, including $142.5 million for family-planning services and $428 million for refugee assistance. *(Regular funding bill, p. 333)*

Legislative Branch: Increased senators' honoraria limit to $30,000 a year, from $22,500, and added $150,000 for a biomedical ethics board and biomedical ethics advisory committee. *(Regular funding bill, p. 326)*

House Committee Action

The House Appropriations Committee reported H J Res 465 Nov. 21 (H Rept 99-403). Approved by voice vote, the bill contained $480 billion for agencies covered by 10 of the 13 regular funding bills that had not been enacted.

As of Nov. 21, the president had signed only two (for energy and water projects and the legislative branch), and had vetoed one, for the Treasury and Postal Service. H J Res 465 included the Treasury-Postal bill and nine others.

Appropriations Chairman Jamie L. Whitten, D-Miss., and ranking Republican Silvio O. Conte, Mass., urged members not to encumber the resolution with miscellaneous projects, and in large part they succeeded.

During markup, the panel refused by one vote to extend a four-year-old moratorium on oil drilling off the California coast and adopted compromise language to make clear that federal family planning funds could not be used to provide or "advocate" abortions.

Oil Drilling Moratorium

The committee rejected — 26-27 — an amendment by Sidney R. Yates, D-Ill., that sought to extend the moratorium on oil and gas drilling off parts of the California coast. The moratorium was due to expire Dec. 12.

The committee's action was a blow to a majority of the California delegation and environmental groups seeking to control offshore drilling. For four years, Congress had included a California drilling ban in Interior appropriations bills. In July, California members opposed to offshore drilling thought they had worked out an agreement with Interior Secretary Donald P. Hodel to allow drilling on 150 of 6,460 tracts, or areas of ocean floor, where drilling was banned. However, in September Hodel said he could not abide by the agreement, which he characterized as tentative. His move angered the Californians and prompted them to seek a continued moratorium. *(Story, p. 208)*

Yates, chairman of the Interior Appropriations subcommittee, said his amendment was necessary to "keep faith with members of the California delegation."

But Ralph Regula, Ohio, ranking subcommittee Republican, and members from Louisiana and Texas, where there already was offshore drilling, vigorously opposed it. Regula said the moratorium could hurt the country's long-range interests. Even if it were lifted, no drilling would begin for probably eight years; to delay it even further could subject the country to an oil shortage, "OPEC blackmail" and "gas lines in the '90s," he said.

Charles Wilson, D-Texas, said California should help supply the nation with oil as other states had.

Family Planning

Jack F. Kemp, R-N.Y., offered an amendment to bar federal family planning funds from being used to provide abortions or to refer pregnant women to clinics or hospitals that performed abortions. But the committee, by a 37-16 vote, adopted a less restrictive substitute offered by Richard J. Durbin, D-Ill.

H J Res 465 provided about $142 million for family planning services under Title X of the 1970 Public Health Services Act (PL 91-572). The program provided funds to more than 5,000 clinics that dispensed family planning information and contraceptive services. The law specifically prohibited use of the money for performing abortions, but counseling and referrals for abortion were permitted.

Kemp and Sen. Orrin G. Hatch, R-Utah, claimed some clinics were encouraging pregnant women to have abortions, in violation of the law, and they sought to restrict the use of funds under the program to bar any mention of abortion in Title X clinics. *(Family planning, p. 300)*

An earlier version of Kemp's amendment would have barred funding for counseling and referrals for abortion. But the Nov. 21 version dropped the counseling prohibition and barred only referrals. Kemp said he supported Title X and the concept of family planning, but said it "should be used to prevent pregnancy, not to terminate pregnancy."

While favored by anti-abortion groups, the amendment drew strong opposition from public health officials, medical associations and family planning groups, who said it would all but destroy the family planning program.

Durbin said the amendment was unconstitutional because it abridged doctors' and health practitioners' freedom of speech. He also said it would subject doctors to malpractice suits if they failed to inform a pregnant woman of all her options, including termination of a pregnancy.

The substitute barred the use of Title X money only for providing or advocating abortions. Durbin said it was consistent with existing Title X regulations, which allowed "non-directive" counseling on abortion.

Kemp said his amendment would not bar anyone from speaking about abortion at a clinic, but only prohibited referrals, which he characterized as "encouragement" to have an abortion. Several members spoke against his proposal, including Conte, an opponent of abortion. Conte said audits of Title X had turned up no violations of the law relating to abortion, adding, "I've always said, if you're against abortion, you gotta be for something."

Foreign Aid, Farm Credit

By voice vote, the committee adopted an amendment by David R. Obey, D-Wis., authorizing $756 million over several years for international development banks, including the World Bank.

The amendment also added $38 million in economic assistance and $13 million in foreign military aid, and raised funding for migration and refugee assistance programs overseas from $292.5 million to $337 million.

The committee adopted report language saying it was "outraged" by the Oct. 8 hijacking of the *Achille Lauro,* the Italian cruise ship, and the actions of Egypt "in facilitating the efforts of the Palestinian terrorists to avoid prosecution." The panel said future funds for Egypt would depend on continued participation in peace efforts with Israel.

After brief debate, the panel agreed to language included in the bill by Whitten, directing the agriculture secretary to use his authority to help financially strapped farmers obtain loans. Whitten chaired the Agriculture Appropriations Subcommittee as well as the full committee. The language would not give the secretary any new powers, but was intended to "reinforce" his authority to provide crop loans, a committee staffer said.

House Floor Action

The House passed H J Res 465 Dec. 4 by a vote of 212-208. *(Vote 389, p. 122-H)*

Members attributed the close vote to Republicans' concern over foreign aid provisions, a potentially costly Whitten provision to help hard-pressed farmers, and the threat of a presidential veto.

The OMB had issued a statement threatening a veto on grounds the bill contained too much money for domestic spending and not enough for defense. OMB officials also said Reagan would veto any bill that exceeded congressional spending targets in any category, even if the bill's total was under the overall congressional budget ceiling.

The administration said both the House and Senate versions of H J Res 465 were $2.6 billion over budget allocations for domestic spending. The House bill was $9.7 billion below the allocation for defense and national security, while the Senate bill was $9.6 billion below, OMB said.

House sponsors of H J Res 465 disputed the administration's figures, claiming that by their accounting, the bill was $5.6 billion under the congressional budget resolution target for domestic spending and $8.4 billion under the target for defense.

Senate Appropriations Chairman Hatfield also strongly disagreed with the administration's position. He said OMB criticism was based on "convoluted reasoning," adding that it appeared administration officials were looking for a reason to veto H J Res 465 regardless of what Congress did.

Floor Debate

House consideration of H J Res 465 was brief and relatively smooth. Debate lasted only three hours, and other than the vote on final passage, the only roll call was on a motion by Conte to send the measure back to the Appropriations Committee. Conte urged the removal of the provisions directing the agriculture secretary to help financially strapped farmers obtain loans. Conte claimed the provisions could cost $10 billion.

Conte's recommittal motion was rejected 200-221. *(Vote 388, p. 122-H)*

The quick House floor action was a result of decisions the Rules Committee made the day before. Although a number of members requested the right to offer amendments, the committee heeded the request of Whitten and Conte to keep the measure free of extraneous amendments. It made in order only one proposal, a compromise worked out between Regula and Leon E. Panetta, D-Calif., on oil and gas drilling off the California coast.

Offshore Oil Compromise. The Regula-Panetta amendment, which the House adopted by voice vote, required Interior Secretary Hodel to meet with a congressional negotiating team every 60 days for the rest of fiscal 1986 to work out an agreement for drilling off the California coast. It established a 19-member committee, including members of Congress from California and from the committees with jurisdiction over oil drilling.

Panetta said the amendment was better than nothing. He said he and his supporters were not sure they had support in the Rules Committee or in the full House to continue the moratorium.

Abortion. A potentially controversial debate on abortion was defused when the Rules Committee, with the approval of key members, deleted the Durbin amendment relating to abortion and federal family planning funds.

At the Rules meeting Dec. 3, Henry J. Hyde, R-Ill., sponsor of the longstanding law that barred most federal funding for abortions, said that because of the way the amendment was worded, it could open the way for allowing federal funding for abortions. Hyde said he would prefer no new restrictions on Title X money to the Durbin language.

Durbin said he would withdraw his language if Kemp was barred from offering his amendment, and Hyde supported that move. The Rules Committee accepted the deal.

Foreign Aid. Kemp sought an open rule for debate on the foreign aid section of the bill. He said the section had not been debated by either chamber of Congress and contended the Appropriations Committee's foreign aid funding bill (HR 3228) had been approved with virtually no GOP support. *(Story, p. 367)*

Kemp's basic criticism of HR 3228, echoed by other conservative Republicans, was that it cut too much in military assistance while providing too much to economic development programs.

Rules members made clear they were not inclined to allow unlimited amendments to the foreign aid section but told Kemp he could offer a substitute section. But Obey, chairman of the Appropriations Subcommittee on Foreign Operations, said if Kemp offered a substitute, he wanted an opportunity to offer one, too.

After mulling the matter over for a few hours, Kemp withdrew his request. Aides said privately that he had been under pressure from the White House to back off. They said that if Kemp provoked a floor fight, Obey would offer an amendment to cut foreign military assistance even more, and would likely prevail.

Trent Lott, R-Miss., asked the committee to make in order an amendment providing assistance to rebels in the southern African country of Angola. Chairman Claude Pepper, D-Fla., supported Lott, but the committee rejected the proposed amendment by voice vote.

Senate Committee

The Senate Appropriations Committee reported a $498 billion version of H J Res 465 Dec. 5 (S Rept 99-210).

The panel worked its way through more than 40

amendments during a 3½-hour markup. Only a handful of them added money to the bill.

While the House and Senate bills had a number of similar provisions, there were important differences in key sections, particularly defense, foreign aid and Interior.

For defense, the Senate committee bill exceeded the House-passed version by about $13.8 billion. The Senate provided $2.96 billion of Reagan's request of $3.7 billion for the SDI, or "star wars," program, while the House provided $2.5 billion. And unlike the House bill, the Senate measure allowed continued ASAT testing.

For foreign aid, the Senate panel provided $15.8 billion, about $1.2 billion more than the House. The two versions also had sharply conflicting priorities in allocating military and economic aid; the House bill gave greater weight to economic aid while the Senate bill put more of its resources into military assistance. The Senate bill provided $70 million in military aid for the troubled government of Philippine President Ferdinand E. Marcos; the House version provided $25 million.

Policy differences also were reflected in funding for the Interior Department. While the House voted to kill the synfuels corporation, James A. McClure, R-Idaho, chairman of the Senate Interior Appropriations Subcommittee, battled to save it. He inserted provisions in H J Res 465 to restructure the program, cutting it from $7.9 billion to about $5.9 billion.

The Senate panel also added $2.4 billion for construction grants for the Environmental Protection Agency, which the president had requested in his budget.

It accepted the House's offshore oil drilling compromise, and concurred with the House Rules Committee decision to drop any new abortion language from the bill.

Foreign Aid. The most significant changes came in foreign aid, where the Appropriations Subcommittee on Foreign Operations was in serious disagreement with the administration and the Foreign Relations Committee.

Subcommittee Chairman Bob Kasten, R-Wis., backed by ranking Democrat Daniel K. Inouye of Hawaii, had inserted a provision in the foreign aid appropriations bill approved by the committee (S 1816) that gave Israel about $500 million in special military benefits. During markup of H J Res 465, Kasten said he had met with Secretary of State George P. Shultz, who vigorously opposed the provision, and had agreed to delete it.

Kasten offered an amendment, adopted by voice vote, taking out the Israel money and making changes in funding for the International Development Association (IDA) and the Export-Import Bank. The amendment put a ceiling of $375 million on U.S. contributions to IDA and limited to $1.8 billion the amount of direct loans by the United States to the Ex-Im Bank. The funding for the bank was about half as much as the administration requested, and less than half the $3.9 billion available to the bank in fiscal 1985.

Another Kasten amendment made several changes to conform the foreign aid appropriation to the foreign aid authorization bill (PL 99-83). Foreign Relations Chairman Richard G. Lugar, R-Ind., had objected to an Appropriations Committee provision that would have overridden several items in the authorizing legislation. *(Foreign aid authorization, p. 41)*

Agriculture. The committee deleted the Whitten provisions in the House version of H J Res 465 aimed at helping financially strapped farmers. Agriculture Appropriations Subcommittee Chairman Thad Cochran, R-Miss., said the provisions were unnecessary because a farm bill under consideration in a conference committee (HR 2100) addressed the issue. *(HR 2100, p. 517)*

At the request of Robert C. Byrd, D-W.Va., the committee added $40 million for the Soil Conservation Service, to help restore areas in West Virginia and elsewhere destroyed by recent flooding.

Commerce, Justice, State. The committee adopted an amendment by Ted Stevens, R-Alaska, adding $20 million for the Commission on the Bicentennial of the Constitution. Stevens said the money was requested by Chief Justice Warren E. Burger, the commission chairman. Congress appropriated $331,000 for the commission in fiscal 1985, but most of the money for the group's activities was expected to be raised from the private sector. Stevens said the private sector would not contribute funds until Congress appropriated more money. *(Story, p. 346)*

By voice vote, the committee accepted an amendment by Alfonse M. D'Amato, R-N.Y., to clarify a provision in anti-crime legislation enacted in 1984 (PL 98-473). The amendment made clear that a mandatory five-year prison sentence for possession of a gun during a crime applied to defendants convicted of major drug offenses. A federal court had said the 1984 law was not explicit on whether the law covered drug crimes. *(1984 Almanac p. 215)*

Defense. The committee adopted an amendment by J. Bennett Johnston, D-La., requiring the Senate and House Armed Services committees to revise the military retirement system. They would have to act before May 1, 1986, to avert substantial cuts in military personnel.

Congress, in the fiscal 1986 defense authorization bill (PL 99-145), put a cap on the amount of money that could be spent for military personnel. Since retirement pay had to be given to all military personnel who qualified, in the absence of legislation limiting such payments the only way to stay within the spending limitation would be to cut military personnel. *(Defense authorization, p. 138)*

Veterans. In the only roll call of the markup, the committee by a 15-11 vote adopted an amendment by Dennis DeConcini, D-Ariz., providing $55 million for emergency job training, primarily for Vietnam veterans. The Senate had passed a bill (S 1887) Dec. 2 reauthorizing the program for one year. *(Story, p. 408)*

Other Amendments. In an effort to meet OMB objections, the committee without debate made changes in the Transportation and Treasury-Postal provisions.

The administration had complained that both chambers' transportation funding bills included too much money for Amtrak and mass transit and not enough for the Federal Aviation Administration (FAA) and Coast Guard. The committee restored $300 million the Senate had cut from the FAA and put back $167 million of the $200 million that was trimmed from the Coast Guard account.

To meet Reagan's objections in the vetoed Treasury-Postal bill, the committee cut $162.1 million, including $72 million in Postal Service subsidies. The other cuts were in funds for the Internal Revenue Service, although the committee said it was acting only because of White House pressure and "wishes to stress that these reductions are not necessarily in the best interests of the nation."

Senate Floor Action

The Senate passed H J Res 465 Dec. 10 by voice vote, after debating it Dec. 6, 9 and 10.

Hatfield had pleaded with his colleagues to withhold extraneous amendments and pass the bill Dec. 6. Lengthy debate would almost assure that Congress would be in session until Christmas, he said, adding that it was "an action of futility" to load the bill with amendments because "we are not really building a signable resolution."

About 50 amendments were considered, but many were technical, and only a handful of generally non-controversial proposals were adopted.

The most troublesome amendment for Senate sponsors was the one that sought to put limits on nuclear exports to China. It was agreed to Dec. 9 by voice vote, after opponents failed by a vote of 28-59 to table it. *(Vote 356, p. 61-S)*

Amendment sponsor John Glenn, D-Ohio, claimed an agreement negotiated between the United States and the People's Republic of China for exporting nuclear materials did not contain enough safeguards to "ensure peaceful uses of U.S. nuclear exports." His amendment added new conditions to the pact designed to make sure that China followed international practices for handling nuclear materials.

Opponents said the language was unnecessary and could undermine a useful agreement.

On another controversial issue, the Senate by a three-vote margin Dec. 6 rejected an amendment by Howard M. Metzenbaum, D-Ohio, and Daniel J. Evans, R-Wash., to kill funding for the Synthetic Fuels Corporation. The vote was 40-43. *(Vote 355, p. 61-S))*

Agreement on a package of defense amendments, which resolved differences between the Appropriations and Armed Services Committees, removed one of the biggest obstacles to Senate passage of the bill.

The Appropriations Subcommittee on Defense, led by Stevens, had provided $7.3 billion for defense programs that had not been authorized by Armed Services. Armed Services members, angry that their turf had been invaded, threatened to hold up the bill because of the appropriation.

After two days of negotiations, Stevens and key Armed Services members reached an agreement. In essence, they left the $7.3 billion in the bill but provided that nearly half of it must be explicitly approved by Armed Services before it could be spent.

Amendments Adopted

Amendments adopted by voice vote were those:

- By William S. Cohen, R-Maine, and Carl Levin, D-Mich., to clarify provisions of the 1978 Ethics in Government Act (PL 95-521) covering financial disclosure for executive branch employees. The amendment authorized the president to require officers and employees in the executive branch to file confidential financial disclosure reports. This would be in addition to public financial disclosure required under the 1978 law and 1982 amendments (PL 97-409). *(1978 Almanac p. 835; 1982 Almanac p. 386)*
- By Byrd, adding $3 million to speed development of a flash-flood warning system for West Virginia, Kentucky, North Carolina, Pennsylvania, Tennessee and Virginia.
- By Frank R. Lautenberg, D-N.J., to suspend a U.S. Parole Commission rule that Lautenberg said was too lenient in granting parole to persons convicted of insider trading on the stock market.

Amendments Derailed

Hatfield and his allies in both parties used a combination of procedural motions to derail many of the amendments that were offered. Rejected were those:

- By Malcolm Wallop, R-Wyo., to provide $50 million for UNITA, the rebel forces in Angola. Ruled not germane by a 39-58 vote. *(Vote 367, p. 62-S)*
- By Edward M. Kennedy, D-Mass., to postpone an automatic increase scheduled for Jan. 1, 1986, in the deductible for hospital care of Medicare patients. The amendment also would have raised the cigarette tax 1 cent a pack for three years to avoid an increase in the deficit from the Medicare proposal. Kennedy's appeal of a ruling by the chair that his amendment was out of order was tabled, 53-37. *(Vote 357, p. 61-S)*
- By John Heinz, R-Pa., to put a cap of $476 on the Medicare hospital deductible. The amendment fell when the Senate, by a vote of 45-41, tabled Heinz' appeal of the ruling that his amendment was legislation on an appropriations bill, and therefore not germane. *(Vote 358, p. 61-S)*
- By John Kerry, D-Mass., to bar use of any nuclear materials in the development or testing of Reagan's SDI anti-missile research program. Tabled 64-32. *(Vote 365, p. 62-S)*

Kerry said that while Reagan described SDI as an effort to nullify nuclear missiles with "non-nuclear" means, it was well known that one approach being explored was the destruction of Soviet missiles with the X-rays produced by a nuclear explosion in outer space.

Only two Republicans joined 30 Democrats in supporting Kerry's amendment.

- By David L. Boren, D-Okla., and Charles E. Grassley, R-Iowa, to bar defense contracts for the General Dynamics Corp. and any of its subsidiaries. General Dynamics was under suspension by the Defense Department for allegedly fraudulent conduct in its dealings with the government. Ruled non-germane 19-77. *(Vote 366, p. 62-S)*
- By Gordon J. Humphrey, R-N.H., and Alan J. Dixon, D-Ill., to establish a special panel on asylum to investigate and study the problem of persons from communist countries seeking political asylum in the United States. Ruled non-germane 46-47. *(Vote 363, p. 62-S)*
- By Glenn, to delete a provision requiring military bases that bought liquor with non-appropriated funds for resale on the base to buy the liquor only from outlets in the state in which the base was located. Tabled 66-29. *(Vote 368, p. 62-S)*

Conference Action

After three days of negotiations Dec. 11-13, conferees thought they had reached a final agreement on H J Res 465. Defense and Interior conferees worked into the weekend Dec. 14-15 putting finishing touches on their sections of the bill, and presented their proposals to the full conference Dec. 16 (H Rept 99-443).

Although he had fought determinedly to save the synfuels corporation, McClure bowed to opposition from the House and the White House and agreed to the agency's termination. In exchange, conferees agreed to put $400 million into the clean-coal program, which was intended to subsidize research and development of technologies for burning coal more cleanly in industrial and utility boilers. Only $100 million would be spent in fiscal 1986, with $150 million available in each of the next two years. The administration had opposed the clean-coal program.

Conferees agreed to provide $282.5 billion in new budget authority for Defense Department programs, about $14 billion more than the House bill provided and nearly identical to the Senate proposal. They also allowed spending of an additional $6.3 billion left over from fiscal 1985.

The conferees agreed to House language barring ASAT

testing as long as the Soviet Union continued its ASAT moratorium, and to provide $2.75 billion for the SDI program. But they refused to accept any House language to tighten up defense procurement procedures.

Conferees by voice vote Dec. 16 accepted the honoraria provision worked out principally by Stevens and Fazio. The honoraria deal was in exchange for dropping a provision, inserted in the Senate bill by Joseph R. Biden Jr., D-Del., restricting members' ability to earn outside income from law practices and business enterprises.

The House had more lenient rules in this area than the Senate, and Fazio said his colleagues could not live with the provision because it would seriously disrupt many members' legitimate activities outside of Congress.

But when Stevens proposed lifting the cap on honoraria completely, Fazio said the House could not go along. They compromised on deleting the Biden provision and raising the honoraria cap to 40 percent of members' annual salary. The agreement would not immediately affect House members, however, because they were bound by a House rule adopted in 1981 setting the limit at 30 percent. To raise the cap, the House would have to alter the rule.

Conferees also agreed to drop the language restricting the export of nuclear materials to China. And after the Senate insisted on deleting the agriculture sections, Whitten agreed to give them up.

House Revolt

When the conference report came to the floor the night of Dec. 16, the Democratic leadership and conferees were surprised by the outpouring of opposition that surfaced. Most of it came from Democrats angry about the defense section, but Republicans also were unhappy. The agreement was rejected, 170-239. *(Vote 420, p. 134-H)*

Republicans voted by more than a 2-to-1 margin against the measure — 119 against, 55 for. Democrats were almost evenly split, 120 against and 115 for.

Several Republicans said they were unhappy with the bill in general and irritated about the way it was handled. They resented being kept in session so long and being pushed into voting on a broad piece of legislation with little time to study its details.

Democratic speakers, led by Barney Frank, Mass., contended conferees gave up too much to the Senate. The Democrats were especially upset about the level of new budget authority for defense, the lack of procurement reform, and funding for chemical weapons.

Several members expressed concern about the effect of the new "Gramm-Rudman-Hollings" budget-cutting law (PL 99-177), which would require across-the-board cuts in non-exempt programs, divided equally between defense and non-defense accounts. Members who wanted to preserve domestic programs were on guard for moves to give the Pentagon a "cushion" against cuts that would be required in 1986. *(Gramm-Rudman-Hollings, p. 459)*

The chemical weapons funding was a sore point even though the House, after three years of opposition, had voted in June to authorize limited production of the new weapons, called "binary munitions." The administration and the armed services insisted the new weapons were needed to replace existing arms that were ineffective and dangerous to handle because of their age.

After the conference report was rejected, Whitten tried by unanimous consent to get an extension of a short-term funding bill that had expired at 6 p.m. (H J Res 476 — PL 99-179). But he was unable to do so. Conte wanted to attach language, which Whitten opposed, barring the synfuels corporation from meeting in the next few days to award contracts for projects in Colorado and Utah.

When it became clear that no agreement could be reached, the Rules Committee hastily convened about 12:45 a.m. Dec. 17 and adopted a rule for another temporary funding bill to last until Dec. 19. That bill (H J Res 491) was passed the morning of Dec. 17, 334-74, with Conte's synfuels ban. It was later approved by the Senate by voice vote. *(Votes 422, 423, p. 134-H)*

New Conference Report

The unexpected House action left conferees no choice but to return to the bargaining table.

They did not formally reconvene Dec. 17. Instead, defense conferees led by Stevens and House Defense Appropriations Subcommittee Chairman Joseph P. Addabbo, D-N.Y., and members Bill Chappell Jr., D-Fla., and Joseph M. McDade, R-Pa., met to work out a new deal.

In the meantime, chemical weapons opponents worked feverishly to get conferees to drop the production money. By Dec. 17, Rep. John Edward Porter, R-Ill., with help from John Isaacs of the Council for a Livable World, got about 140 House members to sign a petition urging House conferees to block the production money.

House conferees voted 15-6 Dec. 18 to insist on their position of no chemical weapons. However, they did reach a tentative agreement with Stevens to trim the Pentagon's new budget authority by $1.3 billion — from $282.5 billion to $281.2 billion. They also agreed that the $6.3 billion in transfer money could be used only for military pay and retirement and for building cargo ships that would be available for wartime use.

Stevens would not yield on the chemical weapons issue and threatened to reopen the entire package, including the previous deals on funding and the ASAT ban.

Conferees broke up for more bargaining, and when they returned, Stevens asked for a vote of Senate conferees. By 8-5, they insisted on their position. Whitten sought another recess, and when House conferees returned, they withdrew their opposition to chemical weapons funding.

But Stevens had one more deal to work. He said the White House wanted the $1.3 billion trim to come from the $6.3 billion in transfer money from fiscal 1985 and not from new budget authority. He suggested that if the House went along with that, he would agree to one of four procurement reforms the House had put in its version of the bill.

House members, some visibly angry, called the tradeoff unacceptable. Obey said it ignored the reality of House concerns over spending levels, and Chappell said the procurement reform likely would be adopted anyway.

After more negotiations, Stevens backed down on the funding request and agreed to accept one of the procurement reforms. This "allowable costs" provision barred contractors from billing the Pentagon for certain kinds of expenses, including entertainment, lobbying and legal fees resulting from charges of contract fraud. Of the four House-passed procurement provisions, this one was nearly identical to a provision already enacted as part of the defense authorization bill.

At Conte's insistence, conferees included language barring the synfuels corporation in its remaining weeks from providing any loan guarantees to any project unless there was a "legally binding" commitment to do so. This apparently allowed a Colorado project (Parachute Creek) to proceed but barred funding for a Utah project (Seep Ridge). Sen. Jake Garn, R-Utah, who had championed that project, angrily protested the action as unfair.

House conferees also agreed to go along with the honoraria provision after insisting that a "statement of managers" accompanying the conference report make clear that the increase applied only to the Senate.

House and Senate passage of the agreement came within 18 hours of the final conference gavel. ∎

Budget Cuts Leave Mark on Foreign Arms Aid

The budget-cutting mood in Congress in 1985 halted President Reagan's steady four-year buildup of military assistance to friendly countries overseas.

Reagan since 1981 had demanded substantial boosts in military aid — most of which financed arms purchases by countries such as Israel and Egypt. That kind of foreign aid, he said, was as important to U.S. national security as defense spending.

But the fiscal 1986 continuing appropriations resolution (H J Res 465 — PL 99-190) approved by Congress on Dec. 19 held the line on all foreign aid spending, including military aid. *(Continuing resolution, p. 360)*

The bill included $15.025 billion for foreign economic, military and development aid programs. Nearly matching Reagan's overall request, that was about $2.7 billion below the comparable amount for fiscal 1985. Almost all the difference was accounted for by a cut in funding for the Export-Import Bank; all other programs were to get the same or slightly less money in 1986 as in 1985. *(Charts, pp. 372, 375)*

This was the fourth year in a row that Congress included foreign aid in an omnibus continuing resolution, rather than passing separate appropriations legislation for those programs. Congress last had enacted a separate aid appropriations bill in 1981. *(1981 Almanac p. 339)*

The foreign aid provisions of the continuing resolution were the same as a complete bill, but because they were folded into an omnibus package, Congress never had to vote separately on them. Foreign aid is one of the most unpopular issues that Congress faces each year, and some leaders said any foreign aid spending bill would have been severely battered if put to up-or-down votes. Congress in August cleared a companion foreign aid authorization bill (S 960 — PL 99-83), but it was politically less controversial because it did not actually appropriate money. *(Foreign aid bill, p. 41)*

Military vs. Economic

Since the beginning of the Reagan administration, foreign aid legislation had been subject to political battling between two groups of patrons on Capitol Hill: moderates and liberals whose primary interests were international development programs and conservatives whose primary interest was military aid to U.S. allies. Each year, the two sides tried to strike a balance in the aid bill.

The fiscal 1986 bill satisfied neither side, but it appeared to give a slight advantage to Rep. David R. Obey, D-Wis., and others who sought to slow down the growth of military aid programs. Obey, chairman of the House Appropriations Subcommittee on Foreign Operations, called the final measure "an exquisitely balanced bill" because it made cuts from Reagan's requests for both military and development aid. The bill's chief virtue, he said, was that it did not "continue the administration's march toward doubling military aid while cutting back on economic."

But Obey's Republican colleagues on the House Foreign Operations Subcommittee sharply disagreed, arguing that the bill slashed too much from military aid and allowed too much for contributions to the World Bank and related programs. All Republican members of the subcommittee except Silvio O. Conte, Mass., refused to sign the foreign aid section of the continuing resolution.

Leaders of the House and Senate Foreign Operations subcommittees, which earlier had drafted separate foreign aid funding bills, negotiated the aid provisions during a private conference meeting on Dec. 11.

In Reagan's first term, military aid was one of the fastest growing parts of the entire federal budget. At the president's request, Congress boosted the three military aid programs an annual average of 20 percent between 1981-85, and Reagan had sought another 15 percent increase in fiscal 1986. The continuing resolution allowed only a 3.9 percent military aid boost.

One administration supporter, Rep. Jack F. Kemp, R-N.Y., insisted that the increase actually amounted to a 10 percent decrease in the amount available for countries other than Israel and Egypt, both of which were to get substantial aid boosts in 1986.

"We have a lot of allies we have to be concerned about. Cutting security assistance undercuts our own interests around the world," Kemp said. "I don't think isolationism is the answer to saving the budget."

Kemp complained that the administration "didn't fight at all" when the House Appropriations Committee moved to cut the military aid budgets. "They're going to rue the day this [continuing resolution] passed," Kemp said.

The continuing resolution allowed slightly more than $6 billion for the three major foreign military aid programs: the Foreign Military Sales financing program ($5.2 billion), which makes loans to help foreign governments buy U.S. weapons and military services; the Military Assistance Program ($782 million), which makes grants for the same purpose; and the International Military Education and Training program ($54.5 million), which trains foreign military officers at U.S. academies and bases.

Of the $5.2 billion set aside for Foreign Military Sales loans, the bill allowed up to $553.9 million to be "concessional" or low-rate loans. Standard foreign military loans carried interest rates of about 12 percent; in recent years the United States had lowered the rate to 5 percent for a few countries facing severe economic problems.

The bill included a lengthy statement calling on the president to propose reforms in the military aid program, especially by replacing loans with outright grants. Written by Sen. Frank H. Murkowski, R-Alaska, the statement said that the current policy of lending billions of dollars to foreign countries for arms purchases had added to their debt problems.

The continuing resolution made absolute cuts in most

economic and development aid programs, both from Reagan's request and from the fiscal 1985 levels.

The Economic Support Fund was set at $3.7 billion, compared with the $3.8 billion level in fiscal 1985 and Reagan's $4 billion request. Coupled with military aid, the Economic Support Fund was part of what the administration called "security assistance": aid intended to bolster the economies and military structures of friendly countries.

Direct, paid-in contributions to the World Bank and other international development banks were to fall to $1.2 billion in fiscal 1986, from $1.55 billion in fiscal 1985.

Development programs directly run by the United States, such as those of the Agency for International Development (AID), were funded at $2.7 billion, a $200 million cut from the previous year. The most severe cut was to be in AID's programs for agriculture and rural development overseas. The agency spent $755 million for those programs in fiscal 1985, and Reagan requested $792 million for 1986. The conference committee approved only $700 million.

Philippines

In what Obey called a message to "that clown in Manila" — President Ferdinand E. Marcos — the bill set a $55 million limit on military aid to the Philippines. Of that amount, $40 million was earmarked for grants by the Military Assistance Program and $15 million was allocated in Foreign Military Sales loans.

Reagan had requested $100 million for military aid to the Philippines, and the Senate had approved $70 million and the House $25 million. The Senate's $70 million figure was taken from the fiscal 1986-87 foreign aid authorizations measure enacted in August.

Congress had used the military aid figure as a means of expressing its dissatisfaction with Marcos' authoritarian rule. Starting in fiscal 1985, Congress reduced Reagan's request for military aid while increasing the amount of economic assistance. Ironically, some critics of that approach noted that Marcos had more freedom to spend the economic money than military aid, which carried numerous restrictions. *(Related story, p. 113)*

The continuing resolution included $125 million in economic aid, thus allowing a total of $180 million in aid related to U.S. use of two major naval and air bases in the Philippines. Under a base accord that took effect in fiscal 1985, Reagan agreed to seek congressional approval for $180 million in aid annually for the Philippines over five years.

Conferees settled the Philippines issue with little controversy, largely because the matter had been worked out in private meetings before the foreign aid conferees began their formal sessions. Sen. Daniel K. Inouye, D-Hawaii, one of the staunchest congressional supporters of Marcos, accepted the $55 million limit readily, according to those who were present.

Obey later said the aid cap was a response to recent events in the Philippines, particularly Marcos' decision to reinstate Gen. Fabian Ver as armed forces chief of staff. Ver was one of 26 military officials acquitted on Dec. 2 of charges relating to the 1983 assassination of opposition leader Benigno S. Aquino Jr. The Reagan administration and leading members of Congress had warned Marcos that reinstating Ver would stir up greater opposition and give fuel to a communist insurgency.

The Ver reinstatement "was a slap in the face by the Philippine government to President Reagan and the Congress," Obey said. "We are sick of being embarrassed by that clown in Manila. All of us are worried we're going to end up with a Marxist victory there, because you've got to have change to win."

Obey added that the aid cut was targeted at Marcos, not his country. "It isn't the Philippines we've lost interest in," he said. "It's Marcos' stupidity we've lost interest in."

Export-Import Bank

From a budget standpoint, the most flexible item in the foreign aid appropriation was the amount for direct loans by the Export-Import Bank, which subsidized exports of U.S.-made products. Ex-Im loans were counted under foreign aid appropriations even though they were not considered as regular foreign aid programs.

In a budget-cutting move, Reagan did not ask Congress to approve any new authority in fiscal 1986 for Ex-Im's direct loan program. The bank received $3.9 billion in direct loan authority in fiscal 1985, but used only about $700 million.

Because it was not clear at the beginning of a fiscal year how much loan authority the bank really would use, Congress often had juggled the Ex-Im account to keep the overall foreign aid figure within budget. That happened in 1985: The House Appropriations Committee approved $784 million for the bank, taking that money from what it cut from Reagan's request for military aid, and the Senate Appropriations Committee approved $1.8 billion.

Conferees compromised at $1.11 billion, the amount needed to keep the total foreign aid bill within the budget and under Reagan's request.

Development Banks

In spite of the general drive for budget austerity, Congress approved a relatively generous contribution to one of the most unpopular of all foreign aid agencies: the World Bank's International Development Association (IDA). The foreign aid section of the continuing resolution included $700 million for IDA, just $50 million less than Reagan's request.

Congressional conservatives long had opposed any U.S. backing for IDA, provider of no-interest, long-term loans to the world's poorest countries. As a negotiating tactic to force a reduced contribution, the Senate Appropriations Committee had voted only $375 million for IDA. But House backers of the agency, especially Obey and Matthew F. McHugh, D-N.Y., fought for the higher amount and won.

The continuing resolution made proportionately larger cuts in fiscal 1986 appropriations for most of the other international development banks. For example, paid-in contributions to the main arm of the World Bank — the International Bank for Reconstruction and Development — were pared to $109.7 million, from Reagan's $182.9 million request. And paid-in contributions to the Inter-American Development Bank, which worked in Latin America, fell to $78 million from the $130.5 million request.

Also included in the continuing resolution were long-term authorizations for increased contributions to several international development banks: $131 million over two years for a selected capital stock increase in the World Bank; $225 million over three years for the African Development Fund; $175.2 million over five years for the World Bank's International Finance Corporation, which boosted private investment overseas; and $225 million for a new, three-year pledge to IDA's "Special Facility for Sub-Saharan Africa."

Those provisions were included in the continuing resolution because the House never took up the legislation (HR 1948, HR 2253) making those authorizations. The authorizations for years after 1986 were subject to follow-up appropriations.

The bill appropriated the first-year installments for those contributions, the most controversial of which was the new Africa program. The Reagan administration was reluctant to contribute to the new program, which IDA established to boost lending for the poorest countries in Africa. Instead, the administration called for increased direct aid programs by the United States aimed at encouraging private business in Africa. *(Related story, p. 102)*

Kemp strongly objected to including the Sub-Saharan funding, saying that the Appropriations Committee never held hearings on the matter and never received a presidential request for the money.

But congressional supporters pushed hard all year for IDA's new program and used their seats on the House Banking and Appropriations committees to advance the legislation mandating the U.S. contribution.

The House bill included a $75 million fiscal 1986 contribution to the Sub-Saharan program and took the money from the Economic Support Fund (ESF) — a provision the State Department opposed because it would have forced a $75 million cut from ESF contributions to other countries. In conference, House negotiators agreed to establish the Africa program as a separate line item, thus freeing up that amount in the ESF account.

Even so, Kemp complained that the money was to come out of U.S. programs that would have gone to Africa anyway. "We're taking the money out of U.S. bilateral programs and putting it into 50-year, no-interest loans," Kemp said.

Middle East

Israel and Egypt — the two biggest recipients of U.S. aid — were among the few countries protected from cuts in the bill. However, aid to both countries faced cuts in 1986 under the automatic budget-slashing procedures of the Gramm-Rudman-Hollings legislation (PL 99-177). *(Related story, p. 459)*

Reagan requested, and the bill approved, $3 billion for Israel, including $1.8 billion in military aid and $1.2 billion in economic aid. That was in addition to the fiscal 1986 portion of a two-year, $1.5 billion "emergency" economic aid package for Israel that had already been enacted into law (PL 99-88).

All aid for both Israel and Egypt was in the form of grants. Aid to most other countries was split between grants and loans that had to be repaid.

The Senate Appropriations Committee had advocated yet another special aid provision for Israel: a $500 million reduction on that country's interest payments to the United States on past military loans. However, the committee on Dec. 5 withdrew that provision, which the Reagan administration and the Senate Budget and Foreign Relations committees had opposed for budget reasons.

As in the preceding two years, Congress earmarked part of Israel's aid program to support research, development and production of a new jet fighter, the Lavi, for that country. The bill set aside $300 million to be spent on the Lavi in Israel and $150 million to be spent in the United States. That brought to $1.4 billion the amount Congress had allocated for the Lavi since fiscal 1984.

The bill contained $1.3 billion in military aid and $815 million in economic aid for Egypt. Of the economic aid, $115 million was to be a no-strings-attached cash transfer, and $200 million was to be used to buy goods from the United States.

Egypt also was to get about $220 million per year in food aid from the United States.

Conferees eliminated from the bill a Senate-passed amendment that would have set a $95 million limit in fiscal 1986 on military loans to Jordan. That provision was aimed at forcing Reagan to return to Congress for supplemental appropriations if he wanted to give Jordan U.S. financing for a pending $1.5 billion-$2 billion arms sale. Obey said he argued against that provision because it was "a gratuitous slap" at Jordan's King Hussein. *(Related story, p. 93)*

The final bill included another Senate-passed provision that would force an early Senate vote on any resolution to block the Jordan arms sale. Congress in October forced Reagan to postpone the sale until March 1, 1986, at the earliest. The provision included in the continuing resolution was to take effect Feb. 1, 1986; it would force Senate floor action as early as 10 days after any legislation had been introduced to prohibit Reagan from carrying out the sale.

The bill also included language from the foreign aid authorization law (PL 99-83) stating congressional opposition to a Jordan arms sale until Middle East peace talks were under way. *(Authorization bill, p. 41)*

Central America

Responding to presidential elections that in January returned an elected civilian to power in Guatemala for the first time since 1954, the conferees agreed to give the administration flexibility to provide economic aid to that country.

Reagan had requested $25 million for economic aid to Guatemala, but the House bill had imposed a $12.5 million limit. The House bill also had barred the use of U.S. funds for Guatemala's rural resettlement program, under which the outgoing military regime had forced thousands of Indians and other rural residents from their homes. Meeting just three days after moderate leader Vinicio Cerezo was elected president, the conferees deleted both provisions.

In their report, conferees called the elections "a significant step forward" for Guatemala and urged the administration to respond quickly to Cerezo's request for aid for his country's ailing economy.

However, the conferees retained House-passed conditions on $10 million in military aid to Guatemala. To provide the money, the president would have to certify to Congress that an elected civilian government was in power in Guatemala and had requested the money. The president also would have to certify that the government had made progress in controlling the security forces, in eliminating kidnappings and in respecting internationally recognized human rights.

In another mild rebuke to the president's aid program for Central America, conferees voted a $250 million limit on development aid for the region. That was $25 million higher than the House-passed amount but $18.5 million below Reagan's request.

The bill placed no other sweeping restrictions on aid to Central America. During the first Reagan term, Congress routinely imposed a wide range of limits on aid to the region, especially on military aid for El Salvador. Largely because of widespread support for Salvadoran President José Napoleón Duarte, Congress was setting few conditions.

The only condition on aid to El Salvador was a requirement that the administration notify the House and Senate Appropriations committees at least 15 days before using U.S. aid to buy helicopters or other aircraft for that country's armed forces.

The same requirement applied to the sale of each aircraft to El Salvador. Under traditional procedures, either Appropriations Committee could then ask the administration not to proceed with its proposed action.

Several human rights groups had charged the Salvadoran military with indiscriminately bombing the countryside in its campaign to wipe out leftist guerrillas.

Greece, Turkey

Both Greece and Turkey would come under the budget ax under the continuing resolution, but Turkey was to suffer more than its traditional rival.

The continuing resolution set military aid limits of $450 million for Greece, a 10 percent cut from Reagan's $500 million request, and $642.8 million for Turkey, a 17 percent cut from Reagan's $780 million request.

The effect of those aid limits was to retain a traditional 7-to-10 ratio for military aid to the two countries: Greece was given $7 for every $10 that Turkey got. Bowing to political pressure by the pro-Greece lobby, Congress for years had kept that ratio as a way of holding down aid to Turkey.

However, foreign aid conferees deleted House-passed language that explicitly specified a 7-to-10 ratio. The Reagan administration, as did its predecessors, had strongly objected to any formal mandate of a 7-to-10 ratio but had acquiesced when Congress merely appropriated funds to conform to that ratio. The administration had argued that aid to the two countries should not be linked formally.

The bill took no position on Reagan's request for $150 million in economic aid to Turkey, but the overall cutbacks in economic aid were expected to force some reductions for that country. Greece did not receive economic aid.

Population Aid

Conferees also adopted a Senate provision, sponsored by Dennis DeConcini, D-Ariz., that required changes in a new Reagan administration policy of giving money to overseas groups that advocated only "natural family-planning" methods, such as abstinence.

In addition to funding government family-planning programs in foreign countries, AID gave money to private agencies that provided counseling and birth control services. Under pressure from conservative groups, M. Peter McPherson, administrator of AID, in July agreed to set aside $40 million over five years for grants to groups that gave advice only on natural family-planning methods. *(Related story, p. 112)*

The DeConcini amendment stated that funds could be given only to agencies that offered "either directly, or through referral to or information about, access to a broad range of family-planning methods." That could force AID to modify its policy, either by banning aid to groups that counseled only natural methods or by pressuring those groups to provide at least some information on other birth control methods.

The continuing resolution contained the so-called "Kemp amendment" barring U.S. contributions to any international agency that "supports or participates in the management of a program of coercive abortion or involuntary sterilization."

Sponsored by Rep. Kemp, that amendment originally was included in a fiscal 1985 supplemental bill (PL 99-88). The Reagan administration used it earlier in the year to block U.S. support of the United Nations Fund for Population Activities because of that agency's alleged ties to China's mandatory family-planning programs.

For the first time in several years, Congress accepted Reagan's recommendation for the amount of funding to family-planning programs overseas: $250 million in fiscal 1986. Reagan requested that amount for fiscal 1985, but Congress appropriated $290 million.

Other Issues

Other foreign aid issues dealt with by the continuing resolution included:

Cambodia. The bill directed the president to provide at least $1.5 million, but no more than $5 million, in economic or military aid for the "non-communist resistance" forces in Cambodia, which was occupied by Vietnam. The House Foreign Affairs Committee had initiated the aid program for Cambodian guerrillas; the Reagan administration had preferred to give any aid secretly rather than publicly. *(Related story, p. 56)*

Military Coups. The original House bill had mandated suspension of foreign aid to El Salvador or Guatemala if the elected head of government were to be deposed by military coup or decree. Instead, conferees adopted a broader Senate measure that would cut off aid to any country where the military ousted the elected government.

Private Agencies. The bill retained a previous requirement that private agencies could not receive U.S. funds for overseas development work unless they got at least 20 percent of their total annual funds from sources other than the U.S. government. Members of the House Appropriations Committee had sought to raise the cutoff level to 25 percent, a step that might have forced curtailment of U.S. funding of several private agencies.

Lebanon. Conferees directed the administration to transfer $22.85 million in unspent economic aid for Lebanon to several other foreign aid accounts: $12.5 million for the Child Survival Fund, which was providing health services for children overseas, $5.35 million for programs by the United Nations Children's Fund and $5 million to the U.S.' international narcotics control program.

Congress in 1983 appropriated $150 million for special aid to Lebanon, as part of the Reagan administration's plan to shore up the shaky government there. But because of continued fighting throughout the country, U.S. agencies were able to spend only about $60 million, and most of the remainder was transferred to other countries or accounts. The latest diversion was to leave about $20 million in the Lebanon account, which conferees said could be spent only with advance notice to Congress.

International Organizations. Among the biggest percentage increases over Reagan's budget request were the amounts allocated to international organizations, most of which were associated with the United Nations. Reagan had requested $196.2 million for those agencies, and the bill provided $277.9 million — a 42 percent increase. The single-biggest recipient was the United Nations Development Program; Reagan had requested $120 million, but the bill set aside $148.5 million.

Pakistan. The bill earmarked $250 million, Reagan's request, for economic aid to Pakistan. It took no formal position on Reagan's request for $325 million in military aid to that country.

Tunisia. The bill earmarked $40 million for military grants and $27 million for military loans to Tunisia.

Narcotics. Conferees dropped Colombia from a House-passed list of countries whose aid was to have been curtailed because of their failure to control narcotics production. The original House bill would have withheld half of all aid destined for Colombia, Jamaica and Peru until the president reported to Congress that the governments of those countries were "sufficiently responsive" to U.S. concerns about controlling narcotics production. Conferees said Colombia had made progress in 1985 and so should not be penalized.

Conferees retained tougher narcotics-related restrictions on aid to Bolivia. The president could give Bolivia up to half of the budgeted aid only by certifying to Congress that the Bolivian government had enacted legislation setting legal limits on production of coca, used to make cocaine. The president would be able to provide the rest of the aid only if he certified that Bolivia had met the targets for eradication of coca crops that it agreed to in 1983.

Opposing U.S. Policies. For the third year in a row, the foreign aid appropriations section required the president to report to Congress on the voting practices in the United Nations of countries that received U.S. aid. The bill also barred the president from giving aid to any country that he determined was engaging in a "consistent pattern of opposition to the foreign policy of the United States" — as shown by the U.N. votes. The administration had supplied the reports in the past, but had not suspended aid to any country solely because of differences over U.N. voting.

Afghan People. At the administration's request, the bill included $15 million for food, medicine and other humanitarian aid to "the Afghan people." That aid was in addition to several hundred million dollars the CIA was providing each year to guerrilla groups battling the Soviet occupation of Afghanistan.

Sudan. Because of an April coup that ousted the pro-U.S. regime in the Sudan, the bill included a provision barring aid to that country if the president determined its new government "is acting in a manner that would endanger the stability of the region or the Camp David peace process."

The new government in July signed a military aid agreement with Libya. Before the coup, Reagan had requested about $200 million in aid for the Sudan, but most aid programs had since been put on hold.

Environmental Programs. The bill directed U.S. representatives to the international development banks to push for an increased emphasis on programs that did not damage the environment. The representatives were ordered to call for special board meetings of those banks to discuss ways of cutting back on environmentally damaging projects.

Child Health. The bill included money and advocacy for increased immunization of children in poor countries. A total of $50 million was earmarked for health programs for children overseas, much of which paid for immunizations. Conferees also called on the president to work toward the goal of universal access to childhood immunization by 1990.

House Committee Bill

The $14.5 billion foreign aid funding bill was reported Aug. 1 by a divided House Appropriations Committee. The panel ordered the measure (HR 3228 — H Rept 99-252) reported by voice vote without much apparent opposition. But the debate before the vote showed that there were deep differences between Democrats and Republicans over the bill's spending priorities.

The stage for argument was set in the Foreign Operations Subcommittee, which approved the measure July 16. There, as in the full committee later, Democrats lined up behind the efforts of subcommittee Chairman Obey to hold down spending chiefly by making reductions in arms aid to other countries.

Even Obey admitted that he probably would have opposed the bill's provisions before he became chairman earlier in the year.

Obey and most of his fellow Democrats said the subcommittee's $14.3 billion measure cut too deeply into overseas development programs. But Obey acknowledged that "this subcommittee can't repeal the results of last November's election," which returned to power an administration that had emphasized military aid to U.S. allies and played down the importance of development aid.

By contrast, some Republicans, led by Kemp, charged that Obey cleverly constructed the bill to favor those development programs at the expense of military aid. Kemp called the bill "seriously flawed" and charged that Obey had forsaken the "bipartisan spirit" that prevailed on the Appropriations subcommittee in recent years.

Administration officials also expressed dismay at the work of the subcommittee, saying the bill could force the suspension of military aid to nearly 20 countries. Obey, one State Department official said, "is a very formidable opponent."

Aside from the argument over funding levels, two important provisions in the bill included a ban on aid to countries that were not enforcing security standards at their airports and a deferment of all aid for family planning programs overseas.

Cutting Back

The Foreign Operations Subcommittee worked on the aid bill during a four-hour, closed-door session the evening of July 16. In the past, the panel conducted its business in open meetings that often were acrimonious. In 1985, members argued that they could work faster if they were not subject to public scrutiny.

Obey said he drafted the aid bill with one goal in mind: making the subcommittee's contribution toward reducing the federal deficit. He calculated that foreign aid's share of the deficit was $2.4 billion, and that cutting that much would require a 17 percent across-the-board reduction in President Reagan's aid request for fiscal 1986.

Obey constructed a complex formula that started with a 17 percent cut. After several exceptions were made, the net cut for foreign aid programs was $1.2 billion, or 8.4 percent. And Obey restored to the bill $784 million for one non-foreign aid program, direct loans by the Export-Import Bank. That made the net cut only $456 million — 3 percent below Reagan's request. Reagan had proposed eliminating the Ex-Im Bank's direct subsidies of some U.S. exports.

The politically popular aid programs for Israel and Egypt were protected from any cutbacks. Reagan had requested $3 billion in military and economic aid for Israel and $2.1 billion for Egypt.

At the request of Charles Wilson, D-Texas, Obey also exempted from cuts Reagan's request for $575 million in aid to Pakistan. Wilson, one of the main proponents in Congress of aid to anti-Soviet guerrillas in Afghanistan,

Foreign Aid Appropriations, Fiscal 1986

The following chart shows President Reagan's request, the House- and Senate-approved amounts, and the final amounts, in new budget authority, for foreign aid appropriations in fiscal 1986. Foreign aid programs were included in a continuing resolution (PL 99-190).

(Figures in parentheses show program limitations that do not count as new budget authority. The figures for individual development banks include only paid-in capital.)

Program	Request	House-Passed Amount	Senate-Passed Amount	Final Amount
Inter-American Development Bank	$ 130,500,983	$ 130,500,983	$ 78,000,983	$ 78,000,983
Inter-American Investment Corporation	13,000,000	11,700,000	13,000,000	11,700,000
World Bank	182,870,597	151,782,596	109,720,549	109,720,549
International Development Association	750,000,000	750,000,000	375,000,000	700,000,000
Special Facility for Sub-Saharan Africa	0	0	0	75,000,000
International Finance Corporation	35,033,000	29,077,390	35,033,000	29,077,390
Asian Development Bank and Fund	143,232,676	141,909,408	113,232,676	111,909,408
African Development Fund	75,000,000	62,250,000	75,000,000	62,250,000
African Development Bank	17,986,678	16,188,910	17,986,678	16,188,910
Total callable capital for development banks	(3,641,746,678)	(3,253,286,650)	(2,889,512,056)	(2,884,116,052)
International Organizations and Programs	196,211,000	298,364,800	287,360,000	277,922,475
Subtotal, multilateral aid	**$ 1,543,834,934**	**$ 1,591,774,087**	**$ 1,104,333,886**	**$ 1,471,769,715**
Agriculture aid	792,352,000	679,995,900	760,000,000	699,995,900
Population aid	250,017,000	261,000,000	250,000,000	250,000,000
Health aid	146,427,000	200,824,200	205,000,000	200,824,200
Child survival fund	0	22,500,000	25,000,000	25,000,000
Education, human resources aid	183,533,000	169,949,700	180,000,000	169,949,700
Energy, selected development aid	210,071,000	174,358,930	190,000,000	174,358,930
Science and technology aid	13,000,000	10,790,000	13,000,000	10,790,000
Private sector revolving fund	(20,000,000)	(18,000,000)	(18,000,000)	(18,000,000)
American schools and hospitals abroad	10,000,000	27,000,000	35,000,000	35,000,000
International disaster aid	25,000,000	22,500,000	25,000,000	22,500,000
Sahel development	80,500,000	87,750,000	80,500,000	80,500,000
Foreign service retirement and disability fund	43,122,000	43,122,000	43,122,000	43,122,000
Rescind Syrian aid account	0	-26,200,000	0	0
Economic Support Fund	4,024,000,000	3,689,286,666	3,745,000,000	3,700,000,000
Agency for International Development (AID) operating expenses	393,700,000	387,000,000	372,200,000	376,350,000
AID reappropriation	0	5,000,000	5,000,000	5,000,000
AID inspector general	0	0	25,200,000	21,050,000
Trade credit insurance program	(200,000,000)	(200,000,000)	(300,000,000)	(250,000,000)
Trade and development program	20,034,000	18,900,000	20,034,000	18,900,000
African Development Foundation	1,012,000	4,000,000	1,012,000	3,872,000
Inter-American Foundation	8,800,000	10,792,800	11,969,000	11,969,000
Peace Corps	125,200,000	128,600,000	130,000,000	130,000,000
International narcotics control	57,709,000	57,529,000	57,529,000	57,529,000
Migration and refugee aid	337,930,000	337,930,000	344,730,000	338,930,000
Anti-terrorism aid	32,000,000	5,000,000	9,840,000	7,420,000
Peace-keeping operations	37,000,000	34,000,000	34,000,000	34,000,000
Subtotal, bilateral aid	**$ 6,791,407,000**	**$ 6,351,629,196**	**$ 6,563,136,000**	**$ 6,417,060,730**
Military Assistance Program grants	976,350,000	764,648,000	805,100,000	782,000,000
International military education and training	65,650,000	54,489,500	56,221,000	54,489,500
Foreign military sales: forgiven loans and direct credits	5,655,000,000	5,058,983,333	5,371,000,000	5,190,000,000
Defense acquisition fund	(345,000,000)	(325,000,000)	(345,000,000)	(325,000,000)
Guarantee Reserve Fund				
Subtotal, military aid	**$ 6,697,000,000**	**$ 5,878,120,833**	**$ 6,282,321,000**	**$ 6,026,489,500**
Housing guaranty program	(45,000,000)	(144,000,000)	(160,000,000)	(152,000,000)
Overseas Private Investment Corporation	(165,000,000)	(148,500,000)	(165,000,000)	(156,750,000)
Export-Import Bank total limitation	(12,018,357,000)	(12,801,879,167)	(13,818,000,000)	(13,128,357,000)
Export-Import Bank direct loans	0	783,879,167	1,800,000,000	1,110,000,000
GRAND TOTAL	**$15,032,241,934**	**$14,605,403,283**	**$15,749,790,886**	**$15,025,319,945**

said that aid would do no good unless there was "confidence and stability in Pakistan."

Obey acknowledged that his proposed bill would anger both Democrats and Republicans. Democrats, he said, would be unhappy about the sharp cuts from fiscal 1985 levels for programs to improve agriculture, education, health and other services in poor countries. And Republicans would be unhappy about the cuts from Reagan's 1986 requests for a substantial increase in military aid.

The subcommittee approved some 30 amendments to Obey's draft bill, but few made substantial changes.

Kemp and Rep. Jerry Lewis, R-Calif., offered a list of particulars against the subcommittee plan. Kemp said that "security assistance for our friends and allies was gouged, if not gutted." Lewis fumed about "prearranged deals behind closed doors" and added: "To walk in there and know you were going to be rolled, you might have stayed home."

Both men complained vigorously that Obey's formula produced no cuts in the World Bank's International Development Association (IDA), which some conservatives had argued promoted socialism and gave too much money to India.

Reagan requested, and the subcommittee approved, $750 million for IDA in fiscal 1986. The IDA appropriation was one of the largest items in the bill for any single agency. Congress had approved $900 million for IDA in 1985; that figure included $150 million to make up for a backlog in previous years' contributions. *(1984 Almanac p. 124)*

Lewis cited the $750 million for IDA figure as evidence that Obey's formula for cutting the aid bill "was designed to give what was desired in economic [aid], and with a bias away from the military."

Obey called such complaints "baloney" and argued that the cutbacks were made fairly. He noted that the bill provided an increase above fiscal 1985 levels for military aid and sharply reduced the development aid programs he favored.

"These sure as hell are not my priorities, and anybody who knows me knows they are not," he said. "I would have more in humanitarian [aid] and less in guns."

Overall Numbers

The Obey subcommittee bill provided $14.3 billion in new budget authority for fiscal 1986, of which $13.5 billion was for foreign economic, military and development aid and $784 million was for direct loans by the Ex-Im Bank.

The total was $456 million below Reagan's request, and about $3.9 billion below what Congress had appropriated to date in fiscal 1985. About $3 billion of the difference between the 1985 and 1986 levels represented a cutback on loans by the Ex-Im Bank. Reagan had proposed eliminating Ex-Im loans.

The bill also was about $500 million below the comparable level for programs in the foreign aid authorizations bill. The appropriations bill included some items, such as the Ex-Im Bank and contributions to international development banks, that were not covered in the authorizations bill.

The biggest category of foreign aid in the appropriations bill was military aid: $5.9 billion, a cut of 11.3 percent from Reagan's request and a slight increase over the 1985 level. Economic aid to key U.S. allies, such as Israel and Egypt, was put at $3.65 billion, a reduction of 9.3 percent from Reagan's request and of 4.6 percent from the 1985 level.

Long-term development aid, including programs administered directly by the U.S. government and contributions to the international development banks, totaled $3.9 billion, a cut of 8.4 percent from Reagan's request and of 5.5 percent from the 1985 amount.

The subcommittee did not include in its figures $261 million for U.S. contributions to family planning programs overseas. That amount was restored Aug. 1 by the full committee, raising the overall level of the bill to $14.5 billion.

Major Provisions

In addition to funding levels, the subcommittee bill included dozens of restrictions on U.S. foreign aid programs. As in past years, many of the restrictions were drafted by Democrats to curtail the Reagan administration's use of military aid to bolster rightist regimes. Other restrictions were aimed at prodding foreign countries to take steps requested by the United States, such as reducing narcotics production or reforming their political systems.

In its major actions, the subcommittee voted to:

- Bar the disbursement of aid to any foreign country until the president had certified to Congress that it had taken "adequate, appropriate steps to provide airport security against potential terrorist activities."

Sponsored by Robert J. Mrazek, D-N.Y., that amendment was an outgrowth of the hijacking of a TWA jet after it left Athens, Greece. The United States charged that the Athens airport, where the hijackers boarded the plane, failed to meet minimum security standards. Mrazek's amendment also could apply to several other countries, especially in Latin America, that allegedly failed to enforce tight security.

- Defer any decision on U.S. aid for family planning programs overseas until Congress and the administration resolved several disputes over how those programs should be administered. Reagan had requested $250 million for overseas population programs, a cut of $40 million from the 1985 level. Obey's formula was to provide $261 million, but that was not included in the bill. "If I'm going to recommend spending some money, I'd like to know how it's going to be spent," he said, referring to conflicting provisions on population programs in various pieces of legislation pending before Congress.

In spite of the deferral, the subcommittee affirmed its support for "informed voluntary family planning" programs overseas. The subcommittee action:

- Barred economic and arms aid to Morocco or the Sudan if the president determined that either country was undermining the stability of Egypt or the Camp David accords between Israel and Egypt. In the past year both countries had signed cooperation agreements with Libya, a country the United States had accused of supporting terrorism and fomenting violence against Israel and Egypt. Kemp sponsored the provision.
- Set a limit of $25 million on military aid to the Philippines. Reagan had requested $100 million. The subcommittee transferred $38 million from military aid to economic aid. That provision tracked earlier action on the aid authorizations bill.

Responding to the authorizations bill, Filipino President Ferdinand E. Marcos on July 18 said his country could do without U.S. aid if necessary. He also threatened to review an agreement allowing two major U.S. bases in the Philippines.

- Made military aid to El Salvador subject to semiannual presidential reports to Congress that the government there had made progress on a variety of fronts, ranging from curbing right-wing death squads to implementing land reform. The panel also barred the United States from providing helicopters or other aircraft to El Salvador unless Congress had been notified, and earmarked $1 million to help the Salvadoran government investigate the June 19 killing of four Marines and two other U.S. citizens.

- Allowed the president to give Colombia, Bolivia, Jamaica and Peru only half of the aid he had planned unless he certified to Congress that they were "sufficiently responsive to U.S. concerns" about drug production and that providing the aid was in the U.S. interest.
- Barred use of money in the bill for military or paramilitary operations in Nicaragua, effectively blocking fiscal 1986 foreign aid funds from going to "contras" who were battling the leftist government in that country. Congress in recent weeks had moved to give the contras non-military aid, under a fiscal 1985 supplemental spending bill (HR 2577). *(Supplemental, p. 350)*
- Directed the president to maintain a traditional ratio under which Greece got $7 in U.S. military aid for every $10 that Turkey got. The administration had opposed that ratio. The bill did not set specific levels for either country.
- Directed that $40 million in unspent economic aid to Lebanon be used instead for narcotics control programs ($10 million) and health care programs overseas ($30.4 million). In effect, that provision was an effort by the subcommittee to head off a pending administration decision to divert the Lebanon money to Grenada and Jamaica.
- Allocated $5 million for economic or military aid to the non-communist resistance forces in Cambodia, and $15 million in relief aid for "the Afghan people." Wilson sponsored both provisions. Obey opposed the Cambodia aid, saying the United States should be aiding the Cambodian rebels secretly rather than openly. Both chambers of Congress had voted to aid the Cambodians, who were fighting Vietnamese forces occupying their country.
- Earmarked $75 million under the Economic Support Fund for a U.S. contribution to a special African aid program run by the World Bank's IDA. The Reagan administration had refused to participate in that program, saying the United States had its own Africa aid programs. Matthew F. McHugh, D-N.Y., sponsored the $75 million earmark.
- Set aside $50 million for a U.S. contribution to the International Fund for Agricultural Development, which promoted small-scale farm programs overseas. The administration had refused to renew U.S. backing for that agency unless Saudi Arabia and other oil-exporting countries kept their promise to support it. Silvio O. Conte, R-Mass., sponsored the provision.
- Set aside up to $400 million of Israeli military aid for research and development on the Lavi, that country's new warplane. Wilson sponsored the provision.

Full Committee Action

Republicans made two major attempts to reverse the priorities in HR 3228 during full committee action July 31 and Aug. 1.

Their first proposal would have expanded funding for country-to-country aid at the expense of contributions to multilateral development programs. It cut $78.6 million from the World Bank, $28.5 million from the United Nations Development Program (UNDP) and $50 million from the U.N.'s agricultural development program. From that savings, $78.6 million was to go for added economic aid to U.S. allies, and $78.5 million for U.S. agricultural development abroad.

Kemp and other Republicans argued that the subcommittee had slighted aid programs under direct U.S. control, while boosting funds for international programs that sometimes aided unfriendly nations. They focused on the UNDP, which they said gave a total of $44 million in 1984 to Nicaragua, Cuba, Laos, Afghanistan, Vietnam, China and North Korea. Republicans hoped to score political points against Democrats who voted for the aid on the House floor.

The amendment, which was rejected 14-26, was seen by backers as a wedge to open up the subcommittee bill to another change that would increase security assistance at the expense of the Export-Import Bank's program of direct loans to foreign purchasers of U.S. goods.

The second proposal offered by Lewis and Kemp added $299 million for loans for foreign arms purchases, $68.5 million for direct military aid and $1.7 million for training of foreign military personnel. Those increases were funded by a $369.2 million cut in the Ex-Im Bank's direct loans to foreign purchasers of U.S. goods.

Debate on the amendment focused on the cuts in Ex-Im, which would have brought the bank's appropriation to less than 20 percent of its 1985 level. Democrats opposing the amendment had a vocal ally, ranking GOP member Silvio O. Conte of Massachusetts, who defended Ex-Im as a vital spur to exports. Backers of the amendment stressed the need for more arms aid, while attacking the Ex-Im loans as corporate subsidies. The amendment was rejected by voice vote.

In other action, the committee:

- Added the $261 million for population programs.
- Refused to increase funding for refugee aid. On a 26-20 vote, the panel accepted an Obey amendment keeping the subcommittee level of $293 million, blocking a Conte amendment to raise the amount to $325 million.
- Rejected, on a 13-30 vote, a Lewis proposal to cut $75 million from the World Bank's International Development Association programs in Africa.
- Rejected, on a 6-23 vote, a Bob Livingston, R-La., amendment to delete language barring use of funds for military actions against Nicaragua.
- Adopted by voice vote an Obey amendment, included at the request of the administration, to drop Laos from the list of communist countries barred from receiving aid. While it had no plans to aid Laos, the administration sought the change in return for that country's cooperation in locating U.S. military personnel missing in action in the Vietnam War.

Disputes With Foreign Affairs Committee

House consideration of HR 3228 was delayed past the Oct. 1 start of the 1986 fiscal year by disputes between the Foreign Affairs and Appropriations committees. Those disputes were resolved, but the bill was further delayed in October because Foreign Operations Subcommittee Chairman Obey was tied up in House-Senate budget negotiations. Foreign aid appropriations were folded into the omnibus continuing appropriations legislation for the fourth straight year.

Leaders of the Foreign Affairs Committee had objected to several foreign policy provisions in HR 3228, which was supposed to be limited to setting amounts of foreign aid spending.

'Security Aid' Totals, Fiscal 1985-86

Following are the amounts for major "security assistance" programs for key countries. Security assistance includes Foreign Military Sales (FMS) loans, Military Assistance Program (MAP) grants and Economic Support Fund (ESF) loans and grants. Not included are military training aid, development aid, food aid or other programs.

The fiscal 1986 "preliminary" figures take into account reductions averaging 4.3 percent that were planned because of the Gramm-Rudman-Hollings budget-cutting procedures.

In both years, foreign aid was included in omnibus continuing appropriations resolutions: PL 98-473 for fiscal 1985 and PL 99-190 for fiscal 1986. *(Figures are in millions of dollars; country totals are in boldface type; fiscal 1984 figures, 1984 Almanac p. 397)*

Country	Fiscal 1985		Fiscal 1986	
	Request	Final	Request	Preliminary
Egypt [1]	**$ 2,240**	**2,240**	**$ 2,365**	**$ 2,275.5**
FMS	1,175	1,175	1,300	1,244.1
ESF	1,065	1,065	1,065	1,031.4
Israel [1]	**3,350**	**3,350**	**3,750**	**3,621**
FMS	1,400	1,400	1,800	1,722.6
ESF	1,950	1,950	1,950	1,898.4
Jordan [1]	**195**	**190**	**215**	**170.9**
FMS [2]	95	90	95	81.3
ESF	100	100	120	89.6
Lebanon	**35**	**18.8**	**10**	**21.9**
FMS	15	0	10	0
ESF[3]	20	18.8	0	21.9
Pakistan	**525**	**525**	**575**	**550.3**
FMS	325	325	325	311
ESF	200	200	250	239.3
Turkey	**930**	**875**	**935**	**734.9**
FMS [2]	525	485	555	409.5
MAP	230	215	230	205.8
ESF	175	175	150	119.6
Greece	**500**	**500**	**500**	**430.7**
FMS [2]	500	500	500	430.7
Cyprus	**3**	**15**	**3**	**14.4**
ESF	3	15	3	14.4
Spain	**412**	**412**	**412**	**394.3**
FMS	400	400	400	382.8
ESF	12	12	12	11.5
Portugal	**205**	**205**	**215**	**186.7**
FMS	55	55	65	43.1
MAP	70	70	70	67
ESF	80	80	80	76.6
South Korea	**230**	**230**	**228**	**162.7**
FMS	230	230	228	162.7
Philippines	**180**	**180**	**195**	**172.3**
FMS [2]	60	15	50	14.4
MAP	25	25	50	38.3
ESF	95	140	95	119.6
Morocco	**65**	**63**	**72.5**	**46**
FMS [2]	10	8	5	1
MAP	40	40	45	33.5
ESF	15	15	22.5	11.5
Tunisia	**68**	**85**	**81.5**	**78.4**
FMS [2]	50	50	43	25.8
MAP	15	15	16	33.5
ESF	3	20	22.5	19.1
Somalia	**75**	**63**	**75**	**45.9**
MAP	40	33	40	23.9
ESF	35	30	35	22
Sudan	**189**	**159**	**173.5**	**78.9**
MAP	69	45	58.5	19.1
ESF	120	114	115	59.8
Zaire	**30**	**17.4**	**25.4**	**16.3**
MAP	15	7	10.4	6.7
ESF	15	10.4	15	9.6
Costa Rica	**169.8**	**171**	**152.5**	**123**
MAP	9.8	11	2.4	2.4
ESF	160	160	150	120.6
El Salvador	**341**	**419.85**	**341**	**302.4**
FMS [2]	15	10	0	0
MAP	116	124.8	131	125.4
ESF	210	285	210	177
Guatemala	**45**	**12.5**	**35**	**52.7**
FMS	10	0	10	0
MAP	0	0	0	4.8
ESF	35	12.5	25	47.9
Honduras	**136.3**	**213.8**	**167**	**119.9**
MAP	61.3	66.3	87	58.7
ESF	75	147.5	80	61.2

[1] *Figures include "emergency" economic aid of $1.5 billion for Israel, $500 million for Egypt, and $250 million for Jordan, appropriated in a supplemental (PL 99-88). Those amounts were spread over fiscal 1985-86 for Egypt and Israel, and over fiscal 1985-87 for Jordan. All aid to those two countries is in grants or forgiven loans.*

[2] *A portion of the FMS aid to these countries is in "concessional" loans carrying below-market interest rates.*

The Appropriations Committee had set conditions on aid for several countries, especially in the Middle East and Central America. The Foreign Affairs Committee said some of those conditions duplicated or contradicted foreign policy provisions that Congress already had enacted in the foreign aid authorization bill (PL 99-83) for fiscal years 1986-87.

Leaders of the two committees negotiated compromises on most of the disputed issues, allowing the appropriations bill to be amended when it reached the House floor.

Senate Bill

When the Senate Appropriations Committee completed its fiscal 1986 foreign aid spending bill (S 1816 — S Rept 99-167) on Oct. 31, it found itself in turf fights of its own — with the Budget and Foreign Relations committees.

At issue was an extra $500 million grant for Israel that was included with the committee bill.

The Budget Committee objected that the addition of the Israel money helped make the measure a "budget buster" that was at least $1.2 billion and possibly $2.5 billion above the amount allowed by the budget resolution (S Con Res 32). The Foreign Relations Committee also objected to the extra Israel money and to another provision that would have repealed several items that Congress had enacted into law in the foreign aid authorization bill (PL 99-83).

Both disputes were ultimately settled Dec. 5, when the Appropriations Committee met to mark up the continuing appropriations resolution (H J Res 465). Bob Kasten, R-Wis., chairman of the Foreign Operations Subcommittee, gave in on both counts, dropping the Israel and authorizations provisions.

As approved by the Appropriations panel on a voice vote, the bill provided $14.8 billion for foreign development, economic and arms aid programs in fiscal 1986. That was $188 million less than Reagan's request and about $6.5 billion below the fiscal 1985 amount. The 1985 figure was higher because it included $3.9 billion for Export-Import Bank loans and $2 billion for supplemental economic aid to Israel and Egypt.

Committee Action: Budget Dispute

The dispute between the Senate Budget and Appropriations committees arose, in large part, because leaders of the Appropriations Subcommittee on Foreign Operations wanted extra money for Israel.

Subcommittee Chairman Kasten and ranking Democrat Daniel K. Inouye, Hawaii, wanted to reduce Israel's interest payments to the United States on past foreign military loans. Israel was paying an average of 11.4 percent a year interest on $9.4 billion in past loans; the subcommittee plan would have cut the rate to 5 percent.

Inouye earlier in 1985 had proposed a permanent cut in Israel's interest rate; doing so would have cost the United States about $3.9 billion. Because that figure was so high, he and Kasten decided on an experimental one-year reduction, costing about $500 million.

The Foreign Operations panel approved the $500 million proposal on Oct. 29, with little debate. That money was on top of $3 billion annually in regular aid to Israel, and in addition to a $1.5 billion economic aid supplemental appropriation (PL 99-88) approved for Israel over fiscal years 1985-86. *(Story, p. 90)*

When the aid bill reached the full Appropriations panel on Oct. 31, Budget Committee leaders attacked the budget strategy Kasten and Inouye had used; it was designed to make room for the Israel aid, as well as for Ex-Im Bank loans to subsidize U.S. exports.

The Kasten-Inouye plan would have allowed the Ex-Im Bank to use, in fiscal 1986-87, $3.2 billion in unspent loan authority that Congress had approved for fiscal 1985. Of that amount, $1.8 billion could have been used in 1986 and the rest in 1987 — enabling the bank to make loans without more appropriations.

To avoid having the $3.2 billion count in the 1986 and 1987 budgets, the Kasten-Inouye plan called for all of it to be counted in fiscal 1985, when it was first appropriated. That maneuver was to make room in the budget for new items — such as the Israel aid.

The drawback was that the Budget panel disagreed with the Kasten-Inouye plan, especially its method of estimating how much of the Ex-Im Bank's loans would create actual outlays, the figure that determined the federal deficit. In a stinging letter to Appropriations Chairman Mark O. Hatfield, R-Ore., Budget panel leaders accused Kasten and Inouye of trying to "deliberately circumvent" the budget process and of exceeding the budget resolution by at least $1.2 billion.

That letter provoked a sharp debate when the Appropriations panel met on Oct. 31. In a break with tradition, Hatfield sided with the Budget Committee, saying that Kasten and Inouye had made the foreign aid bill vulnerable to a deep across-the-board cut. Hatfield also said the Israel aid set a precedent, and that Egypt, South Korea and other nations would be "justified" in seeking similar relief.

Kasten and Inouye refused to budge, saying that a way could be found to keep the Israel aid in the bill while satisfying the Budget panel complaints. If a way could not be found, Kasten agreed to offer a floor amendment cutting other items. With that assurance, Appropriations approved S 1816.

The Israel item also was opposed by Secretary of State George P. Shultz, who wrote to all senators asking for its removal.

Foreign Relations Dispute

In November, the Senate Foreign Relations Committee launched its attack on the Israel aid provision in the foreign operations bill and on the bill's repeal of authorization in the foreign aid bill (PL 99-83).

The issue dividing the two panels was one of power over the multi-million-dollar foreign aid program, one of the primary foreign policy tools of the United States.

Foreign Relations was responsible for authorizing legislation, which set overall policy guidelines for appropriations bills. But from 1982 through 1984, the House and Senate Appropriations committees, and their respective Foreign Operations subcommittees, had wielded most of the congressional power over foreign aid. That was because Congress failed to enact authorization bills but did enact appropriations as part of omnibus continuing resolutions. In the Senate, Foreign Operations Subcommittee Chairman Kasten seemed to relish the power, reportedly telling Reagan officials and lobbyists for foreign governments that he held the purse strings for foreign aid.

After Congress broke that cycle in the summer, enacting a full-scale foreign aid authorization bill, the clout of the Foreign Relations and House Foreign Affairs committees was restored.

Kasten moved to reclaim his authority when the Foreign Operations Subcommittee and the full Appropriations Committee drafted the fiscal 1986 aid spending bill.

With the backing of ranking Democrat Inouye, Kasten inserted the special Israel aid provision.

Kasten also added to the appropriations bill an obscure item, section 523, that would have had the effect of repealing many of the most important provisions of the authorization bill: the "earmarks" and prohibitions that set minimum or maximum amounts of aid that could be given individual countries and groups.

An aide to Kasten said section 523 was a routine effort to clarify "conflicting earmarks" in the authorization and appropriations measures. The Appropriations Committee had taken similar action in the past, he said, although by the less sweeping route of changing the funding levels of individual items. He also noted that most items in the appropriations bill were identical to the authorization bill.

But Foreign Relations Chairman Richard G. Lugar, R-Ind., and ranking Democrat Claiborne Pell, R.I., and their aides saw section 523 as a much broader attack on their committee's authority.

In a statement inserted in the *Congressional Record* on Nov. 21, Lugar said he was concerned about parts of the appropriations bill that "run counter to those which the full Congress and the president agreed to only last summer." He cited in particular section 523. While not mentioning Israel by name, Lugar also referred to the $500 million special aid program, saying the money amounts in the appropriations bill "exceed authorized levels by a substantial amount."

Pell followed with a statement in the Nov. 22 Record, calling section 523 "a gratuitous slap" at his committee.

Kasten, after meeting with Shultz, agreed to drop the extra Israel aid provision. In the Appropriations Committee's Dec. 5 markup, Kasten offered an amendment taking out the Israel money and making changes in the funding for the International Development Association (IDA) and the Export-Import Bank.

The amendment, adopted by voice vote, put a ceiling of $375 million on U.S. contributions to IDA and limited to $1.8 billion the amount of direct loans by the United States to the Export-Import Bank. The funding for the bank was about half the amount requested by the administration, and less than half the $3.9 billion available to the bank in fiscal 1985.

The panel also approved another Kasten amendment, making several changes to conform the foreign aid appropriation to the foreign aid authorization law.

Other Key Provisions

Other provisions in the bill would have:

- Set a $95 million limit on military loans to Jordan, thus forcing Reagan to return to Congress for any special aid to help Jordan pay for a controversial arms package. *(Story, p. 93)*
- Set a $70 million limit on military aid to the Philippines — $30 million more than the fiscal 1985 amount but $30 million less than Reagan wanted.
- Overturned a Reagan administration decision to aid groups that advocated only "natural" family planning methods overseas. The provision allowed aid only for groups that offered "a broad range" of family planning methods. ■

Defense Funds: Drop in Pentagon's Buying Power

For the first time in a decade, Congress voted a defense budget that would result in a significant decline in the Pentagon's purchasing power.

The continuing appropriations resolution (H J Res 465—PL 99-190) cleared and signed by President Reagan on Dec. 19 contained $281.2 billion in new Defense Department budget authority for fiscal 1986, bringing overall defense appropriations for fiscal 1986 to $297.6 billion. *(Continuing resolution, p. 360)*

According to Ted Stevens, R-Alaska, chairman of the Senate Appropriations Subcommittee on Defense, that would amount to a 2 percent decrease in Pentagon purchasing power compared with the fiscal 1985 budget, once the cost of inflation was taken into account.

The defense appropriation faced further cuts under the Gramm-Rudman-Hollings budget-balancing law (PL 99-177). The first automatic spending cuts, affecting the Pentagon as well as a range of domestic programs, were to occur March 1, 1986, under the law's timetable. *(Gramm-Rudman law, p. 459)*

Stevens predicted that the anticipated Gramm-Rudman-Hollings cuts could bring the decline in real defense purchasing power to nearly 7 percent.

Despite the drama inherent in the first declining defense budget in years, the continuing appropriations measure was fundamentally indistinguishable from defense funding bills earlier in Reagan's term.

Once again, House-Senate conferees — like the members of the Appropriations panels who drafted earlier versions of the bill — made hefty trims at the margins of specific programs. But they neither killed any major programs nor reshaped the basic priorities of Reagan's February budget request.

The only clear challenge Congress posed to an important Reagan policy was a ban on tests of the anti-satellite (ASAT) missile against a space target. *(ASAT, p. 162)*

As in 1984, defense funds were folded into the omnibus continuing resolution because Congress failed to enact a separate defense spending bill. The House approved a defense appropriations bill (HR 3629) on Oct. 30, but Senate action on the measure was delayed by farm and budget legislation. *(1984 Almanac p. 399)*

Conference Report

The conference report on the final version of the continuing resolution (H Rept 99-450) was filed Dec. 19; it was agreed to that day by voice vote in the Senate and by 261-137 in the House. *(Vote 433, p. 136-H)*

The $281.2 billion appropriation was $1.5 billion less than the Senate Appropriations Committee had in its version of the defense funding bill and $12.3 million more than the House had originally voted. Supporters of Reagan's defense buildup insisted that the compromise include as much money as possible to help cushion the shock of the Gramm-Rudman budget cuts.

The continuing resolution also identified $6.3 billion left over from amounts appropriated for various projects in earlier years, much of it due to lower-than-anticipated inflation. The bill required the Pentagon to use those funds only for certain purposes, among them: $1.8 billion to pay for the annual military pay raise; $2.9 billion for military pensions if Congress did not quickly adopt pension reform legislation; $852 million for a fund to begin constructing cargo ships to be chartered to commercial firms in peacetime but which could be used for military purposes in case of war; and improvements in the combat readiness of conventional forces.

The resolution barred use of any of the prior-year money to offset the impact of Gramm-Rudman budget cuts. On Dec. 16, the House rejected an earlier version of the continuing resolution that included an additional $1.3 billion in new Pentagon budget authority and did not earmark the $6.3 billion in leftover funds.

One reason the measure was defeated was the complaint of many liberals that the defense appropriation was much closer to the Senate-passed amount than to the House figure, and that the $6.3 billion in prior-year money represented a cushion against Gramm-Rudman cuts.

Strategic Warfare

The House and Senate versions of the bill each included $1.7 billion for 12 MX missiles. The budget request had been for 40 missiles ($3 billion), but the reduction was agreed to as part of a package compromise on the fiscal 1986 defense authorization bill (S1160 — PL 99-145). That deal also included a legislative cap of 50 on the number of MXs to be deployed in existing missile silos. *(MX, p. 119; defense authorization, p. 138)*

The two houses were in basic agreement with the budget request on four other major strategic weapons programs, so the conferees had to resolve little more than some differing budgetary assumptions between Senate and House appropriators:

- For the last 48 B-1 bombers, the conferees approved $5.2 billion.
- For the 13th huge Trident-missile-launching submarine, $1.2 billion was appropriated.
- Conferees voted $2.1 billion to continue developing a larger version of the Trident missile — the D-5 or Trident II — and $582 million to set up a production line for the new weapon.
- To develop an intercontinental missile small enough to be carried in a mobile launcher and carrying a single nuclear warhead — dubbed Midgetman — conferees agreed on the $624 million requested. Another $122 million was approved for research on methods of deploying missiles in very heavily armored silos.

Space Weapons. To continue Reagan's program of research on anti-missile defenses — the "strategic defense initiative" (SDI) or "star wars" — conferees approved $2.75 billion, the ceiling set by the defense authorization bill. Reagan had requested $3.7 billion. *(SDI, p. 130)*

The conferees also retained a Senate provision prohibiting the Pentagon from setting aside some SDI contracts to be awarded only to firms from other countries. Some critics suspected that the administration might do this to win other countries' political support for the project.

The conference report also would ban tests of the anti-satellite (ASAT) missile against targets in space as long as the Soviet Union continued its ongoing ASAT test moratorium.

Ground Combat

The final bill funded 840 M-1 tanks ($1.6 billion) — the number requested and approved by the House — rather than the 720 tanks ($1.3 billion) proposed by the Senate.

On the other hand, the Senate's effort to increase production of Bradley infantry carriers to 761 vehicles ($958 million) was rejected. The conferees approved $931 million for 710 Bradleys, the number included in the budget request and the House bill.

Both houses had approved the request for 144 Apache anti-tank helicopters ($1.1 billion) with minor budgetary differences.

Fiscal 1986 Appropriations for Defense

(in millions of dollars)*

	Reagan Request	House-Passed	Senate-Passed	Final Appropriation
Military personnel	$ 73,425.1	$ 70,139.8	$ 67,783.6	$ 67,906.3
Operations and maintenance	82,450.2	77,222.4	78,835.6	78,664.5
Procurement	106,813.3	86,597.2	98,064.6	97,393.1
(Transfer from other accounts)		(6,827.6)	(3,940.0)	
Research and development	39,280.1	33,152.8	35,984.1	35,337.5
(Transfer from other accounts)		(920.1)	(775.0)	
Special foreign currency program	2.1	2.1	2.1	2.1
Revolving and management funds	1,859.6	1,612.8	1,809.6	1,734.8
Related agencies	123.7	123.5	123.7	123.5
Total, new budget authority	$ 303,954.0	$ 268,850.6	$ 282,703.4	$ 281,161.8
(Transfer from other accounts)		(7,747.7)	(5,547.1)	
Total funding available	$ 303,954.0	$ 276,598.3	$ 288,250.5	$ 281,161.9

* *Totals may not add because of rounding.*

SOURCE: *Congressional Record*

The conferees agreed with a Senate plan to buy 80 Blackhawk troop-carrying helicopters at a cost of $229 million. The budget request was $267 million for 78 Blackhawks, but the conferees — like the Senate — dropped $32 million for some electronic accessories not yet ready for production. The two extra helicopters were to replace two older ones that, in turn, were to be given to the Customs Service for hunting drug smugglers.

To equip "scout" helicopters with target-finding equipment, the conferees agreed on $197 million of the $201 million requested. The Senate had nearly halved the program to $104 million. But the conferees trimmed from 56 to 39 the number of modifications to be made and earmarked the remaining funds for additional maintenance equipment.

The conferees also trimmed funds for development of the LHX, a small helicopter the Army hoped to begin buying in the 1990s to replace more than 7,000 Vietnam War-era choppers. The bill approved $45 million of the $76 million requested for development of the LHX itself, and the conferees warned that Congress might kill the project the following year unless the Army committed itself to a ceiling price for the machine.

Both houses had approved the $71 million requested to develop a new helicopter engine that would be used in the LHX.

DIVAD and Nerve Gas. Both houses had dropped from the bill the $406 million requested to continue production of the Sergeant York (or DIVAD) anti-aircraft gun, which Defense Secretary Caspar W. Weinberger canceled in August. The conference report followed the Senate's lead in earmarking some of those funds to select and begin buying some other anti-aircraft weapon "off the shelf" to replace DIVAD in the Army's lineup. *(DIVAD, p. 154)*

The conferees approved $191 million for the yet-to-be-selected replacement.

To begin production of "binary" chemical weapons, the final version of the bill appropriated $126 million of the $164 million requested. This included $21.7 million to begin production of a binary artillery shell — the first U.S. manufacture of lethal chemical weapons since 1969.

An additional $98.3 million was earmarked to complete construction of a production line for a binary air bomb called Bigeye. The $43.6 million requested for Bigeye production was dropped because of testing problems and $6 million for further development of the weapon was added to the research budget.

Tactical Air Combat

For five of the six types of fighter planes and small bombers currently bought by the Pentagon, the two houses basically approved the budget request, leaving only details to be hammered out by the conference committee:

- For 48 Air Force F-15s, the conferees approved $1.8 billion.
- For 180 F-16s, $2.6 billion was approved. This $253 million reduction from the budget reflected Pentagon decisions to eliminate from the planes several pieces of electronic equipment.
- The conferees approved $649 million for 18 Navy F-14s.
- For 84 F/A-18s, used by the Navy as both a fighter and a small bomber, the bill appropriated $2.3 billion. This was $226 million less than the original request, because of lower than planned prices for some plane components.
- To buy 46 AV-8B Harriers — small vertical-takeoff bombers used by the Marine Corps — the bill included $821 million.

Both houses had included in the bill $200 million to begin buying more than 300 copies of whatever plane won a competition among relatively inexpensive fighters. A stripped-down version of the F-16 was expected to compete with the F-20 for the contract.

The only combat plane over which the two houses had seriously disagreed was the Navy's A-6E carrier-launched bomber. The conferees agreed with the House position providing $293 million for 11 planes, instead of the six requested by the budget and approved by the Senate.

The conference committee also provided $150 million to begin production of the AMRAAM air-to-air missile, which had encountered strong opposition because it had proved more expensive than projected. The budget sought $366 million for AMRAAM and the House provided no funds.

Both houses had approved the $348 million requested to develop an improved version of the F-14 Navy fighter.

The Senate had trimmed the request for an improved A-6E bomber to $188 million, but the conferees approved the $232 million requested.

To develop a new fighter to replace the Air Force F-15 and F-16 beginning in the mid-1990s, the committee approved $170 million of the $243 million requested.

Naval Warfare

To modernize the last of four World War II-era battleships and equip them with long-range cruise missiles, the conference committee approved $469 million.

The administration had requested only $53.5 million to prepare for the conversion, planning to request the rest of the money in the fiscal 1987 budget. The House had approved the use of excess money from prior appropriations to pay for the accelerated program, while the Senate earmarked leftover prior-year money only for the $53.5 million down payment.

The two houses had essentially approved the other major combat ships requested in the budget: four *Los Angeles*-class submarines designed to hunt Soviet subs ($2.1 billion) and four cruisers carrying the Aegis anti-aircraft system ($2.6 billion).

The conferees approved $74 million of the $164 million requested for components that would be used in several smaller Aegis-equipped ships to be funded in the fiscal 1987 budget.

Two large Navy airplane programs the Senate bill would have killed were funded with only minor reductions by the conferees:

- For the first two E-6A airborne radio stations, the entire $297 million request was approved. These were to be versions of Boeing commercial jetliners modified to tow a five-mile-long radio aerial for sending orders to submerged missile-launching submarines.
- Nine additional P-3C long-range anti-submarine patrol planes were approved ($323 million of the $330 million requested). That was in addition to $243 million the Senate had added to its version of the bill to modernize older P-3s already in service.

Airlift and Sealift

The budget request for 16 huge C-5 cargo planes ($1.8 billion) had been approved by both houses.

Conferees agreed to $384 million to develop a smaller aerial transport, the C-17, designed to haul tanks and other large pieces of equipment into primitive airstrips. Originally, the Pentagon had requested $454 million for this program.

Both houses had approved the two large ships included in this Navy budget to help Marine Corps units land on hostile shores: a large helicopter carrier able to haul 2,000 Marines ($1.15 billion); and a so-called LSD designed to carry tanks and other heavy gear and the barges needed to haul them ashore ($403 million).

Also agreed to was $580 million of the $604 million requested to continue development of a hybrid airplane/helicopter called the Osprey (formerly JVX), which was intended to replace the Marines' aging fleet of troop-carrying helicopters.

Both houses had approved the request for $228 million to buy mothballed commercial ships for use as a reserve cargo fleet in case of war.

Personnel Costs and Missions

The conference report cut $695 million from the request for military and civilian personnel costs. This amounted to the bulk of an $808 million reduction made by the Senate to freeze Pentagon manpower costs.

But the conferees included more than $2 billion the administration had not requested for organizations (or missions) that were politically attractive:

- For new equipment for National Guard and reserve units, the bill included $1.5 billion. Congress traditionally had been solicitous of these politically influential organizations. But the Pentagon also had been taking them more seriously, relying on them for important military missions.
- The budget of the Coast Guard — a part of the Treasury Department — was supplemented by $235 million in new budget authority and $140 million in surplus prior-year funds for ships and planes.

An additional $100 million was added to the bill to help pay the Coast Guard's operating expenses. The Coast Guard would operate as part of the Navy in case of war, which was the rationale for these additions. But it also had acquired strong political support in recent years for its role in combating drug smuggling.

Other Provisions

The conference retained $300 million added by the Senate to buy two new airplanes to replace the aging Boeing 707s that had served as "Air Force One."

They also provided $55.1 million to screen recruits for acquired immune deficiency syndrome (AIDS) and an additional $40 million for AIDS research.

In addition, they reaffirmed provisions of the fiscal 1986 intelligence authorization act (PL 99-169) regarding U.S. assistance to "contras," the guerrillas who were battling the leftist government of Nicaragua. *(Intelligence act, p. 96)*

House Committee Action

The House Appropriations Committee on Oct. 24 reported a defense appropriations bill (HR 3629 — Rept 99-332) providing $276.5 billion for Pentagon programs in fiscal 1986. That was to be a reduction of $27.4 billion from the amount requested by the president for this bill.

Of the total, $268.8 billion was in new budget authority and an additional $7.7 billion was drawn from funds that had been appropriated for defense in earlier years but not spent.

The Appropriations panel denied all funds for three major weapons programs: binary munitions, the AMRAAM air-to-air missile and the DIVAD anti-aircraft gun.

The committee made the lion's share of its reductions in those parts of Reagan's request that paid for new weapons. The $107 billion procurement request was cut by 12 percent, to $94 billion; the $39 billion budget for research and development was cut by 13 percent, to $34 billion.

By contrast, the $73 billion requested for military personnel was cut by less than 5 percent to $70 billion. The $82 billion request for day-to-day operations and maintenance for units and facilities was reduced by slightly more than 6 percent to $77 billion.

Manpower

The bulk of the panel's military personnel cut reflected a $2.7 billion reduction in the $18.2 billion requested for military pensions funding. The authorization measure also provided that no pensions then going to retirees would be reduced.

The committee also ordered the Pentagon to find surplus funds in the budget to cover part of the 3 percent military pay raise that had been authorized beginning Oct. 1. The administration had requested $1.9 billion to cover a 3 percent hike starting in July. The panel cut $189 million and set the pay hike for Oct. 1.

Congress had rejected across the board Reagan's proposal to cut civilian federal workers' pay by 5 percent. For the Pentagon's 1.1 million civilians that would have required adding $1 billion to the budget request, most of it in the operations and maintenance accounts. The committee added $550 million, directing the Pentagon to squeeze the remainder out of the rest of its budget.

Reagan requested an increase in active duty military strength of 25,630: from 2,152,470 to 2,178,100. The increase authorized by S 1160 was 14,900 and the Appropriations panel funded that manpower level, a reduction from the request of $125 million.

Reserves, National Guard. The $20 billion requested for National Guard and reserve forces included $4 billion for procurement of some of the newest types of equipment the Army was buying, among them: 60 M-1 tanks, 117 Bradley armored troop carriers and 30 Blackhawk troop-carrying helicopters.

The committee funded that procurement request in full and added to the budget $743 million for National Guard and reserve projects that had not been requested by the administration. Among these add-ons were 14 C-130 transport planes ($270 million). The committee also ordered the Army to hand over to the National Guard 18 of the 144 Apache anti-tank helicopters that were included in the bill.

Congress long had been supportive of the politically influential Guard and reserve forces. But in recent years, the practice had gained momentum as Pentagon planners had assigned increasingly significant roles to reserves.

Because this had resulted in an increase in the number of federal employees and the amount of federal equipment operating in the 2,800 state-owned National Guard armories, the committee proposed that the Pentagon begin contributing the cost of armory operations. It added to the bill $33 million for an interim program of building repair, office renovation and operating cost reimbursement.

The panel suggested that the Pentagon begin picking up 25 percent of the cost of major armory repairs.

Operations and Maintenance

More than 80 percent of the committee's reduction in the request for operations and maintenance funds reflected changes in the marketplace. These economic changes had reduced the cost of planned Pentagon activities, according to the panel:

- $2.9 billion was cut in the expectation that supplies and overhauls would cost less than had been budgeted. Nearly $1 billion of that reduction was intended to be offset by funds that had been appropriated in earlier years in anticipation of higher costs than had materialized.
- $1 billion was cut from the funds budgeted for the operating expenses of U.S. forces deployed overseas because of the dollar's continuing strength against foreign currencies.
- $500 million was cut from the amount requested for fuel, in the expectation that oil would cost less than budget-writers had projected.

All three kinds of reductions already had become routine on Capitol Hill.

The committee added to the bill $144 million to boost funding for overdue routine overhauls of ships, planes and Army vehicles. Under Reagan's request, the backlog of such overhauls would have increased. The committee said the $144 million would hold the Navy and Air Force backlogs at their fiscal 1985 levels while reducing the Army's backlog to zero.

Another $154 million was added to the request for routine upkeep of Pentagon real estate. Under Reagan's budget, the estimated cost of overdue building maintenance would have risen from $3.5 billion in fiscal 1985 to more than $3.6 billion.

Strategic Weapons

Pursuant to a compromise hammered out during debate on the authorization bill, the Appropriations panel approved $1.7 billion for 12 additional MX missiles. The administration had requested 48 missiles ($3 billion).

To continue development of the MX and to begin development of a small, single-warhead missile to complement it — informally referred to as "Midgetman" — the committee approved the $1.55 billion authorized (of $1.58 billion requested).

But the panel said that $65 million of that amount would not need to be appropriated since it could be drawn from funds appropriated for the projects in earlier years but not spent.

The committee approved the huge Trident missile-launching submarine requested by the Navy — which would be the 13th of its class. But the panel appropriated only $816.7 million of the $1.28 billion requested for the ship.

Earlier Trident appropriations had a total of $373.9 million left over that could make up the difference, the committee said. Pointing out that recent contractor bids and the rate of inflation were running below Pentagon predictions, the panel said that $1.19 billion would be enough to build the ship.

The $2.16 billion requested to develop the Trident II sub-launched missile was trimmed by $62 million to $2.1 billion. The new missile was intended to carry more warheads than the existing Trident I and to give them sufficient accuracy to destroy armored enemy missile silos.

Funding for the last 48 of the planned fleet of 100 B-1 bombers was trimmed by $600 million to $4.86 billion. According to the panel, the reduction would not affect the program because contractors were bidding for parts of the project at lower rates than had been anticipated.

The amounts requested and approved for the so-called "stealth" bomber, designed to supplement the B-1, were secret. The stealth was designed to evade enemy detection.

Of the $463 million requested to modernize existing B-52 bombers, the committee approved $416.5 million, with an additional $8 million available from earlier appropriations.

The panel trimmed to $682 million the request for $698 million to put new, more efficient jet engines on the KC-135 tanker planes designed to refuel bombers in mid-air. The fiscal 1985 contract for the project included an option that would provide a lower price on the fiscal 1986 modifications, the panel said.

ASAT, 'Star Wars'

The committee bill contained a provision, which the House had adopted as part of its version of the authorization bill, barring flight tests against space targets of the anti-satellite (ASAT) missile. The moratorium was dependent upon the Soviets continuing their ban on tests of the weapon.

But with President Reagan's summit meeting with Soviet leader Mikhail Gorbachev just weeks away, the Appropriations panel rejected a move to trim $400 million from the anti-missile research program that was at the heart of the two nations' strategic arms debate.

Reagan had requested $3.96 billion for the "strategic defense initiative" (SDI) and the companion defense authorization bill contained $2.75 billion. By a vote of 23-31, the House Appropriations panel voted down an amendment offered by Vic Fazio, D-Calif., to cut the program from $2.5 billion to $2.1 billion.

Before the vote, the White House had strenuously lobbied Appropriations members to close ranks behind President Reagan before the Nov. 19-20 summit and the campaign evidently paid off. *(Summit, p. 109)*

Eight Appropriations Committee members who had voted for $2.1 billion on the House floor in June switched on Oct. 24 and opposed the new SDI trim. They included four of the committee's senior Democrats: Chairman Jamie L. Whitten, Miss., and three subcommittee chairmen: Edward P. Boland, Mass.; William H. Natcher, Ky.; and Neal Smith, Iowa. The other Democrats who switched to oppose $2.1 billion were Ronald D. Coleman, Texas; Bill Boner, Tenn.; and Wes Watkins, Okla. Moderate Republican Carl D. Pursell, Mich., followed the same pattern.

Nerve Gas

The committee on Oct. 24 adopted 26-24 an amendment deleting all $163 million requested to begin production of binary weapons.

Each year from 1982 to 1984, the House had blocked Reagan's proposal to end the nerve gas production moratorium, which had begun in 1969. In 1985, the House had authorized binary funding but with some stringent conditions attached. For instance, production would not begin until fiscal 1987 and then only if NATO formally requested it.

Those conditions were substantially diluted in the defense authorization conference report (S 1160 — H Rept 99-235).

John Edward Porter, R-Ill., who offered the binary amendment in the Appropriations Committee, later said that he had gained votes because some members were unhappy that the authorization conferees had relaxed the binary restrictions.

Ground Combat

The committee's proposal for each of the Army's two principal types of combat vehicles illustrated the range of bookkeeping adjustments that the panel used to trim hundreds of millions of dollars from major arms programs without reducing the number of weapons purchased.

For instance, it approved purchase of 840 M-1 tanks, but recommended an appropriation of only $1.48 billion rather than the $1.75 billion requested. Of the $271.2 million difference, the committee said that $77.9 million could be transferred from available funds in earlier budget years. The remaining $193.3 million, the panel said, was unnecessary because of lower than anticipated contract bids and other savings.

The $1 billion request for 716 Bradley armored infantry carriers was reduced by $97.7 million, using similar logic. In this case, the panel said that $21.7 million could be transferred from earlier appropriations and the remaining $76 million dropped because of low contractor bids and dispensable contract frills.

Similar trimming was applied to the Army's major helicopter projects:

- The request for 144 Apache anti-tank helicopters was cut by $40.9 million to $1.14 billion.
- To modernize 56 small "scout" helicopters to find targets for the Apaches, the panel recommended $146.8 million of the $158.8 million requested.
- The committee reduced by $46.2 million (to $220.8 million) the request for 78 Blackhawk troop carriers. In this case, $32.2 million of the cut was for a secret modification the committee rejected.
- A total of $378.1 million, requested to rebuild Chinook cargo helicopters, was trimmed to $347.3 million. Prior-year funds would offset $11.2 million of the $30.8 million reduction.

Anti-tank Weapons. No reduction was made in the $305.8 million requested for Hellfire laser-guided anti-tank missiles carried by Apaches and some other helicopters. To boost anti-tank firepower, the committee added $20 million to equip some troop helicopters with the Hellfire, a move the Army had resisted, partly for fear that it would encourage Congress to cut back purchases of the more costly Apache.

The committee reduced from nearly 25,000 to less than 17,000 the number of TOW anti-tank missiles to be purchased, insisting that this would even out planned fluctuations in annual TOW purchases. The TOW appropriation was set at $203.8 million, a reduction of $67.6 million from the request.

The panel reiterated its longstanding complaint that the Pentagon was developing too many anti-tank weapons with similar missions. "No tradeoffs between competing programs have been demanded and no difficult choices have been forced," it said.

The committee supported in large measure development of a long-range rocket (called JTACMS) that would rain down conventional warheads on tank columns tens of miles behind an enemy's front line, guided by an airborne radar called Joint STARS. The panel nearly doubled the Joint STARS budget from $47 million to $93.8 million. It trimmed the JTACMS request by $24.8 million, to $130 million.

Anti-aircraft Weapons. Defense Secretary Caspar W. Weinberger's cancellation in August of the trouble-plagued DIVAD anti-aircraft gun yielded one of the three major weapons for which the Appropriations panel denied all funds in Reagan's February request.

Counting production and research funds, ammunition and unspent appropriations from earlier years that now could be diverted to other projects, the total reduction related to DIVAD was $1.25 billion.

The committee estimated that an additional $130 million to $150 million would become available as current DIVAD contracts were canceled. It said it would allot those funds for any replacement weapon the Army could justify.

But the panel approved only $37.2 million of the $110.4 million requested for production of a new version of the Chaparral short-range anti-aircraft missile — one of the weapons the DIVAD was intended to replace. Production of the new version was premature, it said.

The request for Patriot long-range anti-aircraft missiles was trimmed by $16 million, to $967.4 million in anticipation of lower than predicted bids.

Aerial Warfare

The requests for the principal tactical combat planes used by the Navy and Air Force were cut by more than $1.2 billion, with no reduction in the number of aircraft. In terms of new budget authority, the committee recommended:

- 18 of the Navy's long-range F-14 fighters for $553.6 million, a reduction of $100 million.
- 84 Navy F-18s, used by the Navy both as a fighter and a small bomber, for $2.1 billion, a $340 million reduction.
- 46 AV-8Bs, a vertical takeoff jet used by the Marine Corps as a light bomber, for $637.3 million, a reduction of $255.2 million.
- 48 F-16 Air Force fighters for $1.76 billion, a $145 million reduction.
- 180 smaller F-16 Air Force fighters for $2.48 billion, $351.6 million less than the request.

Delays in the production of a new radar jammer intended to equip some of the planes accounted for a sizable fraction of the reductions. But the bulk of the aircraft cutbacks reflected the committee's judgment that contract bids would continue to run low, as in previous years.

An additional $320.8 million was dropped because of the problems in producing a radar warning device intended for several types of planes.

The committee also sliced $1.5 billion from the $4.9 billion requested for Air Force spare parts, complaining that the service was routinely overestimating the number of parts it would use up during normal peacetime training.

New Planes. The committee included in the bill $200 million, not requested by the Air Force, to begin buying some relatively inexpensive fighter planes in addition to the more expensive F-15s and F-16s. The new plane was to be selected by a competition that likely would include the Northrop F-20 and a stripped-down version of the General Dynamics F-16.

The panel also approved $20 million to test a modernized version of the Vietnam War-era Phantom jet.

The panel approved most of the funds requested for three major programs intended to develop combat planes for the 1990s:

- For an improved model of the F-14, $348 million, the amount requested.
- For an A-6F model to replace the Navy's A-6E bomber, $232 million, a reduction of $5.9 million.

• For a so-called advanced tactical fighter to replace the F-15 and F-16, $169.8 million of the $242.8 million requested.

The entire $432.4 million requested to begin production of the AMRAAM air-to-air missile was refused by the committee. The panel noted that this was the third consecutive budget in which the Air Force had claimed initially that the new missile was ready to begin production only to reverse its position because of continued cost increases and technical problems with the missile.

Naval Combat

The only ships the Navy requested that the committee denied outright were four mine sweepers of a class that had had production problems and delivery delays. The committee denied the $334.1 million request.

For the second year in a row, the Navy would rebuild a battleship — this time, the *Wisconsin* — a year ahead of schedule and without any appropriation of new budget authority. The $469 million project could be paid for entirely from surplus funds left over from earlier ship building appropriations, the committee said.

This was the last of four World War II battlewagons being equipped with long-range Tomahawk cruise missiles, like several more modern surface ships and submarines. The committee approved the $670 million requested for 249 Tomahawks.

The committee recommended $2.1 billion of the $2.8 billion requested for three Aegis cruisers intended to protect fleets against swarms of attacking cruise missiles. Of the $693.4 million reduction, $585.2 million should be made up from leftover prior-year Aegis appropriations, it said.

It denied $9.8 million requested to develop a nuclear-armed anti-aircraft missile for use by the Aegis cruiser and other ships, and ordered that the nuclear project be canceled. The Navy had some existing nuclear anti-aircraft missiles, but the committee objected that the weapons might be used without proper civilian authorization and might damage the ships they were being fired to protect.

The Navy requested $44.7 million to begin production of the RAM short-range missile, designed as a last-ditch defense for ships against cruise missiles, but the committee maintained that production was premature in light of some test failures. The panel approved $15 million to set up the RAM production line and $10.9 million to continue development.

Submarine Hunting. For four *Los Angeles*-class submarines, designed chiefly to hunt Soviet subs, the committee recommended $1.95 billion of the $2.12 billion requested. An additional $159.2 million was available from earlier appropriations.

The panel approved $371.7 million — $17.6 million less than requested — to continue work on a new class of anti-sub submarine, the so-called SSN-21. It complained that the project was being pushed too fast.

It also slashed to $90.1 million the $205.2 million requested for an electronic targeting system to be used on the new sub and on later copies of the current *Los Angeles* class.

Like most other Navy aircraft programs, the two types of small anti-submarine helicopters that were carried aboard most surface ships likely could be bought for less per copy than the budget request assumed, the committee said:

• For 18 LAMPS IIIs, the panel recommended $203 million of the $316 million requested, with an additional $47 million to be reallocated from earlier appropriations.

• For the smaller LAMPS I, the committee recommended $61 million of the $70 million requested.

Airlift and Sealift

Of the $1.94 billion requested for 16 huge C-5B cargo planes, the committee approved $1.59 million. An additional $354 million could be transferred from earlier appropriations, it said. The reduction reflected lowered inflation estimates and the denial of some management reserve funds the committee deemed excessive.

Lower inflation also accounted for much of the $71.2 million reduction (to $375.8 million) in the appropriation for the year's installment of a multi-year contract to buy KC-10 midair refueling tankers.

To buy mothballed commercial cargo ships as a reserve fleet for use in wartime, the committee recommended a total of $228.4 million, instead of the $203.4 million requested. But it approved only $173.1 million in new budget authority, allocating surplus funds from earlier budgets to make up the balance.

The committee also made financing adjustments in the request for amphibious assault ships designed to land Marine Corps units under fire:

• The panel approved $1.28 billion of the $1.51 billion requested for a so-called LHD: an aircraft carrier able to haul 2,000 troops and their transport helicopters. This included funds for components that would be used in future ships of the same type.

• For two LSD transports, designed to carry tanks and other heavy equipment and the barges to haul them ashore, the committee approved $384.5 million of the $414.4 million requested and added $18.9 million left over from earlier appropriations.

The panel approved $572 million of the $609 million requested for development of the Osprey (formerly JVX), a hybrid airplane/helicopter the Marines would use to haul troops ashore from distant amphibious fleets.

Other Provisions

The committe bill would have barred both direct and indirect lethal military assistance to the "contra" guerillas fighting Nicaragua's leftist government. This limitation had been incorporated into the House-passed version of the intelligence authorization bill (HR 2419). *(Nicaragua, p. 61)*

The committee approved $15 million to station Coast Guard officers aboard Navy ships steaming in areas that were heavily used by seaborne drug smugglers. Unlike military personnel, Coast Guard officers had the legal authority to arrest drug smugglers at sea.

But the panel turned down a proposed $300 million appropriation to buy equipment for the Coast Guard, which was part of the Treasury Department.

The Army requested $34 million for a new program to screen for acquired immune deficiency syndrome (AIDS) new recruits and military personnel who donated blood. But the committee approved only $15 million, arguing that the cost estimate was based on too sketchy a plan.

In hopes of reducing the number of personnel investigations requested from the Pentagon by other federal agencies and by private industry, the committee ordered the Pentagon to begin charging for security investigations, beginning in fiscal 1987. Many of the security clearances currently requested were unnecessary, the committee said.

Funding for Major Defense Programs, Fiscal 1986

Following is a comparison of the amounts Congress authorized and appropriated for major defense programs in fiscal 1986. Amounts for weapons procurement included some funds for components of items to be bought in future budgets.

(amounts in millions of dollars)

	Reagan Request		Enacted Authorization (HR 5167)		Enacted Appropriation (H J Res 648)	
	Number	Amount	Number	Amount	Number	Amount
Strategic Weapons						
MX missile	48	$23,037	12	$1,746	21	$1,746
B-1 bomber	48	5,462	48	5,462	48	5,162
Trident submarine	1	1,532	1	1,482	1	1,355
Trident II missile (including R&D)		2,748		2,713		2,699
Strategic defense initiative ("star wars")		3,713		2,750		2,750
Ground Combat						
M-1 tank	840	2,109	840	1,923	840	1,873
Bradley troop carrier	716	1,035	716	1,010	716	953
Apache anti-tank helicopter	144	1,234	144	1,234	144	1,193
"Deep Strike" weapons (JTACMS and JSTARS)		418		373		333
Sergeant York anti-aircraft gun (DIVAD)	117	418	72	221	0	150[1]
Patriot anti-aircraft missile	585	983	585	983	585	963
Naval Warfare						
Battleship modernization		54		54	1	469
Aegis cruiser	3	2,766	3	2,766	3	2,653
Sub-hunting submarine	4	2,708	4	2,708	4	2,610
Anti-submarine helicopters (LAMPS I and LAMPS III)	24	440	24	436	24	366
P-3C anti-submarine plane	9	486	9	429	9	429
Tactical Air Combat						
F-15 fighter	48	2,139	48	2,041	48	1,967
F-16 fighter	180	3,390	180	3,179	180	3,132
F-14 carrier fighter	18	802	18	678	18	773
F-18 carrier fighter	84	2,762	84	2,690	84	2,478
A-6E carrier bomber	6	214	11	314	11	314
AV-8B vertical-takeoff bomber	46	979	46	934	46	908
Airlift and Sealift						
LHD helicopter ship	1	1,507	1	1,314	1	1,314
LSD amphibious ship	2	414	2	414	2	403
Purchase of commercial ships for reserve cargo fleet		203		228		228
C-5 transport plane	16	2,268	16	2,166	16	2,135
KC-10 tanker-cargo plane	12	447	12	447	12	432
C-17 cargo plane R&D		454		374		384

[1] The Sergeant York (DIVAD) was canceled in August; $150 million was earmarked to buy an unspecified replacement.

House Floor Action

After the shortest floor debate on any defense appropriations bill in years, the House Oct. 30 passed a measure freezing the defense budget for fiscal 1986 at the $292 billion appropriated for fiscal 1985.

The bill (HR 3629) was passed by a vote of 359-67. *(Vote 343, p. 106-H)*

But the debate's brevity — less than four hours from start to finish — belied a dense web of political battles enmeshing the bill: President Reagan's soon-to-happen Nov. 19 summit meeting with Soviet leader Gorbachev; Washington's ongoing melee over cutting the federal deficit; and the extreme unhappiness of some congressional Republicans over Reagan's approach to farm money problems.

Steeped in this rich political bouillon, the defense appropriations bill yielded a floor fight, but not the one that had been expected.

There was no effort on the House floor by arms control advocates to cut back Reagan's program to develop anti-missile defenses, as they had tried unsuccessfully to do when the Appropriations Committee marked up the bill Oct. 24.

Nor did administration allies try to reverse the committee's decision, by a narrow vote, to deny funds that would have resumed production of lethal chemical weapons for the first time since 1969.

Those two issues had been the focus of intensive lobbying by the administration and its opponents before the committee's markup and had been at the heart of the panel's battles over the bill.

But on Oct. 30, those issues went unraised on the House floor. In each case, the side that lost the committee round concluded that it would fare no better on the floor.

Instead, the House exhumed an old political chestnut: the MX missile.

For upwards of two hours, a laboriously negotiated compromise agreed to in June seemed to have come apart, with the House voting 211-208 to drop from the appropriations bill $1.7 billion earmarked to buy 12 MXs in fiscal 1986. *(Vote 341, p. 106-H)*

But after the White House and the House GOP leadership rounded up their troops, the House reversed itself, rejecting the amendment 210-214. *(Vote 342, p. 106-H)*

Of the House bill's other elements, the most controversial were:

- A ban on tests against a target in space of the anti-satellite (ASAT) missile, so long as the Soviet Union continued its ASAT test moratorium.
- Denial of the $163.6 million requested to begin chemical weapons production for the first time since 1969.
- Four provisions aimed at changing the way the Pentagon bought goods and services. Substantially the same provisions were in the House-passed version of the companion defense authorization bill (S 1160). Senate conferees on that measure had insisted on revisions which, in general, gave Pentagon managers more slack that the original House-passed versions. *(Procurement reform, p. 164)*

MX Resurgence

The amendment to cut MX funds was offered by Barney Frank, D-Mass., a fervent opponent of MX. Frank offered the amendment without any preliminary publicity, later telling reporters that he wanted to give members a chance to vote on MX without being lobbied by the administration.

But a more fundamental part of Frank's strategy was his exploitation of the strong pressure for deficit reductions that had been generated by the so-called Gramm-Rudman amendment to the bill raising the national debt limit.

That measure, sponsored by Republican Sens. Phil Gramm, Texas, and Warren B. Rudman, N.H., would force automatic reductions in federal spending unless the budget were balanced by fiscal 1991.

Frank insisted that the 40 MXs that could be deployed from funds already appropriated would be just as significant militarily as the 50 that would be deployed if additional missiles were built in fiscal 1986.

That argument won over at least one Republican who previously had backed MX: Toby Roth, Wis.

House Armed Services Committee Chairman Les Aspin, D-Wis., was one of several senior Democrats who later described the vote to kill MX as a political response to White House rhetoric on the deficit: "They can't play politics on deficits and not have it come back and bite them," he said.

But Minority Whip Trent Lott, R-Miss., a Gramm-Rudman backer, dismissed that explanation, pointing out that MX votes always had been close in the House.

"All it says to me is that we have a large group of very liberal members" who want to cut defense budgets, Lott told reporters.

But he conceded that there was at least one group of members who voted "aye" on Frank to twist the administration's tail on another issue: This was a small number of farm-state Republicans who wanted to signal to the White House their frustration with administration farm policy. *(Farm bill, p. 517)*

"Sometimes one vote is adequate to send a message," said Rod Chandler, R-Wash., one of Frank's farm-state supporters.

Also contributing to Frank's surprising win were a few pro-MX Republicans who did not make it to the floor in time to vote "nay."

Immediately after the amendment was adopted, the White House and MX backers rounded up enough votes to defeat the amendment on a second try. Bill Chappell Jr., for one, the hawkish Florida Democrat who was managing the bill, urged Claude Pepper, D-Fla., who had supported MX in most earlier votes, to reconsider his vote for Frank.

Pepper later told reporters that he found Chappell's case persuasive: "We're on the eve of the summit . . . and the administration was pleading not to be interfered with."

After the second vote overturned his amendment, Frank said that the House had shown its unwillingness to follow through with the kind of cuts Gramm-Rudman backers claimed to favor. "It shows we have a couple of hundred fakers when it comes to cutting the deficit," he said.

Anti-Missile Defense

Appropriations Committee members and arms control lobbyists who had hoped to trim back anti-missile research funds from the $2.5 billion approved by the panel to $2.1 billion saw no chance of winning the fight on the House floor after their 24-31 defeat in the committee on Oct. 24.

Their assessment was that Congress would make no further cuts in the "strategic defense initiative" (SDI) before the Geneva summit, because both Reagan and the Russians had invested so much political capital in the issue.

During floor debate, after the first House vote on MX, Robert S. Walker, R-Pa., offered an amendment increasing

SDI funds to $2.75 billion, the authorized limit. But other SDI backers sharply attacked the amendment, warning that any effort to increase funding in the existing political climate was hopeless.

Walker withdrew the amendment.

Chemical Weapons

Proponents of the new chemical weapons — called binary munitions — gave up without a floor fight only after a longer effort.

On Oct. 28, Beryl Anthony Jr., D-Ark., in whose district the new arms would be manufactured, announced that he would offer a floor amendment to restore the funds cut in committee. The same day, Thomas J. Welch, the Defense Department's senior chemical warfare expert, laid on the case for the new weapons to Pentagon reporters.

The Soviet chemical weapons arsenal was expanding, Welch said, while existing U.S. stockpiles were technically inadequate and dangerous for U.S. troops to handle.

On Oct. 29, when the House Rules Committee was considering the procedures that would govern floor debate on the defense appropriations measure, binary weapons proponents sought a rule that would have allowed them to present an amendment adding binary funds in the most politically promising form.

Under the proposed rule, the House would have voted first on adding the money for binary production but with several conditions attached that emphasized the proponents' claim that the new weapons would be safer for U.S. troops to handle and store than existing chemical weapons.

The Rules Committee rejected that proposal, so the binary proponents would have had to ask members to vote to add $163 million to the bill while deficit-cutting rhetoric was resounding throughout the Capitol.

Under those circumstances, binary proponents in Congress and the administration decided to bank on keeping binary funding in the Senate defense bill and keeping some of it alive in the Senate-House conference.

Coast Guard

During floor action on the bill, the House adopted by voice vote an amendment offered by Silvio O. Conte, R-Mass., adding $100 million to funding for the Coast Guard.

The Appropriations Committee had turned down a proposed $300 million appropriation to buy equipment for the Coast Guard.

Senate Committee Action

A day after approving it by voice vote, the Senate Appropriations Committee on Nov. 6 reported HR 3629 (S Rept 99-176). The measure provided $288,065,856,000 for the Defense Department in fiscal 1986. This was some $15.9 billion less than the amount Reagan had requested in the bill and about $11.5 billion more than the House had approved.

Counting programs not covered by this bill, the Senate committee's measure would have brought the overall defense budget to more than $302 billion, roughly enough of an increase over the fiscal 1985 defense budget to cover the cost of inflation.

Prior-Year Funds. Of the $288.1 billion in funding provided by the Senate panel's bill, $282.5 billion was new budget authority.

The remaining $5.6 billion was money that had been appropriated for defense programs in prior years, but had not been spent for its original purpose. For example, of that amount, $850 million was to be used to construct cargo ships to be leased to commercial operators but available for military service in an emergency.

The House version of the bill included $7.7 billion of such prior-year savings reallocated to allow corresponding reductions in new budget authority.

This kind of fund transfer — routine in defense appropriations bills — was made possible when production of a weapon had been slowed down by technical problems or when contractors' bids turned out to be lower than anticipated.

But the Reagan budgets also provided the congressional defense panels with large amounts left over from prior-year appropriations, because inflation was running lower than the appropriations assumed.

Such inflation overestimates accounted for a hefty chunk of the $5.6 billion in prior-year funds drawn on by the Senate committee. But the panel warned that the House had gone overboard in assuming how much could be trimmed from the budget request because of reduced inflation assumptions.

Economic Facts of Life. The House also went further than the Senate committee in assuming how much could be trimmed from the budget request without affecting Pentagon programs because of revised estimates about prices and other economic facts of life:

- For fuel costs, the Senate committee sliced $362.6 million from the request. The House bill, assuming a faster drop in oil prices, cut an additional $137.4 million.
- Because the dollar's continued strength against foreign currencies reduced the operating expenses of U.S. forces garrisoned overseas, the House bill cut $1 billion. But the Senate panel, citing a recent turnaround in the trend, cut only $868 million.
- By assuming that myriad small parts and supplies would cost less than expected, the Senate committee cut the bill by $1.4 billion. The corresponding House reduction was $428.9 million larger.

Manpower

The committee sliced $807.7 million from the bill's personnel-related accounts and ordered the Pentagon to freeze its military and civilian manpower at fiscal 1985 levels.

The Pentagon could stay within that manpower cap simply by attrition. But the committee emphasized that it wanted the department instead to cut out layers of bureaucracy that did not contribute directly to combat strength. Warren B. Rudman, R-N.H., had been promoting this approach for nearly a year.

Without ordering specific reorganizations, the panel cited some examples of seemingly superfluous bureaucracy. One instance was the existence of separate Navy and Air Force space commands in addition to the Defense Department's joint, or "multi-service," space command.

As had both Armed Services committees, the panel assumed the military pension system would be amended to allow a $2.9 billion cut in the request for the retirement trust fund.

SDI, ASAT

In marking up the defense spending bill on Oct. 30, the Appropriations Subcommittee on Defense recommended $2.96 billion for SDI, Reagan's anti-missile program. That was $200 million above the level contained in S 1160, the companion authorization bill, which cleared Congress on Oct. 29.

Defense Subcommittee Chairman Ted Stevens, R-Alaska, wanted the higher number to give Senate conferees bargaining leverage in an eventual conference with the House. Stevens hoped that the appropriations conference would approve the entire $2.75 billion authorized by Congress for SDI.

Before approving the bill on Nov. 5, the full committee rejected 13-15 an amendment by J. Bennett Johnston, D-La., that would have established a blue-ribbon commission to analyze the cost and technical feasibility of SDI.

Johnston had prepared another amendment that would have trimmed SDI funding to $2.1 billion. But after the committee rejected the SDI study panel, Johnston dropped the funding amendment.

As had been the case during House action on the defense bill, SDI critics evidently were handicapped by the imminence of Reagan's summit meeting with Soviet leader Gorbachev.

The vote on Johnston's SDI study proposal split basically along party lines. Republicans opposed the amendment, except Appropriations Chairman Mark O. Hatfield, Ore., and Lowell P. Weicker Jr., Conn., who voted "aye."

Democrats supported it, except John C. Stennis, Miss., and Ernest F. Hollings, S.C., who voted "nay" and Lawton Chiles, Fla., who favored the amendment but did not vote.

The committee's bill also approved three tests against a target in space of the anti-satellite missile, as approved by Congress in the authorization bill. The House-passed appropriations bill banned ASAT target tests.

Strategic Warfare

The committee approved 12 MX missiles ($1.7 billion) of the 48 requested ($3 billion). Those were the compromise figures worked out between the White House and congressional moderates during conferees' negotiations on the defense authorization bill.

The Senate appropriators also recommended $784 million to continue MX development, the amount requested. An additional $163.9 million was appropriated — $10 million less than requested — to develop modifications for long-range ballistic missiles like MX. Among these modifications were decoys and other devices to help missile warheads get past anti-missile defenses.

The committee also ordered the Air Force to equip 800 launch silos for existing Minuteman missiles with special batteries that would let them operate for days after a commercial power cutoff. The remaining 200 Minuteman silos already were so equipped.

Small ICBM. To develop a small, single-warhead missile — called "Midgetman" — to supplement the 10-warhead MX, the committee approved $624.5 million, the amount requested. But the panel recommended only $368.5 million of that amount in new budget authority, making up the balance with prior year savings.

The panel dropped $100 million the House had added to the Midgetman appropriation, denying that the added funds would accelerate the program, scheduled for its first deployments in late 1992.

Among the small missile's warmest supporters had been some congressional moderates — including Sen. Albert Gore Jr., D-Tenn., and House Armed Services Committee Chairman Les Aspin, D-Wis. — who helped the administration secure congressional approval of MX in return for signs of flexibility in earlier administration arms control negotiating positions.

Gore and Aspin had urged that the small missile be based in a mobile launcher, thus making a Soviet attack impossible. But the Reagan administration made a new arms control proposal that included a ban on mobile ICBMs including Midgetman and two Soviet missiles that were just being deployed. *(Arms control, p. 175)*

On the heels of that blow, supporters of a mobile Midgetman took another hit from Senate Appropriations, which warned of the cost and manpower that would be needed to carry several hundred small missiles in mobile launchers. It asked the Air Force to report on the feasibility of splitting the Midgetman deployment between mobile launchers and underground silos.

Bomber Weapons. Of the $5.46 billion requested for the last 48 of 100 planned B-1 bombers, the committee approved $5.26 billion, a $200 million reduction. The House had cut a total of $600 million from the fiscal 1986 request and from prior-year funds it said had proven superfluous.

The Senate panel agreed that such savings might be realized once the last plane was completed, but argued that it was premature to assume that so much could be cut from the program when only the first three of 100 planes had been delivered.

The budget request as well as the committee's action regarding another new bomber were secret. This was the "stealth" bomber, designed to evade enemy detection.

The panel approved $35 million of $79 million requested to develop an improved version of the SRAM missile, a nuclear-tipped weapon with a range of about 100 miles carried by bombers to shoot their way through the Soviet Union's dense network of anti-aircraft defenses.

The committee insisted that the new missile's cost be kept down. As it did in other cases, it suggested cutting the program's near-term cost by picking one of the competing designs sooner than had been planned.

To modernize existing B-52 bombers, the panel approved $459.5 million, all but $4.1 million of the request. But it allowed only $36 million of the $72 million requested to develop gear that would make B-52s more effective in attacking targets at very long ranges with non-nuclear arms.

The committee approved $852.5 million of the $868.1 million requested to continue replacing the old jet engines on KC-135 tanker planes — similar to the commercial Boeing 707 jetliner — which were used to refuel bombers in midair.

Sub-launched Missiles. For the 13th Trident missile-launching submarine, the committee recommended $1.2 billion, an $87 million reduction from the request.

The panel also recommended $2.13 billion — $35 million less than the request — to continue development of the Trident II missile, designed to be the first submarine-launched weapon accurate enough to destroy armored, underground missile launchers. Approved without change was the $582 million requested to prepare for Trident II production, scheduled to begin in fiscal 1987 with the first missiles to enter service in 1989.

The committee rejected the request for $356 million to begin buying a fleet of 15 four-engine jets called E-6As, similar to Boeing 707s, equipped with powerful radios to communicate with submerged missile-launching submarines. The mission, which involved towing a five-mile-long wire antenna, had been performed with converted C-130 transport planes.

According to the committee, the C-130s were far from wearing out. Theoretically, because the new planes could fly farther from their bases, U.S. subs could roam over a much larger ocean area and still keep in touch with their headquarters.

But the panel argued that the E-6As' range could not be exploited. Because of limitations in other parts of the communications chain, the E-6As could not go much farther than the C-130s if they were to receive messages to be relayed to the subs.

As one step toward eventually using the E-6As' longer range, the committee added to the bill $150 million to begin improving other planes in the airborne communications network.

Ground Combat

For the third consecutive year, the committee recommended slowing down the budgeted production rate for the Army's M-1 tank, this time approving 720 tanks ($1.35 billion) of the 840 requested ($1.75 billion).

The panel replaced $77.9 million of the $401.4 million cut with leftover funds from earlier budgets. The House also approved 840 M-1s.

According to the committee, $1 billion requested for 716 Bradley armored troop carriers was $115.3 million more than needed. Equipped with anti-tank missiles and a small cannon, the Bradley was designed as a fighting vehicle, not just a troop transport.

The committee recommended that $66.4 million of the surplus be used to buy an additional 60 Bradleys and the rest be cut from the bill.

The panel denied $65 million requested to begin production of the M-9 armored bulldozer. The M-9 was designed to move at high speed on roads — to keep up with M-1s and Bradleys — and then dig defensive barricades and cut roads through rough terrain.

The key to the M-9 was a transmission designed to move the 18-ton vehicle at speeds up to 30 miles per hour on highways, while still being able to function as an earthmover. The panel said that production should await transmission tests.

Helicopters. For 144 Apache, missile-armed anti-tank helicopters, the committee approved $1.14 billion of the $1.18 billion requested.

The panel recommended 80 Blackhawk troop-carrying helicopters ($260.9 million) instead of the 78 requested ($267 million). The committee assumed that the appropriation could be trimmed and still pay for two additional Blackhawks to replace two already in service that it ordered handed over to the Customs Service for drug interdiction.

Reacting to testing problems with another helicopter program, the panel cut a total of $106.8 million from the $210.6 million requested to continue modernizing existing OH-58 scout helicopters. The helicopters were to be equipped with a television camera and laser, rising above the rotor blades like a giant golf ball on a tee. The plan was for the helicopter to hide behind trees and ridges, spot targets with the camera, and beam the laser on them for laser-guided missiles to home in on.

Pentagon weapons testers had approved use of the modified OH-58s only for some of the planned missions. In tests, other missions had been unsuccessful, not because the modified helicopters had failed but because their test crews had not been properly trained. By slowing down the modification program, the committee said, Congress would be in a position either to cut it off or resume the planned buildup, depending on further test results.

The panel also approved $106 million of the $146 million requested to continue development of a new small helicopter, designated LHX. The Army hoped to begin building the new helicopter in the mid-1990s to replace more than 7,000 Vietnam War-era choppers currently used for scout, ground attack and transport missions. The program was the focus of intense interest in the aerospace industry because it was the only new, large helicopter production contract on the horizon.

The committee endorsed the goal of replacing the old helicopters but warned that this might become impossible if the LHX did not meet two of its cost goals:

- A price tag of no more than $5.3 million per copy (in fiscal 1984 dollars).
- Lower operating and repair costs than the models it was to replace.

In hopes of reducing the program's initial cost, the committee called for selecting one helicopter design and one engine design from among the competing proposals at an earlier stage than had been planned.

Anti-tank Weapons. The panel approved $286 million, $20 million less than requested, for Hellfire laser-guided anti-tank missiles carried by Apaches and some other helicopters.

The Army and Marine Corps requested a total of $287 million for Copperhead laser-guided artillery shells. The committee approved $168 million but demanded that it all be drawn from unused funds appropriated in prior years.

According to the panel, the Army and Marine Corps together had requested more TOW anti-tank missiles than could be built in one year's production run. The most widely used U.S. anti-tank weapon, TOWs were fired from helicopters, various ground vehicles and small, tripod-mounted tubes. The panel trimmed the $271 million request to $211 million.

For a smaller anti-tank missile, the Swedish-designed AT-4, the committee recommended $59 million — $10 million more than was authorized — on grounds that that would buy the smallest number of missiles that could efficiently be built in a year.

The panel approved nearly $370 million of the $410 million requested to develop two systems for the 1990s designed to decimate enemy tanks while still far behind their own lines:

- The panel approved $240 million of the $260 million requested for Joint STARS, an airborne radar to detect tank columns tens of miles behind enemy lines.
- It recommended $130 million of the $155 million requested for TACMs, a missile to be guided by Joint STARS and spew anti-tank warheads over enemy convoys.

Communications. The panel approved $238 million of the $335 million requested to begin buying a French-designed communications system for Army units in the field, called RITA. The panel said surplus funds from prior years would cover the $238 million. The committee wanted to hold down the production rate until certain tests had been completed.

The lobbying battle between manufacturers of RITA and builders of the competing, British-designed Ptarmagin was ferocious. Late in the contest, British Prime Minister Margaret Thatcher weighed in on behalf of Ptarmagin — unsuccessfully — with a personal appeal to President Reagan.

Testing delays also were cited as the reason why the

panel approved only $102 million of the $231 million requested for a network of smaller, portable field radios (called SINCGARS).

Tactical Air Warfare

Like the House, the Senate panel approved the number of new fighter planes requested by the Air Force, but recommended a reduction in the amount budgeted, citing various technical reasons why prices should be lower than anticipated. The committee approved:

- 48 F-15s ($1.76 billion), including the first eight of the "E" models designed to attack ground targets at night or in bad weather. The amount was $146 million less than requested.
- 180 smaller F-16s ($2.58 billion), a $253 million reduction.

The committee also concurred with the House in approving $200 million to begin a competition to select the manufacturer of 318 budget-priced fighter planes that would be used on certain missions.

The competition was expected to pit a stripped-down version of General Dynamics' F-16 against Northrop Corp.'s F-20. But the panel told the Air Force to consider all suitable planes, including a proposed updated version of the F-4 Phantom of Vietnam War-vintage. However, unlike the House, the Senate committee did not add to the $22 million to develop the improved Phantom.

Like the House, the committee approved the bulk of the $206 million requested to continue production of a new basic training jet — the T-46A — which the Air Force might abandon under budget-cutting pressure.

But whereas the House recommended new budget authority for the plane, the Senate panel proposed use of $189 million in surplus funds from prior years.

The panel also cut nearly half a billion dollars from the budget because of problems with two devices intended to protect U.S. fighters from enemy radar detection:

- Because the Air Force canceled one item, designed to warn pilots that they were being tracked by radar, the committee cut $220 million.
- Delays in production of a radar jammer accounted for reductions totaling $272 million.

Naval Aircraft. For 18 of the Navy's big F-14 fighter, designed to be flown from aircraft carriers, the panel approved $649 million, $4.5 million less than the request. The House had trimmed $95 million more from the budget, noting that F-14 prices were running below the budgeted level.

But the Senate panel predicted that those anticipated savings would be eaten up by congressional insistence that all F-14s built in fiscal 1986 use a new, more powerful type of engine, requiring design modifications.

However, the panel agreed with large savings the House predicted in the price of the smaller F/A-18, flown from Navy carriers as both a fighter and a light bomber. The committee approved $2.27 billion for 84 F/A-18s, a reduction of $226 million from the amount requested to cover 84 planes.

The Navy had recently decided to deploy fewer F/A-18s than had been planned so that carriers could haul more A-6E bombers, which carried larger bomb loads and had electronic gear to let them find ground targets at night and in bad weather. But the service had not yet adjusted its plan for future purchases of the two planes, which would leave it with a surplus of F/A-18s and a shortage of A-6Es. The committee demanded an explanation.

The panel approved the $202.6 million requested for six A-6Es, but insisted that the amount be taken from prior year leftover funds.

It proposed the same source for $321 million to buy six E-2Cs — small versions of the AWACS radar plane designed to take off from carriers and quarterback a fleet's air defenses. The budget requested $328 million.

For 46 Harriers — small, vertical takeoff jets used as bombers by the Marine Corps — the committee recommended $421.5 million. The $71 million reduction from the budget request was made possible because the dollar's strength on the international market had reduced the price of British-built components of the planes.

The committee added to the bill $110 million to buy up to 16 commercial jetliners for conversion to midair refueling tankers. The idea was that these planes could rendezvous with carrier planes to let them range farther from the carrier. Heretofore, the Navy had used small carrier-based tanker planes for this purpose.

Aerial Missiles. The panel approved the requested $441.5 million for Sparrow air-to-air missiles. But because of anticipated savings, it said the funds could buy 2,445 missiles instead of the 2,297 requested.

It also recommended $180 million, the amount authorized, to begin producing a new air-to-air missile, called AMRAAM, intended as a successor to the Sparrow. The $101 million requested to continue AMRAAM development also was approved. The new missile was much lighter than the Sparrow, and could be borne by F-16s, which did not carry the current missile.

The panel recommended $207 million for nearly 3,000 shorter-range Sidewinder missiles, an increase of $78 million and nearly 1,000 missiles, which the House also approved.

For the long-range Phoenix missile, carried only by Navy F-14s, the committee recommended the $382 million requested, of which $93 million was earmarked to set up a second contractor to compete for future contracts with Phoenix manufacturer Hughes Aircraft.

The panel approved $691 million for more than 2,600 HARM missiles, designed to be fired from Air Force and Navy planes and home in on enemy radars. This was a $46 million reduction from the request, which reflected the panel's decision to block expansion of HARM production.

Future Fighter Planes. The panel approved $237 million, all but $15 million of the requested amount, to continue development of the electronics-packed "E" model of the F-15.

For development of a new fighter plane to succeed the F-15 and F-16 in the late 1990s, the committee approved $140 million of the $242 million requested. But it warned against letting the plane get so expensive that the Air Force would have to disband some squadrons to afford the new planes. It recommended that the new plane's price per unit be held to not more than 20 percent above the cost of an F-15.

The committee approved $345 million, a $3.1 million reduction, to develop an improved version of the F-14 — the so-called F-14D.

But it trimmed $50 million from the request to develop an improved A-6E — the A-6F — recommending $188 million. The Navy discovered that the wings of its A-6Es were wearing out much sooner than expected, and paying to replace the wings was a much higher priority than improving the plane's performance, the panel said.

Naval Forces

The panel approved $52 million of the $133 million requested for components to be used in a major rebuilding of the carrier *Kitty Hawk*. The bulk of the cost, likely more than half a billion dollars, was to be covered in the fiscal 1987 budget.

This was to be the fourth of six 1960s-vintage carriers to have its planned service life extended from 30 years to 45 years by a major overhaul. The work was to include replacement of much of the electronic gear and machinery. The $81.4 million reduction was consistent with a change in the overhaul schedule, the panel said.

The panel approved the $53.5 million requested as a down payment on modernizing the *Wisconsin*, to be the last of four World War II battleships taken out of mothballs and equipped with modern electronic gear and long-range cruise missiles. But it told the Navy to take the funds from leftover prior-year appropriations.

The House told the Navy to use prior-year money to cover the entire cost of the modification — $469 million — and to begin it in fiscal 1986 instead of a year later as planned. But the funds the House earmarked for the *Wisconsin* were allocated to cover other projects by the Senate committee, which said there was no need to accelerate the battleship program.

For 249 Tomahawk cruise missiles, to equip the battleships, most other large surface warships and the newest types of submarines, the committee approved the $670 million requested. Equipped with a non-nuclear warhead, the missile had a range of about 300 miles. With a nuclear warhead, it could reach upwards of 1,500 miles.

The only ships requested for which the panel denied funding were two of four mine sweepers. The committee approved $197 million of the $334 million requested for four ships. But it also transferred to the fiscal 1986 account $81 million appropriated in fiscal 1985 for a mine sweeper that had to be delayed until fiscal 1986.

Submarine Warfare. The Senate committee recommended $2.6 billion of the $2.7 billion requested for four *Los Angeles*-class submarines, designed to hunt other subs. It also approved the amount authorized ($369 million) to develop a new hunter sub designed to carry more weapons and to operate under the Arctic ice pack, where Soviet missile subs patrolled.

The panel recommended $190 million, a $164 million boost over the budget, to convert a retired missile-launching submarine into a training site for crewmen of nuclear subs.

For 18 of the LAMPS III anti-submarine helicopters carried by most of the Navy's modern surface warships, the committee recommended $250 million, a $65.5 million reduction from the request. It also approved $61 million for six of the smaller LAMPS I helicopters, used by older warships.

The budget requested $486 million to buy nine more P-3C long-range submarine hunters — based on the 1950s-vintage Electra airliner — and to buy components that would be used in additional planes to be funded in fiscal 1987. But the committee told the Navy to stop buying new copies of the plane and to accelerate its plans to modernize the sub-hunting gear on P-3Bs and Cs already in the fleet.

The committee added $240 million to the amount requested for P-3 modernization.

Cruise Missile Defense. The panel approved $2.6 billion for three cruisers carrying the Aegis anti-aircraft system — radars and missiles controlled by powerful computers designed to fight off Soviet cruise missiles attacking a U.S. fleet. This was $114 million less than was requested.

It also recommended $14.7 million — $149 million less than the request — for components to be used in two smaller Aegis-equipped destroyers that would be requested in the fiscal 1987 budget. The funding was not necessary, the committee said.

The panel denied the entire amount requested — $76.7 million — to begin producing a short-range missile called RAM and the launcher for it. The committee maintained that production was being delayed by test failures of the missile, which was intended as a last-ditch defense for ships against cruise missiles.

The committee approved $25 million of $41.5 million requested to develop a very-long-range missile that could pick off Soviet bombers before they launched cruise missiles at a U.S. fleet. The Navy had been debating whether to develop a new missile or upgrade the existing Standard anti-aircraft missile, which would provide a smaller improvement, but would be available sooner.

The committee came down foursquare in favor of the near-term improvement, ordering the Navy to concentrate on improving the so-called SM-2 version of the Standard.

Airlift and Sealift

The panel recommended modest cuts in funding for the two major programs to modernize the air cargo fleet:

- For 16 huge C-5Bs in fiscal 1986 and components that would be used in future C-5B purchases, it approved $2.17 billion of the $2.27 billion requested.
- To continue production of KC-10s — DC-10 jetliners modified to haul cargo and refuel other planes in midair — it recommended $399 million of $439 million requested.

It recommended $384 million to continue development of the C-17 cargo plane, designed to haul tanks and other large pieces of equipment into primitive airstrips. Originally, the Pentagon had requested $454 million for this program, but that later was reduced to the $384 million.

Sea Transport. The committee approved the $1.15 billion requested for an aircraft carrier (called an LHD) designed to carry 2,000 marines and 30 troop-carrying helicopters.

The panel approved $681 million for two other major programs for amphibious landing ships, only a minor reduction from the requests:

- Two transports (called LSDs) to carry tanks and the barges to haul them ashore ($405 million).
- 12 air-cushion landing barges able to carry a 60-ton tank at upwards of 40 miles per hour ($276 million).

But the committee provided no new budget authority for the two projects, telling the Navy to draw the funds from unspent amounts in prior year appropriations.

It also told the Navy to use prior year funds for the $203 million requested to buy mothballed commercial vessels to add to the reserve fleet of cargo ships. This program was separate from the committee's proposed cargo ship construction fund.

Other Provisions

The committee rejected four House-passed provisions that would impose significant changes in the way the Pentagon bought goods and services.

It also rejected a House provision that would bar any funding through the Defense Department or the CIA of guerrillas battling the government of Nicaragua.

The committee bill also:

- Included $10 million to transport non-lethal aid to guerrillas fighting Soviet occupation forces in Afghanistan.
- Earmarked $280 million in surplus funds from prior appropriations to buy two wide-body jetliners to replace the two aging planes used by the president. When the president was aboard one of the planes, it was referred to as "Air Force One."
- Added to the budget $67.6 million to test recruits for acquired immune deficiency syndrome (AIDS) and $52.6 million to conduct research on ways to combat the disease.

Continuing Resolution

With farm and budget legislation consuming floor time in November, action on the defense spending bill was delayed in the Senate. Eventually, in December, the House and Senate defense measures were incorporated into an omnibus continuing appropriations resolution (H J Res 465) for fiscal 1986.

In the meantime, the Senate's two defense funding panels dueled to a draw in another episode of their long-running jurisdictional fight over spending levels.

At stake this time was some $7.6 billion, spread across nearly 100 defense programs. In each case, the Senate Appropriations Subcommittee on Defense had approved more than had been allowed by the Senate Armed Services Committee.

A compromise was adopted by voice vote on Dec. 10, in an amendment to the continuing resolution. That agreement made the Armed Services ceilings binding for broad categories of programs — such as Army research and development or Air Force missile procurement — but not for specific projects.

Any funds appropriated for the categories — or "accounts" — above the level set by the authorization bill (S 1160) could not be spent until Congress enacted separate legislation authorizing the funds.

One of the Appropriations Committee's add-ons was specifically exempted from the requirement for authorization: $375 million for aircraft and patrol ships to beef up the Coast Guard, which would operate as part of the Navy in time of war.

Armed Services Committee members declared that the compromise reaffirmed their power to set ceilings on defense appropriations.

"We do not have a monopoly on expertise," said Sam Nunn, Ga., senior Democrat on the panel. "But we do believe that, in the final analysis, we have every right and expectation to be consulted with as these matters come down to the wire."

However, because the authorizations were made binding for accounts rather than specific projects, only about $3.2 billion of the $7.6 billion would require separate authorization.

Military Retirement System

Earlier, on Dec. 5, the Senate appropriations panel by voice vote adopted an amendment by Johnston requiring the House and Senate Armed Services committees to revise the military retirement system. The committees would have to act before May 1 in order to avert substantial cuts in military personnel.

In the fiscal 1986 defense authorization bill, Congress put a cap on the amount of money that could be spent for military personnel. Since retirement pay would have to be given to all military personnel who qualified, in the absence of legislation limiting such payments, the only way to stay within the spending limitation would be to cut military personnel.

House Rebellion

The House passed the continuing resolution Dec. 4 and the Senate followed suit Dec. 10. After three days of negotiations Dec. 11-13, House-Senate conferees thought they had reached a final agreement on the bill. But defense issues contributed to a revolt that ended in House rejection of the conference report on Dec. 16.

The conferees had agreed to provide $282.5 billion in new budget authority for Defense Department programs, about $14 million more than the house version of H J Res 465 provided and nearly identical to the Senate proposal. They also allowed spending of an additional $6.3 billion left over from fiscal 1985.

The conferees agreed to House language barring ASAT testing as long as the Soviets continued their ASAT moratorium, and to provide $2.75 billion for the SDI program. But conferees refused to accept any House language to tighten up defense procurement procedures.

When the conference report (H Rept 99-443) came to the floor, the Democratic leadership and conferees were surprised by the outpouring of opposition that surfaced. Most of it came from Democrats angry about the defense section, but Republicans were unhappy with the way the bill was handled. It was rejected 170-239. *(Vote 420, p. 134-H)*

Democratic speakers, led by Barney Frank, Mass., contended that conferees gave up too much to the Senate. They were especially upset about the level of new budget authority for defense, the lack of procurement reform, and funding for chemical weapons.

Frank called the ASAT ban "the most expensive piece of arms control we have ever seen in the world, because we paid about $10 billion [in higher defense spending] for it."

After the vote, Leon E. Panetta, D-Calif., a respected five-term veteran, said he voted against the conference report because defense spending was too high. "It cushioned defense against Gramm-Rudman," he said, adding that the following year "the real hit" would be in domestic programs.

The chemical weapons funding also was a sore point even though the House, after three years of solid opposition, voted in June to authorize limited production of the new binary munitions.

Revising Defense Package

The unexpected House action left conferees no choice but to return to the bargaining table.

Defense conferees led by Stevens and House Defense Appropriations Subcommittee Chairman Joseph P. Addabbo, D-N.Y., and members Bill Chappell Jr., D-Fla., and McDade, met on Dec. 17 to work out a new deal.

In the meantime, chemical weapons opponents worked to exert pressure on the conferees to drop the production money. Rep. John Edward Porter, R-Ill., with help from John Isaacs of the Council for a Livable World, got about 140 House members to sign a petition urging House conferees to block the production money.

House conferees took a poll among themselves during a midday meeting of the conference Dec. 18, voting 15-6 to insist on their position of no chemical weapons. They did, however, reach a tentative agreement with Stevens to trim the Pentagon's new budget authority by $1.3 billion —

from $282.5 billion to $281.2 billion. They also agreed that the $6.3 billion in transfer money could be used only for military pay and retirement and for building cargo ships that would be available for wartime use.

Throughout the bargaining, the administration was an unseen partner. White House Chief of Staff Donald T. Regan had telephoned Senate Appropriations Chairman Hatfield on Dec. 18 to say that the White House would accept the $1.3 billion defense cut if conferees would trim $300 million from domestic programs.

Stevens would not yield on the chemical weapons issue and threatened to reopen the entire package, including the previous deals on funding and the ASAT ban.

Conferees broke up for another round of bargaining, and when they returned, Stevens asked for a vote of Senate conferees. By 8-5, they insisted on their position. House Appropriations Chairman Jamie L. Whitten, D-Miss., asked for another brief recess, and when House conferees returned, they withdrew their opposition to the chemical weapons funding.

But Stevens had one more deal to work. He said the White House wanted the $1.3 billion trim to come from the $6.3 billion in transfer money from fiscal 1985 and not from new budget authority. Stevens suggested that if the House went along with that, he would agree to one of four procurement reforms the House had put in its version of H J Res 465.

House members said the trade-off was unacceptable. David R. Obey, D-Wis., claimed it ignored the reality of House concerns over spending levels. Chappell said he thought the procurement reform would be acceptable anyway, once the Senate Armed Services Committee agreed on the language.

After another round of negotiations, conferees reached agreement. Stevens backed down on the funding request and agreed to give the House one of the four procurement reforms that had the blessing of Senate Armed Services Chairman Barry Goldwater, R-Ariz.

This "allowable costs" provision barred contractors from billing the Pentagon for certain kinds of expenses including entertainment, lobbying and legal fees resulting from charges of contract fraud. Of the four House-passed procurement provisions, this one was nearly identical to a provision already enacted as part of the defense authorization bill.

With the hurdles on defense and other issues, the measure was cleared by Congress and signed by the president on Dec. 19. ▮

Military Construction Funds

A budget-conscious Congress chopped nearly 20 percent from the Reagan administration's military construction spending in fiscal 1986.

President Reagan had requested $10.3 billion for Pentagon construction projects. A compromise version of the military construction spending bill (HR 3327 — PL 99-173) appropriated $8.5 billion. That was some $700 million less than members of Congress approved in the companion authorization bill (S 1042 — PL 99-167). *(Authorization bill, p. 182)*

And it was just $100 million more than Capitol Hill approved for military construction spending in fiscal 1985. *(1984 Almanac p. 407)*

The conferees' agreement on the fiscal 1986 appropriations bill was adopted by the House by voice vote Nov. 20; the Senate followed suit in the session that began Nov. 21. Reagan signed the measure Dec. 10.

At the same time that members were making cuts, however, they implicitly gave the Navy the go-ahead to start building a network of new bases for its expanding fleet.

Major Provisions

The conference report on the construction appropriations bill was filed Nov. 19 (H Rept 99-380).

The measure included $15.9 million for the GLCM base in the Netherlands and $10.8 million for a binary munitions facility at Pine Bluff, Ark. *(Nerve gas, military construction pp. 138, 182)*

New Navy Facilities

HR 3327 appropriated $79 million to begin work on two new home ports: a base for a battleship and several escorts at Staten Island, just north of the Verrazano-Narrows Bridge at the mouth of New York harbor, and a base for an aircraft carrier and its escorts at Everett, Wash., at the north end of Puget Sound.

The authorization measure, however, authorized only $33 million for the two new facilities. It also barred use of those funds until 90 days after submission by the Navy of a report justifying the proposed development of new bases.

Despite the lower amount authorized for the two new bases, the entire $79 million appropriated could be expended. And the Navy report ordered by the authorization conferees was delivered on Nov. 12, a week before the conference report was cleared for the president.

Accordingly, the 90-day waiting period would expire sometime in February 1986.

On Nov. 21, Pentagon spokesman Bob Sims said that unless Congress moved to block the New York battleship project before February, the Navy would begin work on it.

Another battleship group was earmarked for San Francisco, while a third battleship would be based at Corpus Christi, Texas, with its escorts at several other Gulf Coast ports. But no funds for those projects were requested in fiscal 1986.

The appropriations conferees approved $61 million for the facilities at Staten Island.

According to sources, the funds were added in deference to Joseph P. Addabbo, D-N.Y., a member of the House Appropriations Subcommittee on Military Construction and chairman of the Subcommittee on Defense. Addabbo had been absent from Capitol Hill since August because of a kidney ailment.

Though he had been for years one of the most effective advocates of paring back the Pentagon budget, Addabbo, representing a district in Queens, had been a staunch advocate of the Staten Island home port.

The Navy justified the new ports on grounds that existing bases were overcrowded, and would become more so with the expansion of the fleet envisioned by the Reagan administration.

Moreover, the Navy cited military advantages in having battle groups stationed closer to potential trouble spots in the northern Atlantic and Pacific.

Opponents charged that the Navy was spreading its ships around to develop new pork-barrel constituencies for its expanded fleet. And some critics of the administration's nuclear weapons program saw a more subtle political mo-

Military Construction Appropriations

	Administration Request	House-Passed	Senate-Passed	Final Appropriation
		(in thousands of dollars)		
Army	$2,020,900	$1,646,152	$1,558,710	$1,602,982
Navy	2,085,200	1,703,705	1,632,620	1,705,370
Air Force	2,082,000	1,585,140	1,751,623	1,663,225
Defense Agencies	309,600	124,955	233,290	181,375
NATO Infrastructure	98,000	—	38,000	10,000
Guard and Reserve	428,600	383,331	358,522	389,631
Family Housing	3,282,900 [1]	2,929,447 [1]	3,147,588	2,945,276
Miscellaneous	33,000	—	—	—
TOTAL	**$10,340,200 [1]**	**$8,372,730**	**$8,720,353**	**$8,497,859 [1]**

[1] *Does not include $45,601,000 requested and approved for family housing debt reduction.*

tive in the plan to deploy in New York and San Francisco ships that are equipped to carry nuclear weapons.

Last-Minute Questions

The exact amount appropriated by the compromise bill was uncertain up to the time the Senate approved the conference report at 1 a.m. Nov. 22. This was because the conferees could not agree on two issues that were to be separately voted on by each house at the time it considered the conference report.

One of the items left unsettled was $21.6 million approved by the Senate but denied by the House for a convocation center at the Naval Academy in Annapolis, Md.

The other disputed appropriations issue was a Senate provision authorizing the sale of 45 acres of land at Fort DeRussey, an Army facility that contained a military recreation area — including a hotel — on Waikiki Beach in Honolulu.

For years, the annual military construction appropriations bill had contained a provision barring sale or transfer of the Fort DeRussey property. However, in 1985 the Senate proposed transfer of 45 acres (of a total of 68 acres) that were separated from the beach by a highway.

Before adopting the conference report on HR 3327 Nov. 20, the House by voice vote reaffirmed its initial position on the two provisions: denying the funds for Annapolis and retaining the ban on selling land from Fort DeRussey.

The Senate conceded the two House positions and then agreed to the conference report, all by voice vote.

House Action

Citing acute budgetary stringency, the House Appropriations Committee slashed some $2 billion from the Pentagon's military construction spending request.

The military construction appropriations bill (HR 3327 — H Rept 99-275) was reported Sept. 18. The committee recommended $8.39 billion, a reduction of 19 percent from the administration's $10.34 billion budget request.

The committee's bill put the fiscal 1986 construction budget nearly $15 million less than the amount appropriated for construction in fiscal 1985.

As had become routine, the panel denied funds for several projects it said should be paid for by allies who would be defended by U.S. units using those facilities.

The committee also ordered the Pentagon to report on the possibility of closing seven bases in Europe, but emphasized that it was not calling for their closure.

But the burden-sharing and base-closing issues accounted for only about $125 million of the committee's reduction. The panel approved $1.2 billion worth of projects in Europe and $200 million worth in Japan and Korea — the areas with the largest U.S. military presence.

Most cuts were based on budgetary judgments rather than military or diplomatic strategy. For instance:

- About $265 million was cut because the panel denied all funds for facilities the panel deemed non-essential, such as libraries, swimming pools and religious education centers.
- $175 million was pared from dozens of projects found to be overpriced.
- $125 million was cut on the assumption that in fiscal 1986, as in past years, slow times in the construction business would lead to lower-than-budgeted bids for many projects.

Even before the Appropriations panel began work on its bill, $600 million worth of cuts had, in effect, been imposed by the companion military construction authorization bill. *(Story, p. 182)*

Awaiting House action and a Senate-House conference on that measure, the Appropriations panel considered only projects as reported by the House Armed Services Committee.

Along with the reductions, the Appropriations panel also funded $190 million worth of projects that had been added to the administration's request by the House authorization bill.

The appropriations bill was ordered reported Sept. 18 by voice vote after the full committee made minor changes in the version approved by its Military Construction Subcommittee.

Overseas Base Issues

For years the committee had called for allied governments to pay more of the cost of stationing U.S. forces on their territory, on the grounds that the host countries received improved defense without the cost of enlarging their own military.

In its report on the appropriations bill, the committee reiterated that argument, along with a related one: that the United States, which relied on Persian Gulf sources for less than 10 percent of its oil, was unilaterally bearing the cost of deploying forces and building bases intended to keep open the oil routes from the gulf to Japan and Western Europe. These countries made no direct contribution to the U.S. effort but depended on the Persian Gulf for 70 percent of their oil.

One way Congress had tried to force the NATO allies to pull more of the load since 1982 was by limiting the number of U.S. troops stationed on the continent. But the committee objected that the Pentagon was circumventing that limitation by replacing military personnel with civilians for some jobs and then assigning the military members to new missions.

Arms Control Issues

The panel denied $10.8 million requested for a factory at the arsenal in Pine Bluff, Ark., that would be used to build controversial new lethal binary munitions. The conference on the defense authorization bill watered down some of the conditions the House had attached to binary production and the House was facing a potential vote on proceeding with production. The Appropriations panel decided that construction funding could await authorization. *(Story, p. 182)*

On the other hand, the bill provided $14.9 million requested for facilities at Langley Air Force Base, near Norfolk, Va., that would be used to deploy the anti-satellite (ASAT) guided missile. Arms control advocates had battled for two years to stave off deployment of that weapon which, they argued, would open a new round in the arms race. *(ASAT, p. 162)*

Approved as requested was $62.5 million for construction associated with deployment of MX missiles. The bulk of this amount, $53 million, was for roads and other facilities at Warren Air Force Base, near Cheyenne, Wyo., where the missiles were to be deployed. *(MX, p. 119)*

New Sites

The committee approved construction (or substantial expansion) at three sites in the United States to house newly formed U.S. combat units. The bill included:

- $72.3 million for a naval base on Staten Island, N.Y., to be home port for a renovated battleship and its escorts. This was $65.4 million more than the Pentagon requested.
- $18.6 million for a base in Everett, Wash., to be home port for an aircraft carrier and other ships.
- $86 million for new facilities at Fort Drum in northern New York, due to house one of the Army's new "light" infantry divisions. Some of the 16 existing Army divisions were being trimmed in size and stripped of their heavy vehicles so they could more easily be airlifted to distant trouble spots. In addition, formation of at least two new light divisions was planned, one to be based at Fort Drum.

The House version of the construction authorization bill added to the budget $1 million to alleviate the impact on the local community of basing another new light division at Fort Wainwright in Alaska. But the Appropriations panel provided no funds, saying that plans for the deployment were in too early a stage.

Floor Action

The House passed the $8.4 billion military construction appropriations bill (HR 3327) for fiscal 1986 on Oct. 17 by a vote of 373-36. *(Vote 327, p. 102-H)*

Several amendments were adopted on the House floor, but they made only minor changes in the version reported by the House Appropriations Committee.

An amendment by George E. Brown Jr., D-Calif., deleted $14.2 million for construction of facilities that would be used to deploy the anti-satellite (ASAT) guided missile. Brown and other liberal arms control advocates had opposed ASAT deployment on grounds that it would escalate the arms race with Moscow. He argued that, even if he lost his fight against ASAT, construction of the facilities was premature.

Senate Action

The Senate Appropriations Committee on Oct. 31 reported its version of the military construction spending bill (HR 3327 — S Rept 99-168), containing $8.64 billion.

The bill included $10.8 million for a factory at Pine Bluff, Ark., to manufacture controversial new types of lethal chemical weapons, called binary munitions.

The committee denied $14.9 million for facilities associated with deployment of the anti-satellite (ASAT) missile. But it said this was because funds would not be needed until fiscal 1987 due to ASAT production delays.

The committee approved $56 million the Pentagon requested after the budget was drawn up to improve security around the European sites housing Pershing II ballistic missiles. The panel approved $10.3 million of the $13.3 million requested for a ground-launched cruise missile (GLCM) base in Belgium. The money could only be spent after the Belgian Parliament approved GLCM deployment.

Davis-Bacon Wage Rules

Like its counterpart authorization bill, the Senate Appropriations measure included a provision that would have exempted much of the Pentagon's construction budget from the Davis-Bacon Act, which controlled wages on federal building projects.

The Davis-Bacon Act required that construction workers on federal projects be paid the locally prevailing wage for their type of work. That law was jealously guarded by organized labor. But it long had been a target of conservatives who claimed that, because of the way its rules were administered, it inflated construction wages above those actually prevailing in many places.

The Senate committee's provision would have increased from $2,000 to $1 million the value below which Pentagon building projects would be exempt from Davis-Bacon requirements.

A similar provision had been included in the Senate version of the defense authorization bill (S 1160), but was dropped in conference after lobbying by labor organizations. *(Story, p. 138)*

Floor Action

The Senate passed the $8.7 billion military construction bill on Nov. 7, by a vote of 94-1. *(Vote 287, p. 51-S)*

The Senate adopted several floor amendments that, in the aggregate, added $75.2 million to the amount appropriated by the bill as reported.

As passed, the Senate bill appropriated $1.62 billion

less than Reagan's $10.3 billion military construction request. It provided $348 million more than the House-passed version of the bill.

Before final approval of the bill, however, senators stripped away the Appropriations Committee's provision that would have exempted many Pentagon construction projects from Davis-Bacon Act wage controls.

Edward M. Kennedy, D-Mass., raised a point of order against the Davis-Bacon provision, contending that it violated the Senate's rule against including legislative provisions in an appropriations bill.

On a procedural vote — in effect, on whether to waive the rule — the Senate voted against inclusion of the Davis-Bacon provision 45-49. *(Vote 286, p. 51-S)*

Soviet Sailor

By voice vote, the Senate adopted an amendment to the bill expressing the sense of the Senate that the government take "all legal and legitimate means ... in arriving at a just resolution" of the case of Miroslav Medvid. Medvid was a seaman who swam ashore from a Soviet cargo ship near New Orleans on Oct. 24 in what some observers contended was an attempt to defect.

Philippine Bases

The bill included $104 million of the $121 million requested for construction at U.S. bases in the Philippines, including the huge facilities at Clark Air Force Base and Subic Bay Naval Base near Manila.

Jim Sasser, D-Tenn., the senior Democrat on the Appropriations Subcommittee on Military Construction, had called for a moratorium on further Pentagon construction in the Philippines.

Citing a report by staff aides, Sasser argued that social upheaval in the Philippines, exacerbated by the rule of President Ferdinand E. Marcos, threatened long-term U.S. access to the bases. Sasser called for the funding halt as part of U.S. pressure on Marcos to make fundamental reforms in hopes of damping down the domestic unrest and halting a growing communist insurgency. *(Philippines, p. p. 113)*

But Sasser decided not to offer an amendment cutting funds for the Philippine bases, citing Marcos' decision to hold a presidential election early in 1986. ▮

Africa Relief Supplemental

Congress April 2 completed action on a fiscal 1985 supplemental appropriations bill (HR 1239 — PL 99-10) providing $784 million for Africa emergency relief. President Reagan signed the measure April 4, even though it provided more than three times as much money as he sought. Reagan had asked Congress to provide $235 million by early March.

As cleared, the bill appropriated $609 million for food and gave the administration authority to use another $16 million carried over from fiscal 1984. It also provided $175 million for non-food aid to Africa, such as seeds for farmers and clothing and shelter for refugees.

Congress had authorized the non-food aid in S 689 (PL 99-8), cleared March 21. The food aid amounts in HR 1239 did not require additional authorizations.

HR 1239 was passed by the House (H Rept 99-2) Feb. 28 and the Senate (S Rept 99-8) March 20. Both chambers adopted the conference report (H Rept 99-29) April 2. *(Details of authorization and appropriations action, p. 102)*

The United States previously had provided about $600 million in food and other emergency aid to Africa since Oct. 1, 1984, the start of the 1985 fiscal year. ▮

Stopgap Bill Had $36.3 Billion for Agriculture

Congress approved a $36.3 billion appropriation for agriculture programs as part of the fiscal 1986 continuing resolution (H J Res 465 — PL 99-190).

The separate agriculture appropriations bill (HR 3037) had passed both House and Senate and a conference agreement on the bill had been reached Dec. 12. Soon after, the agriculture funding was included in the continuing resolution, and no further action was taken on HR 3037. President Reagan signed H J Res 465 on Dec. 19. *(Continuing resolution, p. 360)*

The conference agreement on HR 3037 (H Rept 99-439) provided somewhat greater agriculture spending than included in H J Res 465. In order to meet spending limits set by the fiscal 1986 budget resolution (S Con Res 32), the funding levels in HR 3037 were pared by .6 percent, or about $200 million, when they were included in the continuing resolution. *(Budget resolution, p. 441)*

H J Res 465 as cleared provided across-the-board reductions in the funding levels contained in HR 3037 for all programs except child nutrition and special milk.

Provisions

As signed into law, H J Res 465 provided the following amounts for the Department of Agriculture and related programs as compared with fiscal 1985 appropriations:

	Fiscal 1985 Appropriation	Final Amount
Agriculture Programs		
Office of the Secretary	$ 1,732,000	$ 1,739,000
Assistant Secretary for Administration	479,000	481,000
Standard Level User Charges	66,754,000	70,826,000
Advisory Committees	1,385,000	1,315,000
Departmental Administration	24,868,000	24,979,000
Assistant Secretary for Governmental and Public Affairs	375,000	335,000
Governmental and Public Affairs	7,615,000	7,673,000
Inspector General	30,142,000	30,571,000
General Counsel	14,929,000	14,987,000
Assistant Secretary for Economics	413,000	415,000
Economic Research Service	47,098,000	46,027,000
Statistical Reporting Service	58,287,000	58,725,000
World Agricultural Outlook Board	1,676,000	1,670,000
Assistant Secretary for Science and Education	367,000	369,000
Agricultural Research Service	523,156,000	509,319,000
Cooperative State Research Service	290,776,000	288,680,000
Extension Service	343,727,000	304,120,000
National Agricultural Library	11,464,000	11,272,000

	Fiscal 1985 Appropriation	Final Amount
Assistant Secretary for Marketing and Inspection Services	343,000	345,000
Animal and Plant Health Inspection Service	300,918,000	318,624,000
Food Safety and Inspection Service	364,635,000	362,079,000 [1]
Federal Grain Inspection Service	6,994,000	7,003,000
Agricultural Cooperative Service	4,675,000	4,685,000
Agricultural Marketing Service	34,537,000	35,450,000
Packers and Stockyards Administration	9,035,000	9,146,000
Under Secretary for International Affairs and Commodity Programs	501,000	499,000
Agricultural Stabilization & Conservation Service	50,957,000	99,000
Federal Crop Insurance Corporation	473,502,000	353,216,000
Commodity Credit Corporation	12,285,790,000	9,140,069,000 [2]
Subtotal	$14,957,630,000	$11,604,718,000
Rural Development Programs		
Under Secretary for Small Community and Rural Development	410,000	785,000
Office of Rural Development Policy	2,345,000	0
Farmers Home Administration	4,043,172,000	3,994,558,000
Rural Electrification Administration	31,505,000	32,000,000
Assistant Secretary for Natural Resources and Environment	381,000	384,000
Soil Conservation Service	620,082,000	617,256,000
Agricultural Stabilization & Conservation Service	211,300,000	210,032,000
Subtotal	$ 4,909,195,000	$ 4,855,015,000
Domestic Food Programs		
Assistant Secretary for Food and Consumer Services	$ 346,000	$ 348,000
Child Nutrition Programs	1,474,861,000	177,533,000 [3]
Special Milk Program	17,600,000	11,500,000
Women, Infants & Children (WIC) Program	1,500,000,000	1,560,580,000
Commodity Supplemental Food Program	24,918,000	36,777,000
Food Stamps	11,768,856,000	11,820,221,000
Nutrition Assistance for Puerto Rico	825,000,000	820,050,000
Food Donations Programs	139,546,000	193,405,000
Temporary Emergency Food Assistance	57,000,000	49,700,000
Food Program Administration	84,187,000	82,007,000
Nutrition Information	7,533,000	13,481,000
Subtotal	$15,899,847,000	$14,765,602,000
International Programs		
Foreign Agricultural Service	83,622,000	83,046,000
Food for Peace (PL 480)	1,964,000,000	1,299,158,000
Office of International Cooperation & Development	5,038,000	5,384,000
Subtotal	$ 2,052,660,000	$ 1,387,588,000
Related Agencies		
Food and Drug Administration	414,679,000	421,747,000
Commodity Futures Trading Commission	27,564,000	29,240,000
Subtotal	$ 442,243,000	$ 450,987,000
TOTAL (New Budget Authority)	$38,261,575,000	$33,063,910,000
Section 32 Transfers	2,335,964,000	3,277,785,000
Total Obligational Authority	$40,597,539,000	$36,341,695,000

Loan Authorization: The bill also provided the following loan authorizations:

- $7,608,000,000 in direct and insured loans (fiscal 1985 authorization: $8,473,000,000).
- $3,031,000,000 in guaranteed loans (fiscal 1985 authorization: $2,031,000,000).

[1] *An additional $5,735,000 was to be available upon submission of a budget request from the administration.*
[2] *An additional $4,000,000,000 was to be available upon submission of a budget request from the administration. (The president had requested a permanent, indefinite appropropriation for the Commodity Credit Corporation, which in prior years required multibillion-dollar supplemental appropriations. The Senate voted for an annual, indefinite appropriation for the agency, but conferees agreed to a definite appropriation.)*
[3] *An additional $665,015,000 was to be available upon submission of a budget request from the administration.*

House Committee Action

The House Appropriations Committee July 18 deliberated 20 minutes and approved a subcommittee-drafted version of HR 3037 that generally froze anticipated agriculture outlays at 1985 levels, but maintained current service levels for most major farm and nutrition programs.

The committee approved $33.12 billion in new budget authority for the department, $5.13 billion less than the fiscal 1985 appropriation. Committee staff said the bill met budget targets in the House-passed version of S Con Res 32.

The committee bill (H Rept 99-211) fell short of the administration's budget request by $22.4 million. The bill appropriated about $200 million less than the administration requested for basic farm and rural development programs, but $180 million more for domestic food programs.

At the time of the committee action, the House and Senate Agriculture committees were in the midst of a wholesale rewrite of federal farm policy, but neither had yet agreed to an approach that could give specific guidance to the Appropriations panel. In addition, after a decade of farm expansion in the 1970s, farmers as a whole were suffering serious financial difficulties and many were in deep debt as a result of rising interest rates, falling land values, and diminished exports. *(Farm bill, p. 517; farm credit veto, p. 542)*

In issuing its report on HR 3037, the Appropriations panel was sharply critical of many of the Reagan administration's 1986 budget proposals for the department, particularly in light of the severe financial problems encountered by American farmers.

The administration had called for deep reductions in farm spending, to be achieved by providing farmers and their rural neighbors with significantly less help from the federal government. The budget proposed that rural residents be required to pay for many farm-related services that were free or generously subsidized, including crop insurance, federal loans, electric and telephone service and information about agricultural markets.

HR 3037 as reported by the Appropriations Committee appropriated $9.2 billion for the Commodity Credit Corporation (CCC), $3.1 billion less than the agency's fiscal 1985 appropriation. The agency distributed benefits to farmers and bought surplus farm commodities. The bill assumed that existing farm programs would continue at current levels, but at reduced cost, because part of the CCC's fiscal 1985 appropriation was to pay for programs that had since expired.

The bill appropriated nearly $4 billion in fiscal 1986 for the Farmers Home Administration (FmHA), about the same as in fiscal 1985 but nearly $500 million less than requested by the administration.

The bill included $2.3 billion for FmHA loans in fiscal 1986 for low-income housing — the same as in fiscal 1985. The administration had requested only $30 million. Another $900 million was earmarked for rural rental housing loans, a program the administration wanted to end immediately.

And the bill authorized $900 million in direct loans and $975 million in guaranteed loans by the Rural Electrification Administration (REA), which helped to finance telephone and electric service in rural areas. The administration had asked for only $575 million in direct loans and $300 million in guaranteed loans.

Overall, the bill authorized $8 billion in direct loans for rural development programs of the FmHA and the REA. The administration had requested only $3.3 billion in loan authority, intending to abolish most direct farm lending by the FmHA and REA and most rural housing and other rural development programs.

The bill earmarked $1.31 billion in fiscal 1986 for the Food for Peace program, also known as Public Law 480, about $650 million less than the $1.96 billion appropriated in fiscal 1985. The committee report said that $167 million in fiscal 1985 carryover funds and $225 million in fiscal 1985 emergency reserve funds for African famine relief could be applied to fiscal 1986.

The committee said the administration would have to submit new requests for emergency relief funds if famine conditions continued in sub-Saharan Africa. *(Story p. 102)*

The committee bill appropriated $14.85 billion for domestic food programs, including food stamps and child nutrition services. That was a $1.05 billion decrease from 1985, but $180.1 million more than requested by the administration. Budget authority for food stamps increased by $122.7 million, to $11.9 billion.

Most of the decrease in direct appropriations for child nutrition was to be made up by a comparable increase in so-called section 32 transfer funds earmarked for the programs. Under section 32 of a law enacted in 1935, 30 percent of all tariff receipts on imports collected by the U.S. Customs Service were transferred to the Agriculture Department, primarily to purchase surplus domestic foodstuffs for supplementary food programs for low-income persons.

The committee agreed to appropriate another $665 million for child nutrition programs if the administration specifically requested it.

The committee included $1.57 billion for a supplemental program for low-income women and their infant children, known as WIC, an increase of $70 million over fiscal 1985. The administration had asked for $1.48 billion and wanted to merge the WIC program with the commodity supplemental food program for children up to six years old.

But the committee reaffirmed its support for keeping the WIC program separate from other supplemental food services. The committee report said the WIC program "may be the most effective nutrition assistance program administered by the Department."

House Floor Action

The House passed HR 3037, essentially unchanged, by a 354-71 vote July 24. *(Vote 230, p. 74-H)*

Although sponsors said new budget authority in the bill would come in under the limits set in the House version of S Con Res 32, some Republicans charged, as they had in past years, that the bill was drafted to conform to the budget resolution rather than to the actual requirements of the Agriculture Department.

They said Congress had traditionally underfunded Agriculture Department programs, continually forcing members to pass substantial supplemental appropriations bills to cover the department's year-end shortfalls.

"I used to be on the Appropriations Committee, so I know all the tricks," said House Minority Leader Robert H. Michel, R-Ill. "They pass enough funding for 10 months or nine months, then they come back and beg for a [supplemental] request. We're going to have one whopping supplemental bill next year."

The full House took less than an hour in debate and acted on only one amendment, introduced by Jamie L. Whitten, D-Miss., chairman of the Appropriations Committee and its Agriculture Subcommittee.

Whitten asked for an additional $2.1 million in budget authority for a Food and Drug Administration program to develop and improve a screening test for acquired immune deficiency syndrome (AIDS). That amendment, which Whitten said was sanctioned by the Reagan administration, was approved by voice vote and raised the FDA's budget authority to $419.7 million from $417.6 million.

No other amendments were introduced on the House floor and no member registered objections to any of the spending provisions.

Senate Committee Action

The Senate Appropriations Committee reported its version of HR 3037 Sept. 24 (S Rept 99-137).

The committee bill reduced spending for farm and nutrition programs by an estimated $3.1 billion, and sought to eliminate a perennial need for end-of-the-year supplemental appropriations for federal price-support programs.

The panel also agreed, on a 15-12 vote, to strike out an Agriculture Subcommittee provision that would have forced Agriculture Secretary John R. Block to reduce sugar import quotas far below the level he had announced Sept. 13.

Including so-called section 32 transfers, the Senate committee bill provided $28.1 billion for the Agriculture Department and related programs in fiscal 1986.

The Senate committee, however, recommended against including specific appropriations for the CCC. Instead, the panel recommended giving the CCC unlimited budget authority on a year-to-year basis, thereby reducing the total appropriation in the bill.

The panel approved $24.8 billion in new budget authority, $13.5 billion less than appropriated for fiscal 1985 and $8.4 billion less than in the House-passed version of the bill.

The House bill, however, had included $9.2 billion in CCC budget authority. If the Senate panel's $9.4 billion estimate of fiscal 1986 CCC spending were added to its version of HR 3037, new budget authority actually would have been $34.2 billion, about $1.1 billion more than contained in the House bill and $3.1 billion less than fiscal 1985 spending.

As justification for the unlimited CCC appropriation, Senate panel members cited the unpredictability of weather conditions and other production and economic variables. An unlimited appropriation would have allowed the CCC to continue funding its price-support programs through the end of the fiscal year even if budget authority needs exceeded estimates made at the time appropriations were enacted.

Of the $12.9 billion appropriated to the CCC for fiscal 1985, $3.9 billion came in two year-end supplemental appropriations bills (H J Res 342 — PL 99-71; HR 2577 — PL 99-88). The first was needed because the CCC ran out of cash and stopped payments to farmers. *(Supplemental appropriations, p. 350)*

Senate committee members contended that the House bill achieved "paper" savings of $973 million by underestimating spending for CCC and FmHA programs, thus increasing the likelihood for supplemental appropriations requests before the end of fiscal 1986.

The Senate committee approved nearly $1 billion more in budget authority than requested by the administration. That included $808 million more than the administration requested for basic farm and rural development programs, and $185 million more for domestic food programs.

Committee members said their recommendations would achieve $800 million in savings from various direct appropriations, as required in the final version of S Con Res 32. In addition, the committee followed the budget resolution assumption of a cut of 40 percent in the budget authority for rural housing loan programs, setting a limit of $1.9 billion for direct loans, compared with a $3.2 billion loan level in fiscal 1985.

Like the House, the Senate panel appropriated $14.85 billion for domestic food programs, including food stamps and child nutrition services. That was $1.05 billion less than fiscal 1985 appropriations, but much of that decrease was to be offset by a $941.7 million increase in section 32 transfers.

Also like the House, the Senate committee included new budget authority of $842.5 million for child nutrition programs, of which $665 million would be available only if requested later by the administration.

Senate Floor Action

The Senate passed HR 3037 by an 81-14 vote Oct. 16. But before approving the measure, the Senate rejected two attempts to make large-scale reductions in farm and nutrition programs. *(Vote 226, p. 43-S)*

Senators voted 66-28 to kill an amendment by William Proxmire, D-Wis., to make 4 percent cuts in each of the bill's spending accounts. *(Vote 223, p. 43-S)*

Proxmire, arguing that farmers would benefit the most from a reduction in the federal deficit, said an across-the-board reduction, totaling about $1.1 billion, would bring the bill in line with the administration's total budget request, yet maintain the spending ratios set by the Appropriations Committee for the various programs in the bill.

Thad Cochran, R-Miss., chairman of the Appropriations Subcommittee on Agriculture, defended the bill's spending totals as consistent with the budget limits of S Con Res 32.

By a similar margin, the Senate voted 68-27 to kill an amendment by Agriculture Committee Chairman Jesse Helms, R-N.C., to cut FmHA and food stamp funding. *(Vote 224, p. 43-S)*

Helms maintained that a $1.8 billion anomaly existed between spending and borrowing limits in the appropriations bill and the pending reauthorization bill (S 1714) for farm and nutrition programs that had been approved by his committee but not yet passed by the Senate.

Helms' amendment would have cut $1.6 billion in borrowing authority for direct farm ownership and operating loans and rural water and sewer loans; $75 million in borrowing authority for direct community facility loans; $100 million from guaranteed industrial development loans; $115 million in spending authority from rural water and sewer grants; and $166.6 million in spending authority from the food stamp program.

Helms' amendment would have added, however, $150 million in loan guarantees for producing and distributing ethanol in rural areas.

Cochran said the Appropriations Committee could not assume that the Senate Agriculture Committee's funding recommendations would become law, and in the meantime abided by the limitations of current law. He said any farm reauthorization bill that was enacted would take precedence.

In the end, the Senate gave Cochran approval for most of his original subcommittee recommendations, adding only $5.6 million to the Food and Drug Administration (FDA) budget for research grants to study AIDS and to develop drugs for rare diseases.

Albert Gore Jr., D-Tenn., also won approval to require the FDA to complete a safety evaluation of sulfiting agents (chemicals used to preserve some foods) by June 1, 1986, two months earlier than scheduled. Cochran had argued that the amendment did not belong on an appropriations bill, but his motion to kill the amendment failed, 18-77. *(Vote 225, p. 43-S)*

Conference Action

The key dispute settled by conferees on HR 3037 concerned the method of funding the CCC.

The House bill would have given the CCC $9.2 billion to reimburse it for expenses incurred during fiscal 1986 and previous years. The administration estimated that at least $9.4 billion would be required for the agency.

The Senate bill, by contrast, sought to remove the CCC from the direct appropriations process, by giving it unlimited budget authority during the entire year. That would have allowed the Agriculture Department to continue funding its price-support programs through the end of the fiscal year even if CCC budget authority needs exceeded estimates made at the time appropriations were enacted.

Cochran and other Republicans charged that the House Appropriations Committee had purposely understated the need for programs such as the CCC, in order to increase funding for programs that were more vulnerable to budget cuts.

Conferees agreed to retain a definite appropriation of $9.2 billion for the CCC. But they also agreed to make an additional $4 billion available without a special supplemental appropriation, if requested by the administration. ∎

GENERAL GOVERNMENT

CQ

General Government

Federal employee groups began 1985 expecting major battles in Congress over pay and benefits. Members of the Reagan administration, led by Donald J. Devine, Reagan's combative director of the Office of Personnel Management (OPM), had criticized employee benefits as too generous, and sought the first pay cut since the Great Depression. In addition, Devine for years had tried to change the way workers earned raises, focusing on performance rather than seniority.

By the end of the year, Devine was out of office, the victim of his own style. His successor, Constance Horner, smoothly negotiated a change in the merit pay system that satisfied both the administration and congressional supporters of federal workers. And workers had, for the most part, staved off cuts in pay and benefits.

Nevertheless, like most interest groups, federal employees considered the Gramm-Rudman-Hollings plan to balance the federal budget in five years to be the most significant piece of legislation Congress enacted in 1985.

The legislation had an immediate impact on federal retirees, canceling the 3.1 percent cost-of-living allowance (COLA) that was due Jan. 1, 1986. In response, a union and a group representing retirees sued to overturn the new law.

Also, the Gramm-Rudman-Hollings plan absorbed most of Congress' attention as the end of the session neared, leaving until 1986 the settlement of differences on an important bill creating a new retirement system for federal employees.

The deficit-cutting law could have an impact on the retirement bill, which was aimed at providing supplemental benefits for workers hired after Jan. 1, 1984, who were covered by the Social Security system. Critics of the current retirement program, including the Reagan administration, wanted the new plan to reduce future costs by raising the retirement age and limiting COLAs. The Senate-passed bill would cut costs, though not as much as the administration would prefer.

Employee groups and their supporters in Congress backed the measure approved by the House Post Office and Civil Service Committee, which would maintain features of the current system allowing workers to retire with full benefits at age 55 and providing annual COLAs equal to the rise in the Consumer Price Index.

While Congress debated the new proposal, it rejected changes in the existing system. And Congress rejected Reagan's proposal to cut federal wages by 5 percent but agreed to freeze wages in fiscal 1986.

Devine Nomination

Confronted by almost certain rejection by the Republican-controlled Senate Governmental Affairs Committee, Devine withdrew his name from consideration for a second four-year term as OPM director. Horner, a former associate director of the Office of Management and Budget, was confirmed with little debate.

Devine's relations with Congress and federal employee groups often were stormy, and during his confirmation hearings, he sparred with Democrats who accused him of being partisan while running the civil service agency. But even some of his supporters objected to a memorandum he wrote on his last day in office delegating to himself authority to run the agency while he served as executive assistant to the acting director. After the acting director, Loretta Cornelius, testified that Devine had asked her to say she knew about the memo when in fact she had not, he withdrew his name.

Devine later became consulting director of Campaign America, a political action committee founded by Senate Majority Leader Robert Dole, R-Kan.

Pay Equity Study

The House, for the second year in a row, passed a bill requiring a study of the federal work force to determine if differences in pay arose because of sex discrimination. House action came as several states and cities moved to adjust their pay scales to address past discrimination. In the Senate, the Governmental Affairs Subcommittee on Civil Service held hearings, but no further action was taken.

In January 1986, the state of Washington reached a $106.5 million agreement with unions representing state employees to raise wages of jobs dominated by females. If approved by the state Legislature and U.S. District Court for the Western District of Washington, the settlement could end a lawsuit that critics said could cost the state up to $1 billion. In 1983, the court found that the state had discriminated against women employees, but that decision was overturned by a three-judge panel of the 9th U.S. Circuit Court of Appeals.

Los Angeles and Chicago also reached agreements with city workers to raise wages in female-dominated jobs.

Congressional sponsors of a federal pay equity study, led by Mary Rose Oakar, D-Ohio, argued that the U.S. work force had not been studied since 1923, when attitudes about "women's work" were different from what they were currently. And she noted that more than 40 states and many cities, after studying their own work forces, adjusted pay scales to reflect the results of the studies.

But critics, led by business groups and the Reagan administration, contended that it was impossible to determine the relative wages of dissimilar jobs.

Small Business, Veterans

Despite budget-cutting pressures, Congress resisted Reagan's proposal to abolish the Small Business Administration (SBA), an agency former budget director David A. Stockman said served no useful public purpose. Both the House and Senate passed separate legislation reauthorizing the SBA for three years, at sharply reduced funding levels.

Budget questions also dominated most discussion of veterans' issues in Congress in 1985. Disabled veterans received a 3.1 percent COLA, the same as the amount Social Security recipients received, despite efforts by the House to give them a bigger COLA. The House wanted to make up for the fact that disabled veterans received a smaller COLA in fiscal 1985 than Social Security recipients received, but senators successfully held out for the lower figure.

Congress and the administration sought ways to reduce the expected rise in Veterans Administration (VA) health care costs.

Under existing law, veterans over 65 were entitled to free VA care if space was available; the number of veterans over 65 was expected to triple in the next decade as millions of World War II veterans grew older.

In an effort at holding down costs, both the House and the Senate voted to impose a means test on veterans receiving VA health care. The means test, which would require veterans with injuries unrelated to service with incomes exceeding $20,000 annually to pay for care, would be less stringent than a means test proposed by the Reagan administration. Reagan would have restricted access to health care to veterans with incomes below $15,000.

Also, Reagan signed legislation making it easier for the VA to use less-expensive forms of care, and to improve the quality of care. The bill also called on the VA to plan for future construction needs.

However, the Gramm-Rudman-Hollings deficit-reduction measure would protect VA health care from automatic cuts, limiting reductions to 1 percent in fiscal 1986 and 2 percent thereafter.

To curb spending in another VA program, the Senate passed a bill overhauling the VA's home loan guarantee program, which had cost taxpayers more than $500 million since 1984 because of an unusually high default rate.

—By Robert Rothman

VA Health Cost Containment Bill Clears

Legislation aimed at keeping down the cost of Veterans Administration (VA) health care and improving the delivery of services was signed into law by President Reagan Dec. 3.

The measure (HR 505 — PL 99-166) was aimed at helping the VA to prepare for an influx of older veterans and to reduce the expected increase in VA health care costs as millions of World War II veterans turned 65. Eleven million veterans were to reach that age in the next decade. At age 65, under existing law, veterans were entitled to free care in VA hospitals and nursing homes, if space was available.

The Reagan administration had proposed restricting the number of older veterans using VA facilities by imposing a means test. Although that approach was rejected in the congressional budget resolution (S Con Res 32) passed by Congress, a means test was included in a budget reconciliation measure (HR 3128) that did not clear before adjournment. *(Story, p. 498)*

HR 505 would make it easier for veterans to get treatment in non-VA facilities or to receive outpatient care, freeing expensive hospital beds for patients who needed them most. It was designed to improve the quality of VA care by prohibiting the VA from reducing the number of mid-level health care employees, and by strengthening quality assurance programs.

The final version did not include Senate provisions setting up pilot programs to evaluate non-hospital care and to provide community-based psychiatric treatment for chronic mentally ill veterans, or a House provision clarifying the VA's authority to provide respite, or intermittent, care for veterans who could stay home most of the time.

These provisions were aimed at encouraging the VA to use lower-cost treatment. House and Senate Veterans' Affairs committee members said that in 1986 they would examine those issues and the existing VA authority to provide such treatment.

Also dropped was a Senate amendment that would have required the VA to make its expertise in psychological stress counseling available to agencies that dealt with persons taken hostage by Shiite Moslems during the hijacking of TWA Flight 847 in June, as well as other citizens taken hostage. *(Hijacking, p. 416)*

The final version did not include a Senate provision extending, until March 1, 1986, the deadline for veterans to enroll in a job training program. However, separate legislation (S 1671 — PL 99-108) extended the deadline until July 1, 1986.

HR 505 was reported by the House Veterans' Affairs Committee May 15 (H Rept 99-114) and passed by voice vote of the House without amendment May 21. The Senate version (S 876) was reported July 8 by the Veterans' Affairs Committee (S Rept 99-101). After amending that bill on the floor July 30, the Senate substituted its language for that of HR 505 and passed HR 505 by voice vote.

To prevent several programs covered by the bill from expiring at the end of the fiscal year Sept. 30, Congress cleared an interim extension of authority (S 1671 — PL 99-108) for their operation while staff continued to work to resolve disagreements.

Most differences were resolved in an agreement approved by the House by voice vote Oct. 30. The Senate concurred Nov. 13, adding an amendment clearing up a remaining dispute over the possible purchase of a private hospital in Mobile, Ala. Final action came when the House by voice vote Nov. 14 accepted the Senate amendment. The amendment required a study of the feasibility of the VA's buying the hospital but did not mandate the purchase, as the Senate bill originally stipulated.

Provisions

As signed into law, major provisions of HR 505:

- Extended through Sept. 30, 1988, authority for the VA to contract with non-VA halfway houses for drug and alcohol abuse treatment and required a report to Congress by Feb. 1, 1988, on the program, including information on its results and cost.
- Made permanent the VA authority to contract for hospital and outpatient services in the Virgin Islands but phased out contract authority in Puerto Rico after three years.
- Extended through fiscal 1989 eligibility for health care for veterans exposed to the herbicide Agent Orange.
- Allowed veterans receiving nursing home or domiciliary care to be eligible for VA outpatient care for up to 12 months following discharge. Under existing law, only veterans receiving hospital care were eligible for outpatient care.
- Established a three-year pilot program of providing additional services at 10 existing Vietnam readjustment centers, including job counseling, referral for drug and alcohol abuse, and counseling for VA and other federal benefits. The centers were to be known as Vietnam Veterans Resource Centers.
- Required the VA to provide, upon request, counseling to any veteran who was a former prisoner of war.
- Authorized the VA to transfer patients from a VA nursing home directly to a non-VA nursing home, without having to be admitted to a VA hospital as existing law required.
- Directed the VA to set up a pilot program of providing chiropractic services to veterans who received treatment in a VA hospital in the previous 12 months for a neuromusculoskeletal condition of the spine. Charges for the services would be consistent with the Medicare schedule for such services, and the VA would be limited to spending $2 million a year on the demonstration. The VA would report on the program by April 1, 1989.
- Prohibited the VA from withholding the disclosure of statistical information on health care programs, as long as the information did not identify VA patients or employees.
- Expanded from 15 to 25 the number of Geriatric Research, Education and Clinical Centers, which studied and treated diseases related to aging.
- Required the VA to conduct a program to monitor and evaluate the quality of its health care and required the inspector general to monitor the quality assurance program. The Department of Medicine and Surgery would be required to establish and maintain mortality and morbidity standards, collect data on mortality and morbidity rates for each surgical procedure, and compile those data for each case of VA cardiac surgery, heart transplant and renal transplant. Further required the VA to compare the data with the standards, analyze deviations and make recommendations, and to report to Congress on plans for monitoring the credentials of VA health care professionals.

- Required the VA to defer approval of funding to build a state veterans' home if, by July 1 following notice of federal approval, state financial support had not been provided. A House provision authorizing $40 million in fiscal 1986 for matching-fund grants to build the state homes was dropped.
- Directed the VA to prescribe uniform guidelines for the handling of cases involving the proposed reduction or revocation of clinical privileges of VA health professionals.
- Required that any law appropriating funds to build a major VA medical facility specify which facility was being built and how much was appropriated. Also prohibited appropriations from exceeding the estimated cost.
- Ordered the VA to submit annually to Congress a five-year operating plan, including an assessment of medical operation and construction needs. Required that, as part of a prospectus for a new or replacement medical facility, the administrator report to Congress on the consideration given to leasing or buying an existing facility. A Senate provision prohibiting the construction of a hospital containing more than 700 beds was dropped.
- Increased from $35,000 to $50,000 the maximum coverage of the Serviceman's Group Life Insurance/Veterans' Group Life Insurance programs and made such insurance available to the reserves and inactive National Guard.
- Extended through Sept. 30, 1988, authority to operate a VA office in the Republic of the Philippines.
- Prohibited the VA from implementing a systematic grade reduction to reduce average salary costs of certain categories of VA employees — approximately 13,750 employees at the time the measure was signed — without first submitting to Congress a detailed plan and justification for the proposed reduction.
- Required the administrator to conduct a feasibility study, and if indicated by the study, establish a plan to buy a medical facility located in an urban area that was suitable for furnishing hospital and nursing home care and met the current and projected needs of the VA. The plan could not have the effect of making infeasible plans to build a facility in the Florida Panhandle or to expand the Biloxi-Gulfport VA medical center.

House Action

The House May 21 by voice vote passed the bill as approved by the Veterans' Affairs Committee May 7.

The need for the legislation was outlined by Committee Chairman G. V. "Sonny" Montgomery, D-Miss., who said: "In 1980, three million veterans were over the age of 65. By 1990, this number will more than double, reaching 7.2 million.... They will be coming to the VA for health care more often because of their age and they will stay longer."

The measure as passed clarified the VA's authority, based on medical need, to provide respite, or intermittent, care for veterans suffering from long-term chronic illnesses, allowing them to receive some treatment at home. The bill also allowed certain veterans currently in nursing homes to receive outpatient care, and encouraged the VA to transfer patients from VA-run nursing homes to non-VA homes.

In addition, it allowed the VA to expand to 25, from 15, the number of Geriatric Research, Education and Clinical Centers (GRECCs), which conducted research and treatment of diseases affecting older veterans.

It also extended for three years the VA's authority to contract with halfway houses and community centers for treatment of alcohol or drug abuse problems.

The bill authorized $40 million in grants to state-run homes for veterans and required grants to be directed to states with the greatest need. And it established a pilot program to test the cost-efficiency of instituting chiropractic care in VA hospitals.

Senate Action

The version approved by the Senate July 30 also was aimed at making VA health care more efficient by establishing new quality assurance measures, encouraging less costly care and limiting the size of new hospitals.

The Senate bill also extended authority for veterans to apply for job training programs, restricted the ability of the VA to reduce the number of health care employees in middle civil-service grades and encouraged the VA to share its expertise in psychological counseling with agencies providing aid to U.S. citizens who had been taken hostage.

To encourage cost savings, the Senate bill established four-year pilot programs to evaluate non-hospital care. The VA would provide medical and rehabilitative services for certain veterans at home or in boarding homes that would provide some care. It also could contract with non-VA facilities to treat chronically mentally ill veterans.

Alan Cranston, D-Calif., ranking minority member of the Veterans Affairs Committee, said the programs would address the needs of older patients while reducing costs. The bill limited the cost to 60 percent of what it would have cost to provide VA nursing home care.

The Senate bill also required the VA to establish a program to monitor the quality of VA surgery, by directing the chief medical director to compile national mortality and morbidity statistics for all types of surgical procedures.

And it urged the VA to plan for future construction needs and limited the size of new and replacement hospitals to 700 beds; under existing law, there was no limit.

Amendments

The Senate adopted an amendment adding several provisions. One would ensure that the VA share its expertise in psychological stress counseling with other agencies that provided aid to the hostages taken in TWA Flight 847, which was hijacked in June by Shiite Moslem militiamen, as well as to other citizens taken hostage. Another would extend by six months, until March 1, 1986, the deadline for a veteran to apply for a job training program for Vietnam and Korean War veterans (PL 98-77). ∎

D.C. Vote Amendment Dies

A constitutional amendment giving the District of Columbia voting representation in Congress died Aug. 22, when its statutory deadline for ratification expired. Since Congress approved the measure in 1978, only 16 state legislatures had ratified the amendment — well short of the 38 needed. *(1978 Almanac p. 793)*

The District had no senators and only one non-voting member of the House, Democrat Walter E. Fauntroy. The amendment would have given it two senators and at least one House member.

Voting to ratify the amendment were Connecticut, Delaware, Hawaii, Iowa, Louisiana, Maine, Maryland, Massachusetts, Michigan, Minnesota, New Jersey, Ohio, Oregon, Rhode Island, West Virginia and Wisconsin.

Fauntroy and Sen. Edward M. Kennedy, D-Mass., introduced legislation (HR 325, S 293) to make the District a state, which also would give residents voting representation. Congress did not act on the proposals.

Missing Children's Bill

A bill permitting photographs and biographies of missing children to appear on federal and congressional mail was signed into law (S 1195 — PL 99-87) by President Reagan Aug. 9.

The House cleared the measure Aug. 1 by voice vote, after the Senate July 31 added a technical amendment to the version passed by the House two days before.

As originally passed by the Senate by voice vote May 22, the bill would have required 75 percent of agency mail and 50 percent of congressional mail to carry the pictures and information. As reported by the House Post Office and Civil Service Committee July 25 (H Rept 99-226) and passed by voice vote by the House July 29, the bill authorized agencies and members to use the information on their mail but did not require it. The program would run for two and one-half years and then be evaluated.

Committee Chairman William D. Ford, D-Mich., said the Senate version would have created administrative problems because a lot of congressional mail, such as newsletters, did not require envelopes and some agency mail, such as Social Security checks, was sent in small envelopes.

Estimates placed the number of missing children from 30,000 to 1.5 million. Efforts by grocery stores and milk companies displaying photos of missing children on bags and cartons had helped locate some missing children.

Federal executive agencies send two billion to four billion pieces of mail a year and members of Congress 640 million, according to the Government Printing Office.

NBS Authorization Cleared

President Reagan July 29 signed into law legislation (HR 1617 — PL 99-73) that kept alive two agencies he wanted to abolish.

The measure, a fiscal 1986 authorization for the National Bureau of Standards (NBS), also included funding of $5.8 million for the Center for Fire Research and $3.9 million for the Center for Building Technology. The administration sought to kill the agencies for the third year in a row because it believed the research performed by them was more properly the role of private industry or state and local governments.

Both chambers rejected the administration proposal, contending the research had been valuable and necessary. The Senate had authorized slightly lower amounts for the two agencies; conferees accepted the House funding.

Final action on the bill came July 15 when first the House and then the Senate by voice vote approved a conference report (H Rept 99-187) on the measure.

As cleared, the bill authorized $127.8 million in fiscal 1986 for NBS and related agencies, the same amount provided in fiscal 1985.

Legislative History

House. Before approving the bill April 18, the House narrowly rejected a cut and voted to freeze spending by the NBS at fiscal 1985 levels.

The bill as reported April 16 by the Science and Technology Committee (H Rept 99-43) authorized $143.86 million for NBS and related agencies. But Doug Walgren, D-Pa., chairman of the Subcommittee on Science, Research and Technology, offered a floor amendment to freeze spending at the fiscal 1985 level of $127.8 million.

Robert S. Walker, R-Pa., noting that Reagan requested $123 million for NBS, offered a substitute amendment authorizing that amount. Walker's substitute also would have shifted some of the administration's priorities.

Walker argued that to reduce the deficit, Congress must cut programs, not merely freeze them at the previous year's levels. "If you can't cut $5 million from the National Bureau of Standards to get below the freeze," he asked, "where can you cut?"

The House rejected Walker's substitute amendment, 196-201, and then adopted the Walgren freeze amendment, 398-2. The House passed the bill, 282-103. *(Votes 51, 52, 53, p. 20-H)*

Senate. A companion measure reported April 16 by the Senate Commerce, Science and Transportation Committee (S 796 — S Rept 99-31) authorized higher funding levels: $133.5 million for NBS and the agencies.

During floor debate April 23, the Senate by voice vote adopted an amendment by Albert Gore Jr., D-Tenn., authorizing $50,000 for the NBS to make available data on structural failures, such as the one that caused the skywalk in the Hyatt Regency Hotel in Kansas City, Mo., to collapse in 1981.

The Senate substituted the text of S 796 for the House bill before passing HR 1617 by voice vote.

The amendment was retained by conferees.

NASA Authorization

Congress cleared a $7.67 billion fiscal 1986 authorization bill Nov. 21 for the National Aeronautics and Space Administration (NASA).

The measure (HR 1714 — PL 99-170) was $220 million below President Reagan's budget request for the agency and about $150 million above the fiscal 1985 authorization.

The Senate by voice vote adopted the conference report on the bill Nov. 21, and the House cleared the bill by voice vote later that day.

In passing HR 1714 on April 3, the House had frozen NASA spending at the fiscal 1985 level of $7.5 billion, overriding administration and committee proposals to spend more on space programs.

The Senate version, passed June 27, totaled $7.65 billion, which sponsors described as a freeze, except for three "augmentations" that addressed problems not raised by the administration budget.

Before conferees finished work on HR 1714, Congress cleared an appropriations bill containing $7.65 billion for NASA. The total was included in HR 3038 (PL 99-160), the fiscal 1986 funding bill for the Department of Housing and Urban Development, which was signed by the president Nov. 25. *(Story, p. 317)*

Conference Action, Major Provisions

As reported by House-Senate conferees (H Rept 99-379) Nov. 19 and cleared by Congress Nov. 21, HR 1714 authorized funding as follows:

Of the $150 million increase over fiscal 1985 levels, $42 million was for civil service pay. The administration budget request had assumed a 5 percent pay cut.

HR 1714 included $205 million for developing a manned space station in the 1990s, $25 million less than requested. The House had authorized the full $230 million request; the Senate, $200 million.

The bill stated the space station "may be used only for peaceful purposes," and prohibited it from being used "to carry or place in orbit any nuclear weapon or any other weapon of mass destruction."

The measure also allowed $2.67 billion for the space shuttle, $620 million for physics and astronomy research, and $354 million for planetary exploration. The total authorization for research and development was $95 million less than the budget request.

The administration budgeted money for 14 flights of space shuttles during fiscal 1986, as well as delivery of the fourth shuttle, *Atlantis*, but did not propose funds for any others. HR 1714, however, required NASA to maintain "production readiness" for a fifth vehicle.

HR 1714 authorized two interplanetary launches planned by NASA for May 1986: the Galileo mission to Jupiter, and the Ulysses mission to study the sun and solar system. Other major projects slated by NASA for fiscal 1986 included the launch of the Hubble space telescope, and operational use of a space shuttle launching site at Vandenberg Air Force Base north of Los Angeles, which would enable NASA to place the shuttle into polar orbit.

The legislation also directed NASA to include a physically disabled American in the shuttle program. According to Rep. Manuel Lujan Jr. of New Mexico, ranking Republican on the Science and Technology Committee, "NASA has been in the forefront in developing new technology to assist the handicapped."

One of more controversial sections of HR 1714 concerned a proposal by Rep. Robert S. Walker, R-Pa., designed to promote commercial space projects through establishment of a pricing policy for use of the shuttle. The compromise bill set a base price of $74 million per flight to be charged to each commercial or foreign customer using the space shuttle, starting in 1989.

NASA was given wide latitude, however, to set a lower base price to attract customers or to auction off flights to the highest bidder if demand increased.

NASA currently charged $71 million per launch.

Bill Nelson, D-Fla., chairman of the Space Science Subcommittee, and others argued that the price should be as low as possible to make the shuttle competitive with a French government-led space launch firm. But Walker wanted NASA to be able to charge more to enable private U.S. companies with their own launch vehicles to compete with the shuttle. The House adopted a Walker amendment to allow prices to range between $45 million and $105 million.

The Senate bill had required the president to inform congressional committees of his policy.

House Action

The House Science and Technology Committee, in reporting the authorization March 28 (H Rept 99-32), went along with the administration's request to increase NASA's budget to $7.9 billion from the fiscal 1985 level of $7.5 billion. Within the total, however, the panel changed specific programs.

As requested, the committee included $25 million for a new orbital maneuvering vehicle, designed to be used during space shuttle flights to retrieve or deploy satellites in higher orbits than the shuttles could currently fly.

The panel also accepted the $230 million to continue research into a permanent manned space station that the president had asked for in his 1984 State of the Union message. The $230 million would go toward the development of a design for the station.

But the panel cut $10 million of $30 million requested for research into the commercial use of space, and $15 million requested for space transportation research.

The panel also authorized $45 million more than was requested for the space shuttle program, primarily to buy spare parts to prepare for a possible fifth shuttle vehicle.

Floor Action. When the bill reached the floor, the House by a 369-36 vote, adopted an amendment by Bruce A. Morrison, D-Conn., to keep spending at $7.5 billion. The House then passed the bill 395-3. *(Votes 46, 47, p. 18-H)*

"If you don't stop spending more money, it's an endless battle to try to end the deficit," said Morrison.

Nelson argued against freezing NASA spending, an ironic position since he had sponsored an unsuccessful across-the-board budget freeze as an amendment to the fiscal 1985 budget resolution. *(1984 Almanac p. 156)*

He said he would support an across-the-board freeze again in 1985. But until a freeze was adopted government-wide, he said, the House should not single out NASA.

Morrison, who supported Nelson's 1984 freeze amendment, said an across-the-board freeze meant NASA, too: "You can't say, 'Not my program,' or 'Not until something else.' "

As passed by the House, HR 1714:

- Authorized $2.86 billion for fiscal 1986 for research and development, $3.53 billion for space flight, control and data analysis, $148.3 million for construction of space flight facilities and $1.3 million for research and program management.
- Set $7.52 billion as a spending cap for the agency in fiscal 1986, but left undetermined which program areas would be reduced.
- Set a policy for determining the cost to foreign and commercial users of the space shuttle, charging them between $45 million and $105 million per flight.
- Authorized $586,000 in fiscal 1986 for the Office of Commercial Space Transportation in the Department of Transportation.

Amendments. Jan Meyers, R-Kan., noting that NASA Administrator James M. Beggs had written that the additional $45 million for spare parts was unnecessary, proposed an amendment cutting the $45 million added by the committee and adding $25 million to other programs cut by the committee.

Meyers unsuccessfully offered a similar amendment in committee.

But Walker, ranking minority member of the Space Science Subcommittee, proposed instead leaving intact the extra $45 million for shuttle spare parts and cutting $45 million from NASA's administrative budget. Walker's substitute to Meyers' amendment was adopted 288-127. The Meyers amendment, as amended, was adopted by voice vote. *(Vote 44, p. 16-H)*

Another major controversy erupted on the floor over how much to charge private companies and other countries that used the space shuttle to launch satellites.

The committee bill allowed the agency to charge between $45 million and $71.4 million, which committee staff said would recover the operating costs, plus allow for some recovery of depreciation costs for the shuttles.

Nelson and others said the price should be as low as possible to be competitive.

But Walker offered an amendment, which the House adopted 206-201, that would allow prices to range between $45 million and $105 million. *(Vote 45, p. 18-H)*

Senate Action

The Commerce, Science and Transportation Committee reported the bill June 24 (S Rept 99-91), and it was passed intact by the Senate June 27 by voice vote.

The bill provided a total of $7.65 billion for fiscal 1986, which Slade Gorton, R-Wash., chairman of the Subcommittee on Science, Technology and Space, argued constituted a "freeze," except for three "augmentations." The increases over fiscal 1985 totaled $142 million: $52 million for the Centaur upper stage program; $48 million for problems related to a tracking and data relay satellite system; and $42 million to restore the 5 percent pay cut assumed in the administration's request.

As passed by the Senate, the bill authorized:

- $200 million for NASA's permanently manned space station.
- $10 million for the orbital maneuvering vehicle, NASA's only new start for the fiscal year.
- $1.025 million for space science programs.
- $508 million for space applications.
- $16.5 million for the Commercial Use of Space Program.
- $350 million for aeronautical research and technology.
- $3.39 million for space shuttle production, operations and tracking capability.

Flexitime Extended

With the threat of controversial amendments blocking bills to make permanent the option of flexible work schedules for federal employees, Congress three times temporarily extended the "flexitime" program before voting late in the session to make the authorization permanent.

Flexitime allowed workers to stagger their hours or to work 10-hour days, as long as they put in a 40-hour week. First enacted in 1978 (PL 95-390), flexitime was temporarily extended in 1982 and was to expire July 23, 1985. *(1978 Almanac p. 790; 1982 Almanac p. 516)*

The House May 20 had passed legislation (HR 1534 — H Rept 99-82) to extend the program permanently. It was reported July 11 (no written report) by the Senate Governmental Affairs Committee.

But when Sen. Ted Stevens, R-Alaska, chairman of the Subcommittee on Civil Service, tried to bring that measure to the floor, Orrin G. Hatch, R-Utah, chairman of the Labor and Human Resources Committee, proposed attaching controversial amendments authorizing flexitime for federal contractors and reducing the minimum wage for teenagers in summer jobs. Both were hotly contested issues and held up action on HR 1534.

Faced with a shutdown of the program on July 23, Congress July 18 cleared a bill (S 1455) extending it through Sept. 30.

The measure, which bypassed committees in both chambers, was approved by voice vote by the Senate July 17 and cleared by the House by voice vote the next day. It was signed into law (PL 99-69) July 22.

A second extension (HR 3414) carrying the program through Oct. 31 was passed by the House Sept. 26, cleared by the Senate later in the day and signed into law Sept. 30 (PL 99-109).

The third bill (HR 3605) authorizing the program through Dec. 31 was passed by the House Oct. 24, cleared by the Senate the next day and signed into law Oct. 31 (PL 99-140).

Finally, on Dec. 11 the Senate cleared the original bill (HR 1534 — PL 99-196). It was signed Dec. 23.

Travel Expenses

The House Dec. 19 by voice vote passed a bill (S 1840 — PL 99-234) lifting the cap on per diem rates of reimbursement for federal employees' travel expenses, clearing the measure for the president. The Senate passed the bill earlier that day.

Currently, federal workers and contractors traveling for the government could receive up to $75 per day in high-cost areas, and $50 a day in other areas. That rate, which was set by Congress, had not been raised since 1980. Members of Congress said it was too low, forcing employees to pay expenses out of their own pockets.

S 1840 authorized the administrator of the General Services Administration (GSA) to prescribe a method for reimbursement. GSA could provide employees with a per diem allowance, or could pay actual expenses, or both. The allowance would be based on a survey of travel costs.

VA Mortgage Overhaul

Alarmed by a high foreclosure rate in the Veterans Administration (VA) home loan guarantee program that had cost taxpayers more than $500 million in the past two years, the Senate Dec. 2 approved a bill (S 1887) overhauling the program.

The bill, passed by voice vote, would require the VA to tighten credit standards. It also would improve appraisals and increase the amount of a loan the VA could guarantee in order to draw more private lenders into the program.

There was no further action before adjournment because the House objected to accepting the loan guarantee revisions without hearings of its own, according to Frank H. Murkowski, R-Alaska, chairman of the Senate Veterans' Affairs Committee.

The committee reported the bill (S Rept 99-200) Nov. 26.

Loan Guarantees

The bill essentially was the same as approved by the Veterans' Affairs panel Oct. 31.

It was pushed through by Murkowski in response to what he considered to be shortcomings in the VA's home loan guarantee program.

The VA insured 60 percent of a home mortgage made by a private lender to a veteran, up to $27,500. Because of the guarantee, the interest rate was lower than the market rate and most veterans were not required to make a down payment.

However, the program had been plagued by a ballooning foreclosure rate that was running at about 2,500 a month, more than twice as many as in 1979 when the housing market was at a high point.

The foreclosure rate was expensive because it cost the

VA about $15,000 for every home foreclosure, both in payments to private lenders and the costs of maintaining homes it held. To shore up the loan guarantee fund, Congress approved a transfer of $1.3 billion from 1978 through 1984 from a direct VA loan fund to the guarantee fund. In addition, Congress appropriated $566 million in fiscal 1984 and 1985 to keep the guarantee fund solvent.

The Reagan administration proposed raising the fee that borrowers were charged from 1 percent of the loan to 5 percent. Congress, however, rejected that plan, arguing that it would discourage the making of VA loans and hurt veterans who needed them.

Summary of Housing Provisions

Under the bill, the VA would be required to issue regulations on credit underwriting standards to ensure that only credit-worthy veterans received mortgages insured by a VA guarantee.

In response to complaints that some VA appraisals were too high, the bill would authorize lenders to use their own appraisers in place of VA personnel to better ensure that loans would be based on the market value of the house.

The bill also would raise the cap for the VA guarantee from $27,500 to $33,500, offering a greater incentive for private lenders to issue VA loans.

To improve the management of loans in arrears, the bill would require lenders to notify the VA when a loan was two months overdue so the VA would be aware of the problem, and to institute foreclosure after four payments were missed.

In addition, S 1788 would establish a pilot program of contracting with private lenders to manage and dispose of foreclosed homes the VA held.

Miscellaneous Provisions

As passed by the Senate, S 1887 also:

- Authorized $55 million in fiscal 1986 for a job training program for Vietnam and Korean War veterans, and extended it for one year.
- Provided space in national cemeteries for upright grave markers.
- Expanded the definition of "Vietnam era" to include veterans who served in Vietnam between Feb. 21, 1961, and Aug. 5, 1964, for purposes of receiving VA benefits.
- Required a study of the health status of female Vietnam veterans.
- Required a plan for locating seven regional offices in VA medical centers.
- Authorized a 3.1 percent cost-of-living allowance effective Dec. 1, 1985, for veterans' disability compensation and survivor benefits. *(Story, this page)* ∎

New War Memorials

The House unanimously voted Nov. 6 to authorize three memorials to be built in the nation's capital honoring war veterans whose contributions sponsors said had been forgotten.

A bill (HR 2205 — H Rept 99-341) to authorize a memorial to Korean War veterans was passed 406-0. Also approved were H J Res 36 (H Rept 99-342), by 405-0, to authorize a memorial to women who served in the armed forces and H J Res 142 (H Rept 99-340), 408-0, for a memorial to black Revolutionary War veterans. The measures were reported Oct. 29 by the House Administration Committee. *(Votes 356, 355, 357, p. 110-H)*

Each measure required private financing for the memorials and mandated that designs be approved by the Commission of Fine Arts and the National Capital Planning Commission.

While the fund-raising and construction of memorials honoring women and black veterans would be overseen by private foundations, HR 2205 assigned those responsibilities for the Korean War veterans' memorial to the American Battle Monuments Commission, a federal agency.

Members said that placing authority with the monument commission could reduce administrative costs and would provide federal oversight of what was expected to be the largest memorial of the three.

Inspiration for the Korean War memorial seemed to come from the Vietnam Veterans' Memorial dedicated in 1982. It had become one of Washington's most-visited attractions and was credited with creating an outpouring of national sympathy for the contributions and problems of veterans who served in that war.

But some members saw a potential problem in the method used to raise funds and build the Vietnam project, for which private foundations raised $10 million. They preferred using public funds for the Korean War memorial. ∎

Veterans' COLA Clears

The House Dec. 19 by voice vote cleared for the president a bill (HR 1538 — PL 99-238) authorizing a 3.1 percent fiscal 1986 cost-of-living allowance (COLA) for veterans receiving disability compensation and families receiving survivors' benefits.

The Senate had passed the bill earlier that day, adding an amendment authorizing a job training program for Vietnam-era and Korean War veterans for an additional year.

House members had wanted to give disabled veterans a higher COLA because in fiscal 1985 they received an amount that was less than Social Security recipients got. Members included a 3.7 percent veterans' COLA increase in their budget reconciliation bill (HR 3128) that was passed Oct. 24. *(Reconciliation, p. 498)*

After it had been established that Social Security recipients would receive a 3.1 percent COLA and when it appeared that reconciliation legislation might be stalled in conference over other issues, the House passed HR 1538 establishing a 3.4 percent adjustment. That figure, members said, would make up for the previous shortfall. The bill, reported (H Rept 99-337) Oct. 29 by the Veterans' Affairs Committee, was passed Dec. 9.

The Senate, however, insisted on the lower figure, which it had included in a bill it had passed earlier (S 1887), and the House went along.

The job-training amendment represented a compromise between the Senate-passed S 1887 and a bill (HR 1408 — H Rept 99-108) passed May 20 by the House. The compromise authorized funding of $65 million for fiscal 1986, to be available through fiscal 1988. The program, the Emergency Veterans' Job Training Act (PL 98-77), provided cash incentives to employers to hire and train certain long-term Vietnam-era and Korean-conflict veterans. It had expired Feb. 28. *(1983 Almanac p. 599)* ∎

Veterans' Court Review

The Senate for the fourth time passed a bill allowing veterans to appeal to federal courts decisions by the Veterans Administration (VA) denying claims for benefits.

The measure (S 367 — S Rept 99-100) was approved by voice vote July 30, but there was no further action before adjournment. Similar bills passed in 1979, 1982 and 1983 were blocked in the House Veterans' Affairs Committee because its chairman, G. V. "Sonny" Montgomery, D-Miss., opposed judicial review. *(1979 Almanac p. 391)*

The Senate bill would eliminate the existing limit of $10 on fees for attorneys representing veterans before the VA and allow the VA to set "reasonable fees" of up to $500.

Sen. Frank H. Murkowski, R-Alaska, chairman of the Veterans' Affairs Committee, said passage was especially important because of two court decisions. On March 22 the U.S. Circuit Court of Appeals for the District of Columbia held that current law barred judicial review of VA regulations implementing benefits. Also, on June 28, the U.S. Supreme Court upheld the limit on attorneys' fees.

Sen. Gary Hart, D-Colo., author of the legislation, said the VA was one of the few federal agencies whose benefit decisions were not subject to court review. The VA opposed the bill, contending that the Board of Veterans Appeals adequately reviewed VA decisions. ∎

Military Crash Benefits

Congress cleared a bill (HR 3974 — PL 99-227) Dec. 19 giving a three-month military housing allowance to survivors of the 248 members of the 101st Airborne Division killed in a plane crash in Gander, Newfoundland, a week before.

Under existing law, survivors of armed services members who died on duty received a gratuity of $3,000 to help defray expenses. But their military housing allowances stopped, and they were required to pay rent.

The bill allowed survivors to stay in military housing and receive housing allowances for three months after a member of the armed services died. The measure was retroactive to Dec. 11, to include the families of those who died in the crash. The bill also made those families eligible for an increase in the maximum amount of insurance in the Serviceman's Group Life Insurance program.

The House passed the bill by voice vote Dec. 18, immediately after adopting, by a 401-0 vote, a resolution (H Res 345) expressing sympathy for the families. The Senate passed the bill later that day, adding an amendment extending the allowance from two months to three. The House accepted the Senate amendment the next day. *(Vote 430, p. 136-H)* ∎

Landsat Commercialization

A measure authorizing $295 million to enable a private company to develop and deploy satellites to take pictures of the Earth was signed into law (HR 2800 — PL 99-62) July 11.

The Senate cleared the measure for the president June 27. The House had passed it by voice vote June 24.

Congress in 1984 (PL 98-365) authorized sale of existing Landsat satellites and receiving stations to a private firm, and authorized $75 million for development of a successor satellite. Landsat data were used by the government and were available to the public for mineral exploration, cartography and agriculture.

Late in 1984, the Commerce Department accepted a bid from Earth Observation Satellite Inc. (Eosat), a joint venture between RCA Corp. and the Hughes Aircraft Corp., to buy the operation. The government agreed to pay for two new satellites, a receiving station, and launching the satellites on the space shuttle.

HR 2800 enabled the federal government to meet the terms of the agreement. It specified that only $125 million be available through fiscal 1986. *(1984 Almanac p. 195)*

The bill had been reported June 20 (H Rept 99-177) by the House Science and Technology Committee. A companion measure (S 1279 — S Rept 99-86) was reported June 14 by the Senate Commerce, Science and Technology Committee. The Senate June 26 amended the text of S 1279 to HR 2800; the next day, it vacated that action and accepted the House-passed version. ∎

Whistleblower Awards

The House Feb. 26 voted to extend through September 1988 authority for the president and agency inspectors general to give cash awards to employees who disclosed waste, fraud and abuse in federal programs.

The bill (HR 607) passed on a vote of 413-1, but there was no action in the Senate. *(Vote 14, p. 6-H)*

HR 607 was virtually identical to a bill that passed both the House and Senate in 1984. That bill (HR 5646) died when the House refused to accept an amendment added on the Senate floor that would have given federal courts jurisdiction over complaints that whistleblowers had been harassed on the job for reporting waste or fraud. That provision was not included in HR 607. *(1984 Almanac p. 185)*

Authority for the awards, created by the Omnibus Budget Reconciliation Act of 1981 (PL 97-35) as a trial program, expired Sept. 30, 1984. During the three years the program was in place, inspectors general granted only a few awards — worth about $8,800 for cost-savings estimated at more than $1 million. The president gave no awards. *(Reconciliation Act, 1981 Almanac p. 396)*

As passed by the House, HR 607 would:

- Authorize agency inspectors general to award $10,000 or 1 percent of the cost-saving to an employee who disclosed waste or fraud.
- Authorize the president to make up to 50 awards of $20,000 a year.
- Authorize the Defense Department's inspector general to reward whistleblowers who were members of the armed services.
- Require the General Accounting Office to review the program by March 16, 1988.

Rep. Patricia Schroeder, D-Colo., called the Pentagon whistleblower provision "killer ammunition against the horrendous cost overruns and price gougings that have plagued the military." Schroeder was chairman of the Post Office and Civil Service Subcommittee on Civil Service.

HR 607 bypassed committee, and Schroeder said that the report on the 1984 bill (H Rept 98-1053) should be considered as the legislative history for the new bill. ∎

Members Extend New Pension Plan Deadline

Because of the crush of end-of-session business, House and Senate conferees were unable to meet to reconcile differences on a new pension system for federal employees hired after Jan. 1, 1984.

However, members included in the fiscal 1986 continuing resolution (H J Res 465 — PL 99-190) a provision extending the deadline for enactment of a plan from Dec. 31, 1985, to April 30, 1986.

If the Dec. 31 deadline had lapsed, federal workers hired since Jan. 1, 1984, would have been forced to pay 7 percent of their salaries toward the existing retirement system, on top of the 5.7 percent they paid into Social Security. A 1983 law aimed at shoring up the Social Security system included federal employees hired after that date in the system. Workers hired before that date paid no Social Security taxes but contributed 7 percent of their pay to their retirement plan. The newer workers were covered under a temporary system and were not required to contribute to the retirement plan that covered more senior employees. *(1983 Almanac p. 573)*

The Senate passed a bill establishing a new retirement system, and the House Post Office and Civil Service Committee, after approving its version, agreed to bypass floor action and go directly to conference.

Both bills would give the newer workers benefits from three sources: Social Security, a basic pension in which benefits would be based on salary and years of service, and a new thrift plan patterned after so-called 401(k) tax-deferred savings accounts that enabled workers to set aside before taxation a portion of their wages toward retirement, with an employer contribution.

The bills differed mainly on cost. The Senate bill would reduce the government's expense from 25 percent of payroll to 21.9 percent, while the House version would raise it to 25.4 percent. The Reagan administration wanted to lower costs to 20 percent of payroll.

In addition, the Senate bill would give workers a choice of two pension plans, while the House measure offered only one.

Background

After Social Security and Medicare, the civil service retirement system was the largest entitlement program in the federal government, costing taxpayers about $20 billion a year.

That total was about half of all federal pensions. The government also had retirement systems for the military, costing about $14 billion a year; foreign service workers, $200 million; and railroad employees, $5 billion.

The federal retirement system, established in 1920, was one of the chief benefits offered to workers, including employees of the Postal Service and the legislative branch. In 1985, 2.7 million workers contributed, through payroll deductions, 7 percent of their salaries into the civil service retirement fund. Taxpayers matched that amount through federal agencies' budgets.

In addition, the Treasury was expected to pay an additional $4.37 billion into the fund as its fiscal 1985 contribution from general revenues to cover unfunded future liabilities caused by an anticipated gap between contributions received and benefits owed.

Benefits for the 1.9 million annuitants averaged about $14,000 a year, according to the Office of Personnel Management (OPM). Most workers were entitled to full pensions if they retired at age 55 with 30 years' service; at age 60 with 20 years' service; and age 62 with five years' service. Certain employees, including air traffic controllers and members of Congress, could retire earlier with more liberal benefits.

Annuities — annual benefit payments — were based on the highest three consecutive years of earnings, and were adjusted annually for inflation. Benefits were fully taxable.

Critics called the system overly generous compared with private plans and recommended cutting federal benefits. But employee union officials and their supporters in Congress argued that private employees actually received greater retirement benefits than federal workers.

In part, the dispute over the relative value of pension systems involved different ways of measuring benefits.

Rep. William E. Dannemeyer of California, ranking Republican on the House Post Office Compensation and Employee Benefits Subcommittee, acknowledged that private pensions were more generous than civil service benefits, if annuities at the time of retirement were compared.

But, he said, the proper basis of comparison should be the so-called "normal cost": the percentage of payroll that would have to be set aside from every paycheck over a career to pay for lifetime pension benefits.

According to a study released Jan. 16 by the Congressional Research Service, the normal cost of the civil service retirement system was 24.7 percent of payroll, while private-sector plans ranged between 14.8 percent of payroll and 19 percent of payroll.

The civil service system cost more, the report explained, because it allowed workers to retire with full benefits earlier than most private plans and because benefits were indexed for inflation.

However, the report also noted that private employers enjoyed a tax subsidy because earnings on pension trust funds were tax-exempt and contributions to the funds were deductible in the year in which they were made. Those tax advantages, the report explained, significantly reduced the costs of private plans.

The sharpest attack on the federal system came from the President's Private Sector Survey on Cost Control, better known as the Grace commission after its chairman, industrialist J. Peter Grace.

The commission said that if Congress had set up military and civil service retirement plans equal to a typical plan in a *Fortune* 500 company, over the last 10 years it "would have cost taxpayers $103 billion less than it actually did. Over the next 10 years taxpayers would have saved $314 billion."

To lower costs, the Grace commission recommended raising the retirement age and scaling back cost-of-living adjustments (COLAs).

Union Reaction

Unions fought pension reductions, arguing that cuts would break faith with employees, who worked in expectation of receiving certain benefits at a certain time.

L. J. Andolsek, president of the National Association of Retired Federal Employees, accused the administration of treating the retirement system as a welfare system. On the contrary, Andolsek said, "We're not asking for anything that doesn't belong to us."

Other supporters of employees attacked the criticism. A pamphlet entitled "Ten Myths About Civil Service Retirement," published by the Federal Government Service Task Force, a congressional group chaired by Rep. Michael D. Barnes, D-Md., outlined objections to the critics.

The task force noted, for example, that most private-sector employees received greater retirement benefits than federal workers. Beyond pensions, most private employees were covered under Social Security and qualified for other benefits, such as the 401(k) tax-exempt savings plans, the report noted. And, most private-sector plans were fully paid by employers, while federal workers paid 7 percent of their salaries toward retirement.

Moreover, while federal retirees could retire at 55, most retired later, the task force noted. It said the average retirement age of federal retirees (60.7) was similar to the average retirement age of private-sector employees (61.8).

These findings were corroborated by a July 1984 study by the General Accounting Office.

President's Proposal

The president's fiscal 1986 budget proposed major changes in the retirement system, many of which Congress had rejected in prior years. The proposals, based primarily on the recommendations of the Grace commission, would:

- Withhold the COLA scheduled for January 1986 and limit future COLAs.
- Limit COLAs to 55 percent of the scheduled amount for annuities that exceeded $10,000. The $10,000 base would be adjusted for inflation each year.
- Raise the retirement age for full benefits to 65. Employees with 30 years of service could still retire at 55, but their annuities would be cut by 5 percent for each year of early retirement. That provision would be phased in over 10 years.
- Change the base on which benefits were computed from the average of the highest three years of salary to the average of the highest five years.
- Phase out the retirement credit for unused sick leave.

In addition, the budget proposed that the Postal Service and the District of Columbia contribute an amount equal to their employees' contributions to the system.

Senate Action

Legislation (S 1527) to set up the new retirement system was introduced July 30 by Sens. William V. Roth Jr., R-Del., chairman of the Governmental Affairs Committee, and Ted Stevens, R-Alaska, chairman of the Governmental Affairs Civil Service Subcommittee.

They contended that their legislation would cost the federal government 17 percent less than the current system, largely by raising the retirement age and reducing COLAs.

Under the bill, the government would contribute fully to the basic pension plan. But benefits would be based on 1 percent of the average of a worker's highest five years of salary, compared with the highest three years under the current system.

In addition, workers could receive full benefits only after age 62, instead of at age 55 after 30 years' service.

The bill would reduce the annual COLA by 2 percentage points, instead of allowing a COLA based on the full Consumer Price Index (CPI).

Committee Action

Members of the Governmental Affairs Committee changed the bill substantially before approving it Oct. 2 by a 13-0 vote. The report (S Rept 99-166) was filed Oct. 30.

Under the revised proposal, new workers would continue to be covered by Social Security but would choose between two supplemental retirement plans. Both options would offer benefits from three sources: Social Security; a basic pension, in which benefits would be based on salary and length of service; and the voluntary thrift plan.

Workers could choose a pension plan that would be fully funded by the government. However, the age at which they could retire at full benefits would be raised from 55 to 62, and COLAs for those who retired before age 67 would be reduced. That option would allow a 10 percent employee contribution to the thrift plan, matched by up to 5 percent in government contributions.

Or, workers could choose a plan that allowed retirement with full benefits at age 55 and full COLAs after age 62. However, those employees would contribute a small portion of their salary to the pension plan and could contribute up to 6 percent of their salary to the thrift plan.

The original plan had come under fire from employee unions, which argued that it granted the most substantial benefits to a minority of workers who could afford to set aside a large portion of their wages for the thrift plan. Most workers would depend on benefits from the pension plan, and would suffer from the higher retirement age and reduced COLAs, the unions argued.

Roth and Stevens changed their bill to give workers a choice. But committee Democrats argued that the revised plan, which would have cost 20.8 percent of payroll and limited COLAs, still came up short of their ideal.

As Thomas F. Eagleton, D-Mo., ranking minority member of the committee, explained, both sides agreed to make changes before the Oct. 2 markup in order to develop a package both sides could support.

"You on the Republican side of the aisle," Eagleton said, "have swallowed hard to agree to both an overall cost of 21.9 percent of payroll and a full COLA after age 67 [in the first option], while we on the Democratic side have made a major concession by agreeing to break with our party's philosophy that a full COLA is inviolate at all times for all persons."

Despite the widespread agreement on the basic design of the compromise, committee members differed over a provision that would allow workers to choose whether to invest their thrift plan in government securities, private stocks, or a mixture.

Lawton Chiles, D-Fla., proposed an amendment requiring that the government contribution be invested in government securities, which might yield less than private stocks but would carry less risk of loss.

But Roth argued that restricting investments limited workers' freedom of choice. Further, Roth added, the bill was designed to make the federal retirement system comparable to private-sector plans, which allowed workers to choose where to invest.

Chiles' amendment was rejected, 5-8. The administration, however, said the proposal still cost too much and it objected to offering some retirees full COLAs.

The Senate tried to expedite enactment of the plan and force a quick conference with the House by attaching the text of S 1527 to a House-passed bill (HR 2672) renaming a road to a New Jersey mail center after a deceased postal worker.

Before passing HR 2672 by a vote of 96-1 Nov. 7, the Senate adopted amendments adding workers at the Central Intelligence Agency and Foreign Service to the new retirement system. *(Vote 289, p. 51-S)*

House Action

The House Post Office and Civil Service Committee, after approving its version of a new retirement plan Nov. 14, decided to bypass floor action and go directly to conference with the Senate.

Under the committee bill, approved by voice vote, workers could retire at age 55 after 30 years' service and get annual COLAs equal to the increase in the CPI.

Although critics said those provisions would drive the cost of the retirement system up, William D. Ford, D-Mich., chairman of the Post Office Committee, said they would ensure that new workers received the same benefits as older workers. The bill (HR 3660) had been introduced by Ford and Mary Rose Oakar, D-Ohio, chairman of the Subcommittee on Compensation and Employee Benefits.

Both the committee and Senate bills would provide benefits from Social Security, a basic pension and a thrift plan. However, the Senate bill would offer workers a choice of two retirement systems and would reduce the government's cost, mostly by raising the retirement age and reducing COLAs for some workers.

Besides maintaining the early retirement age and full COLAs, the committee bill would preserve the feature that based benefits on the average of the highest three years of salary. The Senate bill would base benefits on the highest five years of salary. The Senate bill would include members of Congress, the Foreign Service and the CIA; the House bill excluded those workers.

In addition, the Senate version would allow workers covered by the existing retirement system to join the new plan. Ford said that his bill prohibited older workers from joining the new system to avoid having the bill referred to the Ways and Means Committee, which had jurisdiction over Social Security. ■

Congress Staves Off Reagan Plan to Ax SBA

Congress staved off the Reagan administration's efforts to kill the Small Business Administration (SBA) and took steps in the first session to protect the agency, though with a sharply trimmed budget.

Reagan originally had proposed abolishing SBA and transferring some functions to the Commerce Department, but his plan met strong opposition in both chambers. As part of negotiations on the Senate-passed budget resolution (S Con Res 32), however, Reagan agreed to preserve the agency with reduced spending. *(Story, p. 441)*

The budget reconciliation bill (HR 3128) that stalled before adjournment would have reauthorized the SBA for three years, while cutting projected spending by $2.5 billion. Primarily, the savings would have come from eliminating most direct loans to businesses and prohibiting farmers from receiving SBA disaster loans.

The conference report (H Rept 99-453) recommended funding authorizations of $515 million in fiscal 1986, $605 million in 1987 and $634 million in 1988. *(Reconciliation, p. 498)*

The Senate July 16 had voted 94-3 to pass a reauthorization for the agency (S 408 — S Rept 99-20), and included those provisions in its reconciliation measure. The House added to its budget package the version (HR 2540 — H Rept 99-222, Part I) of a reauthorization reported by the Small Business Committee July 23. *(Vote 155, p. 31-S)*

Administration Proposal

Budget director David A. Stockman Feb. 28 explained the administration proposal to the Senate Small Business Committee chaired by Lowell P. Weicker Jr., R-Conn.

When Stockman made his case for abolishing the agency, Weicker told him: "You'll lose."

The administration plan would transfer some SBA functions, such as minority set-asides and advocacy, which helped small businesses obtain government contracts, to the Commerce Department.

Stockman argued that although the SBA helped some businesses, particularly in retail and service sectors, many others in the same industries had thrived without federal aid. And, he added, the SBA had done little to aid so-called "sunrise" industries in high-technology fields.

Further, he said it was unfair for companies that made it without SBA assistance to compete with companies benefiting from federal subsidies.

"SBA," Stockman concluded, "conducts a $3 [billion] to $4 billion annual lending program which indiscriminately sprays a faint mist of subsidized credit into the weakest and most prosaic nooks and crannies of the nation's $4 trillion economy. In the process, it serves almost no rigorously defined public policy purpose."

Weicker responded first by showing the committee and Stockman a videotape of Reagan, in which the president told SBA Administrator James C. Sanders, "Keep up the good work."

Weicker said Stockman's information was "either wrong or incomplete or misleading."

Dale Bumpers, D-Ark., ranking minority member of the committee, said several companies, including Federal Express Corp. and Apple Computer Inc., benefited from SBA assistance and had since paid the government millions of dollars in taxes.

Senate Action

The committee voted 16-3 March 26 to report a bill (S 408 — S Rept 99-20) that reauthorized SBA programs for three years, while making cuts totaling $851 million in outlays and $1.1 billion in budget authority. The panel turned back an amendment that would have further reduced spending.

Although the committee's action would cut the agency's budget, it was nevertheless an outright rejection of the administration's proposal to abolish the SBA, as well as the Senate Budget Committee's plan to make deep cuts in the SBA budget.

The Budget Committee had recommended that several SBA programs be eliminated and that its loan portfolio be sold to private investors at 25 cents on the dollar. In the budget resolution, the Budget panel proposed cutting the

SBA's budget authority by $4.7 billion over three years.

As ordered reported, the SBA bill would authorize $690 million for fiscal 1986 but would reduce direct lending from $257 million to $86 million, and reduce the amount of a loan that could be guaranteed by the SBA from 90 percent to 80 percent. S 408 would increase the fee charged to borrowers of SBA-guaranteed loans from 1 percent to 2 percent.

Disaster loans no longer would be available for so-called "non-physical" misfortunes. The existing program gave aid to firms harmed by the devaluation of the Mexican peso. Disaster loans would still be available for physical calamities such as floods and hurricanes.

The bill would freeze spending for salaries and expenses and for guaranteed business loans at their respective fiscal 1985 levels of $234 million and $3.4 billion.

But Rudy Boschwitz, R-Minn., a member of both the Small Business and Budget committees, said S 408 did not go far enough to achieve savings. He offered an amendment, which was defeated 4-15, to save an additional $1.4 billion in outlays over three years, mostly by converting direct loan programs to loan guarantees. Loan guarantees cost the federal government less in outlays than direct loans because the government only paid when a borrower defaulted, whereas each direct loan required an outlay of federal funds.

Boschwitz, Slade Gorton, R-Wash., and Paul S. Trible Jr., R-Va., voted against S 408.

Senate Floor

Majority Leader Robert Dole, R-Kan., called the Senate's overwhelming vote July 16 passing S 408 the first test of budget restraint. As approved by 94-3, the bill cut more deeply into SBA programs than the version reported March 28 by the committee. *(Vote 155, p. 31-S)*

The committee bill would have trimmed $851 million from what would have been spent over the three fiscal years if the current rate of spending were maintained. To push the savings to $2.5 billion, Weicker offered an amendment making additional cuts.

One change would require Small Business Investment Companies (SBIC) to raise funds in private capital markets, rather than the federal Treasury. SBICs raised venture capital for new small businesses by selling debentures, which were backed by an SBA guarantee. This change was expected to save $529 million.

But the major change, expected to save $817 million, would bar farmers from the SBA disaster loan program, a change critics had sought for years. In 1984, Congress passed a bill (PL 98-369) requiring farmers to seek disaster loans first from the Farmers Home Administration (FmHA) in the Department of Agriculture, before qualifying for SBA aid. *(1984 Almanac p. 148)*

Weicker said that farmers should seek aid from FmHA, which he said was better able to tend to their needs.

But Bumpers, ranking minority member of the Small Business Committee, said that under S Con Res 32, the FmHA disaster loan program would be sharply curtailed. He offered an amendment that would allow farmers to continue to receive SBA disaster loans. However, Bumpers would cap the disaster loan program at $500 million over three years.

Weicker argued against the amendment, noting that the provision barring farmers from SBA aid represented about a third of the proposed savings called for in the budget resolution. Bumpers' change would require deep program cuts to make up the difference, he said.

The Senate rejected the Bumpers amendment, 45-52. *(Vote 153, p. 31-S)*

Senators also rejected an amendment by Daniel Patrick Moynihan, D-N.Y., that would have set up a pilot project of selling loans owned by FmHA to the private sector. It would require FmHA to sell to private banks $10 billion worth of loans in each of fiscal 1986-88, at 80 percent of face value. The government thus could receive an additional $24 billion, which could be invested with interest. As a result, Moynihan said, his proposal could provide the government with $30 billion.

It was rejected, 24-73. *(Vote 154, p. 31-S)*

House Committee Action

The House Small Business Committee July 10 ordered reported a bill (HR 2540) that would cut SBA spending on direct loans to businesses to 15 percent below the fiscal 1985 level of $206 million and would freeze salaries and expenses at the fiscal 1985 level of $205 million.

HR 2540 would reduce the authorized level of guaranteed loans by 10 percent. And the bill would eliminate a loan program for so-called "non-physical disasters" that in the past had compensated businesses that suffered losses as a result of the devaluation of the Mexican peso.

The bill also would cap individual direct loans at $150,000, and would require businesses receiving direct loans to borrow from other sources as well. Current law capped direct loans at $350,000 each.

Chairman Parren J. Mitchell, D-Md., said that HR 2540 would make significant reductions in SBA spending.

HR 2540 was substantially similar to Weicker's bill. As introduced by Mitchell, HR 2540 would have reduced spending for direct loans and disaster loans, and would have frozen spending in most other programs.

But the committee, by a 20-19 vote, adopted an amendment by John Hiler, R-Ind., that would reduce the SBA's authority to guarantee repayment of privately financed loans by 10 percent, from $3.18 billion to $2.86 billion.

And, by a single 21-19 vote, the panel adopted two amendments by Joseph M. McDade, R-Pa., that would eliminate the non-physical disaster loan program, and require farmers to seek FmHA disaster loans, rather than through SBA. The panel agreed to recommend to the Agriculture Committee that FmHA interest rates be set to match SBA rates.

The panel also adopted, by voice vote, a Hiler amendment that would increase from 1 percent to 3 percent the fee charged to borrowers of SBA loans. The Senate bill would raise the fee to borrowers from 1 percent to 2 percent.

By an 18-22 vote, the panel rejected a Hiler amendment that would have lowered the ceiling on the amount of a privately financed loan guaranteed by SBA from 90 percent to 75 percent of the loan's principal. S 408 would reduce the amount of the loan guaranteed by SBA to 80 percent.

Silvio O. Conte, R-Mass., offered an amendment, adopted by voice vote, that would impose user fees on certain SBA services, such as publications, and require a $100 application fee from borrowers. ■

House Passes Pay Equity

The House Oct. 9 passed a bill (HR 3008 — H Rept 99-232) authorizing a study of the federal work force to determine if differences in pay arose because of discrimination on the basis of sex, race or national origin.

However, there was no action in the Senate other than hearings on a similar bill (S 519) by the Governmental Affairs Subcommittee on the Civil Service.

The House margin of passage, 259-162, was considerably smaller than in 1984, when a similar study measure was passed 413-6. The study provision was knocked out that year by the Senate in an agreement to hold off action until the General Accounting Office (GAO) laid the groundwork for the study. *(Vote 318, p. 100-H; 1984 Almanac p. 201)*

Sponsors attributed the smaller margin to an intense lobbying campaign by business groups and the Reagan administration, which strongly opposed the bill. The critics argued that the bill would require comparisons of the relative value of dissimilar jobs, a concept known as "comparable worth," which President Reagan had dismissed as "a harebrained idea."

Sharon Spigelmyer, director of human resources and equal opportunity for the National Association of Manufacturers, said the bill represented an intrusion by the federal government into the labor market. "The business community would not have been involved with this bill if it had been a simple evaluation of the federal government," she said.

But sponsors noted that the federal work force had not been studied since 1923, when women and minorities comprised 5 percent of the work force. They also said that women were clustered in the lower grades of the federal pay scales, while men dominated the upper grades.

"This isn't anything radical or crazy or weird or looney," said Mary Rose Oakar, D-Ohio, chairman of the Post Office and Civil Service Subcommittee on Compensation and Employee Benefits. "It is something any rational employer does for its employees."

House Action

HR 3008 was approved July 24 by the Post Office and Civil Service Committee by an 18-4 vote. Its report (H Rept 99-232) was filed July 29.

The House began debate on the measure Aug. 1, but action was held up until after the August recess, in part because critics had threatened to offer more than 100 amendments, a threat they ultimately did not carry out.

As passed by the House, HR 3008 followed the recommendation of the March 1 GAO report that a non-government agent conduct the study and that it examine both job content and economic factors, such as education and experience.

The bill would establish an 11-member commission, consisting of representatives from the administration, Congress, federal employee unions, and women's and civil rights organizations. The commission would oversee an 18-month study, performed by a consultant, of the federal pay and classification system, as well as hiring and promotion practices.

The study would look at job content, considering factors such as skill, effort and responsibility required, as well as economic factors such as education and seniority. The commission would report its findings to the president and Congress, including whether and to what extent the classification and wage systems were affected by sex, race or national origin. It also would make recommendations for legislative or administrative changes.

Critics of the bill said it would require a study of comparable worth, and argued that this concept would require the federal government to determine the value of a job, which should be established by the free market.

"Make no mistake about it, [this] leads us in the direction of socialism," said Dan Burton, R-Ind.

Burton proposed a substitute, which the House rejected by a 142-277 vote, that would have required a study to determine whether pay and classification systems complied with Title VII of the Civil Rights Act of 1964, which prohibited discrimination on the basis of race or sex. *(Vote 317, p. 100-H)*

On another point, Burton argued that enactment could lead to a lawsuit forcing the government to pay billions of dollars in back pay and pay raises. In 1983, a federal district judge in Washington ordered the state to pay about $1 billion in back pay and raises to 33,000 state workers because of sex discrimination. That ruling was overturned in September by a three-judge panel of the 9th U.S. Circuit Court of Appeals.

But Oakar and others countered that numerous states and cities had negotiated adjustments in their pay scales to eliminate sex-based discrimination without going to court. For example, the city of Los Angeles reached a $12 million settlement with the American Federation of State, County and Municipal Employees, calling for pay raises for female-dominated jobs such as librarian and secretary.

Also, the House earlier had adopted an amendment by Gerry Sikorski, D-Minn., clarifying that the study's conclusions would be advisory only.

"There is nothing, absolutely nothing in this bill that would give any sanction, any reason whatsoever for a lawsuit," said John T. Myers, R-Ind., ranking minority member of the Subcommittee on Compensation and Employee Benefits.

Amendments Defeated

Sponsors fought off other attempts by critics to amend the bill. Burton contended that the commission, because its members would be appointed from certain groups, would be predisposed toward finding bias. He offered an amendment to establish a 14-member commission, with seven members appointed by Democrats and seven by Republicans. It was rejected 150-272. *(Vote 315, p. 100-H)*

Dick Armey, R-Texas, proposed that the commission select three consultants, appointed by the president, GAO and federal employee unions, to perform separate studies. That was rejected by voice vote.

Joe L. Barton, R-Texas, objected to a provision that stated that the commission could not recommend that anyone's pay be lowered. He offered an amendment that would have struck that provision and required the commission to list the cost of each of its recommendations. It was was rejected, 148-276. *(Vote 316, p. 100-H)* ▮

Presidential Libraries

A bill (HR 1349) aimed at slowing the increasing cost to the federal government of operating libraries for former presidents was passed by the House and approved by a

Senate committee, but it was not enacted in 1985.

The measure was ordered reported Oct. 2 by the Senate Governmental Affairs Committee, but no report was filed before adjournment. The bill, reported May 15 by the House Government Operations Committee (H Rept 99-125), was passed June 4 by the House.

Both versions would require private foundations that build the libraries to establish an endowment, equal to 20 percent of construction costs, that would help defray the cost of maintaining the libraries of future presidents. Currently, groups built libraries with private funds and donated them to the federal government, which paid the operating costs. In fiscal 1985, the government paid about $15 million to run former presidents' libraries, and in fiscal 1986, the cost was expected to jump to $20.5 million.

The legislation also would designate the archivist of the United States as responsible for overseeing the library program and require the archivist to establish design standards for construction.

The committee bill would limit the size of future libraries to 70,000 square feet, unless the endowment would pay costs associated with larger space.

Both versions would affect libraries for presidents succeeding Ronald Reagan. Sen. Albert Gore Jr., D-Tenn., questioned why Reagan's library, which had not yet been planned, should be excluded. "To saddle the taxpayers with the maintenance of this president's library while all other future presidents' libraries will be maintained with private funds seems a little unfair," Gore said.

But Ted Stevens, R-Alaska, noted that Reagan would be the president who would have to sign the bill and said that he was excluded in order to ensure that it would be signed. "We've had other bills affecting incumbent presidents," he said. "You'd be surprised how slowly those bills move."

The House passed a similar bill (HR 5584) in 1984, but the Senate Governmental Affairs Committee reported out a more far-reaching bill (S 563 — S Rept 98-637). *(1984 Almanac p. 192)* ∎

Earthquake, Fire Programs

The House Sept. 17 by voice vote agreed to Senate amendments to two bills (S 817 — PL 99-105, S 818 — PL 99-97) authorizing federal earthquake hazard and fire control programs, clearing the measures for the president.

The Senate had originally passed the bills on April 17; the House, June 24. The Senate July 31 adopted minor amendments agreed to informally by House-Senate staffs.

S 817 authorized $69.4 million in fiscal 1986 and $72.5 million in 1987 for earthquake hazard reduction programs in the Federal Emergency Management Agency, the U.S. Geological Survey, the National Science Foundation and the National Bureau of Standards. The 1986 total was about $500,000 above the president's request, but less than fiscal 1985 spending.

The Senate Commerce, Science and Transportation Committee reported S 817 April 15 (S Rept 99-29). In the House, the Interior and Insular Affairs Committee reported its version May 14 and the Science and Technology Committee reported it May 21 (H Rept 99-90 Part I, II).

S 818 authorized $22 million in fiscal 1986 for the U.S. Fire Administration and the National Fire Academy, $2.7 million over the president's request.

It was reported April 15 (S Rept 99-30) by the Senate Commerce, Science and Transportation Committee and by the House Science and Technology Committee May 21 (H Rept 99-135). ∎

Limiting Smoking

Smoking in federal offices — including Capitol Hill and the courts — would be limited to designated areas under legislation approved Nov. 19 by the Senate Governmental Affairs Committee.

The bill (S 1937 — S Rept 99-220), approved by voice vote, would direct the General Services Administration (GSA) to consult with the surgeon general and develop regulations to specify smoking areas in U.S. buildings. Agency heads would be required to issue rules to implement the GSA regulations.

Guidelines for congressional offices would be established by the Senate Rules and Administration Committee and the House Committee on House Administration; the Administrative Office of the U.S. Courts would issue rules for the judiciary.

The bill was in response to medical evidence that nonsmokers suffered adverse health effects from exposure to tobacco smoke. Several federal employees filed suit against the government claiming disability resulting from exposure to smoke.

Some 36 states and the District of Columbia had enacted laws restricting smoking in public places.

The tobacco industry opposed the bill, contending that it would cost millions in lost productivity, redesigning buildings and posting signs. ∎

Pay Rules Modified

Toward the end of the first session of the 99th Congress, members reached a compromise with the Office of Personnel Management (OPM) over pay-for-performance rules for federal employees, and they dropped plans to block the regulations with legislation.

OPM had tried since 1983 to implement rules that would give more weight to performance than to seniority in determining raises and protecting workers from layoffs. The regulations, a top priority of OPM Director Donald J. Devine, were to replace the existing approach that relied chiefly on seniority in awarding raises and protecting workers from layoffs.

Reps. Steny H. Hoyer, D-Md., and Frank R. Wolf, R-Va., arguing that the proposed rules did not protect senior workers adequately, successfully sponsored amendments blocking them.

A congressional ban on putting the rules into effect expired in July, but Congress, in the Treasury/Postal Service appropriations bill (HR 3036), voted again to block the rules until May. *(Appropriations bill, p. 329)*

When President Reagan vetoed the bill, Wolf and Hoyer planned to add the ban to a stopgap funding bill for various government agencies.

They agreed to drop their efforts the week of Nov. 30 when OPM came up with a set of new rules that they said protected senior workers and gave employees a voice in the process of setting performance standards. ∎

Hostage Compensation

A bill authorizing benefits to government employees held hostage at home or abroad was approved by two House committees but did not reach the floor in 1985.

The measure (HR 2851 — H Rept 99-201, Parts I and II) was reported July 15 by the Post Office and Civil Service Committee and Nov. 18 by the Foreign Affairs Committee. The bill would authorize compensation and medical and educational benefits to civilian federal employees and their families.

The proposal gained impetus from the growing number of terrorist incidents abroad.

The House Post Office and Civil Service Committee acted on the bill while 40 American passengers of Trans World Airlines Flight 847 were held hostage in Beirut by Shiite Moslems.

And while the world awaited news of the estimated 400 persons taken hostage by Palestinians aboard a Mediterranean cruise ship, the House Foreign Affairs Subcommittee on International Operations by voice vote approved the bill Oct. 8. Several Americans were on board and one was killed before the crisis was over.

In addition to providing benefits to current federal employees and their families, the bill would authorize payment to the 52 Americans who were held hostage in Iran for 444 days from November 1979 to January 1981.

"Terrorism is here to stay," said International Operations Chairman Daniel A. Mica, D-Fla. "Of course, we all know that in light of today's events."

Added Olympia J. Snowe, R-Maine, the panel's ranking minority member, "The urgency of this bill is one of the tragedies of our time."

Mica, Snowe and Mary Rose Oakar, D-Ohio, chairman of the Post Office Subcommittee on Compensation and Employee Benefits, sponsored the bill.

Hostage Benefits

HR 2851 would authorize agency heads to place captive employees' salaries in interest-bearing accounts, and authorize the president to award additional payments based on the amount of time they were held in captivity.

Also, it would grant medical and educational benefits to the families of hostages, and would entitle family members to compensation for death or disability caused to the hostage by terrorist actions.

The measure would suspend civil lawsuits and judgments against any employee held captive.

HR 2851 was modeled after a 1980 law (PL 96-449) that authorized benefits for the 52 U.S. Embassy employees held in Iran from 1979 to 1981. That legislation authorized agencies to place salaries of the captives in interest-bearing accounts, and provided medical and educational benefits to their families. In addition, it exempted hostages' earnings from taxation while in captivity. *(1980 Almanac p. 351)*

By the agreement that paved the way for their release, those hostages were barred from suing the government of Iran for damages.

A presidential commission, appointed after the Iranian government released the hostages, recommended that the hostages receive $12.50 per day for the time they were held in Iran, but no legislation was introduced. The $12.50 figure was based on the amount Vietnam and other recent prisoners of war had received, adjusted for inflation.

Federal Pay Freeze

Faced by bipartisan opposition in Congress, President Reagan dropped his call for a 5 percent pay cut for federal employees and ordered instead that pay for civilian workers be frozen in fiscal 1986.

Reagan had included an across-the-board pay cut of 5 percent in his fiscal 1986 budget, the first time federal workers had been asked to take a pay cut since the Great Depression. Some 2.7 million civilian employees would have been affected. The plan would have reduced spending by $3.4 billion in fiscal 1986 and $15.6 billion over three years from the levels it would have been.

The initial congressional reaction was strong and negative.

"Reprehensible," said Rep. Mary Rose Oakar, D-Ohio, chairman of the Post Office and Civil Service Subcommittee on Compensation and Employee Benefits.

Sen. William V. Roth Jr., R-Del., chairman of the Governmental Affairs Committee, said the pay cut could drive away "our best managers and professionals."

Congress included a one-year freeze in the fiscal 1986 budget resolution (S Con Res 32) it adopted Aug. 1. Reagan, in responding to an annual report required by law on how large a pay raise would be necessary to bring federal workers up to levels comparable with private industry, Aug. 29 ordered a 15-month freeze through January 1987. If the president had not offered the freeze as an alternative, the 19.15 percent increase recommended by an advisory commission would have taken effect automatically.

In addition, both the House and Senate included a one-year freeze in their budget reconciliation bills, but Congress adjourned without taking final action on the conference report (HR 3128 — H Rept 99-453). *(Reconciliation, p. 498)*

As reported by the Post Office Committee, HR 2851 expressed the sense of Congress that $12.50 per day was unacceptable. However, the Foreign Affairs subcommittee adopted an amendment dropping that language. Snowe argued that it was inappropriate and eliminating it would ensure bipartisan support for the legislation.

In addition, the subcommittee deleted a Post Office provision granting the Iran hostages a one-time payment of $50,000 each.

Instead, the subcommittee proposed that all hostages — both the Iran captives and those taken prisoner in the future — receive a payment equal to the worldwide average per diem allowance for federal employees. The allowance, which was adjusted monthly to reflect changes in living costs, was currently $74 per day.

While the Iran hostages were in captivity, the worldwide average per diem was between $62 and $70; thus the Iran hostages each would receive $29,000.

John McCain, R-Ariz., argued against using that formula. "The relationship between a per diem and compensation for hostages is beyond me," he said.

McCain, making the same argument used by the presidential commission on Iran hostages, proposed instead that hostages should receive as compensation the same amount prisoners of war received. Adjusted for inflation, that amount would now be $20 per day, McCain said. McCain also wanted to adjust the level according to the Consumer Price Index.

In addition, McCain's amendment sought to eliminate a provision that would have allowed the president to determine that a hostage deserved a different amount based on the harshness of treatment received.

McCain, a prisoner of war in North Vietnam for almost six years, received $5 per day for the time he was in captivity. "And I was a little embarrassed to take that," he said.

Under McCain's amendment, the Iran hostages each would have received $8,880, an amount members said was too low. "For me," said Mica, "$8,000 for 444 days does not ring correct." McCain's amendment was defeated by voice vote.

Military Personnel

McCain also said that military personnel should be covered by the bill, arguing that they suffered at least as much as civilians when taken hostage. He noted that the only American killed when TWA Flight 847 was captured by Shiite Moslems in June was a Navy diver, Robert Stethem.

The full committee adopted an amendment by McCain to include military personnel. ∎

Museum Funds Denied

Although no one spoke in opposition, the House Nov. 19 rejected a bill (S 583) that would have authorized $11.5 million to expand the Cooper-Hewitt Museum, also known as the National Museum of Design of the Smithsonian Institution.

The rejection, by a 177-234 vote, surprised sponsors, especially since the Senate had passed the bill by voice vote without debate Nov. 12. Rep. Bill Green, R-N.Y., chief advocate of the measure, said he thought members did not want to spend the money at a time of high deficits. *(Vote 373, p. 118-H)*

The bill would have authorized money for a new building but prohibited federal funds from being spent until the museum raised an equivalent amount privately. Silvio O. Conte, R-Mass., a regent of the Smithsonian and a sponsor of similar legislation (HR 1609), said the museum already had raised $3 million.

The museum, located in New York City, was devoted to the study of historical and contemporary design. The Senate measure had been reported Nov. 4 by the Senate Rules and Administration Committee (S Rept 99-172). ∎

Office Closing Notice

The House by voice vote July 8 passed a bill (HR 2401) requiring agencies to notify Congress 120 days before closing any of the 22,000 federal field and regional offices around the country.

The bill was introduced in response to a Reagan administration proposal to reduce the number of federal field offices, outlined in a February report to Congress from the Office of Management and Budget (OMB). Rep. Patricia Schroeder, D-Colo., said that her Post Office and Civil Service Subcommittee on Civil Service tried to elicit details about the plan, but received little response from agencies.

Schroeder said HR 2401 would not bar agencies from closing or consolidating offices, but would require them to justify their decisions.

The Reagan administration strongly opposed the bill, arguing that the measure reduced its flexibility.

The House Post Office and Civil Service Committee had approved the bill June 26 and filed its report (H Rept 99-186) the next day.

Sen. William V. Roth Jr., R-Del., chairman of the Senate Governmental Affairs Committee, sponsored a bill (S 1206) that would declare a 270-day moratorium on any field office changes, and require OMB to report to Congress on the field office structure and plans to change it. There was no action in 1985. ∎

Ex-Presidents' Benefits

The Senate Governmental Affairs Committee Nov. 19 voted to curb some benefits for ex-presidents.

It approved a bill (S 1047) to cap staff allowances for former presidents at $300,000 a year, which would be reduced to $200,000 a year over a nine-year period. It also would prohibit the use of the funds for profit-making or partisan activity.

In fiscal 1984, Congress provided $1.2 million for offices and staff. There was no current ceiling on the allowance.

S 1047 would limit around-the-clock Secret Service protection for former presidents to the first five years out of office. After that, the secretary of the Treasury would have to certify to Congress that additional protection was warranted. Protection currently was provided for life.

The panel adopted an amendment by Thomas F. Eagleton, D-Mo., giving Secret Service protection to spouses and children of former presidents for two years. The bill would have provided security for spouses and children only if they were with the former president.

The committee also had approved a House-passed bill (HR 1349 — H Rept 99-125) limiting the cost of operating libraries of former presidents. *(Story, p. 414)* ∎

Veterans' Job Preference

The House July 22 passed by voice vote a bill (HR 1802 — H Rept 99-204) that would assure certain veterans they would not lose their federal jobs when the government contracted out their services to the private sector.

The Senate took no action on the bill. In 1984, it had declined to act on an identical House bill. *(1984 Almanac p. 503)*

Under a 1944 law (PL 78-359) that gave preference in federal employment to veterans, the jobs of guard, elevator operator, messenger and custodian were reserved for veterans, as long as qualified workers were available. Supporters of the bill, however, said that directives from the Office of Management and Budget circumvented the intent of that law and endangered the job preference for veterans.

The bill would prohibit contracting for those services if it would mean that a veteran in one of those positions would lose his job. Agencies could transfer veterans to another job in the veterans' commuting area and must first seek workers from a sheltered workshop for the blind and severely handicapped. The administration opposed the bill. ∎

Nominations: Major Changes in Reagan Team

The first year of President Reagan's second term saw a major upheaval in administration ranks, as new appointees took over seven Cabinet departments and other key executive branch positions.

Senate committees killed two of President Reagan's major 1985 nominations, apparently the first such actions involving a major post since 1981. One Cabinet appointee whose nomination stalled in committee in 1984 finally won confirmation in 1985. *(1984 appointments, 1984 Almanac p. 21-A)*

Reagan's recess appointments sparked a bitter two-month controversy early in the fall. Senate Democrats charged that the president was misusing his authority to make temporary appointments during congressional recesses to avoid the constitutional requirement of advice and consent by the Senate. In protest, they held up confirmation of thousands of military promotions and executive branch and judicial nominations. The "hold" was lifted Oct. 16, when the White House agreed to give the Senate advance notice of all future recess appointments.

Another logjam was averted when Democratic and Republican members of the Senate Judiciary Committee worked out procedures for handling judicial nominations in 1986. Democrats had complained that Republican members were trying to move too many judgeship nominations through the committee too fast. They said their staffs were not getting enough time to investigate nominees for the lifetime appointments. Dozens of judicial nominations were expected in the remaining three years of Reagan's term, most of them the result of a 1984 law (PL 98-353) that created 85 new judgeships. *(Reagan judicial appointments, p. 246)*

As in previous years, Sen. Jesse Helms, R-N.C., and a few of his colleagues used the Senate confirmation process to press their conservative views. Complaining that Secretary of State George P. Shultz was conducting a "purge" of conservatives in the State Department, Helms and his allies held up nominations for foreign policy posts until the administration gave assurances of job security for several favored diplomats. *(Box, p. 419)*

Another perennial controversy subsided in June with Senate confirmation of all 11 members of the board of the Legal Services Corporation (LSC). The corporation, which Reagan had tried repeatedly to abolish, had been run since 1981 by directors appointed by the president during congressional recesses. *(Legal Services Corporation, p. 244)*

In all, the president sent 3,719 civilian nominations to the Senate in 1985, and the Senate confirmed 3,603. Seven nominations were withdrawn by the White House.

Cabinet Changes

In a series of second-term shuffles early in the year, White House Chief of Staff James A. Baker III traded jobs with Treasury Secretary Donald T. Regan; Energy Secretary Donald P. Hodel replaced Interior Secretary William P. Clark, who resigned; and White House personnel director John S. Herrington replaced Hodel as energy secretary. William J. Bennett, chairman of the National Endowment for the Humanities, succeeded T. H. Bell at the Education Department.

Presidential adviser Edwin Meese III was confirmed as attorney general Feb. 23 after a 13-month wait. His nomination had run into trouble in 1984 when questions arose about some of his personal financial transactions.

In other Cabinet changes, William E. Brock III was confirmed April 26 as secretary of labor. He succeeded Raymond J. Donovan, who resigned March 15 to stand trial on charges of larceny and fraud. And on Dec. 12, the Senate confirmed Otis R. Bowen as secretary of health and human services (HHS). Bowen replaced Margaret M. Heckler, who agreed under administration pressure to become ambassador to Ireland.

Treasury. Baker was the first of the second-term Cabinet nominees to win confirmation. The Senate Jan. 29 unanimously approved his nomination as secretary of the Treasury. The vote was 95-0. *(Vote 1, p. 2-S)*

The 54-year-old Baker had spent most of his professional life as a corporate attorney in Houston. He had served as under secretary of commerce in the Ford administration and as campaign chairman for fellow Texan George Bush's unsuccessful race for the Republican presidential nomination in 1980.

Baker became President Reagan's chief of staff in 1981. During his four years in that post, he was a crucial player in backroom negotiations with Congress on politically sensitive tax and budget legislation. He provided a bridge between an ideological president and House and Senate Republicans trying to win a majority of votes in a diverse, two-party Congress.

The Baker-Regan job swap became official when Baker was sworn in as Treasury secretary. Regan did not require confirmation to his White House post. Before entering the Reagan Cabinet in 1981, Regan had headed Merrill Lynch & Co. Inc., one of the world's largest financial services firms.

Education. The Senate confirmed Bennett as secretary of education Feb. 6, 93-0. *(Vote 2, p. 3-S; story, p. 293)*

The Labor and Human Resources Committee had approved the nomination Feb. 1, but only after demanding and receiving a letter from President Reagan assuring members that he did not plan to renew his efforts to dismantle the Department of Education.

Prior to becoming chairman of the humanities endowment in 1982, Bennett, 41, was president of the National Humanities Center in North Carolina. He earlier taught philosophy and law at a number of universities.

Interior, Energy. Both Hodel and Herrington were confirmed Feb. 6 by votes of 93-1. William Proxmire, D-Wis., was the sole dissenter. *(Votes 3, 4, p. 3-S)*

All of the senators debating Hodel's nomination praised his qualifications for heading the Interior Department, where he had served as under secretary in 1981-82.

Herrington had served as assistant secretary of the Navy from 1981 to 1983, when he became assistant to the president for presidential personnel. *(Hodel, Herrington background, 1984 Almanac p. 345)*

Justice. The Senate Feb. 23 confirmed Meese as attorney general by a 63-31 vote. All of the negative votes were cast by Democrats, who raised questions about Meese's ethical conduct and his fitness for office. *(Vote 9, p. 4-S; story, p. 236)*

Meese was first nominated on Jan. 23, 1984, but questions about his financial dealings held up confirmation. The controversy centered on whether Meese helped get federal jobs for people who provided him with financial assistance. Although a special prosecutor requested by

Helms, Allies Delay Confirmation of Envoys

Backed by a handful of fellow conservatives, Sen. Jesse Helms, R-N.C., tried to bring pressure on the administration in 1985 by holding hostage President Reagan's nominations for various diplomatic posts.

The role was not a new one for Helms, a master of parliamentary obstruction. In previous years, he frequently had opposed nominees whose positions did not square with his own conservative views.

Burt and the Group of 29

Objections by Helms and eight other conservative senators held up action at midyear on 29 nominations for ambassadorships and other foreign policy positions. The nominees were confirmed after the administration gave assurances that it would find posts for four conservative officeholders favored by Helms and his allies. Helms had complained that Secretary of State George P. Shultz was conducting a "purge" of conservatives in the State Department.

The controversy ended July 16 with Senate confirmation of the last three nominations that had been held up by the Helms group: Edwin G. Corr, as ambassador to El Salvador, on a 89-8 vote; Rozanne L. Ridgway, as assistant secretary of state for European and Canadian affairs, on an 88-9 vote; and Richard R. Burt, as ambassador to West Germany, on an 88-10 vote. The conservatives had permitted the other 26 nominees to be confirmed by voice votes earlier in July. *(Votes 150-152, p. 31-S)*

Burt appeared to be the key target of Helms and his allies. They complained the nominee was too eager to reach a nuclear arms control pact with the Soviet Union. Ridgway, who was to succeed Burt as assistant secretary of state for European affairs, was faulted as a Carter administration holdover.

Helms for months had lobbied within the administration against Burt's nomination for the ambassadorship to West Germany. Unable to block the appointment, he launched a publicity campaign against Burt after the nomination was submitted to the Senate in June. Meanwhile, he and his allies held hostage the other diplomatic nominations until the administration promised that conservatives at the State Department would not be fired or would be given other jobs.

The four officials for whom Helms and his allies sought protection were John Gavin, ambassador to Mexico; James L. Malone, assistant secretary of state for oceans and international environmental and scientific affairs; Thomas Aranda Jr., ambassador to Uruguay; and Arthur H. Davis Jr., ambassador to Paraguay.

Lord, Spain Confirmations

The Senate on Nov. 5 confirmed Reagan's nomination of Winston Lord as U.S. ambassador to China by a vote of 87-7, with Helms and six other conservative Republicans voting no. *(Vote 283, p. 50-S)*

Helms had delayed Lord's nomination for several weeks as a tactic to pressure the administration into accepting his interpretation of a 1985 spending bill provision (PL 99-88) dealing with U.S. aid to overseas population programs. Helms said that provision, barring aid to agencies tied to involuntary family planning, required ending all U.S. support for the United Nations Fund for Population Activities (UNFPA). The UNFPA worked in China, which Helms said conducted forced abortions. *(Population control, p. 112)*

Helms said he received the assurances he wanted directly from President Reagan on Nov. 5, and so he allowed the Lord nomination to proceed.

The Senate also confirmed on Nov. 5, by voice vote, the nomination of James W. Spain to be ambassador to Sri Lanka. Helms had delayed that nomination because Spain had made statements critical of the process by which ambassadors were selected and confirmed. Helms and Rudy Boschwitz, R-Minn., met with Spain on Nov. 5, and both said Spain apologized.

Meese found "no basis" for criminal prosecution, the Senate did not act on the nomination in 1984. Meese was renominated Jan. 3, 1985, and approved by the Judiciary Committee Feb. 5, 12-6.

The 53-year-old Meese, a close friend of President Reagan, was sworn in on Feb. 25. He succeeded William French Smith, who returned to private law practice in California.

Labor. Brock won Senate confirmation as secretary of labor by voice vote April 26. The post was vacated by Donovan March 15 after a New York Supreme Court judge refused to dismiss charges concerning financial dealings of his construction company before he joined the Cabinet.

A Tennessean, Brock had served 14 years in Congress (House, 1963-71; Senate, 1971-77) and a stint as chairman of the Republican National Committee (1977-81). He had been U.S. trade representative since 1981. *(Story, p. 474)*

Health and Human Services. Bowen was confirmed as secretary of health and human services Dec. 12 by a 93-2 vote. *(Vote 373, p. 63-S; story, p. 300)*

Bowen, 67, was a professor of family medicine at the Indiana University School of Medicine and a former two-term governor of Indiana (1973-81). He was nominated Dec. 4 to succeed Heckler, who was widely reported to have been edged out of HHS at the urging of senior White House officials, critical of her job performance and her commitment to conservative social causes. The president denied the reports as "malicious gossip."

The Senate Finance Committee unanimously recommended approval of Bowen's nomination. Members said he was particularly well suited for the HHS job because of his work in 1982-84 as chairman of a federal advisory council studying Medicare, the federal health insurance program for the elderly and disabled.

Other Nominations

Other Senate action on major 1985 nominations included the following:

Office of Management and Budget. David A.

Stockman, the architect of President Reagan's 1981 budget-cutting plan, resigned as director of the Office of Management and Budget (OMB) Aug. 1. *(Story, p. 448)*

The Senate confirmed his successor, James C. Miller III Oct. 4 by a 90-2 vote. Miller, 43, was chairman of the Federal Trade Commission (FTC) at the time of his nomination to succeed Stockman. He had served as administrator of OMB's Office of Information and Regulatory Affairs for nine months in 1981 before moving to the FTC.

Stockman left OMB after four and a half years as budget director to join the New York investment firm of Salomon Brothers Inc.

Environmental Protection Agency. Without dissent, the Senate Feb. 7 by voice vote confirmed the nomination of Lee M. Thomas to be administrator of the Environmental Protection Agency (EPA).

Thomas, 40, succeeded William D. Ruckelshaus, who took over the top EPA post in 1983 following the resignation under fire of President Reagan's first appointee, Anne M. Burford.

Thomas had served as assistant administrator of EPA under Ruckelshaus and had been acting director of EPA since Ruckelshaus left the agency Jan. 5 . He had headed the agency's hazardous-waste programs since early 1983 when his predecessor, Rita M. Lavelle, was fired in a controversy over management of the "superfund" hazardous-waste program. *(Background, 1984 Almanac p. 372)*

United Nations. The Senate by voice vote May 16 confirmed the nomination of Vernon A. Walters as the U.S. representative to the United Nations.

Walters, a retired Army lieutenant general and former deputy director of the CIA, had served the Reagan administration as a trouble-shooting ambassador-at-large. He succeeded Jeane J. Kirkpatrick, who announced in January her resignation to return to teaching. Kirkpatrick stuck to her decision even though her conservative supporters wanted her to remain in the administration and Reagan said he was looking for a post to offer her.

Trade Representative. Clayton K. Yeutter was confirmed as U.S. trade representative by voice vote of the Senate June 27.

Yeutter was head of the Chicago Mercantile Exchange at the time he was nominated to succeed Brock as the nation's top trade negotiator. He had served as deputy special trade representative during the Ford administration and as assistant secretary of agriculture during the Nixon administration.

Federal Reserve. Martha Seger June 13 won Senate confirmation, by voice vote, as a member of the Federal Reserve Board for a term expiring in 1998.

When Seger was initially appointed in 1984, Democrats on the Senate Banking Committee objected that she was unqualified for the important job. The committee approved the nomination on a 10-8 party-line vote, but Congress recessed in July 1984 before the full Senate could vote. President Reagan then named her to the board as a recess appointee, allowing her to serve until the end of the 1985 session. In May 1985, the Banking Committee returned to the nomination and voted 11-4 for confirmation.

Seger, a conservative economist and an active Republican, was a former commissioner for state-chartered banks in Michigan, a staff economist for the Fed and a professor of finance.

Council of Economic Advisers. The Senate April 17 confirmed the nomination of former Treasury Under Secretary Beryl W. Sprinkel as a member of the president's Council of Economic Advisers (CEA). President Reagan Feb. 22 named Sprinkel to head the three-member board. He succeeded Martin S. Feldstein, who left the CEA chairmanship in July 1984 after continued disagreement with the White House over economic policy.

Office of Personnel Management. The Senate Aug. 1 by voice vote confirmed the nomination of Constance J. Horner, an associate director of OMB, to succeed Donald J. Devine as director of the Office of Personnel Management (OPM).

In March, Reagan had nominated Devine to serve a second four-year term, but Devine withdrew his name June 6 when it became apparent that he lacked support in the Senate Governmental Affairs Committee. Members objected to a memorandum Devine signed on his last day in office that delegated to himself authority to run the agency, while he served as an executive assistant to the acting director, Loretta Cornelius. *(Details, p. 401)*

National Labor Relations Board. On May 23, the Senate gave voice vote approval to two Reagan nominees for the National Labor Relations Board (NLRB). Confirmation of Marshall B. Babson and Wilford W. Johansen brought the five-man board to full strength for the first time since August 1983.

In earlier action, the Senate April 4 by voice vote confirmed Rosemary M. Collyer to be NLRB general counsel. Collyer had been serving on a recess appointment since the previous October. *(Story, p. 474)*

Nominations Killed

Reynolds. The Senate Judiciary Committee June 27 effectively killed the nomination of William Bradford Reynolds to be associate attorney general, the third-ranking post in the Justice Department. The committee first refused, 8-10, to report the nomination favorably. It then tied 9-9 on separate motions to report the nomination without a recommendation or with an unfavorable recommendation. *(Story, p. 237)*

Reynolds retained his existing post as assistant attorney general in charge of the department's civil rights division. Civil rights activists had criticized his role there, charging that Reynolds failed to enforce civil rights laws and misapplied federal court decisions to suit his own policy ends. Questions about Reynolds' credibility arose during confirmation hearings, as conflicts emerged between his testimony and that of other witnesses.

Curran. The Senate Labor and Human Resources Committee Nov. 19 blocked President Reagan's nomination of Edward A. Curran, deputy director of the Peace Corps, to be chairman of the National Endowment for the Humanities, succeeding Bennett.

The committee refused, on an 8-8 vote, to report the nomination favorably to the Senate floor. It then defeated, on another 8-8 tie, a motion to report the nomination without recommendation. One Republican — Robert T. Stafford, R-Vt. — joined the panel's seven Democrats in opposing Curran as lacking qualifications for the job.

Curran was named to the Peace Corps in 1982, following a stormy tenure as director of the Education Department's research arm, the National Institute of Education (NIE). He was ousted from that post by then-Education Secretary T. H. Bell after he wrote to President Reagan calling for abolition of the institute. NIE had been a frequent target of conservative criticism. *(Story, p. 292)* ▮

Membership of Federal Regulatory Agencies, 1985

Commodity Futures Trading Commission

(Five members appointed for five-year terms; not more than three members from one political party.)

Member	Party	Term Expires	Confirmed by Senate
Susan M. Phillips (C)	R	4/13/90	10/16/85
Kalo A. Hineman	R	6/19/86	12/16/81
Fowler C. West	D	4/13/87	10/1/82
William E. Seale	D	4/13/88	11/15/83
Robert R. Davis	R	4/13/89	9/28/84

Consumer Product Safety Commission

(Five members appointed for seven-year terms; not more than three members from one political party.)

Member	Party	Term Expires	Confirmed by Senate
Carol G. Dawson (C)	R	10/26/92	11/21/85
Stuart M. Statler	R	10/26/86	7/26/79
Terrence M. Scanlon	D	10/28/89	3/23/83
Saundra B. Armstrong	D	10/26/90	11/18/83
Anne Graham	R	10/26/91	12/17/85

Equal Employment Opportunity Commission

(Five members appointed for five-year terms; not more than three members from one political party.)

Member	Party	Term Expires	Confirmed by Senate
Clarence Thomas (C)	R	7/1/86	5/6/82
William A. Webb	R	7/1/87	10/1/82
Fred W. Alvarez	D	7/1/88	5/11/84
Tony E. Gallegos	D	7/1/89	9/26/84
Rosalie Gaull Silberman	R	7/1/90	5/23/85

Federal Communications Commission

(Five members appointed for seven-year terms; not more than three members from one political party.)

Member	Party	Term Expires	Confirmed by Senate
Mark S. Fowler (C)	R	6/30/86	5/14/81
James H. Quello	D	6/30/91	6/15/84
Mary Ann Weyforth-Dawson	R	6/30/88	6/4/81
Dennis R. Patrick	R	6/30/92	7/19/85
Vacancy			

Federal Election Commission

(Six members appointed for six year terms; not more than three members from one political party.)

Member	Party	Term Expires	Confirmed by Senate
John W. McGarry (C)	D	4/30/89	7/29/83
Danny Lee McDonald	D	4/30/87	7/1/82
Lee Ann Elliott	R	4/30/87	7/1/82
Joan D. Aikens	R	4/30/89	7/29/83
Thomas E. Harris	D	4/30/85†	6/19/79
Thomas J. Josefiak	R	4/30/91	*

** Member sitting on commission pending Senate confirmation.*
† Member sitting on commission pending presidential action.

Federal Energy Regulatory Commission

(Five members appointed to staggered four-year terms; not more than three members from one political party.)

Member	Party	Term Expires	Confirmed by Senate
Raymond J. O'Connor (C)	R	10/20/87	10/28/83
Anthony G. Sousa	R	10/20/88	10.18/85
Charles G. Stalon	D	10/20/87	6/21/84
Charles A. Trabandt	R	10/20/88	11/1/85
C. M. Naeve	D	10/20/89	11/1/85

Federal Reserve System Governors

(Seven members appointed for 14-year terms; no statutory limitation on political party membership.)

Member	Party	Term Expires	Confirmed by Senate
Paul A. Volcker (C)	D	1/31/92	8/2/79
J. Charles Partee	I	1/31/86	12/19/75
Henry C. Wallich	R	1/31/88	2/8/74
Emmett J. Rice	D	1/31/90	6/12/79
Wayne D. Angell	R	1/31/94	*
Preston Martin	R	1/31/96	3/30/82
Martha Seger	R	1/31/98	6/13/85

** Member sitting on board pending Senate confirmation.*

Federal Trade Commission

(Five members appointed for seven-year terms; not more than three members from one political party.)

Member	Party	Term Expires	Confirmed by Senate
Terry Calvani (Acting Chairman)	R	9/25/90	11/16/83
Patricia P. Bailey	R	9/25/87	6/26/80
Mary L. Azcuenaga	I	9/25/91	3/18/85
2 Vacancies			

Interstate Commerce Commission

(Membership was being reduced gradually under a 1982 law, PL 97-253. As of Jan. 1, 1986, the ICC was scheduled to have five members; not more than three from one political party. Members would serve five-year terms.)

Member	Party	Term Expires	Confirmed by Senate
Heather J. Gradison (C)	R	12/31/88	6/16/82
Frederic N. Andre	R	12/31/87	3/16/82
Malcolm M. B. Sterrett	R	12/31/87	2/9/82
Andrew J. Strenio	D	12/31/85 †	9/6/84
J.J. Simmons III	D	12/31/85 †	9/6/84
Paul H. Lamboley	D	12/31/89	*

** Member sitting on commission pending Senate confirmation.*
† Position scheduled for elimination.

Nuclear Regulatory Commission

(Five members appointed for five-year terms; not more than three members from one political party.)

Member	Party	Term Expires	Confirmed by Senate
Nunzio J. Palladino (C)	R	6/30/86	6/19/81
Thomas M. Roberts	R	6/30/90	7/8/85
James K. Asselstine	I	6/30/87	5/13/82
Frederick M. Bernthal	R	6/30/88	8/4/83
Lando W. Zech Jr.	I	6/30/89	3/5/85

Securities and Exchange Commission

(Five members appointed for five-year terms; not more than three members from one political party.)

Member	Party	Term Expires	Confirmed by Senate
John S. R. Shad (C)	R	6/5/86	4/8/81
Edward H. Fleischman	R	6/5/87	12/16/85
Charles C. Cox	R	6/5/88	11/18/83
Aulana L. Peters	D	6/5/89	5/22/84
Joseph A. Grundfest	D	6/5/90	10/25/85

Uniform Poll-Closing Time

The House Administration Committee Oct. 30 reported a bill (HR 3525 — H Rept 99-348) setting a uniform poll-closing time for national elections throughout the continental United States. (The House passed the bill Jan. 29, 1986, by a vote of 204-171.)

Under the bill, all polls except those in Alaska and Hawaii would close at 9 p.m. Eastern Standard Time for presidential elections. To keep polls open until 7 p.m. in the Pacific time zone, some states would stay on daylight-saving time until the Sunday after a presidential election.

The measure, sponsored by Al Swift, D-Wash., chairman, and William M. Thomas, R-Calif., ranking minority member of the House Administration Subcommittee on Elections, was in response to complaints that the television networks had discouraged voter turnout in 1980 and 1984 by projecting the winners before polls had closed in the West. The increased use of exit polling had enabled networks to make projections earlier than in the past.

In 1984 the major networks agreed not to predict the outcome in any one state until its polls had closed, but President Reagan's landslide victory still was projected long before voting had stopped in the West. ∎

Federal Health Benefits Veto

Citing concerns about increased government personnel costs, President Reagan Jan. 17, 1986, vetoed and returned to Congress a bill (HR 3384) to revise health insurance benefits for federal employees.

HR 3384 had cleared Dec. 19, 1985, the day before adjournment of the 99th Congress' first session. The House originally had passed HR 3384 (H Rept 99-292) Sept. 30; the Senate had passed an amended version Dec. 11. Final action occurred when the Senate approved further changes voted by the House Dec. 16.

Congress made no attempt to override Reagan's veto, which came four days before the second session convened. Instead, lawmakers approved a stripped-down version of the legislation (HR 4061), dropping two provisions that had led Reagan to veto the earlier measure.

The veto of HR 3384 was Reagan's sixth of a public bill during the 99th Congress. While returning the bill to Congress for possible override action, Reagan asserted his right, during an adjournment, to prevent it from becoming law simply by withholding his approval. The administration was challenging before the Supreme Court a 1984 federal appeals court ruling that such "pocket vetoes" could not be used between sessions of the same Congress. *(Vetoes, box, p. 6; background, 1984 Almanac p. 204)*

Reagan Objections

In his veto message, Reagan objected to HR 3384 because it would eliminate an existing cap on the government's share of federal workers' health insurance premiums. Reagan said eliminating that ceiling, which was set at 75 percent of the premiums, would increase the government's costs by $90 million in fiscal 1986 and $173 million in 1987. *(Veto message text, p. 42-D)*

Rep. Mary Rose Oakar, D-Ohio, a leading proponent of the measure, countered that the bill would save money in the long run by giving workers new incentives to participate in lower-cost health plans.

Reagan also objected to a provision of the bill that would require federal employees' health insurance to make direct payments to nurses and nurse-midwives without requiring supervision or referral by a physician. Insurance companies currently were allowed to require physician involvement before reimbursing for nurses' services.

Reagan said requiring direct payment to nurses was a "major departure" from established practice. But the bill's backers said it would expand employees' access to professionals who generally provided services at a lower cost than physicians charged. Oakar maintained that opposition to the provision by physicians' lobbyists was a "key factor" in the veto.

Reagan said he fully supported another important provision of HR 3384 that would allow federal retirees, as well as current employees, to receive a rebate of health insurance premiums by their insurance carriers. This provision was included in the revised bill cleared in 1986.

Federal employees were due to receive refunds from excess reserves that had built up in the health benefits program. Those extra funds had accumulated in part because workers had not been using their health benefits as much as in the past. Existing law already allowed the refunds to federal employees, but legislation was needed to authorize rebates to retirees still enrolled in the program. ∎

Bicentennial of Constitution

Two years after Congress authorized it, the Commission on the Bicentennial of the Constitution began operations. The 23-member panel held three meetings and issued its first report Sept. 17.

The commission was created in 1983 (PL 98-101) to coordinate the commemoration of the 200th anniversary of the Constitution. *(1983 Almanac p. 324)*

Its initial recommendations included special events, films and projects to educate the public about the history and principles behind the Constitution; a national holiday on Sept. 17, 1987, the 200th anniversary of the signing of the document, and the minting of gold and silver coins to help finance the observance. ∎

Official U.S. Flower

The Senate Sept. 16 passed a resolution declaring that the rose should be the official flower of the United States.

Pushing the resolution (S J Res 159) were J. Bennett Johnston, D-La., and his wife Mary, of Shreveport, La., home of the American Rose Society. After Johnston signed up 52 colleagues — more than half the Senate — as cosponsors, the Judiciary Committee reported S J Res 159. It was brought to the floor when few members were present, and breezed through by voice vote.

In the House, companion legislation (H J Res 385) was referred to the Post Office and Civil Service Subcommittee on Census and Population. To emerge, it must win the cosponsorship of 218 House members.

The issue of a national flower stemmed from the failed crusade of Everett McKinley Dirksen, R-Ill. (House 1933-49; Senate 1951-69), to make the marigold the "official floral emblem" of the United States. Dirksen, who died in 1969, introduced his marigold bill in every Congress for three decades, but it never passed. ∎

ECONOMIC POLICY

CQ

Economic Policy

In 1985 Congress voted to raise the limit on the federal debt to an extraordinary $2 trillion, more than double what it had been when President Reagan first took office. The increase in the government's debt, which represented years' worth of accumulated deficit spending, bore heavy freight. Congress amended the debt measure to include radical changes in budgeting procedures, with the goal of forcing the federal deficit down to zero within five years.

The new anti-deficit law set maximum allowable deficits, declining to zero by fiscal 1991, and required uniform "automatic" cuts in federal spending in years when Congress and the president failed to meet the deficit targets through conventional legislative action. The law was dubbed "Gramm-Rudman-Hollings," for its three original Senate sponsors, Republicans Phil Gramm of Texas and Warren B. Rudman of New Hampshire, and Democrat Ernest F. Hollings of South Carolina. Its unprecedented provision for automatic spending cuts was immediately attacked in courts, by a dozen members of the House and several federal employees' groups, as fundamentally unconstitutional.

The year had begun with budget director David A. Stockman warning that 1985 offered the "last, best chance" for a real strike against the huge federal deficit. Stockman reasoned that politically painful decisions to slash spending, raise taxes, or both — the only options apart from continued borrowing — were increasingly unlikely as members faced the upcoming 1986 congressional elections, the waning influence of a lame-duck president, and the devastating consequences of continued $200 billion deficits.

By the end of the year, however, neither deficit-caused disasters nor, with one exception, significant steps to actually cut spending had materialized. Congress and the president, in enacting the Gramm-Rudman-Hollings law, promised instead that they would get down to eliminating the deficit the next year — in 1986. That was when the new law took effect.

And Stockman, architect of five years of Reagan administration economic policy, left the government for a position with a private investment banking firm. He was replaced by James C. Miller III as director of the Office of Management and Budget.

In 1985 Congress unilaterally made one decision with a significant immediate impact on deficit spending. It rejected Reagan's desired 6 percent growth rate for defense spending, opting instead for zero growth for fiscal 1986. This decision was important because of the enormity of military spending, which comprised nearly a third of the federal budget. The White House was displeased with the erosion of its defense buildup but was surprisingly quiet about it.

Apart from the defense decision, Congress and the president failed to make much real headway against the deficit, and instead reiterated conflicting positions, with Reagan insisting that taxes not be raised to help reduce the deficit, and key members of both parties saying it could not be otherwise.

Tax Overhaul: Reagan's No. 1 Priority

The president said his top priority was the "revenue-neutral" overhaul of the income tax code, and he repudiated suggestions that the massive tax overhaul legislation that finally cleared the House could become a vehicle for some deficit-reducing extra revenues. The tax "reform" drive had begun in late 1984 when the Treasury Department released a far-reaching proposed revision of tax laws. Its intention was to reduce across-the-board the rate of taxation, simplify the bewildering number of different tax rates and eliminate most special breaks for businesses and individuals.

The goals of tax reformers were multiple: Some stressed a need to counteract Americans' growing cynicism about the tangled, seemingly unfair tax code; others, notably fiscal conservatives, contended that the reform efforts would stimulate the economy, or that simplification of the code would weigh against future tax increases by making them more conspicuous.

It seemed that many members of Congress did not share Reagan's belief that overhauling the tax code should be the top economic priority. In the autumn months, members' frustration with the continued budget impasse, and their dismay that the federal debt was cresting above $2 trillion, boiled up and pushed through the Gramm-Rudman-Hollings plan with surprising haste.

Despite the uncertainty as to whether the measure's pivotal feature of automatic cuts would survive court tests, its enactment was a notable event. It signaled widespread belief that nothing effective would be done to curb the deficit without aggressive presidential leadership on the issue, or an economic crisis. In the absence of either, the legislation appeared to say, members had opted for an artificially created legislative crisis in the form of severe automatic cuts.

Congress had, in fact, adopted a budget resolution on Aug. 1, calling for more cuts in the growth of federal programs than ever before. But then members became so mesmerized by Gramm-Rudman-Hollings that they failed to complete follow-up budget "reconciliation" legislation, which would actually have made the spending cuts recommended by the budget resolution. The defense spending decision, however, was not lost because it was reflected in reduced defense appropriations.

On another front, rhetoric ran far ahead of accomplishment on trade legislation. There was very strong, bipartisan support in Congress for protectionist remedies against the flood of competitively priced foreign products, and the deteriorating U.S. trade position abroad. But much talk about retaliating against aggressive trading practices of U.S. competitors came to nothing: No major trade bill was enacted, and Reagan vetoed a bill that would have limited textile imports.

One of the major causes — and symptoms — of the U.S. trade problem was the value of the dollar, which was disproportionately high compared to other major currencies when the year began. The effect of this overvaluation was to push up the cost of goods priced in dollars, and to artificially slash prices of goods in other currencies. On Sept. 22, top government officials of the United States and four other major industrialized nations announced they would act jointly to even out the differential between the dollar and other currencies. The five — the United States, France, Germany, Japan and the United Kingdom — indicated that they would intervene in currency markets in a coordinated manner, and also pledged reforms of their monetary and fiscal policies. Their goal was to reduce disparities among the different economies that had translated into severe trade and currency imbalances.

The U.S. participation in the joint effort was something of an about-face. Reagan had lauded the high value of the dollar as a sign of the nation's economic strength. The administration's action was part of an effort to stall protectionist trade bills in Congress.

State of the Economy

The nation's economy continued to perform moderately well, seemingly in defiance of expectations that the massive government borrowing necessitated by the deficit would result in devastatingly high interest, inflation and unemployment. Inflation for the year rose at 3.8 percent, making 1985 the fourth year in a row that inflation had stayed at or below 4 percent.

In early January 1986, the Commerce Department reported that the economy grew 2.3 percent in 1985. That was the worst rate of growth since the 1982 recession, and substantially below the 3.9 percent growth rate projected by the president's budget in February. By contrast, the real gross national product (GNP) had grown 6.6 percent in 1984 and 3.4 percent in 1983, after declining 2.5 percent in 1982.

One factor mitigating the impact of the large-scale federal borrowing was the continued inflow of foreign capital, drawn to the United States by high real U.S. interest rates, by comparatively lower investment advantages elsewhere, and by the nation's political stability. By some estimates, the net capital inflow into the nation topped $100 billion in 1984 and continued to rise in 1985.

There were signs of trouble as the year went along — a steep run-up in the already-high value of the doller in the early months, an ominously large trade deficit of $150 billion, and slowing economic growth by the years' end. The agricultural economy, bypassed by the overall economic recovery, continued in severe straits. Bank failures, numbering 120, were the highest since the Depression. Some 62 of the failed institutions were agricultural banks. The year's 6.9 percent unemployment rate was the lowest registered since 1980, yet still quite high by historic standards. According to a December AFL-CIO statement, more than 5 million workers had been unemployed for so long they had exhausted unemployment benefits.

Even so, during 1985 the nation escaped precipitous economic disaster and its deficit spending seemed primarily to be laying up debt for the coming generation to pay off. Members commonly remarked that Americans were getting an expensive bargain, receiving about a dollar's worth of government for about 77 cents in taxes and, collectively, borrowing the rest. Interest payments were the fourth largest single item in the federal budget.

—By Elizabeth Wehr

Reagan Budget Highlights Deficit-Cutting Effort

Its general contents widely known for weeks beforehand, President Reagan's $973.7 billion fiscal 1986 budget met with predictable resistance when it was officially submitted to Congress Feb. 4. But the budget brought home a sobering message to legislators about the bleak prospects for controlling federal deficits.

It was clear within a few days that lawmakers would have to accept many of the administration's spending cuts to make a dent in deficits projected by the Congressional Budget Office (CBO) to grow to almost $300 billion annually by the end of the decade.

The president's budget projected deficits at $180 billion, $164.9 billion and $144.4 billion in fiscal years 1986, 1987 and 1988. Those figures far exceeded the administration's announced hope in December 1984 to reduce annual deficits to $100 billion by fiscal 1988.

The biggest rift between Congress and the administration was not over whether cuts should be made, but what their composition should be. *(Program highlights, p. 435)*

Republicans and Democrats in both chambers immediately rejected the president's call for a 5.9 percent inflation-adjusted increase in defense spending authority coupled with deep cuts in domestic programs.

Members told administration officials at budget hearings held throughout the week of Feb. 4 that the entire range of government spending — including defense and Social Security, which the president had promised not to cut — had to be "on the table" at budget negotiations. And they warned that presidential leadership was needed for any package to win congressional approval. *(Budget resolution, p. 441; defense budget, p. 138)*

"My constituents tell me they're willing to take their lumps if everybody else takes theirs," Rep. Silvio O. Conte, R-Mass., told budget director David A. Stockman, Treasury Secretary James A. Baker III, and Council of Economic Advisers member William A. Niskanen when they defended the budget before the House Appropriations Committee Feb. 7. "The deficit is potentially more harmful in the short run than an 'inadequate' defense," he added.

Even the administration appeared divided over where cuts should be made. While defending the budget's defense proposal before the Senate Budget Committee Feb. 5, Stockman suggested Congress should consider reducing the $18 billion-a-year request for military retirement benefits. *(Military retirement, p. 138)*

The retirement system is "a scandal, it's an outrage," he said, admitting he had lost an internal administration battle over trimming the generous benefit plan. "The institutional forces in the military are more concerned about protecting their retirement benefits than they are about protecting the security of the American people."

In addition, angry farmers and farm-state representatives locked horns with the administration the same week the budget was released over a proposed farm credit deal. The White House offered emergency credit assistance to help plant spring crops in exchange for support of its budget proposal to cut farm subsidies. But farmers said they wanted more credit help before they would back the farm program overhaul. *(Farm credit veto, p. 542)*

Stockman said he was discouraged that such attacks on proposed spending restraints had begun so soon after the budget's release.

Meanwhile, Reagan effectively removed tax increases from the budget debate by vowing to submit a proposal later in the year to overhaul the federal tax code. The president, in his State of the Union address Feb. 6, repeated his intention to seek tax reform. *(Tax overhaul, p. 480; State of the Union, text, p. 8-D)*

Democratic Response

Seizing on the budget's proposed reductions in programs that benefit the middle class, House and Senate Democrats said they would try to ensure that the public was aware of the scope of the domestic cuts the president was proposing, including the elimination of the Small Business Administration, the subsidy for Amtrak, general revenue sharing and cuts in student aid.

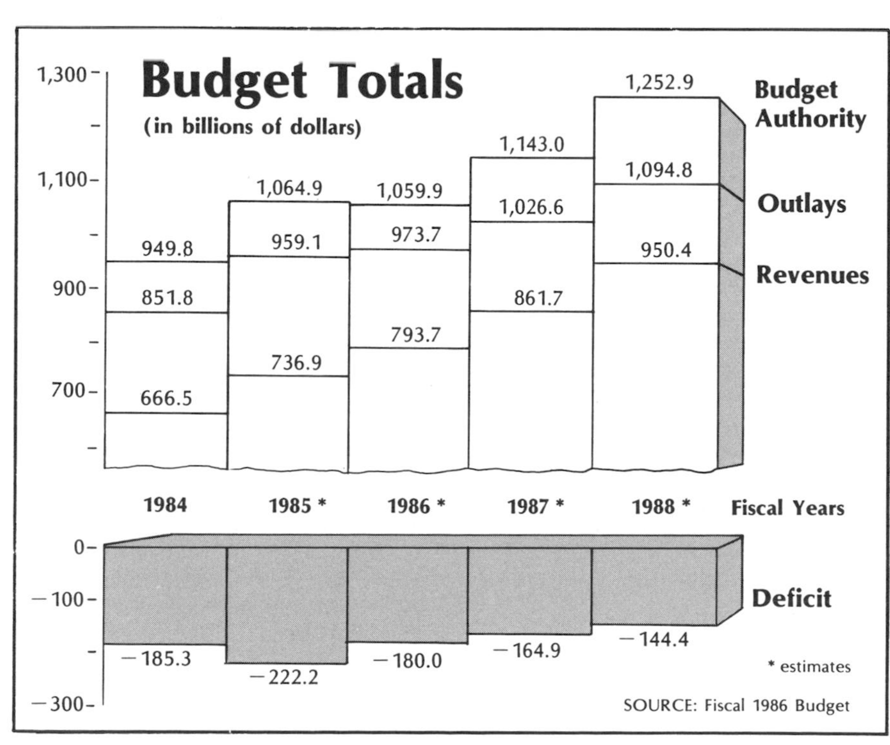

To begin the process, the House Budget Committee held a series of budget hearings around the country in early February, before hearings with administration and other officials began later in the month in Washington.

The president's budget "takes the pain of budget-cutting directly to middle America," said House Speaker Thomas P. O'Neill Jr., D-Mass. "I urge the president to take the time to educate the country on his various budget proposals and to tell people how they will be affected."

GOP Alternative

Republicans also were generally negative about the administration budget. Even before the president's budget request reached Capitol Hill, Senate GOP leaders had set their own agenda for deficit reduction — 2 percent of the gross national product (GNP) by fiscal 1988, a goal embraced the previous December by the White House, but not achieved in the budget request. Such a target assumed a deficit about $45 billion lower than the president projected for fiscal 1988. *(Deficit forecast, chart, p. 427)*

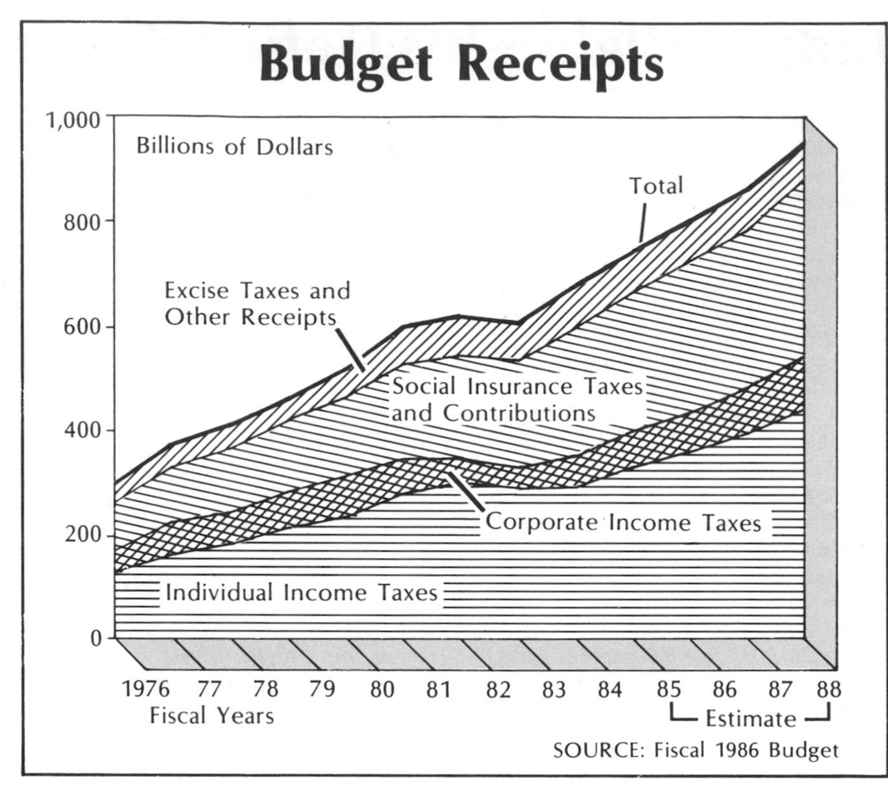

Charging that Reagan's defense figures were bloated at the expense of domestic spending, Republicans at the same time complained that the overall budget did not go far enough to reduce the deficit.

Stockman argued before the Senate Budget Committee that the defense spending request was needed to fund programs, approved by Congress over the past five years, to bolster national security. But his thesis appeared not to hold water for committee members.

Sen. Pete V. Domenici, R-N.M., chairman of the Senate Budget Committee, noted that since Congress had been "extraordinarily generous" on defense spending in the past, "we have enough buffer in our defense spending that this year we cannot give the president the defense request he recommends."

Even some of the most stalwart supporters of the defense budget were reluctant to back the president's request. Sen. John W. Warner, R-Va., said Congress should draw the line at 3 percent inflation-adjusted growth. Senate Armed Services Committee Chairman Barry Goldwater, R-Ariz., told Defense Secretary Caspar W. Weinberger Feb. 4 that defense "will be reduced."

And six Republicans on the House Budget Committee sent Weinberger a letter asking that he give them a detailed explanation of how a one-year "freeze" on defense spending authority could be implemented.

In an appearance before the Senate Budget Committee Feb. 7, Weinberger told senators that such a freeze would "cripple" the nation's defense, but members were leery of his gloomy predictions.

Summary

President Reagan's fiscal 1986 budget proposed a slight overall increase in government spending of fiscal 1985, but continued a trend of the previous four years of shifting expenditures from domestic programs to national defense.

Reagan's plan called for total government outlays of $973.7 billion in fiscal 1986, which ran from Oct. 1, 1985, through Sept. 30, 1986. The budget projected spending of $1,026.6 billion in fiscal 1987 and $1,094.8 billion in fiscal 1988. The budget revised estimates of fiscal 1985 spending to be $959.1 billion. *(Budget totals, chart, p. 427)*

These proposed spending levels assumed cutbacks of $51 billion in fiscal 1986, $83 billion in fiscal 1987 and $105 billion in fiscal 1988.

The bulk of the spending cuts were to come from domestic programs that made up about 60 percent of the federal budget, but whose share would drop to 52 percent by 1990 if the president's program were to be enacted. The rest of the savings were to come from a decrease in the growth rate of defense spending and reductions in the amount of interest payments on the national debt.

Domestic spending cuts in fiscal 1986 of $35.1 billion were to come from a one-year "freeze" in spending for most programs in combination with selective cuts or elimination of dozens of others.

Cost-of-living adjustments (COLAs) were to be delayed one year for some programs, such as military and civilian retirement, but the largest single entitlement program, Social Security, was not to be affected.

Defense spending was to be cut $8.9 billion from the level anticipated by the administration in its August 1984 budget update to $285.7 billion in fiscal 1986. The defense share represented 29 percent of the budget.

But the projected defense savings masked a disagreement between the Office of Management and Budget (OMB) and the CBO over what base was to be used to measure spending changes. According to some congressional estimates, the administration's proposed defense cut was actually an inflation-adjusted increase of about $4 billion.

Reagan's 1986 budget estimated that if no action were taken to lower annual federal deficits, they would rise to $230.3 billion in fiscal 1986, $245.6 billion in 1987 and $247.8 billion by 1988.

Deficit-Reduction Plan

The administration's deficit-reduction plan called for many cuts that had been proposed in prior budgets and rejected by Congress. However, the fiscal 1986 budget also called for deep new reductions in programs that had remained relatively unscathed in previous budget-cutting efforts.

Among the programs slated for elimination were a number that largely aided middle-class taxpayers and powerful interest groups.

The budget would have terminated general revenue sharing for state and local governments, the Small Business Administration, the direct-loan programs of the Export-Import Bank, the subsidy for Amtrak rail passenger service, the Job Corps, Community Services Block Grants and Urban Development Action Grants.

It also called for large reductions in farm price supports and lending programs, Medicare and Medicaid, housing aid, nutrition programs and student loans.

The budget proposed a 5 percent pay cut for federal workers and a 10 percent across-the-board cut for nondefense administrative expenses.

It made relatively small cuts in a number of the programs that were part of the so-called "social safety net." This was done, Stockman said, in recognition of the fact that large cuts were made in these programs over the previous four years.

No changes were proposed for Supplemental Security Income, veterans' pensions or the earned income tax credit for poor working families, nor for Social Security.

Food stamp funding was to remain about the same, with $56 million in savings assumed from a proposal to require able participants to join work programs.

In defense of the proposed domestic spending cuts, Stockman told reporters at a briefing Feb. 4 that a one-year across the board "freeze" of domestic spending, as proposed by some, "simply won't solve the problem ... we have to do more."

He said that Reagan's 1984 reelection was a mandate against new taxes, and justified the administration's defense spending request as necessary to fulfill agreements between the administration and Congress over the past four years to strengthen national defense.

Stockman noted that the president's budget blueprint hit the $50 billion deficit-reduction target that Federal Reserve Board Chairman Paul A. Volcker had said was the minimum needed to convince financial markets that the government was trying to get its fiscal house in order.

The budget director said failure by Congress to act on the deficit quickly would pose an "acute threat to the best economic performance ... we've had in 25 years.... The day of reckoning has arrived."

Revenues

The plan called for no new taxes, as Reagan repeatedly promised, but it did propose some hikes in user fees and other changes in offsetting receipts for a deficit savings of $3.6 billion in fiscal 1986. The president projected total revenues of $793.7 billion in 1986 — $180 billion less than he proposed to spend. *(Composition of federal revenues, chart, this page)*

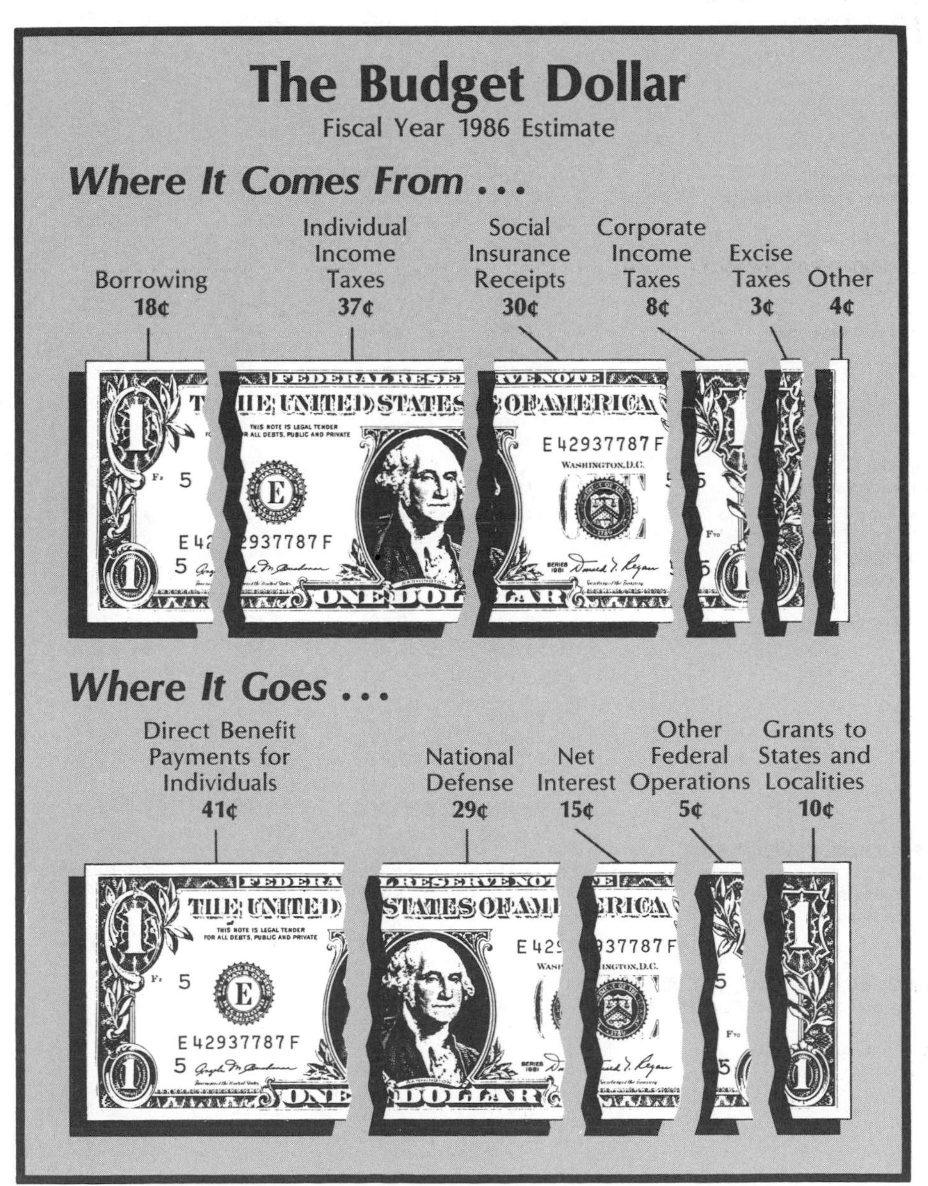

The budget sought to generate $2.3 billion in fiscal 1986 revenues through the imposition of an unprecedented variety of user fees that would have applied to federal program beneficiaries ranging from poultry farmers to yachtsmen. *(Chart, p. 434)*

These new revenues, along with the spending cuts, were expected to lower the cost of servicing the national debt by $3.1 billion in the first year of the three-year budget projection.

The budget forecast a fiscal 1986 debt-service payment of $169.7 billion, more than 17 percent of the budget for that year. The budget predicted that the federal debt, which was $1.577 trillion at the end

Fiscal 1986 Budget by Function: $973.7 Billion in . . .

(in millions of dollars†)

	BUDGET AUTHORITY‡			OUTLAYS		
	1984	1985 est.	1986 est.	1984	1985 est.	1986 est.
NATIONAL DEFENSE						
Military Defense	$258,152	$284,735	$313,705	$220,840	$246,305	$277,505
Atomic Energy Defense Activities	6,555	7,325	8,047	6,120	6,991	7,700
Defense-related Activities	452	493	454	453	533	464
TOTAL	$265,160	$292,553	$322,205	$227,413	$253,830	$285,669
INTERNATIONAL AFFAIRS						
International Security Assistance	$ 8,943	$ 12,854	$ 10,748 *	$ 7,924	$ 10,177	$ 9,213 *
Foreign Economic and Financial Assistance	5,069	5,847	5,343	4,478	5,523	5,278
Conduct of Foreign Affairs	2,025	2,507	2,470	1,882	2,152	2,454
Foreign Information and Exchange Activities	798	897	1,118	682	941	1,041
International Financial Programs	7,718	4,588	891	910	790	364
TOTAL	$ 24,553	$ 26,693	$ 20,569	$ 15,876	$ 19,583	$ 18,349
GENERAL SCIENCE, SPACE AND TECHNOLOGY						
General Science and Basic Research	$ 1,964	$ 2,232	$ 2,260	$ 1,849	$ 2,116	$ 2,237
Space Research and Technology	6,858	6,881	7,264	6,469	6,623	7,048
TOTAL	$ 8,822	$ 9,114	$ 9,524	$ 8,317	$ 8,740	$ 9,285
ENERGY						
Energy Supply	$ 5,345	$ 5,073	$ 4,216	$ 3,252	$ 4,949	$ 3,170
Energy Conservation	455	473	176	527	545	381
Emergency Energy Preparedness	1,268	2,056	6	2,518	1,906	385
Energy Information, Policy and Regulation	796	719	712	790	764	736
TOTAL	$ 7,865	$ 8,321	$ 5,110	$ 7,086	$ 8,164	$ 4,671
NATURAL RESOURCES AND ENVIRONMENT						
Pollution Control and Abatement	$ 4,037	$ 4,257	$ 4,577	$ 4,044	$ 4,387	$ 4,579
Water Resources	3,779	3,916	3,091	4,068	4,293	3,566
Conservation and Land Management	1,389	793	569	1,302	979	719
Recreational Resources	1,453	1,480	1,070	1,581	1,622	1,361
Other Natural Resources	1,622	1,761	1,613	1,595	1,744	1,660
TOTAL	$ 12,280	$ 12,207	$ 10,920	$ 12,591	$ 13,024	$ 11,884
AGRICULTURE						
Farm Income Stabilization	$ 9,945	$ 20,724	$ 11,395	$ 11,877	$ 18,344	$ 10,937
Agricultural Research and Services	1,843	1,845	1,643	1,736	1,821	1,691
TOTAL	$ 11,788	$ 22,569	$ 13,038	$ 13,613	$ 20,165	$ 12,629
COMMERCE AND HOUSING CREDIT						
Mortgage Credit and Deposit Insurance	$ 9,430	$ 7,539	$ 2,473	$ 3,766	$ 2,179	$ −713
Postal Service	1,798	2,443	1,827	1,239	1,361	1,217
Other Advancement of Commerce	2,036	2,455	3,522	1,913	2,447	1,702
TOTAL	$ 13,264	$ 12,437	$ 7,822	$ 6,917	$ 5,987	$ 2,206
TRANSPORTATION						
Ground Transportation	$ 20,685	$ 20,228	$ 17,007	$ 16,158	$ 18,729	$ 17,766
Air Transportation	5,266	5,961	5,697	4,415	4,966	5,175
Water Transportation	3,244	2,928	2,660	3,010	3,176	2,792
Other Transportation	114	126	124	85	123	127
TOTAL	$ 29,309	$ 29,243	$ 25,488	$ 23,669	$ 26,994	$ 25,860
COMMUNITY AND REGIONAL DEVELOPMENT						
Community Development	$ 4,818	$ 4,276	$ 3,504	$ 4,520	$ 4,861	$ 4,616
Area and Regional Development	3,824	3,426	2,190	3,034	3,366	2,792
Disaster Relief and Insurance	257	301	−565	119	326	−84
TOTAL	$ 8,899	$ 8,004	$ 5,129	$ 7,673	$ 8,553	$ 7,323
EDUCATION, TRAINING, EMPLOYMENT, SOCIAL SERVICES						
Elementary, Secondary and Vocational Education	$ 7,243	$ 7,752	$ 7,481	$ 6,520	$ 7,661	$ 7,670
Higher Education	6,956	9,347	6,825	7,383	8,506	7,959
Research and General Education Aids	1,133	1,204	1,029	1,210	1,225	1,187
Training and Employment	8,688	5,117	4,136	4,644	5,298	4,931
Other Labor Services	685	706	674	639	711	679
Social Services	6,937	7,238	6,800	7,185	7,032	6,863
TOTAL	$ 31,642	$ 31,365	$ 26,946	$ 27,579	$ 30,434	$ 29,288

** Does not include aid to Israel, expected to be at least $1.2 billion.*

. . . Expenditures, $1.06 Trillion in Spending Authority

(in millions of dollars†)

	BUDGET AUTHORITY‡			OUTLAYS		
	1984	1985 est.	1986 est.	1984	1985 est.	1986 est.
HEALTH						
Health Care Services	$ 25,241	$ 26,423	$ 28,312	$ 24,522	$ 27,244	$ 28,202
Health Research	4,773	5,396	5,099	4,379	4,961	5,204
Education and Training of Health Care Work Force	461	550	290	388	478	455
Consumer and Occupational Health and Safety	1,156	1,186	1,041	1,129	1,196	1,059
TOTAL	$ 31,630	$ 33,556	$ 34,741	$ 30,417	$ 33,879	$ 34,920
SOCIAL SECURITY AND MEDICARE						
Social Security	$178,512	$199,418	$207,007	$178,223	$191,107	$202,245
Medicare	63,220	71,473	81,698	57,540	66,256	67,158
TOTAL	$241,732	$270,891	$288,705	$235,764	$257,363	$269,404
INCOME SECURITY						
General Retirement and Disability Insurance	$ 8,570	$ 6,886	$ 7,630	$ 5,411	$ 5,504	$ 5,580
Federal Employee Retirement and Disability	53,455	67,331	71,906	38,054	38,641	41,518
Unemployment Compensation	24,320	20,987	21,271	18,421	16,780	16,294
Housing Assistance	12,671	26,401	3,428	11,270	25,355	12,304
Food and Nutrition Assistance	18,235	18,549	18,268	18,055	18,664	18,268
Other Income Security	21,588	21,891	21,643	21,427	22,296	21,806
TOTAL	$138,838	$162,045	$144,147	$112,668	$127,240	$115,769
VETERANS' BENEFITS AND SERVICES						
Income Security	$ 14,884	$ 15,054	$ 15,414	$ 14,400	$ 14,754	$ 15,135
Education, Training and Rehabilitation	1,582	1,232	1,251	1,359	1,295	1,110
Housing	201	307	—	244	358	−288
Hospital and Medical Care	9,078	9,918	9,902	8,861	9,621	9,994
Other Benefits and Services	782	830	825	751	823	817
TOTAL	$ 26,528	$ 27,340	$ 27,393	$ 25,614	$ 26,850	$ 26,769
ADMINISTRATION OF JUSTICE						
Federal Law Enforcement Activities	$ 3,433	$ 3,656	$ 3,652	$ 3,205	$ 3,681	$ 3,610
Federal Litigative and Judicial Activities	1,905	2,198	2,044	1,825	2,192	2,066
Federal Correctional Activities	495	599	593	494	580	632
Criminal Justice Assistance	215	227	252	136	233	280
TOTAL	$ 6,047	$ 6,681	$ 6,542	$ 5,660	$ 6,686	$ 6,587
GENERAL GOVERNMENT						
Legislative Functions	$ 1,443	$ 1,430	$ 1,388	$ 1,319	$ 1,464	$ 1,417
Executive Direction and Management	111	118	113	97	119	112
Central Fiscal Operations	3,469	3,613	3,175	3,254	3,533	3,105
General Property and Records Management	337	248	253	201	376	182
Central Personnel Management	148	149	142	139	153	143
Other General Government	498	597	406	557	586	390
Deductions for Offsetting Receipts	−513	−448	−504	−513	−448	−504
TOTAL	$ 5,494	$ 5,708	$ 4,975	$ 5,053	$ 5,782	$ 4,845
GENERAL PURPOSE FISCAL ASSISTANCE						
General Revenue Sharing	$ 4,574	$ 4,575	$ 6	$ 4,573	$ 4,617	$ 1,168
Other General Purpose Fiscal Assistance	2,223	1,933	1,628	2,197	1,934	1,629
TOTAL	$ 6,797	$ 6,508	$ 1,634	$ 6,770	$ 6,552	$ 2,797
NET INTEREST						
Interest on the Public Debt	$153,822	$180,295	$198,805	$153,822	$180,295	$198,805
Interest Received by Trust Funds	−20,354	−25,554	−29,149	−20,354	−25,554	−29,149
Other Interest	−22,410	−24,315	−27,106	−22,410	−24,315	−27,106
TOTAL	$111,058	$130,426	$142,550	$111,058	$130,426	$142,550
CIVILIAN AGENCY PAY RAISES	—	$ 6	$ 24	—	$ 6	$ 24
CONTINGENCIES	—	$ 1,500	$ 0	—	$ 1,125	$ 375
UNDISTRIBUTED OFFSETTING RECEIPTS	$−31,957	$−32,296	$−37,478	$−31,957	$−32,296	$−37,478
GRAND TOTAL	$949,751	$1,064,870	$1,059,983	$851,781	$959,085	$973,725

† Figures may not add to totals due to rounding. *‡ Primarily appropriations.*

SOURCE: Fiscal 1986 Budget

A Budget Glossary

The federal budget is the president's financial plan for the federal government. It accounts for how government funds have been raised and spent, and it proposes financial policies for the coming **fiscal year** and beyond. Fiscal year 1986 began Oct. 1, 1985, and ended Sept. 30, 1986.

The budget discusses **receipts**, amounts the government expects to raise in taxes and other fees; **budget authority**, amounts federal agencies are allowed to obligate or lend; and **outlays**, amounts actually paid out by the government in cash or checks during the year. Examples of outlays are funds spent to buy equipment or property, to meet the government's liability under a contract or to pay employees' salaries. Outlays also include net lending — the difference between disbursements and repayments under government lending programs.

The budget earmarks funds to cover two kinds of spending. **Mandatory** spending covers **entitlement** programs, such as food stamps, Social Security and agricultural subsidies, that may be used by anyone who meets eligibility criteria. Mandatory spending may not be limited in the annual appropriations process. **Discretionary** spending is set annually in the appropriations process.

The budget has a twofold purpose: to establish governmental priorities among federal programs and to chart U.S. **fiscal policy**, which is the coordinated use of taxes and expenditures to affect the economy.

Congress adopts its version of the budget in the form of a **budget resolution**, which is supposed to be adopted by April 15, starting in 1986, and sets target figures for taxes and spending, broken down among major budget categories called **functions**. It also includes **reconciliation** instructions, directing committees to recommend changes in laws governing programs under their jurisdiction to meet revenue and spending targets.

An **authorization** is an act of Congress that establishes government programs. It defines the scope of programs and sets a ceiling for how much can be spent on them. Authorizations do not actually spend the money. In the case of authority to enter contractual obligations, though, Congress authorizes the administration to make firm commitments for which funds must later be provided. Congress also occasionally includes mandatory spending requirements in an authorization to ensure spending at a certain level.

An **appropriation** provides money for programs within the limits established in authorizations. An appropriation may be for a single year, a specified period of years or an indefinite number of years, according to the restrictions Congress wishes to place on spending for particular purposes.

Appropriations generally take the form of **budget authority**. Budget authority often differs from actual outlays. That is because, in practice, funds actually spent or obligated during a year may be drawn partly from the budget authority conferred in the year in question and partly from budget authority conferred in previous years.

of fiscal 1984, would break the $2 trillion mark by the end of fiscal 1986 and approach $3 trillion by the end of the decade.

In a message to Congress accompanying the budget, Reagan acknowledged that his deficit-reduction package was "a far cry from our goal of a balanced budget, but a significant step in the right direction. . . ." *(Text, p. 4-D)*

While espousing a balanced budget and tax reform, critics pointed out, Reagan's budget called for five tax-break proposals that would cost the Treasury $7.7 billion in fiscal 1986-88. The proposals, all of which had been offered before — and rejected by Congress — were:

- **Tax incentives for higher education.** A parent could exclude from taxable earnings up to $1,000 per child, each year, if the sum was deposited in a savings account reserved for the child's college education. The break would have been less generous for taxpayers who earned more than $40,000 a year; those earning more than $60,000 would have been ineligible.

The proposal, which would have taken effect Jan. 1, 1986, would have cost the Treasury $400 million over three years.

- **Tuition tax credits.** Taxpayers who sent their children to private elementary and secondary schools could get a credit for some tuition expenses of each child — $100 in 1985, $200 in 1986 and $300 in subsequent years.

The credit, effective for expenses after July 31, 1985, would have meant a three-year loss of $1.9 billion.

- **Enterprise zone incentives.** After Jan. 1, 1986, a variety of tax benefits — for property, payroll, construction and equipment — would have been available for investors who developed depressed urban areas designated as "enterprise zones." The plan would have cut Treasury receipts $1.5 billion over three years.
- **Child-care credit.** Taxpayers with incomes up to $60,000 annually would have been able to deduct a larger share of their expenses for child care after Jan. 1, 1986. The proposal would have cost the Treasury $400 million by 1988.
- **Corporate research benefits.** Tax credits for businesses' research and experimentation expenses, scheduled to expire Dec. 31, would have been extended three years, at a cost of $3.5 billion. A Senate proposal to make the credit permanent failed in 1984.

Credit Budget

The administration's budget continued attempts to control federal direct loan and loan guarantee programs, which did not necessarily affect the deficit but placed additional pressures on private credit markets.

The budget request included a credit budget that estimated $24.2 billion in direct loans and $77.2 billion in loan guarantees, for a total of $101.4 billion in fiscal year 1986, almost $25 billion below the estimated level for fiscal 1985.

Reductions in credit activity were tied for the most part to the administration's proposed eliminations and scalebacks of the Export-Import Bank direct loan program, the Farmers Home Administration and low-rent public housing assistance.

The administration also predicted a similar level of credit activities through fiscal 1988 — $101.3 billion in fiscal year 1987 and $100.8 billion in fiscal 1988.

However, the budget reported that total credit activities would be $125.9 billion in fiscal year 1985, $16 billion over the 1984 level. The jump was largely due to higher-than-anticipated loan guarantees by the Federal Housing

Administration because of the introduction of a new type of mortgage called an adjustable rate mortgage, according to the budget document.

1985 Revisions

The administration's fiscal 1985 deficit estimate of more than $222 billion was about $56 billion higher than the $166.9 billion it predicted in its mid-session budget review in August 1984. *(Fiscal 1985 deficit, p. 439)*

One reason for the difference was the inclusion of so-called "off-budget" items in the budget totals. These programs, which added to the federal debt, included a number of federal loan and other programs that traditionally had not been included in overall budget spending figures, often for political reasons.

The administration proposed to include these items in the fiscal 1986 budget to portray a more accurate picture of federal activities. Their inclusion increased the projected deficit $12.5 billion in fiscal 1985 and $1.5 billion in fiscal 1986, but reduced the deficit projection by $3.2 billion in fiscal 1987 and $4.3 billion in fiscal 1988.

The reductions resulted from the administration's effort to cut back on many off-budget programs, including elimination of many Federal Financing Bank loan programs and a freeze on funding for the Strategic Petroleum Reserve.

At the Feb. 4 briefing, Stockman said that the difference between the budget's fiscal 1985 estimate and those made the previous year also resulted from the unexpected, one-time purchase of $13 billion in outstanding housing securities mandated by the Deficit Reduction Act of 1984 (PL 98-369).

Another $11.2 billion of the difference was attributed to changes due to economic assumptions. Inflation was slightly lower and interest rates slightly higher than had been expected, generally reducing anticipated receipts.

The budget also made a fiscal 1985 supplemental request of $5.8 billion in budget authority, excluding increased costs for federal employee pay. The largest supplemental request — $3.5 billion — was for adjustments in anticipated Social Security payments for retirees with pre-1957 military service. The fiscal 1985 pay supplemental request was $2.5 billion.

Economic Prognosis

Despite the prospects for continued high deficits, the administration remained optimistic about the economic outlook.

Citing a continued strong recovery from the 1981-82 recession, the budget projected low inflation, sustained growth, a slight decline in unemployment and a gradual drop in interest rates throughout the decade.

The budget forecast a continuation of economic growth at a steady pace, contingent upon the Federal Reserve Board's continuing a policy of expanding the money supply without allowing it to become "so rapid as to reignite inflationary expectations."

For GNP, the nation's total output of goods and services, it envisioned 3.9 percent, inflation-adjusted average growth in 1985 and 4 percent in 1986. The Consumer Price Index (CPI) was expected to rise slightly from a 4.1 percent rate in 1985 to 4.3 percent in 1986. Inflation as measured by the GNP price deflator, a broader measure of price changes, was expected to be 3.8 percent in 1985 and 4.4 percent in 1986.

Unemployment was expected to drop slightly from 7 percent in 1985 to 6.9 percent in 1986, and interest rates for three-month Treasury bills were expected to drop from an average of 8.1 percent in 1985 to 7.9 percent in 1986.

Revenues and Outlays

As a Percentage of Gross National Product, 1981-1990

	1981	1986 *	1990 *
Revenue	20.8%	18.9%	19.5%
Outlays			
Defense	5.5	6.8	7.5
Domestic	15.6	13.0	11.0
Net Interest	2.4	3.4	2.4
Outlays Total	23.5	23.2	20.9

* *Estimates*

SOURCE: Office of Management and Budget

Over the long range — through 1990 — the administration forecast continued expansion, assuming enactment of its budget.

The budget forecast inflation-adjusted GNP growth of 4 percent in 1987 and 1988, dropping to 3.6 percent by 1990. It said this lower rate was consistent with projections of a drop in the rate of unemployment to 5.8 percent by 1990.

Interest rates were also expected to decline rapidly to 5 percent for three-month Treasury bills, and the CPI increase was expected to drop to 3.3 percent by 1990.

The budget document played down the impact of record-high deficits on the economy. It claimed that, partly because of an inflow of foreign savings into the United States, government borrowing required to finance the deficit had not greatly reduced the credit available to private investors. But, it warned, the "long-term prospect of continued healthy growth" in capital investment is threatened unless measures are taken to reduce federal deficits.

The document also briefly noted the rising federal trade deficit — which reached an unprecedented $123.3 billion in 1984 — and the expectation that the United States would become a net debtor nation sometime during 1985.

If foreigners cut their purchase of U.S. assets while the federal government continued to run such large deficits, it cautioned, "there could be a rise in interest rates and slower overall economic growth."

On Feb. 6, the CBO released its version of the economic and general budgetary outlook for fiscal years 1986-90.

The office projected that if no actions were taken by Congress, the fiscal 1986 deficit would be $215 billion, rising to $296 billion by fiscal 1990, given existing policies. These figures were approximately $84 billion higher over the five-year period than those projected in the administration's so-called "current services" budget.

The administration was required by the 1974 Budget and Impoundment Control Act (PL 93-344) to estimate outlays and budget authority that would be required to maintain services at current fiscal year levels with no changes in policy. The figures provided a "baseline" against which proposed changes could be compared. *(1974*

The Reagan Budget-Cutting Program

Following are the programs and agencies recommended for cuts or elimination in the Reagan administration's budget for fiscal year 1986 and the spending reductions that would result through fiscal 1988 if Congress accepted each of the president's recommendations. The "savings" are estimated against current services spending, the existing rate of funding for programs, adjusted for inflation.

(Outlays, in millions of dollars)

	1986	1987	1988
I. MAJOR FREEZES AND PROGRAM REFORMS			
Limit on Federal Medicaid Cost Growth	−$1,000	−$2,091	−$3,202
Medicare Savings	−4,063	−6,265	−8,225
Reform Education Department Student Aid	−736	−1,530	−1,698
Reform VA-Medical Care	−361	−902	−1,207
Reform of Child Nutrition Subsidies	−648	−906	−1,007
Reduce Farm Price Supports and Related Subsidies	−2,041	−6,136	−7,900
Power Marketing: Repayment Reform	−988	−912	−907
Agricultural Credit Programs	−2,977	−3,402	−3,679
Moratorium on Strategic Petroleum Reserve	−1,650	−1,758	−1,770
Housing Moratorium and Reform	−3,569	−4,793	−5,486
Civil Service Retirement and Disability Reform	−731	−1,393	−1,978
Postal Service Subsidy Reform	−981	−942	−895
Rural Electric and Telephone Reforms	−176	−580	−1,045
Total Freezes and Reforms	−19,921	−31,610	−38,999
II. MAJOR PROGRAM ELIMINATIONS			
Terminate the Job Corps	−96	−566	−671
Terminate Health Professions Training Subsidy	−49	−227	−236
Rural Development Program Terminations	−55	−251	−413
Eliminate General Revenue Sharing	−3,405	−4,567	−4,567
Terminate Amtrak Subsidies	−574	−807	−840
Terminate Funding for Appalachian Regional Commission	−96	−197	−316
Terminate Urban Development Action Grants	−22	−111	−226
Abolish Small Business Administration	−1,467	−1,904	−1,930
Reduce Urban Mass Transit Assistance	−768	−1,339	−2,127
Terminate Air Carrier Subsidies	−53	−56	−58
Eliminate Direct Loans for Export-Import Bank	−393	−1,409	2,072
Total Program Eliminations	−6,978	−11,434	−13,456
III. USER FEES			
Increase Single Employee Pension Premium	−185	−208	−233
Corps of Engineers Navigation User Fees	−403	−622	−641
Recreation User Fees	−87	−89	−92
Meat and Poultry Inspection User Fees	−136	−253	−372
Increase Coast Guard User Fees	−236	−476	−476
Agency User Fees	−60	−213	−304
Federal Credit Program User Fees	−1,207	−1,324	−1,437
Total User Fees	−2,314	−3,185	−3,555
IV. OTHER PROGRAM SAVINGS			
Reform Welfare Administration Financing	−140	−154	−148
AFDC Reforms	−175	−145	−152
Conservation and Watershed Programs	−184	−581	−647
Phase out EPA Sewage Treatment Grants	—	−30	−160
10% Reduction in Agency Administrative Costs	−584	−620	−641
10% Legislative Branch Cut	−171	−179	−189
Privatize Federal Crop Insurance	−189	−262	−339
Land Management and Forest Service Receipts	−401	−406	−419
Other Program Reductions	−7,781	−15,575	−20,949
Total Other Program Savings	−9,625	−17,952	−23,644
V. DEFENSE AND NET INTEREST	−11,956	−18,481	−25,664
VI. TOTAL BUDGET SAVINGS	**−$50,794**	**−$82,662**	**−$105,318**

SOURCE: Office of Management and Budget

Almanac p. 145)

One reason for the difference between the CBO and OMB figures was the baseline used for expected defense spending, which was difficult to calculate because of the long lag time between the time funds were appropriated and the time they were spent.

The administration based its projections on figures used in its August 1984 mid-session review of the budget, which included estimates for what it called an "adequate defense." CBO based its figures on the lower level of defense spending called for in the fiscal 1985 budget resolution adopted by Congress in October 1984. *(Budget resolution, 1984 Almanac p. 155)*

The difference in deficit estimates between OMB and CBO was also explained by variations in economic assumptions. The CBO economic projections assumed no change in current policies, while OMB's figures assumed enactment of the president's budget.

For 1986, CBO predicted lower inflation-adjusted growth and higher inflation and interest rates than did OMB. CBO projected 3.2 percent GNP growth, after adjusting for inflation, a 4.6 percent inflation rate as measured by the GNP deflator and an 8.7 percent interest rate on three-month Treasury bills.

While CBO's projections for growth and inflation were similar to OMB's in the long run, CBO did not foresee the drop in interest rates envisioned by OMB. CBO said three-month Treasury bills would pay 8.2 percent in 1990, compared with the 5 percent rate projected by OMB.

In testimony before the Senate Budget Committee Feb. 6, CBO Director Rudolph G. Penner warned that the projections involved "considerable uncertainty." He said that if economic conditions proved better, the projected current services deficit could drop to $126 billion by 1990. But, he warned, under more pessimistic assumptions the deficit could balloon to $425 billion by the end of the decade.

Program Highlights

National Defense

Reagan requested a 5.9 percent inflation-adjusted increase in Pentagon spending authority, arguing for a continued strengthening of defense.

The Department of Defense requested budget authority of $313.7 billion for fiscal 1986, with anticipated outlays of $277.5 billion, 8.3 percent larger than projected defense outlays in fiscal 1985.

Total spending authority for national security, which included defense-related nuclear activities of the Energy Department, would have been $322.2 billion, with corresponding outlays of $285.7 billion.

The Pentagon request would have upgraded U.S. units across the board with an emphasis on modernizing the nuclear arsenal. Procurement of weapons and other equipment was the largest component: $106.8 billion, an inflation-adjusted increase of 5.1 percent over the fiscal 1985 appropriation.

The $73.4 billion requested for the 2.2 million active-duty military personnel included funds to expand the force by about 26,000 members, mostly for the Navy and the Air Force.

Taxes

As Reagan promised in his re-election campaign, he asked for no new taxes. However, he did request a number of new user fees in his budget and asked for enactment of several special tax breaks that Congress failed to enact in previous years.

These included tuition tax credits for parents who send their children to private schools and tax breaks for business investment in economically distressed areas, called "enterprise zones."

At the same time, the president reiterated his pledge, also made in his State of the Union address, to submit a revenue-neutral tax "simplification" proposal to Congress later in the year.

The changes were expected to raise anticipated receipts $200 million to $793.7 billion in fiscal 1986 and reduce them $1 billion in fiscal 1987 and $700 million in fiscal 1988.

International Affairs

The administration requested $15.3 billion in spending authority for foreign military, economic and development aid, $800 million below the fiscal 1985 level.

However, the fiscal 1986 figures were deceiving. They did not include anticipated economic aid for Israel, which was expected to exceed $1.2 billion in 1986.

Israel, Egypt and Turkey would have been the prime beneficiaries of an $865 million increase in the proposed budget for foreign military aid. The biggest single increase — $400 million — would have gone to Israel.

While requesting $1.3 billion in budget authority to honor current pledges to the World Bank and other international institutions that aided developing nations, the budget contained no estimates of new donations to be made when existing international agreements expired.

The administration also proposed to end the $3.8 billion direct loan program of the 50-year-old Export-Import Bank, which helped boost overseas purchases of U.S. exports.

Housing

The president proposed a two-year moratorium on new housing assistance, reducing requested budget authority for housing programs from $10 billion in fiscal 1985 to $499 million.

Reagan's budget for the Department of Housing and Urban Development also called for the elimination of Urban Development Action Grants, which provided matching funds to states and local governments to stimulate economic development in distressed inner-city areas.

The budget requested an increase in the up-front borrower's fee for Federal Housing Administration-insured loans, from 3.8 percent to 5 percent, and asked that the premium for loans insured by the Veterans Administration increase from 1 percent to 5 percent.

Energy

The administration proposed a 36 percent cut in civilian energy programs, while the portion of the Department of Energy (DOE) budget related to nuclear weapons was to rise to nearly two-thirds of the departmental budget.

The total DOE budget request was $1.8 billion less than the fiscal 1985 level of $14.3 billion.

Declaring that market conditions reduced the need for a large petroleum stockpile, the administration proposed that no additions be made to the Strategic Petroleum Reserve. Such a moratorium on filling the reserve would have left it at less than two-thirds of the 750 million-barrel

Budget Authority and Outlays by Agency

(in billions of dollars†)

DEPARTMENT OR OTHER UNIT	BUDGET AUTHORITY 1984 actual	BUDGET AUTHORITY 1985 estimate	BUDGET AUTHORITY 1986 estimate	OUTLAYS 1984 actual	OUTLAYS 1985 estimate	OUTLAYS 1986 estimate
Legislative branch[1]	$ 1.8	$ 1.8	$ 1.7	$ 1.6	$ 1.8	$ 1.8
The Judiciary	.9	1.1	1.2	.9	1.0	1.1
Executive Office of the President	.1	.1	.1	.1	.1	.1
Funds appropriated to the president	15.6	14.2	13.4	8.5	11.1	12.1
Agriculture	31.2	42.7	36.9	37.5	45.1	38.5
Commerce[2]	2.0	1.9	1.8	1.9	2.1	2.0
Defense — Military[3]	258.2	284.7	313.7	220.8	246.3	277.5
Defense — Civil	19.2	30.0	32.6	19.5	19.0	20.3
Education	15.4	18.4	15.5	15.5	17.4	16.9
Energy	10.5	11.4	9.7	10.6	11.0	9.3
Health and Human Services	299.4	331.2	348.9	292.3	318.5	330.3
Housing and Urban Development	17.9	31.0	7.0	16.5	28.9	15.4
Interior	4.9	4.8	3.8	4.9	5.0	4.4
Justice	3.5	3.8	3.9	3.2	3.9	4.0
Labor	34.8	27.3	27.3	24.5	23.5	22.8
State	3.0	3.5	3.7	2.4	2.7	3.3
Transportation	28.6	28.5	24.7	23.9	26.2	25.1
Treasury[2]	161.9	185.1	184.3	148.3	176.7	181.0
Environmental Protection Agency	4.1	4.3	4.6	4.1	4.4	4.6
General Services Administration	.3	.2	.2	.2	.4	.1
National Aeronautics and Space Administration	7.3	7.5	7.9	7.0	7.3	7.8
Office of Personnel Management	37.7	40.7	42.7	22.6	23.6	24.8
Small Business Administration[2]	.6	.7	.1	.3	.7	.1
Veterans Administration	26.5	27.2	27.1	25.6	26.8	26.7
Other Agencies[4]	16.7	19.1	14.8	11.3	12.3	10.8
Allowances[5]	—	1.5	*	—	1.1	.4
Undistributed Offsetting Receipts:						
Interest received by trust funds	−20.4	−25.6	−29.1	−20.4	−25.6	−29.1
Interest received from Outer Continental Shelf escrow account	−*	—	−1.0	−*	—	−1.0
Employer share, employee retirement	−25.3	−27.0	−29.0	−25.3	−27.0	−29.0
Rents and royalties on the Outer Continental Shelf	−6.7	−5.3	−7.3	−6.7	−5.3	−7.3
Sale of Conrail	—	—	−1.2	—	—	−1.2
Total undistributed offsetting receipts	−52.3	−57.9	−67.6	−52.3	−57.9	−67.6
Total budget authority and outlays	**$949.8**	**$1,064.9**	**$1,060.0**	**$851.8**	**$959.1**	**$973.7**

† *Figures may not add to totals due to rounding.*
* *Less than $50 million.*
[1] *Includes allowances for 10 percent reduction beginning in 1986 (Executive recommendation).*
[2] *Reflects proposed abolition of the Small Business Administration on Dec. 31, 1985, and the transfer of activities to the Departments of Commerce and Treasury.*
[3] *Includes allowances for civilian and military pay raises for Department of Defense.*
[4] *For all years includes amounts for the National Archives and Records Administration for activities formerly included in the General Services Administration.*
[5] *Includes allowances for civilian agency pay raises, military pay raises for the Coast Guard, and contingencies.*
NOTE: Beginning in 1985, the budget reflects establishment of a military retirement trust fund. Amounts for 1984 are shown on a comparable basis.

SOURCE: Fiscal 1986 Budget

goal established by Congress.

Changes in the way federal hydropower projects repaid their debt would have increased revenues by $1 billion but raised electric rates for many consumers.

The administration also proposed to reduce federal funding for research and development for fossil fuels, conservation, solar energy and other renewable energy resources.

Transportation

The president asked for $3.8 billion less for the Department of Transportation than was available in fiscal 1985. The budget would have eliminated subsidies to Amtrak, which received a $684 million appropriation in fiscal 1985 that accounted for 42 percent of the passenger railroad's revenues.

The budget also would have eliminated all operating assistance to mass transit systems, and would have allowed no contracts for new mass transit systems.

The budget would have ended subsidies for air service to small communities and institute "user fees" for boating services provided by the Coast Guard.

Obligations from the Highway Trust Fund would have been held at the fiscal 1985 level of $13.2 billion.

Education

The administration proposed a $15.5 billion budget for the Education Department — some $2.4 billion less than appropriated for fiscal 1985.

The budget called for a dramatic overhaul of aid to college students, sharply reducing subsidies to middle-income students and those attending expensive private colleges. The administration wanted to set a $4,000 annual cap on the total amount of federal aid a student could receive and bar students from receiving low-interest college loans if family income was more than $32,500 a year.

For other forms of student aid, including grants and work-study subsidies, the annual income eligibility cutoff would have been $25,000.

Spending for higher education programs would have been cut by more than 20 percent, but the budget would have frozen spending at fiscal 1985 levels for major elementary and secondary education programs, including aid for school children who were disadvantaged or handicapped.

Jobs

The Labor Department proposed spending $22.8 billion in fiscal 1986 — down from $23.5 billion in 1985. The drop reflected, in part, an anticipated decline in outlays for unemployment insurance.

For the first time, Reagan proposed shifting to the states the full responsibility for administering state unemployment insurance and employment services.

The president again asked Congress to lower the mimimum wage for teenagers in summer months. He also proposed to cut spending for a program providing summer jobs for youths and to abolish the popular Job Corps for disadvantaged teenagers.

The administration requested $2.8 billion in budget authority for the Job Training Partnership Act, down from $3.7 billion appropriated in 1985.

Human Services

Having weathered heavy budget cuts in the early years of the Reagan administration, many programs for low-income people would have been frozen at fiscal 1985 levels. Among those included in the proposed spending freeze were energy aid for the poor and the Head Start preschool program.

While the administration proposed eliminating the 1986 cost-of-living adjustment for many programs, it would have exempted Social Security payments and benefits to low-income elderly, blind and disabled people under Supplemental Security Income.

It also proposed stronger work requirements for recipients of Aid to Families with Dependent Children, the major federal-state welfare program, and would have denied welfare eligibility to single minor parents who were not living with their parents. The administration resurrected its proposal to eliminate the Community Services Block Grant.

The $11.8 billion in anticipated outlays for food stamps assumed $56 million in savings from requiring able program participants to work.

The budget assumed that spending for child nutrition programs — school lunches and breakfasts, day-care meals — would drop $400 million, to $3.4 billion in fiscal 1986. It proposed ending federal meal subsidies for students from families with incomes above 185 percent of the federal poverty level and canceling a COLA scheduled for 1986.

Agriculture

Some $6.6 billion or 15 percent would have been sliced from Agriculture Department programs in fiscal 1986, with the bulk of the spending reductions coming from farm-related programs.

The budget did not reveal specifics of the administration's ambitious plan to restructure basic price support and related farm programs; however, projections of spending after fiscal 1986 assumed enactment of the plan, with a $3 billion to $5 billion reduction in annual farm program spending levels by 1990, compared with the fiscal 1985 level of $15 billion. *(Farm bill, story, p. 517)*

Also, new user fees would have been charged for such items as federally guaranteed loans to farmers, federally guaranteed loans to foreign buyers of U.S. farm goods, market information services and federal regulation of meat and poultry industries.

Health

To throttle spending in Medicare, the administration wanted a yearlong extension of the physician-fee freeze enacted in 1984 and no increase in the hospital payments set by the new flat-fee system, authorized in 1983. *(1984 Almanac p. 480; 1983 Almanac p. 391)*

These changes in the national health care program for the elderly and disabled, plus increases in out-of-pocket payments by beneficiaries and other money-saving proposals, would have saved $4.2 billion in fiscal 1986 outlays, holding total program expenditures to $73.3 billion.

For Medicaid, the federal-state health program for the poor, the budget revived an altered version of a cap on program spending that Congress flatly rejected in 1981. In fiscal 1986 a $22.2 billion ceiling would have been imposed on federal Medicaid outlays, representing a $1.3 billion reduction from existing spending levels, according to the Department of Health and Human Services. *(1981 Almanac p. 477)*

A one-time "hardship" fund of $300 million would have been available to help states that needed extra money. Starting in 1986, the federal share of program costs would have been allowed to grow at the same rate as increases in health care costs as measured by the medical component of

Reagan Administration Economic Assumptions

(Calendar years; dollar amounts in billions)

	Actual 1983	FORECAST 1984[1]	1985	1986	ASSUMPTIONS 1987	1988	1989	1990
Major Economic Indicators:								
Gross national product (percent change, fourth quarter over fourth quarter):								
Current dollars	10.4	9.3	8.5	8.5	8.3	7.9	7.4	6.9
Constant (1972) dollars	6.3	5.6	4.0	4.0	4.0	4.0	3.8	3.6
GNP deflator (percent change, fourth quarter over fourth quarter)	3.8	3.5	4.3	4.3	4.1	3.8	3.5	3.2
Consumer Price Index (percent change, fourth quarter over fourth quarter)[2]	2.9	3.6	4.2	4.3	4.1	3.8	3.5	3.2
Unemployment rate (percent, fourth quarter)[3]	8.4	7.1	6.9	6.8	6.5	6.2	6.0	5.7
Annual Economic Assumptions:								
Gross national product:								
Current dollars:								
Amount	3,305	3,661	3,948	4,285	4,642	5,017	5,399	5,780
Percent change, year over year	7.7	10.8	7.8	8.5	8.3	8.1	7.6	7.1
Constant (1972) dollars:								
Amount	1,535	1,639	1,702	1,771	1,841	1,915	1,989	2,061
Percent change, year over year	3.7	6.8	3.9	4.0	4.0	4.0	3.9	3.6
Incomes:								
Personal income	2,744	3,013	3,241	3,483	3,747	4,019	4,312	4,596
Wages and salaries	1,659	1,804	1,921	2,065	2,237	2,425	2,624	2,824
Corporate profits before tax	203	234	242	286	336	360	377	396
Price level:								
GNP deflator:								
Level (1972 = 100), annual average	215.3	223.4	231.9	242.0	252.1	262.0	271.4	280.4
Percent change, year over year	3.8	3.7	3.8	4.4	4.2	3.9	3.6	3.3
Consumer Price Index:[2]								
Level (1967 = 100), annual average	297.4	307.6	320.2	334.2	348.1	361.7	374.8	387.2
Percent change, year over year	3.0	3.4	4.1	4.3	4.2	3.9	3.6	3.3
Unemployment rates:								
Total, annual average[3]	9.5	7.4	7.0	6.9	6.6	6.3	6.1	5.8
Insured, annual average[4]	3.9	2.8	2.8	2.8	2.6	2.5	2.3	2.2
Federal pay raise, January (percent):								
Military[5]	—	4.0	4.0	5.2	5.4	5.3	5.0	NA
Civilian	—	4.0	3.5	−5.0	3.0	3.0	3.0	3.0
Interest rate, 91-day Treasury bills (percent)[6]	8.6	9.6	8.1	7.9	7.2	5.9	5.1	5.0
Interest rate, 10-year Treasury notes (percent)	11.1	12.4	11.0	10.3	9.3	7.3	5.7	5.5

[1] *Preliminary actual data.*

[2] *CPI for urban wage earners and clerical workers. Two versions of the CPI are now published. The index shown here is that currently used, as required by law, in calculating automatic cost-of-living increases for indexed federal programs. The manner in which this index measures housing costs changed significantly in January.*

[3] *Percent of total labor force, including armed forces residing in the United States.*

[4] *This indicator measures unemployment under state regular unemployment insurance as a percentage of covered employment under that program. It does not include recipients of extended benefits under that program.*

[5] *A 3.0% military pay raise is projected for July 1985. The 1986 military pay raise is projected for October.*

[6] *Average rate on new issues within period, on a bank discount basis. These projections assume, by convention, that interest rates decline with the rate of inflation. They do not represent a forecast of interest rates.*

SOURCE: Fiscal 1986 Budget

the Consumer Price Index.

As a result, states would have been required to come up with extra money to the extent that program costs outstripped that index, but they would have been given more latitude to adjust such factors as benefits, eligibility and matching rates in order to hold down increases.

Environment

Reagan's fiscal 1986 request for environment and natural resources left the Environmental Protection Agency (EPA) almost unscathed, but chopped some 15 percent from Interior Department programs.

The biggest part of the EPA's $4.67 billion budget was $2.4 billion — the same as in fiscal 1985 — for grants to local governments for building sewage plants. That merely put off until fiscal 1987 the bad news for cities and counties: Reagan planned to phase out the grants altogether by 1990.

The budget also gave the first public glimpse of the proposal on the "superfund" hazardous waste cleanup program Reagan was expected to send to Congress. He asked for $900 million in fiscal 1986, pointing toward a $5.5 billion effort for 1986-90, according to OMB. *(Story, p. 191)*

The biggest cuts at the Department of the Interior included a three-year moratorium on land acquisition for the National Park System and National Wildlife Refuge System, as well as on federal grants to states for their acquisition programs. The budget also would have cut funds for construction of Western water projects.

Also included were two new user-fee proposals. One would have raised entrance or camping fees for national parks and wildlife refuges. The other would have set grazing fees closer to market value.

R&D, Space

The administration proposed a $59.7 billion budget for research and development in fiscal 1986. Of that amount, the Defense Department would have received $39.4 billion.

In the Pentagon's share, $3.7 billion would have been used for the strategic defense initiative, the administration's plan for a space-based shield against nuclear weapons. Another $282 million was earmarked for the project in the Department of Energy's budget.

The budget requested $7.9 billion for the National Aeronautics and Space Administration, including funds for continued research and development spending for a permanent manned space station. The amount was only slightly above fiscal 1985 levels.

Hopes expressed in the fiscal 1985 budget that the station would be in operation by 1992 were diminished, however. Because of a proposed slowdown in spending for the space station, it was not expected to be operational until 1993 or 1994.

Federal Employees

Federal civilian workers would have received a 5 percent pay cut under the budget, the first proposed pay reduction since the Great Depression.

The cut was expected to save $1.3 billion in outlays and $3.4 billion in budget authority in fiscal 1986.

Proposed changes in the civil service retirement system were expected to save $1.4 billion in fiscal 1986 and $4.8 billion over three years. Along with other changes, the budget would have frozen the cost-of-living allowance for retirees for one year, and then reduced the COLA in future years. It also would have increased the contribution the Postal Service and the District of Columbia made to their retirement systems.

Veterans

The budget for the Veterans Administration would have increased slightly, to $27.1 billion. However, the president proposed restricting eligibility for free medical care for veterans over 65, in hope of producing significant savings over the next few years.

The budget granted a 4.1 percent COLA for veterans receiving compensation for service-connected disabilities, effective Dec. 1. Veterans receiving pensions also would have received a 4.1 percent COLA.

The budget also asked that third-party insurers reimburse the Veterans Administration for medical care and treatment for veterans without service-connected disabilities, for an anticipated savings of approximately $65 million in fiscal 1986.

Legislative

By law, budget estimates submitted by the legislative branch were included in the president's budget without change. For 1986, however, Reagan recommended a 10

1985 Deficit Near $212 Billion

The Office of Management and Budget (OMB) and Treasury Department jointly determined that the federal budget deficit was $211.9 billion in fiscal 1985, which ended Sept. 30, 1985.

The deficit total included spending for several so-called off-budget items, among them the Federal Financing Bank, which made loans to certain federal agencies, the Strategic Petroleum Reserve, the Postal Service and the Rural Electrification Administration. Not counting such off-budget spending, OMB and Treasury reported the fiscal 1985 deficit was $202.8 billion.

Previously, the largest federal deficit was in fiscal 1983: $207.8 billion including off-budget spending, and $195.4 billion not including such spending.

The fiscal 1985 figure, though a record, was considerably lower than the $222.2 billion that had been projected in February as part of President Reagan's fiscal 1986 budget request. It was significantly higher, however, than projected in Reagan's fiscal 1985 budget request in February 1984. *(1984 Almanac p. 129)*

OMB's final figures for revenues, outlays and deficits for fiscal years 1984-85 and those projected for fiscal 1986 were *(in billions of dollars)*:

	Actual FY 1984 [1]	Budget FY 1985 [2]	Actual FY 1985 [1]
Budget Receipts	$666.5	$745.1	$734.0
Budget Outlays	841.8	925.5	936.8
Budget Deficit	175.3	180.4	202.8
Off-Budget Deficit	10.0	14.8	9.1
Total Deficit	**$185.3**	**$195.2**	**$211.9**

SOURCES: [1] Final Monthly Treasury Statement for Fiscal 1985; [2] President's Fiscal 1985 Budget Request; [3] OMB Mid-Session Review of the Fiscal 1985 Budget.

Presidents, Congress and the Budget, 1980-86

(in billions of dollars)

	Budget Authority	Outlays	Revenues	Deficit
Fiscal Year 1980				
Carter Budget	615.5	531.6	502.6	−29.0
First Resolution	604.4	532.0	509.0	−23.0
Second Resolution	638.0	547.6	517.8	−29.8
Revised Second Resolution	658.9	572.65	525.7	−46.95
Actual	658.8	576.7	517.1	−59.6
Fiscal Year 1981				
Carter Budget	696.1	615.8	600.0	−15.8
Carter Revisions	691.3	611.5	628.0	+16.5
First Resolution	697.2	613.6	613.8	+ 0.2
Second Resolution	694.6	632.4	605.0	−27.4
Revised Second Resolution	717.5	661.35	603.3	−58.05
Actual	718.4	657.2	599.3	−57.9
Fiscal Year 1982				
Carter Budget	809.8	739.3	711.8	−27.5
Reagan Revision	772.4	695.3	650.3	−45.0
First Resolution[1]	770.9	695.45	657.8	−37.65
Revised Second Resolution	777.67	734.10	628.4	−105.7
Actual	779.9	728.4	617.8	−110.6
Fiscal Year 1983				
Reagan Budget	801.9	757.6	666.1	−91.5
First Resolution[2]	822.39	769.82	665.9	−103.92
Revised Resolution	877.2	807.4	604.3	−203.1
	883.36	812.85		−208.55
Actual	866.7	795.97	600.56	−195.4
Fiscal Year 1984				
Reagan Budget	900.1	848.5	659.7	−188.8
First Resolution[2]	919.5	849.5	679.6	−169.9
	928.73	858.93		−179.33
Revised Resolution	918.9	845.6	672.9	−172.7
Actual	927.4	841.8	666.5	−175.36
Fiscal Year 1985				
Reagan Budget	1,006.5	925.5	745.1	−180.4
First Resolution[2]	1,021.35	932.05	750.9	−181.15
Revised Resolution†	1,062.1	946.3	736.5	−209.8
Actual†	NA	945.9	734.0	−211.9
Fiscal Year 1986				
Reagan Budget†	1,252.9	1,094.8	950.4	−144.4
First Resolution[2]†	1,069.7	967.6	795.7	−171.9

[1] *Second resolution merely reaffirmed figures in first resolution.*
[2] *First resolution became binding at beginning of fiscal year Oct. 1.*
* *Larger figure assumed enactment of 10 programs included in a special $8.5 billion reserve fund.*
† *Includes some items previously excluded from budget totals.*

Sources: Federal budget documents, congressional budget resolutions

percent across-the-board cut in the legislative branch's request. This would have lowered the fiscal 1986 budget authority for the House, Senate and related agencies from $1.9 billion to $1.7 billion.

Law Enforcement

The proposed budget for law enforcement remained about the same as the fiscal 1985 level, although overall spending for the administration of justice — by the Justice Department and a handful of other agencies engaged in law enforcement — was proposed to be up slightly from fiscal 1985.

As in previous years, the president did not request any money for the Legal Services Corporation, which provided legal representation for the poor in civil cases. However, the agency submitted its budget directly to Congress, requesting $305 million.

Other

The budget proposed to eliminate the loan programs of the Small Business Administration, and transfer the remaining functions, such as advocacy, minority small business development and procurement assistance, to the Department of Commerce. Outlays for the agency would have been cut from $1.4 billion in fiscal 1985 to $689 million in fiscal 1986.

The budget also proposed elimination of general revenue sharing, a $4.6 billion program that sent federal money to local governments to be used at their discretion. The program was scheduled to expire in fiscal 1986. ∎

Congress Cuts Budget by More Than $55 Billion

Congress on Aug. 1 adopted a fiscal 1986 budget that called for more cuts in the growth of federal programs than ever before, yet not enough to prevent massive future federal budget deficits.

Hours after House and Senate budget conferees agreed to the compromise fiscal 1986 budget resolution (S Con Res 32 — H Rept 99-249), the House approved it by a 309-119 vote. The Senate then adopted the measure by a 67-32 vote. *(House vote 264, p. 84-H; Senate vote 169, p. 34-S)*

Final passage of the budget culminated a difficult, seven-month struggle between the two chambers, between Republicans and Democrats, between members of the same party from opposite sides of Capitol Hill and between Congress and the president.

The budget resolution assumed that the federal government would spend $967.6 billion in fiscal 1986 while taking in $795.7 billion in revenues, leaving a deficit of $171.9 billion.

Those numbers reflected assumptions, not actually stated in the resolution itself, that Congress would make a number of money-saving changes in military and non-military programs, cutting the fiscal 1986 deficit to $55.5 billion less than what it would have been if no changes were made. For fiscal years 1986-88, the cuts would total about $277 billion, leaving a fiscal 1988 deficit of $113 billion. *(Table, this page)*

As a final sour note in the discord between the two chambers that developed during the protracted budget struggle, the House Budget Committee, calculating from a slightly different spending "baseline," issued marginally different estimates for the resolution, projecting the fiscal 1986 deficit reduction at $57.5 billion.

Meanwhile, Senate Democrats, who complained continually about both committees' use of optimistic, administration-generated economic assumptions, put out estimates based on gloomier Congressional Budget Office (CBO) forecasts of slower growth and higher inflation and interest rates in future years. *(Economic assumptions, p. 444)*

The Senate Democrats' estimates showed fiscal 1986 spending reductions of $39 billion — not $55 billion or $57 billion — and a fiscal 1988 deficit of $161 billion.

Senate Budget Committee Chairman Pete V. Domenici, R-N.M., angrily acknowledging in late July that the economic reality of slower growth had already undercut the optimistic assumptions on which the budget resolution was based, said, "The deficits will be recurring year in, year out, well beyond what we can afford or what our children can afford."

Deficits Fiscal 1986-1988

Estimates of revenues, expenditures and deficits, as contained in the first concurrent budget resolution (S Con Res 32) *(in billions of dollars)*:

	1986	1987	1988
Total Outlays	$967.6	$1,024.1	$1,073.0
Revenues	795.7	869.4	960.1
Deficit	−$171.9	−$ 154.7	−$ 112.9

SOURCE: Conference Report on S Con Res 32

Ultimately, concern over the failure of the budget process to lessen sufficiently the prospect for huge federal deficits led to enactment of a radical measure (H J Res 372 — PL 99-177) that mandated declining deficits over five years, and a balanced budget by the beginning of fiscal 1991. Failure by Congress and the president to meet the deficit targets in the new law was to trigger automatic across-the-board cuts to bring spending in line.

Referred to as Gramm-Rudman-Hollings for its three Senate sponsors — Republicans Phil Gramm of Texas and Warren B. Rudman of Hew Hampshire, and Democrat Ernest F. Hollings of South Carolina — the new budget law occupied much of Congress' time from the first of October until mid-December.

Partly as a result, a so-called reconciliation bill comprising many of the deficit-reducing cuts for fiscal 1986 assumed in the budget resolution failed to clear before Congress adjorned Dec. 20, casting doubt on the possibility of achieving the budget resolution's deficit targets. In fact, in January 1986, the CBO and the Office of Management and Budget (OMB) projected the fiscal 1986 deficit might top $220 billion. *(Gramm-Rudman-Hollings, p. 459; reconciliation, p. 498)*

Fight Began Early

The budget battle began even before the president's budget was released Feb. 4, with Majority Leader Robert

Dole, R-Kan., leading the charge to draft a Senate alternative budget that would be more acceptable in its deficit projections than what was anticipated from the White House. *(President's budget, p. 427)*

That effort stumbled, as did other attempts at compromise during the year, as sharp political disagreements prevented agreement, particularly on the key issues of Social Security and defense spending, and tax increases.

The fight continued long after the Senate on May 10 and the House on May 23 passed different resolutions, preventing a conference agreement for two months. House members considered the final version much closer to their more generous budget, and happily declared victory.

"When you take a look at the House and Senate positions, the Senate didn't come out very good," said Rep. Delbert L. Latta, R-Ohio, ranking minority member of the House Budget Committee.

Members of both parties agreed the budget did not make the sustained reductions in the deficit essential to the nation's economic health. But they also said that congressional budgeteers did the best they could, given political constraints that put most options for massive deficit reductions — notably tax increases and Social Security cuts — out of reach.

On July 29 President Reagan, through his spokesman Larry Speakes, had flatly rejected a Senate compromise proposal — the last in a series of unsuccessful efforts to take a bigger bite out of the deficit by combining moderate revenue increases with comparable reductions in Social Security.

Conferees met only sporadically after convening June 11, and made a few final decisions Aug. 1, but basically ratified a plan drafted in unusual private sessions the two preceding evenings by Domenici; the ranking Senate Budget Committee Democrat, Lawton Chiles, Fla.; House Budget Committee Chairman William H. Gray III, D-Pa.; and Latta.

Conferees agreed to the plan by voice vote, but Hollings, convinced that the resolution was wholly inadequate and telegraphing his role in the landmark Gramm-Rudman-Hollings measure, did not sign the conference agreement.

Adoption of the budget resolution also occurred within hours of the departure of budget director David A. Stockman, who had been an exceptionally forceful and effective advocate of deficit reduction, both with Congress and within the administration. *(Stockman resignation, p. 448)*

Reflecting Bitterness

In what it did not do, the budget negatively reflected the year's bitter political battles.

It included neither major tax increases nor reductions in Social Security cost-of-living adjustments (COLAs), despite the belief of such prominent leaders as Domenici, Chiles and Dole that both were essential for significant deficit reduction.

It also anticipated no growth in 1986 in defense spending, which received only an allowance to offset inflation.

Reagan's budget had requested 6 percent growth in defense beyond inflation, but strong bipartisan majorities in both chambers cut that, angered by reports of wasteful and fraudulent military spending practices, and the refusal of Defense Secretary Caspar W. Weinberger to compromise. *(Defense budget, p. 138; Pentagon procurement troubles, p. 164)*

The budget assumed that Congress would prune as much as 20 to 30 percent from a wide range of non-defense programs other than those assisting the poor. The poverty programs, for the most part, were to be allowed to grow enough to keep pace with inflation.

The budget further assumed that federal revenue sharing would expire at the end of fiscal 1986, but generally omitted outright cancellation of programs, such as Urban Development Action Grants and Export-Import Bank subsidized loans, that Reagan's February budget sought and that the Senate-passed version of the budget retained in modified form.

The budget resolution was, basically, a statement of congressional spending priorities and was not sent to the president for his signature, although its spending targets became binding Oct. 1. Other legislation — authorization, appropriations and reconciliation bills — was supposed to make changes needed to achieve the spending levels for different government functions that were the substance of the budget resolution. *(Spending totals by function, p. 446)*

Major Assumptions

The first concurrent resolution on the budget for fiscal 1986 (S Con Res 32), approved Aug. 1, set the following targets: budget authority, $1,069.7 billion; outlays, $967.6 billion; revenues, $795.7 billion; deficit, $171.9 billion.

The resolution also set preliminary targets for fiscal 1987 and 1988, but omitted appropriations "caps" for those two years that were part of the version passed in May by the Senate.

The Senate Budget Committee calculations assumed reductions of spending in fiscal 1986 of $55.5 billion; the House Budget Committee computed the fiscal 1986 deficit reduction at $57.5 billion. The two panels used slightly different spending baselines to calculate savings.

For fiscal years 1986-88, the resolution assumed spending reductions totaling $276 billion, of which $67.1 billion was to be cut through the so-called reconciliation process, in which laws governing programs were changed to achieve long-term savings. *(Reconciliation, p. 498)*

Following is a summary of major policy assumptions underlying the spending targets of S Con Res 32. These assumptions, not formally part of the budget resolution, were developed by the staffs of the Budget committees in the course of deciding on the spending targets in the resolution.

Savings (the "cuts in anticipated outlays" in the assumptions) or revenue increases were measured against one of two different baselines, one for non-defense programs and one for defense. The result of using the two baselines was that savings ascribed to changes in programs in the two categories were not comparable.

The non-defense baseline reflected spending levels required to maintain existing programs, after adjusting for inflation, if no changes in law were made. In some cases, such as Social Security, adjustments were made for expected increases in the number of beneficiaries.

The defense baseline reflected the so-called "Rose Garden" agreement of 1984, in which Reagan and GOP congressional leaders agreed upon defense increases of 7 percent to 8 percent annually, in addition to inflation. *(1984 Almanac p. 143)*

Defense

- Allowed no growth above inflation in 1986 defense

budget authority. In each of fiscal years 1987 and 1988, increased by 3 percent after adjusting for inflation.

Cuts in anticipated outlays: $27.5 billion in fiscal 1986; $137.3 billion in fiscal 1986-88. Outlays reflected both reductions in budget authority and slower rates of disbursement by the Department of Defense than previously estimated.

Reagan's budget had requested inflation-adjusted growth in defense authority of 5.9 percent in fiscal 1986, 8.2 percent in fiscal 1987 and 8.8 percent in fiscal 1988.

The fiscal 1986 ceiling was virtually the same as the level of the fiscal 1986 defense authorization bill (S 1160). *(Defense authorization, p. 138)*

International Affairs

• Froze the direct loan program of the Export-Import Bank at $1.8 billion in each of fiscal years 1986-88, a 55 percent reduction below the fiscal 1985 spending level. The resolution assumed a fiscal 1986 appropriation of $1.2 billion, but it allowed for an additional appropriation of up to $600 million for the loans. Cuts in anticipated outlays: $200 million in fiscal 1986; $1.7 billion in fiscal 1986-88.

The president's budget had requested that the direct loan program, which helped foreign customers purchase such costly U.S. exports as airplanes, be replaced with a $1.8 billion loan guarantee program, for savings of $2.1 billion in fiscal 1986-88.

• Funded a presidential request for a one-time appropriation in the current fiscal year for military aid to Egypt and Israel. *(Supplemental appropriations bill, p. 350)*

• Funded economic and military assistance programs at the level specified in the foreign aid appropriations bill (HR 3228) approved by the House Appropriations Committee. Cuts in anticipated outlays: $400 million in fiscal 1986; $2.8 billion in fiscal 1986-88. *(Foreign aid appropriations, p. 367)*

• Funded international programs in the fiscal 1986 Commerce, Justice and State departments appropriations bill at 97 percent of the level in HR 2068, the State Department authorization measure. No allowance for an anticipated presidential request to finance security improvements at U.S. embassies, but assumed already authorized increases for this purpose. Increases in anticipated outlays: $1.4 billion in fiscal 1986; $800 million in fiscal 1986-88. *(State Department authorization, p. 104)*

Science and Technology

• One-year overall freeze at fiscal 1985 level; funding increases to match inflation in fiscal years 1987 and 1988. Programs included the National Science Foundation, Department of Energy, general science programs and the National Aeronautics and Space Administration (NASA). Cuts in anticipated outlays: $100 million in fiscal 1986; $700 million in fiscal 1986-88.

Energy

• Continued filling the Strategic Petroleum Reserve, the nation's emergency fuel storehouse, at a rate of 35,000 barrels per day in fiscal years 1986-88. The existing fill rate was 159,000 barrels per day. Cuts in anticipated outlays: $1.4 billion in fiscal 1986; $4 billion in fiscal 1986-88. The Reagan budget would have imposed a moratorium on filling the reserve.

• Funded the low-income weatherization program to keep pace with the rate of inflation in fiscal 1986-88. No cuts in anticipated outlays.

• Funded other discretionary programs, such as energy research and development, at the fiscal 1985 level in fiscal 1986 and allowed to increase at half the inflation rate in fiscal 1987-88. Also reduced anticipated outlays by making changes in the uranium enrichment program, Rural Electrification Administration (REA) loans, Federal Energy Regulatory Commission fees and other energy supply programs. Cuts in anticipated outlays: $500 million in fiscal 1986; $2.6 billion in fiscal 1986-88. Reagan had requested increases in REA subsidized interest rates and a phase-out of the agency.

Natural Resources and Environment

• Funded the federal "superfund" hazardous-waste cleanup program at $7.5 billion in fiscal years 1986-90, and assumed sufficient additional superfund tax revenues to cover outlays. Increases in anticipated outlays: $300 million in fiscal 1986; $1.5 billion in fiscal 1986-88. *(Superfund, p. 191)*

• Reduced water resource, land management, recreational and other national resources programs; added $100 million to fiscal 1986 funding for the National Oceanic and Atmospheric Administration, a 9 percent increase; funded other discretionary programs at fiscal 1985 levels and allowed them to grow at half the rate of inflation in fiscal 1987-88. Cuts in anticipated outlays: $500 million in fiscal 1986; $2.9 billion in fiscal 1986-88.

Agriculture

• Revised crop subsidies and credit programs. Cuts in anticipated outlays: $2.1 billion in fiscal 1986; $11.9 billion in fiscal 1986-88.

• Funded certain farm programs, such as agricultural research, at fiscal 1985 levels in fiscal 1986 and allowed them to grow at half the rate of inflation in fiscal 1987-88. Cuts in anticipated outlays: $200 million in fiscal 1986; $700 million in fiscal 1986-88.

Commerce and Housing Credit

• Reduced Small Business Administration business assistance programs by unspecified across-the-board reductions. The resolution assumed enactment of a Senate proposal to sell Small Business Investment Company loans directly to investors and a House-passed amendment to the Commerce, State, Justice appropriations bill (HR 2965) that reduced Business Loan Investment Fund loans. Cuts in anticipated outlays: $400 million in fiscal 1986; $1.5 billion in fiscal 1986-88. *(Commerce appropriations bill, p. 346)*

• Reduced appropriations for postal rate subsidies. Also, assumed enactment of legislation to more narrowly target the subsidies. Cuts in anticipated outlays: $100 million in fiscal 1986; $500 million in fiscal 1986-88. Reagan's budget had requested postal subsidy cuts of $895 million over three years.

• Funded rural housing programs of the Farmers Home Administration (FmHA) at 40 percent below the fiscal 1985 level in fiscal 1986; increased funding to match inflation in fiscal 1987-88; assumed sale of FmHA mortgages. Cuts in anticipated outlays: $1.1 billion in fiscal 1986; $4.7 billion in fiscal 1986-88.

• Reduced funding for discretionary programs of the Commerce Department by less than $50 million in fiscal 1986, and allowed to grow at half the rate of inflation in fiscal years 1987-88. Cuts in anticipated outlays: $400 million in fiscal 1986-88.

Major Economic Assumptions
Calendar Years 1984-88

Following are the primary economic projections released Aug. 15, 1985, by the Congressional Budget Office (CBO) and those used by the Reagan administration in its February budget request. During budget deliberations, both the House and Senate followed the administration's projections, which also formed the basis for projections in the budget resolution (S Con Res 32) as adopted.

	1984 (Actual)	1985	1986	1987	1988
Inflation-adjusted Gross National Product (annual increase)					
CBO	6.8%	2.6%	3.6%	3.4%	3.5%
Administration	6.8%	3.9%	4.0%	4.0%	4.0%
Civilian unemployment					
CBO	7.5%	7.2%	7.0%	6.8%	6.6%
Administration	7.5%	7.1%	7.0%	6.7%	6.4%
Interest rates (based on 3-month Treasury bill)					
CBO	9.5%	7.6%	7.4%	7.2%	7.2%
Administration	9.5%	8.1%	7.9%	7.2%	5.9%
Inflation (based on GNP Deflator*)					
CBO	3.8%	3.9%	4.3%	4.3%	4.2%
Administration	3.8%	3.8%	4.4%	4.2%	3.9%

* The GNP deflator is considered a broader, more accurate measure of inflation than the Consumer Price Index because it takes into account modified buying patterns.

SOURCES: CBO, conference report on S Con Res 32

Transportation

• Set spending for mass transit programs, primarily urban mass transit subsidies, that were financed with general fund receipts at 15 percent below fiscal 1985 levels in fiscal 1986-88. Froze the mass transit trust fund, which was financed with gasoline tax receipts, at the fiscal 1985 level of $1.1 billion annually in fiscal 1986-88. Cuts in anticipated outlays: $100 million in fiscal 1986; $800 million in fiscal years 1986-88. Reagan's budget proposed to cut urban mass transit assistance by $2.1 billion in fiscal 1986-88.

• Retained subsidies for Amtrak passenger rail service, reducing them by 15 percent in fiscal 1986 and funding them at that reduced level in fiscal years 1987-88. Cuts in anticipated outlays: $100 million in fiscal 1986; $400 million in fiscal 1986-88. Reagan's budget had requested termination of the subsidies, for three-year savings of $840 million.

• Limited 1986 federal highway aid obligations to the 1985 level of $13.25 billion; limited obligations to $13.8 billion in fiscal 1987 and $14.4 billion in fiscal 1988. Cuts in anticipated outlays: $200 million in fiscal 1986; $2.1 billion in fiscal 1986-88.

• Established Coast Guard user fees on commercial mariners and recreational boaters for certain non-emergency services, exempting search and rescue missions from such fees. Cuts in anticipated outlays: $100 million in fiscal 1986; $300 million in fiscal 1986-88.

• Assumed sale of Conrail, the government-owned freight railroad, as requested by Reagan's budget. Cuts in anticipated outlays: $1.2 billion in fiscal 1986.

• Revised ship construction differential subsidies to allow repayment to the federal government of outstanding principal and interest on subsidy loans in return for the permanent right for certain tankers — prohibited from serving domestic routes — to serve those routes. Cuts in anticipated outlays: $200 million in fiscal 1986.

• Terminated the Local Rail Assistance Program, which helped communities maintain branch line rail service. Cuts in anticipated outlays: less than $50 million in fiscal 1986.

• Reduced funding for such other programs as the Federal Aviation Administration, the U.S. Coast Guard and other transportation programs, for cuts in anticipated outlays of $500 million in fiscal 1986; $2.3 billion in fiscal 1986-88.

Community and Regional Development

• Reduced community development block grants 15 percent below the baseline in fiscal 1986; funding increases to match inflation in fiscal years 1987-88. The grants were provided to states and cities to fund economic development and neighborhood revitalization. Cuts in anticipated outlays: less than $50 million in fiscal 1986; $700 million in fiscal 1986-88.

• Reduced Urban Development Action Grants 20 percent below the baseline in fiscal 1986; funding increases to match inflation in fiscal years 1987-88. The grants were designed to stimulate private investment in inner cities. Reagan's budget had requested termination of the grants, for three-year savings of $226 million. Also imposed a two-year moratorium on rental rehabilitation grants, as requested by the president. Continued the Rental Housing Development Grant program (HoDAG), which assisted local governments in financing construction of rental housing. Cuts in anticipated outlays: $100 million in fiscal 1986; $400 million in fiscal 1986-88.

• Terminated Small Business Administration loans for non-physical disasters and made farmers ineligible for SBA disaster loans. Cuts in anticipated outlays: $100 million in fiscal 1986; $1 billion in fiscal 1986-88.

• Reduced the Economic Development Administration (EDA) and Appalachian Regional Commission (ARC) 20 percent below baseline in fiscal 1986, frozen at that level in fiscal years 1987-88. The EDA provided grants and low-interest loans to support public works and economic development; the ARC funded public works, economic development and highway construction in the 13-state Appalachian region. Reagan's budget slated both for elimination. Cuts in anticipated outlays: less than $50 million in fiscal 1986; $100 million in fiscal 1986-88.

• Froze or reduced other programs in this function, including Indian programs, flood insurance and Tennessee Valley Development programs. Cuts in anticipated outlays: less than $50 million in fiscal 1986; $1.3 billion in fiscal 1986-88.

Education, Training, Employment, Social Services

• Reduced funding for Guaranteed Student Loans, primarily through administrative reforms. Cuts in anticipated outlays: $100 million in fiscal 1986; $800 million in fiscal 1986-88.

• Funded education, training and social services programs for low-income individuals at $300 million below the baseline in fiscal 1986, with reductions in funding for the programs not specified. Cuts in anticipated outlays: $300 million in fiscal 1986; $2 billion in fiscal 1986-88.

Health

• Reduced Medicaid spending by increasing collections from private health insurers of Medicaid beneficiaries, but collection efforts were not expected adversely to affect beneficiaries or states that made reasonable efforts in the collections. Cuts in anticipated outlays: $100 million in fiscal 1986; $450 million in fiscal 1986-88. Reagan had requested $3.2 billion in savings in Medicaid in fiscal years 1986-88.

• Reduced funding for discretionary health programs (other than low-income and public health programs such as community health centers, as designated in the House-passed resolution). Called for additional funding for immunizations and set the number of National Institutes of Health research grants at 6,000 (compared with the president's budget request of 5,000). Cuts in anticipated outlays: $200 million in fiscal 1986; $900 million in fiscal 1986-88.

• Transferred to the federal government a portion of the Federal Employees' Health Benefits reserve funds held by insurance companies, a change expected to reduce the government's premium payments. Cuts in anticipated outlays: $800 million in fiscal 1986; $1.1 billion in fiscal 1986-88.

Medicare

Total cuts in anticipated outlays for Medicare, the federal health care system for the elderly and disabled, were estimated at $2.5 billion in fiscal 1986 and $11 billion in fiscal 1986-88. Reagan's budget had requested $8.2 billion in cuts.

The resolution specified that the spending reductions were not to be made by reducing benefits to those enrolled in the program. The assumption underlying the resolution was that the savings would be achieved by freezes on payments to providers such as hospitals, and other program revisions. *(Medicare, p. 302)*

Income Security

Assumed full cost-of-living adjustments (COLAs), as under existing policy, for federal military and civilian retirement programs, railroad retirement programs and black lung benefits. The Senate-passed budget resolution had eliminated the 1986 COLA for the retirement programs.

• Reduced military retirement expenditures by permitting and promoting later retirements from the armed forces. Cuts in anticipated outlays: $100 million in fiscal 1986; $600 million in fiscal 1986-88.

• Increased premiums charged by the Pension Benefit Guaranty Corporation (PBGC), which insured private pension plans, to cover PBGC liabilities. Cuts in anticipated outlays: $300 million in fiscal 1986; $900 million in fiscal 1986-88.

• Funded subsidized housing at $9.8 billion, which would finance about 100,000 additional units, and reduced operating subsidies for public housing. Cuts in anticipated outlays: $100 million in fiscal 1986; $800 million in fiscal 1986-88.

• Assumed enactment of legislation to forgive debt service payments for certain public housing projects, no longer requiring the Department of Housing and Urban Development to repay loans that it had been forced to acquire as a result of the 1984 tax law (PL 98-369). The change meant a reduction from the baseline of $1.6 billion in fiscal 1986 and $4.7 billion in fiscal 1986-88. Because the savings from this change were to be offset by reductions in Treasury receipts, the savings did not reduce the deficit. *(1984 Almanac p. 143)*

• Eliminated direct federal loans to finance public housing construction and modernization. Cuts in anticipated outlays: $2.1 billion in fiscal 1986; $6.9 billion in fiscal 1986-88.

• Increased, by $400 million annually in fiscal years 1986-88, funds for food stamps, child nutrition, the women and infants' nutritional supplement program (WIC) and the special milk program. Spending was to be offset by savings in other programs in the income security category. Funded, as under existing law, with adjustments for inflation and beneficiary increases, programs for needy persons such as Aid to Families with Dependent Children and low-income energy assistance.

Social Security

• Assumed full COLAs for Social Security, as under existing policy. The Senate-passed budget resolution had eliminated the 1986 adjustment for Social Security. The resolution assumed that increased automation and improved management would cut less than $50 billion from outlays in fiscal 1986 and $400 million in fiscal years 1986-88.

Veterans' Programs

• Assumed full COLAs for Veterans' Administration compensation and pension payments, as under existing policy. The Senate-passed budget resolution had eliminated the 1986 COLA for these programs.

• Made unspecified changes in veterans' programs to reduce anticipated spending by $300 million in fiscal 1986 and by $1.2 billion in fiscal years 1986-88.

Administration of Justice

• Increased the number of customs agents and inspectors, at an annual additional cost of $50 million in fiscal years 1986-88; the additional staff was expected to increase tariff collections by $1.5 billion in fiscal years 1986-88, a gain reflected in revenue levels of the budget resolution.

• Funded other programs, including the Legal Services Corporation and juvenile justice, at levels to match inflation in fiscal years 1986-88.

General Government

• Imposed user fees for processing and commercial services provided by the U.S. Customs Service. Cuts in anticipated outlays: $500 million in fiscal 1986; $1.5 billion in fiscal 1986-88.

• Increased funding to improve processing and review of tax returns. Increases in anticipated outlays: less than $50 million in fiscal 1986; $100 million in fiscal 1986-88. The improvements were expected to increase revenue collections by $2 billion in fiscal years 1986-88.

• Reduced legislative branch funding below the baseline in fiscal 1986; increased funding for foreign aid to Micronesian islands (the Compact of Free Association); funded other programs at fiscal 1985 levels in fiscal 1986 and allowed to increase at half the rate of inflation in fiscal 1987-88. Cuts in anticipated outlays: $600 million in fiscal 1986-88. *(Compact of Free Association, p. 99)*

General Purpose Fiscal Assistance

• Funded general revenue sharing fully, at $4.6 billion, in fiscal 1986, to be terminated in fiscal 1987. Cuts in

Fiscal 1986 Budget Totals

(in billions of dollars)

Category	President's Request	Conference Agreement
National Defense		
Budget Authority	$322.2	$302.5
Outlays	285.7	267.1
International Affairs		
Budget Authority	20.6	21.3
Outlays	18.3	18.8
Science and Space		
Budget Authority	9.5	9.1
Outlays	9.3	8.9
Energy		
Budget Authority	5.1	5.9
Outlays	4.7	5.5
Natural Resources		
Budget Authority	10.9	13.1
Outlays	11.9	13.0
Agriculture		
Budget Authority	13.0	18.3
Outlays	12.6	15.5
Commerce and Housing		
Budget Authority	7.8	7.7
Outlays	2.2	3.7
Transportation		
Budget Authority	25.5	26.8
Outlays	25.9	25.8
Community Development		
Budget Authority	5.1	6.9
Outlays	7.3	8.0
Education and Social Services		
Budget Authority	26.9	31.5
Outlays	29.3	30.8
Health		
Budget Authority	34.7	36.0
Outlays	34.9	34.9
Medical Insurance		
Budget Authority	81.7	18.5
Outlays	67.2	69.2
Income Security		
Budget Authority	144.1	155.1
Outlays	115.8	119.0
Social Security		
Budget Authority	207.0	207.2
Outlays	202.2	200.8
Veterans' Benefits		
Budget Authority	27.4	27.4
Outlays	26.8	26.8
Justice		
Budget Authority	6.5	6.9
Outlays	6.6	6.8
General Government		
Budget Authority	5.0	5.5
Outlays	4.8	5.4
General Fiscal Assistance		
Budget Authority	1.6	6.5
Outlays	2.8	6.5
Net Interest		
Budget Authority	142.6	142.3
Outlays	142.6	142.3
Allowances		
Budget Authority	0.1	−2.1
Outlays	0.4	−1.6
Offsetting Receipts		
Budget Authority	−37.5	−39.9
Outlays	−37.5	−39.9
Total		
Budget Authority	$1,060.0	$1,069.7
Outlays	973.3	967.6
Revenues	793.7	795.7
Deficit	180.0	171.9
Deficit Reduction	——	−55.5 *

* *Estimated by the Senate Budget Committee. Using a different baseline, the House Budget Committee estimated the deficit reduction at $57.5 billion.*

SOURCES: Conference report on S Con Res 32, President's fiscal 1986 budget request

anticipated outlays: $8.5 billion in fiscal 1987-88.

Interest

• Total debt service reductions expected as a result of policy changes assumed by the budget resolution: $900 million in fiscal 1986; $22.6 billion in fiscal 1986-88.

Allowances

• Held salaries for federal employees, including members of Congress, at fiscal 1985 levels in fiscal 1986; increased these salaries by 3.8 percent in January 1987 and 4.7 percent in January 1988. Cuts in anticipated outlays: $1.2 billion in fiscal 1986; $5.9 billion in fiscal 1986-88. (Defense Department employees were treated the same, with outlay savings tabulated in the defense budget category.)

• Reduced the federal civilian work force by 44,000 positions, approximately 4 percent, through attrition. Cuts in anticipated outlays: $800 million in fiscal 1986; $3.9 billion in fiscal 1986-88.

• Reduced executive branch agencies' administrative costs by 10 percent. Cuts in anticipated outlays: $600 million in fiscal 1986; $1.8 billion in fiscal 1986-88.

• Continued current practice of using 2,087 hours as a full work year for federal employees. This practice started in 1982 when Congress approved legislation changing the method of computing general schedule pay for federal workers, previously calculated on the basis of 2,080 hours annually. Cuts in anticipated outlays: $200 million in fiscal 1986; $500 million in fiscal 1986-88. *(Background, 1982 Almanac p. 514)*

• Assumed enactment of legislation repealing current requirements, based on the Walsh-Healey Public Contracts Act, that overtime rates be paid for workdays exceeding eight hours. The requirements applied to persons working on certain types of government contracts. Cuts in anticipated outlays: $100 million in fiscal 1986; $900 million in fiscal 1986-88. *(Background, Congress and the Nation Vol. I, p. 633)*

Offsetting Receipts

• Assumed enactment of legislation to settle a dispute between the federal government and several states over allocation of revenues from drilling operations on the Outer Continental Shelf. The settlement was expected to give states a 27 percent share of bonuses and rents currently held in escrow. Cuts in anticipated outlays: $4 billion in fiscal 1986; $1.5 billion in fiscal 1986-88.

• Released $1 billion annually in fiscal 1986-88 of petroleum overcharge funds currently held in escrow. Cuts in anticipated outlays: $3 billion in fiscal 1986-88.

• Adjusted for loss of revenues, caused by a federal pay freeze, which would reduce contributions to civil service and military retirement funds. Increases in anticipated outlays: $600 million in fiscal 1986; $1.3 billion in fiscal 1986-88.

Senate Committee Action

Senate Republican leaders had hoped to reach agreement on the outlines of a budget package by Feb. 1. But they missed that deadline, and a second one was set for late February.

GOP senators were anxious about the federal deficit, knowing that failure to reduce it not only could cause economic harm, but also could be a political liability for the

22 Republican-held Senate seats up in the 1986 elections.

The leadership having failed to reach a consensus, Domenici said Feb. 26 that his Budget Committee would begin crafting a budget March 4, and offered a grim view of what that budget might include.

There was other bad news the same week.

A letter from the 10 Republicans on the Senate Armed Services Committee to Majority Leader Dole said the 10 would "in no case" accept an increase in defense spending less than 4 percent above inflation.

The Armed Service members said they supported the president's fiscal 1986 budget request for a 5.9 percent inflation-adjusted increase in military expenditures, highlighting the continuing dissent over defense spending among Republicans.

And on Feb. 27 CBO reported that if Congress accepted all of Reagan's proposed budget cuts, annual deficits would remain about $186 billion through 1990 — not fall to below $100 billion as the administration predicted. The CBO projection assumed higher interest rates and inflation and slower economic growth than did the administration for the rest of the decade.

'Promised Land' Plan

Domenici announced Feb. 26 that revised economic assumptions meant a projected fiscal 1986 deficit of $215 billion, an amount equal to 5.6 percent of the gross national product (GNP), the total of the nation's production of goods and services. In January the GOP leadership set as their goal reduction of the deficit to 4 percent of GNP in 1986, declining to 2 percent in 1988, about $100 billion.

It had been assumed that cuts of $54 billion in 1986, $94 billion in 1987 and $118 billion in 1988 would suffice.

Domenici estimated, however, that spending would have to be cut $64 billion, $112 billion and $151 billion in the three years to reach what he called the "Promised Land" of the GOP deficit-reduction target.

To reach the "Promised Land," he said, the Senate would have to accept all of the administration's recommendations for elimination or reduction of domestic programs, make cuts in other entitlement programs and scrap a cost-of-living increase for Social Security recipients in 1986. Defense spending would have been allowed only to keep pace with inflation in fiscal 1986, and to increase 3 percent, adjusted for inflation, in 1987 and 1988.

Domenici only proposed spending cuts, reflecting one political reality — strong opposition to tax increases, particularly from Reagan. But many lawmakers had already rejected some proposed domestic cuts, and Reagan was resisting any freeze of defense or Social Security.

Committee Markup

With considerable reservations, the committee March 14 agreed to a budget blueprint that would have trimmed the deficit an estimated $55 billion in fiscal 1986 and $297 billion over three years by making deep cuts in domestic programs and setting limits on defense spending growth.

The budget resolution (S Con Res 32 — S Rept 99-15) was approved by a straight party-line vote of 11-10, after the committee failed, after a week and a half of markup sessions, to find a bipartisan majority willing to back any of several other deficit-reduction plans, including Domenici's "Promised Land" option. The committee had spent the week of March 4 debating and voting on Domenici's plan, but deadlocked on Social Security, and Domenici went in search of a different package.

The committee's resolution envisioned a one-year freeze of domestic spending at fiscal 1985 levels and the elimination of a cost-of-living allowance in fiscal 1986 for Social Security recipients. It called for $16.8 billion in additional domestic spending cuts and would have allowed for a fiscal 1986 increase in defense spending authority only to keep pace with inflation.

Under strong pressure from the White House, the committee agreed not to recommend new taxes.

The committee recommended that three-year ceilings be set on defense and domestic spending bills reported by the Senate Appropriations Committee. A plan to impose binding spending caps was rejected in 1984. *(1984 Almanac p. 143)*

The committee projected its proposal would cut the deficit to $172.3 billion in fiscal 1986, $144.9 billion in fiscal 1987 and $101.8 billion in fiscal 1988.

Besides the Social Security COLA freeze, the plan recommended elimination of cost-of-living increases for most other pension and benefit programs, including federal civilian and military retirement benefits. However, a $300 million fiscal 1986 increase would have been provided for the Supplemental Security Income (SSI) program to help offset the effects of the COLA elimination on the elderly and disabled poor.

Among the few programs to escape the proposed freeze were several geared towards low-income recipients, including SSI, food stamps and Aid to Families with Dependent Children. However, other programs would have been eliminated, as recommended by Reagan. These included the Economic Development Administration, the Appalachian regional development programs, housing loan assistance provided by the Farmers Home Administration, community services block grants, the work incentive program and rental housing subsidies.

Passing the 'Turkey'

Domenici crafted the alternative that won a slim victory in committee only after lengthy closed-door caucuses among the panel's Republicans.

Republican members indicated that the votes did not necessarily reflect their support of all the components of the package, but rather a desire to break the impasse the committee faced on designing a blueprint for reducing the federal deficit.

Mark Andrews, R-N.D., observed that members were "voting for this turkey to get it out of the committee and onto the floor" where they could make additional changes.

Much of the conflict centered on finding an acceptable balance between domestic and defense spending cuts, and the desire of some Democrats and Republicans to raise revenues as part of the deficit-reduction plan.

Democrats complained that deep domestic cuts, especially in Social Security, were unfair when defense spending was allowed to increase with inflation and tax breaks for large corporations were left untouched. Although Reagan had campaigned for re-election against cuts in Social Security, he said he would consider a COLA freeze if there were a bipartisan mandate in Congress to do so.

In a series of votes before adoption of the revised Domenici budget, the committee rejected four alternative budgets — including the one submitted by Reagan — and two proposals to raise taxes.

The committee rejected, 4-18, a plan by Ernest F. Hollings, D-S.C., to raise $159 billion over three years by eliminating indexing of federal income tax brackets in 1986

Miller Replaces 'Young Slasher' Stockman at OMB

Widely praised as an articulate spokesman for the administration's campaign to cut back government spending, budget czar David A. Stockman left his post as director of the Office of Management and Budget (OMB) Aug. 1, the same day Congress completed action on the fiscal 1986 budget resolution (S Con Res 32).

His successor, James C. Miller III, inherited what Stockman himself described as a fiscal crisis.

Stockman's resignation was announced on July 9, as congressional negotiators continued to grapple with ways to cut fiscal 1986 spending by as much as $56 billion; Miller's first task — unknown at the time of his Oct. 4 confirmation — was to cut even deeper to craft a fiscal 1987 budget with a maximum deficit of $144 billion, as required by the Gramm-Rudman-Hollings law. *(Budget resolution, p. 441; Gramm-Rudman-Hollings, p. 459)*

Stockman's Departure

Stockman, a two-term Republican representative from Michigan before going to OMB (1977-81), was hired as a managing director for corporate and government finance for the New York investment banking firm of Salomon Brothers Inc.

He had been dubbed the "young slasher" for his role as architect of the Reagan's administration's budget-cutting efforts. And Stockman's departure worried some in Congress that future efforts to trim the federal budget deficit would be weakened. Many on Capitol Hill — including his ideological opponents — said it would be difficult to find someone who could match Stockman's detailed knowledge of the federal budget and the legislative process.

Stockman's almost singular drive to reduce the federal deficit was often at odds with other White House goals. In the December 1981 issue of *The Atlantic*, after the economy began to sour, Stockman conceded that tax-cutting went too far in Reagan's first year and defense spending should have been restrained.

After the article appeared, Stockman offered his resignation, but instead of accepting it, Reagan took Stockman to the "woodshed" for a verbal beating.

Afterwards, Stockman's role in the administration became more subdued and he had most of his impact in behind-the-scenes negotiations on the budget. In the following three years, he was credited with using his knowledge of the minutiae of the federal budget to help steer through Congress several deficit-reduction measures that cut spending and raised taxes. *(1982 Almanac p. 27; 1984 Almanac p. 127)*

Miller's Nomination

The Senate Oct. 4 approved the nomination of James C. Miller III as director of the Office of Management and Budget (OMB). The vote was 90-2, with Tom Harkin, D-Iowa, and Donald W. Riegle Jr., D-Mich., dissenting. Miller, 43, assumed his post immediately.

Reagan's choice of Miller to succeed Stockman stirred little overt opposition in the Senate. However, William S. Cohen, R-Maine, held up the vote for several days to let the White House know of his dissatisfaction with the administration over an unrelated issue — its reluctance to enforce competitive contracting requirements enacted in the 1984 Deficit Reduction Act. *(1984 Almanac p. 200)*

But an agreement allowing Cohen to talk on the issue for an hour before the Miller vote cleared the way for the nomination.

Miller, who was chairman of the Federal Trade Commission from 1981-85, was expected to be more of an administration "team player" than his predecessor.

During confirmation hearings before the Senate Governmental Affairs Committee Sept. 24, several members warned Miller of their concerns about OMB's growing control over other executive branch agencies.

They especially criticized the office for delaying the implementation of agency regulations needed to enforce legislation. Miller was administrator of OMB's Office of Information and Regulatory Affairs for nine months before moving to the Federal Trade Commission.

---

to offset the effects of inflation, by imposing a 5 percent corporate minimum tax and by limiting investment tax breaks and increasing taxpayer compliance.

It also rejected, by a vote of 4-16, a proposal by Howard M. Metzenbaum, D-Ohio, to limit corporate tax breaks to their current levels and to impose a 15 percent minimum tax on corporate earnings over $50,000, for a three-year tax hike of $44.2 billion.

Domenici noted, however, that taxes might be considered as a "last resort" if Congress failed to adopt proposed spending cuts.

On March 13, the committee overwhelmingly rejected several proposed budgets, including Reagan's, which was defeated by a vote of 4-17.

Domenici said it should be "no shock" that many members would not support the package, since the committee had spent the previous week rejecting almost every major component of the president's plan. Four Republicans voted in favor of the budget, the rest voted against it.

J. James Exon, D-Neb., who offered the package aware that it would be defeated, abstained. He said he hoped the vote would force Reagan to begin compromising with Congress on a more palatable package of budget cuts when it became clear how little support there was for his proposal.

The committee also rejected by votes of 4-18:

- A proposal by Hollings, Andrews and Exon to freeze domestic spending at current levels, with many of the additional spending cuts already approved by the committee. It also would have frozen for one year all cost-of-living increases, including Social Security, and provided for no inflation-adjusted growth in defense spending in fiscal 1986, with 3 percent growth after inflation in fiscal 1987 and 1988. The package would have raised $159 billion in new taxes over three years.
- A plan offered by Democrats Daniel Patrick Moynihan, N.Y., and Frank R. Lautenberg, N.J., to sell more than $200 billion in outstanding federal loans to private investors. The package provided for all domestic spending cuts

approved up to that point by the committee and no inflation-adjusted growth in fiscal 1986 defense spending.

- A proposal by Steven D. Symms, R-Idaho, that would have cut non-defense discretionary programs 10 percent below current spending levels, frozen all government pay at fiscal 1985 levels for three years and eliminated cost-of-living increases in all government programs for three years. Symms would have cut the government work force by 10 percent, but allowed for 3 percent inflation-adjusted spending growth in defense programs other than personnel.

Senate Floor Action

Senate Republicans did not rest easy the week after the Budget Committee approved the fiscal 1986 budget resolution. Although the measure delivered on GOP deficit-reduction goals, and did so without proposing to hike taxes, Republicans felt politically isolated and exposed, having embraced defense cuts and a lid on Social Security.

On March 22 Senate Republicans met with Reagan to ask him either to come to some agreement with them or at least refrain from attacking S Con Res 32 so sharply as to cripple it. The meeting resulted in the creation of an administration-Senate GOP group to work out differences between the Reagan and Senate budgets.

In its bluntest form, their message was that the Senate budget resolution was about the best anybody could do, given existing mathematical and political constraints imposed, in part, by the president himself.

Budget Committee calculations showed that the resolution's changes would reduce the deficit to 4.1 percent of GNP in fiscal 1986 and to 2.1 percent by 1988, near to the GOP's goal.

But beyond the objectionable defense and Social Security freezes, the budget resolution engendered what one budget aide described as "just about universal pain" by chopping heavily into many domestic programs with vocal, middle-class constituencies, such as Amtrak train subsidies, the Small Business Administration, rural utility credit programs and housing and education loans.

GOP, White House Deal

After two weeks of private consultations with administration officials, GOP leaders found agreement with the White House. But the price of presidential support — even deeper cuts in or elimination of popular domestic programs and defense spending increases — made a winning GOP majority on the floor ultimately impossible.

On April 4 Dole and Domenici announced an alternative to the committee's budget plan that achieved roughly the same deficit reduction, but with key changes.

At a White House meeting with Dole and Domenici April 5, the president strongly endorsed the package. Yet Dole, Domenici and budget director Stockman — who negotiated closely with Senate GOP leaders all year — also acknowledged that the package faced hostility in the Republican Senate. The final plan had been presented the afternoon of April 4 to about 25 Republican senators, but no commitments of support were sought.

The negotiators agreed to increase Pentagon spending by 3 percent above inflation; to add substantially to the committee's list of domestic program cancellations; to make deeper cuts in certain other programs; and to permit some increases in Social Security and other federal pension programs in the next three years, but not enough to completely offset inflation if it climbed above 4 percent.

Programs to be eliminated included revenue sharing, Export-Import Bank loans, Amtrak subsidies, small business loans, the Job Corps and Urban Development Action Grants.

The program cancellations in Reagan's original budget were a top administration priority. But despite the wishes of the president, Domenici, to get S Con Res 32 out of his committee, had garnered Republican votes by agreeing to continue some of the candidates for extinction. Many of these agreements were reversed by the April 4 budget compromise.

The compromise envisioned deeper cuts in farm programs than the committee had agreed to, and placed an inflation-related cap on spending for Medicaid, the federal-state medical program for the poor.

The committee had left Medicaid relatively untouched as part of its overall strategy to pare the so-called "middle-class" federal subsidies but generally protect "means-tested" programs for the poor from substantial spending cuts in fiscal 1986.

The compromise did not change committee decisions to let food stamps and SSI benefits rise with inflation and to increase SSI monthly benefits modestly. Nor did it change earlier Medicare decisions.

The program eliminations, the Medicaid cap and the treatment of Social Security and other federal pensions — all of which were to lose their automatic, full COLA increases in coming years under the compromise — were important structural changes that were to guarantee continued and growing savings in the years after 1986. Such "out-year" savings were generally considered essential to rein in the rapidly accelerating national debt and the explosive growth in interest paid to finance that debt. But there were deep divisions in Congress over how best to achieve such savings.

It was with evident satisfaction that Stockman told reporters that the April 4 budget package achieved about 90 percent of the structural changes sought by the administration, and about 75 percent of its desired dollar savings in federal spending.

Floor Fight

The budget compromise came to the floor April 25, but as quickly as debate began Dole halted substantive action. It had become apparent that, despite an April 24 television appeal from Reagan and personal presidential lobbying, there were not enough GOP votes for the plan to pass.

Dole maneuvered the proposal onto the floor, using a complicated procedure of technical and perfecting amendments and his pre-eminent power under Senate rules to gain recognition on the floor. His hope was to fend off potentially disruptive amendments before a first, non-binding vote on the budget.

It was expected that such a vote would reveal the depth of Senate opposition to the plan and prevent the Democrats from seizing the first vote and making it a painful test on the plan's reductions in the future growth of Social Security cost-of-living adjustments or another of the plan's controversial elements.

Dole, however, was outflanked by Minority Leader Robert C. Byrd, D-W.Va. After hours of parliamentary delay Byrd unexpectedly dropped his objections to proceed with consideration of the budget and challenged Dole to call for a vote on the plan. Dole hurriedly conferred with colleagues, and then asked the Senate to adjourn.

The following week, Dole renewed his strategy and the

House, Senate Budget Totals

(in billions of dollars)

	FY 1986	FY 1987	FY 1988
Budget Authority			
House	$1,062.9	$1,134.3	$1,212.8
Senate	1,069.5	1,132.8	1,212.9
Outlays			
House	967.3	1,028.5	1,080.0
Senate	965.0	1,011.1	1,060.2
Revenues			
House	794.1	866.0	955.6
Senate	793.6	866.3	955.9
Deficits			
House	173.2	162.5	124.4
Senate	171.4	144.8	104.3
Deficit Reductions			
House	−56.2	−82.9	−119.9
Senate	−56.0	−99.9	−139.93

SOURCES: House and Senate Budget committees

compromise budget was approved April 30 in a hairline 50-49 vote.

Two Republican senators, Bob Kasten, Wis., and Charles McC. Mathias Jr., Md., joined united Democrats in voting against the plan. Kasten had a number of objections to specific program cuts and eliminations, while Mathias said he believed the plan did not do enough to reduce deficits, and had to include a tax increase toward that end. *(Vote 34, p. 12-S)*

The next day, April 30, Republicans began to dismember the compromise budget with votes restoring full funding for cost-of-living adjustments (COLAs) for Social Security and other federal pension programs, and cutting defense spending far below the amount Reagan requested. Dole had agreed to allow the amendments in order to win votes for the compromise.

Byrd and other Democrats objected strenuously that Dole was abusing his privilege of first recognition to hold the floor for Republican amendments, and freezing out the Democrats. But when given the opportunity May 2 to offer an amendment restoring funds for Medicare and Medicaid, the health programs for the aged and the poor, however, Democrats were unable to agree on how to proceed and left the field to the Republicans.

With Dole offering the amendment, the Senate voted 65-34 May 1 to restore some $22 billion over three years for Social Security to the budget. The amendment had the effect of negating the plan's assumption that Social Security COLAs would be reduced to 2 percentage points below inflation. *(Vote 35, p. 12-S)*

The amendment was offered by Dole for Sens. Alfonse M. D'Amato, R-N.Y., and Paula Hawkins, R-Fla. Both had said they would not vote for the leadership plan unless they could offer the first amendment afterwards to restore Social Security cost-of-living increases. D'Amato and Hawkins, both from states with large populations of Social Security recipients, faced re-election in 1986.

On May 2 by a 48-51 vote the Senate refused to kill an amendment reducing the plan's defense spending by about $3 billion in fiscal 1986 and $18 billion over three years. The reduction meant that Pentagon spending would rise only to offset inflation in 1986 — known as "zero real growth" — with defense growing 3 percent over inflation in 1987 and 1988. The amendment was adopted by voice vote. *(Vote 36, p. 12-S)*

The compromise budget had provided for defense increases 3 percent over inflation for all three years. Reagan's budget had requested inflation plus 5.9 percent growth in fiscal 1986, and 8.2 inflation-adjusted in fiscal 1987 and 8.8 inflation-adjusted in fiscal 1988.

Supporters of the defense amendment, including sponsors Mark O. Hatfield, R-Ore., and Charles E. Grassley, R-Iowa, said it was a watershed vote, signaling disapproval in the nation for wasteful and fraudulent Pentagon spending practices. But Reagan May 3 characterized the Senate vote to slow the defense increase as "an irresponsible act."

The Senate also voted to restore some cuts in Medicare and Medicaid and agreed to a non-binding amendment endorsing a minimum tax for corporations and wealthy individuals to be used to help pay for an overhaul of the tax code. Senators May 3 rejected, 49-49, an amendment offered by Jesse Helms, R-N.C., to cut congressional salaries by 10 percent. *(Vote 41, p. 13-S; tax bill, p. 480)*

Another Deal

Dole's floor strategy included offering a comprehensive substitute budget once all amendments had been disposed of — with the idea of canceling or revising some of those amendments — particularly that restoring the Social Security COLA. In a rare moment of unintended irony, Dole told reporters, "We'll put it all back together like Humpty-Dumpty," the nursery-rhyme character who could not be put back together after a fall.

In effect, Dole's substitute was the fifth GOP effort to construct a budget. Party disagreements caused Reagan's original fiscal 1986 budget to be rejected before it reached the Capitol. Dole and Domenici failed in an attempt to draft an alternative by Feb. 1. The White House next rejected a different budget written by Domenici's committee in March, and that rejection led top GOP senators and White House officials to agree privately on the leadership budget in early April.

Dole succeeded by the thinnest of margins — 50-49 — May 10, with Senate Republicans and Reagan in reluctant accord.

As agreed to by the Senate, the budget compromise eliminated the 1986 Social Security cost-of-living adjustment (COLA), held defense spending to the rate of inflation and eliminated 13 domestic programs. It met the deficit-cutting standards — $50 billion to $60 billion in fiscal 1986 and about $300 billion over three years — widely accepted for the year's budget exercise, providing budget authority of $1,069.5 billion and outlays of $965 billion in fiscal 1986. It cut $56 billion from the projected fiscal 1986 deficit and about $295 billion through fiscal 1988. Under the plan, projected deficits were: $171.4 billion in fiscal 1986, $144.8 billion in fiscal 1987, $104.3 billion in fiscal 1988.

The Senate approved the compromise plan when Vice President George Bush cut short a Western trip for the vote and broke a 49-49 tie. Illness had prevented Republican John P. East, N.C., and Democrat J. James Exon, Neb., from voting. It was the 219th vice presidential tie-breaking vote since 1789. *(Vote 72, p. 17-S)*

The pivotal 50-49 vote on an amendment to the budget resolution incorporating the compromise came in the early morning hours of May 10 after a marathon 15-hour session. All but four Republicans voted "aye," and all but one Democrat voted "no." Republicans voting against the plan were D'Amato, Hawkins, Mathias and Arlen Specter, Pa. Edward Zorinsky, Neb., was the lone Democrat to vote "aye."

D'Amato, Hawkins and Specter objected to the Social Security freeze, while Mathias felt strongly that the budget should have included tax increases to provide extra revenues to balance the budget. Zorinsky was brought over with concessions on farm program spending, Amtrak and impact aid (part B) — federal funds for school districts with large populations of children whose parents live or work on federal property.

The 49-49 tie was achieved by rousing Republican Sen. Pete Wilson, Calif., from a hospital bed, where he was recuperating from an appendectomy.

The way for approval was cleared after Majority Leader Robert Dole, R-Kan., won critical concessions from the administration on defense and Social Security.

The resolution differed markedly from the earlier White House-approved compromise budget. In fact, the final version of S Con Res 32 closely resembled the Budget Committee plan, which also froze Social Security COLAs and defense spending in fiscal 1986, but which had been repudiated by the White House.

As adopted by the Senate, the budget would have terminated 13 domestic programs: trade adjustment assistance, Conrail (to be sold to the private sector), the Appalachian Regional Commission, the Economic Development Administration, general revenue sharing, Export-Import Bank direct loans, community services block grants (after 1986), the Work Incentive (WIN) program, Rental Housing Development Grants (HODAGs), Section 312 rehabilitation loans for rehabilitating single-family, multifamily and commercial properties, the U.S. Travel and Tourism Administration, postal subsidies for for-profit publishers, and Urban Development Action Grants.

Other key new features included retention of Amtrak subsidies and the Small Business Administration at reduced levels, and significant cuts in the growth of other programs, including Medicare and farm subsidies.

Deals — many at the fiscal margins — were made by the GOP leadership to get votes necessary for adoption of the budget, including a $1.1 billion restoration to Medicare and Medicaid that still required that $17.5 billion be cut from the program.

Dole also deployed parliamentary maneuvers to control action on the floor to his advantage. For instance, under an unusual procedure for which he had laid the groundwork the previous week, attempts to amend the much-negotiated "final" GOP budget were not in order until after the 50-49 vote.

Democrats' only direct shots at the package occurred in the small hours of the morning directly after a dramatic show of Republican unity. They offered three unsuccessful amendments to strip out the Social Security freeze, restore Medicare and Medicaid funding and impose a minimum corporate tax.

The Social Security amendment, proposed by Moynihan, was tabled (killed) by a 51-47 vote. The Medicare-Medicaid amendment by Edward M. Kennedy, D-Mass., lost 54-44; the tax amendment, by Metzenbaum, lost 61-37. *(Votes 73-75, pp. 17-S — 18-S)*

After these amendments were defeated, the Senate gave final approval to S Con Res 32 by voice vote at about 3:20 a.m. on May 10, having previously disposed of a chain of technical amendments that Dole had used to secure his procedural advantages. This final Senate legislative "day" on S Con Res 32 had begun at about 10 a.m. May 9. Throughout that day and into the early part of the evening, the Senate rejected some 16 amendments, most of which sought to add back money to various programs, and accepted three: to save Amtrak subsidies from extinction, to partially restore funds cut from the school lunch program, and to tell the Office of Management and Budget (OMB) to release all appropriated fiscal 1985 funds for the supplementary food program (WIC) for poor women, infants and children.

These amendments and those passed on previous days of budget work were to an earlier version of the resolution budget and were effectively wiped out by adoption of the final package. *(Senate votes on the budget, pp. 12-S — 18-S)*

Nevertheless, certain of these amendments, including a May 3 amendment by Finance Committee Chairman Bob Packwood, R-Ore., to restore some Medicare and Medicaid funding, found their way into the final package because of commitments by Dole and Domenici. And other amendments on the final day, including those that failed by relatively narrow margins, functioned as important tests of Senate opinion, guiding last-minute negotiations by Dole and Domenici on the plan that eventually passed.

Zorinsky decided to vote for the plan after Senate GOP leaders and administration negotiators agreed to restore about $3.3 billion in proposed agriculture program cuts. They also promised an additional $1 billion in federal guarantees for farmers' loans and a new export-promotion program that would provide bonuses of government-owned surplus grain to foreign buyers of U.S. farm commodities.

Alternative Budgets Rejected

The Senate rejected three alternative budget plans, all of whose sponsors argued that their proposals spread the burden of sacrifice more fairly across various sectors of society than did the GOP package. These amendments were:

- A Chiles-Hollings budget freezing all retirement COLAs for six months, providing an inflation-only increase for defense in fiscal 1986 and calling for $72 billion in new revenues in fiscal 1986-88. The Senate rejected the amendment 35-63 on May 8. *(Vote 51, p. 14-S)*

The plan retained many programs eliminated by the Republican leadership plan and cut less sharply into farm programs, Medicare, mass transit and Amtrak, veterans' programs and student loans, among others. In fiscal 1986 it would have reduced the deficit by $59 billion, using OMB assumptions and baseline, and in fiscal years 1987-88 it would have cut the deficit by $320 billion.

- A series of changes in the leadership plan, sponsored by Democrats Byrd, Minority Whip Alan Cranston, Calif., and others, that would have allowed full COLAs for Social Security and other retirement programs, eliminated Medicaid reductions and cut back on Medicare reductions, provided 1 percent plus inflation for defense in fiscal 1986, and called for $51 billion in new revenues. The new revenues would have been raised by eliminating tax preferences for corporations and by retaining the existing 16-cents-per-pack tax on cigarettes, which was due to drop to 8 cents on Oct. 1. The Senate rejected this plan 43-54 on May 8. *(Vote 52, p. 14-S)*

- An across-the-board freeze of all federal programs, including defense and Social Security, at fiscal 1985 levels with no increases for inflation, sponsored by Max Baucus, D-Mont.; Joseph R. Biden Jr., D-Del.; Nancy Landon Kassebaum, R-Kan.; and Grassley. The Senate rejected the plan May 9 on a 27-70 vote. *(Vote 57, p. 15-S)*

The plan would have yielded about $40 billion in deficit reduction for fiscal 1986. Sponsors said it was more politically feasible than the other plans because it treated all programs the same without singling out some for extra cuts.

House Committee Action

Less than a week after the Senate passed its record $56 billion deficit-reduction package, the House Budget Committee by a 21-12 vote matched those savings with a fiscal 1986 budget resolution (H Con Res 152 — H Rept 99-133, Part I) approved May 16.

But unlike the Senate plan approved May 10, the committee's budget provided less spending for defense and more for domestic programs, and retained the Social Security COLA.

Both froze spending for most government programs and cut below a freeze in many. But while the Senate proposal eliminated 13 programs, the House document ended just one — general revenue sharing.

The committee's fast action was seen as a personal victory for Chairman Gray, who assumed control of the panel in January. The measure was reported after a two-day markup session otherwise notable for an unprecedented effort to involve committee Republicans in the budget process. In the end, though, the attempt at a bipartisan compromise failed; all Democrats voted for the budget, and all Republicans opposed it, except W. Henson Moore, La.

Moore's support prompted a deadpan Gray to claim a bipartisan victory, which he justified by recalling that Reagan had done so after one Democrat voted for the Senate-passed budget.

Three conservative Democrats — Marvin Leath, Texas; Buddy MacKay, Fla.; and Jim Slattery, Kan. — voted for the budget, but on the condition that they could offer an alternative on the House floor that would cut about $75 billion in 1986 through a combination of spending cuts, tax increases and elimination of the Social Security COLA.

Despite two days of debate, including the first closed-door sessions in the Budget Committee's 10-year history, the final product was unchanged from the proposal Gray offered at the outset.

That budget was the result of weeks of private caucuses in which the 20 committee Democrats debated how to balance cuts in defense and domestic programs, and whether to save $8 billion in fiscal 1986 by eliminating the COLAs for Social Security and other federal retirement programs. By doing so, they argued, Democrats would distinguish their party from Republicans on the politically volatile issue.

Despite the potential political advantage in keeping the COLA, a minority of Democrats said deficits were too great to exempt Social Security. In Budget Committee caucuses, Leath said conservatives could support greater restraint on defense spending as a trade for a Social Security freeze.

Though both the House and Senate plans claimed to cut $56 billion from anticipated fiscal 1986 spending, the House plan projected a $173 billion deficit, $2 billion higher than the Senate's estimate. An anticipated $2 billion supplemental appropriation for foreign aid to Israel and Egypt, which the Senate omitted, accounted for the difference. *(Supplemental, p. 350)*

Because the House plan eliminated only one program and retained COLAs for retirement programs, its savings in fiscal 1987 and 1988 were expected to be less than those in the Senate budget.

Preliminaries

As the Budget Committee prepared in March to draft a budget, members found themselves as divided as their Senate counterparts. Neither Democrats, who controlled the House, nor their Republican colleagues were near a consensus on how to cut the deficit.

As in the Senate, spending for defense and Social Security were the biggest hang-ups, while potential cuts in a host of popular domestic programs caused further splits along regional and ideological lines.

To help find ground for agreement, Budget Committee leaders asked House Democrats at a March 21 caucus to complete a questionnaire on budget options dubbed the "tough choices exercise." The survey was a tool House Democrats used in 1983 and 1984 to craft a budget. *(1983 Almanac p. 436)*

One of the toughest choices, however, was avoided: The questionnaire made no mention of tax options. Some members said the omission was ordered by House Speaker Thomas P. O'Neill Jr., D-Mass., but Gray denied that. He conceded, however, before the committee got down to business, that raising taxes was out of the question, recalling how Reagan had taunted Senate Democrats who discussed increasing taxes.

On March 13, the president had said he had his "veto pen" drawn to block any tax bills, and he teased Democrats to "make my day," in reference to a popular line from a Clint Eastwood detective film.

In addition, Majority Leader Jim Wright, D-Texas, predicted the House would not drop the Social Security COLA. Of 154 respondents to the "tough choices" survey, fewer than 16 said they could support canceling the inflation adjustment.

In the end, the Senate's May 10 vote for a budget that eliminated the COLA reinforced many House Democrats' desire to protect the increase.

House leaders scheduled a party caucus May 14 for a vote on a resolution backing the COLA. O'Neill and Wright predicted Democrats would vote to retain the increase by a 4-to-1 margin. But the caucus broke up without a vote. O'Neill said Democrats had decided a show of hands would only embarrass the few who wanted to eliminate the COLA.

Budget Committee Democrats resumed their discussions. At 8 p.m. May 14, Wright and Gray announced agreement on a $56 billion deficit-cutting plan that exempted the COLA.

Working Behind Closed Doors

The markup began the next day, May 15, amid partisan rancor that marked most House action in 1985. It was delayed an hour after committee Republicans made speeches on the House floor expressing outrage at being asked to mark up a budget they had not seen.

But after four hours of dilatory debate on procedural matters, monetary policy and the economic assumptions underlying the budget, the committee voted 26-3 to meet privately in executive session, reflecting a prior agreement among Democrats and Republicans and hope that private negotiations could lead to compromise.

Gray justified the unprecedented closed-door session by pointing to the Armed Services and Intelligence committees. Those panels often met privately for reasons of national security.

Wright said Republicans wanted to close the meeting. "Obviously, they have something to offer," he said.

The group met for five hours, and agreed to meet again the next day, May 16. Though members said no decisions had been made, Latta told reporters, "There is a hope out there that we haven't had before."

Defense Fight

As members' subsequent accounts showed, that hope was based on confusion over what each side was willing to accept for defense spending.

First, many Republicans agreed that the Social Security COLA should remain in the budget, although most Democrats said the matter was not negotiable. Next, Republicans said they also could accept inflation adjustments in programs for the poor.

Then came defense. Charles E. Schumer, D-N.Y., proposed to add $6 billion to defense outlays, bringing them in line with the $273 billion provided by the Senate. But many Republicans claimed Democrats had offered May 15 to increase budget authority for defense, not outlays.

An increase in outlays — the amount of money actually spent in a year — was not meaningful, some said, because as inflation had dropped in recent years, the Pentagon had had more money than it could spend. Budget authority — what could be obligated to be spent over future years — was more important to the Pentagon since it was used to commit funds to long-term development of weapons.

Gray and Latta conferred after the late-night session. Gray said Democrats would not agree to raise budget authority, while Latta said Republicans could accept nothing less.

The next day after another private session broke up without agreement, the panel resumed the public markup and, within hours, approved the entire resolution.

In a last bid for a bipartisan budget, Tom Loeffler, R-Texas, offered an amendment incorporating the GOP's defense position. He indicated Republicans would accept the entire Democratic package if defense spending authority were raised to the Senate-passed level, with its increase for inflation, and outlays were increased $3 billion for 1986.

Democrats were opposed, saying that spending was not being cut, and that even with a freeze in budget authority outlays would rise $15 billion in 1986 to pay for previous Pentagon commitments. The Loeffler amendment failed, 11-22. All Democrats opposed it, as did Republicans Denny Smith, Ore., and Hank Brown, Colo.

Social Security, Taxes

The Social Security COLA easily survived its only challenge. By voice vote May 16, the panel rejected an amendment by Smith for an across-the-board budget freeze, including the retirement program. The House committee budget also protected scheduled 1986 COLAs for federal military, civilian and railroad retirees.

By voice vote, the committee also agreed to include language in the resolution's report urging the Ways and Means Committee to overhaul the tax code.

The amendment was not very specific, however, unlike the Senate measure, which included language calling for any new revenues from a minimum tax to be used to reduce tax rates.

The committee voted 12-20 against an amendment, sponsored by Brown, to reduce Congress' own budget 10 percent below a freeze. The Senate measure included such a cut.

House Floor Action

The House May 23 approved without change the committee-passed fiscal 1986 budget resolution (H Con Res 152), inviting a confrontation over defense spending with Senate Republicans and the president.

The vote in the House, where Democrats had a 71-member majority, was 258-170. Twenty-four Republicans, mostly moderates, supported the budget resolution, and only 15 Democrats opposed it. *(Vote 120, p. 40-H)*

Gray claimed victory on behalf of the Democratic House for passage of a budget plan he described as more fair and compassionate than the Senate's. In two days of floor debate, House members rejected four alternatives, three from divided Republicans and one from the Congressional Black Caucus. They also defeated two amendments, including one to raise taxes and eliminate the Social Security COLA.

The House action was remarkable for the relative unity among usually fractious Democrats, and a surprising lack of partisanship. Republicans were unable to offer a united opposition, and no group espoused the Senate-White House budget with its politically charged freeze on Social Security.

Options Rejected

Floor debate began May 22, with defense clearly the main issue dividing the parties.

Democrats stressed repeatedly that while their budget would freeze defense budget authority in fiscal 1986, the Pentagon still would have $15 billion more in outlays, due to long-term obligations for previously approved weapons systems. In fiscal 1987-88, they added, the Pentagon would receive a 3 percent increase above inflation — the same level as the Senate budget.

Latta, leading the fight to boost defense spending, unsuccessfully offered an alternative budget for Republicans, a $56.7 billion deficit-reduction package that generally tracked the Senate budget, without eliminating the Social Security COLA.

His was not the only GOP package. William E. Dannemeyer, Calif., offered a substitute for conservatives in the Republican Study Group. And party liberals in the 92 Group, named for their goal of winning a House majority in 1992, had a third option proposing fewer program cuts and eliminations than other GOP budgets, and a defense spending freeze identical to the House Democrats' budget.

Dannemeyer's budget was the first defeated, 39-382, on May 22. It tracked the Senate-passed budget on defense, and on eliminating COLAs for federal and civil service retirement programs in 1986. Dannemeyer proposed to keep the Social Security COLA, but at a level equal to 2 percent below inflation. *(Vote 113, p. 38-H)*

He would have eliminated many domestic programs, and made deeper cuts in others than the Budget Committee, but would not have raised taxes.

Also May 22, the House rejected the 92 Group's substitute, 87-335. *(Vote 114, p. 38-H)*

Before the Budget Committee's May 16 vote approving a budget resolution, the 92 Group Republicans had proposed to freeze defense spending in fiscal 1986 and to allow increases only to match inflation in 1987-88. However, after the Democratic panel allowed 3 percent increases above inflation for the Pentagon in 1987-88, the 92 Group followed suit.

Its plan would have cut funding for 75 domestic programs below a freeze, and eliminated seven. The 92 Group did not take a position on Social Security, though its plan would have eliminated the 1986 COLAs for other federal retirement programs. The budget would not have raised taxes.

Given the plan's similarities to the committee budget, notably on defense, Democrats prefaced their criticism of its specifics with praise for the overall outline. And, it attracted few Republican votes other than those of the 40 group members. Minority Leader Robert H. Michel, Ill., and Minority Whip Trent Lott, Miss., supported it, along with several Democrats.

Latta's substitute drew more votes than any other, but failed May 23, 102-329. One Democrat, Earl Hutto, Fla., voted for it; 79 Republicans, mostly moderates, opposed it. *(Vote 117, p. 40-H)*

Thomas J. Downey, N.Y., a Budget Committee Democrat, said the fact that Latta's budget, like the other GOP alternatives, would not have eliminated the Social Security COLA was proof of that provision's bipartisan support in the House.

Charles W. Stenholm, D-Texas, a Boll Weevil conservative who generally supported higher defense spending, opposed the Latta budget. He said Reagan and Republicans should be willing to support a tax hike to pay for the defense buildup "instead of borrowing on our grandchildren's future to pay for it."

For the fifth year, the 20-member Congressional Black Caucus offered a budget that provided more spending for domestic programs. Its plan was the only one to propose cuts below a freeze in defense, and to rely on tax increases for most of its deficit reduction.

Its budget called for a 25 percent minimum tax on corporations and wealthy individuals, a delay in indexing tax rates to inflation until 1989, and repeal of tax breaks for business enacted in 1981. New tax revenues would have been used both to reduce the deficit and to remove poor people from the federal income tax rolls.

In defense, the caucus proposed savings by ending purchases of Trident II submarines, and the MX, Pershing II and cruise missiles. Its plan retained COLAs for retirement programs, and allowed increases for many domestic programs, particularly those related to jobs, health, education and housing.

The plan was rejected 54-361. Gray, a caucus member, voted present. *(Vote 115, p. 38-H)*

Amendments Defeated

With all substitutes easily defeated, the House turned May 23 to two Democratic amendments. One, offered by Budget Committee members Leath, Slattery and MacKay, combined spending cuts with both tax increases and elimination of the 1986 COLAs for fiscal 1986 savings of $75 billion.

Wright and Chief Deputy Whip Bill Alexander, D-Ark., had led a group supporting an alternative that would have used a corporate minimum tax to reduce the budget deficit. At the request of Alexander and allies Mary Rose Oakar, D-Ohio, and Wes Watkins, D-Okla., a party caucus was held May 21 to discuss the two amendments.

After the caucus showed no clear majority for any position except the general idea of a minimum tax, a compromise was reached allowing Oakar to offer a vague amendment, similar to the provision already in H Con Res 152 calling for a general overhaul of the tax code, that would have directed the Ways and Means Committee to report minimum tax legislation.

The compromise was drafted in time for the May 21 meeting of the Rules Committee to determine a rule guiding floor debate on the budget. Though traditionally only alternative budgets were considered on the floor, and not line-item amendments, O'Neill earlier had promised Leath, Slattery and MacKay that they could push their proposal in return for votes supporting the leadership package in committee.

New Taxes, Cola Cut. Leath, Slattery and MacKay proposed to raise $12 billion in new revenues from unspecified taxes, though they cited cigarette and liquor taxes, oil import fees and minimum taxes as potential sources. Of the savings from eliminating the COLAs, they said 20 percent should be "plowed back" into funding for programs that benefit the elderly poor.

More than a dozen moderate-to-conservative Democrats took turns at speeches endorsing the option, including James R. Jones, Okla., Gray's predecessor as Budget chairman, and Leon E. Panetta, Calif., who had challenged Gray for the job in January.

When Claude Pepper, D-Fla., longtime advocate of the elderly, spoke against the proposal, the Democrats listened in silence while a small group of Republicans opposed to the COLA cut applauded Pepper's defense of what traditionally had been a favorite Democratic program.

The amendment was defeated 56-372. Forty-one Democrats and only 15 Republicans supported it. Gray, who privately had supported eliminating the COLA, voted present. *(Vote 118, p. 40-H)*

Minimum Tax. Support for a minimum tax, which proponents said could have raised $25 billion annually, received a boost May 20 when Dole told reporters the Senate would consider a minimum tax if the House proposed it. O'Neill refused to accept Dole's apparent invitation, in light of Reagan's threatened veto of any tax bill.

House leaders also were split. O'Neill and Dan Rostenkowski, D-Ill., chairman of the tax-writing Ways and Means Committee, opposed attaching revenue proposals to the budget resolution. And Rostenkowski said any new taxes must be part of a tax overhaul, with any new revenues used to offset an across-the-board reduction in tax rates. Like many members, he feared that imposing a minimum tax would derail the tax reform effort.

The half-hour debate on the Oakar tax compromise elicited the first notable partisan bickering of the two-day session. But rather than fight over future proposals to overhaul the tax code, Republicans and Democrats sparred more over blame for the 1981 tax cut, which both sides conceded was too generous to business. *(1981 Almanac p. 91)*

The Oakar amendment was rejected 142-283. Only one Republican, Silvio O. Conte, Mass., voted for it. Afterward, Gray and Latta attributed the defeat to a combination of factors: disgust with the amendment's "vague" and "meaningless" language, and opposition both from tax proponents who wanted revenues specifically tied to deficit reduction or to reducing tax rates. *(Vote 119, p. 40-H)*

Conference Action

Agreement on a budget in conference proved to be as difficult as on the floor of the Senate. No fewer than five alternative budgets were put on the table and rejected over the space of eight weeks, and the compromise that finally won consent was drafted in private by the four principal negotiators.

Though both sides gave something up, in the end the budget much more closely resembled the House-passed version than the Senate's. And the Senate flatly failed in its effort to breach the barriers against Social Security COLA cuts and tax increases built by Reagan and House Democratic leaders.

Starting Point

The savings claimed in the House-passed budget were nearly identical to those claimed by the Senate. But policy changes recommended by the two chambers' budgets exposed the conflicting priorities of the two major parties over defense and domestic spending.

The Republican Senate budget would have allowed an inflation increase for the Pentagon but not for 36 million Social Security recipients in fiscal 1986. The Democratic House plan would have done the opposite, freezing defense spending while protecting a scheduled cost-of-living allowance (COLA) for Social Security.

Also, the Senate budget would have eliminated 13 domestic programs, while the House budget would have ended only the general revenue-sharing program that allocated funds to local governments, no strings attached. Neither measure would have imposed new taxes.

Dole May 3 attacked the House plan for failing to achieve meaningful deficit reduction. And Reagan in a May 24 speech pronounced the House budget resolution "unacceptable," adding that "a further cut in defense spending would ... put the defense of our nation at risk."

For their part, House Democrats said Senate leaders miscalculated in voting to eliminate the Social Security COLA, and said Social Security would be "off the table" in conference talks.

Slow Start

Conferees got off to a slow start the week of June 10. They could not agree on a handful of relatively non-controversial items, and, in their first meetings they did not even discuss the major points of dispute.

By June 21, the end of the second week of conference talks, both sides had offered alternatives to the budgets passed in their chambers. Although the offers were rejected, they sparked the first conference debate on Social Security and defense.

Late on June 19, after a sixth day of dickering over individual programs, Senate Republicans offered a compromise package to reduce the deficit $60 billion in fiscal 1986 by cutting defense outlays, but not budget authority, and by eliminating the 1986 Social Security COLA, but adding $700 million to the budget to aid the low-income elderly. House Democrats rejected the offer without a vote the next day.

On June 21, House conferees presented a counterproposal. Like the senators' offer, the House plan was a step toward the other side's position, but not far enough to be immediately accepted. It, too, was rejected without a vote.

The House conferees offered no change in defense or Social Security. They proposed additional cuts in agriculture and other non-poverty domestic programs, for deficit reduction of $57.8 billion in fiscal 1986.

Strains that had threatened the budget conference before it had begun came to the surface in its second week. Senate Republicans, led by Domenici, repeatedly complained of Democrats' resistance to eliminating the COLA and further cutting domestic programs.

House Democrats objected to Republicans' depictions of their budget as anti-defense and full of accounting gimmicks, especially after senators rejected several early House offers of cuts in individual programs.

Taxes Hit the Table

House and Senate negotiators disbanded indefinitely June 25, split over the Social Security issue. But conferees reconvened briefly June 27 before their July 4th recess, and received a new proposal from a majority of the Senate team — three Republicans: Kassebaum; Slade Gorton, Wash.; and Rudy Boschwitz, Minn.; and three Democrats: Chiles, Hollings and J. Bennett Johnston, La.

The plan combined elimination of the Social Security increase with a call for $59 billion in unspecified new taxes over three years.

Gray was receptive, calling the offer "a new direction,... very significant."

The House was to get a piece of its defense freeze; Pentagon spending authority was to get an inflation increase in fiscal 1986, as the Senate wanted. But $4 billion would be subtracted from the Senate figure to account for funds Defense Secretary Weinberger had said were available in existing accounts.

COLAS for Social Security and other retirement programs were to be eliminated in fiscal 1986, but to address Democrats' complaints that thousands of elderly persons would be forced into poverty, the senators proposed that 20 percent of the savings from dropping the COLA go to increase programs benefiting poor senior citizens.

When Domenici recalled conferees June 27, his initial purpose had not been to let the six senators present their offer but to consider what he thought was grounds for a compromise from House Speaker O'Neill.

In response to reporters' questions June 26, O'Neill had said he supported higher income taxes on Social Security benefits as a revenue-raising alternative to eliminating the COLAs. He said he would expand a 1983 law that, for the first time, required individuals with more than $25,000 in income, and couples with income over $32,000, to pay federal income taxes on half their Social Security benefits. O'Neill said he would tax 85 percent of benefits. *(1983 Almanac p. 219)*

Such a change would have raised an estimated $8.5 billion over three years from about 9 percent of the 36 million Social Security recipients, his aides said.

Dole, meanwhile, had told reporters another $8.3 billion could be raised over three years by requiring state and local government employees to contribute to Social Security.

Domenici had hoped to discuss both ideas. But even before conferees gathered June 27, House members told him O'Neill's remarks did not constitute a negotiating proposal. House Democrats said privately they were concerned about becoming tied to a tax-hike proposal without Reagan's support.

Reagan Weighs In

After the recess, Reagan intervened in the deadlocked, month-old budget negotiations, only to alienate fellow Republicans and to leave conferees as divided as ever.

On July 9, after a cocktail-hour reception at the White House for five congressional leaders, Reagan and O'Neill agreed that the Senate should give up its insistence on eliminating the 1986 Social Security COLA and the House should accept the Senate's inflation adjustment for defense.

Reagan also won assurance that no taxes would be raised to pare the deficit, and a vague understanding that conferees would make more cuts in domestic spending to offset the Social Security and defense add-ons.

This "Oak Tree Framework" for agreement, as the understanding was called since it reportedly was reached during talks held under an oak tree on the White House grounds, was concluded at a testy White House meeting July 10 between Reagan and budget conferees.

The president's acceptance of the defense-for-Social Security swap was viewed on all sides as a major defeat for Senate GOP leaders, particularly Dole and Domenici. It also buried the bipartisan Senate compromise put on the table just before the recess. But, though Gray declared victory for the House, not all Democrats were happy with the proposed framework. Many were angry with their leaders, O'Neill and Majority Leader Wright, for compromising too much on defense.

During the White House meeting, Gray told the president his repeated public attacks on the House budget were not helpful to the budget process. "I told him to keep the rhetoric to a minimum and to get the facts straight," Gray said.

That was only one unfriendly exchange of an often-tense session. Dole and Gray took turns questioning savings claims in each other's budgets. Domenici was steaming about the president's concessions to O'Neill, participants said, particularly since he had not been invited to the cocktail session the night before.

Reagan, who opened the meeting with an admonition against tax increases, interrupted both Chiles and Gorton when they tried to describe their proposal pending before the conference. "Dammit, I can't listen to all of this," Reagan said at one point, according to detailed notes taken by Rep. Thomas J. Downey, D-N.Y.

Most of the anger came from bitter Senate Republicans, who attributed Reagan's move to fellow Republican Jack F. Kemp, N.Y., one of the House conferees.

In recent weeks, Kemp had arranged meetings with Gray, House Minority Whip Lott and White House Chief of Staff Donald T. Regan to break the budget stalemate. Domenici and Dole were unaware of the sessions. Kemp, a proponent of tax cuts to stimulate the economy, suspected the two were about to back tax hikes to cut deficits.

Kemp reportedly persuaded Regan that Reagan should give in on Social Security to get a budget without taxes. Also helpful was a letter from 67 House Republicans, including Kemp and Lott, urging Domenici to drop the Senate position.

Talks Collapse . . . Again

The possibility of achieving agreement fell abruptly following the Oak Tree deal, as conferees could not agree on what the terms of the deal required.

Dole had accused Reagan of "surrendering to the deficit." But, although Dole and other GOP senators stood by their criticisms, they stifled attacks after Reagan had surprise surgery July 13 for removal of a cancerous intestinal tumor. "We're not mad at anybody; we're mad at the deficit," Dole said. *(Reagan's surgery, p. 26)*

The terms were disputed from the start. Senate leaders said they required House conferees to find $28 billion in cuts through 1988, roughly the cost of paying COLAs. House members maintained they had no obligation to propose so high a sum.

When the conference resumed July 15, Domenici spoke of discarding the framework. But, after House negotiators rejected the bipartisan Senate offer that had been lingering since before the Oak Tree agreement, Gray brought to the conference a proposal to cut $24 billion over three years.

Savings through 1988 would have totaled $272.6 billion, narrowing the gap between the House-passed budget's $259 billion total and the Senate's $295 billion. The House also dropped a provision from its original budget that senators had derided as phony. It had assumed $12 billion in savings over three years by reducing contracts with private firms providing government services.

In defense, the House offer provided $298 billion in spending authority, $5.4 billion more than the House budget but $4.5 billion less than the Senate's. Domenici said that was a breach of the White House framework, which he said called for a Social Security-for-defense swap.

Wright, the only conferee present at the White House meeting July 9, said the framework bound the House to "move toward" the Senate's defense spending level, not to adopt it entirely.

House Democrats said the counter-offer was close to their "bottom line." On July 17, the shrinking negotiating room was evident when, at a caucus of all House Democrats, leading members opposed the new cuts. And the defense increase was too high for many members, including conservative Democrats and Republicans.

But Domenici rejected the offer as being insubstantial and was joined by Democrats Chiles and Hollings.

Agreement at Last

The conference broke up for a week after the House offer was rejected, and Domenici reconvened it July 25 to break with the White House and join Democratic senators in a call for new taxes to pare the deficit.

This latest compromise combined tax increases — a fee on imported oil and a delay in 1987 of inflation adjustments in income tax brackets — with delays in inflation adjustments for Social Security and other federal pension programs. The plan, which also included spending compromises between House and Senate positions, was backed by Dole and by all Senate conferees except Jim Sasser, D-Tenn.

There was no immediate consensus and conferees agreed they were stymied unless Reagan and O'Neill made concessions. But Reagan flatly rejected the compromise July 29, driving the conference leaders — Domenici, Chiles, Gray and Latta — into private negotiations to hammer out some kind of budget before Congress left for a month-long August recess.

The conference accepted the final compromise by voice vote. It included no tax increase and no COLA reduction. It also anticipated no growth in 1986 in defense spending beyond inflation and cuts of 20 to 30 percent from a wide range of non-defense programs other than those assisting the poor. The poverty programs, for the most part, would be allowed to grow enough to keep pace with inflation.

In one of their few victories, Senate conferees prodded their House counterparts into increasing the proportion of assumed savings covered by so-called reconciliation instructions, which mandated committee action to achieve specified spending levels. The reconciliation instructions covered $68 billion worth of savings. The Senate-passed budget had sought $37 billion more in reconciled savings, the House-passed budget $33 billion less. ∎

Congress Sets $2.079 Trillion Ceiling on Debt

On Dec. 11, just before adjourning for the year, Congress enacted an increase in the ceiling on the federal debt, raising the limit from $1.824 trillion to $2.079 trillion. The measure raising the debt ceiling (H J Res 372 — PL 99-177) also was the vehicle for a far-reaching amendment requiring a balanced budget by fiscal 1991.

The government's need to borrow to pay its bills threatened by the Oct. 1 start of fiscal 1986 to breach the ceiling set the year before. The balanced-budget amendment, sponsored by Sens. Phil Gramm, R-Texas, Warren B. Rudman, R-N.H., and Ernest F. Hollings, D-S.C., required two months of debate on the floors of both chambers and in two separate conference committees.

As a result of that delay, the Treasury Department was forced to take extraordinary steps, including disinvestment of the Social Security trust funds, to prevent the government from defaulting on its obligations. *(Gramm-Rudman-Hollings measure, p. 459)*

In a further step to prevent default, Congress in November enacted a short-term debt-ceiling increase (HR 3721 — PL 99-155), enabling Treasury to continue borrowing until enactment of the permanent increase.

Permanent Debt-Limit Increase

Fights over raising the ceiling on the federal debt had become *de rigueur* for opponents of federal spending in the late 1970s and 1980s. And the need to raise the debt limit for fiscal 1986 above $2 trillion was expected to draw more than the usual series of budget-cutting amendments, especially in a year when deficits had dominated debate all year.

But while the Senate faced a potentially bitter debate in September, after returning from Congress' month-long August recess, the House avoided the initial struggle. Using an automatic procedure that was the equivalent of parliamentary sleight of hand, the House sent H J Res 372, the resolution raising the debt ceiling to $2.079 trillion, to the Senate. *(Automatic procedure, box, p. 458)*

In the Senate, H J Res 372 quickly became the target for amendments. Both Steven D. Symms, R-Idaho, and William L. Armstrong, R-Colo., expressed interest in reviving budget fights from earlier in the year, when H J Res 372 came to the floor.

And on Sept. 25, Sens. Gramm, Rudman and Hollings introduced a bill (S 1702) setting deficit targets for each of the five succeeding years, requiring a balanced budget by fiscal 1991 and creating a method of automatic spending cuts to meet the targets.

On Oct. 3, the Senate began consideration of H J Res 372, and Majority Leader Robert Dole, R-Kan., immediately offered a version of the Gramm-Rudman-Hollings bill as an amendment to the resolution. The Senate agreed to the amendment Oct. 9, and passed the debt-limit bill by a 51-37 vote the following day. *(Vote 222, p. 42-S)*

To avoid a floor vote on the Senate amendment, which some opponents feared might pass, the House immediately asked for a conference on H J Res 372 in hope of altering the balanced-budget provisions.

There was never any dispute over the provision raising the debt ceiling. The conference, however, failed to reach agreement on the Senate's budget-balancing plan, and the measure came back to the House floor. On Nov. 1, in a surprising show of party unity, House Democrats voted almost unanimously, 249-180, to substitute a markedly different version of the Gramm-Rudman-Hollings amendment in H J Res 372. *(Vote 350, p. 108-H)*

After both chambers voted again Nov. 6 — the Senate adopting a somewhat modified version of its plan, the House insisting on its amendment — a new conference convened. Most of that conference's work was done over the following month by a small handful of members meeting in private. On Dec. 10, conferees agreed to a final version of the budget-balancing plan (H Rept 99-433), and both chambers agreed to the conference report the following day, clearing the measure.

Treasury Maneuvers

The deliberations over the Gramm-Rudman-Hollings amendment prevented enactment of the debt-ceiling increase until long after the deadline set by the U.S. Treasury.

Administration officials had warned of catastrophe if Congress failed to increase the amount it could legally borrow by early October. But Senate leaders, who wanted to hold Congress' feet to the fire on Gramm-Rudman-Hollings, refused for about a month to consider temporary increases in the debt limit. During the extended negotiations on H J Res 372, Treasury on several occasions ran out of money, but pulled the institutional equivalent of finding some spare change in a back pocket.

Federal Financing Bank Switch

On Oct. 9 Treasury went through a complicated maneuver that yielded $5 billion with which to pay the federal government's pressing bills. The same maneuver about two weeks later flushed out another $10 billion, enough to carry the government until the first of November.

Treasury's problem on Oct. 9 was that it had borrowed the full $1.824 trillion allowed by law and had run out of cash reserves with which to pay federal checks, contract obligations and the like.

What it did first was to redeem $5 billion in non-marketable Treasury securities held by the Civil Service Retirement and Disability Fund, thereby lowering its indebtedness by $5 billion. It then sold at auction $5 billion worth of 78-day cash-management Treasury bills. It finally arranged for a little-known Treasury agency, the Federal Financing Bank (FFB), which was not subject to the debt

Automatic Debt-Limit Vote

Under a six-year-old procedure, the House effectively adopted a resolution (H J Res 372) raising the debt ceiling Aug. 1. But the House did not consider the debt-ceiling resolution Aug. 1. What it did that day was adopt the fiscal 1986 budget resolution (S Con Res 32), which contained spending and revenue goals, and a projection of the "appropriate" debt ceiling.

Since 1979, the House had automatically sent a separate debt-ceiling measure to the Senate after it adopted a budget resolution. The House voted on the debt-limit resolution only if the Senate amended it. *(Debt-limit action, p. 457; budget resolution, p. 441)*

The procedure grew from the frustration House Democratic leaders felt at the difficulties they encountered in the 1970s whenever it became necessary to raise the debt ceiling. Often the House defeated such increases, despite the pleas of presidents that they were necessary to keep the government running.

Especially during the Carter administration, when Democrats controlled the White House and Congress, few Republicans would vote for an increase, and many Democrats also preferred to vote against them. In July 1978, for example, only nine Republicans voted for a debt increase that passed 205-202.

In 1979, O'Neill asked Rep. Richard A. Gephardt, D-Mo., to round up the votes to pass the debt-limit increases sought by the Carter administration. After the House defeated a debt increase in February and barely passed a six-month extension in March, Gephardt drafted the current procedure. The method was approved as part of the debt-ceiling increase in September 1979, after the House rejected, 132-283, an amendment to block it. *(1979 Almanac p. 305)*

Prior Year Debt-Limit Votes

With several exceptions, the system succeeded in expediting House action. The most problems the House had had under the system occurred in 1984, when six roll-call votes were needed to pass two debt-ceiling extensions.

But the system still worked in 1984. Because there was a budget resolution by fall, House members did not have to vote again on the debt ceiling just prior to adjourning for the elections. As its last act, however, the Senate voted 14-46 against the increase and voted 37-30 to pass it only after senators who already had left town were flown back. *(1984 Almanac p. 165)*

In 1983, it was the House that as its last act before adjournment in November had to vote to increase the debt ceiling. In that case, the vote was needed because the Senate had added several amendments to the measure, including one lowering the ceiling in the bill. In 1982, there were no House votes on debt-limit increases. *(1983 Almanac p. 239; 1982 Almanac p. 44)*

In February 1981, one of the first substantive House votes of Ronald Reagan's presidency came on the debt ceiling. That vote — 305-104 — produced the widest margin of House approval of a debt-limit increase in years as 150 Republicans, including many who had never voted for increasing the national debt, voted for passage. *(1981 Almanac p. 104)*

limit, to issue $5 billion in its own notes to the Civil Service fund, thereby making good the earlier redemption.

The FFB was created by Congress in 1973 as a central authority through which such agencies as the Rural Electrification Administration could borrow from the public. It was given authority to borrow up to $15 billion from the public by issuing its own securities, and unlimited authority to borrow from the Treasury. The pensioners of the Civil Service fund were considered by Treasury attorneys to be the public, so that the $5 billion issue sold to the fund was deemed to use a third of FFB's authority to borrow from the public.

Late in the day on Oct. 9, after the first vote approving the budget plan, the Senate amended an unrelated bill (HR 3453) to, in effect, ratify the Treasury action. But an hour later, Ways and Means Chairman Dan Rostenkowski, D-Ill., advised the House not to consider it. He argued that the bill would bar Treasury from using the additional $10 billion FFB borrowing authority, and that use of that extra authority would give the House a reasonable amount of time to consider the budget plan. HR 3453 never came up again in the House.

Social Security Disinvestment

The trading of securities with the FFB kept the government solvent for a month, but Nov. 1 Treasury had to resort to another survival tactic, drawing on investments of Social Security and other federal retirement funds to pay pension benefits.

Treasury Secretary James A. Baker III made the Social Security plan known Oct. 22, when he discussed it at the White House with Republican leaders and in a letter to Rostenkowski and other conferees on H J Res 372.

In his letter, Baker announced that Treasury would "reluctantly " move to "disinvest" the Social Security, military retirement, civil service retirement and railroad retirement trust funds to permit benefit payments, beginning Nov. 1, to beneficiaries of those funds.

The federal trust funds were required by law to invest any surplus cash in Treasury securities.

Disinvestment, Treasury officials said, involved taking back from the trust funds some of the Treasury securities that the funds owned, dropping the government's indebtedness below the statutory ceiling.

Treasury then sold an equivalent amount in securities to the public, and used the proceeds to cash November checks for the funds' beneficiaries.

Social Security had been a sticking point in budget fights all year long, as many members of both parties acted to protect the program to avoid angering its politically powerful constituency.

The mere threat of the disinvestment had so disturbed conferees on the budget-balancing plan that they tried, but failed, to finish the legislation before Nov. 1, when Treasury put the tactic to use.

Baker's letter, too, had expressed disapproval of the scheme it outlined and blamed Congress for forcing the unprecedented and easily misunderstood action.

In fact, members learned after the Nov. 1 disinvestment that in September and October of 1984 and 1985, Treasury had partially disinvested the trust funds to cover borrowing shortfalls.

In the final version of H J Res 372, Congress took steps to protect Social Security from future budget fights, prohibit future disinvestment of the trust funds and restore lost interest to the funds. *(Social Security, p. 465)*

Temporary Debt-Limit Increase

After Treasury exhausted its maneuvers to stay solvent, Congress was forced Nov. 14 to enact a temporary increase in the debt limit (HR 3721 — PL 99-155) to buy even more time for the conferees on the balanced-budget measure.

The House by a 300-121 vote passed HR 3721, raising the ceiling on the federal debt to $1.904 trillion, but requiring the ceiling to revert to $1.824 trillion on Dec. 13. The measure also required the Treasury to restore to the Social Security trust funds any disinvested securities. *(Vote 369, p. 114-H)*

The same day the Senate passed the measure, after amending it to change to Dec. 6 the date on which the debt-limit would revert to $1.824 trillion, and to add to the bill the text of HR 3722, a bill extending the cigarette excise tax and other programs. *(Cigarette tax, box, p. 502)*

The following day the House accepted the Senate amendment, clearing the bill. House sponsors determined that despite the Dec. 6 date on which the debt-ceiling would revert, the Treasury would have enough cash on hand to carry the government until at least Dec. 13.

H J Res 372, the permanent debt-limit increase, was signed into law Dec. 12, preventing the need for any additional short-term increases.

Congress Enacts Strict Anti-Deficit Measure

At the end of a year of deep frustration over larger and larger budget deficits, Congress and the president took the historic step of binding themselves to five years of forced deficit reduction, with the goal of balancing the budget by October 1990.

On Dec. 12 President Reagan signed into law a radical revision of budgeting procedures (H J Res 372 — PL 99-177), requiring that the federal deficit be eliminated using conventional legislative means or, failing that, through unprecedented automatic spending cuts. The bill also raised the ceiling on the federal debt to above $2 trillion. *(Previous budget-balancing action, box, p. 460)*

At the time Reagan acted, the deficit for fiscal 1986 was projected to top $200 billion. By mid-January 1986, the Congressional Budget Office (CBO) and Office of Management and Budget (OMB) had agreed the fiscal 1986 deficit would exceed $220 billion.

On a Fast Track

The budget measure swept through Congress with gale force after its introduction in late September by two Senate freshmen, Phil Gramm, R-Texas, and Warren B. Rudman, R-N.H., and their more senior colleague, Ernest F. Hollings, D-S.C. The measure — which came to be known as Gramm-Rudman-Hollings — was enacted without benefit of the usual legislative process of committee hearings and markups. Even the floor action was telescoped, and crucial conference negotiations were conducted in private by House and Senate leaders of both parties.

Many members reported little overt lobbying either for or against the legislation, except for strong, last-minute objections from the Defense Department. Those objections, based on the potential of the plan to make the first real reductions in military spending in more than a decade, had raised the specter of a presidential veto.

Reagan had embraced early versions of the plan, but presidential doubts replaced enthusiasm when his advisers realized that the plan would not only cut defense spending but, because of budgetary peculiarities, do so in a distorted manner.

But in his statement on signing the measure, Reagan lauded the legislation as "an important step toward putting our fiscal house in order." He reiterated his commitment to continued real growth in defense spending, however, and his longstanding aversion to raising taxes to reduce the deficit. *(Text, p. 41-D)*

Much of his statement dealt with potential constitutional problems and virtually invited an early court test of the legislation. Hours after Reagan signed the law, Rep. Mike Synar, D-Okla., filed suit in federal district court in the District of Columbia challenging its key provision, the automatic cuts, on constitutional grounds. A special, three-judge panel upheld Synar's challenge Feb. 7, 1986, but stayed its order, pending an appeal to the Supreme Court. *(Constitutional challenge, p. 461)*

The budget legislation made many members of Congress uneasy, and they often said in private that it was neither wise nor workable. Nevertheless, Gramm-Rudman-Hollings won strong, bipartisan support in both chambers because of members' fears of the economic and political consequences of continued deficit spending.

Sponsor Rudman called it "a bad idea whose time has come."

Budget Plan Highlights

- Required federal budgets with deficits not exceeding $171.9 billion in fiscal 1986, $144 billion in fiscal 1987, $108 billion in fiscal 1988, $72 billion in fiscal 1989, $36 billion in fiscal 1990, zero in fiscal 1991.
- Required across-the-board automatic cuts of non-exempt programs by a uniform percentage to achieve deficit targets if regular budget and appropriations actions failed to reach deficit goals. Divided automatic cuts equally between defense and non-defense accounts.
- Established special rules for fiscal 1986 automatic cuts, which were to go into effect March 1 and were limited to $11.7 billion.
- Exempted from automatic cuts: Social Security, interest on the federal debt, veterans' compensation, veterans' pensions, Medicaid, Aid to Families with Dependent Children, WIC (a food program for women, infants, and children) Supplemental Security Income, food stamps and child nutrition. Limited cuts in five health programs, including Medicare.
- Provided that if courts invalidated the mechanism triggering automatic cuts, the order making those cuts would have to be approved by both houses of Congress and the president to take effect.
- Authorized suspension of automatic cuts during a recession or war.
- Established accelerated budget timetables and new procedures to prevent floor action on over-budget legislation.

Solution or 'Suicide Pact'

Gramm-Rudman-Hollings set annual maximum allowable deficits, declining by $36 billion each year to reach zero by the Oct. 1, 1990, start of fiscal 1991. In any year that Congress and the president did not devise a budget meeting the deficit target for the upcoming fiscal year, federal spending was to be cut automatically by a uniform percent to achieve the target. *(Timetables, pp. 462, 463)*

The measure, as enacted, made significant concessions to House Democrats. They wanted Social Security exempted from the measure entirely and insisted that the automatic cuts occur immediately, not after the 1986 elections as the original bill seemed to require. Democrats also succeeded in exempting completely or partly from future automatic cuts a handful of programs that aided the poor or infirm. *(Social Security, p. 465)*

And a compromise provision that in the end gave Reagan and Defense Secretary Caspar W. Weinberger serious cause for concern — and held the promise of significant long-term consequences — required that the automatic spending cuts would have to come half from military spending and half from domestic.

Because the large expenditures for Social Security and interest on the national debt were exempted, the automatic cuts were projected to affect only about half the budget.

The measure, which amended the 1974 Congressional Budget and Impoundment Control Act (PL 93-344), also strengthened routine budget procedures to be used before any automatic cuts went into effect. *(Budget act, 1974 Almanac p. 145)*

Advocates hoped the threat of automatic cuts would force the president, Congress and Americans jointly to decide to spend less on the government services and subsidies that pervaded the nation's life, or to pay for the government they wanted with higher taxes, or both.

Opponents said the plan was inoperable, or that it improperly shifted power away from the legislative branch, or that it would severely damage the nation's economy, its defense and a host of other sectors including agriculture, research and development, airline safety, law enforcement and medicine.

"It's a suicide pact," warned Sen. Daniel Patrick Moynihan, D-N.Y., who was particularly disturbed by the plan's impact on defense.

Most of those who defended the measure said they could not guarantee that it would have the desired effect, but that it was better than $200 billion-a-year deficits and the political impasse that had blocked solutions to the problem.

"I pray that what we are about to undertake will work," a sober Bob Packwood, R-Ore., told the Senate.

Budget Control: An Old Idea

The 1985 measure crafted by Sens. Phil Gramm, R-Texas, Warren B. Rudman, R-N.H., and Ernest F. Hollings, D-S.C., to require a balanced budget by law was not unique. Just seven years before, Congress actually wrote such a requirement into law — only to ignore it.

In late September 1978, as part of unrelated legislation (PL 95-435) involving the International Monetary Fund (IMF), Congress adopted a requirement that, beginning in fiscal 1981, annual budget outlays of the federal government "shall not exceed" its receipts. The provision, initiated by Sen. Harry F. Byrd Jr., Ind.-Va., was mandatory, but House-Senate conferees sought to soften its effect by specifying that it "may be superseded by the action of future Congresses." *(1978 Almanac p. 424)*

In 1980, in a separate IMF bill (PL 96-389), Congress reaffirmed its intent that the budget be balanced by fiscal 1981, but struck any mandatory requirement. *(1980 Almanac p. 349; history of budget control efforts, Congress and the Nation Vol. IV, pp. 57, 71)*

Another Deficit-Reduction Measure Derailed

Even as Congress was trying to scribe in stone its commitment to reduced deficits, however, the reverse was occurring. Members had agreed in August to historically large spending reductions in the fiscal 1986 budget resolution (S Con Res 32). *(Budget resolution, p. 441)*

Some believed deficit reduction had been thwarted by their colleagues' reluctance to touch such politically sensitive programs as Social Security, farm subsidies and the like. Many were exasperated at Reagan's insistence on the expensive defense buildup and his flat refusals to raise taxes to pay for it. The looming 1986 elections heightened members' sense of urgency about the deficit issue.

But in an ironic twist, Congress' legislative attention was so diverted by the Gramm-Rudman-Hollings debate at the end of 1985 that a major deficit-reduction bill for fiscal 1986 failed to clear before adjournment. This so-called reconciliation bill (HR 3128) would make changes in a large number of existing laws to lower program spending levels in accord with S Con Res 32. *(Reconciliation, p. 498)*

The failure to put the money-saving reconciliation changes into place by Oct. 1, the beginning of fiscal 1986, cost an estimated $50 million a day in savings that would otherwise have been made, according to rough estimates of congressional aides.

Immediate Consequences

Gramm-Rudman-Hollings had its intended effects as well. An immediate impact of the budget measure was that on Jan. 1, 1986, retirees receiving military, civil service and certain other federal pensions did not receive scheduled cost-of-living adjustments (COLAs). The legislation delayed implementation of the scheduled COLAs in anticipation of the first round of automatic spending cuts on March 1, 1986.

But the first major event under the new budget regime was the announcement by CBO and OMB Jan. 15, 1986, of the shape of automatic cuts for fiscal 1986. The law limited the 1986 cut to $11.7 billion, or $5.85 billion each for defense and non-defense accounts.

The cuts were ordered by President Reagan Feb. 1 to take effect March 1, and specified across-the-board domestic spending cuts of 4.3 percent and defense cuts of 4.9 percent. The percentage reduction for defense would have been smaller, but under a special provision for 1986 only, Reagan exempted military personnel and his "strategic defense initiative" from the cuts, forcing other defense programs to absorb a bigger bite.

The net effect of the 1986 automatic cuts was to reduce the projected 1986 deficit from $220 billion to $208 billion.

Constitutionality of Automatic Cuts Challenged

One of the enduring complaints about the Gramm-Rudman-Hollings anti-deficit measure as it was debated in conference was that it violated the Constitution's separation-of-powers doctrine in some important and obvious ways.

The focus of the objections was the provision mandating automatic across-the-board cuts to reduce the deficit, should traditional legislative means falter.

Opponents complained that early Senate versions vested too much legislative power in the president by granting him wide discretion to make cuts from enacted spending legislation; conversely, critics of the House alternative said its provisions giving the Congressional Budget Office (CBO) authority to direct the president in making those cuts went too far the other way.

Ultimately, concern that any automatic procedure canceling enacted law would have to survive a stiff constitutional test led conferees to devise a complex formula for the cuts involving CBO, the Office of Management and Budget (OMB) and the General Accounting Office (GAO). In fact, the law contained provisions inviting an early constitutional test, and providing an alternative method of enacting the across-the-board cuts as law, should the courts find the automatic procedure unconstitutional.

Hybrid Role of GAO Seen as Key

Under the law, CBO and OMB were jointly to estimate the deficit, the amount, if any, by which the deficit exceeded mandatory deficit limits, and the percentages by which defense and non-defense spending would have to be cut to achieve the target. GAO was to review the CBO and OMB figures, adjust them if necessary, and issue a report to the president that, in essence, would become the order mandating the cuts.

The hope was that the hybrid process would pass muster, vesting power as it did in a legislative branch agency (CBO), an executive branch agency (OMB), and one that might be perceived as in between (GAO). The president had no discretion to alter the GAO report.

Nevertheless, President Reagan in signing Gramm-Rudman-Hollings Dec. 12 voiced his concern over its constitutionality, and that same day Rep. Mike Synar, D-Okla., filed suit in federal district court in the District of Columbia, asking to have the automatic cuts procedure thrown out.

Synar was joined in his suit by 11 other members of Congress, and a second suit was brought by the National Treasury Employees Union. The two cases were consolidated by the court. The Senate, the Speaker and a bipartisan leadership group of the House, and the comptroller general, who headed GAO, intervened in the case to defend the law.

A special three-judge federal panel on Feb. 7, 1986, agreed with Synar and the other plaintiffs that the comptroller general could not under the Constitution be responsible for deciding the scope and size of the automatic cuts. The court said the comptroller general could be removed from office by Congress, and therefore was an agent of Congress who could not — under the separation-of-powers doctrine — direct the president.

The decision nullified both the automatic cut procedure and the first round of automatic cuts ordered for fiscal 1986. But the court stayed the effect of its order until an appeal could be heard by the Supreme Court. The Supreme Court accepted the appeal Feb. 24, 1986, setting arguments for April 23. The stay left in effect the fiscal 1986 automatic cuts totaling $11.7 billion, which were ordered Feb. 1 and became final March 1.

The ruling affected only the automatic cut procedure, leaving intact the law's deficit targets, the alternate method for enacting the cuts, and many procedural changes aimed at tightening budgeting procedures.

Delegation Itself Not Improper

The court said, in effect, that there were two basic issues raised by the suits: whether Congress could give away — "delegate" — its authority to make spending decisions, and if so, to whom. The court agreed that Congress could make the delegation of power involved in the automatic spending cut procedure, but not to the comptroller general.

The Justice Department had argued that the delegation of power was not improper because Congress had circumscribed it with precise instructions as to how the automatic cut orders were to be constructed. The court essentially affirmed that view.

During 1985, the hybrid role of GAO was also being tested in court cases in which the Reagan administration argued that GAO was strictly a legislative agency. These cases tested the 1984 Competition in Contracting Act (PL 98-369) which authorized GAO to suspend the awarding of a government contract that was under challenge; but in contrast to the Gramm-Rudman decision, federal district court decisions in those cases upheld the view that GAO could direct executive branch actions. *(Competition in Contracting Act, 1984 Almanac p. 198)*

Alternate Method for Enacting Cuts

The law specified the following alternate method for enacting the cuts as law, should the courts strike down the automatic procedure:

CBO and OMB, as under the automatic procedure, were jointly to prepare a report each August calculating whether the deficit for the upcoming fiscal year would exceed the target in the law, and, if necessary, specifying by what percentage spending would have to be cut to meet the target.

This report, however, was to go not to the GAO and then to the president for promulgation. Instead it was to go to Congress, where a special, joint House-Senate budget committee was to have five days in which to report the CBO-OMB findings as a joint resolution.

That resolution was to come to the floor in both chambers under expedited procedures; it was to take effect only if passed by both and signed by the president. The law specified that the resolution could not be amended, either in committee or on the floor. However, these prohibitions were procedural rules of each chamber that could be changed.

The first round of cuts early in 1986 represented a major victory for House Democrats, who had insisted that the procedure be tested before the 1986 elections. Early versions of the Senate bill had appeared to postpone the first automatic cuts until after the election.

The cuts were triggered because deficit estimates based on economic indicators, federal spending requirements and federal revenues, as of Jan. 10, 1986, exceeded $171.9 billion.

As Gramm-Rudman-Hollings continued to dominate congressional activity in early 1986, the president's budget submitted Feb. 5 claimed spending reductions to achieve the required fiscal 1987 deficit target of $144 billion. The legislation required presidential budgets to achieve specified deficit targets, although there was no statutory penalty for a president who failed to meet the mark.

Altering the Budget Debate

The impact of Gramm-Rudman-Hollings on specific programs was, at the time Congress acted, difficult to gauge. But many members predicted that the law would significantly alter budget debates — particularly the provision that seemed to put defense and non-defense programs on equal footing in competition for scarce resources. And the mandatory deficit targets, even if the automatic cut procedure were ultimately not to survive a court test, were seen carrying significant political weight.

The standard fare of congressional budget action in the budget-cutting Reagan years had often meant only a reduction in anticipated growth. Cuts in growth had permitted many federal programs to continue expanding, albeit at rates that advocates called inadequate for the problems to be addressed. Rep. Leon E. Panetta, D-Calif., said, however, that the measure could, for the first time in recent memory, cause real reductions in federal spending.

And Rep. Les Aspin, D-Ore., chairman of the Armed Services Committee, said the net result for defense spending would be the first absolute reduction since the 1970s, when military expenditures failed to keep pace with raging inflation.

Except for the exempted programs, it was not clear how non-defense spending would fare in the new regime. Some members said the exemptions — of which Social Security was by far the largest — would heavily skew the automatic cuts against remaining "discretionary" programs such as biomedical research supported by the National Institutes of Health, mass transit subsidies, "infrastructure" expenditures on sewer and water systems, agricultural subsidies, education, and research and development.

By some estimates, discretionary programs might suffer cuts of as much as 30 percent to 40 percent. Gramm contended that such Draconian figures ignored estimates that federal revenues would grow by $75 billion in the next five years, thereby reducing the size of necessary cuts.

The least-examined aspects of the legislation were its many changes in congressional budget rules. Most of these procedural changes were lifted wholesale from recommendations developed over several years by a House group chaired by Rep. Anthony C. Beilenson, D-Calif. The most quixotic was a potential prohibition against Fourth of July recesses unless the House had passed all regular appropriations bills and reconciliation. Congress regularly had trouble finishing such legislation before October.

The procedural changes included new, early deadlines to prevent congressional foot-dragging, and checks to prevent floor action on legislation exceeding deficit targets. The measure required budget resolutions to include reconciliation instructions — optional under the 1974 budget act — to bring down deficits to the specified amounts, and expanded budget legislation to include all "off-budget" programs, credit and other obligations.

Major Provisions

The Balanced Budget and Emergency Deficit Control Act of 1985 (H J Res 372 — PL 99-177) amended the Congressional Budget and Impoundment Control Act of 1974 (PL 93-344). The new law:

Debt Limit

- Raised the ceiling on the federal debt to $2.079 trillion from $1.824 trillion.

Deficit Limits

- Established maximum allowable federal budget deficits as follows: for fiscal 1986, $171.9 billion; fiscal 1987, $144 billion; fiscal 1988, $108 billion; fiscal 1989, $72 billion; fiscal 1990, $36 billion; fiscal 1991, zero.

Budget Process Revisions

- Established a new, accelerated timetable for presidential submission of budgets and approval of budget resolutions, reconciliation measures and appropriations legislation.

Budget resolutions were non-binding plans specifying how much money Congress thought should be spent in broad categories, such as defense and agriculture; budget reconciliation legislation actually made changes in existing laws to achieve savings assumed by spending targets in budget resolutions.

Reconciliation instructions in budget resolutions had the effect of requiring committees to recommend changes in laws under their jurisdiction, so as to achieve savings assumed by the budget resolution. In appropriations bills, Congress decided how much might be spent in a given year for specific federal programs.

- Required congressional budget resolutions to provide for deficits not exceeding the annual levels specified by the legislation; also required the resolutions to include recon-

Timetable for Fiscal 1986

"Snapshot" of economic indicators, laws affecting spending and revenues and projected deficit taken by Congressional Budget Office (CBO) and Office of Management and Budget (OMB)	January 10
CBO and OMB report to General Accounting Office (GAO) on deficit and content of the so-called sequester order making automatic spending cuts to achieve deficit targets	January 15
GAO forwards deficit and sequester report to president	January 20
President issues sequester order based on GAO report	February 1
Sequester order takes effect	March 1
GAO issues compliance report on sequester order	April 1

Revisions to Budget Process Timetable

(For Fiscal Years 1987-1991)

Action	Prior Law	PL 99-177
President submits budget request	End of January	First Monday after January 3 [1]
Congressional Budget Office (CBO) reports to Budget committees on fiscal policy and budget priorities	April 1	February 15
Committees submit reports and estimates to Budget committees	March 15	February 25
Senate Budget Committee reports budget resolution to floor	April 15 [2]	April 1
Congress completes action on budget resolution	May 15 [3], September 15 [4]	April 15
House Appropriations Committee reports last regular appropriations bill	—	June 10
Congress completes action on reconciliation bill	September 25	June 15
House completes action on regular appropriations bills	Seventh day after Labor Day [5]	June 30
"Snapshot" of economic indicators, laws affecting spending and revenues and projected deficit taken by CBO and Office of Management and Budget (OMB)	—	August 15
CBO and OMB report to General Accounting Office (GAO) on deficit and content of the so-called sequester order making automatic spending cuts to achieve deficit targets	—	August 20
GAO forwards deficit and sequester report to president	—	August 25
President issues sequester order based on GAO report	—	September 1
Sequester order takes effect	—	October 1
Fiscal year begins	October 1	October 1
CBO and OMB issue revised reports reflecting additional congressional action after earlier reports	—	October 5
GAO issues revised report to the president	—	October 10
Final sequester order, based on revised report, becomes effective	—	October 15
GAO issues compliance report on sequester order	—	November 15

[1] President's budget for fiscal 1987 submitted February 5, 1986
[2] Prior law deadline for Budget committees in both houses to report budget resolutions
[3] Prior law deadline for first budget resolution
[4] Prior law deadline for second, binding budget resolution
[5] Prior law deadline for Congress to complete regular appropriations bills

ciliation instructions as needed to achieve the specified deficit targets.

- Expanded application of existing budget processes to cover federal loan programs. Required all budget resolutions to include so-called "off-budget" programs, except for Social Security, which was newly designated to be off-budget.
- Allowed budget resolutions to prohibit the enrollment of completed measures granting new budget or entitlement authority unless Congress had also completed any required reconciliation legislation. (Enrollment is the process of making a final copy of legislation for the president's signature.)
- Revised rules for debate on budget legislation, and required CBO and committees to provide more information about budgetary and economic impacts of individual bills and aggregate spending trends.
- Restated an existing requirement that budget resolutions divide among committees the amount of total outlays, budget authority, entitlement and credit authority assumed by the resolution.
- Required each committee promptly to divide its allotment, from the budget resolution, among its subcommittees.

Under a new procedure, legislation from committees that had not made the allocations could be prevented, by a point of order, from coming to the floor. The intent of requiring allocations was to facilitate comparisons of legislation with budgetary limits and block over-budget bills.

- Designated the following items to be out of order (ineligible for floor consideration if a member objected by raising a point of order and if the objection was not overruled):

1) Budget legislation, including resolutions and reconciliation, amendments to them and conference reports on them, that would cause projected deficits to exceed specified levels. In the House only, a point of order against these measures, at the conference stage, could be waived only by a three-fifths vote of members present and voting.

2) Legislation from committees that had not made their required subcommittee allocations from the budget resolution.

3) Legislation exceeding a subcommittee's allocation. In the House, this point of order was to apply to bills providing new budget, entitlement or credit authorities; in the Senate, bills providing outlays or new budget authority.

4) Until completion of a budget resolution, any legislation providing new budget authority, increases or decreases in revenues, increases or decreases in the federal debt, new entitlement or credit authority. This point of order was not to apply to bills taking effect in the year after the one to which the budget resolution would apply and, in the House, not to appropriations legislation after May 15, if the appropriations bills were for the next fiscal year.

5) Legislation exceeding the budget resolution (which in turn was not to exceed the specified deficit limit). This point of order was not to apply to a House bill that did not exceed a committee's allocation.

6) Legislation providing new spending authority, broadly defined, unless the legislation limited spending to whatever was actually appropriated.

- Designated out of order a House resolution to recess for more than three days in July, unless the House had passed all regular appropriations bills and reconciliation legislation. (The intent was to require completion of these measures before a Fourth of July recess.)

Waivers, Recession, War

- Provided that points of order might be waived in the Senate only by three-fifths votes of all senators. (Existing practice was to require only a simple majority for waivers.) In the House, with two exceptions, waiver of points of order was to be by a simple majority, as was existing practice. The exceptions applied to conference agreements on budget resolutions or reconciliation measures exceeding deficit goals. In these cases, points of order against such legislation were to be waived only by three-fifths of members present and voting.

President's Budget

- Required the president to submit annual budgets in which the projected deficits did not exceed specified levels.

Automatic Cuts

- Required CBO and OMB jointly to estimate and report by set dates economic growth for each quarter of the upcoming fiscal year (current year for fiscal 1986), and the deficit for that year.

The two agencies were also to determine if the projected deficit for fiscal 1986 would exceed the level set by the legislation, and whether deficits for fiscal years 1987-90 would exceed the set levels by more than $10 billion.

They were also to calculate by what uniform percentage spending in federal programs would have to be cut to reduce the deficit to the specified deficit level. The estimates were to reflect economic indicators and statutes and regulations in effect as of Jan. 10, 1986, and as of Aug. 15 thereafter.

With certain exceptions, the CBO-OMB report was to assume that federal spending and revenues would continue at levels provided by laws in effect as of the dates economic indicators were calculated, and would also assume that expiring laws would not be in effect.

The resulting CBO-OMB "baseline" would be used both for projecting deficits and calculating automatic cuts. It was to assume appropriations at current-year levels, with changes only if regular appropriations or a 12-month continuing resolution for the upcoming fiscal year had been enacted. Spending or tax changes in reconciliation were not to be assumed unless that legislation had been enacted. Expiring excise taxes that went into certain trust funds were to be assumed to continue, however, as were federal farm programs operated by the Commodity Credit Corporation (CCC).

The baseline was to assume the most recent Medicare payment regulations for inpatient hospital payment rates, and was also to assume presidential recommendations for adjustments in pay of federal employees, with no absolute reduction in that pay.

If CBO and OMB differed in their estimates, averages of their different figures were to be used.

- Required the CBO-OMB report be sent to the comptroller general on Jan. 15, 1986, and on Aug. 20 thereafter. Required the comptroller general to verify the report and transmit it to Congress and the president by Jan. 20, 1986, and by Aug. 25 thereafter.

The comptroller general directed the General Accounting Office (GAO), an agency that investigated legal, accounting and related matters, largely for Congress.

- If, in fiscal years 1987-90, the CBO-OMB-GAO report projected a deficit exceeding the level specified for the upcoming fiscal year by $10 billion or more, required the president to issue an emergency "sequester" order reducing all federal spending, with certain exemptions, by a uniform percentage, as spelled out in the report. The order was to be required in fiscal 1986 if the deficit exceeded the specified level.

The order was to be issued Feb. 1, 1986, and Sept. 1 thereafter, and was to take effect, permanently canceling the required spending authority as of March 1, 1986, and Oct. 1 thereafter.

- The cuts were to be divided equally, taking half the total from defense programs and half from non-military programs not explicitly exempted by the legislation. In the aggregate, the reductions were to bring the projected deficit down to the specified level.

The defense category was to consist of all military accounts plus half of all federal retirement cost-of-living adjustments (COLAs).

The non-defense category was to include all expenditures considered to be controllable and the other half of the federal retirement COLAs.

- Exempted the following from the automatic cuts: Social Security, interest on the federal debt; earned income tax credit; certain federal insurance trusts, federal payments to retirement funds and other items excluded for technical reasons; veterans' compensation; veterans' benefits; and these low-income programs: Medicaid, Aid to Families with Dependent Children, WIC (a food program for women, infants, and young children), Supplemental Security Income, food stamps and child nutrition.
- Required the sequester order to make sufficient reductions in budget authority, loan obligations and other types of financial obligations so as to yield the required percentage reduction in outlays for programs. (Outlays were what was actually spent in a given year; budget authority referred to the maximum amount that Congress appropriated to be spent in a given year. Depending on program rates of spending, not all budget authority was always used up by outlays in a given fiscal year.)
- Provided special instructions for calculating the de-

Social Security: Much-Discussed Fiscal Topic

Whenever Congress in 1985 pondered questions of spending and deficits, the talk seemed inevitably to turn to a discussion of the Social Security system. Schemes to reduce the federal deficit by slowing payment of Social Security inflation adjustments and the Treasury Department's manipulation of the system's trust fund to ward off federal default weakened partisan loyalties and spurred congressional-administration ill will.

Social Security's status as the most politically untouchable domestic program was confirmed by broad congressional agreement to exempt the system from the across-the-board cuts mandated by the Gramm-Rudman-Hollings budget-balancing measure. Gramm-Rudman-Hollings also contained provisions placing the system beyond the reach of budget-cutters. *(Gramm-Rudman-Hollings, p. 459)*

The fights over Social Security took place against the background of the 1982 elections, when House Republicans lost 26 seats after a campaign in which Democrats tarred the GOP as intent on destroying Social Security. In 1985, all members sought to portray themselves as staunch supporters of Social Security to fend off potential opponents' charges in the 1986 elections.

The Budget Fight

In May, the Senate approved a budget resolution that would have eliminated the 1986 cost-of-living adjustment (COLA) for the 36 million Social Security recipients, while providing an inflation increase for the Pentagon. The House passed a package freezing military spending and protecting COLAs for Social Security and other retirement programs. *(Budget resolution, p. 441)*

The Reagan administration initially backed the Senate budget, but House Republicans rapidly ran from it. Eventually, President Reagan reversed himself and supported the House position on Social Security.

The switch embittered Senate Republicans, who were keenly aware of their political peril in the 1986 elections, when they would have to defend 22 Republican-held seats, an unusually large number, at a time when Democrats needed a net gain of just four to retake control of the chamber. Despite that, most Republicans had voted for the Senate budget's Social Security savings, in what GOP leaders characterized as a dramatic, statesmanlike act to reduce federal deficits.

In a letter June 27, House Minority Whip Trent Lott, Miss., and 66 other House Republicans urged Senate leaders to quit opposing the 1986 benefits increase. At the same time, Rep. Jack F. Kemp, R-N.Y., initiated private talks with House Budget Committee Chairman William H. Gray III, D-Pa., Lott and White House Chief of Staff Donald T. Regan. The meetings, of which Senate leaders were ignorant, helped persuade the administration that House Democrats would not compromise on Social Security. The president July 9 announced he would support the House position on the COLAs, and the provision remained in the final budget resolution.

Enraged Senate Republicans felt the president and Regan had deserted them. But they also blamed Kemp and Lott.

Social Security also accounted for some bitterness between House and Senate Democrats on the conference committee on the budget resolution. But unlike the Republicans' breach, the Democrats' split was limited to the committee. Most Senate Democrats supported the COLAs; a majority of those in the conference did not.

Debt-Limit Debate

Congress again debated Social Security as part of the government's debt crisis at the end of the year. When the government was about to run out of money Nov. 1, Treasury Department officials sold some long-term investments controlled by the Social Security trust fund to tide the government over. *(Debt limit, p. 457)*

Some members of Congress were outraged, not so much because the Treasury officials redeemed some of the system's investments, but because a similar reshuffling of money had occurred before — during debt crises in September and October and in October 1984 — and no one on Capitol Hill had been told.

The shuffling of funds involved the cashing-in of long-term government securities that had been purchased with Social Security surplus funds. Redeeming the securities reduced the government's indebtedness and allowed the Treasury Department to sell new securities to raise cash.

Treasury Secretary James A. Baker III had warned Congress in an Oct. 22 letter that he would take the "extraordinary" step of "disinvestment" if a debt extension had not been enacted. Provisions to make up the losses incurred by the early redemption of the securities were included in a temporary debt-limit measure (PL 99-155) passed Nov. 14 and in the final version of the debt limit/Gramm-Rudman-Hollings measure (PL 99-177). All the funds had been restored by early January 1986, according to Treasury officials.

Gramm-Rudman also removed Social Security from the unified federal budget in fiscal 1986 and thereafter exempted the program from legislated limitations on spending. Congress in 1983 had voted to remove the system from the budget in 1993, but sentiment to do it sooner grew during 1985. *(1983 Almanac p. 219)*

Proponents argued that because the system's trust funds ran a surplus, Social Security did not contribute to the deficit and, therefore, benefits should not be cut to help pay for shortfalls in other federal programs.

However, "removal" of Social Security from the budget had more political than practical implications. The Treasury Department borrowed from the Social Security surplus to help finance the federal debt, and it could continue to do so even if the program were "off budget." As a result, overall government borrowing from the public would remain the same.

Those opposed to putting Social Security off budget argued that the deficit was so serious that all spending programs should be reviewed for possible cuts. They noted that Social Security made up a large portion — approximately one-fifth — of government outlays and removing it from the budget would have presented a distorted view of government activities.

fense cuts, that, among other things, explicitly required unobligated budget authority from previous years to be included in making cuts. The intent was to achieve the required percentage reduction in outlays for the year affected by the sequester order. Other provisions prescribed how to calculate defense outlay rates and special rules for deriving savings from existing military contracts.

The uniform percentage reduction was to apply to eligible federal accounts or sub-accounts — projects, programs and activities — to the extent these were defined by the most recently enacted appropriations bills and committee reports accompanying these bills.

• Limited the amount by which program spending could be reduced in these health programs: Medicare, veterans' health, Indian health, community and migrant health centers.

These programs could be reduced by no more than 1 percent (from any inflation adjustment or from the base level, in the absence of such an adjustment) in fiscal 1986, and by no more than 2 percent thereafter.

• Provided special rules for automatic cuts applying to foster care and adoption assistance, unemployment compensation, child support enforcement, Guaranteed Student Loans, and the CCC. (The CCC, a branch of the Agriculture Department, maintained federal farm price-support programs.)

• Specified that in the case of CCC contracts, which ran for single crop-years, the required cuts were to be made not in contracts in effect at the time of a sequester order, but in contracts signed the following year.

• Specified that any reductions from COLAs would permanently lower the program base from which future calculations would be made.

• Prohibited a sequester order from eliminating any programs, changing program eligibility standards, changing congressionally mandated spending priorities or, in fiscal 1986, closing military bases.

• Provided special rules for fiscal 1986 only, permitting the order to depart, within limits, from uniform percentage reductions in defense accounts and sub-accounts.

The flexibility was to permit the president to shield uniformed military personnel — both numbers of personnel and their salaries — from the automatic cuts, but only if he distributed the percentage reduction from these accounts elsewhere in defense spending.

• Required the president to report fully to Congress on the contents of the emergency order.

• Established a special procedure under which the Senate Budget Committee could initiate a partial or full affirmation of a sequester order under procedures similiar to those used for budget reconciliation. The Senate Budget Committee could require other Senate committees to submit legislative proposals to alter the order and if a committee failed to submit the required alternatives, the Senate Budget Committee could draft the legislation itself.

The House Budget Committee could also initiate an alternative proposal; the intent of adding special Senate rules explicitly was to provide some protection from filibusters and amendments.

• Required a revised CBO-OMB report to GAO on Oct. 5 of every year, noting the impact of any laws enacted after the first report and making adjustments in the deficit estimate and other matters, if needed. Required the GAO by Oct. 10 to forward the revised report to the president, who was to adjust the sequester order to reflect the revised report, if needed.

Social Security

• In addition to exempting Social Security from the automatic cuts, the legislation removed Social Security from the unified federal budget in fiscal 1986 and thereafter exempted the program from any legislated limitations on spending. The bill generally prohibited any measure enacted after it to authorize payments to the Social Security trust funds from the general fund of the Treasury, or payments from the Social Security funds to the Treasury fund.

• Required the secretary of the Treasury to restore to the Social Security trust funds and other federal retirement trust funds the long-term securities that had been redeemed in October 1985 by Treasury, in order to attempt to avoid default and make beneficiary payments, and also required Treasury to restore any interest lost as a result of such maneuvers, and any loss from similar maneuvers in 1984.

Judicial Review

• Authorized members of Congress to bring lawsuits testing the constitutionality of the legislation and authorized members or any person alleged to be injured by the measure to bring lawsuits.

• Provided for direct appeal of preliminary decisions by a special three-judge district court to the Supreme Court and provided for expedited decisions at both levels.

• Provided that if a president, citing his constitutional responsibilities as commander in chief, did not include defense spending in automatic cuts as specified by the legislation, and that if the president's constitutional claim was upheld by the Supreme Court, the entire order making automatic cuts would be invalid.

• Provided that if a court nullified the use of a joint CBO-OMB-GAO report to trigger automatic cut orders, such orders were to go to a special budget committee, comprised of members of Budget committees in both chambers.

The order was to be reported by the special committee within five days as a joint resolution, which must pass each chamber of Congress and be signed by the president (or be passed again over a veto) in order to take effect.

Minimum Corporate Tax

• Directed the House Ways and Means Committee to report, by Oct. 1, 1986, legislation providing for an alternative minimum corporate tax.

Legislative History

After Congress returned from its month-long August recess, a major item on its agenda was raising the ceiling on the federal debt to $2.079 trillion. By the first of October, without that action, the Treasury expected to run out of authority to borrow to pay its bills and federal checks would start bouncing — unprecedented in the nation's history.

Raising the debt limit was always a difficult political vote, because it so directly affirmed Congress' inability to hold spending in line with revenues. The House, therefore, had concocted an automatic procedure whereby adoption of a budget resolution resulted also in adoption of a resolution to raise the debt limit. Using that tool, the House sent the debt-limit resolution (H J Res 372) to the Senate Sept. 9. *(Debt limit, p. 457; automatic procedure, box, p. 458)*

In the Senate, H J Res 372 quickly became the target for amendments. Both Steven D. Symms, R-Idaho, and William L. Armstrong, R-Colo., expressed interest in reviving budget fights from earlier in the year, when the resolution came to the floor.

And on Sept. 25, Gramm, Rudman and Hollings introduced a bill (S 1702) setting deficit targets for each of the five succeeding years, requiring a balanced budget by fiscal 1991 and creating a method of automatic spending cuts to meet the targets.

Senate Moved Fast

On Oct. 3, the Senate began consideration of H J Res 372, and Majority Leader Robert Dole, R-Kan., immediately offered a version of the Gramm-Rudman-Hollings bill as an amendment to the resolution. Though the Senate passed a version of the resolution Oct. 10, a week after Dole called it up on the floor, Congress ultimately wrestled with the measure for more than two months, preventing the needed increase in the debt limit and requiring extraordinary steps to avoid the federal government's first default.

There had been no conventional committee action in either chamber on S 1702, and without the formal economic, procedural or legal analyses that legislation of such importance would ordinarily undergo, members had to rely largely on speculative statements about what the measure would do.

Furthermore, key provisions in the measure were constantly being altered as sponsors negotiated in private to win votes and sort out kinks. The result was a dearth of background material for the floor debate.

On Oct. 4, filibuster threats from a variety of senators among them Lowell P. Weicker Jr., R-Conn., J. Bennett Johnston, D-La., Gary Hart, D-Colo., and Minority Leader Robert C. Byrd, D-W.Va. — prevented a vote on the anti-deficit amendment. They said they needed more time to understand the measure.

Senate GOP leaders had sought, by holding up action on the debt-limit legislation until the first week of October, to create a cash-flow crisis for the government and thereby force quick action. To keep the pressure on, Dole forced the Senate to stay in session Saturday, Oct. 5, and Sunday, Oct. 6, for debate and several procedural votes. One vote on Sunday to cut off debate failed. It was only the third Sunday session since 1981 and the 11th in the Senate's history.

But the Treasury, much to Dole's disgust, on Oct. 9 deflated the pressure he had tried to build with a complicated maneuver to borrow additional funds.

Making Changes

On one of the first days of debate Moynihan had contemptuously pointed out that federal farm price supports, one of the fast-growing, large items in the federal budget, would be almost wholly exempt from any automatic cuts. That was because farmers contracted to participate in the programs and existing contracts were deemed "relatively uncontrollable" expenditures, not subject to the cuts under the bill's terms.

Also shielded for the same reason was an undetermined but substantial portion of the defense budget — multi-year procurement contracts for major weapons.

There were complaints that it was unfair to exempt major sectors of the budget from the risk of harsh cuts because that would mean deeper reductions in programs subject to the cuts. And Hart, a member of the Senate Armed Services Committee, warned that with weapons protected, any automatic cuts would hit military pay and cut into such essential expenditures as practice flights for pilots and ammunition for training.

One multipart, negotiated amendment incorporated into the measure sought to broaden the reach of the automatic cuts, particularly to get at some contract spending. Even with that change, however, it was estimated that as much as 85 percent of agriculture price supports and half of defense procurement expenditures would have been shielded.

In response to concerns that the measure ignored the consequences of an economic downturn, the amendment also changed the bill's trigger mechanism, to allow the president to delay the cuts or suspend other provisions in a recession.

J. James Exon, D-Neb., John Kerry, D-Mass., and Thomas F. Eagleton, D-Mo., sponsored unsuccessful amendments to make cuts much more likely in November 1985. All argued that if the Senate were really serious about deficit reduction it would not want to postpone bill-mandated pressures for deep spending cuts by more than a year. Votes on those two amendments were relatively close, Exon-Kerry losing 46-52 and Eagleton 46-43 (on a tabling motion to kill his amendment). *(Vote 210, p. 41-S; vote 221, p. 42-S)*

But it was by huge, lopsided margins that the Senate rejected a series of Democratic amendments that sponsors said would test their colleagues' resolve to eliminate the deficit.

David L. Boren, D-Okla., one of the Democratic spon sors of Gramm-Rudman-Hollings, offered one of those amendments to subject Social Security cost-of-living adjustments, in part, to any automatic cuts. The amendment was tabled 71-27. *(Vote 215, p. 41-S)*

By voice vote the Senate Oct. 9 accepted a key amendment by Carl Levin, D-Mich., that altered the measure by which automatic cuts were to be computed. The measure originally would have required uniform cuts from OMB spending accounts that often included large numbers of programs. Levin's amendment required that cuts would come from individual programs, projects or activities as defined by the most recently enacted appropriations bills. The change was seen as significantly limiting the president's discretion to shift the burden of automatic cuts within accounts.

The Senate Oct. 9 also rejected 40-59 a Democratic substitute offered by Lawton Chiles, Fla., ranking Democrat on the Budget Committee, and a key participant in negotiations to change Gramm-Rudman-Hollings. *(Vote 211, p. 41-S)*

The same day, by an overwhelming majority of 75-24, the Senate agreed to Dole's amendment adding Gramm-Rudman-Hollings to the debt-limit measure. The following day, after disposing of a double handful of amendments, the Senate adopted the debt-limit resolution by a 51-37 vote, sending the measure back to the House. *(Vote 213, p. 41-S; vote 222, p. 42-S)*

House Asks for Conference

To avoid a floor vote on the Senate amendment, the House Oct. 11 asked for a conference on H J Res 372 in hope of altering the balanced-budget provisions. Congressional pressure for a definitive strike at the deficit was so strong that House Democratic leaders feared a stampede in that chamber to accept the Senate plan, which even advocates said needed much clarification and revision.

Nine senators and 48 representatives were appointed to the conference, which met Oct. 16 and 18, primarily to get answers from sponsors and staff to a wide range of questions about the measure: How would it work; could it be circumvented; did it vest too much power in unelected bureaucrats at the expense of Congress; was it unconstitutional?

Over the following two weeks, conferees met in task forces and discussed emerging differences between the Senate measure and an alternative drafted largely by House Democrats. Key points of contention included how quickly the automatic cuts might kick in (House Democrats wanted them by early 1986), the need for an early court test of the measure's constitutionality, and exemptions for programs that assisted the poor and elderly. In conference, there was never any dispute over the provision raising the debt ceiling.

On Oct. 31, House and Senate conferees submitted formal alternatives to each other. Conference leaders met privately for an hour to review the alternatives and returned declaring the conference deadlocked.

Both alternatives reflected a number of concerns raised during the conference deliberations, such as the constitutionality of the measure and the possibility that the president would simply refuse to cut defense spending by exercising his powers as commander in chief. Both made some allowance to accommodate recessions; both spelled out procedural and substantive details left vague in the original version; both strengthened provisions putting more teeth in the existing budget process that would precede any automatic cuts.

The plans differed in their deficit limits; the House alternative set lower targets for all years, reaching a balanced budget a year earlier than the Senate alternative. They also differed in their reliance on CBO and OMB to calculate deficit projections, and in their treatment of Medicare. The House plan would have limited Medicare cuts — hitting defense harder; the Senate plan took the opposite approach.

House Finally Votes; Conference No. 2

After conferees failed to agree, H J Res 372 came to the House floor Nov. 1. There, in a surprising show of party unity, House Democrats — joined by lone Republican John Paul Hammerschmidt of Arkansas — voted almost unanimously, 249-180, to substitute a markedly different version of the anti-deficit provisions. *(Vote 350, p. 108-H)*

The House version closely resembled the alternative that had been offered by House conferees but rejected by the senators. The Senate Nov. 6 voted again for its version, with some modifications, setting the stage for a second conference.

The second, 66-member conference quickly shrank to a working group of 29 that began meeting Nov. 12 and worked for a month in private sessions to devise a final version acceptable to both chambers. In fact, many of the compromises were forged by an even smaller group of congressional leaders, including Senate Budget Committee Chairman Pete V. Domenici, R-N.M.; Senate Finance Committee Chairman Packwood; House Majority Whip Thomas S. Foley, D-Wash.; House Democratic Caucus Chairman Richard A. Gephardt, Mo.; and Reps. Aspin and Panetta. In addition, the measure's sponsors — principally Gramm — took part in the negotiations.

By its Nov. 21 meeting, the working group of 29 conferees had reviewed a number of compromises that had been agreed to by the four leaders, and staff began converting the agreement into legislative language. The key compromises included:

- The first round of automatic spending cuts would occur in March 1986, not after the November 1986 elections as the Senate bill appeared to provide.
- Half of any automatic cuts would be taken from defense and the other half from remaining programs not explicitly exempted. The original legislation had called for half the cuts to come from automatic cost-of-living increases of certain programs and the other half — or more in certain circumstances — from other programs, including defense.
- A Senate proposal was accepted, requiring congressional approval of an order for automatic cuts if courts nullified a requirement that the CBO, OMB and GAO produce the order.

Other issues remained unresolved, reflecting both policy disputes and reluctance of House GOP leaders to commit themselves, particularly on the sensitive matter of defense spending, without White House accord. Reagan was absent during a key time in the talks, meeting in Geneva with Soviet Leader Mikhail S. Gorbachev. *(Defense policy and the Geneva summit, p. 109)*

After Congress returned from its Thanksgiving recess, the small group of negotiators resumed their private talks, concluding their work at 1 a.m. Dec. 10 with an agreement to give the president a limited degree of flexibility in fiscal 1986 to make defense cuts under the automatic procedure.

Later that day conferees by voice vote agreed to the final version of the plan (H Rept 99-433).

Final Floor Action

Both chambers of Congress gave final approval to the legislation the evening of Dec. 11. The Senate, after some nine hours of speeches, adopted the conference agreement by a 61-31 vote. *(Vote 371, p. 63-S)*

Before the final vote, the Senate easily overturned a point of order, raised by Weicker, that in writing the final compromise conferees had improperly exceeded the boundaries of previously passed versions. The Senate also rejected a motion by Jeremiah Denton, R-Ala., that would have permitted the president to shield defense spending from the automatic spending cuts. *(Votes 369, 370, p. 63-S)*

House passage of the conference agreement, by a 271-154 vote, came at 10:15 p.m. Dec. 11, clearing the legislation for the president's signature on Dec. 12. *(Vote 415, p. 132-H)*

Line-Item Veto Fails

After three failed attempts to stop a weeklong filibuster, the Senate leadership July 24 dropped plans to consider legislation giving the president power to veto spending for individual government programs.

Opponents of the veto — led by Appropriations Committee Chairman Mark O. Hatfield, R-Ore., Rules Committee Chairman Charles McC. Mathias Jr., R-Md., and Senate Minority Leader Robert C. Byrd., D-W.Va. — argued that passage of the bill would have a limited effect on federal spending and would mean a dramatic, unconstitutional shift of power to the president.

But sponsor Mack Mattingly, R-Ga., said the veto

power was needed to bring government spending under control.

The measure died when opponents succeeded in preventing the Senate from voting on a motion to bring the bill to the floor.

"We have stopped what was to be one of the most dangerous proposals that has come up before this Senate during my 19 years," Hatfield said after the final move to end debate on a motion to proceed to S 43 fell two votes short of the needed 60.

Senate approval had seemed possible in 1985, but House action on an identical bill (HR 1247) was thwarted by longstanding objections by that chamber's Democratic leadership.

In 1984, Mattingly came within one vote of winning an important procedural vote when he tried to add his item-veto plan to one version (HR 2163) of the fiscal 1985 deficit reduction bill (PL 98-369). He lost 45-46 on his motion to kill a point of order against his amendment. The Senate then upheld the point of order, thereby ruling out his amendment. *(1984 Almanac p. 153)*

Background

President Reagan repeatedly requested line-item veto authority, and included an appeal for enactment in his February State of the Union address. *(Text, p. 8-D)*

Under existing procedures enumerated in the Constitution, a president had to veto an entire appropriations bill, sometimes containing hundreds of funding items, if he wanted to block spending for an individual program.

Mattingly's item-veto bill would have been similar in effect to proposed constitutional amendments to allow a president to veto individual items in an appropriations bill without vetoing the entire bill. *(1984 Almanac p. 167)*

It would have employed a different procedure, however, providing that once Congress had completed action on an appropriations bill the measure would be divided up by congressional clerks. Each item — a paragraph or a section — was to be packaged as a separate bill for transmission to the White House, and any of the separate bills could have been vetoed.

Authority for this procedure, applicable only to appropriations bills, would have expired after two years.

Hatfield said that, even if the veto authority were granted, it would cover only 11 to 14 percent of the federal budget since most government spending is not provided through appropriations bills. He also argued that Reagan would not want to veto defense spending, which makes up more than half of the money appropriated. *(Controllable and uncontrollable spending, box, this page)*

Mattingly countered that existing procedures to control the budget had failed and that the item veto should at least be given a chance.

Committee and Floor Action

The Senate Rules Committee June 20 decided to let the full Senate determine the fate of S 43, voting 10-0 to report the bill, but with an unfavorable recommendation.

Opponents voted to move the plan to the floor because Mattingly had threatened to offer S 43 as an amendment to the fiscal 1985 supplemental appropriations bill (HR 2577 — PL 99-88) if the committee did not act. The Senate passed HR 2577 June 20, and Mattingly did not offer his amendment.

The full Senate voted three times between July 18 and 24 on cloture — a procedure to shut off debate — when a filibuster prevented floor consideration of the bill. Despite a personal lobbying campaign by Reagan, who was recovering from July 13 surgery to remove a cancerous polyp from his large intestine, only one vote for stopping debate was picked up over the course of the week.

Majority Leader Robert Dole, R-Kan., had said after the first cloture motion, which failed 57-42, that he would not push the bill if it did not pick up support. Cloture required the votes of 60 senators. *(Vote 156, p. 31-S)*

Reagan later made several phone calls to wavering senators, but the second cloture motion July 23 failed by a vote of 57-41. *(Vote 157, p. 32-S)*

Two senators called by Reagan, Arlen Specter, R-Pa., and Howell Heflin, D-Ala., switched their votes to support cloture. But Robert T. Stafford, R-Vt., who had voted for cloture the first time because, he said, he owed Mattingly a political favor, switched to a "nay."

Also, two senators who had voted for cloture the first time — Joseph R. Biden Jr., D-Del., and Paula Hawkins, R-Fla. — were absent for the second vote. Sen. William L. Armstrong, R-Colo., was absent for the first vote, but voted for the second cloture motion.

After the third cloture motion failed the following day 58-40, Dole withdrew the pending motion to proceed to S 43. *(Vote 158, p. 32-S)*

Controllable and Uncontrollable Spending

(in billions of dollars, unadjusted for offsetting receipts)

	Fiscal Year 1986	
Outlays	$ 1,166.3	100.0%
Total, uncontrollable*	861.3	73.8
Controllable†		
Defense	176.9	15.2
Non-defense	128.1	11.0
Total, controllable	305.0	26.2

SOURCE: Senate Rules Committee, based on President Reagan's fiscal 1986 budget recommendations.

* *Uncontrollable spending includes funding for entitlement programs, such as Social Security, and fixed obligations of the federal government, such as payments on the national debt.*
† *Controllable spending is funding for programs whose funding is set each year in the appropriations process.*

Plant-Closing Impact

The House Nov. 21 narrowly rejected watered-down legislation intended to cushion the impact of mass layoffs and plant closings.

The labor-backed bill (HR 1616) fell victim to well-organized opposition from business and deep philosophical differences among members. On the final 203-208 vote, 54 Democrats — 49 from the South — joined 154 Republicans in opposing the revised measure, which would have required employers to give employees advance notice when they intended to close a plant or lay off a large number of workers. Twenty Republicans and 183 Democrats voted for the bill. *(Vote 383, p. 120-H)*

HR 1616 failed to garner majority support even though the revised version was significantly weaker than the original measure. Among other things, the legislation was stripped of a requirement that employers consult with workers before a shutdown and a provision giving employees the right to get a court order halting a shutdown.

Despite the changes, a number of members from both parties bitterly opposed the bill. They argued that while giving advance notice seemed a simple enough requirement, announcing an intent to close down could in fact prevent financially troubled companies from getting credit or working out deals that might keep them afloat.

The defeat of HR 1616 was particularly disappointing for organized labor because a number of its traditional supporters opposed the bill. An AFL-CIO spokesman attributed some defections to a heavy business lobbying effort put together largely by the U.S. Chamber of Commerce. In mailings to local Chamber groups and to House members, Chamber officials painted HR 1616 as a "union bill" and contended that the measure amounted to a foot in the door for union organizing.

At the behest of Republican opponents of the legislation, Labor Secretary William E. Brock III appointed a task force earlier in the year to study the plant-closing issue. The panel was expected to report to Congress by the end of 1986.

Background

The shutdown of plants became a more frequent and prominent source of hardship during the early 1980s, when the economy was wracked by recession and by industrial shifts in the face of accelerating technological change and foreign competition.

According to the Bureau of Labor Statistics, some 11.5 million workers were put out of work from 1979 to 1984 because their plants were shut down or their jobs abolished. That included 5.1 million "displaced" workers who had held their jobs for at least three years — nearly half of them in manufacturing.

Although factory shutdowns were most commonly associated with the decline of the basic industries such as autos and steel in the "Rust Bowl," proponents of plant-closing legislation emphasized that the problem was not confined to the Northeast and Midwest. Indeed, by one count, the state that experienced the most plant closings in 1982 was North Carolina.

While Congress had declined to act on plant-closing proposals, four states had enacted such legislation of their own and 19 others were actively considering such measures in mid-1985. In Maine, for example, employers had to provide two months' notice of plant shutdowns and provide a week of severance pay for each year of a worker's employment.

Proponents said advance notification of closings would give workers time to seek retraining or a new job and would allow state and local governments to anticipate loss of tax revenues and increased demand for social services.

Business groups fought plant-closing legislation, saying it would impose undue restrictions on corporations' ability to invest and allocate resources profitably. But faced with moves to mandate plant-closing guidelines in state and federal law, some business leaders began promoting voluntary efforts to ease the disruption caused by shutdowns.

The National Center on Occupational Readjustment, a business-backed clearinghouse, was set up in 1983 to disseminate information and provide guidance on managing closings to help mitigate adverse effects.

Legislative History

Rep. William D. Ford, Mich., ranking Democrat on the House Education and Labor Subcommittee on Labor-Management Relations, had been working since 1973 to get plant-closing legislation to the floor.

In the 98th Congress, the Labor-Management Subcommittee approved plant-closing legislation (HR 2847), but there was no further action on the measure.

Going far beyond notification requirements, the 1983 bill would have required employers to extend health insurance coverage for laid-off workers and provide up to $25,000 in severance pay per worker. It also authorized an array of federal assistance to finance job training, placement and relocation of workers, to shore up distressed businesses and to help local governments deal with the loss of tax revenues due to a major plant closing.

In 1985, faced with stiff business opposition and a federal budget crunch, Ford said he was persuaded that the legislation would never fly "unless we developed a solution that was no burden to the taxpayer and no burden to responsible business organizations."

House Committee Action

The Education and Labor Committee July 23 approved HR 1616 by a 20-12 vote, with Thomas E. Petri, R-Wis., joining the panel's 19 Democrats in voting for the legislation. All other Republican members opposed it.

As reported Oct. 29 (H Rept 99-336), HR 1616 required employers to provide three months' notice before permanently laying off 50 or more employees. Employers would have to consult with employees in the interim about alternatives to plant closings.

In addition to the notice and consultation requirements, HR 1616 included provisions to:

- Exempt from coverage temporary layoffs, where employees would be recalled in 90 days.
- Allow the three-month notice requirement to be reduced if the business in question demonstrated that "unavoidable business circumstances prevent the employer from withholding the closing or layoff."
- Require an employer, during consultations with a union, to provide workers with "all relevant information" necessary to evaluate alternatives to a plant closing.
- Allow a court to extend the three-month notice period if it determined that the employer refused to meet or consult with a union in good faith.
- Give the Federal Mediation and Conciliation Service authority to help mediate plant-closing disputes.
- Allow the secretary of labor to issue an order barring disclosure of information on a plant closing when disclosure could jeopardize an employer's competitive position.
- Authorize the labor secretary to get a court order within 10 days of determining that there was "reasonable cause to believe" an employer had ordered a plant closing or layoff in violation of the act. The relief available from the court could include reinstatement of workers with back pay and a restoration of operations.
- Allow an employee to file a civil suit in federal court for any layoff in violation of the act. A court could order reinstatement and back pay equal to one day's pay and fringe benefits for each day of layoff that violated the law.

Punitive damages also would be allowed.

- Allow an employer to sue for damages if information protected by a court order were disclosed during the notice period.
- Establish a bipartisan 15-member Commission on Plant Closings and Worker Dislocation to make recommendations about legislation in this area.

House Floor Action

HR 1616 first came to the floor Nov. 14. Knowing it was in trouble, Ford was ready with a substitute that eliminated a number of remedies for laid-off workers but retained the consultation requirement.

The consultation provision was knocked out of the bill by a 215-193 vote, however, prompting Ford to pull the measure off the floor. *(Vote 372, p. 116-H)*

When the bill returned to the floor a week later, James M. Jeffords of Vermont, ranking Republican on the Education and Labor Committee, with Ford's blessing offered a new version that further restricted employees' remedies. Like the original bill, it applied to companies with 50 or more full-time employees but it covered layoffs of 100 employees or more. Employers who intended to close a plant or lay off large numbers of people would have to notify workers 90 days in advance. The Jeffords amendment was adopted 211-201. *(Vote 381, p. 120-H)*

Before rejecting the revised bill 203-208, the House defeated a substitute for Jeffords' proposal that would have reduced the scope of coverage — applying only to employers of at least 200 workers and requiring only 60 days' notice before a shutdown or layoff. The substitute, offered by Buddy Roemer, D-La., failed 109-298. *(Votes 382, 383, p. 120-H)*

Reflecting the view of many members, Roemer said he was "caught between a rock and a hard place" — between "the need to give minimum reasonable notice as soon as possible" and "what can work, what will not work to job disadvantage."

Jeffords defended his proposal as feasible, and Ford said that without a notice provision, "no constructive effort to prevent a shutdown or assist dislocated workers is possible."

But Stan Lundine, D-N.Y., generally a labor supporter, disagreed. Lundine, whose district had suffered a number of plant closings in the past decade, said the bill was misguided. "What we would do by . . . adopting this bill would be simply to put another regulation on at the worst possible time," he asserted. "I am deeply concerned that throughout industrial America, whether it is in the Northeast or the South or the West, we are going to cause a loss of jobs." He said "voluntary cooperation," not regulation, was a better solution. ▮

Public Workers' Overtime

Congress Nov. 7 cleared a bill to ease the impact of a Supreme Court decision requiring overtime pay for state and local government workers.

The measure, signed into law by President Reagan Nov. 13 (S 1570 — PL 99-150), instead allowed public employers to provide time-and-a-half compensatory time off for workers who put in overtime.

The Supreme Court had ruled Feb. 19, in *Garcia v. San Antonio Metropolitan Transit Authority*, that the overtime pay requirements of the Fair Labor Standards Act (FLSA) applied to state and local government workers. The *Garcia* ruling, decided by a 5-4 vote, reversed a 1976 high court decision that exempted state and local government workers from FLSA coverage. *(Garcia decision, p. 15-A)*

Public employer groups — in particular, the National League of Cities, the U.S. Conference of Mayors and the National Association of Counties — sought relief from the *Garcia* ruling, claiming it would cost them more than $1 billion in overtime pay in the next year.

Organized labor, which represented about three million of the nine million state and local government workers, hailed the decision for giving government workers parity with the private sector. Union officials from the AFL-CIO, the Service Employees International Union and the American Federation of State, County and Municipal Employees insisted the public employers were greatly exaggerating the cost of complying with *Garcia.*

But sensing that city and county officials might be able to press Congress into drastically revising the FLSA, a 1938 labor law that set minimum pay and overtime requirements, union lobbyists offered in September to bargain with the public employers. Within days of their first meeting, union and employer negotiators struck a deal. They presented it to key House and Senate members in early October, and by mid-November the proposal had been signed into law. The Labor Department had postponed enforcement of the *Garcia* decision pending congressional action on the bill.

S 1570 revised the FLSA so that state and local governments could give employees compensatory time off for overtime work instead of cash. Employers were required to provide time-and-a-half compensation for any hours worked over 40, although police and firefighters had to work a longer period of time to be eligible for overtime compensation.

Cities, counties and states did not have to start providing time-and-a-half compensatory time until April 16, 1986, giving them another five months to adjust their budgets and personnel practices to comply with the new law.

Provisions

As signed into law Nov. 13, S 1570 (PL 99-150):

- Allowed public employers to give employees time-and-a-half compensatory time off, instead of cash, for each hour of overtime worked over 40 hours. Existing collective bargaining agreements that called for cash payment for overtime or provided employees the option of either cash or time off would not be affected. However, compensatory time after the effective date would have to be at the time-and-a-half rate.
- Established a cap of 480 hours of compensatory time earned for public safety and seasonal employees. Overtime hours worked after this cap would have to be compensated in cash. Other employees, such as clerical workers, would get cash after working 240 hours of overtime.
- Provided that an employee who left a job with unused compensatory time should be paid for the unused time either at the average regular rate received over the last three years of work or at the final regular rate the employee received, whichever was greater.
- Made the bill effective April 15, 1986, giving state and local governments a year from the final decision in *Garcia* to revise their personnel practices.
- Exempted volunteers, such as firefighters, from cover-

age even if the volunteers were paid expense money.

- Exempted state and local legislative staff, except library employees, from FLSA coverage.
- Provided that firefighters and law enforcement employees, including security and prison personnel, who voluntarily did part-time work different from their regular jobs be considered as working two separate jobs. Thus, hours worked at the second job would not be counted toward the overtime limit at the main job. This provision was designed to cover, for example, a firefighter who also worked at a community youth center.
- Barred state and local governments from discriminating against employees by changing wages or other working conditions because the employee asserted that he was covered by the FLSA after the *Garcia* decision.

Background

Key provisions of the Fair Labor Standards Act required time-and-a-half pay for any hours worked beyond 40 per week, although police and firefighters could work a longer period before they had to be compensated for overtime.

Employers could give a worker the option of taking compensatory time instead of cash for overtime, but the time off had to be taken within the same pay period the overtime was earned. The law did not authorize the storing up, or "banking" of compensatory time, a practice used frequently by police, firefighters and other employees whose workload was unpredictable or seasonally varied.

Most state and local workers were not covered by the FLSA until Congress amended it in 1974 (PL 93-259). *(1974 Almanac p. 239)*

The 1974 amendments never went into effect, however, because the League of Cities challenged them in court. That lawsuit resulted in a 1976 decision, *National League of Cities v. Usery,* in which the court ruled 5-4 that the minimum wage and overtime provisions of the FLSA could not constitutionally be applied to "integral governmental functions" at the state and local level. The court specifically found that such functions included fire prevention, police protection, sanitation, public health, and parks and recreation.

In 1979, the Labor Department's Wage and Hour Division made an administrative ruling that certain other state and local services, including public transit, were not integral government functions and thus were subject to the wage and hours law.

San Antonio challenged that determination in federal court and Joe G. Garcia, a city transit operator, countersued. The Supreme Court ultimately used the case as a vehicle for overturning its 1976 *Usery* decision.

Justice Harry A. Blackmun, who switched positions on the FLSA's applicability to state and local workers, wrote for the court in *Garcia*. He said the *Usery* standard had proved "unworkable" and should be abandoned, adding that the "political process ensures that laws that unduly burden the states will not be promulgated."

Legislative History

S 1570 stemmed from an agreement worked out between labor unions and public employer organizations affected by *Garcia*.

Senate. The bill was approved by the Senate Labor and Human Resources Committee by a 16-0 vote Oct. 8. The committee filed its report (S Rept 99-159) Oct. 17, and the bill passed the Senate by voice vote Oct. 24. During the brief Senate floor debate, Pete Wilson, R-Calif. — a former mayor of San Diego — expressed reservations about the bill. He said he feared the compromise legislation would result in higher costs for cities and counties and could result in a reduction of services. It "will come back to haunt us," he predicted.

House. The House Oct. 28 passed a companion bill (HR 3530) by voice vote under suspension of the rules. That measure had been reported by the Education and Labor Committee Oct. 24 (H Rept 99-331).

Conference Action. House and Senate negotiators resolved differences between the bills in a four-hour session Oct. 31. Both chambers adopted the conference report (H Rept 99-357) Nov. 7, completing congressional action.

In a departure from usual practice, Wilson participated actively in the conference even though he was not a member of the committee where the bill originated. Labor Committee Chairman Orrin G. Hatch, R-Utah, gave Wilson virtual veto power over conference report language to clarify a provision that prohibited changing the pay or working conditions of workers who asserted their right to overtime pay. Union representatives were concerned about retaliation against those workers, while city officials worried about facing lawsuits for adjusting job classifications or work schedules to help offset higher pay costs resulting from *Garcia*.

Conferees were able to agree on language to satisfy both sides and Wilson. The conference report stated that the anti-discrimination section "is not intended to prohibit state or local government employers from adjusting rates of pay at some later point in response to fiscal concerns not directly attributable to the impact of extending FLSA coverage to their employees."

Conferees also resolved a disagreement involving the number of overtime hours employees could work before employers would have to give them pay instead of compensatory time off. The Senate bill had a single standard of 480 hours of compensatory time before cash was required. The House bill had a bifurcated plan, requiring overtime pay for public safety and seasonal workers after they had worked 480 hours. Other workers, such as clerical employees, would get overtime after earning 180 hours of overtime.

Conferees kept the House plan but permitted the second group of workers to receive time-and-a-half pay after 240 hours of overtime. ▮

Unemployment Benefits

President Reagan April 4 signed legislation (HR 1866 — PL 99-15) phasing out special assistance for the long-term unemployed, after his repeated veto threats squelched congressional efforts to extend the program.

Reagan had wanted benefits cut off immediately when the federal supplemental unemployment compensation program, enacted in 1982, expired on March 31. But in signing HR 1866, he allowed a more gradual elimination of benefits for those on the rolls.

The House passed the bill April 2, the Senate the next day. Congress was under pressure to act before it began a 10-day recess April 5.

The Democratic-controlled House removed a potential obstacle to quick action when it abandoned a proposed three-month extension of the program. That move embittered some House Democrats who wanted to challenge Senate Republicans and Reagan by pushing an extension.

However, many Democrats, even traditional supporters of aid to the out-of-work, agreed that such benefits were ill-suited to targeting aid to pockets of high unemployment, and suggested the whole system should be revamped.

Provisions

HR 1866 provided that no new beneficiaries could qualify for the supplemental compensation program, which provided up to 14 weeks of additional aid for jobless people who had exhausted regular unemployment benefits.

But to cushion the effects of terminating the program, the bill allowed people already on the rolls to draw their remaining benefits. More than 300,000 persons were receiving benefits under the program.

The cost of the phase-out was estimated at $160 million to $180 million, far less than the $1 billion price tag attached to proposals to keep the program alive for six more months or the $270 million cost of a scaled-down three-month extension urged by a House subcommittee.

Members from high-unemployment districts sought to continue the program; they said the economic recovery had not reached certain areas of the country where unemployment remained far above the national average of 7.3 percent. But Reagan argued that improvements in the economy had eliminated the need for the extra benefits, which were enacted in 1982 as an emergency recession-relief measure and subsequently had been extended three times. He said the long-term unemployed should seek help through job retraining. *(1982 Almanac p. 43; 1983 Almanac p. 274)*

House Action

The House Ways and Means Committee reported HR 1866 April 2 (H Rept 99-36), after rejecting a three-month extension recommended by the Subcommittee on Public Assistance and Unemployment Compensation.

That proposal was dropped in the face of a threat by committee Republicans to delay floor consideration of the bill — possibly until after Congress' recess — if the panel voted to continue the program.

Instead, an amendment offered by Carroll A. Campbell Jr., R-S.C., replacing the extension with the phase-out was approved 20-16. Eight Democrats joined 12 Republicans in supporting the amendment. Only one GOP member, Richard T. Schulze of Pennsylvania, opposed it.

"It's a very difficult decision, but I believe the committee ought to do what's doable," said Ways and Means Chairman Dan Rostenkowski, D-Ill., who voted for the Campbell amendment.

The bill was rushed to the floor later that day and approved by voice vote. Some Democrats argued that the House should not give in so easily to pressure from the White House, but Rostenkowski said the possibility of getting additional relief to current beneficiaries would be jeopardized by pushing a more ambitious proposal with no chance of passage.

"The choices we faced today were whether to help a few or to help no one," he said. "The committee decided to extend help to the few still collecting" benefits.

Senate Action

The Senate passed the House bill without change April 3, 94-0. *(Vote 28, p. 9-S)*

Finance Committee Chairman Bob Packwood, R-Ore., deflected efforts to amend HR 1866, saying changes were certain to stall action or provoke a presidential veto.

The cost-conscious Finance Committee April 2 had approved the proposal to phase out benefits, after rejecting, 3-13, a three-month extension of the program, proposed by John Heinz, R-Pa.

A six-month extension was proposed on the Senate floor by Arlen Specter, R-Pa., but that amendment was rejected, 34-58. *(Vote 26, p. 9-S)*

The Senate also rejected an amendment by Carl Levin, D-Mich., to liberalize another program that provided up to 13 weeks of additional aid to workers in states with very high unemployment rates. The federal-state extended benefits program was sharply restricted in 1981, and only three states qualified. *(1981 Almanac p. 106)*

The Levin amendment, which lost 32-62, would have allowed states to offer extended benefits if their insured unemployment rate, which reflected those receiving benefits, was at least 5 percent — down from the 6 percent threshold set by existing law. *(Vote 27, p. 9-S)* ∎

Conservation Corps

For the third year in a row, the House approved legislation to create an American Conservation Corps (ACC) to put unemployed teenagers to work on conservation projects, primarily rehabilitating public and Indian lands.

However, the measure (HR 99) passed by only a two-vote margin, far short of the support needed to override a veto. The July 11 vote on passage of the bill was 193-191. *(Vote 205, p. 68-H)*

President Reagan pocket-vetoed a similar bill in 1984. Some changes were made in the 1985 version to ease White House opposition, but the administration continued to oppose the legislation. *(1984 Almanac p. 168)*

In past years, the House had voted by wide margins to create the ACC. The hair's-breadth margin of victory for HR 99, achieved only in the last seconds of the roll call, was attributed to pressures to cut federal spending.

Opponents said Congress should not be creating new programs at a time when lawmakers were struggling to rein in spending for existing programs, including popular training programs already on the books such as the Job Corps for disadvantaged youths.

Republicans, only 18 of whom voted for the bill, portrayed the vote as a test of members' seriousness about reducing the federal budget deficit.

But chief sponsor John F. Seiberling, D-Ohio, argued that the new program would be a modest investment in improving the environment and in combating youth unemployment, which he said remained at an "inexcusably high level" of near 40 percent among minority teenagers.

No action was taken on a companion Senate bill (S 27).

House Committee Action. The House Interior Committee approved HR 99 Feb. 27 by a 26-10 vote, and reported it March 14 (H Rept 99-18, Part I). The Interior Committee version would have authorized $75 million a year over three years for the conservation corps.

The committee rejected an amendment by Ron Marlenee, R-Mont., that would have left establishment of the ACC to the discretion of the secretaries of interior and agriculture.

The Education and Labor Committee approved its version of HR 99 April 16 by an 18-11 vote and reported it May 2 (H Rept 99-18, Part II). The only difference between it and the Interior bill was that it set no specific spending ceiling for the program.

The bill passed by the House was the Education and Labor version.

The administration strongly opposed the bill. In a June 3 letter, David A. Stockman, then director of the Office of Management and Budget, called the program "costly, ill conceived and unnecessary for either employment training or for management of the federal public lands.... a make-work program providing temporary jobs involving public sector skills not necessarily in demand by the private sector." Stockman said he would again recommend a veto.

Provisions. As passed by the House, HR 99 authorized such sums as Congress considered necessary in fiscal 1986-88 for the ACC.

The program, modeled on the Civilian Conservation Corps of the 1930s, was designed to provide about 85,000 jobs in the beginning, including year-round jobs for 16-to 25-year-olds and summer jobs for 15-to-21-year-olds. While open to all eligible youths, special efforts would be made to enroll and recruit economically disadvantaged youth.

The bill also provided for educational and training opportunities. States and Indian tribes would have to put up a portion of the funds for the program. ▮

Brock Named Labor Secretary

The Senate by voice vote April 26 confirmed the nomination of the nation's top trade negotiator, William E. Brock III, to be secretary of labor.

Brock succeeded Raymond J. Donovan, who resigned March 15 to stand trial on charges of larceny and fraud in New York. Donovan's resignation, which President Reagan accepted "with deep regret," came five months after a Bronx County, N.Y., grand jury indicted him on charges concerning financial dealings of his construction company before he joined the Cabinet. Donovan had taken leave from his Labor post after he and some of his former business associates were indicted in October 1984. *(Background, 1984 Almanac p. 168)*

Reagan's choice of Brock to succeed Donovan drew praise from organized labor. "While we have not always agreed [with Brock], he has earned our respect," said AFL-CIO President Lane Kirkland. Throughout Donovan's tenure, the Labor Department's budget cuts and allegedly lax enforcement of labor laws had come under steady criticism from union officials, most of whom opposed Reagan's reelection in 1984.

Brock, 54, had been U.S. trade representative since 1981. He was succeeded in that position by Clayton K. Yeutter, head of the Chicago Mercantile Exchange. *(Yeutter confirmation, p. 418)*

Brock Career

A Tennessean, Brock began his career in Congress with four House terms, serving from 1963-1971. He went to the Senate in 1971 after defeating Democratic incumbent Albert Gore.

He built a generally conservative voting record in Congress, earning a 91 percent career support rating from the U.S. Chamber of Commerce. He voted in support of the AFL-CIO's position about 14 percent of the time during his Senate service.

Brock lost his Senate seat in 1976 to Democrat Jim Sasser, whose campaign portrayed Brock as a country-club Republican who represented the banking and insurance industries.

As chairman of the Republican National Committee from 1977-81, Brock earned respect for his organizing skills and for his efforts to broaden the party's base.

Brock was graduated from Washington and Lee University in 1953. After serving three years in the Navy, he returned to work in his family's candy manufacturing business before running for the House. ▮

NLRB Posts Filled

President Reagan tightened his grip on the National Labor Relations Board (NLRB) in 1985 as the Senate confirmed two new board members, as well as the agency's general counsel who had been serving on a recess appointment since 1984.

Three Reagan appointees already served on the five-member board, which investigated and adjudicated unfair labor practices by employers and unions. The board had come under fire from organized labor for an alleged pro-management bias in interpreting labor law.

Collyer. The Senate April 4 by voice vote confirmed the nomination of Rosemary M. Collyer to be general counsel of the NLRB. Confirmation came a year after Reagan tapped her for the influential post. The general counsel, who served a four-year term, supervised much of the day-to-day operations of the agency.

Senate committee action on Collyer's nomination was blocked in 1984 by Democrats who, echoing labor complaints, maintained that the former chairman of the Federal Mine Safety and Health Review Commission did not have enough labor law experience to handle the job. The nomination also became embroiled in parliamentary maneuvering surrounding a controversial civil rights bill pending in the Labor and Human Resources Committee.

After the Senate failed to act on the nomination, Reagan in October 1984 appointed Collyer to the post while Congress was in recess. That recess appointment would have expired at the end of Congress' 1985 session if the Senate had not formally confirmed her.

Board Members. On May 23, the Senate by voice vote confirmed Reagan's nominees to the board, Marshall B. Babson and Wilford W. Johansen.

Babson had been a management attorney in New Haven, Conn. Johansen had been an NLRB attorney for 26 years, serving most recently as the board's regional director in Los Angeles.

Confirmation of the two marked the first time the five-member board had operated at full strength since August 1983, when the term of Howard Jenkins Jr., a Carter administration appointee, expired. The second seat had been vacant since December 1984. Board members served five-year terms. ▮

Union Jobs in Construction

The House Education and Labor Committee July 23 approved legislation aimed at shoring up the collective bargaining rights of construction workers by making it harder for unionized construction firms to set up separate companies to perform similar work on a non-union basis.

Democratic backers of the bill (HR 281 — H Rept 99-311) said the practice, known as "double-breasting," was widely used by construction firms to avoid dealing with their unions or to shift work from a union shop. They said it had been made easier by recent National Labor Relations Board and court decisions.

HR 281 was intended to prohibit the practice by specifying that separate firms performing similar construction work would be considered a single employer if their management or ownership was directly or indirectly in common. The terms of a union contract in one entity of the combined business would be applied to other entities as well.

GOP critics of the bill said construction companies usually resorted to double breasting not to take work away from union employees but to make it possible for them to bid for contracts where union wages would not be competitive. Marge Roukema, R-N.J., said the bill was an attempt to "reverse the recent growth of open-shop construction through legislative fiat." According to Roukema, the volume of construction work handled by union shops declined from 50 percent to 30 percent over the past 10 years.

HR 281 also would strengthen "pre-hire" agreements, under which construction firms and unions signed a contract for a construction job before workers were hired. Democrats claimed recent court decisions had made it too easy for employers to repudiate their "pre-hire" pacts. HR 281 would give the pacts the same binding status as collective bargaining agreements.

Although the committee approved the bill by voice vote July 23, it did not formally report HR 281 until Oct. 17. A supplemental report (H Rept 99-311, Part II) was filed Nov. 20. There was no further action in 1985. ∎

Polygraph Test Restrictions

The House Education and Labor Committee Dec. 5 reported legislation (HR 1524 — H Rept 99-416) that would bar most private employers from requiring employees to take lie detector (polygraph) tests as a condition of getting or keeping a job. (The House passed an amended version of the bill on March 12, 1986.)

The committee had approved HR 1524 by voice vote Oct. 23. The bill, sponsored by Pat Williams, D-Mont., and Matthew G. Martinez, D-Calif., chairman of the Employment Opportunities Subcommittee, exempted state, local and federal government employers from coverage. It also made clear that lie detector tests could be used in counterintelligence work and that persons under contract with the CIA or the National Security Agency would be subject to the tests. Individuals under contract with the FBI also might be subject to polygraph tests when doing counterintelligence work for the bureau.

About 20 states already had some prohibition on the use of polygraph tests for employment, according to the Employment Opportunities Subcommittee. But representatives of organized labor, who had pushed the legislation, said a federal law was necessary because there were abuses.

Lou Gerber, legislative representative for the Communications Workers of America, said some employers used the tests to verify information on a person's application form and as a predictor of future behavior, for which they were unreliable at best. "Our view is that the philosophy of too many employers is 'In God we trust; others we polygraph,' " Gerber said.

During the committee markup, Marge Roukema, R-N.J., sought to exempt private security services from coverage under the bill, but her amendment was rejected, 13-16.

By 20-9, the panel adopted an amendment by Dennis E. Eckart, D-Ohio, allowing companies that manufactured drugs to use lie detector tests under very specific circumstances involving missing or stolen narcotics.

Under HR 1524, an employer could be fined up to $10,000 for violating the law. The Labor Department, which would implement and enforce the law, could seek a court order to restrain an employer from violating it, and individuals would have the right to sue an employer for violations. ∎

Pension Guaranty Program

Legislation to shore up the Pension Benefit Guaranty Corporation (PBGC) was put on hold until 1986 when Congress failed to clear a budget reconciliation bill (HR 3128) in which the proposals were included.

The Senate Dec. 20 sent the bill back to a conference committee to resolve differences over an unrelated matter — how to fund the "superfund" toxic-waste cleanup program. *(HR 3128, p. 498)*

The House Education and Labor Committee, Senate Labor and Human Resources Committee and House Ways and Means Committee all had approved plans for rescuing the PBGC, which was facing a mounting deficit. The plans were all included in HR 3128, and it was left to conferees to pick from among the various provisions.

The conference version of HR 3128 (H Rept 99-453) would increase the annual premiums that employers paid for single-employer pension plans to $8.50 per participant, from $2.60. A premium increase for PBGC had been assumed in the fiscal 1986 budget resolution (S Con Res 32) approved by Congress Aug. 1. *(Story, p. 441)*

Conferees also agreed to require companies to prove financial distress before they could dump their pension liabilities on the government. If a firm remained in business after a plan termination, the PBGC could recover any losses by taking a share of the firm's pretax profits for up to a decade, in addition to its immediate claim under existing law to 30 percent of a company's net worth. A healthy firm could terminate its plan only if the plan had sufficient assets to pay all promised benefits, not just those that were federally guaranteed.

Background

The 1974 Employee Retirement Income Security Act (ERISA — PL 93-406) set federal standards for private pension plans that promised a guaranteed benefit at retirement. If a company went out of business or terminated its pension plan, the PBGC, a federal corporation, guaranteed the benefits of workers and retirees up to certain statutory limits. *(Congress and the Nation Vol. IV, p. 690)*

The law applied to two kinds of pension plans — single-employer and multi-employer. The latter were collectively bargained plans of employers in the same industry who contributed to a single industrywide pension plan. The premiums for those plans were adjusted in 1980 to rise in stages from 50 cents per participant to $2.60 per participant by 1989. The multi-employer insurance fund had a $17 million surplus at the end of fiscal 1984.

But the PBGC was having serious financial problems because of a deficit in the single-employer pension program. In 1984, the agency for the first time had to pay out more in benefits than it collected in premiums, dipping into its reserves to make up the difference. While its ability to pay benefits was not in immediate jeopardy, officials said, the corporation was heading for insolvency and by 1990 would no longer be able to pay benefits when they were due.

At the end of fiscal 1984, the PBGC was responsible for payment of benefits to about 149,000 current and future retirees in 1,100 terminated plans. The program had liabilities of $1.525 billion and assets of $1.063 billion, leaving an accumulated deficit of $462 million. The deficit jumped to over $600 million in July 1985 when Allis-Chalmers Corp., a farm equipment manufacturer, terminated a pension plan with a $165 million shortfall — the largest single claim the PBGC had faced in its 11-year history.

Officials said they feared the deficit could grow to more than $2.4 billion in the next decade unless Congress required higher payments from companies covered by the program and tightened the 1974 law.

The premium employers paid for financing the program was $2.60 per pension plan participant. PBGC requested a hike to $7.50. Opponents said a higher premium could discourage small and medium-sized companies from adopting pension plans.

Critics of the program also said part of PBGC's financial problems could be traced to loopholes in the pension law that allowed companies to dump pension debts on the PBGC even if they were solvent. PBGC officials said one-fifth of the agency's losses could be attributed to companies that took advantage of weaknesses in the law.

Congress had deadlocked for several years over how to restructure the program, which covered about 29 million workers. Since 1982, the PBGC and key members of Congress had proposed tightening the program and raising premiums. But they were unable to gain business and labor support for a reform package. Debate focused on how much the premium should be raised, how to discourage ongoing companies from getting rid of poorly funded pension plans and how much of a company's profits should be taken to cover workers' benefits if it did shut down its plan but stay in business.

The 98th Congress failed to complete work on legislation to crack down on abuses and raise premiums. A House subcommittee and the Senate Labor and Human Resources Committee approved bills, but neither measure went any further. Another House pension bill for public-sector workers included a PBGC premium increase, but it never passed. *(1984 Almanac p. 25)*

Frustrated by the stalemate and concerned about the mounting deficit at the PBGC, members in 1985 dropped or modified many controversial proposals in the earlier legislation, although they retained a requirement that employers prove economic hardship before being allowed to turn pension debts over to the PBGC. Some lawmakers were inclined to settle for simply raising the premium.

Legislative History

The House Ways and Means Committee approved an $8-per-participant premium rate in a deficit-reduction bill (HR 3128 — H Rept 99-241, Part I) reported July 31. The bill contained a "sunset" provision providing that the premium would drop back to $2.60 after Jan. 1, 1989. Committee aides said the provision was designed to keep pressure on Congress to revamp the insurance program.

The Education and Labor Committee reported its version of HR 3128 Sept. 11 (H Rept 99-241, Part II). It called for an $8.50 premium and contained a number of provisions designed to prevent employers from burdening the system in the future with unfunded pension claims.

The Education and Labor provisions also were included in another reconciliation bill (HR 3500) reported by the House Budget Committee Oct. 3 (H Rept 99-300) and passed by the House Oct. 24. The committee estimated its provisions would result in savings of $300 million a year, or $900 million by fiscal 1988, the amount required by the budget resolution. However, the Congressional Budget Office estimated the savings at only $666 million over the three years.

HR 3128 passed the House Oct. 31, and both it and HR 3500 went to conference with the Senate-passed version of HR 3128, which contained a premium increase to $8.10 per participant. ▮

Tax Penalty on Below-Market Deals Relaxed

After a yearlong struggle, Congress resolved a dispute over taxation of below-market, seller-financed real estate transactions.

The Senate Oct. 1 adopted by voice vote the conference report on a bill (HR 2475 — PL 99-121) easing limits on such deals. The vote cleared the bill for President Reagan, who signed it Oct. 11.

The dispute revolved around a seemingly minor provision in the 1984 Deficit Reduction Act (PL 98-369) that would have penalized taxpayers who charge artificially low mortgage interest rates and artificially high property sales prices to avoid taxes. *(1984 Almanac p. 155)*

The measure, which received little attention from Congress when it was enacted, set off a wave of opposition from the real estate industry, farmers and others who often resorted to low-rate, seller financing.

They charged that the "imputed interest" rules so named because the Treasury would impute an interest rate more in line with market rates when taxing real estate deals — would unfairly penalize honest businesses along with those involved in tax-shelter transactions.

Sellers stood to benefit from such low-rate deals because more of their income would be converted into capital gains, which were taxed at lower rates than income from interest payments on loans. Buyers stood to benefit because inflated sales prices would entitle them to larger depreciation and investment tax breaks.

Provisions

As cleared, HR 2475:

- Imputed an interest rate of the lesser of 9 percent, or 100 percent of the "applicable federal rate" (the amount paid on comparable Treasury obligations) in transactions involving seller financing of $2.8 million or less

• Imputed an interest rate equal to the applicable federal rate in transactions involving seller financing of more than $2.8 million, or in any transactions involving investment in new property eligible for an investment tax credit.

• Imputed an interest rate equal to 110 percent of the applicable federal rate in so-called sale-leaseback transactions, which generally transferred tax benefits from a taxpayer who could not use them to one who could.

• Indexed the $2.8 million threshold amount to increase with inflation, beginning in 1990.

• Made the imputed interest provisions effective generally for sales or exchanges made after June 30, 1985.

• Increased from 18 years to 19 years the minimum period over which real estate investments could be depreciated. Low-income housing continued to have a 15-year depreciation period. The change, made to help offset the cost of the imputed interest revisions, was generally effective for property placed in service after May 8, 1985.

• Exempted from tax the interest on entrance fees — considered under the law to be below-market loans — of $90,000 or less made by individuals age 65 and over to so-called life-care facilities.

Background

In 1984, a little-noticed section of the Deficit Reduction Act raised the minimum interest rate a seller could charge without incurring a penalty. It also increased the tax penalty for sellers who charged a lower rate, by permitting the Internal Revenue Service (IRS) to apply a higher interest rate to calculate their tax liability.

The imputed interest provision was included in the bill to combat tax-shelter schemes by ensuring that transactions were taxed as if prevailing mortgage rates applied.

Only after the Deficit Reduction Act had passed both houses in late June 1984, but before it was sent to Reagan, did the real estate and housing interests rally to oppose the imputed interest section. They complained that the limits on seller-financed deals, which were to take effect Jan. 1, 1985, would hurt the housing market.

In October 1984, the unresolved fight threatened to delay Congress' adjournment until members agreed to delay the effective date of the IRS rules until July 1, 1985, for transactions of $2 million or less.

Revised imputed interest rules were aimed at seller-financing arrangements that had become increasingly popular with homeowners, developers, real estate brokers and investors. Sellers made loans at interest rates below those available from banks or other lenders. Buyers, in return, agreed to higher sales prices. Both parties benefited.

A seller could count the income from a loan's principal as a capital gain, which received preferential tax treatment. The larger the loan, the larger the amount of money treated as a capital gain. Income on interest, in contrast, was taxed at regular rates.

On large commercial transactions, a buyer could claim bigger tax breaks from depreciation and investment tax credits based on the exaggerated price of the property.

Such advantages led to widespread tax abuse, according to Treasury Department officials who persuaded sponsors of the Deficit Reduction Act to include the tough imputed interest section.

A number of bills were introduced in early 1985 to reverse or revise the 1984 law. Most of the bills allowed sellers to avoid imputed interest for most sales or calculate taxes on a lower imputed rate, rather than repeal the 1984 tax code revision.

House Action

The House Ways and Means Committee May 14 reported HR 2475 (H Rept 99-87), limiting the reach of the 1984 act.

The Ways and Means bill required the Internal Revenue Service to impute a minimum 9 percent interest rate for transactions of $2 million or less.

Deals involving financing of more than $4 million would have been assigned interest rates equal to or greater than rates on federal securities of a similar duration. For example, rates on a 20-year seller-financed mortgage would have been the same as those on 20-year Treasury notes. Deals between $2 million and $4 million would have been assigned a "blended rate" somewhere between 9 percent and the Treasury rate, based on the amount of the deal.

To pay for the change — estimated to cost the Treasury about $800 million to $900 million through 1990 in lost revenues — the committee agreed to extend from 18 years to 19 years the amount of time over which an investment in a new building could be depreciated. That provision would have covered property placed in service after May 8, unless construction had begun or a binding contract was in force and the property would have been placed in service before Jan. 1, 1987.

By 425-0, the House May 21 passed the Ways and Means bill without amendment. *(Vote 108, p. 38-H)*

Senate Action

The Senate Finance Committee June 13 unanimously reported the bill (S Rept 99-83), after adding several provisions to the House-passed bill, including one to set a ceiling on the rate that Treasury could impute for certain sales, if it could be shown they were not designed to avoid tax payments. The Finance Committee also altered the method of imputing interest rates for deals between $2 million and $4 million.

Ohio Democrat Howard M. Metzenbaum, describing HR 2475 as "giving away the store to the real estate lobby," filibustered the bill when it got to the Senate floor June 25.

Metzenbaum later dropped his objections and the Senate, by voice vote, accepted his amendment requiring interest to be 110 percent of the federal rate on sales of more than $25 million and on sale-leaseback deals.

By voice vote, the Senate also adopted an amendment by John Melcher, D-Mont., allowing sales of farms, ranches and some small businesses up to $9 million to be made at the blended rate. For other loans above $4 million, the entire amount would have been subject to the higher federal rate.

The Senate, 54-43, earlier had rejected a Melcher motion to waive provisions of the 1974 budget act so the Senate could consider his amendment to limit the penalty on sales of farms, ranches and certain small businesses. His proposal would have lost an estimated $1.8 million in tax revenues a year, and the Congressional Budget Act prohibited action on measures that would lose more revenues than provided in a fiscal year's budget resolution. *(Vote 138, p. 28-S)*

After the Senate's acceptance of Metzenbaum's amendment on large sales effectively added $6 million in revenues to the bill, Melcher won reconsideration of his amendment.

John H. Chafee, R-R.I., unsuccessfully opposed the bill's exemption for "continuing care facilities," retirement communities combining independent living and some medical care.

The provision, which was not in the House bill, exempted from the imputed-interest rules deposits up to $90,000 that people 65 or over paid to enter such facilities, at a cost to the Treasury of $44 million in taxes over five years.

Chafee argued that the payments amounted to a loan to a corporation and so should be taxed subject to imputed interest. His amendment to delete the provision was tabled, 73-24. *(Vote 137, p. 28-S)*

The Senate passed HR 2475 by voice vote June 26.

Final Action

Staff from the Ways and Means and Finance Committees met informally over the summer to work out differences between the two bills, particularly over the treatment of more expensive transactions and the Senate provision exempting refundable payments by senior citizens to continuing care facilities.

Just before recessing for August, conferees agreed on a plan that eased tax requirements on transactions of $2.8 million and under, and reduced the penalties on larger transactions, paying for the change by lengthening the depreciation period for real estate holdings.

The House adopted the conference report (H Rept 99-250) by voice vote hours before beginning its summer recess Aug. 1.

Final consideration in the Senate was blocked until October, again by Metzenbaum, who objected to the revenue loss projected in the first few years the measure would be in effect. He also opposed the conferees' decision to drop his amendment retaining a higher tax penalty on transactions of $25 million or more.

In Senate floor debate Oct. 1 on the conference report, Metzenbaum complained about the bill's $115 million cost over the first three years. But Finance Committee Chairman Bob Packwood, R-Ore., noted that over five years the bill would cost only $9 million because of increased revenue from the depreciation change.

A motion by Metzenbaum to delay consideration of the conference report until Oct. 10 to give the Senate Finance Committee time to come up with enough budget savings to cover the $115 million cost lost by a vote of 7-91. *(Vote 199, p. 39-S)*

Metzenbaum and Chafee also criticized the life-care facilities provision, which was expected to cost an estimated $44 million over five years. ▮

Auto Record-Keeping Requirement Repealed

Responding to angry constituents, Congress quickly and overwhelmingly repealed a 1984 law requiring taxpayers to keep daily logs when claiming tax breaks for business use of automobiles, home computers or other equipment.

The Senate by voice vote May 16 cleared the bill (HR 1869 — PL 99-44) repealing the strict new record-keeping requirements. Final action came as the Senate adopted a conference report (H Rept 99-67). The House approved the conference report May 8 by a vote of 426-1. *(Vote 93, p. 32-H)*

The record-keeping rules were required by the Deficit Reduction Act of 1984 (PL 98-369), which was designed to help reduce the federal deficit in part by closing tax loopholes and beefing up compliance with tax laws. *(1984 Almanac p. 143)*

The law mandated that, effective Jan. 1, 1985, taxpayers who claimed business tax breaks would have to keep detailed "contemporaneous" logs of their business and personal use of automobiles and other equipment.

Thousands of taxpayers were outraged by the strict new requirements, set out in detail late in 1984 by the Internal Revenue Service (IRS). Small-business owners and farmers especially complained that the rules, which in some cases mandated multiple daily entries in a log, were burdensome and unnecessarily intrusive.

Members claimed that when they enacted the law they never envisioned the tough record-keeping rules issued by the IRS. Despite the overwhelming support for repeal, a handful of members complained that Congress had buckled under to constituent pressure. They claimed that the less stringent record-keeping requirements would allow more individuals to evade taxes at a time when Congress was considering a complete overhaul of the tax code to eliminate such abuse. *(Tax overhaul, p. 480)*

Under the new record-keeping law, taxpayers were still required to substantiate business use of cars or other vehicles to qualify for deductions or tax credits. But detailed logs or other written records were not necessary.

Nevertheless, the Treasury Department said more than $885 million in tax cheating was likely to result by 1990 from the record-keeping repeal. To help pay for the loss, Congress agreed to limit tax breaks for the business use of luxury cars. That limit was expected to generate more than $1 billion by 1990.

Provisions

As enacted, HR 1869:

- Repealed the requirement that "contemporaneous" records — daily logs detailing every usage or trip — be kept to qualify for tax deductions and credits for business use of automobiles, computers and other equipment.
- Required taxpayers to substantiate claims with "adequate records" or "sufficient evidence," as required prior to passage of the 1984 act. Such evidence could include receipts, expense reports or an employer policy prohibiting personal use of a vehicle.
- Required taxpayers claiming deductions for use of cars to answer several questions on their tax returns about mileage driven and personal use of the vehicle. This provision was to go into effect Jan. 1, 1986.
- Repealed penalties and regulations stemming from the 1984 record-keeping law.
- Repealed a provision of the 1984 law directing tax preparers to inform clients of the new requirements and receive a written statement from clients that they were met.
- Exempted from the substantiation rules vehicles that were unlikely to be used for personal purposes, such as marked police and fire vehicles, single-seat delivery trucks, and hearses.
- Gave employers the option of not withholding taxes from an employee's income for the personal use of a business car if the employee was notified and the value of the benefit was reported to the Treasury Department.

• Lowered the maximum investment tax credit allowed for a business car from $1,000 to $675, and lowered the maximum depreciation on the car in the first year from $4,000 to $3,200 and from $6,000 to $4,800 in each subsequent year. The limits were indexed to increase with inflation, beginning in 1989. The provision, applicable to cars that cost more than $11,250, was to be effective generally for autos placed in service or leased after April 2, 1985. The original limits were enacted in 1984 to prevent large business tax breaks for the use of expensive cars.

House, Senate Action

When — as the 1984 law required — accountants began informing clients of the new IRS record-keeping rules in early 1985, a spontaneous lobbying campaign erupted on Capitol Hill aimed at repealing them.

Phone calls and letters began pouring into congressional offices, and a host of bills were introduced in the opening days of the 99th Congress to soothe constituents.

Meanwhile, the chorus against the new law had become so loud that the IRS announced Jan. 25 that it would relax some of the record-keeping rules. But congressional critics of the new tax law doubted that the IRS would go far enough in scaling back record-keeping requirements and feared that revising the rules would confuse things even further.

The House Ways and Means and Senate Finance committees reported different versions of the measure (HR 1869 — H Rept 99-34; S 245 — S Rept 99-23) April 2.

The House passed HR 1869 April 2 by a vote of 412-1. The following day the Senate passed an amended version of the House bill by a vote of 92-1. *(House vote 41, p. 16-H; Senate vote 25, p. 9-S)*

Under both versions, individuals were required to keep only "adequate" records of their business use of autos and other equipment or to have "substantial corroborating evidence" to back up their claims. The requirement, which was the same as pre-1984 law, was retroactive to Jan. 1, 1985.

The House bill also required that, beginning in 1986, the corroborating evidence be in written form, such as a log, expense report or written employer policy limiting personal use of the vehicle. No record-keeping would be required for vehicles that were unlikely to be used for personal reasons, such as forklifts, cement mixers, ambulances and marked police cars.

Because of the projected cost of repealing the record-keeping rules, the House bill included an unrelated provision to raise offsetting revenues. That provision lowered limits on business tax breaks for expensive, or so-called "luxury," autos enacted in the 1984 deficit-reduction bill.

The Senate bill avoided the requirement of written evidence and steered clear of a tax increase. But the Senate did adopt an amendment that was estimated to raise the cost of the legislation almost sevenfold through fiscal 1988.

The provision, proposed by Malcolm Wallop, R-Wyo., barred taxation of personal use of business vehicles by certain individuals who operated the cars 75 percent or more of the time for business reasons. It was adopted 51-42. *(Vote 23, p. 9-S)*

The exemption would apply only to individuals whose employers required them to take vehicles home or who used them as an integral part of their businesses. Under existing law, personal use of business vehicles was subject to tax as an employee fringe benefit, as well as to record-keeping and tax-withholding requirements.

The Senate narrowly rejected, 46-47, a "sense of Congress" amendment by Howard M. Metzenbaum, D-Ohio, objecting to non-binding language in the Senate Finance Committee report on its version of the bill instructing the Treasury Department to ease rules taxing the personal use of corporate airplanes by top executives. Some members complained that existing rules required excessive tax payments. *(Vote 24, p. 9-S)*

Metzenbaum argued that revising the rules, against the background of Congress' ongoing efforts to reduce deficits, was an unnecessary tax "giveaway." After enactment of HR 1869, Treasury Department officials said they would revise the corporate aircraft regulations.

Conference Action

House and Senate conferees May 1 agreed to repeal the 1984 requirement, generally following the House version of the bill.

Conferees dropped from the bill the costly Senate provision that would have prevented the Treasury from taxing individuals who used business cars for transportation to and from work. They also dropped a House requirement that corroborative evidence of business use of personal cars be in written form, but agreed to retain a requirement for additional information on tax returns.

Conferees agreed to the House provision restricting business tax breaks for so-called "luxury," or expensive, automobiles to offset the cost of the record-keeping repeal. ▮

EDA, ARC Survive

Congress again spared two small community development programs that President Reagan proposed killing.

The agencies were the Economic Development Administration (EDA), which provided grants for public works improvements, and the Appalachian Regional Commission (ARC), which supported public works and highway developments in the 13-state Appalachian region.

Authorization for both agencies, which began during the 1960s war on poverty, expired Sept. 30, 1982. The administration had tried to abolish them each year, arguing that they were limited in scope and should be funded by local or state governments. But Congress had included funding for EDA and ARC in appropriations bills.

For fiscal 1986, EDA received a total of $225 million from the appropriations bill for the Departments of Commerce, Justice and State (HR 2965 — PL 99-180) and the stopgap funding bill for general government agencies (H J Res 465 — PL 99-190). ARC received $120 million in the energy and water development appropriations measure (HR 2959 — PL 99-141).

In addition, the House Sept. 4 passed a bill (HR 10 — H Rept 99-115, Part I) authorizing EDA for three years and ARC for five. The measure, reported May 15 by the House Public Works and Transportation Committee, was passed by a vote of 260-96. *(Vote 266, p. 86-H)*

It was similar to measures the House passed in 1982 and 1983, which died when the Senate failed to act on them. *(1983 Almanac p. 229)*

House sponsors included reforms to answer criticisms raised about EDA. The bill, for example, dropped a controversial loan program. It also tightened the eligibility criteria. Currently, once an area had been designated as eligible for aid, it remained eligible; about 80 percent of the country could receive EDA assistance. ▮

House Approves Major Rewrite of Tax Code

After a year of debate, intense lobbying and the last-minute revolt of nearly its entire Republican membership, the House Dec. 17 passed a sweeping rewrite of the federal tax code that would reduce individual and corporate tax rates and restrict dozens of existing tax breaks.

The Tax Reform Act of 1985 (HR 3838 — H Rept 99-426) was revived from its near death only after a full-court White House lobbying press — including a visit to Capitol Hill by President Reagan — turned around enough Republican votes to bring the measure to the floor.

Reagan had set overhaul and simplification of the tax system as his top domestic goal for his second term. He had initiated the call for tax reform in his 1984 State of the Union address and amplified his message in 1985.

But House Republicans complained that HR 3838, as reported by the Ways and Means Committee, fell short of his tax-reform goals and would hurt the economy. Only five of the 13 Republicans on the committee, but all 25 Democrats, had voted to report the bill favorably. *(Chronology, p. 481; committee vote, p. 492; 1985 State of the Union address, p. 8-D; 1984 State of the Union address, 1984 Almanac p. 6-E)*

On Dec. 11, the House almost buried the bill by voting 202-223 against a rule to allow floor debate. Only 14 of 182 Republicans voted for the rule. *(Vote 411, p. 130-H)*

After the first rule vote failed, the White House lobbying effort reversed what appeared to be a firm GOP resolve to kill the measure, and the rule was adopted Dec. 17, by a 258-168 vote. The House, in an ironic denouement, eight hours later passed the bill by voice vote, having agreed to two relatively minor amendments. *(Vote 425, p. 134-H; switched votes, p. 496)*

Passage of the bill was seen as a personal triumph for House Ways and Means Chairman Dan Rostenkowski, D-Ill., who had carefully shepherded the measure — the first complete rewrite of the Internal Revenue Code since 1954 — through committee.

The panel worked from a draft version Rostenkowski had endorsed, and it ratified compromises preserving tax breaks that he had negotiated as needed to win a majority. Toasting his hard-won victory, Rostenkowski smiled and raised a glass of champagne not only to the accomplishment of the House, but "to a bumpy ride in the Senate."

Veto Threat and Effective Dates

The deal that won Reagan enough GOP votes to pass the bill hung on the president's firm promise to veto any tax measure that was not substantially different from the House bill.

In particular, the president and many in Congress wanted lower maximum tax rates than in the Ways and Means bill and sought to restore incentives for business investment that the bill would eliminate. Reagan made his veto promise in a Dec. 17 letter to House Republicans. *(Text, p. 40-D)*

Republicans also demanded agreement by Democratic leaders that minor changes could be made in a GOP alternative to the committee bill that was to be offered on the floor. The changes were proposed in an effort to pick up the votes of some disaffected Democrats, but the GOP alternative failed by a wide margin, as did a GOP motion to recommit the bill to committee.

The final part of the deal included the promise by the Democratic leadership of a vote on a non-binding resolution concerning the bill's effective dates.

The committee had agreed that most provisions should take effect as of Jan. 1, 1986, to prevent businesses and other taxpayers from taking advantage of anticipated changes in the law. Because the bill clearly could not be enacted until well into 1986, House Republicans argued that the committee bill's effective dates would lead to uncertainty in business decisions and consequent adverse economic impact.

Republicans wanted an understanding that the effective dates would be changed. Immediately after HR 3838 was passed Dec. 17, the House adopted H Res 335, which stated the sense of the House that some unspecified provisions should not take effect until January 1987.

The Senate by voice vote Dec. 19 passed a similar resolution (S Res 281) stating the sense of that chamber that the effective date for almost all provisions should be Jan. 1, 1987.

More Difficulties Ahead

At the start of 1985, Reagan said he hoped the bill could be enacted by the end of the year. But as time passed it became clear that the House — which under the Constitution must generate all revenue bills — would have its hands full completing action before it adjourned for the year. House passage of the tax bill was one of the last major legislative actions of 1985.

Neither the full Senate, nor its Finance Committee, took action on HR 3838 in 1985, although Finance did conduct weeks of fact-gathering hearings throughout the summer at the same time Ways and Means held similar hearings.

The tax bill faced an uncertain future in 1986. Despite Reagan's emphasis on tax reform, public opinion polls throughout 1985 showed little voter interest in it. And, although the bill did promise to shift the burden of about $140 billion in tax payments over five years from individuals to businesses, the lauded goal of simplification — perceived to have some voter appeal — was lost during the House markup, as evidenced by the 1,000-plus page bill that passed.

But Reagan's threat of a veto unless the bill was altered substantially signaled the likelihood of further conflict in the Senate, where Finance Chairman Bob Packwood, R-Ore., predicted that his committee and the full chamber would pass a tax bill in 1986 not unlike the one approved by the House. Senate markup was scheduled to begin in March 1986.

The agreed-upon political goal of keeping the bill "revenue neutral" — so that it generated neither more nor less revenue than the existing tax code — would require Finance to undo deals struck in Ways and Means or find new sources of revenue to pay for the desired changes. Either path would be difficult, Packwood acknowledged.

In addition, the need to increase revenues to alleviate the federal deficit was certain to loom even more threateningly over the tax debate in the Senate. As 1985 wound to a close, members of both parties from both chambers put unavailing pressure on Reagan to adopt deficit reduction as a more pressing priority than the tax bill.

Chronology of Tax Bill

- **August 1982.** Sen. Bill Bradley, D-N.J., and Rep. Richard A. Gephardt, D-Mo., introduce their "Fair Tax" plan (S 409, HR 800) to set individual tax rates at 14, 26 and 30 percent.
- **January 1984.** President Reagan calls in his State of the Union address for simplification of the federal tax system. He directs Treasury Secretary Donald T. Regan to draw up a plan by December 1984, one month following the next presidential election. *(1984 Almanac p. 6-E)*
- **April 1984.** Rep. Jack F. Kemp, R-N.Y., and Sen. Bob Kasten, R-Wis., introduce the "Fair and Simple Tax" (HR 2222, S 1006) to impose a flat 24 percent tax rate.
- **Fall 1984.** Democratic presidential candidate Walter F. Mondale accuses Reagan of having a "secret plan" to raise taxes after the election, and releases his own proposal to raise taxes to reduce the federal deficit.
- **November 1984.** The Treasury Department releases its blueprint for overhauling the federal tax system. Reagan's reaction is lukewarm and he says he is open to suggestions before submitting his own plan.
- **May 1985.** Reagan announces his tax-overhaul plan, which lowers individual and corporate tax rates, limits numerous special tax breaks and raises the same amount of revenue as the current tax system. House Ways and Means Committee Chairman Dan Rostenkowski, D-Ill., says Democrats will work with the president to draw up a bill. A summer of hearings begins in both the Ways and Means and Senate Finance committees.
- **September 1985.** Ways and Means Committee staff draws up a draft tax plan, similar to Reagan's proposal, and the committee begins to mark up a bill.
- **October 1985.** Markup bogs down when Ways and Means Committee members vote to give banks a costly new tax advantage. Rostenkowski breaks the deadlock with back-room negotiations, including informal agreement that the state and local tax deduction will be retained.
- **Nov. 23, 1985.** Committee completes its markup amid growing partisanship. Republicans complain they were shut out of decision making in final hours, and talk of offering a substitute plan.
- **Dec. 4, 1985.** Reagan expresses lukewarm support for the Ways and Means bill and asks Congress to vote for either it or GOP plan to keep the tax-rewrite effort alive.
- **Dec. 11, 1985.** Tax bill is dealt a severe blow when the House votes 202-223 to reject the rule allowing the measure to come to the floor. Of 178 Republicans voting, only 14 voted for the rule.
- **Dec. 17, 1985.** After intense lobbying by the White House, the House reverses its vote on the rule and the Ways and Means tax bill is approved by voice vote.

The week before the House passed HR 3838, Congress enacted the Gramm-Rudman-Hollings anti-deficit legislation, which required a balanced budget by fiscal 1991 and further turned up the heat to find new revenues. *(Gramm-Rudman-Hollings, p. 459)*

Major Provisions

Following are major provisions of HR 3838. Where effective dates were not specified, provisions would take effect Jan. 1, 1986. As passed by the House Dec. 17, HR 3838 would:

Individuals

- **Rates.** Replace individual income tax rates of 11-50 percent with rates of 15, 25, 35 and 38 percent.

For a married couple, taxable income of up to $22,500 would be taxed at the 15 percent rate, income from $22,500 to $43,000 would be taxed at 25 percent, income from $43,000 to $100,000 would be taxed at 35 percent and income in excess of $100,000 would be taxed at 38 percent.

For a single head of household, taxable income up to $16,000 would be taxed at 15 percent, income from $16,000 to $34,000 would be taxed at 25 percent, income from $34,000 to $75,000 would be taxed at 35 percent and income of more than $75,000 would be taxed at 38 percent.

For an individual, income up to $12,500 would be taxed at 15 percent, income from $12,500 to $30,000 would be taxed at 25 percent, income from $30,000 to $60,000 would be taxed at 35 percent and income in excess of $60,000 would be taxed at 38 percent.

The rate cuts would go into effect July 1, 1986.

- **Personal Exemption.** Raise the personal exemption for taxpayers and their dependents from $1,040 (the 1985 rate, scheduled to rise to $1,080 in 1986) to $2,000 for taxpayers who did not itemize their deductions. Taxpayers who itemized would have their personal exemptions effectively reduced to $1,500 by a new provision disallowing the first $500 of their itemized deductions for each exemption claimed.

The increase in the personal exemption would be effective Jan. 1, 1986.

- **Standard Deduction.** Replace the existing zero bracket amount, or the amount below which no taxes were imposed, and replace it with a standard deduction for those who did not itemize their returns. The deduction would be $4,800 for joint returns, $4,200 for single heads of households and $2,950 for individuals. The zero bracket amount in 1986 was expected to be $3,670 for joint returns and $2,480 for single taxpayers.

Under the House bill, the standard deduction would be raised an additional $600 for the elderly and the blind, but there would be no increase for each dependent as Rostenkowski had proposed.

The increase in the standard deduction would be effective Jan. 1, 1987; the increase for the elderly and the blind would be effective Jan. 1, 1986.

- **Earned Income Credit.** Expand the earned income tax credit for working poor families from the existing maximum of $550 to $700. The income level at which the credit would be phased out would be raised from $11,000 to $16,000.
- **Marriage Penalty.** Eliminate the deduction for two-earner couples but make changes in the standard deduction and rate schedules that would provide similar relief for married taxpayers. The deduction was designed to

Tax Liability by Income Class

(As Computed for 1987)

Income Class	Percentage Change In Income Tax Liability: Administration Proposal	House Bill
Less than $10,000	−72.4%	−76.0%
$10,000-$20,000	−18.0	−23.4
$20,000-$30,000	−9.3	−9.9
$30,000-$40,000	−6.6	−9.0
$40,000-$50,000	−7.3	−8.7
$50,000-$75,000	−5.9	−7.4
$75,000-$100,000	−8.9	−5.7
$100,000-$200,000	−10.1	−7.3
$200,000 and above	−15.2	−5.9
TOTAL	−10.5	−9.0

NOTE: These figures did not take into account certain proposals affecting individuals. Thus, the total tax reductions under both the administration proposal and the House bill were expected to be slightly different from what was indicated in this table.

SOURCE: Joint Committee on Taxation

lower taxes for two-earner couples, who otherwise would end up paying higher taxes than if they filed separately as single taxpayers.

• **Child and Dependent Care.** Retain the existing child care tax credit of up to $720 a year for one dependent and up to $1,440 for two dependents.

• **Income Averaging.** Repeal income averaging, which allowed taxpayers with dramatic fluctuations in income to reduce their tax liabilities.

• **Elderly and Disabled.** Retain existing law providing a 15 percent tax credit for elderly taxpayers and those who retired because of permanent and total disability.

• **Unemployment Compensation.** Tax as income all unemployment compensation benefits. Under existing law, such benefits were taxed only for individuals with incomes in excess of $12,000 and couples with incomes in excess of $18,000. The House agreed to retain existing law excluding from taxable income workers' compensation, black lung benefits and certain employer-provided disability benefits.

• **Adoption Expense.** Abolish an existing tax deduction for up to $1,500 in expenses related to the adoption of hard-to-place children and to expand a direct spending program to compensate for the change.

• **Scholarships.** Tax as income scholarships and fellowships that were not used for tuition or equipment required for courses, or were received by students who were not degree candidates. The change would be effective for awards granted after Sept. 25, 1985. All other prizes and awards would be subject to tax.

• **State and Local Taxes.** Retain the deduction for state and local sales, property and income taxes. State and local governments would be required to report to the federal government payments they received from individuals for income and property taxes, beginning Jan. 1, 1987.

• **Charitable Deductions.** Allow those who did not itemize to deduct charitable contributions, but only in excess of $100 a year. Such taxpayers could, under existing law, deduct half of all contributions in 1985 and 100 percent in 1986, but the deduction was due to expire at the end of 1986. Taxpayers who itemized would still be allowed to deduct all of their contributions.

• **Travel and Entertainment.** Allow taxpayers to deduct up to 80 percent of their business-related meals and entertainment expenses. Expenses such as hotel and transportation would remain deductible, as would tickets for certain charitable events. The House also agreed to disallow all deductions for business expenses related to "skyboxes" at such facilities as convention centers or sports arenas.

It also would limit deductions for business travel on luxury cruise ships and disallow deductions for travel taken for educational purposes.

• **Employee Business Expenses.** Allow deductions for certain employee business expenses and several miscellaneous itemized deductions, such as those related to the preparation of tax returns, to the extent they exceeded 1 percent of a taxpayer's adjusted gross income.

• **Home Offices.** Limit deductions for home office expenses to a taxpayer's net income from the business. Under existing law, the deductions could not exceed gross income. However, members agreed that excess deductions could be carried forward and taken against income in future years. The deduction limits would apply to cases, exempt from limitations under existing law, in which a taxpayer leased his home office to his employer.

• **Hobbies.** Expand the definition of "hobbies," for which expense deductions were more limited than for regular businesses. Under the new definition, an activity would be a hobby if it was not profitable in at least three out of five consecutive years, instead of two out of five years as under existing law. The House agreed to exempt horse breeding and racing from the tighter restrictions.

• **Political Contributions.** Allow a taxpayer to claim a credit of up to $100 for 100 percent of contributions to candidates for federal office from the taxpayer's own state. The provision would replace the existing law tax credit of $50 allowed for half of a taxpayer's political contributions.

• **Presidential 'Checkoff.'** Allow taxpayers to continue allocating $1 of their income tax liability to the Presidential Election Campaign Fund.

Fringe Benefits

• Retain existing law allowing the exclusion from income of employer-provided health insurance premiums, the cost of up to $5,000 in death benefits, and the cost of up to $50,000 of group-term life insurance. Limits proposed by Reagan and Rostenkowski on tax-free employee benefits had been strongly opposed by labor groups.

• Extend for two years the existing exclusion from income of employer-provided prepaid legal services and up to $5,000 in education assistance. The exclusions were scheduled to expire at the end of 1985.

• Allow the exclusion for employer-provided van pooling to expire at the end of 1985, as provided by existing law.

• Limit to $5,000 a year the exclusion allowed for employer-provided child care assistance.

Capital Gains

• Raise the top effective individual income tax rate on long-term capital gains (proceeds from the sale of assets held for more than six months) from the existing 20 percent to 22 percent. The change would be effective Jan. 1, 1986.

- Raise the top effective tax rate on capital gains for corporations from 28 percent to 36 percent, effective Jan. 1, 1986.

Depreciation

- Repeal the 10 percent investment tax credit allowed under existing law for investment in certain business assets.

Both Rostenkowski and Reagan had proposed elimination of the credit, which had been repealed and reinstated several times since it was first enacted during the Kennedy administration.

- Replace existing law allowing accelerated depreciation of business assets with a less generous method that would generally lengthen the period of time over which an investment could be written off.

The House agreed to require that assets be depreciated over periods ranging from three to 30 years, compared with the existing three to 19 years, depending on the type of asset. However, the House also agreed in most cases to allow more of an asset's cost to be written off in the earlier years than under existing law.

Real estate would be among the areas hardest hit by the changes, with a depreciation life of 30 years compared with the existing 19 years. Real estate investments also would be written off at a slower pace than under existing law.

Cars and trucks that under existing law could be depreciated over three years would have to be written off over five years.

- Allow the value of depreciated assets to be indexed, beginning in 1988, to offset some of the impact of inflation. The provision would kick into effect only if inflation exceeded 5 percent and, even then, an asset would be indexed to reflect only 50 percent of the increase in inflation above 5 percent.

The administration had proposed that assets be fully indexed.

- Rejected the administration's controversial proposal to impose a tax retroactively on businesses to recapture some of the "windfall" benefits firms would receive from the combined effect of generous depreciation benefits allowed under existing law and a lower corporate tax rate provided by the bill.
- Allow firms with unused investment and other business tax credits to use them to offset their corporate minimum tax liability if they had net operating losses in any two of the last three taxable years prior to 1986.
- Allow firms to continue to write off in one year the costs of removing architectural and transportation barriers for the elderly and handicapped. This provision would expire after two years.

Corporate Taxes

- Lower the maximum corporate rate from 46 percent to 36 percent, effective July 1, 1986.

To help small businesses, corporate income up to $50,000 would be taxed at a rate of 15 percent, income from $50,000 to $75,000 would be taxed at 25 percent, and income above that amount would be taxed at 36 percent. The graduated rates would be phased out so that corporations with taxable income above $350,000 would pay a flat rate of 36 percent.

- Phase in over a 10-year period — beginning in 1987 —

Glossary of Tax Code Terms

Capital gain: Profit made from the sale of a capital asset, such as stocks and bonds, or an individual's home.

Depletion: Similar to depreciation, used by taxpayers with an economic interest in mineral property or timber stands to recover the cost of their investment over the economic life of the property.

Depreciation: Several methods for dividing the cost of an asset by the number of years it was to be used to produce income and deducting these sums from income.

To be depreciable, property had to be used in business, have a useful life of more than one year that could be determined, and wear out or otherwise lose value.

Gross income: Compensation for services, gross income derived from business, interest, rents, alimony and other types of income. **Adjusted gross income** consisted of gross income less trade and business deductions, deductions attributable to rents and royalties, moving expenses, transportation expenses, retirement savings and other deductions specified in the tax laws.

Indexing of tax rates: Adjustment of tax brackets and other provisions of the tax laws based on the value of a price index.

Marginal tax rate: The highest rate of taxation an individual had to pay. For example, under the House-passed tax bill (HR 3838), an individual with taxable income larger than $60,000 would have that portion above $60,000 taxed at 38 percent — the so-called marginal rate. The top marginal rate for an individual under existing law was 50 percent for income above $85,130.

Tax credit: A provision of tax law permitting a taxpayer to subtract certain sums from tax liabilities. It differed from a **deduction** in that it was subtracted after the total tax liability had been calculated.

Tax deduction: Allowed a taxpayer for the payment of certain expenses, such as interest on a home mortgage, deductions were subtracted from adjusted gross income.

If a taxpayer did not itemize deductions, there was a **standard deduction**, known as the **zero bracket amount**, below which income was not taxed.

Tax exemption: A provision permitting a taxpayer to deduct from adjusted gross income specified sums. Exemptions in the tax laws included the taxpayer, his or her spouse and dependents. Other exemptions were available to taxpayers over 65 years of age or those who were blind.

Tax exclusion: A provision permitting taxpayers to exclude certain types of income from their gross income. Fringe benefits (for example, employer contributions to employee pension, accident or health plans), gifts and inheritances and specified portions of retirement income were examples of tax exclusions.

Taxable income: Adjusted gross income less tax exemptions and tax deductions.

a deduction for up to 10 percent of the dividends paid out by a corporation. The deduction would increase by 1 percentage point each year until 1997, when it would be fully in effect. The administration called for the full 10 percent deduction to begin in 1987.

- Repeal the existing exclusion from income of up to $100 in dividends received by an individual ($200 for married couples).
- Make it more difficult for those who acquired a corporation with net operating losses to use those losses to reduce their tax liability. The House agreed to delay, and therefore lessen, the tax benefits from such takeovers.
- Repeal, as of Dec. 31, 1988, several tax incentives enacted in the Deficit Reduction Act of 1984 (PL 98-369) to encourage the financing of employee stock ownership plans. A payroll-based tax credit for employers would be repealed at the end of 1985. It was due to expire at the end of 1987.

Research and Development

- Extend for three years a tax credit for new research and development expenses at a rate of 20 percent. The existing 25 percent tax credit was scheduled to expire at the end of 1985. The House agreed to include language in the bill report to clarify what type of expenses would be eligible for the credit.
- Allow a new 20 percent tax credit for three years for corporate contributions to or contracts with universities or non-profit organizations to conduct new research and development.

The committee had rejected a proposal by Rostenkowski that would no longer have allowed firms to write off in one year, rather than over a longer period of time, the amount of new research and development expenses equal to the tax credit taken that year.

Historic Rehabilitation

- Replace existing tax credits of 15 percent for the rehabilitation of buildings at least 30 years old and 20 percent for buildings at least 40 years old with a 10 percent credit that could be used only for buildings constructed before 1935.
- Reduce from 25 percent to 20 percent the tax credit allowed for rehabilitation of certified historic buildings.

Oil, Gas, Hard Minerals

- Retain the so-called percentage depletion allowance for small, or "stripper," wells owned by independent producers and royalty owners. The allowance would be phased out over three years for other oil and gas properties.

Percentage depletion, one of the key tax breaks for independent producers, allowed taxpayers to deduct up to 15 percent of their gross income each year to cover the cost of depletion of their wells. However, taxpayers could continue to claim the deduction even after they recovered all expenses related to developing and acquiring the property.

Rostenkowski had proposed phasing out the allowance over three years, but his plan was rejected after intense lobbying from oil-state members and Texan James A. Baker III, Treasury secretary and former White House chief of staff.

Reagan would have retained the break for stripper wells, defined as wells that produced 10 barrels or less a day.

- Allow oil, gas and geothermal property operators to write off in one year so-called "intangible drilling costs," such as labor and fuel, before the property became productive. Once wells began producing, intangible drilling costs would have to be amortized over 26 months. Under existing law, all intangible costs could be written off in one year. Committee aides estimated that the change would apply to about one-fourth of all intangible drilling costs.
- Retain existing law allowing a deduction for special injectants used to enhance oil and gas production.
- Reduce to 5 percent by 1988 the depletion allowance for minerals, such as coal and iron ore, from rates ranging up to 22 percent under existing law. Rostenkowski and Reagan had proposed that the allowance be phased out.

The House agreed to retain existing law for stone such as marble and granite and for agricultural minerals such as sulfur and phosphate.

Baker Named to Treasury

The Senate Jan. 29 unanimously confirmed the nomination of White House Chief of Staff James A. Baker III to be secretary of the Treasury. The vote was 95-0. *(Vote 1, p. 2-S; nominations, p. 418)*

Baker was the first of five new Cabinet members to be confirmed by Congress after President Reagan began his second term, and the one most crucial to the president's chief domestic policy initiative of his second term — enactment of a major rewrite of the tax code. *(Tax bill, p. 480)*

Senate Finance Committee Chairman Bob Packwood, R-Ore., noted that tax overhaul was highly controversial. "In order to get that bill passed," Packwood said, "the president is going to need as secretary of the Treasury a man who is very wise to the ways of this Congress, and Jim Baker is that."

Baker replaced Donald T. Regan, who left Treasury to take over Baker's White House job. Regan had presided over the earliest Treasury Department version of the administration's tax initiative.

The job exchange, announced by Reagan Jan. 8, was generally well received on Capitol Hill. Republicans saw it as reinvigorating the administration for the president's second term, and Democrats anticipated little change in current policies.

The Senate Finance Committee on Jan. 23 unanimously recommended Baker's confirmation after a single day of hearings at which the nominee was the only witness. Senators on both sides of the aisle praised Baker before the confirmation vote for the legislative expertise he displayed during his four years as White House chief of staff.

The only negative remarks were made by William Proxmire, D-Wis., who claimed Baker's economics background was inadequate for the Treasury job. But, he added, he would vote for confirmation because "I know that if Mr. Baker should be rejected, the next nominee will be even less qualified."

Earlier the same day, the Senate Finance Committee unanimously approved the nomination of White House aide Richard G. Darman as Baker's deputy secretary at Treasury. Darman had been an assistant to the president and Baker's deputy in the White House. Darman was confirmed by the Senate Jan. 31.

• Phase out over three years special capital gains tax treatment for royalties from coal and domestic iron ore.

Corporate Liquidations

• Tax corporations for the gains from liquidation of their assets, which under existing law were taxed only when distributed as dividends to shareholders. The existing law provision often figured as an incentive for corporate mergers and acquisitions, according to committee aides.

The change, which was expected to raise $4.8 billion over five years, was made to help pay for modifications to Rostenkowski's oil and gas tax proposals. About $500 million of that amount was expected to come from the oil and gas industry.

The change would not apply to closely held corporations.

Energy Credits

• Allow a 15 percent tax credit for residential energy conservation expenses to expire at the end of 1985, as provided by existing law. The existing credit applied to installation of property, such as storm windows or insulation, in a taxpayer's primary residence.

• Allow a 40 percent credit for installation of wind and geothermal energy property in a primary residence to expire at the end of 1985, as provided by existing law. The existing 40 percent credit for installation of solar energy equipment would be extended for three years at a rate of 30 percent in 1986 and 20 percent in 1987 and 1988.

• Allow a number of business energy credits, including those for wind, ocean thermal, intercity buses and small-scale hydroelectric projects, to expire at the end of 1985, as provided by existing law. However, the House agreed to extend a 15 percent business solar energy tax credit for three years at a rate of 15 percent in 1986, 12 percent in 1987 and 8 percent in 1988.

It also agreed to extend the 15 percent credit for business geothermal energy expense for three years at a rate of 15 percent in 1986, and 10 percent in 1987 and 1988.

• Limit a 60-cents-per-gallon credit for alcohol fuels to those produced at plants completed before Jan. 1, 1986, and sold before Jan. 1, 1993.

• Reduce a 9-cents-per-gallon exemption from gasoline excise taxes for alcohol fuels to 6 cents per gallon. The House agreed to retain a 6-cents-per-gallon exemption for alcohol fuel mixtures.

Real Estate, Interest

• Allow taxpayers to take an unlimited mortgage interest deduction for first and second residences. Reagan and Rostenkowski both would have limited such deductions.

The House also agreed that interest on loans that paid for up to six weeks of time sharing for residential resort property would be deductible as if the time-share were a first or second residence.

• Allow individuals to deduct additional interest payments of up to $10,000 ($20,000 for joint returns) plus the amount of net income from investments. This provision would be phased in over 10 years. For example, only 10 percent of interest — with the exception of certain investment interest subject to deduction limits under existing law — would be subject to the limit in the first year.

• Apply to some real estate transactions existing rules preventing investors from deducting losses greater than the amount actually invested. Critics charged that the existing exemption for real estate from so-called "at-risk" rules had provided a major incentive for the proliferation of real estate tax shelters.

The House agreed, however, to exempt real estate transactions involving financing by third parties, such as banks, from the at-risk rules.

Minimum Tax

• Impose a 25 percent minimum tax on individuals and corporations who otherwise would be able to reduce dramatically their tax liabilities through the use of tax breaks retained in the law.

Minimum taxes were imposed under existing law on both individuals (20 percent) and corporations (15 percent), but there were so many loopholes that many taxpayers still escaped paying tax. Under the proposed alternative minimum tax, taxpayers would be required to pay the higher of their normal tax liability or 25 percent of taxable income, plus the value of certain tax advantages they had claimed.

The committee agreed to expand the number of tax breaks, called "preference items," whose value would be added to taxable income. Among the new preference items would be certain deductions for the appreciated value of charitable donations of such items as artwork, deductions investors in tax shelters could take for losses in excess of the amount of cash they had invested, excludable income earned abroad and interest from tax-exempt non-governmental bonds.

Foreign Income

• Revise a complex system of tax credits allowed U.S. corporations to reduce their U.S. tax liability by the amount of foreign taxes they paid on income earned overseas. The changes were designed to prevent companies from investing in low-tax countries to reduce dramatically their U.S. tax liability. The committee had rejected a proposal by Reagan to impose per-country caps on the amount of foreign tax credits firms could claim.

• Retain, with some restrictions, a credit used by firms to eliminate virtually all of their U.S. tax on income earned in Puerto Rico, the Virgin Islands and other U.S. possessions.

Reagan would have repealed the credit and replaced it with a less generous one based on wages, which was designed to encourage employment of island residents.

Rostenkowski would have retained the credit with tighter restrictions than those finally imposed by the committee.

• Reduce from $85,000 to $75,000 the amount of income Americans working overseas could earn tax-free. Rostenkowski had proposed that the exclusion be lowered to $50,000 a year.

Industrial Development Bonds

• Limit the amount of non-governmental bonds that could be issued annually within a state to the greater of $200 million or $175 per resident ($125 after 1987). No more than $150 of the per-resident cap could be used for profitable organizations, in effect reserving at least $25 of the cap for non-profit projects such as hospitals and universities.

A $150 per-resident cap existed under existing law, but applied only to limited kinds of tax-exempt bonds. The bonds could be issued by state or local governments, or their agents, to finance a wide range of private and public projects. Because interest earned on such debt was not subject to federal taxes, developers paid lower interest rates on such loans and trimmed their costs. In effect, the federal government helped to subsidize projects through the tax break.

• Expand the type of bond-financed projects subject to the cap to include multifamily rental housing, mass commuting facilities, sewage disposal facilities, solid-waste disposal facilities, facilities for the furnishing of water, qualified mortgage bonds, qualified veterans' mortgage bonds, veterans' land bonds, qualified student loan bonds, small-issue industrial development bonds and bonds for non-profit organizations. Bonds for airports and port facilities would not be subject to the cap.

Tax-exempt financing could no longer be used for such projects as sports facilities, convention centers, air or water pollution control activities, or the hotels and shops attached to airports.

Reagan had asked for elimination of the tax exemption for all but purely governmental projects, such as schools and roads. Rostenkowski would have allowed tax-exempt bonds for private uses, but would have restricted the kinds of projects eligible for tax-exempt status.

• Define as non-governmental bonds those in which more than 10 percent, or $10 million, whichever was less, was used by a trade or business or more than 5 percent, or $5 million, was used by an individual.

Financial Institutions

• Limit the deduction commercial banks with assets of $500 million or more — about 450 of the nation's largest banks — could take to cover bad loans. Under the plan, the banks could take deductions only when actual losses were incurred.

Banks with assets of less than $500 million would be able to take the more generous deduction allowed under existing law, which was based on a percentage of the bank's outstanding loans or on its past record of bad debts.

Reagan and Rostenkowski had proposed that the deduction be limited for all banks.

• Allow thrift institutions to take bad-debt deductions equal to 5 percent of their taxable income or an amount based on their past experience with bad loans. The deduction would be less generous than what was allowed under existing law, but Rostenkowski and Reagan had proposed that the deductions be limited even further.

• Eliminate a deduction that financial institutions could take under existing law for 80 percent of the interest payments they made on debt used to invest in tax-exempt obligations.

However, the House agreed to allow banks that invested in tax-exempt bonds issued by small jurisdictions for governmental purposes to continue to deduct the interest they paid on money used to purchase the bonds. The banks would have to be located within the jurisdiction and the bond issue could not exceed $3 million.

• Repeal special tax advantages for the reorganization of troubled thrift institutions, including an existing law provision that allowed troubled savings and loans to be acquired tax free.

• Make it easier for individuals to claim losses when their financial institution became bankrupt or insolvent.

• Repeal special rules allowing commercial banks and thrift institutions to deduct their net operating losses in a particular year against income from the preceding 10 taxable years or the succeeding five taxable years. Instead, they would be allowed the less-generous deductions for losses that applied under existing law to other taxpayers.

• Retain existing law exempting credit unions from federal income tax. Rostenkowski and Reagan wanted to repeal the exemption for credit unions with assets of $5 million or more.

Accounting Rules

• Eliminate a special accounting method that allowed defense and building contractors to delay tax payments until work on a project had been completed, and often to reduce dramatically or eliminate their tax liability.

The House decided instead that such contractors would be required to take a percentage of their deductions and to declare a similar percentage of their income during the course of contracts.

The House would provide a special exception for small contractors working on contracts of less than two years' duration.

• Prevent the use of the so-called cash method of accounting for businesses with gross receipts exceeding $5 million a year. But the House exempted from the requirement professionals, such as lawyers and accountants.

The administration argued that cash accounting — where income was declared at the time cash was received and deductions were taken when an expense was actually paid — did not accurately reflect a company's economic circumstances and allowed some firms to delay tax payments.

Instead, companies exceeding the $5 million limit would be required to use accrual accounting, where income and expenses were reported at the time they were earned or incurred, but not necessarily paid.

• Eliminate an accounting scheme that allowed home builders and retailers to borrow against the anticipated proceeds from installment sales of property. They, in effect, could defer paying tax on the gain from such sales, while enjoying the benefits of the loans.

• Agreed to treat payments customers made to utilities for construction of special access lines or other equipment as taxable income to the utility. Under existing law, such payments were not taxed.

Insurance

• Continue the existing treatment of the increased value of life insurance policies, called "inside buildup."

Existing law did not consider inside buildup to be income; Reagan had proposed to tax it. The committee had abandoned the controversial proposal under heavy lobbying pressure from the insurance industry.

• Repeal an existing tax exemption for Blue Cross and Blue Shield. Some members argued that the exemption gave the insurance company an unfair advantage over its competitors. The House retained tax-exempt status for several fraternal organizations, including the Knights of Columbus, which provided insurance benefits to their members.

• Require property and casualty insurance firms to reduce deductions for loss reserves by 10 percent of the interest income they received from new investments in tax-exempt securities. The amount would rise to 15 percent in 1988.

• Impose a stiff new minimum tax on property and casualty insurance firms, beginning in 1988. Rep. Fortney H. "Pete" Stark, D-Calif., described the provision as a "hammer" over the industry to encourage it to cooperate with the committee on a rewrite of property and casualty insurance taxation. Stark, who headed a committee task force on insurance, said there was insufficient time to revamp such a complex area of tax law in this bill.

- Require property and casualty firms to count as income 20 percent of any increases in the value of special reserves used for soliciting premium income in advance of providing insurance coverage.
- Repeal an existing law deduction life insurance firms used to cap their top tax rate at 36.8 percent, instead of the 46 percent top rate paid by other corporations.
- Repeal a $1,000 exclusion survivors could claim under existing law for interest they received on the unpaid proceeds of their spouses' life insurance policies.

Low-Income Housing

- Allow tax-exempt bonds to be issued under the state volume cap for low-income housing if 25 percent or more of the units were rented to families whose incomes were 80 percent of the area median income or below; or if 20 percent or more of the units were rented to families whose incomes were 70 percent of the area median income or below.

Such projects would be depreciated over 30 years, but a larger share of the write-off could be taken in the earlier years than for other real estate projects.

- Allow tax-exempt bond financing for projects where 40 percent or more of the units were rented to families whose incomes were 60 percent of the area median income or below.

Such projects would be depreciated over 20 years, compared with 30 years for other real estate investments.

- Apply the above income requirements to families of four. The requirements would be adjusted to account for family size, which was not done under existing law.
- Require annual certification that projects continued to meet the low-income requirements.
- Allow 20-year depreciation for housing projects too small to qualify for tax-exempt financing, which had 40 percent or more of their units rented to families whose incomes were 60 percent of the area median income or below.
- Allow a five-year write-off for the costs of rehabilitating low-income housing with a maximum amount of new investment per unit of $30,000. The existing law limit was $20,000.

Pensions

- Retain the popular "401(k)" tax-deferred savings plan — named after a section in the Internal Revenue Code — that Reagan had proposed to eliminate.

The House agreed to reduce maximum employer-employee annual contributions to the plans from the lesser of $30,000 or 25 percent of an individual's compensation to $7,000 or 25 percent of compensation.

Under existing law, 401(k) plans were available to more than 20 million workers. They allowed employees to have their employers set aside earnings, tax-free, in a savings plan until they withdrew the money upon retirement or for an emergency. Often, employee contributions were matched by an employer contribution to the plan.

- Continue allowing withdrawals from 401(k) plans in cases of hardship, such as a medical emergency. Both Rostenkowski and Reagan would have restricted the availability of such withdrawals, which were a major attraction of the savings plans.
- Prevent state and local governments and tax-exempt groups from offering 401(k)s, unless they had already received preliminary approval to begin such plans.
- Rejected a Reagan proposal to raise from $2,250 to $4,000 the amount that a worker could contribute to individual retirement accounts (IRAs) for himself or herself and a non-working spouse.

Under existing law, a two-income couple could contribute up to $2,000 each to an IRA every year. Reagan and others argued that it was unfair to penalize non-working spouses by limiting their contributions.

- Increase the tax penalty on early IRA withdrawals from 10 to 15 percent. Reagan had proposed a 20 percent penalty tax. Under existing law, savings in an IRA could not be withdrawn prior to age 59½, death or disability.
- Combine limits on contributions to IRAs and 401(k) plans so that an individual with both kinds of plans could contribute no more than a total of $2,000 — the ceiling on IRA contributions — to the two plans. The change was made to encourage the use of 401(k) plans.
- Reduced from $30,000 to $25,000 the ceiling on the combined employer-employee payments that could be made each year to a defined contribution plan, to which an employer contributed a set amount.
- Reduced from $90,000 to $77,000 the maximum amount of annual benefits an individual could receive from an employer-provided defined benefit plan, a plan to which sufficient contributions were made to produce a specified level of benefits upon retirement.

Trusts, Estates

- Eliminate tax advantages that parents could receive when they passed assets on to a child so that any proceeds, such as interest, would be taxed at the child's lower tax rate. Under the proposal, any unearned income received by a child under age 14 would be taxed at the parents' marginal tax rate to the extent the income was attributable to property received from the parents. Many parents set up custodial accounts for their children to help pay for college educations or other child-rearing expenses.
- Restrict the tax benefits of setting up trusts used to avoid tax payments. The changes would mean the end of so-called Clifford Trusts, in which parents turned over assets to a child for at least 10 years.
- Revise the so-called "generation-skipping tax" imposed on those who tried to avoid paying estate taxes by passing wealth on to their grandchildren, instead of to their children. The changes would make the tax more lenient and allow an exemption for transfers of up to $1 million for each donor with an additional $2 million exemption for each donee. As a result, a couple could pass on $4 million to a grandchild without paying the generation-skipping tax.

Committee aides noted that while the existing tax was more stringent, it was considered so complex that few taxpayers had complied and the Internal Revenue Service had never enforced it. However, some wealthy families, including the Gallo wine family in California, were expected to benefit greatly from the change.

The new tax would apply to transfers after Sept. 25, 1985. The existing tax would be repealed retroactively for earlier transfers, which would still be subject to estate taxes.

Timber

- Repeal special capital gains tax treatment for corporations on the proceeds from timber sales. It would allow individuals to continue treating gains from timber as capital gains, which were taxed at a lower rate than ordinary income.

Reagan and Rostenkowski would have repealed special capital gains tax treatment for both individuals and corporations.

• Require small timber producers (those with 50,000 acres or less of land) to write off certain "pre-productive expenses," over a period of five years, instead of one year, as under existing law. Such expenses would include fertilizer, fire retardants and interest payments.

• Repeal a seven-year write-off and 10 percent tax credit allowed for up to $10,000 a year in reforestation costs.

• Exempt producers of nursery stock and Christmas trees from proposed restrictions on deductions for so-called "pre-productive" costs.

Agriculture

• Retain existing-law accounting rules for farmers. Farmers had complained about a Reagan proposal that businesses with annual gross receipts of more than $5 million could no longer use the cash method of accounting.

• Repeal a one-year write-off allowed under existing law for expenses of clearing land for farming. A special one-year write-off for soil and water conservation costs would be retained but would be limited to conservation activities approved by conservation authorities.

Targeted Jobs

• Extend for two years an existing law tax credit allowed employers who hired disadvantaged or disabled workers, at a cost of $1 billion.

The House agreed, however, to reduce the so-called targeted jobs tax credit from the existing level of 50 percent of the first $6,000 of wages in the first year and 25 percent in the second year to 40 percent in the first year only. The credit would not be available in cases where employment lasted less than 14 days.

A credit of up to 85 percent of the first $3,000 of wages for disadvantaged summer youth employees would also be retained.

Rostenkowski and Reagan would have allowed the credit to expire at the end of 1985, as provided by existing law.

Other

• Repeal rapid write-offs of certain expenditures related to trademarks or trade names, pollution control facilities and land improvements along railroad rights of way.

• Reduce from 85 percent to 75 percent the amount by which businesses could use business tax credits to reduce their tax liability above $25,000. Firms would still be allowed to use business tax credits to reduce all of their tax liability up to $25,000.

• Retain a deduction for funds set aside by shipowners for construction of commercial ships. Rostenkowski and Reagan had both called for elimination of the special tax treatment for these so-called capital construction funds. The House agreed, however, to a number of restrictions on the funds, including a requirement that a contract to build a ship be signed within 10 years of the time money is set aside.

• Extend through 1983 a 50 percent tax credit currently available for clinical testing of certain drugs, called "orphan" drugs, for rare U.S. diseases and conditions. The credit was due to expire at the end of 1987.

• Increase estimated tax payments made by individuals if they did not have enough withheld from their wages. Payments would have to equal at least the lesser of 100 percent of a taxpayer's prior-year tax liability or 90 percent of the current-year liability. Under existing law, such payments had to equal at least the lesser of 100 percent of the previous year's tax liability or 80 percent of the current year's liability.

• Raise the interest rate taxpayers would have to pay the Treasury for late tax payments by 3 percentage points and raise the interest rate on Treasury payments to taxpayers by 2 percentage points.

• Increase penalties for failure to pay taxes and failure to file proper tax information returns.

• Extend for four years a law awarding attorneys' fees of up to $25,000 to taxpayers who won tax cases against the government and could prove the government's position was unreasonable. The provision also would authorize funding for the awards program, which was set to expire at the end of 1985.

• Require a report from the Internal Revenue Service (IRS) within six months of enactment on how it would implement a return-free tax system.

Under such a system, the IRS would calculate a person's tax bill, based on wage and other records it received from such sources as employers and banks. A taxpayer then would receive a bill or refund in the mail.

Reagan's tax plan called for implementation of such a system for those with the simplest tax returns. Use of the system would have been optional under Reagan's proposal.

• Require most taxpayers to go through the IRS administrative appeals process before taking a dispute with the agency to tax court.

• Prohibit the awarding of a federal contract or license to any taxpayer who failed to make tax payments to the IRS after exhausting all appeals procedures.

• Impose a new excise tax on the proceeds television networks received from broadcasting the Olympic games to help support the U.S. Olympic team.

Background

Calls to reform the income tax system — couched most often in terms of achieving simplicity and fairness — were nothing new. But with the president's blessing, the task began in earnest in 1984.

As early as August 1982, Democrats Bill Bradley of New Jersey, a member of the Senate Finance Committee, and Richard A. Gephardt of Missouri, a member of the House Ways and Means Committee, had jointly proposed revising the tax system to curtail sharply most tax breaks and to reduce individual and corporate rates.

And in his January 1984 State of the Union address, Reagan charged the Treasury Department with drafting a plan to simplify the tax code, "so all taxpayers, big and small, are treated more fairly." Such a plan, Reagan said, should broaden the base to lower individual tax rates. And the "underground economy" should be brought "into the sunlight of honest tax compliance." He asked Treasury for a report by December 1984.

After Reagan joined the call for tax reform, the issue took on greater political significance and dozens of plans were introduced in Congress, ranging from flat tax rates to taxes on consumption. Many proposals were similar in approach to Bradley-Gephardt, including its chief rival, introduced in April 1984 by two Republicans, Sen. Robert F. Kasten of Wisconsin and Rep. Jack Kemp of New York.

Evolution of the House-Passed Tax Overhaul Bill

The chart below compares the provisions of existing tax law, the tax overhaul proposal announced May 28 by President Reagan and the version given to House Ways and Means Committee members Sept. 26 by Chairman Dan Rostenkowski, D-Ill., with the version passed by the House Dec. 17.

	Current Law	Reagan Plan	Rostenkowski Plan	House Bill
Individual tax rates	11-50 percent (14 brackets)	15, 25 and 35 percent	15, 25 and 35 percent	15, 25, 35 and 38 percent
Personal exemption	$1,040 (1985)	$2,000	$1,500; plus increase standard deduction of $500	$2,000 for non-itemizers; $1,500 for itemizers
Business tax rates	15-40 percent on first $100,000; 46 percent thereafter	33 percent, with lower rates for income below $75,000	15-30 percent up to $75,000 and 35 percent over $75,000	15-30 percent up to $75,000 and 36 percent over $75,000
Interest payments	Deductions for home mortgage and non-business interest	Unlimited deduction for primary residences; additional interest deductions capped at $5,000	Deduction limited by the greater of $10,000 or the mortgage value of a taxpayer's primary residence, plus the value of a taxpayer's investment income	Unlimited deduction for mortgages on first and second residences; additional deduction of $10,000 plus the value of a taxpayer's investment income
Health benefits	Employer-paid health premiums not taxed; medical expenses deductible if more than 5 percent of adjusted gross income	First $10 a month in employer-paid premiums for individuals ($25 for families) taxed as income; retain existing law for medical deductions	Tax as income health benefits above $120 a month for individuals ($300 for families); retain existing law for medical deductions	Retain existing law on taxation of health benefits and medical deductions
Charitable donations	Deductible	Unlimited deductions for itemizers, none for non-itemizers	Unlimited deductions for itemizers, none for non-itemizers	No change for itemizers; non-itemizers could deduct amount above $100
State and local taxes	Deductible	Deduction eliminated	No deduction for sales and personal property taxes; taxpayers could deduct the greater of $500 or the amount of income and real property taxes in excess of 5 percent of adjusted gross income	No change from existing law
Depreciation	3-19-year recovery periods with accelerated write-off	More generous write-off over 4-28 years; value adjusted for inflation	3-30-year recovery periods; not indexed for inflation	3-30-year recovery periods; partially indexed
Capital gains	60 percent exclusion; top effective rate of 20 percent	Top effective rate of 17.5 percent, but assets eligible would be limited	Top effective rate of 21 percent	42 percent exclusion; top effective rate of 22 percent
Investment tax credit	6-10 percent	Repealed	Repealed	Repealed
Oil and gas	Allow percentage depletion, and expensing of intangible drilling costs	Repeal oil depletion allowance for all but small wells; keep "intangible" drilling breaks, but subject to minimum tax	Repeal percentage depletion allowance; retain one-year expensing of intangible drilling costs for non-producing wells; three-year write-off for producing wells	Repeal percentage depletion allowance for all but small wells; allow expensing of intangible drilling costs for non-producing wells; 26-month write-off for producing wells
Business expenses	Deductible	Deduction for entertainment repealed; limit on meals	Deduction of 75 percent of business meals and 50 percent of entertainment costs	Deduction of 80 percent of business meals and 80 percent of entertainment costs

SOURCES: Treasury Department, House Ways and Means Committee

Neither Kasten nor Kemp served on the tax-writing committees.

During the 1984 presidential campaign, Democratic challenger Walter F. Mondale also called for a "fairer" tax code. But he also asked for higher taxes on middle- and upper-income taxpayers to help reduce the deficit and predicted Reagan would do likewise.

Reagan, however, refused to play along and cast in stone his objections to raising taxes — tying that promise to his future insistence that no tax increase would be acceptable in the guise of tax reform.

Treasury I: The Administration's First Shot

The long-awaited Treasury proposal was released Nov. 27, 1984, to a lukewarm reception from Capitol Hill and the White House. The White House was besieged with complaints about specific features of the Treasury proposal, particularly from businesses, which stood to lose considerably, and Reagan declined to embrace it. He said he would listen to comments before submitting his own version in early 1985.

Both Packwood and Rostenkowski said deficit reduction should take precedence over tax overhaul, a refrain that dominated budget debates into 1986. But Rostenkowski's concern did not prevent him from making tax overhaul a personal cause in 1985.

The plan, presented by Treasury Secretary Donald T. Regan, incorporated three individual tax rates of 15, 25 and 35 percent, curtailment of many tax breaks and repeal of accelerated depreciation, the centerpiece of the Reagan administration's 1981 tax cut, which was designed to spur business investment. Under existing law, individuals were taxed at rates ranging from 11 to 50 percent. *(Glossary, p. 483; 1981 tax bill, 1981 Almanac p. 91)*

It proposed cutting the corporate tax rate to 33 percent from 46 percent and allowing firms to deduct from income half of the stockholder dividends they paid out. Dividends, which were taxed as individual income, were not deductible business expenses under existing law.

Overall, under the plan, which became known as Treasury I, individuals would have paid 8.5 percent less, and businesses 24 percent more.

Even Regan said the proposal was only a starting point; many key provisions, such as revisions to the depreciation schedule, were not final in Treasury I.

On Jan. 8, 1985, the president announced that Regan was switching jobs with White House Chief of Staff Baker. A month later, Reagan renewed his pitch for simplification of the tax code in his State of the Union address Feb. 6. In the speech he called on Baker to work with congressional leaders to produce a bipartisan bill, but he offered no specifics about what he might favor, or when he might send his own proposal to Congress. *(Baker nomination, p. 484)*

Meanwhile, the leading congressional advocates of tax reform announced the reintroduction of their plans at a joint press conference Jan. 30. Kemp and Kasten sponsored bills to eliminate most special tax breaks and to lower income tax rates across the board to 24 percent. Gephardt and Bradley proposed similar bills to impose tax rates of 14, 26 and 30 percent.

The four played down the differences in their packages and said they planned to work together to keep Congress on the track toward tax reform.

Treasury II: Reagan Submits His Own Plan

It was not until May 28 that Reagan, in a nationally televised speech, revealed his own blueprint for a new tax system. Though modeled closely after Treasury I, the plan differed in some key respects. *(Text, p. 20-D)*

Under the president's plan, most taxpayers would have paid taxes below or at the same level they paid under existing law. About one in five individuals and many corporations would have paid more.

Reagan said that families of four with annual incomes of about $12,000 or less would have paid no taxes, compared with about $9,500 under existing law.

The plan held to the rate structure of Treasury I: three individual tax rates of 15, 25 and 35 percent and a top corporate tax rate of 33 percent.

Reagan proposed retaining deductions for charitable contributions and interest payments on primary residences, but eliminating many other breaks, including the deduction allowed for state and local tax payments. Deductions for other interest payments, including those on second homes, would have been limited and a portion of employer-paid health insurance premiums taxed.

Reagan's plan called for limits on the use of some investment tax breaks, but he sought more generous treatment of capital gains income to encourage investment in new industries. He proposed a 20 percent minimum tax so that the most profitable corporations and wealthy individuals would pay at least some tax.

The plan also called for an eventual return-free tax system for more than half of all taxpayers, who could have their taxes calculated directly by the Internal Revenue Service in lieu of filing a return.

White House figures showed that the changes envisioned would have shifted some of the tax burden from corporations to individuals, but not by as much as Treasury I. Corporations would have paid 23 percent more taxes than under existing law by 1990. Individuals would have paid 5 percent less. The administration estimated, however, that the corporate tax burden would be only 9 percent more and the individual share 7 percent less when the proposal was fully phased in after about 40 years.

Selling the Idea to Congress and the Nation

Democratic and Republican adherents of tax reform hoped to find political gain in the issue, but in early 1985 public opinion was mixed, at best, and many members continued to report throughout the year that their constituents showed little interest in it.

Rostenkowski, who delivered the Democratic response to Reagan's speech announcing the tax plan, offered a ringing endorsement of the reform ideal, and welcomed Reagan to the fold of politicians seeking "fair treatment for all" in the tax code. He added that Democrats would not "give the president's reform plan a rubber stamp.... We will make some changes — correct some imbalances — seek to make it fairer."

But Rostenkowski cautioned that "the battle for reform will be long and tough." He noted that Congress faced the problems of a diverse membership and pressures from legions of special-interest lobbyists, who had been preparing for battle for months and now had a specific target for their assault.

Sensing the need to generate a public groundswell, Reagan made a series of speeches across the country in the weeks after revealing his plan. But the hoped for public clamor never developed.

Congressional reaction was generally upbeat. "Looking at the proposal as a whole, the prospects for passage this

Prior 'Reforms' Sometimes Have Gone Awry

For as long as it had been in existence, the income tax was the target of schemes to "reform" it.

The first tax on income, a Civil War-era emergency measure, lasted from 1862-1871. The existing income tax was established after the ratification of the 16th Amendment to the Constitution.

The amendment, ratified on Feb. 25, 1913, states, "The Congress shall have power to lay and collect taxes on incomes, from whatever source derived, without apportionment among the several states and without regard to any census or enumeration."

That power was exercised often. The income tax code itself was last rewritten in 1954, but modified regularly after that. *(Congress and the Nation Vol. I, p. 416)*

Beginning in the mid-1960s efforts were made to bring order and fairness to a tax system that had become increasingly unwieldy. Often, however, changes made in the name of reform led to more of the confusion and perceived inequity that were the target of congressional and White House reform efforts in 1985. Previous attempts included:

- **Revenue Act of 1964 (PL 88-272).** President John F. Kennedy in 1963 proposed massive cuts in tax rates to help stimulate economic growth. They were to be financed by placing restrictions on several existing tax breaks. His plan included a limit on total itemized deductions and reductions in tax breaks for the oil and gas industry.

Congress enacted the tax cuts, but many of Kennedy's "reform" proposals fell by the wayside.

Kennedy made initial proposals to close tax loopholes in 1961. But they also were rejected by Congress when it passed the Revenue Act of 1962 (PL 87-834), which created a new tax credit for business investment. *(Congress and the Nation Vol. I, pp. 429, 437)*

- **Tax Reform Act of 1969 (PL 91-172).** Spurred by widespread discontent with inequities in the federal tax system, Congress passed legislation eliminating or restricting a number of tax breaks, such as the investment tax credit, and allowing the poorest Americans to avoid paying income taxes. Nonetheless, loopholes remained and some of the provisions in the original legislation, such as a proposed reduction in the oil depletion allowance, were watered down before the bill was enacted. *(Congress and the Nation Vol. III, p. 79)*

- **Tax Reform Act of 1976 (PL 94-455).** After two years of turbulent tax debate, Congress agreed to legislation restricting oil and gas, real estate and other tax shelters, increasing minimum taxes on corporations and individuals and setting limits on business expense deductions. The legislation also expanded investment incentives, raised the standard deduction and created a number of miscellaneous special interest tax breaks. *(Congress and the Nation Vol. IV, p. 99)*

- **Revenue Act of 1978 (PL 95-600).** President Jimmy Carter proposed an ambitious tax program that included many changes similar to those being considered in 1985. He recommended a 2 percent cut in tax rates, restrictions on preferential capital gains treatment and elimination of a number of widely used tax breaks. He urged limits on business expense deductions for entertainment, meals and travel.

But the time and politics were not ripe for Carter, and his proposals were rejected. Congress instead enacted a wide range of tax cuts, many of which benefited middle- and upper-income taxpayers. *(Congress and the Nation Vol. V, p. 238)*

- **Tax Equity and Fiscal Responsibility Act of 1982 (97-248).** Although not advertised as tax reform, this bill went a long way toward reducing existing tax loopholes and improving tax collections and compliance with existing law. It included provisions to limit generous business tax breaks enacted in 1981, require withholding of interest and dividend income (later repealed) and impose a more comprehensive minimum tax on wealthy individuals. But the legislation, aimed primarily at raising revenues to reduce the deficit, also added hundreds of provisions to the tax code and further complicated an already complex law. *(1982 Almanac p. 29)*

- **Deficit Reduction Act of 1984 (PL 98-369).** This legislation also was designed to raise revenue to help reduce an ever-growing budget deficit. It attempted to close additional loopholes, including restricting tax breaks for expensive automobiles and placing limits on tax-exempt industrial development bonds. But, as in 1982, the legislation added greatly to the complexity of the law. *(1984 Almanac p. 143)*

Widespread dissatisfaction with the confusion caused by these two bills, and the shifting of the tax burden from corporations onto individuals in a major tax-cut bill enacted in 1981, helped to fuel the sentiment for a clean sweep of the tax code. *(1981 Almanac p. 91)*

year are excellent," Packwood said. Bradley said Reagan's plan "moves the whole process and chance for tax reform a giant step forward."

But behind the praise were criticisms of individual components of the plan that foreshadowed many battles to come.

Gephardt complained that taxpayers in the $20,000-$50,000 range would not fare as well as under Treasury's original proposal. Kemp and Kasten denounced the president's call for a top tax rate of 35 percent and said they could only support a maximum rate of 30 percent or lower.

Members were especially concerned that in its revision of Treasury I the administration had restored tax breaks that favored certain groups — especially the oil and gas industry — at the expense of others.

The original Treasury proposal would have eliminated a generous oil and gas depletion allowance and the one-year write-off of certain "intangible" drilling costs, such as the cost of preparing well sites. Reagan's plan retained the depletion allowance for small wells and the intangible drilling break, arguing that a strong domestic energy industry was vital for national defense.

Rostenkowski and others charged that restoration of such breaks had established a precedent that would make it more difficult for Congress to resist pressure from other interest groups.

House Committee Action

The legislative wheels began to turn immediately after Reagan released his tax plan, with Baker testifying about it before Ways and Means on May 30.

Both Ways and Means and Finance held marathon hearings through June and July so House markup could begin after Congress returned from its August recess. Meanwhile, Ways and Means staff began drafting alternatives to provisions in Reagan's plan.

Ways and Means held the first of 26 days of markup on the tax bill Sept. 18. But the first few days were devoted entirely to deciding on markup procedures and the starting point from which they would work. On the opening day, panel members decided that any amendments would have to be "revenue neutral"; if an amendment would cost money, another would have to be made to cover the loss.

The discipline was supposed to ensure that the final product would raise the same amount of revenue as the existing tax system. But many members became increasingly uneasy about the constraint when they realized how difficult it would be to make changes.

The staff-drafted alternative to Reagan's proposal was given to committee members Sept. 26, and Rostenkowski proposed that it serve as the basis for marking up a bill.

After several days of reviewing the staff alternative, members agreed Oct. 2 to work instead from existing law. That meant elimination of any tax break would have to be specifically approved by the panel; working from a draft rewrite of the code would instead put the burden on members who wanted to restore tax breaks the draft eliminated.

The committee also agreed that although the final bill would have to be revenue neutral, individual amendments would not.

Rostenkowski Weighs In

The following day, panel members decided that they had made a mistake and reversed the procedure again. Rostenkowski formally embraced the staff draft as his own, and it became the basis for the markup. *(Evolution of tax bill, p. 489)*

While retaining a top tax rate of 35 percent, as proposed by Reagan, Rostenkowski's plan attempted to shift more of the tax burden away from lower- and middle-income taxpayers to those with the highest incomes. It did so through changes in the zero bracket amount, a toughened minimum tax and other provisions.

The proposal made an attempt to compromise on one of the most controversial provisions in Reagan's plan, the elimination of deductions for state and local tax payments. It also eased proposed taxation of employee health benefits and life insurance policies.

It would have cut the top corporate tax rate from 46 percent to 35 percent, instead of 33 percent as proposed by Reagan. It called for less generous depreciation of investment in plant and equipment, and would have increased taxes paid by independent oil producers, whose tax breaks would have been spared by Reagan.

In addition, Rostenkowski would have increased taxes on capital-gains income, paid for the most part by wealthy individuals. Reagan had called for a capital gains tax cut.

After finally resolving most procedural issues, panel members — who conducted all their business behind closed doors — began Oct. 3 and 4 to make tentative decisions on a number of relatively minor matters. These included agreements to tax all unemployment compensation benefits and to eliminate income averaging for those with fluctuating incomes.

But in the first of a series of decisions that threatened to bog down the markup, members agreed to retain existing law that excluded from taxable income workers compensation, black lung and other employer-provided disability benefits.

The decision to reject Rostenkowski's proposal to tax most of those benefits put the committee $3.4 billion in the hole over five years against its goal of revenue neutrality.

Political Difficulties

Republicans and Democrats on the panel initially were working together to produce a bipartisan bill. But underlying the deliberations were increasing concerns that partisan pressures from outside the committee could tear apart any agreement. Members had returned from their August vacation convinced that constituents were far more interested in the budget deficit and trade problems than the more amorphous issue of tax reform. And the House Democratic Caucus met Oct. 2 to discuss the issue.

Members of the Democratic Study Group (DSG), the organization of liberal House Democrats who requested the meeting, argued that revenues raised by closing tax loopholes should be used to help reduce the deficit, instead of to lower tax rates as both Rostenkowski and Reagan wanted.

"Ronald Reagan's view of tax reform is not necessarily the majority view of the caucus," said DSG member Matthew F. McHugh, D-N.Y. "Our view of tax reform is to make sure everyone pays their fair share of taxes and to use some of the revenue to reduce the deficit. That's the message we want to deliver."

Others argued that the committee should limit itself to reporting a less-extensive bill that provided some tax breaks for the poor while imposing a tough minimum tax to ensure that wealthy individuals and businesses did not entirely escape taxation through tax loopholes.

Committee Vote on Tax Bill

Following is the breakdown of the Dec. 3 House Ways and Means Committee's 28-8 vote to report the tax bill (HR 3838).

For Reporting the Bill Favorably:

Democrats. Anthony, Ark.; Coyne, Pa.; Donnelly, Mass.; Dorgan, N.D.; Downey, N.Y.; Flippo, Ala.; Ford, Tenn.; Fowler, Ga.; Gephardt, Mo.; Gibbons, Fla.; Guarini, N.J.; Heftel, Hawaii; Jacobs, Ind.; Jenkins, Ga.; Jones, Okla.; Kennelly, Conn.; Matsui, Calif.; Pease, Ohio; Pickle, Texas; Rangel, N.Y.; Rostenkowski, Ill.; Russo, Ill.; Stark, Calif.

Republicans. Campbell, S.C.; Daub, Neb.; Gradison, Ohio; McGrath, N.Y.; Vander Jagt, Mich.

Against Reporting the Bill Favorably:

Democrats. None.

Republicans. Archer, Texas; Crane, Ill.; Duncan, Tenn.; Frenzel, Minn.; Gregg, N.H.; Moore, La.; Schulze, Pa.; Thomas, Calif.

The strong opposition expected at the caucus never materialized, however, and Rostenkowski was given a tentative "go-ahead" to proceed with markup, if only to prevent Reagan from blaming the Democrats for killing the effort.

Republicans, meanwhile, had their own intra-party squabble with which to contend. Kemp and 36 other House Republicans sent a letter to Reagan Sept. 27, urging him to oppose any bill that did not include top tax rates of 35 percent, a $2,000 personal exemption for all individuals and their dependents, and other key elements, such as generous business depreciation tax breaks.

The 13 GOP members of Ways and Means responded with a strongly worded letter to Reagan asserting that some compromises would have to be made to pass a bipartisan bill. They reminded the president that he had requested a "revenue-neutral" bill, and called this a major constraint to fashioning a measure that would cut tax rates while appeasing other interests.

Compounding the tension, in late September, the Republican National Committee sent a targeted mailing to constituents of eight Ways and Means members, mostly Republicans, asking them to urge their members to support Reagan's tax plan against "special interest lobbyists bent on scuttling the President's reform proposal to protect their own selfish interests."

One member whose district was targeted, Raymond J. McGrath, R-N.Y., had been a leader on the committee in opposing Reagan's plan to eliminate the deduction for state and local taxes, which would particularly hurt New York taxpayers.

McGrath was "outraged" by the mailing, and members reportedly complained about the letters to Deputy Treasury Secretary Richard G. Darman, who was attending the committee's private markup sessions in an effort to keep the bill bipartisan.

The dispute reflected a disagreement within the administration and among some congressional Republicans on how much the administration should compromise with Congress to win passage of a bill. It was this concern that contributed to the GOP revolt on the House floor in December that nearly scuttled the bill.

Markup Progreses Slowly; Stalls Over Banks

Ways and Means continued to plod for several weeks through its markup, keeping its decisions tentative and postponing action on most controversial issues as it tried to keep its bipartisan effort intact. Further detracting from the committee's effort were simultaneous conference negotiations on Gramm-Rudman-Hollings; 16 of the 36 Ways and Means members served on that conference committee.

Some decisions were made; Reagan's proposal to increase the personal exemption for each taxpayer and dependent from $1,040 to $2,000 was rejected Oct. 8 on a near party-line 12-24 vote, but the panel failed to agree on an alternative.

The committee endorsed proposals to expand the earned income tax credit for working poor families and to provide additional tax assistance for single parents. It also approved provisions to beef up taxpayer compliance and to restrict a number of smaller tax breaks, including those for home office expenses and hobbies. But an amendment by Republican Bill Frenzel of Minnesota to retain existing law allowing full deductions for business meal and entertainment expenses was defeated by voice vote.

The most serious threat to the success of the markup came on votes Oct. 15 to give a large tax cut to commercial banks and to retain a tax deduction for non-itemizers who made charitable donations.

The bank vote was a major setback to Rostenkowski, who with Reagan wanted to restrict deductions banks took for reserves held to cover bad debts. Democrat Ronnie G. Flippo of Alabama proposed to expand the deduction. His amendment, which passed 17-13, was projected to cost $4.8 billion more than existing law and $7.6 billion more than the Rostenkowski plan over five years.

Cutting Deals to Save the Bill

The markup was nearly derailed by the bank vote, which along with decisions made earlier, left the panel $13.5 billion short of producing a revenue-neutral tax bill. And in a dramatic attempt to put things back on track, Rostenkowski met privately during the week of Oct. 21 with each of the committee's 22 other Democrats. Baker held one-on-one meetings with the panels' 13 Republicans.

Both Democrats and Republicans on the committee had complained that they did not have enough input in crafting the tax bill. Some members said the bank vote the week before sent a message that the bill was in deep trouble unless there were negotiations to address members' concerns about specific components of the package.

As a consequence of the private sessions Rostenkowski agreed to drop one of the most controversial elements of his draft bill, a limit on deductions for state and local tax payments, and the committee voted to reverse the previous week's banking decision.

After intense lobbying by Rostenkowski and Baker, the committee agreed Oct. 23 to reconsider its earlier vote. It adopted, 14-7, an amendment by Democrat Fortney H. "Pete" Stark of California to limit the bad-debt deduction for banks with assets of more than $500 million. Under the amendment, smaller banks would be able to take a more generous deduction allowed under existing law.

Committee aides estimated the changes would raise about $2 billion more over the next five years than existing law, a marked change from the revenue loss predicted after the earlier vote.

Markup Begins to Gather Steam

Once over the state-local deduction and banking hurdles the committee began bearing down on its task, holding a three-day weekend markup session Oct. 25-27, during which it made more decisions than it had made during the previous month.

The committee agreed to restrict existing tax breaks for the timber industry, farmers, trusts and estates, and the construction of low-income housing. It also agreed to limit the use of tax-exempt bonds for non-governmental purposes. But, in almost all cases, the panel did not go as far as either Rostenkowski or Reagan had proposed.

The committee also agreed to lower tax rates for small businesses and to allow corporations to deduct up to 10 percent of the dividends they paid to shareholders.

In addition, several new tax breaks were approved, including a 20 percent tax credit for small manufacturers to help with start-up costs. And the committee retroactively repealed a complex generation-skipping estate tax for the wealthy and agreed to impose a more lenient tax in its place on future transfers.

On Nov. 6, the panel made some key decisions on pensions and accounting rules. It agreed to retain the popular "401(k)" tax-deferred savings plan — named after a section in the Internal Revenue Code — that Reagan had proposed to eliminate, but with lower limits on maximum annual contributions. The committee also voted to reject a Reagan proposal to raise from $2,250 to $4,000 the amount that a worker could contribute to IRAs for him or herself and a non-working spouse.

And the committee agreed to eliminate a special accounting method that allowed defense and building contractors to delay tax payments until work on a project had been completed, thereby dramatically reducing or eliminating their tax liability. Instead, such contractors would be required to take deductions and to declare income during the course of the contract.

Ways and Means' more rapid progress was helped by Rostenkowski's appointment of bipartisan task forces to hash out agreements on complex issues. Each task force would reach agreement on a package of proposals and then present it to the full committee, which in most cases adopted the recommendations with few alterations.

Reagan Raises New Doubts

But Reagan for the first time criticized the direction of the Ways and Means bill Nov. 6, raising new worries that he might not support the panel's final product. He told a group of Republican campaign workers meeting at the White House, "We need the kind of tax reform that we originally proposed and not with some of the waterings down that are taking place as they discuss it up there" on Capitol Hill.

Although Reagan had not publicly criticized the committee, administration officials had privately expressed concern that the bill was veering too far from Reagan's proposal. Particularly, there was concern that the retention of special tax breaks would prevent the lowering of the top individual income tax rate from 50 percent to 35 percent, a key component of the Reagan plan. But administration officials were reluctant to be too critical because Rostenkowski was Reagan's closest congressional ally on the tax bill.

Rostenkowski did not respond, but committee members, many of whom acknowledged that the bill was falling far short of the administration's goals, said they saw Reagan's remarks as an initial warning, not a serious setback. But Reagan's remarks excited growing doubts in the House about the committee's work. A group of 38 conservative House Republicans, led by Vin Weber, Minn., and Newt Gingrich, Ga., had written Reagan Nov. 1 asking him to abandon the committee bill.

Meanwhile, lukewarm business backing for tax reform began to disintegrate into outright opposition from some groups to the Ways and Means bill.

The National Association of Manufacturers (NAM), the U.S. Chamber of Commerce and the Business Roundtable all told committee members that the panel's effort was headed in the wrong direction.

Pressure to set the corporate tax rate above 35 percent to pay for the retention of existing tax breaks for both individuals and corporations was the focus of the growing business community dissent.

Representatives of one of the largest business groups to support the tax-overhaul effort, the Tax Reform Action Coalition (TRAC), were told by top Ways and Means staffers in a private meeting Nov. 14 that Rostenkowski would try to keep the top corporate rate at 35 percent. But the business representatives were warned that they would have to step up their lobbying efforts with other members of the committee for Rostenkowski to succeed.

The Home Stretch

In eight consecutive days of formal and informal sessions beginning Nov. 15, the panel completed markup on the bill, making the tough decisions it had postponed for nearly two months. The last decisions were made about 4 a.m Nov. 23, at the end of a session that began the day before.

In meetings Nov. 16-23, the committee agreed to:

- Repeal the 10 percent tax credit allowed under existing law for investment in certain business assets. Rostenkowski and Reagan had proposed elimination of the credit, which had been repealed and reinstated several times since it was first enacted during the Kennedy administration.
- Replace current law allowing accelerated depreciation of business assets with a less generous method that would generally lengthen the period of time during which an investment could be written off.
- Allow the value of depreciated assets to be indexed, beginning in 1988, to offset some, but not all, of the impact of inflation.
- Retain the so-called percentage depletion allowance for small, or "stripper," wells owned by independent producers and royalty owners.
- Allow oil, gas and geothermal property operators to write off in one year so-called "intangible drilling costs," such as labor and fuel, before the property became productive.

The committee rejected, 21-13, a motion by Democrat James R. Jones of Oklahoma to retain existing law related to the oil and gas industry.

- Allow taxpayers to deduct up to 80 percent of their business-related meals and entertainment expenses.
- Disallow any business deduction for "skyboxes" at such facilities as convention centers or sports arenas, but allow full deductions for tickets to certain charitable sports or entertainment events.
- Impose a 25 percent minimum tax on individuals and corporations who otherwise would be able to reduce dramatically their tax liabilities through the use of tax breaks retained in the law.
- Extend for three years a tax credit for new research and development expenses at a rate of 20 percent.
- Allow taxpayers to take an unlimited mortgage interest deduction for first and second residences.

The committee rejected the administration's controversial proposal to impose a tax retroactively on businesses to recapture some of the "windfall" benefits firms would receive from the combined effect of generous depreciation benefits allowed under existing law and the lower corporate tax rate provided by the bill.

The panel also rejected an amendment creating a new individual tax credit for campaign contributions. That amendment ultimately was one of two that were allowed and accepted on the House floor.

Final Decisions

In the final hours, many of the conflicts and strains that had plagued the tax-rewrite effort since the beginning came to a head as the committee grappled with some of its most crucial decisions — on tax rates, the personal exemption, taxation of fringe benefits and the deduction for state and local tax payments.

Rostenkowski offered a package deal to resolve these issues, which included a top corporate tax rate of 35 percent, a top individual tax rate of 38 percent, a personal exemption of $2,000, a new $500 (per personal exemption) floor on itemized deductions, retention of the deduction for state and local tax payments and taxation of some employer-provided fringe benefits.

During a caucus of committee Democrats, several members urged that fringe benefits remain tax exempt, and that the top corporate tax rate be set at 36 percent to pay for the change. They reasoned that the amount of business support for the bill was small to begin with and an increase in the corporate rate would carry little political risk, despite Rostenkowski's longstanding promise to hold to a top rate of 35 percent.

Republicans, annoyed at being asked to consider such crucial issues as part of a last-minute package, wanted to call for a politically difficult record vote on the chairman's plan to tax some fringe benefits.

At that point, Rostenkowski agreed to go along with the change, and separate amendments to Rostenkowski's package were adopted along party lines to leave fringe benefits tax free and to raise the corporate rate.

But the increase in the rate to 36 percent, plus a decision several hours earlier to raise the top effective tax rate on capital gains from 20 percent to 22 percent to help pay for a $16 billion shortfall in the bill, only intensified Republican opposition to the measure.

"It got a little testy at the end," said McGrath. "Some of those [Republicans] who may have voted for the bill probably had their minds changed that night."

Republicans' Last Gasp; Committee's Last Act

The Ways and Means Committee voted 28-8 Dec. 3 to report the bill, which finally acquired a number: HR 3838. Final action had been delayed for more than a week to allow committee staff to draft the complex legislation from the rough working papers used in markup.

Before the final vote, Republicans proposed an alternative package almost identical to one later offered on the House floor. Unlike the floor version, however, it called for a limit on deductions for charitable contributions.

The proposal was defeated by a party-line vote of 12-24. The only Republican to vote against the plan was McGrath, who opposed limits it would place on state and local tax deductions.

The GOP alternative followed the general outlines of the Ways and Means bill, but would have shifted only about $105 billion in taxes from individuals to corporations over five years, compared with more than $140 billion under the committee bill.

The proposal had a top individual rate of 37 percent that would have been further reduced to 35 percent in 1991. The personal exemption for taxpayers and their dependents would have been $2,000 for about 90 percent of all taxpayers, but lower for those in the upper brackets. The existing 20 percent top effective tax rate for capital gains would have been retained.

To pay for the extra tax advantages, the GOP proposal would have limited deductions for state and local income and property tax payments, and eliminated the deduction for state and local sales taxes.

To help businesses, the GOP plan would have lowered gradually the top corporate tax rate to 33 percent by 1991. It would have allowed somewhat more generous depreciation benefits, and retained a 5 percent tax credit for investment in domestically produced manufacturing equipment used in the United States.

House Floor Action

In the two weeks after the Ways and Means Committee voted to report HR 3838, many business groups shifted gears from trying to influence committee deliberations to trying to kill the measure outright. Although grass-roots support for the tax bill was limited, some business opponents feared the momentum that the measure could develop as the 1986 elections drew nearer.

The bill was expected to shift a significant amount of the income tax burden from individuals to corporations, and as a result draw support for its "populist" appeal. Congressional tax analysts said the bill would provide a tax cut to three-fourths of all individual taxpayers and take as many as six million poor people off the tax rolls altogether.

And, importantly, not all business organizations were opposed.

Business Opposition and Support

The lines dividing corporate America over revision of the tax code had been drawn since Reagan announced his tax package in May and Rostenkowski followed with his modified proposal in September.

Opponents included capital-intensive, heavy manufacturing businesses that were favored under the existing code, with its investment tax credit, accelerated depreciation and foreign tax credit provisions. The committee bill — which would not be subject to amendment on the floor — would repeal the investment credit and provide less generous depreciation and foreign credit provisions.

Supporters included small businesses and labor-intensive firms in the service, retail, consumer goods, food processing and high-technology sectors, which tended not to benefit from investment incentives and generally paid higher effective tax rates under the existing code.

For many, the bill's proposal to reduce the maximum corporate tax rate from 46 percent to 36 percent was sufficient reason for support. For the opponents, in contrast, the lowered tax rate ceiling was less important since existing deductions had allowed many manufacturers to slash their tax bills or eliminate them altogether.

Not surprisingly, on Nov. 26, the Chamber announced its mobilization to defeat the bill after its board voted 42-7 against it. Chamber President Richard L. Lesher conceded that small businesses would gain under the bill, but said the overall effect of the package could be to "deindustrialize America." Allied with the Chamber were the NAM and the Business Roundtable.

Meanwhile, other business groups that consistently had backed Rostenkowski, largely based on his commitment to a maximum 35 percent corporate tax rate, remained supportive despite the last-hour increase to 36 percent.

The percentage point increase initially shook supporters. TRAC had an endorsement ready for release the night of Ways and Means' final drafting, but pulled it when the top corporate rate went to 36 percent. But after a Nov. 26 meeting, the group, whose members included 250 businesses and associations ranging from small retailers and wholesalers to IBM Corp. and General Motors Corp., reiterated its support in a letter to Reagan.

Two of TRAC's founding groups, the National Federation of Independent Business (NFIB) and the American Business Conference, had such problems with the bill that they planned to work apart from TRAC to seek improvements. But neither group was so opposed that members

Switched Votes on the Tax Overhaul Bill Rule

The following list shows the 58 Republicans and 23 Democrats who switched their votes on the rule allowing House floor consideration of the Ways and Means Committee's tax-overhaul bill (HR 3838). The rule was rejected 202-223 on the first vote, Dec. 11; it was adopted 258-168 on the second vote, Dec. 17. A dash (—) indicates that a member did not vote. *(Vote 411, p. 130-H; vote 425, p. 134-H)*

Republicans

	First Vote	Second Vote		First Vote	Second Vote
Badham, Calif.	N	Y	Hyde, Ill.	N	Y
Bateman, Va.	N	Y	Ireland, Fla.	N	Y
Bentley, Md.	N	Y	Kemp, N.Y.	N	Y
Bilirakis, Fla.	N	Y	Latta, Ohio	N	Y
Broomfield, Mich.	N	Y	Lent, N.Y.	N	Y
Callahan, Ala.	N	Y	Lujan, N.M.	N	Y
Carney, N.Y.	N	Y	McDade, Pa.	N	Y
Chappie, Calif.	—	N	McKernan, Maine	N	Y
Clinger, Pa.	N	Y	McMillan, N.C.	N	Y
Coats, Ind.	N	Y	Michel, Ill.	N	Y
Conte, Mass.	N	Y	Miller, Ohio	N	Y
Courter, N.J.	N	Y	O'Brien, Ill.	N	Y
Davis, Mich.	N	Y	Porter, Ill.	N	Y
DeWine, Ohio	N	Y	Pursell, Mich.	N	Y
Dornan, Calif.	N	Y	Regula, Ohio	N	Y
Eckert, N.Y.	N	Y	Ritter, Pa.	N	Y
Evans, Iowa	N	Y	Rogers, Ky.	—	Y
Fawell, Ill.	N	Y	Roukema, N.J.	N	Y
Gekas, Pa.	N	Y	Rowland, Conn.	N	Y
Gilman, N.Y.	N	Y	Schneider, R.I.	N	Y
Goodling, Pa.	N	Y	Schuette, Mich.	N	Y
Grotberg, Ill.	N	Y	Skeen, N.M.	N	Y
Gunderson, Wis.	N	Y	Smith, Neb.	N	Y
Hammerschmidt, Ark.	N	Y	Snowe, Maine	N	Y
Hendon, N.C.	N	Y	Taylor, Mo.	N	Y
Henry, Mich.	N	Y	Vander Jagt, Mich.	N	Y
Hillis, Ind.	N	—	Whitehurst, Va.	N	Y
Holt, Md.	N	Y	Wolf, Va.	N	Y
Hopkins, Ky.	—	Y	Young, Fla.	N	Y

Democrats

	First Vote	Second Vote
Beilenson, Calif.	—	Y
Boner, Tenn.	Y	N
Brooks, Texas	—	N
Bustamante, Texas	Y	N
Byron, Md.	N	Y
Daschle, S.D.	N	Y
Dellums, Calif.	N	Y
Eckart, Ohio	N	Y
Feighan, Ohio	Y	N
Fowler, Ga.	N	Y
Gray, Ill.	Y	—
Hall, R., Texas	Y	N
Hawkins, Calif.	N	Y
Kolter, Pa.	Y	N
Lowry, Wash.	N	Y
Mazzoli, Ky.	Y	N
Mitchell, Md.	N	Y
Oakar, Ohio	Y	N
Ortiz, Texas	Y	N
Roybal, Calif.	Y	N
Savage, Ill.	N	Y
Tallon, S.C.	N	Y
Young, Mo.	N	—

wanted to join the Chamber forces against the entire bill.

Various provisions, including the toughened minimum tax on individuals, were seen as affecting small-business owners adversely. And, the bill's reduction in the maximum corporate tax rate was not viewed as important to many NFIB members who were individual entrepreneurs not in high business tax brackets.

Rule Debate

Ultimately, a key focus of discontent over the bill — which nearly led to its demise — was the rule governing floor debate.

The Rules Committee agreed Dec. 10 to a resolution (H Res 336) that allowed three hours of debate on the bill, two hours on a Republican alternative, and two amendments: one providing a 100 percent tax credit for limited political contributions to congressional candidates, and one on the taxation of U.S. possessions.

Requests to allow votes on a number of other amendments and alternative tax plans, including a minimum tax on individuals and corporations and the Kemp-Kasten tax-overhaul bill, were denied. Many Republicans wanted a vote on Kemp-Kasten, because they did not support the planned GOP alternative.

In a crucial decision, Rules also refused to allow an amendment that would have deleted a provision in the bill requiring public employees to pay higher taxes on their pensions immediately upon retirement.

Opponents of the provision — Republicans and Democrats — charged that it would place an unfair and unanticipated tax burden on public employees already facing budget cutbacks. They predicted that the proposed tax change would cause a wave of early retirements in the public sector before the provision could take effect. Under existing law, public employees who made mandatory, non-tax-exempt contributions to their retirement plans did not have to pay taxes on their pensions until the amount they received exceeded their total lifetime contributions to the plan.

HR 3838 would spread out the tax-exempt portion of the pensions over the anticipated life expectancy of the retiree, requiring retirees to pay higher taxes in the earlier years of retirement. The provision, which had been proposed by Reagan, was expected to raise $7.5 billion in new revenues over five years.

The Rules Committee did agree to alter the bill to treat members of Congress and their staffs the same as other public employees under the pension provision. Under the committee version of HR 3838, congressional employees had been exempted from the pension change.

First Floor Vote: Rule Defeated

The bill came to the floor the following day, Dec. 11, facing strong opposition, particularly from Republicans who did not like the impact on business and who complained that Reagan had effectively sold out to Rostenkowski during committee markup.

The rule's limitations on amendments generated additional opposition, but it was help from unexpected quarters that led GOP leaders to decide during debate on the rule that they had an opportunity to kill the rule, and possibly the bill as well.

Several Democrats, among them a visibly angry Steny Hoyer of Maryland, took to the floor to attack the bill for its provision taxing public employee pensions. GOP strategists, sensing a victory, hit hard on the pension issue during the floor fight, and won enough Democrats and wavering Republicans to defeat the rule.

The vote was 202-223 against the rule, and many supporters of the bill feared that the numbers signaled a death knell for HR 3838. Only 14 Republicans had supported the rule, and the 188 Democrats who did so amounted to the anticipated base level of Democratic support for the bill. Even if the vote on the rule could be turned around, there did not seem to be enough votes to pass HR 3838. *(Vote 411, p. 130-H)*

Republican leaders immediately claimed victory; Minority Leader Robert H. Michel of Illinois said the vote provided "an opportunity to give new life to tax reform ... an opportunity to go back [to committee] and get something more that we can support."

But Democratic leaders also declared a win. They noted that they had delivered their promised votes, and reiterated what they said all year: They could not pass a tax-overhaul measure without Republican support.

"If the president really cares about tax reform, then he will deliver the votes," said Speaker Thomas P. O'Neill Jr., D-Mass. "Otherwise, Dec. 11 at 12 noon will be remembered as the date that Ronald Reagan became a 'lame duck' on the floor of the House."

Salvage Mission

Administration officials, lobbyists and others backing the bill found in the days following the rule defeat that the procedural vote had masked the deep-seated reluctance of many members to pass any sweeping tax-overhaul bill.

And O'Neill set what appeared to be an improbably high price on the administration's request that the House try again. He said Reagan would have to guarantee at least 50 Republican votes for adoption of a rule and passage of the bill before it would be brought back to the floor.

It was not clear that any compromise would guarantee the needed GOP votes. And there were worries that Democratic defections would scuttle a second attempt to bring the bill to the floor, jeopardizing the party's moral victory of having done their part to give Reagan a tax overhaul bill.

In a Dec. 12 meeting with House Republican leaders — described alternately by members as "acrimonious" and "encouraging" — Treasury Secretary Baker and White House Chief of Staff Regan discussed possible maneuvers to win more Republican votes. At that meeting a letter from Reagan promising a veto unless the House bill were altered by the Senate was offered as a drawing card for GOP votes.

Republican leaders also discussed with the White House, Rostenkowski and O'Neill the possibility of changing the rule to allow a vote increasing the personal exemption for individual taxpayers; the committee bill allowed a $2,000 exemption for taxpayers who did not itemize, but effectively only $1,500 for itemizers. The proposal included further limits on deductions for consumer interest payments to offset the revenue loss from the personal exemption change.

Rostenkowski, however, said such an amendment would not be acceptable to the committee bill. Democrats were reluctant to allow further amendments to the bill, for fear of losing the votes of Democrats from oil and gas, timber and steel-producing states who had their own concerns with the bill.

Reagan Appeals in Person

Reagan made an unusual trip to Capitol Hill Dec. 16 to meet with recalcitrant Republicans. He reportedly told GOP members assembled in the Rayburn House Office Building, "If tax reform is killed, if it doesn't pass the House in any form, then there will be no tax reform. I just can't accept we would let this historic initiative slip through our fingers."

But Reagan's personal appeal appeared to have less influence than his letter the following day vowing a veto of the tax measure, if it was not changed. The letter outlined Reagan's "minimum requirements" for a tax bill that he would sign, including lower tax rates, a higher personal exemption and more tax incentives for industry.

Republican leaders also won concessions from Democratic leaders the evening of Reagan's visit to make what amounted to little more than face-saving changes to the rule. After intense negotiations with Baker and Michel, O'Neill and Rostenkowski agreed to allow a change in a substitute tax plan Republicans wanted to offer on the floor. Under the revised rule, the controversial public employee pension provision automatically was to be deleted from the substitute.

They also agreed that upon passage of the bill, the rule would allow Michel to offer a non-binding "sense of the House" resolution (H Res 335) that new, Jan. 1, 1987, effective dates should be announced by the end of the year for several provisions in the bill.

With the agreement, O'Neill received a phone call from Reagan telling him that he had rounded up at least 50 Republican votes for both the rule and passage.

Several GOP leaders who had opposed the measure Dec. 11 changed their positions. Michel said he would vote for the rule, although he still opposed the bill. Kemp said he would vote for the bill.

About Face: House Adopts Rule

The new rule (H Res 343) was reported by the Rules Committee Dec. 17, and taken to the floor that afternoon. But despite the president's assurances to O'Neill, the outcome remained in doubt.

The morning of Dec. 17 some members complained in a private Democratic caucus that they had won a political victory with the first vote and that the bill should not be brought back to the floor "to bail out the president," according to one member present.

Several members indicated that they would not vote

for the rule again and a last-minute head count showed only 165 firm Democratic votes for it, according to one committee aide. *(Switched votes, p. 496)*

On the Republican side, other trouble was brewing. Some Republican leaders, including Minority Whip Trent Lott, Miss.; Chief Deputy GOP Whip Tom Loeffler, Texas; and GOP Policy Committee Chairman Dick Cheney, Wyo., had decided to continue fighting the bill with the help of outside business groups opposed to the legislation.

Shortly before the second rule vote, Loeffler said he had won over a few of the 50 Republican votes Reagan had promised. But in the end, he later acknowledged, the "powerful alliance" of the White House and the House majority could not be beaten.

In an impassioned speech before a full chamber, O'Neill asked members of both parties to vote for the rule to keep the bill alive.

"It is a vote for the working people of America over the special interests. It is a vote for the individual taxpayer over the well-financed corporations," he said. "It is a vote to restore the confidence of our neighbor in the tax code."

With 70 Republicans joining 188 Democrats, the rule was adopted by a vote of 258-168. *(Vote 425, p. 134-H)*

Passage of the Bill

With approval of the rule, the tide began to change.

By voice vote, the House adopted an amendment by Morris K. Udall, D-Ariz., to a provision in the bill allowing American Samoa, Guam, the Northern Mariana Islands and the Virgin Islands to come up with new local tax systems. The amendment would require that the new systems raise the same amount of revenue over the next five years as the islands' current tax laws.

The House also agreed by a vote of 230-196 to an amendment by McHugh that would allow taxpayers to claim a credit for up to $100 a year in contributions to congressional candidates in their home states. *(Vote 426, p. 134-H)*

In debate on the overall bill, Republicans and some Democrats charged that HR 3838 would hurt the economy by eliminating tax incentives for new business investment. And they complained that the 1,379-page Ways and Means bill did little to simplify existing tax law and was rife with the kinds of special-interest provisions that "tax reform" was intended to repeal.

Republicans argued that their own alternative, which called for slightly lower tax rates and the retention of more business tax breaks, would be better for the economy and provide a larger share of tax cuts to those in the lower income levels. However, the overall individual income tax cut was expected to be smaller than under the Ways and Means bill.

But Republicans had problems with their own alternative, which would have reduced by 30 percent the value of many tax deductions, including the one for state and local tax payments. As anticipated, the GOP plan was turned down, by a vote of 133-294. *(Vote 427, p. 136-H)*

Democrats defended the Ways and Means proposal as imperfect, but a great improvement over current tax law, which had been widely criticized as unfair and complex.

Supporters noted that, under the plan, the burden of paying about $141 billion in taxes would be shifted from individuals to corporations over the next five years. They also claimed it would remove 6.3 million low-income individuals from the tax rolls and cut taxes for remaining taxpayers by an average of 9 percent, with most of the cut going to the middle- and lower-income classes.

By a vote of 171 to 256, the House rejected a motion by Philip M. Crane, R-Ill., to recommit the bill to committee, a move that effectively would have killed the measure. *(Vote 428, p. 136-H)*

No Roll Call

Then, in an anticlimactic finale to the emotional tax debate, the House approved the Ways and Means bill without a recorded vote. In the confusing and noisy atmosphere on the House floor following the recommittal motion, members apparently missed their opportunity to ask for a roll-call vote, and Speaker O'Neill gaveled the measure through to passage.

When they realized what had happened, some Republicans who had wanted to be recorded voting against the bill jumped from their seats in protest. But O'Neill angrily insisted he had looked "with deliberation" for someone to recognize, and most Republicans later acknowledged that the whole affair was little more than a mix-up. ▮

Deficit-Reduction Bill Fails to Clear at the Wire

Congress adjourned for 1985 without enacting what one member called "the crowning element" of a year's work on the budget — a $74 billion deficit-reduction package — after the House resisted a Senate provision that would tax manufacturers to pay for a toxic-waste cleanup program.

The deadlock over the three-year package of spending cuts and tax increases (HR 3128) occurred a week after Congress cleared the Gramm-Rudman-Hollings legislation (PL 99-177) promising future cuts to balance the budget within five years. *(Gramm-Rudman-Hollings, p. 459)*

By failing to agree to the long-pending savings proposals in HR 3128, members underscored the difficulty they faced in trying to reach the ambitious new deficit targets of Gramm-Rudman.

HR 3128, known as a reconciliation bill, was the product of a complicated budget process in which committees proposed spending cuts and revenue increases in programs under their jurisdictions to "reconcile" them with deficit targets set in the annual budget resolution.

The fiscal 1986 resolution (S Con Res 32), approved Aug. 1, called for a total of at least $75.5 billion in reconciliation savings over three years, fiscal 1986-88. S Con Res 32 called for about $200 billion more to be cut through the annual appropriations process. *(Budget resolution, p. 441; reconciliation instructions, p. 500)*

Most committee recommendations were received by the Budget committees by the Sept. 27 deadline established by S Con Res 32. That left no time, however, to enact reconciliation before the Oct. 1 start of the fiscal year to which most cuts would apply.

When the bill did not clear before adjournment, it marked the second time in three years that Congress failed to meet its statutory requirement of enacting a prescribed reconciliation bill. In 1983, Congress failed to clear legislation to meet the mandate of $85.3 billion in deficit reduction for fiscal years 1984-86. Parts of the 1983 package were cleared in 1984. HR 3128, in turn, cleared in 1986.*(1983 Almanac p. 231; 1984 Almanac pp. 143, 160)*

Two House Bills, One in the Senate

The House passed two reconciliation bills (HR 3128, HR 3500), including sometimes overlapping and sometimes conflicting provisions from 14 committees. Provisions from HR 3500 were added to HR 3128 for conference with the Senate. The Senate included provisions from 11 committees in one bill (S 1730), which was renumbered HR 3128 for the conference.

The conference agreement on HR 3128 made revisions in the Medicare health care program, restricting both payments for doctors and hospitals and the benefits for elderly patients to cut spending $11.2 billion through fiscal 1988.

In addition, the measure cut spending for student loans, highways, small businesses, housing and veterans, and raised revenues from customs fees, federal pension insurance premiums and a new import tax.

The conference agreement generated objections and veto threats because of several controversial elements, not least of which was the manufacturers' tax to pay for the "superfund" hazardous-waste cleanup program. *(Superfund, p. 191)*

A plan to share offshore oil leasing revenues with coastal states also drew fire, as did extension of a 16-cents-per-pack excise tax on cigarettes, which was worth $4.9 billion over three years. The tax was opposed by cigarette manufacturers and President Reagan, but separate provisions overhauling the federal price-support program for tobacco growers were included largely to appeal to the cigarette industry.

The cigarette tax had been due to revert to 8 cents per pack Sept. 30, 1985, and some members were concerned that states would raise their own cigarette taxes if the federal levy was not extended. So several times during the lengthy committee, floor and conference action on HR 3128, Congress voted to extend the tax temporarily, along with other expiring programs. *(Tax extensions, p. 502)*

Though the savings in the deficit-reduction bill were said to be the second-greatest ever, for weeks the package was in danger of abandonment in Congress' rush to adjourn for the year. Leaders were preoccupied with the budget-balancing measure, appropriations for the federal government and a bill to overhaul the tax code (HR 3838). *(Continuing appropriations resolution, p. 360; tax bill, p. 480)*

But Congress' delay in finishing those "must" measures bought time for final agreement on the deficit-reduction bill. More than 240 House and Senate conferees — believed to be the second largest conference committee ever — began working in 31 groups Dec. 6. They settled the differences in their chambers' versions of the bill and reported the conference agreement Dec. 19 (H Rept 99-453).

The record for reconciliation savings was set in 1981, when Congress approved legislation reducing the deficit an estimated $130.6 billion for fiscal years 1982-84. That bill also was the product of the largest conference committee on record, 280 members meeting in 55 subgroups. *(1981 Almanac p. 257)*

Conference Report: A Ping-Pong Ball

On Dec. 19, the Senate overwhelmingly adopted, 78-1, the conference report approved only hours before by House and Senate negotiators. *(Vote 379, p. 64-S)*

But the House sent the package back to the Senate after voting 205-151 to extract the superfund tax. *(Vote 436, p. 138-H)*

Each chamber then by voice vote rejected the other's position in turn, as the parliamentary test of wills between the two houses continued into the early morning hours of Dec. 20.

Later on Dec. 20, just before adjourning for the year, the Senate tried one last time to find an acceptable compromise. When that failed, the Democrats twice moved to agree to the House position, which would have sent the bill to Reagan, but they lost 29-35 and 30-35. *(Votes 380, 381, p. 65-S)*

Finally, senators by voice vote sent the bill back to conference. The House did not respond before adjourning, leaving the issue to be resolved in the second session of the 99th Congress.

During the first three months of 1986, members sought to find ways to revive the bill. Both chambers offered concessions, and the Senate early on dropped its insistence on the superfund tax, but administration objections continued and the compromise offers threatened not to take hold. The Senate offered one last compromise March 14, 1986, largely on behalf of the administration. The House rejected that offer March 18. But two days later members yielded to pressure from tobacco- and coastal-states members who desperately wanted the bill enacted, and the House accepted the Senate compromise March 20, clearing the bill.

Eventually, the savings claimed in HR 3128 began to deteriorate. According to Reagan's Office of Management and Budget (OMB), the bill never would have achieved the savings that sponsors claimed. OMB said the Senate-passed version would have saved $22.2 billion over three years, not $85.7 billion as claimed; the House version would have saved $17.5 billion rather than an estimated $80.6 billion. Not all of the House savings was claimed in HR 3128; part was contained in an omnibus farm programs reauthorization bill (HR 2100) and part in a superfund reauthorization bill (HR 2817).

As time passed after the Oct. 1 start of fiscal 1986, when most savings were to take effect, congressional sources said the bill's expected savings were shrinking by $50 million a day. When the conference reported the measure Dec. 19, sponsors claimed the measure would save $74 billion through fiscal 1988. By the time the bill cleared, it was expected to save only $18.2 billion over three years. Some of the lost savings had been achieved through enactment of other laws and administrative actions, however.

Superfund Standoff

In large part, HR 3128 fell victim in 1985 to a stubborn, high-stakes standoff that began in conference, involving the chairmen of Congress' tax-writing committees: Bob Packwood, R-Ore., of the Senate Finance Committee, and Dan Rostenkowski, D-Ill., of the House Ways and Means Committee.

Packwood's allies mainly were oil-state members, who favored the Senate's proposed excise tax on manufacturers as a way to expand the superfund cleanup program without adding to the taxes that petrochemical companies paid to support the fund.

He insisted on their position over the opposition of Senate Majority Leader Robert Dole, R-Kan. For oil-state members, the stand for a manufacturers' tax was costly: Without a bill, they would lose the separate provision giving seven coastal states a generous share of offshore oil

Reconciliation Instructions to Senate, House Committees

The conference agreement on the fiscal 1986 budget resolution (S Con Res 32 — H Rept 99-249) directed 11 Senate committees and 14 House committees to alter program authorizations and entitlements to achieve the cuts in budget authority and outlays detailed below.

These so-called reconciliation spending cuts totaled $67.1 billion. In addition, new revenues of $8.4 billion were required through reconciliation to achieve total deficit reduction of $75.5 billion for fiscal years 1986-88. The required new revenues show only on the Senate chart below (indicated as positive numbers). Furthermore, the House deficit-reduction figures add to more than $75.5 billion, owing to overlapping jurisdiction among committees.

(Figures in millions of dollars)

	FY86		FY87		FY88		FY 86-88	
	Budget Authority	Outlays	Budget Authority	Outlays	Budget Authority	Outlays	Budget Authority	Outlays
Senate Committees								
Agriculture, Nutrition and Forestry	--	$ −1,250	--	$ −2,050	--	$ −4,600	--	$ −7,900
Armed Services	--	−100	--	−200	--	−300	--	−600
Banking, Housing and Urban Affairs	−2,374	−2,814	−2,828	−3,685	−2,998	−3,821	−8,200	−10,320
Commerce, Science and Transportation	−328	−310	−133	−119	−135	−130	−596	−559
Energy and Natural Resources	−5,485	−5,403	+291	+147	−337	−314	−5,531	−5,570
Environment and Public Works	--	−200	--	−850	--	−1,050	--	−2,100
Finance	--	−3,307	--	−7,951	--	−10,908	--	−22,166
Finance (new revenues)	--	1,800	--	3,000	--	3,600	--	8,400
Governmental Affairs	--	−3,219	--	−4,421	--	−4,986	--	−12,626
Labor and Human Resources	−670	−170	−860	−535	−1,085	−960	−2,615	−1,665
Small Business	−448	−509	−564	−972	−1,060	−998	−2,072	−2,479
Veterans' Affairs	−300	−300	−400	−400	−450	−450	−1,150	−1,150
House Committees								
Agriculture	--	$ −1,250	--	$ −2,050	--	$ −4,600	--	$ −7,900
Armed Services	--	−100	--	−200	--	−300	--	−600
Banking, Finance and Urban Affairs	−2,374	−2,814	−2,828	−3,685	−2,998	−3,821	−8,200	−10,320
Energy and Commerce	−1,513	−3,947	−1,246	−5,008	−1,401	−6,512	−4,160	−15,467
Education and Labor	−670	−470	−860	−835	−1,085	−1,260	−2,615	−2,565
Government Operations	--	--	--	−3,526	--	−4,956	--	−8,482
Interior and Insular Affairs	−4,000	−4,000	+1,504	+1,504	+1,029	+1,029	−1,467	−1,467
Judiciary	−570	−70	−610	−285	−635	−510	−1,815	−865
Merchant Marine and Fisheries	−300	−300	−100	−100	−100	−100	−500	−500
Post Office and Civil Service	--	−3,219	--	−4,421	--	−4,986	--	−12,626
Public Works and Transportation	--	−200	--	−850	--	−1,050	--	−2,100
Small Business	−448	−509	−564	−972	−1,060	−998	−2,072	−2,479
Veterans' Affairs	−300	−300	−400	−400	−450	−450	−1,150	−1,150
Ways and Means	--	−5,027	--	−7,245	--	−9,362	--	−21,634

SOURCE: Conference report on S Con Res 32

lease revenues. *(Offshore leasing revenues, p. 203)*

Rostenkowski's stand against the tax had the support of a House coalition that included not only many of his fellow Democrats, who were a majority in the House, but also about half the House Republicans, who reflected the president's opposition to the tax and openly rebelled against their GOP colleagues in the Senate.

Just a week before the final floor impasse, on Dec. 10, the House had voted 220-206 for an amendment to the superfund reauthorization bill that rejected the broad-based manufacturers' tax in favor of a combination of existing petrochemical industry taxes and general revenues. *(Vote 406, p. 128-H)*

Highlights

Following are highlights of the major provisions of HR 3128, as agreed to by conferees Dec. 19 (H Rept 99-453):

Agriculture

Farm Bill Savings. The Senate version had included savings generated by changes in farm program provisions relating to food stamps, exports and agricultural credit. The conference agreement agreed to count savings contained in the 1985 farm bill (HR 2100 — PL 99-198). *(Farm bill, p. 517)*

Tobacco Program. As part of a deal extending the cigarette tax, the Senate had included a new tobacco price-support program in its bill, which was retained by the conference. The provisions were crafted with the help of cigarette manufacturuers and would reduce price-support levels, while working to eliminate existing government-owned tobacco surpluses. Manufacturers would have to share in the cost of financing the price-support program, but could buy the surpluses at up to a 90 percent discount. They would also be authorized to help set quotas for growers. *(Tobacco program, p. 539)*

Energy

User Fees. The conference agreement would authorize user fees to be imposed on interstate pipeline carriers of oil, gas and hazardous liquids to cover the cost of federal pipeline safety programs.

Strategic Petroleum Reserve. The measure would authorize continued filling of the Strategic Petroleum Reserve, but at reduced rates, while continuing the goal of 750 million barrels for the reserve. *(Strategic Petroleum Reserve, p. 211)*

Synfuels. The bill would terminate the Synthetic Fuels Corporation and transfer its responsibilities to the secretary of the Treasury. *(Synfuels, p. 212)*

Guaranteed Student Loans

Conferees agreed to extend the Guaranteed Student Loan program for two years, through fiscal 1987. The conference agreement would require future loan payments to borrowers to be made in multiple disbursements rather than lump sums, and that checks be mailed to schools rather than to students.

The measure also would require lenders and state agencies to seek to collect loans for 270 days before declaring a loan in default (existing law was 120 days). And it would require enhanced collection efforts.

The conference agreement also would allow borrowers with loans totaling more than $5,000 to consolidate those loans at 10 percent interest.

House conferees agreed to drop a provision requiring a needs test for all loan applicants, and Senate conferees dropped a provision that would have reduced special allowance payments made to banks as an incentive to issue Guaranteed Student Loans. *(Higher education programs reauthorization, p. 294)*

Housing

Spending Cuts, Debt Forgiveness. The conference agreement included provisions to reduce spending for rural housing, community development programs and operating costs of public housing projects, by capping authorizations and prohibiting the Federal Financing Bank from purchasing direct or guaranteed rural housing loans or Community Development Block Grant-guaranteed obligations. It also proposed to forgive the federal debt on outstanding notes issued by local public housing authorities, which had been used for construction since 1937. The result would be a reduction of new budget authority, some of which would be rescinded.

Housing Reauthorization. Conferees struck a major, omnibus reauthorization for housing programs (HR 1) that would extend various housing and community programs and create several new programs, including one for the homeless. The House had agreed to let the housing bill piggyback on reconciliation at the urging of its Banking, Finance and Urban Affairs Committee, which said the tactic was necessary to force the Senate Banking, Housing and Urban Affairs Committee to consider a housing measure. *(Housing programs reauthorization, p. 303)*

Medicare

Hospital Payment Freeze. The conference agreement would grant a 1 percent increase in hospitals' Medicare repayment rates, which would take effect March 1, 1986.

Physician Fee Freeze. It also would continue a freeze in payments to "non-participating" physicians through Dec. 31, 1986, but would allow physicians the opportunity to choose to participate in the Medicare assignment program during January 1986. Customary and prevailing rates paid to participating physicians would be updated as of Feb. 1, 1986, and participating physicians would receive a one-time, 1 percent upward adjustment to compensate for no increase in prevailing rates from Oct. 1, 1985, until Feb. 1, 1986.

'Prospective Payment' Delay. The measure also would delay, for one year, a scheduled change in the way hospitals are reimbursed under Medicare; a 1983 law (PL 98-21) called for a shift from a system that paid hospitals for their actual costs of care to one that repaid them based on so-called "prospective payment" set in advance. The law provided for a three-year transition period for putting the new system in place by Oct. 1, 1986. The conference agreement would extend the transition period one year. *(Medicare fee freeze, p. 302; PL 98-21, 1983 Almanac, p. 391)*

Coverage of State and Local Employees. The measure would make Medicare coverage of newly hired state and local government employees mandatory, and voluntary for previously hired workers. Workers covered by Medicare would pay the payroll tax that finances the program.

Offshore Oil Revenues

Conferees agreed to resolve a longstanding dispute over the sharing of $5.8 billion in past rents and $1 billion in royalties collected from offshore oil leases that straddled the boundary between state and federally controlled offshore lands.

The agreement would give the federal Treasury 73 percent of future receipts and 73 percent of the $6.8 billion, which was held in escrow. The remaining 27 percent of past and future collections would be split between seven coastal states. This agreement, particularly the provision including royalties (bonuses paid by bidders) with the rents, led to a serious dispute with the administration, and a veto threat.

Pension Benefit Guaranty Corp.

The measure would aid and overhaul the financially troubled Pension Benefit Guaranty Corporation (PBGC), a federal entity that insured workers' retirement benefits in case employers terminated their pension plans. The corporation was burdened with a growing number of unfunded pension claims, including many inherited from firms that dropped their plans but remained in business.

Complicating the usual conference process of negotiating differences between House and Senate bills was the fact that the House bill included contrary proposals from two rival committees, the Education and Labor and Ways and Means panels. The Senate and the Education and Labor Committee were closer to agreement on the issue than were the two House panels, and in most instances the conference followed the Education and Labor Committee's provisions.

The conference agreement would require companies to prove financial distress before they could dump their pension liabilities on the government. If a firm remained in business after a plan termination, the PBGC and the firm would be required to work out "commercially reasonable terms" for payment of those liabilities in excess of the PBGC's immediate claim under existing law to 30 percent of the firm's net worth. A healthy firm could terminate its plan only if the plan had sufficient assets to pay all promised benefits, not just those that were federally guaranteed.

Cigarette Tax, Medicare Fee Limits Extended

Several tax and spending programs expired at midnight Dec. 19 in a pre-adjournment power struggle between the House and Senate. But Congress cleared legislation (HR 4006 — PL 99-201) extending two of them until midnight March 15, 1986: federal excise taxes on cigarettes and limits on Medicare payments to physicians and hospitals.

Authorization was not extended for two other programs: Trade Adjustment Assistance, which helped workers and companies hurt by foreign imports, and railroad unemployment insurance, which needed continued borrowing authority to pay benefits to unemployed railroad workers.

Long-term extensions or revisions for all four programs were contained in the deficit-cutting budget reconciliation bill (HR 3128) that failed to clear before adjournment. *(Reconciliation, p. 498)*

Congress had temporarily extended the four programs three other times between Sept. 30, when their authorizations had first expired, and Dec. 19.

Late on Dec. 19 it became apparent that the reconciliation bill would not clear in time and House leaders brought to the floor HR 4006, a short-term extension of the four previously extended programs. HR 4006 also included extensions for 12 tax provisions that had been extended or revised in the House-passed tax overhaul bill (HR 3838), but were otherwise due to expire at the end of 1985. *(Tax overhaul, p. 480)*

The tax provisions included several popular tax breaks — for research and development, for employer-provided educational benefits, for removing architectural barriers to the handicapped, and special filing rules for spouses of U.S. personnel missing in action in Vietnam.

The bill passed the House Dec. 19 by voice vote. Later that day the Senate stripped out all but the extensions for cigarette taxes, Medicare physician payment limits (after striking the payment limit for hospitals), trade adjustment and railroad retirement, and then passed the measure.

The House Dec. 20 by voice vote further amended HR 4006 to extend only the cigarette tax and the Medicare hospital and physician fee provisions, and returned the bill to the Senate, which concurred, clearing the measure.

The 16-cents-per-pack federal excise tax on cigarettes dropped to 8 cents as of 12:01 a.m. Dec. 20, and at least 10 states had tax "triggers" that automatically would have raised their own taxes on cigarettes by 8 cents per pack when the federal tax lapsed. Those were Arizona, Connecticut, Maryland, Massachusetts, Minnesota, Mississippi, Nevada, Rhode Island, Utah and Wisconsin. As cleared, however, HR 4006 made extension of the cigarette tax retroactive to Dec. 19, and none of the state tax increases took effect.

Earlier Extensions

The House and Senate passed the first emergency extension of the cigarette tax (HR 3452 — PL 99-107) Sept 30. The measure included a 45-day extension, through Nov. 14, of not only the tax, but also the Medicare payment limits, Trade Adjustment Assistance and borrowing authority for the railroad workers' unemployment fund.

Though top administration officials predicted until late into the evening of Sept. 30 that because President Reagan opposed extending the cigarette tax he would veto the bill, he signed it shortly before midnight.

White House aides said Reagan continued to oppose the tax, which was to be permanently extended in the reconciliation bill, and left open the chance he would veto that bill as a result.

Sen. Jesse Helms, R-N.C., had lobbied for Reagan's support for the tax extension at the last minute, because another provision of the reconciliation bill would have revised the tobacco price-support program. Helms was the sponsor of that provision and was concerned that its fate might be tied to the cigarette excise tax. The cigarette tax had been increased from 8 cents to 16 cents in 1982 to help cut the deficit, but the provision was to expire after three years as a concession to Helms. *(Tobacco price supports, p. 539; cigarette tax, 1982 Almanac p. 32)*

Congress Nov. 14 cleared a second round of temporary extensions through Dec. 14 for the four programs (HR 3721 — PL 99-155).

The House Nov. 13 had passed HR 3721, a bill temporarily raising the ceiling on the public debt, and a second bill (HR 3722) extending the four programs. The Senate Nov. 13 amended HR 3721 to include the provisions of HR 3722, and passed the bill. The House accepted the Senate version Nov. 14. *(Debt-limit extensions, p. 457)*

The House and Senate both passed a third bill (HR 3918 — PL 99-181) Dec. 12, extending the four programs until midnight Dec. 19.

The measure would increase the annual premiums that employers paid for single-employer pension plans. (Separate federal funds were maintained for single-employer plans, which covered individual firms, and for multi-employer plans, which covered many firms within a single industry, such as steel.)

The fee would rise from $2.60 per employee to $8.50, effective Dec. 31, 1985, but the PBGC would be required to study the premium structure and report to Congress within a year. *(PBGC, p. 175)*

Small Business

The measure would reauthorize the Small Business Administration (SBA) for three years, through fiscal 1988, at $515 million, $605 million and $634 million. Direct loans would be capped for the three years at $101 million, $111 million and $116 million. Guaranteed loans would be capped at $3.2 billion, $3.4 billion and $3.5 billion. The measure also would raise the fee for guaranteed loans from 1 percent to 2 percent.

Under the conference agreement, the Federal Financing Bank would no longer be authorized to purchase securities to finance Small Business Investment Company loans.

And the measure would prevent agricultural enterprises from qualifying for SBA disaster loans after fiscal 1985. It would eliminate the existing law authorization for non-physical disasters, which in the past was used to aid firms along the Mexican border who suffered financial loss due to the devaluation of the peso. And it would eliminate the authorization cap on disaster relief. *(Small Business Administration reauthorization, p. 412)*

Medicaid

The measure would extend Medicaid coverage to pregnant women in two-parent families where the chief wage earner was employed, but the family met the income standards for federal welfare assistance. Under existing law, Medicaid, the federal-state health care program for the poor, covered such women only if the wage earner was unemployed.

It also would reduce federal spending for Medicaid by requiring states to recover funds from private insurers if beneficiaries had their own health insurance policies.

Welfare

For Aid to Families with Dependent Children (AFDC), which was the principal federal-state welfare program, conferees accepted a House provision mandating that all states offer aid to needy two-parent families in which the principal wage earner was unemployed. Such aid was optional under existing law, and about 18 states provided assistance only to single-parent families, forcing some couples to separate. The provision would take effect Jan. 1, 1988.

Conferees struck a House provision authorizing $150 million over two years for grants to help states start programs to reduce teenage pregnancy and to help young parents become self-sufficient. *(AFDC, p. 308)*

Superfund

The measure would reauthorize the "superfund" toxic-waste cleanup program for five years and extend the taxes that petrochemical industries pay to support it. Also, it would impose a new excise tax on other manufacturers to finance the cleanup program. Both House and Senate had passed separate superfund bills (HR 2817), and the form of taxes to pay for the program was a major issue left to settle in conference on that bill, as well as the reason that HR 3128 failed to clear in 1985. *(Superfund, p. 191)*

Taxes

Cigarette Tax. The 16-cents-a-pack cigarette tax would be extended permanently, rather than revert to 8 cents. The measure also would establish a new tax of 8 cents per pound on chewing tobacco and 24 cents per pound on snuff. A House provision to earmark one penny of the cigarette tax to help finance an existing tobacco price-support program was dropped in lieu of the new, Senate-proposed tobacco program.

Coal Tax. The measure would increase by 10 percent taxes on coal-mining companies. The taxes financed a trust fund that paid benefits either to miners suffering from black lung disease or to their survivors.

Income Averaging. Taxpayers who were full-time students in the three years prior to filing a tax return would be prevented from averaging their income for those years to reduce their tax liability, under the conference agreement.

Trade Adjustment Assistance

The bill would extend for six years authorization of the Trade Adjustment Assistance program, which aided workers and some firms who could show they had lost their jobs or business because of low-cost competing imports. To finance the program, the measure would impose a new tax on all imports within two years. The administration wanted to eliminate the program and the fee provision was among its chief objections to the bill. *(1983 Almanac p. 251)*

Transportation

Amtrak. The measure would reauthorize the national passenger railroad for three years, despite administration calls for deep cuts, at $600 million, $606.1 million and $603.5 million in fiscal years 1986-88.

Highways. It would pare authorized spending from the Highway Trust Fund, which financed major highway programs, to $13.125 billion in fiscal 1986; $13.525 billion in 1987; and $14.1 billion for 1988. Spending was to rise to $14.45 billion in 1986 under a 1982 law (PL 97-424). *(Amtrak, highway authorizations, p. 280; PL 97-424, 1982 Almanac p. 317)*

Veterans

The measure would mandate the first-ever income test on veterans using Veterans Administration (VA) hospitals. Those with incomes exceeding $20,000 annually ($25,000 if they had one dependent) would receive care if space was available and if they paid a new fee.

Also, the measure would entitle veterans — except those with non-service-connected disabilities — to hospital care regardless of their ability to pay. Veterans with non-service-connected disabilities, who also had incomes above $15,000 ($18,000 if they had one dependent) could be provided with care if facilities were available. *(Veterans' health care bill, p. 403)*

House Committee Action: HR 3128

The House Ways and Means Committee July 24 approved a broad package of spending cuts and revenue hikes (HR 3128 — H Rept 99-241, Part I) to whittle about $19 billion from the federal deficit over three years.

The committee bill, approved by a largely party-line vote of 22-14, would have made about $10 billion in cuts in fiscal 1986-88 in Medicare, the federal health-care program for the elderly, and raise some $9 billion in fees and revenues.

The bill was reported before Congress approved the budget resolution setting reconciliation requirements, in large part because Chairman Dan Rostenkowski, D-Ill., wanted to clear the Ways and Means agenda to begin markup of the tax overhaul bill. The same day Ways and Means approved HR 3128, the House adopted a resolution (H Res 231) along party lines, 242-184, instructing committees to begin making reconciliation recommendations based on totals in the House-passed budget resolution. *(Vote 227, p. 72-H)*

The committee's largest revenue-raising proposal was to extend the current 16-cents-per-pack tax on cigarettes — and to earmark 1 cent of the tax for subsidies for tobacco farmers.

The package also would have raised miscellaneous revenues and fees in pension, unemployment and trade programs. But another controversial revenue-raiser was shelved when the committee rejected a proposal to extract larger out-of-pocket payments from wealthier Medicare beneficiaries than from the elderly poor.

Despite the emphasis on deficit reduction, the committee squeezed into the package proposals to increase federal welfare spending by roughly $620 million over three years. Committee member Bill Gradison, R-Ohio, charged that the bill lost GOP support on the final roll call because its deficit-reduction tag was seen as a "fig leaf" for tax and spending increases.

Bill Failed to Reach Budget Targets

The committee approved its package at the end of two days of closed-door sessions July 23-24.

The estimated $19 billion in deficit reductions for fiscal 1986-88 approved by the committee fell about $2.5 billion short of the $21.5 billion in savings the committee was asked to achieve under the House budget resolution. The final budget resolution instructed the committee to find $21.6 billion in savings. Ultimately, the failure to reach the savings target delayed floor action for more than a month. *(Reconciliation instructions, p. 500)*

Debate over extending the cigarette tax focused primarily on proposals to tie strings to the revenues brought in by keeping the tax at 16 cents.

The amendment to earmark 1 cent of the excise tax for tobacco price supports was introduced by Charles B. Rangel, D-N.Y., chairman of the Ways and Means Subcommittee on Select Revenue Measures. The plan represented a compromise reached between Rangel and certain tobacco-state lawmakers, led by Charlie Rose, D-N.C., chairman of the Agriculture Subcommittee on Tobacco and Peanuts, who had sought a 2-cent set-aside of the tax for tobacco subsidies.

The tax set-aside proposal had put Rose at odds with Senate Agriculture Committee Chairman Jesse Helms, R-N.C., who had proposed the new tobacco price-support program that was added to the Senate reconciliation bill by the Finance Committee.

Some members suggested that Rangel's support for the tobacco set-aside was gauged to help him win support for his expected bid for the job of Democratic House whip in 1987. Rangel said he backed the set-aside as a matter of "fair play and equity," and said it represented a kind of "users' fee" by financing tobacco programs with revenues raised from smokers.

Before approving the bill, the committee rejected, on a tie vote, a proposal by Andrew Jacobs Jr., D-Ind., to earmark 1 cent of the cigarette tax for the trust fund that financed Medicare's hospital insurance program.

The panel also rejected a Gradison amendment to dedicate 7 cents of the tax to support cancer research. Gradison said he offered the proposal to make the point that earmarking revenues would set a bad precedent and represented a "hidden means of jacking up spending."

Medicare Proposals

The proposed Medicare savings were to come from a wide range of changes recommended July 15 by the Ways and Means Subcommittee on Health, including a proposal to limit increases in payments to hospitals to 1 percent in fiscal 1986. Existing law otherwise would allow an increase of more than 5 percent. The administration had proposed regulations to freeze fiscal 1986 hospital reimbursements at 1985 levels.

No change was made in the subcommittee's proposal to require state and local government workers hired after Jan. 1, 1986, to participate in Medicare.

The only major subcommittee recommendation rejected by the full committee was a proposal to require wealthier people to pay more than the elderly poor for coverage under Part B of Medicare, which provided optional insurance coverage for doctors' bills and other non-hospital costs. Part B was financed in part by premiums paid by beneficiaries, under existing law $15.50 a month.

The subcommittee proposal would have charged all beneficiaries a $16 premium, but would have levied a tax on individual participants with annual gross adjusted incomes over $20,000, and couples earning more than $40,000. The change would have been a fundamental shift in Medicare, which had never based charges, benefits or eligibility on beneficiaries' income.

Some members objected to the proposal because they saw it as a new tax and said it would further complicate income tax forms. But Fortney H. "Pete" Stark, D-Calif., chairman of the Health Subcommittee and a backer of the proposal, emphasized that participation in Part B was not mandatory, and that the "tax" was a fee the elderly would voluntarily assume.

Despite stiff opposition by the American Medical Association, the committee accepted a one-year extension of the existing freeze on Medicare payments for most doctors, which was supposed to be lifted Oct. 1. The freeze was to be continued for doctors who did not commit themselves to accepting all Medicare patients on "assignment" — that is, to accept Medicare reimbursement as payment in full and not charge patients additional fees. However, fee increases were to be given to doctors who did agreed to accept what Medicare provided as full payment for all their elderly patients.

Welfare Liberalized

Overriding Republican objections, the committee approved a significant change in AFDC, the principal federal-state welfare program. The proposal from the Ways and Means Subcommittee on Public Assistance required states to provide benefits to needy two-parent families where the principal wage earner was unemployed.

Under existing law states had the option of providing benefits to such families, and 23 states had done so. The committee rejected a GOP amendment to drop the proposal making such coverage mandatory.

The committee also accepted a proposal from the public assistance subcommittee to authorize a new program of state block grants to combat teenage pregnancy, after adopting an amendment barring the use of funds to provide abortion counseling or perform abortions.

Joint Referral of the Ways and Means Bill

In advance of floor action on HR 3128, Ways and Means' package of spending cuts and tax hikes was reviewed and amended by three other committees that shared jurisdiction over elements of the bill:

- The Judiciary Committee Sept. 10 recommended changes in provisions imposing stiff new penalties on hospitals and doctors who failed to provide emergency care for indigent patients (H Rept 99-241, Part III).
- A provision to hike the premium employers pay to finance a pension insurance program was revised Sept. 11 by the Education and Labor Committee, which added provisions overhauling the insurance program to close loopholes (H Rept 99-241, Part II).
- A package of cost-cutting Medicare proposals (HR

3101 — H Rept 99-265, Part I) was approved Aug. 1 by the Energy and Commerce Committee, which also included provisions liberalizing eligibility for Medicaid, the federal-state health care program for the poor. Energy and Commerce did not issue a separate report on HR 3128.

Hospital Emergency Care

Provisions of HR 3128 that set standards for hospitals' emergency care for the indigent fell under the purview of the Judiciary Committee because the bill proposed new criminal and civil penalties for hospitals and doctors that failed to comply with the bill's requirements.

The committee voted to drop the criminal penalties that Ways and Means wanted to impose on irresponsible doctors. But Judiciary members, by a 16-18 vote, rejected an amendment to drop the civil penalties as well.

As approved by both Ways and Means and Judiciary, HR 3128 required hospital emergency rooms to screen patients for medical conditions requiring urgent treatment and to provide stabilizing treatment for those found to be emergency cases. It also set limits on the circumstances in which it is appropriate to transfer emergency patients to other hospitals.

Under HR 3128, hospitals that failed to comply with the bill's requirements could lose Medicare funds and faced civil penalties of up to $25,000 per violation. The bill also gave individuals the right to file civil suits if hospitals failed to provide the required care. Judiciary provided for civil monetary penalties against irresponsible doctors as well as hospitals that failed to comply with the bill.

Pension Insurance

HR 3128 came under review by the Education and Labor Committee because it included a proposal to bail out the PBGC's deficit-ridden pension insurance program, which protected workers against the loss of retirement benefits if their pension plans fold.

Education and Labor shared jurisdiction over pension matters with Ways and Means, which included a provision in HR 3128 to raise the annual premium employers paid PBGC to finance the program from $2.60 per pension plan participant to $8.

However, the administration and key Education and Labor members wanted to tie the premium increase to a broad package of structural changes in the PBGC's insurance program for single-employer pensions. The Education and Labor Subcommittee on Labor-Management Relations Aug. 1 approved such a package (HR 2811) to raise the premium to $8.50 and make it harder for companies to take advantage of the insurance program by passing off their pension debts even if they were solvent.

In considering HR 3128, Education and Labor voted to attach the provisions of HR 2811, with only minor modifications. Key provisions specified that only companies in severe financial distress could terminate underfunded pension plans and pass off responsibility for funding workers' benefits to the PBGC. The bill also required companies that remained in business after terminating a pension plan to contribute 10 percent of their net profits for up to 10 years to make up for funding shortfalls.

House Floor Action: HR 3128

The bill was temporarily blocked on its way to the House floor. On Sept. 17, the Rules Committee refused to grant a rule to guide floor debate, protesting that HR 3128, with its $19.5 billion in three-year savings, was short of the $21.6 billion target the committee was instructed to meet by the budget resolution.

Rules agreed to reconsider the bill Oct. 29, after Ways and Means approved the superfund reauthorization bill with an estimated $3.1 billion in new revenues — even though the revenues were earmarked for the superfund program rather than deficit reduction. Budget Committee Chairman William H. Gray III, in a letter to Rules, said Ways and Means should get credit for the additional revenues in the still-unpassed bill.

The maneuver, which Butler Derrick, D-S.C., a member of Rules and Budget, acknowledged as "unusual," brought Ways and Means' proposed savings to $22.6 billion — $1 billion over target.

Closed Rule Approved

By a party-line 9-4 vote Oct. 29, Rules approved a closed rule (H Res 301) barring floor amendments to HR 3128. Also by party-line votes, members rejected five requests from Republicans to offer amendments.

An amendment proposed by Gradison would have stripped eight provisions that provided $954 million in new spending through fiscal 1988, most of it for AFDC. A second proposal, by Thomas N. Kindness, R-Ohio, would have killed a provision mandating that state and local government employees hired after Jan. 1, 1986, contribute payroll taxes for Medicare coverage. Ohio was one of seven states whose public employees were covered by a state retirement system. Ohioan Tony P. Hall was the only Rules Democrat who supported Kindness' amendment.

The bill, as sent to the floor by Rules, included the text of a new bill (HR 3290) that amalgamated the Medicare program changes agreed to by Ways and Means, Energy and Commerce, and Judiciary.

It also also included Ways and Means' PBGC provisions. Contradictory PBGC provisions proposed by the Education and Labor Committee were included in the companion reconciliation package, HR 3500, which went to the House floor and was passed before HR 3128.

Floor Fight: Frustrated Republicans

Frustrated Republicans took their gripes to the floor when the bill came up Oct. 31. Delbert L. Latta of Ohio, ranking Republican on Budget and a member of Rules, groused, "It's a gag rule." By a close procedural vote, 219-205, with not a single Republican voting in favor, the House indicated support for the rule. The rule then was approved by voice vote. *(Vote 345, p. 108-H)*

During debate on the bill, some members, mostly Republicans, objected to the provision dedicating one penny of the cigarette tax to the tobacco price-support program. Judd Gregg, R-N.H., said the money would be better spent for research on cancer and other smoking-related health problems.

Though Gradison's amendment to strike new spending provisions was not permitted, Republicans singled them out for attention nonetheless. Edward R. Madigan, R-Ill., complained that the deficit-cutting bill was no place to hide spending increases. But Henry A. Waxman, D-Calif., stressed that the bill created no new programs, only "improvements or expansions of existing programs."

Gradison moved to recommit the bill to Ways and Means, with instructions that it delete the additions. His motion failed, 183-238. On a mostly party-line vote, the bill was then passed, 245-174. *(Votes 346, 347, p. 108-H)*

House Committee Action: HR 3500

The House Budget Committee Oct. 3 packaged reconciliation recommendations from most House committees into a bill (HR 3500 — H Rept 99-300) that was projected to save an estimated $61.1 billion over three years. Excluded from the bill were recommendations from Agriculture, which were included in the farm bill, and Ways and Means, which were included in HR 3128.

But although the bottom line of the omnibus measure met savings targets from the budget resolution, some of its provisions to increase spending or start new programs caused trouble later in the Rules Committee and on the House floor.

The panel approved the package by a party-line 18-10 vote. Republicans opposed the bill and complained they had not been consulted before the vote. Democrats retorted that the panel had authority under the 1974 budget act only to combine committees' proposals, not to change them.

After that partisan note, the panel united in grousing over new programs and spending increases included with offsetting spending cuts. Two panels — Public Works and Transportation, and Banking, Finance and Urban Affairs — were singled out for criticism.

Housing Bill Added; Trust Funds Taken Off Budget

What most provoked the ire of some Budget members was the Banking Committee's decision to attach a $14.3 billion housing programs reauthorization (HR 1) to its reconciliation recommendations. The Banking panel more than met its savings target, however, proposing reductions of $12.6 billion in housing programs over three years.

Republicans complained that HR 1 created several new programs, including aid for the homeless and home ownership assistance for moderate-income families. Banking members adopted the gambit of welding their bill onto reconciliation out of frustration at Senate inaction on the housing measure.

Derrick defended the strategy, saying Banking members had made enough cuts in other areas to comply with their deficit-reduction instructions.

Members of both parties opposed a provision inserted by the Public Works Committee — along with recommendations to reduce highway spending — to remove spending from trust funds for federal highways, mass transit and airports from the federal budget, starting in fiscal 1987.

Privately, members said the move was aimed at ending Public Works' regular turf battles with the Appropriations Committee; Public Works, as the panel that authorized transportation programs, would have been able to control spending from the trust funds if they were off-budget, and the Appropriations Committee no longer would have shared authority.

Other Key Committee Recommendations

Other significant committee recommendations included:

- **Guaranteed Student Loans and PBGC.** The House Education and Labor Committee Sept. 19 voted to reduce spending for subsidized loans to college students by about $865 million in fiscal 1986-88. Most of the savings were to be achieved through administrative changes, but the committee agreed to require all applicants for Guaranteed Student Loans to pass a financial needs test in order to qualify.

Under existing law, students from families with more than $30,000 in annual income had to pass a financial needs test to qualify. Extending the needs test to all students was expected to save $335 million over five years.

The committee's recommendations incorporated into HR 3500 included those to overhaul the PBGC that had been dropped from HR 3128 in favor of competing provisions recommended by Ways and Means.

- **Synfuels and Strategic Petroleum Reserve.** The Energy and Commerce Committee Sept. 18 voted to abolish the U.S. Synthetic Fuels Corporation, as part of an effort to cut spending by $5.9 billion over three years.

Members of the committee said quick action to abolish the synfuels corporation was needed to prevent it from spending millions of dollars before Congress finally decided its fate. The committee included a provision designed to void contracts the corporation signed after July 31.

As part of the fiscal 1986 Interior Department appropriations bill (HR 3011), the House had voted July 31 to rescind all but $500 million of $7.4 billion in previously appropriated funds for the corporation. *(Interior appropriations, p. 337)*

The greatest savings approved by the committee came from a proposal to reduce the rate at which oil was purchased for the Strategic Petroleum Reserve. Cutting purchases from 159,000 barrels a day to 35,000 barrels was projected to save $4 billion over three years.

- **Offshore Oil Revenues.** Coastal oil states used the reconciliation process to pull off a coup in the Interior and Insular Affairs Committee Sept. 18, which recommended that they get a greater share of disputed revenues from offshore oil and gas drilling.

Under instructions to come up with $4 billion in savings for fiscal 1986, the Interior panel found the entire amount in an escrow fund set up under section 8(g) of the Outer Continental Shelf Lands Act Amendment of 1978 (PL 95-372). For oil and gas formations that straddled the border between state and federal offshore lands, revenues were to be divided in whatever way agreed on by federal and state governments. While coastal states and the federal government fought over how to split revenues from the drilling, $5.8 billion had accumulated in the escrow fund. *(1978 Almanac p. 668)*

Most states were asking for 37.5 percent and the Reagan administration was offering 16⅔ percent. The fiscal 1986 budget resolution included a compromise of 27 percent for the states.

Before Interior began its reconciliation markup, new squabbling broke out over whether future revenues would be subject to the same 27 percent split, which the coastal states wanted. Interior Chairman Morris K. Udall, D-Ariz., proposed dividing future royalties by the actual amount of oil or gas drained from the common pool. But Jerry Huckaby, D-La., proposed the 27 percent formula, which would give Louisiana $635 million, Texas $424 million, California $375 million, Alabama $73 million, Alaska $56 million, Mississippi $15 million and Florida $30,000.

Huckaby bested Udall in a series of close votes. At one point, his amendment was defeated on a 20-20 tie. But Huckaby rounded up enough votes to win, 22-17, a motion to reconsider the earlier vote. His proposal was then adopted by voice vote.

The following week the Merchant Marine and Fisheries Committee followed suit recommending similar provisions to share receipts from offshore oil leases.

- **Veterans.** The Veterans' Affairs Committee voted

14-12 Sept. 11 to impose a means test on veterans using Veterans Administration (VA) hospitals. Under the proposal, a veteran with an annual income above $19,000 ($25,000 if the veteran had a dependent) would pay $476 a year for medical service. The committee also voted to bill private insurance companies for services to these veterans if they had insurance.

Besides saving money, the means test was aimed at clarifying eligibility for VA health care. Under existing law, veterans over 65 were entitled to free medical care in VA facilities if space was available. Studies by the VA and others had projected that the number of older veterans would triple as World War II veterans turned 65, putting a strain on the system.

To prepare for that, the Reagan administration in its fiscal 1986 budget proposed to limit access to VA facilities by older veterans without service-related injuries to those with annual incomes below $15,000.

House Floor Action: HR 3500

The House Oct. 24 passed HR 3500, after agreeing to a strict rule against most amendments. With comparative ease, the measure passed 228-199 after two days of debate. *(Vote 336, p. 104-H)*

After minor changes were made in the measure, its projected three-year savings was $60.9 billion, slightly less than the amount projected for the committee bill. Additional, and in some cases duplicative, savings were contained in HR 3128, and reauthorization bills for farm programs and superfund.

The major obstacles to House passage of the bill were the housing provisions and a turf battle between the Public Works and Appropriations committees over the highway, airport and mass transit trust funds. The Rules Committee arbitrated some of those differences Oct. 16 when it approved a rule (H Res 296) to guide floor debate, but its decision inevitably angered some members. The losers sought to defeat the rule and, failing that, the bill.

The rule, however, passed 230-190 on Oct. 23, with mixed support from Republicans and from Democrats who had prevailed in the jurisdictional disputes. During the vote, members of the various factions stood at each side of the House chamber, competing vigorously to lobby colleagues as they arrived. *(Vote 332, p. 104-H)*

One Amendment Defeated, Two Adopted

Many Republicans wanted the rule because one of the three permissible amendments, sponsored by Latta, would give them a chance to strike a variety of program additions and expansions from the bill, primarily the housing provisions from HR 1. Latta said his amendment would have saved $3.5 billion more over three years, but Democrats on the Budget Committee disputed that. On Oct. 24, despite a last-minute revision Latta made to pick up support from Public Works and Transportation Committee members, his amendment lost, 209-219. *(Vote 334, p. 104-H)*

Initially, Latta's amendment would have deleted the Public Works-sponsored provision to take the highway, mass transit and airport trust funds out of the budget process. Just before the vote, Latta changed his amendment so it would remove the funds from the budget in fiscal 1989.

Public Works' leaders supported the change as a more acceptable alternative to a pending amendment from Vic Fazio, D-Calif., a member of the Appropriations and Budget panels, to strike the Public Works provision, thus keeping the trust funds in the budget process.

Latta needed unanimous consent to change his amendment. He won it early Oct. 24, when few members were on the floor besides Public Works' chairman, James J. Howard, D-N.J., and its senior Republican, Gene Snyder, Ky. Presiding at the moment was Majority Leader Jim Wright, D-Texas, a former Public Works member and a supporter of taking trust funds out of the budget.

The change angered Budget and Appropriations members. But Wright said afterward, "It is the responsiblity of members to be on the floor to protect their own business."

After the Latta amendment's narrow defeat, the House adopted Fazio's amendment, 222-205. *(Vote 335, p. 104-H)*

Fazio argued that he was not trying to fight the usual Public Works vs. Appropriations battle, but instead was concerned that members were using must-pass legislation like reconciliation to win approval for proposals that could not pass alone.

Despite his disclaimer of a turf fight, Public Works and Appropriations members faced off in floor debate. Public Works members urged the House to remove the funds from the budget. They billed the idea as a "truth-in budgeting" step because the trust funds, which were running surpluses, made the deficit look smaller.

By voice vote, the House approved the only other amendment allowed under the rule. The proposal, sponsored by James J. Florio, D-N.J., inserted the text of a House-passed reauthorization for the Amtrak rail system (HR 2266).

Florio, chairman of the Energy and Commerce Committee's transportation subcommittee, said the amendment was needed to protect the House in conference on reconciliation, because the Senate's companion bill to HR 3500 contained Amtrak provisions.

Points of Order Sustained

Three points of order against the bill were sustained, reducing its total savings from about $61.1 billion to $60.9 billion.

Two involved minor tax-related provisions, to which Ways and Means Chairman Rostenkowski successfully objected, arguing that his committee should have been granted jurisdiction but in this case had not.

The other struck a provision making a $500 million appropriation for an alternative synthetic fuels program within the Department of Energy, which was authorized in a separate section as a replacement for the Synthetic Fuels Corporation. The Appropriations Committee had not been granted jurisdiction for this provision.

Finally, the House rejected by voice vote Latta's motion to send the reconciliation bill back to the Budget Committee and the bill was passed.

Senate Committee Action: S 1730

On Oct. 2, the Senate Budget Committee reported its omnibus budget reconciliation bill (S 1730 — S Rept 99-146). The measure, as required by the 1974 Congressional Budget and Impoundment Control Act (PL 93-344), incorporated without change recommendations to reduce spending from the 11 Senate panels that authorized federal programs. All but one panel met or exceeded the targets Congress set for itself in the fiscal 1986 budget resolution (S Con Res 32). *(Reconciliation targets, p. 500)*

Through cuts in spending levels for a wide range of

programs, and some revenue increases, the bill claimed to reduce the deficit by $21.6 billion in fiscal 1986 and by $85.7 billion over three years, $10.2 billion above the target.

Budget Committee aides said most panels generally followed the budget resolution's policy blueprint for deficit reductions, although many also added amendments not directly related to reconciliation.

The bill was approved 18-0, with four members not voting: Mark Andrews, R-N.D.; Ernest F. Hollings, D-S.C.; Gary Hart, D-Colo., and Howard M. Metzenbaum, D-Ohio.

Major Authorizing Committee Recommendations

The only Senate panel not to achieve its reconciliation target was the Armed Services Committee, which fell $186 million short. Budget Committee Chairman Pete V. Domenici, R-N.M., said he would not challenge Armed Services on the floor for its failure to meet the target.

Armed Services, which was supposed to make $600 million in cuts over three years, not only fell short numerically but also did not approve the long-term structural change in military retirement programs assumed by the budget resolution. Instead, it recommended revisions in military medical programs and a one-month delay in a military pay raise, which achieved savings by delaying the extra cost until the following fiscal year.

Other committees made their recommendations with relatively little difficulty. Among the recommendations were:

- **Offshore Oil Leases and Synfuels.** The Energy and Natural Resources Committee Sept. 26 approved the plan to split offshore oil lease revenues with seven coastal states. Approval came on an 11-7 vote to accept a motion by J. Bennett Johnston, D-La., giving the states 27 percent of past and future rents and royalties. The deal also would give about $4 billion — the amount of the panel's deficit-reduction target — to the Treasury in past revenues that had been held in escrow.

The committee defeated 6-12 an amendment by Metzenbaum to kill the synfuels corporation.

- **Housing and Community Development.** The Senate Banking, Housing and Urban Affairs Committee Oct. 1 recommended $8.2 billion in three-year savings from housing and community development programs.

The savings included reducing operating aid to local public housing authorities by $100 million, and cutting rural housing loan authority by 40 percent from the fiscal 1985 level. Also, the panel agreed to finance public housing construction and modernization with tax-exempt notes, as had been done from 1937 until the tax exemption was questioned in 1984. The change would save money because the government would pay investors lower interest than it would pay on taxable notes.

It also preserved the Community Development Block Grant loan guarantee program, which the budget resolution assumed would be eliminated. However, the recommendation would achieve the same saving by requiring that funds to cover defaults came from private insurance, rather than from the Federal Financing Bank.

Besides the savings recommendations, the panel voted to change the funding formula of the Urban Development Action Grant (UDAG) program, which provided money on a competitive basis to spur investment in economically distressed areas. Under the change, funds would be distributed from two pots: two-thirds of the grants would be awarded to the most economically and physically distressed cities, and one-third would be awarded according to the quality of the project, including the number of jobs created and the amount of private investment attracted.

Senators, knowing that the House Banking, Finance and Urban Affairs Committee had included in its reconciliation recommendations provisions from a bill (HR 1) to reauthorize housing programs, drew up their own housing bill and scheduled a markup Sept. 24. But several members objected to parts of the bill and proposed three dozen amendments.

Chairman Jake Garn, R-Utah, saying he was not certain of the budget and policy implications of the amendments, adjourned the markup and decided to send reconciliation instructions to the Budget Committee without a housing authorization.

- **Student Loans, Walsh-Healey and PBGC.** The Senate Labor and Human Resources Committee Sept. 27 approved recommendations that would save $1.7 billion in outlays over three years by trimming student loan spending and cutting labor costs under federal contracts.

Most savings from the Guaranteed Student Loan program would be achieved through administrative changes, not through new eligibility restrictions on students. The recommendations also included changes in the Walsh-Healey Public Contracts Act to repeal the requirement that overtime rates be paid for workdays exceeding eight hours. Eliminating the requirement, which applied to persons working on certain types of government contracts, was expected to reduce outlays by $865 million over three years. Similar provisions became part of the defense authorization bill. *(Defense authorization, p. 138)*

Other provisions of the Labor Committee's package would overhaul the financially ailing pension insurance program run by the federal Pension Benefit Guaranty Corporation and impose stiff new penalties on hospitals that refused to provide emergency medical care for people lacking insurance or the money to pay their bills. The "anti-dumping" provisions were drawn from legislation (S 1615) introduced by Edward M. Kennedy of Massachusetts, ranking Democrat on the committee.

Major Fight in Finance

Proposals forwarded Sept. 20 by voice vote from the Finance Committee to trim some $38 billion from the deficit over three years — $22 billion in outlay cuts and $16 billion in new revenues — accounted for the largest share of the Senate bill's savings. But the committee also added two of the most controversial provisions, the manufacturers' tax to pay for the superfund program and the revised tobacco price-support system.

Most of the committee's recommendations were easily approved Sept. 17.

The committee voted to bring in $5 billion in new revenues through the payroll tax that financed Medicare, by requiring state and local government employees for the first time to be covered by Medicare. The committee also approved proposals expected to cut projected spending for Medicare by $12 billion over three years.

And the panel projected $8.5 billion in savings in 1987-88 by eliminating federal revenue sharing with local governments, which was scheduled to expire at the end of fiscal 1986.

The panel added the superfund tax provisions with barely any debate. At the time the Senate was debating on the floor a bill to reauthorize superfund, and the tax provisions were also part of that bill.

But action on the cigarette tax and the tobacco program Sept. 18-20 was more difficult.

Lawmakers from tobacco-producing states had vigorously opposed extending the cigarette tax. So to ease the political pain of its almost certain passage, Agriculture Committee Chairman Helms and other tobacco-state senators persuaded Finance members to include a bill (S 1418) to revamp the tobacco subsidy program.

The motion to piggyback the tobacco price-support provisions on the reconciliation bill was made by Dole, a member of both the Finance and Agriculture committees. The provisions were a product of negotiations with cigarette manufacturers and tobacco growers, and had bipartisan support from tobacco-state senators. But critics regarded the proposal as a bailout that provided more help for cigarette companies than tobacco farmers.

The measure would lower price support levels while reducing huge surpluses accumulating in government warehouses and maintained at the expense of growers. Dole's amendment also would impose new taxes on "smokeless tobacco" — 8 cents per pound on chewing tobacco and 24 cents a pound on snuff.

Dole and Packwood portrayed the inclusion of the tobacco provisions as a quid pro quo for tobacco-state senators' agreement to the cigarette tax extension. However, other members countered that the cigarette tax would easily be enacted without the support of tobacco-state members.

Indeed, an effort to double the cigarette tax, although defeated, received a surprisingly strong show of support. An amendment by John H. Chafee, R-R.I., to hike the tax to 32 cents was rejected on an 8-10 vote.

The maneuver also drew howls of protest from Democrats who said Finance was in no position to judge the merits of a major agriculture bill. The move initially drew fire from David L. Boren, D-Okla., a Finance member who also sat on Agriculture, where members had been struggling over a bill to reauthorize farm programs. But Boren dropped his opposition after Helms allowed the Agriculture Committee Dec. 19 to report a Democratic-sponsored farm bill.

The victory came Sept. 20, when Finance approved Dole's amendment by a show of hands, with only four senators voting against it — Chafee, Bill Bradley, D-N.J., Daniel Patrick Moynihan, D-N.Y., and Max Baucus, D-Mont.

After adopting the Dole package, the committee rejected, 8-9, a Bradley amendment to increase the tax to 20 cents. The committee also rejected a Chafee amendment to set the "smokeless" tobacco taxes far higher than Dole proposed — $1.20 a pound for snuff and 40 cents a pound for chewing tobacco.

The committee also voted Sept. 20 to wrap in another bill (S 1544) to overhaul the Trade Adjustment Assistance program, after adopting an amendment by William V. Roth Jr., R-Del., that would change the way the program was financed. The amendment called for levying a small fee on all imports. The fee would be capped at 1 percent, but it was expected that far less would be needed — less than one-tenth of a percent — to finance the $200 million-a-year program.

Senate Floor Action: S 1730

The Senate overwhelmingly approved its bill to reduce the deficit by $85.7 billion over three years, without making any of the changes the Reagan administration had demanded in return for the president's approval.

The 625-page package was approved 93-6 Nov. 14, after a month of stop-and-start debate. It included several provisions to which the president objected, including three taxes: extension of the cigarette excise tax and two new levies — import duties to finance Trade Adjustment Assistance and the new superfund tax. The administration also opposed the proposed tobacco price support program and the provision giving coastal states a share of offshore oil lease revenues. The cigarette tax and offshore oil provisions had also been adopted by the House.

After the Senate vote, Domenici acknowledged the possibility of a veto, but he expressed hope that Reagan would "not ignore the savings" when making a decision. And the margin of victory on passage was far more than the 67 votes needed to override a veto.

Senate Republican leaders made no public effort to revise the bill to Reagan's liking. Instead, it was Metzenbaum, one of the Senate's most liberal members, who led the fight against the oil-revenues and tobacco program provisions.

No senator tried to halve the cigarette tax, as Reagan wanted, but two unsuccessful attempts were made in October to raise the tax. As for the import and manufacturers' taxes, administration-supported challenges by two Republicans were easily swatted down in debate Nov. 12.

Floor Action: Round One

Though the measure came to the floor Oct. 15, action was repeatedly delayed so members could debate appropriations and other bills. Nevertheless, Majority Leader Dole allowed the clock to run on the bill, even when members were not on the floor, eating up half the 20 hours provided. The 1974 Budget Act limited Senate floor action on reconciliation bills, primarily to prevent filibusters.

In the first real debate on reconciliation Oct. 22-23, members approved several minor amendments and rejected two others that would have raised taxes on tobacco products.

As he had in committee, Chafee proposed Oct. 22 to increase the cigarette tax from 16 cents a pack to 24 cents, raising $4 billion more over three years. Packwood objected, citing the deal that linked the 16-cent tax to the new tobacco price-support program. Chafee unavailingly countered by citing the health costs of cigarette smoking to both individuals and government medical programs.

By a 66-30 vote, the Senate supported a parliamentary motion against Chafee's proposal. That cleared the way for Domenici to seek a point of order against the amendment and it was ruled non-germane. *(Vote 240, p. 45-S)*

Next, George J. Mitchell, D-Maine, offered an amendment to delay for one year a provision requiring state and local government employees to pay taxes toward the government's Medicare health program for the elderly. To make up the $2.2 billion cost to the Treasury in fiscal 1986, Mitchell proposed a 20-cents-a-pack cigarette tax for three years.

Mitchell's amendment was divided for the vote. The first part on Medicare coverage was tabled, or killed, by a 66-25 vote, and the second part, increasing cigarette taxes, lost by voice vote. *(Vote 241, p. 45-S)*

'Extraneous Provisions'

While the Senate debated amendments to the deficit-reduction package, Dole, Domenici, Minority Leader Robert C. Byrd, D-W.Va., and Lawton Chiles of Florida, ranking Democrat on the Budget Committee, met privately to decide how to deal with what they called "extraneous provisions" in the measure. The list included 129 items, ranging from minor program changes to the tobacco price-support program.

Both the Republican and Democratic leaders were intent on somehow separating the extraneous matter for debate and votes, to alleviate the precedent of unrelated matter piggybacking on the important reconciliation bill. Dole reportedly wanted any debate on the extraneous provisions to count against the 20-hour limit for reconciliation debate, while Democrats wanted up to 15 hours more.

Then on Oct. 24, senators from textile-manufacturing states, joined by those from states that made shoes, tried to attach an amendment limiting textile, apparel and shoe imports. By votes of 38-55 and 57-39, sponsors of the amendment overcame objections that the measure was not germane. Then a procedural vote of 54-42 indicated majority support for it. *(Votes 251, 252, 253, p. 46-S)*

"This is just another good reason [for the president] to veto the whole reconciliation bill," Dole said, warning that attaching the textile amendment would open the gate for further amendments on the volatile issues of civil rights, abortion, prayer in school and line-item veto.

Byrd then won, 96-0, approval of an amendment to restrict amendments to reconciliation bills in the future. Not only was the budget process threatened, he argued, but senators' historic right to filibuster also was endangered. *(Vote 254, p. 46-S)*

The Byrd amendment, which applied only to Senate floor action, was cosponsored by Dole, Domenici, Chiles and Ted Stevens, R-Alaska. It would require a three-fifths vote, rather than a majority vote, to overturn a ruling that an amendment to a reconciliation bill was extraneous or not germane and was retained in conference.

After the Senate agreed to the Byrd amendment, Dole pulled S 1730 from the floor, along with its pending textile amendment.

Round Two: Finishing Up

The Senate finally completed action Nov. 12 and 14, after a two-week stall provoked by the import-limiting amendment. A compromise Nov. 7 allowed the import measure to be passed separately, clearing the way for final action on S 1730. *(Trade protection, p. 255)*

When the Senate resumed debate on the deficit-reduction bill Nov. 12, just one hour and 12 minutes remained for debate and amendments. By noon, all time had run out except for that required to vote on numerous amendments.

For weeks, Senate leaders had tried to negotiate an agreement to provide additional debate time. But such a move required unanimous consent, and various members objected.

Some would not agree to a time extension that allowed debate on two Metzenbaum amendments attacking the bill's proposed new tobacco program, while Metzenbaum would not consent to an agreement that did not provide for his amendments. Coastal-state senators objected to a pending amendment from Metzenbaum and Daniel J. Evans, R-Wash., opposing the offshore oil revenues settlement.

Chiles and other Democrats objected to debate on a proposed amendment by Mack Mattingly, R-Ga., that would empower the president to veto individual items in an appropriations bill. And some Democrats opposed extra time if Helms were permitted to offer amendments limiting food stamps.

The Senate finally reached an agreement Nov. 14 permitting debate on 11 amendments, including Metzenbaum's. The impasse was broken the day before when Metzenbaum, angry at members' refusal to allow him debate time, pointed out that he would get it eventually. Before final passage, he noted, the Senate bill would have to be amended onto the House-passed bill since the Constitution did not allow the Senate to send revenue-raising bills to the House. At that point, he explained, the Senate bill would no longer be subject to limits on debate time for reconciliation bills.

Amendments Rejected

Though the Senate considered about four dozen amendments and adopted many of those, few major changes were made in the package. Some changes increased spending slightly, but Domenici said the net result was $94 million in additional three-year savings.

The Senate rejected several proposed changes in the bill. It voted:

- To support the bill's new tax on imports to help finance Trade Adjustment Assistance. By voice vote Nov. 12, the Senate rejected an amendment, by Phil Gramm, R-Texas, to kill the tax. Gramm argued, as the administration had, that it would violate international trade agreements.
- To support the superfund tax on manufacturers. Helms, with administration support, proposed a "sense of the Senate" amendment calling for a new funding source, but it failed Nov. 12, 32-66. *(Vote 296, p. 52-S)*
- To endorse a provision giving seven coastal states 27 percent of all future rents, bonuses and royalties from oil production in a three-mile offshore strip straddling the boundaries between state and federal lands. The provision, which would settle a longstanding state-federal legal dispute, also would give states $1.8 billion of $6.8 billion that had accumulated in an escrow fund pending resolution of the dispute.

Evans and Metzenbaum proposed dropping most royalties from the agreement, and requiring that lease and bonus revenues to states be pro-rated according to the portion of an oil field tract that lied in the three-mile zone. They echoed administration complaints that the bill would provide "a massive windfall" to coastal states, but their amendment was tabled, or killed, 54-45, Nov. 14. *(Vote 308, p. 53-S)*

- To retain a provision allowing the major cigarette companies to buy surplus federal stocks of tobacco at discounts of up to 90 percent. The industry-backed provision also would lower federal price supports for tobacco growers. Those prices had been so high that many manufacturers imported tobacco, forcing the government to buy and store the domestic crop.

Metzenbaum proposed to delete the provision, citing administration figures that the industry "bailout" would cost $1.1 billion. But Dole countered that lower price supports would save $235 million over three years, and his motion to table Metzenbaum's amendment passed, 66-33, Nov. 14. *(Vote 310, p. 54-S)*

Afterward, the Senate also rejected a more limited Metzenbaum amendment to strike the bill's exemption from antitrust laws for manufacturers who had agreed to buy the discounted tobacco. The vote to table was 57-42. *(Vote 311, p. 54-S)*

- To keep a provision allowing large, multinational firms to deduct research expenses from income subject to U.S. taxes, even if the research related to the firm's foreign operations, until Aug. 1, 1986. Metzenbaum proposed to strike the provision, saying it would cost $287 million in lost tax revenues, but his amendment was tabled, 53-32, Nov. 12. *(Vote 293, p. 52-S)*

- To maintain a provision imposing sanctions on states with high error rates in their food stamp programs, which would raise an estimated $900 million over three years. Evans proposed a two-year moratorium on sanctions, but his amendment was tabled, 52-45, Nov. 13. *(Vote 306, p. 53-S)*
- To reject an amendment from Dale Bumpers, D-Ark., allowing Medicare coverage for liver transplants in patients 18 or older. Existing federal policy limited coverage to children. Domenici argued the change would cost $125 million a year, and his motion to table Bumpers' proposal succeeded, 51-47, Nov. 14. Bumpers then won voice-vote passage of a "sense of the Senate" provision directing the Department of Health and Human Services to consider extending coverage to adults. *(Vote 312, p. 54-S)*
- To retain a provision increasing certain Medicare reimbursements for nursing homes that changed ownership. Metzenbaum and John Glenn, D-Ohio, tried to strike the provision, in order to save $70 million over three years. Their amendment was tabled, 71-27, Nov. 14. *(Vote 313, p. 54-S)*

Amendments Accepted

The Senate did agree to some changes, including:

- A provision, added by voice vote Nov. 12, that would make permanent a 1984 law (PL 98-363) reducing federal highway funds to states that did not set 21 as the minimum drinking age. Sponsor Frank R. Lautenberg, D-N.J., said some states had raised the drinking age, but timed their laws to expire when the federal sanctions were supposed to, on Oct. 1, 1988.
- An amendment, by Dole, striking a provision that would have reduced mail subsidies for political groups. It was adopted by voice vote Nov. 12.
- Two amendments striking provisions that would have required federal benefits for energy assistance and job training to be counted as income when determining food stamp eligibility. Dole tried to table an amendment to strike the energy assistance provision, sponsored by Robert T. Stafford, R-Vt., saying the provision would save $165 million over three years. His motion lost, 37-59, and the Senate adopted Stafford's amendment, 60-37, on Nov. 12. *(Votes 294, 295, p. 52-S)*

The job-training amendment was adopted by voice vote Nov. 13.

- A limit on proposed Customs Service user fees. The bill would have imposed charges of $5 per truck or train car, and $25 per private aircraft or boat, each time they entered the United States. By voice vote Nov. 12, the Senate adopted an amendment by Dennis DeConcini, D-Ariz., to cap the fees at $100 a year for trucks and freight cars, and $500 annually for private boats and aircraft.
- A provision, added Nov. 12 by voice vote, requiring that the Social Security trust fund be reimbursed about $1.3 billion, for interest lost because the Treasury, since 1984, had sold $30.5 billion of the trust fund's government securities.
- Addition of a provision increasing coverage under Medicaid for respirator-dependent persons and certain foster children, and for demonstration projects on home-care alternatives for the elderly.

The provision, by John Heinz, R-Pa., initially was struck down on a point of order by Domenici, who said it was not germane and would cost $225 million. After some redrafting, the amendment was offered again and Domenici's motion to table it failed, 25-73. The amendment was adopted by voice vote Nov. 12. *(Vote 297, p. 52-S)*

Conference Action

Following Senate passage of S 1730 Nov. 14, the text of the Senate bill was substituted for that of HR 3128 in order to get the bills to conference. Conference action was delayed, however, by the Thanksgiving recess and congressional attention on Gramm-Rudman-Hollings. On Dec. 3, the House Rules Committee reported a measure (H Res 330) to combine the texts of HR 3500 and the House version of HR 3128, and to request a conference on the latter bill. The House by voice vote adopted the resolution Dec. 5 and the conference began the next day.

Even though the possibility of an impasse over the superfund tax loomed from the start of conference negotiations — as had other objections to the bill — by the end of the first week about two dozen of the 31 conference subgroups had settled, and final agreement looked possible.

It had been relatively easy to reach accord on most issues, including reduced spending for student loans, small businesses and veterans, and reauthorization for six years of Trade Adjustment Assistance. Conferees agreed to a Senate proposal to finance Trade Adjustment Assistance with a new fee on imports that was strongly opposed by the administration.

Conferees also agreed without much difficulty to accept the Senate's new tobacco price-support program — dropping in the process a House provision that would have earmarked one penny of the cigarette tax to pay for the existing tobacco price-support program. And they moved rapidly toward agreement on conflicting provisions concerning the federal pension insurance program and the Medicaid health program that served the poor.

But the subgroup of conferees from Finance and Ways and Means snagged Dec. 13 on the superfund tax issue, when Rostenkowski suggested dropping the tax from the bill and Packwood objected.

Pressure to finish built with each day as more members began leaving for the holidays. By midweek, even Domenici had left town, though he returned Dec. 20 to try to salvage the bill.

Before going, Domenici had predicted conferees would soon agree. He indicated senators might drop the superfund tax to get a bill, particularly in light of Reagan's opposition.

Veto Threats

Reagan's advisers had listed numerous grounds for a veto, including the manufacturers' tax, extension of the cigarette tax, and the tax on imports to fund trade adjustment.

The administration also criticized the proposed split of offshore oil revenues as a multibillion-dollar giveaway to coastal states, and complained that both the House and Senate bills claimed inflated savings from cuts that were either "phony" or else duplicated in existing laws or administrative rules.

Packwood dismissed the administration's veto threats, and he refused to budge from the superfund tax. Without it, he said Dec. 18, "there will be no reconciliation." During conference meetings, Packwood repeatedly chastised Reagan aides for opposing the tax without proposing alternatives. And he rejected ideas, like the House-passed superfund bill, that would rely on general Treasury revenues and thus add to the deficit.

Opponents of the manufacturers' tax, including Rostenkowski, said the question of financing and expanding superfund should be left to a separate House-Senate conference on the program in 1986. But Packwood said the reconciliation conference, where he enjoyed majority support among both House and Senate negotiators, was his only hope for enacting the manufacturers' tax.

Senate Conferees Offer a Compromise

In his subgroup, Packwood was in control of the votes on the tax issue, and Rostenkowski and his Ways and Means allies did not attend a scheduled conference meeting Dec. 18. Instead, he abruptly convened Ways and Means to mark up a bill temporarily extending the cigarette tax and other programs.

With Rostenkowski and other Ways and Means members missing, Packwood offered a Senate compromise on the various provisions the group was supposed to settle. His offer retained the Senate's superfund tax, at a level sufficient to fund a $7.5 billion program over five years. By comparison, the House-passed superfund bill called for a $10 billion program, and Reagan wanted $5.3 billion.

The Senate's main concession involved a provision mandating that state and local government employees be covered by Medicare, thereby requiring them and their employers to contribute to the program through payroll taxes.

The Senate-passed bill had applied to all public employees, raising $4.7 billion over three years. But the House bill pertained only to workers hired after Jan. 1, 1986, for savings of $4.2 billion less.

Packwood had insisted that all workers be covered, arguing that it was only fair since nearly all would be eligible for Medicare benefits anyway by virtue of marriage to a beneficiary. But his compromise moved the effective date from Oct. 1, 1986, to July 1, 1987, giving states more time to prepare for the added costs.

The conference did not vote on the compromise and Packwood said he never talked to Rostenkowski about it; Ways and Means staff later told him their boss did not want to meet, indicating it was not acceptable.

A Second Compromise

The next day, Dec. 19, the conference met and Packwood made a second offer. Again, it kept the superfund tax but receded to the House on the Medicare issue. The offer also called for dropping a House-passed program to help poor teenage parents. Packwood, a staunch supporter of a woman's right to an abortion, opposed anti-abortion language that House conferees had added to avoid a floor challenge from anti-abortion members in the House.

Ways and Means conferees huddled privately and voted 9-4 for the offer with its superfund tax. Afterward, Rostenkowski said if he had blocked the agreement any longer, "I'd be blamed for hanging up the conference." Grinning, he added, "You've got to lose some." However, he vowed to push for defeat of the superfund tax on the floor — even if it meant killing the bill.

Final Floor Action

Soon after the conference concluded Dec. 19, the Senate gave its 78-1 approval. Only Barry Goldwater, R-Ariz., voted no. *(Vote 379, p. 64-S)*

The House Rules Committee later the same day approved a rare sort of rule (H Res 349) for consideration of the conference report. If passed, it meant rejection of the agreement and approval of an amendment that was, in effect, the conference agreement stripped of the Senate superfund tax. The House vote was 205-151 for the rule. *(Vote 436, p. 138-H)*

Quickly, the Senate by voice vote rejected the House proposal, added the superfund tax and sent the measure back.

At about 11 p.m., restive House Republicans began pushing to adjourn, fearful that Democratic leaders would give in to their fellow Democrats in the Senate on the tax. Trying to put responsibility for the $74 billion deficit-cutting package in the senators' hands, "It's their problem," Minority Whip Trent Lott, Miss., said. A GOP motion to adjourn was defeated first by a division vote of 61-110 and then a motion to table (kill) the concurrent resolution was agreed to by a recorded vote of 229-107. A motion to adjourn subsequently was adopted by voice vote on Dec. 20.*(Vote 438, p. 138-H)*

Then Budget Committee Chairman Gray moved to accept the Senate version. Gray's motion was easily defeated, 137-211, and the House voted a second time, by voice vote, to reject the Senate position and return the measure without the tax yet again. *(Vote 439, p. 138-H)*

"How many times do we have to tell the other body that we do not want a [manufacturers' tax]?" asked Latta, the senior Republican on Budget.

Expiring Provisions

Midnight passed without extension of the cigarette tax, Trade Adjustment Assistance, railroad unemployment and Medicare laws that were all due to expire. Lapse of the cigarette tax was especially crucial, since some states had laws to trigger tobacco tax hikes if the federal tax fell to 8 cents.

Before midnight, Rostenkowski had unsuccessfully tried to win House passage of three bills (HR 3992-94) extending the four provisions and a dozen other tax laws. Republicans led opposition to the rule (H Res 350) for the first bill, saying the bill would not only extend current law but also change it. The vote for the rule was 210-142, but that was short of the two-thirds vote needed. *(Vote 437, p. 138-H)*

Instead, the House by voice vote passed a bill (HR 4006) extending the 16 provisions, unchanged from current laws. Then the Senate rejected all but the four extensions covering cigarette taxes, Medicare pay freezes, trade adjustment and railroad unemployment, and sent the amended bill back to the House.

The volleying continued later in the day Dec. 20. The House returned the tax-extension bill to the Senate, with only the cigarette and Medicare provisions. At day's end, as one of its last acts after returning the reconciliation bill to conference, the Senate agreed to the two temporary extensions. *(Box, p. 502)* ∎

AGRICULTURE

CQ

Agriculture

In a year when nearly all federal farm programs were due to expire, the Reagan administration stepped up its running dispute with Congress over the federal role in agriculture.

The 1985 farm bill debate opened with philosophical questions on whether the government, after 50 years of protecting farmers from the vagaries of production and price, was indeed responsible for their financial well-being. But this wide-scale discourse soon gave way to closely fought arguments among competing special interests. The congressional agenda eventually ground down to a paralyzing, session-long contest of partisan gamesmanship.

At issue was long-term food and nutrition policy as written in enabling legislation of 1933 and 1949, and as revised and reauthorized at least every four years since then — most recently in 1981. Administration officials and members of Congress saw 1985 as their best (and possibly last) opportunity to chart a new course for agriculture through the rest of the century. There was a rather broad consensus that the current policy was not working despite the government's record subsidies to the rural economy since 1982. But agreement on how to correct that policy proved elusive, for political as well as ideological reasons.

At stake were the hearts, minds and pocketbooks of 3 percent of the nation's population who lived and worked on farms, but who were viewed, nonetheless, as a pivotal voting bloc by members of both Democratic and Republican parties. Democrats, in particular, made farm issues an early rallying point for the upcoming 1986 congressional elections, when 22 GOP Senate seats — including seven from bedrock farm states — would be up for re-election. Republicans, who held a tenuous 53-47 majority in the Senate, were torn immediately between the conservative mandate of fiscal responsibility and a more populist appeal to increase farmers' benefits.

Austere Blueprint

President Reagan, ever conscious of his political base in the Midwestern breadbasket, had waited until after the November 1984 elections to offer his own austere blueprint for long-term farm policy. His proposal was openly designed to phase out many New Deal-era programs and begin immediately to apply his "free-market" philosophy to an industry that had relied greatly on friendly government intervention since the Great Depression.

But a continually worsening economic climate in the Farm Belt — and its potentially ominous repercussions for Republicans in 1986 — combined instead to put the White House and the GOP-controlled Senate on the defensive through most of 1985. Farm Belt Republicans began defecting in significant numbers from party ranks on the first major piece of farm legislation to come before the Senate, an emergency credit measure cleared in early March that was designed to help debt-ridden farmers through another spring planting season.

The administration claimed that the credit bill was nothing more than an unwarranted bailout for bankers who had made unwise loans to farmers during the boom years of agriculture in the late 1970s. David A. Stockman, director of the Office of Management and Budget, railed against that notion at a Feb. 5 hearing of the Senate Budget Committee: "For the life of me, I cannot figure out why the taxpayers of this country have the responsibility to go in and refinance bad debt that was willingly incurred by consenting adults."

But farm-state Republicans had a hard time defending that view, particularly after the entire South Dakota legislature flew to Washington Feb. 26 to press Congress for more farm benefits. It was an unprecedented and well-televised visit by a predominately Republican group, highlighting intensive lobbying by large contingents from other Midwestern legislatures, including those of North Dakota, Nebraska and Kansas.

Reagan eventually vetoed the emergency credit bill as too costly, but eight Senate Republicans, by voting for the measure, served early notice that the administration would find few friends for many of its more drastic policy reforms.

Democrats, for their part, took no time in laying claim to farm issues in an effort to show they were more concerned than Republicans about the fate of American farmers. House Agriculture Committee members staged hearings in the spring with movie stars Jane Fonda, Jessica Lange and Sissy Spacek, on the pretext that the latter two had special insights on the issue after appearing in "Country" and "The River," films that evoked a gritty image of family farmers struggling to survive against the twin nemeses of big business and bad weather.

Many Republicans criticized the hearings as blatant, political hype, foisted on Congress by electioneering Democrats. Yet by the end of the summer the political climate surrounding the farm bill debate had gotten so hot that many GOP senators joined their Democratic colleagues in another "media event" with country music recording artists Willie Nelson, Neil Young and John Conlee, organizers of a benefit concert called "Farm Aid." The musicians came to Capitol Hill to ask senators for "advice" on how to spend the millions of dollars the Sept. 22 concert eventually would raise for destitute farm families.

"No one's talking about how the Farm Aid concert is being politicized," noted a Republican staff member at the time, reflecting a concern among Republican leaders that the farm policy debate had gotten further and further away from their original agenda of fiscal restraint. Members of both parties were being drawn into a political cyclone of having to prove the extent of their commitment to farmers.

"Sooner or later," complained Senate Majority Leader

Robert Dole, R-Kan., "we're going to have to decide who's the self-appointed protector of the farmer."

Legislative Gridlock

Complicating the usual political pressure points, however, was an unusually stark budget picture for the entire federal government. In an era of rising federal deficits, traditional methods of crafting federal farm policy no longer worked. Members simply could not afford to tally up requests from various special-interest lobbies and fashion farm programs to cover each group's particular desires.

Faced with competing requests for more money, Congress and the major farm lobby organizations eventually worked themselves into a legislative gridlock. Also working against them was the paradoxical alliance between the conservative White House and urban liberals who resented any effort to pump more money into agriculture at the expense of benefits for the poor.

Economic realities tossed two further problems into the web. History had proven that the government could not keep propping up prices for domestic farm products while foreign producers undercut U.S. goods in overseas markets. At the same time, however, any action to reduce farm prices might cut sharply into farm incomes, handicapping many struggling farmers at a time when their cash was already low and their credit was drying up.

The Catch-22 for farm-state legislators was obvious from the start. Members of the House and Senate Agriculture committees struggled for the better part of the year to come up with a new farm subsidy formula that would at once lower farm prices, bolster farmers' incomes and cut government expenses. Stuffing all three into one package proved impossible. A sense of helplessness pervaded both panels as members learned just before the August recess that their nearly completed bills came nowhere close to meeting the stringent spending requirements set down in each chamber's budget resolutions for fiscal 1986.

Not until December would the stalemate resolve itself in legislative compromise — a new, five-year reauthorization bill for most of the farm and nutrition programs run by the federal government, and a companion bill to shore up the nation's huge, agricultural lending network known as the Farm Credit System. The White House eventually caved in on many of its ideological points as well as its stated spending limits. Democrats, in turn, had to concede that farm incomes could not be subsidized forever at the existing high rates. When the final deal was cut, however, it served mainly to postpone the expected political backlash in farm country for some time later in 1986.

—*By David Rapp*

Farm Bill Granted a Limited 'Win' to All Sides

President Reagan signed a $169.2 billion farm and nutrition measure (HR 2100 — PL 99-198) Dec. 23, defusing a political powder keg that had threatened to explode under Congress all year.

The president signed the five-year bill despite his vocal reservations about many of its key tenets, and despite the estimated $52 billion three-year cost for the price- and income-support sections of the bill. He had threatened to veto any bill over $50 billion.

Reagan's ultimate blessing for HR 2100, announced Dec. 19 by Agriculture Secretary John R. Block, brought the tense standoff between the White House and Congress to a classic "win-win" conclusion: The results pleased few in Congress or the administration, but, more important politically, they angered fewer.

"It didn't leave here as a partisan document," said Senate Majority Leader Robert Dole, R-Kan., moments after House and Senate negotiators Dec. 14 unanimously approved a compromise conference agreement.

The administration, which fought all year to cut the tether that connected farmers and the federal government, won a bill that immediately lowered basic price supports and promised within five years to reduce by half the annual federal outlays for agriculture.

An election-conscious Congress, swayed by powerful sentiment for struggling "family farmers," won a bill that would subsidize farmers' incomes at record levels for at least three years — and two congressional elections.

Both chambers approved the measure in quick order Dec. 18. The conference report (H Rept 99-447) was adopted by the House on a 325-96 vote; Senate action came hours later on a 55-38 vote. *(Vote 431, p. 136-H; vote 378, p. 64-S)*

Divisive Pattern Scrapped

The wide margin of approval in the House, coupled with the emergence of a bipartisan alliance voting for the bill in the Senate, represented a sharp break from the divisive pattern set in both chambers early in the summer that continued through the final conference negotiations.

For the Senate, where the GOP majority hung in the balance with 22 seats up for re-election in 1986, the bill provided farm-state Republicans a measure of distance from the administration's anti-farm image back home.

In the House, Democrats won assurance that farm policy would continue on the path of protective federal intervention begun 50 years earlier in President Franklin D. Roosevelt's New Deal.

However, that course was far from certain over the five-year life of the bill, depending on the administration's use of broad new discretionary powers to set price-support rates for major crops, and the ultimate success of a number of experimental policies spelled out for key commodity programs.

Enactment of the bill defused, if only momentarily, the partisan politics surrounding farm debates, and, congressional leaders said, granted the U.S. farmer a little room to survive the worst economic depression in agriculture since the 1930s.

"The program is compassionate," Block said. "It may give some farmers in trouble a chance to recover. But at the same time, agriculture will be moving in the direction we want it to be moving . . . toward a market-based economy," he said.

For the most part, members of Congress expressed the same notion with a slightly different twist. "The truth is," summed up one Democratic conferee, "we got the money, and the secretary got a little bit of principle."

Cost Breakdown

HR 2100 contained a variety of farm programs expected to cost $100.6 billion over the next five years, according to Agriculture Department estimates. Food assistance programs, including food stamps, were expected to cost another $68.6 billion. *(Food stamps, p. 305)*

One-third of the farm programs' cost came from the Farmers Home Administration and other agriculture credit agencies ($10.2 billion over five years), and agricultural export, research and conservation programs ($21 billion).

As was typical, however, the bulk of the cost stemmed from the price- and income-support programs for major crops, such as wheat, corn, cotton, rice and soybeans. Their price tag was projected to total $69.4 billion over five years.

The Agriculture Department's expected yearly cost breakdown for price and income supports was $16.6 billion in fiscal 1986, $15.7 billion in 1987, $16.5 billion in 1988, $12.9 billion in 1989 and $7.7 billion in 1990.

Support programs in the expired four-year farm bill (PL 97-98) cost $54.7 billion over the life of that measure, including $16.8 billion in fiscal 1985. Before 1981, price- and income-support programs averaged less than $3 billion a year. *(Previous farm bill, 1981 Almanac p. 535)*

Grappling for Benefits

While partisan politics became an overriding component of farm policy debate in 1985, budget reduction also was a pervasive theme throughout the year, particularly for the key commodity groups that were forced to grapple for dwindling federal benefits.

Both House and Senate Agriculture committees spent months trying to whittle the programs to a size that would take care of the special commodity interests of each member and still cut costs enough to ward off a congressional revolt against farm programs by urban members.

The administration, often allying itself with urban Democrats, fired several unsuccessful broadsides at some of the more treasured farm benefits, such as high price supports for dairy, sugar, honey and peanuts, and unlimited income subsidies.

But the Democratic House leadership made the package reported by the Agriculture Committee a leadership issue, arguing that every piece of the farm mosaic had to remain intact to put added pressure on Reagan and the Republican Party.

The farm coalition held fast and won all but one key vote: an alternative plan to let farmers themselves vote on strict production controls for their crops. As it turned out, that was the one issue on which the House leadership itself was divided, and it was summarily defeated on the floor before the bill was passed Oct. 8.

Senate GOP Defections

Partisan emotions were much more intense — and chaotic — in the Senate, particularly after farm-state Re-

Organic Farming Study

Organic farming, which utilized no chemical fertilizers or pesticides, was to be studied as an alternative to conventional farming techniques under legislation that had languished in Congress for years but cleared in 1985.

The House July 11 passed by voice vote a bill (HR 1383) requiring the Agriculture Department to study how using organic farming methods could reduce costs to farmers for pesticides, fertilizer, energy and farm equipment. The bill had been reported by the House Agriculture Committee May 15 (H Rept 99-126), and was a scaled-back version of a bill that passed the House in 1984. *(1984 Almanac p. 366)*

In a surprise move the same day the House passed HR 1383, the Senate Agriculture Committee agreed to include similar provisions in a bill (S 616) reauthorizing federal farm programs. Efforts to promote organic farming had been blocked in the Senate committee for more than two years. The provisions eventually found their way into the five-year farm bill that cleared Dec. 18 (HR 2100 — PL 99-198). *(Story, p. 517)*

The legislation was approved over strong opposition from the Reagan administration, which had opposed the study since 1982 as too expensive and duplicative of work the department already was doing.

The provisions authorized research projects to examine whether farmers could improve crop yields and reduce costs — as well as protect their land — by using organic farming systems that eschewed pesticides and chemical fertilizers. House sponsor James Weaver, D-Ore., said alternative farming methods could help farmers with high production costs who suffered from declining prices for their crops.

The measure as cleared did not specify a spending level but Weaver estimated the program would cost $7.2 million over five years.

publicans on the Agriculture Committee helped to report a Democrat-drafted bill.

The Republicans nearly lost control on the Senate floor, as well, when 12 GOP senators quickly defected and voted with farm-state Democrats against an administration-backed plan to cut the cost of the bill by lowering income subsidies.

Those income subsidies, or deficiency payments, covered the difference between actual market prices and higher "target" prices set in farm law. Although Democrats generally accepted the administration's plan to begin reducing the price supports that put a floor on crop prices, they made deficiency payments a symbolic point of departure.

Whether to freeze existing target prices for the life of the bill, or begin reducing them in 1987, was the question that dominated Senate debate.

That immediately put Dole on the defensive, as majority leader responsible to the Republican Party, as a senior member of the Agriculture Committee with allegiance to his Kansas farm constituency, and as one of those GOP senators facing re-election in 1986.

Dole cast his damage-control mission simply: Stake out the middle ground and fashion a bill that could pass Congress before the end of the year, and still avoid a presidential veto. Throughout the Senate committee and floor debates, and well into the 10-day conference with the House, it was never certain he could accomplish such an agenda.

The bill emerged from the Senate Nov. 23 with an effective one-year freeze on target prices but with other "sweeteners" for nearly every commodity group, reflecting the compromises Dole made with key Democrats to win enough votes for his middle-of-the-road approach.

Dole-Foley Handiwork

Thomas S. Foley, D-Wash., had assumed a similar role as pragmatic mediator in the House. As majority whip and chairman of the Agriculture Subcommittee on Wheat, Soybeans and Feed Grains, he was the chief architect of the central section of the House bill, which effectively set a five-year freeze on target prices for all major commodities.

Although Foley was unable to attend early House-Senate conference sessions because of a conflict with conferences on the Gramm-Rudman-Hollings anti-deficit bill, the final farm bill reflected his handiwork as well as Dole's. *(Gramm-Rudman-Hollings, p. 459)*

When the two finally met face-to-face Dec. 11, they hammered out a compromise package within hours. The key section on target prices — providing a two-year freeze and only a 2 percent reduction in the third year — was ratified quickly by the full conference the next day.

The White House had drawn its line at capping the three-year cost of farm programs at $50 billion, on reducing target prices, on eliminating a House provision to assess dairy producers, and on giving the president wide discretion to increase sugar imports from debt-ridden Caribbean nations.

Instead, what it got was a $52 billion three-year bill, a freeze on target prices, an assessment on milk producers and a directive to cut sugar imports.

Beyond that, Congress assured itself of further partisan battles over basic farm policy by setting a political time bomb: Instead of a traditional four-year reauthorization, conferees agreed to make HR 2100 a five-year bill, expiring in the presidential election year of 1990.

Major Provisions

As cleared, the 1985 omnibus farm bill (PL 99-198) extended and revised federal agriculture and nutrition programs for five years, expiring at the end of fiscal 1990. As in the past, the bill amended and added to — but did not repeal — permanent farm policy legislation of 1938 and 1949.

It authorized programs for commodity price and income supports, including new lower rates for crop loans that helped determine the prices for wheat, corn, cotton, rice, peanuts, soybeans, honey and wool, and a more gradual drop in the target prices that determined federal income subsidies to individual farmers.

Also included were program authorizations for agricultural exports, soil conservation, agricultural research and federal farm credit agencies, such as the Farmers Home Administration. And, as in the past, the measure included reauthorization for federal food assistance programs to low-income persons, including food stamp benefits and other nutrition programs.

Following is a summary of the major sections of the

bill and the significant changes it made in the most recent four-year authorization law (PL 97-98) that expired Sept. 30, 1985.

Wheat and Feed Grains

• Maintained the existing system of offering crop loans to farmers at harvest, with farmers using their crops as collateral and having the option of repaying the loans plus interest, or defaulting on the loans, keeping the principal and leaving the government with no recourse except to take possession of the crops.

• Reduced the rate for these "non-recourse" loans to $3 a bushel for wheat and $2.40 a bushel for corn in 1986, down from their respective 1985 rates of $3.30 and $2.55. Thereafter, the agriculture secretary was authorized to set the rate between 75 and 85 percent of the average domestic market price for the crops of three of the previous five years (disregarding the highest and lowest years), although the basic loan rate could not be reduced by more than 5 percent from the previous year.

• Required the secretary to reduce loan rates by 10 percent in 1986, and gave him authority through 1990 to reduce rates up to 20 percent in any one year, if the average market price of wheat or feed grains in the previous marketing year was less than 110 percent of the loan rate for that year, or if it was necessary to provide competitive prices on the world market.

• Authorized the secretary to permit repayment of crop loans at a rate equal to the prevailing world market price for wheat or feed grains if that rate was lower than the effective loan rate. Repayment could not be less than 70 percent of the loan rate.

• Maintained a system of offering "deficiency" payments to farmers to make up any shortfall between the national weighted average market sale prices received by farmers and certain "target" prices. The bill also froze existing target prices of $4.38 a bushel for wheat and $3.03 a bushel for corn through 1987. For 1988 through 1990, it set target prices at the following percentages of the existing levels: 98 percent in 1988; 95 percent in 1989; and 90 percent in 1990, although target prices could not be reduced below $4.00 a bushel for wheat and $2.75 for corn.

• Maintained the existing $50,000 limit on deficiency payments to individual producers, except that any payments resulting from the secretary's use of 10-20 percent loan-rate reductions, or any gains realized by repaying a loan at a level less than the original loan level, were exempt from the ceiling. In addition, a producer who planted at least 50 percent of his permitted program acres, and who devoted more acres than required under the acreage-reduction program to approved conservation uses or non-program crops, was eligible to receive deficiency payments on 92 percent of the permitted acres.

• Set acreage-reduction requirements for producers as a condition of receiving price-support loans and deficiency payments. In the 1986 crop year, participating wheat producers had to hold acreage to at least 15 percent below their farms' established wheat bases if previous surplus stocks exceeded 1 billion bushels nationwide. The minimum was 20 percent in 1987 through 1990. The secretary had the authority to increase the acreage-reduction requirement to a maximum of 25 percent in 1986, 27½ percent in 1987 and 30 percent in 1988-1990, but if maximum limits were set in 1986 farmers were to receive the equivalent of 2½ percent in government-owned commodities. For wheat producers who planted prior to final announcement of the 1986 program, the secretary had to offer $2 a bushel for up to 10 percent of any acreage base that had been diverted beyond the maximum 25 percent reduction. For feed grains, the minimum acreage reduction was 12½ percent in 1986 through 1990 if annual surplus stocks exceeded 2 billion bushels. The secretary was authorized to increase the acreage-reduction requirement for feed grains to a maximum of 20 percent in any one year, but if maximum limits were set in 1986, farmers received the equivalent of 2½ percent in government-owned commodities.

• Gave the secretary discretion to issue export certificates to wheat and feed grains producers for the percentage of the crop estimated to be sold on foreign markets. The secretary could issue certificates with no cash value, but exporters were required to hold certificates when they exported grain. The secretary could give certificates with a cash value, and redeem them from exporters to give producers a possible source of income, if the secretary were to reduce deficiency payments 13 cents a bushel for wheat and 6 cents a bushel for corn.

• Authorized the secretary to make in-kind payments available to wheat and feed grain producers who did not obtain loans, who did not receive deficiency payments, who did not plant wheat or feed grains for harvest in excess of the farm acreage base reduced by one-half of any acreage limitation, and who otherwise complied with the provisions of the bill. Payments were made in the form of wheat and feed grains owned by the Commodity Credit Corporation (CCC), subject to availability.

• Gave the secretary discretion to increase wheat target prices for 1986 through 1988 on a sliding scale tied to reduced plantings. Also gave the secretary discretion to base target prices on a graduated scale of production with increased payments targeted to family farmers.

• Determined the quantity eligible for deficiency payments by multiplying the established yield times 100 percent of the farm acreage base, less the announced acreage-reduction program. Operators had to plant at least 50 percent of the farm acreage base, less the announced acreage-reduction program, to qualify for deficiency payments.

• Calculated the acreage base for wheat and feed grains as the average acreage planted in the five immediately preceding crop years. The yield was based on average program yields for 1981 through 1985 (disregarding highest and lowest years). In 1988 through 1990, the secretary had the discretion to recompute the yield by taking an average of the program yields of the five preceding years (disregarding the highest and lowest yields), but using the actual yields for 1987 and following years.

• Required prevented-planting and reduced-yield disaster payments for producers for whom federal crop insurance was not available. Similar payments had to be made in cases where no insurance was available and yields were below 75 percent of normal. The secretary had further authority to make payments if disaster created an economic emergency for producers.

• Required state Agriculture Soil Conservation boards to allow haying and grazing in 1986, and grazing at state request through 1990, of the wheat acreage diverted or otherwise devoted to conservation uses. Haying was discretionary from 1987 through 1990.

• Required the secretary to make preliminary announcements of program conditions for wheat growers by June 1, with adjustments made by July 31, and for corn growers by Sept. 30, with adjustments made by Nov. 15.

• Required the secretary by July 1, 1986, to conduct an

Short-Term Farm Extensions

Three times between the Sept. 30 expiration of existing farm program authorizations and the Dec. 13 enactment of a new farm bill Congress was forced to pass temporary extensions of dairy price-support and other programs.

All three temporary measures (HR 3454 — PL 99-114; S 1851 — PL 99-157; HR 3919 — PL 99-182) extended the dairy program and delayed a requirement that Puerto Rico must convert to a non-cash benefit program under its food stamps block grant.

The 1985 farm bill, which cleared Dec. 18 (HR 2100 — PL 99-198), extended the dairy program for five years and repealed the non-cash benefit requirement for Puerto Rico. *(Story, p. 517)*

House and Senate leaders said the dairy price-support extensions were necessary to prevent the program from reverting to permanent farm law dating to the 1930s and 1940s. Under existing law the government purchased milk products at $11.60 per hundred pounds of milk equivalent (about 12 gallons). Under permanent 1949 law, dairy price supports would have been about $16.22 per hundred pounds.

Both the House and Senate passed HR 3454 Sept. 30, extending dairy price supports and delaying the food stamp requirement. The bill also delayed a requirement that the agriculture secretary announce the 1986 loan level for extra-long staple cotton by Nov. 1.

S 1851, passed by the Senate Nov. 13 and the House Nov. 14, extended the dairy and food stamp provisions through Dec. 13. It also put off a requirement for farmer referendums on marketing quotas for cotton and peanuts until 31 days after Congress adjourned for 1985.

An amendment offered by Jesse Helms, R-N.C., Senate Agriculture Committee chairman, and accepted by voice vote, reduced price-support levels for the 1985 crop of burley tobacco, grown primarily in Kentucky. The amendment lowered the federal price-support level by 30 cents per pound, and reduced by 26 cents per pound the assessment farmers had to pay into the price-support program.

The House and Senate Dec. 12 passed HR 3919, extending the dairy and food stamp provisions through Dec. 31. The bill also delayed announcement of the national marketing quota for the 1986 crop of flue-cured tobacco.

advisory poll/referendum of all wheat producers whose bases exceeded 40 acres, to determine whether they would favor using a producer referendum to decide if the secretary should implement mandatory production controls and marketing quotas for their crops. The secretary also had discretion to poll feed grain producers.

Soybeans

- Set the price-support loan rate in 1986 and 1987 at the existing rate of $5.02 a bushel. In 1988 through 1990, set the loan rate at 75 percent of the average market price for three of the past five years (disregarding the highest and lowest years), provided that no annual adjustment exceeded 5 percent of the previous year's level, or fell below $4.50 a bushel. The secretary was permitted to make further reductions of up to 5 percent if he determined that the initial rate would not make the crop competitive on world markets.
- Authorized the secretary to permit repayment of crop loans at less than the effective loan rate.
- Set no limit on non-recourse price-support loans to individual producers. There were no target prices or acreage-control provisions.
- Authorized the secretary to make disaster payments for prevented planting and reduced yields caused by drought, flood or other natural disaster on the 1985 crop, and on the 1986 through 1990 crops.

Cotton

- Maintained the existing loan-rate formula at 85 percent of average market prices, limiting reductions to a maximum of 5 percent a year. Placed a floor of 55 cents on 1986 loan rates and a floor of 50 cents from 1987 through 1990.
- Required the secretary to implement one of the following two options whenever upland cotton was not competitive in world markets: either (1) announce by Nov. 1 a one-time reduction in the loan level of up to 20 percent of the original loan, combined (as necessary) with a market certificate program if the adjusted loan rate still exceeded the world price; or (2) periodically establish repayment rates at levels equal to the world price whenever the original loan rate exceeded the world price, although the secretary was allowed to use market certificates to make up part of the difference. The certificates could be redeemed for government-owned surplus commodities.
- Froze target prices at 81 cents a pound in 1986. For 1987 through 1990, set the target prices at the following percentages of existing levels: 98 percent in 1987, 95 percent in 1988, 92 percent in 1989 and 90 percent in 1990.
- Maintained the existing $50,000 cap on deficiency payments to individual growers, but any payments generated by the optional methods of reducing the rates more than 5 percent a year was not subject to payment limitations. In addition, a producer who planted at least 50 percent of his permitted program acres, and who devoted more acres than required under the acreage-reduction program to approved conservation uses or non-program crops, was eligible to receive deficiency payments on 92 percent of the permitted acres.
- Authorized the secretary to set acreage-reduction requirements in 1986 through 1990 of up to 25 percent as a condition for farmers to receive program benefits. The secretary also had authority to require cross-compliance only to the extent that producers who participated in any acreage-reduction program could not expand acreage of another crop for which there was an acreage-reduction program in effect.
- Determined the quantity eligible for deficiency payments by multiplying the established yield times 100 percent of the farm-acreage base, less the announced acreage-reduction program. Operators had to plant at least 50 percent of the farm acreage base, less the announced acreage-reduction program, to qualify for deficiency payments.
- Calculated the acreage base for cotton as the average acreage planted in the five immediately preceding crop years, where history was available. Individual crop acreage bases (including allowance for crops produced under double-crop systems) could not add up to more than the acres

in the total farm acreage base. The crop yield was to be based on average program yields for 1981 through 1985 (disregarding highest and lowest years). In 1988 through 1990, the secretary had the discretion to recompute the yield by taking an average of the program yields of the five preceding years (disregarding the highest and lowest yields), but using the actual yields for 1987 and following years. The secretary had to announce any such program by Nov. 1.

- Authorized the secretary to make payments available to producers who did not obtain loans. The payment rate was to be the difference between the original loan rate and the loan repayment rate, with payments made in amounts equal to the original loan rate multiplied by the amount of upland cotton the producer was otherwise eligible to place under loan.
- Authorized the secretary to make in-kind payments available to producers who did not obtain loans, who did not receive deficiency payments, who did not plant upland cotton for harvest in excess of the farm acreage base reduced by one-half of any acreage limitation, and who otherwise complied with the provisions of the bill. Payments were to be made in the form of cotton owned by the CCC, subject to availability.
- Required prevented-planting and reduced-yield disaster payments of up to $100,000 for cotton producers for whom federal crop insurance was not available. Similar payments were to be made in cases where no insurance was available and yields were below 75 percent of normal. The secretary had further authority to make payments if disaster created an economic emergency for producers.
- Set the minimum loan rate through 1990 for extra-long staple cotton at 85 percent of the average market price during three of the preceding five years (disregarding the high and low years). Each year's loan rate had to be announced by Dec. 1 of the previous year.

Rice

- Reduced the loan rate in 1986 to $7.20 per hundred pounds from the existing level of $8. From 1987 through 1990, the bill set a new loan-rate formula of 85 percent of average market prices in three of the five preceding years (disregarding the high and low years), although annual reductions were limited to a maximum of 5 percent, and could not be set below $6.50 per hundred pounds.
- Required the secretary to set loan repayment conditions at a rate equal to the prevailing world market price for the 1985 crop, but not less than 50 percent of the original loan rate for the 1986 and 1987 crops, 60 percent for the 1988 crop and 70 percent for the 1989 and 1990 crops. The secretary was authorized to provide up to one-half the differential between the loan rate and redemption rate in negotiable certificates redeemable in government-owned commodities.
- Froze target prices at $11.90 per hundred pounds in 1986, and set target prices at the following percentages of existing levels for 1988 through 1990: 98 percent in 1987; 95 percent in 1988, 92 percent in 1989 and 90 percent in 1990.
- Maintained the existing $50,000 cap on deficiency payments to individual growers, but any payments caused by reducing repayment rates below the original loan rate were not subject to payment limitations. In addition, a producer who planted at least 50 percent of his permitted program acres, and who devoted more acres than required under the acreage-reduction program to approved conservation uses or non-program crops, was eligible to receive deficiency payments on 92 percent of the permitted acres.
- Authorized the secretary to set acreage-reduction requirements in 1986 through 1990 of up to 35 percent as a condition for farmers to receive program benefits. The secretary also had authority to require cross-compliance only to the extent that producers who participated in any acreage-reduction program could not expand acreage of another crop for which there was an acreage-reduction program in effect.
- Determined the quantity eligible for deficiency payments by multiplying the established yield times 100 percent of the farm acreage base, less the announced acreage-reduction program. Operators had to plant at least 50 percent of the farm-acreage base, less the announced acreage-reduction program, to qualify for deficiency payments.
- Calculated the acreage base for rice as the average acreage planted in the five immediately preceding crop years, where history was available. The yield was to be based on average program yields for 1981 through 1985 (disregarding highest and lowest years). In 1988 through 1990, the secretary had discretion to recompute the yield by taking an average of the program yields of the five preceding years (disregarding the highest and lowest yields), but using the actual yields for 1987 and following years. The secretary had to announce any such program by Jan. 31.
- Required the secretary to issue marketing certificates to handlers of rice if the world market price for a class of rice fell below the domestic market price for that class. The certificates could be redeemed for government-owned surplus commodities.
- Authorized the secretary to make payments available to producers who did not obtain loans. The payment rate was to be the difference between the original loan rate and the loan-repayment rate, with payments made in amounts equal to the original loan rate multiplied by the amount of rice the producer was otherwise eligible to place under loan.
- Authorized the secretary to make in-kind payments available to producers who did not obtain loans, who did not receive deficiency payments, who did not plant rice for harvest in excess of the farm-acreage base reduced by one-half of any acreage limitation, and who otherwise complied with the provisions of the bill. Payments were to be made in the form of rice owned by the CCC, subject to availability.
- Required prevented-planting and reduced-yield disaster payments of up to $100,000 for rice producers for whom federal crop insurance was not available. Similar payments were to be made in cases where no insurance was available and yields were below 75 percent of normal. The secretary had further authority to make payments if disaster created an economic emergency for producers.

Dairy

- Maintained the system of government purchases of surplus milk products (butter, cheese, dry milk) from processors to ensure a minimum price to producers during periods of oversupply.
- Retained the existing milk price support at $11.60 per hundred pounds of milk equivalent through calendar year 1986. The secretary was authorized to reduce the rate by 25 cents to $11.35 on Jan. 1, 1987, and another 25 cents to $11.10 on Oct. 1, 1987. In 1988 through 1990 calendar years, the secretary had to reduce the support price by 50 cents per hundred pounds a year if government purchases were

Wheat Referendum

Congress cleared a bill (S 822 — PL 99-63) June 27 authorizing the secretary of agriculture to postpone a scheduled referendum among the nation's wheat farmers on the question of mandatory crop controls.

Agriculture Secretary John R. Block had announced plans to conduct the referendum in late July, in advance of fall wheat planting. The referendum would have been required by permanent farm law enacted in 1938. Existing farm law suspended the referendum requirement, but was set to expire Sept. 30. The administration and critics in Congress variously estimated that a referendum would cost between $700,000 and $8 million.

If the referendum had been held, wheat growers would have decided whether to accept a national acreage allotment of 54 million acres — substantially below 1985 production levels. House and Senate versions of a bill to extend farm program authorizations were tied up in committee markup, and the administration hoped the threat of holding the referendum would expedite farm bill action. *(Story, p. 517)*

The House Agriculture Committee reported a bill (HR 1614 — H Rept 99-146) May 23 similar to S 822. The bill passed the House by voice vote June 4. The Senate panel reported S 822 on June 3 (S Rept 99-77); the Senate passed the bill by voice vote June 21. The House took up S 822 on June 26, and by voice vote substituted the language of HR 1614, requiring that the referendum be postponed. The House then passed S 822 and sent it back to the Senate.

The next day Agriculture Secretary Block announced he would defer the referendum if authorized. The Senate then again amended the bill by voice vote to authorize the secretary to defer the referendum until 31 days after Congress adjourned. The House accepted the Senate amendment that same day by voice vote, clearing the bill.

projected to exceed 5 billion pounds. The secretary had to raise support prices an equivalent amount if government purchases were projected to be less than 2.5 billion pounds.

- Required the secretary by April 1, 1986, to offer bids for a period of 18 months to producers willing to take entire herds of dairy cattle out of production. Qualifying farmers had to sell their herds, including bulls and calves, either for slaughter or export and agree to stay out of dairy farming for three to five years. All price cuts after Jan. 1, 1987, were to be suspended unless whole herd buyouts exceeded 12 billion pounds, or the secretary certified that reasonable offers were made but insufficient bids were submitted.
- Assessed all milk producers 40 cents per hundred pounds of milk produced from April 1 to Dec. 31, 1986, and assessed 25 cents per hundred pounds until Sept. 30, 1987, to cover the cost of the whole herd buyout plan.
- Required the secretary to increase government purchases of red meat by 400 million pounds during the 18-month buyout program. Of that amount, 200 million pounds had to be used for government domestic programs, such as school lunch programs, and 200 million pounds had to be sold for export or used in U.S. military programs overseas. Also required "orderly marketing" of dairy cattle culled in the buyout program to encourage a higher rate of dairy cattle to be slaughtered during months when slaughtering of beef cattle slackened.
- Required the secretary to increase payment differentials in 33 of 45 regional marketing-order districts set up to guarantee locally produced supplies of milk. The differentials were designed mainly to benefit Southeastern producers.
- Required the CCC to offer for bid from government surplus stocks at lease 1 million pounds a year of nonfat dry milk for the manufacture of casein, and allowed the CCC to accept bids at lower than the resale price otherwise required in the bill. The provision was designed to restrict casein imports. The secretary also was required to conduct a study on the impact of imported casein on the U.S. dairy price-support program.

Sugar

- Continued the existing system of giving price-support loans to sugar processors (who agreed to share the support price with sugar cane and beet producers), using sugar as collateral with the option of forfeiting the sugar to the government if domestic prices did not exceed the loan rate.
- Maintained 1985 loan rates of 18 cents a pound for raw cane sugar for the 1986 through 1990 crops. Loan rates for beet sugar were to be based on the cane sugar level, as in the past.
- Maintained, under authority of other laws, the existing system of import quotas and duties to keep domestic market prices above a "price objective." The price objective was set at 21.57 cents in 1984-85. The duty was set at a maximum allowable level of 2.8125 cents.
- Authorized the secretary to make annual adjustments in the support prices, based on changes in inflation and production costs over the two preceding years.
- Required the president at the end of the existing quota year to use all available authority to enable the sugar program to be operated at no cost (except administrative costs), effectively forcing the president to impose stricter import quotas in order to keep domestic prices above the price-support loan rate. Before making adjustments in a previously established sugar quota, the president had to use all available legal means to dispose of accumulated stocks of sugar through sale, tender, loan or donation.
- Required the secretary either (1) to extend the existing quota year (Dec. 1, 1985, through Sept. 30, 1986) by at least three months to Dec. 31, 1986, or (2) to administer the sugar import program in such a way as to result in at least the equivalent reduction in loan forfeitures.
- Authorized the secretary to make disaster payments for prevented planting and reduced yields caused by drought, flood or other natural disaster on the 1985 crops of sugar cane and sugar beets, and on the 1986 through 1990 crops.
- Prohibited import quotas beginning in 1987 for countries that were net importers of sugar unless they verified that they did not import Cuban sugar.

Peanuts

- Extended the existing peanut-stabilization program under which growers who held marketing quotas for domestic sales had to comply with those quotas in order to qualify for price supports. The total national quota for 1986 was maintained at a minimum of 1.1 million tons, the 1985 quota.

• Maintained price-support rates for the 1986 crop at the 1985 rate of $559 a ton, and the additional support level at $148 a ton, allowing for adjustments for increases in producer costs. The support level for the 1987-90 quota crops was to be based on the previous year's level, although increases were limited to 6 percent a year.

• Allowed farms which did not have a quota in 1985, but which produced peanuts in at least two of the three preceding years, to get quotas if the poundage quota for a state in any marketing year was above the quota for the preceding year. The state increase was to be divided equally between "old" and "new" quota holders.

• Continued a program that allowed any farmer, with or without a quota, to grow peanuts for world markets or non-food uses. The agriculture secretary was given discretion to provide price supports for these "additional peanuts," but at a lower rate than quota peanuts to avoid any government losses.

Honey

• Reduced the price-support loan rate for honey producers to 64 cents a pound in 1986 and 63 cents a pound in 1987, with reductions thereafter limited to a maximum of 5 percent a year through 1990. The 1985 rate was 65.3 cents a pound.

• Authorized the secretary to permit repayment of price-support loans at less than the effective loan rate.

Wool and Mohair

• Extended the price-support program for wool and mohair for five years, freezing the wool price support at 77.5 percent of an amount formulated from production costs, and continuing the support level for pulled wool and mohair in relation to the level for shorn wool.

Food for Peace

• Extended the export sales and grant program under the Food for Peace program (PL 480) for five years through fiscal 1990, and extended the existing authorization ceiling for grant programs at $1 billion a year.

• Required that at least 10 percent of the value of sales in PL 480 agreements be made in foreign currencies. The foreign currency generated by these sales was to be converted into U.S. dollars over a 10- to 30-year period, beginning 10 years after the sale of the commodities.

• Authorized the agriculture secretary to lend the foreign currency generated from commodity sales in a developing country to a financial intermediary in that country, for the purpose of making loans to finance private enterprise investment at reasonable rates of interest.

• Maintained the minimum for donations of surplus grains at 1.8 million metric tons a year in fiscal 1986, and increasing to 1.9 million metric tons a year in 1989 through 1990. The president was authorized to waive the ceiling if that was necessary to undertake programs of assistance to meet urgent humanitarian needs. At least 1.425 million metric tons a year had to be distributed through non-profit voluntary agencies.

• Broadened the secretary's authority to distribute eligible commodities under Section 416 of the Agriculture Act of 1949 to include all commodities and products acquired by the CCC.

• Required the secretary to donate up to 650,000 metric tons a year of eligible Section 416 commodities in fiscal 1986-89, including not less than 150,000 tons a year of dairy products, and 500,000 tons a year of grains and oil seeds.

• Required 75,000 to 500,000 tons a year to be distributed under a new Food for Progress program to promote private free enterprise policy and development in the recipient country.

• Lowered the aggregate minimum value of Food for Development agreements from 15 percent to 10 percent of the aggregate value of all regular Food for Peace sales agreements.

• Required that at least 5 percent of donations made under Section 416 and PL 480 programs be made available to private voluntary organizations and cooperatives to convert into cash to support their programs.

• Required the president to designate a special assistant for food aid, to assist and advise the president on U.S. domestic and foreign food assistance programs, and to recommend ways to increase and encourage the use and consumption of U.S. agricultural commodities through food assistance.

Exports

• Required that at least $2 billion of CCC-owned commodities be used to enhance and encourage the export sales of U.S. agricultural commodities during fiscal years 1986 through 1988. The secretary was encouraged, to the maximum extent practicable, to spread the use of such commodities equally during the three fiscal years.

• Required the agriculture secretary to use at least $325 million a year of CCC funds or CCC commodities in fiscal years 1986-88, and such funds and commodities as the secretary deemed necessary for each of the fiscal years 1989-91, for export assistance for U.S. commodities adversely affected by the price or credit subsidies or unfair marketing arrangements used by other countries.

• Required the CCC to make available at least $5 billion a year in short-term export credit guarantees.

• Required the secretary to sell at least 150,000 metric tons a year of CCC-owned dairy products in fiscal years 1986-88 for export.

• Broadened the existing program of loan guarantees for intermediate-term (three to 10 years) export credits. The secretary was required to make at least $500 million a year available in the intermediate credit program through 1988, and up to $1 billion in 1989.

• Extended through 1990 authority for creation of an agricultural export credit revolving fund, which was to be fed by repayments of direct CCC export credit loans.

Cargo Preference

• Exempted certain Agriculture Department export financing programs from requirements that half of specified cargoes had to be shipped on U.S.-flag vessels. Exemptions included those programs that used CCC stocks to enhance U.S. agriculture exports, those under which CCC guarantees of commercial credit were blended with CCC direct credits, short-term credit programs, and those undertaken for the purpose of promoting U.S. agriculture exports if the secretary determined that such activities were necessary to keep U.S. commodities competitive in international trade.

• Increased from 50 percent to 75 percent the cargo preference requirements for the Agriculture Department's concessional programs, such as Food for Peace (PL 480), to be phased in over three years and with funding for the increase to be charged to the budget of the Transportation Department. The Agriculture Department's total cost of ocean freight and the ocean freight differential was not to exceed 20 percent of the total cost of the export programs covered by cargo preference; the excess costs were to be charged to the Transportation Department.

● Guaranteed that Great Lakes ports would receive the same percentage share or metric tonnage (whichever was lower) in 1986 through 1989 of cargo preference commodities as they received in 1984. The secretary of transportation was required to administer the cargo preference requirements to maintain to the fullest extent possible the historical port range share of cargoes exported from each of the four seacoasts.

● Required that the above provisions be revoked and existing law reinstated if funding for cargo preference was not available from the Transportation Department within 90 days.

Credit

● Consolidated the FmHA farm ownership and farm operating loan programs, but required that existing ratios of real estate and operating loans be maintained. The bill also authorized $4 billion a year for fiscal 1986-88, apportioned as follows: in fiscal 1986, $2 billion for direct loans and $2 billion for guarantees; in fiscal 1987, $1.5 billion for direct and $2.5 billion for guarantees; in fiscal 1988, $1 billion for direct and $3 billion for guarantees. The secretary could shift up to 25 percent of the funds for loan guarantees into the direct loan funds.

● Required the secretary to establish a three-year interest rate buy-down program for FmHA guaranteed loans, funded at a level of $490 million over three years. Eligible guaranteed loan borrowers could receive up to a 2 percentage point buy-down if commercial lenders of guaranteed loans agreed to reduce interest rates by a comparable 2 percentage points.

● Required the department to give emergency disaster loans to farmers who qualified regardless of whether a producer's entire home county had been designated a disaster area. Disaster emergency loans could be made only to family-sized farms, removing existing authority for making such loans to larger farms, and after 1986 only to eligible producers who suffered physical losses and who did not have access to federal crop insurance. Emergency disaster loans were restricted to $1.3 billion in 1986, $700 million in 1987 and $600 million a year in 1988, 1989 and 1990.

● Retained the cap on emergency disaster loans at the existing level of $500,000 per disaster.

● Required that emergency disaster loans be made available to producers in disaster counties who grew double crops if they experienced a 50 percent loss on one crop.

● Amended the FmHA water and waste-disposal program to require a graduated system of grant rates geared to giving higher rates to smaller and poorer communities. The bill also revised the loan program to give poorer communities access to 5 percent loans. For fiscal 1986 through 1990, $340 million would be authorized for insured water and waste-disposal facility loans, $250 million for industrial development loans and $115 million for insured community facility loans.

● Prevented the agriculture secretary from prohibiting first-time borrowers from applying for direct loans.

● Forbade the Agriculture Department to sell land acquired through foreclosures on FmHA loans if the sales would depress local farm land values. The bill also required that any sales as far as practicable be made in family-sized units. It also required the department, when leasing or operating foreclosed land, to grant leases on a competitive bid basis, giving priority to former owners of the land, family farmers and beginning farmers.

● Stipulated that if the interest that each family member had in a farming operation was alone small enough to fit the definition of a family farm, then the entire farm operation was eligible for FmHA operating and ownership loans, even though the entire farm operation might exceed the definition of a family farm.

● Eliminated the farm products exemption in the Uniform Commercial Code. The bill also provided "clear title" protection for buyers of agricultural products against previous liens on those products, unless purchasers were given direct notice that liens existed, or liens were listed in a state central filing system. The provision was to take effect after 12 months to give states time to set up optional central filing systems. It also provided for fines of up to $5,000, or 15 percent of the value of the product (whichever was greater) for sellers convicted of making "off-list" sales without notifying lenders or repaying the loans.

Research

● Authorized spending ceilings for federal agricultural research of $600 million for fiscal 1986, rising in $10 million annual increments to $640 million in fiscal 1990.

● Authorized ceilings for federal contribution to cooperative research at state agricultural experiment stations of $270 million for fiscal 1986, rising in $10 million annual increments to $310 million in 1990.

● Authorized ceilings for federal contribution to cooperative extension educational programs in states of $370 million in fiscal 1986, rising in $10 million annual increments to $420 million in 1990. The bill also authorized $10 million annually for extension facilities at "1890 institutions," a group of predominately black schools.

● Provided 50-50 matching grants to states to establish and operate international trade development centers.

● Classified as high-priority research, in considering competitive research grants, studies on the impact on agriculture of emerging technologies and economic, social and environmental developments. The bill also urged giving high priority in competitive research grants to biotechnology research.

● Authorized the secretary to enter into cooperative agreements with private agencies, organizations and individuals on a cost-sharing or cost-reimbursement basis for the development of new agricultural technology, up to $3 million a year. The provision included research to develop new and alternative industrial uses for agricultural crops as high-priority research for competitive grants, and designated the Agriculture Department as the lead agency for establishing appropriate controls for the development and use of the application of biotechnology to agriculture.

● Authorized the Agriculture Department to engage in research designed to test and develop organic farming techniques to improve agricultural productivity and efficiency, and enhance soil, water and energy conservation practices. *(Organic farming, box, p. 518)*

Conservation

● Provided a "sodbuster" program to discourage future cultivation of fragile soils. Farmers who planted crops on land designated as "highly erodible" were to lose price supports, crop insurance protection, FmHA loans and other federal benefits for all of their crops. In addition, farmers who plowed highly erodible land between 1981 and 1985 had to begin applying approved conservation plans on that land by 1990, or two years after completion of a soil survey of the land, and complete such plans by 1995, in order to remain eligible for farm program benefits.

- Provided a "swampbuster" program to deny federal benefits to producers who converted designated wetlands to crop use.
- Established a long-term conservation reserve program for at least 40 million acres and up to 45 million acres of fragile land already in crop use, requiring the agriculture secretary to offer farmers cash contracts to take erosion-prone land out of production for 10 to 15 years. No more than 5 million acres could go into the reserve in the 1986 crop year, no less than 10 million acres each in 1987 through 1989, and 5 million acres in 1990, although the secretary had authority to reduce the minimum amounts by 25 percent a year if it would make the program less expensive in the following year. In return for a landowner's agreement, the secretary would provide aid covering up to 50 percent of the cost of installing approved cover crops, although there was a $50,000 limit on annual payments to farmers under reserve contracts.

Food Assistance

- Required state agencies to provide a method for distributing food stamps to the homeless.
- Revised the definition of "disabled" to allow for special treatment in determining eligibility and benefits for: certain disabled persons who received state-financed Supplemental Security Income (SSI) payments, but who did not receive the basic federal SSI benefits; recipients of public disability retirement pensions who had permanent disabilities; veterans receiving pensions for non-service-connected disabilities; and certain railroad retirement disability annuitants.
- Prohibited states from charging sales taxes on food stamp purchases. This provision was to take effect at the beginning of the fiscal year following the first session of the state legislature.
- Made households automatically eligible for the food stamp program if members already received benefits under the program for Aid to Families with Dependent Children (AFDC) or under SSI. In addition, the bill prohibited the automatic denial of eligibility or termination of food stamp benefits if a recipient was denied AFDC or SSI benefits.
- Emphasized that any federal Pell Grant not used for tuition and mandatory school fees was to be counted as income for food stamp eligibility purposes, and any origination fees or insurance premiums that reduced the amount of a student loan would not be counted as income for food stamp purposes.
- Permitted farmers and other self-employed persons to deduct business losses when determining net income for food stamp eligibility.
- Required that payments to third parties by state and local governments would count as income, including student grants, loans and scholarships, but excepting medical assistance, energy assistance, child care and other basic assistance programs comparable to general assistance.
- Required that all allowances, earnings and payments received under the Job Training Partnership Act be counted as income.
- Allowed states to exclude from income the first $50 a month of child support received by an AFDC recipient family, if the state were to reimburse the federal government for the estimated food stamp benefit cost of doing so.
- Increased the "earned income deduction" from 18 percent to 20 percent to increase food stamp benefits available to low-income working families, effective May 1, 1986. The bill also increased the deduction for shelter expenses from $139 a month to $147 a month, and created a separate deduction of up to $160 a month for child-care costs. The deductions were to be subtracted from gross income to arrive at the net income on which stamp benefits were based.
- Prohibited households receiving low-income energy assistance from taking deductions for utility costs, if the amount of the energy assistance were to exceed the utility allowance. States were given the option of establishing a separate utility allowance for families receiving energy assistance.
- Required states to have households with earnings or recent work history, except for migrant farm workers and families with elderly and handicapped members, report monthly on factors affecting their eligibility, but allowed the requirement to be waived if the state were to show that it would result in unwarranted administrative expenses.
- Raised liquid asset limits on most eligible households from $1,500 to $2,000 in fiscal 1987. For households with one or more members, at least one of whom was elderly, the limit was set at $3,000. The existing level was $3,000 for households of two or more with one elderly member and $1,500 for others. Excluded from assets were property with liens or related to maintenance; or use of a vehicle used to produce income or transport a disabled person; and burial plots.
- Disqualified a household if the head of the household failed to comply with food stamp work requirements; made subject to work requirements heads of households 16 or older not attending school half-time or more.
- Required states to set up job training and employment programs for employable food stamp recipients, designed by the state. A state could exempt recipients from participation if the state determined that it would be impractical or not cost-effective to require them to participate in job programs. States could exempt entire geographic areas and persons receiving food stamps for less than 30 days, but participation could not exceed 50 percent through fiscal 1989. The bill also authorized $40 million in fiscal 1986, $50 million in fiscal 1987, $60 million in fiscal 1988, and $75 million in fiscal 1989 and 1990 in grants to states to carry out their employment and training programs. If states were to incur greater costs, the federal government would share in 50 percent of the additional cost.
- Permitted issuance of food stamp benefits at various times during a month, providing that no more than 40 days elapsed between issuances.
- Permitted federally insured credit unions with wholesale or retail grocers within their field of membership to redeem food stamps.
- Prohibited financial institutions from imposing or collecting from retail food stores a fee or other charge for redemption of coupons.
- Required one adult member of a household to attest, under penalty of perjury, that the household's statements on the food stamp application was true, and required states to verify income and other eligibility factors.
- Required that in areas serving more than 5,000 food stamp households, states would have to set up fraud detection units to investigate and assist in the prosecution of fraud.
- Required that if a disqualified store were sold, the previous owner would be subject to a civil money penalty to reflect the remaining disqualification period.

• Required a study of the quality-control and error-rate sanction system, and prohibited the collection of sanctions from states for six months, pending the results of the study.

• Required the secretary to develop, in consultation with states, a plan by Feb. 1, 1987, for the use of an automated data processing and information retrieval system to administer the food stamp program. States were required to develop a plan based on the secretary's model by Oct. 1, 1987, to improve computer operations, and to implement it by Oct. 1, 1988.

• Authorized for the food stamp program up to $13.037 billion in fiscal 1986, $13.936 billion in 1987, $14.741 billion in 1988, $15.435 billion in 1989 and $15.970 billion in 1990.

• Authorized for the Puerto Rico nutrition assistance block grant $825 million in fiscal 1986, $853 million in fiscal 1987, $880 million in 1988, $908 million in 1989 and $937 million in 1990.

• Extended the Temporary Emergency Food Assistance Program for two years, and authorized $50 million a year for state and local administrative costs. The bill also required states to match 80 percent of the federal contribution, and allowed the match to include in-kind contributions. It also reauthorized the Commodity Supplemental Food Program, and allowed local officials operating the program to serve elderly persons within available funding if the local agencies determined that the funds were in excess of what was necessary to serve eligible women, infants and children.

• Required the cooperative extension services of states to carry out an expanded program of nutrition and consumer education for low-income individuals, and authorized $5 million in fiscal 1986, $6 million in fiscal 1987 and $8 million in fiscal 1988, 1989 and 1990 for the program.

Miscellaneous

• Required the secretary, in any year in which an acreage-reduction program was in effect, to make part of the season's estimated deficiency payments to producers on an advance basis after the producer signed up. In making advance payments, the secretary could issue up to 5 percent of the total deficiency payment in the form of government-owned surplus commodities.

• Provided new authority for farmer-funded beef and pork promotion programs, with referendums among handlers within 22 to 30 months on whether to continue the programs. The beef checkoff was to be $1 per head (including imported beef), with a credit of up to 50 cents for assessments of state beef councils. The pork checkoff was to be 0.25 percent of the sale price of hogs and imported pork. Producers could receive refunds of checkoff contributions during the period between the start of the program and the referendums.

• Prohibited the secretary from terminating any marketing order that was in effect as of Jan. 15, 1986, for a non-price-supported crop, without the concurrence of a majority of the affected producers. Maximum penalties for handlers who violated marketing order regulations were raised from $500 to $5,000.

• Prohibited the Agriculture Department from making commercial sales of government-owned grains and cotton at less than 115 percent of existing price-support loan rates.

• Authorized the CCC to make its surplus stocks available free or at reduced cost to encourage the purchase of such commodities for the production of liquid fuels (ethanol) and agricultural commodity byproducts.

• Changed the federal Virus-Serum-Toxin Act to give the Agriculture Department control over intrastate as well as interstate sales of veterinary biologics, but allowed states that had effective regulatory systems to retain them.

• Maintained existing authority for operation of the farmer-owned grain reserve, the food security wheat reserve and other reserves. The bill also required that reserve loans be repaid in not less than three years, and authorized the secretary to set ceilings on wheat storage of 30 percent and feed grains storage of 15 percent of total annual domestic and export use.

• Made individuals convicted of growing or cultivating controlled substances, such as marijuana, ineligible for program benefits for five years.

• Prohibited the importation of flue-cured and burley tobacco that did not pass U.S. pesticide residue tests used for U.S.-grown tobacco. Tobacco importers, in addition to reporting the country of origin of the product, had to identify the intended U.S. purchaser, which would be filed on public record with U.S. Customs.

• Set standards for the treatment and welfare of laboratory animals, requiring the secretary to upgrade research facility standards to minimize animal pain and distress, and requiring each research facility to establish a three-member committee, made up of a veterinarian and at least one person not affiliated with the facility, to inspect animal study areas twice a year and to file a report for the Agriculture Department. Maximum penalties for violations of the Animal Welfare Act were raised from $1,000 to $2,500 for each violation.

• Required the secretary to conduct a study on the effect of ethanol imports from Brazil on domestic prices and to study the merits of a strategic ethanol reserve.

• Required the secretary to control grasshoppers and Mormon crickets on federal range land.

• Expanded eligibility for rural utilities to borrow from the Banks for Cooperatives of the Farm Credit System.

Background

Overlaying the year's farm policy debate was the financial crisis that threatened the entire agricultural economy. Four years of low profits, caused by global trade problems, high domestic interest rates on loans and collapsing land values had upset the fragile balance between farmers and their creditors and suppliers.

And, although farm-state legislators concentrated their attention on the farm bill — specifically income protection for farmers — the economic concerns resulted in congressional action on credit fronts as well, including measures to grant farmers emergency spring-planting credit and relief from parts of the bankruptcy code, to a bailout plan for some farmlenders. *(Emergency farm credit, p. 542; Farm Credit System bailout, p. 543; bankruptcy, p. 545)*

The credit crisis — though most acute in the Midwest — was viewed as a symptom of larger, systemic problems in the agricultural economy, problems that Agriculture Secretary Block believed could be cured only through austere measures. The administration sought to put U.S. agriculture on a "market-oriented" track, by providing minimal aid to farmers and thereby, indirectly, forcing lower market prices for their goods. The assumption was that reductions in per-unit prices would be made up by greater volumes of sales.

Administration's Farm Bill Proposal

To achieve its aim, the Reagan administration Feb. 22 officially asked Congress to eliminate or radically curtail the economic network of income supplements, production controls and loans.

The administration's bill would have sharply lowered the commodity loan rates that traditionally set minimum market prices. And it would have virtually ended deficiency payments that supplemented farmers' incomes, by phasing them down to the same level as loan rates.

The proposal also differed from previous "omnibus" farm bill reauthorizations in that it was a plan for permanent law. For years Congress had written multi-year amendments to so-called permanent farm law, dating to the Agricultural Adjustment Act of 1933, which was recodified and substantially amended in 1938 and 1949.

Underscoring the administration's desire to reverse course from the New Deal, when the federal government set itself up as the major force in determining how much farmers should produce and what they should be paid, the administration titled its bill the Agricultural Adjustment Act of 1985, bearing — but for the year — the same title as the Depression-era farm law it would have repealed.

The bill had two key aims. The administration argued that the protective and expensive array of existing farm programs had perversely harmed global demand for U.S. farm goods, and that only by stripping away many of these programs could U.S. farmers again compete aggressively for crucial foreign markets.

Equally important to the administration, though, was reducing the record high costs of farm programs. Like entitlement programs for the poor such as food stamps, farm program costs rose when the farm economy was in trouble, because more people turned to them for help.

The proposal's release was a bit untimely, coming in the same week Congress was knotted in debate over the emergency credit bill.

And though few members disagreed with the long-term goal of "getting the government out of agriculture," one of the most durable slogans of farm politics, most believed withdrawing governmental support was politically impossible if not economically unreasonable. Farm groups, too, although they uniformly disliked the administration bill, were divided on what ought to be done instead.

In the Senate, Agriculture Committee Chairman Jesse Helms, R-N.C., introduced the bill (S 501) "by request" Feb. 22, a phrase indicating that he did not personally support the administration measure.

In the House, Rep. Edward R. Madigan, R-Ill., ranking minority member of the Agriculture Committee, did likewise (HR 1420) March 5. Madigan said he would have preferred to "avoid the honor," likening the experience to being ridden out of town on a rail.

Exports: A Dominant Theme

No small part of the Farm Belt's economic woes was attributed to the failure of U.S. crops to compete on world markets. Varying reasons were cited for the problem — high domestic prices, boosted by federal price supports, and the strong value of the U.S. dollar, chief among them.

Some agricultural economists also complained about subsidized exports from other nations that undercut the United States in world competition.

And a long-running battle erupted between farm-state legislators who wanted cheaper exports and members representing the maritime industry and related labor unions, who were concerned about the flagging economic health of the American merchant marine. That battle focused on so-called cargo preference requirements — federal law stipulating that a percentage of U.S. exports had to be carried on more expensive U.S.-flag ships.

Both export subsidies and cargo preference were to capture Congress' attention in 1985.

In 1983 the Senate Agriculture Committee had approved legislation creating an export-subsidy plan for U.S. commodities, in which government-owned surpluses would be given away to foreign purchasers as an inducement. Neither the full Senate nor the House Agriculture Committee ever acted on the 1983 bill. *(1983 Almanac p. 385)*

In 1985, the first farm bill markup decisions on both sides of Capitol Hill involved subsidies to increase foreign sales, signaling the near-universal intention to make export assistance a centerpiece of the year's action.

The Senate Agriculture Committee, in its first days of markup on the farm bill beginning May 14, adopted a long list of "congressional findings" that spelled out its concerns over worldwide trading practices: "Failure to find multilateral or bilateral solutions to international trade problems will increase the likelihood of U.S. unilateral action," read one finding.

The same day Senate markup began, a House Agriculture subcommittee adopted an export subsidy title to be included in the House farm bill.

Members were putting pressure on the administration, however, even before markup got started. The White House had resisted export subsidies on the ground that they violated its free-market approach to agriculture. But during Senate negotiations on the fiscal 1986 budget resolution (S Con Res 32), the administration agreed to implement a subsidy program in return for several key votes, including that of Edward Zorinsky of Nebraska, the ranking Democrat on the Agriculture panel. The budget resolution was adopted in the Senate by a one-vote margin May 10. *(Budget resolution, p. 441)*

On May 15, the administration announced its three-year, $2 billion export subsidy program. Under the plan the government was to offer surplus commodities as free bonuses to U.S. exporting companies or foreign purchasers to induce them to buy more U.S. agricultural products.

The commodities were to come from stocks owned and stored by the CCC, which received them from farmers who defaulted on crop loans secured by the products they grew.

The administration's plan was targeted to overseas markets taken over by competing nations thought to be using unfair trading practices, according to Block, including countries in the European Economic Community.

House Committee Action

Riding a wave of "protectionist" sentiment in Congress, the House Agriculture Committee Sept. 10 approved and sent to the floor a new five-year farm policy authorization bill that included an optional provision for guaranteeing lucrative domestic markets for U.S.-grown grain.

The panel by voice vote approved the omnibus farm bill (HR 2100 — H Rept 99-271, Part I) moments after voting 22-18 in favor of letting wheat and feed grain farmers themselves vote on a program of strict government controls for their crops and a sharp increase in federal price supports.

The committee earlier had approved $11.8 billion in budget cuts recommended by a special task force of members appointed Sept. 4 by Chairman E. "Kika" de la Garza, D-Texas.

De la Garza said the budget cuts — which were spread throughout the bill but not to the basic commodity price-support programs approved by the committee in August — brought the bill within the target set forth in the fiscal 1986 budget resolution, according to committee calculations.

Long Road in House Markup

De la Garza had introduced HR 2100 April 17 as a vehicle for the committee's markup. Soon after, the eight Agriculture subcommittees began meeting, but because no decisions had been made yet on the fiscal 1986 budget, initial markup moved slowly.

Most subcommittees eventually reported what amounted to straight extensions of existing law. Major exceptions to that rule involved programs for wheat and other grain farmers, dairy operators, exports and conservation.

On April 23, the Conservation subcommittee endorsed a so-called "sodbuster" program to protect fragile, highly erodible soil. The provisions required that farmers who planted such land would lose price supports and other federal farm benefits for their entire crop production.

The Department Operations subcommittee gave tentative bipartisan support May 8 to a mandatory export subsidy program aimed at making U.S. agricultural products more attractive on the world market.

Under the export plan, drafted by subcommittee Chairman Berkley Bedell, D-Iowa, and Rep. Pat Roberts, R-Kan., surplus commodities, which were acquired by the federal government from farmers who defaulted on crop loans, were to be given as bonuses to U.S. exporters and food processors, and to foreign purchasers, as an inducement to buy U.S. agricultural products. The subcommittee ratified its earlier decision May 14, going beyond a discretionary plan proposed by de la Garza.

Trouble on Loan Rates

As a signal of the difficulties both Agriculture panels — and both chambers — would have crafting new farm policy in 1985, there were early battles in the House over how deep to cut the crop loan rates that effectively set the market floor for certain crops.

Democratic House leaders, including Foley, who was majority whip as well as chairman of the Wheat subcommittee, were willing to restructure loan rates to keep them more attuned to market fluctuations, but they pushed to ensure only modest reductions, not the 25 percent cut favored by the administration.

Two early votes illustrated House members' search for a middle ground. The Wheat subcommittee voted 6-9 May 23 against a proposal by Cooper Evans, R-Iowa, to reduce commodity loan rates in 1986 to 90 percent of average market prices. But the subcommittee voted 8-9 June 4 against an amendment by Glenn English, D-Okla., to retain wheat loan rates at the 1985 rate of $3.30 a bushel.

Foley supported instead setting loan rates at 95 percent of 1985 levels for fiscal 1986, with maximum 5 percent reductions in each succeeding year through 1988. And a similar provision was approved by the Cotton, Rice and Sugar Subcommittee, headed by Jerry Huckaby, D-La., whose members unanimously adopted proposals to hinge the loan rates for cotton and rice to 85 percent of average market prices, but with year-to-year reductions restricted to no more than 5 percent.

Wheat Panel Adopts Three Concepts

The slow pace of farm-bill action began to pressure wheat-state legislators, as planting season for winter crops approached. Also, Agriculture Secretary Block threatened to hold a referendum among wheat growers July 19-26 unless Congress showed progress on the farm bill. The referendum, required by law if new farm programs were not enacted before Sept. 30, would have asked farmers to choose between mandatory planting quotas or no farm program at all.

Democratic House leaders wanted to force Block to delay the referendum, and Block agreed after Senate Majority Leader Dole engineered a deadline for Senate committee action on the farm bill. On June 27, Congress cleared a bill (S 822) giving Block discretion to postpone the referendum. *(Wheat referendum, p. 522)*

That did not keep the Wheat subcommittee from choosing three distinctive and different approaches for reauthorizing programs for their farmers.

By voice vote June 20, members of the Wheat subcommittee agreed to a "market-oriented" plan that most likely would serve to cut prices and help make U.S. commodities more competitive in world markets.

The plan also had the virtue, in the view of most subcommittee members, of protecting farmers against any drop in income. It would have continued direct income subsidies to farmers and instituted a new program of "marketing loans" to assure them of breaking even on expenses.

Marketing loans differed from existing commodity loans. Instead of allowing farmers to default and turn over their crops but keep the loan money, marketing loans had to be repaid, but only at the price their crops brought at market, which could be significantly lower than the loan rate.

Yet, after voting overwhelmingly in favor of marketing loans, subcommittee members reversed themselves June 25, and voted to strip the plan of its substance by, among other things, allowing farmers to continue defaulting on their loans and giving the secretary of agriculture the discretion to implement the program.

Arlan Stangeland, R-Minn., sponsor of the marketing loan idea, said adding the default provision would make the program useless and virtually guaranteed that the Agriculture Department would never implement it.

In place of marketing loans, the committee approved a less radical but still controversial formula for gradually lowering price supports to conform more closely to actual market influences. As proposed by Foley, loan rates generally could not be reduced more than 5 percent a year.

The subcommittee also approved a third option, a so-called "supply-management" referendum — similar to proposals being debated in the Senate Agriculture Committee — by which farmers could choose whether to institute a supply management program of higher subsidies with huge, mandatory crop reductions. The referendum proposal was seen as a political fallback for members who did not want to appear in favor of lower price supports.

Dairy Program Zips Through

Meanwhile, the Dairy subcommittee held one day of markup action and reported its provisions to the full committee June 26. Subcommittee Chairman Tony Coelho, D-Calif., had guided the panel through weeks of private talks trying to cut $700 million from a program that was costing about $1.7 billion a year.

The subcommittee agreed to continue a controversial "diversion" program of paying dairy farmers not to produce milk — at a cost charged to farmers themselves — but also allowing for increases in price supports over five years as milk surpluses were gradually depleted.

Southeastern dairy farmers generally opposed paying for the diversion program because the Southeast did not produce milk at a surplus. So Coelho included a provision to add "differentials," or geographical bonuses to the support payments made to farmers in the Southeast at the expense of other regions.

The differentials, however, were opposed by farmers from other regions. And James M. Jeffords of Vermont, ranking Republican on the subcommittee, voted for an amendment to kill the differential plan, which failed 5-11.

Committee Ratifies Most Recommendations

The Agriculture panel began full committee markup sessions July 9 and, in most cases, accepted subcommittee recommendations for HR 2100, including those for research, conservation, cotton, rice and dairy programs.

De la Garza deferred debate on price supports for wheat and feed grains until last, however, because members of the Wheat subcommittee had not agreed on how the program should be structured.

As in the Dairy subcommittee, the full committee rejected efforts by Republican members to reduce milk price supports and make them apply equally to all regions of the country. The committee retained the regional differentials. Coelho's effort to achieve "dairy unity" in the bill included a $200 million concession to the livestock industry, which wanted price protection from dairy farmers who culled their herds in a diversion program, sending thousands of dairy cows to slaughter.

The committee approved a plan to have the government buy up to 200 million pounds of red meat a year, and also to require staggered slaughtering of dairy cows to lessen the impact on beef markets.

Price-Support Plan Accepted

The committee July 25, on a 26-16 vote, finally agreed to a price-support system for wheat, corn and other feed grains that would have allowed farm prices for 1986 crops to drop sharply to match world market levels, but required that farmers be compensated in direct federal subsidies for any losses they incurred.

The proposal, offered by Foley, would have allowed loan rates for wheat, corn and other feed grains to be reduced at the agriculture secretary's discretion a maximum of 25 percent in 1986 but no more than 5 percent each year thereafter.

To compensate farmers for immediate losses in income, the Foley provision would have increased direct payments to farmers by freezing existing target prices for two years, and then allowing no more than a 5 percent reduction each year thereafter. A $50,000 cap on direct payments was to be removed if the agriculture secretary was to reduce the loan rate by the full 25 percent.

A major component of the proposal would have required wheat producers who participated in the loan program to idle 30 percent of their crop land and feed grain producers to idle 20 percent of their land.

The House committee approved the Foley compromise after narrowly defeating a competing proposal for marketing loans and by a wider margin rejecting the farmer referendum.

Offered by Stangeland, the marketing loan concept had the support of a majority of Democrats on the panel, but it was ultimately defeated, 20-22, July 24. And, after a long debate July 25, the panel voted 24-17 to delete a subcommittee recommendation to let grain farmers choose in a nationwide referendum if price supports should be raised, rather than lowered, at the cost of stiff, mandatory production controls.

Budget Concerns Stall Markup

Although the committee had effectively finished its work, budget worries and continued bickering over reductions in price-support loan rates prevented a final vote on HR 2100 before Congress adjourned for August.

The panel was under pressure to act, to clear its docket for action on proposals affecting the ailing Farm Credit System, a federally regulated network of farmer-owned agriculture banks, and because existing farm programs were to expire Sept. 30. *(Farm Credit System bailout, p. 543)*

When existing farm law expired, permanent law kicked in, but for most farmers that meant no immediate consequences. There was some urgency regarding dairy price supports, however, which would have jumped Oct. 1 by nearly a half — from $11.60 a hundredweight (what the government paid for surplus butter, cheese and dry milk to ensure a minimum price) to $16.22 a hundredweight.

Ultimately, Congress had to vote several extensions of the dairy program to prevent the change in price supports from taking effect. *(Dairy extensions, p. 520)*

Hanging over the committee and preventing it from reporting the bill was uncertainty over spending targets. The fiscal 1986 budget resolution had not been adopted until Aug. 1, hampering the panel's ability to guess how much it might have to cut to meet its targets.

The budget resolution specified that farm spending would have to be reduced $7.9 billion over three years through reconciliation, the process of changing laws to make cuts. *(Reconciliation, p. 498)*

In its deliberations up to Aug. 1, the House panel had voted to reduce outlays for commodity price supports alone by several billion dollars, but new programs for farm export subsidies, land conservation incentives and direct income payments to farmers had put the bill's projected cost $3.9 billion above existing spending levels, and $11.8 billion above the reconciliation target.

As a result, when the committee returned to work Sept. 4 de la Garza appointed a 12-member task force to recommend places where the committee might cut.

The task force achieved that reduction through a number of devices, some designed merely to delay expenses beyond the three fiscal years covered by the budget resolution. Other savings were achieved by limiting application for emergency disaster loans to the year of a declared disaster. The task force recommendations were adopted Sept. 10.

Surprise Vote: Referendum Resurrected

As its last act, the committee put a production control program back into the bill. Several key Democrats, nervous about lowering price supports, had favored taking another vote on the mandatory controls referendum.

James Weaver, D-Ore., a leading proponent of mandatory controls, sponsored an amendment to restore the referendum to the bill, but the committee turned him down 19-22 after debating the issue for nearly four hours. At that point, referendum supporters had picked up only two votes from their defeat in July.

Bedell then proposed an amendment in what seemed to be a final desperation move. He billed it as a "voluntary," rather than mandatory, production control program because farmers would not have to comply with acreage cutbacks as long as they sold their grain for export or fed it to their own livestock.

The proposal picked up three votes, and passed 22-18.

The favorable vote came as something of a shock, even to Bedell, who acknowledged that the vote turned on the influential support of Foley, who had argued strongly against mandatory controls but voted for Bedell's voluntary program.

Foley had been unable to generate widespread support for provisions in HR 2100 to reduce price supports but maintain income subsidies. Many of the committee's ranking Democrats were promising to challenge the bill on the floor unless it included provisions to expand, rather than reduce, price-support benefits.

Despite the so-called voluntary nature of Bedell's referendum, the administration immediately attacked it and promised a veto if it were not struck on the floor.

Cargo Preference: The Last Trouble Spot

Once approved by the Agriculture panel, HR 2100 faced one last obstacle to floor consideration. The bill had been referred to the Merchant Marine panel after Agriculture reported it with a provision exempting government-assisted export programs from cargo preference rules.

Cargo preference laws required that half of all government-generated agricultural exports be shipped on U.S.-flag vessels. Farm groups had insisted on a full exemption from those laws for agricultural export sales that involved government subsidies and credits. Merchant Marine members, however, maintained that the nation's dwindling merchant marine fleet needed government subsidies to survive.

The exemption was included in HR 2100 by the Agriculture panel with the understanding that a compromise had been worked out between farm groups and merchant marine interests. But some members balked at the agreement, and Walter B. Jones, D-N.C., chairman of the Merchant Marine Committee, pledged to hold up the farm bill in his committee until the deal was resolved.

Jones' committee reported the bill Sept. 18, after substituting for the Agriculture Committee's provision, new language protecting the status quo (H Rept 99-271, Part II).

In drafting a rule for floor debate, the Rules Committee decided to defer to the Merchant Marine Committee and sent the bill to the floor Sept. 19 with the status quo intact.

House Floor Action

After seven days of debate spread over two weeks, the House Oct. 8 spurned administration budget-cutting demands and passed HR 2100, a $141 billion measure to extend federal farm and nutrition programs for five years. Keeping the administration's original agriculture proposals far out of view, a bipartisan coalition of members voted 282-141 for the bill, crafted mainly by the House Democratic leadership and established farm organizations. *(Vote 314, p. 100-H)*

For farm programs, the House bill provided $70 billion through fiscal 1990 for a variety of benefits designed to prop up farmers' incomes and expand their ability to borrow money. That figure also included programs for soil conservation, agricultural research and foreign trade.

The bill also authorized $71 billion in spending through fiscal 1990 for the Agriculture Department's nutrition programs, including food stamps.

The main thrust of the bill was cast Oct. 3, when the House voted against allowing farmers to decide whether the government should implement mandatory controls as a way to guarantee higher prices for major grain crops. Left intact, however, were most of the commodity programs adopted in the Agriculture Committee, including provisions designed to shore up farmers' incomes that were sponsored by Foley and supported by most commodity groups and agribusiness organizations.

Opening Salvos at the Administration

The House Sept. 26 began working on amendments to the bill by soundly rejecting two administration-backed proposals to shave federal subsidies for the dairy and sugar industries.

On a 142-263 vote, it spurned an amendment to scale down sugar price supports over three years. Later, on a 166-244 vote, the House defeated an amendment to make annual reductions in dairy price supports and to prevent the revival of a "diversion" program that would pay farmers not to produce milk. *(Votes 289, 290, p. 92-H)*

Republican leaders conceded that the Reagan administration, as a result of the votes, lost considerable ground in its efforts to scale back price- and income-support benefits in the remaining sections of the bill.

The administration had forged an unusual alliance with consumer groups in an effort to reduce the government's involvement in sugar, dairy and peanut production. But the margins of defeat surprised even committee members, who recalled that an amendment to eliminate the sugar program had passed the House in 1981, only to be knocked out later in a conference with the Senate.

Agriculture Secretary Block had appeared on Capitol Hill for some last-minute lobbying of Republicans. But, as it turned out, 74 Republicans broke ranks with the administration and voted against cutting dairy price supports, and 103 Republicans voted against cutting sugar supports.

Sugar Fight

House Speaker Thomas P. O'Neill Jr. D-Mass., and Majority Whip Foley predicted that any amendment to change the substance of the bill would face an uphill fight, a promise that was proved on the first roll call — the vote to reduce sugar price supports.

The government supported the price by buying U.S. sugar at 18 cents a pound from refiners who agreed to pass on the benefits to growers. The government also placed strict quotas on imported sugar to protect U.S. growers against foreign exporters who "dumped" their own surplus sugar on the world market at heavily subsidized prices.

Thomas J. Downey, D-N.Y., and Bill Gradison, R-Ohio, proposed to reduce the sugar price support by 1 cent a pound per year until it reached 15 cents a pound for the 1988 crop. They also wanted to eliminate a "transportation" factor in current law that added about 2.5 cents a pound to the support price.

Downey said the sugar program had pushed the domestic price of sugar past that in nearly all other nations.

And Gradison argued that reducing the support price would open U.S. markets to Caribbean sugar-producing nations that needed money to repay debts to U.S. banks.

But Agriculture Committee members successfully changed the course of the debate by insisting that sugar price supports were assuring a steady price to sugar manufacturers, and, in the process, protecting U.S jobs. "This will be the first vote on whether we protect American producers and manufacturers this year," said de la Garza in an impassioned floor speech.

"This may well be the beginning of a war, and we are going to have a trade war. You cannot desert this industry at its worst hour. We have to fly the flag."

Dairy Program

The biggest winner of the day may have been Coelho, who was widely criticized for the way he pushed an industry-written dairy bill through committee. As Dairy subcommittee chairman, he managed the bill on the floor without participating in the debate himself. Instead he nervously stalked the chamber in search of votes while other members of dairy states spoke in favor of the bill.

The House bill continued the diversion program that expired in March 1985 as a way to reduce the massive surpluses of dairy products that the government had been required to buy up through the price-support program. Farmers themselves paid the cost of the diversion program through assessments on the milk products they sold at market.

Dairy-state members won a further victory, however, when the House by voice vote approved an amendment to limit the assessments to 50 cents per hundred pounds of milk equivalent (cheese, butter and dry milk). Any diversion costs that exceeded that limit were to be borne by the government.

The bill also permitted the agriculture secretary to buy out whole herds of dairy cows and send them to slaughter, to reduce milk production. But as a concession to the livestock industry, which feared a market glut of beef, the committee included a provision to require the government to buy up $200 million worth of red meat.

The House by voice vote increased that figure to $250 million in a compromise between Coelho and Doug Bereuter, R-Neb.

Marketing Loans Dumped

Dan Glickman, D-Kan., accused the House of "institutional conservatism" for resisting several changes in farm policy, principally the referendum on production controls and Glickman's own proposal for mandatory marketing loans that would have allowed farmers to repay their loans at the market rate, not the rate at which the money was borrowed.

Glickman and Stangeland, among other junior members of the Agriculture Committee, had pushed marketing loans as a way to make U.S. grain exports competitive. They lost in committee on a 20-22 vote, but later won a compromise to give the agriculture secretary discretionary authority to establish marketing loans.

On the floor, Stangeland proposed combining a mandatory marketing loan program with another amendment to the wheat section of the bill to establish a "tiered system" of income subsidies that would increase the target prices for the first 15,000 bushels of a farmer's crop.

The amendment failed on a close 200-228 vote Oct. 1. *(Vote 293, p. 94-H)*

Referendum Rejected

Responding to intense lobbying by agriculture organizations and the administration, the House Oct. 3 rejected a proposal to let farmers vote on what direction government price-support programs should take. The referendum rejection represented the administration's first major victory on the floor.

By 251-174, the House eliminated a section calling for a referendum on imposing strict federal marketing controls on the production and sale of grain. *(Vote 301, p. 96-H)*

The marketing controls — if approved by 60 percent of the nation's grain producers — would have required large-scale reductions in wheat and corn production as a way to guarantee higher prices for those crops.

Without those acreage reductions, prices were virtually guaranteed to fall under the remaining provisions of the bill, which allowed reductions in price supports to bring U.S. farm prices more in line with world market levels.

The proposal to give farmers direct control over the structure of federal agriculture policy had developed slowly over the summer. The idea was to let farmers vote either to accept the traditional voluntary commodity price-support programs as authorized by Congress, or to submit instead to a mandatory program as specified in the referendum proposal.

The mandatory program, if approved in the referendum, would require all farmers to cut back on production to limit supply and thereby increase prices. The government would be required to impose acreage quotas, even for farmers who chose not to participate in federal price-support programs.

The Agriculture panel at first rejected the referendum proposal. But a grass-roots campaign supporting it won the votes of some members during August and bolstered key Democratic backers.

Foley strongly opposed mandatory controls, but several other panel Democrats threatened to mutiny unless such a provision was in the bill. And Foley eventually accepted a "compromise" referendum amendment during committee markup offered by Bedell that was billed as a "voluntary" program of marketing controls and export subsidies. If approved in a referendum, farmers who did not agree to cut production could sell their crops only on foreign markets or use them as feed grain but they would not be allowed to sell them in the United States.

When the Bedell provision came up on the floor Oct. 1, Madigan moved to strike it. Referendum proponents, backed by O'Neill and Majority Leader Jim Wright, D-Texas, believed they could sustain the referendum section on a close vote, but they were undermined by a series of setbacks.

First, Ways and Means Committee Chairman Dan Rostenkowski, D-Ill., in a letter to all members, opposed certain language in the referendum provision covering import restrictions that Rostenkowski believed should be handled by his panel. He also said the bill was "bad trade policy." The Agriculture Committee tried to accommodate Rostenkowski with technical amendments but his continued opposition indicated that the House leadership remained divided on the issue.

Second, debate was stalled on the issue over two days, giving administration and agribusiness lobbyists time to marshal forces against the referendum plan.

When the vote neared on Oct. 3, Madigan was confident he had the votes to knock the Bedell provision out of the bill. Foley and de la Garza, who had been insisting that the entire committee bill remain intact, offered only mild defense of the referendum. In the end, 82 Democrats deserted the leadership and voted for the Madigan amendment. Many were from so-called agriculture districts, including the entire Indiana delegation.

Madigan held onto all but 10 Republican votes.

Cargo Preference Wins Reprieve

A second major vote Oct. 3 pitted two committees against each other in a battle over how the government subsidized agriculture exports. By 179-245, members rejected an attempt by the Agriculture panel to amend cargo preference language added to HR 2100 by the Merchant Marine and Fisheries Committee. *(Vote 303, p. 96-H)*

Efforts during the year to reach a compromise between farm and merchant marine interests had failed, as did a last-minute attempt on the floor.

Immediately after winning on the cargo-preference exemption vote, Merchant Marine Committee leaders prevailed again, 151-269, on an attempt to charge off the cost of cargo preference subsidies for agriculture exports to the Department of Transportation, rather than Agriculture. *(Vote 304, p. 96-H)*

"We were stronger, and we happened to be right," said Mario Biaggi, D-N.Y., chairman of the Merchant Marine Subcommittee. "We put the problem of cargo preference to rest."

Peanuts, Honey, Tobacco Survive

The House Oct. 3 defeated 195-228 an amendment by Stan Lundine, D-N.Y., to phase out the price-support program for peanuts, and turned back on a technicality an attempt by Silvio O. Conte, R-Mass., to eliminate a price-support program for honey producers. *(Vote 302, p. 96-H)*

On Oct. 7, the House defeated by voice vote another attempt by Conte to abolish the honey program.

Consumer advocates won a significant victory the same day, however, when the House voted 340-65 to place an annual $250,000 cap on the amount of price-support loans available to individual commercial beekeepers. There were no limits in existing law on the price supports beekeepers could receive from the government. *(Vote 308, p. 98-H)*

During the final day of debate, Oct. 8, committee members beat back efforts to eliminate the price-support program for tobacco, rejecting by a 195-230 vote an amendment by Thomas E. Petri, R-Wis. *(Vote 310, p. 98-H)*

Finally, the House rejected a last-minute effort to combine two previously defeated proposals: a farmer referendum on mandatory controls and marketing loans.

The marketing loan proposal, again sponsored by Stangeland, was reintroduced as a substitute to another referendum proposal. The mandatory controls referendum was sponsored by Bill Alexander, D-Ark., who hoped an alliance of mandatory control and marketing loan supporters would generate enough votes for passage.

But the twin proposals instead generated severe criticism from members who complained that they had no time to study the 500-page Stangeland substitute under a time deadline for debate that had been agreed to earlier. Stangeland's marketing loan substitute was summarily rejected, 52-371, and Alexander's mandatory controls referendum was similarly defeated, 59-368. *(Votes 311, 312, p. 98-H)*

Senate Committee Action

The Senate Agriculture Committee, under the firm control of minority Democrats and renegade Republicans, Sept. 19 approved a farm bill that sought to lower the prices of major crops, but protect direct subsidies to farmers.

The panel, on a 10-6 vote, ordered the four-year omnibus farm bill (S 1714 — S Rept 99-145) sent to the Senate floor after a deal involving the Agriculture and Finance committees was forged between wheat-state and tobacco-state senators.

S 1714 was an original bill introduced by Helms Sept. 30 that incorporated the decisions made by the panel since markup began May 14. The committee had worked from a different bill, S 616, which Helms introduced March 7. He called S 616 an attempt to strike a balance between the administration's call for a radical change in farm programs and the need to slowly wean farmers from their support system.

Clearing the Way

S 616 had been locked in committee since July, when Republicans won approval to lower price supports for major crops. Democrats, however, held fast against reducing income subsidies, and Helms and Dole were unable to fashion a compromise capable of winning bipartisan support.

It was a deal involving tobacco price supports that were contained in a separate bill that opened the door for the committee to report a farm bill — but not the bill Helms and Dole wanted.

In a key 10-7 vote taken moments before the bill's final approval, two Republican defectors — Mark Andrews, N.D., and Mitch McConnell, Ky. — joined the committee's eight Democrats in support of slightly increasing and then freezing direct subsidies for farmers at existing levels through the life of the four-year bill.

Andrews previously had joined the Democrats in insisting that direct subsidies be maintained for four years, rather than allowing gradual reductions after one year as favored by committee Republicans. Freshman McConnell, on the other hand, had sat silently through three months of markup action on the farm bill, faithfully voting with Helms and Dole on every provision.

McConnell changed his vote after Dole struck a deal to save the price-support system for tobacco, the main agricultural product from McConnell's home state.

"My only interest is in the 150,000 people in Kentucky who grow tobacco," McConnell said afterward, adding that his commitment to the Democrats was only temporary. "I have cooperated in getting [the farm bill] out on the floor. I'm not bound by that vote on the floor," he said.

The tobacco plan, which included provisions designed to aid both tobacco growers and cigarette manufacturers, was offered as an amendment by Dole to a deficit-reduction bill being marked up in the Finance panel, where Dole was also a member. In an unexpected move Sept. 18, Dole introduced the plan as part of a package amendment — combined with a permanent extension of the 16-cents-per-pack cigarette tax — to the so-called budget reconciliation bill (S 1730). *(Tobacco program, p. 539; reconciliation, p. 498)*

The ploy took most Agriculture Democrats by surprise. But David L. Boren, D-Okla., and David Pryor, D-Ark., who also sat on both Agriculture and Finance, agreed to drop their opposition to Dole's tobacco amendment; in return, they won McConnell's vote for their farm package and a promise from Helms not to stand in the way of reporting a Democratic-sponsored farm bill to the floor. Helms voted against reporting the bill.

Over Budget; Veto Threatened

S 1714, as reported, provided an estimated $73.8 billion over four years for farm programs and $53.1 billion for nutrition programs, including food stamps. The Congressional Budget Office estimated the cost over three years would be at least $9 billion above the limit set in the fiscal 1986 budget resolution, primarily owing to the income-subsidy freeze.

Agriculture Secretary Block said revised projections of 1985 crop surpluses further boosted the cost of the bill by $5 billion to $15 billion, and he threatened to recommend a veto if the cost was not brought down.

Markup Begins; Few Decisions

During its first days of markup, which opened May 14, the committee began wading through that section of the bill devoted to exports.

Despite Block's announcement that the administration would initiate an export-subsidy program on its own, the committee tentatively agreed to require one. Senators also spent several days looking for ways to expand exports using the Food for Peace program — known as PL 480 — through which the United States donated surplus food overseas.

Through May and most of June, however, markup moved fitfully. Although senators finished working on exports, the committee often was unable to find a quorum to meet, and members dodged the central question of price supports.

But as Congress recessed for a 10-day Fourth of July break, Agriculture members returned home promising that they would meet a July 15 deadline to send a farm bill to the Senate floor. The deadline was set June 27 at Dole's urging, during the panel's last meeting before the recess.

No small degree of Dole's concern was the unease felt by wheat farmers, including those from his home state of Kansas, as planting season for the winter crop approached and the federal program for wheat farmers was about to expire. Dole got the committee to agree to a markup deadline in return for Block's support for a delay in a scheduled referendum on mandatory wheat planting quotas. *(Wheat referendum, p. 522)*

Before agreeing to the deadline, the committee took a series of straw votes on general policy concepts, practically all of which were inconclusive.

The panel demonstrated the general lack of consensus on Capitol Hill and among farm groups on how to restructure farm programs when it deadlocked 8-8 in a straw vote June 26 on the broad concept of setting farm price support rates anywhere between 75 and 85 percent of prevailing market prices. The vote hinged on lowering loan rates and target prices, or just lowering loan rates.

The committee then turned to another broad concept of holding referendums on some form of mandatory quotas that would determine how much farmers would be allowed to grow and market each year. Edward Zorinsky, D-Neb., offered a plan to hold a referendum on wheat quotas; Tom Harkin, D-Iowa, offered a similar proposal for feed grains and soybeans, as well as wheat.

The Zorinsky and Harkin plans, known as "supply management" programs, were designed to raise price supports even higher than existing rates, to assure profits to farmers who were forced to cut back significantly on production, to reduce surpluses, to raise the floor on domestic prices, and to decrease the government's cost.

The committee defeated the supply management referendum concepts on two 5-11 straw votes.

Deadlock Continues; 'Sodbuster' Plan Approved

Returning from the July 4th recess, committee members were no closer to agreeing on price supports and income subsidies. But reflecting a desire to reduce massive surpluses of U.S. crops that burdened the industry and depressed prices, the panel voted to put up to 30 million acres of the country's most erodible farm land into a conservation reserve, paying farmers to take the land out of production.

Mirroring a House Agriculture Committee decision of July 9, the Senate panel the same week approved "sodbuster" provisions to disqualify farmers who cultivated highly erodible land from receiving any federal price-support benefits. The committee went a step further than its House counterpart, proposing to ban aid after 1988 to farmers who did not set up government-approved conservation plans on land they were currently planting.

Then, in an attempt to get bipartisan support for the core price-support provisions, Dole began trying to combine the main ideas of several senators, courting Democrats Zorinsky, Boren and Alan J. Dixon of Illinois as potential crossover votes on a committee that Republicans controlled 9-to-8.

In a series of fast-breaking committee meetings, alternately in public and behind closed doors, Dole engineered a compromise during the week of July 15 that seemed to protect most of the interests of the committee's senior members — and for a time seemed certain to make it out of committee.

Zorinsky-Dole Compromise Accepted

Dole, joined by Zorinsky, offered a proposal that earned for a time majority support, even though it cast aside budget demands that farm spending be cut. Committee staff estimated the plan's farm programs would have cost $40.5 billion over three years — only $1 billion less than if existing programs were extended without change.

Using the Zorinsky-Dole compromise as a "framework," and working in quick fashion July 18 and 19, Dole got agreements from committee members on how to set commodity price supports for cotton, rice, sugar, peanuts and milk.

That cleared the way for expected agreement on price supports for wheat and corn, and, Dole hoped, floor action before the August recess.

The Zorinsky-Dole plan would have overhauled the crop loan system by allowing loan rates to be reduced as market prices fell. The plan would have made an immediate 30-cent reduction in the loan rate for wheat, dropping it to $3 a bushel, and a 15-cent reduction in the rate for corn, down to $2.40 a bushel.

In succeeding crop years the plan would have allowed 5 percent decreases each year, if market prices continued to decline. And a further 20 percent reduction in any one year would have been allowed if farmers continued to default on their loans.

To protect farmers' incomes, Zorinsky-Dole would have frozen deficiency payments for one year and allowed 5 percent reductions thereafter. If the one-time 20 percent loan-rate cut were instituted, an existing $50,000 cap on deficiency payments that applied to each participating farmer's crop would have been lifted.

Similar to the recommendation of the House Wheat subcommittee, Zorinsky-Dole included in its package discretionary marketing loans for wheat, corn, cotton and rice. And it would have allowed a referendum among wheat farmers on the question of mandatory production controls in return for higher price supports.

In another concession to a ranking Democratic member, the committee also approved a dairy plan submitted by Sen. Patrick J. Leahy, D-Vt., that would have retained price supports for milk solids at the 1985 level of $11.60 a pound for one year, then allowed a 50-cent reduction in January 1987.

Zorinsky-Dole Plan Undone

A successful maneuver by committee Democrats July 24 threatened to add $8 billion more to the cost of the bill, as the committee began voting on the programs for wheat and other grains. Democrats proposed to extend the freeze on target prices to four years. The motion passed 9-8, with Andrews joining all eight Democrats.

The vote, which dramatically raised the cost of the bill, restored the panel's stalemate. Helms threatened to vote against reporting the bill favorably, and Dole threatened to break out the wheat section and bring it to the Senate floor separately.

The impasse lasted well into the next week, although committee members managed to work on other sections of the bill. Then it appeared July 31 that the Democrats and Andrews were about to prevail, and report the bill with the four-year target-price freeze. Helms called a recess and Dole reiterated his threat to call up a separate farm export bill on the floor and attach his own farm bill to it.

But after delaying his move late into the night, Dole finally backed off from his threat. The next day Helms announced that the committee would continue working in September, following a recess for the month of August.

Committee members returned to work Sept. 10 after a five-week hiatus, still deadlocked on price- and income-support sections of the bill. The committee spent the balance of its first week back finishing action on credit, exports and food stamps.

Then came the arrangement between Dole, Helms, and the Democrats that allowed the tobacco program to be attached to reconciliation. That in turn allowed the committee to report the bill Sept. 19.

Senate Floor Action

The Senate Nov. 23 passed a four-year reauthorization of farm programs after a tense, all-night showdown Nov. 22 between Dole and three farm-state Democrats. The vote was 61-28. *(Vote 343, p. 58-S)*

Dole was forced to strike a last-minute compromise with the Democrats to pass a bill before Congress' Thanksgiving recess. After the deal was reached, senators accepted a Dole substitute that incorporated all changes previously made in the bill. Floor fights over S 1714, the Senate Agriculture Committee's bill, had consumed 12 days over a month's time. In the end, the amended version of S 1714 was substituted for the text of the House-passed farm bill (HR 2100).

The bargain that led to passage of the Senate bill centered on deficiency payments, farmer income subsidies that covered the difference between market prices for major commodities and higher target prices set by Congress. The Senate-passed measure called for a one-year freeze on target prices for wheat, corn, cotton and rice, and then annual 5 percent reductions. That was the basic formula favored all along by Dole and the Reagan administration but opposed by Democrats and farm-state Republicans.

The compromise required that the 5 percent reductions in 1987 be made up to farmers by payments-in-kind of government-owned commodities, which farmers were free to sell. In 1988, target prices were to be decreased another 5 percent, reducing cash payments to 90 percent of 1985 levels, but payments-in-kind were to keep total payments at 95 percent of existing rates. In 1989, target prices were to be reduced another 5 percent, but no payments-in-kind were to be allowed.

Although the final Senate version of the bill had one position on income subsidies, three days before the bill passed Dole had engineered adoption of a bizarre compromise that contained two blatantly conflicting positions on the issue. Nevertheless, that vote had ended a three-week gridlock that threatened to derail the bill.

With his eyes on the calendar — and a fear that further delay would prevent enactment of the farm bill in 1985 — Dole had offered a catchall package that he acknowledged to be contradictory and over-budget, but that at the same time placated the various interests whose disagreement had blocked the bill. By offering a plan with something for everyone, Dole avoided both an embarrassing defeat for conservative Republicans and the administration, and a prolonged filibuster by Democrats.

His previous threat to pull the bill from the floor until 1986 did little to budge senators from their stalemate. So Dole instead crafted a comprehensive compromise amendment that included both of the opposing positions that divided the Senate over target prices — a one-year freeze vs. a four-year freeze — to which he added a number of "sweeteners" for key commodity interests. The contradictions, he said, could be worked out in negotiations with House conferees.

Dole swept a series of three crucial votes Nov. 20, as the Senate adopted his amendment, 56-41, and turned back two Democratic attempts to amend it. *(Vote 319, p. 55-S)*

Democratic leaders eventually conceded defeat, although they were able to force some changes in the bill with their 11th-hour tactics. After nearly a month of delay and inaction, the Senate breezed through the remaining sections of the omnibus measure.

Debate Begins; Hangs Up Immediately

Under renewed threats of a veto over its cost and approach, the Senate began debate Oct. 25 on the committee version of S 1714, which had been reported over the objections of the administration and the Senate GOP leadership by a majority comprised of the panel's eight Democrats joined by two Republicans.

And partisan emotions and parliamentary gamesmanship combined to frustrate Senate action from the beginning. By the end of the first week, Nov. 1, Republicans and Democrats had fought to a standoff on the major issue in the bill, setting levels for price supports and income subsidies for major farm commodities.

Each side claimed partial victory on two key votes designed to show, in Dole's words, "where the votes are hiding." On Oct. 30 the Senate rejected, 48-51, an amendment by Richard G. Lugar, R-Ind., to cut income subsidies after 1986. But on a Nov. 1 procedural vote, senators went on record, 49-45, in favor of a modified version of that idea offered by Dole. *(Vote 266, p. 48-S; vote 276, p. 49-S)*

Democrats, who had gotten the Agriculture Committee to maintain a four-year freeze on income subsidies, said the first vote gave them an upper hand on the issue in the chamber, where the GOP held a 53-47 majority. But the closeness of that vote, and the succeeding one, showed new evidence of the shifting allegiances on farm issues within each party, adding geographical confusion to political uncertainty.

Twelve Republicans defected from party ranks and voted against the Lugar cuts. Ten of the 12 were from Farm Belt states. On the other hand, eight Democrats split from their party line and voted for the cuts. Most of the defecting Democrats were from Eastern states where farm issues had little or no constituency. Two days later, however, only four Republicans crossed party lines to vote with the Democrats against the Dole plan, illustrating the fragile nature of the farm coalition and setting the stage for Dole's something-for-everyone compromise.

Immediately after the second vote Nov. 1, the Senate stopped work on the farm bill, not to resume until Nov. 18.

Cargo Preference Compromise

The only major progress that first week on the substance of the bill involved cargo preference requirements for U.S.-subsidized agricultural exports.

The Senate approved a compromise to exempt government-financed commercial exports from the requirement that half be shipped on U.S.-flag vessels. At the same time, the plan expanded such rules for government-donated exports. But that compromise opened a parliamentary gambit that entangled the entire farm bill in a series of technical countermoves.

Cargo preference had been a contentious issue between agriculture and maritime groups for some time. Existing law dated to 1954, when Congress tried to protect the U.S. merchant marine fleet from cheaper foreign competition with the cargo preference rule.

A Feb. 21 court ruling expanded the law to cover an Agriculture Department program that blended government credit with private export sales. Following the decision, farm groups began trying to exempt all such programs from cargo preference, with key agriculture organizations going so far as to reject all attempts at a compromise.

Maritime groups won a major victory, however, when the House voted Oct. 3 to reject efforts by the Agriculture Committee to write in widespread exemptions from cargo preference requirements for most agricultural exports.

After that vote, Sen. Thad Cochran, R-Miss., renegotiated a previous agreement between farm and maritime groups that exempted all government-generated commercial sales, such as those in the "blended credit" program; but in exchange, U.S. merchant marine companies would get assurances of shipping contracts for 75 percent of all government-donated export programs, such as Food for Peace (PL 480). The increase from the existing 50 percent requirement was to be paid for by the Transportation Department, rather than Agriculture.

In an effort to speed the delicate package through the Senate without amendment, Cochran, Ted Stevens, R-Alaska, and Daniel K. Inouye, D-Hawaii, colluded in a parliamentary maneuver of amending their own amendments with minor technical changes, thus blocking further amendments until the Senate went on record on the basic merits of the plan.

That tactic resulted in a tentative 70-30 vote Oct. 29 for the compromise, but also brought on the wrath of Dixon, Rudy Boschwitz, R-Minn., and other Midwestern senators, who felt the new plan would limit the shipping traffic in the shallow-water, inland ports on the Great Lakes, accessible only by the St. Lawrence Seaway. *(Vote 259, p. 47-S)*

Dixon and Boschwitz led a "filibuster by amendment," offering six amendments designed to protect Great Lakes shipping interests, and forcing time-consuming roll-call votes on each. *(Votes 260-265, pp. 47-S, 48-S)*

Although Dixon and Boschwitz, at best, picked up only four more votes, they forced a face-saving compromise that encouraged the government to maintain the level of export traffic in Great Lakes ports that PL 480 shipments generated in 1984. Cochran continued to oppose the Dixon compromise, but Stevens and Inouye agreed to go along and it was eventually approved 53-43. *(Vote 269, p. 48-S)*

Income Subsidy Battle

Even as the cargo preference compromise was coming to fruition, however, senators were positioning themselves for the next battle. While Dixon negotiated his deal off the floor on Oct. 30, the original "amendment tree" on cargo preference constructed by Cochran, Stevens and Inouye was temporarily set aside.

In the meantime, the Senate debated, and narrowly defeated, Lugar's subsidy-cutting amendment.

Both Republicans and Democrats read the vote as an indication that, while the Senate was not prepared to make full-scale cuts on income subsidies, some kind of budget-cutting measure would probably succeed. Each side then scrambled to come up with spending cuts that would protect its own members' interests and preserve the fragile chemistry of urban-rural, Republican-Democratic votes needed for any plan.

Dole held up the threat of an amendment to cut maximum income subsidies from $50,000 per farm to $25,000. That put a scare into Southern Democrats from cotton and rice states, where the $50,000 payment limit was considered sacrosanct.

On the other side, John Melcher, D-Mont., circulated a package he said would save $7.6 billion over three years, enough to bring the bill in line with the budget resolution without touching income subsidies.

Dole, calling Melcher's plan "smoke and mirrors," unveiled his own package for making $7.6 billion in budget cuts over three years, blending Lugar's amendment to cut income subsidies with some of Melcher's ideas. Dole also "dusted off" a program he introduced in 1978. Called "flexible parity," it would have created a sliding scale of higher benefits for wheat farmers who agreed to cut production. The more land set aside, the more subsidies farmers would get for commodities actually produced.

In 1978, Dole based his sliding scale on the concept of parity, an index of farmers' incomes based on the boom years of agriculture in 1910-1914. It passed the Senate but was thrown out in conference with the House, which voted 224-167 to instruct its conferees to reject the plan. *(1978 Almanac p. 437)*

In reintroducing the plan, Dole took parity out of the equation and replaced it with a sliding scale based on farmers' productions costs, rather than historic incomes.

Each senator wanted to be the first to introduce his budget-cutting amendment on the floor, but Dole engaged in a two-day parliamentary test of wills with his Democratic counterpart, Minority Leader Robert C. Byrd of West Virginia, had ultimately engineered the Nov. 1 procedural vote on his amendment that proved GOP discipline was strong enough for Dole to control debate.

Byrd complimented Dole for his stratagem: "So this is the game in the game-playing."

"It's a small one," Dole responded. "I haven't learned to play the big ones yet."

Contradictory Provisions

With the Senate deadlocked on the farm bill, and its attention diverted by other matters, action on S 1714 was suspended until Nov. 18. Two days later Dole got the chamber moving again in earnest when he offered the compromise containing both a one-year and a four-year target price freeze.

First, however, Dole had to untangle the amendment knot he had tied three weeks before. Unwittingly, Democrat Harkin obliged by moving Nov. 19 to table the Dole flexible parity proposal that had been the pending business since Nov. 1. Harkin's motion carried 88-8, freeing space in Dole's amendment tree for his latest compromise. *(Vote 318, p. 55-S)*

Democrats and farm-state Republicans had showed their intention to hold out for a four-year freeze of target prices. But some GOP leaders and the administration, anxious to cut the cost of farm subsidies, wanted to freeze target prices for one year and begin cutting them in 1987.

Early in the week of Nov. 18, Dole garnered the agreement of budget director James C. Miller III that he would endorse a bill whose three-year farm program cost was about $50 billion. Various estimates put the cost of the Senate committee bill $10 billion to $15 billion above that figure. But even with that concession, Dole said he needed some middle ground for bargaining with the House, so his compromise included in each section of the bill dealing with commodity target prices two provisions — a one-year freeze acceptable to the administration and conservative Republicans, and a four-year freeze acceptable to many farm-state Republicans.

But six farm-state Republicans continued to balk and voted against the Dole package: James Abdnor and Larry Pressler of South Dakota, Dave Durenberger of Minnesota, Charles E. Grassley of Iowa, Bob Kasten of Wisconsin and Don Nickles of Oklahoma.

To make up for their defections, Dole resorted to old-fashioned horse trading among senators who represented various commodity interests.

He induced some fiscally conservative Democrats to vote for several cost-saving devices, including one to increase the amount of land taken out of production. And he brought over rice-state senators with three new provisions designed to expand benefits for rice producers, including one to cover the 1985 crop that technically would not have been part of a new farm bill.

He won votes from sugar-producing states with a plan that effectively lowered the amount of sugar imported into the country. Dole also increased authority for giving disaster benefits to Gulf-state farmers whose crops were ruined in 1985 by hurricanes. And he gave corn-state senators a provision to guarantee farmers a certain income subsidy regardless of how market prices turned.

He included a section written by the American Soybean Association to give soybean farmers a flat payment of $30 an acre, and a payment-in-kind of $5 an acre worth of government-owned stocks. And in a final bow to Andrews, who had been a consistent ally of Democrats on farm policy issues, Dole added $35-per-acre payments to sunflower producers, most of whom were in North Dakota and not eligible for other farm programs.

With those sweeteners, Dole's strange compromise passed. He lured 11 Democrats to vote for the package: Pryor, Lloyd Bentsen of Texas, Dale Bumpers of Arkansas, Russell B. Long and J. Bennett Johnston of Louisiana, Lawton Chiles of Florida, Alan Cranston of California, Dennis DeConcini of Arizona, Spark M. Matsunaga of Hawaii, Sam Nunn of Georgia and William Proxmire of Wisconsin.

He also won over six Republicans who earlier had voted against a one-year freeze: Andrews, Boschwitz, John C. Danforth of Missouri, Jeremiah Denton of Alabama, Slade Gorton of Washington and Nancy Landon Kassebaum of Kansas.

Defeating Democrats

Dole held only a tenuous victory, however, until Harkin played into his hands with an amendment to add another four-year freeze provision to the bill. The defeat of Harkin's amendment finally put the Senate on record as being opposed to the four-year freeze.

The Democratic strategy to that point had been to offer another cost-cutting amendment to allay the concerns of urban Democrats who were reluctant to vote for any bill that expanded the ballooning cost of farm programs. But Dole had blocked Melcher from introducing the Democrats' proposal.

Harkin then introduced his four-year freeze plan before Melcher could offer his proposal, and 10 Democrats joined forces with 45 Republicans, for a 55-42 vote approving Dole's motion to kill the Harkin amendment. The strength of that vote gave Dole the leverage he needed to defeat Melcher's cost-cutting amendment, 50-46, on a nearly strict party-line vote. Andrews was the only Republican to vote with Melcher. *(Votes 320, 323, p. 55-S)*

The cumulative effect of all three votes was a defeat for the Democratic strategy and at least one recorded vote in favor of a one-year freeze. Dole said he would be able to go to conference with the House and negotiate with strength against a four-year freeze on target prices.

Zorinsky, ranking Democrat on the Agriculture Committee, predicted that the final outcome of the conference would be a compromise between the two poles. "It's all over for the four-year freeze," Zorinsky said. "We'll end up [in conference] with a two-year freeze."

Administration Won and Lost

In one major defeat for the administration, the Senate Nov. 19 voted 50-47 to kill an amendment by Paula Hawkins, R-Fla., to cut the dairy price-support rate by 50 cents at the beginning of 1986. *(Vote 317, p. 55-S)*

That left intact an Agriculture Committee provision that would maintain until at least January 1987 the existing rate of $11.60 per hundred pounds that the government agreed to pay dairy farmers to buy butter, cheese and nonfat dry milk, in effect providing a guaranteed price for their milk.

But the administration scored a small victory Nov. 22, when the Senate rejected, 36-60, a motion to kill an amendment by Dan Quayle, R-Ind., to phase out the price-support program for honey producers over three years. Quayle's amendment was eventually approved by voice vote. *(Vote 334, p. 57-S)*

Marathon Session

At midnight Nov. 22, when all miscellaneous amendments had been resolved and Dole was ready to press for final passage of the bill, Democrats Melcher, Harkin and J. James Exon of Nebraska threw up a final roadblock, continuing their fight against the one-year target price freeze.

All three had been left out of Dole's previous deal-making sessions, and they forced a showdown by turning Dole's own parliamentary maneuvers against him. Despite pressure by senators of both parties to allow the chamber to recess for Thanksgiving, the three Democrats insisted that the two contradictory provisions on target prices were unacceptable. By keeping the chamber trapped in its own maze of rules, they forced Dole to keep the Senate in session overnight into Nov. 23.

When it became apparent that Melcher, Exon and Harkin would not relent, Dole agreed to meet with them later that day to work out the final compromise that became the Senate-passed bill. The session ended at 3:45 a.m.

It was doubtful that the Democrats won much in the compromise. The final Senate bill was slightly more generous than Dole and the administration originally had wanted, but it no longer provided for a four-year freeze, as reported by the committee.

"I hardly think we [capitulated]," Dole said afterwards. "We got what we [originally] wanted in committee. I think we've got a good document to prepare for conference."

"It is not a good farm bill," Exon acknowledged. "But it's about one-third better than the Republican bill they tried to shove down our throats."

Harkin voted against the bill on final passage. So did Helms, who fulfilled a prophecy he made earlier in the year that he would become the first Agriculture chairman to vote against a farm bill.

Conference Action

Congress returned Dec. 2 from its Thanksgiving recess, and the conference on the farm bill got under way Dec. 5. But on the first day conferees reached only token agreements before adjourning to back rooms to haggle over major differences.

The conference stalled almost as soon as it began over price-support programs for sugar, dairy and wool producers. Conferees and their staffs then split up into separate commodity-interest groups that met privately to avoid further public bickering on even more controversial programs for wheat, corn, rice, cotton and dairy farmers.

They returned only for a brief, half-hour session Dec. 6, to give tentative approval to staff recommendations for reauthorizing non-controversial agricultural research programs.

Part of the early hang-up was the House conferees' readiness to accept Senate-drafted limits on imported sugar that Dole had accepted on the Senate floor to win support for the bill from Southern Democrats.

The Reagan administration, which wanted to open U.S. sugar markets to debt-ridden Latin American countries, opposed the quotas. The White House then jumped further into the fray by sending notice of its other "minimum tests" for the president's approval, including its long-sought $50 billion cap on the bill's three-year cost for farm programs. The House version would have cost $56 billion; the Senate's $58 billion, according to Agriculture Department estimates. Veto threats were hurled at potential conference compromises until the final agreement was cut.

Agriculture Secretary Block also was particularly insistent on changes in the dairy program, quickly nixing one potential conference deal to eliminate a House dairy diversion program to pay farmers not to produce milk, in exchange for Senate approval of a federal buyout plan for whole herds of milk cows.

Block rejected the compromise because it did not include a dairy price-support cut before January 1987. But attempts to make cuts earlier than that had been rejected in floor action by both chambers.

First Compromise: Income Subsidies

The separate groups continued meeting, but meanwhile an impasse-breaking compromise on farmers' income subsidies helped move the conference toward agreement. It was the first major accomplishment of the conference.

Dole and Foley got together Dec. 11 and hammered out an agreement that gave both sides a claim to victory. The next day, with the grudging acceptance of the Reagan administration, conferees accepted the agreement, which was to split the difference between the income-support provisions in the two versions of the bill.

The Foley-Dole proposal met with general favor from conferees, but as soon as the income-subsidy plan was accepted, senators began to complain about provisions in the deal involving increased acreage-reduction requirements, or "set-asides," imposed on wheat and corn farmers who received price- and income-support payments.

Senate Democrats complained that since the minimum set-aside requirements in the Foley-Dole plan would effectively reduce crop-production capacity, they also would reduce the total federal payments farmers received on those crops. Staff members went back to work to develop a compromise for set-aside requirements.

Despite weeklong efforts in various sub-conferences to resolve differences in the dairy, cotton and rice programs, major debates bubbled to the surface whenever members tried to put their private agreements to a public vote. But by Dec. 13, as Congress moved closer to adjournment, those subgroups began to come together.

Dole engineered a compromise on sugar imports Dec. 12, gaining agreement for provisions to force the Agriculture Department to implement stricter quotas, even though the administration threatened a veto over that section alone.

Dole also was involved in a deal to lower price supports for honey producers. The Senate bill would have phased out the program in three years, and although the House bill included a $250,000 limit on federal loans to honey producers, the full House rejected efforts to lower the rates at which the government guaranteed to buy up honey.

The compromise reduced the existing 65.3-cents-per-pound loan rate to 64 cents in 1986, 63 cents in 1987 and then another 5 percent a year in 1988 through 1990.

One of the final points of contention was a continuing disagreement among House conferees on cargo preference. The Senate-passed bill contained a tenuous compromise generally supported by maritime interests and Senate farm panel members that would exempt government-financed commercial exports from the requirement. House Merchant Marine Committee conferees tried to adopt the Senate language and ran into opposition from other House conferees with agriculture interests.

Ultimately, however, the Senate amendment was accepted by conferees.

Major Compromises

The full conference unanimously ratified the conference agreement Dec. 14. Following are descriptions of the major conference compromises:

Wheat, Feed Grains

The package of price- and income-supports for grain farmers crafted by Dole and Foley was a careful compromise between the administration's goals of reducing the artificial floor the government put on wheat and corn prices, and giving struggling farmers some cash security if prices continued to plummet below the cost of production.

The bill reduced sharply the rates the government set for crop loans, which in practice set a floor on domestic prices. In the past, Congress had arbitrarily set loan rates on a rising scale, keeping an eye on inflation, with the result that existing rates were generally higher than prices on most world markets. That had led farmers to forfeit much of their crops to the government.

Under HR 2100, the basic wheat loan rate, set at $3.30 a bushel under existing law, was to drop 10 percent to $3 in 1986, and another 5 percent a year through 1990. The corn rate was to drop in similar fashion, from $2.55 a bushel to $2.40 in 1986.

But the agriculture secretary had authority to reduce the rate another 20 percent a year, lowering the 1986 rate for wheat down to $2.40 a bushel.

That price was much closer to the prevailing market price, which gave agriculture officials hope that foreign nations would have much more difficulty underselling U.S. grain on overseas markets. Nearly half of domestic grains were at the time grown for export.

Cutting the loan rates, however, only served to widen the gap between market prices and target prices, which meant the government would have to pay more in income subsidies.

The Foley-Dole compromise, which froze existing target prices for wheat at $4.38 a bushel (and for corn at $3.03 a bushel) for two years, allowed the rates to drop a total of 10 percent over the remaining three years of the bill, in annual increments of 2 percent, 3 percent and 5 percent.

Allowing no major cuts until the fourth year created another problem, however. Lawmakers were afraid the agriculture secretary might not use his full authority to lower crop loan rates beyond the basic rate — or might not be allowed to by White House budget officials. To force the administration's hand, the bill required the secretary to lower loan rates by at least 10 percent in 1986.

Some Democrats maintained that a two- to three-year freeze would reduce farmers' incomes, mainly because the bill also allowed the secretary to impose harsher production controls on farmers participating in the federal program, giving them lower potential crop yields on which to earn benefits.

The Democrats' continuing doubts, and promises of a filibuster in the Senate, threatened to scuttle the Foley-Dole agreement as soon as it was introduced.

But recognizing the politically symbolic importance of a target price freeze in itself, Foley insisted that conferees vote on that section and then go back to the bargaining table to work out the details of the acreage-reduction issue.

By the time the conference wrapped up the other provisions of the bill and returned to the topic of acreage reduction on the afternoon of Dec. 14, weary members had lost most of their partisan mettle. What had been a political debate on income subsidies suddenly turned to a pragmatic discussion of how to make ends meet. A deal was pounded out with relative ease.

Cotton, Rice

Although cotton and rice farmers were a smaller group than other commodity interests, legislators representing Southern states where cotton and rice were grown played a proportionately larger role in the debate than any other special interest. As a result, the cotton and rice programs contained some of the most radical — and possibly expensive — provisions in the entire package.

Southern senators, in particular, held swing votes in committee and on the floor, forcing Dole to acquiesce in their pet projects in order to win over their votes for his wheat package.

Sens. Cochran and Pryor, along with Rep. Huckaby, parlayed their senior positions on the respective Agriculture panels into a powerful alliance in conference for a marketing loan program for cotton and rice farmers.

Rather than allowing farmers to default on their loans if prices did not rise above the loan rate, the agriculture secretary had to allow rice farmers, and had the option of allowing cotton farmers, the opportunity to pay back loans only at the rate available at market. The farmer-borrower who sold his crop at a rate lower than he borrowed would keep the remaining principal. The concept of mandatory marketing loans for grain farmers had been rejected in the House committee and on the House floor, although the secretary had authority to implement it.

As a further benefit for rice farmers, whose crops in 1985 were earning only half of the existing loan rate of $8 per hundred pounds, the marketing loan took effect for the already-harvested 1985 crop.

Dairy

House Democrats won their biggest victory over the administration when Senate conferees finally gave in on a new program to reduce milk surpluses by requiring the government to buy up entire herds of dairy cows.

The administration, despite losing floor votes in both the House and Senate, continued to fight in the conference for an immediate cut in the dairy price-support rate. (The government bought milk solids, such as cheese, butter and nonfat dry milk, from dairy processors in the latter part of 1985 at a rate of $11.60 per hundred pounds.)

After a week of private negotiations by dairy-state conferees, a compromise package on milk price supports emerged Dec. 14.

The bill required the agriculture secretary to offer bids to dairy producers to send to slaughter or sell for export their entire dairy herds, calves and bulls included. The farmers had to agree to stay out of the dairy business for three to five years.

House Dairy subcommittee Chairman Coelho said the 18-month program would remove 800,000 of the nation's 11 million dairy cows from milk production, reducing current government surplus of 16.5 million pounds down to less than 5 million pounds.

Block steadfastly resisted efforts to assess dairy producers for the herd buyout scheme. Reagan had often referred to the assessment as a "milk tax." Boschwitz, who was leading the conference negotiations for the Senate, said the president and those around him were more "dug in" on dairy provisions than any other commodity. "It's simpler to understand," he said.

The Senate bill contained a straightforward one-year freeze on dairy price supports, with a 50-cent cut in 1987. The House bill contained a hike in the support rate, the whole-herd buyout plan, plus a revival of a diversion plan to pay producers to cut back on their production. The buyout and diversion plans, to be paid for by farmer assessments, were inserted at the insistence of the dairy industry.

Coelho gave up on the diversion plan when Dole agreed to the buyout "experiment," financed by 40-cent-per-hundred-pound assessments in 1986 and a 25-cent assessment in 1987. In return, Coelho agreed to a graduated cut in price-supports in 1987 — 25-cents per hundred pounds on Jan. 1 and another 25 cents on Oct. 1 — if surpluses were not reduced below five billion pounds a year.

The assessments and price cuts combined put the effective price support at $11.20 in 1986 and $11.10 through 1987.

Sugar

Part of Dole's deal with Southern Democrats and farm-state Republicans also involved the sugar program, which supported sugar cane growers in the Gulf States and Hawaii, as well as sugar beet growers in Midwestern states, such as North and South Dakota.

Much to the chagrin of the State Department, Dole agreed to a provision on the Senate floor that effectively forced the White House to reduce the flow of imported sugar. The administration had been trying to increase the flow of sugar from Caribbean nations that needed hard U.S. currency to pay off massive U.S. bank debts.

After the House rebuffed Senate efforts to drop the sugar provision, Dole agreed to a compromise that delayed the effect of the plan until later in 1986.

The only remaining dispute involved a turf battle among House conferees from the Agriculture and Ways and Means committees. Huckaby said House conferees finally worked out compromise wording that carefully skirted the issue of tariffs, which were the sole province of Ways and Means.

Conservation

Conferees had no trouble reaching agreement on the conservation section, which included two new programs that had the potential of becoming the most popular in the entire bill.

A tough sodbuster provision denied federal farm benefits to farmers who tilled highly erodible soil. A similar "swampbuster" program gave like protection to much of the nation's wetlands.

To further encourage farmers to take fragile land out of crop production, the bill also established a "conservation reserve" of at least 40 million acres. Over five years, the agriculture secretary was to offer bids to farmers to place farm land in the reserve for 10 to 15 years, and had to help pay for the expense of planting grass, trees or other covering.

The Senate and House had passed sodbuster bills in 1983 and 1984, but differences were not resolved in conference. *(1984 Almanac p. 364)*

In 1985, the Senate, with the administration's blessing and added pressure from environmental groups, passed even more restrictive conservation provisions than the House. ∎

Tobacco Price-Support Overhaul Left Hanging

Congress' failure to clear a far-reaching deficit-reduction bill (HR 3128) left hanging a plan to restructure the federal price-support program for tobacco growers.

Provisions overhauling the tobacco program had been included in the Senate Finance Committee version of HR 3128, the so-called reconciliation bill that was written to enact a major part of the spending cuts and tax increases assumed in the fiscal 1986 budget resolution (S Con Res 32). Inclusion of the tobacco provisions in what was assumed to be a must-pass bill was seen as a way of ensuring their enactment. *(Reconciliation, p. 498)*

Furthermore, giving tobacco-state legislators room in the omnibus bill for a rewrite of the price-support program helped guarantee support for a permanent extension of the 16-cents-per-pack federal excise tax on cigarettes, one of the biggest revenue-raisers in the measure. Tobacco-state members had threatened to derail the cigarette tax extension if the price-support provisions were not included in the bill.

Although conferees on the reconciliation bill agreed Dec. 19, the day before Congress adjourned for the year, House members and senators disagreed over a provision establishing a new broad-based tax on manufacturers to pay for the "superfund" toxic-waste cleanup program.

The disagreement prevented adoption of the conference report by the House, which voted to strike the superfund tax. The Senate would not go along and Congress adjourned before clearing the bill.

Background

The provisions in HR 3128 grew out of a negotiated agreement, engineered by Senate Agriculture Committee Chairman Jesse Helms, R-N.C., to roll back government loan rates and assess cigarette companies as well as tobacco growers for all of the subsidy program's cost. Since 1982, growers had been charged assessments to finance the price-support system. The agreement included modifying the existing system of setting quotas for how much growers could sell each year, giving manufacturers a direct role in setting those quotas.

And it entailed a manufacturer buyout from growers and the government of 1.2 billion pounds of surplus tobacco at 10 to 90 percent discounts. The buyout was estimated by the Office of Management and Budget to cost the government as much as $1.1 billion.

Helms' deal was concluded late June 4 when cigarette manufacturers agreed to pay half the assessments charged growers to maintain price supports for tobacco.

Tobacco subsidies, similar to price supports for other commodities, allowed growers to borrow money to plant their crops and use their harvest as collateral. Growers could default on their loans and turn their crops over to the government if they could not get a price better than the cost of repaying the loan.

Growers had been paying for the program since 1982, when Congress stipulated that the price-support system be run at no net cost to taxpayers, other than administrative expenses. The legislation (PL 97-218), sponsored by Rep. Charlie Rose, D-N.C., represented a critical victory for tobacco advocates, who hoped it would defuse criticism of the controversial program. *(1982 Almanac p. 357)*

But government-held surpluses continued to mount as prices plunged on world markets and more and more growers defaulted on their loans. As a consequence, assessments charged to growers were rising so fast that many industry analysts predicted that growers, who under existing law were to vote on whether to continue to pay for the program, might choose to eliminate price supports altogether.

In return for sharing the program's costs, Helms' deal gave manufacturers effective control over the acreage allotment and tobacco quota system that governed how much growers could plant and sell each year. Allotments were first issued to tobacco growers as a result of the Agricultural Adjustment Act of 1938, which included penalties for growers who exceeded government-designated quotas. Most allotments remained under the control of the original grantees, who leased them to tobacco growers.

Rose Excluded, Opposed the Deal

Although several other tobacco-state legislators were included in the discussions that led to the agreement, Helms specifically excluded Rose, who chaired the House Agriculture Subcommittee on Tobacco and Peanuts.

Rose and Helms had been political adversaries for years. In October 1982, Rose filed a complaint with the Federal Election Commission challenging the legality of the political activities of an arm of the National Congressional Club, a Raleigh, N.C., conservative political action committee headed by Helms.

In an outgrowth of Rose's complaint, the FEC in early 1985 filed suit against the Congressional Club and its political consulting arm, Jefferson Marketing, Inc.

Rose was critical of Helms' agreement because he said it did not place any restrictions on manufacturers who had been importing increasing amounts of foreign tobacco, which was cheaper than U.S.-grown leaf, and because it gave manufacturers so much control over quotas.

Helms' staff charged Rose with trying to sabotage the negotiations that led to the agreement by introducing a bill to use 2 cents of the current 16-cent excise tax on cigarettes to pay for the tobacco price-support program. Rose and Sen. Albert Gore Jr., D-Tenn., concurrently introduced the excise tax bill (HR 2600, S 1205) on May 23.

Helms introduced his proposal to restructure the price-support system July 10 (S 1418).

Conference Provisions

The following are tobacco price-support provisions from the conference report on HR 3128 (H Rept 99-453). The bill would:

- Maintain the current method of price support by offering loans, with tobacco held as collateral, through producers' associations (cooperatives) that were under Commodity Credit Corporation (CCC) contract.

The cooperatives handled all operations connected with making loan advances to producers, and arranged for receiving, redrying, packing, storing and eventually selling the tobacco under loan. Tobacco not sold at the support rate was consigned to the cooperative, which paid the producer with money borrowed from the CCC. The cooperative reimbursed the CCC, with interest, for the loan advances upon sale of the tobacco.

- Set the price-support level for the 1986 and subsequent crops of flue-cured and burley tobacco by (1) giving two-thirds weight to the difference between the immediately preceding year's support level and the average market price of three of the five preceding years, with the high and low years excluded; (2) giving one-third weight to an index of production costs incurred by tobacco farmers; and (3) allowing the agriculture secretary to adjust the price support from 65 to 100 percent of the annual increase or decrease resulting from the formula.
- Repeal the secretary's authority to reduce the price support on certain low quality grades of flue-cured tobacco.
- Maintain the existing method of supply control through mandatory marketing quotas on growers of each kind of tobacco, if such quotas were approved in a referendum vote by a two-thirds majority of all producers. The marketing quota was translated into a national allotment, and each tobacco farm, based on its historical production, was given a pro rata share of the national allotment.
- Require the secretary to set a national marketing quota for flue-cured and burley tobacco within 3 percent of the combined total of (1) a confidential estimate by cigarette manufacturers of the amount of flue-cured or burley tobacco they intended to purchase at auction during the next marketing year, (2) the average annual exports for the three preceding years, and (3) the amount needed to maintain a reserve stock level.
- Establish reserve stock levels at the greater of (1) 100 million pounds for flue-cured and 50 million pounds for burley tobacco, or (2) 15 percent of the effective national marketing quotas.
- Reduce from 110 percent to 103 percent of the farm-marketing quota, the amount of flue-cured and burley tobacco that could be marketed without penalty.
- Require each cigarette manufacturer to purchase at least 90 percent of the flue-cured and burley tobacco the manufacturer intended to buy when quotas were determined. Failure would subject the manufacturer to a double assessment for each pound below 90 percent of intended purchases.
- Revise the existing system of requiring producers to pay an assessment into a capital fund (called a "no net cost" account) from which CCC losses on loans were repaid. Assessments would be collected from producers and purchasers in a way to ensure that they shared equally. However, future assessments on burley tobacco would be determined without regard to any losses of the CCC from the 1983 crop of burley tobacco.
- Authorize cigarette manufacturers to purchase existing surplus inventories of flue-cured tobacco over an eight-year period and burley tobacco over a five-year period, with each manufacturer purchasing a percentage of the stocks that was at least equal to its share of the cigarette market for the previous year.
- Require the flue-cured association to offer surplus inventories from the 1976-81 crop years at a 90 percent discount from their existing base prices, and the 1982-84 crops at a 10 percent discount. The bill also would require the burley association to offer surplus inventories from the 1982 crop at the base price in effect on July 1, 1985, and the surplus from the 1984 crop at the association's costs on the date of the bill's enactment.
- Require the CCC to take title to remaining surpluses from the 1983 burley crop and offer the stocks for sale on terms and conditions the CCC deemed appropriate. Any

stocks not sold within two years could be offered for sale at a 90 percent discount.

Legislative History

House Committee Action on HR 3128

The House Ways and Means Committee, in voting to make permanent the expiring 16-cents-per-pack cigarette tax, also deferred to Rose, who opposed the tax unless something were done to protect tobacco growers from rising assessments.

During committee markup July 24 on the Ways and Means reconciliation bill (HR 3128), Charles B. Rangel, D-N.Y., chairman of the Ways and Means Subcommittee on Select Revenue Measures, moved to earmark 1 cent of the excise tax to pay for tobacco price supports. Rangel's amendment amounted to a compromise with Rose, who had proposed earmarking 2 cents for price supports.

The cigarette industry was adamantly opposed to earmarking tobacco taxes for particular programs for fear that Congress might designate revenues from cigarette taxes for Medicare or other health programs, in express recognition of the link between smoking and various diseases. Such a proposal failed on a tie vote during Ways and Means markup on HR 3128.

Nonetheless, Rose said lobbyists for the Tobacco Institute, the industry's major trade group, said they would agree to the 1-cent earmark for price supports as long as cigarette taxes did not rise above 16 cents per pack.

The committee reported the bill July 31 with the earmarked tax included (H Rept 99-241, Part I).

House Floor Action on HR 3128

The bill came to the House floor Oct. 31 under a rule governing floor consideration that allowed for no amendments. Some Republicans had objected to the one penny tobacco-tax set-aside in the Rules Committee, arguing that the money would be better spent on medical research. Efforts to allow floor amendments were rejected by party-line votes in committee.

A close procedural vote of 219-205, with not a single Republican voting in favor, gave support to the rule. The House then approved the rule by voice vote. On a mostly party-line vote, the bill was then passed, 245-174. *(Votes 345, 347, p. 108-H)*

Senate Committee Action on S 1730

The Senate Finance Committee by voice vote approved its contribution to the reconciliation bill Sept. 20, with the tobacco provisions added. Along with recommendations from 10 other Senate committees, those from Finance were reported by the Budget Committee Oct. 2 (S 1730 — S Rept 99-146).

As in the House, extension of the cigarette tax had been vigorously opposed. And the Finance Committee's action on the tax and price-support provisions was among its most controversial on the bill.

The motion to attach the tobacco price-support provisions from S 1418 was offered by Senate Majority Leader Robert Dole, R-Kan., a member of both the Finance and Agriculture committees. Dole's amendment also included new taxes on "smokeless tobacco" — 8 cents per pound on chewing tobacco and 24 cents per pound on snuff.

Dole and Finance Committee Chairman Bob Packwood, R-Ore., portrayed the inclusion of S 1418 in the deficit-reduction package as a quid pro quo for tobacco-state senators' agreement to the cigarette tax extension.

Supporters of S 1418 claimed it would reduce federal outlays for the tobacco program by $523 million over five years. But critics complained that those estimates did not account for losses the government would have to absorb by allowing cigarette manufacturers to buy up tobacco surpluses at a discount.

The maneuver drew howls of protest from Democrats who said the Finance Committee was in no position to judge the merits of a major agriculture bill. Among those protesting was David L. Boren, D-Okla., another Finance member who also sat on the Agriculture Committee.

The Agriculture panel had been struggling to rewrite federal farm programs affecting commodities other than tobacco at a time of tight fiscal constraints. Boren objected that some farmers might have to take cuts in their subsidies, while the tobacco provisions amounted to a bailout.

Boren dropped his opposition after Helms allowed the Agriculture Committee on Sept. 19 to report a Democratic-sponsored farm bill. In an ironic development, Helms had sought to attach the tobacco provisions to the reconciliation bill instead of the farm bill in part because he thought the former had a better chance of being enacted. The farm bill cleared Dec. 18. *(Farm bill, p. 517)*

After debating the Dole amendment for two days, the Finance Committee adopted it Sept. 20 without a roll-call vote. The proposal was approved by a show of hands, with only four senators voting against it — Bill Bradley, D-N.J., John H. Chafee, R-R.I., Daniel Patrick Moynihan, D-N.Y., and Max Baucus, D-Mont. Some members said Democrats were reluctant to force a roll-call vote in deference to colleagues like Wendell Ford, D-Ky., who might be politically undermined by opposition to the tobacco program.

Senate Floor Action on S 1730

The Senate took up its reconciliation bill Oct. 15, but became ensnared in a variety of conflicts unrelated to the tobacco provisions. The price-support provisions did come under attack from Howard M. Metzenbaum, D-Ohio, who offered two amendments to the tobacco section of S 1730 and argued that the price-support changes were opposed by the Reagan administration. Both efforts failed.

Metzenbaum first proposed to delete the price-support provisions, citing administration figures that the industry "bailout" would cost more than $1 billion. But Dole countered that lower price supports would save $235 million over three years, and his motion to table Metzenbaum's amendment passed, 66-33, Nov. 14. *(Vote 310, p. 54-S)*

Afterward, the Senate also rejected a more limited Metzenbaum amendment to strike the bill's exemption from antitrust laws for manufacturers who had agreed to buy the discounted tobacco. The vote to table was 57-42. *(Vote 311, p. 54-S)*

After calling up the House-passed bill, and substituting the text of S 1730, as amended, the Senate passed HR 3128 the same day. *(Vote 314, p. 54-S)*

Conference Action

Under pressure to preserve the deal with tobacco-state legislators to alter the price-support program in return for extension of the cigarette tax, conferees on HR 3128 had little difficulty agreeing.

The conference agreement retained the Senate provisions, and dropped the House-passed one penny set-aside for the existing price-support program. ∎

Reagan Vetoes Emergency Farm Credit Bill

A high-speed drive to get extra loan money to farmers to finance their spring plantings failed March 6 when President Reagan killed an emergency farm credit bill, vetoing it in a nationally televised appearance.

The vetoed bill (HR 1096) was a $175 million authorization of non-food emergency aid for African nations, to which farm credit provisions had been added on the Senate floor Feb. 27.

The House cleared the bill for the president March 5 by a 255-168 vote. Democratic leaders in the House had decided on an expedited procedure of accepting the bill as amended by the Senate, instead of going to conference on HR 1096 and a House-passed farm credit bill (HR 1035) that did not include Africa aid. *(Vote 25, p. 10-H)*

The day after the veto, Senate Minority Leader Robert C. Byrd, D-W.Va., tried to resurrect the farm credit fight when he objected to further consideration of African relief legislation.

His objections stalled consideration of an Africa aid authorization bill (S 457) identical to the vetoed measure, whose text had been substituted by the Senate for that in HR 1096 and was still on the Senate calendar. Byrd also prevented consideration of a separate Africa aid appropriations bill (HR 1239).

There was no override attempt on the farm credit veto and objections to HR 1239, the Africa aid appropriations bill, ultimately were lifted and the bill cleared April 2. *(Africa aid, pp. 102, 395)*

Provisions

The vetoed bill would have added $1.85 billion to a $650 million loan-guarantee program, provided $100 million to reduce interest rates on private loans guaranteed by the program, revised some eligibility rules for the guarantees, and allowed farmers to get early advances on crop loans that they normally received in the fall.

Reagan criticized the measure as "a massive new bailout that would add billions to the deficit," while coming too late to offer any help to farmers. Advocates of more farm aid had said that action by early or mid-March was essential, to enable farmers to get crops in the ground on time. *(Veto text, p. 11-D)*

In his veto message, Reagan also asserted that severe financial problems afflicted only a small minority of farmers, and that "96 percent do not have liquidity problems." But some members called attention March 7 to an unpublished Agriculture Department report estimating that 17 to 18 percent of American farms — about 386,000 — had severe financial problems.

The Congressional Budget Office estimated the bill's net cost at $254 million over six years. It would, however, have required $7.3 billion in immediate fiscal year 1985 outlays, to be recouped as the loans were repaid.

Tying the bill to larger budget questions, Reagan said Congress "failed" its first major test of bringing spending under control.

Neither the House nor the Senate, in passing the bill, had shown the two-thirds majority support needed to overturn a presidential veto. Although 84 Republicans had voted for HR 1035, the first farm credit measure to reach the House floor, on final passage, HR 1069 drew support from only 30 Republicans.

Though initially strong in the House, Republican support had waned as Democrats forcefully laid claim to the credit measure, declaring that it proved they cared more about farmers than did Reagan, for whom farmers had voted in overwhelming numbers in 1984.

Farm Crisis

The credit aid bills basically would have instructed the administration to do what it had broad authority to do under existing law. But farmer advocates in Congress doubted that administration announcements of additional assistance held much promise.

The administration, concerned with the increasingly high costs of farm price-support and related programs since 1982, had been reluctant to address the worsening credit problems of farmers and opposed bills in 1982 and 1983 that would have eased Farmers Home Administration (FmHA) loan repayment terms. *(1983 Almanac p. 384)*

By 1984, the phenomenon of farmers too strapped to qualify for continuing credit to operate their farms had spread well beyond the clients of the FmHA. The agency served only farmers that could not qualify for loans from private banks or from the Farm Credit System, a quasi-public network of cooperative farm lending institutions.

These private lenders held an increasing volume of "non-performing" farm loans, ones on which payments were not being made. The lenders — faced with an excess of bad debts — were being confronted with regulatory difficulties and, in some cases, failure. The Farm Credit System eventually needed a bailout in late 1985. *(Farm Credit System bailout, p. 543)*

The credit crisis, compounded by years of low farm profits and collapsing land values, was most acute and widespread among several hundred thousand mid-sized family farms in Midwestern breadbasket states, including Iowa, Nebraska, the Dakotas, Minnesota and Kansas.

In September 1984 the administration had abruptly stopped claiming that no special action was needed, and announced a two-part emergency credit program that became the focus of congressional action in early 1985. *(1984 Almanac p. 363)*

In an unsuccessful bid to buy Senate Republican support for its austere omnibus farm bill proposal, the administration Feb. 6 offered an extended version of the September credit plan.

The offer failed to satisfy critics — or win support for the farm bill — which was formally released Feb. 22. Sen. Mark Andrews, R-N.D., said the timing of the bill's release was "nuts," considering the ongoing credit crisis. *(Farm bill, p. 517)*

Legislative Action

Both the House and Senate on Feb. 27 approved emergency credit aid for cash-short farmers despite repeated veto threats and strong warnings from Republican leaders that the action would wreck their drive for significant across-the-board reductions in deficit spending.

The votes came during a week when the plight of debt-ridden farmers was brought to members' attention by visiting delegations of farm-state legislators and governors, and by a massive rally in Ames, Iowa.

The first legislative action came when the Senate, in

an unusual Saturday session Feb. 23, unanimously approved a non-binding resolution (S Res 79) restating the Reagan administration's commitments to ease the credit problem. *(Vote 11, p. 4-S)*

The Senate action signaled the end of a weeklong filibuster by farm-state Democrats of all Senate business. The filibuster was tacitly supported by a handful of farm-state Republicans.

The next step came Feb. 27 when the House voted 318-103 to pass a bill (HR 1035) providing for advances in the spring of federal crop loans that farmers usually received at harvest time. *(Vote 17, p. 8-H)*

The bill was reported from the House Agriculture Committee Feb. 25 and Feb. 26 (H Rept 99-6, Parts I and II). It would have made additional changes in FmHA rules for guaranteeing repayment of restructured loans, and also would have authorized an extra $3 billion for the guarantees. The six-year net cost of the bill, according to the Congressional Budget Office, would have been $455 million.

Several hours later that day, the Senate in a pivotal 54-45 vote agreed to add similar FmHA loan guarantee provisions to a bill (S 457) providing emergency, non-food aid to drought- and famine-stricken parts of Africa. The vote was on a substitute amendment by Sens. John Melcher, D-Mont., and Mark Andrews, R-N.D., to an amendment by Sen. Edward Zorinsky, D-Neb., which was then adopted by an identical 54-45 vote. *(Votes 13-14, p. 5-S)*

In those Senate votes, Majority Leader Robert Dole, R-Kan., was handed his first significant defeat as leader when eight Republicans broke ranks to vote with Democrats. Dole had made the votes an issue of party loyalty and of commitment to deficit reduction.

By a 50-48 vote the Senate then agreed to an amendment by Sen. Alan J. Dixon, D-Ill., adding the advance crop loan authority to the famine relief bill. It rejected 43-55 an amendment by Sen. Phil Gramm, R-Texas, that would have barred implementation of the farm credit amendments if they would add to the federal deficit.

The Senate then substituted the language of S 457, as amended, for that in a House-passed famine bill (HR 1096) and passed HR 1096 by a 62-35 vote. *(Votes 15-17, p. 5-S)*

The following day, Feb. 28, the House, by a 294-115 vote, passed a farm credit appropriations bill (HR 1189), which would have added $1 billion to the FmHA loan guarantee program, and targeted those loans to the most financially stressed farmers — those whose debts exceeded 75 percent of their assets. That bill was reported by the House Appropriations Committee Feb. 21 (H Rept 99-1). It never came to the Senate floor. *(Vote 20, p. 8-H)* ▮

Farm Credit System Bailout Measure Clears

After tying up one last item of controversy, Congress Dec. 18 cleared a bill (S 1884 — PL 99-205) to reorganize and rescue the Farm Credit System, a financially troubled network of agricultural lenders.

Nearly identical bills moved on a fast track through the House and Senate after the Sept. 5 public confirmation of private reports that the system faced serious losses.

The only issue that divided the two chambers involved a running dispute between healthy and not-so-healthy banks in the 37-bank system. House and Senate Agriculture leaders agreed to a compromise, however, dividing the influence of financially strong and weak banks on a new board that was to have the power to redistribute funds throughout the system. With that change, the Senate passed the measure by voice vote Dec. 17 and the House followed suit the next day.

The measure created a new institution, called the Farm Credit System Capital Corp., which was to have wide-ranging powers to take over bad loans in the system and centralize about $7 billion in surplus reserves.

If those surpluses dried up — an odds-on prospect within two years, system officials said — the bill allowed the Treasury secretary to begin pumping federal funds into the capital corporation to keep the system afloat.

At the insistence of the Reagan administration, which had maintained that the system could take care of itself if the reorganization measures in the bill were put into effect, sponsors agreed to require enactment of a separate appropriations bill to enable a Treasury bailout of the system.

Rep. Ed Jones, D-Tenn., chairman of the Agriculture credit subcommittee, predicted that system officials could return to Capitol Hill as early as the end of 1986 with requests for assistance.

Regulation of the system was to be the responsibility of a realigned Farm Credit Administration (FCA), the independent federal agency that supervised the system's institutions. A new three-member board of directors — including a chairman who was to be chief executive officer of the FCA — was to be appointed by the president rather than by the directors of the banks. The new board's role was to be similar to that of the Federal Deposit Insurance Corp., which regulated commercial banks.

Provisions

The major provisions of S 1884, as cleared, included changes in three broad areas of the Farm Credit Act of 1971 (PL 92-181):

Farm Credit Administration

- The FCA would be run by a three-member board of directors nominated by the president and confirmed by the Senate. They would serve staggered six-year terms and be limited to single terms. The president would designate a chairman to replace the FCA governor (under existing law appointed by the board) as chief executive officer of the agency. Not more than two board members were to be of the same political party.
- The existing board of directors, consisting of 13 representatives from the banking districts of the Farm Credit System, would be an advisory panel only.
- The FCA could set loan security requirements; approve bond issues and their interest rates; regulate transfers of funds between system institutions; and require annual, independent audits of each institution. The FCA also could conduct examinations of system institutions at the chairman's discretion, under the same rules as commercial bank examiners. The FCA could establish and enforce minimum levels of capital reserves for each institution, and require mergers of individual institutions.

- The FCA would be able to issue cease-and-desist orders against officers or institutions for violations of regulations, with power to correct those violations, including removal of directors and officers.

Farm Credit System

- The bill established a federally chartered capital corporation, owned and controlled by the system institutions, that would have the power to redistribute capital resources among institutions to resolve financial problems. The capital corporation was empowered to assess system institutions to cover losses within the system and repay any notes purchased by the Treasury.
- The capital corporation would have a five-member board of directors, including three members elected by the farm credit banks that owned the voting stock in the corporation (one member from "net contributors," one from "net recipients" and one at large), and two members appointed by the FCA chairman. If the Treasury secretary infused federal funds into the capital corporation, two members would be added to the board: one appointed by the secretary of agriculture and the other appointed by the other six board members. The seventh board member would be independent of both the system and the government.
- The capital corporation's authority to redistribute funds and assess institutions would expire Dec. 31, 1990.
- Member-owned associations within a district were allowed to merge voluntarily into a single districtwide association on a vote by a majority of stockholders of each association within the district, although in a state in which two-thirds of the stockholders voted against such mergers, an association in that state would not be required to merge into a districtwide association. Any association that continued as an independent association could not be charged higher assessments or otherwise be discriminated against by a district bank.
- Salaries of system directors and officials would be frozen as long as the system owed money to the U.S. Treasury. Salary increases would be approved by the FCA chairman.

Financial Assistance

- The secretary of the Treasury, at his discretion, was authorized to purchase obligations issued by the capital corporation, under terms and conditions set by the secretary.
- Financial assistance would be authorized only after the FCA had certified that the system's capital and reserve resources had been fully committed to the extent that additional contributions by the system institutions would prevent them from making loans to eligible borrowers at reasonable terms.
- Purchase of capital corporation obligations by the secretary of the Treasury would be approved in advance through enactment of an appropriations bill.

Background

Although the Farm Credit System was created and originally funded by Congress, its diffuse network of hundreds of farmer-owned cooperatives had been self-sustaining since the late 1960s.

The system was divided into 12 districts with a total of 37 banks: 12 land banks, which made long-term real estate loans; 12 intermediate credit banks, which made short- and intermediate-term operating loans; and 13 banks for rural cooperatives. Each bank served several cooperative lending associations that were run by the borrowers themselves.

The banks raised money by selling bonds to private investors, channeling the revenue to the more than 700 local cooperative associations. That meant the associations controlled most of the capital reserves that comprised the $9.2 billion net worth of the entire system in 1985.

The local control made it difficult and time-consuming to shore up financially troubled districts with capital infusions from healthier banks. But only in recent years had some experienced deep financial trouble. The hardest hit were in the Midwest, where agriculture had been sliding into a severe economic depression. With most of the Farm Credit System's debt load in real estate, the continuing rapid decline of farm land values had particularly undermined the system's financial foundation. Taken together, the associations in the Farm Credit System held $70.1 billion in loans outstanding to farmers in mid-1985, a third of the nation's $213 billion in total farm debt.

Bailout Requested

FCA Governor Donald E. Wilkinson had privately warned members of Congress in mid-1985 that the system's finances were headed for trouble. He went public with the story in September 1985 after news reports and rumors about the system's fiscal problems began to swirl on Wall Street.

The problems were further confirmed Oct. 23 when a financial statement revealed that the system's banks incurred net losses of $522.5 million in the third quarter of 1985. That left the system $426.3 million in the red for the nine months ending Sept. 30, leading officials to project the first net operating loss in the system's history.

Repayment of Farm Credit System bonds sold on Wall Street was not guaranteed by the government, but the bonds had benefited from the image of being very secure, historically trading at interest rates only slightly above U.S. Treasury securities.

With reports of trouble in the system, the spread between Treasury and Farm Credit System securities began widening in the summer of 1985.

At his Sept. 5 news conference, Wilkinson said the system would require a rescue package totaling "multi-billions of dollars" within 18 to 24 months, either in federal guarantees or direct subsidies.

Legislative Action

Farm Credit System officials first faced skeptical members of Congress Oct. 30-31 and made a public plea for a $5 billion to $6 billion bailout of the faltering agriculture lending network.

Wilkinson outlined his long-awaited recommendations to the House Agriculture Subcommittee on Conservation, Credit and Rural Development Oct. 30, and to the Senate Agriculture Committee a day later, asking for a "line of credit" to help the system cover as much as $6 billion in bad farm loans.

Although some Reagan administration officials supported assistance for the system, the specific bailout proposal failed to win the president's personal blessing following an Oct. 29 Cabinet meeting. House Democratic leaders, unwilling to take sole blame for encouraging such a large taxpayer expense, said the president's support for any bailout plan was necessary before Congress would act.

Senate Floor, House Committee

Despite the administration's reservations, rescue legislation moved quickly, as members sought to complete action before Congress adjourned for the year. Nearly identical bills (HR 3792, S 1884) were introduced in the House Nov. 20 and in the Senate Nov. 22.

Without waiting for its Agriculture Committee to act on the bill, the Republican-controlled Senate, after only four hours of debate Dec. 3, passed S 1884 by a vote of 57-34. But at the encouragement of the Reagan administration, which maintained that no bailout would be necessary, the Senate by voice vote added a provision requiring Congress to appropriate specifically any money before the Treasury secretary could spend it. *(Vote 351, p. 59-S)*

Senate sponsors of S 1884, Jesse Helms, R-N.C., and Edward Zorinsky, D-Neb., were able to defeat nearly every attempt to change their basic package. They were helped by a threat from Majority Leader Robert Dole, R-Kan., to pull the bill from the floor if any major changes were adopted. *(Votes 345-350, p. 59-S)*

The day after the Senate acted, the House Agriculture Committee approved HR 3792 (H Rept 99-425). Unlike the Senate bill, HR 3792 would not have required further congressional action if the administration were to decide to provide the system with federal aid.

House Agriculture Chairman E. "Kika" de la Garza, D-Texas, said the slowness of using the appropriations process to provide assistance would kill any positive effect of the bill.

De la Garza, who sponsored the House bill along with other committee leaders, managed to keep major changes out of HR 3792 as it sailed through markup sessions of the Agriculture Credit Subcommittee Dec. 2 and Dec. 3, and then through a full-committee markup session Dec. 3.

Committee members soundly defeated attempts by James M. Jeffords, R-Vt., and Charles W. Stenholm, D-Texas, to put a limit on the amount of new capital the corporation could take from healthy banks to help out insolvent institutions.

Texas and New England were the two healthiest districts in the 12-region system. Similar amendments by Patrick J. Leahy, D-Vt., and Lloyd Bentsen, D-Texas, had been defeated in the Senate.

House Floor

The House, Dec. 10 by a vote of 393-32, passed S 1884 and amended it to include the text of the House committee bill. The amendment, however, included the Senate provision requiring a separate bailout appropriation. *(Vote 404, p. 128-H)*

House Agriculture leaders, who at first insisted on placing no restrictions on administration spending authority, were forced by internal House politics to keep the bailout provision firmly under the control of Congress. De la Garza said the appropriation requirement was added to satisfy objections raised by Appropriations Chairman Jamie L. Whitten, D-Miss., as well as leaders of the Budget and Banking committees.

With resolution of the disagreement over the appropriations provision, the only difference to be reconciled between the two versions of S 1884 was the control of the new capital corporation set up to redistribute assets between financially healthy and struggling banks in the system.

The House bill would have set up a five-member board — four members to be elected by banks that contributed money to the capital corporation, and one member to be appointed by administration officials.

The Senate bill would have put only two of the five board members under the control of the contributing banks. The other three would be appointed by the administration.

House and Senate negotiators by Dec. 13 had reached a compromise on the makeup of the board, enabling the bill to go back to both chambers the week of Dec. 16. ∎

Farm Bankruptcy Revisions

As a continuing statement of congressional concern over the economic plight of U.S. agriculture, the House June 24 passed a bill (HR 2211 — H Rept 99-178) that would allow financially strapped farmers to file for bankruptcy with less danger of losing their farms.

Neither the Senate Judiciary Committee, nor the full Senate showed any intention of acting on the bill.

HR 2211 would allow "family farmers" — defined as persons whose debts were at least 80 percent farm-connected — to reorganize under Chapter 13 of the U.S. Bankruptcy Code.

Chapter 13 allowed creditors to attach future earnings on a specified repayment schedule, and its provisions were viewed as simpler and more flexible for debtors. Under existing law Chapter 13 filings were limited to persons whose unsecured debts were less than $100,000 and secured debts less than $350,000.

Because of those limits, most farmers had to file under Chapter 11, which allowed the forced sale of a farmer's land to pay off debts. As passed by the House, HR 2211 would raise the limit for family farmers filing under Chapter 13 to $1 million in secured and unsecured debts.

The bill also would give farmers up to 10 years to repay their debts, rather than the three to five years allowed under existing law. And it would exempt family farmers from existing requirements that mortgage loans secured by family residences could not be modified.

Sponsors said the bill would benefit creditors, who would not be forced to accept the limited value of liquidated farm assets under Chapter 11, and instead could hope to receive full value over time.

Although Congress enacted significant changes in bankruptcy law in 1984 (PL 98-353), including some provisions to aid farmers in their dealings with bankrupt grain elevators, that measure made no provision for farmers who themselves faced bankruptcy. *(1984 Almanac p. 263)*

Legislative History

Two bills similar to HR 2211 were introduced by House Judiciary Committee Chairman Peter W. Rodino Jr., D-N.J., and Rep. Mike Synar, D-Okla., on March 5, the day before President Reagan vetoed an emergency farm credit bill (HR 1097). *(Farm credit veto, p. 542)*

Following March hearings by a House Judiciary subcommittee, Rodino introduced a revised version of those bills as HR 2211. By a vote of 32-0, the committee ordered the bill reported June 18 and the bill came to the House floor June 24. It was passed by voice vote under suspension of the rules, a special procedure that prevented amendments and required a two-thirds majority. ∎

SUPREME COURT

CQ

No Clear Trends as Court Takes a 'Breather'

The 1984-85 Supreme Court term, which ended July 2, was remarkable primarily for what didn't happen.

The court didn't put prayer back in the public schools. It didn't authorize public school teachers to go into parochial schools to teach secular subjects. It didn't permit police to shoot fleeing, unarmed felony suspects. It didn't declare some aliens outside the protection of the Constitution, or allow Congress to limit spending by political action committees. And it didn't defer with any consistency to the wishes of the Reagan administration.

Furthermore, even though five members of the court were age 76 or older, no justice resigned to give Ronald Reagan another chance to name someone of his choice to the nation's highest bench.

A year earlier, as the court ended its 1983-84 term, it appeared to have taken a sharp turn to the right, endorsing the Reagan administration's positions on issues ranging from criminal law and civil rights to antitrust issues and church-state relationships.

But the court displayed little of this conservative activism in its 1984-85 term. Indeed, the legal landscape at the end of the term looked much like it did at the beginning.

A Pause for 'Percolation'

This term was an interim period, a "breather," suggested Russell W. Galloway Jr., a professor of constitutional law at the University of Santa Clara in California. Galloway spent the term at the court, studying its operations close up.

"Often after big breakthroughs, the court pauses to allow consolidation and some 'percolation' of its decisions in the lower courts," Galloway said.

The next term could be quite different, he cautioned, noting that the court had already taken on a sizable number of controversial issues for argument, including abortion, legislative apportionment, affirmative action and "equal access" for student religious groups seeking to use public school facilities.

Its decisions on those matters could either confirm the conservative trend of 1983-84, or show it to have been an aberration.

The Reagan administration no doubt hoped that this term was the aberration. It suffered "severe defeats on social, civil rights and federalism issues," even though it continued to win most of its arguments in criminal cases, said Bruce E. Fein, a former administration official who in 1985 was an adjunct scholar at the conservative-leaning Heritage Foundation and at the American Enterprise Institute.

Overall, Fein characterized the term as "either a misfortune or a calamity for those hoping for a coherent, principled jurisprudence to distinguish the judiciary from the political branches of the government."

Many of the term's rulings, especially in the school prayer and "parochiaid" cases, reflected an unpredictable "jurisprudence of idiosyncrasy," Fein said.

Church-State: Drawing the Line

The court heard arguments in an extraordinary number of First Amendment cases during the term. Nineteen of the 150 cases argued involved some aspect of that constitutional guarantee.

Attention focused on church-state cases, because the court in 1984 seemed to move away from its longstanding demand for strict separation of church and state, endorsing government "accommodation" of religion.

In 1985, however, the court drew the line. Its emphasis was not on accommodation of religion, but on government "neutrality" toward any and all faiths.

By 6-3, the court struck down an Alabama law authorizing a moment of silence in public schools for "meditation or voluntary prayer." Instead, it reaffirmed its controversial school prayer decisions of the 1960s, insisting that "government must pursue a course of complete neutrality toward religion."

This stance was reinforced June 26, as the justices by 8-1 struck down a Connecticut law requiring employers to give devout workers their Sabbath day off. The First Amendment, the court said, requires the government to "take pains not to compel people to act in the name of any religion."

And on July 1, a more divided court ruled 5-4 that sending public school teachers into the parochial schools to provide instruction on purely secular subjects fostered excessive "entanglement" between church and state.

Individual Rights

Individuals claiming that their rights had been violated did far better this term than in the preceding one, winning a number of free speech, age bias and criminal cases.

In more than half of its free-speech decisions, the court rejected government restrictions on that freedom.

For example, it struck down a $1,000 federal limit on independent expenditures by political action committees in presidential campaigns. This limit, wrote Justice William H. Rehnquist, effectively negated the First Amendment's free speech guarantee, "like allowing a speaker in a public hall to express his views while denying him the use of an amplifying system."

But the court declined to extend constitutional protection to libel suits between private parties that involved no issues of public concern, and it rejected the effort of the magazine *The Nation* to use freedom of the press as a defense against charges that it infringed the copyright of President Gerald R. Ford's memoirs by unauthorized publication of excerpts from that book before it was published.

The right to petition the government for a redress of grievances is the First Amendment freedom least often invoked in cases reaching the Supreme Court, and the justices did nothing this term to encourage its more frequent use. They rejected the argument that this right provided an absolute shield against libel suits based on the contents of letters to public officials. And the court found nothing unconstitutional about an 1862 law — still on the books — that limited to $10 the amount a veteran could pay an attorney to press benefit claims before the Veterans Administration.

One group that fared extremely well during the term was older workers. In three rulings, the court gave a broad interpretation to a federal law banning employment discrimination based on age. The justices made clear that employers must meet a heavy burden of proof if they sought to force workers to retire before age 70.

The court was generally receptive to the arguments of police and prosecutors for more leeway in fighting crime, but the justices refused to go so far as to authorize police to shoot any fleeing suspect. Justice Byron R. White bluntly declared that police had asked too much. "A police officer may not seize an unarmed, non-dangerous suspect by shooting him dead. It is not better that all felony suspects die than that they escape."

In similar fashion, the court unanimously refused to allow prosecutors to force a burglary suspect to undergo surgery to remove possible evidence — a bullet — from his body. And it told police they could not detain a man without an arrest warrant just to get his fingerprints.

Despite the Reagan administration's argument that some illegal aliens were entirely outside the Constitution's protection, the justices declined to issue such a ruling, reprimanding a lower court for addressing that point.

On the other hand, the court deferred to administration arguments and upheld a ruling by the newly conservative National Labor Relations Board denying unions the power to discipline members who resign during a strike.

The most significant change in the law during the term came when the court overturned its 1976 decision that Congress could not constitutionally tell state and local governments how much to pay their employees. Both that ruling and its reversal came by 5-4 votes. Justice Harry A. Blackmun changed his mind between 1976 and 1985, and that made all the difference.

Powell: The Pivotal Vote

This turnabout demonstrated how fragile the balance on the court was, a point driven home by the long absence of Justice Lewis F. Powell Jr., who underwent surgery for prostate cancer in early January and did not return to the bench until late March.

Powell held a pivotal middle position in the court's ideological lineup. No justice had been more in step with the court's rulings over the preceding decade; no justice had dissented less.

Because of his illness, Powell missed oral arguments in 56 cases, more than one-third of those decided in the term.

Fifty-two of those cases were disposed of without his vote, but in eight — including three controversial First Amendment cases — his absence resulted in a 4-4 tie. When the court divides evenly, it simply upholds the challenged lower court ruling. No precedent is set.

Powell's absence also led the court to order reargument during the term of four cases, a highly unusual occurrence. Powell cast the deciding vote in one of those, as the court ruled 5-4 that unions could not punish their members for resigning during a strike to return to work. (The other three cases were resolved by votes of 9-0 and 6-3.)

Nineteen rulings this term came on 5-4 votes. Powell was in the majority in 14 of those, more than any other justice. The cases in which he provided the crucial fifth vote included the two "parochiaid" cases decided July 1, and the libel case in which the court refused to extend the First Amendment's protection to "private issue" libel suits.

Supreme Court in 1985

The members of the Supreme Court in 1985 were:

- Chief Justice Warren E. Burger, named to that post by President Nixon. Burger, born in 1907, marked his 15th anniversary as chief justice in June 1984.
- Justice William J. Brennan Jr., born in 1906, appointed by President Eisenhower in 1956.
- Justice Byron R. White, born in 1915, appointed by President Kennedy in 1962.
- Justice Thurgood Marshall, born in 1908, appointed by President Johnson in 1967.
- Justice Harry A. Blackmun, born in 1908, appointed by President Nixon in 1970.
- Justice Lewis F. Powell Jr., born in 1907, appointed by President Nixon in 1971.
- Justice William H. Rehnquist, born in 1924, appointed by President Nixon in 1971.
- Justice John Paul Stevens, born in 1920, appointed by President Ford in 1975.
- Justice Sandra Day O'Connor, born in 1930, appointed by President Reagan in 1981.

Deference

Deference to Congress and the executive branch was again a recurring theme at the court, which upheld five of the six federal laws challenged as unconstitutional.

State laws did not fare as well. Only four of 17 challenged survived the justices' scrutiny.

"Judging the constitutionality of an act of Congress is properly considered 'the gravest and most delicate duty that this court is called upon to perform,'" wrote Justice Rehnquist in the case involving the $10 limit on fees veterans could pay an attorney to press benefit claims.

While some considered the law anachronistic, Rehnquist saw its age as cause for upholding it. "If anything," he wrote, "more deference is called for here: The statute in question ... has been on the books for over 120 years."

The decisions of administrative agencies also received considerable judicial deference this term. In the most dramatic illustration, the court, citing the "special competence" of the National Labor Relations Board (NLRB), upheld its ruling that unions could not punish workers who resigned during or just before a strike.

Concurring in that decision, Justice White made an especially deep bow to administrative expertise, declaring that because the law was murky, he would have voted for the board's position, even if it had ruled exactly the opposite way.

The NLRB's ruling was sensible, and thus should be upheld, White said. But he acknowledged that the law could reasonably be construed as the unions urged. "Therefore, were the board arguing for that interpretation of the act, I would accord its view appropriate deference," he said.

The four dissenters accused the majority of "supinely" deferring to the NLRB, and warned that the "deference owed to an expert tribunal cannot be allowed to slip into a judicial inertia."

—By Elder Witt

Supreme Court Decisions, 1984-85 Term

CRIMINAL LAW

Search and Seizure

United States v. Hensley, decided by a 9-0 vote, Jan. 8, 1985. O'Connor wrote the opinion.

Police may stop and briefly detain a person whom they recognize from a "wanted" flyer from another jurisdiction. Such brief stops, during which police can ascertain whether an arrest warrant has been issued, are permissible when a person is suspected of participating in a completed crime.

New Jersey v. T.L.O., decided by votes of 9-0 and 6-3, Jan. 15, 1985. White wrote the opinion; Brennan, Marshall and Stevens dissented.

Students in public schools are protected by the Fourth Amendment from unreasonable searches. But school officials do not need a search warrant or probable cause to suspect a crime in order to conduct a reasonable search of a student. School officials may search a student "when there are reasonable grounds for suspecting that the search will turn up evidence that the student has violated or is violating either the law or the rules of the school."

United States v. Johns, decided by a vote of 7-2, Jan. 21, 1985. O'Connor wrote the opinion; Brennan and Marshall dissented.

United States v. Ross (1982) permits officers with probable cause to conduct a warrantless search of a vehicle they have lawfully stopped, and to search any container found inside the vehicle and capable of containing the object of their search. Under that rule, government agents acted properly when they searched, without a warrant, packages taken from a vehicle three days after the packages and the vehicle were seized.

United States v. Sharpe, decided by a 7-2 vote, March 20, 1985. Burger wrote the opinion; Brennan and Stevens dissented.

The court eased its rules about the length of time that police may detain a suspect without a warrant or probable cause — rules first set out in its 1968 "stop and frisk" decision in *Terry v. Ohio.*

In assessing the propriety of such a detention, the court explained that judges should consider whether police during the period of the detention were diligently pursuing an investigation that would quickly confirm or dispel their suspicions.

The court held it was not unreasonable or unconstitutional for police to detain for 20 minutes the driver of a car stopped on the highway and suspected of transporting drugs while other law enforcement agents located a truck that had been traveling with the car and confirmed their suspicions that it was carrying narcotics.

Hayes v. Florida, decided by an 8-0 vote, March 20, 1985. White wrote the opinion; Powell did not participate.

Police may not detain a suspect, without his consent or a warrant, long enough to take him to police headquarters to fingerprint him, the court held. Such a detention is unreasonable and unconstitutional under the Fourth Amendment guarantee against unreasonable seizures.

Winston v. Lee, decided by a 9-0 vote, March 20, 1985. Brennan wrote the opinion.

Law enforcement officials in most instances cannot force a robbery suspect to undergo surgery for removal of a bullet that could be used as evidence against him. Only a compelling reason, such as the absence of any other incriminating or exonerating evidence, could justify such an intrusion into an individual's body.

Tennessee v. Garner, decided by a 6-3 vote, March 27, 1985. White wrote the opinion; O'Connor, Burger and Rehnquist dissented.

Police may not use deadly force to stop a fleeing felon unless they have reason to believe that he might kill or seriously injure persons nearby. "A police officer may not seize an unarmed, non-dangerous suspect by shooting him dead," wrote White for the majority.

The court's ruling came in a Tennessee case involving an unarmed 15-year-old boy who was shot and killed by police as he was fleeing a burglarized house. "The use of deadly force to prevent the escape of all felony suspects, whatever the circumstances, is constitutionally unreasonable," wrote White.

Oklahoma v. Castleberry, affirmed by a 4-4 vote, April 1, 1985. Per curiam opinion; Powell did not participate.

The evenly divided court left standing an Oklahoma court's ruling that police officers who had probable cause to believe that suspects had narcotics in their suitcases should have obtained a search warrant before searching the suitcases found in the trunk of a car in which the suspects were arrested.

California v. Carney, decided by a 6-3 vote, May 13, 1985. Burger wrote the opinion; Brennan, Marshall and Stevens dissented.

A motor home that can easily be moved is a vehicle that may be searched without a search warrant. It comes within the "automobile exception" to the constitutional requirement that most searches be authorized by a warrant.

Maryland v. Macon, decided by a 7-2 vote, June 17, 1985. O'Connor wrote the opinion; Brennan and Marshall dissented.

Police undercover agents do not engage in an unreasonable search or seizure when they purchase an allegedly obscene magazine from a bookstore, return, arrest the employee who sold it to them and take their money back. The magazine may be used as evidence against the employee.

United States v. Montoya de Hernandez, decided by a

7-2 vote, July 1, 1985. Rehnquist wrote the opinion; Brennan and Marshall dissented.

It was not unreasonable or unconstitutional for customs agents to detain a traveler at the border because of a reasonable suspicion, based on all the facts surrounding the individual and her trip, that she was carrying contraband in her stomach. This detention to await the natural emptying of her alimentary canal was not unreasonable, even though it lasted almost 24 hours, including 16 hours during which she was held incommunicado and no warrant had been sought.

Exclusionary Rule

Board of License Commissioners of the Town of Tiverton v. Pastore, dismissed as moot without dissent, Jan. 8, 1985, per curiam opinion.

The court dismissed as moot a case from Rhode Island that raised the question of whether the exclusionary rule — barring use of illegally obtained evidence — applied in civil proceedings to revoke a liquor license. The case was moot, the court said, because the tavern involved had gone out of business.

Self-Incrimination

Shea v. Louisiana, decided by a vote of 5-4, Feb. 20, 1985. Blackmun wrote the opinion; White, Burger, Rehnquist and O'Connor dissented.

The Supreme Court's 1981 decision in *Edwards v. Arizona* applies retroactively to cases that were pending on appeal when it was announced. The *Edwards* ruling barred further questioning of a suspect once he says he wants a lawyer, unless the suspect himself initiates the added conversation with police.

Oregon v. Elstad, decided by a vote of 6-3, March 4, 1985. O'Connor wrote the opinion; Brennan, Marshall and Stevens dissented.

If a suspect confesses before he is informed of his constitutional rights to remain silent and to have the aid of a lawyer, prosecutors may use a later confession by the suspect after he has been advised of his rights.

In *Miranda v. Arizona* (1966) the court forbade the use of statements obtained from suspects who had not been so advised of their rights. But in this case, the court held that an initial unwarned admission of guilt — if given voluntarily in a non-coercive environment — does not fatally taint any subsequent confession, even though the first admission could not, under *Miranda,* be used.

Double Jeopardy

Fugate v. New Mexico, affirmed by a 4-4 vote, March 26, 1985. Per curiam opinion; Powell did not participate.

The evenly divided court upheld a decision by the New Mexico Supreme Court that a defendant convicted in city court of drunken driving can be prosecuted in a higher state court on vehicular homicide charges based on the same incident without violating the guarantee against double jeopardy.

Garrett v. United States, decided by a 5-3 vote, June 3, 1985. Rehnquist wrote the opinion; Stevens, Brennan and Marshall dissented; Powell did not participate.

Congress in 1970 made it a crime to engage in a continuing criminal enterprise as well as to violate various federal laws concerning the importation, manufacture, sale and distribution of narcotics. Congress intended the continuing criminal enterprise offense to be a separate crime, for which punishment would be imposed in addition to any punishment resulting from a conviction on drug charges.

Thus, it does not violate the guarantee against double jeopardy for someone to be prosecuted first on drug charges and then on a continuing criminal enterprise charge.

Indictment

United States v. Miller, decided by an 8-0 vote, April 1, 1985. Marshall wrote the opinion; Powell did not participate.

It is not unconstitutional for prosecutors to obtain a conviction on charges narrower than those originally made against a defendant by a grand jury. But it is unconstitutional for someone to be convicted of charges not set out in the indictment.

Impeachment

Luce v. United States, decided by an 8-0 vote, Dec. 10, 1984. Burger wrote the opinion; Stevens did not participate in the decision.

A defendant who does not testify at trial cannot win appellate review of the judge's decision to permit the jury to hear evidence about his prior criminal record by claiming that such evidence improperly impeached his credibility. Without some testimony, a reviewing court cannot properly evaluate that claim.

United States v. Abel, decided by a 9-0 vote, Dec. 10, 1984. Rehnquist wrote the opinion.

A witness can be impeached by a showing of bias. A federal judge acted properly in permitting prosecutors to discredit a witness' testimony by evidence that the witness and the defendant were members of a prison gang whose members agreed to perjure themselves to protect each other.

Right to Counsel

Evitts v. Lucey, decided by a 7-2 vote, Jan. 21, 1985. Brennan wrote the opinion; Burger and Rehnquist dissented.

Defendants have a right to the effective aid of counsel in appealing a conviction. An attorney's failure to file a statement of appeal by the deadline for such a notice constitutes evidence that his client did not have the effective aid of counsel, as the Constitution requires.

Fair Trial

United States v. Young, decided by votes of 8-1 and 5-4, Feb. 20, 1985. Burger wrote the opinion; Stevens dissented, joined in part by Brennan, Marshall and Blackmun.

A prosecutor erred when he used his closing argument to express his personal belief in the defendant's guilt. Taken in context, however, that error did not undermine the fundamental fairness of the trial in question and did not require reversal of the conviction obtained.

Ake v. Oklahoma, decided by an 8-1 vote, Feb. 26,

1985. Marshall wrote the opinion; Rehnquist dissented.

Indigents seeking to defend themselves with a claim of insanity are entitled to the aid of a court-appointed psychiatrist, paid for by the government.

Defendants in capital cases also must be provided psychiatric counsel when the sentence depends in part upon a finding that they pose a future danger to the community.

Francis v. Franklin, decided by a 5-4 vote, April 29, 1985. Brennan wrote the opinion; Rehnquist, O'Connor, Powell and Burger dissented.

The due process guarantee requires that the state prove, beyond a reasonable doubt, every element of a crime charged.

A trial judge impermissibly shifted the burden of proof to a defendant by instructing the jury in a murder trial that the "acts of a person of sound mind and discretion are presumed to be the product of a person's will, but the presumption may be rebutted" and that a "person of sound mind and discretion is presumed to intend the natural and probable consequences of his acts, but the presumption may be rebutted."

Tennessee v. Street, decided by an 8-0 vote, May 13, 1985. Burger wrote the opinion; Powell did not participate.

A defendant's right to confront witnesses against him was not violated when a trial judge admitted as evidence a confession by a non-testifying co-defendant in a murder case — and instructed the jury that its admission was for the limited purpose of disproving the defendant's claim that his confession was a coerced imitation of the co-defendant's confession.

United States v. Bagley, decided by a 5-3 vote, July 2, 1985. Blackmun wrote the opinion; Brennan, Marshall and Stevens dissented; Powell did not participate.

The government's failure to disclose requested impeachment evidence for a defendant's use in cross-examining a prosecution witness requires reversal of the defendant's conviction only if the suppressed evidence can reasonably be viewed as having made a difference in the outcome of the trial.

Capital Punishment

Wainwright v. Witt, decided by a 7-2 vote, Jan. 21, 1985. Rehnquist wrote the opinion; Brennan and Marshall dissented.

The court set out a new test that made it easier to exclude a prospective juror because of his views on capital punishment: A juror may be excluded from a capital case when his views would "prevent or substantially impair the performance of his duties as a juror in accordance with his instructions and oath."

This new test replaced one used since the 1968 decision in *Witherspoon v. Illinois*, in which the court said that a juror could be excluded because of his views on capital punishment only if it was unmistakably clear that he would automatically vote against capital punishment without regard to any evidence developed at the trial, or that his views on capital punishment would prevent his making an impartial decision on the defendant's guilt.

Caldwell v. Mississippi, decided by a 5-3 vote, June 11, 1985. Marshall wrote the opinion; Burger, Rehnquist and White dissented; Powell did not participate in the decision.

The court nullified a convicted murderer's death sentence because the prosecutor in his closing statement minimized the role of the jury in deciding whether the defendant would die, emphasizing that any death sentence would automatically be reviewed by the state Supreme Court.

"It is constitutionally impermissible to rest a death sentence on a determination made by a sentencer who has been led to believe that the responsibility for determining the appropriateness of the defendant's death rests elsewhere," wrote Marshall.

Baldwin v. Alabama, decided by a 6-3 vote, June 17, 1985. Blackmun wrote the opinion; Stevens, Brennan and Marshall dissented.

A convicted murderer's court-imposed death sentence is valid even though it was imposed under an Alabama law, which has since been since repealed, that required the jury to impose the death penalty on anyone found guilty of this type of murder.

The court found the sentence valid because the judge also sentenced the man to die, but only after conducting a sentencing proceeding that comported with the Supreme Court's rulings on fair procedures in capital cases.

Due Process

Black v. Romano, decided by an 8-0 vote, May 20, 1985. O'Connor wrote the opinion; Powell did not participate.

The constitutional guarantee of due process does not require a sentencing court to indicate for the record that it has considered alternatives to incarceration before revoking a convict's probation when he is charged with another crime.

Detainers

Carchman v. Nash, decided by a 6-3 vote, July 2, 1985. Blackmun wrote the opinion; Brennan, Marshall and Stevens dissented.

The Interstate Agreement on Detainers, which gives a prisoner imprisoned in one state the right to demand speedy treatment of any untried indictment or complaint that is the basis of a detainer against him by another state, does not not apply to detainers based on charges that he violated probation.

General

United States v. Powell, decided by a 9-0 vote, Dec. 10, 1984. Rehnquist wrote the opinion.

The fact that a jury has found a defendant not guilty of some charges but guilty of other related charges is no reason to vacate the resulting conviction.

"Inconsistent verdicts," stated the court "present a situation where 'error' . . . most certainly has occurred, but it is unclear whose ox has been gored." Because the government is precluded by the Constitution's double jeopardy guarantee from challenging the acquittal, it would not be satisfactory to grant the defendant a new trial on the charges that brought a conviction solely because the verdicts were inconsistent.

Garcia v. United States, decided by a 6-3 vote, Dec. 10,

1984. Rehnquist wrote the opinion; Stevens, Brennan and Marshall dissented.

The federal law that makes it a crime to assault or rob any custodian of "mail matter, or of any money or other property" of the United States applies to federal agents such as Secret Service agents, as well as to Postal Service employees.

Ball v. United States, affirmed by a 4-4 vote, March 26, 1985. Per curiam opinion; Powell did not participate.

A convicted felon in possession of a firearm cannot be convicted and sentenced to prison terms for both receiving that firearm and possessing that firearm in violation of federal law. Even if the prison sentences are to run concurrently, Congress did not intend to inflict a double sentence on a person for one crime.

Ramirez v. Indiana, affirmed by a 4-4 vote, April 1, 1985. Per curiam opinion; Powell did not participate.

The evenly divided court affirmed a ruling by an Indiana court that a Michigan inmate who agreed to be returned to Indiana for trial on relatively minor charges may, upon his return, be tried for more serious offenses, even if they did not arise out of the same event.

Liparota v. United States, decided by a 6-2 vote, May 13, 1985. Brennan wrote the opinion; Burger and White dissented; Powell did not participate.

Persons charged with food stamp fraud may be convicted of purchasing food stamps illegally only if it is proved that they knew they were acting in a way contrary to law.

Russell v. United States, decided by a 9-0 vote, June 3, 1985. Stevens wrote the opinion.

Federal law making it a crime to maliciously damage with fire or explosives any building used "in any activity affecting interstate or foreign commerce" applies to the attempted arson of an apartment building.

Dowling v. United States, decided by a 6-3 vote, June 28, 1985. Blackmun wrote the opinion; Powell, Burger and White dissented.

The National Stolen Property Act, which makes it illegal to transport in interstate or foreign commerce any stolen goods, wares or merchandise worth $5,000 or more, does not cover interstate transportation of "bootleg" phonograph record albums produced and distributed without consent of the owners of the copyrights of the musical compositions included on the records.

Sedima S.P.R.L. v. Imrex Co. Inc., decided by a 5-4 vote, July 1, 1985. White wrote the opinion; Brennan, Blackmun, Marshall and Powell dissented.

A business need not be convicted of a "mobster-type" crime before it can be the target of a civil suit for triple damages under the 1970 Racketeer Influenced and Corrupt Organizations (RICO) Act.

The court upheld broad use of this law, which was originally designed to strip organized crime of the protection and profits it derived from infiltrating legitimate businesses. The court held that nothing in the history, language or policy of RICO required a criminal conviction before triple-damage civil suits could be filed.

American National Bank and Trust Co. of Chicago v. Haroco Inc., affirmed by a 5-4 vote, July 1, 1985. Per curiam opinion. Brennan, Blackmun, Marshall and Powell dissented.

A bank need not be convicted of a "mobster-type" crime before it can be the target of a civil suit for triple damages under the 1970 Racketeer Influenced and Corrupt Organizations Act.

INDIVIDUAL, CIVIL RIGHTS

Age Discrimination

Trans World Airlines, Inc. v. Thurston, Air Line Pilots Association, International v. Thurston, decided by a 9-0 vote, Jan. 8, 1985. Powell wrote the opinion.

Employers may not make it harder for older workers to change jobs within a company than it is for younger workers. Such a policy violates the Age Discrimination in Employment Act.

Federal regulations require airline pilots to relinquish the controls at age 60 but permit them to remain in the cockpit as flight engineers. TWA discriminated against older pilots by making it difficult for them to transfer to flight engineer jobs upon becoming 60, while such transfers were granted automatically to younger pilots with other disabilities that required them to change jobs.

In this case, however, there was no evidence that TWA's discrimination was "willful" enough to justify an award of double damages to the older pilots who brought the suit. To prove willful discrimination, plaintiffs must show that the employer knew he was violating the law or that he acted in reckless disregard of it.

Western Air Lines Inc. v. Criswell, decided by an 8-0 vote, June 17, 1985. Stevens wrote the opinion; Powell did not participate.

Under the Age Discrimination in Employment Act, employers must have substantial evidence to justify requiring workers to retire early. Employees must be dealt with on an individual basis, not as a group, in determining whether they can continue to hold their jobs as they age.

A provision of the law that treats youth as a bona fide occupational qualification (BFOQ) in some circumstances is to be construed narrowly. Such an exception is permitted only when youth is shown to be a reasonably necessary qualification for carrying out the particular business and when there is a factual basis for believing that most persons over the qualifying age cannot safely and efficiently perform the particular job at issue.

Johnson v. Mayor and City Council of Baltimore, Equal Employment Opportunity Commission v. Mayor and City Council of Baltimore, decided by a 9-0 vote, June 17, 1985. Marshall wrote the opinion.

The decision of Congress to retain a federal law mandating retirement at age 55 for federal firefighters does not establish youth as a bona fide qualification for all firefighters. Baltimore may not invoke the federal rule as a complete justification for its own similar rule.

Discrimination Against Handicapped

Alexander v. Choate, decided by a 9-0 vote, Jan. 9, 1985. Marshall wrote the opinion.

It is not necessary to prove an intent to discriminate in

order to establish a violation of Section 504 of the Rehabilitation Act, which prohibits discrimination based on handicap in any program receiving federal funds.

In this case, however, Tennessee did not violate Section 504 by limiting to 14 days the annual inpatient hospital care covered by Medicaid. This limit was a neutral one, making the same hospital coverage accessible to handicapped and non-handicapped persons.

School Committee of the Town of Burlington, Mass. v. Massachusetts Department of Education, decided by a 9-0 vote, April 29, 1985. Rehnquist wrote the opinion.

Parents who unilaterally place a handicapped child in a private school do not necessarily lose their right to be reimbursed by the local public school system.

Congress, in the Education for All Handicapped Children Act (PL 94-142), guaranteed all handicapped children a "free, appropriate public education" and required public schools to draw up an individualized educational plan for each handicapped child. Federal courts can order school officials to reimburse parents for private school costs if state officials or the courts ultimately decide that such placement is best for the child. Parents risk, but do not waive, their right to reimbursement when they unilaterally shift a child to a private school before a final resolution of any dispute with public school officials over the child's educational plan.

Sex Discrimination

Anderson v. Bessemer City, N.C., decided by a 9-0 vote, March 19, 1985. White wrote the opinion.

An appeals court may not reverse a district court's finding of sex discrimination simply because it would have weighed the evidence differently and reached a different conclusion. There must be clear error to justify reversal.

The justices reinstated a district court's finding that a woman applicant for a job was the victim of sex discrimination when a man 15 years her junior and with no work experience was hired as a city recreation director. The appeals court that overturned that ruling erred; appeals courts should not second-guess the factual findings of district courts unless they are clearly erroneous.

Voting Rights

NAACP v. Hampton County Election Commission, decided by a 9-0 vote, Feb. 27, 1985. White wrote the opinion.

Counties subject to the "pre-clearance" requirements of the Voting Rights Act must seek federal approval of a decision to hold a special election for school board officials and to limit candidates in that election to those who had qualified to run prior to the last general election.

Hunter v. Underwood, decided by an 8-0 vote, April 16, 1985. Rehnquist wrote the opinion; Powell did not participate.

A provision of Alabama's Constitution denying the right to vote to people convicted of certain non-prison offenses involving moral turpitude was adopted in 1901 with racially discriminatory intent and operates in a racially discriminatory manner. It therefore violates the Equal Protection Clause of the U.S. Constitution.

Aliens

Immigration and Naturalization Service v. Rios-Pineda, decided by an 8-0 vote, May 13, 1985. White wrote the opinion; Powell did not participate.

The attorney general has complete discretion to deny an alien's request to suspend deportation based on the alien's seven years of continuous presence in the United States and claim of extreme hardship if denied a chance to remain. Although immigration law permits suspension in those cases, it does not require it. The attorney general can refuse suspension, particularly when the seven years passed while the alien brought baseless appeals from immigration board decisions concerning his flagrant violation of immigration laws.

Jean v. Nelson, decided by a 6-2 vote, June 26, 1985. Rehnquist wrote the opinion; Brennan and Marshall dissented; Powell did not participate.

A federal appeals court erred in addressing the question of whether "excludable aliens" apprehended at or near the U.S. border have any constitutional right to challenge their detention while immigration officials decide whether to admit or deport them.

The court expressed confidence that new immigration regulations, adopted after the beginning of this case, prevented officials from using race or national origin as a basis for deciding whether to detain or "parole" such aliens pending a decision on admission into the United States.

Attorneys' Fees

Webb v. County Board of Education of Dyer County, Tenn., decided by votes of 8-0 and 6-2, April 17, 1985. Stevens wrote the opinion; Marshall did not participate; Brennan and Blackmun dissented.

The Civil Rights Attorneys' Fees Awards Act of 1976 does not authorize a fee award for attorneys' services rendered in optional state administrative proceedings before commencement of a civil rights damage suit.

Marek v. Chesny, decided by a 6-3 vote, June 27, 1985. Burger wrote the opinion; Brennan, Marshall and Blackmun dissented.

Federal Rule of Civil Procedure 68 limits the extent to which successful plaintiffs in civil rights cases can be reimbursed for their attorneys' fees. The rule holds that if a party rejects a settlement offer and wins a less favorable judgment, that party must pay all costs accruing after the settlement offer. Such costs include attorneys' fees.

Kentucky v. Graham, decided by a 9-0 vote, June 28, 1985. Marshall wrote the opinion.

A state may not be ordered to pay attorneys' fees incurred by a citizen who successfully sues state employees for violating his constitutional rights — unless the state itself was held liable for the violation.

Attorneys' fees may not be awarded, under the 1976 Civil Rights Attorneys' Fee Awards Act, against a party not held at fault. When a government employee is sued in his personal, not official, capacity, a judgment against him cannot result in an order that the government employer pay the plaintiffs' attorneys' fees.

Damage Suits

Brandon v. Holt, decided by an 8-1 vote, Jan. 21, 1985. Stevens wrote the opinion; Rehnquist dissented.

When a damage judgment is entered against the head

of a city police department in his official capacity, the award is essentially against the city itself and the city must pay it — even if the city was not explicitly named as a defendant in the suit. A city is not entitled to the shield of qualified immunity in such cases.

Wilson v. Garcia, decided by a 7-1 vote, April 17, 1985. Stevens wrote the opinion; Powell did not participate; O'Connor dissented.

Cases brought under the Civil Rights Act of 1871 against state and local officials charged with violating someone's federal or constitutional rights should be considered personal injury suits subject to whatever statute of limitations state law imposes upon those suits. Most states permit such cases to be filed within two or three years of the alleged violation.

Springfield Township School District v. Knoll, decided by an 8-0 vote, April 17, 1985. Per curiam (unsigned) opinion. Powell did not participate.

The court sent back to the 3rd U.S. Circuit Court of Appeals, for reconsideration in light of the decision in *Wilson v. Garcia* (above), a case in which a teacher's suit against school district officials charging them with sex discrimination was dismissed because it was not brought within six months of the challenged action.

Oklahoma City v. Tuttle, decided by a 7-1 vote, June 3, 1985. Rehnquist wrote the opinion; Stevens dissented; Powell did not participate.

A single incident of the use of excessive force by a city police officer, even one resulting in the death of a citizen, is insufficient basis for a civil rights damage suit against the city.

Food Stamps

Atkins v. Parker, Parker v. Block, decided by a 7-2 vote, June 4, 1985. Stevens wrote the opinion; Brennan and Marshall dissented.

The Massachusetts Department of Public Welfare gave adequate notice to the state's food stamp recipients of a change in the law that lowered to 18 percent from 20 percent the amount of earned income to be disregarded in determining eligibility for stamps. This change meant lower benefits for many people and termination of benefits for some.

The notice was challenged because it did not give specific information concerning the impact of the change on each recipient nor supply the recipient information so that he could make the calculation himself. Nevertheless, the court held the notice sufficient to permit anyone who did not understand the impact of the change to seek clarification.

Due Process

Ponte v. Real, decided by a 6-2 vote, May 20, 1985; Rehnquist wrote the opinion; Marshall and Brennan dissented; Powell did not participate.

The due process guarantee does not require prison officials to place in the record of a disciplinary hearing their reasons for refusing to call witnesses requested by an inmate. The due process guarantee does require that the officials at some point state their reasons, however, either in the record or in later testimony to a court if their decision is challenged.

Superintendent, Massachusetts Correctional Institute at Walpole v. Hill, decided by votes of 9-0 and 6-3, June 17, 1985. O'Connor wrote the opinion; Brennan, Marshall and Stevens dissented in part.

The decision by a prison disciplinary committee to revoke an inmate's good time credits is justifiable under the due process guarantee so long as there is some evidence in the record to support the board's decision.

Cleveland Board of Education v. Loudermill, decided by an 8-1 vote, March 19, 1985. White wrote the decision; Rehnquist dissented.

Before a tenured public employee may be fired, he has a constitutional due-process right to a hearing at which he may respond to charges against him. A worker is entitled to oral or written notice of the charges, an explanation of the evidence supporting the charges, and a chance to present his side of the story.

Mentally Retarded/Zoning

City of Cleburne, Texas v. Cleburne Living Center Inc., decided by votes of 9-0 and 6-3, July 1, 1985. White wrote the opinion; Brennan, Marshall and Stevens dissented in part.

Laws that treat the mentally retarded differently from other citizens are constitutional so long as they are a rational means to a legitimate end. Using that "rational basis" test, the court unanimously struck down Cleburne's use of its zoning ordinance to deny a special use permit for a group home for mentally retarded adults in a residential neighborhood.

"Mental retardation is a characteristic that the government may legitimately take into account in a wide range of decisions," the court said. But in this case — in which the city required a permit for this group home, but not for apartment houses, fraternity houses or hospitals — the permit requirement was based on "an irrational prejudice against the mentally retarded," an impermissible basis for the city's action.

FIRST AMENDMENT

Freedom of Speech

Federal Election Commission v. National Conservative Political Action Committee, Democratic Party of the United States v. National Conservative Political Action Committee, decided by votes of 5-4 and 7-2, March 18, 1985. Rehnquist wrote the opinion; Marshall and White dissented; Brennan and Stevens dissented in part.

Congress cannot limit independent spending by political action committees (PACs) in presidential campaigns, the court ruled 7-2. The court held unconstitutional, as a violation of the First Amendment guarantee of free speech, a provision of the Federal Election Campaign Act Amendments (PL 93-443) that limited to $1,000 the amount a PAC could spend independently to promote or prevent the election of publicly funded presidential candidates.

In the context of a national presidential campaign, the majority found this limit curtailed freedom of speech in the same way as "allowing a speaker in a public hall to express his views while denying him the use of an amplifying system."

By 5-4, the court held that Congress did not intend to permit one private group, the Democratic Party, to sue another, the National Conservative Political Action Committee, for violating the $1,000 limit. Only the Federal Election Commission can move to enforce the law against NCPAC or another party in such circumstances without first going through administrative proceedings.

Wayte v. United States, decided by a 7-2 vote, March 19, 1985. Powell wrote the opinion; Brennan and Marshall dissented.

The court upheld the government's temporary use of a "passive enforcement policy" for the draft registration law, under which it initially prosecuted for failing to register with the Selective Service System only men who publicized their non-compliance or were reported by others to be in non-compliance.

This policy had been challenged as violating the First Amendment rights of vocal non-registrants, penalizing them for exercising their right to speak out to inform the government of their defiance. The court found that the government treated all reported non-registrants similarly and did not submit those who spoke out to any special burden.

Board of Education of the City of Oklahoma City v. National Gay Task Force, affirmed by a 4-4 vote, March 26, 1985. Per curiam opinion; Powell did not participate.

The evenly divided court affirmed a ruling by the 10th U.S. Circuit Court of Appeals invalidating, as a violation of the First Amendment guarantee of free speech, an Oklahoma law that prohibited schoolteachers from advocating or promoting public or private homosexual activity.

Zauderer v. Office of Disciplinary Counsel of the Supreme Court of Ohio, decided by votes of 5-3 and 6-2, May 28, 1985. White wrote the opinion; O'Connor, Rehnquist and Burger dissented in part; Brennan and Marshall dissented in part. Powell did not take part in the decision.

The First Amendment does not permit a state to discipline an attorney for advertising that his services are available to clients bringing a specific sort of suit against a particular target, or for using an accurate line drawing or other illustration in that ad.

The attorney was properly reprimanded by the state for an ad that failed to make clear that clients might have to pay some legal costs even if they paid no legal fees, and for a deceptive ad offering to represent people charged with drunken driving.

Lowe v. Securities and Exchange Commission, decided by an 8-0 vote, June 10, 1985. Stevens wrote the opinion; Powell did not participate.

The Securities and Exchange Commission (SEC) lacks the power to halt publication of an investment advisory newsletter, even though its author had his registration as an investment adviser revoked by the SEC after his conviction for securities-related crimes.

Five justices — Stevens, Brennan, Marshall, Blackmun and O'Connor — held that this individual was not an "investment adviser" within the meaning of the Investment Advisers Act, because the advice he gave in his newsletter was general in nature, not personalized for particular investors. Thus, he qualified for exemption from SEC regulation as a "bona fide newspaper, news magazine or business or financial publication of general and regular circulation."

Three justices — Burger, White and Rehnquist — disagreed with this narrow definition of "investment adviser" and argued that instead the court should deny the SEC this power on the grounds that such a restraint on publication violated the First Amendment freedom of speech and the press.

United States v. Albertini, decided by a 6-3 vote, June 24, 1985. O'Connor wrote the opinion; Brennan, Marshall and Stevens dissented.

A protestor's First Amendment rights were not violated when he was convicted and sentenced to jail for going to an "open house" at a military base from which he had been officially barred nine years earlier. Exclusion of this individual from the military base, even during this sort of "open house," promotes the government's interest in assuring the security of military installations.

In re Snyder, decided by an 8-0 vote, June 24, 1985. Burger wrote the opinion; Blackmun did not participate in the decision.

An attorney should not be suspended from practicing in the federal courts of his home region for a single incident of "disrespect" for the circuit court of appeals and its presiding judge. The attorney's written criticism of the appeals court's administration of a certain program and his refusal to apologize for that letter was not sufficient reason to suspend him from practice.

Dun & Bradstreet, Inc. v. Greenmoss Builders, Inc., decided by a 5-4 vote, June 26, 1985. Powell announced the court's decision, joined in his opinion by two justices, O'Connor and Rehnquist; Burger and White concurred; Brennan, Marshall, Blackmun and Stevens dissented.

Unless a libel case involves a matter of public concern, the First Amendment does not preclude awards of both actual and punitive damage — even without proof of malice on the part of the libeler.

The court thereby upheld a Vermont jury's award of $300,000 in punitive damages, as well as $50,000 in compensatory damages, to Greenmoss, a building company which Dun & Bradstreet had incorrectly reported to have declared bankruptcy.

Cornelius v. NAACP Legal Defense and Educational Fund, Inc., decided by a 4-3 vote, July 2, 1985. O'Connor wrote the opinion; Brennan, Blackmun and Stevens dissented; Marshall and Powell did not participate.

The First Amendment permits exclusion of legal and political advocacy groups from the Combined Federal Campaign, the annual charity drive among federal government employees, if the exclusion has a reasonable basis. "Nothing in the Constitution requires the government freely to grant access to all who wish to exercise their right to free speech on every type of government property."

The reason for such exclusion, however, may not be a mere cover story for government discrimination against certain viewpoints. The lower court must take a second look at this case, the court held, to ensure that the exclusion was not motivated by the government's disagreement with the points of view advocated by the groups involved.

Free Press/Copyright

Harper & Row, Publishers, Inc. v. Nation Enterprises, decided by a 6-3 vote, May 20, 1985. O'Connor wrote the opinion; Brennan, White and Marshall dissented.

The First Amendment does not shield the press from suits for copyright infringement in cases involving extensive use of quotations from unpublished copyrighted material without the permission of the copyright holder.

The court held that *The Nation* magazine violated federal copyright law when it used significant quotations from President Gerald R. Ford's then-unpublished memoirs in an April 1979 article about Ford's decision to pardon his predecessor, Richard M. Nixon.

This use of Ford's material did not come within the "fair use" exception to the copyright law for "criticism, comment, news reporting, teaching, scholarship or research," the court held. The magazine could have reported on the information in the Ford book without risk, but it had no right to quote large segments from the memoirs without authorization.

Church and State

Board of Trustees of the Village of Scarsdale v. McCreary, affirmed by a 4-4 vote, March 27, 1985. Per curiam opinion; Powell did not participate.

The evenly divided court affirmed a ruling by the 2nd U.S. Circuit Court of Appeals that a city cannot rely on the First Amendment's ban on state action establishing religion as its reason for denying a request from a citizens' group that a crèche be displayed in a public park during the Christmas season.

Tony and Susan Alamo Foundation v. Secretary of Labor, decided by a 9-0 vote, April 23, 1985. White wrote the opinion.

Commercial enterprises of churches or religious foundations are subject to minimum wage, overtime and record-keeping requirements of the Fair Labor Standards Act. They cannot claim exemption from such laws by citing First Amendment freedom of religion guarantees.

Even if employees consider themselves associates, rather than employees, and are paid in benefits, not cash wages, the federal law applies. This law must be applied broadly to accomplish its goal of outlawing goods produced under conditions that do not meet minimum standards of decency.

Wallace v. Jaffree, decided by a 6-3 vote, June 4, 1985. Stevens wrote the opinion; Burger, Rehnquist and White dissented.

Moment-of-silence laws intended to restore prayer to the nation's public schools are unconstitutional. The court struck down an Alabama law that permitted a moment of silence for prayer or meditation at the beginning of each school day.

The legislative history of the law made clear that it had no secular purpose, but was specifically designed to endorse religion and to encourage students to pray. Such state endorsement of religion is unconstitutional, a violation of the First Amendment ban on state action establishing religion.

Jensen v. Quaring, affirmed by a 4-4 vote, June 17, 1985. Per curiam opinion; Powell did not participate.

The evenly divided court affirmed a decision by the 8th U.S. Circuit Court of Appeals that Nebraska violated the First Amendment rights of a qualified motorist by denying her a driver's license after she refused, based on her religious beliefs, to have her photograph taken for the license.

Estate of Thornton v. Caldor, Inc., decided by an 8-1 vote, June 26, 1985. Burger wrote the opinion; Rehnquist dissented.

It is not constitutional for states to require employers to give workers a day off on their Sabbath. The court invalidated a Connecticut law that gave all employees the right to refuse with impunity to work on their Sabbath.

By giving workers this unqualified right, the state elevated religious concerns over all other interests that might be involved in setting work schedules. Thus a primary effect of the law was to advance a religious practice, in violation of the First Amendment ban on establishment of religion.

Grand Rapids School District v. Ball, decided by votes of 7-2 and 5-4, July 1, 1985. Brennan wrote the opinion; White and Rehnquist dissented; Burger and O'Connor dissented in part.

Grand Rapids, Mich., school officials violated the First Amendment ban on establishment of religion by providing remedial and enrichment classes to students at 41 non-public schools, all but one religiously affiliated.

These classes were either conducted during the regular school day by public school teachers in a "shared time" program, or after school by parochial school teachers who were paid for this extra work from public funds.

By 7-2, the justices held that the school-day classes were impermissible, primarily because the "symbolic union of church and state inherent in the provision of secular, state-provided instruction in the religious school buildings threatens to convey a message of state support for religion." Burger and O'Connor agreed that this program was unconstitutional.

By 5-4, the justices held the after-school classes similarly impermissible.

Aguilar v. Felton, decided by a 5-4 vote, July 1, 1985. Brennan wrote the opinion; Burger, White, Rehnquist and O'Connor dissented.

New York's system for providing Title I remedial and counseling services to disadvantaged students who attend non-public schools violates the First Amendment, because the city uses federal funds to send teachers and other educational personnel into private and parochial schools to provide these services to these students during the regular school day.

The New York system, like the Grand Rapids system, effectively advanced religion symbolically and practically, by providing services the private or parochial school would otherwise have had to provide. In addition, New York actively monitored its program to ensure that participating personnel were not involved in religious activities, but that monitoring itself inevitably entangled church and state too far, the court held.

Right of Petition

McDonald v. Smith, decided by an 8-0 vote, June 19, 1985. Burger wrote the opinion; Powell did not participate.

The First Amendment right to petition the government does not shield those who exercise it from being sued for libel by persons who allege that they are defamed by the petition or letter.

Walters v. National Association of Radiation Survivors, decided by a 6-3 vote, June 28, 1985. Rehnquist wrote the opinion; Brennan, Marshall and Stevens dissented.

Congress did not deny veterans due process, nor did it limit their right effectively to petition the government for redress of grievances, when it limited to $10 the amount that a veteran can pay an attorney for representing him in pursuing death or disability claims before the Veterans Administration.

The court upheld the 1862 law, emphasizing that Congress did not intend for such benefit disagreements to become adversary proceedings.

Obscenity

Brockett v. Spokane Arcades, Eikenberry v. J-R Distributors, decided by a 6-2 vote, June 19, 1985. White wrote the opinion; Brennan and Marshall dissented. Powell did not participate.

The First Amendment does not permit a state to ban material merely because it incites "lust."

The portion of Washington state's anti-obscenity law permitting regulation or banning of such material is unconstitutional because it covers material that "does no more than arouse 'good, old-fashioned, healthy' interest in sex." But the appeals court went too far in striking down the entire law as unconstitutional; only the "lust" provision is invalid.

BUSINESS LAW

Antitrust

Marrese v. American Academy of Orthopaedic Surgeons, decided by a 7-0 vote, March 4, 1985. O'Connor wrote the opinion; Blackmun and Stevens did not participate.

Although federal antitrust claims are within the exclusive jurisdiction of the federal courts, a federal court hearing such a claim cannot ignore state law and automatically hold that federal courts are barred from hearing that claim by a prior state judgment arising out of the same facts but resolving a differently based claim.

Town of Hallie v. City of Eau Claire, decided by a 9-0 vote, March 27, 1985. Powell wrote the opinion.

Allegedly anti-competitive conduct by a city, if authorized by state law, is immune from challenge under antitrust laws as "state action" — even if the state does not actively supervise the city's implementation of its policy. Such active supervision is necessary only when a private party is carrying out a state policy and hopes to claim the protection of the "state action" exemption from antitrust laws.

Southern Motor Carriers Rate Conference Inc. v. United States, decided by a 7-2 vote, March 27, 1985. Powell wrote the opinion; Stevens and White dissented.

Collective ratemaking by common carrier rate bureaus for submission to state public service commissions is protected from federal antitrust challenge under the "state action" exemption so long as the activities are authorized by states in which the rate bureaus operate.

Northwest Wholesale Stationers, Inc. v. Pacific Stationery and Printing Co., decided by a 7-0 vote, June 11, 1985. Brennan wrote the opinion; Powell and Marshall did not participate.

A wholesale purchasing cooperative does not commit a per se violation of Section 1 of the Sherman Antitrust Act — which declares every restraint of trade illegal — when it expels a member without notice, hearing or the opportunity to challenge the expulsion decision.

Such action is not clearly a group boycott or concerted refusal to deal in violation of Section 1, but should be reviewed under the "rule of reason" standard to determine whether it constitutes an unreasonable restraint of trade.

Aspen Skiing Co. v. Aspen Highlands Skiing Corp., decided by an 8-0 vote, June 19, 1985. Stevens wrote the opinion; White did not participate.

Evidence in an antitrust case that a firm with monopoly power exercised that power in violation of the Sherman Act by refusing to deal with a competitor is sufficient to justify a jury's conclusion that an antitrust violation did occur.

Mitsubishi Motors Corp. v. Soler Chrysler-Plymouth Inc., decided by a 5-3 vote, July 2, 1985. Blackmun wrote the opinion; Brennan, Marshall and Stevens dissented. Powell did not participate.

American courts have power to order international arbitration of antitrust disputes between foreign manufacturers and their distributors in the United States. Antitrust claims by a Puerto Rican car dealer against a Japanese manufacturer and another foreign distributor are arbitrable under the arbitration clause of their sales agreement.

Aviation

Air France v. Saks, decided by an 8-0 vote, March 4, 1985. O'Connor wrote the opinion; Powell did not participate.

A passenger who suffers a permanent hearing loss as a result of normal and usual operation of the aircraft's pressurization system is not injured by an accident within the meaning of the Warsaw Convention, which governs the liability of air carriers to their passengers, and thus may not sue the airlines for damages under it.

Regional Banking

Northeast Bancorp Inc. v. Board of Governors of Federal Reserve System, decided by an 8-0 vote, June 10, 1985. Rehnquist wrote the opinion; Powell did not participate.

Existing regional banking agreements — under which states permit acquisition of in-state banks by banks located in some, but not all, other states — are neither illegal nor unconstitutional.

The Douglas Amendment to the Bank Holding Company Act generally prohibits interstate banking but permits state legislatures to lift that barrier by specifically authorizing interstate bank acquisitions. The language of the amendment permits states to permit some or all interstate bank acquisitions.

Because Congress specifically gave states this power, laws permitting regional banking are immune from challenge as unconstitutional impediments to the flow of interstate commerce.

Bankruptcy

Commodity Futures Trading Commission v. Weintraub, decided by an 8-0 vote, April 29, 1985. Marshall wrote the opinion; Powell did not participate.

The trustee of a bankrupt corporation has the authority to waive the corporation's attorney-client privilege with regard to conversations that occurred before the bankruptcy filing.

Music Copyrights

Mills Music Inc. v. Snyder, decided by a 5-4 vote, Jan. 8, 1985. Stevens wrote the opinion; White, Brennan, Marshall and Blackmun dissented.

A music publisher may continue to receive some royalties from its recordings of a copyrighted song that qualify as derivative works within the meaning of the 1976 Copyright Act even after the heirs to one of the song's writers have reacquired the copyright from the publisher. The song involved in this case was "Who's Sorry Now?"

Railroads

National Railroad Passenger Corp. v. Atchison, Topeka and Santa Fe Railway Co., decided by an 8-0 vote, March 18, 1985. Marshall wrote the opinion; Powell did not participate.

Congress acted within constitutional limits when it amended the Rail Passenger Service Act to require privately owned railroads to reimburse Amtrak for the free or reduced-fare travel that Amtrak provides for the employees of the private railroads and their families.

Pesticide Regulation

Thomas v. Union Carbide Agricultural Products Co., decided by a 9-0 vote, July 1, 1985. O'Connor wrote the opinion.

The Federal Insecticide, Fungicide and Rodenticide Act does not violate the Constitution in permitting the Environmental Protection Agency to use data submitted by one company in support of a second company's application for registration of a pesticide, so long as the second company agrees to compensate the first for use of the data — and insofar as the law provides for binding arbitration, with limited judicial review, of any dispute over the amount of compensation.

Securities

Dean Witter Reynolds Inc. v. Byrd, decided by a 9-0 vote, March 4, 1985. Marshall wrote the opinion.

A federal district court faced with a case in which there are claims of federal securities law violations and claims which under state law may be settled by arbitration must grant a motion to compel arbitration of the state claims while the federal court hears the securities complaint.

Landreth Timber Co. v. Landreth, Gould v. Ruefenacht, decided by an 8-1 vote, May 28, 1985. Powell wrote the opinions; Stevens dissented.

Federal securities law applies to the sale of stock in a closely held company even when the purpose of the sale is the purchase of the entire business. The court rejected the argument that the "sale of business" doctrine left resolution of disputes arising out of such transactions to state courts.

Schreiber v. Burlington Northern Inc., decided by a 7-0 vote, June 4, 1985. Burger wrote the opinion; Powell and O'Connor did not participate.

Federal securities law may not be used to challenge tender offers that are simply "unfair." Securities lawsuits charging fraud in a tender offer must show that a company's management misrepresented or failed to disclose certain crucial information.

Bateman Eichler, Hill Richards Inc. v. Berner, decided by an 8-0 vote, June 11, 1985. Brennan wrote the opinion; Marshall did not participate.

Investors may pursue a private damages suit under federal securities law charging corporate officials and securities brokers with inducing them to buy stocks by giving them false "inside information" — even though the investors themselves, by trading on such information, also violated the law.

Taxation

Paulsen v. Commissioner of Internal Revenue, decided by a 6-2 vote, Jan. 8, 1985. Rehnquist wrote the opinion; O'Connor and Burger dissented; Powell did not participate.

The merger of a stock savings and loan association with a mutual savings and loan association, in which the stockholders in the first exchanged their stock for accounts and certificates of deposit in the second, is not a tax-free reorganization under federal tax laws. The shareholders involved must pay income tax on the gain they realize through the exchange of stock for accounts and certificates.

United States v. Boyle, decided by a 9-0 vote, Jan. 9, 1985. Burger wrote the opinion.

A taxpayer who files a late estate tax return is not excused from the penalty for late filing because he relied on his attorney to meet the deadlines.

Tiffany Fine Arts Inc. v. United States, decided by a 9-0 vote, Jan. 9, 1985. Marshall wrote the opinion.

When the IRS serves a summons on a holding company and its subsidiaries with the dual purpose of obtaining information about their tax liabilities and the tax liabilities of unnamed persons they have licensed to sell a certain device, the IRS is not required to obtain prior judicial approval for the summons.

Prior judicial approval is required only when the IRS seeks information on the tax liability of unnamed taxpayers, not when the person to whom the summons is issued is also a target of such an investigation.

United States v. National Bank of Commerce, decided by a 5-4 vote, June 26, 1985. Blackmun wrote the opinion; Powell, Brennan, Marshall and Stevens dissented.

The Internal Revenue Service may seize the assets of a delinquent taxpayer contained in a joint bank account, even if only one of the account holders is delinquent in paying his taxes.

Trademarks

Park 'N Fly Inc. v. Dollar Park And Fly, Inc., decided by an 8-1 vote, Jan. 8, 1985. O'Connor wrote the opinion; Stevens dissented.

A person charged with infringing upon the use of a trademark may not defend himself against that charge by arguing that the allegedly infringing practice simply describes his business.

LABOR LAW

National Labor Relations Board (NLRB) v. Action Automotive Inc., decided by a 6-3 vote, Feb. 19, 1985. Burger wrote the opinion; Stevens, Rehnquist and O'Connor dissented.

Unions do not have to represent employees who are close relatives of management. The NLRB acted within its powers when it excluded from a union representation election employees who were related to the owner of the employer corporation.

Herb's Welding Inc. v. Gray, decided by a 5-4 vote, March 18, 1985. White wrote the opinion; Marshall, Brennan, Blackmun and O'Connor dissented.

Workers on offshore drilling platforms in state waters are not engaged in maritime employment within the meaning of the Longshoremen's and Harbor Workers' Compensation Act and so are not covered by that law's death and disability benefits.

Allis-Chalmers Corp. v. Lueck, decided by an 8-0 vote, April 16, 1985. Blackmun wrote the opinion; Powell did not participate.

An employee who feels that his employer violated state law by exhibiting bad faith in handling his claim for disability insurance provided in a collective bargaining agreement cannot sue his employer in state courts. Such a suit must either be dismissed as pre-empted by the Labor Management Relations Act, which governs claims alleging violations of labor contracts, or be treated as a claim arising under that law and subject to arbitration.

Central States, Southeast and Southwest Areas Pension Fund v. Central Transport Inc., decided by votes of 9-0 and 6-3, June 19, 1985. Marshall wrote the opinion; Burger, Rehnquist and Stevens dissented.

Officials of a multi-employer benefit plan regulated by the Employee Retirement Income Security Act have the right to audit the records of participating companies to ensure that contributions are being made for all eligible workers.

Cornelius v. Nutt, decided by a 6-2 vote, June 24, 1985. Blackmun wrote the opinion; Marshall and Brennan dissented; Powell did not participate.

The same standard — "harmful error" — applies to review of a federal agency's decision to discipline an employee whether or not that employee belongs to a union.

If the employee belongs to a union, that review is usually conducted by an arbitrator; if he does not, the review is by the Merit Systems Protection Board. Either way, the standard to be used is the same — the action should be overturned only if there is a showing of "substantial prejudice" to the individual employee's rights.

Massachusetts Mutual Life Insurance Co. v. Russell, decided by a vote of 9-0, June 27, 1985. Stevens wrote the opinion.

The provision of the Employee Retirement Income Security Act that makes the fiduciaries of an employee benefit plan personally liable "to such plan" for any losses to it resulting from a breach of fiduciary duties does not give workers with complaints about the payment of benefits under the plan the right to sue the plan administrators for damages.

National Labor Relations Board v. International Longshoremen's Association (ILA), decided by a 6-3 vote, June 27, 1985. Brennan wrote the opinion; Rehnquist, Burger and O'Connor dissented.

ILA rules requiring that most containers to be loaded on ships must be loaded and unloaded by longshoremen if the process takes place within 50 miles of port are a valid work-preservation agreement.

The court overturned an NLRB ruling that the rules, adopted to preserve work for ILA members in the face of increasing containerization of freight, were invalid because they acquired for longshoremen work traditionally done by others.

Pattern Makers' League of North America, AFL-CIO v. National Labor Relations Board, decided by a 5-4 vote, June 27, 1985. Powell wrote the opinion; Blackmun, Brennan, Stevens and Marshall dissented.

Unions violate the 1947 Taft-Hartley Act and the national policy of "voluntary unionism" when they discipline members who resign during a strike and return to work in violation of union rules.

The court upheld the NLRB's finding that it was illegal for unions to enforce rules forbidding members to resign during a strike.

ENVIRONMENT

Ohio v. Kovacs, decided by a 9-0 vote, Jan. 9, 1985. White wrote the opinion.

A businessman's obligation, under a state court order, to clean up a hazardous-waste disposal site is a debt that can be discharged if the businessman declares bankruptcy. Congress did not include such obligations as one of the specific categories of obligations that are exempt from discharge under the bankruptcy law.

Chemical Manufacturers Association v. Natural Resources Defense Council (NRDC), Environmental Protection Agency v. NRDC, decided by a 5-4 vote, Feb. 27, 1985. White wrote the opinion; Marshall, Blackmun, O'Connor and Stevens dissented.

The Environmental Protection Agency may grant individual plants exceptions from the industrywide Clean Water Act standards requiring pre-treatment of toxic wastes before they are dumped into a sewage system. Such variances are granted to plants that are in some way fundamentally different from others in the industry, and for whom compliance with the industrywide standard is particularly difficult.

United States v. Locke, decided by a 6-3 vote, April 1, 1985. Marshall wrote the opinion; Powell, Stevens and Brennan dissented.

The Federal Land Policy and Management Act, which deems unpatented mining claims abandoned if the owner does not file a timely claim with state and federal officials each year of his intention to hold the claim or evidence of work on claim, is not unconstitutional. The law's requirement that this claim must be filed "prior to December 31" makes clear that claims must be filed on or before December 30 — and thus owners filing December 31 have not met the filing deadline.

SOCIAL SECURITY

Heckler v. Turner, decided by a 9-0 vote, Feb. 27, 1985. Blackmun wrote the opinion.

States must use a family's gross income, not its take-home pay after mandatory payroll deductions, in calculating benefits under the Aid to Families with Dependent Children (AFDC) welfare program. Under AFDC, a larger income base means a smaller benefit payment.

The Deficit Reduction Act of 1984 (PL 98-369) declared that "gross earned income, prior to any deductions for taxes or for any other purposes," should be used in calculating AFDC benefits.

Connecticut Department of Income Maintenance v. Heckler, decided by a 9-0 vote, May 20, 1985. Stevens wrote the opinion.

The federal government has authority to deny Medicaid funds to states that use nursing homes and other "intermediate care facilities" to treat mentally ill patients under the age of 65.

Medicaid does not reimburse states for the care of mentally ill persons under 65; it does reimburse them for the care of mentally ill persons over 65. A state may not obtain reimbursement for the younger mentally ill patients just because they are placed in intermediate-care facilities rather than traditional mental hospitals.

STATE POWERS

Federal Payments

Lawrence County v. Lead-Deadwood School District No. 40-1, decided by a 7-2 vote, Jan. 9, 1985. White wrote the opinion; Rehnquist and Stevens dissented.

A state may not dictate to local governments the manner in which they must allocate federal payments received under the Payment in Lieu of Taxes Act. Congress specifically gave local governments complete discretion in deciding how to spend this money, which is intended to defray some of the costs associated with the existence of large units of federally owned land within local government boundaries.

Bennett v. Kentucky Department of Education, decided by an 8-0 vote, March 19, 1985. O'Connor wrote the opinion; Powell did not participate.

States that use federal funds provided under Title I of the Elementary and Secondary Education Act to supplant, rather than supplement, state and local expenditures for education are liable for reimbursement of those funds to the federal government.

Bennett v. New Jersey, decided by a 6-2 vote, March 19, 1985. O'Connor wrote the opinion; Stevens and Marshall dissented, Powell did not participate.

The 1978 Amendments to Title I of the Elementary and Secondary Education Act, which relaxed eligibility requirements for receipt of Title I funds, do not apply retroactively to excuse states from paying back previously misspent Title I funds.

Pre-emption

Metropolitan Life Insurance Co. v. Massachusetts, Travelers Insurance Co. v. Massachusetts, decided by a vote of 8-0, June 3, 1985. Blackmun wrote the opinion. Powell did not participate.

Neither the National Labor Relations Act nor the Employee Retirement Income Security Act pre-empts state laws requiring employee health care plans to include certain minimum mental health care benefits.

Hillsborough County, Florida v. Automated Medical Laboratories Inc., decided by a 9-0 vote, June 3, 1985. Marshall wrote the opinion.

Food and Drug Administration regulations setting minimum federal standards for plasma collection do not pre-empt county ordinances or regulations governing collection of blood plasma in a county.

Privileges and Immunities

Garcia v. San Antonio Metropolitan Transit Authority, decided by a 5-4 vote, Feb. 19, 1985. Blackmun wrote the opinion; Rehnquist, Powell, O'Connor and Burger dissented.

Neither the 10th Amendment nor any other specific provision of the Constitution limits Congress when it exercises its power to regulate commerce in such a fashion as to curtail the power of the states.

The court held that the federal minimum wage and overtime law, the Fair Labor Standards Act, applies to employees of a city-owned and operated transit system. With Justice Blackmun switching positions, the court overruled its 1976 decision in *National League of Cities v. Usery,* which found that the 10th Amendment forbade the application of this law to employees of state and local governments.

By overruling the 1976 decision, the court cleared the way for enforcement of the minimum wage law to cover all such employees.

The framers of the Constitution, the majority held, intended for the political process and the structure of the federal government to protect state prerogatives. States and cities chafing under federal interference must use their political power to persuade Congress, not the courts, to change the laws they find burdensome, the majority said.

Supreme Court of New Hampshire v. Piper, decided by an 8-1 vote, March 4, 1985. Powell wrote the opinion; Rehnquist dissented.

A New Hampshire rule that denies admission to the state bar to attorneys not residing in the state at the time of their admission violates the Constitution's provision that "the citizens of each state shall be entitled to all privileges and immunities of citizens in the several states."

Spencer v. South Carolina Tax Commission, affirmed by a 4-4 vote, March 27, 1985. Per curiam opinion; Powell did not participate.

The evenly divided court affirmed a decision by the South Carolina Supreme Court denying attorneys' fees to taxpayers who successfully challenged a state tax regulation as violating the Privileges and Immunities Clause. The denial of fees was based on the state court's view that state law prohibited such an award.

Atascadero State Hospital v. Scanlon, decided by a 5-4 vote, June 28, 1985. Powell wrote the opinion; Brennan, Marshall, Blackmun and Stevens dissented.

A state cannot be sued in federal court by an individual alleging that the state violated the federal ban on discrimination against the handicapped that is contained in the Rehabilitation Act of 1973. The 11th Amendment gives the state immunity from this sort of suit and neither

Congress nor California, the state in this case, overrode or waived this immunity.

Public Lands

Cory v. Western Oil & Gas Association, affirmed by a 4-4 vote, March 27, 1985. Per curiam opinion. Powell did not participate.

The evenly divided court affirmed a ruling by the 9th U.S. Circuit Court of Appeals that California's method of calculating the rent that oil companies owe for their leases of state lands for pipelines was unconstitutional.

State Courts

Phillips Petroleum Co. v. Shutts, decided by votes of 7-1 and 8-0, June 26, 1985. Rehnquist wrote the opinion; Stevens dissented in part; Powell did not participate.

State courts handling class action suit can exercise jurisdiction over class members and claims that have no contact with the state whose court is hearing the suit.

The court upheld the decision of Kansas courts to permit a nationwide class of 28,000 owners of oil and gas leases to sue Phillips Petroleum for unpaid interest. The leases were in 11 states, including Kansas; the owners lived in all 50 states, plus several foreign countries. Had the court denied the state court jurisdiction, the class members would have had to sue in many different courts.

The court held that the Kansas court erred, however, in applying Kansas law to resolve all the claims, particularly since Kansas law conflicts in significant ways with the laws of Texas, where many of the leases were located. Justice Stevens dissented on this point.

Taxation

First National Bank of Atlanta v. Bartow County Board of Tax Assessors, decided by a 9-0 vote, March 19, 1985. Blackmun wrote the opinion.

States do not have to deduct the full value of a bank's holdings of tax-exempt U.S. obligations when determining the basis upon which to tax the bank's property.

The court in a 1983 ruling, *American Bank & Trust Co. v. Dallas County,* held that federal law prohibited states from imposing a property tax on bank shares when the tax was computed on the basis of a bank's net worth without deducting for its holdings of tax-exempt U.S. notes and bonds. The 1985 decision made clear that the deduction required may be less than the full value of the U.S. obligations.

Metropolitan Life Insurance Co. v. Ward, decided by a 5-4 vote, March 26, 1985. Powell wrote the opinion; O'Connor, Rehnquist, Brennan and Marshall dissented.

Alabama, by taxing out-of-state insurance firms at a higher rate than in-state insurance companies, violates the constitutional guarantee of equal protection. Neither of the state's stated objectives for the tax differential — encouraging formation of new companies in Alabama and capital investment in the state by out-of-state companies — is sufficient to justify such discriminatory treatment of out-of-state firms.

Williams v. Vermont, decided by a 5-3 vote, June 4, 1985. White wrote the opinion; Blackmun, Rehnquist and O'Connor dissented; Powell did not participate.

Vermont's preferential treatment of its own residents in connection with certain sales and use taxes violates the Constitution's guarantee of equal protection. The state allowed its own residents who purchased cars in other states to reduce the amount of use tax owed to Vermont at the time the car was registered by the amount of any sales or use tax paid to the other state. However, it did not grant similar treatment to persons who purchased automobiles outside of Vermont before becoming Vermont residents.

Hooper v. Bernalillo County Assessor, decided by a 5-3 vote, June 24, 1985. Burger wrote the opinion; Stevens, Rehnquist and O'Connor dissented; Powell did not participate.

New Mexico violated the equal protection guarantee by giving an annual property tax exemption to Vietnam War veterans who were state residents before May 8, 1976, but not to veterans who became residents after that date.

That distinction bears no rational relationship to the state's asserted objective of encouraging Vietnam veterans to move to New Mexico, but instead creates permanent distinctions between classes of residents based on when they came to the state to live. The Constitution does not permit such distinctions.

Zoning Powers

Williamson County Regional Planning Commission v. Hamilton Bank of Johnson City, decided by a 7-1 vote, June 28, 1985. Blackmun wrote the opinion; White dissented; Powell did not participate.

A developer who sued a county for damages for diminishing the value of its property by delaying a proposed development because it was not in compliance with zoning requirements should have done more to win county approval for its development before suing for compensation.

The justices held that it was premature to decide the primary question presented by the case — whether a county could be held liable for this sort of property "loss."

FEDERAL COURTS

Heckler v. Chaney, decided by a 9-0 vote, March 20, 1985. Rehnquist wrote the opinion.

A federal agency's decision not to prosecute or enforce a law is generally considered a decision within its discretion and immune from judicial review.

The Food and Drug Administration's decision not to take enforcement actions with regard to drugs used by states to inflict capital punishment by lethal injection is not subject to judicial review.

Florida Power & Light Co. v. Lorion, decided by an 8-1 vote, March 20, 1985. Brennan wrote the opinion; Stevens dissented.

Federal appeals courts may review a decision by the Nuclear Regulatory Commission to deny a citizen's petition for an agency hearing on the continued operation of a nuclear power plant. Appeals from such denials may go directly to the appeals court without first obtaining a ruling from a federal district court.

Lindahl v. Office of Personnel Management, decided by a 5-4 vote, March 20, 1985. Brennan wrote the opinion; White, Burger, Rehnquist and O'Connor dissented.

Appeals courts have limited power to review disagreements over retirement benefits among federal workers, the Office of Personnel Management (OPM) and the Merit Systems Protection Board (MSPB).

Factual decisions by OPM and the MSPB are not reviewable by federal courts, but questions of law and procedure are reviewable by those courts.

Burger King Corp. v. Rudzewicz, decided by a 6-2 vote, May 20, 1985. Brennan wrote the opinion; Powell did not participate; Stevens and White dissented.

A federal court located in one state (Florida) may use that state's laws to claim jurisdiction over a person in another state (Michigan) holding a franchise from a company headquartered in Florida when the franchise holder has received fair notice from franchise documents that he might be subject to suit in Florida for breach of his franchise contract.

Richardson-Merrell Inc. v. Koller, decided by a 7-1 vote, June 17, 1985. O'Connor wrote the opinion; Stevens dissented. Powell did not participate.

A federal district court order granting a motion to disqualify the attorney serving as counsel in a civil case cannot be immediately appealed. Such an order does not come within the "collateral order" exception to the general rule barring appeals from any but final judgments.

INDIANS

United States v. Dann, decided by a 9-0 vote, Feb. 20, 1985. Brennan wrote the opinion.

The court rejected the claim of two Shoshone Indians that they still own more than 5,000 acres in Nevada even though Congress appropriated money in 1979 to compensate them for loss of that land.

The Indian Claims Commission had found that the Shoshones had lost their original title to more than 24 million acres in California and Nevada and awarded them $26 million in compensation. Congress appropriated that money in 1979 and set it aside in trust for the Indians, who had not received it because they refused to cooperate in developing a plan for its distribution. The two Indians bringing this case argued that because they had received no money, they still owned 5,000 acres of the land. The court held that they had effectively been paid at the time the money was appropriated, terminating their claim.

County of Oneida v. Oneida Indian Nation of New York State, decided by a 5-4 vote, March 4, 1985. Powell wrote the opinion; Stevens, Burger, White and Rehnquist dissented.

The court cleared the way for a damage suit brought by the Oneida Indian Nation against two New York counties seeking partial reimbursement for the use of land taken illegally by the state from the Indians in 1795.

The court found no statute of limitations barring this suit, despite the passage of almost 200 years since the illegal taking.

Kerr-McGee Corp. v. Navajo Tribe of Indians, decided by an 8-0 vote, April 16, 1985. Burger wrote the opinion; Powell did not participate.

Indian tribes do not need federal approval from the secretary of the interior before they impose taxes on the value of leasehold interests in tribal lands and on any oil or gas extracted from those lands. Such federal approval is not required by the 1934 Indian Reorganization Act or the 1938 Indian Mineral Leasing Act.

National Farmers Union Insurance Cos. v. Crow Tribe of Indians, decided by a 9-0 vote, June 3, 1985. Stevens wrote the opinion.

Federal courts have jurisdiction to determine whether a tribal court exceeded the limits of its jurisdiction in trying a tort suit against a non-Indian concerning injuries suffered on state land within a reservation. Before a federal district court acts, however, non-Indian parties must exhaust remedies available in tribal court.

Montana v. Blackfeet Tribe of Indians, decided by a 6-3 vote, June 3, 1985. Powell wrote the opinion; White, Rehnquist and Stevens dissented.

States may not tax a tribe's interest in oil and gas produced by non-Indians leasing oil and gas lands from a tribe under the 1938 Indian Mineral Leasing Act. A 1924 law authorizing states to tax such interests does not apply to leases issued under the 1938 law.

Mountain States Telephone & Telegraph Co. v. Pueblo of Santa Ana, decided by a 5-3 vote, June 10, 1985. Stevens wrote the opinion; Brennan, Marshall and Blackmun dissented; Powell did not participate.

The court found valid an easement for a telephone line on Pueblo lands that was granted in 1928 and approved by the secretary of the interior, but not by Congress. The easement had been challenged as a trespass by the Pueblo, citing the Pueblo Lands Act of 1924, which provided that any such conveyance of Pueblo lands must be approved by both the secretary and Congress.

Oregon Department of Fish and Wildlife v. Klamath Indian Tribe, decided by a 6-2 vote, July 2, 1985. Stevens wrote the opinion; Brennan and Marshall dissented; Powell did not participate.

The Klamath Indian Tribe, which retained fishing rights in 1864 when it agreed to the treaty creating its reservation, surrendered those rights in a 1901 agreement giving part of that land to the United States. Oregon therefore may regulate the Indians' hunting, fishing and trapping on the portion of former reservation lands that is now part of national forests and parks.

MISCELLANEOUS

Eminent Domain, Tort Claims

United States v. 50 Acres of Land, decided by a 9-0 vote, Dec. 4, 1984. Stevens wrote the opinion.

When the federal government exercises its power of eminent domain to condemn a city's sanitary landfill, just compensation is the amount equal to the fair market value of the landfill, not the cost of acquiring a substitute facility.

United States v. Shearer, decided by an 8-0 vote, June 27, 1985. Burger wrote the opinion; Powell did not participate.

The Feres doctrine, announced in a 1950 decision, that servicemen cannot sue the U.S. government under the Federal Tort Claims Act for injuries arising out of or in the course of activity incident to military service, applies to bar a suit brought by the mother of a serviceman who was murdered by a fellow serviceman while off duty and away from the military base.

Freedom of Information

U.S. Department of Justice v. Provenzano, Shapiro v. Drug Enforcement Administration, decided by votes of 8-1 and 9-0, Nov. 26, 1984. Per curiam (unsigned) opinion. Stevens dissented in *Provenzano.*

The court vacated two lower court rulings and sent back for reconsideration in light of the Central Intelligence Information Act, PL 98-477, two cases in which individuals invoked the Freedom of Information Act in an effort to obtain copies of criminal investigation files concerning them. The government had cited the Privacy Act in refusing to disclose those files. PL 98-477 declared that the Privacy Act could not be used to limit disclosure under the Freedom of Information Act.

Central Intelligence Agency v. Sims, Sims v. Central Intelligence Agency, decided by votes of 9-0 and 7-2, April 16, 1985. Burger wrote the opinion; Brennan and Marshall dissented in part.

In creating the Central Intelligence Agency in 1947, Congress gave its director authority to see that intelligence methods and sources are protected from unauthorized disclosure. This provision of the National Security Act serves as an appropriate and sufficient basis for the CIA's refusal to release the names of individuals participating in a CIA project code-named MKULTRA. When these names were sought under the Freedom of Information Act, the CIA refused to disclose them, citing Exemption 3 to that act, which permits withholding of information "specifically exempted from disclosure by statute."

The court unanimously rejected a definition of "intelligence source" adopted by the U.S. Circuit Court of Appeals for the District of Columbia, which limited that category to individuals who would supply intelligence only if promised confidentiality.

The court, 7-2, adopted the CIA's broad definition of an intelligence source as including "all sources of intelligence that provide, or are engaged to provide, information the agency needs to perform its statutory duties with respect to foreign intelligence" — even some information that appeared innocuous but might enable someone to discover the identity of an intelligence source.

Official Immunity

Mitchell v. Forsyth, decided by a 5-2 vote, June 19, 1985. White wrote the opinion; Brennan and Marshall dissented; Rehnquist and Powell did not participate.

The attorney general does not have absolute immunity from damage suits by individuals who charge that they were injured by his actions taken in the name of national security.

The attorney general does have qualified immunity against such suits. That immunity protects former Attorney General John N. Mitchell against a suit by a man who was overheard on a warrantless national security wiretap in 1970, because not until 1971 did the Supreme Court rule that such wiretaps must be approved by a warrant.

Interstate Boundaries

United States v. Maine, exceptions overruled and report of special master confirmed by a vote of 9-0, Feb. 19, 1985. Blackmun announced the court's decision.

Long Island, N.Y., is legally part of mainland New York, and the Block Island Sound is a bay, an internal state waterway. New York and Rhode Island may continue to require ships using the sound to have state-licensed pilots.

The federal government had argued that Long Island, which is surrounded by water, should be considered an island, and Block Island Sound therefore part of the high seas not subject to state regulation.

The court rejected that argument however, holding that Long Island functions as a peninsula, an extension of the mainland, forming the southern headland of Block Island Sound.

United States v. Louisiana, exceptions to report of special master overruled and report confirmed by a vote of 8-0, Feb. 26, 1985. Blackmun announced the court's decision; Marshall did not participate.

Mississippi Sound is a historic bay that belongs entirely to the states of Alabama and Mississippi and contains no high seas to be claimed by the federal government. ▮

POLITICAL REPORT

CQ

1985 Elections: New Directions for Parties?

Political professionals spent much of 1985 hashing out a question that arose from President Reagan's resounding 1984 re-election victory: "Is the GOP becoming the majority party?"

But the year's two most important elections were interesting because they posed a new and possibly more significant question: "In what directions might the parties turn in the post-Reagan era?"

In Virginia, Democrats retained the governorship in 1985 with Gerald L. Baliles, who studiously mimicked the moderate philosophy of popular outgoing Democratic Gov. Charles S. Robb, the son-in-law of former President Lyndon B. Johnson. During his tenure in office, Robb upheld his party's traditional commitment to social services while still exercising spending restraint and encouraging private sector growth. The victory of Baliles — who served as state attorney general under Robb — prompted many Democrats to suggest that the national Democratic Party could shed its image as excessively liberal by following the centrist "Robb model."

Virginia's election put two other politicians in the national spotlight: Running with Baliles, 45, on the Democratic ticket and winning as well were state Sen. L. Douglas Wilder, 54, elected to the lieutenant governorship, and state Rep. Mary Sue Terry, 38, elected to be state attorney general. Wilder's win made him the first black since Reconstruction to capture a major state office in the South, and Terry's victory made her the first woman ever to win statewide office in Virginia.

The Republican ticket — a trio of strong conservatives led by former state Rep. Wyatt B. Durrette — tried to portray the Democratic ticket as a captive of special interests. But Wilder and Terry took particular care to target their campaigns at a broad audience and, like Baliles, they said nothing that voters regarded as dangerously liberal.

In the same way that the Virginia Democrats prospered as purveyors of a moderate Democratic Party, New Jersey Republican Gov. Thomas H. Kean thrived at the polls by positioning himself as more moderate than his party's national image. A narrow winner in 1981, Kean took a second term in 1985 by an overwhelming margin, partly because as governor he made an effort to reach out to blacks, labor unions and other groups that had been unsympathetic to the GOP in the Reagan era. Thanks to Kean's popularity, the GOP captured control of the state Assembly for the first time since 1971.

Because neither of the gubernatorial elections produced a partisan shift, the nationwide party lineup of governors remained at 34 Democrats and 16 Republicans — unchanged from 1984.

There was little activity in congressional elections during 1985, with no Senate vacancies occurring and only two vacancies in the House. However, one of the House special elections did receive extensive national publicity because it represented a GOP effort to capture a historically Democratic Southern district, the Texas 1st. Republican officials in Washington lavished resources and attention on party nominee Edd Hargett, but he lost narrowly to Democrat Jim Chapman. National Democratic officials trumpeted Chapman's win as a sign that Reagan's popularity was not touching off a massive Southern voter realignment. But Hargett's strong showing in the "yellow-dog" Democratic 1st enabled Republicans to claim that their party was making significant progress.

At the end of 1985, there were 253 Democrats and 182 Republicans in the House, and Republicans controlled the Senate 53-47.

Gubernatorial Results

Virginia

After their landslide loss in 1984's presidential election, many Democrats were left wondering, "Where's the base?" That question became one for Virginia Republicans to ponder after Democrats swept the state's three top offices Nov. 5.

Republicans had dominated statewide races in Virginia throughout the 1970s by positioning themselves in the state's conservative mainstream against unmistakably liberal Democratic candidates. Robb upset that GOP victory formula in 1981 by hugging the political center, combining appeals to blacks and organized labor with a courtship of the conservative business and political establishment.

Virginia's one-term-and-out law prevented Robb from seeking re-election in 1984. But Baliles and his ticketmates followed Robb's centrist strategy; they also benefited from a prosperous economy and the broadly acceptable image Robb created for the state Democratic Party.

Robb lent his personal prestige to the Democratic campaign, raising money, rounding up endorsements and touting the historic nature of the party's ticket. By Election Day, polls showed Baliles, Wilder and Terry all running ahead of their opponents.

Official results in the gubernatorial contest:

Baliles	741,438	55.2 %
Durrette	601,652	44.8

When the campaign began, a Democratic sweep did not seem likely. At that point, the common wisdom was that while Baliles was an even bet to beat Durrette, the combination of Wilder and Terry was too venturesome for an electorate regarded as tradition-bound and one of the more conservative in the country. With blacks comprising less than one-fifth of the state population, it was widely thought that Wilder would score a moral victory if he reached 40 percent.

But it was the Republicans' campaign that bogged down, not the Democrats'. The GOP boasted that its ticket was homogeneously conservative, but critics called it bland and inexperienced. Durrette had not won any office in 10 years, and his running mates — state Sen. John H. Chichester and state Rep. W. R. "Buster" O'Brien — had languished on the minority side in the Legislature, gaining less publicity than Wilder or Terry.

Once it became clear that the issues of race and gender would not put the Democrats on the defensive, the Republicans seemed unsure of how to proceed. Former GOP Gov. Mills E. Godwin Jr. led conservatives within the campaign urging Durrette to mount sharper attacks against Baliles and the Robb administration; moderates encouraged Durrette to keep his message positive and upbeat. Durrette denounced Baliles as a big-spending liberal, but generally

Kirk Chosen to Head DNC

The Democratic National Committee (DNC) Feb. 1 elected Paul G. Kirk Jr. as the party's national chairman, rejecting arguments that the former Kennedy campaign official was too closely tied to labor and other liberal special interests.

Members of the DNC took just one ballot to elect Kirk, a Washington, D.C., attorney who had been serving as party treasurer. He succeeded Charles T. Manatt of California, and would serve until 1988.

Kirk won by more than 50 votes over former North Carolina Gov. Terry Sanford, even after two other candidates — former party Executive Director Robert Keefe and former California Democratic Chairman Nancy Pelosi — withdrew from the race and threw their support to Sanford.

The race for DNC chairman was seen as the first important move in the struggle of the Democrats to regain their status as national majority party. They had lost four of the last five presidential elections.

Kirk, a former top aide to Sen. Edward M. Kennedy, D-Mass., was viewed by some as too closely tied to traditional party leadership and constituent groups. But Kirk quickly set out to counter the widespread impression that liberal special interest groups exercised too much influence on the Democratic Party agenda.

At Kirk's urging, the DNC Executive Committee revoked official recognition of seven party caucuses representing specific groups, such as homosexuals, Asian-Pacific Americans and blacks. Kirk also convinced the full DNC to abolish the party's midterm conference, which originally was created in 1972 at the behest of liberals.

In addition, Kirk's influence led a party panel assessing delegate selection procedures for 1988 to recommend to the DNC that party and elected officials be given a greater role in the selection process.

shied away from the harsher rhetoric the Godwin group wanted.

The Republicans made several forays against Wilder, attempting to paint him as a liberal unfit to hold high office in Virginia. Wilder admitted that he supported issues of concern to his predominantly black legislative constituency in Richmond, but pointed out that he was a veteran legislative insider who had won the support of a number of conservative legislative colleagues, including state House Speaker A. L. Philpott. Wilder also stressed his military service in Korea — where he won a Bronze Star — and his support from law enforcement groups. One particularly effective Wilder television ad featured a husky Southern sheriff offering him the endorsement of a statewide police organization.

On Election Day, only Wilder's race was close; he took 52 percent of the vote. But it was not a racially polarized vote. Wilder won seven of Virginia's 10 congressional districts and in four of those he carried, blacks amounted to no more than 12 percent of the population. Even in the three districts Wilder lost — the Richmond-area 3rd, the rural "Southside" 5th and the "apple country" 7th — he took well over 40 percent.

Baliles and Terry did even better, sweeping every congressional district in the state. Terry, a protégé of Philpott from rural Patrick County, led the Democratic ticket with 61 percent of the vote. Like Wilder, Terry pointed to her support within the conservative Democratic establishment. But unlike Wilder, she also had broad support in Virginia's business community.

In contrast to the victorious Democrats, the Republican candidates had trouble carrying their home areas. O'Brien lost his hometown of Virginia Beach, normally a GOP stronghold. Chichester carried his home base of Fredericksburg but lost the vote-rich suburbs of nearby Northern Virginia.

Durrette lost in suburban Northern Virginia — where he lived until 1983 — and in the Richmond area, where he moved in 1983. When Durrette narrowly lost to Baliles in the 1981 attorney general race, the Republican capitalized on regional affinity to sweep the two Northern Virginia districts — the 8th and 10th. But with weaker ties to the northern suburbs in 1985, Durrette trailed in the 8th and 10th. Richmond-based Baliles won not only the older Democratic suburbs of Arlington and Alexandria, but also easily carried fast-growing and GOP-leaning Fairfax County, the state's most populous county.

Durrette tried to win votes by tying himself closely to President Reagan, who swept Virginia in 1984 with 62 percent. Reagan appeared at a lucrative fund-raiser for the GOP ticket in early October and hosted Durrette at the White House the day before the election. A photo of the two was featured on a Durrette campaign poster that was prominently displayed outside polling places on Election Day.

But many Republicans probably missed the picture because they stayed at home. While Baliles' total vote was less than 20,000 votes lower than Robb's total in 1981, Durrette's vote was nearly 60,000 votes lower than the GOP gubernatorial total in 1981. Heavy rain and flooding disrupted voting in parts of western Virginia, but turnout was down in virtually every congressional district.

The loss was an especially bitter pill for the GOP to swallow because the party had started the campaign with high hopes that it could win. In the previous five presidential elections and in three of its previous four gubernatorial contests, Virginia had voted Republican.

In assessing blame for their defeat, Republicans pointed in different directions. Chichester blamed "press bias"; he claimed that any comment he made on Wilder's record opened him to "charges of racism and mudslinging .... It's like running against a brick wall."

Conservative Republicans complained that the ticket allocated resources ineptly and never focused on a central message. But moderate Republicans, relegated to the sidelines in 1985, claimed that the ticket lost because the state GOP had lost touch with the political mainstream. They contended the party drifted too far right in an effort to gain support from religious fundamentalists, New Right conservatives and remnants of the rural conservative courthouse machine that once controlled Virginia politics at the behest of Sen. Harry F. Byrd (1933-65).

New Jersey

The enormous re-election margin posted by Republican Gov. Thomas H. Kean put him in New Jersey's political record book for the second time. In 1981, he won the governorship with less than one tenth of a percentage point separating him from Democratic Rep. James J. Florio — the slimmest margin in state history.

Kean's 70 percent showing against his 1985 Democratic opponent, Essex County Executive Peter Shapiro, was the biggest winning percentage in New Jersey history. The previous record was held by Democrat Brendan T. Byrne, who won the governorship with 67 percent in 1973. Kean, 50, won every New Jersey city, including Democratic bastions such as Newark and Trenton.

Official results:

Kean	1,372,631	70.4 %
Shapiro	578,402	29.6

A broad-based Republican Party was what Kean set out to build when he took office; he pursued that goal by demonstrating a commitment to economic opportunity for minorities, by backing enterprise zones in depressed areas and by signing a bill pulling state investment out of companies doing business in South Africa.

Kean also was boosted by the robust state of New Jersey's economy. By election time, unemployment was well below the national average, high-technology investment in the state had grown and the construction industry had been flooded with state money for public works projects. In addition, growing state revenues allowed Kean to bankroll a wide range of social programs and to allocate generous funding to public education.

Shapiro, 33, had a difficult time making headway against voters' satisfaction with the status quo. He stood by helplessly as the state AFL-CIO, black ministers and other traditional sources of Democratic support leaked away to Kean, taking with them campaign manpower and money Shapiro needed badly. His campaign had trouble raising money, a severe handicap in New Jersey, where electoral success depends on buying advertising in the prohibitively expensive New York and Philadelphia media markets.

The GOP poured more than $1 million into legislative contests, and much of Kean's attention in the closing weeks of the campaign centered on helping his party's candidates. His strength helped pull 15 new Republicans into the state Assembly, giving the GOP a 50-30 advantage. Democrats controlled the Senate 23-17; senators did not face re-election until 1987.

Special House Elections

Texas

Thwarting Republican hopes of making a bold strike for partisan realignment, Democrat Jim Chapman carved out a narrow runoff victory over Republican Edd Hargett in Texas' 1st District special election Aug. 3.

The national Republican Party placed a high priority on capturing Texas' northeasternmost district, which the GOP never had held. The party spent more than $1 million trying to elect Hargett as the successor to Democratic Rep. Sam B. Hall Jr., who was named to a federal judgeship by President Reagan. Hall, a conservative, had represented the 1st since 1976.

The GOP's resources had helped Hargett, a 38-year-old Linden rancher and engineer, finish first in the initial round of balloting June 29. But in the Aug. 3 runoff, Chapman, a 40-year-old former district attorney from Sulphur Springs, frustrated GOP hopes of a historic breakthrough by appealing for loyalty to the 1st's Democratic heritage.

Official results:

Chapman	52,665	50.9 %
Hargett	50,741	49.1

Chapman's success was a blow to Republican momentum in Texas. The GOP enjoyed a banner year there in 1984, capturing a record 10 U.S. House seats and winning by huge margins in the presidential and senatorial campaigns.

Chapman overcame some significant hurdles. One of six Democrats in the eight-person primary field, he had trouble securing early commitments because many Democratic officials were waiting for a front-runner to emerge. Also, in the early stages of the campaign, Chapman labored in Hargett's shadow. As the lone Republican in the race and a local football hero — he led Texas A&M to its 1968 Cotton Bowl victory — Hargett had no trouble attracting publicity. Another problem for Chapman was the unsavory reputation of the national Democratic Party; in the 1984 election, many voters in the district viewed the Democrats as too soft on defense, too quick to raise taxes and too eager to embrace causes such as gay rights.

Buoyed by financial and technical assistance from the national GOP, as well as by visits from Vice President George Bush and Texas Sen. Phil Gramm, Hargett netted over 40 percent in the primary, finishing well ahead of the pack but falling short of the majority needed to avoid a runoff. Chapman was second with less than one-third of the vote.

During the runoff campaign, however, Chapman began to wear Hargett down. He reassured voters that he would vote as "a conservative Democratic congressman in the East Texas tradition," and repeatedly he questioned Hargett's qualifications to serve in Congress. Chapman was aided on that count when Hargett was quoted in a local newspaper as saying, "I don't know what trade policies have to do with bringing jobs to East Texas." Chapman accused Hargett of not knowing about layoffs at a local steel plant that Chapman said were caused by steel imports allowed by a flawed administration trade policy.

Hargett countered by questioning Chapman's integrity, pointing to allegations that Chapman supporters had tampered with runoff absentee ballots and complaining that Democratic mailings on the Social Security issue looked like official government documents. But he could not overcome Chapman's momentum. Boosted by strong support from courthouse Democrats, elements of organized labor and trial lawyers, Chapman eked out a victory. He was sworn in as a House member Sept. 4.

Louisiana

Relying more on her late husband's political popularity than on any intensive campaigning of her own, Democrat Cathy (Mrs. Gillis) Long won the March 30 special election to fill Louisiana's 8th District House seat. Rep. Gillis W. Long (1963-65, 1973-85) had died of a heart attack Jan. 20, as he was starting his eighth House term.

By taking just 52 percent of the primary vote, Long came perilously close to being forced into a runoff. If she had fallen below 50 percent, she would have faced a runoff with second-place finisher John E. "Jock" Scott, a three-term Democratic state representative. The compressed, two-month campaign period worked to Long's advantage: In that short time, Scott could not come close to matching Long's districtwide name recognition.

Long, 61, relied heavily on stressing her husband's service to the 8th and generally avoided discussion of controversial issues. Asked about deficit reduction at one point in the campaign, she told a reporter, "If the best economic brains can't answer that question, I can't either right now."

Early in the campaign, Scott was wary of attacking the widow of a popular congressman, and instead he stressed his work in the Legislature, particularly on economic development. Two weeks before the election, however, he abandoned that strategy and started criticizing Long for refusing to take positions on substantive issues. But Gillis Long's supporters among labor unions and in the black community stood with Cathy Long. Those forces were determined to stop Scott because he had contemplated challenging Gillis Long at various times in the past and because he accused Cathy Long of being too liberal.

The only Republican in the contest, Forest Hill nurseryman Clyde C. Holloway, placed third; Democrats Daniel E. Becnel Jr. and Frank James McTopy brought up the rear.

Long was sworn in on April 4. Just over six months later, on Oct. 14, she announced she would not be a candidate for re-election in 1986.

Official returns:

Long	61,791	55.7 %
Scott	27,138	24.5
Holloway	18,013	16.3
Becnel	3,305	3.0
McTopy	503	0.5

VOTING STUDIES

CQ

Compromises Tempered Key 1985 Decisions

In a notable turnabout from his historically successful first year in office in 1981, Ronald Reagan began his second term in 1985 with an increasingly independent Congress that demanded -- and got — substantial changes on key domestic and foreign policy questions.

But Reagan's willingness to compromise enabled him repeatedly to claim victory in the face of otherwise certain setbacks, on votes involving trade and farm policy, South African racism, military aid to Nicaraguan rebels, funding for an anti-missile defense system known popularly as "star wars," and an overhaul of the tax code that Reagan had made the domestic centerpiece of his new term.

On other issues, such as deficit reduction, Congress took the lead but Reagan quickly jumped aboard, allowing him to win a share of the credit for the resulting legislation.

A major test of Congress' relations with the president occurred early in 1985 on the MX intercontinental missile. The year before, Congress had deadlocked on the issue and put off to March a vote on fiscal 1985 funding. Initially, opponents were confident of killing the weapon. But in the meantime, Reagan and Soviet leader Mikhail S. Gorbachev scheduled arms control talks for late 1985 and Reagan successfully argued that an anti-MX vote would undercut his bargaining position.

On March 19, the Senate voted $1.5 billion for continued production of 21 missiles. The House followed suit a week later. Although the promise of arms control talks had braked the momentum for killing MX, it did not translate to full support for Reagan's nuclear policy. Congress later voted to cap the number of MXs to be deployed in existing missile silos at 50, or half the arsenal that Reagan wanted.

The bipartisan support for strengthening Reagan's hand against the Soviets also led Congress to increase funding for his proposed space-based anti-missile system, known popularly as "star wars." But the increase was still $1 billion less than Reagan's $3.7 billion request.

Meanwhile, opponents won a small victory when Congress voted to block for a year the administration's planned tests of a related space weapon, the anti-satellite (ASAT) missile.

Throughout the year, Congress reacted to reports of widespread misery among farmers and a growing U.S. trade deficit by calling on the president to change his longstanding free-market, hands-off policies toward agriculture and imports. Democrats took the lead in both areas, sensing a chance for political advantage in the 1986 elections. But Republicans from farm states and from districts with industries hurt by foreign competition were among those most critical of the president's inaction.

Within weeks of convening in 1985, both chambers had voted overwhelmingly for emergency advances of federal crop-loan payments to hard-hit farmers.

President Reagan vetoed that bill March 6, but by year's end he was forced to accept a five-year farm programs authorization bill that was more expensive than he had said he would accept.

The main product of Congress' growing protectionist mood was a bill limiting textile and apparel imports that passed overwhelmingly. Reagan vetoed the bill Dec. 17, and supporters put off a veto-override vote until August 1986. The president had succeeded in eroding some support for the measure, but only after he had been pressured to respond with a new trade policy that called for attacks against countries with unfair trading practices and for action to reduce the dollar's value so U.S. exports would be affordable.

Also under congressional pressure, Reagan revised his policies toward the white-minority government controlling South Africa. Since the 1984 elections, civil rights protests had built public support for sanctions. When House and Senate negotiators compromised on a remarkably strong sanctions bill, Reagan acted. The only way to avoid the slap at his foreign policy was to impose limited sanctions of his own, which the president did Sept. 9.

In 1985, opposition to Reagan's policy of assisting rebels against Nicaragua's government continued to grow. In April, the House rejected his bid for renewed aid to the "contras." This time, however, it was no action by Reagan that turned the tide; ironically, Nicaraguan President Daniel Ortega did so when he flew to Moscow to visit Soviet leaders within days of the House vote, embarrassing House Democratic leaders. In the end, Congress approved $27 million in non-military aid to the rebels for fiscal 1985.

Another vote illustrated Congress' renewed willingness to aid anti-communist forces. In July, the House went along with the Senate and voted to repeal a law barring U.S. intervention in foreign nations unless vital interests were threatened. The vote opened the way for revived aid to Angolan rebels fighting that country's Marxist regime.

How Votes Were Selected

Congressional Quarterly each year selects a series of key votes on major issues.

Selection of Issues. An issue is judged by the extent it represents one or more of the following:

- A matter of major controversy.
- A matter of presidential or political power.
- A decision of potentially great impact on the nation and lives of Americans.

Selection of Votes. For each group of related votes on an issue, one key vote usually is chosen. This is the vote that, in the opinion of Congressional Quarterly editors, was important in determining the outcome.

In the description of the key votes, the designation "ND" denotes Northern Democrats and "SD" denotes Southern Democrats.

Senate Key Votes

1. Emergency Farm Credit

In an early show of bipartisan opposition to Reagan administration farm policy, the Senate Feb. 27 voted in favor of advancing crop-loan payments to financially strapped farmers. The vote came on a measure providing emergency, non-food assistance to drought- and famine-stricken areas in Africa (HR 1096).

Years of low farm profits and collapsing land values, particularly in the Midwest, had created a credit crisis for many farm communities.

The administration had been pressing for scaled back federal aid to farmers, and argued that it had done enough to help out farmers with serious debts. Notwithstanding the administration's veto threat, and attempts by Majority Leader Robert Dole, R-Kan., to hold the Senate to a goal of serious deficit reduction, eight Republicans voted with all but one Democrat to add the farm credit provisions to the Africa aid bill.

The Senate then passed HR 1096, with the farm-credit provisions, 62-35: R 16-34; D 46-1 (ND 32-1, SD 14-0).

The House accepted the Senate version March 5, and, true to his promise, President Reagan vetoed the bill March 6, calling it a "massive new bailout that would add billions to the deficit." Only a small minority of farmers were in need, Reagan said, despite unpublished Agriculture Department studies that showed 17 to 18 percent of U.S. farms with severe financial problems.

Neither chamber attempted to override the veto, but the Senate coalition of Democrats and farm-state Republicans continued to dominate as Congress worked to rewrite basic farm policy until the end of the 1985 session. And ultimately, Dole had to offer a contradictory amalgam of "sweeteners" to win away enough votes to get a farm bill passed in the Senate. *(Senate key vote 14)*

2. MX Missile Production

The Senate struck a major blow against a coalition of opponents of the MX intercontinental missile March 19 when it approved continued production of the controversial weapon by an unexpectedly large margin.

In 1984, the Senate had cast a tie vote on an amendment that would have blocked MX production, and the missile survived only because of Vice President George Bush's tie-breaking vote in favor. But in the key vote less than a year later — on a joint resolution (S J Res 71) approving procurement of 21 missiles in the fiscal 1985 budget — production was approved March 19, 55-45: R 45-8; D 10-37 (ND 3-30; SD 7-7).

Since MX became the central symbolic battle over Reagan administration nuclear arms policy in early 1983, liberal arms controllers had concentrated their anti-MX lobbying effort in the Democratically controlled House. So when they nearly won in the Senate in 1984 — partly because the particular amendment offered by moderate Democrat Lawton Chiles, Fla., was unexpected — it came as a great morale booster to opponents.

By the same token, their decisive Senate defeat in 1985 hit opponents hard and set the stage for Reagan's companion MX win in the House a week later. *(House key vote 1)*

After the House also approved the fiscal 1985 MX production, an influential group of moderate Democrats led by Sam Nunn, Ga. — all of whom had voted for production on March 19 — called for a legislative cap of 40 on the total number of MXs deployed in existing missile silos, compared with the 100 Reagan had proposed. This formula — with the cap raised to 50 — helped resolve the MX issue in 1985.

3. Budget Resolution

The Senate's new majority leader, Robert Dole, R-Kan., made deficit reduction a top priority during his first months in office. In the early morning hours of May 10, Dole engineered a cliffhanger vote to adopt a sweeping fiscal 1986 budget plan (S Con Res 32) that called for the largest reductions in the spending growth in the nation's history. The vote was 50-49: R 48-4; D 1-45 (ND 1-31, SD 0-14).

The 15-minute deadline for a vote, often bent in the Senate, was stretched well beyond custom as the Senate waited for Pete Wilson, R-Calif., en route by ambulance from a suburban hospital where he had undergone an appendectomy the day before.

An ashen Wilson, garbed in pajamas and robe and still receiving intravenous fluids, finally appeared in a wheelchair and cast his "aye" while senators of both parties cheered. His vote made for a 49-49 tie, which was then broken by Vice President George Bush. (Illness prevented two other senators, Republican John P. East, N.C., and Democrat J. James Exon, Neb., from voting.)

The vote was an important victory for Dole. He had had to persuade GOP senators, particularly 22 skittish colleagues up for re-election in 1986, that constituents were so concerned about the deficit that an "aye" would be a political asset, even though the legislation made substantial reductions in a number of popular programs and froze politically sensitive Social Security spending for a year.

Dole also had to convince the White House not to torpedo the legislation, even though it cut into the president's top-priority buildup in defense spending.

The narrow 53-47 Republican majority in the Senate had forced Dole and Senate Budget Committee Chairman Pete V. Domenici, R-N.M., to struggle hard for every vote. The two spent months in exhaustive, private negotiations with Senate Republicans and the White House. Dole did not turn to Democrats for help, except at the last minute when concessions on farm spending won an "aye" from Edward Zorinsky, D-Neb.

4. Anti-Missile Defense

The Senate approved a reduction in President Reagan's request for anti-missile research that was recommended by its Armed Services Committee for budgetary reasons. It did so after rejecting several amendments that would have sliced more money from the project.

The deeper reductions in the so-called "strategic defense initiative" (SDI) or "star wars" anti-missile defense program were proposed by arms control advocates who warned that the project would end any hope of an agreement to sharply reduce the number of U.S. and Soviet long-range nuclear missiles.

The critics' best effort came on an amendment to the fiscal 1986 defense authorization bill (S 1160) that would have trimmed the SDI ceiling from the $2.96 billion recommended by the Armed Services Committee to $1.9 billion. The amendment was rejected June 4, 38-57: R 6-45; D 32-12 (ND 25-7; SD 7-5).

President Reagan had requested $3.96 billion for the anti-missile defense program.

Other amendments proposing larger and smaller reductions from the committee-recommended level were rejected by larger margins.

5. Nicaraguan 'Contras'

President Reagan's policy of aiding Nicaragua's anti-government guerrillas, called "contras," long had enjoyed wide bipartisan support in the Senate. But that support weakened in 1984 following revelations of the CIA's bungled attempt to mine harbors in Nicaragua, and Congress suspended arms shipments and all other aid to the contras.

Members of both parties in 1985 complained that the administration appeared to have no long-term policy for ending the civil war in Nicaragua. Reagan's request for renewed aid to the contras was rejected by the House in April — but a few days later Nicaraguan President Daniel Ortega angered many in Congress by flying to Moscow for meetings with top Soviet leaders.

Reagan once again sought congressional approval for renewed aid to the contras. The Senate complied on June 6, approving an amendment to a State Department authorizations bill (S 1003) authorizing $24 million for new "humanitarian" aid to the guerrillas and releasing conditions on another $14 million.

The vote was 55-42: R 41-10; D 14-32 (ND 4-28, SD 10-4).

Although the aid was supported by members of both parties, the vote demonstrated for the first time that the overwhelming majority of Senate Democrats had joined their House counterparts in opposing U.S. involvement in Nicaragua's wars. *(House key vote 5)*

Nearly two months later, Congress gave final approval to $27 million in non-military aid to the contras in fiscal 1985.

6. United Nations Budget

With its frequently anti-American slant and seemingly out-of-control budget, the United Nations had been the target of growing congressional criticism over the years. That criticism came to a head in 1985, with Congress approving a provision threatening a major pullback in U.S. support for the world forum.

"The United Nations can no longer be a sacred cow," said Kansas Republican Nancy Landon Kassebaum, who followed up on her views with a key Senate amendment to restrict U.S. support for the U.N. budget. Kassebaum's proposal was added to the 1985 State Department authorizations bill (S 1003) June 7 by a vote of 71-13: R 41-4; D 30-9 (ND 18-8, SD 12-1).

A modified version of it cleared Congress in the final version of the bill.

Kassebaum and many of her allies said that they were not opposed to a strong U.S. role in the world body. But, they argued, the United States could no longer continue to provide a substantial share of the funding for a U.N. budget that had tripled in the preceding decade without gaining a greater voice in how the money was spent. So Kassebaum's amendment called for a reduction in U.S. contributions to the U.N. operating budget unless the institution moved to a system of proportional voting, which would give the United States voting clout on budget matters equal to its financial contribution.

7. Gun Control

Almost since the day the 1968 Gun Control Act was enacted, Westerners in Congress, urged on by the National Rifle Association (NRA), had been trying to undo major elements of the law. On July 9 in the Senate, they took a large step toward that goal.

The Senate handily approved a bill (S 49) relaxing many of the provisions in the 1968 law, including allowing interstate sales of rifles, shotguns and handguns. The vote was 79-15: R 49-2; D 30-13 (ND 18-13, SD 12-0).

The wide margin demonstrated the political clout of the NRA, which was able to overcome strong opposition from major police organizations that claimed the bill would undercut law enforcement efforts. James A. McClure, R-Idaho, chief sponsor of S 49, said the overwhelming vote for his bill was in part a reaction to "abusive enforcement" of the law since 1968 by the federal government.

Edward M. Kennedy, D-Mass., the Senate's leading gun-control advocate, tried to strengthen the bill by banning interstate sales of small handguns and by requiring a 14-day waiting period for gun purchases. But his efforts were rejected by substantial margins.

8. Line-Item Veto

President Reagan suffered a defeat in the Senate when the Republican leadership was prevented from bringing to the floor a measure (S 43) granting Reagan authority to veto individual items in appropriations bills. The attempt was blocked by a bipartisan filibuster, led by Appropriations Committee Chairman Mark O. Hatfield, R-Ore.

Hatfield and others argued that the so-called "line-item veto" would result in an unnecessary and dangerous transfer of power from the legislative branch to the executive branch of government. Under existing law, the president could only veto an entire appropriations bill if he did not like one or two individual items within it.

Sponsor Mack Mattingly, R-Ga., argued that ongoing attempts to trim the federal deficit had been unsuccessful, and that Congress should give the new veto authority a chance. Reagan, who had asked repeatedly for the line-item veto to control government spending, lobbied hard to get the measure to the floor. From his hospital bed at the Bethesda Naval Medical Center in Maryland where he was recuperating from cancer surgery, Reagan made a number of personal calls and wrote a letter to all senators asking for their support.

But three attempts by Republican leaders to cut off debate on the motion to proceed to S 43 failed to get the required 60 votes. After the final cloture motion was rejected July 24, 58-40: R 46-7; D 12-33 (ND 8-24, SD 4-9), Senate Majority Leader Robert Dole, R-Kan., withdrew the pending motion to proceed to the bill.

9. School Prayer

Advocates of organized, recited public school prayer suffered their worst defeat in seven years when the Senate Sept. 10 decisively rejected a bill designed to allow prayer in the schools. The vote on the motion to table, and thus kill, the measure (S 47) was 62-36: R 24-28; D 38-8 (ND 31-1, SD 7-7).

The legislation, sponsored by Jesse Helms, R-N.C., would have barred the federal courts, including the Supreme Court, from hearing any case involving school prayer. Thus, if a state or local government chose to adopt a policy allowing public school prayer, opponents would have no means of challenging it in federal court.

The Senate had voted on similar legislation 10 times in the past seven years. But the Sept. 10 vote marked the lowest level of support for the measure since 1979, when the Senate passed it.

Helms said the vote demonstrated that, although Republicans controlled the chamber, "this is really a liberal Senate." But Lowell P. Weicker Jr., R-Conn., the leading opponent of the bill, contended that there had been "a change in sentiment" about the prayer issue. He said the vote demonstrated that the public was "becoming more sensitive" to the issues involved and that citizens were encouraging their representatives to vote against measures that were "bringing government into religion."

10. Seasonal Workers

Heavy lobbying by Western agricultural growers convinced the Senate Sept. 17 to add a new foreign "guest-worker" program to an overhaul of the nation's immigration laws (S 1200).

The vote to adopt the program, sponsored by Pete Wilson, R-Calif., was 51-44: R 36-15; D 15-29 (ND 6-25, SD 9-4). It reversed the Senate's action Sept. 12 when a similar Wilson amendment was killed, 50-48.

Immigration reform, which the Senate had passed three times since 1982, would create a new system of penalties against employers who knowingly hired illegal aliens. Western growers, who relied heavily on an illegal work force, said they would support the sanctions provisions, but they had insisted on new guarantees of sufficient labor to harvest crops.

The Sept. 17 vote was a blow to Alan K. Simpson, R-Wyo., the chief sponsor of S 1200. He had been unalterably opposed to any guest-worker program, and accused the growers of being greedy in their quest for foreign labor.

The guest-worker program also had repercussions in the House Judiciary Committee, where members were deeply divided about the issue. Although the House Subcommittee on Immigration, Refugees and International Law approved an immigration bill (HR 3080), it bypassed the farm worker issue to give a group of Democrats, led by committee member Charles E. Schumer, D-N.Y., more time to develop a compromise that could be presented to the full committee early in 1986.

11. Toxic-Waste Victims' Aid

A decision to limit the federal role in aiding victims of toxic-waste dumps was settled in a close vote Sept. 24 during debate on Senate passage of the "superfund" hazardous-waste cleanup bill (S 51).

The vote came on a motion by William V. Roth Jr., R-Del., to strike from the bill a provision establishing a demonstration program for medical aid to victims of toxic spills and leaks. The vote in favor of the Roth amendment was 49-45: R 40-11; D 9-34 (ND 3-28, SD 6-6).

Although titled the Comprehensive Environmental Response, Compensation and Liability Act, the superfund program never included liability or compensation provisions for victims. Sponsors dropped those provisions in the closing days of the 96th Congress to get superfund enacted, but vowed to try again in 1985 when the law came up for renewal.

The "Victim Assistance Demonstration Program," proposed by George J. Mitchell, D-Maine, was added to the bill during markup by the Senate Environment and Public Works Committee. Mitchell had drastically pared down earlier victim aid schemes in hopes of picking up enough support.

The program would have been funded at $30 million annually for 1986-90 and have been conducted in five to 10 geographic areas around the country, which could qualify only if scientific studies showed that toxic exposure caused health threats. The U.S. government would have paid only medical expenses not covered by other insurance.

But Roth and other opponents charged that individual victims would not have had to prove that their ailments were specifically caused by a certain toxic release. They said it would be politically difficult to keep the program from expanding.

12. Gramm-Rudman-Hollings

Anger at the prospect of continued high federal deficits, exacerbated by the upcoming 1986 congressional elections, drove Congress to approve a radical overhaul of budgetary procedures with remarkable speed.

First introduced in September, the legislation received emphatic approval on Oct. 9 when the Senate voted to add it to a measure raising the ceiling on the federal debt (H J Res 372). The vote was 75-24: R 48-4; D 27-20 (ND 15-18, SD 12-2).

The following day, Oct. 10, the debt bill bearing the budget amendment passed the Senate by a 51-37 vote, with Republicans voting 38-8 in favor of the measure, and Democrats registering a negative 13-29 vote.

Advocates said that the plan, by requiring forced deficit reductions for a period of five years, would eliminate the federal budget deficit by the beginning of fiscal 1991. Opponents warned that it would have perverse and damaging effects on the nation's economy, on key priorities including defense, and that it entailed an unconstitutional shift of power away from Congress.

Those voting for the plan ranged from conservatives, such as sponsors Phil Gramm, R-Texas, Ernest F. Hollings, D-S.C., and Warren B. Rudman, R-N.H., to liberals such as Edward M. Kennedy, D-Mass.

Each bloc of supporters believed that the plan would foster its own preferred solution to the deficit. Gramm's agenda was to shrink the federal government; others argued that the plan would force defense spending reductions and protect social programs. A strong theme was that the measure would confront President Reagan with a choice of defense spending cuts or higher taxes, and that would make Reagan finally agree to a tax hike.

13. Textile Import Limits

Legislation (HR 1562) limiting textile imports was the most prominent of the many trade bills that drew increasing congressional interest in 1985. Despite strong lobbying support from domestic textile manufacturers and unions, however, sponsors of the measure had to fight tooth-and-nail for nearly two months to get their proposal through the Senate.

The complex interplay of regional and economic factors influencing congressional action on trade legislation was clearly illustrated by the intense maneuvering over the textile bill. Not content with winning just a majority of the

Senate, bill backers worked to expand their base of support by bringing in other trade interests in order to secure the two-thirds majority needed to override President Reagan's expected veto of the bill.

The first move of bill sponsors was to add import protections for shoes to the House-passed textile bill. That helped shore up support from members from shoe-producing states. Another change scaled back the House bill's import limits, in an effort to allay concerns that the application of deep cutbacks on Chinese products would damage trade relations with that country. Those shifts brought the proposal to a comfortable majority, but still well short of two-thirds; sponsors won key procedural votes by margins of 53-42 and 54-42. *(House key vote 10)*

Two other moves lifted the bill somewhat closer to its goal. Sponsors finally secured a promise from the GOP leadership for an up-or-down vote on the House-passed bill, thus avoiding a threatened filibuster as well as quieting objections from the backers of the unrelated bills to which textile forces earlier had sought to attach their proposal as amendments. Finally, an amendment aiding hard-pressed copper producers added strength among Western senators, bringing the bill to its high-water mark. The vote on final passage Nov. 13 was 60-39: R 25-28; D 35-11 (ND 23-10; SD 12-1).

14. Farm Bill

Stymied by an alliance of Democrats and farm-state Republicans, Majority Leader Robert Dole, R-Kan., took personal reins of a farm programs reauthorization measure (S 1714) on the Senate floor and fashioned a catchall compromise that managed to placate the various interests whose disagreement had blocked the bill, and kept the door open for an administration proposal to reduce price- and income-supports for farmers.

Dole put together a package that he acknowledged to be contradictory and over budget, but with its passage managed to avoid both an embarrassing defeat for the administration and a prolonged filibuster by Democrats.

The Agriculture Committee, dominated by an alliance of Democrats and farm-state Republicans, had reported out a bill with a four-year freeze on the "target" prices that determined government income subsidies for farmers. The administration had insisted on no more than a one-year freeze on target prices, although neither a one-year freeze nor a four-year freeze could garner a majority of votes in the full Senate.

To break the logjam, Dole substituted a dual system of income supports, putting both a one-year provision and a four-year provision in the bill, adding other "sweeteners" for nearly every special farm interest in the Senate, and prohibiting the Democrats from attempts to amend it to their advantage.

Dole won over 11 Democrats, mainly from sugar- and rice-producing states, and lost only six farm-state Republicans. The Nov. 20 vote on Dole's package was 56-41: R 45-6; D 11-35 (ND 4-28, SD 7-7).

Dole's maneuver, coupled with some tactical missteps by the Democrats, effectively blunted the organized opposition to his bill and put the GOP firmly back in control of the Senate. He later had to strike a last-minute compromise with three maverick Democrats who continued to hold out the threat of a filibuster. But the product of that deal, a one-year freeze with in-kind payments making up the slack in the second year, gave Dole all the leverage he needed to negotiate a compromise with the House, which had passed a bill containing a five-year freeze on target prices.

The final version of the bill contained a two-year freeze on target prices, with only a 2 percent cut in the third year and a total reduction of 10 percent over the five-year life of the bill.

House Key Votes

1. MX Missile Production

In what may have been the last significant vote of a battle that dominated the congressional defense debate for nearly three years, the House March 26 cleared the way for production of the MX missile.

The vote came on a joint resolution (S J Res 71) that approved spending $1.5 billion in fiscal 1985 to build 21 MXs. This roundabout way of settling the question of MX production had been agreed to in October 1984 by the White House and the House Democratic leadership — which opposed the missile — after conferees on the fiscal 1985 defense authorization bill deadlocked on the issue.

The House approved the resolution by the same kind of narrow margin by which it had resolved MX battles since late 1983. Production was approved 219-213: R 158-24; D 61-189 (ND 15-154; SD 46-35).

Designed to carry 10 nuclear warheads, each with enough accuracy and explosive power to destroy a Soviet missile silo, MX had become by 1983 the central political symbol of President Reagan's nuclear weapons policy. Arms control advocates warned that it would escalate the arms race with Moscow, while Reagan and his allies contended that it was needed to counterbalance Soviet missiles powerful enough to destroy U.S. missiles in a first strike.

Reagan gave his opponents a major political advantage late in 1981 when he stripped the missile of one of its central technical justifications: He rejected the mobile basing method that the Air Force and Presidents Gerald R. Ford and Jimmy Carter had proposed to protect the new missiles against Soviet attack.

Beginning in early 1983, arms controllers organized a powerful grass-roots lobbying campaign that brought them within striking distance of a House vote against the missile. What finally swung the balance was the increasing involvement of the Democratic leaders, who saw MX as a way to crystallize public frustration with Reagan's expensive defense buildup, and widespread concern over his confrontational approach toward the Soviet Union.

Reagan was supported by a small but influential group of Democratic defense specialists who backed limited MX production in return for changes in the administration's arms control policy.

After more than a year of legislative battles, MX opponents eked out a narrow House victory in late May 1984, thus setting the stage for the final compromise that led to the March 26, 1985, House vote. Reagan won that final test by insisting that a vote against MX would undermine U.S. bargaining leverage in arms control talks with the Russians — a message carried to House members by Max M. Kampelman, Reagan's chief arms control negotiator.

In the fiscal 1986 defense bills, Congress seemed to end the MX fight — at least for the next several years — by capping the total MX deployment at 50 missiles, though more would be purchased to allow for testing.

2. McIntyre-McCloskey Contested Election

The winner of the 1984 election in Indiana's 8th Congressional District was not settled until May 1, when the House voted to seat Democrat Frank McCloskey instead of Republican Richard D. McIntyre, who had been certified the winner by Indiana.

The decision to declare McCloskey the winner followed four months of acrimony between Democrats and Republicans over what appeared to be the closest House contest in this century. Republicans, outnumbered 182-252 in the House, charged that Democrats stole the election. Democrats claimed there were inconsistencies in the Indiana ballot-counting and said a recount was necessary.

After the Nov. 6, 1984, election, incumbent McCloskey appeared to win by 72 votes. But in two precincts in one of the district's 15 counties, ballots had been counted twice. Correction of that arithmetical error gave McIntyre an apparent 34-vote victory. On that basis, the Indiana secretary of state certified McIntyre as the winner on Dec. 14.

When the House convened Jan. 3, members voted along party lines to hold vacant the Indiana 8th seat, pending an investigation of alleged election irregularities by the House Administration Committee. Three times after that, Republicans pushed the seating of McIntyre to a vote, but they lost to the Democratic majority.

After conducting its own recount, a House Administration Committee task force concluded April 18, on a 2-to-1 partisan split, that McCloskey had won by four votes.

On April 30, Republicans tried to get a new election by declaring the seat vacant. This was the key vote in the controversy — the best chance Republicans had and the one in which the most Democrats sided with the GOP. The vote on the Republican attempt (H Res 148) was 200-229: R 181-0; D 19-229 (ND 6-161, SD 13-68).

The recommendation of House Administration to seat McCloskey (H Res 146 — H Rept 99-58) came to a vote May 1. The House passed the resolution 236-190, with 10 Democrats voting against it. As Democrats prepared to swear in McCloskey immediately after the vote, Republicans stormed out of the House chamber in protest.

3. South Africa Sanctions

During his first term, one of President Reagan's most controversial foreign policies was his "constructive engagement" approach to South Africa — friendly persuasion of the white minority government to ease its repressive racial system and to participate in regional peace-making efforts.

Constructive engagement came under increased scrutiny in 1985 as civil rights groups staged well-publicized protests at Pretoria's embassy in Washington and as racial violence mounted in South Africa.

To force a change in U.S. policy, congressional activists drew up legislation imposing economic sanctions against South Africa. The idea of sanctions drew broad bipartisan support in both chambers of Congress, with the main debate centering over how tough they should be.

On June 5, the Foreign Affairs Committee took to the House floor HR 1460, which would have imposed immediate sanctions on South Africa, including a ban on bank loans to the government and prohibitions against the sale of computers and nuclear power supplies. Subject to review by the president and Congress, the bill also would have barred new U.S. investment in South Africa and prohibited imports of South African coins called Krugerrands. Over the administration's opposition, the House passed the bill 295-127: R 56-121; D 239-6 (ND 166-0, SD 73-6).

The Senate later passed its own, somewhat weaker sanctions legislation, and on July 31 a House-Senate conference committee produced a surprisingly strong sanctions bill. Rather than face outright congressional repudiation of his policy, Reagan on Sept. 9 imposed his own limited set of sanctions, including a ban on Krugerrand imports, derailing the legislation.

4. Water Projects

On a cliffhanger vote June 6, the House signaled its unwillingness to fund politically popular water projects without program reform that would cut federal costs.

The key vote came on an amendment to the fiscal 1985 supplemental appropriations bill (HR 2577 — PL 99-88) having to do with funds to start construction on new water projects. The amendment, offered by Bob Edgar, D-Pa., cut from $150 million to $51 million the amount in the bill for new Army Corps of Engineers projects. It passed by one vote, 203-202: R 108-69; D 95-133 (ND 80-75, SD 15-58).

Authorization, funding and construction of new water projects had been stalled for almost a decade over how to divide costs between the federal government and local beneficiaries. The federal government had traditionally paid most of the cost, but reformers said fewer wasteful projects would be built if users had to put up a bigger share.

Although authorizing legislation had not been enacted, the House Appropriations Committee put funds for new construction starts into HR 2577. It contained 62 new projects, 31 of which had not yet been authorized. The unauthorized projects had been removed from the bill on the House floor by a point of order, and Edgar's amendment, in effect, blocked the funding that went with them.

The vote was an expression of fiscal austerity. But it also upheld the jurisdiction of the authorizing committee, Public Works and Transportation, whose leaders had jealously opposed what they saw as an effort to short-circuit the authorizing process. Because the omnibus water projects authorizing bill contained many projects not in the supplemental, committee leaders could call on the loyalty of a considerable number of members.

The demonstration of strength by reformers made its mark on the legislation as cleared. The final bill contained $48.8 million for 41 new Army Corps of Engineers projects (21 of them unauthorized), but under the condition that funds could not be spent on the unauthorized projects until Congress passed authorizing legislation (which did not happen in 1985) or the administration reached a cost-sharing agreement with local sponsors of individual projects.

5. Nicaraguan 'Contras'

Since President Reagan took office, no foreign policy question had caused such deep divisions within Congress, and between Congress and the administration, as U.S. involvement in the war in Nicaragua. Reagan in 1981 ordered the CIA to organize a paramilitary force that would harass the leftist Sandinista government in Managua. By 1983, that force had grown to several thousand guerrillas who were receiving about $40 million a year worth of weapons and other supplies from the CIA.

Responding to a bungled CIA attempt to mine Nicaraguan harbors, Congress in 1984 ordered a halt to all U.S.

backing for the guerrillas, widely known as "contras." Reagan early in 1985 asked Congress to renew U.S. aid to the guerrillas. The House, long the center of opposition to intervention in Nicaragua, rebuffed that request April 23-24. A few days later, Nicaraguan President Daniel Ortega flew to Moscow for a meeting with top Soviet officials. That trip angered many House Democrats who had voted against aiding the contras; they said Ortega had forfeited a chance for political reconciliation between his government and the anti-communist guerrillas.

In a new political atmosphere caused by the Ortega trip, Reagan once again sought aid for the contras, promising that it would be used only for "humanitarian" or non-military purposes. The House approved that request in a stunning turnaround on June 12, during consideration of a fiscal 1985 supplemental appropriations bill (HR 2577).

The key House vote came on an amendment by Edward P. Boland, D-Mass., who sought to continue indefinitely his 1984 "Boland amendment" barring aid to the contras by any U.S. intelligence agencies. Democratic opponents of the contra aid saw that amendment as their best shot at defeating Reagan's request. The House rejected Boland's new amendment 196-232: R 7-174; D 189-58 (ND 156-11, SD 33-47). The House then approved $27 million in non-military assistance to the contras. That aid, with some strings attached, was included in the final version of the supplemental spending bill (PL 99-88).

6. Chemical Weapons

After blocking the move for three years, the House June 19 finally gave conditional approval to President Reagan's request to resume production of lethal chemical weapons for the first time since 1969.

The key vote came on an amendment to the fiscal 1986 defense authorization bill (HR 1872) that authorized $124 million for production of the so-called binary chemical weapons, provided they were formally requested by the NATO alliance. The amendment — which, in effect, substituted for a proposed amendment that would have continued the ban on binary production — was agreed to 229-196: R 143-34; D 86-162 (ND 30-138; SD 56-24).

According to the administration, new weapons were needed to replace the existing chemical weapons which, it warned, were militarily ineffective and were in danger of leaking because of age. Moreover, it argued, a U.S. chemical weapons modernization plan would induce the Russians to agree to a mutual ban on chemical weapons.

Opponents warned the weapons were unnecessary since existing chemical weapons were safe and militarily adequate. Moreover, they argued, chemical weapons are particularly repugnant and production would erode U.S. influence with its allies. The amendment skirted that diplomatic argument by making production contingent on NATO approval.

7. Anti-Missile Defense

The effort of liberal arms control advocates to rein in development of anti-missile defenses reached its high-water mark on June 20. The House rejected an effort to trim the project — called the "strategic defense initiative" (SDI) or "star wars" — to $2.1 billion for fiscal 1986.

President Reagan had requested $3.96 billion for SDI in the fiscal 1986 defense budget and the House Armed Services Committee recommended a funding ceiling of $2.5 billion in its version of the fiscal 1986 defense authorization bill (HR 1872). The key vote came on an amendment to cut the figure to $2.1 billion, which was rejected 195-221: R 12-167; D 183-54 (ND 147-11; SD 36-43).

Reagan touted SDI as a way to make nuclear weapons "impotent and obsolete," implying that the program was intended to produce a leakproof shield over the country. But most administration officials set a more modest goal: a defense that could disrupt any Soviet attack on the U.S. nuclear force, and that would thus dissuade Moscow from making such an attack.

Arms controllers argued that Reagan's impenetrable shield would prove physically unattainable and anything less effective would spur a Soviet offensive buildup to swamp U.S. defenses.

8. Repeal of Clark Amendment

In late 1975 and early 1976, reacting to the war in Vietnam and revelations of CIA misdeeds in the guise of "covert operations," Congress halted a Ford administration program of aiding one of the three guerrilla groups then battling for the control of Angola. Sponsored by Sen. Dick Clark, D-Iowa (1973-79), the Clark amendment stopped what was supposed to be secret CIA aid to rebels, called the Union for the Total Independence of Angola (UNITA).

In subsequent years, the Clark amendment became a symbol of congressional intervention in foreign policy; except for a short-lived 1984-85 ban on CIA action in Nicaragua, the Clark amendment was the only law specifically excluding U.S. intervention in a foreign country. To liberals it was a statement that the United States would step into foreign civil wars only when its vital interests were at stake and when the goals were clearly defined to the American public. Conservatives, including President Reagan, said the amendment showed that the United States no longer had the stomach to confront communist expansionism.

Congress weakened the Clark amendment in 1980, while retaining its essential thrust. Reagan persistently demanded its outright repeal, but Democrats in the House fought to retain it.

The time for change came in July 1985, shortly after the House had reversed itself and approved renewed aid for the contras in Nicaragua. When the House was considering the fiscal 1986-87 foreign aid authorizations bill (HR 1555), a coalition of Democrats and Republicans banded together to offer a floor amendment to repeal the entire Clark measure. Their leading spokesman was Claude Pepper, D-Fla., chairman of the House Rules Committee.

The House July 10 adopted the Clark amendment repealer by a surprisingly wide margin of 236-185: R 176-6; D 60-179 (ND 14-150, SD 46-29). The vote was one of several actions the House took on the foreign aid bill demonstrating a new willingness to aid anti-communist insurgents. The Senate a month before had voted a similar measure, and the repealer was included with little controversy in the final version of the foreign aid authorizations bill (PL 99-83) cleared in August.

9. Farm Bill

The administration, generally rebuffed in its efforts in the House to reform federal farm price-support programs, successfully lobbied against a measure to let farmers vote on what direction federal farm programs should take.

The House stripped a provision from the farm programs reauthorization bill (HR 2100 — PL 99-198) calling for a referendum among wheat and feed grain farmers on the question of instituting strict marketing controls in place of the government's regular price supports.

The proposal to give farmers direct control over the structure of federal agriculture policy developed slowly over the summer. The referendum was put into the Agriculture Committee bill at the last minute to keep mutinous Democrats from voting against a bill that would lower price-support protection for major crops, while freezing the "target" prices that determined income subsidies.

The referendum was a compromise version of a plan that would let farmers impose mandatory acreage cutbacks themselves as a way to reduce supply and drive up prices. The compromise, "voluntary" plan would place controls on production for domestic consumption and allow farmers to grow as much as they wanted for export.

On the floor, Democratic leaders hoped to keep the referendum in the bill as a "populist" proposal to embarrass President Reagan's administration in key farm states where House members planned to challenge Republican senators in the 1986 elections. The president vowed to veto the bill if it contained a referendum, and several Democratic members saw political advantage in that prospect.

But on Oct. 3, after intense lobbying against the referendum by agriculture organizations and the administration, the House voted in favor of a motion to strike the referendum by Edward R. Madigan, Ill., ranking Republican on Agriculture. The vote was 251-174: R 169-10; D 82-164 (ND 53-112, SD 29-52).

The Senate-passed bill also contained a referendum measure after Republican leaders included it to buy Democratic votes for their package of price- and income-support cuts. It was quickly dropped in conference, however. And the five-year farm bill shaped up as a compromise between the administration's hard-line stance against price supports and Democrats' equally fervent desire to maintain an income "safety net."

10. Textile Import Limits

Worried about the prospect of a record international trade deficit of nearly $150 billion in 1985, members of Congress shifted sharply in favor of a tougher stance in dealing with America's trading partners. The cutting edge of that surge of "protectionist" sentiment was legislation (HR 1562) to force substantial reductions in the quantities of clothing and other textiles imported from Taiwan, South Korea, Hong Kong and other Third World nations.

The textile bill had strong support from textile manufacturers and unions, who warned that their industry faced a bleak future if something was not done to stem the tide of low-cost imports. But an equally important factor in rounding up overwhelming initial support for the legislation — some 290 House members signed on as cosponsors — was the widespread irritation over President Reagan's "free-trade" policies. Reagan enraged many members by refusing to provide import relief for the shoe industry and other hard-pressed domestic producers.

Unfortunately for backers of the bill, however, Reagan shifted to a more activist trade stance before they could get their bill through Congress. Reagan's new policy, announced in late September, had two key elements — attacks on unfair trading practices of other countries and joint efforts with other leading industrialized countries to bring down the high value of the U.S. dollar.

Reagan's moves were enough to take some of the wind out of the textile bill's sails. The measure passed the House Oct. 10 by a comfortable margin, 262-159: R 75-97; D 187-62 (ND 118-49; SD 69-13). But it lacked the two-thirds majority needed to override an anticipated veto.

Congress later cleared a version of the bill that was considerably less restrictive than the original measure, but support remained inadequate to surmount Reagan's Dec. 17 veto. House sponsors decided to put off an override vote until August 1986, in hopes of pressuring the administration to pursue a tough line in international textile negotiations.

11. Latta Amendment on Reconciliation

When the House considered an omnibus deficit-reduction package (HR 3500) Oct. 24, the rule for debate permitted only three amendments, one of which was a controversial proposal to strike all provisions authorizing new or increased spending. The amendment failed by a close vote, 209-219: R 166-15; D 43-204 (ND 15-151, SD 28-53).

Republicans made the amendment a referendum on who was serious about cutting $200 billion deficits. All but 15 Republicans voted for the amendment, agreeing with sponsor Delbert L. Latta of Ohio, senior Republican on the House Budget Committee, that a deficit-reduction bill was no place to attach spending items, no matter how desirable.

Latta's main target was a package of housing program authorizations that had been added to the bill with bipartisan support in the House Banking, Finance and Urban Affairs Committee.

Another provision called for many states to receive $150 million in 1988 from a new block-grant program for coastal resources. Another authorized 5 percent pay raises in fiscal 1987 and 1988 for federal civilian employees — including members of Congress; some members said they supported the Latta amendment out of fear that otherwise they would be accused of sneaking in a pay raise, even though it required later approval through appropriations.

Latta estimated his amendment would save an additional $3.5 billion over three years beyond the $60.9 billion that the bill would cut. Technically, however, the authorizations would not have added to the deficit since the programs would have required appropriations.

The budget-cutting package, known as a reconciliation bill, combined proposals for spending cuts from most committees to achieve the deficit goals set in the annual budget resolution. The Banking Committee had included the text of a pending housing bill (HR 1) with its proposed spending cuts, after whittling costs elsewhere so it could meet its required savings target.

Committee members argued that without allowing the housing bill to piggyback on the important reconciliation bill, the Senate Banking, Housing and Urban Affairs Committee would never consider housing programs.

After defeating Latta's amendment, the House went on to approve HR 3500 by a 228-199 vote. A second, revenue-raising reconciliation bill (HR 3128) passed a week later, on Oct. 31. The two bills ultimately were combined and the Senate passed its version of HR 3128 Nov. 14, by a 93-6 vote.

In the last days of the 1985 session, a conference agreement on HR 3128 became snared in a House-Senate dispute over a Senate tax provision and Congress adjourned without clearing what would have been the second-largest deficit-reduction package ever.

12. Gramm-Rudman-Hollings

House Democrats cheered themselves when, in a rare moment of unity, all but two voted Nov. 1 for an amended version of the Senate-passed Gramm-Rudman-Hollings plan to balance the federal budget by fiscal 1991 (H J Res 372 — PL 99-177). The vote to substitute the Democratic alternative was 249-180: R 1-178; D 248-2 (ND 167-2, SD 81-0).

The party-line vote and the cheering did not denote any great fondness among House Democrats for the budget plan itself. Nor did the Republican vote signify that members of that party opposed the concept of the legislation. House leaders of both parties had made the vote a matter of partisan loyalty. The procedural vote clearing the way for floor consideration of the Senate measure — which passed 288-134 with 131 Democrats voting against — was a better gauge of outright support or opposition.

But House Democratic leaders had faced a stampede by their own members toward the Senate's budget measure. Conservative Democrats were philosophically in tune with the legislation, and there was very strong pressure from members representing marginal House districts. This group believed that, given the concern in the nation about federal deficits, they could not vote against the very conspicuous budget plan and survive the 1986 elections.

The Democratic leadership rallied its troops at the last moment, arguing among other things that the Senate version was deeply flawed and should not become law without some improvements reflecting Democratic priorities. The House alternative called for forced deficit reductions immediately, in fiscal 1986, so as to expose sponsors to any political fallout from spending cuts. It also exempted several anti-poverty programs from automatic spending cuts mandated by the legislation.

13. Plant Closings

By a five-vote margin Nov. 21, the House rejected a compromise version of a bill (HR 1616) designed to cushion the effect of plant closings and mass layoffs. Organized labor, which had tried for 11 years to get plant-closing legislation to the House floor, suffered a disappointing defeat in the close vote of 203-208: R 20-154; D 183-54 (ND 153-5, SD 30-49).

The bill would have required employers to give employees advance notice of intent to close plants or lay off large numbers of workers. A strong business lobby led by the U.S. Chamber of Commerce and deep philosophical differences among members about this labor-management issue led to the bill's defeat.

The final version of HR 1616 was substantially weaker than the original version. Gone from the bill was a requirement that employers consult with employees before closing plants and the right of employees to get court orders halting shutdowns. But some members said even the notice provision could be burdensome for financially troubled companies trying to find lenders to stay in business.

14. 'Superfund' Petrochemical Tax

A vote that set business against business and House against Senate came Dec. 10 when the House chose a method of paying for the "superfund" hazardous-waste cleanup program. The House voted to increase the existing tax on petroleum and chemical raw materials instead of imposing a new excise tax on a broader base of general manufacturers and producers of raw goods.

A bitterly divided Ways and Means Committee had sent to the floor a tax package that relied largely on the broad-based tax to finance superfund (HR 2817, later renumbered as HR 2005), similar to a Senate-passed tax. Opponents called it a "value-added tax" — a tax on the increase in value of a product at each stage of production.

The vote came on a proposal by Thomas J. Downey, D-N.Y., to increase the tax on oil and chemicals. The vote was structured so that if Downey's amendment were defeated, the broad-based tax automatically would have been adopted. The vote for the Downey amendment was 220-206: R 73-105; D 147-101 (ND 127-42, SD 20-59).

Oil and chemical companies lobbied hard for the broader tax and against Downey's amendment, claiming that it would harm their ability to compete with overseas producers and cost American jobs. On the other side were Republican fiscal conservatives who feared that once a value-added tax got started, Congress would turn to it again and again as a way of raising revenue. Administration officials warned of a veto of any new tax.

Senate backers of the broad-based tax attached their superfund taxing package to the fiscal 1986 budget reconciliation bill (HR 3128). Conferees on HR 3128 agreed to accept the proposal, but the House refused to pass HR 3128 with the tax and the bill failed to clear.

15, 16. Tax Overhaul

In what could have been a devastating blow to President Reagan and his tax-overhaul initiative, almost every House Republican joined a minority of Democrats Dec. 11 to defeat a rule allowing a Ways and Means Committee tax bill (HR 3838) to come to the floor. The rule was rejected 202-223: R 14-164; D 188-59 (ND 135-33, SD 53-26).

The size of the Republican defection on the president's top domestic priority came as a shock to just about everyone, including Republicans. Reagan had said he was not completely happy with the Ways and Means rewrite of the tax code, but had urged members to support it to keep the "process" moving so that improvements could be made in the Senate.

But White House lobbyists had failed to detect widespread unhappiness about the tax bill among the GOP ranks. Republicans complained that they had been virtually ignored by the administration during markup of the bill in the Democrat-controlled Ways and Means Committee. They also felt slighted because Reagan appeared to ignore their earlier warnings that few GOP members were excited about overhauling the tax code.

In addition, many Republicans were unhappy with what they saw as HR 3838's anti-business cast. And they had little confidence that their Republican colleagues in the Senate would be able to reshape the bill to their liking.

The startling vote finally got House Republicans the attention they sought. With Democrats refusing to bring the bill back to the floor without at least 50 Republican votes confirmed, the administration got to work. Reagan finally won his way after he made an unusual visit to Capitol Hill to assure wavering Republicans he would veto any bill that did not include several significant changes to HR 3838.

By a vote of 258-168: R 70-110; D 188-58 (ND 138-28, SD 50-30), the House Dec. 17 approved a slightly modified rule. Later that day, it passed HR 3838 by voice vote and sent the bill to the Senate. ∎

	1	2	3	4	5	6	7
ALABAMA							
Denton	Y	Y	Y	N	Y	Y	Y
Heflin	Y	Y	N	N	Y	Y	Y
ALASKA							
Murkowski	Y	Y	Y	N	Y	Y	Y
Stevens	Y	Y	Y	N	Y	Y	Y
ARIZONA							
Goldwater	?	Y	Y	N	?	Y	Y
DeConcini	Y	Y	N	Y	Y	Y	Y
ARKANSAS							
Bumpers	Y	N	N	Y	N	?	Y
Pryor	Y	N	N	Y	N	Y	Y
CALIFORNIA							
Wilson	N	Y	Y	N	Y	Y	Y
Cranston	Y	N	N	Y	N	?	N
COLORADO							
Armstrong	N	Y	Y	N	Y	?	?
Hart	Y	N	N	Y	N	N	N
CONNECTICUT							
Weicker	Y	N	Y	Y	N	N	Y
Dodd	Y	N	N	Y	N	Y	N
DELAWARE							
Roth	N	Y	Y	N	Y	Y	Y
Biden	Y	N	N	#	N	N	Y
FLORIDA							
Hawkins	Y	Y	N	N	Y	Y	Y
Chiles	Y	N	N	Y	Y	Y	Y
GEORGIA							
Mattingly	N	Y	Y	N	Y	Y	Y
Nunn	Y	Y	N	N	Y	Y	Y
HAWAII							
Inouye	Y	N	N	Y	N	N	N
Matsunaga	Y	N	N	Y	N	N	N
IDAHO							
McClure	N	Y	Y	N	Y	Y	Y
Symms	N	Y	Y	N	Y	Y	Y
ILLINOIS							
Dixon	Y	N	N	N	Y	Y	Y
Simon	Y	N	N	Y	N	?	?
INDIANA							
Lugar	N	Y	Y	N	Y	Y	Y
Quayle	N	Y	Y	N	Y	Y	Y
IOWA							
Grassley	Y	N	Y	Y	Y	Y	Y
Harkin	Y	N	N	Y	N	Y	Y
KANSAS							
Dole	N	Y	Y	N	Y	Y	Y
Kassebaum	N	N	Y	Y	Y	Y	Y
KENTUCKY							
McConnell	N	Y	Y	N	Y	?	Y
Ford	Y	N	N	Y	Y	Y	Y
LOUISIANA							
Johnston	Y	N	N	Y	Y	Y	Y
Long	Y	Y	N	N	Y	N	?
MAINE							
Cohen	N	Y	Y	N	N	?	Y
Mitchell	Y	N	N	Y	N	Y	Y
MARYLAND							
Mathias	Y	Y	N	Y	N	N	N
Sarbanes	Y	N	N	Y	N	N	N
MASSACHUSETTS							
Kennedy	Y	N	N	Y	N	?	N
Kerry	Y	N	N	Y	N	N	N
MICHIGAN							
Levin	Y	N	N	Y	N	Y	N
Riegle	Y	N	N	Y	N	Y	Y
MINNESOTA							
Boschwitz	N	Y	Y	N	Y	Y	Y
Durenberger	Y	N	Y	N	Y	Y	Y
MISSISSIPPI							
Cochran	N	Y	Y	N	Y	Y	Y
Stennis	Y	Y	N	?	Y	Y	?
MISSOURI							
Danforth	Y	Y	Y	N	Y	Y	Y
Eagleton	Y	N	N	Y	N	Y	Y
MONTANA							
Baucus	Y	N	N	Y	N	Y	Y
Melcher	Y	N	N	Y	N	?	Y
NEBRASKA							
Exon	Y	N	+	N	Y	Y	Y
Zorinsky	Y	Y	Y	N	N	Y	Y
NEVADA							
Hecht	N	Y	Y	N	Y	Y	Y
Laxalt	N	Y	Y	N	Y	?	Y
NEW HAMPSHIRE							
Humphrey	N	Y	Y	N	Y	Y	Y
Rudman	N	Y	Y	N	Y	?	Y
NEW JERSEY							
Bradley	Y	N	N	N	N	?	?
Lautenberg	Y	N	N	Y	N	Y	N
NEW MEXICO							
Domenici	N	Y	Y	N	Y	Y	Y
Bingaman	Y	N	N	N	N	Y	Y
NEW YORK							
D'Amato	Y	Y	N	N	Y	Y	Y
Moynihan	Y	N	N	Y	N	N	N
NORTH CAROLINA							
East	N	Y	+	?	Y	Y	Y
Helms	N	Y	Y	N	Y	Y	Y
NORTH DAKOTA							
Andrews	Y	N	Y	N	Y	Y	Y
Burdick	Y	N	N	Y	N	Y	Y
OHIO							
Glenn	Y	N	N	N	N	Y	Y
Metzenbaum	Y	N	N	Y	N	Y	N
OKLAHOMA							
Nickles	N	Y	Y	N	Y	Y	Y
Boren	Y	Y	N	X	Y	Y	Y
OREGON							
Hatfield	Y	N	Y	Y	N	N	+
Packwood	N	Y	Y	N	N	Y	Y
PENNSYLVANIA							
Heinz	N	Y	Y	N	Y	Y	Y
Specter	Y	Y	N	?	N	Y	Y
RHODE ISLAND							
Chafee	N	Y	Y	Y	N	N	N
Pell	Y	N	N	Y	N	N	N
SOUTH CAROLINA							
Thurmond	N	Y	Y	N	Y	Y	Y
Hollings	Y	N	N	N	Y	Y	Y
SOUTH DAKOTA							
Abdnor	Y	Y	Y	N	Y	Y	Y
Pressler	Y	N	Y	N	Y	Y	Y
TENNESSEE							
Gore	Y	Y	N	Y	N	Y	Y
Sasser	Y	N	N	Y	N	Y	Y
TEXAS							
Gramm	N	Y	Y	N	Y	Y	Y
Bentsen	Y	Y	N	N	Y	Y	Y
UTAH							
Garn	-	Y	Y	N	Y	Y	Y
Hatch	N	Y	Y	N	Y	Y	Y
VERMONT							
Stafford	N	N	Y	N	N	Y	Y
Leahy	Y	N	N	Y	N	?	Y
VIRGINIA							
Trible	N	Y	Y	N	Y	Y	Y
Warner	N	Y	Y	N	Y	Y	Y
WASHINGTON							
Evans	N	Y	Y	N	N	Y	Y
Gorton	N	Y	Y	N	N	+	Y
WEST VIRGINIA							
Byrd	Y	Y	N	N	Y	Y	Y
Rockefeller	Y	N	N	Y	+	?	Y
WISCONSIN							
Kasten	Y	Y	Y	N	Y	?	Y
Proxmire	N	N	N	Y	N	Y	Y
WYOMING							
Simpson	N	Y	Y	N	Y	Y	Y
Wallop	?	Y	Y	N	+	+	Y

KEY

- Y Voted for (yea).
- # Paired for.
- + Announced for.
- N Voted against (nay).
- X Paired against.
- \- Announced against.
- P Voted "present."
- C Voted "present" to avoid possible conflict of interest.
- ? Did not vote or otherwise make a position known.

Democrats ***Republicans***

ND - Northern Democrats SD - Southern Democrats (Southern states - Ala., Ark., Fla., Ga., Ky., La., Miss., N.C., Okla., S.C., Tenn., Texas, Va.)

1. HR 1096. African Relief/Farm Credit. Passage of the bill to authorize $175 million in non-food aid for emergency relief to Africa, to authorize $100 million to offset interest on restructured private farm loans guaranteed by the Farmers Home Administration (FmHA), to increase the FmHA loan guarantee program by $1.85 billion and revise certain eligibility rules and to authorize advances to eligible farmers of Commodity Credit Corporation commodity price-support loans. Passed 62-35: R 16-34; D 46-1 (ND 32-1, SD 14-0), Feb. 27, 1985. A "nay" was a vote supporting the president's position.

2. S J Res 71. MX Missile Authorization. Passage of the joint resolution to reaffirm the authorization of $1.5 billion in the fiscal 1985 defense budget to purchase 21 MX missiles. Passed 55-45: R 45-8; D 10-37 (ND 3-30, SD 7-7), March 19, 1985. A "yea" was a vote supporting the president's position.

3. S Con Res 32. First Budget Resolution, Fiscal 1986. Dole, R-Kan., perfecting amendment to the Dole-Domenici, R-N.M., amendment to the instructions of the Dole motion to recommit the concurrent resolution to the Budget Committee, to set budget targets for the fiscal year ending Sept. 30, 1986, as follows: budget authority, $1,069.5 billion; outlays, $965 billion; revenues, $793.6 billion; deficit, $171.4 billion. The amendment also established dual, annual caps on defense appropriations and on non-defense, discretionary (non-entitlement) appropriations as follows: fiscal 1986, defense, $303.2 billion, non-defense, $140.8 billion; 1987, defense, $324.1 billion, non-defense, $143.8 billion; 1988, defense, $347.6 billion, non-defense, $149.3 billion. It revised budget levels for fiscal 1985, and included reconciliation instructions requiring the Budget committees to recommend legislative savings to meet the budget targets by June 30, 1985. Adopted 50-49: R 48-4; D 1-45 (ND 1-31, SD 0-14), with Vice President George Bush casting a "yea" vote to break the 49-49 tie, in the session that began May 9, 1985. (The effect of this Dole amendment was to substitute, for the Senate GOP-White House budget package approved April 30, a revised version of that package providing, among other things, for $17.7 billion less in defense spending in fiscal 1986-88, and $15.7 billion more in domestic program spending for those three fiscal years.) (S Con Res 32, as amended by the Dole plan, subsequently was adopted by voice vote.)

4. S 1160. Department of Defense Authorization, Fiscal 1986. Proxmire, D-Wis., amendment to reduce from $2.96 billion to $1.9 billion the authorization for research on anti-missile defenses. Rejected 38-57: R 6-45; D 32-12 (ND 25-7, SD 7-5), June 4, 1985.

5. S 1003. State Department Authorizations, Fiscal 1986-87. Nunn, D-Ga., amendment to authorize $24 million for fiscal year 1986 for humanitarian assistance to the Nicaraguan rebels and to direct the National Security Council to monitor the use of the funds. The amendment also releases the $14 million approved for fiscal 1985 for the rebels but restricts the use of those funds to humanitarian assistance, and it urges the president to lift the economic sanctions on Nicaragua if that country agrees to a cease-fire and talks with the rebels, to call upon the rebels to remove from their ranks any individuals who have engaged in human rights abuses, and to resume bilateral negotiations with the government of Nicaragua. Adopted 55-42: R 41-10; D 14-32 (ND 4-28, SD 10-4), June 6, 1985. A "yea" was a vote supporting the president's position.

6. S 1003. State Department Authorizations, Fiscal 1986-87. Kassebaum, R-Kan., amendment to limit U.S. contributions to the United Nations and related organizations to 20 percent of those organizations' annual budgets, unless the secretary of state certified to Congress that such organizations had adopted procedures for proportionate voting on budgetary matters and had adopted plans to reduce employee salaries and pensions to levels comparable to those of the U.S. Civil Service. Adopted 71-13: R 41-4; D 30-9 (ND 18-8, SD 12-1), June 7, 1985.

7. S 49. Firearm Owners' Protection. Passage of the bill to revise the Gun Control Act of 1968 to exempt many gun collectors from licensing requirements, remove the ban on interstate sales of rifles, shotguns and handguns, require advance notice for routine compliance inspections, and impose a mandatory five-year sentence on anyone convicted of using a firearm in a violent federal crime. Passed 79-15: R 49-2; D 30-13 (ND 18-13, SD 12-0), July 9, 1985. A "yea" was a vote supporting the president's position.

	8	9	10	11	12	13	14
ALABAMA							
Denton	Y	N	Y	Y	Y	Y	Y
Heflin	Y	N	Y	Y	Y	Y	N
ALASKA							
Murkowski	Y	N	Y	Y	Y	N	Y
Stevens	Y	Y	Y	Y	Y	N	Y
ARIZONA							
Goldwater	Y	Y	Y	Y	Y	N	Y
DeConcini	#	Y	Y	N	Y	Y	Y
ARKANSAS							
Bumpers	N	Y	Y	N	Y	Y	Y
Pryor	N	Y	Y	N	Y	Y	Y
CALIFORNIA							
Wilson	Y	Y	Y	Y	Y	N	Y
Cranston	N	Y	N	N	N	N	Y
COLORADO							
Armstrong	Y	N	Y	Y	Y	N	Y
Hart	N	Y	N	N	N	N	N
CONNECTICUT							
Weicker	N	Y	N	Y	N	Y	Y
Dodd	N	Y	N	N	Y	Y	N
DELAWARE							
Roth	Y	N	N	Y	Y	Y	Y
Biden	Y	Y	N	N	Y	Y	N
FLORIDA							
Hawkins	Y	N	Y	Y	Y	Y	Y
Chiles	N	Y	N	N	N	?	Y
GEORGIA							
Mattingly	Y	N	Y	Y	Y	Y	Y
Nunn	Y	Y	Y	Y	Y	Y	Y
HAWAII							
Inouye	N	Y	?	N	N	N	?
Matsunaga	N	Y	N	N	N	N	Y
IDAHO							
McClure	Y	N	Y	Y	Y	Y	Y
Symms	Y	N	Y	Y	Y	N	Y
ILLINOIS							
Dixon	Y	Y	N	N	Y	Y	N
Simon	N	Y	N	N	Y	Y	N
INDIANA							
Lugar	Y	Y	Y	Y	Y	N	Y
Quayle	Y	N	Y	Y	Y	N	Y
IOWA							
Grassley	Y	N	N	Y	Y	N	N
Harkin	N	Y	N	N	N	N	N
KANSAS							
Dole	Y	N	Y	Y	Y	Y	Y
Kassebaum	Y	Y	Y	Y	N	N	Y
KENTUCKY							
McConnell	Y	N	Y	Y	Y	Y	Y
Ford	N	N	N	N	Y	Y	N
LOUISIANA							
Johnston	N	N	N	Y	N	Y	Y
Long	X	N	N	Y	Y	Y	Y
MAINE							
Cohen	Y	Y	N	N	Y	Y	Y
Mitchell	N	Y	Y	N	N	Y	N
MARYLAND							
Mathias	N	Y	N	N	?	Y	Y
Sarbanes	N	Y	N	N	N	Y	N
MASSACHUSETTS							
Kennedy	Y	Y	N	N	Y	Y	N
Kerry	N	Y	N	N	Y	Y	N
MICHIGAN							
Levin	N	Y	N	N	Y	Y	N
Riegle	N	Y	Y	N	N	Y	N
MINNESOTA							
Boschwitz	Y	Y	Y	Y	Y	N	Y
Durenberger	N	Y	N	N	Y	N	N
MISSISSIPPI							
Cochran	Y	N	Y	Y	Y	Y	Y
Stennis	N	N	?	?	Y	Y	N
MISSOURI							
Danforth	Y	Y	N	Y	Y	N	Y
Eagleton	N	Y	N	N	N	Y	N
MONTANA							
Baucus	N	Y	Y	-	Y	N	N
Melcher	N	Y	N	N	Y	Y	N
NEBRASKA							
Exon	Y	N	Y	N	N	N	N
Zorinsky	Y	Y	X	Y	Y	N	N
NEVADA							
Hecht	Y	N	Y	Y	Y	N	Y
Laxalt	Y	N	Y	Y	Y	Y	Y
NEW HAMPSHIRE							
Humphrey	Y	N	Y	N	Y	N	Y
Rudman	Y	Y	Y	Y	Y	Y	Y
NEW JERSEY							
Bradley	N	Y	N	N	N	N	N
Lautenberg	N	Y	N	N	N	Y	N
NEW MEXICO							
Domenici	Y	Y	Y	Y	Y	Y	Y
Bingaman	N	Y	N	Y	N	Y	N
NEW YORK							
D'Amato	Y	Y	Y	N	Y	Y	Y
Moynihan	N	Y	N	?	N	Y	N
NORTH CAROLINA							
East	Y	?	#	?	Y	Y	?
Helms	Y	N	Y	Y	Y	Y	Y
NORTH DAKOTA							
Andrews	N	Y	N	?	Y	N	Y
Burdick	N	+	N	N	Y	N	N
OHIO							
Glenn	N	Y	N	Y	N	Y	N
Metzenbaum	N	Y	N	N	N	Y	N
OKLAHOMA							
Nickles	Y	N	Y	Y	Y	N	N
Boren	Y	Y	Y	?	Y	N	N
OREGON							
Hatfield	N	Y	+	Y	N	N	Y
Packwood	N	Y	N	N	Y	N	Y
PENNSYLVANIA							
Heinz	Y	Y	N	N	Y	Y	Y
Specter	Y	Y	Y	N	Y	Y	Y
RHODE ISLAND							
Chafee	Y	Y	N	N	Y	N	Y
Pell	Y	Y	N	N	N	Y	N
SOUTH CAROLINA							
Thurmond	Y	N	Y	Y	Y	Y	Y
Hollings	Y	Y	Y	Y	Y	Y	N
SOUTH DAKOTA							
Abdnor	Y	N	Y	Y	Y	N	N
Pressler	Y	N	N	Y	Y	N	N
TENNESSEE							
Gore	N	Y	Y	N	Y	Y	N
Sasser	N	N	Y	N	Y	Y	N
TEXAS							
Gramm	Y	N	Y	Y	Y	N	Y
Bentsen	N	N	Y	Y	Y	Y	Y
UTAH							
Garn	Y	N	Y	Y	Y	Y	Y
Hatch	Y	Y	Y	N	Y	Y	Y
VERMONT							
Stafford	N	Y	N	N	N	N	?
Leahy	Y	Y	Y	N	Y	Y	N
VIRGINIA							
Trible	Y	N	Y	Y	Y	Y	Y
Warner	Y	N	Y	Y	Y	Y	Y
WASHINGTON							
Evans	Y	Y	Y	Y	Y	N	Y
Gorton	Y	Y	Y	Y	Y	N	Y
WEST VIRGINIA							
Byrd	N	Y	N	N	N	Y	N
Rockefeller	N	Y	N	N	Y	Y	N
WISCONSIN							
Kasten	Y	N	N	Y	Y	Y	N
Proxmire	Y	Y	N	N	Y	Y	Y
WYOMING							
Simpson	Y	N	N	Y	Y	N	Y
Wallop	Y	N	Y	Y	Y	N	Y

KEY

- Y Voted for (yea).
- # Paired for.
- + Announced for.
- N Voted against (nay).
- X Paired against.
- - Announced against.
- P Voted "present."
- C Voted "present" to avoid possible conflict of interest.
- ? Did not vote or otherwise make a position known.

Democrats *Republicans*

ND - Northern Democrats SD - Southern Democrats (Southern states - Ala., Ark., Fla., Ga., Ky., La., Miss., N.C., Okla., S.C., Tenn., Texas, Va.)

8. S 43. Line-Item Veto. Dole, R-Kan., motion to invoke cloture (thus limiting debate) on the Dole motion to proceed to consideration of the bill to give the president power to veto individual spending items by requiring that appropriations bills be split by paragraph or section into separate bills before being sent to the White House. Motion rejected 58-40: R 46-7; D 12-33 (ND 8-24, SD 4-9), July 24, 1985. A three-fifths majority vote (60) of the total Senate is required to invoke cloture. A "yea" was a vote supporting the president's position.

9. S 47. School Prayer. Weicker, R-Conn., motion to table (kill) the bill to bar the federal courts, including the Supreme Court, from considering cases involving prayer in public schools. Motion agreed to 62-36: R 24-28; D 38-8 (ND 31-1, 7-7), Sept. 10, 1985. (The effect of the bill would have been to restore the right of states or local communities to permit prayer in public schools without being subject to challenges in the federal courts.)

10. S 1200. Immigration Reform and Control Act. Wilson, R-Calif., amendment to create a "seasonal worker" program to allow foreign workers into the country for up to nine months each year for agricultural work, with a cap allowing no more than 350,000 of these workers in the United States at any one time. Adopted 51-44: R 36-15; D 15-29 (ND 6-25, SD 9-4), Sept. 17, 1985.

11. S 51. Superfund Reauthorization, Fiscal 1986-90. Roth, R-Del., amendment to strike from the bill a section establishing a new demonstration program to pay for medical expenses of victims of hazardous-substance releases, and to authorize appropriations of $30 million annually during fiscal 1986-90 for that purpose. Adopted 49-45: R 40-11; D 9-34 (ND 3-28, SD 6-6), Sept. 24, 1985. A "yea" was a vote supporting the president's position.

12. H J Res 372. Public Debt Limit. Dole, R-Kan. (for Gramm, R-Texas, Rudman, R-N.H., Hollings, D-S.C.), amendment to set maximum allowable federal deficits for fiscal years 1986-91, declining annually to zero in 1991, and to require the president, if projected deficits exceed those allowed, to issue an emergency order reducing all federal spending except for Social Security, interest on the federal debt and existing contractual obligations, by enough to reduce deficits to the maximum established by the bill. The amendment also revises congressional budgeting procedures and removes Social Security from the unified federal budget in fiscal 1986 and thereafter. Adopted 75-24: R 48-4; D 27-20 (ND 15-18, SD 12-2), Oct. 9, 1985. A "yea" was a vote supporting the president's position.

13. HR 1562. Textile Import Quotas. Passage of the bill to establish a worldwide system of quotas for imports of textiles and apparel, limit shoe imports to 60 percent of the domestic shoe market and require negotiations leading to an international agreement limiting copper production. Passed 60-39: R 25-28; D 35-11 (ND 23-10, SD 12-1), Nov. 13, 1985. A "nay" was a vote supporting the president's position.

14. S 1714. Farm Programs Reauthorization, Fiscal 1986-89. Dole, R-Kan., perfecting amendment to the Dole amendment to the Dole motion to recommit the bill to the Agriculture, Nutrition and Forestry Committee with instructions, to freeze current target prices for wheat, feed grains, cotton and rice titles for the life of the bill; to freeze target prices for corn, cotton and rice in fiscal 1986 and allow maximum 5 percent annual reductions thereafter; to provide a sliding scale of target prices for wheat based on levels of production; to authorize the agriculture secretary to increase the maximum acreage limitation for wheat, feed grains, cotton and rice by 5 percent; to reduce the conservation reserve in 1986 and require some of the reserve to be devoted to trees; to change provisions dealing with loans for rice; to provide for payments to soybean and sunflower farmers; to expand disaster payments to farmers of soybeans, sugar cane and sugar beets; and to require the president to operate the sugar program at no cost to the government. Adopted 56-41: R 45-6; D 11-35 (ND 4-28, SD 7-7), Nov. 20, 1985.

1. S J Res 71. MX Missile Authorization. Passage of the joint resolution to approve authorization of $1.5 billion to procure 21 MX missiles in fiscal 1985. Passed 219-213: R 158-24; D 61-189 (ND 15-154, SD 46-35), March 26, 1985. A "yea" was a vote supporting the president's position.

2. H Res 148. Indiana 8th District Seat. Adoption of the resolution to declare a vacancy in the 99th Congress from the 8th District of Indiana. Rejected 200-229: R 181-0; D 19-229 (ND 6-161, SD 13-68), April 30, 1985.

3. HR 1460. Anti-Apartheid Act. Passage of the bill to impose sanctions immediately against South Africa, including a ban on bank loans to the South African government, and prohibitions against the sale of computer goods and nuclear power equipment and supplies to that country. Subject to review by the president and Congress, the bill also would bar new U.S. business investment in South Africa and prohibit the importation into the United States of South African gold coins, called Krugerrands. Passed 295-127: R 56-121; D 239-6 (ND 166-0, SD 73-6), June 5, 1985. A "nay" was a vote supporting the president's position.

4. HR 2577. Supplemental Appropriations, Fiscal 1985. Edgar, D-Pa., amendment to the Whitten, D-Miss., amendment, to reduce from $150 million to $51 million the funds added for water projects of the U.S. Army Corps of Engineers. Adopted 203-202: R 108-69; D 95-133 (ND 80-75, SD 15-58), June 6, 1985. (The Whitten amendment was subsequently adopted.)

5. HR 2577. Supplemental Appropriations, Fiscal 1985. Boland, D-Mass., amendment to the McDade, R-Pa., amendment to continue indefinitely the prohibition of any funding by U.S. intelligence agencies that would support, directly or indirectly, military or paramilitary operations in Nicaragua. Rejected 196-232: R 7-174; D 189-58 (ND 156-11, SD 33-47), June 12, 1985. A "nay" was a vote supporting the president's position.

6. HR 1872. Department of Defense Authorization, Fiscal 1986. Skelton, D-Mo., amendment to the Porter, R-Ill., amendment, to authorize the appropriation of $124 million to produce binary chemical weapons subject to certain conditions. Adopted 229-196: R 143-34; D 86-162 (ND 30-138, SD 56-24), June 19, 1985. A "yea" was a vote supporting the president's position.

7. HR 1872. Department of Defense Authorization, Fiscal 1986. Dicks, D-Wash., amendment to the Price, D-Ill., amendment, to reduce from $2.5 billion to $2.1 billion the authorization for the strategic defense initiative. Rejected 195-221: R 12-167; D 183-54 (ND 147-11, SD 36-43), June 20, 1985. A "nay" was a vote supporting the president's position.

8. HR 1555. Foreign Assistance Authorization, Fiscal 1986. Stratton, D-N.Y., amendment to repeal the so-called "Clark amendment" to the International Security and Development Cooperation Act of 1980, prohibiting assistance for military or paramilitary operations in Angola. Adopted 236-185: R 176-6; D 60-179 (ND 14-150, SD 46-29), July 10, 1985. A "yea" was a vote supporting the president's position.

KEY

- Y Voted for (yea).
- # Paired for.
- + Announced for.
- N Voted against (nay).
- X Paired against.
- \- Announced against.
- P Voted "present."
- C Voted "present" to avoid possible conflict of interest.
- ? Did not vote or otherwise make a position known.

Democrats ***Republicans***

	1	2	3	4	5	6	7	8
ALABAMA								
1 ***Callahan***	Y	Y	N	N	N	Y	N	Y
2 ***Dickinson***	Y	Y	N	N	N	Y	N	Y
3 Nichols	Y	N	N	N	N	Y	N	Y
4 Bevill	Y	N	Y	N	N	Y	N	Y
5 Flippo	Y	N	Y	N	N	Y	N	?
6 Erdreich	Y	N	Y	N	N	N	N	Y
7 Shelby	Y	N	Y	N	N	Y	N	Y
ALASKA								
AL ***Young***	Y	Y	Y	N	N	Y	N	Y
ARIZONA								
1 ***McCain***	Y	Y	N	N	N	Y	N	Y
2 Udall	N	?	Y	N	Y	?	Y	N
3 ***Stump***	Y	Y	N	N	N	Y	N	Y
4 ***Rudd***	Y	Y	N	N	N	Y	N	Y
5 ***Kolbe***	Y	Y	N	N	N	Y	N	Y
ARKANSAS								
1 Alexander	N	N	Y	N	Y	Y	N	N
2 Robinson	Y	N	Y	Y	N	Y	N	Y
3 ***Hammerschmidt***	Y	Y	N	Y	N	Y	N	Y
4 Anthony	N	N	Y	N	Y	Y	Y	Y
CALIFORNIA								
1 Bosco	N	N	Y	Y	?	Y	Y	N
2 ***Chappie***	Y	Y	N	N	N	Y	N	Y
3 Matsui	N	N	Y	?	Y	N	Y	N
4 Fazio	Y	N	Y	N	Y	Y	Y	N
5 Burton	N	N	Y	N	Y	N	Y	N
6 Boxer	N	N	Y	?	Y	N	Y	N
7 Miller	N	N	?	?	Y	N	Y	N
8 Dellums	N	N	Y	N	Y	N	Y	N
9 Stark	N	N	Y	?	Y	N	?	?
10 Edwards	N	N	Y	Y	Y	N	Y	N
11 Lantos	N	N	Y	Y	Y	N	Y	N
12 ***Zschau***	N	Y	N	Y	N	Y	N	Y
13 Mineta	N	N	Y	N	Y	N	Y	N
14 ***Shumway***	Y	Y	N	Y	N	Y	N	Y
15 Coelho	N	N	Y	N	Y	N	Y	N
16 Panetta	N	N	Y	N	Y	N	Y	N
17 ***Pashayan***	Y	Y	N	N	N	Y	N	Y
18 Lehman	N	N	Y	?	Y	N	Y	N
19 ***Lagomarsino***	Y	Y	N	N	N	Y	N	Y
20 ***Thomas***	Y	Y	-	Y	N	Y	N	Y
21 ***Fiedler***	Y	Y	N	?	N	Y	N	Y
22 ***Moorhead***	Y	Y	N	Y	N	Y	N	Y
23 Beilenson	N	N	Y	Y	Y	N	Y	N
24 Waxman	N	N	Y	Y	Y	N	Y	?
25 Roybal	N	N	Y	N	Y	N	Y	N
26 Berman	N	N	Y	Y	Y	N	Y	N
27 Levine	N	N	Y	Y	Y	N	Y	N
28 Dixon	N	N	Y	N	Y	X	?	N
29 Hawkins	N	N	Y	N	?	N	Y	N
30 Martinez	N	N	Y	Y	Y	N	Y	N
31 Dymally	N	N	Y	Y	Y	N	Y	N
32 Anderson	Y	N	Y	Y	Y	Y	Y	Y
33 ***Dreier***	Y	Y	N	Y	N	Y	N	Y
34 Torres	N	N	Y	N	Y	N	Y	N
35 ***Lewis***	Y	Y	Y	N	N	Y	N	Y
36 Brown	N	N	Y	Y	Y	N	Y	N
37 ***McCandless***	Y	Y	N	N	N	Y	N	Y
38 ***Dornan***	Y	Y	N	N	N	Y	N	Y
39 ***Dannemeyer***	Y	Y	N	Y	N	Y	N	Y
40 ***Badham***	Y	Y	N	N	N	Y	N	Y
41 ***Lowery***	Y	Y	N	N	N	Y	N	Y
42 ***Lungren***	Y	Y	N	Y	N	Y	N	Y
43 ***Packard***	Y	Y	N	Y	N	Y	N	Y
44 Bates	N	N	Y	Y	Y	Y	Y	N
45 ***Hunter***	Y	Y	N	N	N	Y	N	Y
COLORADO								
1 Schroeder	N	N	Y	+	Y	N	Y	N
2 Wirth	N	N	Y	?	Y	N	Y	N
3 ***Strang***	Y	Y	N	N	N	+	X	Y
4 ***Brown***	Y	Y	Y	Y	N	N	N	Y
5 ***Kramer***	Y	Y	N	N	N	Y	N	Y
6 ***Schaefer***	Y	Y	N	Y	N	?	N	Y
CONNECTICUT								
1 Kennelly	N	N	Y	Y	Y	N	Y	N
2 Gejdenson	N	N	Y	Y	Y	N	Y	N
3 Morrison	N	N	Y	?	Y	N	Y	N
4 ***McKinney***	N	Y	Y	Y	N	N	Y	N
5 ***Rowland***	Y	Y	Y	Y	N	Y	N	Y
6 ***Johnson***	N	Y	Y	Y	N	Y	N	Y
DELAWARE								
AL Carper	N	N	Y	Y	Y	N	Y	Y
FLORIDA								
1 Hutto	Y	Y	N	?	N	Y	N	Y
2 Fuqua	Y	N	Y	Y	N	Y	N	Y
3 Bennett	N	N	Y	N	Y	Y	N	N
4 Chappell	Y	N	Y	N	N	Y	N	Y
5 ***McCollum***	Y	Y	N	Y	N	Y	N	Y
6 MacKay	N	N	Y	Y	Y	N	Y	N
7 Gibbons	N	N	Y	N	N	Y	Y	N
8 ***Young***	Y	Y	N	N	N	Y	N	Y
9 ***Bilirakis***	Y	Y	N	?	N	Y	N	Y
10 ***Ireland***	Y	Y	N	Y	N	Y	N	Y
11 Nelson	Y	N	Y	N	N	Y	N	#
12 ***Lewis***	Y	Y	N	N	N	N	N	Y
13 ***Mack***	Y	Y	N	Y	N	Y	N	Y
14 Mica	N	N	Y	N	N	Y	Y	Y
15 ***Shaw***	Y	Y	N	Y	N	Y	N	Y
16 Smith	N	N	Y	N	Y	N	#	Y
17 Lehman	N	N	Y	N	Y	N	Y	N
18 Pepper	Y	N	Y	N	Y	#	#	Y
19 Fascell	N	N	Y	N	N	N	Y	Y
GEORGIA								
1 Thomas	Y	N	Y	N	N	Y	N	Y
2 Hatcher	Y	N	Y	?	N	Y	N	Y
3 Ray	Y	Y	Y	Y	N	Y	N	Y
4 ***Swindall***	Y	Y	N	Y	N	Y	N	Y
5 Fowler	N	N	Y	Y	Y	N	N	Y
6 ***Gingrich***	Y	Y	N	Y	N	Y	N	Y
7 Darden	Y	N	Y	N	N	Y	N	Y
8 Rowland	Y	N	Y	N	N	Y	N	Y
9 Jenkins	N	N	Y	N	N	Y	N	Y
10 Barnard	Y	Y	Y	N	N	Y	N	Y
HAWAII								
1 Heftel	N	N	Y	Y	N	Y	Y	?
2 Akaka	N	N	Y	N	Y	Y	Y	N
IDAHO								
1 ***Craig***	Y	Y	N	N	N	Y	N	Y
2 Stallings	N	Y	?	?	Y	N	Y	N
ILLINOIS								
1 Hayes	N	N	Y	Y	Y	N	Y	N
2 Savage	N	N	Y	Y	Y	N	?	N
3 Russo	N	N	Y	N	Y	N	Y	N
4 ***O'Brien***	Y	Y	N	N	N	?	X	Y
5 Lipinski	Y	N	Y	Y	N	Y	?	N
6 ***Hyde***	Y	Y	N	Y	N	Y	N	Y
7 Collins	N	N	Y	Y	Y	N	Y	N
8 Rostenkowski	N	N	Y	N	Y	N	?	N
9 Yates	N	N	Y	Y	Y	N	Y	N
10 ***Porter***	Y	Y	Y	Y	N	N	Y	Y
11 Annunzio	N	N	Y	Y	Y	N	N	N
12 ***Crane***	Y	Y	N	N	N	Y	N	Y
13 ***Fawell***	Y	Y	N	Y	N	Y	N	Y
14 ***Grotberg***	Y	Y	N	Y	N	Y	N	Y
15 ***Madigan***	Y	Y	Y	Y	N	Y	N	Y
16 ***Martin***	Y	Y	Y	Y	N	N	N	Y
17 Evans	N	N	Y	Y	Y	N	Y	N
18 ***Michel***	Y	Y	N	Y	N	Y	N	Y
19 Bruce	N	N	Y	N	Y	N	Y	N
20 Durbin	N	N	Y	N	Y	N	Y	N
21 Price	Y	N	Y	N	Y	Y	Y	N
22 Gray	N	N	Y	Y	Y	Y	N	X
INDIANA								
1 Visclosky	N	N	Y	N	Y	N	Y	N
2 Sharp	N	N	Y	Y	Y	N	Y	Y
3 ***Hiler***	Y	Y	Y	Y	N	Y	N	Y
4 ***Coats***	Y	Y	Y	Y	N	N	N	Y
5 ***Hillis***	Y	Y	N	?	N	Y	N	Y

ND - Northern Democrats SD - Southern Democrats

	1	2	3	4	5	6	7	8
6 ***Burton***	Y	Y	N	Y	N	Y	N	Y
7 ***Myers***	Y	Y	N	N	N	Y	N	Y
8 McCloskey *			Y	N	Y	N	Y	Y
9 Hamilton	N	N	Y	N	Y	Y	Y	Y
10 Jacobs	N	N	Y	Y	Y	N	Y	N
IOWA								
1 ***Leach***	N	Y	Y	Y	Y	N	Y	N
2 ***Tauke***	N	Y	Y	Y	N	N	Y	Y
3 ***Evans***	N	Y	Y	Y	N	Y	N	N
4 Smith	N	N	Y	N	Y	N	Y	N
5 ***Lightfoot***	Y	Y	Y	Y	N	Y	N	Y
6 Bedell	N	N	Y	Y	Y	N	Y	N
KANSAS								
1 ***Roberts***	N	Y	N	Y	N	Y	N	Y
2 Slattery	N	N	Y	Y	N	Y	Y	Y
3 ***Meyers***	Y	Y	N	Y	N	Y	N	Y
4 Glickman	N	N	Y	Y	Y	Y	Y	Y
5 ***Whittaker***	Y	Y	N	Y	N	Y	N	Y
KENTUCKY								
1 Hubbard	Y	N	Y	N	N	Y	N	Y
2 Natcher	N	N	Y	N	Y	N	Y	Y
3 Mazzoli	N	Y	Y	N	N	N	Y	N
4 ***Snyder***	Y	Y	N	Y	N	Y	N	Y
5 ***Rogers***	Y	Y	N	N	N	Y	N	Y
6 ***Hopkins***	Y	Y	Y	Y	N	Y	N	Y
7 Perkins	N	N	Y	N	Y	N	Y	N
LOUISIANA								
1 ***Livingston***	Y	Y	Y	N	N	Y	N	Y
2 Boggs	N	N	Y	N	Y	N	Y	Y
3 Tauzin	Y	N	Y	N	N	Y	N	Y
4 Roemer	Y	N	Y	Y	N	Y	N	Y
5 Huckaby	Y	?	Y	?	N	N	N	Y
6 ***Moore***	Y	Y	Y	N	N	Y	N	Y
7 Breaux	Y	N	Y	N	N	Y	N	Y
8 Long		N	Y	N	N	N	Y	Y
MAINE								
1 ***McKernan***	Y	Y	Y	Y	N	N	N	Y
2 ***Snowe***	Y	Y	Y	Y	N	N	N	Y
MARYLAND								
1 Dyson	Y	N	Y	N	N	Y	N	Y
2 ***Bentley***	Y	Y	N	Y	N	Y	N	Y
3 Mikulski	N	N	Y	N	Y	N	Y	N
4 ***Holt***	Y	Y	N	N	N	Y	N	Y
5 Hoyer	Y	N	Y	N	Y	Y	Y	N
6 Byron	Y	N	Y	N	N	Y	Y	Y
7 Mitchell	N	N	Y	Y	?	N	Y	N
8 Barnes	N	N	Y	Y	Y	N	Y	N
MASSACHUSETTS								
1 ***Conte***	N	Y	Y	Y	Y	N	N	N
2 Boland	N	N	Y	?	Y	N	Y	N
3 Early	N	N	Y	Y	Y	N	Y	N
4 Frank	N	Y	Y	Y	Y	N	Y	N
5 Atkins	N	N	Y	Y	Y	N	Y	N
6 Mavroules	N	N	Y	Y	Y	N	Y	N
7 Markey	N	N	Y	Y	Y	N	Y	N
8 O'Neill								
9 Moakley	N	N	Y	Y	Y	N	Y	N
10 Studds	N	N	Y	Y	Y	N	Y	N
11 Donnelly	N	N	Y	Y	Y	N	Y	N
MICHIGAN								
1 Conyers	N	N	Y	Y	Y	N	Y	N
2 ***Pursell***	Y	Y	?	?	N	Y	Y	Y
3 Wolpe	N	N	Y	Y	Y	N	Y	N
4 ***Siljander***	Y	Y	N	Y	N	Y	N	Y
5 ***Henry***	N	Y	N	Y	N	N	N	Y
6 Carr	N	N	Y	N	Y	N	Y	N
7 Kildee	N	N	Y	Y	Y	N	Y	N
8 Traxler	N	N	Y	N	Y	N	Y	N
9 ***Vander Jagt***	Y	Y	N	Y	N	Y	N	Y
10 ***Schuette***	Y	Y	N	Y	N	Y	N	Y
11 ***Davis***	Y	Y	Y	Y	N	Y	N	Y
12 Bonior	N	N	Y	Y	Y	N	Y	N
13 Crockett	N	N	Y	N	Y	N	N	N
14 Hertel	N	N	Y	Y	Y	N	Y	N
15 Ford	N	N	?	N	Y	N	Y	N
16 Dingell	N	N	?	Y	Y	Y	Y	N
17 Levin	N	N	Y	Y	Y	N	Y	N
18 ***Broomfield***	Y	Y	N	Y	N	Y	N	Y
MINNESOTA								
1 Penny	N	Y	Y	Y	Y	N	Y	N
2 ***Weber***	Y	Y	Y	Y	N	N	N	Y
3 ***Frenzel***	Y	Y	N	Y	N	Y	Y	Y
4 Vento	N	N	Y	Y	Y	N	Y	N
5 Sabo	N	N	Y	N	Y	N	Y	N
6 Sikorski	N	N	Y	Y	Y	N	Y	N
7 ***Stangeland***	Y	Y	N	Y	N	Y	N	Y
8 Oberstar	N	N	Y	Y	Y	N	Y	N
MISSISSIPPI								
1 Whitten	N	N	Y	N	Y	N	Y	Y
2 ***Franklin***	Y	Y	N	N	N	N	N	Y
3 Montgomery	Y	Y	N	N	N	Y	N	Y
4 Dowdy	Y	N	Y	N	N	Y	Y	N
5 ***Lott***	Y	Y	N	N	N	Y	N	Y
MISSOURI								
1 Clay	N	N	Y	Y	Y	N	Y	N
2 Young	N	N	Y	N	Y	Y	N	N
3 Gephardt	N	N	Y	N	Y	Y	Y	N
4 Skelton	Y	N	Y	N	N	Y	Y	Y
5 Wheat	N	N	Y	Y	Y	N	Y	N
6 ***Coleman***	Y	Y	Y	N	N	Y	N	Y
7 ***Taylor***	Y	Y	N	N	N	Y	N	Y
8 ***Emerson***	Y	Y	?	N	N	?	N	Y
9 Volkmer	N	N	Y	N	Y	Y	Y	Y
MONTANA								
1 Williams	N	N	Y	Y	Y	Y	Y	N
2 ***Marlenee***	Y	Y	N	N	N	Y	N	Y
NEBRASKA								
1 ***Bereuter***	N	Y	N	N	N	Y	N	Y
2 ***Daub***	Y	Y	Y	Y	N	Y	N	Y
3 ***Smith***	N	Y	N	N	N	Y	N	Y
NEVADA								
1 Reid	Y	N	Y	N	Y	N	N	N
2 ***Vucanovich***	Y	Y	N	N	N	Y	N	Y
NEW HAMPSHIRE								
1 ***Smith***	Y	Y	N	Y	N	Y	N	Y
2 ***Gregg***	Y	Y	Y	Y	N	N	N	Y
NEW JERSEY								
1 Florio	N	N	Y	Y	Y	N	Y	N
2 Hughes	N	N	Y	Y	Y	Y	Y	N
3 Howard	N	N	Y	Y	Y	N	Y	N
4 ***Smith***	N	Y	Y	Y	N	N	N	Y
5 ***Roukema***	N	Y	Y	Y	Y	N	Y	Y
6 Dwyer	N	N	Y	N	Y	N	Y	N
7 ***Rinaldo***	Y	Y	Y	Y	N	N	N	Y
8 Roe	N	N	Y	Y	Y	N	Y	?
9 Torricelli	N	N	Y	Y	Y	N	Y	N
10 Rodino	N	N	Y	Y	Y	N	Y	N
11 ***Gallo***	Y	Y	Y	Y	N	Y	N	Y
12 ***Courter***	Y	Y	Y	Y	N	Y	N	Y
13 ***Saxton***	Y	Y	Y	Y	N	Y	N	Y
14 Guarini	N	N	Y	Y	Y	N	Y	N
NEW MEXICO								
1 ***Lujan***	Y	Y	N	Y	N	Y	N	Y
2 ***Skeen***	Y	Y	N	N	N	Y	N	Y
3 Richardson	N	N	Y	Y	Y	N	Y	N
NEW YORK								
1 ***Carney***	Y	Y	N	N	N	Y	N	Y
2 Downey	N	N	Y	N	Y	N	Y	N
3 Mrazek	N	N	Y	Y	Y	N	Y	N
4 ***Lent***	Y	Y	Y	N	N	Y	N	Y
5 ***McGrath***	Y	Y	Y	N	N	Y	N	Y
6 Addabbo	N	N	Y	N	Y	N	Y	N
7 Ackerman	N	N	Y	Y	Y	N	Y	N
8 Scheuer	N	N	Y	N	Y	N	?	N
9 Manton	N	N	Y	Y	Y	N	?	N
10 Schumer	N	N	Y	Y	Y	N	Y	N
11 Towns	N	N	Y	Y	Y	N	?	N
12 Owens	N	N	Y	N	Y	N	N	N
13 Solarz	N	N	Y	?	Y	N	Y	N
14 ***Molinari***	Y	Y	Y	N	N	N	N	Y
15 ***Green***	N	Y	Y	Y	Y	N	Y	Y
16 Rangel	N	N	Y	N	Y	N	Y	N
17 Weiss	N	N	Y	Y	Y	N	Y	N
18 Garcia	N	N	Y	N	Y	N	?	N
19 Biaggi	N	N	Y	N	Y	N	N	N
20 ***DioGuardi***	N	Y	Y	N	N	Y	N	Y
21 ***Fish***	Y	Y	Y	N	N	N	Y	Y
22 ***Gilman***	Y	Y	Y	N	N	Y	N	Y
23 Stratton	Y	N	Y	N	N	Y	N	Y
24 ***Solomon***	Y	Y	N	Y	N	Y	N	Y
25 ***Boehlert***	Y	Y	Y	N	N	Y	N	Y
26 ***Martin***	Y	Y	Y	N	N	Y	N	Y
27 ***Wortley***	Y	Y	Y	Y	N	N	N	Y
28 McHugh	N	N	Y	N	Y	N	Y	N
29 ***Horton***	Y	Y	Y	N	N	N	N	N
30 ***Eckert***	Y	Y	N	Y	N	Y	N	Y
31 ***Kemp***	Y	Y	N	N	N	Y	N	Y
32 LaFalce	N	Y	Y	N	Y	N	Y	N
33 Nowak	N	N	Y	N	Y	N	Y	N
34 Lundine	N	N	Y	Y	Y	N	Y	N
NORTH CAROLINA								
1 Jones	N	N	Y	N	Y	N	Y	N
2 Valentine	Y	N	Y	N	N	Y	N	Y
3 Whitley	Y	N	Y	N	Y	Y	N	Y
4 ***Cobey***	Y	Y	N	N	N	Y	N	Y
5 Neal	Y	N	Y	?	Y	Y	Y	N
6 ***Coble***	Y	Y	N	N	N	Y	N	Y
7 Rose	N	N	Y	N	Y	Y	Y	?
8 Hefner	Y	N	Y	N	Y	Y	N	?
9 ***McMillan***	Y	Y	N	Y	N	Y	N	Y
10 ***Broyhill***	Y	Y	N	Y	N	Y	N	Y
11 ***Hendon***	Y	Y	N	Y	N	Y	N	Y
NORTH DAKOTA								
AL Dorgan	N	N	Y	N	Y	N	Y	N
OHIO								
1 Luken	N	N	Y	N	Y	N	?	N
2 ***Gradison***	N	Y	?	Y	N	N	N	Y
3 Hall	N	N	Y	Y	Y	N	Y	?
4 ***Oxley***	Y	Y	N	Y	N	Y	N	Y
5 ***Latta***	Y	Y	N	Y	N	Y	N	Y
6 ***McEwen***	Y	Y	N	Y	N	Y	N	Y
7 ***DeWine***	Y	Y	N	Y	N	Y	N	Y
8 ***Kindness***	Y	Y	N	Y	N	Y	N	Y
9 Kaptur	N	N	Y	N	Y	N	Y	N
10 ***Miller***	Y	Y	N	N	N	Y	N	Y
11 Eckart	N	N	Y	N	Y	N	Y	N
12 ***Kasich***	Y	Y	Y	N	N	Y	N	Y
13 Pease	N	N	Y	N	Y	N	Y	N
14 Seiberling	N	N	Y	Y	Y	N	Y	N
15 ***Wylie***	Y	Y	Y	?	N	Y	N	Y
16 ***Regula***	Y	Y	N	Y	N	N	N	Y
17 Traficant	N	N	Y	Y	Y	N	Y	N
18 Applegate	N	Y	Y	N	Y	N	Y	N
19 Feighan	N	N	Y	N	Y	N	Y	N
20 Oakar	N	N	Y	N	Y	N	Y	N
21 Stokes	N	N	Y	?	Y	N	Y	N
OKLAHOMA								
1 Jones	N	N	Y	N	N	Y	Y	Y
2 Synar	N	N	Y	N	Y	N	Y	N
3 Watkins	Y	N	Y	N	N	N	Y	Y
4 McCurdy	Y	N	Y	N	N	Y	N	Y
5 ***Edwards***	Y	?	?	N	N	Y	N	Y
6 English	Y	Y	Y	N	N	Y	N	Y
OREGON								
1 AuCoin	N	N	Y	N	Y	N	Y	N
2 ***Smith, R.***	Y	Y	N	Y	N	N	N	Y
3 Wyden	N	N	Y	N	Y	N	Y	N
4 Weaver	N	?	Y	?	Y	N	Y	N
5 ***Smith, D.***	Y	Y	N	Y	N	Y	N	Y
PENNSYLVANIA								
1 Foglietta	N	N	Y	Y	Y	N	Y	N
2 Gray	N	N	Y	Y	Y	N	Y	N
3 Borski	N	N	Y	Y	Y	N	Y	N
4 Kolter	N	N	Y	N	Y	N	Y	N
5 ***Schulze***	Y	Y	Y	Y	?	Y	N	Y
6 Yatron	Y	N	Y	N	Y	N	Y	N
7 Edgar	N	N	Y	Y	Y	N	Y	N
8 Kostmayer	N	N	Y	Y	Y	N	Y	N
9 ***Shuster***	Y	Y	N	Y	N	Y	N	Y
10 ***McDade***	Y	Y	Y	N	N	N	Y	Y
11 Kanjorski	N	N	Y	N	Y	N	Y	N
12 Murtha	Y	N	Y	N	N	Y	N	Y
13 ***Coughlin***	N	Y	Y	Y	N	N	Y	Y
14 Coyne	N	N	Y	Y	Y	N	Y	N
15 ***Ritter***	Y	Y	N	Y	N	Y	N	Y
16 ***Walker***	Y	Y	N	Y	N	N	N	Y
17 ***Gekas***	Y	Y	Y	Y	N	Y	N	Y
18 Walgren	N	N	Y	N	Y	Y	Y	N
19 ***Goodling***	N	Y	Y	Y	N	Y	N	Y
20 Gaydos	N	N	Y	N	Y	N	?	N
21 ***Ridge***	N	Y	N	Y	N	Y	Y	Y
22 Murphy	N	N	Y	N	N	Y	Y	N
23 ***Clinger***	Y	Y	N	Y	Y	N	N	Y
RHODE ISLAND								
1 St Germain	N	N	Y	?	Y	N	Y	N
2 ***Schneider***	N	Y	Y	Y	Y	N	Y	Y
SOUTH CAROLINA								
1 ***Hartnett***	Y	Y	N	Y	N	Y	N	Y
2 ***Spence***	Y	Y	N	N	N	Y	N	Y
3 Derrick	N	N	Y	?	Y	N	Y	N
4 ***Campbell***	Y	Y	N	N	N	Y	N	Y
5 Spratt	N	N	+	+	Y	Y	Y	Y
6 Tallon	N	N	Y	Y	N	Y	N	Y
SOUTH DAKOTA								
AL Daschle	N	N	Y	N	Y	N	?	N
TENNESSEE								
1 ***Quillen***	Y	Y	N	N	N	Y	N	Y
2 ***Duncan***	Y	Y	Y	N	N	Y	N	Y
3 Lloyd	Y	Y	Y	N	N	Y	N	Y
4 Cooper	Y	N	Y	Y	N	N	Y	N
5 Boner	Y	N	Y	N	N	Y	Y	N
6 Gordon	N	N	Y	N	N	N	Y	N
7 ***Sundquist***	Y	Y	N	Y	N	Y	N	Y
8 Jones	Y	N	Y	N	Y	Y	N	N
9 Ford	N	N	Y	Y	Y	N	Y	N
TEXAS								
1 Chapman								
2 Wilson	Y	N	?	?	N	Y	N	Y
3 ***Bartlett***	Y	Y	N	Y	N	Y	N	Y
4 Hall, R.	Y	Y	N	N	N	Y	N	Y
5 Bryant	N	N	Y	Y	Y	Y	Y	N
6 ***Barton***	Y	Y	N	Y	N	Y	N	Y
7 ***Archer***	Y	Y	N	Y	N	Y	N	Y
8 ***Fields***	Y	Y	N	Y	N	Y	N	Y
9 Brooks	N	N	Y	N	Y	Y	Y	N
10 Pickle	N	N	Y	N	Y	N	N	Y
11 Leath	Y	Y	N	?	N	Y	N	Y
12 Wright	N	N	Y	N	Y	Y	Y	?
13 ***Boulter***	Y	Y	N	N	N	Y	N	Y
14 ***Sweeney***	Y	Y	N	Y	N	Y	N	Y
15 de la Garza	Y	N	Y	Y	N	Y	N	N
16 Coleman	N	N	Y	N	Y	Y	Y	N
17 Stenholm	Y	Y	Y	Y	N	Y	N	Y
18 Leland	N	N	Y	Y	Y	N	Y	N
19 ***Combest***	Y	Y	N	Y	N	Y	N	Y
20 Gonzalez	N	N	Y	N	Y	N	Y	N
21 ***Loeffler***	Y	Y	N	N	N	Y	N	Y
22 ***DeLay***	Y	Y	N	N	N	Y	N	Y
23 Bustamante	Y	N	Y	N	?	Y	Y	N
24 Frost	Y	N	Y	N	Y	Y	Y	N
25 Andrews	Y	N	Y	Y	Y	Y	Y	Y
26 ***Armey***	Y	Y	N	Y	N	N	N	Y
27 Ortiz	Y	N	Y	N	N	Y	Y	N
UTAH								
1 ***Hansen***	Y	Y	N	Y	N	Y	N	Y
2 ***Monson***	Y	Y	N	Y	N	Y	N	Y
3 ***Nielson***	Y	Y	N	Y	N	Y	N	Y
VERMONT								
AL ***Jeffords***	N	Y	Y	Y	Y	?	?	N
VIRGINIA								
1 ***Bateman***	Y	Y	N	N	N	Y	N	Y
2 ***Whitehurst***	Y	Y	N	N	N	Y	N	Y
3 ***Bliley***	Y	Y	Y	N	N	Y	N	Y
4 Sisisky	N	N	Y	N	N	Y	N	N
5 Daniel	Y	Y	N	N	N	Y	N	?
6 Olin	N	Y	Y	Y	Y	N	N	N
7 ***Slaughter***	Y	Y	N	N	N	Y	N	Y
8 ***Parris***	Y	Y	N	Y	N	Y	N	Y
9 Boucher	N	N	Y	N	Y	Y	Y	N
10 ***Wolf***	Y	Y	N	Y	N	Y	N	Y
WASHINGTON								
1 ***Miller***	N	Y	Y	Y	N	Y	N	Y
2 Swift	N	N	Y	N	Y	N	Y	N
3 Bonker	N	N	Y	N	Y	N	Y	N
4 ***Morrison***	Y	Y	Y	N	N	Y	N	Y
5 Foley	N	N	Y	N	Y	N	Y	N
6 Dicks	Y	N	Y	N	Y	Y	Y	N
7 Lowry	N	N	Y	Y	Y	N	Y	N
8 ***Chandler***	Y	Y	N	Y	N	Y	N	Y
WEST VIRGINIA								
1 Mollohan	Y	N	Y	N	N	Y	N	Y
2 Staggers	N	N	Y	N	Y	N	Y	N
3 Wise	N	Y	Y	?	Y	N	Y	N
4 Rahall	N	N	Y	N	Y	N	Y	N
WISCONSIN								
1 Aspin	Y	N	Y	N	Y	Y	Y	N
2 Kastenmeier	N	N	Y	Y	Y	N	Y	N
3 ***Gunderson***	Y	Y	N	Y	N	N	N	Y
4 Kleczka	N	N	Y	N	Y	N	Y	N
5 Moody	N	N	Y	Y	Y	N	Y	N
6 ***Petri***	N	Y	N	Y	N	Y	N	Y
7 Obey	N	N	Y	N	Y	N	Y	N
8 ***Roth***	Y	Y	N	N	N	N	N	Y
9 ***Sensenbrenner***	N	Y	N	Y	N	N	N	Y
WYOMING								
AL ***Cheney***	Y	Y	N	N	N	Y	N	Y

Southern states - Ala., Ark., Fla., Ga., Ky., La., Miss., N.C., Okla., S.C., Tenn., Texas, Va.

9. HR 2100. Farm Programs Reauthorization, Fiscal 1986-90. Madigan, R-Ill., amendment to strike the wheat and feed grain farmer referendum section from the bill. The farmer referendum would have been on the question of establishing a marketing certificate and export subsidy program for domestic wheat and feed grain production. Adopted 251-174: R 169-10; D 82-164 (ND 53-112, SD 29-52), Oct. 3, 1985. A "yea" was a vote supporting the president's position.

10. HR 1562. Textile Import Quotas. Passage of the bill to impose new quota restrictions on textile imports. Passed 262-159: R 75-97; D 187-62 (ND 118-49, SD 69-13), Oct. 10, 1985. A "nay" was a vote supporting the president's position.

11. HR 3500. Omnibus Budget Reconciliation, Fiscal 1986. Latta, R-Ohio, amendment to eliminate new programs and increased spending authorized in the bill, to remove transportation trust funds from the budget in fiscal year 1989, and to reduce proposed salary increases for federal civilian employees. Rejected 209-219: R 166-15; D 43-204 (ND 15-151, SD 28-53), Oct. 24, 1985.

12. H J Res 372. Public Debt Limit. Rostenkowski, D-Ill., motion to recede from the House position and concur with the Senate amendment to the bill to increase the public debt limit, with a substitute amendment to provide for declining annual statutory limits on the federal debt, automatic deficit reduction and, under certain circumstances, procedural revisions in the congressional budget process. Motion agreed to 249-180: R 1-178; D 248-2 (ND 167-2, SD 81-0), Nov. 1, 1985.

13. HR 1616. Plant Closing Notification. Passage of the bill to require employers of at least 50 full-time employees to give workers 90 days' notice of any plant shutdown or layoff involving at least 100 employees or 30 percent of the work force. Rejected 203-208: R 20-154; D 183-54 (ND 153-5, SD 30-49), Nov. 21, 1985.

14. HR 2817. Superfund Reauthorization, Fiscal 1986-90. Downey, D-N.Y., amendment to strike provisions for a broad-based or "value-added" tax and to provide $10 billion over five years for the "superfund" hazardous-waste cleanup program through increased taxes on chemical feedstocks, petroleum and hazardous-waste disposal and through general revenues. Adopted 220-206: R 73-105; D 147-101 (ND 127-42, SD 20-59), Dec. 10, 1985.

15. HR 3838. Tax Overhaul. Adoption of the rule (H Res 336) to provide for House floor consideration of the bill to restructure the income tax laws; reduce tax rates for individuals and corporations; increase the personal exemption and standard deduction; eliminate the investment tax credit; eliminate or curtail a variety of other deductions and credits; create a new alternative minimum tax for individuals and corporations; and make other changes. Rejected 202-223: R 14-164; D 188-59 (ND 135-33, SD 53-26), Dec. 11, 1985. A "yea" was a vote supporting the president's position.

16. HR 3838. Tax Overhaul. Adoption of the rule (H Res 343) to provide for House floor consideration of the bill to revise the federal income tax system by: lowering individual and corporate tax rates; increasing the personal exemption and standard deduction; eliminating the investment tax credit; eliminating or curtailing a variety of other deductions and credits; creating a new alternative minimum tax for individuals and corporations; and making other changes. Adopted 258-168: R 70-110; D 188-58 (ND 138-28, SD 50-30), Dec. 17, 1985. A "yea" was a vote supporting the president's position.

KEY

- Y Voted for (yea).
- # Paired for.
- + Announced for.
- N Voted against (nay).
- X Paired against.
- \- Announced against.
- P Voted "present."
- C Voted "present" to avoid possible conflict of interest.
- ? Did not vote or otherwise make a position known.

Democrats ***Republicans***

	9	10	11	12	13	14	15	16
ALABAMA								
1 ***Callahan***	N	Y	Y	N	N	N	N	Y
2 ***Dickinson***	N	Y	Y	N	N	N	N	N
3 Nichols	N	Y	Y	Y	N	N	Y	Y
4 Bevill	N	Y	N	Y	Y	N	Y	Y
5 Flippo	Y	Y	N	Y	N	N	Y	Y
6 Erdreich	N	Y	N	Y	N	N	Y	Y
7 Shelby	N	Y	Y	Y	N	N	N	N
ALASKA								
AL ***Young***	Y	Y	N	N	Y	N	N	N
ARIZONA								
1 ***McCain***	Y	N	Y	N	N	Y	N	N
2 Udall	N	N	N	Y	Y	N	Y	Y
3 ***Stump***	Y	N	Y	N	N	N	N	N
4 ***Rudd***	Y	?	Y	N	N	Y	N	N
5 ***Kolbe***	Y	N	Y	N	N	N	N	N
ARKANSAS								
1 Alexander	N	Y	N	Y	Y	N	Y	Y
2 Robinson	N	Y	Y	Y	Y	Y	N	N
3 ***Hammerschmidt***	Y	Y	Y	Y	N	N	N	Y
4 Anthony	N	Y	N	Y	N	N	Y	Y
CALIFORNIA								
1 Bosco	N	N	N	Y	Y	N	Y	Y
2 ***Chappie***	Y	N	Y	N	X	X	?	N
3 Matsui	N	N	N	Y	Y	Y	Y	Y
4 Fazio	N	Y	N	Y	Y	N	N	N
5 Burton	N	Y	N	Y	Y	Y	Y	Y
6 Boxer	N	Y	N	Y	Y	Y	Y	Y
7 Miller	N	N	N	Y	Y	N	Y	Y
8 Dellums	N	Y	N	Y	Y	Y	N	Y
9 Stark	N	N	N	Y	Y	Y	Y	Y
10 Edwards	N	Y	N	Y	Y	Y	Y	Y
11 Lantos	N	Y	N	Y	Y	Y	Y	Y
12 ***Zschau***	Y	N	Y	N	N	Y	N	N
13 Mineta	N	N	N	Y	Y	Y	Y	Y
14 ***Shumway***	Y	N	Y	N	N	N	N	N
15 Coelho	N	Y	?	Y	Y	N	Y	Y
16 Panetta	N	N	N	Y	Y	Y	Y	Y
17 ***Pashayan***	Y	Y	Y	N	N	Y	N	N
18 Lehman	N	Y	N	Y	Y	Y	Y	Y
19 ***Lagomarsino***	Y	N	Y	N	N	N	Y	Y
20 ***Thomas***	Y	Y	Y	N	N	N	N	N
21 ***Fiedler***	Y	Y	Y	N	N	N	N	N
22 ***Moorhead***	Y	N	Y	N	N	N	N	N
23 Beilenson	N	N	N	Y	Y	Y	?	Y
24 Waxman	Y	N	N	Y	Y	Y	Y	Y
25 Roybal	N	N	N	Y	Y	Y	Y	N
26 Berman	?	N	N	Y	Y	Y	Y	Y
27 Levine	Y	N	N	Y	Y	Y	Y	Y
28 Dixon	N	Y	N	Y	Y	Y	Y	Y
29 Hawkins	N	Y	N	Y	#	Y	N	Y
30 Martinez	N	Y	N	Y	Y	Y	Y	Y
31 Dymally	N	N	N	Y	?	Y	Y	X
32 Anderson	Y	N	N	Y	Y	N	Y	Y
33 ***Dreier***	Y	N	Y	N	N	N	N	N
34 Torres	N	Y	N	Y	Y	Y	Y	Y
35 ***Lewis***	Y	N	N	N	N	N	N	N
36 Brown	N	Y	X	Y	?	Y	Y	Y
37 ***McCandless***	Y	N	Y	N	N	N	N	N
38 ***Dornan***	Y	N	Y	N	N	N	N	Y
39 ***Dannemeyer***	Y	N	Y	N	N	N	N	N
40 ***Badham***	Y	N	Y	?	N	N	N	Y
41 ***Lowery***	Y	N	Y	N	N	N	N	N
42 ***Lungren***	Y	?	Y	N	N	Y	N	N
43 ***Packard***	Y	N	Y	N	N	N	N	N
44 Bates	Y	Y	N	Y	Y	Y	Y	Y
45 ***Hunter***	Y	Y	Y	N	N	N	N	N
COLORADO								
1 Schroeder	Y	N	N	Y	N	Y	N	N
2 Wirth	N	N	N	Y	Y	N	Y	Y
3 ***Strang***	Y	-	Y	N	N	N	N	N
4 ***Brown***	Y	N	Y	N	N	N	N	N
5 ***Kramer***	Y	N	Y	N	?	N	N	N
6 ***Schaefer***	Y	N	Y	N	N	N	N	N
CONNECTICUT								
1 Kennelly	Y	Y	N	Y	Y	Y	Y	Y
2 Gejdenson	N	Y	N	Y	Y	Y	Y	Y
3 Morrison	N	Y	N	Y	Y	Y	Y	Y
4 ***McKinney***	Y	Y	N	N	?	?	?	?
5 ***Rowland***	Y	N	Y	N	N	Y	N	Y
6 ***Johnson***	Y	N	Y	N	N	Y	Y	Y
DELAWARE								
AL Carper	Y	Y	N	Y	Y	N	Y	Y
FLORIDA								
1 Hutto	Y	Y	Y	Y	N	N	N	N
2 Fuqua	Y	Y	N	Y	N	N	Y	Y
3 Bennett	N	N	N	Y	Y	Y	N	N
4 Chappell	Y	Y	N	Y	N	N	Y	Y
5 ***McCollum***	Y	N	Y	N	N	N	N	N
6 MacKay	Y	N	Y	Y	N	Y	Y	Y
7 Gibbons	Y	N	N	Y	N	N	Y	Y
8 ***Young***	Y	N	Y	N	N	Y	N	Y
9 ***Bilirakis***	Y	Y	Y	N	N	Y	N	Y
10 ***Ireland***	Y	N	Y	N	N	Y	N	Y
11 Nelson	Y	N	#	Y	X	#	+	#
12 ***Lewis***	Y	N	Y	N	N	N	N	N
13 ***Mack***	Y	N	Y	N	N	Y	N	N
14 Mica	N	N	Y	Y	N	Y	Y	Y
15 ***Shaw***	Y	N	Y	N	N	Y	N	N
16 Smith	N	Y	Y	Y	Y	Y	Y	Y
17 Lehman	Y	Y	N	Y	Y	Y	Y	Y
18 Pepper	N	Y	N	Y	Y	Y	Y	Y
19 Fascell	N	Y	N	Y	Y	Y	Y	Y
GEORGIA								
1 Thomas	Y	Y	Y	Y	N	N	Y	Y
2 Hatcher	N	Y	Y	Y	N	N	Y	Y
3 Ray	Y	Y	Y	Y	N	N	N	N
4 ***Swindall***	Y	Y	Y	N	N	N	N	N
5 Fowler	N	Y	N	Y	N	N	N	Y
6 ***Gingrich***	Y	Y	Y	N	N	N	N	N
7 Darden	N	Y	Y	Y	N	Y	N	N
8 Rowland	Y	Y	Y	Y	N	N	Y	Y
9 Jenkins	Y	Y	Y	Y	N	N	Y	Y
10 Barnard	Y	Y	Y	Y	N	Y	Y	Y
HAWAII								
1 Heftel	Y	N	N	Y	Y	N	Y	Y
2 Akaka	N	N	N	Y	Y	Y	Y	Y
IDAHO								
1 ***Craig***	Y	N	Y	N	N	N	N	N
2 Stallings	N	N	Y	Y	#	Y	Y	Y
ILLINOIS								
1 Hayes	N	Y	N	Y	Y	Y	Y	Y
2 Savage	N	Y	N	Y	Y	Y	N	Y
3 Russo	N	Y	N	Y	Y	N	Y	Y
4 ***O'Brien***	Y	?	Y	N	N	N	N	Y
5 Lipinski	N	Y	N	Y	Y	Y	Y	Y
6 ***Hyde***	Y	X	Y	N	N	Y	N	Y
7 Collins	N	Y	N	Y	Y	Y	Y	Y
8 Rostenkowski	Y	N	N	Y	Y	Y	Y	Y
9 Yates	Y	N	N	Y	Y	Y	Y	Y
10 ***Porter***	Y	-	Y	N	N	Y	N	Y
11 Annunzio	N	Y	N	Y	Y	Y	Y	Y
12 ***Crane***	Y	N	Y	N	X	N	N	N
13 ***Fawell***	Y	N	Y	N	N	Y	N	Y
14 ***Grotberg***	Y	N	Y	N	N	N	N	Y
15 ***Madigan***	Y	N	Y	N	Y	Y	N	N
16 ***Martin***	Y	?	Y	N	N	Y	N	N
17 Evans	N	Y	N	Y	Y	Y	Y	Y
18 ***Michel***	Y	N	Y	N	N	Y	N	Y
19 Bruce	Y	Y	Y	Y	Y	N	Y	Y
20 Durbin	Y	Y	Y	Y	Y	Y	Y	Y
21 Price	N	Y	N	Y	?	?	?	?
22 Gray	Y	Y	N	Y	Y	N	Y	?
INDIANA								
1 Visclosky	Y	Y	N	Y	Y	N	Y	Y
2 Sharp	Y	N	Y	Y	Y	Y	Y	Y
3 ***Hiler***	Y	N	Y	N	N	Y	N	N
4 ***Coats***	Y	N	Y	N	N	Y	N	Y
5 ***Hillis***	Y	Y	Y	N	?	N	N	?

ND - Northern Democrats SD - Southern Democrats

	9	10	11	12	13	14	15	16
6 ***Burton***	Y	N	Y	N	N	N	N	N
7 ***Myers***	Y	N	Y	N	N	N	N	N
8 McCloskey	Y	Y	N	Y	Y	Y	Y	Y
9 Hamilton	Y	N	Y	Y	Y	Y	N	N
10 Jacobs	Y	N	N	Y	Y	N	N	N
IOWA								
1 ***Leach***	Y	N	Y	N	Y	Y	Y	Y
2 ***Tauke***	Y	N	Y	N	N	Y	N	Y
3 ***Evans***	N	N	Y	N	N	Y	N	Y
4 Smith	Y	N	N	Y	?	Y	Y	Y
5 ***Lightfoot***	Y	N	Y	N	N	Y	N	N
6 Bedell	N	C	Y	Y	Y	Y	Y	Y
KANSAS								
1 ***Roberts***	Y	N	Y	N	N	N	N	N
2 Slattery	N	N	Y	Y	Y	N	Y	Y
3 ***Meyers***	Y	N	Y	N	N	Y	Y	Y
4 Glickman	N	N	Y	Y	Y	N	Y	Y
5 ***Whittaker***	Y	N	Y	N	N	N	N	N
KENTUCKY								
1 Hubbard	Y	Y	N	Y	?	N	N	N
2 Natcher	N	Y	N	Y	Y	N	Y	Y
3 Mazzoli	Y	N	N	Y	Y	N	Y	N
4 ***Snyder***	Y	Y	Y	N	N	N	Y	Y
5 ***Rogers***	Y	Y	Y	N	N	N	-	Y
6 ***Hopkins***	Y	Y	Y	N	N	Y	?	Y
7 Perkins	N	Y	N	Y	Y	N	Y	Y
LOUISIANA								
1 ***Livingston***	Y	?	Y	N	N	N	N	N
2 Boggs	Y	Y	N	Y	Y	N	Y	Y
3 Tauzin	Y	Y	N	Y	N	N	N	N
4 Roemer	Y	N	Y	Y	N	N	N	N
5 Huckaby	N	Y	N	Y	N	N	N	N
6 ***Moore***	Y	N	Y	N	N	N	N	N
7 Breaux	Y	Y	N	Y	Y	N	N	N
8 Long	Y	Y	N	Y	Y	N	N	N
MAINE								
1 ***McKernan***	Y	Y	Y	N	N	Y	N	Y
2 ***Snowe***	Y	Y	Y	N	N	Y	N	Y
MARYLAND								
1 Dyson	Y	Y	N	Y	Y	Y	N	N
2 ***Bentley***	Y	Y	Y	N	N	N	N	Y
3 Mikulski	Y	Y	N	Y	Y	Y	N	N
4 ***Holt***	Y	N	N	N	N	Y	N	Y
5 Hoyer	N	Y	N	Y	Y	Y	N	N
6 Byron	Y	Y	N	Y	N	Y	N	Y
7 Mitchell	N	Y	N	Y	Y	Y	N	Y
8 Barnes	Y	Y	N	Y	Y	Y	N	N
MASSACHUSETTS								
1 ***Conte***	Y	Y	N	N	Y	Y	N	Y
2 Boland	Y	Y	N	Y	Y	N	Y	Y
3 Early	Y	Y	N	Y	Y	Y	Y	Y
4 Frank	Y	Y	N	Y	Y	Y	Y	Y
5 Atkins	N	Y	N	Y	?	Y	Y	Y
6 Mavroules	N	Y	N	Y	Y	Y	Y	Y
7 Markey	Y	Y	N	Y	Y	Y	Y	Y
8 O'Neill								
9 Moakley	N	Y	N	Y	Y	Y	Y	Y
10 Studds	Y	Y	N	Y	Y	Y	Y	Y
11 Donnelly	N	Y	N	Y	Y	Y	Y	Y
MICHIGAN								
1 Conyers	N	Y	X	Y	?	Y	N	N
2 ***Pursell***	Y	N	Y	N	N	Y	N	Y
3 Wolpe	N	Y	N	Y	Y	Y	Y	Y
4 ***Siljander***	Y	N	Y	N	N	N	N	N
5 ***Henry***	Y	Y	Y	N	N	Y	N	Y
6 Carr	Y	Y	Y	Y	Y	Y	N	N
7 Kildee	N	#	N	Y	Y	Y	N	N
8 Traxler	N	Y	N	Y	Y	Y	Y	Y
9 ***Vander Jagt***	Y	N	Y	N	N	N	N	Y
10 ***Schuette***	N	Y	Y	N	N	N	N	Y
11 ***Davis***	Y	Y	Y	N	Y	Y	N	Y
12 Bonior	N	Y	N	Y	#	Y	Y	Y
13 Crockett	N	N	N	N	Y	Y	Y	Y
14 Hertel	N	Y	N	Y	Y	Y	Y	Y
15 Ford	?	Y	N	Y	Y	Y	Y	Y
16 Dingell	N	Y	N	Y	Y	N	Y	Y
17 Levin	N	Y	N	Y	Y	Y	Y	Y
18 ***Broomfield***	Y	N	Y	N	N	Y	N	Y
MINNESOTA								
1 Penny	N	N	Y	Y	Y	Y	Y	Y
2 ***Weber***	N	N	Y	N	N	#	N	N
3 ***Frenzel***	Y	N	Y	N	N	Y	N	N
4 Vento	N	Y	N	Y	Y	Y	Y	Y
5 Sabo	N	N	N	Y	Y	Y	Y	Y
6 Sikorski	N	Y	N	Y	Y	Y	Y	Y
7 ***Stangeland***	Y	N	Y	N	N	N	Y	Y
8 Oberstar	N	Y	N	Y	Y	Y	Y	Y
MISSISSIPPI								
1 Whitten	N	Y	N	Y	Y	Y	Y	Y
2 ***Franklin***	Y	Y	Y	N	N	N	N	N
3 Montgomery	Y	Y	Y	Y	N	N	Y	Y
4 Dowdy	N	Y	Y	Y	N	N	N	N
5 ***Lott***	Y	Y	Y	N	N	N	N	N
MISSOURI								
1 Clay	?	Y	N	Y	Y	Y	N	N
2 Young	N	Y	N	Y	Y	N	N	?
3 Gephardt	N	Y	N	Y	Y	N	Y	Y
4 Skelton	N	Y	N	Y	Y	Y	N	N
5 Wheat	N	Y	N	Y	Y	Y	Y	Y
6 ***Coleman***	N	N	Y	N	N	Y	N	N
7 ***Taylor***	Y	Y	Y	N	N	Y	N	Y
8 ***Emerson***	Y	Y	Y	N	N	N	N	N
9 Volkmer	N	Y	Y	Y	Y	N	Y	Y
MONTANA								
1 Williams	N	Y	N	Y	Y	N	Y	Y
2 ***Marlenee***	Y	N	Y	?	N	N	N	N
NEBRASKA								
1 ***Bereuter***	N	N	Y	N	N	N	N	N
2 ***Daub***	Y	N	Y	N	N	N	Y	Y
3 ***Smith***	N	N	Y	N	N	N	N	Y
NEVADA								
1 Reid	Y	Y	N	Y	Y	Y	Y	Y
2 ***Vucanovich***	Y	N	Y	N	N	Y	N	N
NEW HAMPSHIRE								
1 ***Smith***	Y	Y	Y	N	N	Y	N	N
2 ***Gregg***	Y	Y	Y	N	N	Y	N	N
NEW JERSEY								
1 Florio	N	Y	N	Y	Y	Y	Y	Y
2 Hughes	Y	Y	N	Y	Y	Y	N	N
3 Howard	N	Y	N	Y	Y	Y	Y	Y
4 ***Smith***	Y	Y	N	N	Y	Y	N	N
5 ***Roukema***	Y	Y	Y	N	N	N	N	Y
6 Dwyer	N	Y	N	Y	Y	Y	Y	Y
7 ***Rinaldo***	Y	Y	N	N	Y	Y	N	N
8 Roe	N	Y	N	Y	Y	N	N	N
9 Torricelli	N	Y	N	Y	Y	Y	Y	Y
10 Rodino	?	Y	N	Y	Y	Y	Y	Y
11 ***Gallo***	Y	N	Y	N	N	N	N	N
12 ***Courter***	Y	N	Y	N	N	N	N	Y
13 ***Saxton***	Y	N	Y	N	N	N	N	N
14 Guarini	N	Y	N	Y	Y	Y	Y	Y
NEW MEXICO								
1 ***Lujan***	Y	N	Y	N	N	N	N	Y
2 ***Skeen***	Y	Y	Y	N	N	N	N	Y
3 Richardson	N	Y	N	Y	Y	N	Y	Y
NEW YORK								
1 ***Carney***	Y	Y	Y	N	N	N	N	Y
2 Downey	N	N	N	Y	Y	Y	Y	Y
3 Mrazek	Y	Y	Y	Y	Y	Y	Y	Y
4 ***Lent***	Y	Y	Y	N	N	N	N	Y
5 ***McGrath***	Y	Y	Y	N	N	Y	Y	Y
6 Addabbo	?	?	?	?	?	Y	Y	Y
7 Ackerman	Y	Y	N	Y	Y	Y	Y	Y
8 Scheuer	N	N	N	Y	Y	Y	Y	Y
9 Manton	N	Y	N	Y	Y	N	Y	Y
10 Schumer	Y	N	N	Y	Y	Y	Y	Y
11 Towns	N	Y	N	Y	Y	Y	Y	Y
12 Owens	N	Y	N	Y	Y	Y	Y	Y
13 Solarz	Y	N	N	Y	Y	Y	Y	Y
14 ***Molinari***	Y	N	N	N	N	Y	N	N
15 ***Green***	Y	N	N	N	N	Y	N	N
16 Rangel	N	Y	N	Y	Y	Y	Y	Y
17 Weiss	N	Y	N	Y	Y	Y	Y	Y
18 Garcia	N	Y	N	Y	Y	Y	Y	Y
19 Biaggi	Y	Y	N	Y	#	Y	Y	Y
20 ***DioGuardi***	Y	Y	Y	N	N	N	N	N
21 ***Fish***	Y	Y	N	N	Y	Y	N	N
22 ***Gilman***	Y	Y	N	N	Y	N	N	Y
23 Stratton	Y	Y	Y	Y	Y	Y	Y	Y
24 ***Solomon***	Y	?	Y	N	N	Y	N	N
25 ***Boehlert***	Y	Y	Y	N	Y	Y	N	N
26 ***Martin***	Y	Y	Y	N	N	Y	N	N
27 ***Wortley***	Y	N	Y	N	N	Y	N	N
28 McHugh	N	N	N	Y	Y	Y	Y	Y
29 ***Horton***	Y	Y	N	N	#	Y	N	N
30 ***Eckert***	Y	N	Y	N	N	N	N	Y
31 ***Kemp***	Y	N	Y	N	N	N	N	Y
32 LaFalce	Y	N	N	Y	Y	Y	Y	Y
33 Nowak	Y	Y	N	Y	Y	Y	Y	Y
34 Lundine	Y	Y	N	Y	N	Y	Y	Y
NORTH CAROLINA								
1 Jones	N	Y	N	Y	N	N	Y	Y
2 Valentine	N	Y	N	Y	N	Y	N	N
3 Whitley	N	Y	N	Y	N	Y	Y	Y
4 ***Cobey***	Y	Y	Y	N	N	N	N	N
5 Neal	N	Y	N	?	N	Y	Y	Y
6 ***Coble***	Y	Y	Y	N	N	N	N	N
7 Rose	N	Y	N	Y	?	N	Y	Y
8 Hefner	N	Y	N	Y	N	N	Y	Y
9 ***McMillan***	Y	Y	Y	N	N	N	N	Y
10 ***Broyhill***	Y	Y	Y	N	N	N	N	N
11 ***Hendon***	Y	Y	Y	N	N	N	N	Y
NORTH DAKOTA								
AL Dorgan	N	N	N	Y	Y	Y	Y	Y
OHIO								
1 Luken	Y	N	N	Y	Y	Y	Y	Y
2 ***Gradison***	?	N	Y	N	N	N	Y	Y
3 Hall	N	Y	N	Y	Y	Y	Y	Y
4 ***Oxley***	Y	N	Y	N	N	N	N	N
5 ***Latta***	Y	N	Y	N	N	Y	N	Y
6 ***McEwen***	?	N	Y	N	N	Y	N	N
7 ***DeWine***	Y	N	Y	N	N	Y	N	Y
8 ***Kindness***	?	Y	Y	N	N	Y	N	N
9 Kaptur	Y	Y	N	Y	Y	Y	N	N
10 ***Miller***	Y	Y	Y	N	N	?	N	Y
11 Eckart	Y	Y	N	Y	Y	N	N	Y
12 ***Kasich***	Y	N	Y	N	N	N	N	N
13 Pease	Y	N	N	Y	Y	Y	Y	Y
14 Seiberling	N	N	N	Y	Y	Y	Y	Y
15 ***Wylie***	Y	Y	Y	N	N	Y	Y	Y
16 ***Regula***	Y	Y	Y	N	N	Y	N	Y
17 Traficant	N	Y	N	Y	Y	Y	N	N
18 Applegate	Y	Y	N	Y	Y	Y	N	N
19 Feighan	N	Y	N	Y	Y	N	Y	N
20 Oakar	N	Y	N	Y	Y	N	Y	N
21 Stokes	N	Y	N	Y	Y	Y	N	N
OKLAHOMA								
1 Jones	N	N	Y	Y	N	N	N	N
2 Synar	N	N	N	Y	N	N	Y	Y
3 Watkins	N	N	N	Y	N	N	N	N
4 McCurdy	N	N	Y	Y	N	N	N	N
5 ***Edwards***	N	N	Y	N	N	N	N	N
6 English	N	N	Y	Y	N	N	N	N
OREGON								
1 AuCoin	Y	N	N	Y	N	Y	N	N
2 ***Smith, R.***	Y	N	Y	N	X	N	N	N
3 Wyden	Y	N	N	Y	N	Y	N	N
4 Weaver	N	Y	N	Y	Y	Y	Y	Y
5 ***Smith, D.***	Y	N	#	N	N	Y	N	N
PENNSYLVANIA								
1 Foglietta	N	Y	N	Y	Y	N	Y	Y
2 Gray	N	Y	N	Y	Y	N	Y	Y
3 Borski	N	Y	N	Y	Y	N	Y	Y
4 Kolter	N	Y	N	Y	Y	N	Y	N
5 ***Schulze***	Y	Y	Y	N	N	N	N	N
6 Yatron	Y	Y	Y	Y	Y	Y	Y	Y
7 Edgar	N	Y	N	Y	Y	Y	Y	Y
8 Kostmayer	Y	Y	Y	Y	Y	N	Y	Y
9 ***Shuster***	Y	Y	Y	N	N	Y	N	N
10 ***McDade***	Y	Y	Y	N	Y	Y	N	Y
11 Kanjorski	Y	Y	N	N	Y	Y	Y	Y
12 Murtha	N	Y	N	Y	Y	N	Y	Y
13 ***Coughlin***	Y	Y	Y	N	Y	N	N	N
14 Coyne	N	Y	N	Y	Y	Y	Y	Y
15 ***Ritter***	Y	Y	Y	N	Y	N	N	Y
16 ***Walker***	Y	N	Y	N	N	Y	N	N
17 ***Gekas***	Y	Y	Y	N	N	Y	N	Y
18 Walgren	N	Y	N	Y	Y	N	Y	Y
19 ***Goodling***	Y	Y	Y	N	N	Y	N	Y
20 Gaydos	N	Y	N	Y	Y	N	N	N
21 ***Ridge***	Y	Y	Y	N	Y	N	N	N
22 Murphy	N	Y	N	Y	Y	N	N	N
23 ***Clinger***	Y	Y	Y	N	Y	N	N	Y
RHODE ISLAND								
1 St Germain	N	Y	N	Y	Y	Y	Y	Y
2 ***Schneider***	Y	Y	Y	N	Y	Y	N	Y
SOUTH CAROLINA								
1 ***Hartnett***	Y	Y	Y	N	N	N	N	N
2 ***Spence***	Y	Y	Y	N	N	N	N	N
3 Derrick	N	Y	N	Y	N	N	Y	Y
4 ***Campbell***	Y	Y	Y	N	N	N	N	N
5 Spratt	Y	Y	N	Y	N	N	Y	Y
6 Tallon	N	Y	N	Y	N	N	N	Y
SOUTH DAKOTA								
AL Daschle	N	N	N	Y	?	Y	N	Y
TENNESSEE								
1 ***Quillen***	Y	Y	Y	N	N	N	Y	Y
2 ***Duncan***	Y	Y	Y	N	N	N	Y	Y
3 Lloyd	N	Y	N	Y	Y	Y	Y	Y
4 Cooper	N	Y	N	Y	Y	Y	Y	Y
5 Boner	N	Y	N	Y	N	?	Y	N
6 Gordon	N	Y	Y	Y	Y	Y	Y	Y
7 ***Sundquist***	Y	Y	Y	N	N	N	N	N
8 Jones	N	Y	N	Y	N	Y	Y	Y
9 Ford	N	Y	N	Y	Y	N	Y	Y
TEXAS								
1 Chapman	Y	Y	Y	Y	N	N	N	N
2 Wilson	N	Y	N	Y	Y	N	N	N
3 ***Bartlett***	Y	N	Y	N	N	N	N	N
4 Hall, R.	N	Y	Y	Y	N	N	Y	N
5 Bryant	N	Y	N	Y	Y	N	N	N
6 ***Barton***	Y	N	Y	N	N	N	N	N
7 ***Archer***	Y	N	Y	N	X	N	N	N
8 ***Fields***	Y	N	Y	N	N	N	N	N
9 Brooks	N	Y	N	Y	Y	X	?	N
10 Pickle	Y	N	N	Y	N	N	Y	Y
11 Leath	N	Y	Y	Y	N	N	N	N
12 Wright	?	Y	N	Y	Y	N	Y	Y
13 ***Boulter***	Y	N	Y	N	N	N	N	N
14 ***Sweeney***	Y	N	Y	N	N	N	N	N
15 de la Garza	N	Y	N	Y	Y	N	Y	Y
16 Coleman	N	Y	N	Y	Y	N	Y	Y
17 Stenholm	Y	Y	Y	Y	N	N	N	N
18 Leland	N	Y	N	Y	Y	N	Y	Y
19 ***Combest***	Y	Y	Y	N	N	N	N	N
20 Gonzalez	N	Y	N	Y	Y	N	Y	Y
21 ***Loeffler***	Y	Y	Y	N	N	N	N	N
22 ***DeLay***	Y	N	Y	N	N	N	N	N
23 Bustamante	N	Y	N	Y	Y	N	Y	N
24 Frost	N	Y	N	Y	Y	N	P	P
25 Andrews	Y	Y	Y	Y	N	N	N	N
26 ***Armey***	Y	N	Y	N	N	N	N	N
27 Ortiz	N	Y	N	Y	Y	N	Y	N
UTAH								
1 ***Hansen***	Y	N	Y	?	N	N	Y	Y
2 ***Monson***	Y	Y	Y	N	N	N	N	N
3 ***Nielson***	Y	N	Y	N	N	N	N	N
VERMONT								
AL ***Jeffords***	Y	Y	N	N	Y	Y	N	N
VIRGINIA								
1 ***Bateman***	Y	Y	Y	N	N	N	N	Y
2 ***Whitehurst***	Y	N	Y	N	N	N	N	Y
3 ***Bliley***	Y	Y	Y	N	N	N	N	N
4 Sisisky	N	Y	N	Y	N	N	Y	Y
5 Daniel	Y	Y	Y	Y	N	Y	Y	Y
6 Olin	Y	Y	Y	Y	N	N	Y	Y
7 ***Slaughter***	Y	Y	Y	N	N	N	N	N
8 ***Parris***	Y	Y	N	N	N	Y	N	N
9 Boucher	Y	Y	N	Y	N	Y	Y	Y
10 ***Wolf***	Y	N	N	N	N	Y	N	Y
WASHINGTON								
1 ***Miller***	Y	N	Y	N	N	Y	N	N
2 Swift	N	N	N	Y	Y	Y	Y	Y
3 Bonker	Y	N	N	Y	Y	Y	Y	Y
4 ***Morrison***	Y	N	Y	N	Y	Y	N	N
5 Foley	N	N	N	Y	Y	Y	Y	Y
6 Dicks	Y	N	N	Y	Y	Y	N	N
7 Lowry	N	N	N	Y	Y	Y	Y	Y
8 ***Chandler***	Y	N	Y	N	N	Y	N	N
WEST VIRGINIA								
1 Mollohan	N	Y	N	Y	Y	N	Y	Y
2 Staggers	Y	Y	N	Y	Y	N	Y	Y
3 Wise	N	Y	N	Y	Y	N	Y	Y
4 Rahall	N	Y	N	Y	Y	N	Y	Y
WISCONSIN								
1 Aspin	N	Y	N	Y	Y	Y	Y	Y
2 Kastenmeier	N	Y	N	Y	Y	Y	Y	Y
3 ***Gunderson***	N	N	Y	N	Y	N	Y	Y
4 Kleczka	N	N	N	Y	Y	Y	Y	Y
5 Moody	N	Y	N	Y	Y	Y	Y	Y
6 ***Petri***	Y	N	Y	N	Y	Y	Y	Y
7 Obey	N	Y	N	Y	Y	Y	Y	Y
8 ***Roth***	Y	?	Y	N	N	Y	N	N
9 ***Sensenbrenner***	Y	N	Y	N	N	Y	N	N
WYOMING								
AL ***Cheney***	Y	N	Y	N	N	N	N	N

Southern states - Ala., Ark., Fla., Ga., Ky., La., Miss., N.C., Okla., S.C., Tenn., Texas, Va.

Hill Backing for Reagan Continues to Decline

Although President Reagan tried to brush off the "lame duck" label in the first year of his second term, congressional support for the president's positions dropped in 1985 to the lowest level since he took office.

Congress agreed with Reagan on 59.9 percent of the roll-call votes on which he staked out a position, according to Congressional Quarterly's annual study of legislators' backing for presidential positions.

Reagan's legislative success rate was down almost 6 percentage points from 1984. The drop accelerated the decline in support that had occurred since 1981, when Reagan won a stunning series of legislative victories on key parts of his economic program.

Until 1985, the decline in congressional backing had been slowing to the point that 1984 presidential support dropped only 1 percentage point.

At year's end in 1985, Reagan dismissed charges of "lame-duckery" after the House passed legislation (HR 3838) overhauling the tax code, a top Reagan priority for his second term.

But in analysis of votes taken throughout the year, Congressional Quarterly found that Reagan lost more votes than he won in the House. Reagan prevailed in 45 percent of the House roll-call votes where he had declared a clear, well-known stand. That is down from a 52 percent success rate in the House in 1984.

In the Senate, Reagan's roll-call victories dropped to 72 percent, as the GOP-dominated chamber parted ways with the president on a variety of issues, among them trade and farm policy. In 1984, the Senate supported Reagan on 86 percent of the roll calls considered by the Congressional Quarterly study.

The drop in Reagan's congressional support was in keeping with the experience of recent past presidents. Every president since Dwight D. Eisenhower who remained in office more than four years saw a drop in congressional support in his fifth year in the White House.

Reagan's score marked the sixth time in the 33 years since CQ began the vote study that congressional support for a president had dipped below 60 percent. *(Charts, this page, p. 19-C)*

Success Rate

Following are the annual percentages of presidential victories since 1953 on congressional votes where the presidents took a clear-cut position:

Year	Percent
Eisenhower	
1953	89.0%
1954	82.8
1955	75.0
1956	70.0
1957	68.0
1958	76.0
1959	52.0
1960	65.0
Kennedy	
1961	81.0%
1962	85.4
1963	87.1
Johnson	
1964	88.0%
1965	93.0
1966	79.0
1967	79.0
1968	75.0
Nixon	
1969	74.0%
1970	77.0
1971	75.0
1972	66.0
1973	50.6
1974	59.6
Ford	
1974	58.2%
1975	61.0
1976	53.8
Carter	
1977	75.4%
1978	78.3
1979	76.8
1980	75.1
Reagan	
1981	82.4%
1982	72.4
1983	67.1
1984	65.8
1985	59.9

Words of Caution

The CQ study was based on the results of 182 roll-call votes for which the president had a clearly stated position. Of those, 102 of the roll calls were in the Senate and 80 were in the House. *(Ground rules, box, p. 20-C)*

The analysis was a good indication of the White House's increasing political problems in Congress, but it did not measure how much of the president's program was enacted. As an indicator of a member's loyalty to the president, the study should be used with caution, and readers should keep several caveats in mind.

First, the study included only issues that were brought to a roll-call vote on the House or Senate floor. Not taken into account were elements of the White House agenda that were shelved before they got to the floor, extensively revised or compromised in private or whisked through by voice vote.

For example, because the House approved its tax-overhaul bill by voice vote, Reagan's 1985 support score was unaffected by the final vote on the most important item on the president's domestic agenda.

Second, the study took account only of votes in which the president's support or opposition was clear and known to members.

Third, all votes were given equal weight, regardless of whether they involved momentous or trivial issues, narrow or resounding margins, administration proposals or congressional initiatives.

So, for example, the unanimous Senate vote to confirm James A. Baker III to be secretary of the Treasury was given the same weight as a cliffhanger Senate vote to approve a sweeping fiscal 1986 budget plan (S Con Res 32), when Vice President George Bush was called in to break a 49-49 tie.

Finally, issues that were the subject of many roll-call votes may have influenced the study more than questions that were the subject of a single vote. One of the most

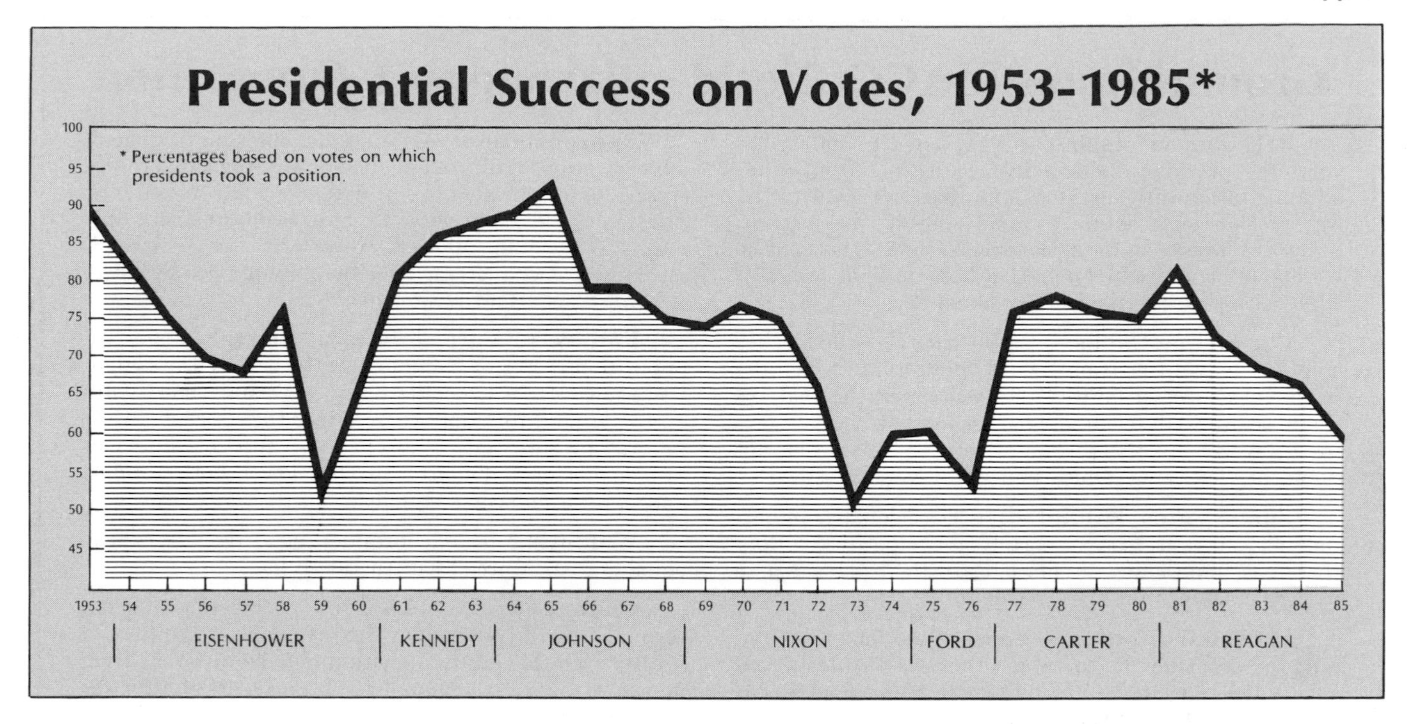

striking examples was in 1978, when President Carter's congressional support rating was bolstered dramatically by 55 winning roll-call votes, mostly procedural, on ratification of the Panama Canal treaties.

In 1985, the House took 20 roll-call votes during debate on legislation rewriting federal farm policy, and 11 of those tallies were considered in the CQ study. But in debate over an extraordinary budget-process overhaul designed to eliminate federal deficits by fiscal 1991, there was only one House roll-call vote where the president's position was clear enough to be considered in the study.

A reporter or researcher interested in how an individual lawmaker voted on the various parts of the Reagan program is advised to look at the specifics of the member's legislative actions, including his or her record on CQ's selection of key votes. *(Key votes, p. 3-C)*

Within those limitations, the presidential support rating is a rough gauge of the relationship between the president and Congress. Over time, the score reflects the rises and drops in those relations, and individuals' ratings show how particular members fit the trends.

The study was begun in 1953, President Eisenhower's first year in office, and has long been considered a yardstick of presidential success on Capitol Hill. A careful reading of the study's ground rules shows its limitations as a measure of executive clout, but not all readers have used the figures with care.

During the 1980 presidential campaign, President Carter's supporters cited his 77 percent support score in 1979 as evidence that Congress had passed four-fifths of the president's program. A Carter aide later conceded that CQ's statistics had been "mistranslated or misused."

Patterns Within Parties, Regions

As might be expected of a Republican president, Reagan was supported more often by GOP lawmakers than by Democrats.

Among Democrats in the Senate, support for the president dipped to 35 percent. That was down from 41 percent in 1984, an election year when more Democrats may have been wary of opposing a president as popular as Reagan.

House Democrats backed Reagan 30 percent of the time, down 4 points from 1984.

Senate Republicans supported the president 75 percent of the time, about the same as in 1984.

The only quarter from which Reagan drew increased support was among House Republicans. Although tensions between the House GOP and Reagan reached a breaking point over the 1985 tax overhaul bill, which Republicans helped sidetrack temporarily, they increasingly backed his positions on earlier votes.

The support score for House Republicans climbed 7 points to 67 percent, almost reversing the 10-point decline in support these members registered in 1984.

An analysis of voting patterns by party and region (East, West, South, Midwest) shows that support for Reagan waned among Democrats from all regions. The largest drop was registered among senators from the South, who in 1984 had been more likely than not to support the president's positions. Southern senators' support score dropped to 44 percent in 1985, from 52 percent.

Among Republicans, Reagan lost support among Western and Southern senators, but gained ground in other regions. Nonetheless, Southern Republicans remained among Reagan's most reliable backers in the Senate, supporting his position 78 percent of the time.

Top Senate Friends, Foes

The president's two most reliable supporters in the Senate came from the top of the new leadership team: Majority Leader Robert Dole of Kansas headed the list, backing the president 92 percent of the time, followed by Assistant Majority Leader Alan K. Simpson, R-Wyo., who racked up a 90 percent support score.

A key player in the year's ongoing debate about deficit reduction, Budget Committee Chairman Pete V. Domenici, R-N.M., was no longer among the president's top 10 Senate supporters as he was in 1984. Domenici, who helped draft a

Ground Rules for CQ Presidential Support-Opposition

Presidential Issues — CQ tries to determine what the president personally, as distinct from other administration officials, does and does not want in the way of legislative action by analyzing his messages to Congress, press conference remarks and other public statements and documents. Members must be aware of the position when the vote is taken.

Borderline Cases — By the time an issue reaches a vote, it may differ from the original form in which the president expressed himself. In such cases, CQ analyzes the measure to determine whether, on balance, the features favored by the president outweigh those he opposed or vice versa. Only then is the vote classified.

Some Votes Excluded — Occasionally, important measures are so extensively amended on the floor that it is impossible to characterize final passage as a victory or defeat for the president.

Procedural Votes — Votes on motions to recommit, to reconsider or to table often are key tests that govern the legislative outcome. Such votes are necessarily included in the presidential support tabulations.

Appropriations — Generally, votes on passage of appropriations bills are not included in the tabulations, since it is rarely possible to determine the president's position on the revisions Congress almost invariably makes in the sums allowed. However, votes on amendments to cut or increase specific amounts requested in the president's budget are included.

Failure to Vote — In tabulating the support or opposition scores of members on the selected presidential-issue votes, CQ counts only "yea" and "nay" votes on the ground that only these affect the outcome. Most failures to vote reflect absences because of illness or official business. Failures to vote lower both support and opposition scores equally.

Weighting — All presidential-issue votes have equal statistical weight in the analysis.

Changed Positions — Presidential support is determined by the position of the president at the time of a vote, even though that position may be different from an earlier position, or may have been reversed after the vote was taken.

budget that reordered Reagan's spending priorities, supported the president 82 percent of the time, down from 88 percent in 1984.

The Republican who was most likely to oppose Reagan was, for the second year in a row, Lowell P. Weicker Jr. of Connecticut. He parted ways with the president on 53 percent of the roll-call votes considered.

The president's top Democratic supporters continued to come largely from the South. But they registered lower levels of support than in 1984.

In 1985, Sam Nunn of Georgia voted with the president 58 percent of the time — more often than any other Senate Democrat. But that was down from his 1984 support score of 69 percent.

The support score of Howell Heflin of Alabama fell sharply to 54 percent, down from 75 percent in 1984 when he was the Democrat most likely to back the president.

Gary Hart of Colorado, the former presidential candidate who was expected to make a second run for the White House in 1988, was among the three Democrats who opposed Reagan most often. Hart posted a 77 percent opposition score, as did Spark M. Matsunaga of Hawaii and freshman Tom Harkin of Iowa.

House Support, Opposition Ratings

The member of Congress who voted most often with the president in 1985 was freshman Fred J. Eckert, R-N.Y., who supported Reagan 94 percent of the time.

Texas sent to Congress some of Reagan's most reliable backers. Half of Reagan's top 10 supporters in the House were Republicans from the Lone Star State. Also among the 10 top House backers was Minority Leader Robert H. Michel, R-Ill., who had an 85 percent support rating.

Majority Leader Jim Wright, D-Texas, the leading contender to be the next House Speaker, put himself increasingly at odds with the president. Wright opposed Reagan 68 percent of the time in 1985, up from 47 percent in 1984.

As in past years, the Republicans most likely to part ways with the president were generally from the Northeast. The Republican most likely to oppose Reagan, Frank Horton of New York, was at odds with the president 68 percent of the time — up from 45 percent in 1984.

Horton was more prone to oppose the president than many senior Democrats — including Ways and Means Chairman Dan Rostenkowski of Illinois and Armed Services Chairman Les Aspin of Wisconsin, who had opposition ratings of 61 percent and 60 percent, respectively.

Average Scores

Following are composites of Democratic and Republican scores for 1985 and 1984:

	1985		1984	
	Dem.	Rep.	Dem.	Rep.
SUPPORT				
Senate	35%	75%	41%	76%
House	30	67	34	60
OPPOSITION				
Senate	61%	19%	49%	18%
House	66	30	58	33

Regional Averages

SUPPORT

Regional presidential support scores for 1985; scores for 1984 are in parentheses:

	East		West		South		Midwest	
DEMOCRATS								
Senate	31%	(35)	27%	(32)	44%	(52)	34%	(40)
House	26	(31)	23	(28)	41	(43)	25	(30)
REPUBLICANS								
Senate	67%	(63)	77%	(79)	78%	(84)	78%	(76)
House	58	(54)	72	(65)	72	(62)	66	(60)

OPPOSITION

Regional presidential opposition scores for 1985; scores for 1984 are in parentheses:

	East		West		South		Midwest	
DEMOCRATS								
Senate	66%	(57)	69%	(52)	52%	(37)	62%	(53)
House	70	(61)	72	(64)	55	(48)	72	(63)
REPUBLICANS								
Senate	29%	(30)	16%	(14)	16%	(10)	20%	(19)
House	39	(40)	24	(28)	26	(30)	31	(33)

(CQ defines regions of the United States as follows: **East:** *Conn., Del., Maine, Md., Mass., N.H., N.J., N.Y., Pa., R.I., Vt., W.Va.* **West:** *Alaska, Ariz., Calif., Colo., Hawaii, Idaho, Mont., Nev., N.M., Ore., Utah, Wash., Wyo.* **South:** *Ala., Ark., Fla., Ga., Ky., La., Miss., N.C., Okla., S.C., Tenn., Texas, Va.* **Midwest:** *Ill., Ind., Iowa, Kan., Mich., Minn., Mo., Neb., N.D., Ohio, S.D., Wis.)*

Highest Scorers — Support

Highest individual scorers in presidential support — those who voted most often for Reagan's position in 1985:

SENATE

Democrats		Republicans	
Nunn, Ga.	58%	Dole, Kan.	92%
Heflin, Ala.	54	Simpson, Wyo.	90
Zorinsky, Neb.	53	Lugar, Ind.	89
Long, La.	52	Hecht, Nev.	89
Hollings, S.C.	52	Quayle, Ind.	88
Bentsen, Texas	50	Thurmond, S.C.	87
Proxmire, Wis.	48	Gramm, Texas	87
Boren, Okla.	47	Boschwitz, Minn.	87

HOUSE

Democrats [1]		Republicans	
Daniel, Va.	66%	Eckert, N.Y.	94%
Stenholm, Texas	66	Bartlett, Texas	89
Roemer, La.	66	Archer, Texas	88
Montgomery, Miss.	66	Armey, Texas	88
Nichols, Ala.	61	Cheney, Wyo.	86
Stratton, N.Y.	59	DeLay, Texas	85
Hubbard, Ky.	59	Mack, Fla.	85
Hall, Ralph M., Texas	58	Fawell, Ill.	85
English, Okla.	58	Michel, Ill.	85
Ray, Ga.	56	Barton, Texas	85
Hutto, Fla.	56	Latta, Ohio	85

[1] *Rep. Sam B. Hall Jr., D-Texas, who was sworn in as a federal judge May 28, 1985, had the highest House Democratic presidential support score with 69 percent.*

1985 Presidential Position Votes

Following is a list of all Senate and House recorded votes in 1985 on which President Reagan took a position. The votes, listed by CQ vote number, appear in the vote charts starting on p. 2-S.

Senate Votes (102)

Presidential Victories (73) — 1, 2, 3, 4, 9, 11, 19, 20, 26, 27, 30, 31, 34, 51, 52, 61, 62, 63, 64, 68, 71, 72, 73, 74, 76, 80, 85, 89, 90, 93, 95, 107, 108, 109, 110, 111, 112, 113, 114, 117, 123, 124, 127, 130, 139, 140, 141, 142, 150, 151, 152, 153, 155, 171, 173, 191, 193, 202, 204, 213, 222, 249, 283, 288, 315, 334, 337, 352, 354, 359, 371, 373, 377.

Presidential Defeats (29) — 13, 14, 16, 17, 28, 35, 36, 37, 115, 126, 156, 157, 158, 180, 229, 231, 244, 253, 266, 296, 305, 308, 310, 314, 317, 321, 325, 356, 379.

House Votes (80)

Presidential Victories (36) — 21, 32, 34, 36, 89, 122, 140, 141, 142, 143, 147, 151, 155, 156, 157, 159, 160, 162, 196, 197, 198, 199, 251, 291, 293, 301, 311, 312, 329, 330, 335, 342, 365, 415, 425, 428.

Presidential Defeats (44) — 17, 25, 31, 40, 58, 60, 61, 120, 130, 145, 152, 153, 161, 170, 178, 185, 192, 205, 211, 225, 226, 266, 269, 289, 290, 294, 302, 303, 307, 309, 318, 320, 336, 341, 347, 358, 359, 364, 370, 379, 386, 389, 391, 411.

High Scorers — Opposition

Highest individual scorers in presidential opposition — those who voted most often against Reagan's position in 1985:

SENATE

Democrats		Republicans	
Matsunaga, Hawaii	77%	Weicker, Conn.	53%
Hart, Colo.	77	Mathias, Md.	44
Harkin, Iowa	77	Hatfield, Ore.	40
Riegle, Mich.	74	Andrews, N.D.	39
Sarbanes, Md.	74	Grassley, Iowa	34
Melcher, Mont.	74	Specter, Pa.	34
Kerry, Mass.	73	Heinz, Pa.	31
Burdick, N.D.	73		
Levin, Mich.	73		
Cranston, Calif.	73		

HOUSE

Democrats		Republicans	
Evans, Ill.	86%	Horton, N.Y.	68%
Boxer, Calif.	86	Leach, Iowa	64
Traficant, Ohio	85	Schneider, R.I.	61
Oberstar, Minn.	84	Green, N.Y.	61
Wheat, Mo.	84	Conte, Mass.	60
Hayes, Ill.	84	Boehlert, N.Y.	59
Sabo, Minn.	84	McKinney, Conn.	56
Obey, Wis.	84	Jeffords, Vt.	56
Kastenmeier, Wis.	84	Gilman, N.Y.	55
Savage, Ill.	84	Smith, N.J.	55
		Evans, Iowa	55

Presidential Support and Opposition: House

1. Reagan Support Score, 1985. Percentage of 80 Reagan-issue recorded votes in 1985 on which representative voted "yea" or "nay" *in agreement* with the president's position. Failures to vote lower both Support and Opposition scores.

2. Reagan Opposition Score, 1985. Percentage of 80 Reagan-issue recorded votes in 1985 on which representative voted "yea" or "nay" *in disagreement* with the president's position. Failures to vote lower both Support and Opposition scores.

1. Rep. Frank McCloskey, D-Ind., was sworn in May 1, 1985, following a House vote to seat him necessitated by a dispute over the outcome of the 1984 general election. The seat was vacant from Jan. 3 to May 1, 1985.

2. Rep. Cathy (Mrs. Gillis) Long, D-La., was sworn in April 4, 1985. She succeeded Gillis W. Long, D, who died Jan. 20, 1985; none of the votes used in this study had been taken by that date.

3. Rep. Thomas P. O'Neill Jr., D-Mass., as Speaker, votes at his discretion.

4. Rep. Jim Chapman, D-Texas, was sworn in Sept. 4, 1985, to succeed Sam B. Hall Jr., D, who was sworn in as a federal judge May 28, 1985. Hall's presidential support score for 1985 was 69 percent. His opposition score was 23 percent.

KEY

† Not eligible for all recorded votes in 1985 (sworn in after Jan. 3, died or resigned during session, or voted "present" to avoid possible conflict of interest).

Democrats *Republicans*

	1	2
ALABAMA		
1 ***Callahan***	74	26
2 ***Dickinson***	63	36
3 Nichols	61	36
4 Bevill	54	39
5 Flippo	45	46
6 Erdreich	52	48
7 Shelby	52	41
ALASKA		
AL ***Young***	51	46
ARIZONA		
1 ***McCain***	68	25
2 Udall	16	73
3 ***Stump***	84	16
4 ***Rudd***	79	14
5 ***Kolbe***	78	23
ARKANSAS		
1 Alexander	25	68
2 Robinson	45	51
3 ***Hammerschmidt***	64	34
4 Anthony	28	71
CALIFORNIA		
1 Bosco	26	66
2 ***Chappie***	59	30
3 Matsui	20	80
4 Fazio	26	65
5 Burton	15	80
6 Boxer	11	86
7 Miller	16	76
8 Dellums	16	83
9 Stark	18	73
10 Edwards	20	80
11 Lantos	19	70
12 ***Zschau***	70	30
13 Mineta	21	76
14 ***Shumway***	79	18
15 Coelho	20	78
16 Panetta	20	79
17 ***Pashayan***	59	33
18 Lehman	16	74
19 ***Lagomarsino***	80	19
20 ***Thomas***	61	33
21 ***Fiedler***	74	26
22 ***Moorhead***	80	20
23 Beilenson	23	69
24 Waxman	28	71
25 Roybal	16	78
26 Berman	24	68
27 Levine	24	75
28 Dixon	18	75
29 Hawkins	14	73
30 Martinez	19	75
31 Dymally	15	78
32 Anderson	39	60
33 ***Dreier***	84	14
34 Torres	18	75
35 ***Lewis***	65	28
36 Brown	20	68
37 ***McCandless***	74	21
38 ***Dornan***	80	16
39 ***Dannemeyer***	78	16
40 ***Badham***	61	23
41 ***Lowery***	71	24
42 ***Lungren***	80	18
43 ***Packard***	75	24
44 Bates	30	70
45 ***Hunter***	74	20
COLORADO		
1 Schroeder	30	69
2 Wirth	21	71
3 ***Strang***	63	24
4 ***Brown***	70	29
5 ***Kramer***	80	20
6 ***Schaefer***	76	20
CONNECTICUT		
1 Kennelly	23	78
2 Gejdenson	23	78
3 Morrison	28	70
4 ***McKinney***	28	56
5 ***Rowland***	71	29
6 ***Johnson***	50	50
DELAWARE		
AL Carper	43	58
FLORIDA		
1 Hutto	56	43
2 Fuqua	52	44
3 Bennett	35	65
4 Chappell	52	43
5 ***McCollum***	80	19
6 MacKay	40	56
7 Gibbons	50	45
8 ***Young***	74	25
9 ***Bilirakis***	75	24
10 ***Ireland***	80	19
11 Nelson	55	19
12 ***Lewis***	66	34
13 ***Mack***	85	15
14 Mica	41	51
15 ***Shaw***	70	25
16 Smith	30	61
17 Lehman	23	78
18 Pepper	26	48
19 Fascell	34	63
GEORGIA		
1 Thomas	50	50
2 Hatcher	49	45
3 Ray	56	43
4 ***Swindall***	79	19
5 Fowler	24	65
6 ***Gingrich***	68	30
7 Darden	51	46
8 Rowland	50	50
9 Jenkins	48	50
10 Barnard	54	41
HAWAII		
1 Heftel	35	52
2 Akaka	26	68
IDAHO		
1 ***Craig***	75	24
2 Stallings	41	58
ILLINOIS		
1 Hayes	15	84
2 Savage	13	84
3 Russo	23	78
4 ***O'Brien***	58	25
5 Lipinski	36	59
6 ***Hyde***	71	19
7 Collins	16	76
8 Rostenkowski	28	61
9 Yates	31	68
10 ***Porter***	68	30
11 Annunzio	29	71
12 ***Crane***	80	11
13 ***Fawell***	85	15
14 ***Grotberg***	80	19
15 ***Madigan***	60	35
16 ***Martin***	61	35
17 Evans	14	86
18 ***Michel***	85	11
19 Bruce	29	71
20 Durbin	28	73
21 Price	33	52
22 Gray	26	65
INDIANA		
1 Visclosky	30	70
2 Sharp	43	56
3 ***Hiler***	80	18
4 ***Coats***	74	26
5 ***Hillis***	65	25

ND Northern Democrats SD Southern Democrats

	1	2
6 ***Burton***	80	16
7 ***Myers***	69	28
8 McCloskey [1]	29†	71†
9 Hamilton	38	63
10 Jacobs	35	65
IOWA		
1 ***Leach***	34	64
2 ***Tauke***	52	46
3 ***Evans***	41	55
4 Smith	30	66
5 ***Lightfoot***	63	38
6 Bedell	21†	79†
KANSAS		
1 ***Roberts***	63	38
2 Slattery	43	58
3 ***Meyers***	68	31
4 Glickman	36	63
5 ***Whittaker***	58	40
KENTUCKY		
1 Hubbard	59	36
2 Natcher	30	70
3 Mazzoli	48	52
4 ***Snyder***	65	33
5 ***Rogers***	64	34
6 ***Hopkins***	61	38
7 Perkins	20	80
LOUISIANA		
1 ***Livingston***	74	24
2 Boggs	28	68
3 Tauzin	54	43
4 Roemer	66	33
5 Huckaby	49	49
6 ***Moore***	68	33
7 Breaux	49	44
8 Long [2]	33†	64†
MAINE		
1 ***McKernan***	50	50
2 ***Snowe***	48	52
MARYLAND		
1 Dyson	55	44
2 ***Bentley***	64	34
3 Mikulski	18	83
4 ***Holt***	69	23
5 Hoyer	29	71
6 Byron	52	43
7 Mitchell	15	78
8 Barnes	25	73
MASSACHUSETTS		
1 ***Conte***	36	60
2 Boland	28	65
3 Early	28	69
4 Frank	25	74
5 Atkins	20	79
6 Mavroules	20	76
7 Markey	23	76
8 O'Neill [3]		
9 Moakley	23	65
10 Studds	21	78
11 Donnelly	26	74
MICHIGAN		
1 Conyers	13	68
2 ***Pursell***	56	35
3 Wolpe	21	76
4 ***Siljander***	73	23
5 ***Henry***	60	40
6 Carr	29	68
7 Kildee	18	78
8 Traxler	26	74
9 ***Vander Jagt***	65	25
10 ***Schuette***	68	33
11 ***Davis***	49	49
12 Bonior	19	76
13 Crockett	19	70
14 Hertel	29	71
15 Ford	16	76
16 Dingell	23	71
17 Levin	23	78
18 ***Broomfield***	73	24
MINNESOTA		
1 Penny	25	75
2 ***Weber***	64	33
3 ***Frenzel***	63	35
4 Vento	21	78
5 Sabo	16	84
6 Sikorski	23	78
7 ***Stangeland***	65	33
8 Oberstar	16	84
MISSISSIPPI		
1 Whitten	33	68
2 ***Franklin***	68	29
3 Montgomery	66	34
4 Dowdy	36	59
5 ***Lott***	73	24
MISSOURI		
1 Clay	15	80
2 Young	26	66
3 Gephardt	26	71
4 Skelton	44	46
5 Wheat	15	84
6 ***Coleman***	56	40
7 ***Taylor***	66	29
8 ***Emerson***	60	36
9 Volkmer	30	70
MONTANA		
1 Williams	18	80
2 ***Marlenee***	61	26
NEBRASKA		
1 ***Bereuter***	58	43
2 ***Daub***	74	26
3 ***Smith***	58	43
NEVADA		
1 Reid	44	55
2 ***Vucanovich***	70	29
NEW HAMPSHIRE		
1 ***Smith***	84	16
2 ***Gregg***	70	25
NEW JERSEY		
1 Florio	25	73
2 Hughes	30	70
3 Howard	21	76
4 ***Smith***	45	55
5 ***Roukema***	49	50
6 Dwyer	25	75
7 ***Rinaldo***	50	45
8 Roe	18	76
9 Torricelli	24	71
10 Rodino	16	69
11 ***Gallo***	63	38
12 ***Courter***	70	28
13 ***Saxton***	61	39
14 Guarini	21	79
NEW MEXICO		
1 ***Lujan***	71	29
2 ***Skeen***	68	31
3 Richardson	25	71
NEW YORK		
1 ***Carney***	68	28
2 Downey	21	75
3 Mrazek	24	70
4 ***Lent***	65	33
5 ***McGrath***	64	33
6 Addabbo	6	45
7 Ackerman	20	74
8 Scheuer	19	73
9 Manton	23	71
10 Schumer	28	64
11 Towns	11	75
12 Owens	16	76
13 Solarz	24	69
14 ***Molinari***	64	36
15 ***Green***	35	61
16 Rangel	16	75
17 Weiss	23	76
18 Garcia	21	75
19 Biaggi	38	52
20 ***DioGuardi***	60	39
21 ***Fish***	45	46
22 ***Gilman***	44	55
23 Stratton	59	41
24 ***Solomon***	70	20
25 ***Boehlert***	41	59
26 ***Martin***	59	40
27 ***Wortley***	65	30
28 McHugh	25	73
29 ***Horton***	31	68
30 ***Eckert***	94	5
31 ***Kemp***	79	18
32 LaFalce	30	66
33 Nowak	23	76
34 Lundine	23	74
NORTH CAROLINA		
1 Jones	20	74
2 Valentine	46	52
3 Whitley	43	55
4 ***Cobey***	80	19
5 Neal	36	64
6 ***Coble***	69	30
7 Rose	28	70
8 Hefner	35	49
9 ***McMillan***	79	20
10 ***Broyhill***	68	29
11 ***Hendon***	64	35
NORTH DAKOTA		
AL Dorgan	23	78
OHIO		
1 Luken	33	58
2 ***Gradison***	65	30
3 Hall	29	68
4 ***Oxley***	75	24
5 ***Latta***	85	15
6 ***McEwen***	69	26
7 ***DeWine***	78	23
8 ***Kindness***	73	21
9 Kaptur	26	70
10 ***Miller***	70	24
11 Eckart	24	76
12 ***Kasich***	74	26
13 Pease	28	71
14 Seiberling	19	73
15 ***Wylie***	68	31
16 ***Regula***	60	40
17 Traficant	13	85
18 Applegate	29	69
19 Feighan	29	71
20 Oakar	18	79
21 Stokes	15	83
OKLAHOMA		
1 Jones	40	60
2 Synar	25	75
3 Watkins	43	56
4 McCurdy	44	56
5 ***Edwards***	71	25
6 English	58	43
OREGON		
1 AuCoin	24	69
2 ***Smith, B.***	63	33
3 Wyden	26	74
4 Weaver	14	78
5 ***Smith D.***	76	18
PENNSYLVANIA		
1 Foglietta	20	75
2 Gray	15	78
3 Borski	24	74
4 Kolter	28	69
5 ***Schulze***	64	33
6 Yatron	44	54
7 Edgar	18	74
8 Kostmayer	29	70
9 ***Shuster***	66	34
10 ***McDade***	59	38
11 Kanjorski	33	63
12 Murtha	52	46
13 ***Coughlin***	50	49
14 Coyne	19	79
15 ***Ritter***	75	23
16 ***Walker***	80	20
17 ***Gekas***	73	28
18 Walgren	25	74
19 ***Goodling***	61	38
20 Gaydos	28	65
21 ***Ridge***	44	54
22 Murphy	36	63
23 ***Clinger***	50	48
RHODE ISLAND		
1 St Germain	20	73
2 ***Schneider***	34	61
SOUTH CAROLINA		
1 ***Hartnett***	65	26
2 ***Spence***	61	39
3 Derrick	29	69
4 ***Campbell***	63	35
5 Spratt	41	58
6 Tallon	41	56
SOUTH DAKOTA		
AL Daschle	16	71
TENNESSEE		
1 ***Quillen***	68	29
2 ***Duncan***	65	35
3 Lloyd	52	45
4 Cooper	43	55
5 Boner	44	54
6 Gordon	33	66
7 ***Sundquist***	75	23
8 Jones	45	54
9 Ford	18	78
TEXAS		
1 Chapman [4]	42†	56†
2 Wilson	40	43
3 ***Bartlett***	89	11
4 Hall, R.	58	39
5 Bryant	23	78
6 ***Barton***	85	15
7 ***Archer***	88	11
8 ***Fields***	74	21
9 Brooks	24	74
10 Pickle	40	59
11 Leath	52	45
12 Wright	23	68
13 ***Boulter***	78	21
14 ***Sweeney***	78	21
15 de la Garza	34	59
16 Coleman	31	68
17 Stenholm	66	31
18 Leland	20	80
19 ***Combest***	75	25
20 Gonzalez	21	74
21 ***Loeffler***	60	23
22 ***DeLay***	85	13
23 Bustamante	34	64
24 Frost	26	69
25 Andrews	39	59
26 ***Armey***	88	11
27 Ortiz	36	61
UTAH		
1 ***Hansen***	81	15
2 ***Monson***	78	21
3 ***Nielson***	84	16
VERMONT		
AL ***Jeffords***	30	56
VIRGINIA		
1 ***Bateman***	69	31
2 ***Whitehurst***	70	26
3 ***Bliley***	74	26
4 Sisisky	39†	58†
5 Daniel	66	25
6 Olin	41	58
7 ***Slaughter***	74	25
8 ***Parris***	64	33
9 Boucher	29	68
10 ***Wolf***	70	30
WASHINGTON		
1 ***Miller***	64	36
2 Swift	26	73
3 Bonker	23	64
4 ***Morrison***	59	40
5 Foley	29	71
6 Dicks	35	61
7 Lowry	18	79
8 ***Chandler***	61	35
WEST VIRGINIA		
1 Mollohan	40	60
2 Staggers	29	70
3 Wise	26	74
4 Rahall	20	79
WISCONSIN		
1 Aspin	33	60
2 Kastenmeier	16	84
3 ***Gunderson***	50	50
4 Kleczka	28	71
5 Moody	20	79
6 ***Petri***	61	39
7 Obey	15	84
8 ***Roth***	55	36
9 ***Sensenbrenner***	68	33
WYOMING		
AL ***Cheney***	86	11

	1	2
ALABAMA		
Denton	75	17
Heflin	54	45
ALASKA		
Murkowski	82	11
Stevens	75	16
ARIZONA		
Goldwater	72	14
DeConcini	45	49
ARKANSAS		
Bumpers	32	62
Pryor	32	66
CALIFORNIA		
Wilson	75	14
Cranston	25	73
COLORADO		
Armstrong	72	12
Hart	21	77
CONNECTICUT		
Weicker	42	53
Dodd	34	64
DELAWARE		
Roth	84	16
Biden	31	64
FLORIDA		
Hawkins	73	24
Chiles	40	46
GEORGIA		
Mattingly	84	16
Nunn	58	42
HAWAII		
Inouye	20	72
Matsunaga	22	77
IDAHO		
McClure	78	20
Symms	81	18
ILLINOIS		
Dixon	46	50
Simon	25	67
INDIANA		
Lugar	89	10
Quayle	88	11
IOWA		
Grassley	66	34
Harkin	22	77
KANSAS		
Dole	92	7
Kassebaum	76	19
KENTUCKY		
McConnell	85	14
Ford	39	60
LOUISIANA		
Johnston	45	53
Long	52	40
MAINE		
Cohen	63	27
Mitchell	33	67
MARYLAND		
Mathias	43	44
Sarbanes	22	74
MASSACHUSETTS		
Kennedy	27	69
Kerry	26	73
MICHIGAN		
Levin	25	73
Riegle	24	74
MINNESOTA		
Boschwitz	87	13
Durenberger	70	21
MISSISSIPPI		
Cochran	80	14
Stennis	41	41
MISSOURI		
Danforth	81	17
Eagleton	30	63
MONTANA		
Baucus	30	68
Melcher	20	74
NEBRASKA		
Exon	43	45
Zorinsky	53	44
NEVADA		
Hecht	89	11
Laxalt	82	8
NEW HAMPSHIRE		
Humphrey	80	14
Rudman	84	14
NEW JERSEY		
Bradley	33	59
Lautenberg	28	69
NEW MEXICO		
Domenici	82	15
Bingaman	33	66
NEW YORK		
D'Amato	71	28
Moynihan	33	65
NORTH CAROLINA		
East	36	10
Helms	79	21
NORTH DAKOTA		
Andrews	59	39
Burdick	25	73
OHIO		
Glenn	42	56
Metzenbaum	26	72
OKLAHOMA		
Nickles	82	18
Boren	47	45
OREGON		
Hatfield	45	40
Packwood	72	25
PENNSYLVANIA		
Heinz	64†	31†
Specter	61	34
RHODE ISLAND		
Chafee	72	26
Pell	29	67
SOUTH CAROLINA		
Thurmond	87	13
Hollings	52	48
SOUTH DAKOTA		
Abdnor	77	23
Pressler	74	25
TENNESSEE		
Gore	34	66
Sasser	33	67
TEXAS		
Gramm	87	13
Bentsen	50	46
UTAH		
Garn	73	11
Hatch	82	16
VERMONT		
Stafford	69	27
Leahy	29	68
VIRGINIA		
Trible	86	13
Warner	82	18
WASHINGTON		
Evans	84	15
Gorton	77	19
WEST VIRGINIA		
Byrd	37	63
Rockefeller	31	61
WISCONSIN		
Kasten	74	26
Proxmire	48	52
WYOMING		
Simpson	90	10
Wallop	73	14

KEY

† Not eligible for all recorded votes in 1985 (sworn in after Jan. 3, died or resigned during session, or voted "present" to avoid possible conflict of interest).

Democrats *Republicans*

Presidential Support and Opposition: Senate

1. Reagan Support Score, 1985. Percentage of 102 Reagan-issue recorded votes in 1985 on which senator voted "yea" or "nay" *in agreement* with the president's position. Failures to vote lower both Support and Opposition scores.

2. Reagan Opposition Score, 1985. Percentage of 102 Reagan-issue recorded votes in 1985 on which senator voted "yea" or "nay" *in disagreement* with the president's position. Failures to vote lower both Support and Opposition scores.

Partisanship in Congress Up Sharply in 1985

1985 was the most partisan year in Congress in more than two decades, with well over half of all recorded votes in the House and Senate dividing along party lines.

Much of the House partisanship stemmed from a bitterly contested election in Indiana's 8th District, which the Democratic majority ultimately resolved by seating the Democratic candidate. The dispute led to dozens of party-line votes.

According to a Congressional Quarterly vote analysis, a majority of voting Democrats opposed a majority of voting Republicans on 56 percent of all recorded votes during the first session of the 99th Congress.

That marked a sharp jump from the 44 percent level of partisan voting in 1984, and it was the highest proportion since 1961, when 58 percent of all roll calls in Congress split along party lines.

CQ's annual vote study also found that in Congress as a whole, Democrats achieved their highest degree of party unity in 26 years. The composite party unity score, which takes account of votes in both the House and Senate, showed that the average Democrat voted with the majority of his party on 79 percent of all partisan votes in 1985 — 5 percentage points more than in 1984, and a level not equaled since 1959.

Republicans stuck together on 75 percent of all partisan votes in 1985, up 3 percentage points from 1984 and their best showing since 1981, President Reagan's first year in office, when the average GOP member voted with his party majority on 76 percent of partisan votes.

Party-Line Issues

Partisan voting was most pronounced in the House, where a majority of Democrats voted against a majority of Republicans on 61 percent of all recorded votes — up 14 percentage points from 1984. In the Senate, that happened on 50 percent of all recorded votes, up 10 points from 1984.

House Democrats were the most unified, with the average member voting with his party majority against the GOP on 80 percent of the partisan votes, up 6 percentage points from 1984. House Republicans increased their party unity average by 4 points, to 75 percent.

The average Senate Democrat toed the party line 75 percent of the time, up 7 points. Only Senate Republicans, who had 22 seats up for election in 1986, showed a slight drop in party unity from 1984, down 2 points to 76 percent.

In the House, the year's most partisan issue was the contested election between Republican Richard D. McIntyre and Democrat Frank McCloskey in Indiana's 8th District.

The House Democratic majority, citing election irregularities, refused to seat McIntyre, the state-certified victor; a subsequent recount by a Democratic-controlled House panel found McCloskey had won by four votes.

Republicans walked out of the House in protest when Democrats voted to seat McCloskey, and repeatedly demanded roll calls on minor procedural votes throughout the year to express their seething anger. Democrats maintained the recount was fair, and accused Republicans of being sore losers. Of the 268 recorded partisan votes that pitted a majority of voting Democrats against a majority of voting Republicans in the House in 1985, 71 of them (or 26 percent) related to the McIntyre-McCloskey dispute — more than any other issue.

In the Senate, economic issues were the most divisive. Of the Senate's 189 partisan roll calls in 1985, 71 (or 39 percent) related to the annual budget resolution, stopgap funding measures, taxes or deficits.

There also were numerous partisan votes during the year on defense and foreign policy issues, such as cutting the number of MX nuclear missiles below Reagan's request, blocking further tests of the anti-satellite (ASAT) missile, forcing Reagan to change his "constructive engagement" policy toward the apartheid system of racial segregation in South Africa, and limiting U.S. assistance to Nicaraguan "contra" rebels to non-lethal humanitarian aid.

Party Dissenters

Continuing a well-established pattern, Southern Democrats showed the least party unity. The average Southern Democrat split with his party majority on 30 percent of the partisan Senate votes in 1985 and on 22 percent of the partisan votes in the House.

However, Southern Democrats in both chambers still voted the party line far more often in 1985 than the year before. On partisan Senate roll calls, Southern Democrats voted with their party majority 64 percent of the time in 1985, an increase of 9 percentage points from 1984. Southern Democrats in the House voted the party line 71 percent of the time, up 10 percentage points.

Northern Republicans also continued their trend of intraparty opposition, voting against GOP positions on 21 percent of the partisan votes in the House and 20 percent of the partisan votes in the Senate.

Definitions

Party Unity Votes. Recorded votes in the Senate and House that split the parties, with a majority of voting Democrats opposing a majority of voting Republicans.

Party Unity Scores. Percentage of Party Unity votes on which a member votes "yea" or "nay" *in agreement* with a majority of his party. Failure to vote, even if a member announced his stand, lowers his score.

Opposition-to-Party Scores. Percentage of Party Unity votes on which a member votes "yea" or "nay" *in disagreement* with a majority of his party. A member's Party Unity and Opposition-to-Party scores add up to 100 percent only if he voted on all Party Unity votes.

Rep. Buddy Roemer, D-La., posted the highest opposition-to-party score (72 percent) of any member of Congress; GOP Rep. Frank Horton of New York was second, with 66 percent. Two retiring senators, Russell B. Long, D-La., and Charles McC. Mathias Jr., R-Md., led the Senate opposition-to-party list with scores of 52 percent and 51 percent, respectively. Right behind Mathias, with a 50 percent opposition score, was Sen. Lowell P. Weicker Jr., R-Conn., the only senator to make the top half-dozen on the opposition list for each of the last five years.

Other Northern Republicans who often opposed their party included Pennsylvania's GOP Sens. Arlen Specter (43 percent) and John Heinz (40 percent). Rep. Silvio O. Conte, Mass., who posted the top GOP opposition score of 70 percent in 1984, dropped to 53 percent in 1985.

Party Loyalists

The Senate Republican who most consistently supported his party in 1985 was Chic Hecht of Nevada, who posted a 98 percent party unity score. Next in line were Phil Gramm, R-Texas, (95 percent) and Jesse Helms, R-N.C., (94 percent). Also among the top scorers, with 92 percent, was Strom Thurmond, R-S.C., who had made the highest-score list each of the last five years.

Among Democrats, Sen. Gary Hart, D-Colo., considered the front-running Democratic candidate for president in 1988, shared the highest party unity score (91 percent) with freshman John Kerry, D-Mass. Hart said Jan. 4, 1986, that he would not seek re-election to the Senate in 1986.

Democratic Sens. Paul S. Sarbanes of Maryland (90 percent) and Carl Levin of Michigan (89 percent) also were among the top scorers, for the fifth consecutive year.

The most loyal Democrat in the House was Martin Olav Sabo, Minn., who scored 98 percent on party unity. Sabo was seeking the Democratic whip's post in 1986. Reps. Alan Wheat, D-Mo.; Don Edwards, D-Calif.; Sander M. Levin, D-Mich.; and Bernard J. Dwyer, D-N.J., all posted 97 percent party unity scores.

Carlos J. Moorhead, Calif., supported his party more often than any other House Republican, on 96 percent of all partisan votes, followed by John Hiler of Indiana, at 95 percent.

Party Unity Scoreboard

The following table shows the proportion of Party Unity recorded votes in recent years:

	Total Recorded Votes	Party Unity Recorded Votes	Percentage of Total
1985			
Both Chambers	820	457	56%
Senate	381	189	50
House	439	268	61
1984			
Both Chambers	683	302	44
Senate	275	110	40
House	408	192	47
1983			
Both Chambers	869	439	51
Senate	371	162	44
House	498	277	56
1982			
Both Chambers	924	369	40
Senate	465	202	43
House	459	167	36
1981			
Both Chambers	836	363	43
Senate	483	231	48
House	353	132	37
1980			
Both Chambers	1,135	470	41
Senate	531	243	46
House	604	227	38
1979			
Both Chambers	1,169	550	47
Senate	497	232	47
House	672	318	47
1978			
Both Chambers	1,350	510	38
Senate	516	233	45
House	834	277	33
1977			
Both Chambers	1,341	567	42
Senate	635	269	42
House	706	298	42
1976			
Both Chambers	1,349	493	37
Senate	688	256	37
House	661	237	36
1975			
Both Chambers	1,214	584	48
Senate	602	288	48
House	612	296	48
1974			
Both Chambers	1,081	399	37
Senate	544	241	44
House	537	158	29
1973			
Both Chambers	1,135	463	41
Senate	594	237	40
House	541	226	42
1972			
Both Chambers	861	283	33
Senate	532	194	36
House	329	89	27
1971			
Both Chambers	743	297	40
Senate	423	176	42
House	320	121	38
1970			
Both Chambers	684	219	32
Senate	418	147	35
House	266	72	27
1969			
Both Chambers	422	144	34
Senate	245	89	36
House	177	55	31

1985 Victories, Defeats

	Senate	House	Total
Democrats won, Republicans lost	65	214	279
Republicans won, Democrats lost	124	54	178
Democrats voted unanimously	8	8	16
Republicans voted unanimously	11	18	29

Party Scores

Party Unity and Opposition-to-Party scores below are composites of individual scores and show the percentage of time the average Democrat and Republican voted with his party majority in disagreement with the other party's majority. Failures to vote lower both Party Unity and Opposition-to-Party scores. Averages are closer to House figures because the House has more members.

	1985		1984	
	Dem.	Rep.	Dem.	Rep.
Party Unity	79%	75%	74%	72%
Senate	75	76	68	78
House	80	75	74	71
Opposition	14%	19%	17%	21%
Senate	20	18	23	16
House	13	19	17	21

Sectional Support, Opposition

SENATE	Support	Opposition
Northern Democrats	80%	16%
Southern Democrats	64	30
Northern Republicans	74	20
Southern Republicans	81	12

HOUSE	Support	Opposition
Northern Democrats	84%	9%
Southern Democrats	71	22
Northern Republicans	73	21
Southern Republcians	80	15

Party Unity History

Composite Party Unity scores showing the percentage of time the average Democrat and Republican voted with his party majority in partisan votes in recent years:

Year	Democrats	Republicans
1985	79%	75%
1984	74	72
1983	76	74
1982	72	71
1981	69	76
1980	68	70
1979	69	72
1978	64	67
1977	67	70
1976	65	66

Individual Scores

Highest Party Unity Scores. Those who in 1985 most consistently voted with their party majority against the majority of the other party:

SENATE

Democrats		Republicans	
Hart, Colo.	91%	Hecht, Nev.	98%
Kerry, Mass.	91	Gramm, Texas	95
Sarbanes, Md.	90	Helms, N.C.	94
Harkin, Iowa	90	Quayle, Ind.	93
Simon, Ill.	89	Lugar, Ind.	92
Levin, Mich.	89	Dole, Kan.	92
Melcher, Mont.	88	Thurmond, S.C.	92

HOUSE

Democrats		Republicans	
Sabo, Minn.	98%	Moorhead, Calif.	96%
Wheat, Mo.	97	Hiler, Ind.	95
Edwards, Calif.	97	Burton, Ind.	94
Levin, Mich.	97	Armey, Texas	94
Dwyer, N.J.	97	Lagomarsino, Calif.	94
Evans, Ill.	96	Barton, Texas	94
Lehman, Fla.	95	Swindall, Ga.	93
Mineta, Calif.	95	Walker, Pa.	93
Burton, Calif.	95	Stump, Ariz.	93
Vento, Minn.	95	Bartlett, Texas	93

Highest Opposition-to-Party Scores. Those who in 1985 most consistently voted against their party majority:

SENATE

Democrats		Republicans	
Long, La.	52%	Mathias, Md.	51%
Zorinsky, Neb.	48	Weicker, Conn.	50
Proxmire, Wis.	44	Specter, Pa.	43
Heflin, Ala.	43	Andrews, N.D.	42
Nunn, Ga.	41	Heinz, Pa.	40
Hollings, S.C.	41	Cohen, Maine	38

HOUSE

Democrats		Republicans	
Roemer, La.	72%	Horton, N.Y.	66%
Stenholm, Texas	64	Green, N.Y.	62
Leath, Texas	49	Schneider, R.I.	57
Penny, Minn.	47	Jeffords, Vt.	53
Ralph M. Hall, Texas	46	Conte, Mass.	53
Daniel, Va.	45	Smith, N.J.	53
English, Okla.	44	Gilman, N.Y.	53
Hubbard, Ky.	44	Rinaldo, N.J.	51
Jacobs, Ind.	44	Johnson, Conn.	51
Ray, Ga.	44	McKinney, Conn.	49
Montgomery, Miss.	44	McDade, Pa.	47

Party Unity and Party Opposition: House

1. Party Unity, 1985. Percentage of 268 House Party Unity recorded votes in 1985 on which representative voted "yea" or "nay" *in agreement* with a majority of his party. (Party unity roll calls are those on which a majority of voting Democrats opposed a majority of voting Republicans. Failures to vote lower both Party Unity and Party Opposition scores.)

2. Party Opposition, 1985. Percentage of 268 House Party Unity recorded votes in 1985 on which representative voted "yea" or "nay" *in disagreement* with a majority of his party.

1. Rep. Frank McCloskey, D-Ind., was sworn in May 1, 1985, following a House vote to seat him necessitated by a dispute over the outcome of the 1984 general election. The seat was vacant from Jan. 3 to May 1, 1985.

2. Rep. Cathy (Mrs. Gillis) Long, D-La., was sworn in April 4, 1985, to succeed Gillis W. Long, D, who died Jan. 20, 1985. Gillis Long's party unity score for 1985 was 100 percent. Opposition was 0 percent.

3. Rep. Thomas P. O'Neill Jr., D-Mass., as Speaker, votes at his discretion.

4. Rep. Jim Chapman, D-Texas, was sworn in Sept. 4, 1985, to succeed Sam B. Hall Jr., D, who was sworn in as a federal judge May 28, 1985. Hall's party unity score for 1985 was 59 percent. Opposition was 25 percent.

KEY

† Not eligible for all recorded votes in 1985 (sworn in after Jan. 3, died or resigned during session, or voted "present" to avoid possible conflict of interest).

Democrats *Republicans*

	1	2
ALABAMA		
1 ***Callahan***	82	16
2 ***Dickinson***	76	17
3 Nichols	55	34
4 Bevill	66	22
5 Flippo	69	24
6 Erdreich	68	28
7 Shelby	60	31
ALASKA		
AL ***Young***	62	32
ARIZONA		
1 ***McCain***	81	13
2 Udall	84	4
3 ***Stump***	93	6
4 ***Rudd***	63	25
5 ***Kolbe***	86	11
ARKANSAS		
1 Alexander	84	7
2 Robinson	66	29
3 ***Hammerschmidt***	71	27
4 Anthony	81	14
CALIFORNIA		
1 Bosco	74	12
2 ***Chappie***	75	7
3 Matsui	94	2
4 Fazio	90	6
5 Burton	95	1
6 Boxer	88	3
7 Miller	84	5
8 Dellums	91	3
9 Stark	89	3
10 Edwards	97	2
11 Lantos	88	4
12 ***Zschau***	82	13
13 Mineta	95	3
14 ***Shumway***	88	9
15 Coelho	88	3
16 Panetta	88†	8†
17 ***Pashayan***	75	18
18 Lehman	83	3
19 ***Lagomarsino***	94	5
20 ***Thomas***	79	15
21 ***Fiedler***	86	7
22 ***Moorhead***	96	3
23 Beilenson	88	4
24 Waxman	86	3
25 Roybal	89	3
26 Berman	91	3
27 Levine	94	3
28 Dixon	84	1
29 Hawkins	81	2
30 Martinez	88	2
31 Dymally	63	6
32 Anderson	84	12
33 ***Dreier***	92	4
34 Torres	90	1
35 ***Lewis***	75	18
36 Brown	84	5
37 ***McCandless***	89	4
38 ***Dornan***	79	10
39 ***Dannemeyer***	89	3
40 ***Badham***	82	4
41 ***Lowery***	74	16
42 ***Lungren***	87	7
43 ***Packard***	85	10
44 Bates	79	14
45 ***Hunter***	75	12
COLORADO		
1 Schroeder	58	39
2 Wirth	81	10
3 ***Strang***	83	8
4 ***Brown***	87	11
5 ***Kramer***	87	7
6 ***Schaefer***	84	10
CONNECTICUT		
1 Kennelly	91	5
2 Gejdenson	92	4
3 Morrison	89	4
4 ***McKinney***	29	49
5 ***Rowland***	76	21
6 ***Johnson***	45	51
DELAWARE		
AL Carper	75	22
FLORIDA		
1 Hutto	56	40
2 Fuqua	65	20
3 Bennett	82	18
4 Chappell	70	23
5 ***McCollum***	82	13
6 MacKay	76	17
7 Gibbons	69	20
8 ***Young***	80	14
9 ***Bilirakis***	84	10
10 ***Ireland***	88	6
11 Nelson	47	26
12 ***Lewis***	85	12
13 ***Mack***	91	7
14 Mica	78	17
15 ***Shaw***	88	8
16 Smith	88	5
17 Lehman	95	2
18 Pepper	81	5
19 Fascell	88	6
GEORGIA		
1 Thomas	75	25
2 Hatcher	73	17
3 Ray	54	44
4 ***Swindall***	93	3
5 Fowler	73	13
6 ***Gingrich***	84	7
7 Darden	67	31
8 Rowland	75	25
9 Jenkins	69	26
10 Barnard	53	37
HAWAII		
1 Heftel	55	18
2 Akaka	86	7
IDAHO		
1 ***Craig***	91	5
2 Stallings	69	24
ILLINOIS		
1 Hayes	93	1
2 Savage	85	3
3 Russo	82	11
4 ***O'Brien***	46	30
5 Lipinski	78	12
6 ***Hyde***	75	17
7 Collins	87	1
8 Rostenkowski	82	6
9 Yates	93	4
10 ***Porter***	71	25
11 Annunzio	89	7
12 ***Crane***	79	5
13 ***Fawell***	79	18
14 ***Grotberg***	87	9
15 ***Madigan***	71	19
16 ***Martin***	84	11
17 Evans	96	1
18 ***Michel***	78†	15†
19 Bruce	89	10
20 Durbin	79	19
21 Price	73	10
22 Gray	75	10
INDIANA		
1 Visclosky	90	9
2 Sharp	76	21
3 ***Hiler***	95	3
4 ***Coats***	81	17
5 ***Hillis***	61	20

ND - Northern Democrats SD - Southern Democrats

	1	2
6 ***Burton***	94	2
7 ***Myers***	58	39
8 McCloskey [1]	89†	10†
9 Hamilton	82	18
10 Jacobs	53	44
IOWA		
1 ***Leach***	53	40
2 ***Tauke***	77	21
3 ***Evans***	69	27
4 Smith	85	11
5 ***Lightfoot***	85	14
6 Bedell	87†	9†
KANSAS		
1 ***Roberts***	83	10
2 Slattery	71	27
3 ***Meyers***	68	26
4 Glickman	76	22
5 ***Whittaker***	79	13
KENTUCKY		
1 Hubbard	48	44
2 Natcher	87	13
3 Mazzoli	74	25
4 ***Snyder***	60	33
5 ***Rogers***	75	21
6 ***Hopkins***	71	25
7 Perkins	94	6
LOUISIANA		
1 ***Livingston***	81	15
2 Boggs	82	9
3 Tauzin	55	37
4 Roemer	27	72
5 Huckaby	51	38
6 ***Moore***	66	32
7 Breaux	53	36
8 Long [2]	77†	12†
MAINE		
1 ***McKernan***	67	32
2 ***Snowe***	56	43
MARYLAND		
1 Dyson	66	29
2 ***Bentley***	74	19
3 Mikulski	89	4
4 ***Holt***	63	23
5 Hoyer	93	5
6 Byron	63	30
7 Mitchell	74	14
8 Barnes	92	3
MASSACHUSETTS		
1 ***Conte***	43	53
2 Boland	82	6
3 Early	82	6
4 Frank	91	4
5 Atkins	86	4
6 Mavroules	87	6
7 Markey	90	4
8 O'Neill [3]		
9 Moakley	80	4
10 Studds	93	3
11 Donnelly	90	6
MICHIGAN		
1 Conyers	69	6
2 ***Pursell***	57	32
3 Wolpe	91	6
4 ***Siljander***	84	6
5 ***Henry***	69	29
6 Carr	81	14
7 Kildee	94	3
8 Traxler	83	5
9 ***Vander Jagt***	74	18
10 ***Schuette***	85	13
11 ***Davis***	55	41
12 Bonior	90	3
13 Crockett	78	5
14 Hertel	88	12
15 Ford	71	2
16 Dingell	76	5
17 Levin	97	3
18 ***Broomfield***	67	28
MINNESOTA		
1 Penny	53	47
2 ***Weber***	79	12
3 ***Frenzel***	72	19
4 Vento	95	3
5 Sabo	98	1
6 Sikorski	70†	28†
7 ***Stangeland***	82	14
8 Oberstar	91	3
MISSISSIPPI		
1 Whitten	79	13
2 ***Franklin***	72	19
3 Montgomery	53	44
4 Dowdy	66	21
5 ***Lott***	82	9
MISSOURI		
1 Clay	73	18
2 Young	81	10
3 Gephardt	84	6
4 Skelton	66	25
5 Wheat	97	1
6 ***Coleman***	76	19
7 ***Taylor***	76	18
8 ***Emerson***	78	17
9 Volkmer	77	21
MONTANA		
1 Williams	76	4
2 ***Marlenee***	71	16
NEBRASKA		
1 ***Bereuter***	74	22
2 ***Daub***	91	9
3 ***Smith***	65	32
NEVADA		
1 Reid	87	13
2 ***Vucanovich***	87	9
NEW HAMPSHIRE		
1 ***Smith***	91	8
2 ***Gregg***	78	13
NEW JERSEY		
1 Florio	89	5
2 Hughes	76	23
3 Howard	94	3
4 ***Smith***	43	53
5 ***Roukema***	56	41
6 Dwyer	97	2
7 ***Rinaldo***	43	51
8 Roe	89	6
9 Torricelli	87	4
10 Rodino	80	3
11 ***Gallo***	80	19
12 ***Courter***	76	18
13 ***Saxton***	81	19
14 Guarini	93	3
NEW MEXICO		
1 ***Lujan***	73	24
2 ***Skeen***	81	17
3 Richardson	89	6
NEW YORK		
1 ***Carney***	75	16
2 Downey	91	4
3 Mrazek	87	7
4 ***Lent***	72	25
5 ***McGrath***	62	25
6 Addabbo	57	1
7 Ackerman	87	3
8 Scheuer	90	3
9 Manton	88	5
10 Schumer	84	7
11 Towns	81	3
12 Owens	86	1
13 Solarz	89	4
14 ***Molinari***	74	26
15 ***Green***	34	62
16 Rangel	89	1
17 Weiss	93	3
18 Garcia	82	1
19 Biaggi	75	10
20 ***DioGuardi***	69	26
21 ***Fish***	42	45
22 ***Gilman***	43	53
23 Stratton	74	25
24 ***Solomon***	86	5
25 ***Boehlert***	54	44
26 ***Martin***	66	26
27 ***Wortley***	62	30
28 McHugh	92	4
29 ***Horton***	25	66
30 ***Eckert***	81	12
31 ***Kemp***	71	17
32 LaFalce	77	15
33 Nowak	89	4
34 Lundine	82	9
NORTH CAROLINA		
1 Jones	76	7
2 Valentine	71	25
3 Whitley	77	20
4 ***Cobey***	90	8
5 Neal	72	17
6 ***Coble***	87	9
7 Rose	84	10
8 Hefner	63	12
9 ***McMillan***	81	15
10 ***Broyhill***	68	25
11 ***Hendon***	80	15
NORTH DAKOTA		
AL Dorgan	83	15
OHIO		
1 Luken	74	17
2 ***Gradison***	63	31
3 Hall	81	12
4 ***Oxley***	88	6
5 ***Latta***	88	8
6 ***McEwen***	79	13
7 ***DeWine***	87	9
8 ***Kindness***	82	9
9 Kaptur	84	9
10 ***Miller***	79	11
11 Eckart	88	10
12 ***Kasich***	90	7
13 Pease	93	7
14 Seiberling	76	4
15 ***Wylie***	61	32
16 ***Regula***	57	42
17 Traficant	87	7
18 Applegate	63	23
19 Feighan	88	9
20 Oakar	94	3
21 Stokes	93	1
OKLAHOMA		
1 Jones	67	29
2 Synar	88	10
3 Watkins	73	22
4 McCurdy	68	27
5 ***Edwards***	79	10
6 English	53	44
OREGON		
1 AuCoin	71	19
2 ***Smith, R.***	82	14
3 Wyden	84	14
4 Weaver	74	7
5 ***Smith D.***	87	7
PENNSYLVANIA		
1 Foglietta	90	4
2 Gray	82	3
3 Borski	94	4
4 Kolter	80	12
5 ***Schulze***	68	23
6 Yatron	80	17
7 Edgar	88	4
8 Kostmayer	90	8
9 ***Shuster***	86	10
10 ***McDade***	44	47
11 Kanjorski	80	17
12 Murtha	77	20
13 ***Coughlin***	63	33
14 Coyne	94	2
15 ***Ritter***	71	22
16 ***Walker***	93	5
17 ***Gekas***	85	15
18 Walgren	89	5
19 ***Goodling***	74	19
20 Gaydos	78	14
21 ***Ridge***	60	35
22 Murphy	78	20
23 ***Clinger***	54	38
RHODE ISLAND		
1 St Germain	82	6
2 ***Schneider***	31	57
SOUTH CAROLINA		
1 ***Hartnett***	74	12
2 ***Spence***	84	13
3 Derrick	74	17
4 ***Campbell***	76	15
5 Spratt	79	17
6 Tallon	69	25
SOUTH DAKOTA		
AL Daschle	83	9
TENNESSEE		
1 ***Quillen***	56	35
2 ***Duncan***	60	37
3 Lloyd	56	39
4 Cooper	85	13
5 Boner	81	16
6 Gordon	79	13
7 ***Sundquist***	87	10
8 Jones	78	19
9 Ford	87	2
TEXAS		
1 Chapman [4]	59†	32†
2 Wilson	63	15
3 ***Bartlett***	93	4
4 Hall, R.	45	46
5 Bryant	89	8
6 ***Barton***	94	3
7 ***Archer***	80	15
8 ***Fields***	89	4
9 Brooks	87	5
10 Pickle	82	15
11 Leath	46	49
12 Wright	81	5
13 ***Boulter***	87	6
14 ***Sweeney***	79	13
15 de la Garza	75	14
16 Coleman	89	9
17 Stenholm	35	64
18 Leland	90	2
19 ***Combest***	89	11
20 Gonzalez	94	3
21 ***Loeffler***	70	5
22 ***DeLay***	87	7
23 Bustamante	85	10
24 Frost	83	9
25 Andrews	77	21
26 ***Armey***	94	4
27 Ortiz	76	14
UTAH		
1 ***Hansen***	85	9
2 ***Monson***	92	4
3 ***Nielson***	89	10
VERMONT		
AL ***Jeffords***	37	53
VIRGINIA		
1 ***Bateman***	67	30
2 ***Whitehurst***	69	20
3 ***Bliley***	83	15
4 Sisisky	76	22
5 Daniel	46	45
6 Olin	72	25
7 ***Slaughter***	90	9
8 ***Parris***	69	25
9 Boucher	87	7
10 ***Wolf***	72	25
WASHINGTON		
1 ***Miller***	65	32
2 Swift	93	5
3 Bonker	81	6
4 ***Morrison***	72	25
5 Foley	90	3
6 Dicks	85	9
7 Lowry	91	5
8 ***Chandler***	72	22
WEST VIRGINIA		
1 Mollohan	82	17
2 Staggers	88	9
3 Wise	84	9
4 Rahall	88	6
WISCONSIN		
1 Aspin	82	9
2 Kastenmeier	91	4
3 ***Gunderson***	74	22
4 Kleczka	87	6
5 Moody	89	5
6 ***Petri***	60	35
7 Obey	93	4
8 ***Roth***	76	13
9 ***Sensenbrenner***	87	11
WYOMING		
AL ***Cheney***	90	3

	1	2
ALABAMA		
Denton	83	13
Heflin	56	43
ALASKA		
Murkowski	78	14
Stevens	71	21
ARIZONA		
Goldwater	68	11
DeConcini	62	31
ARKANSAS		
Bumpers	79	17
Pryor	79	15
CALIFORNIA		
Wilson	74	13
Cranston	80	16
COLORADO		
Armstrong	87	5
Hart	91	6
CONNECTICUT		
Weicker	41	50
Dodd	83	14
DELAWARE		
Roth	81	19
Biden	77	16
FLORIDA		
Hawkins	74	20
Chiles	59	20
GEORGIA		
Mattingly	88	12
Nunn	57	41
HAWAII		
Inouye	80	7
Matsunaga	84	12
IDAHO		
McClure	91	7
Symms	91	7
ILLINOIS		
Dixon	69	29
Simon	89	4
INDIANA		
Lugar	92	8
Quayle	93	5
IOWA		
Grassley	64	35
Harkin	90	8
KANSAS		
Dole	92	6
Kassebaum	79	17
KENTUCKY		
McConnell	82	16
Ford	76	23
LOUISIANA		
Johnston	63	33
Long	43	52
MAINE		
Cohen	55	38
Mitchell	87	13
MARYLAND		
Mathias	33	51
Sarbanes	90	5
MASSACHUSETTS		
Kennedy	81	7
Kerry	91	7
MICHIGAN		
Levin	89	6
Riegle	87	10
MINNESOTA		
Boschwitz	87	13
Durenberger	59	34
MISSISSIPPI		
Cochran	81	14
Stennis	46	32
MISSOURI		
Danforth	77	20
Eagleton	83	9
MONTANA		
Baucus	83	15
Melcher	88	9
NEBRASKA		
Exon	54	30
Zorinsky	46	48
NEVADA		
Hecht	98	2
Laxalt	82†	6†
NEW HAMPSHIRE		
Humphrey	87	8
Rudman	80	17
NEW JERSEY		
Bradley	69	23
Lautenberg	85	14
NEW MEXICO		
Domenici	90	6
Bingaman	75	24
NEW YORK		
D'Amato	69	28
Moynihan	81	13
NORTH CAROLINA		
East	34	3
Helms	94	6
NORTH DAKOTA		
Andrews	55	42
Burdick	87	10
OHIO		
Glenn	79	18
Metzenbaum	87	10
OKLAHOMA		
Nickles	79	20
Boren	52	39
OREGON		
Hatfield	49	35
Packwood	67	26
PENNSYLVANIA		
Heinz	54	40
Specter	51	43
RHODE ISLAND		
Chafee	68	30
Pell	82	14
SOUTH CAROLINA		
Thurmond	92	7
Hollings	59	41
SOUTH DAKOTA		
Abdnor	77	22
Pressler	72	24
TENNESSEE		
Gore	86	14
Sasser	87	13
TEXAS		
Gramm	95	5
Bentsen	54	40
UTAH		
Garn	83	7
Hatch	85	12
VERMONT		
Stafford	62	30
Leahy	83	16
VIRGINIA		
Trible	85	11
Warner	82	18
WASHINGTON		
Evans	79	18
Gorton	79	17
WEST VIRGINIA		
Byrd	81	19
Rockefeller	83	12
WISCONSIN		
Kasten	68	32
Proxmire	56	44
WYOMING		
Simpson	91	9
Wallop	88	5

KEY

† Not eligible for all recorded votes in 1985 (sworn in after Jan. 3, died or resigned during session, or voted "present" to avoid possible conflict of interest).

Democrats *Republicans*

Party Unity and Party Opposition: Senate

1. Party Unity, 1985. Percentage of 189 Senate Party Unity votes in 1985 on which senator voted "yea"or "nay" *in agreement* with a majority of his party. (Party Unity roll calls are those on which a majority of voting Democrats opposed a majority of voting Republicans. Failures to vote lower both Party Unity and Party Opposition score.)

2. Party Opposition, 1985. Percentage of 189 Senate Party Unity votes in 1985 on which senator voted "yea" or "nay" *in disagreement* with a majority of his party.

Hill Voting Participation Hits 33-Year High

Members of Congress missed fewer roll-call votes in 1985 than in any of the 33 years that Congressional Quarterly had been keeping tabs on the subject.

On the average, members voted on 94 percent of the roll-call votes, 2 percentage points more than the previous mark, which was recorded in 1983 and 1981.

Both chambers had their highest voting percentage ever in the study: 95 percent for the Senate and 94 percent for the House. Seven senators scored 100 percent, the most since 1958. Four representatives had perfect scores.

Voting scores generally are higher when members are not running for re-election. In 1984, when there was a general election, the score was 91 percent.

The high participation might reflect the aftermath of several 1984 races in which an incumbent's attendance was an issue. Particularly bitter was the Senate race in Kentucky in which Republican underdog Mitch McConnell defeated incumbent Democrat Walter D. Huddleston (1973-85). McConnell featured TV ads showing a bloodhound unsuccessfully trying to find the senator. Huddleston scored 94 percent in 1983 but only 77 percent in 1984. McConnell's score in 1985 was 99 percent.

The leadership in each chamber tries to schedule votes at times convenient for members, principally midweek. In the Senate, only 4 percent of roll-call votes took place on Mondays and 15 percent on Fridays.

The voting participation study is the closest approach to an attendance record for Congress, but it is only an approximation. *(Definition, box, p. 32-C)*

Senate Democrats recorded a position slightly more often than Republicans, 95 percent vs. 94 percent, but House Republicans edged Democrats, 94 percent to 93 percent. For both chambers combined, Republicans answered roll calls 94 percent of the time, Democrats 93 percent. In 1984, Republicans outscored Democrats 92 percent to 90 percent.

820 Recorded Votes

There were 820 recorded votes in Congress in 1985, more than the 683 in 1984 but far fewer than the 1,350 votes in 1978. There were 381 Senate roll calls, compared with 275 in 1984, but well below the record 688 in 1976. In the House, members answered 439 recorded votes, 31 more than 1984 but 395 fewer than the record 834 in 1978.

Senate Democrats pushed their score up from 90 percent in 1984 to 95 percent in 1985. Senate Republicans' scores went from 93 percent to 94 percent.

In the House, Republicans raised their score from 92 percent in 1984 to 94 percent in 1985; Democrats raised theirs from 90 percent to 93 percent.

In addition to four House members with 100 percent, there were 43 with scores of 99 percent. That was considerably more than 1983, the last non-election year, when 26 members had scores of 99 or 100 percent.

For the 32nd year in a row, William H. Natcher, D-Ky., scored 100 percent. He had not missed a recorded vote since his election to Congress in 1953 and had answered 10,358 consecutive roll calls. Charles E. Bennett, D-Fla., scored 100 percent for the sixth consecutive year; Timothy J. Penny, D-Minn., scored 100 percent for the second year. Also recording a perfect mark was freshman Carl C. Perkins, D-Ky., whose late father, Rep. Carl D. Perkins (1949-84), frequently scored 100 percent.

Sen. William Proxmire, D-Wis., brought his string of consecutive roll-call votes to 9,103 over 19 years.

Several former Democratic presidential candidates brought their Senate voting records up from campaign year 1984. Gary Hart, Colo., went from 37 percent to 97 percent; Ernest F. Hollings, S.C., from 79 percent to 100 percent; John Glenn, Ohio, from 80 percent to 97 percent; and Alan Cranston, Calif., from 78 percent to 96 percent.

The lowest-scoring senator, Republican John P. East of North Carolina, was present for 46 percent of the roll-call votes. In September 1985 he announced that he would not run for re-election because of health problems. In the House, the score of Joseph P. Addabbo, D-N.Y., fell from 88 percent in 1984 to 58 percent in 1985 because of illness.

Absences

Among members of Congress absent for a day or more in 1985 because they were sick or because of illness or death in their families were:

Senate Democrats: Baucus, Mont.; Chiles, Fla.; Exon, Neb.; Levin, Mich.; Melcher, Mont.; Moynihan, N.Y.; Zorinsky, Neb.

Senate Republicans: East, N.C.; Goldwater, Ariz.; Wilson, Calif.

House Democrats: Ackerman, N.Y.; Addabbo, N.Y.; Bevill, Ala.; Boland, Mass.; Brooks, Texas; Byron, Md.; Chapman, Texas; Chappell, Fla.; Dellums, Calif.; Dingell, Mich.; Fuqua, Fla.; Gray, Ill.; Ralph M. Hall, Texas; Hefner, N.C.; Walter B. Jones, N.C.; Ed Jones, Tenn.; Kastenmeier, Wis.; Kildee, Mich.; Kleczka, Wis.; Lehman, Calif.; Levin, Mich.; Lloyd, Tenn.; Luken, Ohio; Neal, N.C.; McHugh, N.Y.; Ortiz, Texas; Owens, N.Y.; Rodino, N.J.; Rangel, N.Y.; Traficant, Ohio; Weaver, Ore.; Yates, Ill.; Young, Mo.

House Republicans: Badham, Calif.; Campbell, S.C.; Fish, N.Y.; Gunderson, Wis.; Hartnett, S.C.; Hunter, Calif.; Lagomarsino, Calif.; Marlenee, Mont.; Martin, Ill.; McKinney, Conn.; McDade, Pa.; Pursell, Mich.; Roukema, N.J.; Rudd, Ariz.; Solomon, N.Y.; Strang, Colo.

Failure to vote often is due to conflicting duties. Members frequently have to be away from Washington on official business. Leaves of absence, not listed here, are granted members for these purposes.

Party Scores

Composites of Democratic and Republican voting participation scores for 1985 and 1984:

	1985		1984	
	Dem.	Rep.	Dem.	Rep.
Senate	95%	94%	90%	93%
House	93	94	90	92

Regional Scores

Regional voting participation breakdowns for 1985, with 1984 scores in parentheses:

	East	West	South	Midwest
DEMOCRATS				
Senate	96% (92)	95% (84)	94% (88)	96% (93)
House	93 (90)	91 (90)	93 (90)	94 (92)
REPUBLICANS				
Senate	94% (93)	92% (92)	93% (93)	97% (93)
House	94 (93)	94 (91)	95 (91)	94 (92)

(CQ defines regions of the United States as follows: **East:** *Conn., Del., Maine, Md., Mass., N.H., N.J., N.Y., Pa., R.I., Vt., W.Va.* **West:** *Alaska, Ariz., Calif., Colo., Hawaii, Idaho, Mont., Nev., N.M., Ore., Utah, Wash., Wyo.* **South:** *Ala., Ark., Fla., Ga., Ky., La., Miss., N.C., Okla., S.C., Tenn., Texas, Va.* **Midwest:** *Ill., Ind., Iowa, Kan., Mich., Minn., Mo., Neb., N.D., Ohio, S.D., Wis.)*

Highest Scorers

SENATE

Democrats		Republicans	
Sasser, Tenn.	100%	Hecht, Nev.	100%
Hollings, S.C.	100	Simpson, Wyo.	100
Proxmire, Wis.	100	Warner, Va.	100
Byrd, W.Va.	100	Thurmond, S.C.	99
Gore, Tenn.	99	Lugar, Ind.	99
Mitchell, Maine	99	Nickles, Okla.	99
Ford, Ky.	99	Boschwitz, Minn.	99
Heflin, Ala.	99	Mattingly, Ga.	99
Metzenbaum, Ohio	99	Kasten, Wis.	99
		Abdnor, S.D.	99
		Helms, N.C.	99
		Dole, Kan.	99
		Grassley, Iowa	99
		McConnell, Ky.	99

HOUSE

Democrats		Republicans	
Natcher, Ky.	100%	Saxton, N.J.	99%
Bennett, Fla.	100	Snowe, Maine	99
Perkins, Ky.	100	Lightfoot, Iowa	99
Penny, Minn.	100	Gekas, Pa.	99
Thomas, Ga.	99	Combest, Texas	99
Pease, Ohio	99	Callahan, Ala.	99
Hamilton, Ind.	99	Stump, Ariz.	99
Hertel, Mich.	99	Mack, Fla.	99
Hughes, N.J.	99	Tauke, Iowa	99
Dwyer, N.J.	99	Daub, Neb.	99
Bruce, Ill.	99	Smith, N.H.	99
Visclosky, Ind.	99	Lagomarsino, Calif.	99
Rowland, Ga.	99	Nielson, Utah	99
McCloskey, Ind. [1]	99	Gallo, N.J.	99
Wheat, Mo.	99	Bliley, Va.	99
Reid, Nev.	99	Slaughter, Va.	99
Edwards, Calif.	99	Moorhead, Calif.	99
Slattery, Kan.	99	Henry, Mich.	99
Wyden, Ore.	99	Molinari, N.Y.	99
Andrews, Texas	99	Walker, Pa.	99
Roemer, La.	99		
Eckart, Ohio	99		
Levin, Mich.	99		
Stenholm, Texas	99		
Mollohan, W.Va.	99		
Cooper, Tenn.	99		
Sabo, Minn.	99		

Definition

Voting Participation. Percentage of recorded votes on which a member voted "yea" or "nay." Failures to vote "yea" or "nay" lower scores — even if the member votes "present," enters a live pair or announces his stand in the *Congressional Record.* Only votes of "yea" or "nay" directly affect the outcome of a vote. Voting participation is the closest approach to an attendance record, but it is only an approximation. A member may be present and nevertheless decline to vote "yea" or "nay" — usually because he has entered a live pair with an absent member.

Lowest Scorers

SENATE

Democrats		Republicans	
Stennis, Miss.	73%	East, N.C.	46%
Chiles, Fla.	83	Goldwater, Ariz.	77
Inouye, Hawaii	87	Mathias, Md.	83
Kennedy, Mass.	89	Hatfield, Ore.	85
Exon, Neb.	90	Laxalt, Nev.	86
Eagleton, Mo.	91	Armstrong, Colo.	88
Bradley, N.J.	91	Stevens, Alaska	90
		Garn, Utah	90
		Murkowski, Alaska	90

HOUSE

Democrats		Republicans	
Addabbo, N.Y.	58%	Loeffler, Texas	76%
Hefner, N.C.	73	O'Brien, Ill.	77
Nelson, Fla.	73	McKinney, Conn.	77
Wilson, Texas	74	Hillis, Ind.	80
Heftel, Hawaii	75	Chappie, Calif.	82
Conyers, Mich.	75	Holt, Md.	84
Dymally, Calif.	76	Crane, Ill.	84
Ford, Mich.	79	Badham, Calif.	85

[1] *Rep. Frank McCloskey, D-Ind., was sworn in May 1, 1985, following a House vote to seat him necessitated by a dispute over the outcome of the 1984 general election. The seat was vacant from Jan. 3 to May 1, 1985.*

Voting Participation Scores: Senate

Voting Participation, 1985. Percentage of 381 roll calls in 1985 on which senator voted "yea" or "nay."

KEY

† Not eligible for all recorded votes in 1985 (sworn in after Jan. 3, died or resigned during session, or voted "present" to avoid possible conflict of interest).

Member absent a day or more in 1985 due to illness or illness or death in family.

Democrats *Republicans*

Senator	Score
ALABAMA	
Denton	94
Heflin	99
ALASKA	
Murkowski	90
Stevens	90
ARIZONA	
Goldwater	77#
DeConcini	94
ARKANSAS	
Bumpers	97
Pryor	95
CALIFORNIA	
Wilson	91#
Cranston	96
COLORADO	
Armstrong	88
Hart	97
CONNECTICUT	
Weicker	91
Dodd	96
DELAWARE	
Roth	98
Biden	92
FLORIDA	
Hawkins	94
Chiles	83#
GEORGIA	
Mattingly	99
Nunn	98
HAWAII	
Inouye	87
Matsunaga	97
IDAHO	
McClure	97
Symms	97
ILLINOIS	
Dixon	96
Simon	93
INDIANA	
Lugar	99
Quayle	98
IOWA	
Grassley	99
Harkin	98
KANSAS	
Dole	99
Kassebaum	95
KENTUCKY	
McConnell	99
Ford	99
LOUISIANA	
Johnston	95
Long	93
MAINE	
Cohen	93
Mitchell	99
MARYLAND	
Mathias	83
Sarbanes	97
MASSACHUSETTS	
Kennedy	89
Kerry	98
MICHIGAN	
Levin	96#
Riegle	98
MINNESOTA	
Boschwitz	99
Durenberger	92
MISSISSIPPI	
Cochran	95
Stennis	73
MISSOURI	
Danforth	96
Eagleton	91
MONTANA	
Baucus	98#
Melcher	95#
NEBRASKA	
Exon	90#
Zorinsky	95#
NEVADA	
Hecht	100
Laxalt	86†
NEW HAMPSHIRE	
Humphrey	94
Rudman	97
NEW JERSEY	
Bradley	91
Lautenberg	98
NEW MEXICO	
Domenici	96
Bingaman	98
NEW YORK	
D'Amato	97
Moynihan	96#
NORTH CAROLINA	
East	46#
Helms	99
NORTH DAKOTA	
Andrews	96
Burdick	98
OHIO	
Glenn	97
Metzenbaum	99
OKLAHOMA	
Nickles	99
Boren	92
OREGON	
Hatfield	85
Packwood	93
PENNSYLVANIA	
Heinz	94†
Specter	94
RHODE ISLAND	
Chafee	97
Pell	97
SOUTH CAROLINA	
Thurmond	99
Hollings	100
SOUTH DAKOTA	
Abdnor	99
Pressler	95
TENNESSEE	
Gore	99
Sasser	100
TEXAS	
Gramm	98
Bentsen	94
UTAH	
Garn	90
Hatch	97
VERMONT	
Stafford	93
Leahy	98
VIRGINIA	
Trible	97
Warner	100
WASHINGTON	
Evans	98
Gorton	97
WEST VIRGINIA	
Byrd	100
Rockefeller	93
WISCONSIN	
Kasten	99
Proxmire	100
WYOMING	
Simpson	100
Wallop	91

Voting Participation Scores: House

Voting Participation, 1985. Percentage of 439 recorded votes in 1985 on which representative voted "yea" or "nay."

1. Rep. Frank McCloskey, D-Ind., was sworn in May 1, 1985, following a House vote to seat him necessitated by a dispute over the outcome of the 1984 general election. The seat was vacant from Jan. 3 to May 1, 1985.

2. Rep. Cathy (Mrs. Gillis) Long, D-La., was sworn in April 4, 1985, to succeed Gillis W. Long, D, who died Jan. 20, 1985. Gillis Long's voting participation score for 1985 was 100 percent.

3. Rep. Thomas P. O'Neill Jr., D-Mass., as Speaker, votes at his discretion.

4. Rep. Jim Chapman, D-Texas, was sworn in Sept. 4, 1985, to succeed Sam B. Hall Jr., D, who was sworn in as a federal judge May 28, 1985. Hall's voting participation score for 1985 was 82 percent.

KEY

† Not eligible for all recorded votes in 1985 (sworn in after Jan. 3, died or resigned during session, or voted "present" to avoid possible conflict of interest).

\# Member absent a day or more in 1985 due to illness or illness or death in family.

Democrats *Republicans*

Member	Score
ALABAMA	
1 ***Callahan***	99
2 ***Dickinson***	93
3 Nichols	91
4 Bevill	91#
5 Flippo	93
6 Erdreich	97
7 Shelby	92
ALASKA	
AL ***Young***	94
ARIZONA	
1 ***McCain***	95
2 Udall	89
3 ***Stump***	99
4 ***Rudd***	87#
5 ***Kolbe***	97
ARKANSAS	
1 Alexander	90
2 Robinson	95
3 ***Hammerschmidt***	98
4 Anthony	94
CALIFORNIA	
1 Bosco	84
2 ***Chappie***	82
3 Matsui	96
4 Fazio	95
5 Burton	95
6 Boxer	91
7 Miller	89
8 Dellums	94#
9 Stark	91
10 Edwards	99
11 Lantos	93
12 ***Zschau***	95
13 Mineta	97
14 ***Shumway***	97
15 Coelho	92
16 Panetta	96†
17 ***Pashayan***	94
18 Lehman	86#
19 ***Lagomarsino***	99#
20 ***Thomas***	92
21 ***Fiedler***	95
22 ***Moorhead***	99
23 Beilenson	92
24 Waxman	89
25 Roybal	91
26 Berman	93
27 Levine	97
28 Dixon	85
29 Hawkins	82
30 Martinez	91
31 Dymally	76
32 Anderson	96
33 ***Dreier***	98
34 Torres	92
35 ***Lewis***	91
36 Brown	90
37 ***McCandless***	94
38 ***Dornan***	92
39 ***Dannemeyer***	91
40 ***Badham***	85#
41 ***Lowery***	91
42 ***Lungren***	96
43 ***Packard***	96
44 Bates	96
45 ***Hunter***	91#
COLORADO	
1 Schroeder	97
2 Wirth	92
3 ***Strang***	92#
4 ***Brown***	98
5 ***Kramer***	93
6 ***Schaefer***	96
CONNECTICUT	
1 Kennelly	97
2 Gejdenson	96
3 Morrison	92
4 ***McKinney***	77#
5 ***Rowland***	97
6 ***Johnson***	97
DELAWARE	
AL Carper	98
FLORIDA	
1 Hutto	97
2 Fuqua	87#
3 Bennett	100
4 Chappell	92#
5 ***McCollum***	96
6 MacKay	94
7 Gibbons	91
8 ***Young***	93
9 ***Bilirakis***	94
10 ***Ireland***	94
11 Nelson	73
12 ***Lewis***	97
13 ***Mack***	99
14 Mica	95
15 ***Shaw***	97
16 Smith	94
17 Lehman	96
18 Pepper	86
19 Fascell	94
GEORGIA	
1 Thomas	99
2 Hatcher	89
3 Ray	98
4 ***Swindall***	97
5 Fowler	86
6 ***Gingrich***	92
7 Darden	98
8 Rowland	99
9 Jenkins	96
10 Barnard	92
HAWAII	
1 Heftel	75
2 Akaka	91
IDAHO	
1 ***Craig***	96
2 Stallings	94
ILLINOIS	
1 Hayes	95
2 Savage	88
3 Russo	94
4 ***O'Brien***	77
5 Lipinski	90
6 ***Hyde***	92
7 Collins	87
8 Rostenkowski	88
9 Yates	95#
10 ***Porter***	96
11 Annunzio	97
12 ***Crane***	84
13 ***Fawell***	98
14 ***Grotberg***	95
15 ***Madigan***	92
16 ***Martin***	95#
17 Evans	97
18 ***Michel***	94†
19 Bruce	99
20 Durbin	98
21 Price	81
22 Gray	86#
INDIANA	
1 Visclosky	99
2 Sharp	97
3 ***Hiler***	98
4 ***Coats***	98
5 ***Hillis***	80

ND - Northern Democrats SD - Southern Democrats

6 ***Burton***	95
7 ***Myers***	96
8 McCloskey [1]	99†
9 Hamilton	99
10 Jacobs	95
IOWA	
1 ***Leach***	95
2 ***Tauke***	99
3 ***Evans***	96
4 Smith	96
5 ***Lightfoot***	99
6 Bedell	96†
KANSAS	
1 ***Roberts***	95
2 Slattery	99
3 ***Meyers***	96
4 Glickman	98
5 ***Whittaker***	94
KENTUCKY	
1 Hubbard	92
2 Natcher	100
3 Mazzoli	97
4 ***Snyder***	94
5 ***Rogers***	96
6 ***Hopkins***	98
7 Perkins	100
LOUISIANA	
1 ***Livingston***	95
2 Boggs	92
3 Tauzin	94
4 Roemer	99
5 Huckaby	89
6 ***Moore***	98
7 Breaux	89
8 Long [2]	91†
MAINE	
1 ***McKernan***	98
2 ***Snowe***	99
MARYLAND	
1 Dyson	97
2 ***Bentley***	92
3 Mikulski	95
4 ***Holt***	84
5 Hoyer	98
6 Byron	92#
7 Mitchell	87
8 Barnes	95
MASSACHUSETTS	
1 ***Conte***	97
2 Boland	88#
3 Early	88
4 Frank	95
5 Atkins	93
6 Mavroules	94
7 Markey	95
8 O'Neill [3]	
9 Moakley	86
10 Studds	96
11 Donnelly	96
MICHIGAN	
1 Conyers	75
2 ***Pursell***	91#
3 Wolpe	97
4 ***Siljander***	92
5 ***Henry***	99
6 Carr	94
7 Kildee	97#
8 Traxler	89
9 ***Vander Jagt***	91
10 ***Schuette***	98
11 ***Davis***	95
12 Bonior	91
13 Crockett	85
14 Hertel	99
15 Ford	79
16 Dingell	85#
17 Levin	99#
18 ***Broomfield***	94
MINNESOTA	
1 Penny	100
2 ***Weber***	92
3 ***Frenzel***	92
4 Vento	97
5 Sabo	99
6 Sikorski	98†
7 ***Stangeland***	96
8 Oberstar	96
MISSISSIPPI	
1 Whitten	92
2 ***Franklin***	92
3 Montgomery	98
4 Dowdy	86
5 ***Lott***	93
MISSOURI	
1 Clay	90
2 Young	91#
3 Gephardt	91
4 Skelton	93
5 Wheat	99
6 ***Coleman***	95
7 ***Taylor***	94
8 ***Emerson***	97
9 Volkmer	98
MONTANA	
1 Williams	85
2 ***Marlenee***	88#
NEBRASKA	
1 ***Bereuter***	98
2 ***Daub***	99
3 ***Smith***	97
NEVADA	
1 Reid	99
2 ***Vucanovich***	96
NEW HAMPSHIRE	
1 ***Smith***	99
2 ***Gregg***	92
NEW JERSEY	
1 Florio	94
2 Hughes	99
3 Howard	97
4 ***Smith***	97
5 ***Roukema***	98#
6 Dwyer	99
7 ***Rinaldo***	94
8 Roe	94
9 Torricelli	92
10 Rodino	86#
11 ***Gallo***	99
12 ***Courter***	94
13 ***Saxton***	99
14 Guarini	95
NEW MEXICO	
1 ***Lujan***	97
2 ***Skeen***	98
3 Richardson	95
NEW YORK	
1 ***Carney***	91
2 Downey	95
3 Mrazek	94
4 ***Lent***	96
5 ***McGrath***	89
6 Addabbo	58#
7 Ackerman	90#
8 Scheuer	93
9 Manton	94
10 Schumer	93
11 Towns	84
12 Owens	87#
13 Solarz	93
14 ***Molinari***	99
15 ***Green***	96
16 Rangel	90#
17 Weiss	97
18 Garcia	84
19 Biaggi	87
20 ***DioGuardi***	96
21 ***Fish***	87#
22 ***Gilman***	96
23 Stratton	98
24 ***Solomon***	91#
25 ***Boehlert***	97
26 ***Martin***	91
27 ***Wortley***	93
28 McHugh	96#
29 ***Horton***	89
30 ***Eckert***	94
31 ***Kemp***	88
32 LaFalce	92
33 Nowak	96
34 Lundine	92
NORTH CAROLINA	
1 Jones	85#
2 Valentine	97
3 Whitley	97
4 ***Cobey***	98
5 Neal	90#
6 ***Coble***	97
7 Rose	95
8 Hefner	73#
9 ***McMillan***	98
10 ***Broyhill***	93
11 ***Hendon***	96
NORTH DAKOTA	
AL Dorgan	97
OHIO	
1 Luken	90#
2 ***Gradison***	95
3 Hall	94
4 ***Oxley***	95
5 ***Latta***	95
6 ***McEwen***	93
7 ***DeWine***	97
8 ***Kindness***	91
9 Kaptur	94
10 ***Miller***	91
11 Eckart	99
12 ***Kasich***	97
13 Pease	99
14 Seiberling	84
15 ***Wylie***	92
16 ***Regula***	98
17 Traficant	94#
18 Applegate	91
19 Feighan	97
20 Oakar	97
21 Stokes	93
OKLAHOMA	
1 Jones	96
2 Synar	98
3 Watkins	96
4 McCurdy	95
5 ***Edwards***	91
6 English	97
OREGON	
1 AuCoin	89
2 ***Smith, R.***	96
3 Wyden	99
4 Weaver	80#
5 ***Smith D.***	94
PENNSYLVANIA	
1 Foglietta	94
2 Gray	86
3 Borski	97
4 Kolter	92
5 ***Schulze***	91
6 Yatron	97
7 Edgar	91
8 Kostmayer	98
9 ***Shuster***	97
10 ***McDade***	91#
11 Kanjorski	98
12 Murtha	95
13 ***Coughlin***	96
14 Coyne	97
15 ***Ritter***	93
16 ***Walker***	99
17 ***Gekas***	99
18 Walgren	95
19 ***Goodling***	93
20 Gaydos	94
21 ***Ridge***	96
22 Murphy	97
23 ***Clinger***	92
RHODE ISLAND	
1 St Germain	88
2 ***Schneider***	91
SOUTH CAROLINA	
1 ***Hartnett***	86#
2 ***Spence***	98
3 Derrick	92
4 ***Campbell***	92#
5 Spratt	97
6 Tallon	96
SOUTH DAKOTA	
AL Daschle	92
TENNESSEE	
1 ***Quillen***	89
2 ***Duncan***	97
3 Lloyd	95#
4 Cooper	99
5 Boner	95
6 Gordon	93
7 ***Sundquist***	97
8 Jones	95#
9 Ford	90
TEXAS	
1 Chapman [4]	91†#
2 Wilson	74
3 ***Bartlett***	98
4 Hall, R.	92#
5 Bryant	97
6 ***Barton***	94
7 ***Archer***	95
8 ***Fields***	95
9 Brooks	91#
10 Pickle	97
11 Leath	95
12 Wright	87
13 ***Boulter***	95
14 ***Sweeney***	94
15 de la Garza	89
16 Coleman	98
17 Stenholm	99
18 Leland	94
19 ***Combest***	99
20 Gonzalez	95
21 ***Loeffler***	76
22 ***DeLay***	95
23 Bustamante	93
24 Frost	93
25 Andrews	99
26 ***Armey***	98
27 Ortiz	90#
UTAH	
1 ***Hansen***	94
2 ***Monson***	95
3 ***Nielson***	99
VERMONT	
AL ***Jeffords***	91
VIRGINIA	
1 ***Bateman***	97
2 ***Whitehurst***	89
3 ***Bliley***	99
4 Sisisky	97†
5 Daniel	91
6 Olin	96
7 ***Slaughter***	99
8 ***Parris***	95
9 Boucher	94
10 ***Wolf***	98
WASHINGTON	
1 ***Miller***	97
2 Swift	98
3 Bonker	87
4 ***Morrison***	98
5 Foley	93
6 Dicks	95
7 Lowry	97†
8 ***Chandler***	94
WEST VIRGINIA	
1 Mollohan	99
2 Staggers	98
3 Wise	95
4 Rahall	94
WISCONSIN	
1 Aspin	89
2 Kastenmeier	97#
3 ***Gunderson***	97#
4 Kleczka	94#
5 Moody	94
6 ***Petri***	97
7 Obey	97
8 ***Roth***	89
9 ***Sensenbrenner***	98
WYOMING	
AL ***Cheney***	93

Conservative Strength Is High but Infrequent

Congressional Republicans and Southern Democrats joined forces less often in 1985 as a voting bloc against Northern Democrats, but when the so-called "conservative coalition" did appear it registered nearly as much success as ever.

A Congressional Quarterly vote analysis showed the coalition emerged in only 14 percent of the recorded votes in 1985, equaling its lowest rate of appearances since 1962 and, before that, 1957.

Despite its decreasing visibility, however, the coalition won 89 percent of the votes in which it appeared in 1985, approaching the 92 percent success rate of 1981 and continuing a high rate of victories scored throughout Ronald Reagan's presidency.

The conservative coalition, as defined for the Congressional Quarterly study, does not refer to any organized group or to an ideological definition of conservatism. It refers instead to a voting alliance that occurs when a majority of Republicans and Southern Democrats vote against a majority of Northern Democrats. *(Definitions, box, this page)*

Congressional Quarterly began studying the voting patterns of this conservative coalition in 1957. Since Reagan took office, Republicans and Southern Democrats had joined forces in opposition to Northern Democrats less often, particularly in comparison with the number of appearances scored during the 1970s.

The coalition appeared in 30 percent of recorded votes in 1971, its highest rate since the survey began, but since 1978 it had appeared no more than 21 percent of the time.

Definitions

Conservative Coalition. As used in this study, the term "conservative coalition" means a voting alliance of Republicans and Southern Democrats against the Northern Democrats in Congress. This meaning, rather than any philosophic definition of the "conservative coalition" position, provides the basis for CQ's selection of coalition votes.

Conservative Coalition Vote. Any vote in the Senate or the House on which a majority of voting Southern Democrats and a majority of voting Republicans opposed the stand taken by a majority of voting Northern Democrats. Votes on which there is an even division within the ranks of voting Northern Democrats, Southern Democrats or Republicans are not included.

Southern States. The Southern states are Alabama, Arkansas, Florida, Georgia, Kentucky, Louisiana, Mississippi, North Carolina, Oklahoma, South Carolina, Tennessee, Texas and Virginia. The other 37 states are grouped as the North in this study.

Conservative Coalition Support Score. Percentage of conservative coalition votes on which member votes "yea" or "nay" *in agreement* with the position of the conservative coalition. Failures to vote, even if a member announces a stand, lower the score.

Conservative Coalition Opposition Score. Percentage of conservative coalition votes on which a member votes "yea" or "nay" *in disagreement* with the position of the conservative coalition.

Senate, House Votes

Of 820 roll-call votes in 1985, the conservative coalition appeared in 60 Senate votes and 55 House votes. All but four of the Senate votes and nine of the House votes were coalition victories over Northern Democrats.

The coalition showed up most frequently in roll calls on defense and foreign affairs issues. In the House, a combined 14 of 46 victories were scored on increased funding for the MX missile and the "strategic defense initiative," the president's space-based anti-missile program also known as "star wars," and aid to anti-government rebels in Nicaragua.

In the Senate, six of the coalition's 56 victories came on funding for the Nicaraguan rebels, and eight wins came on defense issues. Another six wins were scored in the Senate on a bill to revamp immigration laws and control the flow of illegal aliens into the country.

In the House, the coalition did better than in previous years, winning 84 percent of the votes in which it appeared. This was its highest rate of success since 1981, when the coalition won 88 percent of its votes.

The coalition continued its nearly unchallenged strength in the Senate by winning 93 percent of the votes in which it appeared — a decline of only 1 percentage point from 1984.

Republican support for the coalition of 77 percent in the Senate actually dipped 3 percentage points from 1984, but Northern Democrats helped to make up that difference by increasing their support for the coalition by 4 percentage points to 29 percent.

In the House, support for the coalition increased slightly from all three groups.

The coalition's success in the House was also helped by increased support from Western members, Democrat and Republican alike, and from Republicans in all regions, particularly Southern members who supported it at a 90 percent rate.

However, the group with the highest level of opposition to the coalition remained Western House Democrats, who voted against the coalition 74 percent of the time. Still, this represented a decline from a 77 percent support rate in 1984.

Individual Scores

The conservative coalition found its most consistent allies in two House Republicans, Dan Burton of Indiana and John E. Grotberg of Illinois, who each voted with the coalition 100 percent of the time.

House Democratic supporters of the coalition were led

by Richard Ray of Georgia and G. V. "Sonny" Montgomery of Mississippi. Each voted with the coalition 98 percent of the time.

Among Northern Democrats voting with the coalition in the House, Ike Skelton of Missouri gave his support 85 percent of the time.

In the Senate, Republicans Strom Thurmond of South Carolina and Jesse Helms of North Carolina voted with the coalition 97 percent of the time. Sam Nunn of Georgia and Howell Heflin of Alabama were the leading Democratic supporters, each voting with the coalition 88 percent of the time.

For the fifth year in a row, Edward Zorinsky of Nebraska led all Northern Democrats in support of the coalition by voting with it 67 percent of the time. His Nebraska colleague, J. James Exon, voted with the coalition at a 65 percent rate.

House opponents of the coalition were led by Massachusetts Democrat Edward J. Markey, who voted against the coalition 98 percent of the time. Jim Leach of Iowa was the leading House Republican to oppose the coalition, voting against it at a 78 percent rate. Mickey Leland of Texas topped all House Democrats from the South in voting against the coalition 89 percent of the time.

Colorado Democrat Gary Hart led all senators in voting against the coalition, opposing it at a 95 percent rate. Charles McC. Mathias Jr. of Maryland, who voted against the coalition 58 percent of the time, was the leading Senate Republican opponent.

Coalition Appearances

Following is the percentage of the recorded votes for both houses of Congress on which the coalition appeared:

1966	25%	1976	24
1967	20	1977	26
1968	24	1978	21
1969	27	1979	20
1970	22	1980	18
1971	30	1981	21
1972	27	1982	18
1973	23	1983	15
1974	24	1984	16
1975	28	1985	14

Coalition Victories

Year	Total	Senate	House
1966	45%	51%	32%
1967	63	54	73
1968	73	80	63
1969	68	67	71
1970	66	64	70
1971	83	86	79
1972	69	63	79
1973	61	54	67
1974	59	54	67
1975	50	48	52
1976	58	58	59
1977	68	74	60
1978	52	46	57
1979	70	65	73
1980	72	75	67
1981	92	95	88
1982	85	90	78
1983	77	89	71
1984	83	94	75
1985	89	93	84

Average Scores

Following are the composite conservative coalition support and opposition scores for 1985 (scores for 1984 are in parentheses):

	Southern Democrats	Republicans	Northern Democrats
Coalition Support			
Senate	68% (67)	77% (80)	29% (25)
House	64 (63)	81 (79)	22 (21)
Coalition Opposition			
Senate	26% (23)	17% (14)	67% (67)
House	31 (29)	15 (15)	73 (72)

Regional Scores

Following are the parties' coalition support and opposition scores by region for 1985 (scores for 1984 are in parentheses):

SUPPORT

	East	West	South	Midwest
DEMOCRATS				
Senate	23% (20)	32% (23)	68% (67)	33% (31)
House	22 (22)	20 (17)	64 (63)	23 (24)
REPUBLICANS				
Senate	60% (60)	80% (84)	86% (92)	80% (81)
House	68 (66)	86 (83)	90 (86)	81 (80)

OPPOSITION

	East	West	South	Midwest
DEMOCRATS				
Senate	73% (75)	62% (60)	26% (23)	63% (61)
House	73 (71)	74 (77)	31 (29)	72 (70)
REPUBLICANS				
Senate	33% (34)	13% (9)	7% (3)	17% (15)
House	28 (30)	10 (9)	8 (8)	16 (14)

(CQ defines regions of the United States as follows: **East:** *Conn., Del., Maine, Md., Mass., N.H., N.J., N.Y., Pa., R.I., Vt., W.Va.* **West:** *Alaska, Ariz., Calif., Colo., Hawaii, Idaho, Mont., Nev., N.M., Ore., Utah, Wash., Wyo.* **South:** *Ala., Ark., Fla., Ga., Ky., La., Miss., N.C., Okla., S.C., Tenn., Texas, Va.* **Midwest:** *Ill., Ind., Iowa, Kan., Mich., Minn., Mo., Neb., N.D., Ohio, S.D., Wis.)*

Individual Scores

SUPPORT

Highest Coalition Support Scores. Those who voted with the conservative coalition most consistently in 1985:

SENATE

Southern Democrats		Republicans	
Nunn, Ga.	88%	Thurmond, S.C.	97%
Heflin, Ala.	88	Helms, N.C.	97
Long, La.	80	Hecht, Nev.	93
Bentsen, Texas	75	McClure, Idaho	93
Hollings, S.C.	75	Dole, Kan.	92
Boren, Okla.	75	Symms, Idaho	92
Ford, Ky.	68	Boschwitz, Minn.	92
Johnston, La.	68	Warner, Va.	92
Stennis, Miss.	68	Trible, Va.	92

Northern Democrats

Zorinsky, Neb.	67%
Exon, Neb.	65
DeConcini, Ariz.	63
Byrd, W.Va.	55
Dixon, Ill.	50
Baucus, Mont.	47
Rockefeller, W.Va.	47

HOUSE

Southern Democrats		Republicans	
Ray, Ga.	98%	Burton, Ind.	100%
Montgomery, Miss.	98	Grotberg, Ill.	100
Stenholm, Texas	96	McCandless, Calif.	98
Rowland, Ga.	96	Moore, La.	98
English, Okla.	95	McMillan, N.C.	98
Chapman, Texas	94	Kasich, Ohio	98
Hutto, Fla.	93		
Thomas, Ga.	93		

Northern Democrats

Skelton, Mo.	85%
Byron, Md.	80
Stratton, N.Y.	78
Murtha, Pa.	75
Dyson, Md.	71
Mollohan, W.Va.	69
Slattery, Kan.	65
Stallings, Idaho	58
Volkmer, Mo.	55
Glickman, Kan.	53
Carper, Del.	51
Young, Mo.	49
Murphy, Pa.	49
Price, Ill.	49
Yatron, Pa.	49

OPPOSITION

Highest Coalition Opposition Scores. Those who voted against the conservative coalition most consistently in 1985:

SENATE

Southern Democrats		Republicans	
Gore, Tenn.	50%	Mathias, Md.	58%
Sasser, Tenn.	48	Weicker, Conn.	47
Bumpers, Ark.	45	Chafee, R.I.	47
Pryor, Ark.	42	Hatfield, Ore.	42
Ford, Ky.	28	Specter, Pa.	37
Johnston, La.	27	Stafford, Vt.	37

Northern Democrats

Hart, Colo.	95%
Pell, R.I.	92
Lautenberg, N.J.	92
Sarbanes, Md.	87
Kerry, Mass.	87

HOUSE

Southern Democrats		Republicans	
Leland, Texas	89%	Leach, Iowa	78%
Lehman, Fla.	85	Green, N.Y.	67
Ford, Tenn.	85	Conte, Mass.	62
Gonzalez, Texas	78	Schneider, R.I.	62
Perkins, Ky.	73	Jeffords, Vt.	55
Bryant, Texas	67	McKinney, Conn.	53
Smith, Fla.	65	Coughlin, Pa.	45
Boucher, Va.	64	Fish, N.Y.	44
Cooper, Tenn.	60	Boehlert, N.Y.	44
Fascell, Fla.	58	Smith, N.J.	44
MacKay, Fla.	58	Evans, Iowa	44
		Petri, Wis.	40
		Roukema, N.J.	40

Northern Democrats

Markey, Mass.	98%
Kildee, Mich.	96
Sabo, Minn.	95
Ackerman, N.Y.	95
Wheat, Mo.	95
Studds, Mass.	95
Weiss, N.Y.	95

1985 Coalition Votes

Following is a list of all 1985 Senate and House votes on which the conservative coalition appeared. The votes are listed by CQ vote number and may be found in the vote charts starting on p. 2-S.

SENATE VOTES (60)

Coalition Victories (56) — 9, 23, 26, 27, 31, 45, 47, 68, 76, 83, 85, 89, 90, 95, 99, 109, 111, 112, 113, 114, 119, 123, 139, 141, 154, 164, 166, 177, 178, 179, 184, 186, 187, 191, 213, 235, 240, 241, 245, 255, 261, 285, 308, 310, 311, 313, 315, 351, 352, 357, 358, 362, 365, 369, 371, 378.

Coalition Defeats (4) — 176, 194, 244, 353.

HOUSE VOTES (55)

Coalition Victories (46) — 34, 36, 56, 97, 119, 122, 140, 141, 142, 143, 144, 151, 156, 157, 159, 160, 162, 164, 171, 176, 181, 187, 189, 193, 197, 199, 200, 202, 209, 213, 214, 221, 232, 240, 256, 276, 293, 332, 342, 349, 372, 373, 383, 407, 415, 418.

Coalition Defeats (9) — 95, 138, 303, 341, 381, 396, 406, 408, 436.

KEY

Democrats *Republicans*

	1	2
ALABAMA		
Denton	88	3
Heflin	88	12
ALASKA		
Murkowski	90	2
Stevens	90	3
ARIZONA		
Goldwater	72	8
DeConcini	63	28
ARKANSAS		
Bumpers	52	45
Pryor	50	42
CALIFORNIA		
Wilson	87	10
Cranston	18	78
COLORADO		
Armstrong	78	5
Hart	3	95
CONNECTICUT		
Weicker	43	47
Dodd	27	73
DELAWARE		
Roth	72	27
Biden	18	75
FLORIDA		
Hawkins	83	13
Chiles	60	13
GEORGIA		
Mattingly	90	10
Nunn	88	10
HAWAII		
Inouye	20	58
Matsunaga	32	62
IDAHO		
McClure	93	7
Symms	92	7
ILLINOIS		
Dixon	50	47
Simon	10	78
INDIANA		
Lugar	88	12
Quayle	90	10
IOWA		
Grassley	78	22
Harkin	17	82
KANSAS		
Dole	92	5
Kassebaum	75	22
KENTUCKY		
McConnell	90	8
Ford	68	28
LOUISIANA		
Johnston	68	27
Long	80	13
MAINE		
Cohen	55	32
Mitchell	30	70
MARYLAND		
Mathias	28	58
Sarbanes	8	87
MASSACHUSETTS		
Kennedy	17	73
Kerry	13	87
MICHIGAN		
Levin	25	72
Riegle	22	75
MINNESOTA		
Boschwitz	92	8
Durenberger	62	25
MISSISSIPPI		
Cochran	87	5
Stennis	68	10
MISSOURI		
Danforth	70	20
Eagleton	17	75
MONTANA		
Baucus	47	52
Melcher	33	63
NEBRASKA		
Exon	65	28
Zorinsky	67	30
NEVADA		
Hecht	93	7
Laxalt	88†	3†
NEW HAMPSHIRE		
Humphrey	72	22
Rudman	78	20
NEW JERSEY		
Bradley	17	73
Lautenberg	7	92
NEW MEXICO		
Domenici	88	8
Bingaman	37	60
NEW YORK		
D'Amato	88	8
Moynihan	27	67
NORTH CAROLINA		
East	45	0
Helms	97	3
NORTH DAKOTA		
Andrews	67	27
Burdick	30	70
OHIO		
Glenn	42	57
Metzenbaum	17	83
OKLAHOMA		
Nickles	87	12
Boren	75	18
OREGON		
Hatfield	32	42
Packwood	63	28
PENNSYLVANIA		
Heinz	60	33
Specter	58	37
RHODE ISLAND		
Chafee	52	47
Pell	7	92
SOUTH CAROLINA		
Thurmond	97	3
Hollings	75	25
SOUTH DAKOTA		
Abdnor	90	8
Pressler	78	15
TENNESSEE		
Gore	50	50
Sasser	52	48
TEXAS		
Gramm	88	12
Bentsen	75	23
UTAH		
Garn	72	13
Hatch	85	15
VERMONT		
Stafford	53	37
Leahy	27	73
VIRGINIA		
Trible	92	3
Warner	92	8
WASHINGTON		
Evans	73	25
Gorton	70	27
WEST VIRGINIA		
Byrd	55	45
Rockefeller	47	47
WISCONSIN		
Kasten	75	25
Proxmire	37	63
WYOMING		
Simpson	85	15
Wallop	83	5

Conservative Coalition Support and Opposition: Senate

1. Conservative Coalition Support, 1985. Percentage of 60 conservative coalition votes in 1985 on which senator voted "yea" or "nay" *in agreement* with the position of the conservative coalition. Failures to vote lower both support and opposition scores.

2. Conservative Coalition Opposition, 1985. Percentage of 60 conservative coalition votes in 1985 on which senator voted "yea" or "nay" *in disagreement* with the position of the conservative coalition. Failures to vote lower both support and opposition scores.

Conservative Coalition Support and Opposition: House

1. Conservative Coalition Support, 1985. Percentage of 55 conservative coalition recorded votes in 1985 on which representative voted "yea" or "nay" *in agreement* with the position of the conservative coalition. Failures to vote lower both support and opposition scores.

2. Conservative Coalition Opposition, 1985. Percentage of 55 conservative coalition recorded votes in 1985 on which representative voted "yea" or "nay" *in disagreement* with the position of the conservative coalition. Failures to vote lower both support and opposition scores.

1. Rep. Frank McCloskey, D-Ind., was sworn in May 1, 1985, following a House vote to seat him necessitated by a dispute over the outcome of the 1984 general election. The seat was vacant from Jan. 3 until May 1, 1985.

2. Rep. Cathy (Mrs. Gillis) Long, D-La., was sworn in April 4, 1985, to succeed Gillis W. Long, D, who died Jan. 20, 1985. Gillis Long's conservative coalition support and opposition scores for 1985 were 0 percent.

3. Rep. Thomas P. O'Neill Jr., D-Mass., as Speaker, votes at his discretion.

4. Rep. Jim Chapman, D-Texas, was sworn in Sept. 4, 1985, to succeed Sam B. Hall Jr., D, who was sworn in as a federal judge May 28, 1985. Hall's conservative coalition support score for 1985 was 83 percent. His opposition score was 0 percent.

KEY

† Not eligible for all recorded votes in 1985 (sworn in after Jan. 3, died or resigned during session, or voted "present" to avoid possible conflict of interest).

Democrats *Republicans*

	1	2
ALABAMA		
1 ***Callahan***	96	4
2 ***Dickinson***	85	9
3 Nichols	87	4
4 Bevill	80	15
5 Flippo	76	13
6 Erdreich	76	22
7 Shelby	85	13
ALASKA		
AL ***Young***	82	18
ARIZONA		
1 ***McCain***	84	13
2 Udall	16	75
3 ***Stump***	96	4
4 ***Rudd***	82	9
5 ***Kolbe***	91	9
ARKANSAS		
1 Alexander	36	56
2 Robinson	73	25
3 ***Hammerschmidt***	95	4
4 Anthony	58	36
CALIFORNIA		
1 Bosco	35	56
2 ***Chappie***	75	4
3 Matsui	9	89
4 Fazio	35	65
5 Burton	7	89
6 Boxer	2	93
7 Miller	9	84
8 Dellums	5	91
9 Stark	2	91
10 Edwards	7	93
11 Lantos	27	71
12 ***Zschau***	75	24
13 Mineta	13	85
14 ***Shumway***	91	5
15 Coelho	24	69
16 Panetta	25	71
17 ***Pashayan***	84	15
18 Lehman	20	71
19 ***Lagomarsino***	96	4
20 ***Thomas***	84	11
21 ***Fiedler***	85	11
22 ***Moorhead***	93	5
23 Beilenson	11	84
24 Waxman	11	84
25 Roybal	7	84
26 Berman	9	85
27 Levine	7	91
28 Dixon	11	67
29 Hawkins	4	65
30 Martinez	15	76
31 Dymally	9	82
32 Anderson	36	62
33 ***Dreier***	91	9
34 Torres	11	82
35 ***Lewis***	84	11
36 Brown	9	76
37 ***McCandless***	98	0
38 ***Dornan***	82	13
39 ***Dannemeyer***	87	7
40 ***Badham***	82	9
41 ***Lowery***	84	11
42 ***Lungren***	89	11
43 ***Packard***	91	9
44 Bates	25	73
45 ***Hunter***	87	11
COLORADO		
1 Schroeder	24	76
2 Wirth	20	73
3 ***Strang***	76	9
4 ***Brown***	82	18
5 ***Kramer***	84	5
6 ***Schaefer***	91	4
CONNECTICUT		
1 Kennelly	22	78
2 Gejdenson	7	89
3 Morrison	9	87
4 ***McKinney***	25	53
5 ***Rowland***	80	18
6 ***Johnson***	67	33
DELAWARE		
AL Carper	51	49
FLORIDA		
1 Hutto	93	7
2 Fuqua	82	9
3 Bennett	51	49
4 Chappell	82	13
5 ***McCollum***	91	9
6 MacKay	40	58
7 Gibbons	49	45
8 ***Young***	87	9
9 ***Bilirakis***	87	11
10 ***Ireland***	89	7
11 Nelson	60	11
12 ***Lewis***	87	11
13 ***Mack***	91	9
14 Mica	71	27
15 ***Shaw***	89	9
16 Smith	27	65
17 Lehman	11	85
18 Pepper	27	56
19 Fascell	40	58
GEORGIA		
1 Thomas	93	7
2 Hatcher	78	13
3 Ray	98	2
4 ***Swindall***	95	2
5 Fowler	55	38
6 ***Gingrich***	89	9
7 Darden	87	13
8 Rowland	96	4
9 Jenkins	76	22
10 Barnard	87	5
HAWAII		
1 Heftel	42	36
2 Akaka	35	58
IDAHO		
1 ***Craig***	96	2
2 Stallings	58	36
ILLINOIS		
1 Hayes	4	93
2 Savage	2	87
3 Russo	24	75
4 ***O'Brien***	76	11
5 Lipinski	45	49
6 ***Hyde***	85	9
7 Collins	2	89
8 Rostenkowski	18	73
9 Yates	7	91
10 ***Porter***	73	25
11 Annunzio	33	62
12 ***Crane***	76	9
13 ***Fawell***	78	22
14 ***Grotberg***	100	0
15 ***Madigan***	84	16
16 ***Martin***	84	16
17 Evans	5	93
18 ***Michel***	91	7
19 Bruce	25	75
20 Durbin	20	78
21 Price	49	31
22 Gray	40	51
INDIANA		
1 Visclosky	33	67
2 Sharp	36	62
3 ***Hiler***	91	9
4 ***Coats***	80	20
5 ***Hillis***	84	2

ND Northern Democrats SD - Southern Democrats

	1	2
6 ***Burton***	100	0
7 ***Myers***	91	9
8 McCloskey [1]	27†	73†
9 Hamilton	42	56
10 Jacobs	27	71
IOWA		
1 ***Leach***	22	78
2 ***Tauke***	64	36
3 ***Evans***	55	44
4 Smith	35	62
5 ***Lightfoot***	84	16
6 Bedell	16	82
KANSAS		
1 ***Roberts***	80	16
2 Slattery	65	35
3 ***Meyers***	78	18
4 Glickman	53	45
5 ***Whittaker***	84	13
KENTUCKY		
1 Hubbard	76	15
2 Natcher	56	44
3 Mazzoli	62	36
4 ***Snyder***	85	13
5 ***Rogers***	89	9
6 ***Hopkins***	84	15
7 Perkins	27	73
LOUISIANA		
1 ***Livingston***	96	4
2 Boggs	38	55
3 Tauzin	91	5
4 Roemer	85	15
5 Huckaby	89	7
6 ***Moore***	98	2
7 Breaux	89	5
8 Long [2]	42†	51†
MAINE		
1 ***McKernan***	73	27
2 ***Snowe***	69	31
MARYLAND		
1 Dyson	71	27
2 ***Bentley***	85	13
3 Mikulski	18	82
4 ***Holt***	69	15
5 Hoyer	29	71
6 Byron	80	13
7 Mitchell	5	85
8 Barnes	7	91
MASSACHUSETTS		
1 ***Conte***	31	62
2 Boland	25	69
3 Early	11	78
4 Frank	5	91
5 Atkins	13	82
6 Mavroules	13	87
7 Markey	2	98
8 O'Neill [3]		
9 Moakley	11	85
10 Studds	5	95
11 Donnelly	24	73
MICHIGAN		
1 Conyers	7	67
2 ***Pursell***	75	20
3 Wolpe	7	93
4 ***Siljander***	89	4
5 ***Henry***	65	35
6 Carr	38	56
7 Kildee	4	96
8 Traxler	16	71
9 ***Vander Jagt***	87	5
10 ***Schuette***	93	5
11 ***Davis***	78	18
12 Bonior	5	84
13 Crockett	5	80
14 Hertel	16	84
15 Ford	7	87
16 Dingell	27	64
17 Levin	13	87
18 ***Broomfield***	84	13
MINNESOTA		
1 Penny	35	65
2 ***Weber***	73	18
3 ***Frenzel***	80	16
4 Vento	4	91
5 Sabo	5	95
6 Sikorski	20	78
7 ***Stangeland***	89	9
8 Oberstar	7	93
MISSISSIPPI		
1 Whitten	55	35
2 ***Franklin***	91	2
3 Montgomery	98	0
4 Dowdy	76	15
5 ***Lott***	89	5
MISSOURI		
1 Clay	4	91
2 Young	49	49
3 Gephardt	31	65
4 Skelton	85	15
5 Wheat	5	95
6 ***Coleman***	89	5
7 ***Taylor***	89	9
8 ***Emerson***	95	2
9 Volkmer	55	44
MONTANA		
1 Williams	7	87
2 ***Marlenee***	80	11
NEBRASKA		
1 ***Bereuter***	78	18
2 ***Daub***	87	11
3 ***Smith***	82	18
NEVADA		
1 Reid	40	60
2 ***Vucanovich***	91	7
NEW HAMPSHIRE		
1 ***Smith***	82	18
2 ***Gregg***	73	25
NEW JERSEY		
1 Florio	22	75
2 Hughes	40	60
3 Howard	9	89
4 ***Smith***	55	44
5 ***Roukema***	60	40
6 Dwyer	18	82
7 ***Rinaldo***	71	29
8 Roe	24	73
9 Torricelli	18	78
10 Rodino	5	87
11 ***Gallo***	82	18
12 ***Courter***	84	13
13 ***Saxton***	76	24
14 Guarini	15	80
NEW MEXICO		
1 ***Lujan***	85	13
2 ***Skeen***	93	4
3 Richardson	33	65
NEW YORK		
1 ***Carney***	89	7
2 Downey	9	87
3 Mrazek	16	80
4 ***Lent***	89	9
5 ***McGrath***	75	20
6 Addabbo	15	56
7 Ackerman	4	95
8 Scheuer	7	91
9 Manton	24	69
10 Schumer	7	84
11 Towns	2	87
12 Owens	4	82
13 Solarz	11	87
14 ***Molinari***	69	31
15 ***Green***	33	67
16 Rangel	7	91
17 Weiss	5	95
18 Garcia	4	87
19 Biaggi	38	51
20 ***DioGuardi***	80	20
21 ***Fish***	44	44
22 ***Gilman***	60	38
23 Stratton	78	22
24 ***Solomon***	82	13
25 ***Boehlert***	56	44
26 ***Martin***	75	18
27 ***Wortley***	75	18
28 McHugh	11	87
29 ***Horton***	51	36
30 ***Eckert***	87	7
31 ***Kemp***	85	11
32 LaFalce	22	73
33 Nowak	11	89
34 Lundine	25	73
NORTH CAROLINA		
1 Jones	38	49
2 Valentine	84	13
3 Whitley	80	20
4 ***Cobey***	93	7
5 Neal	60	33
6 ***Coble***	91	9
7 Rose	53	42
8 Hefner	60	7
9 ***McMillan***	98	2
10 ***Broyhill***	91	5
11 ***Hendon***	95	4
NORTH DAKOTA		
AL Dorgan	22	78
OHIO		
1 Luken	24	60
2 ***Gradison***	75	22
3 Hall	33	56
4 ***Oxley***	96	4
5 ***Latta***	91	7
6 ***McEwen***	87	11
7 ***DeWine***	87	11
8 ***Kindness***	93	4
9 Kaptur	27	69
10 ***Miller***	85	7
11 Eckart	35	65
12 ***Kasich***	98	2
13 Pease	20	80
14 Seiberling	11	85
15 ***Wylie***	85	9
16 ***Regula***	82	18
17 Traficant	11	89
18 Applegate	45	51
19 Feighan	24	76
20 Oakar	11	89
21 Stokes	5	93
OKLAHOMA		
1 Jones	71	29
2 Synar	33	65
3 Watkins	67	29
4 McCurdy	85	15
5 ***Edwards***	91	5
6 English	95	4
OREGON		
1 AuCoin	31	64
2 ***Smith, R.***	84	11
3 Wyden	36	64
4 Weaver	7	82
5 ***Smith D.***	85	7
PENNSYLVANIA		
1 Foglietta	13	80
2 Gray	13	73
3 Borski	20	78
4 Kolter	38	60
5 ***Schulze***	82	15
6 Yatron	49	51
7 Edgar	5	91
8 Kostmayer	20	80
9 ***Shuster***	87	11
10 ***McDade***	67	29
11 Kanjorski	47	53
12 Murtha	75	22
13 ***Coughlin***	55	45
14 Coyne	9	89
15 ***Ritter***	76	20
16 ***Walker***	85	15
17 ***Gekas***	87	13
18 Walgren	16	75
19 ***Goodling***	69	24
20 Gaydos	47	44
21 ***Ridge***	58	36
22 Murphy	49	49
23 ***Clinger***	65	31
RHODE ISLAND		
1 St Germain	16	78
2 ***Schneider***	25	62
SOUTH CAROLINA		
1 ***Hartnett***	80	13
2 ***Spence***	93	7
3 Derrick	60	35
4 ***Campbell***	89	5
5 Spratt	73	27
6 Tallon	84	16
SOUTH DAKOTA		
AL Daschle	33	55
TENNESSEE		
1 ***Quillen***	80	11
2 ***Duncan***	87	11
3 Lloyd	82	16
4 Cooper	40	60
5 Boner	71	25
6 Gordon	42	56
7 ***Sundquist***	91	7
8 Jones	75	18
9 Ford	7	85
TEXAS		
1 Chapman [4]	94†	0†
2 Wilson	60	22
3 ***Bartlett***	91	9
4 Hall, R.	84	5
5 Bryant	31	67
6 ***Barton***	91	5
7 ***Archer***	87	7
8 ***Fields***	91	9
9 Brooks	35	56
10 Pickle	64	29
11 Leath	91	4
12 Wright	36	47
13 ***Boulter***	93	4
14 ***Sweeney***	91	7
15 de la Garza	60	36
16 Coleman	51	47
17 Stenholm	96	2
18 Leland	7	89
19 ***Combest***	96	4
20 Gonzalez	15	78
21 ***Loeffler***	78	4
22 ***DeLay***	96	4
23 Bustamante	51	44
24 Frost	47	47
25 Andrews	84	16
26 ***Armey***	93	5
27 Ortiz	64	33
UTAH		
1 ***Hansen***	96	2
2 ***Monson***	95	4
3 ***Nielson***	89	9
VERMONT		
AL ***Jeffords***	33	55
VIRGINIA		
1 ***Bateman***	89	11
2 ***Whitehurst***	89	4
3 ***Bliley***	87	13
4 Sisisky	78	20
5 Daniel	80	7
6 Olin	60	36
7 ***Slaughter***	95	5
8 ***Parris***	76	20
9 Boucher	35	64
10 ***Wolf***	75	24
WASHINGTON		
1 ***Miller***	62	36
2 Swift	29	69
3 Bonker	18	73
4 ***Morrison***	84	15
5 Foley	29	69
6 Dicks	44	53
7 Lowry	7	89
8 ***Chandler***	76	22
WEST VIRGINIA		
1 Mollohan	69	31
2 Staggers	33	65
3 Wise	27	71
4 Rahall	25	75
WISCONSIN		
1 Aspin	44	49
2 Kastenmeier	5	93
3 ***Gunderson***	73	25
4 Kleczka	24	75
5 Moody	11	85
6 ***Petri***	60	40
7 Obey	7	91
8 ***Roth***	73	24
9 ***Sensenbrenner***	69	31
WYOMING		
AL ***Cheney***	95	2

PRESIDENTIAL MESSAGES

CQ

President Reagan's 2nd Inaugural Address

Following is the Congressional Record *text of President Reagan's inaugural address as delivered Jan. 21.*

Senator Mathias, Chief Justice Burger, Vice President Bush, Speaker O'Neill, Senator Dole, Reverend Clergy, members of my family and friends, and my fellow citizens:

This day has been made brighter with the presence here of one who, for a time, has been absent — Senator John Stennis.

God bless you and welcome back.

There is, however, one who is not with us today: Representative Gillis Long of Louisiana left us last night. I wonder if we could all join in a moment of silent prayer.*

[Moment of silent prayer.]

Amen.

There are no words adequate to express my thanks for the great honor that you have bestowed on me. I will do my utmost to be deserving of your trust.

This is, as Senator Mathias told us, the 50th time that we the people have celebrated this historic occasion. When the first President, George Washington, placed his hand upon the Bible, he stood less than a single day's journey by horseback from raw, untamed wilderness.

There were 4 million Americans in a union of 13 States. Today we are 60 times as many in a union of 50 States. We have lighted the world with our inventions, gone to the aid of mankind wherever in the world there was a cry for help, journeyed to the Moon and safely returned.

So much has changed. And yet we stand together as we did two centuries ago.

When I took this oath 4 years ago, I did so in a time of economic stress. Voices were raised saying we had to look to our past for the greatness and glory. But we, the present-day Americans, are not given to looking backward. In this blessed land, there is always a better tomorrow.

Four years ago, I spoke to you of a new beginning and we have accomplished that. But in another sense, our new beginning is a continuation of that beginning created two centuries ago when, for the first time in history, government, the people said, was not our master, it is our servant; its only power that which we the people allow it to have.

That system has never failed us, but, for a time, we failed the system. We asked things of government that government was not equipped to give. We yielded authority to the National Government that properly belonged to States or to local governments or to the people themselves. We allowed taxes and inflation to rob us of our earnings and savings and watched the great industrial machine that had made us the most productive people on Earth slow down and the number of unemployed increase.

By 1980, we knew it was time to renew our faith, to strive with all our strength toward the ultimate in individual freedom consistent with an orderly society.

We believed then and now: There are no limits to growth and human progress when men and women are free to follow their dreams. And we were right.

And we were right to believe that. Tax rates have been reduced, inflation cut dramatically, and more people are employed than ever before in our history.

We are creating a nation once again vibrant, robust, and alive. But there are many mountains yet to climb. We will not rest until every American enjoys the fullness of freedom, dignity, and opportunity as our birthright. It is our birthright as citizens of this great Republic.

And, if we meet this challenge, these will be years when Americans have restored their confidence and tradition of progress; when our values of faith, family, work, and neighborhood were restated for a modern age; when our economy was finally freed from government's grip; when we made sincere efforts at meaningful arms reduction, rebuilding our defenses, our economy, and developing new technologies, and helped preserve peace in a troubled world; when Americans courageously supported the struggle for liberty, self-government, and free enterprise throughout the world, and turned the tide of history away from totalitarian darkness and into the warm sunlight of human freedom.

My fellow citizens, our Nation is poised for greatness. We must do what we know is right and do it with all our might. Let history say of us, these were golden years — when the American Revolution was reborn, when freedom gained new life, when America reached for her best.

Our two-party system has served us well over the years, but never better than in those times of great challenge when we came together not as Democrats or Republicans, but as Americans united in a common cause.

Two of our Founding Fathers, a Boston lawyer named Adams and a Virginia planter named Jefferson, members of that remarkable group who met in Independence Hall and dared to think they could start the world over again, left us an important lesson. They had become political rivals in the Presidential election of 1800. Then years later, when both were retired, and age had softened their anger, they began to speak to each other again through letters. A bond was reestablished between those two who had helped create this Government of ours.

In 1826, the 50th anniversary of the Declaration of Independence, they both died. They died on the same day, within a few hours of each other, and that day was the Fourth of July.

In one of those letters exchanged in the sunset of their lives, Jefferson wrote:

> It carries me back to the times when, beset with difficulties and dangers, we were fellow laborers in the same cause, struggling for what is most valuable to man, his right to self-government. Laboring always at the same oar, with some wave ever ahead threatening to overwhelm us, and yet passing harmless ... we rode through the storm with heart and hand.

Well, with heart and hand, let us stand as one today: One people under God determined that our future shall be worthy of our past. As we do, we must not repeat the well-intentioned errors of our past. We must never again abuse the trust of working men and women, by sending their earnings on a futile chase after the spiraling demands of a bloated Federal establishment. You elected us in 1980 to end this prescription for disaster, and I don't believe you reelected us in 1984 to reverse course.

At the heart of our efforts is one idea vindicated by 25 straight months of economic growth: Freedom and incentives unleash the drive and entrepreneurial genius that are the core of human progress. We have begun to increase the rewards for work, savings, and investment, reduce the increase in the cost and size of government and its interference in people's lives.

We must simplify our tax system, make it more fair, and bring the rates down for all who work and earn. We must think anew and move with a new boldness, so every American who seeks work can find work; so the least among us shall have an equal chance to achieve the greatest things — to be heroes who heal our sick, feed the hungry, protect peace among nations, and leave this world a better place.

The time has come for a new American Emancipation — a great national drive to tear down economic barriers and liberate the spirit of enterprise in the most distressed areas of our country. My friends, together we can do this, and do it we must, so help me God.

From new freedom will spring new opportunities for growth, a more productive, fulfilled and united people, and a stronger America — an America that will lead the technological revolution, and also open its mind and heart and soul to the treasures of literature, music and poetry, and the values of faith, courage, and love.

A dynamic economy, with more citizens working and paying taxes, will be our strongest tool to bring down budget deficits. But an almost unbroken 50 years of deficit spending has finally brought us to a time of reckoning.

** The president referred to Sen. John C. Stennis, D-Miss., who had his leg amputated Nov. 30, 1984, because of cancer, and Rep. Gillis W. Long, D-La., who died Jan. 20.*

We have come to a turning point, a moment for hard decisions. I have asked the Cabinet and my staff a question, and now I put the same question to all of you: If not us, who? And if not now, when? It must be done by all of us going forward with a program aimed at reaching a balanced budget. We can then begin reducing the national debt.

I will shortly submit a budget to the Congress aimed at freezing Government program spending for the next year. Beyond that, we must take further steps to permanently control Government's power to tax and spend.

We must act now to protect future generations from Government's desire to spend its citizens' money and tax them into servitude when the bills come due. Let us make it unconstitutional for the Federal Government to spend more than the Federal Government takes in.

We have already started returning to the people and to State and local governments responsibilities better handled by them. Now, there is a place for the Federal Government in matters of social compassion. But our fundamental goals must be to reduce dependency and upgrade the dignity of those who are infirm or disadvantaged. And here a growing economy and support from family and community offer our best chance for a society where compassion is a way of life, where the old and infirm are cared for, the young and, yes, the unborn protected, and the unfortunate looked after and made self-sufficient.

And there is another area where the Federal Government can play a part. As an older American, I remember a time when people of different race, creed, or ethnic origin in our land found hatred and prejudice installed in social custom and, yes, in law. There is no story more heartening in our history than the progress that we have made toward the "brotherhood of man" that God intended for us. Let us resolve there will be no turning back or hesitation on the road to an America rich in dignity and abundant with opportunity for all our citizens.

Let us resolve that we the people will build an American opportunity society in which all of us — white and black, rich and poor, young and old — will go forward together arm in arm. Again, let us remember that though our heritage is one of blood lines from every corner of the Earth, we are all Americans pledged to carry on this last, best hope of man on Earth.

National Security

I have spoken of our domestic goals and the limitations which we should put on our National Government. Now let me turn to a task which is the primary responsibility of National Government — the safety and security of our people.

Today we utter no prayer more fervently than the ancient prayer for peace on Earth. Yet history has shown that peace will not come nor will our freedom be preserved by good will alone. There are those in the world who scorn our vision of human dignity and freedom. One nation, the Soviet Union, has conducted the greatest military buildup in the history of man, building arsenals of awesome offensive weapons.

We have made progress in restoring our defense capability. But much remains to be done. There must be no wavering by us, nor any doubts by others, that America will meet her responsibilities to remain free, secure, and at peace.

There is only one way safely and legitimately to reduce the cost of national security, and that is to reduce the need for it. And this we are trying to do in negotiations with the Soviet Union. We are not just discussing limits on a further increase of nuclear weapons. We seek, instead, to reduce their number. We seek the total elimination one day of nuclear weapons from the face of the Earth.

Now, for decades, we and the Soviets have lived under the threat of mutual assured destruction; if either resorted to the use of nuclear weapons, the other could retaliate and destroy the one who had started it. Is there either logic or morality in believing that if one side threatens to kill tens of millions of our people, our only recourse is to threaten killing tens of millions of theirs?

I have approved a research program to find, if we can, a security shield that would destroy nuclear missiles before they reach their target. It wouldn't kill people, it would destroy weapons. It wouldn't militarize space, it would help demilitarize the arsenals of Earth. It would render nuclear weapons obsolete. We will meet with the Soviets, hoping that we can agree on a way to rid the world of the threat of nuclear destruction.

We strive for peace and security, heartened by the changes all around us. Since the turn of the century, the number of democracies in the world has grown fourfold. Human freedom is on the march, and nowhere more so than in our own hemisphere. Freedom is one of the deepest and noblest aspirations of the human spirit. People worldwide hunger for the right of self-determination, for those inalienable rights that make for human dignity and progress.

America must remain freedom's staunchest friend, for freedom is our best ally —

And it is the world's only hope, to conquer poverty and preserve peace. Every blow we inflict against poverty will be a blow against its dark allies of oppression and war. Every victory for human freedom will be a victory for world peace.

So we go forward today, a Nation still mighty in its youth and powerful in its purpose. With our alliances strengthened, with our economy leading the world to a new age of economic expansion, we look forward to a world rich in possibilities. And all this because we have worked and acted together, not as members of political parties, but as Americans.

My friends, we live in a world that is lit by lightning. So much is changing and will change, but so much endures, and transcends time.

History is a ribbon, always unfurling; history is a journey. And as we continue our journey, we think of those who traveled before us. We stand together again at the steps of this symbol of our democracy — or we would have been standing at the steps if it hadn't gotten so cold. Now we are standing inside this symbol of our democracy. Now we hear again the echoes of our past.

A General falls to his knees in the hard snow of Valley Forge; a lonely President paces the darkened halls, and ponders his struggle to preserve the Union; the men of the Alamo call out encouragement to each other; a settler pushes west and sings a song, and the song echoes out forever and fills the unknowing air.

It is the American sound. It is hopeful, big-hearted, idealistic, daring, decent, and fair. That's our heritage; that is our song. We sing it still. For all our problems, our differences, we are together as of old, as we raise our voices to the God who is the Author of this most tender music. And may He continue to hold us close as we fill the world with our sound — sound in unity, affection, and love. One people under God, dedicated to the dream of freedom that He has placed in the human heart, called upon now to pass that dream on to a waiting and hopeful world.

God bless you and may God bless America. ∎

President's Budget Message

Following is the text of President Reagan's Feb. 4 budget message to Congress.

TO THE CONGRESS OF
THE UNITED STATES:

In the past 2 years we have experienced one of the strongest economic recoveries of the post-war period. The prospect of a substantially brighter future for America lies before us. As 1985 begins, the economy is growing robustly and shows considerable upward momentum. Favorable financial conditions presage a continuation of the expansion. Production, productivity, and employment gains have been impressive, and inflation remains well under control. I am proud of the state of our economy. Let me highlight a few points:

- The economy expanded at a 6.8% rate in 1984 and at a 6% annual rate over the 2 years since the recession trough at the end of 1982 — faster than any other upturn since 1951.

- Confidence in the economy has prompted business firms to expand their capital facilities. Real investment in new plant and equipment has grown 15.4% annually since the end of 1982 — faster than in any other post-war recovery.
- The ratio of real investment to real GNP has reached its highest level in the post-war period.
- Industrial production is 23% above its level at the recession trough in November 1982 — a greater advance than in any other recovery since 1958.
- Corporate profits have risen nearly 90% since the recession trough in 1982 — the fastest 8-quarter increase in 37 years.
- Civilian employment has grown 7.2 million over the past 25 months and the number of unemployed has fallen by 3.7 million. In the last 4 months alone, more than 1.1 million Americans have found jobs.
- Inflation remains well under control. The December 1984 CPI was 4% higher than a year earlier, about a third of the rate of inflation this administration inherited. The GNP deflator, the broadest measure of inflation, increased only 3.5% last year and at only a 2.4% annual rate in the fourth quarter.
- The prime rate of interest is now only half of what it was when I took office.

Contrast our current circumstances with the situation we faced just 4 years ago. Inflation was raging at double-digit rates. Oil prices had soared. The prime rate of interest was over 20%. The economy was stagnating. Unemployment had risen sharply and was to rise further. America's standing in world opinion was at low ebb.

All that, mercifully, is behind us now. The tremendous turnaround in our fortunes did not just happen. In February 1981, I presented the four fundamentals of my economic program. They were:

- Reducing the growth of overall Federal spending by eliminating activities that are beyond the proper sphere of Federal Government responsibilities and by restraining the growth of spending for other activities.
- Limiting tax burdens to the minimum levels necessary to finance only essential government services, thereby strengthening incentives for saving, investment, work, productivity, and economic growth.
- Reducing the Federal regulatory burden where the Federal Government intrudes unnecessarily into our private lives, the efficient conduct of private business, or the operations of State and local governments.
- Supporting a sound and steady monetary policy, to encourage economic growth and bring inflation under control.

Four Years of Accomplishment

These policies were designed to restore economic growth and stability. They succeeded.

The past 4 years have also seen the beginning of a quiet but profound revolution in the conduct of our Federal Government. We have halted what seemed at the time an inexorable set of trends toward greater and greater Government intrusiveness, more and more regulation, higher and higher taxes, more and more spending, higher and higher inflation, and weaker and weaker defense. We have halted these trends in our first 4 years.

- The rate of Federal spending growth was out of control at 17.4% a year in 1980. Under my budget proposals the growth of programmatic spending — that is, total Federal spending except for debt service — will be zero next year — frozen at this year's levels.
- Further, spending will grow only 30% over the 4 years from 1982 to 1986, compared to its record pace of 66% between 1977 and 1981, and this despite legislated additions to my program and the needed rebuilding of our defense capabilities.
- The Federal tax system was changed for the better — marginal tax rates were reduced and depreciation reform introduced. These reforms were designed to increase incentives for work, training and education, saving, business growth, and capital expansion. Tax loopholes have been closed, improving the equity of the system.
- Domestic spending, which previously grew faster than any other major part of the budget (nearly four-fold in real terms between 1960 and 1980), will have been virtually frozen from 1981 to 1985.
- Our defense capabilities are now getting back to a level where we can protect our citizens, honor our commitments to our allies, and participate in the long-awaited arms control talks from a position of respected strength.
- Federal credit programs, which had also grown out of control, have been cut back, and their management has been vastly improved.
- The rapid growth of regulations and red tape has also been halted. The number of Federal rules published by agencies has fallen by over 35% during the past 4 years, and many unnecessary old rules have been eliminated. For the first time, the *Federal Register* of new regulatory actions has grown shorter for 4 consecutive years; it is now 41% shorter than it was in 1980.
- Major management improvement initiatives are underway that will fundamentally change the way the Federal Government operates. The President's Private Sector Survey on Cost Control has completed its report, and many of its recommendations are included in this budget. The President's Council on Integrity and Efficiency has reported $46 billion in improved use of funds through reduction of waste and fraud.
- The Federal nondefense work force has been reduced by over 78,000.

The proposals contained in this budget will build on the accomplishments of the last 4 years and put into action a philosophy of government that is working and that has received the overwhelming endorsement of the American people.

The 1986 Budget Program

If we took no action to curb the growth of spending, Federal outlays would rise to over a trillion dollars in 1986. This would result in deficits exceeding $200 billion in each of the next 5 years. This is unacceptable. The budget I propose, therefore, will reduce spending by $51 billion in 1986, $83 billion in 1987, and $105 billion in 1988. Enactment of these measures would reduce the deficit projected for 1988 to $144 billion — still a far cry from our goal of a balanced budget, but a significant step in the right direction and a 42% reduction from the current services level projected for that year.

Last year my administration worked with Congress to come up with a downpayment on reducing the deficit. This budget commits the Government to a second installment. With comparable commitments to further reductions in the next two budgets, and, I hope, other spending reduction ideas advanced by the Congress, we can achieve our goal in an orderly fashion.

The budget proposes a 1-year freeze in total spending other than debt service. This will be achieved through a combination of freezes, reforms, terminations, cutbacks, and management improvements in individual programs. For a number of reasons, a line-by-line budget freeze is not possible or desirable. Further, such an approach would assume that all programs are of equal importance. Taken together, the specific proposals in this budget hold total Federal spending excluding debt service constant in 1986 at its 1985 level.

The budget proposals provide for substantial cost savings in the medicare program, in Federal payroll costs, in agricultural and other subsidies to business and upper-income groups, in numerous programs providing grants to State and local governments, and in credit programs. A freeze is proposed in the level of some entitlement program benefits, other than social security, means-tested programs, and programs for the disabled, that have hitherto received automatic "cost-of-living adjustments" every year. The budget proposes further reductions in defense spending below previously reduced mid-year levels.

Despite the reforms of the past 4 years, our Federal tax system remains complex and inequitable. Tax rates are still so high that they distort economic decisions, and this reduces economic growth from what it otherwise could be. I will propose, after further consultation with the Congress, further tax simplification and reform. The proposals will not be a scheme to raise taxes — only to distribute their burden more fairly and to simplify the entire system. By broadening the base, we can lower rates.

There will be substantial political resistance to every deficit reduction measure proposed in this budget. Every dollar of current Federal spending benefits someone, and that person has a vested self-interest in seeing these benefits perpetuated and expanded. Prior to my administration, such interests had been dominant and their expectations and demands had been met, time and time again.

At some point, however, the question must be raised: "Where is the political log-rolling going to stop?" At some point, the collective demands upon the public Treasury of all the special interests combined exceed the public's ability and willingness to pay. The single most difficult word for a politician to utter is a simple, flat "No." The patience of the American people has been stretched as far as it will go. They want action; they have demanded it.

We said "no" frequently in 1981, and real spending for discretionary domestic programs dropped sharply. But we did not accomplish enough. We now have no choice but to renew our efforts with redoubled vigor. The profusion of Federal domestic spending programs must be reduced to an acceptable, appropriate, and supportable size.

It will require political courage of a high order to carry this program forward in the halls of Congress, but I believe that with good faith and goodwill on all sides, we can succeed. If we fail to reduce excessive Federal benefits to special interest groups, we will be saddled either with larger budget deficits or with higher taxes — either of which would be of greater harm to the American economy and people.

1986 Management and Regulatory Program

Not only must both the scope and scale of Federal spending be drastically cut back to reduce the deficit: we must also institute comprehensive management improvements and administrative reforms to make sure that we use available funds as efficiently as possible.

Tough but necessary steps are being taken throughout the Federal Government to reduce the costs of management and administration. Substantial savings in overhead costs have been achieved under provisions of the Deficit Reduction Act of 1984. A 5% Federal civilian employee salary cut has been proposed; a 10% reduction in administrative overhead has been ordered; termination of programs that have outlived their usefulness is proposed; outmoded, inefficient agency field structures that have evolved over the past half-century are being consolidated and streamlined to take advantage of efficiencies made possible by modern transportation, communication, and information technology.

Administration of Federal agencies is being made more efficient through the adoption of staffing standards, automation of manual processes, consolidation of similar functions, and reduction of administrative overhead costs. A program to increase productivity by 20% by 1992 in all appropriate Government functions is being instituted, as are improved cash and credit management systems and error rate reduction programs.

This management improvement program will result in a leaner and more efficient Federal structure and will be described in a management report that I am submitting to the Congress for the first time shortly after my annual budget submission.

We have also made a great deal of progress in reducing the costs imposed on businesses and State and local governments by Federal regulations. These savings are estimated to total $150 billion over a 10-year period. We have reduced the number of new regulations in every year of my first term and have eliminated or reduced paperwork requirements by over 300 million hours each year. In addition, the regulations are more carefully crafted to achieve the greatest protection for the least cost, and wherever possible to use market forces instead of working against them.

A recent Executive Order will strengthen the executive branch coordination that has made these accomplishments possible. For the first time, we will publish an annual program of the most significant regulatory activities, including those that precede the publication of a proposed rule. This will give Congress and the public an earlier opportunity to understand the administration's regulatory policies and priorities.

Conclusion

The key elements of the program I set out 4 years ago are in place and working well. Our national security is being restored; so, I am happy to report, is our economy. Growth and investment are healthy; and inflation, interest rates, tax rates, and unemployment are down and can be reduced further. The proliferation of unnecessary regulations that stifled both economic growth and our individual freedoms has been halted. Progress has been made toward the reduction of unwarranted and excessive growth in domestic spending programs.

But we cannot rest on these accomplishments. If we are to attain a new era of sustained peace, prosperity, growth, and freedom, Federal domestic spending must be brought firmly under control. This budget presents the steps that I believe must be taken. I do not exclude other economies that Congress may devise, so long as they do not imperil my fundamental constitutional responsibilities to look after the national defense and the general welfare of the American people.

Let us get on with the job. The time for action is now.

RONALD REAGAN

February 4, 1985 ∎

Reagan's Economic Report

Following is the text of President Reagan's Economic Report sent to Congress Feb. 5.

TO THE CONGRESS OF
THE UNITED STATES:

In 1981, when I first assumed the duties of the Presidency, our Nation was suffering from declining productivity and the highest inflation in the postwar period — the legacy of years of government overspending, overtaxing, and overregulation.

We bent all of our efforts to correct these problems, not by unsustainable short-run measures, but by measures that would increase long-term growth without renewed inflation. We removed unnecessary regulations, cut taxes, and slowed the growth of Federal spending, freeing the private sector to develop markets, create jobs, and increase productivity. With conviction in our principles, with patience and hard work, we restored the economy to a condition of healthy growth without substantial inflation.

Although employment is now rising, business opportunities are expanding, and interest rates and inflation are under control, we cannot relax our economic vigilance. A return to the policies of excessive government spending and control that led to the economic "malaise" of the late seventies would quickly draw us back into that same disastrous pattern of inflation and recession. Now is the time to recommit ourselves to the policies that broke that awful pattern: policies of reduced Federal spending, lower tax rates, and less regulation to free the creative energy of our people and lead us to an even better economic future through strong and sustained economic growth.

Major Economic Developments, 1981-1984

The Program for Economic Recovery that we initiated in February 1981 had four key elements:

- Budget reform to cut the rate of growth in Federal spending,
- Reductions in personal and business taxes,
- A far-reaching program of regulatory relief, and
- Restoration of a stable currency and a healthy financial market through sound monetary policy.

The success of this program is now obvious — the U.S. economy is experiencing the strongest recovery in 30 years:

- Real business fixed investment in plant and equipment is higher, relative to real gross national product, than at any time in the postwar period.
- Productivity growth in the business sector has averaged 2.2 percent since the fourth quarter of 1980, compared with a rate of less than 0.3 percent over the prior 4 years.
- The inflation rate is now about one-third the rate in 1980, and short-term interest rates are less than one-half their peak 1981 levels.

But the quantitative record alone does not tell the full story. Four years ago, there was a widespread and growing anxiety about the economy. Many thought that the Nation had entered a condition of permanent economic decline, and that we would have to live with permanent double-digit inflation unless we were willing to suffer massive long-term unemployment.

We did not share this pessimism. It was clear to us that the Nation's economic problems were not the product of the economic system, but of the onerous influence of government on that system. The creative potential of the American people, choosing their own economic futures, was more constrained than helped by the increasingly heavy hand of government. Nor did we share the negative views that a reduction of inflation would increase long-term unemployment; that economic growth, by itself, would increase inflation; and that the government had to protect a "fragile" market system by regulating oil prices and interest rates.

The primary economic responsibility of the Federal Government is not to make choices for people, but to provide an environment in which people can make their own choices. The performance of the economy in the past 2 years under our Program for Economic Recovery fully justifies our faith in the Nation's basic economic health. In 1983 and 1984 the economy generated about 300,000 new jobs per month without an increase in inflation. Real gross national product increased 5.6 percent during 1984, and the unemployment rate declined from 8.1 percent to 7.1 percent. Inflation was steady at its lowest level in more than a decade, and most interest rates are now lower than a year ago. Yet while the U.S. economy grew rapidly in 1984, it maintains the potential for continued strong growth. The inventory/sales ratio is low by historical standards, and capacity utilization rates in most industries are well below prior peak rates.

Economic conditions in 1984 were more favorable than during the second year of a typical recovery, and we see none of the warning signs that usually precede the end of an expansion. The temporary slowing of economic growth starting in July — reflecting the combination of a minor adjustment of consumer spending and inventories and little growth of the basic money supply — seems to have ended in November. These conditions, plus an expectation that the Federal Reserve System will maintain sufficient money growth, support our forecast that the present recovery will continue. *The thriving venture capital market is financing a new American revolution of entrepreneurship and technological change. The American economy is once again the envy of the world.*

The Economic Outlook

For the years 1985 through 1988, we assume real gross national product growth of 4 percent per year, slowing slightly in 1989-90. We know that economic recoveries have not been stable in either duration or magnitude, in part because monetary and fiscal policies have often been erratic. We may not be able to eliminate recessions entirely, but a sustained commitment to policies that promote long-term growth and stability can reduce their frequency and severity. Our forecast that the unemployment rate, the inflation rate, and interest rates will decline gradually in the years ahead reflects this commitment to sound, sustainable, and predictable policies.

The Task Ahead: A Program For Growth and Opportunity

Our 1981 Program for Economic Recovery was designed for the long run with priority attention to the major problems we faced at that time. Our second-term Program for Growth and Opportunity represents a continuation and expansion of the earlier program, with priority attention to the major problems we face in 1985 and beyond. Our objectives — economic growth, stability of the general price level, and increased individual economic opportunity — have not changed. Federal economic policy will continue to be guided by the four key elements of the earlier program. Our progress in solving the most important economic problems we inherited in 1981, however, has allowed us to refocus our attention on the remaining problems and to shift our priorities and resources toward their solution.

Several significant problems remain to be addressed. The rate of growth of Federal spending has been substantially reduced from the rate projected in the budget we inherited in fiscal 1981, but spending growth continues to outpace the economy. Spending too much has left us with a large budget deficit that must and will be reduced. In our efforts to reduce the deficit, we must not forget that the cause of the deficit is increased spending and insufficient growth, not decreased taxes. Federal tax receipts are now almost the same share of gross national product as in the late 1970s, even after the substantial reduction in tax rates that we initiated in 1981.

Another economic problem demanding resolution is unemployment and its effects on the Nation's workers and families. Despite significant progress, much remains to be done. More than 6 million more Americans are now employed than in January 1981, but the unemployment rate is still too high. We will not be satisfied until every American who wants a job is employed at a wage that reflects the market value of his or her skills. Another aspect of this problem is that the poverty rate remains stubbornly high, despite a strong recovery and a continued increase in government assistance. Also, although the inflation rate has been reduced substantially, it is still higher than during most of our peacetime history prior to 1965. We will not be satisfied until we have totally and permanently wrung inflation out of our economy.

Work also remains to be done in the areas of regulatory and monetary policy. Many Federal regulations still impose a substantial cost to the economy. In addition, we need to strengthen the commitment to a sound monetary policy that never again retards economic growth, or reaccelerates inflation.

Our trade deficit, another area of concern, has been caused in large part by a stronger dollar. Investors around the world have bid up the dollars as they have become increasingly confident in our economy. That confidence is an asset and not a liability. However, the conditions that have led to the trade deficit have increased the obstacles faced by some important industries. Agriculture, one of our most productive export sectors, has been harmed by a combination of rigid and outdated Federal agricultural policies and subsidized foreign competition and the strong dollar. In one respect the trade deficit is like the budget deficit; both are too large to be sustained, but there are both beneficial and detrimental ways to reduce them. Our goal is a system of free and fair trade in goods, services, and capital. We will work toward this goal through both bilateral and multilateral agreements.

Economic conditions during the past 4 years are best characterized as transitional — from a period of low productivity growth to a period of high productivity growth; from a period of high inflation and interest rates to a period of much lower inflation and interest rates; from a period of economic "malaise" to a period of economic opportunity. Our task is to consolidate and extend these gains.

Federal Spending and the Deficit

The rate of growth of Federal spending has been reduced from 14.8 percent in fiscal 1981 to an average rate of 9.1 percent in fiscal years 1982 through 1985. During this period, however, current dollar gross national product has increased at an average rate of 7.6 percent. The continued growth of the Federal spending share of gross national product and lost revenues from the recession are the main reasons we are now faced with such large Federal deficits.

The projected Federal deficits are much too large, and they must be reduced. As explained in the accompanying report, however, the economic consequences of reducing these deficits depend critically on how they are reduced. A sustained reduction of the growth of Federal spending will contribute to economic growth, while an increase in tax rates would constrain economic growth. Federal spending on many programs is far larger than necessary, and far larger than desired by most Americans.

My fiscal 1986 budget proposal will protect the social safety net and essential programs, such as defense, for which the Federal Government has a clear constitutional responsibility, and will reform or eliminate many programs that have proven ineffective or nonessential. With no resort to a tax increase, this budget will reduce the deficit to about 4 percent of gross national product in fiscal 1986 and to a steadily lower percentage in future years. Additional spending reductions will probably be necessary in future years to achieve a balanced budget by the end of the decade.

The problems of excessive spending and deficits are not new. In the absence of fundamental reform, they may recur again and again in the future. I therefore support two important measures — one to authorize the President to veto individual line items in comprehensive spending bills, and another to constrain the federal authority to borrow or to increase spending in the absence of broad congressional support. These structural changes are *not* substitutes for the hard fiscal choices that will be necessary in 1985 and beyond, nor for the need to simplify our tax system to stimulate greater growth; but they are important to provide the mechanisms and discipline for longer term fiscal health.

The case for a line-item veto should by now be obvious. The Governors of 43 States have used this authority effectively, and such authority has only once been withdrawn, only later to be reinstated. For over a century, Presidents of both parties have requested such authority.

The proposed constitutional amendment providing for a balanced budget and a tax limitation would constrain the long-run growth of Federal spending and the national debt. In 1982 a proposed amendment to constrain Federal authority to spend and borrow was approved by more than two-thirds of the Senate and by more than a majority of the House of Representatives; a balanced budget amendment has also been endorsed by the legislatures of 32 States. Approval of the proposed balanced budget/tax limitation amendment would ensure that fiscal decisions by future Presidents and Members of Congress are more responsive to the broad interests of the American population.

Federal Taxation

The Economic Recovery Tax Act of 1981 was one of the most important accomplishments of my first term. Individual income tax rates were reduced nearly 25 percent, effective tax rates on the income from new investment were substantially reduced, and beginning this year tax brackets are adjusted for inflation.

But more needs to be done. Personal tax rates should be reduced further to encourage stronger economic growth which, in itself, is our best tool for putting deficits on a steady downward path. Our tax system needs basic reform. It is extraordinarily complicated; it leads to substantial economic inefficiency; and it is widely perceived to be unfair.

At my request, the Treasury Department has developed a comprehensive proposal to simplify and reform the Federal tax system, one that for expected economic conditions would yield about the same revenues as the present system. This proposal, by substantially broadening the tax base, would permit a significant further reduction of marginal tax rates. Shortly, I will be submitting my own proposal for tax simplification, and will urge the Congress to give serious sustained attention to tax simplification — in order to enact a program that will increase fairness and stimulate future savings, investment, and growth.

Federal Regulation

We have made major efforts in the past 4 years to reduce and eliminate Federal regulation of economic activity. Executive Office review of new regulations was streamlined. Oil prices were deregulated by Executive authority early in 1981. New legislation was approved to reduce regulation of banking and to largely eliminate regulation of interstate bus travel.

Regulatory reform, however, has been painfully slow. The Congress failed to approve our proposals to further deregulate banking and natural gas prices, and to reform the regulation of private pensions. In addition, the reauthorization of several major environmental laws has been delayed for several years.

I urge the Congress to consider further deregulation efforts in several areas. The experience with deregulation of oil prices makes clear that continued regulation of natural gas prices is not appropriate. Reform of nuclear licensing requirements also deserves attention. Further deregulation of the banking system should be paired with a major reform of the deposit insurance systems. Some changes in the single-employer pension law and an increased premium are necessary to preserve the pension insurance system. We should also seriously consider eliminating the remaining Federal regulation of trucking and railroads. Finally, I remain hopeful that the Administration and the Congress can work together to reauthorize the major environmental laws in a way that serves our common environmental and economic goals.

Monetary Policy

The Constitution authorizes the Congress "To coin Money (and) regulate the Value thereof," and Congress has delegated this authority to the Federal Reserve System. The role of the executive branch is restricted to advising the Congress and the Federal Reserve about the conduct of monetary policy, and to nominating members of the Board of Governors as positions become vacant.

During my first term, the Federal Reserve reduced the rate of money growth relative to the high rates of the late 1970s. This change in policy, assisted by the related strong increase in the exchange value of the dollar, helped produce a substantial reduction of inflation and market interest rates. On occasion, however, the rate of money growth has been quite volatile, contributing to instability in interest rates and a decline in economic activity. The sharp reduction in money growth through mid-1982, for example, undoubtedly added to the length and severity of the 1981-1982 recession. And a similar reduction in money growth in the second half of 1984 contributed to the temporary slowing of economic growth late in the year.

We reaffirm our support for a sound monetary policy that contributes to strong, steady economic growth and price stability. Moreover, we expect to cooperate closely with the Federal Reserve in defining and carrying out a prudent and predictable monetary policy.

Conclusion

The Federal Government has only a few important economic responsibilities. Given a proper conduct of these important roles, additional Federal intervention is more often a part of the problem than a part of the solution. We should continue to reduce the many less-important economic activities of the Federal Government so that individuals, private institutions, and State and local governments will have more resources and more freedom to pursue their own interests. Good stewardship of our constitutional responsibilities and the creative energies of the American people will ensure a future of continued economic growth and opportunity.

RONALD REAGAN

February 5, 1985

State of the Union Address

Following is the Congressional Record *text of President Reagan's State of the Union address to a joint session of Congress Feb. 6.*

Mr. Speaker, Mr. President, distinguished Members of the Congress, honored guests, and fellow citizens. I come before you to report on the state of our Union. And I am pleased to report that, after 4 years of united effort, the American people have brought forth a Nation renewed — stronger, freer and more secure than before.

Four years ago, we began to change — forever, I hope — our assumptions about Government and its place in our lives. Out of that change has come great and robust growth — in our confidence, our economy, and our role in the world.

Tonight, America is stronger because of the values that we hold dear. We believe that faith and freedom must be our guiding stars, for they show us truth, they make us brave, give us hope, and leave us wiser than we were. Our progress began not in Washington, D.C., but in the hearts of our families, communities, workplaces, and voluntary groups which, together, are unleashing the invincible spirit of one great Nation under God.

Four years ago, we said we would invigorate our economy by giving people greater freedom and incentives to take risks, and letting them keep more of what they earned.

We did what we promised, and a great industrial giant is reborn. Tonight we can take pride in 25 straight months of economic growth, the strongest in 34 years; a three-year inflation average of 3.9 percent, the lowest in 17 years; and 7.3 million new jobs in two years, with more of our citizens working than ever before.

New freedom in our lives has planted the rich seeds for future success:

For an America of wisdom that honors the family, knowing that as the family goes, so goes our civilization;

For an America of vision that sees tomorrow's dreams in the learning and hard work we do today;

For an America of courage whose servicemen and women, even as we meet, proudly stand watch on the frontiers of freedom;

For an America of compassion that opens its heart to those who cry out for help.

We have begun well. But it's only a beginning. We are not here to congratulate ourselves on what we have done, but to challenge ourselves to finish what has not yet been done.

We are here to speak for millions in our inner cities who long for real jobs, safe neighborhoods, and schools that truly teach. We are here to speak for the American farmer, the entrepreneur, and every worker in industries fighting to modernize and compete. And, yes, we are here to stand, and proudly so, for all who struggle to break free from totalitarianism; for all who know in their hearts that freedom is the one true path to peace and human happiness.

Proverbs tells us, without a vision the people perish. When asked what great principle holds our Union together, Abraham Lincoln said, "Something in (the) Declaration giving liberty, not alone to the people of this country, but hope to the world for all future time."

We honor the giants of our history, not by going back, but forward to the dreams their vision foresaw. My fellow citizens, this Nation is poised for greatness. The time has come to proceed toward a great new challenge — a Second American Revolution of hope and opportunity; a revolution carrying us to new heights of progress by pushing back frontiers of knowledge and space; a revolution of spirit that taps the soul of America, enabling us to summon greater strength than we have ever known; and, a revolution that carries beyond our shores the golden promise of human freedom in a world at peace.

Let us begin by challenging our conventional wisdom: There are no constraints on the human mind, no walls around the human spirit, no barriers to our progress except those we ourselves erect. Already, pushing down tax rates has freed our economy to vault forward to record growth.

In Europe, they are calling it "the American Miracle." Day by day, we are shattering accepted notions of what is possible. When I was growing up, we failed to see how a new thing called radio would transform our marketplace. Well, today many have not yet seen how advances in technology are transforming our lives.

In the late 1950s, workers at the AT&T semiconductor plant in Pennsylvania produced five transistors a day for $7.50 apiece. They now produce over a million for less than a penny apiece.

New laser techniques could revolutionize heart bypass surgery, cut diagnosis time for viruses linked to cancer from weeks to minutes, reduce hospital costs dramatically, and hold out new promise for saving human lives.

Our automobile industry has overhauled assembly lines, increased worker productivity, and is competitive once again.

We stand on the threshold of a great ability to produce more, do more, be more. Our economy is not getting older and weaker, it is getting younger and stronger. It doesn't need rest and supervision, it needs new challenge and greater freedom. And that word, freedom, is the key to the Second American Revolution that we mean to bring about.

Tax Simplification

Let us move together with a historic reform of tax simplification for fairness and growth. Last year I asked then Treasury Secretary Regan to develop a plan to simplify the tax code, so all taxpayers would be treated more fairly, and personal tax rates could come further down.

We have cut tax rates by almost 25 percent, yet the tax system remains unfair and limits our potential for growth. Exclusions and exemptions cause similar incomes to be taxed at different levels. Low-income families face steep tax barriers that make hard lives even harder. The Treasury Department has produced an excellent reform plan whose principles will guide the final proposal that we will ask you to enact.

One thing that tax reform will not be is a tax increase in disguise. We will not jeopardize the mortgage interest deduction that families need. We will reduce personal tax rates as low as possible by removing many tax preferences. We will propose a top rate of not more than 35 percent, and possibly lower. And we will propose reducing corporate rates while maintaining incentives for capital formation.

To encourage opportunity and jobs rather than dependency and welfare, we will propose that individuals living at or near the poverty line be totally exempt from Federal income tax. To restore fairness to families, we will propose increasing significantly the personal exemption.

And tonight, I am instructing Treasury Secretary James Baker — I have to get used to saying that — to begin working with congressional authors and committees for bipartisan legislation conforming to these principles. We will call upon the American people for support and upon every man and woman in this chamber. Together we can pass, this year, a tax bill for fairness, simplicity and growth, making this economy the engine of our dreams, and America the investment capital of the world. So let us begin.

Enterprise, Not Dependency

Tax simplification will be a giant step toward unleashing the tremendous pent-up power of our economy. But a Second American Revolution must carry the promise of opportunity for all. It is time to liberate the spirit of enterprise in the most distressed areas of our country.

This Government will meet its responsibility to help those in need. But policies that increase dependency, break up families and destroy self-respect are not progressive, they are reactionary. Despite our strides in civil rights, blacks, Hispanics, and all minorities will not have full and equal power until they have full economic power.

We have repeatedly sought passage of enterprise zones to help those in the abandoned corners of our land find jobs, learn skills, and build better lives. This legislation is supported by a majority of you. Mr. Speaker, I know we agree that there must be no forgotten Americans. Let us place new dreams in a million hearts and create a new generation of entrepreneurs by passing enterprise zones this year.

And "Tip," you could make that a birthday present.

Nor must we lose the chance to pass our Youth Employment Opportunity Wage proposal. We can help teenagers who have the highest unemployment rate find summer jobs, so they can know the pride of work, and have confidence in their futures.

We will continue to support the Job Training Partnership Act, which has a nearly two-thirds job placement rate. Credits and education and health care vouchers will help working families shop for services they need.

Our Administration is already encouraging certain low-income public housing residents to own and manage their own dwellings. It is time that all public housing residents have that opportunity of ownership.

The Federal Government can help create a new atmosphere of freedom. But States and localities, many of which enjoy surpluses from the recovery, must not permit their tax and regulatory policies to stand as barriers to growth.

Let us resolve that we will stop spreading dependency and start spreading opportunity; that we will stop spreading bondage and start spreading freedom.

Cutting Government Spending

There are some who say that growth initiatives must await final action on deficit reductions. Well, the best way to reduce deficits is through economic growth. More businesses will be started, more investments made, more jobs created, and more people will be on payrolls paying taxes.

The best way to reduce Government spending is to reduce the need for spending by increasing prosperity. Each added percentage point per year of real GNP growth will lead to a cumulative reduction in deficits of nearly $200 billion over five years.

To move steadily toward a balanced budget we must also lighten Government's claim on our total economy. We will not do this by raising taxes. We must make sure that our economy grows faster than the growth in spending by the Federal Government. In our Fiscal Year 1986 budget, overall Government program spending will be frozen at the current level; it must not be one dime higher than Fiscal Year 1985. And three points are key:

First, the social safety net for the elderly, the needy, the disabled, and unemployed will be left intact. Growth of our major health care programs, Medicare and Medicaid, will be slowed, but protections for the elderly and needy will be preserved.

Second, we must not relax our efforts to restore military strength just as we near our goal of a fully equipped, trained, and ready professional corps. National security is Government's first responsibility, so, in past years, defense spending took about half the Federal budget. Today it takes less than a third.

We have already reduced our planned defense expenditures by nearly $100 billion over the past 4 years, and reduced projected spending again this year. You know, we only have a military industrial complex until a time of danger. Then it becomes the arsenal of democracy. Spending for defense is investing in things that are priceless: peace and freedom.

Third, we must reduce or eliminate costly Government subsidies. For example, deregulation of the airline industry has led to cheaper airfares, but on Amtrak taxpayers pay about $35 per passenger every time an Amtrak train leaves the station. It's time we ended this huge Federal subsidy.

Our farm program costs have quadrupled in recent years. Yet I know from visiting farmers, many in great financial distress, that we need an orderly transition to a market-oriented farm economy. We can help farmers best, not by expanding Federal payments, but by making fundamental reforms, keeping interest rates heading down, and knocking down foreign trade barriers to American farm exports.

We are moving ahead with Grace Commission reforms to eliminate waste, and improve Government's management practices. In the long run, we must protect the taxpayers from Government. And I ask again that you pass, as 32 States have now called for, an amendment mandating the Federal Government spend no more than it takes in. And I ask for the authority used responsibly by 43 Governors to veto individual items in appropriations bills. Senator Mattingly has introduced a bill permitting a 2-year trial run of the line-item veto. I hope you will pass and send that legislation to my desk.

Nearly 50 years of Government living beyond its means has brought us to a time of reckoning. Ours is but a moment in history. But one moment of courage, idealism, and bipartisan unity can change American history forever.

Sound monetary policy is key to long-running economic strength and stability. We will continue to cooperate with the Federal Reserve Board, seeking a steady policy that ensures price stability, without keeping interest rates artificially high or needlessly holding down growth.

Reducing unneeded red tape and regulations, and deregulating the energy, transportation, and financial industries, have unleashed new competition, giving consumers more choices, better services, and lower prices. In just one set of grant programs we have reduced 905 pages of regulations to 31.

We seek to fully deregulate natural gas to bring on new supplies and bring us closer to energy independence. Consistent with safety standards, we will continue removing restraints on the bus and railroad industries; we will soon send up legislation to return Conrail to the private sector, where it belongs; and we will support further deregulation of the trucking industry.

Every dollar the Federal Government does not take from us, every decision it does not make for us, will make our economy stronger, our lives more abundant, our future more free.

The New Frontier: Space

Our Second American Revolution will push on to new possibilities not only on Earth, but in the next frontier of space. Despite budget restraints, we will seek record funding for research and development.

We have seen the success of the space shuttle. Now we are going to develop a permanently manned Space Station, and new opportunities for free enterprise because in the next decade Americans and our friends around the world will be living and working together in space.

In the zero gravity of space we could manufacture in 30 days lifesaving medicines it would take 30 years to make on Earth. We can make crystals of exceptional purity to produce super computers, creating jobs, technologies, and medical breakthroughs beyond anything we ever dreamed possible.

As we do all this, we will continue to protect our natural resources. We will seek reauthorization and expanded funding for the Superfund program, to continue cleaning up hazardous waste sites which threaten human health and the environment.

Rediscovery of Values

Now, there is another great heritage to speak of this evening. Of all the changes that have swept America the past four years, none brings greater promise than our rediscovery of the values of faith, freedom, family, work, and neighborhood.

We see signs of renewal in increased attendance in places of worship; renewed optimism and faith in our future; love of country rediscovered by our young who are leading the way. We have rediscovered that work is good in and of itself; that it ennobles us to create and contribute no matter how seemingly humble our jobs. We have seen a powerful new current from an old and honorable tradition — American generosity.

From thousands answering Peace Corps appeals to help boost food production in Africa, to millions volunteering time, corporations adopting schools, and communities pulling together to help the neediest among us at home, we have refound our values. Private sector initiatives are crucial to our future.

I thank the Congress for passing equal access legislation giving religious groups the same right to use classrooms after school that other groups enjoy. But no citizen should tremble, nor the world shudder, if a child stands in a classroom and breathes a prayer. We ask you again — give children back a right they had for a century and a half or more in this country.

The question of abortion grips our Nation. Abortion is either the taking of a human life or it isn't; and if it is — and medical technology is increasingly showing it is — it must be stopped.

It is a terrible irony that while some turn to abortion, so many others who cannot become parents cry out for children to adopt. We have room for these children; we can fill the cradles of those who want a child to love. Tonight I ask you in the Congress to move this year on legislation to protect the unborn.

In the area of education, we are returning to excellence and again the heroes are our people, not government. We are stressing basics of discipline, rigorous testing, and homework, while helping children become computer smart as well. For 20 years Scholastic Aptitude Test scores of our high school students went down. But now they have gone up two of the last three years.

We must go forward in our commitment to the new basics, giving parents greater authority and making sure good teachers are rewarded for hard work and achievement through merit pay.

Violence and Crime

Of all the changes in the past 20 years, none has more threatened our sense of national well-being than the explosion of violent crime. One does not have to be attacked to be a victim. The woman who must run to her car after shopping at night is a victim; the couple draping their door with locks and chains are victims; as is the tired, decent cleaning woman who can't ride a subway home without being afraid.

We do not seek to violate the rights of defendants. But shouldn't we feel more compassion for the victims of crime than for those who commit crime? For the first time in 20 years the crime index has fallen two years in a row; we have convicted over 7,400 drug offenders, and put them, as well as leaders of organized crime, behind bars in record numbers.

But we must do more. I urge the House

to follow the Senate and enact proposals permitting use of all reliable evidence that police officers acquire in good faith. These proposals would also reform the habeus corpus laws and allow, in keeping with the will of the overwhelming majority of Americans, the use of the death penalty where necessary.

There can be no economic revival in ghettos when the most violent among us are allowed to roam free. It is time we restored domestic tranquility. And we mean to do just that.

Working for Peace

Just as we are positioned as never before to secure justice in our economy, we are poised as never before to create a safer, freer, more peaceful world.

Our alliances are stronger than ever. Our economy is stronger than ever. We have resumed our historic role as a leader of the free world — and all of these together are a great force for peace.

Since 1981 we have been committed to seeking fair and verifiable arms agreements that would lower the risk of war and reduce the size of nuclear arsenals. Now our determination to maintain a strong defense has influenced the Soviet Union to return to the bargaining table. Our negotiators must be able to go to that table with the united support of the American people. All of us have no greater dream than to see the day when nuclear weapons are banned from this Earth forever.

Each Member of the Congress has a role to play in modernizing our defenses, thus supporting our chances for a meaningful arms agreement. Your vote this spring on the Peacekeeper missile will be a critical test of our resolve to maintain the strength we need and move toward mutual and verifiable arms reductions.

For the past 20 years we have believed that no war will be launched as long as each side knows it can retaliate with a deadly counterstrike. Well, I believe there is a better way of eliminating the threat of nuclear war.

It is a Strategic Defense Initiative aimed ultimately at finding a non-nuclear defense against ballistic missiles. It is the most hopeful possibility of the nuclear age. But it is not well understood.

Some say it will bring war to the heavens — but its purpose is to deter war, in the heavens and on Earth. Some say the research would be expensive. Perhaps, but it could save millions of lives, indeed humanity itself. Some say if we build such a system the Soviets will build a defense system of their own. Well, they already have strategic defenses that surpass ours; a civil defense system, where we have almost none; and a research program covering roughly the same areas of technology we are exploring. And finally, some say the research will take a long time. The answer to that is: "Let's get started."

Aid and Trade

Harry Truman once said that ultimately our security and the world's hopes for peace and human progress, "lie not in measures of defense or in the control of weapons, but in the growth and expansion of freedom and self-government."

Tonight we declare anew to our fellow citizens of the world: Freedom is not the sole prerogative of a chosen few; it is the universal right of all God's children. Look to where peace and prosperity flourish today. It is in homes that freedom built. Victories against poverty are greatest and peace most secure where people live by laws that ensure free press, free speech, and freedom to worship, vote, and create wealth.

Our mission is to nourish and defend freedom and democracy and to communicate these ideals everywhere we can.

America's economic success is freedom's success; it can be repeated a hundred times in a hundred different nations. Many countries in East Asia and the Pacific have few resources other than the enterprise of their own people. But through low tax rates and free markets they have soared ahead of centralized economies. And now China is opening up its economy to meet its needs.

We need a stronger and simpler approach to the process of making and implementing trade policy and will be studying potential changes in that process in the next few weeks.

We have seen the benefits of free trade and lived through the disasters of protectionism. Tonight I ask all our trading partners, developed and developing alike, to join us in a new round of trade negotiations to expand trade and competition, and strengthen the global economy — and to begin it in this next year.

There are more than 3 billion human beings living in Third World Countries with an average per capita income of $650 a year. Many are victims of dictatorships that impoverish them with taxation and corruption. Let us ask our allies to join us in a practical program of trade and assistance that fosters economic development through personal incentives to help these people climb from poverty on their own. We cannot play innocents abroad in a world that is not innocent. Nor can we be passive when freedom is under siege. Without resources, diplomacy cannot succeed. Our security assistance programs help friendly governments defend themselves, and give them confidence to work for peace. And I hope that you in the Congress will understand that dollar for dollar security assistance contributes as much to global security as our own defense budget.

We must stand by all our democratic allies. And we must not break faith with those who are risking their lives on every continent, from Afghanistan to Nicaragua, to defy Soviet-supported aggression and secure rights which have been ours from birth.

The Sandinista dictatorship of Nicaragua, with full Cuban Soviet-bloc support, not only persecutes its people, the church, and denies a free press, but arms and provides bases for communist terrorists attacking neighboring states. Support for freedom fighters is self-defense, and totally consistent with the OAS [Organization of American States] and U.N. Charters. It is essential that the Congress continue all facets of our assistance to Central America. I want to work with you to support the democratic forces whose struggle is tied to our own security.

Two American Heroes

Tonight I have spoken of great plans and great dreams. They are dreams we can make come true. Two hundred years of American history should have taught us that nothing is impossible.

Ten years ago a young girl left Vietnam with her family, part of the exodus that followed the fall of Saigon. They came to the United States with no possessions and not knowing a word of English, 10 years ago. The young girl studied hard, learned English, and finished high school in the top of her class. And this May, May 22 to be exact, is a big date on her calendar. Just 10 years from the time she left Vietnam she will graduate from the United States Military Academy at West Point.

I though you might like to meet an American hero named Jean Nguyen.

Now, there is someone else here tonight — born 79 years ago. She lives in the inner city where she cares for infants born of mothers who are heroin addicts. The children born in withdrawal are sometimes even dropped at her doorstep. She helps them with love.

Go to her house some night and maybe you will see her silhouette against the window as she walks the floor, talking softly, soothing a child in her arms. Mother Hale of Harlem, and she, too, is an American hero.

Jean, Mother Hale, your lives tell us that the oldest American saying is new again — anything is possible in America if we have the faith, the will, and the heart.

History is asking us once again to be a force for good in the world. Let us begin — in unity, with justice and love.

Thank you and God bless you. ∎

Farm Credit/Africa Aid Veto

Following is the White House text of President Reagan's March 6 message accompanying his veto of HR 1096, to authorize emergency relief for famine victims in Africa and emergency farm credit relief. It was Reagan's first veto of a public bill during the 99th Congress.

TO THE HOUSE OF REPRESENTATIVES:

I am returning without my approval H. R. 1096, a bill to authorize emergency relief for victims of famine in Africa and to establish additional farm credit programs that would add a minimum of $2.5 billion to the deficit over the next several years.

I should note at the outset that my veto of this bill will not interfere with the African relief effort now under way. Using authority in existing law, we can continue to provide relief in the near term, but I urge the Congress to act expeditiously on the request for additional relief authority I submitted earlier this year.

My disapproval of this bill is based on objections to the farm credit provisions, which are completely unacceptable and unnecessary in view of measures already instituted by my Administration.

Title II of the bill would alter the regulations governing the special Debt Adjustment Program that I announced last September. The bill would institute a series of changes that would primarily benefit banks at the expense of farmers and taxpayers. Another of its provisions would establish a new program to pay banks to reduce the interest rate on loans to certain farmers. This program, although initially limited to $100 million, would soon grow into an uncontrollable, multi-billion dollar annual spending spree. A third section of this title would require bank regulatory agencies to refrain, under a vaguely delineated standard, from classifying adversely delinquent loans to farmers and ranchers. This provision would inject uncertainty into the authority of the regulatory agencies charged with ensuring the soundness of our banking system, provoke needless litigation, and possibly jeopardize the interests of depositors in banks that have made agricultural loans.

Title III of the bill would require establishment of a program of "advance loans" from the Commodity Credit Corporation of up to $50,000 per farmer. This provision would have added a minimum of $7 billion to fiscal year 1985 outlays, only part of which would be returned in 1986. By distorting the purpose of the basic Federal mechanism for stabilizing farm prices, this provision risks serious disruption at harvest time as well as long-term damage to the soundness of Federal farm programs.

I share the concern for problems facing certain of our farmers this year. That is why I have taken a number of steps to strengthen existing programs and to institute a new Debt Adjustment Program to help financially strapped farmers refinance their existing debt.

It is time to get on with the job of making these programs work. That will require the cooperation of all concerned, but most important of all, it will require an end to the uncertainty that would be created by hasty legislation requiring massive changes in rules just as the planting season begins.

RONALD REAGAN

The White House,
March 6, 1985

Reagan's April 15 Remarks on Nicaragua

Following is the White House text of President Reagan's April 15 remarks on Nicaragua, made at a dinner for the Nicaraguan Refugee Fund, at the J. W. Marriott Hotel, in Washington, D.C.

THE PRESIDENT: I want to begin by saying that I'm honored to be in the presence of those who are here from Nicaragua and all the rest of you, too. Many of you have been driven from the land of your birth by a sad turn of history, but you've refused to forget your homeland or abandon your fellow Nicaraguans. And for this, you deserve, and you have, both our high regard and our thanks.

Six years ago, many of you were part of the fight to overthrow an oppressive regime that had ruled your country for decades. You succeeded, the regime fell. And many rejoiced, knowing that true freedom and true democracy would finally rise to take its place.

But the new regime became not a democracy but a dictatorship. Communism was embraced and Nicaragua moved into the Soviet orbit. The best of the revolution, members of the original revolutionary government who had fought for high ideals, left the country. In all, more than a quarter of a million souls fled Nicaragua, and they're fleeing still. Many of the refugees are the poorest of the poor, Indians and peasants and terrified mothers and children. All of them need our help. But even more, perhaps, they need the attention of the world. After nearly six years, attention must be paid.

There's so much I want to discuss tonight, from the plight of the refugees to why they're fleeing. I want to talk about what is at stake in Central America, what is at issue and what it means to all of us in this room, in this country and in the West.

I'll start with Nicaragua now, Nicaragua on April 15, 1985.

As you know, the Sandinista dictatorship has taken absolute control of the government and the armed forces. It is a communist dictatorship. It has done what communist dictatorships do, created a repressive state security and secret police organization assisted by Soviet, East German and Cuban advisors; harassed, and in many cases, expunged the political opposition and rendered the democratic freedoms of speech, press and assembly punishable by officially-sanctioned harassment and imprisonment or death.

But the communists are not unopposed. They are facing great resistance from the people of Nicaragua, resistance from the patriots who fight for freedom and their unarmed allies from the pro-democracy movement.

There is growing evidence of Sandinista brutality. We've recently learned that 10 or 11 members of the Social Christian Party have been rounded up and jailed. The Sandinistas are trying to get them to confess to being counter-revolutionaries. And you might be interested in knowing one way the communists are coercing these confessions. They have also arrested more than a hundred relatives of the political prisoners. And according to our most recent information, the Social Christian Party members are being held in the dark in small, over-heated cells. Prisoners are served meals at irregular intervals, after 12 hours, for instance, and then the next in another two. The purpose is to disorient them and wear them down. Where do they get that idea? This same method has been used against political prisoners in Cuba.

Now, we do not know the exact number of political prisoners in Nicaragua today. But we get an indication from the testimony of Jose Gonzalez, a former Vice President of the Social Democratic Party. Gonzalez told Pope John Paul II there were about 8,000 political prisoners in 1981. He also told the Pope the Sandinistas practice "repression and torture." Gonzalez, as you know, was arrested when he returned from Rome. He left Nicaragua and now lives in exile.

But the most compelling evidence of Sandinista brutality and of why people are fleeing is the Sandinistas' scorched-earth policy.

We know the Sandinistas have ordered and are carrying out the forced relocation of tens of thousands of peasants. We have reports that 20,000 peasants have been moved in the past two months from their homes to relocation camps. Peasants who have escaped call themselves "hostages" and call the relocation camps "concentration camps." The communists themselves had admitted they're engaged in the forced resettlement of an estimated 65,000 people. Peasants and journalists tell of entire villages, homes, stores and churches being burnt to the ground. They tell of animals slaughtered, crops burned and villagers taken away at gunpoint in government trucks. Why are the communists doing this? Massed forced relocations are a common feature of modern communist tyrannies. But there are other purposes here, for the people of many villages are supporting, actively supporting the freedom fighters, and so the communists have decided to put more and more of the people of Nicaragua into closely-guarded pens, and that way it will be easier for the regime to stalk the freedom fighters in the countryside. A Sandinista security chief has explained, "Anyone still in the hills is a guerrilla."

While all this is terrible, it can hardly come as a surprise to those who know what was done to the Miskito Indians.

As you know, the Miskitos supported the Sandinistas against Somoza. But shortly after taking power, the Sandinistas attempted to indoctrinate the Miskitos in Marxist dogma and the Indians resisted. The Sandinistas tried to put their own people in as leaders of the Miskito community and the Indians resisted, so much that the Sandinistas labeled them "bourgeois," and, therefore, enemies of the people. They began to arrest Indian leaders. Some were murdered. Some were tortured. One Miskito leader told our AFL-CIO that Thomas Borge and other leaders of the Sandinistas " — came into my cell and warned me that Sandinismo would be established on the Atlantic Coast even if every single Miskito Indian had to be eliminated."

Well, the Sandinistas came close. There were massacres. Eyewitnesses said some Miskitos were buried alive. Ten thousand Indians were force-marched to relocation camps. Miskito villages were burned down. They're still being burned down. Miskito villages were bombed and shelled. And they are still being bombed and shelled. In the name of humanity, these atrocities must be stopped.

Twenty thousand Indians are known to be incarcerated in relocation camps. About half are currently being held at the Tasba Pri Relocation Camps. Tasba Pri, by the way, means "free land." Well, above one "free land" camp, a *New York Times* reporter noted a sign that said, "Work that unites us is a revolutionary force."

In all, tens of thousands of Miskitos have been forced to flee Nicaragua, to free the land they lived on for over a thousand years. Many now live as refugees in Honduras.

Unfortunately, it's widely believed outside Nicaragua that the Sandinistas enjoy the support of the people inside. But you know this is completely untrue. We know this from many sources, even recently, the American press.

A few months ago, *The New Republic* carried a report by Robert Leiken, who had long been sympathetic to the Sandinistas and who had formerly testified in Congress against aid to the Contras. He wrote, "One of the most common means of sustaining the myth of popular support is the Sandinistas' use of the rationing system as a lever — Ration cards are confiscated for nonattendance at Sandinista meetings." And talk of inflation is branded as "counter-revolutionary plot." Sympathy with the Contras, he said, is more and pervasive. In fact, the peasants now call them "Los Muchacho[s]," the affectionate term they once used exclusively for the Sandinistas. And what do they now call the Sandinistas? Well, the latest workers chant is "the Sandinistas and Somoza are the same thing."

In spite of all this, the Sandinista government retains its defenders in this country and in the West. They look at all the evidence that the Sandinistas have instituted a communist regime, all the pictures of dictator Ortega embracing Castro and visiting Moscow, all the Soviet-Bloc advisors and all the Sandinista votes in the U.N., such as their decision in line with the Soviet Bloc to refuse the credentials of Israel, they look at this and they say, "The Sandinistas aren't communists, or aren't real communists. Why, they're only nationalists, only socialists."

But these defenders admit there is a problem in Nicaragua. The problem, they say, is the freedom fighters. Well, just a few weeks ago, the whole world was treated to a so-called "independent investigation" of charges that the freedom fighters have committed atrocities. It spoke of these so-called "atrocities" in a rather riveting manner. And the report received great attention on television and in leading newspapers and publications. The report ignored communist brutality, the murder of the Indians and the arrest, torture and murder of political dissidents. But we really shouldn't be surprised by that, because, as our State Department discovered and *Time* magazine reported, this so-called independent investigation was the work of one of dictator Ortega's supporters, a sympathizer who has openly embraced Sandinismo and who was shepherded through Nicaragua by Sandinista operatives.

The truth is, there are atrocities going on in Nicaragua. But they're largely the work of the institutionalized cruelty of the Sandinista government. This cruelty is the natural expression of a communist government, a cruelty that flows naturally from the heart of totalitarianism. The truth is, Somoza was bad, but so many of the people of Nicaragua know the Sandinistas are infinitely worse.

We have here this evening many individuals who know these truths first hand. Some of you may know of Bayardo Santaeliz. He is a 29-year-old Nicaraguan refugee and a former lay preacher of the Pentecostal Missionary Church in Nicaragua.

And this is his story, a story told in sworn testimony before a Honduran civil rights commission. A few years ago, the Sandinistas began pressuring Bayardo to stop preaching and start fighting for the revolution. And one night after holding a prayer session in a home on the slopes of the Momotombo Volcano, Bayardo went to bed. He was awakened by Sandinista soldiers who asked if he was an evangelical preacher. Bayardo said yes. The Sandinistas arrested him, accused him of counter-revolutionary activity, verbally abused him and then tied him and two others to a pillar. Then the Sandinistas doused the house with gasoline and threw in a match. The room went up in flames, but they burned the rope that bound Bayardo and he escaped with his clothes in flames and his body burned. He hid in the countryside and was rescued by Campesinos who got him to a hospital where he lied about the causes of his injuries. And not long after, he left Nicaragua.

Bayardo, I wonder if you could rise for a moment, wherever you are here in the room.

You know, I was going to ask all of you fellows with the cameras if you wouldn't kind of turn them off me and on him, but then he came up here, so I didn't ask you that. He's just one of the many who've suffered.

He knows things and has experienced things that many of us in this country can barely imagine. And I think America has to see — America has to see the true face of Nicaragua. Thank you, Bayardo.

Some people say this isn't America's problem. Why should we care if Nicaragua is a democracy or not? Well, we should care for a whole host of reasons.

Democracy has its own moral imperatives, as you well know. But it also has advantages that are profoundly practical. Democratic states do not attack their neighbors and destabilize regions. Democratic states do not find it easy to declare and carry out war. Democratic states are not by their nature militaristic. Democracies are traditionally reluctant to spend a great deal of money on arms. Democratic states have built-in controls on aggressive, expansionist behavior, because democratic states must first marshal wide popular support before they move.

None of these characteristics applies to totalitarian states, however. And so totalitarian Nicaragua poses a threat to us all.

The Sandinistas have been engaged for some time in spreading their communist revolution beyond their borders. They're providing arms, training and a headquarters to the communist guerrillas who are attempting to overthrow the democratically-elected Duarte government of El Salvador. The Sandinistas have been caught supporting similar anti-democratic movements in Honduras and Costa Rica. Guatemala, too, is threatened. If these governments fall, as Nicaragua has fallen, it will send millions of refugees north, as country after country collapses. Already, the refugee situation is building to unacceptable levels. More than a quarter of a million refugees have fled Nicaragua since the Sandinistas took control. Some weeks, a hundred Nicaraguans a day stream into Costa Rica alone. It must be noted here that many of these refugees carry no papers, register in no official camps and wind up on no one's official list of those who've fled. They simply cross the border of one country or another and settle where they can.

And let me emphasize a very important point: These refugees are not simply people caught in the middle of a war. They're people fleeing for their lives from the Sandinista police state. They are fleeing from people who are burning down their villages, forcing them into concentration camps and forcing their children into military service.

The refugees come into camps in Honduras with no food and no money. Many are sick with parasites and malaria. And the great tragedy is that these people are the innocents of the war, people without politics, people who had never presumed to govern or to tell the world how to turn. They are both innocents and victims.

And I want to take a moment to thank the people, you who are helping the refugees. Woody Jenkins, Diane Jenkins and so many people in this room. While the world was turning away, you were helping. People like you are America at its best.

If the communists continue unfettered by the weight of world opinion, there will be more victims, victims of a long march north. We've seen this before. We've seen the Boat People leaving Southeast Asia in terror. We saw the streams of refugees leave East Berlin before the wall was built. We've seen these sad, lost armies fleeing in the night. We cannot allow it to happen again.

You know of our efforts to end the tragedy in Nicaragua. We want the killing and the bloodshed and the brutality to end. We've put forth a proposal for peace. We've asked for a cease-fire. We're asking the Sandinistas to join the democratic opposition in a Church-mediated dialogue. The Church itself a year ago independently asked the Sandinistas for this dialogue. We're asking the Sandinistas to take steps to hold truly democratic elections and restore freedom of speech, press and assembly.

Nicaragua's neighbors, El Salvador and Honduras and Costa Rica, have embraced this proposal. President Duarte, President Suazo, President Monge have all personally written to me to express support for this peace plan. And who bears better witness to the merits of this plan than Nicaragua's own neighbors?

As part of our proposal, we've asked the Congress of the United States to release $14 million for food, medicine and other support to help the patriots who believe in democracy survive in the hills of Nicaragua. This has been called a controversial request and it's garnered some opposition in the Congress. I believe the reasons for this must be addressed.

Some claim that the freedom fighters are simply former Somozistas who want to reimpose a dictatorship. That is simply not true. Listen to the roll call of their leaders: Adolpho Calero, a Nicaraguan businessman who was imprisoned by Somoza. Alfonso Robelo, a member of the original Sandinista government, now leading freedom fighters in the south. Arturo Cruz, another former member of the Sandinista government who is supporting the freedom fighters. Eden Pastora, the famed Commander Zero, a hero of the anti-Somoza revolution.

These men are not putting their lives on the line to restore a dictatorship of the past. These men are fighting for freedom. Already they control large sections of the countryside. And, as for their level of support, there are now three times as many freedom fighters fighting the Sandinistas as there were Sandinistas fighting Somoza.

There are those who say America's attempt to encourage freedom in Nicaragua interferes with the right of self-determination of the Nicaraguan people. Self-determination, you wonder what the ghosts of the Miskito Indians would say to that. You wonder what the journalists who cannot print the truth and the political prisoners who cannot speak it would say about self-determination and the Sandinistas. Ithink they would say that when a small communist clique seizes a country there is no self-determination, and no chance of it.

I believe that a vote against this aid is more than a rejection of the freedom fighters. It is a rejection of all the forces of moderation from the Church to the Contadora countries, which have called for freedom and democracy in Nicaragua.

I believe one inevitable outcome of a rejection of this aid would be that it would remove all pressure on the Sandinistas to change. And if no constraints are put on the Sandinistas, I believe the brutality and abuse they already aim at their own country and their neighbors may well be magnified a thousandfold.

I truly believe — the history of this century forces me to believe that to do nothing in Central America is to give the first communist stronghold on the North American continent a green light to spread its poison throughout this free and increasingly democratic hemisphere. (Applause) I — thank you. Thank you. I truly believe that this not only imperils the United States and its allies, but a vote against this proposal is literally a vote against peace because it invites the conditions that will lead to more fighting, new wars, and new bloodshed.

This vote — this vote is more than an appropriation of money. Through this vote, America will declare her commitment to peace. And through this aid, we will say to the free people of Central America, "We will not betray you. We will not leave you. And we will not allow you to become victims of some so-called historic inevitability."

No evil is inevitable unless we make it so. We cannot have the United States walk away from one of the greatest moral challenges in post-war history. I pledge to you that we will do everything we can to win this great struggle.

And, so, we're hopeful. We will fight on. We'll win this struggle for peace. Thank you for inviting me.

Viva Nicaragua Libre. Thank you, and God bless you.

And, now, I want to help Ambassador Davis, who I believe is going to give the first ever "Nicaraguan Refugee Fund Humanitarian Award." And it goes this year to the Executive Director of "Friends of the Americas," Diane Jenkins.

Diane, if you will come up here.

(The presentation is made.) ■

Reagan's Letters to Congress On Aid to Nicaraguan Rebels

Following are the Congressional Record *texts of the April 23 letter from President Reagan to Senate Majority Leader Robert Dole, R-Kan., and of the April 24 letter from President Reagan to House Speaker Thomas P. O'Neill Jr., D-Mass., and House Minority Leader Robert H. Michel, R-Ill., concerning the House and Senate votes on aid to the Nicaraguan rebels.*

Letter to Senate

DEAR SENATOR DOLE:

I announced on April 4 a proposal to promote peace in Central America by fostering a dialogue between the Government of Nicaragua and the democratic resistance, accompanied by a ceasefire in the conflict between them. My proposal was intended, in the words of the Contadora Document of Objectives agreed to by Nicaragua and its neighbors, "to promote national reconciliation efforts . . . , with a view to fostering participation in democratic political processes in accordance with the law."

Since April 4, I have had the benefit of many fruitful discussions with Latin American leaders and with members of the Congress. I have been encouraged by these discussions, which have shown that a broad consensus exists on the need for reconciliation in Nicaragua, based on democratic principles, as an essential aspect of achieving peace in Central America.

Today the Senate will vote on a resolution, S J Res 106, the test [*sic*] of which is required by a law enacted last October. That text purports to release appropriated funds and free the Executive Branch from restrictions against the support of military or paramilitary action in Nicaragua. However, my intentions are founded on a different approach. Accordingly, I want to make clear to the Senate, as it approaches this important vote, how I will proceed in pursuit of peace if S J Res 106 is enacted.

First, I will provide assistance to the democratic resistance only for food, medicine, clothing, and other assistance for their survival and well-being — and not for arms, ammunition, and weapons of war. Second, I will not use more than the $14 million already appropriated during the current fiscal year for such assistance. No other U.S. Government funds would be spent for such material assistance to the armed democratic resistance. I will personally establish thorough procedures for the detailed management and accountability of the program in order to assure that these limitations on both the nature and amount of U.S. assistance are scrupulously observed.

I recognize the importance some Senators have attached to bilateral talks between the United States and Nicaragua and the establishment of a ceasefire. I have considered these views and believe that such steps could help to promote the internal reconciliation called for by Contadora and endorsed by so many Latin American leaders.

Therefore, I intend to resume bilateral talks with the Government of Nicaragua and will instruct our representatives in those talks to press for a ceasefire as well as a church-mediated dialogue between the contending Nicaraguan factions. I must emphasize, however, that such bilateral talks must be in support of the Contadora process and the internal dialogue and cannot become a substitute for these efforts to achieve a comprehensive, verifiable agreement among all the nations of Central America. Also, as I said on April 4, peace negotiations must not become a cover for deception and delay. If the Sandinista government shows bad faith by seeking to gain unilateral advantage, for example, through a further arms buildup during a ceasefire or intransigence in negotiations, I would feel obligated to respond accordingly in our diplomatic efforts and would not expect the democratic resistance to continue to observe a ceasefire which was unfairly working to their disadvantage.

I will report to the Congress no later than September 1, 1985, on the progress made in achieving a verifiable peace and reconciliation in Nicaragua based on democratic principles. Such report shall also include an accounting for the funds obligated or expended under this joint resolution and may include such recommendations as I deem appropriate with respect to Nicaragua. I shall expect any recommendations for additional legislation for further assistance or sanctions to receive expedited handling.

While economic sanctions are unlikely by themselves to create sufficient pressure to change Nicaragua's behavior, the Sandinistas should not benefit from their present access to the U.S. market while continuing their intransigence on issues affecting our national security. The Administration will favorably consider economic sanctions against the Government of Nicaragua and will undertake multilateral consultations with other Central American states in this regard.

The U.S. condemns atrocities by either side in the strongest possible terms. We will use our assistance to help ensure against wrongful acts by those who seek our help and we will urge them to take steps to investigate allegations of such acts and take appropriate actions against those found to be guilty.

The United States now stands at a moment of judgment. Experience has shown that a policy of support for democracy, economic opportunity, and security will best serve the people of Central America and the national interests of the United States. If we show consistency of purpose, if we are firm in our conviction [t]hat the promising developments over the past year in El Salvador, Honduras, Costa Rica, and Guatemala also show the way for a better future for Nicaragua, then over time we can help the democratic center prevail over tyrants of the left or the right. But if we abandon democracy in Nicaragua, if we tolerate the consolidation of a surrogate state in Central America, responsive to Cuba and the Soviet Union, we will see the progress that has been achieved begin to unravel under the strain of continuing conflict, attempts at subversion, and loss of confidence in our support.

There can be a more democratic, more prosperous, and more peaceful Central America. I am prepared to devote my energies toward that end. But, I also need the support of the Congress. I hope that you will give me your support today.

Sincerely,

RONALD REAGAN

Letter to House

DEAR MR. SPEAKER:

I announced on April 4 a proposal to promote peace in Central America by fostering a dialogue between the Government of Nicaragua and the democratic resistance, accompanied by a ceasefire in the conflict between them. My proposal was intended, in the words of the Contadora Document of Objectives agreed to by Nicaragua and its neighbors, "to promote national reconciliation efforts . . . , with a view to fostering participation in democratic political processes in accordance with the law."

Since April 4, I have had the benefit of many fruitful exchanges with Latin American leaders and with members of the Congress. I have been encouraged by these discussions, which have shown that a broad consensus exists on the need for reconciliation in Nicaragua, based on democratic principles, as an essential aspect of achieving peace in Central America.

Today the House will vote on competing proposals on how to proceed with our policy in Central America. The choice to be made is a fundamental one that will have a lasting effect on the prospects for democracy, economic opportunity, and peace in this vital region.

The proposal to be offered by Mr. Barnes and Mr. Hamilton would divert funds from existing economic assistance and refugee accounts for humanitarian assistance to refugees outside Nicaragua and for the expenses of implementing an eventual Contadora agreement. Members of Congress should be under no illusion about this proposal. Its adoption would damage our national security and foreign policy interests. By providing a financial inducement for members of the resistance to leave Nicaragua and become refugees in other countries, it relieves pressure on the Sandinistas while, at the same time, it increases the burdens imposed on the neighboring democracies. As a result, fragile democracies would be weakened, their economic recovery would be stalled, their security would be diminished — and the civil war in Nicaragua would go on.

The other proposal before the House, to be offered by Mr. Michel, would appropriate $14 million in new funds to enable the Agency for International Development to provide humanitarian aid for the Nicaraguan democratic opposition. This alternative meets most of the objectives in my effort to promote a dialogue within Nicaragua which regional leaders have recognized is essential for peace in Central America. Rather than abandon the opposition, the Michel proposal would help to sustain it, giving peace a chance.

If Congress approves $14 million for assistance during the current fiscal year, no other U.S. Government funds would be spent for such material assistance to the armed democratic resistance. I will personally establish thorough procedures for the detailed management and accountability of the program in order to assure that these limitations on both the nature and amount of U.S. assistance are scrupulously observed.

I recognize the importance some members have attached to bilateral talks with the Government of Nicaragua. I am instructing my representatives to meet with representatives of the Government of Nicaragua. In their talks, the U.S. representative will press for a ceasefire as well as a church-mediated dialogue between the Sandinistas and the united democratic opposition. I must emphasize, however, that such bilateral talks must be in support of the Contadora process and cannot become a substitute for these efforts to achieve a comprehensive, verifiable agreement among all the nations of Central America. Also, as I said on April 4, peace negotiations must not become a cover for deception and delay. If the Sandinista government shows bad faith by seeking to gain unilateral advantage, for example, through a further arms buildup during a ceasefire or intransigence in negotiations, I would feel constrained to respond accordingly in our diplomatic efforts and would not expect the democratic resistance to continue to observe a ceasefire which was unfairly working to their disadvantage.

While economic sanctions are unlikely by themselves to create sufficient pressure to change Nicaragua's behavior, the Sandinistas should not benefit from their present access to the U.S. market while continuing their intransigence on issues affecting our national security. The Administration will favorably consider economic sanctions against the Government of Nicaragua and will undertake multilateral consultations with other Central American states in this regard.

The U.S. condemns atrocities by either side in the strongest possible terms. We will use our assistance to help ensure against wrongful acts by those who seek our help and we will urge them to take steps to investigate allegations of such acts and take appropriate actions against those found to be guilty.

The United States now stands at a moment of judgment. Experience has shown that a policy of support for democracy, economic opportunity, and security will best serve the people of Central America and the national interests of the United States. If we show consistency of purpose, if we are firm in our conviction that the promising developments over the past year in El Salvador, Honduras, Costa Rica, and Guatemala also show the way for a better future for Nicaragua, then over time we can help see the democratic center prevail over tyrants of the left or the right. But if we abandon democracy in Nicaragua, if we tolerate the consolidation of a surrogate state in Central America responsive to Cuba and the Soviet Union, we will see the progress that has been achieved begin to unravel under the strain of continuing conflict, attempts at subversion, and loss of confidence in our support.

There can be a more democratic, more prosperous, and more peaceful Central America. I am prepared to devote my energies toward that end. But, I also need the support of the Congress. Yesterday, the Senate in a bipartisan vote for peace and democracy confirmed the commitment of the United States to those who struggle for liberty. I urge that the House of Representatives support such a measure today.

Sincerely,

RONALD REAGAN ∎

Statement on Nicaragua Trade Embargo

Following is the White House text of President Reagan's May 1 statement to Congress that he was imposing an embargo on trade with the leftist Sandinista government of Nicaragua.

TO THE CONGRESS OF THE UNITED STATES:

Pursuant to section 204(b) of the International Emergency Economic Powers Act, 50 U.S.C. 1703, I hereby report to the Congress that I have exercised my statutory authority to declare a national emergency and to prohibit: (1) all imports into the United States of goods and services of Nicaraguan origin; (2) all exports from the United States of goods to or destined for Nicaragua except those destined for the organized democratic resistance; (3) Nicaraguan air carriers from engaging in air transportation to or from points in the United States; and (4) vessels of Nicaraguan registry from entering into United States ports.

These prohibitions will become effective as of 12:01 a.m., Eastern Daylight Time, May 7, 1985.

I am enclosing a copy of the Executive Order that I have issued making this declaration and exercising these authorities.

1. I have authorized these steps in response to the emergency situation created by the Nicaraguan Government's aggressive activities in Central America. Nicaragua's continuing efforts to subvert its neighbors, its rapid and destabilizing military buildup, its close military and security ties to Cuba and the Soviet Union and its imposition of Communist totalitarian internal rule have been described fully in the past several weeks. The current visit by Nicaraguan President Ortega to Moscow underscores this disturbing trend. The recent rejection by Nicaragua of my peace initiative, viewed in the light of the constantly rising pressure that Nicaragua's military buildup places on the democratic nations of the region, makes clear the urgent threat that Nicaragua's activities represent to the security of the region and, therefore, to the security and foreign policy of the United States. The activities of Nicaragua, supported by the Soviet Union and its allies, are incompatible with normal commercial relations.

2. In taking these steps, I note that during this month's debate on U.S. policy toward Nicaragua, many Members of Congress, both supporters and opponents of my proposals, called for the early application of economic sanctions.

3. I have long made clear that changes in Sandinista behavior must occur if peace is to be achieved in Central America. At this time, I again call on the Government of Nicaragua:

- to halt its export of armed insurrection, terrorism, and subversion in neighboring countries;
- to end its extensive military relationship with Cuba and the Soviet Bloc and remove their military and security personnel;
- to stop its massive arms buildup and help restore the regional military balance; and
- to respect, in law and in practice, democratic pluralism and observance of full political and human rights in Nicaragua.

4. U.S. application of these sanctions should be seen by the Government of Nicaragua, and by those who abet it, as unmistakable evidence that we take seriously the obligation to protect our security interests and those of our friends. I ask the Government of Nicaragua to address seriously the concerns of its neighbors and its own opposition and to honor its solemn commitments to non-interference, non-alignment, respect for democracy, and peace. Failure to do so will only diminish the prospects for a peaceful settlement in Central America. ∎

Reagan's Address to European Parliament

Following is the White House text of President Reagan's address to a special session of the European Parliament as delivered May 8, in Strasbourg, France, on the occasion of the 40th anniversary of the end of World War II in Europe.

THE PRESIDENT: Thank you, ladies and gentlemen. It is an honor to be with you on this day.

We mark today the anniversary of the liberation of Europe from tyrants who had seized this continent and plunged it into a terrible war. Forty years ago today, the guns were stilled and peace began, a peace that has become the longest of this century.

On this day 40 years ago, they swarmed onto the boulevards of Paris, rallied under the Arc de Triomphe and sang the "Marseillaise." In the — they were out there in the open and free air. And now on this day 40 years ago, Winston Churchill walked out onto a balcony in Whitehall and said to the people of Britain, "This is your victory." And the crowd yelled back, in an unforgettable moment of love and gratitude, "No — it is yours." Londoners tore the blackout curtains from their windows, put floodlights on the great symbols of English history. And for the first time in nearly six years, Big Ben, Buckingham Palace and St. Paul's Cathedral were illuminated against the sky.

Across the ocean, a half a million New Yorkers flooded Times Square and laughed and posed for the cameras. In Washington, our new President Harry Truman called reporters into his office and said, "The flags of freedom fly all over Europe."

On that day 40 years ago, I was at my post in an Army Air Corps installation in Culver City, California. Passing a radio, I heard the words, "Ladies and gentlemen, the war in Europe is over." I felt a chill, as if a gust of cold wind had just swept past and even though for America, there was still a war in the Pacific Front, I realized I would never forget that moment.

This day can't help but be emotional, for in it we feel the long tug of memory. We're reminded of shared joy and shared pain. A few weeks ago, an old soldier with tears in his eyes said, "It was such a different world then. It's almost impossible to describe it to someone who wasn't there. But when they finally turned the lights on in the cities again, it was like being reborn."

If it is hard to communicate the happiness of those days, it is even harder to communicate, to those who did not share it, the depth of Europe's agony. So much of it lay in ruins. Whole cities had been destroyed. Children played in the rubble and begged for food.

And by this day 40 years ago, over 40 million lay dead and the survivors, they composed a continent of victims. And to this day we wonder: How did this happen? How did civilization take such a terrible turn? After all the books and documentaries, after all the histories and studies, we still wonder: How?

Hannah Arendt spoke of the "banality of evil" — the banality of the little men who did the terrible deeds. We know they were totalitarians who used the state, which they had elevated to the level of a god, to inflict war on peaceful nations and genocide on innocent peoples. We know of the existence of evil in the human heart, and we know that in Nazi Germany that evil was institutionalized, given power and direction by the state and those who did its bidding. And we also know that early attempts to placate the totalitarians did not save us from war. They didn't save us from war, in fact they guaranteed it. There are lessons to be learned in this and never forgotten.

But there is a lesson, too, in another thing we saw in those days, and perhaps we can call it the "commonness of virtue." The common men and women who somehow dug greatness from within their souls, the people who sang to the children during the blitz, who joined the resistance and said "no" to tyranny, the people who had the courage — who had the courage to hide and save the Jews and the dissidents — the people who became for a moment the repositories of all the courage of the West, from a child named Anne Frank to a hero named Raoul Wallenberg. These names shine. They give us heart forever. The glow of their memories lit Europe in her darkest days.

The Atlantic Alliance

Who can forget the hard days after the war? We cannot help but look back and think — life was so vivid then. There was the sense of purpose, the joy of shared effort, and, later, the impossible joy of our triumph. Those were the days when the West rolled up its sleeves and repaired the damage that had been done, the days when Europe rose in glory from the ruins. Old enemies were reconciled with the European family. Together, America and Western Europe created and put into place the Marshall Plan to rebuild from the rubble. Together we created an Atlantic Alliance, which proceeded not from transient interests of state, but from shared ideals. Together we created the North Atlantic Treaty Organization, a partnership aimed at seeing that the kind of tyrants that had tormented Europe would never torment her again.

NATO was a triumph of organization and effort, but it was also something very new and very different. For NATO derived its strength directly from the moral values of the people it represented, from their high ideals, their love of liberty, and their commitment to peace. But perhaps the greatest triumph of all was not in the realm of a sound defense or material achievement. No, the greatest triumph after the war is that in spite of all of the chaos, poverty, sickness, and misfortune that plagued this continent, the people of Western Europe resisted the call of new tyrants and the lure of their seductive ideologies. Your nations did not become the breeding ground for new extremist philosophies. You resisted the totalitarian temptation. Your people embraced democracy, the dream the fascists could not kill. They chose freedom.

And today we celebrate the leaders who led the way — Churchill and Monnet, Adenauer and Schuman, De Gasperi and Spaak, Truman and Marshall. And we celebrate too the free political parties that contributed their share of greatness — the Liberals and the Christian Democrats, the Social Democrats and Labour and the Conservatives. Together they tugged at the same oar and the great and mighty ship of Europe moved on.

If any doubt their success, let them look at you. In this room are those who fought on opposite sides 40 years ago, and their sons and daughters. Now you work together to lead Europe democratically, you buried animosity and hatred in the rubble. There is no greater testament to reconciliation and to the peaceful unity of Europe than the men and women in this chamber.

In the decades after the war, Europe knew great growth and power, amazing vitality in every area of life, from fine arts to fashion, from manufacturing to science to the world of ideas. Europe was robust and alive, and none of this was an accident. It was the natural result of freedom, the natural fruit of the democratic ideal. We in America look at Europe and called her what she was: an economic miracle.

America's European Heritage

And we could hardly be surprised. When we Americans think about our European heritage, we tend to think of your cultural influences and the rich ethnic heritage you gave us. But the industrial revolution that transformed the American economy came from Europe. The guiding intellectual lights of our democratic system — Locke, Montesquieu, and Adam Smith — came from Europe. And the geniuses who ushered in the modern industrial-technological age came from — well, I think you know, but two examples will suffice. Alexander Graham Bell, whose great invention maddens every American parent whose child insists on phoning his European pen pal rather than writing to him — and he was a Scotsman. And Guglielmo Marconi, who invented the radio — thereby providing a living for a young man from Dixon, Illinois, who later went into politics. I guess I should explain — that's me. Blame Marconi. And Marconi, as you know, was born in Italy.

Tomorrow will mark the 35th anniversary of the Schuman Plan, which led to the European Coal and Steel Community, the first block in the creation of a united Europe. The purpose was to tie French and German — and European — industrial production so tightly together that war between them "becomes not merely unthinkable, but materially impossible." Those are the words of Robert Schuman; the Coal and Steel Community was the child of his genius. And if we here today were today — I believe if he were here today, I believe he would say: We have only just begun!

European Unity

I'm here to tell you that America remains, as she was 40 years ago, dedicated to the unity of Europe. We continue to see a strong and unified Europe not as a rival but as an even stronger partner. Indeed, John F. Kennedy, in his ringing "Declaration of Interdependence" in the Freedom Bell city of Philadelphia 23 years ago, explicitly made this objective a key tenet of postwar American policy; that policy saw the New World and the Old as twin pillars of a larger democratic community. We Americans still see European unity as a vital force in that historic process. We favor the expansion of the European Community; we welcome the entrance of Spain and Portugal into that Community — for their presence makes for a stronger Europe, and a stronger Europe is a stronger West.

'Europessimism'

Yet despite Europe's economic miracle which brought so much prosperity to so many, despite the visionary ideas of the European leaders, despite the enlargement of democracy's frontiers within the European community itself, I'm told that a more doubting mood is upon Europe today. I hear words like "Europessimism" and "Europaralysis." I'm told that Europe seems to have lost that sense of confidence that dominated that postwar era. Well, if there is something of a lost quality these days, is it connected to the fact that some in the past few years have begun to question the ideals and philosophies that have guided the West for centuries; that some have even come to question the moral and intellectual worth of the West?

Lessons of History

I wish to speak, in part, to that questioning today. And there is no better place to do it than Strasbourg — where Goethe studied, where Pasteur taught, where Hugo knew inspiration. This has been a lucky city for questioning and finding valid answers. It is also a city for which some of us feel a very sweet affection. You know that our Statue of Liberty was a gift from France, and its sculptor, Auguste Bartholdi, was a son of France. I don't know if you've ever studied the face of the statue, but immigrants entering New York Harbor used to strain to see it, as if it would tell them something about their new world. It's a strong, kind face. It is the face of Bartholdi's mother, a woman of Alsace. And so, among the many things we Americans thank you for, we thank you for her.

The Statue of Liberty — made in Europe, erected in America — helps remind us not only of past ties but present realities. It is to those realities we must look in order to dispel whatever doubts may exist about the course of history and the place of free men and women within it.

We live in a complex, dangerous, divided world; yet a world which can provide all of the good things we require — spiritual and material — if we but have the confidence and courage to face history's challenge.

We in the West have much to be thankful for — peace, prosperity, and freedom. If we are to preserve these for our children and for theirs, today's leaders must demonstrate the same resolve and sense of vision which inspired Churchill, Adenauer, De Gasperi, and Schuman. Their challenge was to rebuild. The challenge was to rebuild a democratic Europe under the shadow of Soviet power. Our task, in some ways even more daunting, is to keep the peace with an ever more powerful Soviet Union, to introduce greater stability in our relationship with it and to live together in a world in which our values can prosper.

The leaders and people of postwar Europe had learned the lessons of their history from the failures of their predecessors. They learned that aggression feeds on appeasement and that weakness itself can be provocative.

We, for our part, can learn from the success of our predecessors. We know that both conflict and aggression can be deterred, that democratic nations are capable of the resolve, the sacrifices, and the consistency of policy needed to sustain such deterrence.

Soviet Aggression

From the creation of NATO in 1949 through the early 1970s, Soviet aggression was effectively deterred. The strength of Western economies, the vitality of our societies, the wisdom of our diplomacy all contributed to Soviet restraint; but certainly the decisive factor must have been the countervailing power — ultimately, military, and above all, nuclear power, which the West was capable of bringing to bear in the defense of its interests. It was in the early 1970s that the United States lost that superiority over the Soviet Union in strategic nuclear weapons, which had characterized the postwar era. In Europe, the effect of this loss was not quickly perceptible, but seen globally, Soviet conduct changed markedly and dangerously, first in Angola in 1975, then when the West failed to respond, in Ethiopia, in South Yemen, in Kampuchea and ultimately in Afghanistan, the Soviet Union began courting more risks and expanding its influence — expanding its influence through the indirect and direct application of military power. Today, we see similar Soviet efforts to profit from and stimulate regional conflicts in Central America.

They haven't been there. I have.

The ineffectual Western response to Soviet adventurism of the late 1970s had many roots, not least the crisis of self-confidence within the American body politic wrought by the Vietnam experience. But just as Soviet decision-making in the earlier postwar era had taken place against a background of overwhelming American strategic power, so the decisions of the late '70s were taken in Moscow, as in Washington and throughout Europe, against a background of growing Soviet and stagnating Western nuclear strength.

Nuclear Arms Race

One might draw the conclusion from these events that the West should reassert that nuclear superiority over the Soviet Union upon which our security and our strategy rested through the postwar era. That is not my view. We cannot and should not seek to build our peace and freedom perpetually upon the basis of expanding nuclear arsenals.

In the short run, we have no alternative but to compete with the Soviet Union in this field, not in the pursuit of superiority, but merely of balance. It is thus essential that the United States maintain a modern and survivable nuclear capability in each leg of the strategic triad — sea, land and air-based. It is similarly important that France and Britain maintain and modernize their independent strategic capabilities.

Now, the Soviet Union, however, does not share our view of what constitutes a stable nuclear balance. It has chosen instead to build nuclear forces clearly designed to strike first and thus disarm their adversary. The Soviet Union is now moving toward deployment of new mobile MIRVed missiles which have these capabilities, plus the potential to avoid detection, monitoring or arms control verification. In doing this, the Soviet Union is undermining stability and the basis for mutual deterrence.

One can imagine several possible responses to the continued Soviet buildup of nuclear forces. On the one hand, we can ask the Soviet Union to reduce its offensive systems through equitable, verifiable arms control measures. We are pressing that case in Geneva. Thus far, however, we've heard nothing new from the other side.

A second possibility would be for the West to step up our current modernization effort to keep up with constantly accelerating Soviet deployments, not to regain superiority, but merely to keep up with Soviet deployments. But is this really an acceptable alternative? Even if this course could be sustained by the West, it would produce a less stable strategic balance than the one we have today. Must we accept an endless process of nuclear arms competition? I don't think so. We need a better guarantee of peace than that.

Strategic Defense Initiative

And fortunately, there is a third possibility. It is to offset the continued Soviet offensive buildup in destabilizing weapons by developing defenses against these weapons. In 1983, I launched a new research program — the Strategic Defense Initiative.

The state of modern technology may soon make possible, for the first time, the ability to use non-nuclear systems to defeat ballistic missiles. The Soviets themselves have long recognized the value of defensive systems and have invested heavily in them. Indeed, they have spent as much on defensive systems as they have on offensive systems for more than 20 years.

Now, this research program will take time. As we proceed with it, we will remain within existing treaty constraints. We will also consult in the closest possible fashion with our allies. And when the time for decisions on the possible production and deployment of such systems comes, we must and will discuss and negotiate these issues with the Soviet Union.

Both for the short and the long term I'm confident that the West can maintain effective military deterrence. But surely we can aspire to more than maintaining a state of highly-armed truce in international politics.

During the 1970s we went to great lengths to restrain unilaterally our strategic weapons programs out of the conviction that the Soviet Union would adhere to certain rules in its conduct — rules such as neither side seeking to gain unilateral advantage at the expense of the other. Those efforts of the early 1970s resulted in some improvements in Europe, the Berlin Quadripartite Agreement being the best example. But the hopes for a broader and lasting moderation of the East-West competition foundered in Angola, Ethiopia, Afghanistan, and Nicaragua.

U.S.-Soviet Cooperation

The question before us today is whether we have learned — had we learned from those mistakes and can we undertake a stable and peaceful relationship with the Soviet Union based upon effective deterrence and the reduction of tensions. I believe we can. I believe we've learned that fruitful cooperation with the Soviet Union must be accompanied by successful competition in areas, particularly Third World areas where the Soviets are not yet prepared to act with restraint.

[At this point, some members of the audience walked out in protest.]

You know, I've learned something useful. Maybe if I talk long enough in my own Congress, some of those will walk out.

But let me talk about the reflections which have molded our policy toward the Soviet Union. That policy embodies the following basic elements: While we maintain deterrence to preserve the peace, the United States will make a steady, sustained effort to reduce tensions and solve problems in its relations with the Soviet Union.

The United States is prepared to conclude fair, equitable, verifiable agreements for arms reduction, above all, with regard to offensive nuclear weapons.

The United States will insist upon compliance with past agreements, both for their own sake and to strengthen confidence in the possibility of future accords.

The United States seeks no unilateral advantages, and, of course, can accept none on the Soviet side. The United States will proceed in full consultation with its allies, recognizing that our fates are intertwined and we must act in unity. The United States does not seek to undermine or change the Soviet system nor to impinge upon the security of the Soviet Union. At the same time it will resist attempts by the Soviet Union to use or threaten force against others, or to impose its system on others by force.

Ultimately, I hope the leaders of the Soviet Union will come to understand that they have nothing to gain from attempts to achieve military superiority or to spread their dominance by force, but have much to gain from joining the West in mutual arms reduction and expanding cooperation.

I have directed the Secretary of State to engage with the Soviet Union on an extended agenda of problem solving. Yet even as we embark upon new efforts to sustain a productive dialogue with the Soviet Union, we're reminded of the obstacles posed by our so fundamentally different concepts of humanity, of human rights, of the value of human life. The murder of Major Nicholson by a Soviet soldier in East Germany, and the Soviet Union's refusal to accept responsibility for this act, is only the latest reminder.

If we're to succeed in reducing East-West tensions, we must find means to ensure against the arbitrary use of lethal force in the future — whether against individuals like Major Nicholson, or against groups, such as the passengers on a jumbo jet.

It is for that reason that I would like to outline for you today what I believe would be a useful way to proceed. I propose that the United States and the Soviet Union take four practical steps.

First, that our two countries make a regular practice of exchanging military observers at military exercises and locations. We now follow this practice with many other nations, to the equal benefit of all parties.

Second, as I believe it is desirable for the leaders of the United States and Soviet Union to meet and tackle problems, I am also convinced that the military leaders of our nations could benefit from more contact. I therefore propose that we institute regular, high-level contacts between Soviet and American military leaders, to develop better understanding and to prevent potential tragedies from occurring.

Third, I urge that the Conference on Disarmament in Europe act promptly and agree on the concrete confidence-building measures proposed by the NATO countries. The United States is prepared to discuss the Soviet proposal on non-use of force in the context of Soviet agreement to concrete confidence-building measures.

Fourth, I believe a permanent military-to-military communications link could serve a useful purpose in this important area of our relationship. It could be the channel for exchanging notifications and other information regarding routine military activities, thereby reducing the chances of misunderstanding and misinterpretation. And over time, it might evolve into a "risk-reduction" mechanism for rapid communication and exchange of data in times of crisis.

These proposals are not cure-alls for our current problems. They will not compensate for the deaths which have occurred.

But as terrible as past events have been, it would be more tragic if we were to make no attempt to prevent even larger tragedies from occurring through lack of contact and communication.

We in the West have much to do — and we must do it together. We must remain unified in the face of attempts to divide us and strong in spite of attempts to weaken us. And we must remember that our unity and strength are not a mere impulse of like-minded allies, but the natural result of our shared love for liberty.

Triumph of Democracy

Surely, we have no illusions that convergence of the communist system and the free societies of the West is likely. We're in for an extended period of competition of ideas. It is up to us in the West to answer whether or not we will make available the resources, ideas, and assistance necessary to compete with the Soviet Union in the Third World. We have much in our favor, not least the experience of those states which have tried Marxism and are looking for an alternative.

We do not aspire to impose our system on anyone, nor do we have pat answers for all the world's ills. But our ideals of freedom and democracy —

AUDIENCE: Nicaragua. Nicaragua.

THE PRESIDENT: Is there an echo in here?

Our ideals of freedom and democracy and our economic systems have proven their ability to meet the needs of our people. Our adversaries can offer their people only economic stagnation and the corrupt hand of a state and party bureaucracy which ultimately satisfy neither material nor spiritual needs.

Western Unity

I want to reaffirm to the people of Europe the constancy of the American purpose. We were at your side through two great wars; we have been at your side through 40 years of a sometimes painful peace. We're at your side today because, like you, we have not veered from the ideals of the West — the ideals of freedom, liberty, and peace. Let no one — no one — doubt our purpose.

The United States is committed not only to the security of Europe, we're committed to the re-creation of a larger and more genuinely European Europe. The United States is committed not only to a partnership with Europe, the United States is committed to an end to the artificial division of Europe.

We do not deny any nation's legitimate interest in security. We share the basic aspirations of all of the peoples of Europe — freedom, prosperity, and peace. But when families are divided, and people are not allowed to maintain normal human and cultural contacts, this creates international tension. Only in a system in which all feel secure and sovereign can there be a lasting and secure peace.

For this reason, we will support and will encourage movement toward the social, humanitarian and democratic ideals shared in Europe. The issue is not one of state boundaries, but of insuring the right of all nations to conduct their affairs as their peoples desire. The problem of a divided Europe, like others, must be solved by peaceful means. Let us rededicate ourselves to the full implementation of the Helsinki Final Act in all its aspects.

As we seek to encourage democracy, we must remember that each country must struggle for democracy within its own culture. Emerging democracies have special problems and require special help. Those nations whose democratic institutions are newly emerged and whose confidence in the process is not yet deeply rooted need our help. They should have an established community of their peers, other democratic countries to whom they can turn for support or just advice.

In my address to the British Parliament in 1982, I spoke of the need for democratic governments to spread the message of democracy throughout the world. I expressed my support for the Council of Europe's effort to bring together delegates from many nations for this purpose. I am encouraged by the product of that conference, the Strasbourg Initiative.

We in our country have launched a major effort to strengthen and promote democratic ideals and institutions. Following a pattern first started in the Federal Republic of Germany, the United States Congress approved the National Endowment for Democracy. This organization subsequently established institutes of labor, business, and political parties dedicated to programs of cooperation with democratic forces around the world. I hope other democracies will join in this effort and contribute their wisdom and talents to this cause.

Here in Western Europe you have created a multinational democratic community in which there is a free flow of people, of information, of goods, and of culture. West Europeans move frequently in all directions, sharing and partaking of each other's ideas and culture. It is my hope that in the 21st century, which is only fifteen years away, all Europeans, from Moscow to Lisbon, will be able to travel without a passport and the free flow of people and ideas will include the other half of Europe. It is my fervent wish that in the next century there will be one free Europe.

I do not believe, those who say the people of Europe today are paralyzed and pessimistic. And I would say to those who think this, Europe, beloved Europe, you are greater than you know. You are the treasury of centuries of Western thought and Western culture. You are the father of Western ideals and the mother of Western faith. Europe, you have been the power and the glory of the West, and you are a moral success. In the horrors after World War II, you rejected totalitarianism, you rejected the lure of the new "Superman" and a "New Communist Man." You proved that you were and are a moral triumph.

You in the West are a Europe without illusions, a Europe firmly grounded in the ideals and traditions that made her greatness, a Europe unbound and unfettered by a bankrupt ideology. You are today a new Europe on the brink of a new century — a democratic community with much to be proud of.

We have so much to do. The work ahead is not unlike the building of a great cathedral. The work is slow, complicated and painstaking. It's passed on with pride from generation to generation. It's the work not only of leaders, but of ordinary people. The cathedral evolves as it is created, with each generation adding its own vision. But the initial ideal remains constant. And the faith that drives the vision persists. The results may be slow to see, but our children and their children will trace in the air the emerging arches and spires and know the faith and dedication and love that produced them. My friends, Europe is the cathedral. And it is illuminated still.

And if you doubt your will and your spirit and your strength to stand for something, think of those people 40 years ago who wept in the rubble, who laughed in the streets, who paraded across Europe, who cheered Churchill with love and devotion, who sang the "Marseillaise" down the boulevards. Spirit like that does not disappear. It cannot perish. It will not go. There is too much left unsung within it.

I would like to just conclude with one line, if I could, and say we've seen evidence here of your faith in democracy, in the ability of some to speak up freely, as they preferred to speak. And yet I can't help but remind all of us that some who take advantage of that right of democracy seem unaware that if the government that they would advocate became reality, no one would have that freedom to speak up again.

Thank you all for your graciousness on this great day. Thank you and God bless you all. Thank you. ■

President Proposes Federal Tax Reform

Following is the White House text of President Reagan's address on his proposal to reform the federal tax system, as delivered May 28 from the Oval Office.

My fellow citizens, I'd like to speak to you tonight about our future, about a great historic effort to give the words "freedom," "fairness" and "hope" new meaning and power for every man and woman in America.

Specifically, I want to talk about taxes, about what we must do as a nation this year to transform a system that's become an endless source of confusion and resentment into one that is clear, simple and fair for all; a tax code that no longer runs roughshod over Main Street America, but ensures your families and firms incentives and rewards for hard work and risk-taking in an American future of strong economic growth.

No other issue goes so directly to the heart of our economic life. No other issue will have more lasting impact on the well-being of your families and your future.

In 1981, our critics charged that letting you keep more of your earnings would trigger an inflationary explosion, send interest rates soaring and destroy our economy. Well, we cut your tax rates anyway, by nearly 25 percent. And what that helped trigger was falling inflation, falling interest rates and the strongest economic expansion in 30 years.

The Need to Reform

We have made one great dramatic step together. We owe it to ourselves now to take another. For the sake of fairness, simplicity and growth, we must radically change the structure of a tax system that still treats our earnings as the personal property of the Internal Revenue Service, radically change a system that still treats people's earnings, similar incomes, much differently, regarding the tax that they pay. And, yes, radically change a system that still causes some to invest their money, not to make a better mousetrap, but simply to avoid a tax trap.

Over the course of this century, our tax system has been modified dozens of times and in hundreds of ways. Yet, most of those changes didn't improve the system. They made it more like Washington itself: complicated, unfair, cluttered with gobbledygook and loopholes designed for those with the power and influence to hire high-priced legal and tax advisors.

But there's more to it than that.

Some years ago, an historian I believe, said that every time in the past when a government began taxing above a certain level of the people's earnings, trust in government began to erode. He said it would begin with efforts to avoid paying the full tax. This would become outright cheating, and eventually a distrust and contempt of government itself, until there would be a breakdown in law and order.

Well, how many times have we heard people brag about clever schemes to avoid paying taxes or watched luxuries casually written off to be paid for by somebody else — that somebody being you? I believe that in both spirit and substance, our tax system has come to be un-American.

'A Second American Revolution'

Death and taxes may be inevitable, but unjust taxes are not. The first American Revolution was sparked by an unshakable conviction — taxation without representation is tyranny. Two centuries later, a second American revolution for hope and opportunity is gathering force again — a peaceful revolution, but born of popular resentment against a tax system that is unwise, unwanted and unfair.

I've spoken with and received letters from thousands of you — Republicans, Democrats, and Independents. I know how hungry you are for change. Make no mistake — we, the sons and daughters of those first brave souls who came to this land to give birth to a new life in liberty, we can change America. We can change America forever. So let's get started. Let's change the tax code to make it fairer and change tax rates so they're lower.

The proposal I'm putting forth tonight for America's future will free us from the grip of special interests and create a binding commitment to the only special interest that counts — you, the people who pay America's bills. It will create millions of new jobs for working people and it will replace the politics of envy with a spirit of partnership — the opportunity for everyone to hitch their wagon to a star and set out to reach the American Dream.

I'll start by answering one question on your minds. Will our proposal help you? You bet it will. We call it America's Tax Plan because it will reduce tax burdens on the working people of this country, close loopholes that benefit a privileged few, simplify a code so complex even Albert Einstein reportedly needed help on his 1040 form, and lead us into a future of greater growth and opportunity for all.

We want to cut taxes, not opportunity. As you can see, the percentage of income tax owed would come down, way down, for those earning less than $15,000; down for earnings between $15,000 and $30,000; down for earnings between $30,000 and $50,000; and down for those earning more than $50,000.

A Three-Bracket System

How would the proposal work? The present tax system has 14 different brackets of tax rates ranging from 11 to 50 percent. We would take a giant step toward an ideal system by replacing all that with a simple three-bracket system — with tax rates of 15, 25, and 35 percent.

Now, let me point out right here that under our plan, by taking the basic deductions, the average family earning up to $12,000 or any blind or elderly American living at or below the poverty level would be dropped completely from the tax rolls — not one penny of tax to pay.

After taking the basic deductions, the first tax rate of 15 percent would apply to each dollar of taxable income up to $29,000 on a joint return. The second rate, 25 percent, would apply, and only apply to taxable income above $29,000 up to a maximum of $70,000. The same principle applies throughout. Only taxable income above $70,000 would be taxed at the third and highest rate of 35 percent. Then no matter how much more you earned, you would pay 35 cents on any dollar to Uncle Sam. That is the top — 35 percent — down from 50 percent today.

By lowering everyone's tax rates all the way up the income scale, each of us will have a greater incentive to climb higher, to excel, to help America grow.

A Pro-Family Initiative

I believe the worth of any economic policy must be measured by the strength of its commitment to American families — the bedrock of our society. There is no instrument of hard work, savings, and job creation as effective as the family. There is no cultural institution as ennobling as family life. And there is no superior, indeed, no equal means to rear the young, protect the weak, or attend the elderly. None.

Yet past government policies betrayed families and family values. They permitted inflation to push families relentlessly into higher and higher tax brackets. And not only did the personal exemption fail to keep pace with inflation. In real dollars its actual value dropped dramatically over the last thirty years.

The power to tax is the power to destroy. For three decades, families have paid the freight for the special interests. Now families are in trouble. As one man from Memphis, Tennessee, recently wrote, "The taxes that are taken out of my check is money that I need, not extra play money. Please do all that you can to make the tax system more equitable toward the family." Well, sir, that is just what we intend to do — to pass the strongest pro-family initiative in post-war history.

In addition to lowering your tax rates further, we will virtually double the personal exemption, raising it by next year to $2,000 for every taxpayer and every dependent. And that $2,000 exemption will be indexed to protect against inflation. Further, we will increase the standard deduction, raising it to $4,000 for joint returns.

Beyond this, we intend to strengthen families' incentives to save through individual retirement accounts, IRAs, by nearly doubling — to $4,000 — the amount all couples can deduct from their taxable income. From now on, each spouse could put up to $2,000 a year into his or her IRA and invest the money however they want. And the value of the IRA would not be taxable until they approach retirement.

Some families could save more, others less. But whether it's $400 or $4,000, every dollar saved up to $4,000 each year would be fully deductible from taxable earnings. Let me add that we would also raise by nearly a full third the special tax credit for low-income working Americans. That special incentive, a credit to reduce the tax they owe, would be raised from the present $550 to a maximum level of over $700.

Effects of Reform

Now, let's look at some examples of families in different income groups to illustrate how dramatically these incentives could help you to better your lives.

Take a family of four, struggling at a poverty-level existence, with an annual income of $12,000. By nearly doubling the personal exemption and raising the standard deduction, we will, as I said before, guarantee that that family pays no income tax at all.

But what if, being industrious, they go out and earn more, say $5,000 more, how much tax would they pay? Only 15 cents on each dollar of the additional $5,000. They would thus pay a total tax of only $750 on $17,000 of earnings. That's less than 5 percent on their total income.

We're offering a ladder of opportunity for every family that feels trapped, a ladder of opportunity to grab hold of and to climb out of poverty forever.

Now, let's take a larger working family, husband, wife, and four children earning an income of $26,000 a year. Right away, under our plan, the value of that family's personal exemptions would be $12,000. Add to this the new higher standard deduction, and, if they save a single IRA, this family could reduce the amount of income subject to tax by $18,000. On earnings of $26,000, they would pay only $1,200, again, an effective tax rate of less than 5 percent. And now, they could earn $17,000 more and it would be taxed at only 15 cents on the dollar.

Higher income couples would also see their effective tax rates lowered. A young married couple earning $40,000 and taking deductions could find themselves paying an effective tax rate of barely 10 percent.

The power of these incentives would send one, simple, straightforward message to an entire nation: America, go for it.

Simplifying Personal Deductions

We're reducing tax rates by simplifying the complex system of special provisions that favor some at the expense of others. Restoring confidence in our tax system means restoring and respecting the principle of fairness for all. This means curtailing some business deductions now being written off. It means ending several personal deductions, including the state and local tax deduction, which actually provides a special subsidy for high-income individuals, especially in a few high-tax states.

Two-thirds of Americans don't even itemize, so they receive no benefit from the state and local tax deduction. But they're being forced to subsidize the high-tax policies of a handful of states. This is truly taxation without representation.

But other deductions widely used, deductions central to American values, will be maintained. The mortgage interest deduction on your home would be fully retained. And on top of that, no less than $5,000 in other interest expenses would still be deductible. The itemized deductions for your charitable contributions will remain intact. The deductions for your medical expenses will be protected and preserved. Deductions for casualty losses would be continued; so, too, would the current preferential treatment of Social Security. Military allowances will not be taxed. And veterans' disability payments will remain totally exempt from federal taxation. These American veterans have already paid their dues.

The number of taxpayers who need to itemize would be reduced to one in four. We envision a system where more than half of us would not even have to fill out a return. We call it the "return-free system." And it would be totally voluntary. If you decided to participate, you would automatically receive your refund or a letter explaining any additional tax you owe.

Should you disagree with this figure, you would be free to fill out your taxes using the regular form.

We believe most Americans would go from the long form or the short form to no form.

Comparing the distance between the present system and our proposal is like comparing the distance between a Model T and the space shuttle. And I should know, I've seen both.

I've spoken of our proposed changes to help individuals and families. Let me explain how we would complement them with proposals for business — proposals to ensure fairness by eliminating or modifying special privileges that are economically unjustifiable and to strengthen growth by preserving incentives for investment, research, and development.

We begin with a basic recognition — the greatest innovations for new jobs, technologies and economic vigor today come from a small but growing circle of heroes, the small business people, American entrepreneurs, the men and women of faith, intellect, and daring who take great risks to invest in and invent our future. The majority of the 8 million new jobs created over the last two and a half years were created by small enterprises — enterprises often born in the dream of one human heart.

To young Americans wondering tonight, where will I go, what will I do with my future, I have a suggestion. Why not set out with your friends on the path of adventure and try to start up your own business? Follow in the footsteps of those two college students who launched one of America's great computer firms from the garage behind their house. You, too, can help us unlock the doors to a golden future. You, too, can become leaders in this great new era of progress — the Age of the Entrepreneur.

Promoting Business Formation

My goal is an America bursting with opportunity; an America that celebrates freedom every day by giving every citizen an equal chance; an America that is once again the youngest nation on Earth — her spirit unleashed and breaking free. For starters, lowering personal tax rates will give a hefty boost to the nearly 15 million small businesses which are individual proprietorships or partnerships.

To further promote business formation, we propose to reduce the maximum corporate tax rate — now 46 percent — to 33 percent, and most small corporations would pay even lower rates. So with lower rates, small business can lead the way in creating jobs for all who want to work.

To these incentives we would add another — a reduction in the tax on capital gains. Since the capital gains tax rates were cut in 1978 and 1981, capital raised for new ventures has increased by over 100-fold. That old tired economy, wheezing from neglect in the 1970s, has been swept aside by a young powerful locomotive of progress carrying a trainload of new jobs, higher incomes, and opportunities for more and more Americans of average means.

So, to marshal more venture capital for more new industries, the kind of efforts that begin with a couple of partners setting out to create and develop a new product, we intend to lower the maximum capital gains tax rate to 17.5 percent.

Oil Depletion Allowance

Under our new tax proposal the oil and gas industry will be asked to pick up a larger share of the national tax burden. The old oil depletion allowance will be dropped from the tax code except for wells producing less than ten barrels per day. By eliminating this special preference, we will go a long way toward ensuring that those that earn their wealth in the oil industry will be subject to the same taxes as the rest of us. This is only fair. To continue our drive for energy independence, the current treatment of the costs of exploring and drilling for new oil will be maintained.

We are determined to cut back on special preferences that have too long favored some industries at the expense of others. We would repeal the investment tax credit and reform the depreciation system. Incentives for research and experimentation, however, would be preserved.

There is one group of losers in our tax plan — those individuals and corporations who are not paying their fair share, or for that matter, any share. These abuses cannot be tolerated. From now on, they shall pay a minimum tax. The free rides are over.

This, then, is our plan — America's tax plan — a revolutionary first for fairness in our future; a long overdue commitment to help working Americans and their families and a challenge to our entire nation to excel — a challenge to give the USA the lowest overall marginal rates of taxation of any major industrial democracy. And, yes, a challenge to lift us into a future of unlimited promise, an endless horizon lit by the star of freedom, guiding America to supremacy in jobs, productivity, growth, and human progress.

The tax system is crucial, not just to our personal material well-being and our nation's economic well-being. It must also reflect and support our deeper values and highest aspirations. It must promote opportunity, lift up the weak, strengthen the family, and perhaps most importantly, it must be rooted in that unique American quality, our special commitment to fairness. It must be an expression of both America's eternal frontier spirit and all the virtues from the heart and soul of a good and decent people — those virtues held high by the Statue of Liberty standing proudly in New York Harbor.

Need for Bipartisan Cooperation

A great national debate now begins. It should not be a partisan debate, for the authors of tax reform come from both parties, and all of us want greater fairness, incentives, and simplicity in taxation. I'm heartened by the cooperation and serious interest already shown by key Congressional leaders, including the Chairman of the Senate Finance Committee, Republican Bob Packwood, and the Chairman of the House Ways and Means Committee, Democrat Dan Rostenkowski.

Prospects for Reform

The pessimists will give a hundred reasons why this historic proposal won't pass and can't work. Well, they've been opposing progress and predicting disaster for four years. Yet, here we are tonight a stronger, more united, more confident nation than at any time in recent memory.

Remember, there are no limits to growth and human progress when men and women are free to follow their dreams. The American Dream belongs to you; it lives in millions of different hearts; it can be fulfilled in millions of different ways. And with you by our side, we're not going to stop moving and shaking this town until that dream is real — for every American, from the sidewalks of Harlem to the mountaintops of Hawaii.

My fellow citizens, let's not let this magnificent moment slip away. Tax relief is in sight. Let's make it a reality. Let's not let prisoners of mediocrity wear us down. Let's not let the special interest raids of the few rob us of all our dreams.

In these last four years, we've made a fresh start together. In these next four, we can begin a new chapter in our history — freedom's finest hour. We can do it. And if you help, we will do it this year.

Thank you. God bless you. And good night. ∎

Reagan's Statement on Salt II Arms-Limitation Agreement

Following is the White House text of President Reagan's June 10 statement regarding U.S. compliance with the unratified SALT II arms-limitation agreement.

In 1982, on the eve of the Strategic Arms Reductions Talks (START), I decided that the United States would not undercut the expired SALT I agreement or the unratified SALT II agreement as long as the Soviet Union exercised equal restraint. Despite my serious reservations about the inequities of the SALT I agreement and the serious flaws of the SALT II agreement, I took this action in order to foster an atmosphere of mutual restraint conducive to serious negotiation as we entered START.

Since then, the United States has not taken any actions which would undercut existing arms control agreements. The United States has fully kept its part of the bargain. However, the Soviets have not. They have failed to comply with several provisions of SALT II, and we have serious concerns regarding their compliance with the provisions of other accords.

The pattern of Soviet violations, if left uncorrected, undercuts the integrity and viability of arms control as an instrument to assist in ensuring a secure and stable future world. The United States will continue to pursue vigorously with the Soviet Union the resolution of our concerns over Soviet noncompliance. We cannot impose upon ourselves a double standard that amounts to unilateral treaty compliance.

We remain determined to pursue a productive dialogue with the Soviet Union aimed at reducing the risk of war through the adoption of meaningful measures which improve security, stability and predictability. Therefore, I have reached the judgment that, despite the Soviet record over the last years, it remains in our interest to establish an interim framework of truly mutual restraint on strategic offensive arms as we pursue with renewed vigor our goal of real reductions in the size of existing nuclear arsenals in the ongoing negotiations in Geneva. Obtaining such reductions remains my highest priority.

The U.S. cannot establish such a framework alone. It will require the Soviet Union to take the positive, concrete steps to correct its noncompliance, resolve our other compliance concerns, and reverse its unparalleled and unwarranted military buildup. So far, the Soviet Union has not chosen to move in this direction. However, in the interest of ensuring that every opportunity to establish the secure, stable future we seek is fully explored, I am prepared to go the extra mile in seeking an interim framework of truly mutual restraint.

Therefore, to provide the Soviets the opportunity to join us in establishing such a framework which could support ongoing negotiations, I have decided that the United States will continue to refrain from undercutting existing strategic arms agreements to the extent that the Soviet Union exercises comparable restraint and provided that the Soviet Union actively pursues arms reduction agreements in the currently ongoing Nuclear and Space Talks in Geneva.

As an integral part of this policy, we will also take those steps required to assure the national security of the United States and our allies which were made necessary by Soviet noncompliance. Appropriate and proportionate responses to Soviet noncompliance are called for to ensure our security, to provide incentives to the Soviets to correct their noncompliance, and to make it clear to Moscow that violations of arms control obligations entail real costs.

Certain Soviet violations are, by their very nature, irreversible. Such is the case with respect to the Soviet Union's flight-testing and steps towards deployment of the SS-X-25 missile, a second new type of ICBM prohibited by the unratified SALT II agreement. Since the noncompliance associated with the development of this missile cannot be corrected by the Soviet Union, the United States reserves the right to respond in a proportionate manner at the appropriate time. The MIDGETMAN small ICBM program is particularly relevant in this regard.

Other Soviet activities involving noncompliance may be reversible and can be corrected by Soviet action. In these instances, we will provide the Soviet Union additional time to take such required corrective action. As we monitor Soviet actions for evidence of the positive, concrete steps needed on their part to correct these activities, I have directed the Department of Defense to conduct a comprehensive assessment aimed at identifying specific actions which the United States could take to augment as necessary the U.S. strategic modernization program as a proportionate response to, and as a hedge against the military consequences of, those Soviet violations of existing arms agreements which the Soviets fail to correct.

To provide adequate time for the Soviets to demonstrate by their actions a commitment to join us in an interim framework of true mutual restraint, we will plan to deactivate and dismantle according to agreed procedures an existing POSEIDON SSBN as the seventh U.S. *Ohio*-class submarine puts to sea later this year. However, the United States will keep open all programmatic options for handling such milestones as they occur in the future. As these later milestones are reached, I will assess the overall situation in light of Soviet actions correcting their noncompliance and promoting progress in Geneva and make a final determination of the U.S. course of action on a case-by-case basis.

I firmly believe that if we are to put the arms reduction process on a firm and lasting foundation, and obtain real reductions, our focus must remain on making best use of the promise provided by the currently ongoing negotiations in Geneva. Our policy, involving the establishment of an interim framework for truly mutual restraint and proportionate U.S. response to uncorrected Soviet noncompliance, is specifically designed to go the extra mile in giving the Soviet Union the opportunity to join us in this endeavor.

My hope is that if the Soviets will do so, we will be able jointly to make progress in framing equitable and verifiable agreements involving real reductions in the size of existing nuclear arsenals in the Geneva negotiations. Such an achievement would not only provide the best and most permanent constraint on the growth of nuclear arsenals, but it would take a major step towards reducing the size of these arsenals and creating a safer future for all nations. ■

Letter to Rep. Dave McCurdy On Aid to Nicaraguan Rebels

Following is the text of the letter sent June 11 by President Reagan to Rep. Dave McCurdy, D-Okla., regarding aid to the anti-government rebels in Nicaragua.

Dear Congressman McCurdy:

I am writing to express my strongest support for your bipartisan proposal to assist the forces of democracy in Nicaragua. It is essential to a peaceful resolution of the conflict in Central America that the House of Representatives pass that proposal, without any weakening amendments.

My Administration is determined to pursue political, not military, solutions in Central America. Our policy for Nicaragua is the same as for El Salvador and all of Central America: to support the democratic center against the extremes of both the right and left, and to secure democracy and lasting peace through national dialogue and regional negotiations. We do not seek the military overthrow of the Sandinista government or to put in its place a government based on supporters of the old Somoza regime.

Just as we support President Duarte in his efforts to achieve reconciliation in El Salvador, we also endorse the unified democratic opposition's March 1, 1985, San Jose Declaration which calls for national reconciliation through a church-mediated dialogue. We oppose a sharing of political power based on military force rather than the will of the people expressed through free and fair elections. That is the position of President Duarte. It is also the position of the Nicaraguan opposition leaders, who have agreed that executive authority in Nicaragua should change only through elections.

It is the guerrillas in El Salvador — and their mentors in Managua, Havana, and Moscow — who demand power-sharing without elections. And it is the Sandinistas in Nicaragua who stridently reject national reconciliation through democratic processes. Our assistance has been crucial to ensuring that democracy has both the strength and will to work in El Salvador. In Nicaragua, our support is also needed to enable the forces of democracy to convince the Sandinistas that real democratic change is necessary. Without the pressure of a viable and democratic resistance, the Sandinistas will continue to impose their will through repression and military force, and a regional settlement based on the Contadora principles will continue to elude us.

I understand that two "perfecting" amendments will be offered that will seek to nullify the intent of your proposal. One, supported by Ed Boland, would prohibit the exchange of information with the democratic resistance and permanently deny even humanitarian assistance because it would "have the effect" of supporting "directly or indirectly" the military efforts of the resistance. The other, supported by Dick Gephardt, would prohibit humanitarian assistance for at least six months and then continue the prohibition until Congress votes yet again.

The Boland Amendment is clearly intended to have the same effect as the Barnes Amendment that was rejected by the House in April. If the Boland prohibitions are enacted, the only way humanitarian assistance could be provided would be for the recipients to abandon their struggle and become refugees. The Gephardt proposal, guaranteeing the Sandinistas six additional months without effective pressure, would send a signal of irresolution to friends and adversaries, while denying the democratic resistance help that it so desperately needs. These amendments would prevent us from providing humanitarian assistance and exchanging information to sustain and preserve the democratic resistance. They would effectively remove the resistance as a source of pressure for dialogue and internal reconciliation. If those struggling for democracy are not supported, or worse, forced to become refugees, the Sandinistas will be encouraged to press their military advantage and the prospects for a peaceful resolution will be diminished.

I take very seriously your concern about human rights. The U.S. condemns, in the strongest possible terms, atrocities by either side. We are committed to helping the democratic resistance in applying strict rules regarding proper treatment of prisoners and the civilian population. And we urge their leaders to investigate allegations of past human rights abuses and take appropriate actions to prevent future abuses.

I recognize the importance that you and others attach to bilateral talks between the United States and Nicaragua. It is possible that in the proper circumstances, such discussions could help promote the internal reconciliation called for by Contadora and endorsed by many Latin American leaders. Therefore, I intend to instruct our special Ambassador to consult with the governments of Central America, the Contadora countries, other democratic governments, and the unified Nicaraguan opposition as to how and when the U.S. could resume useful direct talks with Nicaragua. However, such talks cannot be a substitute for a church-mediated dialogue between the contending factions and the achievement of a workable Contadora agreement. Therefore, I will have our representatives meet again with representatives of Nicaragua only when I determine that such a meeting would be helpful in promoting these ends.

Experience has shown that a policy of support for democracy, economic opportunity, and security will best serve the people of Central America and the national interests of the United States. If we show consistency of purpose, if we are firm in our conviction, we can help the democratic center prevail over tyrants of the left or the right. But if we abandon democracy in Nicaragua, if we tolerate the consolidation of a surrogate state in Central America responsive to Cuba and the Soviet Union, we will see the progress that has been achieved in neighboring countries begin to unravel under the strain of continuing conflict, attempts at subversion, and loss of confidence in our support.

There can be a more democratic, more prosperous, and more peaceful Central America. I will continue to devote my energies toward that end, but I also need the support of the Congress. I hope the House will support your legislation.

Sincerely,

Ronald Reagan

Reagan's Address on World-Wide Terrorism

Following are excerpts from the White House text of President Reagan's July 8 address on terrorism, as delivered before the convention of the American Bar Association, in Washington, D.C.

I'm delighted to be able to speak today, not just to the largest voluntary professional association in the world, but one whose exclusive concern is a starting point for any free society, a concern that is at the heart of civilized life: the law — our courts and legal system — justice itself.

Now, I want to be very candid with you this morning and tell you I'd been planning to come here today to speak on a number of legal issues — the problems of our courts, our administration's enforcement of antitrust and civil rights laws, as well as our ongoing attack on the drug trade and organized crime in general. But I'm afraid this discussion will now have to wait for another occasion, for it's been overtaken by events of an international nature — events that I feel compelled as President to comment on today. And yet, I think these matters will be of interest to you, not only because you're Americans, but because, as lawyers, you are also concerned with the rule of law and the danger posed to it by criminals of both a domestic and international variety.

The reason we haven't had time to discuss the issues that I had originally hoped to address this morning has to do with our hostages — and what all of America have been through during recent weeks.

Escalation of Worldwide Terrorism

Yet my purpose today goes even beyond our concern over the recent outrages in Beirut, El Salvador, or the Air India tragedy, the Narita bombing, or the Jordanian Airlines hijacking. We must look beyond these events because I feel it is vital not to allow them, as terrible as they are, to obscure an even larger and darker terrorist menace.

There is a temptation to see the terrorist act as simply the erratic work of a small group of fanatics. We make this mistake at great peril, for the attacks on America, her citizens, her allies, and other democratic nations in recent years do form a pattern of terrorism that has strategic implications and political goals. And only by moving our focus from the tactical to the strategic perspective, only by identifying the pattern of terror and those behind it, can we hope to put into force a strategy to deal with it.

So, let us go to the facts. Here is what we know. In recent years, there has been a steady and escalating pattern of terrorist acts against the United States and our allies and Third World nations friendly toward our interests. The number of terrorist acts rose from about 500 in 1983 to over 600 in 1984. There were 305 bombings alone last year — that works out to an average of almost one a day.

And some of the most vicious attacks were directed at Americans or United States property and installations. And this pattern has continued throughout 1985, and in most cases, innocent civilians are the victims of the violence.

At the current rate, as many as 1,000 acts of terrorism will occur in 1985. Now, that's what we face unless civilized nations act together to end this assault on humanity.

In recent years, the Mideast has been one principal point of focus for these attacks — attacks directed at the United States, Israel, France, Jordan and the United Kingdom. Beginning in the summer of 1984 and culminating in January and February of this year, there was also a series of apparently coordinated attacks and assassinations by left-wing terrorist groups in Belgium, West Germany and France —

attacks directed against American and NATO installations or military and industrial officials of those nations.

Iranian and Libyan Involvement

Now, what do we know about the sources of those attacks and the whole pattern of terrorist assaults in recent years? Well, in 1983 alone, the Central Intelligence Agency either confirmed or found strong evidence of Iranian involvement in 57 terrorist attacks. While most of these attacks occurred in Lebanon, an increase in activity by terrorists sympathetic to Iran was seen throughout Europe: Spain and France have seen such incidents, and in Italy, seven pro-Iranian Lebanese students were arrested for plotting an attack on the U.S. Embassy; and this violence continues.

It will not surprise any of you to know that, in addition to Iran, we have identified another nation, Libya, as deeply involved in terrorism. We have evidence which links Libyan agents or surrogates to at least 25 incidents last year. Colonel Qaddafi's outrages against civilized conduct are, of course, as infamous as those of the Ayatollah Khomeini. The gunning down last year — from inside the Libyan Embassy — of a British policewoman is only one of many examples.

Since September 1984, Iranian-backed terrorist groups have been responsible for almost 30 attacks, and, most recently, the Egyptian government aborted a Libyan-backed plot to bomb our Embassy in Cairo. It was this pattern of state-approved assassination and terrorism by Libya that led the United States a few years ago to expel Libyan diplomats and has forced other nations to take similar steps since then. But let us, in acknowledging his commitment to terrorism, at least give Colonel Qaddafi his due. The man is candid: He said recently that Libya was — and I quote — "capable of exporting terrorism to the heart of America. We are also capable of physical liquidation and destruction and arson inside America."

And, by the way, it's important to note here that the recognition of this deep and ongoing involvement of Iran and Libya in international terrorism is hardly confined to our own government. Most police forces in Europe now take this involvement for granted; and this is not even to mention the warnings issued by world leaders. For example, the Jordanian leadership has publicly noted that Libyan actions caused the destruction of the Jordanian Embassy in Tripoli.

Now three other governments, along with Iran and Libya, are actively supporting a campaign of international terrorism against the United States, her allies, and moderate Third World states.

North Korean Involvement

First, North Korea. The extent and crudity of North Korean violence against the United States and our ally, South Korea, are a matter of record. Our aircraft have been shot down; our servicemen have been murdered in border incidents; and two years ago, four members of the South Korean Cabinet were blown up in a bombing in Burma by North Korean terrorists — a failed attempt to assassinate President Chun. This incident was just one more of an unending series of attacks directed against the Republic of Korea by North Korea.

Now, what is not readily known or understood is North Korea's wider links to the international terrorist network. There is not time today to recount all of North Korea's efforts to foster separatism, violence, and subversion in other lands, well beyond its immediate borders, but to cite one example, North Korea's efforts to spread separatism and terrorism in the free and prosperous nation of Sri Lanka are a deep and continuing source of tension in South Asia.

And this is not even to mention North Korea's involvement here in our own hemisphere, including a secret arms agreement with the former communist government in Grenada. I will also have something to say about North Korea's involvement in Central America in a moment.

Cuban Involvement

And then there is Cuba, a nation whose government has, since the 1960s, openly armed, trained, and directed terrorists operating on at least three continents. This has occurred in Latin America. The OAS has repeatedly passed sanctions against Castro for sponsoring terrorism in places and countries too numerous to mention.

This has also occurred in Africa. President Carter openly accused the Castro government of supporting and training Katangan terrorists from Angola in their attacks on Zaire. And even in the Middle East, Castro himself has acknowledged that he actively assisted the Sandinistas in the early 70s when they were training in the Middle East with terrorist factions of the PLO.

Nicaraguan Involvement

And finally there is the latest partner of Iran, Libya, North Korea and Cuba in a campaign of international terror — the communist regime in Nicaragua. The Sandinistas not only sponsor terror in El Salvador, Costa Rica, and Honduras — terror that led recently to the murder of four United States Marines, two civilians, and seven Latin Americans. They provide one of the world's principal refuges for international terrorists.

Members of the Italian government have openly charged that Nicaragua is harboring some of Italy's worst terrorists. And when we have evidence that, in addition to Italy's Red Brigades, other elements of the world's most vicious terrorist groups — West Germany's Baader-Meinhoff Gang, the Basque ETA, the PLO, the Tupamaros, and the IRA have found a haven in Nicaragua and support from that country's communist dictatorship.

In fact, the communist regime in Nicaragua has made itself a focal point for the terrorist network and a case study in the extent of its scope.

Consider for just a moment that in addition to establishing strong international alliances with Cuba and Libya, including the receipt of enormous amounts of arms and ammunition, the Sandinistas are also receiving extensive assistance from North Korea. Nor are they reluctant to acknowledge their debt to the government of North Korea dictator Kim Il-Sung. Both Daniel and Humberto Ortega have recently paid official and state visits to North Korea to seek additional assistance and more formal relations.

So we see the Nicaraguans tied to Cuba, Libya, and North Korea. And that leaves only Iran. What about ties to Iran? Well, yes, only recently the Prime Minister of Iran visited Nicaragua, bearing expressions of solidarity from the Ayatollah for the Sandinista communists.

Shared Objectives

Now, I spoke a moment ago about the strategic goals that are motivating these terrorist states. In a minute I will add some comments of my own, but for the moment, why don't we let the leaders of these outlaw governments speak for themselves about their objectives? During his state visit to North Korea, Nicaragua's Sandinista leader, Daniel Ortega, heard Kim Il-Sung say this about the mutual objectives of North Korea and Nicaragua: "If the peoples of the revolutionary countries of the world put pressure on and deal blows at United States imperialism in all places where it stretches its talons of aggression, they will make it powerless and impossible to behave as dominator any longer." And Colonel Qaddafi, who has a formal alliance with North Korea, echoed Kim Il-Sung's words when he laid out the agenda for the terrorist network: "We must force America to fight on a hundred fronts all over the Earth. We must force it to fight in Lebanon, to fight in Chad, to fight in Sudan, and to fight in El Salvador."

So there we have it. Iran, Libya, North Korea, Cuba, Nicaragua — continents away, tens of thousands of miles apart — but the same goals and objectives. I submit to you that the growth in terrorism in recent years results from the increasing involvement of these states in terrorism in every region of the world. This is terrorism that is part of a pattern, the work of a confederation of terrorist states. Most of the terrorists who are kidnapping and murdering American citizens and attacking American installations are being trained, financed, and directly or indirectly controlled by a core group of radical and totalitarian governments — a new, international version of "Murder, Incorporated." And all of these states are united by one, simple, criminal phenomenon — their fanatical hatred of the United States, our people, our way of life, our international stature.

And the strategic purpose behind the terrorism sponsored by these outlaw states is clear: to disorient the United States, to disrupt or alter our foreign policy, to sow discord between ourselves and our allies, to frighten friendly Third World nations working with us for peaceful settlements of regional conflicts, and finally, to remove American influence from those areas of the world where we're working to bring stable and democratic government. In short, to cause us to retreat, retrench, to become "Fortress America." Yes, their real goal is to expel America from the world.

And that is the reason these terrorist nations are arming, training, and supporting attacks against this nation. And that is why we can be clear on one point: These terrorist states are now engaged in acts of war against the government and people of the United States. And under international law, any state which is the victim of acts of war has the right to defend itself.

History of U.S. Retaliation

Now, for the benefit of these outlaw governments who are sponsoring international terrorism against our nation, I'm prepared to offer a brief lesson in American history. A number of times in America's past, foreign tyrants, warlords and totalitarian dictators have misinterpreted the well-known likability, patience and generosity of the American people as signs of weakness or even decadence. Well, it's true. We are an easy-going people, slow to wrath, hesitant to see danger looming over every horizon. But it's also true that when the emotions of the American people are aroused, when their patriotism and their anger are triggered, there are no limits to their national valor nor their consuming passion to protect this nation's cherished tradition of freedom. Teddy Roosevelt once put it this way: "The American people are slow to wrath, but when the wrath is once kindled it burns like a consuming flame." And it was another leader, this time a foreign adversary, Admiral Yamamoto, who warned his own nation after its attack on Pearl Harbor that he feared, quote, "We have only awakened a sleeping giant and his reaction will be terrible."

Yes, we Americans have our disagreements, sometimes noisy ones, almost always in public — that's the nature of our open society. But no foreign power should mistake disagreement for disunity. Those who are tempted to do so should reflect on our national character and our history, a history littered with the wreckage of regimes who made the mistake of underestimating the vigor and will of the American people.

So, let me today speak for a united people. Let me say simply: We're Americans. We love this country. We love what she stands for. And we will always defend her. Thank you very much. Thank you. God bless you. Thank you and God bless you. We live for freedom — our own, our children's — and we will always stand ready to sacrifice for that freedom.

So the American people are not — I repeat, not — going to tolerate intimidation, terror and outright acts of war against this nation and its people. And we're especially not going to tolerate these attacks from outlaw states run by the strangest collection of misfits, looney tunes and squalid criminals — since the advent of the Third Reich.

Now, I've taken your time today to outline the nature of this network of terrorist states, so that we might, as a nation, know who it is we're up against and identify the long-term goals motivating this confederation of criminal governments.

Do not for a moment, however, think that this discussion has been all-inclusive. First of all — though their strength does not match that of the groups supported by the terrorist network I've already mentioned — there are some terrorist organizations that are indigenous to certain localities or countries which are not necessarily tied to this international network. And second, the countries I have mentioned today are not necessarily the only ones that support terrorism against the United States and its allies. Those which I've described are simply the ones that can be most directly implicated.

Soviet Role

Now, the question of the Soviet Union's close relationship with almost all of the terrorist states that I have mentioned and the implications of these Soviet ties on bilateral relations with the United States and other democratic nations must be recognized. So, too, Secretary of State Shultz, in his speech of June 24th of last year, openly raised the question of Soviet support for terrorist organizations, as did Secretary Haig before him.

With regard to the Soviet Union, there is one matter that I cannot let go unaddressed today. During the recent hostage crisis in Beirut, 39 Americans were brutally kidnapped; an American sailor was viciously beaten; another American sailor stomped and shot to death; the families and loved ones of these hostages undergo indescribable suffering and a sense of distress, anger and outrage spreading through our nation like a prairie fire. The Soviet Union made some official comments through its government-controlled press. The Soviet government suggested that the United States was not sincerely concerned about this crisis, but that we were, instead, in the grip of — and I use the Soviets' word here — "hysteria." The Soviet Union also charged that the United States was only looking for a — and, again, I use their word — "pretext" for a military — and, again, I use their word — "invasion."

Well, now, ladies and gentlemen of the American Bar, there is a non-Soviet word for that kind of talk. It's an extremely useful, time-tested, original American word, one with deep roots in our rich agricultural and farming tradition.

Now, much needs to be done by all of us in the community of civilized nations. We must act against the criminal menace of terrorism with the full weight of the law — both domestic and international. We will act to indict, apprehend and prosecute those who commit the kind of atrocities the world has witnessed in recent weeks.

We can act together as free peoples who wish not to see our citizens kidnapped, or shot, or blown out of the skies — just as we acted together to rid the seas of piracy at the turn of the last century. And incidentally, those of you who are legal scholars will note the law's description of pirates — "hostis humanis" — "the enemies of all mankind." There can be no place on Earth left where it is safe for these monsters to rest, or train, or practice their cruel and deadly skills. We must act together, or unilaterally, if necessary, to ensure that terrorists have no sanctuary anywhere. Vice President Bush returned from Europe last week after intense consultations with our allies on practical steps to combat terrorism. He'll be heading up a government-wide task force to review and recommend improvements in our efforts to halt terrorism.

For those countries which sponsor such acts or fail to take action against terrorist criminals, the civilized world needs to ensure that their nonfeasance and malfeasance are answered with actions that demonstrate our unified resolve that this kind of activity must cease. For example, I've informed our allies and others that the Beirut International Airport, through which have passed 15 percent of the world's hijackings since 1970, must be made safe. And until that time, the airport should be closed.

Finally, I want you to accept a challenge — to become part of the solution to the problem of terrorism. You have a fundamental concern for the law, and it's upon the law that terrorists trample. You need to address this problem in conferences and conventions that will lead us to a better domestic and international legal framework for dealing with terrorism. You must help this government and others to deal legally with lawlessness. Where legislation must be crafted to allow appropriate authorities to act, you should help to craft or change it. In the past, lawyers have helped when civilization was threatened by lawbreakers. And now is the time to do so again.

What I place before you this morning is not pleasant, nor will the solution be easy. The answer to the threat of international terrorism is difficult, but it can be found. It is to be found in a clear understanding of the problem and our — the expression of our national will to do something about it. It's always been so with any important cause; it's why our Declaration of Independence was more important to our Revolution than any one military maneuver or single battle. And that is why we do not today engage in policy discussions or focus on strategic options, but simply state the facts about the nature of international terrorism and affirm America's will to resist it.

Terrorists' Real Motive

But there is another point that needs to be made here — the point I made at the start of this discussion. That in taking a strategic, not just a tactical view of terrorism, we must understand that the greatest hope the terrorists and their supporters harbor — the very reason for their cruelty and viciousness of their tactics — is to disorient the American people, to cause disunity, to disrupt or alter our foreign policy, to keep us from the steady pursuit of our strategic interests, to distract us from our very real hope that someday the nightmare of totalitarian rule will end and self-government and personal freedom will become the birthright of every people on Earth.

And here, my fellow Americans, is where we find the real motive behind the rabid and increasing anti-Americanism of the international terrorist network. I have been saying for some years now that the cause of totalitarian ideology is on the wane; that all across the world, there is an uprising of mind and will, a tidal wave of longing for freedom and self-rule.
Well, no one senses this better than those who now stand atop totalitarian states, especially those nations on the outer periphery of the totalitarian world like Iran, Libya, North Korea, Cuba and Nicaragua. Their rulers are frightened; they know that freedom is on the march and when it triumphs, their time in power is over.

Fragility of Totalitarianism

You see, it's true that totalitarian governments are very powerful and, over the short term, may be better organized than the democracies. But it's also true — and no one knows this better than totalitarian rulers themselves — that these regimes are weak in a way that no democracy can ever be weak. For the fragility of totalitarian government is the fragility of any regime whose hold on its people is limited to the instruments of police-state repression.

That is why the stakes are so high, and why we must persevere. Freedom itself is the issue — our own and the entire world's. Yes, America is still a symbol to a few — a symbol that is feared and hated. But to more — many millions more — a symbol that is loved, a country that remains a shining city on a hill.

Teddy Roosevelt — and he is a good President to quote in these circumstances — put it so well: "We, here in America, hold in our hands the hope of the world, the fate of the coming years; and shame and disgrace will be ours if in our eyes the light of high resolve is dimmed, if we trail in the dust those golden hopes of man."

And that light of high resolve, those golden hopes, are now ours to preserve and protect, and with God's help, to pass on to generations to come.

I can't close without telling you one little incident here. When I say, "We are a symbol of hope," I have on my desk at home a letter signed by 10 women in the Soviet Union. They are all in a prison camp in that Union — a labor camp. The letter is no more than 2½ inches wide, and just an inch high, and yet, by hand, they wrote a complete letter, signed their 10 names to it, smuggled that and another document just a little bigger — about a three-inch square of paper — that is the chart of the hunger strikes they have endured. And they smuggled it out to be sent to me because they wanted to tell me and all of you that the United States, where they are, in that prison, still remains their hope that keeps them going — their hope for the world. ■

First Regulatory Message to Congress

Following is the text of President Reagan's first Regulatory Message to Congress, as printed in the first annual "Regulatory Program of the United States Government, April 1, 1985-March 31, 1986."

TO THE CONGRESS OF
THE UNITED STATES:

The publication of *The Regulatory Program of the United States Government* marks a major milestone in our continuing effort to make government more accountable to the American people and more responsive to their needs. This document presents, for the first time, a comprehensive program of regulatory policy to be carried out over the coming year.

Regulations are a feature of almost every government program. Though many regulations accomplish worthwhile ends, we should not forget the huge hidden costs they entail. The Federal government mandates tens of billions of dollars of expenditures every year — dollars paid for by the people but not included in any of the Federal budget accounts, not appropriated by the Congress, and not constrained by any spending limits.

Before 1980, these regulatory expenditures had grown out of control. More pages were published in the *Federal Register* in 1980 than during the entire period between 1936 and 1945 — the first 10 years of the *Register.* Paperwork burdens had grown such that by 1980, almost two billion hours were expended annually by businesses and individuals to satisfy the Federal government. Estimates are that Federal government regulations imposed costs of over $100 billion annually by 1980, adding significantly to the burden imposed on the economy by excessive Federal spending. It has become essential that tools be developed to plan the rational evolution of Federal regulatory requirements.

In 1981, I issued Executive Order No. 12291 setting forth my regulatory principles and, under the Paperwork Reduction Act, my Administration mounted an attack to reduce the paperwork burden. These efforts have helped to reverse the trend of more intrusive and burdensome Federal regulations and paperwork. But more wasneeded.

The Regulatory Program is a critical step in this process. In order to see that the laws are faithfully executed, and that the policies of this Administration are reflected in the regulations issued under those laws, I issued Executive Order No. 12498 initiating this Regulatory Program. The Program covers the decisions that are within the scope of discretion afforded to the executive agencies by law, and describes the underlying policies and priorities that will influence those decisions.

To set goals and priorities for different programs, government officials must choose the right regulatory tools and identify legitimate needs for regulation as opposed to those that merely benefit special interests. Because some complex regulations take years to develop, involving studies, surveys, and the identification and selection of regulatory options, it is important that senior Federal officials be able to review regulatory options early in the rulemaking process and plan regulatory actions over a longer time horizon. It is also important that they examine and reexamine the nearly 200 volumes of existing regulations to see what regulations need to be modified or have outlived their usefulness.

This year's Regulatory Program is the first in an annual series that will document the efforts of my Administration to manage Federal regulatory programs. This should lead to an increased level of predictability, consistency, accountability, and rationality in Federal regulatory activity.

The objectives of the Regulatory Program are to:

- Create a coordinated process for developing on an annual basis the Administration's Regulatory Program;
- Establish Administration regulatory priorities;
- Increase the accountability of agency heads for the regulatory actions of their agencies;
- Provide for Presidential oversight of the regulatory process;
- Reduce the burdens of existing and future regulations;
- Minimize duplication and conflict of regulations; and
- Enhance public and congressional understanding of the Administration's regulatory objectives.

All of this cannot be accomplished simply by publishing a book. This Regulatory Program is the end product of a long process of agencies planning their regulatory activities: gathering and reviewing information, evaluating past progress and program effectiveness, and setting goals and priorities. The publication of the Regulatory Program for 1985 is, however, only the first step in this annual planning process. The next step is for each agency to implement its part of this first Program, as planned and on schedule.

My goal remains to have a government that regulates only where necessary and as efficiently and fairly as possible.

RONALD REAGAN

The White House,
August 1985

South Africa Sanctions

Following is the White House text of President Reagan's Sept. 9 statement accompanying his executive order regarding economic sanctions on the government of South Africa, followed by the White House text of the executive order.

I want to speak this morning about South Africa — about what America can do to help promote peace and justice in that country so troubled and tormented by racial conflict.

The system of apartheid means deliberate, systematic, institutionalized racial discrimination, denying the black majority their God-given rights. America's view of apartheid is simple and straightforward: We believe it is wrong. We condemn it. And we are united in hoping for the day when apartheid will be no more.

Our influence over South African society is limited. But we do have some influence, and the question is, how to use it. Many people of good will in this country have differing views. In my view, we must work for peaceful evolution and reform. Our aim cannot be to punish South Africa with economic sanctions that would injure the very people we are trying to help.

I believe we must help all those who peacefully oppose apartheid; and we must recognize that the opponents of apartheid using terrorism and violence will bring not freedom and salvation, but greater suffering, and more opportunities for expanded Soviet influence within South Africa and in the region. What we see in South Africa is a beginning of a process of change. The changes in policy so far are inadequate — but ironically they have been enough to raise expectations and stimulate demands for more far-reaching, immediate change. It is the growing economic power of the black majority that has put them in a position to insist on political change.

South Africa is not a totalitarian society. There is a vigorous opposition press. And every day we see examples of outspoken protest and access to the international media that would never be possible in many parts of Africa, or in the Soviet Union for that matter. But it is our active engagement — our willingness to try — that gives us influence.

Yes, we in America — because of what we are and what we stand for — have influence to do good. We also have immense potential to make things worse. Before taking fateful steps, we must ponder the key question: Are we helping to change the system? Or are we punishing the blacks whom we seek to help?

American policy through several administrations has been to use our influence and our leverage against apartheid, not against innocent people who are the victims of apartheid.

Being true to our heritage does not mean quitting, but reaching out; expanding our help for black education and community development, calling for political dialogue; urging South Africans of all races to seize the opportunity for peaceful accommodation before it's too late.

I respect and share the goals that have motivated many in Congress to send a message of U.S. concern about apartheid. But in doing so, we must not damage the economic well-being of millions of people in South and southern Africa. If we genuinely wish — as I do — to develop a bipartisan basis of consensus in support of U.S. policies, this is the basis on which to proceed.

Therefore, I am signing today an Executive Order that will put in place a set of measures designed and aimed against the machinery of apartheid, without indiscriminately punishing the people who are victims of that system — measures that will disassociate the United States from apartheid but associate us positively with peaceful change.

These steps include:

- A ban on all computer exports to agencies involved in the enforcement of apartheid and to the security forces.

- A prohibition on exports of nuclear goods or technology to South Africa, except as is required to implement nuclear proliferation safeguards of the International Atomic Energy Agency or those necessary for humanitarian reasons to protect health and safety.

- A ban on loans to the South African government, except certain loans which improve economic opportunities, or educational, housing, and health facilities that are open and accessible to South Africans of all races.

- I am directing the Secretary of State and the United States Trade Representative to consult with our major trading partners regarding banning the importation of Krugerrands. I am also instructing the Secretary of the Treasury to report to me within 60 days on the feasibility of minting an American gold coin which could provide an alternative to the Krugerrand for our coin collectors.

I want to encourage ongoing actions by our Government and by private Americans to improve the living standards of South Africa's black majority. The Sullivan Code — devised by a distinguished black minister from Philadelphia, the Reverend Leon Sullivan — has set the highest standards of labor practices for progressive employers throughout South Africa. I urge all American companies to participate in it, and I am instructing the American Ambassador to South Africa to make every effort to get companies which have not adopted them to do so.

In addition, my Executive Order will ban U.S. Government export assistance to any American firm in South Africa, employing more than 25 persons, which does not adhere to the comprehensive fair employment principles stated in the order by the end of this year.

I am also directing the Secretary of State to increase substantially the money we provide for scholarships to South Africans disadvantaged by apartheid, and the money our embassy uses to promote human rights programs in South Africa.

Finally, I have directed Secretary Shultz to establish an Advisory Committee of distinguished Americans to provide recommendations on measures to encourage peaceful change in South Africa. The Advisory Committee shall provide its first report within 12 months.

I believe the measures I am announcing here today will best advance our goals. If the Congress sends me the present bill as reported by the Conference Committee, I would have to veto it. That need not happen. I want to work with the Congress to advance bipartisan support for America's policy toward South Africa. That is why I have put forward this Executive Order today.

Three months ago, I recalled our Ambassador in South Africa for consultations so that he could participate in the intensive review of the southern African situation that we have been engaged in. I am now sending him back, with a message to State President Botha underlining our grave view of the current crisis, and our assessment of what is needed to restore confidence abroad and move from confrontation to negotiation at home. The problems of South Africa were not created overnight and will not be solved overnight, but there is no time to waste. To withdraw from this drama — or to fan its flames — will serve neither our interests nor those of the South African people.

If all Americans join together behind a common program, we can have so much more influence for good. So let us go forward with a clear vision and an open heart, working for justice and brotherhood and peace.

By the authority vested in me as President by the Constitution and laws of the United States of America, including the International Emergency Economic Powers Act (50 U.S.C. 1701 *et seq.*), the National Emergencies Act (50 U.S.C. 1601 *et seq.*), the Foreign Assistance Act (22 U.S.C. 2151 *et seq.*), the United Nations Participation Act (22 U.S.C. 287), the Arms Export Control Act (22 U.S.C. 2751 *et seq.*), the Export Administration Act (50 U.S.C. App. 2401 *et seq.*), the Atomic Energy Act (42 U.S.C. 2011 *et seq.*), the Foreign Service Act (22 U.S.C. 3901 *et seq.*), the Federal Advisory Committee Act (5 U.S.C. App. I), Section 301 of Title 3 of the United States Code, and considering the measures which the United Nations Security Council has decided on or recommended in Security Council Resolutions No. 418 of November 4, 1977, No. 558 of December 13, 1984, and No. 569 of July 26, 1985, and considering that the policy and practice of apartheid are repugnant to the moral and political values of democratic and free societies and run counter to United States policies to promote democratic governments throughout the world and respect for human rights, and the policy of the United States to influence peaceful change in South Africa, as well as the threat posed to United States interests by recent events in that country,

I, RONALD REAGAN, President of the United States of America, find that the policies and actions of the Government of South Africa constitute an unusual and extraordinary threat to the foreign policy and economy of the United States and hereby declare a national emergency to deal with that threat.

Section 1. Except as otherwise provided in this section, the following transactions are prohibited effective October 11, 1985:

(a) The making or approval of any loans by financial institutions in the United States to the Government of South Africa or to entities owned or controlled by that Government. This prohibition shall enter into force on November 11, 1985. It shall not apply to (i) any loan or extension of credit for any educational, housing, or health facility which is available to all persons on a nondiscriminatory basis and which is located in a geographic area accessible to all population groups without any legal or administrative restriction; or (ii) any loan or extension of credit for which an agreement is entered into before the date of this Order.

The Secretary of the Treasury is hereby authorized to promulgate such rules and regulations as may be necessary to carry out this subsection. The initial rules and regulations shall be issued within sixty days. The Secretary of the Treasury may, in consultation with the Secretary of State, permit exceptions to this prohibition only if the Secretary of the Treasury determines that the loan or extension of credit will improve the welfare or expand the economic opportunities of persons in South Africa disadvantaged by the apartheid system, provided that no exception may be made for any apartheid enforcing entity.

(b) All exports of computers, computer software, or goods or technology intended to service computers to or for use by any of the following entities of the Government of South Africa:

(1) The military;

(2) The police;

(3) The prison system;

(4) The national security agencies;

(5) ARMSCOR and its subsidiaries or the weapons research activities of the Council for Scientific and Industrial Research;

(6) The administering authorities for the black passbook and similar controls;

(7) Any apartheid enforcing agency;

(8) Any local or regional government or "homeland" entity which performs any function of any entity described in paragraphs (1) through (7).

The Secretary of Commerce is hereby authorized to promulgate such rules and regulations as may be necessary to carry out this subsection and to implement a system of end use verification to ensure that any computers exported directly or indirectly to South Africa will not be used by any entity set forth in this subsection.

(c) (1) Issuance of any license for the export to South Africa of goods or technology which are to be used in a nuclear production or utilization facility, or which, in the judgment of the Secretary of State, are likely to be diverted for use in such a facility; any authorization to engage, directly or indirectly, in the production of any special nuclear material in South Africa; any license for the export to South Africa of component parts or other items or substances especially relevant from the standpoint of export control because of their significance for nuclear explosive purposes; and any approval of retransfers to South Africa of any goods, technology, special nuclear material, components, items, or substances described in this section. The Secretaries of State, Energy, Commerce, and Treasury are hereby authorized to take such actions as may be necessary to carry out this subsection.

(2) Nothing in this section shall preclude assistance for International Atomic Energy Agency safeguards or IAEA programs generally available to its member states, or for technical programs for the purpose of reducing proliferation risks, such as for reducing the use of highly enriched uranium and activities envisaged by section 223 of the Nuclear Waste Policy Act (42 U.S.C. 10203) or for exports which the Secretary of State determines are necessary for humanitarian reasons to protect the public health and safety.

(d) The import into the United States of any arms, ammunition, or military vehicles produced in South Africa or of any manufacturing data for such articles. The Secretaries of State, Treasury, and Defense are hereby authorized to take such actions as may be necessary to carry out this subsection.

Sec. 2. (a) The majority of United States firms in South Africa have voluntarily adhered to fair labor principles which have benefited those in South Africa who have been disadvantaged by the apartheid system. It is the policy of the United States to encourage strongly all United States firms in South Africa to follow this commendable example.

(b) Accordingly, no department or agency of the United States may intercede after December 31, 1985, with any foreign government regarding the export marketing activity in any country of any national of the United States employing more than 25 individuals in South Africa who does not adhere to the principles stated in subsection (c) with respect to that national's operations in South Africa. The Secretary of State shall promulgate regulations to further define the employers that will be subject to the requirements of this subsection and procedures to ensure that such nationals may register that they have adhered to the principles.

(c) The principles referred to in subsection (b) are as follows:

(1) Desegregating the races in each employment facility;

(2) Providing equal employment opportunity for all employees without regard to race or ethnic origin;

(3) Assuring that the pay system is applied to all employees without regard to race or ethnic origin;

(4) Establishing a minimum wage and salary structure based on the appropriate local minimum economic level which takes into account the needs of employees and their families;

(5) Increasing by appropriate means the number of persons in managerial, supervisory, administrative, clerical, and technical jobs who are disadvantaged by the apartheid system for the purpose of significantly increasing their representation in such jobs;

(6) Taking reasonable steps to improve the quality of employees' lives outside the work environment with respect to housing, transportation, schooling, recreation, and health;

(7) Implementing fair labor practices by recognizing the right of all employees, regardless of racial or other distinctions, to self-organization and to form, join, or assist labor organizations, freely and without penalty or reprisal, and recognizing the right to refrain from any such activity.

(d) United States nationals referred to in subsection (b) are encouraged to take reasonable measures to extend the scope of their influence on activities outside the workplace, by measures such as supporting the right of all businesses, regardless of the racial character of their owners or employees, to locate in urban areas, by influencing other companies in South Africa to follow the standards specified in subsection (c) and by supporting the freedom of mobility of all workers, regardless of race, to seek employment opportunities wherever they exist, and by making provision for adequate housing for families of employees within the proximity of the employee's place of work.

Sec. 3. The Secretary of State and the head of any other department or agency of the United States carrying out activities in South Africa shall promptly take, to the extent permitted by law, the necessary steps to ensure that the labor practices described in section (2)(c) are applied to their South African employees.

Sec. 4. The Secretary of State and the head of any other department or agency of the United States carrying out activities in South Africa shall, to the maximum extent practicable and to the extent permitted by law, in procuring goods or services in South Africa, make affirmative efforts to assist business enterprises having more than 50 percent beneficial ownership by persons in South Africa disadvantaged by the apartheid system.

Sec. 5. (a) The Secretary of State and the United States Trade Representative are directed to consult with other parties to the General Agreement on Tariffs and Trade with a view toward adopting a prohibition on the import of Krugerrands.

(b) The Secretary of the Treasury is directed to conduct a study to be completed within sixty days regarding the feasibility of minting and issuing gold coins with a view toward expeditiously seeking legislative authority to accomplish the goal of issuing such coins.

Sec. 6. In carrying out their respective functions and responsibilities under this Order, the Secretary of the Treasury and the Secretary of Commerce shall consult with the Secretary of State. Each such Secretary shall consult, as appropriate, with other government agencies and private persons.

Sec. 7. The Secretary of State shall establish, pursuant to appropriate legal authority, an Advisory Committee on South Africa to provide recommendations on measures to encourage peaceful change in South Africa. The Advisory Committee shall provide its initial report within twelve months.

Sec. 8. The Secretary of State is directed to take the steps necessary pursuant to the Foreign Assistance Act and related legislation to (a) increase the amount of internal scholarships provided to South Africans disadvantaged by the apartheid system up to $8 million from funds made available for Fiscal Year 1986, and (b) increase the amount allocated for South Africa from funds made available for Fiscal Year 1986 in the Human Rights Fund up to $1.5 million. At least one-third of the latter amount shall be used for legal assistance for South Africans. Appropriate increases in the amounts made available for these purposes will be considered in future fiscal years.

Sec. 9. This Order is intended to express and implement the foreign policy of the United States. It is not intended to create any right or benefit, substantive or procedural, enforceable at law by a party against the United States, its agencies, its officers, or any person.

RONALD REAGAN

The White House,
September 9, 1985.

Text of President's Remarks on U.S. Trade

Following is the White House text of President Reagan's Sept. 23 remarks on U.S. trade, as delivered to business leaders and members of the president's Export Council and Advisory Committee for Trade Negotiations.

Thank you very much, and welcome to the White House. I'm pleased to have this opportunity to be with you to address the pressing question of America's trade challenge for the '80s and beyond. And let me say at the outset that our trade policy rests firmly on the foundation of free and open markets — free trade.

I, like you, recognize the inescapable conclusion that all of history has taught: the freer the flow of world trade, the stronger the tides for human progress and peace among nations.

Benefits of Free Markets

I certainly don't have to explain the benefits of free and open markets to you. They produce more jobs, a more productive use of our nation's resources, more rapid innovation and a higher standard of living. They strengthen our national security because our economy, the bedrock of our defense, is stronger.

I'm pleased that the United States has played the critical role of ensuring and promoting an open trading system since World War II. And I know that if we ever faltered in the defense and promotion of the worldwide free trading system, that system will collapse, to the detriment of all.

Trading Partners' Responsibility

But our role does not absolve our trading partners from their major responsibility — to support us in seeking a more open trading system. No nation, even one as large and as powerful as the United States, can, by itself, ensure a free trading system. All that we and others have done to provide for the free flow of goods and services and capital is based on cooperation. And our trading partners must join us in working to improve the system of trade that has contributed so much to economic growth and the security of our allies and of ourselves.

And may I say right here to the leaders of industry that my admiration for business in the United States is stronger than ever. You know, sometimes in Washington, there are some who seem to forget what the economy is all about. They give me reports saying the economy does this and the economy will do that. But they never talk about business. And somewhere along the way, these folks in Washington have forgotten that the economy is business. Business creates new products and new services. Business creates jobs. Business creates prosperity for our communities and our nation as a whole. And business is the people that make it work — from the CEO to the workers in the factories.

Free Trade Is Fair Trade

I know, too, that American business has never been afraid to compete. I know that when a trading system follows the rules of free trade, when there is equal opportunity to compete, American business is as innovative, efficient and competitive as any in the world. I also know that the American worker is as good and productive as any in the world.

And that's why to make the international trading system work, all must abide by the rules. All must work to guarantee open markets. Above all else, free trade is, by definition, fair trade.

When domestic markets are closed to the exports of others, it is no longer free trade. When governments subsidize their manufacturers and farmers so that they can dump goods in other markets, it is no longer free trade.

When governments permit counterfeiting or copying of American products, it is stealing our future and it is no longer free trade.

When governments assist their exporters in ways that violate international laws, then the playing field is no longer level, and there is no longer free trade.

When governments subsidize industries for commercial advantage and underwrite costs, placing an unfair burden on competitors, that is not free trade.

I have worked for four years at Versailles and Williamsburg and London and last at Bonn to get our trading partners to dismantle their trade barriers, eliminate their subsidies and other unfair trade practices, enter into negotiations to open markets even further and strengthen GATT, the international accord that governs worldwide trade. I will continue to do these things.

But I also want the American people and our trading partners to know that we will take all the action that is necessary to pursue our rights and interests in international commerce, under our laws and the GATT, to see that other nations live up to their obligations and their trade agreements with us.

I believe that if trade is not fair for all, then trade is "free" in name only.

Combating Unfair Trade Practices

I will not stand by and watch American businesses fail because of unfair trading practices abroad. I will not stand by and watch American workers lose their jobs because other nations do not play by the rules.

We have put incentives into our own economy to make it grow and create jobs. And, as you know, business has prospered. We have created over eight million new jobs in the last 33 months. Just since 1980, manufacturing production has increased 17 percent.

But I'm not unmindful that within this prosperity, some industries and workers face difficulties. To the workers who have been displaced by industrial shifts within our society, we are committed to help.

To those industries that are victims of unfair trade, we will work unceasingly to have those practices eliminated.

Just a few weeks ago, I asked the United States Trade Representative to initiate unfair trade practice investigations. It's the first time a President has done this. And, as you know, we have self-initiated three such cases that will investigate a Korean law that prohibits fair competition for U.S. insurance firms, a Brazilian law restricting the sale of U.S. high technology products, and Japanese restrictions on the sale of U.S. tobacco products. I have also ordered the United States Trade Representative to accelerate the ongoing cases of Common Market restrictions of canned fruit, and Japanese prohibitions on imports of our leather and leather footwear.

New Loan Fund

But I believe more must be done. I am, therefore, today announcing that: I have instructed Ambassador Yeutter to maintain a constant watch and to take action in those instances of unfair trade that will disadvantage American businesses and workers; I have directed the Secretary of the Treasury to work with the Congress to establish a $300 million fund that will support up to a billion dollars in mixed credit loans. These funds will counter our loss of business to trading partners who use what, in effect, are subsidies to deprive U.S. companies of fair access to world markets. And I've asked that these initiatives be continued until unfair credit subsidies by our trading partners are eliminated through negotiations with them.

I have further instructed Treasury Secretary Jim Baker to inform the participants at the International Monetary Fund and World Bank conferences in Seoul that we will take into consideration the trading practices of other nations in our deliberations and decision-making.

A major factor in the growth of our trade deficit has been the combination of our very strong economic performance and the weak economic performance of our major trading partners over the last four years. This has limited our exports and contributed to the weakening of other currencies relative to the dollar, thereby encouraging additional imports by the United States and discouraging our exports.

Trade Negotiations

Yesterday, I authorized Treasury Secretary Baker to join his counterparts from other major industrial countries to announce measures to promote stronger and more balanced growth in our economies and, thereby, the strengthening of foreign currencies. This will provide better markets for U.S. products and improve the competitive position of our industry, agriculture and labor.

I have ordered the Secretary of State to seek time limits on negotiations under way to open up markets in specific product areas in Japan.

I have instructed the United States Trade Representative to accelerate negotiations with any and all countries where the counterfeiting and piracy of U.S. goods has occurred to bring these practices to a quick end. And I look forward to working with the Congress to increase efforts to protect patents, copyrights, trademarks, and other intellectual property rights.

And, finally, I am today directing that a strike force be established among the relevant agencies in our government whose task it will be to uncover unfair trading practices used against us and develop and execute strategies and programs to promptly counter and eliminate them.

Prospective Legislation

I am also looking forward to working with the Congress to put into place any necessary legislation that would help us promote free and fair trade and secure jobs for American workers. Among the topics that we should jointly consider are authority to support our new trade negotiating initiatives that would, among other things, reduce tariffs and attempt to dismantle all other trade barriers; to protect intellectual property rights, including trade in articles that infringe U.S. process patents; longer terms for agricultural chemicals, and eliminating Freedom of Information Act abuses that will help our businesses protect their proprietary property. To improve our antidumping and countervailing duty laws so that a predictable pricing test covers nonmarket economies, enabling our companies to have protection against unfair dumping from those countries. We should also improve these laws so that business can have full and rapid protection in receiving help against unfair imports.

To amend our trade laws to put a deadline on dispute settlement and to conduct a fast-track procedure for perishable items. We should no longer tolerate 16-year cases, and settlements so costly and time-consuming that any assistance is ineffective.

I am also directing the Secretary of Labor to explore ways of assisting workers who lose jobs to find gainful employment in other industries, and I look forward to working with Congress in this vital task.

Additionally, I welcome the suggestions of the members of Congress on other potential legislation that has as its object the promotion of free and fair trade. I will work with them to see that good legislation is passed. Conversely, I will strongly oppose and will veto measures that I believe will harm economic growth, cause loss of jobs, and diminish international trade.

Hazards of Protectionism

But I do not want to let this discussion pass without reminding all of our ultimate purpose — the expansion of free and open markets everywhere. There are some, well-meaning in motive, who have proposed bills and programs that are purely protectionist in nature. These proposals would raise the costs of the goods and services that American consumers across the land would have to pay. They would invite retaliation by our trading partners abroad, would in turn lose jobs for those American workers in industries that would be the victims of such retaliation, would rekindle inflation, would strain international relations, and would impair the stability of the international financial and trading systems.

The net result of these counterproductive proposals would not be to protect consumers or workers or farmers or businesses. In fact, just the reverse would happen. We would lose markets, we would lose jobs, and we would lose our prosperity.

To reduce the impediments to free markets we will accelerate our efforts to launch a new GATT negotiating round with our trading partners. And we hope that the GATT members will see fit to reduce barriers for trade and agricultural products, services, technologies, investments, and in mature industries. We will seek effective dispute settlement techniques in these areas.

But if these negotiations are not initiated or if insignificant progress is made, I'm instructing our trade negotiators to explore regional and bilateral agreements with other nations.

Here at home we will continue our efforts to reduce excessive government spending and to promote our tax reform proposal that is essential to strengthening our own economy and making U.S. business more competitive in international markets.

Further, we will encourage our trading partners, as agreed upon at the Bonn summit, to accelerate their own economic growth by removing rigidities and imbalances in their economies. And we will encourage them to provide sound fiscal and monetary policies to have them fully participate in the growth potential that is there for all.

We will seek to strengthen and improve the operation of the international monetary system and we will encourage the debt-burdened, less-developed countries of the world to reduce and eliminate impediments to investments and eliminate internal restrictions that discourage their own economic growth.

Commitment to Free Trade

Let me summarize. Our commitment to free trade is undiminished. We will vigorously pursue our policy of promoting free and open markets in this country and around the world. We will insist that all nations face up to their responsibilities of preserving and enhancing free trade everywhere. But let no one mistake our resolve to oppose any and all unfair trading practices. It is wrong for the American worker and American businessman to continue to bear the burden imposed by those who abuse the world trading system.

We do not want a trade war with other nations; we want other nations to join us in enlarging and enhancing the world trading system for the benefit of all.

We do not want to stop other nations from selling goods in the United States; we want to sell more of our goods to other nations.

We do not dream of protecting America from other success; we seek to include everyone in the success of the American dream. ■

President Reagan's United Nations Address

Following is the White House text of President Reagan's address to the U.N. General Assembly, as delivered Oct. 24 at the commemoration of the 40th anniversary of the United Nations.

Mr. President, Mr. Secretary General, honored guests and distinguished delegates, thank you for the honor of permitting me to speak on this anniversary for the United Nations.

Forty years ago, the world awoke daring to believe hatred's unyielding grip had finally been broken — daring to believe the torch of peace would be protected in liberty's firm grasp.

Forty years ago, the world yearned to dream again innocent dreams, to believe in ideals with innocent trust. Dreams of trust are worthy, but in these 40 years too many dreams have been shattered, too many promises have been broken, too many lives have been lost. The painful truth is that the use of violence to take, to exercise, and to preserve power remains a persistent reality in much of the world.

The Vision and the Reality

The vision of the U.N. Charter — to spare succeeding generations this scourge of war — remains real. It still stirs our soul and warms our hearts, but it also demands of us a realism that is rockhard, clear-eyed, steady and sure — a realism that understands the nations of the United Nations are not united.

I come before you this morning preoccupied with peace, with ensuring that the differences between some of us not be permitted to degenerate into open conflict. And I come offering for my own country a new commitment, a fresh start.

On this U.N. anniversary, we acknowledge its successes: the decisive action during the Korean War; negotiation of the Non-Proliferation Treaty; strong support for decolonization; and the laudable achievements by the United Nations' High Commissioner for Refugees.

Nor must we close our eyes to this organization's disappointments: its failure to deal with real security issues; the total inversion of morality in the infamous Zionism-is-racist — racism resolution, the politicization of too many agencies, the misuse of too many resources.

The U.N. is a political institution and politics requires compromise. We recognize that. But let us remember from those first days, one guiding star was supposed to light our path toward the U.N. vision of peace and progress — a star of freedom.

The Universal Right to Freedom

What kind of people will we be 40 years from today? May we answer — free people, worthy of freedom and firm in the conviction that freedom is not the sole prerogative of a chosen few, but the universal right of all God's children.

This is the universal declaration of human rights set forth in 1948. And this is the affirming flame the United States has held high to a watching world. We champion freedom not only because it is practical and beneficial, but because it is morally right and just.

Free people whose governments rest upon the consent of the governed do not wage war on their neighbors. Free people blessed by economic opportunity and protected by laws that respect the dignity of the individual are not driven toward the domination of others.

We readily acknowledge that the United States is far from perfect. Yet we have endeavored earnestly to carry out our responsibilities to the Charter these past 40 years, and we take national pride in our contributions to peace.

We take pride in 40 years of helping avert a new world war and pride in our alliances that protect and preserve us and our friends from aggression. We take pride in the Camp David agreements and our efforts for peace in the Middle East, rooted in resolutions 242 and 338; in supporting Pakistan, target of outside intimidation; in assisting El Salvador's struggle to carry forward its democratic revolution; in answering the appeal of our Caribbean friends in Grenada; in seeing Grenada's representative here today voting the will of its own people. And we take pride in our proposals to reduce the weapons of war.

We submit this history as evidence of our sincerity of purpose. But today, it is more important to speak to you about what my country proposes to do in these closing years of the 20th century — to bring about a safer, a more peaceful, a more civilized world.

U.S.-Soviet Differences

Let us begin with candor — with words that rest on plain and simple facts. The differences between America and the Soviet Union are deep and abiding.

The United States is a democratic nation. Here the people rule. We build no walls to keep them in, nor organize any system of police to keep them mute. We occupy no country. The only land abroad we occupy is beneath the graves where our heroes rest. What is called the West is a voluntary association of free nations, all of whom fiercely value their independence and their sovereignty. And as deeply as we cherish our beliefs, we do not seek to compel others to share them.

When we enjoy these vast freedoms as we do, it's difficult for us to understand the restrictions of dictatorships which seek to control each institution and every facet of people's lives, the expression of their beliefs, their movements and their contacts with the outside world. It's difficult for us to understand the ideological premise that force is an acceptable way to expand a political system.

We Americans do not accept that any government has the right to command and order the lives of its people, that any nation has an historic right to use force to export its ideology. This belief — regarding the nature of man and the limitations of government — is at the core of our deep and abiding differences with the Soviet Union, differences that put us into natural conflict and competition with one another.

Now, we would welcome enthusiastically a true competition of ideas, welcome a competition of economic strength and scientific and artistic creativity, and, yes, welcome a competition for the good will of the world's people. But we cannot accommodate ourselves to the use of force and subversion to consolidate and expand the reach of totalitarianism.

U.S.-Soviet Summit

When Mr. Gorbachev and I meet in Geneva next month, I look to a fresh start in the relationship of our two nations. We can and should meet in the spirit that we can deal with our differences peacefully. And that is what we expect.

The only way to resolve differences is to understand them. We must have candid and complete discussions of where dangers exist and where peace is being disrupted. Make no mistake; our policy of open and vigorous competition rests on a realistic view of the world. And therefore, at Geneva, we must review the reasons for the current level of mistrust.

Reasons for Mistrust

For example, in 1972 the international community negotiated in good faith a ban on biological and toxin weapons; in 1975 we negotiated the Helsinki accords on human rights and freedoms; and during the decade just past, the United States and Soviet Union negotiated several agreements on strategic weapons. And yet, we feel it will be necessary at Geneva to discuss with the Soviet Union what we believe are violations of a number of the provisions in all of these agreements. Indeed, this is why it is important that we have this opportunity to air our differences through face-to-face meetings — to let frank talk substitute for anger and tension.

The United States has never sought treaties merely to paper over differences. We continue to believe that a nuclear war is one that cannot be won and must never be fought. And that is why we have sought for nearly 10 years, still seek, and will discuss in Geneva radical, equitable, verifiable reductions in these vast arsenals of offensive nuclear weapons.

Soviet Arms Proposal

At the beginning of the latest round of the ongoing negotiations in Geneva, the Soviet Union presented a specific proposal involving numerical values. We are studying the Soviet counterproposal carefully. I believe that within their proposal there are seeds which we should nurture, and in the coming weeks we will seek to establish a genuine process of give-and-take.

The United States is also seeking to discuss with the Soviet Union in Geneva the vital relationship between offensive and defensive systems, including the possibility of moving toward a more stable and secure world in which defenses play a growing role.

Role of Defensive Weapons

The ballistic missile is the most awesome, threatening, and destructive weapon in the history of man. Thus, I welcome the interest of the new Soviet leadership in the reduction of offensive strategic forces. Ultimately, we must remove this menace, once and for all, from the face of the Earth.

Until that day, the United States seeks to escape the prison of mutual terror by research and testing that could, in time, enable us to neutralize the threat of these ballistic missiles and, ultimately, render them obsolete.

How is Moscow threatened if the capitals of other nations are protected? We do not ask that the Soviet leaders — whose country has suffered so much from war — to leave their people defenseless against foreign attack. Why then do they insist that we remain undefended? Who is threatened if Western research — and Soviet research that is itself well-advanced — should develop a non-nuclear system which would threaten not human beings, but only ballistic missiles?

Surely, the world will sleep more secure when these missiles have been rendered useless, militarily and politically, when the Sword of Damocles that has hung over our planet for too many decades is lifted by Western and Russian scientists working to shield their citizens and one day shut down space as an avenue of weapons of mass destruction.

If we're destined by history to compete, militarily, to keep the peace, then let us compete in systems that defend our societies rather than weapons which can destroy us both and much of God's creation along with us.

Some 18 years ago, then-Premier Aleksei Kosygin was asked about a moratorium on the development of an anti-missile defense system. The official news agency, TASS, reported that he replied with these words:

"I believe the defensive systems, which prevent attack, are not the cause of the arms race, but constitute a factor preventing the death of people. Maybe an antimissile system is more expensive than an offensive system, but it is designed not to kill people, but to preserve human lives." — quoting Aleksei Kosygin.

Preserving lives — no peace is more fundamental than that. Great obstacles lie ahead, but they should not deter us. Peace is God's commandment. Peace is the holy shadow cast by men treading on the path of virtue.

But just as we all know what peace is, we certainly know what peace is not.

Peace based on repression cannot be true peace and is secure only when individuals are free to direct their own governments.

Peace based on partition cannot be true peace. Put simply: nothing can justify the continuing and permanent division of the European continent. Walls of partition and distrust must give way to greater communication for an open world. Before leaving for Geneva, I shall make new proposals to achieve this goal.

Peace based on mutual fear cannot be true peace because staking our future on a precarious balance of terror is not good enough. The world needs a balance of safety.

And finally, a peace based on averting our eyes from trouble cannot be true peace. The consequences of conflict are every bit as tragic when the destruction is contained within one country.

Real peace is what we seek, and that is why today the United States is presenting an initiative that addresses what will be a central issue in Geneva — the issue of regional conflicts in Africa, Asia and Central America.

Our own position is clear: as the oldest nation of the New World, as the first anticolonial power, the United States rejoiced when decolonization gave birth to so many new nations after World War II. We have always supported the right of the people of each nation to define their own destiny. We have given $300 billion since 1945 to help people of other countries, and we've tried to help friendly governments defend against aggression, subversion and terror.

Soviet Record of Aggression

We have noted with great interest similar expressions of peaceful intent by leaders of the Soviet Union. I am not here to challenge the good faith of what they say. But isn't it important for us to weigh the record as well?

In Afghanistan, there are 118,000 Soviet troops prosecuting war against the Afghan people.

In Cambodia, 140,000 Soviet-backed Vietnamese soldiers wage a war of occupation.

In Ethiopia, 1,700 Soviet advisers are involved in military planning and support operations along with 2,500 Cuban combat troops.

In Angola, 1,200 Soviet military advisers involved in planning and supervising combat operations, along with 35,000 Cuban troops.

In Nicaragua, some 8,000 Soviet-bloc and Cuban personnel, including about 3,500 military and secret police personnel.

All of these conflicts — some of them under way for a decade — originate in local disputes, but they share a common characteristic: they are the consequence of an ideology imposed from without, dividing nations and creating regimes that are, almost from the day they take power, at war with their own people. And in each case, Marxism Leninism's war with the people becomes war with their neighbors.

These wars are exacting a staggering human toll and threaten to spill across national boundaries and trigger dangerous confrontations. Where is it more appropriate than right here at the United Nations to call attention to Article II of our Charter which instructs members to refrain "from the use or threat or use of force against the territorial integrity or political independence of any state . . ."?

During the past decade, these wars played a large role in building suspicions and tensions in my country over the purpose of Soviet policy. This gives us an extra reason to address them seriously today.

A Regional Peace Process

Last year, I proposed from this podium that the United States and Soviet Union hold discussions on some of these issues, and we have done so. But I believe these problems need more than talk.

For that reason, we are proposing and are fully committed to support a regional peace process that seeks progress on three levels:

First, we believe the starting point must be a process of negotiation among the warring parties in each country I've mentioned — which, in the case of Afghanistan, includes the Soviet Union. The form of these talks may and should vary. But negotiations and an improvement of internal political conditions are essential to achieving an end to violence, the withdrawal of foreign troops and national reconciliation.

There is a second level: once negotiations take hold and the parties directly involved are making real progress, representatives of the United States and the Soviet Union should sit down together. It is not for us to impose any solutions in this separate set of talks. Such solutions would not last. But the issue we should address is how best to support the ongoing talks among the warring parties. In some cases, it might well be appropriate to consider guarantees for any agreements already reached. But in every case, the primary task is to promote this goal: verified elimination of the foreign military presence and restraint on the flow of outside arms.

And finally, if these first two steps are successful, we could move on to the third — welcoming each country back into the world economy so its citizens can share in the dynamic growth that other developing countries, countries that are at peace, enjoy. Despite past differences with these regimes, the United States would respond generously to their democratic reconciliation with their own people, their respect for human rights and their return to the family of free nations.

Of course, until such time as these negotiations result in definitive progress, America's support for struggling democratic resistance forces must not and shall not cease.

This plan is bold, it is realistic. It is not a substitute for existing peace-making efforts; it complements them. We're not trying to solve every conflict in every region of the globe and we recognize that each conflict has its own character. Naturally, other regional problems will require different approaches. But we believe that the recurrent pattern of conflict that we see in these five cases ought to be broken as soon as possible.

We must begin somewhere, so let us begin where there is great need and great hope. This will be a clear step forward to help people choose their future more freely. Moreover, this is an extraordinary opportunity for the Soviet side to make a contribution to regional peace which, in turn, can promote future dialogue and negotiations on other critical issues.

With hard work and imagination, there is no limit to what, working together, our nations can achieve. Gaining a peaceful resolution of these conflicts will open whole new vistas of peace and progress — the discovery that the promise of the future lies not in measures of military defense, or the control of weapons, but in the expansion of individual freedom and human rights.

Prosperity Out of Freedom

Only when the human spirit can worship, create and build, only when people are given a personal stake in determining their own destiny and benefiting from their own risks, do societies become prosperous, progressive, dynamic and free.

We need only open our eyes to the economic evidence all around us. Nations that deny their people opportunity — in Eastern Europe, Indochina, southern Africa, and Latin America — without exception are dropping further behind in the race for the future.

But where we see enlightened leaders who understand that economic freedom and personal incentive are key to development, we see economies striding forward. Singapore, Taiwan, and South Korea — India, Botswana, and China. These are among the current and emerging success stories because they have the courage to give economic incentives a chance.

Let us all heed the simple eloquence in Andrei Sakharov's Nobel Peace Prize message: "International trust, mutual understanding, disarmament and international security are inconceivable without an open society with the freedom of information, freedom of conscience, the right to publish and the right to travel and choose the country in which one wishes to live."

At the core, this is an eternal truth. Freedom works. That is the promise of the open world and awaits only our collective grasp. Forty years ago, hope came alive again for a world that hungered for hope. I believe fervently that hope is still alive.

The United States has spoken with candor and conviction today, but that does not lessen these strong feelings held by every American. It's in the nature of Americans to hate war and its destructiveness. We would rather wage our struggle to rebuild and renew, not to tear down. We would rather fight against hunger, disease, and catastrophe. We would rather engage our adversaries in the battle of ideals and ideas for the future.

These principles emerge from the innate openness and good character of our people, and from our long struggle and sacrifice for our liberties and the liberties of others. Americans always yearn for peace. They have a passion for life. They carry in their hearts a deep capacity for reconciliation.

Last year at this General Assembly, I indicated there was every reason for the United States and the Soviet Union to shorten the distance between us. In Geneva, the first meeting between our heads of government in more than six years, Mr. Gorbachev and I will have that opportunity.

So, yes, let us go to Geneva with both sides committed to dialogue. Let both sides go committed to a world with fewer nuclear weapons, and some day with none. Let both sides go committed to walk together on a safer path into the 21st century and to lay the foundation for an enduring peace.

Time to Act

It is time, indeed, to do more than just talk of a better world. It is time to act. And we will act when nations cease to try to impose their ways upon others. And we will act when they realize that we, for whom the achievement of freedom has come dear, will do what we must to preserve it from assault.

America is committed to the world because so much of the world is inside America. After all, only a few miles from this very room is our Statue of Liberty, past which life began anew for millions, where the peoples from nearly every country in this hall joined to build these United States.

The blood of each nation courses through the American vein and feeds the spirit that compels us to involve ourselves in the fate of this good Earth. It is the same spirit that warms our heart in concern to help ease the desperate hunger that grips proud people on the African continent.

The Miracle of Life

It is the internationalist spirit that came together last month when our neighbor, Mexico, was struck suddenly by an earthquake. Even as the Mexican nation moved vigorously into action, there were heartwarming offers by other nations offering to help and glimpses of people working together, without concern for national self-interest or gain.

And if there was any meaning to salvage out of that tragedy, it was found one day in a huge mound of rubble that was once the Juarez Hospital in Mexico City.

A week after that terrible event, and as another day of despair unfolded, a team of workers heard a faint sound coming from somewhere in the heart of the crushed concrete. Hoping beyond hope, they quickly burrowed toward it.

And as the late afternoon light faded, and racing against time, they found what they had heard, and the first of three baby girls, newborn infants, emerged to the safety of the rescue team.

And let me tell you the scene through the eyes of one who was there. "Everyone was so quiet when they lowered that little baby down in a basket covered with blankets. The baby didn't make a sound either. But the minute they put her in the Red Cross ambulance, everybody just got up and cheered."

Well, amidst all that hopelessness and debris came a timely and timeless lesson for us all. We witnessed the miracle of life.

It is on this that I believe our nations can make a renewed commitment. The miracle of life is given by One greater than ourselves. But once given, each life is ours to nurture and preserve, to foster, not only for today's world, but for a better one to come.

There is no purpose more noble than for us to sustain and celebrate life in a turbulent world. And that is what we must do now. We have no higher duty, no greater cause as humans. Life and the preservation of freedom to live it in dignity is what we are on this Earth to do.

Everything we work to achieve must seek that end so that some day our prime ministers, our premiers, our presidents and our general secretaries will talk not of war and peace, but only of peace.

We've had 40 years to begin. Let us not waste one more moment to give back to the world all that we can in return for this miracle of life.

Thank you all. God bless you all. ■

Reagan's NIH Veto Message

Following is the White House text of President Reagan's Nov. 8 message accompanying his veto of HR 2409, to reauthorize the National Institutes of Health. It was Reagan's second veto of a public bill during the 99th Congress.

TO THE HOUSE OF REPRESENTATIVES:

I am returning herewith without my approval H.R. 2409, the "Health Research Extension Act of 1985," which would extend and amend the biomedical research authorities of the National Institutes of Health (NIH).

My action on this bill should in no way be interpreted as a lessening of this Administration's strong commitment to the biomedical research endeavors of NIH. In fact, I want to underscore my personal support and the support of my Administration for biomedical research and for the NIH. For over 40 years, the NIH has enjoyed unparalleled success. Enormous progress in research and the improved health of the American people attest to that success. An appropriations bill or a continuing resolution will provide uninterrupted funding for NIH activities in fiscal year 1986.

I believe that instead of fostering a strong Federal biomedical research effort, H.R. 2409 would adversely affect the pursuit of research excellence at NIH by:

- imposing numerous administrative and program requirements that would interfere with the ability to carry forward our biomedical research activities in the most cost-effective manner and would misallocate scarce financial and personnel resources;
- establishing unneeded new organizations, which would lead to unnecessary coordination problems and administrative expenses while doing little to assist the biomedical research endeavors of NIH; and
- imposing a uniform set of authorities on all the research institutes, thus diminishing our administrative flexibility to respond to changing biomedical research needs.

Although H.R. 2409 is overloaded with objectionable provisions that seriously undermine and threaten the ability of NIH to manage itself and is therefore unacceptable, I recognize there are areas in which the Administration can step forward to strengthen specific research efforts.

As Senator Hatch pointed out when introducing the NIH reauthorization bill in the Senate in June of this year, arthritis afflicts some 49 million of this Nation's citizens and "all of us suffer, at some time in our life, from some form of arthritis." Further, arthritis, along with musculoskeletal and skin diseases, "collectively result in an extraordinary loss to our economy from lost productivity as well as from medical expense."

In recognition of the plight of the millions of arthritis victims and society's costs, I have directed the Secretary of Health and Human Services to establish administratively a separate National Institute of Arthritis and Musculoskeletal and Skin Diseases that will meet the continuing need for coordinated research in this important area. This directive is consistent with the Department's recommendation to me that this Institute be established.

At the same time, I do not believe that the establishment of a nursing research center at NIH is appropriate, for a very basic reason — there is a lack of compatibility between the mission of such a center and the mission of NIH. The biomedical research activities of NIH are concerned with discovering the etiology of and treatment for diseases. In contrast, nursing research uses substantive scientific information and methodology and focuses on their relevance to nursing practice and administration. This research is important, but neither it nor disease-oriented research are served by the provisions of the bill.

H.R. 2409 manifests an effort to exert undue political control over decisions regarding scientific research, thus limiting the ability of the NIH to set this Nation's biomedical research agenda. I do not believe that it is either necessary or wise to restrict the flexibility under which the NIH has operated so successfully. In 1984, I rejected a very similar bill, and once again I find no reasonable justification for the extensive changes to the NIH mandated by H.R. 2409. In order to allow NIH to continue to provide excellence in biomedical research and in its management, I am disapproving this bill.

RONALD REAGAN

The White House,
November 8, 1985

President's Nov. 15 Message On Treasury-Postal Service Veto

Following is the Congressional Record *text of President Reagan's Nov. 15 message accompanying his veto of HR 3036, the fiscal 1986 Treasury, Postal Service and general government appropriations bill. It was Reagan's third veto of a public bill during the 99th Congress.*

TO THE HOUSE OF REPRESENTATIVES:

I am returning herewith without my approval H.R. 3036, making appropriations for the Treasury Department, the United States Postal Service and certain Independent Agencies for the fiscal year 1986.

In my budget last February I proposed reforms, reductions, and terminations in some 50 domestic programs to start us on a sensible path to lower budget deficits. Because Congress has accepted very few of these proposals, it is now clear that all of the non-defense appropriations bills will be far above my budget.

However, in the interest of accommodation, I have indicated that I would accept appropriations bills, even if above my budget, that were within the limits set by Congress' own budget resolution. This bill does not meet that test.

For discretionary programs the bill provides $900 million more than my budget and is $180 million above the level for budget authority and other discretionary resources implied in the budget resolution. For example, my budget proposed a major paring of the remaining postal subsidies, and the Congressional budget resolution envisaged a lesser saving. This bill provides $820 million for these subsidies, which represents little saving from current levels and is $72 million above the budget resolution level.

Apart from its spending levels, this bill contains a number of language provisions that are highly objectionable. Among them are provisions blocking performance-based regulations for civil servants issued by the Office of Personnel Management, curbing the authority of the General Services Administration to contract out certain services to the private sector, forbidding review by the Office of Management and Budget of marketing orders for agricultural products, and one section of the bill raises serious constitutional concerns with respect to presidential appointments.

The presidential veto is an instrument to be used with care. But until the Congress comes to grips with the problem of the large budget deficit, it is an instrument that I shall not hesitate to employ.

RONALD REAGAN

The White House,
November 15, 1985

Reagan's Statement on Balanced Budget Bill

Following is the White House text of President Reagan's Dec. 12 statement on his signing of H J Res 372 (PL 99-177), which raised the public debt ceiling and included provisions to balance the federal budget by fiscal 1991.

Today I have signed H J Res 372, which increases the statutory limit on the public debt and includes the Balanced Budget and Emergency Deficit Control Act of 1985, also known as the Gramm-Rudman-Hollings Amendment. With the passage of this landmark legislation, the Congress has made an important step toward putting our fiscal house in order. Deficit reduction is no longer simply our hope and our goal — deficit reduction is now the law. From here to the end of the decade, mandated cuts can put the deficit on a declining path and eliminate governmental overspending by 1991. It is my hope that we will move even one step further to secure the gains we have made by adopting a balanced budget amendment to the Constitution.

Deficits have threatened our economic well-being for too long. For years the Congress has talked about the deficit and now it has done something about it. But the tough work of controlling Federal spending still lies ahead. It is important that we now cooperate in good faith toward building a solid fiscal foundation for economic growth. This legislation mandates that the President and the Congress work together to eliminate the deficit over the next five years. The first step in that process will begin early next year. At that time I anticipate that we will have to take some significant across-the-board reductions in a wide range of programs. That means cutting back on the expansion of government — an expansion which has slowed but which still continues apace. Whether increased government spending is financed through taxes or borrowing, it imposes a heavy burden on the private economy — the source of our prosperity and the foundation of our hopes for the future. That is why increasing taxes is not an option: deficit reduction must mean spending reductions.

We must also never lose sight of the necessity to maintain a strong national defense. Restoring our defenses has been vital not only to our security, but to the cause of freedom. Today, our once ailing alliances are stronger than before. America is looked upon with renewed admiration around the world, and the principles of human freedom that we embody are no longer in retreat. I am confident that implementing our previous agreements with Congress for steady real growth in defense will keep our defenses secure.

In signing this bill, I am mindful of the serious constitutional questions raised by some of its provisions. The bill assigns a significant role to the Director of the Congressional Budget Office and the Comptroller General in calculating the budget estimates that trigger the operative provisions of the bill. Under the system of separated powers established by the Constitution, however, executive functions may only be performed by officers in the Executive branch. The Director of the Congressional Budget Office and the Comptroller General are agents of Congress, not officers in the Executive branch.

The bill itself recognizes this problem, and provides procedures for testing the constitutionality of the dubious provisions. The bill also provides a constitutionally valid alternative mechanism should the role of the Director of the Congressional Budget Office and the Comptroller General be struck down. It is my hope that these outstanding constitutional questions can be promptly resolved.

Similar constitutional concerns are raised by a provision in the bill authorizing the President to terminate or modify defense contracts for deficit reduction purposes, but only if the action is approved by the Comptroller General. Under our constitutional system, an agent of Congress may not exercise such supervisory authority over the President. As the Supreme Court made clear in its *Chadha* decision, Congress can "veto" Presidential action only through the constitutionally established procedure of passing a bill through both Houses and presenting it to the President.

My Administration alerted Congress to these various problems throughout the legislative process, in an effort to achieve a bill free of constitutionally suspect provisions. Although we were unsuccessful in this goal, I am nonetheless signing the bill. In doing so I am in no sense dismissing the constitutional problems or acquiescing in a violation of the system of separated powers carefully crafted by the framers of the Constitution. Rather, it is my hope that the constitutional problems will be promptly resolved so that the vitally important business of deficit reduction can proceed.

Deficit Reduction

In addition the legislation also increases the debt ceiling so that the Federal government can continue to meet its financial obligations.

The many Senators and Representatives whose hard work has borne fruit in this bill are to be commended. The American people expect their elected officials to take action now to reduce the size of government and to set upon a reasonable and equitable course to eliminate Federal budget deficits. I am unequivocally committed to that goal. I am hopeful and confident that Congress will act responsibly in meeting its obligations under the bill and thus in future years will render implementation of the automatic budget reduction mechanism unnecessary. Deficit reduction is on the horizon. We are embarked on this promising new path together, and together we will make it work. ▮

Text of the Joint Statement At End of U.S.-Soviet Summit

Following is the White House text of the joint statement issued Nov. 21 by President Reagan and Soviet leader Mikhail S. Gorbachev at the conclusion of the U.S.-Soviet summit, in Geneva, Switzerland.

By mutual agreement, President of the United States Ronald Reagan and General Secretary of the Central Committee of the Communist Party of the Soviet Union Mikhail Gorbachev met in Geneva November 19-21. Attending the meeting on the U.S. side were Secretary of State George Shultz; Chief of Staff Donald Regan; Assistant to the President Robert McFarlane; Ambassador to the USSR Arthur Hartman; Special Advisor to the President and the Secretary of State for Arms Control Paul H. Nitze; Assistant Secretary of State for European Affairs Rosanne Ridgway; Special Assistant to the President for National Security Affairs Jack Matlock. Attending on the Soviet side were Member of the Politburo of the Central Committee of the CPSU, Minister of Foreign Affairs E. A. Shevardnadze; First Deputy Foreign Minister G. M. Korniyenko; Ambassador to the United States A. F. Dobrynin; Head of the Department of Propaganda of the Central Committee of the CPSU, A. N. Yakovlev; Head of the Department of International Information of the Central Committee of the CPSU, L. M. Zamyatin; Assistant to the General Secretary of the Central Committee of the CPSU, A. M. Aleksandrov.

These comprehensive discussions covered the basic questions of U.S.-Soviet relations and the current international situation. The meetings were frank and useful. Serious differences remain on a number of critical issues.

While acknowledging the differences in their systems and approaches to international issues, some greater understanding of each side's view was achieved by the two leaders. They agreed about the need to improve U.S.-Soviet relations and the international situation as a whole.

In this connection the two sides have confirmed the importance of an ongoing dialogue, reflecting their strong desire to seek common ground on existing problems.

They agreed to meet again in the nearest future. The General Secretary accepted an invitation by the President of the United States to visit the United States of America and the President of the United States accepted an invitation by the General Secretary of the Central Committee of the CPSU to visit the Soviet Union. Arrangements for and timing of the visits will be agreed upon through diplomatic channels.

In their meetings, agreement was reached on a number of specific issues. Areas of agreement are registered on the following pages:

Security

The sides, having discussed key security issues, and conscious of the special responsibility of the USSR and the U.S. for maintaining peace, have agreed that a nuclear war cannot be won and must never be fought. Recognizing that any conflict between the USSR and the U.S. could have catastrophic consequences, they emphasized the importance of preventing any war between them, whether nuclear or conventional. They will not seek to achieve military superiority.

Nuclear and Space Talks

The President and the General Secretary discussed the negotiations on nuclear and space arms.

They agreed to accelerate the work at these negotiations, with a view to accomplishing the tasks set down in the Joint U.S.-Soviet Agreement of January 8, 1985, namely to prevent an arms race in space and to terminate it on Earth, to limit and reduce nuclear arms and enhance strategic stability.

Noting the proposals recently tabled by the U.S. and the Soviet Union, they called for early progress, in particular in areas where there is common ground, including the principle of 50 percent reductions in the nuclear arms of the U.S. and the USSR appropriately applied, as well as the idea of an interim INF agreement.

During the negotiation of these agreements, effective measures for verification of compliance with obligations assumed will be agreed upon.

Risk Reduction Centers

The sides agreed to study the question at the expert level of centers to reduce nuclear risk taking into account the issues and developments in the Geneva negotiations.

They took satisfaction in such recent steps in this direction as the modernization of the Soviet-U.S. hotline.

Nuclear Non-Proliferation

General Secretary Gorbachev and President Reagan reaffirmed the commitment of the USSR and the U.S. to the Treaty on the Non-Proliferation of Nuclear Weapons and their interest in strengthening together with other countries the non-proliferation regime, and in further enhancing of the Treaty, inter alia by enlarging its membership.

They note with satisfaction the overall positive results of the recent Review Conference of the Treaty on the Non-Proliferation of Nuclear Weapons.

The USSR and the U.S. reaffirm their commitment, assumed by them under the Treaty on the Non-Proliferation of Nuclear Weapons, to pursue negotiations in good faith on matters of nuclear arms limitation and disarmament in accordance with Article VI of the Treaty.

The two sides plan to continue to promote the strengthening of the International Atomic Energy Agency and to support the activities of the Agency in implementing safeguards as well as in promoting the peaceful uses of nuclear energy.

They view positively the practice of regular Soviet-U.S. consultations on non-proliferation of nuclear weapons which have been businesslike and constructive and express their intent to continue this practice in the future.

Chemical Weapons

In the context of discussing security problems, the two sides reaffirmed that they are in favor of a general and complete prohibition of chemical weapons and the destruction of existing stockpiles of such weapons.

They agreed to accelerate efforts to conclude an effective and verifiable international convention in this matter.

The two sides agreed to intensify bilateral discussions on the level of experts on all aspects of such a chemical weapons ban, including the question of verification. They agreed to initiate a dialogue on preventing the proliferation of chemical weapons.

MBFR

The two sides emphasized the importance they attach to the Vienna (MBFR) negotiations and expressed their willingness to work for positive results.

CDE

Attaching great importance to the Stockholm Conference on Confidence and Security Building Measures and Disarmament in Europe and noting the progress made there, the two sides stated their intention to facilitate, together with the other participating states, an early and successful completion of the work of the conference. To this end, they reaffirmed the need for a document which would include mutually acceptable confidence and security building measures and give concrete expression and effect to the principle of non-use of force.

Process of Dialogue

President Reagan and General Secretary Gorbachev agreed on the need to place on a regular basis and intensify dialogue at various levels. Along with meetings between the leaders of the two countries, this envisages regular meetings between the USSR Minister of Foreign Affairs and the U.S. Secretary of State, as well as between the heads of other Ministries and Agencies. They agree that the recent visits of the heads of Ministries and Departments in such fields as agriculture, housing and protection of the environment have been useful.

Recognizing that exchanges of views on regional issues on the expert level have proven useful, they agreed to continue such exchanges on a regular basis.

The sides intend to expand the programs of bilateral cultural, educational and scientific-technical exchanges, and also to develop trade and economic ties. The President of the United States and the General Secretary of the Central Committee of the CPSU attended the signing of the Agreement on Contacts and Exchanges in Scientific, Educational and Cultural Fields.

They agreed on the importance of resolving humanitarian cases in the spirit of cooperation.

They believe that there should be greater understanding among our peoples and that to this end they will encourage greater travel and people-to-people contact.

Northern Pacific Air Safety

The two leaders also noted with satisfaction that, in cooperation with the Government of Japan, the United States and the Soviet Union have agreed to a set of measures to promote safety on air routes in the North Pacific and have worked out steps to implement them.

Civil Aviation/Consulates

They acknowledged that delegations from the United States and the Soviet Union have begun negotiations aimed at resumption of air services. The two leaders expressed their desire to reach a mutually beneficial agreement at an early date. In this regard, an agreement was reached on the simultaneous opening of Consulates General in New York and Kiev.

Environmental Protection

Both sides agreed to contribute to the preservation of the environment — a global task — through joint research and practical measures. In accordance with the existing U.S.-Soviet agreement in this area, consultations will be held next year in Moscow and Washington on specific programs of cooperation.

Exchange Initiatives

The two leaders agreed on the utility of broadening exchanges and contacts including some of their new forms in a number of scientific, educational, medical and sports fields (inter alia, cooperation in the development of educational exchanges and software for elementary and secondary school instruction; measures to promote Russian language studies in the United States and English language studies in the USSR; the annual exchange of professors to conduct special courses in history, culture and economics at the relevant departments of Soviet and American institutions of higher education; mutual allocation of scholarships for the best students in the natural sciences, technology, social sciences and humanities for the period of an academic year; holding regular meets in various sports and increased television coverage of sports events). The two sides agreed to resume cooperation in combating cancer diseases.

The relevant agencies in each of the countries are being instructed to develop specific programs for these exchanges. The resulting programs will be reviewed by the leaders at their next meeting.

Fusion Research

The two leaders emphasized the potential importance of the work aimed at utilizing controlled thermonuclear fusion for peaceful purposes and, in this connection, advocated the widest practicable development of international cooperation in obtaining this source of energy . . . for the benefit of all mankind. ∎

Reagan's Remarks on U.S.- Soviet Summit

Following is the White House text of President Reagan's Nov. 21 remarks on the U.S.-Soviet summit meeting, as delivered to a joint session of Congress.

Mr. Speaker, Mr. President, members of the Congress, distinguished guests, my fellow Americans:

It's great to be home, and Nancy and I thank you for this wonderful homecoming. And before I go on, I want to say a personal thank you to Nancy. She was an outstanding ambassador of good will for all of us. She didn't know I was going to say that.

Mr. Speaker, Senator Dole, I want you to know that your statements of support here were greatly appreciated. You can't imagine how much it means in dealing with the Soviets to have the Congress, the allies, and the American people firmly behind you.

I guess you know that I have just come from Geneva and talks with General Secretary Gorbachev. In the past few days, we spent over 15 hours in various meetings with the General Secretary and the members of his official party. And approximately five of those hours were talks between Mr. Gorbachev and myself, just one on one. That was the best part — our fireside summit.

There will be, I know, a great deal of commentary and opinion as to what the meetings produced and what they were like. There were over 3,000 reporters in Geneva, so it's possible there will be 3,000 opinions on what happened, so — maybe it's the old broadcaster in me but I decided to file my own report directly to you.

'A Constructive Meeting'

We met, as we had to meet. I had called for a fresh start — and we made that start. I can't claim we had a meeting of the minds on such fundamentals as ideology or national purpose — but we understand each other better, and that's the key to peace. I gained a better perspective; I feel he did, too.

It was a constructive meeting. So constructive, in fact, that I look forward to welcoming Mr. Gorbachev to the United States next year. And I have accepted his invitation to go to Moscow the following year. We arranged that out in the parking lot.

I found Mr. Gorbachev to be an energetic defender of Soviet policy. He was an eloquent speaker, and a good listener. Our subject matter was shaped by the facts of this century.

Summit's Historic Background

These past 40 years have not been an easy time for the West or for the world. You know the facts; there is no need to recite the historical record. Suffice it to say that the United States cannot afford illusions about the nature of the USSR. We cannot assume that their ideology and purpose will change. This implies enduring competition. Our task is to assure that this competition remains peaceful. With all that divides us, we cannot afford to let confusion complicate things further. We must be clear with each other, and direct. We must pay each other the tribute of candor.

When I took the oath of office for the first time, we began dealing with the Soviet Union in a way that was more realistic than in, say, the recent past. And so, in a very real sense, preparations for the summit started not months ago but five years ago when, with the help of Congress, we began strengthening our economy, restoring our national will, and rebuilding our defenses and alliances. America is once again strong — and our strength has given us the ability to speak with confidence and see that no true opportunity to advance freedom and peace is lost. We must not now abandon policies that work. I need your continued support to keep America strong.

That is the history behind the Geneva summit, and that is the context in which it occurred. And may I add that we were especially eager that our meetings give a push to important talks already under way on reducing nuclear weapons. On this subject it would be foolish not to go the extra mile or in this case the extra 4,000 miles.

We discussed the great issues of our time. I made clear that before the first meeting that no question would be swept aside, no issue buried, just because either side found it uncomfortable or inconvenient.

I brought these questions to the summit and put them before Mr. Gorbachev.

Nuclear Arms Reduction - 1

We discussed nuclear arms and how to reduce them. I explained our proposals for equitable, verifiable, and deep reductions. I outlined my conviction that our proposals would make not just for a world that feels safer but one that really is safer.

I am pleased to report tonight that General Secretary Gorbachev and I did make a measure of progress here. While we still have a long way to go, we're still heading in the right direction. We moved arms control forward from where we were last January, when the Soviets returned to the table. We are both instructing our negotiators to hasten their vital work. The world is waiting for results.

Specifically, we agreed in Geneva that each side should move to cut offensive nuclear arms by 50 percent in appropriate categories. In our joint statement we called for early progress on this, turning the talks toward our chief goal, offensive reductions. We called for an interim accord on intermediate-range nuclear forces, leading, I hope, to the complete elimination of this class of missiles. And all this with tough verification.

We also made progress in combating together the spread of nuclear weapons, an arms control area in which we've cooperated effectively over the years. We are also opening a dialogue on combating the spread and use of chemical weapons, while moving to ban them altogether. Other arms control dialogues — in Vienna on conventional forces, and in Stockholm on lessening the chances for a surprise attack in Europe — also received a boost. And finally, we agreed to begin work on risk reduction centers, a decision that should give special satisfaction to Senators Nunn and Warner who so ably promoted this idea.

'Strategic Defense Initiative' - 1

I described our Strategic Defense Initiative — our research effort that envisions the possibility of defensive systems which could ultimately protect all nation[s] against the danger of nuclear war. This discussion produced a very direct exchange of views.

Mr. Gorbachev insisted that we might use a strategic defense system to put offensive weapons into space and establish nuclear superiority.

I made it clear that SDI has nothing to do with offensive weapons; that, instead, we are investigating non-nuclear defensive systems that would only threaten offensive missiles, not people. If our research succeeds, it will bring much closer the safer, more stable world we seek. Nations could defend themselves against missile attack, and mankind, at long last, escape the prison of mutual terror. And this is my dream.

Nuclear Arms Reduction - 2

So I welcomed the chance to tell Mr. Gorbachev that we are a nation that defends, rather than attacks, that our alliances are defensive, not offensive. We don't seek nuclear superiority. We do not seek a first strike advantage over the Soviet Union.

Indeed, one of my fundamental arms control objectives is to get rid of first-strike weapons altogether. And this is why — this is why we've proposed a 50 percent reduction in the most threatening nuclear weapons, especially those that could carry out a first strike.

'Strategic Defense Initiative' - 2

I went further in expressing our peaceful intentions. I described our proposal in the Geneva negotiations for a reciprocal program of open laboratories and strategic defense research. We're offering to permit Soviet experts to see first-hand that SDI does not involve offensive weapons. American scientists would be allowed to visit comparable facilities of the Soviet strategic defensive program, which, in fact, has involved much more than research for many years.

Finally, I reassured Mr. Gorbachev on another point. I promised that if our research reveals that a defense against nuclear missiles is possible, we would sit down with our allies and the Soviet Union to see how together we could replace all strategic ballistic missiles with such a defense, which threatens no one.

Regional Peace Process

We discussed threats to the peace in several regions of the world. I explained my proposals for a peace process to stop the wars in Afghanistan, Nicaragua, Ethiopia, Angola, and Cambodia — those places where insurgencies that speak for the people are pitted against regimes which obviously do not represent the will or the approval of the people. I tried to be very clear about where our sympathies lie; I believe I succeeded.

Human Rights

We discussed human rights. We Americans believe that history teaches no clearer lesson than this: Those countries which respect the rights of their own people tend, inevitably, to respect the rights of their neighbors. Human rights, therefore, is not an abstract moral issue — it is a peace issue.

Increased Cultural Exchanges

Finally, we discussed the barriers to communication between our societies, and I elaborated on my proposals for real people-to-people contacts on a wide scale.

Americans should know the people of the Soviet Union — their hopes and fears and the facts of their lives. And citizens of the Soviet Union need to know of America's deep desire for peace and our unwavering attachment to freedom.

As you can see, our talks were wide-ranging. And let me at this point tell you what we agreed upon and what we didn't.

We remain far apart on a number of issues, as had to be expected. However, we reached agreement on a number of matters, and, as I mentioned, we agreed to continue meeting and this is important and very good. There's always room for movement, action, and progress when people are talking to each other instead of talking about each other.

We've concluded a new agreement designed to bring the best of America's artists and academics to the Soviet Union. The exhibits that will be included in this exchange are one of the most effective ways for the average Soviet citizen to learn about our way of life. This agreement will also expand the opportunities for Americans to experience the Soviet people's rich cultural heritage — because their artists and academics will be coming here.

We've also decided to go forward with a number of people-to-people initiatives that will go beyond greater contact not only between the political leaders of our two countries, but our respective students, teachers and others as well. We have emphasized youth exchanges. And this will help break down stereotypes, build friendships and, frankly, provide an alternative to propaganda.

Other Agreements

We've agreed to establish a new Soviet Consulate in New York and a new American Consulate in Kiev. This will bring a permanent U.S. presence to the Ukraine for the first time in decades.

And we have also, together with the government of Japan, concluded a Pacific Air Safety Agreement with the Soviet Union. This is designed to set up cooperative measures to improve civil air safety in that region of the Pacific. What happened before must never be allowed to happen there again.

And as a potential way of dealing with the energy needs of the world of the future, we have also advocated international cooperation to explore the feasibility of developing fusion energy.

All of these steps are part of a long-term effort to build a more stable relationship with the Soviet Union. No one ever said it could be easy. But we've come a long way.

Soviet Expansionism

As for Soviet expansionism in a number of regions of the world — while there is little chance of immediate change, we will continue to support the heroic efforts of those who fight for freedom. But we have also agreed to continue — and to intensify — our meetings with the Soviets on this and other regional conflicts and to work toward political solutions.

A Worthwhile Meeting

We know the limits as well as the promise of summit meetings. This is, after all, the 11th summit of the postwar era — and still the differences endure. But we believe continued meetings between the leaders of the United States and the Soviet Union can help bridge those differences.

The fact is, every new day begins with possibilities; it's up to us to fill it with the things that move us toward progress and peace. Hope, therefore, is a realistic attitude — and despair an uninteresting little vice.

And so: Was our journey worthwhile?

Well, thirty years ago, when Ike — President Eisenhower — had just returned from a summit in Geneva, he said, "... the wide gulf that separates so far East and West is wide and deep." Well, today, three decades later, that is still true.

But, yes, this meeting was worthwhile for both sides. A new realism spawned the summit, the summit itself was a good start; and now our byword must be: Steady as we go.

Hopes for the Future

I am, as you are, impatient for results. But good will and good hopes do not always yield lasting results. And quick fixes don't fix big problems.

Just as we must avoid illusions on our side, so we must dispel them on the Soviet side. I have made it clear to Mr. Gorbachev that we must reduce the mistrust and suspicions between us if we are to do such things as reduce arms, and this will take deeds, not words alone. I believe he is in agreement.

Where do we go from here? Well, our desire for improved relations is strong. We're ready and eager for step-by-step progress. We know that peace is not just the absence of war. We don't want a phony peace or a frail peace; we didn't go in pursuit of some kind of illusory détente. We can't be satisfied with cosmetic improvements that won't stand the test of time. We want real peace.

As I flew back this evening, I had many thoughts. In just a few days families across America will gather to celebrate Thanksgiving. And again, as our forefathers who voyaged to America, we traveled to Geneva with peace as our goal and freedom as our guide. For there can be no greater good than the quest for peace and no finer purpose than the preservation of freedom.

It is 350 years since the first Thanksgiving, when Pilgrims and Indians huddled together on the edge of an unknown continent. And now here we are gathered together on the edge of an unknown future — but, like our forefathers, really not so much afraid, but full of hope, and trusting in God, as ever.

Thank you for allowing me to talk to you this evening and God bless you all. ∎

Reagan's Tax Bill Letter

Following is the New York Times *text of the letter President Reagan sent to House Republicans Dec. 17 asking them to support the tax-overhaul bill (HR 3838).*

In my recent letter on tax reform, I strongly urged all members "to vote for tax reform — the Republican alternative or, should it not prevail, the Ways and Means bill." I stated then what seems to me to be the straightforward case: A vote against moving a House bill forward would doom our efforts to achieve real tax reform for the American people. We must not allow that to happen.

I understand the concern that many members have with a strategy that depends upon improvement of the House bill in the Senate. From my perspective, it would be totally inappropriate to give up at this stage — to fail to seek improvement in the Senate. But in order to help reduce concern about this approach, let me state my position with respect to the type of bill I might ultimately accept.

Like you, I believe that increasing incentives for economic growth and jobs, and greater fairness for individual Americans and their families, are fundamental objectives toward which our tax reform deliberations must be oriented. I will veto any tax bill that fails to meet these objectives.

In order that there can be no misunderstanding concerning my views on any ultimate bill, let me say that the minimum requirements for a tax reform bill I am willing to sign are as follows: a full $2,000 personal exemption for both itemizers and non-itemizers, at least for those individuals in the lower and middle income tax brackets; basic tax incentives for American industries, including those which depend upon heavy capital investment in equipment and machinery; effective dates which erase doubt and apprehension in the minds of those who must begin now to plan for 1986 investments; a minimum tax which allows no individual or business to escape paying a fair share of the overall tax burden; a rate structure with a maximum rate no higher than in my proposal; and tax brackets that are fully consistent with our desire to reduce taxes for middle-income working Americans.

These requirements can be met, and should be met as the legislative process moves forward. Getting a bill out of the House is now the essential step we must take in order to keep the process alive, and preserve the chance to achieve true tax reform. I ask for your support.

Sincerely,

RONALD REAGAN ∎

Textile Quotas Veto

Following is the White House text of President Reagan's Dec. 17 message accompanying his veto of HR 1562, the bill to limit textile, apparel and shoe imports and to call for negotiations leading to voluntary reductions in world copper production. It was Reagan's fourth veto of a public bill during the 99th Congress.

TO THE HOUSE OF REPRESENTATIVES:

I am returning herewith without my approval HR 1562. It is my firm conviction that the economic and human costs of such a bill run far too high — costs in foreign retaliation against U.S. exports, loss of American jobs, losses to American businesses, and damage to the world trading system upon which our prosperity depends.

At the same time, I am well aware of the difficulties of the apparel, textile, copper, and shoe industries, and deeply sympathetic about the job layoffs and plant closings that have affected many workers in these industries.

As I stated in my trade speech in September, I will not stand by and watch American businesses fail because of unfair trading practices abroad. I will not stand by and watch American workers lose their jobs because other nations do not play by the rules.

I am directing Secretary of the Treasury Baker, as Chairman Pro Tempore of the Economic Policy Council, to investigate the import levels of textiles and apparel to determine if these imports have exceeded those limits agreed upon in international negotiations. I have directed that he report back to me within 60 days and recommend changes in existing administrative and enforcement procedures, if necessary, so that corrective action is taken.

Also, I am directing the Office of the United States Trade Representative to most aggressively renegotiate the Multi-Fiber Arrangement (MFA) on terms no less favorable than present. Our trading partners must be put on notice that we will not allow unfair trading practices to continue. I am further directing Ambassador Yeutter to closely consult with the U.S. textile and apparel industry to ensure that their views will be fully represented during the negotiations.

Finally, I have directed Secretary of Labor Brock to work with the Congress to provide an additional $100 million increase in funds appropriated to help retrain and relocate displaced workers under the Job Training Partnership Act. The Job Training Partnership Act is a more effective way than Trade Adjustment Assistance for the Secretary of Labor to target those American workers and geographic areas most affected. This is the way we can best help dislocated workers — and without pitting one American worker against another.

Free and fair trade policies have helped create nearly 9 million new jobs in the last 3 years and given us the highest rate of employment in our Nation's history. Still, for some workers in troubled industries, these are difficult times. The personal distress of those who lose their jobs is very real. None of us wants to see American workers lose their jobs or American businesses suffer. I pledge to you to do everything possible to combat unfair trade practices. But in so doing we must take wise and positive steps to redress wrongs. To do otherwise would be counterproductive.

Unfortunately, HR 1562 would invite immediate retaliation against our exports resulting in a loss of American jobs in other areas. Because this bill is so sweeping in its provisions, we could expect that retaliation to be extensive. The United States exported tens of billions of dollars' worth of goods to the countries which would be most affected by this measure, including approximately a third of our farm exports. Workers in agriculture, aerospace, high-tech electronics, chemicals, and pharmaceuticals would be the first to feel the retaliatory backlash, but the damaging effects would soon be felt by every American in the form of lost jobs, higher prices, and shrinking economic growth.

We are pursuing an aggressive trade policy, based on the knowledge that American know-how is still number one and that American industry thrives on fair competition. Where U.S. industries are hurt by unfair practices, we will continue to take vigorous actions. Where foreign trade barriers lock out U.S. exports, we will do everything in our power to knock those barriers down. Our philosophy will always be to increase trade, increase economic growth, and increase jobs. We want to open markets abroad, not close them at home. In a fair and open world market, we know that America can out-produce and out-compete anybody.

RONALD REAGAN

The White House,
December 17, 1985 ∎

Reagan's Remarks on Gramm-Rudman-Hollings

Following is the White House text of President Reagan's remarks on the Gramm-Rudman-Hollings balanced-budget amendment, as delivered Dec. 18 at a White House ceremony for the legislation to which the amendment was attached, H J Res 372, the bill raising the public debt limit.

Good morning and welcome to the White House. There's good news for the American people in the paper this morning. Tax reform is alive and well and kicking. What's that I heard about lame duckery?

Congratulations are due to all of those in the House who worked so long and hard to bring us to this point. And we can now look forward to a lot more hard work, but today, America can feel almost a true tax reform is within its grasp.

We must not disappoint the American people. We must move forward from here with all deliberate speed to pass a tax reform bill that will spur economic growth, create jobs and give America's families the long overdue tax relief that they deserve.

In this last week, we have begun to put into place a solid pro-growth framework of lowered marginal tax rates and spending restraints. And together, they promise to make our economy fit and trim and competitive for the future.

Now, Phil, Warren and Fritz, you who have given your names to [the] Gramm-Rudman-Hollings bill, also deserve our congratulations. From now on when the public hears the names, Gramm, Rudman or Hollings, they'll think deficit reduction. And Connie Mack and Dick Cheney, who followed quite quickly in the House, you deserve our thanks.

All of you here today who have given so much time and hard work to this bill have earned your country's thanks. The government gargantua has been gorging on taxpayer dollars for too long. We plan to get it slimmed down into shape by the end of the decade.

For years we've been warning that the growing deficit reflects a dangerous increase in the size of the government. Polls, too, demonstrate public concern. Now, Gramm-Rudman-Hollings locks in a long-term commitment to lowering and eventually eliminating deficits. It's my hope that history will record last week as the time when the relentless expansion of the federal government was finally halted and put into reverse.

But we can't afford to be complacent. It's going to take a lot more hard work and many more difficult decisions if we are to live up to the promise of this moment. The law now puts a time limit on governmental overspending. It mandates a balanced budget.

But while Gramm-Rudman-Hollings gives us some guidelines and directions, it doesn't take us to our destination. It's essential as we embark on this journey toward a balanced budget that we keep a clear sense of our priorities and hold our first purposes firmly in mind. We must not allow Gramm-Rudman-Hollings to become an excuse to avoid the tough decisions entailed in cutting back on runaway domestic spending.

We will not only be held responsible for cutting the deficit; ultimately, we will be judged on how we reduce the deficit. Will we, for instance, continue to fund welfare for the rich? Will we continue to insist that low-income taxpayers subsidize programs for people who make 10 or 11 times as much money as they do? Will we fund wasteful pork-barrel programs at the expense of essential defense requirements? Will we stifle economic growth and kill off our new-found prosperity with a tax increase?

Gramm-Rudman-Hollings won't make our decisions any easier, but it will make our choices crystal-clear for all to see. Last year, for instance, we said the United States government had no business running a railroad — and running it, by the way, hundreds of millions of dollars in the red. We proposed eliminating federal subsidies to Amtrak, but intense lobbying pressure kept money flowing. Next time around, no program will get a free ride. We can abide by the letter of the Gramm-Rudman-Hollings law and still violate its spirit.

If we try to accomplish deficit reduction by tax increases or through just deep cuts in defense that endanger our national security, we will have failed in our paramount duty to the American people, the duty of good and responsible government.

Raising taxes in order to reduce the deficit is robbing Peter to pay Paul, and Peter went bankrupt a long time ago. Whether excess spending is financed through taxes or borrowing, it puts a heavy burden on the private economy and slows the engines of prosperity. In fact, by slowing economic growth, a tax increase might well make the deficit bigger, not smaller. And I want you all to know that when I sat at my desk in the Oval Office and signed Gramm-Rudman-Hollings, I kept my veto pen ready in the top drawer. It's sitting there right now waiting for any tax increase that might come my way.

We should also remember that when we passed Gramm-Rudman-Hollings, we didn't absolve ourselves of our first responsibility as the elected representatives of this country to provide for the national defense. The last thing we want to do is return our country to the weakened, vulnerable state in which we found it in 1980.

It was a stronger and reinvigorated national defense that allowed the United States to move swiftly and confidently, liberating Grenada from communism and bringing the terrorist murderers of Leon Klinghoffer to justice. It was this renewed sense of purpose and commitment that gave confidence to friends and allies around the globe, and particularly to those struggling for freedom against Soviet-imposed regimes.

And it was our determination to proceed with the modernization of our nuclear deterrent that, through Geneva, has improved the prospects for real arms reduction. Maintaining a strong national defense is not only our obligation to America, it's our duty as the last best hope of mankind to the cause of human freedom.

I feel confident that if Congress abides by its already established agreement for real growth in defense, we can meet our national security requirements. We will meet the Gramm-Rudman-Hollings targets in the budgets that we submit to Congress and we'll do it the right way — by cutting or eliminating wasteful and unnecessary programs.

I hope that each of us will pledge to follow through in the spirit of Gramm-Rudman-Hollings to see that government does only that which it must do and no more. And I hope that we'll all work together to secure the deficit-cutting gains that we make by adopting a balanced-budget amendment to the Constitution.

So, as I said, the real work of controlling federal spending has only just begun. We've taken a dramatic step forward; let's keep the momentum going.

Thank you all for coming down here and God bless you all. ■

Wildlife Refuge Veto

Following is the White House text of President Reagan's Jan. 14 message accompanying his veto of HR 1404, the bill to establish the Eastern Shore of Virginia National Wildlife Refuge and the National Fish and Wildlife Service Training Center at Cape Charles, Va. It was his fifth veto of a public bill during the 99th Congress.

TO THE HOUSE OF REPRESENTATIVES:

Since the adjournment of the Congress has prevented my return of HR 1404 within the meaning of Article I, section 7, clause 2 of the Constitution, my withholding of approval from the bill precludes its becoming law. Notwithstanding what I believe to be my constitutional power regarding the use of the "pocket veto" during an adjournment of Congress, however, I am sending HR 1404 to the House of Representatives with my objections, consistent with the Court of Appeals decision in *Barnes v. Kline*, 759 F.2d 21 (D.C. Cir. 1985), *cert. pending sub. nom. Burke v. Barnes*, No. 85-781.

I have no objection to statutory recognition of the refuge at Cape Charles. This is a significant resting and wintering area for migratory birds along the Atlantic Flyway and an important habitat for the bald eagle and peregrine falcon, two endangered species. I am pleased to note that, in recognition of the area's importance, the U.S. Fish and Wildlife Service has already administratively acquired land at this site and established the Eastern Shore of Virginia National Wildlife Refuge. The Service will continue to operate and maintain the existing refuge and intends to expand it as fiscal conditions permit.

Unfortunately, HR 1404 does not simply provide protection for this valuable habitat. It would also require the Secretary of the Interior to develop a training center at the refuge for use by the Service, other Federal and State agencies, educational institutions, and private organizations and individuals.

In this time of fiscal constraint, the Federal government must limit its expenditures to matters of significant national concern. The provisions of HR 1404 requiring establishment of a training facility do not meet this test. The Service has fully adequate training facilities already in place, including a facility at Leetown, West Virginia, as well as the use of various private sector facilities. In addition, the Service is actively supporting the effort to clean up the Chesapeake Bay by designating an existing Service field station in Annapolis, Maryland, as its primary center for work on this important program. I believe that it would be more appropriate for State or private entities to fund and develop a training center if they consider it essential.

For these reasons, I must return HR 1404 without my approval.

RONALD REAGAN

The White House,
January 14, 1986.

Transfer of Presidential Powers

Following are the White House texts of President Reagan's July 13 letters to the president pro tempore of the Senate, Strom Thurmond, R-S.C., and Speaker of the House Thomas P. O'Neill Jr., D-Mass., in which Reagan temporarily transferred his powers to Vice President George Bush while he underwent surgery for cancer. *(Story, p. 26)*

Dear Mr. President (Mr. Speaker):

I am about to undergo surgery during which time I will be briefly and temporarily incapable of discharging the Constitutional powers and duties of the Office of the President of the United States.

After consultations with my Counsel and the Attorney General, I am mindful of the provisions of Section 3 of the 25th Amendment to the Constitution and of the uncertainties of its application to such brief and temporary periods of incapacity. I do not believe that the drafters of this Amendment intended its application to situations such as the instant one.

Nevertheless, consistent with my longstanding arrangement with Vice President George Bush, and not intending to set a precedent binding anyone privileged to hold this Office in the future, I have determined and it is my intention and direction that Vice President George Bush shall discharge those powers and duties in my stead commencing with the administration of anesthesia to me in this instance.

I shall advise you and the Vice President when I determine that I am able to resume the discharge of the Constitutional powers and duties of this Office.

May God bless this Nation and us all.

Sincerely,

Ronald Reagan

Dear Mr. President (Mr. Speaker):

Following up on my letter to you of this date, please be advised I am able to resume the discharge of the Constitutional powers and duties of the Office of the President of the United States. I have informed the Vice President of my determination and my resumption of those powers and duties.

Sincerely,

Ronald Reagan

Federal Workers' Benefits Veto

Following is the White House text of President Reagan's Jan. 17 message accompanying his veto of HR 3384, the Federal Employees Benefits Improvement Act. It was his sixth veto of a public bill during the 99th Congress.

TO THE HOUSE OF REPRESENTATIVES:

Since the adjournment of the Congress has prevented my return of HR 3384 within the meaning of Article I, section 7, clause 2 of the Constitution, my withholding of approval from the bill precludes its becoming law. Notwithstanding what I believe to be my constitutional power regarding the use of the "pocket veto" during an adjournment of Congress, however, I am sending HR 3384 to the House of Representatives with my objections, consistent with the Court of Appeals decision in *Barnes v. Kline*, 759 F.2d 21 (D.C. Cir. 1985), *cert. pending sub nom. Burke v. Barnes*, No. 85-781.

HR 3384 contains some desirable features, particularly a change in the Federal employees health benefits law recommended by my Administration that would allow anticipated rebates of health insurance premiums to be paid by insurance carriers to Federal annuitants, as is already allowed for active employees. I fully support the proposed rebates, but I could not approve the bill, especially because of one seriously objectionable feature. That feature would eliminate the current 75 percent ceiling on the Government's share of the premiums of any individual health insurance plan of employees and annuitants.

Elimination of the ceiling would add to Government costs and increase the Federal budget deficit at the very time that there is a critical need for fiscal restraint. In order to comply with the deficit reduction mandated by the Gramm-Rudman-Hollings Act, spending for most Government programs will have to be cut. Under those circumstances, this is not the time to raise the Government's personnel costs.

Lifting the 75 percent "cap" by itself would directly increase Government costs for many Federal Employees Health Benefits (FEHB) premiums, since the Government would now pay for costs previously paid by employees. OPM has estimated that this will result in adding almost $90 million to the Federal deficit in fiscal year 1986 and another $173 million in 1987. Over the six-year period 1986 through 1991, the Federal deficit would increase by an estimated $1.2 billion. Some proponents of this provision will claim that it would save money because it will induce employees to shift to low-cost plans. However, any such savings must be weighed against the substantial Federal cost increases projected over the next six years.

Health benefits reform legislation proposed by the Administration included lifting the cap as one of its elements. In our proposal, however, that provision was linked with structural inprovements in the Federal employees health insurance program, including a change in the way the Government's contribution is established, that would reduce the cost of the program for both employees and the Government. HR 3384 ignores that essential linkage by simply lifting the cap without program reform, resulting in an unacceptable shift in costs from employees to the Government. I look forward to working with the Congress early in the session to develop a suitable package of structural reforms that would include lifting the cap.

In addition, the provision requiring direct access to and permitting direct payment for the services of nurses and nurse-midwives, without supervision or referral by another health practitioner, deserves full evaluation, including hearings by the Congress. In its present form, it is a major departure from established health care practice and may be counter to many State laws.

In the meantime, I urge the Congress to act as soon as possible to enact acceptable legislation that will permit Federal annuitants to receive rebates of health insurance premiums without undue further delay.

RONALD REAGAN

The White House,
January 17, 1986.

LOBBY REGISTRATIONS

CQ

October 1984 Registrations

Trade Associations

SOLAR ENERGY INDUSTRIES ASSOCIATION, 1717 Massachusetts Ave. N.W., Washington, D.C. 20036. Filed for self 10/31/84. Legislative interest — "All legislation relating to the promotion of solar energy including Department of Energy Authorization Bills, Department of Energy Appropriations Bills, Tax bills relating to solar investment tax credits, and funding and implementation of the Small Business Energy Loan Program, Solar Energy & Energy Conservation Bank, federal renewable energy procurement and export and loan programs." Lobbyist — Scott Sklar.

Miscellaneous

THE WILDERNESS SOCIETY, 1901 Pennsylvania Ave. N.W., Washington, D.C. 20006. Filed for self 10/22/84. Legislative interest — "Wilderness/Generic legislation affecting national park system." Lobbyist — Clay E. Peters.

November 1984 Registrations

Corporations and Businesses

APPLIED ENERGY SERVICES INC., Arlington, Va. Lobbyist — Chadbourne, Parke, Whiteside & Wolff, 1101 Vermont Ave. N.W., Washington, D.C. 20005. Filed 11/19/84. Legislative interest — "Tax Reform Act of 1984."

BALCOR/AMERICAN EXPRESS INC., 4849 Golf Road, Skokie, Ill. 60077. Filed for self 11/1/84. Legislative interest — "Taxation and Banking Legislation." Lobbyists — Sheila A. Consaul, Dallas E. Gwynn.

THE CLOROX CO., Oakland, Calif. Lobbyist — Buchanan Ingersoll, 1667 K St. N.W., Washington, D.C. 20006. Filed 11/9/84. Legislative interest — "... legislative proposals affecting bleach or related chemicals. This includes HR 746 and S 1080."

DENNY MILLER ASSOCIATES, 203 Maryland Ave. N.E., Washington, D.C. 20002. Filed for self 11/16/84. Legislative interest — Not specified. Lobbyist — Timothy Lovain.

EBASCO SERVICES INC., Two World Trade Center, New York, N.Y. 10048. Filed for self 11/20/84. Legislative interest — "... include tax, energy regulation, international trade, appropriations, authorizations, government operations, environmental & safety legislative matters. ..." Lobbyist — Thomas D. Pestorius, 1025 Connecticut Ave. N.W., Washington, D.C. 20036.

EXPRESS FOODS CO. INC., Louisville, Ky. Lobbyist — Buchanan Ingersoll, 1667 K St. N.W., Washington, D.C. 20006. Filed 11/9/84. Legislative interest — "All legislation affecting the marketing of modified whey products."

GENERAL INSTRUMENT CORP., New York, N.Y. Lobbyist — Buchanan Ingersoll, 1667 K St. N.W., Washington, D.C. 20006. Filed 11/9/84. Legislative interest — Not specified.

GOVERNMENT EMPLOYEES INSURANCE CO., Washington, D.C. Lobbyist — Delaney, Migdail & Young, 1629 K St. N.W., Washington, D.C. 20006. Filed 11/2/84. Legislative interest — "All legislation and statutes pertaining to the taxation of insurance companies. ... All relevant sections of the Internal Revenue Code of 1954."

INTEGRATED RESOURCES INC., New York, N.Y. Lobbyist — Daniel J. Piliero II, 1750 Pennsylvania Ave. N.W., Washington, D.C. 20006. Filed 11/19/84. Legislative interest — "... tax legislation affecting investment and capital formation. Specifically ... the possible effects of the various flat tax and modified flat tax proposals pending before Congress."

KIAWAH ISLAND CO. LTD., P.O. Box 12910, Charleston, S.C. 29412. Filed for self 11/5/84. Legislative interest — "... proposed legislation relating to federal flood insurance and coastal barriers ... draft legislation that may impact on the availability of tax deductions for resort or second homes ... proposed Preservation of Wetlands and Duck Resources Act. ..." Lobbyist — Charles Franklin Daoust.

THE MARYLAND SAVINGS SHARE INSURANCE CORP., Baltimore, Md. Lobbyist — Delaney, Migdail & Young, 1629 K St. N.W., Washington, D.C. 20006. Filed 11/2/84. Legislative interest — "... Internal Revenue Code Section 501(c)."

MICHIGAN KNIFE CO., Big Rapids, Mich. Lobbyist — Kirkpatrick & Lockhart, 1900 M St. N.W., Washington, D.C. 20036. Filed 11/7/84. Legislative interest — "International Trade, particularly legislation to extend duty-free treatment to imports of chipper knife steel."

MOCATTA METALS CORP., New York, N.Y. Lobbyist — Cadwalader, Wickersham & Taft, 1333 New Hampshire Ave. N.W., Washington, D.C. 20036. Filed 11/13/84. Legislative interest — "... regulation of commodity futures exchanges, commodity options and commodity futures trading, including the tax treatment of commodity transactions and the establishment of futures market margins. ..."

NEW YORK LIFE INSURANCE CO., New York, N.Y. Lobbyist — Finley, Kumble, Wagner, Underberg, Manley & Casey, 1120 Connecticut Ave. N.W., Washington, D.C. 20036. Filed 11/26/84. Legislative interest — "HR 4170."

NORTHERN TELECOM INC., 600 Maryland Ave. S.W., Washington, D.C. 20024. Filed for self 11/13/84. Legislative interest — "... legislation impacting on the telecommunications industry, high technology, or management of large corporations." Lobbyist — Norman L. Dobyns.

PROVIDENT MUTUAL LIFE INSURANCE CO., Philadelphia, Pa. Lobbyist — Butler & Binion, 1747 Pennsylvania Ave. N.W., Washington, D.C. 20006. Filed 11/19/84. Legislative interest — "Appropriation for United Education Foundation; H J Res 492."

SIEMENS CORPORATE RESEARCH & SUPPORT INC., Iselin, N.J. Lobbyist — Arnold & Porter, 1200 New Hampshire Ave. N.W., Washington, D.C. 20036. Filed 11/5/84. Legislative interest — "The inclusion of certain language in the legislative history of Semiconductor Chip Protection Act of 1984 (HR 5525 and companion Senate legislation)."

TELEFLEX INC., King of Prussia, Pa. Lobbyist — Butler & Binion, 1747 Pennsylvania Ave. N.W., Washington, D.C. 20006. Filed 11/19/84. Legislative interest — "FY 85 DOD Authorization & Appropriation."

U.S. TRUST CORP., New York, N.Y. Lobbyist — Davis, Polk & Wardwell, 1575 I St. N.W., Washington, D.C. 20005. Filed 11/1/84. Legislative interest — "Matters affecting domestic bank holding companies generally; seeking legislative language to permit U.S. Trust to continue to own its Florida trust company subsidiary."

WINTHROP FINANCIAL, Boston, Mass. Lobbyist — Thomas A. Davis, 499 South Capitol St. S.W., Washington, D.C. 20003. Filed 11/16/84. Legislative interest — "Tax Legislation after Sale-Leasebacks ... Deficit Reduction Act 1984 ... HR 4170 Section 74. ..."

State and Local Governments

HATTIESBURG, CITY OF, Hattiesburg, Miss. Lobbyist

— Cassidy & Associates Inc., 955 L'Enfant Plaza S.W., Washington, D.C. 20024. Filed 11/16/84. Legislative interest — "All legislative and regulatory matters pertaining to economic and industrial development."

WESTERN GOVERNORS' ASSOCIATION, Denver, Colo. Lobbyist — Crowell & Moring, 1100 Connecticut Ave. N.W., Washington, D.C. 20036. Filed 11/14/84. Legislative interest — "... legislation on natural resources and environmental matters."

Trade Associations

AMERICAN PETROLEUM INSTITUTE, 1220 L St. N.W., Washington, D.C. 20005. Filed for self 11/8/84. Legislative interest — Not specified. Lobbyist — R. G. McBride, Mississippi Petroleum Council, P.O. Box 42, Jackson, Miss. 39205.

FEDERAL JUDGES ASSOCIATION, San Francisco, Calif. Lobbyist — Blum, Nash & Railsback, 1015 18th St. N.W., Washington, D.C. 20036. Filed 11/14/84. (Former U.S. Rep. Tom Railsback, R-Ill., 1967-81, was listed as agent for this client.) Legislative interest — Not specified.

THE FERTILIZER INSTITUTE, 1015 18th St. N.W., Washington, D.C. 20036. Filed for self 11/14/84. Legislative interest — "Agriculture Farm Bill of 1985." Lobbyist — Ford B. West.

GETTY NORTHEAST JOBBERS & DISTRIBUTORS ASSOCIATION, Washington, D.C. Lobbyist — Blum, Nash & Railsback, 1015 18th St. N.W., Washington, D.C. 20036. Filed 11/21/84. Legislative interest — "Legislation relating to petroleum mergers, all antitrust legislation and the FTC authorization act."

GROCERY MANUFACTURERS OF AMERICA INC., Washington, D.C. Lobbyist — Buchanan Ingersoll, 1667 K St. N.W., Washington, D.C. 20006. Filed 11/9/84. Legislative interest — "... proposals affecting grocery manufacturers, including proposals affecting packaging and sealing; product safety and quality or procedures for regulating."

INSTITUTO BRASILEIRO DE SIDERURGIA, Rio de Janeiro, Brazil. Lobbyist — Anderson, Hibey, Nauheim & Blair, 1708 New Hampshire Ave. N.W., Washington, D.C. 20009. Filed 11/13/84. Legislative interest — "Legislation limiting steel imports...."

NATIONAL ASSOCIATION OF INDEPENDENT COLLEGES AND UNIVERSITIES, 122 C St. N.W., Washington, D.C. 20001. Filed for self 11/8/84. Legislative interest — "All legislative matters affecting independent colleges and universities, including but not limited to reauthorization of the Higher Education Act of 1965; and tax, budget, and appropriations legislation." Lobbyist — Peter Rogoff.

NATIONAL AUTOMOBILE DEALERS ASSOCIATION, 8400 Westpark Drive, McLean, Va. 22102. Filed for self 11/21/84. Legislative interest — Not specified. Lobbyist — H. Thomas Greene, 412 First St. S.E., Washington, D.C. 20003.

NATIONAL FOOD PROCESSORS ASSOCIATION, 1401 New York Ave. N.W., Washington, D.C. 20005. Filed for self 11/8/84. Legislative interest — "All legislation directly affecting fruit, vegetable, seafood, and meat processing for human consumption including but not limited to food surveillance, food labeling, fish inspection and development, and the Clean Water Act." Lobbyist — Lawrence T. Graham.

SHEET METAL AIR CONDITIONING CONTRACTORS' NATIONAL ASSOCIATION, 8224 Old Courthouse Road, Tysons Corner, Va. 22180. Filed for self 11/13/84. Legislative interest — "... include issues of interest to construction industry i.e., infrastructure, business taxes, ERISA, small business programs." Lobbyist — Donald C. Clark, Dana S. Thompson.

SOCIETY OF AMERICAN FLORISTS, 1601 Duke St., Alexandria, Va. 22314. Filed for self 11/28/84. Legislative interest — "All legislative matters of interest to floriculture, horticulture, and agriculture, including ... human relations and resources, education, transportation, commerce, industry, labor, etc." Lobbyists — Elaine Acevedo; Raymond W. Roper. Filed for self 11/29/84.

SPECIAL COMMITTEE FOR U.S. EXPORTERS, Washington, D.C. Lobbyist — Thomas A. Davis, 499 South Capitol St. S.W., Washington, D.C. 20003. Filed 11/16/84. Legislative interest — "Tax legislation concerning Foreign Sales Corp.... HR 4170 Section 2163 ... Support modification."

STEEL SERVICE CENTER INSTITUTE, 1919 Pennsylvania Ave. N.W., Washington, D.C. 20006. Filed for self 11/13/84. Legislative interest — Not specified. Lobbyist — Philip M. Ola.

WHEY PRODUCTS INSTITUTE, Chicago, Ill. Lobbyist — Buchanan Ingersoll, 1667 K St. N.W., Washington, D.C. 20006. Filed 11/9/84. Legislative interest — "... legislative proposals affecting whey products production and marketing. Including proposals to amend the Federal Food, Drug and Cosmetic Act, 21 USC section 301, *et seq.*"

Miscellaneous

ALEXANDER GRAHAM BELL ASSOCIATION, Washington, D.C. Lobbyist — Cassidy & Associates Inc., 955 L'Enfant Plaza S.W., Washington, D.C. 20024. Filed 11/16/84. Legislative interest — "All legislation pertaining to special education, bio-medical research related to hearing impairments and neurological disorders."

AMERICAN ASSOCIATION OF RETIRED PERSONS, 1909 K St. N.W., Washington, D.C. 20049. Filed for self 11/9/84. Legislative interest — "... support of: Improved Medicare/Medicaid benefits ... Health care cost containment ... Improved nursing home standards ... Improved housing, transportation of older persons ... Improved tax treatment of older persons.... Lobbyist — Theresa Varner. Filed for self 11/2/84. Legislative interest — "Support of: Federal Deficit Reductions ... Improved Social Security and Medicare/Medicaid Laws ... Health Care Cost Containment ... Tax Reforms ... Improved Nursing Home Standards ... Consumer Protection Legislation ... Employment of Older Workers ... Housing for the Elderly ... Improved Low-Income Assistance Programs." Lobbyist — John C. Rother.

COMMITTEE FOR FARMWORKER PROGRAMS, Washington, D.C. Lobbyist — MMB Associates Inc., 122 C St. N.W., Washington, D.C. 20001. Filed 11/9/84. Legislative interest — "Job Training Partnership Act, Community Services Block Grant Act, Labor/HHS Appropriations Act."

COMMON CAUSE, 2030 M St. N.W., Washington, D.C. 20036. Filed for self 11/21/84. Legislative interest — "... open government, campaign finance reform, Federal Election Commission, lobby disclosure, government ethics, Senate confirmation process, extension of the Clean Air Act, court jurisdiction issues, congressional budget process, congressional reform, freedom of information, waste in government, merit selection of Federal judges and U.S. attorneys, regulatory reform, public participation in federal agency proceedings, Legal Services Corporation, civil rights, the Equal Rights Amendment, nuclear arms control, and military spending ... supported legislation to reform congressional campaign financing, including creating a new 100 percent tax credit, PAC limits and response time on independent expenditures (HR 4428) ... opposed production funds for the MX missile and supported a proposal by Senator Nunn to establish nuclear risk reduction centers in Washington and Moscow (S Res 239 and HR 408) ... supported a moratorium on the testing of anti-satellite weapons against objects in space, a $407 million cut in the President's Strategic Defense Initiative program and two amendments to the FY 85 DoD Authorization bill offered in the Senate. One of the amendments called for the U.S. to continue its current policy of not undercutting the terms of existing arms control agreements and the other directed the President to seek immediate resumption of U.S.-Soviet negotiations for a comprehensive test ban treaty ... favored investigation by the House Foreign Affairs Committee of the President's possible violation of the War Powers Resolution of 1973 and opposed covert aid in Nicaragua ... supported legislation intended to limit prepublication review requirements and polygraph examinations imposed on Federal employees (HR 4681) ... worked for stronger lobby disclosure laws, opposed the nomination of Edwin Meese III as Attorney General and urged the Senate Ethics Committee to investigate possible conflict of interest violations by Senator Mark Hatfield ... urged the House Energy and Commerce Committee and Senate Labor

Committee to investigate the process by which the FDA approved aspartame ... supported legislation that would limit the value of tax treatment for luxury cars and maintain a one-year holding period on capital gains ... favored legislation (S 2468) to broaden interpretation of the Civil Rights Act in response to a Supreme Court decision regarding Grove City College, and the 1985 appropriations bill for the Legal Services Corporation." Lobbyist — LeeAnn Pelham.

PERRY COMO DENBY, Box 7000, Texarkana, Texas 75501. Filed for self 11/19/84. Legislative interest — "Criminal justice administration, pardon, parole, commutation, etc."

ENVIRONMENTAL POLICY INSTITUTE, 218 D St. S.E., Washington, D.C. 20003. Filed for self 11/13/84. Legislative interest — "Legislation relating to farm and food policy, rural energy and rural electric cooperatives, energy facility siting, and agricultural land protection." Lobbyist — Jeanne Richards.

FEDERATION FOR AMERICAN AFGHAN ACTION, P.O. Box 881, Centreville, Va. 22020. Filed for self 11/15/84. Legislative interest — "... for S Con Res 74 ... for H Con Res 237 ... for H Res 547 - Condemning Soviet Bombing of Afghanistan."

FEDERATION OF AIDS-RELATED ORGANIZATIONS/AIDS ACTION COUNCIL, 1115½ Independence Ave. S.E., Washington, D.C. 20003. Filed for self 11/6/84. Legislative interest — "... increased funding ... for AIDS-related research ... AIDS-related public health education and training, and/or any other legislative activities that benefit efforts to combat AIDS in the National Institutes of Health, Public Health Service, Centers for Disease Control and other Federal agencies deriving funding from Congress." Lobbyist — Gary B. MacDonald.

NATIONAL COMMITTEE AGAINST REPRESSIVE LEGISLATION, 201 Massachusetts Ave. N.E., Washington, D.C. 20002. Filed for self 11/6/84. Legislative interest — "To prevent passage of legislation which conflicts with First Amendment rights of free speech, press and association ... opposed to HR 48 and HR 218 and some sections of S 1762." Lobbyist — Lisa Collins.

December 1984 Registrations

Corporations & Businesses

BROWN & ROOT INC., P.O. Box 3, Houston, Texas 77001. Filed for self 12/18/84. Legislative interest — "Taxes; natural gas issues; Powerplant and Industrial Fuel Use Act Repeal; OCS revenue sharing; other OCS issues." Lobbyist — C. Kyle Simpson.

FREEPORT-McMoRAN INC., New York, N.Y. Lobbyist — James D. Massie, 1730 Rhode Island Ave. N.W., Washington, D.C. 20036. Filed 12/17/84. Legislative interest — "For amendments to the Clean Air Act to exclude fugitive dust from PSD increments; For legislation to correct inequities in the NGPA; For legislation to reauthorize existing Superfund law; Against legislation to reduce percentage depletion for hard rock mining or for independent oil and gas producers; against legislation to eliminate expensing of intangible drilling costs and against legislation to limit the deductibility of interest expenses for investment borrowing; Against any provisions in legislation to violate the sanctity of contracts for the purchase of natural gas or sale of natural gas ... Interest in any legislation to amend RCRA, Clean Water Act, Safe Drinking Water Act, the Clean Air Act, and Superfund."

GENERAL DYNAMICS CORP., 1745 Jefferson Davis Highway, Arlington, Va. 22202. Filed for self 12/3/84. Legislative interest — "Defense and NASA authorization and appropriation, foreign military sales, taxes, foreign aid authorization and appropriation." Lobbyists — Karl F. Lauenstein, W.H.L. Mullins, John J. Stirk, Robert L. Whitmire.

GLOBETROTTERS ENGINEERING CORP., Chicago, Ill. Lobbyist — Gold and Liebengood Inc., 1050 Connecticut Ave. N.W., Washington, D.C. 20036. Filed 12/3/84. Legislative interest — Not specified.

GOLD AND LIEBENGOOD INC., 1050 Connecticut Ave. N.W., Washington, D.C. 20036. Filed for self 12/3/84. Legislative interest — Not specified. Lobbyists — Janice L. Burch, Peter B. Slone.

HOFFMANN-LA ROCHE INC., 340 Kingsland St., Nutley, N.J. 07110. Filed for self 12/5/84. Legislative interest — "... matters affecting health, health education, research, welfare, drug abuse education and rehabilitation, environmental pollution, consumer protection and other legislative activity pertaining to health care delivery systems, patent legislation and economics in general." Lobbyist — Gerald D. Lore, 1050 Connecticut Ave. N.W., Washington, D.C. 20036.

INTERNATIONAL LEISURE HOSTS LTD., Phoenix, Ariz. Lobbyist — Van Ness, Feldman, Sutcliffe, Curtis & Levenberg, 1050 Thomas Jefferson St. N.W., Washington, D.C. 20007. Filed 12/6/84. Legislative interest — "For a Congressional appropriation or reprogramming of funds to purchase concessioner owned assets at Flagg Ranch, part of the John D. Rockefeller, Jr. Memorial Parkway."

KEMPER FINANCIAL SERVICES INC., 120 South LaSalle St., Chicago, Ill. 60603. Filed for self 12/3/84. Legislative interest — "... including but not limited to financial services integration or deregulation." Lobbyist — Paul R. Knapp.

LANGASCO ENERGY CORP., Pittsburgh, Pa. Lobbyist — Buchanan Ingersoll, 1667 K St. N.W., Washington, D.C. 20006. Filed 12/26/84. Legislative interest — "General in nature relating to federal tax legislation."

THE LTV CORP., P.O. Box 225003, Dallas, Texas 75265. Filed for self 12/6/84. Legislative interest — "Legislation affecting employer's subsidiary steel company and related interest ... including, but not limited to, tax, environment, labor, budget, energy, trade, critical materials, Buy American, antitrust, and election campaign measures." Lobbyist — Harold V. Kelly, 1101 15th St. N.W., Washington, D.C. 20005.

MUTUAL OF OMAHA, Omaha, Neb. Lobbyist — Gray and Co., 3255 Grace St. N.W., Washington, D.C. 20007. Filed 12/10/84. Legislative interest — "Including but not limited to tax legislation."

PENNSYLVANIA SHIPBUILDING CO., P.O. Box 498, Chester, Pa. 19016. Filed for self 12/21/84. Legislative interest — "Department of Defense Authorizations and Appropriations Bills; Maritime Legislation." Lobbyist — Tim Colton.

STROH BREWERY CO., Detroit, Mich. Lobbyist — Gray and Co., 3255 Grace St. N.W., Washington, D.C. 20007. Filed 12/10/84. Legislative interest — "Including but not limited to the Malt Beverage Interbrand Competition Act and other legislation affecting the beer industry."

Labor Organizations

AMERICAN FEDERATION OF TEACHERS, 555 New Jersey Ave. N.W., Washington, D.C. 20001. Filed for self 12/7/84. Legislative interest — Not specified. Lobbyist — Elaine Shocas.

State and Local Governments

SOUTH CAROLINA STATE BUDGET AND CONTROL BOARD, Columbia, S.C. Lobbyist — Adams, Quackenbush, Herring & Stuart, P.O. Box 394, Columbia, S.C. 29202. Filed 12/10/84. Legislative interest — "... secure exemption of 'Mills-Babcock Complex' from new Federal Tax Package."

Trade Associations

AMERICAN ACADEMY OF FAMILY PHYSICIANS, 1740 W. 92nd St., Kansas City, Mo. 64114. Filed for self 12/19/84. Legislative interest — "... health related legislation. Particular interest in Social Security Act, especially Title XVIII and XIX, the Federal Food, Drug and Cosmetic Act and the Public Health Service Act. Legislation currently being considered by Congress, including HHS Appropriations, Medicare and Medicaid reform, legislation amending the Food, Drug and Cosmetic Act, cost containment. Legislation extending the Health Professions Educational Assistance Act." Lobbyist — Lois Holwerda Hoyt, 600 Maryland Ave. S.W., Washington, D.C. 20024.

ASSOCIATION OF PRIVATE PENSION AND WELFARE PLANS, 1201 Pennsylvania Ave. N.W., Washington, D.C. 20004. Filed for self 12/19/84. Legislative interest — "Fair Insurance Practice Act; Pension Equity Acts; Single Employer Termination; Tax Reform Act of 1984 . . . HR 100; S 372; S 19, S 888; HR 3525; HR 3930: S 1227; HR 4170. . . ." Lobbyist — Stuart J. Brahs.

COALITION FOR THE ADVANCEMENT OF INDUSTRIAL TECHNOLOGY, Washington, D.C. Lobbyist — Preston, Thorgrimson, Ellis & Holman, 1735 New York Ave. N.W., Washington, D.C. 20006. Filed 12/14/84. Legislative interest — "Legislation to be introduced on January 3, 1985. Predecessor bills were S 2165, 98th Congress."

GREATER WASHINGTON/MARYLAND SERVICE STATION ASSOCIATION, 9200 Edmonston Rd., Greenbelt, Md. 20770. Filed for self 12/31/84. Legislative interest — ". . . legislation dealing with taxes, small business, regulation of small business, environmental issues, and other concerns as required . . . Product Liability - S 44 (98th Cong.); FLSA Amendment - S 2009 (98th Cong.); RCRA, CERCLA - PL 98-369; Clean Air Act Amendments." Lobbyists — Roy E. Littlefield, Michael Francis DeSanto.

GROCERY MANUFACTURERS OF AMERICA INC., 1010 Wisconsin Ave. N.W., Washington, D.C. 20007. Filed for self 12/18/84. Legislative interest — Not specified. Lobbyist — Kurt Charles McMillan.

NATIONAL ASSOCIATION OF INDEPENDENT INSURERS, Des Plains, Ill. Lobbyist — Delaney, Migdail & Young, 1629 K St. N.W., Washington, D.C. 20006. Filed 12/3/84. Legislative interest — "All legislation and statutes pertaining to the taxation of insurance companies . . . all relevant sections of the Internal Revenue Code of 1954. . . ."

NATIONAL ASSOCIATION OF SOCIAL WORKERS, 7981 Eastern Ave., Silver Spring, Md. 20910. Filed for self 12/21/84. Legislative interest — Not specified. Lobbyists — Alice I. Cohan, Susan Hoechstetter.

NATIONAL AUTOMOBILE DEALERS ASSOCIATION, 8400 Westpark Drive, McLean, Va. 22102. Filed for self 12/10/84. Legislative interest — Not specified. Lobbyist — Charles E. Ing, 412 First St. S.E., Washington, D.C. 20003.

Miscellaneous

COMMITTEE FOR HUMANE LEGISLATION, 400 First St. N.W., Washington, D.C. 20001. Filed for self 12/3/84. Legislative interest — "Animal Welfare Legislation." Lobbyist — Holly Elisabeth Hazard.

FRIENDS OF ANIMALS INC., 400 First St. N.W., Washington, D.C. 20001. Filed for self 12/3/84. Legislative interest — "Animal Welfare Legislation." Lobbyist — Holly Elisabeth Hazard.

LEE F. HOLDMANN, 7315 Wisconsin Ave., Bethesda, Md. 20814. Filed for self 12/3/84. Legislative interest — "Taxation - November, 1984, Treasury Department Report to the President on Tax Reform for fairness, simplicity and economic growth; TRA - 1984. . . ."

INTERNATIONAL FUND FOR ANIMAL WELFARE, Yarmouth Port, Mass. Lobbyist — Nancy Wallace Inc., 6404 Camrose Terrace, Bethesda, Md. 20817. Filed 12/20/84. Legislative interest — ". . . international environment, ocean conservation . . . HR 5032 . . . North Pacific Fur Seal Treaty . . . for fish labeling; against NPFS Treaty."

THE STATUE OF LIBERTY-ELLIS ISLAND FOUNDATION INC., New York, N.Y. Lobbyist — Debevoise & Plimpton, 875 Third Ave., New York, N.Y. 10022. Filed 12/18/84. Legislative interest — "Amend 36 U.S.C. section 1 *et seq.* to provide a Federal Charter for The Statue of Liberty-Ellis Island Foundation Inc. . . ."

January 1985 Registrations

Corporations and Businesses

THE ALGOMA STEEL CORP. LTD., 503 Queen St. East, Sault Ste. Marie, Ontario, Canada P6A 5P2. Filed for self 1/24/85. Legislative interest — ". . . Trade and Tariff Act of 1984; . . . HR 3398; . . . PL 573; . . . In opposition to any legislation which restricts U.S. imports of steel mill products from Canada." Lobbyist — William J. Kissick.

ALLNET COMMUNICATIONS SERVICES INC., Chicago, Ill. Lobbyist — Steven F. Stockmeyer, 1120 20th St. N.W., Washington, D.C. 20036. Filed 1/15/85. Legislative interest — ". . . legislation affecting telecommunications particularly as it relates to long distance telephone service."

ALLSTATE INSURANCE CO., Northbrook, Ill. Lobbyist — Camp, Carmouche, Barsh, Hunter, Gray, Hoffman & Gill, 2550 M St. N.W., Washington, D.C. 20037. Filed 1/15/85. Legislative interest — ". . . taxation of insurance companies and their products."

ALPHA 21 CORP., Midland, Texas. Lobbyist — Kuykendall Co., 517 3rd St. S.E., Washington, D.C. 20003. Filed 1/11/85. (Former U.S. Rep. Dan H. Kuykendall, R-Tenn., 1967-75, was listed as agent for this client.) Legislative interest — Not specified.

AMERICAN CYANAMID CO., One Cyanamid Plaza, Wayne, N.J. 07470. Filed for self 1/31/85. Legislative interest — ". . . agriculture-related legislation, i.e., bills relating to antibiotics in animal feed, animal welfare, FIFRA, patent term, farm policy, biotechnology, appropriations, transportation, FOI, imports, cargo preference." Lobbyist — Debra J. Vanderbeek, 1575 I St. N.W., Washington, D.C. 20005.

AMERICAN HOSPITAL SUPPLY CORP., One American Plaza, Evanston, Ill. 60201. Filed for self 1/24/85. Legislative interest — ". . . tax, trade, transportation, antitrust, health, benefits, product liability. . . ." Lobbyist — John L. Noble.

ATLANTIC RICHFIELD CO., 515 S. Flower St., Los Angeles, Calif. 90071. Filed for self 1/10/85. Legislative interest — Not specified. Lobbyist — James E. Ford, 1333 New Hampshire Ave. N.W., Washington, D.C. 20036.

BAITY & JOSEPH, Los Angeles, Calif. Lobbyist — James C. Corman, 1420 16th St. N.W., Washington, D.C. 20036. Filed 1/11/85. (Former U.S. representative, D-Calif., 1961-81.) Legislative interest — ". . . tax consequences of tort recoveries and structured settlements."

BALCOR/AMERICAN EXPRESS INC., Skokie, Ill. Lobbyist — R. Duffy Wall & Associates Inc., 1317 F St. N.W., Washington, D.C. 20004. Filed 1/22/85. Legislative interest — "Issues relating to real estate taxation."

BARNETT & ALAGIA, 1000 Thomas Jefferson St. N.W., Washington, D.C. 20007. Filed for self 1/15/85. Legislative interest — "All legislation affecting agriculture generally and dairy specifically." Lobbyist — Marion Hopkins.

BEAR, STEARNS AND CO., New York, N.Y. Lobbyist — Chambers Associates Inc., 1411 K St. N.W., Washington, D.C. 20005. Filed 1/10/85. Legislative interest — "Infrastructure finance."

BECHTEL GROUP INC., San Francisco, Calif. Lobbyist — Morgan, Lewis & Bockius, 1800 M St. N.W., Washington, D.C. 20036. Filed 1/24/85. Legislative interest — "Proposed amendments to U.S.C. Title 26, Subtitle A."

BETHLEHEM STEEL CORP., Bethlehem, Pa. 18016. Filed for self 1/9/85. Legislative interest — Not specified. Lobbyist — Catherine L. Imus, 1000 16th St. N.W., Washington, D.C. 20036.

BIXBY RANCH CO., Los Angeles, Calif. Lobbyist — Clair W. Burgener, P.O. Box 8186, Rancho Santa Fe, Calif. 92067. Filed 1/2/85. (Former U.S. representative, R-Calif., 1973-83.) Legislative interest — "Land Use/Condemnation Problem With Bixby Ranch Company Owned Land Adjacent To Vandenberg Air Force Base."

D BORATYN LTD., 3711 Reservoir Rd. N.W., Washington, D.C. 20003. Filed for self 1/21/85. Legislative interest — "Fiscal

Year 1986 budget." Lobbyist — Diane Boratyn.

BREED CORP., Lincoln Park, N.J. Lobbyist — Lesnik & Co., 14701 Gov. Oden Bowie Dr., Upper Marlboro, Md. 20772. Filed 1/12/85. Legislative interest — "Appropriations and other legislation respecting research, demonstration, development, usage of automobile air bag systems and defense programs."

BROYHILL FURNITURE INDUSTRIES, Lenoir, N.C. Lobbyist — Kuykendall Co., 517 3rd St. S.E., Washington, D.C. 20003. Filed 1/11/85. (Former U.S. Rep. Dan H. Kuykendall, R-Tenn., 1967-75, was listed as agent for this client.) Legislative interest — Not specified.

BROYHILL MANAGEMENT CORP., Lenoir, N.C. Lobbyist — Kuykendall Co., 517 3rd St. S.E., Washington, D.C. 20003. Filed 1/11/85. (Former U.S. Rep. Dan H. Kuykendall, R-Tenn., 1967-75, was listed as agent for this client.) Legislative interest — Not specified.

BURLINGTON NORTHERN INC., Washington, D.C. Lobbyist — Jones and Winburn, 1101 15th St. N.W., Washington, D.C. 20005. Filed 1/15/85. Legislative interest — "... Tax Issues pertaining to the Railroad Industry."

CHRYSLER CORP., 12000 Chrysler Dr., Highland Park, Mich. 48288. Filed for self 1/14/85. Legislative interest — Not specified. Lobbyist — Robert G. Liberatore, 1100 Connecticut Ave. N.W., Washington, D.C. 20036.

CROWLEY MARITIME CORP., San Francisco, Calif. Lobbyist — Bill Hecht and Associates Inc., 499 South Capitol St. S.W., Washington, D.C. 20003. Filed 1/30/85. Legislative interest — "... to include but not limited to Senate pre-filed amendment #4277, intended to be offered to HR 5505, amending Title XII of the Merchant Marine Act, 1936."

DETROIT & MACKINAC RAILWAY CO., Tawas City, Mich. Lobbyist — RJA Inc., 1250 I St. N.W., Washington, D.C. 20005. Filed 1/9/85. Legislative interest — Not specified.

DICKSTEIN, SHAPIRO & MORIN, Washington, D.C. Lobbyist — William T. Murphy Jr., 1225 19th St. N.W., Washington, D.C. 20036. Filed 1/24/85. Legislative interest — Not specified.

ELECTRONIC DATA SYSTEMS, Washington, D.C. Lobbyist — Gold and Liebengood Inc., 1050 Connecticut Ave. N.W., Washington, D.C. 20036. Filed 1/10/85. Legislative interest — "... health care costs, various tax issues, and telecommunications issues."

ENERGY RESEARCH CORP., Washington, D.C. Lobbyist — Gold and Liebengood Inc., 1050 Connecticut Ave. N.W., Washington, D.C. 20036. Filed 1/10/85. Legislative interest — "... appropriations and budget process as it relates to funding for energy research and development."

EQUITABLE LIFE ASSURANCE SOCIETY OF THE UNITED STATES, New York, N.Y. Lobbyist — Gold and Liebengood Inc., 1050 Connecticut Ave. N.W., Washington, D.C. 20036. Filed 1/10/85. Legislative interest — Not specified.

FARMLAND INDUSTRIES INC., P.O. Box 7305, Kansas City, Mo. 64116. Filed for self 1/7/85. Legislative interest — "... agriculture, international trade, and farmer cooperatives." Lobbyists — David A. Fulton, G. Mark Mayfield.

FEDERATED INVESTORS INC., Pittsburgh, Pa. Lobbyist — Gold and Liebengood Inc., 1050 Connecticut Ave. N.W., Washington, D.C. 20036. Filed 1/10/85. Legislative interest — "... banking and tax matters."

JACK FERGUSON ASSOCIATES INC., Washington, D.C. Lobbyist — John Vogt, 4414 Macomb St. N.W., Washington, D.C. 20016. Filed 1/7/85. Legislative interest — Not specified.

47th STREET PHOTO, New York, N.Y. Lobbyist — Morris J. Amitay, 444 North Capitol St. N.W., Washington, D.C. 20001. Filed 1/9/85. Legislative interest — "... parallel imports."

GTE SERVICE CORP., Stamford, Conn. Lobbyist — Dewey, Ballantine, Bushby, Palmer & Wood, 1775 Pennsylvania Ave. N.W., Washington, D.C. 20006. Filed 1/14/85. Legislative interest — "Miscellaneous tax legislative matters."

GENERAL MOTORS CORP., 3044 W. Grand Blvd., Detroit, Mich. 48202. Filed for self 1/14/85. Legislative interest — "... prospective legislation in the areas of environmental, occupational safety and health and telecommunications law." Lobbyist — Thomas C. Woods, 1660 L St. N.W., Washington, D.C. 20036.

GEODESCO, Northbrook, Ill. Lobbyist — Tendler & Biggins, 1110 Vermont Ave. N.W., Washington, D.C. 20005. Filed 1/14/85. Legislative interest — "... solar and wind energy tax credits."

GEORGIA PACIFIC CORP., Washington, D.C. Lobbyist — Camp, Carmouche, Barsh, Hunter, Gray, Hoffman & Gill, 2550 M St. N.W., Washington, D.C. 20037. Filed 1/15/85. Legislative interest — Not specified.

GLOBAL COMMUNICATIONS, Williamston, Mich. Lobbyist — RJA Inc., 1250 I St. N.W., Washington, D.C. 20005. Filed 1/9/85. Legislative interest — Not specified.

HOUSTON NATURAL GAS, Houston, Texas. Lobbyist — Nancy Whorton George, 499 South Capitol St. S.W., Washington, D.C. 20003. Filed 1/9/85. Legislative interest — "... energy and tax."

HUCHENG INTERNATIONAL CO., Olney, Md. Lobbyist — Larry Meyers, 412 First St. S.E., Washington, D.C. 20003. Filed 1/10/85. Legislative interest — "General Trade Legislation."

IRWIN AND LESSE, 2011 I St. N.W., Washington, D.C. 20006. Filed for self 1/25/85. Legislative interest — "... all legislative actions affecting the telecommunications field." Lobbyist — David A. Irwin.

JMB REALTY CORP., Chicago, Ill. Lobbyist — R. Duffy Wall & Associates Inc., 1317 F St. N.W., Washington, D.C. 20004. Filed 1/21/85. Legislative interest — "Issues relating to real estate taxation."

JOHNSON & JOHNSON, New Brunswick, N.J. Lobbyist — Perito, Duerk & Pinco, 1140 Connecticut Ave. N.W., Washington, D.C. 20036. Filed 1/21/85. Legislative interest — "... general health care policy matters."

SAM KANE PACKING, Corpus Christi, Texas. Lobbyist — Larry Meyers, 412 First St. S.E., Washington, D.C. 20003. Filed 1/10/85. Legislative interest — "... Agriculture."

KMS INDUSTRIES INC., Ann Arbor, Mich. Lobbyist — James D. Hittle, 3137 S. 14th St., Arlington, Va. 22204. Filed 1/16/85. Legislative interest — "... matters relating to inertial fusion."

KUYKENDALL CO., 517 3rd St. S.E., Washington, D.C. Filed for self 1/11/85. Legislative interest — Not specified. Lobbyist — Dan H. Kuykendall. (Former U.S. representative, R-Tenn., 1967-75.)

LAKE VIEW TRUST & SAVINGS BANK, Chicago, Ill. Lobbyist — Hopkins & Sutter, Three First National Plaza, Chicago, Ill. 60602. Filed 1/16/85. Legislative interest — "Increase federal deposit insurance to provide parity between small and large banks."

LEMA PROPERTIES INC., Lubbock, Texas. Lobbyist — Larry Meyers, 412 First St. S.E., Washington, D.C. 20003. Filed 1/10/85. Legislative interest — "General Real Estate."

LIBERTY NATIONAL LIFE INSURANCE CO., Birmingham, Ala. Lobbyist — R. Duffy Wall & Associates Inc., 1317 F St. N.W., Washington, D.C. 20004. Filed 1/22/85. Legislative interest — "Issues relating to life insurance taxation."

MARRIOTT GROUP/MARRIOTT CORP., Washington, D.C. Lobbyist — Gold and Liebengood Inc., 1050 Connecticut Ave. N.W., Washington, D.C. 20036. Filed 1/10/85. Legislative interest — "... tax legislation."

J. W. MARRIOTT INVESTOR GROUP, Bethesda, Md. Lobbyist — Hill, Betts & Nash, 1220 19th St. N.W., Washington, D.C. 20036. Filed 1/25/85. Legislative interest — "... legislative activity in connection with the possible acquisition of Conrail."

J. W. MARRIOTT JR., Washington, D.C. Lobbyist — Palomar Corp., 1716 N St. N.W., Washington, D.C. 20036. Filed 1/4/85. Legislative interest — "... proposals yet to be introduced dealing with the purchase of Consolidated Rail Corporation."

MASSACHUSETTS MUTUAL LIFE INSURANCE CO., Springfield, Mass. Lobbyist — O'Connor and Hannan, 1919 Pennsylvania Ave. N.W., Washington, D.C. 20006. Filed 1/15/85. Legislative interest — "Tax legislative matters. Antitrust, banking regulation and bankruptcy issues."

MCI COMMUNICATIONS CORP., 1133 19th St. N.W., Washington, D.C. 20036. Filed for self 1/11/85. Legislative interest

— "... any bill similar to HR 5158 as introduced in the last Congress. MCI supports the provision of those bills which promote competition in the provision of telecommunications services, but opposes other provisions which would burden the competing carriers." Lobbyist — Gerald J. Kovach.

MORGAN GUARANTY TRUST CO., New York, N.Y. Lobbyist — R. Duffy Wall & Associates Inc., 1317 F St. N.W., Washington, D.C. 20004. Filed 1/22/85. Legislative interest — "Issues relating to general tax legislation." Filed 1/28/85. Legislative interest — "Issues relating to general tax legislation."

MUSE AIR CORP., Dallas, Texas. Lobbyist — Kuykendall Co., 517 3rd St. S.E., Washington, D.C. 20003. Filed 1/11/85. (Former U.S. Rep. Dan H. Kuykendall, R-Tenn., 1967-75, was listed as agent for this client.) Legislative interest — Not specified.

MUTUAL OF AMERICA, New York, N.Y. Lobbyist — Verner, Liipfert, Bernhard, McPherson & Hand, 1660 L St. N.W., Washington, D.C. 20036. Filed 1/15/85. Legislative interest — "To amend Sections 403(b) and 415 of Internal Revenue Code; to expand the benefits available to employees of health and human service organizations to match those available to employees of education institutions and hospitals."

NABISCO BRANDS INC., Nabisco Brands Plaza, 7 Campus Dr., Parsippany, N.J. 07054. Filed for self 1/14/85. Legislative interest — Not specified. Lobbyist — Jeffrey T. Miller.

NEWMONT MINING CORP., 1090 Vermont Ave. N.W., Washington, D.C. 20005. Filed for self 1/25/85. Legislative interest — "... basic minerals industry; specifically, amendments to Clean Air, Clean Water, Safe Drinking Water and Superfund Acts, international trade, and strategic minerals." Lobbyists — Mary Elizabeth Donnelly, James H. Boyd.

NORTH AMERICAN VAN LINES INC., P.O. Box 988, Fort Wayne, Ind. 46801. Filed for self 1/29/85. Legislative interest — Not specified. Lobbyist — George G. Mead.

NORTHBROOK TRUST & SAVINGS BANK, Northbrook, Ill. Lobbyist — Hopkins & Sutter, Three First National Plaza, Chicago, Ill. 60602. Filed 1/16/85. Legislative interest — "Increase federal deposit insurance to provide parity between small and large banks."

NORTHROP CORP., 1000 Wilson Blvd., Arlington, Va. 22209. Filed for self 1/28/85. Legislative interest — "... authorization and appropriations for programs concerning Foreign Military Sales, plus general legislation which impacts on Northrop business with specific interest in tax legislation." Lobbyist — R. B. Wackerle.

NORTHWEST NATIONAL BANK OF CHICAGO, Chicago, Ill. Lobbyist — Hopkins & Sutter, Three First National Plaza, Chicago, Ill. 60602. Filed 1/16/85. Legislative interest — "Increase federal deposit insurance to provide parity between small and large banks."

OCEANTRAWL CORP., New York, N.Y. Lobbyist — Bogle and Gates, One Thomas Circle N.W., Washington, D.C. 20005. Filed 1/7/85. Legislative interest — "Amendments to the Magnuson Fishery Conservation and Management Act."

PACIFIC-SIERRA RESEARCH CORP., Arlington, Va. Lobbyist — Kojm Associates, 2906 S. Grant St., Arlington, Va. 22202. Filed 1/7/85. Legislative interest — Not specified.

PEREGRINE RESOURCES INC., San Antonio, Texas. Lobbyist — Kuykendall Co., 517 3rd St. S.E., Washington, D.C. 20003. Filed 1/11/85. (Former U.S. Rep. Dan H. Kuykendall, R-Tenn., 1967-75, was listed as agent for this client.) Legislative interest — Not specified.

THE PILLSBURY CO., The Pillsbury Center, Minneapolis, Minn. 55402. Filed for self 1/15/85. Legislative interest — "... tax, food safety, environment, international trade, etc." Lobbyist — Raymond R. Krause.

PIONEER BANK & TRUST CO., Chicago, Ill. Lobbyist — Hopkins & Sutter, Three First National Plaza, Chicago, Ill. 60602. Filed 1/16/85. Legislative interest — "Increase federal deposit insurance to provide parity between small and large banks."

PRYOR, CASHMAN, SHERMAN & FLYNN, 410 Park Ave., New York, N.Y. 10022. Filed for self 1/14/85. Legislative interest — "Private bill for the relief of O. Edmund Clubb." Lobbyist — Gideon Cashman. Filed for self 1/14/85. Legislative interest — "Population planning programs." Lobbyist — Gideon Cashman.

SATELLITE BUSINESS SYSTEMS, 8283 Greensboro Dr., McLean, Va. 22102. Filed for self 1/21/85. Legislative interest — "... Federal regulation of voice data, video telecommunications; regulation and administration of satellite launch services, pricing and construction." Lobbyist — Lawrence E. Siegel.

SEIDMAN & SEIDMAN/BDO, 15 Columbus Circle, New York, N.Y. 10023. Filed for self 1/22/85. Legislative interest — "Legislation affecting emerging and midsized businesses, in particular: ... Small Business Consumed Income Tax Act ... HR 6376 and S 3090 ... In favor. ..." Lobbyist — Helio Fred Garcia.

THE SIGNAL COMPANIES, Hampton, N.H. Lobbyist — J. William W. Harsch, 1825 K St. N.W., Washington, D.C. 20006. Filed 1/25/85. Legislative interest — "Supportive of continued funding for the research and development of synthetic fuels."

SMITHKLINE BECKMAN CORP., Washington, D.C. Lobbyist — O'Connor and Hannan, 1919 Pennsylvania Ave. N.W., Washington, D.C. 20006. Filed 1/15/85. Legislative interest — "... tax work concerning Sections 936 and 861 of the Internal Revenue Code."

SOLARGISTICS CORP., Northbrook, Ill. Lobbyist — Tendler & Biggins, 1110 Vermont Ave. N.W., Washington, D.C. 20005. Filed 1/14/85. Legislative interest — "... solar and wind energy tax credits."

SOLV-EX CORP., Albuquerque, N.M. Lobbyist — J. William W. Harsch, 1825 K St. N.W., Washington, D.C. 20006. Filed 1/25/85. Legislative interest — "Supportive of continued funding for the research and development of synthetic fuels."

SUN CO. INC., 100 Matsonford Rd., Radnor, Pa. 19087. Filed for self 1/10/85. Legislative interest — "Legislation affecting the coal industry including, but not limited to, acid rain, leasing and transportation; legislation affecting development of alternative energy resources (especially geothermal and synthetic fuels such as shale oil); general business legislation (especially trucking and real estate)." Lobbyist — Albert B. Knoll, 1800 K St. N.W., Washington, D.C. 20006.

TECHNICUM INTERNATIONAL CORP., Falls Church, Va. Lobbyist — Kojm Associates, 2906 S. Grant St., Arlington, Va. 22202. Filed 1/7/85. Legislative interest — Not specified.

TENNESSEE GAS PIPELINE CO., P.O. Box 2511, Houston, Texas 77001. Filed for self 1/30/85. Legislative interest — "General educational functions concerning natural gas pricing and deregulation, port development relocation assistance and Clean Air Act. HR 511, HR 624, HR 124, S 51, S 52, S 53, and other related bills." Lobbyist — Richard L. Gruber.

WEDTECH CORP., Bronx, N.Y. Lobbyist — RJA Inc., 1250 I St. N.W., Washington, D.C. 20005. Filed 1/9/85. Legislative interest — Not specified.

WESTVACO CORP., 299 Park Ave., New York, N.Y. 10171. Filed for self 1/14/85. Legislative interest — "President's Economic Program (support)." Lobbyist — Ned W. Massee.

International Relations

HAITI, REPUBLIC OF, Port-au-Prince, Haiti. Lobbyist — Shea & Gould, 330 Madison Ave., New York, N.Y. 10017. Filed 1/14/85. Legislative interest — Not specified.

Labor Organizations

BROTHERHOOD OF LOCOMOTIVE ENGINEERS, 8213 S. Richmond St., Chicago, Ill. 60652. Filed for self 1/4/85. Legislative interest — Not specified. Lobbyist — Donald Lindsey.

SHEET METAL WORKERS INTERNATIONAL ASSOCIATION, 1750 New York Ave. N.W., Washington, D.C. 20006. Filed for self 1/8/85. Legislative interest — "All labor legislation HR 5154, HR 5174, S 2851." Lobbyist — Ellen Scott.

State and Local Governments

DADE COUNTY INTERNATIONAL AIRPORT, Miami, Fla. Lobbyist — Cramer, Haber & Lukis, 818 Connecticut

Ave. N.W., Washington, D.C. 20006. (Former U.S. Rep. William C. Cramer, R-Fla., 1955-71, was listed among agents for this client.) Filed 1/14/85; 1/28/85; 1/31/85. Legislative interest — "Any legislation, including budget authorization or appropriation, which may affect federal funding or federal programs for Dade County International Airport."

DILLINGHAM, CITY OF, Dillingham, Alaska. Lobbyist — R/R Associates, 2 Marine Way, Juneau, Alaska 99801. Filed 1/7/85. Legislative interest — "... fish taxes, shared revenues with local government, capital projects to benefit community."

NEW YORK STATE HOUSING FINANCE AGENCY, New York, N.Y. Lobbyist — Liz Robbins Associates, 132 D St. S.E., Washington, D.C. 20003. Filed 1/10/85. Legislative interest — "... Preservation of housing financial incentives."

PUERTO RICO, U.S.A. FOUNDATION, Washington, D.C. Lobbyist — Groom and Nordberg, 1775 Pennsylvania Ave. N.W., Washington, D.C. 20006. Filed 1/7/85. Legislative interest — "Federal legislation affecting Title 26 of U.S.C."

SEATTLE METRO, Seattle, Wash. Lobbyist — Bogle and Gates, One Thomas Circle N.W., Washington, D.C. 20005. Filed 1/28/85. Legislative interest — "Clean Water Act amendments."

Trade Associations

AMERICAN ASSOCIATION OF ADVERTISING AGENCIES, 666 Third Ave., New York, N.Y. 10017. Filed for self 1/11/85. Legislative interest — "... consumer and advertising legislation such as Class Action and Consumer Representation." Lobbyist — Bradley H. Roberts, 1899 L St. N.W., Washington, D.C. 20036.

AMERICAN ASSOCIATION OF HOMES FOR THE AGING, 1050 17th St. N.W., Washington, D.C. 20036. Filed for self 1/10/85. Legislative interest — "Federal health and housing programs serving the elderly and other issues of concern to the aging (for example, Social Security, Medicaid and Medicare legislation and the Older Americans Act)." Lobbyist — Dean Sagar.

AMERICAN ASSOCIATION OF ZOOLOGICAL PARKS AND AQUARIUMS, Washington, D.C. Lobbyist — George Steele Associates, 1110 Vermont Ave. N.W., Washington, D.C. 20005. Filed 1/10/85. Legislative interest — "... zoos and zoological animals."

AMERICAN AUTOMOTIVE LEASING ASSOCIATION, Milwaukee, Wis. Lobbyist — Jones and Winburn, 1101 15th St. N.W., Washington, D.C. 20005. Filed 1/15/85. Legislative interest — "Tax Reform Act of 1984...."

AMERICAN BUS ASSOCIATION, Washington, D.C. Lobbyist — O'Connor and Hannan, 1919 Pennsylvania Ave. N.W., Washington, D.C. 20006. Filed 1/15/85. Legislative interest — "Tax legislation."

AMERICAN COUNCIL OF LIFE INSURANCE INC., 1850 K St. N.W., Washington, D.C. 20006. Filed for self 1/10/85. Legislative interest — "Proposed legislation which affects the life insurance industry; with emphasis on tax and labor legislation affecting employee benefits." Lobbyist — Michael J. Romig.

AMERICAN ELECTRONICS ASSOCIATION, Washington, D.C. Lobbyist — Powell, Goldstein, Frazer & Murphy, 1110 Vermont Ave. N.W., Washington, D.C. 20005. Filed 1/21/85. Legislative interest — "Research and Development Tax Credit Reauthorization - I.R.C. Section 30."

AMERICAN FARM BUREAU FEDERATION, 225 Touhy Ave., Park Ridge, Ill. 60068. Filed for self 1/29/85. Legislative interest — "... Natural resources; agricultural research and extension; pest control." Lobbyist — Mark A. Maslyn, 600 Maryland Ave. S.W., Washington, D.C. 20024. Filed for self 1/29/85. Legislative interest — "... Farm price support and adjustment programs; agricultural marketing and services; surplus disposal; labeling and standards and grades." Lobbyist — Robert I. Nooter, 600 Maryland Ave. S.W., Washington, D.C. 20024.

AMERICAN HOSPITAL ASSOCIATION, 840 N. Lake Shore Dr., Chicago, Ill. 60611. Filed for self 1/15/85. Legislative interest — Not specified. Lobbyist — Michael J. Rock, 444 North Capitol St. N.W., Washington, D.C. 20001.

AMERICAN HOTEL & MOTEL ASSOCIATION, 888 Seventh Ave., New York, N.Y. 10019. Filed for self 1/22/85. Legislative interest — "... bills impacting on the industry in the energy field, tax, labor/management areas. Specific bills of interest ...: Immigration - HR 1510; Labor - S 281; and Environment - HR 2248." Lobbyist — Thomas F. Youngblood, 1819 L St. N.W., Washington, D.C. 20036.

AMERICAN MEDICAL ASSOCIATION, 535 N. Dearborn St., Chicago, Ill. 60610. Filed for self 1/31/85. Legislative interest — Not specified. Lobbyists — Richard A. Deem, Randolph B. Fenninger, Dorothy J. Moss, 1101 Vermont Ave. N.W., Washington, D.C. 20005.

AMERICAN OSTEOPATHIC ASSOCIATION, 122 C St. N.W., Washington, D.C. 20001. Filed for self 1/9/85. Legislative interest — "Legislation relating to health, including Medicare, Medicaid, Peer Review, Medical Education and Health Planning." Lobbyist — Paul K. Eyer.

AMERICAN PAPER INSTITUTE, New York, N.Y. Lobbyist — Chadbourne, Parke, Whiteside & Wolff, 1101 Vermont Ave. N.W., Washington, D.C. 20005. Filed 1/15/85. Legislative interest — "Amendments to Section 280F of the Internal Revenue Code."

AMERICAN PROTESTANT HEALTH ASSOCIATION, Schaumburg, Ill. Lobbyist — Perito, Duerk & Pinco, 1140 Connecticut Ave. N.W., Washington, D.C. 20036. Filed 1/21/85. Legislative interest — "... general health care policy matters; including tax-exempt bond financing for not-for-profit hospitals and Medicare and Medicaid."

AMERICAN PUBLIC POWER ASSOCIATION, Washington, D.C. Lobbyist — Patton, Boggs & Blow, 2550 M St. N.W., Washington, D.C. 20037. Filed 1/9/85. Legislative interest — "Preserve public preference in hydroelectric relicensing."

AMERICAN REAL ESTATE COMMITTEE, Washington, D.C. Lobbyist — Williams & Jensen, 1101 Connecticut Ave. N.W., Washington, D.C. 20036. Filed 1/30/85. Legislative interest — "... investment in real estate."

AMERICAN SOCIETY OF ANESTHESIOLOGISTS, 1201 Pennsylvania Ave. N.W., Washington, D.C. 20004. Filed for self 1/10/85. Legislative interest — "... practice of anesthesiology in general including particularly, various proposals for third-party reimbursement of non-physician practitioners, national health insurance, medical manpower legislation, Medicare/Medicaid reform, budget reconciliation, malpractice reform, and the jurisdiction of the FTC over the professions." Lobbyist — Thomas L. Adams.

AMERICAN SOCIETY OF ASSOCIATION EXECUTIVES, Washington, D.C. Lobbyist — O'Connor and Hannan, 1919 Pennsylvania Ave. N.W., Washington, D.C. 20006. Filed 1/15/85. Legislative interest — "General tax legislation issues."

AMERICAN SOCIETY FOR PHARMACOLOGY AND EXPERIMENTAL THERAPEUTICS, Bethesda, Md. Lobbyist — Perito, Duerk & Pinco, 1140 Connecticut Ave. N.W., Washington, D.C. 20036. Filed 1/21/85. Legislative interest — "Legislation supporting biomedical research and responsible use of animals and research subjects."

AMERICAN SOYBEAN ASSOCIATION, 600 Maryland Ave. S.W., Washington, D.C. 20024. Filed for self 1/10/85. Legislative interest — Not specified. Lobbyist — Randy Green.

AMERICAN TEXTILE MANUFACTURERS INSTITUTE INC., Washington, D.C. Lobbyist — Jack McDonald Associates Inc. 1120 20th St. N.W., Washington, D.C. 20036. Filed 1/14/85. Legislative interest — "... import of textiles or textile related products into the U.S." Filed 1/15/85. Legislative interest — "... import of textiles or textile related products into the U.S."

THE ASSOCIATED GENERAL CONTRACTORS OF AMERICA, 1957 E St. N.W., Washington, D.C. 20006. Filed for self 1/7/85. Legislative interest — "Compressed workweek - support." Lobbyist — Stephen E. Sandherr.

THE CANADIAN TUBULAR PRODUCERS ASSOCIATION, P.O. Box 2030, Hamilton, Ontario, Canada. Lobbyist — Dow, Lohnes & Albertson, 1255 23rd St. N.W., Washington, D.C. 20037. Filed 1/30/85; filed for self 1/24/85. Legislative interest — "... Trade and Tariff Act of 1984; ... HR 3398; ... PL 573; ... In opposition to any legislation which restricts U.S. imports of tubular steel mill products from Canada." Lobbyists — Ian O'Connor, William J. Kissick, Frank M. Christensen, Donald K. Belch, John A. Armstrong, Barry Sonshine, Dennis Smyth.

CHAMBER OF COMMERCE OF THE UNITED STATES, 1615 H St. N.W., Washington, D.C. 20062. Filed for self 1/9/85. Legislative interest — Not specified. Lobbyist — Virginia B. Lamp. Filed for self 1/25/85. Legislative interest — "... Food and Agriculture Policy." Lobbyist — Stuart B. Hardy.

COALITION FOR THE ADVANCEMENT OF INDUSTRIAL TECHNOLOGY, Washington, D.C. Lobbyist — Jack McDonald Associates Inc., 1120 20th St. N.W., Washington, D.C. 20036. Filed 1/14/85. Legislative interest — "Legislation to extend R&D tax credit." Filed 1/15/85. Legislative interest — "Legislation to extend R&D tax credit."

COALITION ON BEVERAGE ISSUES, Washington, D.C. Lobbyist — Brand, Lowell & Dole, 923 15th St. N.W., Washington, D.C. 20005. Filed 1/24/85. Legislative interest — Not specified.

DISTILLED SPIRITS COUNCIL OF THE U.S., 1250 I St. N.W., Washington, D.C. 20005. Filed for self 1/15/85. Legislative interest — "Legislation dealing with taxes, warning labels, alcohol abuse and any other legislation affecting the distilled spirits industry." Lobbyist — Tim Dudgeon.

EDISON ELECTRIC INSTITUTE, 1111 19th St. N.W., Washington, D.C. 20036. Filed for self 1/31/85. Legislative interest — "... Internal Revenue Code ... TVA Act ... Atomic Energy Act ... Federal Power Act ... Rural Electrification Act ... Bonneville Power Act ... Reclamation Acts ... Flood Control Act ... Appropriation Acts ... Rivers and Harbors and Flood Control Authorization Acts ... Federal Water Pollution Control Act ... Clean Air Act ... Occupation Health and Safety Act ... Equal Employment Opportunity Act ... Employee Retirement Income Security Act ... Wild and Scenic Rivers Act ... National Energy Act." Lobbyist — Thomas R. Kuhn.

THE FARMERS' EDUCATIONAL AND CO-OPERATIVE UNION OF AMERICA (NATIONAL FARMERS UNION), 12025 E. 45th Ave., Denver, Colo. 80251. Filed for self 1/14/85. Legislative interest — "... all federal legislation, bills, resolutions, appropriations and other legislative, executive and administrative actions or proceedings affecting American agriculture, farms, farmers, farm families, farm labor, either directly or indirectly. Among those bills or resolutions ... those dealing with the authorities of and the appropriations for the Department of Agriculture, bills relating to labor, health and medical care, welfare, taxation, revenue, tariffs, farm price supports, crop insurance, farm credit, REA, public power, natural resources, marketing and distribution of farm commodities, exportation and importation of agricultural products, foreign aid, defense, reclamation, education, marketing and consumer cooperatives, social security, reciprocal trade agreements, transportation, and antitrust legislation." Lobbyist — Robert A. Denman, 600 Maryland Ave. S.W., Washington, D.C. 20024.

FEDERAL LAND BANK ASSOCIATIONS OF TEXAS STOCKHOLDERS' DEFENSE FUND. Lobbyist — Vinson & Elkins, 1101 Connecticut Ave. N.W., Washington, D.C. 20036. Filed 1/24/85. Legislative interest — "Amendments to the Farm Credit Act of 1971, as amended." Filed 1/25/85. Legislative interest — "Amendments to the Farm Credit Act of 1971, as amended."

THE FERTILIZER INSTITUTE, 1015 18th St. N.W., Washington, D.C. 20036. Filed for self 1/4/85. Legislative interest — S 1715, HR 1760 ... Proposals to modify the Natural Gas Policy Act; ... S 822 ... Enhance agricultural Exports; ... S 24, HR 1190 ... Amend FmHA loan Program; ... S 757, HR 2867 ... RCRA Reauthorization; ... S 431 ... Clean Water Act Reauthorization; ... S 816, HR 2478 ... Amend and reauthorize the Comprehensive Environmental Response Compensation and Liability Act of 1980; ... S 48 ... Authorize the National Transportation Commission; ... S 865 ... Authorize the collection and disbursement of Port User Fees; ... HR 1242, S 1000, H Con Res 136 ... Proposal to require the use of U.S. vessels for the import and export of bulk cargo; ... S 917 ... Authorize Victims Compensation Trust Fund; ... HR 2142, S 1475 ... Diesel Fuel Tax; ... S 121 ... Create Department of International Trade and Industry; ... S 1904, HR 3810 ... Create Foreign Sales Corporation; ... HR 5640 ... Superfund Reauthorization; ... S 2417 ... Rail Monopoly; ... H J Res 600 ... Export Commission." Lobbyist — Michael J. McAdams.

FOOTWEAR RETAILERS OF AMERICA, Washington, D.C. Lobbyist — R. Duffy Wall & Associates Inc., 1317 F St. N.W., Washington, D.C. 20004. Filed 1/22/85. Legislative interest — "Issues relating to the restrictions on the importation of new rubber footwear."

GROCERY MANUFACTURERS OF AMERICA INC., Washington, D.C. Lobbyist — Wallace & Edwards, 212 East Capitol St. N.E., Washington, D.C. 20003. Filed 1/9/85. Legislative interest — "Legislation affecting pesticides."

GROUP HEALTH ASSOCIATION OF AMERICA INC., 624 9th St. N.W., Washington, D.C. 20001. Filed for self 1/25/85. Legislative interest — "All bills relating to prepayment of health care, comprehensive health care, group practice medicine and matters relating to consumer health care services." Lobbyist — Pat Billings.

JAPAN AUTOMOBILE MANUFACTURERS ASSOCIATION, 1050 17th St. N.W., Washington, D.C. 20036. Filed for self 1/28/85. Legislative interest — "... importing and marketing of automobiles in the United States." Lobbyist — William C. Duncan.

MAN-MADE FIBER PRODUCERS ASSOCIATION INC., 1150 17th St. N.W., Washington, D.C. 20036. Filed for self 1/8/85. Legislative interest — "Trade reform legislation; export & import legislation, tariff legislation." Lobbyist — Paul T. O'Day.

MOTOR VEHICLE MANUFACTURERS ASSOCIATION OF THE U.S. INC., 300 New Center Building, Detroit, Mich. 48202. Filed for self 1/28/85. Legislative interest — "... auto industry." Lobbyist — Anne E. Carlson, 1620 I St. N.W., Washington, D.C. 20006.

NATIONAL APARTMENT ASSOCIATION, 1101 14th St. N.W., Washington, D.C. 20005. Filed for self 1/29/85. Legislative interest — "All legislation that affects the real estate industry, particularly the multifamily housing industry. Specifically, legislation in areas affecting taxes and housing." Lobbyist — Charles H. Fritts.

NATIONAL ASSOCIATION OF ASCS COUNTY OFFICE EMPLOYEES, Caldwell, Idaho. Lobbyist — Jones and Winburn, 1101 15th St. N.W., Washington, D.C. 20005. Filed 1/15/85. Legislative interest — "... issues surrounding federal civil servant employees as they affect the National Association of ASCS County Office Employees."

NATIONAL ASSOCIATION OF ALCOHOLISM TREATMENT PROGRAMS INC., Irvine, Calif. Lobbyist — Perito, Duerk & Pinco, 1140 Connecticut Ave. N.W., Washington, D.C. 20036. Filed 1/21/85. Legislative interest — "... Medicare prospective payment system generally, alcoholism treatment specifically, and Federal Employees Health Benefits Program."

NATIONAL ASSOCIATION OF HOME BUILDERS OF THE UNITED STATES, 15th & M Sts. N.W., Washington, D.C. 20005. Filed for self 1/24/85. Legislative interest — Not specified. Lobbyists — Virginia Brown, William T. Slider, James P. Scala.

NATIONAL ASSOCIATION OF MANUFACTURERS, 1776 F St. N.W., Washington, D.C. 20006. Filed for self 1/11/85. Legislative interest — "... Product Liability, Comparable Worth, Tax Reform, Superfund, Deficit Reduction." Lobbyist — Jane S. Stone, 1719 Route 10, Parsippany, N.J. Filed for self 1/16/85. Legislative interest — "Taxation of employee benefits; amendments to the Employee Retirement Income Security Act of 1974 (ERISA), including plan termination insurance; operations of qualified pension and welfare plans; development of retirement income security policy." Lobbyist — F. Patricia Callahan.

NATIONAL ASSOCIATION OF PRIVATE PSYCHIATRIC HOSPITALS, 1319 F St. N.W., Washington, D.C. 20004. Filed for self 1/14/85. Legislative interest — "... mental health, hospitals, manpower, and patients." Lobbyist — Roy Bussewitz.

NATIONAL ASSOCIATION OF REALTORS, 777 14th

St. N.W., Washington, D.C. 20005. Filed for self 1/7/85. Legislative interest — "... housing and community revitalization issues that affect the real estate industry, including: government-assisted housing programs, Housing Authorization and Appropriations legislation, Farmers Home Administration programs, property management, rent control, public buildings policy, condominium conversion issues, housing vouchers, and enterprise zones." Lobbyist — Peter Denis Morgan.

NATIONAL ASSOCIATION OF RETIRED FEDERAL EMPLOYEES, Washington, D.C. Lobbyist — Chambers Associates Inc., 1411 K St. N.W., Washington, D.C. 20005. Filed 1/10/85. Legislative interest — "Civil Service Retirement...."

NATIONAL COAL ASSOCIATION, 1130 17th St. N.W., Washington, D.C. 20036. Filed for self 1/11/85. Legislative interest — "... bituminous coal industry...." Lobbyist — William D. Fay.

NATIONAL COTTON COUNCIL OF AMERICA, Memphis, Tenn. Lobbyist — Wallace & Edwards, 232 East Capitol St. N.E., Washington, D.C. 20003. Filed 1/9/85. Legislative interest — Not specified.

NATIONAL COUNCIL OF COMMUNITY MENTAL HEALTH CENTERS, Rockville, Md. Lobbyist — Liz Robbins Associates, 132 D St. S.E., Washington, D.C. 20003. Filed 1/10/85. Legislative interest — "Preservation of Mental Health Block Grant."

NATIONAL FEDERATION OF INDEPENDENT BUSINESS, 600 Maryland Ave. S.W., Washington, D.C. 20024. Filed for self 1/21/85. Legislative interest — "... small business and the economic well-being of the country, including taxes, bankruptcy, telephone access charges, regulations, and balanced budget." Lobbyist — Dwight R. Fisher.

NATIONAL MASS RETAILING INSTITUTE, 1901 Pennsylvania Ave. N.W., Washington, D.C. 20006. Filed for self 1/31/85. Legislative interest — "Tax, Trade, Antitrust issues specifically." Lobbyist — Robert J. Verdisco.

NATIONAL RESTAURANT ASSOCIATION, 311 First St. N.W., Washington, D.C. 20001. Filed for self 1/9/85. Legislative interest — "... small business, labor laws, wages and hours, taxation, consumer protection, food marketing and economic stabilization." Lobbyists — Colette R. Coleman, Richard L. Crawford, Thomas F. Kelley III, Shannon B. Tuel.

NATIONAL RETAIL MERCHANTS ASSOCIATION, 100 W. 31st St., New York, N.Y. 10001. Filed for self 1/10/85. Legislative interest — "... advertising, antitrust, conditions and terms of employment, consumer affairs and credit, corporate and individual taxes, crime prevention, energy conservation, environmental protection, foreign trade, health care, housing, land use, national economic recovery, pensions, postal rates and services, prices, regulatory reform, small business, telecommunications and transportation." Lobbyist — Michael J. Altier, 1000 Connecticut Ave. N.W., Washington, D.C. 20036.

NATIONAL TELEPHONE COOPERATIVE ASSOCIATION, 2626 Pennsylvania Ave. N.W., Washington, D.C. 20037. Filed for self 1/30/85. Legislative interest — "... rural telephone program provided for in the Rural Electrification Act of 1936, ... telecommunications and amendments to the Communications Act of 1934, ... the Rural Telephone Bank of 1971, and any other legislation affecting rural telecommunication." Lobbyist — Helane L. Goldstein.

NATURAL GAS SUPPLY ASSOCIATION, Washington, D.C. Lobbyist — William T. Murphy Jr., 1225 19th St. N.W., Washington, D.C. 20036. Filed 1/24/85. Legislative interest — Not specified.

OIL INVESTMENT INSTITUTE, Washington, D.C. Lobbyist — Gold and Liebengood Inc., 1050 Connecticut Ave. N.W., Washington, D.C. 20036. Filed 1/10/85. Legislative interest — "Tax reform legislation."

PACIFIC SEAFOOD PROCESSORS ASSOCIATION, Seattle, Wash. Lobbyist — Dennis J. Phelan, One Thomas Circle N.W., Washington, D.C. 20005. Filed 1/10/85. Legislative interest — "All fisheries and trade legislation during the 99th Congress."

PHARMACEUTICAL MANUFACTURERS ASSOCIATION, Washington, D.C. Lobbyist — R. Duffy Wall & Associates Inc., 1317 F St. N.W., Washington, D.C. 20004. Filed 1/22/85. Legislative interest — "... changes in the Internal Revenue Code of 1954."

SOLAR ENERGY INDUSTRIES ASSOCIATION, Washington, D.C. Lobbyist — Morris J. Amitay, 444 North Capitol St. N.W., Washington, D.C. 20001. Filed 1/9/85. Legislative interest — "... extension of renewable energy tax credits."

TEXAS CATTLEFEEDERS ASSOCIATION, Amarillo, Texas. Lobbyist — Gold and Liebengood Inc., 1050 Connecticut Ave. N.W., Washington, D.C. 20036. Filed 1/10/85. Legislative interest — "Matters involving cost basis of accounting, tax shelter provisions, uniform commercial code, agriculture exemptions 'from sales in the ordinary course of business' rule."

TEXAS SHRIMP ASSOCIATION, 1110 Vermont Ave. N.W., Washington, D.C. 20005. Filed for self 1/10/85. Legislative interest — "... the U.S. Gulf shrimp harvesting industry." Lobbyist — Kristin Lea Vehrs.

UNITED STATES BREWERS ASSOCIATION INC., 1750 K St. N.W., Washington, D.C. 20006. Filed for self 1/8/85. Legislative interest — "... environmental legislation ... Clean Water Act; Clean Air Act; Resource Conservation and Recovery Act; Comprehensive Environmental Response, Compensation, and Liability Act; Safe Drinking Water Act; Federal Insecticide, Fungicide, and Rodenticide Act; and Toxic Substances Control Act...." Lobbyist — Catherine A. Marshall.

U.S. LEAGUE OF SAVINGS INSTITUTIONS, Washington, D.C. Lobbyist — Joseph G. Minish, 66 Sheridan Ave., West Orange, N.J. 07052. Filed 1/15/85. (Former U.S. representative, D-N.J., 1963-85.) Legislative interest — "Banking Committee Matters."

WATER AND WASTEWATER EQUIPMENT MANUFACTURERS ASSOCIATION INC., P.O. Box 17402, Dulles International Airport, Washington, D.C. 20041. Filed for self 1/8/85. Legislative interest — "Safe Drinking Water Act, Clean Water Act, water resources, business practices, small business, agriculture, budget, environment, product liability, authorizations." Lobbyist — Fern Summer.

WINE & SPIRITS WHOLESALERS OF AMERICA INC., Washington, D.C. Lobbyist — R. Duffy Wall & Associates Inc., 1317 F St. N.W., Washington, D.C. 20004. Filed 1/22/85. Legislative interest — "... general tax legislation."

Miscellaneous

AMERICAN ACADEMY OF ARTS AND SCIENCES, Cambridge, Mass. Lobbyist — Chester L. Cooper, 7514 Vale St., Chevy Chase, Md. 20815. Filed 1/21/85. Legislative interest — "Support for International Institute for Applied Systems Analysis (IIASA) ... Austria ... Appropriation Bills for National Academy of Sciences and Smithsonian Institution."

AMERICAN COLLEGE OF NEUROPSYCHOPHARMACOLOGY, VANDERBILT UNIVERSITY, Nashville, Tenn. Lobbyist — Perito, Duerk & Pinco, 1140 Connecticut Ave. N.W., Washington, D.C. 20036. Filed 1/21/85. Legislative interest — "Legislation supporting biomedical research and the responsible use of animals and research subjects in furtherance of biomedical research."

AMERICANS FOR DEMOCRATIC ACTION, 1411 K St. N.W., Washington, D.C. 20005. Filed for self 1/24/85. Legislative interest — "... Domestic, Foreign and Military Policy ... the federal budget; nuclear disarmament; full employment; civil rights; civil liberties; human rights; social security; energy; education; housing; the environment; gun control; other women's issues; other labor issues; South Africa; election law." Lobbyists — Ann F. Lewis, Amy F. Isaacs.

ARMENIAN NATIONAL COMMITTEE OF AMERICA, 1901 Pennsylvania Ave. N.W., Washington, D.C. 20006. Filed for self 1/16/85. Legislative interest — "Commemorative resolutions pertaining to remembrance of victims of the Armenian Genocide." Lobbyist — Berdj Karapetian, 1816 New Hampshire Ave. N.W., Washington, D.C. 20009.

BROWN UNIVERSITY, Providence, R.I. Lobbyist — Cassidy and Associates Inc., 955 L'Enfant Plaza S.W., Washington, D.C. 20024. Filed 1/10/85. Legislative interest — "Legislation relating to federal research, education and development programs."

COALITION TO KEEP ALASKA OIL, Washington, D.C. Lobbyist — Howard Marlowe, 655 15th St. N.W., Washington, D.C. 20005. Filed 1/28/85. Legislative interest — "Extension of restrictions on Alaska Oil exports contained in the Export Administration Act, 50 U.S.C. App. section 2406(d), The Energy Policy and Conservation Act, 42 U.S.C. section 6212, the Mineral Leasing Act, 30 U.S.C. section 185(u), The Outer Continental Shelf Lands Act, 43 U.S.C., section 1354 and other legislation affecting this issue."

COMMITTEE FOR EQUITABLE COMPENSATION, 1825 I St. N.W., Washington, D.C. 20006. Filed for self 1/10/85. Legislative interest — Not specified. Lobbyist — Lewis D. Andrews Jr.

COMMITTEE FOR FAIRNESS IN REAL ESTATE TAXATION, Washington, D.C. Lobbyist — Williams & Jensen, 1101 Connecticut Ave. N.W., Washington, D.C. 20036. Filed 1/30/85. Legislative interest — "... taxation of real estate."

THE COMMITTEE ON PROBLEMS OF DRUG DEPENDENCE INC., Boston, Mass. Lobbyist — Perito, Duerk & Pinco, 1140 Connecticut Ave. N.W., Washington, D.C. 20036. Filed 1/21/85. Legislative interest — "Legislation concerning biomedical research; the responsible use of animals and research subjects in furtherance of biomedical research; the assessment of therapeutic agents for abuse potential; and drug dependence."

CONGRESS WATCH, 215 Pennsylvania Ave. S.E., Washington, D.C. 20003. Filed for self 1/30/85. Legislative interest — Not specified. Lobbyists — Joseph Goffman, Franci Livingston.

FOOD RESEARCH AND ACTION CENTER, 1319 F St. N.W., Washington, D.C. 20004. Filed for self 1/11/85. Legislative interest — "Federal domestic food programs and related programs for low-income people such as: all bills relating to the Food Stamp Act of 1964 (7 U.S.C. sections 2011 et seq.); National School Lunch Act (42 U.S.C. sections 1771 et seq.); Child Nutrition Act of 1966 (42 U.S.C. sections 1771 et seq.); surplus commodities and commodity donations legislation (7 U.S.C. sections 612c, 1431 and 1446a-1); Title VII of the Older Americans Act of 1965 (42 U.S.C. sections 3045 et seq.); and portions of the Social Security Act." Lobbyist — Michael R. Lemov.

FRIENDSHIP HILL ASSOCIATION, P.O. Box 24, New Geneva, Pa. 15467. Filed for self 1/15/85. Legislative interest — Not specified. Lobbyist — Quinten S. Baker, P.O. Box 8091, Falls Church, Va. 22041.

GULF & CARIBBEAN FOUNDATION, Washington, D.C. Lobbyist — Kuykendall Co., 517 3rd St. S.E., Washington, D.C. 20003. Filed 1/11/85. (Former U.S. Rep. Dan H. Kuykendall, R-Tenn., 1967-75, was listed as agent for this client.) Legislative interest — Not specified.

HANDGUN CONTROL INC., 1400 K St. N.W., Washington, D.C. 20005. Filed for self 1/7/85. Legislative interest — "To promote passage of legislation to control handguns including but not limited to ... Kennedy-Rodino Handgun Crime Act - For ... Moynihan-Biaggi Law Enforcement Officers Protection Act - For ... McClure-Volkmer Firearms Owners Protection Act - Against." Lobbyist — Mary Louise Westmoreland. Filed for self 1/31/85. Legislative interest — "Law Enforcement Officers Protection Act S 104, HR 4 - For ... Federal Firearms Owners Protection Act S 49 - Against ... Handgun Crime Control Act of 1985 - For ... General legislative interest in promoting legislation to reduce number of handgun deaths and injuries." Lobbyist — Charles A. Acquard.

LUTHERAN BROTHERHOOD, Minneapolis, Minn. Lobbyist — Covington & Burling, 1201 Pennsylvania Avenue N.W., P.O. Box 7566, Washington, D.C. 20044. Filed 1/25/85. Legislative interest — "Tax exemptions of fraternal beneficiary societies ... in favor of retaining 26 U.S.C. section 501(c)(8)."

MARCH OF DIMES BIRTH DEFECTS FOUNDATION, 1275 Mamaroneck Ave., White Plains, N.Y. 10605. Filed for self 1/7/85. Legislative interest — "Protection of Maternal & Child Health Block Grant ... Protection of WIC program ... Protection of Medicaid funding." Lobbyist — Anne Harrison-Clark, 1707 H St. N.W., Washington, D.C. 20006.

NATIONAL AUDUBON SOCIETY, 950 Third Ave., New York, N.Y. 10022. Filed for self 1/29/85. Legislative interest — "Water resource issue in general ... appropriations, specifically Energy and Water appropriations, in favor of some aspects, opposed to others." Lobbyist — Connie Mahan, 645 Pennsylvania Ave. S.E., Washington, D.C. 20003.

NATIONAL COALITION FOR SCIENCE & TECHNOLOGY, 2000 P St. N.W., Washington, D.C. 20036. Filed for self 1/24/85. Legislative interest — "Issues bearing on science, technology and engineering...." Lobbyists — Dr. Philip Speser, Deborah A. Cohn.

NATIONAL PUBLIC RADIO, 2025 M St. N.W., Washington, D.C. 20036. Filed for self 1/11/85. Legislative interest — "... to pursue legislation which is consistent with the public interest, First Amendment and full development of public radio ... FY 85 Rescission for Public Broadcasting, CPB Authorization Bill, CPB Appropriations Bill for FY88, Public Telecommunications Facility Program Appropriations for FY 86, AM Daytimers Legislation and Cable Copyright." Lobbyist — Johanna S. R. Mendelson.

NATIONAL RIFLE ASSOCIATION OF AMERICA, 1600 Rhode Island Ave. N.W., Washington, D.C. 20036. Filed for self 1/31/85. Legislative interest — "... all aspects of the acquistion, possession, and use of firearms and ammunition as well as legislation relating to hunting and wildlife conservation." Lobbyist — G. Ray Arnett.

PHOENIX HOUSE, New York, N.Y. Lobbyist — Liz Robbins Associates, 132 D St. S.E., Washington, D.C. 20003. Filed 1/10/85. Legislative interest — "... drug and alcohol related legislation."

PLANNED PARENTHOOD FEDERATION OF AMERICA INC., 2010 Massachusetts Ave. N.W., Washington, D.C. 20036. Filed for self 1/24/85. Legislative interest — "Foreign aid legislation as it pertains to family planning, population assistance and reproductive health; also legislation pertaining to policies and regulations regarding matters of personal health and reproduction." Lobbyist — Vivian Escobar Stack.

POLYTECHNIC INSTITUTE OF NEW YORK, Brooklyn, N.Y. Lobbyist — Cassidy and Associates Inc., 955 L'Enfant Plaza S.W., Washington, D.C. 20024. Filed 1/10/85. Legislative interest — "Legislation relating to federal research, education and development programs."

ROCHESTER INSTITUTE OF TECHNOLOGY, Rochester, N.Y. Lobbyist — Cassidy and Associates Inc., 955 L'Enfant Plaza S.W., Washington, D.C. 20024. Filed 1/10/85. Legislative interest — "Legislation relating to federal research, education and development programs."

ROBERT THOMPSON, Greenville, S.C. Lobbyist — Kuykendall Co., 517 3rd St. S.E., Washington, D.C. 20003. Filed 1/11/85. (Former U.S. Rep. Dan H. Kuykendall, R-Tenn., 1967-75, was listed as agent for this client.) Legislative interest — Not specified.

UNITED STATES DEFENSE COMMITTEE, 3238 Wynford Dr., Fairfax, Va. 22031. Filed for self 1/11/85. Legislative interest — "... defense and foreign policy...." Lobbyist — Robin A. Cooper.

February Registrations

Corporations and Businesses

ADVANCED CELLULAR PHONE CO., Los Angeles, Calif. Lobbyist — Tendler & Biggins, 1110 Vermont Ave. N.W., Washington, D.C. 20005. Filed 2/11/85. Legislative interest — "... communications, telecommunications, and cellular phone industries."

ALABAMA POWER CO., Birmingham, Ala. Lobbyist — Charls E. Walker Associates Inc., 1730 Pennsylvania Ave. N.W., Washington, D.C. 20006. Filed 2/12/85. Legislative interest — "... issues relating to federal environmental, tax, or licensing issues of interest to electric utility companies."

ALLIS CHALMERS ENERGY AND MINERALS SYSTEMS CO., Milwaukee, Wis. Lobbyist — Craft & Richards, 1050 Thomas Jefferson St. N.W., Washington, D.C. 20007. Filed 2/7/85. Legislative interest — "... appropriation for KILnGAS project continuation."

AMERICAN AIRLINES, Washington, D.C. Lobbyist — Wexler, Reynolds, Harrison & Schule Inc., 1317 F St. N.W., Washington, D.C. 20004. Filed 2/15/85. Legislative interest — "... airline computer reservations systems."

AMFAC INC., San Francisco, Calif. Lobbyist — McCutchen, Doyle, Brown & Enersen, Three Embarcadero Center, San Francisco, Calif. 94111. Filed 2/25/85. Legislative interest — "... environmental legislation. Specific legislative amendments in reauthorization of the Comprehensive Environmental Response, Compensation, and Liability Act of 1980 (CERCLA)."

AQUA-CHEM INC., Milwaukee, Wis. Lobbyist — Franklin R. Silbey Associates Inc., 1919 Pennsylvania Ave. N.W., Washington, D.C. 20006. Filed 2/11/85. Legislative interest — "... (for) ... S 2723 ... (authorization)...."

ASSOCIATES CORPORATION OF NORTH AMERICA, Dallas, Texas. Lobbyist — Riddell, Holroyd & Butler, 1331 Pennsylvania Ave. N.W., Washington, D.C. 20004. Filed 2/25/85. Legislative interest — "... banking, insurance, and financial fields, including commercial lending."

BALCOR/AMERICAN EXPRESS INC., Skokie, Ill. Lobbyist — Bell, Boyd & Lloyd, 70 W. Madison, Chicago, Ill. 60602. Filed 2/19/85. Legislative interest — "... plan asset regulations of the Department of Labor issued pursuant to the Employee Retirement Income Security Act of 1974...."

BANK OF NEW ENGLAND, Boston, Mass. Lobbyist — O'Neill & Haase, 1333 New Hampshire Ave. N.W., Washington, D.C. 20036. Filed 2/14/85. Legislative interest — "Interstate Banking."

BENEFICIAL CORP., Wilmington, Del. Lobbyist — Riddell, Holroyd & Butler, 1331 Pennsylvania Ave. N.W., Washington, D.C. 20004. Filed 2/25/85. Legislative interest — "... bank holding company, truth-in-lending and commercial lending."

BERG & ASSOCIATES, 641 Indiana Ave. N.W., Washington, D.C. 20004. Filed for self 2/19/85. Legislative interest — "Defense and small business." Lobbyist — Peter E. Berg.

BOEING ENGINEERING CO. SOUTHEAST INC., Oak Ridge, Tenn. Lobbyist — Craft & Richards, 1050 Thomas Jefferson St. N.W., Washington, D.C. 20007. Filed 2/7/85. Legislative interest — "... Uranium Enrichment or Strategic Petroleum Reserve."

C.I.T. FINANCIAL CORP., Livingston, N.J. Lobbyist — Riddell, Holroyd & Butler, 1331 Pennsylvania Ave. N.W., Washington, D.C. 20004. Filed 2/25/85. Legislative interest — "... banking, insurance and financial fields, including commercial lending."

CAROLINA POWER & LIGHT CO., 411 Fayetteville St. Mall, Raleigh, N.C. 27601. Filed for self 2/11/85. Legislative interest — "... electric power industry in general ... ["For and against various provisions" of:] Clean Air Act Amendments ... Clean Water Act Amendments ... Construction Work in Progress ... Hydroelectric Relicensing ... Low Income Energy Assistance ... Public Utility Holding Company Act ... Transmission Access ... Staggers Act Amendments ... Nuclear and other energy related authorization bills ... Nuclear Licensing Reform ... Coal Slurry ... Low Level Radioactive Waste Compacts ... Price Anderson Act ... Dividend Reinvestment ... Normalization ... Regulatory Reform...." Lobbyist — S. M. Henry Brown Jr.

CASTLE & COOKE INC., San Francisco, Calif. Lobbyist — McCutchen, Doyle, Brown & Enersen, Three Embarcadero Center, San Francisco, Calif. 94111. Filed 2/25/85. Legislative interest — "... environmental legislation. Specific legislative amendments in reauthorization of the Comprehensive Environmental Response, Compensation, and Liability Act of 1980 (CERCLA)."

CENTRAL AND SOUTH WEST CORP., Dallas, Texas. Lobbyist — Van Ness, Feldman, Sutcliffe, Curtis & Levenberg, 1050 Thomas Jefferson St. N.W., Washington, D.C. 20007. Filed 2/15/85. Legislative interest — "... matters affecting requirements applicable to registered holding companies under the Public Utility Holding Company Act of 1935."

CHAMPION INTERNATIONAL CORP., Washington, D.C. Lobbyist — Charls E. Walker Associates Inc., 1730 Pennsylvania Ave. N.W., Washington, D.C. 20006. Filed 2/12/85. Legislative interest — "... may concern proposals which alter, amend or otherwise affect the Internal Revenue Code as it relates to the activities of corporations."

COMMUNICATIONS COUNSEL INC., Washington, D.C. Lobbyist — Landon Parvin, 5410 Connecticut Ave. N.W., Washington, D.C. 20015. Filed 2/12/85. Legislative interest — Not specified.

COMPUTER HORIZONS CORP., Vienna, Va. Lobbyist — Francis X. Carroll, 5400 85th Ave., New Carrollton, Md. 20784. Filed 2/15/85. Legislative interest — "... Government Vendor Contracts."

CONNECTICUT BANK & TRUST CORP., Hartford, Conn. Lobbyist — O'Neill and Haase, 1333 New Hampshire Ave. N.W., Washington, D.C. 20036. Filed 2/14/85. Legislative interest — "Interstate banking."

DIAMOND SHAMROCK CORP., 717 N. Harwood, Dallas, Texas 75201. Filed for self 2/19/85. Legislative interest — "... Domestic integrated oil and gas...." Lobbyist — Edlu J. Thom, 919 18th St. N.W., Washington, D.C. 20006.

E. I. du PONT de NEMOURS & CO., Wilmington, Del. Lobbyist — Charls E. Walker Associates Inc., 1730 Pennsylvania Ave. N.W., Washington, D.C. 20006. Filed 2/12/85. Legislative interest — "... may concern proposals which alter, amend or otherwise affect the Internal Revenue Code as it relates to the activities of corporations."

EMOND & VINES, Birmingham, Ala. Lobbyist — Sirote, Permutt, Friend, Friedman, Held & Apolinsky, 2222 Arlington Ave. South, Birmingham, Ala. 35205. Filed 2/19/85. Legislative interest — "Amendment of 26 U.S.C., section 104 (a)(2) as regards taxation of wrongful death awards ... nontaxability of such awards."

FIRST MARYLAND BANCORP, 25 S. Charles St., Baltimore, Md. 21201. Lobbyist — Piper & Marbury, 36 S. Charles St., Baltimore, Md. 21201. Filed 2/1/85. Legislative interest — "... banking and financial matters, such as bank deregulation and interstate and reciprocal banking issues." Filed for self 2/19/85. Legislative interest — "... banking and financial matters, such as bank deregulation and interstate and reciprocal banking issues." Lobbyist — James D. Lucas.

FIRST NATIONAL BANK OF MARYLAND, 25 S. Charles St., Baltimore, Md. 21201. Lobbyist — Piper & Marbury, 36 S. Charles St., Baltimore, Md. 21201. Filed 2/1/85. Legislative interest — "... banking and financial matters, such as bank deregulation and interstate and reciprocal banking issues." Filed for self 2/19/85. Legislative interest — "... banking and financial matters, such as bank deregulation and interstate and reciprocal banking issues." Lobbyist — John D. Lucas.

FLORIDA POWER CORP., P.O. Box 14042, St. Petersburg, Fla. 33733. Filed for self 2/6/85. Legislative interest — "... electric utilities, energy, environmental and taxes related to utilities." Lobbyist — Sue P. Purvis.

FORESIGHT CONSULTING INC., 1310 Hwy. 96, St. Paul, Minn. 55140. Filed for self 2/21/85. Legislative interest — "U.S. Dept. of Interior Authorizations & Appropriations." Lobbyist — Michael F. Priesnitz.

GA TECHNOLOGIES INC., Washington, D.C. Lobbyist — Craft & Richards, 1050 Thomas Jefferson St. N.W., Washington, D.C. 20007. Filed 2/7/85. Legislative interest — "All legislation affecting GA Programs including but not limited to the High Temperature Gas Reactor and fusion programs."

GENCORP, Akron, Ohio. Lobbyist — Verner, Liipfert, Bernhard, McPherson & Hand, 1660 L St. N.W., Washington, D.C. 20036. Legislative interest — Not specified.

GETTY SYNTHETIC FUELS INC., Signal Hill, Calif. Lobbyist — Donald C. Alexander, 1800 M St. N.W., Washington, D.C. 20036. Filed 2/28/85. Legislative interest — "... production energy credits."

GUARDIAN LIFE INSURANCE CO. OF AMERICA,

New York, N.Y. Lobbyist — Marriott & Co., 900 Kennecott Building, Salt Lake City, Utah 84133. Filed 2/12/85. (Former U.S. Rep. Dan Marriott, R-Utah, 1977-85, was listed as agent for this client.) Legislative interest — "Taxation of life insurance companies and policies."

INDUSTRIAL DATA LINK, San Diego, Calif. Lobbyist — The William Chasey Organization, 1800 K St. N.W., Washington, D.C. 20006. Filed 2/25/85. Legislative interest — Not specified.

INTEGRATED RESOURCES INC., New York, N.Y. Lobbyist — Dewey, Ballantine, Bushby, Palmer & Wood, 1775 Pennsylvania Ave. N.W., Washington, D.C. 20006. Filed 2/26/85. Legislative interest — "... tax matters."

INTERNATIONAL TELECOMMUNICATIONS SATELLITE ORGANIZATION, Washington, D.C. Lobbyist — Bogle & Gates, 1 Thomas Circle N.W., Washington, D.C. 20005. Filed 2/4/85. (Former U.S. Rep. Joel Pritchard, R-Wash., 1973-85, was listed as agent for this client.) Legislative interest — "FCC Deregulation."

KIMBERLY-CLARK CORP., 401 N. Lake St., Neenah, Wis. 54956. Filed for self 2/26/85. Legislative interest — "... tax, trade, environmental, energy, transportation, antitrust, health, benefits, labor, consumer and other legislative proposals which directly affect the Corporation, its employees or its stockholders." Lobbyist — Alexander H. Jordan, 1201 Pennsylvania Ave. N.W., Washington, D.C. 20004.

KOOTZNOOWOO INC., Angoon, Alaska. Lobbyist — Perkins, Coie, Stone, Olsen & Williams, 1110 Vermont Ave. N.W., Washington, D.C. 20005. Filed 2/14/85. Legislative interest — "Represent corporate interests in resource, tax and appropriation matters."

LTV AEROSPACE & DEFENSE CO., Dallas, Texas. Lobbyist — Campbell-Raupe Associates Inc., 1015 15th St. N.W., Washington, D.C. 20005. Filed 2/6/85. Legislative interest — "Defense related authorizing initiatives ... appropriation measures for defense...."

LEWIS, WHITE & CLAY, 1300 First National Building, Detroit, Mich. 48226. Filed for self 2/8/85. Legislative interest — Not specified.

LINCOLN SAVINGS, Phoenix, Ariz. Lobbyist — Parry and Romani Associates Inc., 1140 Connecticut Ave. N.W., Washington, D.C. 20036. Filed 2/12/85. Legislative interest — "The application of Federal regulations to state-chartered savings and loans institutions."

MAINE YANKEE - CENTRAL MAINE POWER CO., Augusta, Maine. Lobbyist — Norman J. Temple, 155 Dresden Ave., Gardiner, Maine 04345. Filed 2/21/85. Legislative interest — "Internal Revenue Code ... TVA Act ... Atomic Energy Act ... Federal Power Act ... Rural Electrification Act ... Flood Control Act ... Appropriation Acts ... Rivers and Harbors and Flood Control Authorization Acts ... Federal Water Pollution Control Act ... Clean Air Act ... Occupational Health and Safety Act ... Equal Employment Opportunity Act ... Employee Retirement Income Security Act ... Wild and Scenic Rivers Act ... National Energy Act."

MARTIN MARIETTA AEROSPACE, Bethesda, Md. Lobbyist — D L Associates Inc., 1730 Rhode Island Ave. N.W., Washington, D.C. 20036. Filed 2/28/85. Legislative interest — "Defense issues...."

MARTIN MARIETTA CORP., Bethesda, Md. Lobbyist — Gold and Liebengood Inc., 1050 Connecticut Ave. N.W., Washington, D.C. 20036. Filed 2/20/85. Legislative interest — Not specified.

MARYLAND SAVINGS-SHARE INSURANCE CORP., Baltimore, Md. Lobbyist — Venable, Baetjer and Howard, Two Hopkins Plaza, Baltimore, Md. 21201. Filed 2/1/85. Legislative interest — "... securing remedial legislation specifically exempting Maryland Savings-Share Insurance Corporation from being taxed on its income."

NEW ENGLAND LIFE, Boston, Mass. Lobbyist — Campbell-Raupe Associates Inc., 1015 15th St. N.W., Washington, D.C. 20005. Filed 2/6/85. Legislative interest — "Tax Issues."

NORFOLK SOUTHERN CORP., Washington, D.C. Lobbyist — William H. Harsha & Associates Inc., P.O. Box 24157, Washington, D.C. 20024. Filed 2/12/85. (Former U.S. Rep. William H. Harsha, R-Ohio, 1961-81, was listed as agent for this client.) Legislative interest — "Conrail Sale, in support of." Lobbyist — Edward Hidalgo, 2435 California St. N.W., Washington, D.C. 20008. Filed 2/21/85. Legislative interest — "Advance interest of Norfolk Southern Corporation in legislation regarding its acquisition of Consolidated Rail Corporation (CONRAIL)."

OCCIDENTAL CHEMICAL CORP., 1747 Pennsylvania Ave. N.W., Washington, D.C. 20006. Filed for self 2/21/85. Legislative interest — "Federal Issues: International Trade, Environment, Energy, Transportation." Lobbyist — Julie Archuleta.

ORMAT SYSTEMS INC., Sparks, Nev. Lobbyist — Perkins, Coie, Stone, Olsen & Williams, 1110 Vermont Ave. N.W., Washington, D.C. 20005. Filed 2/14/85. Legislative interest — "Represent corporate interests in legislation and appropriations concerning the federal Geothermal Loan Guarantee Program."

PFIZER INC., 235 E. 42nd St., New York, N.Y. 10017. Filed for self 2/14/85. Legislative interest — Not specified. Lobbyist — Robert M. Sherwood, 1700 Pennsylvania Ave. N.W., Washington, D.C. 20006.

PHILIP MORRIS INTERNATIONAL, New York, N.Y. Lobbyist — The Laxalt Corp., 214 Massachusetts Ave. N.E., Washington, D.C. 20002. Filed 2/28/85. Legislative interest — "U.S. tobacco interests as they relate to Asia."

PHILIP MORRIS U.S.A., New York, N.Y. Lobbyist — Communications Management Inc., 1925 N. Lynn St., Arlington, Va. 22209. Filed 2/14/85. Legislative interest — "... supporting or opposing legislation affecting the current and proposed business operations of PM Inc., including without limitation legislation relating to federal excise taxes on tobacco products."

PHILLIPS PETROLEUM CO., Bartlesville, Okla. Lobbyist — Napier & Jennings, P.O. Drawer 995, Bennettsville, S.C. 29512. Filed 2/11/85. (Former U.S. Rep. John L. Napier, R-S.C., 1981-83, was listed as agent for this client.) Legislative interest — "S 998."

PROFESSIONAL ASSET MANAGEMENT INC., Delmar, Calif. Lobbyist — The William Chasey Organization, 1800 K St. N.W., Washington, D.C. 20006. Filed 2/25/85. Legislative interest — "HR 107."

ROHR INDUSTRIES, Chula Vista, Calif. Lobbyist — McCutchen, Doyle, Brown & Enersen, Three Embarcadero Center, San Francisco, Calif. 94111. Filed 2/25/85. Legislative interest — "... environmental legislation ... reauthorization of the Comprehensive Environmental Response, Compensation, and Liability Act of 1980 (CERCLA)."

RUSSELL CORP., Alexander City, Ala. Lobbyist — Augustine D. Tantillo, 1726 M St. N.W., Washington, D.C. 20036. Filed 2/4/85. Legislative interest — "All legislation dealing with the American textile apparel industry."

SCHNITZER STEEL PRODUCTS CO., Oakland, Calif. Lobbyist — Benner, Burnett & Coleman, 1401 New York Ave. N.W., Washington, D.C. 20005. Filed 2/26/85. Legislative interest — "... certain aspects of the Oakland Inner Harbor Deep Draft Project, a water improvement project affected by the following bills: S 366, HR 6, HR 45, HR 50."

JOSEPH E. SEAGRAM & SONS INC., Washington, D.C. Lobbyist — Dewey, Ballantine, Bushby, Palmer & Wood, 1775 Pennsylvania Ave. N.W., Washington, D.C. 20006. Filed 2/26/85. Legislative interest — "... tax and international trade matters."

SYNCROTECH SOFTWARE CORP., Clinton, Md. Lobbyist — The William Chasey Organization, 1800 K St. N.W., Washington, D.C. 20006. Filed 2/25/85. Legislative interest — "Provide national marketing to secure software contracts for SSC."

TEXAS AIR CORP., Washington, D.C. Lobbyist — Campbell-Raupe Associates, 1015 15th St. N.W., Washington, D.C. 20005. Filed 2/6/85. Legislative interest — Not specified.

TEXAS UTILITIES SERVICE, Washington, D.C. Lobbyist — Campbell-Raupe Associates, 1015 15th St. N.W., Washington, D.C. 20005. Filed 2/6/85. Legislative interest — "Various nuclear matters."

TICOR TITLE INSURANCE CO., Los Angeles, Calif.

Lobbyist — Gold and Liebengood Inc., 1050 Connecticut Ave. N.W., Washington, D.C. 20036. Filed 2/22/85. Legislative interest — Not specified.

U.S. STEEL CORP., Washington, D.C. Lobbyist — O'Neill and Haase, 1333 New Hampshire Ave. N.W., Washington, D.C. 20036. Filed 2/14/85. Legislative interest — "Tax issues."

VALMONT INDUSTRIES INC., Valley, Neb. Lobbyist — Kutak, Rock & Campbell, 1101 Connecticut Ave. N.W., Washington, D.C. 20036. Filed 2/25/85. Legislative interest — "Remedial legislation for leases of agricultural equipment."

WESTINGHOUSE CORP., Washington, D.C. Lobbyist — Campbell-Raupe Associates Inc., 1015 15th St. N.W., Washington, D.C. 20005. Filed 2/6/85. Legislative interest — "Peaceful uses of atomic energy, primarily for the generation of electric power; tariff and trade legislation; export-import bank appropriations; tax reform and/or corporate tax increases...."

International Relations

TURKEY, REPUBLIC OF, Ankara, Turkey. Lobbyist — Gray & Co., 3255 Grace St. N.W., Washington, D.C. 20007. Filed 2/15/85. Legislative interest — "Including but not limited to obtaining information and assistance on foreign operations appropriations legislation."

Labor Organizations

FOOD AND ALLIED SERVICE TRADES DEPARTMENT (AFL-CIO), 815 16th St. N.W., Washington, D.C. 20006. Filed for self 2/8/85. Legislative interest — "Polygraphs: Support the ban of polygraphs in employment. Natonal Health Insurance: Support a national health insurance program. Food Stamps/Child Nutrition: Support food stamps and child nutrition programs. Food Labeling and Safety: Support. FTC: Support the investigation of monopolies and job impact studies in FTC actions. Oppose anti-trust exemptions for professions. Consumer Protection: Support. Civil Rights: Support ERA, National Voting Rights, D.C. Voting Rights. Nutrition: Support programs to provide better nutrition for low income citizens and school children. Fringe Benefits: Oppose taxation of fringe benefits. Balanced Budget: Oppose a constitutional amendment requiring a balanced budget. Tobacco: Oppose attempts to segregate smokers/non-smokers in public areas. International Trade: Oppose Caribbean Basin Initiative, support Domestic Content legislation. Labor Standards: Support higher minimum wage; oppose subminimum wage youth and part-time employees; oppose efforts to exploit child labor. Plant Closings: Oppose plant closing without investigation of alternative. Successorship: Support maintaining existing contracts for unions when company ownership changes. Bottle Bill: Oppose mandatory returnable bottles. Tourism: Support tourism promotion programs. Energy: Support gasohol programs. Oppose deregulation of gas. Bankruptcy Law: Support consumer interests. Taxation: Oppose new excise taxes, support AFL-CIO Tax Reform Measure. Credit Control Act: Support extension and amendments. Immigration: Support employer sanctions coupled with a standard identifier, adjustment of status and humane refugee policy. Oppose guestworker programs. Hazardous Substances and Regulatory Reform: Support attempts to make corporations liable for toxic substances in environment. Electrical Code Standard for OSHA: Support. Grain Standards for Export Elevators (HR 5528): Support. Grain Safety Research: Support. Retirement Security: Support through reporting requirements for employee pension plans. Freedom of Information Act: Support strong disclosure language." Lobbyist — Daniel J. O'Grady.

NATIONAL EDUCATION ASSOCIATION, 1201 16th St. N.W., Washington, D.C. 20036. Filed for self 2/21/85. Legislative interest — Not specified. Lobbyist — Ruby King-Williams.

UNITED BROTHERHOOD OF CARPENTERS AND JOINERS OF AMERICA, 101 Constitution Ave. N.W., Washington, D.C. 20001. Filed for self 2/7/85. Legislative interest — Not specified. Lobbyist — Ed Durkin.

State and Local Governments

ILLINOIS DEPARTMENT OF ENERGY AND NATURAL RESOURCES, Springfield, Ill. Lobbyist — Craft & Richards, 1050 Thomas Jefferson St. N.W., Washington, D.C. 20007. Filed 2/7/85. Legislative interest — "... coal program funding and high energy physics projects."

LOS ANGELES COUNTY, Los Angeles, Calif. Lobbyist — Jones, Day, Reavis & Pogue, 655 15th St. N.W., Washington, D.C. 20005. Filed 2/6/85. Legislative interest — "... recordkeeping of fringe benefits."

NEW YORK STATE HOUSING FINANCE AGENCY, New York, N.Y. Lobbyist — Liz Robbins Associates, 132 D St. S.E., Washington, D.C. 20003. Filed 2/22/85. Legislative interest — "... preservation of housing and health care financial incentives."

SEATTLE METRO, Seattle, Wash. Lobbyist — Bogle & Gates, 1 Thomas Circle N.W., Washington, D.C. 20005. Filed 2/4/85. (Former U.S. Rep. Joel Pritchard, R-Wash., 1973-85, was listed as agent for this client.) Legislative interest — "Clean Water Act Amendments."

Trade Associations

AIR TRAFFIC CONTROL ASSOCIATION INC., Arlington, Va. Lobbyist — Suzette Matthews, 1726 M St. N.W., Washington, D.C. 20036. Filed 2/21/85. Legislative interest — "... air traffic control, aviation, aviation safety, and matters affecting personnel including federal employees who develop, install, maintain and operate ATC facilities."

AMERICAN ACADEMY OF ACTUARIES, 1835 K St. N.W., Washington, D.C. 20006. Filed for self 2/12/85. Legislative interest — "All legislation having actuarial impact (including pensions and insurance)." Lobbyist — Gary D. Simms.

AMERICAN ASSOCIATION OF HOMES FOR THE AGING, 1050 17th St. N.W., Washington, D.C. 20036. Filed for self 2/19/85. Legislative interest — "Federal health and housing programs serving the elderly and other issues of concern to the aging (for example, Social Security, Medicare and Medicaid legislation and the Older Americans Act)." Lobbyists — Steven Hornburg, Mary Webb.

AMERICAN CEMENT TRADE ALLIANCE INC., 1201 Pennsylvania Ave. N.W., Washington, D.C. 20004. Filed for self 2/26/85. Legislative interest — "... international trade in cement." Lobbyist — Michael Scott.

AMERICAN MEAT INSTITUTE, Arlington, Va. Lobbyist — Wallace & Edwards, 232 E. Capitol St. N.E., Washington, D.C. 20003. Filed 2/7/85. Legislative interest — "Support legislation to provide clear title to purchasers of agricultural products and related matters."

AMERICAN PSYCHOLOGICAL ASSOCIATION, 1200 17th St. N.W., Washington, D.C. 20036. Filed for self 2/19/85. Legislative interest — "... relating to psychology ... support for reform of Medicare and Medicaid; and support for programs relating to Alzheimer's Disease, and programs of concern to the aging." Lobbyist — Pamela R. West.

AMERICAN TRUCKING ASSOCIATIONS INC., 2200 Mill Road, Alexandria, Va. 22314. Filed for self 2/11/85. Legislative interest — Not specified. Lobbyists — Thomas J. Donohue, Jerald V. Halvorsen, Joseph L. Rosso.

AMERICAN WIND ENERGY ASSOCIATION, 1516 King St., Alexandria, Va. 22314. Filed for self 2/15/85. Legislative interest — "Energy tax credits, Dept. of Energy budgets." Lobbyist — David S. Pate.

AMERICAN WOOD PRESERVERS INSTITUTE, 1945 Old Gallows Road, Vienna, Va. 22180. Filed for self 2/8/85. Legislative interest — "... any bills to amend the following laws: Clean Air Act, FIFRA, Clean Water Act, Occupational Safety and Health Act, RCRA, Safe Drinking Water Act, CERCLA, TSCA, Used Oil Recycling Act of 1980. AWPI is interested in environmental legislation." Lobbyist — Robert G. Smerko.

AMUSEMENT AND MUSIC OPERATORS ASSOCI-

ATION, Oakbrook, Ill. Lobbyist — Wexler, Reynolds, Harrison & Schule Inc., 1317 F St. N.W., Washington, D.C. 20004. Filed 2/15/85. Legislative interest — "Coin-Operated Phonorecord Player Copyright Act of 1983; ... S 1734 & HR 3858; ... 17 U.S.C. section 116; ... Support S 1734 & HR 3858."

ASSOCIATION OF AMERICAN RAILROADS, 1920 L St. N.W., Washington, D.C. 20036. Filed for self 2/4/85. Legislative interest — "... issues of concern to the railroad industry; including railroad regulation, railroad safety, Federal-Aid Highway Program, highway safety, waterways and ports, and related tax measures." Lobbyist — Paul C. Oakley.

ASSOCIATION OF PROGRESSIVE RENTAL ORGANIZATIONS, Austin, Texas. Lobbyist — J. Samuel Choate Jr., 2033 M St. N.W., Washington, D.C. 20036. Filed 2/13/85. Legislative interest — "... the rent-to-own industry."

AUTOMOBILE IMPORTERS OF AMERICA INC., Arlington, Va. Lobbyist — Busby, Rehm and Leonard, 1629 K St. N.W., Washington, D.C. 20006. Filed 2/14/85. Legislative interest — "Legislation affecting importation, distribution and sale of foreign automobiles."

BURLEY & DARK LEAF TOBACCO EXPORT ASSOCIATION, 1100 17th St. N.W., Washington, D.C. 20036. Filed for self 2/27/85. Legislative interest — "... all legislation affecting tobacco, particularly Burley, Dark Air-Cured, Dark Fire-Cured and cigar types." Lobbyist — Benjamin F. Reeves.

CHEMICAL MANUFACTURERS ASSOCIATION, Washington, D.C. Lobbyist — Gold and Liebengood Inc., 1050 Connecticut Ave. N.W., Washington, D.C. 20036. Filed 2/20/85. Legislative interest — "Superfund legislation, S 51."

THE COALITION FOR THE ADVANCEMENT OF INDUSTRIAL TECHNOLOGY, Washington, D.C. Lobbyist — Hogan & Hartson, 815 Connecticut Ave. N.W., Washington, D.C. 20006. Filed 2/13/85. Legislative interest — "To stimulate industrial research by companies and universities, including modification of the U.S. Tax Code for that purpose. Specifically, its goal is improvement in the existing tax credit for research and development and equipment donations and making the R&D credit permanent — in particular enactment of S 58 and its companion bill to be introduced in the House of Representatives."

EDISON ELECTRIC INSTITUTE, 1111 19th St. N.W., Washington, D.C. 20036. Lobbyist — Craft and Richards, 1050 Thomas Jefferson St., Washington, D.C. 20007. Filed 2/7/85. Legislative interest — "All legislation which affects the electric utility industry including Hydroelectric Relicensing and the Clean Coal Technology Reserve." Filed for self 2/1/85. Legislative interest — "Tax legislation." Lobbyist — Marian E. McDowell. Filed for self 2/11/85. Legislative interest — "... includes but is not limited to ... Internal Revenue Code ... TVA Act ... Atomic Energy Act ... Federal Power Act ... Rural Electrification Act ... Bonneville Power Act ... Reclamation Acts ... Flood Control Act ... Appropriation Acts ... Rivers and Harbors and Flood Control Authorization Acts ... Federal Water Pollution Control Act ... Clean Air Act ... Occupational Health and Safety Act ... Equal Employment Opportunity Act ... Employee Retirement Income Security Act ... Wild and Scenic Rivers Act ... National Energy Act ... Staggers Rail Act." Lobbyist — Lynn H. LeMaster.

THE FARM CREDIT COUNCIL, 1800 Massachusetts Ave. N.W., Washington, D.C. 20036. Filed for self 2/8/85. Legislative interest — Not specified. Lobbyist — Kenneth E. Auer.

GROUP HEALTH ASSOCIATION OF AMERICA INC., 624 9th St. N.W., Washington, D.C. 20001. Filed for self 2/1/85. Lobbyists — Leslie Rose, Pat Billings. Filed for self 2/26/85. Legislative interest — "All bills relating to prepayment of health care, comprehensive health care, group practice medicine and matters relating to consumer health care services."

HARD MINERALS CONSORTIUM, Washington, D.C. Lobbyist — Herrick & Smith, 1800 Massachusetts Ave. N.W., Washington, D.C. 20036. Filed 2/5/85. Legislative interest — "... Outer Continental Shelf Lands Act, Deep Seabed Hard Minerals Resource Act ... 94 Stat. 553, 96 Stat. 2084 ... For an amendment to the Outer Continental Shelf Lands Act."

JAPAN ECONOMIC INSTITUTE OF AMERICA, 1000 Connecticut Ave. N.W., Washington, D.C. 20036. Filed for self 2/25/85. Legislative interest — "... monitors developments affecting U.S. tariff and trade policy, foreign investment and banking activity in the U.S., American exports and export financing, and U.S.-Japan economic relations." Lobbyist — William J. Barnds.

MORTGAGE BANKERS ASSOCIATION OF AMERICA, 1125 15th St. N.W., Washington, D.C. 20005. Filed for self 2/1/85. Legislative interest — "... all legislation affecting the mortgage lending, banking, and construction industries." Lobbyist — Linda Knell Bumbalo.

NATIONAL ASSOCIATION OF MANUFACTURERS, 1776 F St. N.W., Washington, D.C. 20006. Filed for self 2/5/85. Legislative interest — "Medicare reform; taxation of employee benefits; health legislation including access to data, medical malpractice reform, health care technology and rate regulation; Social Security." Lobbyist — Sharon F. Canner. Filed for self 2/27/85. Legislative interest — "... corporate finance, management & competition laws. S 286, HR 1074, FTC Reauthorization, RICO Act, Foreign Corrupt Practices Amendments, Hart-Scott-Rodino Act, Criminal Code legislation when affecting corporate management, SEC and antitrust legislation." Lobbyist — John H. Pilcher.

NATIONAL ASSOCIATION OF MUTUAL INSURANCE COMPANIES, 3707 Woodview Trace, Indianapolis, Ind. 46268. Lobbyist — Collier, Shannon, Rill & Scott, 1055 Thomas Jefferson St. N.W., Washington, D.C. 20007. Filed 2/22/85. Legislative interest — Not specified. Lobbyist — Larry Forrester.

NATIONAL ASSOCIATION OF REALTORS, 777 14th St. N.W., Washington, D.C. 20005. Filed for self 2/15/85; 2/20/85. Legislative interest — "... real estate industry, tax incentives for savings, FHA-HUD authorizations, mortgage revenue bonds, federal budget, restructuring financial institutions, enterprise zones, FHA-HUD negotiated interest rates, environment/land development, imputed interest, cable TV legislation, tax reform legislation." Lobbyists — Ellen L. Maitland, Peter T. Madigan.

NATIONAL CABLE TELEVISION ASSOCIATION, Washington, D.C. Lobbyist — Parry and Romani Associates Inc., 1140 Connecticut Ave. N.W., Washington, D.C. 20036. Filed 2/12/85. Legislative interest — "Cable Deregulation Bill (PL 98-549)."

NATIONAL COUNCIL OF COMMUNITY MENTAL HEALTH CENTERS, Rockville, Md. Lobbyist — Liz Robbins Associates, 132 D St. S.E., Washington, D.C. 20003. Filed 2/22/85. Legislative interest — "... Preservation of Mental Health Block Grant."

NATIONAL RESTAURANT ASSOCIATION, 311 First St. N.W., Washington, D.C. 20001. Filed for self 2/11/85. Legislative interest — "... small business, labor laws, wages and hours, taxation, consumer protection, food marketing and economic stabilization." Lobbyist — Keith Keener.

NATIONAL VEHICLE LEASING ASSOCIATION, Los Angeles, Calif. Lobbyist — Kirby, Gillick, Schwartz & Tuohey, 1220 L St. N.W., Washington, D.C. 20005. Filed 2/6/85. Legislative interest — "Tax Code revision, Federal Motor Vehicle regulations. ..."

NATURAL GAS SUPPLY ASSOCIATION, 1730 Rhode Island Ave. N.W., Washington, D.C. 20036. Filed for self 2/14/85. Legislative interest — "... oversight of the Natural Gas Policy Act of 1978, and amending same with a view toward consumer and national defense." Lobbyist — Melinda M. Zimmerman.

PHARMACEUTICAL MANUFACTURERS ASSOCIATION, 1100 15th St. N.W., Washington, D.C. 20005. Filed for self 2/21/85. Legislative interest — Not specified. Lobbyist — Gerald J. Mossinghoff.

RENEWABLE FUELS ASSOCIATION, 499 South Capitol St. S.W., Washington, D.C. 20003. Filed for self 2/14/85. Legislative interest — Not specified. Lobbyist — Eric Vaughn.

SMALL BUSINESS COUNCIL OF AMERICA INC., Columbus, Ga. Lobbyist — David P. Stang, 1629 K St. N.W., Washington, D.C. 20006. Filed 2/14/85. Legislative interest — "Tax and pension issues related to small businesses."

U.S. LEAGUE OF SAVINGS INSTITUTIONS, 111 E. Wacker Drive, Chicago, Ill 60601. Filed 2/6/85. Legislative interest — "... savings and loans, housing, home financing, thrift and financial institutions." Lobbyists — Susan Carr, Michael D. Solomon, 1709 New York Ave. N.W., Washington, D.C. 20006.

Miscellaneous

AMERICAN ASSOCIATION OF UNIVERSITY WOMEN, 2401 Virginia Ave. N.W., Washington, D.C. 20037. Filed for self 2/15/85. Legislative interest — "... economic and educational equity measures. Specific bills include Civil Rights Restoration Act of 1985 (HR 700, S 431); Student Assistance Equity Act, Economic Equity Act, pay equity legislation." Lobbyists — Kristin Stelck, Patricia Smith.

AMERICAN NUCLEAR ENERGY COUNCIL, Washington, D.C. Lobbyist — Campbell-Raupe Associates Inc., 1015 15th St. N.W., Washington, D.C. 20005. Filed 2/6/85. Legislative interest — Not specified.

CENTER FOR RURAL AFFAIRS, P.O. Box 405, Walthill, Neb. 68067. Filed for self 2/25/85; 2/26/85. Legislative interest — "... Farmers Home Administration legislation, and ... 'The Farm Bill,' and ... income tax legislation." Lobbyist — Jay P. Sherman.

CENTER FOR SCIENCE IN THE PUBLIC INTEREST, 1501 16th St. N.W., Washington, D.C. 20036. Filed for self 2/15/85. Legislative interest — "... restrictions on marketing of alcoholic beverages, excise taxes on alcoholic beverages, and ingredient and caloric labeling of alcoholic beverages...." Lobbyist — George Hacker.

CITIZEN'S CHOICE INC., 1615 H St. N.W., Washington, D.C. 20062. Filed for self 2/19/85. Legislative interest — Not specified. Lobbyist — David Michael Staton (Former U.S. rep., R-W.Va., 1981-83).

CONSTITUTIONAL RIGHTS FOUNDATION, Los Angeles, Calif. Lobbyist — Dechert, Price & Rhoads, 1730 Pennsylvania Ave. N.W., Washington, D.C. 20006. Filed 2/27/85. Legislative interest — "Youth, education and delinquency prevention legislation."

CONSUMERS UNITED FOR RAIL EQUITY, Washington, D.C. Lobbyist — Craft & Richards, 1050 Thomas Jefferson St. N.W., Washington, D.C. 20007. Filed 2/7/85. Legislative interest — "All legislation ... relating to Staggers Rail Act Amendments."

FRIENDSHIP HILL ASSOCIATION, New Geneva, Pa. Lobbyist — Gail DeLoach, P.O. Box 8091, Falls Church, Va. 22041. Filed 2/28/85. Legislative interest — Not specified.

FRANCIS J. GIST, 1511 K St. N.W., Washington, D.C. 20005. Filed for self 2/21/85. Legislative interest — "Immigration issues, Edwin Meese confirmation debates and related matters."

MARY SCOTT GUEST, 1919 Pennsylvania Ave. N.W., Washington, D.C. 20006. Filed for self 2/27/85. Legislative interest — "Tax, banking, securities legislation - 1985 Tax Bill, 1985 Budget Bill, Banking Deregulation 1985."

THE HUMANE SOCIETY OF THE UNITED STATES, Washington, D.C. Lobbyist — Foley, Hoag & Eliot, 1 Post Office Square, Boston, Mass. 02109. Filed 2/7/85. Legislative interest — "... to oppose renewal of the Interim Convention on the conservation of North Pacific Fur Seals which is subject to Senate ratification this year."

W. K. KELLOGG FOUNDATION, Battle Creek, Mich. Lobbyist — Riddell, Holroyd & Butler, 1331 Pennsylvania Ave. N.W., Washington, D.C. 20004. Filed 2/25/85. Legislative interest — "Any legislation amending the Internal Revenue Code with respect to the excess business holdings of private foundations and any other legislation affecting private foundations."

DALE RODNEY KETCHAM, 223 Columbia Drive, Cape Canaveral, Fla. 32920. Filed for self 2/6/85. Legislative interest — "... promotion of State of Florida and maintenances of quality of life of same...."

LAW IN A FREE SOCIETY, Calabasas, Calif. Lobbyist — Dechert, Price & Rhoads, 1730 Pennsylvania Ave. N.W., Washington, D.C. 20006. Filed 2/27/85. Legislative interest — "Youth, education and delinquency prevention legislation."

MARIST COLLEGE, Poughkeepsie, N.Y. Lobbyist — Gold and Liebengood Inc., 1050 Connecticut Ave. N.W., Washington, D.C. 20036. Filed 2/27/85. Legislative interest — "... Title III education grants."

MASSACHUSETTS SOCIETY FOR THE PREVENTION OF CRUELTY TO ANIMALS, Framingham Centre, Mass. Lobbyist — Foley, Hoag & Eliot, 1 Post Office Square, Boston, Mass. 02109. Filed 2/7/85. Legislative interest — "... to oppose renewal of the Interim Convention on the conservation of North Pacific Fur Seals which is subject to Senate ratification this year."

NATIONAL INSTITUTE FOR CITIZEN EDUCATION IN THE LAW, Washington, D.C. Lobbyist — Dechert, Price & Rhoads, 1730 Pennsylvania Ave. N.W., Washington, D.C. 20006. Filed 2/27/85. Legislative interest — "Youth, education and delinquency prevention legislation."

NATIONAL WOMEN'S POLITICAL CAUCUS, 1275 K St. N.W., Washington, D.C. 20005. Filed for self 2/28/85. Legislative interest — "Abortion: opposed to all bills and amendments to restrict abortion ... Budget: opposed to block grants and cuts in domestic spending and entitlements ... Civil Rights: support the Civil Rights Restoration Act of 1985 ... Title X: support ... Equal Rights Amendment: support ... Economic Equity: support Economic Equity Act and related bills ... Child Care: support ... Education: support efforts to expand opportunities for women in education; support efforts to eliminate sex discrimination in education." Lobbyist — Rebecca G. Bown.

NEW GENERATION LOBBY, 410 Eighth Ave., Dayton, Ky. 41074. Filed for self 2/11/85. Legislative interest — "... Promoting Small Business ... Advocating Sentencing Alternatives." Lobbyists — Luis Eduardo Castaneda, Christopher Lynn Meyer.

TEXANS FOR A RESPONSIBLE AMERICA, 1300 Main St., Houston, Texas 77002. Filed for self 2/26/85. Legislative interest — "1986 Federal Budget." Lobbyist — Rob Mosbacher.

UNION OF CONCERNED SCIENTISTS, 1346 Connecticut Ave. N.W., Washington, D.C. 20016. Filed for self 2/20/85. Legislative interest — "DOD Authorizations ... DOD Appropriations." Lobbyist — Peter F. Dioisheim.

U.S. PUBLIC INTEREST RESEARCH GROUP, 215 Pennsylvania Ave. S.E., Washington, D.C. 20003. Filed for self 2/4/85, 2/13/85. Legislative interest — "Various bills concerning telecommunications policy, product liability, and legal services for the poor." Lobbyist — Pamela Gilbert. Filed for self 2/4/85. Legislative interest — "Support for legislation to control and clean up hazardous chemicals and toxic wastes." Lobbyists — Rick Hind, Gene Karpinski. Filed for self 2/13/85. Legislative interest — "Support for election law reform, campaign finance reform, and utility rate reform." Lobbyist — Gene Karpinski.

THE WILDERNESS SOCIETY, 1400 I St. N.W., Washington, D.C. 20005. Filed for self 2/11/85. Legislative interest — Not specified. Lobbyist — Barry Flamm. Filed for self 2/14/85. Legislative interest — Not specified. Lobbyist — Madeline Fishel.

WORLD ZIONIST ORGANIZATION, Jerusalem, Israel. Lobbyist — Cole & Corette, 1110 Vermont Ave. N.W., Washington, D.C. 20005. Filed 2/12/85. Lobbyist — Laventhol & Horwath, 1901 L St., N.W., Washington, D.C. 20036. Filed 2/12/85. Lobbyists — Isadore Hamlin, Bernice Tannenbaum, 515 Park Ave., New York, N.Y. 10022. Filed for self 2/12/85. Legislative interest — "Legislation which would effect an amendment to the definitions of 'non-resident alien' and 'resident alien' in section 7701(e) of the Internal Revenue Code, as amended."

March Registrations

Corporations and Businesses

ADAPSO, 1300 N. 17th St., Arlington, Va. 22209. Filed for self 3/7/85. Legislative interest — Not specified. Lobbyist — Karen M. Greiner.

AIR PRODUCTS & CHEMICALS INC., Allentown, Pa. Lobbyist — Skadden, Arps, Slate, Meagher & Flom, 919 18th St. N.W., Washington, D.C. 20006. Filed 3/14/85. Legislative interest — "Superfund Legislation."

ALGONQUIN GAS TRANSMISSION, Brighton, Mass.

Lobbyist — Campbell-Raupe Associates Inc., 1015 15th St. N.W., Washington, D.C. 20005. Filed 3/7/85. Legislative interest — "... natural gas transmission and energy related business."

ALLIED CORP., 1150 Connecticut Ave. N.W., Washington, D.C. 20036. Filed for self 3/11/85. Legislative interest — "... mergers, international trade, and product liability." Lobbyist — Elvira J. Orly. Filed for self 3/18/85. Legislative interest — "Health, labor, transportation and other matters affecting Allied Corporation." Lobbyist — Michael W. Naylor.

ALLIED CORP., P.O. Box 3000-R, Morristown, N.J. 07960. Filed for self 3/18/85. Legislative interest — "Health, labor, transportation and other matters...." Lobbyist — Michael W. Naylor, 1150 Connecticut Ave. N.W., Washington, D.C. 20036.

AMERICAN CYANAMID CO., Wayne, N.J. Lobbyist — Wilmer, Cutler & Pickering, 1666 K St. N.W., Washington, D.C. 20006. Filed 3/11/85. Legislative interest — "... legislation that would create a mechanism for resolving claims for vaccine-related injuries and place reasonable limits on awards therefor."

ANCHOR INN RESTAURANT INC., Murrells Inlet, S.C. Lobbyist — Kilpatrick & Cody, 2501 M St. N.W., Washington, D.C. 20037. Filed 3/21/85. Legislative interest — "Technical corrections to Tax Reform Act of 1984; IRC section 280B; for modification of transition rule."

APPLE COMPUTER INC., Cupertino, Calif. Lobbyist — Robert H. Scarborough, 1700 Pennsylvania Ave. N.W., Washington, D.C. 20006. Filed 3/22/85. Legislative interest — "... federal income taxation. Specifically, lobbying for modification of section 179 of PL 98-369 (Sections 280F and 274(d) of the Internal Revenue Code), and lobbying in support of HR 531."

ATCHISON, TOPEKA, SANTA FE RAILROAD CO., Chicago, Ill. Lobbyist — Piper & Marbury, 888 16th St. N.W., Washington, D.C. 20006. Filed 3/25/85. Legislative interest — "For amendments to IRC secs. 4051-3 to extend, and to make technical changes to, expiring reduction in rate of excise tax on the retail sale of railroad piggyback equipment."

SANFORD C. BERNSTEIN & CO. INC., New York, N.Y. Lobbyist — Morgan, Lewis & Bockius, 1800 M St. N.W., Washington, D.C. 20036. Filed 3/4/85. Legislative interest — "Amendment of IRC to permit charities to own stock of U.S. corporations."

THE BOEING CO., Seattle, Wash. Lobbyist — Perkins, Coie, 1110 Vermont Ave. N.W., Washington, D.C. 20005. Filed 3/14/85. Legislative interest — "... product liability and related legislation."

BOWATER INDUSTRIES P.L.C., London, England. Lobbyist — Paul H. DeLaney Jr., 1120 20th St. N.W., Washington, D.C. 20036. Filed 3/14/85. Legislative interest — "Possible further changes to the Foreign Investment in Real Property Tax Act of 1980."

BROADHEAD INVESTMENTS INC., Meridian, Miss. Lobbyist — Cassidy & Associates Inc., 955 L'Enfant Plaza S.W., Washington, D.C. 20024. Filed 3/14/85. Legislative interest — "... agriculture and agricultural research."

BURKE, HARTMAN, HALLBERG & CONKLING, 655 15th St. N.W., Washington, D.C. 20005. Filed for self 3/4/85. Legislative interest — "... trade, energy, agriculture and business taxes." Lobbyists — Charles D. Hartman, David E. Hallberg, Paul T. Burke, Raymond F. Conkling.

CCS AUTOMATION SYSTEMS INC., El Segundo, Calif. Lobbyist — Corman Law Offices, 1420 16th St. N.W., Washington, D.C. 20036. Filed 3/28/85. Legislative interest — "... HR 528, and S 120 ... to modify present federal law concerning tax-exempt travel benefits for employees."

CSX CORP., Richmond Va. Lobbyist — McGuire, Woods & Battle, 1400 Ross Building, Richmond, Va. 23219. Filed 3/14/85. Legislative interest — "... transportation and natural resources including the proposed sale of Conrail." Lobbyist — Arnold & Porter, 1200 New Hampshire Ave. N.W., Washington, D.C. 20036. Filed 3/19/85; 3/22/85. Legislative interest — "... opposing legislation to authorize sale of Conrail to Norfolk-Southern Railroad."

CHICAGO TITLE INSURANCE CO., Chicago, Ill. Lobbyist — Gray & Co., 3255 Grace St. N.W., Washington, D.C. 20007. Filed 3/14/85. Legislative interest — "Antitrust legislation relating to the title insurance industry."

CHRYSLER CORP., 12000 Chrysler Drive, Highland Park, Mich. 48288. Filed for self 3/8/85. Legislative interest — Not specified. Lobbyist — Robert G. Liberatore, 1100 Connecticut Ave. N.W., Washington, D.C. 20036.

CONSOLIDATED RAIL CORP., Washington, D.C. Lobbyist — O'Connor & Hannan, 1919 Pennsylvania Ave. N.W., Washington, D.C. 20006. Filed 3/27/85. Legislative interest — "... sale of Consolidated Rail Corporation."

CONTINENTAL GRAIN CO., New York, N.Y. Lobbyist — Paul H. DeLaney Jr., 1120 20th St. N.W., Washington, D.C. 20036. Filed 3/14/85. Legislative interest — "Possible technical corrections to the Tax Reform Act of 1984."

DATA GENERAL CORP., 4400 Computer Drive, Westboro, Mass. 01580. Filed for self 3/4/85. Legislative interest — "... tax reform, amendments to existing tax law, trade, intellectual property rights, and other legislative and oversight activities affecting high technology industries." Lobbyist — John W. Moriarty.

DOW CHEMICAL CO., Midland, Mich. Lobbyist — Barnes, Richardson & Colburn, 1819 H St. N.W., Washington, D.C. 20006. Filed 3/21/85. Legislative interest — "... Trade and Tariff Act of 1984; ... HR 3398, Amend. 4281; HR 6064, Section 117; HR 4232; HR 5455; ... TSUS, 19 USC 1202; ... opposed to tariff reclassification and import quota on naphtha used as petrochemical feedstock."

FIRST AMERICAN TITLE INSURANCE CO., Troy, Mich. Lobbyist — Gray & Co., 3255 Grace St. N.W., Washington, D.C. 20007. Filed 3/14/85. Legislative interest — "Antitrust legislation relating to the title insurance industry."

FIRST DATA RESOURCES, 7301 Pacific St., Omaha, Neb. 68114. Filed for self 3/18/85. Legislative interest — "To monitor immigration reform legislation and appropriations for the INS." Lobbyist — David C. Runnell.

THE FLYING TIGER LINE INC., Los Angeles, Calif. Lobbyist — Manatt, Phelps, Rothenberg & Tunney, 1200 New Hampshire Ave. N.W., Washington, D.C. 20036. Filed 3/21/85. Legislative interest — "... civil aviation negotiations with foreign governments."

GSX CORP., Boston, Mass. Lobbyist — Mintz, Levin, Cohn, Ferris, Glovsky & Popeo, 1825 I St. N.W., Washington, D.C. 20006. Filed 3/29/85. Legislative interest — "... solid and hazardous waste industry."

GLOBAL DEFENSE & SPACE INC., 2550 M St. N.W., Washington, D.C. 20037. Filed for self 3/12/85. Legislative interest — Not specified. Lobbyist — Thomas W. Battaglia.

GRAND TRUNK CORP., Detroit, Mich. Lobbyist — Hamel & Park, 888 16th St. N.W., Washington, D.C. 20006. Filed 3/20/85. Legislative interest — "... regulation of transportation companies and impacting rail transportation services, including the Conrail Sale Amendments Act of 1985."

GREENWOOD MILLS MARKETING CO., 111 W. 40th St., New York, N.Y. 10018. Filed for self 3/12/85. Legislative interest — "... imports of textiles and apparel products." Lobbyist — Robert F. Eisen.

GRUMMAN CORP., Bethpage, N.Y. 11714. Filed for self 3/22/85. Legislative interest — "... the aerospace industry ...." Lobbyist — George L. Brown, 1000 Wilson Blvd., Arlington, Va. 22209.

GULF & WESTERN INDUSTRIES INC., New York, N.Y. Lobbyist — Akin, Gump, Strauss, Hauer & Feld, 1333 New Hampshire Ave. N.W., Washington, D.C. 20036. Filed 3/1/85. Legislative interest — "HR 15, 'Depository Institutions Act of 1985'; HR 20, 'Bank Definition Act of 1985' ... the banking industry." Lobbyist — Dutko and Associates, 412 First St. S.E., Washington, D.C. 20003. Filed 3/19/85. Legislative interest — "... HR 20 and other Banking legislation." Filed for self 3/21/85. Legislative interest — "... domestic commerce, including general trade matters, publishing, motion pictures and financial services." Lobbyist — Lawrence E. Levinson.

THE HARTFORD FIRE INSURANCE GROUP, Hartford, Conn. Lobbyist — Jones & Winburn, 50 E St. S.E., Washington, D.C. 20003. Filed 3/20/85. Legislative interest — "... taxation of life insurance companies."

KIDDER PEABODY & CO. INC., New York, N.Y. Lobbyist — Sullivan & Cromwell, 1775 Pennsylvania Ave. N.W., Washington, D.C. 20006. Filed 3/4/85. Legislative interest — "Technical amendments to provisions of the Tax Reform Act of 1984, PL 98-369, relating to distributions to corporate shareholders. . . ."

LAWYERS TITLE INSURANCE CO., Richmond, Va. Lobbyist — Gray & Co., 3255 Grace St. N.W., Washington, D.C. 20007. Filed 3/14/85. Legislative interest — "Antitrust legislation relating to the title insurance industry."

LEADING EDGE PRODUCTS INC., Wellesley, Mass. Lobbyist — Foley, Hoag & Eliot, 1 Post Office Square, Boston, Mass. 02109. Filed 3/26/85. (Former U.S. Sen. Paul E. Tsongas, D-Mass., 1979-85, was listed among agents for this client.) Legislative interest — ". . . amend Section 301 of the 1974 Trade Act."

LIFE OF VIRGINIA, Richmond, Va. Lobbyist — R. Duffy Wall & Associates Inc., 1317 F St. N.W., Washington, D.C. 20004. Filed 3/14/85. Legislative interest — ". . . life insurance taxation."

LINCOLN SAVINGS & LOAN ASSOCIATION, Irvine, Calif. Lobbyist — Bricker & Eckler, 888 17th St. N.W., Washington, D.C. 20006. Filed 3/12/85. Legislative interest — "Financial Institutions. . . ."

LOTUS DEVELOPMENT CORP., Cambridge, Mass. Lobbyist — Cole & Corette, 1110 Vermont Ave. N.W., Washington, D.C. 20005. Filed 3/6/85. Legislative interest — "Preservation of tax credits for U.S. possessions under section 936 of the Internal Revenue Code of 1954, as amended."

MEMEL, JACOBS, PIERNO, GERSH & ELLSWORTH, 1800 M St. N.W., Washington, D.C. 20036. Filed for self 3/11/85, 3/29/85. Legislative interest — "Healthcare. . . ." Lobbyist — Anne Gallagher.

MERCEDES-BENZ OF NORTH AMERICA INC., Montvale, N.J. Lobbyist — Charles G. Hardin, 815 Connecticut Ave. N.W., Washington, D.C. 20006. Filed 3/25/85. Legislative interest — ". . . amending the National Traffic and Motor Vehicle Safety Act of 1966 with respect to the importation of 'gray market' passenger automobiles that do not conform with U.S."

MOORE McCORMACK RESOURCES, Washington, D.C. Lobbyist — Lipsen, Hamberger, Whitten & Hamberger, 1725 DeSales St. N.W., Washington, D.C. 20006. Filed 3/4/85. Legislative interest — ". . . transportation."

NORANDA MINING INC., Juneau, Alaska. Lobbyist — Robertson, Monagle, Eastaugh & Bradley, 21 Dupont Circle, Washington, D.C. 20036. Filed 3/18/85. Legislative interest — ". . . Alaska Public Land Issues and . . . Admiralty Island National Monument."

NORFOLK SOUTHERN CORP., Washington, D.C. Lobbyist — Lipsen, Hamberger, Whitten & Hamberger, 1725 DeSales St. N.W., Washington, D.C. 20036. Filed 3/4/85. Legislative interest — "Sale of Conrail." Lobbyist — Williams & Jensen, 1101 Connecticut Ave. N.W., Washington, D.C. 20036. Filed 3/5/85. Legislative interest — ". . . approval of proposed Norfolk Southern acquisition of Conrail." Lobbyist — James A. Johnson, 2550 M St. N.W., Washington, D.C. 20037. Filed 3/18/85. Legislative interest — ". . . the federal government's efforts to sell Conrail." Lobbyist — Edward Hidalgo, 1828 L St. N.W., Washington, D.C. 20036. Filed 3/14/85. Legislative interest — "Acquisition of Conrail by Norfolk Southern pursuant to bid submitted to and approved by Dept. of Transportation."

NORFOLK SOUTHERN CORP., Norfolk, Va. Lobbyist — Verner, Liipfert, Bernhard, McPherson & Hand, 1660 L St. N.W., Washington, D.C. 20036. Filed 3/12/85. Legislative interest — ". . . railroad industry, including proposed Conrail sale." Lobbyist — Dewey, Ballantine, Bushby, Palmer & Wood, 1775 Pennsylvania Ave. N.W., Washington, D.C. 20006. Filed 3/20/85. Legislative interest — "Tax issues related to the acquisition of the Consolidated Rail Corporation ('Conrail')."

OCEAN THERMAL CORP., New York, N.Y. Lobbyist — Skadden, Arps, Slate, Meagher & Flom, 919 18th St. N.W., Washington, D.C. 20006. Filed 3/14/85. Legislative interest — "Tax legislation affecting ocean thermal energy conversion."

PFIZER INC., Washington, D.C. Lobbyist — Rogers & Wells, 1737 H St. N.W., Washington, D.C. 20006. Filed 3/6/85. Legislative interest — "Revision of Temporary Regulations on Fringe Benefits (T.D. 8004)."

PHILLIPS PETROLEUM CO., Bartlesville, Okla. Lobbyist — D L Associates Inc., 1730 Rhode Island Ave. N.W., Washington, D.C. 20036. Filed 3/7/85. Legislative interest — "HR 1100 and S 476." Lobbyist — Royer & Shacknai, 1747 Pennsylvania Ave. N.W., Washington, D.C. 20006. Filed 3/18/85. Legislative interest — ". . . oil & gas industry. . . ." Lobbyist — Gold and Liebengood Inc., 1050 Connecticut Ave. N.W., Washington, D.C. 20036. Filed 3/22/85. Legislative interest — "S 476, amending the Internal Revenue Code of 1954 relative to hostile takeovers and acquisitions. . . ."

ROBERT A. RAPOZA ASSOCIATES, 2001 S St. N.W., Washington, D.C. 20007. Filed for self 3/14/85, 3/28/85. Legislative interest — "Matters necessary to provision of representation and legislative choice with respect to low income housing and community development issues." Lobbyist — Robert A. Rapoza.

ROHM AND HAAS CO., Philadelphia, Pa. Lobbyist — Robin W. McClung, 1667 K St. N.W., Washington, D.C. 20006. Filed 3/28/85. Legislative interest — ". . . manufacture, use, and sale of chemicals and allied products. Clean Air . . . Clean Water . . . Groundwater . . . OSHA Amendments . . . Patent Term Restoration . . . Port Development/User Fees . . . Product Liability . . . R&D/Antitrust Issues . . . Risk Assessment . . . Superfund . . . Tax Issues (Research and Development) . . . Toxic Substances Control Act."

SCM CORP., New York, N.Y. Lobbyist — Vorys, Sater, Seymour & Pease, 1828 L St. N.W., Washington, D.C. 20036. Filed 3/18/85. Legislative interest — ". . . corporate governance issues including HR 1100, HR 5914, HR 960, HR 998, HR 1074; S 217, S 286, S 414, S 420, S 473; and others."

SKW ALLOYS INC., Niagara Falls, N.Y. Lobbyist — Powell, Goldstein, Frazer & Murphy, 1110 Vermont Ave. N.W., Washington, D.C. 20005. Filed 3/11/85. Legislative interest — ". . . securing a breakpoint pricing system in Congress."

SAFECO TITLE INSURANCE CO., Seattle, Wash. Lobbyist — Gray & Co., 3255 Grace St. N.W., Washington, D.C. 20007. Filed 3/14/85. Legislative interest — "Antitrust legislation relating to the title insurance industry."

SANTA FE INTERNATIONAL CORP., 1819 L St. N.W., Washington, D.C. 20036. Filed for self 3/7/85. Legislative interest — "Petroleum Import Fees, Tax & Natural Resource Legislation. . . ." Lobbyists — Barbara Diane Gorra, James K. Walton.

SANTA FE SOUTHERN PACIFIC CORP., Chicago, Ill. Lobbyist — Piper & Marbury, 888 16th St. N.W., Washington, D.C. 20006. Filed 3/25/85. Legislative interest — "For amendments to IRC secs. 4051-3 to extend, and to make technical changes to, expiring reduction in rate of excise tax on the retail sale of railroad piggyback equipment."

SHEARSON LEHMAN BROTHERS, New York, N.Y. Lobbyist — James A. Johnson, 2550 M St. N.W., Washington, D.C. 20037. Filed 3/18/85. Legislative interest — ". . . the federal government's efforts to sell Conrail."

SOUTHERN PACIFIC TRANSPORTATION CO., San Francisco, Calif. Lobbyist — Piper & Marbury, 888 16th St. N.W., Washington, D.C. 20006. Filed 3/25/85. Legislative interest — "For amendments to IRC secs. 4051-3 to extend, and to make technical changes to, expiring reduction in rate of excise tax on the retail sale of railroad piggyback equipment."

J. P. STEVENS & CO., 1185 Avenue of the Americas, New York, N.Y. 10036. Filed for self 3/26/85. Legislative interest — ". . . textile and apparel industries, including . . . the importation of textiles and apparel products into the United States." Lobbyist — James R. Franklin.

STEWART TITLE GUARANTY CO., Houston, Texas. Lobbyist — Gray & Co., 3255 Grace St. N.W., Washington, D.C. 20007. Filed 3/14/85. Legislative interest — "Antitrust legislation relating to the title insurance industry."

TRANSAMERICA INTERWAY INC., New York, N.Y. Lobbyist — Piper & Marbury, 888 16th St. N.W., Washington, D.C. 20006. Filed 3/25/85. Legislative interest — "For amendments to IRC secs. 4051-3 to extend, and to make technical changes to, expiring reduction in rate of excise tax on the retail sale of railroad piggyback equipment."

UNION MUTUAL LIFE INSURANCE CO., 2211 Congress St., Portland, Maine 04122. Filed for self 3/18/85. Legislative interest — "... life & health insurance industry." Lobbyist — Donna T. Mundy.

UNIQUE ATHLETES INC., 3 Woodland Ave., Westhampton Beach, N.Y. 11978. Filed for self 3/28/85. Legislative interest — Not specified.

UNITED STATES FOOTBALL LEAGUE, New York, N.Y. Lobbyist — Anderson, Hibey, Nauheim & Blair, 1708 New Hampshire Ave. N.W., Washington, D.C. 20009. Filed 3/26/85. Legislative interest — "... broadcast coverage of professional football."

U.S. WEST INC., 1819 L St. N.W., Washington, D.C. 20036. Filed for self 3/15/85; 3/18/85. Legislative interest — "Telecommunications and tax legislation including, but not limited to, the Treasury Department's Tax Simplification and Reform Proposals, the 'Lifeline Telephone Service Act of 1985' (HR 151) and the 'Telecommunications Policy Coordination Act of 1985' (HR 642)." Lobbyists — Debra T. Yarbrough, Wayne G. Allcott, James A. Smith.

WESTINGHOUSE ELECTRIC CORP., Westinghouse Building, Gateway Center, Pittsburgh, Pa. 15222. Filed for self 3/21/85. Legislative interest — "... taxation, nuclear and fossil energy, international trade and trade regulations, labor-management relations, Government procurement, pension plans and patents." Lobbyist — John K. Rayburn, 1801 K St. N.W., Washington, D.C. 20006.

WISCONSIN DAIRIES, Reedsburg, Wis. Lobbyist — Leonard & McGuan, 900 17th St. N.W., Washington, D.C. 20006. Filed 3/28/85. Legislative interest — "Dairy Legislation."

International Relations

TURKEY, REPUBLIC OF, Ankara, Turkey. Lobbyist — Gray & Co., 3255 Grace St. N.W., Washington, D.C. 20007. Filed 3/14/85. Legislative interest — "... economic assistance and security issues."

SAUDI ARABIA, ROYAL EMBASSY OF, Washington, D.C. Lobbyist — The Hannaford Co. Inc., 655 15th St. N.W., Washington, D.C. 20005. Filed 3/18/85. Legislative interest — Not specified.

Labor Organizations

AMERICAN FEDERATION OF STATE, COUNTY AND MUNICIPAL EMPLOYEES, AFL-CIO, 1625 L St. N.W., Washington, D.C. 20036. Filed for self 3/13/85. Legislative interest — "... the welfare of the country generally and state, county and municipal workers specifically." Lobbyists — Diane B. Burke, Lynn Rosinsky.

INTERNATIONAL UNION OF POLICE ASSOCIATIONS, AFL-CIO, Washington, D.C. Lobbyist — Leonard & McGuan, 900 17th St. N.W., Washington, D.C. 20016. Filed 3/27/85. Legislative interest — "Exemption of certain police crime prevention programs - Police Personal Motor Vehicle Program - from the mandate of the fringe benefits and record keeping requirements of the Tax Reform Act of 1984."

State and Local Governments

GRANT COUNTY PUBLIC UTILITY DISTRICT, Ephrata, Wash. Lobbyist — Preston, Thorgrimson, Ellis & Holman, 1735 New York Ave. N.W., Washington, D.C. 20006. Filed 3/1/85. Legislative interest — "... to amend Section 103 of the Internal Revenue Code and ... pending bills for tax reform: HR 800, HR 1040 and S 325."

SAVANNAH - CHATHAM COUNTY BOARD OF EDUCATION, Savannah, Ga. Lobbyist — Fisher & Phillips, Two Peachtree St. N.W., Atlanta, Ga. 30383. Filed 3/22/85. Legislative interest — "... education legislation (S 415 and HR 1523)."

Trade Associations

AIR TRAFFIC CONTROL ASSOCIATION INC., Arlington, Va. Lobbyist — Suzette Matthews, 1726 M St. N.W., Washington, D.C. 20036. Filed 3/11/85. Legislative interest — "... proposals ... which relate to air traffic control, aviation, aviation safety, and matters affecting personnel including federal employees who develop, install, maintain and operate ATC facilities."

ALLIANCE FOR MEDICAL NUTRITION, Washington, D.C. Lobbyist — Memel, Jacobs, Pierno, Gersh & Ellsworth, 1800 M St. N.W., Washington, D.C. 20036. Filed 3/6/85. Legislative interest — "Health legislation affecting parenteral and/or enteral nutrition, including but not limited to legislation modifying Medicare & Medicaid reimbursement and coverage of such services, budgetary issues affecting health in general, nutrition in particular."

AMERICAN CONGRESS ON REAL ESTATE, 145 E. Center St., Provo, Utah 84601. Filed for self 3/14/85. Legislative interest — "... real estate and budget considerations ... imputed interest provisions - against ... Treasury Tax reform proposal - against." Lobbyist — Paul T. Mero.

AMERICAN INSURANCE ASSOCIATION, New York, N.Y. Lobbyist — Hunton & Williams, P.O. Box 1535, Richmond, Va. 23212. Filed 3/29/85. Legislative interest — "Hazardous substance liability — Comprehensive Environmental Response, Compensation and Liability Act of 1980 42 U.S.C. section 9601; et seq.; S 494, Comprehensive Environmental Response, Compensation and Liability Act Amendments of 1985; with changes."

AMERICAN PETROLEUM INSTITUTE, 1220 L St. N.W., Washington, D.C. 20005. Lobbyist — Bishop, Liberman, Cook, Purcell & Reynolds, 1200 17th St. N.W., Washington, D.C. 20036. Filed 3/14/85. Legislative interest — "... energy matters, tax matters, and the oil industry in general." Filed for self 3/26/85. Legislative interest — "OCS Legislation; CZM Legislation; CERCLA Reauthorization." Lobbyist — J. Ross Martin, Kansas Petroleum Council, Eighth & Jackson, Topeka, Kan. 66612.

AMERICAN PSYCHIATRIC ASSOCIATION, 1400 K St. N.W., Washington, D.C. 20005. Filed for self 3/29/85. Legislative interest — "Federal Employees' Health Benefits Program, Indian Health, Health Care Financing, Veteran's Health." Lobbyist — Patricia Ryan.

AMERICAN TEXTILE MANUFACTURERS INSTITUTE INC., 1101 Connecticut Ave. N.W., Washington, D.C. 20036. Filed for self 3/1/85, 3/7/85. Legislative interest — "... the welfare of the textile industry — such as domestic and foreign trade policy, tax policy, consumer issues, environmental control, energy and lobbying legislation." Lobbyist — Carlos Moore.

AMERICAN TRUCKING ASSOCIATIONS INC., Alexandria, Va. Lobbyist — O'Connor & Hannan, 1919 Pennsylvania Ave. N.W., Washington, D.C. 20006. Filed 3/8/85. Legislative interest — "... amend the Employees Retirement Securities Act."

AMERICAN WOOD PRESERVERS INSTITUTE, 1945 Old Gallows Rd., Vienna, Va. 22180. Filed for self 3/22/85. Legislative interest — "... Clean Air Act, FIFRA, Clean Water Act, Occupational Safety and Health Act, RCRA, Safe Drinking Water Act, CERCLA, TSCA, Used Oil Recycling Act of 1980 ... environmental legislation." Lobbyist — Robert G. Smerko.

THE ASPIRIN FOUNDATION OF AMERICA INC., Scarsdale, N.Y. Lobbyist — Paul, Hastings, Janofsky & Walker, 1050 Thomas Jefferson St. N.W., Washington, D.C. 20007. Filed 3/6/85. Legislative interest — "... aspirin labeling (S 538; HR 1381)."

BURLEY & DARK LEAF TOBACCO EXPORT ASSOCIATION, 1100 17th St. N.W., Washington, D.C. 20036. Filed for self 3/11/85. Legislative interest — "... tobacco, particularly Burley, Dark Air-Cured, Dark Fire-Cured and cigar types." Lobbyist — Benjamin F. Reeves.

CAPITAL MARKETS GROUP, New York, N.Y. Lobbyist — John R. Evans, 9208 Seven Locks Road, Bethesda, Md. 20817. Filed 3/27/85. Legislative interest — "...to oppose prohibition or severe restrictions on corporate takeovers."

CHAMBER OF COMMERCE OF THE UNITED STATES, 1615 H St. N.W., Washington, D.C. 20062. Filed for self

3/4/85. Legislative interest — Not specified. Lobbyist — Dorothy D. Allen. Filed for self 3/27/85. Legislative interest — "... small business legislation...." Lobbyist — Donald C. Berno.

CHELSEA PROPERTY OWNERS, Newark, N.J. Lobbyist — Windels, Marx, Davis & Ives, 51 W. 51st St., New York, N.Y. 10019. Filed 3/28/85. Legislative interest — "ICC appropriation bills."

THE CONSUMER BANKERS ASSOCIATION, 1300 N. 17th St., Arlington, Va. 22209. Filed for self 3/20/85. Legislative interest — "... financial institutions." Lobbyists — Joe Belew, Carl A. Modecki, Craig Ulrich.

DAIRY FARMER-DISTRIBUTORS OF AMERICA INC., Chittenango, N.Y. Lobbyist — John Benjamin Carroll, 100 E. Washington St., Syracuse, N.Y. 13202. Filed 3/4/85. Legislative interest — "All Dairy Bills — for exemption for farmers processing their own milk." Filed 3/14/85. Legislative interest — "All Dairy Bills — for exemption for farmers processing their own milk."

DEALER BANK ASSOCIATION COMMITTEE ON GLASS-STEAGALL REFORM, Washington, D.C. Lobbyist — Wexler, Reynolds, Harrison & Schule, 1317 F St. N.W., Washington, D.C. 20004. Filed 3/8/85. Legislative interest — "To support legislative reforms of the Glass-Steagall Act."

THE FEDERAL LAND BANK ASSOCIATIONS OF TEXAS STOCKHOLDERS' DEFENSE FUND, Washington, D.C. Lobbyist — Ernest Wittenberg Associates Inc., 1616 H St. N.W., Washington, D.C. 20006. Filed 3/12/85. Legislative interest — "Supporting HR 1217, the Farm Credit Private Ownership Restoration Act...."

MANUFACTURED HOUSING INSTITUTE, 1745 Jefferson Davis Highway, Arlington, Va. 22202. Filed for self 3/13/85. Legislative interest — "... manufactured housing." Lobbyist — Michael F. Thompson.

MOTOR VEHICLE MANUFACTURERS ASSOCIATION, Washington, D.C. Lobbyist — Miller & Chevalier, 655 15th St. N.W., Washington, D.C. 20005. Filed 3/11/85. Legislative interest — "... Title 26 of the U.S. Code."

NATIONAL ASSOCIATION FOR STOCK CAR AUTO RACING INC., 1801 Speedway Blvd., Daytona Beach, Fla. 32015. Filed for self 3/7/85. Legislative interest — "Sports Franchise Legislation, including S Bills 172, 259, 287, 298, and HR Bills 510, 751, 785, and 956." Lobbyist — Les Richter.

NATIONAL ASSOCIATION OF DEVELOPMENT COMPANIES, 1511 K St. N.W., Washington, D.C. 20005. Filed for self 3/19/85. Legislative interest — "... Small Business Administration in general, and the loan program established by Sec. 503 of the Small Business Investment Act ... support for: S 408, to amend the Small Business Act to provide program levels, salary and expense levels, and authorization for the Small Business Administration's programs for fiscal years 1986, 1987 and 1988, and for other purposes. HR 1281, to authorize the appropriation of funds to the Small Business Administration. Public Law 85-536, the Small Business Act. Public Law 85-699, the Small Business Investment Act." Lobbyist — Jeanne L. Morin.

NATIONAL ASSOCIATION OF GOVERNMENT GUARANTEED LENDERS INC., San Francisco, Calif. Lobbyist — Dickstein, Shapiro & Morin, 2101 L St. N.W., Washington, D.C. 20037. Filed 3/4/85. Legislative interest — "... the Small Business Administration and its loan guarantee program."

NATIONAL ASSOCIATION OF HOME BUILDERS OF THE UNITED STATES, 15th & M Streets N.W., Washington, D.C. 20005. Filed for self 3/1/85. Legislative interest — Not specified. Lobbyists — Jordan Clark, Floyd L. Williams.

NATIONAL ASSOCIATION OF MANUFACTURERS, 1776 F St. N.W., Washington, D.C. 20006. Filed for self 3/11/85. Legislative interest — "House and Senate Budget Resolutions ... HR 5665, HR 5692, S 2651 - Debt limit ... All Appropriations bills." Lobbyists — Peggy L. Duxbury, Robert N. Mottice.

NATIONAL MOTORSPORTS COMMITTEE OF ACCUS, FIA, INC., Northbrook, Ill. Lobbyist — Les Richter, 1801 Speedway Blvd., Daytona Beach, Fla. 32015. Filed 3/7/85. Legislative interest — "Tax reform and revision as it applies to sports and entertainment business, including the Department of the Treasury's Report to the President on Tax Reform."

NATIONAL RURAL TELECOM ASSOCIATION, 1638 Lincoln St., Blair, Neb. 68008. Filed for self 3/8/85. Legislative interest — "... REA telephone programs, administered by the Rural Electrification Administration ... any amendments which may be offered to the Rural Electrification Act of 1936, as amended (7 USC 901-950b). Supporting REA telephone loan program provisions of Agriculture Appropriations and Budget Authority legislation for FY 1986." Lobbyist — Margaret R. Murray, 600 New Hampshire Ave. N.W., Washington, D.C. 20037.

NATIONAL SOFT DRINK ASSOCIATION, Washington, D.C. Lobbyist — Bayh, Tabbert & Capehart, 1575 I St. N.W., Washington, D.C. 20005. Filed 3/7/85. Legislative interest — "S 484 and related legislation."

NeoRx, Seattle, Wash. Lobbyist — Cassidy & Associates Inc., 955 L'Enfant Plaza S.W., Washington, D.C. 20024. Filed 3/14/85. Legislative interest — "... biotechnology and federal funding for research."

OHIO OIL & GAS ASSOCIATION, Granville, Ohio. Lobbyist — Buchanan Ingersoll, 1667 K St. N.W., Washington, D.C. 20006. Filed 3/1/85. Legislative interest — "... federal tax legislation. HR 1040; Kemp-Kasten; Bradley-Gephardt."

REINSURANCE ASSOCIATION OF AMERICA, 1025 Connecticut Ave. N.W., Washington, D.C. 20036. Filed for self 3/11/85. Legislative interest — "... reinsurance industry. Catastrophic earthquake insurance coverage legislation, taxation of insurance companies, hazardous waste, McCarran-Ferguson antitrust...." Lobbyists — Daniel J. Conway, André Maisonpierre.

RENEWABLE FUELS ASSOCIATION, 499 S. Capitol St. S.W., Washington, D.C. 20003. Filed for self 3/28/85. Legislative interest — Not specified. Lobbyist — Eric Vaughn.

S.O.S. SMALL BUSINESS JOBS, P.O. Box 65761, Washington, D.C. 20035. Filed for self 3/14/85. Legislative interest — Not specified. Lobbyist — Sara L. Loveland.

SMOKELESS TOBACCO COUNCIL INC., Washington, D.C. Lobbyist — Hannaford Co. Inc., 655 15th St. N.W., Washington, D.C. 20005. Filed 3/18/85. Legislative interest — Not specified.

TOWING AND RECOVERY ASSOCIATION OF AMERICA INC., Winter Park, Fla. Lobbyist — Alvin M. Guttman, 818 Connecticut Ave. N.W., Washington, D.C. 20006. Filed 3/29/85. Legislative interest — "... IRC section 274(d)(4) ... opposed...."

UNITED STATES BREWERS ASSOCIATION INC., 1750 K St. N.W., Washington, D.C. 20006. Filed for self 3/28/85. Legislative interest — "General Interest: alcohol beverage issues: ... Advertising; alcohol abuse; excise taxes; drinking and driving; social security and Medicare...." Lobbyist — Anne L. Vignovic. Filed for self 3/28/85. Legislative interest — "Alcoholic Beverage Issues — Advertising, Mandatory Deposits, Excise Taxes, Social Security and Medicare, Food Safety." Lobbyist — Donald B. Shea.

Miscellaneous

AMERICAN RED CROSS, 17th & D Streets N.W., Washington, D.C. 20006. Filed for self 3/1/85. Legislative interest — "Tax treatment of charitable giving; health issues; preventive health care; fund raising by charities; postal rates." Lobbyist — Llewellyn H. Gerson.

JAMES GRAHAM BROWN FOUNDATION, Louisville, Ky. Lobbyist — Taft, Stettinius & Hollister, 21 Dupont Circle N.W., Washington, D.C. 20036. Filed 3/19/85. Legislative interest — "The status of certain hazardous waste clean up expenditures as charitable payments for the purpose of section 4942 of the Internal Revenue Code." Filed 3/26/85. (Former U.S. Sen. Robert Taft Jr., R-Ohio, 1971-76; House, 1963-65, 1967-71, was listed as agent for this client.) Legislative interest — "The status of certain hazardous waste clean up expenditures as charitable payments for the purpose of section 4942 of the Internal Revenue Code."

CENTER FOR LAW AND EDUCATION INC., 236 Massachusetts Ave. N.E., Washington, D.C. 20002. Filed 3/4/85. Legislative interest — "Advocacy ... on behalf of parents and students, particularly low income individuals, on matters concerning education, civil rights, and provision of legal services to low income persons ... HR 650; HR 901, HR 747, S 2422 and HR 7." Lobbyist — Claudia Waller.

CENTER FOR SCIENCE IN THE PUBLIC INTEREST, 1501 16th St. N.W., Washington, D.C. 20036. Filed for self 3/29/85. Legislative interest — "... restrictions on marketing of alcoholic beverages, excise taxes on alcoholic beverages, and ingredient and caloric labeling of alcoholic beverages...." Lobbyist — Deborah Schechter.

COMMITTEE FOR CAPITAL FORMATION THROUGH DIVIDEND REINVESTMENT, Washington, D.C. Lobbyist — David P. Stang, 1629 K St. N.W., Washington, D.C. 20006. Filed 3/18/85. Legislative interest — "HR 654, relating to the tax treatment of qualified dividend reinvestment plans."

CONSUMER FEDERATION OF AMERICA, 1424 16th St. N.W., Washington, D.C. 20036. Filed for self 3/4/85. Legislative interest — "... HR 4102, Universal Telephone Service Act: For ... Auto Theft: For ... HR 3535, Demand Deposit Equity Act: For ... S 44, Product Liability Act: Against ... Natural Gas Decontrol: Against ... HR 555, Construction Work in Progress Act: For ... HR 2668, Consumer Product Safety Comm. Reauth: For ... HR 4103, Cable Communications Act: For...." Lobbyist — Gene Kimmelman.

ENVIRONMENTAL ACTION INC., 1346 Connecticut Ave. N.W., Washington, D.C. 20036. Filed for self 3/6/85. Legislative interest — "... Comprehensive Environmental Response Compensation & Liability Act of 1980 — extension, for; Federal Insecticide, Fungicide and Rodenticide Act amendments and extension, for; Safe Drinking Water Act, reauthorization and strengthening, for; EPA appropriations, interest, acid rain control, for; Florio right to know and emergency response bills, for." Lobbyist — Daniel F. Becker.

ENVIRONMENTAL POLICY INSTITUTE, 218 D St. S.E., Washington, D.C. 20003. Filed for self 3/28/85. Legislative interest — "... ground water issues." Lobbyist — Velma Smith. Filed for self 3/28/85. Legislative interest — "... Chesapeake Bay, Clean Water Act, related agriculture and Soil Conservation Service legislation." Lobbyist — Chuck Fox. Filed for self 3/28/85. Legislative interest — "... nuclear energy and health effects of radiation." Lobbyist — Caroline Petti.

LOUIS F. FINCH, 2001 Jefferson Davis Highway, Arlington, Va. 22202. Filed for self 3/21/85. Legislative interest — "... Department of Defense Authorization and Appropriation Bills ... Trade Administration Act."

THE HIGH FRONTIER GROUP, P.O. Box 5768, Charlottesville, Va. 22905. Filed for self 3/28/85. Legislative interest — "... FOR Peacekeeper missile authorization and appropriations." Lobbyist — Fred Polli.

JAMES E. JOHNSON, 11510 Georgia Ave., Wheaton, Md. 20902. Filed for self 3/27/85. Legislative interest — "Small Businesses, Social Legislation, Farm Legislation, Oil and other natural resources ... moral issues."

NATURAL RESOURCES DEFENSE COUNCIL INC., New York, N.Y. Lobbyist — W. J. Chandler Associates, 1511 K St. N.W., Washington, D.C. 20005. Filed 3/5/85. Legislative interest — "Highway beautification, outdoor advertising control, environmental protection; and tax appropriations bills affecting these subjects."

OKLAHOMA STATE UNIVERSITY, Stillwater, Okla. Lobbyist — Dutko and Associates, 412 First St. S.E., Washington, D.C. 20003. Filed 3/19/85. Legislative interest — "... Appropriations and Budget bills, 1st Concurrent Budget Resolution."

PLANNED PARENTHOOD FEDERATION OF AMERICA INC., 2010 Massachusetts Ave. N.W., Washington, D.C. 20036. Filed for self 3/21/85. Legislative interest — "Foreign aid legislation as it pertains to family planning, population assistance and reproductive health ... policies and regulations regarding matters of personal health and reproduction." Lobbyist — Vivian Escobar Stack.

RAINBOW ALLIANCE, 1010 Vermont Ave. N.W., Washington, D.C. 20005. Filed for self 3/22/85. Legislative interest — Not specified. Lobbyist — Nancy Ross.

SIERRA CLUB, 530 Bush St., San Francisco, Calif. 94108. Filed for self 3/1/85. Legislative interest — "Clean Air; Clean Water; Superfund; Agricultural Lands." Lobbyist — Christian Ballantyne, 214 N. Henry St., Madison, Wis. 53703.

H. DONALD STEWART, 182 W. Main St., Penns Grove, N.J. 08069. Filed for self 3/15/85. Legislative interest — Not specified.

UNIVERSITY OF SYRACUSE, Syracuse, N.Y. Lobbyist — Lipsen, Hamberger, Whitten & Hamberger, 1725 DeSales St. N.W., Washington, D.C. 20036. Filed 3/4/85. Legislative interest — "... education and transportation."

WOMEN'S ACTION FOR NUCLEAR DISARMAMENT EDUCATION FUND INC., 691 Massachusetts Ave., Arlington, Mass., 02174. Filed for self 3/1/85. Legislative interest — "Support for nuclear weapons freeze legislation and for economic conversion legislation. Opposition to legislation granting authority or appropriations for nuclear weapons and delivery systems, anti-satellite weapons testing, production or deployment, chemical weapons, and the 'strategic defense initiative.' Possible Bill numbers are S Res 1, H J Res 441, HR 4805, HR 229 and H J Res 3." Lobbyist — Nancy A. Donaldson, 110 Maryland Ave. N.E., Washington, D.C. 20002.

April Registrations

Corporations and Businesses

ACACIA MUTUAL LIFE INSURANCE CO., 51 Louisiana Ave. N.W., Washington, D.C. 20001. Filed for self 4/11/85. Legislative interest — "... life insurance, banking, and securities industries; in particular the following tax bills, HR 1040, S 409, HR 800, HR 77, S 325, and the following banking bills, HR 20, HR 1513, HR 15, HR 52. Also, opposed to taxing the inside build-up of life insurance policies." Lobbyist — Lisa Andrews.

ALLIED CORP., 1150 Connecticut Ave. N.W., Washington, D.C. 20036. Filed for self 4/11/85. Legislative interest — "... mergers, international trade, and product liability." Lobbyist — Elvira J. Orly.

ALLNET COMMUNICATIONS SERVICES INC., Chicago, Ill. Lobbyist — Surrey & Morse, 1250 I St. N.W., Washington, D.C. 20005. Filed 4/12/85. Legislative interest — "... communication-related legislation of interest to the competitive long distance telephone industry ... HR 957, a bill providing for continued competition in the long distance telephone industry ... supports."

AMERICA WEST AIRLINES INC., Tempe, Ariz. Lobbyist — Kirby, Gillick, Schwartz & Tuohey, 1220 L St. N.W., Washington, D.C. 20005. Filed 4/18/85. Legislative interest — "Aviation, regulation and tax legislation...."

AMERICAN SUN INC., 2075 S. Atlantic Blvd., Commerce, Calif. 90040. Filed for self 4/15/85. Legislative interest — Not specified. Lobbyist — Mary Elizabeth Gregory.

ARTHUR ANDERSEN & CO., Washington, D.C. Lobbyist — Charls E. Walker Associates Inc., 1730 Pennsylvania Ave. N.W., Washington, D.C. 20006. Filed 4/10/85. Legislative interest — "... issues of general interest to the accounting profession."

APPLE COMPUTER INC., Cupertino, Calif. Lobbyist — Eric R. Fox, 1700 Pennsylvania Ave. N.W., Washington, D.C. 20006. Filed 4/9/85. Legislative interest — "... federal income taxation. Specifically, lobbying for modification of section 179 of PL 98-369 (Sections 280F and 274(d) of the Internal Revenue Code), and lobbying in support of HR 531."

ARKANSAS BEST FREIGHT, Fort Smith, Ark. Lobbyist — Jack L. Williams, 451 New Jersey Ave. S.E., Washington, D.C. 20003. Filed 4/18/85. Legislative interest — Not specified.

ARKANSAS-LOUISIANA GAS CO., Little Rock, Ark. Lobbyist — Jack L. Williams, 451 New Jersey Ave. S.E., Washington, D.C. 20003. Filed 4/18/85. Legislative interest — Not specified.

ATCHISON, TOPEKA & SANTA FE, Chicago, Ill. Lobbyist — Edward D. Heffernan, 1513 16th St. N.W., Washington,

D.C. 20036. Filed 4/5/85. Legislative interest — "... federal excise tax on retail sale of heavy trucks and trailer equipment."

ATLANTIC RICHFIELD CO., 515 S. Flower St., Los Angeles, Calif. 90071. Filed for self 4/12/85. Legislative interest — "... the petroleum industry." Lobbyist — Deborah A. White, 1333 New Hampshire Ave. N.W., Washington, D.C. 20036.

AVTEX FIBERS INC., P.O. Box 880, Valley Forge, Pa. 19482. Filed for self 4/5/85. Legislative interest — "S 680, HR 1562, Textile & Apparel Trade Enforcement Act of 1985. For both bills." Lobbyist — Richard H. Hughes.

BALDWIN SECURITIES CORP., New York, N.Y. Lobbyist — Seward & Kissel, 919 18th St. N.W., Washington, D.C. 20006. Filed 4/9/85. Legislative interest — "... HR 1800 and S 814 concerning technical corrections to the Deficit Reduction Act of 1984, PL 98-369 (the 'Act'). Specifically, provisions of the Act concerning the election of a personal holding company to be treated for tax purposes as a regulated investment company."

BALTIMORE GAS & ELECTRIC CO., Baltimore, Md. Lobbyist — Reid & Priest, 1111 19th St. N.W., Washington, D.C. 20036. Filed 4/4/85. Legislative interest — "... Repeal of Public Utility Holding Company Act ... 15 U.S.C. section 79 et seq. ... for repeal."

BANK OF VERMONT, Burlington, Vt. Lobbyist — Thacher, Proffitt & Wood, 1140 Connecticut Ave. N.W., Washington, D.C. 20036. Filed 4/12/85. Legislative interest — "HR 15 and HR 20, financial reform legislation (proposed), affecting Federal savings banks and thrift institutions."

BARBER BLUE SEA LINE, New York, N.Y. Lobbyist — Billig, Sher & Jones, 2033 K St. N.W., Washington, D.C. 20006. Filed 4/10/85. Legislative interest — "... companies operating vessels in international commerce, specifically including draft proposals before the House Merchant Marine and Fisheries Committee to revise maritime liability laws."

BECHTEL POWER CORP., San Francisco, Calif. Lobbyist — Milton Levenson, 21 Politzer Drive, Menlo Park, Calif. 94025. Filed 4/22/85. Legislative interest — Not specified.

BENEFICIAL FINANCIAL CORP., Peapack, N.J. Lobbyist — Dewey, Ballantine, Bushby, Palmer & Wood, 1775 Pennsylvania Ave. N.W., Washington, D.C. 20006. Filed 4/11/85. Legislative interest — "Tax Legislative Matters."

BETHLEHEM STEEL, Washington, D.C. Lobbyist — Black, Manafort, Stone & Kelly, 324 N. Fairfax St., Alexandria, Va. 22314. Filed 4/10/85. Legislative interest — "S 11 Amendment to Steel Stabilization Act."

BLUE CROSS AND BLUE SHIELD ASSOCIATION, Chicago, Ill. Lobbyist — Miller & Chevalier, 655 15th St. N.W., Washington, D.C. 20005. Filed 4/18/85. Legislative interest — "... Titles 5, 10, 26 and 38 of the U.S. Code."

JACQUES BOREL ENTERPRISES INC., New York, N.Y. Lobbyist — Butler & Binion, 1747 Pennsylvania Ave. N.W., Washington, D.C. 20006. Filed 4/29/85. Legislative interest — "Tax Legislation Regarding Section 119 of the IRC."

BRUNSWICK CORP., Skokie, Ill. Lobbyist — Mayer, Brown & Platt, 2000 Pennsylvania Ave. N.W., Washington, D.C. 20006. Filed 4/9/85. Legislative interest — "... amendments to the Internal Revenue Code."

CNA FINANCIAL CORP., Chicago, Ill. Lobbyist — Scribner, Hall & Thompson, 1875 I St. N.W., Washington, D.C. 20006. Filed 4/8/85. Legislative interest — "... taxation of property and casualty insurance companies. ..."

CSX CORP., Washington, D.C. Lobbyist — Edward D. Heffernan, 1513 16th St. N.W., Washington, D.C. 20036. Filed 4/5/85. Legislative interest — "... railroads."

CSX CORP., Richmond, Va. Lobbyist — Wagner & Baroody Inc., 1100 17th St. N.W., Washington, D.C. 20036. Filed 4/9/85. Legislative interest — "Against the Department of Transportation proposal to sell Conrail to Norfolk Southern Railroad." Lobbyist — Garvey, Schubert, Adams & Barer, 1000 Potomac St. N.W., Washington, D.C. 20007. Filed 4/16/85. (Former U.S. Rep. Brock Adams, D-Wash., 1965-77, and transportation secretary, 1977-79, was listed as agent for this client.) Legislative interest — "... sale of Conrail, including but not limited to HR 1455, HR 1930 and S 638."

CAMP, CARMOUCHE, BARSH, HUNTER, GRAY & HOFFMAN, Washington, D.C. Lobbyist — Foreman & Co., 1826 Jefferson Place N.W., Washington, D.C. 20036. Filed 4/22/85. Legislative interest — "Support legislation authorizing operation of 'Consumer Banks.'"

CARLSON COMPANIES INC., Minneapolis, Minn. Lobbyist — Patton, Boggs & Blow, 2550 M St. N.W., Washington, D.C. 20037. Filed 4/10/85. Legislative interest — "Revision of rules affecting consolidated federal income tax returns. HR 1045. Internal Revenue Code. For HR 1045."

CENTRAL ILLINOIS LIGHT CO., Peoria, Ill. Lobbyist — Reid & Priest, 1111 19th St. N.W., Washington, D.C. 20036. Filed 4/4/85. Legislative interest — "... Repeal of Public Utility Holding Company Act ... 15 U.S.C. section 79 et seq. ... for repeal."

CHAMPION INTERNATIONAL CORP., 1875 I St. N.W., Washington, D.C. 20006. Filed for self 4/10/85. Legislative interest — "Tax issues, hostile takeover issue." Lobbyist — Jeanne K. Connelly.

CHICAGO NORTHWESTERN TRANSPORTATION CO., Washington, D.C. Lobbyist — Bible, Santini, Hoy & Miller, 900 17th St. N.W., Washington, D.C. 20006. Filed 4/14/85. Legislative interest — "Consideration of the Milwaukee Railroad acquisition."

CHICAGO TITLE INSURANCE CO., Chicago, Ill. Lobbyist — Gray & Co., 3255 Grace St. N.W., Washington, D.C. 20007. Filed 4/10/85. Legislative interest — "... antitrust legislation relating to the title insurance industry."

CITIBANK N.A., 399 Park Ave., New York, N.Y. 10043. Filed for self 4/9/85. Legislative interest — "... Tax Legislation affecting banks and bank holding companies ... Comprehensive tax reform proposals such as HR 777, HR 800 and HR 1040, etc. ... Targeted jobs tax credit, HR 983. ..." Lobbyist — John F. Rolph III, 1200 New Hampshire Ave. N.W., Washington, D.C. 20036.

LIZ CLAIBORNE INC., New York, N.Y. Lobbyist — Rogers & Wells, 1737 H St. N.W., Washington, D.C. 20006. Filed 4/2/85. Legislative interest — "Tariff and tax legislation regarding textiles and apparel generally, and specifically S 680 and HR 1562."

COMMONWEALTH EDISON CO., Chicago, Ill. Lobbyist — Reid & Priest, 1111 19th St. N.W., Washington, D.C. 20036. Filed 4/4/85. Legislative interest — "... Repeal of Public Utility Holding Company Act ... 15 U.S.C. section 79 et seq. ... for repeal."

CONSOLIDATED RAIL CORP., Philadelphia, Pa. Lobbyist — Bricker & Eckler, 888 17th St. N.W., Washington, D.C. 20006. Filed 4/11/85. Legislative interest — "... sale of Conrail by the government." Filed 4/15/85. Legislative interest — "Government's disposition of its ownership in Conrail."

CONTRACTORS BONDING & INSURANCE CO., Seattle, Wash. Lobbyist — Garvey, Schubert, Adams & Barer, 1000 Potomac St. N.W., Washington, D.C. 20007. Filed 4/16/85. Legislative interest — "Small Business Administration Authorizations, regulation or any legislation impacting small business surety bonds or insurance."

COOPER COMMUNITIES, Bella Vista, Ark. Lobbyist — Jack L. Williams, 451 New Jersey Ave. S.E., Washington, D.C. 20003. Filed 4/18/85. Legislative interest — Not specified.

CORNING ASSOCIATES, Corning, N.Y. Lobbyist — Butler & Binion, 1747 Pennsylvania Ave. N.W., Washington, D.C. 20006. Filed 4/29/85. Legislative interest — "Gift and Estate Tax Matter."

DILLON, READ & CO. INC., 535 Madison Ave. New York, N.Y. 10022. Lobbyist — Vinson & Elkins, 1101 Connecticut Ave. N.W., Washington, D.C. 20036. Filed 4/15/85. Legislative interest — "... corporate mergers and acquisitions." Filed for self 4/18/85. Legislative interest — "... corporate mergers and acquisitions."

DOREMUS AND CO., Washington, D.C. Lobbyist — Gold and Liebengood Inc., 1050 Connecticut Ave. N.W., Washington, D.C. 20036. Filed 4/12/85. Legislative interest — "Legislation affecting student loans and related matters."

DREXEL BURNHAM LAMBERT INC., New York, N.Y.

Lobbyist — Skadden, Arps, Slate, Meagher & Flom, 919 18th St. N.W., Washington, D.C. 20006. Filed 4/10/85. Legislative interest — "... corporate finance."

THE DREYFUS CORP., New York, N.Y. Lobbyist — Rogers & Wells, 1737 H St. N.W., Washington, D.C. 20006. Filed 4/11/85. Legislative interest — "Amendment to section 904(d)(3) of the Internal Revenue Code."

DUKE POWER CO., Charlotte, N.C. Lobbyist — Reid & Priest, 1111 19th St. N.W., Washington, D.C. 20036. Filed 4/4/85. Legislative interest — "... Repeal of Public Utility Holding Company Act ... 15 U.S.C. section 79 et seq. ... for repeal."

ENSERCH CORP., 30 S. St. Paul St., Dallas, Texas 75201. Filed for self 4/11/85. Legislative interest — "... nuclear power issues ... Natural gas issues ... Energy technology research and development issues...." Lobbyist — William W. Turner, 1025 Connecticut Ave. N.W., Washington, D.C. 20036.

ETHYL CORP., 330 Fourth St., Richmond, Va. 23219. Filed for self 4/10/85. Legislative interest — "... fuel additives." Lobbyist — John J. Adams, 2000 Pennsylvania Ave. N.W., Washington, D.C. 20006.

EXXON CORP., 1251 Avenue of the Americas, New York, N.Y. 10020. Filed for self 4/17/85. Legislative interest — Not specified. Lobbyist — Charles Rowton, 1899 L St. N.W., Washington, D.C. 20036.

FIRST AMERICAN TITLE INSURANCE CO., Troy, Mich. Lobbyist — Gray & Co., 3255 Grace St. N.W., Washington, D.C. 20007. Filed 4/10/85. Legislative interest — "... antitrust legislation relating to the title insurance industry."

FIRST COLONY LIFE INSURANCE, Lynchburg, Va. Lobbyist — Bishop, Liberman, Cook, Purcell & Reynolds, 1200 17th St. N.W., Washington, D.C. 20036. Filed 4/24/85. (Former U.S. Rep. David E. Satterfield III, D-Va., 1965-81, was listed as agent for this client.) Legislative interest — "... enlargement of the applicability of section 217(c) — Deficit Reduction Act of 1984 to include corporations domiciled in or having principal place of business in all states instead of four states as now provided."

FIRST SOUTH SAVINGS AND LOAN, Pine Bluff, Ark. Lobbyist — Jack L. Williams, 451 New Jersey Ave. S.E., Washington, D.C. 20003. Filed 4/18/85. Legislative interest — Not specified.

FLUOR CORP., 1627 K St. N.W., Washington, D.C. 20006. Filed for self 4/18/85. Legislative interest — "Product liability, General Tax Legislation, Environmental Legislation, International Trade Legislation." Lobbyist — James R. Byron.

CARL M. FREEMAN ASSOCIATES, Potomac, Md. Lobbyist — Jones, Day, Reavis & Pogue, 655 15th St. N.W., Washington, D.C. 20005. Filed 4/10/85. Legislative interest — "... coastal areas."

GARRETT CORP., Washington, D.C. Lobbyist — Ginn & Edington Inc., 121 S. Columbus St., Alexandria, Va. 22314. Filed 4/12/85. Legislative interest — "Department of Defense Authorization and Appropriations Bills."

GENERAL DYNAMICS, 1745 Jefferson Davis Highway, Arlington, Va. 22202. Filed for self 4/15/85. Legislative interest — "Defense and NASA authorization and appropriation, taxes, labor relations." Lobbyist — Christopher W. Hansen. Filed for self 4/15/85. Legislative interest — "Defense and NASA authorization and appropriation, foreign military sales, taxes." Lobbyist — William W. Maurer.

GOLDMAN, SACHS & CO., Washington, D.C. Lobbyist — Mayer, Brown & Platt, 2000 Pennsylvania Ave. N.W., Washington, D.C. 20006. Filed 4/9/85. Legislative interest — "... amendments to the Internal Revenue Code."

GRANADA MANAGEMENT CORP., Houston, Texas. Lobbyist — Reynolds, Allen & Cook, 1667 K St. N.W., Washington, D.C. 20006. Filed 4/18/85. Legislative interest — "... flat-tax, modified flat-tax, or simplified tax proposals in the Congress."

GRAY & CO., Washington, D.C. Lobbyist — Foreman & Co., 1826 Jefferson Place N.W., Washington, D.C. 20036. Filed 4/23/85. Legislative interest — "HR 5026 and S 2336 Credit Card Surcharges, oppose."

GREAT WESTERN FINANCIAL CORP., Beverly Hills, Calif. Lobbyist — Leff & Mason, 1700 Pennsylvania Ave. N.W., Washington, D.C. 20006. Filed 4/11/85. Legislative interest — "... financial institutions, housing, international finance and public agency legislation...."

GREENE, O'REILLY, AGNEW & BROILLET, Los Angeles, Calif. Lobbyist — Foreman & Co., 1826 Jefferson Place N.W., Washington, D.C. 20036. Filed 4/24/85. Legislative interest — "Opposed S 44."

HEWLETT-PACKARD CO., 3000 Hanover St., Palo Alto, Calif. 94304. Filed for self 4/14/85. Legislative interest — "Legislation in product areas. This includes, but is not limited to international trade (amendments to the Export Administration Act; and legislation affecting access to U.S. and foreign markets; tax (legislation to amend and extend the tax credit for R&D such as HR 1188), and more general tax reform legislation and procurement such as legislation affecting commercial vendors' data rights)." Lobbyist — Eben S. Tisdale, 1550 Wilson Blvd., Arlington, Va. 22209.

HOMESTAKE MINING CO., San Francisco, Calif. Lobbyist — Bible, Santini, Hoy & Miller, 900 17th St. N.W., Washington, D.C. 20006. Filed 4/14/85. Legislative interest — "Monitoring and reporting on public lands issues and Nevada wilderness legislation."

HOUSTON NATURAL GAS CORP., P.O. Box 1188, Houston, Texas 77001. Filed for self 4/5/85. Legislative interest — "... natural gas pricing, transportation and use ... the Outer Continental Shelf; all budget revenue legislation relating to natural gas ... exploration and production of natural gas." Lobbyist — Edward Joseph Hillings, 1700 N. Moore St., Arlington, Va. 22209.

ISL VENTURES INC., Wallace, Idaho. Lobbyist — Bible, Santini, Hoy & Miller, 900 17th St. N.W., Washington, D.C. 20006. Filed 4/14/85. Legislative interest — "Monitoring and reporting on advanced in-situ leaching project with DOI and Congress."

ILLINOIS POWER CO., Decatur, Ill. Lobbyist — Reid & Priest, 1111 19th St. N.W., Washington, D.C. 20036. Filed 4/4/85. Legislative interest — "... Repeal of Public Utility Holding Company Act ... 15 U.S.C. section 79 et seq. ... for repeal."

INTEGRATED RESOURCES INC., 666 Third Ave., New York, N.Y. 10017. Filed for self 4/11/85. Legislative interest — "... tax legislation affecting investment and capital formation, insurance, annuities and related issues. Specifically, ... the adverse effects of the various flat tax and modified flat tax proposals pending before Congress on capital formation." Lobbyists — Richard Rosenbaum and Daniel J. Piliero II.

INTERNATIONAL TELECOMMUNICATIONS SATELLITE ORGANIZATION (INTELSAT), Washington, D.C. Lobbyist — Preston, Thorgrimson, Ellis & Holman, 1735 New York Ave. N.W., Washington, D.C. 20006. Filed 4/4/85. (Former U.S. Rep. Lloyd Meeds, D-Wash., 1965-79, was listed as agent for this client.) Legislative interest — "... protecting Intelsat from a unilateral decision by the U.S. to allow additional International Telecommunications System." Lobbyist — Powell, Goldstein, Frazer & Murphy, 1110 Vermont Ave. N.W., Washington, D.C. 20005. Filed 4/18/85. Legislative interest — Not specified. Lobbyist — Neill & Company Inc., 900 17th St. N.W., Washington, D.C. 20006. Filed 4/24/85. Legislative interest — "Promoting the legislative interests of the International Telecommunications Satellite Organization in relation to the United States obligation to the INTELSAT Agreements of 1964 (TIAS 7532) and the Communications Satellite Act of 1962 (U.S.C. 701)." Lobbyist — Hunton & Williams, 2000 Pennsylvania Ave. N.W., Washington, D.C. 20006. Filed 4/24/85; 4/29/85. Legislative interest — "... international communications satellite systems."

IOWA POWER AND LIGHT CO., Des Moines, Iowa. Lobbyist — Reid & Priest, 1111 19th St. N.W., Washington, D.C. 20036. Filed 4/4/85. Legislative interest — "... Repeal of Public Utility Holding Company Act ... 15 U.S.C. section 79 et seq. ... for repeal."

J. E. JOHNSON & ASSOCIATES INC., 11510 Georgia Ave., Wheaton, Md. 20902. Filed for self 4/17/85. Legislative interest — "Small Businesses, Social Legislation, Farm Legislation, Oil and other natural resources. Lobbying for moral issues." Lobbyist — James E. Johnson.

JOHNSON & JOHNSON, Washington, D.C. Lobbyist —

Black, Manafort, Stone & Kelly, 324 N. Fairfax St., Alexandria, Va. 22314. Filed 4/10/85. Legislative interest — "... Treasury Department tax reform proposal."

KALAMA CHEMICAL INC., Seattle, Wash. Lobbyist — Bogle & Gates, One Thomas Circle N.W., Washington, D.C. 20005. Filed 4/4/85. Legislative interest — "Tariffs."

KANSAS CITY POWER & LIGHT CO., Kansas City, Mo. Lobbyist — Reid & Priest, 1111 19th St. N.W., Washington, D.C. 20036. Filed 4/4/85. Legislative interest — "... Repeal of Public Utility Holding Company Act ... 15 U.S.C. section 79 et seq. ... for repeal."

KELSO & CO., New York, N.Y. Lobbyist — James C. Corman, 1420 16th St. N.W., Washington, D.C. 20036. Filed 4/10/85. (Former U.S. representative, D-Calif., 1961-81.) Legislative interest — "To monitor federal legislative actions regarding employee stock ownership plans (ESOPs)."

KILPATRICK LIFE INSURANCE CO., Shreveport, La. Lobbyist — Bishop, Liberman, Cook, Purcell & Reynolds, 1200 17th St. N.W., Washington, D.C. 20036. Filed 4/24/85. (Former U.S. Rep. David E. Satterfield III, D-Va., 1965-81, was listed as agent for this client.) Legislative interest — "... to effect enlargement of the applicability of section 217(c) - Deficit Reduction Act of 1984 to include corporations domiciled in or having principal place of business in all states instead of four states as now provided."

KOGOVSEK & ASSOCIATES INC., 3600 S. Yosemite, Denver, Colo. 80237. Filed for self 4/30/85. Legislative interest — "General legislation of interest to Colorado." Lobbyist — Joseph L. Coppola.

JAMES D. & LOIS M. LaROSA, Clarksburg, W.Va. Lobbyist — Cole & Corette, 1110 Vermont Ave. N.W., Washington, D.C. 20005. Filed 4/10/85. Legislative interest — "... pending tax reform legislation, specifically HR 1067 and the companion Senate Bill. ..."

JAMES J. LaROSA, Bridgeport, W.Va. Lobbyist — Cole & Corette, 1110 Vermont Ave. N.W., Washington, D.C. 20005. Filed 4/10/85. Legislative interest — "... pending tax reform legislation, specifically HR 1067 and the companion Senate Bill. ..."

LAWYERS TITLE INSURANCE CO., Richmond, Va. Lobbyist — Gray & Co., 3255 Grace St. N.W., Washington, D.C. 20007. Filed 4/10/85. Legislative interest — "... antitrust legislation relating to the title insurance industry."

LIBERTY NATIONAL, Birmingham, Ala. Lobbyist — R. Duffy Wall & Associates Inc., 1317 F St. N.W., Washington, D.C. 20004. Filed 4/8/85. Legislative interest — "... life insurance taxation."

LIFE OF VIRGINIA, Richmond, Va. Lobbyist — R. Duffy Wall & Associates Inc., 1317 F St. N.W., Washington, D.C. 20004. Filed 4/8/85. Legislative interest — "... life insurance taxation."

MAERSK LINE, New York, N.Y. Lobbyist — Billig, Sher & Jones, 2033 K St. N.W., Washington, D.C. 20006. Filed 4/10/85. Legislative interest — "Legislation affecting companies operating vessels in international commerce, specifically including draft proposals before the House Merchant Marine and Fisheries Committee to revise maritime liability laws."

MANVILLE CORP., Littleton, Colo. Lobbyist — Davis, Polk & Wardwell, 1575 I St. N.W., Washington, D.C. 20005. Filed 4/3/85. Legislative interest — "HR 1626 - Legislation establishing an asbestos compensation program."

MICHAEL McGEHEE & ASSOCIATES, 1411 E. Abingdon Drive, Alexandria, Va. 22314. Filed for self 4/16/85. Legislative interest — "National Eye Institute, appropriate appropriation bills." Lobbyist — Michael McGehee.

MERRILL LYNCH & CO. INC., 1828 L St. N.W., Washington, D.C. 20036. Filed for self 4/10/85. Legislative interest — "Financial, banking, securities, taxation, real estate and related legislation." Lobbyist — Janelle Morris.

MILLIKEN & CO., Spartanburg, S.C. Lobbyist — John Francis Nash Jr., 17 N. Greenbrier St., Arlington, Va. 22203. Filed 4/9/85. Legislative interest — "... domestic textile industry."

MINNESOTA POWER & LIGHT CO., Duluth, Minn. Lobbyist — Reid & Priest, 1111 19th St. N.W., Washington, D.C. 20036. Filed 4/4/85. Legislative interest — "... Repeal of Public Utility Holding Company Act ... 15 U.S.C. section 79 et seq. ... for repeal."

THE MONEY STORE, Springfield, N.J. Lobbyist — Manatt, Phelps, Rothenberg & Tunney, 1200 New Hampshire Ave. N.W., Washington, D.C. 20036. Filed 4/26/85. Legislative interest — "... Small Business Administration guaranteed loan program (Sec. 7(a))."

MONTANA-DAKOTA UTILITIES CO., Bismarck, N.D. Lobbyist — Reid & Priest, 1111 19th St. N.W., Washington, D.C. 20036. Filed 4/4/85. Legislative interest — "... Repeal of Public Utility Holding Company Act ... 15 U.S.C. section 79 et seq. ... for repeal."

MONUMENTAL LIFE INSURANCE CO., Baltimore, Md. Lobbyist — Bishop, Liberman, Cook, Purcell & Reynolds, 1200 17th St. N.W., Washington, D.C. 20036. Filed 4/24/85. (Former U.S. Rep. David E. Satterfield III, D-Va., 1965-81, was listed as agent for this client.) Legislative interest — "... to effect enlargement of the applicability of section 217(c) - Deficit Reduction Act of 1984 to include corporations domiciled in or having principal place of business in all states instead of four states as now provided."

MURCHISON OIL & GAS INC., Dallas, Texas. Lobbyist — D'Amico, Luedtke, Demarest & Golden, 1920 N St. N.W., Washington, D.C. 20036. Filed 4/11/85. Legislative interest — "Natural Gas Legislation, tariff and trade legislation, and tax legislation affecting the interests of the company."

MUTUAL OF OMAHA, Omaha, Neb. Lobbyist — Gray & Co., 3255 Grace St. N.W., Washington, D.C. 20007. Filed 4/10/85. Legislative interest — "... tax issues."

NEDLLOYD LINES, New York, N.Y. Lobbyist — Billig, Sher & Jones, 2033 K St. N.W., Washington, D.C. 20006. Filed 4/10/85. Legislative interest — "Legislation affecting companies operating vessels in international commerce, specifically including draft proposals before the House Merchant Marine and Fisheries Committee to revise maritime liability laws."

NORFOLK SOUTHERN, Norfolk, Va. Lobbyist — Verner, Liipfert, Bernhard, McPherson & Hand, 1660 L St. N.W., Washington, D.C. 20036. Filed 4/15/85. Legislative interest — "... railroad industry, including proposed Conrail sale."

NORFOLK SOUTHERN CORP., Washington, D.C. Lobbyist — Buchanan Ingersoll, 1667 K St. N.W., Washington, D.C. 20006. Filed 4/11/85. Legislative interest — "... legislation to authorize the sale of Conrail."

NORTHERN INDIANA PUBLIC SERVICE CO., Hammond, Ind. Lobbyist — Reid & Priest, 1111 19th St. N.W., Washington, D.C. 20036. Filed 4/4/85. Legislative interest — "... Repeal of Public Utility Holding Company Act ... 15 U.S.C. section 79 et seq. ... for repeal."

OPTICAL COATING LABORATORY INC., Santa Rosa, Calif. Lobbyist — O'Connor & Hannan, 1919 Pennsylvania Ave. N.W., Washington, D.C. 20006. Filed 4/14/85. Legislative interest — "... HR 48."

ORBITAL SCIENCES CORP., Vienna, Va. Lobbyist — Hunton & Williams, 2000 Pennsylvania Ave. N.W., Washington, D.C. 20006. Filed 4/29/85. Legislative interest — "... defense procurement matters."

PACIFIC GAS AND ELECTRIC CO., 77 Beale St., San Francisco, Calif. 94106. Lobbyist — Reid & Priest, 1111 19th St. N.W., Washington, D.C. 20036. Filed 4/4/85. Legislative interest — "... Repeal of Public Utility Holding Company Act ... 15 U.S.C. section 79 et seq. ... for repeal." Filed for self 4/1/85. Legislative interest — "... the generation, transmission and distribution of electric energy ... the procurement or development and distribution of natural gas." Lobbyist — Leland M. Gustafson, 1050 17th St. N.W., Washington, D.C. 20036.

PACIFIC LIGHTING CORP., Los Angeles, Calif. Lobbyist — Reid & Priest, 1111 19th St. N.W., Washington, D.C. 20036. Filed 4/4/85. Legislative interest — "... Repeal of Public Utility Holding Company Act ... 15 U.S.C. section 79 et seq. ... for repeal."

PACIFIC POWER & LIGHT CO., 920 S.W. Sixth Ave., Portland, Ore. 97204. Filed for self 4/10/85. Legislative interest — "... sources, generation, transmission and distribution of electric power, federal power marketing, Department of Energy matters, and minerals mining and transportation." Lobbyist — Ed Grosswiler.

PACIFICORP, Portland, Ore. Lobbyist — Stoel, Rives, Boley, Fraser & Wyse, 1730 M St. N.W., Washington, D.C. 20036. Filed 4/10/85. Legislative interest — "... sources, generation, transmission and distribution of electric power, federal power marketing, Department of Energy matters, and minerals mining and transportation."

PINKERTON TOBACCO CO., Owensboro, Ky. Lobbyist — Webster & Sheffield, 1200 New Hampshire Ave. N.W., Washington, D.C. 20036. Filed 4/11/85. Legislative interest — "... the sale and taxation of smokeless tobacco products."

PITNEY BOWES, Stamford, Conn. Lobbyist — Campbell-Raupe Associates, 1015 15th St. N.W., Washington, D.C. 20005. Filed 4/17/85; 4/18/85. Legislative interest — "Tax issues, including opposition to the repeal of the investment tax credit."

POGO PRODUCING CO., Houston, Texas. Lobbyist — Webster & Sheffield, 1200 New Hampshire Ave. N.W., Washington, D.C. 20036. Filed 4/17/85. Legislative interest — "... the imposition of tariffs on the importation of crude oil and refined petroleum products, taxes in general and matters relating to the budget."

POTOMAC ELECTRIC POWER CO., Washington, D.C. Lobbyist — Reid & Priest, 1111 19th St. N.W., Washington, D.C. 20036. Filed 4/4/85. Legislative interest — "... Repeal of Public Utility Holding Company Act ... 15 U.S.C. section 79 et seq. ... for repeal."

PUBLIC SERVICE ELECTRIC & GAS CO., Newark, N.J. Lobbyist — Reid & Priest, 1111 19th St. N.W., Washington, D.C. 20036. Filed 4/4/85. Legislative interest — "... Repeal of Public Utility Holding Company Act ... 15 U.S.C. section 79 et seq. ... for repeal."

RAYBURN COUNTRY ELECTRIC COOPERATIVE INC., Kaufman, Texas. Lobbyist — Verner, Liipfert, Bernhard, McPherson & Hand, 1660 L St. N.W., Washington, D.C. 20036. Filed 4/11/85. Legislative interest — "... electric cooperatives in general, Rayburn Country in particular."

RICELAND FOODS, Stuttgart, Ark. Lobbyist — Jack L. Williams, 451 New Jersey Ave. S.E., Washington, D.C. 20003. Filed 4/18/85. Legislative interest — Not specified.

RIFFE PETROLEUM CO., Jacksonville, Fla. Lobbyist — Campbell-Raupe Associates Inc., 1015 15th St. N.W., Washington, D.C. 20005. Filed 4/10/85; 4/17/85. Legislative interest — "... Transportation issues."

ROCK-OLA MANUFACTURING CORP., Chicago, Ill. Lobbyist — Wexler, Reynolds, Harrison & Schule Inc., 1317 F St. N.W., Washington, D.C. 20004. Filed 4/18/85. Legislative interest — "... trade laws and regulations affecting importing and exporting. ..."

ROCKWELL INTERNATIONAL CORP., Arlington, Va. Lobbyist — Ginn & Edington Inc., 121 S. Columbus St., Alexandria, Va. 22314. Filed 4/12/85. Legislative interest — "Department of Defense Authorization and Appropriations Bills."

SACO DEFENSE INC., Saco, Maine. Lobbyist — Dickstein, Shapiro & Morin, 2101 L St. N.W., Washington, D.C. 20037. Filed 4/10/85. Legislative interest — "Department of Defense authorizations and appropriations."

SAFECO TITLE INSURANCE CO., Seattle, Wash. Lobbyist — Gray & Co., 3255 Grace St. N.W., Washington, D.C. 20007. Filed 4/10/85. Legislative interest — "... antitrust legislation relating to the title insurance industry."

SANTA FE SOUTHERN PACIFIC CORP., Chicago, Ill. Lobbyist — Edward D. Heffernan, 1513 16th St. N.W., Washington, D.C. 20036. Filed 4/5/85. Legislative interest — "... federal excise tax on retail sale of heavy trucks and trailer equipment."

SAVAGE INDUSTRIES, Orem, Utah. Lobbyist — Bible, Santini, Hoy & Miller, 900 17th St. N.W., Washington, D.C. 20006. Filed 4/14/85. Legislative interest — "Monitoring and reporting on Congressional hearings on Emery Mining disaster."

SCOTT PAPER CO., 1726 M St. N.W., Washington, D.C. 20036. Filed for self 4/8/85. Legislative interest — "HR 800/S 409 Tax simplification - oppose certain provisions ... HR 1359 Repeal Section 861 Tax Regs. - support ... S 51 Superfund - support certain provisions ... S 53/HR 8 Clean Water Act - support." Lobbyist — Betty-Grace Terpstra.

SEA-LAND CORP., Iselin, N.J. Lobbyist — Skadden, Arps, Slate, Meagher & Flom, 919 18th St. N.W., Washington, D.C. 20006. Filed 4/3/85. Legislative interest — "Superfund Legislation."

G. D. SEARLE, Skokie, Ill. Lobbyist — Palumbo & Cerrell Inc., 11 Dupont Circle N.W., Washington, D.C. 20036. Filed 4/25/85. Legislative interest — "Laws relating to the labeling and composition of foods."

THE SIGNAL COMPANIES, Washington, D.C. Lobbyist — Black, Manafort, Stone & Kelly, 324 N. Fairfax St., Alexandria, Va. 22314. Filed 4/10/85. Legislative interest — "... issues emanating from Treasury Department tax reform proposal."

SIMUFLITE TRAINING INTERNATIONAL INC., Dallas/Fort Worth Regional Airport, Texas. Lobbyist — Charls E. Walker Associates Inc., 1730 Pennsylvania Ave. N.W., Washington, D.C. 20006. Filed 4/10/85. Legislative interest — "... federal requirements for pilot training."

SINCLAIR OIL CORP., P.O. Box 31825, Salt Lake City, Utah 84131. Filed for self 4/17/85. Legislative interest — "... the oil industry, including regulation of prices, policies, and practices affecting the exploration, development, transportation, refining and marketing of petroleum products, and ... matters pertaining to hotel and resort operations." Lobbyist — Clinton W. Ensign, 2600 Virginia Ave. N.W., Washington, D.C. 20037.

SOUTH CAROLINA ELECTRIC & GAS CO., Columbia, S.C. Lobbyist — Reid & Priest, 1111 19th St. N.W., Washington, D.C. 20036. Filed 4/4/85. Legislative interest — "... Repeal of Public Utility Holding Company Act ... 15 U.S.C. section 79 et seq. ... for repeal."

SOUTHERN PACIFIC TRANSPORTATION CO., San Francisco, Calif. Lobbyist — Edward D. Heffernan, 1513 16th St. N.W., Washington, D.C. 20036. Filed 4/5/85. Legislative interest — "... federal excise tax on retail sale of heavy trucks and trailer equipment."

STEWART TITLE GUARANTY CO., Houston, Texas. Lobbyist — Gray & Co., 3255 Grace St. N.W., Washington, D.C. 20007. Filed 4/10/85. Legislative interest — "... antitrust legislation relating to the title insurance industry."

STORER COMMUNICATIONS INC., Washington, D.C. Lobbyist — Wexler, Reynolds, Harrison & Schule Inc., 1317 F St. N.W., Washington, D.C. 20004. Filed 4/18/85. Legislative interest — "... mergers and acquisitions affecting mass media companies and FCC policy." Lobbyist — Koteen & Naftalin, 1150 Connecticut Ave. N.W., Washington, D.C. 20036. Filed 4/24/85. Legislative interest — "... efforts to take over control of a publicly held broadcast company by way of hostile tender offers, proxy contests or otherwise and the responsibility of the FCC in this field."

STRATTON HATS INC., Bellwood, Ill. Lobbyist — Barnes, Richardson & Colburn, 1819 H St. N.W., Washington, D.C. 20006. Filed 4/22/85. Legislative interest — "Proposal to make permanent the elimination of duties on hatters' fur ... (Item 186.20, Tariff Schedules of the United States) ... support. ..."

SUNDSTRAND CORP., Arlington, Va. Lobbyist — John L. Hills, Route 1, Box 645, Purcellville, Va. 22132. Filed 4/1/85. Legislative interest — Not specified.

TRW INC., Arlington, Va. Lobbyist — George R. Moses, 1341 G St. N.W., Washington, D.C. 20005. Filed 4/8/85. Legislative interest — "Legislative and oversight activities affecting government contracting."

TACOMA BOAT BUILDING CO./AT-SEA INCINERATION, Tacoma, Wash. Lobbyist — Jack Ferguson Associates Inc., 203 Maryland Ave. N.E., Washington, D.C. 20002. Filed 4/26/85. Legislative interest — "FY '86 Budget & Appropriation Measures."

TAMPA ELECTRIC POWER CO., Tampa, Fla. Lobbyist — Reid & Priest, 1111 19th St. N.W., Washington, D.C. 20036. Filed 4/4/85. Legislative interest — "... Repeal of Public Utility Holding Company Act ... 15 U.S.C. section 79 et seq. ... for repeal."

TEXACO INC., 2000 Westchester Ave., White Plains, N.Y.

10650. Filed for self 4/11/85. Legislative interest — "... Federal taxation...." Lobbyist — Anthony J. Sagese Jr., 1050 17th St. N.W., Washington, D.C. 20036.

TEXAS UTILITIES CO., Dallas, Texas. Lobbyist — Reid & Priest, 1111 19th St. N.W., Washington, D.C. 20036. Filed 4/4/85. Legislative interest — "... Repeal of Public Utility Holding Company Act ... 15 U.S.C. section 79 et seq. ... for repeal."

TIME INC., Washington, D.C. Lobbyist — Blum, Nash & Railsback, 1133 15th St. N.W., Washington, D.C. 20005. Filed 4/29/85. Legislative interest — "Legislation affecting antitrust cases against municipalities (S 578 and HR 5993)."

TRANSAMERICA INTERWAY INC., New York, N.Y. Lobbyist — Edward D. Heffernan, 1513 16th St. N.W., Washington, D.C. 20036. Filed 4/5/85. Legislative interest — "... federal excise tax on retail sale of heavy trucks and trailer equipment."

TRANSPACE CARRIERS INC., Greenbelt, Md. Lobbyist — Pillsbury, Madison & Sutro, 1667 K St. N.W., Washington, D.C. 20006. Filed 4/10/85. Legislative interest — "... space shuttle pricing policies."

TURNER BROADCASTING SYSTEMS INC., Washington, D.C. Lobbyist — Wexler, Reynolds, Harrison & Schule Inc., 1317 F St. N.W., Washington, D.C. 20004. Filed 4/8/85. Legislative interest — "... mergers and acquisitions in the broadcasting industry and/or FCC policy regarding mergers and acquisitions in the broadcasting industry...."

TYSON FOODS, Springdale, Ark. Lobbyist — Jack L. Williams, 451 New Jersey Ave. S.E., Washington, D.C. 20003. Filed 4/18/85. Legislative interest — Not specified.

UNION MUTUAL LIFE INSURANCE CO., 2211 Congress St., Portland, Maine 04122. Filed for self 4/8/85. Legislative interest — Not specified. Lobbyist — William T. Christian.

UNION OIL COMPANY OF CALIFORNIA, 461 S. Boylston St., Los Angeles, Calif. 90017. Filed for self 4/10/85. Legislative interest — Not specified. Lobbyist — Gary R. Balzhiser, 1050 Connecticut Ave. N.W., Washington, D.C. 20036.

UNION PACIFIC, Washington, D.C. Lobbyist — Black, Manafort, Stone & Kelly, 324 N. Fairfax St., Alexandria, Va. 22314. Filed 4/10/85. Legislative interest — "... Treasury Department tax reform proposal."

UNITED AIRLINES INC., Chicago, Ill. Lobbyist — Wilkinson, Barker, Knauer & Quinn, 1735 New York Ave. N.W., Washington, D.C. 20036. Filed 4/29/85. Legislative interest — "... airline ownership of computerized reservations systems and other legislation affecting the air transportation industry."

UNITED FAMILY LIFE INSURANCE CO., Atlanta, Ga. Lobbyist — Hansell & Post, 1667 K St. N.W., Washington, D.C. 20006. Filed 4/10/85. Legislative interest — "... taxation of the U.S. life insurance industry."

UNITED NUCLEAR CORP., 7700 Leesburg Pike, Falls Church, Va. 22043. Filed for self 4/19/85. Legislative interest — "... to assist in the passage of uranium mining and milling legislation." Lobbyist — E. B. White.

UNITED TELEVISION INC., Minneapolis, Minn. Lobbyist — Kaye, Scholer, Fierman, Hays & Handler, 1575 I St. N.W., Washington, D.C. 20005. Filed 4/17/85. Legislative interest — "... TV stations and the communications industry."

UNOCAL CORP., Los Angeles, Calif. Lobbyist — Charls E. Walker Associates Inc., 1730 Pennsylvania Ave. N.W., Washington, D.C. 20006. Filed 4/17/85. Legislative interest — "... merger or acquisition activities."

VIACOM INTERNATIONAL INC., New York, N.Y. Lobbyist — Wexler, Reynolds, Harrison & Schule Inc., 1317 F St. N.W., Washington, D.C. 20004. Filed 4/18/85. Legislative interest — "... cable television industry generally; broadcasting deregulation (HR 1977); advertising of alcohol on radio and television; the must carry regulations (S 584)."

VIRGINIA ELECTRIC & POWER CO., Richmond, Va. Lobbyist — Reid & Priest, 1111 19th St. N.W., Washington, D.C. 20036. Filed 4/4/85. Legislative interest — "... Repeal of Public Utility Holding Company Act ... 15 U.S.C. section 79 et seq. ... for repeal."

WASTE MANAGEMENT INC., 600 Maryland Ave. S.W., Washington, D.C. 20024. Filed for self 4/12/85. Legislative interest — "... solid waste, hazardous waste industry ... Resource Recovery and Conservation Act amendments, Superfund amendments." Lobbyists — James T. Banks, William Y. Brown.

WEST POINT PEPPERELL, Box 71, West Point, Ga. 31833. Filed for self 4/24/85. Legislative interest — "HR 1562, S 680 Textile and Apparel Trade Enforcement Act of 1985, Support...." Lobbyist — Conrad M. Fowler.

International Relations

THE BAHAMAS, GOVERNMENT OF, Nassau, Bahamas. Lobbyist — Black, Manafort, Stone & Kelly, 324 N. Fairfax St., Alexandria, Va. 22314. Filed 4/10/85. Legislative interest — "Foreign economic and security assistance proposals, Caribbean Basin Initiative issues, trade, textiles, tourism. HR 961 Caribbean Infrastructure Assistance Act, HR 1158, Caribbean Higher Education Act, HR 5119, International Security and Development Cooperation Act of 1984, HR 962, PL 98-164, Hawkins Amendment."

CANADIAN FOREST INDUSTRIES COUNCIL, Ottawa, Ontario, Canada. Lobbyist — Arnold & Porter, 1200 New Hampshire Ave. N.W., Washington, D.C. 20036. Filed 4/24/85. Legislative interest — "To oppose efforts to restrict imports of lumber products from Canada."

GUAM POWER AUTHORITY, Agana, Guam. Lobbyist — Duncan, Weinberg & Miller, 1775 Pennsylvania Ave. N.W., Washington, D.C. 20006. Filed 4/4/85. Legislative interest — "... annual omnibus Territories bills and amendments to the Clean Air Act or Federal Water Pollution Control Act...."

HONG KONG TRADE DEVELOPMENT COUNCIL, Hong Kong. Lobbyist — French & Co., 1317 F St. N.W., Washington, D.C. 20004. Filed 4/5/85. Legislative interest — Not specified.

PUERTO RICO, COMMONWEALTH OF, San Juan, Puerto Rico. Lobbyist — Covington & Burling, 1201 Pennsylvania Ave. N.W., Washington, D.C. 20044. Filed 4/5/85. Legislative interest — "... preserve section 936 of the Internal Revenue Code."

SUDAN, DEMOCRATIC REPUBLIC OF, Khartoum, Sudan. Lobbyist — Neill & Co. Inc., 900 17th St. N.W., Washington, D.C. 20006. Filed 4/8/85. Legislative interest — "Promoting the passage of the Administration's military and economic assistance programs insofar as it may relate to the Democratic Republic of Sudan, including the foreign assistance authorization and appropriations bills."

Labor Organizations

ALASKA TEAMSTERS-EMPLOYER WELFARE TRUST, Anchorage, Alaska. Lobbyist — Birch, Horton, Bittner, Pestinger & Anderson, 1155 Connecticut Ave. N.W., Washington, D.C. 20036. Filed 4/11/85. Legislative interest — "Employee benefits taxation issues."

AMERICAN FEDERATION OF GOVERNMENT EMPLOYEES, Washington, D.C. Lobbyist — David Joel Schlein, 545 4th St. S.E., Washington, D.C. 20003. Filed 4/5/85. Legislative interest — "Budget of the United States Government, Civil Service Reform Act of 1978 ... Federal Employees Flexible and Compressed Work Schedules Act PL 97-221 - for."

AMERICAN FEDERATION OF LABOR-CONGRESS OF INDUSTRIAL ORGANIZATIONS, 815 16th St. N.W., Washington, D.C. 20006. Filed for self 4/16/85. Legislative interest — "Federal and Postal Employees Issues: Federal Budget, Authorizations & Appropriations, Compensation, Agency Budgets & Government Reorganizations, Civil Service Retirement, Disability Benefits, Health Benefits, Contracting-Out, and Employee Rights...." Lobbyist — Paula D. Lucak. Filed 4/10/85. Legislative interest — Not specified. Lobbyist — Vincent Trivelli.

State and Local Governments

AVALON, CITY OF, Avalon, Calif. Lobbyist — Cliff Madison, P.O. Box 3482, Granada Hills, Calif. 91344. Filed 4/23/85. Legislative interest — "Clean Water Act Amendments - For."

BURBANK-GLENDALE-PASADENA AIRPORT AUTHORITY, Burbank, Calif. Lobbyist — Cliff Madison, P.O. Box 3482, Granada Hills, Calif. 91344. Filed 4/23/85. Legislative interest — "Transportation Appropriations - For."

CHICAGO CITY COLLEGES, Chicago, Ill. Lobbyist — Dow, Lohnes & Albertson, 1255 23rd St. N.W., Washington, D.C. 20037. Filed 4/16/85. Legislative interest — "... Omnibus Defense Authorization Act for FY 86 ... S 694, HR 1872 ... In support of legislation assuring equality of treatment of community colleges in the provision of education services in the treatment of military personnel."

CHICAGO RTA, Chicago, Ill. Lobbyist — Black, Manafort, Stone & Kelly, 324 N. Fairfax St., Alexandria, Va. 22314. Filed 4/10/85. Legislative interest — "Mass Transit matters. . . ."

ILLINOIS ENVIRONMENTAL PROTECTION AGENCY, Springfield, Ill. Lobbyist — Craft & Richards, 1050 Thomas Jefferson St. N.W., Washington, D.C. 20007. Filed 4/25/85. Legislative interest — "... superfund and ground water protection. . . ."

MARYLAND, STATE OF, Annapolis, Md. Lobbyist — Finley, Kumble, Wagner, Heine, Underberg, Manley & Casey, 1120 Connecticut Ave. N.W., Washington, D.C. 20036. Filed 4/29/85. Legislative interest — "... the rights of Maryland Sports Fans, Maryland Municipalities, and the State of Maryland in their relationship to the National Football League and Professional Sports in general. Legislation increasing the power and control of the National Football League by broadening its Antitrust Exemptions: S 172, against ... S 298, against ... HR 510, against ... HR 1124, against ... Legislation protecting Sports Fans, State and Municipalities from continued abuse by certain National Football League Owners: S 187, for ... HR 885, for."

NEW ORLEANS, CITY OF, New Orleans, La. Lobbyist — Verner, Liipfert, Bernhard, McPherson & Hand, 1660 L St. N.W., Washington, D.C. 20036. Filed 4/11/85. Legislative interest — Not specified.

ORANGE COUNTY SANITATION DISTRICTS, Fountain Valley, Calif. Lobbyist — Leff & Mason, 1700 Pennsylvania Ave. N.W., Washington, D.C. 20006. Filed 4/17/85. Legislative interest — "Interference from Mexican radio transmitters with client's pre-existing radio system."

PURGATOIRE RIVER WATER CONSERVANCY DISTRICT, Trinidad, Colo. Lobbyist — Gold and Liebengood Inc., 1050 Connecticut Ave. N.W., Washington, D.C. 20036. Filed 4/12/85. Legislative interest — "... authorization of water resource funding."

Trade Associations

AD-HOC MORTGAGE-BACKED SECURITIES LEGISLATIVE AND REGULATORY ASSOCIATION, Avenue of the Arts Building, Philadelphia, Pa. 19107. Filed for self 4/1/85. Legislative interest — "Mortgage-backed securities. . . ." Lobbyist — Bruce Johnson.

AGRICULTURAL PRODUCERS, Valencia, Calif. Lobbyist — Harris Miller & Associates, 100 Wilson Blvd., Arlington, Va. 22209. Filed 4/2/85. Legislative interest — "Immigration reform legislation, specifically relating to temporary worker programs."

AIR LINE PILOTS ASSOCIATION, 1625 Massachusetts Ave. N.W., Washington, D.C. 20036. Filed for self 4/9/85. Legislative interest — Not specified. Lobbyist — Brendan M. Kenny.

AIR TRAFFIC CONTROL ASSOCIATION, 2020 N. 14th St., Arlington, Va. 22201. Filed for self 4/11/85. Legislative interest — "... air traffic control, aviation, aviation safety, and matters affecting personnel including federal employees who develop, install, maintain and operate ATC facilities." Lobbyist — Gabriel A. Hartl.

AMERICAN ACADEMY OF PHYSICIAN ASSISTANTS, 1117 N. 19th St., Arlington, Va. 22209. Filed for self 4/11/85. Legislative interest — "... reauthorization of Health Professions Educational Assistance Act (FOR); FY 86 appropriation for physician assistant program educational assistance (FOR); coverage of physician assistant services under Part 1 of Medicare (FOR)." Lobbyist — William A. Finerfrock.

AMERICAN BAKERS ASSOCIATION, Washington, D.C. Lobbyist — Corman Law Offices, 1420 16th St. N.W., Washington, D.C. 20036. Filed 4/25/85. Legislative interest — "... imposition and administration of the Highway Motor Vehicle Use Tax and the Diesel Fuel Excise Tax. . . ."

AMERICAN BANKERS ASSOCIATION, 1120 Connecticut Ave. N.W., Washington, D.C. 20036. Filed for self 4/12/85. Legislative interest — "... the banking industry, specifically agricultural banks, HR 1096, HR 1035." Lobbyist — Rusty L. Jesser. Filed for self 4/10/85. Legislative interest — Same as above. Lobbyist — Floyd E. Stoner.

AMERICAN CEMENT TRADE ALLIANCE INC., 1331 Pennsylvania Ave. N.W., Washington, D.C. 20004. Filed for self 4/10/85. Legislative interest — "... the production and sale of cement in the United States and affecting international trade in cement. . . ." Lobbyist — Lauren J. Cronin.

AMERICAN ELECTRONICS ASSOCIATION, Washington, D.C. Lobbyist — Powell, Goldstein, Frazer & Murphy, 1110 Vermont Ave. N.W., Washington, D.C. 20005. Filed 4/3/85. Legislative interest — "Research and Development Tax Credit Reauthorization - I.R.C. Section 30."

AMERICAN FARM BUREAU FEDERATION, 225 Touhy Ave., Park Ridge, Ill. 60068. Filed for self 4/11/85. Legislative interest — "... International Affairs." Lobbyist — Paul A. Drazek, 600 Maryland Ave. S.W., Washington, D.C. 20024.

AMERICAN INSTITUTE OF ARCHITECTS, 1735 New York Ave. N.W., Washington, D.C. 20006. Filed for self 4/9/85. Legislative interest — "... tax reform, historic preservation, federal procurement, design and construction and housing and community development." Lobbyist — John E. Lynn.

AMERICAN MINING CONGRESS, 1920 N St. N.W., Washington, D.C. 20036. Filed for self 4/12/85. Legislative interest — "... income taxation, social security, public lands, monetary policy, mine safety, stockpiling, environmental quality control, etc." Lobbyists — Peter W. Tooker, George F. Fenton Jr.

AMERICAN NEWSPAPER PUBLISHERS ASSOCIATION, Washington, D.C. Lobbyist — James H. Davidson, 2000 L St. N.W., Washington, D.C. 20036. Filed 4/5/85. Legislative interest — "Tax Legislation before the House Ways and Means Committee."

AMERICAN OPTOMETRIC ASSOCIATION, 600 Maryland Ave. S.W., Washington, D.C. 20024. Filed for self 4/9/85. Legislative interest — Not specified. Lobbyist — Keith R. Krueger.

AMERICAN PSYCHOLOGICAL ASSOCIATION, 1200 17th St. N.W., Washington, D.C. 20036. Filed for self 4/12/85. Legislative interest — "... behavioral and social science research and training ... authorizations and appropriations for the National Science Foundation, National Institutes of Health and the National Institute of Mental Health." Lobbyist — Don White.

AMERICAN PUBLIC POWER ASSOCIATION, 2301 M St. N.W., Washington, D.C. 20037. Filed for self 4/4/85. Legislative interest — "... publicly owned utilities and the federal power marketing agencies ... the Federal Power Act; Energy and Water Development appropriations. . . ." Lobbyist — Deborah Sliz.

AMERICAN ROAD & TRANSPORTATION BUILDERS ASSOCIATION, 525 School St. S.W., Washington, D.C. 20024. Filed for self 4/29/85. Legislative interest — "Bills Dealing With Federal-aid Highways - 23 U.S. Code ... Tax laws affecting highway contractors. . . ." Lobbyist — Richard M. Harris. Filed for self 4/29/85. Legislative interest — Not specified. Lobbyist — Daniel J. Hanson Sr.

AMERICAN SOCIETY OF ANESTHESIOLOGISTS, 1201 Pennsylvania Ave. N.W., Washington, D.C. 20004. Filed for self 4/10/85. Legislative interest — "... various proposals for third-party reimbursement of non-physician practitioners, national health insurance, medical manpower legislation, Medicare/Medicaid reform, budget reconciliation, malpractice reform, and the jurisdiction of the FTC over the profession." Lobbyist — Thomas L. Adams.

AMERICAN SOCIETY OF MECHANICAL ENGINEERS, 345 E. 47th St., New York, N.Y. 10017. Filed for self 4/5/85. Legislative interest — "Codes and Standards, consumer legislation, energy legislation, environmental legislation, metric conversion, occupational safety & health, transportation and mass transit and other areas that would affect the profession of mechanical engineers." Lobbyist — Philip W. Hamilton, 1825 K St. N.W., Washington, D.C. 20006.

AMERICAN VETERINARY MEDICAL ASSOCIATION, 1522 K St. N.W., Washington, D.C. 20005. Filed for self 4/11/85. Legislative interest — "The advancement of veterinary medical science. USDA appropriations (no bill - support research, education, and animal disease research programs). USDA authorization (S 501, HR 1420, S 616 - support maintenance of research, education, and animal disease programs at present levels). Tax Reform Act of 1984, PL 98-369 (support HR 1869 repeal of contemporaneous recordkeeping requirement to substantiate business use of automobiles). Laboratory animal welfare (HR 1145 - no position). Use of antibiotics in animals (HR 616 - no position). Animal disease control (S 715 - no position). Federal Food, Drug, and Cosmetic Act, 21 USC Section 301 et seq., amendments (no bill - support). Virus-Serum-Toxin Act, 21 USC Section 151 et seq., amendments (no bill - support). Patent term restoration (no bill - support). State inspection of meat products (S 192 - no position)." Lobbyist — Paul F. Peters.

ANIMAL HEALTH INSTITUTE, 119 Oronoco St., Alexandria, Va. 22313. Filed for self 4/12/85. Legislative interest — "... animal health products industry." Lobbyists — Fred H. Holt, John W. Thomas.

APPALACHIAN ENERGY GROUP, Buffalo, N.Y. Lobbyist — Bracewell & Patterson, 1825 I St. N.W., Washington, D.C. 20006. Filed 4/8/85. Legislative interest — "To protect producer interests in tax bill."

ASSOCIATED GENERAL CONTRACTORS OF AMERICA, 1957 E St. N.W., Washington, D.C. 20006. Filed for self 4/3/85. Legislative interest — "Continued funding for the U.S. Synthetic Fuel Corporation - support." Lobbyist — Craig D. Dart.

ASSOCIATION OF AMERICAN VETERINARY MEDICAL COLLEGES, 1522 K St. N.W., Washington, D.C. 20005. Filed for self 4/11/85. Legislative interest — "... veterinary medical education and research. USDA appropriations (no bill - support education and research programs). USDA authorization (S 501, HR 1420, S 616 - support maintenance of education and research programs at current levels). Health Professions Education Assistance Legislation (support). Laboratory animal welfare (HR 1145 - no position). HHS appropriations (no bill - support health manpower and NIH programs). Reauthorization of Higher Education Act (no bill)." Lobbyist — Paul F. Peters.

ASSOCIATION OF EXECUTIVE SEARCH CONSULTANTS INC., Greenwich, Conn. Lobbyist — Butler & Binion, 1747 Pennsylvania Ave. N.W., Washington, D.C. 20006. Filed 4/29/85. Legislative interest — Not specified.

ASSOCIATION OF SCIENCE-TECHNOLOGY CENTERS, 1413 K St. N.W., Washington, D.C. 20005. Filed for self 4/17/85. Legislative interest — "... federal grant programs for science education, teacher training, and grants specifically for museum operation. National Science Foundation, for-increased approp. for SEE directorate ... Education for Economic Security Act, PL 98-377 (and like bills), for-increased funding and inclusion of science centers and museums as eligible recipients. Institute for Museum Services, for-continuation of program funding levels." Lobbyist — Ellen Griffee.

AUTO IMPORTERS COMPLIANCE ASSOCIATION, Washington, D.C. Lobbyist — Manatt, Phelps, Rothenberg & Tunney, 1200 New Hampshire Ave. N.W., Washington, D.C. 20036. Filed 4/26/85. Legislative interest — "HR 1006 and S 863."

AUTOMOTIVE DISMANTLERS & RECYCLERS ASSOCIATION INC., Washington, D.C. Lobbyist — Jones, Day, Reavis & Pogue, 655 15th St. N.W., Washington, D.C. 20005. Filed 4/10/85. Legislative interest — "Motor vehicle theft prevention and hazardous waste legislation."

BUSINESS ROUNDTABLE, Washington, D.C. Lobbyist — Morgan, Lewis & Bockius, 1800 M St. N.W., Washington, D.C. 20036. Filed 4/12/85. Legislative interest — "Monitoring of legislation addressing tender offers including S 631, S 286 and S 706."

CHAMBER OF COMMERCE OF THE UNITED STATES, 1615 H St. N.W., Washington, D.C. 20062. Lobbyist — O'Connor & Hannan, 1919 Pennsylvania Ave. N.W., Washington, D.C. 20006. Filed 4/12/85; Lobbyist — Daniel Costello, 12321 La Plata St., Silver Spring, Md. 20904. Filed 4/11/85; Filed for self 4/10/85. Lobbyist — Barry H. Bauman. Legislative interest — Not specified in any filing.

CHELSEA PROPERTY OWNERS, Newark, N.J. Lobbyist — Patton, Boggs & Blow, 2550 M St. N.W., Washington, D.C. 20037. Filed 4/10/85. Legislative interest — "ICC appropriations bills."

CHEMICAL MANUFACTURERS ASSOCIATION, 2501 M St. N.W., Washington, D.C. 20037. Filed for self 4/11/85. Legislative interest — "... environmental legislation specifically RCRA and the Safe Drinking Water Act affecting the chemical industry." Lobbyist — Ginny Grenham.

CLEAN COAL TECHNOLOGY COALITION, Washington, D.C. Lobbyist — Van Ness, Feldman, Sutcliffe & Curtis, 1050 Thomas Jefferson St. N.W., Washington, D.C. 20007. Filed for self 4/14/85. Legislative interest — "... funding and implementation of clean coal program and the clean coal technology reserve as authorized by PL 98-473."

COALITION FOR THE ADVANCEMENT OF INDUSTRIAL TECHNOLOGY, Washington, D.C. Lobbyist — Jack McDonald Co., 1800 M St. N.W., Washington, D.C. 20036. Filed 4/16/85. Legislative interest — "... extend R&D tax credit."

CONTRACTORS LIABILITY AND INDEMNIFICATION ALLIANCE, Arlington, Va. Lobbyist — Crowell & Moring, 1100 Connecticut Ave. N.W., Washington, D.C. 20036. Filed 4/5/85. Legislative interest — "... contribution and indemnification for government contractors."

FIBER, FABRIC & APPAREL COALITION FOR TRADE, Washington, D.C. Lobbyist — Jack McDonald Co., 1800 M St. N.W., Washington, D.C. 20036. Filed 4/16/85. Legislative interest — "... the import of textiles or textile related products into the United States."

FOOD MARKETING INSTITUTE, 1750 K St. N.W., Washington, D.C. 20006. Filed for self 4/10/85. Legislative interest — "... tax legislation." Lobbyist — Thomas W. Little.

FOOTWEAR INDUSTRIES OF AMERICA, Philadelphia, Pa. Lobbyist — Black, Manafort, Stone & Kelly, 324 N. Fairfax St., Alexandria, Va. 22314. Filed 4/10/85. Legislative interest — "Petition before the International Trade Commission - S 201."

INDEPENDENT STAINLESS STEEL WIRE REDRAWERS, Washington, D.C. Lobbyist — Pillsbury, Madison & Sutro, 1667 K St. N.W., Washington, D.C. 20006. Filed 4/10/85. Legislative interest — "... importation of stainless steel wire rod."

INDUSTRY COUNCIL FOR TANGIBLE ASSETS, 214 Massachusetts Ave. N.E., Washington, D.C. 20002. Filed for self 4/17/85. Legislative interest — "Tax legislative matters...." Lobbyist — Howard Segermark.

INTERNATIONAL FRANCHISE ASSOCIATION, 1025 Connecticut Ave. N.W., Washington, D.C. 20036. Filed for self 4/12/85. Legislative interest — "General Franchise Legislation." Lobbyists — Susan Strauss, Herbert A. Hedden.

INTERNATIONAL TAXICAB ASSOCIATION, 3849 Farragut Ave., Kensington, Md. 20895. Lobbyist — Webster, Chamberlain & Bean, 1747 Pennsylvania Ave. N.W., Washington, D.C. 20006. Filed 4/9/85. Legislative interest — "... HR 1354 concerning taxicab exemption from federal excise tax on gasoline (for exemption)." Filed for self 4/9/85. Legislative interest — "... HR 1354 concerning taxicab exemption from federal excise tax on gasoline (for exemption)." Lobbyist — C. Michael Deese.

LOS ANGELES ALLIANCE FOR EQUITABLE CUSTOMS STAFFING, Los Angeles, Calif. Lobbyist — Daniel C. Maldonado, 10000 Falls Road, Potomac, Md. 20854. Filed 4/30/85. Legislative interest — "Treasury appropriations and legislative bills affecting the U.S. Customs Service."

MORTGAGE BANKERS ASSOCIATION OF AMERICA, 1125 15th St. N.W., Washington, D.C. 20005. Filed for self 4/8/85. Legislative interest — "... the mortgage lending, banking, and construction industries ... HR 242 TAXATION-At Risk ... HR 591 MORTGAGE CREDIT-Usury ... HR 592 MORTGAGE CREDIT-Foreclosure Relief ... HR 756 VA-Home Loan Guarantee Amount ... HR 1040 TAXATION-Code Reform ... S 9 VA-Home Loan Guaranty ... S 56 TAXATION-Imputed Interest ... S 71 TAXATION-Imputed Interest ... S 409 TAXATION-Code Revision (1985) ... S 411 TAXATION-Code Revision (1985)." Lobbyist — Brian D. Cooney.

MOTION PICTURE ASSOCIATION OF AMERICA INC., 1600 I St. N.W., Washington, D.C. 20006. Filed 4/18/85. Legislative interest — "... amendments to Copyright Act of 1976, HR 384; satellite transmission, HR 1769, HR 1840, S Res 35; S Res 36; and miscellaneous bills relating to trade, network cross-ownership of cable systems, tax, censorship of motion pictures and audiovisual works, and other issues affecting films and television programs." Lobbyist — Barbara A. Dixon.

NATIONAL ASSOCIATION FOR UNIFORMED SERVICES, 5535 Hempstead Way, Springfield, Va. 22151. Filed for self 4/12/85. Legislative interest — "... support measures which will uphold the security of the United States, sustain the morale and provide equitable consideration for all members of the uniformed services — active, reserve, and retired. Specific bills of interest are: HR 752 — to improve the new GI Bill (FOR); HR 597 — to repeal Social Security offset to SBP (FOR); HR 344 — to improve support for military families (FOR); HR 400 — to remove time limitation on use of Vietnam-era GI Bill (FOR); HR 62 — to provide SBP benefits for surviving spouses whose husbands died prior to 9/21/72. S Con Res 32 — First Concurrent Resolution (AGAINST so much of S Con Res 32 as pertains to COLA freeze and CPI-2%)." Lobbyist — James C. Pennington.

NATIONAL ASSOCIATION OF BROADCASTERS, Washington, D.C. Lobbyist — Hoag & Associates, 1877 Broadway, Boulder, Colo. 80302. Filed 4/26/85. Legislative interest — "Communication legislation."

NATIONAL ASSOCIATION OF CONVENIENCE STORES, Falls Church, Va. Lobbyist — Chwat/Weigend Associates, 400 First St. N.W., Washington, D.C. 20001. Filed 4/10/85. Legislative interest — "Tax matters including tax simplification legislation, and agricultural matters including food stamp legislation."

NATIONAL ASSOCIATION OF CRIMINAL DEFENSE LAWYERS, Washington, D.C. Lobbyist — Edward D. Heffernan, 1513 16th St. N.W., Washington, D.C. 20036. Filed 4/5/85. Legislative interest — "Promote amendment to Section 6050 (I) of the Internal Revenue Code (which was added by Section 146 of Title I of the Deficit Reduction Act of 1984) to exempt transactions arising out of the attorney-client relationship."

NATIONAL ASSOCIATION OF FLEET ADMINISTRATORS INC., New York, N.Y. Lobbyist — Kent & O'Connor Inc., 1919 Pennsylvania N.W., Washington, D.C. 20006. Filed 4/10/85. Legislative interest — Not specified.

NATIONAL ASSOCIATION OF MANUFACTURERS, 1776 F St. N.W., Washington, D.C. 20006. Filed for self 4/12/85. Legislative interest — "... topics of concern to small manufacturers, including S 100." Lobbyist — Christian N. Braunlich.

NATIONAL ASSOCIATION OF PRIVATE PSYCHIATRIC HOSPITALS, 1319 F St. N.W., Washington, D.C. 20004. Filed for self 4/12/85. Legislative interest — "Issues affecting mental health, hospitals, manpower, and patients." Lobbyist — Roy Bussewitz.

NATIONAL ASSOCIATION OF PUBLIC TELEVISION STATIONS, 21 Dupont Circle N.W., Washington, D.C. 20036. Filed for self 4/3/85. Legislative interest — "... appropriations for the Corporation for Public Broadcasting (Labor-HHS Appropriation Bill), and for the Public Telecommunications Facilities Program (State, Justice, Commerce Appropriation Bill) and legislative amendments to the Communications Act of 1934 which affect public broadcasting." Lobbyist — Michelle C. Tessier.

NATIONAL ASSOCIATION OF REAL ESTATE INVESTMENT TRUSTS INC., 1101 17th St. N.W., Washington, D.C. 20036. Filed for self 4/12/85. Legislative interest — "... taxation, securities law, pension plan regulation...." Lobbyist — Mark O. Decker.

NATIONAL ASSOCIATION OF REALTORS, 777 14th St. N.W., Washington, D.C. 20005. Filed for self 4/17/85. Legislative interest — "... housing and community revitalization issues that affect the real estate industry, including: government-assisted housing programs, Housing Authorization and Appropriations legislation, Farmers Home Administration programs, property management, rent control, public buildings policy, condominium conversion issues, housing vouchers, and enterprise zones." Lobbyist — John Butts.

NATIONAL ASSOCIATION OF RETAIL DRUGGISTS, 205 Daingerfield Rd., Alexandria, Va. 22314. Filed for self 4/4/85. Legislative interest — "... federal health insurance, drug regulation, reform legislation and small business legislation." Lobbyist — Charles M. West.

NATIONAL ASSOCIATION OF SOCIAL WORKERS, 7981 Eastern Ave., Silver Spring, Md. 20910. Filed for self 4/24/85. Legislative interest — Not specified. Lobbyists — Alice I. Cohan, Susan Hoechstetter.

NATIONAL BROILER COUNCIL, Washington, D.C. Lobbyist — Hansell & Post, 1667 K St. N.W., Washington, D.C. 20006. Filed 4/10/85. Legislative interest — "Opposition to proposed imposition of meat and poultry inspection user fees."

NATIONAL BUSINESS AIRCRAFT ASSOCIATION, Washington, D.C. Lobbyist — Paul, Hastings, Janofsky & Walker, 1050 Connecticut Ave. N.W., Washington, D.C. 20036. Filed 4/25/85. Legislative interest — "S 245/HR 1869...."

NATIONAL COTTON COUNCIL OF AMERICA, P.O. Box 12285, Memphis, Tenn. 39112. Filed for self 4/29/85. Legislative interest — Not specified. Lobbyist — Keith Heard, 1030 15th St. N.W., Washington, D.C. 20005.

NATIONAL ELECTRICAL MANUFACTURERS ASSOCIATION, Washington, D.C. Lobbyist — Kutak, Rock & Campbell, 1101 Connecticut Ave. N.W., Washington, D.C. 20036. Filed 4/3/85. Legislative interest — "Legislation affecting imports of Korean steel and steel producers."

NATIONAL FEDERATION OF INDEPENDENT BUSINESS, 600 Maryland Ave. S.W., Washington, D.C. 20024. Filed for self 4/9/85. Legislative interest — "All legislation affecting small business and the economic well-being of the country, including tax bills, spending cuts, regulation bills, balancing budget bills and paperwork reduction bills." Lobbyist — Mark P. Bolduc.

NATIONAL FOREST PRODUCTS ASSOCIATION, 1619 Massachusetts Ave. N.W., Washington, D.C. 20036. Filed for self 4/14/85. Legislative interest — "... Forest Service appropriations, Federal land management policies, Wilderness proposals, housing and mortgage finance, public financing, lobby law reform, RARE II, Regulatory and Taxation and Federal Timber Contracts legislation." Lobbyists — Mark Gallant, Susan Tatum.

NATIONAL FRATERNAL CONGRESS OF AMERICA, Chicago, Ill. Lobbyist — Zuckert, Scoutt, Rasenberger & Johnson, 888 17th St. N.W., Washington, D.C. 20006. Filed 4/11/85. Legislative interest — "Proponent of retaining Section 501(c)(8) of the Internal Revenue Code."

NATIONAL MULTI HOUSING COUNCIL, 1150 17th St. N.W., Washington, D.C. 20036. Filed for self 4/12/85. Legislative interest — "Legislation affecting the development of rental apartments and condominiums. Specifically imputed interest, original issue discount legislation and provisions of the Treasury Tax Proposal regarding multifamily housing." Lobbyist — Deborah L. Shannon. Filed for self 4/11/85. Legislative interest — Same as above. Lobbyist — Desiree C. Anderson.

NATIONAL PARKS AND CONSERVATION ASSOCIATION, Washington, D.C. Lobbyist — Steven C. Whitney, 27 Sunset Dr., Alexandria, Va. 22301. Filed 4/12/85. Legislative interest — "General legislative interests relating to natural resource conservation and sound management of the National Park System."

NATIONAL RETAIL MERCHANTS ASSOCIATION,

New York, N.Y. Lobbyist — French & Co., 1317 F St. N.W., Washington, D.C. 20004. Filed 4/1/85. Legislative interest — "... Federal taxation and international trade."

NATIONAL SOCIETY OF PROFESSIONAL ENGINEERS, 1420 King St., Alexandria, Va. 22314. Filed for self 4/10/85. Legislative interest — "Federal Trade Commission ... Engineering Education ... Public Works Financing, S 652, Favors ... Capital Budget ... Technology Policy ... Defense Production Act ... Clean Water, S 652, Favors (w/amendment) ... Water Resources ... Hazardous Waste, S 51, Favors (w/amendment) ... Professional Liability ... Procurement Policy ... Federal Employee Liability ... Patents ... Government Control of Technology Exports ... Davis-Bacon ... Immigration ... Product Liability ... National Science Foundation, HR 1210, Favors." Lobbyist — Brian L. Connor.

NATIONAL SOFT DRINK ASSOCIATION, Washington, D.C. Lobbyist — Hogan & Hartson, 815 Connecticut Ave. N.W., Washington, D.C. 20006. Filed 4/10/85. Legislative interest — "... legislation to amend the Saccharin Study and Labeling Act, S 484."

NATIONAL WOOL GROWERS ASSOCIATION, San Angelo, Texas. Lobbyist — Wallace & Edwards, 1150 Connecticut Ave. N.W., Washington, D.C. 20036. Filed 4/10/85. Legislative interest — "Extension of Wool Act."

NORTHERN AIR CARGO, Anchorage, Alaska. Lobbyist — Birch, Horton, Bittner, Pestinger & Anderson, 1155 Connecticut Ave. N.W., Washington, D.C. 20036. Filed 4/11/85. Legislative interest — "Alaskan aviation issues."

POTATO CHIP/SNACK FOOD ASSOCIATION, 1711 King St., Alexandria, Va. 22314. Filed for self 4/12/85. Legislative interest — "... the snack food industry, including energy, agricultural, and nutrition legislation." Lobbyist — John R. Cady.

PUBLIC SECURITIES ASSOCIATION, Washington, D.C. Lobbyist — Charls E. Walker Associates Inc., 1730 Pennsylvania Ave. N.W., Washington, D.C. 20006. Filed 4/2/85. Legislative interest — "... issues relating to the tax treatment accorded to debt securities issued by agencies of state and local governments."

REINSURANCE ASSOCIATION OF AMERICA, 1025 Connecticut Ave. N.W., Washington, D.C. 20036. Filed for self 4/8/85. Legislative interest — "Hazardous waste, pollution, asbestos, insurance taxation." Lobbyist — Mindy Pollack.

RETAIL INDUSTRY TRADE ACTION COALITION, Washington, D.C. Lobbyist — Patton, Boggs & Blow, 2550 M St. N.W., Washington, D.C. 20037. Filed 4/10/85. Legislative interest — "... opposed to increased restrictions on apparel imports of the Textile quota bill."

SMOKELESS TOBACCO COUNCIL INC., 1925 K St. N.W., Washington, D.C. 20006. Filed for self 4/12/85. Legislative interest — Not specified. Lobbyist — Michael J. Kerrigan.

SOCIETY OF AMERICAN FLORISTS, 1601 Duke St., Alexandria, Va. 22314. Filed for self 4/8/85. Legislative interest — "... floriculture, horticulture, and agriculture, including those matters dealing with human relations and resources, education, transportation, commerce, industry, labor, etc." Lobbyist — Nancy Jacks Montgomery. Filed for self 4/12/85. Legislative interest — Same as above. Lobbyist — Deborah Gahs.

SOUTHEAST COMPACT COMMISSION, Raleigh, N.C. Lobbyist — Sutherland, Asbill & Brennan, 1666 K St. N.W., Washington, D.C. 20006. Filed 4/4/85. Legislative interest — "To help secure Congressional approval of the Southeast Compact bill (HR 1261, S 44) and any necessary amendments to the Low-Level Radioactive Waste Policy Act of 1980."

TEXAS CITRUS AND VEGETABLE IMPORT ASSOCIATION, Hidalgo, Texas. Lobbyist — Barnes, Richardson & Colburn, 1819 H St. N.W., Washington, D.C. 20006. Filed 4/29/85. Legislative interest — "Proposal to make permanent the elimination of duties on fresh cantaloupes imported during the months when there is no domestic production. HR 2075, introduced April 18, 1985, supports that proposal."

TOBACCO INSTITUTE, 1875 I St. N.W., Washington, D.C. 20006. Lobbyist — Black, Manafort, Stone & Kelly, 324 N. Fairfax St., Alexandria, Va. 22314. Filed 4/10/85. Legislative interest — "Cigarette excise tax." Filed for self 4/10/85. Legislative interest — Not specified. Lobbyist — Judy A. Wiedemeier.

U.S. TUNA FOUNDATION, Washington, D.C. Lobbyist — Patton, Boggs & Blow, 2550 M St. N.W., Washington, D.C. 20037. Filed 4/10/85. Legislative interest — "... legislation to equalize tariff on canned tuna at 35 percent ... Tariff Schedules of the United States, 112.30, 112.34."

WATER QUALITY ASSOCIATION, 1518 K St. N.W., Washington, D.C. 20005. Filed for self 4/10/85. Legislative interest — "... bills which affect the interests of water treatment equipment manufacturers, dealers and suppliers, (specifically bills designed to either exclude or promote the point of use water quality improvement industry including the Safe Drinking Water Act, Clean Water Act, Comprehensive Environmental Response Compensation and Liability Act and Farmers Home Administration reauthorization)." Lobbyist — Donna M. Cirolia.

WEST COAST FABRICATORS AND STEEL INDUSTRY ASSOCIATION, 2324 Navy Drive, Stockton, Calif. 95206. Filed for self 4/22/85. Legislative interest — Not specified. Lobbyist — Joseph L. Lang, 1121 L St., Sacramento, Calif. 95814.

WESTERN FOREST INDUSTRIES ASSOCIATION, Portland, Ore. Lobbyist — Stephen A. Evered, 21 5th St. S.E., Washington, D.C. 20003. Filed 4/10/85. Legislative interest — "Interior Appropriations bill for FY '86."

Miscellaneous

ALLIANCE FOR JUSTICE, JUDICIAL SELECTION PROJECT, 600 New Jersey Ave. N.W., Washington, D.C. 20001. Filed for self 4/14/85. Legislative interest — "Consultation with Senate Judiciary Committee staff regarding judicial selection and confirmation procedures." Lobbyist — Susan Liss.

AMERICAN BUSINESS PRESS, New York, N.Y. Lobbyist — Wagner & Baroody Inc., 1100 17th St. N.W., Washington, D.C. 20036. Filed 4/9/85. Legislative interest — "In favor of changes in the revenue forgone postal subsidy."

AMERICAN CAMPING ASSOCIATION, Bradford Woods, Martinsville, Ind. 46151. Filed for self 4/18/85. Legislative interest — "Paragraph (3) of Section 276(b) of the Tax Equity and Fiscal Responsibility Act of 1982 (26 U.S.C. 3306 note); In support of repeal of the sunset provision." Lobbyist — David C. Gray.

THE AMERICAN LEGION, 700 N. Pennsylvania St., Indianapolis, Ind. 46204. Filed for self 4/12/85. Legislative interest — "Support National Flag Day/Pause for the Pledge ... Enforce laws prohibiting private citizens from conducting negotiations with foreign governments ... Internal Security of the United States ... Restoration of the House Internal Security Committee ... Memorial Day ... American Legion support for CIA and FBI ... Oppose amnesty for illegal aliens ... Support English as the official national language ... Promote school prayer ... American Legion policy regarding employment of illegal aliens ... Designate May 7 as 'Vietnam Veterans Recognition Day' ... Support special immigrant status for Filipino alien veterans and their families ... Declare George Washington's birthday as a national holiday ... Amend U.S. Flag Code ... Support pro-active delinquency prevention programs ... Support enforcement of child pornography laws ... Support full funding for child immunization programs ... Catastrophic illness among children ... Designate Thanksgiving week as National Family Week ... Support Reye's Syndrome legislation ... Support special adoptive programs ... Support special youth employment opportunity wage ... Support changes in management of Local Veterans Employment Representative activities ... Support Older Veterans Employment Tax Incentive Program ... Support requirement that Local Veterans Employment Representatives be veterans ... Support extension of VRA ... American Legion policy on the VA Home Loan Program ... Support extension of the Targeted Jobs Tax Credit ... Support full funding for the Office of the Assistant Secretary of Labor for Veterans Employment ... Support increased staffing for the Employment Service ... Support extension of the Emergency Veterans Jobs Training Program ... Oppose contracting out of federal jobs reserved for veterans ... Support legislation establishing Regional Veterans Employment Representatives ... Support reallocation of Disabled Veterans Outreach Program staff for outreach purposes ... Support employment programs for all veterans ... Support enforcement of affirmative action for veterans in federal contracts ... Support veterans preference in federal employment ... Support National Employ the Older Worker Week ... Support strengthening prohibitions on transferring U.S. military technology ... Support humanitarian and military aid to Afghan refugees and Freedom fighters ... Support improved U.S./Mexican relations ... Support amendment of FOIA to allow withholding of sensitive information ... American Legion policy on terrorism ... Support the National Endowment for Democracy ... American Legion policy toward Cuba ... American Legion policy supporting El Salvador ... American Legion policy on nuclear arms control ... Support Caribbean Basin Initiative implementation ... Support Central American Democracy, Peace and Development Initiative ... American Legion policy toward Nicaragua ... Support the Republic of China ... Support aid for Turkey ... Support Republic of Korea ... Seek the reestablishment of diplomatic relations with the Republic of China ... Support sale of necessary military hardware to the Republic of China ... Support friendly relations between France and the United States ... Support aid for Guatemala ... Support aid for Honduras ... American Legion policy toward Mexico ... American Legion comprehensive Middle East policy ... American Legion policy toward Japanese defense and trade practices ... Support for Brazil ... Support aid for Costa Rica ... Support effective use of foreign aid ... Korean Conflict POW/MIA ... Support NATO ... Oppose diplomatic recognition of Vietnam ... American Legion policy on South Africa ... Indochina POW/MIA ... Law of the Sea Treaty policy ... Support stabilized postage rates ... Oppose internment of civilians ... Support retention of Senate Veterans Affairs Committee ... Support Latin American regional training programs ... The American Legion policy on the compulsory registration of firearms ... Support expansion of the reserve force program of the Selective Service System ... Support U.S. Army strategic mobility improvements ... Support development of binary munitions ... Support the peaceful and military use of space ... Support development and deployment of the B1-B Bomber and Advanced Technology Bomber (ATB) ... Support retention of military commissary system ... The American Legion policy on the military retirement program ... Support U.S. Air Force/Air Reserve Force mix ... Support armed forces spare parts acquisition ... Support development of increased strategic offensive capabilities ... Support development and procurement of the C-17 air transport ... Support the development of an antiballistic missile capability ... Support total force policy ... Support modernization of the U.S. Air Force ... Support modernization of U.S. Merchant Marine fleet ... Support a strong national defense ... Support development and deployment of Peacekeeper missile ... Support reestablishment of the military draft ... Seek increased PCS mileage allowances and weight limits ... Support modernization of the U.S. Navy ... Support improved U.S. Civil Defense capabilities ... Support improved educational incentives for active and reserve forces ... Support modernization of national defense industrial base ... Support modernization of the U.S. Coast Guard ... Support the National Space Program ... Support for strong U.S. Naval and Marine Corps reserve ... Oppose taxation of military quarters allowance ... Support extension of Vietnam War G.I. Bill delimiting date for certain active duty forces ... Support full funding for the Selective Service System ... Support Panama Canal Act of 1912 and its merger prohibition ... Support redocumentation of the Cunard *Princess* and Cunard *Countess* as U.S. flag vessels ... Support improved Great Lakes/St. Lawrence Seaway system ... Support national organ donor registration program ... Oppose all further reductions in veterans benefits programs ... Support restoration of VA personnel to pre-1981 levels ... Support permanent VA disability ratings held for 10 or more years ... Sponsor and support including the loss of one lung or loss of one kidney on the list of anatomical loss or loss of use disabilities ... Oppose measures to divert resources from veterans benefits ... Sponsor and support increase in burial plot allowance ... Support expansion of the GRECC program ... Support waiver of one year presumptive period and one year retroactive compensation limit for disabilities related to Agent Orange ... The American Legion policy on National Cemetery System and burial benefits ... Support treatment and care of non service-connected disabilities ... Support full funding for veterans programs ... Oppose 'Grace Commission' recommendations adversely affecting veterans ... Legion policy regarding GS 11-15 'Bulge' ... Support VA filling of prescriptions written by non-VA physicians ... Support legislation providing special Government Life Insurance program for Vietnam Era veterans ... Sponsor and support a special WWI pension ... Support two year presumptive period for psychosis for certain veterans ... Support adequate funding for VA medical research ... Sponsor and support exempting compensation as income from work incentive programs ... The American Legion policy on National Health Insurance ... Sponsor and support improved disability and death pension ... The American Legion policy on 'mainstreaming' veterans services ... Rename VAMC, Poplar Bluff, Missouri after John J. Pershing ... Oppose denial of beneficiary travel allowances ... Support use of VA funds for acquisition and rehabilitation of state veterans homes ... Support Veterans Administration as an Executive Department ... Support increase in the monthly rates of D.I.C. ... Oppose consolidation of VA Regional Offices ... Support VA health care construction program ... Oppose reductions in federal benefits by off-setting VA compensation ... Oppose third party reimbursement for VA medical care ... Sponsor and support restoration of burial allowances ... Support increasing disability compensation ... Support increase in Chapter 34 education allowances ... Sponsor and support service connection for Lupus Erythematosus ... Support grants-in-aid and nursing home care to the VAMC in the Philippines ... The American Legion policy on Agent Orange ... The American Legion policy on radiation exposure ... Support VA medical treatment for radiation exposure victims ... Support clothing allowance for certain skin conditions ... Sponsor and support increase in pensions for certain veterans ... Sponsor and support removal of restrictions against concurrent receipt of military longevity retirement and VA compensation ... Support annual review and revision of VA rates of reimbursement for state home care ... Oppose transfer of VA jurisdiction for veterans programs to other government agencies ... Sponsor and support a seven year presumptive period for Syringomyelia ... Support priority funding for VA alcohol, drug treatment and rehabilitation programs ... Support VA compensation, pension and readjustment allowances as veterans rights. ..." Lobbyist — David C. Daniels, 1608 K St. N.W., Washington, D.C. 20006.

AMERICANS FOR IMMIGRATION CONTROL INC., P.O. Box 11839, Alexandria, Va. 22312. Filed for self 4/5/85. Legislative interest — "Support enforcement of immigration laws and employer sanctions. Oppose amnesty for illegal aliens." Lobbyist — Robert H. Goldsborough, 5508 Lombardy Place, Baltimore, Md. 21210. Filed for self 4/8/85. Legislative interest — "Support enforcement of immigration laws and employer sanctions. Oppose amnesty for illegal aliens." Lobbyists — Robert H. Goldsborough, Louis March.

ASSOCIATION OF O&C COUNTIES, Roseburg, Ore. Lobbyist — Stoel, Rives, Boley, Fraser & Wyse, 1730 M St. N.W., Washington, D.C. 20036. Filed 4/10/85. Legislative interest — "... management of Federal lands, including but not limited to wilderness legislation, legislation affecting timber receipts on federal lands, taxation of timber harvested on federal or private lands, and regulatory matters concerning the harvest of timber from federal lands."

CENTER FOR ENVIRONMENTAL EDUCATION, Washington, D.C. Lobbyist — O'Connor & Hannan, 1919 Pennsylvania Ave. N.W., Washington, D.C. 20006. Filed 4/2/85. Legislative interest — "... the Endangered Species Act."

COMMITTEE FOR A RESPONSIBLE TAX POLICY INC., 1750 Pennsylvania Ave. N.W., Washington, D.C. 20006. Filed for self 4/10/85. Legislative interest — "... tax legislation affecting investment and capital formation ... various flat tax and modified flat tax proposals pending. ..." Lobbyist — Richard Rosenbaum.

COMMITTEE FOR FUTURE INVESTMENT IN AMERICA'S PAST, Washington, D.C. Lobbyist — Dewey,

Ballantine, Bushby, Palmer & Wood, 1775 Pennsylvania Ave. N.W., Washington, D.C. 20006. Filed 4/29/85. Legislative interest — "Legislation affecting incentives for rehabilitation projects."

COMMON CAUSE, 2030 M St. N.W., Washington, D.C. 20036. Filed for self 4/19/85. Legislative interest — "... open government, campaign finance reform, the Federal Election Commission, lobby disclosure, government ethics, Senate confirmation process, extension of the Clean Air Act, court jurisdiction issues, congressional budget process, congressional reform, freedom of information, energy policy, waste in government, regulatory reform, public participation in federal agency proceedings, Legal Services Corporation, the Equal Rights Amendment, War Powers Act, nuclear arms control, and military spending." Lobbyist — Jane Mentzinger.

DISABLED AMERICAN VETERANS, 3725 Alexandria Pike, Cold Spring, Ky. 41076. Filed for self 4/16/85. Legislative interest — "... all legislation affecting war veterans, their dependents and survivors of deceased veterans. VA Disability Compensation - Chapter 11, Title 38, USC ... HR 85 - support passage ... HR 1487 - support passage ... HR 1490 - support passage ... HR 1492 - support passage ... H Con Res 69 - support passage ... H J Res 191 - support passage ... H Res 47 - support passage ... S 85 - support passage ... S Con Res 20 - support passage ... VA Hospital and Medical Care - Chapter 17, Title 38, USC ... HR 505 - support passage ... HR 1491 - support passage ... HR 1494 - support passage ... HR 1501 - support passage ... S 6 (sec. 3) - support passage ... S 82 - support passage ... S 875 - support passage ... S 876 (sec. 2) - support passage ... Veterans Employment Benefits - Chapters 41 & 42, Title 38, USC ... HR 1122 - support passage ... HR 1408 - support passage ... HR 1505 - support passage ... HR 1506 - support passage ... Miscellaneous Veteran-Related Legislation ... HR 185 - support passage ... HR 513 - support passage ... HR 597 - support passage ... HR 659 - support passage ... HR 756 - support passage ... HR 759 - support passage ... HR 1141 - support passage ... HR 1476 - support passage ... HR 1485 - support passage ... HR 1486 - support passage ... HR 1493 - support passage ... HR 1516 - support passage ... H Con Res 37 - support passage ... H Con Res 40 - support passage ... H J Res 105 - support passage ... S 190 - support passage ... S 232 - support passage ... S 402 - support passage ... S 622 - support passage ... S 675 - support passage...." Lobbyist — Richard F. Schultz, 807 Maine Ave. S.W., Washington, D.C. 20024.

ROBERT J. EVANS, 2060 Canterbury Rd., Kingsport, Tenn. 37660. Filed for self 4/4/85. Legislative interest — "... to defeat legislation which encroaches on personal freedom."

FUND FOR ASSURING AN INDEPENDENT RETIREMENT, Washington, D.C. Lobbyist — Gold and Liebengood Inc., 1050 Connecticut Ave. N.W., Washington, D.C. 20036. Filed 4/12/85. Legislative interest — "Legislative proposals which affect federal employees retirement plan."

HISTORIC LANDMARKS FOR LIVING, Philadelphia, Pa. Lobbyist — O'Connor & Hannan, 1919 Pennsylvania Ave. N.W., Washington, D.C. 20006. Filed 4/29/85. Legislative interest — "... preservation of investment tax credits for residential historic restoration."

HOUSTON CLEARING HOUSE ASSOCIATION, Houston, Texas. Lobbyist — Arter & Hadden, 1919 Pennsylvania Ave. N.W., Washington, D.C. 20006. Filed 4/12/85. Legislative interest — "... monitor banking bills ... such as legislation regulating the availability of funds, HR 687, etc...."

INSTITUTE FOR PUBLIC INTEREST REPRESENTATION, 600 New Jersey Ave. N.W., Washington, D.C. 20001. Filed for self 4/26/85. Legislative interest — "... Soon to be introduced bill to amend the Federal Insecticide, Fungicide and Rodenticide Act (FIFRA) ... 7 U.S.C. section 136 et seq. ... For the bill to amend FIFRA." Lobbyist — Stephen E. Meili.

L5 SOCIETY, 1060 E. Elm, Tucson, Ariz. 85719. Filed for self 4/4/85. Legislative interest — "National Aeronautics and Space Administration Authorization Act, 1986. HR 1714." Lobbyist — Sandra Lee Adamson, P.O. Box 44026, Washington, D.C. 20026.

LEAGUE OF WOMEN VOTERS OF THE UNITED STATES, 1730 M St. N.W., Washington, D.C. 20036. Filed for self 4/10/85. Legislative interest — "... Human Resources — SUPPORT ... CETA Reauthorization and budgeting ... Civil Rights ... Day Care ... Education ... Employment ... Food Stamps ... HUD Authorizations and Appropriations ... Unemployment Compensation ... Vocational Education ... Human Resources — OPPOSE ... Legislation to rescind IRS regulations on private school non-profit status ... Tuition Tax Credits ... Anti-Busing Legislation ... International Relations — SUPPORT ... International Development Banks ... Foreign Economic Development Assistance ... Free flow in international trade/reduction of trade barriers ... Natural Resources — SUPPORT ... Clean Air Act ... Clean Water Act ... Energy Conservation ... Sound Land Use Legislation ... Surface Mining Control and Reclamation Act ... Low Income Energy Assistance ... Environmental Protection Measures Generally ... Representative Government — SUPPORT ... D.C. Representation ... Looking into problems of early projections ... Voting Rights Act Reauthorization ... Miscellaneous — SUPPORT ... Urban Mass Transit ... Economic Development Administration ... CDBG/UDAG ... General Revenue Sharing...." Lobbyist — Jennifer Vasiloff.

WARNER LeROY, New York, N.Y. Lobbyist — Dewey, Ballantine, Bushby, Palmer & Wood, 1775 Pennsylvania Ave. N.W., Washington, D.C. 20006. Filed 4/2/85. Legislative interest — "... Interior and related agencies appropriations act."

MARLENE C. McGUIRL, Washington, D.C. Lobbyist — Bible, Santini, Hoy & Miller, 900 17th St. N.W., Washington, D.C. 20006. Filed 4/14/85. Legislative interest — "Resolution of EEOC case."

NATIONAL RURAL HOUSING COALITION, Washington, D.C. Lobbyist — Robert A. Rapoza Associates Inc., 2001 S St. N.W., Washington, D.C. 20009. Filed for self 4/2/85. Legislative interest — "... low income housing and community development...."

NATIONAL TELEPHONE COOPERATIVE ASSOCIATION, 2626 Pennsylvania Ave. N.W., Washington, D.C. 20037. Filed for self 4/11/85. Legislative interest — "... the rural telephone program provided for in the Rural Electrification Act of 1936 ... telecommunications ... amendments to the Communications Act of 1934 ... the Rural Telephone Bank of 1971 ... rural telecommunications." Lobbyist — Michael E. Brunner.

NORTHEASTERN UNIVERSITY, Boston, Mass. Lobbyist — Hale & Dorr, 1201 Pennsylvania Ave. N.W., Washington, D.C. 20004. Filed 4/10/85. Legislative interest — Not specified.

RELIGIOUS COALITION FOR ABORTION RIGHTS INC., 100 Maryland Ave. N.E., Washington, D.C. 20002. Filed for self 4/11/85. Legislative interest — Not specified. Lobbyist — Mark A. Bartner.

RETIRED OFFICERS ASSOCIATION, 201 N. Washington St., Alexandria, Va. 22314. Filed for self 4/10/85. Legislative interest — "Any and all legislation pertinent to the rights, benefits, privileges and obligations of retired officers, male and female, Regular and Reserve, and their dependents and survivors, of whatever nature, dealing with personnel matters, pay and retirement benefits and pensions, studying and analyzing bills, preparing statements for presentation to the cognizant committees, and principally the committees on Armed Services, the committees on Veterans Affairs, and the committees dealing with various privileges, opportunities and obligations of the personnel involved." Lobbyist — Paul W. Arcari.

S.O.S., P.O. Box 65761, Washington, D.C. 20035. Filed for self 4/2/85. Legislative interest — Not specified. Lobbyist — Sara L. Loveland.

RAYMOND ST. CONKLING, 1600 S. Lynn St., Arlington, Va. 22202. Filed for self 4/10/85. Legislative interest — Not specified.

SIERRA CLUB, San Francisco, Calif. Lobbyist — Tom Cosgrove, 37 Trumbull St., New Haven, Conn. 06511. Filed 4/30/85. Legislative interest — Not specified.

TEMPLE UNIVERSITY, Philadelphia, Pa. Lobbyist — Ballard, Spahr, Andrews & Ingersoll, 1850 K St. N.W., Washington, D.C. 20006. Filed 4/12/85. Legislative interest — "... higher education and hospitals."

U.S. PUBLIC INTEREST RESEARCH GROUP, 215 Pennsylvania Ave. S.E., Washington, D.C. 20003. Filed for self 4/10/85. Legislative interest — "Support for removal of liability limits on nuclear power plants; support energy conservation and renewable energy sources; support student financial aid." Lobbyist — Kathleen Welch. Filed for self 4/10/85. Legislative interest — "Support for Safe Drinking Water Act, Clean Air Act, and bottle bill." Lobbyist — Reid Wilson.

UNITED WAY OF INDIANAPOLIS/COMMUNITY SERVICE COUNCIL OF METROPOLITAN INDIANAPOLIS, 1828 N. Meridian St., Indianapolis, Ind. 46202. Filed for self 4/2/85. Legislative interest — "... To make permanent the deduction for charitable contributions by nonitemizers ... S 361 and HR 587 ... Amend the Internal Revenue Code of 1954 ... In favor." Lobbyist — J. Byron Jensen.

VILLERS FOUNDATION, Washington, D.C. Lobbyist — Hale & Dorr, 1201 Pennsylvania Ave. N.W., Washington, D.C. 20004. Filed 4/10/85. Legislative interest — Not specified.

WASHINGTON BUREAU FOR THE REPRESENTATION OF THE SOCIETIES FOR THE DEFENSE OF TRADITION, FAMILY AND PROPERTY INC., 4301 Columbia Pike, Arlington, Va. 22204. Filed for self 4/4/85. Legislative interest — "... encourage the adoption of any legislation which promotes the perennial Christian values of tradition, family and private property and oppose any legislation that detracts from or interferes with such values." Lobbyist — Mario Navarro da Costa. Filed for self 4/4/85. Legislative interest — Not specified. Lobbyists — Mario Navarro da Costa, Luis Daniel Merizalde.

May Registrations

Corporations and Businesses

AMALGAMATED BANK OF NEW YORK, New York, N.Y. Lobbyist — Shaw, Pittman, Potts & Trowbridge, 1800 M St. N.W., Washington, D.C. 20036. Filed 5/23/85. Legislative interest — "... amendments to the Bank Holding Company Act."

AMERICAN GENERAL LIFE INSURANCE CO., Houston, Texas. Lobbyist — Davis & Harman, 655 15th St. N.W., Washington, D.C. 20005. Filed 5/24/85. Legislative interest — Not specified.

AMERICAN PETROFINA INC., P.O. Box 2159, Dallas, Texas 75221. Filed for self 5/1/85. Legislative interest — "... construction differential subsidies for ships." Lobbyist — Joe A. Moss.

APACHE CORP., Minneapolis, Minn. Lobbyist — Davis & Harman, 655 15th St. N.W., Washington, D.C. 20005. Filed 5/24/85. Legislative interest — "... tax treatment of publicly traded partnerships."

APPLIED ENERGY SERVICES INC., Arlington, Va. Lobbyist — The Capitol Group Inc., 2550 M St. N.W., Washington, D.C. 20037. Filed 5/10/85. Legislative interest — "... Public Utilities Regulatory legislation ... Tax Simplification." Lobbyist — Chadbourne, Parke, Whiteside & Wolff, 1101 Vermont Ave. N.W., Washington, D.C. 20005. Filed 5/31/85. Legislative interest — "Tax Reform Legislation."

ARIANESPACE S.A., Evry, France. Lobbyist — DGA International Inc., 1818 N St. N.W., Washington, D.C. 20036. Filed 5/13/85. Legislative interest — "Monitor general legislation, making available authorizations and appropriations reports for NASA, and specifically following provisions that would establish a pricing policy for the NASA shuttle program. Specific legislation includes HR 1714, National Aeronautics and Space Administration Authorization Act, 1986."

ARROWHEAD METALS LTD., 260 Eighth St., Toronto, Ontario, Canada M8V 3E1. Lobbyist — Dow, Lohnes & Albertson, 1255 23rd St. N.W., Washington, D.C. 20037. Filed 5/14/85. Legislative interest — "... U.S. Mint Authorization Bill ... HR 2148 ... in opposition to legislation that may adversely affect imports of coinage blanks from Canada." Filed for self 5/14/85. Legislative interest — Same as above. Lobbyist — Robert A. Kay.

ASARCO CORP., New York, N.Y. Lobbyist — Webster & Sheffield, 1200 New Hampshire Ave. N.W., Washington, D.C. 20036. Filed 5/2/85. Legislative interest — "... hostile takeovers, the taxation of mergers and acquisition and other related matters."

AVCO LYCOMING, Washington, D.C. Lobbyist — Cambridge International Inc., 10057 Maclura Court, Fairfax, Va. 22032. Filed 5/1/85. Legislative interest — "Support of annual Department of Defense Authorization Act."

BALDWIN-UNITED CORP., Philadelphia, Pa. Lobbyist — Cadwalader, Wickersham & Taft, 1333 New Hampshire Ave. N.W., Washington, D.C. 20036. Filed 5/23/85. Legislative interest — "Federal tax legislation matters."

THE BOEING CO., P.O. Box 3707, Seattle, Wash. 98124. Lobbyist — Perkins, Coie, 1110 Vermont Ave. N.W., Washington, D.C. 20005. Filed 5/15/85. Legislative interest — "HR 1787 and related legislation affecting U.S. trade and exports." Filed for self 5/13/85. Legislative interest — "... Government procurement — funding and policies ... Revenue issues ... Regulation of transportation: air, surface and water ... Industrial relations issues ... International trade regulation ... Energy resources. ..." Lobbyist — E. W. Baragar, 1700 N. Moore St., Arlington, Va. 22209.

CECOS INTERNATIONAL, P.O. Box 3151, Houston, Texas 77253. Filed for self 5/14/85. Legislative interest — "... Hazardous Waste: Treatment, Transportation, Disposal ... Solid Waste: Collection, Transportation, Disposal." Lobbyist — H. Anthony Breard Jr.

CHAD THERAPEUTICS INC., Woodland Hills, Calif. Lobbyist — Wood, Lucksinger & Epstein, 2000 M St. N.W., Washington, D.C. 20036. Filed 5/31/85. Legislative interest — "All health care related legislation."

CNA INSURANCE, Chicago, Ill. Lobbyist — Davis & Harman, 655 15th St. N.W., Washington, D.C. 20005. Filed 5/24/85. Legislative interest — "Legislation affecting the property casualty insurance industry."

CSX CORP., Richmond, Va. Lobbyist — Thompson, Mann & Hutson, 1730 Pennsylvania Ave. N.W., Washington, D.C. 20006. Filed 5/9/85. Legislative interest — "... Conrail Sale ... S 638 ... 45 U.S.C. section 701 et seq.; 45 U.S.C. section 801 et seq.; 45 U.S.C. section 1101 et seq. ... opposing." Lobbyist — Hansell & Post, 1667 K St. N.W., Washington, D.C. 20006. Filed 5/15/85. Legislative interest — "Opposition to the proposed DOT approved sale of the Consolidated Rail Corp. to the Norfolk-Southern Railway Co."

CAPITOL HOLDING CORP., Louisville, Ky. Lobbyist — Davis & Harman, 655 15th St. N.W., Washington, D.C. 20005. Filed 5/24/85. Legislative interest — "S 814 & HR 1800."

COLT INDUSTRIES INC., 1901 L St. N.W., Washington, D.C. 20036. Filed for self 5/24/85. Legislative interest — "Legislation affecting corporate taxation, defense appropriations, aerospace, product liability and trade." Lobbyists — Larry Ayres, Thomas E. Bass.

CONSOLIDATED RAIL CORP., P.O. Box 23451, Washington, D.C. 20026. Filed for self 5/9/85. Legislative interest — "Conrail Sale." Lobbyists — Alvin J. Arnett, James J. Kelly.

CURTIN, MAHONEY & CAIRNS, Washington, D.C. Lobbyist — Wexler, Reynolds, Harrison & Schule Inc., 1317 F St. N.W., Washington, D.C. 20004. Filed 5/15/85. Legislative interest — "Any potential legislation regarding Postal Rates, especially S Con Res 32. ..."

DEAN WITTER REALTY, New York, N.Y. Lobbyist — John D. Raffaelli, 499 S. Capitol St. S.W., Washington, D.C. 20003. Filed 5/16/85. Legislative interest — "... real estate taxation."

DONOHOE CONSTRUCTION CO. INC., Washington, D.C. Lobbyist — Hill, Betts & Nash, 1818 N St. N.W., Washington, D.C. 20036. Filed 5/17/85. Legislative interest — "... Congressional approval of certain leasing arrangements for the Executive branch."

DOW CORNING CORP., P.O. Box 994, Midland, Mich. 48686. Filed for self 5/24/85. Legislative interest — "... taxes, energy, environment, etc." Lobbyist — Ralph D. Schumack, 1800 M St. N.W., Washington, D.C. 20036.

J. P. DOYLE ENTERPRISES INC., 8600 Boundbrook Lane, Alexandria, Va. 22309. Filed for self 5/17/85. Legislative interest — "... DOD Authorization and Appropriations Bill for FY '86; NASA Authorization and Appropriations for FY '86." Lobbyist — John P. Doyle Jr.

EARTH SATELLITE CORP., Chevy Chase, Md. Lobbyist — Anderson, Hibey, Nauheim & Blair, 1708 New Hampshire Ave. N.W., Washington, D.C. 20009. Filed 5/6/85. Legislative interest — "Support appropriations for commercialization of the Land Remote Sensing System."

FAIC SECURITIES INC., Miami, Fla. Lobbyist — Bruce Johnson, Avenue of the Arts Building, Philadelphia, Pa. 19107. Filed 5/13/85. Legislative interest — "HR 107, HR 1833, HR 792 — deposit broker regulatory legislation."

FMC, Washington, D.C. Lobbyist — Cambridge International Inc., 10057 Maclura Court, Fairfax, Va. 22032. Filed 5/1/85. Legislative interest — "Support of annual Department of Defense Authorization Act."

FARM CREDIT SERVICES, 375 Jackson St., St. Paul, Minn. 55101. Filed for self 5/20/85. Legislative interest — "Issues that affect the ability of Farm Credit Services to extend credit and related services to their owner-borrowers." Lobbyist — Judith M. Goff.

FLORIDA POWER & LIGHT, Juno Beach, Fla. Lobbyist — Davis & Harman, 655 15th St. N.W., Washington, D.C. 20005. Filed 5/24/85. Legislative interest — "Tax legislation affecting public utilities, including nuclear decommissioning."

GEICO CORP., Washington, D.C. Lobbyist — Akin, Gump, Strauss, Hauer & Feld, 1333 New Hampshire Ave. N.W., Washington, D.C. 20036. Filed 5/24/85. Legislative interest — "... taxation of corporations."

GENERAL DYNAMICS LAND SYSTEMS, Arlington, Va. Lobbyist — Cambridge International Inc., 10057 Maclura Court, Fairfax, Va. 22032. Filed 5/1/85. Legislative interest — "Support of annual Department of Defense Authorization Act."

GENERAL ELECTRIC CREDIT CORP., 260 Long Ridge Rd., Stamford, Conn. 06902. Filed for self 5/24/85. Legislative interest — "Tax, trade, banking, budget and other general legislative matters." Lobbyist — Anne C. Canfield, 1331 Pennsylvania Ave. N.W., Washington, D.C. 20004.

GENERAL MOTORS CORP., Detroit, Mich. Lobbyist — Wald, Harkrader & Ross, 1300 19th St. N.W., Washington, D.C. 20036. Filed 5/21/85. Legislative interest — "Amendments to Motor Vehicle Safety Act."

GENERAL MOTORS CORP., Washington, D.C. Lobbyist — Akin, Gump, Strauss, Hauer & Feld, 1333 New Hampshire Ave. N.W., Washington, D.C. 20036. Filed 5/24/85. Legislative interest — "... the automobile industry."

HERBALIFE INTERNATIONAL, Los Angeles, Calif. Lobbyist — Dickstein, Shapiro & Morin, 2101 L St. N.W., Washington, D.C. 20037. Filed 5/21/85. Legislative interest — "Legislation affecting nutrition and food supplements."

HENNESSY ASSOCIATES, 152 Washington Ave., Albany, N.Y. 12210. Filed for self 5/20/85. Legislative interest — "The representation of the views of Conrail before the Senate and House of Representatives on the sale of Conrail." Lobbyist — William C. Hennessy.

HILL & KNOWLTON INC., 420 Lexington Ave., New York, N.Y. 10017. Filed for self 5/6/85. Legislative interest — Not specified. Lobbyists — Katherine Krell, George M. Worden, 1201 Pennsylvania Ave. N.W., Washington, D.C. 20004. Filed for self 5/22/85. Legislative interest — Not specified. Lobbyist — John M. Cross, 1201 Pennsylvania Ave. N.W., Washington, D.C. 20004.

INTERNATIONAL TELECOMMUNICATIONS SATELLITE ORGANIZATION, Washington, D.C. Lobbyist — Hunton & Williams, 2000 Pennsylvania Ave. N.W., Washington, D.C. 20006. Filed 5/17/85. Legislative interest — "... international communications satellite systems." Lobbyist — Gilbert A. Robinson Inc., 1825 K St. N.W., Washington, D.C. 20008. Filed 5/23/85. Legislative interest — Not specified. Lobbyist — F/P Research Associates, 1700 K St. N.W., Washington, D.C. 20006. Filed 5/20/85. Legislative interest — Not specified.

JACKSONVILLE ELECTRIC AUTHORITY, Jacksonville, Fla. Lobbyist — Davis & Harman, 655 15th St. N.W., Washington, D.C. 20005. Filed 5/24/85. Legislative interest — "Tax legislation affecting consumer loan bonds."

JOHNSON & JOHNSON, New Brunswick, N.J. Lobbyist — Finley, Kumble, Wagner, Heine, Underberg, Manley & Casey, 1140 Connecticut Ave. N.W., Washington, D.C. 20036. Filed 5/22/85. Legislative interest — "... general health care policy matters."

JURIKA & ASSOCIATES INC., 649 Mission St., San Francisco, Calif. 94105. Filed for self 5/24/85. Legislative interest — "... National Infrastructure Act ... HR 1776 ... For the Legislation." Lobbyist — Thomas W. Jurika Jr.

KIDDER PEABODY, New York, N.Y. Lobbyist — Liz Robbins Associates, 132 D St. S.E., Washington, D.C. 20003. Filed 5/28/85. Legislative interest — "Banking legislation."

KOGOVSEK & ASSOCIATES INC., 3600 S. Yosemite, Denver, Colo. 80237. Filed for self 5/20/85. Legislative interest — "General legislation of interest to Colorado." Lobbyist — Christine Ann Mulick.

LINCOLN NATIONAL LIFE INSURANCE CO., Fort Wayne, Ind. Lobbyist — Davis & Harman, 655 15th St. N.W., Washington, D.C. 20005. Filed 5/24/85. Legislative interest — Not specified.

LOCKHEED-GEORGIA CO., Washington, D.C. Lobbyist — Cambridge International Inc., 10057 Maclura Court, Fairfax, Va. 22032. Filed 5/1/85. Legislative interest — "Support of annual Department of Defense Authorization Act."

LONG ISLAND LIGHTING CO., Hicksville, N.Y. Lobbyist — Hunton & Williams, 2000 Pennsylvania Ave. N.W., Washington, D.C. 20036. Filed 5/21/85. (Former U.S. Rep. John J. Rhodes, R-Ariz., 1953-83, was listed among agents for this client.) Legislative interest — "... all issues affecting the gas distribution and electric utility business, including but not limited to: Tax Simplification Acts (HR 777, HR 800, HR 1040, HR 1377, HR 2222, HR 2424, S 409, S 556, S 1006); Nuclear Facilities Licensing and Standardization bills (HR 1029, HR 1447, S 836); Price-Anderson Act bills (HR 51, HR 445, S 445); DOE Authorization bill (HR 2041), NRC Authorization bills (HR 1711, S 895); Nuclear Plant Security bills (S 274, S 890); Nuclear Plant Personnel Training bill (S 16); Technical Corrections Act bills (HR 1800, S 814)."

THE LUBRIZOL CORP., Wickliffe, Ohio. Lobbyist — The Capitol Group Inc., 2550 M St. N.W., Washington, D.C. 20037. Filed 5/10/85. Legislative interest — "... Highway Authorization Bill ... FY 1986 Transportation Appropriations."

MAI BASIC FOUR INC., Tustin, Calif. Lobbyist — Tendler & Biggins, 1110 Vermont Ave. N.W., Washington, D.C. 20005. Filed 5/31/85. Legislative interest — "... export licenses and trade matters for high technology to European countries."

MAJOR INDOOR SOCCER LEAGUE, Bala-Cynwyd, Pa. Lobbyist — Baraff, Koerner, Olender & Hochberg, 2033 M St. N.W., Washington, D.C. 20036. Filed 5/20/85. Legislative interest — "... legislation dealing with sports. Specifically ... dealing with sports franchise movements; see S 172, S 259, S 287, and S 298."

MARRIOTT CORP., Bethesda, Md. Lobbyist — Dewey, Ballantine, Bushby, Palmer & Wood, 1775 Pennsylvania Ave. N.W., Washington, D.C. 20006. Filed 5/28/85. Legislative interest — "... tax matters."

WILLIAM M. MERCER-MEIDINGER INC., New York, N.Y. Lobbyist — Peter Small & Associates Inc., 295 Madison Ave., New York, N.Y. 10017. Filed 5/3/85. Legislative interest — Not specified.

MESA PETROLEUM, Amarillo, Texas. Lobbyist — The Laxalt Corp., 214 Massachusetts Ave. N.W., Washington, D.C. 20002. Filed 5/3/85. Legislative interest — "... mergers and acquisitions."

MORGAN STANLEY & CO. INC., New York, N.Y. Lobbyist — Wexler, Reynolds, Harrison & Schule Inc., 1317 F St. N.W., Washington, D.C. 20004. Filed 5/15/85. Legislative interest — "... the sale of the U.S. Government's interest in Conrail, including, but not limited to, S 638." Lobbyist — Timmons & Co. Inc., 1850 K St. N.W., Washington, D.C. 20006. Filed 5/6/85. Legislative interest — "Legislation related to capital formation, including but not limited to amendments to the Williams Act, amendments to the Glass-Steagall Act, and other matters affecting the sale of investment securities."

NATIONWIDE INSURANCE COS., 1 Nationwide Plaza, Columbus, Ohio. 43216. Filed for self 5/31/85. Legislative interest — "In opposition to federal bills mandating taxation of employee fringe benefits, and other insurance issues." Lobbyist — David F. Snyder, 1000 Nationwide Drive, Harrisburg, Pa. 17105.

NEDERLANDER THEATRES, New York, N.Y. Lobbyist — Akin, Gump, Strauss, Hauer & Feld, 1333 New Hampshire Ave. N.W., Washington, D.C. 20036. Filed 5/24/85. Legislative interest — "Hearings and legislation relating to taxation of corporations."

NORDEN SYSTEMS INC., Norwalk, Conn. Lobbyist — Cambridge International Inc., 10057 Maclura Court, Fairfax, Va. 22032. Filed 5/1/85. Legislative interest — "Support of annual Department of Defense Authorization Act."

OMNINET CORP., Los Angeles, Calif. Lobbyist — Benner, Burnett & Coleman, 1401 New York Ave. N.W., Washington, D.C. 20005. Filed 5/23/85. Legislative interest — "... Comsat Divestiture legislation and NASA Act revisions for 1985, 1986. FCC Authorization; Amendments to Communications Act."

ORBITAL SCIENCES CORP., Vienna, Va. Lobbyist — Hunton & Williams, 2000 Pennsylvania Ave. N.W., Washington, D.C. 20006. Filed 5/17/85. Legislative interest — "... defense procurement matters."

PAINE, WEBBER, JACKSON & CURTIS INC., New York, N.Y. Lobbyist — Liz Robbins Associates, 132 D St. S.E., Washington, D.C. 20003. Filed 5/28/85. Legislative interest — "Banking Legislation."

PANAMSAT, New York, N.Y. Lobbyist — Bendixen & Law, 1029 Vermont Ave. N.W., Washington, D.C. 20005. Filed 5/23/85. Legislative interest — "FCC supplemental budget authorization."

THE PENN CENTRAL CORP., 500 W. Putnam Ave., Greenwich, Conn. 06830. Filed for self 5/8/85. Legislative interest — HR 1440 ... OCS Leasing Moratoria - Support with amendments ... HR 641 ... Coastal Zone Management Act of 1972 - Support ... Sale of National Visitors Center Union Station Completion Act - amend to Support ... Appropriation measures affecting the DOD - Support with amendments ... Corps of Engineers Authorization & Appropriations on basin dredging projects - Support ... Authorization & Appropriations relative to international terrorism - Support." Lobbyist — Colise G. Medved, 1701 Pennsylvania Ave. N.W., Washington, D.C. 20006.

GILBERT A. ROBINSON INC., Washington, D.C. Lobbyist — Scott Cohen, 1750 New York Ave. N.W., Washington, D.C. 20006. Filed 5/30/85. Legislative interest — "... INTELSAT."

SANTA CRUZ PROPERTIES INC., Cathedral City, Calif. Lobbyist — William Ferguson Jr., 1875 I St. N.W., Washington, D.C. 20006. Filed 5/1/85. Legislative interest — "... for continued funding for Central Arizona Project in Energy and Water Development Appropriations bill; for education and training funding for Indian Tribes."

SECURITY LIFE OF DENVER INSURANCE CO., Denver, Colo. Lobbyist — Scribner, Hall & Thompson, 1875 I St. N.W., Washington, D.C. 20006. Filed 5/9/85. Legislative interest — "S 973 - Alternative Minimum Tax on Corporations (Bentsen/Danforth) ... S 956 - Minimum Tax Reform Act of 1985 (Moynihan/Chafee) ... S 663 - Alternative Minimum Tax Modifications (Metzenbaum) ... S 411 - Broad Based Enhanced Savings Tax Act (Roth/Cong. Moore) ... S 409 - Fair Tax Act of 1985 (Bradley/Gephardt) ... HR 2222/S 1006 - Fair & Simple Tax Act (Kemp/Kasten) ... Against altering the Federal income tax rules relating to: (1) net operating losses and net operating loss deductions, (2) inside buildup under life insurance and annuity policies, (3) the treatment of policy loans and the interest thereon."

THE SHUBERT ORGANIZATION INC., New York, N.Y. Lobbyist — Murray & Scheer, 2550 M St. N.W., Washington, D.C. 20037. Filed 5/1/85. Legislative interest — Not specified.

SPRINGS INDUSTRIES INC., P.O. Box 70, Fort Mill, S.C. 29715. Filed for self 5/21/85. Legislative interest — "... import of textiles or textile related products into the U.S. ... the textile industry generally." Lobbyist — Robert L. Thompson Jr.

STEPAN CORP., Northfield, Ill. Lobbyist — Donald C. Evans Jr., 655 15th St. N.W., Washington, D.C. 20005. Filed 5/2/85. Legislative interest — "Tax matter...."

DONALD T. STERLING & ASSOCIATES, Beverly Hills, Calif. Lobbyist — Manatt, Phelps, Rothenberg & Tunney, 1200 New Hampshire Ave. N.W., Washington, D.C. 20036. Filed 5/2/85. Legislative interest — "Legislation regarding sports franchises."

SYSTEMS AND APPLIED SCIENCES CORPORATION TECHNOLOGIES, Springhill, Va. Lobbyist — Corman Law Offices, 1420 16th St. N.W., Washington, D.C. 20036. Filed 5/15/85. Legislative interest — "To support legislation favorable to small businesses engaged in contracting with the Federal Government."

TRW, Arlington, Va. Lobbyist — Verner, Liipfert, Bernhard, McPherson & Hand, 1660 L St. N.W., Washington, D.C. 20036. Filed 5/1/85. Legislative interest — Not specified.

TRAILWAYS INC., Washington, D.C. Lobbyist — Garvey, Schubert, Adams & Barer, 1000 Potomac St. N.W., Washington, D.C. 20007. Filed 5/6/85. Legislative interest — "Authorization and appropriation measures re funding or elimination of funding for AMTRAK, including, but not limited to Senate Congressional Resolution 32, Budget for Fiscal Year 1986."

TRANS WORLD AIRLINES INC., New York, N.Y. Lobbyist — Garvey, Schubert, Adams & Barer, 1000 Potomac St. N.W., Washington, D.C. 20007. Filed 5/28/85. (Former U.S. Rep. Brock Adams, D-Wash., 1965-77; transportation secretary, 1977-79, was listed as agent for this client.) Legislative interest — "Legislation regarding airline regulation of domestic and international carriers. HR 2575 and other similar legislation."

UNITED STATES BANKNOTE CORP., New York, N.Y. Lobbyist — Anderson, Benjamin & Read Inc., 1776 K St. N.W., Washington, D.C. 20006. Filed 5/21/85. Legislative interest — Not specified.

UNITED STATES SURGICAL CORP., Norwalk, Conn. Lobbyist — Joseph H. Macaulay, 655 15th St. N.W., Washington, D.C. 20005. Filed 5/31/85. Legislative interest — "Animal Welfare Act amendments."

U.S. WEST INC., 1819 L St. N.W., Washington, D.C. 20036. Filed for self 5/8/85. Legislative interest — "Telecommunications and tax legislation including, but not limited to, the Treasury Department's Tax Simplification and Reform Proposals, the 'Lifelinc Telephone Service Act of 1985' (HR 151) and the 'Telecommunications Policy Coordination Act of 1985.' (HR 642); But will follow mostly tax legislation." Lobbyists — Wayne Allcott, Kim M. Oboz, Jim Smith, Debra Yarborough.

WALK-HAYDEL INC., New Orleans, La. Lobbyist — James E. Guirard Jr., 1730 Rhode Island Ave. N.W., Washington, D.C. 20036. Filed 5/29/85. Legislative interest — "Energy legislation; major federal construction projects from DoD, DoE, GSA; Budget resolutions affecting strategic petroleum reserve."

WINTHROP FINANCIAL ASSOCIATION, Boston, Mass. Lobbyist — Davis & Harman, 655 15th St. N.W., Washington, D.C. 20005. Filed 5/24/85. Legislative interest — "... the real estate industry."

WOLVERINE WORLD WIDE INC., Rockford, Mich. Lobbyist — Kirkpatrick & Lockhart, 1900 M St. N.W., Washington, D.C. 20036. Filed 5/30/85. Legislative interest — "International trade matters, including creation of a new tariff classification for pigskin footwear, e.g., HR 2303."

WOODSTREAM CORP., Lititz, Pa. Lobbyist — Davis & Harman, 655 15th St. N.W., Washington, D.C. 20005. Filed 5/24/85. Legislative interest — "Legislation affecting the fishing equipment manufacturing industry."

International Relations

HONG KONG, GOVERNMENT OF, Hong Kong. Lobbyist — Mudge, Rose, Guthrie, Alexander & Ferdon, 2121 K St. N.W., Washington, D.C. 20036. Filed 5/10/85. Legislative interest — "... trade between Hong Kong and the United States."

TURKEY, REPUBLIC OF, Ankara, Turkey. Lobbyist — Gray & Co., 3255 Grace St. N.W., Washington, D.C. 20007. Filed 5/23/85. Legislative interest — Not specified.

State and Local Governments

ANAHEIM, CITY OF, PUBLIC UTILITIES DEPARTMENT, Anaheim, Calif. Lobbyist — Clinton Reilly Campaigns, 1738 Bush St., San Francisco, Calif. 94109. Filed 5/13/85. Legislative interest — "To oppose efforts to repeal or amend the public preference provisions of the Federal Power Act."

AVALON, CITY OF, Avalon, Calif. Lobbyist — Government Relations Inc., P.O. Box 3482, Granada Hills, Calif. 91344. Filed 5/24/85. Legislative interest — "Clean Water Act Amendments - For."

AZUSA, CITY OF, ELECTRIC UTILITY DEPARTMENT, Azusa, Calif. Lobbyist — Clinton Reilly Campaigns, 1738 Bush St., San Francisco, Calif. 94109. Filed 5/13/85. Legislative interest — "To oppose efforts to repeal or amend the public preference provisions of the Federal Power Act."

BALDWIN PARK, CITY OF, Baldwin Park, Calif. Lobbyist — William Ferguson Jr., 1875 I St. N.W., Washington, D.C. 20006. Filed 5/1/85. Legislative interest — "... to restore social program funding in federal budget."

BANNING, CITY OF, BANNING ELECTRIC DEPARTMENT, Banning, Calif. Lobbyist — Clinton Reilly Campaigns, 1738 Bush St., San Francisco, Calif. 94109. Filed 5/13/85. Legislative interest — "To oppose efforts to repeal or amend the public preference provisions of the Federal Power Act."

BURBANK-GLENDALE-PASADENA AIRPORT AUTHORITY, Burbank, Calif. Lobbyist — Government Relations Inc., P.O. Box 3482, Granada Hills, Calif. 91344. Filed 5/24/85. Legislative interest — "Transportation Appropriations - For."

COLORADO STATE DEPARTMENT OF HIGHWAYS, Denver, Colo. Lobbyist — Linton, Mields, Reisler & Cottone, 1015 18th St. N.W., Washington, D.C. 20036. Filed 5/30/85. Legislative interest — Not specified.

COLTON, CITY OF, COLTON ELECTRIC DEPARTMENT, Colton, Calif. Lobbyist — Clinton Reilly Campaigns, 1738 Bush St., San Francisco, Calif. 94109. Filed 5/13/85. Legislative interest — "To oppose efforts to repeal or amend the public preference provisions of the Federal Power Act."

IMPERIAL IRRIGATION DISTRICT, Imperial, Calif. Lobbyist — William Ferguson Jr., 1875 I St. N.W., Washington, D.C. 20006. Filed 5/1/85. Legislative interest — "... for passage of Clean Water Act amendments ... increased funding for salinity control programs in Federal Budget bill."

INGLEWOOD, CITY OF, Inglewood, Calif. Lobbyist — William Ferguson Jr., 1875 I St. N.W., Washington, D.C. 20006. Filed 5/1/85. Legislative interest — "... appropriation for vocational education programs and HR 1."

MICHIGAN DEPARTMENT OF TRANSPORTATION, Lansing, Mich. Lobbyist — Linton, Mields, Reisler & Cottone, 1015 18th St. N.W., Washington, D.C. 20036. Filed 5/30/85. Legislative interest — Not specified.

NORTHERN CALIFORNIA POWER AGENCY, Citrus Heights, Calif. Lobbyist — Clinton Reilly Campaigns, 1738 Bush St., San Francisco, Calif. 94109. Filed 5/13/85. Legislative interest — "To oppose efforts to repeal or amend the public preference provisions of the Federal Power Act."

OCEANSIDE, CITY OF, Oceanside, Calif. Lobbyist — William Ferguson Jr., 1875 I St. N.W., Washington, D.C. 20006. Filed 5/1/85. Legislative interest — "... passage of Omnibus Water bill; passage of HR 1."

OCEANSIDE REDEVELOPMENT AGENCY, Oceanside, Calif. Lobbyist — William Ferguson Jr., 1875 I St. N.W., Washington, D.C. 20006. Filed 5/1/85. Legislative interest — "... for passage of Omnibus Water bill."

PROVO, CITY OF, Provo, Utah. Lobbyist — William Ferguson Jr., 1875 I St. N.W., Washington, D.C. 20006. Filed 5/1/85. Legislative interest — "... for passage of HR 1; for passage of Omnibus Water bill."

REDONDO BEACH, CITY OF, Redondo Beach, Calif. Lobbyist — William Ferguson Jr., 1875 I St. N.W., Washington, D.C. 20006. Filed 5/1/85. Legislative interest — "... passage of HR 1 and passage of the Omnibus Water bill."

RIVERSIDE, CITY OF, UTILITY DEPARTMENT, Riverside, Calif. Lobbyist — Clinton Reilly Campaigns, 1738 Bush St., San Francisco, Calif. 94109. Filed 5/13/85. Legislative interest — "To oppose efforts to repeal or amend the public preference provisions of the Federal Power Act."

SACRAMENTO MUNICIPAL UTILITY DISTRICT, Sacramento, Calif. Lobbyist — Clinton Reilly Campaigns, 1738 Bush St., San Francisco, Calif. 94109. Filed 5/13/85. Legislative interest — "To oppose efforts to repeal or amend the public preference provisions of the Federal Power Act."

SANTA CLARA, CITY OF, Santa Clara, Calif. Lobbyist — Clinton Reilly Campaigns, 1738 Bush St., San Francisco, Calif. 94109. Filed 5/13/85. Legislative interest — "To oppose efforts to repeal or amend the public preference provisions of the Federal Power Act."

SOUTH SALT LAKE, CITY OF, South Salt Lake, Utah. Lobbyist — William Ferguson Jr., 1875 I St. N.W., Washington, D.C. 20006. Filed 5/1/85. Legislative interest — "... for HR 1 ... for Federal Budget bill."

Trade Associations

AEROSPACE INDUSTRIES ASSOCIATION OF AMERICA INC., Washington, D.C. Lobbyist — Perkins, Coie, Stone, Olsen & Williams, 1110 Vermont Ave. N.W., Washington, D.C. 20005. Filed 5/6/85. Legislative interest — "... air travel compensation."

AIR CONDITIONING CONTRACTORS OF AMERICA, 1228 17th St. N.W., Washington, D.C. 20036. Filed for self 5/15/85. Legislative interest — "... Davis-Bacon Act reform, RCS/CACS and utility competition, the Clean Air Act, ERISA, tax reform measures dealing with vehicle recordkeeping and employee benefits, and general issues which impact small business." Lobbyist — Joanne M. Amorosi.

AMERICAN ASSOCIATION OF EXPORTERS & IMPORTERS-TEXTILE AND APPAREL GROUP, New York, N.Y. Lobbyist — Mudge, Rose, Guthrie, Alexander & Ferdon, 2121 K St. N.W., Washington, D.C. 20037. Filed 5/10/85. Legislative interest — "... textile and apparel imports."

AMERICAN DENTAL ASSOCIATION, 1111 14th St. N.W., Washington, D.C. 20005. Filed for self 5/28/85. Legislative interest — "General issues of interest to dental health providers, the delivery of health care and the welfare of patients." Lobbyist — Kenneth P. Yale.

AMERICAN HORSE COUNCIL, Washington, D.C. Lobbyist — Davis & Harman, 655 15th St. N.W., Washington, D.C. 20005. Filed 5/24/85. Legislative interest — "Legislation affecting the equine industry."

AMERICAN LAND DEVELOPMENT ASSOCIATION, Washington, D.C. Lobbyist — Boyd, Veigel, Gay & McCall Inc., 499 S. Capitol St. S.W., Washington, D.C. 20003. Filed 5/9/85. Legislative interest — "Tax issues."

AMERICAN OPTOMETRIC ASSOCIATION, 600 Maryland Ave. S.W., Washington, D.C. 20024. Filed for self 5/30/85. Legislative interest — Not specified. Lobbyist — Nancy Garland.

AMERICAN ROAD & TRANSPORTATION BUILDERS ASSOCIATION, 525 School St. S.W., Washington, D.C. 20024. Filed for self 5/20/85. Legislative interest — "All Transportation Construction Issues." Lobbyist — Daniel J. Hanson Sr.

ANNUAL CHARGES POLICY GROUP, Vacaville, Calif. Lobbyist — Rose, Schmidt, Chapman, Duff & Hasley, 1825 I St. N.W., Washington, D.C. 20006. Filed 5/6/85. Legislative interest — Not specified.

ASSOCIATION FOR A BETTER NEW YORK, New York, N.Y. Lobbyist — Farker, Chapin, Flattau & Klimpl, 1211 Avenue of the Americas, New York, N.Y. 10036. Filed 5/10/85. (Former U.S. Sen. Jacob K. Javits, R-N.Y., 1957-81; House, 1947-54, was listed among agents for this client.) Legislative interest — "... the Tax Simplification Plan of the Treasury Department. ..."

ASSOCIATION OF TELEPHONE, TELEGRAPH & RELATED TELEMATICS INDUSTRIES, Paris, France.

Lobbyist — O'Melveny & Myers, 1800 M St. N.W., Washington, D.C. 20036. Filed 5/15/85. Legislative interest — "Oppose or amend legislation to inhibit U.S. imports of telecommunications equipment from France, such as S 942, the 'Telecommunications Trade Act of 1985.'"

BEER INDUSTRY LEAGUE OF LOUISIANA, Baton Rouge, La. Lobbyist — Chwat/Weigend Associates, 400 First St. N.W., Washington, D.C. 20001. Filed 5/1/85. Legislative interest — "... the sale and distribution of alcoholic beverages."

THE CANADIAN TUBULAR PRODUCERS ASSOCIATION, Hamilton, Ontario, Canada. Lobbyist — Robert C. Varah, 1330 Burlington St. E., Hamilton, Ontario, Canada L8N 3J5. Filed 5/9/85. Legislative interest — "... Trade and Tariff Act of 1984 ... HR 3398 ... PL 98-573 ... in opposition to any legislation which restricts U.S. imports of tubular steel mill products from Canada."

CHEESE IMPORTERS ASSOCIATION OF AMERICA INC., New York, N.Y. Lobbyist — Harris & Berg, 1100 15th St. N.W., Washington, D.C. 20005. Filed 5/3/85. (Former U.S. Rep. Herbert E. Harris II, D-Va., 1975-81, was listed as agent for this client.) Legislative interest — "... cheese imports and the U.S. dairy program, including HR 1420 and S 501."

COMMITTEE OF ANNUITY INSURERS, Washington, D.C. Lobbyist — Davis & Harman, 655 15th St. N.W., Washington, D.C. 20005. Filed 5/24/85. Legislative interest — "Tax and Security proposals affecting the annuity insurers."

CREDIT UNION NATIONAL ASSOCIATION INC., 1730 Rhode Island Ave. N.W., Washington, D.C. 20036. Filed for self 5/15/85. Legislative interest — "Supporting revision of Tax Reform/Simplification Bills, Individual Retirement Account bills, Non-bank Bank loophole closing bills, Depository Institution Act of 1985, Broker Deposit Restrictions, Lifeline Services Legislation, Truth-in-Lending, Truth-in-Savings, Delayed Funds Availability, Shared ATM legislation, Credit Card Surcharge Ban, Mandatory Insurance for Banks, Interstate Banking, Constitution Amendment for a Balanced Budget, Federally Insured Credit Union Authority to Redeem Food Stamps." Lobbyist — Richard "Sandy" Beach.

DEALER ACTION ASSOCIATION, Bethesda, Md. Lobbyist — Patton, Boggs & Blow, 2550 M St. N.W., Washington, D.C. 20037. Filed 5/21/85. Legislative interest — "Imported automobiles, specifically the National Highway Traffic Safety Authorization Bill, Section 6 of HR 2248 and Title IV of S 683. 15 U.S.C. Sections 1391, 1397, and 1403. For."

ELECTRONIC INDUSTRIES ASSOCIATION/CONSUMER ELECTRONICS GROUP, 2001 I St. N.W., Washington, D.C. 20006. Filed for self 5/6/85. Legislative interest — Not specified. Lobbyist — Thomas L. Conrad.

FLORIDA SUGAR CANE LEAGUE, Clewiston, Fla. Lobbyist — Davis & Harman, 655 15th St. N.W., Washington, D.C. 20005. Filed 5/24/85. Legislative interest — "... the sugar cane industry."

GENERAL AVIATION MANUFACTURERS ASSOCIATION, Washington, D.C. Lobbyist — King & Spalding, 1730 Pennsylvania Ave. N.W., Washington, D.C. 20006. Filed 5/21/85. Legislative interest — "... proposed fringe benefit regulations."

GROCERY MANUFACTURERS OF AMERICA INC., 1010 Wisconsin Ave. N.W., Washington, D.C. 20007. Lobbyist — Rogers & Wells, 1737 H St. N.W., Washington, D.C. 20006. Filed 5/23/85. Legislative interest — "26 U.S.C. section 11 (Reduction of Corporate Tax Rates) and Deduction for Corporate Dividends paid to shareholders." Filed for self 5/28/85. Legislative interest — Not specified. Lobbyist — Mariana E. Griesmer.

HELICOPTER ASSOCIATION INTERNATIONAL, 1110 Vermont Ave. N.W., Washington, D.C. 20005. Filed for self 5/24/85. Legislative interest — Not specified. Lobbyist — Frank L. Jensen Jr.

HOSPITAL ASSOCIATION OF NEW YORK STATE, 15 Computer Drive W., Albany, N.Y. 12205. Filed for self 5/28/85. Legislative interest — "... health care facilities." Lobbyist — David F. Perry.

INTERNATIONAL TAXI ASSOCIATION, Kensington, Md. Lobbyist — Akin, Gump, Strauss, Hauer & Feld, 1333 New Hampshire Ave. N.W., Washington, D.C. 20036. Filed 5/24/85. Legislative interest — "... federal motor fuels taxes, including, but not limited to, HR 1354."

JAPAN LUMBER IMPORTERS ASSOCIATION, Tokyo, Japan. Lobbyist — Mudge, Rose, Guthrie, Alexander & Ferdon, 2121 K St. N.W., Washington, D.C. 20036. Filed 5/10/85. Legislative interest — "... exportation of lumber from the United States to Japan."

KANSAS ELECTRIC COOPERATIVES INC., P.O. Box 4267, Topeka, Kan. 66604. Filed for self 5/20/85. Legislative interest - "... H Res 144 & S Res 148 - 50th Anniversary Commemoration of REA ... HR 1140 & S 447 - Railroad antimonopoly act ... HR 1190 & S 477 - Consumer Rail Equity Act of 1985 ... HR 1615 & S 896 - 401(k) defined contribution plans for RECs ... Acid rain legislation ... Price-Anderson Act reauthorization." Lobbyist — Randy R. Debenham.

MORTGAGE BANKERS ASSOCIATION OF AMERICA, 1125 15th St. N.W., Washington, D.C. 20005. Filed for self 5/10/85. Legislative interest — "... the mortgage lending, banking, and construction industries ... HR 242 Taxation - At Risk ... HR 591 Mortgage Credit - Usury ... HR 592 Mortgage Credit - Foreclosure Relief ... HR 756 VA - Home Loan Guarantee Amount ... HR 1040 Taxation - Code Reform ... S 9 VA - Home Loan Guaranty ... S 56 Taxation - Imputed Interest ... S 71 Taxation - Imputed Interest ... S 409 Taxation - Code Revision (1985) ... S 411 Taxation - Code Revision (1985)." Lobbyist — Warren Lasko.

NATIONAL APARTMENT ASSOCIATION, Washington, D.C. Lobbyist — O'Connor & Hannan, 1919 Pennsylvania Ave. N.W., Washington, D.C. 20006. Filed 5/16/85. Legislative interest — "Provisions of tax reform proposals affecting rental housing industry."

NATIONAL ASSOCIATION OF ALCOHOLISM TREATMENT PROGRAMS INC., Irvine, Calif. Lobbyist — Finley, Kumble, Wagner, Heine, Underberg, Manley & Casey, 1140 Connecticut Ave. N.W., Washington, D.C. 20036. Filed 5/22/85. Legislative interest — "Legislation affecting medicare prospective payment system generally, alcoholism treatment specifically, and Federal Employees Health Benefits Program."

NATIONAL ASSOCIATION OF BROADCASTERS, Washington, D.C. Lobbyist — Robert E. Juliano Associates, 1099 22nd St. N.W., Washington, D.C. 20037. Filed 5/14/85. Legislative interest — "Beer and Wine Advertising Legislation."

NATIONAL ASSOCIATION OF REAL ESTATE INVESTMENT TRUSTS, 1101 17th St. N.W., Washington, D.C. 20036. Filed for self 5/14/85. Legislative interest — "Amendments of Sections 856-860 of The Internal Revenue Code." Lobbyist — G. N. Buffington, 2230 California St. N.W., Washington, D.C. 20008.

NATIONAL ASSOCIATION OF REALTORS, 777 14th St. N.W., Washington, D.C. 20005. Filed for self 5/9/85. Legislative interest — "... tax relief; independent contractor; restructuring of financial institutions; enterprise zone legislation; coastal barrier protection; emergency tax proposals to spur housing; and the 1985 budget." Lobbyist — Lou Ann Burney.

NATIONAL AUTOMOBILE DEALERS ASSOCIATION, McLean, Va. Lobbyist — Shaw, Pittman, Potts & Trowbridge, 1800 M St. N.W., Washington, D.C. 20036. Filed 5/23/85. Legislative interest — "Seek amendment of withholding rules on income from fringe benefits; seek technical correction to Tax Reform Act of 1984."

NATIONAL CATTLEMEN'S ASSOCIATION, Englewood, Colo. Lobbyist — Davis & Harman, 655 15th St. N.W., Washington, D.C. 20005. Filed 5/24/85. Legislative interest — "... the cattle industry."

NATIONAL GRAIN AND FEED ASSOCIATION, 725 15th St. N.W., Washington, D.C. 20005. Filed for self 5/9/85. Legislative interest — "... the grain and feed industry. ..." Lobbyists — Randall C. Gordon, Kendell W. Keith.

NATIONAL RESTAURANT ASSOCIATION, 311 First St. N.W., Washington, D.C. 20001. Filed for self 5/17/85. Legislative interest — "... the restaurant and foodservice industries ... small business, labor laws, wages and hours, taxation, consumer protection, food marketing and economic stabilization." Lobbyist — Dennis B. Clark.

NATIONAL SMALL BUSINESS ASSOCIATION, 1604 K St. N.W., Washington, D.C. 20006. Filed for self 5/23/85. Legislative interest — Not specified. Lobbyist — Senga Howat.

NATIONAL TELEPHONE COOPERATIVE ASSOCIATION, 2626 Pennsylvania Ave. N.W., Washington, D.C. 20037. Filed for self 5/20/85. Legislative interest — "All legislation affecting the rural telephone program provided for in the Rural Electrification Act of 1936, all legislation affecting telecommunications and amendments to the Communications Act of 1934, all legislation affecting the Rural Telephone Bank of 1971; and any other legislation affecting rural telecommunications." Lobbyist — Michael E. Brunner.

NATIONAL VENTURE CAPITAL ASSOCIATION, Arlington, Va. Lobbyist — Weil, Gotshal & Manges, 1101 14th St. N.W., Washington, D.C. 20005. Filed 5/16/85. Legislative interest — "Tax legislation. . . ."

OUTDOOR ADVERTISING ASSOCIATION OF AMERICA INC., 1899 L St. N.W., Washington, D.C. 20036. Filed for self 5/17/85. Legislative interest — ". . . statutes and bills which may have a direct or indirect effect on the business interests of the owners of standard outdoor advertising signs. Specific interests relate to legislation pending before the Public Works & Transportation Committee and the Energy & Commerce Committee in the House, and the Commerce, Science & Transportation Committee and Environment & Public Works Committee in the Senate." Lobbyist — Diane K. Maresco.

PHARMACEUTICAL MANUFACTURERS ASSOCIATION, Washington, D.C. Lobbyist — Williams & Jensen, 1101 Connecticut Ave. N.W., Washington, D.C. 20036. Filed 5/14/85. Legislative interest — "Product liability & related legislation."

PROPERTY/CASUALTY GROUP, Washington, D.C. Lobbyist — Davis & Harman, 655 15th St. N.W., Washington, D.C. 20005. Filed 5/24/85. Legislative interest — ". . . property/casualty insurance industry."

ROADSIDE BUSINESS ASSOCIATION, 1629 K St. N.W., Washington, D.C. 20006. Filed for self 5/24/85. Legislative interest — ". . . statutes and bills which may have a direct or indirect effect on the business interests of the owners and users of roadside advertising signs. . . ." Lobbyist — Richard R. Roberts.

SMALL BUSINESS UNITED, Waltham, Mass. Lobbyist — Neece, Cator & Associates, 1050 17th St. N.W., Washington, D.C. 20036. Filed 5/2/85. Legislative interest — "S Con Res 32, Budget Resolution Reauthorization of the Equal Access to Justice Act . . . S 100 - Product Liability Act . . . S 408 - SBA Reauthorization Bill."

SMOKELESS TOBACCO COUNCIL, Washington, D.C. Lobbyist — Collier, Shannon, Rill & Scott, 1055 Thomas Jefferson St. N.W., Washington, D.C. 20007. Filed 5/13/85. Legislative interest — Not specified.

SOCIETY OF REAL ESTATE APPRAISERS, Chicago, Ill. Lobbyist — Finley, Kumble, Wagner, Heine, Underberg, Manley & Casey, 1140 Connecticut Ave. N.W., Washington, D.C. 20036. Filed 5/22/85. Legislative interest — "Legislation which may impact on appraisers' First Amendment Rights to consider and report all relevant factors in estimation of value."

STOCK INFORMATION GROUP, Washington, D.C. Lobbyist — Davis & Harman, 655 15th St. N.W., Washington, D.C. 20005. Filed 5/24/85. Legislative interest — "Tax legislation affecting the life insurance industry."

SUGAR AND ALCOHOL INSTITUTE, Rio de Janeiro, Brazil. Lobbyist — Arter & Hadden, 1919 Pennsylvania Ave. N.W., Washington, D.C. 20006. Filed 5/29/85. Legislative interest — ". . . monitor legislation affecting the market for Brazilian Sugar and Alcohol including HR 1566, 1567, 1720 and S 575 and 576; as well as general Farm Bill legislation."

TELOCATOR, Washington, D.C. Lobbyist — Barbara Phillips, 4817 36th St. N.W., Washington, D.C. 20008. Filed 5/9/85. Legislative interest — "Telecommunications issues."

URANIUM PRODUCERS OF AMERICA, Washington, D.C. Lobbyist — Covington & Burling, 1201 Pennsylvania Ave. N.W., Washington, D.C. 20044. Filed 5/29/85. Legislative interest — "Uranium Mill Tailings Financing Act, S 1004 and HR 2236 (in favor); all legislation affecting domestic uranium industry generally."

Miscellaneous

AMERICAN COLLEGE OF NEUROPSYCHOPHARMACOLOGY, VANDERBILT UNIVERSITY, Nashville, Tenn. Lobbyist — Finley, Kumble, Wagner, Heine, Underberg, Manley & Casey, 1140 Connecticut Ave. N.W., Washington, D.C. 20036. Filed 5/22/85. Legislative interest — "Legislation supporting biomedical and behavioral research and the responsible use of animals and research subjects in furtherance of such research."

AMERICAN PROTESTANT HEALTH ASSOCIATION, Schaumburg, Ill. Lobbyist — Finley, Kumble, Wagner, Heine, Underberg, Manley & Casey, 1140 Connecticut Ave. N.W., Washington, D.C. 20036. Filed 5/22/85. Legislative interest — "Legislation affecting general health care policy matters, including tax-exempt bond financing for not-for-profit hospitals and Medicare and Medicaid."

AMERICAN RED CROSS NATIONAL HEADQUARTERS, 17th and D Sts. N.W., Washington, D.C. 20008. Filed for self 5/15/85. Legislative interest — "Legislation affecting the homeless . . . Amendment to the Housing and Community Development Act of 1974, S 394 . . . To establish a National Endowment for the Homeless, S 739 . . . Amendment to extend certain laws relating to housing, and for other purposes; HR 1." Lobbyist — Steven Tasgal.

AMERICANS FOR DEMOCRATIC ACTION/FOREIGN POLICY ADVOCATES, 1411 K St. N.W., Washington, D.C. 20005. Filed for self 5/3/85. Legislative interest — "Foreign aid legislation, specifically: aid to El Salvador, covert operations in Nicaragua, military aid to Guatemala." Lobbyist — Susan Alberts.

AMERICAN SOCIETY OF PHARMACOLOGY AND EXPERIMENTAL THERAPEUTICS, Bethesda, Md. Lobbyist — Finley, Kumble, Wagner, Heine, Underberg, Manley & Casey, 1140 Connecticut Ave. N.W., Washington, D.C. 20036. Filed 5/22/85. Legislative interest — "Legislation supporting biomedical research and responsible use of animals and research subjects in furtherance of biomedical research."

AMERICAN SPACE FOUNDATION, 214 Massachusetts Ave. N.E., Washington, D.C. 20002. Filed for self 5/2/85. Legislative interest — "(1) Establishing a permanent manned space station by the 500th anniversary of America's discovery. (2) Encouraging private sector space development through the promotion of research, creation of incentives and elimination of burdensome taxes and regulations. (3) Resuming manned missions to the moon and establishing a lunar base. (4) Providing a space-based defense system as a means to prevent nuclear war. (5) Sending Americans to the planet Mars before the end of the century and returning them safely." Lobbyists — Melody V. Vetro, Robert R. Weed.

APPALACHIAN REGIONAL COMMISSION, Washington, D.C. Lobbyist — The Capitol Group Inc., 2550 M St. N.W., Washington, D.C. 20037. Filed 5/10/85. Legislative interest — ". . . In support of authorization under the Appalachian Regional Development Act of 1965, as amended . . . FY 1986 Budget Resolution . . . FY 1986 Energy & Water Appropriations . . . All other legislation affecting economic development in the thirteen state Appalachian Region."

CITIZEN ACTION, 1300 Connecticut Ave. N.W., Washington, D.C. 20036. Filed for self 5/16/85. Legislative interest — ". . . toxic waste, specifically: the Comprehensive Environmental Response Compensation and Liability Act; Toxic Substances Control Act; and the Safe Drinking Water Act . . . health care and energy issues. . . ." Lobbyists — Robert Brandon, Cathy Hurwit, Michael Podhorzer.

CITIZENS AGAINST MIDSHIPMEN IMPRESSMENT, 1292 Goodrich, St. Paul, Minn. 55105. Filed for self 5/22/85. Legislative interest — "Interested in PL 98-525, The Omnibus Defense Authorization Act for 1985, section 541, Clarification of Authority to order certain Cadets and Midshipmen to Active Duty. This section amends the U.S. Code, Title X sections 4348, 6959, and 9348. In favor of no change in this section." Lobbyist — Alan B. Lawhead.

GEORGE E. CLIFFORD JR., 146 Grafton St., Chevy Chase, Md. 20815. Filed for self 5/15/85. Legislative interest — "... Tax revision."

COALITION TO STOP GOVERNMENT WASTE, 499 S. Capitol St. S.W., Washington, D.C. 20003. Filed for self 5/28/85. Legislative interest — "... in support of ... Creeping Capitalism Bill, Revolving Door Legislation, and the Procurement Safeguard Amendment." Lobbyist — Ann Martino, 2200 Columbia Pike, Arlington, Va. 22204. Filed for self 5/21/85. Legislative interest — Same as above. Lobbyist — Loebe Julie, 211 W. 61 St., New York, N.Y. 10023.

NINA COHEN, McLean, Va. Lobbyist — Williams & Connolly, 839 17th St. N.W., Washington, D.C. 20006. Filed 5/16/85. Legislative interest — "Technical Corrections Bill to Retirement Equity Act of 1984 (REA), and any other legislation amending REA; HR 2110; PL 98-397."

COMMITTEE AGAINST REVISING STAGGERS, Palos Heights, Ill. Lobbyist — Sutherland, Asbill & Brennan, 1666 K St. N.W., Washington, D.C. 20006. Filed 5/6/85. Legislative interest — "Opposition to legislation, such as HR 1190 and S 477, that would directly or indirectly modify the Staggers Rail Act of 1980."

THE COMMITTEE ON PROBLEMS OF DRUG DEPENDENCE INC., Boston, Mass. Lobbyist — Finley, Kumble, Wagner, Heine, Underberg, Manley & Casey, 1140 Connecticut Ave. N.W., Washington, D.C. 20036. Filed 5/22/85. Legislative interest — "Legislation concerning biomedical research; the responsible use of animals and research subjects in furtherance of biomedical research; the assessment of the therapeutic agents for abuse potential; and drug dependence."

COMMON CAUSE, 2030 M St. N.W., Washington, D.C. 20036. Filed for self 5/24/85. Legislative interest — "... open government, campaign finance reform, the Federal Election Commission, lobby disclosure, government ethics, Senate confirmation process, extension of the Clean Air Act, court jurisdiction issues, congressional budget process, congressional reform, freedom of information, energy policy, waste in government, regulatory reform, public participation in federal agency proceedings, Legal Services Corporation, the Equal Rights Amendment, War Powers Act, nuclear arms control, and military spending." Lobbyist — Julie Abbot.

CONSUMER FEDERATION OF AMERICA, 1424 16th St. N.W., Washington, D.C. 20036. Filed for self 5/15/85. Legislative interest — "Banking legislation ... Product Safety legislation ... Indoor Air Pollution ... Tax Legislation." Lobbyist — Alan Fox. Filed for self 5/15/85. Legislative interest — "Energy and utility issues." Lobbyist — Mark Cooper.

DICKINSON BUSINESS SCHOOL, Freehold, N.J. Lobbyist — Baker & Daniels, 1920 N St. N.W., Washington, D.C. 20036. Filed 5/9/85. Legislative interest — "Budget Act and legislation affecting student aid programs. S Con Res 32."

EQUITY FOR NATIONAL GUARD TECHNICIANS, Alexandria, Va. Lobbyist — Fensterwald, Alcorn & Bowman, 1000 Wilson Blvd., Arlington, Va. 22209. Filed 5/23/85. Legislative interest — "Obtaining retroactive retirement credit for former National Guard Technicians."

FARM CREDIT SURVIVAL COALITION, 8118 Orville St., Alexandria, Va. 22309. Filed for self 5/30/85. Legislative interest — "Farming and Banking ... S 1151 (for)." Lobbyist — Carson K. Killen.

L5 SOCIETY, 1060 E. Elm, Tucson, Ariz. 85719. Filed for self 5/28/85. Legislative interest — "National Aeronautics and Space Administration Authorization Act, 1986 ... HR 1714." Lobbyist — Greg Barr.

LEGAL SERVICES CORP., 733 15th St. N.W., Washington, D.C. 20005. Filed for self 5/9/85. Legislative interest — "... will represent the Corporation in connection with its annual appropriation and Congressional actions directly affecting the activities of the Corporation, particularly the appropriations bills of the House and Senate Appropriations Subcommittees on State, Justice, Commerce, the Judiciary and Related Agencies containing funds for the Corporation and bills of the House Judiciary Subcommittee on Courts, Civil Liberties and the Administration of Justice and the Senate Labor and Human Resources Subcommittee on Aging, Family and Human Services regarding reauthorization of the Corporation." Lobbyist — Thomas J. Opsut.

LEGISLATIVE STUDIES INSTITUTE INC., 3471 N. Federal Highway, Fort Lauderdale, Fla. 33306. Filed for self 5/15/85. Legislative interest — "Support corporate tax incentives for employment; primarily Targeted Jobs Tax Credits, Job Training Partnership Act, Emergency Veterans Job Training Act, Federal E.Z. and other similar proposed or existing bills."

THE NATIONAL ASSOCIATION OF TOWN WATCH, Havertown, Pa. Lobbyist — The Capitol Group Inc., 2550 M St. N.W., Washington, D.C. 20037. Filed 5/10/85. Legislative interest — "... FY 1986 State, Commerce, Justice appropriation ... Justice Assistance Act of 1984."

NATIONAL AUDUBON SOCIETY, 930 Third Ave., New York, N.Y. 10022. Filed for self 5/16/85. Legislative interest — "... wildlife and wildlife appropriations." Lobbyists — Jay Copeland, P. Whitney Fosburgh Jr., 645 Pennsylvania Ave. S.E., Washington, D.C. 20003. Filed for self 5/9/85. Legislative interest — Same as above.Lobbyist — Cynthia R. Lenhart, 645 Pennsylvania Ave. S.E., Washington, D.C. 20003.

NATIONAL CENTER FOR DRUNK DRIVING CONTROL, 15837-A Crabbs Branch Way, Rockville, Md. 20855. Filed for self 5/21/85. Legislative interest — "Drunk Driving legislation." Lobbyist — Charles B. Fitzgerald IV. Filed for self 5/24/85. Legislative interest — Same as above. Lobbyist — Cassandra Opperman.

NATIONAL COMMITTEE TO PRESERVE SOCIAL SECURITY & MEDICARE, Washington, D.C. Lobbyist — Richard L. Sinnott, 1 Thomas Circle N.W., Washington, D.C. 20005. Filed 5/13/85. Legislative interest — "Social Security and Medicare matters."

NATURAL RESOURCES DEFENSE COUNCIL INC., 1350 New York Ave. N.W., Washington, D.C. 20005. Filed for self 5/10/85. Legislative interest — "Legislation concerning the environmental and biological consequences of nuclear weapons and nuclear war; legislation concerning the study of such issues by agencies of the federal government." Lobbyist — Diane S. Nine. Filed for self 5/15/85. Legislative interest — "Air Quality Issues ... Clean Air Act." Lobbyist — Deborah A. Sheiman.

WILLIE ERVINE NORMAN, P.O. Box 1010, Bastrop, Texas 78602. Filed for self 5/9/85. Legislative interest — "Criminal Justice Administration, Pardon, Parole ... Commutation, etc. ..."

THE PRESBYTERIAN ASSOCIATION ON AGING, Oakmont, Pa. Lobbyist — Coan, Couture, Lyons & Moorhead, 1625 I St. N.W., Washington, D.C. 20006. Filed 5/17/85. Legislative interest — "HR 1 and related housing legislation affecting HUD elderly housing projects, and various aspects thereof including such issues as meals programs in such projects."

KEVIN JOSEPH PRICE, 3408 Toledo Terrace, Hyattsville, Md. 20782. Filed for self 5/3/85. Legislative interest — Not specified.

PROFESSIONALS' COALITION FOR NUCLEAR ARMS CONTROL, 1346 Connecticut Ave. N.W., Washington, D.C. 20036. Filed for self 5/30/85. Legislative interest — "... arms control issues, specifically, in support of a nuclear freeze and a comprehensive test ban, and in opposition to the MX missile and Space Weapons development." Lobbyists — David Cohen, Richard Mark.

PUBLIC EMPLOYER BENEFITS COUNCIL, Washington, D.C. Lobbyist — O'Melveny & Myers, 1800 M St. N.W., Washington, D.C. 20036. Filed 5/21/85. Legislative interest — "To ensure that the views of public employers (e.g., states, municipalities, etc.) are taken into consideration in formulating federal pension policy, particularly with respect to the tax reform measures currently being considered."

June Registrations

Corporations and Businesses

ACCOR NORTH AMERICAN INC., Scarsdale, N.Y. Lobbyist — Butler & Binion, 1747 Pennsylvania Ave. N.W., Washington, D.C. 20006. Filed 6/6/85. Legislative interest — "Tax Legislation Regarding Section 119 of the Internal Revenue Code."

ACF INDUSTRIES INC., New York, N.Y. Lobbyist — Weil, Gotshal & Manges, 767 Fifth Ave., New York, N.Y. 10153. Filed 6/12/85. Legislative interest — "Opposition to legislation which would further regulate airline industry, e.g., HR 2575."

AMAX INC., Washington, D.C. Lobbyist — Richard W. Bliss, 3242 Grace St. N.W., Washington, D.C. 20007. Filed 6/17/85. Legislative interest — "All legislation affecting environmental issues."

AMERICA FIRST FEDERALLY GUARANTEED MORTGAGE FUND II & LIMITED PARTNERSHIP, Omaha, Neb. Lobbyist — Kutak, Rock & Campbell, 1101 Connecticut Ave. N.W., Washington, D.C. 20036. Filed 6/12/85. Legislative interest — "Tax Simplification Legislation."

ANGLO AMERICAN AUTO AUCTIONS INC., 2 International Plaza Drive, Nashville, Tenn. 37217. Lobbyists — Hughes, Hubbard & Reed, 1201 Pennsylvania Ave. N.W., Washington, D.C. 20004; Filed 6/3/85. Gary Alan Dickinson. Filed for self 6/3/85. Legislative interest — "To bring to the attention of the relevant committees, members and staff of the House and Senate positions on legislation concerning odometer tampering and odometer fraud including S 475, HR 750 and HR 2248."

APEX MARINE CORP., Lake Success, N.Y. Lobbyist — Robertson, Monagle, Eastaugh & Bradley, 21 Dupont Circle N.W., Washington, D.C. 20036. Filed 6/19/85. Legislative interest — "... Maritime Administration and authorization bills ... S 679, S 102 ... Against CDS amendments."

ARCO TRANSPORTATION CO., Long Beach, Calif. Lobbyist — Robertson, Monagle, Eastaugh & Bradley, 21 Dupont Circle N.W., Washington, D.C. 20036. Filed 6/19/85. Legislative interest — "... Maritime Administration and authorization bills ... S 679, S 102 ... Against CDS amendments."

ATLANTIC RICHFIELD CO., Los Angeles, Calif. Lobbyist — Kominers, Fort, Schlefer & Boyer, 1401 New York Ave. N.W., Washington, D.C. 20005. Filed 6/26/85. Legislative interest — "... Capital construction fund legislation and construction-differential subsidy legislation ... (CDS legislation) - S 102, HR 2485, HR 2550."

BASKIN-ROBBINS, Glendale, Calif. Lobbyist — Kadison, Pfaelzer, Woodard, Quinn & Rossi, 2000 Pennsylvania Ave. N.W., Washington, D.C. 20036. Filed 6/17/85. Legislative interest — "Legislative interests center around Senate Amendment SP218 to the Fiscal Year 1986 Department of Defense Authorization Bill."

BEAR, STEARNS & CO., New York, N.Y. Lobbyist — Cleary, Gottlieb, Steen & Hamilton, 1752 N St. N.W., Washington, D.C. 20036. Filed 6/19/85. Legislative interest — "Proposed legislation relating to trust companies (HR 20, S 716, S 736)."

BODINE'S INC. FOOD PRODUCTS, Chicago, Ill. Lobbyist — Campbell-Raupe Associates Inc., 1015 15th St. N.W., Washington, D.C. 20005. Filed 6/26/85. Legislative interest — "Legislation affecting the juice, drinks & concentrate industry."

JACQUES BOREL ENTERPRISES INC., New York, N.Y. Lobbyist — Butler & Binion, 1747 Pennsylvania Ave. N.W., Washington, D.C. 20006. Filed 6/6/85. Legislative interest — "Tax Legislation Regarding Section 119 of the Internal Revenue Code."

BRINKS INC., Darien, Conn. Lobbyist — R. Duffy Wall & Associates Inc., 1317 F St. N.W., Washington, D.C. 20004. Filed 6/11/85. Legislative interest — Not specified.

CBS INC., New York, N.Y. Lobbyist — Wiley & Rein, 1776 K St. N.W., Washington, D.C. 20006. Filed 6/11/85. Legislative interest — "... legislation affecting takeovers of broadcast companies." Lobbyist — Michael K. Deaver & Associates Inc., 1025 Thomas Jefferson St. N.W., Washington, D.C. 20007. Filed 6/20/85. Legislative interest — "... legislation relating to corporate acquisitions."

CALFED INC., Los Angeles, Calif. Lobbyist — Gibson, Dunn & Crutcher, 1050 Connecticut Ave. N.W., Washington, D.C. 20036. Filed 6/5/85. Legislative interest — "... HR 15; HR 20; HR 1513; S 716 ... Amendments to various sections of Title 12, United States Code including 12 U.S.C. sections 78, 377, 378 (Banking Act of 1933), 1730a (Savings and Loan Holding Company Act), and 1941 et seq. (Bank Holding Company Act)...."

CAPITAL CITIES COMMUNICATIONS INC., New York, N.Y. Lobbyist — Wilmer, Cutler & Pickering, 1666 K St. N.W., Washington, D.C. 20006. Filed 6/12/85. Legislative interest — "... broadcast, cable or print media; amendments to Communications Act of 1934."

CHICAGO TITLE INSURANCE CO., Chicago, Ill. Lobbyist — Gray & Co., 3255 Grace St. N.W., Washington, D.C. 20007. Filed 6/25/85. Legislative interest — "Antitrust legislation relating to the title insurance industry."

CITIZENS & SOUTHERN GEORGIA CORP., Atlanta, Ga. Lobbyist — Gibson, Dunn & Crutcher, 1050 Connecticut Ave. N.W., Washington, D.C. 20036. Filed 6/5/85. Legislative interest — "... HR 15; HR 20; HR 1513; S 716 ... Amendments to various sections of Title 12, United States Code including 12 U.S.C. sections 78, 377, 378 (Banking Act of 1933), 1730a (Savings and Loan Holding Company Act), and 1941 et seq. (Bank Holding Company Act)...."

CONNECTICUT NATIONAL BANK, Hartford, Conn. Lobbyist — Manatt, Phelps, Rothenberg & Tunney, 1200 New Hampshire Ave. N.W., Washington, D.C. 20036. Filed 6/5/85. Legislative interest — "Regional Interstate Banking Legislation."

CONSOLIDATED RAIL CORP., Philadelphia, Pa. Lobbyist — Piper & Marbury, 888 16th St. N.W., Washington, D.C. 20006. Filed 6/5/85. Legislative interest — "Tax aspects of sale of U.S. interests in Conrail (HR 1449, HR 1930 and S 638)." Lobbyist — Morgan, Lewis & Bockius, 1800 M St. N.W., Washington, D.C. 20036. Filed 6/17/85. Legislative interest — "Proposed sale of Conrail by Dept. of Transportation."

CORNING ASSOCIATES, Corning, N.Y. Lobbyist — Butler & Binion, 1747 Pennsylvania Ave. N.W., Washington, D.C. 20006. Filed 6/6/85. Legislative interest — "Gift and Estate Tax Matter."

CROWLEY MARITIME CORP., San Francisco, Calif. Lobbyist — Kominers, Fort, Schlefer & Boyer, 1401 New York Ave. N.W., Washington, D.C. 20005. Filed 6/26/85. Legislative interest — "Capital Construction Fund Legislation."

DSC COMMUNICATIONS, Richardson, Texas. Lobbyist — Dutko & Associates, 412 First St. S.E., Washington, D.C. 20003. Filed 6/12/85. Legislative interest — "... International Trade, S 942, S 728."

DIMENSIONS INC., Reading, Pa. Lobbyist — O'Connor & Hannan, 1919 Pennsylvania Ave. N.W., Washington, D.C. 20006. Filed 6/10/85. Legislative interest — "To renew the tariff schedules to continue duty-free treatment of needlecraft display models."

DISTRICT HEATING DEVELOPMENT CO., St. Paul, Minn. Lobbyist — Kutak, Rock & Campbell, 1101 Connecticut Ave. N.W., Washington, D.C. 20036. Filed 6/12/85. Legislative interest — "HR 1507 and tax simplification."

ESSELTE BUSINESS SYSTEMS INC., Garden City, N.J. Lobbyist — Sullivan & Cromwell, 1775 Pennsylvania Ave. N.W., Washington, D.C. 20006. Filed 6/10/85. Legislative interest — "Legislation related to Comprehensive tax reform."

FIRST AMERICAN TITLE INSURANCE CO., Troy, Mich. Lobbyist — Gray & Co., 3255 Grace St. N.W., Washington, D.C. 20007. Filed 6/25/85. Legislative interest — "Antitrust legislation relative to the title insurance industry."

GRANGER ASSOCIATES, Santa Clara, Calif. Lobbyist — Dutko & Associates, 412 First St. S.E., Washington, D.C. 20003. Filed 6/12/85. Legislative interest — "... International Trade, S 942, S 728."

HARRIS STEEL GROUP INC., 20 Queen St. West, Toronto, Ontario, Canada. Lobbyist — Dow, Lohnes & Albertson, 1255 23rd St. N.W., Washington, D.C. 20037. Filed 6/5/85. Legislative interest — "... Trade and Tariff Act of 1984 ... PL 98-573 ... in opposition to legislation which restricts U.S. imports of steel mill products from Canada. . . ." Filed for self 6/6/85. Legislative interest — ". . . Trade and Tariff Act of 1984 . . . PL 98-573 . . . in opposition to legislation which restricts U.S. imports of steel mill products from Canada. . . ." Lobbyist — Milton E. Harris.

HILL & KNOWLTON INC., 420 Lexington Ave., New York, N.Y. 10017. Filed for self 6/13/85. Legislative interest — Not specified. Lobbyist — George M. Worden, 1201 Pennsylvania Ave. N.W., Washington, D.C. 20004. Filed for self 6/24/85. Legislative interest — Not specified. Lobbyist — Katherine Krell, 1201 Pennsylvania Ave. N.W., Washington, D.C. 20004.

INDIANA HI-RAIL CORP., Rural Route 1, Box 242, Connersville, Ind. 47331. Filed for self 6/12/85. Legislative interest — ". . . sale of the U.S. government's interest in Conrail, including S 638, HR 1449, and similar bills." Lobbyist — Felix Powell.

INTERNATIONAL BUSINESS MACHINES CORP., Old Orchard Rd., Armonk, N.Y. 10504. Filed for self 6/14/85. Legislative interest — ". . . issues relating to our South Africa business operation." Lobbyist — Charles E. Taylor, 1801 K St. N.W., Washington, D.C. 20006.

INTERNATIONAL MEDICAL CENTERS, 1505 N.W. 167th St., Miami, Fla. 33169. Filed for self 6/21/85. Legislative interest — "All matters relating to Health Maintenance Organizations."

LAWYERS TITLE INSURANCE CO., Richmond, Va. Lobbyist — Gray & Co., 3255 Grace St. N.W., Washington, D.C. 20007. Filed 6/25/85. Legislative interest — "Antitrust legislation relating to the title insurance industry."

LIBERTY BANK & TRUST OF NEW JERSEY, Gibbsboro, N.J. Lobbyist — Bracewell & Patterson, 1825 I St. N.W., Washington, D.C. 20006. Filed 6/17/85. Legislative interest — "To get grandfather clause date moved to December 31, 1984."

MARRIOTT CORP., Washington, D.C. Lobbyist — Shaw, Pittman, Potts & Trowbridge, 1800 M St. N.W., Washington, D.C. 20036. Filed 6/4/85. Legislative interest — "The organization which is filing this report will seek an amendment to the pending Imputed Interest Bill (HR 2475) and other tax related bills. . . ."

MATSON NAVIGATION CO., San Francisco, Calif. Lobbyist — Kominers, Fort, Schlefer & Boyer, 1401 New York Ave. N.W., Washington, D.C. 20005. Filed 6/26/85. Legislative interest — "Capital Construction Fund legislation."

MERCEDES-BENZ OF NORTH AMERICA, Montvale, N.J. Lobbyist — Winston & Strawn, 2550 M St. N.W., Washington, D.C. 20037. Legislative interest — "Lobbying in favor gray market legislation in the House (HR 2248) and the Senate (S 863)."

MERCHANTS BANK, 702 Hamilton Mall, Allentown, Pa. 18101. Filed for self 6/3/85. Legislative interest — "General banking legislation . . . Nonbank-banks, lifeline banking, Truth in Savings, Interstate banking. . . ." Lobbyist — Kurt D. Zwikl.

MERRILL LYNCH CAPITAL MARKETS, Chicago, Ill. Lobbyist — Mayer, Brown & Platt, 2000 Pennsylvania Ave. N.W., Washington, D.C. 20006. Filed 6/19/85. Legislative interest — "Registrant's interest is limited to amendments to the Internal Revenue Code."

MOORE McCORMACK BULK TRANSPORT INC., Stamford, Conn. Lobbyist — Robertson, Monagle, Eastaugh & Bradley, 21 Dupont Circle N.W., Washington, D.C. 20036. Filed 6/19/85. Legislative interest — ". . . Maritime Administration and authorization bills . . . S 679, S 102 . . . Against CDS amendments."

NAPP CHEMICALS INC., Lodi, N.J. Lobbyist — Chadbourne, Parke, Whiteside & Wolff, 1101 Vermont Ave. N.W., Washington, D.C. 20005. Filed 6/19/85. Legislative interest — "HR 2313 and any companion legislation introduced in the Senate."

PB-KBB INC., Houston, Texas. Lobbyist — Richard W. Bliss, 3242 Grace St. N.W., Washington, D.C. 20007. Filed 6/17/85. Lobbyist — ". . . disposal of hazardous waste into solution mined salt formations."

PAN AMERICAN SATELLITE CORP., New York, N.Y. Lobbyist — Leventhal & Senter, 1001 22nd St. N.W., Washington, D.C. 20037. Filed 6/24/85. Legislative interest — "Matters involving alternative satellite communications systems including but not limited to . . . Appropriations legislation and State Department authorization . . . HR 2577; S 1003; HR 2068 . . . in favor of alternative satellite systems; against restrictions on such systems."

PENNSYLVANIA SHIPBUILDING CO., Chester, Pa. Lobbyist — Reid & Priest, 1111 19th St. N.W., Washington, D.C. 20036. Filed 6/11/85. Legislative interest — "FY 1986 Defense and Transportation Authorization and Appropriations."

THE PRUDENTIAL BANK & TRUST CO., Atlanta, Ga. Lobbyist — Gibson, Dunn & Crutcher, 1050 Connecticut Ave. N.W., Washington, D.C. 20036. Filed 6/5/85. Legislative interest — ". . . HR 15; HR 20; HR 1513; S 716 . . . Amendments to various sections of Title 12, United States Code including 12 U.S.C. sections 78, 377, 378 (Banking Act of 1933), 1730a (Savings and Loan Holding Company Act), and 1941 et seq. (Bank Holding Company Act). . . ."

THE PYRAMID COS., Boston, Mass. Lobbyist — O'Connor & Hannan, 1919 Pennsylvania Ave. N.W., Washington, D.C. 20006. Filed 6/4/85. Legislative interest — ". . . matters of interest to the client including, but not limited to, the Clean Water Act."

HOWARD ROSE CO., Los Angeles, Calif. Lobbyist — Sutherland, Asbill & Brennan, 1666 K St. N.W., Washington, D.C. 20006. Filed 6/18/85. Legislative interest — "To change the effective date provided in Section 104(e)(3) of the Technical Corrections Act and IRC Section 312(N)(7)."

RUSSELL CORP., Washington, D.C. Lobbyist — Claire H. Austin, 8701 Triumph Ct., Alexandria, Va. 22308. Filed 6/26/85. Legislative interest — "S 680 - Textile Trade Enforcement Act."

SAFECO TITLE INSURANCE CO., Seattle, Wash. Lobbyist — Gray & Co., 3255 Grace St. N.W., Washington, D.C. 20007. Filed 6/25/85. Legislative interest — "Antitrust legislation relating to the title insurance industry."

SPERRY CORP., 2000 L St. N.W., Washington, D.C. 20036. Filed for self 6/20/85. Legislative interest — "General legislative interests include taxes, telecommunications, agriculture, international affairs and regulations . . . Export Administration Act legislation (HR 3231 & S 979) . . . for renewal of Act with certain requirements; Joint R&D bill . . . for passage." Lobbyist — John W. Lampmann.

STELCO INC., Toronto, Ontario, Canada. Lobbyist — G. G. Pagonis Associates, 1120 Connecticut Ave. N.W., Washington, D.C. 20036. Filed 6/20/85. Legislative interest — ". . . Trade and Tariff Act of 1984 . . . PL 98-573 . . . in opposition to legislation which restricts U.S. imports of steel mill products from Canada. . . ."

STEWART TITLE INSURANCE CO., Houston, Texas. Lobbyist — Gray & Co., 3255 Grace St. N.W., Washington, D.C. 20007. Filed 6/25/85. Legislative interest — "Antitrust legislation relating to the title insurance industry."

TANADGUSIX CORP., St. Paul Island, Alaska. Lobbyist — Randolph & Truitt, 1752 N St. N.W., Washington, D.C. 20036. Filed 6/5/85. Legislative interest — ". . . in support of ratification by the Senate of the 1984 Interim Convention for the Protection of the North Pacific Fur Seal."

TELEFLEX INC., King of Prussia, Pa. Lobbyist — Reid & Priest, 1111 19th St. N.W., Washington, D.C. 20036. Filed 6/11/85. Legislative interest — "FY 1986 Defense Authorization and Appropriations."

TRANS WORLD AIRLINES INC., New York, N.Y. Lobbyist — Michael K. Deaver & Associates Inc., 1025 Thomas Jefferson St. N.W., Washington, D.C. 20007. Filed 6/20/85. Legislative interest — ". . . legislation relating to corporate acquisitions."

VARIAN EIMAC, San Carlos, Calif. Lobbyist — Richard W. Bliss, 3242 Grace St. N.W., Washington, D.C. 20007. Filed 6/17/85. Legislative interest — "All legislation affecting international broadcasting."

WASHINGTON MUTUAL SAVINGS BANK, Seattle, Wash. Lobbyist — Gibson, Dunn & Crutcher, 1050 Connecticut Ave. N.W., Washington, D.C. 20036. Filed 6/5/85. Legislative interest — ". . . HR 15; HR 20; HR 1513; S 716 . . . Amendments to various sections of Title 23, United States Code including 12 U.S.C. sections 78, 377, 378 (Banking Act of 1933), 1730a (Savings and Loan Holding Company Act), and 1941 et seq. (Bank Holding Company Act). . . ."

WESTERN SAVINGS & LOAN ASSOCIATION, Phoenix, Ariz. Lobbyist — Miller & Chevalier, 655 15th St. N.W., Washington, D.C. 20005. Filed 6/7/85. Legislative interest — "Legislation affecting the powers of state-chartered savings and loan associations."

WHITEHALL CORP., Dallas, Texas. Lobbyist — Boyd, Veigel, Gay & McCall Inc., 499 S. Capitol St. S.W., Washington, D.C. 20003. Filed 6/4/85. Legislative interest — "Authorization and appropriations/defense."

ZOND SYSTEMS INC., Tehachapi, Calif. Lobbyist — David P. Stang, 1629 K St. N.W., Washington, D.C. 20006. Filed 6/10/85. Legislative interest — "HR 2001 & S 1220, Renewable Energy and Conservation Transition Act of 1985."

International Relations

SEYCHELLES, PERMANENT MISSION OF THE REPUBLIC OF, New York, N.Y. Lobbyist — Reichler & Appelbaum, 888 17th St. N.W., Washington, D.C. 20006. Filed 6/28/85. Legislative interest — "Foreign assistance and other legislation affecting the Seychelles."

TURKEY, REPUBLIC OF, Washington, D.C. Lobbyist — Gray & Co., 3255 Grace St. N.W., Washington, D.C. 20007. Filed 6/4/85. Legislative interest — "Any legislation of interest to the Republic of Turkey."

Labor Organizations

NATIONAL ASSOCIATION OF LETTER CARRIERS, 100 Indiana Ave. N.W., Washington, D.C. 20001. Filed for self 6/6/85. Legislative interest — Not specified. Lobbyist — Roger Blacklow.

SERVICE EMPLOYEES INTERNATIONAL UNION, Washington, D.C. Lobbyist — Spiegel & McDiarmid, 1350 New York Ave. N.W., Washington, D.C. 20005. Filed 6/24/85. Legislative interest — "Asbestos in schools and other public and commercial buildings."

State and Local Governments

NEVADA, STATE OF, Carson City, Nev. Lobbyist — Sutherland, Asbill & Brennan, 1666 K St. N.W., Washington, D.C. 20006. Filed 6/10/85. Legislative interest — "Passage of Low Level Waste Compact legislation and any necessary amendments to Low Level Waste Policy Act of 1980, such as proposals in HR 1083."

PHILADELPHIA, CITY OF, Philadelphia, Pa. Lobbyist — Reid & Priest, 1111 19th St. N.W., Washington, D.C. 20036. Filed 6/11/85. Legislative interest — "FY 1986 Defense and Military Construction Authorizations and Appropriations; Conrail sale legislation."

WASHINGTON, STATE OF, Olympia, Wash. Lobbyist — Sutherland, Asbill & Brennan, 1666 K St. N.W., Washington, D.C. 20006. Filed 6/10/85. Legislative interest — "Passage of Low Level Waste Compact legislation and any necessary amendments to Low Level Waste Policy Act of 1980, such as proposals in HR 1083."

Trade Associations

AIR TRAFFIC CONTROL ASSOCIATION INC., 2020 N. 14th St., Arlington, Va. 22201. Filed 6/21/85. Legislative interest — "General legislative interests will include any proposals submitted to, or pending before Congress which relate to air traffic control, aviation, aviation safety, & matters affecting personnel including federal employees who develop, install, maintain and operate ATC facilities." Lobbyist — Suzette Matthews.

AMERICAN SOCIETY OF PLASTIC & RECONSTRUCTIVE SURGERY, Chicago, Ill. Lobbyist — Kent & O'Connor Inc., 1919 Pennsylvania Ave. N.W., Washington, D.C. 20006. Filed 6/11/85. Legislative interest — "Graduate medical education (S 1157)."

ASSOCIATION FOR REGULATORY REFORMS, 1331 Pennsylvania Ave. N.W., Washington, D.C. Filed for self 6/13/85. Legislative interest — "... housing industry." Lobbyist — Danny Ghorbani, 10506 Cavalcade St., Great Falls, Va. 22066. Filed for self 6/21/85. Legislative interest — "In general all legislation, statutes, bills etc. that pertain to the housing industry." Lobbyist — Danny Ghorbani, 10506 Cavalcade St., Great Falls, Va. 22066.

ASSOCIATION OF EXECUTIVE SEARCH CONSULTANTS INC., Greenwich, Conn. Lobbyist — Butler & Binion, 1747 Pennsylvania Ave. N.W., Washington, D.C. 20006. Filed 6/6/85. Legislative interest — "Legislation Affecting Executive Search Industry."

ASSOCIATION OF PRIVATE PENSION & WELFARE PLANS INC., 1331 Pennsylvania Ave. N.W., Washington, D.C. 20004. Filed for self 6/7/85. Legislative interest — "All legislation of general interest to the private pension and employee benefits community." Lobbyist — Frances Ann Kenkel.

N. CHAPMAN ASSOCIATION INC., Washington, D.C. Lobbyist — Olsson & Frank, 1029 Vermont Ave. N.W., Washington, D.C. 20005. Filed 6/27/85. Legislative interest — "Temporary Emergency Food Assistance, HR 2422, PL 98-92 amendment to statute/bill."

FLORIDA FRUIT & VEGETABLE ASSOCIATION, Orlando, Fla. Lobbyist — Harris Miller & Associates, 1000 Wilson Blvd., Arlington, Va. 22209. Filed 6/13/85. Legislative interest — "Immigration reform legislation, specifically relating to temporary worker programs. S 1200."

INDUSTRIAL BIOTECHNOLOGY ASSOCIATION, 2115 E. Jefferson St., Rockville, Md. 20852. Filed for self 6/17/85. Legislative interest — "Generally, promotion of commercial biotechnology companies. Specifically, in favor of legislation to modify FDA authority to allow export of drugs approved for commercial use outside of the U.S." Lobbyist — Harvey S. Price.

JAPAN ECONOMIC INSTITUTE OF AMERICA, 1000 Connecticut Ave. N.W., Washington, D.C. 20036. Filed for self 6/11/85. Legislative interest — "... monitors developments affecting U.S. tariff and trade policy, foreign investment and banking activity in the U.S., American exports and export financing, and U.S.-Japan economic relations." Lobbyist — Sheri L. Hoptman.

MIAMI CHAMBER OF COMMERCE, Miami, Fla. Lobbyist — Gray & Co., 3255 Grace St. N.W., Washington, D.C. 20007. Filed 6/17/85. Legislative interest — "Included but not limited to legislation relating to targeted refugee assistance."

NATIONAL ARMORED CAR ASSOCIATION INC., Rochester, N.Y. Lobbyist — Craft & Richards, 1050 Thomas Jefferson St. N.W., Washington, D.C. 20007. Filed 6/19/85. Legislative interest — "Any legislation to amend the National Labor Relations Act 9(b)(3)." Filed 6/20/85. Legislative interest — "Any legislation to amend the National Labor Relations Act 9(b)(3)."

NATIONAL ASSOCIATION OF LIFE UNDERWRITERS, Washington, D.C. Lobbyist — Miller, Cassidy, Larroca & Lewin, 2555 M St. N.W., Washington, D.C. 20037. Filed 6/6/85. Legislative interest — "Advising representatives ... about the relationship between proposals to amend the Bank Holding Company Act or the National Bank Act and pending or potential litigation or administrative actions construing those Acts. Of particular interest are proposals relating to participation of banks, and their affiliates, in various aspects of the insurance business, e.g., HR 15, HR 428, HR 1513, S 716."

NATIONAL ASSOCIATION OF MANUFACTURERS, 1776 F St. N.W., Washington, D.C. 20006. Filed for self 6/5/85. Legislative interest — "... matters that focus on regulatory reform, transportation, and telecommunications. S 150, HR 1882, FCC matters, Motor Carrier Act amendments, Staggers Act amendments, Freedom of Information Act amendments, S 950, HR 151, HR 2037, HR 1339." Lobbyist — Lawrence A. Fineran.

NATIONAL ASSOCIATION OF MARGARINE MANUFACTURERS, Washington, D.C. Lobbyist — Olsson & Frank, 1029 Vermont Ave. N.W., Washington, D.C. 20005. Filed 6/18/85. Legislative interest — "Matters affecting the U.S. margarine industry, including agricultural legislation and legislation to eliminate the displacement of commercial margarine sales by donation of government commodities." Lobbyist — Olsson & Frank, 1029 Vermont Ave. N.W., Washington, D.C. 20005. Filed 6/27/85. Legislative interest — "Temporary Emergency Food Assistance, HR 2422, PL 98-92 amendment to statute/bill."

NATIONAL ASSOCIATION OF PROFESSIONAL INSURANCE AGENTS, 400 N. Washington St., Alexandria, Va. 22314. Lobbyist — Miller, Cassidy, Larroca & Lewin, 2555 M St. N.W., Washington, D.C. 20037. Filed 6/6/85. Legislative interest — "Advising representatives ... about the relationship between proposals to amend the Bank Holding Company Act or the National Bank Act and pending or potential litigation or administrative actions construing those Acts. Of particular interest are proposals relating to participation of banks, and their affiliates, in various aspects of the insurance business, e.g., HR 15, HR 428, HR 1513, S 716." Filed for self 6/10/85. Legislative interest — "... to cover insurance matters and legislation relating to the welfare of local property and casualty insurance agents." Lobbyist — Jay Harris Berman, 419 10th St. N.E., Washington, D.C. 20002.

NATIONAL ASSOCIATION OF REALTORS, 777 14th St. N.W., Washington, D.C. 20005. Filed for self 6/10/85. Legislative interest — "Any and all legislation affecting the real estate industry including specifically, tax relief; independent contractor; restructuring of financial institutions; enterprise zone legislation; coastal barrier protection; emergency tax proposals to spur housing; and the 1985 budget." Lobbyist — Lou Ann Burney. Filed for self 6/10/85. Legislative interest — "Any legislation dealing with housing and community revitalization issues that affect the real estate industry, including: government-assisted housing programs, Housing Authorization and Appropriations legislation, Farmers Home Administration programs, property management, rent control, public buildings policy, condominium conversion issues, housing vouchers, and enterprise zones. Also, mortgage finance issues including: bank holding companies legislation, financial institutions legislation, and finance reform legislation." Lobbyist — Keith R. Small.

NATIONAL AUTOMOBILE DEALERS ASSOCIATION, 8400 Westpark Drive, McLean, Va. 22102. Filed for self 6/3/85. Legislative interest — "... generally confined to issues that affect the retail automobile and truck industry. Current interest is in the area of odometer and gray market legislation." Lobbyist — Frank E. McCarthy.

NATIONAL BEER WHOLESALERS' ASSOCIATION INC., 5205 Leesburg Pike, Falls Church, Va. 22041. Filed for self 6/3/85. Legislative interest — "Legislation affecting the business interests of small businessmen involved in beer wholesaling. Specifically, alcohol excise taxes, funding for the Department of Treasury's Bureau of Alcohol, Tobacco and Firearms, any amendments to the Federal Alcohol Administration Act, the Malt Beverage Interbrand Competition Act." Lobbyist — John F. Stasiowski.

NATIONAL BICYCLE DEALERS ASSOCIATION INC., 25255 Cabot Rd., Laguna Hills, Calif. 92653. Filed for self 6/3/85. Legislative interest — "HR 2226. To [amend] the tariff schedules of the United States for imported bicycles."

NATIONAL BUILDING GRANITE QUARRIES ASSOCIATION, Barre, Vt. Lobbyist — Baker & McKenzie, 815 Connecticut Ave. N.W., Washington, D.C. 20006. Filed 6/20/85. (Former U.S. Rep. Robert McClory, R-Ill., 1963-83, was listed as agent for this client.) Legislative interest — "Interest relates to certain provisions of proposed Tax Reform legislation."

NATIONAL CLUB ASSOCIATION, Washington, D.C. Lobbyist — O'Connor & Hannan, 1919 Pennsylvania Ave. N.W., Washington, D.C. 20006. Filed 6/20/85. Legislative interest — "... including, but not limited to tax reform proposals affecting deductions for club expenses."

NATIONAL ELECTRICAL MANUFACTURERS ASSOCIATION, Washington, D.C. Lobbyist — Morrison & Foerster, 2000 Pennsylvania Ave. N.W., Washington, D.C. 20006. Filed 6/5/85. Legislative interest — "The legislative interests are related to proposed amendments to CERCLA, including S 51, HR 1342, HR 1775, HR 2018, HR 2022, HR 2206, and HR 2560. The employer is in favor of some provisions and opposed to other provisions."

NATIONAL PAINT & COATINGS ASSOCIATION, Washington, D.C. Lobbyist — Richard W. Bliss, 3242 Grace St. N.W., Washington, D.C. 20007. Filed 6/17/85. Legislative interest — "... environmental issues."

NATIONAL SOFT DRINK ASSOCIATION, Washington, D.C. Lobbyist — Parry & Romani Associates Inc., 1140 Connecticut Ave. N.W., Washington, D.C. 20036. Filed 6/20/85. Legislative interest — "Saccharin Legislation."

THE NEW ENGLAND COUNCIL INC., 1800 Massachusetts Ave. N.W., Washington, D.C. 20036. Filed for self 6/18/85. Legislative interest — "... matters of interest to the Council and the New England region, and business interests in general." Lobbyist — Nicholas P. Koskores.

PETROLEUM MARKETERS ASSOCIATION OF AMERICA, 1120 Vermont Ave. N.W., Washington, D.C. 20005. Filed for self 6/10/85. Legislative interest — "... matters affecting the business interests of its members as small independent businessmen in the oil industry." Lobbyist — Alan J. Cobb. Filed for self 6/12/85. Legislative interest — "... matters affecting the business interests of its members as small independent businessmen in the oil industry." Lobbyist — C. Richard Cahoon.

SEMICONDUCTOR INDUSTRY ASSOCIATION, San Jose, Calif. Lobbyist — Hogan & Hartson, 815 Connecticut Ave. N.W., Washington, D.C. 20006. Filed 6/12/85. Legislative interest — "Legislative activities will be undertaken on behalf of the Semiconductor Industry Association on legislation affecting environmental matters. Current legislation of interest includes HR 2560 and S 51. The Association disapproves of certain funding mechanisms proposed in connection with the reauthorization of the Comprehensive Environmental Response, Compensation and Liability Act insofar as the mechanisms would impose broad-based taxes on all industries, without regard to the generation of hazardous wastes."

SUGAR AND ALCOHOL INSTITUTE, Rio de Janeiro, Brazil. Lobbyist — Arter & Hadden, 1919 Pennsylvania Ave. N.W., Washington, D.C. 20006. Filed 6/3/85. Legislative interest — "During the 99th Congress, to monitor legislation affecting the market for Brazilian Sugar and Alcohol including HR 1566, 1567, 1720 and S 575 and 576; as well as general Farm Bill legislation."

THE SYNTHETIC ORGANIC CHEMICAL MANUFACTURERS ASSOCIATION, 1330 Connecticut Ave. N.W., Washington, D.C. 20036. Filed for self 6/27/85. Legislative interest — "Reauthorization of the Comprehensive Environmental Response, Compensation, and Liability Act (PL 96-510), S 596, S 51, HR 2560, HR 2022 ... In support of reauthorization; generally favor S 596 with certain reservations." Lobbyist — Andrew B. Waldo.

Miscellaneous

ALASKA FEDERATION OF NATIVES, Anchorage, Alaska. Lobbyist — Gerard, Byler & Associates, 1100 17th St. N.W., Washington, D.C. 20036. Filed 6/6/85. Legislative interest — "General work on legislation and appropriations matters ... HR 1, S 667 - HUD amendments and reauthorizations; for, with amendments."

AMERICAN ASSOCIATION OF RETIRED PERSONS, 1909 K St. N.W., Washington, D.C. 20049. Filed for self 6/14/85. Legislative interest — "... in support of: ... legislation protecting statutory policy against age discrimination (HR 700) ... Improved treatment and protection of older persons. ..." Lobbyist — Kevin J. Donnellan.

AMERICAN-EUROPEAN ACID RAIN PROHIBITION, 11573 Embers Ct., Reston, Va. 22091. Filed for self 6/17/85. Legislative interest — Not specified. Lobbyist — Jerry Lindell.

ZALMAN C. BERNSTEIN, New York, N.Y. Lobbyist — Scott Hodes, 180 N. LaSalle St., Chicago, Ill. 60601. Filed 6/14/85. Legislative interest — "... Tax Legislation, S 514 ... In favor. ..."

ROBERT W. BRADFORD, 1900 W. Sunshine St., Springfield, Mo. 65808. Filed for self 6/17/85. Legislative interest — Not specified.

CENTER FOR CIVIC EDUCATION, Calabasas, Calif. Lobbyist — Dechert, Price & Rhoads, 1730 Pennsylvania Ave. N.W., Washington, D.C. 20006. Filed 6/21/85. Legislative interest — "Youth education programs and projects in civic responsibility."

COMMITTEE FOR THE ELECTRIC CONSUMERS PROTECTION ACT, 1000 Potomac St. N.W., Washington, D.C. 20007. Filed for self 6/6/85. Legislative interest — "... support efforts to pass the Electric Consumers Protection Act (HR 44/S 426)."

CONSUMERS UNITED FOR RAIL EQUITY, Washington, D.C. Lobbyist — Craft & Richards, 1050 Thomas Jefferson St. N.W., Washington, D.C. 20007. Filed 6/12/85. Legislative interest — "... Staggers Rail Act Amendments."

ENVIRONMENTAL SCIENCE & ENGINEERING, Baton Rouge, La. Lobbyist — Richard W. Bliss, 3242 Grace St. N.W., Washington, D.C. 20007. Filed 6/17/85. Legislative interest — "... disposal of hazardous waste into solution mined salt formations."

FARMWORKER JUSTICE FUND INC., 2001 S St. N.W., Washington, D.C. 20009. Filed for self 6/21/85. Legislative interest — "... general legislative interest in matters directly affecting FJF clients, as well as those which impact on farmworkers in the U.S. ... The Simpson-Mazzoli Immigration Reform and Control Act of 1983; FY 1984 Appropriations for the Departments of State, Justice, Commerce and Related Agencies; FIFRA Reform Act Amendments of 1983; Appropriations rider(s) to the FY 1984 Labor-HHS Appropriations bill (and supplemental appropriations); the Omnibus Budget and Reconciliation Act; various proposals to amend the Fair Labor Standards Act ... 8 USC section 1101(a)(15)(H)(ii); 42 USC sections 2996 et seq.; 7 USC sections 136a-k; 29 USC sections 651 et seq. 29 USC 201 et seq.. ..." Lobbyist — Garry Geffert.

FRIENDS OF THE RURAL DEVELOPMENT LOAN FUND, 2025 I St. N.W., Washington, D.C. 20006. Filed for self 6/10/85. Legislative interest — "To help rural development organizations improve the administrative and regulatory operation of the Rural Development Loan Fund."

HALT INC. AMERICANS FOR LEGAL REFORM, 201 Massachusetts Ave. N.E., Washington, D.C. 20001. Filed for self 6/20/85. Legislative interest — "... FTC re-authorization (S 1714, HR 2970) in favor ... tort reform (S 44 Uniform Product Liability Act) opposed ... HR 3175 Occupational Disease Compensation Act, in favor ... Crime victim's compensation act (HR 3498) in favor ... D.C. small claims court increased jurisdictional ceiling increase (S 6007) in favor." Lobbyist — Wilson Reynolds.

DAVID M. HIGGINS, 333 S. Grand Ave., Los Angeles, Calif. 90071. Filed for self 6/5/85. Legislative interest — "Protection of interests of recipients of compensation excludable under section 104 of Internal Revenue Code and section 130 of the Internal Revenue Code."

L5 SOCIETY, 1060 E. Elm, Tucson, Ariz. 85719. Filed for self 6/14/85. Legislative interest — "National Aeronautics and Space Administration Authorization Act, 1986. HR 1714." Lobbyist — Sandra Lee Adamson, P.O. Box 44026, Washington, D.C. 20026.

PLANNED PARENTHOOD FEDERATION OF AMERICA INC., 2010 Massachusetts Ave. N.W., Washington, D.C. 20036. Filed for self 6/13/85. Legislative interest — "General health legislation as it pertains to family planning and reproductive health; also legislation pertaining to regulations or restrictions upon the rights of individuals to exercise choice and individual discretion on matters of personal health and reproduction. Also tax, budget and appropriations affecting the operations of non-profit 501(c)3 corporations." Lobbyist — Ronald James Fitzsimmons.

RAUSCHENBERG OVERSEAS CULTURAL INTERCHANGE, Tampa, Fla. Lobbyist — Gray & Co., 3255 Grace St. N.W., Washington, D.C. 20007. Filed 6/26/85. Legislative interest — "Including but not limited to seeking legislation to amend the Arts and Artifacts Indemnities Act of 1975."

SOLAR LOBBY, 1001 Connecticut Ave. N.W., Washington, D.C. 20036. Filed for self 6/24/85. Legislative interest — "... To promote the use of renewable energy sources ... HR 2001, S 1220 ... for both bills." Lobbyist — William Holmberg.

July Registrations

Corporations and Businesses

AEROJET-GENERAL INC., Sacramento, Calif. Lobbyist — Heron, Burchette, Ruckert & Rothwell, 1025 Thomas Jefferson St. N.W., Washington, D.C. 20007. Filed 7/10/85. Legislative interest — "... proposed amendments to the 'Superfund' Law ... Superfund Improvement Act of 1985 ... S 51 ... U.S.C. 9601 et seq. ... modification."

H. F. AHMANSON & CO., Los Angeles, Calif. Lobbyist — Riddell, Holroyd & Butler, 1331 Pennsylvania Ave. N.W., Washington, D.C. 20004. Filed 7/29/85. Legislative interest — "The President's Tax Proposals and the effect of any legislation on thrift institutions."

AMERICAN AUTOMAR CORP., Washington, D.C. Lobbyist — Bowman, Conner, Touhey & Petrillo, 2828 Pennsylvania Ave. N.W., Washington, D.C. 20007. Filed 7/29/85. Legislative interest — "Taxation of lessors of foreign-built U.S. flag ships ... Internal Revenue Code of 1954 ... 26 U.S.C. Section 861 (d). ..."

AMERICAN CYANAMID CO., Washington, D.C. Lobbyist — Murray & Scheer, 2550 M St. N.W., Washington, D.C. 20037. Filed 7/17/85. Legislative interest — Not specified.

AMERICAN ELECTRONIC LABORATORIES INC., Lansdale, Pa. Lobbyist — Dawson Mathis & Associates, 1800 M St. N.W., Washington, D.C. 20036. Filed 7/12/85. (Former U.S. Rep. Dawson Mathis, D-Ga., 1971-81, was listed as agent for this client.) Legislative interest — "Defense authorizations and appropriations."

AMERICAN GENERAL CORP., 2929 Allen Parkway, Houston, Texas 77019. Filed for self 7/24/85. Legislative interest — "... Tax proposals relating to insurance and retirement savings ... Financial services deregulation including HR 20 ... Insurance risk classification ... Securities regulation. ..." Lobbyist — William C. Phelps.

AMERICAN PETROFINA INC., P.O. Box 2159, Dallas, Texas 75221. Filed for self 7/8/85. Legislative interest — "... House Appropriations bill for Commerce, State, and the Judiciary, and any and all amendments which relate to construction differential subsidies for ships." Lobbyist — Gary W. Bruner.

ANDERSON, HIBEY, NAUHEIM & BLAIR, Washington, D.C. Lobbyist — Charles G. Hardin Associates Inc., 815 Connecticut Ave. N.W., Washington, D.C. 20006. Filed 7/2/85. Legislative interest — "... airport funding and fees."

ARCHER DANIELS MIDLAND CORP., Decatur, Ill. Lobbyist — Mark A. Siegel & Associates, 400 N. Capitol St., Washington, D.C. 20001. FIled 7/24/85. Legislative interest — Not specified.

ASARCO INC., New York, N.Y. Lobbyist — Gray & Co., 3255 Grace St. N.W., Washington, D.C. 20007. Filed 7/10/85. Legislative interest — "... the copper industry." Lobbyist — Heron, Burchette, Ruckert & Rothwell, 1025 Thomas Jefferson St. N.W., Washington, D.C. 20007. Filed 7/10/85. Legislative interest — "... proposed amendments to the 'Superfund' Law ... Superfund Improvement Act of 1985 ... S 51 ... U.S.C. 9601 et seq. ... modification."

ASUNTOS INTERNACIONALES A.C., Mexico City, Mexico. Lobbyist — Arnold & Porter, 1200 New Hampshire Ave. N.W., Washington, D.C. 20036. Filed 7/16/85. Legislative interest — "Against proposals which would change the U.S. countervailing duty law to treat Mexico's pricing of oil and gas products as a countervailable subsidy."

BEAR WEST CO. INC., Salt Lake City, Utah. Lobbyist — Dennis J. Earhart, 2001 Wisconsin Ave. N.W., Washington, D.C. 20007. Filed 7/17/85. Legislative interest — "Clean Air, public land policy, and coal leasing. ..."

BELL ATLANTIC MANAGEMENT SERVICES, Philadelphia, Pa. Lobbyist — Gray & Co., 3255 Grace St. N.W., Washington, D.C. 20007. Filed 7/11/85. Legislative interest — "Including but not limited to information and assistance on communications legislation."

BETHLEHEM STEEL, Washington, D.C. Lobbyist — Davis & Harman, 655 15th St. N.W., Washington, D.C. 20005. Filed 7/8/85. Legislative interest — "Tax Legislative proposals relating to the steel industry."

BLOUNT INC., Montgomery, Ala. Lobbyist — Ivins, Phillips & Barker, 1700 Pennsylvania Ave. N.W., Washington, D.C. 20006. Filed 7/10/85. Legislative interest — "Tax reform proposals affecting the development of waste-to-energy facilities."

BURLINGTON COAT FACTORY, New York, N.Y. Lobbyist — Management & Government Resources, 1305 Mount Holly Road, Burlington, N.J. 08016. Filed 7/10/85. Legislative interest — "For H Con Res 128 & HR 1467 ... Evidentiary Standards (Rudman & Metzenbaum)."

CBS INC., Washington, D.C. Lobbyist — Wellford, Wegman, Krulwich & Hoff, 1775 Pennsylvania Ave. N.W., Washington, D.C. 20006. Filed 7/8/85. Legislative interest — "Securing support for S 1312, HR 2904 and related legislation."

CHAD THERAPEUTICS, 6324 Variel Ave., Woodland Hills, Calif. 91367. Filed for self 7/13/85. Legislative interest — "... health care...." Lobbyists — Charles Adams, Frank R. Fleming.

CPC INTERNATIONAL INC., Englewood Cliffs, N.J. Lobbyist — Heron, Burchette, Ruckert & Rothwell, 1025 Thomas Jefferson St. N.W., Washington, D.C. 20007. Filed 7/10/85. Legislative interest — "... proposed amendments to the 'Superfund' Law ... Superfund Improvement Act of 1985 ... S 51 ... U.S.C. 9601 et seq. ... modification."

CPEX PACIFIC INC., St. Helens, Ore. Lobbyist — Larry Meyers, 412 First St. S.E., Washington, D.C. 20003. Filed 7/10/85. Legislative interest — "General Farm Issues."

CPM ENERGY CORP., Wilmington, Del. Lobbyist — Washington Energy Trade & Agriculture Group, 655 15th St. N.W., Washington, D.C. 20005. Filed 7/13/85. Legislative interest — "Energy & Tax Legislation...."

CRS SIRRINE INC., Houston, Texas. Lobbyist — McNair, Glenn, Konduros, Corley, Singletary, Porter & Dibble, 1155 15th St. N.W., Washington, D.C. 20005. Filed 7/25/85. Legislative interest — "Tax legislative issues ... construction and architectural design industries."

CANTOR, FITZGERALD & CO. INC., Beverly Hills, Calif. Lobbyist — R. Duffy Wall & Associates Inc., 1317 F St. N.W., Washington, D.C. 20004. Filed 7/12/85. Legislative interest — "... tax legislation."

CHANCELLOR CORP., Boston, Mass. Lobbyist — Jones & Winburn, 50 E St. S.E., Washington, D.C. 20003. Filed 7/25/85. Legislative interest — "... tax laws affecting the capital equipment leasing industry."

CHICAGO TITLE INSURANCE CO., Chicago, Ill. Lobbyist — Gray & Co., 3255 Grace St. N.W., Washington, D.C. 20007. Filed 7/10/85. Legislative interest — "... antitrust legislation relating to the title insurance industry."

CHILDREN'S HOSPITAL, Boston, Mass. Lobbyist — Dickstein, Shapiro & Morin, 2101 L St. N.W., Washington, D.C. 20037. Filed 7/31/85. Legislative interest — "... pediatric hospitals."

CIBA-GEIGY CORP., Ardsley, N.Y. Lobbyist — David P. Drake, 1747 Pennsylvania Ave. N.W., Washington, D.C. 20006. Filed 7/13/85. Legislative interest — "... the chemical industry, including but not limited to Superfund (S 51, HR 2817); the Clean Air Act (HR 2576); and the Clean Water Act."

CIRCLE ENERGIES INC., Wichita, Kan. Lobbyist — Washington Energy Trade & Agriculture Group, 655 15th St. N.W., Washington, D.C. 20005. Filed 7/13/85. Legislative interest — "Energy & Tax Legislation...."

THE COCA-COLA CO., Atlanta, Ga. Lobbyist — O'Connor & Hannan, 1919 Pennsylvania Ave. N.W., Washington, D.C. 20006. Filed 7/10/85. Legislative interest — "... matters involving ... the soft drink industry."

COMINCO ALASKA, Anchorage, Alaska. Lobbyist — Van Ness, Feldman, Sutcliffe & Curtis, 1050 Thomas Jefferson St. N.W., Washington, D.C. 20007. Filed 7/10/85. Legislative interest — "... public lands in Alaska, including support of S 444 and HR 1092."

CRAY RESEARCH INC., Minneapolis, Minn. Lobbyist — Cassidy & Associates Inc., 955 L'Enfant Plaza S.W., Washington, D.C. 20024. Filed 7/9/85. Legislative interest — "Legislation relating to federal procurement activities and federal research."

CROWLEY MARITIME CORP., San Francisco, Calif. Lobbyist — Dawson Mathis & Associates, 1800 M St. N.W., Washington, D.C. 20036. Filed 7/30/85. (Former U.S. Rep. Dawson Mathis, D-Ga., 1971-81, was listed as agent for this client.) Legislative interest — "... retention of Capital Construction Fund (Maritime)."

DAEWOO INTERNATIONAL CORP., Washington, D.C. Lobbyist — Wagner & Baroody Inc., 1100 17th St. N.W., Washington, D.C. 20036. Filed 7/16/85. Legislative interest — "To monitor trade legislation ... at this time, no specific legislative interests."

ECONOMICS LABORATORY INC., St. Paul, Minn. Lobbyist — Hogan & Hartson, 815 Connecticut Ave. N.W., Washington, D.C. 20006. Filed 7/16/85. Legislative interest — "... the application of section 280G of the Internal Revenue Code to closely-held corporations."

EQUITY PROGRAMS INVESTMENT CORP., Falls Church, Va. Lobbyist — Lane & Mittendorf, 1750 K St. N.W., Washington, D.C. 20006. Filed 7/13/85. Legislative interest — "General legislative interest: tax reform proposals ... Specific legislative interests: 'Fair and Simple Tax Act of 1985' (HR 777/S 325); 'Fair Tax Act of 1985' (HR 800/S 409); 'Tax Equity and Simplification Act of 1985' (HR 1040); and President's Tax Proposals to Congress, May 1985. Against all bills and Treasury Department Report."

ESKATON HEALTH CORP., Carmichael, Calif. Lobbyist — Memel, Jacobs, Pierno, Gersh & Ellsworth, 1800 M St. N.W., Washington, D.C. 20036. Filed 7/13/85. Legislative interest — "Health Legislation."

ESSELTE BUSINESS SYSTEMS INC., Garden City, N.Y. Lobbyist — R. Duffy Wall & Associates Inc., 1317 F St. N.W., Washington, D.C. 20004. Filed 7/12/85. Legislative interest — "... tax legislation."

FIRST AMERICAN TITLE INSURANCE CO., Troy, Mich. Lobbyist — Gray & Co., 3255 Grace St. N.W., Washington, D.C. 20007. Filed 7/10/85. Legislative interest — "... antitrust legislation relating to the title insurance industry."

FIRST INTERSTATE BANCORP, Los Angeles, Calif. Lobbyist — Stuart A. Lewis, 1919 Pennsylvania Ave. N.W., Washington, D.C. 20006. Filed 7/12/85. Legislative interest — "Financial legislation - HR 2707."

GENERAL DYNAMICS CORP., Arlington, Va. Lobbyist — D L Associates Inc., 1730 Rhode Island Ave. N.W., Washington, D.C. 20036. Filed 7/9/85. Legislative interest — "Defense issues...."

GENERAL MOTORS CORP., ALLISON GAS TURBINE DIVISION, Indianapolis, Ind. Lobbyist — Snyder, Ball, Kriser & Associates Inc., 499 S. Capitol St. S.W., Washington, D.C. 20003. Filed 7/23/85. Legislative interest — "Portions of Defense Authorization and Appropriation Bills."

GROUP HEALTH ASSOCIATION OF AMERICA INC., 624 Ninth St. N.W., Washington, D.C. 20001. Filed for self 7/24/85. Legislative interest — "... prepayment of health care, comprehensive health care, group practice medicine and matters relating to consumer health care services." Lobbyist — Pat Billings.

HEALTHCARE SERVICES OF AMERICA INC., Birmingham, Ala. Lobbyist — Sirote, Permutt, Friend, Friedman, Held & Apolinsky, 2222 Arlington Ave. South, Birmingham, Ala. 35255. Filed 7/29/85. Legislative interest — "President's Proposal for Tax Reform for Fairness, Growth and Simplicity."

HITACHI AMERICA LTD., New York, N.Y. Lobbyist — Gray & Co., 3255 Grace St. N.W., Washington, D.C. 20007. Filed 7/10/85. Legislative interest — "Seeking legislation affecting a contract dispute with the U.S. Army Corps of Engineers."

THE HOLDEN GROUP INC., 11365 W. Olympic Blvd., Los Angeles, Calif. 90064. Filed for self 7/29/85. Legislative interest — "To ensure that the views of public employers (e.g., states, municipalities, etc.) are taken into consideration in formulating federal pension policy, particularly with respect to the various tax reform measures currently being considered." Lobbyist — P. Daniel Demko.

FLOYD H. HYDE ASSOCIATES, 719 Eighth St. S.E., Washington, D.C. 20003. Filed for self 7/24/85. Legislative interest — "... local government ... housing and community development ... general revenue sharing ... in support such legislation."

ICAHN & CO. INC., New York, N.Y. Lobbyist — Verner, Liipfert, Bernhard, McPherson & Hand, 1660 L St. N.W., Washington, D.C. 20036. Filed 7/13/85. Legislative interest — Not specified.

INTERAND CORP., 3200 West Peterson Ave., Chicago, Ill. 60659. Filed for self 7/24/85. Legislative interest — "... Defense authorization and appropriation legislation ... Telecommunications legislation." Lobbyist — Frederic William Corle, 1828 L St. N.W., Washington, D.C. 20036.

KAISER FOUNDATION HEALTH PLAN, 900 17th St. N.W., Washington, D.C. 20006. Filed for self 7/12/85. Legislative interest — "... organizing, providing, delivering, and paying for medical care. ..." Lobbyist — JoAnne Glisson.

KRAFT INC., 1100 17th St. N.W., Washington, D.C. 20036. Filed for self 7/24/85. Legislative interest — "Tax Reform; USDA Reauthorization; South Africa Disinvestment Legislation." Lobbyist — Linda L. Bartlett.

LANE INDUSTRIES, Northbrook, Ill. Lobbyist — Gray & Co., 3255 Grace St. N.W., Washington, D.C. 20007. Filed 7/12/85. Legislative interest — "... antitrust legislation affecting consolidated income tax returns."

LAWYERS TITLE INSURANCE CO., Richmond, Va. Lobbyist — Gray & Co., 3255 Grace St. N.W., Washington, D.C. 20007. Filed 7/10/85. Legislative interest — "... antitrust legislation related to the title insurance industry."

LONZA INC., Fairlawn, N.J. Lobbyist — Cleary, Gottlieb, Steen & Hamilton, 1752 N St. N.W., Washington, D.C. 20036. Filed 7/3/85. Legislative interest — "Potential legislation to reduce tariffs on the imports of certain chemicals."

LYNG AND LESHER INC., 517 C St. N.E., Washington, D.C. 20002. Filed for self 7/20/85. Legislative interest — "General agriculture, budget, tax and trade issues before the Congress." Lobbyists — Delores A. Flowers, William Gene Lesher, Richard E. Lyng.

MASSACHUSETTS MUTUAL LIFE INSURANCE CO., Springfield, Mass. Lobbyist — Dawson Mathis & Associates, 1800 M St. N.W., Washington, D.C. 20036. Filed 7/12/85. (Former U.S. Rep. Dawson Mathis, D-Ga., 1971-81, was listed as agent for this client.) Legislative interest — "Life insurance taxation."

McABEE CONSTRUCTION INC., Tuscaloosa, Ala. Lobbyist — Sirote, Permutt, Friend, Friedman, Held & Apolinsky, 2222 Arlington Ave. South, Birmingham, Ala. 35255. Filed 7/29/85. Legislative interest — "President's Proposal for Tax Reform for Fairness, Growth and Simplicity."

McDERMOTT INC., New Orleans, La. Lobbyist — David P. Stang, 1629 K St. N.W., Washington, D.C. 20006. Filed 7/8/85. Legislative interest — "... Longshoremen's and Harbor Workers' Compensation Act."

McNEILL & CO., 1217 Elm St., Denver, Colo. 80220. Filed for self 7/3/85. Legislative interest — "... international interest." Lobbyist — Cynthia A. McNeill.

THE MEAD CORP., Courthouse Plaza N.E., Dayton, Ohio 45463. Filed for self 7/10/85. Legislative interest — "... Environment, Labor, Taxation, Economics, Pensions, Trade, Natural Resources, Transportation, Consumerism. ..." Lobbyist — Jane Scherer Haake, 1667 K St. N.W., Washington, D.C. 20006.

MEDTRONIC INC., 3055 Old Highway Eight, Minneapolis, Minn. 55440. Filed for self 7/8/85. Legislative interest — "... health care, prospective payment, Medicare/Medicaid changes, Social Security Act, product liability, trade, hazardous waste, Caribbean Trade Plan, research, tax measures, etc." Lobbyists — David Levy, George Gregory Raab.

HERMAN MILLER INC., 8500 Byron Road, Zeeland, Mich. 49464. Filed for self 7/26/85. Legislative interest — Not specified. Lobbyist — Kris Pathuis.

THE MONEY STORE, Sacramento, Calif. Lobbyist — Mark A. Siegel & Associates, 400 N. Capitol St. N.W., Washington, D.C. 20001. Filed 7/24/85. Legislative interest — Not specified.

NATIONAL INVESTMENT DEVELOPMENT CORP., Los Angeles, Calif. Lobbyist — Washington Resources & Strategy Inc., 220 I St. N.E., Washington, D.C. 20002. Filed 7/23/85. Legislative interest — "President Reagan's tax proposal."

NATIONAL MEDICAL CARE, Waltham, Mass. Lobbyist — Heron, Burchette, Ruckert & Rothwell, 1025 Thomas Jefferson St. N.W., Washington, D.C. 20007. Filed 7/10/85. Legislative interest — "... the health industry."

NATIONWIDE INSURANCE CO., Columbus, Ohio. Lobbyist — Bricker & Eckler, 888 17th St. N.W., Washington, D.C. 20006. Filed 7/26/85. Legislative interest — "Tax and insurance related legislation."

NEW WORLD PICTURES, Los Angeles, Calif. Lobbyist — Manatt, Phelps, Rothenberg & Tunney, 1200 New Hampshire Ave. N.W., Washington, D.C. 20036. Filed 7/25/85. Legislative interest — "HR 2783, S 1314."

NORFOLK SOUTHERN CORP., Norfolk, Va. Lobbyist — Finley, Kumble, Wagner, Heine, Underberg, Manley & Casey, 1120 Connecticut Ave. N.W., Washington, D.C. 20036. Filed 7/26/85. Legislative interest — "Advocating the acquisition of Conrail by the Norfolk Southern Corporation."

NORFOLK SOUTHERN CORP., Washington, D.C. Lobbyist — Bregman, Abell, Kay & Simon, 1156 15th St. N.W., Washington, D.C. 20005. Filed 7/24/85. Legislative interest — "... support of S 638 and HR 1449."

NORWOOD CLINIC INC., Birmingham, Ala. Lobbyist — Sirote, Permutt, Friend, Friedman, Held & Apolinsky, 2222 Arlington Ave. South, Birmingham, Ala. 35255. Filed 7/29/85. Legislative interest — "President's Proposal for Tax Reform for Fairness, Growth and Simplicity."

PACIFIC GAS & ELECTRIC, San Francisco, Calif. Lobbyist — Dawson Mathis & Associates, 1800 M St. N.W., Washington, D.C. 20036. Filed 7/12/85. (Former U.S. Rep. Dawson Mathis, D-Ga., 1971-81, was listed as agent for this client.) Legislative interest — "... licensing of hydro-electric facilities."

THE PACIFIC STOCK EXCHANGE INC., San Francisco, Calif. Lobbyist — John McElroy Atkisson, 1717 K St. N.W., Washington, D.C. 20036. Filed 7/29/85. Legislative interest — "... securities and exchanges, securities markets and regulation thereof, and oversite of American regional securities markets."

PAN AMERICAN SATELLITE CORP., 460 W. 42nd St., New York, N.Y. 10036. Lobbyist — Holland & Knight, 888 17th St. N.W., Washington, D.C. 20006. Filed 7/8/85. Legislative interest — "Matters involving alternative satellite communications systems ... Appropriations legislation and State Department authorization ... HR 2577; S 1003; HR 2068 ... in favor of alternative satellite systems; against restrictions on such systems." Filed for self 7/10/85. Legislative interest — Same as above. Lobbyist — Frederick Landman.

J. C. PENNEY CO. INC., New York, N.Y. Lobbyist — Russell H. Pearson, 1156 15th St. N.W., Washington, D.C. 20005. Filed 7/23/85. Legislative interest — "... labor law, antitrust, taxation, energy, foreign trade, inflation, and social security."

THE PEORIA JOURNAL STAR INC., Peoria, Ill. Lobbyist — Sidley & Austin, 1722 I St. N.W., Washington, D.C. 20006. Filed 7/29/85. Legislative interest — "The President's Tax Simplification Proposals of May, 1985. Against ESOP and section 401(k) portions of Proposals."

THE PILLSBURY CO., Pillsbury Center, Minneapolis, Minn. 55402. Lobbyist — Lipsen, Hamberger, Whitten & Hamberger, 1725 DeSales St. N.W., Washington, D.C. 20036. Filed 7/29/85. Legislative interest — "... agriculture." Filed for self 7/13/85. Legislative interest — "... Reagan's Tax Proposal ... for some portions of proposal and against some portions. ..." Lobbyist — Kenneth A. Johnson, 4524 N. Hillsboro Ave., Minneapolis, Minn. 55428.

PRIMARK CORP., 2021 K St. N.W., Washington, D.C.

20006. Filed for self 7/11/85. Legislative interest — "... health care, natural gas, and environment." Lobbyist — William L. Lucas. Filed for self 7/16/85. Legislative interest — "... the natural gas, health care, and banking industry." Lobbyist — Kenneth W. Thompson.

PROVIDENT LIFE & ACCIDENT INSURANCE CO., Chattanooga, Tenn. Lobbyist — Vinson & Elkins, 1101 Connecticut Ave. N.W., Washington, D.C. 20036. Filed 7/10/85. Legislative interest — "General tax matters relating to the treatment under the Internal Revenue Code of insurance companies and insurance products."

PROVIDENT MUTUAL LIFE INSURANCE CO. OF PHILADELPHIA, Philadelphia, Pa. Lobbyist — Murray & Scheer, 2550 M St. N.W., Washington, D.C. 20037. Filed 7/17/85. Legislative interest — Not specified.

PUBLIC SERVICE CO. OF COLORADO, 2121 K St. N.W., Washington, D.C. 20037. Filed for self 7/12/85. Legislative interest — "... regulated electric and gas utility." Lobbyist — David R. Toll.

RICE BELT WAREHOUSE INC., El Campo, Texas. Lobbyist — Larry Meyers, 412 First St. S.E., Washington, D.C. 20003. Filed 7/10/85. Legislative interest — "General Farm issues affecting Rice Issues."

ROCKY MOUNTAIN ENERGY, Washington, D.C. Lobbyist — Cassidy & Associates Inc., 955 L'Enfant Plaza S.W., Washington, D.C. 20024. Filed 7/9/85. Legislative interest — "... energy issues and mineral rights."

ROCKY MOUNTAIN ENERGY CO., Broomfield, Colo. Lobbyist — Bear West Co. Inc., 9 Exchange Place, Salt Lake City, Utah 84111. Filed 7/16/85. Legislative interest — "Clean air, public land policy, and coal leasing. ..."

ROYAL SILK, Clifton, N.J. Lobbyist — Paul S. Forbes, 7700 Leesburg Pike, Falls Church, Va. 22043. Filed 7/13/85. Legislative interest — "Duration of consideration of HR 1562 and S 608, re: the Multi-Fiber Arrangement, in opposition to restraints on the importation of silk."

SCM CORP., New York, N.Y. Lobbyist — Jones, Day, Reavis & Pogue, 655 15th St. N.W., Washington, D.C. 20005. Filed 7/15/85. Legislative interest — "Trade legislation relating to duty-free treatment for imports of synthetic rutile."

SAFECO TITLE INSURANCE CO., Seattle, Wash. Lobbyist — Gray & Co., 3255 Grace St. N.W., Washington, D.C. 20007. Filed 7/10/85. Legislative interest — "... antitrust legislation relating to the title insurance industry."

SEARS, ROEBUCK & CO., Chicago, Ill. Lobbyist — Burson-Marsteller, 1825 I St. N.W., Washington, D.C. 20006. Filed 7/12/85. Legislative interest — "... regulation and ownership of financial institutions, security firms, real estate companies, insurance companies, holding companies possessing an interest in these and other businesses, including HR 20 and HR 2707."

SINAI HOSPITAL OF BALTIMORE INC., Baltimore, Md. Lobbyist — Gordon, Feinblatt, Rothman, Hoffberger & Hollander, 233 E. Redwood St., Baltimore, Md. 21202. Filed 7/16/85. Legislative interest — "... Medicare reimbursement of physicians in teaching hospitals ... Senate Finance Committee Bill providing for recomputation of customary profiles for some hospital-based physicians currently reimbursed by Medicare under Compensation Related Customary Charge screens. (Support) ... Senate budget resolution providing for discontinuation of Medicare "freeze" for participating physicians. (Support) ... Congressional action to require immediate implementation of Section 2307 of the Deficit Reduction Act of 1984, dealing with reimbursement of physicians in teaching hospitals. (Support)."

SPERRY CORP., 2000 L St. N.W., Washington, D.C. 20036. Filed for self 7/17/85. Legislative interest — "... taxes, telecommunications, agriculture, international affairs and regulations ... Export Administration Act legislation (HR 3231 & S 979); ... for renewal of Act with certain requirements; Joint R&D bill ... for passage." Lobbyist — John W. Lampmann.

STEWART TITLE GUARANTY CO., Houston, Texas. Lobbyist — Gray & Co., 3255 Grace St. N.W., Washington, D.C. 20007. Filed 7/10/85. Legislative interest — "... antitrust legislation relating to the title insurance industry."

SUN LIFE ASSURANCE CO. OF CANADA, Wellesley Hills, Mass. Lobbyist — Covington & Burling, 1201 Pennsylvania Ave. N.W., Washington, D.C. 20044. Filed 7/29/85. Legislative interest — "... President's Tax Proposals concerning the taxation of life insurance companies and their products ... Against."

TEXAS INSTRUMENTS INC., Dallas, Texas. Lobbyist — William B. Driggers, 1745 Jefferson Davis Highway, Arlington, Va. 22202. Filed 7/23/85. Legislative interest — "Matters affecting conduct of business, including but not limited to taxation, telecommunications, Defense, Trade, Energy and government relations."

TEX-LA, Nacogdoches, Texas. Lobbyist — Heron, Burchette, Ruckert & Rothwell, 1025 Thomas Jefferson St. N.W., Washington, D.C. 20007. Filed 7/10/85. Legislative interest — "Support amendment to water resources bill regarding Dennison Dam."

3M INC., St. Paul, Minn. Lobbyist — Heron, Burchette, Ruckert & Rothwell, 1025 Thomas Jefferson St. N.W., Washington, D.C. 20007. Filed 7/10/85. Legislative interest — "... proposed amendments to the 'Superfund' Law ... Superfund Improvement Act of 1985 ... S 51 ... U.S.C. 9601 et seq. ... modification."

TIFFANY & CO., New York, N.Y. Lobbyist — Crowell & Moring, 1100 Connecticut Ave. N.W., Washington, D.C. 20036. Filed 7/25/85. Legislative interest — "... amendments in connection with fringe benefit provisions of the Internal Revenue Code and S 743."

TOSHIBA AMERICA INC., Lebanon, Tenn. Lobbyist — Arent, Fox, Kintner, Plotkin & Kahn, 1050 Connecticut Ave. N.W., Washington, D.C. 20036. Filed 7/3/85. Legislative interest — "HR 2349 (against)."

TRAILWAYS BUS CO., Dallas, Texas. Lobbyist — Hagedorn-Cando Inc., 1704 S. 23rd St., Arlington, Va. 22202. Filed 7/10/85. (Former U.S. Rep. Tom Hagedorn, R-Minn., 1975-83, was listed as agent for this client.) Legislative interest — "Reduce AMTRAK subsidy."

TURNER BROADCASTING SYSTEM INC., Washington, D.C. Lobbyist — Verner, Liipfert, Bernhard, McPherson & Hand, 1660 L St. N.W., Washington, D.C. 20036. Filed 7/13/85. Legislative interest — Not specified.

UNITED AIRLINES, Chicago, Ill. Lobbyist — Gray & Co., 3255 Grace St. N.W., Washington, D.C. 20007. Filed 7/10/85. Legislative interest — "... airline routes and computer reservation systems." Filed 7/15/85. Legislative interest — "... airline routes and computer reservation systems."

UNITED HOSPITALS, Cheltenham, Pa. Lobbyist — Cassidy & Associates Inc., 955 L'Enfant Plaza S.W., Washington, D.C. 20024. Filed 7/9/85. Legislative interest — "... health care, financing and administration."

U.S. REPEATING ARMS CO., New Haven, Conn. Lobbyist — Cassidy & Associates Inc., 955 L'Enfant Plaza S.W., Washington, D.C. 20024. Filed 7/3/85. Legislative interest — "... economic development."

VALLEY GREEN INTERNATIONAL TRADING CORP., New Orleans, La. Lobbyist — Washington Energy Trade & Agriculture Group, 655 15th St. N.W., Washington, D.C. 20005. Filed 7/13/85. Legislative interest — "Energy & Tax Legislation. ..."

WARBURG, PINCUS CAPITAL CORP., New York, N.Y. Lobbyist — Vinson & Elkins, 1101 Connecticut Ave. N.W., Washington, D.C. 20036. Filed 7/10/85. Legislative interest — "... general changes to the Internal Revenue Code affecting corporations and partnerships."

WARNER AMEX CABLE COMMUNICATIONS INC., New York, N.Y. Lobbyist — Vinson & Elkins, 1101 Connecticut Ave. N.W., Washington, D.C. 20036. FIled 7/10/85. Legislative interest — "Tax legislation concerning Section 280G of the Internal Revenue Code."

WESTERN SAVINGS & LOAN ASSOCIATION, Phoenix, Ariz. Lobbyist — John Daniel Reaves, 910 16th St. N.W., Washington, D.C. 20006. Filed 7/26/85. Legislative interest — "HR 20 Opposed to Section 4(e)."

WESTINGHOUSE CORP., Washington, D.C. Lobbyist —

Dawson Mathis & Associates, 1800 M St. N.W., Washington, D.C. 20036. Filed 7/12/85. (Former U.S. Rep. Dawson Mathis, D-Ga., 1971-81, was listed as agent for this client.) Legislative interest — "... energy policies."

THE WILLIAMS COS., P.O. Box 2400, Tulsa, Okla. 74102. Filed for self 7/30/85. Legislative interest — "... fertilizer, energy or other matters ... promotion of U.S. exports, deregulation of natural gas; importation of anhydrous ammonia from U.S.S.R.; petroleum pipeline regulatory reform; corporate taxation matters; and extension of the Export Administration Act." Lobbyist — Sandra Zeune Harris, 1120 20th St. N.W., Washington, D.C. 20036.

WILLIAMS TECHNOLOGIES INC., Tulsa, Okla. Lobbyist — Kendall & Associates Inc., 50 E St. S.E., Washington, D.C. 20003. Filed 7/10/85. Legislative interest — "... energy legislation and specifically appropriations bills dealing with energy."

YANKEE ENERGY CO., Boston, Mass. Lobbyist — Hagedorn-Cando Inc., 1704 S. 23rd St., Arlington, Va. 22202. Filed 7/10/85. (Former U.S. Rep. Tom Hagedorn, R-Minn., 1975-83, was listed as agent for this client.) Legislative interest — "... methanol fuel production."

Foreign Governments

ECUADOR, EMBASSY OF, Washington, D.C. Lobbyist — O'Connor & Hannan, 1919 Pennsylvania Ave. N.W., Washington, D.C. 20006. Filed 7/2/85. Legislative interest — "Foreign assistance legislation."

MOROCCO, KINGDOM OF, Rabat, Morocco. Lobbyist — Gray & Co., 3255 Grace St. N.W., Washington, D.C. 20007. Filed 7/10/85. Legislative interest — "Seeking legislation memorializing U.S.-Moroccan friendship."

TURKEY, REPUBLIC OF, Ankara, Turkey. Lobbyist — Gray & Co., 3255 Grace St. N.W., Washington, D.C. 20007. Filed 7/12/85. Legislative interest — "... economic assistance and security issues."

State and Local Governments

MASSPORT/COMMONWEALTH OF MASSACHUSETTS, Boston, Mass. Lobbyist — Heron, Burchette, Ruckert & Rothwell, 1025 Thomas Jefferson St. N.W., Washington, D.C. 20007. Filed 7/10/85. Legislative interest — "... transportation in Massachusetts."

NAPA COUNTY, Napa, Calif. Lobbyist — A-K Associates Inc., 1225 Eighth St., Sacramento, Calif. 95814. Filed 7/31/85. Legislative interest — "Funding for County Jail facilities."

NEW YORK STATE COMPTROLLER, Albany, N.Y. Lobbyist — Willkie, Farr & Gallagher, 818 Connecticut Ave. N.W., Washington, D.C. 20006. Filed 7/15/85. Legislative interest — "Support of legislation protecting the interests of the New York State Employee's Retirement System, specifically the inclusion of a clause preempting state and local statutes in Federal legislation concerning South Africa and monitoring tax and pension legislation."

NEW YORK STATE POWER AUTHORITY, New York, N.Y. Lobbyist — Mark A. Siegel & Associates, 400 N. Capitol St. N.W., Washington, D.C. 20001. Filed 7/24/85. Legislative interest — Not specified.

PHILADELPHIA, CITY OF, Philadelphia, Pa. Lobbyist — Ballard, Spahr, Andrews & Ingersoll, 1850 K St. N.W., Washington, D.C. 20006. Filed 7/12/85. Legislative interest — "Tax Issues ... Rehab Tax Credits, Tax-exempt financing, etc."

PUERTO RICO, COMMONWEALTH OF, San Juan, Puerto Rico. Lobbyist — Mark A. Siegel & Associates, 400 N. Capitol St. N.W., Washington, D.C. 20001. Filed 7/24/85. Legislative interest — Not specified.

Labor Organizations

AMALGAMATED TRANSIT UNION, AFL-CIO, 5025 Wisconsin Ave. N.W., Washington, D.C. 20016. Filed for self 7/13/85. Legislative interest — Not specified. Lobbyist — Ellis B. Franklin.

BROTHERHOOD OF LOCOMOTIVE ENGINEERS, Engineers Building, Cleveland, Ohio 44114. Filed for self 7/11/85. Legislative interest — "... rail labor and transportation." Lobbyist — Paul T. Kerrigan, 400 First St. N.W., Washington, D.C. 20001.

NATIONAL FEDERATION OF FEDERAL EMPLOYEES, 2020 K St. N.W., Washington, D.C. 20006. Filed for self 7/10/85. Legislative interest — "... First and Second Concurrent Budget Resolutions, Agency Appropriations and Authorizations, Budget Reconciliation, Social Security Benefits, Mandatory Social Security coverage, contracting out (OMB circular A-76) Federal Employees Compensation Act, Civil Service Reform Act (U.S.C. Title V), overall compensation and working conditions for Federal employees and retirees. Specific legislative interests include: Fiscal Year 1986 appropriations (support or oppose) ... HR 27 to eliminate wage discrimination in the Federal workforce (support) ... HR 917 to grant greater appeal rights to excepted service Federal employees ... Greater asbestos control ... Private Sector Survey on Cost Control recommendation cutting Federal pay/benefit/workforce (oppose) ... Office of Personnel Management's revised personnel regulations (oppose) ... Supplemental Federal Retirement System." Lobbyist — Beth Moten.

Trade Associations

ABRAFE, São Paulo, Brazil. Lobbyist — Wald, Harkrader & Ross, 1300 19th St. N.W., Washington, D.C. 20036. Filed 7/13/85. Legislative interest — "... the preservation of the ferroalloy industry in the United States; Fair Trade in Ferroalloys Act ... S 262; HR 976 ... Against."

AIR TRANSPORT ASSOCIATION, Washington, D.C. Lobbyist — Cadwalader, Wickersham & Taft, 1333 New Hampshire Ave. N.W., Washington, D.C. 20036. Filed 7/26/85. Legislative interest — "Federal Taxation matters." Lobbyist — Lipsen, Hamberger, Whitten & Hamberger, 1725 DeSales St. N.W., Washington, D.C. 20036. Filed 7/29/85. Legislative interest — "Assistance in tax legislation."

AMERICAN BAKERS ASSOCIATION, 1111 14th St. N.W., Washington, D.C. 20005. Filed for self 7/9/85. Legislative interest — Not specified. Lobbyist — Victor A. Sherlock.

AMERICAN BANKERS ASSOCIATION, 1120 Connecticut Ave. N.W., Washington, D.C. 20036. Lobbyist — Manatt, Phelps, Rothenberg & Tunney, 1200 New Hampshire Ave. N.W., Washington, D.C. 20036. Filed 7/23/85. Legislative interest — "... relating to the taxation of financial institutions, HR 2874, S 1263, on bad debt reserves." Filed for self 7/10/85. Legislative interest — "... banking industry." Lobbyist — Donald G. Ogilvie.

AMERICAN CONSULTING ENGINEERS COUNCIL, 1015 15th St. N.W., Washington, D.C. 20005. Filed for self 7/22/85. Legislative interest — "... public works; transportation; the environment; pollution control; housing; equal employment opportunity; public health and safety; economy and efficiency in government; energy and small business...." Lobbyists — Vicki R. Keenan, Lori A. Marsden.

AMERICAN FURNITURE MANUFACTURERS ASSOCIATION, P.O. Box HP-7, High Point, N.C. 27261. Filed for self 7/12/85. Legislative interest — "... Clean Air Act ... Sales Representatives Contractual Relations Act ... Resource Conservation and Recovery Act ... Tariff negotiations on furniture products." Lobbyist — David C. Frankil.

AMERICAN INSTITUTE OF CERTIFIED PUBLIC ACCOUNTANTS, Washington, D.C. Lobbyist — Hughes, Hubbard & Reed, 1201 Pennsylvania Ave. N.W., Washington, D.C. 20004. Filed 7/8/85. Legislative interest — "To bring to the attention of the relevant committees, members and staff of the House and Senate positions on legislation concerning the Racketeer Influenced and Corrupt Organizations Act."

AMERICAN LAND DEVELOPMENT ASSOCIATION, Washington, D.C. Lobbyist — Washington Resources &

Strategy Inc., 220 I St. N.E., Washington, D.C. 20002. Filed 7/8/85. Legislative interest — "President Reagan's Tax Proposal...."

AMERICAN MEAT INSTITUTE, 1700 N. Moore St., Arlington, Va. 22209. Filed for self 7/15/85. Legislative interest — "Legislation affecting the food industry in general and particularly the livestock and meat industry — including, but not limited to: livestock production and feeding, animal diseases, meat inspection, food additives, labeling, transportation, environmental protection, safety, trade practices, consumer protection, energy, food safety, regulatory reform." Lobbyists — Robert G. Hibbert, Jerry Welcome, P.O. Box 3556, Washington, D.C. 20007.

AMERICAN MEDICAL CARE AND REVIEW ASSOCIATION, 5410 Grosvenor Lane, Bethesda, Md. 20814. Filed for self 7/9/85. Legislative interest — "... with PL 92-333, PL 97-248 and with potential legislation concerning Preferred Provider Organizations (PPOs), Health Maintenance Organizations (HMOs) or Peer Review Organizations (PROs) ... will continue as long as laws are in effect and there is legislation or potential legislation concerning these organizations." Lobbyist — Ronald A. Hurst.

AMERICAN NUCLEAR ENERGY COUNCIL, 410 First St. S.E., Washington, D.C. 20003. Filed for self 7/9/85. Legislative interest — "... the Atomic Energy Act of 1954 (42 U.S.C. 2011 et seq.), the Energy Reorganization Act of 1974 (88 Stat. 1233) and related legislation in effect and pending.... HR 28 ... Roth; Foreign Affairs; to reauthorize the Export Administration Act of 1979.... HR 51 ... Price; Interior & Insular Affairs; to amend and extend the Price-Anderson Act.... HR 445 ... Seiberling; Interior & Insular Affairs; to amend the Price-Anderson Act to remove the limitation on liability.... HR 621 ... Whitehurst; Government Operations, Energy & Commerce and Rules; to terminate the DOE.... HR 632 ... Roemer; Banking, Finance & Urban Affairs and Foreign Affairs; to prohibit U.S. banks from making loans to enterprises in South Africa and to ban new investments by U.S. corporations to South Africa and other purposes (including limiting nuclear exports) in order to distance the U.S. from the abhorrent apartheid policies of the South African Government and to send a clear signal to that regime to modify those racist policies or face further economic isolation.... HR 862 ... Akaka; Interior & Insular Affairs and Energy & Commerce; to grant the consent of Congress to the Northwest Interstate Compact on Low-Level Radioactive Waste Management.... HR 903 ... Wolpe; Foreign Affairs; to amend the Nuclear Non-Proliferation Act of 1978 and to promote the nuclear non-proliferation policies of the U.S..... HR 1029 ... Broyhill; Energy & Commerce and Interior & Insular Affairs; to encourage the development and use of standardized plant designs and improve the nuclear licensing and regulatory process.... HR 1046 ... Glickman; Energy & Commerce and Interior & Insular Affairs; to grant the consent of Congress to the Central Interstate Compact on Low-Level Radioactive Waste Management.... HR 1083 ... Udall; Energy & Commerce and Interior & Insular Affairs; to improve procedures for the implementation of compacts providing for the establishment and generation of regional disposal facilities for low-level radioactive waste.... HR 1098 ... Fauntroy; Foreign Affairs, Banking, Finance & Urban Affairs; Ways & Means, Science & Technology; Public Works & Transportation; and Rules; to prohibit new loans by U.S. persons to the Government of South Africa, to prohibit new investments in business enterprises in South Africa, to prohibit the importation of South African krugerrands or other gold and silver coins, to prohibit the importation of coal and uranium from South Africa, to prohibit exports to South Africa of nuclear items and to prohibit exports of goods or technology to or for the use by the South African Government.... HR 1105 ... Biaggi; Public Works & Transportation; to amend the Hazardous Materials Transportation Act to restrict the transportation of radioactive materials through large cities.... HR 1133 ... Rangel; Foreign Affairs; to prohibit the export or other transfer to the Republic of South Africa of nuclear material, equipment, and technology.... HR 1135 ... Rangel; Foreign Affairs; to prohibit the import of coal and certain articles of uranium if the product of South Africa or Namibia.... HR 1221 ... Moakley; Energy & Commerce, Interior & Insular Affairs and Rules; to modify House & Senate proceedings for consideration of fee adjustment proposed by the Secretary of Energy and to establish an Advisory Commission on Nuclear Waste Finance.... HR 1267 ... Derrick; Energy & Commerce and Interior & Insular Affairs; to provide Congressional consent to the Southeast Interstate Low-Level Radioactive Waste Management Compacts.... HR 1287 ... Wirth; Energy and Commerce; to transfer to the Department of Health & Human Services DoE's authority for epidemiological studies of radiation effects.... HR 1447 ... Udall; Energy & Commerce and Interior & Insular Affairs; NRC bill to improve the nuclear power plant siting and licensing process.... HR 1613 ... Evans; Veterans; to provide disability and death benefits allowances, compensation, health care, and other benefits to veterans and the survivors of veterans who participated in Atomic tests or the occupation of Hiroshima and Nagasaki and suffer from diseases that may be attributable to ionizing radiation.... HR 1619 ... Gibbons; Ways & Means; to allow deductions for additions to reserves established for decommissioning costs associated with nuclear power-plants.... HR 1695 ... Oakar; Public Works & Transportation, Energy & Commerce and Interior and Insular Affairs; 'The Nuclear Waste Transportation Safety Act of 1985' to establish restrictions on the transportation of radioactive waste & spent fuel.... HR 1711 ... Udall; Interior & Insular Affairs; to authorize FY86-87 NRC appropriations.... HR 1786 ... Bonker; Foreign Affairs; clean version of HR 28 to reauthorize the Export Administration Act.... HR 1799 ... Fuqua; Interior & Insular, Energy & Commerce and Science & Technology; to authorize DoE civilian energy programs.... HR 1843 ... Weaver; Interior & Insular and Energy & Commerce; to enable States primarily affected by the siting of repositories for high-level radioactive waste or spent nuclear fuel to participate effectively in the site selection review and approval process.... HR 2009 ... Luken; Energy & Commerce; to clarify the jurisdiction of EPA over the regulations of solid waste mixed with radioactive materials at DoE facilities.... HR 2026 ... Madigan; Energy & Commerce and Interior & Insular Affairs; to grant the consent of Congress to the Central Midwest Interstate Low-Level Waste Compact.... HR 2040 ... Udall; Interior & Insular Affairs and Energy & Commerce; to authorize FY86-87 appropriations to DoE for expenditures from the nuclear waste fund for activities under Title 1 of the Nuclear Waste Policy Act of 1982.... HR 2041 ... Udall; Interior & Insular Affairs and Energy & Commerce and Science & Technology; to authorize FY86-87 appropriations to DoE for civilian energy programs.... HR 2094 ... Lujan; Government Operations and Interior; to prohibit the purchase of non-domestic uranium by federal agencies.... HR 2439 ... Neal; Energy & Commerce and Interior & Insular Affairs; to remove the limitation on the quantity of radioactive waste that may be emplaced in the first repository for the disposal of high-level radioactive waste and spent nuclear fuel.... HR 2488 ... Broyhill; Energy & Commerce and Interior & Insular Affairs; to encourage the standardization of nuclear power plants, to improve the nuclear licensing and regulatory process.... HR 2524 ... Morrison; Energy & Commerce and Interior & Insular Affairs; to establish liability and indemnification for nuclear incidents arising out of Federal storage, disposal or related transportation of high-level radioactive waste.... HR 2593 ... Wyden; Armed Services, Energy & Commerce and Public Works and Transportation; to require EPA to establish certain standards for radioactive emissions from atomic energy defense facilities of the DoE and to monitor radioactive and non-radioactive emissions from such facilities.... HR 2635 ... Vento; Energy & Commerce and Interior & Insular Affairs; to grant the consent of Congress to the Midwest Interstate Low-Level Radioactive Waste Compact.... HR 2665 ... Weiss; Interior & Insular Affairs; to modify certain limitations on the amount of financial protection required with respect to nuclear incidents, to remove the limitations on the aggregate liability for a single nuclear incident, to limit financial obligations of the U.S. with respect to such incidents.... HR 2702 ... Wirth; Energy & Commerce and Interior & Insular Affairs; to grant the consent of Congress to the Rocky Mountain Low-Level Radioactive Waste Compact.... HR 2743 ... Eckart; Interior & Insular Affairs; to require NRC to certain standards in the conduct of meetings.... S 16 ... Moynihan; Environment & Public Works; Nuclear Power Plant Personnel Training Act to establish the National Academy for Nuclear Power Safety.... S 44 ... Thurmond; Judiciary; to provide Congressional consent to the Southeast Interstate Low-Level Radioactive Waste Management Compacts.... S 147 ... Proxmire; Foreign Relations; to prohibit U.S. banks from making loans to enterprises in South Africa and to ban new investments by U.S. corporations to South Africa and other purposes (including limiting nuclear exports) in order to distance the U.S. from the abhorrent apartheid policies of the South African Government and to send a clear signal to that regime to modify those racist policies or face further economic isolation.... S 274 ... Denton; Judiciary; Anti-Nuclear Terrorism Act to allow reactor licensees access to certain FBI criminal history files.... S 356 ... Gorton; Judiciary; to grant the consent of Congress to the Northwest Interstate Compact on Low-Level Radioactive Waste Management.... S 442 ... Simpson; Judiciary; to grant the consent of Congress to the Rocky Mountain Low-Level Radioactive Waste Compact.... S 445 ... Hart; Environment & Public Works; to amend the Price-Anderson Act to remove the limitation for nuclear accidents to provide better economic protection for the people living near nuclear power plants and nuclear transportation routes.... S 525 ... Glenn; Government Affairs; to transfer to the Department of Health & Human Services DoE's authority for epidemiological studies of radiation effects.... S 655 ... Dole; Judiciary; to grant the consent of Congress to the Central Interstate Low-Level Radioactive Waste Compact.... S 707 ... Simpson; Veterans; to provide disability and death benefits allowances, compensation, health care, and other benefits to veterans and the survivors of veterans who participated in Atomic tests or the occupation of Hiroshima and Nagasaki and suffer from diseases that may be attributable to ionizing radiation.... S 802 ... Dixon; Judiciary; to grant the consent of Congress to the Central Midwest Interstate Compact on Low-Level Radioactive Waste Management.... S 836 ... Simpson; Environment & Public Works; NRC bill to improve the nuclear power plant siting and licensing process.... S 883 ... Heinz; simple extension of the Export Administration Act.... S 890 ... Simpson; Environment & Public Works; to provide applicants for, or holders of a production facility license, or a utilization facility license with access to certain federal criminal history records.... S 891 ... Simpson; Environment & Public Works; to clarify notification requirements for non-compliance.... S 892 ... Glenn; Environment & Public Works; to clarify the jurisdiction of EPA over the regulations of solid waste mixed with radioactive materials at DoE facilities.... S 895 ... Simpson; Environment & Public Works; to authorize FY86-87 NRC appropriations.... S 899 ... Grassley; Judiciary; to grant the consent to Congress to the Midwest Interstate Compact on Low-Level Radioactive Waste Management.... S 1162 ... Hart; Environment & Public Works; to amend the Nuclear Waste Policy Act of 1982 to require the Secretary of Energy to incorporate transportation impacts into the selection process for repositories of high-level radioactive waste.... S 1198 ... Mitchell; Environment & Public Works; to establish within EPA a program of research on indoor air quality.... S 1225 ... Simpson and McClure; Energy & Natural Resources and Environment & Public Works; to establish a comprehensive equitable, reliable and efficient mechanism for full compensation of the public in the event of an accident resulting from activities undertaken by Nuclear Regulatory Commission licensees involving nuclear materials.... S 1235 ... Simpson; Environment & Public Works; to reorganize the functions of the NRC by abolishing the Commission, and, in its place, establishing the Nuclear Regulation Agency, in order to promote more effective and efficient nuclear licensing regulation.... S 1254 ... Grassley; Judiciary; to provide for equitable reduction of liability of contractors with the U.S. in certain cases, to provide for a comprehensive system for indemnification by the U.S. for its contractors for liability in excess of reasonably available financial protection." Lobbyist — Thomas J. Price. Filed for self 7/17/85. Lobbyist — Richard H. Bornemann.

AMERICAN PAPER INSTITUTE INC., 260 Madison Ave., New York, N.Y. 10016. Filed for self 7/30/85. Legislative interest — "... the pulp, paper and paperboard industry, its operation, practices and properties; environmental legislation, air, water and energy." Lobbyist — Josephine S. Cooper, 1619 Massachusetts Ave. N.W., Washington, D.C. 20036.

AMERICAN PETROLEUM INSTITUTE, 1229 L St. N.W., Washington, D.C. 20005. Filed for self 7/8/85. Legislative interest — "... OCS legislation, HR 5973, S 2463; Superfund Reauthorization HR 5640; CERCLA Reauthorization S 51, S 596." Lobbyist — John F. Holtz, 170 W. State St., Trenton, N.J. 08608; Filed for self 7/8/85. Legislative interest — "OCS Legislation ... CERCLA Reauthorization." Lobbyist — Gary B. Patterson, P.O. Box 1429, Dover, Del. 19902.

AMERICAN PHARMACEUTICAL ASSOCIATION, 2215 Constitution Ave. N.W., Washington, D.C. 20037. Filed for self 7/2/85. Legislative interest — "... medicaid drug reimbursement; opposition to HR 1597, the Compassionate Pain Relief Act." Lobbyist — Dorothy A. Keville.

AMERICAN PSYCHOLOGICAL ASSOCIATION, 1200 17th St. N.W., Washington, D.C. 20036. Filed for self 7/22/85. Legislative interest — "... health care." Lobbyist — Anne Marie O'Keefe.

AMERICAN RETAIL FEDERATION, 1616 H St. N.W., Washington, D.C. 20006. Filed for self 7/29/85. Legislative interest — "Financial Services HR 20, 52, 514, 636, 683, 916; Credit Card HR 24, 286, 425, 1001, S 212, 440; Comparable Worth HR 27, 375, S 5; Contract Sanctity HR 28; National Health Insurance HR 212; Shelf Price HR 291; Trade Reorganization HR 320, S 21; First Sale Doctrine HR 384; OSHA Amendments HR 963, 965, 966, 967; Gray Market HR 1006; Tariff/Surcharge HR 1139, S 761, 770; Textile and Apparel Trade Enforcement Act HR 1562, S 680; Reauthorize Export Administraton Act HR 1786; International Trade & Investment Act HR 1808; Youth Subminimum Wage HR 1811, S 790; Car Log Repeal HR 1869, S 245; Footwear Recovery Act of 1985 HR 1973, S 848; Hazardous Waste-Superfund S 51, 494, 596; Products Liability S 100; Trade Expansion S 234. Lobbyist — Joseph P. O'Neill.

AMERICAN SOCIETY OF ASSOCIATION EXECUTIVES, 1575 I St. N.W., Washington, D.C. 20005. Filed for self 7/8/85. Legislative interest — "HR 1800 ... HR 1732 ... HR 1040 ... HR 1356 ... S 260 ... S 558 Treasury II proposal and issues relating to fringe benefits and tax-exempt associations." Lobbyist — Ernestine S. Robinson.

AMERICAN TEXTILE MANUFACTURERS INSTITUTE INC., Washington, D.C. Lobbyist — Ivins, Phillips & Barker, 1700 Pennsylvania Ave. N.W., Washington, D.C. 20006. Filed 7/10/85. Legislative interest — "Tax reform ... S 409, HR 800 and similar bills."

ANTITRUST REMEDIES REFORM GROUP, Toledo, Ohio. Lobbyist — Weil, Gotshal & Manges, 767 Fifth Ave., New York, N.Y. 10153. Filed 7/8/85. Legislative interest — "... amending the antitrust laws to provide for individual treble damage responsibility including S 1300."

ASSOCIATION OF AMERICAN RAILROADS, Washington, D.C. Lobbyist — Taggart & Associates Inc., 1015 15th St. N.W., Washington, D.C. 20005. Filed 7/11/85. Legislative interest — "Regulatory legislation."

ASSOCIATION OF TRIAL LAWYERS OF AMERICA, 1050 31st St. N.W., Washington, D.C. 20007. Filed for self 7/10/85. Legislative interest — "... admiralty, automobile reparation, aviation, consumer protection, criminal law, the environment, health, the administration of justice, legal services, and workers' compensation...." Lobbyist — Robert A. Lembo.

AUTOMOBILE IMPORT COMPLIANCE ASSOCIATION, Washington, D.C. Lobbyist — Heron, Burchette, Ruckert & Rothwell, 1025 Thomas Jefferson St. N.W., Washington, D.C. 20007. Filed 7/10/85. Legislative interest — "Support HR 2598."

THE BUSINESS ROUNDTABLE, Washington, D.C. Lobbyist — Hogan & Hartson, 815 Connecticut Ave. N.W., Washington, D.C. 20006. Filed 7/9/85. Legislative interest — "HR 2735, a bill to amend the Clayton Act. Against."

CALIFORNIA HOSPITAL ASSOCIATION, Sacramento, Calif. Lobbyist — Hanson, Bridgett, Marcus & Vlahos, 333 Market St., San Francisco, Calif. 94105. Filed 7/30/85. Legislative interest — "... support of the fiscal year 1986 Medicare budget as passed by the Health Subcommittee of the House of Representatives on July 16, 1985."

CHAMBER OF COMMERCE OF THE UNITED STATES, 1615 H St. N.W., Washington, D.C. 20062. Filed for self 7/24/85. Legislative interest — Not specified. Lobbyists — Lori C. Consadori, John Howard, Harry H. Westbay III.

CHEMICAL SPECIALTIES MANUFACTURERS ASSOCIATION INC., 1001 Connecticut Ave. N.W., Washington, D.C. 20036. Filed for self 7/10/85. Legislative interest — "... household, industrial and personal care chemical specialty products ... aerosols, detergents and cleaning compounds, antimicrobial products, pesticides, automotive chemicals, and waxes, polishes and floor finishes ... HR 2630, Consumer Product Safety Commission Amendments. Generally oppose." Lobbyist — Lawrence A. Levin.

CHICAGO BOARD OF TRADE, Washington, D.C. Lobbyist — Davis & Harman, 655 15th St. N.W., Washington, D.C. 20005. Filed 7/8/85. Legislative interest — "... the commodity industry."

COMPETITIVE TELECOMMUNICATIONS ASSOCIATION, 308 E. Capitol St. S.E., Washington, D.C. 20003. Filed for self 7/30/85. Legislative interest — Not specified. Lobbyist — Jerry McAndrew.

DREDGING INDUSTRY SIZE STANDARD COALITION, Oak Brook, Ill. Lobbyist — Patton, Boggs & Blow, 2550 M St. N.W., Washington, D.C. 20037. Filed 7/29/85. Legislative interest — "HR 1178, for."

EMPLOYEE RELOCATION COUNCIL, Washington, D.C. Lobbyist — Ivins, Phillips & Barker, 1700 Pennsylvania Ave. N.W., Washington, D.C. 20006. Filed 7/10/85. Legislative interest — "Tax reform legislation, generally, and other tax legislation such as HR 2475 (imputed interest) and HR 1800 and S 814 (Tech. Corrections) which has an impact on the purchase and sale of homes by employers and other employee relocation matters."

FIBER, FABRIC & APPAREL COALITION FOR TRADE, Washington, D.C. Lobbyist — Jack McDonald Co., 1800 M St. N.W., Washington, D.C. 20036. Filed 7/12/85. (Former U.S. Rep. Dawson Mathis, D-Ga., 1971-81, was listed as agent for this client.) Legislative interest — "... the import of textiles or textile related products into the United States."

GROCERY MANUFACTURERS OF AMERICA INC., Washington, D.C. Lobbyist — Heron, Burchette, Ruckert & Rothwell, 1025 Thomas Jefferson St. N.W., Washington, D.C. 20007. Filed 7/10/85. Legislative interest — "Seeking food production and marketing uniformity amendment for 1985."

HOSPITAL CORPORATION OF AMERICA, Washington, D.C. Lobbyist — McNair, Glenn, Konduros, Corley, Singletary, Porter & Dibble, 1155 15th St. N.W., Washington, D.C. 20005. Filed 7/29/85. Legislative interest — "Tax, Medicare and Medic Aid legislative issues."

INDEPENDENT BANKERS ASSOCIATION OF AMERICA, 1168 S. Main St., Sauk Centre, Minn. 56378. Filed for self 7/11/85. Legislative interest — "S 1609 Financial Institution Deregulation Act... For... S 2181 Financial Service Competitive Equity Act ... Against." Lobbyist — Stephen J. Verdier, 1625 Massachusetts Ave. N.W., Washington, D.C. 20036.

INTELLECTUAL PROPERTY OWNERS INC., Washington, D.C. Lobbyist — McNair, Glenn, Konduros, Corley, Singletary, Porter & Dibble, 1155 15th St. N.W., Washington, D.C. 20005. Filed 7/29/85. Legislative interest — "Patent legislation."

INTERNATIONAL ASSOCIATION OF AMUSEMENT PARKS AND ATTRACTIONS, Washington, D.C. Lobbyist — John McElroy Atkisson, 1717 K St. N.W., Washington, D.C. 20036. Filed 7/29/85. Legislative interest — "... federal safety legislation concerning fixed site amusement parks and attractions."

INTERNATIONAL FOOTWEAR ASSOCIATION, 19 W. 34th St., New York, N.Y. 10019. Filed for self 7/24/85. Legislative interest — "... S 848, 'American Footwear Industry Recovery Act of 1985' ... oppose ... importing into the U.S. in general, such as ... HR 2941 (Pease), to extend the authority to grant Adjustment Assistance ... support."

INVESTMENT COMPANY INSTITUTE, 1600 M St. N.W., Washington, D.C. 20036. Filed for self 7/15/85. Legislative interest — "HR 15 Depository Institutions Act of '85 ... HR 20 Bank Definition Act of '85 ... HR 428 Banking Integrity Act of 1985 ... HR 1346 Securities Investor Protection Act ... HR 1513 Financial Authorities Equity Act ... HR 1514 Depository Institutions Interstate Competition Act ... S 409 Fair Tax Act ... S 411 Broad-Based Enhanced Savings Act ... S 510 Interstate Banking Act '85." Lobbyist — Susan P. Hart.

IOWA PORK PRODUCERS ASSOCIATION, Clive, Iowa. Lobbyist — Gray & Co., 3255 Grace St. N.W., Washington, D.C. 20007. Filed 7/16/85. Legislative interest — "... the pork industry."

JOINT MARITIME CONGRESS, Washington, D.C. Lobbyist — Gray & Co., 3255 Grace St. N.W., Washington, D.C. 20007. Filed 7/12/85. Legislative interest — "... maritime legislation to permit foreign built passenger vessels entering U.S. passenger cruise trade."

MORTGAGE BANKERS ASSOCIATION OF AMERICA, 1125 15th St. N.W., Washington, D.C. 20005. Filed for self 7/15/85. Legislative interest — "... the mortgage lending, banking, and construction industries ... HR 20 Banking - Deregulation (1985) ... HR 242 Taxation - At Risk ... HR 591 Mortgage Credit - Usury ... HR 592 Mortgage Credit - Foreclosure Relief ... HR 756 VA - Home Loan Guarantee Amount ... HR 1040 Taxation - Code Reform ... HR 2801 VA - Foreclosure ... S 9 VA - Home Loan Guaranty ... S 43 Appropriations - Line Item Veto ... S 56 Taxation - Imputed Interest ... S 71 Taxation - Imputed Interest ... S 409 Taxation - Code Revision (1985) ... S 411 Taxation - Code Revision (1985) ... S 1214 Banking - Bribery." Lobbyist — Philip A. Brooks.

NATIONAL ASSOCIATION OF BROADCASTERS, 1771 N St. N.W., Washington, D.C. 20036. Filed for self 7/11/85. Legislative interest — Not specified. Lobbyist — Thomas McCoy.

THE NATIONAL ASSOCIATION OF LIFE UNDERWRITERS, Washington, D.C. Lobbyist — Miller, Cassidy, Larroca & Lewin, 2555 M St. N.W., Washington, D.C. 20037. Filed 7/13/85. Legislative interest — "... proposals relating to participation of banks, and their affiliates, in various aspects of the insurance business, e.g., HR 15, HR 428, HR 1513, S 716."

NATIONAL ASSOCIATION OF MANUFACTURERS, Washington, D.C. Lobbyist — Heron, Burchette, Ruckert & Rothwell, 1025 Thomas Jefferson St. N.W., Washington, D.C. 20007. Filed 7/13/85. Legislative interest — "... proposed amendments to the 'Superfund' Law ... Superfund Amendments of 1985 ... HR 2817, S 51 ... 42 U.S.C. Section 9601 et seq. ... modification." Lobbyist — David C. Luttrell, 1422 W. Peachtree St. N.W., Atlanta, Ga. 30309. Filed 7/29/85. Legislative interest — "... international trade, taxation & fiscal policy, employee benefits, and environmental issues."

NATIONAL ASSOCIATION OF PROFESSIONAL INSURANCE AGENTS, Alexandria, Va. Lobbyist — Miller, Cassidy, Larroca & Lewin, 2555 M St. N.W., Washington, D.C. 20037. Filed 7/13/85. Legislative interest — "... proposals relating to participation of banks, and their affiliates, in various aspects of the insurance business, e.g., HR 15, HR 428, HR 1513, S 716."

NATIONAL COUNCIL OF SAVINGS INSTITUTIONS, 1101 15th St. N.W., Washington, D.C. 20005. Filed for self 7/26/85. Legislative interest — "Support of bills to improve facilities of savings institutions for encouragement of thrift and home financing. Oppose any legislation adverse to thrift and home financing." Lobbyist — John H. Rousselot (former U.S. representative, R-Calif., 1961-63, 1970-83).

NATIONAL FEDERATION OF INDEPENDENT BUSINESS, 600 Maryland Ave. S.W., Washington, D.C. 20024. Filed for self 7/2/85. Legislative interest — "... small business ... labor and pensions." Lobbyist — Frank V. Toti Jr. Filed for self 7/2/85. Legislative interest — "... small business ... tax, budget and trade." Lobbyist — Abraham Schneier. Filed for self 7/2/85. Legislative interest — "... small business ... regulated industries and general commerce issues." Lobbyist — Leslie Christensen. Filed for self 7/2/85. Legislative interest — "... small business ... regulatory issues, and procurement." Lobbyist — Sally L. Douglas.

THE NATIONAL GRANGE, 1616 H St. N.W., Washington, D.C. 20006. Filed for self 7/10/85. Legislative interest — Not specified. Lobbyist — Leroy Watson.

NATIONAL RURAL LETTER CARRIERS ASSOCIATION, Alexandria, Va. Lobbyist — Lipsen, Hamberger, Whitten & Hamberger, 1725 DeSales St. N.W., Washington, D.C. 20036. Filed 7/29/85. Legislative interest — "Assistance in tax legislation."

NATIONAL TELEPHONE COOPERATIVE ASSOCIATION, 2626 Pennsylvania Ave. N.W., Washington, D.C. 20037. Filed for self 7/24/85. Legislative interest — "... the rural telephone program provided for in the Rural Electrification Act of 1936, all legislation affecting telecommunications and amendments to the Communications Act of 1934 ... the Rural Telephone Bank of 1971 ... rural telecommunications." Lobbyist — Stuart E. Proctor Jr.

NATURAL GAS SUPPLY ASSOCIATION, 1730 Rhode Island Ave. N.W., Washington, D.C. 20036. Filed for self 7/9/85. Legislative interest — "... oversight of the Natural Gas Policy Act of 1978, and amending same with a view toward consumer and national defense." Lobbyist — Walter J. Sczudio.

NEW YORK COTTON EXCHANGE, New York, N.Y. Lobbyist — H. Wesley McAden, 1155 15th St. N.W., Washington, D.C. 20005. Filed 7/2/85. Legislative interest — "... production, distribution and marketing of Cotton."

NEW YORK STATE BANKERS ASSOCIATION, New York, N.Y. Lobbyist — R. Duffy Wall & Associates Inc., 1317 F St. N.W., Washington, D.C. 20004. Filed 7/16/85. Legislative interest — "... general tax legislation."

NOR-CAL FEDERAL COALITION, P.O. Box 161, North Highlands, Calif. 95660. Filed for self 7/12/85. Legislative interest — "... HR 283, HR 68 - Legislation to reform Hatch Act restrictions ... HR 1336 - Legislation to repeal Social Security coverage of federal employees starting after 1 Jan. 84 ... HR 1964 - Legislation to pay overtime to TDY travel periods, weekends, and Holidays." Lobbyist — John M. Ellis, 1120 Fairfield Ave., Roseville, Calif. 95678.

PHOSPHATE ROCK EXPORT ASSOCIATION, Tampa, Fla. Lobbyist — Jane A. Golden, 1775 Pennsylvania Ave. N.W., Washington, D.C. 20006. Filed 7/30/85. Legislative interest — "... the Railroad Antimonopoly Act of 1985 (HR 1140; S 447) ... the application of the antitrust laws to railroads."

REINSURANCE ASSOCIATION OF AMERICA, Washington, D.C. Lobbyist — Preston, Thorgrimson, Ellis & Holman, 1735 New York Ave. N.W., Washington, D.C. 20006. Filed 7/23/85. Legislative interest — "Opposition to the President's tax proposal affecting property/casualty insurance."

RETAIL TOBACCO DEALERS OF AMERICA INC., Rockville Centre, N.Y. Lobbyist — Chwat/Weigend Associates, 400 First St. N.W., Washington, D.C. 20001. Filed 7/9/85. Legislative interest — "Unfair Sales Legislation, antitrust issues, Section 3 of the Robinson-Patman Act (15 USC 13a), FTC Act (15 USC 41), Clayton Act (15 USC 13), and predatory pricing."

ROCHESTER TAX COUNCIL, Rochester, N.Y. Lobbyist — Ivins, Phillips & Barker, 1700 Pennsylvania Ave. N.W., Washington, D.C. 20006. Filed 7/10/85. Legislative interest — "Tax reform legislation, generally, including S 409, HR 800 and similar bills; and legislation relating to section 30 of the Internal Revenue Code, including S 53 and HR 1188."

SOCIETY OF AMERICAN FLORISTS, 1601 Duke St., Alexandria, Va. 22314. Filed for self 7/20/85. Legislative interest — "... floriculture, horticulture, and agriculture, including those matters dealing with human relations and resources, education, transportation, commerce, industry, labor, etc." Lobbyist — Channing W. Daniel.

SOUTHEASTERN DREDGE OWNERS ASSOCIATION, Jacksonville, Fla. Lobbyist — Walter Larke Sorg, 1625 I St. N.W., Washington, D.C. 20006. Filed 7/17/85. Legislative interest — "... Amending the small business size standard ... HR 1178 ... Against. ..."

SOUTHEASTERN PEANUT ASSOCIATION, Albany, Ga. Lobbyist — Dawson Mathis & Associates, 1800 M St. N.W., Washington, D.C. 20036. Filed 7/12/85. (Former U.S. Rep. Dawson Mathis, D-Ga., 1971-81, was listed as agent for this client.) Legislative interest — "... Federal peanut program."

SUPIMA ASSOCIATION OF AMERICA, Phoenix, Ariz. Lobbyist — H. Wesley McAden, 1155 15th St. N.W., Washington, D.C. 20005. Filed 7/2/85. Legislative interest — "... production, distribution and marketing of Extra Long Staple Cotton."

TELEVISION OPERATORS CAUCUS INC., 1730 M St. N.W., Washington, D.C. 20036. Filed for self 7/16/85. Legislative interest — "... television station owners ... HR 2526." Lobbyist — Margita E. White.

Miscellaneous

AMERICAN ASSOCIATION OF RETIRED PERSONS, 1909 K St. N.W., Washington, D.C. 20049. Filed for self 7/8/85. Legislative interest — "Support of: ... Improved Tax Treatment of Older Americans ... Improved Social Security and Medicare/Medicaid Laws ... Improved Nursing Home Standards ... Consumer Protection Legislation ... Employment of Older Workers ... National Health Insurance ... Transportation of the Elderly ... Housing for the Elderly." Lobbyist — Judy Schub.

AMERICAN HORSE PROTECTION ASSOCIATION INC., Washington, D.C. Lobbyist — Russell J. Gaspar, 2555 M St. N.W., Washington, D.C. 20037. Filed 7/3/85. Legislative interest — "... the humane treatment of horses and other equine animals ... amending 16 U.S.C. section 1331 et seq. ... oppose most aspects of any legislation introduced to amend 16 U.S.C. section 1331 et seq., but to favor legislation advancing the protection or humane treatment of equines."

AMERICAN RED CROSS RETIREMENT SYSTEM, Alexandria, Va. Lobbyist — Willkie, Farr & Gallagher, 818 Connecticut Ave. N.W., Washington, D.C. 20006. Filed 7/15/85. Legislative interest — "Generally following and supporting HR 2811."

AMERICANS FOR THE HIGH FRONTIER, 1010 Vermont Ave. N.W., Washington, D.C. 20005. Filed for self 7/23/85. Legislative interest — "98th Congress HR 215, S 100 (for), Interest in any legislation relative to SDI." Lobbyist — Robert C. Richardson III.

ANIMAL HEALTH INSTITUTE, 119 Oronoco St., Alexandria, Va. 22313. Filed for self 7/17/85. Legislative interest — "... animal health products industry." Lobbyist — Martha A. Vanier.

THE ASSOCIATION FOR THE PRESERVATION OF HISTORIC COASTAL PROPERTIES INC., Myrtle Beach, S.C. Lobbyist — Hunton & Williams, 2000 Pennsylvania Ave. N.W., Washington, D.C. 20036. Filed 7/8/85. Legislative interest — "... issues affecting the preservation of traditional management regions and uses of coastal properties on the South Carolina, North Carolina and Georgia coastlines, and specifically relate, inter alia, to implementation of section 404 of the Clean Water Act, 33 U.S.C. section 466 et seq., the Coastal Zone Management Act, 16 U.S.C. section 1451 et seq., the Coastal Barriers Resource Act, 16 U.S.C. section 3809 et seq. and related legislation."

BOAT OWNERS ASSOCIATION OF THE UNITED STATES, 880 S. Pickett St., Alexandria, Va. 22304. Filed for self 7/9/85. Legislative interest — "... water pollution, recreational boating and other legislation impacting on boating and boat owners ... amendments to the Federal Safe Boating Act ... Coast Guard and NOAA Budgets." Lobbyist — Elaine Dickinson.

JAMES GRAHAM BROWN FOUNDATION, Louisville, Ky. Lobbyist — Taft, Stettinius & Hollister, First National Bank Center, Cincinnati, Ohio 45202. Filed 7/25/85. Legislative interest — "The status of certain hazardous waste clean up expenditures as charitable payments for the purpose of section 4942 of the Internal Revenue Code."

CALIFORNIA STUDENT LOAN FINANCE CORP., Los Angeles, Calif. Lobbyist — Heron, Burchette, Ruckert & Rothwell, 1025 Thomas Jefferson St. N.W., Washington, D.C. 20007. Filed 7/10/85. Legislative interest — "Support legislation to protect the formula for student loan guarantees."

COALITION AGAINST DOUBLE TAXATION INC., Washington, D.C. Lobbyist — Hale & Dorr, 60 State St., Boston, Mass. 02109. Filed 7/8/85. (Former U.S. Rep. James M. Shannon,

D-Mass., 1979-85, was listed among agents for this client.) Legislative interest — "Preserving the deductibility of state and local taxes as currently provided under Federal tax law. Focus on deletion or modification of provisions of the President's tax reform proposal seeking repeal of deductibility."

COALITION FOR ALTERNATIVES IN NUTRITION & HEALTHCARE INC., P.O. Box B12, Richlandtown, Pa. 18955. Filed for self 7/8/85. Legislative interest — "To advocate nutrition and alternate healthcare as means to improve healthcare system and reduce costs in USA along with ancillary relevant issues regarding healthcare, i.e., pure water, food irradiation, etc. Will support these Bills: HR 616, 1383, 1589, 1819, 1877 . . . Do not support these Bills: S 288, HR 696." Lobbyist — Catherine J. Frompovich.

COALITION FOR CLEAN WATER, Seattle, Wash. Lobbyist — Bogle & Gates, One Thomas Circle N.W., Washington, D.C. 20005. Filed 7/10/85. Legislative interest — "Clean Water Act Amendments."

COALITION FOR JOBS, GROWTH AND INTERNATIONAL COMPETITIVENESS, 1730 Pennsylvania Ave. N.W., Washington, D.C. 20006. Filed for self 7/23/85. Legislative interest — ". . . federal taxation affecting capital formation and jobs, growth and international competitiveness."

COALITION FOR THE ADVANCEMENT OF INDUSTRIAL TECHNOLOGY, Washington, D.C. Lobbyist — Jack McDonald Co., 1800 M St. N.W., Washington, D.C. 20036. Filed 7/12/85. (Former U.S. Rep. Dawson Mathis, D-Ga., 1971-81, was listed as agent for this client.) Legislative interest — ". . . extend R&D tax credit."

COMMITTEE FOR FINANCING PUBLIC TRANSPORTATION FACILITIES, Washington, D.C. Lobbyist — McNair, Glenn, Konduros, Corley, Singletary, Porter & Dibble, 1155 15th St. N.W., Washington, D.C. 20005. Filed 7/25/85. Legislative interest — "Tax issues."

COMMITTEE FOR REASONABLE INVENTORY ACCOUNTING RULES, Washington, D.C. Lobbyist — Ivins, Phillips & Barker, 1700 Pennsylvania Ave. N.W., Washington, D.C. 20006. Filed 7/10/85. Legislative interest — "Tax reform proposals affecting rules for accounting for inventory costs." Filed 7/31/85. Legislative interest — "Tax reform proposals affecting rules for accounting for inventory costs."

COMMITTEE FOR TAX EQUITY, Washington, D.C. 20006. Lobbyist — Bregman, Abell, Kay & Simon, 1156 15th St. N.W., Washington, D.C. 20005. Filed 7/24/85. Legislative interest — ". . . tax issues."

COMMON CAUSE, 2030 M St. N.W., Washington, D.C. 20036. Filed for self 7/17/85. Legislative interest — ". . . open government, campaign finance reform, the Federal Election Commission, lobby disclosure, government ethics, Senate confirmation process, extension of the Clean Air Act, court jurisdiction issues, congressional budget process, congressional reform, freedom of information, energy policy, waste in government, regulatory reform, public participation in federal agency proceedings, Legal Services Corporation, the Equal Rights Amendment, War Powers Act, nuclear arms control, military spending and tax reform . . . supported a freeze on military spending, opposed funds for the further deployment of the MX missile system, supported reductions in funding for the Strategic Defense Initiative, and supported continuation of the ban on anti-satellite weapons testing . . . supported the resumption of negotiations for a comprehensive test ban treaty and continued adherence to the SALT II treaty . . . urged the Senate and House to curb the 'revolving door' practices between the Pentagon and defense contractors and to reform longstanding defense contractor practices of billing the government for extraneous costs . . . opposed covert aid to the contras in Nicaragua, and supported legislation barring the use of funds to commit combat troops to Nicaragua without prior Congressional approval . . . supported legislation to reform congressional campaign financing and opposed the repeal of the dollar tax check-off for public financing of presidential campaigns . . . supported legislation to broaden interpretation of the Civil Rights Act in response to a Supreme Court decision regarding Grove City College . . . reiterated . . . support for tax reform in testimony before the House Ways and Means and Senate Finance Committees . . . opposed the Balanced Budget constitutional amendment and legislation to give the President line item veto authority over appropriations bills." Lobbyists — Michael Mawby, Linda Yeldezian.

CONGRESS WATCH, 215 Pennsylvania Ave. S.E., Washington, D.C. 20003. Filed for self 7/16/85. Legislative interest — "Malt Beverage Interbrand Competition Act, Consumer Product Safety Commission reauthorization." Lobbyist — Priscilla R. Budeiri.

DEVILS LAKE SIOUX TRIBE, Fort Totten, N.D. Lobbyist — Sonosky, Chambers & Sachse, 1050 31st St. N.W., Washington, D.C. 20007. Filed 7/15/85. Legislative interest — ". . . HR 1156, HR 526, HR 1920, HR 2404, S 277, S 400, S 15, S 902."

DREXEL UNIVERSITY, Philadelphia, Pa. Lobbyist — Cassidy & Associates Inc., 955 L'Enfant Plaza S.W., Washington, D.C. 20024. Filed 7/3/85. Legislative interest — ". . . funding of education programs, including student aid."

FEDERAL NATIONAL MORTGAGE ASSOCIATION, 3900 Wisconsin Ave. N.W., Washington, D.C. 20016. Filed for self 7/3/85. Legislative interest — "Residential mortgage, housing, banking, tax issues." Lobbyist — Annette P. Fribourg.

HOOPA VALLEY INDIANS, Hoopa, Calif. Lobbyist — Gray & Co., 3255 Grace St. N.W., Washington, D.C. 20007. Filed 7/10/85. Legislative interest — ". . . Indian tribal management and authority." Filed 7/12/85. Legislative interest — ". . . Indian tribal management and authority."

INVEST TO COMPETE ALLIANCE, Washington, D.C. Lobbyist — Mayer, Brown & Platt, 2000 Pennsylvania Ave. N.W., Washington, D.C. 20006. Filed 7/10/85. Legislative interest — ". . . amendments to the Internal Revenue Code." Lobbyist — Campbell Raupe Associates, 1015 15th St. N.W., Washington, D.C. 20005. Filed 7/15/85. Legislative interest — "Retention of the Investment Tax Credit."

MARTIN MAYFIELD, 3408 Toledo Terrace, Hyattsville, Md. 20782. Filed for self 7/25/85. Legislative interest — Not specified.

NATIONAL ASSOCIATION OF ATOMIC VETERANS, Eldon, Mo. Lobbyist — Alvin M. Guttman, 818 Connecticut Ave. N.W., Washington, D.C. 20006. Filed 7/9/85. Legislative interest — ". . . supporting H J Res 295, to designate July 16, 1985 as 'National Atomic Veterans Day'; S 707 & HR 1613, 'Atomic Veterans Relief Act of 1985.' "

NATIONAL ASSOCIATION OF FOREIGN STUDENT AFFAIRS, Washington, D.C. Lobbyist — Harris Miller & Associates, 1000 Wilson Blvd., Arlington, Va. 22209. Filed 7/31/85. Legislative interest — ". . . the admission and immigration status of foreign students."

NATIONAL ASSOCIATION OF RAILROAD PASSENGERS, 417 New Jersey Ave. S.E., Washington, D.C. 20003. Filed for self 7/15/85. Legislative interest — ". . . railroads and transportation . . . rail passenger service . . . in support of bills which would improve and expand such service." Lobbyists — John Lagomarcino, Anthony D. Perl.

NATIONAL AUDUBON SOCIETY, New York, N.Y. Lobbyist — Whitney C. Tilt, 645 Pennsylvania Ave. S.E., Washington, D.C. 20003. Filed 7/23/85. Legislative interest — ". . . wildlife and natural resources."

NATIONAL CLEAN AIR COALITION, 530 7th St. S.E., Washington, D.C. 20003. Filed for self 7/11/85. Legislative interest — ". . . to preserve, restore, and insure the rational use of the ecosphere, particularly legislation dealing with clean air issues such as Acid Rain bills (HR 2679, HR 2918, HR 1414, S 283, S 52, S 503); Tall Stacks bill, HR 2900; and Toxic Air bill, HR 2576." Lobbyist — Robert Bingaman Jr.

NATIONAL COALITION TO BAN HANDGUNS, 100 Maryland Ave. N.E., Washington, D.C. 20002. Filed for self 7/10/85. Legislative interest — ". . . availability and use of firearms . . . 'Firearms Owners' Protection Act,' HR 954 & S 49, against . . . 'Law Enforcement Officers Protection Act of 1985,' HR 4, for. . . . HR 2024, for." Lobbyist — D. Michael Hancock.

NATIONAL CONSUMER LAW CENTER, 11 Beacon St., Boston, Mass. 02108. Filed for self 7/15/85. Legislative interest

— "Support legislative efforts on behalf of low-income consumers on energy issues . . . low-income energy assistance, weatherization, conservation, and alternative energy sources . . . HR 2422, S 1142, S 969, S Con Res 32, HR 152, HR 1 etc. . . . Low-income Home Energy Assistance Act, 42 USC 6861, et. seq. Food Stamp Act, etc. . . . For certain provisions; against certain provisions." Lobbyist — Helen C. Gonzales, 236 Massachusetts Ave N.E., Washington, D.C. 20002.

NATIONAL EMPLOYEE BENEFITS INSTITUTE, Washington, D.C. Lobbyist — Reinhart, Boerner, Van Deuren, Norris & Rieselbach, 111 E. Wisconsin Ave., Milwaukee, Wis. 53202. Filed 7/12/85. Legislative interest — ". . . deferred compensation and employee fringe benefits . . . Homemakers Equity (S 200), Kasten Tax (S 325), Bradley Broad Tax (S 409), Chafee Tax (S 556), Flat Tax (HR 200), Rangel Treas. Bill (HR 1040) and Stark Tax (HR 1377)."

NATIONAL TAX POLICY INSTITUTE FOR THE PUBLIC INTEREST, 933 President St., Brooklyn, N.Y. 11215. Filed for self 7/8/85. Legislative interest — ". . . Tax Reform . . . Internal Revenue Code . . . For certain provisions; Against others." Lobbyist — Michael Dinnerstein, 1600 S. Eads St., Arlington, Va. 22202.

NEW ENGLAND COLLEGE OF OPTOMETRY, Boston, Mass. Lobbyist — Cassidy & Associates Inc., 955 L'Enfant Plaza S.W., Washington, D.C. 20024. Filed 7/9/85. Legislative interest — ". . . funding of optometry programs, including student aid."

OBERLIN COLLEGE, Oberlin, Ohio. Lobbyist — Ivins, Phillips & Barker, 1700 Pennsylvania Ave. N.W., Washington, D.C. 20006. Filed 7/10/85. Legislative interest — "Tax reform proposals affecting qualified tuition reductions plans under I.R.C. section 117(d)."

PARALYZED VETERANS OF AMERICA, Washington, D.C. Lobbyist — Bingham, Dana & Gould, 1724 Massachusetts Ave. N.W., Washington, D.C. 20036. Filed 7/9/85. Legislative interest — "Veterans affairs . . . through passage of First Concurrent Budget Resolution for FY 86 and HUD-Independent Agencies Appropriations Act for FY 1986 . . . 38 U.S.C. Section 5010; in favor."

PREVENTION OF CRUELTY TO ANIMALS, 354 Longacre Ave., Woodmere, N.Y. 11598. Filed for self 7/8/85. Legislative interest — ". . . re-ratification of the North Pacific Fur Seal Treaty . . . opposed." Lobbyist — Dr. Debra L. Schultz.

PUBLIC EMPLOYER BENEFITS COUNCIL, 1800 M St. N.W., Washington, D.C. 20036. Filed for self 7/26/85. Legislative interest — "To ensure that the views of public employers (e.g., states, municipalities, etc.) are taken into consideration in formulating federal pension policy, particularly with respect to the various tax reform measures currently being considered." Lobbyist — P. Daniel Demko.

RULE OF LAW COMMITTEE, Washington, D.C. Lobbyist — Steptoe & Johnson, 1330 Connecticut Ave. N.W., Washington, D.C. 20036. Filed 7/25/85. Legislative interest — ". . . A bill to amend title 9 of the U.S.C. regarding arbitral awards . . . S 1395 . . . For."

SECTION 936 STEERING COMMITTEE, Hato Rey, Puerto Rico. Lobbyist — Vinson & Elkins, 1101 Connecticut Ave. N.W., Washington, D.C. 20036. Filed 7/10/85. Legislative interest — ". . . Section 936 of the Internal Revenue Code."

SOLAR LOBBY, 1001 Connecticut Ave. N.W., Washington, D.C. 20036. Filed for self 7/2/85. Legislative interest — ". . . To promote the use of renewable energy sources . . . HR 2001, S 1220 . . . for both bills." Lobbyist — Joan Moody.

MELVIN L. STARK, 1025 Connecticut Ave. N.W., Washington, D.C. 20036. Filed for self 7/8/85. Legislative interest — "Superfund Legislation (S 51)."

UNIFICATION CHURCH, McLean, Va. Lobbyist — Casey, Scott & Canfield, 1331 Pennsylvania Ave. N.W., Washington, D.C. 20004. Filed 7/11/85. Legislative interest — Not specified.

UNITED INTERNATIONAL CONSULTANTS, 1800 Diagonal Road, Alexandria, Va. 22314. Filed for self 7/26/85. Legislative interest — "Foreign policy and foreign commerce . . . Anti-Apartheid Action Act of 1985 . . . S 995 . . . Against." Lobbyist — Michael D. Hathaway.

U.S. COALITION FOR FAIR CANADIAN LUMBER IMPORTS, Dewey, Ballantine, Bushby, Palmer & Wood, 1775 Pennsylvania Ave. N.W., Washington, D.C. 20006. Filed 7/17/85. Legislative interest — Not specified.

UNIVERSITY OF BRIDGEPORT, Bridgeport, Conn. Lobbyist — Cassidy & Associates Inc., 955 L'Enfant Plaza S.W., Washington, D.C. 20024. Filed 7/3/85. Legislative interest — ". . . funding of education programs, including student aid."

UNIVERSITY OF GUADALAJARA ALUMNI ASSOCIATION, San Antonio, Texas. Lobbyist — Medical-Dental Diversified Services Inc., 5372 Fredericksburg Road, San Antonio, Texas 78229. Filed 7/30/85. Legislative interest — ". . . graduates of foreign medical schools, including but not limited to S 1210."

UNIVERSITY OF MARYLAND, College Park, Md. Lobbyist — White, Fine & Verville, 1156 15th St. N.W., Washington, D.C. 20005. Filed 7/12/85. Legislative interest — ". . . contracting for educational services, including but not limited to S 1029 and HR 1872."

UNIVERSITY OF NEVADA/LAS VEGAS — RESEARCH CENTER, Las Vegas, Nev. Lobbyist — Heron, Burchette, Ruckert & Rothwell, 1025 Thomas Jefferson St. N.W., Washington, D.C. 20007. Filed 7/10/85. Legislative interest — "Support appropriations funding for Research Center."

UNIVERSITY OF SOUTHERN MISSISSIPPI, Hattiesburg, Miss. Lobbyist — Cassidy & Associates Inc., 955 L'Enfant Plaza S.W., Washington, D.C. 20024. Filed 7/3/85. Legislative interest — ". . . funding of education programs, including student aid."

VILLERS ADVOCACY FOUNDATION, Washington, D.C. Lobbyist — Hale & Dorr, 1201 Pennsylvania Ave. N.W., Washington, D.C. 20005. Filed 7/10/85. Legislative interest — Not specified.

August Registrations

Corporations and Businesses

ADLER & SHAYKIN, New York, N.Y. Lobbyist — Akin, Gump, Strauss, Hauer & Feld, 1333 New Hampshire Ave. N.W., Washington, D.C. 20036. Filed 8/16/85. Legislative interest — ". . . regulation of banking and securities industries."

AKER ASSOCIATES, 1341 G St. N.W., Washington, D.C. 20005. Filed for self 8/14/85. Legislative interest — ". . . relief from importation of gasoline and any other refined petroleum products." Lobbyists — G. Colburn Aker, Scott Richardson.

ALAMO RENT-A-CAR INC., Ft. Lauderdale, Fla. Lobbyist — Anderson, Hibey, Nauheim & Blair, 1708 New Hampshire Ave. N.W., Washington, D.C. 20009. Filed 8/27/85. Legislative interest — "Airport Program and Funding Legislation."

AMERICAN CYANAMID CO., Washington, D.C. Lobbyist — Wexler, Reynolds, Harrison & Schule Inc., 1317 F St. N.W., Washington, D.C. 20004. Filed 8/15/85. Legislative interest — ". . . establishment of a national no-fault childhood vaccine injury compensation system, including HR 1780 (The National Childhood Vaccine-Injury Compensation Act of 1985), and S 827 (National Childhood Vaccine Injury Compensation Act)."

AMERICAN INTERNATIONAL KNITTERS CORP., Saipan, Commonwealth of the Northern Mariana Islands. Lobbyist — Barnes, Richardson & Colburn, 1819 H St. N.W., Washington, D.C. 20006. Filed 8/16/85. Legislative interest — ". . . Textile and Apparel Trade Enforcement Bill . . . S 680, HR 1562 . . . favor excluding insular possessions from coverage of bill."

AMERICAN TRADING TRANSPORTATION CO. INC., New York, N.Y. Lobbyist — Bogle & Gates, One Thomas Circle N.W., Washington, D.C. 20005. Filed 8/7/85. Legislative interest — ". . . opposes Administration's Rule to lift domestic trading restrictions on vessels built with construction-differential subsidy upon repayment of such subsidy . . . opposes Administration efforts to allow existing foreign-built ships to engage in carriage of U.S. preference cargoes without waiting three (3) years from date of U.S. registry. . . ."

APEX MARINE CORP., Lake Success, N.Y. Lobbyist — Robertson, Monagle, Eastaugh & Bradley, 21 Dupont Circle N.W., Washington, D.C. 20036. Filed 8/13/85. Legislative interest — ". . . Maritime Administration and authorization bills . . . S 679, S 102 . . . Against CDS amendments."

ARTISTS PRODUCTIONS CELEBRITY DEVELOPMENT, 8881 Rosemont, Detroit, Mich. 48228. Filed for self 8/12/85. Legislative interest — ". . . for the proper developing for disadvantaged individuals whom have talent, but unable to pay normal fees. (Performing artists — drama or musical (singers))." Lobbyist — Diane E. Smith.

ATLANTIC RICHFIELD CO., 515 S. Flower St., Los Angeles, Calif. 90071. Filed for self 8/14/85. Legislative interest — ". . . the petroleum industry." Lobbyist — Richard N. Sawaya, 1333 New Hampshire Ave. N.W., Washington, D.C. 20036.

AT-SEA INCINERATION INC., Fort Newark, N.J. Lobbyist — Broadhurst, Brook, Mangham & Hardy, 1730 Pennsylvania Ave. N.W., Washington, D.C. 20006. Filed 8/21/85. Legislative interest — "Proposed Legislation (S 1039, HR 1295)."

AVON PRODUCTS INC., 9 W. 57th St., New York, N.Y. 10019. Filed for self 8/1/85. Legislative interest — ". . . government regulation of the manufacture and distribution of products, the environment and taxation." Lobbyist — Diana Berardocco, 1660 L St. N.W., Washington, D.C. 20036.

BATUS D.C. INC., 1825 K St. N.W., Washington, D.C. 20006. Filed for self 8/2/85. Legislative interest — Not specified. Lobbyists — Susan G. Flack, Mark S. Knouse, Wilson W. Wyatt Jr.

BRIGHT & CO., Dallas, Texas. Lobbyist — Bill Hecht & Associates Inc., 499 S. Capitol St. S.W., Washington, D.C. 20003. Filed 8/5/85. Legislative interest — Not specified.

BROWNING-FERRIS INDUSTRIES, P.O. Box 3151, Houston, Texas 77253. Filed for self 8/21/85. Legislative interest — "Legislation impacting waste service industry." Lobbyist — Fred C. Himes.

CSX CORP., Baltimore, Md. Lobbyist — Blum, Nash & Railsback, 1133 15th St. N.W., Washington, D.C. 20005. Filed 8/1/85. (Former U.S. Rep. Tom Railsback, R-Ill., 1967-83, was listed as agent for this client.) Legislative interest — ". . . sale of Conrail . . . S 638, S 447, HR 1140, HR 1190, HR 1449."

CSX CORP., Richmond, Va. Lobbyist — Broadhurst, Brook, Mangham & Hardy, 1730 Pennsylvania Ave. N.W., Washington, D.C. 20006. Filed 8/5/85. Legislative interest — "Proposed Conrail Legislation (S 638, HR 1930)."

CAMP, CARMOUCHE, BARSH, HUNTER, GRAY, HOFFMAN & GILL, Washington, D.C. Lobbyist — The Fox Group, USA Ltd., P.O. Box 1831, Charleston, S.C. 29402. Filed 8/22/85. Legislative interest — ". . . the regulation and ownership of financial institutions, security firms, real estate companies, insurance companies, holding companies possessing an interest in these and other businesses, including HR 20 and HR 2707." Lobbyist — Lewis, Babcock, Gregory & Pleicones, P.O. Box 11208, Columbia, S.C. 29211. Filed 8/22/85. Legislative interest — Same as above. Lobbyist — Miller, Hamilton, Snider & Odom, 256 State St., Mobile, Ala. 36603. Filed 8/26/85. Legislative interest — Same as above.

THE CHASE MANHATTAN BANK, Washington, D.C. Lobbyist — McNair, Glenn, Konduros, Corley, Singletary, Porter & Dibble, 1155 15th St. N.W., Washington, D.C. 20005. Filed 8/28/85. Legislative interest — "All banking legislation."

CITY OF HOPE NATIONAL MEDICAL CENTER & REHABILITATION HOSPITAL, Los Angeles, Calif. Lobbyist — Memel, Jacobs, Pierno, Gersh & Ellsworth, 1800 M St. N.W., Washington, D.C. 20036. Filed 8/15/85. Legislative interest — "ERISA pre-emption legislation."

COMMONWEALTH GARMENT MANUFACTURING, Chalan Piao, Saipan, Commonwealth of the Northern Mariana Islands. Lobbyist — Barnes, Richardson & Colburn, 1819 H St. N.W., Washington, D.C. 20006. Filed 8/16/85. Legislative interest — ". . . Textile and Apparel Trade Enforcement Bill . . . S 680, HR 1562 . . . favor excluding insular possessions from coverage of bill."

CREST TANKERS INC., St. Louis, Mo. Lobbyist — Bogle & Gates, One Thomas Circle N.W., Washington, D.C. 20005. Filed 8/7/85. Legislative interest — ". . . opposes Administration's Rule to lift domestic trading restrictions on vessels built with construction-differential subsidy upon repayment of such subsidy . . . opposes Administration efforts to allow existing foreign-built ships to engage in carriage of U.S. preference cargoes without waiting three (3) years from date of U.S. registry. . . ."

DART AND KRAFT INC., Washington, D.C. Lobbyist — McNair, Glenn, Konduros, Corley, Singletary, Porter & Dibble, 1155 15th St. N.W., Washington, D.C. 20005. Filed 8/28/85. Legislative interest — ". . . international trade."

DOCTOR'S HOSPITAL, Detroit, Mich. Lobbyist — Gnau & Associates Inc., 44 E. Long Lake Rd., Bloomfield Hills, Mich. 48013. Filed 8/20/85. Legislative interest — Not specified.

DRIFTWOOD DAIRIES, El Monte, Calif. Lobbyist — Latham, Watkins & Hills, 1333 New Hampshire Ave. N.W., Washington, D.C. 20036. Filed 8/14/85. Legislative interest — "In favor of Dairy Unity Bill, HR 2100."

FORD AEROSPACE & COMMUNICATIONS CORP., Palo Alto, Calif. Lobbyist — Gnau & Associates Inc., 44 E. Long Lake Rd., Bloomfield Hills, Mich. 48013. Filed 8/20/85. Legislative interest — Not specified.

GULF & WESTERN INDUSTRIES INC., 1 Gulf & Western Plaza, New York, N.Y. 10023. Filed for self 8/5/85. Legislative interest — ". . . communications, copyrights, banking, tax reform and other matters generally affecting private industry." Lobbyist — David H. Lissy.

HNG/INTERNORTH, 2223 Dodge St., Omaha, Neb. 68102. Filed for self 8/8/85. Legislative interest — "Superfund, Pipeline Safety Act, Tax reform legislation and any natural gas legislation." Lobbyist — Edward Joseph Hillings, 1015 15th St. N.W., Washington, D.C. 20005. Filed for self 8/19/85. Legislative interest — "Superfund, Pipeline Safety Act, Tax reform legislation and any natural gas legislation." Lobbyist — Edward Joseph Hillings, 1015 15th St. N.W., Washington, D.C. 20005.

BILL HECHT & ASSOCIATES INC., 499 S. Capitol St. S.W., Washington, D.C. 20003. Filed for self 8/5/85. Legislative interest — Not specified. Lobbyists — Craig R. Helsing, G. Franklin West.

HOME INSURANCE CO., New York, N.Y. Lobbyist — Finley, Kumble, Wagner, Heine, Underberg, Manley & Casey, 1120 Connecticut Ave. N.W., Washington, D.C. 20036. Filed 8/12/85. Legislative interest — "S 51, 'Superfund Improvement Act of 1985,' support in part, seeking an amendment; also interested in the tax legislation in connection with the administration's tax proposal."

INSURANCE SERVICING AND INFORMATION SYSTEMS CORP., Rockville, Md. Lobbyist — Arent, Fox, Kintner, Plotkin & Kahn, 1050 Connecticut Ave. N.W., Washington, D.C. 20036. Filed 8/28/85. Legislative interest — "For extension of Federal Crime Insurance Program; for HR 1, Sec. 122 (as reported H Rept 99-230)."

INTECH SYSTEMS, Hampton, Va. Lobbyist — Gnau & Associates Inc., 44 E. Long Lake Rd., Bloomfield Hills, Mich. 48013. Filed 8/20/85. Legislative interest — Not specified.

INTERGY INC., Brecksville, Ohio. Lobbyist — Gnau & Associates Inc., 44 E. Long Lake Rd., Bloomfield Hills, Mich. 48013. Filed 8/20/85. Legislative interest — Not specified.

THE IRVINE CO., Newport Beach, Calif. Lobbyist — Bill Hecht & Associates Inc., 499 S. Capitol St. S.W., Washington, D.C. 20003. Filed 8/5/85. Legislative interest — Not specified.

KEYSTONE SHIPPING CO., Philadelphia, Pa. Lobbyist — Bogle & Gates, One Thomas Circle N.W., Washington, D.C. 20005. Filed 8/7/85. Legislative interest — ". . . opposes Administration's Rule to lift domestic trading restrictions on vessels built with construction-differential subsidy upon repayment of such subsidy . . . opposes Administration efforts to allow existing foreign-built ships to engage in carriage of U.S. preference cargoes without waiting three (3) years from date of U.S. registry. . . ."

KOHLBERG, KRAVIS, ROBERTS & CO., New York,

N.Y. Lobbyist — Akin, Gump, Strauss, Hauer & Feld, 1333 New Hampshire Ave. N.W., Washington, D.C. 20036. Filed 8/16/85. Legislative interest — "... regulation of the banking and securities industries."

LITTON INDUSTRIES, Beverly Hills, Calif. Lobbyist — Patton, Boggs & Blow, 2550 M St. N.W., Washington, D.C. 20037. Filed 8/1/85. Legislative interest — "General tax matters regarding employee benefits."

MANAGEMENT INSIGHTS INC., Dallas, Texas. Lobbyist — Bill Hecht & Associates Inc., 499 S. Capitol St. S.W., Washington, D.C. 20003. Filed 8/5/85. Legislative interest — "... HR 983 (for)."

MARITZ INC., Fenton, Mo. Lobbyist — Arnold & Porter, 1200 New Hampshire Ave. N.W., Washington, D.C. 20036. Filed 8/12/85. Legislative interest — "Tax Reform Proposals."

MARRIOTT CORP., Washington, D.C. Lobbyist — Anderson, Hibey, Nauheim & Blair, 1708 New Hampshire Ave. N.W., Washington, D.C. 20009. Filed 8/27/85. Legislative interest — "Tax legislation — the Technical Corrections Act."

McDONNELL DOUGLAS CORP., Arlington, Va. Lobbyist — Jones & Winburn, 50 E St. S.E. Washington, D.C. 20003. Filed 8/28/85. Legislative interest — "... the Tax Reform Act of 1984...."

MILLER & CHEVALIER, Washington, D.C. Lobbyist — Barbara S. Blaine, 910 16th St. N.W., Washington, D.C. 20006. Filed 8/2/85. Legislative interest — "HR 20 ... Opposed to Section 4(e)."

NORFOLK SOUTHERN CORP., Washington, D.C. Lobbyist — Bartley M. O'Hara, 1919 Pennsylvania Ave. N.W., Washington, D.C. 20006. Filed 8/13/85. Legislative interest — "Support for sale of government's interest in the Consolidated Rail Corporation (CONRAIL), as provided in [S] 638 and HR 1449."

NYNEX CORP., Washington, D.C. Lobbyist — Dewey, Ballantine, Bushby, Palmer & Wood, 1775 Pennsylvania Ave. N.W., Washington, D.C. 20006. Filed 8/5/85. Legislative interest — "... taxation and regulation...."

OVERSEAS VESSEL CONVERSION, Washington, D.C. Lobbyist — Broadhurst, Brook, Mangham & Hardy, 1730 Pennsylvania Ave. N.W., Washington, D.C. 20006. Filed 8/21/85. Legislative interest — "Proposed Legislation (HR 1362)."

PATLEX CORP., Westfield, N.J. Lobbyist — Washington Resources & Strategy Inc., 220 I St. N.E., Washington, D.C. 20002. Filed 8/22/85. Legislative interest — Not specified.

J. C. PENNEY CO. INC., 1301 Avenue of the Americas, New York, N.Y. 10019. Filed for self 8/14/85. Legislative interest — "... labor law, antitrust, taxation, energy, foreign trade, inflation and social security." Lobbyist — James G. Tetirick, 1156 15th St. N.W., Washington, D.C. 20005.

THE PILLSBURY CO., Pillsbury Center M.S. 3771, Minneapolis, Minn. 55402. Filed for self 8/5/85. Legislative interest — "... tax, food safety, environment, international trade, etc." Lobbyist — Patricia A. Jensen.

PRIMARK CORP., Washington, D.C. Lobbyist — Gnau & Associates Inc., 44 E. Long Lake Rd., Bloomfield Hills, Mich. 48013. Filed 8/20/85. Legislative interest — Not specified.

PRODUCER'S GAS CO., Dallas, Texas. Lobbyist — The Hannaford Co. Inc., 655 15th St. N.W., Washington, D.C. 20005. Filed 8/27/85. Legislative interest — Not specified.

PGA TOUR INC., Ponte Vedra, Fla. Lobbyist — NS & MG, 1919 Pennsylvania Ave. N.W., Washington, D.C. 20006. Filed 8/1/85. Legislative interest — "... President's Tax Proposals to the Congress for Fairness, Growth and Simplicity ... Opposed to certain provisions...."

RECOGNITION EQUIPMENT INC., Irvine, Texas. Lobbyist — Gnau & Associates Inc., 44 E. Long Lake Rd., Bloomfield Hills, Mich. 48013. Filed 8/20/85. Legislative interest — Not specified.

REED, ROBERTS TAX CREDIT ASSISTANCE CORP., Uniondale, N.Y. Lobbyist — Bill Hecht & Associates Inc., 499 S. Capitol St. S.W., Washington, D.C. 20003. Filed 8/5/85. Legislative interest — "... HR 983 (for)."

REHABILITATION INSTITUTE OF CHICAGO, Chicago, Ill. Lobbyist — Capitol Associates Inc., 1156 15th St. N.W., Washington, D.C. 20005. Filed 8/14/85. Legislative interest — "... health research."

RES-CARE INC., Louisville, Ky. Lobbyist — Rice, Porter & Seiller, 2200 Meidinger Tower, Louisville, Ky. 40202. Filed 8/15/85. Legislative interest — "Support adequate FY 1986 funding for Job Corps (Title IV - B PL 97-300) ... First concurrent Budget Resolution for FY 1986; FY 1986 Labor - HHS - Education Appropriations Bills ... S Con Res 32, H Con Res 153, Conf. Rpt. 99-249 ... Support...."

ROYAL SILK LTD., Clifton, N.J. Lobbyist — Heron, Burchette, Ruckert & Rothwell, 1025 Thomas Jefferson St. N.W., Washington, D.C. 20007. Filed 8/8/85. Legislative interest — "Oppose bills of protectionist legislation — harmful to the silk industry."

STATLEY CONTINENTAL, Rolling Meadows, Ill. Lobbyist — Paul H. DeLaney Jr., 1120 20th St. N.W., Washington, D.C. 20036. Filed 8/14/85. Legislative interest — "... changes to United States tax law in the context of the ongoing United States tax reform process."

SUN TRANSPORT INC., Aston, Pa. Lobbyist — Bogle & Gates, One Thomas Circle N.W., Washington, D.C. 20005. Filed 8/7/85. Legislative interest — "... opposes Administration's Rule to lift domestic trading restrictions on vessels built with construction-differential subsidy upon repayment of such subsidy ... opposes Administration efforts to allow existing foreign-built ships to engage in carriage of U.S. preference cargoes without waiting three (3) years from date of U.S. registry...."

TRINIDAD CORP., Philadelphia, Pa. Lobbyist — Bogle & Gates, One Thomas Circle N.W., Washington, D.C. 20005. Filed 8/7/85. Legislative interest — "... opposes Administration's Rule to lift domestic trading restrictions on vessels built with construction-differential subsidy upon repayment of such subsidy ... opposes Administration efforts to allow existing foreign-built ships to engage in carriage of U.S. preference cargoes without waiting three (3) years from date of U.S. registry...."

TRIPLE A SHIPYARDS, San Francisco, Calif. Lobbyist — The Hannaford Co. Inc., 655 15th St. N.W., Washington, D.C. 20005. Filed 8/27/85. Legislative interest — Not specified.

U. C. CONSULTANTS, Nashville, Tenn. Lobbyist — Bill Hecht & Associates Inc., 499 S. Capitol St. S.W., Washington, D.C. 20003. Filed 8/5/85. Legislative interest — "... HR 983 (for)."

UNION STATION VENTURE, Washington, D.C. Lobbyist — Mayer, Brown & Platt, 2000 Pennsylvania Ave. N.W., Washington, D.C. 20006. Filed 8/13/85. Legislative interest — "... amendments to the Internal Revenue Code."

UNITED COMPANIES LIFE INSURANCE CO., Baton Rouge, La. Lobbyist — Jones & Winburn, 50 E St. S.E., Washington, D.C. 20003. Filed 8/28/85. Legislative interest — "... taxation of Life Insurance Companies."

VENEZOLANA DE CEMENTOS CA, Caracas, Venezuela. Lobbyist — Arnold & Porter, 1200 New Hampshire Ave. N.W., Washington, D.C. 20230. Filed 8/5/85. Legislative interest — "Against proposals which would change the U.S. countervailing duty law to treat Mexico's pricing of oil and gas products as a countervailable subsidy."

VENTURE DEVELOPMENT CORP., Miami, Fla. Lobbyist — Kaye, Scholer, Fierman, Hays & Handler, 1575 I St. N.W., Washington, D.C. 20005. Filed 8/26/85. Legislative interest — "... tax legislation affecting the real estate industry."

VICTORY CARRIERS INC., New York, N.Y. Lobbyist — Bogle & Gates, One Thomas Circle N.W., Washington, D.C. 20005. Filed 8/7/85. Legislative interest — "... opposes Administration's Rule to lift domestic trading restrictions on vessels built with construction-differential subsidy upon repayment of such subsidy ... opposes Administration efforts to allow existing foreign-built ships to engage in carriage of U.S. preference cargoes without waiting three (3) years from date of U.S. registry...."

WARREN REAL ESTATE GROUP INC., Lansing, Mich. Lobbyist — Gnau & Associates Inc., 44 E. Long Lake Rd., Bloomfield Hills, Mich. 48013. Filed 8/20/85. Legislative interest — Not specified.

WESTERN GROWERS ASSURANCE TRUST, Irvine, Calif. Lobbyist — Bill Hecht & Associates Inc., 499 S. Capitol St.

S.W., Washington, D.C. 20003. Filed 8/5/85. Legislative interest — Not specified.

WESTERN SAVINGS & LOAN ASSOCIATION, Phoenix, Ariz. Lobbyist — Hunton & Williams, 2000 Pennsylvania Ave. N.W., Washington, D.C. 20006. Filed 8/7/85. (Former U.S. Rep. John J. Rhodes, R-Ariz., 1953-83, was listed as agent for this client.) Legislative interest — "... amendments pertaining to HR 20."

WORCESTER BUSINESS DEVELOPMENT CORP., Worcester, Mass. Lobbyist — Capitol Associates Inc., 1156 15th St. N.W., Washington, D.C. 20005. Filed 8/14/85. Legislative interest — "For legislation affecting health research."

Labor Organizations

INTERNATIONAL UNION OF BRICKLAYERS AND ALLIED CRAFTSMEN, Washington, D.C. Lobbyist — Bartley M. O'Hara, 1919 Pennsylvania Ave. N.W., Washington, D.C. 20006. Filed 8/13/85. Legislative interest — "... retention of laws such as the Davis Bacon Act."

State and Local Governments

TURLOCK IRRIGATION DISTRICT, Turlock, Calif. Lobbyist — Damrell, Damrell & Nelson, 1625 I St., Modesto, Calif. 95354. Filed 8/12/85. Legislative interest — "... hydroelectric developments in California."

Trade Associations

ALIGNPAC, Portland, Ore. Lobbyist — McNair, Glenn, Konduros, Corley, Singletary, Porter & Dibble, 1155 15th St. N.W., Washington, D.C. 20005. Filed 8/28/85. Legislative interest — "Tax reform & fringe benefits issues."

ALLIANCE FOR FAIR TRADE, Washington, D.C. Lobbyist — Bogle & Gates, One Thomas Circle N.W., Washington, D.C. 20005. Filed 8/1/85. (Former U.S. Rep. Joel Pritchard, R-Wash., 1973-85, was listed among agents for this client.) Legislative interest — "HR 1562 (against); S 680 (against)."

AMERICAN ACADEMY OF OPHTHALMOLOGY, Washington, D.C. Lobbyist — Gold & Liebengood Inc., 1050 Connecticut Ave. N.W., Washington, D.C. 20036. Filed 8/5/85. Legislative interest — Not specified.

AMERICAN COUNCIL OF LIFE INSURANCE INC., 1850 K St. N.W., Washington, D.C. 20006. Filed for self 8/21/85. Legislative interest — "... the life insurance industry ... pension and tax legislation...." Lobbyist — William T. Gibb.

AMERICAN FAIR TRADE COUNCIL, San Francisco, Calif. Lobbyist — Bogle & Gates, One Thomas Circle N.W., Washington, D.C. 20005. Filed 8/1/85. (Former U.S. Rep. Joel Pritchard, R-Wash., 1973-85, was listed among agents for this client.) Legislative interest — "HR 1562 (against); S 680 (against)."

AMERICAN PAPER INSTITUTE INC., 260 Madison Ave., New York, N.Y. 10016. Filed for self 8/19/85. Legislative interest — "... the pulp, paper and paperboard industry, its operation, practices and properties; tax legislation and environmental legislation — air, water and energy." Lobbyist — Terry L. Serie, 1619 Massachusetts Ave. N.W., Washington, D.C. 20036.

AMERICAN PETROLEUM INSTITUTE, Washington, D.C. Lobbyist — Florida Petroleum Council, 325 John Knox Rd., Tallahassee, Fla. 32303. Filed 8/20/85. Legislative interest — Not specified.

ASSOCIATION FOR A BETTER NEW YORK, 355 Lexington Ave., New York, N.Y. 10017. Lobbyist — Kriegel Communications, 437 Madison Ave., New York, N.Y. 10022. Filed 8/7/85. Legislative interest — "... Tax Simplification Plan of the Treasury Department as it affects the State and City of New York and their citizens & residents." Filed for self 8/13/85. Legislative interest — "... Tax Simplification Plan of the Treasury Department as it affects the State and City of New York and their citizens & residents." Lobbyist — Lewis Rudin.

ASSOCIATION OF AMERICAN RAILROADS, Washington, D.C. Lobbyist — Bill Hecht & Associates Inc., 499 S. Capitol St. S.W., Washington, D.C. 20003. Filed 8/5/85. Legislative interest — Not specified.

THE BUSINESS ROUNDTABLE, Washington, D.C. Lobbyist — Hogan & Hartson, 815 Connecticut Ave. N.W., Washington, D.C. 20006. Filed 8/5/85. Legislative interest — "S 1300, a bill to provide individual liability for antitrust damages. For."

CALIFORNIA HOSPITAL ASSOCIATION, Sacramento, Calif. Lobbyist — Jones & Winburn, 50 E St. S.E., Washington, D.C. 20003. Filed 8/28/85. Legislative interest — "... Medicare Budget Issues."

CALIFORNIA LEAGUE OF SAVINGS INSTITUTIONS, Los Angeles, Calif. Lobbyist — Arnold & Porter, 1200 New Hampshire Ave. N.W., Washington, D.C. 20036. Filed 8/12/85. Legislative interest — "Tax proposals affecting savings & loan institutions."

CANADIAN FOREST INDUSTRIES COUNCIL, Ottawa, Ontario, Canada. Lobbyist — APCO Associates, 1200 New Hampshire Ave. N.W., Washington, D.C. 20036. Filed 8/1/85. Legislative interest — "To oppose efforts to restrict imports of lumber products from Canada, including HR 2451 and S 1292."

COLORADO MUNICIPAL BOND DEALERS ASSOCIATION, Denver, Colo. Lobbyist — Bartley M. O'Hara, 1919 Pennsylvania Ave. N.W., Washington, D.C. 20006. Filed 8/12/85. Legislative interest — "Support for elimination of proposals to tax advanced refundings of public purpose municipal bonds."

FAIR MARKETING COALITION, New York, N.Y. Lobbyist — Akin, Gump, Strauss, Hauer & Feld, 1333 New Hampshire Ave. N.W., Washington, D.C. 20036. Filed 8/16/85. Legislative interest — "... beer and wine advertising on broadcast media, including but not limited to HR 2526...."

FEDERATION OF BEHAVIORAL, PSYCHOLOGICAL AND COGNITIVE SCIENCES, 1200 17th St. N.W., Washington, D.C. 20036. Filed for self 8/8/85. Legislative interest — "... research in behavioral and cognitive sciences ... authorization and appropriations for the National Science Foundation, National Institute of Education, National Institute of Mental Health, and National Institutes of Health." Lobbyists — Claudia Feller, Cynthia H. Null.

FINANCIAL EXECUTIVES INSTITUTE, 1050 17th St. N.W., Washington, D.C. 20036. Filed for self 8/14/85. Legislative interest — "Budget, Tax, DoD Authorizations/Appropriations, and general business issues." Lobbyist — Michael J. Quaranta.

GROCERY MANUFACTURERS OF AMERICA INC., 1010 Wisconsin Ave. N.W., Washington, D.C. 20007. Filed for self 8/2/85. Legislative interest — Not specified. Lobbyist — Heather S. Richards.

HOUSING AMERICA FOUNDATION, Washington, D.C. Lobbyist — O'Neill & Haase, 1333 New Hampshire Ave. N.W., Washington, D.C. 20036. Filed 8/8/85. Legislative interest — "... tax legislation and FmHA Rural Housing Program."

INVESTMENT COMPANY INSTITUTE, Washington, D.C. Lobbyist — Daniel J. Piliero II, 1750 Pennsylvania Ave. N.W., Washington, D.C. 20006. Filed 8/13/85. Legislative interest — "... amend Subchapter M of the Internal Revenue Code to modify existing rules pertaining to the tax treatment of mutual funds to shareholders and other related tax issues."

LABOR-INDUSTRY COALITION FOR INTERNATIONAL TRADE, Washington, D.C. Lobbyist — Dewey, Ballantine, Bushby, Palmer & Wood, 1775 Pennsylvania Ave. N.W., Washington, D.C. 20006. Filed 8/29/85. Legislative interest — "... Eximbank budget and authorization, trade reform legislation, trade reorganization and other International trade legislation, industrial policy legislation."

LUGGAGE & LEATHER GOODS MANUFACTURERS OF AMERICA INC., New York, N.Y. Lobbyist — Economic Consulting Services Inc., 1320 19th St. N.W., Washington, D.C. 20036. Filed 8/22/85. Legislative interest — "Trade legislation...."

MASTER MARKETERS ASSOCIATION OF AMERICA, Alexandria, Ind. Lobbyist — Bishop, Liberman, Cook, Purcell & Reynolds, 1200 17th St. N.W., Washington, D.C. 20036. Filed 8/15/85. Legislative interest — "... Federal Crop Insurance Corporation."

NATIONAL APARTMENT ASSOCIATION, 1101 14th St. N.W., Washington, D.C. 20005. Filed for self 8/6/85. Legislative interest — "... the real estate industry ... taxes and housing." Lobbyist — Marlana Chickos.

NATIONAL ASSOCIATION FOR BIOMEDICAL RESEARCH, Washington, D.C. Lobbyist — Pierson, Ball & Dowd, 1200 18th St. N.W., Washington, D.C. 20036. Filed 8/26/85. Legislative interest — "... laboratory animal research."

NATIONAL ASSOCIATION OF METAL FINISHERS, Chicago, Ill. Lobbyist — Smith, Bucklin & Associates, 1101 Connecticut Ave. N.W., Washington, D.C. 20036. Filed 8/14/85. Legislative interest — "Clean Water Act, Superfund."

NATIONAL ASSOCIATION OF REALTORS, 777 14th St. N.W., Washington, D.C. 20005. Filed for self 8/23/85. Legislative interest — "... the real estate industry, including specifically, tax relief; independent contractor; restructuring of financial institutions; enterprise zones; coastal barrier protection; emergency tax proposals; spur housing; budget; fair housing; tax reform; and imputed interest." Lobbyists — Byron Anderson, Martin L. DePoy, Patricia A. English, Daniel P. Lucas, Walter J. Witek Jr.

NATIONAL ASSOCIATION OF WHEAT GROWERS — AD HOC COALITION OF NATIONAL FARM GROUPS ON CARGO PREFERENCE LEGISLATION, Washington, D.C. Lobbyist — Bishop, Liberman, Cook, Purcell & Reynolds, 1200 17th St. N.W., Washington, D.C. 20036. Filed 8/15/85. Legislative interest — "Cargo Preference Legislation — S 721, and cargo preference provisions of HR 2100 and other comparable bills — attempting to achieve a compromise."

NATIONAL COMMERCIAL FINANCE ASSOCIATION, 225 W. 34th St., New York, N.Y. 10001. Filed for self 8/20/85. Legislative interest — "HR 2517 & HR 2943 (R.I.C.O.); HR 2617, HR 2839, S 1214 (Bank Bribery); HR 1591 & S 744 (Clear Title)." Lobbyist — Linda S. Eisnaugle.

NATIONAL COUNCIL OF FARMER COOPERATIVES, 1800 Massachusetts Ave. N.W., Washington, D.C. 20036. Filed for self 8/15/85. Legislative interest — Not specified. Lobbyist — Terry N. Barr.

NATIONAL COUNCIL ON COMPENSATION INSURANCE, New York, N.Y. Lobbyist — Preston, Thorgrimson, Ellis & Holman, 1735 New York Ave. N.W., Washington, D.C. 20006. Filed 8/28/85. Legislative interest — "To oppose the President's proposal to tax workers' compensation and black lung benefits."

NATIONAL KNITWEAR & SPORTSWEAR ASSOCIATION, New York, N.Y. Lobbyist — Economic Consulting Services Inc., 1320 19th St. N.W., Washington, D.C. 20036. Filed 8/22/85. Legislative interest — "Trade legislation affecting the textile and apparel industry."

NATIONAL LICENSED BEVERAGE ASSOCIATION, Alexandria, Va. Lobbyist — Chwat/Weigend Associates, 400 First St. N.W., Washington, D.C. 20001. Filed 8/7/85. Legislative interest — "HR 3129, S 1529, S 1428 Minimum Drinking Age; HR 1054 excise taxes; S 412, HR 1108, Malt Beverage International Competition Act; HR 2526, Alcohol Advertising Act; HR 2656, Alcoholic Beverage Labeling Act; S 1120, S 1553 National Bottle Law; any other issues which might affect the Retail Beverage Industry, such as 'Dram Shop' Laws."

NECKWEAR ASSOCIATION OF AMERICA INC., New York, N.Y. Lobbyist — Economic Consulting Services Inc., 1320 19th St. N.W., Washington, D.C. 20036. Filed 8/22/85. Legislative interest — "Trade legislation affecting the textile and apparel industry."

NORTHWEST APPAREL AND TEXTILE ASSOCIATION, Seattle, Wash. Lobbyist — Bogle & Gates, One Thomas Circle N.W., Washington, D.C. 20005. Filed 8/1/85. (Former U.S. Rep. Joel Pritchard, R-Wash., 1973-85, was listed among agents for this client.) Legislative interest — "HR 1562 (against); S 680 (against)."

PHARMACEUTICAL MANUFACTURERS ASSOCIATION, 1100 15th St. N.W., Washington, D.C. 20005. Filed for self 8/30/85. Legislative interest — "All matters relating to health care, and, particularly, prescription medicines." Lobbyist — E. Geoffrey Littlehale.

POTATO CHIP/SNACK FOOD ASSOCIATION, 1711 King St., Alexandria, Va. 22314. Filed for self 8/22/85. Legislative interest — "... snack food industry, including energy, agricultural, and nutrition legislation." Lobbyist — Stephen E. Eure.

PUBLIC EMPLOYEES' RETIREMENT ASSOCIATION OF COLORADO, Denver, Colo. Lobbyist — McDermott, Will & Emery, 1850 K St. N.W., Washington, D.C. 20006. Filed 8/5/85. Legislative interest — "Mandatory coverage of state and local government employees under Social Security."

SEMICONDUCTOR INDUSTRY ASSOCIATION, San Jose, Calif. Lobbyist — Dewey, Ballantine, Bushby, Palmer & Wood, 1775 Pennsylvania Ave. N.W., Washington, D.C. 20006. Filed 8/29/85. Legislative interest — "... trade matters and tax matters."

SERVICE INDUSTRIES' COALITION TO PRESERVE CASH METHOD ACCOUNTING, Washington, D.C. Lobbyist — Sutherland, Asbill & Brennan, 1666 K St. N.W., Washington, D.C. 20006. Filed 8/14/85. Legislative interest — "To oppose the proposed requirement that providers of services be required to change from the cash method of accounting to an accrual method under Chapter 8.03 of the President's Tax Proposals to the Congress for Fairness, Growth and Simplicity."

SMOKELESS TOBACCO COUNCIL INC., Washington, D.C. Lobbyist — Dutko & Associates, 412 First St. S.E., Washington, D.C. 20003. Filed 8/2/85. Legislative interest — "HR 2950, HR 760, HR 3064, HR 3078."

THE SOCIETY OF THE PLASTICS INDUSTRY INC., 1025 Connecticut Ave. N.W., Washington, D.C. 20036. Filed for self 8/22/85. Legislative interest — "... the plastics industry ... petrochemical feedstocks, workplace and product safety and health, food safety, energy, transportation, international trade, and the economy." Lobbyist — Margaret Rogers.

U.S. TUNA FOUNDATION, Washington, D.C. Lobbyist — O'Connor & Hannan, 1919 Pennsylvania Ave. N.W., Washington, D.C. 20006. Filed 8/9/85. Legislative interest — "... trade and tariff issues."

WESTERN GROWERS ASSOCIATION, Irvine, Calif. Lobbyist — Bill Hecht & Associates Inc., 499 S. Capitol St. S.W., Washington, D.C. 20003. Filed 8/5/85. Legislative interest — Not specified.

Miscellaneous

AMERICAN ACADEMY OF ALLERGY AND IMMUNOLOGY/ASTHMA & ALLERGY FOUNDATION OF AMERICA, Milwaukee, Wis. Lobbyist — Capitol Associates Inc., 1156 15th St. N.W., Washington, D.C. 20005. Filed 8/14/85. Legislative interest — "... health research."

AMERICAN SECURITY COUNCIL, Boston, Va. Lobbyist — Bill Hecht & Associates Inc., 499 S. Capitol St. S.W., Washington, D.C. 20003. Filed 8/5/85. Legislative interest — Not specified.

CITIZENS COMMITTEE FOR MEDICAL RESEARCH AND HEALTH EDUCATION, New York, N.Y. Lobbyist — Capitol Associates Inc., 1156 15th St. N.W., Washington, D.C. 20005. Filed 8/14/85. Legislative interest — "... health research."

CITIZENS UNITED FOR REHABILITATION OF ERRANTS, 11 15th St. N.E., Washington, D.C. 20002. Filed 8/26/85. Legislative interest — "PL 98-473 especially sentencing commission appointments T.J.T.C. Targeted Jobs Tax Credit — especially for ex-convicts. Appropriations to Federal Bureau of Prisons — relating to programs for incarcerated mothers." Lobbyists — Pauline Sullivan, Charles S. Sullivan.

COALITION AGAINST DOUBLE TAXATION, New York, N.Y. Lobbyist — Dutko & Associates, 412 First St. S.E., Washington, D.C. 20003. Filed 8/19/85. Legislative interest — "President's proposed tax bill."

THOMAS JEFFERSON CURREY, 1900 W. Sunshine St., Springfield, Mo. 65808. Filed for self 8/19/85. Legislative interest — Not specified.

EMORY UNIVERSITY MEDICAL SCHOOL, Atlanta, Ga. Lobbyist — Capitol Associates Inc., 1156 15th St. N.W., Washington, D.C. 20005. Filed 8/14/85. Legislative interest — "... health research."

THE ENDOCRINE SOCIETY, Bethesda, Md. Lobbyist — Capitol Associates Inc., 1156 15th St. N.W., Washington, D.C. 20005. Filed 8/14/85. Legislative interest — "... health research."

EYE BANK ASSOCIATION OF AMERICA, Washington, D.C. Lobbyist — Gold & Liebengood Inc., 1050 Connecticut Ave. N.W., Washington, D.C. 20036. Filed 8/5/85. Legislative interest — "... HR 3010, Medicare Vision Reform Act and similar legislation."

FEDERATION FOR AMERICAN IMMIGRATION REFORM, 1424 16th St. N.W., Washington, D.C. 20036. Filed for self 8/6/85. Legislative interest — "Pro immigration reform legislation such as S 1200. Working to stop illegal immigration to the U.S. and to place a ceiling on legal immigration that reflects the economic & environmental realities of the 1980's." Lobbyist — Kateri A. Callahan, 102 E. Del Ray Ave., Alexandria, Va. 22301.

TERRI GOTTHELF LUPUS RESEARCH INSTITUTE, Ridgefield, Conn. Lobbyist — Capitol Associates Inc., 1156 15th St. N.W., Washington, D.C. 20005. Filed 8/14/85. Legislative interest — "... health research."

HOWARD HUGHES MEDICAL INSTITUTE, Bethesda, Md. Lobbyist — Paul H. DeLaney Jr., 1120 20th St. N.W., Washington, D.C. 20036. Filed 8/16/85. Legislative interest — "Possible legislative and interpretive changes to United States tax law in the context of the ongoing United States tax reform process."

LET THE PEOPLE BE HEARD COMMITTEE, P.O. Box 26818, Santa Ana, Calif. 92799. Filed for self 8/23/85. Legislative interest — "... Airport and Airway Development Act, also A. and A. Revenue Act and A. and A. Trust Fund ... Civil Rights Amendments." Lobbyist — John Henry Leach II.

JOHN EDWARD McNALLY, 11417 Orleans Way, Kensington, Md. 20895. Filed for self 8/5/85. Legislative interest — Not specified.

NATIONAL CONGRESS OF PARENTS AND TEACHERS, 700 N. Rush St., Chicago, Ill. 60611. Filed for self 8/2/85. Legislative interest — "... the welfare of children and youth in education, social and economic well-being, health, child labor, juvenile protection, world understanding, consumer protection and environmental concerns...." Lobbyist — Millie Waterman, 5256 Corduroy Rd., Mentor, Ohio 44060.

NATIONAL CONSUMERS LEAGUE, 600 Maryland Ave. S.W., Washington, D.C. 20024. Filed for self 8/29/85. Legislative interest — "Medicare costs, health care cost containment legislation." Lobbyist — Linda F. Golodner.

NATIONAL MULTIPLE SCLEROSIS SOCIETY, New York, N.Y. Lobbyist — Capitol Associates Inc., 1156 15th St. N.W., Washington, D.C. 20005. Filed 8/14/85. Legislative interest — "... health research."

THE NOBEL FOUNDATION, Stockholm, Sweden. Lobbyist — Arnold & Porter, 1200 New Hampshire Ave. N.W., Washington, D.C. 20036. Filed 8/12/85. Legislative interest — "Tax proposals regarding the taxation of prizes."

PROJECT ORBIS, New York, N.Y. Lobbyist — Anderson, Hibey, Nauheim & Blair, 1708 New Hampshire Ave. N.W., Washington, D.C. 20009. Filed 8/19/85. Legislative interest — "Bills to amend the Foreign Assistance Act of 1961: S 960, HR 1650."

RULE OF LAW COMMITTEE, Washington, D.C. Lobbyist — Steptoe & Johnson, 1330 Connecticut Ave. N.W., Washington, D.C. 20036. Filed for self 8/12/85. Legislative interest — "... A bill to amend title 9 of the U.S.C. regarding arbitral awards ... S 1395 ... For."

TEXAS EDUCATION FOUNDATION, San Marcos, Texas. Lobbyist — Rice, Porter & Seiller, 2200 Meidinger Tower, Louisville, Ky. 40202. Filed 8/14/85. Legislative interest — "Support adequate FY 1986 funding for Job Corps (Title IV - B PL 97-300) ... First concurrent Budget Resolution for FY 1986; FY 1986 Labor - HHS - Education Appropriations Bills ... S Con Res 32, H Con Res 153, Conf. Rpt. 99-249 ... Support...."

THE WILDERNESS SOCIETY, 1400 Eye St. N.W., Washington, D.C. 20005. Filed for self 8/19/85. Legislative interest — "HR 2577 - 1985 Supplemental Appropriations Bill (for); HR 3011 - Interior Appropriations Bill (for) 1986; HR 2790, S 1406 - Grazings Fee Bill (Against)." Lobbyist — Norbert J. Riedy Jr. Filed for self 8/22/85. Legislative interest — "White Mountains National Forest, New Hampshire and Maine." Lobbyist — Sarah Muyskens.

September Registrations

Corporations and Businesses

AMERICAN PETROFINA, Dallas, Texas. Lobbyist — Manatt, Phelps, Rothenberg, Tunney & Evans, 1200 New Hampshire Ave. N.W., Washington, D.C. 20036. Filed 9/13/85. (Former U.S. Rep. Thomas B. Evans Jr., R-Del., 1977-83, was listed as agent for this client.) Legislative interest — "... promoting the promulgation of a rule allowing permanent payback of construction differential subsidies, and other matters."

AMERICAN REF-FUEL, Houston, Texas. Lobbyist — Karalekas, McCahill, Wilson & Iovino, 1250 Connecticut Ave. N.W., Washington, D.C. 20036. Filed 9/13/85. Legislative interest — "... tax exemption for interest on Industrial Development Bonds."

BALLARD, SPAHR, ANDREWS & INGERSOLL, 1850 K St. N.W., Washington, D.C. 20006. Filed for self 9/23/85. Legislative interest — "... Tax Exempt Bonds, Amend. RICO Act." Lobbyist — Laurie Michel.

BASKIN & STEINGUT, 818 Connecticut Ave. N.W., Washington, D.C. 20006. Filed for self 9/12/85. Legislative interest — "... Norfolk Southern Corporation." Lobbyist — G. Kent Woodman.

BROWNING-FERRIS INDUSTRIES, P.O. Box 3151, Houston, Texas 77253. Filed for self 9/16/85. Legislative interest — "... waste service industry." Lobbyist — Fred C. Himes.

CADILLAC FAIRVIEW U.S. INC., White Plains, N.Y. Lobbyist — Craig Hackler, 412 First St. S.E., Washington, D.C. 20003. Filed 9/30/85. Legislative interest — "Tax reform legislation ... 'Tax Reform for Fairness, Simplicity and Economic Growth' (Treasury I) ... Generally, For."

CARNIVAL CRUISE LINES, Miami, Fla. Lobbyist — Alcalde, Henderson, O'Bannon & Rousselot, 1901 N. Ft. Myer Dr., Arlington, Va. 22209. Filed 9/20/85. Legislative interest — "... business and tax issues ... Part C of Section 251 of HR 3128 (ag) and HR 277 (position not yet determined)."

CHRONAR CORP., Princeton, N.J. Lobbyist — Manatt, Phelps, Rothenberg, Tunney & Evans, 1200 New Hampshire Ave. N.W., Washington, D.C. 20036. Filed 9/13/85. (Former U.S. Rep. Thomas B. Evans Jr., R-Del., 1977-83, was listed as agent for this client.) Legislative interest — "... tax issues affecting solar energy."

COMMUNICATIONS SATELLITE CORP., 950 L'Enfant Plaza S.W., Washington, D.C. 20024. Filed for self 9/13/85. Legislative interest — "... communications, especially the Communications Act of 1934 and the Communications Satellite Act of 1962." Lobbyist — Thomas Andrew Scully. Filed for self 9/25/85. Legislative interest — "... Matters pertaining to telecommunications and related fields ... HR 1175 introduced by Rep. Markey, International Telecommunications Act of 1985; Communications Act of 1934 and the Communications Satellite Act of 1962." Lobbyist — Richard L. McGraw.

COMPUTERLAND CORP., Oakland, Calif. Lobbyist — Patton, Boggs & Blow, 2550 M St. N.W., Washington, D.C. 20037. Filed 9/16/85. Legislative interest — "... tax reform...."

THE CONWOOD CORP., Memphis, Tenn. Lobbyist — Baker, Worthington, Crossley, Stansberry & Woolf, P.O. Box 2866, Nashville, Tenn. 37219. Filed 9/30/85. Legislative interest — "... tobacco issues."

CROWLEY MARITIME CORP., San Francisco, Calif. Lobbyist — Patton, Boggs & Blow, 2550 M St. N.W., Washington, D.C. 20037. Filed 9/16/85. Legislative interest — "Opposition to tax reform proposal to repeal capital construction fund provisions contained in section 607 of Merchant Marine Act."

DOMINION PROPERTY CO., Santa Monica, Calif. Lobbyist — Corman Law Offices, 1420 16th St. N.W., Washington, D.C. 20036. Filed 9/18/85. Legislative interest — "... proposed changes in the Internal Revenue Code affecting real estate transactions."

EAGLE ENGINEERING INC., Houston, Texas. Lobbyist — A. B. Virkler, 77 Sycamore Circle, Ormond Beach, Fla. 32074. Filed 9/25/85. Legislative interest — Not specified.

ENSERCH, Washington, D.C. Lobbyist — McNair, Glenn, Konduros, Corley, Singletary, Porter & Dibble, 1155 15th St. N.W., Washington, D.C. 20005. Filed 9/3/85. Legislative interest — "Energy & legislative tax issues."

ESPERANZA ENERGY CO., Dallas, Texas. Lobbyist — McNair, Glenn, Konduros, Corley, Singletary, Porter & Dibble, 1155 15th St. N.W., Washington, D.C. 20005. Filed 9/3/85. Legislative interest — "Energy & legislative tax issues."

FEDERATED COST MANAGEMENT SYSTEMS, Pittsburgh, Pa. Lobbyist — Barrett, Montgomery & Murphy, 2555 M St. N.W., Washington, D.C. 20037. Filed 9/30/85. Legislative interest — "... money market funds."

FIRST PENNSYLVANIA BANK, Philadelphia, Pa. Lobbyist — Manatt, Phelps, Rothenberg, Tunney & Evans, 1200 New Hampshire Ave. N.W., Washington, D.C. 20036. Filed 9/13/85. (Former U.S. Rep. Thomas B. Evans Jr., R-Del., 1977-83, was listed as agent for this client.) Legislative interest — "... the FDIC."

FLINT INDUSTRIES, Tulsa, Okla. Lobbyist — Patton, Boggs & Blow, 2550 M St. N.W., Washington, D.C. 20037. Filed 9/16/85. Legislative interest — "... tax reform ... proposals affecting related party insurance."

HOGAN & HARTSON, Washington, D.C. Lobbyist — Kendall & Associates, 50 E St. S.E., Washington, D.C. 20003. Filed 9/27/85. Legislative interest — "Quota bills on shoe imports (S 848) — opposed."

E. F. HUTTON INC., New York, N.Y. Lobbyist — Winthrop, Stimson, Putnam & Roberts, 1155 Connecticut Ave. N.W., Washington, D.C. 20036. Filed 9/24/85. Legislative interest — Not specified.

INSURANCE SERVING AND INFORMATION SYSTEMS CORP., Rockville, Md. Lobbyist — Neill, Mullenholz, Shaw & Seeger, 900 17th St. N.W., Washington, D.C. 20006. Filed 9/19/85. Legislative interest — "... extending federal crime insurance, more specifically, HR 1 and other related bills in support of."

THE IRVINE CO., Newport Beach, Calif. Lobbyist — Leon G. Billings Inc., 1660 L St. N.W., Washington, D.C. 20036. Filed 9/27/85. Legislative interest — "Securing a provision in the Clean Water Act of 1985 for Irvine Ranch Water District ocean outfall ... relating to water and toxic wastes."

ISHAM, LINCOLN & BEALE, 1120 Connecticut Ave. N.W., Washington, D.C. 20036. Filed for self 9/12/85. Legislative interest — "... Norfolk Southern Corporation." Lobbyist — J. Paul Molloy.

KAISER ALUMINUM & CHEMICAL CORP., Oakland, Calif. Lobbyist — Patton, Boggs & Blow, 2550 M St. N.W., Washington, D.C. 20037. Filed 9/16/85. Legislative interest — "General tax reform proposals affecting capital cost recovery and proposed corporate minimum tax."

LOAN AMERICA FINANCIAL CORP., Miami, Fla. Lobbyist — Patton, Boggs & Blow, 2550 M St. N.W., Washington, D.C. 20037. Filed 9/16/85. Legislative interest — "Opposed to S 1314 and HR 2783, which would impose uniform listing standards respecting classes of stock with disparate voting rights."

MCI COMMUNICATIONS CORP., 1133 19th St. N.W., Washington, D.C. 20036. Filed for self 9/26/85. Legislative interest — "Legislation affecting competition in telecommunications." Lobbyist — Robert D. Swezey Jr.

MATSON NAVIGATION CO., San Francisco, Calif. Lobbyist — Patton, Boggs & Blow, 2550 M St. N.W., Washington, D.C. 20037. Filed 9/16/85. Legislative interest — "Opposition to tax reform proposal to repeal capital construction fund provisions contained in section 607 of Merchant Marine Act."

MESSERSCHMITT, BOLKOW-BLOHM GMBH, Munich, West Germany. Lobbyist — Benner, Burnett & Coleman, 1401 New York Ave. N.W., Washington, D.C. 20005. Filed 9/30/85. Legislative interest — "... space commerce and exploration, and Space Station ... Outer Space Inventions Act ... HR 3112 ... for bill."

NORTHWESTERN MUTUAL LIFE INSURANCE CO., Milwaukee, Wis. Lobbyist — McNair, Glenn, Konduros, Corley, Singletary, Porter & Dibble, 1155 15th St. N.W., Washington, D.C. 20005. Filed 9/3/85. Legislative interest — "Tax reform & fringe benefits issues."

NORWEGIAN CARIBBEAN LINES, Miami, Fla. Lobbyist — Alcalde, Henderson, O'Bannon & Rousselot, 1901 N. Ft. Myer Dr., Arlington, Va. 22209. Filed 9/20/85. Legislative interest — "... business and tax issues ... Part C of Section 251 of HR 3128 (ag) and HR 277 (position not yet determined)."

O'CONNOR & ASSOCIATES, Chicago, Ill. Lobbyist — Barrett, Montgomery & Murphy, 2555 M St. N.W., Washington, D.C. 20037. Filed 9/30/85. Legislative interest — "Legislation affecting options traders."

OMNINET CORP., Los Angeles, Calif. Lobbyist — Benner, Burnett & Coleman, 1401 New York Ave. N.W., Washington, D.C. 20005. Filed 9/30/85. Legislative interest — "FCC authorization, appropriations and oversight; legislation affecting telecommunications."

PACIFIC RESOURCES INC., P.O. Box 3379, Honolulu, Hawaii 96813. Filed for self 9/23/85. Legislative interest — Not specified. Lobbyists — Christine M. Boris, Richard F. Hall, 2501 M St. N.W., Washington, D.C. 20037.

PECHINEY CORP., Greenwich, Conn. Lobbyist — Ivins, Phillips & Barker, 1700 Pennsylvania Ave. N.W., Washington, D.C. 20006. Filed 9/30/85. Legislative interest — "Tax reform legislation, specifically, changes affecting present tax treatment of '80/20' companies."

PHILADELPHIA PORT CORP., Philadelphia, Pa. Lobbyist — Burson-Marsteller, 1825 I St. N.W., Washington, D.C. 20006. Filed 9/26/85. Legislative interest — "User Fee Legislation."

PHILIP MORRIS INC., 1875 I St. N.W., Washington, D.C. 20006. Filed for self 9/27/85. Legislative interest — "... the manufacture and sale of tobacco products, beer and soft drinks, and community development." Lobbyists — Kathleen M. Linehan, Amy J. Millman, Gregory R. Scott.

PROVIDENT LIFE & ACCIDENT INSURANCE CO., Chattanooga, Tenn. Lobbyist — Scribner, Hall & Thompson, 1875 I St. N.W., Washington, D.C. 20006. Filed 9/27/85. Legislative interest — "... taxation of insurance companies...."

THE PYRAMID COS., Boston, Mass. Lobbyist — Manatt, Phelps, Rothenberg, Tunney & Evans, 1200 New Hampshire Ave. N.W., Washington, D.C. 20036. Filed 9/13/85. (Former U.S. Rep. Thomas B. Evans Jr., R-Del., 1977-83, was listed as agent for this client.) Legislative interest — "... the Clean Water Act."

RLC CORP., Wilmington, Del. Lobbyist — Manatt, Phelps, Rothenberg, Tunney & Evans, 1200 New Hampshire Ave. N.W., Washington, D.C. 20036. Filed 9/13/85. (Former U.S. Rep. Thomas B. Evans Jr., R-Del., 1977-83, was listed as agent for this client.) Legislative interest — Not specified.

R/S/M INC., 1012 Pennsylvania Ave. S.E., Washington, D.C. 20003. Filed for self 9/4/85. Legislative interest — "Taxation, Health, Energy Issues...." Lobbyist — Cleve Benedict (former U.S. representative, R-W.Va., 1981-83).

ROLLINS ENVIRONMENTAL SERVICES, Wilmington, Del. Lobbyist — Manatt, Phelps, Rothenberg, Tunney & Evans, 1200 New Hampshire Ave. N.W., Washington, D.C. 20036. Filed 9/13/85. (Former U.S. Rep. Thomas B. Evans Jr., R-Del., 1977-83, was listed as agent for this client.) Legislative interest — Not specified.

ROYAL CARIBBEAN CRUISE LINE, Miami, Fla. Lobbyist — Alcalde, Henderson, O'Bannon & Rousselot, 1901 N. Ft. Myer Dr., Arlington, Va. 22209. Filed 9/20/85. Legislative interest — "... business and tax issues ... Part C of Section 251 of HR 3128 (ag) and HR 277 (position not yet determined)."

SABINE CORP., Dallas, Texas. Lobbyist — McNair, Glenn, Konduros, Corley, Singletary, Porter & Dibble, 1155 15th St. N.W., Washington, D.C. 20005. Filed 9/3/85. Legislative interest — "Energy & legislative tax issues."

SANDOZ CHEMICALS CORP., Charlotte, N.C. Lobbyist — Edith W. Marsh, 200 W. Morgan St., Raleigh, N.C. 27601. Filed 9/18/85. Legislative interest — "Superfund Legislation."

SECURITY FIRST GROUP, Los Angeles, Calif. Lobbyist — Manatt, Phelps, Rothenberg, Tunney & Evans, 1200 New Hampshire Ave. N.W., Washington, D.C. 20036. Filed 9/25/85. Legislative interest — ". . . tax treatment of employees' retirement plans."

SONAT INC., Birmingham, Ala. Lobbyist — Luther J. Strange III, 1100 15th St. N.W., Washington, D.C. 20005. Filed 9/30/85. Legislative interest — ". . . interstate natural gas transmission, offshore drilling, oil and gas exploration and production, forest products and marine transportation."

SOUTH JERSEY PORT CORP., Camden, N.J. Lobbyist — Burson-Marsteller, 1825 I St. N.W., Washington, D.C. 20006. Filed 9/26/85. Legislative interest — "User Fee Legislation."

SUN CO., Radnor, Pa. Lobbyist — David P. Stang, 1629 K St. N.W., Washington, D.C. 20006. Filed 9/26/85. Legislative interest — "HR 3179, a bill to amend IRC of 1954 to provide that employees may make certain contributions to provide for cost-of-living protection under a defined benefit plan."

TEKTRONIX INC., P.O. Box 500, Beaverton, Ore. 97077. Filed for self 9/3/85. Legislative interest — "Tax Policy - Treasury II . . . International Trade - EAA . . . Environmental Issues . . . Intellectual Property Rights . . . R&D Investments . . . Employee Fringe Benefits . . . Government Contracting . . . Commercial Vendor . . . Educational Issues. . . ." Lobbyist — Gary L. Conkling.

TEMPLE-INLAND, Diboll, Texas. Lobbyist — J. Lem Anderson, 4111 Franconia Rd., Alexandria, Va. 22310. Filed 9/3/85. Legislative interest — "The Tax Bill, Canadian Forest Products Importation Bill."

TEXAS OIL & GAS CORP., Dallas, Texas. Lobbyist — McNair, Glenn, Konduros, Corley, Singletary, Porter & Dibble, 1155 15th St. N.W., Washington, D.C. 20005. Filed 9/3/85. Legislative interest — "Energy & legislative tax issues."

TRAWEEK INVESTMENT CO. INC., Marina Del Rey, Calif. Lobbyist — Manatt, Phelps, Rothenberg, Tunney & Evans, 1200 New Hampshire Ave. N.W., Washington, D.C. 20036. Filed 9/23/85. Legislative interest — "Legislative tax issues pertaining to real estate."

UNIVERSAL HOVERCRAFT, Reno, Nev. Lobbyist — Dickstein, Shapiro & Morin, 2101 L St. N.W., Washington, D.C. 20037. Filed 9/19/85. Legislative interest — ". . . operation of hovercraft."

WESSLEY ENERGY CORP., Dallas, Texas. Lobbyist — McNair, Glenn, Konduros, Corley, Singletary, Porter & Dibble, 1155 15th St. N.W., Washington, D.C. 20005. Filed 9/3/85. Legislative interest — "Tax reform issues."

WILLARD & ARNOLD COMMUNICATIONS, 405 Capitol St., Charleston, W.Va. 25301. Filed for self 9/20/85. Legislative interest — "Norfolk Southern Corp. - Conrail acquisition legislation - for NS purchase . . . Sears Roebuck Co. - family/consumer banking legislation - in favor of (legislation not yet introduced)."

Foreign Governments

GOVERNMENT OF CYPRUS, Washington, D.C. Lobbyist — Manatt, Phelps, Rothenberg, Tunney & Evans, 1200 New Hampshire Ave. N.W., Washington, D.C. 20036. Filed 9/13/85. (Former U.S. Rep. Thomas B. Evans Jr., R-Del., 1977-83, was listed as agent for this client.) Legislative interest — ". . . monitoring foreign assistance legislation and promoting the best interests of Cyprus in the formulation of economic support funding and military assistance legislation affecting that country."

GOVERNMENT OF JAMAICA, Kingston, Jamaica. Lobbyist — Manatt, Phelps, Rothenberg, Tunney & Evans, 1200 New Hampshire Ave. N.W., Washington, D.C. 20036. Filed 9/13/85. (Former U.S. Rep. Thomas B. Evans Jr., R-Del., 1977-83, was listed as agent for this client.) Legislative interest — ". . . monitoring foreign assistance legislation and promoting the best interests of Jamaica in the formulation of economic support funding and other foreign assistance legislation affecting that country."

JAMAICA BROADCASTING CORP., Kingston, Jamaica. Lobbyist — Manatt, Phelps, Rothenberg, Tunney & Evans, 1200 New Hampshire Ave. N.W., Washington, D.C. 20036. Filed 9/13/85. (Former U.S. Rep. Thomas B. Evans Jr., R-Del., 1977-83, was listed as agent for this client.) Legislative interest — ". . . copyright law."

Labor Organizations

INTERNATIONAL UNION OF OPERATING ENGINEERS, 1125 17th St. N.W., Washington, D.C. 20036. Filed for self 9/5/85. Legislative interest — ". . . organized labor." Lobbyist — J. C. Turner.

NATIONAL TREASURY EMPLOYEES UNION, 1730 K St. N.W., Washington, D.C. 20006. Filed for self 9/4/85. Legislative interest — "All matters before the Appropriations committees; Trade issues before Ways & Means and Finance committees and all Federal Civil Service issues before Post Office & Civil Service and Governmental Affairs committees." Lobbyist — Paul W. Newton, 6060 Hollow Hill Lane, Springfield, Va. 22152. Filed for self 9/5/85. Legislative interest — "Civil Service pay and benefits legislation, federal occupational safety and health, Department of Health and Human Services appropriations. HR 1534, HR 3008, S 519." Lobbyist — Cathy E. Overly. Filed for self 9/5/85. Legislative interest — "All matters before Appropriations committees; Ways & Means and Finance committees, all civil service issues before Post Office & Civil Service and Governmental Affairs committees." Lobbyist — James R. Lawrence, 1004 Markham St., Silver Spring, Md. 20901.

SHEET METAL WORKERS' INTERNATIONAL ASSOCIATION, Washington, D.C. Lobbyist — Dewey, Ballantine, Bushby, Palmer & Wood, 1775 Pennsylvania Ave. N.W., Washington, D.C. 20006. Filed 9/18/85. Legislative interest — "Tax legislative matters. . . ."

State and Local Governments

CITY OF PHILADELPHIA, Philadelphia, Pa. Lobbyist — Burson-Marsteller, 1825 I St. N.W., Washington, D.C. 20006. Filed 9/26/85. Legislative interest — "Tax Legislation."

COMMUNITY REDEVELOPMENT AGENCY, CITY OF LOS ANGELES, Los Angeles, Calif. Lobbyist — Latham, Watkins & Hills, 1333 New Hampshire Ave. N.W., Washington, D.C. 20036. Filed 9/12/85. Legislative interest — ". . . Administration's various tax reform bills . . . Favor modifications in these bills."

COUNTY OF NAPA, Napa, Calif. Lobbyist — A-K Associates Inc., 1225 8th St., Sacramento, Calif. 95814. Filed 9/19/85. Legislative interest — "Funding for County Jail facilities."

Trade Associations

AGRICULTURE FOR MARKET ORIENTED POLICIES, Washington, D.C. Lobbyist — Gray & Co., 3255 Grace St. N.W., Washington, D.C. 20007. Filed 9/5/85. Legislative interest — ". . . lobbying on behalf of marketing orders and the citrus industry."

AMERICAN ASSOCIATION OF EXPORTERS AND IMPORTERS, New York, N.Y. Lobbyist — International Business & Economic Research Corp., 2121 K St. N.W., Washington, D.C. 20037. Filed 9/12/85. Legislative interest — "Proposals to restrict textile imports, e.g., HR 1562, S 680."

AMERICAN INSTITUTE OF CERTIFIED PUBLIC ACCOUNTANTS, 1211 Avenue of the Americas, New York, N.Y. 10036. Filed for self 9/10/85. Legislative interest — ". . .

traditional accounting & auditing practices, or independent public accountants." Lobbyist — Mary Frances Widner, 1620 I St. N.W., Washington, D.C. 20006.

AMERICAN MEDICAL INTERNATIONAL, Beverly Hills, Calif. Lobbyist — Rebecca L. Kupper, 655 15th St. N.W., Washington, D.C. 20005. Filed 9/19/85. Legislative interest — "... the health and health insurance industries."

AMERICAN SOCIETY OF ANESTHESIOLOGISTS, Park Ridge, Ill. Lobbyist — Daniel C. Maldonado, 10000 Falls Rd., Potomac, Md. 20854. Filed 9/20/85. Legislative interest — "... reimbursement for services and patient care by anesthesiologists."

ASSOCIACAO COMERCIAL E INDUSTRIAL DE NOVO HAMBURGO, Novo Hamburgo, Brazil. Lobbyist — Wald, Harkrader & Ross, 1300 19th St. N.W., Washington, D.C. 20036. Filed 9/30/85. Legislative interest — "... import restrictions on nonrubber footwear."

ASSOCIACAO INDUSTRIAS DE CALCADOS DE RIO GRANDE DO SUL, Novo Hamburgo, Brazil. Lobbyist — Wald, Harkrader & Ross, 1300 19th St. N.W., Washington, D.C. 20036. Filed 9/30/85. Legislative interest — "... import restrictions on nonrubber footwear."

ASSOCIATION OF GREYHOUND TRACK OPERATORS OF AMERICA, North Miami, Fla. Lobbyist — Barrett, Montgomery & Murphy, 2555 M St. N.W., Washington, D.C. 20037. Filed 9/30/85. Legislative interest — "... gambling on Indian Reservations."

CAMARA DE LA INDUSTRIA DE TRANSFORMACION DE NUEVO LEON, Monterrey, Mexico. Lobbyist — Brownstein, Zeidman & Schomer, 1401 New York Ave. N.W., Washington, D.C. 20005. Filed 9/30/85. Legislative interest — "... international trade, e.g., HR 2345, S 1292; against such bills."

CELLULAR TELECOMMUNICATIONS INDUSTRY ASSOCIATION, 1150 17th St. N.W., Washington, D.C. 20036. Filed for self 9/3/85. Legislative interest — "... telecommunications privacy." Lobbyist — Robert W. Maher.

CHAMBER OF COMMERCE OF THE UNITED STATES, 1615 H St. N.W., Washington, D.C. 20062. Filed for self 9/12/85. Legislative interest — Not specified. Lobbyists — Robert L. Martin, William D. Kelleher.

CHEMICAL MANUFACTURERS ASSOCIATION, Washington, D.C. Lobbyist — Barrett, Montgomery & Murphy, 2555 M St. N.W., Washington, D.C. 20037. Filed 9/30/85. Legislative interest — "Superfund Legislation."

THE COMPUTER & BUSINESS EQUIPMENT MANUFACTURERS ASSOCIATION, 311 First St. N.W., Washington, D.C. 20001. Filed for self 9/17/85. Legislative interest — Not specified. Lobbyist — Susan Stuebing.

COUNCIL FOR PERIODICAL DISTRIBUTORS ASSOCIATION, New York, N.Y. Lobbyist — Sidley & Austin, 1722 I St. N.W., Washington, D.C. 20006. Filed 9/26/85. Legislative interest — "The President's Tax Reform Proposal. Working Against Repeal of Section 458 of Tax Code."

DAIRY FARMERS FOR RESPONSIBLE FARM POLICY, 517 C St. N.E., Washington, D.C. 20002. Filed for self 9/13/85. Legislative interest — "Legislation that would regulate or support the production and processing of dairy products, including but not limited to HR 2100." Lobbyists — Robert Feenstra, Joseph Lang.

EDISON ELECTRIC INSTITUTE, Washington, D.C. Lobbyist — Aycock Associates, 1899 L St. N.W., Washington, D.C. 20036. Filed 9/20/85. Legislative interest — "Energy tax issues/utility industry, decommissioning, tax reform proposal. Generally in favor of tax reform with specific concerns relating to capital formation incentives, accelerated depreciation, investment tax credit, normalization and employee benefits."

ELECTRONIC FUNDS TRANSFER ASSOCIATION, 1726 M St. N.W., Washington, D.C. 20036. Filed for self 9/23/85. Legislative interest — Not specified. Lobbyist — James Callan.

FEDERATION OF AMERICAN HOSPITALS, 1111 19th St. N.W., Washington, D.C. 20036. Lobbyist — Dewey, Ballantine, Bushby, Palmer & Wood, 1775 Pennsylvania Ave. N.W., Washington, D.C. 20006. Filed 9/18/85. Legislative interest — "Tax legislative matters...." Filed for self 9/25/85. Legislative interest — "Specifically Medicare, National Health Insurance and Hospital Cost Containment Legislation." Lobbyist — Lynn S. Hart.

FIBER, FABRIC & APPAREL COALITION FOR TRADE, 1800 M St. N.W., Washington, D.C. 20036. Filed for self 9/16/85. Legislative interest — "... import of textiles or textile related products into the United States." Lobbyist — Park R. Davidson.

GROCERY MANUFACTURERS OF AMERICA INC., 1010 Wisconsin Ave. N.W., Washington, D.C. 20007. Filed for self 9/30/85. Legislative interest — "VAT Tax/Superfund." Lobbyist — Jo Anne Singley Sharlack. Filed for self 9/30/85. Legislative interest — "... Tax Reform." Lobbyist — Richard P. Swigart.

HOUSING AMERICA FOUNDATION, Washington, D.C. Lobbyist — Manatt, Phelps, Rothenberg, Tunney & Evans, 1200 New Hampshire Ave. N.W., Washington, D.C. 20036. Filed 9/13/85. (Former U.S. Rep. Thomas B. Evans Jr., R-Del., 1977-83, was listed as agent for this client.) Legislative interest — "... tax issues related to multi-family housing."

INTERNATIONAL ASSOCIATION OF AUDITORIUM MANAGERS, Chicago, Ill. Lobbyist — Akin, Gump, Strauss, Hauer & Feld, 1333 New Hampshire Ave. N.W., Washington, D.C. 20036. Filed 9/5/85. Legislative interest — "... deductibility of business entertainment expenses and legislation relating to the applicability of the Fair Labor Standards Act to public employees."

KOREAN FOOTWEAR EXPORTERS ASSOCIATION, Seoul, South Korea. Lobbyist — Oppenheimer, Wolff, Foster, Shepard & Donnelly, 1317 F St. N.W., Washington, D.C. 20004. Filed 9/12/85. Legislative interest — "Defeat legislation imposing quotas or other restraints on U.S. footwear imports, such as S 848, the 'American Footwear Industry Recovery Act of 1985.'"

MILK PRODUCERS COUNCIL, Ontario, Calif. Lobbyist — Dairy Farmers for Responsible Dairy Policy, 517 C St. N.E., Washington, D.C. 20002. Filed 9/13/85. Legislative interest — "Legislation that would regulate or support the production and processing of dairy products, including but not limited to HR 2100."

NATIONAL FOOD BROKERS ASSOCIATION, 1010 Massachusetts Ave. N.W., Washington, D.C. 20001. Filed for self 9/13/85. Legislative interest — "Food industry issues, tax issues, antitrust issues and small business issues ... 'Fair Tax Act of 1985' and 'Fair and Simple Tax Act of 1985' ... HR 800, HR 2222, S 409 and S 325 ... For some sections and against some sections." Lobbyist — Wilbur H. Hamilton III.

NATIONAL PORK PRODUCERS COUNCIL, Des Moines, Iowa. Lobbyist — Thompson, Hine & Flory, 1920 N St. N.W., Washington, D.C. 20036. Filed 9/20/85. Legislative interest — "... treatment of agricultural products, under the trade laws. S 1629."

NEW YORK STATE BANKERS ASSOCIATION, New York, N.Y. Lobbyist — R. Duffy Wall & Associates Inc., 1317 F St. N.W., Washington, D.C. 20004. Filed 9/17/85. Legislative interest — "... general tax legislation."

PETROLEUM EQUIPMENT SUPPLIERS ASSOCIATION, 9225 Katy Freeway, Houston, Texas 77024. Filed for self 9/4/85. Legislative interest — "... the oilfield service industry including tax reform, energy, and trade." Lobbyist — J. Stephen Larkin.

Miscellaneous

ALLIANCE FOR A COMPETITIVE AMERICA, Washington, D.C. Lobbyist — Manatt, Phelps, Rothenberg, Tunney & Evans, 1200 New Hampshire Ave. N.W., Washington, D.C. 20036. Filed 9/13/85. (Former U.S. Rep. Thomas B. Evans Jr., R-Del., 1977-83, was listed as agent for this client.) Legislative interest — "... issues relating to high yield bonds."

AMERICAN COLLEGE OF EMERGENCY PHYSICIANS, 1125 Executive Circle, Irving, Texas 75038. Filed for self 9/3/85. Legislative interest — "Health care legislation ... the

Social Security Act Titles XVIII and XIX (Medicare and Medicaid) and the Public Health Service Act . . . Medicare and Medicaid reform, graduate medical education financing, and Medicare budget reconciliation provision relating to hospital and physician responsibilities in emergency cases." Lobbyist — Virginia L. Pitcher, 2000 L St. N.W., Washington, D.C. 20036.

ASSOCIATION OF UNIVERSITY PROGRAMS IN OCCUPATIONAL HEALTH AND SAFETY, Berkeley, Calif. Lobbyist — Daniel C. Maldonado, 10000 Falls Rd., Potomac, Md. 20854. Filed 9/20/85. Legislative interest — "Superfund legislation, primarily HR 2817 and S 51."

CARNEGIE-MELLON UNIVERSITY, 5000 Forbes Ave., Pittsburgh, Pa. 15213. Filed for self 9/30/85. Legislative interest — ". . . authorization and appropriation of funds for Departments of Agriculture, Commerce, Defense, Education, Energy, Health & Human Services, Housing and Urban Development, Interior, Justice, Labor, State, Treasury and independent agencies (NSF, EPA, NASA) . . . funding for university research activities." Lobbyist — Margaret M. McCormick.

CHILDREN'S DEFENSE FUND, 122 C St. N.W., Washington, D.C. 20001. Filed for self 9/30/85. Legislative interest — "Health legislation affecting children (Medicaid, Title V, Maternal and Child Health Block Grant)." Lobbyist — Kay Johnson.

COMMON CAUSE, 2030 M St. N.W., Washington, D.C. 20036. Filed for self 9/5/85. Legislative interest — "HR 323: To establish an office of the Attorney General for the District of Columbia, to transfer prosecutorial authority for local offenses to the D.C. government, and to provide for the local appointment of judges for the D.C. courts . . . HR 324: To amend the D.C. Self-Government Act to provide for autonomy for the D.C. government over expenditure of funds derived from D.C. revenues . . . HR 2639: To transfer the ownership of RFK Stadium to the District of Columbia . . . HR 2642: To establish a formula based Federal payment for the District . . . HR 2717: To establish an independent jury system for the District of Columbia." Lobbyist — Kurt Vorndran.

DEVELOPMENT CORPORATION FOR ISRAEL, New York, N.Y. Lobbyist — Finley, Kumble, Wagner, Heine, Underberg, Manley & Casey, 1120 Connecticut Ave. N.W., Washington, D.C. 20036. Filed 9/30/85. Legislative interest — "Seeking legislation to exempt Israel bonds from Section 7872 of IRS Code."

EMBRY-RIDDLE AERONAUTICAL UNIVERSITY, Bunnell, Fla. Lobbyist — A. B. Virkler, 77 Sycamore Circle, Ormond Beach, Fla. 32074. Filed 9/25/85. Legislative interest — Not specified.

ENVIRONMENTAL POLICY INSTITUTE, 218 D St. S.E., Washington, D.C. 20003. Filed for self 9/26/85. Legislative interest — ". . . energy and environmental policy." Lobbyist — Heidi Hanson. Filed for self 9/26/85. Legislative interest — ". . . energy conservation, fuel efficiency, mass transportation, and highway maintenance." Lobbyist — Arnita Hannon.

JOHN B. FRANZ, P.O. Box 10568, Pompano Beach, Fla. 33061. Filed for self 9/20/85. Legislative interest — "Art and Fine Arts."

FRIENDS OF THE COLUMBIA RIVER GORGE, Portland, Ore. Lobbyist — Riddell, William, Bullitt & Walkinshaw, 4400 Seattle First National Bank Bldg., Seattle, Wash. 98154. Filed 9/24/85. Legislative interest — "A federal bill for management of the Columbia River Gorge area sponsored by the Senators from Oregon & Washington."

GRASSROOTS, NATIONAL ASSOCIATION OF FARM CREDIT SYSTEM STOCKHOLDERS, 501 Alabama St., Jacksonville, Texas 75766. Filed for self 9/5/85. Legislative interest — "Passage of a Farm Credit Bill to amend 1971 Act." Lobbyist — Luman W. Holman.

ISIAH CARL GREEN, P.O. Box 38, Huntsville, Texas 77344. Filed for self 9/18/85. Legislative interest — "Criminal Justice Administration, Pardon, Parole, Etc."

INTERNATIONAL ORGANIZATION OF CONSUMER UNIONS, The Hague, Netherlands. Lobbyist — Esther Peterson, 7714 13th St. N.W., Washington, D.C. 20012. Filed 9/17/85. Legislative interest — ". . . consumer issues before the United Nations. . . ."

JOINT MARITIME CONGRESS, 444 North Capitol St. N.W., Washington, D.C. 20001. Filed for self 9/4/85. Legislative interest — "Transportation and maritime related legislation." Lobbyists — Bruce J. Carlton, Julie S. Lee.

KHA GROUP APPEAL LEGAL FUND, Louisville, Ky. Lobbyist — Rice, Porter & Seiller, 2200 Meidinger Tower, Louisville, Ky. 40202. Filed 9/19/85. Legislative interest — "To protect the interest of various non-profit Ky. hospitals in prospective legislation affecting the Medicare Program . . . Medicare and Medicaid Budget Reconciliation Amendments of 1985; Health Care Financing Cost Reduction Amendments of 1985 . . . HR 3128; HR 3101; HR 3290; HR 3084; S 1550 . . . 42 USC Section 1395 et seq. . . . Support and oppose various provisions. . . ."

NATIONAL ASSOCIATION FOR HOME CARE, Washington, D.C. Lobbyist — Williams & Jensen, 1101 Connecticut Ave. N.W., Washington, D.C. 20036. Filed 9/24/85. Legislative interest — "Medicare legislation."

NATIONAL COMMITTEE AGAINST REPRESSIVE LEGISLATION, 201 Massachusetts Ave. N.E., Washington, D.C. 20002. Filed for self 9/16/85. Legislative interest — ". . . First Amendment rights." Lobbyist — Esther Herst.

NEW GENERATION LOBBY, Dayton, Ky. Lobbyist — Raymond C. Janus, P.O. Box 888, Ashland, Ky. 41101. Filed 9/13/85. Legislative interest — "Small business . . . sentencing alternatives."

OPPOSE-COLORADO PUBLIC EMPLOYEE RETIREMENT ASSOCIATION, Denver, Colo. Lobbyist — Endicott Peabody, 71 Spit Brook Rd., Nashua, N.H. 03060. Filed 9/3/85. Legislative interest — "Opposition to Budget Committee's recommendation to include state and local employees in Medicare and Social Security."

ST. ELLA LTD. INC., 11510 Georgia Ave., Wheaton, Md. 20902. Filed for self 9/17/85. Legislative interest — ". . . moral issues, social legislation." Lobbyist — Ross L. McCall.

U.S. PUBLIC INTEREST RESEARCH GROUP, 215 Pennsylvania Ave. S.E., Washington, D.C. 20003. Filed for self 9/20/85. Legislative interest — ". . . unfair banking practices." Lobbyist — Michael Caudell-Feagan. ■

LOBBY REGISTRATION INDEX

A

H

I

O

S

T

U

V

W

X, Y, Z

PUBLIC LAWS

CQ

Public Laws, 99th Congress, 1st Session

PL 99-1 (S J Res 6) Extend the time within which the president may transmit the budget message and the Economic Report to Congress, and extend the time within which the Joint Economic Committee shall file its report. Introduced by DOLE, R-Kan., Jan. 3, 1985. Senate passed Jan. 3. House passed Jan. 3. President signed Jan. 9, 1985.

PL 99-2 (S J Res 36) Designate the week of Feb. 10-16, 1985, as "National DECA Week." Introduced by SIMPSON, R-Wyo., Jan. 31, 1985. Senate passed Jan. 31. House Post Office and Civil Service discharged. House passed Feb. 7. President signed Feb. 11, 1985.

PL 99-3 (H J Res 50) Designate the week beginning March 3, 1985, as "Women's History Week." Introduced by BOXER, D-Calif., Jan. 3, 1985. House Post Office and Civil Service discharged. House passed Feb. 28. Senate passed March 6. President signed March 8, 1985.

PL 99-4 (HR 1251) Apportion one-half of the funds for construction of the National System of Interstate and Defense Highways for fiscal years 1985 and 1986 and substitute highway and transit projects for fiscal years 1984 and 1985. Introduced by HOWARD, D-N.J., Feb. 25, 1985. House Public Works and Transportation reported Feb. 27 (H Rept 99-11). House passed Feb. 28. Senate passed March 5. President signed March 13, 1985.

PL 99-5 (HR 1093) Give effect to the treaty between the government of the United States and the government of Canada concerning Pacific salmon, signed at Ottawa, Jan. 28, 1985. Introduced by BREAUX, D-La., Feb. 7, 1985. House Merchant Marine and Fisheries reported Feb. 28 (H Rept 99-16). House passed, under suspension of the rules, March 5. Senate passed March 7. President signed March 15, 1985.

PL 99-6 (H J Res 85) Designate the week of March 24-30, 1985, as "National Skin Cancer Prevention and Detection Week." Introduced by SHELBY, D-Ala., Jan. 22, 1985. House Post Office and Civil Service discharged. House passed March 7. Senate passed March 18. President signed March 22, 1985.

PL 99-7 (S 592) Provide that the chairmanship of the Commission on Security and Cooperation in Europe shall rotate between members appointed from the House of Representatives and members appointed from the Senate. Introduced by DOLE, R-Kan., March 6, 1985. Senate passed March 6. House passed, under suspension of the rules, March 19. President signed March 27, 1985.

PL 99-8 (S 689) Authorize funds for famine relief and recovery in Africa. Introduced by LUGAR, R-Ind., March 19, 1985. Senate passed March 19. House passed March 21. President signed April 2, 1985.

PL 99-9 (H J Res 134) Authorize and request the president to designate the week of March 10-16, 1985, as "National Employ the Older Worker Week." Introduced by ROYBAL, D-Calif., Feb. 6, 1985. House Post Office and Civil Service discharged. House passed March 7. Senate Judiciary reported March 26. Senate passed March 28. President signed April 3, 1985.

PL 99-10 (HR 1239) Appropriate urgent supplemental funds for the fiscal year ending Sept. 30, 1985, for emergency famine relief and recovery in Africa. Introduced by WHITTEN, D-Miss., Feb. 21, 1985. House Appropriations reported Feb. 21 (H Rept 99-2). House Appropriations reported Feb. 25 (H Rept 99-2, Part II). House passed Feb. 28. Senate Appropriations reported March 5 (S Rept 99-8). Senate passed, amended, March 20. House agreed to conference report April 2 (H Rept 99-29). Senate agreed to conference report April 2. President signed April 4, 1985.

PL 99-11 (S J Res 79) Designate the month of April 1985 as "Fair Housing Month." Introduced by MATHIAS, R-Md., March 14, 1985. Senate Judiciary reported March 26. Senate passed March 28. House Post Office and Civil Service discharged. House passed April 2. President signed April 4, 1985.

PL 99-12 (S J Res 62) Commemorate the 25th anniversary of the U.S. weather satellites. Introduced by GORTON, R-Wash., Feb. 22, 1985. Senate Judiciary reported March 26. Senate passed March 28. House Post Office and Civil Service discharged. House passed April 2. President signed April 4, 1985.

PL 99-13 (H J Res 121) Designate the month of April 1985 as "National Child Abuse Prevention Month." Introduced by HILER, R-Ind., Jan. 31, 1985. House Post Office and Civil Service discharged. House passed March 7. Senate Judiciary reported March 26. Senate passed March 28. President signed April 4, 1985.

PL 99-14 (H J Res 160) Designate March 22, 1985, as "National Energy Education Day." Introduced by TAUZIN, D-La., Feb. 21, 1985. House Post Office and Civil Service discharged. House passed March 7. Senate Judiciary reported March 26. Senate passed March 28. President signed April 4, 1985.

PL 99-15 (HR 1866) Phase out the federal supplemental compensation program for the long-term unemployed. Introduced by ROSTENKOWSKI, D-Ill., April 2, 1985. House Ways and Means reported April 2 (H Rept 99-36). House passed, under suspension of the rules, April 2. Senate passed April 3. President signed April 4, 1985.

PL 99-16 (S J Res 50) Designate the week of April 1-7, 1985, as "World Health Week," and designate April 7, 1985, as "World Health Day." Introduced by RIEGLE, D-Mich., Feb. 19, 1985. Senate Judiciary reported March 26. Senate passed March 28. House Post Office and Civil Service discharged. House passed April 2. President signed April 4, 1985.

PL 99-17 (S J Res 71) Approve the obligation of funds made available by PL 98-473 for the procurement of 21 MX missiles in fiscal 1985. Introduced by GOLDWATER, R-Ariz., March 5, 1985. Senate Armed Services reported March 18. Senate passed March 19. House passed March 26. President signed April 4, 1985.

PL 99-18 (H J Res 181) Approve the obligation and availability of prior year unobligated balances made available for fiscal year 1985 for the procurement of 21 additional operational MX missiles. Introduced by McDADE, R-Pa., March 5, 1985. House Appropriations reported March 20 (H Rept 99-22). House passed March 28. Senate passed March 28. President signed April 4, 1985.

PL 99-19 (H J Res 186) Designate April 2, 1985, as "Education Day, U.S.A." Introduced by MICHEL, R-Ill., March 7, 1985. House Post Office and Civil Service discharged. House passed March 28. Senate passed April 1. President signed April 4, 1985.

PL 99-20 (H J Res 74) Designate the week of Sept. 8, 1985, as "National Independent Retail Grocer Week." Introduced by CAMPBELL, R-S.C., Jan. 22, 1985. House Post Office and Civil Service discharged. House passed March 28. Senate passed April 2. President signed April 14, 1985.

PL 99-21 (S J Res 35) Authorize and request the president to issue a proclamation designating April 21-27, 1985, as "National Organ Donation Awareness Week." Introduced by GORTON, R-Wash., Jan. 31, 1985. Senate Judiciary reported March 26. Senate passed March 28. House Post Office and Civil Service discharged. House passed April 2. President signed April 14, 1985.

PL 99-22 (HR 1847) Amend title 28, U.S. Code, with respect to the U.S. Sentencing Commission. Introduced by CONYERS, D-Mich., April 1, 1985. House passed, under suspension of the rules, April 2. Senate passed April 3. President signed April 15, 1985.

PL 99-23 (HR 730) Declare that the United States holds in trust for the Cocopah Indian Tribe of Arizona certain lands in Yuma County, Ariz. Introduced by UDALL, D-Ariz., Jan. 24, 1985. House Interior and Insular Affairs reported March 21 (H Rept 99-24). House passed April 1. Senate passed April 3. President signed April 15, 1985.

PL 99-24 (S 781) Amend the Biomass Energy and Alcohol Fuels Act of 1980 to clarify the intention of section 221 of the act by extending the eligibility for federal assistance of four projects designed to make alcohol fuel from farm crops. Introduced by EXON, D-Neb., March 28, 1985. Senate passed March 28. House Banking, Finance and Urban Affairs discharged. House passed April 2. President signed April 16, 1985.

PL 99-25 (H J Res 236) Commemorate the 24th anniversary of the Bay of Pigs invasion to liberate Cuba from communist tyranny. Introduced by PEPPER, D-Fla., April 4, 1985. House Post Office and Civil Service discharged. House passed April 16. Senate passed April 17. President signed April 19, 1985.

PL 99-26 (S J Res 17) Authorize and request the president to issue a proclamation designating the week of April 21-28, 1985, as "Jewish Heritage Week." Introduced by D'AMATO, R-N.Y., Jan. 21, 1985. Senate Judiciary reported March 26. Senate passed March 28. House Post Office and Civil Service discharged. House passed April 4. President signed April 19, 1985.

PL 99-27 (S J Res 109) Designate the week of April 14, 1985, as "Crime Victims Week." Introduced by DOLE, R-Kan., April 15, 1985. Senate passed April 15. House Post Office and Civil Service discharged. House passed April 18. President signed April 19, 1985.

PL 99-28 (S J Res 63) Designate the week of April 21-27, 1985, as "National DES Awareness Week." Introduced by RIEGLE, D-Mich., Feb. 22, 1985. Senate Judiciary reported April 3. Senate passed April 15. House Post Office and Civil Service discharged. House passed April 18. President signed April 25, 1985.

PL 99-29 (S J Res 15) Designate May 7, 1985, as "Helsinki Human Rights Day." Introduced by DeCONCINI, D-Ariz., Jan. 3, 1985. Senate Judiciary reported March 26. Senate passed March 28. House passed, under suspension of the rules, April 16. President signed April 25, 1985.

PL 99-30 (H J Res 33) Authorize and request the president to issue a proclamation designating May 1985 as "National Child Safety Awareness Month." Introduced by LEWIS, R-Fla., Jan. 3, 1985. House Post Office and Civil Service discharged. House passed April 4. Senate passed, amended, April 23. House agreed to Senate amendments April

24. President signed April 30, 1985.

PL 99-31 (S J Res 64) Designate the week beginning May 5, 1985, as "National Correctional Officers Week." Introduced by RIEGLE, D-Mich., Feb. 26, 1985. Senate Judiciary reported May 2. Senate passed May 3. House Post Office and Civil Service discharged. House passed May 7. President signed May 14, 1985.

PL 99-32 (S J Res 83) Designate the week beginning May 5, 1985, as "National Asthma and Allergy Awareness Week." Introduced by DOLE, R-Kan., March 18, 1985. Senate Judiciary reported May 2. Senate passed May 3. House Post Office and Civil Service discharged. House passed May 7. President signed May 14, 1985.

PL 99-33 (H J Res 258) Designate May 6, 1985, as "Dr. Jonas Salk Day." Introduced by SCHEUER, D-N.Y., April 24, 1985. House Post Office and Civil Service discharged. House passed May 2. Senate passed May 3. President signed May 14, 1985.

PL 99-34 (H J Res 195) Designate May 1985 as "Older Americans Month." Introduced by McCOLLUM, R-Fla., March 19, 1985. House Post Office and Civil Service discharged. House passed April 4. Senate Judiciary reported May 2. Senate passed May 3. President signed May 14, 1985.

PL 99-35 (S J Res 128) Designate May 7, 1985, as "Vietnam Veterans' Recognition Day." Introduced by BYRD, D-W.Va., April 30, 1985. Senate passed May 2. House Post Office and Civil Service discharged. House passed May 7. President signed May 14, 1985.

PL 99-36 (S 597) Make technical and conforming changes to certain provisions of title 46, U.S. Code, to clarify the wage penalty provisions for coastwise commerce, to repeal duplicate provisions regarding the requirement for exposure suits on U.S. vessels, and to clarify the limited application of dangerous cargo provisions to certain fishing industry vessels. Introduced by STEVENS, R-Alaska, March 6, 1985. Senate Commerce, Science and Transportation reported April 10 (S Rept 99-26). Senate passed April 17. House passed, under suspension of the rules, May 6. President signed May 15, 1985.

PL 99-37 (S J Res 65) Designate November 1985 as "National Alzheimer's Disease Month." Introduced by EAGLETON, D-Mo., Feb. 27, 1985. Senate Judiciary reported March 26. Senate passed March 28. House Post Office and Civil Service discharged. House passed May 7. President signed May 15, 1985.

PL 99-38 (S J Res 53) Authorize and request the president to designate June 1985 as "Youth Suicide Prevention Month." Introduced by DENTON, R-Ala., Feb. 20, 1985. Senate Judiciary reported March 26. Senate passed March 28. House Post Office and Civil Service discharged. House passed May 7. President signed May 15, 1985.

PL 99-39 (S J Res 94) Designate the week beginning May 12, 1985, as "National Digestive Diseases Awareness Week." Introduced by GORE, D-Tenn., March 26, 1985. Senate Judiciary reported April 3. Senate passed April 15. House Post Office and Civil Service discharged. House passed May 7. President signed May 15, 1985.

PL 99-40 (S J Res 60) Designate the week of May 12-18, 1985, as "Senior Center Week." Introduced by NUNN, D-Ga., Feb. 21, 1985. Senate Judiciary reported March 26. Senate passed March 28. House Post Office and Civil Service discharged. House passed May 7. President signed May 15, 1985.

PL 99-41 (S J Res 59) Designate the week of May 12-18, 1985, as "National Science Week." Introduced by HATCH, R-Utah, Feb. 21, 1985. Senate Judiciary reported May 2. Senate passed May 3. House Post Office and Civil Service discharged. House passed May 9. President signed May 17, 1985.

PL 99-42 (S J Res 61) Designate the week of May 20-26, 1985, as "National Osteoporosis Awareness Week." Introduced by GRASSLEY, R-Iowa, Feb. 22, 1985. Senate Judiciary reported March 26. Senate passed March 28. House Post Office and Civil Service discharged. House passed, amended, May 7. Senate agreed to House amendments May 14. President signed May 20, 1985.

PL 99-43 (S J Res 103) Designate May 1985 as "Very Special Arts U.S.A. Month." Introduced by PELL, D-R.I., April 3, 1985. Senate Judiciary reported May 2. Senate passed May 3. House Post Office and Civil Service discharged. House passed May 15. President signed May 21, 1985.

PL 99-44 (HR 1869) Repeal the contemporaneous record-keeping requirements added to the Tax Reform Act of 1984. Introduced by ROSTENKOWSKI, D-Ill., April 2, 1985. House Ways and Means reported April 2 (H Rept 99-34). House passed, under suspension of the rules, April 2. Senate passed, amended, April 3. House agreed to conference report May 8 (H Rept 99-67). Senate agreed to conference report May 16. President signed May 24, 1985.

PL 99-45 (S 661) Designate the air traffic control tower at the Medford/Jackson County (Ore.) Airport as the "George Milligan Control Tower." Introduced by PACKWOOD, R-Ore., March 11, 1985. Senate Commerce, Science and Transportation reported April 10. Senate passed April 15. House Public Works and Transportation discharged. House passed May 14. President signed May 24, 1985.

PL 99-46 (S 484) Amend the Saccharin Study and Labeling Act to extend the period during which the secretary of health and human services may not take certain actions to restrict the continued use of saccharin or of any food, drug or cosmetic containing saccharin. Introduced by HATCH, R-Utah, Feb. 20, 1985. Senate Labor and Human Resources reported April 22 (S Rept 99-36). Senate passed May 7. House passed May 14. President signed May 24, 1985.

PL 99-47 (HR 2268) Approve and implement the Free Trade Area Agreement between the United States and Israel. Introduced by WRIGHT, D-Texas, April 29, 1985. House Ways and Means reported May 6 (H Rept 99-64). House passed, under suspension of the rules, May 7. Senate passed May 23. President signed June 11, 1985.

PL 99-48 (S J Res 93) Designate May 1985 as "Better Hearing and Speech Month." Introduced by METZENBAUM, D-Ohio, March 26, 1985. Senate Judiciary reported May 2. Senate passed May 3. House Post Office and Civil Service discharged. House passed June 4. President signed June 12, 1985.

PL 99-49 (S J Res 66) Designate June 14, 1985, as "Baltic Freedom Day." Introduced by D'AMATO, R-N.Y., Feb. 27, 1985. Senate Judiciary reported May 2. Senate passed May 3. House Post Office and Civil Service discharged. House passed June 11. President signed June 13, 1985.

PL 99-50 (S J Res 142) Designate June 12, 1985, as "Anne Frank Day." Introduced by LEVIN, D-Mich., May 23, 1985. Senate Judiciary reported June 7. Senate passed June 10. House Post Office and Civil Service discharged. House passed June 12. President signed June 14, 1985.

PL 99-51 (H J Res 25) Designate the week beginning June 2, 1985, as "National Theatre Week." Introduced by GREEN, R-N.Y., Jan. 3, 1985. House Post Office and Civil Service discharged. House passed June 4. Senate passed June 10. President signed June 14, 1985.

PL 99-52 (H J Res 64) Designate Mother's Day, May 12, 1985, to Father's Day, June 16, 1985, as "Family Reunion Month." Introduced by RAY, D-Ga., Jan. 3, 1985. House Post Office and Civil Service discharged. House passed May 15. Senate Judiciary reported June 7. Senate passed June 10. President signed June 14, 1985.

PL 99-53 (HR 873) Amend title 5, U.S. Code, to provide that employee organizations that are not eligible to participate in the federal employee health benefits program solely because of the requirement that applications for approval be filed before Jan. 1, 1980, may apply to become so eligible. Introduced by DICKS, D-Wash., Jan. 31, 1985. House Post Office and Civil Service reported May 9 (H Rept 99-72). House passed, under suspension of the rules, May 13. Senate passed June 3. President signed June 17, 1985.

PL 99-54 (H J Res 211) Recognize the pause for the Pledge of Allegiance as part of national Flag Day activities. Introduced by MIKULSKI, D-Md., March 26, 1985. House Post Office and Civil Service discharged. House passed June 11. Senate passed June 13. President signed June 20, 1985.

PL 99-55 (HR 14) Designate the federal building and U.S. Courthouse in Ashland, Ky., as the "Carl D. Perkins Federal Building and United States Courthouse." Introduced by NATCHER, D-Ky., Jan. 3, 1985. House Public Works and Transportation reported Feb. 27 (H Rept 99-10). House passed Feb. 28. Senate Environment and Public Works reported May 7. Senate passed June 18. President signed June 26, 1985.

PL 99-56 (S J Res 125) Designate the week of June 23-29, 1985, as "Helen Keller Deaf-Blind Awareness Week." Introduced by LEAHY, D-Vt., April 26, 1985. Senate Judiciary reported June 7. Senate passed June 10. House Post Office and Civil Service discharged. House passed June 19. President signed June 26, 1985.

PL 99-57 (S J Res 87) Designate July 19, 1985, as "National P.O.W./M.I.A. Recognition Day." Introduced by MURKOWSKI, R-Alaska, March 19, 1985. Senate Judiciary reported May 2. Senate passed May 3. House Post Office and Civil Service discharged. House passed June 19. President signed June 27, 1985.

PL 99-58 (HR 1699) Amend the Energy Policy and Conservation Act to extend the expiration date of title I from June 30, 1985, to June 30, 1989, and to extend the expiration date of title II from June 30, 1985, to June 30, 1987, to help the U.S. respond to a future oil crisis. Introduced by SHARP, D-Ind., March 25, 1985. House Energy and Commerce reported June 3 (H Rept 99-152). House passed, under suspension of the rules, June 4. Senate passed, amended, June 18. Senate receded from its amendment and concurred with a further amendment June 27. House agreed to Senate amendment June 27. President signed July 2, 1985.

PL 99-59 (S 413) Extend the provisions of title XII of the Merchant Marine Act of 1936, relating to war risk insurance. Introduced by STEVENS, R-Alaska, Feb. 6, 1985. Senate Commerce, Science and Transportation reported March 19 (S Rept 99-13). Senate passed June

6. House passed, under suspension of the rules, June 24. President signed July 3, 1985.

PL 99-60 (H J Res 159) Commemorate the 75th anniversary of the Boy Scouts of America. Introduced by STALLINGS, D-Idaho, Feb. 20, 1985. House Post Office and Civil Service discharged. House passed June 4. Senate Judiciary reported June 20. Senate passed June 21. President signed July 3, 1985.

PL 99-61 (HR 47) Provide for the minting of coins in commemoration of the centennial of the Statue of Liberty. Introduced by ANNUNZIO, D-Ill., Jan. 3, 1985. House passed, under suspension of the rules, March 5. Senate Banking, Housing and Urban Affairs reported May 7. Senate passed, amended, June 21. House agreed to Senate amendments June 25. President signed July 9, 1985.

PL 99-62 (HR 2800) Authorize funds for activities under the Land Remote-Sensing Commercialization Act of 1985. Introduced by SCHEUER, D-N.Y., June 18, 1985. House Science and Technology reported June 20 (H Rept 99-177). House passed, under suspension of the rules, June 24. Senate passed June 27. President signed July 11, 1985.

PL 99-63 (S 822) Extend the time for conducting the referendum with respect to the national marketing quota for wheat for the marketing year beginning June 1, 1986. Introduced by ZORINSKY, D-Neb., April 1, 1985. Senate Agriculture, Nutrition and Forestry reported June 3 (S Rept 99-77). Senate passed June 21. House passed, amended, June 26. Senate agreed to House amendment with an amendment June 27. House agreed to Senate amendment June 27. President signed July 11, 1985.

PL 99-64 (S 883) Extend the Export Administration Act of 1979 until June 15, 1985. Introduced by HEINZ, R-Pa., April 3, 1985. Senate passed April 3. House passed, amended, April 16. House agreed to conference report June 27 (H Rept 99-180). Senate agreed to conference report June 27. President signed July 12, 1985.

PL 99-65 (S 1141) Amend title 2, U.S. Code, to require the sergeant-at-arms of the Senate to provide senators with telephone service in their state offices, except services for which the charge is based on the amount of time the service is used. Introduced by MATHIAS, R-Md., May 15, 1985. Senate Rules and Administration reported May 15 (S Rept 99-52). Senate passed June 6. House Administration discharged. House passed June 25. President signed July 12, 1985.

PL 99-66 (H J Res 325) Designate July 13, 1985, as "Live Aid Day." Introduced by CARR, D-Mich., June 25, 1985. House Post Office and Civil Service discharged. House passed July 11. Senate passed July 11. President signed July 17, 1985.

PL 99-67 (S J Res 154) Designate July 20, 1985, as "Space Exploration Day." Introduced by GARN, R-Utah, June 27, 1985. Senate Judiciary discharged. Senate passed July 16. House Post Office and Civil Service discharged. House passed July 18. President signed July 19, 1985.

PL 99-68 (HR 1373) Designate the wilderness in the Point Reyes National Seashore in California as the Phillip Burton Wilderness. Introduced by SEIBERLING, D-Ohio, Feb. 28, 1985. House Interior and Insular Affairs reported March 28 (H Rept 99-31). House passed, under suspension of the rules, April 2. Senate Energy and Natural Resources reported June 27 (S Rept 99-95). Senate passed July 9. President signed July 19, 1985.

PL 99-69 (S 1455) Extend the authority to establish and administer flexible and compressed work schedules for federal government employees. Introduced by DOLE, R-Kan., July 17, 1985. Senate passed July 17. House passed July 18. President signed July 22, 1985.

PL 99-70 (H J Res 198) Provide for the appointment of Barnabas McHenry as a citizen regent of the Board of Regents of the Smithsonian Institution. Introduced by CONTE, R-Mass., March 20, 1985. House Administration reported June 21 (H Rept 99-179). House passed June 25. Senate Rules and Administration discharged. Senate passed July 11. President signed July 22, 1985.

PL 99-71 (H J Res 342) Authorize urgent supplemental appropriations for the fiscal year ending Sept. 30, 1985, for the Department of Agriculture. Introduced by WHITTEN, D-Miss., July 18, 1985. House passed July 18. Senate passed July 19. President signed July 24, 1985.

PL 99-72 (S J Res 40) Designate October 1985 as "National Down [*sic*] Syndrome Month." Introduced by LUGAR, R-Ind., Feb. 5, 1985. Senate Judiciary reported May 9. Senate passed May 15. House Post Office and Civil Service discharged. House passed July 11. President signed July 24, 1985.

PL 99-73 (HR 1617) Authorize funds to the secretary of commerce for the programs of the National Bureau of Standards for fiscal year 1986. Introduced by FUQUA, D-Fla., March 20, 1985. House Science and Technology reported April 16 (H Rept 99-43). House passed April 18. Senate passed, amended, April 23. House agreed to conference report July 15 (H Rept 99-187). Senate agreed to conference report July 15. President signed July 29, 1985.

PL 99-74 (S J Res 86) Designate the week of July 25-31, 1985, as "National Disability in Entertainment Week." Introduced by WILSON, R-Calif., March 19, 1985. Senate Judiciary reported June 27. Senate passed July 8. House Post Office and Civil Service discharged. House passed July 24. President signed July 29, 1985.

PL 99-75 (S J Res 144) Authorize the printing and binding of a revised edition of Senate Procedure. Introduced by BYRD, D-W.Va., May 24, 1985. Senate passed May 24. House Administration discharged. House passed July 16. President signed July 29, 1985.

PL 99-76 (H J Res 106) Designate August 1985 as "Polish American Heritage Month." Introduced by BORSKI, D-Pa., Jan. 30, 1985. House Post Office and Civil Service discharged. House passed July 11. Senate Judiciary reported July 18. Senate passed July 19. President signed July 31, 1985.

PL 99-77 (S J Res 57) Designate the week of Oct. 20-26, 1985, as "Lupus Awareness Week." Introduced by CHILES, D-Fla., Feb. 20, 1985. Senate Judiciary reported May 9. Senate passed May 15. House Post Office and Civil Service discharged. House passed July 24. President signed Aug. 2, 1985.

PL 99-78 (H J Res 164) Designate Aug. 4, 1985, as "Freedom of the Press Day." Introduced by LANTOS, D-Calif., Feb. 21, 1985. House Post Office and Civil Service discharged. House passed July 11. Senate Judiciary reported July 25. Senate passed July 26. President signed Aug. 2, 1985.

PL 99-79 (S J Res 180) Commemorate the 10th anniversary of the signing of the Helsinki Final Act. Introduced by SIMPSON, R-Wyo. (in behalf of D'AMATO, R-N.Y.), July 29, 1985. Senate passed July 29. House passed July 30. President signed Aug. 2, 1985.

PL 99-80 (HR 2378) Amend section 504 of title 5, U.S. Code, and section 2412 of title 28, U.S. Code, with respect to awards of expenses of certain agency and court proceedings. Introduced by KASTENMEIER, D-Wis., May 7, 1985. House Judiciary reported May 15 (H Rept 99-120). Supplemental report filed June 13 (H Rept 99-120, Part II). House passed, under suspension of the rules, June 24. Senate passed July 24. President signed Aug. 5, 1985.

PL 99-81 (S J Res 161) Appeal for the release of Soviet Jewry. Introduced by DOLE, R-Kan., July 11, 1985. Senate Foreign Relations reported July 17. Senate passed July 18. House Foreign Affairs discharged. House passed July 25. President signed Aug. 6, 1985.

PL 99-82 (S J Res 168) Designate Aug. 13, 1985, as "National Neighborhood Crime Watch Day." Introduced by TRIBLE, R-Va., July 23, 1985. Senate Judiciary reported July 25. Senate passed July 26. House Post Office and Civil Service discharged. House passed Aug. 1. President signed Aug. 7, 1985.

PL 99-83 (S 960) Amend the Foreign Assistance Act of 1961, the Arms Export Control Act and other acts to authorize funds for fiscal year 1986 for international security and development assistance, the Peace Corps and the Inter-American Development Foundation. Introduced by LUGAR, R-Ind., April 19, 1985. Senate Foreign Relations reported April 19 (S Rept 99-34). Senate passed May 15. House passed, amended, July 11. Senate agreed to conference report July 30 (H Rept 99-237). House agreed to conference report July 31. President signed Aug. 8, 1985.

PL 99-84 (S J Res 137) Designate the week of Dec. 15-21, 1985, as "National Drunk and Drugged Driving Awareness Week." Introduced by HUMPHREY, R-N.H., May 16, 1985. Senate Judiciary reported June 7. Senate passed June 10. House Post Office and Civil Service discharged. House passed Aug. 1. President signed Aug. 8, 1985.

PL 99-85 (S J Res 108) Authorize the secretary of defense to provide to the Soviet Union, on a reimbursable basis, equipment and services necessary for an improved United States-Soviet Union Direct Communication Link for crisis control. Introduced by WARNER, R-Va., April 4, 1985. Senate Armed Services reported May 14 (S Rept 99-49). Senate passed May 16. House Armed Services reported June 4 (H Rept 99-156). House passed July 29. President signed Aug. 8, 1985.

PL 99-86 (H J Res 251) Provide that a special gold medal honoring George Gershwin be presented to his sister, Frances Gershwin Godowsky, and a special gold medal honoring Ira Gershwin be presented to his widow, Lenore Gershwin, and provide for the production of bronze duplicates of such medals for sale to the public. Introduced by YATES, D-Ill., April 23, 1985. House passed, under suspension of the rules, July 15. Senate Banking, Housing and Urban Affairs reported Aug. 1. Senate passed Aug. 1. President signed Aug. 9, 1985.

PL 99-87 (S 1195) Require that a portion of the mail of Congress and the executive branch include a photograph and biography of a missing child. Introduced by METZENBAUM, D-Ohio, May 22, 1985. Senate passed May 22. House Post Office and Civil Service reported July 25 (H Rept 99-226, Part I). House passed, amended, under suspension of the rules, July 29. Senate agreed to House amendments with amendments July 31. House agreed to Senate amendments Aug. 1. President signed Aug. 9, 1985.

PL 99-88 (HR 2577) Appropriate supplemental funds for the fiscal year ending Sept. 30, 1985. Introduced by WHITTEN, D-Miss., May 22, 1985. House Appropriations reported May 22 (H Rept 99-142). House passed June 12. Senate Appropriations reported June 13 (S Rept 99-82). Senate passed, amended, June 20. House agreed to conference report July 31 (H Rept 99-236). Senate agreed to conference report Aug. 1. President signed Aug. 15, 1985.

PL 99-89 (HR 2908) Amend title XI of the Education Amendments of 1978, relating to Indian education programs. Introduced by KILDEE, D-Mich., June 27, 1985. House Education and Labor reported July 26 (H Rept 99-231). House passed, under suspension of the rules, July 29. Senate passed July 30. President signed Aug. 15, 1985.

PL 99-90 (S J Res 98) Condemn the passage of resolution 3379, in the United Nations General Assembly on Nov. 10, 1975, and urge the U.S. ambassador and U.S. delegation to take all appropriate actions necessary to erase the resolution from the record of the United Nations. Introduced by D'AMATO, R-N.Y., March 28, 1985. Senate Foreign Relations reported June 27. Senate passed July 9. House Foreign Affairs discharged. House passed Aug. 1. President signed Aug. 15, 1985.

PL 99-91 (S 1147) Amend the orphan drug provisions of the Federal Food, Drug and Cosmetic Act and related laws. Introduced by DOLE, R-Kan. (in behalf of HATCH, R-Utah), May 15, 1985. Senate passed May 23. House passed, amended, June 18. Senate agreed to House amendment with amendments July 25. House agreed to Senate amendments to House amendment July 31. President signed Aug. 15, 1985.

PL 99-92 (HR 2370) Amend the Public Health Service Act to extend the programs of assistance for nurse education. Introduced by WAXMAN, D-Calif., May 6, 1985. House Energy and Commerce reported June 5 (H Rept 99-161). House passed, under suspension of the rules, July 15. Senate passed, amended, July 22. House agreed to Senate amendment July 31. President signed Aug. 16, 1985.

PL 99-93 (HR 2068) Authorize funds for the Department of State, the U.S. Information Agency, the Board for International Broadcasting and the National Endowment for Democracy for fiscal years 1986 and 1987. Introduced by MICA, D-Fla., April 17, 1985. House passed May 9. Senate passed, amended, June 11. Senate agreed to conference report July 31 (H Rept 99-240). House agreed to conference report Aug. 1. President signed Aug. 16, 1985.

PL 99-94 (S J Res 31) Designate the week of Nov. 24-30, 1986, as "National Family Week." Introduced by BURDICK, D-N.D., Jan. 29, 1985. Senate Judiciary reported March 26. Senate passed March 28. House Post Office and Civil Service discharged. House passed, amended, Aug. 1. Senate agreed to House amendments Sept. 10. President signed Sept. 19, 1985.

PL 99-95 (H J Res 128) Designate October 1985 as "National High-Tech Month." Introduced by DYMALLY, D-Calif., Feb. 6, 1985. House Post Office and Civil Service discharged. House passed May 15. Senate Judiciary reported Sept. 12. Senate passed Sept. 12. President signed Sept. 23, 1985.

PL 99-96 (S 444) Confirm and ratify a land exchange between NANA Regional Corp. Inc. and the United States through the secretary of the interior for lands within Cape Krusenstern National Monument, in Alaska. Introduced by MURKOWSKI, R-Alaska, Feb. 7, 1985. Senate Energy and Natural Resources reported June 27 (S Rept 99-97). Senate passed July 18. House Interior and Insular Affairs discharged. House passed, amended, July 29. Senate agreed to House amendment with an amendment Aug. 1. House agreed to Senate amendment Sept. 12. President signed Sept. 25, 1985.

PL 99-97 (S 818) Authorize appropriations for activities under the Federal Fire Prevention and Control Act of 1974. Introduced by GORTON, R-Wash., March 28, 1985. Senate Commerce, Science and Transportation reported April 15 (S Rept 99-30). Senate passed April 17. House Science and Technology reported May 21 (H Rept 99-135). House passed, amended, under suspension of the rules, June 24. Senate agreed to House amendment with an amendment July 31. House agreed to Senate amendment Sept. 17. President signed Sept. 26, 1985.

PL 99-98 (S J Res 141) Designate the week beginning May 18, 1986, as "National Tourism Week." Introduced by SASSER, D-Tenn., May 23, 1985. Senate Judiciary reported Sept. 12. Senate passed Sept. 13. House passed Sept. 19. President signed Sept. 26, 1985.

PL 99-99 (S J Res 173) Designate September 1985 as "National Sewing Month." Introduced by EAST, R-N.C., July 24, 1985. Senate Judiciary reported Sept. 12. Senate passed Sept. 13. House Post Office and Civil Service discharged. House passed Sept. 19. President signed Sept. 26.

PL 99-100 (S J Res 186) Designate the week of Sept. 23-29, 1985, as "National Historically Black Colleges Week." Introduced by THURMOND, R-S.C., Aug. 1, 1985. Senate Judiciary reported Sept. 12. Senate passed Sept. 13. House Post Office and Civil Service discharged. House passed Sept. 24. President signed Sept. 27, 1985.

PL 99-101 (H J Res 218) Designate the week beginning Sept. 15, 1985, as "National Dental Hygiene Week." Introduced by PORTER, R-Ill., March 28, 1985. House Post Office and Civil Service discharged. House passed Sept. 19. Senate passed Sept. 19. President signed Sept. 27, 1985.

PL 99-102 (H J Res 229) Designate the week beginning Sept. 22, 1985, as "National Adult Day Care Center Week." Introduced by HERTEL, D-Mich., April 3, 1985. House Post Office and Civil Service discharged. House passed Aug. 1. Senate Judiciary reported Sept. 19. Senate passed Sept. 19. President signed Sept. 27, 1985.

PL 99-103 (H J Res 388) Make continuing appropriations for fiscal year 1986. Introduced by WHITTEN, D-Miss., Sept. 17, 1985. House Appropriations reported Sept. 17 (H Rept 99-272). House passed Sept. 18. Senate Appropriations reported Sept. 24 (S Rept 99-142). Senate passed Sept. 25. President signed Sept. 30, 1985.

PL 99-104 (S 1514) Approve the Interstate Cost Estimate and the Interstate Substitute Cost Estimate of the Department of Transportation. Introduced by SYMMS, R-Idaho, July 29, 1985. Senate Environment and Public Works reported July 29. Senate passed July 30. House passed Sept. 19. President signed Sept. 30, 1985.

PL 99-105 (S 817) Authorize appropriations under the Earthquake Hazards Reduction Act of 1977 for fiscal years 1986 and 1987. Introduced by GORTON, R-Wash., March 28, 1985. Senate Commerce, Science and Transportation reported April 15 (S Rept 99-29). Senate passed April 17. House Interior and Insular Affairs reported May 14 (H Rept 99-90, Part I). House Science and Technology reported May 21 (H Rept 99-90, Part II). House passed, amended, under suspension of the rules, June 24. Senate agreed to House amendments with amendments July 31. House agreed to Senate amendments Sept. 17. President signed Sept. 30, 1985.

PL 99-106 (S J Res 127) Grant the consent of Congress to certain additional powers conferred upon the Bi-State Development Agency by the states of Missouri and Illinois. Introduced by DANFORTH, R-Mo., April 30, 1985. Senate Judiciary reported May 20. Senate passed May 23. House Judiciary reported Sept. 19 (H Rept 99-278). House passed, under suspension of the rules, Sept. 26. President signed Sept. 30, 1985.

PL 99-107 (HR 3452) Extend for 45 days the application of tobacco excise taxes, trade adjustment assistance, certain Medicare reimbursement provisions and borrowing authority under the railroad unemployment insurance program. Introduced by ROSTENKOWSKI, D-Ill., Sept. 30, 1985. House Energy and Commerce discharged. House Ways and Means discharged. House passed Sept. 30. Senate passed Sept. 30. President signed Sept. 30, 1985.

PL 99-108 (S 1671) Amend title 38, U.S. Code, to provide interim extension of the authority of the Veterans Administration to operate a regional office in the Republic of the Philippines, to contract for hospital care and outpatient services in Puerto Rico and the Virgin Islands, and to contract for treatment and rehabilitation services for alcohol and drug dependence and abuse disabilities, and to amend the Emergency Veterans' Job Training Act of 1983, to extend the period for entering into training under such act. Introduced by STAFFORD, R-Vt. (in behalf of MURKOWSKI, R-Alaska), Sept. 19, 1985. Senate passed Sept. 20. House passed Sept. 26. President signed Sept. 30, 1985.

PL 99-109 (HR 3414) Provide that the authority to establish and administer flexible and compressed work schedules for federal government employees be extended through Oct. 31, 1985. Introduced by ACKERMAN, D-N.Y., Sept. 23, 1985. House Post Office and Civil Service discharged. House passed Sept. 26. Senate passed Sept. 26. President signed Sept. 30, 1985.

PL 99-110 (H J Res 299) Recognize the accomplishments over 50 years resulting from the passage of the Historic Sites Act of 1935. Introduced by BUSTAMANTE, D-Texas, June 4, 1985. House Interior and Insular Affairs reported July 29 (H Rept 99-233). House passed July 29. Senate passed Sept. 12. President signed Oct. 1, 1985.

PL 99-111 (H J Res 305) Recognize both Peace Corps volunteers and the Peace Corps on the agency's 25th anniversary, 1985-86. Introduced by HENRY, R-Mich., June 5, 1985. House Post Office and Civil Service discharged. House passed July 24. Senate Judiciary reported Sept. 19. Senate passed Sept. 19. President signed Oct. 1, 1985.

PL 99-112 (S J Res 67) Designate the week of Oct. 6-12, 1985, as "Mental Illness Awareness Week." Introduced by QUAYLE, R-Ind., Feb. 28, 1985. Senate Judiciary reported April 3. Senate passed April 15. House Post Office and Civil Service discharged. House passed Sept. 19. President signed Oct. 1, 1985.

PL 99-113 (S J Res 111) Designate October 1985 as "National Spina Bifida Month." Introduced by DIXON, D-Ill., April 16, 1985. Senate Judiciary reported June 20. Senate passed June 21. House Post Office and Civil Service discharged. House passed Sept. 19. President signed Oct. 1, 1985.

PL 99-114 (HR 3454) Extend temporarily certain provisions of the Agricultural Act of 1949 (7 U.S.C. 1466(d)(1)(B)). Introduced by de la GARZA, D-Texas, Sept. 30, 1985. House Agriculture discharged. House passed Sept. 30. Senate passed Sept. 30. President signed Oct. 1, 1985.

PL 99-115 (H J Res 287) Designate October 1985 as "Learning Disabilities Awareness Month." Introduced by BROWN, D-Calif., May 14, 1985. House Post Office and Civil Service discharged. House passed Sept. 19. Senate passed Sept. 23. President signed Oct. 4, 1985.

PL 99-116 (H J Res 394) Reaffirm our historic solidarity with the people of Mexico following the devastating earthquake of Sept. 19, 1985. Introduced by WRIGHT, D-Texas, Sept. 20, 1985. House passed Sept. 20. Senate passed Sept. 20. President signed Oct. 4, 1985.

PL 99-117 (S 1689) Amend various provisions of the Public Health Service Act. Introduced by STAFFORD, R-Vt. (in behalf of HATCH, R-Utah), Sept. 20, 1985. Senate passed Sept. 23. House passed Sept. 24. President signed Oct. 7, 1985.

PL 99-118 (S J Res 115) Designate 1985 as the "Oil Heat Centennial Year." Introduced by LEAHY, D-Vt., April 17, 1985. Senate Judiciary reported June 27. Senate passed July 8. House Post Office and Civil Service discharged. House passed Sept. 19. President signed Oct. 7, 1985.

PL 99-119 (HR 1042) Grant a federal charter to the Pearl Harbor Survivors Association. Introduced by DWYER, D-N.J., Feb. 7, 1985. House Judiciary reported May 8 (H Rept 99-71). House passed, under suspension of the rules, May 13. Senate Judiciary reported July 15 (S Rept 99-103). Senate passed, amended, July 18. House agreed to Senate amendments Sept. 20. President signed Oct. 7, 1985.

PL 99-120 (H J Res 393) Provide for the temporary extension of certain programs relating to housing and community development programs. Introduced by GONZALEZ, D-Texas, Sept. 19, 1985. House Banking, Finance and Urban Affairs discharged. House passed Sept. 20. Senate passed, amended, Oct. 2. House agreed to Senate amendment Oct. 3. President signed Oct. 8, 1985.

PL 99-121 (HR 2475) Amend the Internal Revenue Code of 1954 to simplify the imputed interest rules of sections 1274 and 483. Introduced by ROSTENKOWSKI, D-Ill., May 14, 1985. House Ways and Means reported May 14 (H Rept 99-87). House passed, under suspension of the rules, May 21. Senate Finance reported June 13 (S Rept 99-83). Senate passed, amended, June 26. House agreed to conference report Aug. 1 (H Rept 99-250). Senate agreed to conference report Oct. 1. President signed Oct. 11, 1985.

PL 99-122 (S J Res 72) Designate Oct. 16, 1985, as "World Food Day." Introduced by DANFORTH, R-Mo., March 5, 1985. Senate Judiciary reported March 26. Senate passed March 28. House Post Office and Civil Service discharged. House passed Oct. 9. President signed Oct. 16, 1985.

PL 99-123 (S J Res 183) Provide for the designation of the week of Oct. 6-12, 1985, as "Myasthenia Gravis Awareness Week." Introduced by BYRD, D-W.Va., July 31, 1985. Senate passed Aug. 1. House Post Office and Civil Service discharged. House passed Oct. 9. President signed Oct. 16, 1985.

PL 99-124 (S J Res 197) Designate the week of Oct. 6-13, 1985, as "National Housing Week." Introduced by HECHT, R-Nev., Sept. 12, 1985. Senate Judiciary reported Sept. 19. Senate passed Sept. 19. House Post Office and Civil Service discharged. House passed Oct. 9. President signed Oct. 16, 1985.

PL 99-125 (S J Res 155) Designate November 1985 as "National Hospice Month." Introduced by PACKWOOD, R-Ore., July 8, 1985. Senate Judiciary reported Sept. 12. Senate passed Sept. 23. House Post Office and Civil Service discharged. House passed Oct. 9. President signed Oct. 18, 1985.

PL 99-126 (S J Res 175) Designate the week of Oct. 20-26, 1985, as "National CPR Awareness Week." Introduced by PROXMIRE, D-Wis., July 25, 1985. Senate Judiciary reported Sept. 19. Senate passed Sept. 19. House Post Office and Civil Service discharged. House passed Oct. 9. President signed Oct. 18, 1985.

PL 99-127 (S J Res 194) Designate the week beginning Oct. 1, 1985, as "National Buy American Week." Introduced by METZENBAUM, D-Ohio, Sept. 11, 1985. Senate Judiciary reported Sept. 19. Senate passed Sept. 19. House Post Office and Civil Service discharged. House passed Oct. 9. President signed Oct. 18, 1985.

PL 99-128 (S J Res 158) Designate October 1985 as "National Community College Month." Introduced by MURKOWSKI, R-Alaska, July 11, 1985. Senate Judiciary reported Sept. 26. Senate passed Sept. 30. House passed Oct. 9. President signed Oct. 22, 1985.

PL 99-129 (HR 2410) Amend the Public Health Service Act, relating to health professions training assistance. Introduced by WAXMAN, D-Calif., May 7, 1985. House Energy and Commerce reported May 23 (H Rept 99-145). House passed, under suspension of the rules, July 15. Senate passed, amended, July 19. House agreed to Senate amendment with an amendment Oct. 3. Senate agreed to House amendment Oct. 4. President signed Oct. 22, 1985.

PL 99-130 (S 1349) Provide for the use and distribution of funds awarded in docket 363 to the Mdewakanton and Mahpekute Eastern or Mississippi Sioux before the U.S. Court of Claims. Introduced by ABDNOR, R-S.D., June 25, 1985. Senate Select Indian Affairs reported July 26 (S Rept 99-115). Senate passed, amended, July 31. House Interior and Insular Affairs reported Oct. 2 (H Rept 99-298). House passed Oct. 9. President signed Oct. 28, 1985.

PL 99-131 (S J Res 92) Designate October 1985 as "National Foster Grandparents Week." Introduced by DENTON, R-Ala., March 26, 1985. Senate Judiciary reported May 2. Senate passed May 3. House Post Office and Civil Service discharged. House passed Oct. 17. President signed Oct. 28, 1985.

PL 99-132 (S J Res 104) Proclaim Oct. 23, 1985, as "A Time of Remembrance for All Victims of Terrorism Throughout the World." Introduced by DENTON, R-Ala., April 3, 1985. Senate Judiciary reported May 2. Senate passed May 3. House Post Office and Civil Service discharged. House passed Oct. 22. President signed Oct. 28, 1985.

PL 99-133 (HR 2174) Provide for the transfer to the Colville Business Council of any undistributed portion of amounts appropriated in satisfaction of certain judgments awarded the Confederated Tribes of the Colville Reservation before the Indian Claims Commission. Introduced by FOLEY, D-Wash., April 23, 1985. House Interior and Insular Affairs reported Sept. 12 (H Rept 99-270). House passed Oct. 7. Senate passed Oct. 15. President signed Oct. 28, 1985.

PL 99-134 (H J Res 79) Designate the week beginning Oct. 6, 1985, as "National Children's Week." Introduced by FOWLER, D-Ga., Jan. 22, 1985. House Post Office and Civil Service discharged. House passed Oct. 9. Senate Judiciary discharged. Senate passed Oct. 18. President signed Oct. 28, 1985.

PL 99-135 (H J Res 386) Designate Nov. 24, 1985, as "National Day of Fasting to Raise Funds to Combat Hunger." Introduced by PACKARD, R-Calif., Sept. 12, 1985. House Post Office and Civil Service discharged. House passed Oct. 9. Senate passed Oct. 16. President signed Oct. 28, 1985.

PL 99-136 (H J Res 407) Designate the 12-month period ending on Oct. 28, 1986, as the "Centennial Year of Liberty in the United States." Introduced by FORD, D-Mich., Oct. 2, 1985. House Post Office and Civil Service discharged. House passed Oct. 9. Senate Judiciary discharged. Senate passed Oct. 21. President signed Oct. 28, 1985.

PL 99-137 (H J Res 308) Designate the week beginning Oct. 20, 1985, as "Benign Essential Blepharospasm Awareness Week." Introduced by BROOKS, D-Texas, June 6, 1985. House Post Office and Civil Service discharged. House passed Oct. 17. Senate Judiciary reported Oct. 24. Senate passed Oct. 25. President signed Oct. 30, 1985.

PL 99-138 (H J Res 322) Designate October 1985 as "National Sudden Infant Death Syndrome Awareness Month." Introduced by MILLER, D-Calif., June 20, 1985. House Post Office and Civil Service discharged. House passed Oct. 9. Senate Judiciary reported Oct. 24. Senate passed Oct. 25. President signed Oct. 30, 1985.

PL 99-139 (S 1726) Repeal section 121(b) of the International Security and Development Cooperation Act of 1985 (PL 99-83), relating to funding for the Special Defense Acquisition Fund. Introduced by DOLE, R-Kan. (in behalf of LUGAR, R-Ind.), Oct. 1, 1985. Senate passed Oct. 10. House passed Oct. 17. President signed Oct. 30, 1985.

PL 99-140 (HR 3605) Provide that the authority to establish and administer flexible and compressed work schedules for federal government employees be extended through Dec. 31, 1985. Introduced by ACKERMAN, D-N.Y., Oct. 23, 1985. House Post Office and Civil Service discharged. House passed Oct. 24. Senate passed Oct. 25. President signed Oct. 31, 1985.

PL 99-141 (HR 2959) Appropriate funds for energy and water development for fiscal year 1986. Introduced by BEVILL, D-Ala., July 10, 1985. House Appropriations reported July 10 (H Rept 99-195). House passed July 16. Senate Appropriations reported July 25 (S Rept 99-110). Senate passed, amended, Aug. 1. House agreed to conference report Oct. 17 (H Rept 99-307). Senate agreed to conference report Oct. 17. President signed Nov. 1, 1985.

PL 99-142 (S J Res 145) Designate November 1985 as "National Diabetes Month." Introduced by DURENBERGER, R-Minn., June 13, 1985. Senate Judiciary reported July 18. Senate passed July 19. House Post Office and Civil Service discharged. House passed Oct. 30. President signed Nov. 5, 1985.

PL 99-143 (H J Res 126) Designate the week of Nov. 3-9, 1985, as "National Drug Abuse Education Week." Introduced by BENNETT, D-Fla., Feb. 6, 1985. House Post Office and Civil Service discharged. House passed Oct. 30. Senate passed Nov. 4. President signed Nov. 7, 1985.

PL 99-144 (S J Res 227) Commend the people and the sovereign confederation of the neutral nation of Switzerland for their contributions to freedom, international peace and understanding on the occasion of the meeting between the leaders of the United States and the Soviet Union on Nov. 19-20, 1985, in Geneva, Switzerland. Introduced by LUGAR, R-Ind., Oct. 24, 1985. Senate Foreign Relations reported Oct. 24. Senate passed Oct. 25. House passed Oct. 29. President signed Nov. 8, 1985.

PL 99-145 (S 1160) Authorize funds for the military functions of the Department of Defense and prescribe personnel levels for the Department of Defense for fiscal year 1986, authorize certain construction at military installations for 1986, and authorize funds for the Department of Energy for national security programs for 1986. Introduced by GOLDWATER, R-Ariz., May 16, 1985. Senate Armed Services reported May 16. Senate passed June 5. House passed, amended, June 27. Senate agreed to conference report July 30 (H Rept 99-235). House agreed to conference report Oct. 29. President signed Nov. 8, 1985.

PL 99-146 (HR 1903) Provide for the use and distribution of funds appropriated in satisfaction of judgments awarded to the Chippewas of Lake Superior in dockets numbered 18-A, 18-U, 18-C and 18-T before the Indian Claims Commission. Introduced by OBERSTAR, D-Minn., April 2, 1985. House Interior and Insular Affairs reported Sept. 12 (H Rept 99-268). House passed Oct. 7. Senate passed Oct. 29. President signed Nov. 11, 1985.

PL 99-147 (H J Res 282) Designate the week beginning Oct. 27, 1985, as "National Alopecia Areata Awareness Week." Introduced by KOSTMAYER, D-Pa., May 8, 1985. House Post Office and Civil Service discharged. House passed Oct. 30. Senate Judiciary discharged. Senate passed Nov. 4. President signed Nov. 12, 1985.

PL 99-148 (S J Res 29) Designate the week of Nov. 11-17, 1985, as "National Reye's Syndrome Week." Introduced by GLENN, D-Ohio, Jan. 24, 1985. Senate Judiciary reported March 26. Senate passed March 28. House Post Office and Civil Service discharged. House passed, amended, Oct. 30. Senate agreed to House amendments with an amendment Nov. 5. House agreed to Senate amendments Nov. 6. President signed Nov. 12, 1985.

PL 99-149 (S J Res 130) Designate the week beginning Nov. 10, 1985, as "National Blood Pressure Awareness Week." Introduced by QUAYLE, R-Ind., May 3, 1985. Senate Judiciary reported Oct. 31. Senate passed Nov. 4. House Post Office and Civil Service discharged. House passed Nov. 6. President signed Nov. 12, 1985.

PL 99-150 (S 1570) Amend the Fair Labor Standards Act of 1938 to provide rules for overtime compensatory time off for certain public agency employees, and to clarify the application of that act to volunteers. Introduced by NICKLES, R-Okla., Aug. 1, 1985. Senate Labor and Human Resources reported Oct. 17 (S Rept 99-159). Senate passed Oct. 24. House passed, amended, Oct. 28. House agreed to conference report Nov. 7 (H Rept 99-357). Senate agreed to conference report Nov. 7. President signed Nov. 13, 1985.

PL 99-151 (HR 2942) Appropriate funds for the legislative branch for fiscal year 1986. Introduced by FAZIO, D-Calif., July 10, 1985. House Appropriations reported July 10 (H Rept 99-194). House passed July 18. Senate Appropriations reported July 25 (S Rept 99-111). Senate passed, amended, July 31. House agreed to conference report Oct. 29 (H Rept 99-321). Senate agreed to conference report Oct. 29. President signed Nov. 13, 1985.

PL 99-152 (S J Res 47) Designate the week beginning Nov. 10, 1985, as "National Women Veterans Recognition Week." Introduced by CRANSTON, D-Calif., Feb. 7, 1985. Senate Judiciary reported April 3. Senate passed April 15. House Post Office and Civil Service discharged. House passed Nov. 6. President signed Nov. 13, 1985.

PL 99-153 (S J Res 51) Designate the week beginning Nov. 24, 1985, as "National Adoption Week." Introduced by HATCH, R-Utah, Feb. 19, 1985. Senate Judiciary reported July 18. Senate passed July 19. House Post Office and Civil Service discharged. House passed Nov. 6. President signed Nov. 14, 1985.

PL 99-154 (H J Res 441) Make further continuing appropriations for fiscal year 1986, until Dec. 12, 1985. Introduced by WHITTEN, D-Miss., Nov. 5, 1985. House passed Nov. 12. Senate passed Nov. 13. President signed Nov. 14, 1985.

PL 99-155 (HR 3721) Temporarily increase the limit on the public debt and restore the investments of the Social Security trust funds and other trust funds. Introduced by ROSTENKOWSKI, D-Ill., Nov. 12, 1985. House passed Nov. 13. Senate passed, amended, Nov. 13. House agreed to Senate amendment Nov. 14. President signed Nov. 14, 1985.

PL 99-156 (H J Res 449) Provide for the temporary extension of certain programs relating to housing and community development. Introduced by GONZALEZ, D-Texas, Nov. 12, 1985. House Banking, Finance and Urban Affairs discharged. House passed Nov. 14. Senate passed Nov. 14. President signed Nov. 15, 1985.

PL 99-157 (S 1851) Extend temporarily the dairy price support program and certain food stamp program provisions. Introduced by HELMS, R-N.C., Nov. 13, 1985. Senate passed Nov. 13. House passed Nov. 14. President signed Nov. 15, 1985.

PL 99-158 (HR 2409) Amend the Public Health Service Act to revise and extend the authorities under the act relating to the National Institutes of Health and National Research Institutes. Introduced by WAXMAN, D-Calif., May 7, 1985. House Energy and Commerce reported June 4 (H Rept 99-158). House passed, under suspension of the rules, June 17. Senate passed, amended, July 19. Senate agreed to conference report Oct. 18 (H Rept 99-309). House agreed to conference report Oct. 23. President vetoed Nov. 8. House passed over presidential veto Nov. 12. Senate passed over presidential veto Nov. 20. Became public law without presidential approval Nov. 20, 1985.

PL 99-159 (HR 1210) Authorize funds for the National Science Foundation for fiscal year 1986. Introduced by FUQUA, D-Fla., Feb. 21, 1985. House Science and Technology reported April 16 (H Rept 99-44). House passed April 17. Senate passed, amended, Sept. 26. House agreed to Senate amendment with an amendment Oct. 24. Senate agreed to House amendment Nov. 1. President signed Nov. 22, 1985.

PL 99-160 (HR 3038) Appropriate funds for the Department of Housing and Urban Development, and for sundry independent agencies, boards, commissions, corporations and offices for fiscal year 1986. Introduced by BOLAND, D-Mass., July 18, 1985. House Appropriations reported July 18 (H Rept 99-212). House passed July 25. Senate Appropriations reported Aug. 28 (S Rept 99-129). Senate passed, amended, Oct. 18. House agreed to conference report Nov. 13 (H Rept 99-363). Senate agreed to conference report Nov. 13. President signed Nov. 25, 1985.

PL 99-161 (HR 3447) Amend and extend the Congressional Award Act. Introduced by WILLIAMS, D-Mont., Sept. 26, 1985. House Education and Labor reported Oct. 24 (H Rept 99-327). House passed, under suspension of the rules, Oct. 28. Senate Governmental Affairs discharged. Senate passed, amended, Nov. 13. House agreed to Senate amendments Nov. 14. President signed Nov. 25, 1985.

PL 99-162 (S J Res 228) Provide that, prior to March 1, 1986, no letter of acceptance to sell advanced weapons to Jordan (pursuant to Oct. 21 notification) is valid unless direct and meaningful peace negotiations between Israel and Jordan are under way. Introduced by LUGAR, R-Ind. (in behalf of DOLE, R-Kan.), Oct. 24, 1985. Senate passed Oct. 24. House Foreign Affairs reported Nov. 12 (H Rept 99-364). House passed, under suspension of the rules, Nov. 12. President signed Nov. 25, 1985.

PL 99-163 (S J Res 174) Designate Nov. 18, 1985, as "Eugene Ormandy Appreciation Day." Introduced by HEINZ, R-Pa., July 24, 1985. Senate Judiciary reported Oct. 3. Senate passed Oct. 4. House Post Office and Civil Service discharged. House passed Nov. 14. President signed Nov. 25, 1985.

PL 99-164 (H J Res 259) Designate Nov. 30, 1985, as "National Mark Twain Day." Introduced by VOLKMER, D-Mo., April 24, 1985. House Post Office and Civil Service discharged. House passed Oct. 9. Senate Judiciary reported Nov. 14. Senate passed Nov. 18. President signed Nov. 26, 1985.

PL 99-165 (S J Res 139) Designate the week of Dec. 1-7, 1985, as "National Home Care Week." Introduced by HATCH, R-Utah, May 21, 1985. Senate Judiciary reported Sept. 12. Senate passed Sept. 13. House Post Office and Civil Service discharged. House passed Nov. 21. President signed Dec. 3, 1985.

PL 99-166 (HR 505) Amend title 38, U.S. Code, to improve the delivery of health care services by the Veterans Administration. Introduced by EDGAR, D-Pa., Jan. 7, 1985. House Veterans' Affairs reported May 15 (H Rept 99-114). House passed, under suspension of the rules, May 21. Senate passed, amended, July 30. House concurred in Senate amendment to text of bill with an amendment Oct. 30. House agreed to Senate amendment to title of bill Oct. 30. Senate concurred in House amendment to Senate amendment to text of bill with amendments Nov. 13. House agreed to Senate amendments Nov. 14. President signed Dec. 3, 1985.

PL 99-167 (S 1042) Authorize funds for certain construction at military installations for fiscal year 1986. Introduced by GOLDWATER, R-Ariz., May 1, 1985. Senate Armed Services reported May 1. Senate passed June 5. House passed, amended, Oct. 16. Senate agreed to conference report Nov. 12 (H Rept 99-366). House agreed to conference report Nov. 19. President signed Dec. 3, 1985.

PL 99-168 (S J Res 195) Designate the week of Dec. 1-7, 1985, as "National Temporary Services Week." Introduced by KASTEN, R-Wis., Sept. 11, 1985. Senate Judiciary discharged. Senate passed Oct. 18. House Post Office and Civil Service discharged. House passed, amended, Nov. 6. Senate agreed to House amendments Nov. 23. President signed Dec. 3, 1985.

PL 99-169 (HR 2419) Authorize funds for fiscal year 1986 for the intelligence activities of the U.S. government, the Intelligence Community Staff, and the Central Intelligence Agency Retirement and Disability System. Introduced by HAMILTON, D-Ind., May 8, 1985. House Select Intelligence reported May 15 (H Rept 99-106, Part I). House Armed Services reported May 23 (H Rept 99-106, Part II). House passed July 18. Senate passed, amended, Sept. 26. House agreed to conference report Nov. 19 (H Rept 99-373). Senate agreed to conference report Nov. 21. President signed Dec. 4, 1985.

PL 99-170 (HR 1714) Authorize funds to the National Aeronautics and Space Administration for research and development, space flight, control and data communications, construction of facilities, and research and program management. Introduced by FUQUA, D-Fla., March 26, 1985. House Science and Technology reported March 28 (H Rept 99-32). House passed April 3. Senate Commerce, Science and

Transportation reported June 24 (S Rept 99-91). Senate passed, amended, June 27. Senate agreed to conference report Nov. 21 (H Rept 99-379). House agreed to conference report Nov. 21. President signed Dec. 5, 1985.

PL 99-171 (HR 3235) Authorize the administrator of the National Aeronautics and Space Administration to accept title to the Mississippi Technology Transfer Center to be constructed by the state of Mississippi at the National Space Technologies Laboratories in Hancock County, Miss. Introduced by LOTT, R-Miss., Sept. 4, 1985. House Science and Technology reported Oct. 23 (H Rept 99-322). House passed, under suspension of the rules, Oct. 28. Senate Commerce, Science and Transportation reported Nov. 18 (S Rept 99-187). Senate passed Nov. 21. President signed Dec. 9, 1985.

PL 99-172 (HR 1806) Recognize the organization known as the Daughters of Union Veterans of the Civil War 1861-1865. Introduced by KINDNESS, R-Ohio, March 28, 1985. House Judiciary reported May 8 (H Rept 99-70). House passed, under suspension of the rules, May 13. Senate Judiciary reported Nov. 12 (S Rept 99-179). Senate passed Nov. 21. President signed Dec. 9, 1985.

PL 99-173 (HR 3327) Appropriate funds for military construction for the Department of Defense for fiscal year 1986. Introduced by HEFNER, D-N.C., Sept. 18, 1985. House Appropriations reported Sept. 18 (H Rept 99-275). House passed Oct. 17. Senate Appropriations reported Oct. 31 (S Rept 99-168). Senate passed, amended, Nov. 7. House agreed to conference report Nov. 20 (H Rept 99-380). Senate agreed to conference report Nov. 21. President signed Dec. 10, 1985.

PL 99-174 (H J Res 459) Reaffirm the friendship of the people of the United States with the people of Colombia following the devastating volcanic eruption of Nov. 13, 1985. Introduced by FASCELL, D-Fla., Nov. 19, 1985. House passed Nov. 19. Senate passed Nov. 23. President signed Dec. 11, 1985.

PL 99-175 (S J Res 206) Authorize and request the president to designate December 1985 as "Made in America Month." Introduced by THURMOND, R-S.C., Sept. 24, 1985. Senate Judiciary reported Sept. 26. Senate passed Sept. 30. House Post Office and Civil Service discharged. House passed Nov. 21. President signed Dec. 11, 1985.

PL 99-176 (H J Res 473) Waive the printing on parchment of the enrollment of H J Res 372, increasing the statutory limit on the public debt. Introduced by FOLEY, D-Wash., Dec. 10, 1985. House passed Dec. 10. Senate passed Dec. 10. President signed Dec. 11, 1985.

PL 99-177 (H J Res 372) Increase the statutory limit on the public debt. This law includes the Gramm-Rudman-Hollings legislation setting maximum allowable federal deficits for fiscal years 1986-91, declining annually by $36 billion to zero in fiscal 1991. Introduced by O'NEILL, D-Mass., Aug. 1, 1985. House passed Aug. 1. Senate Finance reported Sept. 26 (S Rept 99-144). Senate passed, amended, Oct. 10. Senate agreed to conference report Dec. 11 (H Rept 99-433). House agreed to conference report Dec. 11. President signed Dec. 12, 1985.

PL 99-178 (HR 3424) Appropriate funds for the Departments of Labor, Health and Human Services, and Education and related agencies for fiscal year 1986. Introduced by NATCHER, D-Ky., Sept. 26, 1985. House Appropriations reported Sept. 26 (H Rept 99-289). House passed Oct. 2. Senate Appropriations reported Oct. 4 (S Rept 99-151). Senate passed, amended, Oct. 22. House agreed to conference report Dec. 5 (H Rept 99-402). Senate agreed to conference report Dec. 6. President signed Dec. 12, 1985.

PL 99-179 (H J Res 476) Make further continuing appropriations for fiscal year 1986, until Dec. 16, 1985. Introduced by WHITTEN, D-Miss., Dec. 12, 1985. House passed Dec. 12. Senate passed Dec. 12. President signed Dec. 13, 1985.

PL 99-180 (HR 2965) Appropriate funds for the Departments of Commerce, Justice and State, the judiciary and related agencies for fiscal year 1986. Introduced by SMITH, D-Iowa, July 11, 1985. House Appropriations reported July 11 (H Rept 99-197). House passed July 17. Senate Appropriations reported Oct. 4 (S Rept 99-150). Senate passed, amended, Nov. 1. House agreed to conference report Dec. 5 (H Rept 99-414). Senate agreed to conference report Dec. 6. President signed Dec. 13, 1985.

PL 99-181 (HR 3918) Extend until Dec. 18, 1985, the application of certain tobacco excise taxes, trade adjustment assistance, certain Medicare reimbursement provisions, and borrowing authority under the railroad unemployment insurance program. Introduced by ROSTENKOWSKI, D-Ill., Dec. 12, 1985. House Ways and Means discharged. House passed Dec. 12. Senate passed Dec. 12. President signed Dec. 13, 1985.

PL 99-182 (HR 3919) Extend temporarily the dairy price support program and certain food stamp program provisions. Introduced by de la GARZA, D-Texas, Dec. 12, 1985. House Agriculture discharged. House passed Dec. 12. Senate passed Dec. 12. President signed Dec. 13, 1985.

PL 99-183 (S J Res 238) Relating to the approval and implementation of the proposed agreement for nuclear cooperation between the United States and the People's Republic of China. Introduced by LUGAR, R-Ind., Nov. 14, 1985. Senate Foreign Relations reported Nov. 14. Senate passed Nov. 21. House passed Dec. 11. President signed Dec. 16, 1985.

PL 99-184 (H J Res 491) Make further continuing appropriations for fiscal year 1986, until Dec. 19, 1985. Introduced by WHITTEN, D-Miss., Dec. 16, 1985. House passed Dec. 17. Senate passed Dec. 17. President signed Dec. 17, 1985.

PL 99-185 (S 1639) Authorize the minting of gold bullion coins. Introduced by EXON, D-Neb., Sept. 12, 1985. Senate Banking, Housing and Urban Affairs reported Nov. 13. Senate passed Nov. 14. House passed, under suspension of the rules, Dec. 2. President signed Dec. 17, 1985.

PL 99-186 (S 727) Clarify the application of the Public Utility Holding Company Act of 1935 to encourage "cogeneration" activities by gas utility holding company systems. Introduced by HEINZ, R-Pa., March 20, 1985. Senate Banking, Housing and Urban Affairs reported Nov. 13. Senate passed Nov. 14. House Energy and Commerce discharged. House passed Dec. 6. President signed Dec. 18, 1985.

PL 99-187 (S 1116) Amend the act of Oct. 15, 1982, to designate the Mary McLeod Bethune Council House in Washington, D.C., as a national historic site. Introduced by WARNER, R-Va., May 9, 1985. Senate Energy and Natural Resources reported Nov. 18 (S Rept 99-181). Senate passed Dec. 3. House passed, under suspension of the rules, Dec. 9. President signed Dec. 18, 1985.

PL 99-188 (H J Res 485) Waive the printing on parchment of enrolled bills and joint resolutions during the remainder of the first session of the 99th Congress. Introduced by WRIGHT, D-Texas, Dec. 16, 1985. House passed Dec. 16. Senate passed Dec. 18. President signed Dec. 18, 1985.

PL 99-189 (HR 3981) Extend until Dec. 19, 1985, the application of certain tobacco excise taxes, trade adjustment assistance, certain Medicare reimbursement provisions, and borrowing authority under the railroad unemployment insurance program. Introduced by GIBBONS, D-Fla., Dec. 18, 1985. House Ways and Means discharged. House passed Dec. 18. Senate passed Dec. 18. President signed Dec. 18, 1985.

PL 99-190 (H J Res 465) Make further continuing appropriations for fiscal year 1986. Introduced by WHITTEN, D-Miss., Nov. 21, 1985. House Appropriations reported Nov. 21 (H Rept 99-403). House passed Dec. 4. Senate Appropriations reported Dec. 5 (S Rept 99-210). Senate passed, amended, Dec. 10. House rejected conference report Dec. 16 (H Rept 99-443). House agreed to conference report Dec. 19 (H Rept 99-450). Senate agreed to conference report Dec. 19. President signed Dec. 19, 1985.

PL 99-191 (HR 1789) Relating to the authorization of appropriations for certain components of the National Wildlife Refuge System. Introduced by BREAUX, D-La., March 28, 1985. House Merchant Marine and Fisheries reported May 15 (H Rept 99-100). House passed, under suspension of the rules, July 29. Senate passed Dec. 5. President signed Dec. 19, 1985.

PL 99-192 (HR 3735) Designate the pedestrian walkway crossing the Potomac River at Harpers Ferry National Historic Park as the "Goodloe E. Byron Memorial Pedestrian Walkway." Introduced by HOLT, R-Md., Nov. 12, 1985. House Interior and Insular Affairs reported Dec. 4 (H Rept 99-412). House passed Dec. 6. Senate Energy and Natural Resources discharged. Senate passed Dec. 11. President signed Dec. 19, 1985.

PL 99-193 (H J Res 424) Designate 1986 as the "Year of the Flag." Introduced by COBEY, R-N.C., Oct. 22, 1985. House Post Office and Civil Service discharged. House passed Dec. 3. Senate passed Dec. 5. President signed Dec. 19, 1985.

PL 99-194 (S 1264) Amend the National Foundation on the Arts and Humanities Act of 1965, the Museum Services Act and the Arts and Artifacts Indemnity Act, and extend the authorization of appropriations for the acts. Introduced by QUAYLE, R-Ind., June 7, 1985. Senate Labor and Human Resources reported Aug. 1 (S Rept 99-125). Senate passed Oct. 3. House passed, amended, Oct. 10. Senate agreed to House amendments with an amendment Dec. 3. House agreed to Senate amendment Dec. 4. President signed Dec. 20, 1985.

PL 99-195 (HR 664) Amend the Panama Canal Act of 1979 with respect to the payment of interest on U.S. investment. Introduced by FIELDS, R-Texas, Jan. 24, 1985. House Merchant Marine and Fisheries reported April 22 (H Rept 99-53). House passed, under suspension of the rules, May 6. Senate Armed Services reported Dec. 3 (S Rept 99-205). Senate passed Dec. 11. President signed Dec. 23, 1985.

PL 99-196 (HR 1534) Convert the temporary authority to allow federal employees to work on a flexible or compressed schedule under title 5, U.S. Code, into permanent authority. Introduced by ACKERMAN, D-N.Y., March 19, 1985. House Post Office and Civil Service reported May 13 (H Rept 99-82). House passed, under suspension of the rules, May 20. Senate Governmental Affairs reported July 11. Senate passed Dec. 11. President signed Dec. 23, 1985.

PL 99-197 (HR 1627) Designate certain national forest system lands in

Kentucky for inclusion in the National Wilderness Preservation System and release other forest lands for multiple-use management. Introduced by PERKINS, D-Ky., March 20, 1985. House Interior and Insular Affairs reported Dec. 4 (H Rept 99-411, Part I). House passed, under suspension of the rules, Dec. 9. Senate passed Dec. 12. President signed Dec. 23, 1985.

PL 99-198 (HR 2100) Revise agriculture programs and extend them through fiscal year 1990; modify price supports by reducing loan rates in 1986 and thereafter; maintain income supports by freezing target prices at fiscal 1985 levels through fiscal 1987 and reduce them by a total of 10 percent over the remaining three years of the bill; provide for agricultural export, soil conservation, farm credit and agricultural research programs; and continue food assistance to low-income persons through fiscal year 1990. Introduced by de la GARZA, D-Texas, April 17, 1985. House Agriculture reported Sept. 13 (H Rept 99-271, Part I). House Merchant Marine and Fisheries reported Sept. 18 (H Rept 99-271, Part II). House passed Oct. 8. Senate passed, amended, Nov. 23. House agreed to conference report Dec. 18 (H Rept 99-447). Senate agreed to conference report Dec. 18. President signed Dec. 23, 1985.

PL 99-199 (HR 2976) Direct the secretary of agriculture to release the condition requiring that a parcel of land conveyed to New York state be used for public purposes and convey U.S. mineral interests in the parcel to New York state. Introduced by LUNDINE, D-N.Y., July 11, 1985. House Agriculture reported Dec. 6 (H Rept 99-424). House passed, under suspension of the rules, Dec. 9. Senate passed Dec. 11. President signed Dec. 23, 1985.

PL 99-200 (HR 3085) Clear title to certain lands along the California-Nevada boundary. Introduced by LEHMAN, D-Calif., July 25, 1985. House Interior and Insular Affairs reported Nov. 20 (H Rept 99-385). House passed Dec. 9. Senate passed Dec. 11. President signed Dec. 23, 1985.

PL 99-201 (HR 4006) Extend until March 15, 1986, the application of certain tobacco excise taxes, trade adjustment assistance, certain Medicare reimbursement provisions, and borrowing authority under the railroad unemployment insurance program, and amend the Internal Revenue Code of 1954 to extend for a temporary period certain tax provisions of current law that would otherwise expire at the end of 1985. Introduced by ROSTENKOWSKI, D-Ill., Dec. 19, 1985. House Energy and Commerce discharged. House Ways and Means discharged. House passed Dec. 19. Senate passed, amended, Dec. 19. House agreed to Senate amendments with amendments Dec. 20. Senate agreed to House amendments Dec. 20. President signed Dec. 23, 1985.

PL 99-202 (H J Res 436) Designate 1986 as "Save for the U.S.A. Year." Introduced by KAPTUR, D-Ohio, Oct. 30, 1985. House Banking, Finance and Urban Affairs discharged. House passed Dec. 12. Senate Judiciary discharged. Senate passed Dec. 16. President signed Dec. 23, 1985.

PL 99-203 (H J Res 450) Authorize and request the president to issue a proclamation designating April 20-26, 1986, as "National Organ and Tissue Donor Awareness Week." Introduced by MORRISON, R-Wash., Nov. 12, 1985. House Post Office and Civil Service discharged. House passed Nov. 14. Senate Judiciary reported Dec. 12. Senate passed Dec. 13. President signed Dec. 23, 1985.

PL 99-204 (S 947) Amend the Foreign Assistance Act of 1961 to renew and extend the authority of the Overseas Private Investment Corporation to issue insurance, reinsurance, and guarantees for projects in friendly developing nations. Introduced by LUGAR, R-Ind., April 18, 1985. Senate Foreign Relations reported Oct. 10 (S Rept 99-156). Senate passed Nov. 14. House passed, amended, Dec. 3. House agreed to conference report Dec. 11 (H Rept 99-428). Senate agreed to conference report Dec. 12. President signed Dec. 23, 1985.

PL 99-205 (S 1884) Reorganize the Farm Credit System to enable individual institutions to pool resources and sell assets to resolve financial problems affecting individual institutions; create a capital corporation within the system to take over non-performing loans and obligations of member institutions; restructure the federal Farm Credit Administration to perform as an independent regulating agency of the system; and authorize the secretary of the Treasury to purchase obligations of the capital corporation. Introduced by HELMS, R-N.C., Nov. 22, 1985. Senate Agriculture, Nutrition and Forestry discharged. Senate passed Dec. 3. House passed, amended, under suspension of the rules, Dec. 10. Senate agreed to House amendment with amendments Dec. 17. House agreed to Senate amendments Dec. 18. President signed Dec. 23, 1985.

PL 99-206 (S J Res 32) Authorize and request the president to designate Sept. 21, 1986, as "Ethnic American Day." Introduced by PRESSLER, R-S.D., Jan. 29, 1985. Senate Judiciary reported May 9. Senate passed May 16. House Post Office and Civil Service discharged. House passed Dec. 12. President signed Dec. 23, 1985.

PL 99-207 (S J Res 70) Proclaim March 20, 1986, as "National Agriculture Day." Introduced by HELMS, R-N.C., Feb. 28, 1985. Senate Judiciary reported March 26. Senate passed March 28. House Post Office and Civil Service discharged. House passed, amended, Dec. 3. Senate agreed to House amendments Dec. 11. President signed Dec. 23, 1985.

PL 99-208 (S J Res 213) Designate Jan. 19-25, 1986, as "National Jaycee Week." Introduced by FORD, D-Ky., Oct. 4, 1985. Senate Judiciary reported Oct. 31. Senate passed Nov. 4. House Post Office and Civil Service discharged. House passed Dec. 12. President signed Dec. 23, 1985.

PL 99-209 (HR 729) Amend the Panama Canal Act of 1979, in order that claims for vessels damaged outside the locks may be resolved in the same manner as those for vessels damaged inside the locks. Introduced by TAUZIN, D-La., Jan. 24, 1985. House Merchant Marine and Fisheries reported June 27 (H Rept 99-184). House passed, under suspension of the rules, July 22. Senate Armed Services reported Dec. 3 (S Rept 99-206). Senate passed Dec. 11. President signed Dec. 23, 1985.

PL 99-210 (HR 2694) Designate the U.S. post office building located at 300 Packerland Drive, Green Bay, Wis., as the "John W. Byrnes Post Office and Federal Building." Introduced by ROTH, R-Wis., June 6, 1985. House Post Office and Civil Service discharged. House passed July 8. Senate Governmental Affairs reported Dec. 12. Senate passed Dec. 13. President signed Dec. 23, 1985.

PL 99-211 (HR 2391) Authorize the administrator of general services to collect additional contributions of money provided for him by private individuals or organizations for the Nancy Hanks Center. Introduced by HOWARD, D-N.J., May 7, 1985. House Public Works and Transportation discharged. House passed Dec. 11. Senate passed Dec. 18. President signed Dec. 26, 1985.

PL 99-212 (HR 2542) Designate the building located at 125 S. State St., Salt Lake City, Utah, as the "Wallace F. Bennett Federal Building." Introduced by MONSON, R-Utah, May 16, 1985. House Public Works and Transportation discharged. House passed Dec. 11. Senate passed Dec. 18. President signed Dec. 26, 1985.

PL 99-213 (HR 2698) Designate the U.S. Courthouse in Tucson, Ariz., as the "James A. Walsh United States Courthouse." Introduced by UDALL, D-Ariz., June 6, 1985. House Public Works and Transportation reported July 18 (H Rept 99-209). House passed Oct. 7. Senate Environment and Public Works discharged. Senate passed Dec. 18. President signed Dec. 26, 1985.

PL 99-214 (HR 2903) Designate the federal building and U.S. post office located in Philadelphia, Pa., as the "Robert N. C. Nix Sr. Building." Introduced by FOGLIETTA, D-Pa., June 27, 1985. House Public Works and Transportation discharged. House passed Dec. 11. Senate passed Dec. 18. President signed Dec. 26, 1985.

PL 99-215 (HR 3003) Authorize the secretary of the interior to convey certain land located in Maryland to the Maryland-National Capital Park and Planning Commission. Introduced by HOYER, D-Md., July 16, 1985. House Interior and Insular Affairs reported Oct. 17 (H Rept 99-313). House passed Oct. 23. Senate Energy and Natural Resources reported Nov. 18 (S Rept 99-186). Senate passed, amended, Dec. 3. House agreed to Senate amendment Dec. 6. President signed Dec. 26, 1985.

PL 99-216 (HR 3718) Waive the period of congressional review for certain District of Columbia acts authorizing the issuance of revenue bonds. Introduced by FAUNTROY, D-D.C., Nov. 8, 1985. House District of Columbia reported Nov. 13 (H Rept 99-372). House passed Nov. 19. Senate Governmental Affairs reported Dec. 11 (S Rept 99-227). Senate passed, amended, Dec. 19. House agreed to Senate amendments Dec. 19. President signed Dec. 26, 1985.

PL 99-217 (HR 3837) Extend the deadline for the submission of the initial set of sentencing guidelines by the U.S. Sentencing Commission. Introduced by CONYERS, D-Mich., Dec. 3, 1985. House passed, under suspension of the rules, Dec. 16. Senate passed Dec. 18. President signed Dec. 26, 1985.

PL 99-218 (HR 3914) Preserve the authority of the Supreme Court police to provide protective services for justices and court personnel. Introduced by GLICKMAN, D-Kan., Dec. 11, 1985. House Judiciary discharged. House passed Dec. 12. Senate passed, amended, Dec. 12. House agreed to Senate amendment Dec. 17. President signed Dec. 26, 1985.

PL 99-219 (H J Res 495) Provide for the temporary extension of certain programs relating to housing and community development. Introduced by St GERMAIN, D-R.I., Dec. 19, 1985. House Banking, Finance and Urban Affairs discharged. House passed Dec. 19. Senate passed Dec. 20. President signed Dec. 26, 1985.

PL 99-220 (S J Res 189) Designate the week beginning Jan. 12, 1986, as "National Fetal Alcohol Syndrome Awareness Week." Introduced by HATCH, R-Utah, Aug. 1, 1985. Senate Judiciary reported Sept. 26. Senate passed Sept. 30. House Post Office and Civil Service discharged. House passed Dec. 18. President signed Dec. 26, 1985.

PL 99-221 (S 1728) Authorize the Cherokee Nation of Oklahoma to lease certain lands held in trust for up to 99 years. Introduced by NICKLES, R-Okla., Oct. 2, 1985. Senate Select Indian Affairs reported Nov. 19 (S Rept 99-191). Senate passed Dec. 3. House Interior and Insular Affairs discharged. House Post Office and Civil Service discharged. House Ways and Means discharged. House passed Dec. 17. President signed Dec. 26, 1985.

PL 99-222 (HR 1603) Amend the Securities Exchange Act of 1934 to authorize the Securities and Exchange Commission to subject banks, associations and other entities that exercise fiduciary powers to the same regulations as broker-dealers, pursuant to section 14(b) of the act. Introduced by WIRTH, D-Colo., March 20, 1985. House Energy and Commerce reported June 26 (H Rept 99-181). House passed, under suspension of the rules, July 22. Senate passed Dec. 18. President signed Dec. 28, 1985.

PL 99-223 (HR 1784) Authorize appropriations for fiscal year 1986 for the operation and maintenance of the Panama Canal. Introduced by LOWRY, D-Wash., March 28, 1985. House Merchant Marine and Fisheries reported April 29 (H Rept 99-59). House passed May 14. Senate Armed Services reported Dec. 3 (S Rept 99-207). Senate passed, amended, Dec. 12. House agreed to Senate amendments Dec. 17. President signed Dec. 28, 1985.

PL 99-224 (HR 1890) Provide for an equitable waiver in the compromise and collection of federal claims. Introduced by SAM B. HALL JR., D-Texas, April 2, 1985. House Judiciary reported May 15 (H Rept 99-102). House passed, under suspension of the rules, July 15. Senate Judiciary reported Dec. 6. Senate passed, amended, Dec. 11. House agreed to Senate amendments with amendments Dec. 17. Senate agreed to House amendments Dec. 18. President signed Dec. 28, 1985.

PL 99-225 (HR 2962) Remove certain restrictions on the availability of office space for former Speakers of the House of Representatives. Introduced by GRAY, D-Ill., July 10, 1985. House Public Works and Transportation discharged. House passed Dec. 11. Senate passed Dec. 18. President signed Dec. 28, 1985.

PL 99-226 (HR 3608) Amend the Small Business Investment Act of 1958, to clarify certain provisions in current law that establish the permissable interest rates that a small-business investment company may charge to a small-business borrower. Introduced by MITCHELL, D-Md., Oct. 23, 1985. House Small Business reported Nov. 14 (H Rept 99-376). House passed, under suspension of the rules, Nov. 19. Senate passed Dec. 18. President signed Dec. 28, 1985.

PL 99-227 (HR 3974) Provide for temporary family housing or temporary housing allowances for dependents of members of the armed forces who die on or after Dec. 12, 1985. Introduced by SCHROEDER, D-Colo., Dec. 17, 1985. House Armed Services discharged. House passed Dec. 18. Senate passed, amended, Dec. 18. House agreed to Senate amendments Dec. 19. President signed Dec. 28, 1985.

PL 99-228 (S 1621) Amend title 25, U.S. Code, relating to Indian education programs. Introduced by MELCHER, D-Mont., Sept. 11, 1985. Senate Select Indian Affairs reported Nov. 13 (S Rept 99-180). Senate passed Dec. 13. House passed Dec. 16. President signed Dec. 28, 1985.

PL 99-229 (S 1706) Authorize the architect of the Capitol, in cooperation with the Union Station Redevelopment Corporation, to design a building or buildings adjacent to Union Station, in Washington, D.C. Introduced by STAFFORD, R-Vt., Sept. 26, 1985. Senate Environment and Public Works reported Oct. 16 (S Rept 99-158). Senate passed Oct. 29. House Public Works and Transportation discharged. House passed, amended, Dec. 10. Senate agreed to House amendments Dec. 19. President signed Dec. 28, 1985.

PL 99-230 (S 1918) Change the date for transmittal of a report relating to the International Security and Development Cooperation Act of 1985 on the employee stock ownership plan in business enterprises in the Caribbean. Introduced by LUGAR, R-Ind., Dec. 10, 1985. Senate Foreign Relations discharged. Senate passed Dec. 16. House passed Dec. 18. President signed Dec. 28, 1985.

PL 99-231 (S J Res 198) Designate 1986 as the "Sesquicentennial Year of the National Library of Medicine." Introduced by MATHIAS, R-Md., Sept. 12, 1985. Senate Judiciary reported Nov. 21. Senate passed Nov. 23. House Post Office and Civil Service discharged. House passed Dec. 18. President signed Dec. 28, 1985.

PL 99-232 (S J Res 235) Designate the week of Jan. 26-Feb. 1, 1986, as "Truck and Bus Safety Week." Introduced by DANFORTH, R-Mo., Nov. 6, 1985. Senate Judiciary reported Dec. 12. Senate passed Dec. 13. House Post Office and Civil Service discharged. House passed Dec. 18. President signed Dec. 28, 1985.

PL 99-233 (S J Res 255) Provide for the convening of the second session of the 99th Congress. Introduced by DOLE, R-Kan., Dec. 19, 1985. Senate passed Dec. 19. House passed Dec. 20. President signed Dec. 28, 1985.

PL 99-234 (S 1840) Amend title 5, U.S. Code, to revise the authority relating to the payment of subsistence and travel allowances to government employees for official travel, and to prescribe standards for the allowability of the cost of subsistence and travel of contractor personnel under government contracts. Introduced by STEVENS, R-Alaska, Nov. 7, 1985. Senate Governmental Affairs discharged. Senate passed Dec. 19. House passed Dec. 19. President signed Jan. 2, 1986.

PL 99-235 (HR 2651) Amend section 504 of the Alaska National Interest Lands Conservation Act to promote the development of mineral wealth in Alaska. Introduced by YOUNG, R-Alaska, June 3, 1985. House Interior and Insular Affairs reported Dec. 12 (H Rept 99-436). House passed Dec. 12. Senate Energy and Natural Resources discharged. Senate passed Dec. 19. President signed Jan. 9, 1986.

PL 99-236 (HR 3931) Designate the General Services Administration building known as the "United States Appraiser's Stores Building" in Boston, Mass., as the "Captain John Foster Williams Coast Guard Building." Introduced by MOAKLEY, D-Mass., Dec. 12, 1985. House Public Works and Transportation discharged. House passed Dec. 18. Senate passed Dec. 19. President signed Jan. 9, 1986.

PL 99-237 (H J Res 440) Designate the week of Dec. 1-7, 1985, as "National Autism Week." Introduced by BIAGGI, D-N.Y., Nov. 1, 1985. House Post Office and Civil Service discharged. House passed Dec. 3. Senate passed Dec. 6. President signed Jan. 13, 1986.

PL 99-238 (HR 1538) Amend title 38, U.S. Code, to provide a 3.1 percent increase in the rates of disability compensation and of dependency and indemnity compensation paid by the Veterans Administration, and to make improvements in veterans' job training programs. Introduced by APPLEGATE, D-Ohio, March 19, 1985. House Veterans' Affairs reported Oct. 29 (H Rept 99-337, Part I). House Ways and Means discharged. House passed, under suspension of the rules, Dec. 9. Senate passed, amended, Dec. 19. House agreed to Senate amendments Dec. 19. President signed Jan. 13, 1986.

PL 99-239 (H J Res 187) Approve the Compact of Free Association negotiated by the United States and the Republic of the Marshall Islands and the Federated States of Micronesia. Introduced by FASCELL, D-Fla., March 7, 1985. House Foreign Affairs reported July 1 (H Rept 99-188, Part I). House Interior and Insular Affairs reported July 15 (H Rept 99-188, Part II). House Merchant Marine and Fisheries reported July 19 (H Rept 99-188, Part III). House Armed Services discharged. House Judiciary discharged. House Ways and Means reported July 22 (H Rept 99-188, Part IV). House passed July 25. Senate passed, amended, Nov. 14. House agreed to Senate amendments with an amendment Dec. 11. Senate agreed to House amendment Dec. 13. President signed Jan. 14, 1986.

PL 99-240 (HR 1083) Amend the Low-Level Radioactive Waste Policy Act to improve procedures for the implementation of compacts providing for the establishment and operation of regional disposal facilities for low-level radioactive waste, and to grant the consent of Congress to certain interstate compacts on low-level radioactive waste. Introduced by UDALL, D-Ariz., Feb. 7, 1985. House Interior and Insular Affairs reported Oct. 22 (H Rept 99-314, Part I). House Energy and Commerce reported Dec. 4 (H Rept 99-314, Part II). House passed, under suspension of the rules, Dec. 9. Senate passed, amended, Dec. 19. House agreed to Senate amendment with an amendment Dec. 19. Senate agreed to House amendment Dec. 19. President signed Jan. 15, 1986. ■

CONGRESS and Its MEMBERS

CQ

Characteristics of the 99th Congress

Following is a compilation of information about individual members of the 99th Congress — their birth dates, occupations, religion and seniority.

Senate and House seniority lists begin on page 12-G.

The average age of members of the new Congress was 50, slightly higher than in the two previous Congresses.

As in previous years, the biggest single occupational group in Congress was lawyers. Nearly half the members — 251 — listed law as their profession. Businessmen and bankers comprised the next largest category, with 174 members falling into those groups.

Roman Catholic members made up the largest religious group, followed by Methodists and Episcopalians. The lists below include Frank McCloskey (D) as representative of the 8th Congressional District of Indiana. That seat was contested and declared vacant when Congress convened Jan. 3. The issue was not settled until May 1, when the House voted to seat McCloskey.

Senate—Birth Dates, Occupations, Religions, Seniority

(Seniority rank is within the member's party.)

ALABAMA

Heflin (D)—June 19, 1921. Occupation: lawyer, judge. Religion: Methodist. Seniority: 35.

Denton (R)—July 15, 1924. Occupation: naval officer, educator, broadcasting executive. Religion: Roman Catholic. Seniority: 34.

ALASKA

Murkowski (R)—March 28, 1933. Occupation: banker. Religion: Roman Catholic. Seniority: 41.

Stevens (R)—Nov. 18, 1923. Occupation: lawyer. Religion: Episcopalian. Seniority: 3.

ARIZONA

DeConcini (D)—May 8, 1937. Occupation: lawyer. Religion: Roman Catholic. Seniority: 28.

Goldwater (R)—Jan. 1, 1909. Occupation: author, department store executive. Religion: Episcopalian. Seniority: 4.

ARKANSAS

Bumpers (D)—Aug. 12, 1925. Occupation: farmer, hardware company executive, lawyer, governor. Religion: Methodist. Seniority: 19.

Pryor (D)—Aug. 29, 1934. Occupation: newspaper publisher, lawyer, governor. Religion: Presbyterian. Seniority: 32.

CALIFORNIA

Cranston (D)—June 19, 1914. Occupation: author, journalist, real estate executive. Religion: Protestant. Seniority: 11.

Wilson (R)—Aug. 23, 1933. Occupation: lawyer. Religion: Protestant. Seniority: 49.

COLORADO

Hart (D)—Nov. 28, 1936. Occupation: author, educator, lawyer. Religion: Presbyterian. Seniority: 20.

Armstrong (R)—March 16, 1937. Occupation: broadcasting executive. Religion: Lutheran. Seniority: 28.

CONNECTICUT

Dodd (D)—May 27, 1944. Occupation: lawyer. Religion: Roman Catholic. Seniority: 39.

Weicker (R)—May 16, 1931. Occupation: lawyer. Religion: Episcopalian. Seniority: 9.

DELAWARE

Biden (D)—Nov. 20, 1942. Occupation: lawyer. Religion: Roman Catholic. Seniority: 16.

Roth (R)—July 22, 1921. Occupation: lawyer. Religion: Episcopalian. Seniority: 8.

FLORIDA

Chiles (D)—April 3, 1930. Occupation: lawyer. Religion: Presbyterian. Seniority: 13.

Hawkins (R)—June 24, 1927. Occupation: vitamin retailer, public official. Religion: Mormon. Seniority: 33.

GEORGIA

Nunn (D)—Sept. 8, 1938. Occupation: farmer, lawyer. Religion: Methodist: Seniority: 14.

Mattingly (R)—Jan. 7, 1931. Occupation: corporate executive. Religion: Episcopalian. Seniority: 41.

HAWAII

Inouye (D)—Sept. 7, 1924. Occupation: lawyer. Religion: Methodist. Seniority: 8.

Matsunaga (D)—Oct. 8, 1916. Occupation: lawyer. Religion: Episcopalian. Seniority: 25.

IDAHO

McClure (R)—Dec. 27, 1924. Occupation: lawyer. Religion: Methodist. Seniority: 11.

Symms (R)—April 23, 1938. Occupation: fruit grower, fitness club owner. Religion: Methodist. Seniority: 36.

ILLINOIS

Dixon (D)—July 7, 1927. Occupation: lawyer. Religion: Presbyterian. Seniority: 40.

Simon (D)—Nov. 29, 1928. Occupation: author, newspaper editor and publisher. Religion: Lutheran. Seniority: 44.

INDIANA

Lugar (R)—April 4, 1932. Occupation: farmer, educator, tool company executive. Religion: Methodist. Seniority: 19.

Quayle (R)—Feb. 4, 1947. Occupation: lawyer, newspaper publisher. Religion: Presbyterian. Seniority: 39.

IOWA

Grassley (R)—Sept. 17, 1933. Occupation: farmer, educator. Religion: Baptist. Seniority: 38.

Harkin (D)—Nov. 19, 1939. Occupation: lawyer. Religion: Roman Catholic. Seniority: 44.

KANSAS

Dole (R)—July 22, 1923. Occupation: lawyer. Religion: Methodist. Seniority: 5.

Kassebaum (R)—July 29, 1932. Occupation: broadcasting executive. Religion: Episcopalian. Seniority: 23.

KENTUCKY

Ford (D)—Sept. 8, 1924. Occupation: insurance executive, governor. Religion: Baptist. Seniority: 18.

McConnell (R)—Feb. 20, 1942. Occupation: county judge/executive. Religion: Baptist. Seniority: 53.

LOUISIANA

Johnston (D)—June 10, 1932. Occupation: lawyer. Religion: Baptist. Seniority: 15.

Long (D)—Nov. 3, 1918. Occupation: lawyer. Religion: Methodist. Seniority: 2.

MAINE

Mitchell (D)—Aug. 20, 1933. Occupation: lawyer, judge. Religion: Roman Catholic. Seniority: 38.

Cohen (R)—Aug. 28, 1940. Occupation: author, educator, lawyer. Religion: Unitarian. Seniority: 28.

MARYLAND

Sarbanes (D)—Feb. 3, 1933. Occupation: lawyer. Religion: Greek Orthodox. Seniority: 27.

Mathias (R)—July 24, 1922. Occupation: lawyer. Religion: Episcopalian. Seniority: 5.

MASSACHUSETTS

Kennedy (D)—Feb. 22, 1932. Occupation: author, lawyer. Religion: Roman Catholic. Seniority: 7.

Kerry (D)—Dec. 11, 1943. Occupation: lawyer. Religion: Roman Catholic. Seniority: 43.

MICHIGAN

Levin (D)—June 28, 1934. Occupation: lawyer. Religion: Jewish. Seniority: 35.

Riegle (D)—Feb. 4, 1938. Occupation: pricing analyst, professor. Religion: Methodist. Seniority: 24.

MINNESOTA

Boschwitz (R)—Nov. 7, 1930. Occupation: plywood company owner, lawyer. Religion: Jewish. Seniority: 25.

Durenberger (R)—Aug. 19, 1934. Occupation: adhesive manufacturing company executive, lawyer. Religion: Roman Catholic. Seniority: 22.

MISSISSIPPI

Stennis (D)—Aug. 3, 1901. Occupation: lawyer, judge. Religion: Presbyterian. Seniority: 1.

Cochran (R)—Dec. 7, 1937. Occupation: lawyer. Religion: Baptist. Seniority: 24.

MISSOURI

Eagleton (D)—Sept. 4, 1929. Occupation: lawyer. Religion: Roman Catholic. Seniority: 10.

Danforth (R)—Sept. 5, 1936. Occupation: lawyer, clergyman. Religion: Episcopalian. Seniority: 16.

MONTANA

Baucus (D)—Dec. 11, 1941. Occupation: lawyer. Religion: United Church of Christ. Seniority: 31.

Melcher (D)—Sept. 6, 1924. Occupation: veterinarian, cattle feedlot operator. Religion: Roman Catholic. Seniority: 26.

NEBRASKA

Exon (D)—Aug. 9, 1921. Occupation: office equipment retailer, governor. Religion: Episcopalian. Seniority: 33.

Zorinsky (D)—Nov. 11, 1928. Occupation: tobacco and candy wholesaler. Religion: Jewish. Seniority: 22.

NEVADA

Hecht (R)—Nov. 30, 1928. Occupation: clothing store owner. Religion: Jewish. Seniority: 49.

Laxalt (R)—Aug. 2, 1922. Occupation: hotel casino owner, lawyer, governor. Religion: Roman Catholic. Seniority: 14.

NEW HAMPSHIRE

Humphrey (R)—Oct. 9, 1940. Occupation: airline pilot. Religion: Baptist. Seniority: 30.

Rudman (R)—May 13, 1930. Occupation: lawyer. Religion: Jewish. Seniority: 32.

NEW JERSEY

Bradley (D)—July 28, 1943. Occupation: author, professional basketball player. Religion: Protestant. Seniority: 35.

Lautenberg (D)—Jan. 23, 1924. Occupation: computer firm executive. Religion: Jewish. Seniority: 41.

NEW MEXICO

Bingaman (D)—Oct. 3, 1943. Occupation: lawyer. Religion: Methodist. Seniority: 42.

Domenici (R)—May 7, 1932. Occupation: lawyer. Religion: Roman Catholic. Seniority: 12.

NEW YORK

Moynihan (D)—March 16, 1927. Occupation: author, government professor. Religion: Roman Catholic. Seniority: 28.

D'Amato (R)—Aug. 1, 1937. Occupation: lawyer, public official. Religion: Roman Catholic. Seniority: 41.

NORTH CAROLINA

East (R)—May 5, 1931. Occupation: author, college professor. Religion: Methodist. Seniority: 41.

Helms (R)—Oct. 18, 1921. Occupation: journalist, banking association director, broadcasting executive. Religion: Baptist. Seniority: 12.

NORTH DAKOTA

Burdick (D)—June 19, 1908. Occupation: lawyer. Religion: United Church of Christ. Seniority: 5.

Andrews (R)—May 9, 1926. Occupation: farmer. Religion: Episcopalian. Seniority: 35.

OHIO

Glenn (D)—July 18, 1921. Occupation: astronaut, soft drink company executive. Religion: Presbyterian. Seniority: 17.

Metzenbaum (D)—June 4, 1917. Occupation: newspaper publisher, parking lot executive, lawyer. Religion: Jewish. Seniority: 23.

OKLAHOMA

Boren (D)—April 21, 1941. Occupation: lawyer, professor, governor. Religion: Methodist. Seniority: 33.

Nickles (R)—Dec. 6, 1948. Occupation: machine company executive. Religion: Roman Catholic. Seniority: 41.

OREGON

Hatfield (R)—July 12, 1922. Occupation: associate professor, author, governor. Religion: Baptist. Seniority: 2.

Packwood (R)—Sept. 11, 1932. Occupation: lawyer. Religion: Unitarian. Seniority: 7.

PENNSYLVANIA

Heinz (R)—Oct. 23, 1938. Occupation: management consultant, lecturer. Religion: Episcopalian. Seniority: 18.

Specter (R)—Feb. 12, 1930. Occupation: lawyer. Religion: Jewish. Seniority: 41.

RHODE ISLAND

Pell (D)—Nov. 22, 1918. Occupation: investment executive. Religion: Episcopalian. Seniority: 6.

Chafee (R)—Oct. 22, 1922. Occupation: lawyer, governor. Religion: Episcopalian. Seniority: 17.

SOUTH CAROLINA

Hollings (D)—Jan. 1, 1922. Occupation: lawyer, governor. Religion: Lutheran. Seniority: 9.

Thurmond (R)—Dec. 5, 1902. Occupation: lawyer, judge, governor. Religion: Baptist. Seniority: 1.

SOUTH DAKOTA

Abdnor (R)—Feb. 23, 1923. Occupation: rancher. Religion: Methodist. Seniority: 36.

Pressler (R)—March 29, 1942. Occupation: lawyer. Religion: Roman Catholic. Seniority: 30.

TENNESSEE

Sasser (D)—Sept. 30, 1936. Occupation: lawyer. Religion: Methodist. Seniority: 28.

Gore (D)—March 31, 1948. Occupation: journalist, home builder. Religion: Baptist. Seniority: 46.

TEXAS

Bentsen (D)—Feb. 11, 1921. Occupation: finance holding institution executive, lawyer, judge. Religion: Presbyterian. Seniority: 12.

Gramm (R)—July 8, 1942. Occupation: economics professor. Religion: Episcopalian. Seniority: 52.

UTAH

Garn (R)—Oct. 12, 1932. Occupation: insurance executive. Religion: Mormon. Seniority: 15.

Hatch (R)—March 22, 1934. Occupation: lawyer. Religion: Mormon. Seniority: 19.

VERMONT

Leahy (D)—March 31, 1940. Occupation: lawyer. Religion: Roman Catholic. Seniority: 20.

Stafford (R)—Aug. 8, 1913. Occupation: lawyer, governor. Religion: Congregationalist. Seniority: 10.

VIRGINIA

Trible (R)—Dec. 29, 1946. Occupation: lawyer. Religion: Episcopalian. Seniority: 48.

Warner (R)—Feb. 18, 1927. Occupation: lawyer, farmer. Religion: Episcopalian. Seniority: 27.

WASHINGTON

Gorton (R)—Jan. 8, 1928. Occupation: lawyer. Religion: Episcopalian. Seniority: 41.

Evans (R)—Oct. 16, 1925. Occupation: education, engineer. Religion: Congregationalist. Seniority: 51.

WEST VIRGINIA

Byrd (D)—Nov. 20, 1917. Occupation: lawyer. Religion: Baptist. Seniority: 4.

Rockefeller (D)—June 18, 1937. Occupation: governor. Religion: Protestant. Seniority: 47.

WISCONSIN

Proxmire (D)—Nov. 11, 1915. Occupation: author, journalist, printing company executive. Religion: United Church of Christ. Seniority: 3.

Kasten (R)—June 19, 1942. Occupation: shoe manufacturing company executive. Religion: Episcopalian. Seniority: 39.

WYOMING

Simpson (R)—Sept. 2, 1931. Occupation: lawyer. Religion: Episcopalian. Seniority: 26.

Wallop (R)—Feb. 27, 1933. Occupation: rancher, meatpacking plant executive. Religion: Episcopalian. Seniority: 19.

House — Birth Dates, Occupations, Religions, Seniority

(Seniority rank is within the member's party.)

ALABAMA

1 **Callahan (R)**—Sept. 11, 1932. Occupation: commercial real estate company president, public official. Religion: Roman Catholic. Seniority: 155.

2 **Dickinson (R)**—June 5, 1925. Occupation: railroad executive, lawyer, judge. Religion: Methodist. Seniority: 9.

3 **Nichols (D)**—Oct. 16, 1918. Occupation: cotton gin company president, fertilizer manufacturing company executive. Religion: Methodist. Seniority: 36.

4 **Bevill (D)**—March 27, 1921. Occupation: lawyer. Religion: Baptist. Seniority: 36.

5 **Flippo (D)**—Aug. 15, 1937. Occupation: accountant. Religion: Church of Christ. Seniority: 105.

6 **Erdreich (D)**—Dec. 9, 1938. Occupation: lawyer. Religion: Jewish. Seniority: 188.

7 **Shelby (D)**—May 6, 1934. Occupation: lawyer. Religion: Presbyterian. Seniority: 134.

ALASKA

AL **Young (R)**—June 9, 1933. Occupation: elementary school teacher, river boat captain. Religion: Episcopalian. Seniority: 40.

ARIZONA

1 **McCain (R)**—Aug. 29, 1936. Occupation: naval officer, beer distributor. Religion: Episcopalian. Seniority: 128.

2 **Udall (D)**—June 15, 1922. Occupation: author, professional basketball player, lawyer. Religion: Mormon. Seniority: 18.

3 **Stump (R)**—April 4, 1927. Occupation: farmer. Religion: Seventh-Day Adventist. Seniority: 51.

4 **Rudd (R)**—July 15, 1920. Occupation: lawyer, FBI agent. Religion: Roman Catholic. Seniority: 51.

5 **Kolbe (R)**—June 28, 1942. Occupation: consultant. Religion: Methodist. Seniority: 155.

ARKANSAS

1 **Alexander (D)**—Jan. 16, 1934. Occupation: lawyer. Religion: Episcopalian. Seniority: 40.

2 **Robinson (D)**—March 7, 1942. Occupation: sheriff. Religion: Methodist. Seniority: 243.

3 **Hammerschmidt (R)**—May 4, 1922. Occupation: lumber company executive. Religion: Presbyterian. Seniority: 13.

4 **Anthony (D)**—Feb. 21, 1938. Occupation: lawyer. Religion: Episcopalian. Seniority: 134.

CALIFORNIA

1 **Bosco (D)**—July 28, 1946. Occupation: lawyer. Religion: Episcopalian. Seniority: 188.

2 **Chappie (R)**—March 28, 1920. Occupation: rancher. Religion: Roman Catholic. Seniority: 90.

3 **Matsui (D)**—Sept. 17, 1941. Occupation: lawyer. Religion: Methodist. Seniority: 134.

4 **Fazio (D)**—Oct. 11, 1942. Occupation: journalist, public official. Religion: Episcopalian. Seniority: 134.

5 **Burton (D)**—April 1, 1925. Occupation: political activist. Religion: Jewish. Seniority: 237.

6 **Boxer (D)**—Nov. 11, 1940. Occupation: stockbroker, journalist. Religion: Jewish. Seniority: 188.

7 **Miller (D)**—May 17, 1945. Occupation: lawyer. Religion: Roman Catholic. Seniority: 74.

8 **Dellums (D)**—Nov. 24, 1935. Occupation: social worker, consultant. Religion: Protestant. Seniority: 51.

9 **Stark (D)**—Nov. 11, 1931. Occupation: banker. Religion: Unitarian. Seniority: 60.

10 **Edwards (D)**—Jan. 6, 1915. Occupation: insurance company executive, lawyer, FBI agent. Religion: Unitarian. Seniority: 20.

11 **Lantos (D)**—Feb. 1, 1928. Occupation: professor, economist. Religion: Jewish. Seniority: 164.

12 **Zschau (R)**—Jan. 6, 1940. Occupation: microcomputer executive, business professor. Religion: Congregationalist. Seniority: 128.

13 **Mineta (D)**—Nov. 12, 1931. Occupation: insurance executive. Religion: Methodist. Seniority: 74.

14 **Shumway (R)**—July 28, 1934. Occupation: lawyer. Religion: Mormon. Seniority: 63.

15 **Coelho (D)**—June 15, 1942. Occupation: congressional aide. Religion: Roman Catholic. Seniority: 134.

16 **Panetta (D)**—June 28, 1938. Occupation: lawyer. Religion: Roman Catholic. Seniority: 105.

17 **Pashayan (R)**—March 27, 1941. Occupation: lawyer, tire retailer. Religion: Protestant. Seniority: 63.

18 **Lehman (D)**—July 20, 1948. Occupation: legislative aide. Religion: Lutheran. Seniority: 188.

19 **Lagomarsino (R)**—Sept. 4, 1926. Occupation: lawyer. Religion: Roman Catholic. Seniority: 41.

20 **Thomas (R)**—Dec. 6, 1941. Occupation: political science professor. Religion: Baptist. Seniority: 63.

21 **Fiedler (R)**—April 22, 1937. Occupation: author, interior decorator, drugstore owner. Religion: Jewish. Seniority: 90.

22 **Moorhead (R)**—May 6, 1922. Occupa-

tion: lawyer. Religion: Presbyterian. Seniority: 30.
23 **Beilenson (D)**—Oct. 26, 1932. Occupation: lawyer. Religion: Jewish. Seniority: 105.
24 **Waxman (D)**—Sept. 12, 1939. Occupation: lawyer. Religion: Jewish. Seniority: 74.
25 **Roybal (D)**—Feb. 10, 1916. Occupation: social worker, public health teacher. Religion: Roman Catholic. Seniority: 20.
26 **Berman (D)**—April 15, 1941. Occupation: lawyer. Religion: Jewish. Seniority: 188.
27 **Levine (D)**—June 7, 1943. Occupation: lawyer. Religion: Jewish. Seniority: 188.
28 **Dixon (D)**—Aug. 8, 1934. Occupation: legislative aide, lawyer. Religion: Episcopalian. Seniority: 134.
29 **Hawkins (D)**—Aug. 31, 1907. Occupation: real estate salesman. Religion: Methodist. Seniority: 20.
30 **Martinez (D)**—Feb. 14, 1929. Occupation: public official. Religion: Roman Catholic. Seniority: 185.
31 **Dymally (D)**—May 12, 1926. Occupation: author, special education teacher, data processing executive. Religion: Episcopalian. Seniority: 164.
32 **Anderson (D)**—Feb. 21, 1913. Occupation: savings and loan executive. Religion: Episcopalian. Seniority: 40.
33 **Dreier (R)**—July 5, 1952. Occupation: public relations executive. Religion: Christian Scientist. Seniority: 90.
34 **Torres (D)**—Jan. 27, 1930. Occupation: international trade executive. Religion: unspecified. Seniority: 188.
35 **Lewis (R)**—Oct. 21, 1934. Occupation: public official, insurance executive. Religion: Presbyterian. Seniority: 63.
36 **Brown (D)**—March 6, 1920. Occupation: management consultant. Religion: Methodist. Seniority: 58.
37 **McCandless (R)**—July 23, 1927. Occupation: automobile dealer. Religion: Protestant. Seniority: 128.
38 **Dornan (R)**—April 3, 1933. Occupation: public official. Religion: Roman Catholic. Seniority 153.
39 **Dannemeyer (R)**—Sept. 22, 1929. Occupation: lawyer. Religion: Lutheran. Seniority: 63.
40 **Badham (R)**—June 9, 1929. Occupation: hardware company executive. Religion: Lutheran. Seniority: 51.
41 **Lowery (R)**—May 2, 1947. Occupation: public relations executive. Religion: Roman Catholic. Seniority: 90.
42 **Lungren (R)**—Sept. 22, 1946. Occupation: lawyer. Religion: Roman Catholic. Seniority: 63.
43 **Packard (R)**—Jan. 19, 1931. Occupation: dentist. Religion: Mormon. Seniority: 128.
44 **Bates (D)**—July 21, 1941. Occupation: marketing analyst. Religion: Protestant. Seniority: 188.
45 **Hunter (R)**—May 31, 1948. Occupation: lawyer. Religion: Baptist. Seniority: 90.

COLORADO

1 **Schroeder (D)**—July 30, 1940. Occupation: lawyer, law instructor. Religion: Congregationalist. Seniority: 60.
2 **Wirth (D)**—Sept. 22, 1939. Occupation: corporate executive. Religion: Episcopalian. Seniority: 74.
3 **Strang (R)**—June 17, 1929. Occupation: rancher. Religion: Episcopalian. Seniority: 155.
4 **Brown (R)**—Feb. 12, 1940. Occupation: meatpacking company executive, lawyer. Religion: United Church of Christ. Seniority: 90.
5 **Kramer (R)**—Feb. 19, 1942. Occupation: lawyer. Religion: Jewish. Seniority: 63.
6 **Schaefer (R)**—Jan. 25, 1936. Occupation: consultant, history and political science teacher. Religion: Roman Catholic. Seniority: 151.

CONNECTICUT

1 **Kennelly (D)**—July 10, 1936. Occupation: public official. Religion: Roman Catholic. Seniority: 184.
2 **Gejdenson (D)**—May 20, 1948. Occupation: dairy farmer. Religion: Jewish. Seniority: 164.
3 **Morrison (D)**—Oct. 8, 1944. Occupation: lawyer. Religion: Lutheran. Seniority: 188.
4 **McKinney (R)**—Jan. 30, 1931. Occupation: tire retailer. Religion: Episcopalian. Seniority: 22.
5 **Rowland (R)**—May 24, 1957. Occupation: insurance agent. Religion: Roman Catholic. Seniority: 155.
6 **Johnson (R)**—Jan. 5, 1935. Occupation: civic volunteer. Religion: Unitarian. Seniority: 128.

DELAWARE

AL **Carper (D)**—Jan. 23, 1947. Occupation: public official. Religion: Presbyterian. Seniority: 188.

FLORIDA

1 **Hutto (D)**—May 12, 1926. Occupation: advertising executive. Religion: Baptist. Seniority: 134.
2 **Fuqua (D)**—Aug. 20, 1933. Occupation: farmer. Religion: Presbyterian. Seniority: 20.
3 **Bennett (D)**—Dec. 2, 1910. Occupation: author, lawyer. Religion: Disciples of Christ. Seniority: 3.
4 **Chappell (D)**—Feb. 3, 1922. Occupation: lawyer. Religion: Methodist. Seniority: 40.
5 **McCollum (R)**—July 12, 1944. Occupation: lawyer. Religion: Episcopalian. Seniority: 90.
6 **MacKay (D)**—March 22, 1933. Occupation: lawyer, citrus grower. Religion: Presbyterian. Seniority: 188.
7 **Gibbons (D)**—Jan. 20, 1920. Occupation: lawyer. Religion: Presbyterian. Seniority: 20.
8 **Young (R)**—Dec. 16, 1930. Occupation: insurance executive. Religion: Methodist. Seniority: 22.
9 **Bilirakis (R)**—July 16, 1930. Occupation: lawyer, businessman. Religion: Greek Orthodox. Seniority: 128.
10 **Ireland (R)**—Aug. 23, 1930. Occupation: banker. Religion: Episcopalian. Seniority: 51.
11 **Nelson (D)**—Sept. 29, 1942. Occupation: lawyer. Religion: Episcopalian. Seniority: 134.
12 **Lewis (R)**—Oct. 26, 1924. Occupation: real estate broker, aircraft testing specialist. Religion: Methodist. Seniority: 128.
13 **Mack (R)**—Oct. 29, 1940. Occupation: banker. Religion: Roman Catholic. Seniority: 128.
14 **Mica (D)**—Feb. 4, 1944. Occupation: junior high school teacher, congressional aide. Religion: Roman Catholic. Seniority: 134.
15 **Shaw (R)**—April 19, 1939. Occupation: nurseryman, lawyer, judge. Religion: Roman Catholic. Seniority: 90.
16 **Smith (D)**—April 25, 1941. Occupation: lawyer. Religion: Jewish. Seniority: 188.
17 **Lehman (D)**—Oct. 5, 1913. Occupation: high school English teacher, automobile dealer. Religion: Jewish. Seniority: 60.
18 **Pepper (D)**—Sept. 8, 1900. Occupation: lawyer. Religion: Baptist. Seniority: 20.
19 **Fascell (D)**—March 9, 1917. Occupation: lawyer. Religion: Protestant. Seniority: 9.

GEORGIA

1 **Thomas (D)**—Nov. 20, 1943. Occupation: farmer, investment banker. Religion: Methodist. Seniority: 188.
2 **Hatcher (D)**—July 1, 1939. Occupation: lawyer. Religion: Episcopalian. Seniority: 164.
3 **Ray (D)**—Feb. 2, 1927. Occupation: exterminator, legislative aide. Religion: Methodist. Seniority: 188.
4 **Swindall (R)**—Oct. 18, 1950. Occupation: lawyer and businessman. Religion: Presbyterian. Seniority: 155.

5 **Fowler (D)**—Oct. 6, 1940. Occupation: lawyer. Religion: Presbyterian. Seniority: 132.
6 **Gingrich (R)**—June 17, 1943. Occupation: history professor. Religion: Baptist. Seniority: 63.
7 **Darden (D)**—Nov. 22, 1943. Occupation: lawyer. Religion: Methodist. Seniority: 239.
8 **Rowland (D)**—Feb. 3, 1926. Occupation: physician. Religion: Methodist. Seniority: 188.
9 **Jenkins (D)**—Jan. 4, 1933. Occupation: lawyer. Religion: Baptist. Seniority: 105.
10 **Barnard (D)**—March 20, 1922. Occupation: banker. Religion: Baptist. Seniority: 105.

HAWAII

1 **Heftel (D)**—Sept. 30, 1924. Occupation: broadcasting executive. Religion: Mormon. Seniority: 105.
2 **Akaka (D)**—Sept. 11, 1924. Occupation: elementary school teacher, public official. Religion: Congregationalist. Seniority: 105.

IDAHO

1 **Craig (R)**—July 20, 1945. Occupation: real estate salesman, cattle and grain farmer. Religion: Methodist. Seniority: 90.
2 **Stallings (D)**—Oct. 7, 1940. Occupation: history professor. Religion: Mormon. Seniority: 243.

ILLINOIS

1 **Hayes (D)**—Feb. 17, 1918. Occupation: labor official, packinghouse worker. Religion: Baptist. Seniority: 238.
2 **Savage (D)**—Oct. 30, 1925. Occupation: journalist, newspaper publisher. Religion: Baptist. Seniority: 164.
3 **Russo (D)**—Jan. 23, 1944. Occupation: lawyer. Religion: Roman Catholic. Seniority: 74.
4 **O'Brien (R)**—June 17, 1917. Occupation: lawyer. Religion: Roman Catholic. Seniority: 30.
5 **Lipinski (D)**—Dec. 22, 1937. Occupation: public official. Religion: Roman Catholic. Seniority: 188.
6 **Hyde (R)**—April 18, 1924. Occupation: lawyer. Religion: Roman Catholic. Seniority: 42.
7 **Collins (D)**—Sept. 24, 1931. Occupation: auditor, accountant. Religion: Baptist. Seniority: 69.
8 **Rostenkowski (D)**—Jan. 2, 1928. Occupation: insurance executive. Religion: Roman Catholic. Seniority: 13.
9 **Yates (D)**—Aug. 27, 1909. Occupation: lawyer. Religion: Jewish. Seniority: 27.
10 **Porter (R)**—June 1, 1935. Occupation: lawyer. Religion: Presbyterian. Seniority: 88.
11 **Annunzio (D)**—Jan. 12, 1915. Occupation: high school industrial arts teacher, labor union executive. Religion: Roman Catholic. Seniority: 28.
12 **Crane, Philip M. (R)**—Nov. 3, 1930. Occupation: American history professor, author. Religion: Methodist. Seniority: 21.
13 **Fawell (R)**—March 25, 1929. Occupation: lawyer. Religion: Methodist. Seniority: 155.
14 **Grotberg (R)**—March 21, 1925. Occupation: consultant. Religion: Methodist. Seniority: 155.
15 **Madigan (R)**—Jan. 13, 1936. Occupation: automobile leasing company executive. Religion: Roman Catholic. Seniority: 30.
16 **Martin (R)**—Dec. 26, 1939. Occupation: English teacher. Religion: Roman Catholic. Seniority: 90.
17 **Evans (D)**—Aug. 4, 1951. Occupation: lawyer. Religion: Roman Catholic. Seniority: 188.
18 **Michel (R)**—March 2, 1923. Occupation: congressional aide. Religion: Apostolic Christian. Seniority: 1.
19 **Bruce (D)**—March 25, 1944. Occupation: farmer, lawyer, public official. Religion: Methodist. Seniority: 243.
20 **Durbin (D)**—Nov. 21, 1944. Occupation: lawyer. Religion: Roman Catholic. Seniority: 188.
21 **Price (D)**—Jan. 1, 1905. Occupation: journalist. Religion: Roman Catholic. Seniority: 2.
22 **Gray (D)**—Nov. 14, 1924. Occupation: auto dealer, pilot, public official. Religion: Baptist. Seniority: 242.

INDIANA

1 **Visclosky (D)**—Aug. 13, 1949. Occupation: lawyer. Religion: Roman Catholic. Seniority: 243.
2 **Sharp (D)**—July 15, 1942. Occupation: political science professor, congressional aide. Religion: Methodist. Seniority: 74.
3 **Hiler (R)**—April 24, 1953. Occupation: foundry executive. Religion: Roman Catholic. Seniority: 90.
4 **Coats (R)**—May 16, 1943. Occupation: lawyer. Religion: Baptist. Seniority: 90.
5 **Hillis (R)**—March 6, 1926. Occupation: lawyer. Religion: Presbyterian. Seniority: 22.
6 **Burton (R)**—June 21, 1938. Occupation: insurance and real estate agent. Religion: Protestant. Seniority: 128.
7 **Myers (R)**—Feb. 8, 1927. Occupation: banker, farmer. Religion: Episcopalian. Seniority: 13.
8 **McCloskey (D)**—June 12, 1939. Occupation: lawyer, journalist. Religion: Roman Catholic. Not seated until May 1; not included in seniority ranking. Service began Jan. 3, 1983.
9 **Hamilton (D)**—April 20, 1931. Occupation: lawyer. Religion: Methodist. Seniority: 28.
10 **Jacobs (D)**—Feb. 24, 1932. Occupation: lawyer. Religion: Roman Catholic. Seniority: 72.

IOWA

1 **Leach (R)**—Oct. 15, 1942. Occupation: propane gas marketer. Religion: Episcopalian. Seniority: 51.
2 **Tauke (R)**—Oct. 11, 1950. Occupation: lawyer. Religion: Roman Catholic. Seniority: 63.
3 **Evans (R)**—May 26, 1924. Occupation: farmer, engineer. Religion: Methodist. Seniority: 90.
4 **Smith (D)**—March 23, 1920. Occupation: farmer, lawyer. Religion: Methodist. Seniority: 13.
5 **Lightfoot (R)**—Sept. 27, 1939. Occupation: businessman, journalist. Religion: Roman Catholic. Seniority: 155.
6 **Bedell (D)**—March 5, 1921. Occupation: fishing tackle manufacturer. Religion: Methodist. Seniority: 74.

KANSAS

1 **Roberts (R)**—April 20, 1936. Occupation: congressional aide. Religion: Methodist. Seniority: 90.
2 **Slattery (D)**—Aug. 4, 1948. Occupation: lawyer, real estate agent. Religion: Roman Catholic. Seniority: 188.
3 **Meyers (R)**—July 20, 1928. Occupation: homemaker, public official. Religion: Methodist. Seniority: 155.
4 **Glickman (D)**—Nov. 24, 1944. Occupation: lawyer. Religion: Jewish. Seniority: 105.
5 **Whittaker (R)**—Sept. 18, 1939. Occupation: optometrist. Religion: Christian Church. Seniority: 63.

KENTUCKY

1 **Hubbard (D)**—July 7, 1937. Occupation: lawyer. Religion: Baptist. Seniority: 74.
2 **Natcher (D)**—Sept. 11, 1909. Occupation: lawyer. Religion: Baptist. Seniority: 8.
3 **Mazzoli (D)**—Nov. 2, 1932. Occupation: lawyer. Religion: Roman Catholic. Seniority: 51.
4 **Snyder (R)**—Jan. 26, 1928. Occupation: farmer, real estate salesman, lawyer. Religion: Lutheran. Seniority: 12.
5 **Rogers (R)**—Dec. 31, 1937. Occupation: lawyer. Religion: Baptist. Seniority: 90.

6 **Hopkins (R)**—Oct. 25, 1933. Occupation: stockbroker. Religion: Methodist. Seniority: 63.

7 **Perkins (D)**—Aug. 6, 1954. Occupation: lawyer, public official. Religion: Baptist. Seniority: 241.

LOUISIANA

1 **Livingston (R)**—April 30, 1943. Occupation: lawyer. Religion: Episcopalian. Seniority: 61.

2 **Boggs (D)**—March 13, 1916. Occupation: high school teacher. Religion: Roman Catholic. Seniority: 68.

3 **Tauzin (D)**—June 14, 1943. Occupation: lawyer. Religion: Roman Catholic. Seniority: 162.

4 **Roemer (D)**—Oct. 4, 1943. Occupation: farmer, banker, data processing executive. Religion: Methodist. Seniority: 164.

5 **Huckaby (D)**—July 19, 1941. Occupation: farmer, engineer, corporate executive. Religion: Methodist. Seniority: 105.

6 **Moore (R)**—Oct. 4, 1939. Occupation: lawyer. Religion: Episcopalian. Seniority: 49.

7 **Breaux (D)**—March 1, 1944. Occupation: lawyer. Religion: Roman Catholic. Seniority: 57.

8 **Long (D)**—May 4, 1923. Occupation: lawyer, farmer, investment broker. Religion: Baptist. Seniority: 59.

MAINE

1 **McKernan (R)**—May 20, 1948. Occupation: lawyer. Religion: Protestant. Seniority: 128.

2 **Snowe (R)**—Feb. 21, 1947. Occupation: public official. Religion: Greek Orthodox. Seniority: 63.

MARYLAND

1 **Dyson (D)**—Nov. 15, 1948. Occupation: lumber company executive. Religion: Roman Catholic. Seniority: 164.

2 **Bentley (R)**—Nov. 28, 1923. Occupation: public official. Religion: Greek Orthodox. Seniority: 155.

3 **Mikulski (D)**—July 20, 1936. Occupation: social work professor, social worker. Religion: Roman Catholic. Seniority: 105.

4 **Holt (R)**—Sept. 17, 1920. Occupation: lawyer. Religion: Presbyterian. Seniority: 30.

5 **Hoyer (D)**—June 14, 1939. Occupation: lawyer. Religion: Baptist. Seniority: 182.

6 **Byron (D)**—July 27, 1932. Occupation: civic volunteer. Religion: Episcopalian. Seniority: 134.

7 **Mitchell (D)**—April 29, 1922. Occupation: sociology professor. Religion: Episcopalian. Seniority: 51.

8 **Barnes (D)**—Sept. 3, 1943. Occupation: lawyer. Religion: Protestant. Seniority: 134.

MASSACHUSETTS

1 **Conte (R)**—Nov. 9, 1921. Occupation: lawyer. Religion: Roman Catholic. Seniority: 3.

2 **Boland (D)**—Oct. 1, 1911. Occupation: public official. Religion: Roman Catholic. Seniority: 5.

3 **Early (D)**—Jan. 31, 1933. Occupation: teacher, basketball coach. Religion: Roman Catholic. Seniority: 74.

4 **Frank (D)**—March 31, 1940. Occupation: public official. Religion: Jewish. Seniority: 164.

5 **Atkins (D)**—April 14, 1948. Occupation: public official. Religion: Unitarian. Seniority: 243.

6 **Mavroules (D)**—Nov. 1, 1929. Occupation: personnel supervisor. Religion: Greek Orthodox. Seniority: 134.

7 **Markey (D)**—July 11, 1946. Occupation: lawyer. Religion: Roman Catholic. Seniority: 103.

8 **O'Neill (D)**—Dec. 9, 1912. Occupation: insurance broker. Religion: Roman Catholic. Seniority: 5.

9 **Moakley (D)**—April 27, 1927. Occupation: lawyer. Religion: Roman Catholic. Seniority: 60.

10 **Studds (D)**—May 12, 1937. Occupation: high school teacher. Religion: Episcopalian. Seniority: 60.

11 **Donnelly (D)**—March 2, 1946. Occupation: high school teacher. Religion: Roman Catholic. Seniority: 134.

MICHIGAN

1 **Conyers (D)**—May 16, 1929. Occupation: lawyer. Religion: Baptist. Seniority: 28.

2 **Pursell (R)**—Dec. 19, 1932. Occupation: publisher, high school teacher, real estate salesman, office equipment retailer. Religion: Baptist. Seniority: 51.

3 **Wolpe (D)**—Nov. 2, 1939. Occupation: author, political science professor, congressional aide. Religion: Jewish. Seniority: 134.

4 **Siljander (R)**—June 11, 1951. Occupation: restaurant executive. Religion: unspecified Christian. Seniority: 126.

5 **Henry (R)**—July 9, 1942. Occupation: public official. Religion: Christian Reformed. Seniority: 155.

6 **Carr (D)**—March 27, 1943. Occupation: lawyer. Religion: Baptist. Seniority: 186.

7 **Kildee (D)**—Sept. 16, 1929. Occupation: Latin teacher. Religion: Roman Catholic. Seniority: 105.

8 **Traxler (D)**—July 21, 1931. Occupation: lawyer. Religion: Episcopalian. Seniority: 71.

9 **Vander Jagt (R)**—Aug. 26, 1931. Occupation: lawyer. Religion: Presbyterian. Seniority: 11.

10 **Schuette (R)**—Oct. 13, 1953. Occupation: lawyer. Religion: Episcopalian. Seniority: 155.

11 **Davis (R)**—July 31, 1932. Occupation: funeral director. Religion: Episcopalian. Seniority: 63.

12 **Bonior (D)**—June 6, 1945. Occupation: public official. Religion: Roman Catholic. Seniority: 105.

13 **Crockett (D)**—Aug. 10, 1909. Occupation: lawyer, judge. Religion: Baptist. Seniority: 163.

14 **Hertel (D)**—Dec. 7, 1948. Occupation: lawyer. Religion: Roman Catholic. Seniority: 164.

15 **Ford (D)**—Aug. 6, 1927. Occupation: lawyer. Religion: United Church of Christ. Seniority: 28.

16 **Dingell (D)**—July 8, 1926. Occupation: lawyer. Religion: Roman Catholic. Seniority: 11.

17 **Levin (D)**—Sept. 6, 1931. Occupation: lawyer. Religion: Jewish. Seniority: 188.

18 **Broomfield (R)**—April 28, 1922. Occupation: insurance salesman. Religion: Presbyterian. Seniority: 1.

MINNESOTA

1 **Penny (D)**—Nov. 19, 1951. Occupation: sales representative. Religion: Lutheran. Seniority: 188.

2 **Weber (R)**—July 24, 1952. Occupation: newspaper publisher. Religion: Roman Catholic. Seniority: 90.

3 **Frenzel (R)**—July 31, 1928. Occupation: warehouse company executive. Religion: unspecified. Seniority: 22.

4 **Vento (D)**—Oct. 7, 1940. Occupation: science teacher. Religion: Roman Catholic. Seniority: 105.

5 **Sabo (D)**—Feb. 28, 1938. Occupation: public official. Religion: Lutheran. Seniority: 134.

6 **Sikorski (D)**—April 26, 1948. Occupation: lawyer. Religion: Roman Catholic. Seniority: 188.

7 **Stangeland (R)**—Feb. 8, 1930. Occupation: farmer. Religion: Lutheran. Seniority: 60.

8 **Oberstar (D)**—Sept. 10, 1934. Occupation: congressional aide. Religion: Roman Catholic. Seniority: 74.

MISSISSIPPI

1 **Whitten (D)**—April 18, 1910. Occupation: author, lawyer, grammar school teacher and principal. Religion: Presbyterian. Seniority: 1.

2 **Franklin (R)**—Dec. 13, 1941. Occupation: lawyer. Religion: Episcopalian. Seniority: 128

3 **Montgomery (D)**—Aug. 5, 1920. Occu-

pation: insurance executive. Religion: Episcopalian. Seniority: 36.

4 **Dowdy (D)**—July 27, 1943. Occupation: broadcasting executive, lawyer. Religion: Methodist. Seniority: 183.

5 **Lott (R)**—Oct. 9, 1941. Occupation: lawyer. Religion: Baptist. Seniority: 30.

MISSOURI

1 **Clay (D)**—April 30, 1931. Occupation: real estate broker, insurance company executive. Religion: Roman Catholic. Seniority: 40.

2 **Young (D)**—Nov. 27, 1923. Occupation: pipefitter. Religion: Roman Catholic. Seniority: 105.

3 **Gephardt (D)**—Jan. 31, 1941. Occupation: lawyer. Religion: Baptist. Seniority: 105.

4 **Skelton (D)**—Dec. 20, 1931. Occupation: lawyer. Religion: Christian Church. Seniority: 105.

5 **Wheat (D)**—Oct. 16, 1951. Occupation: public official. Religion: Church of Christ. Seniority: 188.

6 **Coleman (R)**—May 29, 1943. Occupation: lawyer. Religion: Protestant. Seniority: 50.

7 **Taylor (R)**—Feb. 10, 1928. Occupation: automobile dealer. Religion: Methodist. Seniority: 30.

8 **Emerson (R)**—Jan. 1, 1938. Occupation: corporate executive. Religion: Presbyterian. Seniority: 90.

9 **Volkmer (D)**—April 4, 1931. Occupation: lawyer. Religion: Roman Catholic. Seniority: 105.

MONTANA

1 **Williams (D)**—Oct. 30, 1937. Occupation: elementary and secondary school teacher. Religion: Roman Catholic. Seniority: 134.

2 **Marlenee (R)**—Aug. 8, 1935. Occupation: rancher. Religion: Lutheran. Seniority: 51.

NEBRASKA

1 **Bereuter (R)**—Oct. 6, 1939. Occupation: residential and commercial development consultant, automobile and hardware dealer. Religion: Lutheran. Seniority: 63.

2 **Daub (R)**—April 23, 1941. Occupation: lawyer, feed company executive. Religion: Presbyterian. Seniority: 90.

3 **Smith (R)**—June 30, 1911. Occupation: farmer. Religion: Methodist. Seniority: 42.

NEVADA

1 **Reid (D)**—Dec. 2, 1939. Occupation: lawyer. Religion: Mormon. Seniority: 188.

2 **Vucanovich (R)**—June 22, 1921. Occupation: congressional aide. Religion: Roman Catholic. Seniority: 128.

NEW HAMPSHIRE

1 **Smith (R)**—March 30, 1941. Occupation: realtor. Religion: Congregationalist. Seniority: 155.

2 **Gregg (R)**—Feb. 14, 1947. Occupation: lawyer. Religion: Protestant. Seniority: 90.

NEW JERSEY

1 **Florio (D)**—Aug. 29, 1937. Occupation: lawyer. Religion: Roman Catholic. Seniority: 74.

2 **Hughes (D)**—Oct. 17, 1932. Occupation: lawyer. Religion: Episcopalian. Seniority: 74.

3 **Howard (D)**—July 24, 1927. Occupation: elementary school teacher. Religion: Roman Catholic. Seniority: 28.

4 **Smith (R)**—March 4, 1953. Occupation: sporting goods wholesaler. Religion: Roman Catholic. Seniority: 90.

5 **Roukema (R)**—Sept. 19, 1929. Occupation: high school history and government teacher. Religion: Protestant. Seniority: 90.

6 **Dwyer (D)**—Jan. 24, 1921. Occupation: insurance salesman. Religion: Roman Catholic. Seniority: 164.

7 **Rinaldo (R)**—Sept. 1, 1931. Occupation: industrial relations consultant. Religion: Roman Catholic. Seniority: 30.

8 **Roe (D)**—Feb. 28, 1924. Occupation: corporate executive. Religion: Roman Catholic. Seniority: 50.

9 **Torricelli (D)**—Aug. 26, 1951. Occupation: lawyer. Religion: Methodist. Seniority: 188.

10 **Rodino (D)**—June 7, 1909. Occupation: lawyer. Religion: Roman Catholic. Seniority: 3.

11 **Gallo (R)**—Nov. 23, 1935. Occupation: real estate broker. Religion: Methodist. Seniority: 155.

12 **Courter (R)**—Oct. 14, 1941. Occupation: lawyer. Religion: Methodist. Seniority: 63.

13 **Saxton (R)**—Jan. 22, 1943. Occupation: realty company owner, public official. Religion: Protestant. Seniority: 152.

14 **Guarini (D)**—Aug. 20, 1924. Occupation: lawyer. Religion: Roman Catholic. Seniority: 134.

NEW MEXICO

1 **Lujan (R)**—May 12, 1928. Occupation: insurance broker. Religion: Roman Catholic. Seniority: 17.

2 **Skeen. (R)**—June 30, 1927. Occupation: rancher. Religion: Roman Catholic. Seniority: 90.

3 **Richardson (D)**—Nov. 15, 1947. Occupation: business consultant. Religion: Roman Catholic. Seniority: 188.

NEW YORK

1 **Carney (R)**—July 1, 1942. Occupation: heavy equipment sales representative. Religion: Roman Catholic. Seniority: 63.

2 **Downey (D)**—Jan. 28, 1949. Occupation: public official. Religion: Methodist. Seniority: 74.

3 **Mrazek (D)**—Nov. 6, 1945. Occupation: public official. Religion: Methodist. Seniority: 188.

4 **Lent (R)**—March 23, 1931. Occupation: lawyer. Religion: Methodist. Seniority: 22.

5 **McGrath (R)**—March 27, 1942. Occupation: public official. Religion: Roman Catholic. Seniority: 90.

6 **Addabbo (D)**—March 17, 1925. Occupation: lawyer. Religion: Roman Catholic. Seniority: 16.

7 **Ackerman (D)**—Nov. 19, 1942. Occupation: advertising executive, newspaper publisher, teacher. Religion: Jewish. Seniority: 236.

8 **Scheuer (D)**—Feb. 6, 1920. Occupation: lawyer. Religion: Jewish. Seniority: 72.

9 **Manton (D)**—Nov. 3, 1932. Occupation: police officer, public official. Religion: Roman Catholic. Seniority: 243.

10 **Schumer (D)**—Nov. 23, 1950. Occupation: lawyer. Religion: Jewish. Seniority: 164.

11 **Towns (D)**—July 21, 1934. Occupation: social worker. Religion: Presbyterian. Seniority: 188.

12 **Owens (D)**—June 28, 1936. Occupation: librarian. Religion: Baptist. Seniority: 188.

13 **Solarz (D)**—Sept. 12, 1940. Occupation: public official. Religion: Jewish. Seniority: 74.

14 **Molinari (R)**—Nov. 23, 1928. Occupation: lawyer. Religion: Roman Catholic. Seniority: 90.

15 **Green (R)**—Oct. 16, 1929. Occupation: lawyer. Religion: Jewish. Seniority: 62.

16 **Rangel (D)**—June 11, 1930. Occupation: lawyer. Religion: Roman Catholic. Seniority: 51.

17 **Weiss (D)**—Sept. 17, 1927. Occupation: lawyer. Religion: Jewish. Seniority: 105.

18 **Garcia (D)**—Jan. 9, 1933. Occupation: computer engineer. Religion: Pentecostal. Seniority: 133.

19 **Biaggi (D)**—Oct. 26, 1917. Occupation: lawyer, police detective. Religion: Roman Catholic. Seniority: 40.

20 **DioGuardi (R)**—Sept. 20, 1940. Occupation: accountant. Religion: Roman Catholic. Seniority: 155.

21 **Fish (R)**—June 3, 1926. Occupation: lawyer. Religion: Episcopalian. Seniority: 17.

22 Gilman (R)—Dec. 6, 1922. Occupation: lawyer. Religion: Jewish. Seniority: 30.
23 Stratton (D)—Sept. 27, 1916. Occupation: public official, radio and television announcer and newscaster. Religion: Presbyterian. Seniority: 13.
24 Solomon (R)—Aug. 14, 1930. Occupation: investment and insurance broker. Religion: Presbyterian. Seniority: 63.
25 Boehlert (R)—Sept. 28, 1936. Occupation: congressional aide. Religion: Roman Catholic. Seniority: 128.
26 Martin (R)—April 26, 1944. Occupation: lawyer. Religion: Roman Catholic. Seniority: 90.
27 Wortley (R)—Dec. 8, 1926. Occupation: newspaper publisher. Religion: Roman Catholic. Seniority: 90.
28 McHugh (D)—Dec. 6, 1938. Occupation: lawyer. Religion: Roman Catholic. Seniority: 74.
29 Horton (R)—Dec. 12, 1919. Occupation: lawyer. Religion: Presbyterian. Seniority: 5.
30 Eckert (R)—May 6, 1941. Occupation: public official, public relations executive. Religion: Roman Catholic. Seniority: 155.
31 Kemp (R)—July 13, 1935. Occupation: professional football player, radio and television commentator. Religion: Presbyterian. Seniority: 22.
32 LaFalce (D)—Oct. 6, 1939. Occupation: lawyer. Religion: Roman Catholic. Seniority: 74.
33 Nowak (D)—Feb. 21, 1935. Occupation: lawyer. Religion: Roman Catholic. Seniority: 74.
34 Lundine (D)—Feb. 4, 1939. Occupation: lawyer. Religion: Protestant. Seniority: 101.

NORTH CAROLINA

1 Jones (D)—Aug. 19, 1913. Occupation: office supply company executive. Religion: Baptist. Seniority: 35.
2 Valentine (D)—March 15, 1926. Occupation: lawyer. Religion: Baptist. Seniority: 188.
3 Whitley (D)—Jan. 3, 1927. Occupation: congressional aide. Religion: Baptist. Seniority: 105.
4 Cobey (R)—May 13, 1939. Occupation: management consultant. Religion: Independent Bible Church. Seniority: 155.
5 Neal (D)—Nov. 7, 1934. Occupation: newspaper publisher, mortgage banker. Religion: Episcopalian. Seniority: 74.
6 Coble (R)—March 18, 1931. Occupation: lawyer. Religion: Presbyterian. Seniority: 155.
7 Rose (D)—Aug. 10, 1939. Occupation: lawyer. Religion: Presbyterian. Seniority: 60.
8 Hefner (D)—April 11, 1930. Occupation: broadcasting executive. Religion: Baptist. Seniority: 74.
9 McMillan (R)—May 9, 1932. Occupation: business executive. Religion: Presbyterian. Seniority: 155.
10 Broyhill (R)—Aug. 19, 1927. Occupation: furniture manufacturing executive. Religion: Baptist. Seniority: 5.
11 Hendon (R)—Nov. 9, 1944. Occupation: business underwriter. Religion: Episcopalian. Seniority: 154.

NORTH DAKOTA

AL Dorgan (D)—May 14, 1942. Occupation: public official. Religion: Lutheran. Seniority: 164.

OHIO

1 Luken (D)—July 9, 1925. Occupation: lawyer. Religion: Roman Catholic. Seniority: 104.
2 Gradison (R)—Dec. 28, 1928. Occupation: investment broker. Religion: Jewish. Seniority: 42.
3 Hall (D)—Jan. 16, 1942. Occupation: real estate broker. Religion: Presbyterian. Seniority: 134.
4 Oxley (R)—Feb. 11, 1944. Occupation: FBI agent, lawyer. Religion: Lutheran. Seniority: 127.
5 Latta (R)—March 5, 1920. Occupation: lawyer. Religion: Church of Christ. Seniority: 3.
6 McEwen (R)—Jan. 12, 1950. Occupation: real estate developer. Religion: Protestant. Seniority: 90.
7 DeWine (R)—Jan. 5, 1947. Occupation: lawyer. Religion: Roman Catholic. Seniority: 128.
8 Kindness (R)—Aug. 26, 1929. Occupation: lawyer. Religion: Presbyterian. Seniority: 42.
9 Kaptur (D)—June 17, 1946. Occupation: urban planner. Religion: Roman Catholic. Seniority: 188.
10 Miller (R)—Nov. 1, 1917. Occupation: electrical engineer. Religion: Methodist. Seniority: 13.
11 Eckart (D)—April 6, 1950. Occupation: lawyer. Religion: Roman Catholic. Seniority: 164.
12 Kasich (R)—May 13, 1952. Occupation: legislative aide. Religion: Roman Catholic. Seniority: 128.
13 Pease (D)—Sept. 26, 1931. Occupation: editor. Religion: Protestant. Seniority: 105.
14 Seiberling (D)—Sept. 8, 1918. Occupation: lawyer. Religion: Presbyterian. Seniority: 51.
15 Wylie (R)—Nov. 23, 1920. Occupation: lawyer. Religion: Methodist. Seniority: 13.
16 Regula (R)—Dec. 3, 1924. Occupation: lawyer. Religion: Episcopalian. Seniority: 30.
17 Traficant (D)—May 8, 1941. Occupation: county sheriff. Religion: Roman Catholic. Seniority: 243.
18 Applegate (D)—March 27, 1928. Occupation: salesman, real estate broker. Religion: Presbyterian. Seniority: 105.
19 Feighan (D)—Oct. 22, 1947. Occupation: lawyer. Religion: Roman Catholic. Seniority: 188.
20 Oakar (D)—March 5, 1940. Occupation: high school English and drama teacher. Religion: Roman Catholic. Seniority: 105.
21 Stokes (D)—Feb. 23, 1925. Occupation: lawyer. Religion: African Methodist Episcopal Zion. Seniority: 40.

OKLAHOMA

1 Jones (D)—May 5, 1939. Occupation: lawyer. Religion: Roman Catholic. Seniority: 60.
2 Synar (D)—Oct. 17, 1950. Occupation: lawyer, rancher, real estate broker. Religion: Episcopalian. Seniority: 134.
3 Watkins (D)—Dec. 15, 1938. Occupation: real estate broker, homebuilder. Religion: Presbyterian. Seniority: 105.
4 McCurdy (D)—March 30, 1950. Occupation: lawyer. Religion: Lutheran. Seniority: 164.
5 Edwards (R)—July 12, 1937. Occupation: author, journalist, lawyer. Religion: Episcopalian. Seniority: 51.
6 English (D)—Nov. 30, 1940. Occupation: petroleum landman. Religion: Methodist. Seniority: 74.

OREGON

1 AuCoin (D)—Oct. 21, 1942. Occupation: journalist, public relations officer, architectural firm administrator. Religion: Protestant. Seniority 74.
2 Smith, Bob (R)—June 16, 1931. Occupation: cattle rancher. Religion: Presbyterian. Seniority: 128.
3 Wyden (D)—May 3, 1949. Occupation: lawyer. Religion: Jewish. Seniority: 164.
4 Weaver (D)—Aug. 8, 1927. Occupation: homebuilder. Religion: Protestant. Seniority: 74.
5 Smith, Denny (R)—Jan. 19, 1938. Occupation: newspaper publisher, airline pilot. Religion: Protestant. Seniority: 90.

PENNSYLVANIA

1 Foglietta (D)—Dec. 3, 1928. Occupation: lawyer. Religion: Roman Catholic. Seniority: 164.
2 Gray (D)—Aug. 20, 1941. Occupation: clergyman. Religion: Baptist. Seniority: 134.

3 Borski (D)—Oct. 20, 1948. Occupation: stockbroker. Religion: Roman Catholic. Seniority: 188.

4 Kolter (D)—Sept. 3, 1926. Occupation: accountant. Religion: Roman Catholic. Seniority: 188.

5 Schulze (R)—Aug. 7, 1929. Occupation: household appliance retailer, public official. Religion: Presbyterian. Seniority: 42.

6 Yatron (D)—Oct. 16, 1927. Occupation: professional boxer, ice cream manufacturer. Religion: Greek Orthodox. Seniority: 40.

7 Edgar (D)—May 29, 1943. Occupation: clergyman. Religion: Methodist. Seniority: 74.

8 Kostmayer (D)—Sept. 27, 1946. Occupation: public relations consultant. Religion: Episcopalian. Seniority: 187.

9 Shuster (R)—Jan. 23, 1932. Occupation: corporate executive. Religion: United Church of Christ. Seniority: 30.

10 McDade (R)—Sept. 29, 1931. Occupation: lawyer. Religion: Roman Catholic. Seniority: 5.

11 Kanjorski (D)—April 2, 1937. Occupation: lawyer. Religion: Roman Catholic. Seniority: 243.

12 Murtha (D)—June 17, 1932. Occupation: car wash operator. Religion: Roman Catholic. Seniority: 70.

13 Coughlin (R)—April 11, 1929. Occupation: lawyer. Religion: Episcopalian. Seniority: 17.

14 Coyne (D)—Aug. 24, 1936. Occupation: accountant. Religion: Roman Catholic. Seniority: 164.

15 Ritter (R)—Oct. 21, 1940. Occupation: engineering consultant and professor. Religion: Unitarian. Seniority: 63.

16 Walker (R)—Dec. 23, 1942. Occupation: high school teacher, congressional aide. Religion: Presbyterian. Seniority: 51.

17 Gekas (R)—April 14, 1930. Occupation: lawyer. Religion: Greek Orthodox. Seniority: 128.

18 Walgren (D)—Dec. 28, 1940. Occupation: lawyer. Religion: Roman Catholic. Seniority: 105.

19 Goodling (R)—Dec. 5, 1927. Occupation: public school superintendent. Religion: Methodist. Seniority: 42.

20 Gaydos (D)—July 3, 1926. Occupation: lawyer. Religion: Roman Catholic. Seniority: 39.

21 Ridge (R)—Aug. 26, 1945. Occupation: lawyer. Religion: Roman Catholic. Seniority: 128.

22 Murphy (D)—June 17, 1927. Occupation: lawyer. Religion: Roman Catholic. Seniority: 105.

23 Clinger (R)—April 4, 1929. Occupation: lawyer. Religion: Presbyterian. Seniority: 63.

RHODE ISLAND

1 St Germain (D)—Jan. 9, 1928. Occupation: lawyer. Religion: Roman Catholic. Seniority: 16.

2 Schneider (R)—March 25, 1947. Occupation: television producer and moderator. Religion: Roman Catholic. Seniority: 90.

SOUTH CAROLINA

1 Hartnett (R)—Aug. 7, 1941. Occupation: businessman. Religion: Roman Catholic. Seniority: 90.

2 Spence (R)—April 9, 1928. Occupation: lawyer. Religion: Lutheran. Seniority: 22.

3 Derrick (D)—Sept. 30, 1936. Occupation: lawyer. Religion: Episcopalian. Seniority: 74.

4 Campbell (R)—July 24, 1940. Occupation: farmer, real estate broker, parking lot president, restaurant executive. Religion: Episcopalian. Seniority: 63.

5 Spratt (D)—Nov. 1, 1942. Occupation: lawyer. Religion: Presbyterian. Seniority: 188.

6 Tallon (D)—Aug. 8, 1946. Occupation: clothing store executive. Religion: Methodist. Seniority: 188.

SOUTH DAKOTA

AL Daschle (D)—Dec. 9, 1947. Occupation: congressional aide. Religion: Roman Catholic. Seniority: 134.

TENNESSEE

1 Quillen (R)—Jan. 11, 1916. Occupation: newspaper publisher, real estate and insurance salesman. Religion: Methodist. Seniority: 5.

2 Duncan (R)—March 24, 1919. Occupation: lawyer. Religion: Presbyterian. Seniority: 9.

3 Lloyd (D)—Jan. 3, 1929. Occupation: radio station manager. Religion: Church of Christ. Seniority: 74.

4 Cooper (D)—June 19, 1954. Occupation: lawyer. Religion: Episcopalian. Seniority: 188.

5 Boner (D)—Feb. 14, 1945. Occupation: high school and college teacher and coach, banker, lawyer. Religion: Methodist. Seniority: 134.

6 Gordon (D)—Jan. 24, 1949. Occupation: lawyer. Religion: Methodist. Seniority: 243.

7 Sundquist (R)—March 15, 1936. Occupation: marketing and printing company owner. Religion: Lutheran. Seniority: 128.

8 Jones (D)—April 20, 1912. Occupation: agricultural representative. Religion: Presbyterian. Seniority: 48.

9 Ford (D)—May 20, 1945. Occupation: mortician. Religion: Baptist. Seniority: 74.

TEXAS

1 Hall, Sam B. Jr. (D)—Jan. 11, 1924. Occupation: lawyer. Religion: Church of Christ. Seniority: 102.

2 Wilson (D)—June 1, 1933. Occupation: lumberyard executive. Religion: Methodist. Seniority: 60.

3 Bartlett (R)—Sept. 19, 1947. Occupation: tool and plastics company owner. Religion: Presbyterian. Seniority: 128.

4 Hall, Ralph M. (D)—May 3, 1923. Occupation: feed company executive, banker, lawyer, judge. Religion: Methodist. Seniority: 164.

5 Bryant (D)—Feb. 22, 1947. Occupation: lawyer. Religion: Methodist. Seniority: 188.

6 Barton (R)—Sept. 15, 1949. Occupation: consultant, engineer. Religion: Methodist. Seniority: 155.

7 Archer (R)—March 22, 1928. Occupation: lawyer, feed company executive. Religion: Roman Catholic. Seniority: 22.

8 Fields (R)—Feb. 3, 1952. Occupation: lawyer, cemetery executive. Religion: Baptist. Seniority: 90.

9 Brooks (D)—Dec. 18, 1922. Occupation: lawyer. Religion: Methodist. Seniority: 5.

10 Pickle (D)—Oct. 11, 1913. Occupation: public relations and advertising executive. Religion: Methodist. Seniority: 26.

11 Leath (D)—May 6, 1931. Occupation: banker. Religion: Presbyterian. Seniority: 134.

12 Wright (D)—Dec. 22, 1922. Occupation: advertising executive. Religion: Presbyterian. Seniority: 9.

13 Boulter (R)—Feb. 23, 1942. Occupation: lawyer. Religion: Independent Bible Church. Seniority: 155.

14 Sweeney (R)—Sept. 15, 1955. Occupation: public official. Religion: Methodist. Seniority: 155.

15 De la Garza (D)—Sept. 22, 1927. Occupation: lawyer. Religion: Roman Catholic. Seniority: 28.

16 Coleman (D)—Nov. 29, 1941. Occupation: lawyer. Religion: Presbyterian. Seniority: 188.

17 Stenholm (D)—Oct. 26, 1938. Occupation: cotton grower. Religion: Lutheran. Seniority: 134.

18 Leland (D)—Nov. 27, 1944. Occupation: pharmacist. Religion: Roman Catholic. Seniority: 134.

19 Combest (R)—March 20, 1945. Occupation: wholesale distributor. Religion: Methodist. Seniority: 155.

20 Gonzalez (D)—May 3, 1916. Occupation: lawyer, public official. Religion: Roman Catholic. Seniority: 19.

21 Loeffler (R)—Aug. 1, 1946. Occupation: rancher, lawyer. Religion: Lutheran. Seniority: 63.
22 DeLay (R)—April 8, 1947. Occupation: pest control company owner. Religion: Baptist. Seniority: 155.
23 Bustamante (D)—April 8, 1935. Occupation: judge. Religion: Roman Catholic. Seniority: 243.
24 Frost (D)—Jan. 1, 1942. Occupation: lawyer. Religion: Jewish. Seniority: 134.
25 Andrews (D)—Feb. 7, 1944. Occupation: lawyer. Religion: Methodist. Seniority: 188.
26 Armey (R)—July 7, 1940. Occupation: economics professor. Religion: Presbyterian. Seniority: 155.
27 Ortiz (D)—June 3, 1937. Occupation: law enforcement official. Religion: Methodist. Seniority: 188.

UTAH

1 Hansen (R)—Aug. 14, 1932. Occupation: insurance executive, land developer. Religion: Mormon. Seniority: 90.
2 Monson (R)—June 20, 1945. Occupation: accountant, public official. Religion: Mormon. Seniority: 155.
3 Nielson (R)—Sept. 12, 1924. Occupation: statistics professor. Religion: Mormon. Seniority: 128.

VERMONT

AL Jeffords (R)—May 11, 1934. Occupation: lawyer. Religion: Congregationalist. Seniority: 42.

VIRGINIA

1 Bateman (R)—Aug. 7, 1928. Occupation: lawyer. Religion: Presbyterian. Seniority: 128.
2 Whitehurst (R)—March 12, 1925. Occupation: history professor, broadcast journalist. Religion: Methodist. Seniority: 17.
3 Bliley (R)—Jan. 28, 1932. Occupation: funeral director, public official. Religion: Roman Catholic. Seniority: 90.
4 Sisisky (D)—June 9, 1927. Occupation: beer and soft drink distributor. Religion: Jewish. Seniority: 188.
5 Daniel (D)—May 12, 1914. Occupation: textile company executive. Religion: Baptist. Seniority: 40.
6 Olin (D)—Feb. 28, 1920. Occupation: corporate executive. Religion: Unitarian. Seniority: 188.
7 Slaughter (R)—May 20, 1925. Occupation: lawyer. Religion: Episcopalian. Seniority: 155.
8 Parris (R)—Sept. 9, 1929. Occupation: automobile dealer, commercial pilot, banker. Religion: Episcopalian. Seniority: 89.
9 Boucher (D)—Aug. 1, 1946. Occupation: lawyer. Religion: Methodist. Seniority: 188.
10 Wolf (R)—Jan. 30, 1939. Occupation: lawyer. Religion: Presbyterian. Seniority: 90.

WASHINGTON

1 Miller (R)—May 23, 1938. Occupation: public official, television and radio commentator. Religion: Jewish. Seniority: 155.
2 Swift (D)—Sept. 12, 1935. Occupation: broadcaster. Religion: Unitarian. Seniority: 134.
3 Bonker (D)—March 7, 1937. Occupation: auditor. Religion: Presbyterian. Seniority: 74.
4 Morrison (R)—May 13, 1933. Occupation: fruit grower, nurseryman. Religion: Methodist. Seniority: 90.
5 Foley (D)—March 6, 1929. Occupation: lawyer. Religion: Roman Catholic. Seniority: 28.
6 Dicks (D)—Dec. 14, 1940. Occupation: lawyer, congressional aide. Religion: Lutheran. Seniority: 105.
7 Lowry (D)—March 8, 1939. Occupation: public official. Religion: Baptist. Seniority: 134.
8 Chandler (R)—July 13, 1942. Occupation: public relations consultant, television newsman. Religion: Protestant. Seniority: 128.

WEST VIRGINIA

1 Mollohan (D)—May 14, 1943. Occupation: lawyer. Religion: Baptist. Seniority: 188.
2 Staggers (D)—Feb. 22, 1951. Occupation: lawyer. Religion: Roman Catholic. Seniority: 188.
3 Wise (D)—Jan. 6, 1948. Occupation: lawyer. Religion: Episcopalian. Seniority: 188.
4 Rahall (D)—May 20, 1949. Occupation: broadcasting executive, travel agent. Religion: Presbyterian. Seniority: 105.

WISCONSIN

1 Aspin (D)—July 21, 1938. Occupation: economics professor. Religion: Episcopalian. Seniority: 51.
2 Kastenmeier (D)—Jan. 24, 1924. Occupation: lawyer. Religion: Unspecified. Seniority: 12.
3 Gunderson (R)—May 10, 1951. Occupation: public official. Religion: Lutheran. Seniority: 90.
4 Kleczka (D)—Nov. 26, 1943. Occupation: accountant. Religion: Roman Catholic. Seniority: 240.
5 Moody (D)—Sept. 2, 1935. Occupation: economist. Religion: Protestant. Seniority: 188.
6 Petri (R)—May 28, 1940. Occupation: lawyer. Religion: Lutheran. Seniority: 87.
7 Obey (D)—Oct. 3, 1938. Occupation: real estate broker. Religion: Roman Catholic. Seniority: 49.
8 Roth (R)—Oct. 10, 1938. Occupation: real estate broker. Religion: Roman Catholic. Seniority. 63.
9 Sensenbrenner (R)—June 14, 1943. Occupation: lawyer. Religion: Episcopalian. Seniority: 63.

WYOMING

AL Cheney (R)—Jan. 30, 1941. Occupation: financial consultant. Religion: Methodist. Seniority: 63. ∎

Seniority in the 99th Congress

Senate Seniority

Senate rank generally is determined according to the official date of the beginning of a member's service, which is Jan. 3, except in the case of new members sworn in at times other than the beginning of a Congress. For those appointed or elected to fill unexpired terms, the date of the appointment, certification or swearing-in determines the senator's rank.

When members are sworn in on the same day, custom decrees that those with prior political experience take precedence. Counted as political experience, in order of importance, is senatorial, House and gubernatorial service. Information on prior experience is given where applicable. The dates following senators' names refer to the beginning of their present service.

REPUBLICANS

1. Thurmond—Nov. 7, 1956[1]
2. Hatfield—Jan. 10, 1967
3. Stevens—Dec. 24, 1968
4. Goldwater (ex-senator)—Jan. 3, 1969
5. Dole (ex-representative, four House terms)—Jan. 3, 1969
   Mathias (ex-representative, four House terms)—Jan. 3, 1969
7. Packwood—Jan. 3, 1969
8. Roth—Jan. 1, 1971
9. Weicker—Jan. 3, 1971
10. Stafford—Sept. 16, 1971
11. McClure (ex-representative)—Jan. 3, 1973
12. Helms—Jan. 3, 1973

Domenici—Jan. 3, 1973
14. Laxalt—Dec. 18, 1974
15. Garn—Dec. 21, 1974
16. Danforth—Dec. 27, 1976
17. Chafee—Dec. 29, 1976
18. Heinz (ex-representative)—Jan. 3, 1977
19. Hatch—Jan. 3, 1977
Lugar—Jan. 3, 1977
Wallop—Jan. 3, 1977
22. Durenberger—Nov. 8, 1978
23. Kassebaum—Dec. 23, 1978
24. Cochran—Dec. 27, 1978
25. Boschwitz—Dec. 30, 1978
26. Simpson—Jan. 1, 1979
27. Warner—Jan. 2, 1979
28. Armstrong (ex-representative, three House terms)—Jan. 3, 1979
Cohen (ex-representative, three House terms)—Jan. 3, 1979
30. Pressler (ex-representative, two House terms)—Jan. 3, 1979
Humphrey—Jan. 3, 1979
32. Rudman—Dec. 29, 1980
33. Hawkins—Jan. 1, 1981
34. Denton—Jan. 2, 1981
35. Andrews (ex-representative, eight and one-half House terms)—Jan. 3, 1981
36. Abdnor (ex-representative, four House terms)—Jan. 3, 1981
Symms (ex-representative, four House terms)—Jan. 3, 1981
38. Grassley (ex-representative, three House terms)—Jan. 3, 1981
39. Kasten (ex-representative, two House terms)—Jan. 3, 1981
Quayle (ex-representative, two House terms)—Jan. 3, 1981
41. D'Amato—Jan. 3, 1981
East—Jan. 3, 1981
Gorton—Jan. 3, 1981
Mattingly—Jan. 3, 1981
Murkowski—Jan. 3, 1981
Nickles—Jan. 3, 1981
Specter—Jan. 3, 1981
48. Trible (ex-representative)—Jan. 3, 1983
49. Hecht—Jan. 3, 1983
Wilson—Jan. 3, 1983
51. Evans—Sept. 12, 1983
52. Gramm (ex-representative)—Jan. 3, 1985
53. McConnell—Jan. 3, 1985

DEMOCRATS

1. Stennis—Nov. 5, 1947
2. Long—Dec. 31, 1948
3. Proxmire—Aug. 28, 1957
4. Byrd—Jan. 3, 1959
5. Burdick—Aug. 8, 1960
6. Pell—Jan. 3, 1961
7. Kennedy—Nov. 7, 1962
8. Inouye—Jan. 3, 1963
9. Hollings—Nov. 9, 1966
10. Eagleton—Dec. 28, 1968
11. Cranston—Jan. 3, 1969
12. Bentsen (ex-representative)—Jan. 3, 1971
13. Chiles—Jan. 3, 1971
14. Nunn—Nov. 8, 1972
15. Johnston—Nov. 14, 1972
16. Biden—Jan. 3, 1973
17. Glenn—Dec. 24, 1974
18. Ford—Dec. 28, 1974
19. Bumpers (ex-governor)—Jan. 3, 1975
20. Hart—Jan. 3, 1975
Leahy—Jan. 3, 1975
22. Zorinsky—Dec. 28, 1976
23. Metzenbaum—Dec. 29, 1976
24. Riegle—Dec. 30, 1976
25. Matsunaga (ex-representative, seven House terms)—Jan. 3, 1977
26. Melcher (ex-representative, three and one-half House terms)—Jan. 3, 1977
27. Sarbanes (ex-representative, three House terms)—Jan. 3, 1977
28. DeConcini—Jan. 3, 1977
Moynihan—Jan. 3, 1977
Sasser—Jan. 3, 1977
31. Baucus—Dec. 15, 1978
32. Pryor (ex-representative, three and one-half House terms; ex-governor)—Jan. 3, 1979
33. Boren (ex-governor)—Jan. 3, 1979
Exon (ex-governor)—Jan. 3, 1979
35. Bradley—Jan. 3, 1979
Heflin—Jan. 3, 1979
Levin—Jan. 3, 1979
38. Mitchell—May 19, 1980
39. Dodd (ex-representative)—Jan. 3, 1981
40. Dixon—Jan. 3, 1981
41. Lautenberg—Dec. 27, 1982
42. Bingaman—Jan. 3, 1983
43. Kerry—Jan. 2, 1985
44. Harkin (ex-representative, five House terms)—Jan. 3, 1985
Simon (ex-representative, five House terms)—Jan. 3, 1985
46. Gore (ex-representative, four House terms)—Jan. 3, 1985
47. Rockefeller (ex-governor)—Jan. 15, 1985

1. Thurmond began his Senate service Nov. 7, 1956, as a Democrat. He became a Republican Sept. 16, 1964. The Republican Conference allowed his seniority to count from his 1956 election to the Senate.

House Seniority

House rank generally is determined according to the official date of the beginning of a member's service, which is Jan. 3, except in the case of members elected to fill vacancies, in which instance the date of election determines rank.

When members enter the House on the same day, those with prior House experience take precedence, starting with those with the longest consecutive service. Experience as a senator or governor is disregarded. Information on prior experience is given where applicable. The dates following members' names refer to the beginning of their present service.

DEMOCRATS

1. Whitten (Miss.)—Nov. 4, 1941
2. Price (Ill.)—Jan. 3, 1945
3. Bennett (Fla.)—Jan. 3, 1949
Rodino (N.J.)—Jan. 3, 1949
5. Boland (Mass.)—Jan. 3, 1953
Brooks (Texas)—Jan. 3, 1953
O'Neill (Mass.)—Jan. 3, 1953
8. Natcher (Ky.)—Aug. 1, 1953
9. Fascell (Fla.)—Jan. 3, 1955
Wright (Texas)—Jan. 3, 1955
11. Dingell (Mich.)—Dec. 13, 1955
12. Kastenmeier (Wis.)—Dec. 13, 1959
13. Rostenkowski (Ill.)—Jan. 3, 1959
Smith (Iowa)—Jan. 3, 1959
Stratton (N.Y.)—Jan. 3, 1959
16. Addabbo (N.Y.)—Jan. 3, 1961
St Germain (R.I.)—Jan. 3, 1961
18. Udall (Ariz.)—May 2, 1961
19. Gonzalez (Texas)—Nov. 4, 1961
20. Edwards (Calif.)—Jan. 3, 1963
Fuqua (Fla.)—Jan. 3, 1963
Gibbons (Fla.)—Jan. 3, 1963
Hawkins (Calif.)—Jan. 3, 1963
Pepper (Fla.)—Jan. 3, 1963
Roybal (Calif.)—Jan. 3, 1963
26. Pickle (Texas)—Dec. 21, 1963
27. Yates (Ill.) (seven terms previously)—Jan. 3, 1965
28. Annunzio (Ill.)—Jan. 3, 1965
Conyers (Mich.)—Jan. 3, 1965
de la Garza (Texas)—Jan. 3, 1965
Foley (Wash.)—Jan. 3, 1965
Ford (Mich.)—Jan. 3, 1965
Hamilton (Ind.)—Jan. 3, 1965
Howard (N.J.)—Jan. 3, 1965
35. Jones (N.C.)—Feb. 5, 1966
36. Bevill (Ala.)—Jan. 3, 1967
Montgomery (Miss.)—Jan. 3, 1967
Nichols (Ala.)—Jan. 3, 1967
39. Gaydos (Pa.)—Nov. 5, 1968
40. Alexander (Ark.)—Jan. 3, 1969
Anderson (Calif.)—Jan. 3, 1969
Biaggi (N.Y.)—Jan. 3, 1969
Chappell (Fla.)—Jan. 3, 1969
Clay (Mo.)—Jan. 3, 1969
Daniel (Va.)—Jan. 3, 1969
Stokes (Ohio)—Jan. 3, 1969
Yatron (Pa.)—Jan. 3, 1969
48. Jones (Tenn.)—March 25, 1969
49. Obey (Wis.)—April 1, 1969
50. Roe (N.J.)—Nov. 4, 1969
51. Aspin (Wis.)—Jan. 3, 1971
Dellums (Calif.)—Jan. 3, 1971
Mazzoli (Ky.)—Jan. 3, 1971
Mitchell (Md.)—Jan. 3, 1971
Rangel (N.Y.)—Jan. 3, 1971
Seiberling (Ohio)—Jan. 3, 1971
57. Breaux (La.)—Sept. 30, 1972
58. Brown (Calif.) (four terms previously)—Jan. 3, 1973
59. Long (La.) (one term previously)—Jan. 3, 1973
60. Jones (Okla.)—Jan. 3, 1973

Lehman (Fla.)—Jan. 3, 1973
Moakley (Mass.)—Jan. 3, 1973
Rose (N.C.)—Jan. 3, 1973
Schroeder (Colo.)—Jan. 3, 1973
Stark (Calif.)—Jan. 3, 1973
Studds (Mass.)—Jan. 3, 1973
Wilson (Texas)—Jan. 3, 1973
68. Boggs (La.)—March 20, 1973
69. Collins (Ill.)—June 5, 1973
70. Murtha (Pa.)—Feb. 5, 1974
71. Traxler (Mich.)—April 16, 1974
72. Jacobs (Ind.) (four terms previously)—Jan. 3, 1975
Scheuer (N.Y.) (four terms previously)—Jan. 3, 1975
74. AuCoin (Ore.)—Jan. 3, 1975
Bedell (Iowa)—Jan. 3, 1975
Bonker (Wash.)—Jan. 3, 1975
Derrick (S.C.)—Jan. 3, 1975
Downey (N.Y.)—Jan. 3, 1975
Early (Mass.)—Jan. 3, 1975
Edgar (Pa.)—Jan. 3, 1975
English (Okla.)—Jan. 3, 1975
Florio (N.J.)—Jan. 3, 1975
Ford (Tenn.)—Jan. 3, 1975
Hefner (N.C.)—Jan. 3, 1975
Hubbard (Ky.)—Jan. 3, 1975
Hughes (N.J.)—Jan. 3, 1975
LaFalce (N.Y.)—Jan. 3, 1975
Lloyd (Tenn.)—Jan. 3, 1975
McHugh (N.Y.)—Jan. 3, 1975
Miller (Calif.)—Jan. 3, 1975
Mineta (Calif.)—Jan. 3, 1975
Neal (N.C.)—Jan. 3, 1975
Nowak (N.Y.)—Jan. 3, 1975
Oberstar (Minn.)—Jan. 3, 1975
Russo (Ill.)—Jan. 3, 1975
Sharp (Ind.)—Jan. 3, 1975
Solarz (N.Y.)—Jan. 3, 1975
Waxman (Calif.)—Jan. 3, 1975
Weaver (Ore.)—Jan. 3, 1975
Wirth (Colo.)—Jan. 3, 1975
101. Lundine (N.Y.)—March 2, 1976
102. Hall, Sam B. Jr. (Texas)—June 19, 1976
103. Markey (Mass.)—Nov. 2, 1976
104. Luken (Ohio) (one term previously)—Jan. 3, 1977
105. Akaka (Hawaii)—Jan. 3, 1977
Applegate (Ohio)—Jan. 3, 1977
Barnard (Ga.)—Jan. 3, 1977
Beilenson (Calif.)—Jan. 3, 1977
Bonior (Mich.)—Jan. 3, 1977
Dicks (Wash.)—Jan. 3, 1977
Flippo (Ala.)—Jan. 3, 1977
Gephardt (Mo.)—Jan. 3, 1977
Glickman (Kan.)—Jan. 3, 1977
Heftel (Hawaii)—Jan. 3, 1977
Huckaby (La.)—Jan. 3, 1977
Jenkins (Ga.)—Jan. 3, 1977
Kildee (Mich.)—Jan. 3, 1977
Mikulski (Md.)—Jan. 3, 1977
Murphy (Pa.)—Jan. 3, 1977
Oakar (Ohio)—Jan. 3, 1977
Panetta (Calif.)—Jan. 3, 1977
Pease (Ohio)—Jan. 3, 1977
Rahall (W.Va.)—Jan. 3, 1977
Skelton (Mo.)—Jan. 3, 1977
Vento (Minn.)—Jan. 3, 1977
Volkmer (Mo.)—Jan. 3, 1977
Walgren (Pa.)—Jan. 3, 1977
Watkins (Okla.)—Jan. 3, 1977
Weiss (N.Y.)—Jan. 3, 1977
Whitley (N.C.)—Jan. 3, 1977
Young (Mo.)—Jan. 3, 1977
132. Fowler (Ga.)—April 5, 1977
133. Garcia (N.Y.)—Feb. 14, 1978
134. Anthony (Ark.)—Jan. 3, 1979
Barnes (Md.)—Jan. 3, 1979
Boner (Tenn.)—Jan. 3, 1979
Byron (Md.)—Jan. 3, 1979
Coelho (Calif.)—Jan. 3, 1979
Daschle (S.D.)—Jan. 3, 1979
Dixon (Calif.)—Jan. 3, 1979
Donnelly (Mass.)—Jan. 3, 1979
Fazio (Calif.)—Jan. 3, 1979
Frost (Texas)—Jan. 3, 1979
Gray (Pa.)—Jan. 3, 1979
Guarini (N.J.)—Jan. 3, 1979
Hall (Ohio)—Jan. 3, 1979
Hutto (Fla.)—Jan. 3, 1979
Leath (Texas)—Jan. 3, 1979
Leland (Texas)—Jan. 3, 1979
Lowry (Wash.)—Jan. 3, 1979
Matsui (Calif.)—Jan. 3, 1979
Mavroules (Mass.)—Jan. 3, 1979
Mica (Fla.)—Jan. 3, 1979
Nelson (Fla.)—Jan. 3, 1979
Sabo (Minn.)—Jan. 3, 1979
Shelby (Ala.)—Jan. 3, 1979
Stenholm (Texas)—Jan. 3, 1979
Swift (Wash.)—Jan. 3, 1979
Synar (Okla.)—Jan. 3, 1979
Williams (Mont.)—Jan. 3, 1979
Wolpe (Mich.)—Jan. 3, 1979
162. Tauzin (La.)—May 17, 1980
163. Crockett (Mich.)—Nov. 4, 1980
164. Coyne (Pa.)—Jan. 3, 1981
Dorgan (N.D.)—Jan. 3, 1981
Dwyer (N.J.)—Jan. 3, 1981
Dymally (Calif.)—Jan. 3, 1981
Dyson (Md.)—Jan. 3, 1981
Eckart (Ohio)—Jan. 3, 1981
Foglietta (Pa.)—Jan. 3, 1981
Frank (Mass.)—Jan. 3, 1981
Gejdenson (Conn.)—Jan. 3, 1981
Hall, Ralph M. (Texas)—Jan. 3, 1981
Hatcher (Ga.)—Jan. 3, 1981
Hertel (Mich.)—Jan. 3, 1981
Lantos (Calif.)—Jan. 3, 1981
McCurdy (Okla.)—Jan. 3, 1981
Roemer (La.)—Jan. 3, 1981
Savage (Ill.)—Jan. 3, 1981
Schumer (N.Y.)—Jan. 3, 1981
Wyden (Ore.)—Jan. 3, 1981
182. Hoyer (Md.)—May 19, 1981
183. Dowdy (Miss.)—July 7, 1981
184. Kennelly (Conn.)—Jan. 12, 1982
185. Martinez (Calif.)—July 13, 1982
186. Carr (Mich.) (three terms previously)—Jan. 3, 1983
187. Kostmayer (Pa.) (two terms previously)—Jan. 3, 1983
188. Andrews (Texas)—Jan. 3, 1983
Bates (Calif.)—Jan. 3, 1983
Berman (Calif.)—Jan. 3, 1983
Borski (Pa.)—Jan. 3, 1983
Bosco (Calif.)—Jan. 3, 1983
Boucher (Va.)—Jan. 3, 1983
Boxer (Calif.)—Jan. 3, 1983
Bryant (Texas)—Jan. 3, 1983
Carper (Del.)—Jan. 3, 1983
Coleman (Texas)—Jan. 3, 1983
Cooper (Tenn.)—Jan. 3, 1983
Durbin (Ill.)—Jan. 3, 1983
Erdreich (Ala.)—Jan. 3, 1983
Evans (Ill.)—Jan. 3, 1983
Feighan (Ohio)—Jan. 3, 1983
Kaptur (Ohio)—Jan. 3, 1983
Kolter (Pa.)—Jan. 3, 1983
Lehman (Calif.)—Jan. 3, 1983
Levin (Mich.)—Jan. 3, 1983
Levine (Calif.)—Jan. 3, 1983
Lipinski (Ill.)—Jan. 3, 1983
MacKay (Fla)—Jan. 3, 1983
Mollohan (W.Va.)—Jan. 3, 1983
Moody (Wis.)—Jan. 3, 1983
Morrison (Conn.)—Jan. 3, 1983
Mrazek (N.Y.)—Jan. 3, 1983
Olin (Va.)—Jan. 3, 1983
Ortiz (Texas)—Jan. 3, 1983
Owens (N.Y.)—Jan. 3, 1983
Penny (Minn.)—Jan. 3, 1983
Ray (Ga.)—Jan. 3, 1983
Reid (Nev.)—Jan. 3, 1983
Richardson (N.M.)—Jan. 3, 1983
Rowland (Ga.)—Jan. 3, 1983
Sikorski (Minn.)—Jan. 3, 1983
Sisisky (Va.)—Jan. 3, 1983
Slattery (Kan.)—Jan. 3, 1983
Smith (Fla.)—Jan. 3, 1983
Spratt (S.C.)—Jan. 3, 1983
Staggers (W.Va.)—Jan. 3, 1983
Tallon (S.C.)—Jan. 3, 1983
Thomas (Ga.)—Jan. 3, 1983
Torres (Calif.)—Jan. 3, 1983
Torricelli (N.J.)—Jan. 3, 1983
Towns (N.Y.)—Jan. 3, 1983
Valentine (N.C.)—Jan. 3, 1983
Wheat (Mo.)—Jan. 3, 1983
Wise (W.Va.)—Jan. 3, 1983
236. Ackerman (N.Y.)—March 1, 1983
237. Burton (Calif.)—June 21, 1983
238. Hayes (Ill.)—Aug. 23, 1983
239. Darden (Ga.)—Nov. 8, 1983
240. Kleczka (Wis.)—April 3, 1984
241. Perkins (Ky.)—Nov. 6, 1984
242. Gray (Ill.) (10 terms previously)—Jan. 3, 1985
243. Atkins (Mass.)—Jan. 3, 1985
Bruce (Ill.)—Jan. 3, 1985
Bustamante (Texas)—Jan. 3, 1985
Gordon (Tenn.)—Jan. 3, 1985
Kanjorski (Pa.)—Jan. 3, 1985
Manton (N.Y.)—Jan. 3, 1985
Robinson (Ark.)—Jan. 3, 1985
Stallings (Idaho)—Jan. 3, 1985
Traficant (Ohio)—Jan. 3, 1985

Visclosky (Ind.)—Jan. 3, 1985

REPUBLICANS

1. Broomfield (Mich.)—Jan. 3, 1957
Michel (Ill.)—Jan. 3, 1957
3. Conte (Mass.)—Jan. 3, 1959
Latta (Ohio)—Jan. 3, 1959
5. Broyhill (N.C.)—Jan. 3, 1963
Horton (N.Y.)—Jan. 3, 1963
McDade (Pa.)—Jan. 3, 1963
Quillen (Tenn.)—Jan. 3, 1963
9. Dickinson (Ala.)—Jan. 3, 1965
Duncan (Tenn.)—Jan. 3, 1965
11. Vander Jagt (Mich.)—Nov. 8, 1966
12. Snyder (Ky.) (one term previously)—Jan. 3, 1967
13. Hammerschmidt (Ark.)—Jan. 3, 1967
Miller (Ohio)—Jan. 3, 1967
Myers (Ind.)—Jan. 3, 1967
Wylie (Ohio)—Jan. 3, 1967
17. Coughlin (Pa.)—Jan. 3, 1969
Fish (N.Y.)—Jan. 3, 1969
Lujan (N.M.)—Jan. 3, 1969
Whitehurst (Va.)—Jan. 3, 1969
21. Crane, Philip M. (Ill.)—Nov. 25, 1969
22. Archer (Texas)—Jan. 3, 1971
Frenzel (Minn.)—Jan. 3, 1971
Hillis (Ind.)—Jan. 3, 1971
Kemp (N.Y.)—Jan. 3, 1971
Lent (N.Y.)—Jan. 3, 1971
McKinney (Conn.)—Jan. 3, 1971
Spence (S.C.)—Jan. 3, 1971
Young (Fla.)—Jan. 3, 1971
30. Gilman (N.Y.)—Jan. 3, 1973
Holt (Md.)—Jan. 3, 1973
Lott (Miss.)—Jan. 3, 1973
Madigan (Ill.)—Jan. 3, 1973
Moorhead (Calif.)—Jan. 3, 1973
O'Brien (Ill.)—Jan. 3, 1973
Regula (Ohio)—Jan. 3, 1973
Rinaldo (N.J.)—Jan. 3, 1973
Shuster (Pa.)—Jan. 3, 1973
Taylor (Mo.)—Jan. 3, 1973
40. Young (Alaska)—March 6, 1973
41. Lagomarsino (Calif.)—March 5, 1974
42. Goodling (Pa.)—Jan. 3, 1975
Gradison (Ohio)—Jan. 3, 1975
Hyde (Ill.)—Jan. 3, 1975
Jeffords (Vt.)—Jan. 3, 1975
Kindness (Ohio)—Jan. 3, 1975
Schulze (Pa.)—Jan. 3, 1975
Smith (Neb.)—Jan. 3, 1975
49. Moore (La.)—Jan. 7, 1975
50. Coleman (Mo.)—Nov. 2, 1976
51. Badham (Calif.)—Jan. 3, 1977
Edwards (Okla.)—Jan. 3, 1977
Ireland (Fla.)—Jan. 3, 1977*
Leach (Iowa)—Jan. 3, 1977
Marlenee (Mont.)—Jan. 3, 1977
Pursell (Mich.)—Jan. 3, 1977
Rudd (Ariz.)—Jan. 3, 1977
Stump (Ariz.)—Jan. 3, 1977*
Walker (Pa.)—Jan. 3, 1977
60. Stangeland (Minn.)—Feb. 22, 1977
61. Livingston (La.)—Aug. 27, 1977
62. Green (N.Y.)—Feb. 14, 1978
63. Bereuter (Neb.)—Jan. 3, 1979
Campbell (S.C.)—Jan. 3, 1979
Carney (N.Y.)—Jan. 3, 1979
Cheney (Wyo.)—Jan. 3, 1979
Clinger (Pa.)—Jan. 3, 1979
Courter (N.J.)—Jan. 3, 1979
Dannemeyer (Calif.)—Jan. 3, 1979
Davis (Mich.)—Jan. 3, 1979
Gingrich (Ga.)—Jan. 3, 1979
Hopkins (Ky.)—Jan. 3, 1979
Kramer (Colo.)—Jan. 3, 1979
Lewis (Calif.)—Jan. 3, 1979
Loeffler (Texas)—Jan. 3, 1979
Lungren (Calif.)—Jan. 3, 1979
Pashayan (Calif.)—Jan. 3, 1979
Ritter (Pa.)—Jan. 3, 1979
Roth (Wis.)—Jan. 3, 1979
Sensenbrenner (Wis.)—Jan. 3, 1979
Shumway (Calif.)—Jan. 3, 1979
Snowe (Maine)—Jan. 3, 1979
Solomon (N.Y.)—Jan. 3, 1979
Tauke (Iowa)—Jan. 3, 1979
Thomas (Calif.)—Jan. 3, 1979
Whittaker (Kan.)—Jan. 3, 1979
87. Petri (Wis.)—April 3, 1979
88. Porter (Ill.)—Jan. 22, 1980
89. Parris (Va.) (one term previously)—Jan. 3, 1981
90. Bliley (Va.)—Jan. 3, 1981
Brown (Colo.)—Jan. 3, 1981
Chappie (Calif.)—Jan. 3, 1981
Coats (Ind.)—Jan. 3, 1981
Craig (Idaho)—Jan. 3, 1981
Daub (Neb.)—Jan. 1981
Dreier (Calif.)—Jan. 3, 1981
Emerson (Mo.)—Jan. 3, 1981
Evans (Iowa)—Jan. 3, 1981
Fiedler (Calif.)—Jan. 3, 1981
Fields (Texas)—Jan. 3, 1981
Gregg (N.H.)—Jan. 3, 1981
Gunderson (Wis.)—Jan. 3, 1981
Hansen (Utah)—Jan. 3, 1981
Hartnett (S.C.)—Jan. 3, 1981
Hiler (Ind.)—Jan. 3, 1981
Hunter (Calif.)—Jan. 3, 1981
Lowery (Calif.)—Jan. 3, 1981
Martin (N.Y.)—Jan. 3, 1981
Martin (Ill.)—Jan. 3, 1981
McCollum (Fla.)—Jan. 3, 1981
McEwen (Ohio)—Jan. 3, 1981
McGrath (N.Y.)—Jan. 3, 1981
Molinari (N.Y.)—Jan. 3, 1981
Morrison (Wash.)—Jan. 3, 1981
Roberts (Kan.)—Jan. 3, 1981
Rogers (Ky.)—Jan. 3, 1981
Roukema (N.J.)—Jan. 3, 1981
Schneider (R.I.)—Jan. 3, 1981
Shaw (Fla.)—Jan. 3, 1981
Skeen (N.M.)—Jan. 3, 1981
Smith (N.J.)—Jan. 3, 1981
Smith, Denny (Ore.)—Jan. 3, 1981
Weber (Minn.)—Jan. 3, 1981
Wolf (Va.)—Jan. 3, 1981
Wortley (N.Y.)—Jan. 3, 1981
126. Siljander (Mich.)—April 21, 1981
127. Oxley (Ohio)—June 25, 1981
128. Bartlett (Texas)—Jan. 3, 1983
Bateman (Va.)—Jan. 3, 1983
Bilirakis (Fla.)—Jan. 3, 1983
Boehlert (N.Y.)—Jan. 3, 1983
Burton (Ind.)—Jan. 3, 1983
Chandler (Wash.)—Jan. 3, 1983
DeWine (Ohio)—Jan. 3, 1983
Franklin (Miss.)—Jan. 3, 1983
Gekas (Pa.)—Jan. 3, 1983
Johnson (Conn.)—Jan. 3, 1983
Kasich (Ohio)—Jan. 3, 1983
Lewis (Fla.)—Jan. 3, 1983
Mack (Fla.)—Jan. 3, 1983
McCain (Ariz.)—Jan. 3, 1983
McCandless (Calif.)—Jan. 3, 1983
McKernan (Maine)—Jan. 3, 1983
Nielson (Utah)—Jan. 3, 1983
Packard (Calif.)—Jan. 3, 1983
Ridge (Pa.)—Jan. 3, 1983
Smith, Bob (Ore.)—Jan. 3, 1983
Sundquist (Tenn.)—Jan. 3, 1983
Vucanovich (Nev.)—Jan. 3, 1983
Zschau (Calif.)—Jan. 3, 1983
151. Schaeffer (Colo.)—March 29, 1983
152. Saxton (N.J.)—Nov. 6, 1984
153. Dornan (Calif.) (three terms previously)—Jan. 3, 1985
154. Hendon (N.C.) (one term previously)—Jan. 3, 1985
155. Armey (Texas)—Jan. 3, 1985
Barton (Texas)—Jan. 3, 1985
Bentley (Md.)—Jan. 3, 1985
Boulter (Texas)—Jan. 3, 1985
Callahan (Ala.)—Jan. 3, 1985
Cobey (N.C.)—Jan. 3, 1985
Coble (N.C.)—Jan. 3, 1985
Combest (Texas)—Jan. 3, 1985
DeLay (Texas)—Jan. 3, 1985
DioGuardi (N.Y.)—Jan. 3, 1985
Eckert (N.Y.)—Jan. 3, 1985
Fawell (Ill.)—Jan. 3, 1985
Gallo (N.J.)—Jan. 3, 1985
Grotberg (Ill.)—Jan. 3, 1985
Henry (Mich.)—Jan. 3, 1985
Kolbe (Ariz.)—Jan. 3, 1985
Lightfoot (Iowa)—Jan. 3, 1985
McMillan (N.C.)—Jan. 3, 1985
Meyers (Kan.)—Jan. 3, 1985
Miller (Wash.)—Jan. 3, 1985
Monson (Utah)—Jan. 3, 1985
Rowland (Conn.)—Jan. 3, 1985
Schuette (Mich.)—Jan. 3, 1985
Slaughter (Va.)—Jan. 3, 1985
Smith (N.H.)—Jan. 3, 1985
Strang (Colo.)—Jan. 3, 1985
Sweeney (Texas)—Jan. 3, 1985
Swindall (Ga.)—Jan. 3, 1985

** Ireland and Stump began their House service Jan. 3, 1977, as Democrats, later switched parties. The Republican Conference let their seniority count from 1977.*

Committees Are Where the Work Is Done

The bulk of congressional work is done in committees, not on the floor of the House or Senate.

Legislation is written by committees; hearings are held by committees; oversight investigations are conducted by committees.

Especially in the House, influence often is closely related to the committee or committees on which a member serves. Assignment to a powerful committee virtually guarantees plentiful campaign contributions.

While many members seek a particular committee because they have an interest in issues within that panel's jurisdiction, others' preferences are based on political need.

Members from large agricultural districts gravitate toward the Agriculture committees. Those from districts with major military installations often seek out the Armed Services panels.

But just wanting to be on a committee is not good enough. In most cases members have to fight for assignments to the best committees. In each chamber, a few committees are considered glamorous and powerful and are difficult to get on. But some are quite the opposite; congressional leaders often have to go looking for "volunteers" to serve on lesser panels.

Traditionally, the premier committees sought by representatives have been Appropriations, Ways and Means and Rules, although Rules has lost its attraction in recent years. In the last several years, members have also scrapped for postings to Energy and Commerce, Budget and Banking, Finance and Urban Affairs.

In the Senate, where members serve on more panels, the most popular committees have traditionally been Appropriations and Finance. Both the Budget Committee and Armed Services also have been in demand.

Although veteran members do switch committees, most keep their assignments throughout their careers.

Influence Measured By Assignments

Major vs. Minor

In both chambers, committees are ranked as major and minor. In the House, Energy and Commerce is a major committee, while Post Office and Civil Service is a minor committee.

Agriculture, Nutrition and Forestry is a major committee in the Senate, while Small Business is minor.

In most cases the distinction is based on the traditional importance of the panel. But both House and Senate Budget committees are classified as minor, even though they have been in the limelight in recent years.

The House also has three "exclusive" committees — Appropriations, Rules and Ways and Means — whose members generally may not serve on other committees. In addition to these three, the House has eight major committees and 10 minor committees.

In the Senate, there are 12 major committees and 10 minor committees. While representatives generally serve on only two panels, sometimes just one, senators often serve on four. The feeling that senators were stretched too thin by serving on too many panels led Senate leaders to seek strict enforcement in 1985 of the Senate rule that limits senators to two major committees and one minor panel.

In the 98th Congress, 31 senators served on three major committees. Despite the pleas of Senate leaders, these senators were not anxious to give up assignments that they felt were important to their constituents. Internal fighting over the issue delayed the Senate from organizing until late February. In the end, 14 senators kept three major committees each.

While floor fights on tough issues such as the MX missile can be nasty, the internal battles over knocking a senator off a committee can be worse. According to one Senate aide involved in the process: "I spent a year in Vietnam, I lived through a Guatemalan earthquake, and I've been through a divorce. But this was the most nerve-racking experience I've ever gone through. It wasn't pretty."

The Senate was not alone in producing high-pitched committee battles in 1985. In January, House Democrats on a 118-121 vote deposed Armed Services Committee Chairman Melvin Price, D-Ill., who, at 80, was viewed as too infirm to do the job. Then Democrats bypassed several more-senior committee members to elect Les Aspin, D-Wis., as chairman.

But this was an exception to the norm. Most often, particularly in the Senate, the chairman of a committee is the member of the majority party with the most committee seniority.

Assignments of members to committees are made by the political parties in each chamber. Those assignments are then packaged into resolutions and routinely ratified by the full House or Senate. The specific process varies by chamber and party.

Senate

The number of senators on each committee, as well as the ratio of Republicans to Democrats, is generally determined through negotiations between leaders of the parties. However, the majority party, the Republicans, clearly holds the upper hand.

Republicans fill committee vacancies strictly by seniority, with senior members picking first.

Although senators who had three major committees in the 98th Congress came under pressure in 1985 to give one up, they also came under opposing pressure from organized lobbies. For example, labor and education lobbyists were anxious to keep Sen. Lowell P. Weicker Jr., R-Conn., on the Labor and Human Resources Committee, where his is a swing vote.

Weicker kept all three major committee seats.

Democratic senators are assigned to committee openings by the Democratic Steering Committee, chaired by Minority Leader Robert C. Byrd of West Virginia. This panel generally bases its assignments on members' desires and seniority.

Although Senate custom generally precludes senators from the same state and party from serving together on the same committee, Democrats broke that tradition in 1985. They put freshman John Kerry, Mass., on Labor

Key to Listings, Abbreviations

ORDER OF LISTS — In the Senate Committee section, Republicans are listed on the left in roman type. Democrats are on the right in italics. In the House, Democrats are listed on the left in roman type and Republicans are on the right in italics.

Members of legislative committees and subcommittees are listed in order of their seniority on those panels.

Members of party committees are listed alphabetically.

An index of members' committee assignments begins on p. 77-G.

ROOM AND TELEPHONE NUMBERS — Phone and room numbers are listed in the body of the book for each committee and subcommittee. All mail should be addressed to main committee rooms.

To reach the U.S. Capitol switchboard, call (202) 224-3121.

BUILDINGS, ADDRESSES, ZIP CODES — The following abbreviations are used for congressional office buildings:

- SD — Dirksen Senate Office Building;
- SH — Hart Senate Office Building;
- SR — Russell Senate Office Building;
- CHOB — Cannon House Office Building;
- LHOB — Longworth House Office Building;
- RHOB — Rayburn House Office Building.
- HOB Annex #1 — House Office Building Annex #1;
- HOB Annex #2 — House Office Building Annex #2.

A map of Capitol Hill showing the location of each building appears on page 84-G.

The ZIP code for all mail addressed to offices of the Senate is 20510; for the House, 20515.

and Human Resources along with Edward M. Kennedy.

House

In recent years, Republicans have bitterly complained that Democrats have not given them enough seats on House committees. Some Republicans in 1985 called for a boycott of committees unless they were given more seats.

The numbers of members on panels and the party ratios are negotiated by leaders of the two parties; in 1985 they were decided by Majority Leader Jim Wright, D-Texas, and Minority Leader Robert H. Michel, R-Ill.

They worked out a deal to give Republicans 30 more seats on standing committees than they had had in the 98th Congress, even though the GOP had gained only 14 seats in the 1984 elections. Democrats gave up 21 seats on standing committees.

Several Republicans said they were happy with the change, adding that there was still room for improvement. "We were starving to death, and we've now gotten some mush. But we're not quite at steak yet," said Lynn Martin, R-Ill., vice chairman of the Republican Conference.

Even with the extra seats, partisan skirmishing over ratios broke out on two committees. Unhappy with the way they were treated on subcommittee ratios, Republicans walked out of meetings of both the Judiciary Committee and of Energy and Commerce. Eventually, Democrats gave them more subcommittee seats and the Republicans returned.

Democrats are assigned to House committees by the 31-member Democratic Steering and Policy Committee, chaired by Speaker Thomas P. O'Neill Jr. of Massachusetts. The committee consists of 12 members elected by region, eight appointed by O'Neill and 11 who hold other leadership jobs.

A member seeking a particular committee must be nominated by a member of Steering and Policy, so it helps to have a patron on the inside. Members of Steering and Policy are heavily lobbied for their support.

In 1985, the biggest fights were over assignments to Appropriations, Ways and Means and Budget, all of which are central arenas in efforts to deal with the federal budget deficit.

For example, seven candidates ran for two Democratic openings on Appropriations and it took seven ballots to fill the slots. Much of the competition was among regions.

In the end, though, states with the most Steering and Policy members and the most powerful leaders — Texas and Illinois — produced the winners on Appropriations, Ronald D. Coleman of Texas and Richard J. Durbin of Illinois.

Coleman was helped by Wright and Jack Brooks of Texas, while Durbin was aided by Ways and Means Chairman Dan Rostenkowski of Illinois, plus two other Illinois members on Steering and Policy.

The only freshman Democrat to get on one of these "money" committees was Chester G. Atkins, Mass. In O'Neill, Atkins had the best patron of all to land his spot on Budget.

House Republicans are assigned to committees by the executive committee of the Republican Committee on Committees, chaired by Michel. There are 21 voting members of the executive committee, elected by state or region to represent fellow Republicans. The number of votes a member has varies according to the number of Republicans he represents. For example, Jerry Lewis, Calif., represents his state on the panel and has 18 votes, the number of California Republicans.

Among Republicans in 1985, the toughest competition was for seats on Energy and Commerce, Budget, Agriculture and Armed Services. The contests for these slots often involved competition between small and large states. And, while Democrats had given Republicans 30 more seats, the 31 GOP freshmen had to fight for them with more senior members who had been limited in previous years. ∎

Senate Committee Assignments, 99th Congress

As of May 15, 1985

Agriculture, Nutrition and Forestry

Phone: 224-2035 Room: SR-328A

Agriculture in general; animal industry and diseases; crop insurance and soil conservation; farm credit and farm security; food from fresh waters; food stamp programs; forestry in general; home economics; human nutrition; inspection of livestock, meat and agricultural products; pests and pesticides; plant industry, soils and agricultural engineering; rural development, rural electrification and watersheds; school nutrition programs; matters relating to food, nutrition, hunger and rural affairs. Chairman and ranking minority member are members *ex officio* of all subcommittees of which they are not regular members. ***Party Ratio: R 9 - D 8***

Jesse Helms
Chairman

Edward Zorinsky
Ranking Member

Republicans	Democrats
Jesse Helms, N.C.	*Edward Zorinsky, Neb.*
Robert Dole, Kan.	*Patrick J. Leahy, Vt.*
Richard G. Lugar, Ind.	*John Melcher, Mont.*
Thad Cochran, Miss.	*David Pryor, Ark.*
Rudy Boschwitz, Minn.	*David L. Boren, Okla.*
Paula Hawkins, Fla.	*Alan J. Dixon, Ill.*
Mark Andrews, N.D.	*Howell Heflin, Ala.*
Pete Wilson, Calif.	*Tom Harkin, Iowa*
Mitch McConnell, Ky.	

SUBCOMMITTEES

Agricultural Credit and Rural Electrification

Phone: 224-6901 Room: SR-328A

Hawkins — chairman

Andrews	*Boren*
Helms	*Zorinsky*
Cochran	*Heflin*

Agricultural Production, Marketing and Stabilization of Prices

Phone: 224-6901 Room: SR-328A

Cochran — chairman

McConnell	*Leahy*
Dole	*Pryor*
Boschwitz	*Harkin*
Andrews	*Zorinsky*
Wilson	*Melcher*
	Dixon

Agricultural Research, Conservation, Forestry and General Legislation

Phone: 224-6901 Room: SR-328A

Lugar — chairman

Cochran	*Melcher*
Helms	*Heflin*
Wilson	*Pryor*
McConnell	*Boren*
	Harkin

Foreign Agricultural Policy

Phone: 224-6901 Room: SR-328A

Boschwitz — chairman

Wilson	*Dixon*
Lugar	*Heflin*
McConnell	*Zorinsky*
Dole	*Boren*
Hawkins	

Nutrition

Phone: 224-6901 Room: SR-328A

Dole — chairman

Hawkins	*Harkin*
Lugar	*Dixon*
Boschwitz	*Melcher*

Rural Development, Oversight and Investigations

Phone: 224-6901 Room: SR-328A

Andrews — chairman

Helms	*Pryor*

Appropriations

Phone: 224-3471 Room: SD-118

Appropriation of revenue for support of the government; rescission of appropriations; new spending authority under the Congressional Budget Act. Chairman and ranking minority member are members *ex officio* of all subcommittees of which they are not regular members. **Party Ratio: R 15 - D 14**

Mark O. Hatfield
Chairman

John C. Stennis
Ranking Member

Mark O. Hatfield, Ore.	*John C. Stennis, Miss.*
Ted Stevens, Alaska	*Robert C. Byrd, W.Va.*
Lowell P. Weicker Jr., Conn.	*William Proxmire, Wis.*
James A. McClure, Idaho	*Daniel K. Inouye, Hawaii*
Paul Laxalt, Nev.	*Ernest F. Hollings, S.C.*
Jake Garn, Utah	*Lawton Chiles, Fla.*
Thad Cochran, Miss.	*J. Bennett Johnston, La.*
Mark Andrews, N.D.	*Quentin N. Burdick, N.D.*
James Abdnor, S.D.	*Patrick J. Leahy, Vt.*
Bob Kasten, Wis.	*Jim Sasser, Tenn.*
Alfonse M. D'Amato, N.Y.	*Dennis DeConcini, Ariz.*
Mack Mattingly, Ga.	*Dale Bumpers, Ark.*
Warren B. Rudman, N.H.	*Frank R. Lautenberg, N.J.*
Arlen Specter, Pa.	*Tom Harkin, Iowa*
Pete V. Domenici, N.M.	

SUBCOMMITTEES

Agriculture, Rural Development and Related Agencies

Phone: 224-7240 Room: SD-140

Cochran — chairman

McClure	*Burdick*
Andrews	*Stennis*
Abdnor	*Chiles*
Kasten	*Sasser*
Mattingly	*Bumpers*
Specter	*Harkin*

Commerce, Justice, State, the Judiciary and Related Agencies

Phone: 224-0336 Room: S-146A Capitol

Laxalt — chairman

Stevens	*Hollings*
Weicker	*Inouye*
Rudman	*Bumpers*
Hatfield	*Chiles*
Specter	*Lautenberg*

Defense

Phone: 224-7255 Room: SD-122

Stevens — chairman

Weicker	*Stennis*
Garn	*Proxmire*
McClure	*Inouye*
Andrews	*Hollings*
Kasten	*Chiles*
D'Amato	*Johnston*
Rudman	*Byrd*
Cochran	*Sasser*

District of Columbia

Phone: 224-2727 | Room: SD-129

Specter — chairman

Mattingly	*Lautenberg*
Domenici	*Harkin*

Energy and Water Development

Phone: 224-7260 | Room: SD-142

Hatfield — chairman

McClure	*Johnston*
Garn	*Stennis*
Cochran	*Byrd*
Abdnor	*Hollings*
Kasten	*Burdick*
Mattingly	*Sasser*
Domenici	*DeConcini*

Foreign Operations

Phone: 224-7250 | Room: S-125 Capitol

Kasten — chairman

Hatfield	*Inouye*
D'Amato	*Johnston*
Rudman	*Leahy*
Specter	*DeConcini*

HUD - Independent Agencies

Phone: 224-7210 | Room: SD-123

Garn — chairman

Weicker	*Leahy*
Laxalt	*Stennis*
D'Amato	*Proxmire*
Abdnor	*Johnston*
Domenici	*Lautenberg*

Interior and Related Agencies

Phone: 224-7257 | Room: SD-114

McClure — chairman

Stevens	*Byrd*
Laxalt	*Johnston*
Garn	*Leahy*
Cochran	*DeConcini*
Andrews	*Burdick*
Rudman	*Bumpers*
Weicker	*Hollings*

Labor, Health and Human Services, Education and Related Agencies

Phone: 224-7283 | Room: SD-131

Weicker — chairman

Hatfield	*Proxmire*
Stevens	*Byrd*
Andrews	*Hollings*
Rudman	*Chiles*
Specter	*Burdick*
McClure	*Inouye*
Domenici	*Harkin*

Legislative Branch

Phone: 224-7287 | Room: S-129 Capitol

D'Amato — chairman

Hatfield	*Bumpers*
Stevens	*Harkin*

Military Construction

Phone: 224-7271 | Room: SD-129

Mattingly — chairman

Laxalt	*Sasser*
Garn	*Inouye*

Transportation and Related Agencies

Phone: 224-7281 | Room: SD-156

Andrews — chairman

Cochran	*Chiles*
Abdnor	*Stennis*
Kasten	*Byrd*
D'Amato	*Lautenberg*

Treasury, Postal Service and General Government

Phone: 224-2726 | Room: SD-188

Abdnor — chairman

Laxalt	*DeConcini*
Mattingly	*Proxmire*

Armed Services

Phone: 224-3871 Room: SR-222

Defense and defense policy generally; aeronautical and space activities peculiar to or primarily associated with the development of weapons systems or military operations; maintenance and operation of the Panama Canal, including the Canal Zone; military research and development; national security aspects of nuclear energy; naval petroleum reserves (except Alaska); armed forces generally; Selective Service System; strategic and critical materials. Chairman and ranking minority member are members *ex officio* of all subcommittees of which they are not regular members.
Party Ratio: R 10 - D 9

Barry Goldwater
Chairman

Sam Nunn
Ranking Member

Barry Goldwater, Ariz.	*Sam Nunn, Ga.*
Strom Thurmond, S.C.	*John C. Stennis, Miss.*
John W. Warner, Va.	*Gary Hart, Colo.*
Gordon J. Humphrey, N.H.	*J. James Exon, Neb.*
William S. Cohen, Maine	*Carl Levin, Mich.*
Dan Quayle, Ind.	*Edward M. Kennedy, Mass.*
John P. East, N.C.	*Jeff Bingaman, N.M.*
Pete Wilson, Calif.	*Alan J. Dixon, Ill.*
Jeremiah Denton, Ala.	*John Glenn, Ohio*
Phil Gramm, Texas	

SUBCOMMITTEES

Defense Acquisition Policy

Phone: 224-8634 Room: SR-222

Quayle — chairman

Goldwater	*Levin*
Warner	*Bingaman*
Humphrey	*Dixon*
Gramm	*Glenn*

Manpower and Personnel

Phone: 224-9348 Room: SR-232A

Wilson — chairman

Thurmond	*Glenn*
Cohen	*Nunn*
East	*Exon*
Denton	*Kennedy*

Military Construction

Phone: 224-8631 Room: SR-222

Thurmond — chairman

Warner	*Bingaman*
Humphrey	*Stennis*
East	*Hart*

Preparedness

Phone: 224-8639 Room: SR-222

Humphrey — chairman

Goldwater	*Dixon*
East	*Levin*
Denton	*Kennedy*
Gramm	*Glenn*

Sea Power and Force Projection

Phone: 224-8630 Room: SR-222

Cohen — chairman

Quayle	*Exon*
Wilson	*Nunn*
Denton	*Stennis*
Gramm	*Hart*

Strategic and Theater Nuclear Forces

Phone: 224-9349 Room: SR-222

Warner — chairman

Goldwater	*Hart*
Thurmond	*Nunn*
Cohen	*Stennis*
Quayle	*Exon*
Wilson	*Levin*

Banking, Housing and Urban Affairs

Phone: 224-7391 Room: SD-534

Banks, banking and financial institutions; price controls; deposit insurance; economic stabilization and growth; defense production; export and foreign trade promotion; export controls; federal monetary policy, including Federal Reserve System; financial aid to commerce and industry; issuance and redemption of notes; money and credit, including currency and coinage; nursing home construction; public and private housing, including veterans' housing; renegotiation of government contracts; urban development and mass transit; international economic policy. Chairman and ranking minority member are members *ex officio* of all subcommittees of which they are not regular members.
Party Ratio: R 8 - D 7

Jake Garn
Chairman

William Proxmire
Ranking Member

Jake Garn, Utah
John Heinz, Pa.
William L. Armstrong, Colo.
Alfonse M. D'Amato, N.Y.
Slade Gorton, Wash.
Mack Mattingly, Ga.
Chic Hecht, Nev.
Phil Gramm, Texas

William Proxmire, Wis.
Alan Cranston, Calif.
Donald W. Riegle Jr., Mich.
Paul S. Sarbanes, Md.
Christopher J. Dodd, Conn.
Alan J. Dixon, Ill.
Jim Sasser, Tenn.

SUBCOMMITTEES

Economic Policy

Phone: 224-7391 Room: SD-534

Mattingly — chairman

Armstrong	*Dodd*
Gramm	*Dixon*

Financial Institutions and Consumer Affairs

Phone: 224-7391 Room: SD-534

Gorton — chairman

Garn	*Sarbanes*
Hecht	*Proxmire*
Gramm	*Cranston*
D'Amato	*Dodd*

Housing and Urban Affairs

Phone: 224-5404 Room: SD-535

Hecht — chairman

Garn	*Riegle*
Heinz	*Sarbanes*
Armstrong	*Proxmire*
D'Amato	*Cranston*
Gorton	*Dodd*
Mattingly	*Dixon*
Gramm	*Sasser*

International Finance and Monetary Policy

Phone: 224-7391 Room: SD-534

Heinz — chairman

Garn	*Proxmire*
Armstrong	*Dixon*
Gorton	*Sasser*
Mattingly	*Riegle*
Hecht	*Sarbanes*

Securities

Phone: 224-7391 Room: SD-534

D'Amato — chairman

Heinz	*Cranston*
Hecht	*Sasser*
Gramm	*Riegle*

Budget

Phone: 224-0642 Room: SD-621

Federal budget generally; concurrent budget resolutions; Congressional Budget Office. ***Party Ratio: R 12 - D 10***

Pete V. Domenici
Chairman

Lawton Chiles
Ranking Member

Pete V. Domenici, N.M.
William L. Armstrong, Colo.
Nancy Landon Kassebaum, Kan.
Rudy Boschwitz, Minn.
Orrin G. Hatch, Utah
Mark Andrews, N.D.
Steven D. Symms, Idaho
Charles E. Grassley, Iowa
Bob Kasten, Wis.
Dan Quayle, Ind.
Slade Gorton, Wash.
John C. Danforth, Mo.

Lawton Chiles, Fla.
Ernest F. Hollings, S.C.
J. Bennett Johnston, La.
Jim Sasser, Tenn.
Gary Hart, Colo.
Howard M. Metzenbaum, Ohio
Donald W. Riegle Jr., Mich.
Daniel Patrick Moynihan, N.Y.
J. James Exon, Neb.
Frank R. Lautenberg, N.J.

No standing subcommittees.

Commerce, Science and Transportation

Phone: 224-5115 Room: SD-508

Interstate commerce and transportation generally; Coast Guard; coastal zone management; communications; highway safety; inland waterways, except construction; marine fisheries; Merchant Marine and navigation; non-military aeronautical and space sciences; oceans, weather and atmospheric activities; interoceanic canals generally; regulation of consumer products and services; science, engineering and technology research, development and policy; sports; standards and measurement; transportation and commerce aspects of Outer Continental Shelf lands. Chairman and ranking minority member are members *ex officio* of all subcommittees of which they are not regular members. ***Party Ratio: R 9 - D 8***

John C. Danforth
Chairman

Ernest F. Hollings
Ranking Member

John C. Danforth, Mo.
Bob Packwood, Ore.
Barry Goldwater, Ariz.
Nancy Landon Kassebaum, Kan.
Larry Pressler, S.D.
Slade Gorton, Wash.
Ted Stevens, Alaska
Bob Kasten, Wis.
Paul S. Trible Jr., Va.

Ernest F. Hollings, S.C.
Russell B. Long, La.
Daniel K. Inouye, Hawaii
Wendell H. Ford, Ky.
Donald W. Riegle Jr., Mich.
J. James Exon, Neb.
Albert Gore Jr., Tenn.
John D. Rockefeller IV, W.Va.

SUBCOMMITTEES

Aviation

Phone: 224-4852 Room: SH-428

Kassebaum — chairman

Goldwater
Stevens
Trible

Exon
Inouye
Ford

Business, Trade and Tourism

Phone: 224-8170 Room: SH-427

Pressler — chairman

Packwood

Gore

Communications

Phone: 224-8144 Room: SH-227

Goldwater — chairman

Packwood	*Hollings*
Pressler	*Inouye*
Stevens	*Ford*
Gorton	*Gore*

Consumer

Phone: 224-4768 Room: SH-227

Kasten — chairman

Danforth	*Ford*

Merchant Marine

Phone: 224-4766 Room: SH-425

Stevens — chairman

Gorton	*Inouye*
Kasten	*Long*
Trible	*Rockefeller*

Science, Technology and Space

Phone: 224-8172 Room: SH-427

Gorton — chairman

Goldwater	*Riegle*
Kassebaum	*Gore*
Trible	*Rockefeller*

Surface Transportation

Phone: 224-4852 Room: SH-428

Packwood — chairman

Pressler	*Long*
Kassebaum	*Riegle*
Kasten	*Exon*
Danforth	*Rockefeller*

National Ocean Policy Study

Phone: 224-8170 Room: SH-427

The National Ocean Policy Study is technically not a subcommittee of the Commerce, Science and Transportation Committee; no legislation is referred to it. Numerous *ex officio* members from other Senate committees and from the Senate at large serve on it.

Danforth — chairman
Stevens — vice chairman

Packwood	*Hollings*
Gorton	*Long*
Kasten	*Inouye*
Trible	

Energy and Natural Resources

Phone: 224-4971 Room: SD-358

Energy policy, regulation, conservation, research and development; coal; energy-related aspects of deep-water ports; hydroelectric power, irrigation and reclamation; mines, mining and minerals generally; national parks, recreation areas, wilderness areas, wild and scenic rivers, historic sites, military parks and battlefields; naval petroleum reserves in Alaska; non-military development of nuclear energy; oil and gas production and distribution; public lands and forests; solar energy systems; territorial possessions of the United States. Chairman and ranking minority member are members *ex officio* of all subcommittees of which they are not regular members. ***Party Ratio: R 10 - D 8***

James A. McClure
Chairman

J. Bennett Johnston
Ranking Member

James A. McClure, Idaho	*J. Bennett Johnston, La.*
Mark O. Hatfield, Ore.	*Dale Bumpers, Ark.*
Lowell P. Weicker Jr., Conn.	*Wendell H. Ford, Ky.*
Pete V. Domenici, N.M.	*Howard M. Metzenbaum, Ohio*
Malcolm Wallop, Wyo.	*John Melcher, Mont.*
John W. Warner, Va.	*Bill Bradley, N.J.*
Frank H. Murkowski, Alaska	*Jeff Bingaman, N.M.*
Don Nickles, Okla.	*John D. Rockefeller IV, W.Va.*
Chic Hecht, Nev.	
Daniel J. Evans, Wash.	

SUBCOMMITTEES

Energy Regulation and Conservation

Phone: 224-5205 Room: SD-306

Nickles — chairman

Hatfield	*Metzenbaum*
Domenici	*Ford*
Warner	*Bradley*
Hecht	*Bingaman*
Evans	*Rockefeller*

Energy Research and Development

Phone: 224-4431 Room: SD-317

Domenici — chairman

Warner	*Ford*
Hecht	*Bumpers*
Evans	*Metzenbaum*
Wallop	*Rockefeller*

Natural Resources Development and Production

Phone: 224-5205 Room: SD-306

Warner - chairman

Weicker	*Melcher*
Wallop	*Bumpers*
Murkowski	*Bingaman*
Nickles	*Rockefeller*

Public Lands, Reserved Water and Resource Conservation

Phone: 224-0613 Room: SD-308

Wallop — chairman

Weicker	*Bumpers*
Hecht	*Melcher*
Hatfield	*Bradley*
Domenici	*Bingaman*
Murkowski	

Water and Power

Phone: 224-2366 Room: SH-212

Murkowski — chairman

Hatfield	*Bradley*
Evans	*Ford*
Nickles	*Metzenbaum*
Weicker	*Melcher*

Environment and Public Works

Phone: 224-6176 Room: SD-410

Environmental policy, research and development; air, water and noise pollution; construction and maintenance of highways; environmental aspects of Outer Continental Shelf lands; environmental effects of toxic substances, other than pesticides; fisheries and wildlife; flood control and improvements of rivers and harbors; non-military environmental regulation and control of nuclear energy; ocean dumping; public buildings and grounds; public works, bridges and dams; regional economic development; solid waste disposal and recycling; water resources. ***Party Ratio: R 8 - D 7***

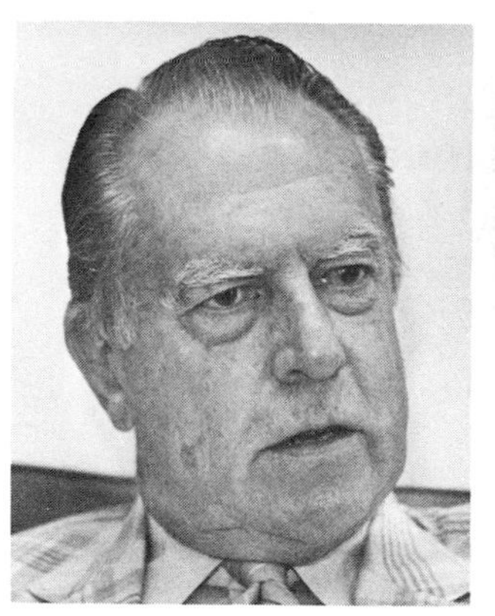

Robert T. Stafford
Chairman

Lloyd Bentsen
Ranking Member

Robert T. Stafford, Vt.	*Lloyd Bentsen, Texas*
John H. Chafee, R.I.	*Quentin N. Burdick, N.D.*
Alan K. Simpson, Wyo.	*Gary Hart, Colo.*
James Abdnor, S.D.	*Daniel Patrick Moynihan, N.Y.*
Steven D. Symms, Idaho	*George J. Mitchell, Maine*
Gordon J. Humphrey, N.H.	*Max Baucus, Mont.*
Pete V. Domenici, N.M.	*Frank R. Lautenberg, N.J.*
Dave Durenberger, Minn.	

SUBCOMMITTEES

Environmental Pollution

Phone: 224-6691 Room: SH-408

Chafee — chairman

Simpson	*Mitchell*
Symms	*Hart*
Durenberger	*Moynihan*
Humphrey	*Lautenberg*

Nuclear Regulation

Phone: 224-2991 Room: SH-415

Simpson — chairman

Domenici	*Hart*
Symms	*Moynihan*

Regional and Community Development

Phone: 224-7857 Room: SD-410

Humphrey — chairman

Domenici	*Lautenberg*
Chafee	*Burdick*

Toxic Substances and Environmental Oversight

Phone: 224-5761 Room: SD-410

Durenberger — chairman

Simpson	*Baucus*
Abdnor	*Burdick*
Humphrey	*Hart*

Transportation

Phone: 224-7863 Room: SH-415

Symms — chairman

Chafee	*Burdick*
Abdnor	*Mitchell*
Stafford	*Bentsen*

Water Resources

Phone: 224-2867 Room: SH-508

Abdnor — chairman

Domenici	*Moynihan*
Durenberger	*Baucus*

Finance

Phone: 224-4515 Room: SD-219

Revenue measures generally; taxes; tariffs and import quotas; foreign trade agreements; customs; revenue sharing; federal debt limit; Social Security; health programs financed by taxes or trust funds. Chairman and ranking minority member are members *ex officio* of all subcommittees of which they are not regular members. ***Party Ratio: R 11 - D 9***

Bob Packwood
Chairman

Russell B. Long
Ranking Member

Bob Packwood, Ore.	*Russell B. Long, La.*
Robert Dole, Kan.	*Lloyd Bentsen, Texas*
William V. Roth Jr., Del.	*Spark M. Matsunaga, Hawaii*
John C. Danforth, Mo.	*Daniel Patrick Moynihan, N.Y.*
John H. Chafee, R.I.	*Max Baucus, Mont.*
John Heinz, Pa.	*David L. Boren, Okla.*
Malcolm Wallop, Wyo.	*Bill Bradley, N.J.*
Dave Durenberger, Minn.	*George J. Mitchell, Maine*
William L. Armstrong, Colo.	*David Pryor, Ark.*
Steven D. Symms, Idaho	
Charles E. Grassley, Iowa	

SUBCOMMITTEES

Energy and Agricultural Taxation

Phone: 224-4515 Room: SD-219

Wallop — chairman

Durenberger	*Bradley*
Symms	*Bentsen*
Grassley	*Matsunaga*

Estate and Gift Taxation

Phone: 224-4515 Room: SD-219

Symms — chairman

Boren

Health

Phone: 224-4515 Room: SD-219

Durenberger — chairman

Dole	*Baucus*
Roth	*Mitchell*
Chafee	*Boren*
Wallop	*Bradley*
Heinz	*Long*

International Trade

Phone: 224-4515 Room: SD-219

Danforth — chairman

Roth	*Bentsen*
Chafee	*Matsunaga*
Heinz	*Baucus*
Armstrong	*Boren*
Symms	*Bradley*
Grassley	*Moynihan*
	Mitchell

Oversight of the Internal Revenue Service

Phone: 224-4515 Room: SD-219

Dole — chairman

Grassley	*Pryor*

Savings, Pensions and Investment Policy

Phone: 224-4515 Room: SD-219

Heinz — chairman

Roth	*Mitchell*
Chafee	*Long*

Social Security and Income Maintenance Programs

Phone: 224-4515 Room: SD-219

Armstrong — chairman

Danforth	*Moynihan*
Durenberger	*Pryor*
	Long

Taxation and Debt Management

Phone: 224-4515 Room: SD-219

Chafee — chairman

Dole	*Matsunaga*
Roth	*Bentsen*
Danforth	*Moynihan*
Wallop	*Pryor*
Armstrong	*Baucus*

Foreign Relations

Phone: 224-4651 Room: SD-446

Relations of the United States with foreign nations generally; treaties; foreign economic, military, technical and humanitarian assistance; foreign loans; diplomatic service; International Red Cross; international aspects of nuclear energy; International Monetary Fund; intervention abroad and declarations of war; foreign trade; national security; oceans and international environmental and scientific affairs; protection of U.S. citizens abroad; United Nations; World Bank and other development assistance organizations. Chairman and ranking minority member are members *ex officio* of all subcommittees of which they are not regular members. ***Party Ratio: R 9 - D 8***

Richard G. Lugar
Chairman

Claiborne Pell
Ranking Member

Richard G. Lugar, Ind.
Jesse Helms, N.C.
Charles McC. Mathias Jr., Md.
Nancy Landon Kassebaum, Kan.
Rudy Boschwitz, Minn.
Larry Pressler, S.D.
Frank H. Murkowski, Alaska
Paul S. Trible Jr., Va.
Daniel J. Evans, Wash.

Claiborne Pell, R.I.
Joseph R. Biden Jr., Del.
Paul S. Sarbanes, Md.
Edward Zorinsky, Neb.
Alan Cranston, Calif.
Christopher J. Dodd, Conn.
Thomas F. Eagleton, Mo.
John Kerry, Mass.

SUBCOMMITTEES

African Affairs

Phone: 224-4651 Room: SD-423

Kassebaum — chairman

Helms	*Kerry*
Mathias	*Sarbanes*
Pressler	*Pell*

East Asian and Pacific Affairs

Phone: 224-4651 Room: SD-423

Murkowski — chairman

Helms	*Cranston*
Evans	*Zorinsky*
Lugar	*Dodd*

European Affairs

Phone: 224-4651 Room: SD-423

Pressler — chairman

Mathias	*Biden*
Boschwitz	*Sarbanes*
Trible	*Zorinsky*
Lugar	*Eagleton*

International Economic Policy, Oceans and Environment

Phone: 224-4651 Room: SD-423

Mathias — chairman

Boschwitz	*Dodd*
Murkowski	*Eagleton*
Trible	*Kerry*
Evans	*Pell*

Near Eastern and South Asian Affairs

Phone: 224-4651 Room: SD-423

Boschwitz — chairman

Kassebaum	*Sarbanes*
Pressler	*Cranston*
Lugar	*Pell*

Western Hemisphere Affairs

Phone: 224-3866 Room: SH-521

Helms — chairman

Kassebaum	*Zorinsky*
Murkowski	*Dodd*
Trible	*Eagleton*
Evans	*Kerry*

Governmental Affairs

Phone: 224-4751 Room: SD-340

Budget and accounting measures; census and statistics; federal civil service; congressional organization; intergovernmental relations; government information; District of Columbia; organization and management of nuclear export policy; executive branch reorganization; Postal Service; efficiency, economy and effectiveness of government. Chairman and ranking minority member are members *ex officio* of all subcommittees of which they are not regular members. ***Party Ratio: R 7 - D 6***

William V. Roth Jr.
Chairman

Thomas F. Eagleton
Ranking Member

William V. Roth Jr., Del.
Ted Stevens, Alaska
Charles McC. Mathias Jr., Md.
William S. Cohen, Maine

Thomas F. Eagleton, Mo.
Lawton Chiles, Fla.
Sam Nunn, Ga.
John Glenn, Ohio
Carl Levin, Mich.

Dave Durenberger, Minn.
Warren B. Rudman, N.H.
Thad Cochran, Miss.

Albert Gore Jr., Tenn.

SUBCOMMITTEES

Civil Service, Post Office and General Services

Phone: 224-2254 Room: SH-601

Stevens — chairman

Mathias	*Gore*
Durenberger	*Levin*

Energy, Nuclear Proliferation and Government Processes

Phone: 224-9515 Room: SH-605

Cochran — chairman

Cohen	*Glenn*

Governmental Efficiency and the District of Columbia

Phone: 224-4161 Room: SH-442

Mathias — chairman

Rudman	*Eagleton*

Intergovernmental Relations

Phone: 224-4718 Room: SH-432

Durenberger — chairman

Stevens	*Chiles*
Cochran	*Nunn*

Oversight of Government Management

Phone: 224-5538 Room: SD-326

Cohen — chairman

Rudman	*Levin*
Durenberger	*Chiles*

Permanent Subcommittee on Investigations

Phone: 224-3721 Room: SR-100

Roth — chairman

Rudman	*Nunn*
Mathias	*Chiles*
Cohen	*Glenn*
Cochran	*Levin*
Stevens	*Gore*

Judiciary

Phone: 224-5225 Room: SD-224

Civil and criminal judicial proceedings generally; penitentiaries; bankruptcy, mutiny, espionage and counterfeiting; civil liberties; constitutional amendments; apportionment of representatives; government information; immigration and naturalization; interstate compacts generally; claims against the United States; patents, copyrights and trademarks; monopolies and unlawful restraints of trade; holidays and celebrations. ***Party Ratio: R 10 - D 8***

Strom Thurmond
Chairman

Joseph R. Biden Jr.
Ranking Member

Strom Thurmond, S.C.	*Joseph R. Biden Jr., Del.*
Charles McC. Mathias Jr., Md.	*Edward M. Kennedy, Mass.*
Paul Laxalt, Nev.	*Robert C. Byrd, W.Va.*
Orrin G. Hatch, Utah	*Howard M. Metzenbaum, Ohio*
Alan K. Simpson, Wyo.	*Dennis DeConcini, Ariz.*
John P. East, N.C.	*Patrick J. Leahy, Vt.*
Charles E. Grassley, Iowa	*Howell Heflin, Ala.*
Jeremiah Denton, Ala.	*Paul Simon, Ill.*
Arlen Specter, Pa.	
Mitch McConnell, Ky.	

SUBCOMMITTEES

Administrative Practice and Procedure

Phone: 224-7703 Room: SH-229

Grassley — chairman

Specter	*Metzenbaum*
East	*Heflin*

Constitution

Phone: 224-8191 Room: SD-212

Hatch — chairman

Thurmond	*DeConcini*
Grassley	*Simon*

Courts

Phone: 224-6791 Room: SD-163

East — chairman

Thurmond	*Heflin*
Simpson	*DeConcini*
Laxalt	

Criminal Law

Phone: 224-2951 Room: SD-148

Laxalt — chairman

Thurmond	*Biden*
Specter	*Kennedy*
Mathias	*Metzenbaum*

Immigration and Refugee Policy

Phone: 224-7877 Room: SD-518

Simpson — chairman

Grassley	*Kennedy*
Denton	*Simon*

Juvenile Justice

Phone: 224-8178 Room: SH-327

Specter — chairman

Denton	*Simon*
Mathias	*Metzenbaum*
McConnell	

Patents, Copyrights and Trademarks

Phone: 224-5617 Room: SD-137

Mathias — chairman

Laxalt	*Leahy*
Hatch	*Metzenbaum*
Simpson	*DeConcini*

Security and Terrorism

Phone: 224-6136 Room: SR-198

Denton — chairman

Hatch	*Leahy*
East	*DeConcini*
McConnell	

Labor and Human Resources

Phone: 224-5375 Room: SD-428

Education, labor, health and public welfare generally; aging; arts and humanities; biomedical research and development; child labor; convict labor; American National Red Cross; equal employment opportunity; handicapped individuals; labor standards and statistics; mediation and arbitration of labor disputes; occupational safety and health; private pension plans; public health; railway labor and retirement; regulation of foreign laborers; student loans; wages and hours. Chairman and ranking minority member are members *ex officio* of all subcommittees of which they are not regular members. **Party Ratio: R 9 - D 7**

Orrin G. Hatch
Chairman

Edward M. Kennedy
Ranking Member

Orrin G. Hatch, Utah	*Edward M. Kennedy, Mass.*
Robert T. Stafford, Vt.	*Claiborne Pell, R.I.*
Dan Quayle, Ind.	*Howard M. Metzenbaum, Ohio*
Don Nickles, Okla.	*Spark M. Matsunaga, Hawaii*
Paula Hawkins, Fla.	*Christopher J. Dodd, Conn.*
Strom Thurmond, S.C.	*Paul Simon, Ill.*
Lowell P. Weicker Jr., Conn.	*John Kerry, Mass.*
Malcolm Wallop, Wyo.	
Charles E. Grassley, Iowa	

SUBCOMMITTEES

Aging

Phone: 224-3239 Room: SH-404

Grassley — chairman

Hawkins	*Matsunaga*
Thurmond	*Pell*
Wallop	*Metzenbaum*

Children, Family, Drugs and Alcoholism

Phone: 224-5630 Room: SH-639

Hawkins — chairman

Quayle	*Dodd*
Grassley	*Kerry*
Nickles	*Metzenbaum*

Education, Arts and the Humanities

Phone: 224-2962 Room: SH-625

Stafford — chairman

Hatch	*Pell*
Quayle	*Kennedy*
Weicker	*Dodd*
Wallop	*Matsunaga*
Thurmond	*Simon*

Employment and Productivity

Phone: 224-6306 Room: SH-607

Quayle — chairman

Hawkins	*Simon*
Hatch	*Pell*
Grassley	*Dodd*

Handicapped

Phone: 224-6265 Room: SH-113

Weicker — chairman

Stafford	*Kerry*
Nickles	*Simon*
Thurmond	*Kennedy*

Labor

Phone: 224-5546 Room: SH-608

Nickles — chairman

Hatch	*Metzenbaum*
Stafford	*Kennedy*
Wallop	*Matsunaga*

Rules and Administration

Phone: 224-6352 Room: SR-305

Senate administration generally; corrupt practices; qualifications of senators; contested elections; federal elections generally; Government Printing Office; *Congressional Record;* meetings of Congress and attendance of members; presidential succession; the Capitol, congressional office buildings, the Library of Congress, the Smithsonian Institution and the Botanic Garden. **Party Ratio: R 8 - D 7**

Charles McC. Mathias Jr.
Chairman

Wendell H. Ford
Ranking Member

Charles McC. Mathias Jr., Md.	*Wendell H. Ford, Ky.*
Mark O. Hatfield, Ore.	*Claiborne Pell, R.I.*
James A. McClure, Idaho	*Robert C. Byrd, W.Va.*
Jesse Helms, N.C.	*Daniel K. Inouye, Hawaii*
John W. Warner, Va.	*Dennis DeConcini, Ariz.*
	Paul Simon, Ill.

Robert Dole, Kan.
Ted Stevens, Alaska
Jake Garn, Utah

Albert Gore Jr., Tenn.

No standing subcommittees.

Select Ethics

Phone: 224-2981 Room: SH-220

Studies and investigates standards and conduct of Senate members and employees and may recommend remedial action. ***Party Ratio: R 3 - D 3***

Warren B. Rudman
Chairman

Howell Heflin
Vice Chairman

Warren B. Rudman, N.H.
Jesse Helms, N.C.
Nancy Landon Kassebaum, Kan.

Howell Heflin, Ala.
David Pryor, Ark.
Russell B. Long, La.

No standing subcommittees.

Select Indian Affairs

Phone: 224-2251 Room: SH-838

Problems and opportunities of Indians, including Indian land management and trust responsibilities, education, health, special services, loan programs and Indian claims against the United States. ***Party Ratio: R 5 - D 4***

Mark Andrews
Chairman

John Melcher
Ranking Member

Mark Andrews, N.D.
Barry Goldwater, Ariz.
Slade Gorton, Wash.
Frank H. Murkowski, Alaska
James Abdnor, S.D.

John Melcher, Mont.
Daniel K. Inouye, Hawaii
Dennis DeConcini, Ariz.
Quentin N. Burdick, N.D.

No standing subcommittees.

Select Intelligence

Phone: 224-1700 Room: SH-211

Legislative and budgetary authority over the Central Intelligence Agency, the Defense Intelligence Agency, the National Security Agency and intelligence activities of the Federal Bureau of Investigation and other components of the federal intelligence community. ***Party Ratio: R 8 - D 7***

Dave Durenberger
Chairman

Patrick J. Leahy
Vice Chairman

Dave Durenberger, Minn.
William V. Roth Jr., Del.
William S. Cohen, Maine

Patrick J. Leahy, Vt.
Lloyd Bentsen, Texas
Sam Nunn, Ga.

Orrin G. Hatch, Utah	*Thomas F. Eagleton, Mo.*
Frank H. Murkowski, Alaska	*Ernest F. Hollings, S.C.*
Arlen Specter, Pa.	*David L. Boren, Okla.*
Chic Hecht, Nev.	*Bill Bradley, N.J.*
Mitch McConnell, Ky.	

No standing subcommittees.

Small Business

Phone: 224-5175 Room: SR-428A

Problems of small business; Small Business Administration. **Party Ratio: R 10 - D 9**

Lowell P. Weicker Jr.
Chairman

Dale Bumpers
Ranking Member

Lowell P. Weicker Jr., Conn.	*Dale Bumpers, Ark.*
Rudy Boschwitz, Minn.	*Sam Nunn, Ga.*
Slade Gorton, Wash.	*Jim Sasser, Tenn.*
Don Nickles, Okla.	*Max Baucus, Mont.*
Warren B. Rudman, N.H.	*Carl Levin, Mich.*
Alfonse M. D'Amato, N.Y.	*Alan J. Dixon, Ill.*
Bob Kasten, Wis.	*David L. Boren, Okla.*
Larry Pressler, S.D.	*Tom Harkin, Iowa*
Barry Goldwater, Ariz.	*John Kerry, Mass.*
Paul S. Trible Jr., Va.	

SUBCOMMITTEES

Entrepreneurship and Special Problems Facing Small Business

Phone: 224-3099 Room: SR-428A

Kasten — chairman

Boschwitz	*Sasser*
Goldwater	*Baucus*

Export Promotion and Market Development

Phone: 224-0840 Room: SR-428A

Boschwitz — chairman

Kasten	*Baucus*
Pressler	*Nunn*
Trible	*Harkin*

Government Procurement

Phone: 224-5175 Room: SR-428A

Nickles — chairman

Goldwater	*Levin*
Rudman	*Sasser*

Innovation and Technology

Phone: 224-3099 Room: SR-428A

Rudman — chairman

Trible	*Boren*
Gorton	*Kerry*

Productivity and Competition

Phone: 224-3099 Room: SR-428A

Gorton — chairman

Weicker	*Bumpers*

Small Business: Family Farm

Phone: 224-5175 Room: SR-428A

Pressler — chairman

Nickles	*Nunn*
D'Amato	*Levin*

Urban and Rural Economic Development

Phone: 224-5175 Room: SR-428A

D'Amato — chairman

Weicker	*Dixon*

Special Aging

Phone: 224-5364 Room: SD-G33

Problems and opportunities of older people including health, income, employment, housing and care and assistance. Reports findings and makes recommendations to the Senate, but cannot report legislation. ***Party Ratio: R 10 - D 9***

John Heinz
Chairman

John Glenn
Ranking Member

John Heinz, Pa.
William S. Cohen, Maine
Larry Pressler, S.D.
Charles E. Grassley, Iowa
Pete Wilson, Calif.
John W. Warner, Va.
Daniel J. Evans, Wash.
Jeremiah Denton, Ala.
Don Nickles, Okla.
Paula Hawkins, Fla.

John Glenn, Ohio
Lawton Chiles, Fla.
John Melcher, Mont.
David Pryor, Ark.
Bill Bradley, N.J.
Quentin N. Burdick, N.D.
Christopher J. Dodd, Conn.
J. Bennett Johnston, La.
Jeff Bingaman, N.M.

No standing subcommittees.

Veterans' Affairs

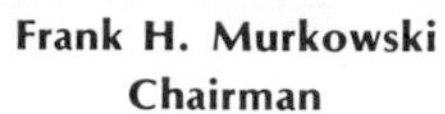

Frank H. Murkowski
Chairman

Alan Cranston
Ranking Member

Phone: 224-9126 Room: SR-414

Veterans' measures generally; compensation; armed forces life insurance; national cemeteries; pensions; readjustment benefits; veterans' hospitals, medical care and treatment; vocational rehabilitation and education. ***Party Ratio: R 7 - D 5***

Frank H. Murkowski, Alaska
Alan K. Simpson, Wyo.
Strom Thurmond, S.C.
Robert T. Stafford, Vt.
Arlen Specter, Pa.
Jeremiah Denton, Ala.
Rudy Boschwitz, Minn.

Alan Cranston, Calif.
Spark M. Matsunaga, Hawaii
Dennis DeConcini, Ariz.
George J. Mitchell, Maine
John D. Rockefeller IV, W.Va.

No standing subcommittees.

House Committee Assignments, 99th Congress

As of May 15, 1985

Agriculture

Phone: 225-2171 Room: 1301 LHOB

Agriculture generally; production, marketing and stabilization of agricultural prices; animal industry and diseases of animals; crop insurance and soil conservation; dairy industry; farm credit and security; forestry in general; human nutrition; home economics; inspection of livestock and meat products; plant industry, soils and agricultural engineering; rural electrification; commodities exchanges; rural development. Chairman and ranking minority member are members *ex officio* of all subcommittees of which they are not regular members. ***Party Ratio: D 26 - R 17***

E. "Kika" de la Garza
Chairman

Edward R. Madigan
Ranking Member

E. "Kika" de la Garza, Texas
Thomas S. Foley, Wash.
Walter B. Jones, N.C.
Ed Jones, Tenn.
George E. Brown Jr., Calif.
Charlie Rose, N.C.
James Weaver, Ore.
Berkley Bedell, Iowa
Glenn English, Okla.
Leon E. Panetta, Calif.
Jerry Huckaby, La.
Dan Glickman, Kan.
Charles Whitley, N.C.
Tony Coelho, Calif.
Thomas A. Daschle, S.D.
Charles W. Stenholm, Texas
Harold L. Volkmer, Mo.
Charles Hatcher, Ga.
Robin Tallon, S.C.
Harley O. Staggers Jr., W.Va.
Lane Evans, Ill.
Robert Lindsay Thomas, Ga.
James R. Olin, Va.
Timothy J. Penny, Minn.
Richard H. Stallings, Idaho
Terry L. Bruce, Ill. *

Edward R. Madigan, Ill.
James M. Jeffords, Vt.
E. Thomas Coleman, Mo.
Ron Marlenee, Mont.
Larry J. Hopkins, Ky.
Arlan Stangeland, Minn.
Pat Roberts, Kan.
Bill Emerson, Mo.
Sid Morrison, Wash.
Steve Gunderson, Wis.
Cooper Evans, Iowa
Gene Chappie, Calif.
Webb Franklin, Miss.
Tom Lewis, Fla.
Robert F. Smith, Ore.
Larry Combest, Texas
Bill Schuette, Mich.

* Member appointed only for the first session of the 99th Congress.

SUBCOMMITTEES

Conservation, Credit and Rural Development

Phone: 225-1867 Room: 1336 LHOB

Jones (Tenn.) — chairman

Weaver	*Coleman*
Glickman	*Jeffords*
Daschle	*Morrison*
Stenholm	*Gunderson*
Tallon	*Evans (Iowa)*
Evans (Ill.)	*Franklin*
Thomas	
Stallings	
Brown	

Cotton, Rice and Sugar

Phone: 225-1867 Room: 1336 LHOB

Huckaby — chairman

Coelho	*Stangeland*
Jones (Tenn.)	*Emerson*
Rose	*Chappie*
English	*Franklin*
Whitley	*Lewis*
Tallon	*Combest*
Stallings	
Stenholm	
Panetta	

Department Operations, Research and Foreign Agriculture

Phone: 225-1867 Room: 1336 LHOB

Bedell — chairman

Brown
Staggers
Panetta
Hatcher
Penny
Foley
Volkmer

Roberts
Morrison
Gunderson
Evans (Iowa)
Combest

Domestic Marketing, Consumer Relations and Nutrition

Phone: 225-0301 Room: 1430 LHOB

Panetta — chairman

Glickman
Staggers
Huckaby
Coelho
Olin
Foley

Emerson
Coleman
Chappie
Lewis

Forests, Family Farms and Energy

Phone: 225-0301 Room: 1301 LHOB

Whitley — chairman

Foley
Weaver
Huckaby
Olin
Stallings
Panetta
Hatcher

Morrison
Marlenee
Chappie
Smith
Schuette

Livestock, Dairy and Poultry

Phone: 225-0301 Room: 1430 LHOB

Coelho — chairman

Volkmer
Olin
Penny
Rose
Stenholm
Daschle
Jones (Tenn.)
Bedell
English

Jeffords
Hopkins
Stangeland
Gunderson
Lewis
Smith

Tobacco and Peanuts

Phone: 225-8906 Room: 1534 LHOB

Rose — chairman

Jones (N.C.)
Hatcher
English
Whitley
Tallon
Thomas
Stenholm

Hopkins
Roberts
Franklin
Combest
Vacancy

Wheat, Soybeans and Feed Grains

Phone: 225-1867 Room: 1336 LHOB

Foley — chairman

English
Bedell
Daschle
Volkmer
Evans (Ill.)
Glickman
Penny
Rose
Whitley
Bruce

Marlenee
Stangeland
Roberts
Emerson
Evans (Iowa)
Smith
Schuette

Appropriations

Phone: 225-2771 Room: H-218 Capitol

Appropriation of revenue for support of the federal government; rescissions of appropriations; transfers of unexpended balances; new spending authority under the Congressional Budget Act. Chairman and ranking minority member are members *ex officio* of all subcommittees of which they are not regular members. ***Party Ratio: D 35 - R 22***

Jamie L. Whitten
Chairman

Silvio O. Conte
Ranking Member

Jamie L. Whitten, Miss.
Edward P. Boland, Mass.
William H. Natcher, Ky.
Neal Smith, Iowa
Joseph P. Addabbo, N.Y.

Silvio O. Conte, Mass.
Joseph M. McDade, Pa.
John T. Myers, Ind.
Clarence E. Miller, Ohio
Lawrence Coughlin, Pa.

Sidney R. Yates, Ill.
David R. Obey, Wis.
Edward R. Roybal, Calif.
Louis Stokes, Ohio
Tom Bevill, Ala.
Bill Chappell Jr., Fla.
Bill Alexander, Ark.
John P. Murtha, Pa.
Bob Traxler, Mich.
Joseph D. Early, Mass.
Charles Wilson, Texas
Lindy (Mrs. Hale) Boggs, La.
Norman D. Dicks, Wash.
Matthew F. McHugh, N.Y.
William Lehman, Fla.
Martin Olav Sabo, Minn.
Julian C. Dixon, Calif.
Vic Fazio, Calif.
W.G. "Bill" Hefner, N.C.
Les AuCoin, Ore.
Daniel K. Akaka, Hawaii
Wes Watkins, Okla.
William H. Gray III, Pa.
Bernard J. Dwyer, N.J.
Bill Boner, Tenn.
Steny H. Hoyer, Md.
Bob Carr, Mich.
Robert J. Mrazek, N.Y.
Richard J. Durbin, Ill.
Ronald D. Coleman, Texas

C.W. Bill Young, Fla.
Jack F. Kemp, N.Y.
Ralph Regula, Ohio
George M. O'Brien, Ill.
Virginia Smith, Neb.
Eldon Rudd, Ariz.
Carl D. Pursell, Mich.
Mickey Edwards, Okla.
Bob Livingston, La.
Bill Green, N.Y.
Tom Loeffler, Texas
Jerry Lewis, Calif.
John Edward Porter, Ill.
Harold Rogers, Ky.
Joe Skeen, N.M.
Frank R. Wolf, Va.
Bill Lowery, Calif.

SUBCOMMITTEES

Agriculture, Rural Development and Related Agencies

Phone: 225-2638 Room: 2362 RHOB

Whitten — chairman

Traxler
McHugh
Natcher
Akaka
Watkins
Durbin
Smith, Iowa

Smith, Neb.
Myers
Rogers
Skeen

Commerce, Justice, State and Judiciary

Phone: 225-3351 Room: H-309 Capitol

Smith, Iowa — chairman

Alexander
Early
Dwyer
Carr
Boland

O'Brien
Regula
Rogers

Defense

Phone: 225-2847 Room: H-144 Capitol

Addabbo — chairman

Chappell
Murtha
Dicks
Wilson
Hefner
AuCoin

McDade
Young
Miller
Livingston

District of Columbia

Phone: 225-5338 Room: H-302 Capitol

Dixon — chairman

Natcher
Stokes
Wilson
Sabo
Hoyer

Coughlin
Green
Wolf

Energy and Water Development

Phone: 225-3421 Room: 2362 RHOB

Bevill — chairman

Boggs
Chappell
Fazio
Watkins
Boner

Myers
Smith, Neb.
Rudd

Foreign Operations

Phone: 225-2041 Room: H-307 Capitol

Obey — chairman

Yates
McHugh
Lehman
Wilson
Dixon
Gray
Mrazek

Kemp
Edwards
Lewis
Porter

HUD - Independent Agencies

Phone: 225-3241 Room: H-143 Capitol

Boland — chairman

Traxler

Green

Stokes	*Coughlin*
Boggs	*Lewis*
Sabo	
Boner	

Interior

Phone: 225-3081 Room: B308 RHOB

Yates — chairman

Murtha	*Regula*
Dicks	*McDade*
Boland	*Loeffler*
AuCoin	
Bevill	

Labor - Health and Human Services - Education

Phone: 225-3508 Room: 2358 RHOB

Natcher — chairman

Smith, Iowa	*Conte*
Obey	*O'Brien*
Roybal	*Pursell*
Stokes	*Porter*
Early	*Young*
Dwyer	
Hoyer	

Legislative Branch

Phone: 225-5338 Room: H-301 Capitol

Fazio — chairman

Obey	*Lewis*
Alexander	*Conte*
Murtha	*Myers*
Traxler	*Porter*
Boggs	

Military Construction

Phone: 225-3047 Room: B300 RHOB

Hefner — chairman

Bevill	*Edwards*
Alexander	*Loeffler*
Coleman	*Rudd*
Addabbo	*Lowery*
Chappell	
Early	

Transportation

Phone: 225-2141 Room: 2358 RHOB

Lehman — chairman

Sabo	*Coughlin*
Gray	*Conte*
Carr	*Pursell*
Durbin	*Wolf*
Mrazek	

Treasury - Postal Service - General Government

Phone: 225-5834 Room: H-164 Capitol

Roybal — chairman

Addabbo	*Skeen*
Akaka	*Lowery*
Hoyer	*Wolf*
Coleman	
Yates	

Armed Services

Phone: 225-4151 Room: 2120 RHOB

Common defense generally; Department of Defense; ammunition depots; forts; arsenals; Army, Navy and Air Force reservations and establishments; naval petroleum and oil shale reserves; scientific research and development in support of the armed services; Selective Service System; strategic and critical materials; military applications of nuclear energy; soldiers' and sailors' homes. **Party Ratio: D 27 - R 19 †**

Les Aspin
Chairman

William L. Dickinson
Ranking Member

Les Aspin, Wis.	*William L. Dickinson, Ala.*
Melvin Price, Ill.	*G. William Whitehurst, Va.*

Charles E. Bennett, Fla.	*Floyd Spence, S.C.*
Samuel S. Stratton, N.Y.	*Marjorie S. Holt, Md.*
Bill Nichols, Ala.	*Elwood Hillis, Ind.*
Dan Daniel, Va.	*Robert E. Badham, Calif.*
G. V. "Sonny" Montgomery, Miss.	*Bob Stump, Ariz.*
Ronald V. Dellums, Calif.	*Jim Courter, N.J.*
Patricia Schroeder, Colo.	*Larry J. Hopkins, Ky.*
Beverly B. Byron, Md.	*Robert W. Davis, Mich.*
Nicholas Mavroules, Mass.	*Ken Kramer, Colo.*
Earl Hutto, Fla.	*Duncan L. Hunter, Calif.*
Ike Skelton, Mo.	*Thomas F. Hartnett, S.C.*
Marvin Leath, Texas	*David O'B. Martin, N.Y.*
Dave McCurdy, Okla.	*John R. Kasich, Ohio*
Thomas M. Foglietta, Pa.	*William Carney, N.Y.*
Roy Dyson, Md.	*Lynn Martin, Ill.*
Dennis M. Hertel, Mich.	*Herbert H. Bateman, Va.*
Marilyn Lloyd, Tenn.	*Mac Sweeney, Texas*
Norman Sisisky, Va.	*Ben Blaz, Guam †*
Richard Ray, Ga.	
John M. Spratt Jr., S.C.	
Frank McCloskey, Ind.	
Solomon P. Ortiz, Texas	
George "Buddy" Darden, Ga.	
Tommy F. Robinson, Ark.	
Albert G. Bustamante, Texas	

† Party ratios do not include delegates or resident commissioner.

SUBCOMMITTEES

Investigations

Phone: 225-4221 Room: 2339 RHOB

Nichols — chairman

Byron	*Hopkins*
Mavroules	*Stump*
McCurdy	*Kasich*
Spratt	*Martin (Ill.)*
Aspin	*Carney*
Stratton	

Military Installations and Facilities

Phone: 225-7120 Room: 2120 RHOB

Dellums — chairman

Montgomery	*Kramer*
Hutto	*Whitehurst*
Leath	*Dickinson*
Hertel	*Hartnett*
Sisisky	*Martin (N.Y.)*
Ray	*Martin (Ill.)*
Ortiz	*Blaz*
Robinson	

Military Personnel and Compensation

Phone: 225-7560 Room: 2120 RHOB

Aspin — chairman

Montgomery	*Hillis*
Schroeder	*Holt*
Skelton	*Bateman*
Sisisky	*Sweeney*
Robinson	*Hunter*
Bustamante	
Bennett	

Procurement and Military Nuclear Systems

Phone: 225-7160 Room: 2120 RHOB

Stratton — chairman

Byron	*Holt*
Mavroules	*Badham*
Skelton	*Courter*
Leath	*Kramer*
Dyson	*Davis*
Lloyd	*Hopkins*
Ray	*Hunter*
Spratt	
Bustamante	

Readiness

Phone: 225-7991 Room: 2120 RHOB

Daniel — chairman

Hutto	*Whitehurst*
Leath	*Spence*
Foglietta	*Kasich*
Hertel	*Martin (N.Y.)*
Ray	*Sweeney*
Darden	
Nichols	

Research and Development

Phone: 225-3168 Room: 2120 RHOB

Price — chairman

McCurdy	*Dickinson*
Hertel	*Courter*
Darden	*Badham*
Bennett	*Davis*
Nichols	*Stump*
Dellums	

Seapower and Strategic and Critical Materials

Phone: 225-6704 Room: 2343 RHOB

Bennett — chairman

Foglietta	*Spence*
Dyson	*Hartnett*
Lloyd	*Hunter*
Sisisky	*Carney*
Ortiz	*Bateman*
Bustamante	*Blaz*
Price	

Banking, Finance and Urban Affairs

Phone: 225-4247 Room: 2129 RHOB

Banks and banking including deposit insurance and federal monetary policy; money and credit; currency; issuance and redemption of notes; gold and silver; coinage; valuation and revaluation of the dollar; urban development; private and public housing; economic stabilization; defense production; renegotiation; price controls; international finance; financial aid to commerce and industry. ***Party Ratio: D 28 - R 19†***

Fernand J. St Germain
Chairman

Chalmers P. Wylie
Ranking Member

Fernand J. St Germain, R.I.	*Chalmers P. Wylie, Ohio*
Henry B. Gonzalez, Texas	*Stewart B. McKinney, Conn.*
Frank Annunzio, Ill.	*Jim Leach, Iowa*
Parren J. Mitchell, Md.	*Norman D. Shumway, Calif.*
Walter E. Fauntroy, D.C. †	*Stan Parris, Va.*
Stephen L. Neal, N.C.	*Bill McCollum, Fla.*
Carroll Hubbard Jr., Ky.	*George C. Wortley, N.Y.*
John J. LaFalce, N.Y.	*Marge Roukema, N.J.*
Stan Lundine, N.Y.	*Doug Bereuter, Neb.*
Mary Rose Oakar, Ohio	*David Dreier, Calif.*
Bruce F. Vento, Minn.	*John Hiler, Ind.*
Doug Barnard Jr., Ga.	*Tom Ridge, Pa.*
Robert Garcia, N.Y.	*Steve Bartlett, Texas*
Charles E. Schumer, N.Y.	*Toby Roth, Wis.*
Barney Frank, Mass.	*Rod Chandler, Wash.*
Buddy Roemer, La.	*Al McCandless, Calif.*
Richard H. Lehman, Calif.	*John E. Grotberg, Ill.*
Bruce A. Morrison, Conn.	*Jim Kolbe, Ariz.*
Jim Cooper, Tenn.	*J. Alex McMillan, N.C.*
Marcy Kaptur, Ohio	
Ben Erdreich, Ala.	
Sander M. Levin, Mich.	
Thomas R. Carper, Del.	
Esteban Edward Torres, Calif.	
Gerald D. Kleczka, Wis.	
Bill Nelson, Fla.	
Paul E. Kanjorski, Pa.	
Bart Gordon, Tenn.	
Thomas J. Manton, N.Y.	
Jaime B. Fuster, Puerto Rico †	

† Party ratios do not include delegates or resident commissioner.

Mike Lowry, D-Wash., is on leave from the committee but retains his seniority behind Garcia, D-N.Y.

SUBCOMMITTEES

Consumer Affairs and Coinage

Phone: 226-3280 Room: 212 HOB Annex #1

Annunzio — chairman

St Germain	*Hiler*
Gonzalez	*Wylie*
Mitchell	*Ridge*
Neal	*Roth*
Barnard	*Kolbe*
Morrison	

Domestic Monetary Policy

Phone: 226-7315 Room: 109 HOB Annex #2

Fauntroy — chairman

Neal	*McCollum*
Barnard	*Hiler*
Hubbard	*Leach*
Roemer	*Bartlett*
Cooper	*Ridge*
Carper	*Chandler*
Erdreich	

Economic Stabilization

Phone: 225-7145 Room: 2220 RHOB

LaFalce — chairman

Lundine	*Shumway*
Vento	*McKinney*
Oakar	*Wortley*
Schumer	*Bereuter*
Roemer	*Ridge*
Cooper	*Dreier*
Kaptur	*McCandless*
Erdreich	*Grotberg*
Levin	*McMillan*
Torres	
Carper	
Kanjorski	
Gordon	

Financial Institutions Supervision, Regulation and Insurance

Phone: 225-2926 Room: B303 RHOB

St Germain — chairman

Annunzio	*Wylie*
Hubbard	*Leach*
Barnard	*McKinney*
LaFalce	*Shumway*
Oakar	*McCollum*
Vento	*Wortley*
Garcia	*Dreier*
Schumer	*Parris*
Frank	*Roukema*
Lehman	*Bereuter*
Cooper	*Bartlett*
Roemer	*Roth*
Kaptur	
Nelson	
Kanjorski	
Gordon	
Manton	

General Oversight and Investigations

Phone: 225-2828 Room: B304 RHOB

Hubbard — chairman

Gonzalez	*Parris*
Annunzio	*Wortley*
Barnard	*Dreier*
Garcia	*Bartlett*
Kaptur	*Chandler*
Kleczka	*McCandless*
Kanjorski	
Gordon	
Fuster	

Housing and Community Development

Phone: 225-7054 Room: 2129 RHOB

Gonzalez — chairman

St Germain	*McKinney*
Fauntroy	*Wylie*
Lundine	*Roukema*
Oakar	*Wortley*
Vento	*McCollum*
Garcia	*Bereuter*
Mitchell	*Dreier*
Schumer	*Hiler*
Frank	*Ridge*
Lehman	*Bartlett*
Morrison	*Roth*
Cooper	*Chandler*
Kaptur	*McCandless*
Erdreich	*Grotberg*
Levin	*Kolbe*
Carper	*McMillan*
Torres	
Roemer	
Kleczka	
Kanjorski	
Manton	
Fuster	

International Development Institutions and Finance

Phone: 226-7511 Room: 604 HOB Annex #1

Lundine — chairman

LaFalce	*Bereuter*
Oakar	*Roukema*
Levin	*McCandless*
Torres	*Kolbe*
Fauntroy	*McMillan*
Morrison	

International Finance, Trade and Monetary Policy

Phone: 225-1271 Room: 139 HOB Annex #2

Neal — chairman

LaFalce	*Leach*
Levin	*Shumway*
Fauntroy	*Parris*
Schumer	*McCollum*
Frank	*Chandler*
Morrison	*Grotberg*
Kleczka	*Kolbe*
Nelson	*McMillan*
Manton	
Fuster	

Budget

Phone: 226-7200 Room: 214 HOB Annex #1

Federal budget generally; concurrent budget resolutions; Congressional Budget Office. Chairman and ranking minority member are members *ex officio* of all task forces of which they are not regular members. The majority leader is a member *ex officio* of all task forces. ***Party Ratio: D 20 - R 13***

William H. Gray III
Chairman

Delbert L. Latta
Ranking Member

William H. Gray III, Pa.
Jim Wright, Texas
W. G. "Bill" Hefner, N.C.
Thomas J. Downey, N.Y.
Mike Lowry, Wash.
Butler Derrick, S.C.
George Miller, Calif.
Pat Williams, Mont.
Howard Wolpe, Mich.
Martin Frost, Texas
Vic Fazio, Calif.
Marty Russo, Ill.
Ed Jenkins, Ga.
Michael D. Barnes, Md.
Marvin Leath, Texas
Charles E. Schumer, N.Y.
Barbara Boxer, Calif.
Buddy MacKay, Fla.
Jim Slattery, Kan.
Chester G. Atkins, Mass.

Delbert L. Latta, Ohio
Jack F. Kemp. N.Y.
Lynn Martin, Ill.
Bobbi Fiedler, Calif.
Bill Gradison, Ohio
Tom Loeffler, Texas
Connie Mack, Fla.
Bill Goodling, Pa.
W. Henson Moore, La.
Denny Smith, Ore.
Vin Weber, Minn.
Hank Brown, Colo.
Beau Boulter, Texas

TASK FORCES

Budget Process

Derrick — chairman

Frost
MacKay
Atkins

Martin
Kemp
Gradison
Smith
Boulter

Community and Natural Resources

Wolpe — chairman

Fazio
Jenkins
MacKay
Slattery
Atkins

Loeffler
Fiedler
Goodling
Moore
Brown

Defense and International Affairs

Downey — chairman

Hefner
Wolpe
Fazio
Russo
Barnes
Leath
Schumer
Boxer
Slattery

Fiedler
Kemp
Loeffler
Brown
Boulter

Economic Policy

Lowry — chairman

Derrick
Russo
Leath
Schumer
MacKay

Kemp
Martin
Gradison
Loeffler
Mack

Health

Frost — chairman

Leath
MacKay

Gradison
Fiedler
Goodling
Weber

Human Resources

Williams — chairman

Lowry
Atkins

Goodling
Martin
Moore
Weber

Income Security

Fazio — chairman

Barnes	*Moore*
Boxer	*Gradison*
	Mack
	Smith

State and Local Government

Miller — chairman

Jenkins	*Mack*
Schumer	*Smith*
Boxer	*Weber*
Atkins	*Brown*
	Boulter

District of Columbia

Phone: 225-4457 Room: 1310 LHOB

Municipal affairs of the District of Columbia. **Party Ratio: D 7 - R 4†**

Ronald V. Dellums
Chairman

Stewart B. McKinney
Ranking Member

Ronald V. Dellums, Calif.	*Stewart B. McKinney, Conn.*
Walter E. Fauntroy, D.C. †	*Stan Parris, Va.*
Romano L. Mazzoli, Ky.	*Thomas J. Bliley Jr., Va.*
Fortney H. "Pete" Stark, Calif.	*Vacancy*
William H. Gray III, Pa.	
Michael D. Barnes, Md.	
Mervyn M. Dymally, Calif.	
Alan Wheat, Mo.	

† Party ratios do not include delegates or resident commissioner.

SUBCOMMITTEES

Fiscal Affairs and Health

Phone: 225-4457 Room: 1310 LHOB

Fauntroy — chairman

Dellums	*McKinney*
Stark	*Parris*
Gray	*Bliley*
Vacancy	

Government Operations and Metropolitan Affairs

Phone: 225-4457 Room: 1310 LHOB

Barnes — chairman

Gray	*Parris*
Stark	*McKinney*
Fauntroy	*Vacancy*
Vacancy	

Judiciary and Education

Phone: 225-4457 Room: 1310 LHOB

Dymally — chairman

Mazzoli	*Bliley*
Barnes	*Vacancy*
Wheat	*Vacancy*
Vacancy	

Education and Labor

Phone: 225-4527 Room: 2181 RHOB

Education and labor generally; child labor; convict labor; labor standards and statistics; mediation and arbitration of labor disputes; regulation of foreign laborers; school food programs; vocational rehabilitation; wages and hours; welfare of miners; work incentive programs; Indian education; juvenile delinquency; human services programs; Gallaudet College; Howard University. Chairman and ranking minority member are members *ex officio*, with vote, of all subcommittees of which they are not regular members, except in the case of the Subcommittee on Elementary, Secondary and Vocational Education, where the ranking minority member has designated a substitute. **Party Ratio: D 19 - R 13**

Augustus F. Hawkins
Chairman

James M. Jeffords
Ranking Member

Augustus F. Hawkins, Calif.	*James M. Jeffords, Vt.*
William D. Ford, Mich.	*Bill Goodling, Pa.*
Joseph M. Gaydos, Pa.	*E. Thomas Coleman, Mo.*
William L. Clay, Mo.	*Thomas E. Petri, Wis.*
Mario Biaggi, N.Y.	*Marge Roukema, N.J.*
Austin J. Murphy, Pa.	*Steve Gunderson, Wis.*
Dale E. Kildee, Mich.	*Steve Bartlett, Texas*
Pat Williams, Mont.	*Rod Chandler, Wash.*
Matthew G. Martinez, Calif.	*Tom Tauke, Iowa*
Major R. Owens, N.Y.	*John R. McKernan Jr., Maine*
Frederick C. Boucher, Va.	*Dick Armey, Texas*
Charles A. Hayes, Ill.	*Harris W. Fawell, Ill.*
Carl C. Perkins, Ky.	*Paul B. Henry, Mich.*
Terry L. Bruce, Ill.	
Stephen J. Solarz, N.Y. *	
Mervyn M. Dymally, Calif. *	
Dennis E. Eckart, Ohio *	
Timothy J. Penny, Minn. *	
Chester G. Atkins, Mass. *	

* Members appointed only for the first session of the 99th Congress.

George Miller, D-Calif., is on leave from the committee but retains his seniority behind Biaggi, D-N.Y.

SUBCOMMITTEES

Elementary, Secondary and Vocational Education

Phone: 225-4368 Room: B346-C RHOB

Hawkins — chairman

Ford	*Goodling*
Kildee	*Fawell*
Williams	*Chandler*
Boucher	*McKernan*
Owens	*Armey*
Martinez	*Gunderson (ex officio)*
Perkins	
Solarz	
Eckart	

Employment Opportunities

Phone: 226-7594 Room: 518 HOB Annex #1

Martinez — chairman

Williams	*Gunderson*
Hayes	*Henry*
Atkins	

Health and Safety

Phone: 225-6876 Room: B345-A RHOB

Gaydos — chairman

Murphy	*Chandler*
Ford	*Roukema*
Hayes	

Human Resources

Phone: 225-1850 Room: 402 CHOB

Kildee — chairman

Bruce	*Tauke*
Martinez	*Coleman*
Perkins	*Petri*
Eckart	

Labor - Management Relations

Phone: 225-5768 Room: 2451 RHOB

Clay — chairman

Ford	*Roukema*
Kildee	*Chandler*
Biaggi	*Armey*
Hayes	*Bartlett*
Dymally	*Fawell*
Atkins	
Owens	

Labor Standards

Phone: 225-1927 Room: B346-A RHOB

Murphy — chairman

Clay	*Petri*
Martinez	*Bartlett*
Williams	

Postsecondary Education

Phone: 225-8881 Room: 320 CHOB

Ford — chairman

Owens	*Coleman*
Williams	*Gunderson*
Biaggi	*McKernan*
Hayes	*Henry*
Perkins	*Goodling*
Bruce	*Petri*
Solarz	*Roukema*
Dymally	*Tauke*
Eckart	
Penny	
Atkins	
Gaydos	

Select Education

Phone: 226-7532 Room: 617 HOB Annex #1

Williams — chairman

Biaggi	*Bartlett*
Hayes	*Goodling*
Eckart	*Coleman*
Martinez	

Energy and Commerce

Phone: 225-2927 Room: 2125 RHOB

Interstate and foreign commerce generally; national energy policy generally; exploration, production, storage, supply, marketing, pricing and regulation of energy resources; nuclear energy; solar energy; energy conservation; generation and marketing of power; inland waterways; railroads and railway labor and retirement; communications generally; securities and exchanges; consumer affairs; travel and tourism; public health and quarantine; health care facilities; biomedical research and development. Chairman and ranking minority member are members *ex officio* of all subcommittees of which they are not regular members.
Party Ratio: D 25 - R 17

John D. Dingell
Chairman

James T. Broyhill
Ranking Member

John D. Dingell, Mich.	*James T. Broyhill, N.C.*
James H. Scheuer, N.Y.	*Norman F. Lent, N.Y.*
Henry A. Waxman, Calif.	*Edward R. Madigan, Ill.*
Timothy E. Wirth, Colo.	*Carlos J. Moorhead, Calif.*
Philip R. Sharp, Ind.	*Matthew J. Rinaldo, N.J.*
James J. Florio, N.J.	*William E. Dannemeyer, Calif.*
Edward J. Markey, Mass.	*Bob Whittaker, Kan.*
Thomas A. Luken, Ohio	*Tom Tauke, Iowa*
Doug Walgren, Pa.	*Don Ritter, Pa.*
Barbara A. Mikulski, Md.	*Dan Coats, Ind.*
Al Swift, Wash.	*Thomas J. Bliley Jr., Va.*
Mickey Leland, Texas	*Jack Fields, Texas*
Richard C. Shelby, Ala.	*Michael G. Oxley, Ohio*
Cardiss Collins, Ill.	*Howard C. Nielson, Utah*
Mike Synar, Okla.	*Michael Bilirakis, Fla.*
W. J. "Billy" Tauzin, La.	*Dan L. Schaefer, Colo.*
Ron Wyden, Ore.	*Fred J. Eckert, N.Y.*
Ralph M. Hall, Texas	
Dennis E. Eckart, Ohio	
Wayne Dowdy, Miss.	
Bill Richardson, N.M.	
Jim Slattery, Kan.	
Gerry Sikorski, Minn.	
John Bryant, Texas	
Jim Bates, Calif.	

SUBCOMMITTEES

Commerce, Transportation and Tourism

Phone: 226-3160 Room: 151 HOB Annex #2

Florio — chairman

Mikulski	*Lent*
Eckart (Ohio)	*Tauke*
Richardson	*Ritter*
Hall	*Coats*
Sharp	*Fields*
Tauzin	*Schaefer*
Dowdy	
Slattery	
Sikorski	

Energy Conservation and Power

Phone: 226-2424 Room: 316 HOB Annex #2

Markey — chairman

Swift	*Moorhead*
Bryant	*Oxley*
Leland	*Nielson*
Shelby	*Bilirakis*
Wyden	*Eckert (N.Y.)*
Hall	
Eckart (Ohio)	
Sikorski	

Fossil and Synthetic Fuels

Phone: 226-2500 Room: 331 HOB Annex #2

Sharp — chairman

Walgren	*Dannemeyer*
Shelby	*Whittaker*
Synar	*Coats*
Hall	*Fields*
Tauzin	*Oxley*
Dowdy	*Schaefer*
Richardson	
Slattery	
Bryant	

Health and the Environment

Phone: 225-4952 Room: 2415 RHOB

Waxman — chairman

Scheuer	*Madigan*
Walgren	*Dannemeyer*
Shelby	*Whittaker*
Wyden	*Tauke*
Sikorski	*Ritter*
Wirth	*Bliley*
Florio	*Nielson*
Luken	*Bilirakis*
Mikulski	*Eckert (N.Y.)*
Leland	
Collins	
Richardson	
Bates	

Oversight and Investigations

Phone: 225-4441 Room: 2323 RHOB

Dingell — chairman

Wyden	*Broyhill*
Eckart (Ohio)	*Whittaker*
Slattery	*Bliley*
Sikorski	*Oxley*
Scheuer	*Bilirakis*
Florio	*Schaefer*
Luken	*Eckert (N.Y.)*
Bryant	
Waxman	
Shelby	

Telecommunications, Consumer Protection and Finance

Phone: 225-9304 Room: B331 RHOB

Wirth — chairman

Swift	*Rinaldo*
Leland	*Moorhead*
Collins	*Tauke*
Bryant	*Ritter*
Bates	*Coats*
Luken	*Bliley*
Synar	*Fields*
Tauzin	*Oxley*
Dowdy	*Nielson*
Slattery	
Scheuer	
Waxman	
Markey	

Foreign Affairs

Phone: 225-5021 Room: 2170 RHOB

Relations of the United States with foreign nations generally; foreign loans; international conferences and congresses; intervention abroad and declarations of war; diplomatic service; foreign trade; neutrality; protection of Americans abroad; Red Cross; United Nations; international economic policy; export controls including nonproliferation of nuclear technology and hardware; international commodity agreements; trading with the enemy; international financial and monetary organizations. Chairman and ranking minority member are non-voting members *ex officio* of all subcommittees of which they are not regular members. ***Party Ratio: D 25 - R 17***

Dante B. Fascell
Chairman

William S. Broomfield
Ranking Member

Dante B. Fascell, Fla.	*William S. Broomfield, Mich.*
Lee H. Hamilton, Ind.	*Benjamin A. Gilman, N.Y.*
Gus Yatron, Pa.	*Robert J. Lagomarsino, Calif.*
Stephen J. Solarz, N.Y.	*Jim Leach, Iowa*
Don Bonker, Wash.	*Toby Roth, Wis.*
Gerry E. Studds, Mass.	*Olympia J. Snowe, Maine*
Daniel A. Mica, Fla.	*Henry J. Hyde, Ill.*
Michael D. Barnes, Md.	*Gerald B. H. Solomon, N.Y.*
Howard Wolpe, Mich.	*Doug Bereuter, Neb.*
George W. Crockett Jr., Mich.	

Sam Gejdenson, Conn.
Mervyn M. Dymally, Calif.
Tom Lantos, Calif.
Peter H. Kostmayer, Pa.
Robert G. Torricelli, N.J.
Larry Smith, Fla.
Howard L. Berman, Calif.
Harry Reid, Nev.
Mel Levine, Calif.
Edward F. Feighan, Ohio
Ted Weiss, N.Y.
Gary L. Ackerman, N.Y.
Buddy MacKay, Fla.
Morris K. Udall, Ariz.
Robert Garcia, N.Y. *

Mark D. Siljander, Mich.
Ed Zschau, Calif.
Bob Dornan, Calif.
Christopher H. Smith, N.J.
Connie Mack, Fla.
Michael DeWine, Ohio
Dan Burton, Ind.
John McCain, Ariz.

* Member appointed only for the first session of the 99th Congress.

Bill Goodling, R-Pa., is on leave from the committee but retains his seniority behind Lagomarsino, R-Calif.

SUBCOMMITTEES

Africa

Phone: 226-7807 Room: 705 HOB Annex #1

Wolpe — chairman

Crockett
Solarz
Berman
Weiss
Garcia

Siljander
DeWine
Burton
Dornan

Arms Control, International Security and Science

Phone: 225-8926 Room: 2103 RHOB

Fascell — chairman

Berman
Udall
Hamilton
Solarz
Studds
Barnes
Lantos

Broomfield
Hyde
Leach
Snowe
Dornan

Asian and Pacific Affairs

Phone: 226-7801 Room: 707 HOB Annex #1

Solarz — chairman

Dymally
Torricelli
Udall
Barnes
Gejdenson

Leach
Roth
Solomon
Bereuter

Europe and the Middle East

Phone: 225-3345 Room: B359 RHOB

Hamilton — chairman

Lantos
Torricelli
Smith (Fla.)
Levine
Reid
Feighan
Ackerman

Gilman
Siljander
Zschau
Dornan
Smith (N.J.)

Human Rights and International Organizations

Phone: 226-7825 Room: B358 RHOB

Yatron — chairman

Ackerman
Bonker
Lantos
Feighan
Crockett

Solomon
Smith (N.J.)
Siljander
Burton

International Economic Policy and Trade

Phone: 226-7820 Room: 702 HOB Annex #1

Bonker — chairman

Mica
Wolpe
Gejdenson
Berman
Levine
Feighan
MacKay

Roth
Bereuter
Mack
Lagomarsino
Zschau

International Operations

Phone: 225-3424 Room: 703 HOB Annex #1

Mica — chairman

Yatron
Kostmayer
Smith (Fla.)
Weiss
MacKay

Snowe
Gilman
Mack
McCain

Western Hemisphere Affairs

Phone: 226-7812 Room: 709 HOB Annex #1

Barnes — chairman

Studds	*Lagomarsino*
Gejdenson	*DeWine*
Kostmayer	*Burton*
Dymally	*McCain*
Weiss	*Hyde*
MacKay	
Reid	

Government Operations

Phone: 225-5051 Room: 2157 RHOB

Budget and accounting measures; overall economy and efficiency in government including federal procurement; executive branch reorganization; general revenue sharing; intergovernmental relations; National Archives. Chairman and ranking minority member are members *ex officio* of all subcommittees of which they are not regular members.
Party Ratio: D 23 - R 16

Jack Brooks
Chairman

Frank Horton
Ranking Member

Jack Brooks, Texas	*Frank Horton, N.Y.*
Don Fuqua, Fla.	*Thomas N. Kindness, Ohio*
John Conyers Jr., Mich.	*Robert S. Walker, Pa.*
Cardiss Collins, Ill.	*William F. Clinger Jr., Pa.*
Glenn English, Okla.	*Al McCandless, Calif.*
Henry A. Waxman, Calif.	*Larry E. Craig, Idaho*
Ted Weiss, N.Y.	*Howard C. Nielson, Utah*
Mike Synar, Okla.	*H. James Saxton, N.J.*
Stephen L. Neal, N.C.	*Pat Swindall, Ga.*
Doug Barnard Jr., Ga.	*Thomas D. DeLay, Texas*
Barney Frank, Mass.	*David S. Monson, Utah*
Tom Lantos, Calif.	*Joseph J. DioGuardi, N.Y.*
Bob Wise, W.Va.	*John G. Rowland, Conn.*
Barbara Boxer, Calif.	*Dick Armey, Texas*
Sander M. Levin, Mich.	*Jim Lightfoot, Iowa*
Major R. Owens, N.Y.	*John R. Miller, Wash.*
Edolphus Towns, N.Y.	
John M. Spratt Jr., S.C.	
Joe Kolter, Pa.	
Ben Erdreich, Ala.	
Gerald D. Kleczka, Wis.	
Albert G. Bustamante, Texas	
Matthew G. Martinez, Calif.	

SUBCOMMITTEES

Commerce, Consumer and Monetary Affairs

Phone: 225-4407 Room: B377 RHOB

Barnard — chairman

Spratt	*Craig*
Kolter	*Swindall*
Erdreich	*Saxton*
Bustamante	

Employment and Housing

Phone: 225-6751 Room: B349-A RHOB

Frank — chairman

Levin	*Nielson*
Owens	*Rowland*
Lantos	*Lightfoot*
Martinez	

Environment, Energy and Natural Resources

Phone: 225-6427 Room: B371-B RHOB

Synar — chairman

Wise	*Clinger*
Boxer	*DeLay*
Kolter	*Armey*
Towns	*Miller*
Bustamante	

Government Activities and Transportation

Phone: 225-7920 Room: B350-A RHOB

Collins — chairman

Owens	*McCandless*
Lantos	*Swindall*
Kleczka	*DeLay*
Martinez	

Government Information, Justice and Agriculture

Phone: 225-3741 Room: B349-C RHOB

English — chairman

Kleczka	*Kindness*
Neal	*Lightfoot*
Wise	*DioGuardi*
Towns	*Miller*
Spratt	

Intergovernmental Relations and Human Resources

Phone: 225-2548 Room: B372 RHOB

Weiss — chairman

Levin	*Walker*
Erdreich	*Rowland*
Conyers	*Monson*
Waxman	*Armey*
Boxer	

Legislation and National Security

Phone: 225-5147 Room: B373 RHOB

Brooks — chairman

Fuqua	*Horton*
Waxman	*Saxton*
Neal	*Monson*
Lantos	*DioGuardi*
Conyers	

House Administration

Phone: 225-2061 Room: H-326 Capitol

House administration generally; contested elections; federal elections generally; corrupt practices; qualifications of members of the House; *Congressional Record;* the Capitol; Library of Congress; Smithsonian Institution; Botanic Garden. Chairman and ranking minority member are members *ex officio* of all subcommittees of which they are not regular members. **Party Ratio: D 12 - R 7**

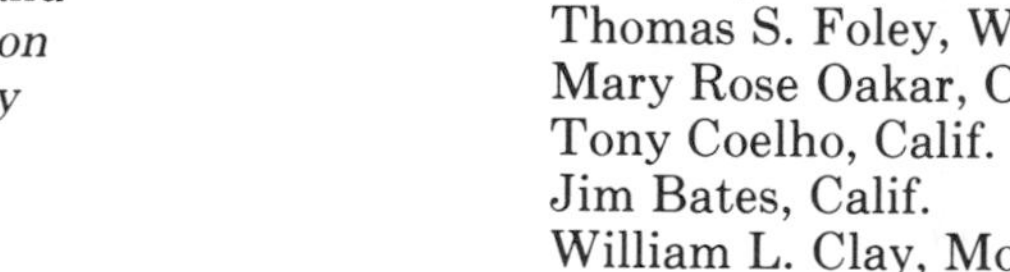

Frank Annunzio
Chairman

Bill Frenzel
Ranking Member

Frank Annunzio, Ill.	*Bill Frenzel, Minn.*
Joseph M. Gaydos, Pa.	*William L. Dickinson, Ala.*
Ed Jones, Tenn.	*Robert E. Badham, Calif.*
Charlie Rose, N.C.	*Newt Gingrich, Ga.*
Leon E. Panetta, Calif.	*William M. Thomas, Calif.*
Al Swift, Wash.	*Barbara F. Vucanovich, Nev.*
Thomas S. Foley, Wash.	*Pat Roberts, Kan.*
Mary Rose Oakar, Ohio	
Tony Coelho, Calif.	
Jim Bates, Calif.	
William L. Clay, Mo.	
Sam Gejdenson, Conn.	

SUBCOMMITTEES

Accounts

Phone: 226-7540 Room: 611 HOB Annex #1

Gaydos — chairman

Swift	*Badham*
Foley	*Thomas*
Oakar	*Roberts*
Coelho	*Vucanovich*
Clay	
Gejdenson	

Elections

Phone: 226-7616 Room: 802 HOB Annex #1

Swift — chairman

Gaydos	*Thomas*
Rose	*Vucanovich*
Panetta	*Roberts*
Oakar	*Frenzel*
Clay	
Gejdenson	

Office Systems

Phone: 225-1608 Room: 722 HOB Annex #1

Rose — chairman

Foley	*Thomas*
Clay	*Dickinson*

Personnel and Police

Phone: 226-2307 Room: 612 HOB Annex #1

Panetta — chairman

Coelho	*Roberts*
Bates	*Gingrich*

Procurement and Printing

Phone: 226-7310 Room: 720 HOB Annex #1

Foley — chairman

Gaydos	*Gingrich*
Jones	*Badham*

Services

Phone: 225-4568 Room: 105 CHOB

Jones — chairman

Oakar	*Dickinson*
Bates	*Vucanovich*

TASK FORCE

Libraries and Memorials

Phone: 226-7641 Room: 103 HOB Annex #1

Oakar — chairman

Bates	*Gingrich*
Clay	*Frenzel*

Interior and Insular Affairs

Phone: 225-2761 Room: 1324 LHOB

Public lands, parks and natural resources generally; Geological Survey; interstate water compacts; irrigation and reclamation; Indian affairs; minerals, mines and mining; petroleum conservation on public lands; regulation of domestic nuclear energy industry including waste disposal; territorial affairs of the United States. Chairman and ranking minority member are non-voting members *ex officio* of all subcommittees of which they are not regular members.
Party Ratio: D 22 - R 15 †

Morris K. Udall
Chairman

Don Young
Ranking Member

Morris K. Udall, Ariz.
John F. Seiberling, Ohio
James Weaver, Ore.
George Miller, Calif.
Philip R. Sharp, Ind.
Edward J. Markey, Mass.
Austin J. Murphy, Pa.
Nick J. Rahall II, W.Va.
Bruce F. Vento, Minn.
Jerry Huckaby, La.
Dale E. Kildee, Mich.
Tony Coelho, Calif.
Beverly B. Byron, Md.
Ron de Lugo, Virgin Islands †
Sam Gejdenson, Conn.
Peter H. Kostmayer, Pa.
Jim Moody, Wis.
Alan B. Mollohan, W.Va.
Richard H. Lehman, Calif.
Bill Richardson, N.M.
Fofō I. F. Sunia, American Samoa †
George "Buddy" Darden, Ga.
Peter J. Visclosky, Ind.
Jaime B. Fuster, Puerto Rico †
Mel Levine, Calif.

Don Young, Alaska
Manuel Lujan Jr., N.M.
Robert J. Lagomarsino, Calif.
Ron Marlenee, Mont.
Dick Cheney, Wyo.
Charles Pashayan Jr., Calif.
Larry E. Craig, Idaho
Denny Smith, Ore.
James V. Hansen, Utah
Bill Emerson, Mo.
John McCain, Ariz.
Barbara F. Vucanovich, Nev.
Bill Hendon, N.C.
Mike Strang, Colo.
Ben Blaz, Guam †
Joe L. Barton, Texas

† Party ratios do not include delegates or resident commissioner.

Pat Williams, D-Mont., is on leave from the committee but retains his seniority behind Huckaby, D-La. Hank Brown, R-Colo., is on leave from the committee but retains his seniority behind Craig, R-Idaho.

SUBCOMMITTEES

Energy and the Environment

Phone: 225-8331 Room: 1327 LHOB

Udall — chairman

Seiberling	*Lujan*
Miller	*Young*
Sharp	*Marlenee*
Markey	*Craig*
Murphy	*Smith*
Rahall	*McCain*
Huckaby	*Vucanovich*
Byron	*Hendon*
Gejdenson	*Strang*
Kostmayer	*Barton*
Moody	
Mollohan	
Sunia	
Darden	
Levine	

General Oversight, Northwest Power and Forest Management

Phone: 225-1661 Room: 1626 LHOB

Weaver — chairman

Udall	*Pashayan*
Seiberling	*Smith*
Moody	*Hansen*
Visclosky	*McCain*
Levine	*Blaz*

Mining and Natural Resources

Phone: 226-7761 Room: 819 HOB Annex #1

Rahall — chairman

Murphy	*Craig*
Huckaby	*Emerson*
Mollohan	*Vucanovich*
Fuster	

National Parks and Recreation

Phone: 226-7736 Room: 818 HOB Annex #1

Vento — chairman

Seiberling	*Lagomarsino*
Murphy	*Marlenee*
Kildee	*Cheney*
Coelho	*Pashayan*
Byron	*Smith*
de Lugo	*Hansen*
Gejdenson	*Emerson*
Kostmayer	*Hendon*
Mollohan	*Blaz*
Lehman	
Darden	
Visclosky	
Fuster	

Public Lands

Phone: 226-7734 Room: 812 HOB Annex #1

Seiberling — chairman

Weaver	*Marlenee*
Markey	*Lagomarsino*
Vento	*Cheney*
Kildee	*Craig*
de Lugo	*Hansen*
Kostmayer	*Emerson*
Moody	*Vucanovich*
Lehman	*Strang*
Richardson	*Blaz*
Sunia	
Darden	
Fuster	
Levine	

Water and Power Resources

Phone: 225-6042 Room: 1522 LHOB

Miller — chairman

Udall	*Cheney*
Weaver	*Pashayan*
Sharp	*McCain*
Markey	*Strang*
Coelho	*Barton*
Lehman	
Richardson	

Judiciary

Phone: 225-3951 Room: 2137 RHOB

Civil and criminal judicial proceedings generally; federal courts and judges; bankruptcy, mutiny, espionage and counterfeiting; civil liberties; constitutional amendments; immigration and naturalization; interstate compacts; claims against the United States; apportionment of representatives; meetings of Congress and attendance of members; penitentiaries; patents, copyrights and trademarks; presidential succession, monopolies and unlawful restraints of trade; internal security. **Party Ratio: D 21 - R 14**

Peter W. Rodino Jr.
Chairman

Hamilton Fish Jr.
Ranking Member

Peter W. Rodino Jr., N.J.	*Hamilton Fish Jr., N.Y.*
Jack Brooks, Texas	*Carlos J. Moorhead, Calif.*
Robert W. Kastenmeier, Wis.	*Henry J. Hyde, Ill.*
Don Edwards, Calif.	*Thomas N. Kindness, Ohio*
John Conyers Jr., Mich.	*Dan Lungren, Calif.*
John F. Seiberling, Ohio	*F. James Sensenbrenner Jr., Wis.*
Romano L. Mazzoli, Ky.	*Bill McCollum, Fla.*
William J. Hughes, N.J.	*E. Clay Shaw Jr., Fla.*
Mike Synar, Okla.	*George W. Gekas, Pa.*
Patricia Schroeder, Colo.	*Michael DeWine, Ohio*
Dan Glickman, Kan.	*William E. Dannemeyer, Calif.*
Barney Frank, Mass.	*Hank Brown, Colo.*
George W. Crockett Jr., Mich.	*Pat Swindall, Ga.*
Charles E. Schumer, N.Y.	*Howard Coble, N.C.*
Bruce A. Morrison, Conn.	
Edward F. Feighan, Ohio	
Larry Smith, Fla.	
Howard L. Berman, Calif.	
Frederick C. Boucher, Va.	
Harley O. Staggers Jr., W.Va.	
John Bryant, Texas	

SUBCOMMITTEES

Administrative Law and Governmental Relations

Phone: 225-5741 Room: B351-A RHOB

Glickman — chairman

Crockett	*Kindness*
Frank	*Brown*
Berman	*Swindall*
Staggers	*Coble*
Boucher	

Civil and Constitutional Rights

Phone: 226-7680 Room: 806 HOB Annex #1

Edwards — chairman

Kastenmeier	*Sensenbrenner*
Conyers	*DeWine*
Schroeder	*Dannemeyer*
Schumer	

Courts, Civil Liberties and Administration of Justice

Phone: 225-3926 Room: 2137 RHOB

Kastenmeier — chairman

Brooks	*Moorhead*
Synar	*Hyde*
Schroeder	*Kindness*
Glickman	*DeWine*
Mazzoli	*Swindall*
Morrison	*Coble*
Berman	
Boucher	

Crime

Phone: 225-1695 Room: 207 CHOB

Hughes — chairman

Morrison	*McCollum*
Feighan	*Lungren*
Smith	*Shaw*
Staggers	*Gekas*
Mazzoli	

Criminal Justice

Phone: 226-2406 Room: 362 HOB Annex #2

Conyers — chairman

Edwards	*Gekas*
Frank	*Swindall*
Berman	*Coble*
Boucher	
Bryant	

Immigration, Refugees and International Law

Phone: 225-5727 Room: 2137 RHOB

Mazzoli — chairman

Frank	*Lungren*
Crockett	*Fish*
Schumer	*Sensenbrenner*
Berman	*McCollum*
Bryant	

Monopolies and Commercial Law

Phone: 225-2825 Room: B353-B RHOB

Rodino — chairman

Brooks	*Fish*
Edwards	*Shaw*
Seiberling	*Dannemeyer*
Glickman	*Brown*
Hughes	*Moorhead*
Synar	*Hyde*
Feighan	
Smith	

Merchant Marine and Fisheries

Phone: 225-4047 Room: 1334 LHOB

Merchant marine generally; oceanography and marine affairs including coastal zone management; Coast Guard; fisheries and wildlife; regulation of common carriers by water and inspection of merchant marine vessels, lights and signals, lifesaving equipment and fire protection; navigation; Panama Canal, Canal Zone and interoceanic canals generally; registration and licensing of vessels; rules and international arrangements to prevent collisions at sea; international fishing agreements; Coast Guard and Merchant Marine academies and state maritime academies. Chairman and ranking minority member are members *ex officio* of all subcommittees of which they are not regular members. **Party Ratio: D 25 - R 17**

Walter B. Jones
Chairman

Norman F. Lent
Ranking Member

Walter B. Jones, N.C.
Mario Biaggi, N.Y.
Glenn M. Anderson, Calif.
John B. Breaux, La.
Gerry E. Studds, Mass.
Carroll Hubbard Jr., Ky.
Don Bonker, Wash.
James L. Oberstar, Minn.
William J. Hughes, N.J.
Barbara A. Mikulski. Md.
Mike Lowry, Wash.
Earl Hutto, Fla.
W. J. "Billy" Tauzin, La.
Thomas M. Foglietta, Pa.
Dennis M. Hertel, Mich.
Roy Dyson, Md.
William O. Lipinski, Ill.
Robert A. Borski, Pa.
Thomas R. Carper, Del.
Douglas H. Bosco, Calif.
Robin Tallon, S.C.
Robert Lindsay Thomas, Ga.
Solomon P. Ortiz, Texas
Charles E. Bennett, Fla.
Thomas J. Manton, N.Y.

Norman F. Lent, N.Y.
Gene Snyder, Ky.
Don Young, Alaska
Robert W. Davis, Mich.
William Carney, N.Y.
Norman D. Shumway, Calif.
Jack Fields, Texas
Claudine Schneider, R.I.
Herbert H. Bateman, Va.
John R. McKernan Jr., Maine
Webb Franklin, Miss.
Thomas F. Hartnett, S.C.
Gene Chappie, Calif.
H. James Saxton, N.J.
Sonny Callahan, Ala.
John R. Miller, Wash.
Helen Delich Bentley, Md.

Barbara Boxer, D-Calif., is on leave from the committee but retains her seniority behind Thomas, D-Ga.

SUBCOMMITTEES

Coast Guard and Navigation

Phone: 226-3533 Room: 543 HOB Annex #2

Studds — chairman

Hughes	*Davis*
Hutto	*Snyder*
Tauzin	*Young*
Biaggi	*Franklin*
Borski	*Hartnett*
Carper	*Callahan*
Thomas	*Miller*
Hubbard	
Mikulski	
Bennett	

Fisheries and Wildlife Conservation and the Environment

Phone: 226-3522 Room: 544 HOB Annex #2

Breaux — chairman

Bonker	*Young*
Oberstar	*Carney*
Carper	*Fields*
Bosco	*Schneider*
Thomas	*Bateman*
Manton	*McKernan*
Anderson	*Franklin*
Studds	*Chappie*

Hughes
Lowry
Hutto
Hertel
Dyson
Ortiz
Bennett

Saxton
Callahan
Miller

Merchant Marine

Phone: 226-3500 Room: 531 HOB Annex #2

Biaggi — chairman

Anderson
Foglietta
Hertel
Dyson
Lipinski
Borski
Tallon
Ortiz
Bennett
Hubbard
Bonker
Mikulski
Breaux
Bosco
Thomas

Snyder
Young
Davis
Carney
Shumway
Fields
Bateman
McKernan
Hartnett
Saxton
Bentley

Oceanography

Phone: 226-3513 Room: 541 HOB Annex #2

Mikulski — chairman

Breaux
Tauzin
Foglietta
Tallon
Manton
Studds
Hughes
Lowry

Shumway
Schneider
Bateman
McKernan
Saxton
Miller

Oversight and Investigations

Phone: 225-4047 Room: 1334 LHOB

Jones — chairman

Oberstar
Lipinski
Foglietta

Carney
McKernan
Bentley

Panama Canal and Outer Continental Shelf

Phone: 226-3508 Room: 542 HOB Annex #2

Lowry — chairman

Hubbard
Bosco
Anderson
Tauzin
Hertel
Borski
Ortiz
Manton
Biaggi
Breaux
Studds

Fields
Young
Davis
Shumway
Franklin
Chappie
Callahan
Bentley

Post Office and Civil Service

Phone: 225-4054 Room: 309 CHOB

Postal and federal civil services; census and the collection of statistics generally; Hatch Act; holidays and celebrations. ***Party Ratio: D 13 - R 8 †***

William D. Ford
Chairman

Gene Taylor
Ranking Member

William D. Ford, Mich.
William L. Clay, Mo.
Patricia Schroeder, Colo.
Stephen J. Solarz, N.Y.
Robert Garcia, N.Y.
Mickey Leland, Texas
Gus Yatron, Pa.
Mary Rose Oakar, Ohio
Gerry Sikorski, Minn.
Frank McCloskey, Ind.
Gary L. Ackerman, N.Y.
Mervyn M. Dymally, Calif.
Ron de Lugo, Virgin Islands * †
Morris K. Udall, Ariz. *

Gene Taylor, Mo.
Benjamin A. Gilman, N.Y.
Charles Pashayan Jr., Calif.
Frank Horton, N.Y.
John T. Myers, Ind.
Don Young, Alaska
James V. Hansen, Utah
Dan Burton, Ind.

* Members appointed only for the first session of the 99th Congress.

† Party ratios do not include delegates or resident commissioner.

SUBCOMMITTEES

Census and Population

Phone: 226-7523 Room: 219 CHOB

Garcia — chairman

Oakar
Ackerman

Hansen
Myers

Civil Service

Phone: 225-4025 Room: 122 CHOB

Schroeder — chairman

Sikorski
McCloskey
Dymally

Pashayan
Horton

Compensation and Employee Benefits

Phone: 226-7546 Room: 406 CHOB

Oakar — chairman

Leland
Solarz

Myers
Young

Human Resources

Phone: 225-2821 Room: 511 HOB Annex #1

Ackerman — chairman

Yatron
Foley

Burton
Gilman

Investigations

Phone: 225-6295 Room: 608 HOB Annex #1

Sikorski — chairman

Ford
Yatron

Taylor
Gilman

Postal Operations and Services

Phone: 225-9124 Room: 209 CHOB

Leland — chairman

Clay
Garcia
de Lugo

Horton
Pashayan
Hansen

Postal Personnel and Modernization

Phone: 226-7520 Room: 603 HOB Annex #1

McCloskey — chairman

Clay
Dymally

Young
Burton

Public Works and Transportation

Phone: 225-4472 Room: 2165 RHOB

Flood control and improvement of rivers and harbors; construction and maintenance of roads; oil and other pollution of navigable waters; public buildings and grounds; public works for the benefit of navigation including bridges and dams; water power; transportation, except railroads; Botanic Garden; Library of Congress; Smithsonian Institution. Chairman and ranking minority member are members *ex officio* of all subcommittees of which they are not regular members. ***Party Ratio: D 27 - R 19 †***

James J. Howard
Chairman

Gene Snyder
Ranking Member

James J. Howard, N.J.
Glenn M. Anderson, Calif.
Robert A. Roe, N.J.
John B. Breaux, La.
Norman Y. Mineta, Calif.
James L. Oberstar, Minn.
Henry J. Nowak, N.Y.
Bob Edgar, Pa.
Robert A. Young, Mo.
Nick J. Rahall II, W.Va.
Douglas Applegate, Ohio
Ron de Lugo, Virgin Islands †
Gus Savage, Ill.
Fofō I. F. Sunia, American Somoa †

Gene Snyder, Ky.
John Paul Hammerschmidt, Ark.
Bud Shuster, Pa.
Arlan Stangeland, Minn.
Newt Gingrich, Ga.
William F. Clinger Jr., Pa.
Guy V. Molinari, N.Y.
E. Clay Shaw Jr., Fla.
Bob McEwen, Ohio
Thomas E. Petri, Wis.
Don Sundquist, Tenn.
Nancy L. Johnson, Conn.
Ron Packard, Calif.
Sherwood Boehlert, N.Y.

Douglas H. Bosco, Calif.	*Thomas D. DeLay, Texas*
Jim Moody, Wis.	*Sonny Callahan, Ala.*
Robert A. Borski, Pa.	*Dean A. Gallo, N.J.*
Joe Kolter, Pa.	*Helen Delich Bentley, Md.*
Tim Valentine, N.C.	*Jim Lightfoot, Iowa*
Edolphus Towns, N.Y.	
William O. Lipinski, Ill.	
Michael A. Andrews, Texas	
J. Roy Rowland, Ga.	
Bob Wise, W.Va.	
Kenneth J. Gray, Ill.	
Chester G. Atkins, Mass.	
Peter J. Visclosky, Ind.	
James A. Traficant Jr., Ohio	
Cathy (Mrs. Gillis) Long, La.	
Carl C. Perkins, Ky. *	

* Member appointed only for the first session of the 99th Congress.

† Party ratios do not include delegates or resident commissioner.

Vin Weber, R-Minn., and Bobbi Fiedler, R-Calif., are on leave from the committee but retain their seniority behind Petri, R-Wis.

SUBCOMMITTEES

Aviation

Phone: 225-9161 Room: 2251 RHOB

Mineta — chairman

de Lugo	*Hammerschmidt*
Savage	*Shuster*
Bosco	*Stangeland*
Valentine	*Gingrich*
Lipinski	*Molinari*
Rowland	*Shaw*
Wise	*Boehlert*
Anderson	*Lightfoot*
Nowak	
Edgar	
Young	
Rahall	
Sunia	

Economic Development

Phone: 225-6151 Room: B370-A RHOB

Nowak — chairman

Applegate	*Clinger*
Towns	*Shuster*
Visclosky	*Johnson*
Oberstar	*Boehlert*
Borski	*Gallo*
Kolter	*Bentley*
Lipinski	
Wise	
Perkins	

Investigations and Oversight

Phone: 225-3274 Room: B376 RHOB

Oberstar — chairman

Rowland	*Gingrich*
Andrews	*Clinger*
Gray	*Molinari*
Atkins	*Shaw*
Traficant	*McEwen*
Roe	*Sundquist*
Breaux	*Johnson*
Applegate	
Bosco	
Moody	
Perkins	

Public Buildings and Grounds

Phone: 225-9161 Room: 2251 RHOB

Young — chairman

Savage	*Shaw*
Towns	*Stangeland*
Andrews	*Petri*
Gray	*Sundquist*
Traficant	

Surface Transportation

Phone: 225-4472 Room: 2165 RHOB

Anderson — chairman

Edgar	*Shuster*
Rahall	*Hammerschmidt*
Applegate	*Gingrich*
Savage	*Clinger*
Sunia	*Molinari*
Moody	*McEwen*
Borski	*Petri*
Kolter	*Packard*
Valentine	*DeLay*
Lipinski	*Callahan*
Andrews	*Lightfoot*
Gray	
Atkins	
Traficant	
Roe	
Breaux	
de Lugo	
Mineta	

Water Resources

Phone: 225-0060 Room: B376 RHOB

Roe — chairman

Breaux	*Stangeland*
Bosco	*Hammerschmidt*
Towns	*McEwen*
Wise	*Petri*
Visclosky	*Sundquist*
Anderson	*Johnson*
Mineta	*Packard*
Oberstar	*DeLay*
Nowak	*Callahan*
Edgar	*Gallo*
Young	*Bentley*
Rahall	
Sunia	
Moody	
Borski	
Kolter	
de Lugo	
Rowland	
Atkins	

Rules

Phone: 225-9486 Room: H-312 Capitol

Rules and order of business of the House; emergency waivers under the Congressional Budget Act of required reporting date for bills and resolutions authorizing new budget authority; recesses and final adjournments of Congress. **Party Ratio: D 9 - R 4**

Claude Pepper
Chairman

James H. Quillen
Ranking Member

Claude Pepper, Fla.	*James H. Quillen, Tenn.*
Joe Moakley, Mass.	*Delbert L. Latta, Ohio*
Butler Derrick, S.C.	*Trent Lott, Miss.*
Anthony C. Beilenson, Calif.	*Gene Taylor, Mo.*
Martin Frost, Texas	
David E. Bonior, Mich.	
Tony P. Hall, Ohio	
Alan Wheat, Mo.	
Sala Burton, Calif.	

SUBCOMMITTEES

Legislative Process

Phone: 225-1037 Room: H-133 Capitol

Derrick — chairman

Frost	*Lott*
Wheat	*Taylor*
Burton	
Pepper	

Rules of the House

Phone: 225-9091 Room: H-152 Capitol

Moakley — chairman

Beilenson	*Taylor*
Bonior	*Lott*
Hall	
Pepper	

Science and Technology

Phone: 225-6371 Room: 2321 RHOB

Scientific and astronautical research and development including resources, personnel, equipment and facilities; Bureau of Standards, standardization of weights and measures and the metric system; National Aeronautics and Space Administration; National Aeronautics and Space Council; National Science Foundation; outer space including exploration and control; science scholarships; federally owned or operated non-military energy laboratories; civil aviation research and development; energy research, development and demonstration (except nuclear research and development); National Weather Service. Chairman and ranking minority member are members *ex officio* of all subcommittees of which they are not regular members. **Party Ratio: D 24 - R 17**

Don Fuqua
Chairman

Manuel Lujan Jr.
Ranking Member

Don Fuqua, Fla.	*Manuel Lujan Jr., N.M.*
Robert A. Roe, N.J.	*Robert S. Walker, Pa.*
George E. Brown Jr., Calif.	*F. James Sensenbrenner Jr., Wis.*
James H. Scheuer, N.Y.	*Claudine Schneider, R.I.*
Marilyn Lloyd, Tenn.	*Sherwood Boehlert, N.Y.*
Timothy E. Wirth, Colo.	*Tom Lewis, Fla.*
Doug Walgren, Pa.	*Don Ritter, Pa.*
Dan Glickman, Kan.	*Sid Morrison, Wash.*
Robert A. Young, Mo.	*Ron Packard, Calif.*
Harold L. Volkmer, Mo.	*Jan Meyers, Kan.*
Bill Nelson, Fla.	*Robert C. Smith, N.H.*
Stan Lundine, N.Y.	*Paul B. Henry, Mich.*
Ralph M. Hall, Texas	*Harris W. Fawell, Ill.*
Dave McCurdy, Okla.	*Bill Cobey, N.C.*
Norman Y. Mineta, Calif.	*Joe L. Barton, Texas*
Michael A. Andrews, Texas	*D. French Slaughter Jr., Va.*
Tim Valentine, N.C.	*David S. Monson, Utah*
Harry Reid, Nev.	
Robert G. Torricelli, N.J.	
Frederick C. Boucher, Va.	
Terry L. Bruce, Ill.	
Richard H. Stallings, Idaho	
Bart Gordon, Tenn.	
James A. Traficant Jr., Ohio	

Howard Wolpe, D-Mich., is on leave from the committee but retains his seniority behind Volkmer, D-Mo. Buddy MacKay, D-Fla., also on leave, retains his seniority behind Andrews, D-Texas.

SUBCOMMITTEES

Energy Development and Applications

Phone: 225-4494 — Room: B374 RHOB

Fuqua — chairman

Roe	*Sensenbrenner*
Hall	*Schneider*
Boucher	*Packard*
Bruce	*Fawell*
Traficant	*Cobey*
Walgren	*Barton*
Young	*Slaughter*
McCurdy	
Stallings	
Brown	
Mineta	

Energy Research and Production

Phone: 225-8056 — Room: B374 RHOB

Lloyd — chairman

Young	*Morrison*
Stallings	*Fawell*
Roe	*Barton*
Lundine	*Monson*
Valentine	

Investigations and Oversight

Phone: 226-3636 — Room: 822 HOB Annex #1

Volkmer — chairman

Andrews	*Packard*
Traficant	*Sensenbrenner*
Roe	*Morrison*
Reid	

Natural Resources, Agriculture Research and Environment

Phone: 226-6980 — Room: 388 HOB Annex #2

Scheuer — chairman

Wirth	*Schneider*
Valentine	*Ritter*
McCurdy	*Meyers*
Reid	*Smith*
Torricelli	*Henry*
Andrews	

Science, Research and Technology

Phone: 225-8844 — Room: 2319 RHOB

Walgren — chairman

Lundine	*Boehlert*
Mineta	*Ritter*
Brown	*Henry*
Wirth	*Cobey*
Bruce	
Valentine	

Space Science and Applications

Phone: 225-7858 Room: 2324 RHOB

Nelson — chairman

Brown	*Walker*
Andrews	*Meyers*
Torricelli	*Smith*
Gordon	*Barton*
Scheuer	*Slaughter*
Volkmer	*Monson*
Mineta	
Hall	

Transportation, Aviation and Materials

Phone: 225-9662 Room: 2324 RHOB

Brown — chairman

Reid	*Lewis*
Nelson	*Boehlert*
Gordon	*Packard*
Scheuer	

Select Aging

Phone: 226-3375 Room: 712 HOB Annex #1

Problems of older Americans including income, housing, health, welfare, employment, education, recreation and participation in family and community life. Studies and reports findings to House, but cannot report legislation. Chairman and ranking minority member are members *ex officio* of all subcommittees of which they are not regular members. ***Party Ratio: D 38 - R 26 †***

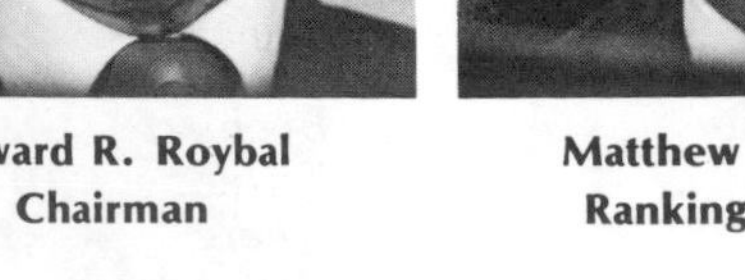

Edward R. Roybal
Chairman

Matthew J. Rinaldo
Ranking Member

Edward R. Roybal, Calif.
Claude Pepper, Fla.
Mario Biaggi, N.Y.
Don Bonker, Wash.
Thomas J. Downey, N.Y.
James J. Florio, N.J.
Harold E. Ford, Tenn.
William J. Hughes, N.J.
Marilyn Lloyd, Tenn.
Stan Lundine, N.Y.
Mary Rose Oakar, Ohio
Thomas A. Luken, Ohio
Beverly B. Byron, Md.
Daniel A. Mica, Fla.
Henry A. Waxman, Calif.
Mike Synar, Okla.
Butler Derrick, S.C.
Bruce F. Vento, Minn.
Barney Frank, Mass.
Tom Lantos, Calif.
Ron Wyden, Ore.
George W. Crockett Jr., Mich.
Bill Boner, Tenn.
Ike Skelton, Mo.
Dennis M. Hertel, Mich.
Robert A. Borski, Pa.
Frederick C. Boucher, Va.
Ben Erdreich, Ala.
Buddy MacKay, Fla.
Harry Reid, Nev.
Norman Sisisky, Va.
Bob Wise, W.Va.
Bill Richardson, N.M.
Harold L. Volkmer, Mo.
Bart Gordon, Tenn.
Thomas J. Manton, N.Y.
Tommy F. Robinson, Ark.
Richard H. Stallings, Idaho

Matthew J. Rinaldo, N.J.
John Paul Hammerschmidt, Ark.
Ralph Regula, Ohio
Norman D. Shumway, Calif.
Olympia J. Snowe, Maine
James M. Jeffords, Vt.
Tom Tauke, Iowa
George C. Wortley, N.Y.
Jim Courter, N.J.
Claudine Schneider, R.I.
Tom Ridge, Pa.
John McCain, Ariz.
George W. Gekas, Pa.
Mark D. Siljander, Mich.
Christopher H. Smith, N.J.
Sherwood Boehlert, N.Y.
H. James Saxton, N.J.
Helen Delich Bentley, Md.
Jim Lightfoot, Iowa
Harris W. Fawell, Ill.
Jan Meyers, Kan.
Ben Blaz, Guam †
Pat Swindall, Ga.
Paul B. Henry, Mich.
Jim Kolbe, Ariz.
Bill Schuette, Mich.
Vacancy

† Party ratios do not include delegates or resident commissioner.

SUBCOMMITTEES

Health and Long-Term Care

Phone: 226-3381 Room: 715 HOB Annex #1

Pepper — chairman

Ford	*Regula*
Oakar	*Wortley*
Luken	*Courter*
Mica	*Schneider*
Waxman	*Ridge*
Synar	*McCain*
Derrick	*Boehlert*
Vento	*Lightfoot*
Frank	*Myers*
Wyden	*Swindall*

Skelton	*Henry*
Hertel	*Kolbe*
Borski	
Erdreich	
MacKay	
Sisisky	

Housing and Consumer Interests

Phone: 226-3344 Room: 717 HOB Annex #1

Bonker — chairman

Lloyd	*Hammerschmidt*
Lundine	*Wortley*
Byron	*Ridge*
Lantos	*Gekas*
Boner	*Smith*
Gordon	*Blaz*
Frank	*Schuette*
Wyden	
Richardson	

Human Services

Phone: 226-3348 Room: 716 HOB Annex #1

Biaggi — chairman

Florio	*Snowe*
Hughes	*Rinaldo*
Richardson	*McCain*
Robinson	*Saxton*
Downey	*Lightfoot*
Synar	*Blaz*
Lantos	*Vacancy*
Erdreich	
Lundine	

Retirement, Income and Employment

Phone: 226-3335 Room: 714 HOB Annex #1

Roybal — chairman

Downey	*Tauke*
Crockett	*Shumway*
Boucher	*Jeffords*
Reid	*Siljander*
Wise	*Saxton*
Volkmer	*Bentley*
Manton	*Fawell*
Stallings	
Oakar	

Select Children, Youth and Families

Phone: 226-7660 Room: 385 HOB Annex #2

Problems of children, youth and families including income maintenance, health, nutrition, education, welfare, employment and recreation. Studies and reports findings to House, but cannot report legislation. Chairman and ranking minority member are members *ex officio* of all task forces. **Party Ratio: D 15 - R 10**

George Miller
Chairman

Dan Coats
Ranking Member

George Miller, Calif.	*Dan Coats, Ind.*
William Lehman, Fla.	*Hamilton Fish Jr., N.Y.*
Patricia Schroeder, Colo.	*Thomas J. Bliley Jr., Va.*
Lindy (Mrs. Hale) Boggs, La.	*Frank R. Wolf, Va.*
Matthew F. McHugh, N.Y.	*Dan Burton, Ind.*
Ted Weiss, N.Y.	*Nancy L. Johnson, Conn.*
Beryl Anthony Jr., Ark.	*John R. McKernan Jr., Maine*
Barbara Boxer, Calif.	*Barbara F. Vucanovich, Nev.*
Sander M. Levin, Mich.	*David S. Monson, Utah*
Bruce A. Morrison, Conn.	*Robert C. Smith, N.H.*
J. Roy Rowland, Ga.	
Gerry Sikorski, Minn.	
Alan Wheat, Mo.	
Matthew G. Martinez, Calif.	
Lane Evans, Ill.	

TASK FORCES

Crisis Intervention

Phone: 226-7660 Room: 385 HOB Annex #2

Boggs — chairman

Anthony	*Burton*
Boxer	*Fish*
Levin	*Johnson*
Rowland	*Monson*
Sikorski	
Evans	

Economic Security

Phone: 226-7660 Room: 385 HOB Annex #2

Schroeder — chairman

Weiss	*Wolf*
Morrison	*Fish*
Wheat	*Bliley*
Martinez	*Johnson*
Evans	
McHugh	

Prevention Strategies

Phone: 226-7660 Room: 385 HOB Annex #2

Lehman — chairman

McHugh	*Bliley*
Weiss	*McKernan*
Anthony	*Vucanovich*
Levin	*Smith*
Schroeder	
Boggs	

Select Hunger

Phone: 226-5470 Room: 507 HOB Annex #2

Comprehensive study and review of hunger and malnutrition, including U.S. development and economic assistance programs; U.S. trade relations with less-developed nations; food production and distribution; agribusiness efforts to further international development; policies of development banks and international development institutions; and food assistance programs in the United States. Review of executive branch recommendations relating to programs affecting hunger and malnutrition, and to recommend legislation or other action with respect to such programs to the appropriate committees of the House. Chairman and ranking minority member are members *ex officio* of all subcommittees of which they are not regular members. ***Party Ratio: D 10 - R 7***

Mickey Leland
Chairman

Marge Roukema
Ranking Member

Mickey Leland, Texas	*Marge Roukema, N.J.*
Tony P. Hall, Ohio	*Bill Emerson, Mo.*
Bob Traxler, Mich.	*Sid Morrison, Wash.*
Leon E. Panetta, Calif.	*Benjamin A. Gilman, N.Y.*
Thomas A. Daschle, S.D.	*Cooper Evans, Iowa*
Vic Fazio, Calif.	*Robert F. Smith, Ore.*
Sam Gejdenson, Conn.	*Doug Bereuter, Neb.*
Peter H. Kostmayer, Pa.	
Sala Burton, Calif.	
Byron L. Dorgan, N.D.	

TASK FORCES

Domestic

Phone: 226-5470 Room: 507 HOB Annex #2

Panetta — chairman

Traxler	*Emerson*
Gejdenson	*Morrison*
Burton	

International

Phone: 226-5470 Room: 507 HOB Annex #2

Hall — chairman

Daschle	*Evans*
Fazio	*Morrison*
Kostmayer	*Gilman*
Gejdenson	*Smith*
Dorgan	*Bereuter*

Select Intelligence

Phone: 225-4121 Room: H-405 Capitol

Legislative and budgetary authority over the Central Intelligence Agency, the Defense Intelligence Agency, the National Security Agency, intelligence activities of the Federal Bureau of Investigation and other components of the federal intelligence community. **Party Ratio: D 10 - R 6**

Lee H. Hamilton
Chairman

Bob Stump
Ranking Member

Lee H. Hamilton, Ind.
Louis Stokes, Ohio
Dave McCurdy, Okla.
Anthony C. Beilenson, Calif.
Robert W. Kastenmeier, Wis.
Dan Daniel, Va.
Robert A. Roe, N.J.
George E. Brown Jr., Calif.
Matthew F. McHugh, N.Y.
Bernard J. Dwyer, N.J.

Bob Stump, Ariz.
Andy Ireland, Fla.
Henry J. Hyde, Ill.
Dick Cheney, Wyo.
Bob Livingston, La.
Bob McEwen, Ohio

SUBCOMMITTEES

Legislation

Phone: 225-7310 Room: H-405 Capitol

Beilenson — chairman

Stokes
Kastenmeier
Brown
Hamilton

Hyde
Livingston
McEwen

Oversight and Evaluation

Phone: 225-5657 Room: H-405 Capitol

McCurdy — chairman

Brown
McHugh
Dwyer
Hamilton

Ireland
Hyde
Stump

Program and Budget Authorization

Phone: 225-7690 Room: H-405 Capitol

Stokes — chairman

Hamilton
Kastenmeier
Daniel
Roe

Stump
Cheney
Livingston

Select Narcotics Abuse and Control

Phone: 226-3040 Room: 234 HOB Annex #2

Problems of narcotics, drug and polydrug abuse and control including opium and its derivatives, other narcotic drugs, psychotropics and other controlled substances; trafficking, manufacturing and distribution; treatment, prevention and rehabilitation; narcotics-related violations of tax laws; international treaties and agreements relating to narcotics and drug abuse; role of organized crime in narcotics and drug abuse; abuse and control in the armed forces and in industry; criminal justice system and narcotics and drug law violations and crimes related to drug abuse. Studies and reports findings to House, but cannot report legislation. **Party Ratio: D 15 - R 10**

Charles B. Rangel
Chairman

Benjamin A. Gilman
Ranking Member

Charles B. Rangel, N.Y.
Peter W. Rodino Jr., N.J.
Fortney H. "Pete" Stark, Calif.
James H. Scheuer, N.Y.
Cardiss Collins, Ill.
Daniel K. Akaka, Hawaii
Frank J. Guarini, N.J.
Robert T. Matsui, Calif.
Dante B. Fascell, Fla.
Walter E. Fauntroy, D.C.
William J. Hughes, N.J.
Mel Levine, Calif.
Solomon P. Ortiz, Texas
Larry Smith, Fla.
Edolphus Towns, N.Y.

Benjamin A. Gilman, N.Y.
Lawrence Coughlin, Pa.
E. Clay Shaw Jr., Fla.
Michael G. Oxley, Ohio
Stan Parris, Va.
Gene Chappie, Calif.
Duncan L. Hunter, Calif.
Joseph J. DioGuardi, N.Y.
Mike Strang, Colo.
John G. Rowland, Conn.

No standing subcommittees.

Ike Skelton, Mo.
Charles W. Stenholm, Texas
Romano L. Mazzoli, Ky.
Nicholas Mavroules, Mass.
Charles Hatcher, Ga.
Ron Wyden, Ore.
Dennis E. Eckart, Ohio
Gus Savage, Ill.
Buddy Roemer, La.
Norman Sisisky, Va.
Esteban Edward Torres, Calif.
Jim Cooper, Tenn.
James R. Olin, Va.
Richard Ray, Ga.
Charles A. Hayes, Ill.
Cathy (Mrs. Gillis) Long, La.
Tommy F. Robinson, Ark. *

D. French Slaughter Jr., Va.
Jim Kolbe, Ariz.
Bill Cobey, N.C.
Robert C. Smith, N.H.
Howard Coble, N.C.
Joseph J. DioGuardi, N.Y.
Jan Meyers, Kan.
Dean A. Gallo, N.J.
J. Alex McMillan, N.C.
John E. Grotberg, Ill.

* Member appointed only for the first session of the 99th Congress.

Small Business

Phone: 225-5821 Room: 2361 RHOB

Assistance to and protection of small business including financial aid; participation of small business enterprises in federal procurement and government contracts. Chairman and ranking minority member are members *ex officio* of all subcommittees of which they are not regular members.
Party Ratio: D 25 - R 17

Parren J. Mitchell
Chairman

Joseph M. McDade
Ranking Member

Parren J. Mitchell, Md.
Neal Smith, Iowa
Joseph P. Addabbo, N.Y.
Henry B. Gonzalez, Texas
John J. LaFalce, N.Y.
Berkley Bedell, Iowa
Henry J. Nowak, N.Y.
Thomas A. Luken, Ohio

Joseph M. McDade, Pa.
Silvio O. Conte, Mass.
William S. Broomfield, Mich.
Andy Ireland, Fla.
John Hiler, Ind.
Vin Weber, Minn.
David Dreier, Calif.

SUBCOMMITTEES

Antitrust and Restraint of Trade Activities Affecting Small Business

Phone: 225-3171 Room: 569 HOB Annex #2

Hatcher — chairman

Gonzalez
Ray

Weber
Slaughter

Energy, Environment and Safety Issues Affecting Small Business

Phone: 225-9368 Room: B363 RHOB

Stenholm — chairman

Wyden
Sisisky
Torres
Vacancy

Broomfield
Cobey
Smith (N.H.)

Export Opportunities and Special Small Business Problems

Phone: 225-9368 Room: B363 RHOB

Skelton — chairman

Eckart

Ireland

Savage	*Cobey*
Olin	*Coble*
Robinson	*Dreier*
Mazzoli	

General Oversight and the Economy

Phone: 225-8944 Room: B363 RHOB

Mavroules — chairman

Bedell	*Conte*
Sisisky	*Dreier*
Cooper	*DioGuardi*
Olin	*Kolbe*
Addabbo	

SBA and SBIC Authority, Minority Enterprise and General Small Business Problems

Phone: 225-5821 Room: 2361 RHOB

Mitchell — chairman

Smith (Iowa)	*McDade*
Addabbo	*Kolbe*
LaFalce	*Gallo*
Wyden	*McMillan*
Savage	*Grotberg*
Hayes	
Torres	

Tax, Access to Equity Capital and Business Opportunities

Phone: 225-7797 Room: B363 RHOB

Luken — chairman

Nowak	*Hiler*
Roemer	*Slaughter*
Eckart	*Smith (N.H.)*
Robinson	*Meyers*
Gonzalez	

Standards of Official Conduct

Phone: 225-7103 Room: HT-2 Capitol

Measures relating to the Code of Official Conduct; conduct of House members and employees; Ethics in Government Act. ***Party Ratio: D 6 - R 6***

Julian C. Dixon
Chairman

Floyd Spence
Ranking Member

Julian C. Dixon, Calif.	*Floyd Spence, S.C.*
Ed Jenkins, Ga.	*John T. Myers, Ind.*
Vic Fazio, Calif.	*James V. Hansen, Utah*
William J. Coyne, Pa.	*G. William Whitehurst, Va.*
Bernard J. Dwyer, N.J.	*Carl D. Pursell, Mich.*
Alan B. Mollohan, W.Va.	*George C. Wortley, N.Y.*

No standing subcommittees.

Veterans' Affairs

Phone: 225-3527 Room: 335 CHOB

Veterans' measures generally; compensation, vocational rehabilitation and education of veterans; armed forces life insurance; pensions; readjustment benefits; veterans' hospitals, medical care and treatment. Chairman and ranking minority member are members *ex officio* of all subcommittees of which they are not regular members. ***Party Ratio: D 20 - R 14***

G. V. "Sonny" Montgomery
Chairman

John Paul Hammerschmidt
Ranking Member

G. V. "Sonny" Montgomery, Miss.
Don Edwards, Calif.
Bob Edgar, Pa.
Douglas Applegate, Ohio
Richard C. Shelby, Ala.
Daniel A. Mica, Fla.
Thomas A. Daschle, S.D.
Wayne Dowdy, Miss.
Lane Evans, Ill.
Marcy Kaptur, Ohio
Alan B. Mollohan, W.Va.
Timothy J. Penny, Minn.
Harley O. Staggers Jr., W.Va.
J. Roy Rowland, Ga.
John Bryant, Texas
James J. Florio, N.J.
Kenneth J. Gray, Ill.
Paul E. Kanjorski, Pa.
Tommy F. Robinson, Ark.
Vacancy

John Paul Hammerschmidt, Ark.
Chalmers P. Wylie, Ohio
Elwood Hillis, Ind.
Gerald B. H. Solomon, N.Y.
Bob McEwen, Ohio
Christopher H. Smith, N.J.
Dan L. Burton, Ind.
Don Sundquist, Tenn.
Michael Bilirakis, Fla.
Nancy L. Johnson, Conn.
Guy V. Molinari, N.Y.
Tom Ridge, Pa.
Bill Hendon, N.C.
John G. Rowland, Conn.

Marvin Leath, D-Texas, is on leave from the committee but retains his seniority after Applegate, D-Ohio. Jim Slattery, D-Kan., also on leave, retains his seniority behind Rowland, D-Ga. Denny Smith, R-Ore., and Bob Stump, R-Ariz., are on leave from the committee but retain their seniority behind Smith, R-N.J.

SUBCOMMITTEES

Compensation, Pension and Insurance

Phone: 225-3527 Room: 335 CHOB

Applegate — chairman

Montgomery	*Solomon*
Mica	*Wylie*
Dowdy	*Hammerschmidt*
Evans	*Burton*
Robinson	*Molinari*

Education, Training and Employment

Phone: 225-3527 Room: 335 CHOB

Daschle — chairman

Evans	*McEwen*
Kaptur	*Wylie*
Bryant	*Solomon*
Florio	*Hendon*
Kanjorski	

Hospitals and Health Care

Phone: 225-3527 Room: 335 CHOB

Edgar — chairman

Mica	*Hammerschmidt*
Dowdy	*Hillis*
Evans	*Solomon*
Kaptur	*McEwen*
Mollohan	*Smith*
Penny	*Bilirakis*
Staggers	*Johnson*
Rowland (Ga.)	*Molinari*
Bryant	*Ridge*
Florio	*Hendon*
Kanjorski	*Rowland (Conn.)*
Robinson	
Daschle	
Vacancy	

Housing and Memorial Affairs

Phone: 225-3527 Room: 335 CHOB

Shelby — chairman

Edgar	*Smith*
Applegate	*Sundquist*
Mollohan	*Bilirakis*
Bryant	*Rowland (Conn.)*
Florio	
Kanjorski	

Oversight and Investigations

Phone: 225-3527 Room: 335 CHOB

Montgomery — chairman

Edwards	*Hillis*
Gray	*Burton*
Penny	*Sundquist*
Rowland (Ga.)	*Johnson*
Robinson	*Ridge*

Ways and Means

Phone: 225-3625 Room: 1102 LHOB

Revenue measures generally; reciprocal trade agreements; customs, collection districts and ports of entry and delivery; bonded debt of the United States; deposit of public moneys; transportation of dutiable goods; tax exempt foundations and charitable trusts; Social Security. Chairman and ranking minority member are members *ex officio* of all subcommittees of which they are not regular members. ***Party Ratio: D 23 - R 13***

Dan Rostenkowski
Chairman

John J. Duncan
Ranking Member

Dan Rostenkowski, Ill.
Sam Gibbons, Fla.
J. J. Pickle, Texas
Charles B. Rangel, N.Y.
Fortney H. "Pete" Stark, Calif.
James R. Jones, Okla.
Andrew Jacobs Jr., Ind.
Harold E. Ford, Tenn.
Ed Jenkins, Ga.
Richard A. Gephardt, Mo.
Thomas J. Downey, N.Y.
Cecil Heftel, Hawaii
Wyche Fowler Jr., Ga.
Frank J. Guarini, N.J.
Marty Russo, Ill.
Don J. Pease, Ohio
Robert T. Matsui, Calif.
Beryl Anthony Jr., Ark.
Ronnie G. Flippo, Ala.
Byron L. Dorgan, N.D.
Barbara B. Kennelly, Conn.
Brian J. Donnelly, Mass.
William J. Coyne, Pa.

John J. Duncan, Tenn.
Bill Archer, Texas
Guy Vander Jagt, Mich.
Philip M. Crane, Ill.
Bill Frenzel, Minn.
Richard T. Schulze, Pa.
Bill Gradison, Ohio
W. Henson Moore, La.
Carroll A. Campbell Jr., S.C.
William M. Thomas, Calif.
Raymond J. McGrath, N.Y.
Hal Daub, Neb.
Judd Gregg, N.H.

SUBCOMMITTEES

Health

Phone: 225-7785 Room: 1114 LHOB

Stark — chairman

Jacobs
Rangel
Donnelly
Coyne
Pickle
Jones

Gradison
Moore
Daub
Gregg

Oversight

Phone: 225-2743 Room: 1105 LHOB

Pickle — chairman

Guarini
Anthony
Flippo
Dorgan
Ford
Heftel

Schulze
Frenzel
Thomas
McGrath

Public Assistance and Unemployment Compensation

Phone: 225-1025 Room: B317 RHOB

Ford — chairman

Stark
Pease
Matsui
Kennelly

Campbell
Frenzel
Gradison

Select Revenue Measures

Phone: 225-9710 Room: 1111 LHOB

Rangel — chairman

Flippo
Dorgan
Kennelly
Fowler
Matsui
Anthony

Vander Jagt
Campbell
Thomas
McGrath

Social Security

Phone: 225-9263 Room: 1101 LHOB

Jones — chairman

Jacobs
Gephardt
Fowler
Donnelly
Coyne
Gibbons

Archer
Crane
Daub
Gregg

Trade

Phone: 225-3943 Room: 1136 LHOB

Gibbons — chairman

Rostenkowski
Jenkins
Downey
Pease
Heftel
Russo
Gephardt
Guarini

Crane
Archer
Vander Jagt
Frenzel
Schulze

Joint Committee Assignments, 99th Congress

As of May 15, 1985

Joint committees are set up to examine specific questions and are established by public law. Membership is drawn from both chambers and both parties. When a senator serves as chairman, the vice chairman is usually a representative, and vice versa. The chairmanship usually rotates from one chamber to the other at the beginning of each Congress. Democrats are listed on the left in roman type; Republicans are listed on the right in italics.

Economic

Phone: 224-5171 Room: SD-G01

Studies and investigates all recommendations in the president's annual Economic Report to Congress. Reports findings and recommendations to the House and Senate.

Rep. David R. Obey
Chairman

Sen. James Abdnor
Vice Chairman

Senate Members

Lloyd Bentsen, Texas
William Proxmire, Wis.
Edward M. Kennedy, Mass.
Paul S. Sarbanes, Md.

James Abdnor, S.D.
William V. Roth Jr., Del.
Steven D. Symms, Idaho
Mack Mattingly, Ga.
Alfonse M. D'Amato, N.Y.
Pete Wilson, Calif.

House Members

David R. Obey, Wis.
Lee H. Hamilton, Ind.
Parren J. Mitchell, Md.
Augustus F. Hawkins, Calif.
James H. Scheuer, N.Y.
Fortney H. "Pete" Stark, Calif.

Chalmers P. Wylie, Ohio
Dan Lungren, Calif.
Olympia J. Snowe, Maine
Bobbi Fiedler, Calif.

Subcommittee assignments were not available.

Library

Phone: 224-0299 Room: SR-309

Management and expansion of the Library of Congress; receipt of gifts for the benefit of the library; development and maintenance of the Botanic Garden; placement of statues and other works of art in the Capitol.

Rep. Frank Annunzio
Chairman

Sen. Charles McC. Mathias Jr.
Vice Chairman

Senate Members

Daniel K. Inouye, Hawaii
Claiborne Pell, R.I.

Charles McC. Mathias Jr., Md.
Mark O. Hatfield, Ore.
John W. Warner, Va.

House Members

Frank Annunzio, Ill.
Al Swift, Wash.
Mary Rose Oakar, Ohio

Newt Gingrich, Ga.
Pat Roberts, Kan.

No standing subcommittees.

Printing

Phone: 224-5241 Room: SH-818

Probes inefficiency and waste in the printing, binding and distribution of federal government publications. Oversees arrangement and style of the *Congressional Record*.

Sen. Charles McC. Mathias Jr.
Chairman

Rep. Frank Annunzio
Vice Chairman

Senate Members

Wendell H. Ford, Ky.
Dennis DeConcini, Ariz.

Charles McC. Mathias Jr., Md.
Mark O. Hatfield, Ore.
Ted Stevens, Alaska

House Members

Frank Annunzio, Ill.
Joseph M. Gaydos, Pa.
Ed Jones, Tenn.

Robert E. Badham, Calif.
Pat Roberts, Kan.

No standing subcommittees.

Taxation

Phone: 225-3621 Room: 1015 LHOB

Operation, effects and administration of the federal system of internal revenue taxes; measures and methods for simplification of taxes.

Rep. Dan Rostenkowski
Chairman

Sen. Bob Packwood
Vice Chairman

Senate Members

Russell B. Long, La.
Lloyd Bentsen, Texas

Bob Packwood, Ore.
Robert Dole, Kan.
William V. Roth Jr., Del.

House Members

Dan Rostenkowski, Ill.
Sam Gibbons, Fla.
J. J. Pickle, Texas

John J. Duncan, Tenn.
Bill Archer, Texas

No standing subcommittees.

Senate Party Committees, 99th Congress

REPUBLICANS

Strom Thurmond
President Pro Tempore

Robert Dole
Majority Leader

Alan K. Simpson
Assistant Majority Leader

John H. Chafee
Conference Chairman

Party Leadership

President Pro Tempore — Strom Thurmond, S.C. 224-5257
Majority Leader — Robert Dole, Kan. 224-3135
Assistant Majority Leader — Alan K. Simpson, Wyo. 224-2708
Chairman of the Conference — John H. Chafee, R.I. 224-2764
Secretary of the Conference — Thad Cochran, Miss. 224-1326

Policy Committee

Phone: 224-2946 Room: SR-347

Scheduling of legislation.

William L. Armstrong, Colo., chairman

Mark Andrews, N.D.
John H. Chafee, R.I.
Thad Cochran, Miss.
John C. Danforth, Mo.
Robert Dole, Kan.
Pete V. Domenici, N.M.
Jake Garn, Utah
Barry Goldwater, Ariz.
Orrin G. Hatch, Utah
Mark O. Hatfield, Ore.
Jesse Helms, N.C.
Richard G. Lugar, Ind.
Charles McC. Mathias Jr., Md.
James A. McClure, Idaho
Frank H. Murkowski, Alaska
Bob Packwood, Ore.
William V. Roth Jr., Del.
Alan K. Simpson, Wyo.
Robert T. Stafford, Vt.
Strom Thurmond, S.C.
Lowell P. Weicker Jr., Conn.

Committee on Committees

Phone: 224-3643 Room: SH-320

Makes Republican committee assignments.

Mack Mattingly, Ga., chairman

James Abdnor, S.D.
Alfonse M. D'Amato, N.Y.
Jeremiah Denton, Ala.
Robert Dole, Kan. †
John P. East, N.C.
Daniel J. Evans, Wash.
Slade Gorton, Wash.
Phil Gramm, Texas
Charles E. Grassley, Iowa
Paula Hawkins, Fla.
Nancy Landon Kassebaum, Kan.
Bob Kasten, Wis.
Paul Laxalt, Nev.
Don Nickles, Okla.
Dan Quayle, Ind.
Warren B. Rudman, N.H.
Arlen Specter, Pa.
Steven D. Symms, Idaho
John W. Warner, Va.
Pete Wilson, Calif.

† Member *ex officio* from the leadership.

National Republican Senatorial Committee

Phone: 224-2351 440 First St. N.W. 20001

Campaign support committee for Republican senatorial candidates.

John Heinz, Pa., chairman

Rudy Boschwitz, Minn.
William S. Cohen, Maine
Dave Durenberger, Minn.
Chic Hecht, Nev.
Gordon J. Humphrey, N.H.
Mitch McConnell, Ky.
Larry Pressler, S.D.
Ted Stevens, Alaska
Paul S. Trible Jr., Va.
Malcolm Wallop, Wyo.

DEMOCRATS

Robert C. Byrd
Minority Leader and Conference Chairman

Alan Cranston
Minority Whip

Daniel K. Inouye
Conference Secretary

Spark M. Matsunaga
Chief Deputy Whip

Party Leadership

Minority Leader — Robert C. Byrd, W.Va. 224-5556
Minority Whip — Alan Cranston, Calif. 224-2158
Chairman of the Conference — Robert C. Byrd, W.Va. 224-5551
Secretary of the Conference — Daniel K. Inouye, Hawaii 224-5551
Chief Deputy Whip — Spark M. Matsunaga, Hawaii 224-6361
Deputy Whips — Max Baucus, Mont.; Alan J. Dixon, Ill.; Christopher J. Dodd, Conn.; J. James Exon, Neb.; Wendell H. Ford, Ky.; John Glenn, Ohio; Patrick J. Leahy, Vt.; David Pryor, Ark.; Donald W. Riegle Jr., Mich.; Paul S. Sarbanes, Md.

Policy Committee

Phone: 224-5551 Room: S-118 Capitol

Scheduling of legislation.

Robert C. Byrd, W.Va., chairman

Quentin N. Burdick, N.D.
Alan Cranston, Calif. †
John Glenn, Ohio
Ernest F. Hollings, S.C.
Daniel K. Inouye, Hawaii †
Claiborne Pell, R.I.

† Member *ex officio* from the leadership.

Legislative Review Committee

Phone: 224-3735 Room: S-208 Capitol

Reviews legislative proposals, provides recommendations.

Dale Bumpers, Ark., chairman

Lloyd Bentsen, Texas
J. James Exon, Neb.
Gary Hart, Colo.
John Melcher, Mont.
Daniel Patrick Moynihan, N.Y.
William Proxmire, Wis.
Paul S. Sarbanes, Md.

Steering Committee

Phone: 224-3735 Room: S-208 Capitol

Makes Democratic committee assignments.

Robert C. Byrd, W.Va., chairman

Joseph R. Biden Jr., Del.
David L. Boren, Okla.
Lawton Chiles, Fla.
Alan Cranston, Calif.
Dennis DeConcini, Ariz.
Christopher J. Dodd, Conn.
Thomas F. Eagleton, Mo.
Wendell H. Ford, Ky.
Daniel K. Inouye, Hawaii †
Edward M. Kennedy, Mass.
Patrick J. Leahy, Vt.
Russell B. Long, La.
Howard M. Metzenbaum, Ohio
George J. Mitchell, Maine
Sam Nunn, Ga.
David Pryor, Ark.
Donald W. Riegle Jr., Mich.
Jim Sasser, Tenn.
John C. Stennis, Miss.
Edward Zorinsky, Neb.

† Member *ex officio* from the leadership.

Democratic Senatorial Campaign Committee

Phone: 224-2447 430 S. Capitol St. S.E. 20003

Campaign support committee for Democratic senatorial candidates.

George J. Mitchell, Maine, chairman
Alan Cranston, Calif., vice chairman

Max Baucus, Mont.
Lloyd Bentsen, Texas
Joseph R. Biden Jr., Del.
Bill Bradley, N.J.
Robert C. Byrd, W.Va. †
Lawton Chiles, Fla.
Christopher J. Dodd, Conn.
Wendell H. Ford, Ky.
Tom Harkin, Iowa
Gary Hart, Colo.
Daniel K. Inouye, Hawaii†
J. Bennett Johnston, La.
Edward M. Kennedy, Mass.
Frank R. Lautenberg, N.J.
Russell B. Long, La.
Daniel Patrick Moynihan, N.Y.
Sam Nunn, Ga.
Donald W. Riegle Jr., Mich.
Paul S. Sarbanes, Md.
Jim Sasser, Tenn.
Paul Simon, Ill.

† Member *ex officio* from the leadership.

House Party Committees, 99th Congress

DEMOCRATS

Thomas P. O'Neill Jr.
Speaker of the House

Jim Wright
Majority Leader

Thomas S. Foley
Majority Whip

Richard A. Gephardt
Caucus Chairman

Party Leadership

Speaker of the House — Thomas P. O'Neill Jr., Mass. 225-5414
Majority Leader — Jim Wright, Texas 225-8040
Majority Whip — Thomas S. Foley, Wash. 225-5604
Chairman of the Caucus — Richard A. Gephardt, Mo. 226-3210
Secretary of the Caucus — Mary Rose Oakar, Ohio 226-3210
Chief Deputy Whip — Bill Alexander, Ark. 225-0080

Deputy Whips — David E. Bonior, Mich.; Norman Y. Mineta, Calif.; Joe Moakley, Mass.; Leon E. Panetta, Calif.; Charles B. Rangel, N.Y.; Marty Russo, Ill.; Charles Whitley, N.C.; Pat Williams, Mont.

At-Large Whips — Les Aspin, Wis.; Les AuCoin, Ore.; Michael D. Barnes, Md.; Tom Bevill, Ala.; Frederick C. Boucher, Va.; Barbara Boxer, Calif.; John B. Breaux, La.; Terry L. Bruce, Ill.; Tony Coelho, Calif.; Ronald D. Coleman, Texas; Thomas A. Daschle, S.D.; Byron L. Dorgan, N.D.; Dennis E. Eckart, Ohio; Vic Fazio, Calif.; William D. Ford, Mich.; Dan Glickman, Kan.; William H. Gray III, Pa.; Steny H. Hoyer, Md.; Carroll Hubbard Jr., Ky.; Ed Jenkins, Ga.; James R. Jones, Okla.; Mike Lowry, Wash.; Parren J. Mitchell, Md.; Robert J. Mrazek, N.Y.; John P. Murtha, Pa.; Mary Rose Oakar, Ohio; Tommy F. Robinson, Ark.; Charlie Rose, N.C.; Dan Rostenkowski, Ill.; Patricia Schroeder, Colo.; Philip R. Sharp, Ind.; Gerry Sikorski, Minn.

Assistant Whips, by zone numbers:

1. Bruce A. Morrison, Conn. — Connecticut, Massachusetts, New Hampshire, Rhode Island
2. Charles E. Schumer, N.Y., and Henry J. Nowak, N.Y. — New York
3. Austin J. Murphy, Pa. — Pennsylvania
4. Robert G. Torricelli, N.J. — Delaware, Maryland, New Jersey
5. Charles Whitley, N.C. — North Carolina, Virginia
6. Charles Hatcher, Ga. — Georgia, South Carolina
7. Dale E. Kildee, Mich. — Michigan
8. David R. Obey, Wis. — Minnesota, Wisconsin
9. Lee H. Hamilton, Ind. — Indiana, Kentucky
10. Don J. Pease, Ohio — Ohio, West Virginia
11. Harold E. Ford, Tenn. — Louisiana, Mississippi, Tennessee
12. Daniel A. Mica, Fla. — Alabama, Florida
13. Harold L. Volkmer, Mo. — Iowa, Missouri
14. Sidney R. Yates, Ill. — Illinois
15. J. J. Pickle, Texas, and Henry B. Gonzalez, Texas — Texas
16. Mike Synar, Okla. — Arkansas, Kansas, Oklahoma
17. Bill Richardson, N.M., and Harry Reid, Nev. — Arizona, Colorado, Montana, Nevada, New Mexico, North Dakota, South Dakota
18. James Weaver, Ore. — Hawaii, Idaho, Oregon, Washington
19. Mel Levine, Calif., and Richard H. Lehman, Calif. — California

The six states not covered — Alaska, Maine, Nebraska, Utah, Vermont, Wyoming — have no Democratic representatives.

Steering and Policy Committee

Phone: 226-3260 Room: 114 HOB Annex #1

Scheduling of legislation and Democratic committee assignments.

Thomas P. O'Neill Jr., Mass., chairman
Jim Wright, Texas, vice chairman
Richard A. Gephardt, Mo., 2nd vice chairman

Bill Alexander, Ark. †
Charles E. Bennett, Fla.
John B. Breaux, La.
Jack Brooks, Texas
William L. Clay, Mo.
Tony Coelho, Calif. †
Cardiss Collins, Ill.
Thomas A. Daschle, S.D.
Norman D. Dicks, Wash.
Joseph D. Early, Mass.
Vic Fazio, Calif.
Thomas S. Foley, Wash. †
Wyche Fowler Jr., Ga.
Robert Garcia, N.Y.
William H. Gray III, Pa. †
Steny H. Hoyer, Md.
Ed Jenkins, Ga.
James R. Jones, Okla.
Paul E. Kanjorski, Pa.
Barbara B. Kennelly, Conn.
John P. Murtha, Pa.
Mary Rose Oakar, Ohio †
Claude Pepper, Fla. †
Dan Rostenkowski, Ill. †
Marty Russo, Ill.
Martin Olav Sabo, Minn.
Henry A. Waxman, Calif.
Jamie L. Whitten, Miss. †

† Member *ex officio* from the leadership.

Personnel Committee

Phone: 225-4068 Room: B343 RHOB

Selects, appoints and supervises Democratic patronage positions.

Membership had not been determined.

Democratic Congressional Campaign Committee

Phone: 863-1500 430 S. Capitol St. S.E. 20003

Campaign support committee for Democratic House candidates.

Tony Coelho, Calif., chairman
Dan Rostenkowski, Ill., vice chairman

Joseph P. Addabbo, N.Y.
Bill Alexander, Ark. †
Frank Annunzio, Ill.
Beryl Anthony Jr., Ark.
Les AuCoin, Ore.
Tom Bevill, Ala.
Don Bonker, Wash.
Thomas R. Carper, Del.
Bill Chappell Jr., Fla.
William L. Clay, Mo.
Thomas A. Daschle, S.D.
Ron de Lugo, Virgin Islands
Butler Derrick, S.C.
John D. Dingell, Mich.
Brian J. Donnelly, Mass.
Byron L. Dorgan, N.D.
Wayne Dowdy, Miss.
Walter E. Fauntroy, D.C.
James J. Florio, N.J.
Thomas S. Foley, Wash. †
Wyche Fowler Jr., Ga.
Jaime B. Fuster, Puerto Rico
Sam Gejdenson, Conn.
Richard A. Gephardt, Mo. †
Dan Glickman, Kan.
Bart Gordon, Tenn.
Lee H. Hamilton, Ind.
Cecil Heftel, Hawaii
Steny H. Hoyer, Md.
James R. Jones, Okla.
John P. Murtha, Pa.
William H. Natcher, Ky.
Mary Rose Oakar, Ohio
James L. Oberstar, Minn.
David R. Obey, Wis.
Thomas P. O'Neill Jr., Mass. †
J. J. Pickle, Texas
Nick J. Rahall II, W.Va.
Harry Reid, Nev.
Bill Richardson, N.M.
Charlie Rose, N.C.
Fernand J. St Germain, R.I.
Patricia Schroeder, Colo.
Norman Sisisky, Va.
Neal Smith, Iowa
Fofō I. F. Sunia, American Samoa
W. J. "Billy" Tauzin, La.
Morris K. Udall, Ariz.
Henry A. Waxman, Calif.
Pat Williams, Mont.
Jim Wright, Texas †

† Member *ex officio* from the leadership.

REPUBLICANS

Robert H. Michel
Minority Leader

Trent Lott
Minority Whip

Jack F. Kemp
Conference Chairman

Lynn Martin
Conference Vice Chairman

Party Leadership

Minority Leader — Robert H. Michel, Ill.	225-0600
Minority Whip — Trent Lott, Miss.	225-0197
Chairman of the Conference — Jack F. Kemp, N.Y.	225-5107
Vice Chairman of the Conference — Lynn Martin, Ill.	225-5107
Secretary of the Conference — Robert J. Lagomarsino, Calif.	225-5107
Chief Deputy Whip — Tom Loeffler, Texas	225-4236
Deputy Whips — Olympia J. Snowe, Maine	225-6306
— Dan Burton, Ind.	225-2276
Sophomore Class Whip — John R. Kasich, Ohio	225-5355
Freshman Class Whip — Dean A. Gallo, N.J.	225-5034

The assistant minority whips are divided into four divisions, each with an overall regional whip and assistant whips in charge of a specific number of members as follows:

Northeast Region - Jim Courter, N.J. (10 states, 39 members):

Judd Gregg, N.H. (9 members)
David O'B. Martin, N.Y. (10 members)
Richard T. Schulze, Pa. (11 members)
Gerald B. H. Solomon, N.Y. (9 members)

Midwest Region - Arlan Stangeland, Minn. (8 states, 41 members):

E. Thomas Coleman, Mo. (11 members)
Carl D. Pursell, Mich. (11 members)
Vin Weber, Minn. (10 members)
Chalmers P. Wylie, Ohio (9 members)

Western Region - Mickey Edwards, Okla. (15 states, 44 members):

Hank Brown, Colo. (11 members)
Duncan L. Hunter, Calif. (11 members)
Manuel Lujan Jr., N.M. (11 members)
Sid Morrison, Wash. (11 members)

Southern Region - Bob Livingston, La. (12 states, 42 members)

Thomas J. Bliley Jr., Va. (10 members)
Steve Bartlett, Texas (10 members)
Carroll A. Campbell Jr., S.C. (11 members)
William L. Dickinson, Ala. (11 members)

The five states not covered — Delaware, Hawaii, North Dakota, South Dakota, West Virginia — have no Republican representatives.

Committee on Committees

Phone: 225-0600 Room: H-230 Capitol

Makes Republican committee assignments.

Robert H. Michel, Ill., chairman

Bill Archer, Texas
Ben Blaz, Guam
William S. Broomfield, Mich.
Hank Brown, Colo.
James T. Broyhill, N.C.
Dan Burton, Ind.
Rod Chandler, Wash.
Dick Cheney, Wyo.
E. Thomas Coleman, Mo.
Silvio O. Conte, Mass.
Jim Courter, N.J.
Larry E. Craig, Idaho
Thomas D. DeLay, Texas
William L. Dickinson, Ala.
John J. Duncan, Tenn.
Mickey Edwards, Okla.
Cooper Evans, Iowa
Bill Frenzel, Minn.
Judd Gregg, N.H.
John Paul Hammerschmidt, Ark.
Marjorie S. Holt, Md.
Frank Horton, N.Y.
James M. Jeffords, Vt.
Delbert L. Latta, Ohio
Virginia Smith, Neb.
Olympia J. Snowe, Maine
Floyd Spence, S.C.
Pat Swindall, Ga.
Barbara F. Vucanovich, Nev.
G. William Whitehurst, Va.
Bob Whittaker, Kan.
C. W. Bill Young, Fla.
Don Young, Alaska
Jerry Lewis, Calif.
Trent Lott, Miss.
Ron Marlenee, Mont.
Joseph M. McDade, Pa.
Stewart B. McKinney, Conn.
W. Henson Moore, La.
John T. Myers, Ind.
Howard C. Nielson, Utah
Thomas E. Petri, Wis.
Harold Rogers, Ky.
Eldon Rudd, Ariz.
Claudine Schneider, R.I.
Joe Skeen, N.M.
Robert F. Smith, Ore.

Personnel Committee

Phone: 225-0833 Room: 1620 LHOB

Selects, appoints and supervises Republican patronage positions.

Membership had not been determined.

Policy Committee

Phone: 225-6168 Room: 1620 LHOB

Advises on party action and policy.

Dick Cheney, Wyo., chairman

Robert E. Badham, Calif.
Steve Bartlett, Texas
Doug Bereuter, Neb.
Beau Boulter, Texas
Dan Coats, Ind.
Silvio O. Conte, Mass.
Thomas D. DeLay, Texas
John J. Duncan, Tenn.
Hamilton Fish Jr., N.Y.
Bill Frenzel, Minn.
Bill Hendon, N.C.
Jack F. Kemp, N.Y.
Robert J. Lagomarsino, Calif.
Delbert L. Latta, Ohio
Jerry Lewis, Calif.
Trent Lott, Miss.
Lynn Martin, Ill.
Bill McCollum, Fla.
Jan Meyers, Kan.
Robert H. Michel, Ill.
W. Henson Moore, La.
Howard C. Nielson, Utah
James H. Quillen, Tenn.
Ralph Regula, Ohio
Bill Schuette, Mich.
Floyd Spence, S.C.
Mike Strang, Colo.
Guy Vander Jagt, Mich.
Barbara F. Vucanovich, Nev.
Vacancy

National Republican Congressional Committee

Phone: 479-7000 320 First St. S.E. 20003

Campaign support committee for Republican House candidates.

Guy Vander Jagt, Mich., chairman

Helen Delich Bentley, Md.
Ben Blaz, Guam
Beau Boulter, Texas
Sonny Callahan, Ala.
Dick Cheney, Wyo. †
Bill Cobey, N.C.
Silvio O. Conte, Mass.
Lawrence Coughlin, Pa.
Larry E. Craig, Idaho
Hal Daub, Neb.
Mickey Edwards, Okla.
Webb Franklin, Miss.
Newt Gingrich, Ga.
Steve Gunderson, Wis.
John Paul Hammerschmidt, Ark.
Thomas F. Hartnett, S.C.
John Hiler, Ind.
Marjorie S. Holt, Md.
Larry J. Hopkins, Ky.
James M. Jeffords, Vt.
Nancy L. Johnson, Conn.
Jack F. Kemp, N.Y. †
Ken Kramer, Colo.
Robert J. Lagomarsino, Calif. †
Norman F. Lent, N.Y.
Jerry Lewis, Calif. †
Bob Livingston, La.
Tom Loeffler, Texas
Trent Lott, Miss. †
Manuel Lujan Jr., N.M.
Connie Mack, Fla.
Edward R. Madigan, Ill.
Ron Marlenee, Mont.
Lynn Martin, Ill. †
Bill McCollum, Fla.
John R. McKernan Jr., Maine
Robert H. Michel, Ill. †
Clarence E. Miller, Ohio
David S. Monson, Utah
Sid Morrison, Wash.
Stan Parris, Va.
Matthew J. Rinaldo, N.J.
Pat Roberts, Kan.
Claudine Schneider, R.I.
Denny Smith, Ore.
Robert C. Smith, N.H.
Bob Stump, Ariz.
Don Sundquist, Tenn.
Tom Tauke, Iowa
Gene Taylor, Mo.
William M. Thomas, Calif.
Guy Vander Jagt, Mich.
Barbara F. Vucanovich, Nev.
Vin Weber, Minn.
Don Young, Alaska

† Member *ex officio* from the leadership.

Index of Senators' Committee Assignments

Abdnor: Appropriations; Environment and Public Works; Select Indian Affairs; Joint Economic.

Andrews: Agriculture, Nutrition and Forestry; Appropriations; Budget; Select Indian Affairs, chairman.

Armstrong: Banking, Housing and Urban Affairs; Budget; Finance.

Baucus: Environment and Public Works; Finance; Small Business.

Bentsen: Environment and Public Works; Finance; Select Intelligence; Joint Economic; Joint Taxation.

Biden: Foreign Relations; Judiciary.

Bingaman: Armed Services; Energy and Natural Resources; Special Aging.

Boren: Agriculture, Nutrition and Forestry; Finance; Select Intelligence; Small Business.

Boschwitz: Agriculture, Nutrition and Forestry; Budget; Foreign Relations; Small Business; Veterans' Affairs.

Bradley: Energy and Natural Resources; Finance; Select Intelligence; Special Aging.

Bumpers: Appropriations; Energy and Natural Resources; Small Business.

Burdick: Appropriations; Environment and Public Works; Select Indian Affairs; Special Aging.

Byrd: Minority Leader; Appropriations; Judiciary; Rules and Administration.

Chafee: Environment and Public Works; Finance.

Chiles: Appropriations; Budget; Governmental Affairs; Special Aging.

Cochran: Agriculture, Nutrition and Forestry; Appropriations; Governmental Affairs.

Cohen: Armed Services; Governmental Affairs; Select Intelligence; Special Aging.

Cranston: Minority Whip; Banking, Housing and Urban Affairs; Foreign Relations; Veterans' Affairs.

D'Amato: Appropriations; Banking, Housing and Urban Affairs; Small Business; Joint Economic.

Danforth: Budget; Commerce, Science and Transportation, chairman; Finance.

DeConcini: Appropriations; Judiciary; Rules and Administration; Select Indian Affairs; Veterans' Affairs; Joint Printing.

Denton: Armed Services; Judiciary; Special Aging; Veterans' Affairs.

Dixon: Agriculture, Nutrition and Forestry; Armed Services; Banking, Housing and Urban Affairs; Small Business.

Dodd: Banking, Housing and Urban Affairs; Foreign Relations; Labor and Human Resources; Special Aging.

Dole: Majority Leader; Agriculture, Nutrition and Forestry; Finance; Rules and Administration; Joint Taxation.

Domenici: Appropriations; Budget, chairman; Energy and Natural Resources; Environment and Public Works.

Durenberger: Environment and Public Works; Finance; Governmental Affairs; Select Intelligence, chairman.

Eagleton: Foreign Relations; Governmental Affairs; Select Intelligence.

East: Armed Services; Judiciary.

Evans: Energy and Natural Resources; Foreign Relations; Special Aging.

Exon: Armed Services; Budget; Commerce, Science and Transportation.

Ford: Commerce, Science and Transportation; Energy and Natural Resources; Rules and Administration; Joint Printing.

Garn: Appropriations; Banking, Housing and Urban Affairs, chairman; Rules and Administration.

Glenn: Armed Services; Governmental Affairs; Special Aging.

Goldwater: Armed Services, chairman; Commerce, Science and Transportation; Select Indian Affairs; Small Business.

Gore: Commerce, Science and Transportation; Governmental Affairs; Rules and Administration.

Gorton: Banking, Housing and Urban Affairs; Budget; Commerce, Science and Transportation; Select Indian Affairs; Small Business.

Gramm: Armed Services; Banking, Housing and Urban Affairs.

Grassley: Budget; Finance; Judiciary; Labor and Human Resources; Special Aging.

Harkin: Agriculture, Nutrition and Forestry; Appropriations; Small Business.

Hart: Armed Services; Budget; Environment and Public Works.

Hatch: Budget; Judiciary; Labor and Human Resources, chairman; Select Intelligence.

Hatfield: Appropriations, chairman; Energy and Natural Resources; Rules and Administration; Joint Library; Joint Printing.

Hawkins: Agriculture, Nutrition and Forestry; Labor and Human Resources; Special Aging.

Hecht: Banking, Housing and Urban Affairs; Energy and Natural Resources; Select Intelligence.

Heflin: Agriculture, Nutrition and Forestry; Judiciary; Select Ethics.

Heinz: Banking, Housing and Urban Affairs; Finance; Special Aging, chairman.

Helms: Agriculture, Nutrition and Forestry, chairman; Foreign Relations; Rules and Administration; Select Ethics.

Hollings: Appropriations; Budget; Commerce, Science and Transportation; Select Intelligence.

Humphrey: Armed Services; Environment and Public Works.

Inouye: Appropriations; Commerce, Science and Transportation; Rules and Administration; Select Indian Affairs; Joint Library.

Johnston: Appropriations; Budget; Energy and Natural Resources; Special Aging.

Kassebaum: Budget; Commerce, Science and Transportation; Foreign Relations; Select Ethics.

Kasten: Appropriations; Budget; Commerce, Science and Transportation; Small Business.

Kennedy: Armed Services; Judiciary; Labor and Human Resources; Joint Economic.

Kerry: Foreign Relations; Labor and Human Resources; Small Business.

Lautenberg: Appropriations; Budget; Environment and Public Works.

Laxalt: Appropriations; Judiciary.

Leahy: Agriculture, Nutrition and Forestry; Appropriations; Judiciary; Select Intelligence.

Levin: Armed Services; Governmental Affairs; Small Business.

Long: Commerce, Science and Transportation; Finance; Select Ethics; Joint Taxation.

Lugar: Agriculture, Nutrition and Forestry; Foreign Relations, chairman.

Mathias: Foreign Relations; Governmental Affairs; Judiciary; Rules and Administration, chairman; Joint Library; Joint Printing, chairman.

Matsunaga: Finance; Labor and Human Resources; Veterans' Affairs.
Mattingly: Appropriations; Banking, Housing and Urban Affairs; Joint Economic.
McClure: Appropriations; Energy and Natural Resources, chairman; Rules and Administration.
McConnell: Agriculture, Nutrition and Forestry; Judiciary; Select Intelligence.
Melcher: Agriculture, Nutrition and Forestry; Energy and Natural Resources; Select Indian Affairs; Special Aging.
Metzenbaum: Budget; Energy and Natural Resources; Judiciary; Labor and Human Resources.
Mitchell: Environment and Public Works; Finance; Veterans' Affairs.
Moynihan: Budget; Environment and Public Works; Finance.
Murkowski: Energy and Natural Resources; Foreign Relations; Select Indian Affairs; Select Intelligence; Veterans' Affairs, chairman.
Nickles: Energy and Natural Resources; Labor and Human Resources; Small Business; Special Aging.
Nunn: Armed Services; Governmental Affairs; Select Intelligence; Small Business.
Packwood: Commerce, Science and Transportation; Finance, chairman; Joint Taxation.
Pell: Foreign Relations; Labor and Human Resources; Rules and Administration; Joint Library.
Pressler: Commerce, Science and Transportation; Foreign Relations; Small Business; Special Aging.
Proxmire: Appropriations; Banking, Housing and Urban Affairs; Joint Economic.
Pryor: Agriculture, Nutrition and Forestry; Finance; Select Ethics; Special Aging.
Quayle: Armed Services; Budget; Labor and Human Resources.
Riegle: Banking, Housing and Urban Affairs; Budget; Commerce, Science and Transportation.
Rockefeller: Commerce, Science and Transportation; Energy and Natural Resources; Veterans' Affairs.
Roth: Finance; Governmental Affairs, chairman; Select Intelligence; Joint Economic; Joint Taxation.
Rudman: Appropriations; Governmental Affairs; Select Ethics, chairman; Small Business.
Sarbanes: Banking, Housing and Urban Affairs; Foreign Relations; Joint Economic.
Sasser: Appropriations; Banking, Housing and Urban Affairs; Budget; Small Business.
Simon: Judiciary; Labor and Human Resources; Rules and Administration.
Simpson: Environment and Public Works; Judiciary; Veterans' Affairs.
Specter: Appropriations; Judiciary; Select Intelligence; Veterans' Affairs.
Stafford: Environment and Public Works, chairman; Labor and Human Resources; Veterans' Affairs.
Stennis: Appropriations; Armed Services.
Stevens: Appropriations; Commerce, Science and Transportation; Governmental Affairs; Rules and Administration; Joint Printing.
Symms: Budget; Environment and Public Works; Finance; Joint Economic.
Thurmond: Armed Services; Judiciary, chairman; Labor and Human Resources; Veterans' Affairs.
Trible: Commerce, Science and Transportation; Foreign Relations; Small Business.
Wallop: Energy and Natural Resources; Finance; Labor and Human Resources.
Warner: Armed Services; Energy and Natural Resources; Rules and Administration; Special Aging; Joint Library.
Weicker: Appropriations; Energy and Natural Resources; Labor and Human Resources; Small Business, chairman.
Wilson: Agriculture, Nutrition and Forestry; Armed Services; Special Aging; Joint Economic.
Zorinsky: Agriculture, Nutrition and Forestry; Foreign Relations.

Index of Representatives' Committee Assignments

Ackerman: Foreign Affairs; Post Office and Civil Service.
Addabbo: Appropriations; Small Business.
Akaka: Appropriations; Select Narcotics Abuse and Control.
Alexander: Appropriations.
Anderson: Merchant Marine and Fisheries; Public Works and Transportation.
Andrews: Public Works and Transportation; Science and Technology.
Annunzio: Banking, Finance and Urban Affairs; House Administration, chairman; Joint Library, chairman; Joint Printing.
Anthony: Select Children, Youth and Families; Ways and Means.
Applegate: Public Works and Transportation; Veterans' Affairs.
Archer: Ways and Means; Joint Taxation.
Armey: Education and Labor; Government Operations.
Aspin: Armed Services, chairman.
Atkins: Budget; Education and Labor; Public Works and Transportation.
AuCoin: Appropriations.
Badham: Armed Services; House Administration; Joint Printing.
Barnard: Banking, Finance and Urban Affairs; Government Operations.
Barnes: Budget; District of Columbia; Foreign Affairs.
Bartlett: Banking, Finance and Urban Affairs; Education and Labor.
Barton: Interior and Insular Affairs; Science and Technology.
Bateman: Armed Services; Merchant Marine and Fisheries.
Bates: Energy and Commerce; House Administration.
Bedell: Agriculture; Small Business.
Beilenson: Rules; Select Intelligence.
Bennett: Armed Services; Merchant Marine and Fisheries.
Bentley: Merchant Marine and Fisheries; Public Works and Transportation; Select Aging.
Bereuter: Banking, Finance and Urban Affairs; Foreign Affairs; Select Hunger.
Berman: Foreign Affairs; Judiciary.
Bevill: Appropriations.
Biaggi: Education and Labor; Merchant Marine and Fisheries; Select Aging.
Bilirakis: Energy and Commerce; Veterans' Affairs.
Blaz: Armed Services; Interior and Insular Affairs; Select Aging.
Bliley: District of Columbia; Energy and Commerce; Select Children, Youth and Families.
Boehlert: Public Works and Transportation; Science and Technology; Select Aging.
Boggs: Appropriations; Select Children, Youth and Families.
Boland: Appropriations.
Boner: Appropriations; Select Aging.
Bonior: Rules.
Bonker: Foreign Affairs; Merchant Marine and Fisheries; Select Aging.
Borski: Merchant Marine and Fisheries; Public Works and Transportation; Select Aging.
Bosco: Merchant Marine and Fisheries; Public Works and Transportation.
Boucher: Education and Labor; Judiciary; Science and Technology; Select Aging.
Boulter: Budget.
Boxer: Budget; Government Operations; Select Children, Youth and Families.
Breaux: Merchant Marine and Fisheries; Public Works and Transportation.
Brooks: Government Operations, chairman; Judiciary.
Broomfield: Foreign Affairs; Small Business.
Brown (Calif.): Agriculture; Science and Technology; Select Intelligence.
Brown (Colo.): Budget; Judiciary.
Broyhill: Energy and Commerce.
Bruce: Agriculture; Education and Labor; Science and Technology.
Bryant: Energy and Commerce; Judiciary; Veterans' Affairs.
Burton (Calif.): Rules; Select Hunger.
Burton (Ind.): Foreign Affairs; Post Office and Civil Service; Select Children, Youth and Families; Veterans' Affairs.
Bustamante: Armed Services; Government Operations.
Byron: Armed Services; Interior and Insular Affairs; Select Aging.
Callahan: Merchant Marine and Fisheries; Public Works and Transportation.
Campbell: Ways and Means.
Carney: Armed Services; Merchant Marine and Fisheries.
Carper: Banking, Finance and Urban Affairs; Merchant Marine and Fisheries.
Carr: Appropriations.
Chandler: Banking, Finance and Urban Affairs; Education and Labor.
Chappell: Appropriations.
Chappie: Agriculture; Merchant Marine and Fisheries; Select Narcotics Abuse and Control.
Cheney: Interior and Insular Affairs; Select Intelligence.
Clay: Education and Labor; House Administration; Post Office and Civil Service.
Clinger: Government Operations; Public Works and Transportation.
Coats: Energy and Commerce; Select Children, Youth and Families.
Cobey: Science and Technology; Small Business.
Coble: Judiciary; Small Business.
Coelho: Agriculture; House Administration; Interior and Insular Affairs.
Coleman (Mo.): Agriculture; Education and Labor.
Coleman (Texas): Appropriations.
Collins: Energy and Commerce; Government Operations; Select Narcotics Abuse and Control.
Combest: Agriculture.
Conte: Appropriations; Small Business.
Conyers: Government Operations; Judiciary.
Cooper: Banking, Finance and Urban Affairs; Small Business.
Coughlin: Appropriations; Select Narcotics Abuse and Control.
Courter: Armed Services; Select Aging.
Coyne: Standards of Official Conduct; Ways and Means.
Craig: Government Operations; Interior and Insular Affairs.
Crane: Ways and Means.
Crockett: Foreign Affairs; Judiciary; Select Aging.
Daniel: Armed Services; Select Intelligence.
Dannemeyer: Energy and Commerce; Judiciary;
Darden: Armed Services; Interior and Insular Affairs
Daschle: Agriculture; Select Hunger; Veterans' Affairs.
Daub: Ways and Means.

Davis: Armed Services; Merchant Marine and Fisheries.
de la Garza: Agriculture, chairman.
DeLay: Government Operations; Public Works and Transportation.
Dellums: Armed Services; District of Columbia, chairman.
de Lugo: Interior and Insular Affairs; Post Office and Civil Service; Public Works and Transportation.
Derrick: Budget; Rules; Select Aging.
DeWine: Foreign Affairs; Judiciary.
Dickinson: Armed Services; House Administration.
Dicks: Appropriations.
Dingell: Energy and Commerce, chairman.
DioGuardi: Government Operations; Select Narcotics Abuse and Control; Small Business.
Dixon: Appropriations; Standards of Official Conduct, chairman.
Donnelly: Ways and Means.
Dorgan: Select Hunger; Ways and Means.
Dornan: Foreign Affairs.
Dowdy: Energy and Commerce; Veterans' Affairs.
Downey: Budget; Select Aging; Ways and Means.
Dreier: Banking, Finance and Urban Affairs; Small Business.
Duncan: Ways and Means; Joint Taxation.
Durbin: Appropriations.
Dwyer: Appropriations; Select Intelligence; Standards of Official Conduct.
Dymally: District of Columbia; Education and Labor; Foreign Affairs; Post Office and Civil Service.
Dyson: Armed Services; Merchant Marine and Fisheries.
Early: Appropriations.
Eckart (Ohio): Education and Labor; Energy and Commerce; Small Business.
Eckert (N.Y.): Energy and Commerce.
Edgar: Public Works and Transportation; Veterans' Affairs.
Edwards (Calif.): Judiciary; Veterans' Affairs.
Edwards (Okla.): Appropriations.
Emerson: Agriculture; Interior and Insular Affairs; Select Hunger.
English: Agriculture; Government Operations.
Erdreich: Banking, Finance and Urban Affairs; Government Operations; Select Aging.
Evans (Ill.): Agriculture; Select Children, Youth and Families; Veterans' Affairs.
Evans (Iowa): Agriculture; Select Hunger.
Fascell: Foreign Affairs, chairman; Select Narcotics Abuse and Control.
Fauntroy: Banking, Finance and Urban Affairs; District of Columbia; Select Narcotics Abuse and Control.
Fawell: Education and Labor; Science and Technology; Select Aging.
Fazio: Appropriations; Budget; Select Hunger; Standards of Official Conduct.
Feighan: Foreign Affairs; Judiciary.
Fiedler: Budget; Joint Economic.
Fields: Energy and Commerce; Merchant Marine and Fisheries.
Fish: Judiciary; Select Children, Youth and Families.
Flippo: Ways and Means.
Florio: Energy and Commerce; Select Aging; Veterans' Affairs.
Foglietta: Armed Services; Merchant Marine and Fisheries.
Foley: Majority Whip; Agriculture; House Administration.
Ford (Mich.): Education and Labor; Post Office and Civil Service, chairman.
Ford (Tenn.): Select Aging; Ways and Means.
Fowler: Ways and Means.
Frank: Banking, Finance and Urban Affairs; Government Operations; Judiciary; Select Aging.
Franklin: Agriculture; Merchant Marine and Fisheries.
Frenzel: House Administration; Ways and Means.
Frost: Budget; Rules.
Fuqua: Government Operations; Science and Technology, chairman.
Fuster: Banking, Finance and Urban Affairs; Interior and Insular Affairs.
Gallo: Public Works and Transportation; Small Business.
Garcia: Banking, Finance and Urban Affairs; Foreign Affairs; Post Office and Civil Service.
Gaydos: Education and Labor; House Administration; Joint Printing.
Gejdenson: Foreign Affairs; House Administration; Interior and Insular Affairs; Select Hunger.
Gekas: Judiciary; Select Aging.
Gephardt: Ways and Means.
Gibbons: Ways and Means; Joint Taxation.
Gilman: Foreign Affairs; Post Office and Civil Service; Select Hunger; Select Narcotics Abuse and Control.
Gingrich: House Administration; Public Works and Transportation; Joint Library.
Glickman: Agriculture; Judiciary; Science and Technology.
Gonzalez: Banking, Finance and Urban Affairs; Small Business.
Goodling: Budget; Education and Labor.
Gordon: Banking, Finance and Urban Affairs; Science and Technology; Select Aging.
Gradison: Budget; Ways and Means.
Gray (Ill.): Public Works and Transportation; Veterans' Affairs.
Gray (Pa.): Appropriations; Budget, chairman; District of Columbia.
Green: Appropriations.
Gregg: Ways and Means.
Grotberg: Banking, Finance and Urban Affairs; Small Business.
Guarini: Select Narcotics Abuse and Control; Ways and Means.
Gunderson: Agriculture; Education and Labor.
Hall, Ralph (Texas): Energy and Commerce; Science and Technology.
Hall, Tony (Ohio): Rules; Select Hunger.
Hamilton: Foreign Affairs; Select Intelligence, chairman; Joint Economic.
Hammerschmidt: Public Works and Transportation; Select Aging; Veterans' Affairs.
Hansen: Interior and Insular Affairs; Post Office and Civil Service; Standards of Official Conduct.
Hartnett: Armed Services; Merchant Marine and Fisheries.
Hatcher: Agriculture; Small Business.
Hawkins: Education and Labor, chairman; Joint Economic.
Hayes: Education and Labor; Small Business.
Hefner: Appropriations; Budget.
Heftel: Ways and Means.
Hendon: Interior and Insular Affairs; Veterans' Affairs.
Henry: Education and Labor; Science and Technology; Select Aging.
Hertel: Armed Services; Merchant Marine and Fisheries; Select Aging.
Hiler: Banking, Finance and Urban Affairs; Small Business.
Hillis: Armed Services; Veterans' Affairs.
Holt: Armed Services.
Hopkins: Agriculture; Armed Services.
Horton: Government Operations; Post Office & Civil Service.

Howard: Public Works and Transportation, chairman.
Hoyer: Appropriations.
Hubbard: Banking, Finance and Urban Affairs; Merchant Marine and Fisheries.
Huckaby: Agriculture; Interior and Insular Affairs.
Hughes: Judiciary; Merchant Marine and Fisheries; Select Aging; Select Narcotics Abuse and Control.
Hunter: Armed Services; Select Narcotics Abuse and Control.
Hutto: Armed Services; Merchant Marine and Fisheries.
Hyde: Foreign Affairs; Judiciary; Select Intelligence.
Ireland: Select Intelligence; Small Business.
Jacobs: Ways and Means.
Jeffords: Agriculture; Education and Labor; Select Aging.
Jenkins: Budget; Standards of Official Conduct; Ways and Means.
Johnson: Public Works and Transportation; Select Children, Youth and Families; Veterans' Affairs.
Jones (N.C.): Agriculture; Merchant Marine and Fisheries, chairman.
Jones (Okla.): Ways and Means.
Jones (Tenn.): Agriculture; House Administration; Joint Printing.
Kanjorski: Banking, Finance and Urban Affairs; Veterans' Affairs.
Kaptur: Banking, Finance and Urban Affairs; Veterans' Affairs.
Kasich: Armed Services.
Kastenmeier: Judiciary; Select Intelligence.
Kemp: Appropriations; Budget.
Kennelly: Ways and Means.
Kildee: Education and Labor; Interior and Insular Affairs.
Kindness: Government Operations; Judiciary.
Kleczka: Banking, Finance and Urban Affairs; Government Operations.
Kolbe: Banking, Finance and Urban Affairs; Select Aging; Small Business.
Kolter: Government Operations; Public Works and Transportation.
Kostmayer: Foreign Affairs; Interior and Insular Affairs; Select Hunger.
Kramer: Armed Services.
LaFalce: Banking, Finance and Urban Affairs; Small Business.
Lagomarsino: Foreign Affairs; Interior and Insular Affairs.
Lantos: Foreign Affairs; Government Operations; Select Aging.
Latta: Budget; Rules.
Leach: Banking, Finance and Urban Affairs; Foreign Affairs.
Leath: Armed Services; Budget.
Lehman (Calif.): Banking, Finance and Urban Affairs; Interior and Insular Affairs.
Lehman (Fla.): Appropriations; Select Children, Youth and Families.
Leland: Energy and Commerce; Post Office and Civil Service; Select Hunger, chairman.
Lent: Energy and Commerce; Merchant Marine and Fisheries.
Levin: Banking, Finance and Urban Affairs; Government Operations; Select Children, Youth and Families.
Levine: Foreign Affairs; Interior and Insular Affairs; Select Narcotics Abuse and Control.
Lewis (Calif.): Appropriations.
Lewis (Fla.): Agriculture; Science and Technology.
Lightfoot: Government Operations; Public Works and Transportation; Select Aging.
Lipinski: Merchant Marine and Fisheries; Public Works and Transportation.
Livingston: Appropriations; Select Intelligence.
Lloyd: Armed Services; Science & Technology; Select Aging.
Loeffler: Appropriations; Budget.
Long: Public Works and Transportation; Small Business.
Lott: Minority Whip; Rules.
Lowery (Calif.): Appropriations.
Lowry (Wash.): Budget; Merchant Marine and Fisheries.
Lujan: Interior and Insular Affairs; Science and Technology.
Luken: Energy and Commerce; Select Aging; Small Business.
Lundine: Banking, Finance and Urban Affairs; Science and Technology; Select Aging.
Lungren: Judiciary; Joint Economic.
Mack: Budget; Foreign Affairs.
MacKay: Budget; Foreign Affairs; Select Aging.
Madigan: Agriculture; Energy and Commerce.
Manton: Banking, Finance and Urban Affairs; Merchant Marine and Fisheries; Select Aging.
Markey: Energy and Commerce; Interior and Insular Affairs.
Marlenee: Agriculture; Interior and Insular Affairs.
Martin (Ill.): Armed Services; Budget.
Martin (N.Y.): Armed Services.
Martinez: Education and Labor; Government Operations; Select Children, Youth and Families.
Matsui: Select Narcotics Abuse and Control; Ways and Means.
Mavroules: Armed Services; Small Business.
Mazzoli: District of Columbia; Judiciary; Small Business.
McCain: Foreign Affairs; Interior and Insular Affairs; Select Aging.
McCandless: Banking, Finance and Urban Affairs; Government Operations.
McCloskey: Armed Services; Post Office and Civil Service.
McCollum: Banking, Finance and Urban Affairs; Judiciary.
McCurdy: Armed Services; Science and Technology; Select Intelligence.
McDade: Appropriations; Small Business.
McEwen: Public Works and Transportation; Select Intelligence; Veterans' Affairs.
McGrath: Ways and Means.
McHugh: Appropriations; Select Children, Youth and Families; Select Intelligence.
McKernan: Education and Labor; Merchant Marine and Fisheries; Select Children, Youth and Families.
McKinney: Banking, Finance and Urban Affairs; District of Columbia.
McMillan: Banking, Finance and Urban Affairs; Small Business.
Meyers (Kan.): Science and Technology; Select Aging; Small Business.
Mica: Foreign Affairs; Select Aging; Veterans' Affairs.
Michel: Minority Leader.
Mikulski: Energy and Commerce; Merchant Marine and Fisheries.
Miller (Calif.): Budget; Interior and Insular Affairs; Select Children, Youth and Families, chairman.
Miller (Ohio): Appropriations.
Miller (Wash.): Government Operations; Merchant Marine and Fisheries.
Mineta: Public Works and Transportation; Science and Technology.
Mitchell: Banking, Finance and Urban Affairs; Small Business, chairman; Joint Economic.
Moakley: Rules.
Molinari: Public Works and Transportation; Veterans' Affairs.
Mollohan: Interior and Insular Affairs; Standards of Official Conduct; Veterans' Affairs.

Monson: Government Operations; Science and Technology; Select Children, Youth and Families.
Montgomery: Armed Services; Veterans' Affairs, chairman.
Moody: Interior and Insular Affairs; Public Works and Transportation.
Moore: Budget; Ways and Means.
Moorhead: Energy and Commerce; Judiciary.
Morrison (Conn.): Banking, Finance and Urban Affairs; Judiciary; Select Children, Youth and Families.
Morrison (Wash.): Agriculture; Science and Technology; Select Hunger.
Mrazek: Appropriations.
Murphy: Education and Labor; Interior and Insular Affairs.
Murtha: Appropriations.
Myers (Ind.): Appropriations; Post Office and Civil Service; Standards of Official Conduct.
Natcher: Appropriations.
Neal: Banking, Finance and Urban Affairs; Government Operations.
Nelson: Banking, Finance and Urban Affairs; Science and Technology.
Nichols: Armed Services.
Nielson: Energy and Commerce; Government Operations.
Nowak: Public Works and Transportation; Small Business.
Oakar: Banking, Finance and Urban Affairs; House Administration; Post Office and Civil Service; Select Aging; Joint Library.
Oberstar: Merchant Marine and Fisheries; Public Works and Transportation.
Obey: Appropriations; Joint Economic, chairman.
O'Brien: Appropriations.
Olin: Agriculture; Small Business.
O'Neill: Speaker of the House.
Ortiz: Armed Services; Merchant Marine and Fisheries; Select Narcotics Abuse and Control.
Owens: Education and Labor; Government Operations.
Oxley: Energy and Commerce; Select Narcotics Abuse and Control.
Packard: Public Works and Transportation; Science and Technology.
Panetta: Agriculture; House Administration; Select Hunger.
Parris: Banking, Finance and Urban Affairs; District of Columbia; Select Narcotics Abuse and Control.
Pashayan: Interior and Insular Affairs; Post Office and Civil Service.
Pease: Ways and Means.
Penny: Agriculture; Education and Labor; Veterans' Affairs.
Pepper: Rules, chairman; Select Aging.
Perkins: Education and Labor; Public Works and Transportation.
Petri: Education and Labor; Public Works and Transportation.
Pickle: Ways and Means; Joint Taxation.
Porter: Appropriations.
Price: Armed Services.
Pursell: Appropriations; Standards of Official Conduct.
Quillen: Rules.
Rahall: Interior and Insular Affairs; Public Works and Transportation.
Rangel: Select Narcotics Abuse and Control, chairman; Ways and Means.
Ray: Armed Services; Small Business.
Regula: Appropriations; Select Aging.
Reid: Foreign Affairs; Science and Technology; Select Aging.
Richardson: Energy and Commerce; Interior and Insular Affairs; Select Aging.
Ridge: Banking, Finance and Urban Affairs; Select Aging; Veterans' Affairs.
Rinaldo: Energy and Commerce; Select Aging.
Ritter: Energy and Commerce; Science and Technology.
Roberts: Agriculture; House Administration; Joint Library; Joint Printing.
Robinson: Armed Services; Select Aging; Small Business; Veterans' Affairs.
Rodino: Judiciary, chairman; Select Narcotics Abuse and Control.
Roe: Public Works and Transportation; Science and Technology; Select Intelligence.
Roemer: Banking, Finance and Urban Affairs; Small Business.
Rogers: Appropriations.
Rose: Agriculture; House Administration.
Rostenkowski: Ways and Means, chairman; Joint Taxation, chairman.
Roth: Banking, Finance and Urban Affairs; Foreign Affairs.
Roukema: Banking, Finance and Urban Affairs; Education and Labor; Select Hunger.
Rowland (Conn.): Government Operations; Select Narcotics Abuse and Control; Veterans' Affairs.
Rowland (Ga.): Public Works and Transportation; Select Children, Youth and Families; Veterans' Affairs.
Roybal: Appropriations; Select Aging, chairman.
Rudd: Appropriations.
Russo: Budget; Ways and Means.
Sabo: Appropriations.
St Germain: Banking, Finance and Urban Affairs, chairman.
Savage: Public Works and Transportation; Small Business.
Saxton: Government Operations; Merchant Marine and Fisheries; Select Aging.
Schaefer: Energy and Commerce.
Scheuer: Energy and Commerce; Science and Technology; Select Narcotics Abuse and Control; Joint Economic.
Schneider: Merchant Marine and Fisheries; Science and Technology; Select Aging.
Schroeder: Armed Services; Judiciary; Post Office and Civil Service; Select Children, Youth and Families.
Schuette: Agriculture; Select Aging.
Schulze: Ways and Means.
Schumer: Banking, Finance and Urban Affairs; Budget; Judiciary.
Seiberling: Interior and Insular Affairs; Judiciary.
Sensenbrenner: Judiciary; Science and Technology.
Sharp: Energy and Commerce; Interior and Insular Affairs.
Shaw: Judiciary; Public Works and Transportation; Select Narcotics Abuse and Control.
Shelby: Energy and Commerce; Veterans' Affairs.
Shumway: Banking, Finance and Urban Affairs; Merchant Marine and Fisheries; Select Aging.
Shuster: Public Works and Transportation.
Sikorski: Energy and Commerce; Post Office and Civil Service; Select Children, Youth and Families.
Siljander: Foreign Affairs; Select Aging.
Sisisky: Armed Services; Select Aging; Small Business.
Skeen: Appropriations.
Skelton: Armed Services; Select Aging; Small Business.
Slattery: Budget; Energy and Commerce.
Slaughter: Science and Technology; Small Business.
Smith, Christopher (N.J.): Foreign Affairs; Select Aging; Veterans' Affairs.
Smith, Denny (Ore.): Budget; Interior and Insular Affairs.
Smith, Larry (Fla.): Foreign Affairs; Judiciary; Select Narcotics Abuse and Control.
Smith, Neal (Iowa): Appropriations; Small Business.
Smith, Robert C. (N.H.): Science and Technology; Select Children, Youth and Families; Small Business.

Smith, Robert F. (Ore.): Agriculture; Select Hunger.
Smith, Virginia (Neb.): Appropriations.
Snowe: Foreign Affairs; Select Aging; Joint Economic.
Snyder: Merchant Marine and Fisheries; Public Works and Transportation.
Solarz: Education and Labor; Foreign Affairs; Post Office and Civil Service.
Solomon: Foreign Affairs; Veterans' Affairs.
Spence: Armed Services; Standards of Official Conduct.
Spratt: Armed Services; Government Operations.
Staggers: Agriculture; Judiciary; Veterans' Affairs.
Stallings: Agriculture; Science and Technology; Select Aging.
Stangeland: Agriculture; Public Works and Transportation.
Stark: District of Columbia; Select Narcotics Abuse and Control; Ways and Means; Joint Economic.
Stenholm: Agriculture; Small Business.
Stokes: Appropriations; Select Intelligence.
Strang: Interior and Insular Affairs; Select Narcotics Abuse and Control.
Stratton: Armed Services.
Studds: Foreign Affairs; Merchant Marine and Fisheries.
Stump: Armed Services; Select Intelligence.
Sundquist: Public Works and Transportation; Veterans' Affairs.
Sunia: Interior and Insular Affairs; Public Works and Transportation.
Sweeney: Armed Services.
Swift: Energy and Commerce; House Administration; Joint Library.
Swindall: Government Operations; Judiciary; Select Aging.
Synar: Energy and Commerce; Government Operations; Judiciary; Select Aging.
Tallon: Agriculture; Merchant Marine and Fisheries.
Tauke: Education and Labor; Energy and Commerce; Select Aging.
Tauzin: Energy and Commerce; Merchant Marine and Fisheries.
Taylor: Post Office and Civil Service; Rules.
Thomas (Calif.): House Administration; Ways and Means.
Thomas (Ga.): Agriculture; Merchant Marine and Fisheries.
Torres: Banking, Finance and Urban Affairs; Small Business.
Torricelli: Foreign Affairs; Science and Technology.
Towns: Government Operations; Public Works and Transportation; Select Narcotics Abuse and Control.
Traficant: Public Works and Transportation; Science and Technology.
Traxler: Appropriations; Select Hunger.
Udall: Foreign Affairs; Interior and Insular Affairs, chairman; Post Office and Civil Service.
Valentine: Public Works and Transportation; Science and Technology.
Vander Jagt: Ways and Means.
Vento: Banking, Finance and Urban Affairs; Interior and Insular Affairs; Select Aging.
Visclosky: Interior and Insular Affairs; Public Works and Transportation.
Volkmer: Agriculture; Science and Technology, Select Aging.
Vucanovich: House Administration; Interior and Insular Affairs; Select Children, Youth and Families.
Walgren: Energy and Commerce; Science and Technology.
Walker: Government Operations; Science and Technology.
Watkins: Appropriations.
Waxman: Energy and Commerce; Government Operations; Select Aging.
Weaver: Agriculture; Interior and Insular Affairs.
Weber: Budget; Small Business.
Weiss: Foreign Affairs; Government Operations; Select Children, Youth and Families.
Wheat: District of Columbia; Rules; Select Children, Youth and Families.
Whitehurst: Armed Services; Standards of Official Conduct.
Whitley: Agriculture.
Whittaker: Energy and Commerce.
Whitten: Appropriations, chairman.
Williams: Budget; Education and Labor.
Wilson: Appropriations.
Wirth: Energy and Commerce; Science and Technology.
Wise: Government Operations; Public Works and Transportation; Select Aging.
Wolf: Appropriations; Select Children, Youth and Families.
Wolpe: Budget; Foreign Affairs.
Wortley: Banking, Finance and Urban Affairs; Select Aging; Standards of Official Conduct.
Wright: Majority Leader; Budget.
Wyden: Energy and Commerce; Select Aging; Small Business.
Wylie: Banking, Finance and Urban Affairs; Veterans' Affairs; Joint Economic.
Yates: Appropriations.
Yatron: Foreign Affairs; Post Office and Civil Service.
Young (Alaska): Interior and Insular Affairs; Merchant Marine and Fisheries; Post Office and Civil Service.
Young (Fla.): Appropriations.
Young (Mo.): Public Works and Transportation; Science and Technology.
Zschau: Foreign Affairs.

Map of Capitol Hill

(Dotted line indicates the city's quadrants, which are noted in the corners of the map)

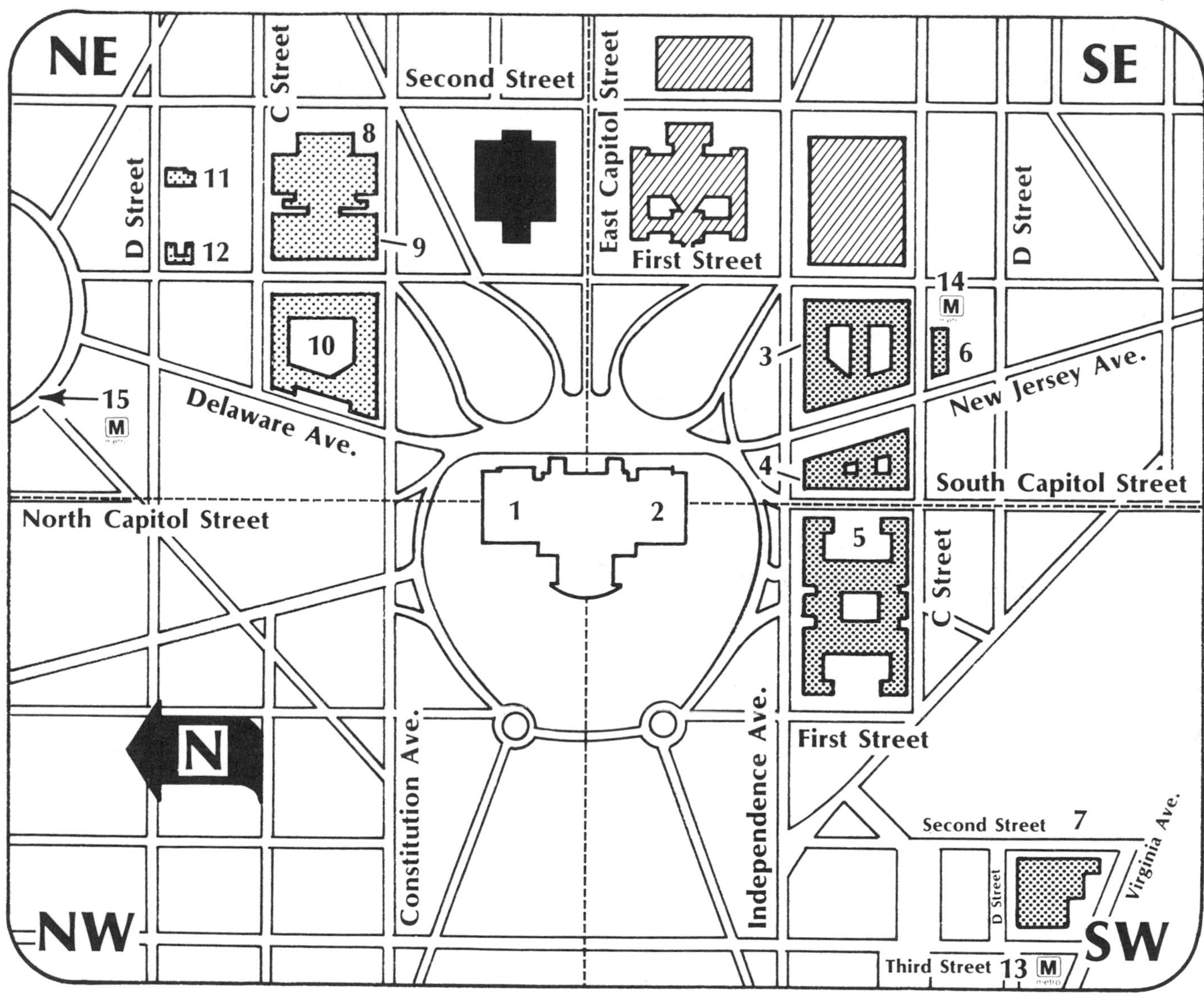

□ U.S. Capitol,
Washington, D.C. 20510 20515*

1 Senate Wing
2 House Wing

▩ House Office Buildings,
Washington, D.C. 20515

3 Cannon
4 Longworth
5 Rayburn
6 House Annex No. 1
7 House Annex No. 2

▩ Senate Office Buildings,
Washington, D.C. 20510

8 Hart
9 Dirksen
10 Russell
11 Immigration Building
12 Plaza Hotel

■ Supreme Court
Washington, D.C. 20543

▨ Library of Congress,
Washington, D.C. 20540

Ⓜ Subway System

13 Federal Center SW Station
14 Capitol South Station
15 Union Station Station

*Mail sent to the U.S. Capitol should bear the ZIP code of the chamber to which it is addressed.

Glossary of Congressional Terms

Act—The term for legislation once it has passed both houses of Congress and has been signed by the president or passed over his veto, thus becoming law. *(See below.)* Also used in parliamentary terminology for a bill that has been passed by one house and engrossed. *(See Engrossed Bill.)*

Adjournment Sine Die—Adjournment without definitely fixing a day for reconvening; literally "adjournment without a day." Usually used to connote the final adjournment of a session of Congress. A session can continue until noon, Jan. 3, of the following year, when, under the 20th Amendment to the Constitution, it automatically terminates. Both houses must agree to a concurrent resolution for either house to adjourn for more than three days.

Adjournment to a Day Certain—Adjournment under a motion or resolution that fixes the next time of meeting. Under the Constitution, neither house can adjourn for more than three days without the concurrence of the other. A session of Congress is not ended by adjournment to a day certain.

Amendment—A proposal of a member of Congress to alter the language, provisions or stipulations in a bill or in another amendment. An amendment usually is printed, debated and voted upon in the same manner as a bill.

Amendment in the Nature of a Substitute—Usually an amendment that seeks to replace the entire text of a bill. Passage of this type of amendment strikes out everything after the enacting clause and inserts a new version of the bill. An amendment in the nature of a substitute also can refer to an amendment that replaces a large portion of the text of a bill.

Appeal—A member's challenge of a ruling or decision made by the presiding officer of the chamber. In the Senate, the senator appeals to members of the chamber to override the decision. If carried by a majority vote, the appeal nullifies the chair's ruling. In the House, the decision of the Speaker traditionally has been final; seldom are there appeals to the members to reverse the Speaker's stand. To appeal a ruling is considered an attack on the Speaker.

Appropriations Bill—A bill that gives legal authority to spend or obligate money from the Treasury. The Constitution disallows money to be drawn from the Treasury "but in Consequence of Appropriations made by Law."

It usually is the case that an appropriations bill provides the actual monies approved by authorization bills, but not necessarily the full amount permissible under the authorization measures. By congressional custom, an appropriations bill originates in the House, and it is not supposed to be considered by the full House or Senate until the related authorization measure is enacted. Under the 1974 Congressional Budget and Impoundment Control Act, general appropriations bills are supposed to be enacted by the seventh day after Labor Day before the start of the fiscal year to which they apply, but in recent years this deadline rarely has been met.

In addition to general appropriations bills, there are two specialized types. *(See Continuing Resolution, Supplemental Appropriations Bill.)*

Authorization—Basic, substantive legislation that establishes or continues the legal operation of a federal program or agency, either indefinitely or for a specific period of time, or which sanctions a particular type of obligation or expenditure. An authorization normally is a prerequisite for an appropriation or other kind of budget authority. Under the rules of both houses, the appropriation for a program or agency may not be considered until its authorization has been considered. An authorization also may limit the amount of budget authority to be provided or may authorize the appropriation of "such sums as may be necessary." *(See also Backdoor Spending.)*

Backdoor Spending—Budget authority provided in legislation outside the normal appropriations process. The most common forms of backdoor spending are borrowing authority, contract authority and entitlements. *(See below.)* In some cases, such as interest on the public debt, a permanent appropriation is provided that becomes available without further action by Congress. The 1974 budget act places limits on the use of backdoor spending.

Bills—Most legislative proposals before Congress are in the form of bills and are designated by HR in the House of Representatives or S in the Senate, according to the house in which they originate, and by a number assigned in the order in which they are introduced during the two-year period of a congressional term. "Public bills" deal with general questions and become public laws if approved by Congress and signed by the president. "Private bills" deal with individual matters such as claims against the government, immigration and naturalization cases, land titles, etc., and become private laws if approved and signed. *(See also Concurrent Resolution, Joint Resolution, Resolution.)*

Bills Introduced—In both the House and Senate, any number of members may join in introducing a single bill or resolution. The first member listed is the sponsor of the bill, and all members' names following his are the bill's cosponsors.

Many bills are committee bills and are introduced under the name of the chairman of the committee or subcommittee. All appropriations bills fall into this category. A committee frequently holds hearings on a number of related bills and may agree to one of them or to an entirely new bill. *(See also Report, Clean Bill, By Request.)*

Bills Referred—When introduced, a bill is referred to the committee or committees that have jurisdiction over the subject with which the bill is concerned. Under the standing rules of the House and Senate, bills are referred by the Speaker in the House and by the presiding officer in the Senate. In practice, the House and Senate parliamentarians act for these officials and refer the vast majority of bills.

Borrowing Authority—Statutory authority that permits a federal agency to incur obligations and make payments for specified purposes with borrowed money. The 1974 budget act sets limits on new borrowing authority, except in certain instances, to the extent or amount provided in appropriations acts.

Budget—The document sent to Congress by the president early each year estimating government revenue and expenditures for the ensuing fiscal year.

Budget Authority—Authority to enter into obligations that will result in immediate or future outlays involving federal funds. The basic forms of budget authority are appropriations, contract authority and borrowing authority. Budget authority may be classified by (1) the period of availability (one-year, multiple-year or without a time limitation), (2) the timing of congressional action (current or permanent), or (3) the manner of determining the amount available (definite or indefinite).

Budget Process—The congressional budget process is organized around two concurrent resolutions. The deadline for approval of the first resolution is May 15. The resolution must be passed before the House and Senate consider appropriations, revenue and entitlement legislation. The deadline for the second budget resolution is Sept. 15, two weeks before the Oct. 1 start of the next fiscal year. (Congress has failed to meet these deadlines in recent years.) The purpose of the budget resolutions is to guide and restrain Congress in its actions on appropriations, spending and revenue bills. A concurrent resolution does not have the force of law. Consequently, Congress cannot appropriate money, impose taxes or directly limit federal expenditures by means of a budget resolution. Unless it otherwise stipulates, Congress is not bound by the targets in the first budget resolution when it acts on appropriations and tax legislation. The second resolution sets a ceiling on new budget authority and outlays and a floor on revenues for the coming year. After its adoption a point of order can be raised against any legislation that would cause expenditures to exceed or revenues to drop below budgeted amounts. Congress can revise its budget decisions at any time during the fiscal year by adopting supplementary budget resolutions.

Budget Reconciliation—The 1974 budget act provides for a "reconciliation" procedure for bringing existing tax and spending laws into conformity with the congressional budget resolutions. Under the procedure, Congress instructs designated legislative committees to approve measures adjusting revenues and expenditures by a certain amount. The committees have a deadline by which they must report the legislation, but they have the discretion of deciding what changes are to be made. The recommendations of the various committees are consolidated without change by the Budget committees into an omnibus reconciliation bill, which then must be considered and approved by both houses of Congress.

By Request—A phrase used when a senator or representative introduces a bill at the request of an executive agency or private organization but does not necessarily endorse the legislation.

Calendar—An agenda or list of business awaiting possible action by each chamber. The House uses five legislative calendars. *(See Consent, Discharge, House, Private and Union Calendar.)*

In the Senate, all legislative matters reported from committee go on one calendar. They are listed there in the order in which committees report them or the Senate places them on the calendar, but may be called up out of order by the majority leader, either by obtaining unanimous consent of the Senate or by a motion to call up a bill. The Senate also uses one non-legislative calendar; this is used for treaties and nominations. *(See Executive Calendar.)*

Calendar Wednesday—In the House, committees, on Wednesdays, may be called in the order in which they appear in Rule X of the House, for the purpose of bringing up any of their bills from either the House or the Union Calendar, except bills that are privileged. General debate is limited to two hours. Bills called up from the Union Calendar are considered in Committee of the Whole. Calendar Wednesday is not observed during the last two weeks of a session and may be dispensed with at other times by a two-thirds vote. This procedure is rarely used and routinely is dispensed with by unanimous consent.

Call of the Calendar—Senate bills that are not brought up for debate by a motion, unanimous consent or a unanimous consent agreement are brought before the Senate for action when the calendar listing them is "called." Bills must be called in the order listed. Measures considered by this method usually are non-controversial, and debate is limited to a total of five minutes for each senator on the bill and any amendments proposed to it.

Chamber—The meeting place for the membership of either the House or the Senate; also the membership of the House or Senate meeting as such.

Clean Bill—Frequently after a committee has finished a major revision of a bill, one of the committee members, usually the chairman, will assemble the changes and what is left of the original bill into a new measure and introduce it as a "clean bill." The revised measure, which is given a new number, then is referred back to the committee, which reports it to the floor for consideration. This often is a timesaver, as committee-recommended changes in a clean bill do not have to be considered and voted on by the chamber. Reporting a clean bill also protects committee amendments that might be subject to points of order concerning germaneness.

Clerk of the House—Chief administrative officer of the House of Representatives, with duties corresponding to those of the secretary of the Senate. *(See also Secretary of the Senate.)*

Cloture—The process by which a filibuster can be ended in the Senate other than by unanimous consent. A motion for cloture can apply to any measure before the Senate, including a proposal to change the chamber's rules.

A cloture motion requires the signatures of 16 senators to be introduced, and to end a filibuster the cloture motion must obtain the votes of three-fifths of the entire Senate membership (60 if there are no vacancies), except that to end a filibuster against a proposal to amend the standing rules of the Senate a two-thirds vote of senators present and voting is required. The cloture request is put to a roll-call vote one hour after the Senate meets on the second day following introduction of the motion. If approved, cloture limits each senator to one hour of debate. The bill or amendment in question comes to a final vote after 100 hours of consideration (including debate time and the time it takes to conduct roll calls, quorum calls and other procedural motions). *(See Filibuster.)*

Committee—A division of the House or Senate that prepares legislation for action by the parent chamber or makes investigations as directed by the parent chamber. There are several types of committees. *(See Standing and Select or Special Committees.)* Most standing committees are divided into subcommittees, which study legislation, hold hearings and report bills, with or without amendments, to the full committee. Only the full committee can report legislation for action by the House or Senate.

Committee of the Whole—The working title of what is formally "The Committee of the Whole House (of Representatives) on the State of the Union." The membership is comprised of all House members sitting as a committee. Any 100 members who are present on the floor of the chamber to consider legislation comprise a quorum of the committee. Any legislation, however, must first have passed through the regular legislative or Appropriations committee and have been placed on the calendar.

Technically, the Committee of the Whole considers only bills directly or indirectly appropriating money, authorizing appropriations or involving taxes or charges on the public. Because the Committee of the Whole need number only 100 representatives, a quorum is more readily attained, and legislative business is expedited. Before 1971, members' positions were not individually recorded on votes taken in Committee of the Whole. *(See Teller Vote.)*

When the full House resolves itself into the Committee of the Whole, it supplants the Speaker with a "chairman." A measure is debated and amendments may be proposed, with votes on amendments as needed. *(See Five-Minute Rule.)* When the committee completes its work on the measure, it dissolves itself by "rising." The Speaker returns, and the chairman of the Committee of the Whole reports to the House that the committee's work has been completed. At this time members may demand a roll-call vote on any amendment *adopted* in the Committee of the Whole. The final vote is on passage of the legislation.

Committee Veto—A requirement added to a few statutes directing that certain policy directives by an executive department or agency be reviewed by certain congressional committees before they are implemented. Under common practice, the government department or agency and the committees involved are expected to reach a consensus before the directives are carried out. *(See also Legislative.)*

Concurrent Resolution—A concurrent resolution, designated H Con Res or S Con Res, must be adopted by both houses, but it is not sent to the president for his signature and therefore does not have the force of law. A concurrent resolution, for example, is used to fix the time for adjournment of a Congress. It also is used as the vehicle for expressing the sense of Congress on various foreign policy and domestic issues, and it serves as the vehicle for coordinated decisions on the federal budget under the 1974 Congressional Budget and Impoundment Control Act. *(See also Bills, Joint Resolution, Resolution.)*

Conference—A meeting between the representatives of the House and the Senate to reconcile differences between the two houses on provisions of a bill passed by both chambers. Members of the conference committee are appointed by the Speaker and the presiding officer of the Senate and are called "managers" for their respective chambers. A majority of the managers for each house must reach agreement on the provisions of the bill (often a compromise between the versions of the two chambers) before it can be considered by either chamber in the form of a "conference report." When the conference report goes to the floor, it cannot be amended, and, if it is not approved by both chambers, the bill may go back to conference under certain situations, or a new conference must be convened. Many rules and informal practices govern the conduct of conference committees.

Bills that are passed by both houses with only minor differences need not be sent to conference. Either chamber may "concur" in the other's amendments, completing action on the legislation. Sometimes leaders of the committees of jurisdiction work out an informal compromise instead of having a formal conference. *(See Custody of the Papers.)*

Confirmations—*(See Nominations.)*

Congressional Record—The daily, printed account of proceedings in both the House and Senate chambers, showing substantially verbatim debate, statements and a record of floor action. Highlights of legislative and committee action are embodied in a Daily Digest section of the Record, and members are entitled to have their extraneous remarks printed in an appendix known as "Extension of Remarks." Members may edit and revise remarks made on the floor during debate, and quotations from debate reported by the press are not always found in the Record.

Beginning on March 1, 1978, the Record incorporated a procedure to distinguish remarks spoken on the floor of the House and Senate from undelivered speeches. Congress directed that all speeches, articles and other matter that members inserted in the Record without actually reading them on the floor were to be set off by large black dots, or bullets. However, a loophole allows a member to avoid the bulleting if he delivers any portion of the speech in person.

In 1985, the House decided on a trial basis, to print undelivered speeches and other material in boldface type.

Congressional Terms of Office—Normally begin on Jan. 3 of the year following a general election and are two years for representatives and six years for senators. Representatives elected in special elections are sworn in for the remainder of a term. A person may be appointed to fill a Senate vacancy and serves until a successor is elected; the successor serves until the end of the term applying to the vacant seat.

Consent Calendar—Members of the House may

place on this calendar most bills on the Union or House Calendar that are considered to be non-controversial. Bills on the Consent Calendar normally are called on the first and third Mondays of each month. On the first occasion that a bill is called in this manner, consideration may be blocked by the objection of any member. The second time, if there are three objections, the bill is stricken from the Consent Calendar. If less than three members object, the bill is given immediate consideration.

A bill on the Consent Calendar may be postponed in another way. A member may ask that the measure be passed over "without prejudice." In that case, no objection is recorded against the bill, and its status on the Consent Calendar remains unchanged. A bill stricken from the Consent Calendar remains on the Union or House Calendar.

Cosponsor—*(See Bills Introduced.)*

Continuing Resolution—A joint resolution drafted by Congress "continuing appropriations" for specific ongoing activities of a government department or departments when a fiscal year begins and Congress has not yet enacted all of the regular appropriations bills for that year. The continuing resolution usually specifies a maximum rate at which the agency may incur obligations. This usually is based on the rate for the previous year, the president's budget request or an appropriation bill for that year passed by either or both houses of Congress, but not cleared.

Contract Authority—Budget authority contained in an authorization bill that permits the federal government to enter into contracts or other obligations for future payments from funds not yet appropriated by Congress. The assumption is that funds will be available for payment in a subsequent appropriation act.

Controllable Budget Items—In federal budgeting this refers to programs for which the budget authority or outlays during a fiscal year can be controlled without changing existing, substantive law. The concept "relatively uncontrollable under current law" includes outlays for open-ended programs and fixed costs such as interest on the public debt, Social Security benefits, veterans' benefits and outlays to liquidate prior-year obligations.

Correcting Recorded Votes—Rules prohibit members from changing their votes after the result has been announced. But, occasionally hours, days or months after a vote has been taken, a member may announce that he was "incorrectly recorded." In the Senate, a request to change one's vote almost always receives unanimous consent. In the House, members are prohibited from changing their votes if tallied by the electronic voting system installed in 1973. If taken by roll call, it is permissible if consent is granted.

Current Services Estimates—Estimated budget authority and outlays for federal programs and operations for the forthcoming fiscal year based on continuation of existing levels of service without policy changes. These estimates of budget authority and outlays, accompanied by the underlying economic and policy assumptions upon which they are based, are transmitted by the president to Congress when the budget is submitted.

Custody of the Papers—To reconcile differences between the House and Senate versions of a bill, a conference may be arranged. The chamber with "custody of the papers" — the engrossed bill, engrossed amendments, messages of transmittal — is the only body empowered to request the conference. By custom, the chamber that asks for a conference is the last to act on the conference report once agreement has been reached on the bill by the conferees.

Custody of the papers sometimes is manipulated to ensure that a particular chamber acts either first or last on the conference report.

Deferrals of Budget Authority—Any action taken by U.S. government officials that withholds, delays or precludes the obligation or expenditure of budget authority. The 1974 budget act requires a special message from the president to Congress reporting a proposed deferral. Deferrals may not extend beyond the end of the fiscal year in which the message reporting the deferral is transmitted. *(See also Rescission Bill.)*

Dilatory Motion—A motion made for the purpose of killing time and preventing action on a bill or amendment. House rules outlaw dilatory motions, but enforcement is largely within the discretion of the Speaker or chairman of the Committee of the Whole. The Senate does not have a rule banning dilatory motions, except under cloture.

Discharge a Committee—Occasionally, attempts are made to relieve a committee from jurisdiction over a measure before it. This is attempted more often in the House than in the Senate, and the procedure rarely is successful.

In the House, if a committee does not report a bill within 30 days after the measure is referred to it, any member may file a discharge motion. Once offered, the motion is treated as a petition needing the signatures of 218 members (a majority of the House). After the required signatures have been obtained, there is a delay of seven days. Thereafter, on the second and fourth Mondays of each month, except during the last six days of a session, any member who has signed the petition must be recognized, if he so desires, to move that the committee be discharged. Debate on the motion to discharge is limited to 20 minutes, and, if the motion is carried, consideration of the bill becomes a matter of high privilege.

If a resolution to consider a bill is held up in the Rules Committee for more than seven legislative days, any member may enter a motion to discharge the committee. The motion is handled like any other discharge petition in the House.

Occasionally, to expedite non-controversial legislative business, a committee is discharged by unanimous consent of the House, and a petition is not required. *(Senate procedure, see Discharge Resolution.)*

Discharge Calendar—The House calendar to which motions to discharge committees are referred when they have the required number of signatures (218) and are awaiting floor action.

Discharge Petition—*(See Discharge a Committee.)*

Discharge Resolution—In the Senate, a special motion that any senator may introduce to relieve a committee from consideration of a bill before it. The resolution can be called up for Senate approval or disapproval in the same manner as any other Senate business. *(House procedure, see Discharge a Committee.)*

Division of a Question for Voting—A practice that is more common in the Senate but also used in the House, a member may demand a division of an amendment or a motion for purposes of voting. Where an amendment or motion can be divided, the individual parts are voted on separately when a member demands a division. This procedure occurs most often during the consideration of conference reports.

Division Vote—*(See Standing Vote.)*

Enacting Clause—Key phrase in bills beginning, "Be it enacted by the Senate and House of Representatives. . . ." A successful motion to strike it from legislation kills the measure.

Engrossed Bill—The final copy of a bill as passed by one chamber, with the text as amended by floor action and certified by the clerk of the House or the secretary of the Senate.

Enrolled Bill—The final copy of a bill that has been passed in identical form by both chambers. It is certified by an officer of the house of origin (clerk of the House or secretary of the Senate) and then sent on for the signatures of the House Speaker, the Senate president pro tempore and the president of the United States. An enrolled bill is printed on parchment.

Entitlement Program—A federal program that guarantees a certain level of benefits to persons or other entities who meet requirements set by law, such as Social Security or unemployment benefits. It thus leaves no discretion with Congress on how much money to appropriate.

Executive Calendar—This is a non-legislative calendar in the Senate on which presidential documents such as treaties and nominations are listed.

Executive Document—A document, usually a treaty, sent to the Senate by the president for consideration or approval. Executive documents are identified for each session of Congress as Executive A, 97th Congress, 1st Session; Executive B, etc. They are referred to committee in the same manner as other measures. Unlike legislative documents, however, treaties do not die at the end of a Congress but remain "live" proposals until acted on by the Senate or withdrawn by the president.

Executive Session—A meeting of a Senate or House committee (or occasionally of either chamber) that only its members may attend. Witnesses regularly appear at committee meetings in executive session — for example, Defense Department officials during presentations of classified defense information. Other members of Congress may be invited, but the public and press are not allowed to attend.

Expenditures—The actual spending of money as distinguished from the appropriation of funds. Expenditures are made by the disbursing officers of the administration; appropriations are made only by Congress. The two are rarely identical in any fiscal year. In addition to some current budget authority, expenditures may represent budget authority made available one, two or more years earlier.

Filibuster—A time-delaying tactic associated with the Senate and used by a minority in an effort to prevent a vote on a bill or amendment that probably would pass if voted upon directly. The most common method is to take advantage of the Senate's rules permitting unlimited debate, but other forms of parliamentary maneuvering may be used. The stricter rules used by the House make filibusters more difficult, but delaying tactics are employed occasionally through various procedural devices allowed by House rules. *(Senate filibusters, see Cloture.)*

Fiscal Year—Financial operations of the government are carried out in a 12-month fiscal year, beginning on Oct. 1 and ending on Sept. 30. The fiscal year carries the date of the calendar year in which it ends. (From fiscal year 1844 to fiscal year 1976, the fiscal year began July 1 and ended the following June 30.)

Five-Minute Rule—A debate-limiting rule of the House that is invoked when the House sits as the Committee of the Whole. Under the rule, a member offering an amendment is allowed to speak five minutes in its favor, and an opponent of the amendment is allowed to speak five minutes in opposition. Debate is then closed. In practice, amendments regularly are debated more than 10 minutes, with members gaining the floor by offering pro forma amendments or obtaining unanimous consent to speak longer than five minutes. *(See Strike Out the Last Word.)*

Floor Manager—A member who has the task of steering legislation through floor debate and the amendment process to a final vote in the House or the Senate. Floor managers are usually chairmen or ranking members of the committee that reported the bill. Managers are responsible for apportioning the debate time granted supporters of the bill. The ranking minority member of the committee normally apportions time for the minority party's participation in the debate.

Frank—A member's facsimile signature, which is used on envelopes in lieu of stamps, for the member's official outgoing mail. The "franking privilege" is the right to send mail postage-free.

Germane—Pertaining to the subject matter of the measure at hand. All House amendments must be germane to the bill being considered. The Senate requires that amendments be germane when they are proposed to general appropriation bills, bills being considered once cloture has been adopted, or, frequently, when proceeding under a unanimous consent agreement placing a time limit on consideration of a bill. The 1974 budget act also requires that amendments to concurrent budget resolutions be germane. In the House, floor debate must be germane, and the first three hours of debate each day in the Senate must be germane to the pending business.

Grandfather Clause—A provision exempting persons or other entities already engaged in an activity from rules or legislation affecting that activity. Grandfather clauses sometimes are added to legislation in order to avoid antagonizing groups with established interests in the activities affected.

Grants-in-Aid—Payments by the federal government to states, local governments or individuals in support of specified programs, services or activities.

Guaranteed Loans—Loans to third parties for which the federal government in the event of default guarantees, in whole or in part, the repayment of principal or interest to a lender or holder of a security.

Hearings—Committee sessions for taking testimony from witnesses. At hearings on legislation, witnesses usually include specialists, government officials and spokesmen for persons or entities affected by the bill or bills under study. Hearings related to special investigations bring forth a variety of witnesses. Committees sometimes use their subpoena power to summon reluctant witnesses. The public and press may attend open hearings, but are barred from closed, or "executive," hearings. The vast majority of hearings are open to the public. *(See Executive Session.)*

Hold-Harmless Clause—A provision added to legislation to ensure that recipients of federal funds do not receive less in a future year than they did in the current year if a new formula for allocating funds authorized in the legislation would result in a reduction to the recipients. This clause has been used most frequently to soften the impact of sudden reductions in federal grants.

Hopper—Box on House clerk's desk where members deposit bills and resolutions to introduce them. *(See also Bills Introduced.)*

Hour Rule—A provision in the rules of the House that permits one hour of debate time for each member on amendments debated in the House of Representatives sitting as the House. Therefore, the House normally amends bills while sitting as the Committee of the Whole, where the five-minute rule on amendments operates. *(See Committee of the Whole, Five-Minute Rule.)*

House—The House of Representatives, as distinct from the Senate, although each body is a "house" of Congress.

House as in Committee of the Whole—A procedure that can be used to expedite consideration of certain measures such as continuing resolutions and, when there is debate, private bills. The procedure only can be invoked with the unanimous consent of the House or a rule from the Rules Committee and has procedural elements of both the House sitting as the House of Representatives, such as the Speaker presiding and the previous question motion being in order, and the House sitting as the Committee of the Whole, such as the five-minute rule pertaining.

House Calendar—A listing for action by the House of public bills that do not directly or indirectly appropriate money or raise revenue.

Immunity—The constitutional privilege of members of Congress to make verbal statements on the floor and in committee for which they cannot be sued or arrested for slander or libel. Also, freedom from arrest while traveling to or from sessions of Congress or on official business. Members in this status may be arrested only for treason, felonies or a breach of the peace, as defined by congressional manuals.

Impoundments —Any action taken by the executive branch that delays or precludes the obligation or expenditure of budget authority previously approved by Congress. *(See also Deferrals of Budget Authority, Rescission Bill.)*

Joint Committee—A committee composed of a specified number of members of both the House and Senate. A joint committee may be investigative or research-oriented, an example of the latter being the Joint Economic Committee. Others have housekeeping duties such as the joint committees on Printing and on the Library of Congress.

Joint Resolution—A joint resolution, designated H J Res or S J Res, requires the approval of both houses and the signature of the president, just as a bill does, and has the force of law if approved. There is no practical difference between a bill and a joint resolution. A joint resolution generally is used to deal with a limited matter such as a single appropriation.

Joint resolutions also are used to propose amendments to the Constitution in Congress. They do not require a presidential signature, but become a part of the Constitution when three-fourths of the states have ratified them.

Journal—The official record of the proceedings of the House and Senate. The *Journal* records the actions taken in each chamber, but, unlike the *Congressional Record*, it does not include the substantially verbatim report of speeches, debates, etc.

Law—An act of Congress that has been signed by the president or passed over his veto by Congress. Public bills, when signed, become public laws, and are cited by the letters PL and a hyphenated number. The two digits before the number correspond to the Congress, and the one or more digits after the hyphen refer to the numerical sequence in which the bills were signed by the president during that Congress. Private bills, when signed, become private laws. *(See also Slip Laws, Statutes at Large, U.S. Code.)*

Legislative Day—The "day" extending from the time either house meets after an adjournment until the time it next adjourns. Because the House normally adjourns from day to day, legislative days and calendar days usually coincide. But in the Senate, a legislative day may, and frequently does, extend over several calendar days. *(See Recess.)*

Legislative Veto—A procedure, no longer allowed, permitting either the House or Senate, or both chambers, to review proposed executive branch regulations or actions and to block or modify those with which they disagreed.

The specifics of the procedure varied, but Congress generally provided for a legislative veto by including in a bill a provision that administrative rules or action taken to implement the law were to go into effect at the end of a designated period of time unless blocked by either or both houses of Congress. Another version of the veto provided for congressional reconsideration and rejection of regulations already in effect.

The Supreme Court ruling of June 23, 1983, struck

down the legislative veto as an unconstitutional violation of the lawmaking procedure provided in the Constitution.

Lobby—A group seeking to influence the passage or defeat of legislation. Originally the term referred to persons frequenting the lobbies or corridors of legislative chambers in order to speak to lawmakers.

The definition of a lobby and the activity of lobbying is a matter of differing interpretation. By some definitions, lobbying is limited to direct attempts to influence lawmakers through personal interviews and persuasion. Under other definitions, lobbying includes attempts at indirect, or "grass-roots," influence, such as persuading members of a group to write or visit their district's representative and state's senators or attempting to create a climate of opinion favorable to a desired legislative goal.

The right to attempt to influence legislation is based on the First Amendment to the Constitution, which says Congress shall make no law abridging the right of the people "to petition the government for a redress of grievances."

Majority Leader—The majority leader is elected by his party colleagues. In the Senate, in consultation with the minority leader and his colleagues, the majority leader directs the legislative schedule for the chamber. He also is his party's spokesman and chief strategist. In the House, the majority leader is second to the Speaker in the majority party's leadership and serves as his party's legislative strategist.

Majority Whip—In effect, the assistant majority leader, in either the House or Senate. His job is to help marshal majority forces in support of party strategy and legislation.

Manual—The official handbook in each house prescribing in detail its organization, procedures and operations.

Marking Up a Bill—Going through the contents of a piece of legislation in committee or subcommittee, considering its provisions in large and small portions, acting on amendments to provisions and proposed revisions to the language, inserting new sections and phraseology, etc. If the bill is extensively amended, the committee's version may be introduced as a separate bill, with a new number, before being considered by the full House or Senate. *(See Clean Bill.)*

Minority Leader—Floor leader for the minority party in each chamber. *(See also Majority Leader.)*

Minority Whip—Performs duties of whip for the minority party. *(See also Majority Whip.)*

Morning Hour—The time set aside at the beginning of each legislative day for the consideration of regular, routine business. The "hour" is of indefinite duration in the House, where it is rarely used.

In the Senate it is the first two hours of a session following an adjournment, as distinguished from a recess. The morning hour can be terminated earlier if the morning business has been completed. Business includes such matters as messages from the president, communications from the heads of departments, messages from the House, the presentation of petitions, reports of standing and select committees and the introduction of bills and resolutions. During the first hour of the morning hour in the Senate, no motion to proceed to the consideration of any bill on the calendar is in order except by unanimous consent. During the second hour, motions can be made but must be decided without debate. Senate committees may meet while the Senate conducts morning hour.

Motion—In the House or Senate chamber, a request by a member to institute any one of a wide array of parliamentary actions. He "moves" for a certain procedure, the consideration of a measure, etc. The precedence of motions, and whether they are debatable, is set forth in the House and Senate manuals. *(See some specific motions above and below.)*

Nominations—Presidential appointments to office subject to Senate confirmation. Although most nominations win quick Senate approval, some are controversial and become the topic of hearings and debate. Sometimes senators object to appointees for patronage reasons — for example, when a nomination to a local federal job is made without consulting the senators of the state concerned. In some situations a senator may object that the nominee is "personally obnoxious" to him. Usually other senators join in blocking such appointments out of courtesy to their colleagues. *(See Senatorial Courtesy.)*

One-Minute Speeches—Addresses by House members at the beginning of a legislative day. The speeches may cover any subject but are limited to one minute's duration.

Override a Veto—If the president disapproves a bill and sends it back to Congress with his objections, Congress may try to override his veto and enact the bill into law. Neither house is required to attempt to override a veto. The override of a veto requires a recorded vote with a two-thirds majority in each chamber. The question put to each house is: "Shall the bill pass, the objections of the president to the contrary notwithstanding?" *(See also Pocket Veto, Veto.)*

Oversight Committee—A congressional committee, or designated subcommittee of a committee, that is charged with general oversight of one or more federal agencies' programs and activities. Usually, the oversight panel for a particular agency also is the authorizing committee for that agency's programs and operations.

Pair—A voluntary arrangement between two lawmakers, usually on opposite sides of an issue. If passage of the measure requires a two-thirds majority vote, a pair would require two members favoring the action to one opposed to it. Pairs can take one of three forms — specific, general and live. The names of lawmakers pairing on a given vote and their stands, if known, are printed in the *Congressional Record.*

The specific pair applies to one or more votes on the same subject. On special pairs, lawmakers usually specify how they would have voted.

A general pair in the Senate, now rarely used, applies to all votes on which the members pairing are on opposite sides. It usually does not specify the positions of the senators pairing. In a general pair in the House, no agreement is involved. A representative expecting to be absent may notify the House clerk he wishes to make a "general" pair. His name then is paired arbitrarily with that of another member desiring a pair, and the list is printed in the *Congressional Record.* He may or may not be paired with a member taking the opposite position. General pairs in the House give no indication of how a member would have voted.

A live pair involves two members, one present for the vote, the other absent. The member present casts his vote and then withdraws it and votes "present." He then announces that he has a live pair with a colleague, identifying how each would have voted on the question. A live pair subtracts the vote of the member in attendance from the final vote tabulation.

Petition—A request or plea sent to one or both chambers from an organization or private citizens' group asking support of particular legislation or favorable consideration of a matter not yet receiving congressional attention. Petitions are referred to appropriate committees.

Pocket Veto—The act of the president in withholding his approval of a bill after Congress has adjourned. When Congress is in session, a bill becomes law without the president's signature if he does not act upon it within 10 days, excluding Sundays, from the time he gets it. But if Congress adjourns sine die within that 10-day period, the bill will die even if the president does not formally veto it. *(See also Veto.)*

Point of Order—An objection raised by a member that the chamber is departing from rules governing its conduct of business. The objector cites the rule violated, the chair sustaining his objection if correctly made. Order is restored by the chair's suspending proceedings of the chamber until it conforms to the prescribed "order of business."

President of the Senate—Under the Constitution, the vice president of the United States presides over the Senate. In his absence, the president pro tempore, or a senator designated by the president pro tempore, presides over the chamber.

President Pro Tempore—The chief officer of the Senate in the absence of the vice president; literally, but loosely, the president for a time. The president pro tempore is elected by his fellow senators, and the recent practice has been to elect the senator of the majority party with the longest period of continuous service.

Previous Question—A motion for the previous question, when carried, has the effect of cutting off all debate, preventing the offering of further amendments, and forcing a vote on the pending matter. In the House, the previous question is not permitted in the Committee of the Whole. The motion for the previous question is a debate-limiting device and is not in order in the Senate.

Printed Amendment—A House rule guarantees five minutes of floor debate in support and five minutes in opposition, and no other debate time, on amendments printed in the *Congressional Record* at least one day prior to the amendment's consideration in the Committee of the Whole.

In the Senate, while amendments may be submitted for printing, they have no parliamentary standing or status. An amendment submitted for printing in the Senate, however, may be called up by any senator.

Private Calendar—In the House, private bills dealing with individual matters such as claims against the government, immigration, land titles, etc., are put on this calendar. The private calendar must be called on the first Tuesday of each month, and the Speaker may call it on the third Tuesday of each month as well.

When a private bill is before the chamber, two members may block its consideration, which recommits the bill to committee. Backers of a recommitted private bill have recourse. The measure can be put into an "omnibus claims bill" — several private bills rolled into one. As with any bill, no part of an omnibus claims bill may be deleted without a vote. When the private bill goes back to the House floor in this form, it can be deleted from the omnibus bill only by majority vote.

Privilege—Privilege relates to the rights of members of Congress and to the relative priority of the motions and actions they may make in their respective chambers. The two are distinct. "Privileged questions" deal with legislative business. "Questions of privilege" concern legislators themselves.

Privileged Questions—The order in which bills, motions and other legislative measures are considered by Congress is governed by strict priorities. A motion to table, for instance, is more privileged than a motion to recommit. Thus, a motion to recommit can be superseded by a motion to table, and a vote would be forced on the latter motion only. A motion to adjourn, however, takes precedence over a tabling motion and thus is considered of the "highest privilege." *(See also Questions of Privilege.)*

Pro Forma Amendment—*(See Strike Out the Last Word.)*

Public Laws—*(See Law.)*

Questions of Privilege—These are matters affecting members of Congress individually or collectively. Matters affecting the rights, safety, dignity and integrity of proceedings of the House or Senate as a whole are questions of privilege in both chambers.

Questions involving individual members are called questions of "personal privilege." A member rising to ask a question of personal privilege is given precedence over almost all other proceedings. An annotation in the House rules points out that the privilege rests primarily on the Constitution, which gives him a conditional immunity from arrest and an unconditional freedom to speak in the House. *(See also Privileged Questions.)*

Quorum—The number of members whose presence is necessary for the transaction of business. In the Senate and House, it is a majority of the membership. A quorum is 100 in the Committee of the Whole House. If a point of order is made that a quorum is not present, the only business that is in order is either a motion to adjourn or a motion to direct the sergeant-at-arms to request the attendance of absentees.

Readings of Bills—Traditional parliamentary procedure required bills to be read three times before they were passed. This custom is of little modern significance. Normally a bill is considered to have its first reading when it is introduced and printed, by title, in the *Congressional Record*. In the House, its second reading comes when floor consideration begins. (This is the most likely point at which there is an actual reading of the bill, if there is any.) The second reading in the Senate is supposed to occur on the legislative day after the measure is introduced, but before it is referred to committee. The third reading (again, usually by title) takes place when floor action has been completed on amendments.

Recess—Distinguished from adjournment *(see above)* in that a recess does not end a legislative day and therefore does not interrupt unfinished business. The rules in each house set forth certain matters to be taken up and disposed of at the beginning of each legislative day. The House usually adjourns from day to day. The Senate often recesses, thus meeting on the same legislative day for several calendar days or even weeks at a time.

Recognition—The power of recognition of a member is lodged in the Speaker of the House and the presiding officer of the Senate. The presiding officer names the member who will speak first when two or more members simultaneously request recognition.

Recommit to Committee—A motion, made on the floor after a bill has been debated, to return it to the committee that reported it. If approved, recommittal usually is considered a death blow to the bill. In the House, a motion to recommit can be made only by a member opposed to the bill, and, in recognizing a member to make the motion, the Speaker gives preference to members of the minority party over majority party members.

A motion to recommit may include instructions to the committee to report the bill again with specific amendments or by a certain date. Or, the instructions may direct that a particular study be made, with no definite deadline for further action. If the recommittal motion includes instructions to "report the bill back forthwith" and the motion is adopted, floor action on the bill continues; the committee does not actually reconsider the legislation.

Reconciliation—*(See Budget Reconciliation.)*

Reconsider a Vote—A motion to reconsider the vote by which an action was taken has, until it is disposed of, the effect of putting the action in abeyance. In the Senate, the motion can be made only by a member who voted on the prevailing side of the original question or by a member who did not vote at all. In the House, it can be made only by a member on the prevailing side.

A common practice in the Senate after close votes on an issue is a motion to reconsider, followed by a motion to table the motion to reconsider. On this motion to table, senators vote as they voted on the original question, which allows the motion to table to prevail, assuming there are no switches. The matter then is finally closed and further motions to reconsider are not entertained. In the House, as a routine precaution, a motion to reconsider usually is made every time a measure is passed. Such a motion almost always is tabled immediately, thus shutting off the possibility of future reconsideration, except by unanimous consent.

Motions to reconsider must be entered in the Senate within the next two days of actual session after the original vote has been taken. In the House they must be entered either on the same day or on the next succeeding day the House is in session.

Recorded Vote—A vote upon which each member's stand is individually made known. In the Senate, this is accomplished through a roll call of the entire membership, to which each senator on the floor must answer "yea," "nay" or, if he does not wish to vote, "present." Since January 1973, the House has used an electronic voting system for recorded votes, including yea-and-nay votes formerly taken by roll calls.

When not required by the Constitution, a recorded vote can be obtained on questions in the House on the demand of one-fifth (44 members) of a quorum or one-fourth (25) of a quorum in the Committee of the Whole. *(See Yeas and Nays.)*

Report—Both a verb and a noun as a congressional term. A committee that has been examining a bill referred to it by the parent chamber "reports" its findings and recommendations to the chamber when it completes consideration and returns the measure. The process is called "reporting" a bill.

A "report" is the document setting forth the committee's explanation of its action. Senate and House reports are numbered separately and are designated S Rept or H Rept. When a committee report is not unanimous, the dissenting committee members may file a statement of their views, called minority views and referred to as a minority report. Members in disagreement with some provisions of a bill may file additional or supplementary views. Sometimes a bill is reported without a committee recommendation.

Adverse reports occasionally are submitted by legislative committees. However, when a committee is opposed to a bill, it usually fails to report the bill at all. Some laws require that committee reports — favorable or adverse — be made.

Rescission Bill—A bill rescinding or canceling budget authority previously made available by Congress. The president may request a rescission to reduce spending or because the budget authority no longer is needed. Under the 1974 budget act, however, unless Congress approves a rescission bill within 45 days of continuous session after receipt of the proposal, the funds must be made available for obligation. *(See also Deferrals of Budget Authority.)*

Resolution—A "simple" resolution, designated H Res or S Res, deals with matters entirely within the prerogatives of one house or the other. It requires neither passage by the other chamber nor approval by the president, and it does not have the force of law. Most resolutions deal with the rules or procedures of one house. They also are used to express the sentiments of a single house such as condolences to the family of a deceased member or to comment on foreign policy or executive business. A simple resolution is the vehicle for a "rule" from the House Rules Committee. *(See also Concurrent and Joint Resolutions, Rules.)*

Rider—An amendment, usually not germane, that its sponsor hopes to get through more easily by including it in other legislation. Riders become law if the bills embodying them are enacted. Amendments providing legislative directives in appropriations bills are outstanding examples of riders, though technically legislation is banned from appropriations bills. The House, unlike the Senate, has a strict germaneness rule; thus, riders usually are Senate devices to get legislation enacted quickly or to bypass lengthy House consideration and, possibly, opposition.

Rules—The term has two specific congressional meanings. A rule may be a standing order governing the conduct of House or Senate business and listed among the permanent rules of either chamber. The rules deal with duties of officers, the order of business, admission to the floor, parliamentary procedures on handling amendments and voting, jurisdictions of committees, etc.

In the House, a rule also may be a resolution reported by its Rules Committee to govern the handling of a particular bill on the floor. The committee may report a "rule," also called a "special order," in the form of a simple resolution. If the resolution is adopted by the House, the temporary rule becomes as valid as any standing rule and lapses only after action has been completed on the measure to which it pertains. A rule sets the time limit on general debate. It also may waive points of order against provisions of the bill in question such as non-germane language or against certain amendments intended to be proposed to the bill from the floor. It may even forbid all amendments or all amendments except those proposed by the legislative committee that handled the bill. In this instance, it is known as a "closed" or "gag" rule as opposed to an "open" rule, which puts no limitation on floor amendments, thus leaving the bill completely open to alteration by the adoption of germane amendments.

Secretary of the Senate—Chief administrative officer of the Senate, responsible for overseeing the duties of Senate employees, educating Senate pages, administering oaths, handling the registration of lobbyists, and handling other tasks necessary for the continuing operation of the Senate. *(See also Clerk of the House.)*

Select or Special Committee—A committee set up for a special purpose and, usually, for a limited time by resolution of either the House or Senate. Most special committees are investigative and lack legislative authority — legislation is not referred to them and they cannot report bills to their parent chamber. *(See also Standing Committees.)*

Senatorial Courtesy—Sometimes referred to as "the courtesy of the Senate," it is a general practice — with no written rule — applied to consideration of executive nominations. Generally, it means that nominations from a state are not to be confirmed unless they have been approved by the senators of the president's party of that state, with other senators following their colleagues' lead in the attitude they take toward consideration of such nominations. *(See Nominations.)*

Sine Die—*(See Adjournment Sine Die.)*

Slip Laws—The first official publication of a bill that has been enacted and signed into law. Each is published separately in unbound single-sheet or pamphlet form. *(See also Law, Statutes at Large, U.S. Code.)*

Speaker—The presiding officer of the House of Representatives, selected by the caucus of the party to which he belongs and formally elected by the whole House.

Special Session—A session of Congress after it has adjourned sine die, completing its regular session. Special sessions are convened by the president.

Spending Authority—The 1974 budget act defines spending authority as borrowing authority, contract authority and entitlement authority *(see above)*, for which budget authority is not provided in advance by appropriation acts.

Sponsor—*(See Bills Introduced.)*

Standing Committees—Committees permanently established by House and Senate rules. The standing committees of the House were last reorganized by the committee reorganization act of 1974. The last major realignment of Senate committees was in the committee system reorganization of 1977. The standing committees are legislative committees — legislation may be referred to them and they may report bills and resolutions to their parent chambers. *(See also Select or Special Committees.)*

Standing Vote—A non-recorded vote used in both the House and Senate. (A standing vote also is called a division vote.) Members in favor of a proposal stand and are counted by the presiding officer. Then members opposed stand and are counted. There is no record of how individual members voted.

Statutes at Large—A chronological arrangement of the laws enacted in each session of Congress. Though indexed, the laws are not arranged by subject matter, and there is not an indication of how they changed previously enacted laws. *(See also Law, Slip Laws, U.S. Code.)*

Strike From the Record—Remarks made on the House floor may offend some member, who moves that the offending words be "taken down" for the Speaker's cognizance, and then expunged from the debate as published in the *Congressional Record.*

Strike Out the Last Word—A motion whereby a House member is entitled to speak for five minutes on an amendment then being debated by the chamber. A member gains recognition from the chair by moving to "strike out the last word" of the amendment or section of the bill under consideration. The motion is pro forma, requires no vote and does not change the amendment being debated.

Substitute—A motion, amendment or entire bill introduced in place of the pending legislative business. Passage of a substitute measure kills the original measure by supplanting it. The substitute also may be amended. *(See also Amendment in the Nature of a Substitute.)*

Supplemental Appropriation Bill—Legislation appropriating funds after the regular annual appropriation bill *(see above)* for a federal department or agency has been enacted. A supplemental appropriation provides additional budget authority beyond original estimates for programs or activities, including new programs authorized after the enactment of the regular appropriation act, for which the need for funds is too urgent to be postponed until enactment of the next year's regular appropriation bill.

Suspend the Rules—Often a time-saving procedure for passing bills in the House. The wording of the motion, which may be made by any member recognized by the Speaker, is: "I move to suspend the rules and pass the bill. . . ." A favorable vote by two-thirds of those present is required for passage. Debate is limited to 40 minutes and no amendments from the floor are permitted. If a two-thirds favorable vote is not attained, the bill may be considered later under regular procedures. The suspension procedure is in order every Monday and Tuesday and is intended to be reserved for non-controversial bills.

Table a Bill—A motion to "lay on the table" is not debatable in either house, and usually it is a method of making a final, adverse disposition of a matter. In the Senate, however, different language sometimes is used. The motion may be worded to let a bill "lie on the table," perhaps for subsequent "picking up." This motion is more flexible, keeping the bill pending for later action, if desired. Tabling motions on amendments are effective debate-ending devices in the Senate.

Teller Vote—This is a largely moribund House procedure in the Committee of the Whole. Members file past tellers and are counted as for, or against, a measure, but they are not recorded individually. In the House, tellers are ordered upon demand of one-fifth of a quorum. This is 44 in the House, 20 in the Committee of the Whole.

The House also has a recorded teller vote, now largely supplanted by the electronic voting procedure, under which the votes of each member are made public just as they would be on a recorded vote. *(See above.)*

Treaties—Executive proposals — in the form of resolutions of ratification — which must be submitted to the Senate for approval by two-thirds of the senators present. Treaties today are normally sent to the Foreign Relations Committee for scrutiny before the Senate takes action. Foreign Relations has jurisdiction over all treaties, regardless of the subject matter. Treaties are read three times and debated on the floor in much the same manner as legislative proposals. After approval by the Senate, treaties are formally ratified by the president.

Trust Funds—Funds collected and used by the federal government for carrying out specific purposes and programs according to terms of a trust agreement or statute such as the Social Security and unemployment compensation trust funds. Such funds are administered by the government in a fiduciary capacity and are not available for the general purposes of the government.

Unanimous Consent—Proceedings of the House or Senate and action on legislation often take place upon the unanimous consent of the chamber, whether or not a rule of the chamber is being violated. Unanimous consent is used to expedite floor action and frequently is used in a routine fashion such as by a senator requesting the unanimous consent of the Senate to have specified members of his staff present on the floor during debate on a specific amendment.

Unanimous Consent Agreement—A device used in the Senate to expedite legislation. Much of the Senate's legislative business, dealing with both minor and controversial issues, is conducted through unanimous consent or unanimous consent agreements. On major legislation, such agreements usually are printed and transmitted to all senators in advance of floor debate. Once agreed to, they are binding on all members unless the Senate, by unanimous consent, agrees to modify them. An agreement may list the order in which various bills are to be considered, specify the length of time bills and contested amendments are to be debated and when they are to be voted upon and, frequently, require that all amendments introduced be germane to the bill under consideration. In this regard, unanimous consent agreements are similar to the "rules" issued by the House Rules Committee for bills pending in the House. *(See above.)*

Union Calendar—Bills that directly or indirectly appropriate money or raise revenue are placed on this House calendar according to the date they are reported from committee.

U.S. Code—A consolidation and codification of the general and permanent laws of the United States arranged by subject under 50 titles, the first six dealing with general or political subjects, and the other 44 alphabetically arranged from agriculture to war. The code is revised every six years, and a supplement is published after each session of Congress. *(See also Law, Slip Laws, Statutes at Large.)*

Veto—Disapproval by the president of a bill or joint resolution (other than one proposing an amendment to the Constitution). When Congress is in session, the president must veto a bill within 10 days, excluding Sundays, after he has received it; otherwise, it becomes law without his signature. When the president vetoes a bill, he returns it to the house of origin along with a message stating his objections. *(See also Pocket Veto, Override a Veto.)*

Voice Vote—In either the House or Senate, members answer "aye" or "no" in chorus, and the presiding officer decides the result. The term also is used loosely to indicate action by unanimous consent or without objection.

Whip—*(See Majority and Minority Whip.)*

Without Objection—Used in lieu of a vote on non-controversial motions, amendments or bills that may be passed in either the House or Senate if no member voices an objection.

Yeas and Nays—The Constitution requires that yea-and-nay votes be taken and recorded when requested by one-fifth of the members present. In the House, the Speaker determines whether one-fifth of the members present requested a vote. In the Senate, practice requires only 11 members. The Constitution requires the yeas and nays on a veto override attempt. *(See Recorded Vote.)*

Yielding—When a member has been recognized to speak, no other member may speak unless he obtains permission from the member recognized. This permission is called yielding and usually is requested in the form, "Will the gentleman yield to me?" While this activity occasionally is seen in the Senate, the Senate has no rule or practice to parcel out time.

How a Bill Becomes Law

This graphic shows the most typical way in which proposed legislation is enacted into law. There are more complicated, as well as simpler, routes, and most bills never become law. The process is illustrated with two hypothetical bills, House bill No. 1 (HR 1) and Senate bill No. 2 (S 2). Bills must be passed by both houses in identical form before they can be sent to the president. The path of HR 1 is traced by a solid line, that of S 2 by a broken line. In practice most bills begins as similar proposals in both houses.

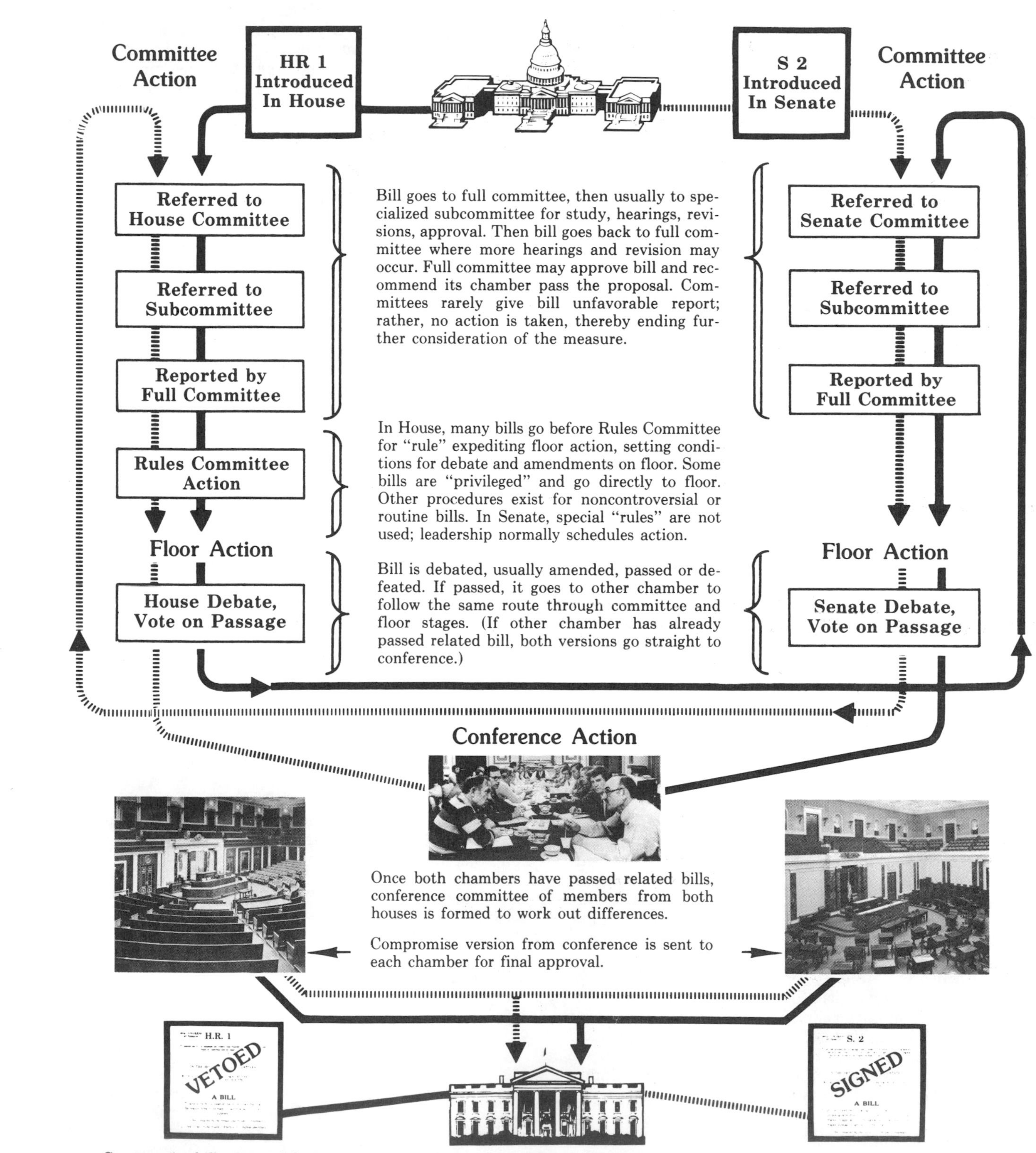

Compromise bill approved by both houses is sent to the president, who can sign it into law or veto it and return it to Congress. Congress may override veto by a two-thirds majority vote in both houses; bill then becomes law without president's signature.

The Legislative Process in Brief

Note: Parliamentary terms used below are defined in the glossary.

Introduction of Bills

A House member (including the resident commissioner of Puerto Rico and non-voting delegates of the District of Columbia, Guam, the Virgin Islands and American Samoa) may introduce any one of several types of bills and resolutions by handing it to the clerk of the House or placing it in a box called the hopper. A senator first gains recognition of the presiding officer to announce the introduction of a bill. If objection is offered by any senator, the introduction of the bill is postponed until the following day.

As the next step in either the House or Senate, the bill is numbered, referred to the appropriate committee, labeled with the sponsor's name, and sent to the Government Printing Office so that copies can be made for subsequent study and action. Senate bills may be jointly sponsored and carry several senators' names. Until 1978, the House limited the number of members who could cosponsor any one bill; the ceiling was eliminated at the beginning of the 96th Congress. A bill written in the executive branch and proposed as an administration measure usually is introduced by the chairman of the congressional committee that has jurisdiction.

Bills—Prefixed with "HR" in the House, "S" in the Senate, followed by a number. Used as the form for most legislation, whether general or special, public or private.

Joint Resolutions—Designated H J Res or S J Res. Subject to the same procedure as bills, with the exception of a joint resolution proposing an amendment to the Constitution. The latter must be approved by two-thirds of both houses and is thereupon sent directly to the administrator of general services for submission to the states for ratification rather than being presented to the president for his approval.

Concurrent Resolutions—Designated H Con Res or S Con Res. Used for matters affecting the operations of both houses. These resolutions do not become law.

Resolutions—Designated H Res or S Res. Used for a matter concerning the operation of either house alone and adopted only by the chamber in which it originates.

Committee Action

A bill is referred to the appropriate committee by a House parliamentarian on the Speaker's order, or by the Senate president. Sponsors may indicate their preferences for referral, although custom and chamber rule generally govern. An exception is the referral of private bills, which are sent to whatever group is designated by their sponsors. Bills are technically considered "read for the first time" when referred to House committees.

When a bill reaches a committee it is placed on the group's calendar. At that time it comes under the sharpest congressional focus. Its chances for passage are quickly determined — and the great majority of bills fall by the legislative roadside. Failure of a committee to act on a bill is equivalent to killing it; the measure can be withdrawn from the group's purview only by a discharge petition signed by a majority of the House membership on House bills, or by adoption of a special resolution in the Senate. Discharge attempts rarely succeed.

The first committee action taken on a bill usually is a request for comment on it by interested agencies of the government. The committee chairman may assign the bill to a subcommittee for study and hearings, or it may be considered by the full committee. Hearings may be public, closed (executive session), or both. A subcommittee, after considering a bill, reports to the full committee its recommendations for action and any proposed amendments.

The full committee then votes on its recommendation to the House or Senate. This procedure is called "ordering a bill reported." Occasionally a committee may order a bill reported unfavorably; most of the time a report, submitted by the chairman of the committee to the House or Senate, calls for favorable action on the measure since the committee can effectively "kill" a bill by simply failing to take any action.

When a committee sends a bill to the chamber floor, it explains its reasons in a written statement, called a report, which accompanies the bill. Often committee members opposing a measure issue dissenting minority statements that are included in the report.

Usually, the committee "marks up" or proposes amendments to the bill. If they are substantial and the measure is complicated, the committee may order a "clean bill" introduced, which will embody the proposed amendments. The original bill then is put aside and the "clean bill," with a new number, is reported to the floor.

The chamber must approve, alter or reject the committee amendments before the bill itself can be put to a vote.

Floor Action

After a bill is reported back to the house where it originated, it is placed on the calendar.

There are five legislative calendars in the House, issued in one cumulative calendar titled *Calendars of the United States House of Representatives and History of Legislation*. The House calendars are:

The Union Calendar to which are referred bills raising revenues, general appropriations bills and any measures directly or indirectly appropriating money or property. It is the Calendar of the Committee of the Whole House on the State of the Union.

The House Calendar to which are referred bills of public character not raising revenue or appropriating money or property.

The Consent Calendar to which are referred bills of a non-controversial nature that are passed without debate when the Consent Calendar is called on the first and third Mondays of each month.

The Private Calendar to which are referred bills for relief in the nature of claims against the United States or private immigration bills that are passed without debate when the Private Calendar is called the first and third Tuesdays of each month.

The Discharge Calendar to which are referred motions to discharge committees when the necessary signatures are signed to a discharge petition.

There is only one legislative calendar in the Senate and one "executive calendar" for treaties and nominations submitted to the Senate. When the Senate Calendar is called, each senator is limited to five minutes' debate on each bill.

Debate. A bill is brought to debate by varying procedures. If a routine measure, it may await the call of the calendar. If it is urgent or important, it can be taken up in the Senate either by unanimous consent or by a majority vote. The policy committee of the majority party in the Senate schedules the bills that it wants taken up for debate.

In the House, precedence is granted if a special rule is obtained from the Rules Committee. A request for a special rule is usually made by the chairman of the committee that favorably reported the bill, supported by the bill's sponsor and other committee members. The request, considered by the Rules Committee in the same fashion that other committees consider legislative measures, is in the form of a resolution providing for immediate consideration of the bill. The Rules Committee reports the resolution to the House where it is debated and voted upon in the same fashion as regular bills. If the Rules Committee should fail to report a rule requested by a committee, there are several ways to bring the bill to the House floor — under suspension of the rules, on Calendar Wednesday or by a discharge motion.

The resolutions providing special rules are important because they specify how long the bill may be debated and whether it may be amended from the floor. If floor amendments are banned, the bill is considered under a "closed rule," which permits only members of the committee that first reported the measure to the House to alter its language, subject to chamber acceptance.

When a bill is debated under an "open rule," amendments may be offered from the floor. Committee amendments are always taken up first, but may be changed, as may all amendments up to the second degree; i.e., an amendment to an amendment to an amendment is not in order.

Duration of debate in the House depends on whether the bill is under discussion by the House proper or before the House when it is sitting as the Committee of the Whole House on the State of the Union. In the former, the amount of time for debate is determined either by special rule or is allocated with an hour for each member if the measure is under consideration without a rule. In the Committee of the Whole the amount of time agreed on for general debate is equally divided between proponents and opponents. At the end of general discussion, the bill is read section by section for amendment. Debate on an amendment is limited to five minutes for each side.

Senate debate is usually unlimited. It can be halted only by unanimous consent by "cloture," which requires a three-fifths majority of the entire Senate except for proposed changes in the Senate rules. The latter requires a two-thirds vote.

The House sits as the Committee of the Whole when it considers any tax measure or bill dealing with public appropriations. It can also resolve itself into the Committee of the Whole if a member moves to do so and the motion is carried. The Speaker appoints a member to serve as the chairman. The rules of the House permit the Committee of the Whole to meet with any 100 members on the floor, and to amend and act on bills with a quorum of the 100, within the time limitations mentioned previously. When the Committee of the Whole has acted, it "rises," the Speaker returns as the presiding officer of the House and the member appointed chairman of the Committee of the Whole reports the action of the committee and its recommendations (amendments adopted).

Votes. Voting on bills may occur repeatedly before they are finally approved or rejected. The House votes on the rule for the bill and on various amendments to the bill. Voting on amendments often is a more illuminating test of a bill's support than is the final tally. Sometimes members approve final passage of bills after vigorously supporting amendments that, if adopted, would have scuttled the legislation.

The Senate has three different methods of voting: an untabulated voice, a standing vote (called a division) and a recorded roll call to which members answer "yea" or "nay" when their names are called. The House also employs voice and standing votes, but since January 1973 yeas and nays have been recorded by an electronic voting device, eliminating the need for time-consuming roll calls.

Another method of voting, used in the House only, is the teller vote. Traditionally, members filed up the center aisle past counters; only vote totals were announced. Since 1971, one-fifth of a quorum can demand that the votes of individual members be recorded, thereby forcing them to take a public position on amendments to key bills. Electronic voting now is commonly used for this purpose.

After amendments to a bill have been voted upon, a vote may be taken on a motion to recommit the bill to committee. If carried, this vote removes the bill from the chamber's calendar. If the motion is unsuccessful, the bill then is "read for the third time." An actual reading usually is dispensed with. Until 1965, an opponent of a bill could delay this move by objecting and asking for a full reading of an engrossed (certified in final form) copy of the bill. After the "third reading," the vote on final passage is taken.

The final vote may be followed by a motion to reconsider, and this motion itself may be followed by a move to lay the motion on the table. Usually, those voting for the bill's passage vote for the tabling motion, thus safeguarding the final passage action. With that, the bill has been formally passed by the chamber. While a motion to reconsider a Senate vote is pending on a bill, the measure cannot be sent to the House.

Action in Second House

After a bill is passed it is sent to the other chamber. This body may then take one of several steps. It may pass the bill as is — accepting the other chamber's language. It may send the bill to committee for scrutiny or alteration, or reject the entire bill, advising the other house of its actions. Or it may simply ignore the bill submitted while it continues work on its own version of the proposed legislation. Frequently, one chamber may approve a version of a bill that is greatly at variance with the version already passed by the other house, and then substitute its amendments for the language of the other, retaining only the latter's bill designation.

A provision of the Legislative Reorganization Act of 1970 permits a separate House vote on any non-germane amendment added by the Senate to a House-passed bill and requires a majority vote to retain the amendment. Previously, the House was forced to act on the bill as a whole; the only way to defeat the non-germane amendment was to reject the entire bill.

Often the second chamber makes only minor changes. If these are readily agreed to by the other house, the bill then is routed to the White House for signing. However, if the opposite chamber basically alters the bill submitted to it, the measure usually is "sent to conference." The chamber that has possession of the "papers" (engrossed bill, engrossed amendments, messages of transmittal) requests a conference and the other chamber must agree to it. If the second house does not agree, the bill dies.

Conference, Final Action

Conference. A conference undertakes to harmonize conficting House and Senate versions of a bill. The conference is usually staffed by senior members (conferees), appointed by the presiding officers of the two houses, from the committees that managed the bills. Under this arrangement the conferees of one house have the duty of trying to maintain their chamber's position in the face of amending actions by the conferees (also referred to as "managers") of the other house.

The number of conferees from each chamber may vary, the range usually being from three to nine members in each group, depending upon the length or complexity of the bill involved. There may be five representatives and three senators on the conference committee, or the reverse. But a majority vote controls the action of each group so that a large representation does not give one chamber a voting advantage over the other chamber's conferees.

Theoretically, conferees are not allowed to write new legislation in reconciling the two versions before them, but this curb sometimes is bypassed. Many bills have been put into acceptable compromise form only after new language was provided by the conferees. The 1970 Reorganization Act attempted to tighten restrictions on conferees by forbidding them to introduce any language on a topic that neither chamber sent to conference or to modify any topic beyond the scope of the different House and Senate versions.

Frequently the ironing out of difficulties takes days or even weeks. Conferences on involved appropriations bills sometimes are particularly drawn out.

As a conference proceeds, conferees reconcile differences between the versions, but generally they grant concessions only insofar as they remain sure that the chamber they represent will accept the compromises. Occasionally, uncertainty over how either house will react, or the positive refusal of a chamber to back down on a disputed amendment, results in an impasse, and the bills die in conference even though each was approved by its sponsoring chamber.

Conferees sometimes go back to their respective chambers for further instructions, when they report certain portions in disagreement. Then the chamber concerned can either "recede and concur" in the amendment of the other house, or "insist on its amendment."

When the conferees have reached agreement, they prepare a conference report embodying their recommendations (compromises). The reports, in document form, must be submitted to each house.

The conference report must be approved by each house. Consequently, approval of the report is approval of the compromise bill.

Final Steps. After a bill has been passed by both the House and Senate in identical form, all of the original papers are sent to the enrolling clerk of the chamber in which the bill originated. He then prepares an enrolled bill, which is printed on parchment paper. When this bill has been certified as correct by the secretary of the Senate or the clerk of the House, depending on which chamber originated the bill, it is signed first (no matter whether it originated in the Senate or House) by the Speaker of the House and then by the president of the Senate. It is next sent to the White House to await action.

If the president approves the bill, he signs it, dates it and usually writes the word "approved" on the document. If he does not sign it within 10 days (Sundays excepted) and Congress is in session, the bill becomes law without his signature.

However, should Congress adjourn before the 10 days expire, and the president failed to sign the measure, it does not become law. This procedure is called a pocket veto.

A president vetoes a bill by refusing to sign it and, before the 10-day period expires, returning it to Congress with a message stating his reasons. The message is sent to the chamber that originated the bill. If no action is taken there on the message, the bill dies. Congress, however, can attempt to override the president's veto and enact the bill, "the objections of the president to the contrary notwithstanding." Overriding of a veto requires a two-thirds vote of those present, who must number a quorum and vote by roll call.

Debate can precede this vote, with motions permitted to lay the message on the table, postpone action on it, or refer it to committee. If the president's veto is overridden by a two-thirds vote in both houses, the bill becomes law. Otherwise it is dead.

When bills are passed finally and signed, or passed over a veto, they are given law numbers in numerical order as they become law. There are two series of numbers, one for public and one for private laws, starting at the number "1" for each two-year term of Congress. They are then identified by law number and by Congress — i.e., Private Law 21, 99th Congress; Public Law 183, 99th Congress (or PL 99-183).

SENATE ROLL-CALL VOTES

CQ

CQ Senate Vote 1

Corresponding to Congressional Record Vote 1

	1
ALABAMA	
Denton	Y
Heflin	Y
ALASKA	
Murkowski	Y
Stevens	Y
ARIZONA	
Goldwater	Y
DeConcini	Y
ARKANSAS	
Bumpers	?
Pryor	Y
CALIFORNIA	
Wilson	Y
Cranston	Y
COLORADO	
Armstrong	Y
Hart	Y
CONNECTICUT	
Weicker	Y
Dodd	Y
DELAWARE	
Roth	Y
Biden	Y
FLORIDA	
Hawkins	Y
Chiles	Y
GEORGIA	
Mattingly	Y
Nunn	Y
HAWAII	
Inouye	Y
Matsunaga	Y
IDAHO	
McClure	Y
Symms	Y
ILLINOIS	
Dixon	+
Simon	Y
INDIANA	
Lugar	Y
Quayle	Y

	1
IOWA	
Grassley	Y
Harkin	Y
KANSAS	
Dole	Y
Kassebaum	Y
KENTUCKY	
McConnell	Y
Ford	Y
LOUISIANA	
Johnston	Y
Long	Y
MAINE	
Cohen	Y
Mitchell	Y
MARYLAND	
Mathias	Y
Sarbanes	Y
MASSACHUSETTS	
Kennedy	Y
Kerry	Y
MICHIGAN	
Levin	Y
Riegle	Y
MINNESOTA	
Boschwitz	Y
Durenberger	Y
MISSISSIPPI	
Cochran	Y
Stennis	+
MISSOURI	
Danforth	Y
Eagleton	Y
MONTANA	
Baucus	Y
Melcher	+
NEBRASKA	
Exon	Y
Zorinsky	Y
NEVADA	
Hecht	Y
Laxalt	Y

	1
NEW HAMPSHIRE	
Humphrey	Y
Rudman	Y
NEW JERSEY	
Bradley	Y
Lautenberg	Y
NEW MEXICO	
Domenici	Y
Bingaman	Y
NEW YORK	
D'Amato	Y
Moynihan	Y
NORTH CAROLINA	
East	Y
Helms	Y
NORTH DAKOTA	
Andrews	Y
Burdick	Y
OHIO	
Glenn	Y
Metzenbaum	Y
OKLAHOMA	
Nickles	Y
Boren	Y
OREGON	
Hatfield	Y
Packwood	Y
PENNSYLVANIA	
Heinz	Y
Specter	Y
RHODE ISLAND	
Chafee	Y
Pell	Y
SOUTH CAROLINA	
Thurmond	Y
Hollings	Y
SOUTH DAKOTA	
Abdnor	Y
Pressler	Y
TENNESSEE	
Gore	Y
Sasser	Y

KEY

Y Voted for (yea).
Paired for.
\+ Announced for.
N Voted against (nay).
X Paired against.
\- Announced against.
P Voted "present".
C Voted "present" to avoid possible conflict of interest.
? Did not vote or otherwise make a position known.

Democrats *Republicans*

	1
TEXAS	
Gramm	Y
Bentsen	Y
UTAH	
Garn	+
Hatch	Y
VERMONT	
Stafford	Y
Leahy	Y
VIRGINIA	
Trible	Y
Warner	Y
WASHINGTON	
Evans	Y
Gorton	Y
WEST VIRGINIA	
Byrd	Y
Rockefeller	Y
WISCONSIN	
Kasten	Y
Proxmire	Y
WYOMING	
Simpson	Y
Wallop	Y

ND - Northern Democrats SD - Southern Democrats (Southern states - Ala., Ark., Fla., Ga., Ky., La., Miss., N.C., Okla., S.C., Tenn., Texas, Va.)

1. Baker Nomination. Confirmation of President Reagan's nomination of James A. Baker III of Texas to be secretary of the Treasury. Confirmed 95-0: R 52-0; D 43-0 (ND 31-0, SD 12-0), Jan. 29, 1985. A "yea" was a vote supporting the president's position.

KEY

- Y Voted for (yea).
- # Paired for.
- + Announced for.
- N Voted against (nay).
- X Paired against.
- - Announced against.
- P Voted "present".
- C Voted "present" to avoid possible conflict of interest.
- ? Did not vote or otherwise make a position known.

Democrats ***Republicans***

	2	3	4
ALABAMA			
Denton	Y	Y	Y
Heflin	Y	Y	Y
ALASKA			
Murkowski	Y	Y	Y
Stevens	Y	Y	Y
ARIZONA			
Goldwater	?	Y	Y
DeConcini	Y	Y	Y
ARKANSAS			
Bumpers	Y	Y	Y
Pryor	Y	Y	Y
CALIFORNIA			
Wilson	Y	Y	Y
Cranston	Y	Y	Y
COLORADO			
Armstrong	Y	Y	Y
Hart	Y	Y	Y
CONNECTICUT			
Weicker	Y	Y	Y
Dodd	Y	Y	Y
DELAWARE			
Roth	Y	Y	Y
Biden	Y	Y	Y
FLORIDA			
Hawkins	Y	Y	Y
Chiles	Y	Y	Y
GEORGIA			
Mattingly	Y	Y	Y
Nunn	Y	Y	Y
HAWAII			
Inouye	Y	Y	Y
Matsunaga	Y	Y	Y
IDAHO			
McClure	Y	Y	Y
Symms	Y	Y	Y
ILLINOIS			
Dixon	Y	Y	Y
Simon	Y	Y	Y
INDIANA			
Lugar	Y	Y	Y
Quayle	Y	Y	Y
IOWA			
Grassley	Y	Y	Y
Harkin	Y	Y	Y
KANSAS			
Dole	Y	Y	Y
Kassebaum	Y	Y	Y
KENTUCKY			
McConnell	Y	Y	Y
Ford	Y	Y	Y
LOUISIANA			
Johnston	Y	Y	Y
Long	Y	Y	Y
MAINE			
Cohen	Y	Y	Y
Mitchell	Y	Y	Y
MARYLAND			
Mathias	?	?	?
Sarbanes	Y	Y	Y
MASSACHUSETTS			
Kennedy	Y	Y	Y
Kerry	Y	Y	Y
MICHIGAN			
Levin	Y	Y	Y
Riegle	Y	Y	Y
MINNESOTA			
Boschwitz	Y	Y	Y
Durenberger	Y	Y	Y
MISSISSIPPI			
Cochran	?	?	?
Stennis	+	+	+
MISSOURI			
Danforth	Y	Y	Y
Eagleton	Y	Y	Y
MONTANA			
Baucus	Y	Y	Y
Melcher	+	+	+
NEBRASKA			
Exon	Y	Y	Y
Zorinsky	Y	Y	Y
NEVADA			
Hecht	Y	Y	Y
Laxalt	Y	Y	Y
NEW HAMPSHIRE			
Humphrey	Y	Y	Y
Rudman	Y	Y	Y
NEW JERSEY			
Bradley	Y	Y	Y
Lautenberg	Y	Y	Y
NEW MEXICO			
Domenici	Y	Y	Y
Bingaman	Y	Y	Y
NEW YORK			
D'Amato	Y	Y	Y
Moynihan	Y	Y	Y
NORTH CAROLINA			
East	+	+	+
Helms	Y	Y	Y
NORTH DAKOTA			
Andrews	Y	Y	Y
Burdick	Y	Y	Y
OHIO			
Glenn	Y	Y	Y
Metzenbaum	Y	Y	Y
OKLAHOMA			
Nickles	Y	Y	Y
Boren	Y	Y	Y
OREGON			
Hatfield	Y	Y	Y
Packwood	Y	Y	Y
PENNSYLVANIA			
Heinz	Y	Y	Y
Specter	Y	Y	Y
RHODE ISLAND			
Chafee	Y	Y	Y
Pell	Y	Y	Y
SOUTH CAROLINA			
Thurmond	Y	Y	Y
Hollings	Y	Y	Y
SOUTH DAKOTA			
Abdnor	Y	Y	Y
Pressler	Y	Y	Y
TENNESSEE			
Gore	Y	Y	Y
Sasser	Y	Y	Y
TEXAS			
Gramm	Y	Y	Y
Bentsen	Y	Y	Y
UTAH			
Garn	+	+	+
Hatch	Y	Y	Y
VERMONT			
Stafford	Y	Y	Y
Leahy	Y	Y	Y
VIRGINIA			
Trible	Y	Y	Y
Warner	Y	Y	Y
WASHINGTON			
Evans	Y	Y	Y
Gorton	Y	Y	Y
WEST VIRGINIA			
Byrd	Y	Y	Y
Rockefeller	Y	Y	Y
WISCONSIN			
Kasten	Y	Y	Y
Proxmire	Y	N	N
WYOMING			
Simpson	Y	Y	Y
Wallop	Y	Y	Y

ND - Northern Democrats SD - Southern Democrats (Southern states - Ala., Ark., Fla., Ga., Ky., La., Miss., N.C., Okla., S.C., Tenn., Texas, Va.)

2. Bennett Nomination. Confirmation of President Reagan's nomination of William J. Bennett of North Carolina to be secretary of education. Confirmed 93-0: R 48-0; D 45-0 (ND 32-0, SD 13-0), Feb. 6, 1985. A "yea" was a vote supporting the president's position.

3. Herrington Nomination. Confirmation of President Reagan's nomination of John S. Herrington of California to be secretary of energy. Confirmed 93-1: R 49-0; D 44-1 (ND 31-1, SD 13-0), Feb. 6, 1985. A "yea" was a vote supporting the president's position.

4. Hodel Nomination. Confirmation of President Reagan's nomination of Donald P. Hodel of Virginia to be secretary of the interior. Confirmed 93-1: R 49-0; D 44-1 (ND 31-1, SD 13-0), Feb. 6, 1985. A "yea" was a vote supporting the president's position.

CQ Senate Votes 5 - 12

Corresponding to Congressional Record Votes 5, 6, 7, 8, 9, 10, 11, 12

	5	6	7	8	9	10	11	12
ALABAMA								
Denton	?	Y	Y	Y	Y	Y	Y	Y
Heflin	Y	Y	Y	Y	Y	Y	Y	Y
ALASKA								
Murkowski	Y	Y	Y	Y	Y	Y	Y	Y
Stevens	?	?	?	?	+	?	?	Y
ARIZONA								
Goldwater	?	N	N	?	+	?	?	N
DeConcini	Y	Y	Y	Y	Y	Y	Y	Y
ARKANSAS								
Bumpers	?	Y	Y	Y	N	Y	Y	Y
Pryor	Y	Y	Y	Y	N	Y	Y	Y
CALIFORNIA								
Wilson	Y	Y	Y	Y	Y	Y	Y	Y
Cranston	Y	Y	Y	Y	N	Y	Y	Y
COLORADO								
Armstrong	Y	Y	Y	Y	Y	Y	Y	Y
Hart	Y	Y	Y	Y	N	Y	Y	Y
CONNECTICUT								
Weicker	N	N	N	N	Y	Y	Y	N
Dodd	Y	Y	Y	Y	N	Y	Y	Y
DELAWARE								
Roth	?	Y	Y	Y	Y	Y	Y	Y
Biden	?	Y	Y	?	N	Y	Y	Y
FLORIDA								
Hawkins	Y	Y	Y	?	Y	Y	Y	Y
Chiles	Y	Y	Y	Y	-	?	?	Y
GEORGIA								
Mattingly	Y	Y	Y	Y	Y	Y	Y	Y
Nunn	Y	Y	?	Y	N	Y	Y	Y
HAWAII								
Inouye	Y	Y	Y	Y	Y	Y	Y	Y
Matsunaga	?	Y	Y	Y	Y	Y	Y	Y
IDAHO								
McClure	?	?	Y	?	Y	Y	Y	Y
Symms	Y	Y	Y	Y	Y	Y	Y	Y
ILLINOIS								
Dixon	Y	Y	Y	Y	N	Y	Y	Y
Simon	Y	Y	Y	Y	N	Y	Y	Y
INDIANA								
Lugar	Y	Y	Y	Y	Y	Y	Y	Y
Quayle	N	N	N	N	Y	Y	Y	N
IOWA								
Grassley	Y	Y	Y	Y	Y	Y	Y	Y
Harkin	Y	Y	Y	Y	N	Y	Y	Y
KANSAS								
Dole	Y	Y	Y	Y	Y	Y	Y	Y
Kassebaum	Y	Y	?	?	Y	Y	Y	Y
KENTUCKY								
McConnell	Y	Y	Y	Y	Y	Y	Y	Y
Ford	Y	Y	Y	Y	Y	Y	Y	Y
LOUISIANA								
Johnston	?	Y	Y	Y	Y	Y	Y	Y
Long	?	?	Y	Y	Y	Y	Y	N
MAINE								
Cohen	?	Y	Y	Y	Y	Y	Y	Y
Mitchell	Y	Y	Y	Y	N	Y	Y	Y
MARYLAND								
Mathias	Y	Y	Y	Y	Y	Y	Y	Y
Sarbanes	Y	Y	Y	Y	N	Y	Y	Y
MASSACHUSETTS								
Kennedy	Y	Y	Y	Y	N	Y	Y	Y
Kerry	Y	Y	Y	Y	N	Y	Y	Y
MICHIGAN								
Levin	Y	Y	Y	Y	N	Y	Y	Y
Riegle	Y	Y	Y	Y	N	Y	Y	Y
MINNESOTA								
Boschwitz	Y	Y	Y	Y	Y	Y	Y	Y
Durenberger	Y	Y	Y	Y	Y	Y	Y	Y
MISSISSIPPI								
Cochran	Y	Y	Y	Y	Y	Y	Y	Y
Stennis	?	?	Y	?	Y	Y	Y	?
MISSOURI								
Danforth	Y	Y	Y	Y	Y	Y	Y	Y
Eagleton	?	?	?	?	N	Y	Y	Y
MONTANA								
Baucus	Y	Y	Y	Y	N	Y	Y	Y
Melcher	Y	Y	Y	Y	N	Y	Y	Y
NEBRASKA								
Exon	Y	Y	Y	Y	Y	Y	Y	Y
Zorinsky	Y	Y	Y	Y	Y	Y	Y	Y
NEVADA								
Hecht	Y	Y	Y	Y	Y	Y	Y	Y
Laxalt	?	Y	Y	Y	Y	Y	Y	Y
NEW HAMPSHIRE								
Humphrey	Y	Y	?	?	+	?	?	Y
Rudman	Y	Y	Y	Y	Y	Y	Y	Y
NEW JERSEY								
Bradley	?	?	Y	Y	N	Y	?	Y
Lautenberg	Y	Y	Y	Y	N	Y	?	Y
NEW MEXICO								
Domenici	Y	Y	Y	Y	Y	Y	Y	Y
Bingaman	Y	Y	Y	Y	N	Y	Y	Y
NEW YORK								
D'Amato	Y	Y	Y	Y	Y	Y	Y	Y
Moynihan	Y	Y	Y	Y	N	Y	Y	Y
NORTH CAROLINA								
East	?	Y	Y	?	+	?	?	Y
Helms	?	Y	Y	Y	Y	Y	Y	Y
NORTH DAKOTA								
Andrews	Y	Y	Y	Y	Y	Y	Y	Y
Burdick	Y	Y	Y	Y	Y	Y	Y	Y
OHIO								
Glenn	Y	Y	Y	Y	N	Y	Y	Y
Metzenbaum	Y	Y	Y	Y	N	Y	Y	Y
OKLAHOMA								
Nickles	Y	Y	Y	Y	Y	Y	Y	Y
Boren	Y	Y	Y	Y	Y	Y	Y	Y
OREGON								
Hatfield	Y	Y	Y	Y	Y	Y	Y	Y
Packwood	Y	Y	?	Y	Y	Y	Y	Y
PENNSYLVANIA								
Heinz	?	Y	Y	Y	Y	Y	Y	Y
Specter	Y	Y	Y	Y	Y	Y	Y	Y
RHODE ISLAND								
Chafee	Y	Y	?	Y	Y	Y	Y	Y
Pell	Y	Y	Y	Y	Y	Y	+	Y
SOUTH CAROLINA								
Thurmond	Y	Y	Y	Y	Y	Y	Y	Y
Hollings	Y	Y	Y	Y	Y	Y	Y	Y
SOUTH DAKOTA								
Abdnor	Y	Y	Y	Y	Y	Y	Y	Y
Pressler	Y	Y	Y	?	Y	Y	Y	Y
TENNESSEE								
Gore	Y	Y	Y	Y	N	Y	Y	Y
Sasser	Y	Y	Y	Y	N	Y	Y	Y
TEXAS								
Gramm	Y	Y	Y	Y	Y	Y	Y	Y
Bentsen	Y	Y	Y	Y	Y	Y	Y	Y
UTAH								
Garn	?	?	?	?	+	?	?	?
Hatch	Y	Y	Y	Y	Y	Y	Y	Y
VERMONT								
Stafford	Y	Y	Y	Y	Y	Y	Y	Y
Leahy	Y	Y	Y	Y	N	Y	Y	Y
VIRGINIA								
Trible	Y	?	Y	Y	Y	Y	Y	Y
Warner	Y	Y	Y	Y	Y	Y	Y	Y
WASHINGTON								
Evans	Y	Y	Y	Y	Y	Y	Y	Y
Gorton	Y	Y	Y	Y	Y	Y	Y	Y
WEST VIRGINIA								
Byrd	Y	Y	Y	Y	N	Y	Y	Y
Rockefeller	Y	Y	Y	Y	N	Y	Y	Y
WISCONSIN								
Kasten	Y	Y	Y	Y	Y	Y	Y	Y
Proxmire	Y	Y	Y	Y	N	Y	Y	Y
WYOMING								
Simpson	Y	Y	Y	Y	Y	Y	Y	Y
Wallop	Y	Y	?	Y	Y	Y	Y	Y

KEY

- Y Voted for (yea).
- # Paired for.
- + Announced for.
- N Voted against (nay).
- X Paired against.
- - Announced against.
- P Voted "present".
- C Voted "present" to avoid possible conflict of interest.
- ? Did not vote or otherwise make a position known.

Democrats *Republicans*

ND - Northern Democrats SD - Southern Democrats (Southern states - Ala., Ark., Fla., Ga., Ky., La., Miss., N.C., Okla., S.C., Tenn., Texas, Va.)

5. Meese Nomination. Simpson, R-Wyo., motion to instruct the sergeant-at-arms to request the attendance of absent senators. Motion agreed to 79-2: R 40-2; D 39-0 (ND 29-0, SD 10-0), Feb. 22, 1985.

6. Meese Nomination. Dole, R-Kan., motion to instruct the sergeant-at-arms to request the attendance of absent senators. Motion agreed to 89-3: R 46-3; D 43-0 (ND 31-0, SD 12-0), Feb. 22, 1985.

7. Meese Nomination. Dole, R-Kan., motion to instruct the sergeant-at-arms to request the attendance of absent senators. Motion agreed to 88-3: R 43-3; D 45-0 (ND 32-0, SD 13-0), Feb. 22, 1985.

8. Meese Nomination. Simpson, R-Wyo., motion to instruct the sergeant-at-arms to request the attendance of absent senators. Motion agreed to 86-2: R 42-2; D 44-0 (ND 31-0, SD 13-0), Feb. 23, 1985.

9. Meese Nomination. Confirmation of President Reagan's nomination of Edwin Meese III of California to be attorney general. Confirmed 63-31: R 48-0; D 15-31 (ND 7-26, SD 8-5), Feb. 23, 1985. A "yea" was a vote supporting the president's position.

10. S 391. Interstate Highway Funding Act. Passage of the bill to release more than $7 billion from the Highway Trust Fund to the states for the second half of fiscal 1984 and all of fiscal 1985 for work on Interstate highways; and to reduce the trust fund obligation ceiling for fiscal 1986, from $14.45 billion to $12.75 billion. Passed 94-0: R 48-0; D 46-0 (ND 33-0, SD 13-0), Feb. 23, 1985.

11. S Res 79. Emergency Farm Credit. Adoption of the resolution expressing the sense of the Senate that adequate funding should be available for Farmers Home Administration (FmHA) loans for farmers' operating expenses and for FmHA guarantees of restructured loans to farmers by private lenders, that a "cash-flow" requirement for FmHA-guaranteed loans be lowered to 100 percent from 110 percent, and that the amount of a loan covered by the FmHA guarantee would, after a certain number of years, be equal to 90 percent of the principal. Adopted 91-0: R 48-0; D 43-0 (ND 30-0, SD 13-0), Feb. 23, 1985. A "yea" was a vote supporting the president's position.

12. S 457. African Relief. Helms, R-N.C., motion to instruct the sergeant-at-arms to request the attendance of absent senators. Motion agreed to 94-4: R 49-3; D 45-1 (ND 33-0, SD 12-1), Feb. 27, 1985.

Corresponding to Congressional Record Votes 13, 14, 15, 16, 17

	13	14	15	16	17
ALABAMA					
Denton	N	N	Y	N	Y
Heflin	Y	Y	N	Y	Y
ALASKA					
Murkowski	N	N	Y	N	Y
Stevens	N	N	Y	N	Y
ARIZONA					
Goldwater	N	N	Y	N	?
DeConcini	Y	Y	N	Y	Y
ARKANSAS					
Bumpers	Y	Y	N	Y	Y
Pryor	Y	Y	N	Y	Y
CALIFORNIA					
Wilson	N	N	Y	N	N
Cranston	Y	Y	N	Y	Y
COLORADO					
Armstrong	N	N	Y	N	N
Hart	Y	Y	N	Y	Y
CONNECTICUT					
Weicker	Y	Y	N	N	Y
Dodd	Y	Y	N	Y	Y
DELAWARE					
Roth	N	N	Y	N	N
Biden	Y	Y	N	Y	Y
FLORIDA					
Hawkins	N	N	Y	N	Y
Chiles	Y	Y	N	Y	Y
GEORGIA					
Mattingly	N	N	Y	N	N
Nunn	Y	Y	N	Y	Y
HAWAII					
Inouye	Y	Y	N	Y	Y
Matsunaga	Y	Y	N	Y	Y
IDAHO					
McClure	N	N	Y	N	N
Symms	N	N	Y	N	N
ILLINOIS					
Dixon	Y	Y	N	Y	Y
Simon	Y	Y	N	Y	Y
INDIANA					
Lugar	N	N	Y	N	N
Quayle	N	N	Y	N	N
IOWA					
Grassley	Y	Y	N	Y	Y
Harkin	Y	Y	N	Y	Y
KANSAS					
Dole	N	N	Y	N	N
Kassebaum	N	N	N	N	N
KENTUCKY					
McConnell	N	N	Y	N	N
Ford	Y	Y	N	Y	Y
LOUISIANA					
Johnston	Y	Y	N	Y	Y
Long	Y	Y	N	Y	Y
MAINE					
Cohen	N	N	Y	N	N
Mitchell	Y	Y	N	Y	Y
MARYLAND					
Mathias	N	N	N	N	Y
Sarbanes	Y	Y	N	Y	Y
MASSACHUSETTS					
Kennedy	Y	Y	N	Y	Y
Kerry	Y	Y	N	Y	Y
MICHIGAN					
Levin	Y	Y	N	Y	Y
Riegle	Y	Y	N	Y	Y
MINNESOTA					
Boschwitz	N	N	Y	N	N
Durenberger	Y	Y	N	N	Y
MISSISSIPPI					
Cochran	N	N	Y	N	N
Stennis	Y	Y	N	Y	Y
MISSOURI					
Danforth	Y	Y	N	Y	Y
Eagleton	Y	Y	N	Y	Y
MONTANA					
Baucus	Y	Y	N	Y	Y
Melcher	Y	Y	N	Y	Y
NEBRASKA					
Exon	Y	Y	N	Y	Y
Zorinsky	Y	Y	N	Y	Y
NEVADA					
Hecht	N	N	Y	N	N
Laxalt	N	N	Y	N	N
NEW HAMPSHIRE					
Humphrey	N	N	Y	N	N
Rudman	N	N	Y	N	N
NEW JERSEY					
Bradley	Y	Y	Y	N	Y
Lautenberg	Y	Y	N	Y	Y
NEW MEXICO					
Domenici	N	N	Y	N	N
Bingaman	Y	Y	N	Y	Y
NEW YORK					
D'Amato	N	N	Y	N	Y
Moynihan	Y	Y	N	Y	Y
NORTH CAROLINA					
East	N	N	Y	N	N
Helms	N	N	Y	N	N
NORTH DAKOTA					
Andrews	Y	Y	N	Y	Y
Burdick	Y	Y	N	Y	Y
OHIO					
Glenn	Y	Y	N	Y	Y
Metzenbaum	Y	Y	N	Y	Y
OKLAHOMA					
Nickles	N	N	Y	N	N
Boren	Y	Y	N	Y	Y
OREGON					
Hatfield	N	N	Y	N	Y
Packwood	N	N	Y	N	N
PENNSYLVANIA					
Heinz	N	N	Y	N	N
Specter	N	N	Y	N	Y
RHODE ISLAND					
Chafee	N	N	Y	N	N
Pell	Y	Y	N	Y	Y
SOUTH CAROLINA					
Thurmond	N	N	Y	N	N
Hollings	Y	Y	N	Y	Y
SOUTH DAKOTA					
Abdnor	Y	Y	N	Y	Y
Pressler	Y	Y	N	Y	Y
TENNESSEE					
Gore	Y	Y	N	Y	Y
Sasser	Y	Y	N	Y	Y
TEXAS					
Gramm	N	N	Y	N	N
Bentsen	Y	Y	N	Y	Y
UTAH					
Garn	-	-	+	-	-
Hatch	N	N	Y	N	N
VERMONT					
Stafford	N	N	Y	N	N
Leahy	Y	Y	N	Y	Y
VIRGINIA					
Trible	N	N	Y	N	N
Warner	N	N	Y	N	N
WASHINGTON					
Evans	N	N	Y	N	N
Gorton	N	N	Y	N	N
WEST VIRGINIA					
Byrd	Y	Y	N	Y	Y
Rockefeller	Y	Y	N	Y	Y
WISCONSIN					
Kasten	Y	Y	N	N	Y
Proxmire	N	N	Y	N	N
WYOMING					
Simpson	N	N	Y	N	N
Wallop	N	N	?	?	?

KEY

- Y Voted for (yea).
- # Paired for.
- + Announced for.
- N Voted against (nay).
- X Paired against.
- - Announced against.
- P Voted "present".
- C Voted "present" to avoid possible conflict of interest.
- ? Did not vote or otherwise make a position known.

Democrats ***Republicans***

ND - Northern Democrats SD - Southern Democrats (Southern states - Ala., Ark., Fla., Ga., Ky., La., Miss., N.C., Okla., S.C., Tenn., Texas, Va.)

13. S 457. African Relief/Farm Credit. Melcher, D-Mont., substitute to the Zorinsky, D-Neb., amendment *(see vote 14, below)*, to authorize $100 million to offset interest reductions by private lenders on restructured loans guaranteed by the Farmers Home Administration (FmHA), to increase FmHA loan guarantee authority by $1.85 billion, and to revise certain eligibility rules for the loan guarantees. (The Melcher amendment was identical to the Zorinsky amendment, except that it omitted a section that would have eliminated a requirement that banks forgive a portion of interest or principal of a farm loan in order to qualify for an FmHA guarantee. The effect of the vote was to leave that requirement intact.) Adopted 54-45: R 8-44; D 46-1 (ND 32-1, SD 14-0), Feb. 27, 1985. A "nay" was a vote supporting the president's position.

14. S 457. African Relief/Farm Credit. Zorinsky, D-Neb., amendment, as amended by the Melcher, D-Mont., substitute *(see vote 13, above)*, to authorize $100 million to offset interest reductions by private lenders on restructured loans guaranteed by the Farmers Home Administration (FmHA), to increase FmHA loan guarantee authority by $1.85 billion, and to revise certain eligibility rules for the loan guarantees. Adopted 54-45: R 8-44; D 46-1 (ND 32-1, SD 14-0), Feb. 27, 1985. A "nay" was a vote supporting the president's position.

15. S 457. African Relief/Farm Credit. Gramm, R-Texas, amendment to bar implementation of any farm credit provisions of the legislation that would increase the federal budget deficit. Rejected 43-55: R 41-10; D 2-45 (ND 2-31, SD 0-14), Feb. 27, 1985.

16. S 457. African Relief/Farm Credit. Dixon, D-Ill., amendment to authorize the Commodity Credit Corporation to advance eligible farmers up to half the commodity price support loans they would be due at harvest time, up to a maximum of $50,000. Adopted 50-48: R 5-46; D 45-2 (ND 31-2, SD 14-0), Feb. 27, 1985. A "nay" was a vote supporting the president's position.

17. HR 1096. African Relief/Farm Credit. Passage of the bill to authorize $175 million in non-food aid for emergency relief to Africa, to authorize $100 million to offset interest on restructured private farm loans guaranteed by the Farmers Home Administration (FmHA), to increase the FmHA loan guarantee program by $1.85 billion and revise certain eligibility rules and to authorize advances to eligible farmers of Commodity Credit Corporation commodity price-support loans. Passed 62-35: R 16-34; D 46-1 (ND 32-1, SD 14-0), Feb. 27, 1985. A "nay" was a vote supporting the president's position.

CQ Senate Vote 18

Corresponding to Congressional Record Vote 18

	18
ALABAMA	
Denton	Y
Heflin	Y
ALASKA	
Murkowski	Y
Stevens	Y
ARIZONA	
Goldwater	Y
DeConcini	Y
ARKANSAS	
Bumpers	Y
Pryor	Y
CALIFORNIA	
Wilson	Y
Cranston	Y
COLORADO	
Armstrong	Y
Hart	Y
CONNECTICUT	
Weicker	Y
Dodd	Y
DELAWARE	
Roth	Y
Biden	Y
FLORIDA	
Hawkins	Y
Chiles	Y
GEORGIA	
Mattingly	Y
Nunn	Y
HAWAII	
Inouye	Y
Matsunaga	Y
IDAHO	
McClure	Y
Symms	+
ILLINOIS	
Dixon	Y
Simon	Y
INDIANA	
Lugar	Y
Quayle	Y

	18
IOWA	
Grassley	Y
Harkin	Y
KANSAS	
Dole	Y
Kassebaum	Y
KENTUCKY	
McConnell	Y
Ford	Y
LOUISIANA	
Johnston	Y
Long	Y
MAINE	
Cohen	Y
Mitchell	Y
MARYLAND	
Mathias	Y
Sarbanes	Y
MASSACHUSETTS	
Kennedy	Y
Kerry	Y
MICHIGAN	
Levin	Y
Riegle	Y
MINNESOTA	
Boschwitz	Y
Durenberger	Y
MISSISSIPPI	
Cochran	Y
Stennis	Y
MISSOURI	
Danforth	Y
Eagleton	Y
MONTANA	
Baucus	+
Melcher	Y
NEBRASKA	
Exon	Y
Zorinsky	Y
NEVADA	
Hecht	Y
Laxalt	Y

	18
NEW HAMPSHIRE	
Humphrey	Y
Rudman	Y
NEW JERSEY	
Bradley	Y
Lautenberg	Y
NEW MEXICO	
Domenici	Y
Bingaman	Y
NEW YORK	
D'Amato	Y
Moynihan	Y
NORTH CAROLINA	
East	Y
Helms	Y
NORTH DAKOTA	
Andrews	Y
Burdick	Y
OHIO	
Glenn	Y
Metzenbaum	Y
OKLAHOMA	
Nickles	Y
Boren	Y
OREGON	
Hatfield	Y
Packwood	Y
PENNSYLVANIA	
Heinz	Y
Specter	Y
RHODE ISLAND	
Chafee	Y
Pell	Y
SOUTH CAROLINA	
Thurmond	Y
Hollings	Y
SOUTH DAKOTA	
Abdnor	?
Pressler	Y
TENNESSEE	
Gore	Y
Sasser	Y

KEY

- Y Voted for (yea).
- # Paired for.
- + Announced for.
- N Voted against (nay).
- X Paired against.
- \- Announced against.
- P Voted "present".
- C Voted "present" to avoid possible conflict of interest.
- ? Did not vote or otherwise make a position known.

Democrats *Republicans*

	18
TEXAS	
Gramm	Y
Bentsen	Y
UTAH	
Garn	Y
Hatch	Y
VERMONT	
Stafford	Y
Leahy	Y
VIRGINIA	
Trible	Y
Warner	Y
WASHINGTON	
Evans	Y
Gorton	Y
WEST VIRGINIA	
Byrd	Y
Rockefeller	?
WISCONSIN	
Kasten	Y
Proxmire	Y
WYOMING	
Simpson	Y
Wallop	Y

ND - Northern Democrats   SD - Southern Democrats (Southern states - Ala., Ark., Fla., Ga., Ky., La., Miss., N.C., Okla., S.C., Tenn., Texas, Va.)

18. Treaty Doc 99-2, 99th Cong, 1st Sess, Pacific Salmon Treaty. Adoption of the resolution of ratification to the Treaty Between the Government of the United States of America and the Government of Canada Concerning Pacific Salmon. Adopted 96-0: R 51-0; D 45-0 (ND 31-0, SD 14-0), March 7, 1985. A two-thirds majority of those present and voting (64 in this case) is required for adoption of resolutions of ratification.

	19	20	21
ALABAMA			
Denton	Y	Y	Y
Heflin	Y	Y	Y
ALASKA			
Murkowski	Y	Y	Y
Stevens	Y	Y	Y
ARIZONA			
Goldwater	Y	Y	N
DeConcini	Y	Y	Y
ARKANSAS			
Bumpers	N	N	Y
Pryor	N	N	Y
CALIFORNIA			
Wilson	Y	Y	Y
Cranston	N	N	Y
COLORADO			
Armstrong	Y	Y	Y
Hart	N	N	Y
CONNECTICUT			
Weicker	N	N	Y
Dodd	N	N	Y
DELAWARE			
Roth	Y	Y	Y
Biden	N	N	Y
FLORIDA			
Hawkins	Y	Y	Y
Chiles	N	N	Y
GEORGIA			
Mattingly	Y	Y	Y
Nunn	Y	Y	Y
HAWAII			
Inouye	N	N	Y
Matsunaga	N	N	Y
IDAHO			
McClure	Y	Y	Y
Symms	Y	Y	Y
ILLINOIS			
Dixon	N	N	Y
Simon	N	N	Y
INDIANA			
Lugar	Y	Y	Y
Quayle	Y	Y	Y
IOWA			
Grassley	N	N	Y
Harkin	N	N	Y
KANSAS			
Dole	Y	Y	Y
Kassebaum	N	N	Y
KENTUCKY			
McConnell	Y	Y	Y
Ford	N	N	Y
LOUISIANA			
Johnston	N	N	Y
Long	Y	Y	Y
MAINE			
Cohen	Y	Y	Y
Mitchell	N	N	Y
MARYLAND			
Mathias	Y	Y	Y
Sarbanes	N	N	Y
MASSACHUSETTS			
Kennedy	N	N	Y
Kerry	N	N	Y
MICHIGAN			
Levin	N	N	Y
Riegle	N	N	Y
MINNESOTA			
Boschwitz	Y	Y	Y
Durenberger	N	N	Y
MISSISSIPPI			
Cochran	Y	Y	Y
Stennis	Y	Y	Y
MISSOURI			
Danforth	Y	Y	Y
Eagleton	N	N	Y
MONTANA			
Baucus	N	N	Y
Melcher	N	N	Y
NEBRASKA			
Exon	N	N	Y
Zorinsky	Y	Y	Y
NEVADA			
Hecht	Y	Y	Y
Laxalt	Y	Y	Y
NEW HAMPSHIRE			
Humphrey	Y	Y	Y
Rudman	Y	Y	Y
NEW JERSEY			
Bradley	N	N	Y
Lautenberg	N	N	Y
NEW MEXICO			
Domenici	Y	Y	Y
Bingaman	N	N	Y
NEW YORK			
D'Amato	Y	Y	Y
Moynihan	N	N	Y
NORTH CAROLINA			
East	Y	Y	Y
Helms	Y	Y	Y
NORTH DAKOTA			
Andrews	N	N	Y
Burdick	N	N	Y
OHIO			
Glenn	N	N	Y
Metzenbaum	N	N	Y
OKLAHOMA			
Nickles	Y	Y	Y
Boren	Y	Y	+
OREGON			
Hatfield	N	N	Y
Packwood	Y	Y	Y
PENNSYLVANIA			
Heinz	Y	Y	Y
Specter	Y	Y	Y
RHODE ISLAND			
Chafee	Y	Y	Y
Pell	N	N	Y
SOUTH CAROLINA			
Thurmond	Y	Y	Y
Hollings	N	N	Y
SOUTH DAKOTA			
Abdnor	Y	Y	Y
Pressler	N	N	Y
TENNESSEE			
Gore	Y	Y	Y
Sasser	N	N	Y
TEXAS			
Gramm	Y	Y	Y
Bentsen	Y	Y	Y
UTAH			
Garn	Y	Y	Y
Hatch	Y	Y	Y
VERMONT			
Stafford	N	N	Y
Leahy	N	N	Y
VIRGINIA			
Trible	Y	Y	Y
Warner	Y	Y	Y
WASHINGTON			
Evans	Y	Y	Y
Gorton	Y	Y	Y
WEST VIRGINIA			
Byrd	Y	Y	Y
Rockefeller	N	N	Y
WISCONSIN			
Kasten	Y	Y	Y
Proxmire	N	N	Y
WYOMING			
Simpson	Y	Y	Y
Wallop	Y	Y	Y

KEY

- Y Voted for (yea).
- # Paired for.
- + Announced for.
- N Voted against (nay).
- X Paired against.
- \- Announced against.
- P Voted "present".
- C Voted "present" to avoid possible conflict of interest.
- ? Did not vote or otherwise make a position known.

Democrats ***Republicans***

ND - Northern Democrats SD - Southern Democrats (Southern states - Ala., Ark., Fla., Ga., Ky., La., Miss., N.C., Okla., S.C., Tenn., Texas, Va.)

19. S J Res 71. MX Missile Authorization. Passage of the joint resolution to reaffirm the authorization of $1.5 billion in the fiscal 1985 defense budget to purchase 21 MX missiles. Passed 55-45: R 45-8; D 10-37 (ND 3-30, SD 7-7), March 19, 1985. A "yea" was a vote supporting the president's position.

20. S J Res 75. MX Missile Appropriation. Passage of the joint resolution to reaffirm the appropriation of $1.5 billion in the fiscal 1985 defense budget to purchase 21 MX missiles. Passed 55-45: R 45-8; D 10-37 (ND 3-30, SD 7-7), March 20, 1985. A "yea" was a vote supporting the president's position.

21. HR 1239. African Famine Relief. Passage of the bill to appropriate $510 million for food aid and $175 million for disaster relief and other non-food aid to African countries suffering from famine. Passed 98-1: R 52-1; D 46-0 (ND 33-0, SD 13-0), March 20, 1985.

CQ Senate Vote 22

Corresponding to Congressional Record Vote 22

	22
ALABAMA	
Denton	Y
Heflin	Y
ALASKA	
Murkowski	Y
Stevens	Y
ARIZONA	
Goldwater	Y
DeConcini	Y
ARKANSAS	
Bumpers	Y
Pryor	Y
CALIFORNIA	
Wilson	Y
Cranston	Y
COLORADO	
Armstrong	Y
Hart	Y
CONNECTICUT	
Weicker	Y
Dodd	Y
DELAWARE	
Roth	Y
Biden	Y
FLORIDA	
Hawkins	Y
Chiles	Y
GEORGIA	
Mattingly	Y
Nunn	Y
HAWAII	
Inouye	Y
Matsunaga	Y
IDAHO	
McClure	Y
Symms	Y
ILLINOIS	
Dixon	Y
Simon	Y
INDIANA	
Lugar	Y
Quayle	Y

	22
IOWA	
Grassley	Y
Harkin	Y
KANSAS	
Dole	Y
Kassebaum	Y
KENTUCKY	
McConnell	Y
Ford	Y
LOUISIANA	
Johnston	Y
Long	Y
MAINE	
Cohen	Y
Mitchell	Y
MARYLAND	
Mathias	?
Sarbanes	Y
MASSACHUSETTS	
Kennedy	Y
Kerry	Y
MICHIGAN	
Levin	Y
Riegle	Y
MINNESOTA	
Boschwitz	Y
Durenberger	Y
MISSISSIPPI	
Cochran	Y
Stennis	Y
MISSOURI	
Danforth	Y
Eagleton	Y
MONTANA	
Baucus	Y
Melcher	+
NEBRASKA	
Exon	Y
Zorinsky	Y
NEVADA	
Hecht	Y
Laxalt	Y

	22
NEW HAMPSHIRE	
Humphrey	Y
Rudman	Y
NEW JERSEY	
Bradley	Y
Lautenberg	Y
NEW MEXICO	
Domenici	Y
Bingaman	Y
NEW YORK	
D'Amato	+
Moynihan	Y
NORTH CAROLINA	
East	+
Helms	Y
NORTH DAKOTA	
Andrews	Y
Burdick	?
OHIO	
Glenn	Y
Metzenbaum	Y
OKLAHOMA	
Nickles	Y
Boren	Y
OREGON	
Hatfield	?
Packwood	Y
PENNSYLVANIA	
Heinz	Y
Specter	Y
RHODE ISLAND	
Chafee	Y
Pell	Y
SOUTH CAROLINA	
Thurmond	Y
Hollings	Y
SOUTH DAKOTA	
Abdnor	Y
Pressler	Y
TENNESSEE	
Gore	Y
Sasser	Y

KEY

- Y Voted for (yea).
- # Paired for.
- \+ Announced for.
- N Voted against (nay).
- X Paired against.
- \- Announced against.
- P Voted "present".
- C Voted "present" to avoid possible conflict of interest.
- ? Did not vote or otherwise make a position known.

Democrats *Republicans*

	22
TEXAS	
Gramm	Y
Bentsen	Y
UTAH	
Garn	Y
Hatch	Y
VERMONT	
Stafford	?
Leahy	?
VIRGINIA	
Trible	Y
Warner	Y
WASHINGTON	
Evans	Y
Gorton	Y
WEST VIRGINIA	
Byrd	Y
Rockefeller	Y
WISCONSIN	
Kasten	Y
Proxmire	Y
WYOMING	
Simpson	Y
Wallop	Y

ND - Northern Democrats SD - Southern Democrats (Southern states - Ala., Ark., Fla., Ga., Ky., La., Miss., N.C., Okla., S.C., Tenn., Texas, Va.)

22. S Con Res 15. United States-Japan Trade. Adoption of the concurrent resolution to urge the president to retaliate against Japan if that country continues unfair trade practices, such as refusing to open its markets to foreign businesses. Adopted 92-0: R 48-0; D 44-0 (ND 30-0, SD 14-0), March 28, 1985.

	23	24	25	26	27	28	29
ALABAMA							
Denton	Y	N	Y	N	N	Y	Y
Heflin	Y	Y	Y	Y	N	Y	Y
ALASKA							
Murkowski	?	?	+	?	?	?	?
Stevens	Y	N	Y	?	N	Y	Y
ARIZONA							
Goldwater	Y	N	Y	N	N	Y	N
DeConcini	Y	Y	Y	N	N	Y	Y
ARKANSAS							
Bumpers	Y	N	Y	N	N	Y	Y
Pryor	Y	N	Y	N	N	Y	Y
CALIFORNIA							
Wilson	Y	N	Y	N	N	Y	Y
Cranston	N	Y	Y	Y	Y	Y	Y
COLORADO							
Armstrong	?	?	?	?	?	?	?
Hart	N	Y	Y	Y	Y	Y	Y
CONNECTICUT							
Weicker	Y	N	Y	N	N	Y	Y
Dodd	Y	Y	Y	Y	Y	Y	Y
DELAWARE							
Roth	N	N	Y	N	N	Y	Y
Biden	N	Y	Y	Y	Y	Y	Y
FLORIDA							
Hawkins	Y	N	Y	N	N	Y	Y
Chiles	N	Y	Y	N	N	Y	Y
GEORGIA							
Mattingly	Y	N	Y	N	N	Y	Y
Nunn	Y	Y	Y	N	N	Y	Y
HAWAII							
Inouye	Y	Y	Y	Y	Y	Y	Y
Matsunaga	Y	Y	Y	N	N	Y	Y
IDAHO							
McClure	Y	N	Y	N	N	Y	Y
Symms	Y	N	Y	N	N	Y	N
ILLINOIS							
Dixon	Y	Y	Y	Y	Y	Y	Y
Simon	N	Y	Y	Y	Y	Y	Y
INDIANA							
Lugar	Y	N	Y	N	N	Y	Y
Quayle	Y	N	Y	N	N	Y	Y
IOWA							
Grassley	N	Y	Y	N	N	Y	Y
Harkin	N	Y	Y	Y	Y	Y	Y
KANSAS							
Dole	N	N	Y	N	N	Y	Y
Kassebaum	Y	N	Y	N	N	Y	Y
KENTUCKY							
McConnell	N	N	Y	N	N	Y	Y
Ford	Y	Y	Y	N	N	Y	Y
LOUISIANA							
Johnston	N	Y	Y	Y	Y	Y	Y
Long	N	N	Y	Y	N	Y	Y
MAINE							
Cohen	Y	Y	Y	N	N	Y	Y
Mitchell	N	Y	Y	N	N	Y	Y
MARYLAND							
Mathias	Y	Y	Y	Y	Y	Y	Y
Sarbanes	Y	Y	Y	Y	Y	Y	Y
MASSACHUSETTS							
Kennedy	N	Y	Y	Y	Y	Y	Y
Kerry	N	Y	Y	Y	Y	Y	Y
MICHIGAN							
Levin	N	Y	Y	Y	Y	Y	Y
Riegle	Y	Y	Y	Y	Y	Y	Y
MINNESOTA							
Boschwitz	N	N	Y	N	N	Y	Y
Durenberger	?	?	?	?	?	?	?
MISSISSIPPI							
Cochran	N	N	Y	N	N	Y	Y
Stennis	N	?	?	N	N	Y	Y
MISSOURI							
Danforth	N	Y	Y	N	N	Y	Y
Eagleton	N	Y	Y	Y	Y	Y	Y
MONTANA							
Baucus	Y	Y	Y	N	Y	Y	Y
Melcher	Y	Y	Y	Y	Y	Y	Y
NEBRASKA							
Exon	Y	Y	Y	N	N	Y	Y
Zorinsky	Y	N	Y	N	N	Y	Y
NEVADA							
Hecht	Y	N	Y	N	N	Y	N
Laxalt	Y	N	Y	N	N	Y	Y
NEW HAMPSHIRE							
Humphrey	?	?	?	?	?	?	?
Rudman	Y	N	Y	N	N	Y	Y
NEW JERSEY							
Bradley	N	Y	Y	Y	Y	Y	Y
Lautenberg	N	Y	Y	?	Y	Y	Y
NEW MEXICO							
Domenici	N	N	Y	N	N	Y	Y
Bingaman	N	Y	Y	N	N	Y	Y
NEW YORK							
D'Amato	Y	N	Y	Y	N	Y	Y
Moynihan	?	Y	Y	Y	Y	Y	Y
NORTH CAROLINA							
East	Y	N	Y	N	N	Y	P
Helms	Y	Y	Y	N	N	Y	N
NORTH DAKOTA							
Andrews	Y	N	Y	N	N	Y	Y
Burdick	Y	Y	Y	Y	Y	Y	Y
OHIO							
Glenn	N	Y	Y	Y	Y	Y	Y
Metzenbaum	N	Y	Y	Y	Y	Y	Y
OKLAHOMA							
Nickles	Y	N	Y	N	N	Y	Y
Boren	Y	N	Y	N	N	Y	Y
OREGON							
Hatfield	-	-	?	+	+	+	+
Packwood	N	N	Y	N	N	Y	Y
PENNSYLVANIA							
Heinz	N	N	Y	Y	Y	Y	Y
Specter	Y	N	Y	Y	Y	Y	Y
RHODE ISLAND							
Chafee	N	Y	Y	N	N	Y	Y
Pell	N	Y	Y	Y	Y	Y	Y
SOUTH CAROLINA							
Thurmond	Y	N	Y	N	N	Y	Y
Hollings	N	N	Y	N	N	Y	Y
SOUTH DAKOTA							
Abdnor	Y	N	Y	N	N	Y	Y
Pressler	Y	N	Y	N	N	Y	Y
TENNESSEE							
Gore	Y	Y	Y	Y	N	Y	Y
Sasser	Y	Y	Y	Y	N	Y	Y
TEXAS							
Gramm	N	N	Y	N	N	Y	Y
Bentsen	N	N	Y	N	N	Y	Y
UTAH							
Garn	?	?	?	?	?	?	?
Hatch	Y	N	Y	N	N	Y	Y
VERMONT							
Stafford	Y	N	Y	N	N	Y	Y
Leahy	Y	N	Y	Y	Y	Y	Y
VIRGINIA							
Trible	N	Y	Y	N	N	Y	Y
Warner	N	Y	Y	N	N	Y	Y
WASHINGTON							
Evans	N	N	Y	N	N	Y	Y
Gorton	N	N	Y	Y	Y	Y	Y
WEST VIRGINIA							
Byrd	N	Y	Y	Y	Y	Y	Y
Rockefeller	N	Y	Y	Y	Y	Y	Y
WISCONSIN							
Kasten	Y	N	Y	N	Y	Y	Y
Proxmire	N	Y	N	N	N	Y	Y
WYOMING							
Simpson	N	N	Y	N	N	Y	Y
Wallop	Y	N	Y	N	N	Y	Y

KEY

- Y Voted for (yea).
- # Paired for.
- + Announced for.
- N Voted against (nay).
- X Paired against.
- \- Announced against.
- P Voted "present".
- C Voted "present" to avoid possible conflict of interest.
- ? Did not vote or otherwise make a position known.

Democrats *Republicans*

ND - Northern Democrats SD - Southern Democrats (Southern states - Ala., Ark., Fla., Ga., Ky., La., Miss., N.C., Okla., S.C., Tenn., Texas, Va.)

23. HR 1869. Automobile Record-keeping Requirements. Wallop, R-Wyo., amendment to prevent the taxation of limited personal use of cars that are used 75 percent or more of the time for business. Adopted 51-42: R 30-17; D 21-25 (ND 13-19, SD 8-6), April 3, 1985.

24. HR 1869. Automobile Record-keeping Requirements. Metzenbaum, D-Ohio, amendment to express the sense of Congress that current Internal Revenue Service regulations governing the taxation of personal use of airplanes by top executives not be eased. Rejected 46-47: R 8-39; D 38-8 (ND 31-2, SD 7-6), April 3, 1985.

25. HR 1869. Automobile Record-keeping Requirements. Passage of the bill to repeal rules requiring detailed "contemporaneous" logs of business and personal use of automobiles and other equipment to qualify for business tax deductions. Passed 92-1: R 47-0; D 45-1 (ND 32-1, SD 13-0), April 3, 1985.

26. HR 1866. Federal Supplemental Compensation. Specter, R-Pa., amendment to extend for six months the federal supplemental unemployment compensation program. Rejected 34-58: R 5-41; D 29-17 (ND 24-8, SD 5-9), April 3, 1985. A "nay" was a vote supporting the president's position.

27. HR 1866. Federal Supplemental Compensation. Levin, D-Mich., amendment to liberalize the federal-state extended benefit program for the long-term unemployed by allowing states to offer extra benefits if their insured unemployment rate was at least 5 percent, rather than 6 percent as in current law. Rejected 32-62: R 5-42; D 27-20 (ND 26-7, SD 1-13), April 3, 1985. A "nay" was a vote supporting the president's position.

28. HR 1866. Federal Supplemental Compensation. Passage of the bill to phase out the federal supplemental compensation program by enrolling no new beneficiaries after the week of March 31, but allowing those already on the rolls to receive their remaining benefits. Passed 94-0: R 47-0; D 47-0 (ND 33-0, SD 14-0), April 3, 1985. A "nay" was a vote supporting the president's position.

29. S J Res 96. Apartheid in South Africa. Passage of the joint resolution to condemn South Africa's racial policy of apartheid and to call on the secretary of state to conduct an investigation of violence there. Passed 89-4: R 42-4; D 47-0 (ND 33-0, SD 14-0), April 3, 1985.

CQ Senate Vote 30

Corresponding to Congressional Record Vote 30

	30
ALABAMA	
Denton	Y
Heflin	Y
ALASKA	
Murkowski	Y
Stevens	?
ARIZONA	
Goldwater	Y
DeConcini	Y
ARKANSAS	
Bumpers	N
Pryor	N
CALIFORNIA	
Wilson	Y
Cranston	Y
COLORADO	
Armstrong	Y
Hart	N
CONNECTICUT	
Weicker	Y
Dodd	Y
DELAWARE	
Roth	Y
Biden	?
FLORIDA	
Hawkins	Y
Chiles	N
GEORGIA	
Mattingly	Y
Nunn	Y
HAWAII	
Inouye	Y
Matsunaga	Y
IDAHO	
McClure	Y
Symms	Y
ILLINOIS	
Dixon	Y
Simon	N
INDIANA	
Lugar	Y
Quayle	Y
IOWA	
Grassley	N
Harkin	N
KANSAS	
Dole	Y
Kassebaum	Y
KENTUCKY	
McConnell	Y
Ford	Y
LOUISIANA	
Johnston	Y
Long	?
MAINE	
Cohen	Y
Mitchell	N
MARYLAND	
Mathias	Y
Sarbanes	N
MASSACHUSETTS	
Kennedy	Y
Kerry	N
MICHIGAN	
Levin	?
Riegle	N
MINNESOTA	
Boschwitz	Y
Durenberger	Y
MISSISSIPPI	
Cochran	Y
Stennis	Y
MISSOURI	
Danforth	Y
Eagleton	?
MONTANA	
Baucus	N
Melcher	N
NEBRASKA	
Exon	Y
Zorinsky	Y
NEVADA	
Hecht	Y
Laxalt	Y
NEW HAMPSHIRE	
Humphrey	Y
Rudman	Y
NEW JERSEY	
Bradley	Y
Lautenberg	Y
NEW MEXICO	
Domenici	Y
Bingaman	?
NEW YORK	
D'Amato	Y
Moynihan	N
NORTH CAROLINA	
East	Y
Helms	Y
NORTH DAKOTA	
Andrews	Y
Burdick	Y
OHIO	
Glenn	Y
Metzenbaum	Y
OKLAHOMA	
Nickles	Y
Boren	N
OREGON	
Hatfield	Y
Packwood	Y
PENNSYLVANIA	
Heinz	Y
Specter	Y
RHODE ISLAND	
Chafee	Y
Pell	Y
SOUTH CAROLINA	
Thurmond	Y
Hollings	Y
SOUTH DAKOTA	
Abdnor	Y
Pressler	Y
TENNESSEE	
Gore	N
Sasser	N
TEXAS	
Gramm	Y
Bentsen	Y
UTAH	
Garn	?
Hatch	Y
VERMONT	
Stafford	Y
Leahy	?
VIRGINIA	
Trible	Y
Warner	Y
WASHINGTON	
Evans	?
Gorton	Y
WEST VIRGINIA	
Byrd	Y
Rockefeller	Y
WISCONSIN	
Kasten	Y
Proxmire	N
WYOMING	
Simpson	Y
Wallop	Y

KEY

- Y Voted for (yea).
- # Paired for.
- + Announced for.
- N Voted against (nay).
- X Paired against.
- - Announced against.
- P Voted "present".
- C Voted "present" to avoid possible conflict of interest.
- ? Did not vote or otherwise make a position known.

Democrats ***Republicans***

ND - Northern Democrats SD - Southern Democrats (Southern states - Ala., Ark., Fla., Ga., Ky., La., Miss., N.C., Okla., S.C., Tenn., Texas, Va.)

30. Krings Nomination. Confirmation of President Reagan's nomination of John E. Krings of Virginia to be director of operational test and evaluation at the Department of Defense. Confirmed 73-18: R 49-1; D 24-17 (ND 17-11, SD 7-6), April 16, 1985. A "yea" was a vote supporting the president's position.

Corresponding to Congressional Record Votes 31, 32

	31	32
ALABAMA		
Denton	Y	Y
Heflin	Y	N
ALASKA		
Murkowski	Y	Y
Stevens	Y	Y
ARIZONA		
Goldwater	Y	Y
DeConcini	N	N
ARKANSAS		
Bumpers	N	N
Pryor	N	N
CALIFORNIA		
Wilson	Y	Y
Cranston	N	N
COLORADO		
Armstrong	Y	Y
Hart	N	N
CONNECTICUT		
Weicker	N	Y
Dodd	N	N
DELAWARE		
Roth	Y	Y
Biden	N	N
FLORIDA		
Hawkins	Y	Y
Chiles	Y	N
GEORGIA		
Mattingly	Y	Y
Nunn	Y	N
HAWAII		
Inouye	N	?
Matsunaga	N	N
IDAHO		
McClure	Y	Y
Symms	Y	Y
ILLINOIS		
Dixon	Y	N
Simon	N	N
INDIANA		
Lugar	Y	Y
Quayle	Y	Y
IOWA		
Grassley	Y	Y
Harkin	N	N
KANSAS		
Dole	Y	Y
Kassebaum	Y	Y
KENTUCKY		
McConnell	Y	Y
Ford	N	N
LOUISIANA		
Johnston	Y	N
Long	Y	N
MAINE		
Cohen	Y	Y
Mitchell	N	N
MARYLAND		
Mathias	N	Y
Sarbanes	N	N
MASSACHUSETTS		
Kennedy	N	N
Kerry	N	N
MICHIGAN		
Levin	N	N
Riegle	N	N
MINNESOTA		
Boschwitz	Y	Y
Durenberger	Y	Y
MISSISSIPPI		
Cochran	Y	Y
Stennis	Y	?
MISSOURI		
Danforth	Y	Y
Eagleton	N	?
MONTANA		
Baucus	N	N
Melcher	N	N
NEBRASKA		
Exon	N	N
Zorinsky	N	N
NEVADA		
Hecht	Y	Y
Laxalt	Y	Y
NEW HAMPSHIRE		
Humphrey	Y	Y
Rudman	Y	Y
NEW JERSEY		
Bradley	N	N
Lautenberg	N	N
NEW MEXICO		
Domenici	Y	Y
Bingaman	N	N
NEW YORK		
D'Amato	Y	Y
Moynihan	N	N
NORTH CAROLINA		
East	?	?
Helms	Y	Y
NORTH DAKOTA		
Andrews	Y	Y
Burdick	N	N
OHIO		
Glenn	N	N
Metzenbaum	N	N
OKLAHOMA		
Nickles	Y	Y
Boren	Y	N
OREGON		
Hatfield	N	Y
Packwood	N	Y
PENNSYLVANIA		
Heinz	Y	Y
Specter	N	Y
RHODE ISLAND		
Chafee	N	Y
Pell	N	N
SOUTH CAROLINA		
Thurmond	Y	Y
Hollings	Y	N
SOUTH DAKOTA		
Abdnor	Y	Y
Pressler	Y	Y
TENNESSEE		
Gore	N	N
Sasser	N	N
TEXAS		
Gramm	Y	Y
Bentsen	Y	N
UTAH		
Garn	Y	Y
Hatch	Y	Y
VERMONT		
Stafford	N	Y
Leahy	N	N
VIRGINIA		
Trible	Y	Y
Warner	Y	Y
WASHINGTON		
Evans	N	Y
Gorton	N	Y
WEST VIRGINIA		
Byrd	N	N
Rockefeller	N	N
WISCONSIN		
Kasten	Y	Y
Proxmire	N	N
WYOMING		
Simpson	Y	Y
Wallop	Y	Y

KEY

- Y Voted for (yea).
- # Paired for.
- + Announced for.
- N Voted against (nay).
- X Paired against.
- - Announced against.
- P Voted "present".
- C Voted "present" to avoid possible conflict of interest.
- ? Did not vote or otherwise make a position known.

Democrats ***Republicans***

ND - Northern Democrats SD - Southern Democrats (Southern states - Ala., Ark., Fla., Ga., Ky., La., Miss., N.C., Okla., S.C., Tenn., Texas, Va.)

31. S J Res 106. Aid to Nicaraguan Rebels. Passage of the joint resolution to approve the release of $14 million in fiscal 1985 for supporting military or paramilitary operations in Nicaragua. Passed 53-46: R 43-9; D 10-37 (ND 1-32, SD 9-5), April 23, 1985. A "yea" was a vote supporting the president's position.

32. Procedural Motion. Dole, R-Kan., motion to recess until Friday, April 26. Motion agreed to 52-44: R 52-0; D 0-44 (ND 0-31, SD 0-13), April 25, 1985. (Dole moved to recess to fend off a vote on the fiscal 1986 budget resolution.)

CQ Senate Votes 33 - 38

Corresponding to Congressional Record Votes 33, 34, 35, 36, 37, 38

	33	34	35	36	37	38
ALABAMA						
Denton	Y	Y	N	Y	N	Y
Heflin	N	N	Y	Y	Y	N
ALASKA						
Murkowski	Y	Y	N	Y	Y	Y
Stevens	Y	Y	N	Y	N	Y
ARIZONA						
Goldwater	Y	Y	N	Y	N	Y
DeConcini	N	N	Y	N	Y	Y
ARKANSAS						
Bumpers	N	N	Y	N	Y	N
Pryor	N	N	Y	N	Y	Y
CALIFORNIA						
Wilson	Y	Y	N	Y	N	Y
Cranston	N	N	Y	N	Y	Y
COLORADO						
Armstrong	Y	Y	N	Y	Y	Y
Hart	N	N	Y	N	Y	Y
CONNECTICUT						
Weicker	Y	Y	Y	N	Y	Y
Dodd	N	N	Y	N	Y	N
DELAWARE						
Roth	Y	Y	N	Y	Y	Y
Biden	N	N	Y	N	Y	Y
FLORIDA						
Hawkins	Y	Y	Y	Y	Y	Y
Chiles	N	N	Y	N	Y	N
GEORGIA						
Mattingly	Y	Y	Y	Y	Y	Y
Nunn	N	N	Y	Y	Y	N
HAWAII						
Inouye	N	N	Y	N	Y	Y
Matsunaga	N	N	Y	N	Y	Y
IDAHO						
McClure	Y	Y	N	Y	Y	Y
Symms	Y	Y	N	Y	N	Y
ILLINOIS						
Dixon	N	N	Y	N	Y	Y
Simon	N	N	Y	N	Y	N
INDIANA						
Lugar	Y	Y	Y	Y	Y	Y
Quayle	Y	Y	Y	Y	Y	Y
IOWA						
Grassley	Y	Y	Y	N	Y	Y
Harkin	N	N	Y	N	Y	Y
KANSAS						
Dole	Y	Y	N	Y	N	Y
Kassebaum	Y	Y	N	N	N	Y
KENTUCKY						
McConnell	Y	Y	Y	Y	Y	Y
Ford	N	N	Y	N	Y	Y
LOUISIANA						
Johnston	N	N	Y	Y	Y	Y
Long	Y	N	Y	Y	Y	Y
MAINE						
Cohen	Y	Y	Y	Y	Y	Y
Mitchell	N	N	Y	N	Y	Y
MARYLAND						
Mathias	Y	N	Y	N	Y	N
Sarbanes	N	N	Y	N	Y	N
MASSACHUSETTS						
Kennedy	N	N	Y	N	Y	Y
Kerry	N	N	Y	N	Y	Y
MICHIGAN						
Levin	N	N	Y	N	Y	Y
Riegle	N	N	Y	N	Y	N
MINNESOTA						
Boschwitz	Y	Y	N	N	N	Y
Durenberger	Y	Y	Y	Y	Y	?
MISSISSIPPI						
Cochran	Y	Y	N	Y	Y	Y
Stennis	N	N	N	Y	Y	?
MISSOURI						
Danforth	Y	Y	N	N	N	Y
Eagleton	N	N	Y	N	?	?
MONTANA						
Baucus	N	N	Y	N	Y	Y
Melcher	N	N	Y	N	Y	Y
NEBRASKA						
Exon	N	N	Y	N	Y	Y
Zorinsky	N	N	Y	Y	Y	Y
NEVADA						
Hecht	Y	Y	N	Y	N	Y
Laxalt	Y	Y	N	Y	N	N
NEW HAMPSHIRE						
Humphrey	Y	Y	N	Y	N	Y
Rudman	Y	Y	N	Y	Y	Y
NEW JERSEY						
Bradley	N	N	Y	Y	Y	Y
Lautenberg	N	N	Y	N	Y	Y
NEW MEXICO						
Domenici	Y	Y	N	Y	Y	Y
Bingaman	N	N	Y	N	Y	Y
NEW YORK						
D'Amato	Y	Y	Y	Y	Y	Y
Moynihan	N	N	Y	N	Y	Y
NORTH CAROLINA						
East	+	?	?	?	?	?
Helms	Y	Y	N	Y	N	Y
NORTH DAKOTA						
Andrews	Y	Y	Y	N	Y	Y
Burdick	N	N	Y	N	Y	Y
OHIO						
Glenn	N	N	Y	Y	Y	N
Metzenbaum	N	N	Y	N	Y	N
OKLAHOMA						
Nickles	Y	Y	N	N	Y	Y
Boren	N	N	Y	N	Y	Y
OREGON						
Hatfield	Y	Y	Y	N	Y	Y
Packwood	Y	Y	Y	Y	Y	Y
PENNSYLVANIA						
Heinz	Y	Y	Y	Y	Y	Y
Specter	Y	Y	Y	Y	Y	Y
RHODE ISLAND						
Chafee	Y	Y	N	N	Y	N
Pell	N	N	Y	N	Y	Y
SOUTH CAROLINA						
Thurmond	Y	Y	N	Y	Y	Y
Hollings	N	N	Y	N	Y	N
SOUTH DAKOTA						
Abdnor	Y	Y	N	N	Y	Y
Pressler	Y	Y	Y	N	Y	Y
TENNESSEE						
Gore	N	N	Y	N	Y	N
Sasser	N	N	Y	N	Y	Y
TEXAS						
Gramm	Y	Y	N	Y	Y	Y
Bentsen	N	N	Y	N	Y	Y
UTAH						
Garn	Y	Y	N	Y	N	Y
Hatch	Y	Y	N	Y	N	N
VERMONT						
Stafford	Y	Y	N	Y	Y	Y
Leahy	N	N	Y	N	Y	Y
VIRGINIA						
Trible	Y	Y	N	Y	Y	Y
Warner	Y	Y	N	Y	Y	Y
WASHINGTON						
Evans	Y	Y	N	Y	N	Y
Gorton	Y	Y	Y	Y	Y	Y
WEST VIRGINIA						
Byrd	Y	N	Y	N	Y	Y
Rockefeller	N	N	Y	N	Y	Y
WISCONSIN						
Kasten	Y	N	Y	Y	Y	Y
Proxmire	N	N	Y	N	N	Y
WYOMING						
Simpson	Y	Y	N	Y	Y	Y
Wallop	Y	Y	N	Y	N	N

KEY

- Y Voted for (yea).
- # Paired for.
- + Announced for.
- N Voted against (nay).
- X Paired against.
- - Announced against.
- P Voted "present".
- C Voted "present" to avoid possible conflict of interest.
- ? Did not vote or otherwise make a position known.

Democrats *Republicans*

ND - Northern Democrats SD - Southern Democrats (Southern states - Ala., Ark., Fla., Ga., Ky., La., Miss., N.C., Okla., S.C., Tenn., Texas, Va.)

33. S Con Res 32. First Budget Resolution, Fiscal 1986. Metzenbaum, D-Ohio, appeal of the chair's ruling that the Metzenbaum motion, to recess for 15 minutes and then reconvene and immediately proceed to a vote on a Democratic amendment to restore existing treatment of Social Security cost-of-living adjustments, was out of order. Ruling of the chair upheld 54-45: R 52-0; D 2-45 (ND 1-32, SD 1-13), April 30, 1985. (The effect of the vote was to ensure that the Senate would vote on the Senate GOP-White House budget before considering any amendments to it.)

34. S Con Res 32. First Budget Resolution, Fiscal 1986. Dole, R-Kan., perfecting amendment to the Dole-Domenici, R-N.M., amendment to the instructions of the Dole motion to recommit the concurrent resolution to the Budget Committee. The instructions ordered the insertion of the text of the Senate GOP-White House budget package. The Senate GOP-White House agreement set budget targets for the fiscal year ending Sept. 30, 1986, as follows: budget authority, $1,076 billion; outlays, $969 billion; revenues, $793.6 billion; deficit, $175.4 billion. The amendment also set preliminary goals for fiscal 1987-88, revised budget levels for fiscal 1985, and included reconciliation instructions requiring House and Senate committees to recommend legislative savings to meet the budget targets. Adopted 50-49: R 50-2; D 0-47 (ND 0-33, SD 0-14), April 30, 1985. (The effect of the vote was to give preliminary approval to the Senate GOP-White House budget.) A "yea" was a vote supporting the president's position.

35. S Con Res 32. First Budget Resolution, Fiscal 1986. Dole, R-Kan., perfecting amendment to the Dole-Domenici, R-N.M., amendment to the instructions of the Dole motion to recommit the concurrent resolution to the Budget Committee, to retain existing Social Security cost-of-living adjustments (COLAs). Adopted 65-34: R 19-33; D 46-1 (ND 33-0, SD 13-1), May 1, 1985. A "nay" was a vote supporting the president's position. (The Senate GOP-White House budget given preliminary Senate approval April 30 *(see vote 34, above)* set COLAs at the greater of 2 percent or the inflation rate minus 2 percentage points. Current law guarantees a full COLA if inflation exceeds 3 percent.) (Dole, using his privilege as majority leader to gain first recognition on the floor, introduced the amendment for Hawkins, R-Fla., and D'Amato, R-N.Y. The effect was to preclude Democratic amendments to the budget resolution.)

36. S Con Res 32. First Budget Resolution, Fiscal 1986. Goldwater, R-Ariz., motion to table (kill) the Dole, R-Kan., perfecting amendment to the Dole-Domenici, R-N.M., amendment to the instructions of the Dole motion to recommit the concurrent resolution to the Budget Committee, to limit budget authority for defense to 0 percent, inflation-adjusted, in fiscal 1986, and 3 percent, inflation-adjusted, in fiscal 1987 and 1988. Motion rejected 48-51: R 40-12; D 8-39 (ND 3-30, SD 5-9), May 2, 1985. A "yea" was a vote supporting the president's position. (Dole, using his privilege as majority leader to gain first recognition on the floor, introduced the amendment for Grassley, R-Iowa, and Hatfield, R-Ore. The effect was to preclude Democratic amendments to the budget resolution.)

37. S Con Res 32. First Budget Resolution, Fiscal 1986. Dole, R-Kan.-Murkowski, R-Alaska, perfecting amendment to the Dole-Domenici, R-N.M., amendment to the instructions of the Dole motion to recommit the concurrent resolution to the Budget Committee, to restore cost-of-living adjustment reductions for non-Social Security retirement programs. Adopted 80-18: R 35-17; D 45-1 (ND 31-1, SD 14-0), May 2, 1985. A "nay" was a vote supporting the president's position.

38. S Con Res 32. First Budget Resolution, Fiscal 1986. Packwood, R-Ore.-Dole, R-Kan.-Rudman, R-N.H., perfecting amendment to the Dole-Domenici, R-N.M., amendment to the instructions of the Dole motion to recommit the concurrent resolution to the Budget Committee, to express the sense of Congress that minimum taxes ought to be imposed on corporations and individuals. Adopted 79-17: R 46-5; D 33-12 (ND 26-6, SD 7-6), May 2, 1985.

	39	40	41	42	43	44
ALABAMA						
Denton	Y	Y	Y	Y	N	Y
Heflin	Y	N	Y	Y	Y	N
ALASKA						
Murkowski	Y	Y	N	Y	N	Y
Stevens	Y	N	N	X	N	Y
ARIZONA						
Goldwater	Y	Y	Y	Y	N	Y
DeConcini	Y	N	Y	Y	N	Y
ARKANSAS						
Bumpers	Y	N	Y	Y	Y	N
Pryor	Y	N	N	Y	Y	N
CALIFORNIA						
Wilson	Y	N	Y	Y	N	Y
Cranston	Y	N	Y	Y	N	Y
COLORADO						
Armstrong	Y	Y	Y	Y	?	Y
Hart	Y	N	N	Y	Y	N
CONNECTICUT						
Weicker	Y	N	N	Y	N	Y
Dodd	Y	N	Y	Y	Y	N
DELAWARE						
Roth	Y	N	N	Y	N	Y
Biden	Y	N	N	?	N	Y
FLORIDA						
Hawkins	Y	N	Y	Y	Y	N
Chiles	Y	N	Y	Y	Y	N
GEORGIA						
Mattingly	Y	Y	Y	Y	N	Y
Nunn	Y	N	N	Y	Y	N
HAWAII						
Inouye	Y	N	N	Y	Y	N
Matsunaga	Y	N	N	Y	?	?
IDAHO						
McClure	N	Y	N	Y	N	Y
Symms	N	Y	Y	#	Y	N
ILLINOIS						
Dixon	Y	N	N	?	N	Y
Simon	Y	N	N	Y	N	Y
INDIANA						
Lugar	Y	N	N	Y	N	Y
Quayle	Y	Y	Y	Y	N	Y
IOWA						
Grassley	Y	Y	Y	Y	N	Y
Harkin	Y	N	Y	Y	Y	Y
KANSAS						
Dole	Y	Y	Y	Y	N	Y
Kassebaum	Y	N	Y	Y	N	Y
KENTUCKY						
McConnell	Y	Y	N	Y	Y	N
Ford	Y	N	Y	Y	Y	N
LOUISIANA						
Johnston	Y	N	N	Y	Y	N
Long	Y	?	N	Y	Y	N
MAINE						
Cohen	Y	N	Y	Y	N	Y
Mitchell	Y	N	Y	Y	Y	N
MARYLAND						
Mathias	Y	N	N	N	Y	N
Sarbanes	Y	N	N	N	Y	N
MASSACHUSETTS						
Kennedy	Y	N	N	Y	Y	Y
Kerry	Y	N	N	Y	Y	Y
MICHIGAN						
Levin	Y	N	N	Y	Y	N
Riegle	Y	N	N	Y	N	Y
MINNESOTA						
Boschwitz	Y	N	N	Y	N	Y
Durenberger	Y	N	N	Y	N	Y
MISSISSIPPI						
Cochran	Y	N	N	Y	N	Y
Stennis	Y	N	Y	?	?	?
MISSOURI						
Danforth	Y	N	Y	Y	N	Y
Eagleton	Y	N	N	Y	Y	N
MONTANA						
Baucus	Y	N	N	Y	Y	N
Melcher	Y	N	N	Y	Y	Y
NEBRASKA						
Exon	Y	Y	Y	?	?	?
Zorinsky	Y	Y	Y	Y	N	Y
NEVADA						
Hecht	Y	N	Y	Y	N	Y
Laxalt	Y	N	N	Y	N	Y
NEW HAMPSHIRE						
Humphrey	N	Y	Y	Y	N	Y
Rudman	Y	N	N	Y	N	Y
NEW JERSEY						
Bradley	Y	N	N	Y	N	Y
Lautenberg	Y	N	N	Y	N	Y
NEW MEXICO						
Domenici	Y	N	Y	Y	N	Y
Bingaman	Y	N	N	Y	N	Y
NEW YORK						
D'Amato	Y	N	Y	Y	N	Y
Moynihan	Y	N	N	Y	Y	N
NORTH CAROLINA						
East	?	?	?	?	?	?
Helms	N	Y	Y	Y	N	Y
NORTH DAKOTA						
Andrews	Y	N	Y	Y	N	Y
Burdick	Y	N	Y	Y	Y	Y
OHIO						
Glenn	Y	N	N	?	Y	N
Metzenbaum	Y	N	N	Y	N	Y
OKLAHOMA						
Nickles	Y	Y	Y	Y	Y	N
Boren	Y	Y	?	Y	Y	N
OREGON						
Hatfield	Y	N	N	Y	Y	N
Packwood	Y	N	N	N	N	Y
PENNSYLVANIA						
Heinz	Y	N	Y	Y	N	Y
Specter	Y	N	Y	N	N	Y
RHODE ISLAND						
Chafee	Y	N	N	Y	N	Y
Pell	Y	N	N	Y	N	Y
SOUTH CAROLINA						
Thurmond	Y	Y	Y	Y	N	Y
Hollings	Y	N	N	Y	Y	Y
SOUTH DAKOTA						
Abdnor	Y	Y	Y	Y	N	Y
Pressler	Y	Y	Y	Y	N	Y
TENNESSEE						
Gore	Y	N	N	Y	Y	N
Sasser	Y	N	N	Y	Y	N
TEXAS						
Gramm	Y	Y	Y	Y	N	Y
Bentsen	Y	Y	Y	Y	Y	N
UTAH						
Garn	Y	Y	Y	Y	N	Y
Hatch	Y	N	Y	Y	N	Y
VERMONT						
Stafford	Y	N	N	?	N	Y
Leahy	Y	N	Y	Y	N	Y
VIRGINIA						
Trible	Y	N	Y	Y	N	Y
Warner	Y	N	Y	Y	Y	N
WASHINGTON						
Evans	Y	N	N	Y	N	Y
Gorton	Y	N	N	Y	N	Y
WEST VIRGINIA						
Byrd	Y	N	N	Y	Y	N
Rockefeller	Y	N	N	Y	Y	N
WISCONSIN						
Kasten	Y	Y	Y	Y	N	Y
Proxmire	N	Y	Y	N	N	Y
WYOMING						
Simpson	Y	Y	Y	Y	N	Y
Wallop	N	Y	Y	Y	Y	N

KEY

- Y Voted for (yea).
- # Paired for.
- \+ Announced for.
- N Voted against (nay).
- X Paired against.
- \- Announced against.
- P Voted "present".
- C Voted "present" to avoid possible conflict of interest.
- ? Did not vote or otherwise make a position known.

Democrats ***Republicans***

ND - Northern Democrats SD - Southern Democrats (Southern states - Ala., Ark., Fla., Ga., Ky., La., Miss., N.C., Okla., S.C., Tenn., Texas, Va.)

39. S Con Res 32. First Budget Resolution, Fiscal 1986. Packwood, R-Ore., perfecting amendment to the Dole, R-Kan.-Domenici, R-N.M., amendment to the instructions of the Dole motion to recommit the concurrent resolution to the Budget Committee, to restore $2.6 billion in funding for Medicare and Medicaid for fiscal years 1986-88. Adopted 93-6: R 47-5; D 46-1 (ND 32-1, SD 14-0), May 3, 1985. (The effect was to set total reductions in the two health programs at $17.5 billion for the three fiscal years, instead of $20.1 billion as called for in the Senate GOP-White House budget.)

40. S Con Res 32. First Budget Resolution, Fiscal 1986. Gramm, R-Texas, perfecting amendment to the Dole, R-Kan.-Domenici, R-N.M., amendment to the instructions of the Dole motion to recommit the concurrent resolution to the Budget Committee, to terminate funding for the Legal Services Corporation and to transfer $300 million, approximately the amount of money saved by the termination, to crop insurance and soil and water conservation programs. Rejected 27-71: R 22-30; D 5-41 (ND 3-30, SD 2-11), May 3, 1985.

41. S Con Res 32. First Budget Resolution, Fiscal 1986. Helms, R-N.C., perfecting amendment to the Dole, R-Kan.-Domenici, R-N.M., amendment to the instructions of the Dole motion to recommit the concurrent resolution to the Budget Committee, to lower the salaries of members of Congress by 10 percent and to use the resulting savings to reduce the federal deficit. Rejected 49-49: R 33-19; D 16-30 (ND 10-23, SD 6-7), May 3, 1985.

42. S Con Res 32. First Budget Resolution, Fiscal 1986. Nickles, R-Okla., perfecting amendment to the Dole, R-Kan.-Domenici, R-N.M., amendment to the instructions of the Dole motion to recommit the concurrent resolution to the Budget Committee, to express the sense of Congress that legislation be enacted to conform overtime payment requirements of the Walsh-Healey Act to those of the Fair Labor Standards Act, and that the resulting savings be used to reduce the federal deficit. Adopted 86-5: R 46-3; D 40-2 (ND 27-2, SD 13-0), May 6, 1985. (The Walsh-Healey Act requires that contractors supplying the federal government with more than $10,000 worth of goods pay workers at overtime rates of time-and-a-half for work in excess of eight hours per day; the Fair Labor Standards Act requires the time-and-a-half pay for work in excess of 40 hours per week.)

43. S Con Res 32. First Budget Resolution, Fiscal 1986. Harkin, D-Iowa, motion to table (kill) the Abdnor, R-S.D., perfecting amendment to the Dole, R-Kan.-Domenici, R-N.M., amendment to the instructions of the Dole motion to recommit the concurrent resolution to the Budget Committee, to express the sense of Congress that legislation be enacted to limit to the national median family income (about $24,600 in 1983) the amount of farm losses that may be deducted from non-farm income for purposes of calculating an individual's federal income tax payments, and that additional revenues provided by such legislation be used to reduce income tax rates for individuals. Motion rejected 38-57: R 8-43; D 30-14 (ND 17-14, SD 13-0), May 7, 1985. (The Abdnor amendment subsequently was adopted *(see vote 44, below)*.)

44. S Con Res 32. First Budget Resolution, Fiscal 1986. Abdnor, R-S.D., perfecting amendment to the Dole, R-Kan.-Domenici, R-N.M., amendment to the instructions of the Dole motion to recommit the concurrent resolution to the Budget Committee, to express the sense of Congress that legislation be enacted to limit to the national median family income (about $24,600 in 1983) the amount of farm losses that may be deducted from non-farm income for purposes of calculating an individual's federal income tax payments, and that additional revenues provided by such legislation be used to reduce income tax rates for individuals. Adopted 64-32: R 44-8; D 20-24 (ND 19-12, SD 1-12), May 7, 1985.

Corresponding to Congressional Record Votes 45, 46, 47, 48, 49, 50, 51, 52

	45	46	47	48	49	50	51	52
ALABAMA								
Denton	N	Y	N	Y	Y	Y	N	N
Heflin	N	Y	N	Y	Y	Y	N	Y
ALASKA								
Murkowski	N	N	N	Y	Y	Y	N	N
Stevens	N	N	N	Y	Y	Y	N	N
ARIZONA								
Goldwater	N	N	N	Y	Y	Y	N	N
DeConcini	N	Y	N	Y	Y	Y	Y	Y
ARKANSAS								
Bumpers	N	Y	N	Y	Y	Y	Y	Y
Pryor	N	Y	N	Y	Y	Y	Y	Y
CALIFORNIA								
Wilson	N	N	N	Y	?	?	?	?
Cranston	Y	N	Y	Y	Y	N	N	Y
COLORADO								
Armstrong	N	N	N	Y	Y	Y	N	N
Hart	Y	N	Y	Y	Y	Y	Y	Y
CONNECTICUT								
Weicker	N	?	?	?	Y	Y	N	N
Dodd	Y	N	Y	Y	Y	Y	Y	Y
DELAWARE								
Roth	N	N	N	Y	Y	Y	N	N
Biden	Y	N	N	Y	Y	Y	Y	Y
FLORIDA								
Hawkins	N	Y	N	Y	Y	Y	N	N
Chiles	N	Y	Y	Y	Y	Y	Y	Y
GEORGIA								
Mattingly	N	Y	N	Y	Y	Y	N	N
Nunn	N	Y	N	Y	Y	Y	Y	N
HAWAII								
Inouye	Y	N	N	Y	Y	N	Y	Y
Matsunaga	Y	N	Y	Y	Y	N	Y	Y
IDAHO								
McClure	N	Y	N	Y	N	Y	N	N
Symms	N	Y	N	Y	N	Y	N	N
ILLINOIS								
Dixon	N	N	N	Y	Y	Y	N	N
Simon	Y	N	Y	Y	Y	Y	Y	Y
INDIANA								
Lugar	N	N	N	Y	Y	Y	N	N
Quayle	N	N	N	Y	Y	Y	N	N
IOWA								
Grassley	N	N	N	Y	Y	Y	N	N
Harkin	N	Y	Y	Y	Y	Y	N	Y
KANSAS								
Dole	N	N	N	Y	Y	Y	N	N
Kassebaum	N	Y	N	Y	Y	Y	Y	N
KENTUCKY								
McConnell	N	N	N	Y	Y	Y	N	N
Ford	N	Y	N	Y	Y	Y	N	Y
LOUISIANA								
Johnston	Y	N	Y	Y	Y	Y	Y	Y
Long	N	Y	Y	Y	Y	Y	N	Y
MAINE								
Cohen	N	N	N	Y	Y	Y	Y	N
Mitchell	Y	Y	N	Y	Y	Y	N	Y
MARYLAND								
Mathias	N	N	Y	Y	Y	N	Y	Y
Sarbanes	Y	N	Y	Y	Y	N	N	Y
MASSACHUSETTS								
Kennedy	Y	N	Y	Y	Y	N	N	Y
Kerry	Y	N	Y	Y	Y	Y	N	Y
MICHIGAN								
Levin	N	N	N	Y	Y	Y	Y	Y
Riegle	Y	N	N	Y	Y	Y	N	Y
MINNESOTA								
Boschwitz	N	N	N	Y	Y	Y	Y	N
Durenberger	N	N	N	Y	Y	Y	N	N
MISSISSIPPI								
Cochran	N	N	N	Y	Y	Y	N	N
Stennis	N	Y	?	?	?	?	Y	Y
MISSOURI								
Danforth	N	N	N	Y	Y	Y	N	N
Eagleton	Y	N	Y	Y	Y	Y	Y	Y
MONTANA								
Baucus	N	Y	N	Y	Y	Y	Y	Y
Melcher	Y	Y	Y	Y	?	+	Y	Y
NEBRASKA								
Exon	?	?	?	?	Y	Y	Y	?
Zorinsky	N	Y	N	Y	Y	Y	Y	Y
NEVADA								
Hecht	N	N	N	Y	Y	Y	N	N
Laxalt	N	Y	N	Y	Y	Y	N	N
NEW HAMPSHIRE								
Humphrey	Y	N	N	Y	Y	Y	N	N
Rudman	N	N	N	Y	Y	Y	N	N
NEW JERSEY								
Bradley	Y	N	N	Y	Y	Y	N	Y
Lautenberg	Y	N	Y	Y	Y	Y	N	Y
NEW MEXICO								
Domenici	N	N	N	Y	Y	Y	N	N
Bingaman	N	Y	N	Y	Y	Y	Y	Y
NEW YORK								
D'Amato	N	Y	N	Y	Y	Y	N	N
Moynihan	Y	N	Y	Y	Y	N	N	Y
NORTH CAROLINA								
East	?	?	?	?	?	?	?	?
Helms	N	Y	N	Y	Y	Y	N	N
NORTH DAKOTA								
Andrews	?	?	?	?	?	Y	Y	N
Burdick	N	Y	Y	Y	Y	Y	Y	Y
OHIO								
Glenn	N	N	Y	Y	Y	Y	Y	Y
Metzenbaum	N	N	Y	Y	Y	N	N	Y
OKLAHOMA								
Nickles	N	Y	N	Y	Y	Y	N	N
Boren	N	Y	N	Y	Y	Y	Y	Y
OREGON								
Hatfield	N	N	Y	Y	Y	Y	Y	N
Packwood	N	N	N	Y	Y	Y	N	N
PENNSYLVANIA								
Heinz	N	N	N	Y	Y	Y	N	N
Specter	N	N	Y	Y	Y	Y	N	N
RHODE ISLAND								
Chafee	N	N	Y	Y	Y	N	N	N
Pell	Y	N	Y	Y	Y	Y	Y	Y
SOUTH CAROLINA								
Thurmond	N	Y	N	Y	Y	Y	N	N
Hollings	N	Y	N	Y	Y	Y	Y	N
SOUTH DAKOTA								
Abdnor	N	Y	N	Y	Y	Y	N	N
Pressler	N	Y	N	Y	Y	Y	N	N
TENNESSEE								
Gore	Y	Y	N	Y	Y	Y	Y	Y
Sasser	Y	Y	N	Y	Y	Y	Y	Y
TEXAS								
Gramm	N	Y	N	Y	Y	Y	N	N
Bentsen	Y	Y	N	Y	Y	Y	Y	Y
UTAH								
Garn	N	Y	N	Y	Y	Y	N	N
Hatch	N	Y	N	Y	Y	N	N	N
VERMONT								
Stafford	N	N	N	Y	Y	Y	N	N
Leahy	Y	N	N	Y	Y	Y	Y	Y
VIRGINIA								
Trible	N	N	N	Y	Y	Y	N	N
Warner	N	N	N	Y	Y	Y	N	N
WASHINGTON								
Evans	N	N	N	Y	Y	Y	N	N
Gorton	N	N	N	Y	Y	Y	N	N
WEST VIRGINIA								
Byrd	Y	Y	Y	Y	Y	Y	N	Y
Rockefeller	Y	N	Y	Y	Y	Y	N	Y
WISCONSIN								
Kasten	N	N	N	Y	Y	Y	N	N
Proxmire	N	Y	Y	N	Y	N	N	N
WYOMING								
Simpson	N	N	N	Y	Y	N	N	N
Wallop	N	Y	N	Y	Y	Y	N	N

KEY

- Y Voted for (yea).
- # Paired for.
- \+ Announced for.
- N Voted against (nay).
- X Paired against.
- \- Announced against.
- P Voted "present".
- C Voted "present" to avoid possible conflict of interest.
- ? Did not vote or otherwise make a position known.

Democrats *Republicans*

ND - Northern Democrats SD - Southern Democrats (Southern states - Ala., Ark., Fla., Ga., Ky., La., Miss., N.C., Okla., S.C., Tenn., Texas, Va.)

45. S Con Res 32. First Budget Resolution, Fiscal 1986. Moynihan, D-N.Y., perfecting amendment to the Dole, R-Kan.-Domenici, R-N.M., amendment to the instructions of the Dole motion to recommit the concurrent resolution to the Budget Committee, to establish a pilot program to sell up to $10 billion annually, in fiscal years 1986-88, of direct government loans to federally chartered entities. The amendment specified that the loans to be sold in fiscal 1986 would be those used to finance rural housing, and that proceeds from this sale would be allotted to the Rural Housing Fund, and that the loans to be sold in the following two fiscal years would be designated by the Office of Management and Budget and the secretary of the Treasury. The amendment also specified that the intent was to provide for the annual sale of $8 billion worth of loans, with $2 billion in "over-collateralization," an arrangement to protect the buyers from uncollectable loans. Rejected 26-71: R 1-50; D 25-21 (ND 21-11, SD 4-10), May 7, 1985.

46. S Con Res 32. First Budget Resolution, Fiscal 1986. Symms, R-Idaho, perfecting amendment to the Dole, R-Kan.-Domenici, R-N.M., amendment to the instructions of the Dole motion to recommit the concurrent resolution to the Budget Committee, to reduce funding for foreign aid by $200 million. Half the reduction would be earmarked for agricultural research; the remaining $100 million would be used to lower deficits. Rejected 40-56: R 17-33; D 23-23 (ND 10-22, SD 13-1), May 7, 1985.

47. S 484. Saccharin Study and Labeling Act. Metzenbaum, D-Ohio, amendment to require special labeling of diet soft drinks containing aspartame, an artificial sweetener, to indicate how much of the additive they contain. Rejected 27-68: R 4-46; D 23-22 (ND 20-12, SD 3-10), May 7, 1985.

48. S 484. Saccharin Study and Labeling Act. Passage of the bill to extend through May 1, 1987, a measure designed to keep saccharin on the market by prohibiting any government action against the sweetener that was based on research findings from before 1978. Passed 94-1: R 50-0; D 44-1 (ND 31-1, SD 13-0), May 7, 1985.

49. S Con Res 32. First Budget Resolution, Fiscal 1986. Kerry, D-Mass., perfecting amendment to the Dole, R-Kan.-Domenici, R-N.M., amendment to the instructions of the Dole motion to recommit the concurrent resolution to the Budget Committee, to express the sense of Congress that the Finance Committee should approve legislation cracking down on tax evaders and increasing voluntary compliance with tax laws. Adopted 93-2: R 48-2; D 45-0 (ND 32-0, SD 13-0), May 8, 1985.

50. S Con Res 32. First Budget Resolution, Fiscal 1986. Mattingly, R-Ga., perfecting amendment to the Dole, R-Kan.-Domenici, R-N.M., amendment to the instructions of the Dole motion to recommit the concurrent resolution to the Budget Committee, to express the sense of Congress that the amount of Social Security benefits paid to non-resident and illegal aliens should be limited. Adopted 84-12: R 47-4; D 37-8 (ND 24-8, SD 13-0), May 8, 1985.

51. S Con Res 32. First Budget Resolution, Fiscal 1986. Chiles, D-Fla.-Hollings, D-S.C., perfecting amendment to the Dole, R-Kan.-Domenici, R-N.M., amendment to the instructions of the Dole motion to recommit the concurrent resolution to the Budget Committee, to replace the Senate GOP-White House budget with an alternative budget setting budget targets for the fiscal year ending Sept. 30, 1986, as follows: budget authority, $1,083 billion; outlays, $977 billion; revenues, $807.7 billion; deficit, $169.3 billion. The amendment also set preliminary goals for fiscal 1987-88, revised budget levels for fiscal 1985, and included reconciliation instructions requiring House and Senate committees to recommend legislative savings to meet the budget targets. Rejected 35-63: R 6-45; D 29-18 (ND 18-15, SD 11-3), May 8, 1985. A "nay" was a vote supporting the president's position.

52. S Con Res 32. First Budget Resolution, Fiscal 1986. Byrd, D-W.Va., perfecting amendment to the Dole, R-Kan.-Domenici, R-N.M., amendment to the instructions of the Dole motion to recommit the concurrent resolution to the Budget Committee, to alter the Senate GOP-White House budget by, among other changes, reducing the rate of growth for defense spending, increasing taxes and reinstating existing law treatment of Social Security cost-of-living adjustments. Rejected 43-54: R 1-50; D 42-4 (ND 30-2, SD 12-2), May 8, 1985. A "nay" was a vote supporting the president's position.

Corresponding to Congressional Record Votes 53, 54, 55, 56, 57, 58, 59, 60

	53	54	55	56	57	58	59	60
ALABAMA								
Denton	N	Y	Y	Y	N	N	N	N
Heflin	Y	N	N	N	N	Y	Y	Y
ALASKA								
Murkowski	N	Y	Y	Y	N	N	Y	N
Stevens	N	Y	Y	Y	N	N	Y	N
ARIZONA								
Goldwater	N	Y	Y	Y	N	N	N	N
DeConcini	Y	N	N	Y	Y	Y	N	Y
ARKANSAS								
Bumpers	Y	N	N	Y	Y	Y	Y	Y
Pryor	Y	N	N	N	Y	Y	Y	Y
CALIFORNIA								
Wilson	?	?	?	?	?	?	?	?
Cranston	N	N	N	N	N	Y	Y	Y
COLORADO								
Armstrong	N	Y	Y	Y	N	N	N	N
Hart	Y	N	N	N	N	Y	Y	Y
CONNECTICUT								
Weicker	Y	Y	N	Y	Y	N	N	N
Dodd	Y	N	N	N	Y	Y	N	Y
DELAWARE								
Roth	Y	Y	Y	Y	N	N	N	N
Biden	Y	N	N	N	Y	Y	Y	Y
FLORIDA								
Hawkins	Y	Y	N	Y	N	Y	Y	N
Chiles	Y	N	N	Y	N	Y	Y	Y
GEORGIA								
Mattingly	N	Y	Y	Y	Y	N	N	N
Nunn	N	N	N	Y	N	N	N	Y
HAWAII								
Inouye	Y	N	N	N	N	Y	Y	Y
Matsunaga	Y	N	N	N	Y	Y	Y	Y
IDAHO								
McClure	N	Y	Y	Y	N	N	N	N
Symms	N	Y	Y	Y	N	N	N	N
ILLINOIS								
Dixon	Y	N	N	N	Y	Y	N	Y
Simon	Y	N	N	N	Y	Y	Y	Y
INDIANA								
Lugar	Y	Y	Y	Y	N	N	N	N
Quayle	Y	Y	Y	Y	N	N	N	N
IOWA								
Grassley	Y	Y	N	N	Y	N	Y	N
Harkin	Y	N	N	N	Y	Y	Y	Y
KANSAS								
Dole	N	Y	Y	Y	N	N	N	N
Kassebaum	N	Y	Y	Y	Y	N	N	N
KENTUCKY								
McConnell	N	Y	Y	N	N	N	N	N
Ford	Y	N	N	N	N	Y	Y	Y
LOUISIANA								
Johnston	N	N	N	N	N	Y	Y	Y
Long	N	N	N	N	N	N	Y	Y
MAINE								
Cohen	N	Y	N	N	N	N	Y	N
Mitchell	Y	N	N	N	N	Y	Y	Y
MARYLAND								
Mathias	#	?	?	?	N	Y	N	N
Sarbanes	Y	N	N	N	N	Y	Y	Y
MASSACHUSETTS								
Kennedy	Y	N	N	N	N	Y	Y	?
Kerry	Y	N	N	N	N	Y	Y	Y
MICHIGAN								
Levin	Y	N	N	N	N	Y	Y	Y
Riegle	Y	N	N	N	N	Y	Y	Y
MINNESOTA								
Boschwitz	N	Y	N	Y	Y	N	N	N
Durenberger	Y	Y	N	Y	N	N	N	N
MISSISSIPPI								
Cochran	N	Y	Y	N	N	N	N	N
Stennis	N	N	N	N	N	Y	Y	Y
MISSOURI								
Danforth	X	Y	N	Y	N	N	N	N
Eagleton	Y	N	N	N	N	Y	Y	Y
MONTANA								
Baucus	Y	N	N	N	Y	Y	Y	Y
Melcher	Y	N	N	N	Y	Y	Y	Y
NEBRASKA								
Exon	?	?	?	?	?	?	?	?
Zorinsky	Y	N	N	N	Y	Y	Y	Y
NEVADA								
Hecht	N	Y	Y	Y	N	N	N	N
Laxalt	N	Y	Y	Y	N	N	N	N
NEW HAMPSHIRE								
Humphrey	N	Y	Y	Y	Y	N	N	N
Rudman	N	Y	Y	Y	N	N	N	N
NEW JERSEY								
Bradley	Y	N	N	Y	N	Y	N	Y
Lautenberg	Y	N	N	N	N	Y	N	Y
NEW MEXICO								
Domenici	N	Y	Y	Y	N	N	N	N
Bingaman	Y	N	N	N	Y	Y	Y	Y
NEW YORK								
D'Amato	Y	Y	N	Y	N	N	Y	N
Moynihan	Y	N	N	N	N	Y	Y	Y
NORTH CAROLINA								
East	?	?	?	?	?	?	?	?
Helms	N	Y	Y	Y	N	N	N	N
NORTH DAKOTA								
Andrews	Y	N	N	Y	Y	Y	Y	N
Burdick	Y	N	N	N	Y	Y	Y	Y
OHIO								
Glenn	Y	N	N	N	N	Y	Y	Y
Metzenbaum	Y	N	N	N	N	Y	Y	Y
OKLAHOMA								
Nickles	N	Y	Y	Y	N	N	N	N
Boren	Y	N	N	Y	Y	Y	Y	Y
OREGON								
Hatfield	N	Y	N	Y	N	N	N	N
Packwood	N	Y	Y	Y	N	N	N	N
PENNSYLVANIA								
Heinz	Y	Y	N	Y	N	N	N	N
Specter	Y	N	Y	N	N	Y	Y	N
RHODE ISLAND								
Chafee	Y	Y	N	Y	N	N	N	N
Pell	Y	N	N	N	Y	Y	N	Y
SOUTH CAROLINA								
Thurmond	N	Y	Y	Y	N	N	N	N
Hollings	Y	N	N	N	Y	Y	Y	Y
SOUTH DAKOTA								
Abdnor	N	Y	Y	Y	N	N	N	N
Pressler	N	Y	Y	Y	N	N	N	N
TENNESSEE								
Gore	Y	N	N	N	Y	Y	Y	Y
Sasser	Y	N	N	N	N	Y	Y	Y
TEXAS								
Gramm	N	Y	Y	Y	N	N	N	N
Bentsen	N	N	N	Y	N	Y	N	Y
UTAH								
Garn	N	Y	Y	Y	N	N	N	N
Hatch	N	Y	Y	Y	N	N	N	N
VERMONT								
Stafford	Y	Y	N	Y	N	N	Y	N
Leahy	Y	N	N	N	N	Y	Y	Y
VIRGINIA								
Trible	?	Y	Y	Y	Y	N	N	N
Warner	Y	Y	Y	Y	N	N	N	N
WASHINGTON								
Evans	N	Y	N	Y	N	N	N	N
Gorton	N	Y	Y	Y	N	N	Y	N
WEST VIRGINIA								
Byrd	Y	N	N	N	N	Y	Y	Y
Rockefeller	Y	N	N	N	N	Y	Y	Y
WISCONSIN								
Kasten	N	Y	N	N	Y	N	N	N
Proxmire	N	Y	Y	Y	N	N	N	Y
WYOMING								
Simpson	N	Y	Y	Y	N	N	N	N
Wallop	N	Y	Y	Y	N	N	N	N

KEY

Y Voted for (yea).
Paired for.
+ Announced for.
N Voted against (nay).
X Paired against.
- Announced against.
P Voted "present".
C Voted "present" to avoid possible conflict of interest.
? Did not vote or otherwise make a position known.

Democrats *Republicans*

ND - Northern Democrats SD - Southern Democrats (Southern states - Ala., Ark., Fla., Ga., Ky., La., Miss., N.C., Okla., S.C., Tenn., Texas, Va.)

53. S Con Res 32. First Budget Resolution, Fiscal 1986. Specter, R-Pa., perfecting amendment to the Dole, R-Kan.-Domenici, R-N.M., amendment to the instructions of the Dole motion to recommit the concurrent resolution to the Budget Committee, to restore funds for Amtrak at a level that is 10 percent less than the fiscal 1985 level. Adopted 53-41: R 14-34; D 39-7 (ND 30-2, SD 9-5), May 9, 1985.

54. S Con Res 32. First Budget Resolution, Fiscal 1986. Domenici, R-N.M., motion to table (kill) the Cranston, D-Calif., perfecting amendment to the Dole, R-Kan.-Domenici amendment to the instructions of the Dole motion to recommit the concurrent resolution to the Budget Committee, to restore $2.3 billion in budget authority for fiscal years 1986-88 for veterans' programs. Motion agreed to 49-47: R 48-2; D 1-45 (ND 1-31, SD 0-14), May 9, 1985.

55. S Con Res 32. First Budget Resolution, Fiscal 1986. Domenici, R-N.M., motion to table (kill) the Hawkins, R-Fla., perfecting amendment to the Dole, R-Kan.-Domenici amendment to the instructions of the Dole motion to recommit the concurrent resolution to the Budget Committee, to restore funding for the school lunch program in fiscal years 1986-88 to the fiscal 1985 level. Motion rejected 36-60: R 35-15; D 1-45 (ND 1-31, SD 0-14), May 9, 1985. (The Hawkins amendment was subsequently adopted by voice vote.)

56. S Con Res 32. First Budget Resolution, Fiscal 1986. Domenici, R-N.M., motion to table (kill) the Sasser, D-Tenn., perfecting amendment to the Dole, R-Kan.-Domenici amendment to the instructions of the Dole motion to recommit the concurrent resolution to the Budget Committee, to restore funding for community and regional development programs such as the Appalachian Regional Commission at fiscal 1985 levels and to restore partially funds for Farmers Home Administration rural housing programs. Motion agreed to 52-44: R 44-6; D 8-38 (ND 3-29, SD 5-9), May 9, 1985.

57. S Con Res 32. First Budget Resolution, Fiscal 1986. Grassley, R-Iowa, perfecting amendment to the Dole, R-Kan.-Domenici, R-N.M., amendment to the instructions of the Dole motion to recommit the concurrent resolution to the Budget Committee, to freeze funding for all federal programs in fiscal 1986 at fiscal 1985 levels, with no allowances for inflation. Rejected 27-70: R 9-42; D 18-28 (ND 13-19, SD 5-9), May 9, 1985.

58. S Con Res 32. First Budget Resolution, Fiscal 1986. Chiles, D-Fla., perfecting amendment to the Dole, R-Kan.-Domenici, R-N.M., amendment to the instructions of the Dole motion to recommit the concurrent resolution to the Budget Committee, to restore funds for Head Start, developmental disability and handicapped education programs, the guaranteed student loan and certain other education and training programs. Rejected 47-50: R 4-47; D 43-3 (ND 31-1, SD 12-2), May 9, 1985.

59. S Con Res 32. First Budget Resolution, Fiscal 1986. Cohen, R-Maine, perfecting amendment to the Dole, R-Kan.-Domenici, R-N.M., amendment to the instructions of the Dole motion to recommit the concurrent resolution to the Budget Committee, to restore funds for rural housing programs of the Farmers Home Administration to 80 percent of the fiscal 1985 level, and to phase in a loan guarantee program. Rejected 47-50: R 10-41; D 37-9 (ND 25-7, SD 12-2), May 9, 1985.

60. Procedural Motion. Byrd, D-W.Va., motion to recess for 30 minutes. Motion rejected 45-51: R 0-51; D 45-0 (ND 31-0, SD 14-0), May 9, 1985. (The purpose of the amendment was to halt temporarily the using up of time allotted to Democrats, for debate, under the 1974 Congressional Budget and Impoundment Control Act, PL 93-344.)

CQ Senate Votes 61 - 68

Corresponding to Congressional Record Votes 61, 62, 63, 64, 65, 66, 67, 68

	61	62	63	64	65	66	67	68
ALABAMA								
Denton	N	Y	N	Y	Y	Y	Y	Y
Heflin	Y	N	Y	N	N	Y	Y	N
ALASKA								
Murkowski	Y	Y	N	Y	N	Y	Y	Y
Stevens	Y	Y	N	Y	N	X	Y	Y
ARIZONA								
Goldwater	N	Y	N	Y	Y	Y	Y	Y
DeConcini	Y	N	N	N	N	Y	Y	N
ARKANSAS								
Bumpers	Y	N	Y	N	N	N	Y	Y
Pryor	Y	N	Y	N	N	N	Y	Y
CALIFORNIA								
Wilson	?	?	?	?	?	?	?	?
Cranston	N	N	N	N	N	N	Y	N
COLORADO								
Armstrong	N	Y	N	Y	Y	Y	Y	Y
Hart	Y	N	Y	N	N	N	Y	N
CONNECTICUT								
Weicker	N	Y	N	Y	N	Y	Y	N
Dodd	Y	N	N	N	N	N	Y	N
DELAWARE								
Roth	N	Y	N	Y	Y	Y	Y	Y
Biden	Y	N	Y	N	N	N	Y	N
FLORIDA								
Hawkins	Y	Y	N	N	N	Y	Y	Y
Chiles	Y	N	N	N	N	N	Y	Y
GEORGIA								
Mattingly	N	Y	N	Y	N	Y	Y	Y
Nunn	Y	N	N	Y	N	Y	Y	Y
HAWAII								
Inouye	Y	N	Y	N	N	N	Y	N
Matsunaga	Y	N	Y	N	N	N	Y	N
IDAHO								
McClure	N	Y	N	Y	Y	Y	Y	Y
Symms	N	Y	N	Y	Y	Y	Y	Y
ILLINOIS								
Dixon	N	N	Y	N	N	N	Y	N
Simon	N	N	Y	N	N	N	Y	N
INDIANA								
Lugar	N	Y	N	Y	N	Y	Y	Y
Quayle	N	Y	N	Y	N	Y	Y	Y
IOWA								
Grassley	N	Y	Y	Y	N	Y	Y	Y
Harkin	N	N	Y	N	N	N	Y	N
KANSAS								
Dole	N	Y	N	Y	Y	Y	Y	Y
Kassebaum	N	Y	N	Y	N	Y	Y	Y
KENTUCKY								
McConnell	N	Y	N	Y	N	Y	Y	Y
Ford	Y	N	Y	N	N	Y	Y	N
LOUISIANA								
Johnston	Y	N	Y	N	N	N	Y	N
Long	Y	N	Y	Y	Y	N	Y	Y
MAINE								
Cohen	N	Y	Y	N	N	N	Y	Y
Mitchell	Y	N	Y	N	N	N	Y	Y
MARYLAND								
Mathias	Y	Y	Y	Y	N	N	Y	N
Sarbanes	Y	N	Y	N	N	N	Y	N
MASSACHUSETTS								
Kennedy	N	N	N	N	N	N	Y	N
Kerry	Y	N	Y	N	N	N	Y	N
MICHIGAN								
Levin	Y	N	Y	N	N	N	Y	N
Riegle	Y	N	Y	N	N	N	Y	N
MINNESOTA								
Boschwitz	N	Y	N	Y	N	N	Y	Y
Durenberger	N	Y	N	Y	N	Y	Y	Y
MISSISSIPPI								
Cochran	N	Y	N	Y	N	Y	Y	Y
Stennis	Y	N	Y	Y	Y	Y	Y	N
MISSOURI								
Danforth	N	Y	N	Y	N	Y	Y	Y
Eagleton	?	N	Y	N	N	N	Y	N
MONTANA								
Baucus	Y	N	N	N	N	N	Y	N
Melcher	Y	N	Y	N	N	N	Y	N
NEBRASKA								
Exon	?	?	?	?	?	?	?	?
Zorinsky	Y	N	Y	N	N	Y	Y	N
NEVADA								
Hecht	N	Y	N	Y	Y	Y	Y	Y
Laxalt	N	Y	N	Y	Y	Y	Y	Y
NEW HAMPSHIRE								
Humphrey	N	Y	N	Y	Y	Y	Y	Y
Rudman	N	Y	N	Y	N	Y	Y	Y
NEW JERSEY								
Bradley	Y	N	Y	N	N	N	Y	N
Lautenberg	Y	N	Y	N	N	N	Y	N
NEW MEXICO								
Domenici	N	Y	N	Y	Y	Y	Y	Y
Bingaman	Y	N	N	N	N	N	Y	Y
NEW YORK								
D'Amato	Y	Y	N	N	N	Y	Y	N
Moynihan	Y	N	Y	N	N	N	Y	N
NORTH CAROLINA								
East	?	?	?	?	?	#	?	?
Helms	N	Y	N	Y	Y	Y	Y	Y
NORTH DAKOTA								
Andrews	Y	N	Y	Y	N	Y	Y	N
Burdick	Y	N	Y	N	N	N	Y	N
OHIO								
Glenn	Y	N	Y	N	N	N	Y	Y
Metzenbaum	N	N	Y	N	N	N	Y	N
OKLAHOMA								
Nickles	Y	Y	N	Y	Y	N	Y	Y
Boren	Y	N	N	N	N	N	Y	Y
OREGON								
Hatfield	N	Y	N	Y	Y	N	Y	Y
Packwood	N	Y	N	Y	N	Y	Y	Y
PENNSYLVANIA								
Heinz	Y	Y	Y	Y	N	N	Y	N
Specter	Y	Y	Y	N	N	Y	Y	N
RHODE ISLAND								
Chafee	N	Y	N	Y	N	N	Y	Y
Pell	Y	N	N	N	N	N	Y	N
SOUTH CAROLINA								
Thurmond	N	Y	N	Y	Y	Y	Y	Y
Hollings	Y	N	Y	N	N	Y	Y	N
SOUTH DAKOTA								
Abdnor	Y	Y	N	Y	Y	Y	Y	Y
Pressler	Y	Y	N	Y	Y	Y	Y	Y
TENNESSEE								
Gore	Y	N	Y	N	N	Y	Y	Y
Sasser	Y	N	Y	N	N	N	Y	Y
TEXAS								
Gramm	N	Y	N	Y	Y	Y	Y	Y
Bentsen	N	N	N	N	N	N	Y	Y
UTAH								
Garn	N	Y	Y	Y	Y	N	Y	Y
Hatch	N	Y	Y	Y	Y	N	Y	Y
VERMONT								
Stafford	N	Y	N	Y	N	Y	Y	Y
Leahy	N	N	Y	N	N	N	Y	N
VIRGINIA								
Trible	Y	Y	N	Y	N	Y	Y	Y
Warner	Y	Y	N	Y	N	Y	Y	Y
WASHINGTON								
Evans	N	Y	N	Y	N	Y	Y	Y
Gorton	N	Y	N	Y	N	Y	Y	Y
WEST VIRGINIA								
Byrd	N	N	Y	N	N	N	Y	N
Rockefeller	N	N	Y	N	N	N	Y	N
WISCONSIN								
Kasten	N	Y	Y	Y	N	Y	Y	N
Proxmire	N	Y	N	Y	Y	N	Y	Y
WYOMING								
Simpson	N	Y	N	Y	Y	Y	Y	Y
Wallop	N	Y	N	Y	Y	Y	Y	Y

KEY

- Y Voted for (yea).
- # Paired for.
- + Announced for.
- N Voted against (nay).
- X Paired against.
- - Announced against.
- P Voted "present".
- C Voted "present" to avoid possible conflict of interest.
- ? Did not vote or otherwise make a position known.

Democrats *Republicans*

ND - Northern Democrats SD - Southern Democrats (Southern states - Ala., Ark., Fla., Ga., Ky., La., Miss., N.C., Okla., S.C., Tenn., Texas, Va.)

61. S Con Res 32. First Budget Resolution, Fiscal 1986. Dole, R-Kan., perfecting amendment to the Dole-Domenici, R-N.M., amendment to the instructions of the Dole motion to recommit the concurrent resolution to the Budget Committee, to restore funding for the impact aid "Part B" program. Rejected 47-49: R 13-38; D 34-11 (ND 21-10, SD 13-1), May 9, 1985. A "nay" was a vote supporting the president's position. (Dole proposed the amendment for Abdnor, R-S.D., for parliamentary reasons.)

62. S Con Res 32. First Budget Resolution, Fiscal 1986. Stevens, R-Alaska, motion to table (kill) the Metzenbaum, D-Ohio, perfecting amendment to the Dole, R-Kan.-Domenici, R-N.M., amendment to the instructions of the Dole motion to recommit the concurrent resolution to the Budget Committee, to restore postal subsidies for charitable and religious organizations, small newspapers and libraries. Motion agreed to 51-46: R 50-1; D 1-45 (ND 1-31, SD 0-14), May 9, 1985. A "yea" was a vote supporting the president's position.

63. S Con Res 32. First Budget Resolution, Fiscal 1986. Kasten, R-Wis., perfecting amendment to the Dole, R-Kan.-Domenici, R-N.M., amendment to the instructions of the Dole motion to recommit the concurrent resolution to the Budget Committee, to restore funding for general revenue sharing in fiscal 1986. Rejected 43-54: R 9-42; D 34-12 (ND 24-8, SD 10-4), May 9, 1985. A "nay" was a vote supporting the president's position.

64. S Con Res 32. First Budget Resolution, Fiscal 1986. Packwood, R-Ore., motion to table (kill) the Kennedy, D-Mass., perfecting amendment to the Dole, R-Kan.-Domenici, R-N.M., amendment to the instructions of the Dole motion to recommit the concurrent resolution to the Budget Committee, to add funding for the Medicare program. Motion agreed to 51-46: R 47-4; D 4-42 (ND 1-31, SD 3-11), May 9, 1985. A "yea" was a vote supporting the president's position.

65. S Con Res 32. First Budget Resolution, Fiscal 1986. Symms, R-Idaho, perfecting amendment to the Dole, R-Kan.-Domenici, R-N.M., amendment to the instructions of the Dole motion to recommit the concurrent resolution to the Budget Committee, to reduce budget authority further for mass transit by $8.2 billion through fiscal 1988. Rejected 25-72: R 22-29; D 3-43 (ND 1-31, SD 2-12), May 9, 1985.

66. S Con Res 32. First Budget Resolution, Fiscal 1986. Dole, R-Kan., motion to table (kill) the Bradley, D-N.J., perfecting amendment to the Dole-Domenici, R-N.M., amendment to the instructions of the Dole motion to recommit the concurrent resolution to the Budget Committee, to offset proposed Medicare premiums increases by continuing the current 16-cents-per-pack cigarette tax, which is due to drop to 8 cents Oct. 1. Motion agreed to 49-47: R 41-9; D 8-38 (ND 2-30, SD 6-8), May 9, 1985.

67. S Con Res 32. First Budget Resolution, Fiscal 1986. DeConcini, D-Ariz., perfecting amendment to the Dole, R-Kan.-Domenici, R-N.M., amendment to the instructions of the Dole motion to recommit the concurrent resolution to the Budget Committee, to express the sense of the Senate that the Office of Management and Budget should immediately release the full 1985 appropriation for the special supplemental food program for women, infants and children (WIC). Adopted 97-0: R 51-0; D 46-0 (ND 32-0, SD 14-0), May 9, 1985.

68. S Con Res 32. First Budget Resolution, Fiscal 1986. Dole, R-Kan., motion to table (kill) the Lautenberg, D-N.J., perfecting amendment to the Dole-Domenici, R-N.M., amendment to the instructions of the Dole motion to recommit the concurrent resolution to the Budget Committee, to restore funding for Amtrak, urban mass transit programs and Urban Development Action Grants. Motion agreed to 57-40: R 44-7; D 13-33 (ND 4-28, SD 9-5), May 9, 1985. A "yea" was a vote supporting the president's position.

	69	70	71	72	73	74
ALABAMA						
Denton	Y	Y	Y	Y	Y	Y
Heflin	Y	Y	Y	N	N	N
ALASKA						
Murkowski	Y	Y	Y	Y	Y	Y
Stevens	Y	X	Y	Y	Y	Y
ARIZONA						
Goldwater	Y	Y	Y	Y	Y	Y
DeConcini	Y	N	Y	N	N	N
ARKANSAS						
Bumpers	N	N	N	N	N	N
Pryor	N	N	N	N	N	N
CALIFORNIA						
Wilson	?	?	?	Y	Y	Y
Cranston	N	N	Y	N	N	N
COLORADO						
Armstrong	Y	Y	Y	Y	Y	Y
Hart	N	Y	Y	N	N	N
CONNECTICUT						
Weicker	Y	Y	Y	Y	Y	Y
Dodd	N	N	Y	N	N	N
DELAWARE						
Roth	Y	Y	Y	Y	Y	Y
Biden	N	N	N	N	N	N
FLORIDA						
Hawkins	Y	Y	Y	N	Y	Y
Chiles	Y	N	Y	N	N	N
GEORGIA						
Mattingly	Y	Y	Y	Y	Y	Y
Nunn	N	N	Y	N	N	Y
HAWAII						
Inouye	N	N	N	N	N	N
Matsunaga	N	N	N	N	N	N
IDAHO						
McClure	Y	Y	Y	Y	Y	Y
Symms	Y	Y	Y	Y	Y	Y
ILLINOIS						
Dixon	N	N	N	N	N	N
Simon	N	N	N	N	N	N
INDIANA						
Lugar	Y	Y	Y	Y	Y	Y
Quayle	Y	Y	Y	Y	Y	Y

	69	70	71	72	73	74
IOWA						
Grassley	Y	Y	Y	Y	Y	Y
Harkin	N	N	N	N	N	N
KANSAS						
Dole	Y	Y	Y	Y	Y	Y
Kassebaum	Y	N	Y	Y	Y	Y
KENTUCKY						
McConnell	Y	Y	Y	Y	Y	Y
Ford	N	Y	N	N	N	N
LOUISIANA						
Johnston	N	N	Y	N	N	N
Long	Y	Y	N	N	N	N
MAINE						
Cohen	N	N	N	Y	Y	Y
Mitchell	Y	N	N	N	N	N
MARYLAND						
Mathias	Y	N	Y	N	N	Y
Sarbanes	N	N	N	N	N	N
MASSACHUSETTS						
Kennedy	N	N	N	N	N	N
Kerry	N	N	N	N	N	N
MICHIGAN						
Levin	N	N	N	N	N	N
Riegle	N	N	N	N	N	N
MINNESOTA						
Boschwitz	Y	N	Y	Y	Y	Y
Durenberger	Y	Y	Y	Y	Y	Y
MISSISSIPPI						
Cochran	Y	Y	Y	Y	Y	Y
Stennis	Y	Y	N	N	Y	N
MISSOURI						
Danforth	Y	Y	Y	Y	Y	Y
Eagleton	N	N	N	N	N	N
MONTANA						
Baucus	Y	N	Y	N	N	N
Melcher	N	N	N	N	N	N
NEBRASKA						
Exon	?	?	?	+	?	?
Zorinsky	Y	Y	N	Y	Y	Y
NEVADA						
Hecht	Y	Y	Y	Y	Y	Y
Laxalt	Y	Y	Y	Y	Y	Y

	69	70	71	72	73	74
NEW HAMPSHIRE						
Humphrey	Y	Y	Y	Y	Y	Y
Rudman	Y	Y	Y	Y	Y	Y
NEW JERSEY						
Bradley	N	N	Y	N	N	N
Lautenberg	N	N	Y	N	N	N
NEW MEXICO						
Domenici	Y	Y	Y	Y	Y	Y
Bingaman	N	N	N	N	N	N
NEW YORK						
D'Amato	N	Y	Y	N	N	Y
Moynihan	N	N	N	N	N	N
NORTH CAROLINA						
East	?	#	?	+	?	?
Helms	Y	Y	Y	Y	Y	Y
NORTH DAKOTA						
Andrews	Y	Y	Y	Y	Y	Y
Burdick	N	N	N	N	N	N
OHIO						
Glenn	Y	N	Y	N	N	N
Metzenbaum	N	Y	N	N	N	N
OKLAHOMA						
Nickles	Y	N	Y	Y	Y	Y
Boren	Y	N	Y	N	N	N
OREGON						
Hatfield	Y	N	Y	Y	Y	Y
Packwood	Y	Y	Y	Y	Y	Y
PENNSYLVANIA						
Heinz	N	N	Y	Y	Y	Y
Specter	N	Y	Y	N	N	N
RHODE ISLAND						
Chafee	Y	N	Y	Y	Y	Y
Pell	N	N	N	N	N	N
SOUTH CAROLINA						
Thurmond	Y	Y	Y	Y	Y	Y
Hollings	N	Y	N	N	N	N
SOUTH DAKOTA						
Abdnor	Y	Y	N	Y	Y	Y
Pressler	Y	N	N	Y	Y	Y
TENNESSEE						
Gore	N	Y	N	N	N	N
Sasser	N	Y	Y	N	N	N

KEY

- Y Voted for (yea).
- # Paired for.
- + Announced for.
- N Voted against (nay).
- X Paired against.
- - Announced against.
- P Voted "present".
- C Voted "present" to avoid possible conflict of interest.
- ? Did not vote or otherwise make a position known.

Democrats ***Republicans***

	69	70	71	72	73	74
TEXAS						
Gramm	Y	Y	Y	Y	Y	Y
Bentsen	Y	N	Y	N	N	N
UTAH						
Garn	Y	N	Y	Y	Y	Y
Hatch	Y	N	Y	Y	Y	Y
VERMONT						
Stafford	Y	Y	Y	Y	Y	Y
Leahy	Y	N	N	N	N	N
VIRGINIA						
Trible	Y	Y	Y	Y	Y	Y
Warner	Y	Y	Y	Y	Y	Y
WASHINGTON						
Evans	Y	Y	Y	Y	Y	Y
Gorton	Y	N	Y	Y	Y	Y
WEST VIRGINIA						
Byrd	Y	Y	N	N	N	N
Rockefeller	Y	Y	N	N	N	N
WISCONSIN						
Kasten	Y	Y	Y	Y	Y	Y
Proxmire	Y	N	Y	N	N	Y
WYOMING						
Simpson	Y	Y	Y	Y	Y	Y
Wallop	Y	Y	Y	Y	Y	Y

ND - Northern Democrats SD - Southern Democrats (Southern states - Ala., Ark., Fla., Ga., Ky., La., Miss., N.C., Okla., S.C., Tenn., Texas, Va.)

69. S Con Res 32. First Budget Resolution, Fiscal 1986. Hatfield, R-Ore., motion to table (kill) the Dixon, D-Ill., perfecting amendment to the Dole, R-Kan.-Domenici, R-N.M., amendment to the instructions of the Dole motion to recommit the concurrent resolution to the Budget Committee, to restore funding for the Summer Youth Employment Program to the fiscal 1985 level of $825 million, an increase from the $665 million assumed in the budget resolution. Motion agreed to 62-35: R 47-4; D 15-31 (ND 9-23, SD 6-8), May 9, 1985.

70. S Con Res 32. First Budget Resolution, Fiscal 1986. Dole, R-Kan., motion to table (kill) the Levin, D-Mich., perfecting amendment to the Dole-Domenici, R-N.M., amendment to the instructions of the Dole motion to recommit the concurrent resolution to the Budget Committee, to retain the current 16-cents-per-pack federal tax on cigarettes instead of letting the tax drop to 8 cents per pack at the end of fiscal 1985, as provided by existing law, and to use the $4.9 billion in revenues (for fiscal years 1986-88) to reduce the federal deficit. Motion agreed to 50-46: R 38-12; D 12-34 (ND 5-27, SD 7-7), May 9, 1985.

71. S Con Res 32. First Budget Resolution, Fiscal 1986. Dole, R-Kan., motion to table (kill) the Hollings, D-S.C.-Bumpers, D-Ark., perfecting amendment to the Dole-Domenici, R-N.M., amendment to the instructions of the Dole motion to recommit the concurrent resolution to the Budget Committee, to restore funding for the Economic Development Administration at an annual level of $200 million in fiscal years 1986-88. Motion agreed to 64-33: R 48-3; D 16-30 (ND 9-23, SD 7-7), in the session that began May 9, 1985. A "yea" was a vote supporting the president's position.

72. S Con Res 32. First Budget Resolution, Fiscal 1986. Dole, R-Kan., perfecting amendment to the Dole-Domenici, R-N.M., amendment to the instructions of the Dole motion to recommit the concurrent resolution to the Budget Committee, to set budget targets for the fiscal year ending Sept. 30, 1986, as follows: budget authority, $1,069.5 billion; outlays, $965 billion; revenues, $793.6 billion; deficit, $171.4 billion. The amendment also established dual, annual caps on defense appropriations and on non-defense, discretionary (non-entitlement) appropriations as follows: fiscal 1986, defense, $303.2 billion, non-defense, $140.8 billion; 1987, defense, $324.1 billion, non-defense, $143.8 billion; 1988, defense, $347.6 billion, non-defense, $149.3 billion. It revised budget levels for fiscal 1985, and included reconciliation instructions requiring the Budget committees to recommend legislative savings to meet the budget targets by June 30, 1985. Adopted 50-49: R 48-4; D 1-45 (ND 1-31, SD 0-14), with Vice President George Bush casting a "yea" vote to break the 49-49 tie, in the session that began May 9, 1985. (The effect of this Dole amendment was to substitute, for the Senate GOP-White House budget package approved April 30, a revised version of that package providing, among other things, for $17.7 billion less in defense spending in fiscal 1986-88, and $15.7 billion more in domestic program spending for those three fiscal years.) (S Con Res 32, as amended by the Dole plan, subsequently was adopted by voice vote.) A "yea" was a vote supporting the president's position.

73. S Con Res 32. First Budget Resolution, Fiscal 1986. Dole, R-Kan., motion to table (kill) the Moynihan, D-N.Y., perfecting amendment to the Dole-Domenici, R-N.M., amendment to the instructions of the Dole motion to recommit the concurrent resolution to the Budget Committee, to restore the full Social Security cost-of-living adjustment (COLA) for fiscal 1986. Motion agreed to 51-47: R 49-3; D 2-44 (ND 1-31, SD 1-13), in the session that began May 9, 1985. A "yea" was a vote supporting the president's position. (The amendment adopted by vote 72 included elimination of the 1986 Social Security COLA.)

74. S Con Res 32. First Budget Resolution, Fiscal 1986. Packwood, R-Ore., motion to table (kill) the Kennedy, D-Mass., perfecting amendment to the Dole, R-Kan.-Domenici, R-N.M., amendment to the instructions of the Dole motion to recommit the concurrent resolution to the Budget Committee, to restore $4.6 billion during fiscal years 1986-88 for Medicare and Medicaid programs. Motion agreed to 54-44: R 51-1; D 3-43 (ND 2-30, SD 1-13), in the session that began May 9, 1985. A "yea" was a vote supporting the president's position.

CQ Senate Votes 75 - 82

Corresponding to Congressional Record Votes 75, 76, 77, 78, 79, 80, 81, 82

	75	76	77	78	79	80	81	82
ALABAMA								
Denton	Y	N	Y	Y	Y	Y	N	Y
Heflin	Y	N	Y	N	N	Y	N	Y
ALASKA								
Murkowski	Y	N	Y	Y	Y	Y	Y	Y
Stevens	Y	N	N	Y	Y	Y	Y	Y
ARIZONA								
Goldwater	Y	N	Y	Y	Y	Y	Y	?
DeConcini	Y	Y	N	Y	N	N	Y	N
ARKANSAS								
Bumpers	N	Y	N	Y	N	N	N	Y
Pryor	N	Y	N	Y	N	N	N	N
CALIFORNIA								
Wilson	Y	?	?	?	?	?	?	?
Cranston	N	Y	N	Y	N	N	N	Y
COLORADO								
Armstrong	Y	N	Y	Y	Y	Y	N	Y
Hart	N	Y	N	Y	N	N	N	Y
CONNECTICUT								
Weicker	N	Y	N	Y	Y	Y	N	Y
Dodd	N	N	N	Y	N	Y	N	Y
DELAWARE								
Roth	Y	N	Y	Y	Y	Y	Y	N
Biden	Y	N	N	Y	N	Y	N	Y
FLORIDA								
Hawkins	Y	?	?	Y	Y	Y	N	Y
Chiles	N	N	N	Y	N	N	N	Y
GEORGIA								
Mattingly	Y	Y	Y	Y	Y	Y	Y	Y
Nunn	N	N	N	Y	N	Y	N	Y
HAWAII								
Inouye	N	Y	N	Y	N	N	N	Y
Matsunaga	N	Y	N	Y	N	N	N	Y
IDAHO								
McClure	Y	Y	Y	N	Y	Y	Y	N
Symms	Y	Y	Y	N	Y	Y	Y	N
ILLINOIS								
Dixon	Y	Y	N	Y	N	N	N	Y
Simon	N	N	N	Y	N	N	N	Y
INDIANA								
Lugar	Y	N	Y	Y	Y	Y	N	Y
Quayle	Y	N	Y	Y	Y	Y	N	Y
IOWA								
Grassley	Y	N	N	Y	Y	N	Y	Y
Harkin	N	Y	N	Y	N	N	Y	Y
KANSAS								
Dole	Y	N	Y	Y	Y	Y	N	Y
Kassebaum	Y	Y	N	Y	Y	Y	Y	Y
KENTUCKY								
McConnell	Y	N	Y	Y	Y	Y	N	Y
Ford	Y	Y	N	Y	N	N	N	N
LOUISIANA								
Johnston	N	N	N	Y	N	N	N	Y
Long	Y	N	N	Y	N	N	N	Y
MAINE								
Cohen	N	N	N	Y	N	Y	N	Y
Mitchell	N	Y	N	Y	N	N	N	Y
MARYLAND								
Mathias	Y	N	N	Y	N	Y	N	?
Sarbanes	N	Y	N	Y	N	Y	N	Y
MASSACHUSETTS								
Kennedy	N	Y	N	Y	N	N	N	Y
Kerry	N	Y	N	Y	N	N	N	Y
MICHIGAN								
Levin	N	Y	N	Y	N	N	N	Y
Riegle	N	?	?	Y	N	N	N	Y
MINNESOTA								
Boschwitz	Y	N	N	Y	N	Y	N	Y
Durenberger	Y	N	N	Y	Y	Y	N	Y
MISSISSIPPI								
Cochran	Y	N	Y	Y	Y	Y	N	Y
Stennis	Y	Y	N	Y	?	?	N	Y
MISSOURI								
Danforth	Y	N	N	Y	N	Y	N	Y
Eagleton	N	N	N	Y	N	N	N	Y
MONTANA								
Baucus	N	Y	N	Y	N	N	N	N
Melcher	N	Y	N	Y	N	N	Y	N
NEBRASKA								
Exon	?	?	?	?	?	?	?	?
Zorinsky	Y	Y	N	Y	N	N	Y	N
NEVADA								
Hecht	Y	N	Y	N	Y	Y	N	Y
Laxalt	Y	N	Y	N	?	Y	N	N
NEW HAMPSHIRE								
Humphrey	Y	Y	Y	Y	Y	Y	N	Y
Rudman	Y	Y	Y	Y	Y	Y	N	Y
NEW JERSEY								
Bradley	Y	N	N	Y	N	N	N	Y
Lautenberg	Y	N	N	Y	N	Y	N	Y
NEW MEXICO								
Domenici	Y	N	Y	Y	Y	Y	N	Y
Bingaman	Y	N	N	Y	N	N	Y	Y
NEW YORK								
D'Amato	Y	N	Y	Y	N	Y	N	Y
Moynihan	N	N	N	Y	N	N	N	Y
NORTH CAROLINA								
East	?	?	+	?	?	?	?	?
Helms	Y	Y	Y	N	Y	Y	N	N
NORTH DAKOTA								
Andrews	Y	Y	Y	Y	Y	Y	Y	Y
Burdick	N	Y	N	Y	N	N	Y	N
OHIO								
Glenn	Y	N	N	Y	N	Y	N	Y
Metzenbaum	N	N	N	Y	N	N	N	Y
OKLAHOMA								
Nickles	Y	Y	Y	Y	N	Y	Y	N
Boren	N	?	?	Y	N	N	N	N
OREGON								
Hatfield	Y	Y	N	Y	N	N	Y	Y
Packwood	Y	N	N	Y	N	Y	N	Y
PENNSYLVANIA								
Heinz	N	Y	N	Y	N	Y	N	Y
Specter	Y	Y	N	Y	N	Y	Y	Y
RHODE ISLAND								
Chafee	Y	?	?	Y	Y	Y	N	Y
Pell	N	Y	N	Y	N	Y	N	Y
SOUTH CAROLINA								
Thurmond	Y	N	Y	Y	Y	Y	Y	Y
Hollings	N	Y	N	Y	N	N	Y	N
SOUTH DAKOTA								
Abdnor	Y	Y	Y	Y	Y	Y	Y	N
Pressler	Y	N	Y	Y	Y	Y	Y	Y
TENNESSEE								
Gore	N	N	N	Y	N	N	N	Y
Sasser	N	Y	N	Y	N	N	N	Y
TEXAS								
Gramm	Y	N	Y	Y	Y	Y	Y	Y
Bentsen	N	N	N	Y	N	N	N	Y
UTAH								
Garn	Y	N	Y	Y	Y	?	Y	Y
Hatch	Y	N	Y	Y	Y	Y	N	Y
VERMONT								
Stafford	Y	N	N	Y	Y	Y	N	Y
Leahy	N	Y	N	Y	N	N	N	Y
VIRGINIA								
Trible	Y	N	N	Y	Y	Y	N	?
Warner	Y	N	N	Y	Y	Y	N	Y
WASHINGTON								
Evans	Y	N	N	Y	Y	Y	N	Y
Gorton	Y	N	N	Y	Y	Y	N	Y
WEST VIRGINIA								
Byrd	N	Y	Y	Y	N	N	N	N
Rockefeller	N	Y	N	Y	N	N	N	Y
WISCONSIN								
Kasten	Y	N	Y	Y	N	Y	N	Y
Proxmire	N	Y	N	Y	N	N	Y	N
WYOMING								
Simpson	Y	N	Y	N	Y	Y	N	Y
Wallop	Y	N	Y	N	Y	Y	Y	N

KEY

- Y Voted for (yea).
- # Paired for.
- + Announced for.
- N Voted against (nay).
- X Paired against.
- - Announced against.
- P Voted "present".
- C Voted "present" to avoid possible conflict of interest.
- ? Did not vote or otherwise make a position known.

Democrats *Republicans*

ND - Northern Democrats SD - Southern Democrats (Southern states - Ala., Ark., Fla., Ga., Ky., La., Miss., N.C., Okla., S.C., Tenn., Texas, Va.)

75. S Con Res 32. First Budget Resolution, Fiscal 1986. Dole, R-Kan., motion to table (kill) the Metzenbaum, D-Ohio, perfecting amendment to the Dole-Domenici, R-N.M., amendment to the instructions of the Dole motion to recommit the concurrent resolution to the Budget Committee, to impose a 15 percent minimum tax on corporate earnings in excess of $50,000 and to use the revenues to reduce the federal deficit. Motion agreed to 61-37: R 49-3; D 12-34 (ND 8-24, SD 4-10), in the session that began May 9, 1985.

76. S 960. Foreign Assistance Authorization, Fiscal 1986. Kassebaum, R-Kan., amendment to delete from the bill the section that authorizes $3.6 billion in economic assistance to Central America for fiscal 1987-89. Rejected 41-52: R 14-35; D 27-17 (ND 21-10, SD 6-7), May 14, 1985. A "nay" was a vote supporting the president's position.

77. S 960. Foreign Assistance Authorization, Fiscal 1986. Helms, R-N.C., amendment to delete from the bill a section authorizing the president to make aid available to governments with land reform programs if the president determines that the programs would further U.S. interests. Rejected 33-60: R 31-18; D 2-42 (ND 1-30, SD 1-12), May 14, 1985. (The effect of the amendment was to eliminate funding for the land reform program in El Salvador.)

78. S 960. Foreign Assistance Authorization, Fiscal 1986. Kerry, D-Mass., amendment to express the sense of the Senate that Congress should give aid to the Philippines only if the government there had made "sufficient progress" in implementing a number of reforms. Adopted 89-8: R 44-7; D 45-1 (ND 32-0, SD 13-1), May 15, 1985.

79. S 960. Foreign Assistance Authorization, Fiscal 1986. Lugar, R-Ind., motion to table (kill) the Bradley, D-N.J., amendment to express the sense of Congress that the secretary of the Treasury and the chairman of the Federal Reserve Board, in concert with U.S. allies, should take necessary steps to lower the value of the dollar. Motion rejected 39-56: R 39-11; D 0-45 (ND 0-32, SD 0-13), May 15, 1985. (The Bradley amendment was subsequently adopted by voice vote.)

80. S 960. Foreign Assistance Authorization, Fiscal 1986. Lugar, R-Ind., motion to table (kill) the Bingaman, D-N.M., amendment to reduce the military assistance program by $100 million, and to transfer that $100 million to the Food for Peace program (PL 480). Motion agreed to 56-39: R 48-2; D 8-37 (ND 6-26, SD 2-11), May 15, 1985. A "yea" was a vote supporting the president's position.

81. S 960. Foreign Assistance Authorization, Fiscal 1986. Murkowski, R-Alaska, amendment to terminate the 30-year Extended Repayment Loan Program under the foreign military sales loan program. Rejected 27-70: R 19-32; D 8-38 (ND 7-25, SD 1-13), May 15, 1985.

82. S 960. Foreign Assistance Authorization, Fiscal 1986. Passage of the bill to make $12.8 billion in authorizations for fiscal years 1986 and 1987 for foreign aid programs. Passed 75-19: R 40-8; D 35-11 (ND 25-7, SD 10-4), May 15, 1985.

	83	84	85	86	87	88	89	90
ALABAMA								
Denton	N	Y	N	Y	N	Y	N	N
Heflin	N	Y	N	Y	Y	Y	N	N
ALASKA								
Murkowski	?	?	N	Y	Y	Y	N	N
Stevens	N	Y	N	Y	Y	Y	N	N
ARIZONA								
Goldwater	N	Y	N	Y	N	Y	N	N
DeConcini	Y	Y	N	Y	Y	Y	N	Y
ARKANSAS								
Bumpers	Y	Y	Y	Y	Y	Y	Y	N
Pryor	Y	Y	Y	Y	Y	?	Y	Y
CALIFORNIA								
Wilson	N	Y	N	Y	Y	Y	N	N
Cranston	?	?	Y	Y	Y	Y	Y	Y
COLORADO								
Armstrong	N	Y	N	Y	Y	Y	N	N
Hart	Y	Y	Y	Y	Y	N	Y	Y
CONNECTICUT								
Weicker	?	?	Y	Y	Y	Y	N	Y
Dodd	N	Y	Y	Y	Y	Y	N	Y
DELAWARE								
Roth	N	Y	N	Y	Y	Y	Y	Y
Biden	?	?	Y	Y	Y	Y	N	Y
FLORIDA								
Hawkins	N	Y	N	Y	Y	Y	N	N
Chiles	?	Y	N	Y	Y	Y	N	N
GEORGIA								
Mattingly	N	Y	N	Y	Y	Y	N	N
Nunn	N	Y	N	Y	Y	Y	Y	N
HAWAII								
Inouye	N	Y	Y	Y	Y	Y	N	Y
Matsunaga	N	Y	Y	Y	Y	Y	N	Y
IDAHO								
McClure	N	Y	N	Y	N	Y	N	N
Symms	N	Y	N	Y	N	Y	N	N
ILLINOIS								
Dixon	?	?	Y	Y	Y	Y	N	N
Simon	Y	Y	Y	Y	Y	Y	Y	Y
INDIANA								
Lugar	N	Y	N	Y	Y	Y	N	N
Quayle	N	Y	N	Y	N	Y	N	N
IOWA								
Grassley	Y	Y	N	Y	Y	Y	N	Y
Harkin	Y	Y	Y	Y	Y	Y	Y	Y
KANSAS								
Dole	N	Y	N	Y	Y	Y	N	N
Kassebaum	N	?	Y	?	?	Y	N	Y
KENTUCKY								
McConnell	N	Y	N	Y	Y	Y	N	Y
Ford	Y	Y	Y	Y	Y	N	N	Y
LOUISIANA								
Johnston	N	Y	Y	Y	Y	Y	N	?
Long	N	Y	N	Y	Y	Y	N	N
MAINE								
Cohen	N	Y	N	Y	Y	Y	N	N
Mitchell	Y	Y	Y	Y	Y	Y	Y	Y
MARYLAND								
Mathias	N	Y	N	Y	Y	Y	N	Y
Sarbanes	N	Y	Y	Y	Y	Y	Y	Y
MASSACHUSETTS								
Kennedy	?	?	Y	Y	Y	Y	Y	Y
Kerry	Y	Y	Y	Y	Y	Y	Y	Y
MICHIGAN								
Levin	N	Y	Y	Y	Y	Y	Y	Y
Riegle	Y	Y	Y	Y	Y	N	Y	Y
MINNESOTA								
Boschwitz	N	Y	N	Y	Y	Y	N	N
Durenberger	N	Y	Y	Y	Y	Y	N	Y
MISSISSIPPI								
Cochran	N	Y	N	Y	N	Y	N	N
Stennis	N	Y	N	Y	?	Y	N	?
MISSOURI								
Danforth	N	Y	N	Y	Y	Y	N	Y
Eagleton	Y	Y	Y	Y	Y	Y	Y	Y
MONTANA								
Baucus	Y	Y	Y	Y	Y	Y	Y	Y
Melcher	Y	Y	Y	Y	Y	Y	Y	Y
NEBRASKA								
Exon	N	Y	Y	Y	Y	Y	Y	N
Zorinsky	N	Y	N	Y	Y	Y	N	N
NEVADA								
Hecht	N	Y	N	Y	N	Y	N	N
Laxalt	N	Y	N	Y	Y	Y	N	N
NEW HAMPSHIRE								
Humphrey	N	Y	N	?	?	Y	N	N
Rudman	N	Y	N	Y	Y	Y	N	N
NEW JERSEY								
Bradley	?	?	Y	Y	Y	Y	Y	Y
Lautenberg	Y	Y	Y	Y	Y	Y	Y	Y
NEW MEXICO								
Domenici	N	Y	N	Y	Y	Y	N	N
Bingaman	N	Y	Y	Y	Y	N	Y	N
NEW YORK								
D'Amato	N	Y	N	Y	Y	Y	N	N
Moynihan	?	?	Y	Y	Y	Y	N	Y
NORTH CAROLINA								
East	?	?	?	?	?	?	?	?
Helms	N	Y	N	Y	N	Y	N	N
NORTH DAKOTA								
Andrews	N	Y	Y	Y	Y	Y	N	Y
Burdick	Y	Y	Y	Y	Y	Y	Y	Y
OHIO								
Glenn	N	Y	Y	Y	Y	N	N	N
Metzenbaum	Y	Y	Y	Y	Y	Y	Y	Y
OKLAHOMA								
Nickles	N	Y	N	Y	Y	Y	N	N
Boren	N	Y	N	Y	Y	?	Y	Y
OREGON								
Hatfield	+	+	Y	Y	Y	Y	N	Y
Packwood	N	Y	?	?	?	?	N	Y
PENNSYLVANIA								
Heinz	N	Y	N	Y	Y	Y	?	Y
Specter	N	Y	N	Y	Y	Y	N	Y
RHODE ISLAND								
Chafee	N	Y	N	Y	Y	Y	Y	Y
Pell	N	Y	Y	Y	Y	Y	Y	Y
SOUTH CAROLINA								
Thurmond	N	Y	N	Y	Y	Y	N	N
Hollings	N	Y	Y	Y	Y	N	N	N
SOUTH DAKOTA								
Abdnor	N	Y	N	Y	Y	Y	N	N
Pressler	N	Y	N	?	?	?	N	N
TENNESSEE								
Gore	N	Y	N	Y	Y	Y	Y	Y
Sasser	Y	Y	Y	Y	Y	N	Y	Y
TEXAS								
Gramm	N	Y	N	Y	N	Y	N	N
Bentsen	N	Y	N	Y	Y	Y	N	N
UTAH								
Garn	N	Y	N	Y	Y	N	N	N
Hatch	N	Y	N	Y	Y	Y	N	N
VERMONT								
Stafford	N	Y	Y	Y	Y	?	N	?
Leahy	Y	Y	Y	Y	Y	N	Y	Y
VIRGINIA								
Trible	N	Y	N	Y	Y	Y	N	N
Warner	N	Y	N	Y	Y	Y	N	N
WASHINGTON								
Evans	N	Y	N	Y	Y	Y	N	Y
Gorton	N	Y	N	Y	Y	Y	N	N
WEST VIRGINIA								
Byrd	Y	Y	N	Y	Y	Y	N	N
Rockefeller	Y	Y	Y	Y	Y	Y	N	N
WISCONSIN								
Kasten	N	Y	N	Y	Y	Y	N	N
Proxmire	Y	Y	Y	Y	Y	Y	Y	Y
WYOMING								
Simpson	N	Y	N	Y	Y	Y	N	N
Wallop	N	Y	N	Y	N	Y	N	N

KEY

- Y Voted for (yea).
- # Paired for.
- + Announced for.
- N Voted against (nay).
- X Paired against.
- - Announced against.
- P Voted "present".
- C Voted "present" to avoid possible conflict of interest.
- ? Did not vote or otherwise make a position known.

Democrats *Republicans*

ND - Northern Democrats SD - Southern Democrats (Southern states - Ala., Ark., Fla., Ga., Ky., La., Miss., N.C., Okla., S.C., Tenn., Texas, Va.)

83. S 1160. Department of Defense Authorization, Fiscal 1986. Pryor, D-Ark., amendment to make changes in Defense Department procurement practices, including barring Pentagon officials from working for firms having contracts over which they exercised responsibility, and requiring congressional authorization of major contracts for which there was only one bid. Rejected 22-67: R 1-48; D 21-19 (ND 17-10, SD 4-9), May 20, 1985.

84. S 1160. Department of Defense Authorization, Fiscal 1986. Goldwater, R-Ariz., amendment to make changes in Defense Department procurement practices, including requiring Pentagon officials to recuse themselves from handling any contract with firms with which they discuss post-retirement employment. The amendment also required a Pentagon purchasing plan for each major weapon that would keep two manufacturers competing for contracts; the requirement could be waived on grounds of cost, delay or "national security." Adopted 89-0: R 48-0; D 41-0 (ND 27-0, SD 14-0), May 20, 1985.

85. S 1160. Department of Defense Authorization, Fiscal 1986. Hart, D-Colo., amendment to delete from the bill $2.1 billion for the production of 21 MX missiles and to prohibit use of funds authorized by the bill for the production or deployment of MX missiles. Rejected 42-56: R 6-45; D 36-11 (ND 30-3, SD 6-8), May 21, 1985. A "nay" was a vote supporting the president's position.

86. S 1160. Department of Defense Authorization, Fiscal 1986. Byrd, D-W.Va.-Heflin, D-Ala., amendment to direct the Defense Department to study what effect the loss of all domestic ferroalloys production capacity would have on the U.S. defense industrial base and on industrial preparedness. Adopted 95-0: R 48-0; D 47-0 (ND 33-0, SD 14-0), May 21, 1985.

87. S 1160. Department of Defense Authorization, Fiscal 1986. Specter, R-Pa., amendment to express the sense of the Senate that the president of the United States and the president of the Soviet Union should meet at the earliest practical time to work toward a mutual, equitable and verifiable reduction in nuclear arms. Adopted 84-10: R 38-10; D 46-0 (ND 33-0, SD 13-0), May 21, 1985.

88. S 1160. Department of Defense Authorization, Fiscal 1986. Goldwater, R-Ariz., motion to table (kill) the Glenn, D-Ohio, amendment to restore $1.8 billion for the Defense Military Retirement Fund and to require the secretary of defense to report to Congress on the impact of potential cuts of 10, 20 and 30 percent in military retirement costs for fiscal 1986. Motion agreed to 85-9: R 48-1; D 37-8 (ND 28-5, SD 9-3), May 21, 1985.

89. S 1160. Department of Defense Authorization, Fiscal 1986. Exon, D-Neb., amendment to delete from the bill $53.5 million for reactivation of the battleship *Wisconsin*, to prohibit future spending to reactivate battleships, and to increase funding for naval munitions by $53.5 million. Rejected 30-68: R 2-49; D 28-19 (ND 22-11, SD 6-8), May 22, 1985. A "nay" was a vote supporting the president's position.

90. S 1160. Department of Defense Authorization, Fiscal 1986. Pryor, D-Ark., amendment to delete from the bill $163 million for the procurement of binary chemical weapons munitions, to prohibit future use of funds for such procurement, and to express the sense of Congress that the president should intensify efforts to achieve an agreement with the Soviet Union for the banning of chemical weapons. Rejected 46-50: R 15-36; D 31-14 (ND 26-7, SD 5-7), May 22, 1985. A "nay" was a vote supporting the president's position.

CQ Senate Votes 91 - 93

Corresponding to Congressional Record Votes 91, 92, 93

	91	92	93
ALABAMA			
Denton	N	N	N
Heflin	Y	Y	Y
ALASKA			
Murkowski	N	N	Y
Stevens	N	N	Y
ARIZONA			
Goldwater	N	N	Y
DeConcini	N	Y	Y
ARKANSAS			
Bumpers	Y	Y	Y
Pryor	Y	Y	Y
CALIFORNIA			
Wilson	N	N	N
Cranston	Y	Y	Y
COLORADO			
Armstrong	N	?	Y
Hart	Y	Y	Y
CONNECTICUT			
Weicker	N	N	N
Dodd	N	Y	Y
DELAWARE			
Roth	N	N	Y
Biden	N	Y	Y
FLORIDA			
Hawkins	N	N	Y
Chiles	Y	Y	Y
GEORGIA			
Mattingly	N	N	Y
Nunn	Y	Y	Y
HAWAII			
Inouye	Y	Y	Y
Matsunaga	Y	Y	Y
IDAHO			
McClure	N	N	N
Symms	N	N	N
ILLINOIS			
Dixon	Y	Y	Y
Simon	Y	Y	Y
INDIANA			
Lugar	N	N	Y
Quayle	N	N	Y
IOWA			
Grassley	N	N	Y
Harkin	N	Y	Y
KANSAS			
Dole	N	N	Y
Kassebaum	N	N	Y
KENTUCKY			
McConnell	N	N	Y
Ford	Y	Y	Y
LOUISIANA			
Johnston	Y	Y	Y
Long	Y	Y	Y
MAINE			
Cohen	N	?	Y
Mitchell	Y	Y	Y
MARYLAND			
Mathias	N	N	Y
Sarbanes	Y	Y	Y
MASSACHUSETTS			
Kennedy	Y	Y	N
Kerry	Y	Y	N
MICHIGAN			
Levin	Y	Y	Y
Riegle	Y	Y	Y
MINNESOTA			
Boschwitz	N	N	Y
Durenberger	Y	Y	Y
MISSISSIPPI			
Cochran	N	N	N
Stennis	Y	Y	Y
MISSOURI			
Danforth	N	N	Y
Eagleton	Y	Y	Y
MONTANA			
Baucus	Y	Y	Y
Melcher	Y	Y	Y
NEBRASKA			
Exon	Y	Y	Y
Zorinsky	N	N	Y
NEVADA			
Hecht	N	N	N
Laxalt	N	N	Y
NEW HAMPSHIRE			
Humphrey	N	N	N
Rudman	N	N	Y
NEW JERSEY			
Bradley	Y	Y	Y
Lautenberg	Y	Y	Y
NEW MEXICO			
Domenici	N	N	Y
Bingaman	Y	Y	Y
NEW YORK			
D'Amato	N	N	Y
Moynihan	N	Y	Y
NORTH CAROLINA			
East	?	?	?
Helms	N	N	N
NORTH DAKOTA			
Andrews	Y	Y	Y
Burdick	Y	Y	N
OHIO			
Glenn	Y	Y	Y
Metzenbaum	N	Y	Y
OKLAHOMA			
Nickles	N	N	N
Boren	Y	Y	Y
OREGON			
Hatfield	N	N	N
Packwood	N	N	Y
PENNSYLVANIA			
Heinz	Y	Y	Y
Specter	Y	Y	Y
RHODE ISLAND			
Chafee	N	N	Y
Pell	Y	Y	Y
SOUTH CAROLINA			
Thurmond	N	N	Y
Hollings	N	N	Y
SOUTH DAKOTA			
Abdnor	N	N	Y
Pressler	N	N	N
TENNESSEE			
Gore	Y	Y	Y
Sasser	Y	Y	Y
TEXAS			
Gramm	N	N	N
Bentsen	N	Y	Y
UTAH			
Garn	N	N	N
Hatch	N	N	N
VERMONT			
Stafford	N	?	?
Leahy	Y	Y	N
VIRGINIA			
Trible	N	N	Y
Warner	N	N	Y
WASHINGTON			
Evans	N	N	Y
Gorton	N	N	Y
WEST VIRGINIA			
Byrd	Y	Y	Y
Rockefeller	Y	Y	Y
WISCONSIN			
Kasten	N	N	Y
Proxmire	N	N	Y
WYOMING			
Simpson	N	N	Y
Wallop	N	N	N

KEY

- Y Voted for (yea).
- # Paired for.
- + Announced for.
- N Voted against (nay).
- X Paired against.
- - Announced against.
- P Voted "present".
- C Voted "present" to avoid possible conflict of interest.
- ? Did not vote or otherwise make a position known.

Democrats *Republicans*

ND - Northern Democrats SD - Southern Democrats (Southern states - Ala., Ark., Fla., Ga., Ky., La., Miss., N.C., Okla., S.C., Tenn., Texas, Va.)

91. S 1160. Department of Defense Authorization, Fiscal 1986. Bumpers, D-Ark., amendment to delete provisions that would simplify current procedures for closing military bases. Rejected 41-58: R 4-48; D 37-10 (ND 25-8, SD 12-2), May 23, 1985.

92. S 1160. Department of Defense Authorization, Fiscal 1986. Bingaman, D-N.M., amendment to retain a streamlined version of current procedures for closing military bases. Rejected 48-48: R 4-45; D 44-3 (ND 31-2, SD 13-1), May 23, 1985.

93. S 1160. Department of Defense Authorization, Fiscal 1986. Nunn, D-Ga., amendment to express the sense of the Senate that no more than 50 MX missiles should be deployed in existing missile silos and to authorize procurement of 12 MX missiles in fiscal 1986. Adopted 78-20: R 35-16; D 43-4 (ND 29-4, SD 14-0), May 23, 1985. A "yea" was a vote supporting the president's position.

	94	95	96
ALABAMA			
Denton	Y	N	Y
Heflin	Y	N	Y
ALASKA			
Murkowski	Y	N	Y
Stevens	Y	N	Y
ARIZONA			
Goldwater	Y	N	Y
DeConcini	?	?	?
ARKANSAS			
Bumpers	Y	Y	Y
Pryor	Y	Y	Y
CALIFORNIA			
Wilson	?	N	N
Cranston	Y	Y	Y
COLORADO			
Armstrong	Y	N	Y
Hart	Y	Y	Y
CONNECTICUT			
Weicker	Y	Y	Y
Dodd	Y	Y	Y
DELAWARE			
Roth	Y	N	Y
Biden	Y	Y	Y
FLORIDA			
Hawkins	Y	N	Y
Chiles	Y	N	?
GEORGIA			
Mattingly	Y	N	Y
Nunn	Y	N	Y
HAWAII			
Inouye	Y	Y	Y
Matsunaga	Y	Y	Y
IDAHO			
McClure	?	N	Y
Symms	Y	N	N
ILLINOIS			
Dixon	?	?	?
Simon	Y	Y	Y
INDIANA			
Lugar	Y	N	Y
Quayle	Y	N	N
IOWA			
Grassley	Y	N	Y
Harkin	Y	+	?
KANSAS			
Dole	Y	N	Y
Kassebaum	Y	N	Y
KENTUCKY			
McConnell	Y	N	Y
Ford	Y	N	Y
LOUISIANA			
Johnston	Y	?	?
Long	?	?	?
MAINE			
Cohen	?	?	?
Mitchell	Y	Y	Y
MARYLAND			
Mathias	Y	Y	Y
Sarbanes	Y	Y	Y
MASSACHUSETTS			
Kennedy	Y	Y	Y
Kerry	Y	Y	Y
MICHIGAN			
Levin	Y	Y	Y
Riegle	Y	Y	Y
MINNESOTA			
Boschwitz	Y	N	Y
Durenberger	Y	N	Y
MISSISSIPPI			
Cochran	Y	N	Y
Stennis	Y	N	Y
MISSOURI			
Danforth	Y	?	?
Eagleton	Y	Y	Y
MONTANA			
Baucus	Y	Y	Y
Melcher	+	+	+
NEBRASKA			
Exon	Y	N	Y
Zorinsky	Y	N	N
NEVADA			
Hecht	Y	N	N
Laxalt	Y	N	?
NEW HAMPSHIRE			
Humphrey	Y	N	Y
Rudman	?	?	?
NEW JERSEY			
Bradley	Y	N	Y
Lautenberg	Y	Y	Y
NEW MEXICO			
Domenici	?	?	?
Bingaman	Y	Y	Y
NEW YORK			
D'Amato	Y	N	?
Moynihan	Y	Y	Y
NORTH CAROLINA			
East	?	?	?
Helms	Y	N	Y
NORTH DAKOTA			
Andrews	Y	N	Y
Burdick	Y	Y	Y
OHIO			
Glenn	Y	N	Y
Metzenbaum	Y	Y	Y
OKLAHOMA			
Nickles	Y	N	Y
Boren	?	?	?
OREGON			
Hatfield	Y	Y	Y
Packwood	?	?	?
PENNSYLVANIA			
Heinz	Y	Y	Y
Specter	Y	Y	Y
RHODE ISLAND			
Chafee	Y	Y	Y
Pell	Y	Y	Y
SOUTH CAROLINA			
Thurmond	Y	N	Y
Hollings	Y	N	N
SOUTH DAKOTA			
Abdnor	Y	N	Y
Pressler	Y	N	Y
TENNESSEE			
Gore	Y	Y	Y
Sasser	Y	Y	Y
TEXAS			
Gramm	Y	N	Y
Bentsen	Y	?	?
UTAH			
Garn	Y	N	N
Hatch	Y	N	N
VERMONT			
Stafford	Y	Y	Y
Leahy	Y	Y	Y
VIRGINIA			
Trible	Y	N	Y
Warner	Y	N	Y
WASHINGTON			
Evans	Y	N	Y
Gorton	Y	N	Y
WEST VIRGINIA			
Byrd	Y	N	Y
Rockefeller	Y	Y	Y
WISCONSIN			
Kasten	Y	N	Y
Proxmire	Y	Y	Y
WYOMING			
Simpson	Y	N	Y
Wallop	Y	N	N

KEY

- Y Voted for (yea).
- # Paired for.
- + Announced for.
- N Voted against (nay).
- X Paired against.
- - Announced against.
- P Voted "present".
- C Voted "present" to avoid possible conflict of interest.
- ? Did not vote or otherwise make a position known.

Democrats *Republicans*

ND - Northern Democrats SD - Southern Democrats (Southern states - Ala., Ark., Fla., Ga., Ky., La., Miss., N.C., Okla., S.C., Tenn., Texas, Va.)

94. S 1160. Department of Defense Authorization, Fiscal 1986. Byrd, D-W.Va., amendment to impose a financial penalty on a contractor that bills the Defense Department for any expense expressly prohibited by law or regulation. Adopted 88-0: R 46-0; D 42-0 (ND 30-0, SD 12-0), May 24, 1985.

95. S 1160. Department of Defense Authorization, Fiscal 1986. Kerry, D-Mass., amendment to bar during fiscal years 1985 and 1986 tests against a target in space of the anti-satellite (ASAT) missile, unless the Soviet Union tests an ASAT. Rejected 35-51: R 7-40; D 28-11 (ND 24-5, SD 4-6), May 24, 1985. A "nay" was a vote supporting the president's position.

96. S 1160. Department of Defense Authorization, Fiscal 1986. Warner, R-Va., amendment to bar any test of the anti-satellite (ASAT) missile against a target in space during fiscal 1986 unless the Soviet Union tests an ASAT or the president certifies to Congress that the test is required for national security and that it would not impair prospects for a treaty limiting ASATs. Adopted 74-9: R 38-7; D 36-2 (ND 28-1, SD 8-1), May 24, 1985.

CQ Senate Votes 97 - 104

Corresponding to Congressional Record Votes 97, 98, 99, 100, 101, 102, 103, 104

	97	98	99	100	101	102	103	104
ALABAMA								
Denton	N	Y	N	N	N	N	Y	N
Heflin	Y	N	N	N	N	N	Y	Y
ALASKA								
Murkowski	Y	N	N	N	N	N	Y	N
Stevens	Y	N	N	N	N	N	N	N
ARIZONA								
Goldwater	N	Y	N	N	N	N	N	N
DeConcini	N	Y	N	Y	Y	Y	N	Y
ARKANSAS								
Bumpers	N	Y	Y	Y	Y	Y	N	Y
Pryor	N	Y	Y	Y	?	?	?	?
CALIFORNIA								
Wilson	N	Y	N	N	N	N	Y	N
Cranston	Y	N	Y	Y	Y	Y	N	Y
COLORADO								
Armstrong	N	Y	N	N	N	N	Y	N
Hart	Y	N	Y	Y	Y	N	N	Y
CONNECTICUT								
Weicker	Y	N	Y	Y	N	Y	N	N
Dodd	Y	N	N	Y	Y	Y	N	Y
DELAWARE								
Roth	N	Y	N	N	N	N	N	N
Biden	Y	N	N	#	Y	N	N	Y
FLORIDA								
Hawkins	N	Y	N	N	N	N	Y	?
Chiles	Y	N	N	Y	Y	Y	N	?
GEORGIA								
Mattingly	N	Y	N	N	N	N	Y	N
Nunn	N	Y	N	N	N	N	N	Y
HAWAII								
Inouye	Y	N	Y	Y	Y	Y	N	?
Matsunaga	Y	N	Y	Y	Y	Y	N	Y
IDAHO								
McClure	N	Y	N	N	N	N	Y	N
Symms	N	Y	N	N	N	N	Y	N
ILLINOIS								
Dixon	Y	N	N	N	N	N	N	Y
Simon	Y	N	Y	Y	Y	Y	N	Y
INDIANA								
Lugar	N	Y	N	N	N	N	Y	N
Quayle	N	Y	N	N	N	N	Y	N
IOWA								
Grassley	N	Y	N	Y	N	N	Y	N
Harkin	Y	N	Y	Y	Y	N	N	Y
KANSAS								
Dole	N	Y	N	N	N	N	N	N
Kassebaum	N	Y	N	Y	N	N	N	N
KENTUCKY								
McConnell	N	Y	N	N	N	N	N	N
Ford	Y	N	N	Y	Y	Y	N	Y
LOUISIANA								
Johnston	N	Y	N	Y	Y	Y	N	Y
Long	Y	N	N	N	N	N	Y	N
MAINE								
Cohen	N	Y	N	N	N	N	N	N
Mitchell	Y	N	N	Y	Y	Y	N	Y
MARYLAND								
Mathias	Y	N	N	Y	?	N	N	Y
Sarbanes	Y	N	Y	Y	Y	Y	N	Y
MASSACHUSETTS								
Kennedy	Y	N	Y	Y	Y	N	N	Y
Kerry	Y	N	Y	Y	Y	N	N	Y
MICHIGAN								
Levin	Y	N	N	Y	Y	Y	N	Y
Riegle	Y	N	Y	Y	Y	Y	N	Y
MINNESOTA								
Boschwitz	N	Y	N	N	N	N	N	N
Durenberger	Y	N	N	N	N	N	N	N
MISSISSIPPI								
Cochran	N	Y	N	N	N	?	?	?
Stennis	Y	N	N	?	?	?	?	?
MISSOURI								
Danforth	Y	N	N	N	N	N	N	N
Eagleton	Y	N	Y	Y	Y	Y	N	?
MONTANA								
Baucus	Y	N	N	Y	Y	Y	N	Y
Melcher	Y	N	Y	Y	Y	Y	N	Y
NEBRASKA								
Exon	N	Y	N	N	N	Y	N	N
Zorinsky	N	Y	N	N	N	N	Y	N
NEVADA								
Hecht	N	Y	N	N	N	N	Y	N
Laxalt	N	Y	N	N	N	N	Y	N
NEW HAMPSHIRE								
Humphrey	N	Y	N	N	N	N	Y	N
Rudman	N	Y	N	N	N	N	Y	?
NEW JERSEY								
Bradley	Y	N	N	N	Y	Y	N	Y
Lautenberg	Y	N	N	Y	Y	Y	N	Y
NEW MEXICO								
Domenici	N	Y	N	N	N	N	Y	N
Bingaman	Y	N	N	N	N	Y	N	Y
NEW YORK								
D'Amato	Y	N	N	N	N	N	Y	N
Moynihan	Y	N	N	Y	Y	Y	N	Y
NORTH CAROLINA								
East	-	#	?	?	?	?	?	?
Helms	N	Y	N	N	N	N	Y	N
NORTH DAKOTA								
Andrews	Y	N	N	N	N	N	N	N
Burdick	Y	N	Y	Y	Y	Y	N	Y
OHIO								
Glenn	Y	N	N	N	N	Y	N	N
Metzenbaum	Y	N	Y	Y	Y	N	N	Y
OKLAHOMA								
Nickles	N	Y	N	N	N	N	Y	N
Boren	N	Y	N	X	N	N	Y	?
OREGON								
Hatfield	N	Y	Y	Y	Y	Y	N	N
Packwood	Y	N	N	N	N	N	N	?
PENNSYLVANIA								
Heinz	Y	X	N	N	N	Y	N	Y
Specter	Y	N	N	?	?	Y	Y	N
RHODE ISLAND								
Chafee	N	Y	N	Y	N	N	N	N
Pell	Y	N	Y	Y	Y	Y	N	Y
SOUTH CAROLINA								
Thurmond	N	Y	N	N	N	N	N	N
Hollings	N	Y	N	N	N	N	Y	N
SOUTH DAKOTA								
Abdnor	N	Y	N	N	N	N	Y	N
Pressler	?	?	N	N	N	N	Y	N
TENNESSEE								
Gore	Y	N	N	Y	Y	Y	N	Y
Sasser	Y	N	N	Y	Y	Y	N	Y
TEXAS								
Gramm	N	Y	N	N	N	N	Y	N
Bentsen	N	Y	N	N	Y	Y	N	?
UTAH								
Garn	N	Y	N	N	N	N	Y	N
Hatch	N	Y	N	N	N	N	Y	N
VERMONT								
Stafford	Y	N	N	N	N	?	?	?
Leahy	Y	N	Y	Y	Y	N	N	Y
VIRGINIA								
Trible	N	Y	N	N	N	N	N	N
Warner	N	Y	N	N	N	N	N	Y
WASHINGTON								
Evans	N	Y	N	N	N	N	N	N
Gorton	N	Y	N	N	N	N	N	N
WEST VIRGINIA								
Byrd	Y	N	N	N	Y	Y	N	Y
Rockefeller	Y	N	N	Y	Y	Y	N	Y
WISCONSIN								
Kasten	N	Y	N	N	N	Y	Y	N
Proxmire	Y	N	Y	Y	Y	Y	N	Y
WYOMING								
Simpson	N	Y	N	N	N	N	Y	N
Wallop	N	Y	N	N	N	N	Y	N

KEY

- Y Voted for (yea).
- # Paired for.
- + Announced for.
- N Voted against (nay).
- X Paired against.
- \- Announced against.
- P Voted "present".
- C Voted "present" to avoid possible conflict of interest.
- ? Did not vote or otherwise make a position known.

Democrats ***Republicans***

ND - Northern Democrats SD - Southern Democrats (Southern states - Ala., Ark., Fla., Ga., Ky., La., Miss., N.C., Okla., S.C., Tenn., Texas, Va.)

97. S 1160. Department of Defense Authorization, Fiscal 1986. Kennedy, D-Mass., amendment to repeal a provision of the bill that would exempt military construction projects from the Davis-Bacon Act, which regulates hourly wages for construction workers on federal projects. Rejected 49-49: R 12-39; D 37-10 (ND 30-3, SD 7-7), June 4, 1985.

98. S 1160. Department of Defense Authorization, Fiscal 1986. Gramm, R-Texas, motion to table (kill) the Dole, R-Kan., motion to reconsider the vote by which the Kennedy, D-Mass., amendment was rejected *(vote 97, above)*. Motion agreed to 49-48: R 39-11; D 10-37 (ND 3-30, SD 7-7), June 4, 1985.

99. S 1160. Department of Defense Authorization, Fiscal 1986. Kerry, D-Mass., amendment to reduce from $2.96 billion to $1.4 billion the authorization for research on anti-missile defenses. Rejected 21-78: R 2-50; D 19-28 (ND 17-16, SD 2-12), June 4, 1985.

100. S 1160. Department of Defense Authorization, Fiscal 1986. Proxmire, D-Wis., amendment to reduce from $2.96 billion to $1.9 billion the authorization for research on anti-missile defenses. Rejected 38-57: R 6-45; D 32-12 (ND 25-7, SD 7-5), June 4, 1985.

101. S 1160. Department of Defense Authorization, Fiscal 1986. Gore, D-Tenn., amendment to reduce from $2.96 billion to $2.5 billion the authorization for research on anti-missile defenses. Rejected 36-59: R 1-49; D 35-10 (ND 28-5, SD 7-5), June 4, 1985.

102. S 1160. Department of Defense Authorization, Fiscal 1986. Glenn, D-Ohio, amendment to reduce from $2.96 billion to $2.8 billion the authorization for research on anti-missile defenses. Rejected 36-59: R 5-45; D 31-14 (ND 24-9, SD 7-5), June 4, 1985.

103. S 1160. Department of Defense Authorization, Fiscal 1986. Wallop, R-Wyo., amendment to earmark $800 million of the amount authorized for research on anti-missile defenses to develop anti-missile weapons that could be deployed within five to seven years. Rejected 33-62: R 28-22; D 5-40 (ND 1-32, SD 4-8), June 4, 1985.

104. S 1160. Department of Defense Authorization, Fiscal 1986. Bumpers, D-Ark., amendment to express the sense of the Senate that an expert panel should be established to advise the Senate on efforts to develop anti-missile defenses and their impact on arms control agreements. Rejected 38-49: R 3-44; D 35-5 (ND 28-3, SD 7-2), in the session that began June 4, 1985.

	105	106	107	108	109	110	111	112
ALABAMA								
Denton	-	+	-	-	-	-	N	Y
Heflin	Y	Y	N	N	N	N	N	Y
ALASKA								
Murkowski	Y	Y	N	N	N	N	N	Y
Stevens	Y	Y	N	N	N	N	N	Y
ARIZONA								
Goldwater	Y	Y	N	N	N	N	N	?
DeConcini	Y	Y	N	Y	N	N	N	Y
ARKANSAS								
Bumpers	Y	Y	N	Y	N	N	N	N
Pryor	Y	Y	N	Y	N	N	Y	N
CALIFORNIA								
Wilson	Y	Y	N	N	N	N	N	Y
Cranston	Y	Y	Y	Y	Y	Y	N	N
COLORADO								
Armstrong	Y	Y	N	?	?	?	N	Y
Hart	Y	Y	Y	Y	Y	Y	Y	N
CONNECTICUT								
Weicker	Y	Y	Y	Y	Y	Y	N	N
Dodd	Y	Y	Y	Y	Y	N	N	N
DELAWARE								
Roth	?	?	N	N	N	N	N	Y
Biden	Y	Y	N	Y	Y	N	Y	N
FLORIDA								
Hawkins	Y	Y	N	N	N	N	N	Y
Chiles	Y	Y	N	Y	N	N	N	Y
GEORGIA								
Mattingly	?	+	N	N	N	N	N	Y
Nunn	Y	Y	N	Y	N	N	N	Y
HAWAII								
Inouye	Y	Y	?	Y	Y	Y	Y	N
Matsunaga	Y	Y	Y	Y	Y	Y	Y	N
IDAHO								
McClure	Y	Y	N	N	N	N	N	Y
Symms	N	Y	N	N	N	N	N	Y
ILLINOIS								
Dixon	Y	Y	N	Y	N	N	Y	Y
Simon	Y	Y	N	Y	Y	Y	Y	N
INDIANA								
Lugar	Y	Y	N	N	N	N	N	Y
Quayle	Y	Y	N	N	N	N	N	Y
IOWA								
Grassley	Y	Y	N	N	N	N	N	Y
Harkin	Y	Y	Y	Y	Y	Y	N	N
KANSAS								
Dole	Y	Y	N	N	N	N	N	Y
Kassebaum	Y	Y	N	N	N	N	N	Y
KENTUCKY								
McConnell	Y	Y	N	N	N	N	N	Y
Ford	Y	Y	N	Y	N	N	N	Y
LOUISIANA								
Johnston	Y	Y	N	Y	N	N	N	Y
Long	Y	Y	N	N	N	N	N	Y
MAINE								
Cohen	Y	Y	N	N	N	N	Y	N
Mitchell	Y	Y	N	Y	Y	N	Y	N
MARYLAND								
Mathias	Y	Y	N	Y	Y	N	N	N
Sarbanes	Y	Y	Y	Y	Y	Y	Y	N
MASSACHUSETTS								
Kennedy	Y	Y	Y	Y	#	Y	N	N
Kerry	Y	Y	Y	Y	Y	N	N	N
MICHIGAN								
Levin	Y	Y	Y	Y	Y	N	Y	N
Riegle	Y	Y	Y	Y	Y	N	Y	N
MINNESOTA								
Boschwitz	Y	Y	N	N	N	N	N	Y
Durenberger	Y	Y	N	N	X	N	N	Y
MISSISSIPPI								
Cochran	Y	Y	N	N	N	N	N	Y
Stennis	Y	Y	N	N	N	N	N	Y
MISSOURI								
Danforth	?	?	N	N	N	N	N	Y
Eagleton	Y	Y	N	Y	Y	N	N	N
MONTANA								
Baucus	Y	Y	N	Y	Y	N	Y	N
Melcher	Y	N	Y	Y	Y	N	Y	N
NEBRASKA								
Exon	Y	Y	N	Y	Y	N	N	Y
Zorinsky	Y	Y	N	Y	N	N	N	N
NEVADA								
Hecht	N	Y	N	N	N	N	N	Y
Laxalt	Y	Y	N	N	N	N	N	Y
NEW HAMPSHIRE								
Humphrey	N	Y	N	N	N	N	N	Y
Rudman	Y	Y	N	N	N	N	N	Y
NEW JERSEY								
Bradley	Y	Y	N	Y	N	N	Y	N
Lautenberg	Y	Y	N	Y	Y	N	Y	N
NEW MEXICO								
Domenici	Y	Y	N	N	N	N	N	Y
Bingaman	Y	Y	N	Y	Y	N	Y	N
NEW YORK								
D'Amato	Y	Y	N	N	N	N	N	Y
Moynihan	Y	Y	N	N	N	N	N	N
NORTH CAROLINA								
East	?	?	?	?	N	N	N	Y
Helms	N	Y	N	N	N	N	N	Y
NORTH DAKOTA								
Andrews	Y	Y	N	N	Y	N	N	Y
Burdick	Y	Y	Y	Y	Y	Y	N	N
OHIO								
Glenn	Y	Y	N	Y	N	N	N	N
Metzenbaum	Y	N	Y	Y	Y	Y	N	N
OKLAHOMA								
Nickles	Y	Y	N	N	N	N	N	Y
Boren	Y	Y	N	Y	N	N	N	Y
OREGON								
Hatfield	Y	N	Y	Y	Y	Y	Y	N
Packwood	Y	Y	N	Y	N	N	N	N
PENNSYLVANIA								
Heinz	Y	Y	N	Y	N	N	N	Y
Specter	Y	Y	N	Y	N	N	N	N
RHODE ISLAND								
Chafee	Y	Y	N	N	N	N	N	N
Pell	Y	Y	Y	Y	Y	Y	Y	N
SOUTH CAROLINA								
Thurmond	Y	Y	N	N	N	N	N	Y
Hollings	Y	Y	N	N	N	N	N	Y
SOUTH DAKOTA								
Abdnor	Y	Y	N	N	N	N	N	Y
Pressler	Y	Y	N	N	N	N	?	Y
TENNESSEE								
Gore	Y	Y	N	Y	Y	N	Y	N
Sasser	Y	Y	N	Y	Y	N	Y	N
TEXAS								
Gramm	Y	Y	N	N	N	N	N	Y
Bentsen	Y	Y	N	Y	N	N	N	Y
UTAH								
Garn	Y	Y	N	N	N	N	N	Y
Hatch	Y	Y	N	N	N	N	N	Y
VERMONT								
Stafford	Y	Y	N	N	Y	N	N	N
Leahy	Y	Y	Y	Y	Y	Y	N	N
VIRGINIA								
Trible	Y	Y	N	N	N	N	N	Y
Warner	Y	Y	N	N	N	N	N	Y
WASHINGTON								
Evans	Y	Y	N	N	N	N	N	N
Gorton	Y	Y	N	N	N	N	N	N
WEST VIRGINIA								
Byrd	Y	Y	N	Y	N	N	Y	Y
Rockefeller	Y	Y	N	Y	N	-	+	+
WISCONSIN								
Kasten	Y	Y	N	N	N	N	N	Y
Proxmire	Y	N	N	Y	Y	Y	N	N
WYOMING								
Simpson	Y	Y	N	N	N	N	N	Y
Wallop	N	Y	-	-	-	?	-	+

KEY

Y Voted for (yea).
Paired for.
\+ Announced for.
N Voted against (nay).
X Paired against.
\- Announced against.
P Voted "present".
C Voted "present" to avoid possible conflict of interest.
? Did not vote or otherwise make a position known.

Democrats *Republicans*

ND - Northern Democrats SD - Southern Democrats (Southern states - Ala., Ark., Fla., Ga., Ky., La., Miss., N.C., Okla., S.C., Tenn., Texas, Va.)

105. S 1160. Department of Defense Authorization, Fiscal 1986. Bumpers, D-Ark., amendment to express the sense of the Senate that the United States should not undercut the 1972 and 1979 U.S.-Soviet strategic arms limitation agreements (SALT I and II), but should be free to take proportionate responses to Soviet actions that undercut the agreements. Adopted 90-5: R 43-5; D 47-0 (ND 33-0, SD 14-0), June 5, 1985.

106. S 1160. Department of Defense Authorization, Fiscal 1986. Passage of the bill to authorize $231,854,402,000 for military programs of the Department of Defense in fiscal year 1986. Passed 91-4: R 47-1; D 44-3 (ND 30-3, SD 14-0), June 5, 1985.

107. S 1003. State Department Authorizations, Fiscal 1986-87. Dodd, D-Conn., amendment to prohibit additional funding for military or paramilitary activities in Central America, to authorize $14 million for fiscal 1985 for the withdrawal and relocation of all U.S.-supported forces and their families outside Nicaragua, and to authorize $10 million to assist regional negotiations. The amendment also declared that the United States is prepared to use military force in Central America if U.S. security interests are jeopardized. Rejected 17-79: R 2-48; D 15-31 (ND 15-17, SD 0-14), June 6, 1985. A "nay" was a vote supporting the president's position.

108. S 1003. State Department Authorizations, Fiscal 1986-87. Division I of the Kennedy, D-Mass., amendment, to express the sense of Congress that the United States should resume bilateral negotiations with the government of Nicaragua. Rejected 48-48: R 6-43; D 42-5 (ND 32-1, SD 10-4), June 6, 1985. A "nay" was a vote supporting the president's position.

109. S 1003. State Department Authorizations, Fiscal 1986-87. Division II of the Kennedy, D-Mass., amendment, to prohibit the introduction of U.S. combat troops into Nicaragua without prior approval of Congress, except if the president determines that troops must be sent to meet a clear threat of attack upon the United States or U.S. citizens, or if Congress has declared war. Rejected 31-64: R 5-44; D 26-20 (ND 24-8, SD 2-12), June 6, 1985. A "nay" was a vote supporting the president's position.

110. S 1003. State Department Authorizations, Fiscal 1986-87. Hart, D-Colo., amendment to restrict the introduction of U.S. combat troops into Central America unless authorized by Congress or if the president determines that troops must be sent to meet a threat of attack upon the United States or U.S. citizens. Rejected 15-81: R 2-48; D 13-33 (ND 13-19, SD 0-14), June 6, 1985. A "nay" was a vote supporting the president's position.

111. S 1003. State Department Authorizations, Fiscal 1986-87. Biden, D-Del., amendment to prohibit funding for military and paramilitary forces in Nicaragua, and to authorize $14 million in fiscal 1985 for non-lethal aid to anti-government rebels there, provided that the aid is independently monitored, the United States resumes bilateral negotiations with the government of Nicaragua, and the rebels and the Nicaraguan government agree to a cease-fire. The amendment also would terminate the trade embargo implemented May 1 on Nicaragua if that government enters into a cease-fire and negotiations, and set preconditions for future aid to the rebels. Rejected 22-75: R 2-49; D 20-26 (ND 17-15, SD 3-11), June 6, 1985. A "nay" was a vote supporting the president's position.

112. S 1003. State Department Authorizations, Fiscal 1986-87. Nunn, D-Ga., amendment to authorize $24 million for fiscal year 1986 for humanitarian assistance to the Nicaraguan rebels and to direct the National Security Council to monitor the use of the funds. The amendment also releases the $14 million approved for fiscal 1985 for the rebels but restricts the use of those funds to humanitarian assistance, and it urges the president to lift the economic sanctions on Nicaragua if that country agrees to a cease-fire and talks with the rebels, to call upon the rebels to remove from their ranks any individuals who have engaged in human rights abuses, and to resume bilateral negotiations with the government of Nicaragua. Adopted 55-42: R 41-10; D 14-32 (ND 4-28, SD 10-4), June 6, 1985. A "yea" was a vote supporting the president's position.

CQ Senate Votes 113 - 120

Corresponding to Congressional Record Votes 113, 114, 115, 116, 117, 118, 119, 120

	113	114	115	116	117	118	119	120
ALABAMA								
Denton	N	N	N	Y	N	Y	Y	Y
Heflin	N	N	Y	N	N	Y	Y	Y
ALASKA								
Murkowski	N	N	N	Y	N	Y	Y	Y
Stevens	N	N	N	Y	N	Y	Y	Y
ARIZONA								
Goldwater	N	N	N	Y	N	Y	Y	N
DeConcini	N	N	Y	N	N	Y	Y	Y
ARKANSAS								
Bumpers	?	?	?	?	?	?	N	Y
Pryor	Y	Y	Y	N	Y	Y	N	Y
CALIFORNIA								
Wilson	N	N	N	Y	N	Y	Y	Y
Cranston	Y	Y	Y	N	Y	?	N	Y
COLORADO								
Armstrong	N	N	Y	Y	N	?	Y	Y
Hart	Y	Y	Y	N	Y	N	N	Y
CONNECTICUT								
Weicker	Y	Y	Y	N	Y	N	N	Y
Dodd	Y	Y	Y	N	N	Y	N	Y
DELAWARE								
Roth	N	N	N	Y	N	Y	Y	Y
Biden	Y	Y	Y	N	N	N	N	N
FLORIDA								
Hawkins	N	N	N	Y	N	Y	Y	Y
Chiles	N	N	+	N	N	Y	Y	Y
GEORGIA								
Mattingly	N	N	N	Y	N	Y	Y	Y
Nunn	N	N	Y	N	N	Y	Y	Y
HAWAII								
Inouye	Y	Y	Y	N	Y	N	N	?
Matsunaga	Y	Y	Y	N	Y	N	N	N
IDAHO								
McClure	N	N	N	Y	N	Y	Y	Y
Symms	N	N	N	Y	N	Y	Y	Y
ILLINOIS								
Dixon	N	N	Y	N	Y	Y	Y	Y
Simon	?	?	?	?	?	?	N	Y
INDIANA								
Lugar	N	N	Y	Y	N	Y	Y	Y
Quayle	N	N	N	Y	N	Y	Y	Y
IOWA								
Grassley	Y	Y	Y	N	N	Y	Y	Y
Harkin	Y	Y	Y	N	Y	Y	N	?
KANSAS								
Dole	N	N	N	Y	N	Y	Y	Y
Kassebaum	N	N	N	Y	N	Y	Y	Y
KENTUCKY								
McConnell	N	N	N	Y	N	?	Y	Y
Ford	Y	Y	Y	N	N	Y	Y	Y
LOUISIANA								
Johnston	N	N	Y	N	N	Y	Y	Y
Long	N	N	N	Y	N	N	Y	Y
MAINE								
Cohen	?	?	?	?	?	?	Y	Y
Mitchell	Y	Y	Y	N	Y	Y	Y	Y
MARYLAND								
Mathias	Y	Y	N	Y	Y	N	N	Y
Sarbanes	?	?	?	?	N	N	N	Y
MASSACHUSETTS								
Kennedy	Y	Y	Y	N	?	?	N	Y
Kerry	Y	Y	Y	N	Y	N	N	Y
MICHIGAN								
Levin	Y	Y	Y	N	N	Y	N	Y
Riegle	Y	Y	Y	N	N	Y	N	Y
MINNESOTA								
Boschwitz	N	N	N	Y	N	Y	Y	Y
Durenberger	N	N	N	Y	N	Y	Y	Y
MISSISSIPPI								
Cochran	N	N	N	Y	N	Y	Y	Y
Stennis	N	N	?	?	N	Y	Y	Y
MISSOURI								
Danforth	N	N	N	Y	Y	Y	?	?
Eagleton	Y	Y	Y	N	N	Y	N	?
MONTANA								
Baucus	Y	N	Y	N	Y	Y	N	Y
Melcher	Y	Y	Y	N	?	?	N	Y
NEBRASKA								
Exon	N	N	Y	N	N	Y	Y	Y
Zorinsky	Y	N	Y	N	N	Y	Y	Y
NEVADA								
Hecht	N	N	N	Y	N	Y	Y	Y
Laxalt	N	N	N	Y	?	?	Y	N
NEW HAMPSHIRE								
Humphrey	N	N	N	Y	N	Y	Y	Y
Rudman	N	N	N	Y	N	?	Y	Y
NEW JERSEY								
Bradley	Y	Y	?	?	?	?	N	N
Lautenberg	Y	Y	Y	N	N	Y	N	Y
NEW MEXICO								
Domenici	N	N	N	Y	N	Y	Y	Y
Bingaman	Y	Y	Y	N	N	Y	N	N
NEW YORK								
D'Amato	N	N	N	Y	N	Y	Y	Y
Moynihan	Y	N	Y	N	N	N	N	Y
NORTH CAROLINA								
East	N	N	N	Y	N	Y	Y	Y
Helms	N	N	N	Y	N	Y	Y	Y
NORTH DAKOTA								
Andrews	N	N	N	Y	N	Y	Y	Y
Burdick	Y	Y	Y	N	Y	Y	N	Y
OHIO								
Glenn	N	N	Y	N	N	Y	N	N
Metzenbaum	Y	Y	Y	N	Y	Y	N	Y
OKLAHOMA								
Nickles	N	N	Y	Y	N	Y	Y	Y
Boren	N	N	Y	N	Y	Y	Y	Y
OREGON								
Hatfield	#	#	#	?	Y	N	N	Y
Packwood	N	N	Y	N	N	Y	?	?
PENNSYLVANIA								
Heinz	N	N	Y	Y	N	Y	Y	Y
Specter	N	N	Y	Y	N	Y	N	Y
RHODE ISLAND								
Chafee	Y	N	N	Y	Y	N	Y	Y
Pell	Y	Y	Y	N	Y	N	N	Y
SOUTH CAROLINA								
Thurmond	N	N	N	Y	N	Y	Y	Y
Hollings	N	N	N	Y	N	Y	Y	Y
SOUTH DAKOTA								
Abdnor	N	N	N	Y	N	Y	Y	Y
Pressler	N	N	N	Y	N	Y	Y	Y
TENNESSEE								
Gore	Y	Y	Y	N	Y	Y	N	Y
Sasser	Y	Y	Y	N	N	Y	Y	Y
TEXAS								
Gramm	N	N	N	Y	N	Y	Y	Y
Bentsen	N	N	Y	N	N	Y	Y	Y
UTAH								
Garn	N	N	N	Y	N	Y	Y	Y
Hatch	N	N	N	Y	N	Y	Y	Y
VERMONT								
Stafford	Y	Y	Y	Y	N	Y	?	Y
Leahy	Y	Y	Y	N	Y	?	N	Y
VIRGINIA								
Trible	N	N	N	Y	N	Y	Y	Y
Warner	N	N	N	Y	N	Y	Y	Y
WASHINGTON								
Evans	N	N	N	Y	N	Y	Y	Y
Gorton	X	X	X	?	-	+	Y	Y
WEST VIRGINIA								
Byrd	Y	N	Y	N	N	Y	Y	Y
Rockefeller	?	?	?	?	?	?	N	Y
WISCONSIN								
Kasten	N	N	N	Y	N	?	Y	Y
Proxmire	Y	Y	Y	N	Y	Y	N	Y
WYOMING								
Simpson	N	N	N	Y	N	Y	Y	Y
Wallop	-	?	?	?	-	+	Y	Y

KEY

- Y Voted for (yea).
- # Paired for.
- + Announced for.
- N Voted against (nay).
- X Paired against.
- - Announced against.
- P Voted "present".
- C Voted "present" to avoid possible conflict of interest.
- ? Did not vote or otherwise make a position known.

Democrats ***Republicans***

ND - Northern Democrats SD - Southern Democrats (Southern states - Ala., Ark., Fla., Ga., Ky., La., Miss., N.C., Okla., S.C., Tenn., Texas, Va.)

113. S 1003. State Department Authorizations, Fiscal 1986-87. Division I of the Harkin, D-Iowa, amendment, to prohibit the expenditure of funds by the CIA or the Department of Defense for "humanitarian" aid to guerrillas battling the government of Nicaragua. Rejected 35-57: R 5-44; D 30-13 (ND 26-4, SD 4-9), June 7, 1985. A "nay" was a vote supporting the president's position.

114. S 1003. State Department Authorizations, Fiscal 1986-87. Division II of the Harkin, D-Iowa, amendment, to prohibit expenditure of funds by any U.S. intelligence agency to support military or paramilitary operations in Nicaragua, unless authorized by the president to respond directly to an unforeseen specific and immediate threat to the United States or its allies. Rejected 30-62: R 4-45; D 26-17 (ND 22-8, SD 4-9), June 7, 1985. A "nay" was a vote supporting the president's position.

115. S 1003. State Department Authorizations, Fiscal 1986-87. Kerry, D-Mass., amendment to prohibit expenditure of funds for activities in Nicaragua that are in violation of international law or of U.S. obligations under the charter of the Organization of American States. Adopted 47-42: R 9-40; D 38-2 (ND 29-0, SD 9-2), June 7, 1985. A "nay" was a vote supporting the president's position. The Senate subsequently voted to reconsider the vote by which the amendment was adopted *(see vote 116, below)* and then adopted, by voice vote, a modified Kerry amendment to allow activities in Nicaragua that were authorized by U.S. law.

116. S 1003. State Department Authorizations, Fiscal 1986-87. Lugar, R-Ind., motion to reconsider the vote by which the Kerry, D-Mass., amendment was adopted *(vote 115, above)*. Motion agreed to 48-42: R 46-3; D 2-39 (ND 0-29, SD 2-10), June 7, 1985. (The Senate subsequently adopted, by voice vote, a modified Kerry amendment to allow activities in Nicaragua that were authorized by U.S. law.)

117. S 1003. State Department Authorizations, Fiscal 1986-87. Dixon, D-Ill., amendment to call upon the president to rescind economic sanctions he had imposed upon Nicaragua on May 1, 1985. Rejected 22-68: R 5-44; D 17-24 (ND 14-14, SD 3-10), June 7, 1985. A "nay" was a vote supporting the president's position.

118. S 1003. State Department Authorizations, Fiscal 1986-87. Kassebaum, R-Kan., amendment to limit U.S. contributions to the United Nations and related organizations to 20 percent of those organizations' annual budgets, unless the secretary of state certified to Congress that such organizations had adopted procedures for proportionate voting on budgetary matters and had adopted plans to reduce employee salaries and pensions to levels comparable to those of the U.S. Civil Service. Adopted 71-13: R 41-4; D 30-9 (ND 18-8, SD 12-1), June 7, 1985.

119. S 1003. State Department Authorizations, Fiscal 1986-87. Symms, R-Idaho, amendment to repeal the section of the 1980 foreign aid authorizations bill (PL 96-533) known as the Clark amendment that prohibited U.S. military aid to anti-government rebels in Angola unless specifically requested by the president and approved by Congress. Adopted 63-34: R 46-4; D 17-30 (ND 6-27, SD 11-3), June 11, 1985.

120. S 1003. State Department Authorizations, Fiscal 1986-87. Byrd, D-W.Va., amendment to express the sense of Congress that Japan should develop and implement a 1986-90 defense plan to acquire and maintain armed forces adequate to defend its land area and surrounding airspace and sea lanes out to a distance of 1,000 miles. In addition, the amendment urged Japan to increase substantially its annual contributions to construct new U.S. military bases in that country and its annual financial contributions to support U.S. forces stationed in Japan, especially by paying more of the costs of Japanese labor hired by the U.S. forces there. Adopted 88-7: R 49-2; D 39-5 (ND 25-5, SD 14-0), June 11, 1985.

	121	122	123	124	125	126
ALABAMA						
Denton	N	Y	Y	Y	Y	Y
Heflin	N	N	Y	Y	N	Y
ALASKA						
Murkowski	N	Y	Y	Y	N	Y
Stevens	Y	Y	Y	Y	N	Y
ARIZONA						
Goldwater	Y	Y	Y	?	N	Y
DeConcini	N	Y	N	N	Y	Y
ARKANSAS						
Bumpers	Y	Y	N	N	?	?
Pryor	Y	Y	Y	Y	Y	Y
CALIFORNIA						
Wilson	Y	Y	Y	Y	N	Y
Cranston	Y	N	N	N	Y	Y
COLORADO						
Armstrong	N	Y	Y	Y	N	Y
Hart	Y	N	N	N	Y	Y
CONNECTICUT						
Weicker	Y	Y	Y	Y	Y	Y
Dodd	Y	N	N	N	Y	Y
DELAWARE						
Roth	N	Y	Y	Y	Y	Y
Biden	Y	Y	N	N	Y	Y
FLORIDA						
Hawkins	N	Y	Y	Y	Y	Y
Chiles	Y	Y	Y	N	Y	Y
GEORGIA						
Mattingly	N	Y	Y	Y	N	Y
Nunn	Y	?	Y	N	N	Y
HAWAII						
Inouye	?	?	N	N	Y	Y
Matsunaga	Y	N	N	N	Y	Y
IDAHO						
McClure	N	N	Y	Y	N	Y
Symms	N	Y	Y	Y	N	Y
ILLINOIS						
Dixon	Y	Y	Y	Y	Y	?
Simon	Y	Y	Y	N	Y	Y
INDIANA						
Lugar	N	Y	Y	Y	Y	Y
Quayle	N	Y	Y	Y	N	Y
IOWA						
Grassley	N	Y	Y	Y	Y	Y
Harkin	?	?	N	N	Y	Y
KANSAS						
Dole	N	Y	Y	Y	Y	Y
Kassebaum	Y	Y	Y	Y	?	?
KENTUCKY						
McConnell	N	Y	Y	Y	N	Y
Ford	N	Y	N	N	Y	Y
LOUISIANA						
Johnston	N	Y	Y	Y	Y	Y
Long	Y	Y	Y	Y	N	Y
MAINE						
Cohen	Y	Y	?	?	Y	Y
Mitchell	Y	Y	N	N	Y	Y
MARYLAND						
Mathias	Y	Y	Y	Y	Y	Y
Sarbanes	Y	Y	N	N	Y	Y
MASSACHUSETTS						
Kennedy	Y	N	N	N	Y	Y
Kerry	Y	N	N	N	Y	+
MICHIGAN						
Levin	Y	N	N	N	Y	Y
Riegle	Y	Y	N	N	Y	Y
MINNESOTA						
Boschwitz	N	Y	Y	Y	Y	Y
Durenberger	N	Y	Y	Y	Y	Y
MISSISSIPPI						
Cochran	N	Y	Y	Y	Y	Y
Stennis	N	Y	Y	Y	?	Y
MISSOURI						
Danforth	N	Y	Y	Y	Y	Y
Eagleton	N	Y	N	N	Y	?
MONTANA						
Baucus	Y	Y	N	N	Y	Y
Melcher	N	N	?	N	Y	Y
NEBRASKA						
Exon	N	N	Y	Y	Y	Y
Zorinsky	N	N	Y	Y	Y	Y
NEVADA						
Hecht	N	Y	Y	Y	N	Y
Laxalt	N	Y	Y	Y	N	Y
NEW HAMPSHIRE						
Humphrey	N	Y	Y	Y	Y	Y
Rudman	Y	Y	Y	Y	Y	Y
NEW JERSEY						
Bradley	Y	Y	N	N	Y	Y
Lautenberg	Y	Y	N	N	Y	Y
NEW MEXICO						
Domenici	N	Y	Y	Y	N	Y
Bingaman	Y	Y	N	N	Y	Y
NEW YORK						
D'Amato	N	Y	Y	Y	Y	Y
Moynihan	Y	Y	N	N	Y	Y
NORTH CAROLINA						
East	N	Y	?	?	?	?
Helms	N	Y	Y	Y	N	Y
NORTH DAKOTA						
Andrews	N	Y	Y	Y	Y	Y
Burdick	Y	N	N	N	Y	Y
OHIO						
Glenn	Y	Y	N	N	Y	Y
Metzenbaum	Y	Y	N	N	Y	Y
OKLAHOMA						
Nickles	N	Y	Y	Y	N	Y
Boren	Y	Y	Y	N	Y	Y
OREGON						
Hatfield	Y	N	Y	Y	N	Y
Packwood	Y	Y	Y	Y	Y	Y
PENNSYLVANIA						
Heinz	Y	Y	?	?	Y	Y
Specter	Y	Y	Y	Y	Y	Y
RHODE ISLAND						
Chafee	Y	Y	Y	Y	Y	Y
Pell	Y	N	N	Y	Y	Y
SOUTH CAROLINA						
Thurmond	N	Y	Y	Y	N	Y
Hollings	Y	Y	N	N	Y	Y
SOUTH DAKOTA						
Abdnor	N	Y	Y	Y	N	Y
Pressler	N	Y	Y	Y	Y	Y
TENNESSEE						
Gore	Y	Y	N	N	Y	Y
Sasser	Y	Y	N	N	Y	Y
TEXAS						
Gramm	N	Y	Y	Y	N	Y
Bentsen	Y	Y	N	N	Y	Y
UTAH						
Garn	N	N	Y	Y	N	Y
Hatch	N	Y	Y	Y	N	Y
VERMONT						
Stafford	Y	Y	Y	Y	Y	Y
Leahy	Y	Y	N	N	Y	Y
VIRGINIA						
Trible	N	Y	Y	Y	Y	Y
Warner	Y	Y	Y	Y	Y	Y
WASHINGTON						
Evans	Y	Y	Y	Y	Y	Y
Gorton	Y	Y	Y	Y	Y	Y
WEST VIRGINIA						
Byrd	Y	Y	N	N	Y	Y
Rockefeller	Y	Y	N	N	Y	Y
WISCONSIN						
Kasten	N	Y	Y	Y	Y	Y
Proxmire	N	N	N	N	Y	Y
WYOMING						
Simpson	Y	Y	Y	Y	N	Y
Wallop	N	Y	Y	Y	N	Y

KEY

- Y Voted for (yea).
- # Paired for.
- + Announced for.
- N Voted against (nay).
- X Paired against.
- - Announced against.
- P Voted "present".
- C Voted "present" to avoid possible conflict of interest.
- ? Did not vote or otherwise make a position known.

Democrats *Republicans*

ND - Northern Democrats SD - Southern Democrats (Southern states - Ala., Ark., Fla., Ga., Ky., La., Miss., N.C., Okla., S.C., Tenn., Texas, Va.)

121. S 1003. State Department Authorizations, Fiscal 1986-87. Kassebaum, R-Kan., motion to table (kill) the Helms, R-N.C., amendment to maintain presidential authority, in connection with funding for population planning, to implement whatever policies the president deems necessary to curb human rights violations such as infanticide, abortion, involuntary sterilization, and racial or ethnic discrimination. Motion agreed to 53-45: R 18-35; D 35-10 (ND 25-6, SD 10-4), June 11, 1985.

122. HR 2068. State Department Authorizations, Fiscal 1986-87. Passage of the bill to authorize appropriations of $3.8 billion in fiscal 1986 and $3.8 billion in fiscal 1987 for the State Department, the U.S. Information Agency, the Board of International Broadcasting, and the Arms Control and Disarmament Agency. Passed 80-17: R 50-3; D 30-14 (ND 18-13, SD 12-1), June 11, 1985. (The Senate had previously moved to delete the House language of HR 2068 and insert instead the language of S 1003, the Senate version of the State Department authorization bill.)

123. Wallace Nomination. Confirmation of President Reagan's nomination of Michael B. Wallace of Mississippi to be a member of the board of directors of the Legal Services Corporation. Confirmed 62-34: R 50-0; D 12-34 (ND 4-28, SD 8-6), June 12, 1985. A "yea" was a vote supporting the president's position.

124. Bernstein Nomination. Confirmation of President Reagan's nomination of LeaAnne Bernstein of Maryland to be a member of the board of directors of the Legal Services Corporation. Confirmed 58-38: R 49-0; D 9-38 (ND 4-29, SD 5-9), June 12, 1985. A "yea" was a vote supporting the president's position.

125. S 1128. Clean Water Act. Chafee, R-R.I., motion to table (kill) the Wallop, R-Wyo., amendment to prohibit the Environmental Protection Agency from pursuing certain enforcement actions against violators of the act when a state has already begun enforcement action. Motion agreed to 70-26: R 28-23; D 42-3 (ND 33-0, SD 9-3), June 13, 1985.

126. S 1128. Clean Water Act. Passage of the bill to amend and reauthorize the Clean Water Act, providing $20,008,000,000 in fiscal 1986-94, including $18 billion for federal grants and capitalization of state revolving funds for construction of local sewage treatment facilities during fiscal 1986-94. The bill authorizes spending levels of $2.879 billion in fiscal 1986, $2.909 billion in 1987, $2.939 billion in 1988, $2.796 billion in 1989, $2.485 billion in 1990, $2.4 billion in 1991, $1.8 billion in 1992, $1.2 billion in 1993, and $600 million in 1994. Passed 94-0: R 51-0; D 43-0 (ND 30-0, SD 13-0), June 13, 1985. A "nay" was a vote supporting the president's position.

CQ Senate Votes 127 - 129

Corresponding to Congressional Record Votes 127, 128, 129

	127	128	129
ALABAMA			
Denton	N	Y	P
Heflin	N	Y	Y
ALASKA			
Murkowski	N	Y	N
Stevens	N	Y	Y
ARIZONA			
Goldwater	N	Y	Y
DeConcini	Y	Y	Y
ARKANSAS			
Bumpers	Y	Y	Y
Pryor	Y	Y	Y
CALIFORNIA			
Wilson	N	Y	N
Cranston	Y	Y	Y
COLORADO			
Armstrong	N	Y	Y
Hart	Y	Y	Y
CONNECTICUT			
Weicker	Y	Y	Y
Dodd	Y	Y	Y
DELAWARE			
Roth	N	Y	Y
Biden	Y	Y	Y
FLORIDA			
Hawkins	N	Y	N
Chiles	Y	Y	Y
GEORGIA			
Mattingly	N	Y	N
Nunn	Y	Y	Y
HAWAII			
Inouye	Y	Y	Y
Matsunaga	Y	Y	Y
IDAHO			
McClure	N	Y	N
Symms	N	Y	N
ILLINOIS			
Dixon	N	Y	Y
Simon	Y	Y	Y
INDIANA			
Lugar	N	Y	Y
Quayle	N	Y	Y
IOWA			
Grassley	N	Y	Y
Harkin	Y	Y	Y
KANSAS			
Dole	N	Y	Y
Kassebaum	N	Y	Y
KENTUCKY			
McConnell	N	Y	Y
Ford	N	Y	Y
LOUISIANA			
Johnston	N	Y	Y
Long	N	Y	Y
MAINE			
Cohen	Y	Y	Y
Mitchell	Y	Y	Y
MARYLAND			
Mathias	Y	Y	Y
Sarbanes	Y	Y	Y
MASSACHUSETTS			
Kennedy	Y	Y	Y
Kerry	Y	Y	Y
MICHIGAN			
Levin	Y	Y	Y
Riegle	Y	Y	Y
MINNESOTA			
Boschwitz	N	Y	Y
Durenberger	N	Y	Y
MISSISSIPPI			
Cochran	N	Y	Y
Stennis	N	Y	Y
MISSOURI			
Danforth	Y	Y	Y
Eagleton	Y	Y	Y
MONTANA			
Baucus	N	Y	Y
Melcher	Y	Y	Y
NEBRASKA			
Exon	Y	Y	Y
Zorinsky	N	Y	N
NEVADA			
Hecht	N	Y	N
Laxalt	N	Y	Y
NEW HAMPSHIRE			
Humphrey	N	Y	N
Rudman	N	Y	Y
NEW JERSEY			
Bradley	Y	N	Y
Lautenberg	Y	Y	Y
NEW MEXICO			
Domenici	N	Y	Y
Bingaman	Y	Y	Y
NEW YORK			
D'Amato	Y	Y	Y
Moynihan	Y	Y	+
NORTH CAROLINA			
East	N	Y	?
Helms	N	Y	N
NORTH DAKOTA			
Andrews	N	Y	Y
Burdick	Y	Y	Y
OHIO			
Glenn	N	Y	Y
Metzenbaum	Y	Y	Y
OKLAHOMA			
Nickles	N	Y	Y
Boren	?	?	?
OREGON			
Hatfield	Y	Y	Y
Packwood	N	Y	Y
PENNSYLVANIA			
Heinz	Y	Y	Y
Specter	Y	Y	Y
RHODE ISLAND			
Chafee	Y	Y	Y
Pell	Y	Y	Y
SOUTH CAROLINA			
Thurmond	N	Y	N
Hollings	N	Y	N
SOUTH DAKOTA			
Abdnor	N	Y	Y
Pressler	N	Y	Y
TENNESSEE			
Gore	Y	Y	Y
Sasser	Y	Y	Y
TEXAS			
Gramm	N	Y	N
Bentsen	Y	Y	Y
UTAH			
Garn	N	Y	N
Hatch	N	Y	N
VERMONT			
Stafford	N	Y	Y
Leahy	Y	Y	Y
VIRGINIA			
Trible	N	Y	Y
Warner	N	Y	Y
WASHINGTON			
Evans	N	Y	Y
Gorton	N	Y	Y
WEST VIRGINIA			
Byrd	Y	Y	Y
Rockefeller	Y	Y	Y
WISCONSIN			
Kasten	N	Y	N
Proxmire	N	Y	Y
WYOMING			
Simpson	N	Y	Y
Wallop	N	Y	N

KEY

- Y Voted for (yea).
- # Paired for.
- + Announced for.
- N Voted against (nay).
- X Paired against.
- \- Announced against.
- P Voted "present".
- C Voted "present" to avoid possible conflict of interest.
- ? Did not vote or otherwise make a position known.

Democrats ***Republicans***

ND - Northern Democrats SD - Southern Democrats (Southern states - Ala., Ark., Fla., Ga., Ky., La., Miss., N.C., Okla., S.C., Tenn., Texas, Va.)

127. S 979. Energy Policy and Conservation. Bradley, D-N.J., amendment to establish a standby block grant program to states to aid low-income citizens in the event of an oil shortage. Rejected 44-55: R 9-44; D 35-11 (ND 28-5, SD 7-6), June 18, 1985. A "nay" was a vote supporting the president's position.

128. HR 1699. Energy Policy and Conservation. Passage of the bill to extend authorization of the Strategic Petroleum Reserve and for U.S. participation in the International Energy Agency. Passed 98-1: R 53-0; D 45-1 (ND 32-1, SD 13-0), June 18, 1985. (The Senate had previously moved to delete the House language of HR 1699 and insert instead the language of S 979, the Senate version of the bill.)

129. HR 2577. Supplemental Appropriations, Fiscal 1985. Lugar, R-Ind., motion to table (kill) the Helms, R-N.C., amendment to provide that no funds appropriated by the bill may be obligated. The effect of the vote was to kill the Helms perfecting amendment to the Helms amendment, to prevent the president from dismantling missiles or submarines to comply with the unratified SALT II treaty. Motion agreed to 79-17: R 36-15; D 43-2 (ND 31-1, SD 12-1), June 19, 1985.

	130	131	132
ALABAMA			
Denton	N	Y	Y
Heflin	Y	Y	Y
ALASKA			
Murkowski	N	Y	?
Stevens	Y	Y	Y
ARIZONA			
Goldwater	N	N	Y
DeConcini	Y	N	N
ARKANSAS			
Bumpers	Y	N	Y
Pryor	Y	N	?
CALIFORNIA			
Wilson	N	Y	Y
Cranston	Y	N	N
COLORADO			
Armstrong	N	N	Y
Hart	Y	N	Y
CONNECTICUT			
Weicker	N	N	Y
Dodd	Y	N	Y
DELAWARE			
Roth	N	Y	Y
Biden	Y	N	Y
FLORIDA			
Hawkins	N	Y	N
Chiles	Y	N	Y
GEORGIA			
Mattingly	N	Y	Y
Nunn	Y	N	Y
HAWAII			
Inouye	Y	N	Y
Matsunaga	Y	N	Y
IDAHO			
McClure	N	Y	Y
Symms	N	Y	Y
ILLINOIS			
Dixon	Y	N	Y
Simon	Y	N	N
INDIANA			
Lugar	N	Y	Y
Quayle	N	Y	Y
IOWA			
Grassley	N	Y	Y
Harkin	Y	Y	Y
KANSAS			
Dole	N	N	Y
Kassebaum	N	Y	Y
KENTUCKY			
McConnell	N	Y	Y
Ford	Y	N	Y
LOUISIANA			
Johnston	Y	N	Y
Long	N	Y	Y
MAINE			
Cohen	N	N	Y
Mitchell	Y	N	Y
MARYLAND			
Mathias	N	N	Y
Sarbanes	Y	N	Y
MASSACHUSETTS			
Kennedy	Y	N	Y
Kerry	Y	N	Y
MICHIGAN			
Levin	Y	N	N
Riegle	Y	N	N
MINNESOTA			
Boschwitz	N	N	Y
Durenberger	N	N	?
MISSISSIPPI			
Cochran	N	N	Y
Stennis	Y	N	Y
MISSOURI			
Danforth	N	N	Y
Eagleton	Y	N	Y
MONTANA			
Baucus	Y	N	Y
Melcher	Y	N	Y
NEBRASKA			
Exon	Y	Y	Y
Zorinsky	Y	N	Y
NEVADA			
Hecht	N	Y	Y
Laxalt	N	Y	Y
NEW HAMPSHIRE			
Humphrey	N	Y	Y
Rudman	Y	Y	Y
NEW JERSEY			
Bradley	Y	N	Y
Lautenberg	Y	N	Y
NEW MEXICO			
Domenici	N	Y	Y
Bingaman	Y	Y	Y
NEW YORK			
D'Amato	N	N	Y
Moynihan	+	-	?
NORTH CAROLINA			
East	N	Y	?
Helms	N	Y	Y
NORTH DAKOTA			
Andrews	Y	N	Y
Burdick	Y	N	Y
OHIO			
Glenn	Y	N	Y
Metzenbaum	Y	N	Y
OKLAHOMA			
Nickles	N	Y	Y
Boren	?	?	?
OREGON			
Hatfield	Y	N	Y
Packwood	N	N	Y
PENNSYLVANIA			
Heinz	N	N	Y
Specter	N	Y	N
RHODE ISLAND			
Chafee	N	N	Y
Pell	Y	N	Y
SOUTH CAROLINA			
Thurmond	N	Y	Y
Hollings	N	Y	Y
SOUTH DAKOTA			
Abdnor	N	Y	Y
Pressler	N	Y	N
TENNESSEE			
Gore	Y	N	Y
Sasser	Y	N	Y
TEXAS			
Gramm	N	Y	?
Bentsen	Y	Y	Y
UTAH			
Garn	N	Y	Y
Hatch	N	Y	Y
VERMONT			
Stafford	N	N	Y
Leahy	Y	N	Y
VIRGINIA			
Trible	N	Y	Y
Warner	Y	Y	Y
WASHINGTON			
Evans	N	N	Y
Gorton	N	N	Y
WEST VIRGINIA			
Byrd	Y	N	Y
Rockefeller	Y	N	Y
WISCONSIN			
Kasten	N	N	Y
Proxmire	Y	N	N
WYOMING			
Simpson	N	Y	Y
Wallop	N	Y	Y

KEY

- Y Voted for (yea).
- # Paired for.
- \+ Announced for.
- N Voted against (nay).
- X Paired against.
- \- Announced against.
- P Voted "present".
- C Voted "present" to avoid possible conflict of interest.
- ? Did not vote or otherwise make a position known.

Democrats *Republicans*

ND - Northern Democrats SD - Southern Democrats (Southern states - Ala., Ark., Fla., Ga., Ky., La., Miss., N.C., Okla., S.C., Tenn., Texas, Va.)

130. HR 2577. Supplemental Appropriations, Fiscal 1985. Byrd, D-W.Va., perfecting amendment to the Byrd amendment to establish a national commission to study espionage. Rejected 48-50: R 5-48; D 43-2 (ND 32-0, SD 11-2), June 20, 1985. A "nay" was a vote supporting the president's position. (The Byrd amendment subsequently was rejected by voice vote.)

131. HR 2577. Supplemental Appropriations, Fiscal 1985. Helms, R-N.C., amendment to allow states to retain 5 percent of funds for the feeding program for women, infants and children from one fiscal year to the next. Rejected 40-58: R 33-20; D 7-38 (ND 3-29, SD 4-9), June 20, 1985.

132. HR 2577. Supplemental Appropriations, Fiscal 1985. Hatfield, R-Ore., motion to table (kill) the DeConcini, D-Ariz., amendment to the Kasten, R-Wis., amendment, to express the sense of Congress that the president should not propose to sell advanced military articles or equipment to Jordan until that country signs a peace treaty with Israel. Motion agreed to 84-9: R 46-3; D 38-6 (ND 26-6, SD 12-0), June 20, 1985. (Subsequently, the Senate adopted by voice vote the Kasten amendment, to provide $250 million in economic aid to Jordan provided that not more than one-third of the funds be spent before Sept. 30, 1985, not more than half before March 31, 1986, not more than two-thirds before Sept. 30, 1986, and not more than 85 percent before March 31, 1987.)

CQ Senate Votes 133 - 138

Corresponding to Congressional Record Votes 133, 134, 135, 136, 137, 138

	133	134	135	136	137	138
ALABAMA						
Denton	?	Y	Y	N	Y	Y
Heflin	?	Y	Y	N	Y	N
ALASKA						
Murkowski	Y	Y	Y	N	Y	Y
Stevens	Y	Y	Y	N	Y	Y
ARIZONA						
Goldwater	?	?	?	?	Y	Y
DeConcini	Y	Y	Y	N	Y	N
ARKANSAS						
Bumpers	Y	Y	Y	N	N	N
Pryor	Y	Y	Y	N	Y	N
CALIFORNIA						
Wilson	Y	Y	Y	N	Y	N
Cranston	Y	Y	Y	N	Y	N
COLORADO						
Armstrong	Y	Y	Y	N	N	N
Hart	Y	Y	Y	N	Y	N
CONNECTICUT						
Weicker	N	N	N	N	N	Y
Dodd	Y	?	?	?	Y	N
DELAWARE						
Roth	Y	Y	Y	N	Y	Y
Biden	Y	Y	Y	N	N	Y
FLORIDA						
Hawkins	Y	Y	Y	N	Y	N
Chiles	Y	Y	Y	N	Y	N
GEORGIA						
Mattingly	Y	Y	Y	N	Y	Y
Nunn	Y	Y	Y	N	N	Y
HAWAII						
Inouye	Y	N	N	N	Y	N
Matsunaga	Y	Y	Y	N	Y	Y
IDAHO						
McClure	Y	Y	Y	N	Y	N
Symms	Y	Y	Y	N	Y	N
ILLINOIS						
Dixon	N	Y	Y	N	Y	N
Simon	Y	Y	Y	N	Y	N
INDIANA						
Lugar	Y	Y	Y	N	Y	Y
Quayle	N	N	N	N	Y	Y
IOWA						
Grassley	Y	Y	Y	N	Y	N
Harkin	Y	Y	Y	N	N	N
KANSAS						
Dole	Y	Y	Y	N	N	Y
Kassebaum	Y	Y	Y	N	Y	Y
KENTUCKY						
McConnell	Y	Y	Y	N	Y	Y
Ford	Y	Y	Y	N	Y	N
LOUISIANA						
Johnston	Y	Y	Y	N	Y	Y
Long	Y	Y	Y	N	Y	Y
MAINE						
Cohen	Y	Y	Y	N	Y	Y
Mitchell	Y	Y	Y	N	N	Y
MARYLAND						
Mathias	Y	Y	Y	N	?	?
Sarbanes	?	Y	Y	N	N	N
MASSACHUSETTS						
Kennedy	Y	Y	Y	Y	N	Y
Kerry	Y	Y	Y	N	Y	N
MICHIGAN						
Levin	Y	?	Y	N	Y	N
Riegle	Y	Y	Y	N	N	N
MINNESOTA						
Boschwitz	Y	Y	Y	N	Y	N
Durenberger	Y	Y	Y	N	Y	N
MISSISSIPPI						
Cochran	Y	Y	Y	N	Y	Y
Stennis	Y	Y	Y	?	Y	Y
MISSOURI						
Danforth	Y	Y	Y	N	Y	Y
Eagleton	Y	Y	Y	N	Y	N
MONTANA						
Baucus	Y	Y	Y	N	N	N
Melcher	Y	Y	Y	N	Y	N
NEBRASKA						
Exon	Y	Y	Y	N	N	N
Zorinsky	Y	Y	Y	N	Y	N
NEVADA						
Hecht	Y	Y	Y	N	Y	Y
Laxalt	Y	Y	Y	N	Y	Y
NEW HAMPSHIRE						
Humphrey	Y	Y	Y	N	Y	Y
Rudman	Y	Y	Y	N	Y	Y
NEW JERSEY						
Bradley	Y	Y	Y	N	N	Y
Lautenberg	Y	Y	Y	N	Y	Y
NEW MEXICO						
Domenici	Y	Y	Y	N	Y	Y
Bingaman	Y	Y	Y	N	Y	Y
NEW YORK						
D'Amato	Y	Y	Y	N	Y	Y
Moynihan	Y	Y	Y	N	N	Y
NORTH CAROLINA						
East	Y	Y	Y	?	?	?
Helms	Y	Y	Y	N	Y	N
NORTH DAKOTA						
Andrews	Y	Y	Y	N	Y	N
Burdick	Y	Y	Y	N	N	N
OHIO						
Glenn	Y	Y	Y	N	Y	Y
Metzenbaum	Y	Y	Y	N	N	Y
OKLAHOMA						
Nickles	Y	Y	Y	N	Y	N
Boren	?	Y	Y	N	Y	N
OREGON						
Hatfield	Y	Y	Y	N	N	Y
Packwood	Y	Y	Y	?	Y	Y
PENNSYLVANIA						
Heinz	Y	Y	Y	N	Y	Y
Specter	Y	Y	Y	N	Y	Y
RHODE ISLAND						
Chafee	Y	Y	Y	N	N	Y
Pell	Y	Y	Y	N	N	Y
SOUTH CAROLINA						
Thurmond	Y	Y	Y	N	Y	Y
Hollings	Y	Y	Y	Y	Y	Y
SOUTH DAKOTA						
Abdnor	Y	Y	Y	N	Y	N
Pressler	Y	Y	Y	N	Y	Y
TENNESSEE						
Gore	Y	Y	Y	N	Y	N
Sasser	Y	Y	Y	N	Y	N
TEXAS						
Gramm	Y	Y	Y	N	Y	Y
Bentsen	Y	Y	Y	N	N	Y
UTAH						
Garn	N	N	Y	N	Y	Y
Hatch	Y	Y	Y	N	Y	Y
VERMONT						
Stafford	Y	Y	Y	N	?	?
Leahy	Y	Y	Y	N	N	N
VIRGINIA						
Trible	Y	Y	Y	N	Y	Y
Warner	Y	Y	Y	N	Y	Y
WASHINGTON						
Evans	Y	Y	Y	N	N	Y
Gorton	Y	Y	Y	N	Y	Y
WEST VIRGINIA						
Byrd	Y	Y	Y	N	Y	N
Rockefeller	Y	Y	Y	N	Y	N
WISCONSIN						
Kasten	Y	Y	Y	N	Y	N
Proxmire	N	N	N	Y	N	Y
WYOMING						
Simpson	Y	Y	Y	N	Y	Y
Wallop	Y	Y	Y	N	Y	N

KEY

- Y Voted for (yea).
- # Paired for.
- + Announced for.
- N Voted against (nay).
- X Paired against.
- \- Announced against.
- P Voted "present".
- C Voted "present" to avoid possible conflict of interest.
- ? Did not vote or otherwise make a position known.

Democrats *Republicans*

ND - Northern Democrats SD - Southern Democrats (Southern states - Ala., Ark., Fla., Ga., Ky., La., Miss., N.C., Okla., S.C., Tenn., Texas, Va.)

133. Procedural Motion. Dole, R-Kan., motion to instruct the sergeant-at-arms to request the attendance of absent senators. Motion agreed to 90-5: R 48-3; D 42-2 (ND 30-2, SD 12-0), June 25, 1985.

134. Procedural Motion. Packwood, R-Ore., motion to instruct the sergeant-at-arms to request the attendance of absent senators. Motion agreed to 92-5: R 49-3; D 43-2 (ND 29-2, SD 14-0), June 25, 1985.

135. Procedural Motion. Packwood, R-Ore., motion to instruct the sergeant-at-arms to request the attendance of absent senators. Motion agreed to 94-4: R 50-2; D 44-2 (ND 30-2, SD 14-0), June 25, 1985.

136. HR 2475. Imputed Interest Rules. Metzenbaum, D-Ohio, motion to instruct the clerk to read into the *Congressional Record* the committee report on HR 2475, a bill to ease provisions of the Deficit Reduction Act of 1984 (PL 98-369) aimed at restricting the use of below-market, seller-financed real estate transactions to avoid tax payments. Motion rejected 3-92: R 0-50; D 3-42 (ND 2-30, SD 1-12), June 25, 1985. (The motion was an effort to block consideration of the legislation.)

137. HR 2475. Imputed Interest Rules. Heinz, R-Pa., motion to table (kill) the Chafee, R-R.I., amendment to remove the bill's provision relating to loans to qualified continuing-care facilities. Motion agreed to 73-24: R 44-6; D 29-18 (ND 18-15, SD 11-3), June 26, 1985.

138. HR 2475. Imputed Interest Rules. Packwood, R-Ore., motion to table (kill) the Melcher, D-Mont., motion to waive the Congressional Budget Act with regard to the Melcher amendment to provide for a "blended" imputed interest rate on seller-financed real estate sales when debt exceeds $2 million for such sales of farms, ranches and property of small businesses. Motion agreed to 54-43: R 36-14; D 18-29 (ND 12-21, SD 6-8), June 26, 1985.

	139	140	141	142	143
ALABAMA					
Denton	Y	Y	Y	Y	Y
Heflin	Y	Y	Y	Y	Y
ALASKA					
Murkowski	Y	Y	Y	Y	Y
Stevens	Y	Y	Y	Y	Y
ARIZONA					
Goldwater	Y	Y	Y	Y	Y
DeConcini	Y	Y	Y	Y	Y
ARKANSAS					
Bumpers	Y	Y	Y	Y	Y
Pryor	Y	Y	Y	Y	Y
CALIFORNIA					
Wilson	Y	Y	Y	Y	Y
Cranston	N	N	N	N	Y
COLORADO					
Armstrong	?	?	?	?	?
Hart	N	Y	N	N	Y
CONNECTICUT					
Weicker	N	Y	N	Y	Y
Dodd	N	N	N	N	Y
DELAWARE					
Roth	Y	Y	Y	Y	Y
Biden	N	Y	Y	Y	Y
FLORIDA					
Hawkins	Y	Y	Y	Y	Y
Chiles	Y	Y	Y	Y	Y
GEORGIA					
Mattingly	Y	Y	Y	Y	Y
Nunn	Y	N	Y	Y	Y
HAWAII					
Inouye	N	N	N	N	Y
Matsunaga	N	N	N	N	Y
IDAHO					
McClure	Y	Y	Y	Y	N
Symms	Y	Y	Y	Y	N
ILLINOIS					
Dixon	N	Y	Y	Y	Y
Simon	?	?	?	?	?
INDIANA					
Lugar	Y	Y	Y	Y	Y
Quayle	Y	Y	Y	Y	Y
IOWA					
Grassley	Y	Y	Y	Y	Y
Harkin	N	N	N	Y	Y
KANSAS					
Dole	Y	Y	Y	Y	Y
Kassebaum	N	Y	N	Y	?
KENTUCKY					
McConnell	Y	Y	Y	Y	Y
Ford	Y	Y	Y	Y	Y
LOUISIANA					
Johnston	Y	Y	Y	Y	Y
Long	?	?	?	?	Y
MAINE					
Cohen	Y	Y	Y	Y	Y
Mitchell	Y	Y	Y	Y	Y
MARYLAND					
Mathias	N	N	N	N	Y
Sarbanes	N	N	N	N	Y
MASSACHUSETTS					
Kennedy	N	N	N	N	Y
Kerry	N	N	N	N	Y
MICHIGAN					
Levin	N	Y	N	N	Y
Riegle	N	Y	Y	Y	Y
MINNESOTA					
Boschwitz	Y	Y	Y	Y	Y
Durenberger	Y	Y	Y	Y	Y
MISSISSIPPI					
Cochran	Y	Y	Y	Y	Y
Stennis	Y	?	?	?	Y
MISSOURI					
Danforth	Y	Y	Y	Y	Y
Eagleton	Y	Y	Y	Y	Y
MONTANA					
Baucus	Y	Y	Y	Y	Y
Melcher	Y	Y	N	Y	Y
NEBRASKA					
Exon	Y	Y	Y	Y	Y
Zorinsky	Y	Y	Y	Y	Y
NEVADA					
Hecht	Y	Y	Y	Y	N
Laxalt	Y	Y	Y	Y	N
NEW HAMPSHIRE					
Humphrey	Y	Y	Y	Y	N
Rudman	Y	Y	Y	Y	Y
NEW JERSEY					
Bradley	?	?	?	?	+
Lautenberg	N	N	N	N	Y
NEW MEXICO					
Domenici	Y	Y	Y	Y	Y
Bingaman	Y	Y	Y	Y	Y
NEW YORK					
D'Amato	Y	Y	Y	Y	Y
Moynihan	N	N	N	N	Y
NORTH CAROLINA					
East	Y	Y	Y	Y	N
Helms	Y	Y	Y	Y	N
NORTH DAKOTA					
Andrews	Y	Y	Y	Y	Y
Burdick	Y	Y	Y	Y	Y
OHIO					
Glenn	N	N	N	Y	Y
Metzenbaum	N	N	N	N	Y
OKLAHOMA					
Nickles	Y	Y	Y	Y	Y
Boren	N	Y	N	Y	Y
OREGON					
Hatfield	?	?	?	+	Y
Packwood	Y	Y	Y	Y	Y
PENNSYLVANIA					
Heinz	Y	Y	Y	Y	Y
Specter	Y	Y	Y	Y	Y
RHODE ISLAND					
Chafee	N	N	N	N	Y
Pell	N	N	N	N	Y
SOUTH CAROLINA					
Thurmond	Y	Y	Y	Y	Y
Hollings	Y	Y	Y	Y	Y
SOUTH DAKOTA					
Abdnor	Y	Y	Y	Y	Y
Pressler	Y	Y	Y	Y	Y
TENNESSEE					
Gore	Y	Y	Y	Y	Y
Sasser	Y	Y	Y	Y	Y
TEXAS					
Gramm	Y	Y	Y	Y	Y
Bentsen	Y	Y	Y	Y	Y
UTAH					
Garn	Y	Y	Y	Y	Y
Hatch	Y	Y	Y	Y	Y
VERMONT					
Stafford	Y	N	Y	Y	Y
Leahy	Y	Y	Y	Y	Y
VIRGINIA					
Trible	Y	Y	Y	Y	Y
Warner	Y	Y	N	Y	Y
WASHINGTON					
Evans	N	N	Y	Y	Y
Gorton	N	Y	Y	Y	Y
WEST VIRGINIA					
Byrd	Y	Y	Y	Y	Y
Rockefeller	Y	Y	Y	Y	Y
WISCONSIN					
Kasten	Y	Y	Y	Y	Y
Proxmire	N	Y	N	Y	Y
WYOMING					
Simpson	Y	Y	Y	Y	Y
Wallop	Y	Y	Y	Y	N

KEY

- Y Voted for (yea).
- # Paired for.
- + Announced for.
- N Voted against (nay).
- X Paired against.
- - Announced against.
- P Voted "present."
- C Voted "present" to avoid possible conflict of interest.
- ? Did not vote or otherwise make a position known.

Democrats *Republicans*

ND - Northern Democrats SD - Southern Democrats (Southern states - Ala., Ark., Fla., Ga., Ky., La., Miss., N.C., Okla., S.C., Tenn., Texas, Va.)

139. S 49. Firearm Owners' Protection. McClure, R-Idaho, motion to table (kill) the Kennedy, D-Mass., amendment to retain the ban in the Gun Control Act of 1968 on the interstate sales of handguns. Motion agreed to 69-26: R 45-6; D 24-20 (ND 12-19, SD 12-1), July 9, 1985. A "yea" was a vote supporting the president's position.

140. S 49. Firearm Owners' Protection. McClure, R-Idaho, motion to table (kill) the Mathias, R-Md., amendment to retain current law allowing federal authorities to conduct all inspections of gun dealers without providing notice of such inspections. Motion agreed to 76-18: R 47-4; D 29-14 (ND 18-13, SD 11-1), July 9, 1985. A "yea" was a vote supporting the president's position.

141. S 49. Firearm Owners' Protection. McClure, R-Idaho, motion to table (kill) the Inouye, D-Hawaii, amendment to require a 14-day waiting period between the purchase of a handgun and its delivery to the buyer. Motion agreed to 71-23: R 46-5; D 25-18 (ND 14-17, SD 11-1), July 9, 1985. A "yea" was a vote supporting the president's position.

142. S 49. Firearm Owners' Protection. Passage of the bill to revise the Gun Control Act of 1968 to exempt many gun collectors from licensing requirements, remove the ban on interstate sales of rifles, shotguns and handguns, require advance notice for routine compliance inspections, and impose a mandatory five-year sentence on anyone convicted of using a firearm in a violent federal crime. Passed 79-15: R 49-2; D 30-13 (ND 18-13, SD 12-0), July 9, 1985. A "yea" was a vote supporting the president's position.

143. S 995. Anti-Apartheid Act. Dole, R-Kan., motion to invoke cloture (thus limiting debate) on the Dole motion to proceed to the consideration of the bill to impose economic sanctions on South Africa on account of its white minority government's racial policies. Motion agreed to 88-8: R 43-8; D 45-0 (ND 31-0, SD 14-0), July 10, 1985. A three-fifths majority (60) of the total Senate is required to invoke cloture.

CQ Senate Votes 144 - 149

Corresponding to Congressional Record Votes 144, 145, 146, 147, 148, 149

	144	145	146	147	148	149
ALABAMA						
Denton	N	N	Y	N	Y	N
Heflin	Y	Y	Y	Y	Y	Y
ALASKA						
Murkowski	?	?	?	?	?	?
Stevens	Y	Y	N	Y	Y	Y
ARIZONA						
Goldwater	N	N	Y	?	?	-
DeConcini	N	Y	Y	Y	Y	Y
ARKANSAS						
Bumpers	Y	Y	N	Y	Y	Y
Pryor	Y	Y	N	Y	Y	Y
CALIFORNIA						
Wilson	N	N	Y	N	Y	Y
Cranston	Y	Y	N	Y	Y	Y
COLORADO						
Armstrong	?	?	?	?	?	?
Hart	Y	Y	N	Y	Y	Y
CONNECTICUT						
Weicker	Y	Y	N	Y	Y	Y
Dodd	Y	Y	N	Y	Y	Y
DELAWARE						
Roth	Y	Y	N	Y	Y	Y
Biden	Y	Y	N	Y	Y	Y
FLORIDA						
Hawkins	?	?	?	?	?	?
Chiles	Y	Y	N	Y	Y	Y
GEORGIA						
Mattingly	N	Y	Y	N	Y	Y
Nunn	Y	Y	N	Y	Y	Y
HAWAII						
Inouye	Y	Y	N	Y	Y	Y
Matsunaga	Y	Y	N	Y	Y	Y
IDAHO						
McClure	N	N	Y	N	Y	N
Symms	N	N	Y	N	Y	N
ILLINOIS						
Dixon	Y	Y	Y	Y	Y	Y
Simon	?	?	?	?	?	?
INDIANA						
Lugar	Y	Y	N	Y	Y	Y
Quayle	Y	Y	N	Y	Y	Y
IOWA						
Grassley	N	Y	Y	N	Y	Y
Harkin	Y	Y	N	Y	Y	Y
KANSAS						
Dole	Y	Y	N	Y	Y	Y
Kassebaum	Y	Y	N	Y	Y	Y
KENTUCKY						
McConnell	Y	Y	N	Y	Y	Y
Ford	Y	Y	N	Y	Y	Y
LOUISIANA						
Johnston	Y	Y	Y	Y	Y	Y
Long	N	Y	Y	Y	Y	Y
MAINE						
Cohen	Y	Y	N	Y	Y	Y
Mitchell	Y	Y	N	Y	Y	Y
MARYLAND						
Mathias	Y	Y	N	Y	Y	Y
Sarbanes	Y	Y	N	Y	Y	Y
MASSACHUSETTS						
Kennedy	Y	Y	N	Y	Y	Y
Kerry	Y	Y	N	Y	Y	Y
MICHIGAN						
Levin	Y	Y	N	Y	Y	Y
Riegle	Y	Y	N	Y	N	Y
MINNESOTA						
Boschwitz	N	N	Y	Y	Y	Y
Durenberger	Y	Y	N	Y	Y	Y
MISSISSIPPI						
Cochran	Y	Y	N	Y	Y	Y
Stennis	Y	Y	?	?	?	?
MISSOURI						
Danforth	Y	Y	N	Y	Y	Y
Eagleton	Y	Y	N	Y	Y	Y
MONTANA						
Baucus	Y	Y	N	Y	Y	Y
Melcher	Y	Y	N	Y	Y	Y
NEBRASKA						
Exon	Y	Y	N	Y	Y	Y
Zorinsky	Y	Y	N	Y	Y	Y
NEVADA						
Hecht	N	N	Y	N	Y	N
Laxalt	N	N	Y	N	Y	N
NEW HAMPSHIRE						
Humphrey	N	N	Y	N	Y	N
Rudman	N	Y	Y	N	Y	Y
NEW JERSEY						
Bradley	Y	Y	N	Y	Y	Y
Lautenberg	Y	Y	N	Y	Y	Y
NEW MEXICO						
Domenici	Y	Y	Y	N	Y	Y
Bingaman	Y	Y	Y	Y	Y	Y
NEW YORK						
D'Amato	Y	Y	Y	Y	Y	Y
Moynihan	Y	Y	N	Y	Y	Y
NORTH CAROLINA						
East	N	N	Y	N	Y	N
Helms	N	N	Y	N	Y	N
NORTH DAKOTA						
Andrews	Y	Y	N	Y	Y	Y
Burdick	Y	Y	N	Y	Y	Y
OHIO						
Glenn	Y	Y	N	Y	?	?
Metzenbaum	Y	Y	N	Y	N	Y
OKLAHOMA						
Nickles	N	N	Y	N	Y	Y
Boren	Y	Y	N	Y	Y	Y
OREGON						
Hatfield	N	Y	Y	Y	Y	Y
Packwood	N	Y	Y	Y	Y	Y
PENNSYLVANIA						
Heinz	Y	Y	N	Y	Y	Y
Specter	Y	Y	Y	Y	Y	Y
RHODE ISLAND						
Chafee	Y	Y	N	Y	Y	Y
Pell	Y	Y	N	Y	Y	Y
SOUTH CAROLINA						
Thurmond	N	N	Y	N	Y	N
Hollings	Y	Y	N	N	Y	Y
SOUTH DAKOTA						
Abdnor	N	Y	Y	N	Y	Y
Pressler	Y	Y	N	Y	Y	Y
TENNESSEE						
Gore	Y	Y	N	Y	Y	Y
Sasser	Y	Y	Y	Y	Y	Y
TEXAS						
Gramm	N	?	?	?	?	?
Bentsen	Y	Y	N	Y	Y	Y
UTAH						
Garn	N	N	Y	N	Y	N
Hatch	N	N	Y	N	Y	N
VERMONT						
Stafford	Y	Y	N	Y	Y	Y
Leahy	Y	Y	N	Y	Y	Y
VIRGINIA						
Trible	N	Y	Y	Y	Y	Y
Warner	N	Y	Y	Y	Y	Y
WASHINGTON						
Evans	Y	Y	N	Y	Y	Y
Gorton	N	Y	Y	Y	Y	Y
WEST VIRGINIA						
Byrd	Y	Y	N	Y	Y	Y
Rockefeller	Y	Y	N	Y	Y	Y
WISCONSIN						
Kasten	N	Y	Y	Y	Y	Y
Proxmire	Y	Y	N	Y	Y	Y
WYOMING						
Simpson	Y	N	Y	N	Y	Y
Wallop	N	N	Y	N	Y	N

KEY

- Y Voted for (yea).
- # Paired for.
- + Announced for.
- N Voted against (nay).
- X Paired against.
- \- Announced against.
- P Voted "present."
- C Voted "present" to avoid possible conflict of interest.
- ? Did not vote or otherwise make a position known.

Democrats *Republicans*

ND - Northern Democrats SD - Southern Democrats (Southern states - Ala., Ark., Fla., Ga., Ky., La., Miss., N.C., Okla., S.C., Tenn., Texas, Va.)

144. S 995. Anti-Apartheid Act. Lugar, R-Ind., motion to table (kill) the Humphrey, R-N.H., amendment to impose sanctions on signatories of the 1975 Helsinki agreement if the president determined they were not in compliance with the agreement's human rights standards. Motion agreed to 67-29: R 23-27; D 44-2 (ND 31-1, SD 13-1), July 11, 1985.

145. S 995. Anti-Apartheid Act. Lugar, R-Ind., motion to table (kill) the Symms, R-Idaho, amendment to block implementation of sanctions against South Africa in the bill if the president or Congress determined that the sanctions would lead to increased unemployment among South African blacks. Motion agreed to 78-17: R 32-17; D 46-0 (ND 32-0, SD 14-0), July 11, 1985.

146. S 995. Anti-Apartheid Act. Wallop, R-Wyo., amendment to extend the sanctions in the bill to the Soviet Union, Poland, Afghanistan, Mozambique, Angola, Ethiopia, East Germany, Libya, Syria, Iran, Cuba, China and any other countries that the president determined had human rights records equal to or worse than that of South Africa, as well as to any countries that have encouraged terrorist attacks on Americans. Rejected 37-57: R 30-19; D 7-38 (ND 3-29, SD 4-9), July 11, 1985.

147. S 995. Anti-Apartheid Act. Lugar, R-Ind., motion to table (kill) the Denton, R-Ala., amendment to declare that the black African National Congress (ANC) organization of South Africa is a terrorist group, and to impose a series of sanctions, such as travel restrictions on ANC members in the United States and a prohibition on the group's U.S. fund-raising activities, until the organization renounces the use of violence and breaks its ties with the South African Communist Party. Motion agreed to 72-21: R 28-20; D 44-1 (ND 32-0, SD 12-1), July 11, 1985.

148. S 995. Anti-Apartheid Act. Wallop, R-Wyo., motion to table (kill) the Wallop amendment to substitute the text of the House-passed bill (HR 1460). Motion agreed to 90-2: R 48-0; D 42-2 (ND 29-2, SD 13-0), July 11, 1985.

149. HR 1460. Anti-Apartheid Act. Passage of the bill to impose sanctions immediately against South Africa, including a ban on bank loans to the South African government, and prohibitions against the sale of computer goods and nuclear materials to that country. The bill also calls for imposition of additional sanctions, such as a ban on new U.S. investment and a prohibition on the importation into the United States of South African gold coins, if South Africa does not reform its racial policies within 18 months. Passed 80-12: R 36-12; D 44-0 (ND 31-0, SD 13-0), July 11, 1985. (Before passing the bill, the Senate substituted the text of S 995 for the House-passed version, HR 1460.)

	150	151	152	153	154	155	156
ALABAMA							
Denton	P	P	N	N	N	Y	Y
Heflin	Y	Y	N	Y	N	Y	N
ALASKA							
Murkowski	Y	Y	Y	N	N	Y	Y
Stevens	?	?	?	?	N	Y	Y
ARIZONA							
Goldwater	Y	Y	N	N	N	Y	Y
DeConcini	Y	Y	Y	Y	N	Y	Y
ARKANSAS							
Bumpers	Y	Y	Y	Y	N	Y	N
Pryor	Y	Y	Y	Y	N	Y	N
CALIFORNIA							
Wilson	Y	N	Y	N	N	Y	Y
Cranston	Y	Y	Y	Y	Y	Y	N
COLORADO							
Armstrong	?	?	?	?	?	?	?
Hart	Y	Y	Y	Y	Y	Y	N
CONNECTICUT							
Weicker	Y	Y	Y	N	N	Y	N
Dodd	Y	Y	Y	N	Y	Y	N
DELAWARE							
Roth	Y	Y	Y	N	N	Y	Y
Biden	Y	Y	Y	Y	Y	Y	Y
FLORIDA							
Hawkins	N	Y	Y	N	N	Y	Y
Chiles	Y	Y	Y	Y	N	Y	N
GEORGIA							
Mattingly	Y	Y	Y	N	N	Y	Y
Nunn	Y	Y	Y	Y	N	Y	Y
HAWAII							
Inouye	Y	Y	Y	Y	Y	Y	N
Matsunaga	Y	Y	Y	Y	Y	Y	N
IDAHO							
McClure	N	N	N	N	N	Y	Y
Symms	N	N	N	N	N	Y	Y
ILLINOIS							
Dixon	Y	Y	Y	Y	N	Y	Y
Simon	Y	Y	Y	Y	Y	Y	N
INDIANA							
Lugar	Y	Y	Y	N	N	Y	Y
Quayle	Y	Y	Y	N	N	Y	Y
IOWA							
Grassley	Y	Y	Y	Y	N	Y	Y
Harkin	Y	Y	Y	Y	N	Y	N
KANSAS							
Dole	Y	Y	Y	N	N	Y	Y
Kassebaum	Y	Y	Y	N	N	Y	Y
KENTUCKY							
McConnell	Y	Y	Y	N	N	Y	Y
Ford	Y	Y	Y	Y	N	Y	N
LOUISIANA							
Johnston	Y	Y	Y	Y	N	Y	N
Long	Y	N	Y	Y	N	Y	N
MAINE							
Cohen	Y	Y	Y	N	N	Y	Y
Mitchell	Y	Y	Y	Y	Y	Y	N
MARYLAND							
Mathias	Y	Y	Y	N	N	Y	N
Sarbanes	Y	Y	Y	Y	Y	Y	N
MASSACHUSETTS							
Kennedy	Y	Y	Y	Y	Y	Y	Y
Kerry	Y	Y	Y	Y	Y	Y	N
MICHIGAN							
Levin	Y	Y	Y	Y	N	Y	N
Riegle	Y	Y	Y	Y	N	Y	N
MINNESOTA							
Boschwitz	Y	Y	Y	N	N	Y	Y
Durenberger	Y	Y	Y	?	?	?	N
MISSISSIPPI							
Cochran	Y	Y	Y	N	N	Y	Y
Stennis	Y	Y	N	Y	N	Y	N
MISSOURI							
Danforth	Y	Y	Y	N	N	Y	Y
Eagleton	Y	Y	Y	Y	Y	Y	N
MONTANA							
Baucus	Y	Y	Y	Y	N	Y	N
Melcher	Y	Y	Y	Y	Y	Y	N
NEBRASKA							
Exon	Y	Y	Y	Y	Y	Y	Y
Zorinsky	Y	Y	N	Y	N	Y	Y
NEVADA							
Hecht	Y	Y	Y	N	N	Y	Y
Laxalt	Y	Y	Y	N	N	Y	Y
NEW HAMPSHIRE							
Humphrey	Y	Y	Y	N	Y	N	Y
Rudman	Y	Y	Y	N	N	Y	Y
NEW JERSEY							
Bradley	Y	Y	Y	N	Y	Y	N
Lautenberg	Y	Y	Y	N	Y	Y	N
NEW MEXICO							
Domenici	Y	Y	Y	N	N	Y	Y
Bingaman	Y	Y	Y	Y	N	Y	N
NEW YORK							
D'Amato	Y	Y	Y	N	N	Y	Y
Moynihan	Y	Y	Y	Y	Y	Y	N
NORTH CAROLINA							
East	N	N	N	N	N	Y	Y
Helms	N	N	N	N	N	N	Y
NORTH DAKOTA							
Andrews	Y	Y	Y	Y	N	Y	N
Burdick	Y	Y	Y	Y	N	Y	N
OHIO							
Glenn	Y	Y	Y	Y	N	Y	N
Metzenbaum	Y	Y	Y	Y	N	Y	N
OKLAHOMA							
Nickles	Y	Y	Y	N	N	Y	Y
Boren	Y	Y	Y	Y	N	Y	Y
OREGON							
Hatfield	Y	Y	Y	N	N	Y	N
Packwood	Y	Y	Y	N	N	Y	N
PENNSYLVANIA							
Heinz	Y	Y	Y	N	N	Y	Y
Specter	Y	Y	Y	Y	N	Y	N
RHODE ISLAND							
Chafee	Y	Y	Y	N	N	Y	Y
Pell	Y	Y	Y	N	Y	Y	Y
SOUTH CAROLINA							
Thurmond	N	Y	Y	N	N	Y	Y
Hollings	Y	Y	Y	Y	N	Y	Y
SOUTH DAKOTA							
Abdnor	Y	Y	Y	Y	N	Y	Y
Pressler	Y	Y	Y	N	N	Y	Y
TENNESSEE							
Gore	Y	Y	Y	Y	N	Y	N
Sasser	Y	Y	Y	Y	Y	Y	N
TEXAS							
Gramm	Y	Y	Y	N	N	Y	Y
Bentsen	Y	Y	Y	N	Y	Y	N
UTAH							
Garn	Y	N	Y	N	N	Y	Y
Hatch	N	N	Y	N	N	Y	Y
VERMONT							
Stafford	Y	Y	Y	N	N	Y	Y
Leahy	Y	Y	Y	N	Y	Y	Y
VIRGINIA							
Trible	Y	Y	Y	N	N	Y	Y
Warner	Y	Y	Y	N	N	Y	Y
WASHINGTON							
Evans	Y	Y	Y	N	N	Y	Y
Gorton	Y	Y	Y	N	N	Y	Y
WEST VIRGINIA							
Byrd	Y	Y	Y	Y	Y	Y	N
Rockefeller	Y	Y	Y	Y	Y	Y	N
WISCONSIN							
Kasten	Y	Y	Y	Y	N	Y	Y
Proxmire	Y	Y	Y	N	N	N	Y
WYOMING							
Simpson	Y	Y	Y	N	N	Y	Y
Wallop	N	N	N	N	?	+	Y

KEY

- Y Voted for (yea).
- # Paired for.
- + Announced for.
- N Voted against (nay).
- X Paired against.
- \- Announced against.
- P Voted "present."
- C Voted "present" to avoid possible conflict of interest.
- ? Did not vote or otherwise make a position known.

Democrats ***Republicans***

ND - Northern Democrats SD - Southern Democrats (Southern states - Ala., Ark., Fla., Ga., Ky., La., Miss., N.C., Okla., S.C., Tenn., Texas, Va.)

150. Corr Nomination. Confirmation of President Reagan's nomination of Edwin G. Corr of Oklahoma to be ambassador to El Salvador. Confirmed 89-8: R 42-8; D 47-0 (ND 33-0, SD 14-0), July 16, 1985. A "yea" was a vote supporting the president's position.

151. Ridgway Nomination. Confirmation of President Reagan's nomination of Rozanne L. Ridgway of the District of Columbia to be assistant secretary of state for European and Canadian affairs. Confirmed 88-9: R 42-8; D 46-1 (ND 33-0, SD 13-1), July 16, 1985. A "yea" was a vote supporting the president's position.

152. Burt Nomination. Confirmation of President Reagan's nomination of Richard R. Burt of the District of Columbia to be ambassador to West Germany. Confirmed 88-10: R 44-7; D 44-3 (ND 32-1, SD 12-2), July 16, 1985. A "yea" was a vote supporting the president's position.

153. S 408. Small Business Administration Authorizations, Fiscal 1986-88. Bumpers, D-Ark., amendment to the Weicker, R-Conn., substitute, to strike the provision of the substitute barring farmers from receiving disaster loans from the Small Business Administration. Rejected 45-52: R 5-45; D 40-7 (ND 27-6, SD 13-1), July 16, 1985. A "nay" was a vote supporting the president's position.

154. S 408. Small Business Administration Authorizations, Fiscal 1986-88. Moynihan, D-N.Y., amendment to the Weicker, R-Conn., substitute, to establish a pilot program to sell to private banks loans from the Farmers Home Administration worth $10 billion in each of the three years. Rejected 24-73: R 1-49; D 23-24 (ND 21-12, SD 2-12), July 16, 1985.

155. S 408. Small Business Administration Authorizations, Fiscal 1986-88. Passage of the bill, as amended by the Weicker, R-Conn., substitute, to authorize $1.66 billion in fiscal 1986-88 for programs of the Small Business Administration, and $228 million in direct loans and $9.25 billion in guaranteed loans in fiscal 1986-88. The bill would also eliminate most direct loans to businesses and loans for non-physical disasters. Passed 94-3: R 48-2; D 46-1 (ND 32-1, SD 14-0), July 16, 1985. A "yea" was a vote supporting the president's position. (The Weicker substitute previously had been adopted by voice vote.)

156. S 43. Line-Item Veto. Quayle, R-Ind., motion to invoke cloture (thus limiting debate) on the Quayle motion to proceed to the consideration of the bill to give the president power to veto individual spending items by requiring that appropriations bills be split by paragraph or section into separate bills before being sent to the White House. Motion rejected 57-42: R 45-7; D 12-35 (ND 9-24, SD 3-11), July 18, 1985. A three-fifths majority vote (60) of the total Senate is required to invoke cloture. A "yea" was a vote supporting the president's position.

CQ Senate Votes 157 - 162

Corresponding to Congressional Record Votes 157, 158, 159, 160, 161, 162

	157	158	159	160	161	162
ALABAMA						
Denton	Y	Y	Y	Y	N	Y
Heflin	Y	Y	Y	N	N	Y
ALASKA						
Murkowski	Y	Y	Y	Y	N	Y
Stevens	Y	Y	Y	Y	Y	Y
ARIZONA						
Goldwater	Y	Y	?	Y	Y	Y
DeConcini	Y	#	Y	N	Y	Y
ARKANSAS						
Bumpers	N	N	Y	?	Y	Y
Pryor	N	N	Y	?	Y	Y
CALIFORNIA						
Wilson	Y	Y	Y	Y	Y	Y
Cranston	N	N	Y	N	Y	Y
COLORADO						
Armstrong	Y	Y	Y	Y	?	?
Hart	N	N	Y	N	Y	Y
CONNECTICUT						
Weicker	N	N	Y	N	N	Y
Dodd	N	N	Y	Y	Y	Y
DELAWARE						
Roth	Y	Y	Y	N	N	Y
Biden	?	Y	Y	N	Y	Y
FLORIDA						
Hawkins	?	Y	Y	Y	Y	Y
Chiles	N	N	N	N	Y	Y
GEORGIA						
Mattingly	Y	Y	Y	Y	Y	Y
Nunn	Y	Y	Y	N	Y	Y
HAWAII						
Inouye	N	N	Y	N	Y	Y
Matsunaga	N	N	Y	N	Y	Y
IDAHO						
McClure	Y	Y	Y	Y	N	Y
Symms	Y	Y	Y	Y	N	Y
ILLINOIS						
Dixon	Y	Y	Y	N	Y	Y
Simon	N	N	Y	N	Y	Y
INDIANA						
Lugar	Y	Y	Y	Y	Y	Y
Quayle	Y	Y	Y	Y	Y	Y
IOWA						
Grassley	Y	Y	Y	Y	N	Y
Harkin	N	N	Y	N	Y	Y
KANSAS						
Dole	Y	Y	Y	Y	Y	Y
Kassebaum	Y	Y	Y	Y	Y	Y
KENTUCKY						
McConnell	Y	Y	Y	Y	N	Y
Ford	N	N	Y	Y	Y	Y
LOUISIANA						
Johnston	N	N	Y	N	N	Y
Long	N	X	?	?	?	Y
MAINE						
Cohen	Y	Y	Y	N	Y	Y
Mitchell	N	N	Y	N	Y	Y
MARYLAND						
Mathias	N	N	Y	N	Y	Y
Sarbanes	N	N	Y	N	Y	Y
MASSACHUSETTS						
Kennedy	Y	Y	Y	N	Y	Y
Kerry	N	N	Y	N	Y	Y
MICHIGAN						
Levin	N	N	Y	N	Y	Y
Riegle	N	N	Y	N	Y	Y
MINNESOTA						
Boschwitz	Y	Y	Y	Y	Y	Y
Durenberger	N	N	Y	Y	Y	Y
MISSISSIPPI						
Cochran	Y	Y	Y	Y	N	Y
Stennis	N	N	?	?	Y	?
MISSOURI						
Danforth	Y	Y	Y	Y	Y	Y
Eagleton	N	N	Y	N	Y	?
MONTANA						
Baucus	N	N	Y	?	Y	Y
Melcher	N	N	Y	N	N	Y
NEBRASKA						
Exon	Y	Y	Y	Y	Y	Y
Zorinsky	Y	Y	Y	Y	N	Y
NEVADA						
Hecht	Y	Y	Y	Y	N	Y
Laxalt	Y	Y	Y	Y	N	Y
NEW HAMPSHIRE						
Humphrey	Y	Y	Y	Y	N	Y
Rudman	Y	Y	Y	N	Y	Y
NEW JERSEY						
Bradley	N	N	Y	?	Y	Y
Lautenberg	N	N	Y	N	Y	Y
NEW MEXICO						
Domenici	Y	Y	Y	Y	Y	Y
Bingaman	N	N	Y	N	Y	Y
NEW YORK						
D'Amato	Y	Y	Y	Y	Y	Y
Moynihan	N	N	Y	N	Y	Y
NORTH CAROLINA						
East	Y	Y	Y	Y	N	Y
Helms	Y	Y	Y	Y	N	Y
NORTH DAKOTA						
Andrews	N	N	Y	Y	N	Y
Burdick	N	N	Y	N	Y	Y
OHIO						
Glenn	N	N	Y	N	Y	Y
Metzenbaum	N	N	Y	N	Y	Y
OKLAHOMA						
Nickles	Y	Y	Y	Y	N	Y
Boren	Y	Y	Y	N	N	Y
OREGON						
Hatfield	N	N	Y	N	Y	Y
Packwood	N	N	Y	Y	Y	Y
PENNSYLVANIA						
Heinz	Y	Y	Y	?	Y	Y
Specter	Y	Y	Y	Y	Y	Y
RHODE ISLAND						
Chafee	Y	Y	Y	Y	Y	Y
Pell	Y	Y	N	N	Y	Y
SOUTH CAROLINA						
Thurmond	Y	Y	Y	Y	Y	Y
Hollings	Y	Y	Y	N	Y	Y
SOUTH DAKOTA						
Abdnor	Y	Y	Y	Y	Y	Y
Pressler	Y	Y	Y	Y	?	?
TENNESSEE						
Gore	N	N	Y	Y	Y	Y
Sasser	N	N	Y	Y	Y	Y
TEXAS						
Gramm	Y	Y	Y	Y	N	Y
Bentsen	N	N	Y	N	Y	Y
UTAH						
Garn	Y	Y	Y	Y	N	Y
Hatch	Y	Y	Y	Y	N	Y
VERMONT						
Stafford	N	N	Y	Y	N	Y
Leahy	Y	Y	Y	N	Y	Y
VIRGINIA						
Trible	Y	Y	Y	Y	Y	Y
Warner	Y	Y	Y	Y	Y	Y
WASHINGTON						
Evans	Y	Y	Y	Y	Y	Y
Gorton	Y	Y	Y	Y	Y	Y
WEST VIRGINIA						
Byrd	N	N	Y	N	Y	Y
Rockefeller	N	N	Y	N	Y	Y
WISCONSIN						
Kasten	Y	Y	Y	Y	Y	Y
Proxmire	Y	Y	Y	N	Y	Y
WYOMING						
Simpson	Y	Y	Y	Y	Y	Y
Wallop	Y	Y	Y	Y	N	Y

KEY

Y Voted for (yea).
Paired for.
+ Announced for.
N Voted against (nay).
X Paired against.
- Announced against.
P Voted "present."
C Voted "present" to avoid possible conflict of interest.
? Did not vote or otherwise make a position known.

Democrats ***Republicans***

ND - Northern Democrats SD - Southern Democrats (Southern states - Ala., Ark., Fla., Ga., Ky., La., Miss., N.C., Okla., S.C., Tenn., Texas, Va.)

157. S 43. Line-Item Veto. Dole, R-Kan., motion to invoke cloture (thus limiting debate) on the Dole motion to proceed to the consideration of the bill to give the president power to veto individual spending items by requiring that appropriations bills be split by paragraph or section into separate bills before being sent to the White House. Motion rejected 57-41: R 45-7; D 12-34 (ND 8-24, SD 4-10), July 23, 1985. A three-fifths majority vote (60) of the total Senate is required to invoke cloture. A "yea" was a vote supporting the president's position.

158. S 43. Line-Item Veto. Dole, R-Kan., motion to invoke cloture (thus limiting debate) on the Dole motion to proceed to the consideration of the bill to give the president power to veto individual spending items by requiring that appropriations bills be split by paragraph or section into separate bills before being sent to the White House. Motion rejected 58-40: R 46-7; D 12-33 (ND 8-24, SD 4-9), July 24, 1985. A three-fifths majority vote (60) of the total Senate is required to invoke cloture. A "yea" was a vote supporting the president's position.

159. S 1487. Equal Access to Justice. Passage of the bill to award attorneys' fees to individuals, small businesses and certain local governments who prevail in legal disputes with the U.S. government. The government could avoid paying the fees if it proved that its position in the matter at issue was "substantially justified." Passed 95-2: R 52-0; D 43-2 (ND 32-1, SD 11-1), July 24, 1985. (The Senate subsequently passed by voice vote HR 2378, the House companion bill to S 1487.)

160. S 1077. Consumer Product Safety Commission Authorizations, Fiscal 1986-87. Danforth, R-Mo., substitute for the Simon, D-Ill., amendment, to establish a commission to study the safety of amusement park rides instead of giving the Consumer Product Safety Commission authority to inspect such rides, as proposed by Simon. Adopted 52-41: R 46-6; D 6-35 (ND 3-28, SD 3-7), July 24, 1985. (The Simon amendment, as amended by the Danforth substitute, was subsequently adopted by voice vote. The bill then was passed by voice vote.)

161. S 1078. Federal Trade Commission Act Amendments. Kasten, R-Wis., motion to table (kill) the McClure, R-Idaho, amendment to prohibit the Federal Trade Commission from using its jurisdiction over unfair or deceptive acts or practices to overrule state laws regarding the licensing, qualifications and permissible duties or tasks of professionals such as lawyers, doctors and dentists. Motion agreed to 71-26: R 30-21; D 41-5 (ND 31-2, SD 10-3), July 25, 1985.

162. HR 2796. Air Traveler Protection Act. Passage of the bill to direct the secretary of transportation to identify and aid in the correction of security problems at foreign airports, to study the need for sky marshals on U.S. carriers, and to authorize $10 million for research into security devices and techniques for identifying explosives. Passed 96-0: R 51-0; D 45-0 (ND 32-0, SD 13-0), July 25, 1985.

CQ Senate Votes 163 - 167

Corresponding to Congressional Record Votes 163, 164, 165, 166, 167

	163	164	165	166	167
ALABAMA					
Denton	Y	N	Y	?	Y
Heflin	Y	N	Y	Y	Y
ALASKA					
Murkowski	Y	N	Y	Y	Y
Stevens	Y	N	Y	Y	Y
ARIZONA					
Goldwater	Y	Y	Y	Y	Y
DeConcini	?	?	?	Y	Y
ARKANSAS					
Bumpers	Y	N	Y	Y	Y
Pryor	Y	N	Y	Y	Y
CALIFORNIA					
Wilson	Y	N	Y	Y	Y
Cranston	Y	N	Y	N	Y
COLORADO					
Armstrong	?	?	?	N	Y
Hart	N	Y	Y	N	Y
CONNECTICUT					
Weicker	?	?	?	?	Y
Dodd	Y	N	Y	Y	Y
DELAWARE					
Roth	Y	N	Y	N	N
Biden	N	Y	Y	?	Y
FLORIDA					
Hawkins	Y	N	Y	Y	Y
Chiles	Y	N	Y	N	Y
GEORGIA					
Mattingly	Y	N	Y	N	Y
Nunn	Y	N	Y	?	Y
HAWAII					
Inouye	Y	Y	Y	Y	Y
Matsunaga	Y	N	Y	N	Y
IDAHO					
McClure	Y	N	N	Y	Y
Symms	Y	N	N	Y	?
ILLINOIS					
Dixon	Y	N	Y	N	Y
Simon	N	Y	Y	N	Y
INDIANA					
Lugar	Y	N	Y	Y	Y
Quayle	Y	Y	Y	Y	Y
IOWA					
Grassley	Y	N	Y	Y	Y
Harkin	Y	N	Y	N	Y
KANSAS					
Dole	Y	N	Y	Y	Y
Kassebaum	N	Y	Y	Y	Y
KENTUCKY					
McConnell	Y	N	Y	Y	Y
Ford	N	Y	Y	Y	Y
LOUISIANA					
Johnston	?	?	?	Y	Y
Long	N	Y	Y	Y	Y
MAINE					
Cohen	Y	N	Y	N	Y
Mitchell	Y	N	Y	N	Y
MARYLAND					
Mathias	N	Y	Y	N	Y
Sarbanes	N	Y	Y	N	Y
MASSACHUSETTS					
Kennedy	N	Y	Y	N	Y
Kerry	Y	N	Y	N	Y
MICHIGAN					
Levin	Y	N	Y	Y	Y
Riegle	Y	N	Y	?	Y
MINNESOTA					
Boschwitz	Y	N	Y	Y	Y
Durenberger	+	Y	Y	N	Y
MISSISSIPPI					
Cochran	?	?	?	Y	Y
Stennis	N	Y	Y	Y	Y
MISSOURI					
Danforth	N	Y	Y	N	Y
Eagleton	Y	Y	Y	N	Y
MONTANA					
Baucus	Y	N	Y	N	Y
Melcher	Y	N	Y	Y	N
NEBRASKA					
Exon	Y	N	Y	Y	Y
Zorinsky	Y	N	Y	N	Y
NEVADA					
Hecht	Y	N	Y	Y	Y
Laxalt	Y	N	Y	N	Y
NEW HAMPSHIRE					
Humphrey	Y	Y	Y	Y	Y
Rudman	Y	Y	Y	N	Y
NEW JERSEY					
Bradley	?	?	?	?	Y
Lautenberg	Y	Y	Y	N	Y
NEW MEXICO					
Domenici	Y	N	Y	Y	Y
Bingaman	?	?	?	?	Y
NEW YORK					
D'Amato	Y	N	Y	Y	Y
Moynihan	Y	Y	Y	?	Y
NORTH CAROLINA					
East	Y	N	Y	Y	Y
Helms	Y	N	N	Y	Y
NORTH DAKOTA					
Andrews	Y	N	Y	Y	Y
Burdick	Y	N	Y	N	Y
OHIO					
Glenn	N	Y	Y	N	Y
Metzenbaum	N	Y	Y	N	N
OKLAHOMA					
Nickles	Y	N	Y	Y	Y
Boren	Y	N	Y	Y	Y
OREGON					
Hatfield	Y	Y	Y	N	N
Packwood	N	Y	Y	N	Y
PENNSYLVANIA					
Heinz	?	?	?	N	Y
Specter	Y	N	Y	N	Y
RHODE ISLAND					
Chafee	N	Y	?	Y	Y
Pell	N	Y	Y	N	Y
SOUTH CAROLINA					
Thurmond	Y	N	Y	Y	Y
Hollings	N	Y	Y	N	Y
SOUTH DAKOTA					
Abdnor	Y	N	Y	Y	Y
Pressler	?	?	?	Y	Y
TENNESSEE					
Gore	Y	N	Y	Y	Y
Sasser	Y	N	Y	Y	Y
TEXAS					
Gramm	Y	N	N	Y	Y
Bentsen	Y	N	Y	N	Y
UTAH					
Garn	?	?	?	Y	Y
Hatch	Y	N	Y	Y	Y
VERMONT					
Stafford	N	N	Y	N	Y
Leahy	Y	Y	Y	N	Y
VIRGINIA					
Trible	Y	N	Y	?	Y
Warner	Y	N	Y	Y	Y
WASHINGTON					
Evans	N	Y	Y	N	Y
Gorton	N	Y	Y	N	Y
WEST VIRGINIA					
Byrd	Y	Y	Y	Y	Y
Rockefeller	N	Y	Y	Y	Y
WISCONSIN					
Kasten	Y	Y	Y	Y	Y
Proxmire	N	Y	N	N	N
WYOMING					
Simpson	Y	N	Y	Y	Y
Wallop	Y	N	Y	Y	Y

KEY

- Y Voted for (yea).
- # Paired for.
- + Announced for.
- N Voted against (nay).
- X Paired against.
- \- Announced against.
- P Voted "present."
- C Voted "present" to avoid possible conflict of interest.
- ? Did not vote or otherwise make a position known.

Democrats *Republicans*

ND - Northern Democrats SD - Southern Democrats (Southern states - Ala., Ark., Fla., Ga., Ky., La., Miss., N.C., Okla., S.C., Tenn., Texas, Va.)

163. S 1078. Federal Trade Commission Act Amendments. Kasten, R-Wis., amendment to allow a regulation of the Federal Trade Commission or the Consumer Product Safety Commission to be vetoed by a joint resolution of Congress signed by the president. Adopted 67-22: R 38-8; D 29-14 (ND 20-10, SD 9-4), July 26, 1985.

164. S 1078. Federal Trade Commission Act Amendments. Kasten, R-Wis., motion to table (kill) the Grassley, R-Iowa, amendment to set up expedited procedures for considering an amendment to appropriations bills for the Federal Trade Commission or the Consumer Product Safety Commission to deny funds to implement a regulation, if the president vetoes a joint resolution disapproving that regulation of those agencies. Motion rejected 34-56: R 14-33; D 20-23 (ND 16-14, SD 4-9), July 26, 1985. (The Grassley amendment was subsequently adopted by voice vote.)

165. S 1078. Federal Trade Commission Act Amendments. Passage of the bill to authorize $65.8 million for the Federal Trade Commission in fiscal 1986, $66.8 million in 1987 and $67.8 million in 1988. Passed 84-5: R 42-4; D 42-1 (ND 29-1, SD 13-0), July 26, 1985.

166. S 410. Conservation Service Reform Act. Dole, R-Kan., motion to table (kill) the Evans, R-Wash., amendment to express the sense of the Senate that the National Highway Traffic Safety Administration should retain the corporate average fuel economy standard for passenger automobiles specified in current law. Motion agreed to 52-39: R 34-16; D 18-23 (ND 8-20, SD 10-3), July 29, 1985.

167. S 1160. Department of Defense Authorization, Fiscal 1986. Adoption of the conference report to authorize $222,992,600,000 for military programs of the Defense and Energy departments in fiscal 1986. Adopted 94-5: R 50-2; D 44-3 (ND 30-3, SD 14-0), July 30, 1985.

CQ Senate Votes 168 - 169

Corresponding to Congressional Record Votes 168, 169

	168	169
ALABAMA		
Denton	N	Y
Heflin	N	Y
ALASKA		
Murkowski	N	Y
Stevens	N	Y
ARIZONA		
Goldwater	?	?
DeConcini	N	Y
ARKANSAS		
Bumpers	N	Y
Pryor	N	Y
CALIFORNIA		
Wilson	N	Y
Cranston	N	N
COLORADO		
Armstrong	N	Y
Hart	N	N
CONNECTICUT		
Weicker	N	N
Dodd	N	Y
DELAWARE		
Roth	N	Y
Biden	N	N
FLORIDA		
Hawkins	N	Y
Chiles	N	Y
GEORGIA		
Mattingly	N	Y
Nunn	N	N
HAWAII		
Inouye	N	Y
Matsunaga	N	Y
IDAHO		
McClure	N	N
Symms	?	N
ILLINOIS		
Dixon	N	Y
Simon	N	Y
INDIANA		
Lugar	N	Y
Quayle	N	Y
IOWA		
Grassley	N	N
Harkin	N	N
KANSAS		
Dole	N	Y
Kassebaum	N	Y
KENTUCKY		
McConnell	N	Y
Ford	N	Y
LOUISIANA		
Johnston	N	Y
Long	N	N
MAINE		
Cohen	N	Y
Mitchell	N	Y
MARYLAND		
Mathias	N	N
Sarbanes	N	N
MASSACHUSETTS		
Kennedy	N	Y
Kerry	N	N
MICHIGAN		
Levin	N	Y
Riegle	N	Y
MINNESOTA		
Boschwitz	N	Y
Durenberger	N	Y
MISSISSIPPI		
Cochran	N	Y
Stennis	?	Y
MISSOURI		
Danforth	N	Y
Eagleton	N	Y
MONTANA		
Baucus	N	N
Melcher	N	N
NEBRASKA		
Exon	N	Y
Zorinsky	N	Y
NEVADA		
Hecht	N	Y
Laxalt	N	Y
NEW HAMPSHIRE		
Humphrey	N	N
Rudman	N	N
NEW JERSEY		
Bradley	N	Y
Lautenberg	N	Y
NEW MEXICO		
Domenici	N	Y
Bingaman	N	Y
NEW YORK		
D'Amato	N	Y
Moynihan	N	N
NORTH CAROLINA		
East	N	Y
Helms	N	N
NORTH DAKOTA		
Andrews	N	N
Burdick	N	N
OHIO		
Glenn	N	N
Metzenbaum	N	N
OKLAHOMA		
Nickles	N	Y
Boren	N	Y
OREGON		
Hatfield	N	Y
Packwood	N	Y
PENNSYLVANIA		
Heinz	N	Y
Specter	N	Y
RHODE ISLAND		
Chafee	N	Y
Pell	N	Y
SOUTH CAROLINA		
Thurmond	N	Y
Hollings	N	N
SOUTH DAKOTA		
Abdnor	N	Y
Pressler	N	N
TENNESSEE		
Gore	N	Y
Sasser	N	Y
TEXAS		
Gramm	N	Y
Bentsen	N	N
UTAH		
Garn	N	N
Hatch	N	N
VERMONT		
Stafford	N	Y
Leahy	N	Y
VIRGINIA		
Trible	N	Y
Warner	N	N
WASHINGTON		
Evans	N	N
Gorton	N	Y
WEST VIRGINIA		
Byrd	N	Y
Rockefeller	N	Y
WISCONSIN		
Kasten	N	Y
Proxmire	N	N
WYOMING		
Simpson	N	Y
Wallop	N	N

KEY

- Y Voted for (yea).
- # Paired for.
- + Announced for.
- N Voted against (nay).
- X Paired against.
- - Announced against.
- P Voted "present."
- C Voted "present" to avoid possible conflict of interest.
- ? Did not vote or otherwise make a position known.

Democrats *Republicans*

ND - Northern Democrats SD - Southern Democrats (Southern states - Ala., Ark., Fla., Ga., Ky., La., Miss., N.C., Okla., S.C., Tenn., Texas, Va.)

168. HR 1460. Anti-Apartheid Act. Weicker, R-Conn., motion to table (kill) the conference report on the bill to impose sanctions against the government of South Africa until it eliminated laws enforcing "apartheid," official racial segregation. Motion rejected 0-97: R 0-51; D 0-46 (ND 0-33, SD 0-13), Aug. 1, 1985. (This was a procedural motion intended to demonstrate support for the bill.)

169. S Con Res 32. First Budget Resolution, Fiscal 1986. Domenici, R-N.M., motion that the Senate concur in the further House amendment to the first concurrent budget resolution for fiscal 1986. That amendment was the text of the conference report on the resolution, which set non-binding spending and taxing levels for the fiscal year ending Sept. 30, 1986, as follows: budget authority $1,069.7 billion; outlays, $967.6 billion; revenues, $795.7 billion; and deficit, $171.9 billion. Motion agreed to 67-32: R 37-15; D 30-17 (ND 20-13, SD 10-4), Aug. 1, 1985.

Corresponding to Congressional Record Votes 170, 171, 172, 173, 174, 175, 176, 177

	170	171	172	173	174	175	176	177
ALABAMA								
Denton	Y	N	N	N	Y	N	N	Y
Heflin	Y	Y	N	Y	N	Y	N	Y
ALASKA								
Murkowski	?	?	N	N	Y	N	N	Y
Stevens	Y	N	Y	N	Y	N	N	Y
ARIZONA								
Goldwater	N	N	Y	N	Y	N	N	Y
DeConcini	?	+	Y	Y	N	Y	N	Y
ARKANSAS								
Bumpers	Y	Y	Y	Y	N	Y	N	N
Pryor	Y	Y	Y	Y	N	Y	?	?
CALIFORNIA								
Wilson	Y	N	Y	?	?	N	N	Y
Cranston	Y	Y	Y	Y	N	N	Y	N
COLORADO								
Armstrong	Y	N	N	N	Y	N	N	Y
Hart	?	+	Y	Y	N	N	Y	N
CONNECTICUT								
Weicker	N	Y	Y	Y	N	Y	Y	N
Dodd	?	+	Y	Y	N	Y	Y	N
DELAWARE								
Roth	Y	N	N	N	Y	N	Y	Y
Biden	?	Y	Y	Y	N	N	Y	N
FLORIDA								
Hawkins	Y	N	N	N	Y	N	N	Y
Chiles	?	Y	Y	Y	N	N	Y	Y
GEORGIA								
Mattingly	Y	Y	N	N	Y	N	N	Y
Nunn	Y	Y	Y	Y	N	N	N	Y
HAWAII								
Inouye	Y	Y	Y	Y	N	N	Y	N
Matsunaga	Y	Y	Y	Y	N	N	Y	N
IDAHO								
McClure	Y	N	N	N	Y	N	N	Y
Symms	Y	N	N	N	Y	N	N	Y
ILLINOIS								
Dixon	Y	Y	Y	Y	N	N	Y	Y
Simon	Y	Y	Y	Y	N	N	Y	N
INDIANA								
Lugar	Y	N	Y	N	Y	N	Y	Y
Quayle	N	N	N	N	Y	N	Y	Y
IOWA								
Grassley	Y	Y	N	Y	Y	N	Y	Y
Harkin	Y	Y	Y	Y	N	N	Y	N
KANSAS								
Dole	Y	N	N	N	Y	N	N	Y
Kassebaum	?	?	Y	N	Y	N	N	Y
KENTUCKY								
McConnell	Y	N	N	N	Y	N	N	Y
Ford	Y	Y	N	Y	N	N	Y	Y
LOUISIANA								
Johnston	Y	Y	N	Y	N	N	Y	N
Long	?	?	N	Y	N	N	N	Y
MAINE								
Cohen	Y	Y	Y	Y	Y	N	Y	Y
Mitchell	Y	Y	Y	Y	N	N	N	N
MARYLAND								
Mathias	Y	Y	Y	Y	N	N	Y	N
Sarbanes	Y	Y	Y	Y	N	N	Y	N
MASSACHUSETTS								
Kennedy	Y	Y	Y	Y	N	N	Y	N
Kerry	Y	Y	Y	Y	N	N	Y	N
MICHIGAN								
Levin	Y	Y	Y	Y	N	N	Y	N
Riegle	?	+	Y	Y	N	N	Y	N
MINNESOTA								
Boschwitz	Y	N	Y	N	Y	N	N	Y
Durenberger	Y	N	Y	N	Y	N	Y	Y
MISSISSIPPI								
Cochran	Y	N	N	N	Y	N	N	Y
Stennis	Y	Y	N	Y	N	N	Y	Y
MISSOURI								
Danforth	Y	N	Y	N	Y	N	Y	Y
Eagleton	Y	Y	Y	Y	N	N	Y	N
MONTANA								
Baucus	Y	Y	Y	Y	N	N	N	N
Melcher	Y	Y	Y	Y	N	N	Y	N
NEBRASKA								
Exon	Y	Y	N	Y	N	N	N	Y
Zorinsky	Y	Y	Y	Y	Y	N	Y	Y
NEVADA								
Hecht	Y	N	N	N	Y	N	N	Y
Laxalt	?	?	N	N	Y	N	N	?
NEW HAMPSHIRE								
Humphrey	Y	N	N	N	Y	N	N	Y
Rudman	Y	N	Y	N	Y	N	Y	Y
NEW JERSEY								
Bradley	Y	Y	Y	Y	N	Y	Y	Y
Lautenberg	?	Y	Y	Y	N	Y	Y	N
NEW MEXICO								
Domenici	Y	N	Y	N	Y	N	N	Y
Bingaman	Y	Y	Y	Y	N	N	Y	N
NEW YORK								
D'Amato	?	Y	Y	Y	Y	N	N	Y
Moynihan	Y	Y	Y	Y	N	N	Y	N
NORTH CAROLINA								
East	?	-	?	?	?	?	?	?
Helms	Y	N	N	N	Y	N	N	Y
NORTH DAKOTA								
Andrews	?	?	Y	N	Y	N	Y	Y
Burdick	?	?	+	Y	N	Y	Y	N
OHIO								
Glenn	Y	Y	Y	Y	N	Y	Y	Y
Metzenbaum	Y	Y	Y	Y	N	N	Y	N
OKLAHOMA								
Nickles	Y	N	N	N	Y	N	N	Y
Boren	Y	Y	Y	Y	N	N	N	N
OREGON								
Hatfield	Y	Y	Y	Y	Y	N	N	N
Packwood	Y	Y	Y	Y	Y	N	Y	Y
PENNSYLVANIA								
Heinz	Y	Y	Y	Y	Y	N	Y	Y
Specter	?	?	Y	N	Y	N	Y	Y
RHODE ISLAND								
Chafee	?	?	Y	Y	Y	N	Y	N
Pell	Y	Y	Y	Y	N	N	Y	N
SOUTH CAROLINA								
Thurmond	Y	N	N	N	Y	N	N	Y
Hollings	Y	Y	Y	Y	N	Y	N	Y
SOUTH DAKOTA								
Abdnor	Y	N	N	N	Y	N	N	Y
Pressler	Y	Y	N	Y	Y	N	Y	Y
TENNESSEE								
Gore	Y	Y	Y	Y	N	N	N	N
Sasser	Y	Y	N	Y	N	N	N	N
TEXAS								
Gramm	Y	N	N	N	Y	N	N	Y
Bentsen	Y	Y	N	Y	N	N	N	Y
UTAH								
Garn	Y	N	N	N	Y	N	N	Y
Hatch	Y	N	Y	N	Y	N	N	Y
VERMONT								
Stafford	Y	Y	Y	N	Y	N	Y	?
Leahy	Y	Y	Y	Y	N	N	N	N
VIRGINIA								
Trible	Y	N	N	N	Y	N	N	Y
Warner	Y	N	N	N	Y	N	N	Y
WASHINGTON								
Evans	?	N	Y	N	Y	N	N	Y
Gorton	Y	N	Y	N	Y	N	N	Y
WEST VIRGINIA								
Byrd	Y	Y	Y	N	N	N	N	Y
Rockefeller	Y	Y	Y	Y	N	N	Y	Y
WISCONSIN								
Kasten	Y	Y	N	Y	Y	N	Y	Y
Proxmire	Y	Y	Y	Y	N	N	Y	N
WYOMING								
Simpson	Y	N	N	N	Y	N	Y	Y
Wallop	Y	N	N	N	Y	N	N	Y

KEY

- Y Voted for (yea).
- # Paired for.
- + Announced for.
- N Voted against (nay).
- X Paired against.
- - Announced against.
- P Voted "present."
- C Voted "present" to avoid possible conflict of interest.
- ? Did not vote or otherwise make a position known.

Democrats *Republicans*

ND - Northern Democrats SD - Southern Democrats (Southern states - Ala., Ark., Fla., Ga., Ky., La., Miss., N.C., Okla., S.C., Tenn., Texas, Va.)

170. Procedural Motion. Dole, R-Kan., motion to instruct the sergeant-at-arms to request the attendance of absent senators. Motion agreed to 79-3: R 41-3; D 38-0 (ND 26-0, SD 12-0), Sept. 9, 1985.

171. HR 1460. Anti-Apartheid Act. Weicker, R-Conn., motion to invoke cloture (thus limiting debate) on the conference report on the bill to impose economic sanctions on South Africa on account of its white minority government's racial policies. Motion rejected 53-34: R 12-34; D 41-0 (ND 28-0, SD 13-0), Sept. 9, 1985. A three-fifths majority (60) of the total Senate is required to invoke cloture. A "nay" was a vote supporting the president's position.

172. S 47. School Prayer. Weicker, R-Conn., motion to table (kill) the bill to bar the federal courts, including the Supreme Court, from considering cases involving prayer in public schools. Motion agreed to 62-36: R 24-28; D 38-8 (ND 31-1, 7-7), Sept. 10, 1985. (The effect of the bill would have been to restore the right of states or local communities to permit prayer in public schools without being subject to challenges in the federal courts.)

173. HR 1460. Anti-Apartheid Act. Kennedy, D-Mass., motion to invoke cloture (thus limiting debate) on the conference report on the bill to impose economic sanctions on South Africa on account of its white minority government's racial policies. Motion rejected 57-41: R 11-40; D 46-1 (ND 32-1, SD 14-0), Sept. 11, 1985. A three-fifths majority (60) of the total Senate is required to invoke cloture. A "nay" was a vote supporting the president's position.

174. HR 1460. Anti-Apartheid Act. Dole, R-Kan., motion to table (kill) the Byrd, D-W.Va., motion to reconsider the vote by which the Kennedy, D-Mass., motion was rejected *(vote 173, above)*. Motion agreed to 50-48: R 49-2; D 1-46 (ND 1-32, SD 0-14), Sept. 11, 1985.

175. HR 1460. Anti-Apartheid Act. Kennedy, D-Mass., motion to invoke cloture (thus limiting debate) on the Kennedy motion to proceed to the consideration of the conference report on the bill to impose economic sanctions on South Africa on account of its white minority government's racial policies. Motion rejected 11-88: R 1-51; D 10-37 (ND 6-27, SD 4-10), Sept. 12, 1985. A three-fifths majority (60) of the total Senate is required to invoke cloture. (Before the vote was taken, Kennedy urged supporters of the motion to vote against it. That request effectively rendered the vote procedural, and precluded a vote on the merits of the motion that may have indicated a slip in support.)

176. S 1200. Immigration Reform and Control Act. Simpson, R-Wyo., motion to table (kill) the Hatch, R-Utah, amendment to create a "seasonal worker" program to allow foreign workers into the country for up to nine months each year for agricultural work. Motion agreed to 50-48: R 19-33; D 31-15 (ND 27-6, SD 4-9), Sept. 12, 1985. (The effect of the motion was to kill both the Hatch amendment and an almost identical amendment that had been appended to the bill by Wilson, R-Calif., which had been offered to preclude additional amendments from being proposed to the Hatch amendment.)

177. S 1200. Immigration Reform and Control Act. Goldwater, R-Ariz., motion to table (kill) the Kerry, D-Mass., amendment to delay testing by the United States of an anti-satellite weapon against an object in space until after the November summit conference between the United States and the Soviet Union. Motion agreed to 62-34: R 46-4; D 16-30 (ND 8-25, SD 8-5), Sept. 12, 1985.

CQ Senate Votes 178 - 185

Corresponding to Congressional Record Votes 178, 179, 180, 181, 182, 183, 184, 185

	178	179	180	181	182	183	184	185
ALABAMA								
Denton	N	N	N	Y	Y	N	Y	Y
Heflin	N	N	Y	Y	Y	N	Y	Y
ALASKA								
Murkowski	N	N	N	Y	Y	Y	Y	Y
Stevens	N	N	Y	Y	Y	Y	Y	Y
ARIZONA								
Goldwater	N	N	Y	Y	Y	Y	Y	N
DeConcini	N	Y	Y	Y	Y	Y	Y	Y
ARKANSAS								
Bumpers	N	N	Y	Y	Y	Y	Y	Y
Pryor	?	?	?	?	Y	N	Y	Y
CALIFORNIA								
Wilson	N	N	Y	Y	N	N	Y	Y
Cranston	Y	Y	Y	N	Y	Y	N	Y
COLORADO								
Armstrong	N	N	Y	Y	Y	N	Y	Y
Hart	Y	Y	Y	Y	Y	Y	N	Y
CONNECTICUT								
Weicker	Y	N	Y	Y	N	Y	Y	Y
Dodd	Y	Y	N	Y	Y	Y	N	N
DELAWARE								
Roth	N	N	Y	Y	N	Y	Y	N
Biden	Y	Y	Y	Y	Y	Y	N	Y
FLORIDA								
Hawkins	N	N	Y	Y	Y	N	Y	Y
Chiles	Y	N	Y	Y	Y	Y	Y	Y
GEORGIA								
Mattingly	N	N	N	Y	N	N	Y	Y
Nunn	N	N	N	Y	Y	Y	Y	Y
HAWAII								
Inouye	Y	Y	N	Y	?	?	?	?
Matsunaga	?	Y	Y	N	Y	Y	N	Y
IDAHO								
McClure	N	N	Y	Y	Y	N	Y	Y
Symms	N	N	Y	Y	Y	N	Y	Y
ILLINOIS								
Dixon	N	Y	Y	Y	Y	Y	Y	N
Simon	Y	Y	Y	N	Y	Y	N	Y
INDIANA								
Lugar	N	N	N	Y	Y	Y	Y	N
Quayle	N	N	Y	Y	Y	Y	Y	Y
IOWA								
Grassley	N	N	N	Y	Y	N	Y	N
Harkin	Y	Y	Y	Y	Y	Y	N	Y
KANSAS								
Dole	N	?	N	Y	Y	Y	Y	Y
Kassebaum	?	?	N	Y	Y	Y	Y	Y
KENTUCKY								
McConnell	N	N	N	Y	Y	N	Y	Y
Ford	?	?	?	?	Y	N	Y	Y
LOUISIANA								
Johnston	N	N	Y	Y	Y	Y	N	Y
Long	N	N	N	Y	Y	N	Y	Y
MAINE								
Cohen	?	?	?	?	Y	N	Y	N
Mitchell	Y	N	N	Y	Y	Y	N	N
MARYLAND								
Mathias	Y	N	N	Y	N	Y	N	Y
Sarbanes	Y	Y	Y	Y	Y	Y	N	Y
MASSACHUSETTS								
Kennedy	Y	Y	Y	Y	Y	Y	N	Y
Kerry	Y	Y	N	Y	Y	Y	N	Y
MICHIGAN								
Levin	Y	Y	Y	N	Y	Y	N	Y
Riegle	N	N	Y	Y	Y	Y	N	Y
MINNESOTA								
Boschwitz	N	N	N	Y	Y	Y	Y	Y
Durenberger	?	N	N	Y	Y	Y	Y	Y
MISSISSIPPI								
Cochran	?	?	?	?	N	Y	Y	Y
Stennis	N	N	Y	Y	Y	?	?	?
MISSOURI								
Danforth	Y	N	N	Y	Y	Y	Y	N
Eagleton	Y	Y	N	?	Y	Y	N	Y
MONTANA								
Baucus	N	N	Y	Y	Y	Y	N	N
Melcher	N	Y	Y	N	Y	Y	N	Y
NEBRASKA								
Exon	N	N	Y	Y	Y	Y	N	Y
Zorinsky	N	N	Y	Y	Y	N	N	N
NEVADA								
Hecht	N	N	Y	Y	Y	N	Y	Y
Laxalt	N	N	?	?	Y	N	Y	Y
NEW HAMPSHIRE								
Humphrey	N	N	Y	Y	N	N	Y	Y
Rudman	N	N	N	Y	N	Y	Y	Y
NEW JERSEY								
Bradley	N	Y	N	Y	N	Y	N	N
Lautenberg	Y	Y	N	Y	Y	Y	N	Y
NEW MEXICO								
Domenici	N	N	Y	Y	Y	Y	Y	Y
Bingaman	N	Y	Y	Y	Y	Y	N	Y
NEW YORK								
D'Amato	N	N	Y	Y	N	N	Y	Y
Moynihan	Y	N	Y	#	Y	Y	N	Y
NORTH CAROLINA								
East	?	?	?	?	?	?	?	?
Helms	N	N	Y	Y	Y	N	Y	Y
NORTH DAKOTA								
Andrews	Y	N	Y	Y	Y	Y	Y	Y
Burdick	N	N	Y	Y	Y	Y	Y	Y
OHIO								
Glenn	N	Y	N	Y	Y	Y	Y	N
Metzenbaum	Y	Y	N	Y	Y	Y	N	Y
OKLAHOMA								
Nickles	N	N	Y	Y	Y	N	Y	Y
Boren	N	N	Y	Y	Y	N	N	Y
OREGON								
Hatfield	Y	N	Y	Y	?	?	-	-
Packwood	Y	N	Y	Y	Y	Y	Y	N
PENNSYLVANIA								
Heinz	N	N	N	Y	Y	Y	Y	Y
Specter	N	N	N	Y	Y	Y	Y	N
RHODE ISLAND								
Chafee	Y	N	N	Y	Y	Y	Y	N
Pell	Y	Y	Y	Y	Y	Y	N	N
SOUTH CAROLINA								
Thurmond	N	N	N	Y	Y	N	Y	Y
Hollings	N	N	N	Y	Y	Y	Y	Y
SOUTH DAKOTA								
Abdnor	N	N	N	Y	Y	N	Y	Y
Pressler	N	N	N	Y	Y	Y	Y	Y
TENNESSEE								
Gore	Y	Y	N	Y	Y	Y	N	Y
Sasser	N	N	Y	Y	Y	Y	Y	Y
TEXAS								
Gramm	N	N	Y	Y	N	N	Y	Y
Bentsen	N	Y	Y	N	Y	Y	Y	Y
UTAH								
Garn	?	?	?	?	Y	N	Y	Y
Hatch	N	N	Y	Y	N	N	Y	Y
VERMONT								
Stafford	?	?	?	?	Y	Y	Y	Y
Leahy	Y	Y	?	X	Y	Y	N	N
VIRGINIA								
Trible	N	N	N	Y	Y	N	Y	Y
Warner	N	N	Y	Y	Y	Y	Y	Y
WASHINGTON								
Evans	Y	N	N	Y	N	Y	Y	Y
Gorton	Y	N	N	Y	N	Y	Y	Y
WEST VIRGINIA								
Byrd	N	N	N	Y	Y	Y	Y	Y
Rockefeller	N	Y	N	Y	Y	Y	Y	N
WISCONSIN								
Kasten	N	N	Y	Y	Y	N	Y	Y
Proxmire	Y	N	N	Y	Y	Y	N	N
WYOMING								
Simpson	Y	N	N	Y	Y	Y	Y	N
Wallop	N	N	?	?	N	N	Y	N

KEY

- Y Voted for (yea).
- # Paired for.
- + Announced for.
- N Voted against (nay).
- X Paired against.
- - Announced against.
- P Voted "present."
- C Voted "present" to avoid possible conflict of interest.
- ? Did not vote or otherwise make a position known.

Democrats *Republicans*

ND - Northern Democrats SD - Southern Democrats (Southern states - Ala., Ark., Fla., Ga., Ky., La., Miss., N.C., Okla., S.C., Tenn., Texas, Va.)

178. S 1200. Immigration Reform and Control Act. Kennedy, D-Mass., motion to table (kill) the Hawkins, R-Fla., amendment to make mandatory nationwide a demonstration program requiring states to verify whether applicants for federal benefit programs were legal U.S. residents. Motion rejected 31-59: R 10-36; D 21-23 (ND 19-13, SD 2-10), Sept. 13, 1985. (The Hawkins amendment subsequently was adopted by voice vote.)

179. S 1200. Immigration Reform and Control Act. Kennedy, D-Mass., amendment to make illegal aliens who were in the United States prior to Jan. 1, 1981, eligible for legal status, and to delete a proposed commission that would study the "legalization" issue. Rejected 26-65: R 0-46; D 26-19 (ND 24-9, SD 2-10), Sept. 13, 1985. (The bill set Jan. 1, 1980, as the eligibility date.)

180. S 1200. Immigration Reform and Control Act. McClure, R-Idaho, amendment to require agents of the Immigration and Naturalization Service to obtain a warrant before searching "open fields" for illegal aliens. Adopted 51-39: R 23-23; D 28-16 (ND 20-12, SD 8-4), Sept. 13, 1985. A "nay" was a vote supporting the president's position.

181. S 1200. Immigration Reform and Control Act. Simpson, R-Wyo., motion to table (kill) the Cranston, D-Calif., amendment to provide that documents such as a rent receipt, bank book, utility bill or affidavit from a priest or other "credible witness" could be used as documentation to establish residence and physical presence in the United States. Motion agreed to 82-6: R 46-0; D 36-6 (ND 25-5, SD 11-1), Sept. 13, 1985. (The bill called for employment records as proof of residence.)

182. S 1200. Immigration Reform and Control Act. Exon, D-Neb., amendment to express the sense of the Senate that the 60-cent-per-gallon tariff on imported ethanol should be implemented immediately. Adopted 82-15: R 37-14; D 45-1 (ND 31-1, SD 14-0), Sept. 17, 1985.

183. S 1200. Immigration Reform and Control Act. Simpson, R-Wyo., motion to table (kill) the Symms, R-Idaho, amendment to provide that no agency of the United States should extend any loan or credit to any country in North America that allows access to its ports to any Soviet vessel capable of delivering nuclear weapons. Motion agreed to 66-30: R 27-24; D 39-6 (ND 31-1, SD 8-5), Sept. 17, 1985.

184. S 1200. Immigration Reform and Control Act. Simpson, R-Wyo., motion to table (kill) the Simon, D-Ill., amendment to change the existing exclusions in immigration law that apply to non-immigrants seeking visas to enter the United States who are members of the Communist Party, are anarchists or advocate the overthrow by force of the U.S. government. Motion agreed to 66-30: R 50-1; D 16-29 (ND 6-26, SD 10-3), Sept. 17, 1985.

185. S 1200. Immigration Reform and Control Act. D'Amato, R-N.Y., amendment to require the federal government to reimburse state governments for the cost of incarcerating in state prisons illegal aliens and "Marielito" Cubans who commit felonies. Adopted 74-22: R 40-11; D 34-11 (ND 21-11, SD 13-0), Sept. 17, 1985.

	186	187	188	189	190	191
ALABAMA						
Denton	Y	Y	Y	N	Y	Y
Heflin	Y	Y	Y	N	Y	N
ALASKA						
Murkowski	Y	Y	Y	N	Y	Y
Stevens	Y	Y	Y	N	N	Y
ARIZONA						
Goldwater	Y	Y	Y	Y	N	N
DeConcini	Y	N	Y	N	Y	N
ARKANSAS						
Bumpers	Y	N	N	N	Y	Y
Pryor	Y	?	?	N	Y	N
CALIFORNIA						
Wilson	Y	N	Y	N	Y	Y
Cranston	N	N	N	N	Y	N
COLORADO						
Armstrong	Y	Y	Y	Y	N	N
Hart	N	N	N	N	Y	N
CONNECTICUT						
Weicker	N	Y	N	Y	Y	Y
Dodd	N	N	N	N	Y	Y
DELAWARE						
Roth	N	Y	N	Y	Y	Y
Biden	N	N	N	N	Y	N
FLORIDA						
Hawkins	Y	Y	Y	N	Y	Y
Chiles	N	Y	N	N	Y	Y
GEORGIA						
Mattingly	Y	Y	Y	N	Y	Y
Nunn	Y	Y	N	N	Y	Y
HAWAII						
Inouye	?	?	N	N	Y	N
Matsunaga	N	N	N	N	Y	Y
IDAHO						
McClure	Y	N	Y	Y	N	N
Symms	Y	N	Y	Y	N	N
ILLINOIS						
Dixon	N	N	N	N	Y	N
Simon	N	N	N	N	Y	N
INDIANA						
Lugar	Y	Y	Y	N	Y	Y
Quayle	Y	Y	Y	N	Y	Y
IOWA						
Grassley	N	Y	N	N	Y	Y
Harkin	N	N	N	N	Y	Y
KANSAS						
Dole	Y	Y	Y	Y	N	Y
Kassebaum	Y	N	N	Y	N	Y
KENTUCKY						
McConnell	Y	Y	Y	N	Y	Y
Ford	N	Y	N	N	Y	Y
LOUISIANA						
Johnston	N	Y	N	Y	Y	Y
Long	N	Y	N	N	Y	Y
MAINE						
Cohen	N	Y	N	N	Y	N
Mitchell	Y	N	N	N	Y	N
MARYLAND						
Mathias	N	Y	N	N	Y	Y
Sarbanes	N	N	N	N	Y	Y
MASSACHUSETTS						
Kennedy	N	N	N	N	Y	N
Kerry	N	N	N	N	Y	N
MICHIGAN						
Levin	N	N	N	N	N	N
Riegle	Y	N	N	N	Y	N
MINNESOTA						
Boschwitz	Y	Y	Y	Y	N	Y
Durenberger	N	Y	N	N	Y	Y
MISSISSIPPI						
Cochran	Y	Y	Y	N	Y	Y
Stennis	?	?	?	Y	Y	Y
MISSOURI						
Danforth	N	Y	N	Y	N	Y
Eagleton	N	N	N	Y	Y	Y
MONTANA						
Baucus	Y	N	N	N	Y	Y
Melcher	N	N	N	N	Y	Y
NEBRASKA						
Exon	Y	N	N	N	Y	Y
Zorinsky	X	Y	N	N	Y	N
NEVADA						
Hecht	Y	Y	Y	N	Y	Y
Laxalt	Y	Y	Y	N	N	Y
NEW HAMPSHIRE						
Humphrey	Y	Y	Y	N	Y	N
Rudman	Y	Y	Y	Y	N	Y
NEW JERSEY						
Bradley	N	N	N	N	Y	N
Lautenberg	N	N	N	N	Y	N
NEW MEXICO						
Domenici	Y	N	Y	Y	N	N
Bingaman	N	N	N	N	Y	N
NEW YORK						
D'Amato	Y	Y	Y	N	Y	Y
Moynihan	N	N	-	N	Y	Y
NORTH CAROLINA						
East	#	?	?	?	?	?
Helms	Y	Y	Y	Y	Y	N
NORTH DAKOTA						
Andrews	N	Y	N	N	Y	Y
Burdick	N	Y	N	N	Y	N
OHIO						
Glenn	N	N	N	N	Y	Y
Metzenbaum	N	N	N	N	Y	Y
OKLAHOMA						
Nickles	Y	Y	Y	N	Y	Y
Boren	Y	N	Y	Y	N	Y
OREGON						
Hatfield	+	-	Y	Y	N	Y
Packwood	N	N	N	N	N	Y
PENNSYLVANIA						
Heinz	N	Y	N	N	Y	Y
Specter	Y	Y	N	N	Y	Y
RHODE ISLAND						
Chafee	N	Y	N	Y	Y	Y
Pell	N	N	N	N	Y	Y
SOUTH CAROLINA						
Thurmond	Y	Y	Y	N	Y	Y
Hollings	Y	Y	Y	N	Y	Y
SOUTH DAKOTA						
Abdnor	Y	Y	Y	N	Y	Y
Pressler	N	Y	N	N	Y	Y
TENNESSEE						
Gore	Y	N	Y	N	Y	Y
Sasser	Y	N	N	N	Y	Y
TEXAS						
Gramm	Y	N	Y	N	N	N
Bentsen	Y	N	N	N	Y	Y
UTAH						
Garn	Y	Y	Y	N	Y	N
Hatch	Y	N	Y	N	Y	N
VERMONT						
Stafford	N	Y	N	N	Y	Y
Leahy	Y	N	N	N	Y	Y
VIRGINIA						
Trible	Y	Y	Y	N	Y	Y
Warner	Y	Y	Y	N	Y	Y
WASHINGTON						
Evans	Y	Y	Y	Y	N	Y
Gorton	Y	Y	Y	Y	N	Y
WEST VIRGINIA						
Byrd	N	Y	N	N	Y	Y
Rockefeller	N	N	N	N	Y	Y
WISCONSIN						
Kasten	N	Y	N	N	Y	Y
Proxmire	N	Y	N	N	Y	Y
WYOMING						
Simpson	N	Y	N	N	Y	Y
Wallop	Y	Y	Y	Y	N	Y

KEY

- Y Voted for (yea).
- # Paired for.
- + Announced for.
- N Voted against (nay).
- X Paired against.
- \- Announced against.
- P Voted "present."
- C Voted "present" to avoid possible conflict of interest.
- ? Did not vote or otherwise make a position known.

Democrats *Republicans*

ND - Northern Democrats SD - Southern Democrats (Southern states - Ala., Ark., Fla., Ga., Ky., La., Miss., N.C., Okla., S.C., Tenn., Texas, Va.)

186. S 1200. Immigration Reform and Control Act. Wilson, R-Calif., amendment to create a "seasonal worker" program to allow foreign workers into the country for up to nine months each year for agricultural work, with a cap allowing no more than 350,000 of these workers in the United States at any one time. Adopted 51-44: R 36-15; D 15-29 (ND 6-25, SD 9-4), Sept. 17, 1985.

187. S 1200. Immigration Reform and Control Act. Simpson, R-Wyo., motion to table (kill) the Levin, D-Mich., amendment to protect from deportation illegal aliens who would qualify for legalization between the date of enactment of the bill and the time the legalization program took effect three years later. Motion agreed to 54-41: R 43-8; D 11-33 (ND 4-28, SD 7-5), Sept. 17, 1985.

188. S 1200. Immigration Reform and Control Act. Wilson, R-Calif., motion to table (kill) the Simon, D-Ill., amendment to terminate the "seasonal worker" program after three years unless Congress votes to continue it. Motion rejected 40-56: R 35-17; D 5-39 (ND 1-31, SD 4-8), Sept. 18, 1985. (The Simon amendment subsequently was adopted by voice vote.)

189. S 1200. Immigration Reform and Control Act. Heinz, R-Pa., motion to table (kill) the Heinz amendment to the Hawkins, R-Fla., amendment to express the sense of the Senate that the Social Security trust funds be removed as a component of the unified federal budget at the earliest possible date. Motion rejected 22-77: R 18-34; D 4-43 (ND 1-32, SD 3-11), Sept. 19, 1985. (The Heinz amendment subsequently was removed as the pending amendment to the bill *(see vote 190, below)*.)

190. S 1200. Immigration Reform and Control Act. Cranston, D-Calif., amendment to the Riegle, D-Mich., amendment to the Cranston motion to commit the bill to the Budget Committee with instructions to report legislation by Oct. 15 that would prevent the use of Social Security benefit reductions to help reduce the federal deficit. The motion also specified that the Budget Committee bill be sequentially referred to the Finance Committee. The Cranston amendment to the Riegle amendment changed from Nov. 2 to Nov. 3, 1985, the date by which the Finance Committee must report the bill. Adopted 79-20: R 34-18; D 45-2 (ND 32-1, SD 13-1), Sept. 19, 1985. (The Riegle amendment, as amended by the Cranston amendment, subsequently was adopted by voice vote. The Cranston motion to commit, as amended by the Riegle and Cranston amendments, then was agreed to by voice vote. The purpose of the motion to commit was to remove the Heinz, R-Pa., amendment on Social Security from the debate on S 1200 *(see vote 189, above)*. The Cranston and Riegle amendments were procedural moves that prevented other senators from altering the substance of the motion.)

191. S 1200. Immigration Reform and Control Act. Passage of the bill to revise U.S. immigration law, creating a new system of penalties for employers who knowingly hire illegal aliens; creating a program, three years after enactment, to grant legal status to millions of illegal aliens already in the country; expanding an existing temporary foreign worker program; and creating a new seasonal foreign worker program expressly for the perishable-crop industry. Passed 69-30: R 41-11; D 28-19 (ND 16-17, SD 12-2), Sept. 19, 1985. A "yea" was a vote supporting the president's position.

CQ Senate Votes 192 - 198

Corresponding to Congressional Record Votes 192, 193, 194, 195, 196, 197, 198

	192	193	194	195	196	197	198
ALABAMA							
Denton	Y	Y	Y	Y	N	N	Y
Heflin	Y	Y	Y	N	N	N	N
ALASKA							
Murkowski	N	Y	Y	N	Y	Y	Y
Stevens	N	Y	Y	Y	Y	Y	Y
ARIZONA							
Goldwater	?	Y	N	N	N	Y	Y
DeConcini	N	N	Y	N	Y	Y	Y
ARKANSAS							
Bumpers	N	N	Y	N	Y	N	Y
Pryor	N	N	Y	N	Y	N	Y
CALIFORNIA							
Wilson	N	Y	Y	N	Y	N	Y
Cranston	N	N	N	N	Y	Y	Y
COLORADO							
Armstrong	?	Y	Y	Y	Y	N	Y
Hart	N	N	N	N	Y	N	Y
CONNECTICUT							
Weicker	N	Y	Y	Y	Y	Y	Y
Dodd	N	N	N	N	Y	Y	Y
DELAWARE							
Roth	N	Y	N	N	Y	N	N
Biden	N	N	?	N	Y	Y	Y
FLORIDA							
Hawkins	N	Y	Y	N	Y	Y	Y
Chiles	N	N	Y	N	Y	N	Y
GEORGIA							
Mattingly	N	Y	Y	N	N	N	Y
Nunn	N	Y	N	N	Y	N	Y
HAWAII							
Inouye	N	N	N	N	Y	Y	Y
Matsunaga	N	N	N	?	Y	Y	Y
IDAHO							
McClure	Y	Y	Y	N	N	Y	Y
Symms	Y	Y	Y	N	N	?	?
ILLINOIS							
Dixon	N	N	Y	N	Y	N	Y
Simon	N	N	N	N	Y	N	Y
INDIANA							
Lugar	N	Y	N	N	Y	N	Y
Quayle	N	Y	N	N	Y	N	Y
IOWA							
Grassley	N	Y	Y	N	Y	N	Y
Harkin	N	N	N	N	Y	Y	Y
KANSAS							
Dole	N	Y	Y	Y	N	N	Y
Kassebaum	Y	Y	N	N	Y	Y	Y
KENTUCKY							
McConnell	N	Y	N	N	Y	N	Y
Ford	N	N	Y	N	Y	Y	Y
LOUISIANA							
Johnston	N	Y	Y	N	Y	N	Y
Long	N	Y	N	N	Y	N	Y
MAINE							
Cohen	N	N	N	N	Y	N	Y
Mitchell	N	N	N	N	Y	N	Y
MARYLAND							
Mathias	N	N	N	Y	Y	N	Y
Sarbanes	N	N	N	N	Y	Y	Y
MASSACHUSETTS							
Kennedy	?	N	N	N	Y	Y	?
Kerry	N	N	N	N	Y	Y	Y
MICHIGAN							
Levin	N	N	Y	N	Y	Y	Y
Riegle	N	N	N	N	Y	N	Y
MINNESOTA							
Boschwitz	N	Y	Y	N	Y	N	Y
Durenberger	N	N	Y	Y	Y	N	Y
MISSISSIPPI							
Cochran	N	Y	Y	Y	Y	Y	Y
Stennis	Y	?	Y	?	Y	Y	Y
MISSOURI							
Danforth	N	Y	N	Y	Y	N	Y
Eagleton	N	N	N	N	Y	N	Y
MONTANA							
Baucus	N	-	+	N	Y	N	Y
Melcher	-	N	Y	N	Y	N	Y
NEBRASKA							
Exon	N	N	Y	N	Y	N	N
Zorinsky	Y	Y	Y	N	N	N	Y
NEVADA							
Hecht	Y	Y	N	N	N	N	Y
Laxalt	Y	Y	Y	Y	Y	?	?
NEW HAMPSHIRE							
Humphrey	N	N	N	Y	Y	N	N
Rudman	N	Y	N	Y	Y	Y	Y
NEW JERSEY							
Bradley	N	N	N	N	Y	N	Y
Lautenberg	N	N	N	N	Y	N	Y
NEW MEXICO							
Domenici	N	Y	Y	Y	Y	N	Y
Bingaman	N	Y	Y	N	Y	N	Y
NEW YORK							
D'Amato	N	N	Y	N	Y	Y	Y
Moynihan	N	?	N	N	Y	Y	Y
NORTH CAROLINA							
East	?	?	?	?	?	?	?
Helms	Y	Y	Y	N	N	N	N
NORTH DAKOTA							
Andrews	N	?	?	N	Y	Y	Y
Burdick	N	N	Y	N	Y	Y	Y
OHIO							
Glenn	N	Y	N	N	Y	?	?
Metzenbaum	N	N	N	N	Y	N	Y
OKLAHOMA							
Nickles	Y	Y	?	N	Y	N	Y
Boren	N	?	?	N	Y	N	Y
OREGON							
Hatfield	-	Y	N	Y	Y	Y	Y
Packwood	N	N	N	N	Y	Y	Y
PENNSYLVANIA							
Heinz	N	N	N	Y	Y	Y	Y
Specter	N	N	N	?	Y	Y	?
RHODE ISLAND							
Chafee	N	N	N	N	Y	N	Y
Pell	N	N	N	N	Y	Y	Y
SOUTH CAROLINA							
Thurmond	N	Y	Y	Y	Y	N	Y
Hollings	N	Y	Y	N	Y	N	Y
SOUTH DAKOTA							
Abdnor	N	Y	Y	Y	Y	Y	Y
Pressler	N	Y	Y	N	Y	Y	Y
TENNESSEE							
Gore	N	N	N	N	Y	N	Y
Sasser	N	N	N	N	Y	Y	Y
TEXAS							
Gramm	Y	Y	N	N	N	N	Y
Bentsen	N	Y	N	N	Y	N	Y
UTAH							
Garn	Y	Y	Y	N	N	N	Y
Hatch	Y	N	Y	Y	N	N	Y
VERMONT							
Stafford	N	N	N	Y	Y	Y	Y
Leahy	N	N	N	N	Y	N	Y
VIRGINIA							
Trible	N	Y	Y	Y	Y	N	Y
Warner	N	Y	Y	Y	Y	N	Y
WASHINGTON							
Evans	N	Y	N	Y	Y	N	Y
Gorton	N	Y	N	Y	Y	N	Y
WEST VIRGINIA							
Byrd	N	N	Y	N	Y	Y	Y
Rockefeller	N	N	N	N	Y	Y	Y
WISCONSIN							
Kasten	N	Y	Y	N	Y	N	Y
Proxmire	N	N	Y	N	Y	N	N
WYOMING							
Simpson	N	Y	Y	Y	Y	N	Y
Wallop	Y	Y	N	N	Y	Y	Y

KEY

- Y Voted for (yea).
- # Paired for.
- + Announced for.
- N Voted against (nay).
- X Paired against.
- \- Announced against.
- P Voted "present."
- C Voted "present" to avoid possible conflict of interest.
- ? Did not vote or otherwise make a position known.

Democrats *Republicans*

ND - Northern Democrats SD - Southern Democrats (Southern states - Ala., Ark., Fla., Ga., Ky., La., Miss., N.C., Okla., S.C., Tenn., Texas, Va.)

192. S 51. Superfund Reauthorization, Fiscal 1986-90. Symms, R-Idaho, amendment to reduce the amount of spending authorized for fiscal 1986-90 to $5.7 billion. (As reported to the Senate, the bill authorized $7.5 billion for the same period.) Rejected 15-79: R 12-37; D 3-42 (ND 1-30, SD 2-12), Sept. 20, 1985.

193. S 51. Superfund Reauthorization, Fiscal 1986-90. Roth, R-Del., amendment to strike from the bill a section establishing a new demonstration program to pay for medical expenses of victims of hazardous substance releases, and to authorize appropriations of $30 million annually during fiscal 1986-90 for that purpose. Adopted 49-45: R 40-11; D 9-34 (ND 3-28, SD 6-6), Sept. 24, 1985. A "yea" was a vote supporting the president's position.

194. S 51. Superfund Reauthorization, Fiscal 1986-90. Abdnor, R-S.D., amendment to exempt fertilizer, animal feed, and any raw material used in their production from the superfund excise tax. Rejected 46-48: R 28-22; D 18-26 (ND 10-21, SD 8-5), Sept. 24, 1985.

195. HR 3036. Treasury, Postal Service and General Government Appropriations, Fiscal 1986. Abdnor, R-S.D., amendment to add $1.5 million to the appropriation for the Office of Management and Budget. The amendment would restore the full amount of the administration's request. Rejected 24-72: R 24-27; D 0-45 (ND 0-32, SD 0-13), Sept. 26, 1985.

196. HR 2005. Superfund Reauthorization, Fiscal 1986-90. Passage of the bill to amend and reauthorize hazardous-waste cleanup programs under the Comprehensive Environmental Response, Compensation and Liability Act of 1980 (PL 96-510), at a spending level of $7.5 billion for fiscal 1986-90. Passed 86-13: R 41-11; D 45-2 (ND 32-1, SD 13-1), Sept. 26, 1985. (The Senate Sept. 24 moved to strike the bill's House language and insert instead the provisions of S 51, the Senate version of the bill.)

197. HR 3036. Treasury, Postal Service and General Government Appropriations, Fiscal 1986. Abdnor, R-S.D., motion to table (kill) the Domenici, R-N.M., amendment to cut spending for discretionary programs in the bill by 2 percent. Motion rejected 38-58: R 19-31; D 19-27 (ND 16-16, SD 3-11), Sept. 26, 1985. (The Domenici amendment was subsequently adopted by voice vote.)

198. HR 3036. Treasury, Postal Service and General Government Appropriations, Fiscal 1986. Passage of the bill to appropriate $12,865,853,960 for fiscal 1986 for the Treasury Department, U.S. Postal Service, Executive Office of the President and a number of independent agencies. Passed 88-6: R 46-3; D 42-3 (ND 29-2, SD 13-1), Sept. 26, 1985. (The president had requested $12,211,347,000 in new budget authority.)

	199	200	201
ALABAMA			
Denton	N	Y	N
Heflin	N	Y	N
ALASKA			
Murkowski	N	Y	N
Stevens	N	Y	Y
ARIZONA			
Goldwater	N	Y	?
DeConcini	Y	Y	N
ARKANSAS			
Bumpers	N	Y	N
Pryor	N	Y	N
CALIFORNIA			
Wilson	N	Y	Y
Cranston	N	Y	Y
COLORADO			
Armstrong	N	Y	Y
Hart	N	N	Y
CONNECTICUT			
Weicker	N	Y	N
Dodd	N	Y	N
DELAWARE			
Roth	N	Y	N
Biden	N	?	?
FLORIDA			
Hawkins	N	?	?
Chiles	N	N	Y
GEORGIA			
Mattingly	N	Y	N
Nunn	N	Y	N
HAWAII			
Inouye	N	Y	Y
Matsunaga	N	Y	Y
IDAHO			
McClure	N	Y	Y
Symms	N	Y	Y
ILLINOIS			
Dixon	N	Y	N
Simon	Y	Y	N
INDIANA			
Lugar	N	Y	Y
Quayle	N	Y	?

	199	200	201
IOWA			
Grassley	N	Y	Y
Harkin	N	Y	N
KANSAS			
Dole	N	Y	N
Kassebaum	N	Y	Y
KENTUCKY			
McConnell	N	Y	N
Ford	N	Y	N
LOUISIANA			
Johnston	N	Y	Y
Long	N	Y	N
MAINE			
Cohen	N	Y	N
Mitchell	N	Y	N
MARYLAND			
Mathias	N	Y	N
Sarbanes	N	Y	N
MASSACHUSETTS			
Kennedy	N	Y	N
Kerry	N	N	N
MICHIGAN			
Levin	N	Y	N
Riegle	N	Y	N
MINNESOTA			
Boschwitz	N	Y	Y
Durenberger	N	Y	Y
MISSISSIPPI			
Cochran	N	Y	N
Stennis	Y	Y	N
MISSOURI			
Danforth	N	N	Y
Eagleton	N	Y	N
MONTANA			
Baucus	N	N	Y
Melcher	N	Y	N
NEBRASKA			
Exon	N	Y	Y
Zorinsky	N	Y	Y
NEVADA			
Hecht	N	Y	Y
Laxalt	N	Y	N

	199	200	201
NEW HAMPSHIRE			
Humphrey	N	N	Y
Rudman	N	Y	N
NEW JERSEY			
Bradley	N	N	Y
Lautenberg	N	Y	N
NEW MEXICO			
Domenici	N	Y	Y
Bingaman	N	Y	Y
NEW YORK			
D'Amato	N	Y	N
Moynihan	N	Y	N
NORTH CAROLINA			
East	?	?	?
Helms	N	Y	N
NORTH DAKOTA			
Andrews	N	Y	Y
Burdick	N	Y	Y
OHIO			
Glenn	N	Y	N
Metzenbaum	Y	Y	N
OKLAHOMA			
Nickles	N	Y	Y
Boren	N	N	Y
OREGON			
Hatfield	N	Y	Y
Packwood	N	Y	Y
PENNSYLVANIA			
Heinz	N	+	N
Specter	N	Y	N
RHODE ISLAND			
Chafee	Y	N	Y
Pell	Y	Y	N
SOUTH CAROLINA			
Thurmond	N	Y	N
Hollings	N	Y	N
SOUTH DAKOTA			
Abdnor	N	Y	Y
Pressler	N	Y	Y
TENNESSEE			
Gore	N	Y	N
Sasser	N	Y	N

KEY

- Y Voted for (yea).
- # Paired for.
- + Announced for.
- N Voted against (nay).
- X Paired against.
- \- Announced against.
- P Voted "present."
- C Voted "present" to avoid possible conflict of interest.
- ? Did not vote or otherwise make a position known.

Democrats *Republicans*

	199	200	201
TEXAS			
Gramm	N	Y	Y
Bentsen	N	Y	Y
UTAH			
Garn	N	Y	Y
Hatch	?	Y	N
VERMONT			
Stafford	N	Y	Y
Leahy	N	Y	N
VIRGINIA			
Trible	N	Y	N
Warner	N	Y	N
WASHINGTON			
Evans	N	Y	Y
Gorton	N	Y	Y
WEST VIRGINIA			
Byrd	N	Y	N
Rockefeller	N	Y	N
WISCONSIN			
Kasten	N	Y	N
Proxmire	Y	Y	N
WYOMING			
Simpson	N	Y	Y
Wallop	N	Y	Y

ND - Northern Democrats SD - Southern Democrats (Southern states - Ala., Ark., Fla., Ga., Ky., La., Miss., N.C., Okla., S.C., Tenn., Texas, Va.)

199. HR 2475. Imputed Interest Rules. Metzenbaum, D-Ohio, motion to postpone consideration of the conference report on the bill until Oct. 10 to allow time for the Finance Committee to agree to budget savings of $115 million over the next three years to cover the initial cost of the bill. Motion rejected 7-91: R 1-50; D 6-41 (ND 5-28, SD 1-13), Oct. 1, 1985.

200. S J Res 77. Compact of Free Association. McClure, R-Idaho, motion to table (kill) the Bradley, D-N.J., amendment to require the International Trade Commission to determine the extent of economic damage from textile imports and impose a 6 percent annual cap on the growth of textile imports. Motion agreed to 87-9: R 47-3; D 40-6 (ND 28-4, SD 12-2), Oct. 2, 1985.

201. S J Res 77. Compact of Free Association. McClure, R-Idaho, motion to table (kill) the Thurmond, R-S.C., amendment to limit importation of foreign textiles and shoes. Motion rejected 42-53: R 28-21; D 14-32 (ND 10-22, SD 4-10), Oct. 2, 1985.

CQ Senate Votes 202 - 209

Corresponding to Congressional Record Votes 202, 203, 204, 205, 206, 207, 208, 209

	202	203	204	205	206	207	208	209
ALABAMA								
Denton	Y	Y	Y	N	N	Y	Y	Y
Heflin	Y	Y	Y	N	Y	Y	Y	Y
ALASKA								
Murkowski	Y	Y	Y	Y	Y	Y	Y	Y
Stevens	Y	Y	Y	Y	Y	Y	Y	Y
ARIZONA								
Goldwater	Y	Y	Y	Y	N	?	?	?
DeConcini	Y	?	?	Y	Y	Y	Y	Y
ARKANSAS								
Bumpers	Y	N	N	Y	Y	N	N	N
Pryor	Y	N	N	Y	Y	N	N	N
CALIFORNIA								
Wilson	Y	Y	Y	Y	Y	Y	Y	Y
Cranston	Y	N	N	Y	Y	N	N	N
COLORADO								
Armstrong	Y	Y	Y	Y	Y	Y	Y	Y
Hart	Y	N	N	Y	Y	N	N	N
CONNECTICUT								
Weicker	Y	N	N	Y	N	N	N	N
Dodd	Y	Y	Y	Y	Y	N	N	N
DELAWARE								
Roth	Y	Y	Y	N	Y	Y	Y	Y
Biden	Y	N	N	Y	Y	N	N	N
FLORIDA								
Hawkins	Y	Y	Y	Y	Y	Y	Y	Y
Chiles	Y	N	N	Y	Y	N	N	N
GEORGIA								
Mattingly	Y	Y	Y	Y	Y	Y	Y	Y
Nunn	Y	Y	Y	Y	Y	Y	Y	N
HAWAII								
Inouye	?	?	?	Y	Y	?	N	N
Matsunaga	Y	N	N	Y	Y	N	N	N
IDAHO								
McClure	Y	Y	Y	Y	Y	Y	Y	Y
Symms	Y	Y	Y	N	Y	?	?	?
ILLINOIS								
Dixon	Y	Y	Y	Y	Y	Y	Y	Y
Simon	Y	N	N	Y	Y	N	N	N
INDIANA								
Lugar	Y	Y	Y	N	Y	Y	Y	Y
Quayle	Y	Y	Y	Y	N	Y	Y	Y
IOWA								
Grassley	Y	Y	Y	Y	Y	Y	Y	Y
Harkin	N	N	N	Y	Y	N	N	N
KANSAS								
Dole	Y	N	Y	Y	Y	Y	Y	Y
Kassebaum	+	Y	Y	Y	Y	Y	Y	Y
KENTUCKY								
McConnell	Y	Y	Y	Y	Y	Y	Y	Y
Ford	Y	N	N	Y	Y	N	N	N
LOUISIANA								
Johnston	Y	N	N	Y	N	N	N	N
Long	Y	N	Y	Y	Y	?	N	N
MAINE								
Cohen	Y	Y	Y	Y	Y	Y	Y	Y
Mitchell	Y	N	N	Y	Y	N	N	N
MARYLAND								
Mathias	Y	N	N	?	?	?	?	?
Sarbanes	Y	N	N	Y	Y	N	N	N
MASSACHUSETTS								
Kennedy	Y	N	N	Y	Y	N	N	N
Kerry	Y	Y	Y	Y	Y	Y	Y	N
MICHIGAN								
Levin	Y	N	N	Y	Y	N	N	N
Riegle	N	N	N	Y	Y	N	N	N
MINNESOTA								
Boschwitz	Y	Y	Y	Y	Y	Y	Y	Y
Durenberger	?	Y	Y	Y	Y	Y	Y	Y
MISSISSIPPI								
Cochran	Y	Y	Y	Y	Y	Y	Y	Y
Stennis	Y	N	N	Y	Y	?	?	?
MISSOURI								
Danforth	Y	Y	Y	Y	Y	Y	Y	Y
Eagleton	?	N	N	Y	Y	N	N	N
MONTANA								
Baucus	Y	N	N	Y	Y	N	N	N
Melcher	Y	N	N	Y	Y	N	N	N
NEBRASKA								
Exon	Y	N	N	Y	Y	N	N	N
Zorinsky	Y	Y	Y	Y	Y	Y	Y	Y
NEVADA								
Hecht	Y	Y	Y	N	Y	Y	Y	Y
Laxalt	Y	Y	Y	N	Y	?	?	?
NEW HAMPSHIRE								
Humphrey	Y	Y	Y	N	Y	Y	Y	Y
Rudman	Y	Y	Y	Y	Y	Y	Y	Y
NEW JERSEY								
Bradley	Y	N	N	Y	Y	N	N	N
Lautenberg	Y	N	N	Y	Y	N	N	N
NEW MEXICO								
Domenici	Y	Y	Y	Y	Y	Y	Y	Y
Bingaman	Y	Y	Y	Y	Y	Y	Y	Y
NEW YORK								
D'Amato	Y	Y	Y	Y	Y	Y	Y	Y
Moynihan	Y	N	N	Y	Y	N	N	N
NORTH CAROLINA								
East	?	?	?	N	?	?	?	?
Helms	Y	Y	Y	Y	Y	Y	Y	Y
NORTH DAKOTA								
Andrews	Y	Y	Y	Y	Y	Y	Y	Y
Burdick	Y	N	N	Y	Y	N	N	N
OHIO								
Glenn	Y	N	N	Y	Y	N	N	N
Metzenbaum	Y	N	N	Y	Y	N	N	N
OKLAHOMA								
Nickles	Y	Y	Y	Y	Y	Y	Y	Y
Boren	Y	Y	Y	Y	Y	Y	Y	N
OREGON								
Hatfield	Y	N	N	Y	N	Y	Y	N
Packwood	?	Y	Y	Y	Y	Y	Y	Y
PENNSYLVANIA								
Heinz	Y	Y	Y	Y	Y	Y	Y	Y
Specter	Y	Y	Y	Y	Y	Y	Y	Y
RHODE ISLAND								
Chafee	Y	Y	Y	Y	Y	Y	Y	Y
Pell	+	?	?	Y	Y	Y	Y	Y
SOUTH CAROLINA								
Thurmond	Y	Y	Y	Y	Y	Y	Y	Y
Hollings	Y	Y	Y	Y	Y	Y	Y	Y
SOUTH DAKOTA								
Abdnor	Y	Y	Y	Y	Y	Y	Y	Y
Pressler	Y	N	Y	Y	Y	?	?	?
TENNESSEE								
Gore	Y	N	N	Y	Y	N	N	N
Sasser	Y	N	N	Y	Y	N	N	N
TEXAS								
Gramm	Y	Y	Y	N	Y	Y	Y	Y
Bentsen	?	?	?	Y	Y	N	N	N
UTAH								
Garn	Y	Y	Y	Y	Y	Y	Y	Y
Hatch	Y	Y	Y	Y	Y	Y	Y	Y
VERMONT								
Stafford	Y	Y	Y	Y	Y	?	?	?
Leahy	Y	Y	N	Y	Y	Y	Y	Y
VIRGINIA								
Trible	Y	Y	Y	Y	Y	?	?	Y
Warner	Y	Y	Y	Y	Y	Y	Y	Y
WASHINGTON								
Evans	Y	Y	Y	Y	Y	Y	Y	Y
Gorton	Y	Y	Y	Y	Y	Y	Y	Y
WEST VIRGINIA								
Byrd	Y	N	N	Y	Y	N	N	N
Rockefeller	Y	N	N	Y	Y	N	N	N
WISCONSIN								
Kasten	Y	Y	Y	Y	Y	Y	Y	Y
Proxmire	Y	N	N	Y	Y	Y	Y	Y
WYOMING								
Simpson	Y	Y	Y	Y	Y	Y	Y	Y
Wallop	Y	Y	Y	N	Y	Y	Y	Y

KEY

- Y Voted for (yea).
- # Paired for.
- + Announced for.
- N Voted against (nay).
- X Paired against.
- - Announced against.
- P Voted "present."
- C Voted "present" to avoid possible conflict of interest.
- ? Did not vote or otherwise make a position known.

Democrats *Republicans*

ND - Northern Democrats   SD - Southern Democrats (Southern states - Ala., Ark., Fla., Ga., Ky., La., Miss., N.C., Okla., S.C., Tenn., Texas, Va.)

202. Miller Nomination. Confirmation of President Reagan's nomination of James C. Miller III to be director of the Office of Management and Budget. Confirmed 90-2: R 49-0; D 41-2 (ND 28-2, SD 13-0), Oct. 4, 1985. A "yea" was a vote supporting the president's position.

203. H J Res 372. Public Debt Limit. Dole, R-Kan., motion to invoke cloture (thus limiting debate) on the Dole (for Gramm, R-Texas, Rudman, R-N.H., Hollings, D-S.C.) amendment to require a balanced budget by fiscal 1991. Motion rejected 57-38: R 47-5; D 10-33 (ND 6-24, SD 4-9), Oct. 6, 1985. A two-thirds majority of those present and voting (64 in this case) is required to invoke cloture on a measure or motion to amend the Senate rules. (The Dole (for Gramm, R-Texas, Rudman, R-N.H., Hollings, D-S.C.) amendment subsequently was adopted *(see vote 213, p. 41-S).*)

204. H J Res 372. Public Debt Limit. Dole, R-Kan., motion to table (kill) the Byrd, D-W.Va., motion to recommit the joint resolution to the Finance Committee with instructions to report the joint resolution with an amendment to extend the limit on federal borrowing until Oct. 18, 1985. Motion agreed to 59-36: R 49-3; D 10-33 (ND 5-25, SD 5-8), Oct. 6, 1985. A "yea" was a vote supporting the president's position.

205. H J Res 372. Public Debt Limit. Boren, D-Okla., amendment to direct the Senate Finance Committee to report, by July 1, 1986, legislation imposing a minimum corporate tax, effective Oct. 1, 1986, with revenues from the tax to be used to reduce the federal deficit. Adopted 88-11: R 42-10; D 46-1 (ND 33-0, SD 13-1), Oct. 8, 1985.

206. Procedural Motion. Domenici, R-N.M., motion to instruct the sergeant-at-arms to request the attendance of absent senators. Motion agreed to 92-6: R 46-5; D 46-1 (ND 33-0, SD 13-1), Oct. 8, 1985.

207. H J Res 372. Public Debt Limit. Dole, R-Kan., motion to proceed to the Dole motion to reconsider the vote by which the Dole motion to invoke cloture (thus limiting debate) on the Dole (for Gramm, R-Texas, Rudman, R-N.H., Hollings, D-S.C.) amendment, to require a balanced budget by fiscal 1991, was rejected *(vote 203, above)*. Motion agreed to 56-33: R 44-1; D 12-32 (ND 8-24, SD 4-8), Oct. 8, 1985. (The Dole (for Gramm, R-Texas, Rudman, R-N.H., Hollings, D-S.C.) amendment subsequently was adopted *(vote 213, p. 41-S)*.)

208. H J Res 372. Public Debt Limit. Dole, R-Kan., motion to reconsider the vote by which the Dole motion to invoke cloture (thus limiting debate) on the Dole (for Gramm, R-Texas, Rudman, R-N.H., Hollings, D-S.C.) amendment to require a balanced budget by fiscal 1991 was rejected *(vote 203, above)*. Motion agreed to 56-35: R 44-1; D 12-34 (ND 8-25, SD 4-9), Oct. 8, 1985. (The Dole (for Gramm, R-Texas, Rudman, R-N.H., Hollings, D-S.C.) amendment subsequently was adopted *(vote 213, p. 41-S)*.)

209. H J Res 372. Public Debt Limit. Dole, R-Kan., motion to invoke cloture (thus limiting debate) on the Dole (for Gramm, R-Texas, Rudman, R-N.H., Hollings, D-S.C.) amendment to require a balanced budget by fiscal 1991. Motion rejected 53-39: R 44-2; D 9-37 (ND 7-26, SD 2-11), in the session that began Oct. 8, 1985. A two-thirds majority of those present and voting (62 in this case) is required to invoke cloture on a measure or motion to amend the Senate rules. (This motion had previously been rejected *(see vote 203, above)*; this vote was taken after the Senate agreed to reconsider the previous vote *(see vote 208, above)*. The Dole (for Gramm, R-Texas, Rudman, R-N.H., Hollings, D-S.C.) amendment subsequently was adopted *(vote 213, p. 41-S)*.)

	210	211	212	213	214	215	216	217
ALABAMA								
Denton	N	N	N	Y	Y	Y	Y	N
Heflin	Y	N	N	Y	Y	Y	N	Y
ALASKA								
Murkowski	N	N	N	Y	Y	Y	N	Y
Stevens	N	N	N	Y	Y	Y	N	Y
ARIZONA								
Goldwater	N	N	N	Y	Y	N	Y	Y
DeConcini	Y	Y	N	Y	Y	Y	N	Y
ARKANSAS								
Bumpers	Y	Y	N	Y	Y	Y	N	Y
Pryor	Y	Y	N	Y	Y	Y	N	Y
CALIFORNIA								
Wilson	N	N	N	Y	Y	Y	N	Y
Cranston	Y	Y	N	N	Y	Y	N	Y
COLORADO								
Armstrong	N	N	N	Y	Y	N	Y	Y
Hart	Y	Y	N	N	Y	Y	N	Y
CONNECTICUT								
Weicker	Y	N	N	N	N	N	N	Y
Dodd	Y	N	N	Y	Y	Y	N	Y
DELAWARE								
Roth	N	N	N	Y	Y	Y	Y	Y
Biden	Y	Y	N	Y	Y	Y	N	Y
FLORIDA								
Hawkins	N	N	N	Y	Y	Y	N	Y
Chiles	Y	Y	N	N	Y	Y	N	Y
GEORGIA								
Mattingly	N	N	N	Y	Y	Y	N	Y
Nunn	Y	Y	N	Y	Y	N	N	Y
HAWAII								
Inouye	Y	Y	N	N	Y	Y	N	Y
Matsunaga	Y	Y	Y	N	N	Y	N	Y
IDAHO								
McClure	N	N	N	Y	Y	N	Y	N
Symms	N	N	N	Y	Y	N	Y	Y
ILLINOIS								
Dixon	Y	Y	N	Y	Y	Y	N	Y
Simon	Y	Y	N	Y	N	Y	N	Y
INDIANA								
Lugar	N	N	N	Y	Y	Y	Y	Y
Quayle	N	N	N	Y	Y	Y	N	Y
IOWA								
Grassley	N	N	N	Y	Y	Y	N	Y
Harkin	Y	Y	N	N	Y	Y	N	Y
KANSAS								
Dole	N	N	N	Y	Y	Y	Y	Y
Kassebaum	N	N	N	N	Y	N	Y	Y
KENTUCKY								
McConnell	N	N	N	Y	Y	Y	Y	Y
Ford	Y	Y	N	Y	Y	Y	N	Y
LOUISIANA								
Johnston	Y	Y	Y	N	Y	Y	N	Y
Long	N	N	N	Y	Y	N	N	Y
MAINE								
Cohen	N	N	N	Y	Y	Y	N	Y
Mitchell	Y	Y	N	N	Y	Y	N	Y
MARYLAND								
Mathias	?	?	?	?	?	?	?	?
Sarbanes	Y	Y	N	N	Y	Y	N	Y
MASSACHUSETTS								
Kennedy	Y	Y	Y	Y	Y	Y	N	Y
Kerry	Y	Y	N	Y	Y	Y	N	Y
MICHIGAN								
Levin	Y	Y	Y	Y	Y	Y	N	Y
Riegle	Y	Y	N	N	Y	Y	N	Y
MINNESOTA								
Boschwitz	N	N	N	Y	Y	N	Y	Y
Durenberger	N	N	N	Y	?	?	N	Y
MISSISSIPPI								
Cochran	N	N	N	Y	Y	Y	Y	Y
Stennis	Y	Y	N	Y	Y	N	N	Y
MISSOURI								
Danforth	N	N	N	Y	Y	N	Y	Y
Eagleton	Y	Y	N	N	Y	N	N	Y
MONTANA								
Baucus	Y	Y	Y	Y	Y	N	N	Y
Melcher	Y	Y	Y	Y	N	Y	N	Y
NEBRASKA								
Exon	Y	Y	Y	N	Y	N	N	Y
Zorinsky	Y	Y	N	Y	Y	Y	N	Y
NEVADA								
Hecht	N	N	N	Y	Y	Y	Y	Y
Laxalt	?	N	?	Y	?	Y	?	?
NEW HAMPSHIRE								
Humphrey	N	N	N	Y	Y	Y	Y	N
Rudman	N	N	N	Y	Y	N	N	Y
NEW JERSEY								
Bradley	N	N	N	N	Y	Y	N	Y
Lautenberg	Y	Y	N	N	Y	Y	N	Y
NEW MEXICO								
Domenici	N	N	N	Y	Y	N	Y	N
Bingaman	Y	Y	N	N	Y	N	N	Y
NEW YORK								
D'Amato	N	N	N	Y	Y	Y	Y	Y
Moynihan	Y	N	N	N	Y	Y	N	Y
NORTH CAROLINA								
East	N	N	N	Y	Y	N	Y	Y
Helms	N	N	N	Y	Y	N	N	Y
NORTH DAKOTA								
Andrews	N	N	N	Y	Y	Y	Y	Y
Burdick	Y	Y	Y	Y	N	Y	N	Y
OHIO								
Glenn	Y	Y	N	N	Y	Y	N	Y
Metzenbaum	Y	Y	N	N	Y	Y	N	Y
OKLAHOMA								
Nickles	Y	N	N	Y	Y	N	Y	Y
Boren	Y	N	Y	Y	Y	N	N	?
OREGON								
Hatfield	N	N	N	N	N	N	N	Y
Packwood	N	N	N	Y	Y	Y	Y	Y
PENNSYLVANIA								
Heinz	N	N	N	Y	Y	Y	Y	Y
Specter	N	N	N	Y	Y	Y	Y	Y
RHODE ISLAND								
Chafee	N	N	N	Y	Y	Y	Y	Y
Pell	Y	Y	Y	N	N	Y	N	Y
SOUTH CAROLINA								
Thurmond	N	N	N	Y	Y	Y	Y	Y
Hollings	N	N	N	Y	Y	Y	N	Y
SOUTH DAKOTA								
Abdnor	N	N	N	Y	Y	Y	Y	Y
Pressler	N	N	N	Y	Y	Y	N	Y
TENNESSEE								
Gore	Y	Y	N	Y	Y	Y	N	Y
Sasser	Y	Y	N	Y	Y	Y	N	Y
TEXAS								
Gramm	N	N	N	Y	Y	N	Y	Y
Bentsen	Y	Y	N	Y	Y	Y	N	Y
UTAH								
Garn	N	N	N	Y	Y	N	Y	Y
Hatch	N	N	N	Y	Y	N	N	Y
VERMONT								
Stafford	N	N	N	N	Y	Y	Y	Y
Leahy	Y	Y	N	Y	Y	Y	N	Y
VIRGINIA								
Trible	N	N	N	Y	Y	Y	Y	Y
Warner	N	N	N	Y	Y	Y	N	Y
WASHINGTON								
Evans	N	N	N	Y	?	Y	N	Y
Gorton	N	N	N	Y	Y	Y	Y	Y
WEST VIRGINIA								
Byrd	Y	Y	N	N	Y	Y	N	Y
Rockefeller	Y	Y	N	Y	Y	Y	N	Y
WISCONSIN								
Kasten	N	N	N	Y	Y	Y	N	Y
Proxmire	Y	Y	N	Y	Y	Y	N	Y
WYOMING								
Simpson	N	N	N	Y	Y	N	Y	Y
Wallop	N	N	N	Y	Y	N	Y	Y

KEY

- Y Voted for (yea).
- # Paired for.
- + Announced for.
- N Voted against (nay).
- X Paired against.
- \- Announced against.
- P Voted "present."
- C Voted "present" to avoid possible conflict of interest.
- ? Did not vote or otherwise make a position known.

Democrats ***Republicans***

ND - Northern Democrats SD - Southern Democrats (Southern states - Ala., Ark., Fla., Ga., Ky., La., Miss., N.C., Okla., S.C., Tenn., Texas, Va.)

210. H J Res 372. Public Debt Limit. Exon, D-Neb., amendment to the Dole, R-Kan. (for Gramm, R-Texas, Rudman, R-N.H., Hollings, D-S.C.), amendment, to require that reports to the president and Congress from the directors of the Congressional Budget Office and the Office of Management and Budget, for the purpose of determining that projected budget deficits were within established target limits, would be due on Oct. 1, Feb. 15 and May 1 of each fiscal year, except for fiscal 1986, when such reports would be due Nov. 1, Feb. 15 and May 1. The Exon amendment also would have established that projections that the fiscal 1986 deficit would exceed the target by 5 percent would trigger procedures requiring automatic reductions in spending. Rejected 46-52: R 2-49; D 44-3 (ND 32-1, SD 12-2), Oct. 9, 1985. (The Dole (for Gramm, R-Texas, Rudman, R-N.H., Hollings, D-S.C.) amendment, which would require a balanced budget by fiscal 1991, subsequently was adopted *(see vote 213, below)*.)

211. H J Res 372. Public Debt Limit. Chiles, D-Fla., amendment to the Dole, R-Kan., amendment to the Dole motion to recommit the joint resolution to the Budget Committee with instructions, to set maximum allowable deficits for fiscal years 1986-90, declining annually to zero in 1990, and to require the president, if projected deficits exceed those allowed, to issue an emergency order reducing federal spending, except for Social Security and means-tested entitlement programs and including defense, reducing projected deficits to the maximum as established by the bill. Rejected 40-59: R 0-52; D 40-7 (ND 30-3, SD 10-4), Oct. 9, 1985.

212. H J Res 372. Public Debt Limit. Melcher, D-Mont., amendment to the Dole, R-Kan. (for Gramm, R-Texas, Rudman, R-N.H., Hollings, D-S.C.), amendment, to impose a 20 percent minimum alternative tax on corporations beginning in 1986. Rejected 10-88: R 0-51; D 10-37 (ND 8-25, SD 2-12), Oct. 9, 1985.

213. H J Res 372. Public Debt Limit. Dole, R-Kan. (for Gramm, R-Texas, Rudman, R-N.H., Hollings, D-S.C.), amendment to set maximum allowable federal deficits for fiscal years 1986-91, declining annually to zero in 1991, and to require the president, if projected deficits exceed those allowed, to issue an emergency order reducing all federal spending except for Social Security, interest on the federal debt and existing contractual obligations, by enough to reduce deficits to the maximum established by the bill. The amendment also revises congressional budgeting procedures and removes Social Security from the unified federal budget in fiscal 1986 and thereafter. Adopted 75-24: R 48-4; D 27-20 (ND 15-18, SD 12-2), Oct. 9, 1985. A "yea" was a vote supporting the president's position.

214. H J Res 372. Public Debt Limit. Goldwater, R-Ariz., motion to table (kill) the Bradley, D-N.J., amendment to reduce fiscal 1987 appropriations for defense programs by 5 percent, to $298.8 billion. Motion agreed to 89-7: R 47-2; D 42-5 (ND 28-5, SD 14-0), Oct. 10, 1985.

215. H J Res 372. Public Debt Limit. Packwood, R-Ore., motion to table (kill) the Boren, D-Okla., amendment to include cost-of-living adjustments for Social Security benefits in any emergency presidential "sequestering" order reducing spending, as provided by the bill (except that the adjustments could not be reduced by more than 3 percentage points). Motion agreed to 71-27: R 32-19; D 39-8 (ND 29-4, SD 10-4), Oct. 10, 1985.

216. H J Res 372. Public Debt Limit. Packwood, R-Ore., motion to table (kill) the Glenn, D-Ohio, amendment to affirm an existing requirement that presidential budgets include proposals for eliminating any gap (deficit) between spending and revenues, and to bar such budgets, beginning in fiscal 1987, from proposing increases in the federal debt for that purpose. Motion rejected 33-65: R 33-18; D 0-47 (ND 0-33, SD 0-14), Oct. 10, 1985. (The Glenn amendment was subsequently adopted *(see vote 217, below)*.)

217. H J Res 372. Public Debt Limit. Glenn, D-Ohio, amendment to affirm an existing requirement that presidential budgets include proposals for eliminating any gap (deficit) between spending and revenues, and to bar such budgets, beginning in fiscal 1987, from proposing increases in the federal debt for that purpose. Adopted 93-4: R 47-4; D 46-0 (ND 33-0, SD 13-0), Oct. 10, 1985.

CQ Senate Votes 218 - 222

Corresponding to Congressional Record Votes 218, 219, 220, 221, 222

	218	219	220	221	222
ALABAMA					
Denton	Y	Y	N	Y	Y
Heflin	Y	Y	N	N	N
ALASKA					
Murkowski	Y	Y	Y	Y	Y
Stevens	Y	Y	N	Y	Y
ARIZONA					
Goldwater	Y	?	N	Y	Y
DeConcini	Y	Y	N	N	N
ARKANSAS					
Bumpers	Y	Y	N	N	N
Pryor	Y	Y	N	N	N
CALIFORNIA					
Wilson	Y	Y	Y	Y	Y
Cranston	Y	N	N	N	N
COLORADO					
Armstrong	Y	Y	Y	Y	Y
Hart	N	Y	N	N	N
CONNECTICUT					
Weicker	N	N	N	N	N
Dodd	Y	Y	N	N	N
DELAWARE					
Roth	Y	N	Y	Y	Y
Biden	Y	Y	N	N	Y
FLORIDA					
Hawkins	Y	Y	Y	Y	Y
Chiles	Y	Y	N	N	Y
GEORGIA					
Mattingly	Y	Y	Y	Y	Y
Nunn	Y	Y	N	N	N
HAWAII					
Inouye	Y	Y	N	N	N
Matsunaga	N	Y	N	N	N
IDAHO					
McClure	Y	Y	?	?	?
Symms	Y	Y	Y	Y	N
ILLINOIS					
Dixon	Y	Y	N	N	?
Simon	Y	Y	N	N	Y
INDIANA					
Lugar	Y	Y	Y	Y	Y
Quayle	Y	Y	Y	Y	Y

	218	219	220	221	222
IOWA					
Grassley	Y	Y	N	Y	N
Harkin	Y	Y	Y	N	N
KANSAS					
Dole	Y	Y	Y	Y	Y
Kassebaum	Y	Y	N	Y	N
KENTUCKY					
McConnell	Y	Y	N	?	?
Ford	Y	Y	N	N	Y
LOUISIANA					
Johnston	Y	Y	N	N	N
Long	Y	Y	N	Y	N
MAINE					
Cohen	Y	Y	N	Y	Y
Mitchell	Y	N	N	N	N
MARYLAND					
Mathias	?	?	?	?	?
Sarbanes	Y	N	N	N	N
MASSACHUSETTS					
Kennedy	Y	Y	N	N	Y
Kerry	Y	Y	N	N	Y
MICHIGAN					
Levin	Y	Y	N	N	Y
Riegle	Y	N	N	N	N
MINNESOTA					
Boschwitz	Y	Y	N	Y	Y
Durenberger	Y	Y	N	+	+
MISSISSIPPI					
Cochran	Y	Y	N	?	?
Stennis	Y	Y	N	?	?
MISSOURI					
Danforth	Y	Y	N	Y	Y
Eagleton	N	N	N	N	Y
MONTANA					
Baucus	Y	Y	N	N	-
Melcher	Y	Y	N	N	N
NEBRASKA					
Exon	Y	Y	Y	N	N
Zorinsky	Y	Y	Y	N	N
NEVADA					
Hecht	Y	Y	N	Y	Y
Laxalt	?	?	?	Y	Y

	218	219	220	221	222
NEW HAMPSHIRE					
Humphrey	Y	N	Y	Y	N
Rudman	Y	Y	N	Y	Y
NEW JERSEY					
Bradley	N	N	N	Y	N
Lautenberg	Y	N	N	N	N
NEW MEXICO					
Domenici	Y	Y	N	Y	Y
Bingaman	Y	Y	N	N	N
NEW YORK					
D'Amato	Y	Y	N	Y	Y
Moynihan	N	N	N	N	N
NORTH CAROLINA					
East	Y	Y	Y	?	?
Helms	Y	Y	Y	Y	Y
NORTH DAKOTA					
Andrews	Y	Y	N	Y	Y
Burdick	Y	Y	N	N	N
OHIO					
Glenn	Y	Y	N	N	Y
Metzenbaum	Y	N	N	?	?
OKLAHOMA					
Nickles	Y	Y	Y	N	N
Boren	Y	Y	N	N	Y
OREGON					
Hatfield	N	N	Y	?	?
Packwood	Y	Y	N	Y	Y
PENNSYLVANIA					
Heinz	Y	Y	N	Y	Y
Specter	Y	Y	N	Y	Y
RHODE ISLAND					
Chafee	Y	Y	N	Y	Y
Pell	N	N	N	+	-
SOUTH CAROLINA					
Thurmond	Y	Y	Y	Y	Y
Hollings	Y	Y	N	Y	Y
SOUTH DAKOTA					
Abdnor	Y	Y	N	Y	Y
Pressler	Y	Y	N	Y	Y
TENNESSEE					
Gore	Y	Y	N	N	Y
Sasser	Y	Y	N	N	N

KEY

- Y Voted for (yea).
- # Paired for.
- + Announced for.
- N Voted against (nay).
- X Paired against.
- - Announced against.
- P Voted "present."
- C Voted "present" to avoid possible conflict of interest.
- ? Did not vote or otherwise make a position known.

Democrats ***Republicans***

	218	219	220	221	222
TEXAS					
Gramm	Y	Y	N	Y	Y
Bentsen	N	Y	N	?	N
UTAH					
Garn	Y	Y	Y	Y	Y
Hatch	Y	Y	Y	Y	Y
VERMONT					
Stafford	Y	Y	N	Y	Y
Leahy	Y	Y	N	N	N
VIRGINIA					
Trible	Y	Y	N	Y	Y
Warner	Y	Y	N	Y	N
WASHINGTON					
Evans	Y	Y	N	Y	Y
Gorton	Y	Y	N	Y	Y
WEST VIRGINIA					
Byrd	Y	N	N	N	N
Rockefeller	Y	N	N	N	Y
WISCONSIN					
Kasten	Y	Y	Y	N	N
Proxmire	Y	Y	N	N	N
WYOMING					
Simpson	Y	Y	N	Y	Y
Wallop	Y	Y	N	Y	Y

ND - Northern Democrats SD - Southern Democrats (Southern states - Ala., Ark., Fla., Ga., Ky., La., Miss., N.C., Okla., S.C., Tenn., Texas, Va.)

218. H J Res 372. Public Debt Limit. Packwood, R-Ore., motion to table (kill) the Bradley, D-N.J., amendment to increase by 18 cents a gallon the federal excise tax on motor fuels. Motion agreed to 89-9: R 49-2; D 40-7 (ND 27-6, SD 13-1), Oct. 10, 1985.

219. H J Res 372. Public Debt Limit. Packwood, R-Ore., motion to table (kill) the Moynihan, D-N.Y., amendment to reduce spending by the Commodity Credit Corporation (which provides federal price-support farm loans) by the same percentage as other programs in the event of an emergency presidential "sequestering" order reducing spending, as provided by the bill. Motion agreed to 81-16: R 46-4; D 35-12 (ND 21-12, SD 14-0), Oct. 10, 1985.

220. H J Res 372. Public Debt Limit. Zorinsky, D-Neb., amendment to make out of order any budget reconciliation legislation in which spending increases are offset by increases in taxes. Rejected 22-75: R 19-31; D 3-44 (ND 3-30, SD 0-14), Oct. 10, 1985. (The effect of the amendment was to require that spending increases be offset with an equivalent amount of reductions in spending in the legislation.)

221. H J Res 372. Public Debt Limit. Packwood, R-Ore., motion to table (kill) the Eagleton, D-Mo., amendment to require joint Office of Management and Budget and Congressional Budget Office projections of deficits on Feb. 15 and May 1 of each year (in addition to dates established by the bill), to set the maximum allowable deficit for fiscal 1986 at $175 billion (instead of $180 billion), and to require an emergency presidential "sequestering" order reducing spending if the fiscal 1986 projected deficit exceeds $175 billion by 5 percent. Motion agreed to 46-43: R 43-3; D 3-40 (ND 1-30, SD 2-10), Oct. 10, 1985.

222. H J Res 372. Public Debt Limit. Passage of the joint resolution to raise the federal debt to $2.079 trillion from $1.824 trillion; to set maximum allowable federal deficits for fiscal years 1986-91, declining annually to zero in 1991; and to require the president, if projected deficits exceed those allowed, to issue an emergency order reducing all federal spending except Social Security, interest on the federal debt and existing contractual obligations, by enough to reduce deficits to the maximum as established by the bill. The joint resolution also revised congressional budgeting procedures and removed Social Security from the unified federal budget in fiscal 1986 and thereafter. Passed 51-37: R 38-8; D 13-29 (ND 8-21, SD 5-8), Oct. 10, 1985. A "yea" was a vote supporting the president's position.

Corresponding to Congressional Record Votes 223, 224, 225, 226, 227, 228, 229, 230

	223	224	225	226	227	228	229	230
ALABAMA								
Denton	Y	N	Y	Y	N	Y	Y	Y
Heflin	Y	Y	N	Y	N	Y	N	Y
ALASKA								
Murkowski	?	?	?	?	N	Y	Y	N
Stevens	Y	Y	N	Y	Y	N	N	N
ARIZONA								
Goldwater	Y	N	N	N	Y	?	?	N
DeConcini	X	Y	N	Y	N	Y	Y	N
ARKANSAS								
Bumpers	Y	Y	N	Y	N	Y	N	Y
Pryor	Y	Y	N	Y	N	Y	Y	N
CALIFORNIA								
Wilson	N	N	N	N	N	Y	N	Y
Cranston	Y	Y	N	Y	Y	N	N	?
COLORADO								
Armstrong	N	N	Y	N	Y	N	Y	Y
Hart	Y	Y	N	Y	N	Y	N	Y
CONNECTICUT								
Weicker	Y	Y	N	Y	Y	N	N	Y
Dodd	Y	Y	N	Y	N	Y	N	N
DELAWARE								
Roth	N	N	N	N	Y	N	Y	Y
Biden	?	?	?	Y	N	Y	N	Y
FLORIDA								
Hawkins	N	N	Y	Y	N	Y	N	Y
Chiles	Y	Y	N	Y	N	Y	N	Y
GEORGIA								
Mattingly	N	N	N	Y	Y	N	Y	Y
Nunn	N	Y	N	Y	N	Y	Y	Y
HAWAII								
Inouye	Y	Y	N	Y	N	Y	N	N
Matsunaga	Y	Y	N	Y	?	Y	N	N
IDAHO								
McClure	Y	N	Y	Y	Y	N	Y	N
Symms	N	N	Y	N	Y	N	Y	N
ILLINOIS								
Dixon	Y	Y	N	Y	N	Y	N	Y
Simon	Y	Y	N	Y	N	Y	N	Y
INDIANA								
Lugar	N	N	N	N	Y	N	Y	Y
Quayle	N	N	N	Y	Y	N	Y	Y
IOWA								
Grassley	Y	Y	N	Y	N	Y	Y	Y
Harkin	#	+	?	Y	N	Y	N	Y
KANSAS								
Dole	Y	N	N	Y	Y	N	Y	Y
Kassebaum	Y	Y	Y	Y	N	Y	Y	N
KENTUCKY								
McConnell	Y	Y	N	Y	Y	N	Y	Y
Ford	Y	Y	N	Y	N	Y	N	Y
LOUISIANA								
Johnston	Y	Y	N	Y	N	Y	N	N
Long	Y	Y	N	?	N	Y	Y	N
MAINE								
Cohen	Y	Y	N	Y	N	Y	N	Y
Mitchell	N	Y	N	Y	N	Y	N	Y
MARYLAND								
Mathias	Y	Y	Y	?	?	?	?	?
Sarbanes	Y	Y	N	Y	N	Y	N	Y
MASSACHUSETTS								
Kennedy	Y	Y	N	Y	N	Y	N	Y
Kerry	Y	Y	N	Y	N	Y	N	Y
MICHIGAN								
Levin	Y	Y	N	Y	?	?	?	?
Riegle	Y	Y	N	Y	N	Y	N	Y
MINNESOTA								
Boschwitz	Y	N	Y	Y	Y	N	Y	Y
Durenberger	Y	Y	N	Y	N	Y	Y	Y
MISSISSIPPI								
Cochran	Y	Y	Y	Y	Y	N	Y	Y
Stennis	Y	Y	N	Y	Y	N	N	N
MISSOURI								
Danforth	Y	Y	N	Y	Y	N	Y	Y
Eagleton	Y	Y	N	Y	Y	N	N	N
MONTANA								
Baucus	N	Y	N	Y	N	Y	N	Y
Melcher	Y	Y	N	Y	N	Y	N	Y
NEBRASKA								
Exon	Y	Y	N	Y	N	Y	Y	Y
Zorinsky	Y	Y	N	Y	N	Y	Y	Y
NEVADA								
Hecht	N	N	Y	N	Y	N	Y	Y
Laxalt	?	?	?	?	?	?	?	?
NEW HAMPSHIRE								
Humphrey	N	N	N	N	Y	N	Y	Y
Rudman	N	N	N	Y	Y	N	Y	Y
NEW JERSEY								
Bradley	N	Y	N	Y	Y	N	N	Y
Lautenberg	Y	Y	N	Y	N	Y	N	Y
NEW MEXICO								
Domenici	Y	N	N	Y	Y	N	Y	Y
Bingaman	N	Y	N	Y	N	Y	N	Y
NEW YORK								
D'Amato	Y	Y	N	Y	N	Y	N	N
Moynihan	N	Y	N	Y	N	Y	N	Y
NORTH CAROLINA								
East	N	N	Y	N	Y	N	Y	Y
Helms	N	N	Y	N	Y	N	Y	Y
NORTH DAKOTA								
Andrews	Y	Y	N	Y	N	Y	N	N
Burdick	Y	Y	N	Y	N	Y	N	Y
OHIO								
Glenn	Y	Y	N	Y	N	Y	N	Y
Metzenbaum	Y	Y	N	Y	N	Y	N	Y
OKLAHOMA								
Nickles	N	Y	Y	Y	Y	N	Y	Y
Boren	N	Y	N	Y	N	Y	Y	N
OREGON								
Hatfield	Y	Y	N	Y	Y	N	N	N
Packwood	Y	Y	N	Y	N	Y	N	Y
PENNSYLVANIA								
Heinz	Y	Y	N	Y	N	Y	N	Y
Specter	Y	Y	N	Y	N	Y	N	Y
RHODE ISLAND								
Chafee	?	?	?	?	Y	N	N	Y
Pell	N	Y	N	N	N	Y	N	Y
SOUTH CAROLINA								
Thurmond	Y	N	N	Y	Y	N	Y	N
Hollings	Y	Y	N	Y	N	Y	N	N
SOUTH DAKOTA								
Abdnor	Y	Y	Y	Y	N	Y	N	N
Pressler	Y	Y	N	Y	N	Y	Y	Y
TENNESSEE								
Gore	Y	Y	N	Y	N	Y	N	Y
Sasser	Y	Y	N	Y	N	Y	Y	N
TEXAS								
Gramm	N	N	Y	N	Y	N	Y	Y
Bentsen	N	Y	N	Y	Y	N	Y	Y
UTAH								
Garn	Y	N	N	Y	N	N	Y	N
Hatch	Y	N	Y	Y	Y	N	Y	N
VERMONT								
Stafford	Y	Y	N	Y	N	Y	N	Y
Leahy	Y	Y	N	Y	N	Y	N	Y
VIRGINIA								
Trible	N	Y	N	Y	Y	N	Y	Y
Warner	N	N	N	Y	Y	N	Y	Y
WASHINGTON								
Evans	Y	Y	N	Y	Y	N	N	Y
Gorton	Y	Y	Y	Y	Y	N	N	Y
WEST VIRGINIA								
Byrd	Y	Y	N	Y	N	Y	N	Y
Rockefeller	Y	Y	N	Y	N	Y	N	Y
WISCONSIN								
Kasten	Y	Y	N	Y	N	Y	Y	Y
Proxmire	N	N	N	N	Y	N	Y	Y
WYOMING								
Simpson	N	N	N	Y	Y	N	Y	N
Wallop	Y	N	Y	N	Y	N	Y	Y

KEY

- Y Voted for (yea).
- # Paired for.
- + Announced for.
- N Voted against (nay).
- X Paired against.
- - Announced against.
- P Voted "present."
- C Voted "present" to avoid possible conflict of interest.
- ? Did not vote or otherwise make a position known.

Democrats *Republicans*

ND - Northern Democrats SD - Southern Democrats (Southern states - Ala., Ark., Fla., Ga., Ky., La., Miss., N.C., Okla., S.C., Tenn., Texas, Va.)

223. HR 3037. Agriculture Appropriations, Fiscal 1986. Cochran, R-Miss., motion to table (kill) the Proxmire, D-Wis., amendment to reduce amounts appropriated or otherwise made available in the bill by 4 percent. Motion agreed to 66-28: R 32-18; D 34-10 (ND 23-7, SD 11-3), Oct. 16, 1985.

224. HR 3037. Agriculture Appropriations, Fiscal 1986. Cochran, R-Miss., motion to table (kill) the Helms, R-N.C., amendment to reduce the farm credit loan authorization levels in accordance with the authorizations contained in S 1714, the farm program reauthorization bill reported by the Agriculture Committee, and to reduce the appropriations for the food stamp program to conform to budget authority levels estimated by the Congressional Budget Office. Motion agreed to 68-27: R 24-26; D 44-1 (ND 30-1, SD 14-0), Oct. 16, 1985.

225. HR 3037. Agriculture Appropriations, Fiscal 1986. Cochran, R-Miss., motion to table (kill) the Gore, D-Tenn., amendment to require the Food and Drug Administration to complete a safety evaluation of sulfiting agents by June 1, 1986. Motion rejected 18-77: R 18-32; D 0-45 (ND 0-31, SD 0-14), Oct. 16, 1985. (The Gore amendment subsequently was adopted by voice vote.)

226. HR 3037. Agriculture Appropriations, Fiscal 1986. Passage of the bill to provide $24,854,204,000 in fiscal 1986 appropriations for programs for agriculture, rural development and related agencies. Passed 81-14: R 37-12; D 44-2 (ND 31-2, SD 13-0), Oct. 16, 1985. (The president had requested $33,233,217,000 in new budget authority.)

227. HR 3038. Department of Housing and Urban Development/Independent Agencies Appropriations, Fiscal 1986. Garn, R-Utah, motion to table (kill) the Durenberger, R-Minn., amendment to restore $570 million for general revenue sharing. Motion rejected 39-57: R 33-18; D 6-39 (ND 4-27, SD 2-12), Oct. 17, 1985. (The Durenberger amendment was subsequently adopted by voice vote.)

228. HR 3038. Department of Housing and Urban Development/Independent Agencies Appropriations, Fiscal 1986. Durenberger, R-Minn., motion to table (kill) the Garn, R-Utah, motion to reconsider the vote by which the Garn motion to table the Durenberger amendment, to restore $570 million for general revenue sharing, was rejected *(vote 227, above)*. Motion agreed to 57-39: R 17-33: D 40-6 (ND 28-4, SD 12-2), Oct. 17, 1985. (The Durenberger amendment was subsequently adopted by voice vote.)

229. HR 3038. Department of Housing and Urban Development/Independent Agencies Appropriations, Fiscal 1986. Proxmire, D-Wis., amendment to implement the Reagan administration's proposed moratorium on assisted housing. Rejected 44-52: R 34-16; D 10-36 (ND 4-28, SD 6-8), Oct. 17, 1985. A "yea" was a vote supporting the president's position.

230. HR 3038. Department of Housing and Urban Development/Independent Agencies Appropriations, Fiscal 1986. Gorton, R-Wash., amendment to strike $7 million earmarked for construction of a demonstration anaerobic wastewater treatment system at a pulp mill in Sitka, Alaska. Adopted 70-26: R 37-14; D 33-12 (ND 26-5, SD 7-7), Oct. 17, 1985.

CQ Senate Votes 231 - 238

Corresponding to Congressional Record Votes 231, 232, 233, 234, 235, 236, 237, 238

	231	232	233	234	235	236	237	238
ALABAMA								
Denton	Y	N	Y	Y	Y	Y	Y	N
Heflin	Y	N	Y	N	N	Y	N	N
ALASKA								
Murkowski	Y	N	Y	Y	Y	N	N	Y
Stevens	Y	N	Y	Y	?	?	N	Y
ARIZONA								
Goldwater	N	?	?	?	Y	Y	Y	Y
DeConcini	Y	N	N	Y	Y	N	N	Y
ARKANSAS								
Bumpers	N	N	Y	Y	N	N	N	Y
Pryor	Y	N	Y	Y	N	N	N	Y
CALIFORNIA								
Wilson	N	N	Y	Y	Y	N	N	Y
Cranston	?	?	?	?	Y	N	N	Y
COLORADO								
Armstrong	N	Y	Y	N	Y	Y	Y	N
Hart	Y	N	?	?	N	N	N	Y
CONNECTICUT								
Weicker	Y	Y	?	?	Y	N	N	Y
Dodd	Y	Y	Y	Y	N	N	N	Y
DELAWARE								
Roth	N	Y	Y	N	Y	Y	Y	N
Biden	Y	N	Y	Y	N	N	N	Y
FLORIDA								
Hawkins	Y	N	Y	Y	?	?	N	Y
Chiles	Y	Y	Y	Y	Y	N	N	Y
GEORGIA								
Mattingly	N	N	Y	Y	Y	Y	Y	Y
Nunn	Y	N	Y	Y	Y	N	Y	Y
HAWAII								
Inouye	Y	N	Y	Y	?	?	?	?
Matsunaga	Y	N	Y	Y	?	?	N	Y
IDAHO								
McClure	N	Y	Y	Y	Y	Y	Y	Y
Symms	N	Y	Y	N	?	?	Y	N
ILLINOIS								
Dixon	Y	N	?	+	N	N	N	Y
Simon	Y	N	Y	Y	N	N	N	Y
INDIANA								
Lugar	N	Y	Y	Y	Y	N	Y	Y
Quayle	N	Y	Y	Y	N	Y	Y	Y
IOWA								
Grassley	Y	N	Y	Y	Y	N	N	Y
Harkin	Y	N	Y	Y	N	N	N	Y
KANSAS								
Dole	N	Y	Y	Y	Y	N	N	Y
Kassebaum	N	Y	Y	Y	Y	N	N	Y
KENTUCKY								
McConnell	N	N	Y	Y	Y	N	N	Y
Ford	Y	N	Y	Y	N	N	N	Y
LOUISIANA								
Johnston	N	Y	Y	Y	Y	N	N	Y
Long	Y	Y	N	Y	?	?	Y	Y
MAINE								
Cohen	Y	N	Y	Y	N	N	N	Y
Mitchell	Y	N	Y	Y	N	N	N	Y
MARYLAND								
Mathias	?	?	?	?	?	?	?	?
Sarbanes	Y	N	Y	Y	N	N	N	Y
MASSACHUSETTS								
Kennedy	Y	N	?	?	?	?	N	Y
Kerry	Y	N	Y	Y	N	N	N	Y
MICHIGAN								
Levin	?	?	?	?	?	?	N	Y
Riegle	Y	N	Y	Y	N	N	N	Y
MINNESOTA								
Boschwitz	N	Y	Y	Y	Y	Y	N	Y
Durenberger	N	Y	Y	Y	N	N	N	Y
MISSISSIPPI								
Cochran	N	Y	Y	Y	Y	N	N	Y
Stennis	Y	?	?	?	Y	N	N	Y
MISSOURI								
Danforth	N	Y	Y	Y	Y	N	N	Y
Eagleton	Y	N	Y	Y	N	N	N	Y
MONTANA								
Baucus	Y	N	Y	Y	Y	N	N	Y
Melcher	Y	N	Y	Y	N	N	N	Y
NEBRASKA								
Exon	Y	Y	Y	N	Y	Y	Y	N
Zorinsky	Y	N	Y	N	N	Y	Y	N
NEVADA								
Hecht	N	Y	Y	Y	Y	Y	Y	Y
Laxalt	?	?	?	?	Y	N	Y	Y
NEW HAMPSHIRE								
Humphrey	N	Y	Y	N	Y	Y	Y	N
Rudman	N	Y	Y	Y	Y	N	N	Y
NEW JERSEY								
Bradley	Y	N	Y	Y	N	N	N	Y
Lautenberg	Y	N	Y	Y	N	N	N	Y
NEW MEXICO								
Domenici	N	Y	Y	Y	Y	N	Y	Y
Bingaman	N	N	Y	Y	Y	N	N	Y
NEW YORK								
D'Amato	Y	N	Y	Y	?	?	N	Y
Moynihan	Y	Y	Y	Y	?	?	N	Y
NORTH CAROLINA								
East	N	Y	Y	Y	Y	Y	Y	N
Helms	N	Y	Y	N	Y	Y	Y	N
NORTH DAKOTA								
Andrews	Y	N	Y	Y	?	?	N	Y
Burdick	Y	N	Y	Y	N	N	N	Y
OHIO								
Glenn	Y	N	Y	Y	N	N	N	Y
Metzenbaum	Y	N	Y	Y	N	N	N	Y
OKLAHOMA								
Nickles	N	N	Y	Y	Y	Y	Y	N
Boren	Y	N	Y	Y	Y	N	Y	Y
OREGON								
Hatfield	Y	Y	Y	Y	Y	N	N	Y
Packwood	N	Y	Y	Y	N	N	N	Y
PENNSYLVANIA								
Heinz	Y	N	Y	Y	N	N	N	Y
Specter	Y	N	Y	Y	N	N	N	Y
RHODE ISLAND								
Chafee	N	N	Y	Y	Y	N	N	Y
Pell	Y	N	+	+	-	-	N	Y
SOUTH CAROLINA								
Thurmond	N	N	Y	Y	Y	Y	Y	Y
Hollings	Y	N	Y	Y	N	N	N	Y
SOUTH DAKOTA								
Abdnor	Y	N	Y	Y	Y	N	N	Y
Pressler	N	N	Y	Y	?	?	N	Y
TENNESSEE								
Gore	Y	N	Y	Y	Y	N	N	Y
Sasser	Y	N	Y	Y	N	N	N	Y
TEXAS								
Gramm	N	Y	?	?	Y	Y	Y	N
Bentsen	N	Y	?	?	Y	N	N	Y
UTAH								
Garn	N	Y	Y	Y	Y	N	Y	N
Hatch	?	?	?	+	N	N	N	Y
VERMONT								
Stafford	N	Y	Y	Y	Y	N	N	Y
Leahy	N	Y	Y	Y	Y	N	N	Y
VIRGINIA								
Trible	N	N	Y	Y	Y	N	Y	Y
Warner	N	N	Y	Y	Y	N	Y	Y
WASHINGTON								
Evans	N	Y	Y	Y	Y	N	N	Y
Gorton	N	Y	Y	Y	Y	N	N	Y
WEST VIRGINIA								
Byrd	Y	N	Y	Y	N	N	N	Y
Rockefeller	Y	?	?	+	N	N	N	Y
WISCONSIN								
Kasten	Y	N	N	Y	Y	N	N	Y
Proxmire	N	Y	Y	N	Y	Y	Y	N
WYOMING								
Simpson	N	N	Y	Y	Y	N	Y	Y
Wallop	N	Y	Y	Y	Y	Y	Y	N

KEY

- Y Voted for (yea).
- # Paired for.
- + Announced for.
- N Voted against (nay).
- X Paired against.
- \- Announced against.
- P Voted "present."
- C Voted "present" to avoid possible conflict of interest.
- ? Did not vote or otherwise make a position known.

Democrats *Republicans*

ND - Northern Democrats SD - Southern Democrats (Southern states - Ala., Ark., Fla., Ga., Ky., La., Miss., N.C., Okla., S.C., Tenn., Texas, Va.)

231. HR 3038. Department of Housing and Urban Development/Independent Agencies Appropriations, Fiscal 1986. Garn, R-Utah, motion to table (kill) the Armstrong, R-Colo., amendment to eliminate the Urban Development Action Grant program. Motion agreed to 53-42: R 14-36; D 39-6 (ND 28-3, SD 11-3), Oct. 17, 1985. A "nay" was a vote supporting the president's position.

232. HR 3038. Department of Housing and Urban Development/Independent Agencies Appropriations, Fiscal 1986. Garn, R-Utah, motion to table (kill) the Murkowski, R-Alaska, amendment to restore $166 million for veterans' health care. Motion rejected 36-56: R 27-22; D 9-34 (ND 5-25, SD 4-9), Oct. 18, 1985. (The Murkowski amendment was subsequently adopted by voice vote.)

233. HR 3038. Department of Housing and Urban Development/Independent Agencies Appropriations, Fiscal 1986. Garn, R-Utah, amendment to restore $100 million for veterans' health care, and to cut $50 million from general revenue sharing; $10 million from Department of Housing and Urban Development management and administration; $10 million from the Environmental Protection Agency salaries and expenses; $10 million from the Federal Emergency Management Agency salaries and expenses; $15 million from the National Aeronautics and Space Administration research; $3 million from Veterans Administration (VA) medical administration; and $15 million from VA general operating expenses. Adopted 82-3: R 46-1; D 36-2 (ND 25-1, SD 11-1), Oct. 18, 1985.

234. HR 3038. Department of Housing and Urban Development/Independent Agencies Appropriations, Fiscal 1986. Passage of the bill to appropriate $55,810,733,381 in fiscal 1986 for the Department of Housing and Urban Development and 17 independent agencies, less a 1.1 percent reduction in non-defense discretionary items. Passed 76-9: R 42-5; D 34-4 (ND 23-3, SD 11-1), Oct. 18, 1985. (The president had requested $50,144,168,000 in new budget authority.)

235. HR 3424. Labor, Health and Human Services, Education Appropriations, Fiscal 1986. Weicker, R-Conn., motion to table (kill) the Dixon, D-Ill., amendment to add $122.5 million to funding for the Job Training Partnership Act, which helps retrain displaced workers. Motion agreed to 53-33: R 39-7; D 14-26 (ND 7-20, SD 7-6), Oct. 21, 1985.

236. HR 3424. Labor, Health and Human Services, Education Appropriations, Fiscal 1986. Proxmire, D-Wis., amendment to terminate the Work Incentive (WIN) Program providing jobs and training services for recipients of Aid to Families with Dependent Children. Rejected 20-66: R 16-30; D 4-36 (ND 3-24, SD 1-12), Oct. 21, 1985.

237. HR 3424. Labor, Health and Human Services, Education Appropriations, Fiscal 1986. Proxmire, D-Wis., amendment to cut 5 percent from all discretionary funding in the bill. Rejected 29-69: R 23-29; D 6-40 (ND 3-29, SD 3-11), Oct. 22, 1985.

238. HR 3424. Labor, Health and Human Services, Education Appropriations, Fiscal 1986. Passage of the bill to provide $105,098,691,000 in fiscal 1986 appropriations for the Departments of Labor, Health and Human Services, and Education, and related agencies. Passed 83-15: R 41-11; D 42-4 (ND 29-3, SD 13-1), Oct. 22, 1985. (The president had requested $100,143,-954,000 in new budget authority.)

Corresponding to Congressional Record Votes 239, 240, 241, 242, 243, 244, 245, 246

	239	240	241	242	243	244	245	246
ALABAMA								
Denton	Y	Y	Y	?	?	?	?	N
Heflin	Y	Y	Y	Y	N	Y	Y	N
ALASKA								
Murkowski	Y	Y	N	N	N	Y	Y	N
Stevens	Y	Y	Y	Y	Y	Y	Y	N
ARIZONA								
Goldwater	Y	Y	?	N	Y	N	Y	N
DeConcini	Y	Y	Y	Y	Y	Y	N	Y
ARKANSAS								
Bumpers	Y	Y	N	Y	Y	N	N	Y
Pryor	Y	Y	Y	Y	N	Y	Y	Y
CALIFORNIA								
Wilson	Y	Y	Y	N	N	Y	Y	Y
Cranston	Y	Y	N	Y	Y	N	Y	Y
COLORADO								
Armstrong	Y	Y	Y	N	N	?	Y	N
Hart	Y	Y	N	Y	N	N	Y	Y
CONNECTICUT								
Weicker	Y	N	Y	Y	N	Y	N	Y
Dodd	Y	Y	N	Y	Y	N	Y	Y
DELAWARE								
Roth	Y	N	Y	Y	Y	N	Y	Y
Biden	Y	Y	N	Y	Y	N	N	Y
FLORIDA								
Hawkins	Y	Y	Y	Y	N	Y	N	N
Chiles	Y	Y	Y	Y	Y	N	Y	N
GEORGIA								
Mattingly	Y	Y	Y	N	Y	N	N	Y
Nunn	Y	Y	Y	Y	Y	N	Y	N
HAWAII								
Inouye	?	?	?	?	?	?	?	?
Matsunaga	Y	Y	Y	Y	Y	N	Y	N
IDAHO								
McClure	Y	Y	Y	N	N	Y	Y	Y
Symms	Y	Y	Y	N	N	Y	Y	Y
ILLINOIS								
Dixon	Y	Y	N	Y	Y	N	N	Y
Simon	Y	N	N	Y	Y	N	N	Y
INDIANA								
Lugar	Y	N	Y	Y	N	Y	Y	N
Quayle	Y	Y	Y	Y	N	Y	N	N
IOWA								
Grassley	Y	Y	Y	Y	N	Y	Y	Y
Harkin	Y	Y	N	Y	Y	N	N	Y
KANSAS								
Dole	Y	Y	Y	N	N	Y	N	N
Kassebaum	Y	Y	Y	Y	Y	Y	Y	N
KENTUCKY								
McConnell	Y	Y	Y	N	N	Y	Y	N
Ford	Y	Y	Y	Y	N	Y	Y	N
LOUISIANA								
Johnston	Y	Y	Y	Y	N	Y	Y	N
Long	Y	Y	Y	Y	N	Y	Y	N
MAINE								
Cohen	Y	N	N	Y	Y	N	N	Y
Mitchell	Y	N	N	Y	Y	N	N	N
MARYLAND								
Mathias	?	?	?	Y	Y	N	N	Y
Sarbanes	Y	N	N	Y	Y	N	N	N
MASSACHUSETTS								
Kennedy	Y	N	N	Y	Y	N	Y	Y
Kerry	Y	Y	N	Y	Y	N	N	Y
MICHIGAN								
Levin	Y	N	N	Y	Y	N	Y	Y
Riegle	Y	Y	Y	Y	N	Y	N	Y
MINNESOTA								
Boschwitz	Y	N	Y	N	Y	N	Y	N
Durenberger	Y	Y	Y	Y	Y	N	N	Y
MISSISSIPPI								
Cochran	Y	Y	Y	Y	Y	Y	N	Y
Stennis	Y	Y	?	Y	N	Y	Y	Y
MISSOURI								
Danforth	Y	?	?	?	?	-	?	?
Eagleton	Y	?	?	?	?	?	?	?
MONTANA								
Baucus	Y	N	Y	Y	Y	N	N	Y
Melcher	Y	Y	Y	Y	N	Y	Y	Y
NEBRASKA								
Exon	Y	Y	Y	Y	N	Y	Y	Y
Zorinsky	Y	Y	Y	Y	Y	N	N	Y
NEVADA								
Hecht	Y	Y	Y	N	N	Y	Y	N
Laxalt	Y	Y	Y	N	?	?	Y	N
NEW HAMPSHIRE								
Humphrey	Y	Y	Y	N	Y	N	N	N
Rudman	Y	Y	Y	N	Y	N	Y	Y
NEW JERSEY								
Bradley	Y	N	N	Y	Y	N	N	Y
Lautenberg	Y	N	N	Y	Y	N	N	Y
NEW MEXICO								
Domenici	Y	Y	Y	N	Y	N	Y	N
Bingaman	Y	N	Y	Y	Y	N	Y	Y
NEW YORK								
D'Amato	Y	Y	N	Y	Y	Y	N	Y
Moynihan	Y	N	Y	Y	Y	N	Y	Y
NORTH CAROLINA								
East	Y	Y	Y	N	N	Y	Y	N
Helms	Y	Y	Y	N	N	Y	Y	N
NORTH DAKOTA								
Andrews	Y	Y	Y	Y	Y	Y	N	Y
Burdick	Y	N	N	Y	N	N	N	Y
OHIO								
Glenn	Y	N	N	Y	N	Y	N	Y
Metzenbaum	Y	Y	N	Y	Y	N	Y	Y
OKLAHOMA								
Nickles	Y	Y	Y	N	N	Y	Y	N
Boren	Y	Y	?	Y	N	Y	Y	Y
OREGON								
Hatfield	Y	N	?	Y	Y	Y	N	Y
Packwood	Y	Y	Y	Y	Y	N	N	N
PENNSYLVANIA								
Heinz	Y	Y	Y	Y	Y	N	Y	Y
Specter	Y	N	?	Y	Y	Y	N	Y
RHODE ISLAND								
Chafee	Y	N	Y	Y	Y	N	Y	Y
Pell	Y	N	N	Y	Y	N	N	Y
SOUTH CAROLINA								
Thurmond	Y	Y	Y	N	N	Y	Y	N
Hollings	Y	Y	Y	Y	Y	N	Y	Y
SOUTH DAKOTA								
Abdnor	Y	Y	N	Y	Y	Y	N	Y
Pressler	Y	Y	Y	Y	N	Y	N	Y
TENNESSEE								
Gore	Y	Y	Y	Y	N	Y	N	Y
Sasser	Y	Y	Y	Y	N	Y	N	Y
TEXAS								
Gramm	Y	Y	Y	N	N	Y	Y	N
Bentsen	Y	N	N	Y	Y	N	Y	N
UTAH								
Garn	Y	N	Y	N	N	Y	Y	N
Hatch	Y	N	Y	Y	N	Y	Y	N
VERMONT								
Stafford	Y	N	Y	Y	Y	N	Y	Y
Leahy	Y	N	N	Y	Y	N	Y	Y
VIRGINIA								
Trible	Y	Y	Y	N	N	Y	N	Y
Warner	Y	Y	Y	Y	N	Y	Y	Y
WASHINGTON								
Evans	Y	N	Y	Y	Y	N	Y	N
Gorton	Y	N	Y	Y	Y	N	Y	N
WEST VIRGINIA								
Byrd	Y	Y	Y	Y	Y	Y	N	Y
Rockefeller	Y	N	Y	Y	Y	N	Y	Y
WISCONSIN								
Kasten	Y	Y	Y	Y	Y	N	N	Y
Proxmire	Y	N	Y	N	Y	N	N	N
WYOMING								
Simpson	Y	Y	Y	N	Y	N	Y	N
Wallop	Y	Y	Y	N	N	Y	Y	Y

KEY

- Y Voted for (yea).
- # Paired for.
- + Announced for.
- N Voted against (nay).
- X Paired against.
- \- Announced against.
- P Voted "present."
- C Voted "present" to avoid possible conflict of interest.
- ? Did not vote or otherwise make a position known.

Democrats *Republicans*

ND - Northern Democrats SD - Southern Democrats (Southern states - Ala., Ark., Fla., Ga., Ky., La., Miss., N.C., Okla., S.C., Tenn., Texas, Va.)

239. Treaty Doc 98-5, 98th Cong, 1st Sess. International Wheat Agreement Extension. Adoption of the resolution of ratification to two treaty protocols for the further extension to June 30, 1986, of the 1971 Wheat Trade Convention and the 1980 Food Aid Convention, which constitute the 1971 International Wheat Agreement. Adopted 98-0: R 52-0; D 46-0 (ND 32-0, SD 14-0), Oct. 22, 1985. A two-thirds majority of those present and voting (66 in this case) is required for adoption of resolutions of ratification. (The protocols were signed on behalf of the United States on April 25, 1983.)

240. S 1730. Omnibus Budget Reconciliation, Fiscal 1986. Domenici, R-N.M., motion to table (kill) the Chafee, R-R.I., motion to waive the germaneness requirement contained in the 1974 Congressional Budget and Impoundment Control Act (PL 93-344) with respect to the Chafee amendment to raise taxes on tobacco products. Motion agreed to 66-30: R 38-13; D 28-17 (ND 15-16, SD 13-1), Oct. 22, 1985. (The chair subsequently upheld the Domenici, R-N.M., point of order that the Chafee amendment was not germane.)

241. S 1730. Omnibus Budget Reconciliation, Fiscal 1986. Dole, R-Kan., motion to table (kill) division 1 of the Mitchell, D-Maine, amendment, to delay for one year implementation of a provision in the bill mandating Medicare coverage for state and local government employees. Motion agreed to 66-25: R 44-4; D 22-21 (ND 12-19, SD 10-2), Oct. 22, 1985. (Division 2 of the Mitchell amendment, to increase the per-pack tax on cigarettes by 4 cents, was subsequently rejected by voice vote.)

242. HR 3244. Transportation Appropriations, Fiscal 1986. Andrews, R-N.D., motion to table (kill) the Armstrong, R-Colo., amendment to eliminate funding for Amtrak. Motion agreed to 71-25: R 27-24; D 44-1 (ND 30-1, SD 14-0), Oct. 23, 1985.

243. HR 3244. Transportation Appropriations, Fiscal 1986. Judgment of the Senate whether the Evans, R-Wash., amendment, to deny automakers credit for meeting automobile fuel-efficiency standards that have been lowered by the Department of Transportation, was germane. Ruled germane 56-39: R 26-24; D 30-15 (ND 25-6, SD 5-9), Oct. 23, 1985. (The Evans amendment was subsequently adopted by voice vote.)

244. HR 3244. Transportation Appropriations, Fiscal 1986. Andrews, R-N.D., motion to table (kill) the Evans, R-Wash., amendment to deny automakers credit for meeting automobile fuel-efficiency standards that have been lowered by the Department of Transportation. Motion rejected 46-48: R 31-18; D 15-30 (ND 6-25, SD 9-5), Oct. 23, 1985. (The Evans amendment was subsequently adopted by voice vote.) A "yea" was a vote supporting the president's position.

245. HR 3244. Transportation Appropriations, Fiscal 1986. Domenici, R-N.M., amendment to add $16.26 million for road improvements near a nuclear-waste storage site in New Mexico. Adopted 56-40: R 32-19; D 24-21 (ND 13-18, SD 11-3), Oct. 23, 1985.

246. HR 3244. Transportation Appropriations, Fiscal 1986. Andrews, R-N.D., motion to table (kill) the Kassebaum, R-Kan., amendment to add funds for the Federal Aviation Administration and the Coast Guard, and reduce funding for other programs. Motion agreed to 59-38: R 25-27; D 34-11 (ND 27-4, SD 7-7), Oct. 23, 1985.

CQ Senate Votes 247 - 254

Corresponding to Congressional Record Votes 247, 248, 249, 250, 251, 252, 253, 254

	247	248	249	250	251	252	253	254
ALABAMA								
Denton	N	?	N	Y	N	Y	Y	Y
Heflin	N	Y	N	Y	N	Y	+	Y
ALASKA								
Murkowski	Y	Y	?	Y	N	Y	Y	Y
Stevens	Y	?	N	Y	#	X	X	Y
ARIZONA								
Goldwater	Y	N	Y	Y	Y	N	N	Y
DeConcini	Y	Y	N	Y	N	Y	Y	Y
ARKANSAS								
Bumpers	Y	Y	N	Y	N	Y	Y	Y
Pryor	Y	Y	N	Y	N	Y	Y	Y
CALIFORNIA								
Wilson	Y	Y	N	Y	N	Y	N	Y
Cranston	Y	Y	Y	Y	Y	N	N	Y
COLORADO								
Armstrong	N	Y	N	Y	Y	N	N	Y
Hart	Y	?	N	Y	Y	N	N	Y
CONNECTICUT								
Weicker	Y	N	Y	Y	?	Y	Y	Y
Dodd	Y	?	Y	N	N	Y	Y	Y
DELAWARE								
Roth	Y	Y	N	Y	N	Y	Y	Y
Biden	Y	Y	N	Y	N	Y	Y	Y
FLORIDA								
Hawkins	Y	Y	N	Y	N	Y	Y	Y
Chiles	N	Y	N	Y	Y	N	N	Y
GEORGIA								
Mattingly	Y	Y	N	Y	N	Y	Y	Y
Nunn	Y	Y	N	Y	N	Y	Y	Y
HAWAII								
Inouye	?	Y	N	Y	N	Y	N	Y
Matsunaga	Y	Y	Y	Y	Y	N	N	Y
IDAHO								
McClure	Y	Y	?	Y	Y	N	N	Y
Symms	Y	Y	?	Y	Y	N	N	Y
ILLINOIS								
Dixon	Y	Y	N	Y	N	Y	Y	Y
Simon	Y	Y	Y	Y	N	Y	Y	?
INDIANA								
Lugar	Y	Y	N	Y	Y	N	N	Y
Quayle	Y	?	N	Y	Y	N	N	Y
IOWA								
Grassley	Y	Y	N	Y	Y	N	N	Y
Harkin	Y	Y	Y	Y	N	Y	N	Y
KANSAS								
Dole	Y	Y	N	Y	Y	N	N	Y
Kassebaum	N	Y	N	Y	Y	N	N	Y
KENTUCKY								
McConnell	Y	Y	N	Y	N	Y	Y	Y
Ford	Y	Y	N	Y	N	Y	Y	Y
LOUISIANA								
Johnston	Y	Y	N	Y	N	Y	Y	Y
Long	Y	Y	N	Y	Y	N	Y	Y
MAINE								
Cohen	N	N	N	Y	N	Y	Y	Y
Mitchell	N	Y	N	Y	N	Y	Y	Y
MARYLAND								
Mathias	Y	?	Y	Y	Y	N	Y	Y
Sarbanes	Y	Y	Y	Y	N	Y	Y	Y
MASSACHUSETTS								
Kennedy	Y	Y	Y	Y	N	Y	Y	Y
Kerry	Y	Y	Y	Y	N	Y	Y	Y
MICHIGAN								
Levin	Y	Y	N	Y	N	Y	Y	Y
Riegle	Y	Y	N	Y	N	Y	Y	Y
MINNESOTA								
Boschwitz	Y	?	N	Y	Y	N	N	Y
Durenberger	Y	Y	N	Y	Y	N	N	Y
MISSISSIPPI								
Cochran	Y	Y	N	Y	N	Y	Y	Y
Stennis	Y	?	Y	Y	N	Y	Y	?
MISSOURI								
Danforth	?	Y	N	Y	Y	N	N	Y
Eagleton	?	Y	N	Y	X	#	#	?
MONTANA								
Baucus	Y	Y	Y	Y	Y	N	N	Y
Melcher	Y	?	N	Y	N	Y	Y	Y
NEBRASKA								
Exon	Y	Y	N	Y	Y	N	N	Y
Zorinsky	Y	Y	N	Y	Y	N	N	Y
NEVADA								
Hecht	Y	Y	N	Y	Y	N	N	Y
Laxalt	Y	Y	N	Y	N	Y	Y	Y
NEW HAMPSHIRE								
Humphrey	N	Y	N	Y	?	N	N	Y
Rudman	Y	Y	N	Y	N	Y	Y	Y
NEW JERSEY								
Bradley	Y	?	?	?	?	?	N	Y
Lautenberg	Y	Y	?	Y	N	Y	Y	Y
NEW MEXICO								
Domenici	Y	Y	N	Y	Y	N	N	Y
Bingaman	Y	Y	N	Y	N	Y	N	Y
NEW YORK								
D'Amato	Y	Y	N	Y	N	Y	Y	Y
Moynihan	Y	Y	Y	Y	N	Y	Y	Y
NORTH CAROLINA								
East	Y	Y	N	Y	N	Y	Y	Y
Helms	N	Y	N	Y	N	Y	Y	Y
NORTH DAKOTA								
Andrews	Y	Y	Y	Y	Y	N	N	Y
Burdick	Y	Y	Y	Y	N	Y	N	Y
OHIO								
Glenn	Y	Y	N	Y	N	Y	Y	Y
Metzenbaum	Y	Y	Y	Y	N	Y	Y	Y
OKLAHOMA								
Nickles	N	Y	N	Y	Y	N	N	Y
Boren	Y	Y	N	Y	Y	N	N	Y
OREGON								
Hatfield	Y	Y	Y	?	+	-	-	?
Packwood	Y	Y	N	Y	Y	N	N	Y
PENNSYLVANIA								
Heinz	Y	Y	N	Y	N	Y	Y	Y
Specter	Y	Y	N	Y	N	Y	Y	Y
RHODE ISLAND								
Chafee	Y	Y	N	Y	Y	N	N	Y
Pell	Y	Y	N	Y	N	Y	Y	Y
SOUTH CAROLINA								
Thurmond	Y	Y	N	Y	N	Y	Y	Y
Hollings	Y	Y	N	Y	N	Y	Y	Y
SOUTH DAKOTA								
Abdnor	Y	Y	N	Y	Y	N	N	Y
Pressler	Y	Y	N	Y	Y	N	N	Y
TENNESSEE								
Gore	Y	Y	Y	Y	N	Y	Y	Y
Sasser	Y	Y	N	Y	N	Y	Y	Y
TEXAS								
Gramm	N	Y	N	Y	Y	N	N	Y
Bentsen	Y	Y	N	Y	Y	N	Y	Y
UTAH								
Garn	Y	Y	N	Y	Y	N	N	Y
Hatch	Y	Y	N	Y	N	Y	Y	Y
VERMONT								
Stafford	Y	Y	N	Y	Y	N	N	Y
Leahy	Y	Y	Y	Y	N	Y	Y	Y
VIRGINIA								
Trible	Y	Y	N	Y	?	Y	Y	Y
Warner	Y	Y	N	Y	N	Y	Y	Y
WASHINGTON								
Evans	Y	?	N	Y	Y	N	N	Y
Gorton	N	Y	N	Y	Y	N	N	Y
WEST VIRGINIA								
Byrd	Y	Y	N	Y	N	Y	Y	Y
Rockefeller	Y	Y	N	Y	N	Y	Y	Y
WISCONSIN								
Kasten	Y	Y	N	Y	N	Y	Y	Y
Proxmire	N	Y	Y	Y	N	Y	Y	Y
WYOMING								
Simpson	Y	Y	N	Y	Y	N	N	Y
Wallop	Y	N	N	Y	Y	N	N	Y

KEY

- Y Voted for (yea).
- # Paired for.
- + Announced for.
- N Voted against (nay).
- X Paired against.
- \- Announced against.
- P Voted "present."
- C Voted "present" to avoid possible conflict of interest.
- ? Did not vote or otherwise make a position known.

Democrats ***Republicans***

ND - Northern Democrats SD - Southern Democrats (Southern states - Ala., Ark., Fla., Ga., Ky., La., Miss., N.C., Okla., S.C., Tenn., Texas, Va.)

247. HR 3244. Transportation Appropriations, Fiscal 1986. Passage of the bill to appropriate $9,877,233,488 for the Department of Transportation and related agencies in fiscal 1986. Passed 84-13: R 43-9; D 41-4 (ND 29-2, SD 12-2), Oct. 23, 1985. (The president had requested $7,888,219,569 in new budget authority.)

248. Procedural Motion. Dole, R-Kan., motion to instruct the sergeant-at-arms to request the attendance of absent senators. Motion agreed to 85-4: R 43-4; D 42-0 (ND 29-0, SD 13-0), Oct. 24, 1985.

249. HR 2965. Commerce, Justice, State and the Judiciary Appropriations, Fiscal 1986. Hatfield, R-Ore., amendment to bar the use of funds under the bill for U.S. payments to international organizations unless the United States rejoined and accepted the compulsory jurisdiction of the International Court of Justice (World Court). Rejected 21-74: R 5-45; D 16-29 (ND 14-17, SD 2-12), Oct. 24, 1985. A "nay" was a vote supporting the president's position.

250. S J Res 228. Jordan Arms Sales. Passage of the joint resolution to prevent the sale of advanced weapons to Jordan prior to March 1, 1986, unless Jordan and Israel have engaged in "direct and meaningful" peace negotiations. Passed 97-1: R 52-0; D 45-1 (ND 31-1, SD 14-0), Oct. 24, 1985.

251. S 1730. Omnibus Budget Reconciliation, Fiscal 1986. Domenici, R-N.M., motion to table (kill) the Hollings, D-S.C., motion to waive the germaneness requirement contained in the 1974 Congressional Budget and Impoundment Control Act (PL 93-344) with respect to the Hollings amendment. Motion rejected 38-55: R 28-20; D 10-35 (ND 6-25, SD 4-10), Oct. 24, 1985. (The Hollings amendment would establish a new system of quotas on textile imports and limit shoe imports to 60 percent of the domestic market over the next eight years.)

252. S 1730. Omnibus Budget Reconciliation, Fiscal 1986. Hollings, D-S.C., motion to waive the germaneness requirement contained in the 1974 Congressional Budget and Impoundment Control Act (PL 93-344) with respect to the Hollings amendment. Motion agreed to 57-39: R 22-29; D 35-10 (ND 25-6, SD 10-4), Oct. 24, 1985. (The Hollings amendment would establish a new system of quotas on textile imports and limit shoe imports to 60 percent of the domestic market over the next eight years.)

253. S 1730. Omnibus Budget Reconciliation, Fiscal 1986. Thurmond, R-S.C., perfecting amendment to the Hollings, D-S.C., amendment to establish a new system of quotas on textile imports and to limit shoe imports to 60 percent of the domestic market over the next eight years. Adopted 54-42: R 22-29; D 32-13 (ND 21-11, SD 11-2), Oct. 24, 1985. A "nay" was a vote supporting the president's position.

254. S 1730. Omnibus Budget Reconciliation, Fiscal 1986. Byrd, D-W.Va., amendment to require, in future years, a three-fifths vote of the Senate to override rulings that provisions of a budget reconciliation bill are extraneous or not germane. Adopted 96-0: R 52-0; D 44-0 (ND 31-0, SD 13-0), Oct. 24, 1985.

	255	256	257	258	259	260	261	262
ALABAMA								
Denton	N	?	Y	Y	Y	Y	Y	Y
Heflin	N	Y	Y	Y	Y	Y	Y	Y
ALASKA								
Murkowski	N	Y	Y	Y	Y	Y	Y	Y
Stevens	Y	?	?	?	Y	Y	Y	Y
ARIZONA								
Goldwater	?	?	?	?	Y	Y	Y	?
DeConcini	N	Y	Y	Y	Y	Y	N	Y
ARKANSAS								
Bumpers	Y	Y	Y	Y	Y	N	N	Y
Pryor	Y	Y	Y	Y	Y	Y	N	Y
CALIFORNIA								
Wilson	N	?	?	?	Y	Y	Y	Y
Cranston	Y	?	?	?	Y	Y	Y	Y
COLORADO								
Armstrong	N	?	?	?	N	N	Y	Y
Hart	Y	Y	Y	N	Y	Y	N	Y
CONNECTICUT								
Weicker	Y	Y	Y	?	Y	Y	Y	Y
Dodd	Y	Y	Y	N	Y	Y	Y	Y
DELAWARE								
Roth	Y	Y	Y	Y	N	N	Y	N
Biden	N	Y	N	Y	Y	Y	N	Y
FLORIDA								
Hawkins	N	Y	Y	Y	Y	N	N	Y
Chiles	N	?	?	?	Y	Y	Y	Y
GEORGIA								
Mattingly	N	Y	Y	Y	Y	Y	Y	Y
Nunn	Y	Y	Y	Y	Y	Y	Y	Y
HAWAII								
Inouye	Y	Y	Y	Y	Y	Y	Y	Y
Matsunaga	Y	Y	Y	Y	Y	Y	Y	Y
IDAHO								
McClure	N	Y	Y	Y	N	N	N	Y
Symms	N	Y	Y	Y	N	N	Y	Y
ILLINOIS								
Dixon	N	Y	Y	Y	N	N	N	N
Simon	?	Y	Y	N	Y	Y	N	N
INDIANA								
Lugar	N	Y	Y	N	N	N	N	N
Quayle	N	Y	Y	Y	N	N	Y	N
IOWA								
Grassley	N	Y	Y	Y	N	N	N	N
Harkin	Y	Y	Y	Y	Y	Y	N	N
KANSAS								
Dole	N	Y	Y	Y	N	N	Y	N
Kassebaum	Y	Y	Y	Y	N	N	Y	Y
KENTUCKY								
McConnell	?	Y	Y	Y	N	N	Y	Y
Ford	N	Y	Y	Y	Y	Y	N	Y
LOUISIANA								
Johnston	N	Y	Y	Y	Y	Y	Y	Y
Long	N	Y	Y	?	Y	Y	Y	Y
MAINE								
Cohen	Y	Y	Y	Y	Y	Y	Y	Y
Mitchell	N	Y	Y	Y	Y	Y	Y	Y
MARYLAND								
Mathias	Y	?	?	?	Y	Y	Y	Y
Sarbanes	Y	Y	Y	N	Y	Y	Y	Y
MASSACHUSETTS								
Kennedy	Y	?	?	?	Y	Y	Y	Y
Kerry	Y	Y	Y	Y	Y	Y	N	Y
MICHIGAN								
Levin	Y	Y	Y	Y	N	Y	Y	N
Riegle	Y	Y	Y	Y	N	Y	N	N
MINNESOTA								
Boschwitz	N	Y	Y	Y	N	N	N	N
Durenberger	N	Y	Y	Y	N	N	N	N
MISSISSIPPI								
Cochran	Y	Y	Y	?	Y	Y	Y	Y
Stennis	?	Y	Y	?	Y	Y	?	?
MISSOURI								
Danforth	N	Y	Y	N	N	N	N	N
Eagleton	?	Y	Y	N	Y	Y	Y	N
MONTANA								
Baucus	Y	Y	Y	Y	Y	Y	N	Y
Melcher	N	Y	Y	Y	Y	Y	N	Y
NEBRASKA								
Exon	N	Y	Y	Y	Y	Y	N	Y
Zorinsky	N	Y	Y	Y	Y	Y	N	Y
NEVADA								
Hecht	N	Y	Y	Y	Y	Y	Y	Y
Laxalt	N	Y	Y	?	Y	Y	Y	Y
NEW HAMPSHIRE								
Humphrey	N	Y	Y	Y	N	N	Y	Y
Rudman	Y	Y	Y	?	Y	N	Y	Y
NEW JERSEY								
Bradley	Y	Y	N	N	Y	Y	N	Y
Lautenberg	Y	Y	N	?	Y	Y	Y	Y
NEW MEXICO								
Domenici	N	Y	Y	Y	Y	N	Y	Y
Bingaman	Y	Y	Y	Y	Y	Y	Y	Y
NEW YORK								
D'Amato	N	Y	Y	Y	Y	Y	Y	Y
Moynihan	Y	Y	Y	N	Y	Y	Y	+
NORTH CAROLINA								
East	?	Y	Y	Y	N	N	Y	?
Helms	N	Y	Y	Y	N	N	Y	N
NORTH DAKOTA								
Andrews	N	Y	Y	Y	Y	Y	N	Y
Burdick	Y	Y	Y	Y	Y	Y	N	Y
OHIO								
Glenn	Y	Y	Y	Y	Y	Y	Y	N
Metzenbaum	Y	Y	Y	Y	Y	Y	N	N
OKLAHOMA								
Nickles	N	Y	Y	Y	N	N	N	N
Boren	N	Y	Y	Y	N	N	N	Y
OREGON								
Hatfield	?	?	?	?	Y	Y	Y	Y
Packwood	Y	?	?	?	Y	Y	Y	Y
PENNSYLVANIA								
Heinz	Y	Y	N	Y	Y	Y	Y	Y
Specter	Y	Y	Y	Y	Y	Y	Y	?
RHODE ISLAND								
Chafee	Y	Y	Y	N	N	N	Y	Y
Pell	Y	Y	Y	N	Y	Y	Y	Y
SOUTH CAROLINA								
Thurmond	N	Y	Y	Y	N	N	Y	Y
Hollings	Y	Y	Y	Y	Y	Y	Y	Y
SOUTH DAKOTA								
Abdnor	N	Y	Y	Y	N	N	N	?
Pressler	?	Y	Y	?	N	N	N	N
TENNESSEE								
Gore	N	Y	Y	N	Y	Y	N	Y
Sasser	Y	Y	Y	Y	Y	Y	N	Y
TEXAS								
Gramm	N	Y	Y	Y	N	N	Y	Y
Bentsen	Y	?	?	?	Y	Y	Y	Y
UTAH								
Garn	N	Y	Y	Y	Y	N	Y	Y
Hatch	N	Y	Y	Y	Y	N	Y	Y
VERMONT								
Stafford	Y	Y	Y	Y	Y	Y	Y	Y
Leahy	Y	Y	Y	?	Y	Y	N	Y
VIRGINIA								
Trible	N	Y	Y	Y	Y	Y	Y	Y
Warner	Y	Y	Y	Y	Y	Y	Y	Y
WASHINGTON								
Evans	Y	Y	Y	N	Y	Y	Y	Y
Gorton	Y	Y	Y	Y	Y	Y	Y	Y
WEST VIRGINIA								
Byrd	Y	Y	Y	Y	Y	Y	Y	Y
Rockefeller	Y	?	?	?	Y	Y	Y	Y
WISCONSIN								
Kasten	N	Y	Y	Y	N	N	N	N
Proxmire	N	Y	Y	Y	N	N	N	N
WYOMING								
Simpson	Y	Y	Y	Y	N	N	N	N
Wallop	N	?	?	?	N	N	?	-

KEY

- Y Voted for (yea).
- # Paired for.
- + Announced for.
- N Voted against (nay).
- X Paired against.
- - Announced against.
- P Voted "present."
- C Voted "present" to avoid possible conflict of interest.
- ? Did not vote or otherwise make a position known.

Democrats *Republicans*

ND - Northern Democrats SD - Southern Democrats (Southern states - Ala., Ark., Fla., Ga., Ky., La., Miss., N.C., Okla., S.C., Tenn., Texas, Va.)

255. HR 2965. Commerce, Justice, State and the Judiciary Appropriations, Fiscal 1986. Rudman, R-N.H., motion to table (kill) the Helms, R-N.C., amendment to prohibit the use of funds for the federal prison system to perform abortions on pregnant inmates, except when the mother's life was in danger. Motion rejected 46-46: R 17-31; D 29-15 (ND 23-8, SD 6-7), Oct. 24, 1985.

256. S 1714. Farm Programs Reauthorization, Fiscal 1986-89. Dixon, D-Ill., amendment to permit the transfer of agricultural products from one licensed warehouse to another warehouse for continued storage. Adopted 86-0: R 44-0; D 42-0 (ND 30-0, SD 12-0), Oct. 25, 1985.

257. S 1714. Farm Programs Reauthorization, Fiscal 1986-89. Mattingly, R-Ga., amendment to make surplus Commodity Credit Corporation stocks available to the secretary of energy for barter purposes to enhance the effort of adding to the Strategic Petroleum Reserve and stimulating foreign purchases of current-crop U.S. agricultural products. Adopted 83-4: R 44-1; D 39-3 (ND 27-3, SD 12-0), Oct. 25, 1985.

258. S 1714. Farm Programs Reauthorization, Fiscal 1986-89. Symms, R-Idaho, amendment to require U.S. representatives to multilateral development agencies to oppose assistance by such institutions for the production of agricultural commodities in competition with U.S.-produced agricultural commodities. Adopted 65-13: R 36-4; D 29-9 (ND 20-8, SD 9-1), Oct. 25, 1985.

259. S 1714. Farm Programs Reauthorization, Fiscal 1986-89. Stevens, R-Alaska, amendment to the Inouye, D-Hawaii, perfecting amendment to the Stevens amendment, to exempt government-generated commercial agricultural exports from cargo preference requirements that half of such exports be carried on U.S.-flag vessels, and to require that 75 percent of government-donated exports be covered by cargo preference. Adopted 70-30: R 28-25; D 42-5 (ND 29-4, SD 13-1), Oct. 29, 1985. (The Inouye amendment was subsequently withdrawn by unanimous consent.)

260. S 1714. Farm Programs Reauthorization, Fiscal 1986-89. Cochran, R-Miss., motion to table (kill) the Boschwitz, R-Minn., amendment to the Inouye, D-Hawaii, perfecting amendment to the Stevens, R-Alaska, amendment, to specify criteria for the determination of fair and reasonable rates to be charged by U.S.-flag commercial vessels. Motion agreed to 66-34: R 23-30; D 43-4 (ND 31-2, SD 12-2), Oct. 29, 1985. (The Inouye amendment was subsequently withdrawn by unanimous consent.)

261. S 1714. Farm Programs Reauthorization, Fiscal 1986-89. Cochran, R-Miss., motion to table (kill) the Harkin, D-Iowa, amendment to the Inouye, D-Hawaii, perfecting amendment to the Stevens, R-Alaska, amendment, to transfer increased costs incurred by revising cargo preference requirements from the Department of Agriculture to the Department of Defense. Motion agreed to 62-36: R 39-13; D 23-23 (ND 16-17, SD 7-6), Oct. 29, 1985. (The Inouye amendment was subsequently withdrawn by unanimous consent.)

262. S 1714. Farm Programs Reauthorization, Fiscal 1986-89. Cochran, R-Miss., motion to table (kill) the Dixon, D-Ill., amendment to the Inouye, D-Hawaii, perfecting amendment to the Stevens, R-Alaska, amendment, to establish the National Advisory Commission on Agricultural Export Transportation Policy, and require the secretaries of agriculture and transportation in administering cargo preference laws to preserve the average share between 1980 and 1983 of government-donated cargoes shipped out of the four coastal ranges. Motion agreed to 71-22: R 35-13; D 36-9 (ND 23-9, SD 13-0), Oct. 29, 1985. (The Inouye amendment was subsequently withdrawn by unanimous consent.)

CQ Senate Votes 263 - 270

Corresponding to Congressional Record Votes 263, 264, 265, 266, 267, 268, 269, 270

	263	264	265	266	267	268	269	270
ALABAMA								
Denton	Y	Y	Y	N	N	Y	N	N
Heflin	Y	Y	Y	N	Y	Y	N	Y
ALASKA								
Murkowski	Y	Y	Y	Y	N	Y	Y	Y
Stevens	Y	Y	Y	Y	N	Y	Y	Y
ARIZONA								
Goldwater	Y	Y	Y	Y	?	?	N	Y
DeConcini	Y	Y	Y	N	Y	N	Y	N
ARKANSAS								
Bumpers	Y	Y	Y	N	Y	Y	N	N
Pryor	Y	Y	Y	N	Y	Y	Y	N
CALIFORNIA								
Wilson	Y	Y	Y	Y	Y	Y	N	N
Cranston	Y	Y	Y	Y	Y	Y	Y	N
COLORADO								
Armstrong	N	N	N	Y	Y	Y	Y	Y
Hart	Y	Y	Y	N	Y	Y	N	Y
CONNECTICUT								
Weicker	Y	Y	Y	Y	N	Y	Y	N
Dodd	Y	Y	Y	Y	Y	Y	Y	N
DELAWARE								
Roth	N	N	N	Y	N	Y	N	N
Biden	?	Y	Y	N	Y	Y	N	N
FLORIDA								
Hawkins	Y	Y	Y	Y	N	Y	N	N
Chiles	Y	Y	Y	N	Y	Y	N	N
GEORGIA								
Mattingly	Y	Y	Y	Y	N	Y	N	N
Nunn	?	Y	Y	N	Y	Y	N	Y
HAWAII								
Inouye	Y	Y	Y	N	Y	Y	Y	Y
Matsunaga	Y	Y	Y	N	Y	Y	Y	Y
IDAHO								
McClure	Y	Y	Y	Y	Y	Y	N	Y
Symms	Y	Y	Y	Y	Y	Y	N	Y
ILLINOIS								
Dixon	N	N	N	N	Y	Y	Y	Y
Simon	N	N	N	N	Y	N	Y	Y
INDIANA								
Lugar	N	N	N	Y	N	Y	Y	N
Quayle	N	N	N	Y	N	Y	Y	N
IOWA								
Grassley	N	Y	Y	N	Y	Y	Y	N
Harkin	Y	Y	Y	N	Y	Y	Y	N
KANSAS								
Dole	Y	Y	Y	Y	Y	Y	Y	N
Kassebaum	N	N	Y	N	Y	Y	Y	N
KENTUCKY								
McConnell	N	N	N	Y	N	Y	Y	Y
Ford	Y	Y	Y	N	Y	Y	Y	Y
LOUISIANA								
Johnston	Y	Y	Y	N	Y	Y	N	Y
Long	Y	Y	Y	N	Y	Y	N	Y
MAINE								
Cohen	Y	Y	Y	Y	N	Y	N	N
Mitchell	Y	Y	Y	Y	N	Y	Y	N
MARYLAND								
Mathias	Y	Y	Y	?	N	Y	N	Y
Sarbanes	Y	Y	Y	N	Y	Y	N	N
MASSACHUSETTS								
Kennedy	Y	Y	Y	N	Y	Y	N	N
Kerry	Y	Y	Y	N	Y	Y	N	N
MICHIGAN								
Levin	N	N	N	N	Y	Y	Y	N
Riegle	N	N	?	N	Y	Y	Y	N
MINNESOTA								
Boschwitz	N	N	N	N	Y	Y	Y	N
Durenberger	N	N	N	N	Y	Y	Y	N
MISSISSIPPI								
Cochran	Y	Y	Y	Y	N	Y	N	N
Stennis	Y	?	?	N	?	?	?	?
MISSOURI								
Danforth	N	N	N	N	N	Y	Y	N
Eagleton	Y	N	Y	N	Y	Y	Y	N
MONTANA								
Baucus	Y	Y	Y	N	Y	Y	Y	N
Melcher	Y	Y	Y	N	Y	Y	Y	N
NEBRASKA								
Exon	Y	Y	Y	N	Y	Y	N	Y
Zorinsky	Y	Y	Y	N	Y	Y	N	Y
NEVADA								
Hecht	Y	Y	Y	Y	N	Y	N	Y
Laxalt	Y	Y	?	Y	N	Y	?	Y
NEW HAMPSHIRE								
Humphrey	N	N	Y	Y	N	Y	N	N
Rudman	Y	Y	Y	Y	N	Y	N	N
NEW JERSEY								
Bradley	Y	Y	Y	Y	Y	Y	?	N
Lautenberg	Y	Y	Y	Y	Y	Y	N	N
NEW MEXICO								
Domenici	Y	Y	Y	Y	N	Y	Y	Y
Bingaman	Y	Y	Y	N	Y	Y	Y	N
NEW YORK								
D'Amato	Y	Y	Y	Y	N	Y	Y	N
Moynihan	Y	N	Y	Y	Y	Y	Y	N
NORTH CAROLINA								
East	Y	N	N	Y	N	Y	N	N
Helms	N	N	N	Y	N	Y	N	N
NORTH DAKOTA								
Andrews	Y	Y	Y	N	Y	Y	Y	Y
Burdick	Y	Y	Y	N	Y	Y	N	Y
OHIO								
Glenn	N	N	N	N	Y	Y	Y	N
Metzenbaum	N	N	Y	N	Y	Y	Y	N
OKLAHOMA								
Nickles	N	N	N	N	Y	Y	Y	N
Boren	N	N	N	N	Y	Y	Y	N
OREGON								
Hatfield	Y	Y	Y	Y	N	Y	N	N
Packwood	Y	Y	Y	Y	N	Y	N	N
PENNSYLVANIA								
Heinz	Y	Y	Y	Y	N	Y	Y	Y
Specter	Y	Y	Y	Y	N	Y	Y	Y
RHODE ISLAND								
Chafee	N	N	Y	Y	N	Y	Y	N
Pell	Y	Y	Y	Y	Y	Y	Y	Y
SOUTH CAROLINA								
Thurmond	Y	Y	N	Y	N	Y	Y	Y
Hollings	Y	Y	Y	N	Y	Y	N	N
SOUTH DAKOTA								
Abdnor	N	N	N	N	N	Y	Y	Y
Pressler	N	N	N	N	N	Y	?	Y
TENNESSEE								
Gore	Y	Y	Y	N	Y	Y	N	Y
Sasser	Y	Y	Y	N	Y	Y	N	Y
TEXAS								
Gramm	Y	Y	Y	Y	N	Y	N	N
Bentsen	Y	Y	Y	N	Y	Y	N	Y
UTAH								
Garn	Y	Y	Y	Y	N	Y	Y	Y
Hatch	Y	Y	Y	Y	N	Y	Y	Y
VERMONT								
Stafford	Y	Y	Y	Y	N	Y	Y	N
Leahy	Y	Y	Y	N	Y	Y	N	N
VIRGINIA								
Trible	Y	Y	?	Y	N	Y	N	Y
Warner	Y	Y	Y	Y	N	Y	N	Y
WASHINGTON								
Evans	Y	Y	Y	Y	Y	Y	N	N
Gorton	Y	Y	Y	N	Y	Y	N	N
WEST VIRGINIA								
Byrd	Y	Y	Y	N	Y	Y	Y	Y
Rockefeller	Y	Y	Y	N	Y	Y	Y	Y
WISCONSIN								
Kasten	N	N	N	N	N	Y	Y	N
Proxmire	N	N	N	Y	N	Y	Y	N
WYOMING								
Simpson	N	N	N	Y	N	Y	Y	N
Wallop	N	N	N	Y	N	Y	Y	Y

KEY

- Y Voted for (yea).
- # Paired for.
- + Announced for.
- N Voted against (nay).
- X Paired against.
- - Announced against.
- P Voted "present."
- C Voted "present" to avoid possible conflict of interest.
- ? Did not vote or otherwise make a position known.

Democrats *Republicans*

ND - Northern Democrats SD - Southern Democrats (Southern states - Ala., Ark., Fla., Ga., Ky., La., Miss., N.C., Okla., S.C., Tenn., Texas, Va.)

263. S 1714. Farm Programs Reauthorization, Fiscal 1986-89. Cochran, R-Miss., motion to table (kill) the Dixon, D-Ill., amendment to the Inouye, D-Hawaii, perfecting amendment to the Stevens, R-Alaska, amendment, to require that agricultural commodities shipped under cargo preference requirements be shipped at the lowest landed cost. Motion agreed to 71-27: R 34-19; D 37-8 (ND 25-7, SD 12-1), Oct. 30, 1985. (The Inouye amendment was subsequently withdrawn by unanimous consent.)

264. S 1714. Farm Programs Reauthorization, Fiscal 1986-89. Cochran, R-Miss., motion to table (kill) the Dixon, D-Ill., amendment to the Inouye, D-Hawaii, perfecting amendment to the Stevens, R-Alaska, amendment, to ensure fair and reasonable participation for all four port ranges in the movement of U.S. government-generated cargo, to establish the Great Lakes and St. Lawrence Seaway Advisory Council, and to require that commodities shipped under cargo preference requirements be shipped at the lowest landed costs. Motion agreed to 70-29: R 34-19; D 36-10 (ND 24-9, SD 12-1), Oct. 30, 1985. (The Inouye amendment was subsequently withdrawn by unanimous consent.)

265. S 1714. Farm Programs Reauthorization, Fiscal 1986-89. Cochran, R-Miss., motion to table (kill) the Dixon, D-Ill., amendment to the Inouye, D-Hawaii, perfecting amendment to the Stevens, R-Alaska, amendment, to specify criteria for the qualified use of U.S.-flag vessels in cargo preference shipments. Motion agreed to 73-23: R 34-17; D 39-6 (ND 27-5, SD 12-1), Oct. 30, 1985. (The Inouye amendment was subsequently withdrawn by unanimous consent.)

266. S 1714. Farm Programs Reauthorization, Fiscal 1986-89. Lugar, R-Ind., amendment to provide a one-year freeze in target prices and a 5 percent annual reduction thereafter for agriculture commodities of wheat, feed grains, cotton and rice. Rejected 48-51: R 40-12; D 8-39 (ND 8-25, SD 0-14), Oct. 30, 1985. A "yea" was a vote supporting the president's position.

267. S 1714. Farm Programs Reauthorization, Fiscal 1986-89. Harkin, D-Iowa, amendment to the Pressler, R-S.D., amendment, to strike the provisions for setting target prices for wheat according to levels of production, but retain provisions for setting target prices for corn according to levels of production. Adopted 57-41: R 13-39; D 44-2 (ND 31-2, SD 13-0), Oct. 30, 1985. (The Pressler amendment was subsequently tabled (killed) *(see vote 268, below)*.)

268. S 1714. Farm Programs Reauthorization, Fiscal 1986-89. Pressler, R-S.D., motion to table (kill) the Pressler amendment, as amended by the Harkin, D-Iowa, amendment *(vote 267, above)*, to set target prices for feed grains according to levels of production. Motion agreed to 96-2: R 52-0; D 44-2 (ND 31-2, SD 13-0), Oct. 30, 1985.

269. S 1714. Farm Programs Reauthorization, Fiscal 1986-89. Dixon, D-Ill., amendment to the Stevens, R-Alaska, amendment, to require the secretary of transportation to preserve as practicable through 1989 the percentage share, or metric tonnage, whichever is lower, of the government-donated commodities that were shipped out of Great Lakes ports in 1984. Adopted 53-43: R 28-23; D 25-20 (ND 22-10, SD 3-10), Oct. 30, 1985.

270. HR 3011. Interior Appropriations, Fiscal 1986. McClure, R-Idaho, motion to table (kill) the Metzenbaum, D-Ohio, amendment to rescind all but $500,000,001 in unobligated funds from the U.S. Synthetic Fuels Corporation (excluding $500 million transferred to the Clean Coal Technology Reserve). Motion rejected 41-58: R 22-31; D 19-27 (ND 11-22, SD 8-5), Oct. 31, 1985.

	271	272	273	274	275	276	277	278
ALABAMA								
Denton	Y	N	Y	Y	Y	N	Y	N
Heflin	Y	N	Y	Y	N	Y	Y	N
ALASKA								
Murkowski	Y	Y	Y	Y	Y	N	?	?
Stevens	?	N	Y	N	Y	N	Y	?
ARIZONA								
Goldwater	N	Y	Y	N	Y	N	N	?
DeConcini	Y	Y	Y	?	?	?	?	?
ARKANSAS								
Bumpers	Y	N	Y	N	Y	Y	Y	Y
Pryor	Y	N	Y	N	Y	Y	Y	?
CALIFORNIA								
Wilson	Y	Y	Y	Y	Y	N	Y	Y
Cranston	Y	Y	Y	N	Y	N	Y	N
COLORADO								
Armstrong	Y	Y	Y	Y	Y	N	Y	N
Hart	Y	N	Y	N	Y	Y	Y	Y
CONNECTICUT								
Weicker	Y	N	Y	N	Y	N	N	?
Dodd	?	N	Y	N	Y	Y	?	Y
DELAWARE								
Roth	Y	Y	Y	Y	N	N	Y	?
Biden	Y	N	Y	Y	?	?	?	?
FLORIDA								
Hawkins	Y	N	Y	Y	Y	N	Y	Y
Chiles	Y	N	Y	N	Y	Y	Y	Y
GEORGIA								
Mattingly	Y	Y	Y	Y	Y	N	Y	N
Nunn	Y	N	Y	N	Y	Y	Y	Y
HAWAII								
Inouye	Y	N	Y	N	Y	Y	Y	?
Matsunaga	?	N	Y	N	Y	Y	Y	Y
IDAHO								
McClure	Y	Y	Y	Y	Y	N	Y	N
Symms	Y	Y	Y	Y	N	N	Y	N
ILLINOIS								
Dixon	Y	N	Y	Y	Y	Y	Y	Y
Simon	Y	N	Y	N	Y	Y	Y	Y
INDIANA								
Lugar	Y	Y	Y	Y	Y	N	Y	Y
Quayle	Y	Y	Y	Y	Y	N	N	?
IOWA								
Grassley	Y	N	Y	Y	Y	Y	Y	N
Harkin	Y	N	Y	N	Y	Y	Y	?
KANSAS								
Dole	Y	Y	Y	Y	Y	N	Y	Y
Kassebaum	Y	Y	Y	N	Y	N	Y	Y
KENTUCKY								
McConnell	Y	Y	Y	Y	Y	N	Y	N
Ford	Y	N	Y	Y	Y	Y	Y	Y
LOUISIANA								
Johnston	?	?	?	?	?	?	?	?
Long	Y	N	Y	?	Y	Y	Y	Y
MAINE								
Cohen	Y	N	Y	N	Y	N	Y	?
Mitchell	Y	N	Y	Y	Y	Y	Y	Y
MARYLAND								
Mathias	N	N	Y	N	Y	N	Y	Y
Sarbanes	Y	N	Y	N	Y	Y	Y	?
MASSACHUSETTS								
Kennedy	Y	N	Y	N	Y	Y	?	?
Kerry	Y	N	Y	N	Y	Y	Y	Y
MICHIGAN								
Levin	Y	N	Y	N	Y	Y	?	Y
Riegle	Y	N	Y	N	Y	Y	Y	Y
MINNESOTA								
Boschwitz	Y	Y	Y	Y	Y	N	Y	Y
Durenberger	Y	N	N	Y	Y	Y	Y	Y
MISSISSIPPI								
Cochran	Y	N	Y	N	Y	N	Y	Y
Stennis	Y	N	Y	N	Y	Y	Y	?
MISSOURI								
Danforth	Y	Y	Y	Y	Y	Y	Y	N
Eagleton	Y	N	Y	Y	Y	Y	Y	?
MONTANA								
Baucus	Y	N	Y	N	Y	Y	?	N
Melcher	?	N	Y	Y	Y	Y	Y	Y
NEBRASKA								
Exon	Y	Y	Y	Y	N	Y	Y	N
Zorinsky	Y	N	Y	Y	N	Y	Y	N
NEVADA								
Hecht	Y	Y	Y	Y	Y	N	Y	Y
Laxalt	Y	Y	Y	Y	Y	N	Y	?
NEW HAMPSHIRE								
Humphrey	Y	?	Y	Y	N	N	Y	N
Rudman	Y	Y	Y	N	Y	N	Y	Y
NEW JERSEY								
Bradley	Y	N	Y	N	Y	Y	Y	Y
Lautenberg	Y	N	Y	N	Y	Y	Y	Y
NEW MEXICO								
Domenici	Y	Y	Y	Y	Y	N	Y	Y
Bingaman	Y	N	Y	N	Y	Y	Y	Y
NEW YORK								
D'Amato	Y	N	Y	Y	Y	N	Y	?
Moynihan	Y	N	Y	N	Y	Y	Y	Y
NORTH CAROLINA								
East	Y	Y	Y	Y	Y	N	Y	?
Helms	Y	Y	Y	Y	N	N	Y	N
NORTH DAKOTA								
Andrews	Y	N	Y	Y	Y	N	?	?
Burdick	Y	N	Y	N	Y	Y	Y	Y
OHIO								
Glenn	Y	Y	Y	N	Y	Y	Y	N
Metzenbaum	Y	N	Y	N	Y	Y	Y	Y
OKLAHOMA								
Nickles	Y	Y	Y	Y	N	Y	Y	N
Boren	Y	Y	Y	Y	Y	Y	Y	N
OREGON								
Hatfield	Y	N	Y	Y	+	?	?	?
Packwood	Y	N	Y	N	Y	N	Y	Y
PENNSYLVANIA								
Heinz	+	N	Y	N	Y	N	Y	Y
Specter	Y	N	Y	N	Y	N	Y	?
RHODE ISLAND								
Chafee	Y	Y	Y	N	Y	N	Y	Y
Pell	Y	N	Y	N	Y	Y	Y	Y
SOUTH CAROLINA								
Thurmond	Y	N	Y	Y	Y	N	Y	Y
Hollings	Y	N	Y	N	Y	Y	Y	Y
SOUTH DAKOTA								
Abdnor	Y	N	Y	Y	Y	N	Y	?
Pressler	Y	Y	Y	Y	Y	N	Y	Y
TENNESSEE								
Gore	Y	N	Y	Y	Y	Y	Y	Y
Sasser	Y	N	Y	N	Y	Y	Y	N
TEXAS								
Gramm	Y	Y	Y	Y	N	N	Y	Y
Bentsen	?	?	?	?	?	?	?	?
UTAH								
Garn	Y	Y	Y	Y	Y	N	Y	Y
Hatch	Y	Y	Y	Y	Y	N	Y	Y
VERMONT								
Stafford	Y	Y	Y	N	Y	N	Y	?
Leahy	Y	N	Y	N	Y	Y	Y	Y
VIRGINIA								
Trible	Y	Y	Y	Y	Y	N	Y	Y
Warner	Y	Y	Y	N	Y	N	Y	Y
WASHINGTON								
Evans	Y	Y	Y	N	Y	N	Y	N
Gorton	Y	Y	Y	N	Y	N	Y	Y
WEST VIRGINIA								
Byrd	Y	N	Y	N	Y	Y	Y	Y
Rockefeller	Y	N	Y	N	Y	Y	Y	Y
WISCONSIN								
Kasten	Y	N	Y	Y	Y	N	Y	N
Proxmire	Y	Y	Y	Y	N	N	Y	N
WYOMING								
Simpson	Y	Y	Y	N	Y	N	Y	Y
Wallop	?	?	?	?	?	?	?	?

KEY

- Y Voted for (yea).
- # Paired for.
- \+ Announced for.
- N Voted against (nay).
- X Paired against.
- \- Announced against.
- P Voted "present."
- C Voted "present" to avoid possible conflict of interest.
- ? Did not vote or otherwise make a position known.

Democrats *Republicans*

ND - Northern Democrats SD - Southern Democrats (Southern states - Ala., Ark., Fla., Ga., Ky., La., Miss., N.C., Okla., S.C., Tenn., Texas, Va.)

271. HR 2965. Commerce, Justice, State and the Judiciary Appropriations, Fiscal 1986. Lautenberg, D-N.J., amendment to prohibit the use of funds for U.S. contributions to international organizations from being used for projects or entities that benefit the Palestine Liberation Organization. Adopted 90-2: R 48-2; D 42-0 (ND 30-0, SD 12-0), Nov. 1, 1985.

272. HR 2965. Commerce, Justice, State and the Judiciary Appropriations, Fiscal 1986. Chafee, R-R.I., amendment to delete funding for the Economic Development Administration except for $15 million for salaries and expenses while terminating the program. Rejected 39-57: R 33-18; D 6-39 (ND 5-28, SD 1-11), Nov. 1, 1985.

273. HR 2965. Commerce, Justice, State and the Judiciary Appropriations, Fiscal 1986. Moynihan, D-N.Y., amendment to require that not less than $1 million of the FBI's fiscal 1986 funding be used for countering Soviet interception of domestic U.S. telecommunications, and to require the FBI director to report to Congress by June 1, 1986, on the bureau's ability to counter the interception of U.S. telecommunications by foreign agents. Adopted 96-1: R 51-1; D 45-0 (ND 33-0, SD 12-0), Nov. 1, 1985.

274. HR 2965. Commerce, Justice, State and the Judiciary Appropriations, Fiscal 1986. Helms, R-N.C., motion to table (kill) the Rudman, R-N.H., point of order that the Helms amendment to bar the use of federal funds for abortions for prison inmates was unconstitutional. Motion rejected 47-48: R 35-17; D 12-31 (ND 8-24, SD 4-7), Nov. 1, 1985. (The Rudman point of order was subsequently upheld by voice vote.)

275. HR 2965. Commerce, Justice, State and the Judiciary Appropriations, Fiscal 1986. Passage of the bill to appropriate $11,928,160,000 for the Commerce, Justice and State departments, the federal judiciary and related agencies in fiscal 1986. Passed 84-10: R 45-6; D 39-4 (ND 28-3, SD 11-1), Nov. 1, 1985. (The president had requested $11,659,270,000 in new budget authority.)

276. S 1714. Farm Programs Reauthorization, Fiscal 1986-89. Dole, R-Kan., motion to table (kill) the Dole perfecting amendment to the Dole amendment to the Dole motion to recommit the bill to the Agriculture, Nutrition and Forestry Committee with instructions to report back forthwith with the Dole amendment to freeze target prices for corn, cotton and rice in fiscal 1986 and allow maximum 5 percent annual reductions thereafter, to freeze target prices for wheat in 1986 and thereafter provide a sliding scale based on levels of production, to create an emergency conservation reserve, to provide numerous cost-saving measures, and to include the Stevens, R-Alaska, amendment dealing with cargo preference, as perfected by Senate action to date. Motion rejected 45-49: R 4-47; D 41-2 (ND 29-2, SD 12-0), Nov. 1, 1985.

277. Procedural Motion. Packwood, R-Ore., motion to instruct the sergeant-at-arms to request the attendance of absent senators. Motion agreed to 85-3: R 46-3; D 39-0 (ND 27-0, SD 12-0), Nov. 1, 1985.

278. HR 3669. Temporary Public Debt Limit Increase. Passage of the bill to raise temporarily the limit on the federal debt by enough to permit the federal government to meet fiscal obligations without accelerated redemptions of Treasury securities from the Social Security trust funds or other federal trust funds, and also to bar such redemptions and direct the secretary of the Treasury to use the increased borrowing authority to restore, with interest, such securities as were redeemed from the Social Security or other trust funds after Oct. 31, 1985, until enactment of the legislation. The legislation would permit the debt limit to increase temporarily to no more than $1.841 trillion, until Nov. 6, 1985, and to revert to its existing level of $1.824 trillion after that date. Passed 51-22: R 24-13; D 27-9 (ND 20-6, SD 7-3), in the session that began Nov. 1, 1985.

CQ Senate Votes 279 - 284

Corresponding to Congressional Record Votes 279, 280, 281, 282, 283, 284

	279	280	281	282	283	284
ALABAMA						
Denton	N	Y	Y	Y	N	Y
Heflin	N	N	Y	N	Y	Y
ALASKA						
Murkowski	Y	Y	Y	Y	Y	Y
Stevens	Y	Y	Y	Y	Y	Y
ARIZONA						
Goldwater	?	Y	Y	Y	?	Y
DeConcini	Y	N	N	N	Y	Y
ARKANSAS						
Bumpers	Y	N	N	N	Y	Y
Pryor	Y	N	N	N	Y	Y
CALIFORNIA						
Wilson	Y	Y	Y	Y	Y	Y
Cranston	Y	N	N	N	Y	Y
COLORADO						
Armstrong	Y	Y	Y	Y	N	Y
Hart	?	N	N	N	Y	N
CONNECTICUT						
Weicker	Y	?	?	?	?	?
Dodd	Y	N	N	Y	Y	Y
DELAWARE						
Roth	N	Y	Y	Y	Y	Y
Biden	Y	N	N	?	?	N
FLORIDA						
Hawkins	Y	N	Y	N	Y	Y
Chiles	Y	N	N	N	Y	Y
GEORGIA						
Mattingly	?	Y	Y	Y	Y	Y
Nunn	Y	Y	N	Y	Y	Y
HAWAII						
Inouye	?	N	N	N	Y	N
Matsunaga	Y	N	N	N	Y	Y
IDAHO						
McClure	N	Y	Y	Y	N	Y
Symms	N	Y	Y	Y	N	Y
ILLINOIS						
Dixon	+	N	N	N	Y	Y
Simon	Y	N	N	N	Y	Y
INDIANA						
Lugar	N	Y	Y	Y	Y	Y
Quayle	Y	Y	Y	Y	?	Y
IOWA						
Grassley	Y	Y	Y	Y	Y	Y
Harkin	Y	N	N	N	Y	N
KANSAS						
Dole	Y	Y	Y	Y	Y	Y
Kassebaum	Y	N	Y	Y	Y	Y
KENTUCKY						
McConnell	Y	Y	Y	Y	Y	Y
Ford	Y	N	Y	N	Y	Y
LOUISIANA						
Johnston	Y	Y	N	N	Y	N
Long	Y	Y	Y	Y	Y	Y
MAINE						
Cohen	Y	Y	Y	Y	Y	Y
Mitchell	Y	N	N	N	Y	Y
MARYLAND						
Mathias	Y	Y	N	Y	Y	N
Sarbanes	Y	N	N	N	Y	N
MASSACHUSETTS						
Kennedy	?	N	N	N	Y	N
Kerry	Y	N	N	N	Y	Y
MICHIGAN						
Levin	Y	N	N	N	Y	Y
Riegle	Y	N	N	N	Y	N
MINNESOTA						
Boschwitz	Y	Y	Y	Y	Y	Y
Durenberger	?	N	Y	Y	Y	Y
MISSISSIPPI						
Cochran	Y	Y	Y	Y	Y	Y
Stennis	Y	Y	N	N	?	N
MISSOURI						
Danforth	Y	Y	Y	Y	Y	Y
Eagleton	Y	N	N	N	Y	N
MONTANA						
Baucus	Y	N	N	N	Y	Y
Melcher	Y	N	N	N	Y	N
NEBRASKA						
Exon	Y	N	N	N	Y	Y
Zorinsky	?	?	?	?	?	?
NEVADA						
Hecht	N	Y	Y	Y	Y	Y
Laxalt	N	Y	Y	Y	Y	Y
NEW HAMPSHIRE						
Humphrey	N	Y	Y	?	Y	Y
Rudman	Y	Y	Y	Y	Y	Y
NEW JERSEY						
Bradley	?	N	Y	N	Y	Y
Lautenberg	Y	N	N	N	Y	Y
NEW MEXICO						
Domenici	Y	Y	Y	Y	Y	Y
Bingaman	?	Y	N	Y	Y	Y
NEW YORK						
D'Amato	Y	Y	Y	Y	Y	Y
Moynihan	Y	N	N	N	Y	N
NORTH CAROLINA						
East	N	Y	Y	Y	N	Y
Helms	N	Y	Y	Y	N	Y
NORTH DAKOTA						
Andrews	?	N	Y	N	Y	Y
Burdick	Y	N	N	N	Y	Y
OHIO						
Glenn	Y	N	N	N	Y	Y
Metzenbaum	Y	N	N	N	Y	Y
OKLAHOMA						
Nickles	Y	Y	N	Y	Y	Y
Boren	Y	Y	N	Y	Y	Y
OREGON						
Hatfield	Y	Y	Y	Y	Y	Y
Packwood	Y	Y	Y	Y	Y	Y
PENNSYLVANIA						
Heinz	Y	N	Y	Y	Y	Y
Specter	Y	N	Y	N	Y	Y
RHODE ISLAND						
Chafee	Y	N	Y	Y	Y	Y
Pell	Y	N	N	N	Y	N
SOUTH CAROLINA						
Thurmond	Y	Y	Y	Y	Y	Y
Hollings	Y	Y	Y	N	Y	Y
SOUTH DAKOTA						
Abdnor	Y	Y	Y	N	Y	Y
Pressler	Y	Y	Y	N	Y	Y
TENNESSEE						
Gore	Y	N	N	N	Y	Y
Sasser	Y	N	N	N	Y	N
TEXAS						
Gramm	N	Y	Y	Y	Y	Y
Bentsen	Y	Y	N	N	Y	Y
UTAH						
Garn	N	Y	Y	Y	Y	Y
Hatch	N	Y	Y	Y	Y	Y
VERMONT						
Stafford	Y	Y	Y	Y	Y	Y
Leahy	Y	N	N	N	Y	Y
VIRGINIA						
Trible	?	Y	Y	Y	Y	Y
Warner	Y	Y	Y	Y	Y	Y
WASHINGTON						
Evans	Y	Y	Y	Y	Y	Y
Gorton	?	Y	Y	Y	Y	Y
WEST VIRGINIA						
Byrd	Y	N	N	N	Y	N
Rockefeller	Y	N	N	N	Y	Y
WISCONSIN						
Kasten	Y	Y	Y	Y	Y	Y
Proxmire	Y	Y	N	Y	Y	Y
WYOMING						
Simpson	Y	Y	Y	Y	Y	Y
Wallop	N	Y	Y	Y	N	Y

KEY

- Y Voted for (yea).
- # Paired for.
- + Announced for.
- N Voted against (nay).
- X Paired against.
- \- Announced against.
- P Voted "present."
- C Voted "present" to avoid possible conflict of interest.
- ? Did not vote or otherwise make a position known.

Democrats ***Republicans***

ND - Northern Democrats SD - Southern Democrats (Southern states - Ala., Ark., Fla., Ga., Ky., La., Miss., N.C., Okla., S.C., Tenn., Texas, Va.)

279. H J Res 372. Public Debt Limit. Metzenbaum, D-Ohio, motion to concur in the House amendment to the Senate amendment, with the Metzenbaum substitute to require the House Ways and Means and Senate Finance committees to report, by April 15, 1986, legislation providing for a minimum tax on corporations, to take effect July 1, 1986, and to specify that revenues from the tax be used to reduce the public debt. Motion agreed to 72-15: R 33-14; D 39-1 (ND 26-0, SD 13-1), Nov. 4, 1985. (The House amendment would have required the Ways and Means Committee to report minimum tax legislation by Oct. 1, 1986, and had not specified how the resulting revenue would be used.)

280. H J Res 372. Public Debt Limit. Packwood, R-Ore., motion to table (kill) the Chiles, D-Fla., amendment to the Packwood amendment to the House amendment to the Senate amendment, to specify that if automatic, across-the-board spending reductions were imposed, as provided by the Packwood amendment, Medicare would be considered to be an indexed program, meaning that any reductions would reduce scheduled automatic increases but not base-level spending in Medicare. Motion agreed to 54-44: R 45-7; D 9-37 (ND 2-30, SD 7-7), Nov. 5, 1985. (The Packwood amendment specified that Medicare would not be considered an indexed program, meaning that reductions could reduce base-level spending. The effect of the Packwood amendment was to reduce the amount that would have to be cut from defense and other "controllable" spending. The effect of the Chiles amendment would have been to increase the amount to be cut from defense and other "controllable" spending. The Packwood amendment set maximum allowable federal deficits for fiscal years 1986-1991, declining to zero by the final year; provided for automatic, across-the-board cuts in federal programs (with certain exceptions) in years when congressional action fails to bring spending for the upcoming fiscal year to the maximum level specified for that year; otherwise revised the congressional budget process; and removed the Social Security program from the unified federal budget. The Packwood amendment subsequently was adopted *(see vote 285, p. 51-S)*.)

281. H J Res 372. Public Debt Limit. Packwood, R-Ore., motion to table (kill) the Riegle, D-Mich., amendment to the Packwood amendment to the House amendment to the Senate amendment, to specify that the projected federal budget deficit in fiscal 1986 may not exceed $171.9 billion, and to require automatic reductions, by a presidential "sequester" order, to reach that figure, prorated for the portion of the fiscal year remaining at the time of enactment. Motion agreed to 55-43: R 50-2; D 5-41 (ND 1-31, SD 4-10), Nov. 5, 1985. (The Packwood amendment specified that the projected federal budget deficit in fiscal 1986 may not exceed $180 billion and required automatic reductions to that figure if the projected deficit were to exceed that figure by more than 5 percent.)

282. H J Res 372. Public Debt Limit. Packwood, R-Ore., motion to table (kill) the Riegle, D-Mich., amendment to the Packwood amendment to the House amendment to the Senate amendment, to exempt veterans' compensation and medical programs from any automatic spending reductions. Motion agreed to 52-44: R 46-5; D 6-39 (ND 3-28, SD 3-11), Nov. 5, 1985.

283. Lord Nomination. Confirmation of President Reagan's nomination of Winston Lord of New York to be ambassador to the People's Republic of China. Confirmed 87-7: R 43-7; D 44-0 (ND 31-0, SD 13-0), Nov. 5, 1985. A "yea" was a vote supporting the president's position.

284. H J Res 372. Public Debt Limit. Packwood, R-Ore., motion to table (kill) the Moynihan, D-N.Y., amendment to the Packwood amendment to the House amendment to the Senate amendment, to exempt from any automatic spending reductions, as provided by the Packwood amendment, all federal agencies, including national security agencies, that provide economic forecasts and related data. Motion agreed to 82-16: R 51-1; D 31-15 (ND 20-12, SD 11-3), Nov. 6, 1985.

Corresponding to Congressional Record Votes 285, 286, 287, 288, 289, 290, 291, 292

	285	286	287	288	289	290	291	292
ALABAMA								
Denton	Y	Y	Y	Y	Y	Y	N	N
Heflin	Y	N	Y	Y	Y	N	Y	N
ALASKA								
Murkowski	Y	N	Y	Y	Y	N	N	Y
Stevens	Y	N	Y	Y	Y	N	Y	Y
ARIZONA								
Goldwater	Y	Y	Y	N	Y	N	Y	Y
DeConcini	Y	N	Y	Y	Y	N	Y	Y
ARKANSAS								
Bumpers	Y	Y	Y	N	Y	N	Y	Y
Pryor	Y	Y	Y	N	Y	N	Y	Y
CALIFORNIA								
Wilson	Y	Y	Y	Y	Y	N	Y	Y
Cranston	N	N	Y	N	Y	N	Y	Y
COLORADO								
Armstrong	Y	Y	Y	Y	Y	Y	N	N
Hart	N	N	Y	N	Y	N	Y	Y
CONNECTICUT								
Weicker	?	N	Y	N	Y	N	Y	Y
Dodd	Y	N	Y	N	Y	N	Y	Y
DELAWARE								
Roth	Y	Y	Y	Y	Y	N	Y	?
Biden	Y	N	Y	N	Y	N	Y	Y
FLORIDA								
Hawkins	Y	Y	Y	Y	Y	Y	N	Y
Chiles	Y	N	Y	N	Y	N	Y	Y
GEORGIA								
Mattingly	Y	Y	Y	Y	Y	Y	N	Y
Nunn	Y	N	Y	N	Y	N	Y	Y
HAWAII								
Inouye	N	N	Y	N	Y	N	Y	Y
Matsunaga	N	?	Y	N	Y	N	Y	Y
IDAHO								
McClure	Y	Y	Y	Y	Y	Y	N	Y
Symms	Y	Y	Y	Y	Y	Y	N	N
ILLINOIS								
Dixon	Y	N	Y	Y	Y	N	Y	Y
Simon	Y	N	Y	N	Y	N	Y	Y
INDIANA								
Lugar	Y	Y	Y	Y	Y	Y	N	Y
Quayle	Y	Y	Y	Y	Y	Y	N	Y
IOWA								
Grassley	Y	Y	Y	Y	Y	Y	N	Y
Harkin	N	N	Y	N	Y	N	Y	Y
KANSAS								
Dole	Y	Y	Y	Y	Y	N	N	Y
Kassebaum	N	Y	Y	Y	Y	N	Y	Y
KENTUCKY								
McConnell	Y	Y	Y	Y	Y	Y	N	Y
Ford	Y	N	Y	N	Y	Y	N	Y
LOUISIANA								
Johnston	N	N	Y	N	Y	Y	N	Y
Long	Y	N	Y	Y	Y	N	N	Y
MAINE								
Cohen	Y	Y	Y	N	Y	N	Y	Y
Mitchell	N	N	Y	N	Y	N	Y	Y
MARYLAND								
Mathias	N	N	Y	Y	Y	N	Y	Y
Sarbanes	N	N	Y	N	Y	N	Y	Y
MASSACHUSETTS								
Kennedy	Y	N	Y	N	Y	N	Y	Y
Kerry	Y	N	Y	N	Y	X	#	+
MICHIGAN								
Levin	Y	N	?	N	Y	N	Y	Y
Riegle	N	N	Y	N	Y	N	Y	Y
MINNESOTA								
Boschwitz	Y	Y	Y	Y	Y	Y	N	Y
Durenberger	Y	N	Y	Y	Y	Y	N	Y
MISSISSIPPI								
Cochran	Y	Y	Y	Y	Y	N	Y	Y
Stennis	Y	N	Y	Y	Y	Y	N	?
MISSOURI								
Danforth	Y	N	Y	Y	Y	Y	N	Y
Eagleton	N	N	Y	N	Y	#	X	Y
MONTANA								
Baucus	Y	N	Y	N	Y	N	Y	N
Melcher	N	N	Y	N	Y	N	N	Y
NEBRASKA								
Exon	N	#	Y	N	Y	N	N	N
Zorinsky	?	?	?	?	?	?	?	?
NEVADA								
Hecht	Y	Y	Y	Y	Y	Y	N	Y
Laxalt	Y	Y	Y	Y	Y	Y	N	Y
NEW HAMPSHIRE								
Humphrey	Y	Y	Y	Y	N	Y	N	N
Rudman	Y	Y	Y	Y	Y	N	Y	Y
NEW JERSEY								
Bradley	N	N	Y	N	Y	N	Y	Y
Lautenberg	N	N	Y	N	Y	N	Y	Y
NEW MEXICO								
Domenici	Y	Y	Y	Y	Y	Y	N	Y
Bingaman	Y	N	Y	N	Y	N	Y	Y
NEW YORK								
D'Amato	Y	N	Y	Y	Y	Y	N	Y
Moynihan	N	N	Y	N	Y	N	Y	Y
NORTH CAROLINA								
East	Y	Y	Y	Y	Y	Y	N	N
Helms	Y	Y	Y	Y	Y	Y	N	N
NORTH DAKOTA								
Andrews	Y	N	Y	Y	Y	N	N	Y
Burdick	N	N	Y	N	Y	N	Y	Y
OHIO								
Glenn	N	N	Y	N	Y	N	Y	Y
Metzenbaum	N	N	Y	N	Y	N	Y	Y
OKLAHOMA								
Nickles	Y	Y	Y	Y	Y	Y	N	N
Boren	Y	Y	Y	N	Y	N	Y	Y
OREGON								
Hatfield	N	Y	N	Y	Y	Y	N	Y
Packwood	Y	N	Y	Y	Y	N	Y	Y
PENNSYLVANIA								
Heinz	Y	-	?	?	?	?	?	?
Specter	Y	N	Y	Y	Y	N	Y	Y
RHODE ISLAND								
Chafee	Y	Y	Y	Y	Y	N	Y	Y
Pell	N	N	Y	N	Y	N	Y	Y
SOUTH CAROLINA								
Thurmond	Y	Y	Y	Y	Y	Y	N	Y
Hollings	Y	Y	Y	N	Y	N	Y	Y
SOUTH DAKOTA								
Abdnor	Y	Y	Y	Y	Y	Y	N	Y
Pressler	Y	Y	Y	Y	Y	Y	N	Y
TENNESSEE								
Gore	Y	N	Y	N	Y	N	Y	Y
Sasser	Y	N	Y	N	Y	N	Y	Y
TEXAS								
Gramm	Y	Y	Y	Y	Y	Y	N	N
Bentsen	Y	Y	Y	N	Y	N	Y	Y
UTAH								
Garn	Y	Y	Y	Y	Y	Y	N	Y
Hatch	Y	Y	Y	Y	Y	Y	N	N
VERMONT								
Stafford	N	N	Y	Y	Y	N	Y	Y
Leahy	Y	N	Y	N	Y	N	Y	Y
VIRGINIA								
Trible	Y	Y	Y	Y	Y	Y	N	Y
Warner	Y	Y	Y	Y	Y	N	Y	Y
WASHINGTON								
Evans	Y	?	Y	Y	Y	N	Y	Y
Gorton	Y	Y	Y	Y	Y	N	Y	Y
WEST VIRGINIA								
Byrd	N	N	Y	N	Y	N	Y	Y
Rockefeller	Y	X	?		+	?	?	+
WISCONSIN								
Kasten	Y	Y	Y	Y	Y	Y	N	Y
Proxmire	Y	N	Y	N	Y	Y	N	N
WYOMING								
Simpson	Y	Y	Y	Y	Y	N	Y	Y
Wallop	Y	Y	?	Y	Y	Y	N	N

KEY

- Y Voted for (yea).
- # Paired for.
- + Announced for.
- N Voted against (nay).
- X Paired against.
- \- Announced against.
- P Voted "present."
- C Voted "present" to avoid possible conflict of interest.
- ? Did not vote or otherwise make a position known.

Democrats ***Republicans***

ND - Northern Democrats SD - Southern Democrats (Southern states - Ala., Ark., Fla., Ga., Ky., La., Miss., N.C., Okla., S.C., Tenn., Texas, Va.)

285. H J Res 372. Public Debt Limit. Domenici, R-N.M., motion to concur in the House amendment to the Senate amendment, with the Packwood, R-Ore., substitute to set maximum allowable federal deficits for fiscal years 1986-1991, declining to zero by the final year; provide for automatic, across-the-board cuts in federal programs (with certain exceptions) in years when congressional action fails to bring spending for the upcoming fiscal year to the maximum level specified for that year; otherwise revise the congressional budget process; and remove the Social Security program from the unified federal budget. Motion agreed to 74-24: R 48-4; D 26-20 (ND 13-19, SD 13-1), Nov. 6, 1985.

286. HR 3327. Military Construction Appropriations, Fiscal 1986. Judgment of the Senate whether the Appropriations Committee amendment to exempt certain military construction projects from provisions of the Davis-Bacon Act was germane to the bill. Ruled non-germane 45-49: R 40-11; D 5-38 (ND 0-29, SD 5-9), Nov. 7, 1985.

287. HR 3327. Military Construction Appropriations, Fiscal 1986. Passage of the bill to appropriate $8,720,353,000 for military construction programs in fiscal 1986. Passed 94-1: R 50-1; D 44-0 (ND 30-0, SD 14-0), Nov. 7, 1985. (The president had requested $10,340,200,000 in new budget authority.)

288. Kozinski Nomination. Confirmation of President Reagan's nomination of Alex Kozinski of California to be U.S. circuit judge for the 9th Circuit. Confirmed 54-43: R 49-3; D 5-40 (ND 2-29, SD 3-11), Nov. 7, 1985. A "yea" was a vote supporting the president's position.

289. HR 2672. Federal Retirement Reform Act. Passage of the bill to establish a new retirement plan for federal employees, postal workers, members of Congress, Foreign Service workers, and CIA employees. Passed 96-1: R 51-1; D 45-0 (ND 31-0, SD 14-0), Nov. 7, 1985.

290. HR 3067. District of Columbia Appropriations, Fiscal 1986. Helms, R-N.C., motion to table (kill) the Appropriations Committee amendment to strike language passed by the House barring the use of any funds in the bill to pay for abortions. Motion rejected 35-60: R 31-21; D 4-39 (ND 1-28, SD 3-11), Nov. 7, 1985. (The committee amendment was subsequently adopted by voice vote.)

291. HR 3067. District of Columbia Appropriations, Fiscal 1986. Simpson, R-Wyo., motion to table (kill) the Humphrey, R-N.H., amendment to bar the use of federal or District funds to pay for abortions, except to save the life of the mother. Motion agreed to 54-41: R 18-34; D 36-7 (ND 26-3, SD 10-4), Nov. 7, 1985.

292. HR 3067. District of Columbia Appropriations, Fiscal 1986. Passage of the bill to provide $549,870,000 in new budget authority in federal funds and $2,706,777,000 in District funds in fiscal 1986. Passed 80-14: R 41-10; D 39-4 (ND 27-3, SD 12-1), Nov. 7, 1985. (The president had requested $532,170,000 in federal funds and $2,689,077,000 in District funds.)

CQ Senate Votes 293 - 300

Corresponding to Congressional Record Votes 293, 294, 295, 296, 297, 298, 299, 300

	293	294	295	296	297	298	299	300
ALABAMA								
Denton	?	Y	N	Y	N	Y	Y	Y
Heflin	Y	Y	Y	Y	N	Y	Y	Y
ALASKA								
Murkowski	Y	N	Y	N	N	Y	Y	Y
Stevens	Y	N	Y	N	N	Y	Y	Y
ARIZONA								
Goldwater	Y	?	N	Y	Y	Y	Y	Y
DeConcini	N	N	Y	N	N	Y	Y	Y
ARKANSAS								
Bumpers	?	N	Y	N	N	Y	Y	Y
Pryor	Y	N	Y	N	N	Y	Y	Y
CALIFORNIA								
Wilson	Y	Y	N	N	N	Y	N	N
Cranston	Y	N	Y	N	N	Y	N	N
COLORADO								
Armstrong	Y	Y	N	Y	Y	Y	N	N
Hart	N	N	Y	N	N	Y	N	N
CONNECTICUT								
Weicker	Y	N	Y	N	N	Y	Y	Y
Dodd	N	N	Y	N	N	?	Y	Y
DELAWARE								
Roth	Y	Y	N	N	N	Y	Y	Y
Biden	Y	N	Y	N	N	Y	Y	Y
FLORIDA								
Hawkins	?	-	+	?	?	?	Y	Y
Chiles	N	N	Y	N	Y	?	?	?
GEORGIA								
Mattingly	N	Y	N	Y	N	Y	Y	Y
Nunn	N	Y	N	N	Y	Y	Y	Y
HAWAII								
Inouye	?	N	Y	N	N	Y	Y	Y
Matsunaga	?	N	Y	N	N	N	N	N
IDAHO								
McClure	Y	Y	N	Y	Y	Y	N	N
Symms	Y	Y	N	Y	N	Y	N	N
ILLINOIS								
Dixon	Y	N	Y	Y	N	Y	N	Y
Simon	N	N	?	N	N	Y	Y	Y
INDIANA								
Lugar	N	Y	N	Y	Y	Y	N	N
Quayle	Y	Y	N	Y	Y	Y	N	N
IOWA								
Grassley	Y	N	Y	N	N	Y	N	N
Harkin	N	N	Y	N	N	Y	Y	N
KANSAS								
Dole	Y	Y	N	Y	Y	Y	N	N
Kassebaum	N	Y	N	N	N	Y	N	N
KENTUCKY								
McConnell	Y	Y	N	Y	Y	Y	Y	Y
Ford	N	N	Y	N	N	Y	Y	Y
LOUISIANA								
Johnston	Y	Y	N	N	Y	Y	Y	Y
Long	Y	Y	N	N	N	Y	Y	Y
MAINE								
Cohen	N	N	Y	N	N	Y	Y	Y
Mitchell	Y	N	Y	N	N	Y	Y	Y
MARYLAND								
Mathias	N	N	Y	N	N	Y	Y	Y
Sarbanes	?	N	Y	N	N	Y	Y	Y
MASSACHUSETTS								
Kennedy	N	N	Y	N	N	Y	Y	Y
Kerry	Y	N	Y	N	N	Y	Y	Y
MICHIGAN								
Levin	N	N	Y	Y	N	Y	Y	Y
Riegle	Y	N	Y	N	N	Y	Y	Y
MINNESOTA								
Boschwitz	Y	Y	N	Y	Y	Y	N	N
Durenberger	N	N	Y	Y	N	Y	N	N
MISSISSIPPI								
Cochran	Y	Y	N	N	N	Y	Y	Y
Stennis	N	N	Y	N	N	Y	Y	Y
MISSOURI								
Danforth	Y	N	Y	N	N	Y	N	N
Eagleton	Y	?	Y	N	N	Y	Y	Y
MONTANA								
Baucus	Y	N	Y	N	N	Y	N	N
Melcher	N	N	Y	N	N	Y	Y	N
NEBRASKA								
Exon	Y	N	Y	N	N	N	N	N
Zorinsky	N	Y	N	Y	Y	Y	N	N
NEVADA								
Hecht	Y	Y	N	Y	N	Y	N	N
Laxalt	Y	Y	N	Y	N	Y	Y	Y
NEW HAMPSHIRE								
Humphrey	Y	N	Y	Y	Y	Y	Y	N
Rudman	?	N	Y	Y	Y	Y	Y	Y
NEW JERSEY								
Bradley	Y	N	Y	N	N	Y	Y	Y
Lautenberg	Y	N	Y	N	N	Y	Y	Y
NEW MEXICO								
Domenici	N	Y	N	N	Y	Y	N	N
Bingaman	Y	N	Y	N	N	Y	N	N
NEW YORK								
D'Amato	?	N	Y	N	N	Y	Y	Y
Moynihan	?	N	Y	N	N	Y	Y	Y
NORTH CAROLINA								
East	Y	Y	N	Y	Y	Y	Y	Y
Helms	Y	Y	N	Y	Y	Y	Y	Y
NORTH DAKOTA								
Andrews	Y	N	Y	Y	N	N	N	N
Burdick	?	N	Y	N	N	N	N	N
OHIO								
Glenn	N	N	Y	N	N	Y	Y	Y
Metzenbaum	N	N	Y	Y	N	Y	Y	Y
OKLAHOMA								
Nickles	Y	Y	N	N	N	N	N	N
Boren	?	?	?	?	?	N	N	N
OREGON								
Hatfield	N	N	Y	N	N	Y	N	N
Packwood	Y	Y	N	N	N	Y	N	N
PENNSYLVANIA								
Heinz	Y	N	Y	N	N	Y	Y	Y
Specter	Y	Y	N	N	N	Y	Y	Y
RHODE ISLAND								
Chafee	Y	N	Y	N	N	Y	Y	Y
Pell	-	N	Y	N	N	Y	Y	Y
SOUTH CAROLINA								
Thurmond	N	Y	N	Y	N	Y	Y	Y
Hollings	N	N	Y	N	Y	Y	Y	Y
SOUTH DAKOTA								
Abdnor	?	N	Y	Y	N	Y	N	N
Pressler	Y	Y	N	Y	Y	Y	N	N
TENNESSEE								
Gore	N	N	Y	N	N	Y	Y	Y
Sasser	N	N	Y	N	N	Y	Y	Y
TEXAS								
Gramm	N	Y	N	N	Y	Y	N	N
Bentsen	Y	Y	N	N	N	Y	Y	Y
UTAH								
Garn	N	Y	N	Y	Y	Y	Y	Y
Hatch	Y	Y	N	Y	N	Y	Y	Y
VERMONT								
Stafford	Y	N	Y	N	N	Y	N	N
Leahy	Y	N	Y	N	N	Y	Y	Y
VIRGINIA								
Trible	Y	N	Y	Y	N	Y	Y	Y
Warner	Y	N	Y	N	N	Y	Y	Y
WASHINGTON								
Evans	Y	Y	N	N	Y	Y	N	N
Gorton	N	Y	N	N	N	Y	N	N
WEST VIRGINIA								
Byrd	N	N	Y	N	N	Y	Y	Y
Rockefeller	?	N	Y	N	N	Y	Y	Y
WISCONSIN								
Kasten	-	N	Y	Y	N	Y	N	N
Proxmire	N	N	Y	Y	Y	Y	Y	Y
WYOMING								
Simpson	Y	Y	N	N	Y	Y	N	N
Wallop	Y	Y	N	N	Y	Y	N	N

KEY

- Y Voted for (yea).
- # Paired for.
- \+ Announced for.
- N Voted against (nay).
- X Paired against.
- \- Announced against.
- P Voted "present."
- C Voted "present" to avoid possible conflict of interest.
- ? Did not vote or otherwise make a position known.

Democrats *Republicans*

ND - Northern Democrats SD - Southern Democrats (Southern states - Ala., Ark., Fla., Ga., Ky., La., Miss., N.C., Okla., S.C., Tenn., Texas, Va.)

293. S 1730. Omnibus Budget Reconciliation, Fiscal 1986. Packwood, R-Ore., motion to table (kill) the Metzenbaum, D-Ohio, amendment to strike a provision in the bill that would extend, until Aug. 1, 1986, a law allowing large, multinational corporations to deduct research expenses from their income subject to U.S. income taxes, even if the research related to the firm's foreign operations. Motion agreed to 53-32: R 35-12; D 18-20 (ND 13-13, SD 5-7), Nov. 12, 1985.

294. S 1730. Omnibus Budget Reconciliation, Fiscal 1986. Helms, R-N.C., motion to table (kill) the Stafford, R-Vt., amendment to strike a provision in the bill requiring that, in determining eligibility for food stamps, any federal assistance for paying energy bills should be counted as income. Motion rejected 37-59: R 31-20; D 6-39 (ND 1-31, SD 5-8), Nov. 12, 1985. (The Stafford amendment subsequently was adopted *(see vote 295, below)*.)

295. S 1730. Omnibus Budget Reconciliation, Fiscal 1986. Stafford, R-Vt., amendment to strike a provision in the bill requiring that, in determining eligibility for food stamps, any federal assistance for paying energy bills should be counted as income. Adopted 60-37: R 20-32; D 40-5 (ND 31-1, SD 9-4), Nov. 12, 1985.

296. S 1730. Omnibus Budget Reconciliation, Fiscal 1986. Helms, R-N.C., amendment to express the sense of the Senate that an alternative funding source should be found to pay for the "superfund" hazardous-waste cleanup program other than the broad-based tax on manufacturers proposed in the bill. Rejected 32-66: R 26-26; D 6-40 (ND 5-28, SD 1-12), Nov. 12, 1985. A "yea" was a vote supporting the president's position.

297. S 1730. Omnibus Budget Reconciliation, Fiscal 1986. Domenici, R-N.M., motion to table (kill) the Heinz, R-Pa., amendment to allow Medicaid reimbursement for respirator-dependent individuals and for foster children, and to allow Medicaid to pay for demonstration projects on home-care alternatives for elderly persons who otherwise would be in institutions. Motion rejected 25-73: R 19-33; D 6-40 (ND 2-31, SD 4-9), Nov. 12, 1985. (The Heinz amendment subsequently was adopted by voice vote.)

298. HR 1562. Textile Import Quotas. Dole, R-Kan., unanimous-consent request to close debate on the bill to restrict textile and apparel imports. The request also provided that the Thurmond, R-S.C., amendment, to establish a worldwide system of quotas for imports of textiles and apparel and limit shoe imports to 60 percent of the domestic shoe market, was germane, and delineated the only other amendments that would be in order. Request agreed to 91-6: R 50-2; D 41-4 (ND 29-3, SD 12-1), Nov. 13, 1985. A three-fifths majority (60) of the Senate was required, under the provisions of the Dole request, for agreement to the unanimous-consent request.

299. HR 1562. Textile Import Quotas. Thurmond, R-S.C., motion to table (kill) the Boschwitz, R-Minn., amendment to the Baucus, D-Mont., amendment to the Thurmond amendment, to bar implementation of the provisions of the bill if the president determined that they would lead to reductions in the quantity of U.S. agricultural exports. Motion agreed to 62-37: R 26-27; D 36-10 (ND 24-9, SD 12-1), Nov. 13, 1985. (The Baucus amendment subsequently was tabled *(see vote 300, below)*. The Thurmond amendment, to establish a worldwide system of quotas for imports of textiles and apparel, limit shoe imports to 60 percent of the domestic shoe market and require negotiations leading to an international agreement limiting copper production, subsequently was adopted by voice vote.)

300. HR 1562. Textile Import Quotas. Thurmond, R-S.C., motion to table (kill) the Baucus, D-Mont., amendment to the Thurmond amendment, to bar implementation of the quotas in the bill on textile and apparel imports from countries that purchase at least $400 million worth of U.S. agricultural products annually. Motion agreed to 60-39: R 25-28; D 35-11 (ND 23-10, SD 12-1), Nov. 13, 1985.

	301	302	303	304	305	306	307	308
ALABAMA								
Denton	Y	Y	Y	Y	Y	Y	Y	Y
Heflin	Y	Y	Y	Y	Y	N	Y	Y
ALASKA								
Murkowski	Y	Y	N	Y	N	N	N	Y
Stevens	N	N	N	Y	N	N	Y	Y
ARIZONA								
Goldwater	N	N	N	Y	N	N	N	Y
DeConcini	Y	Y	N	Y	Y	N	Y	Y
ARKANSAS								
Bumpers	Y	Y	Y	Y	Y	Y	Y	N
Pryor	Y	Y	Y	Y	Y	N	Y	Y
CALIFORNIA								
Wilson	N	N	N	Y	N	Y	Y	Y
Cranston	Y	Y	Y	Y	N	N	Y	Y
COLORADO								
Armstrong	N	N	N	Y	N	?	?	N
Hart	N	Y	N	Y	N	N	Y	N
CONNECTICUT								
Weicker	Y	Y	Y	Y	Y	N	N	N
Dodd	Y	Y	Y	Y	Y	N	Y	N
DELAWARE								
Roth	Y	Y	N	Y	Y	Y	Y	N
Biden	Y	Y	Y	Y	Y	N	Y	N
FLORIDA								
Hawkins	Y	Y	Y	Y	Y	Y	N	Y
Chiles	?	?	?	?	?	?	?	?
GEORGIA								
Mattingly	Y	Y	Y	Y	Y	Y	N	N
Nunn	Y	Y	Y	Y	Y	N	Y	Y
HAWAII								
Inouye	Y	Y	N	Y	N	N	Y	Y
Matsunaga	N	N	N	Y	N	N	Y	Y
IDAHO								
McClure	N	N	N	Y	Y	Y	N	Y
Symms	N	N	N	Y	N	Y	N	Y
ILLINOIS								
Dixon	Y	Y	Y	Y	Y	Y	Y	N
Simon	Y	Y	Y	Y	Y	N	Y	N
INDIANA								
Lugar	N	N	N	Y	N	Y	Y	N
Quayle	N	N	Y	Y	N	Y	Y	Y
IOWA								
Grassley	Y	N	N	Y	N	Y	Y	N
Harkin	Y	Y	N	Y	N	N	Y	Y
KANSAS								
Dole	Y	N	N	Y	Y	Y	Y	N
Kassebaum	Y	Y	Y	Y	N	Y	Y	N
KENTUCKY								
McConnell	Y	Y	Y	Y	Y	Y	Y	Y
Ford	Y	Y	Y	Y	Y	N	N	Y
LOUISIANA								
Johnston	Y	Y	Y	Y	Y	Y	N	Y
Long	Y	Y	Y	Y	Y	Y	N	Y
MAINE								
Cohen	Y	Y	Y	Y	Y	Y	Y	Y
Mitchell	Y	Y	Y	Y	Y	N	Y	N
MARYLAND								
Mathias	Y	Y	Y	Y	Y	N	Y	N
Sarbanes	Y	Y	Y	Y	Y	N	Y	N
MASSACHUSETTS								
Kennedy	Y	Y	Y	Y	Y	N	Y	Y
Kerry	?	Y	Y	Y	Y	N	Y	Y
MICHIGAN								
Levin	Y	Y	Y	Y	Y	N	Y	N
Riegle	Y	Y	Y	Y	Y	N	Y	N
MINNESOTA								
Boschwitz	N	N	N	Y	N	Y	N	N
Durenberger	N	Y	Y	Y	N	N	Y	N
MISSISSIPPI								
Cochran	Y	Y	Y	Y	Y	Y	Y	Y
Stennis	Y	Y	Y	Y	Y	?	?	Y
MISSOURI								
Danforth	Y	Y	N	Y	N	Y	N	N
Eagleton	Y	Y	Y	Y	Y	N	Y	N
MONTANA								
Baucus	N	Y	N	Y	N	N	N	Y
Melcher	Y	Y	Y	Y	Y	Y	Y	Y
NEBRASKA								
Exon	N	N	N	Y	N	N	Y	Y
Zorinsky	N	N	Y	Y	N	Y	N	Y
NEVADA								
Hecht	N	N	N	Y	N	Y	Y	N
Laxalt	Y	Y	Y	Y	Y	Y	Y	Y
NEW HAMPSHIRE								
Humphrey	N	N	N	Y	N	Y	Y	N
Rudman	Y	Y	Y	Y	Y	Y	N	N
NEW JERSEY								
Bradley	Y	Y	Y	Y	N	N	Y	N
Lautenberg	Y	Y	Y	Y	Y	N	Y	N
NEW MEXICO								
Domenici	Y	Y	Y	Y	Y	Y	Y	Y
Bingaman	N	N	Y	Y	Y	N	Y	Y
NEW YORK								
D'Amato	Y	Y	N	Y	Y	N	N	Y
Moynihan	Y	Y	Y	Y	Y	N	Y	N
NORTH CAROLINA								
East	Y	Y	Y	Y	Y	Y	Y	Y
Helms	Y	Y	Y	Y	Y	Y	Y	Y
NORTH DAKOTA								
Andrews	N	N	N	Y	N	Y	Y	Y
Burdick	Y	Y	Y	Y	N	N	Y	Y
OHIO								
Glenn	Y	Y	Y	Y	Y	N	Y	N
Metzenbaum	Y	Y	Y	Y	Y	N	Y	N
OKLAHOMA								
Nickles	N	N	Y	Y	N	Y	Y	Y
Boren	Y	N	Y	Y	N	Y	Y	Y
OREGON								
Hatfield	N	N	N	Y	N	N	Y	Y
Packwood	N	N	Y	Y	N	Y	Y	N
PENNSYLVANIA								
Heinz	Y	Y	Y	Y	Y	Y	Y	N
Specter	Y	Y	Y	Y	Y	Y	Y	N
RHODE ISLAND								
Chafee	Y	Y	N	Y	N	Y	Y	N
Pell	Y	Y	Y	Y	Y	N	Y	N
SOUTH CAROLINA								
Thurmond	Y	Y	Y	Y	Y	Y	Y	Y
Hollings	Y	Y	Y	Y	Y	N	Y	Y
SOUTH DAKOTA								
Abdnor	Y	N	N	Y	N	Y	Y	N
Pressler	Y	N	Y	Y	N	Y	Y	N
TENNESSEE								
Gore	Y	Y	Y	Y	Y	N	Y	N
Sasser	Y	Y	Y	Y	Y	N	Y	Y
TEXAS								
Gramm	N	N	N	Y	N	Y	Y	Y
Bentsen	Y	Y	Y	Y	Y	Y	Y	Y
UTAH								
Garn	N	Y	Y	Y	Y	Y	Y	Y
Hatch	Y	Y	Y	Y	Y	Y	Y	Y
VERMONT								
Stafford	N	N	N	Y	N	Y	Y	N
Leahy	Y	Y	Y	Y	Y	N	Y	N
VIRGINIA								
Trible	Y	Y	Y	Y	Y	Y	Y	Y
Warner	Y	Y	Y	Y	Y	Y	Y	Y
WASHINGTON								
Evans	N	N	N	Y	N	N	Y	N
Gorton	N	N	Y	Y	N	Y	Y	N
WEST VIRGINIA								
Byrd	Y	Y	Y	Y	Y	N	Y	Y
Rockefeller	N	Y	Y	Y	Y	N	Y	Y
WISCONSIN								
Kasten	Y	N	Y	Y	Y	Y	Y	N
Proxmire	Y	Y	Y	Y	Y	Y	Y	N
WYOMING								
Simpson	N	N	N	Y	N	Y	Y	Y
Wallop	N	N	N	Y	N	Y	N	Y

KEY

- Y Voted for (yea).
- # Paired for.
- + Announced for.
- N Voted against (nay).
- X Paired against.
- \- Announced against.
- P Voted "present."
- C Voted "present" to avoid possible conflict of interest.
- ? Did not vote or otherwise make a position known.

Democrats ***Republicans***

ND - Northern Democrats SD - Southern Democrats (Southern states - Ala., Ark., Fla., Ga., Ky., La., Miss., N.C., Okla., S.C., Tenn., Texas, Va.)

301. HR 1562. Textile Import Quotas. Thurmond, R-S.C., motion to table (kill) the Gramm, R-Texas, amendment to the Thurmond amendment, to bar implementation of the quotas in the bill on textile and apparel imports from countries that the president determined had tariffs and quotas on imports that were less restrictive than those imposed by the United States on imports. Motion agreed to 68-30: R 30-23; D 38-7 (ND 25-7, SD 13-0), Nov. 13, 1985.

302. HR 1562. Textile Import Quotas. Thurmond, R-S.C., motion to table (kill) the Gramm, R-Texas, amendment to the Thurmond amendment, to bar implementation of the quotas in the bill on textile and apparel imports from Taiwan if the president determined that the bill would harm the trade treatment of Taiwan more than it harmed the trade treatment of China. Motion agreed to 68-31: R 27-26; D 41-5 (ND 29-4, SD 12-1), Nov. 13, 1985.

303. HR 1562. Textile Import Quotas. Thurmond, R-S.C., motion to table (kill) the Matsunaga, D-Hawaii, amendment to the Thurmond amendment, to add Canada and members of the European Economic Community to the countries subject to the textile and apparel import quotas in the bill. Motion agreed to 67-32: R 28-25; D 39-7 (ND 26-7, SD 13-0), Nov. 13, 1985.

304. S Res 257. Geneva Summit Meeting. Adoption of the resolution to extend full support to President Reagan in his Nov. 19-20 meeting with Soviet leader Mikhail S. Gorbachev, and to encourage him to include certain items on his agenda for the meeting. Adopted 99-0: R 53-0; D 46-0 (ND 33-0, SD 13-0), Nov. 13, 1985.

305. HR 1562. Textile Import Quotas. Passage of the bill to establish a worldwide system of quotas for imports of textiles and apparel, limit shoe imports to 60 percent of the domestic shoe market and require negotiations leading to an international agreement limiting copper production. Passed 60-39: R 25-28; D 35-11 (ND 23-10, SD 12-1), Nov. 13, 1985. A "nay" was a vote supporting the president's position.

306. S 1730. Omnibus Budget Reconciliation, Fiscal 1986. Dole, R-Kan., motion to table (kill) the Evans, R-Wash., amendment to require studies of the error-control system for the food stamp program and to impose a two-year moratorium on federal penalties against states with excessive error rates. Motion agreed to 52-45: R 43-9; D 9-36 (ND 4-29, SD 5-7), Nov. 13, 1985.

307. S 1730. Omnibus Budget Reconciliation, Fiscal 1986. Metzenbaum, D-Ohio, amendment to express the sense of the Senate that 10 minutes of debate time should be provided for each side on all remaining amendments to the bill. Adopted 80-17: R 40-12; D 40-5 (ND 31-2, SD 9-3), Nov. 13, 1985.

308. S 1730. Omnibus Budget Reconciliation, Fiscal 1986. McClure, R-Idaho, motion to table (kill) the Evans, R-Wash., amendment to limit coastal states' share of rent, bonus and royalty revenues from offshore oil tracts in a zone straddling state and federal boundaries. Motion agreed to 54-45: R 28-25; D 26-20 (ND 15-18, SD 11-2), Nov. 14, 1985. A "nay" was a vote supporting the president's position.

CQ Senate Votes 309 - 316

Corresponding to Congressional Record Votes 309, 310, 311, 312, 313, 314, 315, 316

	309	310	311	312	313	314	315	316
ALABAMA								
Denton	N	Y	Y	Y	Y	Y	N	Y
Heflin	N	Y	Y	N	Y	Y	N	Y
ALASKA								
Murkowski	Y	Y	Y	Y	Y	Y	Y	Y
Stevens	N	Y	Y	Y	Y	Y	N	N
ARIZONA								
Goldwater	N	Y	Y	Y	Y	Y	?	?
DeConcini	N	Y	Y	N	N	Y	N	Y
ARKANSAS								
Bumpers	N	Y	N	N	Y	Y	Y	Y
Pryor	N	Y	Y	N	N	Y	Y	N
CALIFORNIA								
Wilson	N	Y	Y	N	Y	Y	N	Y
Cranston	N	Y	Y	N	N	Y	Y	Y
COLORADO								
Armstrong	Y	Y	Y	Y	Y	Y	Y	Y
Hart	N	N	N	N	N	Y	N	N
CONNECTICUT								
Weicker	N	Y	N	N	Y	Y	Y	Y
Dodd	N	N	N	N	N	Y	N	Y
DELAWARE								
Roth	Y	N	N	Y	Y	Y	Y	Y
Biden	N	N	N	N	N	Y	N	Y
FLORIDA								
Hawkins	Y	Y	Y	Y	Y	Y	N	Y
Chiles	?	?	?	?	?	Y	Y	Y
GEORGIA								
Mattingly	N	Y	Y	Y	Y	Y	Y	Y
Nunn	N	Y	Y	N	Y	Y	Y	Y
HAWAII								
Inouye	N	Y	Y	N	N	Y	N	Y
Matsunaga	N	Y	Y	N	N	Y	N	Y
IDAHO								
McClure	Y	Y	Y	Y	Y	Y	Y	Y
Symms	Y	Y	Y	Y	Y	Y	Y	Y
ILLINOIS								
Dixon	N	N	N	N	N	Y	N	Y
Simon	N	N	N	N	N	Y	N	N
INDIANA								
Lugar	Y	Y	Y	Y	Y	Y	Y	Y
Quayle	N	Y	Y	Y	Y	Y	Y	Y
IOWA								
Grassley	Y	Y	Y	Y	Y	Y	N	Y
Harkin	N	Y	N	N	N	N	Y	Y
KANSAS								
Dole	Y	Y	Y	Y	Y	Y	Y	Y
Kassebaum	Y	Y	Y	Y	Y	Y	Y	Y
KENTUCKY								
McConnell	N	Y	Y	Y	Y	Y	N	Y
Ford	N	Y	Y	N	Y	Y	Y	N
LOUISIANA								
Johnston	N	Y	Y	N	Y	Y	Y	Y
Long	N	Y	Y	Y	Y	Y	Y	N
MAINE								
Cohen	Y	N	N	N	Y	Y	Y	Y
Mitchell	N	N	N	N	Y	Y	Y	Y
MARYLAND								
Mathias	N	N	N	N	N	Y	Y	N
Sarbanes	N	N	N	N	N	Y	N	N
MASSACHUSETTS								
Kennedy	N	Y	N	N	N	Y	N	Y
Kerry	N	N	N	N	N	N	N	Y
MICHIGAN								
Levin	N	N	N	N	N	Y	N	N
Riegle	N	N	N	N	N	Y	N	Y
MINNESOTA								
Boschwitz	Y	Y	Y	Y	Y	Y	Y	Y
Durenberger	N	N	N	Y	Y	Y	Y	Y
MISSISSIPPI								
Cochran	Y	Y	Y	Y	Y	Y	Y	Y
Stennis	N	Y	Y	Y	N	Y	?	?
MISSOURI								
Danforth	Y	Y	Y	Y	Y	Y	Y	Y
Eagleton	N	N	N	N	Y	Y	Y	N
MONTANA								
Baucus	N	N	N	N	Y	Y	Y	Y
Melcher	N	Y	Y	N	N	N	N	Y
NEBRASKA								
Exon	N	Y	Y	N	Y	Y	Y	N
Zorinsky	Y	Y	N	Y	N	Y	Y	Y
NEVADA								
Hecht	Y	Y	Y	Y	Y	Y	N	Y
Laxalt	N	Y	Y	Y	Y	Y	N	Y
NEW HAMPSHIRE								
Humphrey	N	Y	Y	Y	Y	Y	N	Y
Rudman	Y	Y	Y	Y	Y	Y	Y	Y
NEW JERSEY								
Bradley	N	N	N	N	Y	Y	Y	N
Lautenberg	N	N	N	N	Y	Y	N	N
NEW MEXICO								
Domenici	Y	Y	Y	Y	Y	Y	N	Y
Bingaman	N	N	N	N	N	Y	N	N
NEW YORK								
D'Amato	N	Y	Y	N	Y	Y	N	Y
Moynihan	N	N	N	Y	Y	Y	Y	Y
NORTH CAROLINA								
East	Y	Y	Y	Y	Y	Y	?	?
Helms	Y	Y	Y	Y	Y	Y	Y	Y
NORTH DAKOTA								
Andrews	Y	Y	Y	Y	Y	N	N	Y
Burdick	N	N	N	N	N	N	N	Y
OHIO								
Glenn	N	N	N	N	N	Y	Y	N
Metzenbaum	N	N	N	N	N	N	Y	Y
OKLAHOMA								
Nickles	Y	Y	N	N	Y	Y	Y	Y
Boren	N	Y	Y	N	Y	Y	Y	N
OREGON								
Hatfield	Y	N	N	?	?	?	?	?
Packwood	Y	Y	Y	Y	Y	Y	Y	Y
PENNSYLVANIA								
Heinz	Y	Y	Y	Y	Y	Y	N	Y
Specter	N	N	N	Y	Y	Y	N	Y
RHODE ISLAND								
Chafee	Y	N	N	N	Y	Y	Y	Y
Pell	Y	N	N	N	N	Y	N	Y
SOUTH CAROLINA								
Thurmond	N	Y	Y	Y	Y	Y	N	Y
Hollings	N	Y	Y	N	N	Y	Y	Y
SOUTH DAKOTA								
Abdnor	N	Y	Y	Y	Y	Y	Y	Y
Pressler	Y	Y	Y	Y	Y	Y	N	Y
TENNESSEE								
Gore	N	Y	Y	N	Y	Y	N	Y
Sasser	N	Y	Y	N	Y	Y	Y	Y
TEXAS								
Gramm	Y	Y	Y	Y	Y	Y	N	Y
Bentsen	N	Y	Y	Y	Y	Y	Y	N
UTAH								
Garn	N	N	N	Y	Y	Y	N	Y
Hatch	N	N	N	Y	Y	Y	N	Y
VERMONT								
Stafford	Y	N	N	Y	Y	Y	Y	Y
Leahy	N	N	N	N	Y	Y	N	Y
VIRGINIA								
Trible	N	Y	Y	Y	Y	Y	?	Y
Warner	Y	Y	Y	Y	Y	Y	Y	Y
WASHINGTON								
Evans	Y	Y	N	Y	Y	Y	Y	Y
Gorton	Y	Y	N	Y	Y	Y	Y	Y
WEST VIRGINIA								
Byrd	N	Y	Y	N	Y	Y	N	Y
Rockefeller	N	Y	Y	N	Y	Y	N	N
WISCONSIN								
Kasten	N	N	N	Y	Y	Y	Y	Y
Proxmire	Y	N	N	Y	N	Y	Y	Y
WYOMING								
Simpson	Y	Y	N	Y	Y	Y	Y	Y
Wallop	Y	Y	Y	Y	Y	Y	Y	Y

KEY

Y Voted for (yea).
Paired for.
+ Announced for.
N Voted against (nay).
X Paired against.
- Announced against.
P Voted "present."
C Voted "present" to avoid possible conflict of interest.
? Did not vote or otherwise make a position known.

Democrats ***Republicans***

ND - Northern Democrats SD - Southern Democrats (Southern states - Ala., Ark., Fla., Ga., Ky., La., Miss., N.C., Okla., S.C., Tenn., Texas, Va.)

309. S 1730. Omnibus Budget Reconciliation, Fiscal 1986. Gorton, R-Wash., motion to table (kill) the DeConcini, D-Ariz., motion to waive the germaneness requirement contained in the 1974 Congressional Budget and Impoundment Control Act (PL 93-344) with respect to the DeConcini amendment to prohibit a reduction in pay in fiscal 1986 for about 800 blue-collar federal workers in the Tucson, Ariz., area. Motion rejected 36-63: R 33-20; D 3-43 (ND 3-30, SD 0-13), Nov. 14, 1985. (The DeConcini amendment subsequently was adopted by voice vote.)

310. S 1730. Omnibus Budget Reconciliation, Fiscal 1986. Dole, R-Kan., motion to table (kill) the Metzenbaum, D-Ohio, amendment to strike provisions making changes in the federal tobacco price-support program to allow discount sales of tobacco in federal stockpiles and to reduce price supports. Motion agreed to 66-33: R 42-11; D 24-22 (ND 11-22, SD 13-0), Nov. 14, 1985. A "nay" was a vote supporting the president's position.

311. S 1730. Omnibus Budget Reconciliation, Fiscal 1986. Dole, R-Kan., motion to table (kill) the Metzenbaum, D-Ohio, amendment to strike provisions exempting from federal antitrust laws major cigarette manufacturers that have agreed to purchase discounted tobacco from federal stockpiles in amounts reflecting their shares of the cigarette market. Motion agreed to 57-42: R 37-16; D 20-26 (ND 8-25, SD 12-1), Nov. 14, 1985.

312. S 1730. Omnibus Budget Reconciliation, Fiscal 1986. Durenberger, R-Minn., motion to table (kill) the Bumpers, D-Ark., amendment to provide Medicare coverage for "reasonable and medically necessary" liver transplants performed on individuals aged 18 and over. Motion agreed to 51-47: R 45-7; D 6-40 (ND 3-30, SD 3-10), Nov. 14, 1985.

313. S 1730. Omnibus Budget Reconciliation, Fiscal 1986. Packwood, R-Ore., motion to table (kill) the Metzenbaum, D-Ohio, amendment to strike a provision increasing Medicaid coverage for certain nursing homes that change ownership. Motion agreed to 71-27: R 51-1; D 20-26 (ND 10-23, SD 10-3), Nov. 14, 1985.

314. HR 3128. Omnibus Budget Reconciliation, Fiscal 1986. Passage of the bill to reduce the deficit by $85.7 billion over fiscal 1986-88 through $69.9 billion in spending cuts and $15.8 billion in added revenues. Passed 93-6: R 51-1; D 42-5 (ND 28-5, SD 14-0), Nov. 14, 1985. (The Senate previously had moved to strike the text of HR 3128, the House version of the bill, and insert instead the provisions of S 1730.) A "nay" was a vote supporting the president's position.

315. S J Res 77. Compact of Free Association. McClure, R-Idaho, motion to table (kill) the Hatch, R-Utah, amendment to create a $150 million trust fund to compensate American victims of nuclear weapons tests in the Southwest. Motion agreed to 53-42: R 30-19; D 23-23 (ND 12-21, SD 11-2), Nov. 14, 1985. A "yea" was a vote supporting the president's position.

316. S J Res 77. Compact of Free Association. McClure, R-Idaho, motion to table (kill) the Hart, D-Colo., amendment to impose a new $10-per-barrel oil import fee. Motion agreed to 78-18: R 48-2; D 30-16 (ND 22-11, SD 8-5), Nov. 14, 1985. (The Senate subsequently moved to strike the language of H J Res 187, the House version of the joint resolution, and insert instead the provisions of S J Res 77. The Senate subsequently passed H J Res 187 by voice vote.)

CQ Senate Votes 317 - 324

Corresponding to Congressional Record Votes 317, 318, 319, 320, 321, 322, 323, 324

	317	318	319	320	321	322	323	324
ALABAMA								
Denton	N	Y	Y	Y	N	Y	N	Y
Heflin	Y	Y	N	N	Y	Y	Y	Y
ALASKA								
Murkowski	N	N	Y	Y	Y	Y	N	Y
Stevens	N	Y	Y	Y	Y	Y	N	Y
ARIZONA								
Goldwater	Y	Y	Y	Y	Y	Y	N	Y
DeConcini	Y	Y	Y	N	Y	Y	Y	Y
ARKANSAS								
Bumpers	Y	Y	Y	N	Y	Y	Y	Y
Pryor	Y	Y	Y	N	Y	Y	Y	Y
CALIFORNIA								
Wilson	N	Y	Y	Y	Y	Y	N	Y
Cranston	Y	Y	Y	Y	Y	Y	Y	Y
COLORADO								
Armstrong	N	Y	Y	Y	Y	Y	N	Y
Hart	Y	Y	N	N	Y	Y	Y	Y
CONNECTICUT								
Weicker	Y	?	Y	Y	Y	Y	N	Y
Dodd	Y	Y	N	Y	Y	Y	Y	Y
DELAWARE								
Roth	N	Y	Y	Y	Y	Y	N	Y
Biden	N	Y	N	N	Y	Y	Y	Y
FLORIDA								
Hawkins	N	N	Y	Y	Y	Y	N	Y
Chiles	N	Y	Y	N	Y	Y	Y	Y
GEORGIA								
Mattingly	N	Y	Y	Y	Y	Y	N	Y
Nunn	N	Y	Y	Y	Y	Y	Y	Y
HAWAII								
Inouye	Y	Y	?	?	?	?	?	?
Matsunaga	Y	Y	Y	N	Y	Y	Y	Y
IDAHO								
McClure	N	Y	Y	Y	Y	Y	N	Y
Symms	N	Y	Y	Y	Y	Y	N	Y
ILLINOIS								
Dixon	Y	Y	N	N	Y	Y	Y	Y
Simon	Y	Y	N	N	Y	Y	Y	Y
INDIANA								
Lugar	N	Y	Y	Y	Y	Y	N	Y
Quayle	N	N	Y	Y	Y	Y	N	Y

	317	318	319	320	321	322	323	324
IOWA								
Grassley	Y	Y	N	N	Y	Y	N	N
Harkin	Y	Y	N	N	Y	Y	Y	N
KANSAS								
Dole	N	Y	Y	Y	Y	Y	N	Y
Kassebaum	N	Y	Y	Y	Y	Y	N	Y
KENTUCKY								
McConnell	Y	Y	Y	Y	Y	Y	N	Y
Ford	Y	Y	N	N	Y	Y	Y	Y
LOUISIANA								
Johnston	Y	Y	Y	N	Y	Y	Y	Y
Long	Y	Y	Y	N	Y	Y	Y	Y
MAINE								
Cohen	Y	N	Y	Y	Y	Y	N	Y
Mitchell	Y	Y	N	Y	Y	Y	Y	Y
MARYLAND								
Mathias	?	?	Y	Y	Y	Y	N	Y
Sarbanes	Y	Y	N	N	Y	Y	Y	Y
MASSACHUSETTS								
Kennedy	N	Y	N	N	Y	Y	Y	Y
Kerry	N	Y	N	N	Y	Y	Y	Y
MICHIGAN								
Levin	Y	Y	N	N	Y	Y	Y	Y
Riegle	Y	Y	N	N	Y	Y	Y	Y
MINNESOTA								
Boschwitz	Y	Y	Y	Y	Y	Y	N	Y
Durenberger	Y	Y	N	N	Y	Y	N	Y
MISSISSIPPI								
Cochran	N	Y	Y	Y	Y	Y	N	Y
Stennis	?	?	N	N	Y	Y	Y	Y
MISSOURI								
Danforth	N	Y	Y	Y	N	Y	N	Y
Eagleton	Y	Y	N	N	Y	Y	Y	Y
MONTANA								
Baucus	Y	Y	N	N	Y	Y	Y	N
Melcher	Y	Y	N	N	Y	Y	Y	Y
NEBRASKA								
Exon	Y	Y	N	N	Y	Y	Y	Y
Zorinsky	N	Y	N	N	Y	Y	Y	Y
NEVADA								
Hecht	N	Y	Y	Y	Y	Y	N	Y
Laxalt	N	N	Y	Y	N	Y	N	Y

	317	318	319	320	321	322	323	324
NEW HAMPSHIRE								
Humphrey	N	Y	Y	Y	N	Y	N	Y
Rudman	N	Y	Y	Y	Y	Y	N	Y
NEW JERSEY								
Bradley	N	Y	N	Y	Y	Y	N	Y
Lautenberg	N	Y	N	Y	Y	Y	Y	Y
NEW MEXICO								
Domenici	N	Y	Y	Y	Y	?	?	?
Bingaman	Y	Y	N	N	Y	Y	Y	Y
NEW YORK								
D'Amato	N	Y	Y	Y	Y	Y	N	Y
Moynihan	N	Y	N	Y	Y	Y	Y	Y
NORTH CAROLINA								
East	?	?	?	?	?	?	?	?
Helms	N	Y	Y	Y	Y	Y	N	Y
NORTH DAKOTA								
Andrews	Y	Y	Y	Y	Y	Y	Y	Y
Burdick	Y	Y	N	N	Y	Y	Y	Y
OHIO								
Glenn	Y	Y	N	N	Y	Y	Y	Y
Metzenbaum	N	Y	N	Y	Y	Y	Y	Y
OKLAHOMA								
Nickles	N	Y	N	N	N	Y	N	Y
Boren	Y	Y	N	N	Y	Y	Y	Y
OREGON								
Hatfield	N	N	Y	Y	Y	Y	N	Y
Packwood	N	Y	Y	Y	Y	Y	N	Y
PENNSYLVANIA								
Heinz	Y	Y	Y	Y	Y	Y	N	Y
Specter	Y	Y	Y	Y	?	Y	N	Y
RHODE ISLAND								
Chafee	N	Y	Y	Y	Y	Y	N	Y
Pell	N	Y	N	Y	Y	N	Y	Y
SOUTH CAROLINA								
Thurmond	N	Y	Y	Y	Y	Y	N	Y
Hollings	N	Y	N	N	Y	Y	Y	Y
SOUTH DAKOTA								
Abdnor	Y	Y	N	N	Y	Y	N	Y
Pressler	Y	Y	N	N	Y	Y	N	N
TENNESSEE								
Gore	Y	Y	N	N	Y	Y	Y	Y
Sasser	Y	Y	N	N	Y	Y	Y	Y

KEY

- Y Voted for (yea).
- # Paired for.
- + Announced for.
- N Voted against (nay).
- X Paired against.
- \- Announced against.
- P Voted "present."
- C Voted "present" to avoid possible conflict of interest.
- ? Did not vote or otherwise make a position known.

Democrats *Republicans*

	317	318	319	320	321	322	323	324
TEXAS								
Gramm	N	Y	Y	Y	N	Y	N	Y
Bentsen	Y	Y	Y	N	Y	Y	Y	Y
UTAH								
Garn	N	Y	Y	Y	Y	Y	N	Y
Hatch	N	Y	Y	Y	Y	Y	N	Y
VERMONT								
Stafford	Y	Y	?	?	?	?	?	?
Leahy	Y	Y	N	N	Y	Y	Y	Y
VIRGINIA								
Trible	N	Y	Y	Y	Y	Y	N	Y
Warner	N	Y	Y	Y	Y	Y	N	Y
WASHINGTON								
Evans	Y	Y	Y	Y	N	Y	N	Y
Gorton	Y	Y	Y	Y	Y	Y	N	Y
WEST VIRGINIA								
Byrd	Y	Y	N	N	Y	Y	Y	Y
Rockefeller	Y	Y	N	N	Y	Y	Y	Y
WISCONSIN								
Kasten	Y	Y	N	N	Y	Y	N	Y
Proxmire	Y	N	Y	Y	Y	Y	Y	Y
WYOMING								
Simpson	N	Y	Y	Y	Y	Y	N	Y
Wallop	N	N	Y	Y	Y	Y	N	Y

ND - Northern Democrats SD - Southern Democrats (Southern states - Ala., Ark., Fla., Ga., Ky., La., Miss., N.C., Okla., S.C., Tenn., Texas, Va.)

317. S 1714. Farm Programs Reauthorization, Fiscal 1986-89. Boschwitz, R-Minn., motion to table (kill) the Hawkins, R-Fla., amendment to reduce the price-support rate for dairy products by 50 cents on Jan. 2, 1986, instead of Jan. 1, 1987, if projected government purchases of surplus dairy products in 1986 is estimated to exceed 10 billion pounds. Motion agreed to 50-47: R 16-35; D 34-12 (ND 24-9, SD 10-3), Nov. 19, 1985. A "nay" was a vote supporting the president's position.

318. S 1714. Farm Programs Reauthorization, Fiscal 1986-89. Harkin, D-Iowa, motion to table (kill) the Dole, R-Kan., perfecting amendment to the Dole amendment to the Dole motion to recommit the bill to the Agriculture, Nutrition and Forestry Committee with instructions to report back forthwith with the Dole amendment to freeze target prices for corn, cotton and rice in fiscal 1986 and allow maximum 5 percent annual reductions thereafter, to provide a sliding scale of target prices for wheat based on levels of production, to create an emergency conservation reserve, to provide numerous cost-saving measures, and to include the Stevens, R-Alaska, amendment dealing with cargo preference, as perfected by Senate action to date. Motion agreed to 88-8: R 43-7; D 45-1 (ND 32-1, SD 13-0), Nov. 19, 1985.

319. S 1714. Farm Programs Reauthorization, Fiscal 1986-89. Dole, R-Kan., perfecting amendment to the Dole amendment to the Dole motion to recommit the bill to the Agriculture, Nutrition and Forestry Committee with instructions, to freeze current target prices for wheat, feed grains, cotton and rice titles for the life of the bill; to freeze target prices for corn, cotton and rice in fiscal 1986 and allow maximum 5 percent annual reductions thereafter; to provide a sliding scale of target prices for wheat based on levels of production; to authorize the agriculture secretary to increase the maximum acreage limitation for wheat, feed grains, cotton and rice by 5 percent; to reduce the conservation reserve in 1986 and require some of the reserve to be devoted to trees; to change provisions dealing with loans for rice; to provide for payments to soybean and sunflower farmers; to expand disaster payments to farmers of soybeans, sugar cane and sugar beets; and to require the president to operate the sugar program at no cost to the government. Adopted 56-41: R 45-6; D 11-35 (ND 4-28, SD 7-7), Nov. 20, 1985.

320. S 1714. Farm Programs Reauthorization, Fiscal 1986-89. Dole, R-Kan., motion to table (kill) the Harkin, D-Iowa, perfecting amendment to the Dole amendment to the Dole motion to recommit the bill to the Agriculture, Nutrition and Forestry Committee with instructions, to freeze target prices for wheat, corn, cotton and rice through the life of the bill. Motion agreed to 55-42: R 45-6; D 10-36 (ND 9-23, SD 1-13), Nov. 20, 1985.

321. HR 2409. National Institutes of Health Authorizations, Fiscal 1986-88. Passage, over President Reagan's Nov. 8 veto, of the bill to reauthorize selected biomedical research activities at the National Institutes of Health through fiscal 1988 and to set up a new arthritis research institute and nursing research center. Passed (thus enacted into law) 89-7: R 43-7; D 46-0 (ND 32-0, SD 14-0), Nov. 20, 1985. A two-thirds majority of those present and voting (64 in this case) of both houses is required to override a veto. (The House Nov. 12 voted to override the veto.) A "nay" was a vote supporting the president's position. *(Vote 364, p. 114-H)*

322. S 1714. Farm Programs Reauthorization, Fiscal 1986-89. Abdnor, R-S.D., perfecting amendment to the Dole, R-Kan., amendment to the Dole motion to recommit the bill to the Agriculture, Nutrition and Forestry Committee with instructions, to require the administrator of the Environmental Protection Agency and the agriculture secretary jointly to conduct a study on the use of unleaded fuel in agricultural machinery. Adopted 95-1: R 50-0; D 45-1 (ND 31-1, SD 14-0), Nov. 20, 1985.

323. S 1714. Farm Programs Reauthorization, Fiscal 1986-89. Melcher, D-Mont., perfecting amendment to the Dole, R-Kan., amendment to the Dole motion to recommit the bill to the Agriculture, Nutrition and Forestry Committee with instructions, to reinstate the farmer-owned grain reserve, to increase the required acreage-reduction program for wheat and feed grains, to provide a paid land-diversion program and to expand the mandatory dairy sales program. Rejected 46-50: R 1-49; D 45-1 (ND 31-1, SD 14-0), Nov. 20, 1985.

324. S 1714. Farm Programs Reauthorization, Fiscal 1986-89. Thurmond, R-S.C., motion to table (kill) the Pressler, R-S.D., perfecting amendment to the Dole, R-Kan., amendment to the Dole motion to recommit the bill to the Agriculture, Nutrition and Forestry Committee with instructions, to allow certain sellers of agricultural products to bring antitrust actions. Motion agreed to 92-4: R 48-2; D 44-2 (ND 30-2, SD 14-0), Nov. 20, 1985.

CQ Senate Votes 325 - 332

Corresponding to Congressional Record Votes 325, 326, 327, 328, 329, 330, 331, 332

	325	326	327	328	329	330	331	332
ALABAMA								
Denton	N	Y	N	Y	Y	Y	Y	Y
Heflin	Y	Y	N	Y	N	Y	N	Y
ALASKA								
Murkowski	N	Y	Y	N	N	N	N	Y
Stevens	Y	Y	Y	N	N	?	N	N
ARIZONA								
Goldwater	N	Y	Y	Y	N	N	N	?
DeConcini	Y	N	Y	N	N	Y	N	N
ARKANSAS								
Bumpers	Y	N	Y	Y	N	Y	N	N
Pryor	Y	N	Y	Y	N	Y	N	N
CALIFORNIA								
Wilson	N	N	Y	N	Y	Y	Y	Y
Cranston	Y	N	Y	N	N	Y	N	N
COLORADO								
Armstrong	N	Y	N	Y	Y	N	Y	Y
Hart	Y	N	Y	N	N	Y	?	N
CONNECTICUT								
Weicker	?	Y	N	N	N	Y	?	?
Dodd	Y	N	Y	N	N	Y	N	N
DELAWARE								
Roth	N	N	Y	N	Y	N	Y	Y
Biden	Y	N	Y	N	N	Y	N	Y
FLORIDA								
Hawkins	Y	N	Y	N	N	Y	Y	Y
Chiles	Y	N	Y	N	N	Y	?	N
GEORGIA								
Mattingly	Y	N	Y	Y	Y	Y	Y	Y
Nunn	Y	Y	N	Y	Y	Y	N	?
HAWAII								
Inouye	Y	N	Y	N	N	Y	N	N
Matsunaga	Y	N	Y	N	N	Y	N	Y
IDAHO								
McClure	N	Y	N	Y	Y	N	Y	Y
Symms	N	Y	N	Y	Y	N	Y	Y
ILLINOIS								
Dixon	Y	N	Y	N	N	Y	N	Y
Simon	Y	N	Y	N	N	Y	N	Y
INDIANA								
Lugar	N	Y	N	N	Y	Y	Y	Y
Quayle	N	Y	N	N	Y	Y	?	N
IOWA								
Grassley	Y	N	Y	Y	N	Y	Y	N
Harkin	Y	N	Y	N	N	Y	N	N
KANSAS								
Dole	N	N	N	N	Y	Y	Y	Y
Kassebaum	N	Y	N	N	Y	Y	N	N
KENTUCKY								
McConnell	N	N	Y	N	Y	N	Y	Y
Ford	Y	N	Y	Y	N	Y	N	Y
LOUISIANA								
Johnston	Y	Y	N	N	Y	Y	Y	Y
Long	N	Y	N	N	Y	Y	?	Y
MAINE								
Cohen	Y	Y	N	N	N	Y	Y	Y
Mitchell	Y	N	Y	N	N	Y	N	Y
MARYLAND								
Mathias	Y	Y	N	N	N	Y	N	Y
Sarbanes	Y	N	N	N	N	Y	N	N
MASSACHUSETTS								
Kennedy	Y	N	Y	N	N	Y	N	?
Kerry	Y	N	Y	N	N	Y	N	Y
MICHIGAN								
Levin	Y	N	Y	N	N	Y	N	Y
Riegle	Y	N	Y	N	N	Y	N	N
MINNESOTA								
Boschwitz	Y	N	Y	N	Y	Y	Y	N
Durenberger	Y	N	Y	N	N	Y	N	N
MISSISSIPPI								
Cochran	Y	N	Y	Y	Y	Y	Y	Y
Stennis	Y	N	N	Y	Y	Y	?	?
MISSOURI								
Danforth	Y	N	Y	N	N	Y	Y	Y
Eagleton	Y	N	Y	N	N	Y	N	?
MONTANA								
Baucus	Y	N	Y	N	N	Y	N	N
Melcher	Y	N	Y	N	N	Y	Y	N
NEBRASKA								
Exon	Y	N	Y	N	N	Y	N	N
Zorinsky	Y	N	Y	N	Y	N	Y	Y
NEVADA								
Hecht	N	Y	N	N	Y	N	Y	Y
Laxalt	N	Y	N	Y	Y	N	Y	Y
NEW HAMPSHIRE								
Humphrey	N	Y	N	Y	N	N	Y	Y
Rudman	N	Y	N	N	N	N	Y	?
NEW JERSEY								
Bradley	Y	Y	N	N	N	Y	N	Y
Lautenberg	Y	Y	N	N	N	Y	N	Y
NEW MEXICO								
Domenici	Y	Y	N	N	Y	Y	Y	Y
Bingaman	Y	Y	N	Y	N	Y	N	N
NEW YORK								
D'Amato	Y	N	Y	N	N	Y	N	N
Moynihan	Y	N	Y	N	N	Y	N	Y
NORTH CAROLINA								
East	?	?	?	?	?	?	?	?
Helms	N	Y	N	N	Y	N	Y	Y
NORTH DAKOTA								
Andrews	Y	N	Y	N	N	Y	N	Y
Burdick	Y	N	Y	N	N	Y	N	Y
OHIO								
Glenn	Y	N	Y	N	N	Y	N	Y
Metzenbaum	Y	N	Y	N	N	Y	N	Y
OKLAHOMA								
Nickles	N	N	Y	Y	Y	N	Y	Y
Boren	Y	N	Y	Y	Y	Y	Y	N
OREGON								
Hatfield	Y	N	N	N	N	Y	N	Y
Packwood	Y	N	Y	N	Y	Y	N	?
PENNSYLVANIA								
Heinz	Y	N	+	N	N	Y	N	N
Specter	Y	N	Y	N	N	Y	N	Y
RHODE ISLAND								
Chafee	Y	Y	N	N	N	Y	Y	Y
Pell	Y	N	Y	N	N	Y	N	N
SOUTH CAROLINA								
Thurmond	N	Y	N	Y	Y	N	Y	Y
Hollings	Y	Y	N	Y	N	Y	N	Y
SOUTH DAKOTA								
Abdnor	Y	N	Y	Y	N	Y	N	N
Pressler	N	N	Y	Y	Y	Y	Y	N
TENNESSEE								
Gore	Y	N	Y	Y	N	Y	N	N
Sasser	Y	N	Y	Y	N	Y	N	Y
TEXAS								
Gramm	N	Y	N	Y	Y	N	Y	Y
Bentsen	Y	N	Y	N	Y	Y	Y	N
UTAH								
Garn	N	Y	N	Y	Y	N	Y	Y
Hatch	N	Y	N	Y	Y	Y	N	Y
VERMONT								
Stafford	Y	N	Y	N	N	Y	N	Y
Leahy	Y	N	Y	N	N	Y	N	Y
VIRGINIA								
Trible	Y	Y	N	N	N	N	Y	N
Warner	N	Y	N	N	N	N	Y	N
WASHINGTON								
Evans	Y	N	N	Y	Y	Y	N	Y
Gorton	Y	Y	N	Y	Y	Y	N	Y
WEST VIRGINIA								
Byrd	Y	N	N	N	N	Y	N	Y
Rockefeller	Y	Y	N	N	N	Y	N	Y
WISCONSIN								
Kasten	N	N	Y	N	N	Y	Y	Y
Proxmire	N	N	Y	N	N	N	Y	Y
WYOMING								
Simpson	N	Y	N	Y	Y	Y	Y	Y
Wallop	N	Y	Y	Y	Y	N	Y	Y

KEY

- Y Voted for (yea).
- # Paired for.
- + Announced for.
- N Voted against (nay).
- X Paired against.
- - Announced against.
- P Voted "present."
- C Voted "present" to avoid possible conflict of interest.
- ? Did not vote or otherwise make a position known.

Democrats *Republicans*

ND - Northern Democrats SD - Southern Democrats (Southern states - Ala., Ark., Fla., Ga., Ky., La., Miss., N.C., Okla., S.C., Tenn., Texas, Va.)

325. S 1714. Farm Programs Reauthorization, Fiscal 1986-89. Harkin, D-Iowa, motion to table (kill) the Helms, R-N.C., perfecting amendment to the Dole, R-Kan., amendment to the Dole motion to recommit the bill to the Agriculture, Nutrition and Forestry Committee with instructions, to allow states the option of receiving food stamp funds in a block grant and designing their own programs. Motion agreed to 68-30: R 23-28; D 45-2 (ND 32-1, SD 13-1), Nov. 21, 1985. A "nay" was a vote supporting the president's position.

326. S 1714. Farm Programs Reauthorization, Fiscal 1986-89. Thurmond, R-S.C., perfecting amendment to the Dole, R-Kan., amendment to the Dole motion to recommit the bill to the Agriculture, Forestry and Nutrition Committee with instructions, to require the approval of a majority of producers voting in a referendum as a prerequisite to the issuance of an order to establish a pork promotion program, and to permit states to continue to operate existing pork promotion programs. Rejected 38-61: R 29-23; D 9-38 (ND 4-29, SD 5-9), Nov. 21, 1985.

327. S 1714. Farm Programs Reauthorization, Fiscal 1986-89. Zorinsky, D-Neb., motion to table (kill) the Thurmond, R-S.C., perfecting amendment to the Dole, R-Kan., amendment to the Dole motion to recommit the bill to the Agriculture, Forestry and Nutrition Committee with instructions, to require the approval of a majority of producers voting in a referendum as a prerequisite to the issuance of an order to establish a pork promotion, research, and consumer information program. Motion agreed to 58-40: R 23-28; D 35-12 (ND 27-6, SD 8-6), Nov. 21, 1985.

328. S 1714. Farm Programs Reauthorization, Fiscal 1986-89. Denton, R-Ala., perfecting amendment to the Dole, R-Kan., amendment to the Dole motion to recommit the bill to the Agriculture, Nutrition and Forestry Committee with instructions, to strike a provision prohibiting states from charging sales taxes on purchases made with food stamps. Rejected 32-67: R 21-31; D 11-36 (ND 1-32, SD 10-4), Nov. 21, 1985.

329. S 1714. Farm Programs Reauthorization, Fiscal 1986-89. Zorinsky, D-Neb., motion to table (kill) the Stafford, R-Vt., perfecting amendment to the Dole, R-Kan., amendment to the Dole motion to recommit the bill to the Agriculture, Nutrition and Forestry Committee with instructions, to strike a provision that would have counted payments made under the low-income energy assistance program as income for calculating food stamp benefits. Motion rejected 36-63: R 29-23; D 7-40 (ND 1-32, SD 6-8), Nov. 21, 1985. (The Stafford amendment subsequently was adopted by voice vote.)

330. S 1714. Farm Programs Reauthorization, Fiscal 1986-89. Pryor, D-Ark., motion to table (kill) the McClure, R-Idaho, perfecting amendment to the Dole, R-Kan., amendment to the Dole motion to recommit the bill to the Agriculture, Nutrition and Forestry Committee with instructions, to reduce states' allowable food stamp error rates from 5 percent to 3 percent. Motion agreed to 77-21: R 32-19; D 45-2 (ND 31-2, SD 14-0), Nov. 21, 1985.

331. S 1714. Farm Programs Reauthorization, Fiscal 1986-89. Cochran, R-Miss., motion to table (kill) the Evans, R-Wash., perfecting amendment to the Dole, R-Kan., amendment to the Dole motion to recommit the bill to the Agriculture, Nutrition and Forestry Committee with instructions, to suspend for two years collection of fiscal sanctions on states for food stamp errors, pending a study of the error rate system. Motion rejected 39-54: R 33-17; D 6-37 (ND 3-29, SD 3-8), Nov. 21, 1985. (The Evans amendment subsequently was adopted by voice vote.)

332. S 1714. Farm Programs Reauthorization, Fiscal 1986-89. Thurmond, R-S.C., motion to table (kill) the Grassley, R-Iowa, perfecting amendment to the Dole, R-Kan., amendment to the Dole motion to recommit the bill to the Agriculture, Forestry and Nutrition Committee with instructions, to provide for additional bankruptcy judges for the northern and southern districts of Iowa, to be appointed for a limited time. Motion agreed to 60-31: R 36-12; D 24-19 (ND 18-13, SD 6-6), Nov. 21, 1985.

Corresponding to Congressional Record Votes 333, 334, 335, 336, 337

	333	334	335	336	337
ALABAMA					
Denton	Y	N	Y	N	N
Heflin	N	Y	Y	N	Y
ALASKA					
Murkowski	Y	N	Y	Y	N
Stevens	Y	N	Y	Y	N
ARIZONA					
Goldwater	?	?	?	?	?
DeConcini	Y	Y	Y	N	N
ARKANSAS					
Bumpers	N	Y	Y	N	Y
Pryor	N	Y	Y	N	Y
CALIFORNIA					
Wilson	Y	N	Y	Y	N
Cranston	N	Y	Y	N	N
COLORADO					
Armstrong	Y	N	N	Y	N
Hart	N	Y	Y	N	Y
CONNECTICUT					
Weicker	?	?	?	?	?
Dodd	N	N	N	N	Y
DELAWARE					
Roth	Y	N	N	Y	N
Biden	N	N	N	N	?
FLORIDA					
Hawkins	Y	Y	Y	Y	N
Chiles	N	Y	Y	Y	Y
GEORGIA					
Mattingly	Y	N	Y	Y	N
Nunn	N	Y	N	N	N
HAWAII					
Inouye	Y	Y	Y	N	Y
Matsunaga	N	Y	Y	N	Y
IDAHO					
McClure	Y	Y	Y	Y	Y
Symms	Y	Y	Y	Y	N
ILLINOIS					
Dixon	N	N	Y	N	N
Simon	N	N	Y	N	Y
INDIANA					
Lugar	Y	N	N	Y	N
Quayle	Y	N	N	Y	N
IOWA					
Grassley	N	Y	Y	N	Y
Harkin	N	Y	Y	N	Y
KANSAS					
Dole	Y	N	Y	Y	N
Kassebaum	Y	N	Y	Y	N
KENTUCKY					
McConnell	Y	N	Y	Y	N
Ford	N	Y	Y	N	Y
LOUISIANA					
Johnston	N	Y	Y	N	Y
Long	N	Y	Y	N	Y
MAINE					
Cohen	Y	N	N	Y	N
Mitchell	N	N	N	N	N
MARYLAND					
Mathias	Y	N	N	Y	N
Sarbanes	N	N	N	N	N
MASSACHUSETTS					
Kennedy	?	N	N	N	?
Kerry	N	N	N	N	Y
MICHIGAN					
Levin	N	N	Y	N	Y
Riegle	Y	N	Y	N	Y
MINNESOTA					
Boschwitz	N	N	Y	Y	N
Durenberger	N	N	Y	Y	N
MISSISSIPPI					
Cochran	Y	Y	Y	N	N
Stennis	?	Y	Y	N	N
MISSOURI					
Danforth	Y	N	N	Y	N
Eagleton	?	N	N	N	Y
MONTANA					
Baucus	N	Y	Y	N	Y
Melcher	N	Y	Y	N	Y
NEBRASKA					
Exon	N	Y	P	N	Y
Zorinsky	N	Y	Y	N	Y
NEVADA					
Hecht	Y	N	Y	Y	N
Laxalt	?	N	Y	Y	N
NEW HAMPSHIRE					
Humphrey	Y	N	N	Y	N
Rudman	Y	N	N	Y	N
NEW JERSEY					
Bradley	Y	N	N	Y	N
Lautenberg	Y	N	N	Y	N
NEW MEXICO					
Domenici	Y	N	?	?	?
Bingaman	N	N	Y	Y	Y
NEW YORK					
D'Amato	Y	N	N	Y	N
Moynihan	N	N	N	Y	Y
NORTH CAROLINA					
East	?	?	?	?	?
Helms	Y	N	Y	Y	N
NORTH DAKOTA					
Andrews	N	Y	Y	Y	N
Burdick	N	Y	Y	N	Y
OHIO					
Glenn	N	Y	?	?	?
Metzenbaum	N	?	N	Y	Y
OKLAHOMA					
Nickles	N	N	N	Y	N
Boren	N	Y	Y	N	Y
OREGON					
Hatfield	Y	Y	Y	Y	N
Packwood	?	N	N	Y	N
PENNSYLVANIA					
Heinz	Y	N	C	Y	N
Specter	Y	N	?	?	?
RHODE ISLAND					
Chafee	Y	N	N	Y	N
Pell	N	N	N	Y	Y
SOUTH CAROLINA					
Thurmond	Y	N	Y	N	N
Hollings	N	Y	Y	N	N
SOUTH DAKOTA					
Abdnor	N	Y	Y	N	N
Pressler	N	Y	Y	N	Y
TENNESSEE					
Gore	N	N	Y	N	Y
Sasser	N	N	Y	N	Y
TEXAS					
Gramm	Y	N	Y	Y	N
Bentsen	Y	Y	Y	N	N
UTAH					
Garn	Y	N	Y	Y	N
Hatch	Y	N	Y	Y	N
VERMONT					
Stafford	Y	N	N	Y	N
Leahy	?	Y	N	N	Y
VIRGINIA					
Trible	Y	N	Y	Y	N
Warner	Y	N	Y	Y	N
WASHINGTON					
Evans	Y	N	N	Y	N
Gorton	Y	N	N	Y	N
WEST VIRGINIA					
Byrd	N	Y	Y	N	Y
Rockefeller	N	Y	Y	N	Y
WISCONSIN					
Kasten	N	N	N	Y	Y
Proxmire	Y	N	N	Y	N
WYOMING					
Simpson	Y	N	Y	Y	N
Wallop	Y	N	Y	Y	N

KEY

- Y Voted for (yea).
- # Paired for.
- + Announced for.
- N Voted against (nay).
- X Paired against.
- - Announced against.
- P Voted "present."
- C Voted "present" to avoid possible conflict of interest.
- ? Did not vote or otherwise make a position known.

Democrats *Republicans*

ND - Northern Democrats SD - Southern Democrats (Southern states - Ala., Ark., Fla., Ga., Ky., La., Miss., N.C., Okla., S.C., Tenn., Texas, Va.)

333. S 1714. Farm Programs Reauthorization, Fiscal 1986-89. Garn, R-Utah, motion to table (kill) the Dixon, D-Ill., perfecting amendment to the Dole, R-Kan., amendment to the Dole motion to recommit the bill to the Agriculture, Nutrition and Forestry Committee with instructions, to permit banks to renegotiate agricultural loans from book value to fair market value and to write off the difference over a period of up to 30 years. Motion agreed to 47-44: R 40-8; D 7-36 (ND 6-24, SD 1-12), Nov. 21, 1985.

334. S 1714. Farm Programs Reauthorization, Fiscal 1986-89. Boren, D-Okla., motion to table (kill) the Quayle, R-Ind., perfecting amendment to the Dole, R-Kan., amendment to the Dole motion to recommit the bill to the Agriculture, Nutrition and Forestry Committee with instructions, to give the agriculture secretary authority to set price-support rates for honey in fiscal years 1986-88 at levels he determines will maintain competitive domestic and export markets for honey after taking into consideration production costs, supply and demand, and world markets, and to terminate price-support programs for honey in 1989. Motion rejected 36-60: R 9-41; D 27-19 (ND 15-17, SD 12-2), Nov. 22, 1985. (The Quayle amendment subsequently was adopted by voice vote.) A "nay" was a vote supporting the president's position.

335. S 1714. Farm Programs Reauthorization, Fiscal 1986-89. Inouye, D-Hawaii, motion to table (kill) the Bradley, D-N.J., perfecting amendment to the Dole, R-Kan., amendment to the Dole motion to recommit the bill to the Agriculture, Nutrition and Forestry Committee with instructions, to set the price-support rate for sugar cane at 18 cents a pound for the 1986 crop, and allow reductions of up to 5 percent a year for the 1987 through 1989 crops, and to set comparable price-support rates for sugar beets. Motion agreed to 60-32: R 30-17; D 30-15 (ND 17-14, SD 13-1), Nov. 22, 1985.

336. S 1714. Farm Programs Reauthorization, Fiscal 1986-89. Wilson, R-Calif., motion to table (kill) the Bumpers, D-Ark., perfecting amendment to the Dole, R-Kan., amendment to the Dole motion to recommit the bill to the Agriculture, Nutrition and Forestry Committee with instructions, to prohibit the agriculture secretary from reducing the price-support rate for soybeans by more than 5 percent a year, and to prohibit the secretary from setting a rate lower than $4.50 a bushel. Motion agreed to 50-44: R 42-6; D 8-38 (ND 7-25, SD 1-13), Nov. 22, 1985.

337. S 1714. Farm Programs Reauthorization, Fiscal 1986-89. Harkin, D-Iowa, perfecting amendment to the Dole, R-Kan., amendment to the Dole motion to recommit the bill to the Agriculture, Nutrition and Forestry Committee with instructions, to establish a marketing certificate program for producers of wheat and feed grains if approved by 60 percent of eligible farmers, including at least 50 percent of wheat farmers and 50 percent of feed grains farmers, voting in a referendum every two years. If the program were approved, crop-support "non-recourse" loan rates for 1986 and 1987 would be set at 70 percent of parity (a formula based on farmers' purchasing power during the years 1910-14), or $4.86 a bushel for wheat and $3.55 a bushel for corn; national acreage-reduction programs could be implemented at no more than 35 percent for wheat and 20 percent for feed grains; and the agriculture secretary would be required to calculate domestic demand for wheat and feed grains and issue marketing certificates governing their supply and sale within the United States, so that only the amount used on the farm of the producer or sold for export could be used or marketed without such a certificate. Rejected 36-56: R 4-44; D 32-12 (ND 22-8, SD 10-4), Nov. 22, 1985. A "nay" was a vote supporting the president's position.

CQ Senate Votes 338 - 343

Corresponding to Congressional Record Votes 338, 339, 340, 341, 342, 343

	338	339	340	341	342	343
ALABAMA						
Denton	N	N	N	N	Y	Y
Heflin	N	N	Y	Y	Y	N
ALASKA						
Murkowski	?	?	?	?	?	?
Stevens	Y	N	Y	N	Y	Y
ARIZONA						
Goldwater	?	?	?	?	?	?
DeConcini	N	Y	N	Y	Y	N
ARKANSAS						
Bumpers	N	Y	N	Y	Y	Y
Pryor	N	Y	N	Y	Y	Y
CALIFORNIA						
Wilson	Y	Y	Y	N	Y	N
Cranston	N	Y	Y	Y	Y	Y
COLORADO						
Armstrong	Y	Y	Y	N	Y	Y
Hart	N	Y	N	Y	Y	Y
CONNECTICUT						
Weicker	N	Y	Y	N	Y	?
Dodd	N	Y	N	Y	Y	N
DELAWARE						
Roth	Y	Y	Y	N	Y	N
Biden	?	?	N	Y	Y	N
FLORIDA						
Hawkins	Y	Y	Y	N	Y	N
Chiles	N	Y	N	Y	Y	Y
GEORGIA						
Mattingly	Y	Y	Y	N	Y	Y
Nunn	Y	Y	N	Y	Y	Y
HAWAII						
Inouye	N	N	N	Y	Y	Y
Matsunaga	N	N	N	Y	Y	Y
IDAHO						
McClure	Y	N	Y	N	Y	?
Symms	Y	N	Y	N	Y	Y
ILLINOIS						
Dixon	N	Y	Y	Y	Y	N
Simon	N	Y	N	Y	Y	N
INDIANA						
Lugar	Y	Y	Y	N	Y	Y
Quayle	Y	Y	Y	N	Y	Y
IOWA						
Grassley	N	Y	N	N	Y	Y
Harkin	N	Y	N	Y	Y	N
KANSAS						
Dole	Y	Y	Y	N	Y	Y
Kassebaum	Y	Y	Y	N	Y	Y
KENTUCKY						
McConnell	Y	Y	Y	N	Y	Y
Ford	N	N	N	Y	Y	Y
LOUISIANA						
Johnston	N	N	?	?	?	Y
Long	Y	Y	Y	N	?	?
MAINE						
Cohen	Y	Y	Y	N	Y	N
Mitchell	N	Y	N	Y	Y	N
MARYLAND						
Mathias	N	Y	Y	N	Y	N
Sarbanes	N	Y	N	Y	Y	Y
MASSACHUSETTS						
Kennedy	?	?	?	?	?	?
Kerry	N	Y	N	Y	Y	?
MICHIGAN						
Levin	N	Y	Y	Y	Y	Y
Riegle	N	Y	N	Y	Y	Y
MINNESOTA						
Boschwitz	Y	Y	Y	N	Y	Y
Durenberger	Y	Y	Y	N	Y	Y
MISSISSIPPI						
Cochran	Y	Y	Y	N	Y	Y
Stennis	?	?	?	?	?	Y
MISSOURI						
Danforth	Y	Y	Y	N	Y	Y
Eagleton	N	Y	N	Y	Y	Y
MONTANA						
Baucus	N	Y	N	Y	Y	Y
Melcher	N	N	N	Y	Y	Y
NEBRASKA						
Exon	N	N	N	Y	Y	Y
Zorinsky	N	N	Y	N	Y	Y
NEVADA						
Hecht	Y	N	Y	N	Y	Y
Laxalt	Y	N	Y	N	Y	Y
NEW HAMPSHIRE						
Humphrey	Y	N	Y	N	Y	?
Rudman	Y	N	Y	N	Y	N
NEW JERSEY						
Bradley	?	Y	Y	Y	Y	N
Lautenberg	N	Y	N	Y	Y	-
NEW MEXICO						
Domenici	?	?	?	?	?	?
Bingaman	N	Y	N	N	Y	N
NEW YORK						
D'Amato	N	Y	Y	N	Y	Y
Moynihan	N	Y	Y	Y	Y	N
NORTH CAROLINA						
East	?	?	?	?	?	?
Helms	Y	N	Y	N	Y	N
NORTH DAKOTA						
Andrews	N	Y	Y	N	Y	Y
Burdick	N	Y	N	Y	Y	Y
OHIO						
Glenn	?	Y	N	Y	Y	Y
Metzenbaum	N	Y	N	Y	Y	N
OKLAHOMA						
Nickles	Y	Y	N	N	Y	Y
Boren	Y	Y	N	Y	Y	Y
OREGON						
Hatfield	Y	N	Y	N	Y	Y
Packwood	Y	Y	Y	N	Y	Y
PENNSYLVANIA						
Heinz	Y	Y	Y	N	Y	Y
Specter	?	?	?	?	?	Y
RHODE ISLAND						
Chafee	Y	Y	Y	N	Y	N
Pell	N	Y	N	N	Y	N
SOUTH CAROLINA						
Thurmond	Y	N	Y	N	Y	Y
Hollings	N	Y	N	N	Y	Y
SOUTH DAKOTA						
Abdnor	N	Y	Y	N	Y	Y
Pressler	N	Y	N	N	Y	Y
TENNESSEE						
Gore	N	Y	N	Y	Y	Y
Sasser	N	Y	N	Y	Y	Y
TEXAS						
Gramm	Y	Y	Y	N	Y	N
Bentsen	N	N	N	Y	Y	Y
UTAH						
Garn	Y	Y	Y	N	Y	N
Hatch	Y	N	Y	N	Y	Y
VERMONT						
Stafford	Y	Y	Y	N	Y	Y
Leahy	N	Y	Y	Y	Y	Y
VIRGINIA						
Trible	Y	Y	Y	N	Y	Y
Warner	Y	Y	Y	N	Y	N
WASHINGTON						
Evans	Y	Y	Y	N	Y	Y
Gorton	Y	Y	Y	N	Y	Y
WEST VIRGINIA						
Byrd	N	Y	N	Y	Y	Y
Rockefeller	N	Y	N	Y	Y	Y
WISCONSIN						
Kasten	N	N	Y	N	Y	N
Proxmire	N	Y	N	N	Y	N
WYOMING						
Simpson	Y	N	Y	N	Y	N
Wallop	Y	Y	Y	N	Y	N

KEY

- Y Voted for (yea).
- # Paired for.
- + Announced for.
- N Voted against (nay).
- X Paired against.
- - Announced against.
- P Voted "present."
- C Voted "present" to avoid possible conflict of interest.
- ? Did not vote or otherwise make a position known.

Democrats *Republicans*

ND - Northern Democrats SD - Southern Democrats (Southern states - Ala., Ark., Fla., Ga., Ky., La., Miss., N.C., Okla., S.C., Tenn., Texas, Va.)

338. S 1714. Farm Programs Reauthorization, Fiscal 1986-89. Boschwitz, R-Minn., perfecting amendment to the Dole, R-Kan., amendment to the Dole motion to recommit the bill to the Agriculture, Nutrition and Forestry Committee with instructions, to establish a six-year price-support program for major commodities; to set loan rates of $2.20 a bushel for wheat, $1.90 a bushel for corn, 50 cents a pound for cotton and $5.50 a hundredweight for rice; to allow repayment of a loan at the lesser of the loan rate or the prevailing world market rate; to repeal authority for acreage-reduction programs; and to provide for direct payments to farmers in 1986 under a formula for acreage bases and crop yields times standard rates of $1.42 a bushel for wheat, 94 cents a bushel for corn, 18 cents a pound for cotton and $4.26 a hundredweight for rice, with those payments reduced 10 percent a year from 1987 through 1991. Rejected 42-48: R 39-9; D 3-39 (ND 0-29, SD 3-10), Nov. 22, 1985.

339. S 1714. Farm Programs Reauthorization, Fiscal 1986-89. Durenberger, R-Minn., motion to table (kill) the Melcher, D-Mont., perfecting amendment to the Dole, R-Kan., amendment to the Dole motion to recommit the bill to the Agriculture, Nutrition and Forestry Committee with instructions, to require that the quota on sugar imports from the Philippines be allocated on a rate not less than the percentage allocated to any other country, effectively increasing the quota by 3 percent, on the condition that the Philippines Sugar Commission use the value of any increased quotas to buy U.S. commodities by barter for feeding programs available to sugar workers and families in the provinces of Negros and Tarlack. Motion agreed to 69-23: R 34-14; D 35-9 (ND 26-5, SD 9-4), Nov. 22, 1985.

340. S 1714. Farm Programs Reauthorization, Fiscal 1986-89. Dole, R-Kan., motion to table (kill) the Harkin, D-Iowa, perfecting amendment to the Dole amendment to the Dole motion to recommit the bill to the Agriculture, Nutrition and Forestry Committee with instructions, to require labeling of imported meat within one year of enactment. Motion agreed to 53-39: R 44-4; D 9-35 (ND 7-25, SD 2-10), Nov. 22, 1985.

341. S 1714. Farm Programs Reauthorization, Fiscal 1986-89. Dole, R-Kan., motion to table (kill) the Dole motion to proceed to the consideration of HR 2100, the House version of the farm bill. Motion rejected 38-54: R 0-48; D 38-6 (ND 28-4, SD 10-2), in the session that began Nov. 22, 1985. (The Dole motion to proceed was subsequently withdrawn.)

342. S 1714. Farm Programs Reauthorization, Fiscal 1986-89. Dole, R-Kan., motion to table (kill) the Dole perfecting amendment to the Dole amendment to the Dole motion to recommit the bill to the Agriculture, Nutrition and Forestry Committee with instructions, to add a provision freezing target prices for wheat, feed grains, cotton and rice at 1985 levels for crop years 1986 through 1988. Motion agreed to 91-0: R 48-0; D 43-0 (ND 32-0, SD 11-0), in the session that began Nov. 22, 1985.

343. HR 2100. Farm Programs Reauthorization, Fiscal 1986-89. Passage of the bill, as amended by the Dole, R-Kan., substitute, which incorporated S 1714 as amended by the Senate to date, to modify target prices by freezing 1985 levels through 1987 and allow 5 percent reductions thereafter; to give the agriculture secretary authority to compensate all reductions in 1987 with in-kind payments of government-owned commodities and partially compensate reductions in 1988 with in-kind payments; to extend and revise other agricultural price-support and related programs; to provide for agricultural export, soil conservation, farm credit and agricultural research programs; and to continue food assistance to low-income persons through fiscal 1989. Passed 61-28: R 32-14; D 29-14 (ND 17-13, SD 12-1), Nov. 23, 1985.

CQ Senate Votes 344 - 351

Corresponding to Congressional Record Votes 344, 345, 346, 347, 348, 349, 350, 351

	344	345	346	347	348	349	350	351
ALABAMA								
Denton	N	N	N	N	N	Y	Y	Y
Heflin	N	N	Y	N	N	Y	N	Y
ALASKA								
Murkowski	N	Y	Y	Y	Y	Y	Y	Y
Stevens	?	?	?	?	?	?	?	?
ARIZONA								
Goldwater	-	?	?	?	?	?	?	?
DeConcini	N	N	Y	Y	N	N	Y	N
ARKANSAS								
Bumpers	N	N	N	Y	N	N	N	N
Pryor	N	N	N	Y	N	N	N	N
CALIFORNIA								
Wilson	N	Y	Y	Y	Y	Y	Y	Y
Cranston	N	N	Y	N	N	N	N	N
COLORADO								
Armstrong	N	Y	Y	Y	Y	Y	Y	Y
Hart	N	N	N	N	N	N	N	N
CONNECTICUT								
Weicker	Y	N	Y	N	N	N	Y	Y
Dodd	N	Y	Y	N	N	N	N	N
DELAWARE								
Roth	N	Y	Y	N	N	Y	Y	Y
Biden	N	Y	Y	N	Y	N	Y	N
FLORIDA								
Hawkins	N	Y	Y	Y	Y	Y	Y	Y
Chiles	-	?	?	?	?	?	?	?
GEORGIA								
Mattingly	N	Y	Y	N	Y	Y	Y	Y
Nunn	N	N	Y	N	N	N	N	Y
HAWAII								
Inouye	N	N	N	N	N	N	N	N
Matsunaga	N	N	N	N	N	N	N	Y
IDAHO								
McClure	N	N	Y	N	Y	Y	Y	Y
Symms	N	Y	Y	N	Y	Y	Y	Y
ILLINOIS								
Dixon	N	N	N	N	N	N	Y	Y
Simon	N	N	N	N	N	N	Y	N
INDIANA								
Lugar	N	Y	Y	Y	Y	Y	Y	Y
Quayle	N	Y	Y	Y	Y	Y	Y	Y
IOWA								
Grassley	N	N	N	Y	Y	N	Y	N
Harkin	N	N	N	Y	N	N	N	N
KANSAS								
Dole	N	Y	Y	Y	Y	Y	Y	Y
Kassebaum	N	Y	Y	Y	Y	Y	Y	Y
KENTUCKY								
McConnell	N	Y	N	Y	Y	Y	N	Y
Ford	N	N	N	Y	N	N	N	Y
LOUISIANA								
Johnston	N	Y	Y	Y	Y	N	N	Y
Long	N	Y	N	Y	Y	Y	Y	Y
MAINE								
Cohen	N	Y	Y	N	N	Y	Y	N
Mitchell	N	N	Y	N	N	N	Y	N
MARYLAND								
Mathias	N	Y	Y	Y	Y	Y	Y	Y
Sarbanes	N	N	N	N	N	N	N	N
MASSACHUSETTS								
Kennedy	N	Y	N	?	?	?	?	?
Kerry	N	Y	N	N	N	N	N	N
MICHIGAN								
Levin	N	N	N	Y	Y	N	?	?
Riegle	N	N	N	Y	Y	N	Y	Y
MINNESOTA								
Boschwitz	N	N	N	Y	Y	N	Y	Y
Durenberger	?	?	?	Y	Y	N	Y	Y
MISSISSIPPI								
Cochran	N	Y	Y	Y	Y	Y	Y	Y
Stennis	N	Y	Y	N	N	Y	N	Y
MISSOURI								
Danforth	N	Y	Y	Y	Y	Y	Y	Y
Eagleton	N	Y	N	Y	Y	Y	N	Y
MONTANA								
Baucus	N	N	N	Y	N	N	N	N
Melcher	N	N	N	Y	N	N	N	Y
NEBRASKA								
Exon	N	N	N	Y	Y	N	N	N
Zorinsky	Y	Y	Y	Y	Y	Y	N	Y
NEVADA								
Hecht	N	Y	Y	Y	Y	Y	Y	Y
Laxalt	N	Y	Y	Y	Y	Y	Y	Y
NEW HAMPSHIRE								
Humphrey	Y	Y	Y	Y	Y	Y	Y	N
Rudman	N	Y	Y	N	N	Y	Y	N
NEW JERSEY								
Bradley	?	?	?	?	?	?	?	?
Lautenberg	N	Y	Y	N	N	Y	Y	N
NEW MEXICO								
Domenici	N	Y	Y	N	Y	Y	N	Y
Bingaman	N	N	Y	N	N	N	N	N
NEW YORK								
D'Amato	N	Y	Y	N	N	Y	Y	Y
Moynihan	N	N	N	N	N	N	Y	N
NORTH CAROLINA								
East	?	?	?	?	?	?	?	?
Helms	Y	Y	Y	Y	Y	Y	Y	Y
NORTH DAKOTA								
Andrews	N	N	N	Y	N	N	N	N
Burdick	N	N	N	Y	N	N	N	N
OHIO								
Glenn	N	Y	N	Y	N	N	N	Y
Metzenbaum	N	N	Y	N	N	N	Y	Y
OKLAHOMA								
Nickles	N	N	N	Y	N	Y	Y	Y
Boren	N	N	N	Y	N	Y	N	Y
OREGON								
Hatfield	-	?	?	?	?	?	?	?
Packwood	?	?	?	?	?	?	?	?
PENNSYLVANIA								
Heinz	N	Y	Y	N	Y	Y	Y	Y
Specter	N	Y	Y	N	Y	Y	Y	Y
RHODE ISLAND								
Chafee	N	Y	Y	N	N	Y	Y	N
Pell	N	N	Y	N	N	N	Y	N
SOUTH CAROLINA								
Thurmond	N	Y	Y	Y	Y	Y	Y	Y
Hollings	N	N	N	N	N	N	N	N
SOUTH DAKOTA								
Abdnor	N	N	N	Y	Y	N	Y	Y
Pressler	N	N	N	Y	Y	N	Y	N
TENNESSEE								
Gore	N	N	N	N	N	N	N	Y
Sasser	N	N	N	N	N	N	N	Y
TEXAS								
Gramm	Y	N	Y	N	N	Y	Y	N
Bentsen	N	N	Y	N	N	N	N	N
UTAH								
Garn	N	Y	Y	Y	Y	Y	Y	N
Hatch	?	Y	Y	Y	Y	Y	Y	Y
VERMONT								
Stafford	N	Y	Y	N	Y	Y	Y	Y
Leahy	N	Y	N	N	N	Y	N	N
VIRGINIA								
Trible	N	Y	Y	Y	Y	Y	Y	Y
Warner	N	Y	Y	Y	Y	Y	Y	Y
WASHINGTON								
Evans	N	Y	Y	Y	Y	Y	Y	Y
Gorton	N	Y	Y	Y	Y	Y	Y	Y
WEST VIRGINIA								
Byrd	N	N	N	N	N	N	N	Y
Rockefeller	N	N	N	N	N	N	N	Y
WISCONSIN								
Kasten	N	N	N	Y	Y	N	Y	Y
Proxmire	N	N	Y	Y	Y	N	Y	Y
WYOMING								
Simpson	Y	Y	Y	Y	Y	Y	Y	N
Wallop	Y	Y	Y	Y	Y	Y	Y	N

KEY

- Y Voted for (yea).
- # Paired for.
- + Announced for.
- N Voted against (nay).
- X Paired against.
- - Announced against.
- P Voted "present."
- C Voted "present" to avoid possible conflict of interest.
- ? Did not vote or otherwise make a position known.

Democrats *Republicans*

ND - Northern Democrats SD - Southern Democrats (Southern states - Ala., Ark., Fla., Ga., Ky., La., Miss., N.C., Okla., S.C., Tenn., Texas, Va.)

344. S 655. Low-Level Radioactive Waste Compact/PAC Spending Limits. Heinz, R-Pa., motion to table (kill) the Boren, D-Okla., amendment to limit spending by political action committees (PACs) in House and Senate campaigns and to require broadcasters to provide free "equal time" to congressional candidates whose opponents are aided by independent expenditures by PACs. Motion rejected 7-84: R 6-40; D 1-44 (ND 1-31, SD 0-13), Dec. 3, 1985.

345. S 1884. Farm Credit System Restructuring. Zorinsky, D-Neb., motion to table (kill) the Baucus, D-Mont., substitute for the Helms, R-N.C., substitute, to require separate five-member boards of directors for each district institution (Federal Intermediate Credit Bank, Federal Land Bank and Bank for Cooperatives). Motion agreed to 48-44: R 36-11; D 12-33 (ND 9-23, SD 3-10), Dec. 3, 1985.

346. S 1884. Farm Credit System Restructuring. Garn, R-Utah, motion to table (kill) the Boschwitz, R-Minn., amendment to require the federal government to subsidize 2 percentage points of interest rates on agricultural loans provided to eligible borrowers by banks, Farm Credit System institutions and other creditors, and to allow states to subsidize 2 percentage points on such loans, if the creditor agrees to forgive 1 percentage point of such loans, and to allow agriculture creditors to write down a nonconforming debt by up to 30 percent, with the difference guaranteed by the Farmers Home Administration over a period of 10 years, that guarantee declining by 10 percent a year. Motion agreed to 54-38: R 38-9; D 16-29 (ND 11-21, SD 5-8), Dec. 3, 1985.

347. S 1884. Farm Credit System Restructuring. Zorinsky, D-Neb., motion to table (kill) the Leahy, D-Vt., amendment to limit any assessments on system institutions as a result of new regulations to ensure that any increase in the interest rates on loans to member-borrowers shall not exceed one-half of 1 percent a year. Motion agreed to 51-41: R 33-15; D 18-26 (ND 12-19, SD 6-7), Dec. 3, 1985.

348. S 1884. Farm Credit System Restructuring. Zorinsky, D-Neb., motion to table (kill) the Baucus, D-Mont., substitute to limit contributions made to the new capital corporation by system institutions to a total of $5 billion, further to limit contributions to no more than 3 percent of any single institution's loan portfolio in any one year, and to require the capital corporation to repay the contributed funds from accumulated surpluses. Motion agreed to 47-45: R 38-10; D 9-35 (ND 7-24, SD 2-11), Dec. 3, 1985.

349. S 1884. Farm Credit System Restructuring. Zorinsky, D-Neb., motion to table (kill) the Harkin, D-Iowa, amendment to require the capital corporation to sell or lease farm land acquired under authority of the bill first to operators of family-sized farms, and to limit the interest rate on any loan owned or made by the capital corporation to no more than the average rate charged by the original system institution. Motion agreed to 48-44: R 40-8; D 8-36 (ND 4-27, SD 4-9), Dec. 3, 1985.

350. S 1884. Farm Credit System Restructuring. Helms, R-N.C., motion to table (kill) the Melcher, D-Mont., amendment to require the Farm Credit Administration to use revolving funds to alleviate losses of borrower-owned stock created as a result of the liquidation of a lending association by loaning money on a "non-recourse" basis to borrowers who pledge to apply the money to outstanding loans made by the association or its successor institution. Motion agreed to 57-34: R 45-3; D 12-31 (ND 11-19, SD 1-12), Dec. 3, 1985.

351. S 1884. Farm Credit System Restructuring. Passage of the bill to reorganize the Farm Credit System to enable individual institutions to pool resources and sell assets to resolve financial problems affecting individual institutions; to create a capital corporation within the system to take over non-performing loans and obligations of member institutions; to restructure the federal Farm Credit Administration to perform as an independent regulating agency of the system; and to authorize the secretary of the Treasury to purchase obligations of the capital corporation. Passed 57-34: R 37-11; D 20-23 (ND 11-19, SD 9-4), Dec. 3, 1985.

CQ Senate Vote 352

Corresponding to Congressional Record Vote 352

	352
ALABAMA	
Denton	Y
Heflin	Y
ALASKA	
Murkowski	Y
Stevens	Y
ARIZONA	
Goldwater	?
DeConcini	Y
ARKANSAS	
Bumpers	Y
Pryor	Y
CALIFORNIA	
Wilson	Y
Cranston	N
COLORADO	
Armstrong	Y
Hart	N
CONNECTICUT	
Weicker	Y
Dodd	N
DELAWARE	
Roth	Y
Biden	N
FLORIDA	
Hawkins	N
Chiles	?
GEORGIA	
Mattingly	Y
Nunn	Y
HAWAII	
Inouye	Y
Matsunaga	?
IDAHO	
McClure	Y
Symms	Y
ILLINOIS	
Dixon	Y
Simon	N
INDIANA	
Lugar	N
Quayle	Y
IOWA	
Grassley	Y
Harkin	N
KANSAS	
Dole	Y
Kassebaum	Y
KENTUCKY	
McConnell	Y
Ford	N
LOUISIANA	
Johnston	Y
Long	Y
MAINE	
Cohen	Y
Mitchell	N
MARYLAND	
Mathias	?
Sarbanes	N
MASSACHUSETTS	
Kennedy	Y
Kerry	N
MICHIGAN	
Levin	N
Riegle	N
MINNESOTA	
Boschwitz	Y
Durenberger	N
MISSISSIPPI	
Cochran	Y
Stennis	Y
MISSOURI	
Danforth	Y
Eagleton	N
MONTANA	
Baucus	N
Melcher	N
NEBRASKA	
Exon	Y
Zorinsky	Y
NEVADA	
Hecht	Y
Laxalt	Y
NEW HAMPSHIRE	
Humphrey	N
Rudman	N
NEW JERSEY	
Bradley	N
Lautenberg	N
NEW MEXICO	
Domenici	Y
Bingaman	N
NEW YORK	
D'Amato	Y
Moynihan	Y
NORTH CAROLINA	
East	?
Helms	Y
NORTH DAKOTA	
Andrews	N
Burdick	Y
OHIO	
Glenn	Y
Metzenbaum	N
OKLAHOMA	
Nickles	Y
Boren	Y
OREGON	
Hatfield	Y
Packwood	?
PENNSYLVANIA	
Heinz	N
Specter	Y
RHODE ISLAND	
Chafee	N
Pell	N
SOUTH CAROLINA	
Thurmond	Y
Hollings	N
SOUTH DAKOTA	
Abdnor	Y
Pressler	Y
TENNESSEE	
Gore	N
Sasser	Y
TEXAS	
Gramm	Y
Bentsen	Y
UTAH	
Garn	Y
Hatch	Y
VERMONT	
Stafford	N
Leahy	N
VIRGINIA	
Trible	Y
Warner	Y
WASHINGTON	
Evans	Y
Gorton	Y
WEST VIRGINIA	
Byrd	Y
Rockefeller	Y
WISCONSIN	
Kasten	N
Proxmire	N
WYOMING	
Simpson	Y
Wallop	Y

KEY

Y Voted for (yea).
Paired for.
+ Announced for.
N Voted against (nay).
X Paired against.
- Announced against.
P Voted "present."
C Voted "present" to avoid possible conflict of interest.
? Did not vote or otherwise make a position known.

Democrats *Republicans*

ND - Northern Democrats SD - Southern Democrats (Southern states - Ala., Ark., Fla., Ga., Ky., La., Miss., N.C., Okla., S.C., Tenn., Texas, Va.)

352. Dawson Nomination. Confirmation of President Reagan's nomination of Robert K. Dawson of Virginia to be assistant secretary of the Army for civil works. Confirmed 60-34: R 39-10; D 21-24 (ND 11-21, SD 10-3), Dec. 4, 1985. A "yea" was a vote supporting the president's position.

	353	354	355	356	357	358	359	360
ALABAMA								
Denton	?	?	?	N	Y	Y	Y	N
Heflin	Y	Y	N	N	Y	N	N	N
ALASKA								
Murkowski	Y	N	?	Y	Y	Y	Y	N
Stevens	Y	N	N	Y	Y	Y	Y	Y
ARIZONA								
Goldwater	?	?	?	N	Y	Y	Y	?
DeConcini	N	N	N	?	?	?	?	?
ARKANSAS								
Bumpers	Y	Y	Y	N	N	N	N	Y
Pryor	N	N	N	N	Y	Y	N	Y
CALIFORNIA								
Wilson	N	N	Y	N	N	N	Y	N
Cranston	?	?	?	Y	N	N	N	Y
COLORADO								
Armstrong	?	Y	N	N	Y	Y	Y	N
Hart	?	?	?	N	N	N	N	Y
CONNECTICUT								
Weicker	Y	Y	?	N	N	N	N	Y
Dodd	N	N	Y	Y	N	N	Y	Y
DELAWARE								
Roth	Y	Y	Y	N	Y	Y	Y	N
Biden	N	Y	Y	N	N	N	Y	?
FLORIDA								
Hawkins	N	N	N	?	N	N	Y	N
Chiles	?	?	?	?	?	?	?	?
GEORGIA								
Mattingly	Y	Y	Y	N	Y	Y	Y	N
Nunn	Y	Y	N	N	Y	Y	N	?
HAWAII								
Inouye	?	?	?	?	?	?	?	?
Matsunaga	N	N	N	N	Y	Y	N	Y
IDAHO								
McClure	Y	Y	N	Y	Y	Y	Y	N
Symms	N	Y	N	Y	Y	Y	Y	N
ILLINOIS								
Dixon	Y	N	N	N	N	N	N	Y
Simon	N	N	N	?	?	?	N	Y
INDIANA								
Lugar	N	N	N	?	Y	Y	Y	Y
Quayle	N	N	Y	N	Y	Y	Y	?
IOWA								
Grassley	Y	N	Y	N	Y	N	Y	N
Harkin	N	Y	Y	N	N	N	N	Y
KANSAS								
Dole	Y	N	Y	Y	Y	?	?	?
Kassebaum	Y	Y	Y	Y	Y	Y	?	?
KENTUCKY								
McConnell	N	N	N	Y	Y	Y	Y	N
Ford	N	N	N	N	Y	Y	N	N
LOUISIANA								
Johnston	Y	N	N	Y	N	Y	Y	Y
Long	Y	Y	N	N	Y	Y	N	?
MAINE								
Cohen	?	?	?	N	N	N	Y	N
Mitchell	N	N	N	N	N	N	N	?
MARYLAND								
Mathias	?	N	N	Y	N	N	Y	Y
Sarbanes	?	?	?	N	N	N	N	?
MASSACHUSETTS								
Kennedy	N	N	?	N	N	N	N	?
Kerry	N	N	?	N	N	N	Y	?
MICHIGAN								
Levin	N	N	Y	N	N	N	N	Y
Riegle	N	N	Y	?	N	N	N	Y
MINNESOTA								
Boschwitz	Y	N	Y	N	Y	Y	Y	Y
Durenberger	N	N	Y	?	?	?	Y	Y
MISSISSIPPI								
Cochran	?	?	?	Y	Y	?	Y	Y
Stennis	Y	Y	N	?	?	Y	Y	?
MISSOURI								
Danforth	N	N	Y	N	Y	Y	Y	Y
Eagleton	N	N	Y	N	N	N	N	Y
MONTANA								
Baucus	Y	Y	Y	N	Y	Y	N	Y
Melcher	N	N	N	N	Y	N	N	Y
NEBRASKA								
Exon	Y	Y	N	N	N	N	N	N
Zorinsky	Y	Y	?	Y	Y	Y	N	N
NEVADA								
Hecht	Y	Y	Y	N	Y	Y	Y	N
Laxalt	C	N	N	?	?	?	?	?
NEW HAMPSHIRE								
Humphrey	Y	N	Y	N	Y	Y	Y	N
Rudman	Y	Y	Y	N	Y	Y	Y	N
NEW JERSEY								
Bradley	N	Y	Y	N	N	N	N	N
Lautenberg	N	N	Y	N	N	N	N	Y
NEW MEXICO								
Domenici	Y	Y	N	Y	Y	Y	Y	N
Bingaman	N	N	Y	N	N	Y	N	Y
NEW YORK								
D'Amato	Y	N	Y	N	Y	?	?	?
Moynihan	N	N	Y	N	N	Y	Y	Y
NORTH CAROLINA								
East	?	?	?	?	?	?	?	?
Helms	Y	Y	Y	N	Y	Y	Y	N
NORTH DAKOTA								
Andrews	Y	N	N	Y	Y	N	Y	N
Burdick	Y	Y	N	N	N	N	N	Y
OHIO								
Glenn	N	N	Y	N	N	?	?	?
Metzenbaum	N	N	Y	N	N	N	N	Y
OKLAHOMA								
Nickles	Y	Y	Y	N	N	N	Y	N
Boren	Y	Y	N	N	N	N	N	N
OREGON								
Hatfield	N	N	N	Y	Y	Y	Y	Y
Packwood	N	N	Y	N	Y	Y	Y	Y
PENNSYLVANIA								
Heinz	N	N	N	Y	N	N	Y	Y
Specter	N	N	N	?	?	?	?	?
RHODE ISLAND								
Chafee	Y	Y	Y	Y	N	N	Y	?
Pell	N	N	N	Y	N	N	N	Y
SOUTH CAROLINA								
Thurmond	N	N	Y	N	Y	Y	Y	N
Hollings	Y	Y	Y	N	Y	N	N	N
SOUTH DAKOTA								
Abdnor	Y	N	N	N	Y	?	Y	N
Pressler	Y	N	N	Y	Y	Y	Y	N
TENNESSEE								
Gore	N	N	N	N	Y	N	N	Y
Sasser	N	N	N	N	Y	N	N	Y
TEXAS								
Gramm	Y	Y	Y	Y	Y	Y	Y	N
Bentsen	N	?	?	N	Y	Y	N	?
UTAH								
Garn	N	N	N	Y	?	?	?	?
Hatch	N	N	N	Y	Y	N	Y	N
VERMONT								
Stafford	Y	N	Y	Y	N	Y	Y	Y
Leahy	N	N	?	?	N	N	N	Y
VIRGINIA								
Trible	Y	N	N	N	Y	Y	Y	N
Warner	Y	Y	N	N	Y	N	Y	N
WASHINGTON								
Evans	N	N	Y	Y	Y	Y	Y	Y
Gorton	N	N	Y	Y	Y	Y	Y	Y
WEST VIRGINIA								
Byrd	Y	Y	N	N	N	N	N	N
Rockefeller	Y	Y	N	N	N	Y	N	Y
WISCONSIN								
Kasten	Y	N	Y	Y	Y	N	Y	Y
Proxmire	Y	Y	Y	N	Y	Y	N	Y
WYOMING								
Simpson	Y	N	N	Y	Y	Y	Y	Y
Wallop	N	N	N	N	Y	Y	Y	N

KEY

- Y Voted for (yea).
- # Paired for.
- + Announced for.
- N Voted against (nay).
- X Paired against.
- - Announced against.
- P Voted "present."
- C Voted "present" to avoid possible conflict of interest.
- ? Did not vote or otherwise make a position known.

Democrats *Republicans*

ND - Northern Democrats SD - Southern Democrats (Southern states - Ala., Ark., Fla., Ga., Ky., La., Miss., N.C., Okla., S.C., Tenn., Texas, Va.)

353. HR 2965. Commerce, Justice, State and the Judiciary Appropriations, Fiscal 1986. Rudman, R-N.H., motion to table (kill) the House amendment to the Senate amendment, to put restrictions on the use of funds from the National Endowment for Democracy by international institutes operated by the Democratic and Republican parties. Motion rejected 43-44: R 27-18; D 16-26 (ND 8-21, SD 8-5), Dec. 6, 1985. (The Senate subsequently moved to concur in the House amendment by voice vote.)

354. HR 2965. Commerce, Justice, State and the Judiciary Appropriations, Fiscal 1986. Hollings, D-S.C., amendment to move that the Senate concur in the House amendment to the Senate amendment, with an amendment to delete all funds for the National Endowment for Democracy. Rejected 32-57: R 15-33; D 17-24 (ND 10-19, SD 7-5), Dec. 6, 1985. (The Senate subsequently moved to concur in the House amendment by voice vote.) A "nay" was a vote supporting the president's position.

355. H J Res 465. Further Continuing Appropriations, Fiscal 1986. Metzenbaum, D-Ohio, amendment to rescind funds for the Energy Security Reserve and return the money to the Treasury. Rejected 40-43: R 24-22; D 16-21 (ND 14-11, SD 2-10), Dec. 6, 1985. (The effect of the amendment would have been to end the Synthetic Fuels Corporation.)

356. H J Res 465. Further Continuing Appropriations, Fiscal 1986. Evans, R-Wash., motion to table (kill) the Glenn, D-Ohio, amendment to prohibit the use of funds in the bill to transfer nuclear equipment, materials or technology to the People's Republic of China unless specified conditions were met. Motion rejected 28-59: R 23-24; D 5-35 (ND 4-24, SD 1-11), Dec. 9, 1985. (The Glenn amendment subsequently was adopted by voice vote.) A "yea" was a vote supporting the president's position.

357. H J Res 465. Further Continuing Appropriations, Fiscal 1986. Packwood, R-Ore., motion to table (kill) the Kennedy, D-Mass., appeal of the chair's ruling that the Kennedy amendment relating to Medicare was legislation on an appropriations measure, and thus not germane. Motion agreed to 53-37: R 39-9; D 14-28 (ND 5-25, SD 9-3), Dec. 9, 1985. (The Kennedy amendment would have delayed until May 15, 1986, an increase in the Medicare inpatient hospital deductible, scheduled to take effect Jan. 1, 1986, and would have increased the cigarette tax by 1 cent for a three-year period to avoid any increase in the deficit due to the Medicare delay.)

358. H J Res 465. Further Continuing Appropriations, Fiscal 1986. Hatfield, R-Ore., motion to table (kill) the Heinz, R-Pa., appeal of the chair's ruling that the Heinz amendment relating to Medicare was legislation on an appropriations measure, and thus not germane. Motion agreed to 45-41: R 31-13; D 14-28 (ND 7-22, SD 7-6), Dec. 9, 1985. (The Heinz amendment would have set a cap of $476 on the Medicare inpatient hospital deductible.)

359. H J Res 465. Further Continuing Appropriations, Fiscal 1986. Kasten, R-Wis., motion to table (kill) the Pryor, D-Ark., amendment to cap spending for military assistance grants at $764,648,000, thus reducing the grants by $40 million in fiscal 1986. Motion agreed to 51-38: R 45-1; D 6-37 (ND 4-26, SD 2-11), Dec. 9, 1985. A "yea" was a vote supporting the president's position.

360. H J Res 465. Further Continuing Appropriations, Fiscal 1986. Hatfield, R-Ore., motion to table (kill) the Wallop, R-Wyo., amendment to limit U.S. voluntary contributions to the United Nations and its agencies to $15 million, the same level as the Soviet Union's contributions. Motion agreed to 42-35: R 16-27; D 26-8 (ND 21-4, SD 5-4), Dec. 9, 1985.

CQ Senate Votes 361 - 368

Corresponding to Congressional Record Votes 361, 362, 363, 364, 365, 366, 367, 368

	361	362	363	364	365	366	367	368
ALABAMA								
Denton	Y	Y	Y	Y	Y	N	Y	N
Heflin	Y	Y	Y	N	Y	N	Y	Y
ALASKA								
Murkowski	Y	Y	N	Y	Y	N	Y	Y
Stevens	?	Y	Y	Y	Y	N	N	Y
ARIZONA								
Goldwater	?	?	?	?	?	?	?	?
DeConcini	?	?	Y	N	Y	Y	N	Y
ARKANSAS								
Bumpers	Y	N	Y	N	N	Y	N	Y
Pryor	?	N	N	N	N	Y	N	Y
CALIFORNIA								
Wilson	Y	Y	Y	Y	Y	N	Y	N
Cranston	Y	N	N	N	N	Y	N	N
COLORADO								
Armstrong	Y	Y	Y	Y	Y	N	Y	Y
Hart	N	N	N	N	N	Y	N	N
CONNECTICUT								
Weicker	Y	Y	N	Y	Y	N	N	Y
Dodd	Y	N	Y	N	N	N	N	Y
DELAWARE								
Roth	N	?	Y	Y	Y	N	N	Y
Biden	?	Y	N	N	N	Y	N	Y
FLORIDA								
Hawkins	Y	Y	N	Y	Y	N	Y	Y
Chiles	?	?	?	?	?	?	?	?
GEORGIA								
Mattingly	Y	N	N	Y	Y	N	Y	Y
Nunn	?	N	N	N	Y	N	N	N
HAWAII								
Inouye	?	?	?	N	N	N	N	Y
Matsunaga	Y	?	N	N	N	N	N	Y
IDAHO								
McClure	Y	Y	Y	Y	Y	N	Y	N
Symms	Y	Y	Y	Y	Y	N	Y	N
ILLINOIS								
Dixon	Y	N	Y	N	Y	N	N	Y
Simon	Y	N	Y	N	N	N	N	Y
INDIANA								
Lugar	Y	Y	N	Y	Y	N	N	Y
Quayle	?	Y	N	Y	Y	N	Y	N
IOWA								
Grassley	Y	Y	Y	Y	Y	Y	Y	Y
Harkin	Y	Y	N	N	N	N	N	Y
KANSAS								
Dole	?	Y	N	Y	Y	N	Y	Y
Kassebaum	?	Y	N	Y	Y	N	N	Y
KENTUCKY								
McConnell	Y	Y	N	?	Y	N	Y	Y
Ford	Y	Y	Y	N	Y	Y	Y	Y
LOUISIANA								
Johnston	Y	Y	N	N	N	N	N	Y
Long	?	N	N	Y	Y	N	N	Y
MAINE								
Cohen	Y	?	N	Y	Y	N	N	N
Mitchell	?	N	Y	N	N	Y	N	N
MARYLAND								
Mathias	Y	N	N	Y	N	N	N	Y
Sarbanes	N	N	Y	N	N	N	N	Y
MASSACHUSETTS								
Kennedy	?	?	?	N	N	N	N	N
Kerry	?	N	Y	N	N	N	N	N
MICHIGAN								
Levin	N	N	Y	N	N	?	N	N
Riegle	Y	N	Y	N	N	N	N	Y
MINNESOTA								
Boschwitz	Y	Y	N	Y	Y	N	Y	Y
Durenberger	?	Y	N	Y	Y	N	N	Y
MISSISSIPPI								
Cochran	Y	Y	N	Y	Y	N	Y	N
Stennis	?	Y	Y	N	?	N	N	?
MISSOURI								
Danforth	Y	N	N	Y	Y	N	Y	Y
Eagleton	N	N	Y	N	N	N	N	Y
MONTANA								
Baucus	Y	N	N	N	N	N	N	Y
Melcher	Y	N	?	N	N	Y	N	Y
NEBRASKA								
Exon	Y	N	Y	N	Y	N	N	N
Zorinsky	Y	N	Y	N	Y	N	N	Y
NEVADA								
Hecht	Y	Y	Y	Y	Y	N	Y	Y
Laxalt	?	Y	N	Y	Y	N	Y	Y
NEW HAMPSHIRE								
Humphrey	Y	Y	Y	Y	Y	Y	Y	N
Rudman	Y	N	Y	?	Y	N	Y	Y
NEW JERSEY								
Bradley	N	N	Y	N	Y	Y	N	N
Lautenberg	N	N	Y	N	N	Y	N	Y
NEW MEXICO								
Domenici	Y	Y	N	Y	Y	N	Y	Y
Bingaman	Y	N	N	N	Y	N	N	Y
NEW YORK								
D'Amato	?	Y	Y	Y	Y	N	Y	Y
Moynihan	N	Y	Y	N	N	N	N	N
NORTH CAROLINA								
East	?	?	?	?	?	?	?	?
Helms	?	Y	Y	Y	Y	N	Y	Y
NORTH DAKOTA								
Andrews	Y	Y	Y	Y	Y	N	Y	Y
Burdick	Y	N	N	N	N	Y	N	Y
OHIO								
Glenn	?	Y	Y	N	Y	N	N	N
Metzenbaum	Y	N	N	N	N	N	N	N
OKLAHOMA								
Nickles	Y	N	Y	Y	Y	Y	Y	N
Boren	Y	Y	Y	N	Y	Y	N	Y
OREGON								
Hatfield	Y	Y	N	Y	Y	N	N	Y
Packwood	Y	Y	Y	Y	Y	N	N	Y
PENNSYLVANIA								
Heinz	N	Y	N	Y	Y	N	N	N
Specter	?	Y	Y	Y	Y	N	N	Y
RHODE ISLAND								
Chafee	?	Y	N	Y	N	N	N	Y
Pell	N	N	N	N	N	N	N	N
SOUTH CAROLINA								
Thurmond	Y	Y	N	Y	Y	N	Y	Y
Hollings	Y	Y	N	N	Y	N	Y	N
SOUTH DAKOTA								
Abdnor	Y	Y	Y	Y	Y	N	Y	Y
Pressler	Y	Y	N	Y	Y	N	Y	Y
TENNESSEE								
Gore	?	N	Y	N	N	N	N	N
Sasser	Y	N	Y	N	N	N	Y	N
TEXAS								
Gramm	Y	Y	N	Y	Y	N	Y	N
Bentsen	?	Y	N	N	Y	N	N	Y
UTAH								
Garn	?	Y	N	Y	Y	N	Y	Y
Hatch	Y	Y	Y	Y	Y	N	Y	Y
VERMONT								
Stafford	Y	Y	N	Y	Y	N	N	Y
Leahy	Y	N	N	N	N	N	N	Y
VIRGINIA								
Trible	Y	Y	N	Y	Y	N	Y	Y
Warner	N	Y	Y	Y	Y	N	Y	Y
WASHINGTON								
Evans	Y	?	?	Y	Y	N	N	Y
Gorton	Y	Y	N	Y	Y	N	Y	N
WEST VIRGINIA								
Byrd	Y	Y	N	N	Y	Y	N	N
Rockefeller	?	Y	N	N	N	Y	N	?
WISCONSIN								
Kasten	Y	N	Y	Y	Y	N	Y	Y
Proxmire	Y	N	Y	N	N	Y	N	Y
WYOMING								
Simpson	Y	Y	N	Y	Y	N	N	Y
Wallop	?	Y	Y	Y	Y	N	Y	Y

KEY

- Y Voted for (yea).
- # Paired for.
- + Announced for.
- N Voted against (nay).
- X Paired against.
- \- Announced against.
- P Voted "present."
- C Voted "present" to avoid possible conflict of interest.
- ? Did not vote or otherwise make a position known.

Democrats ***Republicans***

ND - Northern Democrats SD - Southern Democrats (Southern states - Ala., Ark., Fla., Ga., Ky., La., Miss., N.C., Okla., S.C., Tenn., Texas, Va.)

361. H J Res 465. Further Continuing Appropriations, Fiscal 1986. Hatfield, R-Ore., motion to table (kill) the Heinz, R-Pa., amendment to provide an additional $91.1 million for the Internal Revenue Service. Motion agreed to 60-11: R 36-3; D 24-8 (ND 17-8, SD 7-0), Dec. 9, 1985.

362. H J Res 465. Further Continuing Appropriations, Fiscal 1986. Hatfield, R-Ore., motion to table (kill) the Proxmire, D-Wis., amendment to delete $12 million for a computer facility at Syracuse University. Motion agreed to 55-35: R 42-6; D 13-29 (ND 6-23, SD 7-6), Dec. 10, 1985.

363. H J Res 465. Further Continuing Appropriations, Fiscal 1986. Judgment of the Senate whether the Humphrey, R-N.H., amendment, to establish a special panel on asylum to conduct an investigation on the general problem of people from communist countries who seek political asylum in the United States, was germane. Ruled non-germane 46-47: R 22-28; D 24-19 (ND 17-13, SD 7-6), Dec. 10, 1985.

364. H J Res 465. Further Continuing Appropriations, Fiscal 1986. Gorton, R-Wash., motion to table (kill) the Hart, D-Colo., amendment to express the sense of the Senate that funds should not be used to provide permits for commercial activity within specified areas proposed for wilderness designation in Colorado. Motion agreed to 50-45: R 49-0; D 1-45 (ND 0-33, SD 1-12), Dec. 10, 1985.

365. H J Res 465. Further Continuing Appropriations, Fiscal 1986. Stevens, R-Alaska, motion to table (kill) the Kerry, D-Mass., amendment to bar the use of any nuclear materials in the development of the "strategic defense initiative" program. Motion agreed to 64-32: R 49-2; D 15-30 (ND 8-25, SD 7-5), Dec. 10, 1985.

366. H J Res 465. Further Continuing Appropriations, Fiscal 1986. Judgment of the Senate whether the Boren, D-Okla., amendment relating to General Dynamics was germane. Ruled non-germane 19-77: R 3-48; D 16-29 (ND 12-20, SD 4-9), Dec. 10, 1985. (The amendment would have barred defense contracts for General Dynamics Corp. and any of its subsidiaries, which were under suspension by the Defense Department for allegedly fraudulent conduct in dealing with the federal government, until at least five days after the defense secretary reported to the appropriate committees of Congress that the department intended to lift the suspension.)

367. H J Res 465. Further Continuing Appropriations, Fiscal 1986. Judgment of the Senate whether the Wallop, R-Wyo., amendment, to provide $50 million for UNITA, the anti-communist rebel forces in Angola, was germane. Ruled non-germane 39-58: R 35-16; D 4-42 (ND 0-33, SD 4-9), Dec. 10, 1985.

368. H J Res 465. Further Continuing Appropriations, Fiscal 1986. Hatfield, R-Ore., motion to table (kill) the Glenn, D-Ohio, amendment to delete a provision that would require military bases that buy liquor with non-appropriated funds for resale on the base to buy that liquor only from outlets in the state in which the base is located. Motion agreed to 66-29: R 39-12; D 27-17 (ND 19-13, SD 8-4), Dec. 10, 1985.

CQ Senate Votes 369 - 373

Corresponding to Congressional Record Votes 369, 370, 371, 372, 373

	369	370	371	372	373
ALABAMA					
Denton	N	N	N	Y	Y
Heflin	N	N	Y	N	Y
ALASKA					
Murkowski	N	Y	Y	Y	Y
Stevens	N	N	Y	Y	Y
ARIZONA					
Goldwater	?	?	?	?	?
DeConcini	N	Y	N	N	Y
ARKANSAS					
Bumpers	Y	Y	Y	Y	Y
Pryor	Y	Y	N	N	Y
CALIFORNIA					
Wilson	N	Y	Y	Y	Y
Cranston	Y	Y	N	N	Y
COLORADO					
Armstrong	N	Y	Y	Y	Y
Hart	Y	Y	N	N	Y
CONNECTICUT					
Weicker	Y	Y	N	Y	Y
Dodd	N	Y	Y	Y	Y
DELAWARE					
Roth	Y	Y	N	Y	Y
Biden	N	?	?	Y	Y
FLORIDA					
Hawkins	N	Y	N	Y	Y
Chiles	?	?	#	?	?
GEORGIA					
Mattingly	N	Y	Y	Y	Y
Nunn	N	Y	Y	N	Y
HAWAII					
Inouye	Y	Y	X	N	Y
Matsunaga	Y	Y	N	N	Y
IDAHO					
McClure	N	N	Y	Y	Y
Symms	N	N	Y	Y	Y
ILLINOIS					
Dixon	N	Y	Y	Y	Y
Simon	N	Y	Y	N	Y
INDIANA					
Lugar	N	Y	Y	Y	Y
Quayle	N	N	Y	Y	Y

	369	370	371	372	373
IOWA					
Grassley	N	Y	Y	Y	Y
Harkin	Y	Y	N	N	Y
KANSAS					
Dole	N	Y	Y	Y	Y
Kassebaum	N	Y	N	Y	Y
KENTUCKY					
McConnell	N	Y	Y	Y	Y
Ford	Y	Y	Y	N	Y
LOUISIANA					
Johnston	N	Y	N	N	Y
Long	Y	Y	Y	Y	Y
MAINE					
Cohen	N	Y	Y	Y	Y
Mitchell	N	Y	Y	N	Y
MARYLAND					
Mathias	Y	Y	X	Y	Y
Sarbanes	Y	Y	N	N	Y
MASSACHUSETTS					
Kennedy	N	Y	Y	N	Y
Kerry	N	Y	Y	N	Y
MICHIGAN					
Levin	N	Y	Y	N	Y
Riegle	Y	Y	N	Y	Y
MINNESOTA					
Boschwitz	N	Y	Y	Y	Y
Durenberger	N	Y	Y	Y	Y
MISSISSIPPI					
Cochran	N	Y	Y	Y	Y
Stennis	?	?	Y	?	?
MISSOURI					
Danforth	N	Y	Y	Y	Y
Eagleton	Y	Y	N	N	Y
MONTANA					
Baucus	N	Y	Y	N	Y
Melcher	N	Y	N	N	Y
NEBRASKA					
Exon	Y	N	N	N	Y
Zorinsky	N	Y	N	Y	Y
NEVADA					
Hecht	N	N	Y	Y	Y
Laxalt	N	?	?	Y	Y

	369	370	371	372	373
NEW HAMPSHIRE					
Humphrey	N	N	Y	Y	Y
Rudman	N	Y	Y	Y	Y
NEW JERSEY					
Bradley	Y	Y	N	N	Y
Lautenberg	Y	N	N	N	Y
NEW MEXICO					
Domenici	N	Y	Y	Y	Y
Bingaman	Y	Y	N	N	N
NEW YORK					
D'Amato	N	Y	Y	Y	Y
Moynihan	Y	N	N	N	Y
NORTH CAROLINA					
East	?	?	?	?	?
Helms	N	N	Y	Y	N
NORTH DAKOTA					
Andrews	Y	Y	N	Y	Y
Burdick	Y	Y	N	N	Y
OHIO					
Glenn	Y	N	N	N	Y
Metzenbaum	Y	Y	N	N	Y
OKLAHOMA					
Nickles	N	Y	Y	N	Y
Boren	N	Y	Y	N	Y
OREGON					
Hatfield	Y	Y	N	Y	Y
Packwood	N	Y	Y	Y	Y
PENNSYLVANIA					
Heinz	N	+	#	Y	Y
Specter	N	Y	Y	Y	Y
RHODE ISLAND					
Chafee	N	Y	Y	Y	Y
Pell	Y	Y	N	N	Y
SOUTH CAROLINA					
Thurmond	N	N	Y	Y	Y
Hollings	N	Y	Y	Y	Y
SOUTH DAKOTA					
Abdnor	N	Y	Y	Y	Y
Pressler	N	Y	N	Y	Y
TENNESSEE					
Gore	N	Y	Y	N	Y
Sasser	N	Y	Y	N	Y

KEY

- Y Voted for (yea).
- # Paired for.
- + Announced for.
- N Voted against (nay).
- X Paired against.
- - Announced against.
- P Voted "present."
- C Voted "present" to avoid possible conflict of interest.
- ? Did not vote or otherwise make a position known.

Democrats *Republicans*

	369	370	371	372	373
TEXAS					
Gramm	N	Y	Y	Y	Y
Bentsen	N	Y	Y	Y	Y
UTAH					
Garn	N	N	Y	Y	Y
Hatch	N	Y	Y	+	+
VERMONT					
Stafford	?	Y	N	Y	Y
Leahy	N	Y	Y	N	Y
VIRGINIA					
Trible	N	Y	Y	Y	Y
Warner	N	Y	Y	Y	Y
WASHINGTON					
Evans	N	Y	Y	Y	Y
Gorton	N	Y	Y	Y	Y
WEST VIRGINIA					
Byrd	Y	N	N	N	Y
Rockefeller	N	Y	Y	N	Y
WISCONSIN					
Kasten	N	Y	Y	Y	Y
Proxmire	N	Y	Y	N	Y
WYOMING					
Simpson	N	Y	Y	Y	Y
Wallop	N	N	Y	Y	Y

ND - Northern Democrats SD - Southern Democrats (Southern states - Ala., Ark., Fla., Ga., Ky., La., Miss., N.C., Okla., S.C., Tenn., Texas, Va.)

369. H J Res 372. Public Debt Limit/Balanced Budget. Judgment of the Senate to affirm the chair's ruling sustaining the Weicker, R-Conn., point of order that the conference agreement on the joint resolution violates Senate rules because, in granting flexibility to the president in determining automatic defense spending cuts for fiscal 1986, the conferees exceeded the scope of their authority. Ruling of the chair rejected 27-68: R 5-45; D 22-23 (ND 18-15, SD 4-8), Dec. 11, 1985.

370. H J Res 372. Public Debt Limit/Balanced Budget. Packwood, R-Ore., motion to table (kill) the Denton, R-Ala., motion to recommit the conference report on the joint resolution to the conference committee with instructions to grant authority to the president not to "sequester" funds for defense programs, projects, activities or accounts, provided that he certify to Congress that sequestering such funds would substantially impair the national defense, further providing that such discretionary authority may be suspended for a given fiscal year by a majority vote of both houses of Congress. Motion agreed to 76-17: R 38-11; D 38-6 (ND 27-5, SD 11-1), Dec. 11, 1985.

371. H J Res 372. Public Debt Limit/Balanced Budget. Adoption of the conference report on the joint resolution to raise the ceiling on the federal debt to $2.079 trillion from $1.824 trillion; to set maximum allowable federal deficits for fiscal years 1986-91, declining annually to zero in fiscal 1991; to require the president, if projected deficits exceed those allowed, to issue an emergency order reducing all federal spending by the same percentage amount, to reduce deficits to the maximum allowed, with half of such cuts to come from defense and half from non-defense programs; to exempt Social Security, interest on the national debt and certain poverty programs from such automatic cuts; to limit the size of such cuts as they affect certain health programs; to revise congressional budget procedures; to remove Social Security from the unified federal budget in fiscal 1986 and thereafter; and to replenish the Social Security trust funds of any interest lost due to disinvestment or non-investment of those trust funds during periods in 1985 when the ceiling on the federal debt was about to be breached. Adopted 61-31: R 39-9; D 22-22 (ND 11-20, SD 11-2), Dec. 11, 1985. A "yea" was a vote supporting the president's position.

372. S 1396. White Earth Reservation Land Claim. Boschwitz, R-Minn., motion to table (kill) the Melcher, D-Mont., amendment to extend from six to eighteen months the time for recipients of allocations of land on the White Earth Indian Reservation in Minnesota and their heirs to file claims. Motion agreed to 58-37: R 49-1; D 9-36 (ND 5-28, SD 4-8), Dec. 12, 1985.

373. Bowen Nomination. Confirmation of President Reagan's nomination of Otis R. Bowen of Indiana to be secretary of health and human services. Confirmed 93-2: R 49-1; D 44-1 (ND 32-1, SD 12-0), Dec. 12, 1985. A "yea" was a vote supporting the president's position.

CQ Senate Votes 374 - 379

Corresponding to Congressional Record Votes 374, 375, 376, 377, 378, 379

	374	375	376	377	378	379
ALABAMA						
Denton	Y	Y	Y	Y	Y	Y
Heflin	N	N	N	Y	N	Y
ALASKA						
Murkowski	Y	Y	Y	?	?	?
Stevens	Y	Y	Y	Y	Y	Y
ARIZONA						
Goldwater	?	?	?	Y	N	N
DeConcini	N	N	Y	Y	N	Y
ARKANSAS						
Bumpers	Y	N	Y	Y	Y	Y
Pryor	N	N	N	Y	Y	?
CALIFORNIA						
Wilson	Y	Y	Y	Y	N	Y
Cranston	N	N	N	Y	Y	Y
COLORADO						
Armstrong	Y	Y	Y	Y	Y	Y
Hart	N	N	N	Y	N	Y
CONNECTICUT						
Weicker	Y	Y	Y	N	?	+
Dodd	?	?	Y	N	N	?
DELAWARE						
Roth	Y	Y	N	Y	N	Y
Biden	Y	Y	Y	Y	N	Y
FLORIDA						
Hawkins	Y	Y	Y	Y	Y	Y
Chiles	?	?	?	?	?	?
GEORGIA						
Mattingly	Y	Y	Y	Y	Y	Y
Nunn	N	N	N	Y	Y	Y
HAWAII						
Inouye	N	N	N	N	Y	Y
Matsunaga	N	N	N	N	Y	Y
IDAHO						
McClure	Y	Y	Y	Y	Y	Y
Symms	Y	Y	Y	Y	Y	Y
ILLINOIS						
Dixon	Y	Y	N	Y	N	Y
Simon	N	N	N	Y	N	Y
INDIANA						
Lugar	Y	Y	Y	Y	Y	Y
Quayle	Y	Y	Y	Y	Y	Y
IOWA						
Grassley	Y	Y	Y	Y	N	Y
Harkin	N	N	N	Y	N	Y
KANSAS						
Dole	Y	Y	Y	Y	Y	Y
Kassebaum	?	?	?	Y	Y	?
KENTUCKY						
McConnell	Y	Y	Y	Y	Y	Y
Ford	N	N	N	Y	Y	Y
LOUISIANA						
Johnston	Y	N	Y	Y	Y	Y
Long	Y	N	Y	Y	Y	Y
MAINE						
Cohen	Y	Y	Y	Y	N	?
Mitchell	N	N	N	Y	N	Y
MARYLAND						
Mathias	?	?	?	?	?	?
Sarbanes	N	N	N	Y	Y	?
MASSACHUSETTS						
Kennedy	N	N	N	Y	?	?
Kerry	N	N	N	Y	N	Y
MICHIGAN						
Levin	N	N	N	N	Y	Y
Riegle	N	N	N	N	Y	Y
MINNESOTA						
Boschwitz	Y	Y	Y	Y	Y	Y
Durenberger	Y	Y	Y	Y	Y	?
MISSISSIPPI						
Cochran	Y	Y	Y	Y	Y	Y
Stennis	N	?	N	Y	Y	?
MISSOURI						
Danforth	Y	Y	Y	Y	Y	Y
Eagleton	N	N	Y	Y	Y	Y
MONTANA						
Baucus	N	N	N	N	Y	Y
Melcher	N	N	N	Y	Y	Y
NEBRASKA						
Exon	N	N	N	Y	N	Y
Zorinsky	Y	Y	N	Y	N	?
NEVADA						
Hecht	Y	Y	Y	Y	N	Y
Laxalt	Y	?	?	Y	Y	?
NEW HAMPSHIRE						
Humphrey	Y	Y	Y	Y	N	?
Rudman	Y	Y	Y	Y	N	?
NEW JERSEY						
Bradley	N	N	N	Y	N	Y
Lautenberg	N	N	N	N	N	Y
NEW MEXICO						
Domenici	Y	Y	Y	Y	?	?
Bingaman	Y	Y	Y	Y	N	Y
NEW YORK						
D'Amato	Y	Y	Y	Y	Y	Y
Moynihan	N	N	N	Y	N	Y
NORTH CAROLINA						
East	?	?	?	?	Y	?
Helms	Y	Y	Y	Y	Y	Y
NORTH DAKOTA						
Andrews	N	Y	Y	Y	Y	Y
Burdick	N	N	N	Y	Y	+
OHIO						
Glenn	N	N	N	Y	Y	Y
Metzenbaum	N	N	N	N	Y	Y
OKLAHOMA						
Nickles	Y	Y	Y	Y	N	Y
Boren	N	N	Y	?	N	?
OREGON						
Hatfield	Y	Y	Y	Y	Y	?
Packwood	Y	Y	Y	Y	Y	Y
PENNSYLVANIA						
Heinz	Y	Y	Y	Y	Y	Y
Specter	Y	Y	Y	Y	Y	Y
RHODE ISLAND						
Chafee	Y	Y	Y	Y	N	Y
Pell	N	N	N	Y	N	Y
SOUTH CAROLINA						
Thurmond	Y	Y	?	Y	Y	Y
Hollings	Y	Y	Y	Y	N	Y
SOUTH DAKOTA						
Abdnor	Y	Y	Y	Y	Y	Y
Pressler	Y	Y	Y	Y	N	Y
TENNESSEE						
Gore	N	N	N	Y	N	Y
Sasser	N	N	N	Y	N	Y
TEXAS						
Gramm	Y	Y	Y	Y	N	Y
Bentsen	Y	Y	Y	Y	Y	Y
UTAH						
Garn	Y	Y	Y	Y	N	Y
Hatch	?	?	?	Y	Y	Y
VERMONT						
Stafford	Y	Y	Y	Y	Y	Y
Leahy	N	N	Y	Y	Y	Y
VIRGINIA						
Trible	Y	Y	Y	Y	?	Y
Warner	Y	Y	Y	Y	N	Y
WASHINGTON						
Evans	Y	Y	Y	Y	Y	Y
Gorton	?	?	?	Y	Y	Y
WEST VIRGINIA						
Byrd	N	N	N	N	N	Y
Rockefeller	N	N	N	Y	Y	Y
WISCONSIN						
Kasten	Y	Y	Y	Y	N	Y
Proxmire	Y	Y	N	N	N	Y
WYOMING						
Simpson	Y	Y	Y	Y	Y	Y
Wallop	Y	Y	Y	Y	Y	Y

KEY

Y Voted for (yea).
Paired for.
+ Announced for.
N Voted against (nay).
X Paired against.
- Announced against.
P Voted "present."
C Voted "present" to avoid possible conflict of interest.
? Did not vote or otherwise make a position known.

Democrats ***Republicans***

ND - Northern Democrats SD - Southern Democrats (Southern states - Ala., Ark., Fla., Ga., Ky., La., Miss., N.C., Okla., S.C., Tenn., Texas, Va.)

374. S 1396. White Earth Reservation Land Claim. Durenberger, R-Minn., motion to table (kill) the Melcher, D-Mont., appeal of the chair's ruling that the Melcher amendment, to provide legal advice and assistance to recipients of allocations of land on the White Earth Indian Reservation in Minnesota and their heirs, was not germane. Motion agreed to 56-36: R 46-1; D 10-35 (ND 5-27, SD 5-8), Dec. 13, 1985.

375. S 1396. White Earth Reservation Land Claim. Durenberger, R-Minn., motion to table (kill) the Melcher, D-Mont., amendment to provide for the transfer of certain lands to the White Earth Indian Reservation held by the state of Minnesota that had been taken by the state through tax forfeitures. Motion agreed to 53-37: R 46-0; D 7-37 (ND 5-27, SD 2-10), Dec. 13, 1985.

376. S 1396. White Earth Reservation Land Claim. Passage of the bill to settle unresolved claims relating to certain allotted Indian lands on the White Earth Indian Reservation in Minnesota. Passed 56-35: R 44-1; D 12-34 (ND 6-27, SD 6-7), Dec. 13, 1985.

377. Buckley Nomination. Confirmation of President Reagan's nomination of James L. Buckley of Connecticut to be U.S. circuit judge for the District of Columbia circuit. Confirmed 84-11: R 49-1; D 35-10 (ND 23-10, SD 12-0), Dec. 17, 1985. A "yea" was a vote supporting the president's position.

378. HR 2100. Farm Programs Reauthorization, Fiscal 1986-90. Adoption of the conference report on the bill to revise agriculture programs and extend them through fiscal year 1990; to modify price supports by reducing loan rates in 1986 and thereafter; to maintain income supports by freezing target prices at fiscal 1985 levels through fiscal 1987 and reduce them by a total of 10 percent over the remaining three years of the bill; to provide for agricultural export, soil conservation, farm credit and agricultural research programs; and to continue food assistance to low-income persons through fiscal 1990. Adopted (thus cleared for the president) 55-38: R 33-15; D 22-23 (ND 14-18, SD 8-5), Dec. 18, 1985.

379. HR 3128. Omnibus Budget Reconciliation, Fiscal 1986. Adoption of the conference report on the bill to reduce the deficit by $74 billion over fiscal 1986-88 through spending cuts and added revenues. Adopted 78-1: R 40-1; D 38-0 (ND 28-0, SD 10-0), Dec. 19, 1985. A "nay" was a vote supporting the president's position.

	380	381
ALABAMA		
Denton	?	?
Heflin	Y	Y
ALASKA		
Murkowski	?	?
Stevens	N	N
ARIZONA		
Goldwater	N	N
DeConcini	Y	Y
ARKANSAS		
Bumpers	Y	Y
Pryor	?	?
CALIFORNIA		
Wilson	N	N
Cranston	?	?
COLORADO		
Armstrong	Y	Y
Hart	?	?
CONNECTICUT		
Weicker	?	?
Dodd	?	?
DELAWARE		
Roth	N	N
Biden	?	?
FLORIDA		
Hawkins	-	?
Chiles	?	?
GEORGIA		
Mattingly	N	N
Nunn	?	?
HAWAII		
Inouye	Y	Y
Matsunaga	Y	Y
IDAHO		
McClure	?	?
Symms	N	N
ILLINOIS		
Dixon	?	?
Simon	?	?
INDIANA		
Lugar	N	N
Quayle	N	N
IOWA		
Grassley	?	?
Harkin	Y	Y
KANSAS		
Dole	N	N
Kassebaum	N	N
KENTUCKY		
McConnell	Y	Y
Ford	Y	Y
LOUISIANA		
Johnston	Y	Y
Long	Y	Y
MAINE		
Cohen	?	?
Mitchell	Y	Y
MARYLAND		
Mathias	?	?
Sarbanes	?	Y
MASSACHUSETTS		
Kennedy	?	?
Kerry	Y	Y
MICHIGAN		
Levin	Y	Y
Riegle	?	?
MINNESOTA		
Boschwitz	N	N
Durenberger	?	?
MISSISSIPPI		
Cochran	N	N
Stennis	Y	Y
MISSOURI		
Danforth	N	N
Eagleton	?	?
MONTANA		
Baucus	Y	Y
Melcher	?	?
NEBRASKA		
Exon	Y	Y
Zorinsky	?	?
NEVADA		
Hecht	N	N
Laxalt	N	N
NEW HAMPSHIRE		
Humphrey	?	?
Rudman	N	N
NEW JERSEY		
Bradley	Y	Y
Lautenberg	?	?
NEW MEXICO		
Domenici	N	N
Bingaman	Y	Y
NEW YORK		
D'Amato	N	N
Moynihan	?	?
NORTH CAROLINA		
East	?	?
Helms	N	N
NORTH DAKOTA		
Andrews	N	N
Burdick	+	+
OHIO		
Glenn	Y	Y
Metzenbaum	?	?
OKLAHOMA		
Nickles	Y	Y
Boren	?	?
OREGON		
Hatfield	?	?
Packwood	N	N
PENNSYLVANIA		
Heinz	N	N
Specter	N	N
RHODE ISLAND		
Chafee	N	N
Pell	+	+
SOUTH CAROLINA		
Thurmond	N	N
Hollings	Y	Y
SOUTH DAKOTA		
Abdnor	N	N
Pressler	N	N
TENNESSEE		
Gore	Y	Y
Sasser	Y	Y
TEXAS		
Gramm	N	N
Bentsen	Y	Y
UTAH		
Garn	?	?
Hatch	N	N
VERMONT		
Stafford	N	N
Leahy	Y	Y
VIRGINIA		
Trible	?	?
Warner	N	N
WASHINGTON		
Evans	?	?
Gorton	N	N
WEST VIRGINIA		
Byrd	Y	Y
Rockefeller	Y	Y
WISCONSIN		
Kasten	N	N
Proxmire	Y	Y
WYOMING		
Simpson	N	N
Wallop	N	N

KEY

- Y Voted for (yea).
- # Paired for.
- + Announced for.
- N Voted against (nay).
- X Paired against.
- \- Announced against.
- P Voted "present."
- C Voted "present" to avoid possible conflict of interest.
- ? Did not vote or otherwise make a position known.

Democrats *Republicans*

ND - Northern Democrats SD - Southern Democrats (Southern states - Ala., Ark., Fla., Ga., Ky., La., Miss., N.C., Okla., S.C., Tenn., Texas, Va.)

380. HR 3128. Omnibus Budget Reconciliation, Fiscal 1986. Johnston, D-La., motion to table (kill) the Dole, R-Kan., motion to insist on the Senate amendment to the House amendment to the Senate amendment to the bill. Motion rejected 29-35: R 3-35; D 26-0 (ND 16-0, SD 10-0), Dec. 20, 1985. (The effect of the Dole motion was to restore the original language of the conference report on the bill. The House had earlier voted to amend the conference agreement to strike a provision for a new manufacturers' excise tax to finance the "superfund" toxic-waste cleanup program *(see House vote 436, p. 138-H)*. The Senate then by voice vote had further amended the House amendment, reinstating the superfund provision, returning the bill to the House. The House refused to concur in the new Senate amendment *(see House vote 439, p. 138-H)*, and returned the bill to the Senate. After the Senate declined to table the Dole motion, it refused to recede to the House *(see vote 381, below)*, and agreed by voice vote to insist on its amendment and return the bill to conference.)

381. HR 3128. Omnibus Budget Reconciliation, Fiscal 1986. Johnston, D-La., motion to recede from the Senate amendment to the House amendment to the Senate amendment to the bill. Motion rejected 30-35: R 3-35; D 27-0 (ND 17-0, SD 10-0), Dec. 20, 1985. (The effect of the vote was to let stand a Senate amendment restoring a provision for a new manufacturers' excise tax to finance the "superfund" toxic-waste cleanup program. The Senate by voice vote then insisted on its amendment and returned the bill to conference.)

HOUSE ROLL-CALL VOTES

CQ

1. Election of Speaker. Nominees for Speaker of the House of Representatives for the 99th Congress were Thomas P. O'Neill Jr., D-Mass., the Speaker since 1977, and Robert H. Michel, R-Ill., minority leader since 1981. O'Neill was elected 247-175: R 0-175; D 247-0 (ND 168-0, SD 79-0), Jan. 3, 1985. A "Y" on the chart represents a vote for O'Neill, an "N" a vote for Michel.

2. H Res 1. Indiana 8th District Seat. Adoption of the resolution to provide that neither Republican Richard D. McIntyre nor Democrat Frank McCloskey be seated as a member of the 99th Congress, pending a Committee on House Administration investigation of the contested race. Adopted 238-177: R 0-177; D 238-0 (ND 161-0, SD 77-0), Jan. 3, 1985.

3. H Res 2. Idaho 2nd District Seat. Adoption of the resolution to administer the oath of office to Richard H. Stallings, D-Idaho. Adopted 407-0: R 174-0; D 233-0 (ND 157-0, SD 76-0), Jan. 3, 1985.

4. H Res 7. House Rules. Frost, D-Texas, motion to order the previous question (thus ending debate and the possibility of amendment) on the resolution to adopt the rules of the House of Representatives for the 99th Congress as proposed by the Democratic Caucus. Motion agreed to 238-176: R 0-175; D 238-1 (ND 160-1, SD 78-0), Jan. 3, 1985.

5. H Res 7. House Rules. Lott, R-Miss., motion to recommit the resolution to adopt the rules of the House for the 99th Congress to a select committee for the purpose of directing the Rules Committee to study the congressional budget process, committee operations and the House broadcasting system. Motion rejected 176-237: R 176-0; D 0-237 (ND 0-159, SD 0-78), Jan. 3, 1985.

6. H Res 7. House Rules. Adoption of the resolution to adopt the rules of the House of Representatives for the 99th Congress as proposed by the Democratic Caucus. Adopted 235-174: R 0-174; D 235-0 (ND 159-0, SD 76-0), Jan. 3, 1985.

All members-elect are eligible to vote on election of the Speaker.

† Not yet sworn in and therefore ineligible for CQ votes 2-6.
‡ Because of a seating challenge, Rep.-elect Richard H. Stallings, D-Idaho, was not eligible for CQ votes 2-3.
** The seat in the 8th District of Indiana was declared vacant after a challenge to the seating of Republican Richard McIntyre. The matter was later referred to the House Administration Committee for study.* (See vote 2, above)

KEY

Y Voted for (yea).
\# Paired for.
\+ Announced for.
N Voted against (nay).
X Paired against.
\- Announced against.
P Voted "present".
C Voted "present" to avoid possible conflict of interest.
? Did not vote or otherwise make a position known.

Democrats *Republicans*

	1	2	3	4	5	6
ALABAMA						
1 *Callahan*	N	N	Y	N	Y	N
2 *Dickinson*	N	N	Y	N	Y	N
3 Nichols	Y	Y	Y	Y	N	Y
4 Bevill	Y	Y	Y	Y	N	Y
5 Flippo	Y	Y	Y	Y	N	Y
6 Erdreich	Y	Y	Y	Y	N	Y
7 Shelby	Y	Y	Y	Y	N	Y
ALASKA						
AL *Young*	N	N	+	N	Y	N
ARIZONA						
1 *McCain*	N	N	Y	N	Y	N
2 Udall	Y	Y	Y	Y	N	Y
3 *Stump*	N	N	Y	N	Y	N
4 *Rudd*	N	N	Y	N	Y	N
5 *Kolbe*	N	N	Y	N	Y	N
ARKANSAS						
1 Alexander	Y	Y	Y	Y	N	Y
2 Robinson	Y	Y	Y	Y	N	Y
3 *Hammerschmidt*	N	N	Y	N	Y	N
4 Anthony	Y	Y	Y	Y	N	Y
CALIFORNIA						
1 Bosco	Y	Y	?	Y	?	Y
2 *Chappie*†	?					
3 Matsui	Y	Y	Y	Y	N	Y
4 Fazio	Y	Y	Y	Y	N	Y
5 Burton	Y	Y	Y	Y	N	Y
6 Boxer	Y	Y	Y	Y	N	Y
7 Miller	Y	Y	Y	Y	N	Y
8 Dellums	Y	Y	Y	Y	N	Y
9 Stark	Y	Y	Y	Y	N	Y
10 Edwards	Y	Y	Y	Y	N	Y
11 Lantos	Y	Y	Y	Y	N	Y
12 *Zschau*	N	N	Y	N	Y	N
13 Mineta	Y	Y	Y	Y	N	Y
14 *Shumway*	N	N	Y	N	Y	N
15 Coelho	Y	Y	Y	Y	N	Y
16 Panetta	Y	Y	Y	Y	N	Y
17 *Pashayan*	N	N	Y	N	Y	N
18 Lehman	Y	Y	Y	Y	N	Y
19 *Lagomarsino*	N	N	Y	N	Y	N
20 *Thomas*	N	N	Y	?	Y	N
21 *Fiedler*	N	N	Y	N	Y	N
22 *Moorhead*	N	N	Y	N	Y	N
23 Beilenson	Y	Y	Y	Y	N	Y
24 Waxman	Y	Y	?	Y	N	Y
25 Roybal	Y	Y	Y	Y	N	Y
26 Berman	Y	?	Y	Y	N	Y
27 Levine	Y	Y	Y	Y	N	Y
28 Dixon	Y	Y	Y	Y	N	Y
29 Hawkins	Y	Y	Y	Y	N	Y
30 Martinez	Y	Y	Y	Y	N	Y
31 Dymally	Y	?	?	?	?	?
32 Anderson	Y	Y	Y	Y	N	Y
33 *Dreier*	N	N	Y	N	Y	N
34 Torres	Y	Y	Y	Y	N	Y
35 *Lewis*	N	N	Y	N	Y	N
36 Brown	Y	Y	Y	?	?	?
37 *McCandless*	N	N	Y	N	Y	N
38 *Dornan*	N	?	Y	N	Y	N
39 *Dannemeyer*	N	N	Y	N	Y	N
40 *Badham*	N	N	Y	N	Y	N
41 *Lowery*	N	N	P	N	Y	N
42 *Lungren*	N	N	Y	N	Y	N
43 *Packard*	?	N	Y	N	Y	N
44 Bates	Y	Y	Y	Y	N	Y
45 *Hunter*	N	N	Y	N	Y	N
COLORADO						
1 Schroeder	Y	Y	Y	Y	N	Y
2 Wirth	Y	Y	Y	Y	N	Y
3 *Strang*	N	N	Y	N	Y	N
4 *Brown*	N	N	Y	N	Y	N
5 *Kramer*	N	N	Y	N	Y	N
6 *Schaefer*	N	N	Y	N	Y	?
CONNECTICUT						
1 Kennelly	Y	Y	Y	Y	N	Y
2 Gejdenson	Y	Y	Y	Y	N	Y
3 Morrison	Y	Y	Y	Y	N	Y
4 *McKinney*	N	N	Y	N	Y	N
5 *Rowland*	N	N	Y	N	Y	N
6 *Johnson*	N	N	Y	N	Y	N
DELAWARE						
AL Carper	Y	Y	Y	Y	N	Y
FLORIDA						
1 Hutto	Y	Y	Y	Y	N	Y
2 Fuqua	Y	Y	Y	Y	N	Y
3 Bennett	Y	Y	Y	Y	N	Y
4 Chappell	Y	Y	Y	Y	N	Y
5 *McCollum*	N	N	Y	N	Y	N
6 MacKay	Y	Y	Y	Y	N	Y
7 Gibbons	Y	Y	Y	Y	N	Y
8 *Young*	N	N	Y	N	Y	N
9 *Bilirakis*	N	N	Y	N	Y	N
10 *Ireland*	N	N	Y	N	Y	N
11 Nelson	Y	Y	Y	Y	N	Y
12 *Lewis*	N	N	Y	N	Y	N
13 *Mack*	N	N	Y	N	Y	N
14 Mica	Y	Y	Y	Y	N	Y
15 *Shaw*	N	N	Y	N	Y	N
16 Smith	Y	Y	Y	Y	N	Y
17 Lehman	Y	Y	Y	Y	N	Y
18 Pepper	Y	Y	Y	Y	N	Y
19 Fascell	Y	Y	Y	Y	N	Y
GEORGIA						
1 Thomas	Y	Y	Y	Y	N	Y
2 Hatcher	Y	Y	Y	Y	N	Y
3 Ray	Y	Y	Y	Y	N	Y
4 *Swindall*	N	N	+	N	Y	N
5 Fowler†	?					
6 *Gingrich*	N	N	Y	N	Y	N
7 Darden	Y	Y	Y	Y	N	Y
8 Rowland	Y	Y	Y	Y	N	Y
9 Jenkins	Y	Y	Y	Y	N	Y
10 Barnard	Y	Y	Y	Y	N	Y
HAWAII						
1 Heftel†	?					
2 Akaka	Y	Y	Y	Y	N	Y
IDAHO						
1 *Craig*	N	N	Y	N	Y	N
2 Stallings‡	Y			Y	N	Y
ILLINOIS						
1 Hayes	Y	Y	Y	Y	N	Y
2 Savage	Y	Y	Y	Y	N	Y
3 Russo	Y	Y	Y	Y	N	Y
4 *O'Brien*†	?					
5 Lipinski	Y	?	Y	Y	N	Y
6 *Hyde*	N	N	Y	N	Y	N
7 Collins	Y	Y	Y	Y	N	Y
8 Rostenkowski	Y	Y	Y	Y	N	Y
9 Yates	Y	Y	Y	Y	N	Y
10 *Porter*	N	N	Y	N	Y	N
11 Annunzio	Y	Y	Y	Y	N	Y
12 *Crane, P.*	N	N	Y	N	Y	N
13 *Fawell*	N	N	Y	N	Y	N
14 *Grotberg*	N	N	Y	N	Y	N
15 *Madigan*	N	N	Y	N	Y	?
16 *Martin*	N	N	Y	N	Y	N
17 Evans	Y	Y	Y	Y	N	Y
18 *Michel*	C	N	Y	N	Y	N
19 Bruce	Y	Y	Y	Y	N	Y
20 Durbin	Y	Y	Y	Y	N	Y
21 Price	Y	Y	Y	?	?	?
22 Gray	Y	Y	Y	Y	N	Y
INDIANA						
1 Visclosky	Y	Y	Y	Y	N	Y
2 Sharp	Y	Y	Y	Y	N	Y
3 *Hiler*	N	N	Y	N	Y	N
4 *Coats*	N	N	Y	N	Y	N
5 *Hillis*†	?					

ND - Northern Democrats SD - Southern Democrats

* Corresponding to Congressional Record Votes 2, 3, 4, 5, 6, 7

	1	2	3	4	5	6
6 ***Burton***	N	N	Y	N	Y	N
7 ***Myers***	N	N	Y	N	Y	N
8 ***McIntyre****	N					
9 Hamilton	Y	Y	Y	Y	N	Y
10 Jacobs	Y	Y	Y	N	N	Y
IOWA						
1 ***Leach***	N	N	Y	N	?	?
2 ***Tauke***	N	N	Y	N	Y	N
3 ***Evans***	N	N	Y	N	Y	N
4 Smith	Y	Y	Y	Y	N	Y
5 ***Lightfoot***	N	N	Y	N	Y	N
6 Bedell	Y	Y	Y	Y	N	Y
KANSAS						
1 ***Roberts***	N	N	Y	N	Y	N
2 Slattery	Y	Y	Y	Y	N	Y
3 ***Meyers***	N	N	Y	N	Y	N
4 Glickman	Y	Y	Y	Y	N	Y
5 ***Whittaker***	N	N	Y	N	Y	N
KENTUCKY						
1 Hubbard	Y	Y	Y	Y	N	Y
2 Natcher	Y	Y	Y	Y	N	Y
3 Mazzoli	Y	Y	Y	Y	N	Y
4 ***Snyder***	N	N	Y	N	Y	N
5 ***Rogers***	N	N	Y	N	Y	N
6 ***Hopkins***	N	N	Y	N	Y	N
7 Perkins	Y	Y	Y	Y	N	Y
LOUISIANA						
1 ***Livingston***	N	N	Y	N	Y	N
2 Boggs	Y	Y	Y	Y	N	Y
3 Tauzin	Y	Y	Y	Y	N	?
4 Roemer	Y	Y	Y	Y	N	Y
5 Huckaby	Y	Y	Y	Y	N	Y
6 ***Moore***	N	N	Y	N	Y	N
7 Breaux	Y	Y	Y	Y	N	Y
8 Long	Y	Y	Y	Y	N	Y
MAINE						
1 ***McKernan***	?	N	Y	N	Y	N
2 ***Snowe***	N	N	Y	N	Y	N
MARYLAND						
1 Dyson	Y	Y	Y	Y	N	Y
2 ***Bentley***	N	N	Y	N	Y	N
3 Mikulski	Y	Y	Y	Y	N	Y
4 ***Holt***	N	N	Y	N	Y	N
5 Hoyer	Y	Y	Y	Y	N	Y
6 Byron	Y	Y	Y	Y	N	Y
7 Mitchell	Y	Y	Y	Y	N	Y
8 Barnes	Y	Y	Y	Y	N	Y
MASSACHUSETTS						
1 ***Conte***	N	N	Y	N	Y	N
2 Boland	Y	Y	Y	?	?	?
3 Early	Y	Y	Y	Y	N	Y
4 Frank	Y	Y	Y	Y	N	Y
5 Atkins	Y	Y	Y	Y	N	?
6 Mavroules	Y	Y	?	Y	N	Y
7 Markey	Y	Y	Y	Y	?	Y
8 O'Neill	C					
9 Moakley	Y	Y	?	?	?	?
10 Studds	Y	Y	Y	Y	N	?
11 Donnelly	Y	Y	Y	Y	N	Y
MICHIGAN						
1 Conyers	Y	?	?	Y	N	Y
2 ***Pursell***	N	N	Y	N	Y	N
3 Wolpe	Y	Y	Y	Y	N	Y
4 ***Siljander***	N	N	Y	N	Y	N
5 ***Henry***	N	N	Y	N	Y	N
6 Carr	Y	Y	Y	Y	N	Y
7 Kildee	Y	Y	Y	Y	N	Y
8 Traxler	Y	Y	Y	Y	N	Y
9 ***Vander Jagt***	N	N	Y	N	Y	N
10 ***Schuette***	N	N	Y	N	Y	N
11 ***Davis***	N	N	Y	N	Y	N
12 Bonior	Y	Y	Y	Y	N	Y
13 Crockett	Y	Y	Y	Y	N	Y
14 Hertel	Y	Y	Y	Y	N	Y
15 Ford	Y	Y	Y	Y	N	Y
16 Dingell	Y	?	Y	Y	N	Y
17 Levin	Y	Y	?	Y	N	Y
18 ***Broomfield***	N	N	Y	N	Y	N
MINNESOTA						
1 Penny	Y	Y	Y	Y	N	Y
2 ***Weber***	N	N	Y	N	Y	N
3 ***Frenzel***	N	N	Y	N	Y	N
4 Vento	Y	Y	Y	Y	N	Y
5 Sabo	Y	Y	Y	Y	N	Y
6 Sikorski	Y	Y	Y	Y	N	Y
7 ***Stangeland***	N	N	Y	N	Y	N
8 Oberstar	Y	Y	Y	Y	N	Y
MISSISSIPPI						
1 Whitten	Y	Y	Y	Y	N	Y
2 ***Franklin***	N	N	Y	N	Y	N
3 Montgomery	Y	Y	Y	Y	N	Y
4 Dowdy	Y	Y	Y	?	N	Y
5 ***Lott***	N	N	Y	N	Y	N
MISSOURI						
1 Clay	Y	Y	Y	Y	N	Y
2 Young	Y	Y	Y	Y	N	Y
3 Gephardt	Y	Y	Y	Y	N	Y
4 Skelton	Y	Y	Y	Y	N	Y
5 Wheat	Y	Y	Y	Y	N	Y
6 ***Coleman***	N	N	Y	N	Y	N
7 ***Taylor***	N	N	Y	N	Y	N
8 ***Emerson***	N	N	Y	N	Y	N
9 Volkmer	Y	Y	Y	Y	N	Y
MONTANA						
1 Williams	Y	Y	Y	Y	N	Y
2 ***Marlenee***	?	N	Y	N	Y	N
NEBRASKA						
1 ***Bereuter***	N	N	Y	N	Y	N
2 ***Daub***	N	N	Y	N	Y	N
3 ***Smith***	N	N	Y	N	Y	N
NEVADA						
1 Reid	Y	?	?	Y	N	Y
2 ***Vucanovich***	N	N	Y	N	Y	N
NEW HAMPSHIRE						
1 ***Smith***	N	N	Y	N	Y	N
2 ***Gregg***	N	N	Y	N	Y	N
NEW JERSEY						
1 Florio	Y	Y	Y	Y	N	Y
2 Hughes	Y	Y	Y	Y	N	Y
3 Howard	Y	Y	Y	Y	N	Y
4 ***Smith***	N	N	Y	N	Y	N
5 ***Roukema***	N	N	Y	N	Y	N
6 Dwyer	Y	Y	Y	Y	N	Y
7 ***Rinaldo***	N	N	Y	N	Y	N
8 Roe	Y	Y	Y	Y	N	Y
9 Torricelli	Y	Y	Y	Y	N	Y
10 Rodino	Y	Y	?	Y	N	Y
11 ***Gallo***	N	N	Y	N	Y	N
12 ***Courter***	N	N	Y	N	Y	N
13 ***Saxton***	N	N	Y	N	Y	N
14 Guarini	Y	Y	?	Y	N	?
NEW MEXICO						
1 ***Lujan***	N	N	Y	N	Y	N
2 ***Skeen***	N	N	Y	N	Y	N
3 Richardson	Y	Y	Y	Y	N	Y
NEW YORK						
1 ***Carney***	N	N	Y	N	Y	N
2 Downey	Y	Y	Y	Y	N	Y
3 Mrazek	Y	Y	Y	Y	N	Y
4 ***Lent***	N	N	Y	N	Y	N
5 ***McGrath***	N	N	Y	N	Y	N
6 Addabbo	Y	Y	Y	Y	N	Y
7 Ackerman	Y	Y	Y	Y	N	Y
8 Scheuer	Y	Y	Y	Y	N	Y
9 Manton	Y	Y	Y	Y	N	Y
10 Schumer	Y	Y	Y	?	?	?
11 Towns	Y	Y	Y	Y	N	Y
12 Owens	Y	Y	Y	Y	N	Y
13 Solarz	Y	Y	Y	Y	N	Y
14 ***Molinari***	N	N	Y	N	Y	N
15 ***Green***	N	N	Y	N	Y	N
16 Rangel	Y	Y	Y	Y	N	Y
17 Weiss	Y	Y	Y	Y	N	Y
18 Garcia	Y	Y	Y	Y	N	Y
19 Biaggi	Y	Y	Y	Y	N	Y
20 ***DioGuardi***	N	N	Y	N	Y	N
21 ***Fish***	N	N	Y	N	Y	N
22 ***Gilman***	N	N	Y	N	Y	N
23 Stratton	Y	Y	Y	Y	N	Y
24 ***Solomon***	N	N	Y	N	Y	N
25 ***Boehlert***	N	N	Y	N	Y	N
26 ***Martin***	N	N	Y	N	Y	N
27 ***Wortley***	N	N	Y	N	Y	N
28 McHugh	Y	Y	Y	Y	N	Y
29 ***Horton***	N	N	Y	N	Y	N
30 ***Eckert***	N	N	Y	N	Y	N
31 ***Kemp***	N	N	Y	N	Y	N
32 LaFalce	Y	Y	Y	Y	N	Y
33 Nowak	Y	Y	Y	Y	N	Y
34 Lundine	Y	Y	Y	Y	N	Y
NORTH CAROLINA						
1 Jones	Y	?	?	?	?	?
2 Valentine	Y	?	Y	Y	N	Y
3 Whitley	Y	Y	Y	Y	N	Y
4 ***Cobey***	N	N	Y	N	Y	N
5 Neal	?	?	?	?	?	?
6 ***Coble***	N	N	Y	N	Y	N
7 Rose	Y	Y	Y	Y	N	Y
8 Hefner	Y	Y	Y	Y	N	Y
9 ***McMillan***	N	N	Y	N	Y	N
10 ***Broyhill***	N	N	Y	N	Y	N
11 ***Hendon***	N	N	Y	N	Y	N
NORTH DAKOTA						
AL Dorgan	Y	Y	Y	Y	N	Y
OHIO						
1 Luken	Y	Y	Y	Y	N	Y
2 ***Gradison***	N	N	Y	N	Y	N
3 Hall	Y	Y	Y	Y	N	Y
4 ***Oxley***	N	N	Y	N	Y	N
5 ***Latta***	N	N	Y	N	Y	N
6 ***McEwen***	N	N	Y	N	Y	N
7 ***DeWine***	N	N	Y	N	Y	N
8 ***Kindness***	N	N	Y	N	Y	N
9 Kaptur	Y	Y	Y	Y	N	Y
10 ***Miller***	N	N	Y	N	Y	N
11 Eckart	Y	Y	Y	Y	N	Y
12 ***Kasich***	N	N	Y	N	Y	N
13 Pease	Y	Y	Y	Y	N	Y
14 Seiberling	Y	Y	Y	Y	N	Y
15 ***Wylie***	N	N	Y	N	Y	N
16 ***Regula***	N	N	Y	N	Y	N
17 Traficant	Y	Y	Y	Y	N	Y
18 Applegate	Y	Y	Y	Y	N	Y
19 Feighan	Y	Y	Y	Y	N	Y
20 Oakar	Y	Y	Y	Y	N	Y
21 Stokes	Y	Y	Y	Y	N	Y
OKLAHOMA						
1 Jones	Y	Y	Y	Y	N	Y
2 Synar	Y	Y	Y	Y	N	Y
3 Watkins	Y	Y	Y	Y	N	Y
4 McCurdy	Y	Y	Y	Y	N	Y
5 ***Edwards***	N	N	Y	?	Y	N
6 English	Y	Y	Y	Y	N	Y
OREGON						
1 AuCoin	Y	Y	Y	Y	?	Y
2 ***Smith, R.***	N	N	Y	N	Y	N
3 Wyden	Y	Y	Y	Y	N	Y
4 Weaver	Y	Y	Y	Y	N	Y
5 ***Smith, D.***	N	N	Y	N	Y	N
PENNSYLVANIA						
1 Foglietta	Y	Y	Y	Y	N	Y
2 Gray	Y	Y	Y	Y	N	Y
3 Borski	Y	Y	Y	Y	N	Y
4 Kolter	Y	Y	Y	Y	N	Y
5 ***Schulze***	N	N	Y	N	Y	N
6 Yatron	Y	Y	Y	Y	N	Y
7 Edgar	Y	Y	Y	Y	N	Y
8 Kostmayer	Y	Y	Y	Y	N	Y
9 ***Shuster***	N	N	Y	N	Y	N
10 ***McDade***	N	N	Y	N	Y	N
11 Kanjorski	Y	Y	Y	Y	N	Y
12 Murtha	Y	Y	Y	Y	N	Y
13 ***Coughlin***	N	N	Y	N	Y	N
14 Coyne	Y	Y	Y	Y	N	Y
15 ***Ritter***	N	N	Y	N	Y	N
16 ***Walker***	N	N	Y	N	Y	N
17 ***Gekas***	N	N	Y	N	Y	N
18 Walgren	Y	Y	Y	Y	N	Y
19 ***Goodling***	N	N	Y	N	Y	N
20 Gaydos	Y	Y	Y	?	N	Y
21 ***Ridge***	N	N	Y	N	Y	N
22 Murphy	Y	Y	Y	Y	N	Y
23 ***Clinger***	N	N	Y	N	Y	N
RHODE ISLAND						
1 St Germain	Y	Y	Y	Y	N	Y
2 ***Schneider***	N	N	Y	N	Y	N
SOUTH CAROLINA						
1 ***Hartnett***	N	N	Y	N	Y	?
2 ***Spence***	N	N	Y	N	Y	N
3 Derrick	Y	Y	Y	Y	?	?
4 ***Campbell***	N	N	Y	N	Y	N
5 Spratt	Y	Y	Y	Y	N	Y
6 Tallon	Y	Y	Y	Y	N	Y
SOUTH DAKOTA						
AL Daschle	Y	Y	Y	Y	N	Y
TENNESSEE						
1 ***Quillen***	N	N	Y	N	Y	N
2 ***Duncan***	N	N	Y	N	Y	N
3 Lloyd	Y	Y	Y	Y	N	Y
4 Cooper	Y	Y	Y	Y	N	Y
5 Boner	Y	Y	Y	Y	N	Y
6 Gordon	Y	Y	Y	Y	N	Y
7 ***Sundquist***	N	N	Y	N	Y	N
8 Jones	Y	Y	Y	Y	N	Y
9 Ford	Y	Y	Y	Y	N	Y
TEXAS						
1 Hall, S.	Y	Y	Y	Y	N	Y
2 Wilson	Y	Y	Y	Y	N	?
3 ***Bartlett***	N	N	Y	N	Y	N
4 Hall, R.	P	?	?	Y	N	Y
5 Bryant	Y	Y	Y	Y	N	Y
6 ***Barton***	N	N	?	N	Y	N
7 ***Archer***†	?					
8 ***Fields***	N	N	Y	N	Y	N
9 Brooks	Y	Y	Y	Y	N	Y
10 Pickle	Y	Y	Y	Y	N	Y
11 Leath	Y	Y	?	Y	N	Y
12 Wright	Y	Y	Y	Y	N	Y
13 ***Boulter***	N	N	Y	N	Y	N
14 ***Sweeney***	N	N	Y	N	Y	N
15 de la Garza	Y	Y	Y	Y	N	Y
16 Coleman	Y	Y	Y	Y	N	Y
17 Stenholm	Y	Y	Y	Y	N	Y
18 Leland	Y	Y	Y	Y	N	Y
19 ***Combest***	N	N	Y	N	Y	N
20 Gonzalez	Y	Y	Y	Y	N	Y
21 ***Loeffler***	N	N	Y	N	Y	N
22 ***DeLay***	N	N	Y	N	Y	N
23 Bustamante	Y	Y	Y	Y	N	Y
24 Frost	Y	Y	Y	Y	N	Y
25 Andrews	Y	Y	Y	Y	N	Y
26 ***Armey***	N	N	Y	N	Y	N
27 Ortiz	Y	Y	Y	Y	N	Y
UTAH						
1 ***Hansen***	N	N	Y	N	Y	N
2 ***Monson***	N	N	Y	N	Y	N
3 ***Nielson***	N	N	Y	N	Y	N
VERMONT						
AL ***Jeffords***	N	N	Y	N	Y	N
VIRGINIA						
1 ***Bateman***	N	N	Y	N	Y	N
2 ***Whitehurst***	N	N	Y	N	Y	N
3 ***Bliley***	N	N	Y	N	Y	N
4 Sisisky	Y	Y	Y	Y	N	Y
5 Daniel	Y	Y	?	Y	N	Y
6 Olin	Y	Y	Y	Y	N	Y
7 ***Slaughter***	N	N	Y	N	Y	N
8 ***Parris***	N	N	Y	N	Y	N
9 Boucher	Y	Y	Y	Y	N	Y
10 ***Wolf***	N	N	Y	N	Y	N
WASHINGTON						
1 ***Miller***	N	N	Y	-	+	N
2 Swift	Y	Y	Y	Y	N	Y
3 Bonker	Y	Y	Y	Y	N	Y
4 ***Morrison***	N	N	Y	N	Y	N
5 Foley	Y	Y	Y	Y	N	Y
6 Dicks	Y	Y	Y	Y	N	Y
7 Lowry	Y	Y	Y	Y	N	Y
8 ***Chandler***	N	N	Y	N	Y	N
WEST VIRGINIA						
1 Mollohan	Y	Y	Y	Y	N	Y
2 Staggers	Y	Y	Y	Y	N	Y
3 Wise	Y	Y	Y	Y	N	Y
4 Rahall	Y	Y	Y	Y	N	Y
WISCONSIN						
1 Aspin	Y	Y	Y	Y	N	Y
2 Kastenmeier	Y	Y	Y	Y	N	Y
3 ***Gunderson***	N	N	Y	N	Y	N
4 Kleczka	Y	Y	Y	Y	N	Y
5 Moody	Y	Y	Y	Y	N	Y
6 ***Petri***	N	N	Y	N	Y	N
7 Obey	Y	Y	Y	Y	N	Y
8 ***Roth***	N	N	Y	N	Y	N
9 ***Sensenbrenner***	N	N	Y	N	Y	N
WYOMING						
AL ***Cheney***	N	N	Y	N	Y	N

Southern states - Ala., Ark., Fla., Ga., Ky., La., Miss., N.C., Okla., S.C., Tenn., Texas, Va.

* The *Congressional Record* vote number is different from the CQ vote number because the *Record* includes quorum calls in its tally. CQ does not publish quorum call votes.

7. Procedural Motion. Boulter, R-Texas, motion to approve the House *Journal* of Wednesday, Feb. 6. Motion agreed to 375-17: R 165-7; D 210-10 (ND 141-8, SD 69-2), Feb. 7, 1985.

8. H Res 52. Indiana 8th District Seat. Wright, D-Texas, motion to refer to the Committee on House Administration the resolution to seat Republican Richard D. McIntyre as a member of the 99th Congress, pending an investigation of the contested race by the Committee on House Administration. Motion agreed to 221-180: R 0-175; D 221-5 (ND 151-1, SD 70-4), Feb. 7, 1985.

KEY

- Y Voted for (yea).
- # Paired for.
- + Announced for.
- N Voted against (nay).
- X Paired against.
- \- Announced against.
- P Voted "present".
- C Voted "present" to avoid possible conflict of interest.
- ? Did not vote or otherwise make a position known.

Democrats ***Republicans***

	7	8
ALABAMA		
1 ***Callahan***	Y	N
2 ***Dickinson***	N	N
3 Nichols	?	?
4 Bevill	Y	Y
5 Flippo	P	Y
6 Erdreich	Y	Y
7 Shelby	Y	Y
ALASKA		
AL ***Young***	Y	N
ARIZONA		
1 ***McCain***	Y	N
2 Udall	Y	Y
3 ***Stump***	Y	N
4 ***Rudd***	Y	N
5 ***Kolbe***	Y	N
ARKANSAS		
1 Alexander	Y	Y
2 Robinson	P	Y
3 ***Hammerschmidt***	Y	N
4 Anthony	Y	Y
CALIFORNIA		
1 Bosco	?	?
2 ***Chappie***	P	N
3 Matsui	Y	Y
4 Fazio	Y	Y
5 Burton	Y	Y
6 Boxer	Y	Y
7 Miller	Y	Y
8 Dellums	Y	Y
9 Stark	Y	Y
10 Edwards	Y	Y
11 Lantos	Y	Y
12 ***Zschau***	Y	N
13 Mineta	Y	Y
14 ***Shumway***	Y	N
15 Coelho	Y	Y
16 Panetta	Y	C
17 ***Pashayan***	Y	N
18 Lehman	Y	Y
19 ***Lagomarsino***	Y	N
20 ***Thomas***	Y	N
21 ***Fiedler***	Y	N
22 ***Moorhead***	Y	N
23 Beilenson	Y	Y
24 Waxman	?	?
25 Roybal	Y	Y
26 Berman	Y	Y
27 Levine	Y	Y
28 Dixon	Y	Y
29 Hawkins	N	Y
30 Martinez	Y	Y
31 Dymally	P	Y
32 Anderson	Y	Y
33 ***Dreier***	Y	N
34 Torres	Y	Y
35 ***Lewis***	Y	N
36 Brown	Y	Y
37 ***McCandless***	Y	N
38 ***Dornan***	Y	N
39 ***Dannemeyer***	Y	N
40 ***Badham***	Y	N
41 ***Lowery***	Y	N
42 ***Lungren***	Y	N

	7	8
43 ***Packard***	Y	N
44 Bates	Y	?
45 ***Hunter***	Y	N
COLORADO		
1 Schroeder	N	Y
2 Wirth	Y	Y
3 ***Strang***	Y	N
4 ***Brown***	Y	N
5 ***Kramer***	Y	N
6 ***Schaefer***	Y	N
CONNECTICUT		
1 Kennelly	Y	Y
2 Gejdenson	Y	Y
3 Morrison	Y	Y
4 ***McKinney***	?	?
5 ***Rowland***	Y	N
6 ***Johnson***	Y	N
DELAWARE		
AL Carper	Y	Y
FLORIDA		
1 Hutto	Y	Y
2 Fuqua	Y	Y
3 Bennett	Y	Y
4 Chappell	Y	Y
5 ***McCollum***	Y	N
6 MacKay	Y	Y
7 Gibbons	Y	Y
8 ***Young***	Y	N
9 ***Bilirakis***	Y	N
10 ***Ireland***	Y	N
11 Nelson	Y	Y
12 ***Lewis***	Y	N
13 ***Mack***	Y	N
14 Mica	Y	Y
15 ***Shaw***	Y	N
16 Smith	Y	Y
17 Lehman	Y	Y
18 Pepper	Y	Y
19 Fascell	Y	Y
GEORGIA		
1 Thomas	Y	Y
2 Hatcher	Y	Y
3 Ray	Y	Y
4 ***Swindall***	Y	N
5 Fowler	Y	Y
6 ***Gingrich***	?	?
7 Darden	Y	Y
8 Rowland	Y	Y
9 Jenkins	Y	Y
10 Barnard	?	?
HAWAII		
1 Heftel	?	?
2 Akaka	?	?
IDAHO		
1 ***Craig***	Y	N
2 Stallings	Y	Y
ILLINOIS		
1 Hayes	?	Y
2 Savage	Y	Y
3 Russo	Y	Y
4 ***O'Brien***	Y	N
5 Lipinski	?	?
6 ***Hyde***	Y	N
7 Collins	Y	Y
8 Rostenkowski	?	Y
9 Yates	Y	Y
10 ***Porter***	Y	N
11 Annunzio	Y	Y
12 ***Crane, P.***	Y	N
13 ***Fawell***	Y	N
14 ***Grotberg***	Y	N
15 ***Madigan***	Y	N
16 ***Martin***	Y	N
17 Evans	Y	Y
18 ***Michel***	Y	N
19 Bruce	Y	Y
20 Durbin	N	Y
21 Price	Y	Y
22 Gray	Y	Y
INDIANA		
1 Visclosky	Y	Y
2 Sharp	Y	Y
3 ***Hiler***	Y	N
4 ***Coats***	Y	N
5 ***Hillis***	Y	N

ND - Northern Democrats SD - Southern Democrats

	7	8
6 ***Burton***	Y	N
7 ***Myers***	Y	N
8 Vacancy		
9 Hamilton	Y	Y
10 Jacobs	N	Y
IOWA		
1 ***Leach***	Y	N
2 ***Tauke***	Y	N
3 ***Evans***	N	N
4 Smith	Y	Y
5 ***Lightfoot***	Y	N
6 Bedell	Y	Y
KANSAS		
1 ***Roberts***	Y	N
2 Slattery	Y	Y
3 ***Meyers***	Y	N
4 Glickman	Y	Y
5 ***Whittaker***	Y	N
KENTUCKY		
1 Hubbard	Y	Y
2 Natcher	Y	Y
3 Mazzoli	?	N
4 ***Snyder***	Y	N
5 ***Rogers***	Y	N
6 ***Hopkins***	Y	N
7 Perkins	N	Y
LOUISIANA		
1 ***Livingston***	Y	N
2 Boggs	Y	Y
3 Tauzin	Y	Y
4 Roemer	N	Y
5 Huckaby	Y	Y
6 ***Moore***	Y	N
7 Breaux	Y	Y
8 Vacancy*		
MAINE		
1 ***McKernan***	Y	N
2 ***Snowe***	Y	N
MARYLAND		
1 Dyson	Y	Y
2 ***Bentley***	Y	N
3 Mikulski	Y	Y
4 ***Holt***	N	N
5 Hoyer	Y	Y
6 Byron	Y	Y
7 Mitchell	N	Y
8 Barnes	Y	Y
MASSACHUSETTS		
1 ***Conte***	Y	N
2 Boland	?	?
3 Early	?	?
4 Frank	Y	Y
5 Atkins	Y	Y
6 Mavroules	Y	Y
7 Markey	Y	Y
8 O'Neill		
9 Moakley	?	?
10 Studds	Y	Y
11 Donnelly	Y	Y
MICHIGAN		
1 Conyers	Y	Y
2 ***Pursell***	Y	N
3 Wolpe	Y	Y
4 ***Siljander***	Y	N
5 ***Henry***	Y	N
6 Carr	Y	Y
7 Kildee	Y	Y
8 Traxler	?	?
9 ***Vander Jagt***	Y	N
10 ***Schuette***	Y	N
11 ***Davis***	Y	N
12 Bonior	Y	Y
13 Crockett	Y	Y
14 Hertel	Y	Y
15 Ford	?	Y
16 Dingell	Y	Y
17 Levin	Y	Y
18 ***Broomfield***	Y	N
MINNESOTA		
1 Penny	N	Y
2 ***Weber***	Y	N
3 ***Frenzel***	Y	N
4 Vento	Y	Y
5 Sabo	Y	Y
6 Sikorski	N	Y

	7	8
7 ***Stangeland***	Y	N
8 Oberstar	P	Y
MISSISSIPPI		
1 Whitten	Y	Y
2 ***Franklin***	Y	N
3 Montgomery	Y	Y
4 Dowdy	Y	Y
5 ***Lott***	Y	N
MISSOURI		
1 Clay	?	?
2 Young	?	?
3 Gephardt	Y	Y
4 Skelton	Y	?
5 Wheat	Y	Y
6 ***Coleman***	Y	N
7 ***Taylor***	Y	N
8 ***Emerson***	Y	N
9 Volkmer	Y	Y
MONTANA		
1 Williams	Y	Y
2 ***Marlenee***	Y	N
NEBRASKA		
1 ***Bereuter***	Y	N
2 ***Daub***	Y	N
3 ***Smith***	Y	N
NEVADA		
1 Reid	Y	Y
2 ***Vucanovich***	Y	N
NEW HAMPSHIRE		
1 ***Smith***	Y	N
2 ***Gregg***	Y	N
NEW JERSEY		
1 Florio	Y	Y
2 Hughes	Y	Y
3 Howard	Y	Y
4 ***Smith***	Y	N
5 ***Roukema***	?	?
6 Dwyer	Y	Y
7 ***Rinaldo***	Y	N
8 Roe	Y	Y
9 Torricelli	Y	Y
10 Rodino	Y	Y
11 ***Gallo***	Y	N
12 ***Courter***	?	?
13 ***Saxton***	Y	N
14 Guarini	Y	Y
NEW MEXICO		
1 ***Lujan***	Y	N
2 ***Skeen***	Y	N
3 Richardson	Y	Y
NEW YORK		
1 ***Carney***	Y	N
2 Downey	Y	Y
3 Mrazek	Y	Y
4 ***Lent***	Y	N
5 ***McGrath***	Y	N
6 Addabbo	Y	Y
7 Ackerman	Y	Y
8 Scheuer	Y	Y
9 Manton	Y	Y
10 Schumer	Y	Y
11 Towns	Y	Y
12 Owens	Y	Y
13 Solarz	Y	Y
14 ***Molinari***	Y	N
15 ***Green***	Y	N
16 Rangel	Y	Y
17 Weiss	Y	Y
18 Garcia	Y	Y
19 Biaggi	Y	Y
20 ***DioGuardi***	Y	N
21 ***Fish***	Y	N
22 ***Gilman***	Y	N
23 Stratton	Y	Y
24 ***Solomon***	Y	N
25 ***Boehlert***	Y	N
26 ***Martin***	Y	N
27 ***Wortley***	Y	N
28 McHugh	Y	Y
29 ***Horton***	?	?
30 ***Eckert***	Y	N
31 ***Kemp***	Y	N
32 LaFalce	Y	Y
33 Nowak	Y	Y
34 Lundine	Y	Y

	7	8
NORTH CAROLINA		
1 Jones	Y	Y
2 Valentine	Y	?
3 Whitley	Y	Y
4 ***Cobey***	Y	N
5 Neal	Y	Y
6 ***Coble***	Y	N
7 Rose	P	Y
8 Hefner	Y	Y
9 ***McMillan***	Y	N
10 ***Broyhill***	Y	N
11 ***Hendon***	Y	N
NORTH DAKOTA		
AL Dorgan	Y	Y
OHIO		
1 Luken	Y	Y
2 ***Gradison***	?	N
3 Hall	Y	Y
4 ***Oxley***	Y	N
5 ***Latta***	Y	N
6 ***McEwen***	Y	N
7 ***DeWine***	Y	N
8 ***Kindness***	Y	N
9 Kaptur	Y	Y
10 ***Miller***	N	N
11 Eckart	Y	Y
12 ***Kasich***	Y	N
13 Pease	Y	Y
14 Seiberling	Y	Y
15 ***Wylie***	Y	N
16 ***Regula***	Y	N
17 Traficant	Y	Y
18 Applegate	?	N
19 Feighan	?	?
20 Oakar	Y	Y
21 Stokes	Y	?
OKLAHOMA		
1 Jones	Y	?
2 Synar	Y	Y
3 Watkins	Y	Y
4 McCurdy	Y	Y
5 ***Edwards***	Y	N
6 English	Y	Y
OREGON		
1 AuCoin	N	Y
2 ***Smith, R.***	Y	N
3 Wyden	Y	Y
4 Weaver	Y	Y
5 ***Smith, D.***	Y	N
PENNSYLVANIA		
1 Foglietta	?	?
2 Gray	Y	Y
3 Borski	Y	Y
4 Kolter	Y	Y
5 ***Schulze***	Y	N
6 Yatron	Y	Y
7 Edgar	Y	Y
8 Kostmayer	Y	Y
9 ***Shuster***	Y	N
10 ***McDade***	Y	N
11 Kanjorski	Y	Y
12 Murtha	Y	Y
13 ***Coughlin***	N	N
14 Coyne	Y	Y
15 ***Ritter***	Y	N
16 ***Walker***	N	N
17 ***Gekas***	Y	N
18 Walgren	Y	Y
19 ***Goodling***	N	N
20 Gaydos	Y	Y
21 ***Ridge***	Y	N
22 Murphy	Y	Y
23 ***Clinger***	+	-
RHODE ISLAND		
1 St Germain	Y	Y
2 ***Schneider***	Y	N
SOUTH CAROLINA		
1 ***Hartnett***	Y	N
2 ***Spence***	Y	N
3 Derrick	Y	Y
4 ***Campbell***	Y	N
5 Spratt	Y	Y
6 Tallon	Y	Y
SOUTH DAKOTA		
AL Daschle	P	Y

	7	8
TENNESSEE		
1 ***Quillen***	Y	N
2 ***Duncan***	Y	N
3 Lloyd	Y	Y
4 Cooper	Y	Y
5 Boner	Y	Y
6 Gordon	Y	Y
7 ***Sundquist***	Y	N
8 Jones	Y	Y
9 Ford	Y	Y
TEXAS		
1 Hall, S.	Y	N
2 Wilson	?	?
3 ***Bartlett***	Y	N
4 Hall, R.	Y	N
5 Bryant	?	?
6 ***Barton***	Y	N
7 ***Archer***	Y	N
8 ***Fields***	Y	N
9 Brooks	Y	Y
10 Pickle	Y	Y
11 Leath	Y	Y
12 Wright	Y	Y
13 ***Boulter***	Y	N
14 ***Sweeney***	Y	N
15 de la Garza	?	?
16 Coleman	Y	Y
17 Stenholm	Y	N
18 Leland	Y	Y
19 ***Combest***	Y	N
20 Gonzalez	Y	Y
21 ***Loeffler***	Y	N
22 ***DeLay***	Y	N
23 Bustamante	Y	Y
24 Frost	Y	Y
25 Andrews	Y	Y
26 ***Armey***	Y	N
27 Ortiz	Y	Y
UTAH		
1 ***Hansen***	Y	N
2 ***Monson***	Y	N
3 ***Nielson***	Y	N
VERMONT		
AL ***Jeffords***	Y	N
VIRGINIA		
1 ***Bateman***	Y	N
2 ***Whitehurst***	Y	N
3 ***Bliley***	Y	N
4 Sisisky	Y	Y
5 Daniel	?	Y
6 Olin	Y	Y
7 ***Slaughter***	Y	N
8 ***Parris***	Y	N
9 Boucher	Y	Y
10 ***Wolf***	Y	N
WASHINGTON		
1 ***Miller***	Y	N
2 Swift	Y	Y
3 Bonker	Y	Y
4 ***Morrison***	?	?
5 Foley	Y	Y
6 Dicks	Y	Y
7 Lowry	Y	Y
8 ***Chandler***	Y	N
WEST VIRGINIA		
1 Mollohan	Y	Y
2 Staggers	Y	Y
3 Wise	Y	Y
4 Rahall	Y	Y
WISCONSIN		
1 Aspin	Y	Y
2 Kastenmeier	Y	Y
3 ***Gunderson***	Y	N
4 Kleczka	Y	Y
5 Moody	Y	Y
6 ***Petri***	Y	N
7 Obey	Y	Y
8 ***Roth***	Y	N
9 ***Sensenbrenner***	Y	N
WYOMING		
AL ***Cheney***	?	N

** Rep. Gillis W. Long, D-La., died Jan. 20, 1985. The last vote for which he was eligible was CQ vote 6.*

Southern states - Ala., Ark., Fla., Ga., Ky., La., Miss., N.C., Okla., S.C., Tenn., Texas, Va.

* The *Congressional Record* vote number is different from the CQ vote number because the *Record* includes quorum calls in its tally. CQ does not publish quorum call votes.

9. Procedural Motion. Cobey, R-N.C., motion to approve the House *Journal* of Wednesday, Feb. 20. Motion agreed to 189-144: R 6-136; D 183-8 (ND 124-5, SD 59-3), Feb. 21, 1985.

10. Procedural Motion. Wright, D-Texas, motion that when the House adjourns Feb. 21, it meet again at noon Feb. 25. Motion agreed to 194-137: R 3-137; D 191-0 (ND 128-0, SD 63-0), Feb. 21, 1985. (Republicans voted against the routine motion to protest the House's refusal to seat Richard D. McIntyre in Indiana's 8th District.)

11. Procedural Motion. DeLay, R-Texas, motion to approve the House *Journal* of Thursday, Feb. 21. Motion agreed to 131-86: R 11-81; D 120-5 (ND 75-3, SD 45-2), Feb. 25, 1985.

12. Procedural Motion. Combest, R-Texas, motion to approve the House *Journal* of Monday, Feb. 25. Motion agreed to 224-162: R 9-154; D 215-8 (ND 141-6, SD 74-2), Feb. 26, 1985.

13. HR 1096. African Relief. Wolpe, D-Mich., motion to suspend the rules and pass the bill to authorize $175 million in fiscal year 1985 for disaster and refugee aid for African countries affected by drought and famine. Motion agreed to 391-25: R 151-24; D 240-1 (ND 163-0, SD 77-1), Feb. 26, 1985. A two-thirds majority of those present and voting (278 in this case) is required for passage under suspension of the rules.

14. HR 607. Cost-Savings Disclosure Awards. Schroeder, D-Colo., motion to suspend the rules and pass the bill to authorize the president and agency inspectors general to grant cash awards to employees who disclose waste, fraud and abuse. Motion agreed to 413-1: R 174-1; D 239-0 (ND 161-0, SD 78-0), Feb. 26, 1985. A two-thirds majority of those present and voting (276 in this case) is required for passage under suspension of the rules.

15. Procedural Motion. Combest, R-Texas, motion to approve the House *Journal* of Tuesday, Feb. 26. Motion agreed to 234-167: R 12-158; D 222-9 (ND 148-8, SD 74-1), Feb. 27, 1985.

16. HR 1035. Emergency Farm Credit. Adoption of the rule (H Res 79) providing for House floor consideration of the bill to authorize advance Commodity Credit Corporation crop loans to farmers, to authorize $3 billion in Farmers Home Administration (FmHA) loan guarantees for restructured private loans to farmers, to revise rules for the FmHA loan guarantees and to authorize low-interest federal disaster loans to farmers in certain circumstances. Adopted 331-91: R 87-90; D 244-1 (ND 165-1, SD 79-0), Feb. 27, 1985.

KEY

Y Voted for (yea).
\# Paired for.
\+ Announced for.
N Voted against (nay).
X Paired against.
\- Announced against.
P Voted "present".
C Voted "present" to avoid possible conflict of interest.
? Did not vote or otherwise make a position known.

Democrats *Republicans*

	9	10	11	12	13	14	15	16
ALABAMA								
1 *Callahan*	N	N	?	N	Y	Y	N	Y
2 *Dickinson*	N	Y	N	N	Y	Y	N	Y
3 Nichols	?	Y	Y	Y	Y	Y	Y	Y
4 Bevill	Y	Y	Y	Y	Y	Y	Y	Y
5 Flippo	Y	Y	Y	Y	Y	Y	Y	Y
6 Erdreich	Y	Y	?	Y	Y	Y	Y	Y
7 Shelby	Y	Y	?	Y	Y	Y	Y	Y
ALASKA								
AL *Young*	N	?	N	N	Y	Y	N	Y
ARIZONA								
1 *McCain*	?	?	?	N	Y	Y	N	N
2 Udall	Y	Y	Y	Y	Y	Y	Y	Y
3 *Stump*	N	N	N	N	N	Y	N	N
4 *Rudd*	?	?	Y	N	N	Y	N	N
5 *Kolbe*	?	?	?	N	Y	Y	N	N
ARKANSAS								
1 Alexander	Y	Y	Y	Y	Y	Y	Y	Y
2 Robinson	?	Y	?	?	Y	Y	Y	Y
3 *Hammerschmidt*	N	N	N	N	Y	Y	N	Y
4 Anthony	?	?	Y	Y	Y	Y	?	Y
CALIFORNIA								
1 Bosco	?	?	?	Y	Y	?	Y	Y
2 *Chappie*	?	?	N	N	Y	Y	N	N
3 Matsui	?	?	?	Y	Y	Y	Y	Y
4 Fazio	Y	Y	Y	Y	Y	Y	Y	Y
5 Burton	?	?	Y	Y	Y	Y	Y	Y
6 Boxer	Y	Y	?	Y	Y	Y	Y	Y
7 Miller	Y	Y	Y	Y	Y	Y	Y	Y
8 Dellums	?	?	?	Y	Y	Y	Y	Y
9 Stark	Y	Y	Y	Y	+	Y	Y	Y
10 Edwards	Y	Y	Y	Y	Y	Y	Y	Y
11 Lantos	?	?	?	?	#	?	Y	Y
12 *Zschau*	N	N	N	N	Y	Y	N	Y
13 Mineta	Y	Y	?	Y	Y	Y	Y	Y
14 *Shumway*	N	N	N	N	Y	Y	N	N
15 Coelho	Y	Y	?	Y	Y	Y	Y	Y
16 Panetta	Y	Y	?	Y	Y	Y	Y	Y
17 *Pashayan*	N	N	?	N	Y	Y	Y	Y
18 Lehman	Y	Y	?	Y	Y	Y	Y	Y
19 *Lagomarsino*	N	N	N	N	Y	Y	N	Y
20 *Thomas*	N	N	Y	N	Y	Y	N	Y
21 *Fiedler*	?	?	?	N	Y	Y	N	N
22 *Moorhead*	N	N	N	N	Y	Y	N	N
23 Beilenson	?	?	?	Y	Y	Y	Y	Y
24 Waxman	Y	Y	Y	?	Y	Y	?	Y
25 Roybal	?	?	?	Y	Y	Y	Y	Y
26 Berman	Y	Y	Y	Y	Y	Y	Y	Y
27 Levine	Y	Y	?	Y	Y	Y	Y	Y
28 Dixon	Y	Y	?	Y	Y	Y	Y	Y
29 Hawkins	Y	?	Y	Y	Y	?	Y	Y
30 Martinez	Y	Y	Y	Y	Y	Y	Y	Y
31 Dymally	?	?	?	?	Y	Y	P	Y
32 Anderson	?	?	?	Y	Y	Y	Y	Y
33 *Dreier*	?	?	?	N	Y	Y	N	N
34 Torres	Y	Y	Y	Y	Y	Y	Y	Y
35 *Lewis*	?	?	N	N	Y	Y	N	N
36 Brown	Y	Y	Y	Y	Y	Y	Y	Y
37 *McCandless*	?	?	?	N	Y	Y	N	N
38 *Dornan*	?	?	?	N	Y	Y	N	N
39 *Dannemeyer*	?	?	?	N	N	Y	N	N
40 *Badham*	N	N	N	N	N	Y	N	N
41 *Lowery*	N	N	?	N	Y	Y	N	N
42 *Lungren*	N	N	N	N	Y	Y	N	N
43 *Packard*	N	N	N	N	Y	Y	N	N
44 Bates	Y	Y	Y	Y	Y	Y	Y	Y
45 *Hunter*	N	N	N	N	Y	Y	N	N
COLORADO								
1 Schroeder	N	Y	?	N	Y	Y	N	Y
2 Wirth	Y	Y	Y	Y	Y	Y	Y	Y
3 *Strang*	N	N	N	N	Y	Y	N	N
4 *Brown*	N	N	?	N	N	Y	N	N
5 *Kramer*	?	?	?	N	Y	Y	N	Y
6 *Schaefer*	?	?	?	N	Y	Y	N	N
CONNECTICUT								
1 Kennelly	?	?	Y	Y	Y	Y	Y	Y
2 Gejdenson	Y	Y	?	Y	Y	Y	Y	Y
3 Morrison	?	?	?	Y	Y	Y	Y	Y
4 *McKinney*	?	?	?	N	Y	Y	N	Y
5 *Rowland*	N	N	?	N	Y	Y	N	N
6 *Johnson*	?	?	Y	?	Y	Y	Y	Y
DELAWARE								
AL Carper	Y	Y	?	Y	Y	Y	Y	Y
FLORIDA								
1 Hutto	Y	Y	Y	Y	Y	Y	Y	Y
2 Fuqua	?	?	Y	Y	Y	Y	Y	Y
3 Bennett	Y	Y	Y	Y	Y	Y	Y	Y
4 Chappell	Y	Y	Y	Y	Y	Y	Y	Y
5 *McCollum*	?	?	N	N	Y	Y	N	N
6 MacKay	Y	?	?	Y	Y	Y	Y	Y
7 Gibbons	Y	Y	Y	Y	Y	Y	Y	Y
8 *Young*	?	N	?	N	Y	Y	N	N
9 *Bilirakis*	N	N	?	N	Y	Y	?	N
10 *Ireland*	N	N	N	N	Y	Y	N	N
11 Nelson	Y	Y	Y	Y	Y	Y	Y	Y
12 *Lewis*	N	N	-	N	Y	Y	N	N
13 *Mack*	N	N	N	N	Y	Y	N	N
14 Mica	?	?	Y	Y	Y	Y	Y	Y
15 *Shaw*	N	N	N	N	Y	Y	N	N
16 Smith	Y	Y	Y	?	Y	Y	Y	Y
17 Lehman	Y	Y	Y	Y	Y	Y	Y	Y
18 Pepper	?	Y	?	Y	Y	Y	Y	Y
19 Fascell	Y	?	?	?	?	?	?	?
GEORGIA								
1 Thomas	Y	Y	Y	Y	Y	Y	Y	Y
2 Hatcher	Y	Y	?	?	?	?	Y	Y
3 Ray	Y	Y	?	?	Y	Y	Y	Y
4 *Swindall*	N	N	N	N	N	Y	N	N
5 Fowler	?	?	?	Y	Y	Y	Y	Y
6 *Gingrich*	N	N	N	P	Y	Y	?	N
7 Darden	Y	Y	Y	Y	Y	Y	Y	Y
8 Rowland	Y	Y	Y	Y	Y	Y	Y	Y
9 Jenkins	Y	Y	?	Y	Y	Y	Y	Y
10 Barnard	?	?	Y	Y	Y	Y	Y	Y
HAWAII								
1 Heftel	?	?	?	?	Y	Y	Y	Y
2 Akaka	Y	Y	Y	Y	Y	Y	Y	Y
IDAHO								
1 *Craig*	N	N	N	N	N	Y	N	N
2 Stallings	Y	Y	Y	?	Y	Y	Y	Y
ILLINOIS								
1 Hayes	Y	Y	Y	Y	Y	Y	Y	Y
2 Savage	?	?	?	Y	Y	Y	Y	Y
3 Russo	Y	Y	?	Y	Y	Y	Y	Y
4 *O'Brien*	N	Y	N	N	Y	Y	Y	N
5 Lipinski	?	?	?	Y	Y	Y	Y	Y
6 *Hyde*	N	N	N	N	Y	Y	N	N
7 Collins	Y	Y	?	Y	Y	Y	Y	Y
8 Rostenkowski	Y	Y	?	Y	Y	Y	Y	Y
9 Yates	Y	Y	Y	Y	Y	Y	Y	Y
10 *Porter*	N	N	?	N	Y	Y	N	N
11 Annunzio	?	?	?	?	Y	Y	Y	Y
12 *Crane, P.*	?	?	?	?	X	?	Y	?
13 *Fawell*	?	N	?	N	Y	Y	N	N
14 *Grotberg*	N	-	N	N	Y	Y	N	N
15 *Madigan*	N	N	?	?	?	?	?	?
16 *Martin*	N	N	N	?	?	?	?	?
17 Evans	Y	Y	Y	Y	Y	Y	Y	Y
18 *Michel*	N	N	?	N	Y	Y	N	N
19 Bruce	Y	Y	Y	Y	Y	Y	Y	Y
20 Durbin	Y	Y	Y	Y	Y	Y	Y	Y
21 Price	Y	Y	?	Y	Y	Y	Y	Y
22 Gray	?	?	?	?	?	?	Y	Y
INDIANA								
1 Visclosky	Y	Y	Y	Y	Y	Y	Y	Y
2 Sharp	Y	Y	Y	Y	Y	Y	Y	Y
3 *Hiler*	N	N	?	N	Y	Y	N	N
4 *Coats*	N	N	N	N	Y	Y	N	Y
5 *Hillis*	?	?	?	?	Y	Y	N	Y

ND - Northern Democrats SD - Southern Democrats

* Corresponding to Congressional Record Votes 10, 11, 12, 13, 14, 15, 16, 17

	9	10	11	12	13	14	15	16
6 ***Burton***	N	N	?	N	Y	Y	N	N
7 ***Myers***	N	N	N	N	Y	Y	N	Y
8 Vacancy								
9 Hamilton	Y	Y	Y	Y	Y	Y	Y	Y
10 Jacobs	?	?	N	N	Y	Y	N	Y
IOWA								
1 ***Leach***	N	N	N	N	Y	Y	N	Y
2 ***Tauke***	N	N	?	N	Y	Y	N	Y
3 ***Evans***	N	N	N	N	Y	Y	N	Y
4 Smith	Y	Y	Y	Y	Y	Y	Y	Y
5 ***Lightfoot***	N	N	N	N	Y	Y	N	Y
6 Bedell	?	Y	Y	Y	Y	Y	Y	Y
KANSAS								
1 ***Roberts***	Y	N	N	N	Y	Y	N	Y
2 Slattery	Y	Y	Y	Y	Y	Y	Y	Y
3 ***Meyers***	N	?	N	?	Y	Y	N	N
4 Glickman	Y	Y	Y	Y	Y	Y	Y	Y
5 ***Whittaker***	?	?	?	N	Y	Y	N	Y
KENTUCKY								
1 Hubbard	?	?	?	Y	Y	Y	Y	Y
2 Natcher	Y	Y	Y	Y	Y	Y	Y	Y
3 Mazzoli	Y	Y	Y	Y	Y	Y	Y	Y
4 ***Snyder***	?	?	?	Y	Y	Y	Y	Y
5 ***Rogers***	N	N	?	N	Y	Y	N	Y
6 ***Hopkins***	N	N	?	N	Y	Y	N	Y
7 Perkins	Y	Y	Y	Y	Y	Y	Y	Y
LOUISIANA								
1 ***Livingston***	N	N	?	N	Y	Y	N	N
2 Boggs	Y	Y	?	Y	Y	Y	?	Y
3 Tauzin	Y	Y	?	Y	Y	Y	Y	Y
4 Roemer	N	Y	N	N	Y	Y	N	Y
5 Huckaby	N	Y	Y	N	Y	Y	?	Y
6 ***Moore***	Y	N	Y	N	Y	Y	Y	Y
7 Breaux	Y	Y	Y	Y	Y	Y	Y	Y
8 Vacancy								
MAINE								
1 ***McKernan***	N	N	N	N	Y	Y	N	N
2 ***Snowe***	N	N	N	N	Y	Y	N	Y
MARYLAND								
1 Dyson	Y	Y	Y	Y	Y	Y	Y	Y
2 ***Bentley***	?	?	?	N	Y	Y	N	?
3 Mikulski	Y	Y	?	Y	Y	Y	Y	Y
4 ***Holt***	N	N	Y	?	?	?	Y	N
5 Hoyer	Y	Y	?	Y	Y	Y	Y	Y
6 Byron	Y	Y	Y	Y	Y	Y	Y	Y
7 Mitchell	Y	Y	?	Y	Y	Y	N	Y
8 Barnes	Y	Y	?	Y	Y	Y	Y	Y
MASSACHUSETTS								
1 ***Conte***	N	N	?	N	Y	Y	N	N
2 Boland	Y	Y	Y	Y	Y	Y	Y	Y
3 Early	Y	Y	Y	Y	Y	Y	Y	Y
4 Frank	Y	Y	?	Y	Y	Y	?	Y
5 Atkins	Y	?	?	Y	Y	Y	Y	Y
6 Mavroules	Y	Y	?	?	Y	Y	Y	Y
7 Markey	Y	Y	?	Y	Y	Y	N	Y
8 O'Neill								
9 Moakley	?	?	?	Y	Y	Y	Y	Y
10 Studds	Y	Y	?	Y	Y	Y	Y	Y
11 Donnelly	?	?	?	Y	Y	Y	Y	Y
MICHIGAN								
1 Conyers	?	?	?	P	Y	Y	?	Y
2 ***Pursell***	N	N	?	N	Y	Y	N	Y
3 Wolpe	Y	Y	?	Y	Y	Y	Y	Y
4 ***Siljander***	?	N	?	N	Y	Y	N	Y
5 ***Henry***	N	N	?	N	Y	Y	N	Y
6 Carr	Y	Y	Y	Y	Y	Y	Y	Y
7 Kildee	Y	Y	Y	Y	Y	Y	Y	Y
8 Traxler	Y	Y	?	Y	Y	Y	Y	Y
9 ***Vander Jagt***	N	?	?	?	Y	Y	N	Y
10 ***Schuette***	N	N	N	N	Y	Y	N	Y
11 ***Davis***	N	?	?	N	Y	Y	N	Y
12 Bonior	Y	Y	Y	Y	Y	Y	Y	Y
13 Crockett	?	?	Y	Y	Y	Y	Y	Y
14 Hertel	Y	Y	?	Y	Y	Y	Y	Y
15 Ford	?	?	?	?	Y	?	?	Y
16 Dingell	Y	Y	Y	?	Y	Y	?	Y
17 Levin	Y	Y	?	Y	Y	Y	Y	Y
18 ***Broomfield***	N	N	N	N	Y	Y	N	N
MINNESOTA								
1 Penny	N	Y	N	N	Y	Y	N	Y
2 ***Weber***	N	?	N	N	N	Y	?	Y
3 ***Frenzel***	?	N	?	?	?	?	N	N
4 Vento	Y	Y	Y	Y	Y	Y	Y	Y
5 Sabo	Y	Y	Y	Y	Y	Y	Y	Y
6 Sikorski	N	Y	N	N	Y	Y	N	Y

	9	10	11	12	13	14	15	16
7 ***Stangeland***	Y	N	?	N	Y	Y	N	Y
8 Oberstar	Y	Y	Y	Y	Y	Y	Y	Y
MISSISSIPPI								
1 Whitten	Y	Y	Y	Y	Y	Y	Y	Y
2 ***Franklin***	N	N	?	N	Y	Y	N	Y
3 Montgomery	Y	Y	Y	Y	Y	Y	Y	Y
4 Dowdy	?	?	?	Y	Y	Y	Y	Y
5 ***Lott***	N	N	N	N	Y	Y	N	N
MISSOURI								
1 Clay	?	?	?	N	Y	Y	N	Y
2 Young	Y	Y	?	Y	Y	Y	Y	Y
3 Gephardt	?	?	?	?	Y	Y	?	Y
4 Skelton	Y	Y	?	Y	Y	Y	Y	Y
5 Wheat	?	?	Y	Y	Y	Y	Y	Y
6 ***Coleman***	N	N	?	Y	Y	Y	N	Y
7 ***Taylor***	N	N	?	Y	Y	Y	N	Y
8 ***Emerson***	N	N	?	N	Y	Y	N	Y
9 Volkmer	Y	Y	?	Y	Y	Y	Y	Y
MONTANA								
1 Williams	?	?	Y	Y	Y	Y	?	Y
2 ***Marlenee***	?	N	Y	N	Y	Y	N	Y
NEBRASKA								
1 ***Bereuter***	N	N	N	N	Y	Y	N	Y
2 ***Daub***	N	N	N	N	Y	Y	N	N
3 ***Smith***	N	N	N	N	Y	Y	N	Y
NEVADA								
1 Reid	Y	Y	Y	Y	Y	Y	Y	Y
2 ***Vucanovich***	?	N	Y	N	Y	Y	N	N
NEW HAMPSHIRE								
1 ***Smith***	N	N	?	N	N	Y	N	N
2 ***Gregg***	?	?	?	N	Y	Y	N	N
NEW JERSEY								
1 Florio	Y	?	Y	Y	Y	Y	Y	Y
2 Hughes	Y	Y	Y	Y	Y	Y	Y	Y
3 Howard	Y	Y	Y	Y	Y	Y	Y	Y
4 ***Smith***	N	N	?	N	Y	Y	N	Y
5 ***Roukema***	N	N	?	N	Y	Y	N	Y
6 Dwyer	Y	Y	Y	Y	Y	Y	Y	Y
7 ***Rinaldo***	N	N	?	N	Y	Y	N	Y
8 Roe	Y	Y	?	Y	Y	Y	Y	Y
9 Torricelli	Y	Y	?	Y	Y	Y	Y	?
10 Rodino	Y	Y	?	Y	Y	Y	Y	Y
11 ***Gallo***	N	N	N	N	Y	Y	N	N
12 ***Courter***	N	N	?	?	Y	Y	N	Y
13 ***Saxton***	N	N	N	N	Y	Y	N	N
14 Guarini	Y	Y	?	?	Y	Y	Y	Y
NEW MEXICO								
1 ***Lujan***	N	N	N	N	Y	Y	N	N
2 ***Skeen***	N	N	N	N	Y	Y	N	N
3 Richardson	Y	Y	Y	Y	Y	Y	Y	Y
NEW YORK								
1 ***Carney***	N	N	N	N	Y	Y	?	Y
2 Downey	Y	Y	?	Y	Y	Y	Y	Y
3 Mrazek	Y	Y	?	Y	Y	Y	Y	Y
4 ***Lent***	N	N	N	N	Y	Y	N	Y
5 ***McGrath***	?	?	?	N	Y	Y	N	N
6 Addabbo	Y	Y	Y	Y	Y	Y	Y	Y
7 Ackerman	?	?	?	?	?	?	?	?
8 Scheuer	Y	Y	?	Y	Y	?	Y	Y
9 Manton	Y	Y	Y	Y	Y	Y	Y	Y
10 Schumer	Y	Y	?	Y	Y	Y	Y	Y
11 Towns	?	?	?	?	Y	Y	?	?
12 Owens	?	?	?	Y	Y	Y	Y	Y
13 Solarz	Y	Y	?	Y	Y	Y	Y	Y
14 ***Molinari***	N	N	N	N	Y	Y	N	N
15 ***Green***	N	N	?	N	Y	Y	N	N
16 Rangel	Y	Y	?	Y	Y	?	Y	Y
17 Weiss	Y	Y	?	Y	Y	Y	Y	Y
18 Garcia	Y	Y	?	?	Y	Y	Y	Y
19 Biaggi	Y	Y	?	Y	Y	Y	Y	Y
20 ***DioGuardi***	N	N	?	N	Y	Y	N	N
21 ***Fish***	?	N	N	N	Y	Y	N	Y
22 ***Gilman***	N	N	-	N	Y	Y	?	Y
23 Stratton	Y	Y	Y	Y	Y	Y	Y	Y
24 ***Solomon***	N	N	N	N	Y	Y	N	Y
25 ***Boehlert***	N	N	?	?	?	?	N	Y
26 ***Martin***	?	?	?	N	Y	Y	Y	Y
27 ***Wortley***	N	N	N	N	Y	Y	N	Y
28 McHugh	Y	Y	Y	Y	Y	Y	Y	Y
29 ***Horton***	N	N	Y	Y	Y	Y	Y	Y
30 ***Eckert***	N	N	?	N	Y	Y	N	N
31 ***Kemp***	?	?	?	N	Y	Y	?	Y
32 LaFalce	?	?	?	Y	Y	Y	?	Y
33 Nowak	Y	Y	?	Y	Y	Y	Y	Y
34 Lundine	Y	Y	?	Y	Y	Y	Y	Y

	9	10	11	12	13	14	15	16
NORTH CAROLINA								
1 Jones	?	?	?	Y	Y	Y	Y	Y
2 Valentine	Y	Y	?	Y	Y	Y	Y	Y
3 Whitley	?	?	?	Y	Y	Y	Y	Y
4 ***Cobey***	N	N	?	N	N	Y	N	N
5 Neal	Y	Y	Y	Y	Y	Y	Y	Y
6 ***Coble***	N	N	N	N	N	Y	N	N
7 Rose	Y	Y	?	Y	Y	Y	Y	Y
8 Hefner	Y	?	Y	Y	Y	Y	Y	Y
9 ***McMillan***	N	N	?	?	Y	Y	N	N
10 ***Broyhill***	?	?	?	Y	Y	Y	Y	N
11 ***Hendon***	N	N	?	N	Y	Y	N	N
NORTH DAKOTA								
AL Dorgan	Y	Y	?	Y	Y	Y	Y	Y
OHIO								
1 Luken	N	Y	?	N	Y	Y	N	N
2 ***Gradison***	Y	N	Y	Y	Y	Y	Y	N
3 Hall	Y	Y	Y	Y	Y	Y	Y	Y
4 ***Oxley***	N	N	N	N	Y	Y	N	Y
5 ***Latta***	N	N	?	N	Y	Y	N	Y
6 ***McEwen***	?	?	?	N	Y	Y	N	Y
7 ***DeWine***	N	N	?	N	Y	Y	N	Y
8 ***Kindness***	N	N	?	N	N	Y	N	N
9 Kaptur	Y	Y	?	?	Y	Y	Y	Y
10 ***Miller***	N	N	N	N	Y	Y	N	Y
11 Eckart	Y	Y	Y	Y	#	Y	Y	Y
12 ***Kasich***	N	N	?	N	Y	Y	N	Y
13 Pease	Y	Y	Y	Y	Y	Y	Y	Y
14 Seiberling	Y	Y	?	Y	Y	Y	Y	Y
15 ***Wylie***	N	N	?	N	Y	Y	N	Y
16 ***Regula***	N	?	N	N	Y	Y	N	Y
17 Traficant	?	?	?	?	Y	Y	Y	Y
18 Applegate	Y	Y	?	Y	Y	Y	Y	Y
19 Feighan	Y	Y	?	Y	Y	Y	Y	Y
20 Oakar	Y	Y	Y	Y	Y	Y	Y	Y
21 Stokes	Y	Y	Y	Y	Y	Y	Y	Y
OKLAHOMA								
1 Jones	N	Y	?	Y	Y	Y	Y	Y
2 Synar	Y	Y	Y	Y	Y	Y	Y	Y
3 Watkins	?	Y	Y	Y	Y	Y	Y	Y
4 McCurdy	Y	Y	?	Y	Y	Y	Y	Y
5 ***Edwards***	N	N	N	N	Y	Y	N	Y
6 English	Y	Y	Y	Y	Y	Y	Y	Y
OREGON								
1 AuCoin	Y	Y	?	Y	Y	Y	Y	Y
2 ***Smith, R.***	N	N	N	N	Y	Y	N	N
3 Wyden	Y	Y	Y	Y	Y	Y	Y	Y
4 Weaver	Y	Y	Y	?	Y	Y	Y	Y
5 ***Smith, D.***	N	N	?	N	N	Y	N	N
PENNSYLVANIA								
1 Foglietta	?	?	?	Y	Y	Y	Y	Y
2 Gray	?	?	Y	?	Y	Y	?	Y
3 Borski	Y	Y	Y	Y	Y	Y	Y	Y
4 Kolter	Y	Y	?	Y	?	Y	Y	Y
5 ***Schulze***	N	N	N	N	Y	Y	N	Y
6 Yatron	Y	Y	?	Y	Y	Y	Y	Y
7 Edgar	Y	Y	?	Y	Y	Y	Y	Y
8 Kostmayer	Y	Y	?	?	Y	Y	Y	Y
9 ***Shuster***	?	?	N	N	Y	Y	N	N
10 ***McDade***	N	N	N	N	Y	Y	N	Y
11 Kanjorski	?	Y	?	Y	Y	Y	Y	Y
12 Murtha	Y	Y	Y	Y	Y	Y	Y	Y
13 ***Coughlin***	?	?	N	N	Y	Y	N	N
14 Coyne	?	Y	Y	Y	Y	Y	Y	Y
15 ***Ritter***	N	N	N	N	Y	Y	N	N
16 ***Walker***	N	N	?	N	Y	Y	N	N
17 ***Gekas***	N	N	N	N	Y	Y	N	N
18 Walgren	Y	Y	Y	Y	Y	Y	Y	Y
19 ***Goodling***	N	N	?	N	Y	Y	N	?
20 Gaydos	Y	Y	Y	Y	Y	Y	Y	Y
21 ***Ridge***	N	N	?	?	Y	Y	N	Y
22 Murphy	Y	Y	Y	Y	Y	Y	Y	Y
23 ***Clinger***	N	N	Y	N	Y	Y	N	Y
RHODE ISLAND								
1 St Germain	?	?	?	Y	Y	Y	Y	Y
2 ***Schneider***	N	?	?	Y	Y	Y	N	Y
SOUTH CAROLINA								
1 ***Hartnett***	Y	?	?	?	Y	Y	N	Y
2 ***Spence***	N	N	?	N	Y	Y	N	Y
3 Derrick	Y	?	?	Y	Y	Y	Y	Y
4 ***Campbell***	N	N	?	N	Y	Y	N	Y
5 Spratt	Y	Y	Y	Y	Y	Y	Y	Y
6 Tallon	Y	Y	?	Y	Y	Y	Y	Y
SOUTH DAKOTA								
AL Daschle	Y	Y	Y	Y	Y	Y	Y	Y

	9	10	11	12	13	14	15	16
TENNESSEE								
1 ***Quillen***	N	N	?	N	Y	Y	N	Y
2 ***Duncan***	?	N	Y	N	Y	Y	N	Y
3 Lloyd	Y	Y	?	Y	Y	Y	?	?
4 Cooper	Y	Y	Y	Y	Y	Y	Y	Y
5 Boner	?	?	Y	Y	Y	Y	Y	Y
6 Gordon	Y	Y	Y	Y	Y	Y	Y	Y
7 ***Sundquist***	?	?	?	N	Y	Y	N	Y
8 Jones	Y	Y	Y	Y	Y	Y	Y	Y
9 Ford	Y	Y	?	Y	Y	Y	Y	Y
TEXAS								
1 Hall, S.	Y	Y	Y	Y	Y	Y	Y	Y
2 Wilson	Y	Y	?	Y	Y	Y	?	Y
3 ***Bartlett***	N	N	N	N	Y	Y	N	N
4 Hall, R.	?	?	?	Y	N	Y	Y	Y
5 Bryant	?	?	Y	Y	Y	Y	Y	Y
6 ***Barton***	N	N	?	N	N	Y	N	N
7 ***Archer***	N	N	?	?	N	Y	N	N
8 ***Fields***	?	?	?	N	N	Y	N	N
9 Brooks	?	?	Y	Y	?	Y	Y	Y
10 Pickle	Y	Y	Y	Y	Y	Y	Y	Y
11 Leath	Y	Y	N	Y	Y	Y	Y	Y
12 Wright	Y	Y	?	Y	Y	Y	Y	Y
13 ***Boulter***	N	N	?	?	?	?	?	Y
14 ***Sweeney***	?	?	N	N	N	Y	N	Y
15 de la Garza	?	?	?	Y	Y	Y	Y	Y
16 Coleman	Y	Y	Y	Y	Y	Y	Y	Y
17 Stenholm	Y	Y	Y	Y	Y	Y	Y	Y
18 Leland	Y	Y	?	Y	Y	?	Y	Y
19 ***Combest***	N	N	N	N	N	Y	N	Y
20 Gonzalez	Y	Y	Y	Y	Y	Y	Y	Y
21 ***Loeffler***	N	N	?	N	Y	Y	N	N
22 ***DeLay***	N	N	N	N	N	Y	N	N
23 Bustamante	Y	Y	Y	Y	Y	Y	Y	Y
24 Frost	Y	Y	?	Y	Y	Y	Y	Y
25 Andrews	Y	Y	Y	Y	Y	Y	Y	Y
26 ***Armey***	N	N	?	N	N	N	?	N
27 Ortiz	?	Y	?	Y	Y	Y	Y	Y
UTAH								
1 ***Hansen***	Y	Y	N	N	N	Y	N	N
2 ***Monson***	N	N	N	?	N	Y	N	N
3 ***Nielson***	N	N	N	N	N	Y	N	N
VERMONT								
AL ***Jeffords***	N	N	?	N	Y	Y	N	Y
VIRGINIA								
1 ***Bateman***	N	N	N	N	Y	Y	N	Y
2 ***Whitehurst***	N	N	N	N	Y	Y	?	Y
3 ***Bliley***	N	N	N	N	Y	Y	N	N
4 Sisisky	Y	Y	Y	Y	Y	Y	Y	Y
5 Daniel	Y	Y	?	Y	Y	Y	Y	Y
6 Olin	Y	Y	?	Y	Y	Y	Y	Y
7 ***Slaughter***	N	N	N	N	Y	Y	N	N
8 ***Parris***	N	N	?	Y	Y	Y	Y	Y
9 Boucher	Y	Y	?	Y	Y	Y	Y	Y
10 ***Wolf***	N	N	N	N	Y	Y	N	Y
WASHINGTON								
1 ***Miller***	N	N	N	N	Y	Y	N	N
2 Swift	Y	Y	Y	Y	Y	Y	Y	Y
3 Bonker	Y	Y	Y	Y	Y	Y	Y	Y
4 ***Morrison***	N	N	N	N	Y	Y	N	N
5 Foley	Y	Y	Y	Y	Y	Y	?	Y
6 Dicks	?	?	?	Y	Y	Y	Y	Y
7 Lowry	Y	Y	Y	?	Y	Y	Y	Y
8 ***Chandler***	N	N	?	N	Y	Y	N	Y
WEST VIRGINIA								
1 Mollohan	Y	Y	?	Y	Y	Y	Y	Y
2 Staggers	N	Y	?	Y	Y	Y	Y	Y
3 Wise	+	+	+	Y	Y	Y	Y	Y
4 Rahall	Y	Y	Y	Y	Y	Y	Y	Y
WISCONSIN								
1 Aspin	Y	?	?	Y	Y	Y	Y	Y
2 Kastenmeier	Y	Y	Y	Y	Y	Y	Y	Y
3 ***Gunderson***	N	N	N	N	Y	Y	N	Y
4 Kleczka	Y	Y	?	Y	Y	Y	Y	Y
5 Moody	?	?	?	Y	Y	Y	Y	Y
6 ***Petri***	?	?	N	N	Y	Y	?	Y
7 Obey	Y	Y	Y	Y	Y	Y	Y	Y
8 ***Roth***	N	?	?	?	Y	Y	N	Y
9 ***Sensenbrenner***	N	N	?	N	Y	Y	N	Y
WYOMING								
AL ***Cheney***	N	N	N	N	N	Y	N	N

Southern states - Ala., Ark., Fla., Ga., Ky., La., Miss., N.C., Okla., S.C., Tenn., Texas, Va.

* The *Congressional Record* vote number is different from the CQ vote number because the *Record* includes quorum calls in its tally. CQ does not publish quorum call votes.

17. HR 1035. Emergency Farm Credit. Passage of the bill to authorize advance Commodity Credit Corporation crop loans to farmers, to authorize $3 billion in Farmers Home Administration (FmHA) loan guarantees for restructured private loans to farmers, to revise rules for the FmHA loan guarantees and to authorize low-interest federal disaster loans to farmers in certain circumstances. Passed 318-103: R 84-93; D 234-10 (ND 158-6, SD 76-4), Feb. 27, 1985. A "nay" was a vote supporting the president's position.

18. Procedural Motion. Weber, R-Minn., motion to approve the House *Journal* of Wednesday, Feb. 27. Motion agreed to 227-178: R 8-168; D 219-10 (ND 147-6, SD 72-4), Feb. 28, 1985.

19. HR 1189. Emergency Farm Credit Appropriations. Adoption of the rule (H Res 85) providing for House floor consideration of the bill to appropriate $1 billion for Farmers Home Administration (FmHA) guarantees of restructured farm loans by private lenders, restricted to farmers with debt-to-asset ratios of at least 75 percent, to increase by $17 million appropriations for FmHA salaries and expenses, and to provide $500,000 for a study of the impact of agricultural trade embargos. Adopted 260-149: R 34-137; D 226-12 (ND 158-4, SD 68-8), Feb. 28, 1985.

20. HR 1189. Emergency Farm Credit Appropriations. Passage of the bill to appropriate $1 billion for Farmers Home Administration (FmHA) guarantees of restructured farm loans by private lenders, restricted to farmers with debt-to-asset ratios of at least 75 percent, to increase by $17 million appropriations for FmHA salaries and expenses, and to provide $500,000 for a study of the impact of agricultural trade embargos. Passed 294-115: R 77-95; D 217-20 (ND 152-11, SD 65-9), Feb. 28, 1985.

21. HR 1251. Interstate Highway Funds. Passage of the bill to release to the states more than $7 billion in Interstate highway construction funds for the second half of fiscal 1984 and all of fiscal 1985. Passed 392-4: R 162-4; D 230-0 (ND 160-0, SD 70-0), Feb. 28, 1985. A "yea" was a vote supporting the president's position.

KEY

Y Voted for (yea).
Paired for.
+ Announced for.
N Voted against (nay).
X Paired against.
- Announced against.
P Voted "present".
C Voted "present" to avoid possible conflict of interest.
? Did not vote or otherwise make a position known.

Democrats *Republicans*

	17	18	19	20	21
ALABAMA					
1 ***Callahan***	N	N	Y	N	Y
2 ***Dickinson***	Y	N	N	Y	Y
3 Nichols	Y	Y	N	?	?
4 Bevill	Y	Y	Y	Y	Y
5 Flippo	Y	Y	Y	Y	?
6 Erdreich	Y	Y	N	Y	Y
7 Shelby	Y	Y	Y	Y	Y
ALASKA					
AL ***Young***	N	N	N	N	Y
ARIZONA					
1 ***McCain***	Y	N	Y	N	Y
2 Udall	Y	Y	Y	Y	Y
3 ***Stump***	N	N	N	N	Y
4 ***Rudd***	N	Y	N	N	Y
5 ***Kolbe***	N	N	N	Y	Y
ARKANSAS					
1 Alexander	Y	Y	Y	Y	Y
2 Robinson	Y	Y	Y	Y	Y
3 ***Hammerschmidt***	Y	N	N	N	Y
4 Anthony	Y	Y	Y	Y	Y
CALIFORNIA					
1 Bosco	N	Y	Y	N	Y
2 ***Chappie***	Y	N	N	N	Y
3 Matsui	Y	Y	Y	Y	Y
4 Fazio	Y	Y	Y	Y	Y
5 Burton	Y	Y	Y	Y	Y
6 Boxer	Y	Y	Y	Y	Y
7 Miller	Y	Y	Y	Y	Y
8 Dellums	Y	Y	Y	Y	Y
9 Stark	Y	Y	Y	Y	?
10 Edwards	Y	Y	Y	Y	Y
11 Lantos	Y	Y	Y	Y	Y
12 ***Zschau***	N	N	N	N	Y
13 Mineta	Y	Y	Y	Y	Y
14 ***Shumway***	N	N	N	N	Y
15 Coelho	Y	Y	Y	Y	Y
16 Panetta	Y	Y	Y	Y	Y
17 ***Pashayan***	Y	N	N	Y	Y
18 Lehman	Y	Y	Y	Y	Y
19 ***Lagomarsino***	N	N	N	N	Y
20 ***Thomas***	Y	N	Y	?	?
21 ***Fiedler***	N	N	N	N	Y
22 ***Moorhead***	N	N	N	N	Y
23 Beilenson	Y	Y	Y	Y	Y
24 Waxman	Y	?	Y	Y	Y
25 Roybal	Y	Y	Y	Y	Y
26 Berman	Y	Y	Y	Y	Y
27 Levine	Y	Y	Y	Y	Y
28 Dixon	Y	Y	Y	Y	Y
29 Hawkins	Y	?	Y	Y	Y
30 Martinez	Y	?	Y	Y	Y
31 Dymally	Y	P	Y	Y	Y
32 Anderson	Y	Y	Y	Y	Y
33 ***Dreier***	N	N	N	N	Y
34 Torres	Y	Y	Y	Y	Y
35 ***Lewis***	N	N	?	N	Y
36 Brown	Y	Y	Y	Y	Y
37 ***McCandless***	N	N	N	N	Y
38 ***Dornan***	N	N	N	N	Y
39 ***Dannemeyer***	N	N	N	N	Y
40 ***Badham***	?	?	?	?	?
41 ***Lowery***	N	N	N	N	Y
42 ***Lungren***	N	N	N	N	Y
43 ***Packard***	Y	N	N	N	Y
44 Bates	N	Y	Y	N	Y
45 ***Hunter***	?	N	?	Y	Y
COLORADO					
1 Schroeder	N	N	N	N	Y
2 Wirth	Y	Y	Y	Y	Y
3 ***Strang***	N	N	N	Y	Y
4 ***Brown***	N	N	N	Y	Y
5 ***Kramer***	N	N	N	Y	Y
6 ***Schaefer***	N	N	N	N	Y
CONNECTICUT					
1 Kennelly	Y	Y	Y	Y	Y
2 Gejdenson	Y	Y	Y	Y	Y
3 Morrison	Y	Y	Y	Y	Y
4 ***McKinney***	Y	N	N	N	Y
5 ***Rowland***	N	N	N	N	Y
6 ***Johnson***	N	Y	N	Y	Y
DELAWARE					
AL Carper	N	Y	Y	N	Y
FLORIDA					
1 Hutto	Y	Y	Y	Y	Y
2 Fuqua	Y	Y	Y	Y	Y
3 Bennett	Y	Y	Y	Y	Y
4 Chappell	Y	Y	Y	Y	Y
5 ***McCollum***	N	N	N	N	Y
6 MacKay	Y	Y	Y	Y	Y
7 Gibbons	N	Y	Y	N	Y
8 ***Young***	N	N	N	N	Y
9 ***Bilirakis***	N	N	N	N	Y
10 ***Ireland***	N	N	N	Y	Y
11 Nelson	N	Y	Y	N	Y
12 ***Lewis***	Y	N	N	N	Y
13 ***Mack***	N	N	N	N	Y
14 Mica	Y	Y	Y	Y	Y
15 ***Shaw***	Y	N	N	N	Y
16 Smith	Y	Y	Y	Y	Y
17 Lehman	Y	Y	Y	Y	Y
18 Pepper	Y	Y	Y	Y	Y
19 Fascell	Y	?	?	?	?
GEORGIA					
1 Thomas	Y	Y	Y	Y	Y
2 Hatcher	Y	Y	Y	Y	?
3 Ray	Y	Y	Y	Y	Y
4 ***Swindall***	N	N	N	N	Y
5 Fowler	Y	Y	Y	Y	Y
6 ***Gingrich***	Y	?	?	X	?
7 Darden	Y	Y	Y	Y	Y
8 Rowland	Y	Y	Y	Y	Y
9 Jenkins	Y	Y	N	Y	Y
10 Barnard	Y	Y	N	Y	Y
HAWAII					
1 Heftel	Y	Y	Y	Y	Y
2 Akaka	Y	Y	Y	Y	Y
IDAHO					
1 ***Craig***	N	N	N	N	Y
2 Stallings	Y	Y	Y	N	Y
ILLINOIS					
1 Hayes	Y	Y	Y	Y	Y
2 Savage	Y	Y	Y	Y	Y
3 Russo	Y	Y	Y	N	Y
4 ***O'Brien***	Y	N	N	Y	?
5 Lipinski	Y	Y	Y	Y	Y
6 ***Hyde***	N	N	N	X	?
7 Collins	Y	Y	Y	Y	Y
8 Rostenkowski	Y	Y	Y	Y	Y
9 Yates	Y	Y	Y	Y	Y
10 ***Porter***	N	N	N	N	Y
11 Annunzio	Y	Y	Y	Y	Y
12 ***Crane, P.***	N	N	N	N	Y
13 ***Fawell***	N	N	Y	N	Y
14 ***Grotberg***	Y	N	N	Y	Y
15 ***Madigan***	?	?	?	?	?
16 ***Martin***	?	N	N	Y	Y
17 Evans	Y	Y	Y	Y	Y
18 ***Michel***	N	N	N	Y	?
19 Bruce	Y	Y	Y	Y	Y
20 Durbin	Y	Y	Y	Y	Y
21 Price	Y	Y	Y	Y	Y
22 Gray	Y	Y	Y	Y	Y
INDIANA					
1 Visclosky	Y	Y	Y	Y	Y
2 Sharp	Y	Y	Y	Y	Y
3 ***Hiler***	N	N	N	N	Y
4 ***Coats***	Y	N	N	N	Y
5 ***Hillis***	N	N	Y	Y	Y

ND - Northern Democrats SD - Southern Democrats

* Corresponding to Congressional Record Votes 18, 19, 20, 21, 22

	17	18	19	20	21
6 ***Burton***	N	N	N	N	Y
7 ***Myers***	Y	N	Y	Y	Y
8 Vacancy					
9 Hamilton	Y	Y	Y	Y	Y
10 Jacobs	Y	N	N	Y	Y
IOWA					
1 ***Leach***	Y	N	Y	Y	Y
2 ***Tauke***	Y	N	Y	Y	Y
3 ***Evans***	Y	N	N	Y	Y
4 Smith	Y	Y	Y	Y	Y
5 ***Lightfoot***	Y	N	Y	Y	Y
6 Bedell	Y	Y	Y	Y	Y
KANSAS					
1 ***Roberts***	Y	N	N	N	Y
2 Slattery	Y	Y	Y	Y	Y
3 ***Meyers***	Y	N	Y	N	Y
4 Glickman	Y	Y	Y	Y	Y
5 ***Whittaker***	Y	N	N	N	Y
KENTUCKY					
1 Hubbard	Y	Y	Y	Y	Y
2 Natcher	Y	Y	Y	Y	Y
3 Mazzoli	N	Y	Y	N	Y
4 ***Snyder***	Y	Y	N	Y	Y
5 ***Rogers***	Y	N	Y	Y	Y
6 ***Hopkins***	Y	N	Y	Y	Y
7 Perkins	Y	Y	Y	Y	Y
LOUISIANA					
1 ***Livingston***	N	N	N	N	Y
2 Boggs	Y	Y	Y	Y	Y
3 Tauzin	Y	Y	Y	N	Y
4 Roemer	N	N	N	N	Y
5 Huckaby	Y	N	Y	Y	Y
6 ***Moore***	Y	Y	N	Y	Y
7 Breaux	Y	?	?	#	?
8 Vacancy					
MAINE					
1 ***McKernan***	Y	N	Y	Y	Y
2 ***Snowe***	Y	N	Y	Y	Y
MARYLAND					
1 Dyson	Y	Y	Y	Y	Y
2 ***Bentley***	Y	N	N	Y	Y
3 Mikulski	Y	Y	Y	Y	Y
4 ***Holt***	N	N	N	N	Y
5 Hoyer	Y	Y	Y	Y	Y
6 Byron	Y	Y	Y	Y	Y
7 Mitchell	Y	N	Y	Y	Y
8 Barnes	Y	Y	Y	Y	Y
MASSACHUSETTS					
1 ***Conte***	N	N	N	N	Y
2 Boland	Y	Y	Y	Y	Y
3 Early	Y	?	Y	Y	Y
4 Frank	Y	Y	Y	Y	Y
5 Atkins	Y	Y	Y	Y	Y
6 Mavroules	Y	Y	Y	Y	Y
7 Markey	Y	Y	Y	Y	Y
8 O'Neill					
9 Moakley	Y	Y	Y	Y	Y
10 Studds	Y	Y	Y	Y	Y
11 Donnelly	Y	Y	Y	Y	Y
MICHIGAN					
1 Conyers	Y	Y	Y	Y	Y
2 ***Pursell***	Y	N	Y	N	Y
3 Wolpe	Y	?	Y	Y	Y
4 ***Siljander***	Y	N	Y	Y	?
5 ***Henry***	Y	N	N	Y	Y
6 Carr	Y	?	Y	Y	Y
7 Kildee	Y	Y	Y	Y	Y
8 Traxler	Y	Y	Y	Y	Y
9 ***Vander Jagt***	N	N	N	Y	?
10 ***Schuette***	Y	N	Y	Y	Y
11 ***Davis***	Y	N	N	Y	Y
12 Bonior	Y	Y	Y	Y	Y
13 Crockett	Y	Y	Y	Y	Y
14 Hertel	Y	Y	Y	Y	Y
15 Ford	Y	?	Y	Y	Y
16 Dingell	Y	Y	?	Y	Y
17 Levin	Y	Y	Y	Y	Y
18 ***Broomfield***	N	N	N	N	N
MINNESOTA					
1 Penny	Y	N	Y	Y	Y
2 ***Weber***	Y	N	Y	Y	Y
3 ***Frenzel***	Y	N	Y	Y	Y
4 Vento	Y	Y	Y	Y	Y
5 Sabo	Y	Y	Y	Y	Y
6 Sikorski	Y	N	Y	Y	Y

	17	18	19	20	21
7 ***Stangeland***	Y	N	?	Y	Y
8 Oberstar	Y	Y	Y	Y	Y
MISSISSIPPI					
1 Whitten	Y	Y	Y	Y	Y
2 ***Franklin***	Y	N	N	N	Y
3 Montgomery	Y	Y	Y	N	Y
4 Dowdy	Y	Y	Y	Y	Y
5 ***Lott***	N	N	?	N	Y
MISSOURI					
1 Clay	Y	N	Y	Y	Y
2 Young	Y	Y	Y	Y	Y
3 Gephardt	Y	?	Y	Y	Y
4 Skelton	Y	Y	Y	Y	Y
5 Wheat	Y	Y	Y	Y	Y
6 ***Coleman***	Y	N	Y	?	?
7 ***Taylor***	Y	N	N	Y	Y
8 ***Emerson***	Y	N	N	Y	Y
9 Volkmer	Y	Y	Y	Y	Y
MONTANA					
1 Williams	Y	?	?	Y	Y
2 ***Marlenee***	Y	N	Y	Y	Y
NEBRASKA					
1 ***Bereuter***	Y	N	Y	Y	Y
2 ***Daub***	Y	N	N	Y	Y
3 ***Smith***	Y	N	Y	Y	Y
NEVADA					
1 Reid	Y	Y	Y	N	Y
2 ***Vucanovich***	N	N	N	N	Y
NEW HAMPSHIRE					
1 ***Smith***	N	N	N	N	Y
2 ***Gregg***	N	N	N	N	Y
NEW JERSEY					
1 Florio	Y	?	Y	Y	Y
2 Hughes	Y	Y	Y	Y	Y
3 Howard	Y	Y	Y	Y	Y
4 ***Smith***	Y	N	Y	Y	Y
5 ***Roukema***	N	N	N	N	Y
6 Dwyer	Y	Y	Y	Y	Y
7 ***Rinaldo***	N	N	Y	N	Y
8 Roe	Y	Y	Y	Y	Y
9 Torricelli	?	Y	Y	Y	Y
10 Rodino	Y	Y	Y	Y	Y
11 ***Gallo***	N	N	N	N	Y
12 ***Courter***	N	N	N	?	?
13 ***Saxton***	N	N	N	N	Y
14 Guarini	Y	Y	Y	Y	Y
NEW MEXICO					
1 ***Lujan***	N	N	N	N	Y
2 ***Skeen***	Y	N	Y	N	Y
3 Richardson	Y	Y	Y	Y	Y
NEW YORK					
1 ***Carney***	N	N	N	N	Y
2 Downey	Y	Y	Y	Y	Y
3 Mrazek	N	Y	Y	?	?
4 ***Lent***	N	N	N	N	Y
5 ***McGrath***	?	N	N	N	Y
6 Addabbo	?	Y	Y	#	?
7 Ackerman	?	?	?	?	?
8 Scheuer	Y	Y	Y	Y	Y
9 Manton	?	Y	Y	Y	Y
10 Schumer	Y	Y	Y	N	Y
11 Towns	Y	Y	Y	?	?
12 Owens	Y	Y	Y	Y	Y
13 Solarz	Y	Y	Y	Y	Y
14 ***Molinari***	N	N	N	N	Y
15 ***Green***	N	N	N	N	Y
16 Rangel	Y	Y	Y	Y	?
17 Weiss	Y	Y	Y	Y	Y
18 Garcia	Y	Y	Y	Y	Y
19 Biaggi	Y	?	?	?	?
20 ***DioGuardi***	N	?	?	?	?
21 ***Fish***	Y	N	N	Y	Y
22 ***Gilman***	Y	N	Y	Y	Y
23 Stratton	Y	Y	Y	Y	Y
24 ***Solomon***	N	N	N	N	N
25 ***Boehlert***	Y	Y	N	Y	Y
26 ***Martin***	Y	N	N	Y	Y
27 ***Wortley***	Y	N	?	Y	Y
28 McHugh	Y	Y	Y	Y	Y
29 ***Horton***	Y	Y	Y	Y	Y
30 ***Eckert***	N	N	N	N	Y
31 ***Kemp***	N	N	N	Y	?
32 LaFalce	Y	Y	N	Y	Y
33 Nowak	Y	Y	Y	Y	Y
34 Lundine	Y	Y	Y	Y	Y

	17	18	19	20	21
NORTH CAROLINA					
1 Jones	Y	?	Y	Y	?
2 Valentine	Y	Y	Y	Y	Y
3 Whitley	Y	Y	Y	Y	?
4 ***Cobey***	N	N	N	N	Y
5 Neal	Y	Y	Y	Y	Y
6 ***Coble***	N	N	N	?	Y
7 Rose	Y	Y	Y	Y	Y
8 Hefner	Y	Y	Y	Y	Y
9 ***McMillan***	N	N	N	N	Y
10 ***Broyhill***	N	?	N	N	Y
11 ***Hendon***	Y	N	Y	Y	Y
NORTH DAKOTA					
AL Dorgan	Y	Y	Y	Y	Y
OHIO					
1 Luken	N	Y	Y	N	Y
2 ***Gradison***	N	Y	N	N	Y
3 Hall	Y	Y	Y	Y	Y
4 ***Oxley***	Y	N	N	Y	Y
5 ***Latta***	Y	N	N	N	Y
6 ***McEwen***	Y	N	Y	?	?
7 ***DeWine***	Y	N	N	N	Y
8 ***Kindness***	Y	N	N	Y	N
9 Kaptur	Y	Y	Y	Y	Y
10 ***Miller***	Y	N	N	Y	Y
11 Eckart	Y	Y	Y	Y	Y
12 ***Kasich***	Y	N	N	Y	Y
13 Pease	Y	Y	Y	Y	Y
14 Seiberling	?	Y	Y	Y	Y
15 ***Wylie***	N	N	N	Y	Y
16 ***Regula***	Y	N	N	N	Y
17 Traficant	Y	Y	Y	Y	Y
18 Applegate	Y	?	Y	Y	Y
19 Feighan	Y	Y	Y	Y	Y
20 Oakar	Y	Y	Y	Y	Y
21 Stokes	Y	Y	Y	Y	Y
OKLAHOMA					
1 Jones	Y	N	Y	Y	Y
2 Synar	Y	?	Y	Y	Y
3 Watkins	Y	Y	Y	Y	Y
4 McCurdy	Y	Y	?	Y	Y
5 ***Edwards***	Y	N	?	Y	Y
6 English	Y	Y	Y	Y	Y
OREGON					
1 AuCoin	Y	Y	N	N	Y
2 ***Smith, R.***	N	N	N	Y	Y
3 Wyden	Y	Y	Y	N	Y
4 Weaver	Y	Y	Y	Y	Y
5 ***Smith, D.***	N	N	N	N	Y
PENNSYLVANIA					
1 Foglietta	Y	?	?	?	?
2 Gray	Y	Y	?	Y	Y
3 Borski	Y	Y	Y	Y	Y
4 Kolter	Y	Y	Y	Y	Y
5 ***Schulze***	N	N	N	N	Y
6 Yatron	Y	Y	Y	Y	Y
7 Edgar	Y	Y	Y	Y	Y
8 Kostmayer	Y	Y	Y	Y	Y
9 ***Shuster***	Y	N	N	N	Y
10 ***McDade***	N	N	N	Y	?
11 Kanjorski	Y	Y	Y	Y	Y
12 Murtha	Y	Y	Y	Y	Y
13 ***Coughlin***	N	N	N	N	Y
14 Coyne	Y	Y	Y	Y	Y
15 ***Ritter***	N	N	N	N	Y
16 ***Walker***	N	N	N	N	N
17 ***Gekas***	N	N	N	N	Y
18 Walgren	Y	Y	Y	Y	Y
19 ***Goodling***	N	N	N	N	Y
20 Gaydos	Y	Y	Y	Y	Y
21 ***Ridge***	Y	N	N	Y	Y
22 Murphy	Y	Y	Y	Y	Y
23 ***Clinger***	Y	N	N	Y	Y
RHODE ISLAND					
1 St Germain	Y	Y	Y	Y	?
2 ***Schneider***	N	N	N	N	Y
SOUTH CAROLINA					
1 ***Hartnett***	N	N	N	Y	Y
2 ***Spence***	Y	N	N	Y	Y
3 Derrick	Y	N	Y	Y	Y
4 ***Campbell***	Y	N	N	Y	Y
5 Spratt	Y	Y	Y	Y	Y
6 Tallon	Y	?	Y	Y	Y
SOUTH DAKOTA					
AL Daschle	Y	Y	Y	Y	Y

	17	18	19	20	21
TENNESSEE					
1 ***Quillen***	N	N	N	N	?
2 ***Duncan***	N	N	Y	Y	Y
3 Lloyd	+	Y	Y	Y	Y
4 Cooper	Y	Y	Y	Y	Y
5 Boner	Y	Y	Y	Y	Y
6 Gordon	Y	Y	Y	Y	Y
7 ***Sundquist***	Y	N	N	Y	Y
8 Jones	Y	Y	Y	Y	Y
9 Ford	Y	Y	Y	Y	Y
TEXAS					
1 Hall, S.	Y	Y	Y	Y	Y
2 Wilson	Y	Y	Y	Y	Y
3 ***Bartlett***	N	N	N	N	Y
4 Hall, R.	Y	Y	Y	Y	Y
5 Bryant	Y	Y	Y	Y	Y
6 ***Barton***	N	N	N	N	Y
7 ***Archer***	N	N	N	N	Y
8 ***Fields***	N	N	N	N	Y
9 Brooks	Y	Y	Y	Y	Y
10 Pickle	Y	Y	Y	Y	Y
11 Leath	Y	Y	N	N	Y
12 Wright	Y	Y	Y	Y	Y
13 ***Boulter***	Y	N	N	N	Y
14 ***Sweeney***	Y	N	Y	Y	Y
15 de la Garza	Y	Y	?	?	?
16 Coleman	Y	Y	Y	Y	Y
17 Stenholm	Y	Y	N	N	Y
18 Leland	Y	Y	Y	Y	Y
19 ***Combest***	Y	N	Y	Y	Y
20 Gonzalez	Y	Y	Y	Y	Y
21 ***Loeffler***	N	N	N	N	Y
22 ***DeLay***	N	N	N	N	Y
23 Bustamante	Y	Y	?	?	?
24 Frost	Y	Y	Y	Y	Y
25 Andrews	Y	Y	Y	?	?
26 ***Armey***	N	N	N	N	Y
27 Ortiz	Y	Y	Y	?	?
UTAH					
1 ***Hansen***	N	N	N	N	Y
2 ***Monson***	Y	N	N	N	Y
3 ***Nielson***	N	N	N	N	Y
VERMONT					
AL ***Jeffords***	Y	?	Y	Y	
VIRGINIA					
1 ***Bateman***	N	N	N	Y	Y
2 ***Whitehurst***	Y	N	N	Y	Y
3 ***Bliley***	Y	N	N	Y	Y
4 Sisisky	Y	Y	Y	Y	Y
5 Daniel	Y	Y	N	N	Y
6 Olin	Y	Y	Y	Y	Y
7 ***Slaughter***	Y	N	N	Y	Y
8 ***Parris***	Y	Y	N	Y	Y
9 Boucher	Y	Y	Y	Y	Y
10 ***Wolf***	Y	N	N	Y	Y
WASHINGTON					
1 ***Miller***	N	N	N	N	Y
2 Swift	Y	Y	Y	Y	Y
3 Bonker	Y	Y	Y	Y	Y
4 ***Morrison***	Y	N	N	N	Y
5 Foley	Y	Y	Y	Y	Y
6 Dicks	Y	Y	Y	Y	Y
7 Lowry	Y	Y	Y	Y	Y
8 ***Chandler***	N	N	N	N	Y
WEST VIRGINIA					
1 Mollohan	Y	Y	Y	Y	Y
2 Staggers	Y	Y	Y	Y	Y
3 Wise	Y	Y	Y	Y	Y
4 Rahall	Y	Y	Y	Y	Y
WISCONSIN					
1 Aspin	Y	Y	Y	Y	Y
2 Kastenmeier	Y	Y	Y	Y	Y
3 ***Gunderson***	Y	N	N	Y	Y
4 Kleczka	Y	?	?	Y	Y
5 Moody	Y	Y	Y	Y	Y
6 ***Petri***	Y	N	N	Y	Y
7 Obey	Y	Y	Y	Y	Y
8 ***Roth***	Y	N	?	Y	Y
9 ***Sensenbrenner***	Y	N	N	Y	Y
WYOMING					
AL ***Cheney***	N	N	N	N	Y

Southern states - Ala., Ark., Fla., Ga., Ky., La., Miss., N.C., Okla., S.C., Tenn., Texas, Va.

* The *Congressional Record* vote number is different from the CQ vote number because the *Record* includes quorum calls in its tally. CQ does not publish quorum call votes.

22. Procedural Motion. Walker, R-Pa., motion to approve the House *Journal* of Thursday, Feb. 28. Motion agreed to 202-87: R 67-83; D 135-4 (ND 80-3, SD 55-1), March 4, 1985.

23. H Res 97. Indiana 8th District Seat. Alexander, D-Ark., motion to refer to the Committee on House Administration the resolution to seat Republican Richard D. McIntyre as a member of the 99th Congress, pending an investigation of the contested race by the Committee on House Administration. Motion agreed to 168-167: R 0-163; D 168-4 (ND 110-0, SD 58-4), March 4, 1985.

24. HR 1096. African Famine Relief. Frost, D-Texas, motion to order the previous question (thus ending debate and the possibility of amendment) on the rule (H Res 92) providing for House floor consideration and passage of the bill, together with a Senate amendment, to authorize $175 million in non-food aid for emergency relief to Africa, to authorize $100 million to offset interest on restructured private farm loans guaranteed by the Farmers Home Administration (FmHA), to increase the FmHA loan guarantee program by $1.85 billion and revise certain eligibility rules, and to authorize advances to eligible farmers of Commodity Credit Corporation commodity price-support loans. (The rule provided that a vote for the rule also constituted a vote on agreeing to the Senate amendment and on passage of the bill.) Motion agreed to 239-185: R 3-177; D 236-8 (ND 160-5, SD 76-3), March 5, 1985.

25. HR 1096. African Famine Relief. Adoption of the rule (H Res 92) providing for floor consideration of the bill, together with a Senate amendment, to authorize $175 million in non-food aid for emergency relief to Africa, to authorize $100 million to offset interest on restructured private farm loans guaranteed by the Farmers Home Administration (FmHA), to increase the FmHA loan guarantee program by $1.85 billion and revise certain eligibility rules, and to authorize advances to eligible farmers of Commodity Credit Corporation commodity price-support loans. The rule provided that a vote for the rule also constituted a vote on agreeing to the Senate amendment and on passage of the bill. Adopted (thus clearing the bill for the president) 255-168: R 30-150; D 225-18 (ND 151-12, SD 74-6), March 5, 1985. A "nay" was a vote supporting the president's position.

26. Procedural Motion. Gray, D-Ill., motion to approve the House *Journal* of Tuesday, March 5. Motion agreed to 232-144: R 24-138; D 208-6 (ND 138-4, SD 70-2), March 6, 1985.

27. Procedural Motion. Strang, R-Colo., motion to approve the House *Journal* of Wednesday, March 6. Motion agreed to 244-162: R 20-153; D 224-9 (ND 148-7, SD 76-2), March 7, 1985.

28. H Res 20. Select Committee on Hunger. Adoption of the resolution re-establishing the Select Committee on Hunger in the 99th Congress. Adopted 286-124: R 78-95; D 208-29 (ND 146-12, SD 62-17), March 7, 1985.

29. H Res 22. Select Committee on Narcotics Abuse and Control. Adoption of the resolution re-establishing the Select Committee on Narcotics Abuse and Control in the 99th Congress. Adopted 310-94: R 107-64; D 203-30 (ND 139-18, SD 64-12), March 7, 1985.

KEY

Y Voted for (yea).
\# Paired for.
\+ Announced for.
N Voted against (nay).
X Paired against.
\- Announced against.
P Voted "present".
C Voted "present" to avoid possible conflict of interest.
? Did not vote or otherwise make a position known.

Democrats *Republicans*

	22	23	24	25	26	27	28	29
ALABAMA								
1 *Callahan*	Y	N	N	N	N	N	Y	Y
2 *Dickinson*	N	N	N	N	N	N	N	Y
3 Nichols	Y	Y	Y	Y	?	Y	Y	Y
4 Bevill	?	Y	Y	Y	Y	Y	Y	Y
5 Flippo	Y	Y	Y	Y	Y	Y	N	Y
6 Erdreich	?	?	N	N	Y	Y	Y	Y
7 Shelby	?	?	Y	Y	Y	Y	Y	Y
ALASKA								
AL *Young*	?	?	N	N	N	N	Y	Y
ARIZONA								
1 *McCain*	N	N	N	N	N	N	N	N
2 Udall	Y	Y	Y	Y	Y	Y	Y	P
3 *Stump*	N	N	N	N	N	N	N	N
4 *Rudd*	Y	N	N	N	Y	Y	N	Y
5 *Kolbe*	N	N	N	N	N	N	Y	Y
ARKANSAS								
1 Alexander	Y	Y	Y	Y	Y	Y	Y	Y
2 Robinson	?	?	Y	Y	Y	Y	N	Y
3 *Hammerschmidt*	Y	N	N	N	N	N	N	Y
4 Anthony	Y	Y	Y	Y	Y	Y	N	Y
CALIFORNIA								
1 Bosco	Y	Y	Y	N	Y	Y	N	N
2 *Chappie*	?	N	N	N	?	N	N	Y
3 Matsui	?	Y	Y	Y	Y	Y	Y	Y
4 Fazio	Y	Y	Y	Y	Y	Y	Y	Y
5 Burton	Y	Y	Y	Y	Y	Y	Y	Y
6 Boxer	Y	Y	Y	Y	Y	Y	Y	Y
7 Miller	?	?	Y	Y	Y	Y	Y	Y
8 Dellums	?	Y	Y	Y	Y	Y	Y	Y
9 Stark	?	?	Y	Y	Y	Y	Y	Y
10 Edwards	?	?	Y	Y	Y	Y	Y	Y
11 Lantos	Y	Y	Y	Y	Y	Y	Y	Y
12 *Zschau*	N	N	N	N	N	N	N	N
13 Mineta	Y	Y	Y	Y	Y	Y	Y	Y
14 *Shumway*	N	N	N	N	N	N	N	N
15 Coelho	?	Y	Y	Y	?	Y	Y	Y
16 Panetta	?	?	Y	Y	Y	Y	Y	N
17 *Pashayan*	N	N	N	N	N	?	N	Y
18 Lehman	?	+	?	+	?	Y	Y	Y
19 *Lagomarsino*	N	N	N	N	N	N	Y	Y
20 *Thomas*	N	N	N	Y	N	N	N	N
21 *Fiedler*	Y	N	N	N	N	N	Y	Y
22 *Moorhead*	N	N	N	N	N	N	Y	Y
23 Beilenson	?	Y	Y	N	Y	?	Y	N
24 Waxman	?	?	Y	Y	Y	Y	Y	Y
25 Roybal	?	Y	Y	Y	Y	Y	Y	Y
26 Berman	Y	Y	Y	Y	Y	Y	Y	?
27 Levine	Y	Y	Y	Y	Y	Y	Y	Y
28 Dixon	Y	Y	Y	Y	Y	Y	Y	Y
29 Hawkins	?	?	Y	Y	Y	Y	Y	Y
30 Martinez	?	?	Y	Y	Y	Y	Y	Y
31 Dymally	P	Y	Y	Y	?	P	Y	Y
32 Anderson	?	?	Y	Y	Y	Y	Y	Y
33 *Dreier*	Y	N	N	N	N	N	N	N
34 Torres	+	+	Y	Y	Y	+	+	+
35 *Lewis*	N	N	N	N	N	N	Y	Y
36 Brown	?	Y	Y	Y	Y	Y	Y	Y
37 *McCandless*	Y	N	N	N	N	N	N	N
38 *Dornan*	Y	N	N	N	?	Y	N	Y
39 *Dannemeyer*	N	N	N	N	N	N	N	N
40 *Badham*	Y	N	N	N	N	N	N	N
41 *Lowery*	N	N	N	N	N	N	Y	N
42 *Lungren*	Y	N	N	N	N	N	N	N
43 *Packard*	N	N	N	N	N	?	?	?
44 Bates	?	?	N	N	Y	Y	Y	Y
45 *Hunter*	?	N	N	N	N	?	Y	Y
COLORADO								
1 Schroeder	N	Y	N	Y	N	N	Y	Y
2 Wirth	Y	Y	Y	Y	Y	Y	Y	N
3 *Strang*	N	N	N	N	N	N	N	Y
4 *Brown*	N	N	N	N	N	N	N	N
5 *Kramer*	N	N	N	N	N	N	N	Y
6 *Schaefer*	Y	N	N	N	N	N	Y	N
CONNECTICUT								
1 Kennelly	Y	Y	Y	Y	Y	Y	Y	Y
2 Gejdenson	?	?	Y	Y	?	Y	Y	Y
3 Morrison	Y	Y	Y	N	?	Y	Y	Y
4 *McKinney*	N	N	N	N	N	N	Y	Y
5 *Rowland*	?	N	N	N	N	N	Y	Y
6 *Johnson*	Y	N	N	N	Y	Y	N	N
DELAWARE								
AL Carper	?	?	N	N	Y	Y	Y	Y
FLORIDA								
1 Hutto	?	?	Y	Y	Y	Y	Y	N
2 Fuqua	Y	Y	Y	Y	Y	Y	Y	Y
3 Bennett	Y	Y	Y	Y	Y	Y	Y	Y
4 Chappell	Y	Y	Y	Y	Y	Y	Y	Y
5 *McCollum*	N	N	N	N	N	N	N	N
6 MacKay	Y	Y	Y	Y	Y	Y	N	?
7 Gibbons	Y	Y	Y	Y	Y	Y	N	N
8 *Young*	Y	N	N	N	Y	N	N	Y
9 *Bilirakis*	Y	N	N	N	N	N	N	Y
10 *Ireland*	N	N	N	N	N	Y	Y	Y
11 Nelson	Y	Y	Y	N	Y	Y	Y	Y
12 *Lewis*	N	N	N	N	N	Y	N	Y
13 *Mack*	N	N	N	N	N	N	N	N
14 Mica	Y	Y	Y	Y	Y	Y	Y	Y
15 *Shaw*	Y	N	N	N	N	N	N	Y
16 Smith	?	Y	Y	Y	Y	Y	Y	Y
17 Lehman	Y	Y	Y	Y	Y	Y	Y	Y
18 Pepper	Y	Y	+	+	Y	Y	Y	Y
19 Fascell	Y	Y	Y	Y	?	Y	Y	Y
GEORGIA								
1 Thomas	Y	Y	Y	Y	Y	Y	Y	Y
2 Hatcher	?	?	Y	Y	Y	?	Y	Y
3 Ray	Y	Y	Y	Y	Y	Y	N	N
4 *Swindall*	N	N	N	N	N	N	N	N
5 Fowler	?	?	Y	Y	Y	Y	Y	Y
6 *Gingrich*	N	N	N	N	N	N	Y	Y
7 Darden	Y	Y	Y	Y	Y	Y	Y	Y
8 Rowland	Y	Y	Y	Y	Y	Y	Y	Y
9 Jenkins	?	?	Y	Y	Y	Y	Y	N
10 Barnard	?	?	Y	Y	Y	Y	N	N
HAWAII								
1 Heftel	?	Y	Y	Y	?	?	N	Y
2 Akaka	Y	Y	Y	Y	Y	Y	Y	Y
IDAHO								
1 *Craig*	N	N	N	N	N	N	N	Y
2 Stallings	Y	Y	Y	Y	Y	Y	Y	Y
ILLINOIS								
1 Hayes	?	?	Y	Y	Y	Y	Y	Y
2 Savage	?	?	Y	Y	?	Y	Y	Y
3 Russo	?	?	Y	Y	Y	Y	Y	Y
4 *O'Brien*	N	N	N	N	Y	Y	?	Y
5 Lipinski	?	?	Y	N	Y	Y	Y	Y
6 *Hyde*	?	N	N	N	?	N	N	Y
7 Collins	?	?	Y	Y	Y	?	?	?
8 Rostenkowski	?	?	Y	Y	Y	Y	Y	Y
9 Yates	Y	Y	Y	Y	Y	Y	Y	Y
10 *Porter*	N	N	N	N	?	N	Y	Y
11 Annunzio	?	?	Y	Y	Y	Y	Y	Y
12 *Crane, P.*	N	N	N	N	N	Y	N	N
13 *Fawell*	Y	N	N	N	N	N	Y	Y
14 *Grotberg*	N	N	N	N	-	N	N	N
15 *Madigan*	N	N	N	N	?	N	Y	Y
16 *Martin*	N	N	N	N	N	N	N	N
17 Evans	Y	Y	Y	Y	Y	Y	Y	Y
18 *Michel*	Y	N	N	N	?	N	N	N
19 Bruce	Y	Y	Y	Y	Y	Y	Y	Y
20 Durbin	Y	Y	Y	Y	Y	Y	Y	Y
21 Price	Y	Y	Y	Y	Y	Y	Y	Y
22 Gray	Y	Y	Y	Y	Y	Y	Y	Y
INDIANA								
1 Visclosky	Y	Y	Y	Y	Y	Y	N	N
2 Sharp	Y	Y	Y	Y	Y	Y	Y	Y
3 *Hiler*	N	N	N	N	N	N	N	N
4 *Coats*	N	N	N	N	N	N	Y	Y
5 *Hillis*	?	?	?	?	?	?	?	?

ND - Northern Democrats SD - Southern Democrats

* Corresponding to Congressional Record Votes 23, 24, 26, 27, 28, 29, 30, 31

	22	23	24	25	26	27	28	29
6 ***Burton***	?	N	N	N	N	N	N	Y
7 ***Myers***	Y	N	N	N	Y	Y	Y	Y
8 Vacancy								
9 Hamilton	Y	Y	Y	Y	Y	Y	Y	Y
10 Jacobs	?	?	Y	Y	N	N	Y	N
IOWA								
1 ***Leach***	N	N	Y	Y	N	N	Y	Y
2 ***Tauke***	Y	N	N	Y	N	N	N	N
3 ***Evans***	?	N	N	Y	?	N	Y	Y
4 Smith	Y	Y	Y	Y	Y	Y	Y	Y
5 ***Lightfoot***	Y	N	N	Y	N	N	N	Y
6 Bedell	?	Y	Y	Y	Y	Y	Y	Y
KANSAS								
1 ***Roberts***	?	?	N	Y	N	N	N	N
2 Slattery	Y	Y	Y	Y	Y	Y	N	N
3 ***Meyers***	N	N	N	N	N	N	N	N
4 Glickman	?	Y	Y	Y	Y	Y	N	N
5 ***Whittaker***	N	N	N	N	N	N	N	N
KENTUCKY								
1 Hubbard	?	?	Y	Y	?	Y	N	N
2 Natcher	Y	Y	Y	Y	Y	Y	Y	Y
3 Mazzoli	Y	N	N	N	Y	Y	Y	Y
4 ***Snyder***	Y	N	N	N	Y	Y	Y	Y
5 ***Rogers***	N	N	N	N	N	N	Y	Y
6 ***Hopkins***	?	?	N	N	N	N	N	N
7 Perkins	Y	Y	Y	Y	Y	Y	Y	Y
LOUISIANA								
1 ***Livingston***	N	N	N	N	N	N	N	N
2 Boggs	?	Y	Y	Y	Y	Y	Y	Y
3 Tauzin	Y	Y	Y	Y	Y	?	?	?
4 Roemer	N	Y	N	N	N	N	N	N
5 Huckaby	?	?	Y	Y	Y	N	Y	Y
6 ***Moore***	?	?	N	Y	Y	Y	Y	N
7 Breaux	Y	Y	Y	Y	Y	?	?	?
8 Vacancy								
MAINE								
1 ***McKernan***	N	N	N	N	N	N	Y	Y
2 ***Snowe***	Y	N	N	N	Y	N	Y	Y
MARYLAND								
1 Dyson	Y	Y	Y	Y	Y	Y	N	N
2 ***Bentley***	Y	N	N	Y	N	N	N	Y
3 Mikulski	?	?	Y	Y	Y	Y	Y	Y
4 ***Holt***	Y	N	N	N	N	N	N	N
5 Hoyer	?	Y	Y	Y	Y	Y	Y	Y
6 Byron	Y	Y	Y	Y	Y	Y	N	Y
7 Mitchell	?	Y	Y	Y	?	N	Y	Y
8 Barnes	Y	Y	Y	Y	?	Y	Y	Y
MASSACHUSETTS								
1 ***Conte***	N	N	N	N	?	N	Y	Y
2 Boland	?	?	Y	Y	Y	Y	Y	Y
3 Early	?	Y	Y	Y	Y	Y	N	Y
4 Frank	?	Y	Y	Y	Y	?	?	?
5 Atkins	Y	Y	Y	Y	Y	Y	?	Y
6 Mavroules	?	?	Y	Y	?	Y	Y	Y
7 Markey	?	?	Y	?	?	N	Y	Y
8 O'Neill								
9 Moakley	?	?	?	?	?	?	?	?
10 Studds	?	?	Y	Y	Y	Y	Y	Y
11 Donnelly	?	?	Y	Y	Y	Y	Y	Y
MICHIGAN								
1 Conyers	?	?	Y	Y	Y	Y	Y	Y
2 ***Pursell***	?	?	N	N	N	N	N	Y
3 Wolpe	?	?	Y	Y	Y	Y	Y	Y
4 ***Siljander***	Y	N	N	Y	N	N	Y	Y
5 ***Henry***	Y	N	N	N	N	N	Y	Y
6 Carr	Y	Y	Y	Y	Y	Y	Y	Y
7 Kildee	Y	Y	Y	Y	Y	Y	Y	Y
8 Traxler	?	?	Y	Y	Y	Y	Y	Y
9 ***Vander Jagt***	N	N	?	?	N	N	Y	Y
10 ***Schuette***	N	N	N	Y	N	N	Y	Y
11 ***Davis***	Y	N	N	Y	N	N	Y	Y
12 Bonior	Y	Y	Y	Y	?	Y	Y	Y
13 Crockett	?	?	Y	Y	?	Y	Y	Y
14 Hertel	Y	Y	Y	Y	Y	Y	Y	Y
15 Ford	?	Y	Y	Y	?	?	#	#
16 Dingell	Y	Y	Y	Y	Y	Y	Y	Y
17 Levin	Y	Y	Y	Y	Y	Y	Y	Y
18 ***Broomfield***	Y	N	N	N	?	Y	Y	Y
MINNESOTA								
1 Penny	N	Y	Y	Y	N	N	Y	Y
2 ***Weber***	?	?	Y	Y	N	N	N	N
3 ***Frenzel***	Y	N	N	N	Y	P	N	N
4 Vento	Y	Y	Y	Y	Y	Y	Y	Y
5 Sabo	Y	Y	Y	Y	Y	Y	Y	Y
6 Sikorski	N	Y	Y	Y	N	N	Y	Y

	22	23	24	25	26	27	28	29
7 ***Stangeland***	N	N	Y	Y	N	N	Y	Y
8 Oberstar	P	Y	Y	Y	P	P	Y	N
MISSISSIPPI								
1 Whitten	Y	Y	Y	Y	Y	Y	Y	Y
2 ***Franklin***	?	?	N	N	?	N	N	N
3 Montgomery	Y	Y	Y	Y	Y	Y	N	Y
4 Dowdy	?	?	Y	Y	Y	Y	Y	Y
5 ***Lott***	Y	N	N	N	?	N	N	Y
MISSOURI								
1 Clay	?	Y	Y	Y	P	N	Y	Y
2 Young	Y	?	Y	Y	Y	Y	Y	Y
3 Gephardt	?	Y	Y	Y	?	Y	Y	Y
4 Skelton	Y	Y	Y	Y	Y	Y	Y	Y
5 Wheat	Y	Y	Y	Y	Y	Y	Y	Y
6 ***Coleman***	?	N	N	Y	?	N	Y	Y
7 ***Taylor***	N	N	N	N	N	N	N	Y
8 ***Emerson***	N	N	N	Y	N	N	Y	Y
9 Volkmer	Y	Y	Y	Y	Y	Y	Y	Y
MONTANA								
1 Williams	Y	Y	Y	Y	Y	Y	Y	Y
2 ***Marlenee***	N	N	N	Y	N	N	N	Y
NEBRASKA								
1 ***Bereuter***	?	-	N	Y	N	N	Y	Y
2 ***Daub***	Y	N	N	Y	N	N	N	N
3 ***Smith***	Y	N	N	Y	N	N	Y	Y
NEVADA								
1 Reid	Y	Y	Y	Y	Y	Y	Y	Y
2 ***Vucanovich***	N	N	N	N	N	N	N	Y
NEW HAMPSHIRE								
1 ***Smith***	Y	N	N	N	N	N	N	N
2 ***Gregg***	N	N	N	N	N	N	N	N
NEW JERSEY								
1 Florio	?	?	Y	Y	Y	Y	Y	Y
2 Hughes	Y	Y	N	N	Y	Y	N	Y
3 Howard	?	?	Y	Y	Y	Y	Y	Y
4 ***Smith***	Y	N	N	N	Y	Y	Y	Y
5 ***Roukema***	Y	N	N	N	N	N	Y	Y
6 Dwyer	Y	Y	Y	Y	Y	Y	Y	Y
7 ***Rinaldo***	Y	N	N	N	Y	?	?	?
8 Roe	?	?	Y	Y	Y	Y	Y	Y
9 Torricelli	?	?	Y	Y	Y	Y	Y	Y
10 Rodino	?	?	?	?	?	?	#	#
11 ***Gallo***	N	N	N	N	N	N	Y	Y
12 ***Courter***	Y	N	N	N	N	N	Y	Y
13 ***Saxton***	Y	N	N	N	N	N	Y	N
14 Guarini	Y	Y	Y	Y	Y	Y	Y	Y
NEW MEXICO								
1 ***Lujan***	Y	N	N	N	N	N	Y	N
2 ***Skeen***	Y	N	N	N	N	N	N	Y
3 Richardson	Y	Y	Y	Y	Y	Y	Y	Y
NEW YORK								
1 ***Carney***	N	N	N	N	N	N	N	Y
2 Downey	Y	Y	Y	Y	Y	Y	Y	Y
3 Mrazek	?	?	N	N	Y	Y	Y	Y
4 ***Lent***	N	N	N	N	N	N	Y	Y
5 ***McGrath***	Y	N	N	N	N	N	Y	Y
6 Addabbo	Y	Y	Y	Y	Y	Y	Y	Y
7 Ackerman	?	?	Y	Y	Y	Y	Y	Y
8 Scheuer	Y	Y	Y	Y	Y	Y	Y	Y
9 Manton	?	Y	Y	Y	Y	Y	Y	Y
10 Schumer	?	?	Y	Y	Y	Y	Y	Y
11 Towns	?	?	Y	Y	Y	Y	Y	Y
12 Owens	?	?	Y	Y	Y	Y	Y	Y
13 Solarz	?	Y	Y	Y	Y	Y	?	Y
14 ***Molinari***	N	N	N	N	N	N	Y	Y
15 ***Green***	N	N	N	N	N	N	N	N
16 Rangel	?	Y	Y	Y	Y	Y	Y	Y
17 Weiss	Y	Y	Y	Y	?	Y	Y	Y
18 Garcia	?	?	Y	Y	Y	Y	Y	Y
19 Biaggi	?	?	Y	Y	Y	Y	Y	?
20 ***DioGuardi***	Y	N	N	N	Y	N	N	Y
21 ***Fish***	N	N	N	N	N	N	Y	Y
22 ***Gilman***	N	N	N	Y	N	N	Y	Y
23 Stratton	Y	Y	Y	Y	Y	Y	Y	Y
24 ***Solomon***	N	N	N	N	N	N	N	N
25 ***Boehlert***	Y	N	N	Y	N	Y	Y	Y
26 ***Martin***	Y	N	N	N	Y	Y	Y	Y
27 ***Wortley***	N	N	N	N	N	?	Y	Y
28 McHugh	?	Y	Y	Y	Y	Y	Y	Y
29 ***Horton***	Y	N	N	Y	Y	Y	Y	Y
30 ***Eckert***	?	?	N	N	N	N	N	Y
31 ***Kemp***	?	?	N	N	?	N	Y	Y
32 LaFalce	?	?	Y	Y	P	Y	Y	N
33 Nowak	?	?	Y	Y	P	Y	Y	Y
34 Lundine	Y	Y	Y	Y	Y	Y	Y	Y

	22	23	24	25	26	27	28	29
NORTH CAROLINA								
1 Jones	Y	Y	Y	Y	Y	Y	Y	Y
2 Valentine	?	Y	Y	Y	Y	Y	Y	Y
3 Whitley	?	?	Y	Y	Y	Y	Y	Y
4 ***Cobey***	Y	N	N	N	N	N	Y	Y
5 Neal	?	Y	Y	Y	Y	Y	Y	Y
6 ***Coble***	Y	N	N	N	N	N	N	?
7 Rose	Y	Y	Y	Y	Y	Y	Y	Y
8 Hefner	Y	Y	Y	Y	Y	Y	Y	Y
9 ***McMillan***	Y	N	N	N	N	N	Y	Y
10 ***Broyhill***	Y	N	N	N	Y	Y	N	N
11 ***Hendon***	N	N	N	Y	N	N	Y	?
NORTH DAKOTA								
AL Dorgan	?	?	Y	Y	Y	Y	Y	Y
OHIO								
1 Luken	?	?	Y	N	Y	Y	Y	N
2 ***Gradison***	N	N	N	N	Y	N	N	N
3 Hall	Y	Y	Y	N	Y	Y	Y	N
4 ***Oxley***	N	N	N	N	?	N	N	Y
5 ***Latta***	N	N	N	N	N	N	N	Y
6 ***McEwen***	Y	N	N	N	N	N	Y	Y
7 ***DeWine***	N	N	N	N	N	N	Y	Y
8 ***Kindness***	?	?	N	N	?	N	N	N
9 Kaptur	?	Y	Y	Y	Y	Y	Y	Y
10 ***Miller***	N	N	N	N	N	N	N	N
11 Eckart	?	Y	Y	Y	Y	Y	Y	Y
12 ***Kasich***	N	N	N	N	N	N	Y	Y
13 Pease	Y	Y	Y	N	Y	Y	Y	Y
14 Seiberling	Y	Y	Y	Y	Y	Y	Y	Y
15 ***Wylie***	Y	N	N	N	Y	Y	Y	Y
16 ***Regula***	Y	N	N	N	Y	Y	Y	Y
17 Traficant	Y	Y	Y	Y	Y	Y	Y	Y
18 Applegate	?	Y	Y	Y	?	?	Y	Y
19 Feighan	Y	Y	Y	Y	Y	Y	Y	Y
20 Oakar	Y	Y	Y	Y	Y	Y	Y	Y
21 Stokes	Y	Y	Y	Y	Y	Y	Y	Y
OKLAHOMA								
1 Jones	Y	?	Y	Y	N	Y	N	N
2 Synar	Y	Y	Y	Y	P	Y	N	+
3 Watkins	Y	Y	Y	Y	Y	Y	Y	Y
4 McCurdy	Y	Y	Y	Y	Y	Y	N	Y
5 ***Edwards***	Y	N	N	Y	N	N	Y	Y
6 English	Y	Y	Y	Y	Y	Y	Y	Y
OREGON								
1 AuCoin	Y	Y	Y	N	Y	Y	N	N
2 ***Smith, R.***	N	N	N	N	N	N	Y	N
3 Wyden	Y	Y	Y	Y	Y	Y	Y	Y
4 Weaver	Y	Y	Y	Y	Y	?	Y	N
5 ***Smith, D.***	?	?	N	N	N	N	N	N
PENNSYLVANIA								
1 Foglietta	?	?	Y	Y	Y	Y	Y	Y
2 Gray	?	?	Y	Y	Y	?	Y	Y
3 Borski	Y	Y	Y	Y	Y	Y	Y	Y
4 Kolter	?	?	Y	Y	Y	Y	Y	?
5 ***Schulze***	?	N	N	N	N	N	X	X
6 Yatron	?	?	Y	Y	Y	Y	Y	Y
7 Edgar	?	?	Y	Y	Y	Y	Y	Y
8 Kostmayer	Y	Y	Y	Y	Y	Y	Y	Y
9 ***Shuster***	?	?	N	N	N	N	N	N
10 ***McDade***	N	N	N	Y	N	?	?	?
11 Kanjorski	Y	Y	Y	Y	Y	Y	Y	Y
12 Murtha	?	?	Y	Y	Y	Y	Y	Y
13 ***Coughlin***	?	N	N	N	N	N	Y	Y
14 Coyne	Y	Y	Y	Y	Y	Y	Y	Y
15 ***Ritter***	?	N	N	N	N	N	?	Y
16 ***Walker***	Y	N	N	N	N	N	N	N
17 ***Gekas***	Y	N	N	N	N	N	N	N
18 Walgren	?	Y	Y	Y	Y	Y	Y	Y
19 ***Goodling***	N	N	N	N	N	N	N	N
20 Gaydos	?	?	Y	Y	Y	Y	Y	Y
21 ***Ridge***	Y	N	N	N	N	N	Y	Y
22 Murphy	Y	Y	Y	Y	Y	Y	N	N
23 ***Clinger***	N	N	N	N	N	N	Y	N
RHODE ISLAND								
1 St Germain	?	?	Y	Y	Y	Y	Y	?
2 ***Schneider***	Y	N	N	N	Y	Y	Y	Y
SOUTH CAROLINA								
1 ***Hartnett***	?	?	N	N	Y	N	N	?
2 ***Spence***	N	N	N	N	N	N	N	Y
3 Derrick	?	?	?	Y	Y	Y	Y	Y
4 ***Campbell***	?	N	N	N	N	N	N	Y
5 Spratt	Y	Y	Y	Y	Y	Y	Y	Y
6 Tallon	?	?	Y	Y	Y	Y	Y	Y
SOUTH DAKOTA								
AL Daschle	Y	?	Y	Y	Y	Y	Y	Y

	22	23	24	25	26	27	28	29
TENNESSEE								
1 ***Quillen***	?	?	N	N	N	?	?	?
2 ***Duncan***	?	?	N	N	Y	N	Y	Y
3 Lloyd	Y	Y	Y	Y	Y	Y	Y	Y
4 Cooper	Y	Y	Y	Y	Y	Y	Y	Y
5 Boner	Y	Y	Y	Y	Y	Y	Y	Y
6 Gordon	Y	Y	Y	Y	Y	Y	Y	Y
7 ***Sundquist***	N	N	N	N	N	N	N	N
8 Jones	Y	Y	Y	Y	Y	Y	Y	Y
9 Ford	Y	Y	Y	Y	Y	Y	Y	Y
TEXAS								
1 Hall, S.	?	N	Y	Y	Y	Y	Y	Y
2 Wilson	Y	Y	Y	Y	?	Y	Y	Y
3 ***Bartlett***	?	N	N	N	?	N	N	N
4 Hall, R.	Y	N	Y	Y	Y	Y	Y	Y
5 Bryant	Y	Y	Y	Y	Y	Y	Y	Y
6 ***Barton***	N	N	N	N	N	N	N	Y
7 ***Archer***	N	N	N	N	N	N	N	N
8 ***Fields***	N	N	N	N	N	N	N	N
9 Brooks	Y	Y	Y	Y	Y	Y	Y	Y
10 Pickle	Y	Y	Y	Y	Y	Y	N	N
11 Leath	Y	Y	Y	Y	Y	Y	Y	Y
12 Wright	Y	Y	Y	Y	?	Y	Y	?
13 ***Boulter***	Y	N	N	N	Y	N	N	N
14 ***Sweeney***	?	N	N	Y	N	N	N	Y
15 de la Garza	?	?	Y	Y	?	Y	Y	Y
16 Coleman	Y	Y	Y	Y	Y	Y	Y	Y
17 Stenholm	Y	N	Y	Y	Y	Y	N	N
18 Leland	?	Y	Y	Y	?	Y	Y	Y
19 ***Combest***	Y	N	N	N	N	N	N	N
20 Gonzalez	Y	Y	Y	Y	Y	Y	Y	Y
21 ***Loeffler***	Y	N	N	N	N	N	N	N
22 ***DeLay***	N	N	N	N	N	N	N	N
23 Bustamante	Y	Y	Y	Y	Y	Y	Y	Y
24 Frost	?	?	Y	Y	Y	Y	Y	Y
25 Andrews	Y	Y	Y	Y	Y	Y	Y	Y
26 ***Armey***	Y	N	N	N	N	N	N	N
27 Ortiz	?	?	Y	Y	Y	Y	Y	Y
UTAH								
1 ***Hansen***	N	N	N	N	N	N	N	N
2 ***Monson***	Y	N	N	N	N	N	N	N
3 ***Nielson***	N	N	N	N	Y	N	N	N
VERMONT								
AL ***Jeffords***	?	?	N	Y	N	N	Y	?
VIRGINIA								
1 ***Bateman***	N	N	N	N	N	N	N	Y
2 ***Whitehurst***	Y	N	N	N	N	N	Y	Y
3 ***Bliley***	N	N	N	N	N	N	N	Y
4 Sisisky	Y	Y	Y	Y	Y	Y	Y	Y
5 Daniel	Y	Y	Y	N	Y	Y	N	N
6 Olin	?	?	Y	N	Y	Y	N	N
7 ***Slaughter***	Y	N	N	N	N	N	Y	Y
8 ***Parris***	Y	N	N	Y	?	N	N	Y
9 Boucher	Y	Y	Y	Y	?	Y	Y	Y
10 ***Wolf***	N	N	N	N	N	N	Y	Y
WASHINGTON								
1 ***Miller***	Y	N	N	N	N	N	Y	Y
2 Swift	?	Y	Y	?	Y	Y	N	N
3 Bonker	Y	Y	?	?	?	Y	Y	N
4 ***Morrison***	N	N	N	N	N	N	Y	Y
5 Foley	Y	Y	Y	Y	?	Y	?	Y
6 Dicks	Y	Y	Y	Y	Y	Y	Y	Y
7 Lowry	Y	Y	Y	Y	Y	Y	Y	Y
8 ***Chandler***	?	?	N	N	N	N	Y	Y
WEST VIRGINIA								
1 Mollohan	Y	Y	Y	Y	Y	Y	?	Y
2 Staggers	Y	Y	Y	Y	Y	Y	Y	Y
3 Wise	Y	Y	Y	Y	Y	Y	?	Y
4 Rahall	Y	Y	Y	Y	Y	Y	Y	Y
WISCONSIN								
1 Aspin	?	Y	Y	Y	?	Y	?	?
2 Kastenmeier	?	Y	Y	Y	Y	Y	Y	Y
3 ***Gunderson***	N	N	N	N	N	N	Y	Y
4 Kleczka	?	?	Y	Y	Y	Y	Y	Y
5 Moody	Y	Y	Y	Y	?	Y	Y	Y
6 ***Petri***	Y	N	N	Y	Y	Y	N	Y
7 Obey	Y	Y	Y	Y	Y	Y	Y	Y
8 ***Roth***	N	N	N	Y	?	N	N	Y
9 ***Sensenbrenner***	N	N	N	N	N	N	N	N
WYOMING								
AL ***Cheney***	Y	N	N	N	N	N	X	X

Southern states - Ala., Ark., Fla., Ga., Ky., La., Miss., N.C., Okla., S.C., Tenn., Texas, Va.

* The *Congressional Record* vote number is different from the CQ vote number because the *Record* includes quorum calls in its tally. CQ does not publish quorum call votes.

30. Procedural Motion. Mack, R-Fla., motion to approve the House *Journal* of Thursday, March 7. Motion agreed to 228-154: R 14-146; D 214-8 (ND 141-7, SD 73-1), March 19, 1985.

31. HR 1025. Anadromous Fish Conservation. Jones, D-N.C., motion to suspend the rules and pass the bill to reauthorize at $7.5 million annually for fiscal 1986-88 section 4 of the Anadromous Fish Conservation Act, which established a federal-state cost-sharing program for research, development and management to support anadromous fish. Motion agreed to 268-133: R 62-107; D 206-26 (ND 144-13, SD 62-13), March 19, 1985. A two-thirds majority of those present and voting (268 in this case) is required for passage under suspension of the rules. A "nay" was a vote supporting the president's position.

32. HR 1028. Interjurisdictional Fisheries Research. Jones, D-N.C., motion to suspend the rules and pass the bill to replace the Commercial Fisheries Research and Development Act (PL 88-309) with the Interjurisdictional Fisheries Research Act, a federal-state program of fishery research, and authorize $7.85 million annually for fiscal 1986-88. Motion rejected 252-149: R 52-118; D 200-31 (ND 141-16, SD 59-15), March 19, 1985. A two-thirds majority of those present and voting (268 in this case) is required for passage under suspension of the rules. A "nay" was a vote supporting the president's position.

KEY

Y Voted for (yea).
\# Paired for.
\+ Announced for.
N Voted against (nay).
X Paired against.
\- Announced against.
P Voted "present".
C Voted "present" to avoid possible conflict of interest.
? Did not vote or otherwise make a position known.

Democrats ***Republicans***

	30	31	32
ALABAMA			
1 ***Callahan***	N	N	N
2 ***Dickinson***	N	N	N
3 Nichols	Y	Y	Y
4 Bevill	Y	Y	Y
5 Flippo	Y	Y	Y
6 Erdreich	Y	Y	Y
7 Shelby	Y	Y	Y
ALASKA			
AL ***Young***	N	Y	Y
ARIZONA			
1 ***McCain***	?	?	?
2 Udall	Y	Y	Y
3 ***Stump***	N	N	N
4 ***Rudd***	N	N	N
5 ***Kolbe***	N	N	N
ARKANSAS			
1 Alexander	Y	Y	Y
2 Robinson	?	?	?
3 ***Hammerschmidt***	N	?	?
4 Anthony	Y	Y	Y
CALIFORNIA			
1 Bosco	?	?	?
2 ***Chappie***	N	Y	Y
3 Matsui	Y	Y	Y
4 Fazio	Y	Y	Y
5 Burton	Y	Y	Y
6 Boxer	Y	Y	Y
7 Miller	P	Y	Y
8 Dellums	Y	Y	Y
9 Stark	Y	Y	Y
10 Edwards	Y	Y	Y
11 Lantos	?	?	?
12 ***Zschau***	N	N	N
13 Mineta	Y	Y	Y
14 ***Shumway***	?	?	?
15 Coelho	Y	Y	Y
16 Panetta	Y	Y	Y
17 ***Pashayan***	?	?	?
18 Lehman	Y	Y	Y
19 ***Lagomarsino***	N	Y	N
20 ***Thomas***	N	N	N
21 ***Fiedler***	N	Y	N
22 ***Moorhead***	N	N	N
23 Beilenson	Y	Y	Y
24 Waxman	Y	Y	Y
25 Roybal	Y	Y	Y
26 Berman	Y	Y	Y
27 Levine	Y	Y	Y
28 Dixon	Y	Y	Y
29 Hawkins	Y	Y	Y
30 Martinez	Y	Y	Y
31 Dymally	P	Y	Y
32 Anderson	Y	Y	Y
33 ***Dreier***	N	N	N
34 Torres	Y	Y	Y
35 ***Lewis***	N	N	N
36 Brown	Y	Y	Y
37 ***McCandless***	N	N	N
38 ***Dornan***	?	N	N
39 ***Dannemeyer***	N	N	N
40 ***Badham***	?	?	?
41 ***Lowery***	N	Y	Y
42 ***Lungren***	N	N	N
43 ***Packard***	N	N	N
44 Bates	Y	Y	Y
45 ***Hunter***	N	Y	N
COLORADO			
1 Schroeder	N	N	N
2 Wirth	Y	Y	Y
3 ***Strang***	N	N	N
4 ***Brown***	N	N	N
5 ***Kramer***	N	N	N
6 ***Schaefer***	N	N	N
CONNECTICUT			
1 Kennelly	Y	Y	Y
2 Gejdenson	Y	Y	Y
3 Morrison	Y	Y	Y
4 ***McKinney***	N	Y	Y
5 ***Rowland***	N	Y	N
6 ***Johnson***	Y	Y	Y
DELAWARE			
AL Carper	Y	Y	Y
FLORIDA			
1 Hutto	Y	Y	Y
2 Fuqua	Y	Y	Y
3 Bennett	Y	Y	Y
4 Chappell	Y	Y	Y
5 ***McCollum***	N	N	N
6 MacKay	Y	N	N
7 Gibbons	Y	N	N
8 ***Young***	N	Y	Y
9 ***Bilirakis***	N	N	N
10 ***Ireland***	N	N	N
11 Nelson	Y	Y	Y
12 ***Lewis***	N	N	N
13 ***Mack***	N	N	N
14 Mica	?	#	#
15 ***Shaw***	N	N	N
16 Smith	Y	Y	Y
17 Lehman	Y	Y	Y
18 Pepper	Y	#	#
19 Fascell	Y	Y	Y
GEORGIA			
1 Thomas	Y	Y	Y
2 Hatcher	Y	Y	Y
3 Ray	Y	Y	Y
4 ***Swindall***	N	N	N
5 Fowler	Y	Y	Y
6 ***Gingrich***	N	N	N
7 Darden	Y	Y	Y
8 Rowland	Y	Y	Y
9 Jenkins	Y	Y	N
10 Barnard	Y	Y	Y
HAWAII			
1 Heftel	?	?	?
2 Akaka	?	Y	Y
IDAHO			
1 ***Craig***	N	N	N
2 Stallings	Y	Y	Y
ILLINOIS			
1 Hayes	Y	Y	Y
2 Savage	Y	Y	Y
3 Russo	Y	Y	Y
4 ***O'Brien***	Y	Y	Y
5 Lipinski	?	?	?
6 ***Hyde***	N	N	N
7 Collins	Y	Y	Y
8 Rostenkowski	?	?	?
9 Yates	Y	Y	Y
10 ***Porter***	N	N	N
11 Annunzio	Y	Y	Y
12 ***Crane, P.***	N	N	N
13 ***Fawell***	P	N	N
14 ***Grotberg***	N	N	N
15 ***Madigan***	N	Y	Y
16 ***Martin***	N	N	N
17 Evans	Y	Y	Y
18 ***Michel***	?	N	N
19 Bruce	Y	N	N
20 Durbin	N	Y	Y
21 Price	Y	Y	Y
22 Gray	Y	Y	Y
INDIANA			
1 Visclosky	Y	Y	N
2 Sharp	Y	N	N
3 ***Hiler***	N	N	N
4 ***Coats***	N	N	N
5 ***Hillis***	Y	N	N

ND - Northern Democrats SD - Southern Democrats

* Corresponding to Congressional Record Votes 32, 33, 34

	30	31	32
6 ***Burton***	N	N	N
7 ***Myers***	Y	N	N
8 Vacancy			
9 Hamilton	Y	Y	N
10 Jacobs	N	N	N
IOWA			
1 ***Leach***	?	N	N
2 ***Tauke***	N	N	N
3 ***Evans***	N	?	N
4 Smith	Y	Y	Y
5 ***Lightfoot***	N	N	N
6 Bedell	Y	Y	Y
KANSAS			
1 ***Roberts***	?	N	N
2 Slattery	?	N	N
3 ***Meyers***	N	N	N
4 Glickman	Y	N	N
5 ***Whittaker***	?	N	N
KENTUCKY			
1 Hubbard	Y	N	N
2 Natcher	Y	Y	Y
3 Mazzoli	Y	Y	Y
4 ***Snyder***	Y	N	N
5 ***Rogers***	N	N	N
6 ***Hopkins***	N	N	N
7 Perkins	Y	Y	Y
LOUISIANA			
1 ***Livingston***	N	Y	Y
2 Boggs	Y	Y	Y
3 Tauzin	?	Y	Y
4 Roemer	N	N	N
5 Huckaby	Y	N	N
6 ***Moore***	Y	Y	Y
7 Breaux	Y	Y	Y
8 Vacancy			
MAINE			
1 ***McKernan***	N	Y	Y
2 ***Snowe***	N	Y	Y
MARYLAND			
1 Dyson	Y	Y	Y
2 ***Bentley***	N	Y	Y
3 Mikulski	Y	Y	Y
4 ***Holt***	N	?	?
5 Hoyer	Y	Y	Y
6 Byron	Y	N	N
7 Mitchell	N	Y	Y
8 Barnes	Y	Y	Y
MASSACHUSETTS			
1 ***Conte***	Y	Y	Y
2 Boland	Y	Y	Y
3 Early	Y	Y	Y
4 Frank	Y	Y	Y
5 Atkins	Y	Y	Y
6 Mavroules	Y	Y	Y
7 Markey	Y	Y	Y
8 O'Neill			
9 Moakley	?	?	?
10 Studds	Y	Y	Y
11 Donnelly	Y	Y	Y
MICHIGAN			
1 Conyers	?	?	?
2 ***Pursell***	?	?	?
3 Wolpe	Y	Y	Y
4 ***Siljander***	N	N	N
5 ***Henry***	N	N	N
6 Carr	Y	Y	Y
7 Kildee	Y	Y	Y
8 Traxler	Y	Y	Y
9 ***Vander Jagt***	N	N	Y
10 ***Schuette***	N	N	N
11 ***Davis***	N	Y	Y
12 Bonior	Y	Y	Y
13 Crockett	Y	Y	Y
14 Hertel	Y	Y	Y
15 Ford	?	Y	Y
16 Dingell	?	Y	Y
17 Levin	Y	Y	Y
18 ***Broomfield***	N	N	N
MINNESOTA			
1 Penny	N	N	N
2 ***Weber***	N	N	N
3 ***Frenzel***	N	N	N
4 Vento	Y	Y	Y
5 Sabo	Y	Y	Y
6 Sikorski	N	Y	Y
7 ***Stangeland***	N	N	N
8 Oberstar	P	Y	Y
MISSISSIPPI			
1 Whitten	Y	Y	Y
2 ***Franklin***	N	Y	Y
3 Montgomery	Y	Y	Y
4 Dowdy	?	Y	Y
5 ***Lott***	N	Y	N
MISSOURI			
1 Clay	N	Y	Y
2 Young	Y	Y	Y
3 Gephardt	Y	Y	Y
4 Skelton	?	?	?
5 Wheat	Y	Y	Y
6 ***Coleman***	?	N	N
7 ***Taylor***	N	N	N
8 ***Emerson***	N	N	N
9 Volkmer	Y	Y	Y
MONTANA			
1 Williams	Y	Y	N
2 ***Marlenee***	?	?	?
NEBRASKA			
1 ***Bereuter***	N	N	N
2 ***Daub***	?	N	N
3 ***Smith***	N	N	N
NEVADA			
1 Reid	Y	Y	Y
2 ***Vucanovich***	N	N	N
NEW HAMPSHIRE			
1 ***Smith***	N	N	N
2 ***Gregg***	?	?	?
NEW JERSEY			
1 Florio	Y	Y	Y
2 Hughes	Y	Y	Y
3 Howard	Y	Y	Y
4 ***Smith***	Y	Y	Y
5 ***Roukema***	N	N	N
6 Dwyer	Y	Y	Y
7 ***Rinaldo***	N	Y	Y
8 Roe	Y	Y	Y
9 Torricelli	Y	Y	Y
10 Rodino	?	?	?
11 ***Gallo***	N	Y	Y
12 ***Courter***	N	N	N
13 ***Saxton***	N	Y	Y
14 Guarini	Y	Y	Y
NEW MEXICO			
1 ***Lujan***	N	N	N
2 ***Skeen***	N	Y	Y
3 Richardson	Y	Y	Y
NEW YORK			
1 ***Carney***	N	Y	Y
2 Downey	Y	Y	Y
3 Mrazek	Y	Y	Y
4 ***Lent***	N	Y	Y
5 ***McGrath***	N	Y	Y
6 Addabbo	Y	Y	Y
7 Ackerman	Y	Y	Y
8 Scheuer	Y	Y	Y
9 Manton	?	Y	Y
10 Schumer	Y	Y	N
11 Towns	Y	Y	Y
12 Owens	Y	Y	Y
13 Solarz	Y	Y	Y
14 ***Molinari***	N	Y	Y
15 ***Green***	N	Y	Y
16 Rangel	Y	Y	Y
17 Weiss	Y	Y	Y
18 Garcia	Y	Y	Y
19 Biaggi	Y	Y	Y
20 ***DioGuardi***	N	N	N
21 ***Fish***	N	Y	Y
22 ***Gilman***	N	Y	Y
23 Stratton	Y	Y	Y
24 ***Solomon***	N	N	N
25 ***Boehlert***	N	Y	Y
26 ***Martin***	N	Y	Y
27 ***Wortley***	N	Y	Y
28 McHugh	Y	Y	Y
29 ***Horton***	Y	Y	Y
30 ***Eckert***	N	N	N
31 ***Kemp***	?	?	N
32 LaFalce	Y	Y	Y
33 Nowak	Y	Y	Y
34 Lundine	Y	Y	Y
NORTH CAROLINA			
1 Jones	Y	Y	Y
2 Valentine	Y	Y	Y
3 Whitley	Y	Y	Y
4 ***Cobey***	N	N	N
5 Neal	Y	Y	Y
6 ***Coble***	N	N	N
7 Rose	Y	Y	Y
8 Hefner	Y	Y	Y
9 ***McMillan***	N	N	N
10 ***Broyhill***	Y	N	N
11 ***Hendon***	N	Y	Y
NORTH DAKOTA			
AL Dorgan	Y	Y	N
OHIO			
1 Luken	Y	N	Y
2 ***Gradison***	Y	N	N
3 Hall	Y	N	N
4 ***Oxley***	N	N	N
5 ***Latta***	N	N	N
6 ***McEwen***	N	N	N
7 ***DeWine***	N	Y	Y
8 ***Kindness***	N	N	N
9 Kaptur	Y	Y	Y
10 ***Miller***	N	N	N
11 Eckart	Y	Y	Y
12 ***Kasich***	N	N	N
13 Pease	Y	Y	Y
14 Seiberling	Y	Y	Y
15 ***Wylie***	Y	N	N
16 ***Regula***	N	Y	N
17 Traficant	Y	Y	Y
18 Applegate	?	Y	Y
19 Feighan	Y	N	N
20 Oakar	Y	Y	Y
21 Stokes	Y	Y	Y
OKLAHOMA			
1 Jones	Y	N	N
2 Synar	Y	Y	Y
3 Watkins	Y	N	N
4 McCurdy	Y	N	N
5 ***Edwards***	N	N	N
6 English	Y	N	N
OREGON			
1 AuCoin	?	?	?
2 ***Smith, R.***	N	Y	Y
3 Wyden	Y	Y	Y
4 Weaver	Y	Y	Y
5 ***Smith, D.***	N	N	N
PENNSYLVANIA			
1 Foglietta	Y	Y	Y
2 Gray	Y	Y	Y
3 Borski	Y	Y	Y
4 Kolter	Y	Y	Y
5 ***Schulze***	N	Y	Y
6 Yatron	Y	Y	Y
7 Edgar	Y	Y	Y
8 Kostmayer	Y	Y	Y
9 ***Shuster***	N	N	N
10 ***McDade***	N	Y	Y
11 Kanjorski	?	?	?
12 Murtha	Y	Y	Y
13 ***Coughlin***	N	Y	N
14 Coyne	Y	Y	Y
15 ***Ritter***	N	Y	Y
16 ***Walker***	N	N	N
17 ***Gekas***	N	N	N
18 Walgren	Y	Y	Y
19 ***Goodling***	N	N	N
20 Gaydos	Y	Y	Y
21 ***Ridge***	?	Y	Y
22 Murphy	Y	N	N
23 ***Clinger***	N	Y	N
RHODE ISLAND			
1 St Germain	Y	Y	Y
2 ***Schneider***	Y	Y	Y
SOUTH CAROLINA			
1 ***Hartnett***	N	Y	Y
2 ***Spence***	N	Y	Y
3 Derrick	?	Y	Y
4 ***Campbell***	N	Y	Y
5 Spratt	Y	Y	Y
6 Tallon	?	Y	Y
SOUTH DAKOTA			
AL Daschle	Y	Y	Y
TENNESSEE			
1 ***Quillen***	N	N	N
2 ***Duncan***	N	Y	N
3 Lloyd	Y	Y	Y
4 Cooper	Y	N	N
5 Boner	Y	Y	Y
6 Gordon	Y	Y	?
7 ***Sundquist***	N	N	N
8 Jones	Y	Y	Y
9 Ford	Y	Y	Y
TEXAS			
1 Hall, S.	Y	N	N
2 Wilson	Y	Y	Y
3 ***Bartlett***	N	N	N
4 Hall, R.	Y	N	N
5 Bryant	Y	Y	N
6 ***Barton***	N	N	N
7 ***Archer***	N	N	N
8 ***Fields***	?	?	?
9 Brooks	Y	Y	Y
10 Pickle	Y	Y	Y
11 Leath	Y	Y	Y
12 Wright	Y	Y	Y
13 ***Boulter***	N	N	?
14 ***Sweeney***	?	N	N
15 de la Garza	Y	?	?
16 Coleman	Y	Y	Y
17 Stenholm	Y	X	X
18 Leland	?	Y	Y
19 ***Combest***	N	N	N
20 Gonzalez	Y	Y	Y
21 ***Loeffler***	N	N	N
22 ***DeLay***	?	?	?
23 Bustamante	Y	Y	Y
24 Frost	Y	Y	Y
25 Andrews	Y	Y	Y
26 ***Armey***	N	N	N
27 Ortiz	Y	Y	Y
UTAH			
1 ***Hansen***	N	N	N
2 ***Monson***	N	N	N
3 ***Nielson***	N	N	N
VERMONT			
AL ***Jeffords***	N	Y	N
VIRGINIA			
1 ***Bateman***	N	Y	Y
2 ***Whitehurst***	N	Y	Y
3 ***Bliley***	N	N	N
4 Sisisky	Y	?	?
5 Daniel	Y	N	N
6 Olin	Y	Y	Y
7 ***Slaughter***	?	N	N
8 ***Parris***	N	N	N
9 Boucher	Y	Y	Y
10 ***Wolf***	?	Y	Y
WASHINGTON			
1 ***Miller***	N	Y	Y
2 Swift	Y	Y	Y
3 Bonker	?	?	?
4 ***Morrison***	N	Y	Y
5 Foley	Y	Y	Y
6 Dicks	Y	Y	Y
7 Lowry	Y	Y	Y
8 ***Chandler***	N	Y	Y
WEST VIRGINIA			
1 Mollohan	Y	Y	Y
2 Staggers	Y	Y	Y
3 Wise	Y	N	Y
4 Rahall	Y	Y	Y
WISCONSIN			
1 Aspin	Y	Y	Y
2 Kastenmeier	Y	Y	Y
3 ***Gunderson***	N	Y	N
4 Kleczka	Y	Y	Y
5 Moody	Y	Y	Y
6 ***Petri***	Y	Y	Y
7 Obey	Y	Y	Y
8 ***Roth***	N	Y	Y
9 ***Sensenbrenner***	N	N	N
WYOMING			
AL ***Cheney***	N	N	N

Southern states - Ala., Ark., Fla., Ga., Ky., La., Miss., N.C., Okla., S.C., Tenn., Texas, Va.

* The *Congressional Record* vote number is different from the CQ vote number because the *Record* includes quorum calls in its tally. CQ does not publish quorum call votes.

33. H Res 100. House Committee Funding. Adoption of the resolution authorizing $48 million in fiscal 1985 for the investigative expenses of House committees. The resolution covers about half of committee costs in 1985. Adopted 254-158: R 43-132; D 211-26 (ND 150-10, SD 61-16), March 26, 1985.

34. S J Res 71. MX Missile Authorization. Passage of the joint resolution to approve authorization of $1.5 billion to procure 21 MX missiles in fiscal 1985. Passed 219-213: R 158-24; D 61-189 (ND 15-154, SD 46-35), March 26, 1985. A "yea" was a vote supporting the president's position.

35. Procedural Motion. Loeffler, R-Texas, motion to approve the House *Journal* of Wednesday, March 27. Motion agreed to 271-138: R 48-130; D 223-8 (ND 149-6, SD 74-2), March 28, 1985.

36. H J Res 181. MX Missile Appropriation. Passage of the joint resolution to approve appropriation of $1.5 billion to procure 21 MX missiles in fiscal 1985. Passed 217-210: R 156-23; D 61-187 (ND 15-152, SD 46-35), March 28, 1985. A "yea" was a vote supporting the president's position.

KEY

Y Voted for (yea).
Paired for.
+ Announced for.
N Voted against (nay).
X Paired against.
- Announced against.
P Voted "present".
C Voted "present" to avoid possible conflict of interest.
? Did not vote or otherwise make a position known.

Democrats ***Republicans***

	33	34	35	36
ALABAMA				
1 ***Callahan***	N	Y	Y	Y
2 ***Dickinson***	Y	Y	N	Y
3 Nichols	N	Y	Y	Y
4 Bevill	Y	Y	Y	Y
5 Flippo	Y	Y	Y	Y
6 Erdreich	N	Y	Y	Y
7 Shelby	Y	Y	Y	Y
ALASKA				
AL ***Young***	Y	Y	N	Y
ARIZONA				
1 ***McCain***	N	Y	N	Y
2 Udall	Y	N	Y	N
3 ***Stump***	N	Y	N	Y
4 ***Rudd***	Y	Y	N	Y
5 ***Kolbe***	N	Y	N	Y
ARKANSAS				
1 Alexander	Y	N	Y	N
2 Robinson	N	Y	Y	Y
3 ***Hammerschmidt***	Y	Y	Y	Y
4 Anthony	Y	N	Y	N
CALIFORNIA				
1 Bosco	Y	N	Y	N
2 ***Chappie***	N	Y	N	Y
3 Matsui	Y	N	Y	N
4 Fazio	Y	Y	Y	Y
5 Burton	Y	N	Y	N
6 Boxer	Y	N	P	N
7 Miller	Y	N	Y	N
8 Dellums	Y	N	Y	N
9 Stark	Y	N	Y	N
10 Edwards	Y	N	Y	N
11 Lantos	Y	N	Y	N
12 ***Zschau***	N	N	N	N
13 Mineta	Y	N	Y	N
14 ***Shumway***	N	Y	N	Y
15 Coelho	Y	N	Y	N
16 Panetta	Y	N	Y	N
17 ***Pashayan***	N	Y	N	Y
18 Lehman	Y	N	Y	N
19 ***Lagomarsino***	N	Y	Y	Y
20 ***Thomas***	Y	Y	N	Y
21 ***Fiedler***	N	Y	N	Y
22 ***Moorhead***	N	Y	N	Y
23 Beilenson	Y	N	Y	N
24 Waxman	Y	N	?	N
25 Roybal	Y	N	Y	N
26 Berman	Y	N	Y	N
27 Levine	Y	N	Y	N
28 Dixon	Y	N	?	N
29 Hawkins	Y	N	Y	N
30 Martinez	?	N	Y	N
31 Dymally	?	N	?	X
32 Anderson	Y	Y	Y	Y
33 ***Dreier***	N	Y	N	Y
34 Torres	Y	N	Y	N
35 ***Lewis***	Y	Y	N	Y
36 Brown	Y	N	Y	N
37 ***McCandless***	?	Y	N	Y
38 ***Dornan***	N	Y	?	Y
39 ***Dannemeyer***	N	Y	N	Y
40 ***Badham***	Y	Y	N	Y
41 ***Lowery***	N	Y	N	Y
42 ***Lungren***	N	Y	Y	Y
43 ***Packard***	N	Y	Y	Y
44 Bates	Y	N	Y	N
45 ***Hunter***	N	Y	N	Y
COLORADO				
1 Schroeder	Y	N	N	N
2 Wirth	Y	N	Y	N
3 ***Strang***	N	Y	N	Y
4 ***Brown***	N	Y	N	Y
5 ***Kramer***	N	Y	N	Y
6 ***Schaefer***	N	Y	Y	Y
CONNECTICUT				
1 Kennelly	Y	N	Y	N
2 Gejdenson	Y	N	Y	N
3 Morrison	Y	N	Y	N
4 ***McKinney***	Y	N	Y	N
5 ***Rowland***	N	Y	N	Y
6 ***Johnson***	N	N	Y	N
DELAWARE				
AL Carper	N	N	Y	N
FLORIDA				
1 Hutto	N	Y	Y	Y
2 Fuqua	Y	Y	Y	Y
3 Bennett	Y	N	Y	N
4 Chappell	Y	Y	Y	Y
5 ***McCollum***	N	Y	N	Y
6 MacKay	Y	N	Y	N
7 Gibbons	Y	N	Y	N
8 ***Young***	N	Y	Y	Y
9 ***Bilirakis***	N	Y	N	Y
10 ***Ireland***	N	Y	Y	Y
11 Nelson	Y	Y	Y	Y
12 ***Lewis***	N	Y	N	Y
13 ***Mack***	N	Y	N	Y
14 Mica	Y	N	P	N
15 ***Shaw***	N	Y	N	Y
16 Smith	Y	N	Y	N
17 Lehman	Y	N	Y	N
18 Pepper	Y	Y	Y	Y
19 Fascell	Y	N	Y	N
GEORGIA				
1 Thomas	Y	Y	Y	Y
2 Hatcher	?	Y	P	Y
3 Ray	N	Y	Y	Y
4 ***Swindall***	N	Y	N	Y
5 Fowler	Y	N	Y	N
6 ***Gingrich***	Y	Y	N	Y
7 Darden	Y	Y	Y	Y
8 Rowland	Y	Y	Y	Y
9 Jenkins	Y	N	Y	N
10 Barnard	Y	Y	Y	Y
HAWAII				
1 Heftel	Y	N	?	N
2 Akaka	Y	N	Y	N
IDAHO				
1 ***Craig***	N	Y	Y	Y
2 Stallings	Y	N	?	N
ILLINOIS				
1 Hayes	Y	N	Y	N
2 Savage	Y	N	?	N
3 Russo	Y	N	Y	N
4 ***O'Brien***	Y	Y	Y	Y
5 Lipinski	Y	Y	Y	Y
6 ***Hyde***	N	Y	N	Y
7 Collins	Y	N	Y	N
8 Rostenkowski	Y	N	Y	N
9 Yates	Y	N	Y	N
10 ***Porter***	N	Y	N	Y
11 Annunzio	Y	N	Y	N
12 ***Crane, P.***	N	Y	N	#
13 ***Fawell***	N	Y	N	Y
14 ***Grotberg***	N	Y	N	Y
15 ***Madigan***	Y	Y	N	Y
16 ***Martin***	N	Y	N	Y
17 Evans	Y	N	Y	N
18 ***Michel***	Y	Y	Y	Y
19 Bruce	Y	N	Y	N
20 Durbin	N	N	N	N
21 Price	Y	Y	Y	Y
22 Gray	Y	N	Y	N
INDIANA				
1 Visclosky	Y	N	Y	N
2 Sharp	Y	N	Y	N
3 ***Hiler***	N	Y	N	Y
4 ***Coats***	N	Y	N	Y
5 ***Hillis***	Y	Y	Y	Y

ND - Northern Democrats SD - Southern Democrats

* Corresponding to Congressional Record Votes 35, 37, 38, 39

	33	34	35	36
6 ***Burton***	N	Y	N	Y
7 ***Myers***	Y	Y	Y	Y
8 Vacancy				
9 Hamilton	Y	N	Y	N
10 Jacobs	N	N	N	N
IOWA				
1 ***Leach***	N	N	N	N
2 ***Tauke***	N	N	N	N
3 ***Evans***	N	N	N	N
4 Smith	Y	N	Y	N
5 ***Lightfoot***	N	Y	N	Y
6 Bedell	Y	N	Y	N
KANSAS				
1 ***Roberts***	Y	N	N	N
2 Slattery	N	N	Y	N
3 ***Meyers***	N	Y	N	Y
4 Glickman	N	N	Y	N
5 ***Whittaker***	N	Y	N	Y
KENTUCKY				
1 Hubbard	Y	Y	Y	Y
2 Natcher	Y	N	Y	N
3 Mazzoli	Y	N	Y	N
4 ***Snyder***	Y	Y	Y	Y
5 ***Rogers***	N	Y	N	Y
6 ***Hopkins***	N	Y	N	Y
7 Perkins	Y	N	Y	N
LOUISIANA				
1 ***Livingston***	N	Y	N	Y
2 Boggs	Y	N	Y	N
3 Tauzin	N	Y	Y	Y
4 Roemer	N	Y	N	Y
5 Huckaby	N	Y	Y	Y
6 ***Moore***	N	Y	Y	Y
7 Breaux	Y	Y	Y	Y
8 Vacancy				
MAINE				
1 ***McKernan***	N	Y	N	Y
2 ***Snowe***	N	Y	N	Y
MARYLAND				
1 Dyson	N	Y	Y	Y
2 ***Bentley***	N	Y	N	Y
3 Mikulski	Y	N	P	N
4 ***Holt***	N	Y	N	Y
5 Hoyer	Y	Y	Y	Y
6 Byron	N	Y	Y	Y
7 Mitchell	Y	N	?	N
8 Barnes	Y	N	Y	N
MASSACHUSETTS				
1 ***Conte***	N	N	N	N
2 Boland	Y	N	Y	N
3 Early	N	N	Y	N
4 Frank	Y	N	Y	N
5 Atkins	Y	N	Y	N
6 Mavroules	Y	N	Y	N
7 Markey	Y	N	Y	N
8 O'Neill				
9 Moakley	Y	N	Y	N
10 Studds	Y	N	Y	N
11 Donnelly	Y	N	Y	N
MICHIGAN				
1 Conyers	Y	N	Y	-
2 ***Pursell***	Y	Y	N	Y
3 Wolpe	Y	N	Y	N
4 ***Siljander***	N	Y	?	Y
5 ***Henry***	N	N	N	N
6 Carr	N	N	Y	N
7 Kildee	Y	N	Y	N
8 Traxler	Y	N	Y	N
9 ***Vander Jagt***	?	Y	N	Y
10 ***Schuette***	N	Y	N	Y
11 ***Davis***	Y	Y	N	Y
12 Bonior	Y	N	Y	N
13 Crockett	Y	N	Y	N
14 Hertel	Y	N	Y	N
15 Ford	Y	N	?	N
16 Dingell	Y	N	Y	N
17 Levin	Y	N	Y	N
18 ***Broomfield***	Y	Y	Y	Y
MINNESOTA				
1 Penny	N	N	N	N
2 ***Weber***	N	Y	N	Y
3 ***Frenzel***	Y	Y	Y	Y
4 Vento	Y	N	Y	N
5 Sabo	Y	N	Y	N
6 Sikorski	Y	N	N	N

	33	34	35	36
7 ***Stangeland***	Y	Y	N	Y
8 Oberstar	Y	N	P	N
MISSISSIPPI				
1 Whitten	Y	N	Y	N
2 ***Franklin***	?	Y	N	Y
3 Montgomery	Y	Y	Y	Y
4 Dowdy	?	Y	Y	Y
5 ***Lott***	N	Y	N	Y
MISSOURI				
1 Clay	Y	N	N	N
2 Young	Y	N	Y	N
3 Gephardt	Y	N	?	N
4 Skelton	Y	Y	Y	Y
5 Wheat	Y	N	Y	N
6 ***Coleman***	Y	Y	N	Y
7 ***Taylor***	Y	Y	Y	Y
8 ***Emerson***	N	Y	N	Y
9 Volkmer	Y	N	Y	N
MONTANA				
1 Williams	Y	N	Y	N
2 ***Marlenee***	N	Y	Y	Y
NEBRASKA				
1 ***Bereuter***	-	N	N	N
2 ***Daub***	N	Y	N	Y
3 ***Smith***	N	N	N	N
NEVADA				
1 Reid	Y	Y	Y	Y
2 ***Vucanovich***	Y	Y	N	Y
NEW HAMPSHIRE				
1 ***Smith***	N	Y	N	Y
2 ***Gregg***	N	Y	N	Y
NEW JERSEY				
1 Florio	Y	N	Y	N
2 Hughes	Y	N	Y	N
3 Howard	Y	N	Y	N
4 ***Smith***	N	N	Y	N
5 ***Roukema***	?	N	N	N
6 Dwyer	Y	N	Y	N
7 ***Rinaldo***	Y	Y	Y	Y
8 Roe	Y	N	Y	N
9 Torricelli	Y	N	Y	N
10 Rodino	Y	N	Y	N
11 ***Gallo***	N	Y	N	Y
12 ***Courter***	Y	Y	N	Y
13 ***Saxton***	N	Y	N	Y
14 Guarini	Y	N	Y	N
NEW MEXICO				
1 ***Lujan***	N	Y	N	Y
2 ***Skeen***	N	Y	N	Y
3 Richardson	Y	N	Y	N
NEW YORK				
1 ***Carney***	Y	Y	N	Y
2 Downey	Y	N	Y	N
3 Mrazek	Y	N	Y	N
4 ***Lent***	Y	Y	N	Y
5 ***McGrath***	Y	Y	Y	Y
6 Addabbo	Y	N	Y	N
7 Ackerman	Y	N	Y	N
8 Scheuer	Y	N	Y	N
9 Manton	Y	N	Y	N
10 Schumer	Y	N	Y	N
11 Towns	Y	N	Y	N
12 Owens	Y	N	Y	N
13 Solarz	Y	N	Y	N
14 ***Molinari***	Y	Y	Y	Y
15 ***Green***	N	N	N	N
16 Rangel	?	N	Y	N
17 Weiss	Y	N	Y	N
18 Garcia	Y	N	P	N
19 Biaggi	Y	N	Y	N
20 ***DioGuardi***	N	N	N	N
21 ***Fish***	Y	Y	N	Y
22 ***Gilman***	N	Y	Y	Y
23 Stratton	Y	Y	Y	Y
24 ***Solomon***	N	Y	Y	Y
25 ***Boehlert***	N	Y	Y	Y
26 ***Martin***	N	Y	Y	Y
27 ***Wortley***	?	Y	N	Y
28 McHugh	Y	N	Y	N
29 ***Horton***	Y	Y	Y	Y
30 ***Eckert***	Y	Y	N	Y
31 ***Kemp***	N	Y	N	Y
32 LaFalce	Y	N	Y	N
33 Nowak	Y	N	Y	N
34 Lundine	?	N	Y	N

	33	34	35	36
NORTH CAROLINA				
1 Jones	Y	N	Y	N
2 Valentine	Y	Y	Y	Y
3 Whitley	Y	Y	Y	Y
4 ***Cobey***	N	Y	N	Y
5 Neal	Y	Y	Y	Y
6 ***Coble***	N	Y	N	Y
7 Rose	Y	N	Y	N
8 Hefner	Y	Y	Y	Y
9 ***McMillan***	N	Y	N	Y
10 ***Broyhill***	N	Y	Y	Y
11 ***Hendon***	N	Y	Y	Y
NORTH DAKOTA				
AL Dorgan	Y	N	Y	N
OHIO				
1 Luken	Y	N	Y	N
2 ***Gradison***	N	N	Y	N
3 Hall	Y	N	Y	N
4 ***Oxley***	N	Y	N	Y
5 ***Latta***	N	Y	Y	Y
6 ***McEwen***	N	Y	N	Y
7 ***DeWine***	N	Y	N	Y
8 ***Kindness***	N	Y	N	Y
9 Kaptur	Y	N	Y	N
10 ***Miller***	N	Y	N	Y
11 Eckart	Y	N	Y	N
12 ***Kasich***	N	Y	N	Y
13 Pease	Y	N	Y	N
14 Seiberling	Y	N	Y	N
15 ***Wylie***	?	Y	Y	Y
16 ***Regula***	Y	Y	Y	Y
17 Traficant	Y	N	Y	N
18 Applegate	Y	N	?	N
19 Feighan	?	N	Y	N
20 Oakar	?	N	Y	N
21 Stokes	Y	N	Y	N
OKLAHOMA				
1 Jones	Y	N	N	N
2 Synar	Y	N	Y	N
3 Watkins	Y	Y	Y	Y
4 McCurdy	N	Y	Y	Y
5 ***Edwards***	N	Y	Y	Y
6 English	Y	Y	Y	Y
OREGON				
1 AuCoin	Y	N	Y	N
2 ***Smith, R.***	N	Y	Y	Y
3 Wyden	Y	N	Y	N
4 Weaver	Y	N	Y	N
5 ***Smith, D.***	N	Y	Y	Y
PENNSYLVANIA				
1 Foglietta	Y	N	Y	N
2 Gray	Y	N	Y	N
3 Borski	Y	N	Y	N
4 Kolter	Y	N	Y	N
5 ***Schulze***	Y	Y	N	Y
6 Yatron	Y	Y	Y	Y
7 Edgar	Y	N	Y	N
8 Kostmayer	Y	N	Y	N
9 ***Shuster***	N	Y	N	Y
10 ***McDade***	Y	Y	Y	Y
11 Kanjorski	Y	N	Y	N
12 Murtha	Y	Y	Y	Y
13 ***Coughlin***	N	N	N	N
14 Coyne	?	N	Y	N
15 ***Ritter***	N	Y	N	Y
16 ***Walker***	N	Y	N	Y
17 ***Gekas***	N	Y	Y	Y
18 Walgren	Y	N	Y	N
19 ***Goodling***	N	N	N	N
20 Gaydos	Y	N	Y	N
21 ***Ridge***	Y	N	Y	X
22 Murphy	Y	N	Y	N
23 ***Clinger***	N	Y	N	Y
RHODE ISLAND				
1 St Germain	Y	N	Y	N
2 ***Schneider***	N	N	N	N
SOUTH CAROLINA				
1 ***Hartnett***	N	Y	Y	Y
2 ***Spence***	N	Y	N	Y
3 Derrick	?	N	Y	N
4 ***Campbell***	N	Y	Y	Y
5 Spratt	Y	N	Y	N
6 Tallon	Y	N	Y	N
SOUTH DAKOTA				
AL Daschle	Y	N	Y	N

	33	34	35	36
TENNESSEE				
1 ***Quillen***	Y	Y	Y	Y
2 ***Duncan***	Y	Y	N	Y
3 Lloyd	N	Y	Y	Y
4 Cooper	Y	Y	P	Y
5 Boner	Y	Y	Y	Y
6 Gordon	?	N	Y	N
7 ***Sundquist***	N	Y	N	Y
8 Jones	Y	Y	Y	Y
9 Ford	Y	N	Y	N
TEXAS				
1 Hall, S.	N	Y	Y	Y
2 Wilson	Y	Y	Y	Y
3 ***Bartlett***	N	Y	N	Y
4 Hall, R.	N	Y	Y	Y
5 Bryant	Y	N	Y	N
6 ***Barton***	N	Y	?	Y
7 ***Archer***	N	Y	N	#
8 ***Fields***	N	Y	N	Y
9 Brooks	Y	N	Y	N
10 Pickle	Y	N	Y	N
11 Leath	N	Y	Y	Y
12 Wright	Y	N	Y	N
13 ***Boulter***	N	Y	N	Y
14 ***Sweeney***	N	Y	N	Y
15 de la Garza	Y	Y	Y	Y
16 Coleman	Y	N	Y	N
17 Stenholm	N	Y	Y	Y
18 Leland	Y	N	Y	N
19 ***Combest***	N	Y	N	Y
20 Gonzalez	Y	N	Y	N
21 ***Loeffler***	N	Y	N	Y
22 ***DeLay***	N	Y	N	Y
23 Bustamante	Y	Y	Y	Y
24 Frost	Y	Y	Y	Y
25 Andrews	Y	Y	Y	Y
26 ***Armey***	N	Y	Y	Y
27 Ortiz	Y	Y	P	Y
UTAH				
1 ***Hansen***	N	Y	N	Y
2 ***Monson***	N	Y	N	Y
3 ***Nielson***	N	Y	Y	Y
VERMONT				
AL ***Jeffords***	Y	N	N	N
VIRGINIA				
1 ***Bateman***	N	Y	?	Y
2 ***Whitehurst***	Y	Y	N	Y
3 ***Bliley***	N	Y	N	Y
4 Sisisky	Y	N	P	N
5 Daniel	N	Y	Y	Y
6 Olin	N	N	Y	N
7 ***Slaughter***	N	Y	N	Y
8 ***Parris***	N	Y	N	Y
9 Boucher	Y	N	Y	N
10 ***Wolf***	N	Y	N	Y
WASHINGTON				
1 ***Miller***	N	N	N	N
2 Swift	Y	N	Y	N
3 Bonker	Y	N	Y	N
4 ***Morrison***	Y	Y	N	Y
5 Foley	Y	N	Y	N
6 Dicks	Y	Y	Y	Y
7 Lowry	Y	N	Y	N
8 ***Chandler***	Y	Y	N	Y
WEST VIRGINIA				
1 Mollohan	Y	Y	Y	Y
2 Staggers	Y	N	Y	N
3 Wise	-	N	Y	N
4 Rahall	Y	N	Y	N
WISCONSIN				
1 Aspin	Y	Y	Y	Y
2 Kastenmeier	Y	N	Y	N
3 ***Gunderson***	N	Y	N	Y
4 Kleczka	Y	N	Y	N
5 Moody	?	N	Y	N
6 ***Petri***	N	N	Y	N
7 Obey	Y	N	Y	N
8 ***Roth***	N	Y	N	Y
9 ***Sensenbrenner***	N	N	N	N
WYOMING				
AL ***Cheney***	N	Y	N	Y

Southern states - Ala., Ark., Fla., Ga., Ky., La., Miss., N.C., Okla., S.C., Tenn., Texas, Va.

* The *Congressional Record* vote number is different from the CQ vote number because the *Record* includes quorum calls in its tally. CQ does not publish quorum call votes.

37. Procedural Motion. Kasich, R-Ohio, motion to approve the House *Journal* of Monday, April 1. Motion agreed to 243-161: R 18-151; D 225-10 (ND 152-8, SD 73-2), April 2, 1985.

38. H Res 121. Indiana 8th District Seat. Wright, D-Texas, motion to refer to the Committee on House Administration the resolution to seat Republican Richard D. McIntyre as a member of the 99th Congress representing the 8th District of Indiana. (The effect of the Wright motion was to delay a decision on seating McIntyre pending a recount by a House Administration Committee task force.) Motion agreed to 241-183: R 0-178; D 241-5 (ND 165-1, SD 76-4), April 2, 1985.

39. HR 1239. African Famine Relief. Adoption of the conference report on the bill to appropriate $784 million in fiscal 1985 for food and non-food aid to African countries suffering from famine. Adopted 400-19: R 157-19; D 243-0 (ND 164-0, SD 79-0), April 2, 1985. (The Senate subsequently adopted the conference report by voice vote, thus clearing it for the president.)

40. HR 1373. Phillip Burton Wilderness. Vento, D-Minn., motion to suspend the rules and pass the bill to name a previously designated 25,370-acre wilderness area within the Point Reyes National Seashore in California as the "Phillip Burton Wilderness." Motion agreed to 342-69: R 110-69; D 232-0 (ND 158-0, SD 74-0), April 2, 1985. A two-thirds majority of those present and voting (274 in this case) is required for passage under suspension of the rules. A "nay" was a vote supporting the president's position.

41. HR 1869. Automobile Record-keeping Requirements. Rostenkowski, D-Ill., motion to suspend the rules and pass the bill to repeal rules requiring detailed "contemporaneous" logs of business and personal use of automobiles and other equipment to qualify for business tax deductions, and to lower limits on business tax breaks for expensive automobiles. Motion agreed to 412-1: R 178-0; D 234-1 (ND 160-1, SD 74-0), April 2, 1985. A two-thirds majority of those present and voting (276 in this case) is required for passage under suspension of the rules.

42. H Con Res 107. Unfair Trade Practices of Japan. Rostenkowski, D-Ill., motion to suspend the rules and adopt the concurrent resolution to urge the president either to persuade the Japanese to buy more U.S. goods or to approve tariffs, quotas or other restraints to block Japanese imports. Motion agreed to 394-19: R 160-17; D 234-2 (ND 159-2, SD 75-0), April 2, 1985. A two-thirds majority of those present and voting (276 in this case) is required for adoption under suspension of the rules.

43. Procedural Motion. Strang, R-Colo., motion to approve the House *Journal* of Tuesday, April 2. Motion agreed to 246-155: R 22-146; D 224-9 (ND 152-6, SD 72-3), April 3, 1985.

44. HR 1714. NASA Authorization, Fiscal 1986. Walker, R-Pa., substitute amendment to the Meyers, R-Kan., amendment, to reduce the authorized spending level for research and program management from $1,345,000,000 to $1,300,000,000. (The Meyers amendment would have reduced the authorized spending level for space shuttle production and operation capability from $1,011,500,000 to $976,500,000, and increased the authorized spending level for space transportation capability development from $444,300,000 to $459,300,000.) Adopted 288-127: R 128-48; D 160-79 (ND 85-75, SD 75-4), April 3, 1985. (The Meyers amendment, as amended by the Walker substitute, subsequently was adopted by voice vote.)

KEY

- Y Voted for (yea).
- # Paired for.
- + Announced for.
- N Voted against (nay).
- X Paired against.
- \- Announced against.
- P Voted "present".
- C Voted "present" to avoid possible conflict of interest.
- ? Did not vote or otherwise make a position known.

Democrats ***Republicans***

	37	38	39	40	41	42	43	44
ALABAMA								
1 ***Callahan***	N	N	Y	Y	Y	Y	Y	Y
2 ***Dickinson***	N	N	Y	Y	Y	Y	N	Y
3 Nichols	Y	Y	Y	Y	Y	Y	Y	Y
4 Bevill	Y	Y	Y	Y	Y	Y	Y	Y
5 Flippo	Y	Y	Y	Y	Y	Y	Y	Y
6 Erdreich	Y	Y	Y	Y	Y	Y	Y	Y
7 Shelby	?	Y	Y	Y	Y	Y	N	Y
ALASKA								
AL ***Young***	N	N	Y	Y	Y	Y	N	N
ARIZONA								
1 ***McCain***	N	N	Y	Y	Y	Y	N	Y
2 Udall	Y	Y	Y	Y	Y	Y	Y	Y
3 ***Stump***	N	N	N	N	Y	N	N	Y
4 ***Rudd***	Y	N	N	Y	Y	Y	?	?
5 ***Kolbe***	N	N	Y	N	Y	Y	?	?
ARKANSAS								
1 Alexander	Y	Y	Y	Y	Y	Y	Y	Y
2 Robinson	Y	Y	Y	Y	Y	Y	Y	Y
3 ***Hammerschmidt***	N	N	Y	Y	Y	Y	Y	Y
4 Anthony	Y	Y	Y	Y	Y	Y	Y	Y
CALIFORNIA								
1 Bosco	Y	Y	Y	Y	Y	Y	Y	N
2 ***Chappie***	N	N	Y	N	Y	Y	N	Y
3 Matsui	Y	Y	Y	Y	Y	Y	Y	N
4 Fazio	Y	Y	Y	Y	Y	Y	Y	Y
5 Burton	Y	Y	Y	Y	Y	Y	Y	N
6 Boxer	Y	Y	Y	Y	Y	Y	Y	N
7 Miller	Y	Y	Y	Y	Y	Y	Y	N
8 Dellums	Y	Y	Y	Y	Y	Y	?	?
9 Stark	Y	Y	Y	?	Y	Y	Y	N
10 Edwards	Y	Y	Y	Y	Y	Y	Y	N
11 Lantos	Y	Y	Y	Y	Y	Y	Y	Y
12 ***Zschau***	N	N	Y	N	Y	Y	N	Y
13 Mineta	Y	Y	Y	Y	Y	Y	Y	Y
14 ***Shumway***	N	N	Y	N	Y	N	N	Y
15 Coelho	Y	Y	Y	Y	Y	Y	Y	Y
16 Panetta	Y	C	Y	Y	Y	Y	Y	Y
17 ***Pashayan***	N	N	Y	Y	Y	Y	N	Y
18 Lehman	Y	Y	Y	Y	Y	Y	Y	Y
19 ***Lagomarsino***	N	N	Y	Y	Y	Y	N	Y
20 ***Thomas***	N	N	Y	Y	Y	Y	N	Y
21 ***Fiedler***	N	N	Y	N	Y	Y	N	Y
22 ***Moorhead***	N	N	Y	Y	Y	?	N	N
23 Beilenson	Y	Y	Y	Y	Y	Y	Y	N
24 Waxman	Y	Y	Y	Y	Y	Y	Y	Y
25 Roybal	Y	Y	Y	Y	Y	Y	Y	N
26 Berman	Y	Y	Y	Y	Y	Y	Y	N
27 Levine	Y	Y	Y	Y	Y	Y	Y	Y
28 Dixon	Y	Y	Y	Y	Y	Y	Y	N
29 Hawkins	?	Y	Y	Y	Y	Y	Y	N
30 Martinez	Y	Y	Y	Y	Y	Y	Y	Y
31 Dymally	P	Y	Y	Y	Y	Y	P	N
32 Anderson	Y	Y	Y	Y	Y	Y	Y	Y
33 ***Dreier***	N	N	Y	N	Y	Y	N	Y
34 Torres	Y	Y	Y	Y	Y	N	Y	N
35 ***Lewis***	N	N	Y	Y	Y	Y	Y	Y
36 Brown	Y	Y	Y	Y	Y	Y	Y	N
37 ***McCandless***	N	N	Y	Y	Y	Y	N	Y
38 ***Dornan***	?	X	?	N	Y	Y	N	N
39 ***Dannemeyer***	N	N	N	N	Y	Y	N	Y
40 ***Badham***	N	N	Y	Y	Y	N	N	Y
41 ***Lowery***	N	N	Y	Y	Y	Y	N	Y
42 ***Lungren***	Y	N	Y	N	Y	N	N	Y
43 ***Packard***	N	N	Y	N	Y	Y	N	Y
44 Bates	Y	Y	Y	Y	Y	Y	Y	Y
45 ***Hunter***	N	N	Y	Y	Y	Y	N	Y
COLORADO								
1 Schroeder	N	Y	Y	Y	Y	Y	?	?
2 Wirth	Y	Y	Y	Y	Y	Y	Y	Y
3 ***Strang***	N	N	Y	N	Y	N	N	N
4 ***Brown***	N	N	N	Y	Y	Y	N	Y
5 ***Kramer***	N	N	Y	Y	Y	Y	N	Y
6 ***Schaefer***	Y	N	Y	Y	Y	Y	N	Y
CONNECTICUT								
1 Kennelly	Y	Y	Y	Y	Y	Y	Y	N
2 Gejdenson	Y	Y	Y	Y	Y	Y	Y	Y
3 Morrison	Y	Y	Y	+	+	+	Y	N
4 ***McKinney***	N	N	Y	Y	Y	Y	N	N
5 ***Rowland***	N	N	Y	N	Y	Y	N	Y
6 ***Johnson***	Y	N	Y	Y	Y	Y	Y	N
DELAWARE								
AL Carper	Y	Y	Y	Y	Y	Y	Y	Y
FLORIDA								
1 Hutto	Y	Y	Y	Y	Y	Y	Y	Y
2 Fuqua	Y	Y	Y	Y	Y	Y	Y	Y
3 Bennett	Y	Y	Y	Y	Y	Y	Y	Y
4 Chappell	Y	Y	Y	Y	Y	Y	Y	Y
5 ***McCollum***	N	N	Y	Y	Y	Y	N	?
6 MacKay	Y	Y	Y	Y	Y	Y	Y	Y
7 Gibbons	Y	Y	Y	Y	Y	Y	Y	Y
8 ***Young***	N	N	Y	Y	Y	Y	N	Y
9 ***Bilirakis***	N	N	Y	Y	Y	Y	N	Y
10 ***Ireland***	N	N	Y	Y	Y	Y	N	Y
11 Nelson	Y	Y	Y	Y	Y	Y	Y	Y
12 ***Lewis***	N	N	Y	Y	Y	Y	N	Y
13 ***Mack***	N	N	N	N	Y	N	N	Y
14 Mica	Y	Y	Y	Y	Y	Y	Y	Y
15 ***Shaw***	N	N	Y	Y	Y	Y	N	Y
16 Smith	Y	Y	Y	Y	Y	Y	Y	Y
17 Lehman	Y	Y	Y	Y	Y	Y	Y	Y
18 Pepper	Y	Y	Y	+	+	+	+	Y
19 Fascell	Y	Y	Y	?	?	?	Y	Y
GEORGIA								
1 Thomas	Y	Y	Y	Y	Y	Y	Y	Y
2 Hatcher	Y	Y	Y	Y	Y	Y	Y	Y
3 Ray	Y	Y	Y	Y	Y	Y	Y	Y
4 ***Swindall***	N	N	N	N	Y	Y	N	Y
5 Fowler	Y	Y	Y	Y	Y	Y	Y	Y
6 ***Gingrich***	N	N	Y	N	Y	Y	N	Y
7 Darden	Y	Y	Y	Y	Y	Y	Y	Y
8 Rowland	Y	Y	Y	Y	Y	Y	Y	Y
9 Jenkins	Y	Y	Y	Y	Y	Y	Y	Y
10 Barnard	Y	Y	Y	Y	Y	Y	Y	Y
HAWAII								
1 Heftel	Y	Y	Y	Y	Y	Y	Y	Y
2 Akaka	Y	Y	Y	Y	Y	Y	Y	Y
IDAHO								
1 ***Craig***	N	N	N	Y	Y	Y	Y	Y
2 Stallings	Y	Y	?	Y	Y	Y	Y	Y
ILLINOIS								
1 Hayes	Y	Y	Y	Y	Y	Y	Y	N
2 Savage	Y	Y	Y	Y	Y	Y	Y	Y
3 Russo	Y	Y	Y	Y	Y	Y	Y	N
4 ***O'Brien***	Y	N	Y	Y	Y	Y	Y	N
5 Lipinski	Y	Y	Y	Y	Y	Y	Y	Y
6 ***Hyde***	N	N	Y	Y	Y	Y	N	N
7 Collins	Y	Y	Y	Y	Y	Y	Y	N
8 Rostenkowski	Y	Y	Y	Y	Y	Y	Y	Y
9 Yates	?	#	?	?	?	?	?	?
10 ***Porter***	?	N	Y	Y	Y	Y	N	Y
11 Annunzio	Y	Y	Y	Y	Y	Y	Y	N
12 ***Crane, P.***	N	N	N	N	Y	N	N	Y
13 ***Fawell***	?	N	Y	N	Y	Y	N	N
14 ***Grotberg***	N	N	Y	N	Y	Y	N	Y
15 ***Madigan***	N	N	Y	N	Y	Y	N	N
16 ***Martin***	N	N	Y	N	Y	Y	N	Y
17 Evans	Y	Y	Y	Y	Y	Y	Y	Y
18 ***Michel***	Y	N	Y	N	Y	Y	Y	Y
19 Bruce	Y	Y	Y	Y	Y	Y	Y	Y
20 Durbin	N	Y	Y	Y	Y	Y	N	Y
21 Price	Y	Y	Y	Y	Y	Y	Y	N
22 Gray	Y	Y	Y	Y	Y	Y	Y	N
INDIANA								
1 Visclosky	Y	Y	Y	Y	Y	Y	Y	N
2 Sharp	Y	Y	Y	Y	Y	Y	Y	Y
3 ***Hiler***	N	N	Y	N	Y	Y	N	Y
4 ***Coats***	N	N	Y	N	Y	Y	N	Y
5 ***Hillis***	Y	N	Y	Y	Y	Y	Y	Y

ND - Northern Democrats SD - Southern Democrats

* Corresponding to Congressional Record Votes 40, 41, 42, 43, 44, 45, 46, 48

	37	38	39	40	41	42	43	44
6 ***Burton***	N	N	?	N	Y	Y	N	N
7 ***Myers***	Y	N	Y	Y	Y	Y	Y	Y
8 Vacancy								
9 Hamilton	Y	Y	Y	Y	Y	Y	Y	Y
10 Jacobs	N	Y	Y	Y	Y	Y	N	N
IOWA								
1 ***Leach***	N	N	Y	Y	Y	Y	?	N
2 ***Tauke***	N	N	Y	Y	Y	Y	N	N
3 ***Evans***	N	N	Y	Y	Y	Y	?	N
4 Smith	Y	Y	Y	Y	Y	Y	Y	Y
5 ***Lightfoot***	N	N	Y	N	Y	Y	N	N
6 Bedell	Y	Y	Y	Y	Y	Y	Y	N
KANSAS								
1 ***Roberts***	N	N	Y	Y	Y	Y	N	N
2 Slattery	Y	Y	Y	Y	Y	Y	Y	Y
3 ***Meyers***	N	N	Y	Y	Y	Y	Y	N
4 Glickman	Y	Y	Y	Y	Y	Y	Y	Y
5 ***Whittaker***	?	N	Y	N	Y	Y	N	N
KENTUCKY								
1 Hubbard	Y	Y	Y	Y	Y	Y	Y	Y
2 Natcher	Y	Y	Y	Y	Y	Y	Y	Y
3 Mazzoli	Y	N	Y	Y	Y	Y	Y	Y
4 ***Snyder***	?	N	Y	Y	Y	Y	Y	Y
5 ***Rogers***	N	N	Y	N	Y	Y	N	Y
6 ***Hopkins***	N	N	Y	Y	Y	Y	N	Y
7 Perkins	Y	Y	Y	Y	Y	Y	Y	Y
LOUISIANA								
1 ***Livingston***	N	N	Y	N	Y	Y	N	Y
2 Boggs	Y	Y	Y	?	?	?	Y	Y
3 Tauzin	Y	Y	Y	+	+	Y	Y	Y
4 Roemer	N	Y	Y	Y	Y	Y	N	Y
5 Huckaby	N	Y	Y	Y	Y	?	N	Y
6 ***Moore***	Y	N	Y	Y	Y	Y	Y	Y
7 Breaux	?	Y	Y	Y	Y	Y	Y	Y
8 Vacancy								
MAINE								
1 ***McKernan***	N	N	Y	Y	Y	Y	N	Y
2 ***Snowe***	N	N	Y	Y	Y	Y	N	N
MARYLAND								
1 Dyson	Y	Y	Y	Y	Y	Y	Y	N
2 ***Bentley***	?	N	N	Y	Y	Y	?	N
3 Mikulski	P	Y	Y	Y	Y	Y	?	N
4 ***Holt***	N	N	Y	Y	Y	Y	N	N
5 Hoyer	Y	Y	Y	Y	Y	Y	Y	N
6 Byron	Y	Y	Y	Y	Y	Y	Y	N
7 Mitchell	N	Y	Y	Y	Y	Y	N	N
8 Barnes	Y	Y	Y	Y	Y	Y	Y	N
MASSACHUSETTS								
1 ***Conte***	N	N	Y	Y	Y	Y	N	N
2 Boland	Y	Y	Y	Y	Y	Y	Y	N
3 Early	Y	Y	Y	Y	Y	Y	Y	N
4 Frank	Y	Y	Y	Y	N	Y	Y	N
5 Atkins	Y	Y	Y	Y	Y	Y	Y	Y
6 Mavroules	Y	Y	Y	Y	Y	Y	Y	Y
7 Markey	Y	Y	Y	Y	Y	Y	Y	N
8 O'Neill								
9 Moakley	Y	Y	Y	Y	Y	Y	Y	Y
10 Studds	Y	Y	Y	Y	Y	Y	Y	N
11 Donnelly	Y	Y	Y	Y	Y	Y	Y	Y
MICHIGAN								
1 Conyers	Y	Y	Y	Y	Y	Y	Y	N
2 ***Pursell***	N	N	Y	Y	Y	Y	N	N
3 Wolpe	Y	Y	Y	+	+	+	Y	N
4 ***Siljander***	N	N	Y	Y	Y	Y	N	Y
5 ***Henry***	N	N	Y	Y	Y	Y	N	N
6 Carr	Y	Y	Y	Y	Y	Y	Y	Y
7 Kildee	Y	Y	Y	Y	Y	Y	Y	N
8 Traxler	Y	Y	Y	Y	Y	Y	Y	Y
9 ***Vander Jagt***	N	N	Y	?	?	?	N	Y
10 ***Schuette***	N	N	Y	N	Y	Y	N	Y
11 ***Davis***	N	N	Y	Y	Y	Y	N	Y
12 Bonior	Y	Y	Y	Y	Y	Y	Y	N
13 Crockett	Y	Y	Y	?	?	?	?	N
14 Hertel	Y	Y	Y	Y	Y	Y	Y	Y
15 Ford	?	Y	Y	Y	Y	Y	?	Y
16 Dingell	Y	Y	Y	Y	Y	Y	Y	N
17 Levin	Y	Y	Y	Y	Y	Y	Y	Y
18 ***Broomfield***	Y	N	Y	N	Y	Y	Y	Y
MINNESOTA								
1 Penny	N	Y	Y	Y	Y	Y	N	Y
2 ***Weber***	?	?	?	N	Y	N	N	Y
3 ***Frenzel***	N	N	Y	N	Y	N	?	Y
4 Vento	Y	Y	Y	Y	Y	Y	Y	N
5 Sabo	Y	Y	Y	Y	Y	Y	?	Y
6 Sikorski	N	Y	Y	Y	Y	Y	N	N

	37	38	39	40	41	42	43	44
7 ***Stangeland***	N	N	Y	Y	Y	Y	N	Y
8 Oberstar	P	Y	Y	Y	Y	Y	P	Y
MISSISSIPPI								
1 Whitten	Y	Y	Y	Y	Y	Y	P	Y
2 ***Franklin***	N	N	Y	Y	Y	Y	?	Y
3 Montgomery	Y	Y	Y	Y	Y	Y	Y	Y
4 Dowdy	?	Y	Y	Y	Y	Y	Y	Y
5 ***Lott***	N	N	Y	Y	Y	Y	N	Y
MISSOURI								
1 Clay	N	Y	Y	Y	Y	Y	N	N
2 Young	Y	Y	Y	Y	Y	Y	Y	Y
3 Gephardt	Y	Y	Y	?	?	?	Y	Y
4 Skelton	Y	Y	Y	Y	Y	Y	Y	N
5 Wheat	Y	Y	Y	Y	Y	Y	Y	N
6 ***Coleman***	N	N	Y	Y	Y	Y	N	N
7 ***Taylor***	N	N	Y	Y	Y	Y	N	Y
8 ***Emerson***	N	N	Y	Y	Y	Y	N	Y
9 Volkmer	Y	Y	Y	Y	Y	Y	Y	Y
MONTANA								
1 Williams	?	Y	Y	Y	Y	Y	Y	N
2 ***Marlenee***	?	N	Y	N	Y	Y	N	N
NEBRASKA								
1 ***Bereuter***	N	N	Y	Y	Y	Y	N	Y
2 ***Daub***	N	N	Y	Y	Y	Y	N	Y
3 ***Smith***	N	N	Y	Y	Y	Y	?	Y
NEVADA								
1 Reid	Y	Y	Y	Y	Y	Y	Y	N
2 ***Vucanovich***	N	N	Y	Y	Y	Y	N	Y
NEW HAMPSHIRE								
1 ***Smith***	N	N	Y	N	Y	Y	N	N
2 ***Gregg***	N	N	Y	N	Y	Y	N	Y
NEW JERSEY								
1 Florio	Y	Y	Y	Y	Y	Y	Y	Y
2 Hughes	Y	Y	Y	Y	Y	Y	Y	Y
3 Howard	Y	Y	Y	Y	Y	Y	Y	N
4 ***Smith***	N	N	Y	Y	Y	Y	N	Y
5 ***Roukema***	Y	N	Y	Y	Y	Y	N	Y
6 Dwyer	Y	Y	Y	Y	Y	Y	Y	Y
7 ***Rinaldo***	N	N	Y	Y	Y	Y	N	N
8 Roe	Y	Y	Y	Y	Y	Y	Y	Y
9 Torricelli	Y	Y	Y	Y	Y	Y	Y	Y
10 Rodino	?	Y	Y	Y	Y	Y	Y	N
11 ***Gallo***	N	N	Y	Y	Y	Y	N	N
12 ***Courter***	N	N	Y	Y	Y	Y	?	?
13 ***Saxton***	N	N	Y	Y	Y	Y	N	N
14 Guarini	Y	Y	+	Y	Y	Y	Y	Y
NEW MEXICO								
1 ***Lujan***	N	N	Y	Y	Y	Y	N	N
2 ***Skeen***	N	N	Y	Y	Y	Y	N	N
3 Richardson	N	Y	Y	Y	Y	Y	Y	N
NEW YORK								
1 ***Carney***	N	N	Y	Y	Y	Y	N	N
2 Downey	Y	Y	Y	Y	Y	Y	Y	Y
3 Mrazek	Y	Y	Y	Y	Y	Y	Y	Y
4 ***Lent***	N	N	Y	Y	Y	Y	N	Y
5 ***McGrath***	Y	N	Y	Y	Y	Y	Y	Y
6 Addabbo	Y	Y	Y	Y	Y	Y	Y	N
7 Ackerman	Y	Y	Y	Y	Y	Y	Y	N
8 Scheuer	Y	Y	Y	Y	Y	Y	Y	Y
9 Manton	Y	Y	Y	Y	Y	Y	Y	Y
10 Schumer	Y	Y	Y	Y	Y	Y	Y	Y
11 Towns	Y	Y	Y	Y	Y	Y	Y	N
12 Owens	Y	Y	Y	Y	Y	Y	Y	N
13 Solarz	Y	Y	Y	?	?	?	Y	Y
14 ***Molinari***	N	N	Y	Y	Y	Y	N	Y
15 ***Green***	N	N	Y	Y	Y	Y	N	N
16 Rangel	Y	Y	+	Y	Y	Y	Y	N
17 Weiss	Y	Y	Y	Y	Y	Y	Y	N
18 Garcia	Y	Y	Y	Y	Y	Y	Y	N
19 Biaggi	Y	Y	Y	Y	Y	Y	Y	Y
20 ***DioGuardi***	?	N	Y	Y	Y	Y	?	Y
21 ***Fish***	N	N	Y	Y	Y	Y	N	Y
22 ***Gilman***	Y	N	+	Y	Y	Y	N	Y
23 Stratton	Y	Y	Y	Y	Y	Y	Y	N
24 ***Solomon***	N	N	Y	N	Y	Y	N	Y
25 ***Boehlert***	N	N	Y	Y	Y	Y	N	N
26 ***Martin***	N	N	Y	Y	Y	Y	N	Y
27 ***Wortley***	N	N	Y	N	Y	Y	N	Y
28 McHugh	Y	Y	Y	Y	Y	Y	Y	N
29 ***Horton***	Y	N	Y	Y	Y	Y	Y	Y
30 ***Eckert***	N	N	Y	N	Y	N	N	Y
31 ***Kemp***	N	N	Y	Y	Y	N	N	Y
32 LaFalce	Y	Y	Y	Y	Y	Y	Y	Y
33 Nowak	Y	Y	Y	Y	Y	Y	Y	Y
34 Lundine	Y	Y	Y	Y	Y	Y	Y	?

	37	38	39	40	41	42	43	44
NORTH CAROLINA								
1 Jones	Y	Y	Y	Y	Y	Y	?	Y
2 Valentine	Y	Y	Y	Y	Y	Y	Y	Y
3 Whitley	Y	Y	Y	Y	Y	Y	Y	Y
4 ***Cobey***	N	N	Y	N	Y	Y	N	Y
5 Neal	Y	Y	Y	Y	Y	Y	Y	Y
6 ***Coble***	N	N	N	N	Y	Y	N	Y
7 Rose	Y	Y	Y	Y	Y	Y	Y	Y
8 Hefner	Y	Y	Y	Y	Y	Y	Y	Y
9 ***McMillan***	N	N	Y	N	Y	Y	N	Y
10 ***Broyhill***	N	N	Y	Y	Y	?	N	Y
11 ***Hendon***	N	N	Y	Y	Y	Y	N	Y
NORTH DAKOTA								
AL Dorgan	Y	Y	Y	Y	Y	Y	Y	Y
OHIO								
1 Luken	Y	Y	Y	Y	Y	Y	Y	?
2 ***Gradison***	N	N	Y	Y	Y	Y	N	Y
3 Hall	Y	Y	Y	Y	Y	Y	Y	Y
4 ***Oxley***	N	N	Y	N	Y	Y	N	Y
5 ***Latta***	N	N	Y	N	Y	Y	?	?
6 ***McEwen***	N	N	Y	N	Y	Y	N	Y
7 ***DeWine***	N	N	Y	N	Y	Y	N	N
8 ***Kindness***	N	N	Y	N	?	Y	N	Y
9 Kaptur	Y	Y	Y	Y	Y	Y	Y	N
10 ***Miller***	N	N	N	Y	Y	Y	N	N
11 Eckart	Y	Y	Y	Y	Y	Y	Y	Y
12 ***Kasich***	N	N	Y	Y	Y	Y	N	Y
13 Pease	Y	Y	Y	Y	Y	Y	Y	N
14 Seiberling	Y	Y	Y	Y	Y	Y	Y	N
15 ***Wylie***	Y	N	Y	Y	Y	Y	Y	Y
16 ***Regula***	N	N	Y	Y	Y	Y	N	Y
17 Traficant	Y	Y	Y	Y	Y	Y	Y	Y
18 Applegate	Y	N	Y	Y	Y	Y	Y	Y
19 Feighan	Y	Y	Y	Y	Y	Y	Y	Y
20 Oakar	Y	Y	Y	Y	Y	Y	Y	Y
21 Stokes	Y	Y	Y	Y	Y	Y	Y	N
OKLAHOMA								
1 Jones	Y	Y	Y	Y	Y	Y	Y	Y
2 Synar	Y	Y	Y	Y	Y	Y	Y	Y
3 Watkins	Y	Y	Y	Y	Y	Y	Y	Y
4 McCurdy	Y	Y	Y	Y	Y	Y	Y	Y
5 ***Edwards***	N	N	Y	Y	Y	Y	N	Y
6 English	Y	Y	Y	Y	Y	Y	?	Y
OREGON								
1 AuCoin	Y	Y	Y	?	Y	Y	Y	?
2 ***Smith, R.***	N	N	Y	N	Y	Y	N	N
3 Wyden	Y	Y	Y	Y	Y	Y	Y	Y
4 Weaver	Y	Y	Y	Y	Y	Y	Y	Y
5 ***Smith, D.***	N	N	N	N	Y	Y	N	Y
PENNSYLVANIA								
1 Foglietta	Y	Y	Y	Y	Y	Y	Y	Y
2 Gray	Y	Y	Y	Y	Y	Y	Y	N
3 Borski	Y	Y	Y	Y	Y	Y	Y	Y
4 Kolter	Y	Y	Y	Y	Y	Y	?	?
5 ***Schulze***	N	N	Y	Y	Y	N	N	Y
6 Yatron	Y	Y	Y	Y	Y	Y	Y	Y
7 Edgar	Y	Y	Y	Y	Y	Y	Y	N
8 Kostmayer	Y	Y	Y	Y	Y	Y	Y	N
9 ***Shuster***	N	N	N	Y	Y	Y	Y	Y
10 ***McDade***	N	N	Y	Y	Y	Y	N	Y
11 Kanjorski	Y	Y	Y	+	Y	Y	Y	Y
12 Murtha	Y	Y	Y	Y	Y	Y	Y	?
13 ***Coughlin***	Y	Y	Y	+	+	+	N	Y
14 Coyne	Y	Y	Y	Y	Y	Y	Y	Y
15 ***Ritter***	N	N	Y	N	Y	Y	N	N
16 ***Walker***	N	N	Y	N	Y	N	N	Y
17 ***Gekas***	N	N	Y	Y	Y	Y	N	Y
18 Walgren	Y	Y	Y	Y	Y	Y	Y	N
19 ***Goodling***	N	N	Y	Y	Y	Y	?	Y
20 Gaydos	Y	Y	Y	Y	Y	Y	Y	Y
21 ***Ridge***	N	N	Y	N	Y	Y	N	Y
22 Murphy	Y	Y	Y	Y	Y	Y	Y	Y
23 ***Clinger***	N	N	Y	Y	Y	Y	N	Y
RHODE ISLAND								
1 St Germain	Y	Y	Y	Y	Y	Y	Y	N
2 ***Schneider***	Y	N	Y	Y	Y	Y	?	N
SOUTH CAROLINA								
1 ***Hartnett***	?	X	?	X	?	?	?	?
2 ***Spence***	N	N	Y	Y	Y	Y	N	N
3 Derrick	Y	Y	Y	Y	Y	Y	?	Y
4 ***Campbell***	N	N	Y	Y	Y	Y	N	Y
5 Spratt	Y	Y	Y	Y	Y	Y	Y	Y
6 Tallon	?	Y	Y	Y	Y	Y	Y	Y
SOUTH DAKOTA								
AL Daschle	Y	Y	Y	Y	Y	Y	Y	Y

	37	38	39	40	41	42	43	44
TENNESSEE								
1 ***Quillen***	Y	N	Y	Y	Y	Y	Y	Y
2 ***Duncan***	N	N	Y	Y	Y	Y	Y	Y
3 Lloyd	Y	Y	Y	Y	Y	Y	Y	Y
4 Cooper	Y	Y	Y	Y	Y	Y	Y	Y
5 Boner	Y	Y	Y	Y	Y	Y	Y	Y
6 Gordon	Y	Y	Y	Y	Y	Y	Y	Y
7 ***Sundquist***	N	N	Y	N	Y	Y	N	Y
8 Jones	Y	Y	Y	#	+	Y	Y	Y
9 Ford	Y	Y	Y	Y	Y	Y	Y	N
TEXAS								
1 Hall, S.	Y	N	Y	Y	Y	Y	Y	Y
2 Wilson	Y	Y	Y	Y	Y	Y	Y	?
3 ***Bartlett***	N	N	Y	N	Y	Y	N	Y
4 Hall, R.	Y	N	Y	Y	Y	Y	Y	Y
5 Bryant	Y	Y	?	Y	Y	Y	Y	Y
6 ***Barton***	N	N	N	N	Y	N	N	Y
7 ***Archer***	N	N	Y	N	Y	Y	N	Y
8 ***Fields***	N	N	N	N	Y	Y	N	Y
9 Brooks	Y	#	Y	Y	Y	Y	Y	N
10 Pickle	Y	Y	Y	Y	Y	Y	Y	Y
11 Leath	Y	Y	Y	Y	Y	Y	Y	Y
12 Wright	Y	Y	Y	Y	Y	Y	Y	Y
13 ***Boulter***	Y	N	Y	N	Y	Y	N	Y
14 ***Sweeney***	N	N	N	N	Y	Y	N	Y
15 de la Garza	Y	Y	Y	Y	Y	Y	Y	Y
16 Coleman	Y	Y	Y	Y	Y	Y	Y	Y
17 Stenholm	Y	N	Y	Y	Y	Y	Y	Y
18 Leland	Y	Y	Y	Y	Y	Y	Y	Y
19 ***Combest***	N	N	Y	Y	Y	Y	N	Y
20 Gonzalez	Y	Y	Y	Y	Y	Y	Y	N
21 ***Loeffler***	N	N	Y	Y	Y	Y	N	Y
22 ***DeLay***	N	N	N	N	Y	N	N	Y
23 Bustamante	Y	Y	Y	Y	Y	Y	Y	Y
24 Frost	Y	Y	Y	Y	Y	Y	Y	Y
25 Andrews	Y	Y	Y	Y	Y	Y	Y	Y
26 ***Armey***	N	N	N	N	Y	N	N	Y
27 Ortiz	I	Y	I	#	+	+	+	+
UTAH								
1 ***Hansen***	N	N	N	Y	Y	Y	Y	Y
2 ***Monson***	N	N	Y	N	Y	Y	N	Y
3 ***Nielson***	N	N	Y	N	Y	Y	N	Y
VERMONT								
AL ***Jeffords***	?	N	Y	Y	Y	Y	N	Y
VIRGINIA								
1 ***Bateman***	N	N	Y	Y	Y	Y	N	N
2 ***Whitehurst***	N	N	Y	Y	Y	Y	N	N
3 ***Bliley***	?	N	Y	N	Y	Y	N	Y
4 Sisisky	Y	Y	Y	Y	Y	Y	Y	Y
5 Daniel	?	Y	Y	Y	Y	Y	Y	Y
6 Olin	Y	Y	Y	?	?	?	Y	N
7 ***Slaughter***	N	N	Y	N	Y	Y	N	Y
8 ***Parris***	N	N	Y	N	Y	Y	N	N
9 Boucher	Y	Y	Y	Y	Y	Y	Y	Y
10 ***Wolf***	N	N	Y	Y	Y	Y	N	N
WASHINGTON								
1 ***Miller***	N	N	Y	Y	Y	N	N	N
2 Swift	Y	Y	Y	Y	Y	Y	Y	Y
3 Bonker	?	#	+	+	+	+	Y	Y
4 ***Morrison***	N	N	Y	Y	Y	Y	N	Y
5 Foley	Y	Y	Y	Y	Y	Y	Y	Y
6 Dicks	Y	Y	Y	Y	Y	Y	Y	Y
7 Lowry	Y	Y	Y	Y	Y	N	Y	Y
8 ***Chandler***	N	N	Y	Y	Y	Y	N	N
WEST VIRGINIA								
1 Mollohan	Y	Y	Y	Y	Y	Y	Y	Y
2 Staggers	Y	Y	Y	Y	Y	Y	Y	Y
3 Wise	Y	Y	Y	Y	Y	Y	?	Y
4 Rahall	Y	Y	Y	Y	Y	Y	Y	N
WISCONSIN								
1 Aspin	Y	Y	Y	?	?	?	Y	N
2 Kastenmeier	Y	Y	Y	Y	Y	Y	Y	N
3 ***Gunderson***	N	N	Y	Y	Y	Y	N	N
4 Kleczka	Y	Y	Y	Y	Y	Y	Y	N
5 Moody	Y	Y	Y	Y	Y	Y	Y	?
6 ***Petri***	N	N	Y	Y	Y	Y	N	Y
7 Obey	Y	Y	Y	Y	Y	Y	Y	Y
8 ***Roth***	N	N	Y	N	Y	Y	N	Y
9 ***Sensenbrenner***	N	N	Y	N	Y	Y	N	Y
WYOMING								
AL ***Cheney***	?	X	?	N	Y	Y	N	Y

Southern states - Ala., Ark., Fla., Ga., Ky., La., Miss., N.C., Okla., S.C., Tenn., Texas, Va.

* The *Congressional Record* vote number is different from the CQ vote number because the *Record* includes quorum calls in its tally. CQ does not publish quorum call votes.

45. HR 1714. NASA Authorization, Fiscal 1986. Walker, R-Pa., amendment to allow the National Aeronautics and Space Administration to charge higher prices than the bill would have allowed to private companies and foreign countries that use the space shuttle for satellite launches. Adopted 206-201: R 163-11; D 43-190 (ND 30-126, SD 13-64), April 3, 1985.

46. HR 1714. NASA Authorization, Fiscal 1986. Morrison, D-Conn., amendment to freeze spending for the National Aeronautics and Space Administration at the fiscal 1985 level of $7,510,700,000. Adopted 369-36: R 161-12; D 208-24 (ND 137-20, SD 71-4), April 3, 1985. (The Morrison amendment previously had been adopted in the Committee of the Whole by voice vote.)

47. HR 1714. NASA Authorization, Fiscal 1986. Passage of the bill to authorize $7,510,700,000 in fiscal 1986 for the National Aeronautics and Space Administration and $586,000 in fiscal 1986 for the Office of Space Transportation in the Department of Transportation, and to set a pricing policy for the space shuttle. Passed 395-3: R 169-0; D 226-3 (ND 152-3, SD 74-0), April 3, 1985.

KEY

- Y Voted for (yea).
- # Paired for.
- + Announced for.
- N Voted against (nay).
- X Paired against.
- - Announced against.
- P Voted "present".
- C Voted "present" to avoid possible conflict of interest.
- ? Did not vote or otherwise make a position known.

Democrats *Republicans*

	45	46	47
ALABAMA			
1 ***Callahan***	Y	Y	Y
2 ***Dickinson***	N	Y	Y
3 Nichols	N	Y	Y
4 Bevill	N	Y	Y
5 Flippo	N	Y	Y
6 Erdreich	Y	Y	Y
7 Shelby	N	Y	Y
ALASKA			
AL ***Young***	Y	Y	Y
ARIZONA			
1 ***McCain***	Y	Y	Y
2 Udall	N	Y	Y
3 ***Stump***	Y	Y	Y
4 ***Rudd***	?	?	?
5 ***Kolbe***	Y	Y	Y
ARKANSAS			
1 Alexander	?	?	?
2 Robinson	Y	Y	Y
3 ***Hammerschmidt***	Y	Y	Y
4 Anthony	N	Y	Y
CALIFORNIA			
1 Bosco	N	Y	Y
2 ***Chappie***	Y	Y	Y
3 Matsui	N	Y	Y
4 Fazio	N	Y	Y
5 Burton	N	Y	Y
6 Boxer	N	Y	Y
7 Miller	Y	Y	Y
8 Dellums	?	?	?
9 Stark	N	?	Y
10 Edwards	N	Y	Y
11 Lantos	N	Y	Y
12 ***Zschau***	Y	Y	Y
13 Mineta	N	N	Y
14 ***Shumway***	Y	Y	Y
15 Coelho	N	Y	Y
16 Panetta	N	Y	Y
17 ***Pashayan***	Y	Y	Y
18 Lehman	N	Y	Y
19 ***Lagomarsino***	Y	Y	Y
20 ***Thomas***	Y	Y	Y
21 ***Fiedler***	Y	N	Y
22 ***Moorhead***	Y	N	Y
23 Beilenson	Y	Y	Y
24 Waxman	N	N	Y
25 Roybal	N	Y	Y
26 Berman	N	Y	Y
27 Levine	N	N	Y
28 Dixon	?	Y	Y
29 Hawkins	N	N	Y
30 Martinez	N	Y	Y
31 Dymally	N	Y	Y
32 Anderson	N	N	Y
33 ***Dreier***	Y	Y	Y
34 Torres	N	Y	Y
35 ***Lewis***	Y	N	Y
36 Brown	Y	N	Y
37 ***McCandless***	Y	Y	Y
38 ***Dornan***	Y	Y	Y
39 ***Dannemeyer***	Y	Y	Y
40 ***Badham***	Y	Y	Y
41 ***Lowery***	N	N	Y
42 ***Lungren***	Y	Y	Y
43 ***Packard***	Y	Y	Y
44 Bates	N	Y	Y
45 ***Hunter***	Y	Y	Y
COLORADO			
1 Schroeder	?	?	?
2 Wirth	N	Y	Y
3 ***Strang***	Y	Y	Y
4 ***Brown***	Y	Y	Y
5 ***Kramer***	Y	Y	Y
6 ***Schaefer***	Y	Y	Y
CONNECTICUT			
1 Kennelly	N	Y	Y
2 Gejdenson	Y	Y	Y
3 Morrison	N	Y	Y
4 ***McKinney***	N	Y	Y
5 ***Rowland***	Y	Y	Y
6 ***Johnson***	Y	Y	Y
DELAWARE			
AL Carper	Y	Y	Y
FLORIDA			
1 Hutto	N	Y	Y
2 Fuqua	N	Y	Y
3 Bennett	N	Y	Y
4 Chappell	N	Y	Y
5 ***McCollum***	Y	Y	Y
6 MacKay	N	?	?
7 Gibbons	N	Y	Y
8 ***Young***	Y	N	Y
9 ***Bilirakis***	Y	Y	Y
10 ***Ireland***	Y	Y	Y
11 Nelson	N	N	Y
12 ***Lewis***	Y	Y	Y
13 ***Mack***	Y	Y	Y
14 Mica	N	N	Y
15 ***Shaw***	Y	Y	Y
16 Smith	N	Y	Y
17 Lehman	N	Y	Y
18 Pepper	N	N	+
19 Fascell	N	Y	Y
GEORGIA			
1 Thomas	N	Y	Y
2 Hatcher	N	Y	Y
3 Ray	N	Y	Y
4 ***Swindall***	Y	Y	Y
5 Fowler	N	Y	Y
6 ***Gingrich***	Y	Y	Y
7 Darden	N	Y	Y
8 Rowland	N	Y	Y
9 Jenkins	N	Y	Y
10 Barnard	N	Y	Y
HAWAII			
1 Heftel	N	Y	Y
2 Akaka	N	Y	Y
IDAHO			
1 ***Craig***	Y	Y	Y
2 Stallings	N	Y	Y
ILLINOIS			
1 Hayes	N	Y	Y
2 Savage	?	?	?
3 Russo	Y	Y	Y
4 ***O'Brien***	Y	Y	Y
5 Lipinski	?	?	?
6 ***Hyde***	Y	N	Y
7 Collins	N	Y	Y
8 Rostenkowski	N	Y	Y
9 Yates	?	?	?
10 ***Porter***	Y	Y	Y
11 Annunzio	N	Y	Y
12 ***Crane, P.***	Y	Y	Y
13 ***Fawell***	Y	Y	Y
14 ***Grotberg***	Y	Y	Y
15 ***Madigan***	Y	Y	Y
16 ***Martin***	Y	Y	Y
17 Evans	N	Y	Y
18 ***Michel***	Y	Y	Y
19 Bruce	N	Y	Y
20 Durbin	N	Y	Y
21 Price	N	Y	Y
22 Gray	N	Y	Y
INDIANA			
1 Visclosky	Y	Y	Y
2 Sharp	N	Y	Y
3 ***Hiler***	Y	Y	Y
4 ***Coats***	Y	Y	Y
5 ***Hillis***	?	?	?

ND - Northern Democrats SD - Southern Democrats

* Corresponding to Congressional Record Votes 49, 50, 51

	45	46	47
6 ***Burton***	Y	Y	Y
7 ***Myers***	Y	Y	Y
8 Vacancy			
9 Hamilton	N	Y	Y
10 Jacobs	?	?	?
IOWA			
1 ***Leach***	Y	Y	Y
2 ***Tauke***	Y	Y	Y
3 ***Evans***	Y	Y	Y
4 Smith	N	Y	Y
5 ***Lightfoot***	Y	Y	Y
6 Bedell	Y	Y	Y
KANSAS			
1 ***Roberts***	Y	Y	Y
2 Slattery	N	Y	Y
3 ***Meyers***	Y	Y	Y
4 Glickman	N	Y	Y
5 ***Whittaker***	Y	Y	Y
KENTUCKY			
1 Hubbard	Y	Y	Y
2 Natcher	N	Y	Y
3 Mazzoli	Y	Y	Y
4 ***Snyder***	Y	Y	Y
5 ***Rogers***	Y	Y	Y
6 ***Hopkins***	Y	Y	Y
7 Perkins	N	Y	Y
LOUISIANA			
1 ***Livingston***	Y	N	Y
2 Boggs	N	?	Y
3 Tauzin	Y	Y	Y
4 Roemer	Y	Y	Y
5 Huckaby	N	Y	Y
6 ***Moore***	Y	Y	Y
7 Breaux	Y	Y	Y
8 Vacancy			
MAINE			
1 ***McKernan***	Y	Y	Y
2 ***Snowe***	Y	Y	Y
MARYLAND			
1 Dyson	Y	Y	Y
2 ***Bentley***	Y	?	?
3 Mikulski	N	Y	Y
4 ***Holt***	Y	N	Y
5 Hoyer	N	Y	Y
6 Byron	N	Y	Y
7 Mitchell	?	?	?
8 Barnes	N	N	Y
MASSACHUSETTS			
1 ***Conte***	Y	Y	Y
2 Boland	N	N	Y
3 Early	N	N	Y
4 Frank	Y	Y	Y
5 Atkins	N	Y	Y
6 Mavroules	N	Y	Y
7 Markey	N	N	Y
8 O'Neill			
9 Moakley	N	Y	Y
10 Studds	Y	Y	Y
11 Donnelly	N	N	Y
MICHIGAN			
1 Conyers	N	N	N
2 ***Pursell***	Y	Y	Y
3 Wolpe	Y	Y	Y
4 ***Siljander***	Y	Y	Y
5 ***Henry***	Y	Y	Y
6 Carr	N	Y	Y
7 Kildee	N	N	Y
8 Traxler	N	Y	Y
9 ***Vander Jagt***	Y	Y	Y
10 ***Schuette***	Y	Y	Y
11 ***Davis***	Y	Y	Y
12 Bonior	N	Y	Y
13 Crockett	?	?	?
14 Hertel	N	Y	Y
15 Ford	N	Y	Y
16 Dingell	N	Y	Y
17 Levin	N	Y	Y
18 ***Broomfield***	Y	Y	Y
MINNESOTA			
1 Penny	Y	Y	Y
2 ***Weber***	Y	Y	Y
3 ***Frenzel***	Y	Y	Y
4 Vento	N	Y	Y
5 Sabo	N	Y	Y
6 Sikorski	N	Y	Y
7 ***Stangeland***	Y	Y	Y
8 Oberstar	Y	Y	Y
MISSISSIPPI			
1 Whitten	N	Y	Y
2 ***Franklin***	Y	Y	Y
3 Montgomery	N	Y	Y
4 Dowdy	N	Y	Y
5 ***Lott***	Y	Y	Y
MISSOURI			
1 Clay	N	N	Y
2 Young	N	Y	Y
3 Gephardt	N	Y	Y
4 Skelton	N	Y	Y
5 Wheat	N	Y	Y
6 ***Coleman***	Y	Y	Y
7 ***Taylor***	Y	Y	Y
8 ***Emerson***	Y	Y	Y
9 Volkmer	N	Y	Y
MONTANA			
1 Williams	?	N	Y
2 ***Marlenee***	?	Y	Y
NEBRASKA			
1 ***Bereuter***	Y	Y	Y
2 ***Daub***	Y	Y	Y
3 ***Smith***	Y	Y	Y
NEVADA			
1 Reid	Y	Y	Y
2 ***Vucanovich***	Y	Y	Y
NEW HAMPSHIRE			
1 ***Smith***	Y	Y	Y
2 ***Gregg***	Y	Y	Y
NEW JERSEY			
1 Florio	N	Y	Y
2 Hughes	Y	Y	Y
3 Howard	N	N	Y
4 ***Smith***	N	Y	Y
5 ***Roukema***	Y	Y	Y
6 Dwyer	N	Y	Y
7 ***Rinaldo***	Y	Y	Y
8 Roe	N	Y	Y
9 Torricelli	N	Y	Y
10 Rodino	N	Y	Y
11 ***Gallo***	Y	Y	Y
12 ***Courter***	?	?	?
13 ***Saxton***	Y	Y	Y
14 Guarini	N	Y	Y
NEW MEXICO			
1 ***Lujan***	Y	Y	Y
2 ***Skeen***	Y	Y	Y
3 Richardson	N	Y	Y
NEW YORK			
1 ***Carney***	Y	Y	Y
2 Downey	N	Y	Y
3 Mrazek	N	Y	Y
4 ***Lent***	Y	Y	Y
5 ***McGrath***	N	Y	Y
6 Addabbo	N	Y	Y
7 Ackerman	N	Y	Y
8 Scheuer	N	Y	Y
9 Manton	N	Y	Y
10 Schumer	Y	Y	Y
11 Towns	N	Y	Y
12 Owens	N	Y	Y
13 Solarz	N	Y	Y
14 ***Molinari***	N	Y	Y
15 ***Green***	N	N	Y
16 Rangel	N	Y	Y
17 Weiss	N	Y	Y
18 Garcia	N	N	Y
19 Biaggi	N	Y	Y
20 ***DioGuardi***	Y	Y	Y
21 ***Fish***	N	Y	?
22 ***Gilman***	Y	Y	Y
23 Stratton	N	Y	Y
24 ***Solomon***	Y	Y	Y
25 ***Boehlert***	Y	Y	Y
26 ***Martin***	Y	Y	Y
27 ***Wortley***	Y	Y	Y
28 McHugh	N	Y	Y
29 ***Horton***	?	?	?
30 ***Eckert***	Y	Y	Y
31 ***Kemp***	Y	N	Y
32 LaFalce	Y	Y	Y
33 Nowak	N	Y	Y
34 Lundine	?	?	?
NORTH CAROLINA			
1 Jones	N	Y	Y
2 Valentine	N	Y	Y
3 Whitley	N	Y	Y
4 ***Cobey***	Y	Y	Y
5 Neal	N	Y	Y
6 ***Coble***	Y	Y	Y
7 Rose	N	Y	Y
8 Hefner	N	Y	Y
9 ***McMillan***	Y	Y	Y
10 ***Broyhill***	Y	Y	Y
11 ***Hendon***	Y	Y	Y
NORTH DAKOTA			
AL Dorgan	N	Y	Y
OHIO			
1 Luken	?	?	?
2 ***Gradison***	Y	Y	Y
3 Hall	N	Y	?
4 ***Oxley***	Y	Y	Y
5 ***Latta***	?	?	?
6 ***McEwen***	N	Y	Y
7 ***DeWine***	Y	N	Y
8 ***Kindness***	Y	Y	Y
9 Kaptur	N	Y	Y
10 ***Miller***	Y	Y	Y
11 Eckart	N	Y	Y
12 ***Kasich***	Y	Y	Y
13 Pease	N	Y	Y
14 Seiberling	N	Y	Y
15 ***Wylie***	Y	Y	Y
16 ***Regula***	Y	Y	Y
17 Traficant	N	Y	Y
18 Applegate	N	Y	?
19 Feighan	Y	Y	Y
20 Oakar	N	N	Y
21 Stokes	N	N	Y
OKLAHOMA			
1 Jones	N	Y	Y
2 Synar	N	Y	Y
3 Watkins	N	Y	Y
4 McCurdy	N	Y	?
5 ***Edwards***	Y	Y	Y
6 English	N	Y	Y
OREGON			
1 AuCoin	N	Y	Y
2 ***Smith, R.***	Y	Y	Y
3 Wyden	Y	Y	Y
4 Weaver	Y	Y	N
5 ***Smith, D.***	Y	Y	Y
PENNSYLVANIA			
1 Foglietta	N	Y	Y
2 Gray	N	Y	Y
3 Borski	N	Y	Y
4 Kolter	?	?	?
5 ***Schulze***	?	?	?
6 Yatron	Y	Y	Y
7 Edgar	N	Y	?
8 Kostmayer	Y	Y	Y
9 ***Shuster***	Y	Y	Y
10 ***McDade***	N	Y	Y
11 Kanjorski	N	Y	Y
12 Murtha	N	Y	Y
13 ***Coughlin***	Y	Y	Y
14 Coyne	N	N	Y
15 ***Ritter***	Y	Y	Y
16 ***Walker***	Y	Y	Y
17 ***Gekas***	Y	Y	Y
18 Walgren	N	Y	Y
19 ***Goodling***	Y	Y	?
20 Gaydos	Y	Y	Y
21 ***Ridge***	Y	Y	Y
22 Murphy	Y	Y	Y
23 ***Clinger***	Y	Y	Y
RHODE ISLAND			
1 St Germain	N	Y	Y
2 ***Schneider***	Y	Y	Y
SOUTH CAROLINA			
1 ***Hartnett***	?	?	?
2 ***Spence***	Y	Y	Y
3 Derrick	N	Y	Y
4 ***Campbell***	Y	Y	?
5 Spratt	N	Y	Y
6 Tallon	Y	Y	Y
SOUTH DAKOTA			
AL Daschle	N	Y	Y
TENNESSEE			
1 ***Quillen***	Y	?	?
2 ***Duncan***	Y	Y	Y
3 Lloyd	N	Y	Y
4 Cooper	N	Y	Y
5 Boner	N	Y	Y
6 Gordon	N	Y	Y
7 ***Sundquist***	Y	Y	Y
8 Jones	N	Y	Y
9 Ford	N	Y	Y
TEXAS			
1 Hall, S.	Y	Y	Y
2 Wilson	?	?	?
3 ***Bartlett***	Y	Y	Y
4 Hall, R.	N	Y	Y
5 Bryant	N	Y	Y
6 ***Barton***	Y	Y	Y
7 ***Archer***	Y	Y	Y
8 ***Fields***	Y	Y	Y
9 Brooks	N	Y	Y
10 Pickle	N	Y	Y
11 Leath	N	Y	Y
12 Wright	?	?	?
13 ***Boulter***	Y	Y	Y
14 ***Sweeney***	Y	Y	Y
15 de la Garza	N	Y	Y
16 Coleman	Y	Y	Y
17 Stenholm	Y	Y	Y
18 Leland	N	Y	Y
19 ***Combest***	Y	Y	Y
20 Gonzalez	N	N	Y
21 ***Loeffler***	Y	Y	Y
22 ***DeLay***	Y	Y	Y
23 Bustamante	N	Y	Y
24 Frost	N	Y	Y
25 Andrews	N	Y	Y
26 ***Armey***	Y	N	Y
27 Ortiz	-	+	+
UTAH			
1 ***Hansen***	Y	Y	Y
2 ***Monson***	Y	Y	Y
3 ***Nielson***	Y	Y	Y
VERMONT			
AL ***Jeffords***	N	Y	Y
VIRGINIA			
1 ***Bateman***	Y	Y	Y
2 ***Whitehurst***	Y	Y	Y
3 ***Bliley***	Y	Y	Y
4 Sisisky	N	Y	Y
5 Daniel	Y	Y	Y
6 Olin	Y	Y	Y
7 ***Slaughter***	Y	Y	Y
8 ***Parris***	Y	Y	Y
9 Boucher	N	Y	Y
10 ***Wolf***	Y	Y	Y
WASHINGTON			
1 ***Miller***	Y	Y	Y
2 Swift	N	Y	Y
3 Bonker	N	Y	Y
4 ***Morrison***	Y	Y	Y
5 Foley	N	Y	Y
6 Dicks	N	Y	Y
7 Lowry	Y	Y	Y
8 ***Chandler***	Y	Y	Y
WEST VIRGINIA			
1 Mollohan	N	Y	Y
2 Staggers	N	Y	Y
3 Wise	Y	Y	Y
4 Rahall	N	Y	N
WISCONSIN			
1 Aspin	Y	Y	Y
2 Kastenmeier	N	Y	Y
3 ***Gunderson***	Y	Y	Y
4 Kleczka	N	Y	Y
5 Moody	Y	Y	Y
6 ***Petri***	Y	Y	Y
7 Obey	Y	Y	Y
8 ***Roth***	Y	Y	?
9 ***Sensenbrenner***	Y	Y	Y
WYOMING			
AL ***Cheney***	Y	Y	Y

Southern states - Ala., Ark., Fla., Ga., Ky., La., Miss., N.C., Okla., S.C., Tenn., Texas, Va.

* The *Congressional Record* vote number is different from the CQ vote number because the *Record* includes quorum calls in its tally. CQ does not publish quorum call votes.

48. S J Res 15. Helsinki Human Rights Day. Fascell, D-Fla., motion to suspend the rules and pass the joint resolution to designate May 7, 1985, as "Helsinki Human Rights Day," and to request the president to raise the issue of Soviet and East European human rights violations at every available opportunity. Motion agreed to 390-0: R 168-0; D 222-0 (ND 146-0, SD 76-0), April 16, 1985. A two-thirds majority of those present and voting (260 in this case) is required for passage under suspension of the rules.

49. H Con Res 110. Extradition of Accused Taiwanese. Solarz, D-N.Y., motion to suspend the rules and adopt the concurrent resolution to express the sense of Congress that Taiwan should cooperate in the extradition of any Taiwanese involved in the murder of Henry Liu, a U.S. citizen of Chinese descent, killed in California in 1984. Motion agreed to 387-2: R 166-2; D 221-0 (ND 147-0, SD 74-0), April 16, 1985. A two-thirds majority of those present and voting (260 in this case) is required for passage under suspension of the rules.

50. HR 1210. National Science Foundation Authorization, Fiscal 1986. Walker, R-Pa., amendment to limit authorized spending for the National Science Foundation to the fiscal 1985 level of $1.5 billion. Adopted 407-4: R 179-0; D 228-4 (ND 151-4, SD 77-0), April 17, 1985. (The amendment earlier had been modified by a Science and Technology Committee substitute that adjusted spending priorities for the foundation but kept spending within the $1.5 billion ceiling. The bill subsequently was passed by voice vote.)

51. HR 1617. National Bureau of Standards Authorization, Fiscal 1986. Walker, R-Pa., amendment to the Walgren, D-Pa., amendment to reduce the authorization level for the agency from $127.8 million to $122.6 million, the amount requested by President Reagan. Rejected 196-201: R 157-15; D 39-186 (ND 19-133, SD 20-53), April 18, 1985. (The Walgren amendment was subsequently adopted *(see vote 52, below)*.)

52. HR 1617. National Bureau of Standards Authorization, Fiscal 1986. Walgren, D-Pa., amendment to freeze funding for the agency at the fiscal 1985 level of $127.8 million. Adopted 398-2: R 170-1; D 228-1 (ND 154-1, SD 74-0), April 18, 1985.

53. HR 1617. National Bureau of Standards Authorization, Fiscal 1986. Passage of the bill to authorize $127.8 million in fiscal 1986 for the National Bureau of Standards, the Office of Productivity, Technology and Innovation, and the National Technical Information Services. Passed 282-103: R 68-98; D 214-5 (ND 145-2, SD 69-3), April 18, 1985.

KEY

- Y Voted for (yea).
- # Paired for.
- + Announced for.
- N Voted against (nay).
- X Paired against.
- \- Announced against.
- P Voted "present".
- C Voted "present" to avoid possible conflict of interest.
- ? Did not vote or otherwise make a position known.

Democrats ***Republicans***

	48	49	50	51	52	53
ALABAMA						
1 ***Callahan***	Y	Y	Y	Y	Y	N
2 ***Dickinson***	Y	Y	Y	Y	Y	N
3 Nichols	Y	Y	Y	Y	Y	Y
4 Bevill	Y	Y	Y	N	Y	Y
5 Flippo	Y	Y	Y	N	Y	Y
6 Erdreich	Y	Y	Y	N	Y	Y
7 Shelby	Y	Y	Y	N	Y	Y
ALASKA						
AL ***Young***	Y	Y	Y	Y	Y	Y
ARIZONA						
1 ***McCain***	Y	Y	Y	Y	Y	N
2 Udall	Y	Y	Y	N	Y	Y
3 ***Stump***	Y	N	Y	Y	Y	N
4 ***Rudd***	Y	Y	Y	Y	Y	X
5 ***Kolbe***	Y	Y	Y	Y	Y	N
ARKANSAS						
1 Alexander	Y	?	Y	N	Y	Y
2 Robinson	Y	?	Y	?	?	?
3 ***Hammerschmidt***	Y	Y	Y	Y	Y	N
4 Anthony	Y	Y	Y	N	Y	Y
CALIFORNIA						
1 Bosco	Y	Y	Y	Y	Y	Y
2 ***Chappie***	Y	Y	Y	Y	Y	N
3 Matsui	Y	Y	Y	N	Y	Y
4 Fazio	+	+	Y	N	Y	Y
5 Burton	Y	Y	Y	N	Y	Y
6 Boxer	Y	Y	Y	N	Y	Y
7 Miller	?	?	Y	N	Y	Y
8 Dellums	Y	Y	Y	N	Y	Y
9 Stark	Y	Y	?	N	Y	Y
10 Edwards	Y	Y	Y	N	Y	Y
11 Lantos	Y	Y	Y	N	Y	Y
12 ***Zschau***	Y	Y	Y	Y	Y	N
13 Mineta	Y	Y	Y	N	Y	Y
14 ***Shumway***	Y	Y	Y	Y	Y	N
15 Coelho	Y	Y	Y	N	Y	Y
16 Panetta	Y	Y	Y	N	Y	?
17 ***Pashayan***	Y	Y	Y	Y	Y	Y
18 Lehman	Y	Y	Y	N	Y	Y
19 ***Lagomarsino***	Y	Y	Y	Y	Y	N
20 ***Thomas***	Y	Y	Y	?	?	?
21 ***Fiedler***	Y	Y	Y	Y	Y	N
22 ***Moorhead***	Y	Y	Y	Y	Y	N
23 Beilenson	Y	Y	Y	N	Y	Y
24 Waxman	?	?	Y	?	Y	Y
25 Roybal	Y	Y	Y	N	Y	Y
26 Berman	Y	Y	Y	N	Y	Y
27 Levine	Y	Y	Y	N	Y	Y
28 Dixon	?	?	Y	N	Y	?
29 Hawkins	Y	Y	Y	X	?	#
30 Martinez	Y	Y	Y	N	Y	Y
31 Dymally	Y	Y	Y	N	Y	Y
32 Anderson	Y	Y	Y	N	Y	Y
33 ***Dreier***	Y	Y	Y	Y	Y	N
34 Torres	Y	Y	Y	N	Y	Y
35 ***Lewis***	Y	Y	Y	Y	Y	N
36 Brown	Y	Y	Y	N	Y	N
37 ***McCandless***	Y	Y	Y	Y	Y	N
38 ***Dornan***	Y	Y	Y	Y	Y	N
39 ***Dannemeyer***	Y	Y	Y	Y	Y	N
40 ***Badham***	Y	Y	Y	Y	Y	N
41 ***Lowery***	Y	Y	Y	Y	Y	N
42 ***Lungren***	Y	Y	Y	Y	Y	N
43 ***Packard***	Y	Y	Y	Y	Y	Y
44 Bates	Y	Y	Y	Y	Y	?
45 ***Hunter***	Y	Y	Y	Y	Y	N
COLORADO						
1 Schroeder	Y	Y	Y	Y	Y	Y
2 Wirth	Y	Y	Y	N	Y	Y
3 ***Strang***	Y	Y	Y	Y	Y	N
4 ***Brown***	Y	Y	Y	Y	Y	N
5 ***Kramer***	Y	Y	Y	Y	Y	Y
6 ***Schaefer***	Y	Y	Y	Y	Y	N
CONNECTICUT						
1 Kennelly	Y	Y	Y	N	Y	Y
2 Gejdenson	Y	Y	Y	N	Y	Y
3 Morrison	Y	Y	Y	N	Y	Y
4 ***McKinney***	Y	Y	Y	N	Y	Y
5 ***Rowland***	Y	Y	Y	Y	Y	Y
6 ***Johnson***	Y	Y	Y	Y	Y	Y
DELAWARE						
AL Carper	Y	Y	Y	N	Y	Y
FLORIDA						
1 Hutto	Y	Y	Y	N	Y	Y
2 Fuqua	Y	Y	Y	N	Y	Y
3 Bennett	Y	Y	Y	Y	Y	Y
4 Chappell	Y	Y	Y	Y	Y	Y
5 ***McCollum***	Y	Y	Y	Y	Y	N
6 MacKay	Y	Y	Y	N	Y	Y
7 Gibbons	Y	Y	Y	Y	Y	Y
8 ***Young***	Y	Y	?	Y	Y	N
9 ***Bilirakis***	?	?	Y	Y	Y	N
10 ***Ireland***	Y	Y	Y	Y	Y	Y
11 Nelson	Y	Y	Y	N	Y	Y
12 ***Lewis***	Y	Y	Y	Y	Y	Y
13 ***Mack***	Y	Y	Y	Y	Y	N
14 Mica	Y	Y	Y	N	Y	Y
15 ***Shaw***	Y	Y	Y	Y	Y	N
16 Smith	?	?	Y	N	Y	Y
17 Lehman	Y	Y	Y	N	Y	Y
18 Pepper	Y	Y	+	N	Y	Y
19 Fascell	Y	Y	Y	N	Y	Y
GEORGIA						
1 Thomas	Y	Y	Y	N	Y	Y
2 Hatcher	Y	Y	Y	N	Y	Y
3 Ray	Y	Y	Y	Y	Y	Y
4 ***Swindall***	+	+	Y	Y	Y	N
5 Fowler	Y	Y	Y	N	Y	Y
6 ***Gingrich***	Y	Y	Y	Y	Y	N
7 Darden	Y	Y	Y	Y	Y	Y
8 Rowland	Y	Y	Y	N	Y	Y
9 Jenkins	Y	Y	Y	Y	Y	Y
10 Barnard	Y	Y	Y	Y	Y	Y
HAWAII						
1 Heftel	?	?	Y	Y	Y	Y
2 Akaka	Y	Y	Y	N	Y	Y
IDAHO						
1 ***Craig***	Y	Y	Y	Y	Y	N
2 Stallings	Y	Y	Y	?	?	?
ILLINOIS						
1 Hayes	Y	Y	Y	N	Y	Y
2 Savage	Y	Y	?	?	?	?
3 Russo	?	?	Y	N	Y	Y
4 ***O'Brien***	Y	Y	Y	N	Y	Y
5 Lipinski	Y	Y	Y	N	Y	Y
6 ***Hyde***	Y	Y	Y	Y	Y	Y
7 Collins	?	?	Y	N	Y	Y
8 Rostenkowski	?	?	Y	N	Y	Y
9 Yates	Y	Y	Y	N	Y	Y
10 ***Porter***	Y	Y	Y	Y	Y	Y
11 Annunzio	Y	Y	Y	N	Y	Y
12 ***Crane***	Y	Y	Y	Y	?	X
13 ***Fawell***	Y	Y	Y	Y	Y	Y
14 ***Grotberg***	+	+	+	Y	Y	N
15 ***Madigan***	Y	Y	Y	Y	Y	N
16 ***Martin***	Y	Y	Y	Y	Y	N
17 Evans	Y	Y	Y	N	Y	Y
18 ***Michel***	?	?	Y	Y	Y	N
19 Bruce	Y	Y	Y	N	Y	Y
20 Durbin	Y	Y	Y	N	Y	Y
21 Price	Y	Y	Y	N	Y	Y
22 Gray	Y	Y	Y	N	Y	Y
INDIANA						
1 Visclosky	Y	Y	Y	N	Y	Y
2 Sharp	Y	Y	Y	N	Y	Y
3 ***Hiler***	Y	Y	Y	Y	Y	N
4 ***Coats***	Y	Y	Y	Y	Y	N
5 ***Hillis***	Y	Y	Y	Y	Y	N

ND - Northern Democrats SD - Southern Democrats

* Corresponding to Congressional Record Votes 52, 53, 54, 56, 57, 58

	48	49	50	51	52	53
6 ***Burton***	Y	Y	Y	Y	Y	N
7 ***Myers***	Y	Y	Y	Y	Y	?
8 Vacancy						
9 Hamilton	Y	Y	Y	N	Y	Y
10 Jacobs	Y	Y	Y	N	Y	Y
IOWA						
1 ***Leach***	Y	Y	Y	Y	Y	Y
2 ***Tauke***	Y	Y	Y	Y	Y	Y
3 ***Evans***	Y	Y	Y	Y	Y	Y
4 Smith	Y	Y	Y	Y	Y	Y
5 ***Lightfoot***	Y	Y	Y	Y	Y	Y
6 Bedell	Y	Y	Y	N	Y	Y
KANSAS						
1 ***Roberts***	Y	Y	Y	Y	Y	N
2 Slattery	Y	Y	Y	Y	Y	Y
3 ***Meyers***	Y	Y	Y	Y	Y	?
4 Glickman	Y	Y	Y	?	?	?
5 ***Whittaker***	Y	Y	Y	Y	Y	N
KENTUCKY						
1 Hubbard	Y	Y	Y	Y	Y	N
2 Natcher	Y	Y	Y	N	Y	Y
3 Mazzoli	Y	Y	Y	Y	Y	Y
4 ***Snyder***	Y	Y	Y	Y	Y	N
5 ***Rogers***	Y	Y	Y	Y	Y	N
6 ***Hopkins***	Y	Y	Y	Y	Y	N
7 Perkins	Y	Y	Y	N	Y	Y
LOUISIANA						
1 ***Livingston***	Y	Y	Y	Y	Y	Y
2 Boggs	Y	Y	Y	?	?	?
3 Tauzin	Y	Y	Y	?	Y	Y
4 Roemer	Y	Y	Y	Y	Y	Y
5 Huckaby	Y	Y	Y	Y	Y	Y
6 ***Moore***	Y	Y	Y	Y	Y	Y
7 Breaux	Y	Y	Y	Y	Y	Y
8 Long*	Y	Y	Y	N	Y	Y
MAINE						
1 ***McKernan***	?	?	Y	N	Y	Y
2 ***Snowe***	Y	Y	Y	N	Y	Y
MARYLAND						
1 Dyson	Y	Y	Y	N	Y	Y
2 ***Bentley***	Y	Y	Y	Y	Y	Y
3 Mikulski	Y	Y	Y	N	Y	Y
4 ***Holt***	?	?	Y	Y	Y	Y
5 Hoyer	Y	Y	Y	N	Y	Y
6 Byron	Y	Y	Y	N	Y	Y
7 Mitchell	Y	Y	Y	N	Y	Y
8 Barnes	Y	Y	Y	N	Y	Y
MASSACHUSETTS						
1 ***Conte***	?	?	Y	N	Y	Y
2 Boland	?	?	Y	N	Y	?
3 Early	Y	Y	N	?	?	?
4 Frank	Y	Y	Y	N	Y	Y
5 Atkins	Y	Y	Y	N	Y	Y
6 Mavroules	Y	Y	Y	N	Y	Y
7 Markey	?	?	Y	N	Y	Y
8 O'Neill						
9 Moakley	Y	Y	Y	N	Y	Y
10 Studds	Y	Y	Y	N	Y	Y
11 Donnelly	Y	Y	Y	N	Y	Y
MICHIGAN						
1 Conyers	Y	Y	Y	?	?	?
2 ***Pursell***	Y	Y	Y	N	Y	Y
3 Wolpe	Y	Y	Y	Y	Y	Y
4 ***Siljander***	Y	Y	Y	Y	Y	N
5 ***Henry***	Y	Y	Y	N	Y	Y
6 Carr	Y	Y	Y	Y	Y	Y
7 Kildee	Y	Y	Y	N	Y	Y
8 Traxler	Y	Y	Y	?	?	?
9 ***Vander Jagt***	Y	Y	Y	Y	Y	Y
10 ***Schuette***	Y	Y	Y	Y	Y	N
11 ***Davis***	Y	Y	Y	Y	Y	Y
12 Bonior	Y	Y	Y	N	Y	Y
13 Crockett	Y	Y	Y	N	Y	Y
14 Hertel	Y	Y	Y	N	Y	Y
15 Ford	?	?	?	X	?	#
16 Dingell	Y	Y	?	N	Y	Y
17 Levin	Y	Y	Y	N	Y	Y
18 ***Broomfield***	Y	Y	Y	Y	Y	N
MINNESOTA						
1 Penny	Y	Y	Y	Y	Y	N
2 ***Weber***	Y	Y	Y	Y	Y	N
3 ***Frenzel***	Y	Y	Y	Y	N	N
4 Vento	Y	Y	Y	N	Y	Y
5 Sabo	Y	Y	Y	N	Y	Y
6 Sikorski	Y	Y	Y	Y	Y	Y
7 ***Stangeland***	Y	Y	Y	Y	Y	N
8 Oberstar	Y	Y	Y	N	Y	Y
MISSISSIPPI						
1 Whitten	Y	Y	Y	N	Y	Y
2 ***Franklin***	Y	Y	Y	Y	Y	N
3 Montgomery	Y	Y	Y	?	?	?
4 Dowdy	?	?	Y	N	Y	Y
5 ***Lott***	Y	Y	Y	Y	Y	N
MISSOURI						
1 Clay	Y	Y	Y	?	?	?
2 Young	?	?	Y	N	Y	Y
3 Gephardt	Y	Y	Y	N	Y	Y
4 Skelton	Y	Y	Y	N	Y	Y
5 Wheat	Y	Y	Y	N	Y	Y
6 ***Coleman***	?	?	Y	Y	Y	Y
7 ***Taylor***	Y	Y	Y	Y	Y	N
8 ***Emerson***	Y	Y	Y	N	Y	Y
9 Volkmer	Y	Y	Y	N	Y	Y
MONTANA						
1 Williams	Y	Y	N	N	N	Y
2 ***Marlenee***	Y	Y	Y	Y	Y	Y
NEBRASKA						
1 ***Bereuter***	Y	Y	Y	N	Y	Y
2 ***Daub***	Y	Y	Y	Y	Y	N
3 ***Smith***	Y	Y	Y	Y	Y	Y
NEVADA						
1 Reid	Y	Y	Y	N	Y	Y
2 ***Vucanovich***	Y	Y	Y	Y	Y	N
NEW HAMPSHIRE						
1 ***Smith***	Y	Y	Y	Y	Y	N
2 ***Gregg***	Y	Y	Y	?	?	?
NEW JERSEY						
1 Florio	Y	Y	Y	N	Y	Y
2 Hughes	Y	Y	Y	Y	Y	Y
3 Howard	Y	Y	Y	N	Y	Y
4 ***Smith***	Y	Y	Y	Y	Y	Y
5 ***Roukema***	Y	Y	Y	Y	Y	Y
6 Dwyer	Y	Y	Y	N	Y	Y
7 ***Rinaldo***	?	?	Y	Y	Y	Y
8 Roe	Y	Y	Y	N	Y	Y
9 Torricelli	Y	Y	Y	N	Y	Y
10 Rodino	Y	Y	Y	N	Y	Y
11 ***Gallo***	Y	Y	Y	Y	Y	Y
12 ***Courter***	Y	Y	Y	Y	Y	N
13 ***Saxton***	Y	Y	Y	Y	Y	Y
14 Guarini	?	?	Y	N	Y	Y
NEW MEXICO						
1 ***Lujan***	Y	Y	Y	Y	Y	Y
2 ***Skeen***	Y	Y	Y	Y	Y	N
3 Richardson	Y	Y	Y	N	Y	Y
NEW YORK						
1 ***Carney***	Y	Y	Y	Y	Y	Y
2 Downey	Y	Y	Y	N	Y	Y
3 Mrazek	Y	Y	Y	N	Y	Y
4 ***Lent***	Y	Y	Y	Y	Y	Y
5 ***McGrath***	Y	Y	Y	Y	Y	Y
6 Addabbo	Y	Y	Y	N	Y	Y
7 Ackerman	?	?	?	?	?	?
8 Scheuer	Y	Y	Y	N	Y	Y
9 Manton	?	Y	Y	N	Y	Y
10 Schumer	Y	Y	Y	N	Y	Y
11 Towns	Y	Y	?	N	Y	?
12 Owens	Y	Y	Y	N	Y	Y
13 Solarz	Y	Y	Y	N	Y	Y
14 ***Molinari***	Y	Y	Y	Y	Y	N
15 ***Green***	Y	Y	Y	N	Y	Y
16 Rangel	?	?	Y	N	Y	Y
17 Weiss	Y	Y	Y	N	Y	Y
18 Garcia	Y	Y	Y	N	Y	Y
19 Biaggi	Y	Y	Y	N	Y	Y
20 ***DioGuardi***	Y	Y	Y	Y	Y	Y
21 ***Fish***	Y	Y	Y	Y	Y	Y
22 ***Gilman***	Y	Y	Y	Y	Y	Y
23 Stratton	Y	Y	Y	Y	Y	Y
24 ***Solomon***	Y	Y	Y	#	?	?
25 ***Boehlert***	Y	Y	Y	N	Y	Y
26 ***Martin***	Y	Y	Y	Y	Y	Y
27 ***Wortley***	Y	Y	Y	Y	Y	?
28 McHugh	Y	Y	Y	N	Y	Y
29 ***Horton***	Y	Y	Y	#	?	?
30 ***Eckert***	Y	Y	Y	Y	Y	Y
31 ***Kemp***	Y	Y	Y	Y	Y	N
32 LaFalce	Y	Y	Y	Y	Y	Y
33 Nowak	Y	Y	Y	N	Y	Y
34 Lundine	Y	Y	Y	N	Y	Y
NORTH CAROLINA						
1 Jones	Y	Y	?	?	?	?
2 Valentine	Y	Y	Y	N	Y	Y
3 Whitley	Y	Y	Y	N	Y	Y
4 ***Cobey***	Y	Y	Y	Y	Y	N
5 Neal	Y	Y	Y	N	Y	Y
6 ***Coble***	Y	Y	Y	Y	Y	N
7 Rose	Y	Y	Y	N	Y	?
8 Hefner	Y	Y	Y	N	Y	Y
9 ***McMillan***	Y	Y	Y	Y	Y	N
10 ***Broyhill***	Y	Y	Y	Y	Y	?
11 ***Hendon***	Y	Y	Y	Y	Y	Y
NORTH DAKOTA						
AL Dorgan	?	?	?	?	?	?
OHIO						
1 Luken	Y	Y	Y	N	Y	Y
2 ***Gradison***	Y	Y	Y	Y	Y	Y
3 Hall	Y	Y	Y	Y	Y	Y
4 ***Oxley***	+	+	Y	Y	Y	Y
5 ***Latta***	?	?	Y	Y	Y	N
6 ***McEwen***	Y	Y	Y	Y	Y	N
7 ***DeWine***	Y	Y	Y	Y	Y	N
8 ***Kindness***	Y	Y	Y	Y	Y	N
9 Kaptur	Y	Y	Y	N	Y	Y
10 ***Miller***	Y	Y	Y	Y	Y	N
11 Eckart	Y	Y	?	N	Y	Y
12 ***Kasich***	Y	Y	Y	Y	Y	N
13 Pease	Y	Y	Y	N	Y	Y
14 Seiberling	?	?	?	?	?	?
15 ***Wylie***	Y	Y	Y	?	?	?
16 ***Regula***	?	?	Y	Y	Y	Y
17 Traficant	?	?	?	?	?	?
18 Applegate	Y	Y	Y	Y	Y	Y
19 Feighan	Y	Y	Y	N	Y	Y
20 Oakar	Y	Y	Y	N	Y	Y
21 Stokes	Y	Y	Y	N	Y	Y
OKLAHOMA						
1 Jones	Y	Y	Y	N	Y	Y
2 Synar	Y	Y	Y	N	Y	Y
3 Watkins	Y	Y	Y	N	Y	Y
4 McCurdy	Y	Y	Y	?	?	?
5 ***Edwards***	Y	Y	Y	Y	Y	N
6 English	Y	Y	Y	Y	Y	Y
OREGON						
1 AuCoin	Y	Y	Y	Y	Y	Y
2 ***Smith, R.***	Y	Y	Y	Y	Y	Y
3 Wyden	Y	Y	Y	N	Y	Y
4 Weaver	?	?	Y	Y	Y	?
5 ***Smith, D.***	Y	Y	Y	Y	Y	N
PENNSYLVANIA						
1 Foglietta	Y	Y	?	N	Y	Y
2 Gray	Y	Y	Y	?	Y	Y
3 Borski	Y	Y	Y	N	Y	Y
4 Kolter	Y	Y	Y	N	Y	?
5 ***Schulze***	Y	Y	Y	?	?	?
6 Yatron	Y	Y	Y	N	Y	Y
7 Edgar	+	+	Y	N	Y	Y
8 Kostmayer	Y	Y	Y	N	Y	Y
9 ***Shuster***	Y	Y	Y	Y	Y	N
10 ***McDade***	?	?	Y	Y	Y	Y
11 Kanjorski	Y	Y	Y	Y	Y	Y
12 Murtha	?	?	Y	N	Y	Y
13 ***Coughlin***	Y	Y	Y	Y	Y	Y
14 Coyne	Y	Y	Y	N	Y	Y
15 ***Ritter***	Y	Y	Y	N	Y	Y
16 ***Walker***	Y	Y	Y	Y	Y	N
17 ***Gekas***	Y	Y	Y	Y	Y	N
18 Walgren	Y	Y	Y	N	Y	Y
19 ***Goodling***	Y	Y	Y	Y	Y	N
20 Gaydos	Y	Y	Y	N	Y	Y
21 ***Ridge***	Y	Y	Y	N	Y	Y
22 Murphy	Y	Y	Y	N	Y	Y
23 ***Clinger***	Y	Y	Y	+	+	-
RHODE ISLAND						
1 St Germain	Y	Y	N	N	Y	?
2 ***Schneider***	Y	Y	Y	N	Y	Y
SOUTH CAROLINA						
1 ***Hartnett***	Y	Y	Y	Y	Y	N
2 ***Spence***	Y	Y	Y	Y	Y	N
3 Derrick	Y	Y	Y	?	?	?
4 ***Campbell***	Y	Y	Y	Y	Y	N
5 Spratt	Y	Y	Y	Y	Y	Y
6 Tallon	Y	Y	Y	N	Y	Y
SOUTH DAKOTA						
AL Daschle	Y	Y	Y	?	Y	Y
TENNESSEE						
1 ***Quillen***	Y	Y	Y	#	?	?
2 ***Duncan***	Y	Y	Y	Y	Y	N
3 Lloyd	Y	Y	?	?	?	?
4 Cooper	Y	Y	Y	N	Y	Y
5 Boner	Y	Y	Y	N	Y	Y
6 Gordon	Y	Y	Y	N	Y	Y
7 ***Sundquist***	Y	Y	Y	Y	Y	N
8 Jones	Y	Y	Y	N	Y	?
9 Ford	Y	Y	Y	N	Y	Y
TEXAS						
1 Hall, S.	Y	Y	Y	N	Y	Y
2 Wilson	Y	Y	?	Y	Y	Y
3 ***Bartlett***	Y	Y	Y	Y	Y	N
4 Hall, R.	Y	Y	Y	Y	Y	Y
5 Bryant	?	?	Y	N	Y	Y
6 ***Barton***	Y	Y	Y	Y	Y	N
7 ***Archer***	Y	Y	Y	Y	Y	N
8 ***Fields***	Y	Y	Y	Y	Y	N
9 Brooks	Y	Y	Y	N	Y	Y
10 Pickle	Y	Y	Y	N	Y	Y
11 Leath	Y	Y	Y	Y	Y	N
12 Wright	Y	Y	Y	N	Y	Y
13 ***Boulter***	Y	Y	Y	Y	Y	N
14 ***Sweeney***	?	?	?	Y	Y	N
15 de la Garza	Y	Y	Y	N	Y	Y
16 Coleman	Y	Y	Y	N	Y	Y
17 Stenholm	Y	Y	Y	Y	Y	N
18 Leland	+	+	Y	N	Y	Y
19 ***Combest***	Y	Y	Y	Y	Y	N
20 Gonzalez	Y	Y	Y	N	Y	Y
21 ***Loeffler***	Y	Y	Y	Y	Y	N
22 ***DeLay***	Y	Y	Y	?	?	?
23 Bustamante	+	+	+	X	?	?
24 Frost	Y	Y	Y	N	Y	Y
25 Andrews	Y	Y	Y	N	Y	Y
26 ***Armey***	Y	Y	Y	Y	Y	N
27 Ortiz	Y	Y	Y	N	Y	Y
UTAH						
1 ***Hansen***	Y	Y	Y	Y	Y	N
2 ***Monson***	Y	Y	Y	Y	Y	N
3 ***Nielson***	Y	N	Y	Y	Y	N
VERMONT						
AL ***Jeffords***	Y	Y	Y	?	?	?
VIRGINIA						
1 ***Bateman***	Y	Y	Y	Y	Y	N
2 ***Whitehurst***	Y	Y	Y	Y	Y	Y
3 ***Bliley***	Y	Y	Y	Y	Y	Y
4 Sisisky	?	?	Y	N	Y	Y
5 Daniel	Y	Y	Y	Y	Y	Y
6 Olin	Y	Y	Y	N	Y	Y
7 ***Slaughter***	Y	Y	Y	Y	Y	Y
8 ***Parris***	Y	Y	Y	Y	Y	Y
9 Boucher	Y	Y	Y	N	Y	Y
10 ***Wolf***	Y	Y	Y	Y	Y	Y
WASHINGTON						
1 ***Miller***	Y	Y	Y	Y	Y	N
2 Swift	Y	Y	Y	N	Y	Y
3 Bonker	Y	Y	Y	Y	Y	Y
4 ***Morrison***	Y	Y	Y	N	Y	Y
5 Foley	?	?	?	?	?	?
6 Dicks	Y	Y	Y	N	Y	Y
7 Lowry	Y	Y	Y	N	Y	Y
8 ***Chandler***	Y	Y	Y	Y	Y	Y
WEST VIRGINIA						
1 Mollohan	Y	Y	Y	N	Y	Y
2 Staggers	Y	Y	Y	N	Y	Y
3 Wise	Y	Y	Y	N	Y	Y
4 Rahall	Y	Y	Y	N	Y	Y
WISCONSIN						
1 Aspin	Y	Y	?	N	Y	Y
2 Kastenmeier	Y	Y	N	N	Y	Y
3 ***Gunderson***	Y	Y	Y	Y	Y	Y
4 Kleczka	Y	Y	+	N	Y	Y
5 Moody	Y	Y	Y	N	Y	Y
6 ***Petri***	Y	Y	Y	Y	Y	N
7 Obey	Y	Y	Y	N	Y	Y
8 ***Roth***	Y	Y	Y	Y	Y	Y
9 ***Sensenbrenner***	Y	Y	Y	Y	Y	N
WYOMING						
AL ***Cheney***	Y	Y	Y	Y	Y	N

** Rep. Cathy (Mrs. Gillis) Long, D-La., was sworn in on April 4, 1985. The first vote for which she was eligible was CQ vote 48.*

Southern states - Ala., Ark., Fla., Ga., Ky., La., Miss., N.C., Okla., S.C., Tenn., Texas, Va.

* The *Congressional Record* vote number is different from the CQ vote number because the *Record* includes quorum calls in its tally. CQ does not publish quorum call votes.

54. Procedural Motion. Frenzel, R-Minn., motion to approve the House *Journal* of Thursday, April 18. Motion agreed to 200-61: R 15-53; D 185-8 (ND 124-7, SD 61-1), April 22, 1985.

55. H Res 125. Soviet Killing of Major Nicholson. Hamilton, D-Ind., motion to suspend the rules and adopt the resolution to condemn the government of the Soviet Union for the March 24 shooting in East Germany of U.S. Army Major Arthur D. Nicholson Jr. Motion agreed to 394-2: R 171-0; D 223-2 (ND 155-2, SD 68-0), April 22, 1985. A two-thirds majority of those present and voting (264 in this case) is required for adoption under suspension of the rules.

56. H Con Res 52. Democracy in Chile. Weiss, D-N.Y., motion to suspend the rules and adopt the concurrent resolution to call upon the government of Chile to negotiate with its democratic opposition, and to call upon the United States to continue to deny security aid to the government of Chile, to cease all joint military exercises, to deny economic aid, except for humanitarian and disaster assistance, and to continue to oppose loans and grants to Chile by international institutions. Motion rejected 191-206: R 23-148; D 168-58 (ND 143-14, SD 25-44), April 22, 1985. A two-thirds majority of those present and voting (265 in this case) is required for adoption under suspension of the rules.

57. H J Res 239. Aid to Nicaraguan Rebels. Adoption of the rule (H Res 136) to provide for House floor consideration of the joint resolution to approve the release of $14 million in fiscal 1985 for supporting military or paramilitary operations in Nicaragua. Adopted 286-127: R 55-120; D 231-7 (ND 160-4, SD 71-3), April 23, 1985. (The rule also provided for consideration of Democratic and Republican alternative plans.)

58. H J Res 239. Aid to Nicaraguan Rebels. Passage of the joint resolution to approve the release of $14 million in fiscal 1985 for supporting military or paramilitary operations in Nicaragua. Rejected 180-248: R 140-40; D 40-208 (ND 4-163, SD 36-45), April 23, 1985. A "yea" was a vote supporting the president's position.

59. Procedural Motion. Gingrich, R-Ga., motion to approve the House *Journal* of Monday, April 22, and Tuesday, April 23. Motion agreed to 236-171: R 11-164; D 225-7 (ND 146-6, SD 79-1), April 24, 1985.

60. H J Res 247. Aid to Nicaragua. Hamilton, D-Ind., amendment in the nature of a substitute to provide $4 million for the implementation of a Contadora peace agreement in Nicaragua and $10 million in humanitarian assistance for refugees outside Nicaragua, to be administered through the Red Cross or the United Nations. The amendment also prohibited aid to military or paramilitary groups in Nicaragua until Congress passed a joint resolution repealing the prohibition. Adopted 219-206: R 15-166; D 204-40 (ND 154-9, SD 50-31), April 24, 1985. A "nay" was a vote supporting the president's position.

61. H J Res 247. Aid to Nicaragua. Michel, R-Ill., amendment in the nature of a substitute to provide $14 million for humanitarian assistance for the Nicaraguan anti-government rebels ("contras") to be distributed by the U.S. Agency for International Development. Rejected 213-215: R 167-14; D 46-201 (ND 6-160, SD 40-41), April 24, 1985. A "yea" was a vote supporting the president's position.

KEY

Y Voted for (yea).
\# Paired for.
\+ Announced for.
N Voted against (nay).
X Paired against.
\- Announced against.
P Voted "present".
C Voted "present" to avoid possible conflict of interest.
? Did not vote or otherwise make a position known.

Democrats ***Republicans***

	54	55	56	57	58	59	60	61
ALABAMA								
1 ***Callahan***	?	Y	N	N	Y	N	N	Y
2 ***Dickinson***	N	Y	N	Y	Y	N	N	Y
3 Nichols	?	Y	N	Y	Y	Y	N	Y
4 Bevill	Y	Y	N	Y	Y	Y	N	Y
5 Flippo	Y	?	?	Y	Y	Y	N	Y
6 Erdreich	Y	Y	N	Y	Y	Y	N	Y
7 Shelby	?	?	?	Y	Y	Y	N	Y
ALASKA								
AL ***Young***	N	Y	N	?	Y	N	N	Y
ARIZONA								
1 ***McCain***	N	Y	N	Y	Y	N	N	Y
2 Udall	Y	Y	Y	Y	N	Y	Y	N
3 ***Stump***	?	Y	N	Y	Y	N	N	Y
4 ***Rudd***	+	Y	N	N	Y	Y	N	Y
5 ***Kolbe***	-	Y	Y	Y	N	N	N	Y
ARKANSAS								
1 Alexander	Y	Y	Y	Y	N	Y	Y	N
2 Robinson	Y	Y	N	Y	N	Y	Y	N
3 ***Hammerschmidt***	?	Y	N	Y	Y	N	N	Y
4 Anthony	Y	Y	N	Y	N	Y	N	N
CALIFORNIA								
1 Bosco	?	Y	Y	Y	N	Y	Y	N
2 ***Chappie***	N	Y	N	N	Y	N	N	Y
3 Matsui	?	Y	Y	Y	N	Y	Y	N
4 Fazio	Y	Y	Y	Y	N	Y	Y	N
5 Burton	Y	Y	Y	Y	N	Y	Y	N
6 Boxer	Y	Y	Y	Y	N	Y	Y	N
7 Miller	Y	Y	Y	Y	N	Y	Y	N
8 Dellums	?	Y	Y	Y	N	Y	Y	N
9 Stark	?	Y	Y	Y	N	Y	Y	N
10 Edwards	Y	Y	Y	Y	N	Y	Y	N
11 Lantos	Y	Y	Y	Y	N	Y	Y	N
12 ***Zschau***	-	Y	N	N	N	N	Y	N
13 Mineta	Y	Y	Y	Y	N	Y	Y	N
14 ***Shumway***	N	Y	N	N	Y	N	N	Y
15 Coelho	Y	Y	Y	Y	N	?	Y	N
16 Panetta	Y	Y	Y	Y	N	Y	Y	N
17 ***Pashayan***	Y	Y	N	?	Y	N	N	Y
18 Lehman	Y	Y	Y	Y	N	Y	Y	N
19 ***Lagomarsino***	+	Y	N	N	Y	N	N	Y
20 ***Thomas***	?	Y	N	N	Y	N	N	Y
21 ***Fiedler***	-	Y	N	N	Y	N	N	Y
22 ***Moorhead***	N	Y	N	N	Y	N	N	Y
23 Beilenson	Y	Y	Y	Y	N	Y	Y	N
24 Waxman	?	?	#	Y	N	Y	Y	N
25 Roybal	Y	Y	Y	Y	N	Y	Y	N
26 Berman	Y	Y	Y	Y	N	Y	Y	N
27 Levine	Y	Y	Y	Y	N	Y	Y	N
28 Dixon	Y	Y	Y	Y	N	Y	Y	N
29 Hawkins	Y	Y	Y	Y	N	Y	Y	N
30 Martinez	Y	Y	Y	Y	N	Y	Y	N
31 Dymally	P	Y	Y	N	N	P	Y	N
32 Anderson	?	?	?	Y	N	Y	Y	N
33 ***Dreier***	N	Y	N	N	Y	N	N	Y
34 Torres	Y	Y	Y	Y	N	Y	Y	N
35 ***Lewis***	-	Y	N	N	Y	N	N	Y
36 Brown	Y	Y	Y	Y	N	Y	Y	N
37 ***McCandless***	-	Y	N	N	Y	N	N	Y
38 ***Dornan***	P	Y	N	N	Y	N	N	Y
39 ***Dannemeyer***	?	?	?	N	Y	N	N	Y
40 ***Badham***	-	Y	N	?	#	?	X	#
41 ***Lowery***	-	Y	N	N	Y	N	N	Y
42 ***Lungren***	-	Y	N	N	Y	N	N	Y
43 ***Packard***	?	Y	N	N	Y	N	N	Y
44 Bates	?	?	?	Y	N	Y	Y	N
45 ***Hunter***	-	Y	N	N	Y	N	N	Y
COLORADO								
1 Schroeder	N	Y	Y	Y	N	N	Y	N
2 Wirth	Y	Y	Y	Y	N	Y	Y	N
3 ***Strang***	+	Y	N	N	Y	N	N	Y
4 ***Brown***	N	Y	Y	N	Y	N	N	Y
5 ***Kramer***	N	Y	Y	N	Y	N	N	Y
6 ***Schaefer***	?	Y	N	N	Y	N	N	Y
CONNECTICUT								
1 Kennelly	Y	Y	Y	Y	N	Y	Y	N
2 Gejdenson	Y	Y	Y	Y	N	Y	Y	N
3 Morrison	Y	Y	Y	Y	N	Y	Y	N
4 ***McKinney***	-	Y	N	N	N	N	Y	N
5 ***Rowland***	-	Y	N	N	N	N	N	Y
6 ***Johnson***	?	Y	N	N	N	Y	N	Y
DELAWARE								
AL Carper	Y	Y	N	Y	N	Y	N	N
FLORIDA								
1 Hutto	?	Y	N	Y	Y	Y	N	Y
2 Fuqua	?	?	?	?	N	Y	N	Y
3 Bennett	Y	Y	N	Y	N	Y	Y	Y
4 Chappell	Y	Y	N	Y	Y	Y	N	Y
5 ***McCollum***	-	Y	N	N	Y	N	N	Y
6 MacKay	Y	Y	N	Y	N	Y	Y	N
7 Gibbons	Y	Y	Y	Y	Y	Y	Y	Y
8 ***Young***	Y	Y	N	N	Y	?	N	Y
9 ***Bilirakis***	N	Y	N	N	Y	N	N	Y
10 ***Ireland***	?	Y	N	N	Y	N	N	Y
11 Nelson	+	+	-	+	Y	Y	N	Y
12 ***Lewis***	-	Y	N	N	Y	N	N	Y
13 ***Mack***	-	Y	N	Y	Y	N	N	Y
14 Mica	Y	Y	N	Y	Y	Y	Y	Y
15 ***Shaw***	-	Y	N	N	Y	N	N	Y
16 Smith	Y	Y	Y	Y	Y	Y	Y	Y
17 Lehman	Y	Y	Y	Y	N	Y	Y	N
18 Pepper	Y	Y	Y	Y	Y	Y	Y	Y
19 Fascell	Y	Y	Y	Y	Y	Y	N	N
GEORGIA								
1 Thomas	Y	Y	N	Y	Y	Y	Y	Y
2 Hatcher	?	Y	N	?	Y	Y	Y	Y
3 Ray	Y	Y	N	Y	Y	Y	N	Y
4 ***Swindall***	N	Y	N	N	Y	N	N	Y
5 Fowler	Y	Y	N	Y	N	Y	Y	N
6 ***Gingrich***	?	Y	N	N	Y	N	N	Y
7 Darden	Y	Y	N	Y	Y	Y	N	Y
8 Rowland	Y	Y	N	Y	Y	Y	Y	Y
9 Jenkins	Y	Y	N	Y	Y	Y	N	Y
10 Barnard	Y	Y	N	Y	Y	Y	N	Y
HAWAII								
1 Heftel	?	Y	N	?	N	?	Y	Y
2 Akaka	Y	Y	N	Y	N	Y	Y	N
IDAHO								
1 ***Craig***	-	Y	N	N	Y	N	N	Y
2 Stallings	Y	Y	N	Y	N	Y	Y	N
ILLINOIS								
1 Hayes	Y	Y	Y	Y	N	Y	Y	N
2 Savage	Y	N	Y	N	N	Y	P	N
3 Russo	Y	Y	Y	Y	N	Y	Y	N
4 ***O'Brien***	-	Y	N	N	Y	N	N	Y
5 Lipinski	Y	Y	Y	Y	Y	Y	Y	?
6 ***Hyde***	?	?	?	Y	Y	N	N	Y
7 Collins	Y	Y	Y	Y	N	Y	Y	N
8 Rostenkowski	?	Y	Y	Y	N	Y	Y	N
9 Yates	Y	Y	Y	Y	N	Y	N	N
10 ***Porter***	?	Y	Y	N	Y	N	N	Y
11 Annunzio	Y	Y	Y	Y	N	Y	Y	N
12 ***Crane***	N	Y	N	X	Y	N	N	Y
13 ***Fawell***	N	Y	Y	Y	N	N	N	Y
14 ***Grotberg***	N	Y	N	X	Y	-	N	Y
15 ***Madigan***	N	Y	N	N	N	N	N	Y
16 ***Martin***	-	Y	N	N	N	N	N	Y
17 Evans	Y	Y	Y	Y	N	Y	Y	N
18 ***Michel***	?	Y	N	Y	Y	N	N	Y
19 Bruce	?	Y	Y	Y	N	Y	Y	N
20 Durbin	N	Y	Y	Y	N	N	Y	N
21 Price	Y	Y	Y	Y	N	Y	Y	N
22 Gray	Y	Y	Y	Y	N	Y	Y	N
INDIANA								
1 Visclosky	Y	Y	Y	Y	N	Y	Y	N
2 Sharp	Y	Y	Y	Y	N	Y	Y	N
3 ***Hiler***	-	Y	N	N	Y	N	N	Y
4 ***Coats***	-	Y	N	Y	Y	N	N	Y
5 ***Hillis***	N	Y	N	Y	Y	N	N	Y

ND - Northern Democrats SD - Southern Democrats

* Corresponding to Congressional Record Votes 59, 60, 61, 62, 64, 65, 67, 68

	54	55	56	57	58	59	60	61
6 ***Burton***	-	Y	N	N	Y	N	N	Y
7 ***Myers***	?	Y	N	Y	Y	N	N	Y
8 Vacancy								
9 Hamilton	Y	Y	Y	Y	N	Y	Y	N
10 Jacobs	N	Y	Y	Y	N	N	Y	N
IOWA								
1 ***Leach***	?	Y	Y	Y	N	N	Y	N
2 ***Tauke***	P	Y	N	N	N	N	N	Y
3 ***Evans***	N	?	?	N	N	N	N	N
4 Smith	Y	Y	N	Y	N	Y	N	N
5 ***Lightfoot***	-	Y	N	N	Y	N	N	Y
6 Bedell	?	Y	Y	Y	N	Y	Y	N
KANSAS								
1 ***Roberts***	?	?	?	N	Y	N	N	Y
2 Slattery	?	Y	Y	Y	N	Y	Y	N
3 ***Meyers***	-	Y	N	Y	N	Y	N	Y
4 Glickman	?	Y	Y	Y	N	Y	Y	N
5 ***Whittaker***	-	Y	N	N	Y	N	N	Y
KENTUCKY								
1 Hubbard	?	Y	N	Y	Y	Y	N	Y
2 Natcher	Y	Y	N	Y	N	Y	Y	N
3 Mazzoli	Y	Y	N	Y	N	Y	Y	N
4 ***Snyder***	?	Y	N	N	Y	Y	N	Y
5 ***Rogers***	?	+	X	#	Y	N	N	Y
6 ***Hopkins***	N	Y	N	Y	N	N	N	Y
7 Perkins	Y	Y	Y	Y	N	Y	Y	N
LOUISIANA								
1 ***Livingston***	N	Y	N	Y	Y	N	N	Y
2 Boggs	?	?	?	Y	N	Y	Y	N
3 Tauzin	Y	Y	Y	Y	Y	Y	N	Y
4 Roemer	N	Y	Y	N	Y	N	N	Y
5 Huckaby	?	?	?	Y	Y	Y	N	Y
6 ***Moore***	Y	Y	N	Y	Y	Y	N	Y
7 Breaux	Y	Y	N	Y	Y	Y	N	Y
8 Long	Y	Y	Y	Y	N	Y	Y	N
MAINE								
1 ***McKernan***	?	Y	Y	N	N	N	Y	N
2 ***Snowe***	?	Y	Y	Y	N	Y	Y	N
MARYLAND								
1 Dyson	Y	Y	N	Y	Y	Y	N	Y
2 ***Bentley***	-	Y	N	Y	Y	N	N	Y
3 Mikulski	P	Y	Y	Y	N	Y	Y	N
4 ***Holt***	N	Y	N	Y	Y	N	N	Y
5 Hoyer	Y	Y	Y	Y	N	Y	Y	N
6 Byron	?	?	?	?	?	?	?	Y
7 Mitchell	N	Y	Y	Y	N	?	P	N
8 Barnes	Y	Y	Y	Y	N	Y	Y	N
MASSACHUSETTS								
1 ***Conte***	N	Y	Y	Y	N	N	Y	N
2 Boland	Y	Y	Y	Y	N	Y	Y	N
3 Early	Y	Y	Y	Y	N	Y	Y	N
4 Frank	Y	Y	Y	Y	N	Y	Y	N
5 Atkins	Y	Y	Y	Y	N	Y	Y	N
6 Mavroules	Y	Y	Y	Y	N	Y	Y	N
7 Markey	?	Y	Y	Y	N	Y	Y	N
8 O'Neill								
9 Moakley	Y	Y	Y	Y	N	?	Y	N
10 Studds	Y	Y	Y	Y	N	Y	Y	N
11 Donnelly	Y	Y	Y	Y	N	Y	Y	N
MICHIGAN								
1 Conyers	?	?	?	Y	N	Y	Y	N
2 ***Pursell***	N	Y	Y	Y	Y	N	N	Y
3 Wolpe	Y	Y	Y	Y	N	Y	Y	N
4 ***Siljander***	N	Y	N	N	Y	N	N	Y
5 ***Henry***	-	Y	Y	Y	Y	N	N	Y
6 Carr	Y	Y	Y	Y	N	Y	N	N
7 Kildee	Y	Y	Y	Y	N	Y	Y	N
8 Traxler	Y	Y	Y	Y	N	Y	Y	N
9 ***Vander Jagt***	?	Y	N	Y	?	N	N	Y
10 ***Schuette***	-	Y	N	Y	Y	N	N	Y
11 ***Davis***	N	Y	N	N	N	N	N	Y
12 Bonior	Y	Y	Y	Y	N	Y	Y	N
13 Crockett	Y	N	Y	N	N	Y	Y	N
14 Hertel	Y	Y	Y	Y	N	Y	Y	N
15 Ford	?	Y	Y	Y	N	?	Y	N
16 Dingell	Y	Y	N	Y	N	?	Y	N
17 Levin	Y	Y	Y	Y	N	Y	Y	N
18 ***Broomfield***	Y	Y	N	Y	Y	Y	N	Y
MINNESOTA								
1 Penny	N	Y	Y	Y	N	N	Y	N
2 ***Weber***	-	Y	N	N	Y	?	N	Y
3 ***Frenzel***	?	Y	N	N	N	?	N	Y
4 Vento	Y	Y	Y	Y	N	Y	Y	N
5 Sabo	Y	Y	Y	Y	N	Y	Y	N
6 Sikorski	N	Y	Y	Y	N	N	Y	N
7 ***Stangeland***	?	Y	N	N	Y	N	N	Y
8 Oberstar	P	Y	Y	Y	N	Y	Y	N
MISSISSIPPI								
1 Whitten	Y	Y	N	Y	N	Y	Y	N
2 ***Franklin***	?	?	X	N	Y	N	N	Y
3 Montgomery	Y	Y	N	Y	Y	Y	N	Y
4 Dowdy	?	?	?	?	Y	Y	N	Y
5 ***Lott***	?	Y	N	N	Y	N	N	Y
MISSOURI								
1 Clay	N	Y	Y	Y	N	N	Y	N
2 Young	Y	Y	Y	Y	N	Y	Y	N
3 Gephardt	?	Y	Y	Y	N	Y	Y	N
4 Skelton	Y	Y	N	N	N	Y	Y	Y
5 Wheat	Y	Y	Y	Y	N	Y	Y	N
6 ***Coleman***	N	Y	N	Y	Y	N	N	Y
7 ***Taylor***	P	Y	N	N	Y	N	N	Y
8 ***Emerson***	-	Y	N	N	Y	N	N	Y
9 Volkmer	?	?	?	Y	N	Y	Y	N
MONTANA								
1 Williams	?	Y	Y	Y	N	?	Y	N
2 ***Marlenee***	?	Y	N	N	Y	N	N	Y
NEBRASKA								
1 ***Bereuter***	?	?	?	N	N	N	N	Y
2 ***Daub***	N	Y	N	N	Y	N	N	Y
3 ***Smith***	?	Y	N	Y	N	N	N	Y
NEVADA								
1 Reid	Y	Y	Y	Y	N	Y	Y	N
2 ***Vucanovich***	N	Y	N	N	Y	N	N	Y
NEW HAMPSHIRE								
1 ***Smith***	-	Y	N	N	Y	N	N	Y
2 ***Gregg***	N	Y	N	N	N	N	N	Y
NEW JERSEY								
1 Florio	Y	Y	Y	Y	N	Y	N	N
2 Hughes	Y	Y	Y	Y	N	Y	Y	N
3 Howard	Y	Y	Y	Y	N	Y	Y	N
4 ***Smith***	Y	Y	Y	Y	Y	N	N	Y
5 ***Roukema***	N	Y	N	Y	N	N	N	Y
6 Dwyer	Y	Y	Y	Y	N	Y	Y	N
7 ***Rinaldo***	Y	Y	N	Y	N	N	N	Y
8 Roe	Y	Y	Y	Y	N	Y	Y	N
9 Torricelli	?	Y	Y	Y	N	Y	Y	N
10 Rodino	?	?	#	?	X	?	#	X
11 ***Gallo***	-	Y	N	N	Y	N	N	Y
12 ***Courter***	N	Y	N	N	Y	N	N	Y
13 ***Saxton***	N	Y	N	N	Y	N	N	Y
14 Guarini	Y	Y	Y	Y	N	Y	Y	N
NEW MEXICO								
1 ***Lujan***	N	Y	Y	Y	Y	N	N	Y
2 ***Skeen***	?	Y	N	N	Y	N	N	Y
3 Richardson	?	Y	Y	Y	N	Y	Y	N
NEW YORK								
1 ***Carney***	N	Y	N	N	Y	N	N	Y
2 Downey	Y	Y	Y	Y	N	Y	Y	N
3 Mrazek	Y	Y	Y	Y	N	Y	Y	N
4 ***Lent***	?	Y	N	N	Y	N	N	Y
5 ***McGrath***	?	Y	N	N	Y	?	N	Y
6 Addabbo	Y	Y	Y	Y	N	Y	Y	N
7 Ackerman	?	Y	Y	Y	N	Y	Y	N
8 Scheuer	Y	Y	Y	Y	N	Y	Y	N
9 Manton	Y	Y	Y	Y	N	Y	Y	N
10 Schumer	?	?	?	Y	N	Y	Y	N
11 Towns	?	?	#	Y	N	Y	P	N
12 Owens	Y	Y	Y	Y	N	?	Y	N
13 Solarz	Y	Y	Y	Y	N	Y	Y	N
14 ***Molinari***	?	Y	N	Y	Y	N	N	Y
15 ***Green***	?	Y	Y	Y	N	N	Y	N
16 Rangel	Y	Y	Y	Y	N	Y	Y	N
17 Weiss	Y	Y	Y	Y	N	Y	Y	N
18 Garcia	Y	Y	Y	Y	N	Y	Y	N
19 Biaggi	?	Y	Y	Y	N	Y	Y	Y
20 ***DioGuardi***	-	Y	N	N	Y	N	N	Y
21 ***Fish***	?	Y	N	N	N	N	Y	N
22 ***Gilman***	-	Y	Y	Y	N	N	Y	Y
23 Stratton	Y	Y	N	Y	Y	Y	N	Y
24 ***Solomon***	N	Y	N	N	Y	N	N	Y
25 ***Boehlert***	N	Y	Y	Y	N	N	Y	N
26 ***Martin***	N	Y	N	N	Y	N	N	Y
27 ***Wortley***	N	Y	N	N	Y	N	N	Y
28 McHugh	Y	Y	Y	Y	N	Y	Y	N
29 ***Horton***	?	?	?	Y	N	Y	Y	N
30 ***Eckert***	-	Y	N	N	Y	N	N	Y
31 ***Kemp***	-	Y	N	Y	Y	N	N	Y
32 LaFalce	?	Y	Y	Y	N	Y	Y	N
33 Nowak	Y	Y	Y	Y	N	Y	Y	N
34 Lundine	?	?	?	?	N	?	Y	N
NORTH CAROLINA								
1 Jones	Y	Y	N	Y	N	Y	Y	N
2 Valentine	Y	Y	N	Y	N	Y	Y	N
3 Whitley	Y	Y	N	Y	N	Y	Y	N
4 ***Cobey***	-	Y	Y	N	Y	N	N	Y
5 Neal	Y	Y	Y	Y	N	Y	Y	N
6 ***Coble***	?	Y	N	N	Y	N	N	Y
7 Rose	Y	Y	Y	Y	N	Y	Y	N
8 Hefner	?	?	?	Y	N	?	Y	N
9 ***McMillan***	-	Y	N	N	Y	N	N	Y
10 ***Broyhill***	?	Y	N	Y	Y	Y	N	Y
11 ***Hendon***	N	Y	N	N	Y	N	N	Y
NORTH DAKOTA								
AL Dorgan	Y	Y	Y	Y	N	Y	Y	N
OHIO								
1 Luken	?	Y	Y	Y	N	Y	Y	N
2 ***Gradison***	Y	Y	N	Y	N	N	Y	N
3 Hall	?	Y	Y	Y	N	Y	N	N
4 ***Oxley***	?	Y	N	N	Y	N	N	Y
5 ***Latta***	N	Y	N	N	Y	N	N	Y
6 ***McEwen***	N	Y	N	?	Y	N	N	Y
7 ***DeWine***	-	Y	N	N	Y	N	N	Y
8 ***Kindness***	-	Y	N	N	Y	N	N	Y
9 Kaptur	Y	Y	Y	Y	N	Y	Y	N
10 ***Miller***	?	Y	N	N	Y	N	N	Y
11 Eckart	Y	Y	Y	Y	N	Y	Y	N
12 ***Kasich***	-	Y	N	Y	Y	N	N	Y
13 Pease	Y	Y	Y	Y	N	Y	Y	N
14 Seiberling	?	?	?	?	N	?	Y	N
15 ***Wylie***	?	?	?	N	Y	N	N	Y
16 ***Regula***	N	Y	N	Y	N	Y	N	Y
17 Traficant	Y	Y	Y	Y	N	?	+	-
18 Applegate	?	Y	Y	Y	N	?	N	N
19 Feighan	Y	Y	Y	Y	N	Y	Y	N
20 Oakar	Y	Y	Y	Y	N	Y	Y	N
21 Stokes	Y	Y	Y	Y	N	Y	Y	N
OKLAHOMA								
1 Jones	?	Y	N	Y	N	Y	Y	N
2 Synar	Y	Y	Y	Y	N	Y	Y	N
3 Watkins	Y	Y	N	Y	N	Y	Y	N
4 McCurdy	Y	Y	N	Y	N	Y	Y	N
5 ***Edwards***	?	Y	N	N	Y	N	N	Y
6 English	Y	Y	N	Y	Y	Y	Y	Y
OREGON								
1 AuCoin	?	?	#	Y	N	Y	Y	N
2 ***Smith, R.***	Y	Y	N	N	N	N	N	Y
3 Wyden	Y	Y	Y	Y	N	Y	Y	N
4 Weaver	Y	Y	Y	Y	N	Y	Y	N
5 ***Smith, D.***	-	Y	N	N	Y	N	N	Y
PENNSYLVANIA								
1 Foglietta	Y	Y	Y	Y	N	Y	Y	N
2 Gray	Y	Y	Y	Y	N	Y	Y	N
3 Borski	Y	Y	Y	Y	N	Y	Y	N
4 Kolter	Y	Y	N	Y	N	Y	Y	N
5 ***Schulze***	N	Y	N	Y	Y	N	N	Y
6 Yatron	Y	Y	Y	Y	N	Y	Y	N
7 Edgar	Y	Y	Y	Y	N	Y	Y	N
8 Kostmayer	Y	Y	Y	Y	N	Y	Y	N
9 ***Shuster***	Y	Y	N	N	Y	N	N	Y
10 ***McDade***	?	Y	N	Y	N	?	N	Y
11 Kanjorski	Y	Y	N	Y	N	Y	Y	N
12 Murtha	Y	Y	N	Y	Y	Y	Y	N
13 ***Coughlin***	?	Y	Y	Y	Y	N	Y	Y
14 Coyne	Y	Y	Y	Y	N	Y	Y	N
15 ***Ritter***	N	Y	Y	N	Y	N	N	Y
16 ***Walker***	-	Y	N	N	Y	N	N	Y
17 ***Gekas***	Y	Y	N	N	Y	N	N	Y
18 Walgren	Y	Y	Y	Y	N	Y	Y	N
19 ***Goodling***	N	Y	N	Y	N	N	N	Y
20 Gaydos	Y	Y	N	Y	N	Y	Y	N
21 ***Ridge***	?	?	?	Y	N	N	N	Y
22 Murphy	Y	Y	Y	Y	N	Y	Y	N
23 ***Clinger***	-	Y	N	Y	N	N	Y	Y
RHODE ISLAND								
1 St Germain	?	Y	Y	Y	N	Y	Y	N
2 ***Schneider***	Y	Y	Y	Y	N	Y	Y	N
SOUTH CAROLINA								
1 ***Hartnett***	Y	Y	N	N	Y	N	N	Y
2 ***Spence***	?	Y	N	Y	Y	N	N	Y
3 Derrick	Y	Y	Y	Y	N	Y	Y	N
4 ***Campbell***	?	Y	N	Y	Y	N	N	Y
5 Spratt	Y	Y	N	Y	N	Y	Y	N
6 Tallon	Y	Y	N	Y	Y	Y	N	Y
SOUTH DAKOTA								
AL Daschle	Y	Y	Y	Y	N	Y	Y	N
TENNESSEE								
1 ***Quillen***	Y	Y	N	Y	Y	N	N	Y
2 ***Duncan***	N	Y	N	Y	Y	N	N	Y
3 Lloyd	?	Y	N	Y	N	Y	N	Y
4 Cooper	Y	Y	Y	Y	N	Y	Y	N
5 Boner	Y	Y	N	Y	N	Y	N	N
6 Gordon	P	Y	Y	Y	N	Y	Y	N
7 ***Sundquist***	N	Y	N	N	Y	N	N	Y
8 Jones	Y	Y	N	Y	N	Y	N	N
9 Ford	?	?	?	?	N	Y	Y	N
TEXAS								
1 Hall, S.	Y	Y	N	Y	Y	Y	N	Y
2 Wilson	Y	Y	N	N	Y	Y	N	Y
3 ***Bartlett***	-	Y	N	N	Y	N	N	Y
4 Hall, R.	Y	Y	N	Y	Y	Y	N	Y
5 Bryant	Y	Y	Y	Y	N	Y	Y	N
6 ***Barton***	-	Y	N	N	Y	N	N	Y
7 ***Archer***	N	Y	N	N	Y	N	N	Y
8 ***Fields***	N	Y	N	N	Y	N	N	Y
9 Brooks	Y	Y	Y	Y	N	Y	Y	N
10 Pickle	Y	Y	N	Y	N	Y	Y	Y
11 Leath	?	?	?	Y	Y	Y	N	Y
12 Wright	Y	?	?	Y	N	Y	Y	N
13 ***Boulter***	-	Y	N	N	Y	N	N	Y
14 ***Sweeney***	Y	Y	N	N	Y	N	N	Y
15 de la Garza	Y	Y	N	?	N	Y	Y	Y
16 Coleman	Y	Y	Y	Y	N	Y	Y	N
17 Stenholm	Y	Y	N	N	Y	Y	N	Y
18 Leland	Y	Y	Y	Y	N	Y	Y	N
19 ***Combest***	N	Y	N	N	Y	N	N	Y
20 Gonzalez	Y	Y	Y	Y	N	Y	Y	N
21 ***Loeffler***	?	Y	N	N	Y	N	N	Y
22 ***DeLay***	-	Y	N	N	Y	N	N	Y
23 Bustamante	?	?	?	?	N	Y	Y	N
24 Frost	Y	Y	Y	Y	N	Y	Y	N
25 Andrews	Y	Y	N	Y	N	Y	Y	N
26 ***Armey***	-	Y	N	N	Y	N	N	Y
27 Ortiz	?	?	N	#	Y	Y	Y	Y
UTAH								
1 ***Hansen***	?	Y	N	N	Y	N	N	Y
2 ***Monson***	-	Y	N	N	Y	N	N	Y
3 ***Nielson***	+	+	-	N	Y	N	N	Y
VERMONT								
AL ***Jeffords***	N	Y	Y	N	N	N	N	N
VIRGINIA								
1 ***Bateman***	-	Y	N	N	Y	N	N	Y
2 ***Whitehurst***	?	Y	N	N	Y	N	N	Y
3 ***Bliley***	-	Y	N	N	Y	N	N	Y
4 Sisisky	P	Y	Y	Y	Y	Y	Y	Y
5 Daniel	?	?	?	Y	?	?	?	?
6 Olin	Y	Y	Y	Y	N	Y	Y	N
7 ***Slaughter***	-	Y	N	N	Y	N	N	Y
8 ***Parris***	-	Y	N	Y	Y	N	N	Y
9 Boucher	Y	Y	Y	Y	N	Y	Y	N
10 ***Wolf***	N	Y	N	N	Y	N	N	Y
WASHINGTON								
1 ***Miller***	-	Y	Y	N	Y	N	N	Y
2 Swift	Y	Y	Y	Y	N	Y	Y	N
3 Bonker	Y	Y	Y	Y	N	Y	Y	N
4 ***Morrison***	?	Y	N	N	N	N	N	Y
5 Foley	Y	Y	Y	Y	N	Y	Y	N
6 Dicks	Y	Y	N	Y	N	Y	Y	N
7 Lowry	Y	Y	Y	Y	N	Y	Y	N
8 ***Chandler***	N	Y	N	N	N	N	N	Y
WEST VIRGINIA								
1 Mollohan	Y	Y	Y	Y	N	Y	Y	N
2 Staggers	Y	Y	Y	Y	N	Y	Y	N
3 Wise	Y	Y	Y	Y	N	Y	Y	N
4 Rahall	Y	Y	Y	Y	N	Y	Y	N
WISCONSIN								
1 Aspin	Y	Y	Y	Y	N	Y	Y	N
2 Kastenmeier	Y	Y	Y	Y	N	Y	Y	N
3 ***Gunderson***	-	Y	N	Y	N	N	Y	N
4 Kleczka	Y	Y	Y	Y	N	P	Y	N
5 Moody	Y	Y	Y	Y	N	?	Y	N
6 ***Petri***	-	Y	N	N	Y	N	N	Y
7 Obey	Y	Y	Y	Y	N	Y	Y	N
8 ***Roth***	Y	Y	N	N	Y	N	N	Y
9 ***Sensenbrenner***	N	Y	Y	N	Y	N	N	Y
WYOMING								
AL ***Cheney***	-	Y	N	N	Y	N	N	Y

Southern states - Ala., Ark., Fla., Ga., Ky., La., Miss., N.C., Okla., S.C., Tenn., Texas, Va.

* The *Congressional Record* vote number is different from the CQ vote number because the *Record* includes quorum calls in its tally. CQ does not publish quorum call votes.

62. H J Res 247. Aid to Nicaragua. Passage of the joint resolution to provide $4 million for the implementation of a Contadora peace agreement in Nicaragua and $10 million in humanitarian assistance for refugees outside Nicaragua, to be administered through the Red Cross or the United Nations, and to prohibit aid to military or paramilitary groups in Nicaragua until Congress passes a joint resolution repealing the prohibition. Rejected 123-303: R 17-162; D 106-141 (ND 71-95, SD 35-46), April 24, 1985.

63. Procedural Motion. Frenzel, R-Minn., motion to approve the House *Journal* of Wednesday, April 24. Motion agreed to 216-177: R 8-166; D 208-11 (ND 134-8, SD 74-3), April 25, 1985.

64. Procedural Motion. Walker, R-Pa., motion to permit a member (Walker) to read from the *Congressional Record*. Motion agreed to 351-14: R 161-6; D 190-8 (ND 128-5, SD 62-3), April 25, 1985. (The motion was made and the roll call was ordered to delay House business as part of a Republican protest of the handling of the contested election in the Indiana 8th District.)

65. HR 2068. State, USIA and Board for International Broadcasting Authorizations, Fiscal 1986 and 1987. Adoption of the rule (H Res 137) to provide for House floor consideration of the bill to authorize appropriations for the State Department, the U.S. Information Agency and the Board for International Broadcasting for fiscal years 1986 and 1987. Adopted 383-0: R 166-0; D 217-0 (ND 145-0, SD 72-0), April 25, 1985.

66. HR 2068. State, USIA and Board for International Broadcasting Authorizations, Fiscal 1986 and 1987. Bonior, D-Mich., motion to table (kill) the Walker, R-Pa., motion to reconsider the vote by which the rule (H Res 137, which provided for House floor consideration of HR 2068, the bill to authorize appropriations for the State Department, the U.S. Information Agency and the Board for International Broadcasting for fiscal years 1986 and 1987) was adopted. Motion agreed to 212-157: R 4-156; D 208-1 (ND 139-1, SD 69-0), April 25, 1985. (The roll call was ordered and the motion to reconsider was made to delay House business as part of a Republican protest of the handling of the contested election in the Indiana 8th District.)

67. Procedural Motion. Foley, D-Wash., motion to table (kill) the Weber, R-Minn., appeal of the chair's ruling that the Weber motion to correct the *Congressional Record* was not a privileged motion. Motion agreed to 200-156: R 0-156; D 200-0 (ND 137-0, SD 63-0), April 25, 1985. (The Weber motion and appeal were made and the roll call was ordered to delay House business as part of a Republican protest of the handling of the contested election in the Indiana 8th District.)

68. Procedural Motion. Foley, D-Wash., motion to adjourn. Motion agreed to 201-153: R 5-152; D 196-1 (ND 134-1, SD 62-0), April 25, 1985. (The motion was made because of repeated Republican efforts to delay House business in protest of the handling of the contested election in the Indiana 8th District.)

KEY

- Y Voted for (yea).
- # Paired for.
- + Announced for.
- N Voted against (nay).
- X Paired against.
- \- Announced against.
- P Voted "present".
- C Voted "present" to avoid possible conflict of interest.
- ? Did not vote or otherwise make a position known.

Democrats ***Republicans***

	62	63	64	65	66	67	68
ALABAMA							
1 ***Callahan***	N	N	Y	Y	N	N	N
2 ***Dickinson***	N	N	Y	Y	?	?	?
3 Nichols	N	Y	Y	Y	Y	Y	Y
4 Bevill	N	Y	Y	Y	Y	Y	Y
5 Flippo	N	Y	Y	Y	Y	Y	Y
6 Erdreich	N	Y	Y	Y	Y	Y	Y
7 Shelby	N	?	?	Y	Y	Y	Y
ALASKA							
AL ***Young***	N	N	Y	Y	N	N	N
ARIZONA							
1 ***McCain***	N	N	Y	Y	N	N	N
2 Udall	Y	Y	Y	Y	Y	Y	Y
3 ***Stump***	N	N	Y	Y	N	N	N
4 ***Rudd***	N	Y	Y	Y	N	N	N
5 ***Kolbe***	N	N	Y	Y	N	N	N
ARKANSAS							
1 Alexander	Y	Y	Y	Y	Y	Y	Y
2 Robinson	Y	Y	Y	Y	Y	P	Y
3 ***Hammerschmidt***	N	N	Y	Y	N	N	N
4 Anthony	N	Y	?	?	?	?	?
CALIFORNIA							
1 Bosco	N	?	?	?	?	?	?
2 ***Chappie***	N	N	Y	Y	N	N	N
3 Matsui	N	Y	?	Y	Y	Y	Y
4 Fazio	N	Y	?	Y	Y	Y	Y
5 Burton	N	Y	Y	Y	Y	Y	Y
6 Boxer	N	?	?	?	?	?	?
7 Miller	N	?	?	?	?	?	?
8 Dellums	N	Y	Y	Y	Y	Y	Y
9 Stark	N	Y	Y	Y	Y	Y	Y
10 Edwards	N	Y	Y	Y	Y	Y	Y
11 Lantos	N	Y	Y	Y	Y	Y	Y
12 ***Zschau***	Y	N	N	Y	N	N	N
13 Mineta	N	Y	Y	Y	?	?	?
14 ***Shumway***	N	N	Y	Y	N	N	N
15 Coelho	Y	Y	Y	Y	Y	Y	Y
16 Panetta	N	Y	Y	Y	Y	Y	Y
17 ***Pashayan***	N	N	Y	Y	N	N	N
18 Lehman	N	?	?	?	?	?	?
19 ***Lagomarsino***	N	N	Y	Y	N	N	N
20 ***Thomas***	N	N	Y	Y	N	N	N
21 ***Fiedler***	N	N	Y	Y	N	N	N
22 ***Moorhead***	N	N	Y	Y	N	N	N
23 Beilenson	N	?	Y	Y	Y	Y	Y
24 Waxman	N	Y	Y	Y	Y	Y	Y
25 Roybal	N	Y	Y	Y	Y	Y	Y
26 Berman	N	Y	Y	Y	Y	Y	Y
27 Levine	Y	Y	Y	Y	Y	Y	Y
28 Dixon	N	Y	Y	Y	Y	Y	Y
29 Hawkins	N	Y	Y	Y	Y	Y	Y
30 Martinez	N	Y	Y	Y	Y	Y	Y
31 Dymally	N	?	?	?	?	?	?
32 Anderson	Y	Y	Y	Y	Y	Y	Y
33 ***Dreier***	N	N	Y	Y	N	N	N
34 Torres	N	Y	Y	Y	Y	Y	Y
35 ***Lewis***	N	N	Y	Y	N	N	N
36 Brown	Y	Y	Y	Y	Y	Y	Y
37 ***McCandless***	N	N	Y	Y	N	N	N
38 ***Dornan***	N	N	N	Y	N	N	N
39 ***Dannemeyer***	N	N	Y	Y	N	N	N
40 ***Badham***	?	?	?	?	?	?	?
41 ***Lowery***	N	N	Y	Y	N	N	N
42 ***Lungren***	N	Y	Y	Y	N	N	N
43 ***Packard***	N	N	Y	Y	?	?	?
44 Bates	N	Y	Y	Y	Y	Y	N
45 ***Hunter***	N	N	Y	Y	Y	N	N
COLORADO							
1 Schroeder	N	N	Y	Y	Y	Y	Y
2 Wirth	Y	Y	Y	Y	Y	Y	Y
3 ***Strang***	N	N	Y	Y	N	N	N
4 ***Brown***	N	N	Y	Y	N	N	N
5 ***Kramer***	N	N	Y	Y	N	N	N
6 ***Schaefer***	N	N	Y	Y	N	N	N
CONNECTICUT							
1 Kennelly	N	Y	Y	Y	Y	Y	Y
2 Gejdenson	Y	Y	P	Y	Y	Y	Y
3 Morrison	N	Y	Y	Y	Y	Y	Y
4 ***McKinney***	Y	N	Y	Y	N	N	N
5 ***Rowland***	N	N	Y	Y	N	N	N
6 ***Johnson***	N	Y	Y	Y	N	N	N
DELAWARE							
AL Carper	N	Y	Y	Y	Y	Y	Y
FLORIDA							
1 Hutto	N	Y	Y	Y	Y	Y	Y
2 Fuqua	N	Y	Y	Y	Y	?	?
3 Bennett	Y	Y	Y	Y	Y	Y	Y
4 Chappell	N	Y	?	?	Y	Y	Y
5 ***McCollum***	N	N	Y	Y	N	N	N
6 MacKay	Y	Y	Y	Y	Y	?	?
7 Gibbons	Y	Y	Y	Y	Y	?	?
8 ***Young***	N	N	Y	Y	N	N	N
9 ***Bilirakis***	N	N	Y	Y	N	N	N
10 ***Ireland***	N	N	Y	Y	N	N	N
11 Nelson	N	Y	Y	Y	Y	Y	Y
12 ***Lewis***	N	-	+	Y	N	N	N
13 ***Mack***	N	N	Y	Y	N	N	N
14 Mica	N	Y	Y	Y	Y	Y	Y
15 ***Shaw***	N	N	Y	Y	N	N	N
16 Smith	N	Y	Y	Y	Y	Y	Y
17 Lehman	N	Y	N	Y	Y	Y	Y
18 Pepper	N	Y	N	Y	Y	Y	Y
19 Fascell	N	Y	N	Y	Y	Y	Y
GEORGIA							
1 Thomas	Y	Y	Y	Y	Y	Y	Y
2 Hatcher	Y	Y	?	Y	?	?	?
3 Ray	N	Y	Y	Y	Y	Y	Y
4 ***Swindall***	N	N	Y	Y	N	N	N
5 Fowler	Y	Y	Y	Y	Y	Y	Y
6 ***Gingrich***	N	N	Y	Y	N	N	N
7 Darden	N	Y	Y	Y	Y	Y	Y
8 Rowland	Y	Y	Y	Y	Y	Y	Y
9 Jenkins	N	Y	Y	Y	Y	Y	?
10 Barnard	N	Y	Y	Y	Y	Y	?
HAWAII							
1 Heftel	N	Y	Y	Y	Y	Y	Y
2 Akaka	N	Y	Y	Y	Y	Y	Y
IDAHO							
1 ***Craig***	N	N	Y	Y	N	N	N
2 Stallings	N	Y	?	Y	Y	Y	Y
ILLINOIS							
1 Hayes	N	Y	Y	Y	Y	Y	Y
2 Savage	N	?	?	?	?	?	?
3 Russo	N	?	?	?	?	?	?
4 ***O'Brien***	N	N	Y	?	Y	?	N
5 Lipinski	?	?	?	?	?	?	?
6 ***Hyde***	N	N	Y	Y	N	N	Y
7 Collins	N	?	?	?	?	?	?
8 Rostenkowski	N	Y	?	?	?	?	?
9 Yates	N	Y	Y	Y	Y	Y	Y
10 ***Porter***	N	N	Y	Y	N	N	N
11 Annunzio	N	Y	Y	Y	Y	Y	Y
12 ***Crane***	N	N	Y	Y	N	N	N
13 ***Fawell***	N	N	Y	Y	N	N	N
14 ***Grotberg***	N	-	+	+	-	-	-
15 ***Madigan***	N	N	Y	Y	N	N	N
16 ***Martin***	N	N	Y	Y	N	N	N
17 Evans	N	Y	Y	Y	Y	Y	Y
18 ***Michel***	N	N	Y	Y	N	?	?
19 Bruce	Y	Y	Y	Y	Y	Y	Y
20 Durbin	Y	Y	N	Y	Y	Y	Y
21 Price	Y	Y	Y	Y	Y	Y	Y
22 Gray	N	Y	Y	Y	?	?	?
INDIANA							
1 Visclosky	Y	Y	Y	Y	Y	Y	Y
2 Sharp	Y	Y	Y	Y	Y	Y	Y
3 ***Hiler***	N	N	Y	Y	N	N	N
4 ***Coats***	N	N	?	?	?	?	?
5 ***Hillis***	N	N	Y	Y	N	?	?

ND - Northern Democrats SD - Southern Democrats

* Corresponding to Congressional Record Votes 69, 70, 71, 72, 73, 74, 75

	62	63	64	65	66	67	68
6 ***Burton***	N	Y	Y	Y	N	N	N
7 ***Myers***	N	N	Y	Y	N	N	N
8 Vacancy							
9 Hamilton	Y	Y	Y	Y	Y	Y	Y
10 Jacobs	N	N	Y	Y	Y	Y	Y
IOWA							
1 ***Leach***	Y	Y	Y	Y	N	N	N
2 ***Tauke***	N	N	Y	Y	N	N	N
3 ***Evans***	N	N	Y	Y	N	N	N
4 Smith	N	?	?	Y	Y	Y	Y
5 ***Lightfoot***	N	N	Y	Y	N	N	N
6 Bedell	N	Y	Y	Y	Y	Y	Y
KANSAS							
1 ***Roberts***	N	N	Y	Y	N	N	N
2 Slattery	Y	Y	Y	Y	Y	Y	Y
3 ***Meyers***	N	N	Y	Y	N	N	N
4 Glickman	Y	Y	Y	Y	Y	Y	Y
5 ***Whittaker***	N	N	Y	Y	N	N	N
KENTUCKY							
1 Hubbard	N	Y	Y	Y	Y	Y	Y
2 Natcher	N	Y	Y	Y	Y	Y	Y
3 Mazzoli	N	Y	?	?	Y	Y	Y
4 ***Snyder***	N	N	Y	Y	N	?	?
5 ***Rogers***	N	N	Y	Y	N	N	N
6 ***Hopkins***	N	N	Y	Y	N	N	N
7 Perkins	N	Y	Y	Y	Y	Y	Y
LOUISIANA							
1 ***Livingston***	N	N	N	Y	N	N	N
2 Boggs	N	Y	?	Y	Y	Y	Y
3 Tauzin	N	Y	Y	Y	Y	Y	Y
4 Roemer	N	N	Y	Y	Y	Y	Y
5 Huckaby	N	N	?	Y	Y	Y	Y
6 ***Moore***	N	N	Y	Y	N	N	N
7 Breaux	N	Y	Y	Y	Y	Y	Y
8 Long	N	Y	Y	Y	Y	?	Y
MAINE							
1 ***McKernan***	Y	N	Y	Y	N	N	N
2 ***Snowe***	Y	N	Y	Y	Y	N	N
MARYLAND							
1 Dyson	N	Y	Y	Y	Y	Y	Y
2 ***Bentley***	N	N	Y	Y	N	N	N
3 Mikulski	N	Y	Y	Y	Y	Y	Y
4 ***Holt***	N	N	Y	Y	P	N	Y
5 Hoyer	Y	Y	Y	Y	Y	Y	Y
6 Byron	N	Y	Y	Y	Y	Y	Y
7 Mitchell	N	N	N	Y	Y	Y	Y
8 Barnes	Y	Y	Y	Y	Y	Y	Y
MASSACHUSETTS							
1 ***Conte***	Y	N	Y	Y	N	N	N
2 Boland	Y	?	?	?	?	?	?
3 Early	Y	Y	Y	Y	Y	Y	Y
4 Frank	N	Y	P	Y	Y	Y	Y
5 Atkins	N	Y	Y	Y	?	?	Y
6 Mavroules	Y	Y	?	Y	Y	Y	Y
7 Markey	N	Y	Y	Y	Y	Y	Y
8 O'Neill							
9 Moakley	Y	+	+	+	+	+	+
10 Studds	N	Y	P	Y	Y	Y	Y
11 Donnelly	Y	Y	N	Y	Y	Y	Y
MICHIGAN							
1 Conyers	N	Y	P	Y	Y	Y	Y
2 ***Pursell***	Y	N	Y	Y	N	N	N
3 Wolpe	Y	Y	Y	Y	Y	Y	Y
4 ***Siljander***	N	N	Y	Y	N	N	N
5 ***Henry***	N	N	Y	Y	N	N	N
6 Carr	N	Y	Y	Y	Y	Y	Y
7 Kildee	N	Y	Y	Y	Y	Y	Y
8 Traxler	Y	Y	Y	Y	Y	Y	?
9 ***Vander Jagt***	N	N	Y	Y	N	N	N
10 ***Schuette***	N	N	Y	Y	N	N	N
11 ***Davis***	?	?	Y	Y	N	N	N
12 Bonior	Y	Y	Y	Y	Y	Y	Y
13 Crockett	N	Y	Y	Y	?	?	?
14 Hertel	Y	Y	Y	Y	Y	Y	Y
15 Ford	N	?	?	Y	Y	Y	Y
16 Dingell	N	Y	Y	?	Y	Y	Y
17 Levin	Y	Y	Y	Y	Y	Y	Y
18 ***Broomfield***	N	Y	Y	Y	N	N	Y
MINNESOTA							
1 Penny	Y	N	Y	Y	Y	Y	Y
2 ***Weber***	N	N	Y	Y	N	N	N
3 ***Frenzel***	N	N	Y	Y	N	N	N
4 Vento	Y	Y	Y	Y	Y	Y	Y
5 Sabo	Y	Y	Y	Y	Y	Y	Y
6 Sikorski	Y	N	Y	Y	Y	Y	Y
7 ***Stangeland***	N	N	?	Y	N	N	N
8 Oberstar	N	Y	N	Y	Y	Y	Y
MISSISSIPPI							
1 Whitten	Y	Y	Y	?	?	?	?
2 ***Franklin***	N	N	Y	Y	N	N	N
3 Montgomery	N	Y	Y	Y	?	?	?
4 Dowdy	N	Y	Y	Y	Y	Y	Y
5 ***Lott***	N	N	Y	Y	N	N	N
MISSOURI							
1 Clay	Y	N	Y	Y	Y	Y	?
2 Young	Y	Y	Y	Y	Y	Y	Y
3 Gephardt	Y	Y	?	Y	Y	Y	Y
4 Skelton	Y	Y	Y	Y	Y	Y	Y
5 Wheat	N	Y	Y	Y	Y	Y	Y
6 ***Coleman***	N	N	Y	Y	N	N	N
7 ***Taylor***	N	N	Y	Y	N	N	N
8 ***Emerson***	N	N	Y	Y	N	N	N
9 Volkmer	Y	Y	Y	Y	Y	Y	Y
MONTANA							
1 Williams	N	?	Y	Y	?	Y	Y
2 ***Marlenee***	N	N	Y	Y	N	N	N
NEBRASKA							
1 ***Bereuter***	N	N	Y	Y	Y	N	N
2 ***Daub***	N	N	Y	Y	N	N	N
3 ***Smith***	N	N	Y	Y	N	N	N
NEVADA							
1 Reid	Y	Y	Y	Y	Y	Y	Y
2 ***Vucanovich***	N	Y	Y	Y	N	N	N
NEW HAMPSHIRE							
1 ***Smith***	N	N	Y	Y	N	N	N
2 ***Gregg***	N	N	Y	Y	N	N	N
NEW JERSEY							
1 Florio	N	Y	Y	Y	Y	Y	Y
2 Hughes	Y	Y	Y	Y	Y	Y	Y
3 Howard	Y	Y	Y	Y	?	?	?
4 ***Smith***	N	N	Y	Y	N	N	N
5 ***Roukema***	N	N	Y	Y	N	N	N
6 Dwyer	Y	Y	Y	Y	Y	Y	Y
7 ***Rinaldo***	N	N	Y	Y	N	N	N
8 Roe	Y	Y	?	Y	Y	Y	Y
9 Torricelli	N	Y	Y	Y	Y	Y	Y
10 Rodino	?	?	?	?	?	?	?
11 ***Gallo***	N	N	Y	Y	N	N	N
12 ***Courter***	N	N	Y	Y	N	N	N
13 ***Saxton***	N	N	Y	Y	N	N	N
14 Guarini	Y	Y	Y	Y	Y	?	?
NEW MEXICO							
1 ***Lujan***	N	N	Y	Y	N	N	N
2 ***Skeen***	N	N	Y	Y	N	N	N
3 Richardson	Y	N	Y	?	Y	Y	Y
NEW YORK							
1 ***Carney***	N	N	Y	Y	N	N	N
2 Downey	N	Y	Y	Y	Y	Y	Y
3 Mrazek	Y	Y	Y	Y	Y	Y	?
4 ***Lent***	N	N	Y	Y	N	N	?
5 ***McGrath***	N	?	?	?	?	?	?
6 Addabbo	N	Y	Y	Y	Y	Y	Y
7 Ackerman	N	?	Y	Y	Y	?	?
8 Scheuer	N	?	?	?	?	?	?
9 Manton	Y	Y	Y	Y	Y	Y	Y
10 Schumer	N	Y	Y	Y	Y	Y	Y
11 Towns	N	N	Y	Y	Y	Y	Y
12 Owens	N	Y	Y	Y	Y	Y	Y
13 Solarz	N	Y	Y	Y	Y	Y	Y
14 ***Molinari***	N	N	Y	Y	N	N	N
15 ***Green***	N	?	?	?	?	?	?
16 Rangel	N	Y	Y	Y	Y	Y	Y
17 Weiss	Y	?	Y	Y	Y	Y	Y
18 Garcia	N	?	?	?	?	?	?
19 Biaggi	Y	Y	Y	Y	N	?	?
20 ***DioGuardi***	N	N	Y	Y	N	N	N
21 ***Fish***	Y	N	Y	Y	N	?	?
22 ***Gilman***	Y	N	Y	Y	N	N	N
23 Stratton	N	Y	Y	Y	Y	Y	Y
24 ***Solomon***	N	N	Y	Y	?	N	N
25 ***Boehlert***	Y	N	Y	Y	N	N	N
26 ***Martin***	N	N	Y	?	?	?	?
27 ***Wortley***	N	N	Y	Y	N	N	N
28 McHugh	Y	Y	Y	Y	Y	Y	Y
29 ***Horton***	Y	Y	Y	?	?	?	Y
30 ***Eckert***	N	N	Y	Y	N	N	N
31 ***Kemp***	N	N	Y	Y	N	N	N
32 LaFalce	Y	Y	Y	Y	Y	Y	Y
33 Nowak	Y	Y	Y	Y	?	?	?
34 Lundine	N	Y	Y	Y	Y	Y	Y
NORTH CAROLINA							
1 Jones	N	?	?	?	?	?	?
2 Valentine	Y	Y	Y	Y	Y	Y	Y
3 Whitley	Y	Y	Y	Y	Y	Y	Y
4 ***Cobey***	N	N	Y	Y	N	N	N
5 Neal	Y	Y	?	Y	Y	Y	Y
6 ***Coble***	N	N	Y	Y	N	N	N
7 Rose	N	Y	Y	Y	Y	Y	Y
8 Hefner	Y	Y	?	?	?	?	?
9 ***McMillan***	N	N	Y	Y	N	N	N
10 ***Broyhill***	N	N	Y	Y	N	N	N
11 ***Hendon***	N	N	Y	Y	N	N	N
NORTH DAKOTA							
AL Dorgan	N	Y	Y	Y	Y	Y	Y
OHIO							
1 Luken	N	Y	Y	Y	Y	Y	Y
2 ***Gradison***	Y	N	Y	Y	N	N	N
3 Hall	N	Y	Y	Y	Y	Y	Y
4 ***Oxley***	N	N	Y	Y	N	N	N
5 ***Latta***	N	N	?	?	?	?	?
6 ***McEwen***	N	N	Y	Y	N	N	N
7 ***DeWine***	N	N	Y	Y	N	N	N
8 ***Kindness***	N	N	N	?	N	N	N
9 Kaptur	Y	Y	Y	Y	Y	Y	Y
10 ***Miller***	N	N	Y	Y	N	N	N
11 Eckart	N	Y	Y	Y	Y	Y	Y
12 ***Kasich***	N	N	Y	Y	N	N	N
13 Pease	N	Y	Y	Y	Y	Y	Y
14 Seiberling	Y	?	?	?	?	?	?
15 ***Wylie***	N	N	Y	Y	N	N	Y
16 ***Regula***	N	N	Y	Y	N	N	N
17 Traficant	?	?	?	?	?	?	?
18 Applegate	N	?	Y	Y	Y	Y	Y
19 Feighan	Y	Y	Y	Y	Y	Y	Y
20 Oakar	N	Y	Y	Y	Y	Y	Y
21 Stokes	N	Y	Y	Y	Y	Y	?
OKLAHOMA							
1 Jones	Y	Y	Y	Y	Y	Y	Y
2 Synar	Y	Y	Y	Y	Y	Y	Y
3 Watkins	Y	Y	Y	Y	Y	Y	Y
4 McCurdy	Y	Y	Y	Y	Y	Y	Y
5 ***Edwards***	N	N	Y	Y	?	?	?
6 English	Y	Y	Y	Y	Y	Y	Y
OREGON							
1 AuCoin	N	Y	Y	Y	Y	Y	Y
2 ***Smith, R.***	N	N	Y	Y	N	N	N
3 Wyden	N	Y	Y	Y	Y	Y	Y
4 Weaver	N	?	?	?	?	?	?
5 ***Smith, D.***	N	N	Y	Y	N	N	N
PENNSYLVANIA							
1 Foglietta	Y	Y	Y	Y	Y	Y	Y
2 Gray	N	Y	Y	Y	Y	Y	Y
3 Borski	N	Y	Y	Y	Y	Y	Y
4 Kolter	N	?	?	?	?	?	?
5 ***Schulze***	?	?	?	?	?	?	?
6 Yatron	Y	Y	Y	Y	Y	Y	Y
7 Edgar	N	Y	Y	Y	Y	Y	Y
8 Kostmayer	Y	Y	Y	Y	Y	Y	Y
9 ***Shuster***	N	N	Y	Y	?	?	?
10 ***McDade***	Y	N	?	?	?	?	?
11 Kanjorski	Y	Y	Y	Y	Y	Y	Y
12 Murtha	Y	Y	?	?	?	?	?
13 ***Coughlin***	Y	N	Y	Y	N	N	N
14 Coyne	Y	Y	Y	Y	Y	Y	Y
15 ***Ritter***	N	N	Y	Y	N	N	N
16 ***Walker***	N	N	Y	Y	N	N	N
17 ***Gekas***	N	N	Y	Y	N	N	N
18 Walgren	N	Y	Y	Y	Y	Y	Y
19 ***Goodling***	N	N	?	Y	N	?	N
20 Gaydos	N	Y	Y	Y	Y	Y	Y
21 ***Ridge***	N	N	Y	Y	N	N	N
22 Murphy	N	Y	Y	Y	Y	Y	Y
23 ***Clinger***	Y	N	Y	Y	N	N	N
RHODE ISLAND							
1 St Germain	Y	Y	Y	Y	Y	Y	Y
2 ***Schneider***	Y	N	Y	Y	N	N	N
SOUTH CAROLINA							
1 ***Hartnett***	N	N	Y	Y	N	N	?
2 ***Spence***	N	N	Y	Y	N	N	N
3 Derrick	N	Y	Y	Y	Y	Y	?
4 ***Campbell***	N	N	Y	Y	N	N	N
5 Spratt	Y	Y	Y	Y	Y	Y	Y
6 Tallon	N	Y	Y	Y	Y	Y	Y
SOUTH DAKOTA							
AL Daschle	N	Y	Y	Y	Y	Y	Y
TENNESSEE							
1 ***Quillen***	N	N	Y	?	?	?	?
2 ***Duncan***	N	N	?	Y	N	N	N
3 Lloyd	N	Y	?	Y	Y	Y	Y
4 Cooper	Y	Y	Y	Y	Y	Y	Y
5 Boner	N	Y	Y	Y	Y	Y	Y
6 Gordon	Y	?	Y	Y	Y	Y	Y
7 ***Sundquist***	N	N	Y	Y	N	N	N
8 Jones	N	Y	Y	Y	?	?	?
9 Ford	N	Y	?	?	?	?	?
TEXAS							
1 Hall, S.	N	Y	?	Y	Y	?	?
2 Wilson	N	Y	Y	Y	Y	Y	Y
3 ***Bartlett***	N	N	?	?	?	?	?
4 Hall, R.	N	Y	Y	Y	Y	Y	Y
5 Bryant	Y	Y	Y	Y	Y	Y	Y
6 ***Barton***	N	N	Y	Y	N	N	N
7 ***Archer***	N	N	Y	Y	N	N	N
8 ***Fields***	N	N	Y	Y	N	N	N
9 Brooks	Y	Y	Y	Y	Y	Y	Y
10 Pickle	Y	Y	Y	Y	Y	Y	Y
11 Leath	N	Y	Y	Y	Y	Y	Y
12 Wright	Y	Y	Y	Y	?	?	?
13 ***Boulter***	N	N	Y	Y	N	N	N
14 ***Sweeney***	N	N	Y	Y	N	N	N
15 de la Garza	Y	?	?	?	?	?	?
16 Coleman	Y	Y	Y	Y	Y	Y	Y
17 Stenholm	N	N	Y	Y	Y	Y	Y
18 Leland	N	Y	Y	Y	Y	Y	Y
19 ***Combest***	N	N	Y	Y	N	N	N
20 Gonzalez	N	Y	P	Y	Y	Y	Y
21 ***Loeffler***	N	?	?	?	?	?	?
22 ***DeLay***	N	N	Y	Y	N	N	N
23 Bustamante	Y	Y	Y	Y	Y	Y	Y
24 Frost	Y	Y	?	?	?	?	?
25 Andrews	Y	Y	Y	Y	?	?	?
26 ***Armey***	N	N	Y	Y	N	N	N
27 Ortiz	Y	Y	Y	Y	Y	Y	Y
UTAH							
1 ***Hansen***	N	N	Y	Y	?	?	?
2 ***Monson***	N	N	Y	Y	N	N	N
3 ***Nielson***	N	N	Y	Y	N	N	N
VERMONT							
AL ***Jeffords***	N	N	Y	Y	N	N	N
VIRGINIA							
1 ***Bateman***	N	N	?	?	?	?	?
2 ***Whitehurst***	N	N	Y	Y	?	?	?
3 ***Bliley***	N	N	Y	Y	N	N	N
4 Sisisky	Y	Y	Y	Y	Y	Y	Y
5 Daniel	?	?	?	?	?	?	?
6 Olin	Y	Y	Y	Y	Y	Y	Y
7 ***Slaughter***	N	N	Y	Y	N	N	N
8 ***Parris***	N	N	Y	Y	N	N	N
9 Boucher	Y	Y	Y	Y	Y	Y	Y
10 ***Wolf***	N	N	Y	Y	N	N	N
WASHINGTON							
1 ***Miller***	N	N	Y	Y	N	N	N
2 Swift	Y	Y	Y	Y	Y	Y	Y
3 Bonker	N	?	?	Y	Y	Y	Y
4 ***Morrison***	N	N	Y	Y	N	N	N
5 Foley	Y	Y	Y	Y	Y	Y	Y
6 Dicks	Y	Y	Y	Y	Y	Y	Y
7 Lowry	N	Y	Y	?	?	?	Y
8 ***Chandler***	N	N	Y	Y	N	N	N
WEST VIRGINIA							
1 Mollohan	Y	Y	Y	Y	Y	Y	Y
2 Staggers	Y	Y	Y	Y	Y	Y	Y
3 Wise	N	Y	?	Y	Y	Y	Y
4 Rahall	Y	Y	N	Y	?	?	?
WISCONSIN							
1 Aspin	Y	?	Y	Y	Y	Y	Y
2 Kastenmeier	Y	Y	Y	Y	Y	Y	?
3 ***Gunderson***	N	N	Y	Y	N	N	N
4 Kleczka	Y	Y	Y	Y	Y	?	Y
5 Moody	Y	Y	?	?	Y	Y	Y
6 ***Petri***	Y	N	N	Y	N	N	N
7 Obey	Y	Y	P	Y	Y	Y	Y
8 ***Roth***	N	N	Y	Y	N	N	N
9 ***Sensenbrenner***	N	N	N	Y	N	N	N
WYOMING							
AL ***Cheney***	N	N	Y	Y	N	N	N

Southern states - Ala., Ark., Fla., Ga., Ky., La., Miss., N.C., Okla., S.C., Tenn., Texas, Va.

* The *Congressional Record* vote number is different from the CQ vote number because the *Record* includes quorum calls in its tally. CQ does not publish quorum call votes.

69. Procedural Motion. Dreier, R-Calif., motion to approve the House *Journal* of Thursday, April 25. Motion agreed to 158-130: R 4-125; D 154-5 (ND 98-4, SD 56-1), April 29, 1985.

70. Procedural Motion. Martin, R-Ill., motion to adjourn. Motion rejected 124-168: R 123-8; D 1-160 (ND 1-107, SD 0-53), April 29, 1985. (The motion was made and the roll call was ordered to delay House business as part of a Republican protest of the handling of the contested election in the Indiana 8th District.)

71. S Con Res 37. Jeannette Rankin Statue. Frenzel, R-Minn., demand for a second on the Oakar, D-Ohio, motion to suspend the rules and adopt the concurrent resolution. Second ordered 318-0: R 140-0; D 178-0 (ND 117-0, SD 61-0), April 29, 1985. (The demand was made and the roll call was ordered to delay House business as part of a Republican protest of the handling of the contested election in the Indiana 8th District.) (The resolution was subsequently adopted *(see vote 75, below)*.)

72. H Con Res 130. President's Visit to Bitburg Cemetery. Broomfield, R-Mich., demand for a second on the Fascell, D-Fla., motion to suspend the rules and adopt the concurrent resolution. Second ordered 325-1: R 143-1; D 182-0 (ND 120-0, SD 62-0), April 29, 1985. (The demand was made and the roll call was ordered to delay House business as part of a Republican protest of the handling of the contested election in the Indiana 8th District.) (The resolution was subsequently adopted *(see vote 76, below)*.)

73. Procedural Motion. Saxton, R-N.J., motion to approve the House *Journal* of Monday, April 29. Motion agreed to 231-172: R 7-165; D 224-7 (ND 147-6, SD 77-1), April 30, 1985.

74. H Res 148. Indiana 8th District Seat. Adoption of the resolution to declare a vacancy in the 99th Congress from the 8th District of Indiana. Rejected 200-229: R 181-0; D 19-229 (ND 6-161, SD 13-68), April 30, 1985.

75. S Con Res 37. Jeannette Rankin Statue. Oakar, D-Ohio, motion to suspend the rules and adopt the concurrent resolution to provide for the acceptance of a statue of former Rep. Jeannette Rankin (R-Mont., 1917-19, 1941-43), and for its placement in National Statuary Hall, in the U.S. Capitol. Motion agreed to 424-4: R 178-3; D 246-1 (ND 167-0, SD 79-1), April 30, 1985. A two-thirds majority of those present and voting (286 in this case) is required for adoption under suspension of the rules.

76. H Con Res 130. President's Visit to Bitburg Cemetery. Fascell, D-Fla., motion to suspend the rules and adopt the concurrent resolution to express the sense of Congress that the president should reconsider his scheduled visit to the Bitburg military cemetery in West Germany, and that he should pay tribute to appropriate symbols of that nation's current democracy. Motion agreed to 390-26: R 143-26; D 247-0 (ND 166-0, SD 81-0), April 30, 1985. A two-thirds majority of those present and voting (278 in this case) is required for adoption under suspension of the rules.

KEY

- Y Voted for (yea).
- # Paired for.
- + Announced for.
- N Voted against (nay).
- X Paired against.
- \- Announced against.
- P Voted "present".
- C Voted "present" to avoid possible conflict of interest.
- ? Did not vote or otherwise make a position known.

Democrats ***Republicans***

	69	70	71	72	73	74	75	76
ALABAMA								
1 ***Callahan***	N	Y	Y	Y	Y	Y	Y	Y
2 ***Dickinson***	N	Y	Y	Y	N	Y	Y	P
3 Nichols	Y	N	Y	Y	Y	N	Y	Y
4 Bevill	?	?	Y	Y	Y	N	Y	Y
5 Flippo	Y	N	Y	Y	Y	N	Y	Y
6 Erdreich	?	?	?	?	Y	N	Y	Y
7 Shelby	?	?	?	?	Y	N	Y	Y
ALASKA								
AL ***Young***	N	Y	Y	Y	N	Y	Y	Y
ARIZONA								
1 ***McCain***	N	Y	Y	Y	N	Y	Y	Y
2 Udall	?	?	?	?	?	?	?	?
3 ***Stump***	N	N	Y	Y	N	Y	Y	N
4 ***Rudd***	N	Y	Y	Y	N	Y	Y	Y
5 ***Kolbe***	N	Y	Y	Y	N	Y	Y	Y
ARKANSAS								
1 Alexander	Y	N	Y	Y	Y	N	Y	Y
2 Robinson	Y	N	Y	Y	Y	N	Y	Y
3 ***Hammerschmidt***	N	N	Y	Y	N	Y	Y	Y
4 Anthony	Y	?	Y	Y	Y	N	Y	Y
CALIFORNIA								
1 Bosco	?	?	?	?	Y	N	Y	Y
2 ***Chappie***	N	Y	Y	Y	N	Y	Y	Y
3 Matsui	Y	N	Y	Y	Y	N	Y	Y
4 Fazio	Y	N	?	Y	Y	N	Y	Y
5 Burton	Y	N	Y	?	Y	N	Y	Y
6 Boxer	?	?	?	?	Y	N	Y	Y
7 Miller	?	?	Y	P	Y	N	Y	Y
8 Dellums	?	?	?	?	Y	N	Y	Y
9 Stark	Y	N	Y	Y	?	N	Y	Y
10 Edwards	Y	N	Y	Y	Y	N	Y	Y
11 Lantos	?	?	?	?	Y	N	Y	Y
12 ***Zschau***	N	Y	Y	Y	N	Y	Y	Y
13 Mineta	Y	N	Y	Y	Y	N	Y	Y
14 ***Shumway***	N	Y	Y	Y	N	Y	Y	N
15 Coelho	?	?	?	?	Y	N	Y	Y
16 Panetta	Y	N	Y	Y	Y	N	Y	Y
17 ***Pashayan***	N	Y	Y	Y	N	Y	Y	Y
18 Lehman	?	?	?	?	?	N	Y	Y
19 ***Lagomarsino***	N	Y	Y	Y	N	Y	Y	Y
20 ***Thomas***	N	Y	Y	Y	N	Y	Y	Y
21 ***Fiedler***	N	Y	Y	Y	N	Y	Y	+
22 ***Moorhead***	N	Y	Y	Y	N	Y	Y	Y
23 Beilenson	?	?	?	?	?	N	Y	Y
24 Waxman	?	?	?	?	Y	N	Y	Y
25 Roybal	Y	N	Y	Y	Y	N	Y	Y
26 Berman	Y	N	Y	Y	Y	N	Y	Y
27 Levine	Y	N	Y	Y	Y	N	Y	Y
28 Dixon	Y	N	Y	Y	Y	N	Y	Y
29 Hawkins	N	N	?	?	N	N	Y	Y
30 Martinez	Y	N	Y	Y	Y	N	Y	Y
31 Dymally	?	?	?	?	P	N	Y	Y
32 Anderson	Y	?	?	Y	Y	N	Y	Y
33 ***Dreier***	N	Y	Y	Y	N	Y	Y	Y
34 Torres	Y	N	Y	Y	Y	N	Y	Y
35 ***Lewis***	N	Y	Y	Y	N	Y	Y	Y
36 Brown	Y	N	Y	Y	Y	N	Y	Y
37 ***McCandless***	N	Y	Y	Y	N	Y	Y	P
38 ***Dornan***	N	Y	Y	Y	N	Y	Y	Y
39 ***Dannemeyer***	-	+	+	+	N	Y	Y	N
40 ***Badham***	?	?	?	?	N	Y	Y	N
41 ***Lowery***	N	Y	Y	Y	N	Y	Y	Y
42 ***Lungren***	N	Y	Y	?	N	Y	Y	Y
43 ***Packard***	?	?	?	?	N	Y	Y	Y
44 Bates	Y	N	Y	Y	Y	N	Y	Y
45 ***Hunter***	?	?	?	Y	N	Y	Y	Y
COLORADO								
1 Schroeder	N	N	Y	Y	N	N	Y	Y
2 Wirth	Y	N	Y	Y	Y	N	Y	Y
3 ***Strang***	N	Y	+	Y	N	Y	Y	Y
4 ***Brown***	N	Y	Y	Y	N	Y	Y	Y
5 ***Kramer***	N	Y	Y	Y	N	Y	Y	Y
6 ***Schaefer***	N	Y	Y	Y	N	Y	Y	Y
CONNECTICUT								
1 Kennelly	?	?	?	?	Y	N	Y	Y
2 Gejdenson	P	N	Y	Y	Y	N	Y	Y
3 Morrison	Y	N	Y	Y	Y	N	Y	Y
4 ***McKinney***	?	?	?	?	N	Y	Y	Y
5 ***Rowland***	N	Y	Y	Y	N	Y	Y	Y
6 ***Johnson***	?	?	?	?	Y	Y	Y	Y
DELAWARE								
AL Carper	?	?	?	?	Y	N	Y	Y
FLORIDA								
1 Hutto	Y	N	Y	Y	Y	Y	Y	Y
2 Fuqua	?	?	?	?	Y	N	Y	Y
3 Bennett	Y	N	Y	Y	Y	N	Y	Y
4 Chappell	Y	N	?	Y	?	N	Y	Y
5 ***McCollum***	?	?	?	?	N	Y	Y	Y
6 MacKay	?	?	?	Y	Y	N	Y	Y
7 Gibbons	Y	N	Y	Y	Y	N	Y	Y
8 ***Young***	?	?	?	?	N	Y	Y	Y
9 ***Bilirakis***	N	Y	Y	Y	N	Y	Y	Y
10 ***Ireland***	N	Y	Y	Y	N	Y	Y	Y
11 Nelson	+	-	+	+	Y	N	Y	Y
12 ***Lewis***	N	Y	Y	Y	N	Y	Y	Y
13 ***Mack***	N	Y	Y	Y	?	Y	Y	Y
14 Mica	Y	N	Y	Y	Y	N	Y	Y
15 ***Shaw***	N	Y	Y	Y	N	Y	Y	Y
16 Smith	P	N	Y	Y	Y	N	Y	Y
17 Lehman	Y	N	Y	Y	Y	N	Y	Y
18 Pepper	Y	-	Y	+	Y	N	Y	Y
19 Fascell	Y	N	Y	Y	Y	N	Y	Y
GEORGIA								
1 Thomas	Y	N	Y	Y	Y	N	Y	Y
2 Hatcher	Y	N	Y	Y	Y	N	Y	Y
3 Ray	Y	N	Y	Y	Y	Y	Y	Y
4 ***Swindall***	-	+	Y	Y	N	Y	Y	Y
5 Fowler	Y	N	Y	Y	Y	N	Y	Y
6 ***Gingrich***	?	?	Y	Y	N	Y	Y	Y
7 Darden	Y	N	Y	Y	Y	N	Y	Y
8 Rowland	Y	N	Y	Y	Y	N	Y	Y
9 Jenkins	Y	N	Y	?	Y	N	Y	Y
10 Barnard	Y	N	Y	Y	Y	Y	Y	Y
HAWAII								
1 Heftel	?	?	?	?	?	N	Y	Y
2 Akaka	Y	N	Y	Y	Y	N	Y	Y
IDAHO								
1 ***Craig***	N	Y	Y	Y	N	Y	Y	Y
2 Stallings	Y	N	Y	Y	Y	Y	Y	Y
ILLINOIS								
1 Hayes	?	?	Y	Y	Y	N	Y	Y
2 Savage	?	?	?	?	Y	N	Y	Y
3 Russo	?	?	?	?	Y	N	Y	Y
4 ***O'Brien***	N	Y	Y	Y	N	Y	Y	Y
5 Lipinski	?	?	?	?	Y	N	Y	Y
6 ***Hyde***	?	?	?	?	N	Y	Y	N
7 Collins	Y	N	Y	Y	Y	N	Y	Y
8 Rostenkowski	?	?	?	?	Y	N	Y	Y
9 Yates	Y	N	Y	Y	Y	N	Y	Y
10 ***Porter***	N	Y	Y	Y	N	Y	Y	Y
11 Annunzio	Y	N	?	Y	Y	N	Y	Y
12 ***Crane***	?	?	?	?	N	Y	N	N
13 ***Fawell***	N	Y	Y	Y	N	Y	Y	Y
14 ***Grotberg***	-	+	+	+	-	Y	Y	Y
15 ***Madigan***	?	?	Y	Y	N	Y	Y	Y
16 ***Martin***	N	Y	Y	Y	N	Y	Y	Y
17 Evans	Y	N	Y	Y	Y	N	Y	Y
18 ***Michel***	?	?	Y	Y	N	Y	Y	N
19 Bruce	Y	N	Y	Y	Y	N	Y	Y
20 Durbin	?	?	?	?	Y	N	Y	Y
21 Price	Y	N	Y	?	Y	N	Y	Y
22 Gray	Y	N	Y	Y	Y	N	Y	Y
INDIANA								
1 Visclosky	Y	N	Y	Y	Y	N	Y	Y
2 Sharp	Y	N	Y	Y	Y	N	Y	Y
3 ***Hiler***	N	Y	Y	Y	N	Y	Y	P
4 ***Coats***	N	Y	Y	Y	N	Y	Y	Y
5 ***Hillis***	N	Y	Y	Y	N	Y	Y	N

ND - Northern Democrats SD - Southern Democrats

* Corresponding to Congressional Record Votes 76, 77, 78, 79, 80, 82, 83, 84

	69	70	71	72	73	74	75	76
6 ***Burton***	N	Y	Y	Y	N	Y	Y	N
7 ***Myers***	N	Y	Y	Y	N	Y	Y	N
8 Vacancy								
9 Hamilton	Y	N	Y	Y	Y	N	Y	Y
10 Jacobs	?	?	?	?	N	N	Y	Y
IOWA								
1 ***Leach***	N	Y	Y	Y	N	Y	Y	Y
2 ***Tauke***	N	Y	Y	Y	N	Y	Y	Y
3 ***Evans***	N	Y	Y	Y	N	Y	Y	Y
4 Smith	Y	N	Y	Y	Y	N	Y	Y
5 ***Lightfoot***	N	Y	Y	Y	N	Y	Y	Y
6 Bedell	Y	N	Y	Y	Y	N	Y	Y
KANSAS								
1 ***Roberts***	N	Y	Y	Y	N	Y	Y	Y
2 Slattery	Y	N	Y	Y	Y	N	Y	Y
3 ***Meyers***	N	Y	Y	Y	N	Y	Y	Y
4 Glickman	Y	N	Y	Y	Y	N	Y	Y
5 ***Whittaker***	?	?	Y	Y	N	Y	Y	Y
KENTUCKY								
1 Hubbard	?	?	?	?	Y	N	Y	Y
2 Natcher	Y	N	Y	Y	Y	N	Y	Y
3 Mazzoli	Y	N	Y	Y	Y	Y	Y	Y
4 ***Snyder***	N	N	Y	Y	Y	Y	Y	P
5 ***Rogers***	N	Y	Y	Y	N	Y	Y	Y
6 ***Hopkins***	N	N	Y	Y	Y	Y	Y	Y
7 Perkins	Y	N	Y	Y	Y	N	Y	Y
LOUISIANA								
1 ***Livingston***	N	Y	Y	Y	?	Y	Y	Y
2 Boggs	?	?	?	?	?	N	Y	Y
3 Tauzin	Y	N	Y	Y	Y	N	Y	Y
4 Roemer	-	-	Y	Y	N	N	Y	Y
5 Huckaby	Y	N	Y	Y	?	?	?	?
6 ***Moore***	N	Y	Y	Y	N	Y	Y	Y
7 Breaux	?	?	?	?	Y	N	Y	Y
8 Long	Y	N	Y	Y	Y	N	Y	Y
MAINE								
1 ***McKernan***	N	Y	Y	Y	N	Y	Y	Y
2 ***Snowe***	N	Y	Y	Y	N	Y	Y	Y
MARYLAND								
1 Dyson	Y	N	Y	Y	Y	N	Y	Y
2 ***Bentley***	?	?	?	?	N	Y	Y	Y
3 Mikulski	?	?	?	?	Y	N	Y	Y
4 ***Holt***	Y	Y	Y	Y	N	Y	Y	N
5 Hoyer	Y	N	?	Y	Y	N	Y	Y
6 Byron	Y	N	Y	Y	Y	N	Y	Y
7 Mitchell	P	N	Y	?	?	N	Y	Y
8 Barnes	?	?	?	?	Y	N	Y	Y
MASSACHUSETTS								
1 ***Conte***	N	Y	Y	Y	N	Y	Y	Y
2 Boland	?	N	Y	Y	Y	N	Y	Y
3 Early	Y	N	Y	Y	Y	N	Y	Y
4 Frank	?	?	Y	Y	Y	Y	Y	Y
5 Atkins	?	?	Y	Y	Y	N	Y	Y
6 Mavroules	Y	N	Y	Y	Y	N	Y	Y
7 Markey	?	?	Y	Y	Y	N	Y	Y
8 O'Neill								
9 Moakley	+	?	Y	Y	+	N	Y	Y
10 Studds	?	?	?	?	Y	N	Y	Y
11 Donnelly	?	?	?	?	Y	N	Y	Y
MICHIGAN								
1 Conyers	?	?	?	?	?	N	Y	Y
2 ***Pursell***	N	Y	Y	Y	N	Y	Y	Y
3 Wolpe	Y	N	Y	Y	Y	N	Y	Y
4 ***Siljander***	?	?	?	?	N	Y	Y	Y
5 ***Henry***	N	Y	Y	Y	N	Y	Y	Y
6 Carr	?	?	?	?	Y	N	Y	Y
7 Kildee	Y	N	Y	Y	Y	N	Y	Y
8 Traxler	?	?	?	?	Y	N	Y	Y
9 ***Vander Jagt***	N	Y	Y	Y	N	Y	Y	?
10 ***Schuette***	N	Y	Y	Y	N	Y	Y	Y
11 ***Davis***	N	Y	Y	Y	N	Y	Y	Y
12 Bonior	Y	N	Y	Y	Y	N	Y	Y
13 Crockett	?	?	?	?	Y	N	Y	Y
14 Hertel	Y	N	Y	Y	Y	N	Y	Y
15 Ford	?	?	?	Y	?	N	Y	Y
16 Dingell	Y	N	Y	Y	Y	N	Y	Y
17 Levin	Y	N	Y	Y	Y	N	Y	Y
18 ***Broomfield***	Y	Y	Y	Y	Y	Y	Y	Y
MINNESOTA								
1 Penny	N	Y	Y	Y	N	Y	Y	Y
2 ***Weber***	N	Y	Y	Y	N	Y	Y	Y
3 ***Frenzel***	N	Y	Y	Y	N	Y	Y	Y
4 Vento	Y	N	Y	Y	Y	N	Y	Y
5 Sabo	Y	N	Y	Y	Y	N	Y	Y
6 Sikorski	N	N	Y	Y	N	N	Y	Y

	69	70	71	72	73	74	75	76
7 ***Stangeland***	N	Y	Y	Y	N	Y	Y	Y
8 Oberstar	?	?	Y	Y	Y	N	Y	Y
MISSISSIPPI								
1 Whitten	N	N	Y	Y	Y	N	Y	Y
2 ***Franklin***	?	?	?	?	N	Y	Y	Y
3 Montgomery	Y	N	Y	?	Y	Y	Y	Y
4 Dowdy	Y	N	Y	Y	Y	N	Y	Y
5 ***Lott***	?	?	?	?	N	Y	Y	Y
MISSOURI								
1 Clay	Y	N	Y	Y	N	N	Y	Y
2 Young	Y	N	Y	Y	Y	N	Y	Y
3 Gephardt	?	?	?	?	Y	N	Y	Y
4 Skelton	?	?	?	Y	Y	N	Y	Y
5 Wheat	Y	N	Y	Y	Y	N	Y	Y
6 ***Coleman***	N	Y	Y	Y	N	Y	Y	Y
7 ***Taylor***	?	?	?	?	?	Y	Y	P
8 ***Emerson***	N	Y	Y	Y	N	Y	Y	Y
9 Volkmer	?	?	?	?	Y	N	Y	Y
MONTANA								
1 Williams	Y	N	Y	Y	?	N	Y	Y
2 ***Marlenee***	N	Y	Y	Y	N	Y	Y	Y
NEBRASKA								
1 ***Bereuter***	N	N	Y	Y	N	Y	Y	Y
2 ***Daub***	N	Y	Y	Y	N	Y	Y	Y
3 ***Smith***	?	?	?	?	N	Y	Y	Y
NEVADA								
1 Reid	Y	N	Y	Y	Y	N	Y	Y
2 ***Vucanovich***	?	Y	Y	Y	N	Y	Y	N
NEW HAMPSHIRE								
1 ***Smith***	N	Y	Y	Y	N	Y	N	Y
2 ***Gregg***	?	?	?	?	N	Y	Y	N
NEW JERSEY								
1 Florio	Y	N	Y	Y	Y	N	Y	Y
2 Hughes	Y	N	Y	Y	Y	N	Y	Y
3 Howard	Y	N	Y	Y	Y	N	Y	Y
4 ***Smith***	N	Y	Y	Y	N	Y	Y	Y
5 ***Roukema***	N	Y	Y	Y	N	Y	Y	Y
6 Dwyer	Y	N	Y	Y	Y	N	Y	Y
7 ***Rinaldo***	?	?	?	?	N	Y	Y	Y
8 Roe	?	?	?	?	Y	N	Y	Y
9 Torricelli	Y	N	Y	Y	Y	N	Y	Y
10 Rodino	?	?	?	?	Y	N	Y	Y
11 ***Gallo***	N	Y	Y	Y	N	Y	Y	Y
12 ***Courter***	N	Y	Y	Y	N	Y	Y	Y
13 ***Saxton***	N	Y	Y	Y	N	Y	Y	Y
14 Guarini	Y	N	Y	Y	Y	N	Y	Y
NEW MEXICO								
1 ***Lujan***	?	?	Y	Y	N	Y	Y	Y
2 ***Skeen***	?	Y	Y	Y	N	Y	Y	Y
3 Richardson	Y	N	Y	Y	Y	N	Y	Y
NEW YORK								
1 ***Carney***	?	?	?	?	N	Y	Y	Y
2 Downey	Y	N	Y	Y	Y	N	Y	Y
3 Mrazek	Y	N	Y	Y	Y	N	Y	Y
4 ***Lent***	?	?	?	?	N	Y	Y	Y
5 ***McGrath***	N	Y	Y	Y	N	Y	Y	Y
6 Addabbo	?	?	Y	Y	Y	N	Y	Y
7 Ackerman	Y	N	Y	Y	Y	N	Y	Y
8 Scheuer	?	?	?	?	Y	N	Y	Y
9 Manton	?	?	Y	Y	Y	N	Y	Y
10 Schumer	Y	N	Y	Y	Y	N	Y	Y
11 Towns	?	?	?	Y	?	N	Y	Y
12 Owens	?	N	Y	Y	Y	N	Y	Y
13 Solarz	Y	?	Y	Y	Y	N	Y	Y
14 ***Molinari***	N	N	Y	Y	N	Y	Y	Y
15 ***Green***	N	Y	Y	Y	N	Y	Y	Y
16 Rangel	?	N	Y	Y	Y	N	Y	Y
17 Weiss	?	?	Y	Y	Y	N	Y	Y
18 Garcia	?	?	?	?	Y	N	Y	Y
19 Biaggi	?	?	?	?	Y	N	Y	Y
20 ***DioGuardi***	N	N	Y	Y	N	Y	Y	Y
21 ***Fish***	?	?	?	?	N	Y	Y	Y
22 ***Gilman***	N	Y	Y	Y	N	Y	Y	Y
23 Stratton	Y	N	Y	Y	Y	N	Y	Y
24 ***Solomon***	N	Y	Y	Y	N	Y	Y	Y
25 ***Boehlert***	?	?	?	?	N	Y	Y	Y
26 ***Martin***	?	?	?	?	N	Y	Y	Y
27 ***Wortley***	N	Y	Y	Y	N	Y	Y	Y
28 McHugh	Y	N	Y	?	Y	N	Y	Y
29 ***Horton***	Y	Y	?	Y	N	Y	Y	Y
30 ***Eckert***	?	?	?	?	N	Y	Y	Y
31 ***Kemp***	?	Y	Y	Y	?	Y	Y	Y
32 LaFalce	Y	N	Y	Y	Y	Y	Y	Y
33 Nowak	Y	N	Y	Y	Y	N	Y	Y
34 Lundine	Y	N	Y	Y	Y	N	Y	Y

	69	70	71	72	73	74	75	76
NORTH CAROLINA								
1 Jones	Y	N	Y	Y	Y	N	Y	Y
2 Valentine	?	?	Y	Y	Y	N	Y	Y
3 Whitley	Y	N	Y	Y	Y	N	Y	Y
4 ***Cobey***	N	Y	Y	Y	N	Y	Y	Y
5 Neal	?	?	Y	Y	Y	N	Y	Y
6 ***Coble***	N	Y	Y	Y	N	Y	Y	Y
7 Rose	Y	N	Y	Y	Y	N	Y	Y
8 Hefner	?	?	?	?	Y	N	Y	Y
9 ***McMillan***	N	Y	Y	Y	N	Y	Y	Y
10 ***Broyhill***	N	Y	Y	Y	Y	Y	Y	Y
11 ***Hendon***	N	Y	Y	Y	N	Y	Y	Y
NORTH DAKOTA								
AL Dorgan	Y	N	Y	Y	Y	N	Y	Y
OHIO								
1 Luken	Y	N	Y	Y	Y	N	Y	Y
2 ***Gradison***	N	?	?	Y	N	Y	Y	Y
3 Hall	Y	N	Y	Y	Y	N	Y	Y
4 ***Oxley***	?	?	?	?	N	Y	Y	P
5 ***Latta***	N	Y	Y	Y	N	Y	Y	P
6 ***McEwen***	N	Y	Y	Y	N	Y	Y	Y
7 ***DeWine***	N	Y	Y	Y	N	Y	Y	P
8 ***Kindness***	N	Y	Y	N	N	Y	Y	N
9 Kaptur	Y	N	Y	Y	Y	N	Y	Y
10 ***Miller***	?	?	Y	Y	N	Y	Y	N
11 Eckart	Y	N	Y	Y	Y	N	Y	Y
12 ***Kasich***	N	Y	Y	Y	N	Y	Y	Y
13 Pease	Y	N	Y	Y	Y	N	Y	Y
14 Seiberling	?	?	?	?	?	N	Y	?
15 ***Wylie***	?	?	?	?	N	Y	Y	N
16 ***Regula***	N	Y	Y	Y	N	Y	Y	Y
17 Traficant	Y	N	Y	Y	Y	N	Y	Y
18 Applegate	Y	N	Y	Y	?	Y	Y	Y
19 Feighan	Y	N	Y	Y	Y	N	Y	Y
20 Oakar	Y	N	Y	Y	Y	N	Y	Y
21 Stokes	?	?	?	?	Y	N	Y	Y
OKLAHOMA								
1 Jones	?	?	?	?	Y	N	Y	Y
2 Synar	Y	N	Y	Y	Y	N	Y	Y
3 Watkins	Y	N	Y	Y	Y	N	Y	Y
4 McCurdy	Y	N	Y	Y	Y	N	Y	Y
5 ***Edwards***	N	Y	?	Y	?	?	?	?
6 English	Y	N	Y	Y	Y	Y	Y	Y
OREGON								
1 AuCoin	Y	N	Y	Y	Y	N	Y	Y
2 ***Smith, R.***	N	Y	Y	Y	N	Y	Y	Y
3 Wyden	Y	N	Y	Y	Y	N	Y	Y
4 Weaver	?	?	?	?	?	?	?	?
5 ***Smith, D.***	N	Y	Y	Y	N	Y	Y	N
PENNSYLVANIA								
1 Foglietta	Y	N	Y	Y	Y	N	Y	Y
2 Gray	?	?	?	?	Y	N	Y	Y
3 Borski	?	?	?	?	Y	N	Y	Y
4 Kolter	?	?	?	Y	Y	N	Y	Y
5 ***Schulze***	N	Y	Y	Y	N	Y	Y	Y
6 Yatron	Y	N	Y	Y	Y	N	Y	Y
7 Edgar	Y	N	Y	Y	Y	N	Y	Y
8 Kostmayer	Y	N	Y	Y	Y	N	Y	Y
9 ***Shuster***	N	Y	Y	Y	N	Y	Y	Y
10 ***McDade***	N	Y	Y	Y	?	Y	Y	Y
11 Kanjorski	Y	N	Y	Y	Y	N	Y	Y
12 Murtha	Y	N	Y	Y	Y	N	Y	Y
13 ***Coughlin***	N	Y	Y	Y	N	Y	Y	Y
14 Coyne	?	?	?	?	Y	N	Y	Y
15 ***Ritter***	?	?	?	?	N	Y	Y	Y
16 ***Walker***	N	Y	Y	Y	N	Y	Y	Y
17 ***Gekas***	N	Y	Y	Y	N	Y	Y	Y
18 Walgren	?	N	Y	Y	Y	N	Y	Y
19 ***Goodling***	?	?	?	?	?	Y	Y	Y
20 Gaydos	Y	N	Y	Y	Y	N	Y	Y
21 ***Ridge***	N	Y	Y	Y	N	Y	Y	Y
22 Murphy	?	N	Y	?	Y	N	Y	Y
23 ***Clinger***	N	Y	Y	Y	N	Y	Y	Y
RHODE ISLAND								
1 St Germain	?	?	?	?	Y	N	Y	Y
2 ***Schneider***	?	?	?	?	Y	Y	Y	Y
SOUTH CAROLINA								
1 ***Hartnett***	?	?	Y	Y	N	Y	Y	N
2 ***Spence***	?	?	Y	Y	N	Y	Y	Y
3 Derrick	?	?	?	?	Y	N	Y	Y
4 ***Campbell***	?	?	Y	Y	N	Y	Y	Y
5 Spratt	Y	?	Y	Y	Y	N	Y	Y
6 Tallon	?	?	Y	Y	Y	N	Y	Y
SOUTH DAKOTA								
AL Daschle	Y	N	Y	Y	Y	N	Y	Y

	69	70	71	72	73	74	75	76
TENNESSEE								
1 ***Quillen***	?	?	Y	Y	N	Y	Y	Y
2 ***Duncan***	N	Y	Y	Y	N	Y	Y	Y
3 Lloyd	?	?	?	Y	Y	Y	Y	Y
4 Cooper	Y	N	Y	Y	Y	N	Y	Y
5 Boner	Y	N	Y	Y	Y	N	Y	Y
6 Gordon	?	?	?	?	Y	N	Y	Y
7 ***Sundquist***	N	Y	Y	Y	N	Y	Y	Y
8 Jones	Y	N	?	Y	Y	N	Y	Y
9 Ford	Y	N	Y	Y	Y	N	Y	Y
TEXAS								
1 Hall, S.	Y	N	Y	Y	Y	Y	Y	Y
2 Wilson	?	?	?	?	Y	N	Y	Y
3 ***Bartlett***	N	Y	Y	Y	N	Y	Y	Y
4 Hall, R.	Y	N	Y	Y	Y	Y	N	Y
5 Bryant	Y	N	Y	Y	Y	N	Y	Y
6 ***Barton***	N	Y	Y	?	N	Y	Y	N
7 ***Archer***	?	?	?	?	N	Y	N	Y
8 ***Fields***	?	?	?	?	N	Y	Y	P
9 Brooks	?	?	?	?	Y	N	?	Y
10 Pickle	Y	N	Y	Y	Y	N	Y	Y
11 Leath	Y	N	Y	?	Y	Y	Y	Y
12 Wright	Y	N	Y	Y	Y	N	Y	Y
13 ***Boulter***	N	Y	Y	Y	N	Y	Y	N
14 ***Sweeney***	?	?	Y	Y	N	Y	Y	Y
15 de la Garza	Y	?	?	Y	Y	N	Y	Y
16 Coleman	Y	N	Y	Y	Y	N	Y	Y
17 Stenholm	Y	N	Y	Y	Y	Y	Y	Y
18 Leland	?	?	Y	Y	Y	N	Y	Y
19 ***Combest***	N	Y	Y	Y	N	Y	Y	Y
20 Gonzalez	Y	N	Y	Y	Y	N	Y	Y
21 ***Loeffler***	?	?	?	?	?	Y	Y	Y
22 ***DeLay***	Y	Y	Y	Y	N	Y	Y	N
23 Bustamante	?	?	?	?	Y	N	Y	Y
24 Frost	Y	N	Y	Y	Y	N	Y	Y
25 Andrews	Y	N	Y	Y	Y	N	Y	Y
26 ***Armey***	N	Y	Y	Y	N	Y	Y	N
27 Ortiz	?	?	?	?	?	N	Y	Y
UTAH								
1 ***Hansen***	?	?	?	?	N	Y	Y	N
2 ***Monson***	N	Y	Y	Y	N	Y	Y	Y
3 ***Nielson***	N	Y	Y	Y	N	Y	Y	N
VERMONT								
AL ***Jeffords***	?	?	?	?	?	Y	Y	N
VIRGINIA								
1 ***Bateman***	N	Y	Y	Y	N	Y	Y	P
2 ***Whitehurst***	N	Y	Y	Y	N	Y	Y	Y
3 ***Bliley***	N	Y	Y	Y	N	Y	Y	Y
4 Sisisky	Y	N	Y	Y	Y	N	Y	Y
5 Daniel	Y	?	Y	Y	Y	Y	Y	Y
6 Olin	Y	N	Y	Y	Y	Y	Y	Y
7 ***Slaughter***	N	Y	Y	Y	N	Y	Y	Y
8 ***Parris***	N	Y	Y	Y	N	Y	Y	Y
9 Boucher	?	?	?	?	Y	N	Y	Y
10 ***Wolf***	N	Y	Y	Y	N	Y	Y	Y
WASHINGTON								
1 ***Miller***	?	?	Y	Y	N	Y	Y	Y
2 Swift	Y	N	Y	Y	Y	N	Y	Y
3 Bonker	Y	N	Y	?	Y	N	Y	Y
4 ***Morrison***	N	Y	Y	Y	N	Y	Y	Y
5 Foley	?	?	Y	Y	?	N	Y	Y
6 Dicks	Y	N	Y	Y	Y	N	Y	Y
7 Lowry	Y	N	Y	Y	Y	N	Y	Y
8 ***Chandler***	?	?	?	?	N	Y	Y	Y
WEST VIRGINIA								
1 Mollohan	Y	N	Y	Y	Y	N	Y	Y
2 Staggers	Y	N	Y	Y	Y	N	Y	Y
3 Wise	?	?	?	Y	Y	Y	Y	Y
4 Rahall	Y	N	Y	Y	Y	N	Y	Y
WISCONSIN								
1 Aspin	?	?	Y	Y	Y	N	Y	Y
2 Kastenmeier	Y	N	Y	Y	Y	N	Y	Y
3 ***Gunderson***	N	Y	Y	Y	N	Y	Y	Y
4 Kleczka	Y	N	Y	Y	Y	N	Y	Y
5 Moody	?	?	?	Y	Y	N	Y	Y
6 ***Petri***	?	?	?	?	N	Y	Y	N
7 Obey	?	N	Y	Y	Y	N	Y	Y
8 ***Roth***	N	N	Y	Y	N	Y	Y	Y
9 ***Sensenbrenner***	N	Y	Y	Y	N	Y	Y	Y
WYOMING								
AL ***Cheney***	N	Y	Y	Y	N	Y	Y	Y

Southern states - Ala., Ark., Fla., Ga., Ky., La., Miss., N.C., Okla., S.C., Tenn., Texas, Va.

* The *Congressional Record* vote number is different from the CQ vote number because the *Record* includes quorum calls in its tally. CQ does not publish quorum call votes.

77. H Res 151. Committee Proxy Voting. Foley, D-Wash., motion to table (kill) the resolution to direct the Rules Committee to undertake an investigation concerning voting by proxy in committees. Motion agreed to 231-187: R 1-178; D 230-9 (ND 158-2, SD 72-7), April 30, 1985. (The resolution was introduced and the roll call was ordered to delay House business as part of a Republican protest of the handling of the contested election in the Indiana 8th District.)

78. Procedural Motion. Wright, D-Texas, motion to adjourn. Motion agreed to 239-174: R 3-173; D 236-1 (ND 157-0, SD 79-1), April 30, 1985. (The motion was made because of repeated Republican efforts to delay House business in protest of the handling of the contested election in the Indiana 8th District.)

79. Procedural Motion. Saxton, R-N.J., motion to approve the House *Journal* of Tuesday, April 30. Motion agreed to 227-178: R 3-173; D 224-5 (ND 148-4, SD 76-1), May 1, 1985.

80. Procedural Motion. Cobey, R-N.C., motion to adjourn. Motion rejected 182-243: R 181-0; D 1-243 (ND 0-164, SD 1-79), May 1, 1985. (The motion, part of a Republican protest of the handling of the contested election in Indiana's 8th District, was made just before the House took up a resolution to seat incumbent Democrat Frank McCloskey *(see vote 81, below).*)

81. H Res 146. Indiana 8th District Seat. Panetta, D-Calif., motion to consider the resolution to seat incumbent Democrat Frank McCloskey as the representative from the 8th District of Indiana. Motion agreed to 242-185: R 0-181; D 242-4 (ND 165-0, SD 77-4), May 1, 1985. (Motions to consider are not normally voted upon in the House, but Republicans, protesting the Democrats' decision to seat McCloskey, forced a vote.)

82. H Res 146. Indiana 8th District Seat. Frenzel, R-Minn., motion to recommit the resolution to seat incumbent Democrat Frank McCloskey of Indiana to the House Administration Committee with instructions for the panel to count the remaining absentee ballots in the contested election. Motion rejected 183-246: R 180-0; D 3-246 (ND 2-166, SD 1-80), May 1, 1985.

83. H Res 146. Indiana 8th District Seat. Adoption of the resolution to seat incumbent Democrat Frank McCloskey as the representative from the 8th District of Indiana. Adopted 236-190: R 0-180; D 236-10 (ND 163-3, SD 73-7), May 1, 1985.

84. Procedural Motion. Michel, R-Ill., motion to adjourn. Motion rejected 179-248: R 179-0; D 0-248 (ND 0-167, SD 0-81), May 1, 1985. (The motion was made by Republicans to protest the decision to seat Democrat Frank McCloskey as the representative from the 8th District of Indiana. During the roll call on the motion, Republicans walked out of the House chamber.)

KEY

Y Voted for (yea).
Paired for.
+ Announced for.
N Voted against (nay).
X Paired against.
- Announced against.
P Voted "present".
C Voted "present" to avoid possible conflict of interest.
? Did not vote or otherwise make a position known.

Democrats ***Republicans***

	77	78	79	80	81	82	83	84
ALABAMA								
1 ***Callahan***	N	N	N	Y	N	Y	N	Y
2 ***Dickinson***	N	N	N	Y	N	Y	N	Y
3 Nichols	Y	Y	Y	N	Y	N	Y	N
4 Bevill	Y	Y	Y	N	Y	N	Y	N
5 Flippo	Y	Y	Y	N	Y	N	Y	N
6 Erdreich	Y	Y	Y	N	Y	N	Y	N
7 Shelby	Y	Y	Y	N	Y	N	Y	N
ALASKA								
AL ***Young***	N	N	N	Y	N	Y	N	Y
ARIZONA								
1 ***McCain***	N	N	N	Y	N	Y	N	Y
2 Udall	?	?	Y	N	Y	N	Y	N
3 ***Stump***	N	N	N	Y	N	Y	N	Y
4 ***Rudd***	N	N	N	Y	N	Y	N	Y
5 ***Kolbe***	N	N	N	Y	N	Y	N	Y
ARKANSAS								
1 Alexander	Y	Y	Y	N	Y	N	Y	N
2 Robinson	Y	Y	Y	N	Y	N	Y	N
3 ***Hammerschmidt***	N	N	N	Y	N	Y	N	Y
4 Anthony	Y	Y	Y	N	Y	N	Y	N
CALIFORNIA								
1 Bosco	Y	Y	Y	N	Y	N	Y	N
2 ***Chappie***	N	N	N	Y	N	Y	N	Y
3 Matsui	Y	Y	Y	N	Y	N	Y	N
4 Fazio	Y	Y	Y	N	Y	N	Y	N
5 Burton	Y	Y	Y	N	Y	N	Y	N
6 Boxer	Y	Y	Y	N	Y	N	Y	N
7 Miller	Y	Y	Y	N	Y	N	Y	N
8 Dellums	Y	Y	Y	N	Y	N	Y	N
9 Stark	Y	Y	Y	N	Y	N	Y	N
10 Edwards	Y	Y	Y	N	Y	N	Y	N
11 Lantos	Y	Y	Y	N	Y	N	Y	N
12 ***Zschau***	N	N	N	Y	N	Y	N	Y
13 Mineta	Y	Y	Y	N	Y	N	Y	N
14 ***Shumway***	N	N	N	Y	N	Y	N	Y
15 Coelho	Y	Y	Y	N	Y	N	Y	N
16 Panetta	Y	Y	Y	N	Y	N	Y	N
17 ***Pashayan***	N	N	N	Y	N	Y	N	Y
18 Lehman	Y	Y	Y	N	Y	N	Y	N
19 ***Lagomarsino***	N	N	N	Y	N	Y	N	Y
20 ***Thomas***	N	N	N	Y	N	Y	N	Y
21 ***Fiedler***	N	N	N	Y	N	Y	N	Y
22 ***Moorhead***	N	N	N	Y	N	Y	N	Y
23 Beilenson	Y	Y	Y	N	Y	N	Y	N
24 Waxman	Y	?	Y	N	Y	N	Y	N
25 Roybal	Y	Y	Y	N	Y	N	Y	N
26 Berman	Y	Y	Y	N	Y	N	Y	N
27 Levine	Y	Y	?	N	Y	N	Y	N
28 Dixon	Y	Y	Y	N	Y	N	Y	N
29 Hawkins	Y	Y	Y	N	Y	N	Y	N
30 Martinez	Y	Y	Y	N	Y	N	Y	N
31 Dymally	Y	Y	P	N	Y	N	Y	N
32 Anderson	Y	Y	Y	N	Y	N	Y	N
33 ***Dreier***	N	N	N	Y	N	Y	N	Y
34 Torres	Y	Y	Y	N	Y	N	Y	N
35 ***Lewis***	N	N	N	Y	N	Y	N	Y
36 Brown	?	Y	Y	N	Y	N	Y	N
37 ***McCandless***	N	N	N	Y	N	Y	N	Y
38 ***Dornan***	N	N	N	Y	N	Y	N	Y
39 ***Dannemeyer***	N	N	N	Y	N	Y	N	Y
40 ***Badham***	N	N	N	Y	N	Y	N	Y
41 ***Lowery***	N	?	N	Y	N	Y	N	Y
42 ***Lungren***	N	N	N	Y	N	Y	N	Y
43 ***Packard***	N	N	N	Y	N	Y	N	Y
44 Bates	Y	Y	Y	N	Y	N	Y	N
45 ***Hunter***	N	N	N	Y	N	Y	N	Y
COLORADO								
1 Schroeder	Y	Y	N	N	Y	N	Y	N
2 Wirth	Y	Y	Y	N	Y	N	Y	N
3 ***Strang***	N	N	N	Y	N	Y	N	Y
4 ***Brown***	N	N	N	Y	N	Y	N	?
5 ***Kramer***	N	N	N	Y	N	Y	N	Y
6 ***Schaefer***	N	N	N	Y	N	Y	N	Y
CONNECTICUT								
1 Kennelly	Y	Y	Y	N	Y	N	Y	N
2 Gejdenson	Y	Y	Y	N	Y	N	Y	N
3 Morrison	Y	Y	Y	N	Y	N	Y	N
4 ***McKinney***	N	N	N	Y	N	Y	N	Y
5 ***Rowland***	N	N	N	Y	N	Y	N	Y
6 ***Johnson***	N	N	Y	Y	N	Y	N	Y
DELAWARE								
AL Carper	Y	Y	Y	N	Y	N	Y	N
FLORIDA								
1 Hutto	Y	Y	Y	N	Y	N	Y	N
2 Fuqua	Y	Y	Y	N	Y	N	Y	N
3 Bennett	Y	Y	Y	N	Y	N	Y	N
4 Chappell	Y	Y	Y	N	Y	N	Y	N
5 ***McCollum***	N	N	N	Y	N	Y	N	Y
6 MacKay	Y	Y	Y	N	Y	N	Y	N
7 Gibbons	Y	Y	Y	N	Y	N	Y	N
8 ***Young***	N	N	N	Y	N	Y	N	Y
9 ***Bilirakis***	N	N	N	Y	N	Y	N	Y
10 ***Ireland***	N	N	N	Y	N	Y	N	?
11 Nelson	Y	Y	Y	N	Y	N	Y	N
12 ***Lewis***	N	N	N	Y	N	Y	N	Y
13 ***Mack***	N	N	N	Y	N	Y	N	Y
14 Mica	Y	Y	Y	?	Y	N	Y	N
15 ***Shaw***	N	N	N	Y	N	Y	N	Y
16 Smith	Y	Y	Y	N	Y	N	Y	N
17 Lehman	Y	Y	Y	N	Y	N	Y	N
18 Pepper	Y	Y	Y	N	Y	N	Y	N
19 Fascell	Y	Y	Y	N	Y	N	Y	N
GEORGIA								
1 Thomas	Y	Y	Y	N	Y	N	Y	N
2 Hatcher	Y	Y	Y	N	Y	N	Y	N
3 Ray	N	Y	Y	N	Y	N	Y	N
4 ***Swindall***	N	N	N	Y	N	Y	N	Y
5 Fowler	Y	Y	Y	N	Y	N	Y	N
6 ***Gingrich***	?	N	N	Y	N	Y	N	Y
7 Darden	Y	Y	Y	N	Y	N	Y	N
8 Rowland	Y	Y	Y	N	Y	N	Y	N
9 Jenkins	Y	Y	Y	N	Y	N	Y	N
10 Barnard	Y	Y	Y	N	Y	N	N	N
HAWAII								
1 Heftel	Y	Y	?	N	Y	N	Y	N
2 Akaka	Y	Y	Y	N	Y	N	Y	N
IDAHO								
1 ***Craig***	N	N	N	Y	N	Y	N	Y
2 Stallings	Y	Y	Y	N	Y	N	N	N
ILLINOIS								
1 Hayes	?	?	Y	N	Y	N	Y	N
2 Savage	Y	Y	Y	N	Y	N	Y	N
3 Russo	Y	Y	Y	N	Y	N	Y	N
4 ***O'Brien***	N	?	N	Y	N	Y	N	Y
5 Lipinski	Y	Y	Y	N	Y	N	Y	N
6 ***Hyde***	N	N	N	Y	N	Y	N	Y
7 Collins	Y	Y	Y	N	Y	N	Y	N
8 Rostenkowski	Y	Y	Y	N	Y	N	Y	N
9 Yates	Y	?	Y	N	Y	N	Y	N
10 ***Porter***	N	N	N	Y	N	Y	N	Y
11 Annunzio	Y	Y	Y	N	Y	N	Y	N
12 ***Crane***	N	N	N	Y	N	Y	N	Y
13 ***Fawell***	N	N	N	Y	N	Y	N	Y
14 ***Grotberg***	N	N	N	Y	N	Y	N	Y
15 ***Madigan***	N	N	N	Y	N	Y	N	Y
16 ***Martin***	N	N	N	Y	N	Y	N	Y
17 Evans	Y	Y	Y	N	Y	N	Y	N
18 ***Michel***	N	N	N	Y	N	Y	N	Y
19 Bruce	Y	Y	Y	N	Y	N	Y	N
20 Durbin	Y	Y	Y	N	Y	N	Y	N
21 Price	Y	Y	Y	N	Y	N	Y	N
22 Gray	Y	Y	Y	N	Y	N	Y	N
INDIANA								
1 Visclosky	Y	Y	Y	N	Y	N	Y	N
2 Sharp	Y	Y	Y	N	Y	N	Y	N
3 ***Hiler***	N	N	N	Y	N	Y	N	Y
4 ***Coats***	N	N	N	Y	N	Y	N	Y
5 ***Hillis***	N	N	N	Y	N	Y	N	Y

ND - Northern Democrats SD - Southern Democrats

* Corresponding to Congressional Record Votes 85, 86, 87, 88, 89, 90, 91, 92

	77	78	79	80	81	82	83	84
6 ***Burton***	N	N	P	Y	N	Y	N	Y
7 ***Myers***	N	N	N	Y	N	Y	?	Y
8 Vacancy								
9 Hamilton	Y	Y	Y	N	Y	N	Y	N
10 Jacobs	Y	Y	N	N	Y	N	Y	N
IOWA								
1 ***Leach***	N	N	N	Y	N	?	N	Y
2 ***Tauke***	N	Y	N	Y	N	Y	N	Y
3 ***Evans***	N	N	N	Y	N	Y	N	Y
4 Smith	Y	Y	Y	N	Y	N	Y	N
5 ***Lightfoot***	N	N	N	Y	N	Y	N	Y
6 Bedell	N	Y	?	N	Y	N	Y	N
KANSAS								
1 ***Roberts***	N	N	?	Y	N	Y	N	Y
2 Slattery	Y	Y	Y	N	Y	N	Y	N
3 ***Meyers***	N	N	N	Y	N	Y	N	Y
4 Glickman	Y	Y	Y	N	Y	N	Y	N
5 ***Whittaker***	N	N	N	Y	N	Y	N	Y
KENTUCKY								
1 Hubbard	Y	Y	Y	N	Y	N	Y	N
2 Natcher	Y	Y	Y	N	Y	N	Y	N
3 Mazzoli	Y	Y	Y	N	Y	Y	N	N
4 ***Snyder***	N	N	N	Y	N	Y	N	Y
5 ***Rogers***	N	N	N	Y	N	Y	N	Y
6 ***Hopkins***	N	N	N	Y	N	Y	N	Y
7 Perkins	Y	Y	Y	N	Y	N	Y	N
LOUISIANA								
1 ***Livingston***	N	?	N	Y	N	Y	N	Y
2 Boggs	Y	Y	Y	N	Y	N	Y	N
3 Tauzin	N	Y	Y	N	Y	N	Y	N
4 Roemer	N	N	N	N	Y	N	Y	N
5 Huckaby	?	?	?	?	?	?	?	?
6 ***Moore***	N	N	N	Y	N	Y	N	Y
7 Breaux	Y	Y	Y	Y	Y	N	Y	N
8 Long	Y	Y	Y	N	Y	N	Y	N
MAINE								
1 ***McKernan***	N	N	N	Y	N	Y	N	Y
2 ***Snowe***	N	N	N	Y	N	Y	N	Y
MARYLAND								
1 Dyson	Y	Y	Y	N	Y	N	Y	N
2 ***Bentley***	N	N	N	Y	N	Y	N	Y
3 Mikulski	Y	Y	Y	N	Y	N	Y	N
4 ***Holt***	N	Y	N	Y	N	Y	N	Y
5 Hoyer	Y	?	Y	N	Y	N	Y	N
6 Byron	Y	Y	?	N	Y	N	Y	N
7 Mitchell	Y	Y	P	N	Y	N	Y	N
8 Barnes	Y	Y	Y	N	Y	N	Y	N
MASSACHUSETTS								
1 ***Conte***	N	N	N	Y	N	Y	N	Y
2 Boland	Y	Y	Y	N	Y	N	Y	N
3 Early	Y	Y	Y	N	Y	N	Y	N
4 Frank	Y	Y	Y	N	Y	N	P	N
5 Atkins	Y	Y	Y	N	Y	N	Y	N
6 Mavroules	Y	Y	Y	N	Y	N	Y	N
7 Markey	Y	Y	Y	N	Y	N	Y	N
8 O'Neill								
9 Moakley	Y	Y	Y	N	Y	N	Y	N
10 Studds	Y	Y	Y	N	Y	N	Y	N
11 Donnelly	Y	Y	Y	N	Y	N	Y	N
MICHIGAN								
1 Conyers	?	?	Y	N	Y	N	Y	N
2 ***Pursell***	N	N	N	Y	N	Y	N	Y
3 Wolpe	Y	Y	Y	N	Y	N	Y	N
4 ***Siljander***	N	N	N	Y	N	Y	N	Y
5 ***Henry***	N	N	N	Y	N	Y	N	Y
6 Carr	Y	Y	Y	N	Y	N	Y	N
7 Kildee	Y	Y	Y	N	Y	N	Y	N
8 Traxler	Y	Y	Y	N	Y	N	Y	N
9 ***Vander Jagt***	N	N	N	Y	N	Y	N	Y
10 ***Schuette***	N	N	N	Y	N	Y	N	Y
11 ***Davis***	N	N	N	Y	N	Y	N	Y
12 Bonior	?	Y	Y	N	Y	N	Y	N
13 Crockett	?	?	?	N	Y	N	Y	N
14 Hertel	Y	Y	Y	N	Y	N	Y	N
15 Ford	Y	Y	?	N	Y	N	Y	N
16 Dingell	Y	Y	?	?	?	N	Y	N
17 Levin	Y	Y	Y	N	Y	N	Y	N
18 ***Broomfield***	N	N	Y	Y	N	Y	N	Y
MINNESOTA								
1 Penny	Y	Y	N	N	Y	N	N	N
2 ***Weber***	N	N	N	Y	N	Y	N	Y
3 ***Frenzel***	N	N	N	Y	N	Y	N	Y
4 Vento	Y	Y	Y	N	Y	N	Y	N
5 Sabo	Y	Y	Y	N	Y	N	Y	N
6 Sikorski	Y	Y	N	N	Y	N	Y	N

	77	78	79	80	81	82	83	84
7 ***Stangeland***	N	N	N	Y	N	Y	N	Y
8 Oberstar	Y	Y	Y	N	Y	N	Y	N
MISSISSIPPI								
1 Whitten	Y	Y	Y	N	Y	N	Y	N
2 ***Franklin***	N	?	N	Y	N	Y	N	Y
3 Montgomery	Y	Y	Y	N	Y	N	Y	N
4 Dowdy	Y	Y	Y	N	Y	N	Y	N
5 ***Lott***	N	N	N	Y	N	Y	N	Y
MISSOURI								
1 Clay	Y	Y	Y	N	Y	N	Y	N
2 Young	Y	Y	Y	N	Y	N	Y	N
3 Gephardt	Y	Y	Y	N	Y	N	Y	N
4 Skelton	Y	Y	Y	N	Y	N	Y	N
5 Wheat	Y	Y	Y	N	Y	N	Y	N
6 ***Coleman***	N	N	N	Y	N	Y	N	Y
7 ***Taylor***	N	N	N	Y	N	Y	N	Y
8 ***Emerson***	N	N	N	Y	N	Y	N	Y
9 Volkmer	Y	Y	Y	N	Y	N	Y	N
MONTANA								
1 Williams	Y	Y	?	?	Y	N	Y	?
2 ***Marlenee***	N	N	?	Y	N	Y	N	Y
NEBRASKA								
1 ***Bereuter***	Y	N	N	Y	N	Y	N	Y
2 ***Daub***	N	N	N	Y	N	Y	N	Y
3 ***Smith***	N	N	N	Y	N	Y	N	Y
NEVADA								
1 Reid	Y	Y	Y	N	Y	N	Y	N
2 ***Vucanovich***	N	N	N	Y	N	Y	N	Y
NEW HAMPSHIRE								
1 ***Smith***	N	N	N	Y	N	Y	N	Y
2 ***Gregg***	N	N	N	Y	N	Y	N	Y
NEW JERSEY								
1 Florio	Y	Y	Y	N	Y	N	Y	N
2 Hughes	Y	Y	Y	N	Y	N	Y	N
3 Howard	Y	Y	Y	N	Y	N	Y	N
4 ***Smith***	N	N	N	Y	N	Y	N	Y
5 ***Roukema***	N	N	N	Y	N	Y	N	Y
6 Dwyer	Y	Y	Y	N	Y	N	Y	N
7 ***Rinaldo***	N	N	N	Y	N	Y	N	Y
8 Roe	Y	Y	Y	N	Y	N	Y	N
9 Torricelli	Y	Y	Y	N	Y	N	Y	N
10 Rodino	Y	Y	?	N	Y	N	Y	N
11 ***Gallo***	N	N	N	Y	N	Y	N	Y
12 ***Courter***	N	N	N	Y	N	Y	N	Y
13 ***Saxton***	N	N	N	Y	N	Y	N	Y
14 Guarini	Y	Y	Y	N	Y	N	Y	N
NEW MEXICO								
1 ***Lujan***	N	N	N	Y	N	Y	N	Y
2 ***Skeen***	N	N	N	Y	N	Y	N	Y
3 Richardson	Y	Y	Y	N	Y	N	Y	N
NEW YORK								
1 ***Carney***	N	N	N	Y	N	Y	N	Y
2 Downey	Y	Y	Y	N	Y	N	Y	N
3 Mrazek	Y	?	Y	N	Y	N	Y	N
4 ***Lent***	N	N	N	Y	N	Y	N	Y
5 ***McGrath***	N	N	N	Y	N	Y	N	Y
6 Addabbo	Y	Y	Y	N	Y	N	Y	N
7 Ackerman	Y	Y	Y	N	Y	N	Y	N
8 Scheuer	Y	Y	Y	N	Y	N	Y	N
9 Manton	Y	Y	Y	N	Y	N	Y	N
10 Schumer	Y	Y	Y	N	Y	N	Y	N
11 Towns	Y	Y	Y	N	Y	N	Y	N
12 Owens	Y	Y	Y	N	Y	N	Y	N
13 Solarz	Y	Y	Y	N	Y	N	Y	N
14 ***Molinari***	N	N	N	Y	N	Y	N	Y
15 ***Green***	N	N	N	Y	N	Y	N	Y
16 Rangel	Y	Y	Y	N	Y	N	Y	N
17 Weiss	Y	Y	Y	N	Y	N	Y	N
18 Garcia	Y	Y	Y	N	Y	N	Y	N
19 Biaggi	Y	Y	Y	N	Y	N	Y	N
20 ***DioGuardi***	N	N	N	Y	N	Y	N	Y
21 ***Fish***	N	N	N	Y	N	Y	N	Y
22 ***Gilman***	N	N	N	Y	N	Y	N	Y
23 Stratton	Y	Y	Y	N	Y	N	Y	N
24 ***Solomon***	N	N	N	Y	N	Y	N	Y
25 ***Boehlert***	N	N	N	Y	N	Y	N	Y
26 ***Martin***	N	N	N	Y	N	Y	N	Y
27 ***Wortley***	N	N	N	Y	N	Y	N	Y
28 McHugh	Y	Y	?	N	Y	N	Y	N
29 ***Horton***	N	N	N	Y	N	Y	N	Y
30 ***Eckert***	N	N	N	Y	N	Y	N	Y
31 ***Kemp***	N	N	Y	Y	N	Y	N	Y
32 LaFalce	Y	Y	Y	N	Y	Y	N	N
33 Nowak	Y	Y	Y	N	Y	N	Y	N
34 Lundine	Y	Y	Y	N	Y	N	Y	N

	77	78	79	80	81	82	83	84
NORTH CAROLINA								
1 Jones	?	Y	?	N	Y	N	Y	N
2 Valentine	Y	Y	Y	N	Y	N	Y	N
3 Whitley	Y	Y	Y	N	Y	N	Y	N
4 ***Cobey***	N	N	N	Y	N	Y	N	Y
5 Neal	Y	Y	Y	N	Y	N	Y	N
6 ***Coble***	N	N	N	Y	N	Y	N	Y
7 Rose	Y	Y	Y	N	Y	N	Y	N
8 Hefner	Y	Y	Y	N	Y	N	Y	N
9 ***McMillan***	N	N	N	Y	N	Y	N	Y
10 ***Broyhill***	N	N	N	Y	N	Y	N	Y
11 ***Hendon***	N	N	N	Y	N	Y	N	Y
NORTH DAKOTA								
AL Dorgan	Y	Y	Y	N	Y	N	Y	N
OHIO								
1 Luken	Y	Y	Y	N	Y	N	Y	N
2 ***Gradison***	N	N	N	Y	N	Y	N	Y
3 Hall	Y	Y	Y	N	Y	N	Y	N
4 ***Oxley***	N	N	N	Y	N	Y	N	Y
5 ***Latta***	N	N	N	Y	N	Y	N	Y
6 ***McEwen***	N	N	N	Y	N	Y	N	Y
7 ***DeWine***	N	N	N	Y	N	Y	N	Y
8 ***Kindness***	?	N	N	Y	N	Y	N	Y
9 Kaptur	Y	Y	Y	N	Y	N	Y	N
10 ***Miller***	N	N	N	Y	N	Y	N	Y
11 Eckart	Y	Y	Y	N	Y	N	Y	N
12 ***Kasich***	N	Y	N	Y	N	Y	N	Y
13 Pease	Y	Y	Y	N	Y	N	Y	N
14 Seiberling	?	?	?	?	?	N	Y	N
15 ***Wylie***	N	N	N	Y	N	Y	N	Y
16 ***Regula***	N	N	N	Y	N	Y	N	Y
17 Traficant	Y	Y	Y	N	Y	N	Y	N
18 Applegate	Y	?	?	N	Y	Y	Y	N
19 Feighan	Y	Y	Y	N	Y	N	Y	N
20 Oakar	Y	Y	Y	N	Y	N	Y	N
21 Stokes	Y	Y	Y	N	Y	N	Y	N
OKLAHOMA								
1 Jones	Y	Y	?	N	Y	N	Y	N
2 Synar	Y	Y	Y	N	Y	N	Y	N
3 Watkins	Y	Y	Y	N	Y	N	Y	N
4 McCurdy	Y	Y	Y	N	Y	N	Y	N
5 ***Edwards***	?	?	N	Y	N	Y	N	Y
6 English	Y	Y	Y	N	Y	N	P	N
OREGON								
1 AuCoin	Y	Y	?	N	Y	N	Y	N
2 ***Smith, R.***	N	N	N	Y	N	Y	N	Y
3 Wyden	Y	Y	Y	N	Y	N	Y	N
4 Weaver	?	?	?	?	?	?	?	?
5 ***Smith, D.***	N	N	N	Y	N	Y	N	Y
PENNSYLVANIA								
1 Foglietta	Y	Y	Y	N	Y	N	Y	N
2 Gray	Y	Y	Y	N	Y	N	Y	N
3 Borski	Y	Y	Y	N	Y	N	Y	N
4 Kolter	Y	Y	Y	N	Y	N	Y	N
5 ***Schulze***	N	N	N	Y	N	Y	N	Y
6 Yatron	Y	Y	Y	N	Y	N	Y	N
7 Edgar	?	?	Y	N	Y	N	Y	N
8 Kostmayer	Y	Y	Y	N	Y	N	Y	N
9 ***Shuster***	N	N	N	Y	N	Y	N	Y
10 ***McDade***	N	?	N	Y	N	Y	N	Y
11 Kanjorski	Y	Y	Y	N	Y	N	Y	N
12 Murtha	Y	Y	Y	N	Y	N	Y	N
13 ***Coughlin***	N	N	N	Y	N	Y	N	Y
14 Coyne	Y	Y	Y	N	Y	N	Y	N
15 ***Ritter***	N	N	N	Y	N	Y	N	Y
16 ***Walker***	N	N	N	Y	N	Y	N	Y
17 ***Gekas***	N	N	N	Y	N	Y	N	Y
18 Walgren	Y	Y	Y	N	Y	N	Y	N
19 ***Goodling***	N	N	?	Y	N	Y	N	Y
20 Gaydos	Y	Y	Y	N	Y	N	Y	N
21 ***Ridge***	N	N	N	Y	N	Y	N	Y
22 Murphy	Y	Y	Y	N	Y	N	Y	N
23 ***Clinger***	N	N	N	Y	N	Y	N	Y
RHODE ISLAND								
1 St Germain	Y	Y	Y	N	Y	N	Y	N
2 ***Schneider***	N	N	?	Y	N	Y	N	Y
SOUTH CAROLINA								
1 ***Hartnett***	N	N	N	Y	N	Y	N	Y
2 ***Spence***	N	N	N	Y	N	Y	N	Y
3 Derrick	Y	Y	Y	N	Y	N	Y	N
4 ***Campbell***	N	N	N	Y	N	Y	N	Y
5 Spratt	Y	Y	Y	N	Y	N	Y	N
6 Tallon	Y	Y	Y	N	Y	N	Y	N
SOUTH DAKOTA								
AL Daschle	Y	Y	Y	N	Y	N	Y	N

	77	78	79	80	81	82	83	84
TENNESSEE								
1 ***Quillen***	N	N	N	Y	N	Y	N	Y
2 ***Duncan***	N	N	N	Y	N	Y	N	Y
3 Lloyd	Y	Y	Y	N	Y	N	Y	N
4 Cooper	Y	Y	Y	N	Y	N	Y	N
5 Boner	Y	Y	Y	N	Y	N	Y	N
6 Gordon	Y	Y	Y	N	Y	N	Y	N
7 ***Sundquist***	N	N	N	Y	N	Y	N	Y
8 Jones	Y	Y	Y	N	Y	N	Y	N
9 Ford	Y	Y	Y	N	Y	N	Y	N
TEXAS								
1 Hall, S.	Y	Y	?	N	N	N	N	N
2 Wilson	Y	Y	Y	N	Y	N	Y	N
3 ***Bartlett***	N	N	N	Y	N	Y	N	Y
4 Hall, R.	N	Y	?	N	N	N	N	N
5 Bryant	Y	Y	Y	N	Y	N	Y	N
6 ***Barton***	N	N	N	Y	N	Y	N	Y
7 ***Archer***	N	N	N	Y	N	Y	N	Y
8 ***Fields***	N	N	N	Y	N	Y	N	Y
9 Brooks	Y	Y	Y	N	Y	N	Y	N
10 Pickle	Y	Y	Y	N	Y	N	Y	N
11 Leath	N	Y	Y	N	N	N	N	N
12 Wright	Y	Y	Y	N	Y	N	Y	N
13 ***Boulter***	N	N	N	Y	N	Y	N	Y
14 ***Sweeney***	N	N	N	Y	N	Y	N	Y
15 de la Garza	Y	Y	Y	N	Y	N	Y	N
16 Coleman	Y	Y	Y	N	Y	N	Y	N
17 Stenholm	N	Y	Y	N	N	N	N	N
18 Leland	Y	Y	Y	N	Y	N	Y	N
19 ***Combest***	N	N	N	Y	N	Y	N	Y
20 Gonzalez	Y	Y	Y	N	Y	N	Y	N
21 ***Loeffler***	N	N	N	Y	N	Y	N	Y
22 ***DeLay***	N	N	N	Y	N	Y	N	Y
23 Bustamante	Y	Y	Y	N	Y	N	Y	N
24 Frost	?	?	Y	N	Y	N	Y	N
25 Andrews	Y	Y	Y	N	Y	N	Y	N
26 ***Armey***	N	N	N	Y	N	Y	N	Y
27 Ortiz	Y	Y	Y	N	Y	N	Y	N
UTAH								
1 ***Hansen***	N	N	N	Y	N	Y	N	Y
2 ***Monson***	N	N	N	Y	N	Y	N	Y
3 ***Nielson***	N	N	N	Y	N	Y	N	Y
VERMONT								
AL ***Jeffords***	N	N	N	Y	N	Y	N	Y
VIRGINIA								
1 ***Bateman***	N	N	N	Y	N	Y	N	Y
2 ***Whitehurst***	N	N	N	Y	N	Y	N	Y
3 ***Bliley***	N	N	N	Y	N	Y	N	Y
4 Sisisky	Y	Y	Y	N	Y	N	Y	N
5 Daniel	N	Y	Y	N	Y	N	Y	N
6 Olin	Y	Y	Y	N	Y	N	N	N
7 ***Slaughter***	N	N	N	Y	N	Y	N	Y
8 ***Parris***	N	N	N	Y	N	Y	N	Y
9 Boucher	Y	Y	Y	N	Y	N	Y	N
10 ***Wolf***	N	N	N	Y	N	Y	N	Y
WASHINGTON								
1 ***Miller***	N	N	N	Y	N	Y	N	Y
2 Swift	Y	Y	Y	N	Y	N	Y	N
3 Bonker	Y	Y	Y	N	Y	N	Y	N
4 ***Morrison***	N	N	N	Y	N	Y	N	Y
5 Foley	Y	Y	Y	N	Y	N	Y	N
6 Dicks	Y	Y	Y	N	Y	N	Y	N
7 Lowry	Y	Y	Y	N	Y	N	Y	N
8 ***Chandler***	N	N	N	Y	N	Y	N	Y
WEST VIRGINIA								
1 Mollohan	Y	Y	Y	N	Y	N	Y	N
2 Staggers	Y	Y	Y	N	Y	N	Y	N
3 Wise	Y	Y	Y	N	Y	N	Y	N
4 Rahall	Y	Y	?	?	?	N	Y	N
WISCONSIN								
1 Aspin	Y	Y	Y	N	Y	N	Y	N
2 Kastenmeier	N	Y	Y	N	Y	N	Y	N
3 ***Gunderson***	N	N	-	+	-	+	-	+
4 Kleczka	Y	Y	Y	N	Y	N	Y	N
5 Moody	Y	Y	Y	N	Y	N	?	N
6 ***Petri***	N	N	N	Y	N	Y	N	Y
7 Obey	Y	Y	Y	N	Y	N	Y	N
8 ***Roth***	N	N	N	Y	N	Y	N	Y
9 ***Sensenbrenner***	N	N	N	Y	N	Y	N	Y
WYOMING								
AL ***Cheney***	N	N	N	Y	N	Y	N	Y

Southern states - Ala., Ark., Fla., Ga., Ky., La., Miss., N.C., Okla., S.C., Tenn., Texas, Va.

* The *Congressional Record* vote number is different from the CQ vote number because the *Record* includes quorum calls in its tally. CQ does not publish quorum call votes.

85. Procedural Motion. Cobey, R-N.C., motion to permit a member (Cobey) to read from the *Congressional Record.* Motion agreed to 392-18: R 171-3; D 221-15 (ND 144-13, SD 77-2), May 2, 1985. (The roll call was ordered to delay House business as part of a Republican protest of the handling of the contested election in the Indiana 8th District.)

86. H Res 127. Soviet Jewry. Adoption of the resolution to express the sense of the House that it supports "Solidarity Sunday for Soviet Jewry," on May 5, 1985. Adopted 405-0: R 171-0; D 234-0 (ND 159-0, SD 75-0), May 2, 1985.

87. H J Res 125. National Community College Month. Passage of the joint resolution to designate May 1985 as "National Community College Month." Passed 410-0: R 175-0; D 235-0 (ND 159-0, SD 76-0), May 2, 1985.

KEY

Y Voted for (yea).
\# Paired for.
\+ Announced for.
N Voted against (nay).
X Paired against.
\- Announced against.
P Voted "present".
C Voted "present" to avoid possible conflict of interest.
? Did not vote or otherwise make a position known.

Democrats ***Republicans***

	85	86	87
ALABAMA			
1 ***Callahan***	Y	Y	Y
2 ***Dickinson***	N	Y	Y
3 Nichols	Y	Y	Y
4 Bevill	Y	Y	Y
5 Flippo	Y	Y	Y
6 Erdreich	Y	Y	Y
7 Shelby	Y	Y	Y
ALASKA			
AL ***Young***	Y	Y	Y
ARIZONA			
1 ***McCain***	Y	Y	Y
2 Udall	Y	Y	Y
3 ***Stump***	Y	Y	Y
4 ***Rudd***	?	?	?
5 ***Kolbe***	Y	Y	Y
ARKANSAS			
1 Alexander	Y	Y	Y
2 Robinson	Y	Y	Y
3 ***Hammerschmidt***	Y	Y	Y
4 Anthony	Y	Y	Y
CALIFORNIA			
1 Bosco	Y	?	?
2 ***Chappie***	Y	Y	Y
3 Matsui	N	Y	Y
4 Fazio	Y	Y	Y
5 Burton	N	Y	Y
6 Boxer	N	Y	Y
7 Miller	N	Y	?
8 Dellums	Y	+	Y
9 Stark	Y	Y	Y
10 Edwards	Y	Y	Y
11 Lantos	Y	Y	Y
12 ***Zschau***	Y	Y	Y
13 Mineta	Y	Y	Y
14 ***Shumway***	Y	Y	Y
15 Coelho	Y	Y	Y
16 Panetta	Y	Y	Y
17 ***Pashayan***	Y	Y	Y
18 Lehman	Y	Y	Y
19 ***Lagomarsino***	Y	Y	Y
20 ***Thomas***	Y	Y	Y
21 ***Fiedler***	Y	Y	Y
22 ***Moorhead***	Y	Y	Y
23 Beilenson	Y	Y	Y
24 Waxman	Y	Y	Y
25 Roybal	Y	Y	Y
26 Berman	?	?	?
27 Levine	Y	Y	Y
28 Dixon	?	?	?
29 Hawkins	?	?	?
30 Martinez	Y	Y	Y
31 Dymally	Y	Y	Y
32 Anderson	Y	Y	Y
33 ***Dreier***	Y	Y	Y
34 Torres	Y	Y	Y
35 ***Lewis***	Y	Y	Y
36 Brown	Y	Y	Y
37 ***McCandless***	Y	Y	Y
38 ***Dornan***	Y	Y	Y
39 ***Dannemeyer***	Y	Y	Y
40 ***Badham***	Y	Y	Y
41 ***Lowery***	Y	+	Y
42 ***Lungren***	Y	Y	Y
43 ***Packard***	Y	+	Y
44 Bates	Y	Y	Y
45 ***Hunter***	Y	Y	Y
COLORADO			
1 Schroeder	N	Y	Y
2 Wirth	Y	Y	Y
3 ***Strang***	Y	Y	Y
4 ***Brown***	Y	Y	Y
5 ***Kramer***	Y	Y	Y
6 ***Schaefer***	Y	Y	Y
CONNECTICUT			
1 Kennelly	Y	Y	Y
2 Gejdenson	Y	Y	Y
3 Morrison	Y	Y	Y
4 ***McKinney***	Y	Y	Y
5 ***Rowland***	Y	Y	Y
6 ***Johnson***	Y	Y	Y
DELAWARE			
AL Carper	Y	Y	Y
FLORIDA			
1 Hutto	Y	Y	Y
2 Fuqua	Y	Y	Y
3 Bennett	Y	Y	Y
4 Chappell	Y	?	?
5 ***McCollum***	Y	Y	Y
6 MacKay	Y	Y	Y
7 Gibbons	Y	Y	Y
8 ***Young***	Y	Y	Y
9 ***Bilirakis***	Y	Y	Y
10 ***Ireland***	Y	Y	Y
11 Nelson	Y	Y	Y
12 ***Lewis***	Y	Y	Y
13 ***Mack***	Y	Y	Y
14 Mica	Y	Y	Y
15 ***Shaw***	Y	Y	Y
16 Smith	Y	Y	Y
17 Lehman	Y	Y	Y
18 Pepper	Y	Y	Y
19 Fascell	Y	Y	Y
GEORGIA			
1 Thomas	Y	Y	Y
2 Hatcher	Y	Y	Y
3 Ray	Y	Y	Y
4 ***Swindall***	Y	Y	Y
5 Fowler	N	Y	Y
6 ***Gingrich***	Y	?	Y
7 Darden	Y	Y	Y
8 Rowland	Y	Y	Y
9 Jenkins	Y	Y	Y
10 Barnard	Y	Y	Y
HAWAII			
1 Heftel	?	?	Y
2 Akaka	Y	Y	Y
IDAHO			
1 ***Craig***	Y	Y	Y
2 Stallings	Y	Y	Y
ILLINOIS			
1 Hayes	Y	Y	Y
2 Savage	?	?	?
3 Russo	Y	Y	Y
4 ***O'Brien***	Y	Y	Y
5 Lipinski	Y	Y	Y
6 ***Hyde***	Y	Y	Y
7 Collins	Y	Y	Y
8 Rostenkowski	Y	Y	Y
9 Yates	Y	Y	?
10 ***Porter***	Y	Y	Y
11 Annunzio	Y	Y	Y
12 ***Crane***	Y	Y	Y
13 ***Fawell***	Y	Y	Y
14 ***Grotberg***	Y	Y	Y
15 ***Madigan***	Y	Y	Y
16 ***Martin***	Y	Y	Y
17 Evans	Y	Y	Y
18 ***Michel***	Y	Y	Y
19 Bruce	Y	Y	Y
20 Durbin	N	Y	Y
21 Price	Y	Y	Y
22 Gray	?	Y	Y
INDIANA			
1 Visclosky	Y	Y	Y
2 Sharp	Y	Y	Y
3 ***Hiler***	Y	Y	Y
4 ***Coats***	Y	Y	Y
5 ***Hillis***	Y	Y	Y

ND - Northern Democrats SD - Southern Democrats

* Corresponding to Congressional Record Votes 93, 94, 95

	85	86	87
6 ***Burton***	?	Y	Y
7 ***Myers***	?	?	?
8 McCloskey*	Y	Y	Y
9 Hamilton	Y	Y	Y
10 Jacobs	Y	Y	Y
IOWA			
1 ***Leach***	Y	Y	Y
2 ***Tauke***	Y	Y	Y
3 ***Evans***	Y	Y	Y
4 Smith	Y	Y	Y
5 ***Lightfoot***	Y	Y	Y
6 Bedell	Y	Y	Y
KANSAS			
1 ***Roberts***	Y	Y	Y
2 Slattery	Y	Y	Y
3 ***Meyers***	Y	Y	Y
4 Glickman	N	Y	Y
5 ***Whittaker***	Y	Y	Y
KENTUCKY			
1 Hubbard	Y	Y	Y
2 Natcher	Y	Y	Y
3 Mazzoli	Y	Y	Y
4 ***Snyder***	Y	Y	Y
5 ***Rogers***	Y	Y	Y
6 ***Hopkins***	Y	Y	Y
7 Perkins	Y	Y	Y
LOUISIANA			
1 ***Livingston***	Y	?	?
2 Boggs	Y	Y	Y
3 Tauzin	Y	Y	Y
4 Roemer	Y	Y	Y
5 Huckaby	Y	?	?
6 ***Moore***	Y	Y	Y
7 Breaux	N	Y	Y
8 Long	Y	?	Y
MAINE			
1 ***McKernan***	Y	Y	Y
2 ***Snowe***	Y	Y	Y
MARYLAND			
1 Dyson	?	?	Y
2 ***Bentley***	Y	Y	Y
3 Mikulski	Y	Y	Y
4 ***Holt***	Y	Y	Y
5 Hoyer	N	Y	Y
6 Byron	Y	Y	Y
7 Mitchell	?	Y	Y
8 Barnes	Y	Y	Y
MASSACHUSETTS			
1 ***Conte***	Y	Y	Y
2 Boland	N	Y	Y
3 Early	Y	Y	Y
4 Frank	Y	Y	Y
5 Atkins	Y	Y	Y
6 Mavroules	Y	Y	Y
7 Markey	Y	Y	Y
8 O'Neill			
9 Moakley	Y	Y	Y
10 Studds	Y	Y	Y
11 Donnelly	Y	Y	Y
MICHIGAN			
1 Conyers	?	Y	Y
2 ***Pursell***	Y	Y	Y
3 Wolpe	Y	Y	Y
4 ***Siljander***	Y	Y	Y
5 ***Henry***	Y	Y	Y
6 Carr	Y	Y	Y
7 Kildee	Y	Y	Y
8 Traxler	Y	Y	Y
9 ***Vander Jagt***	?	?	?
10 ***Schuette***	Y	Y	Y
11 ***Davis***	Y	Y	Y
12 Bonior	Y	Y	?
13 Crockett	Y	Y	Y
14 Hertel	Y	Y	Y
15 Ford	Y	Y	Y
16 Dingell	Y	Y	Y
17 Levin	Y	Y	Y
18 ***Broomfield***	Y	Y	Y
MINNESOTA			
1 Penny	Y	Y	Y
2 ***Weber***	Y	Y	Y
3 ***Frenzel***	Y	Y	Y
4 Vento	Y	Y	Y
5 Sabo	Y	Y	Y
6 Sikorski	Y	Y	Y

	85	86	87
7 ***Stangeland***	Y	Y	Y
8 Oberstar	Y	Y	Y
MISSISSIPPI			
1 Whitten	Y	Y	Y
2 ***Franklin***	Y	Y	Y
3 Montgomery	Y	Y	Y
4 Dowdy	Y	Y	Y
5 ***Lott***	Y	Y	Y
MISSOURI			
1 Clay	N	Y	Y
2 Young	Y	Y	Y
3 Gephardt	Y	Y	Y
4 Skelton	Y	Y	Y
5 Wheat	Y	Y	Y
6 ***Coleman***	Y	Y	Y
7 ***Taylor***	Y	Y	Y
8 ***Emerson***	Y	Y	Y
9 Volkmer	Y	Y	Y
MONTANA			
1 Williams	Y	Y	Y
2 ***Marlenee***	Y	Y	Y
NEBRASKA			
1 ***Bereuter***	Y	Y	Y
2 ***Daub***	Y	Y	Y
3 ***Smith***	Y	Y	Y
NEVADA			
1 Reid	N	Y	Y
2 ***Vucanovich***	Y	Y	Y
NEW HAMPSHIRE			
1 ***Smith***	Y	Y	Y
2 ***Gregg***	Y	Y	Y
NEW JERSEY			
1 Florio	Y	Y	Y
2 Hughes	Y	Y	Y
3 Howard	Y	Y	Y
4 ***Smith***	Y	Y	Y
5 ***Roukema***	Y	Y	Y
6 Dwyer	Y	Y	Y
7 ***Rinaldo***	Y	Y	Y
8 Roe	Y	Y	Y
9 Torricelli	Y	Y	Y
10 Rodino	Y	Y	Y
11 ***Gallo***	Y	Y	Y
12 ***Courter***	Y	Y	Y
13 ***Saxton***	Y	Y	Y
14 Guarini	Y	Y	Y
NEW MEXICO			
1 ***Lujan***	Y	Y	Y
2 ***Skeen***	Y	Y	Y
3 Richardson	Y	Y	Y
NEW YORK			
1 ***Carney***	Y	Y	Y
2 Downey	Y	Y	Y
3 Mrazek	Y	Y	Y
4 ***Lent***	Y	Y	Y
5 ***McGrath***	Y	Y	Y
6 Addabbo	Y	Y	Y
7 Ackerman	Y	Y	Y
8 Scheuer	Y	Y	Y
9 Manton	Y	Y	Y
10 Schumer	Y	Y	Y
11 Towns	Y	Y	?
12 Owens	Y	Y	Y
13 Solarz	Y	Y	Y
14 ***Molinari***	Y	Y	Y
15 ***Green***	Y	Y	Y
16 Rangel	Y	Y	Y
17 Weiss	Y	Y	Y
18 Garcia	Y	Y	Y
19 Biaggi	Y	Y	Y
20 ***DioGuardi***	Y	Y	Y
21 ***Fish***	Y	Y	Y
22 ***Gilman***	Y	Y	Y
23 Stratton	Y	Y	Y
24 ***Solomon***	Y	Y	Y
25 ***Boehlert***	Y	Y	Y
26 ***Martin***	Y	Y	Y
27 ***Wortley***	Y	Y	Y
28 McHugh	Y	Y	Y
29 ***Horton***	Y	Y	Y
30 ***Eckert***	Y	Y	Y
31 ***Kemp***	Y	Y	Y
32 LaFalce	Y	Y	Y
33 Nowak	Y	Y	Y
34 Lundine	Y	Y	Y

	85	86	87
NORTH CAROLINA			
1 Jones	Y	Y	Y
2 Valentine	Y	Y	Y
3 Whitley	Y	Y	Y
4 ***Cobey***	Y	Y	Y
5 Neal	Y	Y	Y
6 ***Coble***	Y	Y	Y
7 Rose	Y	Y	Y
8 Hefner	Y	Y	Y
9 ***McMillan***	Y	Y	Y
10 ***Broyhill***	Y	?	Y
11 ***Hendon***	Y	Y	Y
NORTH DAKOTA			
AL Dorgan	Y	Y	Y
OHIO			
1 Luken	Y	Y	Y
2 ***Gradison***	Y	Y	Y
3 Hall	Y	Y	Y
4 ***Oxley***	Y	Y	Y
5 ***Latta***	Y	Y	Y
6 ***McEwen***	Y	Y	Y
7 ***DeWine***	Y	Y	Y
8 ***Kindness***	N	Y	Y
9 Kaptur	Y	Y	Y
10 ***Miller***	Y	Y	Y
11 Eckart	N	Y	Y
12 ***Kasich***	Y	Y	Y
13 Pease	Y	Y	Y
14 Seiberling	?	?	Y
15 ***Wylie***	?	?	Y
16 ***Regula***	Y	Y	Y
17 Traficant	Y	Y	Y
18 Applegate	Y	Y	Y
19 Feighan	Y	Y	Y
20 Oakar	Y	Y	Y
21 Stokes	Y	Y	Y
OKLAHOMA			
1 Jones	Y	Y	Y
2 Synar	Y	Y	Y
3 Watkins	Y	Y	Y
4 McCurdy	Y	Y	Y
5 ***Edwards***	Y	Y	Y
6 English	Y	Y	Y
OREGON			
1 AuCoin	Y	Y	Y
2 ***Smith, R.***	Y	Y	Y
3 Wyden	Y	Y	Y
4 Weaver	?	?	?
5 ***Smith, D.***	Y	Y	Y
PENNSYLVANIA			
1 Foglietta	Y	Y	Y
2 Gray	?	Y	Y
3 Borski	Y	Y	Y
4 Kolter	Y	Y	Y
5 ***Schulze***	Y	Y	Y
6 Yatron	Y	Y	Y
7 Edgar	Y	Y	Y
8 Kostmayer	Y	Y	Y
9 ***Shuster***	Y	Y	Y
10 ***McDade***	Y	Y	?
11 Kanjorski	Y	Y	Y
12 Murtha	Y	Y	Y
13 ***Coughlin***	Y	Y	Y
14 Coyne	Y	Y	Y
15 ***Ritter***	Y	Y	Y
16 ***Walker***	Y	Y	Y
17 ***Gekas***	Y	Y	Y
18 Walgren	Y	Y	Y
19 ***Goodling***	Y	Y	Y
20 Gaydos	Y	Y	Y
21 ***Ridge***	Y	Y	Y
22 Murphy	Y	Y	Y
23 ***Clinger***	Y	Y	Y
RHODE ISLAND			
1 St Germain	Y	Y	Y
2 ***Schneider***	Y	Y	Y
SOUTH CAROLINA			
1 ***Hartnett***	?	?	?
2 ***Spence***	Y	Y	Y
3 Derrick	?	+	?
4 ***Campbell***	Y	Y	Y
5 Spratt	Y	Y	Y
6 Tallon	Y	Y	Y
SOUTH DAKOTA			
AL Daschle	Y	Y	Y

	85	86	87
TENNESSEE			
1 ***Quillen***	Y	Y	Y
2 ***Duncan***	Y	Y	Y
3 Lloyd	Y	Y	Y
4 Cooper	Y	Y	Y
5 Boner	Y	Y	Y
6 Gordon	Y	Y	Y
7 ***Sundquist***	Y	Y	Y
8 Jones	Y	Y	Y
9 Ford	Y	Y	Y
TEXAS			
1 Hall, S.	?	?	?
2 Wilson	Y	?	Y
3 ***Bartlett***	Y	Y	Y
4 Hall, R.	Y	Y	Y
5 Bryant	Y	Y	Y
6 ***Barton***	Y	Y	Y
7 ***Archer***	Y	Y	Y
8 ***Fields***	Y	Y	Y
9 Brooks	Y	Y	Y
10 Pickle	Y	Y	Y
11 Leath	Y	Y	Y
12 Wright	Y	?	?
13 ***Boulter***	Y	Y	Y
14 ***Sweeney***	Y	Y	Y
15 de la Garza	?	Y	Y
16 Coleman	Y	Y	?
17 Stenholm	Y	Y	Y
18 Leland	Y	Y	Y
19 ***Combest***	Y	Y	Y
20 Gonzalez	Y	Y	Y
21 ***Loeffler***	Y	Y	Y
22 ***DeLay***	Y	Y	Y
23 Bustamante	Y	Y	Y
24 Frost	Y	Y	Y
25 Andrews	Y	Y	Y
26 ***Armey***	Y	Y	Y
27 Ortiz	Y	Y	Y
UTAH			
1 ***Hansen***	Y	Y	Y
2 ***Monson***	Y	Y	Y
3 ***Nielson***	Y	Y	Y
VERMONT			
AL ***Jeffords***	Y	Y	Y
VIRGINIA			
1 ***Bateman***	Y	Y	Y
2 ***Whitehurst***	Y	Y	Y
3 ***Bliley***	Y	Y	Y
4 Sisisky	Y	Y	Y
5 Daniel	Y	Y	Y
6 Olin	Y	Y	Y
7 ***Slaughter***	Y	Y	Y
8 ***Parris***	?	?	?
9 Boucher	Y	Y	Y
10 ***Wolf***	Y	Y	Y
WASHINGTON			
1 ***Miller***	Y	Y	Y
2 Swift	Y	Y	Y
3 Bonker	Y	Y	Y
4 ***Morrison***	Y	Y	Y
5 Foley	Y	Y	Y
6 Dicks	Y	Y	Y
7 Lowry	N	Y	Y
8 ***Chandler***	Y	Y	Y
WEST VIRGINIA			
1 Mollohan	Y	P	Y
2 Staggers	Y	Y	Y
3 Wise	Y	Y	Y
4 Rahall	Y	Y	Y
WISCONSIN			
1 Aspin	Y	Y	Y
2 Kastenmeier	Y	Y	Y
3 ***Gunderson***	Y	Y	Y
4 Kleczka	Y	Y	Y
5 Moody	Y	Y	Y
6 ***Petri***	Y	Y	Y
7 Obey	P	Y	?
8 ***Roth***	Y	Y	Y
9 ***Sensenbrenner***	N	Y	Y
WYOMING			
AL ***Cheney***	?	Y	Y

**Rep. Frank McCloskey, D-Ind., was sworn in on May 1, 1985. The first vote for which he was eligible was CQ vote 85.*

Southern states - Ala., Ark., Fla., Ga., Ky., La., Miss., N.C., Okla., S.C., Tenn., Texas, Va.

* The *Congressional Record* vote number is different from the CQ vote number because the *Record* includes quorum calls in its tally. CQ does not publish quorum call votes.

88. Procedural Motion. Strang, R-Colo., motion to approve the House *Journal* of Monday, May 6. Motion agreed to 241-164: R 19-154; D 222-10 (ND 149-9, SD 73-1), May 7, 1985.

89. HR 2268. United States-Israel Free Trade. Rostenkowski, D-Ill., motion to suspend the rules and pass the bill to implement the Free Trade Area Agreement between the United States and Israel. Motion agreed to 422-0: R 181-0; D 241-0 (ND 162-0, SD 79-0), May 7, 1985. A two-thirds majority of those present and voting (282 in this case) is required for passage under suspension of the rules. A "yea" was a vote supporting the president's position.

90. H Res 145. El Salvador Vaccination Program. Yatron, D-Pa., motion to suspend the rules and adopt the resolution to commend El Salvadoran President José Napoleón Duarte and the participating international humanitarian organizations in carrying out the recent immunization campaign in El Salvador. Motion agreed to 420-1: R 179-0; D 241-1 (ND 162-1, SD 79-0), May 7, 1985. A two-thirds majority of those present and voting (281 in this case) is required for adoption under suspension of the rules.

91. Procedural Motion. Emerson, R-Mo., motion to approve the House *Journal* of Tuesday, May 7. Motion agreed to 259-157: R 28-148; D 231-9 (ND 152-7, SD 79-2), May 8, 1985.

92. H Res 163. *Congressional Record* Investigation. Foley, D-Wash., motion to commit to the House Administration Committee the resolution to require a Rules Committee investigation of speeches that were not given on the House floor May 1 but appeared in the *Record* as if they were. Motion agreed to 245-184: R 0-182; D 245-2 (ND 165-1, SD 80-1), May 8, 1985. (The disputed floor debate was over whether to seat Democrat Frank McCloskey as the representative from Indiana's 8th District rather than Republican Richard D. McIntyre. McCloskey was seated May 1, and H Res 163 was part of the continuing Republican protest of that action.)

93. HR 1869. Automobile Record-keeping Requirements. Adoption of the conference report on the bill to repeal a provision of the 1984 Deficit Reduction Act (PL 98-369) requiring "contemporaneous" logs detailing personal and business use of automobiles, home computers and other equipment to qualify for business tax breaks. Adopted 426-1: R 182-0; D 244-1 (ND 163-1, SD 81-0), May 8, 1985.

94. Procedural Motion. Strang, R-Colo., motion to approve the House *Journal* of Wednesday, May 8. Motion agreed to 250-162: R 23-154; D 227-8 (ND 151-5, SD 76-3), May 9, 1985.

95. HR 2068. State Department Authorizations, Fiscal 1986-87. Hutto, D-Fla., amendment to strike a ban on the use of Pentagon funds to repair and expand the headquarters of the Coordinating Committee for Export Controls (COCOM), and delete provisions that would have let only State Department officials serve on the U.S. permanent delegation to COCOM. Rejected 196-222: R 128-48; D 68-174 (ND 23-141, SD 45-33), May 9, 1985.

KEY

Y Voted for (yea).
\# Paired for.
\+ Announced for.
N Voted against (nay).
X Paired against.
\- Announced against.
P Voted "present".
C Voted "present" to avoid possible conflict of interest.
? Did not vote or otherwise make a position known.

Democrats ***Republicans***

	88	89	90	91	92	93	94	95
ALABAMA								
1 ***Callahan***	N	Y	Y	N	N	Y	Y	Y
2 ***Dickinson***	?	Y	Y	N	N	Y	N	Y
3 Nichols	Y	Y	Y	Y	Y	Y	Y	Y
4 Bevill	Y	Y	Y	Y	Y	Y	Y	Y
5 Flippo	Y	Y	Y	Y	Y	Y	Y	Y
6 Erdreich	Y	Y	Y	Y	Y	Y	Y	Y
7 Shelby	Y	Y	Y	Y	Y	Y	Y	Y
ALASKA								
AL ***Young***	N	Y	Y	N	N	Y	N	Y
ARIZONA								
1 ***McCain***	N	Y	Y	N	N	Y	N	Y
2 Udall	Y	Y	Y	Y	Y	Y	Y	N
3 ***Stump***	N	Y	Y	Y	N	Y	Y	Y
4 ***Rudd***	Y	Y	Y	N	N	Y	Y	Y
5 ***Kolbe***	N	Y	Y	N	N	Y	N	N
ARKANSAS								
1 Alexander	Y	Y	Y	Y	?	Y	Y	N
2 Robinson	?	Y	Y	Y	Y	Y	Y	Y
3 ***Hammerschmidt***	N	Y	Y	Y	N	Y	N	Y
4 Anthony	Y	Y	Y	Y	Y	Y	Y	Y
CALIFORNIA								
1 Bosco	Y	Y	Y	Y	Y	Y	Y	N
2 ***Chappie***	N	Y	Y	N	N	Y	N	Y
3 Matsui	Y	Y	Y	N	Y	Y	Y	N
4 Fazio	Y	Y	Y	Y	Y	Y	Y	N
5 Burton	Y	Y	?	Y	Y	Y	Y	N
6 Boxer	Y	Y	Y	Y	Y	Y	Y	N
7 Miller	N	Y	Y	Y	Y	Y	Y	N
8 Dellums	Y	Y	Y	Y	Y	Y	Y	N
9 Stark	Y	Y	Y	Y	Y	Y	Y	N
10 Edwards	Y	Y	Y	Y	Y	Y	Y	N
11 Lantos	Y	Y	Y	Y	Y	Y	Y	N
12 ***Zschau***	N	Y	Y	N	N	Y	N	N
13 Mineta	Y	Y	Y	Y	Y	Y	Y	N
14 ***Shumway***	N	Y	Y	N	N	Y	N	Y
15 Coelho	Y	Y	Y	Y	Y	Y	Y	N
16 Panetta	Y	Y	Y	Y	Y	Y	Y	N
17 ***Pashayan***	N	Y	Y	N	N	Y	N	N
18 Lehman	Y	Y	Y	Y	Y	Y	Y	N
19 ***Lagomarsino***	N	Y	Y	N	N	Y	N	Y
20 ***Thomas***	N	Y	Y	N	N	Y	N	Y
21 ***Fiedler***	N	Y	Y	N	N	Y	N	Y
22 ***Moorhead***	N	Y	Y	N	N	Y	Y	Y
23 Beilenson	?	?	?	?	Y	Y	Y	N
24 Waxman	Y	Y	Y	Y	Y	Y	Y	N
25 Roybal	?	?	?	Y	?	?	?	?
26 Berman	Y	Y	Y	Y	Y	Y	Y	N
27 Levine	Y	Y	Y	Y	Y	Y	Y	N
28 Dixon	?	Y	Y	Y	Y	Y	Y	N
29 Hawkins	Y	Y	Y	Y	Y	?	?	N
30 Martinez	Y	Y	Y	Y	Y	Y	Y	N
31 Dymally	P	Y	Y	P	Y	Y	P	N
32 Anderson	Y	Y	Y	Y	Y	Y	Y	Y
33 ***Dreier***	N	Y	Y	N	N	Y	N	Y
34 Torres	Y	Y	Y	Y	?	Y	Y	N
35 ***Lewis***	N	Y	Y	N	N	Y	N	Y
36 Brown	Y	Y	Y	Y	Y	Y	Y	N
37 ***McCandless***	N	Y	Y	N	N	Y	N	Y
38 ***Dornan***	N	Y	Y	Y	N	Y	N	Y
39 ***Dannemeyer***	N	Y	Y	N	N	Y	N	Y
40 ***Badham***	N	Y	Y	N	N	Y	N	Y
41 ***Lowery***	N	Y	Y	N	N	Y	N	?
42 ***Lungren***	N	Y	Y	N	N	Y	N	Y
43 ***Packard***	N	Y	Y	N	N	Y	N	N
44 Bates	Y	Y	Y	Y	Y	Y	Y	N
45 ***Hunter***	N	Y	Y	N	N	Y	Y	Y
COLORADO								
1 Schroeder	N	Y	Y	N	Y	Y	N	Y
2 Wirth	Y	Y	Y	Y	Y	Y	Y	N
3 ***Strang***	N	Y	Y	N	N	Y	N	N
4 ***Brown***	N	Y	Y	N	N	Y	N	Y
5 ***Kramer***	N	Y	Y	N	N	Y	N	?
6 ***Schaefer***	N	Y	Y	N	N	Y	N	Y
CONNECTICUT								
1 Kennelly	Y	Y	?	Y	Y	Y	Y	N
2 Gejdenson	Y	Y	Y	Y	Y	Y	Y	N
3 Morrison	Y	Y	Y	Y	Y	Y	Y	N
4 ***McKinney***	N	Y	Y	N	N	Y	N	N
5 ***Rowland***	N	Y	Y	N	N	Y	N	?
6 ***Johnson***	Y	Y	Y	Y	N	Y	Y	N
DELAWARE								
AL Carper	?	Y	Y	Y	Y	Y	Y	N
FLORIDA								
1 Hutto	Y	Y	Y	Y	Y	Y	Y	Y
2 Fuqua	Y	Y	Y	Y	Y	Y	Y	N
3 Bennett	Y	Y	Y	Y	Y	Y	Y	Y
4 Chappell	?	Y	Y	Y	Y	Y	Y	Y
5 ***McCollum***	N	Y	Y	N	N	Y	N	Y
6 MacKay	Y	Y	Y	Y	Y	Y	Y	N
7 Gibbons	Y	Y	Y	Y	Y	Y	Y	N
8 ***Young***	N	Y	Y	N	N	Y	N	Y
9 ***Bilirakis***	N	Y	Y	N	N	Y	N	Y
10 ***Ireland***	N	Y	Y	N	N	Y	N	Y
11 Nelson	Y	Y	Y	Y	Y	Y	Y	Y
12 ***Lewis***	N	Y	Y	N	N	Y	N	Y
13 ***Mack***	N	Y	Y	N	N	Y	N	Y
14 Mica	Y	Y	Y	Y	Y	Y	Y	N
15 ***Shaw***	N	Y	Y	N	N	Y	N	Y
16 Smith	Y	Y	Y	Y	Y	Y	Y	N
17 Lehman	Y	Y	Y	Y	Y	Y	Y	N
18 Pepper	Y	Y	Y	+	Y	Y	Y	N
19 Fascell	?	?	?	Y	Y	Y	Y	N
GEORGIA								
1 Thomas	Y	Y	Y	Y	Y	Y	Y	Y
2 Hatcher	Y	Y	Y	Y	Y	Y	Y	Y
3 Ray	Y	Y	Y	Y	Y	Y	Y	Y
4 ***Swindall***	N	Y	Y	N	N	Y	N	Y
5 Fowler	?	Y	Y	Y	Y	Y	Y	N
6 ***Gingrich***	N	Y	Y	N	N	Y	N	Y
7 Darden	Y	Y	Y	Y	Y	Y	Y	Y
8 Rowland	Y	Y	Y	Y	Y	Y	Y	Y
9 Jenkins	Y	Y	Y	Y	Y	Y	Y	Y
10 Barnard	?	?	?	Y	Y	Y	Y	Y
HAWAII								
1 Heftel	Y	Y	Y	?	Y	Y	Y	Y
2 Akaka	Y	Y	Y	Y	Y	Y	Y	N
IDAHO								
1 ***Craig***	N	Y	Y	N	N	Y	N	Y
2 Stallings	Y	Y	Y	Y	Y	Y	Y	N
ILLINOIS								
1 Hayes	Y	Y	Y	Y	Y	Y	Y	N
2 Savage	Y	Y	Y	Y	Y	Y	Y	N
3 Russo	Y	Y	Y	Y	Y	Y	Y	N
4 ***O'Brien***	Y	Y	Y	Y	N	Y	Y	N
5 Lipinski	Y	Y	Y	Y	Y	Y	Y	N
6 ***Hyde***	N	Y	Y	N	N	Y	N	Y
7 Collins	Y	Y	Y	Y	Y	Y	?	?
8 Rostenkowski	Y	Y	Y	Y	Y	Y	Y	N
9 Yates	Y	Y	Y	Y	Y	Y	Y	N
10 ***Porter***	N	Y	Y	N	N	Y	N	N
11 Annunzio	Y	Y	Y	Y	Y	Y	Y	N
12 ***Crane***	N	Y	Y	N	N	Y	N	Y
13 ***Fawell***	N	Y	?	N	N	Y	N	N
14 ***Grotberg***	N	Y	Y	N	N	Y	N	Y
15 ***Madigan***	N	Y	Y	N	N	Y	N	N
16 ***Martin***	N	Y	Y	N	N	Y	N	Y
17 Evans	Y	Y	Y	Y	Y	Y	Y	N
18 ***Michel***	N	Y	Y	Y	N	Y	?	Y
19 Bruce	Y	Y	Y	Y	Y	Y	Y	N
20 Durbin	N	Y	Y	N	Y	Y	Y	N
21 Price	Y	Y	Y	Y	Y	Y	Y	Y
22 Gray	Y	Y	Y	Y	Y	Y	?	N
INDIANA								
1 Visclosky	Y	Y	Y	Y	Y	Y	Y	N
2 Sharp	Y	Y	Y	?	Y	Y	Y	N
3 ***Hiler***	N	Y	Y	N	N	Y	N	Y
4 ***Coats***	N	Y	Y	N	N	Y	N	Y
5 ***Hillis***	N	Y	Y	N	N	Y	N	Y

ND - Northern Democrats SD - Southern Democrats

* Corresponding to Congressional Record Votes 96, 97, 98, 99, 100, 101, 102, 104

	88	89	90	91	92	93	94	95
6 ***Burton***	N	Y	Y	N	N	Y	N	Y
7 ***Myers***	Y	Y	Y	Y	N	Y	Y	Y
8 McCloskey	Y	Y	Y	Y	Y	Y	Y	N
9 Hamilton	Y	Y	Y	Y	Y	Y	Y	N
10 Jacobs	N	Y	Y	N	Y	Y	N	N
IOWA								
1 ***Leach***	N	Y	Y	N	N	Y	N	N
2 ***Tauke***	N	Y	Y	N	N	Y	N	N
3 ***Evans***	N	Y	Y	N	N	Y	N	N
4 Smith	Y	Y	Y	Y	Y	Y	Y	N
5 ***Lightfoot***	N	Y	Y	N	N	Y	N	N
6 Bedell	Y	Y	Y	Y	Y	Y	Y	N
KANSAS								
1 ***Roberts***	N	Y	Y	N	N	Y	N	N
2 Slattery	Y	Y	Y	Y	Y	Y	Y	Y
3 ***Meyers***	Y	Y	Y	N	N	Y	N	N
4 Glickman	Y	Y	Y	Y	N	Y	Y	N
5 ***Whittaker***	?	Y	Y	N	N	Y	N	N
KENTUCKY								
1 Hubbard	Y	Y	Y	Y	Y	Y	Y	Y
2 Natcher	Y	Y	Y	Y	Y	Y	Y	N
3 Mazzoli	Y	Y	Y	Y	Y	Y	Y	N
4 ***Snyder***	Y	Y	Y	Y	N	Y	Y	Y
5 ***Rogers***	N	Y	Y	N	N	Y	N	Y
6 ***Hopkins***	Y	Y	Y	Y	N	Y	Y	Y
7 Perkins	Y	Y	Y	Y	Y	Y	Y	N
LOUISIANA								
1 ***Livingston***	N	Y	Y	N	N	Y	N	Y
2 Boggs	Y	Y	Y	Y	Y	Y	?	N
3 Tauzin	Y	Y	Y	Y	Y	Y	Y	Y
4 Roemer	N	Y	Y	N	N	Y	N	Y
5 Huckaby	Y	Y	Y	Y	Y	Y	Y	Y
6 ***Moore***	N	Y	Y	N	N	Y	Y	N
7 Breaux	?	?	?	Y	Y	Y	Y	Y
8 Long	Y	Y	Y	Y	Y	Y	Y	N
MAINE								
1 ***McKernan***	N	Y	Y	N	N	Y	N	Y
2 ***Snowe***	Y	Y	Y	N	N	Y	N	Y
MARYLAND								
1 Dyson	Y	Y	Y	Y	Y	Y	Y	Y
2 ***Bentley***	N	Y	Y	N	N	Y	N	Y
3 Mikulski	Y	Y	Y	Y	Y	Y	Y	N
4 ***Holt***	N	Y	Y	N	N	Y	N	Y
5 Hoyer	Y	Y	Y	Y	Y	Y	Y	N
6 Byron	Y	Y	Y	Y	Y	Y	Y	Y
7 Mitchell	?	Y	Y	?	Y	Y	P	N
8 Barnes	Y	Y	Y	Y	Y	Y	Y	N
MASSACHUSETTS								
1 ***Conte***	N	Y	Y	?	N	Y	N	Y
2 Boland	Y	Y	Y	Y	Y	Y	Y	N
3 Early	Y	Y	Y	Y	Y	Y	?	?
4 Frank	Y	Y	Y	Y	Y	N	Y	N
5 Atkins	Y	Y	Y	Y	Y	Y	Y	N
6 Mavroules	Y	Y	Y	Y	Y	Y	Y	N
7 Markey	Y	Y	Y	Y	Y	Y	Y	N
8 O'Neill								
9 Moakley	Y	Y	Y	Y	Y	Y	Y	N
10 Studds	Y	Y	Y	Y	Y	Y	Y	N
11 Donnelly	Y	Y	Y	Y	Y	Y	Y	Y
MICHIGAN								
1 Conyers	Y	P	N	Y	Y	Y	Y	N
2 ***Pursell***	N	Y	Y	?	N	Y	N	Y
3 Wolpe	Y	Y	Y	Y	Y	Y	Y	N
4 ***Siljander***	N	Y	Y	?	N	Y	N	Y
5 ***Henry***	N	Y	Y	N	N	Y	N	Y
6 Carr	Y	Y	Y	Y	Y	Y	Y	N
7 Kildee	Y	Y	Y	Y	Y	Y	Y	N
8 Traxler	Y	Y	Y	Y	Y	Y	Y	N
9 ***Vander Jagt***	?	?	?	?	N	Y	?	N
10 ***Schuette***	N	Y	Y	N	N	Y	N	Y
11 ***Davis***	N	Y	Y	N	N	Y	N	Y
12 Bonior	?	P	Y	Y	Y	?	Y	N
13 Crockett	Y	Y	Y	Y	Y	Y	Y	N
14 Hertel	Y	Y	Y	Y	Y	Y	Y	Y
15 Ford	P	Y	Y	Y	Y	Y	?	N
16 Dingell	Y	Y	Y	?	Y	Y	Y	N
17 Levin	Y	Y	Y	Y	Y	Y	Y	N
18 ***Broomfield***	Y	Y	Y	Y	N	Y	Y	Y
MINNESOTA								
1 Penny	N	Y	Y	N	Y	Y	N	N
2 ***Weber***	N	Y	Y	N	N	Y	N	N
3 ***Frenzel***	N	Y	Y	Y	N	Y	Y	N
4 Vento	Y	Y	Y	Y	Y	Y	Y	N
5 Sabo	Y	Y	Y	Y	Y	Y	Y	N
6 Sikorski	N	Y	Y	N	Y	Y	N	N

	88	89	90	91	92	93	94	95
7 ***Stangeland***	N	Y	Y	N	N	Y	N	Y
8 Oberstar	Y	Y	Y	Y	Y	Y	Y	N
MISSISSIPPI								
1 Whitten	Y	Y	Y	Y	Y	Y	Y	Y
2 ***Franklin***	?	Y	Y	Y	N	Y	N	Y
3 Montgomery	Y	Y	Y	Y	Y	Y	Y	Y
4 Dowdy	?	Y	Y	Y	Y	Y	Y	Y
5 ***Lott***	N	Y	Y	N	N	Y	N	Y
MISSOURI								
1 Clay	N	Y	P	N	Y	Y	N	N
2 Young	Y	Y	Y	Y	Y	Y	Y	N
3 Gephardt	Y	Y	Y	Y	Y	Y	?	N
4 Skelton	Y	Y	Y	Y	Y	Y	Y	Y
5 Wheat	Y	Y	Y	Y	Y	Y	Y	N
6 ***Coleman***	N	Y	Y	N	N	Y	N	Y
7 ***Taylor***	N	Y	Y	N	N	Y	N	Y
8 ***Emerson***	N	Y	Y	N	N	Y	N	Y
9 Volkmer	Y	Y	Y	Y	Y	Y	Y	Y
MONTANA								
1 Williams	Y	Y	Y	Y	Y	Y	Y	N
2 ***Marlenee***	N	Y	Y	N	N	Y	N	Y
NEBRASKA								
1 ***Bereuter***	N	Y	Y	N	N	Y	N	N
2 ***Daub***	N	Y	Y	N	N	Y	N	N
3 ***Smith***	N	Y	Y	N	N	Y	N	N
NEVADA								
1 Reid	Y	Y	Y	Y	Y	Y	Y	N
2 ***Vucanovich***	N	Y	Y	N	N	Y	N	Y
NEW HAMPSHIRE								
1 ***Smith***	N	Y	Y	N	N	Y	N	Y
2 ***Gregg***	N	Y	Y	N	N	Y	N	Y
NEW JERSEY								
1 Florio	Y	Y	Y	Y	Y	Y	Y	N
2 Hughes	Y	Y	Y	Y	Y	Y	Y	Y
3 Howard	Y	Y	Y	Y	Y	Y	Y	N
4 ***Smith***	N	Y	Y	N	N	Y	N	Y
5 ***Roukema***	N	Y	Y	Y	N	Y	Y	N
6 Dwyer	Y	Y	Y	Y	Y	Y	Y	N
7 ***Rinaldo***	Y	Y	Y	Y	N	Y	Y	Y
8 Roe	Y	Y	Y	Y	Y	Y	Y	N
9 Torricelli	Y	Y	Y	Y	Y	Y	Y	N
10 Rodino	Y	Y	Y	Y	Y	Y	Y	N
11 ***Gallo***	N	Y	Y	N	N	Y	N	N
12 ***Courter***	N	Y	Y	N	N	Y	N	Y
13 ***Saxton***	N	Y	Y	N	N	Y	N	N
14 Guarini	Y	Y	Y	Y	Y	Y	Y	N
NEW MEXICO								
1 ***Lujan***	N	Y	Y	N	N	Y	N	Y
2 ***Skeen***	N	Y	Y	N	N	Y	N	?
3 Richardson	Y	Y	Y	Y	Y	Y	Y	N
NEW YORK								
1 ***Carney***	N	Y	Y	N	N	Y	N	Y
2 Downey	N	Y	Y	Y	Y	Y	Y	N
3 Mrazek	Y	Y	Y	Y	Y	Y	Y	N
4 ***Lent***	N	Y	Y	Y	N	Y	N	Y
5 ***McGrath***	N	Y	Y	N	N	Y	N	Y
6 Addabbo	?	?	?	?	?	?	?	?
7 Ackerman	Y	?	Y	Y	Y	Y	Y	N
8 Scheuer	Y	Y	Y	Y	Y	Y	Y	N
9 Manton	Y	Y	Y	Y	Y	Y	Y	N
10 Schumer	N	Y	Y	Y	Y	Y	Y	N
11 Towns	Y	Y	Y	?	Y	Y	Y	N
12 Owens	Y	Y	Y	Y	Y	Y	Y	N
13 Solarz	Y	Y	Y	Y	Y	Y	Y	N
14 ***Molinari***	N	Y	Y	N	N	Y	N	Y
15 ***Green***	?	Y	Y	N	N	Y	N	N
16 Rangel	Y	Y	Y	Y	Y	Y	Y	N
17 Weiss	Y	Y	Y	Y	Y	Y	Y	N
18 Garcia	Y	Y	Y	Y	Y	Y	Y	N
19 Biaggi	Y	Y	Y	Y	Y	Y	Y	N
20 ***DioGuardi***	N	Y	Y	N	N	Y	N	Y
21 ***Fish***	N	Y	Y	N	N	Y	N	N
22 ***Gilman***	N	Y	Y	N	N	Y	N	Y
23 Stratton	Y	Y	Y	Y	Y	Y	Y	Y
24 ***Solomon***	N	Y	Y	N	N	Y	N	Y
25 ***Boehlert***	N	Y	Y	N	N	Y	N	N
26 ***Martin***	N	Y	Y	N	N	Y	N	Y
27 ***Wortley***	?	Y	Y	Y	N	Y	N	Y
28 McHugh	Y	Y	Y	Y	Y	Y	Y	N
29 ***Horton***	Y	Y	Y	Y	N	Y	Y	Y
30 ***Eckert***	N	Y	Y	N	N	Y	N	Y
31 ***Kemp***	N	Y	Y	N	N	Y	?	Y
32 LaFalce	Y	Y	Y	Y	Y	Y	Y	N
33 Nowak	Y	Y	Y	Y	Y	Y	Y	N
34 Lundine	Y	Y	Y	Y	Y	Y	Y	N

	88	89	90	91	92	93	94	95
NORTH CAROLINA								
1 Jones	Y	Y	Y	Y	Y	?	Y	Y
2 Valentine	Y	Y	Y	Y	Y	Y	Y	Y
3 Whitley	Y	Y	Y	Y	Y	Y	Y	Y
4 ***Cobey***	N	Y	Y	N	N	Y	N	Y
5 Neal	Y	Y	Y	Y	Y	Y	?	?
6 ***Coble***	N	Y	Y	N	N	Y	N	Y
7 Rose	Y	Y	Y	Y	Y	Y	Y	N
8 Hefner	Y	Y	Y	Y	Y	Y	Y	Y
9 ***McMillan***	N	Y	Y	N	N	Y	N	Y
10 ***Broyhill***	Y	Y	Y	?	N	Y	Y	Y
11 ***Hendon***	N	Y	Y	N	N	Y	N	Y
NORTH DAKOTA								
AL Dorgan	Y	Y	Y	Y	Y	Y	Y	Y
OHIO								
1 Luken	Y	Y	Y	Y	Y	Y	Y	N
2 ***Gradison***	Y	Y	Y	Y	N	Y	N	N
3 Hall	Y	Y	Y	Y	Y	Y	Y	N
4 ***Oxley***	?	Y	Y	N	N	Y	N	Y
5 ***Latta***	Y	Y	Y	N	N	Y	N	Y
6 ***McEwen***	N	Y	Y	N	N	Y	N	Y
7 ***DeWine***	N	Y	Y	N	N	Y	N	Y
8 ***Kindness***	N	Y	Y	N	N	Y	N	Y
9 Kaptur	Y	Y	Y	Y	Y	Y	Y	N
10 ***Miller***	N	Y	Y	N	N	Y	N	Y
11 Eckart	Y	Y	Y	Y	Y	Y	Y	N
12 ***Kasich***	N	Y	Y	N	N	Y	N	Y
13 Pease	Y	Y	Y	Y	Y	Y	Y	N
14 Seiberling	Y	Y	Y	?	Y	Y	Y	N
15 ***Wylie***	Y	Y	Y	Y	N	Y	Y	N
16 ***Regula***	N	Y	Y	N	N	Y	Y	Y
17 Traficant	Y	Y	Y	Y	Y	Y	Y	N
18 Applegate	Y	Y	Y	?	Y	Y	?	Y
19 Feighan	Y	Y	Y	Y	Y	Y	Y	N
20 Oakar	Y	Y	Y	Y	Y	Y	Y	N
21 Stokes	Y	Y	Y	Y	Y	?	Y	N
OKLAHOMA								
1 Jones	Y	Y	Y	Y	Y	Y	Y	N
2 Synar	Y	Y	Y	Y	Y	Y	Y	N
3 Watkins	Y	Y	Y	Y	Y	Y	Y	Y
4 McCurdy	Y	Y	Y	Y	Y	Y	Y	Y
5 ***Edwards***	N	Y	Y	N	N	Y	N	?
6 English	Y	Y	Y	Y	Y	Y	Y	Y
OREGON								
1 AuCoin	Y	Y	Y	Y	Y	Y	Y	N
2 ***Smith, R.***	N	Y	Y	N	N	Y	N	N
3 Wyden	Y	Y	Y	Y	Y	Y	Y	N
4 Weaver	?	?	?	?	?	?	?	?
5 ***Smith, D.***	N	Y	Y	N	N	Y	N	Y
PENNSYLVANIA								
1 Foglietta	Y	Y	Y	Y	Y	Y	Y	Y
2 Gray	Y	Y	Y	Y	Y	Y	Y	?
3 Borski	Y	Y	Y	Y	Y	Y	Y	N
4 Kolter	?	Y	Y	Y	Y	Y	Y	Y
5 ***Schulze***	N	Y	Y	N	N	Y	N	Y
6 Yatron	Y	Y	Y	Y	Y	Y	Y	Y
7 Edgar	Y	Y	Y	Y	Y	Y	?	N
8 Kostmayer	Y	Y	Y	Y	Y	Y	Y	N
9 ***Shuster***	N	Y	Y	N	N	Y	N	Y
10 ***McDade***	N	Y	Y	N	N	Y	N	Y
11 Kanjorski	Y	Y	Y	Y	Y	Y	Y	N
12 Murtha	Y	Y	Y	Y	Y	Y	Y	Y
13 ***Coughlin***	N	Y	Y	N	N	Y	N	Y
14 Coyne	Y	Y	Y	Y	Y	Y	Y	N
15 ***Ritter***	N	Y	Y	N	N	Y	N	Y
16 ***Walker***	N	Y	Y	N	N	Y	N	Y
17 ***Gekas***	N	Y	Y	Y	N	Y	N	Y
18 Walgren	Y	Y	Y	Y	Y	Y	?	N
19 ***Goodling***	N	Y	Y	N	N	Y	N	Y
20 Gaydos	Y	Y	Y	Y	Y	Y	Y	Y
21 ***Ridge***	N	Y	Y	N	N	Y	?	N
22 Murphy	Y	P	Y	Y	Y	Y	Y	Y
23 ***Clinger***	N	Y	Y	N	N	Y	N	N
RHODE ISLAND								
1 St Germain	Y	Y	Y	Y	Y	Y	Y	N
2 ***Schneider***	N	Y	Y	N	N	Y	N	N
SOUTH CAROLINA								
1 ***Hartnett***	N	Y	Y	N	N	Y	N	Y
2 ***Spence***	N	Y	Y	N	N	Y	N	Y
3 Derrick	Y	Y	Y	N	Y	Y	N	Y
4 ***Campbell***	N	Y	Y	N	N	Y	N	Y
5 Spratt	Y	Y	Y	Y	Y	Y	Y	N
6 Tallon	Y	Y	Y	Y	Y	Y	Y	Y
SOUTH DAKOTA								
AL Daschle	Y	Y	Y	Y	Y	Y	Y	N

	88	89	90	91	92	93	94	95
TENNESSEE								
1 ***Quillen***	Y	Y	Y	N	N	Y	Y	?
2 ***Duncan***	Y	Y	Y	Y	N	Y	N	Y
3 Lloyd	Y	Y	Y	Y	Y	Y	Y	Y
4 Cooper	Y	Y	Y	Y	Y	Y	Y	N
5 Boner	Y	Y	Y	Y	Y	Y	Y	N
6 Gordon	Y	Y	Y	Y	Y	Y	Y	N
7 ***Sundquist***	N	Y	Y	N	N	Y	N	Y
8 Jones	Y	Y	Y	Y	Y	Y	Y	?
9 Ford	Y	Y	Y	Y	Y	Y	Y	N
TEXAS								
1 Hall, S.	Y	Y	Y	Y	Y	Y	Y	Y
2 Wilson	Y	Y	Y	Y	Y	Y	?	?
3 ***Bartlett***	N	Y	Y	N	N	Y	N	N
4 Hall, R.	Y	Y	Y	Y	Y	Y	Y	Y
5 Bryant	Y	Y	Y	Y	Y	Y	Y	N
6 ***Barton***	N	Y	Y	N	N	Y	N	Y
7 ***Archer***	N	Y	Y	Y	N	Y	Y	N
8 ***Fields***	N	Y	Y	?	N	Y	N	Y
9 Brooks	Y	Y	Y	Y	Y	Y	Y	N
10 Pickle	Y	Y	Y	Y	Y	Y	Y	Y
11 Leath	Y	Y	Y	Y	Y	Y	Y	Y
12 Wright	Y	Y	Y	Y	Y	Y	Y	N
13 ***Boulter***	N	Y	Y	N	N	Y	N	Y
14 ***Sweeney***	N	Y	Y	N	N	Y	N	Y
15 de la Garza	Y	Y	Y	Y	Y	Y	Y	Y
16 Coleman	?	Y	Y	Y	Y	Y	Y	N
17 Stenholm	Y	Y	Y	Y	Y	Y	N	Y
18 Leland	Y	Y	Y	Y	Y	Y	Y	?
19 ***Combest***	N	Y	Y	N	N	Y	N	Y
20 Gonzalez	Y	Y	Y	Y	Y	Y	Y	N
21 ***Loeffler***	?	Y	Y	N	N	Y	N	Y
22 ***DeLay***	N	Y	Y	N	N	Y	N	Y
23 Bustamante	Y	Y	Y	Y	Y	Y	Y	N
24 Frost	Y	Y	Y	Y	Y	Y	Y	N
25 Andrews	Y	Y	Y	Y	Y	Y	Y	N
26 ***Armey***	Y	Y	Y	N	N	Y	N	Y
27 Ortiz	Y	Y	Y	Y	Y	Y	Y	Y
UTAH								
1 ***Hansen***	N	Y	Y	Y	N	Y	?	Y
2 ***Monson***	N	Y	Y	N	N	Y	N	Y
3 ***Nielson***	N	Y	Y	N	N	Y	N	N
VERMONT								
AL ***Jeffords***	N	Y	?	N	N	Y	N	N
VIRGINIA								
1 ***Bateman***	N	Y	Y	Y	N	Y	Y	Y
2 ***Whitehurst***	?	Y	Y	Y	N	Y	N	Y
3 ***Bliley***	N	Y	Y	N	N	Y	N	Y
4 Sisisky	Y	Y	Y	Y	Y	Y	Y	Y
5 Daniel	Y	Y	Y	Y	Y	Y	Y	Y
6 Olin	Y	Y	Y	Y	Y	Y	Y	N
7 ***Slaughter***	N	Y	Y	N	N	Y	N	Y
8 ***Parris***	N	Y	Y	N	N	Y	N	Y
9 Boucher	Y	Y	Y	Y	Y	Y	Y	N
10 ***Wolf***	N	Y	Y	N	N	Y	N	N
WASHINGTON								
1 ***Miller***	N	Y	Y	N	N	Y	N	Y
2 Swift	Y	Y	Y	Y	Y	Y	Y	N
3 Bonker	Y	Y	Y	Y	Y	Y	Y	N
4 ***Morrison***	N	Y	Y	N	N	Y	N	N
5 Foley	Y	Y	Y	Y	Y	Y	Y	N
6 Dicks	Y	Y	Y	Y	Y	Y	Y	N
7 Lowry	Y	Y	Y	Y	Y	Y	Y	N
8 ***Chandler***	N	Y	Y	N	N	Y	N	N
WEST VIRGINIA								
1 Mollohan	Y	Y	Y	Y	Y	Y	Y	Y
2 Staggers	Y	Y	Y	Y	Y	Y	Y	N
3 Wise	Y	Y	Y	Y	Y	Y	Y	N
4 Rahall	Y	Y	Y	Y	Y	Y	Y	N
WISCONSIN								
1 Aspin	?	Y	Y	Y	Y	Y	Y	Y
2 Kastenmeier	Y	Y	Y	Y	Y	Y	Y	N
3 ***Gunderson***	N	Y	Y	N	N	Y	N	N
4 Kleczka	Y	Y	Y	Y	Y	Y	Y	N
5 Moody	Y	Y	Y	Y	Y	Y	Y	N
6 ***Petri***	Y	Y	Y	N	Y	Y	Y	N
7 Obey	Y	Y	Y	Y	Y	Y	Y	N
8 ***Roth***	N	Y	Y	N	N	Y	N	N
9 ***Sensenbrenner***	N	Y	Y	N	N	Y	N	Y
WYOMING								
AL ***Cheney***	N	Y	Y	N	N	Y	N	Y

Southern states - Ala., Ark., Fla., Ga., Ky., La., Miss., N.C., Okla., S.C., Tenn., Texas, Va.

* The *Congressional Record* vote number is different from the CQ vote number because the *Record* includes quorum calls in its tally. CQ does not publish quorum call votes.

96. HR 2068. State Department Authorizations, Fiscal 1986-87. Broomfield, R-Mich., amendment to express the sense of Congress that the Soviet Union's chief of mission to the United States should be declared persona non grata beginning on June 1 until or unless the president certifies to Congress that the Soviet Union has made a formal apology for the killing of Maj. Arthur D. Nicholson Jr. Adopted 322-93: R 173-2; D 149-91 (ND 82-82, SD 67-9), May 9, 1985.

97. HR 2068. State Department Authorizations, Fiscal 1986-87. Burton, R-Ind., amendment to delete $50,000 for special religious sensitivity instruction for U.S. foreign service officers. Adopted 224-189: R 145-30; D 79-159 (ND 34-128, SD 45-31), May 9, 1985.

98. HR 2068. State Department Authorizations, Fiscal 1986-87. Mica, D-Fla., amendment to reduce the fiscal 1986 State Department authorization level to the fiscal 1985 appropriation level, and reduce the fiscal 1987 authorization level to the fiscal 1985 appropriation level adjusted for inflation. Adopted 398-1: R 169-0; D 229-1 (ND 157-1, SD 72-0), May 9, 1985. (The bill was subsequently passed by voice vote.)

99. Procedural Motion. Slaughter, R-Va., motion to approve the House *Journal* of Monday, May 13. Motion agreed to 246-156: R 26-145; D 220-11 (ND 148-8, SD 72-3), May 14, 1985.

100. HR 1784. Panama Canal Authorization, Fiscal 1986. Walker, R-Pa., amendment to express the sense of Congress that fiscal 1986 expenditures of the Panama Canal Commission be frozen at the fiscal 1985 levels, and that all possible steps be taken to assure that any savings from an actual freeze go into the Treasury. Adopted 241-173: R 168-7; D 73-166 (ND 36-126, SD 37-40), May 14, 1985. (Under the 1978 Panama Canal Treaties (Exec N, 95th Congress, First Session), article XIII, paragraph 4 (c), a direct freeze on expenditures would result in the government of Panama receiving $7 million from tolls and fees collected for the use of the canal. The effect of the Walker amendment is to urge that the treaty be amended to allow the savings to go into the U.S. Treasury, rather than to the government of Panama.) (The bill was subsequently passed by voice vote.)

101. HR 1157. Maritime Programs Authorization, Fiscal 1986. Walker, R-Pa., perfecting amendment to the Jones, D-N.C., substitute to the Walker amendment, to cut the authorization for maritime programs of the Maritime Administration and the Federal Maritime Commission for fiscal 1986 by 10 percent. Rejected 100-318: R 92-84; D 8-234 (ND 7-157, SD 1-77), May 14, 1985. (The Jones amendment, to state that the authorization was not an increase over fiscal 1985 levels, was subsequently adopted by voice vote.)

102. HR 1157. Maritime Programs Authorization, Fiscal 1986. Passage of the bill to authorize maritime programs of the Maritime Administration and the Federal Maritime Commission for fiscal 1986. Passed 371-46: R 135-42; D 236-4 (ND 158-4, SD 78-0), May 14, 1985.

103. HR 2005. Social Security Minor and Technical Changes Act. Rostenkowski, D-Ill., motion to suspend the rules and pass the bill to make minor and technical changes in the Social Security and Disability Insurance programs. Motion agreed to 413-0: R 175-0; D 238-0 (ND 162-0, SD 76-0), May 14, 1985. A two-thirds majority of those present and voting (276 in this case) is required for passage under suspension of the rules.

KEY

Y Voted for (yea).
Paired for.
+ Announced for.
N Voted against (nay).
X Paired against.
- Announced against.
P Voted "present".
C Voted "present" to avoid possible conflict of interest.
? Did not vote or otherwise make a position known.

Democrats *Republicans*

	96	97	98	99	100	101	102	103
ALABAMA								
1 ***Callahan***	Y	Y	Y	Y	Y	N	Y	Y
2 ***Dickinson***	Y	Y	Y	N	Y	N	Y	Y
3 Nichols	Y	Y	Y	Y	Y	N	Y	Y
4 Bevill	Y	N	Y	Y	Y	N	Y	Y
5 Flippo	Y	Y	?	Y	Y	N	Y	Y
6 Erdreich	Y	Y	Y	Y	Y	N	Y	Y
7 Shelby	Y	Y	Y	Y	Y	N	Y	Y
ALASKA								
AL ***Young***	Y	Y	Y	N	Y	N	Y	Y
ARIZONA								
1 ***McCain***	Y	Y	Y	Y	Y	Y	Y	Y
2 Udall	N	N	Y	Y	?	?	?	?
3 ***Stump***	Y	Y	Y	N	Y	Y	N	Y
4 ***Rudd***	Y	Y	Y	Y	Y	Y	N	Y
5 ***Kolbe***	Y	Y	Y	N	Y	Y	Y	Y
ARKANSAS								
1 Alexander	N	N	Y	Y	N	N	Y	Y
2 Robinson	?	?	?	Y	N	N	Y	Y
3 ***Hammerschmidt***	Y	Y	Y	Y	Y	Y	Y	Y
4 Anthony	Y	Y	?	Y	N	N	Y	Y
CALIFORNIA								
1 Bosco	N	N	Y	Y	N	N	Y	Y
2 ***Chappie***	Y	Y	Y	N	Y	N	Y	Y
3 Matsui	N	N	Y	Y	N	N	Y	Y
4 Fazio	N	N	Y	Y	N	N	Y	Y
5 Burton	N	N	Y	Y	N	N	Y	Y
6 Boxer	N	N	Y	Y	N	N	Y	Y
7 Miller	N	N	Y	Y	N	N	Y	Y
8 Dellums	N	N	Y	Y	N	N	Y	Y
9 Stark	N	N	Y	Y	N	?	?	?
10 Edwards	N	N	Y	Y	N	N	Y	Y
11 Lantos	Y	N	Y	Y	N	N	Y	Y
12 ***Zschau***	Y	Y	Y	N	Y	Y	Y	Y
13 Mineta	N	N	Y	Y	N	N	Y	Y
14 ***Shumway***	Y	Y	?	N	N	Y	Y	Y
15 Coelho	Y	N	Y	?	N	N	Y	Y
16 Panetta	N	N	Y	Y	N	N	Y	Y
17 ***Pashayan***	Y	Y	Y	?	Y	Y	Y	Y
18 Lehman	N	N	Y	Y	N	N	Y	Y
19 ***Lagomarsino***	Y	Y	Y	N	Y	Y	Y	Y
20 ***Thomas***	Y	Y	Y	N	Y	N	Y	Y
21 ***Fiedler***	Y	N	Y	N	Y	Y	Y	Y
22 ***Moorhead***	Y	Y	Y	N	Y	Y	Y	Y
23 Beilenson	Y	Y	Y	Y	N	N	Y	Y
24 Waxman	Y	N	?	Y	?	N	Y	Y
25 Roybal	?	?	?	Y	N	N	Y	Y
26 Berman	N	N	Y	Y	N	N	Y	Y
27 Levine	N	N	Y	Y	N	N	Y	Y
28 Dixon	Y	N	?	?	N	N	Y	Y
29 Hawkins	Y	N	Y	Y	N	N	Y	Y
30 Martinez	Y	N	Y	Y	N	N	Y	Y
31 Dymally	N	N	Y	P	N	N	Y	Y
32 Anderson	Y	N	Y	Y	N	N	Y	Y
33 ***Dreier***	Y	Y	Y	N	Y	Y	N	Y
34 Torres	Y	N	Y	Y	N	N	Y	Y
35 ***Lewis***	Y	Y	Y	N	Y	N	Y	Y
36 Brown	N	N	?	Y	Y	N	Y	Y
37 ***McCandless***	Y	Y	Y	N	Y	Y	Y	Y
38 ***Dornan***	Y	N	Y	N	Y	Y	N	Y
39 ***Dannemeyer***	Y	Y	Y	N	Y	Y	N	Y
40 ***Badham***	Y	Y	?	N	Y	Y	Y	Y
41 ***Lowery***	?	?	?	N	Y	N	Y	Y
42 ***Lungren***	Y	Y	Y	N	Y	Y	N	Y
43 ***Packard***	Y	Y	Y	N	Y	Y	Y	Y
44 Bates	N	N	Y	Y	Y	N	Y	Y
45 ***Hunter***	Y	Y	Y	N	Y	N	Y	Y
COLORADO								
1 Schroeder	N	Y	Y	N	N	Y	N	Y
2 Wirth	Y	N	Y	Y	N	Y	Y	Y
3 ***Strang***	Y	Y	Y	N	Y	N	Y	Y
4 ***Brown***	Y	Y	Y	N	Y	Y	N	Y
5 ***Kramer***	?	?	?	N	Y	Y	N	Y
6 ***Schaefer***	Y	Y	Y	N	Y	N	Y	Y
CONNECTICUT								
1 Kennelly	Y	N	Y	Y	N	N	Y	Y
2 Gejdenson	N	N	Y	Y	N	N	Y	Y
3 Morrison	N	N	Y	Y	N	N	Y	Y
4 ***McKinney***	Y	N	Y	N	Y	N	Y	Y
5 ***Rowland***	Y	Y	Y	N	Y	Y	Y	Y
6 ***Johnson***	Y	Y	Y	Y	Y	Y	Y	Y
DELAWARE								
AL Carper	Y	Y	Y	Y	N	N	Y	Y
FLORIDA								
1 Hutto	Y	Y	Y	Y	Y	N	Y	Y
2 Fuqua	Y	Y	Y	Y	N	N	Y	Y
3 Bennett	Y	N	Y	Y	Y	N	Y	Y
4 Chappell	Y	N	Y	Y	N	N	Y	Y
5 ***McCollum***	Y	Y	Y	N	Y	Y	Y	Y
6 MacKay	Y	N	Y	Y	N	N	Y	Y
7 Gibbons	N	N	Y	Y	Y	N	Y	Y
8 ***Young***	Y	Y	Y	N	Y	Y	Y	Y
9 ***Bilirakis***	Y	Y	Y	N	Y	N	Y	Y
10 ***Ireland***	Y	Y	Y	N	Y	Y	Y	Y
11 Nelson	Y	Y	Y	Y	Y	N	Y	Y
12 ***Lewis***	Y	Y	Y	N	Y	Y	Y	Y
13 ***Mack***	Y	Y	Y	N	Y	Y	Y	Y
14 Mica	Y	N	Y	Y	Y	N	Y	Y
15 ***Shaw***	Y	Y	Y	N	Y	N	Y	Y
16 Smith	Y	N	Y	Y	Y	N	Y	Y
17 Lehman	N	N	Y	Y	N	N	Y	Y
18 Pepper	Y	N	Y	Y	-	-	+	+
19 Fascell	N	N	Y	Y	N	N	Y	Y
GEORGIA								
1 Thomas	Y	Y	Y	Y	N	N	Y	Y
2 Hatcher	Y	Y	Y	Y	N	N	Y	Y
3 Ray	Y	Y	Y	?	Y	N	Y	?
4 ***Swindall***	Y	Y	Y	N	Y	Y	N	Y
5 Fowler	Y	Y	Y	Y	Y	?	?	?
6 ***Gingrich***	Y	Y	Y	N	Y	Y	Y	Y
7 Darden	Y	Y	Y	Y	N	N	Y	Y
8 Rowland	Y	Y	Y	Y	N	N	Y	Y
9 Jenkins	Y	Y	Y	Y	Y	N	Y	Y
10 Barnard	Y	Y	Y	Y	Y	N	Y	Y
HAWAII								
1 Heftel	Y	N	Y	Y	Y	N	Y	Y
2 Akaka	Y	N	Y	Y	N	N	Y	Y
IDAHO								
1 ***Craig***	Y	Y	Y	Y	Y	N	N	Y
2 Stallings	Y	N	Y	Y	N	N	Y	Y
ILLINOIS								
1 Hayes	N	N	Y	Y	N	N	Y	Y
2 Savage	N	N	Y	Y	N	N	Y	Y
3 Russo	N	N	Y	Y	N	N	Y	Y
4 ***O'Brien***	Y	Y	Y	?	?	?	?	?
5 Lipinski	Y	N	Y	Y	N	N	Y	Y
6 ***Hyde***	Y	Y	Y	N	N	Y	Y	Y
7 Collins	?	?	?	Y	N	N	Y	Y
8 Rostenkowski	N	N	Y	Y	N	N	Y	Y
9 Yates	N	N	Y	Y	N	N	N	Y
10 ***Porter***	Y	Y	Y	N	Y	Y	Y	Y
11 Annunzio	Y	N	Y	Y	N	N	Y	Y
12 ***Crane***	Y	Y	Y	N	Y	Y	N	Y
13 ***Fawell***	Y	N	Y	N	Y	N	Y	Y
14 ***Grotberg***	Y	Y	Y	N	Y	Y	Y	Y
15 ***Madigan***	Y	Y	Y	N	Y	Y	N	Y
16 ***Martin***	Y	Y	Y	N	Y	Y	N	Y
17 Evans	N	?	Y	?	?	?	?	?
18 ***Michel***	Y	Y	Y	Y	Y	N	Y	Y
19 Bruce	Y	N	Y	Y	Y	N	Y	Y
20 Durbin	Y	N	Y	N	N	N	Y	Y
21 Price	Y	N	Y	Y	N	N	Y	Y
22 Gray	Y	Y	Y	Y	Y	N	Y	Y
INDIANA								
1 Visclosky	N	Y	Y	Y	N	N	Y	Y
2 Sharp	Y	Y	Y	Y	N	Y	Y	Y
3 ***Hiler***	Y	Y	Y	N	Y	Y	Y	Y
4 ***Coats***	Y	Y	Y	N	Y	Y	Y	Y
5 ***Hillis***	Y	Y	Y	N	Y	Y	Y	Y

ND - Northern Democrats SD - Southern Democrats

* Corresponding to Congressional Record Votes 105, 106, 107, 108, 110, 111, 112, 113

	96	97	98	99	100	101	102	103
6 ***Burton***	Y	Y	Y	N	Y	Y	Y	Y
7 ***Myers***	Y	Y	Y	Y	Y	Y	Y	Y
8 McCloskey	Y	Y	Y	Y	N	N	Y	Y
9 Hamilton	N	Y	Y	Y	N	N	Y	Y
10 Jacobs	Y	Y	Y	N	N	Y	N	Y
IOWA								
1 ***Leach***	N	Y	Y	N	Y	Y	N	Y
2 ***Tauke***	Y	N	Y	N	Y	Y	N	Y
3 ***Evans***	Y	N	Y	N	Y	N	Y	Y
4 Smith	N	Y	Y	Y	N	N	Y	Y
5 ***Lightfoot***	Y	Y	Y	N	Y	Y	N	Y
6 Bedell	N	N	Y	Y	N	N	Y	Y
KANSAS								
1 ***Roberts***	Y	Y	Y	?	?	?	?	?
2 Slattery	Y	Y	Y	Y	Y	N	Y	Y
3 ***Meyers***	Y	Y	Y	N	Y	Y	Y	Y
4 Glickman	Y	?	?	Y	Y	N	Y	Y
5 ***Whittaker***	Y	Y	Y	?	Y	Y	N	Y
KENTUCKY								
1 Hubbard	Y	Y	Y	Y	N	N	Y	Y
2 Natcher	Y	Y	Y	Y	Y	N	Y	Y
3 Mazzoli	Y	N	Y	Y	Y	N	Y	Y
4 ***Snyder***	Y	Y	Y	?	Y	N	Y	Y
5 ***Rogers***	Y	Y	Y	N	Y	Y	Y	Y
6 ***Hopkins***	Y	Y	Y	Y	Y	N	Y	Y
7 Perkins	N	N	Y	Y	Y	N	Y	Y
LOUISIANA								
1 ***Livingston***	Y	Y	Y	N	Y	N	Y	Y
2 Boggs	Y	Y	Y	Y	N	N	Y	Y
3 Tauzin	Y	Y	Y	Y	N	N	Y	Y
4 Roemer	Y	Y	Y	N	Y	N	Y	Y
5 Huckaby	Y	Y	Y	?	?	?	?	?
6 ***Moore***	Y	Y	Y	Y	Y	N	Y	Y
7 Breaux	Y	Y	Y	Y	Y	N	Y	Y
8 Long	?	?	?	Y	N	N	Y	Y
MAINE								
1 ***McKernan***	Y	Y	Y	N	Y	N	Y	Y
2 ***Snowe***	Y	N	Y	Y	Y	N	Y	Y
MARYLAND								
1 Dyson	Y	N	Y	Y	Y	N	Y	Y
2 ***Bentley***	Y	Y	Y	?	?	N	Y	Y
3 Mikulski	Y	N	Y	Y	N	N	Y	Y
4 ***Holt***	Y	N	Y	?	?	?	?	?
5 Hoyer	N	N	Y	Y	N	N	Y	Y
6 Byron	Y	Y	Y	Y	Y	N	Y	Y
7 Mitchell	N	N	?	N	N	N	Y	Y
8 Barnes	N	N	Y	Y	N	N	Y	Y
MASSACHUSETTS								
1 ***Conte***	N	N	Y	N	Y	N	Y	Y
2 Boland	N	N	Y	Y	N	N	Y	Y
3 Early	?	?	?	Y	N	N	Y	Y
4 Frank	N	N	Y	Y	N	N	Y	Y
5 Atkins	Y	N	Y	Y	N	N	Y	Y
6 Mavroules	Y	N	Y	Y	N	N	Y	Y
7 Markey	N	N	Y	Y	N	N	Y	Y
8 O'Neill								
9 Moakley	Y	N	Y	Y	N	N	Y	Y
10 Studds	N	N	Y	Y	N	N	Y	Y
11 Donnelly	Y	N	Y	Y	N	N	Y	Y
MICHIGAN								
1 Conyers	N	N	Y	Y	?	?	?	?
2 ***Pursell***	Y	Y	Y	N	Y	N	Y	Y
3 Wolpe	N	N	Y	Y	N	N	Y	Y
4 ***Siljander***	Y	Y	Y	N	Y	N	Y	Y
5 ***Henry***	Y	Y	Y	N	Y	N	Y	Y
6 Carr	Y	Y	Y	Y	Y	N	Y	Y
7 Kildee	N	N	Y	Y	N	N	Y	Y
8 Traxler	?	?	?	Y	Y	N	Y	Y
9 ***Vander Jagt***	Y	Y	Y	?	Y	N	Y	Y
10 ***Schuette***	Y	Y	Y	N	Y	N	Y	Y
11 ***Davis***	?	Y	Y	N	Y	N	Y	Y
12 Bonior	N	N	Y	Y	N	N	Y	Y
13 Crockett	N	N	Y	Y	N	N	Y	Y
14 Hertel	Y	Y	Y	Y	N	N	Y	Y
15 Ford	Y	N	Y	?	N	N	Y	Y
16 Dingell	N	Y	Y	?	N	N	Y	Y
17 Levin	N	N	Y	Y	N	N	Y	Y
18 ***Broomfield***	Y	Y	Y	Y	Y	N	Y	Y
MINNESOTA								
1 Penny	Y	N	Y	N	Y	N	Y	Y
2 ***Weber***	Y	Y	Y	N	Y	Y	N	Y
3 ***Frenzel***	Y	Y	Y	?	?	?	?	?
4 Vento	N	N	Y	Y	N	N	Y	Y
5 Sabo	N	N	Y	Y	N	N	Y	Y
6 Sikorski	Y	N	Y	N	Y	N	Y	Y

	96	97	98	99	100	101	102	103
7 ***Stangeland***	Y	Y	Y	N	Y	N	Y	Y
8 Oberstar	N	N	Y	?	N	N	Y	Y
MISSISSIPPI								
1 Whitten	Y	N	Y	?	?	N	Y	Y
2 ***Franklin***	Y	Y	Y	N	Y	N	Y	Y
3 Montgomery	Y	Y	Y	Y	Y	N	Y	Y
4 Dowdy	Y	Y	?	?	Y	N	Y	Y
5 ***Lott***	Y	Y	Y	N	Y	N	Y	Y
MISSOURI								
1 Clay	N	N	Y	N	N	N	Y	Y
2 Young	Y	Y	Y	Y	N	N	Y	Y
3 Gephardt	N	N	Y	?	N	N	Y	Y
4 Skelton	Y	Y	Y	Y	Y	N	Y	Y
5 Wheat	Y	N	Y	Y	N	N	Y	Y
6 ***Coleman***	Y	N	Y	N	Y	Y	Y	Y
7 ***Taylor***	Y	N	Y	N	Y	Y	Y	Y
8 ***Emerson***	Y	Y	Y	N	Y	N	Y	Y
9 Volkmer	Y	Y	Y	Y	Y	N	Y	Y
MONTANA								
1 Williams	Y	N	N	Y	N	N	Y	Y
2 ***Marlenee***	Y	Y	Y	N	Y	Y	Y	Y
NEBRASKA								
1 ***Bereuter***	Y	Y	Y	N	Y	Y	Y	Y
2 ***Daub***	Y	Y	Y	N	Y	N	Y	Y
3 ***Smith***	Y	Y	Y	Y	Y	Y	N	Y
NEVADA								
1 Reid	Y	N	Y	Y	N	N	Y	Y
2 ***Vucanovich***	Y	Y	Y	N	Y	N	Y	Y
NEW HAMPSHIRE								
1 ***Smith***	Y	Y	Y	N	Y	Y	N	Y
2 ***Gregg***	Y	Y	Y	N	Y	N	Y	Y
NEW JERSEY								
1 Florio	Y	N	Y	Y	N	N	Y	Y
2 Hughes	Y	Y	Y	Y	N	N	Y	Y
3 Howard	Y	N	Y	Y	N	N	Y	Y
4 ***Smith***	Y	Y	Y	N	Y	N	Y	Y
5 ***Roukema***	Y	N	Y	Y	Y	N	Y	Y
6 Dwyer	Y	N	Y	Y	N	N	Y	Y
7 ***Rinaldo***	Y	N	Y	Y	Y	N	Y	Y
8 Roe	Y	N	Y	Y	Y	N	Y	Y
9 Torricelli	Y	N	Y	Y	Y	N	Y	Y
10 Rodino	N	N	Y	Y	N	N	Y	Y
11 ***Gallo***	Y	Y	Y	N	Y	N	Y	Y
12 ***Courter***	Y	Y	Y	N	Y	Y	Y	Y
13 ***Saxton***	Y	Y	Y	N	Y	N	Y	Y
14 Guarini	N	N	Y	Y	N	N	Y	Y
NEW MEXICO								
1 ***Lujan***	Y	Y	Y	N	Y	N	Y	Y
2 ***Skeen***	?	?	?	N	Y	N	Y	Y
3 Richardson	Y	N	Y	Y	Y	N	Y	Y
NEW YORK								
1 ***Carney***	Y	Y	?	N	Y	N	Y	Y
2 Downey	N	N	Y	Y	N	N	Y	Y
3 Mrazek	Y	Y	Y	Y	Y	N	Y	Y
4 ***Lent***	Y	Y	?	N	Y	N	Y	Y
5 ***McGrath***	Y	Y	?	N	Y	N	Y	Y
6 Addabbo	?	?	?	?	?	?	?	?
7 Ackerman	Y	N	Y	Y	N	N	Y	Y
8 Scheuer	N	N	Y	Y	N	N	Y	Y
9 Manton	Y	N	Y	Y	N	N	Y	Y
10 Schumer	Y	N	Y	Y	N	N	Y	Y
11 Towns	N	N	Y	Y	N	N	Y	Y
12 Owens	N	N	Y	Y	N	N	Y	Y
13 Solarz	N	N	Y	Y	N	N	Y	Y
14 ***Molinari***	Y	N	Y	N	Y	N	Y	Y
15 ***Green***	Y	N	Y	N	N	N	Y	Y
16 Rangel	N	N	Y	Y	Y	N	Y	Y
17 Weiss	N	N	Y	Y	N	N	Y	Y
18 Garcia	N	N	Y	Y	N	N	Y	Y
19 Biaggi	Y	N	Y	?	N	N	Y	Y
20 ***DioGuardi***	Y	Y	Y	N	Y	N	Y	Y
21 ***Fish***	Y	N	Y	N	Y	N	Y	Y
22 ***Gilman***	Y	N	Y	N	Y	N	Y	Y
23 Stratton	Y	N	Y	Y	Y	N	Y	Y
24 ***Solomon***	Y	Y	Y	?	?	?	?	?
25 ***Boehlert***	Y	N	Y	N	Y	N	Y	Y
26 ***Martin***	Y	Y	Y	N	Y	N	Y	Y
27 ***Wortley***	Y	Y	Y	Y	Y	N	Y	Y
28 McHugh	N	N	Y	Y	N	N	Y	Y
29 ***Horton***	Y	N	Y	Y	Y	N	Y	Y
30 ***Eckert***	Y	Y	Y	N	Y	Y	Y	Y
31 ***Kemp***	Y	Y	Y	N	Y	N	Y	?
32 LaFalce	N	Y	Y	Y	N	N	Y	Y
33 Nowak	Y	N	Y	Y	N	Y	Y	Y
34 Lundine	N	N	Y	Y	N	N	Y	Y

	96	97	98	99	100	101	102	103
NORTH CAROLINA								
1 Jones	N	N	Y	Y	N	N	Y	?
2 Valentine	Y	Y	Y	Y	Y	N	Y	Y
3 Whitley	Y	Y	Y	Y	Y	N	Y	Y
4 ***Cobey***	Y	Y	Y	N	Y	Y	N	Y
5 Neal	?	?	?	Y	Y	N	Y	Y
6 ***Coble***	Y	Y	Y	N	Y	Y	N	Y
7 Rose	Y	N	Y	Y	N	N	Y	Y
8 Hefner	Y	Y	Y	Y	Y	N	Y	Y
9 ***McMillan***	Y	Y	Y	N	Y	N	Y	Y
10 ***Broyhill***	Y	Y	Y	Y	Y	Y	N	Y
11 ***Hendon***	Y	Y	Y	N	Y	Y	Y	Y
NORTH DAKOTA								
AL Dorgan	Y	Y	Y	Y	Y	Y	Y	Y
OHIO								
1 Luken	Y	N	Y	Y	N	N	Y	Y
2 ***Gradison***	Y	N	Y	Y	Y	Y	Y	Y
3 Hall	Y	Y	Y	Y	N	N	Y	Y
4 ***Oxley***	Y	Y	Y	N	Y	Y	N	Y
5 ***Latta***	Y	?	?	N	Y	Y	N	Y
6 ***McEwen***	Y	Y	Y	N	Y	Y	Y	Y
7 ***DeWine***	Y	Y	Y	N	Y	Y	Y	Y
8 ***Kindness***	Y	Y	Y	N	Y	N	Y	Y
9 Kaptur	Y	N	Y	Y	N	N	Y	Y
10 ***Miller***	Y	Y	Y	N	Y	Y	Y	Y
11 Eckart	Y	Y	Y	Y	Y	N	Y	Y
12 ***Kasich***	Y	Y	Y	N	Y	Y	Y	Y
13 Pease	N	Y	Y	Y	N	N	Y	Y
14 Seiberling	N	N	Y	?	?	N	Y	?
15 ***Wylie***	Y	Y	?	Y	Y	Y	Y	Y
16 ***Regula***	Y	Y	Y	Y	Y	Y	Y	Y
17 Traficant	Y	N	Y	Y	Y	N	Y	Y
18 Applegate	Y	Y	Y	?	Y	N	Y	Y
19 Feighan	Y	N	Y	Y	Y	N	Y	Y
20 Oakar	Y	N	Y	Y	Y	N	Y	Y
21 Stokes	N	N	Y	Y	N	N	Y	Y
OKLAHOMA								
1 Jones	Y	Y	Y	Y	N	N	Y	Y
2 Synar	Y	N	Y	Y	N	N	Y	Y
3 Watkins	Y	Y	Y	Y	N	N	Y	Y
4 McCurdy	Y	Y	Y	Y	N	N	Y	Y
5 ***Edwards***	Y	Y	Y	?	?	?	N	Y
6 English	Y	Y	Y	?	?	?	?	?
OREGON								
1 AuCoin	Y	Y	Y	?	N	N	Y	Y
2 ***Smith, R.***	Y	Y	Y	N	Y	N	Y	Y
3 Wyden	Y	Y	Y	Y	Y	N	Y	Y
4 Weaver	?	?	?	Y	?	N	Y	Y
5 ***Smith, D.***	Y	Y	Y	N	Y	Y	N	Y
PENNSYLVANIA								
1 Foglietta	Y	N	Y	Y	N	N	Y	Y
2 Gray	N	N	Y	Y	N	N	Y	Y
3 Borski	Y	N	Y	Y	N	N	Y	Y
4 Kolter	Y	N	Y	Y	Y	N	Y	Y
5 ***Schulze***	Y	Y	Y	N	Y	N	Y	Y
6 Yatron	Y	N	Y	Y	Y	N	Y	Y
7 Edgar	N	N	Y	Y	N	N	Y	Y
8 Kostmayer	N	N	Y	Y	N	N	Y	Y
9 ***Shuster***	Y	Y	Y	N	Y	Y	N	Y
10 ***McDade***	Y	N	Y	N	Y	N	Y	Y
11 Kanjorski	Y	Y	Y	Y	Y	N	Y	Y
12 Murtha	N	Y	Y	Y	N	N	Y	Y
13 ***Coughlin***	Y	Y	Y	N	Y	N	Y	Y
14 Coyne	N	N	Y	Y	N	N	Y	Y
15 ***Ritter***	Y	Y	Y	N	Y	Y	Y	Y
16 ***Walker***	Y	Y	Y	N	Y	Y	N	Y
17 ***Gekas***	Y	Y	Y	N	Y	Y	N	Y
18 Walgren	Y	N	Y	Y	N	N	Y	Y
19 ***Goodling***	Y	Y	Y	N	Y	Y	Y	Y
20 Gaydos	Y	Y	Y	Y	Y	N	Y	Y
21 ***Ridge***	Y	N	Y	N	Y	N	Y	Y
22 Murphy	Y	Y	Y	N	Y	N	Y	Y
23 ***Clinger***	Y	N	Y	N	Y	N	Y	Y
RHODE ISLAND								
1 St Germain	Y	N	?	Y	N	N	?	Y
2 ***Schneider***	Y	?	?	N	Y	N	Y	Y
SOUTH CAROLINA								
1 ***Hartnett***	Y	Y	Y	N	Y	N	Y	Y
2 ***Spence***	Y	Y	Y	Y	Y	Y	Y	Y
3 Derrick	Y	Y	Y	N	N	N	Y	Y
4 ***Campbell***	Y	Y	Y	N	Y	N	Y	Y
5 Spratt	Y	N	Y	Y	N	N	Y	Y
6 Tallon	Y	Y	Y	?	N	N	Y	Y
SOUTH DAKOTA								
AL Daschle	Y	Y	Y	Y	Y	N	Y	Y

	96	97	98	99	100	101	102	103
TENNESSEE								
1 ***Quillen***	?	?	?	N	Y	N	Y	Y
2 ***Duncan***	Y	Y	Y	Y	Y	N	Y	Y
3 Lloyd	Y	Y	Y	Y	Y	N	Y	Y
4 Cooper	Y	N	Y	Y	N	N	Y	Y
5 Boner	Y	Y	Y	Y	Y	N	Y	Y
6 Gordon	Y	N	Y	Y	Y	N	Y	Y
7 ***Sundquist***	Y	Y	Y	N	Y	N	Y	Y
8 Jones	?	?	?	Y	Y	N	Y	Y
9 Ford	N	N	Y	Y	N	N	Y	Y
TEXAS								
1 Hall, S.	Y	Y	Y	?	Y	N	Y	Y
2 Wilson	?	?	?	Y	N	N	Y	Y
3 ***Bartlett***	Y	N	Y	N	Y	Y	N	Y
4 Hall, R.	Y	Y	Y	Y	Y	N	Y	Y
5 Bryant	Y	N	Y	Y	N	N	Y	Y
6 ***Barton***	?	?	?	N	Y	Y	N	?
7 ***Archer***	Y	Y	Y	Y	Y	Y	N	Y
8 ***Fields***	Y	Y	Y	N	Y	N	Y	Y
9 Brooks	Y	N	Y	Y	N	N	Y	Y
10 Pickle	N	N	Y	Y	N	N	Y	Y
11 Leath	Y	Y	Y	Y	Y	N	Y	Y
12 Wright	Y	N	Y	Y	?	N	Y	Y
13 ***Boulter***	Y	Y	Y	N	Y	Y	Y	Y
14 ***Sweeney***	Y	Y	Y	N	Y	N	Y	Y
15 de la Garza	Y	N	Y	Y	N	N	Y	Y
16 Coleman	Y	Y	Y	Y	N	N	Y	Y
17 Stenholm	Y	Y	Y	N	Y	Y	Y	Y
18 Leland	?	?	?	Y	N	N	Y	Y
19 ***Combest***	Y	Y	Y	N	Y	Y	N	Y
20 Gonzalez	N	N	P	Y	N	N	Y	Y
21 ***Loeffler***	Y	N	Y	N	Y	N	Y	Y
22 ***DeLay***	Y	Y	Y	N	Y	Y	Y	Y
23 Bustamante	Y	N	Y	Y	N	N	Y	Y
24 Frost	Y	N	Y	Y	N	N	Y	Y
25 Andrews	Y	Y	Y	Y	Y	N	Y	Y
26 ***Armey***	Y	Y	Y	N	Y	Y	N	Y
27 Ortiz	Y	N	Y	Y	N	N	Y	Y
UTAH								
1 ***Hansen***	Y	Y	Y	N	Y	Y	N	Y
2 ***Monson***	Y	Y	Y	N	Y	Y	N	Y
3 ***Nielson***	Y	Y	Y	N	Y	Y	N	Y
VERMONT								
AL ***Jeffords***	Y	N	Y	N	N	N	Y	Y
VIRGINIA								
1 ***Bateman***	P	Y	Y	Y	Y	N	Y	Y
2 ***Whitehurst***	Y	Y	Y	N	Y	N	Y	Y
3 ***Bliley***	Y	Y	Y	N	Y	Y	Y	Y
4 Sisisky	Y	Y	Y	Y	Y	N	Y	Y
5 Daniel	Y	Y	Y	Y	Y	N	Y	Y
6 Olin	Y	Y	Y	Y	N	N	Y	Y
7 ***Slaughter***	Y	Y	Y	N	Y	Y	Y	Y
8 ***Parris***	Y	Y	Y	N	Y	N	Y	Y
9 Boucher	Y	N	Y	Y	N	N	Y	Y
10 ***Wolf***	Y	Y	Y	N	Y	N	Y	Y
WASHINGTON								
1 ***Miller***	Y	N	Y	N	N	N	Y	Y
2 Swift	N	N	Y	Y	N	N	Y	Y
3 Bonker	N	N	Y	Y	N	N	?	?
4 ***Morrison***	Y	N	Y	N	Y	N	Y	Y
5 Foley	N	N	Y	Y	N	N	Y	Y
6 Dicks	N	N	Y	Y	N	N	Y	Y
7 Lowry	N	N	Y	Y	N	N	Y	Y
8 ***Chandler***	Y	Y	Y	N	N	N	Y	Y
WEST VIRGINIA								
1 Mollohan	Y	Y	Y	Y	Y	N	Y	Y
2 Staggers	Y	N	Y	Y	Y	N	Y	Y
3 Wise	Y	N	Y	Y	N	N	Y	Y
4 Rahall	N	N	Y	+	+	-	+	+
WISCONSIN								
1 Aspin	N	N	Y	Y	N	N	Y	Y
2 Kastenmeier	N	N	Y	Y	N	Y	N	Y
3 ***Gunderson***	Y	N	Y	N	N	Y	Y	Y
4 Kleczka	N	N	Y	Y	N	N	Y	Y
5 Moody	N	N	Y	Y	N	N	Y	Y
6 ***Petri***	Y	N	Y	Y	Y	Y	N	Y
7 Obey	N	N	Y	Y	N	N	Y	Y
8 ***Roth***	Y	Y	Y	N	Y	Y	N	Y
9 ***Sensenbrenner***	Y	Y	Y	N	Y	Y	N	Y
WYOMING								
AL ***Cheney***	Y	Y	Y	N	Y	Y	N	Y

Southern states - Ala., Ark., Fla., Ga., Ky., La., Miss., N.C., Okla., S.C., Tenn., Texas, Va.

* The *Congressional Record* vote number is different from the CQ vote number because the *Record* includes quorum calls in its tally. CQ does not publish quorum call votes.

104. HR 1555. Foreign Assistance Authorization, Fiscal 1986. Adoption of the rule (H Res 140) to provide for House floor consideration of the bill to authorize $12.8 billion for development and security assistance programs for fiscal year 1986. Adopted 400-2: R 166-2; D 234-0 (ND 156-0, SD 78-0), May 14, 1985.

105. Procedural Motion. Lott, R-Miss., motion to approve the House *Journal* of Tuesday, May 14. Motion agreed to 213-158: R 16-150; D 197-8 (ND 135-4, SD 62-4), May 15, 1985.

106. Procedural Motion. Denny Smith, R-Ore., motion to adjourn. Motion rejected 65-331: R 64-110; D 1-221 (ND 1-151, SD 0-70), May 15, 1985. (The motion was made by Republicans to protest the process by which the fiscal 1986 Democratic budget proposal was being handled in the Budget Committee.)

107. HR 1872. Department of Defense Authorization, Fiscal 1986. Adoption of the rule (H Res 169) to provide for House floor consideration of the bill to authorize $223.8 billion for research and development, weapons procurement, test and evaluation, and operation and maintenance in the Department of Defense for fiscal year 1986. Adopted 366-25: R 146-25; D 220-0 (ND 151-0, SD 69-0), May 15, 1985.

KEY

Y Voted for (yea).
Paired for.
+ Announced for.
N Voted against (nay).
X Paired against.
- Announced against.
P Voted "present".
C Voted "present" to avoid possible conflict of interest.
? Did not vote or otherwise make a position known.

Democrats ***Republicans***

	104	105	106	107
ALABAMA				
1 ***Callahan***	Y	Y	N	Y
2 ***Dickinson***	Y	N	Y	Y
3 Nichols	Y	Y	N	Y
4 Bevill	Y	Y	N	Y
5 Flippo	Y	Y	N	Y
6 Erdreich	Y	Y	N	Y
7 Shelby	Y	Y	N	Y
ALASKA				
AL ***Young***	?	N	Y	Y
ARIZONA				
1 ***McCain***	Y	N	Y	Y
2 Udall	?	Y	N	Y
3 ***Stump***	N	N	N	Y
4 ***Rudd***	Y	N	N	Y
5 ***Kolbe***	Y	N	N	Y
ARKANSAS				
1 Alexander	Y	?	?	?
2 Robinson	Y	Y	N	Y
3 ***Hammerschmidt***	Y	Y	N	Y
4 Anthony	Y	Y	N	Y
CALIFORNIA				
1 Bosco	Y	Y	N	Y
2 ***Chappie***	Y	N	Y	Y
3 Matsui	Y	Y	N	Y
4 Fazio	Y	Y	N	Y
5 Burton	Y	Y	N	Y
6 Boxer	Y	Y	N	Y
7 Miller	Y	Y	N	Y
8 Dellums	Y	Y	N	Y
9 Stark	?	Y	N	Y
10 Edwards	Y	Y	N	Y
11 Lantos	Y	Y	N	Y
12 ***Zschau***	Y	N	N	N
13 Mineta	Y	Y	?	?
14 ***Shumway***	Y	N	Y	Y
15 Coelho	Y	?	N	Y
16 Panetta	Y	Y	N	Y
17 ***Pashayan***	Y	N	Y	Y
18 Lehman	Y	Y	N	Y
19 ***Lagomarsino***	Y	N	Y	Y
20 ***Thomas***	Y	N	Y	Y
21 ***Fiedler***	Y	N	N	Y
22 ***Moorhead***	Y	N	N	Y
23 Beilenson	Y	?	?	?
24 Waxman	Y	Y	N	Y
25 Roybal	Y	Y	N	Y
26 Berman	Y	Y	N	Y
27 Levine	Y	Y	N	Y
28 Dixon	Y	?	N	Y
29 Hawkins	Y	Y	?	?
30 Martinez	Y	?	N	Y
31 Dymally	Y	P	N	Y
32 Anderson	Y	Y	N	Y
33 ***Dreier***	Y	N	Y	N
34 Torres	Y	Y	N	Y
35 ***Lewis***	Y	N	Y	?
36 Brown	Y	Y	N	Y
37 ***McCandless***	Y	N	Y	N
38 ***Dornan***	Y	N	Y	N
39 ***Dannemeyer***	Y	N	N	Y
40 ***Badham***	Y	N	Y	Y
41 ***Lowery***	Y	N	Y	Y
42 ***Lungren***	Y	N	Y	Y
43 ***Packard***	Y	N	N	Y
44 Bates	Y	Y	N	Y
45 ***Hunter***	Y	N	Y	N
COLORADO				
1 Schroeder	Y	N	N	Y
2 Wirth	Y	?	?	?
3 ***Strang***	Y	N	N	Y
4 ***Brown***	Y	N	N	N
5 ***Kramer***	Y	N	N	Y
6 ***Schaefer***	Y	N	N	Y
CONNECTICUT				
1 Kennelly	Y	Y	N	Y
2 Gejdenson	Y	Y	N	Y
3 Morrison	Y	Y	N	Y
4 ***McKinney***	Y	Y	N	Y
5 ***Rowland***	Y	N	N	Y
6 ***Johnson***	Y	Y	N	Y
DELAWARE				
AL Carper	Y	Y	N	Y
FLORIDA				
1 Hutto	Y	?	?	?
2 Fuqua	Y	?	?	?
3 Bennett	Y	Y	N	Y
4 Chappell	Y	?	?	?
5 ***McCollum***	Y	N	N	Y
6 MacKay	Y	Y	N	Y
7 Gibbons	Y	?	N	?
8 ***Young***	Y	N	Y	Y
9 ***Bilirakis***	Y	N	N	Y
10 ***Ireland***	Y	N	N	Y
11 Nelson	Y	#	-	+
12 ***Lewis***	Y	N	N	+
13 ***Mack***	Y	N	N	N
14 Mica	Y	Y	N	Y
15 ***Shaw***	Y	X	?	?
16 Smith	Y	?	?	?
17 Lehman	Y	Y	N	Y
18 Pepper	+	+	-	+
19 Fascell	Y	Y	N	Y
GEORGIA				
1 Thomas	Y	Y	N	Y
2 Hatcher	Y	Y	N	Y
3 Ray	Y	Y	N	Y
4 ***Swindall***	Y	N	N	N
5 Fowler	?	?	?	?
6 ***Gingrich***	Y	N	N	Y
7 Darden	Y	Y	N	Y
8 Rowland	Y	Y	N	Y
9 Jenkins	Y	Y	N	Y
10 Barnard	Y	Y	?	Y
HAWAII				
1 Heftel	Y	Y	N	Y
2 Akaka	Y	?	?	?
IDAHO				
1 ***Craig***	?	N	Y	Y
2 Stallings	Y	Y	N	Y
ILLINOIS				
1 Hayes	Y	Y	N	Y
2 Savage	?	Y	N	Y
3 Russo	Y	Y	N	Y
4 ***O'Brien***	?	?	?	?
5 Lipinski	Y	Y	N	Y
6 ***Hyde***	Y	N	N	Y
7 Collins	Y	Y	N	Y
8 Rostenkowski	Y	Y	N	Y
9 Yates	Y	Y	N	Y
10 ***Porter***	Y	N	N	Y
11 Annunzio	Y	Y	N	Y
12 ***Crane***	Y	N	Y	N
13 ***Fawell***	Y	N	N	Y
14 ***Grotberg***	Y	N	Y	Y
15 ***Madigan***	Y	?	Y	Y
16 ***Martin***	Y	N	Y	N
17 Evans	?	?	?	?
18 ***Michel***	Y	N	Y	Y
19 Bruce	Y	Y	N	Y
20 Durbin	Y	?	?	?
21 Price	Y	Y	N	Y
22 Gray	Y	Y	N	Y
INDIANA				
1 Visclosky	Y	Y	N	Y
2 Sharp	Y	Y	N	Y
3 ***Hiler***	Y	N	Y	Y
4 ***Coats***	Y	N	N	Y
5 ***Hillis***	Y	N	N	Y

ND - Northern Democrats SD - Southern Democrats

* Corresponding to Congressional Record Votes 114, 115, 116, 117

	104	105	106	107
6 ***Burton***	Y	N	N	N
7 ***Myers***	Y	Y	Y	Y
8 McCloskey	Y	Y	N	Y
9 Hamilton	Y	Y	N	Y
10 Jacobs	Y	N	N	Y
IOWA				
1 ***Leach***	Y	N	N	Y
2 ***Tauke***	Y	N	N	Y
3 ***Evans***	Y	N	N	Y
4 Smith	Y	Y	N	Y
5 ***Lightfoot***	Y	N	N	Y
6 Bedell	Y	Y	N	Y
KANSAS				
1 ***Roberts***	?	N	N	Y
2 Slattery	Y	Y	N	Y
3 ***Meyers***	Y	Y	N	Y
4 Glickman	Y	Y	N	Y
5 ***Whittaker***	Y	N	N	Y
KENTUCKY				
1 Hubbard	Y	Y	N	Y
2 Natcher	Y	Y	N	Y
3 Mazzoli	Y	Y	N	Y
4 ***Snyder***	Y	Y	N	Y
5 ***Rogers***	Y	N	Y	Y
6 ***Hopkins***	Y	N	N	Y
7 Perkins	Y	Y	N	Y
LOUISIANA				
1 ***Livingston***	Y	N	Y	?
2 Boggs	Y	Y	N	?
3 Tauzin	Y	Y	N	Y
4 Roemer	Y	N	N	Y
5 Huckaby	?	N	N	Y
6 ***Moore***	Y	Y	N	Y
7 Breaux	Y	Y	N	Y
8 Long	Y	Y	N	Y
MAINE				
1 ***McKernan***	Y	?	N	Y
2 ***Snowe***	Y	N	N	Y
MARYLAND				
1 Dyson	Y	Y	N	Y
2 ***Bentley***	Y	N	N	Y
3 Mikulski	Y	Y	N	Y
4 ***Holt***	?	?	N	Y
5 Hoyer	Y	Y	N	Y
6 Byron	Y	Y	N	Y
7 Mitchell	Y	?	N	Y
8 Barnes	Y	Y	N	Y
MASSACHUSETTS				
1 ***Conte***	Y	?	Y	Y
2 Boland	Y	Y	N	Y
3 Early	Y	Y	N	Y
4 Frank	Y	Y	N	Y
5 Atkins	Y	Y	N	Y
6 Mavroules	?	Y	N	Y
7 Markey	Y	Y	N	Y
8 O'Neill				
9 Moakley	Y	Y	N	Y
10 Studds	Y	Y	N	Y
11 Donnelly	Y	Y	N	Y
MICHIGAN				
1 Conyers	?	?	N	?
2 ***Pursell***	Y	N	N	Y
3 Wolpe	Y	Y	N	Y
4 ***Siljander***	Y	N	Y	N
5 ***Henry***	Y	N	N	Y
6 Carr	Y	?	N	Y
7 Kildee	Y	Y	N	Y
8 Traxler	Y	Y	N	Y
9 ***Vander Jagt***	Y	?	?	?
10 ***Schuette***	Y	?	N	Y
11 ***Davis***	?	Y	N	Y
12 Bonior	?	?	?	?
13 Crockett	Y	Y	N	Y
14 Hertel	Y	Y	N	Y
15 Ford	Y	?	N	Y
16 Dingell	Y	Y	N	Y
17 Levin	Y	Y	N	Y
18 ***Broomfield***	Y	N	Y	Y
MINNESOTA				
1 Penny	Y	N	N	Y
2 ***Weber***	Y	N	N	N
3 ***Frenzel***	?	N	N	N
4 Vento	Y	Y	N	Y
5 Sabo	Y	Y	N	Y
6 Sikorski	Y	N	N	Y

	104	105	106	107
7 ***Stangeland***	Y	N	N	Y
8 Oberstar	Y	Y	N	Y
MISSISSIPPI				
1 Whitten	Y	Y	N	Y
2 ***Franklin***	Y	N	N	Y
3 Montgomery	Y	Y	N	Y
4 Dowdy	Y	Y	N	Y
5 ***Lott***	?	N	N	Y
MISSOURI				
1 Clay	Y	?	N	Y
2 Young	Y	Y	N	Y
3 Gephardt	Y	Y	N	Y
4 Skelton	Y	Y	N	Y
5 Wheat	Y	Y	N	Y
6 ***Coleman***	Y	N	Y	Y
7 ***Taylor***	Y	?	?	?
8 ***Emerson***	Y	N	Y	Y
9 Volkmer	Y	Y	N	Y
MONTANA				
1 Williams	Y	?	N	Y
2 ***Marlenee***	Y	N	Y	Y
NEBRASKA				
1 ***Bereuter***	Y	N	N	Y
2 ***Daub***	N	N	Y	N
3 ***Smith***	Y	N	Y	Y
NEVADA				
1 Reid	Y	Y	N	Y
2 ***Vucanovich***	Y	N	N	Y
NEW HAMPSHIRE				
1 ***Smith***	Y	N	N	N
2 ***Gregg***	Y	N	Y	Y
NEW JERSEY				
1 Florio	Y	Y	N	Y
2 Hughes	Y	Y	N	Y
3 Howard	Y	Y	N	Y
4 ***Smith***	Y	N	N	Y
5 ***Roukema***	Y	Y	N	Y
6 Dwyer	Y	Y	N	Y
7 ***Rinaldo***	Y	Y	Y	Y
8 Roe	Y	Y	N	Y
9 Torricelli	?	Y	N	Y
10 Rodino	Y	Y	N	Y
11 ***Gallo***	Y	N	N	Y
12 ***Courter***	Y	N	Y	Y
13 ***Saxton***	Y	N	N	N
14 Guarini	Y	Y	N	Y
NEW MEXICO				
1 ***Lujan***	Y	N	Y	Y
2 ***Skeen***	Y	N	Y	Y
3 Richardson	Y	Y	N	Y
NEW YORK				
1 ***Carney***	Y	N	N	Y
2 Downey	Y	?	?	?
3 Mrazek	?	Y	N	?
4 ***Lent***	Y	N	N	Y
5 ***McGrath***	Y	N	Y	Y
6 Addabbo	?	?	?	?
7 Ackerman	Y	Y	N	Y
8 Scheuer	Y	?	?	?
9 Manton	Y	?	?	Y
10 Schumer	Y	Y	N	Y
11 Towns	Y	Y	N	Y
12 Owens	Y	Y	N	Y
13 Solarz	Y	Y	N	Y
14 ***Molinari***	Y	N	N	Y
15 ***Green***	Y	N	Y	Y
16 Rangel	Y	?	N	Y
17 Weiss	Y	Y	N	Y
18 Garcia	Y	Y	N	Y
19 Biaggi	Y	?	N	Y
20 ***DioGuardi***	Y	N	N	Y
21 ***Fish***	Y	?	?	?
22 ***Gilman***	Y	N	N	Y
23 Stratton	Y	Y	N	Y
24 ***Solomon***	?	N	Y	Y
25 ***Boehlert***	Y	N	N	Y
26 ***Martin***	?	N	N	Y
27 ***Wortley***	Y	N	N	Y
28 McHugh	Y	Y	N	Y
29 ***Horton***	Y	N	N	Y
30 ***Eckert***	Y	?	Y	N
31 ***Kemp***	?	?	N	Y
32 LaFalce	Y	?	?	?
33 Nowak	Y	Y	N	Y
34 Lundine	Y	Y	N	Y

	104	105	106	107
NORTH CAROLINA				
1 Jones	Y	Y	N	Y
2 Valentine	Y	Y	N	Y
3 Whitley	Y	Y	N	Y
4 ***Cobey***	Y	N	Y	N
5 Neal	Y	?	N	Y
6 ***Coble***	Y	N	Y	Y
7 Rose	Y	Y	N	Y
8 Hefner	Y	Y	N	Y
9 ***McMillan***	Y	N	N	N
10 ***Broyhill***	Y	Y	N	Y
11 ***Hendon***	Y	N	N	Y
NORTH DAKOTA				
AL Dorgan	Y	Y	N	Y
OHIO				
1 Luken	Y	Y	N	Y
2 ***Gradison***	Y	N	Y	Y
3 Hall	Y	Y	N	Y
4 ***Oxley***	?	N	N	Y
5 ***Latta***	Y	N	Y	N
6 ***McEwen***	Y	N	N	Y
7 ***DeWine***	Y	N	Y	Y
8 ***Kindness***	Y	N	N	Y
9 Kaptur	Y	Y	N	Y
10 ***Miller***	Y	N	N	Y
11 Eckart	Y	Y	N	Y
12 ***Kasich***	Y	N	N	Y
13 Pease	Y	Y	N	Y
14 Seiberling	Y	Y	N	Y
15 ***Wylie***	Y	Y	N	Y
16 ***Regula***	Y	?	?	?
17 Traficant	Y	Y	N	Y
18 Applegate	Y	?	?	Y
19 Feighan	Y	Y	N	Y
20 Oakar	Y	?	?	?
21 Stokes	Y	?	?	?
OKLAHOMA				
1 Jones	Y	Y	N	Y
2 Synar	Y	?	?	+
3 Watkins	Y	Y	N	Y
4 McCurdy	Y	?	?	?
5 ***Edwards***	Y	N	N	Y
6 English	?	Y	N	Y
OREGON				
1 AuCoin	Y	?	N	?
2 ***Smith, R.***	Y	N	N	Y
3 Wyden	Y	Y	N	Y
4 Weaver	?	Y	N	Y
5 ***Smith, D.***	Y	N	N	Y
PENNSYLVANIA				
1 Foglietta	Y	Y	N	Y
2 Gray	Y	Y	N	Y
3 Borski	Y	Y	N	Y
4 Kolter	Y	Y	N	Y
5 ***Schulze***	Y	N	N	Y
6 Yatron	Y	Y	N	Y
7 Edgar	Y	Y	N	Y
8 Kostmayer	Y	Y	N	Y
9 ***Shuster***	Y	N	Y	Y
10 ***McDade***	Y	N	N	Y
11 Kanjorski	Y	Y	N	Y
12 Murtha	Y	Y	N	Y
13 ***Coughlin***	Y	N	Y	Y
14 Coyne	Y	Y	N	Y
15 ***Ritter***	Y	N	N	Y
16 ***Walker***	Y	N	Y	N
17 ***Gekas***	Y	N	N	N
18 Walgren	Y	Y	N	Y
19 ***Goodling***	Y	Y	Y	Y
20 Gaydos	Y	Y	N	Y
21 ***Ridge***	Y	N	N	Y
22 Murphy	Y	Y	Y	Y
23 ***Clinger***	Y	N	N	Y
RHODE ISLAND				
1 St Germain	Y	?	N	Y
2 ***Schneider***	Y	N	Y	Y
SOUTH CAROLINA				
1 ***Hartnett***	Y	N	N	Y
2 ***Spence***	Y	N	N	Y
3 Derrick	Y	N	N	Y
4 ***Campbell***	Y	N	Y	Y
5 Spratt	Y	Y	N	Y
6 Tallon	Y	Y	N	Y
SOUTH DAKOTA				
AL Daschle	Y	Y	N	Y

	104	105	106	107
TENNESSEE				
1 ***Quillen***	Y	N	Y	Y
2 ***Duncan***	Y	N	?	?
3 Lloyd	Y	Y	N	Y
4 Cooper	Y	Y	N	Y
5 Boner	Y	Y	N	Y
6 Gordon	Y	Y	N	Y
7 ***Sundquist***	Y	N	N	Y
8 Jones	Y	Y	N	Y
9 Ford	Y	Y	N	Y
TEXAS				
1 Hall, S.	Y	Y	N	Y
2 Wilson	Y	?	N	Y
3 ***Bartlett***	Y	N	N	Y
4 Hall, R.	Y	Y	N	Y
5 Bryant	Y	?	N	Y
6 ***Barton***	?	?	?	?
7 ***Archer***	Y	Y	Y	Y
8 ***Fields***	Y	?	Y	N
9 Brooks	Y	Y	N	Y
10 Pickle	Y	?	?	?
11 Leath	Y	Y	N	Y
12 Wright	Y	Y	N	Y
13 ***Boulter***	Y	N	N	Y
14 ***Sweeney***	Y	N	Y	Y
15 de la Garza	Y	Y	N	Y
16 Coleman	Y	Y	N	Y
17 Stenholm	Y	N	N	Y
18 Leland	Y	?	N	Y
19 ***Combest***	Y	N	N	Y
20 Gonzalez	Y	Y	N	Y
21 ***Loeffler***	Y	N	Y	Y
22 ***DeLay***	Y	N	N	Y
23 Bustamante	Y	Y	N	Y
24 Frost	Y	Y	N	Y
25 Andrews	Y	Y	N	Y
26 ***Armey***	Y	N	N	Y
27 Ortiz	Y	Y	N	Y
UTAH				
1 ***Hansen***	Y	N	N	Y
2 ***Monson***	Y	N	N	Y
3 ***Nielson***	Y	N	N	N
VERMONT				
AL ***Jeffords***	Y	N	Y	Y
VIRGINIA				
1 ***Bateman***	Y	Y	N	Y
2 ***Whitehurst***	?	N	Y	Y
3 ***Bliley***	Y	N	N	Y
4 Sisisky	Y	Y	N	Y
5 Daniel	Y	Y	N	Y
6 Olin	Y	Y	N	Y
7 ***Slaughter***	Y	N	N	Y
8 ***Parris***	Y	N	N	Y
9 Boucher	Y	Y	N	Y
10 ***Wolf***	Y	N	N	Y
WASHINGTON				
1 ***Miller***	Y	N	N	Y
2 Swift	Y	Y	N	Y
3 Bonker	?	?	?	?
4 ***Morrison***	Y	?	N	Y
5 Foley	Y	Y	N	Y
6 Dicks	Y	Y	?	Y
7 Lowry	Y	Y	N	Y
8 ***Chandler***	Y	N	N	Y
WEST VIRGINIA				
1 Mollohan	Y	Y	N	Y
2 Staggers	?	Y	N	Y
3 Wise	Y	Y	N	Y
4 Rahall	+	?	N	?
WISCONSIN				
1 Aspin	Y	?	N	Y
2 Kastenmeier	Y	Y	N	Y
3 ***Gunderson***	Y	N	N	Y
4 Kleczka	Y	Y	N	Y
5 Moody	Y	Y	N	Y
6 ***Petri***	Y	N	N	Y
7 Obey	Y	Y	N	Y
8 ***Roth***	Y	N	N	Y
9 ***Sensenbrenner***	Y	N	Y	Y
WYOMING				
AL ***Cheney***	Y	N	Y	Y

Southern states - Ala., Ark., Fla., Ga., Ky., La., Miss., N.C., Okla., S.C., Tenn., Texas, Va.

* The *Congressional Record* vote number is different from the CQ vote number because the *Record* includes quorum calls in its tally. CQ does not publish quorum call votes.

108. HR 2475. Imputed Interest Rules. Rostenkowski, D-Ill., motion to suspend the rules and pass the bill to ease provisions of the Deficit Reduction Act of 1984 (PL 98-369) aimed at restricting the use of below-market, seller-financed real estate transactions to avoid tax payments. Motion agreed to 425-0: R 178-0; D 247-0 (ND 167-0, SD 80-0), May 21, 1985. A two-thirds majority of those present and voting (284 in this case) is required for passage under suspension of the rules.

109. HR 1460. Anti-Apartheid Act. Adoption of the rule (H Res 174) to provide for House floor consideration of the bill to punish the white minority government of South Africa for its racial policy of apartheid. Adopted 414-4: R 168-4; D 246-0 (ND 166-0, SD 80-0), May 21, 1985.

110. HR 1460. Anti-Apartheid Act. Zschau, R-Calif., amendment to let U.S. firms continue investing in South Africa if their South African units comply with a code of worker rights. Rejected 148-256: R 145-29; D 3-227 (ND 1-156, SD 2-71), May 21, 1985.

111. H Con Res 152. First Budget Resolution, Fiscal 1986. Derrick, D-S.C., motion to order the previous question (thus ending debate and the possibility of amendment) on the rule (H Res 177) to provide for House floor consideration of the concurrent resolution to set budget targets for the fiscal year ending Sept. 30, 1986. Motion agreed to 255-159: R 22-151; D 233-8 (ND 159-3, SD 74-5), May 22, 1985.

112. H Con Res 152. First Budget Resolution, Fiscal 1986. Adoption of the rule (H Res 177) to provide for House floor consideration of the concurrent resolution to set budget targets for the fiscal year ending Sept. 30, 1986, as follows: budget authority, $1,051.5 billion; outlays, $959.1 billion; revenues, $794.1 billion; deficit, $165 billion. The concurrent resolution also revised budget levels for fiscal 1985 and included reconciliation instructions requiring House committees, within 30 days after final approval of the resolution, to submit measures to meet budget targets to the Budget Committee. Adopted 273-141: R 44-129; D 229-12 (ND 154-7, SD 75-5), May 22, 1985.

113. H Con Res 152. First Budget Resolution, Fiscal 1986. Dannemeyer, R-Calif., substitute to set budget targets for the fiscal year ending Sept. 30, 1986, as follows: budget authority, $1,050.9 billion; outlays, $961.3 billion; revenues, $793 billion; deficit, $168.2 billion. The amendment also revised budget levels for fiscal 1985 and included reconciliation instructions requiring House committees, no later than June 30, to submit measures to meet budget targets to the Budget Committee. Rejected 39-382: R 39-135; D 0-247 (ND 0-167, SD 0-80), May 22, 1985.

114. H Con Res 152. First Budget Resolution, Fiscal 1986. Pursell, R-Mich., substitute to set budget targets for the fiscal year ending Sept. 30, 1986, as follows: budget authority, $1,060 billion; outlays, $970.8 billion; revenues, $794.2 billion; deficit, $176.6 billion. The amendment also revised budget levels for fiscal 1985. Rejected 87-335: R 82-94; D 5-241 (ND 4-163, SD 1-78), May 22, 1985.

115. H Con Res 152. First Budget Resolution, Fiscal 1986. Leland, D-Texas, substitute to set budget targets for the fiscal year ending Sept. 30, 1986, as follows: budget authority, $1,056.5 billion; outlays, $989.4 billion; revenues, $816.1 billion; deficit, $173.3 billion. The amendment also revised budget levels for fiscal 1985. Rejected 54-361: R 0-172; D 54-189 (ND 47-118, SD 7-71), May 22, 1985.

KEY

- Y Voted for (yea).
- # Paired for.
- \+ Announced for.
- N Voted against (nay).
- X Paired against.
- \- Announced against.
- P Voted "present".
- C Voted "present" to avoid possible conflict of interest.
- ? Did not vote or otherwise make a position known.

Democrats *Republicans*

	108	109	110	111	112	113	114	115
ALABAMA								
1 *Callahan*	Y	Y	Y	Y	N	N	N	N
2 *Dickinson*	Y	Y	Y	N	Y	N	N	N
3 Nichols	Y	Y	N	Y	Y	N	N	N
4 Bevill	Y	Y	N	Y	Y	N	N	N
5 Flippo	Y	Y	N	Y	Y	N	N	N
6 Erdreich	Y	Y	N	?	#	N	N	N
7 Shelby	Y	Y	N	Y	Y	N	N	N
ALASKA								
AL *Young*	Y	Y	Y	N	Y	?	Y	N
ARIZONA								
1 *McCain*	Y	?	Y	N	N	N	Y	N
2 Udall	Y	Y	?	Y	Y	N	N	N
3 *Stump*	Y	N	Y	N	N	N	N	N
4 *Rudd*	?	?	#	N	Y	Y	N	N
5 *Kolbe*	Y	Y	Y	N	N	N	Y	N
ARKANSAS								
1 Alexander	Y	Y	X	Y	Y	N	N	Y
2 Robinson	Y	Y	N	Y	Y	N	N	N
3 *Hammerschmidt*	Y	Y	Y	N	Y	N	Y	N
4 Anthony	Y	Y	N	Y	Y	?	N	N
CALIFORNIA								
1 Bosco	Y	Y	N	Y	Y	N	N	?
2 *Chappie*	Y	Y	Y	Y	Y	N	N	?
3 Matsui	Y	Y	N	Y	Y	N	N	N
4 Fazio	Y	Y	N	Y	Y	N	N	N
5 Burton	Y	Y	N	Y	Y	N	N	Y
6 Boxer	Y	Y	N	Y	Y	N	N	Y
7 Miller	Y	Y	N	Y	Y	N	N	N
8 Dellums	Y	Y	N	Y	Y	N	N	Y
9 Stark	Y	Y	N	Y	Y	N	N	Y
10 Edwards	Y	Y	N	Y	Y	N	N	Y
11 Lantos	Y	Y	N	Y	Y	N	N	N
12 *Zschau*	Y	Y	Y	N	N	N	N	N
13 Mineta	Y	Y	N	Y	Y	N	N	Y
14 *Shumway*	Y	Y	Y	N	N	Y	N	N
15 Coelho	Y	Y	N	?	Y	N	N	N
16 Panetta	Y	Y	N	Y	Y	N	N	N
17 *Pashayan*	Y	Y	Y	N	N	N	N	N
18 Lehman	Y	Y	N	Y	Y	N	N	N
19 *Lagomarsino*	Y	Y	Y	N	N	N	N	N
20 *Thomas*	Y	Y	Y	N	N	N	Y	?
21 *Fiedler*	Y	Y	Y	N	Y	N	N	N
22 *Moorhead*	Y	Y	Y	N	N	Y	Y	N
23 Beilenson	Y	Y	N	Y	Y	N	N	Y
24 Waxman	Y	Y	N	Y	Y	N	N	N
25 Roybal	Y	Y	N	Y	Y	N	N	Y
26 Berman	Y	Y	N	Y	Y	N	N	Y
27 Levine	Y	Y	N	Y	Y	N	N	N
28 Dixon	Y	Y	N	Y	Y	N	N	Y
29 Hawkins	Y	Y	N	Y	Y	N	N	Y
30 Martinez	Y	Y	N	Y	Y	N	N	N
31 Dymally	Y	Y	N	Y	Y	N	N	Y
32 Anderson	Y	Y	N	Y	Y	N	N	N
33 *Dreier*	Y	Y	Y	N	N	Y	N	N
34 Torres	Y	Y	N	Y	Y	N	N	N
35 *Lewis*	?	?	#	N	N	Y	Y	N
36 Brown	Y	Y	N	Y	Y	N	N	?
37 *McCandless*	Y	Y	Y	Y	N	N	N	N
38 *Dornan*	Y	Y	Y	N	N	Y	N	N
39 *Dannemeyer*	Y	Y	Y	N	N	Y	N	?
40 *Badham*	Y	Y	Y	N	N	Y	N	N
41 *Lowery*	Y	Y	#	-	X	-	-	-
42 *Lungren*	Y	Y	Y	N	N	Y	N	N
43 *Packard*	Y	Y	Y	N	N	Y	Y	N
44 Bates	Y	Y	N	Y	Y	N	N	Y
45 *Hunter*	Y	Y	Y	N	N	N	N	N
COLORADO								
1 Schroeder	Y	Y	N	Y	Y	N	Y	Y
2 Wirth	Y	Y	N	Y	Y	N	N	N
3 *Strang*	Y	?	Y	N	N	Y	N	N
4 *Brown*	Y	Y	Y	N	N	Y	Y	N
5 *Kramer*	Y	Y	Y	N	N	Y	N	N
6 *Schaefer*	Y	Y	Y	N	N	Y	N	N
CONNECTICUT								
1 Kennelly	Y	Y	N	Y	Y	N	N	N
2 Gejdenson	Y	Y	N	Y	Y	N	N	N
3 Morrison	Y	Y	X	Y	Y	N	N	N
4 *McKinney*	Y	Y	N	N	Y	N	Y	N
5 *Rowland*	Y	Y	Y	N	N	N	Y	N
6 *Johnson*	Y	Y	Y	N	N	N	Y	N
DELAWARE								
AL Carper	Y	Y	N	Y	Y	N	Y	N
FLORIDA								
1 Hutto	Y	Y	Y	Y	Y	N	N	N
2 Fuqua	Y	Y	N	Y	Y	N	N	N
3 Bennett	Y	Y	N	Y	Y	N	N	N
4 Chappell	Y	Y	N	Y	Y	N	N	N
5 *McCollum*	Y	Y	Y	N	N	N	N	N
6 MacKay	Y	Y	N	Y	Y	N	N	N
7 Gibbons	Y	Y	N	Y	Y	N	N	N
8 *Young*	Y	Y	Y	N	Y	N	N	N
9 *Bilirakis*	Y	Y	Y	N	N	?	?	?
10 *Ireland*	Y	Y	Y	N	N	?	N	N
11 Nelson	Y	Y	N	N	N	N	N	N
12 *Lewis*	Y	Y	Y	N	N	N	N	N
13 *Mack*	Y	Y	#	N	N	N	N	N
14 Mica	Y	Y	N	Y	Y	N	N	N
15 *Shaw*	Y	Y	Y	N	N	N	N	N
16 Smith	Y	Y	N	Y	Y	N	N	N
17 Lehman	Y	Y	N	Y	Y	N	N	N
18 Pepper	Y	Y	N	Y	Y	N	N	N
19 Fascell	Y	Y	N	Y	Y	N	N	N
GEORGIA								
1 Thomas	Y	Y	N	Y	Y	N	N	N
2 Hatcher	Y	Y	N	Y	Y	N	N	N
3 Ray	Y	Y	N	Y	Y	N	N	N
4 *Swindall*	Y	Y	Y	N	N	N	N	N
5 Fowler	Y	Y	N	Y	Y	N	N	N
6 *Gingrich*	Y	Y	Y	N	N	N	Y	N
7 Darden	Y	Y	N	Y	Y	N	N	N
8 Rowland	Y	Y	N	Y	Y	N	N	N
9 Jenkins	Y	Y	?	Y	Y	N	N	N
10 Barnard	Y	Y	N	Y	Y	N	N	N
HAWAII								
1 Heftel	Y	Y	N	Y	N	N	N	N
2 Akaka	Y	Y	N	Y	Y	N	N	Y
IDAHO								
1 *Craig*	Y	Y	Y	?	?	Y	Y	N
2 Stallings	Y	Y	N	Y	Y	N	N	N
ILLINOIS								
1 Hayes	Y	Y	N	Y	Y	N	N	Y
2 Savage	Y	Y	N	Y	Y	N	N	Y
3 Russo	Y	Y	N	Y	Y	N	N	N
4 *O'Brien*	Y	Y	Y	N	X	N	N	N
5 Lipinski	Y	Y	N	Y	Y	N	N	N
6 *Hyde*	Y	?	Y	N	N	N	N	N
7 Collins	Y	Y	N	Y	Y	N	N	Y
8 Rostenkowski	Y	Y	N	?	?	N	N	?
9 Yates	Y	Y	N	N	Y	N	N	Y
10 *Porter*	Y	Y	Y	N	N	N	N	N
11 Annunzio	Y	Y	N	Y	Y	N	N	N
12 *Crane*	Y	N	Y	N	N	Y	N	N
13 *Fawell*	Y	Y	Y	N	N	N	Y	N
14 *Grotberg*	Y	Y	Y	N	N	N	N	N
15 *Madigan*	Y	Y	Y	N	N	N	Y	N
16 *Martin*	Y	Y	N	N	N	N	Y	N
17 Evans	Y	Y	N	Y	Y	N	N	N
18 *Michel*	Y	Y	?	N	N	N	Y	N
19 Bruce	Y	Y	N	Y	Y	N	N	N
20 Durbin	Y	Y	N	Y	Y	N	N	N
21 Price	Y	Y	N	Y	Y	N	N	N
22 Gray	Y	Y	N	Y	Y	N	N	N
INDIANA								
1 Visclosky	Y	Y	N	Y	Y	N	N	N
2 Sharp	Y	Y	N	Y	Y	N	N	N
3 *Hiler*	Y	Y	Y	N	N	N	Y	N
4 *Coats*	Y	Y	Y	N	N	N	Y	N
5 *Hillis*	Y	Y	Y	N	N	N	Y	?

ND - Northern Democrats SD - Southern Democrats

* Corresponding to Congressional Record Votes 119, 120, 121, 122, 123, 124, 125, 126

Member	108	109	110	111	112	113	114	115
6 ***Burton***	Y	N	Y	N	N	N	N	N
7 ***Myers***	Y	Y	#	N	N	N	N	N
8 McCloskey	Y	Y	N	Y	Y	N	N	N
9 Hamilton	Y	Y	N	Y	Y	N	N	N
10 Jacobs	Y	Y	N	N	N	N	N	N
IOWA								
1 ***Leach***	Y	Y	N	N	N	N	?	N
2 ***Tauke***	Y	Y	Y	N	N	N	Y	N
3 ***Evans***	Y	Y	Y	N	N	N	N	N
4 Smith	Y	Y	N	Y	Y	N	N	N
5 ***Lightfoot***	Y	Y	Y	N	N	N	N	N
6 Bedell	Y	Y	N	Y	Y	N	N	N
KANSAS								
1 ***Roberts***	Y	Y	Y	N	N	N	Y	N
2 Slattery	Y	Y	N	Y	Y	N	N	N
3 ***Meyers***	Y	Y	Y	Y	Y	N	Y	N
4 Glickman	Y	Y	N	Y	Y	N	N	N
5 ***Whittaker***	Y	Y	Y	N	N	N	Y	N
KENTUCKY								
1 Hubbard	Y	Y	N	Y	Y	N	N	N
2 Natcher	Y	Y	N	Y	Y	N	N	Y
3 Mazzoli	Y	Y	N	Y	Y	N	N	N
4 ***Snyder***	Y	Y	Y	N	Y	N	N	N
5 ***Rogers***	Y	Y	Y	N	N	N	N	N
6 ***Hopkins***	Y	Y	N	N	N	N	Y	N
7 Perkins	Y	Y	N	Y	Y	N	N	Y
LOUISIANA								
1 ***Livingston***	Y	Y	Y	N	Y	Y	N	N
2 Boggs	Y	Y	N	Y	Y	N	N	+
3 Tauzin	Y	Y	N	N	N	N	N	N
4 Roemer	Y	Y	N	N	N	N	N	N
5 Huckaby	Y	Y	N	Y	Y	N	N	N
6 ***Moore***	Y	Y	Y	N	Y	N	N	N
7 Breaux	Y	Y	X	Y	Y	N	N	N
8 Long	Y	Y	N	Y	Y	N	N	X
MAINE								
1 ***McKernan***	Y	Y	Y	Y	Y	N	Y	N
2 ***Snowe***	Y	Y	N	Y	Y	N	Y	N
MARYLAND								
1 Dyson	Y	Y	?	Y	Y	N	N	N
2 ***Bentley***	Y	Y	N	?	?	?	?	?
3 Mikulski	Y	Y	N	?	#	N	N	N
4 ***Holt***	?	?	Y	?	X	N	N	N
5 Hoyer	Y	Y	N	Y	Y	N	N	Y
6 Byron	Y	Y	Y	Y	Y	N	N	N
7 Mitchell	Y	Y	N	Y	Y	N	N	Y
8 Barnes	Y	Y	N	Y	Y	N	N	N
MASSACHUSETTS								
1 ***Conte***	Y	Y	N	N	Y	N	Y	N
2 Boland	Y	Y	N	Y	Y	N	N	N
3 Early	Y	Y	N	Y	Y	N	N	Y
4 Frank	Y	Y	N	Y	Y	N	N	N
5 Atkins	Y	Y	N	Y	Y	N	N	N
6 Mavroules	Y	Y	N	Y	Y	N	N	N
7 Markey	Y	Y	N	Y	Y	N	N	Y
8 O'Neill								
9 Moakley	Y	Y	N	Y	Y	N	N	N
10 Studds	Y	Y	N	Y	Y	N	N	N
11 Donnelly	Y	Y	N	Y	Y	N	N	N
MICHIGAN								
1 Conyers	Y	Y	N	Y	Y	N	?	Y
2 ***Pursell***	Y	Y	N	N	Y	N	Y	N
3 Wolpe	Y	Y	N	Y	Y	N	N	N
4 ***Siljander***	Y	Y	Y	N	N	Y	Y	N
5 ***Henry***	Y	Y	Y	N	N	N	Y	N
6 Carr	Y	Y	?	Y	N	N	N	N
7 Kildee	Y	Y	N	Y	Y	N	N	Y
8 Traxler	Y	Y	N	Y	Y	N	N	N
9 ***Vander Jagt***	Y	Y	Y	?	N	Y	Y	N
10 ***Schuette***	Y	+	Y	N	N	N	Y	N
11 ***Davis***	Y	Y	Y	N	N	N	Y	N
12 Bonior	Y	Y	N	Y	Y	N	N	Y
13 Crockett	Y	Y	N	?	?	?	?	#
14 Hertel	Y	Y	N	Y	Y	N	N	N
15 Ford	Y	Y	N	Y	Y	N	N	N
16 Dingell	Y	Y	?	Y	Y	N	N	N
17 Levin	Y	Y	N	Y	Y	N	N	N
18 ***Broomfield***	Y	Y	Y	N	N	N	Y	N
MINNESOTA								
1 Penny	Y	Y	N	N	N	N	N	N
2 ***Weber***	Y	Y	N	N	N	N	N	N
3 ***Frenzel***	Y	Y	Y	?	N	Y	Y	N
4 Vento	Y	Y	N	Y	Y	N	N	N
5 Sabo	Y	Y	N	Y	Y	N	N	N
6 Sikorski	Y	Y	N	Y	Y	N	N	N
7 ***Stangeland***	Y	Y	Y	N	N	N	Y	?
8 Oberstar	Y	Y	N	Y	Y	N	N	Y
MISSISSIPPI								
1 Whitten	Y	Y	?	Y	Y	N	N	N
2 ***Franklin***	Y	Y	Y	N	N	Y	N	N
3 Montgomery	Y	Y	Y	Y	Y	N	N	N
4 Dowdy	Y	Y	N	Y	Y	N	N	N
5 ***Lott***	Y	Y	Y	N	N	N	Y	N
MISSOURI								
1 Clay	Y	Y	N	Y	Y	N	N	Y
2 Young	Y	Y	N	Y	Y	N	N	N
3 Gephardt	Y	Y	N	Y	Y	N	N	N
4 Skelton	Y	Y	N	Y	Y	N	Y	N
5 Wheat	Y	Y	N	Y	Y	N	N	Y
6 ***Coleman***	Y	Y	Y	N	Y	N	Y	N
7 ***Taylor***	Y	Y	Y	Y	Y	N	N	N
8 ***Emerson***	Y	Y	Y	N	N	N	N	N
9 Volkmer	Y	Y	N	Y	Y	N	N	N
MONTANA								
1 Williams	Y	?	?	Y	Y	N	N	N
2 ***Marlenee***	Y	Y	Y	N	N	Y	N	N
NEBRASKA								
1 ***Bereuter***	Y	Y	Y	N	Y	N	Y	N
2 ***Daub***	Y	Y	Y	Y	Y	N	Y	N
3 ***Smith***	Y	Y	Y	N	Y	N	Y	N
NEVADA								
1 Reid	Y	Y	N	Y	Y	N	N	N
2 ***Vucanovich***	Y	Y	Y	Y	N	N	N	N
NEW HAMPSHIRE								
1 ***Smith***	Y	Y	Y	N	N	Y	N	N
2 ***Gregg***	Y	Y	N	N	N	Y	Y	N
NEW JERSEY								
1 Florio	Y	Y	N	Y	Y	N	N	N
2 Hughes	Y	Y	N	Y	N	N	N	N
3 Howard	Y	Y	N	Y	Y	N	N	N
4 ***Smith***	Y	Y	N	N	Y	N	Y	N
5 ***Roukema***	Y	Y	Y	Y	Y	N	Y	N
6 Dwyer	Y	Y	N	Y	Y	N	N	N
7 ***Rinaldo***	Y	Y	N	N	N	N	Y	N
8 Roe	Y	Y	N	Y	Y	N	N	N
9 Torricelli	Y	Y	N	Y	Y	N	N	N
10 Rodino	Y	Y	N	Y	Y	N	N	Y
11 ***Gallo***	Y	Y	Y	N	N	N	N	N
12 ***Courter***	Y	Y	N	N	N	N	N	N
13 ***Saxton***	Y	Y	N	N	N	N	N	N
14 Guarini	Y	Y	N	Y	?	N	N	N
NEW MEXICO								
1 ***Lujan***	Y	Y	Y	N	Y	Y	Y	N
2 ***Skeen***	Y	Y	Y	Y	N	N	N	N
3 Richardson	Y	Y	N	Y	Y	N	N	Y
NEW YORK								
1 ***Carney***	Y	Y	N	N	N	N	N	N
2 Downey	Y	Y	N	Y	Y	N	N	N
3 Mrazek	Y	Y	N	Y	Y	N	N	N
4 ***Lent***	Y	Y	Y	N	Y	N	Y	N
5 ***McGrath***	?	?	?	?	?	?	?	?
6 Addabbo	Y	Y	N	Y	Y	N	N	Y
7 Ackerman	Y	Y	N	Y	Y	N	N	Y
8 Scheuer	Y	Y	N	Y	Y	N	N	N
9 Manton	Y	Y	N	Y	Y	N	N	N
10 Schumer	Y	Y	N	Y	Y	N	N	N
11 Towns	Y	Y	N	Y	Y	N	N	Y
12 Owens	Y	Y	N	Y	Y	N	N	Y
13 Solarz	Y	Y	N	?	?	?	N	N
14 ***Molinari***	Y	Y	N	N	N	N	Y	N
15 ***Green***	Y	Y	Y	Y	Y	N	Y	N
16 Rangel	?	?	N	Y	Y	N	N	Y
17 Weiss	Y	Y	N	Y	Y	N	N	Y
18 Garcia	Y	Y	N	Y	Y	N	N	Y
19 Biaggi	Y	Y	N	?	#	N	N	N
20 ***DioGuardi***	Y	Y	N	N	N	N	N	N
21 ***Fish***	Y	Y	N	N	Y	N	Y	?
22 ***Gilman***	Y	Y	N	-	+	N	N	N
23 Stratton	Y	Y	N	Y	Y	N	N	N
24 ***Solomon***	Y	Y	Y	N	N	N	N	N
25 ***Boehlert***	Y	Y	N	N	N	N	Y	N
26 ***Martin***	Y	?	Y	N	N	N	Y	N
27 ***Wortley***	Y	Y	Y	N	N	N	Y	N
28 McHugh	Y	Y	N	Y	?	N	N	N
29 ***Horton***	Y	Y	N	N	Y	N	Y	N
30 ***Eckert***	Y	Y	Y	N	N	Y	Y	N
31 ***Kemp***	Y	Y	Y	N	N	Y	N	N
32 LaFalce	Y	Y	N	Y	N	?	N	N
33 Nowak	Y	Y	N	Y	Y	N	N	N
34 Lundine	Y	Y	X	Y	Y	N	N	N
NORTH CAROLINA								
1 Jones	?	?	X	?	Y	N	N	N
2 Valentine	Y	Y	N	Y	Y	N	N	N
3 Whitley	Y	Y	N	Y	Y	N	N	N
4 ***Cobey***	Y	Y	Y	N	N	N	N	N
5 Neal	Y	Y	N	Y	Y	N	N	N
6 ***Coble***	Y	?	Y	N	N	N	N	N
7 Rose	Y	Y	N	Y	Y	N	N	N
8 Hefner	Y	Y	N	Y	Y	N	N	N
9 ***McMillan***	Y	Y	Y	N	N	N	N	N
10 ***Broyhill***	Y	Y	Y	N	N	N	N	N
11 ***Hendon***	Y	Y	Y	N	?	N	N	N
NORTH DAKOTA								
AL Dorgan	Y	Y	N	Y	Y	N	N	N
OHIO								
1 Luken	Y	Y	N	Y	Y	N	N	N
2 ***Gradison***	Y	Y	Y	Y	Y	N	Y	N
3 Hall	Y	Y	?	Y	Y	N	N	N
4 ***Oxley***	Y	Y	Y	N	N	N	N	N
5 ***Latta***	Y	Y	Y	Y	Y	N	N	N
6 ***McEwen***	Y	Y	Y	N	N	N	Y	N
7 ***DeWine***	Y	Y	Y	N	N	N	N	N
8 ***Kindness***	Y	N	Y	N	N	Y	Y	N
9 Kaptur	Y	Y	N	Y	Y	N	N	N
10 ***Miller***	Y	Y	Y	N	N	N	Y	N
11 Eckart	Y	Y	N	Y	Y	N	N	N
12 ***Kasich***	Y	Y	Y	Y	Y	N	Y	N
13 Pease	Y	Y	N	Y	Y	N	N	N
14 Seiberling	Y	Y	N	Y	Y	N	N	Y
15 ***Wylie***	Y	Y	N	N	Y	N	Y	N
16 ***Regula***	Y	Y	Y	N	Y	N	Y	N
17 Traficant	Y	Y	N	Y	Y	N	N	N
18 Applegate	Y	Y	N	Y	Y	N	N	N
19 Feighan	Y	Y	N	Y	Y	N	N	N
20 Oakar	Y	Y	N	Y	Y	N	N	Y
21 Stokes	Y	Y	N	Y	Y	N	N	Y
OKLAHOMA								
1 Jones	Y	Y	N	Y	Y	N	N	N
2 Synar	Y	Y	N	N	N	N	N	N
3 Watkins	Y	Y	N	Y	Y	N	N	N
4 McCurdy	Y	Y	N	Y	Y	N	N	N
5 ***Edwards***	Y	Y	N	N	N	N	Y	N
6 English	Y	Y	N	Y	Y	N	N	N
OREGON								
1 AuCoin	Y	Y	N	Y	N	N	-	N
2 ***Smith, R.***	Y	Y	Y	N	N	N	N	N
3 Wyden	Y	Y	N	Y	Y	N	N	N
4 Weaver	Y	Y	N	Y	Y	N	N	Y
5 ***Smith, D.***	Y	Y	Y	N	N	N	N	N
PENNSYLVANIA								
1 Foglietta	Y	Y	N	Y	Y	N	N	N
2 Gray	Y	Y	N	Y	Y	N	N	P
3 Borski	Y	Y	N	Y	Y	N	N	N
4 Kolter	Y	Y	N	Y	Y	N	N	N
5 ***Schulze***	Y	Y	N	N	N	Y	N	N
6 Yatron	?	?	?	?	?	N	N	N
7 Edgar	Y	Y	N	Y	Y	N	N	N
8 Kostmayer	Y	Y	N	Y	Y	N	N	N
9 ***Shuster***	Y	Y	Y	N	Y	N	N	N
10 ***McDade***	Y	Y	N	Y	Y	N	N	N
11 Kanjorski	Y	Y	N	Y	Y	N	N	N
12 Murtha	Y	Y	?	Y	Y	N	N	N
13 ***Coughlin***	Y	Y	N	?	?	N	Y	N
14 Coyne	Y	Y	N	Y	Y	N	N	Y
15 ***Ritter***	Y	Y	?	N	N	N	Y	N
16 ***Walker***	Y	Y	Y	N	N	Y	Y	N
17 ***Gekas***	Y	Y	Y	N	N	N	N	N
18 Walgren	Y	Y	?	Y	Y	N	N	N
19 ***Goodling***	Y	Y	Y	N	N	Y	Y	N
20 Gaydos	Y	Y	N	Y	Y	N	N	N
21 ***Ridge***	Y	Y	Y	N	N	N	Y	N
22 Murphy	Y	Y	N	Y	Y	N	N	N
23 ***Clinger***	Y	Y	Y	N	Y	N	N	N
RHODE ISLAND								
1 St Germain	Y	Y	N	Y	Y	N	N	N
2 ***Schneider***	Y	Y	N	N	Y	N	Y	N
SOUTH CAROLINA								
1 ***Hartnett***	Y	Y	Y	N	N	Y	Y	N
2 ***Spence***	Y	Y	Y	N	N	N	Y	N
3 Derrick	Y	Y	?	Y	Y	N	N	N
4 ***Campbell***	Y	Y	Y	N	N	N	N	N
5 Spratt	Y	Y	N	Y	Y	N	N	N
6 Tallon	Y	Y	N	Y	Y	N	N	N
SOUTH DAKOTA								
AL Daschle	Y	Y	N	Y	Y	N	N	N
TENNESSEE								
1 ***Quillen***	Y	Y	Y	Y	Y	N	N	N
2 ***Duncan***	Y	Y	Y	Y	Y	N	N	N
3 Lloyd	Y	Y	N	Y	Y	N	N	N
4 Cooper	Y	Y	N	Y	Y	N	Y	N
5 Boner	Y	Y	N	Y	Y	N	N	N
6 Gordon	Y	Y	N	Y	Y	N	?	N
7 ***Sundquist***	Y	Y	Y	Y	Y	N	N	N
8 Jones	Y	Y	N	Y	Y	N	N	N
9 Ford	Y	Y	N	Y	Y	N	?	Y
TEXAS								
1 Hall, S.	?	?	?	?	?	?	?	?
2 Wilson	Y	Y	N	Y	Y	N	N	N
3 ***Bartlett***	Y	Y	Y	N	N	Y	Y	N
4 Hall, R.	Y	Y	N	N	N	N	N	N
5 Bryant	Y	Y	N	Y	Y	N	N	N
6 ***Barton***	Y	Y	Y	N	N	Y	N	N
7 ***Archer***	Y	Y	Y	N	N	N	N	N
8 ***Fields***	Y	Y	Y	N	N	N	N	N
9 Brooks	Y	Y	N	Y	Y	N	N	?
10 Pickle	Y	Y	N	Y	Y	N	N	N
11 Leath	Y	Y	N	Y	Y	N	N	N
12 Wright	Y	Y	?	Y	Y	N	N	N
13 ***Boulter***	Y	Y	Y	N	N	N	N	N
14 ***Sweeney***	Y	Y	Y	N	N	?	N	N
15 de la Garza	Y	Y	N	Y	Y	N	N	N
16 Coleman	Y	Y	N	Y	Y	N	N	N
17 Stenholm	Y	Y	N	Y	Y	N	N	N
18 Leland	Y	Y	N	Y	Y	N	N	Y
19 ***Combest***	Y	Y	Y	N	N	N	N	N
20 Gonzalez	Y	Y	N	Y	Y	N	N	Y
21 ***Loeffler***	Y	Y	Y	N	N	N	N	N
22 ***DeLay***	Y	Y	Y	N	N	Y	N	N
23 Bustamante	Y	Y	N	Y	Y	N	N	N
24 Frost	Y	Y	N	Y	Y	N	N	Y
25 Andrews	Y	Y	N	Y	Y	N	N	N
26 ***Armey***	Y	Y	Y	N	N	Y	N	N
27 Ortiz	Y	Y	N	Y	Y	N	N	N
UTAH								
1 ***Hansen***	Y	Y	Y	N	N	Y	N	N
2 ***Monson***	Y	Y	Y	N	N	N	N	N
3 ***Nielson***	Y	Y	Y	N	N	Y	Y	N
VERMONT								
AL ***Jeffords***	Y	Y	N	N	N	N	Y	N
VIRGINIA								
1 ***Bateman***	Y	Y	Y	N	N	N	N	N
2 ***Whitehurst***	Y	Y	Y	N	N	N	N	N
3 ***Bliley***	Y	Y	N	N	N	N	N	N
4 Sisisky	Y	Y	N	Y	Y	N	N	N
5 Daniel	Y	Y	N	Y	Y	N	N	N
6 Olin	Y	Y	N	Y	Y	N	N	N
7 ***Slaughter***	Y	Y	Y	Y	N	N	N	N
8 ***Parris***	Y	Y	Y	Y	Y	N	N	N
9 Boucher	Y	Y	?	Y	Y	N	N	N
10 ***Wolf***	Y	Y	Y	Y	Y	?	N	N
WASHINGTON								
1 ***Miller***	Y	Y	N	N	N	N	Y	N
2 Swift	Y	Y	N	Y	Y	N	N	N
3 Bonker	Y	Y	N	?	?	N	N	N
4 ***Morrison***	Y	Y	Y	N	N	N	N	N
5 Foley	Y	Y	?	Y	Y	N	N	N
6 Dicks	Y	Y	N	Y	Y	N	N	N
7 Lowry	C	Y	N	Y	Y	N	Y	Y
8 ***Chandler***	Y	Y	Y	N	N	N	Y	N
WEST VIRGINIA								
1 Mollohan	Y	Y	N	Y	Y	N	N	N
2 Staggers	Y	Y	N	Y	Y	N	N	N
3 Wise	Y	Y	N	Y	Y	N	N	N
4 Rahall	Y	Y	N	Y	Y	N	N	Y
WISCONSIN								
1 Aspin	Y	?	N	Y	Y	N	N	N
2 Kastenmeier	Y	Y	N	Y	Y	N	N	Y
3 ***Gunderson***	Y	Y	Y	N	Y	N	Y	N
4 Kleczka	Y	Y	N	Y	Y	N	N	N
5 Moody	Y	Y	?	Y	Y	N	N	Y
6 ***Petri***	Y	Y	Y	N	N	N	Y	N
7 Obey	Y	Y	N	Y	Y	N	N	N
8 ***Roth***	Y	Y	Y	N	N	N	?	N
9 ***Sensenbrenner***	Y	Y	Y	N	N	Y	Y	N
WYOMING								
AL ***Cheney***	Y	Y	Y	N	N	Y	Y	N

Southern states - Ala., Ark., Fla., Ga., Ky., La., Miss., N.C., Okla., S.C., Tenn., Texas, Va.

* The *Congressional Record* vote number is different from the CQ vote number because the *Record* includes quorum calls in its tally. CQ does not publish quorum call votes.

116. Procedural Motion. Lott, R-Miss., motion to approve the House *Journal* of Wednesday, May 22. Motion agreed to 257-147: R 31-139; D 226-8 (ND 151-5, SD 75-3), May 23, 1985.

117. H Con Res 152. First Budget Resolution, Fiscal 1986. Latta, R-Ohio, substitute to set budget targets for the fiscal year ending Sept. 30, 1986, as follows: budget authority, $1,064.9 billion; outlays, $966.1 billion; revenues, $793.5 billion; deficit, $172.6 billion. The amendment also revised budget totals for fiscal 1985 and included reconciliation instructions requiring House committees, no later than June 30, to submit measures to meet budget targets to the Budget Committee. Rejected 102-329: R 101-79; D 1-250 (ND 0-170, SD 1-80), May 23, 1985.

118. H Con Res 152. First Budget Resolution, Fiscal 1986. Leath, D-Texas, amendment to reduce the deficit by $75 billion in fiscal 1986, and by $350 billion over fiscal 1986-88, by eliminating increases in cost-of-living adjustments for recipients of Social Security and other federal retirement programs and by raising $12 billion in new taxes, in combination with spending cuts outlined in the concurrent resolution. Rejected 56-372: R 15-165; D 41-207 (ND 18-150, SD 23-57), May 23, 1985.

119. H Con Res 152. First Budget Resolution, Fiscal 1986. Oakar, D-Ohio, amendment to express the sense of the House that the Ways and Means Committee should report legislation imposing a minimum federal income tax, with new revenues to be used to reduce either tax rates or the federal budget deficit. Rejected 142-283: R 1-177; D 141-106 (ND 112-54, SD 29-52), May 23, 1985.

120. H Con Res 152. First Budget Resolution, Fiscal 1986. Adoption of the concurrent resolution to set budget targets for the fiscal year ending Sept. 30, 1986, as follows: budget authority, $1,051.5 billion; outlays, $959.1 billion; revenues, $794.1 billion; deficit, $165 billion. The concurrent resolution also revised budget levels for fiscal 1985 and included reconciliation instructions requiring House committees, within 30 days after final approval of the resolution, to submit measures to meet budget targets to the Budget Committee. Adopted 258-170: R 24-155; D 234-15 (ND 160-8, SD 74-7), May 23, 1985. A "nay" was a vote supporting the president's position.

KEY

- Y Voted for (yea).
- # Paired for.
- + Announced for.
- N Voted against (nay).
- X Paired against.
- \- Announced against.
- P Voted "present".
- C Voted "present" to avoid possible conflict of interest.
- ? Did not vote or otherwise make a position known.

Democrats *Republicans*

	116	117	118	119	120
ALABAMA					
1 ***Callahan***	N	Y	N	N	N
2 ***Dickinson***	N	Y	Y	N	N
3 Nichols	Y	N	N	N	Y
4 Bevill	Y	N	N	N	Y
5 Flippo	Y	N	N	N	Y
6 Erdreich	Y	N	N	N	Y
7 Shelby	Y	N	N	N	Y
ALASKA					
AL ***Young***	N	N	N	N	N
ARIZONA					
1 ***McCain***	Y	Y	N	N	N
2 Udall	Y	N	Y	Y	Y
3 ***Stump***	N	Y	Y	N	N
4 ***Rudd***	Y	Y	Y	N	N
5 ***Kolbe***	N	Y	N	N	N
ARKANSAS					
1 Alexander	Y	N	N	Y	Y
2 Robinson	Y	N	N	Y	Y
3 ***Hammerschmidt***	N	Y	N	N	Y
4 Anthony	Y	N	Y	N	Y
CALIFORNIA					
1 Bosco	Y	N	Y	N	Y
2 ***Chappie***	N	Y	N	N	N
3 Matsui	Y	N	N	Y	Y
4 Fazio	Y	N	Y	Y	Y
5 Burton	Y	N	N	Y	Y
6 Boxer	Y	N	N	Y	Y
7 Miller	Y	N	N	N	Y
8 Dellums	Y	N	N	Y	Y
9 Stark	Y	N	?	Y	Y
10 Edwards	Y	N	N	Y	Y
11 Lantos	Y	N	N	Y	Y
12 ***Zschau***	N	N	N	N	N
13 Mineta	Y	N	N	Y	Y
14 ***Shumway***	N	Y	N	N	N
15 Coelho	Y	N	N	Y	Y
16 Panetta	Y	N	Y	N	Y
17 ***Pashayan***	N	Y	N	N	N
18 Lehman	Y	N	N	N	Y
19 ***Lagomarsino***	N	Y	N	N	N
20 ***Thomas***	N	N	N	N	N
21 ***Fiedler***	N	Y	N	N	N
22 ***Moorhead***	N	Y	N	N	N
23 Beilenson	Y	N	N	N	Y
24 Waxman	Y	N	N	Y	Y
25 Roybal	Y	N	N	Y	Y
26 Berman	Y	N	N	Y	Y
27 Levine	Y	N	N	Y	Y
28 Dixon	?	N	N	Y	Y
29 Hawkins	?	N	N	Y	Y
30 Martinez	Y	N	N	Y	Y
31 Dymally	P	N	N	Y	Y
32 Anderson	Y	N	N	Y	Y
33 ***Dreier***	N	Y	N	N	N
34 Torres	?	N	N	Y	Y
35 ***Lewis***	N	Y	N	N	N
36 Brown	Y	N	N	Y	Y
37 ***McCandless***	N	Y	N	N	N
38 ***Dornan***	Y	Y	N	N	N
39 ***Dannemeyer***	N	N	N	N	N
40 ***Badham***	N	Y	N	N	N
41 ***Lowery***	?	Y	N	N	N
42 ***Lungren***	N	Y	N	N	N
43 ***Packard***	N	Y	N	N	N
44 Bates	Y	N	Y	N	Y
45 ***Hunter***	Y	Y	N	N	N
COLORADO					
1 Schroeder	N	N	N	Y	Y
2 Wirth	Y	N	N	Y	Y
3 ***Strang***	N	Y	N	N	N
4 ***Brown***	N	Y	Y	N	N
5 ***Kramer***	N	N	N	N	N
6 ***Schaefer***	N	N	N	N	N
CONNECTICUT					
1 Kennelly	Y	N	N	N	Y
2 Gejdenson	Y	N	N	Y	Y
3 Morrison	Y	N	N	Y	Y
4 ***McKinney***	N	N	N	N	Y
5 ***Rowland***	Y	Y	N	N	Y
6 ***Johnson***	Y	N	N	N	Y
DELAWARE					
AL Carper	Y	N	Y	N	Y
FLORIDA					
1 Hutto	Y	Y	Y	Y	Y
2 Fuqua	Y	N	N	N	Y
3 Bennett	Y	N	N	Y	Y
4 Chappell	?	N	N	N	Y
5 ***McCollum***	Y	Y	N	N	N
6 MacKay	Y	N	Y	N	Y
7 Gibbons	Y	N	Y	Y	Y
8 ***Young***	N	Y	N	N	N
9 ***Bilirakis***	?	Y	N	N	N
10 ***Ireland***	N	Y	N	N	N
11 Nelson	Y	N	Y	N	N
12 ***Lewis***	N	Y	N	N	N
13 ***Mack***	N	N	N	N	N
14 Mica	Y	N	N	N	Y
15 ***Shaw***	N	N	N	N	N
16 Smith	Y	N	N	Y	Y
17 Lehman	Y	N	N	Y	Y
18 Pepper	Y	N	N	Y	Y
19 Fascell	?	N	N	Y	Y
GEORGIA					
1 Thomas	Y	N	Y	N	Y
2 Hatcher	Y	N	N	N	Y
3 Ray	Y	N	Y	N	N
4 ***Swindall***	N	Y	N	N	N
5 Fowler	Y	N	N	N	Y
6 ***Gingrich***	N	N	N	N	N
7 Darden	Y	N	N	N	Y
8 Rowland	Y	N	Y	N	Y
9 Jenkins	Y	N	N	N	Y
10 Barnard	Y	N	Y	N	Y
HAWAII					
1 Heftel	Y	N	Y	N	Y
2 Akaka	Y	N	N	Y	Y
IDAHO					
1 ***Craig***	N	Y	N	N	N
2 Stallings	Y	N	N	N	Y
ILLINOIS					
1 Hayes	Y	N	N	Y	Y
2 Savage	Y	N	N	Y	Y
3 Russo	Y	N	N	Y	Y
4 ***O'Brien***	Y	Y	N	N	N
5 Lipinski	Y	N	N	Y	Y
6 ***Hyde***	N	Y	N	?	?
7 Collins	Y	N	N	Y	Y
8 Rostenkowski	Y	N	N	Y	Y
9 Yates	Y	N	N	Y	Y
10 ***Porter***	N	N	Y	N	N
11 Annunzio	Y	N	N	Y	Y
12 ***Crane***	?	Y	N	N	N
13 ***Fawell***	N	Y	N	N	N
14 ***Grotberg***	N	Y	N	N	N
15 ***Madigan***	N	Y	N	N	N
16 ***Martin***	N	Y	N	N	N
17 Evans	Y	N	N	Y	Y
18 ***Michel***	N	Y	N	N	N
19 Bruce	Y	N	N	N	Y
20 Durbin	Y	N	N	N	Y
21 Price	Y	N	N	Y	Y
22 Gray	?	N	N	Y	Y
INDIANA					
1 Visclosky	P	N	Y	N	Y
2 Sharp	Y	N	N	N	Y
3 ***Hiler***	N	Y	N	N	N
4 ***Coats***	N	N	N	N	N
5 ***Hillis***	N	Y	N	N	N

ND - Northern Democrats SD - Southern Democrats

	116	117	118	119	120
6 ***Burton***	N	Y	N	N	N
7 ***Myers***	Y	Y	N	N	N
8 McCloskey	Y	N	N	N	Y
9 Hamilton	Y	N	N	N	Y
10 Jacobs	N	N	N	N	Y
IOWA					
1 ***Leach***	N	N	N	N	N
2 ***Tauke***	N	N	N	N	N
3 ***Evans***	N	N	N	N	N
4 Smith	Y	N	N	N	Y
5 ***Lightfoot***	N	N	N	N	N
6 Bedell	Y	N	Y	Y	Y
KANSAS					
1 ***Roberts***	N	N	N	N	N
2 Slattery	Y	N	Y	N	Y
3 ***Meyers***	N	N	N	N	Y
4 Glickman	Y	N	N	N	Y
5 ***Whittaker***	N	N	N	N	N
KENTUCKY					
1 Hubbard	Y	N	N	Y	Y
2 Natcher	Y	N	N	N	Y
3 Mazzoli	Y	N	N	N	Y
4 ***Snyder***	Y	N	N	N	N
5 ***Rogers***	N	N	N	N	Y
6 ***Hopkins***	Y	N	N	N	N
7 Perkins	Y	N	N	Y	Y
LOUISIANA					
1 ***Livingston***	N	Y	N	N	N
2 Boggs	Y	N	N	N	Y
3 Tauzin	Y	N	N	N	Y
4 Roemer	N	N	Y	N	N
5 Huckaby	Y	N	N	N	Y
6 ***Moore***	Y	Y	N	N	Y
7 Breaux	Y	N	N	N	Y
8 Long	Y	N	N	Y	Y
MAINE					
1 ***McKernan***	N	N	N	N	N
2 ***Snowe***	N	N	N	N	N
MARYLAND					
1 Dyson	Y	N	N	N	Y
2 ***Bentley***	N	Y	N	N	N
3 Mikulski	Y	N	N	Y	Y
4 ***Holt***	Y	Y	N	N	N
5 Hoyer	Y	N	N	Y	Y
6 Byron	Y	N	N	N	Y
7 Mitchell	?	N	N	Y	Y
8 Barnes	Y	N	N	Y	Y
MASSACHUSETTS					
1 ***Conte***	N	N	N	Y	Y
2 Boland	Y	N	N	N	Y
3 Early	Y	N	N	Y	Y
4 Frank	Y	N	N	Y	Y
5 Atkins	P	N	N	Y	Y
6 Mavroules	?	N	N	Y	Y
7 Markey	Y	N	N	Y	Y
8 O'Neill					
9 Moakley	Y	N	N	Y	Y
10 Studds	Y	N	N	Y	Y
11 Donnelly	Y	N	N	Y	Y
MICHIGAN					
1 Conyers	Y	N	N	Y	N
2 ***Pursell***	Y	N	N	N	N
3 Wolpe	Y	N	N	Y	Y
4 ***Siljander***	N	N	N	N	N
5 ***Henry***	N	N	N	N	N
6 Carr	Y	N	N	N	N
7 Kildee	Y	N	N	Y	Y
8 Traxler	Y	N	N	Y	Y
9 ***Vander Jagt***	Y	Y	N	N	N
10 ***Schuette***	N	Y	N	N	N
11 ***Davis***	N	N	N	N	Y
12 Bonior	Y	N	N	N	Y
13 Crockett	Y	N	N	?	?
14 Hertel	Y	N	N	N	Y
15 Ford	?	N	N	Y	Y
16 Dingell	?	N	N	Y	Y
17 Levin	Y	N	N	Y	Y
18 ***Broomfield***	Y	N	N	N	N
MINNESOTA					
1 Penny	N	N	Y	N	N
2 ***Weber***	N	N	N	N	N
3 ***Frenzel***	N	N	Y	N	N
4 Vento	Y	N	N	Y	Y
5 Sabo	Y	N	N	Y	Y
6 Sikorski	N	N	N	N	Y
7 ***Stangeland***	N	Y	N	N	N
8 Oberstar	Y	N	N	Y	Y
MISSISSIPPI					
1 Whitten	Y	N	N	N	Y
2 ***Franklin***	N	N	N	N	N
3 Montgomery	Y	N	Y	N	Y
4 Dowdy	Y	N	N	Y	Y
5 ***Lott***	N	Y	N	N	N
MISSOURI					
1 Clay	N	N	N	Y	Y
2 Young	Y	N	N	N	Y
3 Gephardt	Y	N	Y	Y	Y
4 Skelton	Y	N	N	N	Y
5 Wheat	Y	N	N	Y	Y
6 ***Coleman***	?	N	N	N	N
7 ***Taylor***	N	Y	N	N	Y
8 ***Emerson***	N	N	N	N	Y
9 Volkmer	Y	N	N	N	Y
MONTANA					
1 Williams	Y	N	N	Y	Y
2 ***Marlenee***	Y	N	N	N	N
NEBRASKA					
1 ***Bereuter***	N	N	N	N	N
2 ***Daub***	N	N	N	N	N
3 ***Smith***	N	N	N	N	N
NEVADA					
1 Reid	Y	N	N	N	Y
2 ***Vucanovich***	N	Y	N	N	N
NEW HAMPSHIRE					
1 ***Smith***	N	Y	N	N	N
2 ***Gregg***	N	N	Y	N	N
NEW JERSEY					
1 Florio	Y	N	N	Y	Y
2 Hughes	Y	N	N	N	Y
3 Howard	Y	N	N	Y	Y
4 ***Smith***	N	N	N	N	Y
5 ***Roukema***	Y	N	N	N	N
6 Dwyer	Y	N	N	Y	Y
7 ***Rinaldo***	Y	N	N	N	Y
8 Roe	Y	N	N	Y	Y
9 Torricelli	Y	N	N	Y	Y
10 Rodino	Y	N	N	Y	Y
11 ***Gallo***	N	Y	N	N	N
12 ***Courter***	N	Y	N	N	N
13 ***Saxton***	N	Y	N	N	N
14 Guarini	Y	N	N	Y	Y
NEW MEXICO					
1 ***Lujan***	N	Y	Y	N	Y
2 ***Skeen***	N	Y	N	N	N
3 Richardson	Y	N	N	Y	Y
NEW YORK					
1 ***Carney***	N	Y	N	N	N
2 Downey	Y	N	N	Y	Y
3 Mrazek	?	N	N	N	Y
4 ***Lent***	N	N	N	N	N
5 ***McGrath***	?	N	N	N	N
6 Addabbo	Y	N	N	Y	Y
7 Ackerman	Y	N	N	Y	Y
8 Scheuer	Y	N	N	Y	Y
9 Manton	Y	N	N	Y	Y
10 Schumer	Y	N	N	Y	Y
11 Towns	Y	N	N	Y	Y
12 Owens	Y	N	N	Y	Y
13 Solarz	Y	N	N	Y	Y
14 ***Molinari***	N	Y	N	N	N
15 ***Green***	N	N	N	N	Y
16 Rangel	Y	N	N	Y	Y
17 Weiss	Y	N	N	Y	Y
18 Garcia	Y	N	N	Y	Y
19 Biaggi	Y	N	N	Y	Y
20 ***DioGuardi***	N	N	N	N	N
21 ***Fish***	N	N	-	+	-
22 ***Gilman***	N	N	N	N	N
23 Stratton	Y	N	N	N	Y
24 ***Solomon***	N	N	N	N	N
25 ***Boehlert***	N	N	N	N	N
26 ***Martin***	N	N	N	N	N
27 ***Wortley***	Y	N	N	N	N
28 McHugh	Y	N	N	Y	Y
29 ***Horton***	Y	N	N	N	Y
30 ***Eckert***	N	Y	N	N	N
31 ***Kemp***	Y	Y	N	N	N
32 LaFalce	Y	N	N	Y	Y
33 Nowak	Y	N	N	Y	Y
34 Lundine	Y	N	N	Y	Y
NORTH CAROLINA					
1 Jones	Y	N	N	Y	Y
2 Valentine	Y	N	N	N	Y
3 Whitley	Y	N	N	N	Y
4 ***Cobey***	N	Y	N	N	N
5 Neal	Y	N	N	N	Y
6 ***Coble***	N	N	N	N	N
7 Rose	Y	N	N	N	Y
8 Hefner	Y	N	N	N	Y
9 ***McMillan***	N	Y	N	N	N
10 ***Broyhill***	Y	Y	N	N	Y
11 ***Hendon***	N	N	N	N	N
NORTH DAKOTA					
AL Dorgan	Y	N	N	Y	Y
OHIO					
1 Luken	Y	N	Y	N	Y
2 ***Gradison***	?	?	?	?	?
3 Hall	Y	N	N	N	Y
4 ***Oxley***	N	Y	N	N	N
5 ***Latta***	Y	Y	N	N	N
6 ***McEwen***	N	Y	N	N	N
7 ***DeWine***	N	Y	N	N	N
8 ***Kindness***	?	Y	N	N	N
9 Kaptur	Y	N	N	?	Y
10 ***Miller***	N	Y	N	N	N
11 Eckart	Y	N	N	N	Y
12 ***Kasich***	N	Y	N	N	Y
13 Pease	Y	N	Y	Y	Y
14 Seiberling	Y	N	N	?	+
15 ***Wylie***	Y	Y	N	N	Y
16 ***Regula***	Y	N	N	N	N
17 Traficant	Y	N	N	Y	Y
18 Applegate	Y	N	N	N	N
19 Feighan	Y	N	N	N	Y
20 Oakar	Y	N	N	Y	Y
21 Stokes	Y	N	N	Y	Y
OKLAHOMA					
1 Jones	Y	N	Y	N	Y
2 Synar	Y	N	N	N	Y
3 Watkins	Y	N	N	Y	Y
4 McCurdy	Y	N	Y	N	Y
5 ***Edwards***	N	Y	N	?	N
6 English	Y	N	N	N	N
OREGON					
1 AuCoin	Y	N	N	N	Y
2 ***Smith, R.***	N	N	N	N	N
3 Wyden	Y	N	N	N	Y
4 Weaver	Y	N	N	Y	Y
5 ***Smith, D.***	N	N	N	N	N
PENNSYLVANIA					
1 Foglietta	Y	N	N	Y	Y
2 Gray	Y	N	P	P	Y
3 Borski	Y	N	N	Y	Y
4 Kolter	Y	N	N	N	N
5 ***Schulze***	N	N	Y	N	N
6 Yatron	Y	N	N	N	N
7 Edgar	Y	N	N	Y	Y
8 Kostmayer	Y	N	N	N	Y
9 ***Shuster***	N	N	N	N	N
10 ***McDade***	N	N	N	N	N
11 Kanjorski	Y	N	N	N	N
12 Murtha	Y	N	N	N	Y
13 ***Coughlin***	N	Y	N	N	Y
14 Coyne	Y	N	N	Y	Y
15 ***Ritter***	?	N	N	N	N
16 ***Walker***	N	N	N	N	N
17 ***Gekas***	N	N	N	N	N
18 Walgren	?	N	Y	Y	Y
19 ***Goodling***	N	Y	Y	N	N
20 Gaydos	Y	N	N	N	N
21 ***Ridge***	N	N	N	N	N
22 Murphy	Y	N	N	N	Y
23 ***Clinger***	N	N	N	N	Y
RHODE ISLAND					
1 St Germain	Y	N	N	Y	Y
2 ***Schneider***	?	?	N	N	N
SOUTH CAROLINA					
1 ***Hartnett***	N	Y	N	N	N
2 ***Spence***	N	Y	N	N	N
3 Derrick	N	N	N	N	Y
4 ***Campbell***	N	Y	N	N	N
5 Spratt	Y	N	Y	N	Y
6 Tallon	Y	N	N	N	Y
SOUTH DAKOTA					
AL Daschle	Y	N	Y	N	Y
TENNESSEE					
1 ***Quillen***	Y	Y	N	N	Y
2 ***Duncan***	Y	N	N	N	Y
3 Lloyd	Y	N	N	Y	Y
4 Cooper	Y	N	Y	Y	Y
5 Boner	Y	N	N	Y	Y
6 Gordon	Y	N	Y	Y	Y
7 ***Sundquist***	N	N	N	N	N
8 Jones	Y	N	N	Y	Y
9 Ford	Y	N	?	Y	Y
TEXAS					
1 Hall, S.	?	?	?	?	?
2 Wilson	Y	N	Y	Y	Y
3 ***Bartlett***	N	Y	N	N	N
4 Hall, R.	Y	N	N	N	N
5 Bryant	Y	N	N	Y	Y
6 ***Barton***	N	Y	N	N	N
7 ***Archer***	Y	Y	N	N	N
8 ***Fields***	N	Y	N	N	N
9 Brooks	Y	N	N	Y	Y
10 Pickle	Y	N	Y	Y	Y
11 Leath	Y	N	Y	N	Y
12 Wright	Y	N	N	Y	Y
13 ***Boulter***	?	Y	N	N	N
14 ***Sweeney***	N	Y	N	N	N
15 de la Garza	Y	N	N	N	Y
16 Coleman	Y	N	N	N	Y
17 Stenholm	N	N	Y	N	Y
18 Leland	Y	N	N	Y	Y
19 ***Combest***	N	Y	N	N	N
20 Gonzalez	P	N	N	Y	N
21 ***Loeffler***	N	Y	N	N	N
22 ***DeLay***	?	Y	N	N	N
23 Bustamante	Y	N	Y	Y	Y
24 Frost	Y	N	N	N	Y
25 Andrews	Y	N	Y	N	Y
26 ***Armey***	Y	Y	N	N	N
27 Ortiz	Y	N	N	N	Y
UTAH					
1 ***Hansen***	N	Y	N	N	N
2 ***Monson***	N	N	N	N	N
3 ***Nielson***	N	Y	N	N	N
VERMONT					
AL ***Jeffords***	N	N	N	N	N
VIRGINIA					
1 ***Bateman***	Y	Y	Y	N	N
2 ***Whitehurst***	N	Y	Y	N	N
3 ***Bliley***	N	Y	N	N	N
4 Sisisky	Y	N	N	N	Y
5 Daniel	Y	N	N	N	N
6 Olin	Y	N	Y	N	Y
7 ***Slaughter***	N	Y	N	N	N
8 ***Parris***	N	N	N	N	N
9 Boucher	Y	N	N	N	Y
10 ***Wolf***	N	N	N	N	N
WASHINGTON					
1 ***Miller***	N	N	Y	N	N
2 Swift	Y	N	Y	N	Y
3 Bonker	Y	N	N	N	Y
4 ***Morrison***	?	N	Y	N	Y
5 Foley	Y	N	N	Y	Y
6 Dicks	?	N	N	Y	Y
7 Lowry	Y	N	N	N	Y
8 ***Chandler***	N	N	Y	N	N
WEST VIRGINIA					
1 Mollohan	Y	N	N	Y	Y
2 Staggers	Y	N	N	N	Y
3 Wise	Y	N	N	Y	Y
4 Rahall	Y	N	N	Y	Y
WISCONSIN					
1 Aspin	Y	N	N	Y	Y
2 Kastenmeier	Y	N	N	Y	Y
3 ***Gunderson***	N	N	N	N	N
4 Kleczka	Y	N	N	Y	Y
5 Moody	Y	N	Y	Y	Y
6 ***Petri***	N	N	N	N	N
7 Obey	Y	N	N	Y	Y
8 ***Roth***	N	Y	N	N	N
9 ***Sensenbrenner***	N	Y	N	N	N
WYOMING					
AL ***Cheney***	N	Y	N	N	N

Southern states - Ala., Ark., Fla., Ga., Ky., La., Miss., N.C., Okla., S.C., Tenn., Texas, Va.

* The *Congressional Record* vote number is different from the CQ vote number because the *Record* includes quorum calls in its tally. CQ does not publish quorum call votes.

121. Procedural Motion. Dornan, R-Calif., motion to approve the House *Journal* of Monday, June 3. Motion agreed to 250-144: R 36-136; D 214-8 (ND 141-6, SD 73-2), June 4, 1985.

122. H J Res 192. National Day of Remembrance of Man's Inhumanity to Man. Ford, D-Mich., motion to suspend the rules and pass the joint resolution to designate April 24, 1986, as "National Day of Remembrance of Man's Inhumanity to Man," to memorialize all victims of genocide, especially the 1.5 million Armenians killed in Turkey from 1915-1923. Motion rejected 233-180: R 59-117; D 174-63 (ND 144-16, SD 30-47), June 4, 1985. A two-thirds majority of those present and voting (276 in this case) is required for passage under suspension of the rules. A "nay" was a vote supporting the president's position.

123. HR 1460. Anti-Apartheid Act. Zschau, R-Calif., amendment to ban the importation into the United States of South African gold coins, called Krugerrands, only if the prohibition is not inconsistent with U.S. obligations under the General Agreement on Tariffs and Trade (GATT). Rejected 127-292: R 119-59; D 8-233 (ND 3-161, SD 5-72), June 4, 1985. (The effect of the amendment was to allow the administration to kill the ban if it decided that the action constituted a violation of GATT.)

124. HR 1460. Anti-Apartheid Act. Burton, R-Ind., amendment to waive the provisions in the bill restricting new investment in South Africa if the secretary of state determined, based on a poll of non-white South Africans, that a majority of non-white South Africans opposed the restrictions or the divestiture of U.S. investments in South Africa. Rejected 40-379: R 40-138; D 0-241 (ND 0-164, SD 0-77), June 4, 1985.

125. HR 1460. Anti-Apartheid Act. Burton, R-Ind., amendment to waive the provisions in the bill restricting new investment in South Africa if the secretary of state determined, based on an internationally supervised referendum of non-white South Africans, that a majority of non-white South Africans opposed the restrictions. Rejected 30-384: R 30-146; D 0-238 (ND 0-161, SD 0-77), June 4, 1985.

126. HR 1460. Anti-Apartheid Act. Siljander, R-Mich., substitute to establish a commission to study apartheid in South Africa and to recommend, after three years, what sanctions the United States should impose on the South African government. The amendment would also require all U.S. companies doing business in South Africa to adhere to the fair-labor code known as the Sullivan principles. Rejected 108-310: R 102-75; D 6-235 (ND 0-162, SD 6-73), June 5, 1985.

127. HR 1460. Anti-Apartheid Act. Gunderson, R-Wis., substitute to impose sanctions against South Africa if significant progress had not been made toward eliminating apartheid in two years. The amendment would also require all U.S. companies doing business in South Africa to adhere to the fair-labor code known as the Sullivan principles. Rejected 112-313: R 104-75; D 8-238 (ND 0-167, SD 8-71), June 5, 1985.

128. HR 1460. Anti-Apartheid Act. Dellums, D-Calif., substitute to require the immediate withdrawal of all U.S. investment from South Africa and to impose a total ban on U.S. exports to that country. Rejected 77-345: R 0-178; D 77-167 (ND 69-97, SD 8-70), June 5, 1985.

KEY

Y Voted for (yea).
\# Paired for.
\+ Announced for.
N Voted against (nay).
X Paired against.
\- Announced against.
P Voted "present".
C Voted "present" to avoid possible conflict of interest.
? Did not vote or otherwise make a position known.

Democrats ***Republicans***

	121	122	123	124	125	126	127	128
ALABAMA								
1 ***Callahan***	N	N	Y	Y	N	N	N	N
2 ***Dickinson***	N	N	Y	N	N	Y	Y	N
3 Nichols	?	N	N	N	N	Y	N	N
4 Bevill	Y	N	N	N	N	N	N	N
5 Flippo	?	N	N	N	N	N	N	N
6 Erdreich	Y	N	N	N	N	N	N	N
7 Shelby	Y	N	N	N	N	N	N	N
ALASKA								
AL ***Young***	N	Y	N	N	Y	N	N	N
ARIZONA								
1 ***McCain***	?	N	Y	N	N	N	Y	N
2 Udall	?	Y	N	N	N	N	N	N
3 ***Stump***	N	N	Y	Y	Y	Y	Y	N
4 ***Rudd***	Y	N	Y	N	N	N	N	N
5 ***Kolbe***	N	N	Y	N	N	Y	Y	N
ARKANSAS								
1 Alexander	Y	N	N	N	N	N	N	?
2 Robinson	Y	Y	N	N	N	N	N	N
3 ***Hammerschmidt***	Y	N	Y	N	N	Y	Y	N
4 Anthony	Y	N	N	N	N	N	N	N
CALIFORNIA								
1 Bosco	Y	Y	N	N	?	N	N	N
2 ***Chappie***	N	Y	N	N	N	N	Y	N
3 Matsui	Y	Y	N	N	N	N	N	Y
4 Fazio	Y	Y	N	N	N	N	N	Y
5 Burton	Y	Y	N	N	N	N	N	Y
6 Boxer	?	Y	N	N	N	N	N	Y
7 Miller	Y	Y	N	N	N	N	N	Y
8 Dellums	Y	Y	N	N	N	N	N	Y
9 Stark	Y	?	N	N	N	N	N	Y
10 Edwards	Y	Y	N	N	N	N	N	Y
11 Lantos	Y	?	N	N	N	N	N	Y
12 ***Zschau***	N	N	Y	N	N	N	N	N
13 Mineta	Y	Y	N	N	N	N	N	Y
14 ***Shumway***	N	N	Y	N	N	Y	N	N
15 Coelho	Y	Y	N	N	N	N	N	N
16 Panetta	Y	Y	N	N	N	N	N	Y
17 ***Pashayan***	N	Y	N	N	N	Y	Y	N
18 Lehman	Y	Y	N	N	N	N	N	Y
19 ***Lagomarsino***	N	N	Y	N	N	Y	Y	N
20 ***Thomas***	N	Y	Y	N	N	Y	Y	N
21 ***Fiedler***	N	Y	Y	N	N	Y	Y	N
22 ***Moorhead***	N	Y	Y	N	N	Y	Y	N
23 Beilenson	Y	Y	N	N	N	N	N	N
24 Waxman	?	Y	N	N	N	N	N	Y
25 Roybal	Y	Y	N	N	N	N	N	Y
26 Berman	Y	Y	N	N	N	N	N	Y
27 Levine	Y	Y	N	N	?	N	N	Y
28 Dixon	?	Y	N	N	N	N	N	Y
29 Hawkins	Y	Y	N	N	N	?	N	Y
30 Martinez	?	Y	N	N	N	N	N	N
31 Dymally	P	Y	N	N	N	N	N	Y
32 Anderson	Y	Y	N	N	N	N	N	N
33 ***Dreier***	N	Y	Y	N	N	Y	Y	N
34 Torres	Y	Y	N	N	N	N	N	Y
35 ***Lewis***	N	?	N	N	N	N	Y	N
36 Brown	Y	Y	N	N	N	N	N	Y
37 ***McCandless***	N	N	N	N	N	N	N	N
38 ***Dornan***	N	Y	Y	Y	Y	Y	Y	N
39 ***Dannemeyer***	N	Y	Y	Y	Y	Y	Y	N
40 ***Badham***	N	N	Y	Y	Y	Y	Y	N
41 ***Lowery***	N	Y	Y	Y	N	Y	Y	N
42 ***Lungren***	N	Y	Y	N	N	Y	Y	N
43 ***Packard***	N	Y	Y	N	N	Y	N	N
44 Bates	Y	Y	N	N	N	N	N	Y
45 ***Hunter***	N	Y	N	Y	Y	Y	Y	N
COLORADO								
1 Schroeder	N	N	N	N	N	N	N	Y
2 Wirth	Y	Y	N	N	N	N	N	N
3 ***Strang***	N	Y	Y	Y	N	Y	Y	N
4 ***Brown***	N	N	Y	N	N	N	N	N
5 ***Kramer***	N	N	Y	N	N	Y	Y	N
6 ***Schaefer***	N	N	Y	N	N	N	N	N
CONNECTICUT								
1 Kennelly	Y	Y	N	N	N	N	N	N
2 Gejdenson	Y	Y	N	N	N	N	N	Y
3 Morrison	Y	Y	N	N	N	N	N	Y
4 ***McKinney***	Y	Y	N	N	N	N	N	N
5 ***Rowland***	Y	Y	N	N	N	Y	Y	N
6 ***Johnson***	Y	Y	Y	N	N	N	N	N
DELAWARE								
AL Carper	Y	N	N	N	N	N	N	N
FLORIDA								
1 Hutto	Y	N	N	N	N	N	Y	N
2 Fuqua	Y	N	N	N	N	N	N	N
3 Bennett	Y	N	N	N	N	N	N	N
4 Chappell	Y	?	N	N	N	?	N	N
5 ***McCollum***	Y	Y	Y	N	N	Y	N	N
6 MacKay	Y	Y	N	N	N	N	N	N
7 Gibbons	Y	N	N	N	N	N	N	N
8 ***Young***	N	N	N	N	N	Y	Y	N
9 ***Bilirakis***	N	Y	Y	Y	Y	Y	Y	N
10 ***Ireland***	N	Y	Y	N	N	N	N	N
11 Nelson	Y	N	N	N	N	N	N	N
12 ***Lewis***	N	N	N	N	N	N	Y	N
13 ***Mack***	N	N	N	N	N	N	N	N
14 Mica	Y	N	N	N	N	N	N	N
15 ***Shaw***	N	N	Y	N	N	Y	Y	N
16 Smith	Y	Y	N	?	N	N	N	N
17 Lehman	Y	Y	N	N	N	N	N	Y
18 Pepper	Y	Y	N	N	N	N	N	N
19 Fascell	Y	Y	N	N	N	N	N	N
GEORGIA								
1 Thomas	Y	N	N	N	N	N	N	N
2 Hatcher	Y	N	N	N	N	N	N	N
3 Ray	Y	N	N	N	N	N	N	N
4 ***Swindall***	N	N	Y	N	N	Y	Y	N
5 Fowler	?	?	?	?	?	N	N	N
6 ***Gingrich***	?	N	N	N	Y	Y	Y	N
7 Darden	Y	N	N	N	N	N	N	N
8 Rowland	Y	N	N	N	N	N	N	N
9 Jenkins	Y	N	N	N	N	N	Y	N
10 Barnard	Y	N	?	N	N	Y	Y	N
HAWAII								
1 Heftel	Y	Y	N	N	N	N	N	N
2 Akaka	?	Y	N	N	N	N	N	Y
IDAHO								
1 ***Craig***	N	N	Y	N	Y	Y	Y	N
2 Stallings	Y	Y	N	N	N	?	?	?
ILLINOIS								
1 Hayes	Y	Y	N	N	N	N	N	Y
2 Savage	Y	Y	N	N	N	N	N	Y
3 Russo	Y	Y	N	N	N	N	N	Y
4 ***O'Brien***	Y	N	Y	N	N	N	Y	N
5 Lipinski	Y	Y	N	N	N	N	N	N
6 ***Hyde***	N	N	Y	N	N	Y	N	N
7 Collins	?	?	-	-	N	N	N	Y
8 Rostenkowski	Y	Y	N	N	N	?	N	N
9 Yates	Y	Y	N	N	N	N	N	Y
10 ***Porter***	N	Y	N	N	N	N	Y	N
11 Annunzio	Y	Y	N	N	N	N	N	N
12 ***Crane***	N	N	Y	Y	Y	N	N	N
13 ***Fawell***	P	N	N	Y	N	Y	N	N
14 ***Grotberg***	N	N	Y	Y	N	Y	N	N
15 ***Madigan***	N	N	N	N	N	N	N	N
16 ***Martin***	?	N	N	N	N	N	N	N
17 Evans	Y	Y	N	N	N	N	N	Y
18 ***Michel***	N	N	Y	Y	N	Y	Y	N
19 Bruce	Y	Y	N	N	N	N	N	N
20 Durbin	N	Y	N	N	N	N	N	N
21 Price	Y	N	N	N	N	N	N	Y
22 Gray	?	?	?	?	N	N	N	Y
INDIANA								
1 Visclosky	Y	Y	N	N	N	N	N	N
2 Sharp	Y	Y	N	N	N	N	N	N
3 ***Hiler***	N	N	Y	N	N	N	Y	N
4 ***Coats***	N	Y	N	N	N	N	N	N
5 ***Hillis***	N	N	N	N	N	Y	N	N

ND - Northern Democrats SD - Southern Democrats

* Corresponding to Congressional Record Votes 132, 133, 134, 135, 136, 137, 138, 139

	121	122	123	124	125	126	127	128
6 ***Burton***	N	N	Y	Y	Y	Y	Y	N
7 ***Myers***	Y	Y	Y	N	N	Y	Y	N
8 McCloskey	Y	Y	N	N	N	N	N	N
9 Hamilton	Y	Y	N	N	N	N	N	N
10 Jacobs	N	Y	N	N	N	N	N	Y
IOWA								
1 ***Leach***	N	Y	N	N	N	N	N	N
2 ***Tauke***	N	N	Y	N	N	N	Y	N
3 ***Evans***	N	Y	Y	N	N	N	Y	N
4 Smith	Y	N	Y	N	N	N	N	N
5 ***Lightfoot***	N	N	Y	N	N	N	Y	N
6 Bedell	Y	Y	N	N	N	N	N	N
KANSAS								
1 ***Roberts***	N	N	Y	N	N	?	Y	N
2 Slattery	Y	Y	N	N	N	?	N	N
3 ***Meyers***	N	N	N	N	N	N	Y	N
4 Glickman	Y	Y	N	N	N	N	N	N
5 ***Whittaker***	?	?	Y	N	N	N	N	N
KENTUCKY								
1 Hubbard	Y	-	?	?	?	N	N	N
2 Natcher	Y	N	N	N	N	N	N	N
3 Mazzoli	Y	N	Y	N	N	N	N	N
4 ***Snyder***	Y	N	Y	N	N	N	N	N
5 ***Rogers***	N	N	+	N	N	Y	N	N
6 ***Hopkins***	N	N	N	N	N	N	N	N
7 Perkins	Y	N	N	N	N	N	N	Y
LOUISIANA								
1 ***Livingston***	N	N	Y	N	N	Y	Y	N
2 Boggs	?	Y	N	N	N	N	N	N
3 Tauzin	Y	Y	N	N	N	N	N	N
4 Roemer	N	Y	N	N	N	N	N	N
5 Huckaby	Y	N	N	N	N	N	N	N
6 ***Moore***	Y	N	N	N	N	Y	Y	N
7 Breaux	Y	Y	N	N	N	N	N	N
8 Long	Y	Y	N	N	N	N	N	N
MAINE								
1 ***McKernan***	N	Y	N	N	N	N	N	N
2 ***Snowe***	Y	Y	N	N	N	N	N	N
MARYLAND								
1 Dyson	Y	N	N	N	N	N	N	N
2 ***Bentley***	N	N	Y	N	N	Y	Y	N
3 Mikulski	Y	Y	N	N	N	N	N	Y
4 ***Holt***	Y	N	Y	N	?	Y	N	N
5 Hoyer	Y	Y	N	N	N	N	N	N
6 Byron	?	?	?	?	?	?	?	N
7 Mitchell	?	Y	N	N	N	N	N	Y
8 Barnes	Y	Y	N	N	N	N	N	N
MASSACHUSETTS								
1 ***Conte***	N	Y	N	N	N	N	N	N
2 Boland	Y	Y	N	N	N	N	N	N
3 Early	Y	Y	N	N	N	N	N	N
4 Frank	Y	Y	N	N	N	N	N	Y
5 Atkins	Y	Y	N	N	N	N	N	N
6 Mavroules	Y	Y	N	N	N	N	N	N
7 Markey	Y	Y	N	N	N	?	N	Y
8 O'Neill								
9 Moakley	Y	Y	N	N	N	N	N	N
10 Studds	Y	Y	N	N	N	N	N	Y
11 Donnelly	Y	Y	N	N	N	N	N	N
MICHIGAN								
1 Conyers	Y	Y	N	N	N	N	N	Y
2 ***Pursell***	N	Y	Y	N	N	N	Y	N
3 Wolpe	Y	Y	N	N	N	N	N	N
4 ***Siljander***	N	N	Y	Y	Y	Y	Y	N
5 ***Henry***	N	Y	Y	N	N	Y	Y	N
6 Carr	Y	Y	N	N	N	N	N	N
7 Kildee	Y	Y	N	N	N	N	N	Y
8 Traxler	Y	Y	N	N	N	N	N	N
9 ***Vander Jagt***	Y	N	Y	Y	N	Y	Y	N
10 ***Schuette***	N	N	Y	N	N	Y	Y	N
11 ***Davis***	N	Y	Y	N	N	Y	Y	N
12 Bonior	Y	Y	N	N	N	N	N	N
13 Crockett	?	Y	N	N	N	N	N	Y
14 Hertel	Y	Y	N	N	N	N	N	N
15 Ford	?	Y	N	N	N	N	N	?
16 Dingell	?	?	?	?	?	?	?	?
17 Levin	Y	Y	N	N	N	N	N	N
18 ***Broomfield***	Y	Y	N	N	N	Y	Y	N
MINNESOTA								
1 Penny	N	Y	N	N	N	N	N	N
2 ***Weber***	N	N	N	N	Y	N	N	N
3 ***Frenzel***	N	N	Y	N	N	?	Y	N
4 Vento	Y	Y	N	N	?	N	N	N
5 Sabo	Y	Y	N	N	N	N	N	N
6 Sikorski	N	Y	N	N	N	N	N	Y
7 ***Stangeland***	N	N	N	Y	N	Y	Y	N
8 Oberstar	Y	Y	N	N	N	N	N	N
MISSISSIPPI								
1 Whitten	Y	N	N	N	N	N	N	N
2 ***Franklin***	N	N	Y	N	N	Y	Y	N
3 Montgomery	Y	N	Y	N	N	Y	Y	N
4 Dowdy	Y	N	N	N	N	N	N	N
5 ***Lott***	N	N	Y	Y	N	Y	Y	N
MISSOURI								
1 Clay	N	Y	N	N	N	N	N	Y
2 Young	Y	N	N	N	N	N	N	N
3 Gephardt	Y	Y	N	N	N	N	N	N
4 Skelton	Y	N	N	N	N	N	N	N
5 Wheat	Y	Y	N	N	N	N	N	Y
6 ***Coleman***	N	N	N	N	N	N	N	N
7 ***Taylor***	N	N	Y	Y	N	Y	Y	N
8 ***Emerson***	N	N	Y	Y	N	?	?	?
9 Volkmer	Y	Y	N	N	N	N	N	N
MONTANA								
1 Williams	?	Y	N	N	N	N	N	N
2 ***Marlenee***	N	N	N	N	N	Y	Y	N
NEBRASKA								
1 ***Bereuter***	N	N	Y	N	N	N	Y	N
2 ***Daub***	N	N	Y	N	N	Y	Y	N
3 ***Smith***	N	N	Y	N	N	Y	Y	N
NEVADA								
1 Reid	Y	Y	N	N	N	N	N	N
2 ***Vucanovich***	N	Y	N	Y	Y	Y	Y	N
NEW HAMPSHIRE								
1 ***Smith***	N	Y	N	N	N	N	N	N
2 ***Gregg***	N	N	N	N	N	N	N	N
NEW JERSEY								
1 Florio	?	?	?	?	?	N	N	N
2 Hughes	Y	Y	N	N	N	N	N	N
3 Howard	Y	Y	N	N	N	N	N	N
4 ***Smith***	N	Y	N	N	N	N	N	N
5 ***Roukema***	Y	Y	N	N	?	N	Y	N
6 Dwyer	Y	Y	N	N	N	N	N	N
7 ***Rinaldo***	Y	Y	N	N	N	N	N	N
8 Roe	Y	Y	N	N	N	N	N	N
9 Torricelli	?	?	?	?	?	N	N	N
10 Rodino	?	Y	N	N	N	N	N	Y
11 ***Gallo***	N	Y	Y	N	N	N	N	N
12 ***Courter***	N	Y	Y	N	N	N	N	N
13 ***Saxton***	N	Y	Y	N	N	N	Y	N
14 Guarini	Y	Y	N	N	N	N	N	N
NEW MEXICO								
1 ***Lujan***	N	Y	Y	N	N	Y	Y	N
2 ***Skeen***	N	N	Y	N	N	Y	Y	N
3 Richardson	Y	Y	N	N	N	N	N	Y
NEW YORK								
1 ***Carney***	N	N	N	?	?	N	N	N
2 Downey	Y	Y	N	N	N	N	N	Y
3 Mrazek	Y	Y	N	N	N	N	N	N
4 ***Lent***	N	N	Y	N	N	N	N	N
5 ***McGrath***	N	?	?	?	?	N	N	N
6 Addabbo	Y	Y	N	N	N	N	N	Y
7 Ackerman	Y	Y	N	N	N	N	N	Y
8 Scheuer	Y	Y	N	N	N	N	N	N
9 Manton	Y	Y	N	N	N	N	N	N
10 Schumer	Y	Y	N	N	N	N	N	N
11 Towns	?	Y	N	N	N	N	N	Y
12 Owens	Y	Y	N	N	N	N	N	Y
13 Solarz	Y	?	N	N	N	N	N	N
14 ***Molinari***	N	N	N	N	N	N	N	N
15 ***Green***	Y	Y	N	N	N	N	N	N
16 Rangel	Y	Y	N	N	N	N	N	Y
17 Weiss	Y	Y	N	N	N	N	N	Y
18 Garcia	Y	Y	N	N	N	N	N	Y
19 Biaggi	Y	Y	N	N	?	N	N	N
20 ***DioGuardi***	N	N	N	N	N	N	N	N
21 ***Fish***	N	Y	N	N	N	N	N	N
22 ***Gilman***	N	Y	N	N	N	N	N	N
23 Stratton	Y	N	N	N	N	N	N	N
24 ***Solomon***	N	N	Y	Y	Y	Y	N	N
25 ***Boehlert***	N	Y	N	N	N	N	N	N
26 ***Martin***	?	Y	Y	N	N	N	N	N
27 ***Wortley***	Y	Y	Y	N	N	N	N	N
28 McHugh	Y	Y	N	N	N	N	N	N
29 ***Horton***	Y	Y	N	N	N	N	N	N
30 ***Eckert***	N	N	Y	Y	Y	Y	N	N
31 ***Kemp***	Y	N	Y	N	N	Y	N	N
32 LaFalce	Y	Y	Y	N	N	N	N	N
33 Nowak	Y	Y	N	N	N	N	N	N
34 Lundine	Y	N	N	N	N	N	N	N
NORTH CAROLINA								
1 Jones	Y	N	N	N	?	N	N	N
2 Valentine	Y	N	N	N	N	N	N	N
3 Whitley	Y	N	N	N	N	N	N	N
4 ***Cobey***	N	N	N	Y	Y	Y	Y	N
5 Neal	Y	N	N	N	N	N	N	N
6 ***Coble***	N	N	Y	N	Y	Y	Y	N
7 Rose	Y	Y	N	N	N	N	N	N
8 Hefner	Y	N	N	N	N	N	N	N
9 ***McMillan***	Y	N	Y	N	N	Y	N	N
10 ***Broyhill***	Y	N	Y	N	N	Y	Y	N
11 ***Hendon***	N	N	N	Y	Y	Y	Y	N
NORTH DAKOTA								
AL Dorgan	Y	Y	N	N	N	N	N	N
OHIO								
1 Luken	Y	Y	N	N	N	N	N	N
2 ***Gradison***	N	N	Y	N	N	N	?	?
3 Hall	Y	Y	N	N	N	N	N	N
4 ***Oxley***	?	N	N	N	N	Y	Y	N
5 ***Latta***	N	N	Y	N	N	N	Y	N
6 ***McEwen***	N	N	Y	N	N	Y	N	N
7 ***DeWine***	N	N	Y	N	N	Y	Y	N
8 ***Kindness***	N	N	Y	N	N	Y	N	N
9 Kaptur	Y	Y	N	N	N	N	N	N
10 ***Miller***	N	N	Y	N	N	Y	N	N
11 Eckart	?	Y	N	N	N	N	N	N
12 ***Kasich***	N	N	N	N	N	N	N	N
13 Pease	Y	Y	N	N	N	N	N	N
14 Seiberling	Y	Y	N	N	N	N	N	N
15 ***Wylie***	Y	N	N	N	N	N	N	N
16 ***Regula***	Y	N	N	N	N	N	Y	N
17 Traficant	?	Y	N	N	N	N	N	Y
18 Applegate	Y	?	N	N	N	N	N	N
19 Feighan	Y	Y	N	N	N	N	N	N
20 Oakar	Y	Y	N	N	N	N	N	Y
21 Stokes	Y	Y	N	N	N	N	N	Y
OKLAHOMA								
1 Jones	Y	N	N	N	N	N	N	N
2 Synar	Y	Y	N	N	N	N	N	N
3 Watkins	Y	N	N	N	N	N	N	N
4 McCurdy	Y	N	N	N	N	N	N	N
5 ***Edwards***	N	N	N	N	N	?	?	?
6 English	Y	N	N	N	N	N	N	N
OREGON								
1 AuCoin	Y	Y	N	N	N	N	N	N
2 ***Smith, R.***	Y	N	Y	Y	N	Y	Y	N
3 Wyden	Y	Y	N	N	N	N	N	N
4 Weaver	Y	Y	N	N	N	N	N	N
5 ***Smith, D.***	N	N	Y	Y	Y	Y	Y	N
PENNSYLVANIA								
1 Foglietta	?	Y	N	N	N	N	N	Y
2 Gray	Y	Y	N	N	N	N	N	P
3 Borski	Y	Y	N	N	N	N	N	N
4 Kolter	Y	Y	N	N	N	N	N	N
5 ***Schulze***	Y	Y	N	N	N	Y	N	N
6 Yatron	Y	Y	N	N	N	N	N	N
7 Edgar	Y	Y	N	N	N	N	N	Y
8 Kostmayer	Y	Y	N	N	N	N	N	Y
9 ***Shuster***	N	N	Y	Y	N	Y	Y	N
10 ***McDade***	N	N	N	N	N	N	N	N
11 Kanjorski	Y	Y	N	N	N	N	N	N
12 Murtha	Y	N	N	N	N	N	N	N
13 ***Coughlin***	N	Y	N	N	N	N	N	N
14 Coyne	Y	Y	N	N	N	N	N	Y
15 ***Ritter***	N	N	Y	Y	Y	N	N	N
16 ***Walker***	N	N	N	N	Y	Y	Y	N
17 ***Gekas***	N	Y	Y	N	N	Y	Y	N
18 Walgren	Y	Y	N	N	N	N	N	N
19 ***Goodling***	N	N	N	N	N	Y	Y	N
20 Gaydos	Y	Y	N	N	N	N	N	N
21 ***Ridge***	?	?	?	?	?	N	Y	N
22 Murphy	Y	N	N	N	N	N	N	N
23 ***Clinger***	+	+	-	-	N	N	Y	N
RHODE ISLAND								
1 St Germain	Y	Y	N	N	N	N	N	N
2 ***Schneider***	Y	Y	Y	N	N	N	N	N
SOUTH CAROLINA								
1 ***Hartnett***	?	N	Y	N	N	Y	Y	N
2 ***Spence***	Y	Y	Y	Y	N	Y	Y	N
3 Derrick	N	Y	N	N	N	N	N	N
4 ***Campbell***	N	N	Y	N	N	Y	Y	?
5 Spratt	Y	N	N	N	N	N	-	-
6 Tallon	Y	N	N	N	N	N	N	N
SOUTH DAKOTA								
AL Daschle	Y	Y	N	N	N	N	N	N
TENNESSEE								
1 ***Quillen***	Y	N	Y	N	N	Y	Y	N
2 ***Duncan***	Y	N	Y	N	N	N	Y	N
3 Lloyd	Y	N	N	N	N	N	N	N
4 Cooper	Y	Y	N	N	N	N	N	N
5 Boner	Y	N	N	N	N	N	N	N
6 Gordon	Y	Y	N	N	N	N	N	N
7 ***Sundquist***	N	N	Y	N	N	Y	Y	N
8 Jones	Y	Y	N	N	N	N	N	N
9 Ford	Y	Y	N	N	N	N	N	Y
TEXAS								
1 Vacancy*								
2 Wilson	?	?	?	?	?	?	?	?
3 ***Bartlett***	Y	N	Y	Y	Y	Y	N	N
4 Hall, R.	Y	Y	Y	N	N	Y	Y	N
5 Bryant	Y	Y	N	N	N	N	N	Y
6 ***Barton***	N	N	Y	Y	Y	Y	Y	N
7 ***Archer***	Y	N	Y	Y	N	Y	Y	N
8 ***Fields***	N	N	Y	Y	Y	Y	Y	N
9 Brooks	Y	Y	N	N	N	N	N	N
10 Pickle	Y	N	N	N	N	N	N	N
11 Leath	Y	N	Y	N	N	Y	Y	N
12 Wright	Y	Y	N	N	N	N	N	N
13 ***Boulter***	N	N	Y	N	N	N	N	N
14 ***Sweeney***	N	N	Y	N	N	?	N	N
15 de la Garza	Y	Y	N	N	N	N	N	N
16 Coleman	Y	Y	N	N	N	N	N	N
17 Stenholm	?	N	N	N	N	N	Y	N
18 Leland	Y	Y	N	N	N	N	N	Y
19 ***Combest***	N	N	Y	N	N	Y	N	N
20 Gonzalez	Y	Y	N	N	N	N	N	Y
21 ***Loeffler***	N	N	Y	N	N	Y	Y	N
22 ***DeLay***	Y	N	Y	Y	Y	N	N	N
23 Bustamante	Y	N	N	N	N	N	N	Y
24 Frost	Y	Y	N	N	N	N	N	N
25 Andrews	Y	Y	N	N	N	N	N	N
26 ***Armey***	N	N	Y	Y	Y	Y	N	N
27 Ortiz	Y	Y	N	N	N	N	N	Y
UTAH								
1 ***Hansen***	N	N	Y	Y	Y	Y	Y	N
2 ***Monson***	N	N	Y	Y	N	Y	Y	N
3 ***Nielson***	N	N	Y	N	N	Y	Y	N
VERMONT								
AL ***Jeffords***	N	Y	N	N	N	N	N	N
VIRGINIA								
1 ***Bateman***	Y	N	Y	N	N	Y	Y	N
2 ***Whitehurst***	N	N	Y	N	?	Y	Y	N
3 ***Bliley***	N	Y	N	N	N	N	N	N
4 Sisisky	Y	N	N	N	N	N	N	N
5 Daniel	Y	N	N	N	N	Y	Y	N
6 Olin	Y	N	Y	N	N	N	N	N
7 ***Slaughter***	N	N	Y	N	N	Y	N	N
8 ***Parris***	N	Y	Y	N	N	Y	Y	N
9 Boucher	Y	Y	N	N	N	N	N	N
10 ***Wolf***	N	Y	Y	N	N	Y	Y	N
WASHINGTON								
1 ***Miller***	N	Y	N	N	N	N	N	N
2 Swift	Y	N	N	N	N	N	N	N
3 Bonker	?	N	Y	N	?	N	N	N
4 ***Morrison***	Y	?	Y	N	N	Y	Y	N
5 Foley	Y	Y	N	N	N	N	N	N
6 Dicks	Y	N	N	N	N	N	N	N
7 Lowry	Y	Y	N	N	N	N	N	Y
8 ***Chandler***	N	N	Y	N	N	Y	Y	N
WEST VIRGINIA								
1 Mollohan	Y	Y	N	N	N	N	N	N
2 Staggers	Y	N	N	N	N	N	N	N
3 Wise	Y	Y	N	N	N	N	N	Y
4 Rahall	Y	N	N	N	N	?	N	Y
WISCONSIN								
1 Aspin	Y	Y	N	N	N	N	N	N
2 Kastenmeier	Y	Y	N	N	N	N	N	Y
3 ***Gunderson***	N	N	Y	N	N	Y	Y	N
4 Kleczka	Y	Y	N	N	N	N	N	N
5 Moody	Y	Y	N	N	N	N	N	Y
6 ***Petri***	Y	N	Y	Y	Y	Y	Y	N
7 Obey	Y	Y	N	N	N	N	N	N
8 ***Roth***	N	Y	Y	N	Y	Y	Y	N
9 ***Sensenbrenner***	N	N	Y	N	N	N	Y	N
WYOMING								
AL ***Cheney***	N	N	Y	Y	N	Y	Y	N

**Rep. Sam B. Hall Jr., D-Texas, resigned on May 27, 1985. The last vote for which he was eligible was CQ vote 120.*

Southern states - Ala., Ark., Fla., Ga., Ky., La., Miss., N.C., Okla., S.C., Tenn., Texas, Va.

* The *Congressional Record* vote number is different from the CQ vote number because the *Record* includes quorum calls in its tally. CQ does not publish quorum call votes.

129. HR 1460. Anti-Apartheid Act. Crane, R-Ill., motion to recommit the bill to the Foreign Affairs Committee with instructions to amend it to postpone for one year the imposition of any sanctions against South Africa and to permit the president to waive the sanctions if he determined that the African National Congress had not renounced the use of violence. Motion rejected 139-282: R 132-44; D 7-238 (ND 0-166, SD 7-72), June 5, 1985.

130. HR 1460. Anti-Apartheid Act. Passage of the bill to impose sanctions immediately against South Africa, including a ban on bank loans to the South African government, and prohibitions against the sale of computer goods and nuclear power equipment and supplies to that country. Subject to review by the president and Congress, the bill also would bar new U.S. business investment in South Africa and prohibit the importation into the United States of South African gold coins, called Krugerrands. Passed 295-127: R 56-121; D 239-6 (ND 166-0, SD 73-6), June 5, 1985. A "nay" was a vote supporting the president's position.

131. Procedural Motion. Dreier, R-Calif., motion to approve the House *Journal* of Wednesday, June 5. Motion agreed to 266-127: R 48-116; D 218-11 (ND 145-7, SD 73-4), June 6, 1985.

132. HR 2577. Supplemental Appropriations, Fiscal 1985. Adoption of the rule (H Res 186) to provide for House floor consideration of the bill to appropriate $13.49 billion for fiscal 1985. Adopted 267-149: R 56-118; D 211-31 (ND 139-25, SD 72-6), June 6, 1985.

133. HR 2577. Supplemental Appropriations, Fiscal 1985. Edgar, D-Pa., amendment to the Whitten, D-Miss., amendment, to reduce from $150 million to $51 million the funds added for water projects of the U.S. Army Corps of Engineers. Adopted 203-202: R 108-69; D 95-133 (ND 80-75, SD 15-58), June 6, 1985. (The Whitten amendment was subsequently adopted *(see vote 134, below)*.)

134. HR 2577. Supplemental Appropriations, Fiscal 1985. Whitten, D-Miss., amendment as amended by the Edgar, D-Pa., amendment *(vote 133, above)* to add $51 million for water projects of the U.S. Army Corps of Engineers. Adopted 325-74: R 120-56; D 205-18 (ND 136-15, SD 69-3), June 6, 1985.

KEY

- Y Voted for (yea).
- # Paired for.
- + Announced for.
- N Voted against (nay).
- X Paired against.
- \- Announced against.
- P Voted "present".
- C Voted "present" to avoid possible conflict of interest.
- ? Did not vote or otherwise make a position known.

Democrats *__Republicans__*

	129	130	131	132	133	134
ALABAMA						
1 ***Callahan***	Y	N	N	N	N	Y
2 ***Dickinson***	Y	N	N	N	N	Y
3 Nichols	N	N	Y	Y	N	Y
4 Bevill	N	Y	Y	Y	N	Y
5 Flippo	N	Y	Y	Y	N	Y
6 Erdreich	N	Y	Y	Y	N	Y
7 Shelby	N	Y	N	Y	N	Y
ALASKA						
AL ***Young***	Y	Y	N	Y	N	Y
ARIZONA						
1 ***McCain***	Y	N	N	N	N	Y
2 Udall	N	Y	?	Y	N	Y
3 ***Stump***	Y	N	N	N	N	Y
4 ***Rudd***	Y	N	Y	Y	N	Y
5 ***Kolbe***	Y	N	N	N	N	Y
ARKANSAS						
1 Alexander	N	Y	Y	Y	N	Y
2 Robinson	N	Y	Y	Y	Y	Y
3 ***Hammerschmidt***	Y	N	Y	N	Y	Y
4 Anthony	N	Y	Y	Y	N	Y
CALIFORNIA						
1 Bosco	N	Y	Y	Y	Y	Y
2 ***Chappie***	Y	N	N	N	N	Y
3 Matsui	N	Y	Y	Y	?	?
4 Fazio	N	Y	Y	Y	N	Y
5 Burton	N	Y	Y	Y	N	Y
6 Boxer	N	Y	Y	N	?	?
7 Miller	N	?	Y	Y	?	?
8 Dellums	N	Y	Y	N	N	Y
9 Stark	N	Y	?	Y	?	?
10 Edwards	N	Y	Y	Y	Y	Y
11 Lantos	N	Y	Y	Y	Y	Y
12 ***Zschau***	N	N	N	N	Y	N
13 Mineta	N	Y	Y	Y	N	Y
14 ***Shumway***	Y	N	N	N	Y	Y
15 Coelho	N	Y	Y	Y	N	Y
16 Panetta	N	Y	Y	Y	N	Y
17 ***Pashayan***	Y	N	Y	N	N	Y
18 Lehman	N	Y	Y	Y	?	?
19 ***Lagomarsino***	Y	N	N	N	N	Y
20 ***Thomas***	N	-	N	N	Y	?
21 ***Fiedler***	Y	N	N	N	?	Y
22 ***Moorhead***	Y	N	N	N	Y	N
23 Beilenson	N	Y	Y	Y	Y	Y
24 Waxman	N	Y	Y	Y	Y	Y
25 Roybal	N	Y	Y	Y	N	Y
26 Berman	N	Y	Y	N	Y	Y
27 Levine	N	Y	Y	Y	Y	?
28 Dixon	N	Y	Y	Y	N	Y
29 Hawkins	N	Y	Y	Y	N	Y
30 Martinez	N	Y	Y	Y	Y	Y
31 Dymally	N	Y	P	N	Y	Y
32 Anderson	N	Y	Y	Y	Y	Y
33 ***Dreier***	Y	N	N	N	Y	N
34 Torres	N	Y	Y	Y	N	Y
35 ***Lewis***	Y	Y	N	N	N	Y
36 Brown	N	Y	?	Y	Y	Y
37 ***McCandless***	Y	N	N	N	N	Y
38 ***Dornan***	Y	N	?	N	N	Y
39 ***Dannemeyer***	Y	N	N	N	Y	N
40 ***Badham***	Y	N	N	N	N	Y
41 ***Lowery***	Y	N	N	N	N	Y
42 ***Lungren***	Y	N	N	N	Y	Y
43 ***Packard***	Y	N	N	N	Y	Y
44 Bates	N	Y	Y	N	Y	N
45 ***Hunter***	Y	N	?	?	N	Y
COLORADO						
1 Schroeder	N	Y	N	N	+	-
2 Wirth	N	Y	?	?	?	?
3 ***Strang***	Y	N	Y	N	N	Y
4 ***Brown***	N	Y	N	N	Y	N
5 ***Kramer***	N	N	Y	N	N	Y
6 ***Schaefer***	Y	N	N	N	Y	Y
CONNECTICUT						
1 Kennelly	N	Y	Y	Y	Y	Y
2 Gejdenson	N	Y	Y	N	Y	Y
3 Morrison	N	Y	Y	Y	?	?
4 ***McKinney***	N	Y	Y	N	Y	Y
5 ***Rowland***	N	Y	Y	N	Y	Y
6 ***Johnson***	N	Y	Y	Y	Y	Y
DELAWARE						
AL Carper	N	Y	Y	Y	Y	N
FLORIDA						
1 Hutto	N	N	Y	Y	?	?
2 Fuqua	N	Y	Y	Y	Y	Y
3 Bennett	N	Y	Y	Y	N	Y
4 Chappell	Y	Y	Y	Y	N	Y
5 ***McCollum***	Y	N	Y	N	Y	N
6 MacKay	N	Y	Y	Y	Y	N
7 Gibbons	N	Y	Y	N	N	Y
8 ***Young***	Y	N	N	N	N	Y
9 ***Bilirakis***	Y	N	N	N	?	?
10 ***Ireland***	Y	N	N	N	Y	Y
11 Nelson	N	Y	Y	Y	N	Y
12 ***Lewis***	Y	N	-	N	N	Y
13 ***Mack***	Y	N	N	N	Y	N
14 Mica	N	Y	Y	Y	N	Y
15 ***Shaw***	Y	N	N	N	Y	Y
16 Smith	N	Y	Y	Y	N	Y
17 Lehman	N	Y	Y	Y	N	Y
18 Pepper	N	Y	Y	Y	N	Y
19 Fascell	N	Y	Y	Y	N	Y
GEORGIA						
1 Thomas	N	Y	Y	Y	N	Y
2 Hatcher	N	Y	Y	Y	?	?
3 Ray	N	Y	Y	Y	Y	N
4 ***Swindall***	Y	N	N	N	Y	N
5 Fowler	N	Y	Y	Y	Y	Y
6 ***Gingrich***	Y	N	?	?	Y	Y
7 Darden	N	Y	Y	Y	N	Y
8 Rowland	N	Y	Y	Y	N	Y
9 Jenkins	N	Y	Y	Y	N	Y
10 Barnard	Y	Y	Y	Y	N	Y
HAWAII						
1 Heftel	N	Y	?	Y	Y	Y
2 Akaka	N	Y	Y	Y	N	Y
IDAHO						
1 ***Craig***	Y	N	N	N	N	Y
2 Stallings	?	?	?	?	?	?
ILLINOIS						
1 Hayes	N	Y	Y	Y	Y	Y
2 Savage	N	Y	?	Y	Y	Y
3 Russo	N	Y	Y	Y	N	Y
4 ***O'Brien***	Y	N	Y	Y	N	Y
5 Lipinski	N	Y	Y	Y	Y	Y
6 ***Hyde***	Y	N	Y	N	Y	N
7 Collins	N	Y	Y	Y	Y	Y
8 Rostenkowski	N	Y	Y	Y	N	Y
9 Yates	N	Y	Y	Y	Y	Y
10 ***Porter***	?	Y	N	N	Y	N
11 Annunzio	N	Y	Y	Y	Y	Y
12 ***Crane***	Y	N	?	N	N	?
13 ***Fawell***	Y	N	N	N	Y	N
14 ***Grotberg***	Y	N	N	N	Y	N
15 ***Madigan***	Y	Y	?	Y	Y	Y
16 ***Martin***	Y	Y	N	N	Y	N
17 Evans	N	Y	Y	Y	Y	Y
18 ***Michel***	Y	N	Y	Y	Y	N
19 Bruce	N	Y	Y	Y	N	Y
20 Durbin	N	Y	N	Y	N	Y
21 Price	N	Y	Y	Y	N	Y
22 Gray	N	Y	Y	Y	Y	Y
INDIANA						
1 Visclosky	N	Y	Y	Y	N	Y
2 Sharp	N	Y	Y	Y	Y	N
3 ***Hiler***	Y	Y	N	N	Y	N
4 ***Coats***	N	Y	Y	N	Y	N
5 ***Hillis***	Y	N	N	Y	?	?

ND - Northern Democrats SD - Southern Democrats

* Corresponding to Congressional Record Votes 140, 141, 142, 143, 145, 146

	129	130	131	132	133	134
6 ***Burton***	Y	N	N	N	Y	N
7 ***Myers***	Y	N	Y	Y	N	Y
8 McCloskey	N	Y	Y	Y	N	Y
9 Hamilton	N	Y	Y	Y	N	Y
10 Jacobs	N	Y	N	N	Y	N
IOWA						
1 ***Leach***	N	Y	?	N	Y	N
2 ***Tauke***	Y	Y	N	N	Y	N
3 ***Evans***	Y	Y	N	N	Y	N
4 Smith	N	Y	Y	Y	N	Y
5 ***Lightfoot***	Y	Y	N	N	Y	N
6 Bedell	N	Y	Y	Y	Y	N
KANSAS						
1 ***Roberts***	Y	N	N	N	Y	Y
2 Slattery	N	Y	Y	N	Y	Y
3 ***Meyers***	Y	N	N	Y	Y	Y
4 Glickman	N	Y	Y	Y	Y	Y
5 ***Whittaker***	Y	N	N	N	Y	Y
KENTUCKY						
1 Hubbard	N	Y	Y	Y	N	Y
2 Natcher	N	Y	Y	Y	N	Y
3 Mazzoli	N	Y	Y	Y	N	Y
4 ***Snyder***	Y	N	Y	Y	Y	Y
5 ***Rogers***	Y	N	Y	Y	N	Y
6 ***Hopkins***	N	Y	Y	N	Y	Y
7 Perkins	N	Y	Y	Y	N	Y
LOUISIANA						
1 ***Livingston***	Y	Y	N	N	N	N
2 Boggs	N	Y	Y	Y	N	Y
3 Tauzin	N	Y	Y	Y	N	Y
4 Roemer	N	Y	N	N	Y	Y
5 Huckaby	N	Y	?	N	?	?
6 ***Moore***	Y	Y	Y	?	N	Y
7 Breaux	N	Y	Y	Y	N	Y
8 Long	N	Y	Y	Y	N	Y
MAINE						
1 ***McKernan***	N	Y	N	Y	Y	Y
2 ***Snowe***	N	Y	Y	Y	Y	Y
MARYLAND						
1 Dyson	N	Y	Y	Y	N	Y
2 ***Bentley***	Y	N	N	Y	Y	Y
3 Mikulski	N	Y	Y	Y	N	Y
4 ***Holt***	Y	N	Y	N	N	Y
5 Hoyer	N	Y	?	Y	N	Y
6 Byron	N	Y	Y	Y	N	Y
7 Mitchell	N	Y	N	Y	Y	Y
8 Barnes	N	Y	Y	Y	Y	Y
MASSACHUSETTS						
1 ***Conte***	N	Y	N	Y	Y	N
2 Boland	N	Y	Y	Y	?	?
3 Early	N	Y	Y	Y	Y	Y
4 Frank	N	Y	Y	N	Y	Y
5 Atkins	N	Y	Y	Y	Y	Y
6 Mavroules	N	Y	Y	Y	Y	?
7 Markey	N	Y	Y	Y	Y	Y
8 O'Neill						
9 Moakley	N	Y	Y	Y	Y	Y
10 Studds	N	Y	Y	Y	Y	Y
11 Donnelly	N	Y	Y	Y	Y	Y
MICHIGAN						
1 Conyers	N	Y	Y	N	Y	Y
2 ***Pursell***	?	?	?	?	?	?
3 Wolpe	N	Y	Y	N	Y	Y
4 ***Siljander***	Y	N	?	N	Y	N
5 ***Henry***	Y	N	N	N	Y	N
6 Carr	N	Y	Y	Y	N	Y
7 Kildee	N	Y	Y	Y	Y	N
8 Traxler	N	Y	Y	?	N	Y
9 ***Vander Jagt***	Y	N	Y	Y	Y	Y
10 ***Schuette***	Y	N	N	N	Y	Y
11 ***Davis***	Y	Y	Y	Y	Y	Y
12 Bonior	N	Y	Y	Y	Y	Y
13 Crockett	N	Y	P	N	N	Y
14 Hertel	N	Y	Y	Y	Y	N
15 Ford	?	?	?	Y	N	Y
16 Dingell	?	?	?	?	Y	Y
17 Levin	N	Y	Y	Y	Y	Y
18 ***Broomfield***	Y	N	Y	N	Y	N
MINNESOTA						
1 Penny	N	Y	N	N	Y	Y
2 ***Weber***	Y	Y	N	N	Y	N
3 ***Frenzel***	N	N	N	N	Y	Y
4 Vento	N	Y	Y	Y	Y	N
5 Sabo	N	Y	Y	Y	N	Y
6 Sikorski	N	Y	N	N	Y	N

	129	130	131	132	133	134
7 ***Stangeland***	Y	N	N	N	Y	Y
8 Oberstar	N	Y	Y	Y	Y	Y
MISSISSIPPI						
1 Whitten	N	Y	Y	Y	N	Y
2 ***Franklin***	Y	N	N	N	N	Y
3 Montgomery	Y	N	Y	Y	N	Y
4 Dowdy	N	Y	Y	Y	N	Y
5 ***Lott***	Y	N	N	N	N	N
MISSOURI						
1 Clay	N	Y	N	Y	Y	Y
2 Young	N	Y	Y	Y	N	Y
3 Gephardt	N	Y	Y	Y	N	Y
4 Skelton	N	Y	Y	Y	N	Y
5 Wheat	N	Y	Y	N	Y	Y
6 ***Coleman***	Y	Y	N	N	N	Y
7 ***Taylor***	Y	N	N	Y	N	Y
8 ***Emerson***	?	?	?	?	N	Y
9 Volkmer	N	Y	Y	Y	N	Y
MONTANA						
1 Williams	N	Y	Y	Y	Y	Y
2 ***Marlenee***	Y	N	N	Y	N	Y
NEBRASKA						
1 ***Bereuter***	Y	N	N	Y	N	Y
2 ***Daub***	Y	Y	N	N	Y	Y
3 ***Smith***	Y	N	?	Y	N	Y
NEVADA						
1 Reid	N	Y	Y	Y	N	Y
2 ***Vucanovich***	Y	N	N	N	N	Y
NEW HAMPSHIRE						
1 ***Smith***	Y	N	N	N	Y	N
2 ***Gregg***	N	Y	N	N	Y	N
NEW JERSEY						
1 Florio	N	Y	Y	Y	Y	Y
2 Hughes	N	Y	Y	N	Y	Y
3 Howard	N	Y	Y	N	Y	Y
4 ***Smith***	N	Y	N	Y	Y	Y
5 ***Roukema***	N	Y	Y	Y	Y	N
6 Dwyer	N	Y	Y	Y	N	Y
7 ***Rinaldo***	N	Y	Y	Y	Y	Y
8 Roe	N	Y	Y	N	Y	Y
9 Torricelli	N	Y	Y	Y	Y	Y
10 Rodino	N	Y	Y	Y	Y	Y
11 ***Gallo***	N	Y	N	N	Y	Y
12 ***Courter***	N	Y	N	N	Y	Y
13 ***Saxton***	Y	Y	N	N	Y	Y
14 Guarini	N	Y	Y	Y	Y	Y
NEW MEXICO						
1 ***Lujan***	N	N	N	Y	Y	Y
2 ***Skeen***	Y	N	N	Y	N	Y
3 Richardson	N	Y	Y	Y	Y	Y
NEW YORK						
1 ***Carney***	N	N	N	Y	N	Y
2 Downey	N	Y	Y	Y	N	Y
3 Mrazek	N	Y	Y	Y	Y	Y
4 ***Lent***	Y	Y	N	Y	N	Y
5 ***McGrath***	N	Y	N	Y	N	Y
6 Addabbo	N	Y	Y	Y	N	Y
7 Ackerman	N	Y	Y	Y	Y	Y
8 Scheuer	N	Y	Y	Y	N	Y
9 Manton	N	Y	?	Y	Y	Y
10 Schumer	N	Y	Y	Y	Y	Y
11 Towns	N	Y	Y	Y	Y	Y
12 Owens	N	Y	Y	Y	N	Y
13 Solarz	N	Y	?	?	?	?
14 ***Molinari***	N	Y	Y	N	N	Y
15 ***Green***	N	Y	Y	Y	Y	N
16 Rangel	N	Y	?	Y	N	?
17 Weiss	N	Y	Y	N	Y	Y
18 Garcia	N	Y	Y	Y	N	Y
19 Biaggi	N	Y	Y	Y	N	Y
20 ***DioGuardi***	N	Y	N	Y	N	Y
21 ***Fish***	N	Y	Y	N	N	Y
22 ***Gilman***	N	Y	-	+	N	Y
23 Stratton	N	Y	Y	Y	N	Y
24 ***Solomon***	Y	N	N	N	Y	N
25 ***Boehlert***	N	Y	N	Y	N	Y
26 ***Martin***	N	Y	Y	N	N	Y
27 ***Wortley***	N	Y	Y	N	Y	Y
28 McHugh	N	Y	Y	Y	N	Y
29 ***Horton***	N	Y	Y	Y	N	Y
30 ***Eckert***	Y	N	N	N	Y	N
31 ***Kemp***	Y	N	?	Y	N	Y
32 LaFalce	N	Y	Y	Y	N	Y
33 Nowak	?	Y	Y	Y	N	Y
34 Lundine	N	Y	?	Y	Y	Y

	129	130	131	132	133	134
NORTH CAROLINA						
1 Jones	N	Y	Y	Y	N	Y
2 Valentine	N	Y	Y	Y	N	Y
3 Whitley	N	Y	Y	Y	N	Y
4 ***Cobey***	Y	N	N	N	N	Y
5 Neal	N	Y	Y	Y	?	?
6 ***Coble***	Y	N	?	Y	N	Y
7 Rose	N	Y	Y	Y	N	Y
8 Hefner	N	Y	Y	Y	N	Y
9 ***McMillan***	Y	N	N	Y	Y	N
10 ***Broyhill***	Y	N	Y	Y	Y	N
11 ***Hendon***	Y	N	N	?	Y	Y
NORTH DAKOTA						
AL Dorgan	N	Y	Y	Y	N	Y
OHIO						
1 Luken	N	Y	Y	Y	N	Y
2 ***Gradison***	?	?	Y	N	Y	N
3 Hall	N	Y	Y	Y	Y	Y
4 ***Oxley***	Y	N	N	N	Y	Y
5 ***Latta***	Y	N	N	N	Y	N
6 ***McEwen***	Y	N	N	N	Y	Y
7 ***DeWine***	N	N	N	N	Y	Y
8 ***Kindness***	Y	N	N	Y	Y	Y
9 Kaptur	N	Y	Y	Y	N	Y
10 ***Miller***	Y	N	N	N	Y	Y
11 Eckart	N	Y	Y	Y	N	Y
12 ***Kasich***	N	Y	N	Y	N	Y
13 Pease	N	Y	Y	Y	N	Y
14 Seiberling	N	Y	Y	Y	Y	Y
15 ***Wylie***	N	Y	Y	N	?	?
16 ***Regula***	N	N	Y	Y	Y	Y
17 Traficant	N	Y	Y	Y	Y	Y
18 Applegate	N	Y	?	Y	N	N
19 Feighan	N	Y	Y	Y	N	Y
20 Oakar	N	Y	Y	Y	N	Y
21 Stokes	N	Y	Y	Y	?	?
OKLAHOMA						
1 Jones	N	Y	Y	N	N	Y
2 Synar	N	Y	Y	Y	N	Y
3 Watkins	N	Y	Y	Y	N	Y
4 McCurdy	N	Y	Y	Y	N	Y
5 ***Edwards***	?	?	N	N	N	Y
6 English	N	Y	Y	Y	N	Y
OREGON						
1 AuCoin	N	Y	Y	N	N	Y
2 ***Smith, R.***	Y	N	N	N	Y	N
3 Wyden	N	Y	Y	Y	N	Y
4 Weaver	N	Y	Y	N	?	?
5 ***Smith, D.***	Y	N	N	N	Y	N
PENNSYLVANIA						
1 Foglietta	N	Y	Y	Y	Y	Y
2 Gray	N	Y	Y	Y	Y	Y
3 Borski	N	Y	Y	Y	Y	Y
4 Kolter	N	Y	Y	Y	N	Y
5 ***Schulze***	N	Y	Y	Y	N	N
6 Yatron	N	Y	Y	Y	N	Y
7 Edgar	N	Y	Y	Y	Y	N
8 Kostmayer	N	Y	Y	N	Y	Y
9 ***Shuster***	Y	N	N	N	Y	Y
10 ***McDade***	N	Y	N	Y	N	Y
11 Kanjorski	N	Y	Y	?	N	Y
12 Murtha	N	Y	Y	N	N	Y
13 ***Coughlin***	N	Y	N	N	Y	Y
14 Coyne	N	Y	Y	Y	Y	Y
15 ***Ritter***	N	N	Y	N	Y	N
16 ***Walker***	Y	N	N	N	Y	N
17 ***Gekas***	Y	Y	N	N	Y	N
18 Walgren	N	Y	Y	Y	N	Y
19 ***Goodling***	Y	Y	N	N	Y	Y
20 Gaydos	N	Y	Y	Y	N	Y
21 ***Ridge***	Y	N	N	N	Y	Y
22 Murphy	N	Y	Y	Y	N	Y
23 ***Clinger***	Y	N	Y	Y	Y	Y
RHODE ISLAND						
1 St Germain	N	Y	Y	Y	?	?
2 ***Schneider***	N	Y	Y	Y	Y	N
SOUTH CAROLINA						
1 ***Hartnett***	Y	N	N	N	Y	N
2 ***Spence***	Y	N	N	N	N	Y
3 Derrick	N	Y	N	Y	?	?
4 ***Campbell***	?	N	Y	Y	N	Y
5 Spratt	-	+	+	+	+	+
6 Tallon	N	Y	Y	Y	Y	Y
SOUTH DAKOTA						
AL Daschle	N	Y	Y	Y	N	Y

	129	130	131	132	133	134
TENNESSEE						
1 ***Quillen***	Y	N	N	Y	N	Y
2 ***Duncan***	Y	Y	Y	Y	N	Y
3 Lloyd	N	Y	Y	Y	N	Y
4 Cooper	N	Y	Y	Y	Y	Y
5 Boner	N	Y	Y	Y	N	Y
6 Gordon	N	Y	Y	Y	N	Y
7 ***Sundquist***	Y	N	N	N	Y	Y
8 Jones	N	Y	Y	Y	N	Y
9 Ford	N	Y	?	Y	Y	Y
TEXAS						
1 Vacancy						
2 Wilson	?	?	?	?	?	?
3 ***Bartlett***	Y	N	N	N	Y	N
4 Hall, R.	Y	N	Y	N	N	Y
5 Bryant	N	Y	Y	Y	Y	Y
6 ***Barton***	Y	N	N	N	Y	Y
7 ***Archer***	Y	N	Y	N	Y	Y
8 ***Fields***	Y	N	N	N	Y	Y
9 Brooks	N	Y	Y	Y	N	Y
10 Pickle	N	Y	Y	Y	N	Y
11 Leath	Y	N	Y	?	?	?
12 Wright	N	Y	Y	Y	N	Y
13 ***Boulter***	Y	N	N	N	N	N
14 ***Sweeney***	Y	N	?	N	Y	N
15 de la Garza	N	Y	Y	Y	Y	Y
16 Coleman	N	Y	Y	Y	N	Y
17 Stenholm	Y	Y	N	Y	Y	Y
18 Leland	N	Y	Y	N	Y	Y
19 ***Combest***	Y	N	N	N	Y	Y
20 Gonzalez	N	Y	Y	Y	N	Y
21 ***Loeffler***	Y	N	N	N	N	Y
22 ***DeLay***	Y	N	Y	Y	N	Y
23 Bustamante	N	Y	Y	Y	N	Y
24 Frost	N	Y	Y	Y	N	Y
25 Andrews	N	Y	Y	Y	Y	Y
26 ***Armey***	Y	N	?	N	Y	N
27 Ortiz	N	Y	Y	Y	N	Y
UTAH						
1 ***Hansen***	Y	N	Y	?	Y	N
2 ***Monson***	Y	N	?	N	Y	Y
3 ***Nielson***	Y	N	N	N	Y	Y
VERMONT						
AL ***Jeffords***	N	Y	Y	Y	Y	N
VIRGINIA						
1 ***Bateman***	Y	N	Y	N	N	Y
2 ***Whitehurst***	Y	N	Y	Y	N	Y
3 ***Bliley***	N	Y	?	Y	N	Y
4 Sisisky	N	Y	Y	Y	N	?
5 Daniel	Y	N	Y	Y	N	Y
6 Olin	N	Y	Y	Y	Y	N
7 ***Slaughter***	Y	N	N	N	N	Y
8 ***Parris***	Y	N	N	N	Y	Y
9 Boucher	N	Y	Y	Y	N	Y
10 ***Wolf***	Y	N	N	Y	Y	Y
WASHINGTON						
1 ***Miller***	N	Y	N	N	Y	N
2 Swift	N	Y	Y	Y	N	Y
3 Bonker	N	Y	Y	Y	N	Y
4 ***Morrison***	Y	Y	N	Y	N	Y
5 Foley	N	Y	Y	Y	N	Y
6 Dicks	N	Y	Y	Y	N	Y
7 Lowry	N	Y	Y	Y	Y	Y
8 ***Chandler***	Y	N	N	Y	Y	Y
WEST VIRGINIA						
1 Mollohan	N	Y	Y	Y	N	Y
2 Staggers	N	Y	Y	Y	N	Y
3 Wise	N	Y	Y	Y	?	?
4 Rahall	N	Y	Y	Y	N	?
WISCONSIN						
1 Aspin	N	Y	Y	Y	N	Y
2 Kastenmeier	N	Y	Y	N	Y	N
3 ***Gunderson***	Y	N	N	Y	Y	Y
4 Kleczka	N	Y	Y	Y	N	N
5 Moody	N	Y	Y	Y	Y	N
6 ***Petri***	Y	N	Y	N	Y	N
7 Obey	N	Y	?	Y	N	N
8 ***Roth***	Y	N	N	N	N	N
9 ***Sensenbrenner***	Y	N	N	N	Y	N
WYOMING						
AL ***Cheney***	Y	N	N	Y	N	Y

Southern states - Ala., Ark., Fla., Ga., Ky., La., Miss., N.C., Okla., S.C., Tenn., Texas, Va.

* The *Congressional Record* vote number is different from the CQ vote number because the *Record* includes quorum calls in its tally. CQ does not publish quorum call votes.

135. Procedural Motion. Combest, R-Texas, motion to approve the House *Journal* of Monday, June 10. Motion agreed to 254-145: R 35-135; D 219-10 (ND 146-7, SD 73-3), June 11, 1985.

136. HR 2577. Supplemental Appropriations, Fiscal 1985. Brown, R-Colo., amendment to cut $500 million in economic aid for Egypt. Rejected 110-314: R 76-103; D 34-211 (ND 15-151, SD 19-60), June 11, 1985.

137. HR 2577. Supplemental Appropriations, Fiscal 1985. Walker, R-Pa., amendments to cut all supplemental appropriations for the House of Representatives and the executive branch. Rejected en bloc 202-217: R 150-27; D 52-190 (ND 22-142, SD 30-48), June 11, 1985.

138. HR 2577. Supplemental Appropriations, Fiscal 1985. Zschau, R-Calif., amendment to cut all supplemental appropriations for discretionary programs by 5 percent. Rejected 190-226: R 123-54; D 67-172 (ND 26-135, SD 41-37), June 11, 1985.

139. Procedural Motion. McCain, R-Ariz., motion to approve the House *Journal* of Tuesday, June 11. Motion agreed to 251-142: R 40-131; D 211-11 (ND 140-8, SD 71-3), June 12, 1985.

140. HR 2577. Supplemental Appropriations, Fiscal 1985. Boland, D-Mass., amendment to the McDade, R-Pa., amendment, to continue indefinitely the prohibition of any funding by U.S. intelligence agencies that would support, directly or indirectly, military or paramilitary operations in Nicaragua. Rejected 196-232: R 7-174; D 189-58 (ND 156-11, SD 33-47), June 12, 1985. A "nay" was a vote supporting the president's position.

141. HR 2577. Supplemental Appropriations, Fiscal 1985. Gephardt, D-Mo., amendment to the McDade, R-Pa., amendment, to delay expenditure of "humanitarian" assistance to the Nicaraguan rebels until six months after enactment of the bill, to encourage negotiations under the auspices of the "Contadora" countries or through other diplomatic channels. After six months, the assistance would be made available if the president submitted a request to Congress and Congress passed a joint resolution approving his request. Rejected 172-259: R 3-179; D 169-80 (ND 150-19, SD 19-61), June 12, 1985. A "nay" was a vote supporting the president's position.

142. HR 2577. Supplemental Appropriations, Fiscal 1985. McDade, R-Pa., amendment to provide $27 million in "humanitarian" assistance to the Nicaraguan rebels, to be allocated in three equal installments, coinciding with the president's submission of reports every 90 days until March 31, 1986, by a U.S. agency other than the CIA or the Department of Defense. The amendment also provided $2 million for implementation of a Central America peace agreement reached under the auspices of the "Contadora" countries. Adopted 248-184: R 175-7; D 73-177 (ND 14-155, SD 59-22), June 12, 1985. A "yea" was a vote supporting the president's position.

KEY

Y Voted for (yea).
\# Paired for.
\+ Announced for.
N Voted against (nay).
X Paired against.
\- Announced against.
P Voted "present".
C Voted "present" to avoid possible conflict of interest.
? Did not vote or otherwise make a position known.

Democrats ***Republicans***

	135	136	137	138	139	140	141	142
ALABAMA								
1 ***Callahan***	N	N	Y	Y	N	N	N	Y
2 ***Dickinson***	N	Y	N	N	N	N	N	Y
3 Nichols	Y	?	Y	Y	Y	N	N	Y
4 Bevill	Y	N	Y	Y	Y	N	N	Y
5 Flippo	Y	N	Y	Y	Y	N	N	Y
6 Erdreich	Y	N	Y	Y	Y	N	N	Y
7 Shelby	Y	N	N	N	?	N	N	Y
ALASKA								
AL ***Young***	N	N	N	N	N	N	N	Y
ARIZONA								
1 ***McCain***	N	N	Y	Y	N	N	N	Y
2 Udall	Y	N	N	N	Y	Y	Y	N
3 ***Stump***	N	Y	Y	Y	N	N	N	Y
4 ***Rudd***	Y	Y	Y	N	Y	N	N	Y
5 ***Kolbe***	N	N	Y	Y	N	N	N	Y
ARKANSAS								
1 Alexander	Y	N	N	N	Y	Y	Y	N
2 Robinson	Y	Y	Y	Y	Y	N	N	Y
3 ***Hammerschmidt***	N	N	Y	Y	Y	N	N	Y
4 Anthony	Y	N	N	N	Y	Y	Y	N
CALIFORNIA								
1 Bosco	Y	N	N	N	Y	?	Y	N
2 ***Chappie***	N	Y	Y	Y	N	N	N	Y
3 Matsui	Y	N	N	N	Y	Y	Y	N
4 Fazio	Y	N	N	N	Y	Y	Y	N
5 Burton	Y	N	N	N	?	Y	Y	N
6 Boxer	Y	N	N	N	Y	Y	Y	N
7 Miller	Y	N	N	N	Y	Y	Y	N
8 Dellums	Y	N	N	?	Y	Y	Y	N
9 Stark	Y	N	N	N	Y	Y	Y	N
10 Edwards	Y	N	N	N	Y	Y	Y	N
11 Lantos	Y	N	N	N	Y	Y	Y	N
12 ***Zschau***	N	N	Y	Y	N	N	N	Y
13 Mineta	Y	N	N	N	Y	Y	Y	N
14 ***Shumway***	N	Y	Y	Y	N	N	N	Y
15 Coelho	Y	N	N	?	Y	Y	Y	N
16 Panetta	Y	N	N	Y	Y	Y	Y	N
17 ***Pashayan***	N	Y	Y	Y	N	N	N	Y
18 Lehman	Y	N	N	N	Y	Y	Y	N
19 ***Lagomarsino***	N	N	Y	Y	N	N	N	Y
20 ***Thomas***	N	Y	Y	Y	N	N	N	Y
21 ***Fiedler***	N	Y	Y	N	N	N	N	Y
22 ***Moorhead***	N	N	Y	Y	N	N	N	Y
23 Beilenson	Y	N	N	N	Y	Y	Y	N
24 Waxman	Y	N	N	N	?	Y	Y	N
25 Roybal	Y	N	N	N	Y	Y	Y	N
26 Berman	Y	N	N	N	Y	Y	Y	N
27 Levine	Y	N	N	N	Y	Y	Y	N
28 Dixon	Y	N	N	N	?	Y	Y	N
29 Hawkins	?	?	?	?	?	?	?	?
30 Martinez	Y	N	N	N	Y	Y	Y	N
31 Dymally	P	N	N	N	P	Y	Y	N
32 Anderson	Y	Y	N	N	Y	Y	Y	N
33 ***Dreier***	N	Y	Y	Y	N	N	N	Y
34 Torres	Y	N	N	N	Y	Y	Y	N
35 ***Lewis***	N	N	N	N	N	N	N	Y
36 Brown	Y	N	?	?	Y	Y	Y	N
37 ***McCandless***	N	Y	Y	Y	N	N	N	Y
38 ***Dornan***	N	N	?	Y	?	N	N	Y
39 ***Dannemeyer***	N	Y	Y	Y	N	N	N	Y
40 ***Badham***	N	N	Y	Y	N	N	N	Y
41 ***Lowery***	N	N	Y	N	N	N	N	Y
42 ***Lungren***	N	N	Y	Y	N	N	N	Y
43 ***Packard***	N	N	Y	Y	N	N	N	Y
44 Bates	Y	Y	N	Y	Y	Y	Y	N
45 ***Hunter***	N	Y	Y	N	N	N	N	Y
COLORADO								
1 Schroeder	N	Y	N	Y	N	Y	Y	N
2 Wirth	Y	N	N	Y	Y	Y	Y	N
3 ***Strang***	N	Y	Y	Y	N	N	N	Y
4 ***Brown***	N	Y	Y	Y	N	N	N	Y
5 ***Kramer***	N	Y	Y	Y	N	N	N	Y
6 ***Schaefer***	N	Y	Y	Y	N	N	N	Y
CONNECTICUT								
1 Kennelly	Y	N	N	N	Y	Y	Y	N
2 Gejdenson	Y	N	N	N	Y	Y	Y	N
3 Morrison	Y	N	N	N	Y	Y	Y	N
4 ***McKinney***	Y	N	N	N	Y	N	N	Y
5 ***Rowland***	Y	N	Y	Y	?	N	N	Y
6 ***Johnson***	Y	N	Y	N	Y	N	N	Y
DELAWARE								
AL Carper	Y	N	Y	Y	Y	Y	Y	N
FLORIDA								
1 Hutto	Y	N	Y	Y	Y	N	N	Y
2 Fuqua	Y	N	N	N	Y	N	N	Y
3 Bennett	Y	N	Y	Y	Y	Y	N	Y
4 Chappell	Y	N	N	N	Y	N	N	Y
5 ***McCollum***	Y	Y	Y	Y	N	N	N	Y
6 MacKay	Y	N	N	Y	Y	Y	N	Y
7 Gibbons	?	N	N	Y	?	N	N	Y
8 ***Young***	N	N	Y	Y	N	N	N	Y
9 ***Bilirakis***	N	Y	Y	Y	N	N	N	Y
10 ***Ireland***	N	N	Y	Y	N	N	N	Y
11 Nelson	Y	N	Y	Y	Y	N	N	Y
12 ***Lewis***	N	N	Y	Y	N	N	N	Y
13 ***Mack***	N	N	Y	Y	N	N	N	Y
14 Mica	Y	N	N	Y	Y	N	N	Y
15 ***Shaw***	N	N	Y	N	N	N	N	Y
16 Smith	Y	N	N	N	P	Y	N	Y
17 Lehman	Y	N	N	N	Y	Y	Y	N
18 Pepper	Y	N	N	N	?	Y	N	Y
19 Fascell	Y	N	N	N	Y	N	N	Y
GEORGIA								
1 Thomas	Y	N	N	Y	Y	N	N	Y
2 Hatcher	Y	N	N	N	Y	N	N	Y
3 Ray	Y	Y	Y	Y	Y	N	N	Y
4 ***Swindall***	N	Y	Y	Y	N	N	N	Y
5 Fowler	Y	N	N	Y	Y	Y	Y	N
6 ***Gingrich***	?	N	Y	Y	N	N	N	Y
7 Darden	Y	Y	N	Y	Y	N	N	Y
8 Rowland	Y	N	N	Y	Y	N	N	Y
9 Jenkins	Y	Y	N	Y	Y	N	N	Y
10 Barnard	Y	N	N	Y	Y	N	N	Y
HAWAII								
1 Heftel	?	N	Y	Y	?	N	N	Y
2 Akaka	?	?	?	?	Y	Y	Y	N
IDAHO								
1 ***Craig***	N	Y	Y	Y	N	N	N	Y
2 Stallings	Y	N	N	Y	Y	Y	N	Y
ILLINOIS								
1 Hayes	Y	N	N	N	Y	Y	Y	N
2 Savage	Y	N	N	N	Y	Y	Y	N
3 Russo	Y	N	N	Y	Y	Y	Y	N
4 ***O'Brien***	Y	N	N	N	?	N	N	Y
5 Lipinski	Y	N	N	N	Y	N	N	Y
6 ***Hyde***	N	N	N	Y	N	N	N	Y
7 Collins	Y	N	N	N	Y	Y	Y	N
8 Rostenkowski	Y	N	N	N	Y	Y	Y	N
9 Yates	Y	N	N	N	Y	Y	Y	N
10 ***Porter***	N	N	Y	Y	N	N	N	Y
11 Annunzio	Y	N	N	N	Y	Y	Y	N
12 ***Crane***	N	Y	Y	Y	N	N	N	Y
13 ***Fawell***	N	N	Y	Y	N	N	N	Y
14 ***Grotberg***	N	N	Y	Y	-	N	N	Y
15 ***Madigan***	N	N	Y	Y	N	N	N	Y
16 ***Martin***	N	Y	Y	Y	N	N	N	Y
17 Evans	Y	N	N	N	Y	Y	Y	N
18 ***Michel***	N	N	N	N	Y	N	N	Y
19 Bruce	Y	N	N	N	Y	Y	Y	N
20 Durbin	N	N	N	N	N	Y	Y	N
21 Price	Y	N	N	N	Y	Y	Y	Y
22 Gray	Y	Y	N	N	Y	Y	Y	N
INDIANA								
1 Visclosky	Y	N	N	N	Y	Y	Y	N
2 Sharp	Y	N	Y	Y	Y	Y	Y	N
3 ***Hiler***	N	Y	Y	Y	N	N	N	Y
4 ***Coats***	N	Y	Y	Y	N	N	N	Y
5 ***Hillis***	N	Y	Y	Y	?	N	N	Y

ND - Northern Democrats SD - Southern Democrats

* Corresponding to Congressional Record Votes 147, 148, 150, 152, 153, 154, 155, 156

	135	136	137	138	139	140	141	142
6 ***Burton***	N	Y	Y	Y	?	N	N	Y
7 ***Myers***	Y	N	N	Y	Y	N	N	Y
8 McCloskey	Y	N	N	N	Y	Y	Y	N
9 Hamilton	Y	N	N	Y	Y	Y	Y	N
10 Jacobs	N	Y	Y	Y	N	Y	Y	N
IOWA								
1 ***Leach***	N	N	Y	Y	N	Y	Y	N
2 ***Tauke***	N	Y	Y	Y	N	N	N	Y
3 ***Evans***	N	Y	Y	N	?	N	N	N
4 Smith	Y	N	N	N	Y	Y	Y	N
5 ***Lightfoot***	N	Y	Y	Y	N	N	N	Y
6 Bedell	Y	N	Y	N	Y	Y	Y	N
KANSAS								
1 ***Roberts***	N	Y	Y	Y	N	N	N	Y
2 Slattery	Y	N	Y	Y	Y	N	N	N
3 ***Meyers***	Y	N	Y	Y	N	N	N	Y
4 Glickman	Y	N	Y	N	Y	Y	N	N
5 ***Whittaker***	?	Y	Y	Y	N	N	N	Y
KENTUCKY								
1 Hubbard	Y	Y	Y	Y	Y	N	N	Y
2 Natcher	Y	N	N	N	Y	Y	N	N
3 Mazzoli	Y	N	N	N	Y	N	N	Y
4 ***Snyder***	?	Y	Y	Y	Y	N	N	Y
5 ***Rogers***	Y	Y	Y	Y	N	N	N	Y
6 ***Hopkins***	Y	Y	Y	Y	Y	N	N	Y
7 Perkins	Y	N	N	N	Y	Y	Y	N
LOUISIANA								
1 ***Livingston***	N	N	Y	Y	N	N	N	Y
2 Boggs	Y	N	N	N	Y	Y	N	N
3 Tauzin	Y	Y	Y	Y	Y	N	N	Y
4 Roemer	N	Y	Y	Y	N	N	N	Y
5 Huckaby	Y	N	Y	Y	Y	N	N	Y
6 ***Moore***	Y	N	Y	Y	Y	N	N	Y
7 Breaux	Y	Y	Y	Y	Y	N	N	Y
8 Long	Y	N	N	N	Y	N	N	Y
MAINE								
1 ***McKernan***	N	N	Y	Y	N	N	N	Y
2 ***Snowe***	N	N	Y	Y	Y	N	N	Y
MARYLAND								
1 Dyson	Y	Y	Y	Y	?	N	N	Y
2 ***Bentley***	N	N	Y	N	N	N	N	Y
3 Mikulski	Y	N	N	N	Y	Y	Y	N
4 ***Holt***	Y	N	Y	N	Y	N	N	Y
5 Hoyer	Y	N	N	N	Y	Y	Y	N
6 Byron	Y	N	Y	Y	Y	N	N	Y
7 Mitchell	N	N	N	N	N	?	Y	N
8 Barnes	Y	N	N	N	Y	Y	Y	N
MASSACHUSETTS								
1 ***Conte***	N	N	N	N	N	Y	N	N
2 Boland	Y	N	N	N	Y	Y	Y	N
3 Early	Y	Y	Y	N	Y	Y	Y	N
4 Frank	Y	N	N	N	Y	Y	Y	N
5 Atkins	Y	N	N	N	P	Y	Y	N
6 Mavroules	Y	N	N	N	Y	Y	Y	N
7 Markey	Y	N	N	N	Y	Y	Y	N
8 O'Neill								
9 Moakley	?	N	N	N	N	Y	Y	N
10 Studds	?	N	N	N	Y	Y	Y	N
11 Donnelly	Y	Y	N	Y	Y	Y	N	N
MICHIGAN								
1 Conyers	?	N	N	N	Y	Y	Y	N
2 ***Pursell***	Y	N	Y	Y	Y	N	N	Y
3 Wolpe	Y	N	N	N	Y	Y	Y	N
4 ***Siljander***	N	N	Y	N	N	N	N	Y
5 ***Henry***	N	Y	Y	Y	N	N	N	Y
6 Carr	Y	N	N	N	Y	Y	Y	N
7 Kildee	Y	N	N	N	Y	Y	Y	N
8 Traxler	Y	N	N	N	Y	Y	Y	N
9 ***Vander Jagt***	Y	N	Y	Y	Y	N	N	Y
10 ***Schuette***	N	Y	Y	N	N	N	N	Y
11 ***Davis***	Y	Y	N	N	Y	N	N	Y
12 Bonior	Y	N	N	N	Y	Y	Y	N
13 Crockett	Y	N	N	N	Y	Y	Y	N
14 Hertel	Y	N	N	N	Y	Y	Y	N
15 Ford	?	N	N	N	?	Y	Y	N
16 Dingell	Y	N	N	N	?	Y	Y	N
17 Levin	Y	N	N	N	Y	Y	Y	N
18 ***Broomfield***	Y	N	Y	Y	Y	N	N	Y
MINNESOTA								
1 Penny	N	N	Y	Y	N	Y	Y	N
2 ***Weber***	N	N	Y	N	N	N	N	Y
3 ***Frenzel***	N	N	Y	Y	N	N	N	Y
4 Vento	Y	N	N	N	Y	Y	Y	N
5 Sabo	?	N	N	N	Y	Y	Y	N
6 Sikorski	N	N	N	N	N	Y	Y	N
7 ***Stangeland***	N	N	Y	N	N	N	N	Y
8 Oberstar	Y	N	N	N	Y	Y	Y	N
MISSISSIPPI								
1 Whitten	Y	Y	N	N	Y	Y	N	Y
2 ***Franklin***	?	Y	Y	Y	N	N	N	Y
3 Montgomery	Y	Y	Y	Y	Y	N	N	Y
4 Dowdy	?	N	N	N	P	N	N	Y
5 ***Lott***	N	Y	Y	Y	N	N	N	Y
MISSOURI								
1 Clay	N	N	N	N	N	Y	Y	N
2 Young	Y	N	N	N	Y	Y	N	N
3 Gephardt	Y	N	N	N	Y	Y	Y	N
4 Skelton	Y	N	N	Y	Y	N	N	Y
5 Wheat	Y	N	N	N	Y	Y	Y	N
6 ***Coleman***	?	?	?	?	N	N	N	Y
7 ***Taylor***	N	Y	Y	?	N	N	N	Y
8 ***Emerson***	N	Y	Y	Y	N	N	N	Y
9 Volkmer	Y	N	Y	N	?	Y	Y	N
MONTANA								
1 Williams	?	N	N	N	Y	Y	Y	N
2 ***Marlenee***	Y	Y	Y	N	N	N	N	Y
NEBRASKA								
1 ***Bereuter***	N	Y	Y	N	N	N	N	Y
2 ***Daub***	N	Y	Y	Y	N	N	N	Y
3 ***Smith***	Y	Y	Y	N	Y	N	N	Y
NEVADA								
1 Reid	Y	N	N	N	Y	Y	N	N
2 ***Vucanovich***	N	Y	Y	Y	N	N	N	Y
NEW HAMPSHIRE								
1 ***Smith***	N	Y	Y	Y	N	N	N	Y
2 ***Gregg***	N	Y	Y	Y	N	N	N	Y
NEW JERSEY								
1 Florio	Y	N	N	N	Y	Y	Y	N
2 Hughes	Y	N	Y	Y	Y	Y	Y	N
3 Howard	Y	N	N	N	?	Y	Y	N
4 ***Smith***	Y	N	N	N	Y	N	N	Y
5 ***Roukema***	Y	N	Y	N	Y	Y	N	Y
6 Dwyer	Y	N	N	N	Y	Y	Y	N
7 ***Rinaldo***	Y	N	Y	N	Y	N	N	Y
8 Roe	Y	N	N	N	Y	Y	Y	N
9 Torricelli	Y	N	N	?	?	Y	Y	N
10 Rodino	Y	N	N	N	Y	Y	Y	N
11 ***Gallo***	N	N	Y	N	?	N	N	Y
12 ***Courter***	N	N	Y	N	N	N	N	Y
13 ***Saxton***	N	N	Y	Y	N	N	N	Y
14 Guarini	Y	N	N	N	Y	Y	Y	N
NEW MEXICO								
1 ***Lujan***	N	Y	Y	Y	N	N	N	Y
2 ***Skeen***	N	N	Y	Y	N	N	N	Y
3 Richardson	Y	N	N	N	Y	Y	N	Y
NEW YORK								
1 ***Carney***	N	N	N	Y	N	N	N	Y
2 Downey	Y	N	N	?	Y	Y	Y	N
3 Mrazek	Y	N	N	N	Y	Y	Y	N
4 ***Lent***	N	N	N	N	N	N	N	Y
5 ***McGrath***	N	N	N	N	N	N	N	Y
6 Addabbo	Y	N	?	N	Y	Y	Y	N
7 Ackerman	Y	N	N	N	Y	Y	Y	N
8 Scheuer	Y	N	N	N	Y	Y	Y	N
9 Manton	?	N	N	N	Y	Y	Y	N
10 Schumer	Y	N	N	N	Y	Y	Y	N
11 Towns	Y	N	N	N	Y	Y	Y	N
12 Owens	?	N	N	N	Y	Y	Y	N
13 Solarz	P	N	N	N	Y	Y	Y	N
14 ***Molinari***	N	N	N	N	N	N	N	Y
15 ***Green***	Y	N	N	N	Y	Y	Y	N
16 Rangel	Y	N	N	N	Y	Y	Y	N
17 Weiss	Y	N	N	N	Y	Y	Y	N
18 Garcia	Y	N	N	N	?	Y	Y	N
19 Biaggi	Y	N	N	N	Y	N	N	Y
20 ***DioGuardi***	N	N	Y	N	?	N	N	Y
21 ***Fish***	Y	N	N	N	Y	N	N	Y
22 ***Gilman***	N	N	N	N	N	N	N	Y
23 Stratton	Y	N	N	N	?	N	N	Y
24 ***Solomon***	N	Y	Y	Y	N	N	N	Y
25 ***Boehlert***	N	N	Y	Y	N	N	N	N
26 ***Martin***	N	N	?	N	Y	N	N	Y
27 ***Wortley***	Y	N	Y	N	Y	N	N	Y
28 McHugh	Y	N	N	N	Y	Y	Y	N
29 ***Horton***	Y	N	N	N	Y	N	N	Y
30 ***Eckert***	N	N	Y	Y	N	N	N	Y
31 ***Kemp***	?	N	Y	?	N	N	N	Y
32 LaFalce	Y	N	N	Y	Y	Y	Y	N
33 Nowak	Y	N	N	Y	Y	Y	Y	N
34 Lundine	Y	N	N	Y	Y	Y	Y	N
NORTH CAROLINA								
1 Jones	Y	N	N	?	Y	Y	Y	N
2 Valentine	Y	Y	Y	Y	Y	N	N	N
3 Whitley	Y	N	N	Y	Y	Y	N	Y
4 ***Cobey***	N	Y	Y	N	N	N	N	Y
5 Neal	Y	N	N	Y	Y	Y	Y	N
6 ***Coble***	N	Y	Y	Y	N	N	N	Y
7 Rose	Y	N	N	N	Y	Y	Y	N
8 Hefner	Y	Y	N	N	Y	Y	N	Y
9 ***McMillan***	Y	N	Y	Y	N	N	N	Y
10 ***Broyhill***	?	Y	Y	Y	Y	N	N	Y
11 ***Hendon***	N	N	Y	N	N	N	N	Y
NORTH DAKOTA								
AL Dorgan	Y	N	Y	N	Y	Y	Y	N
OHIO								
1 Luken	Y	N	N	N	Y	Y	Y	N
2 ***Gradison***	Y	Y	Y	Y	Y	N	N	Y
3 Hall	Y	N	N	Y	Y	Y	Y	N
4 ***Oxley***	N	N	Y	Y	N	N	N	Y
5 ***Latta***	N	N	Y	Y	N	N	N	Y
6 ***McEwen***	?	?	?	?	?	N	N	Y
7 ***DeWine***	?	N	Y	Y	N	N	N	Y
8 ***Kindness***	N	Y	Y	Y	N	N	N	Y
9 Kaptur	Y	N	Y	N	Y	Y	Y	N
10 ***Miller***	N	Y	Y	Y	N	N	N	Y
11 Eckart	Y	N	Y	N	Y	Y	Y	N
12 ***Kasich***	N	N	Y	Y	?	N	N	Y
13 Pease	Y	N	N	Y	Y	Y	Y	N
14 Seiberling	?	N	N	N	?	Y	Y	N
15 ***Wylie***	Y	N	Y	Y	Y	N	N	Y
16 ***Regula***	Y	N	Y	N	Y	N	N	Y
17 Traficant	Y	N	N	N	Y	Y	Y	N
18 Applegate	?	Y	Y	Y	?	Y	Y	N
19 Feighan	Y	N	N	N	Y	Y	Y	N
20 Oakar	Y	N	N	N	Y	Y	Y	N
21 Stokes	Y	N	N	N	?	Y	Y	N
OKLAHOMA								
1 Jones	Y	N	Y	Y	Y	N	N	Y
2 Synar	P	N	N	N	Y	Y	Y	N
3 Watkins	Y	Y	Y	N	Y	N	N	Y
4 McCurdy	Y	N	Y	Y	Y	N	N	Y
5 ***Edwards***	N	N	Y	N	N	N	N	Y
6 English	Y	Y	Y	Y	Y	N	N	Y
OREGON								
1 AuCoin	Y	N	N	N	?	Y	Y	N
2 ***Smith, R.***	N	Y	Y	Y	N	N	N	Y
3 Wyden	Y	Y	N	N	Y	Y	Y	N
4 Weaver	?	?	?	?	Y	Y	Y	N
5 ***Smith, D.***	N	Y	Y	Y	N	N	N	Y
PENNSYLVANIA								
1 Foglietta	Y	N	N	N	Y	Y	Y	N
2 Gray	Y	N	N	N	Y	Y	Y	N
3 Borski	Y	N	N	N	Y	Y	Y	N
4 Kolter	Y	Y	N	N	Y	Y	Y	N
5 ***Schulze***	N	N	Y	N	N	?	N	Y
6 Yatron	Y	N	Y	N	Y	Y	Y	N
7 Edgar	Y	N	N	N	Y	Y	Y	N
8 Kostmayer	Y	N	N	N	Y	Y	Y	N
9 ***Shuster***	N	Y	Y	Y	N	N	N	Y
10 ***McDade***	N	N	N	N	N	N	N	Y
11 Kanjorski	Y	N	Y	Y	Y	Y	N	Y
12 Murtha	Y	N	N	N	Y	N	N	Y
13 ***Coughlin***	N	N	N	N	N	N	N	Y
14 Coyne	Y	N	N	N	Y	Y	Y	N
15 ***Ritter***	N	Y	Y	Y	N	N	N	Y
16 ***Walker***	N	Y	Y	Y	N	N	N	Y
17 ***Gekas***	N	N	Y	Y	N	N	N	Y
18 Walgren	Y	N	Y	N	Y	Y	Y	N
19 ***Goodling***	N	Y	Y	Y	N	N	N	Y
20 Gaydos	Y	Y	N	N	Y	Y	N	N
21 ***Ridge***	N	N	Y	Y	N	N	Y	Y
22 Murphy	Y	Y	Y	N	Y	N	Y	N
23 ***Clinger***	-	-	+	+	Y	Y	N	Y
RHODE ISLAND								
1 St Germain	Y	N	N	N	Y	Y	Y	N
2 ***Schneider***	Y	N	Y	N	Y	Y	N	N
SOUTH CAROLINA								
1 ***Hartnett***	N	Y	Y	Y	N	N	N	Y
2 ***Spence***	N	N	Y	Y	N	N	N	Y
3 Derrick	N	N	N	Y	N	Y	N	Y
4 ***Campbell***	N	N	Y	Y	N	N	N	Y
5 Spratt	Y	N	N	Y	Y	Y	N	Y
6 Tallon	?	Y	Y	Y	Y	N	N	Y
SOUTH DAKOTA								
AL Daschle	Y	N	N	N	Y	Y	Y	N
TENNESSEE								
1 ***Quillen***	N	N	N	N	Y	N	N	Y
2 ***Duncan***	Y	N	Y	N	Y	N	N	Y
3 Lloyd	Y	Y	Y	Y	Y	N	N	Y
4 Cooper	Y	N	N	Y	Y	N	N	Y
5 Boner	Y	N	Y	Y	Y	N	N	N
6 Gordon	Y	Y	Y	N	Y	N	N	Y
7 ***Sundquist***	N	Y	Y	Y	N	N	N	Y
8 Jones	Y	N	N	N	Y	Y	N	Y
9 Ford	Y	N	?	N	Y	Y	Y	N
TEXAS								
1 Vacancy								
2 Wilson	?	?	?	?	?	N	N	Y
3 ***Bartlett***	N	N	Y	Y	N	N	N	Y
4 Hall, R.	Y	Y	Y	Y	Y	N	N	Y
5 Bryant	Y	N	N	N	Y	Y	Y	N
6 ***Barton***	N	N	Y	Y	N	N	N	Y
7 ***Archer***	Y	Y	Y	Y	Y	N	N	Y
8 ***Fields***	?	Y	Y	Y	N	N	N	Y
9 Brooks	Y	N	N	N	Y	Y	Y	N
10 Pickle	Y	N	N	?	Y	Y	N	Y
11 Leath	Y	N	Y	N	Y	N	N	Y
12 Wright	Y	N	N	N	Y	Y	Y	N
13 ***Boulter***	N	Y	Y	Y	N	N	N	Y
14 ***Sweeney***	?	N	Y	Y	Y	N	N	Y
15 de la Garza	Y	N	N	N	Y	N	Y	Y
16 Coleman	Y	N	N	N	Y	Y	Y	Y
17 Stenholm	N	Y	Y	Y	N	N	N	Y
18 Leland	Y	N	N	N	Y	Y	Y	N
19 ***Combest***	N	Y	Y	Y	N	N	N	Y
20 Gonzalez	Y	N	N	N	Y	Y	P	N
21 ***Loeffler***	N	N	Y	Y	N	N	N	Y
22 ***DeLay***	N	Y	Y	Y	N	N	N	Y
23 Bustamante	Y	N	?	N	Y	?	N	Y
24 Frost	Y	N	N	N	Y	Y	Y	N
25 Andrews	Y	N	Y	Y	Y	Y	N	Y
26 ***Armey***	N	N	Y	Y	N	N	N	Y
27 Ortiz	Y	N	N	N	?	N	N	Y
UTAH								
1 ***Hansen***	N	Y	Y	Y	N	N	N	Y
2 ***Monson***	N	Y	Y	Y	N	N	N	Y
3 ***Nielson***	N	Y	Y	Y	Y	N	N	Y
VERMONT								
AL ***Jeffords***	Y	N	N	Y	Y	Y	N	N
VIRGINIA								
1 ***Bateman***	Y	N	N	N	Y	N	N	Y
2 ***Whitehurst***	N	N	N	N	N	N	N	Y
3 ***Bliley***	N	N	Y	N	N	N	N	Y
4 Sisisky	Y	N	N	N	Y	N	N	Y
5 Daniel	Y	N	Y	Y	Y	N	N	Y
6 Olin	Y	N	Y	Y	Y	Y	Y	N
7 ***Slaughter***	N	N	Y	Y	N	N	N	Y
8 ***Parris***	N	N	N	N	N	N	N	Y
9 Boucher	Y	N	N	N	Y	Y	Y	N
10 ***Wolf***	N	N	N	N	N	N	N	Y
WASHINGTON								
1 ***Miller***	N	N	Y	Y	N	N	N	Y
2 Swift	Y	N	N	N	Y	Y	Y	N
3 Bonker	Y	N	N	N	?	Y	Y	N
4 ***Morrison***	N	N	Y	Y	N	N	N	Y
5 Foley	Y	N	N	N	Y	Y	Y	N
6 Dicks	Y	N	N	N	Y	Y	N	N
7 Lowry	Y	N	N	N	Y	Y	Y	N
8 ***Chandler***	N	N	Y	Y	N	N	N	Y
WEST VIRGINIA								
1 Mollohan	Y	N	N	N	Y	N	N	Y
2 Staggers	?	?	?	?	Y	Y	Y	N
3 Wise	Y	N	Y	N	?	Y	Y	N
4 Rahall	Y	N	N	N	Y	Y	Y	N
WISCONSIN								
1 Aspin	Y	N	N	N	?	Y	Y	Y
2 Kastenmeier	Y	Y	N	Y	Y	Y	Y	N
3 ***Gunderson***	N	N	Y	Y	N	N	N	Y
4 Kleczka	Y	Y	N	N	Y	Y	Y	N
5 Moody	Y	N	N	N	Y	Y	Y	N
6 ***Petri***	Y	Y	Y	Y	Y	N	N	Y
7 Obey	Y	N	N	N	Y	Y	Y	N
8 ***Roth***	N	Y	Y	Y	N	N	N	Y
9 ***Sensenbrenner***	N	Y	Y	Y	N	N	N	Y
WYOMING								
AL ***Cheney***	N	Y	Y	Y	N	N	N	Y

Southern states - Ala., Ark., Fla., Ga., Ky., La., Miss., N.C., Okla., S.C., Tenn., Texas, Va.

* The *Congressional Record* vote number is different from the CQ vote number because the *Record* includes quorum calls in its tally. CQ does not publish quorum call votes.

143. HR 2577. Supplemental Appropriations, Fiscal 1985. Hamilton, D-Ind., amendment to authorize $14 million for aid to Nicaraguan refugees outside Nicaragua, to authorize use of the Economic Support Fund to implement a Central America peace agreement reached under the auspices of the "Contadora" countries, and to extend indefinitely a prohibition on support by any U.S. intelligence agency for military or paramilitary operations in Nicaragua. Rejected 174-254: R 5-175; D 169-79 (ND 143-26, SD 26-53), June 12, 1985. A "nay" was a vote supporting the president's position.

144. HR 2577. Supplemental Appropriations, Fiscal 1985. Passage of the bill to provide $13.4 billion in supplemental appropriations for fiscal 1985. Passed 271-156: R 127-53; D 144-103 (ND 84-85, SD 60-18), June 12, 1985.

145. HR 1452. Refugee Assistance Extension Act. Sensenbrenner, R-Wis., amendment to delete a $50 million authorization for "targeted assistance" to areas with large refugee populations, such as California and Florida. Rejected 104-307: R 86-89; D 18-218 (ND 4-158, SD 14-60), June 13, 1985. A "yea" was a vote supporting the president's position.

146. HR 1452. Refugee Assistance Extension Act. Pursell, R-Mich., amendment to freeze the authorization for refugee social services and medical screening programs at the fiscal 1985 appropriations level plus an adjustment for inflation. Adopted 278-112: R 151-21; D 127-91 (ND 82-67, SD 45-24), June 13, 1985. (The bill was subsequently passed by voice vote.)

KEY

Y Voted for (yea).
Paired for.
+ Announced for.
N Voted against (nay).
X Paired against.
- Announced against.
P Voted "present".
C Voted "present" to avoid possible conflict of interest.
? Did not vote or otherwise make a position known.

Democrats ***Republicans***

	143	144	145	146
ALABAMA				
1 ***Callahan***	N	Y	N	Y
2 ***Dickinson***	N	Y	N	Y
3 Nichols	N	N	Y	Y
4 Bevill	N	Y	Y	Y
5 Flippo	N	Y	?	?
6 Erdreich	N	Y	N	Y
7 Shelby	N	Y	N	N
ALASKA				
AL ***Young***	N	Y	N	?
ARIZONA				
1 ***McCain***	N	Y	N	Y
2 Udall	Y	Y	N	Y
3 ***Stump***	N	Y	Y	Y
4 ***Rudd***	N	Y	?	?
5 ***Kolbe***	N	Y	Y	Y
ARKANSAS				
1 Alexander	Y	N	N	N
2 Robinson	N	Y	N	Y
3 ***Hammerschmidt***	N	Y	N	N
4 Anthony	Y	N	N	N
CALIFORNIA				
1 Bosco	Y	N	N	Y
2 ***Chappie***	N	N	Y	Y
3 Matsui	Y	N	N	N
4 Fazio	Y	N	?	?
5 Burton	Y	Y	N	N
6 Boxer	Y	N	N	?
7 Miller	Y	N	N	?
8 Dellums	N	N	N	N
9 Stark	Y	N	N	N
10 Edwards	Y	N	N	N
11 Lantos	Y	Y	N	Y
12 ***Zschau***	N	N	N	N
13 Mineta	Y	N	N	N
14 ***Shumway***	N	N	Y	Y
15 Coelho	Y	N	N	N
16 Panetta	Y	N	N	Y
17 ***Pashayan***	N	Y	N	N
18 Lehman	Y	N	N	N
19 ***Lagomarsino***	N	N	N	Y
20 ***Thomas***	N	Y	N	Y
21 ***Fiedler***	N	Y	N	Y
22 ***Moorhead***	N	N	Y	Y
23 Beilenson	Y	N	N	Y
24 Waxman	Y	Y	N	?
25 Roybal	Y	N	N	N
26 Berman	Y	Y	N	N
27 Levine	Y	Y	N	N
28 Dixon	Y	Y	N	?
29 Hawkins	?	?	?	?
30 Martinez	Y	N	N	Y
31 Dymally	Y	N	N	N
32 Anderson	Y	Y	N	N
33 ***Dreier***	N	N	Y	Y
34 Torres	Y	N	N	N
35 ***Lewis***	N	Y	N	N
36 Brown	Y	N	N	N
37 ***McCandless***	N	Y	Y	N
38 ***Dornan***	N	Y	N	N
39 ***Dannemeyer***	N	N	Y	Y
40 ***Badham***	N	N	N	N
41 ***Lowery***	N	Y	?	?
42 ***Lungren***	N	N	N	N
43 ***Packard***	N	N	N	Y
44 Bates	Y	N	N	Y
45 ***Hunter***	N	Y	N	Y
COLORADO				
1 Schroeder	Y	N	N	Y
2 Wirth	Y	N	N	Y
3 ***Strang***	N	Y	Y	Y
4 ***Brown***	N	N	Y	Y
5 ***Kramer***	N	Y	Y	Y
6 ***Schaefer***	N	Y	Y	Y
CONNECTICUT				
1 Kennelly	Y	Y	N	Y
2 Gejdenson	Y	N	N	Y
3 Morrison	Y	N	N	Y
4 ***McKinney***	N	Y	N	Y
5 ***Rowland***	N	Y	N	Y
6 ***Johnson***	N	Y	N	Y
DELAWARE				
AL Carper	Y	N	N	Y
FLORIDA				
1 Hutto	N	Y	N	N
2 Fuqua	N	Y	N	N
3 Bennett	N	Y	N	N
4 Chappell	N	Y	N	N
5 ***McCollum***	N	Y	N	N
6 MacKay	N	N	?	?
7 Gibbons	N	Y	N	N
8 ***Young***	N	Y	N	Y
9 ***Bilirakis***	N	Y	N	N
10 ***Ireland***	N	Y	N	N
11 Nelson	N	Y	N	N
12 ***Lewis***	N	Y	N	+
13 ***Mack***	N	N	N	Y
14 Mica	N	Y	N	N
15 ***Shaw***	N	Y	N	N
16 Smith	N	Y	N	N
17 Lehman	Y	Y	N	N
18 Pepper	N	Y	N	N
19 Fascell	N	Y	N	N
GEORGIA				
1 Thomas	N	Y	N	Y
2 Hatcher	N	Y	N	N
3 Ray	N	N	N	Y
4 ***Swindall***	N	Y	Y	Y
5 Fowler	Y	Y	N	Y
6 ***Gingrich***	N	Y	N	Y
7 Darden	N	N	N	Y
8 Rowland	N	Y	N	Y
9 Jenkins	N	N	N	Y
10 Barnard	N	N	N	?
HAWAII				
1 Heftel	N	Y	N	?
2 Akaka	Y	Y	N	N
IDAHO				
1 ***Craig***	N	N	Y	Y
2 Stallings	N	N	N	Y
ILLINOIS				
1 Hayes	Y	N	N	N
2 Savage	Y	N	N	N
3 Russo	Y	N	N	Y
4 ***O'Brien***	N	Y	N	N
5 Lipinski	N	Y	N	N
6 ***Hyde***	N	Y	N	Y
7 Collins	Y	N	N	N
8 Rostenkowski	Y	Y	N	Y
9 Yates	Y	Y	N	N
10 ***Porter***	N	N	#	#
11 Annunzio	Y	Y	N	Y
12 ***Crane***	N	N	Y	Y
13 ***Fawell***	N	Y	Y	Y
14 ***Grotberg***	N	Y	Y	Y
15 ***Madigan***	N	Y	Y	Y
16 ***Martin***	N	N	Y	Y
17 Evans	Y	Y	N	Y
18 ***Michel***	N	Y	Y	Y
19 Bruce	Y	Y	N	Y
20 Durbin	Y	Y	N	Y
21 Price	Y	Y	N	N
22 Gray	Y	Y	N	Y
INDIANA				
1 Visclosky	Y	Y	N	Y
2 Sharp	Y	Y	N	Y
3 ***Hiler***	N	N	Y	Y
4 ***Coats***	N	N	N	Y
5 ***Hillis***	N	Y	N	N

ND - Northern Democrats SD - Southern Democrats

* Corresponding to Congressional Record Votes 157, 158, 159, 160

	143	144	145	146
6 ***Burton***	N	Y	Y	Y
7 ***Myers***	N	Y	Y	Y
8 McCloskey	Y	N	N	Y
9 Hamilton	Y	Y	N	Y
10 Jacobs	N	N	N	Y
IOWA				
1 ***Leach***	Y	N	N	Y
2 ***Tauke***	N	N	Y	Y
3 ***Evans***	N	N	Y	Y
4 Smith	N	Y	N	?
5 ***Lightfoot***	N	N	Y	Y
6 Bedell	Y	N	N	Y
KANSAS				
1 ***Roberts***	N	N	Y	Y
2 Slattery	N	N	N	Y
3 ***Meyers***	N	Y	Y	Y
4 Glickman	Y	Y	N	Y
5 ***Whittaker***	N	N	N	Y
KENTUCKY				
1 Hubbard	N	N	Y	Y
2 Natcher	Y	Y	N	Y
3 Mazzoli	N	Y	N	N
4 ***Snyder***	N	N	N	Y
5 ***Rogers***	N	Y	N	Y
6 ***Hopkins***	N	N	N	Y
7 Perkins	N	Y	N	Y
LOUISIANA				
1 ***Livingston***	N	Y	N	Y
2 Boggs	Y	Y	N	N
3 Tauzin	N	Y	Y	Y
4 Roemer	N	Y	Y	Y
5 Huckaby	N	Y	?	?
6 ***Moore***	N	Y	Y	Y
7 Breaux	N	Y	Y	?
8 Long	N	P	N	N
MAINE				
1 ***McKernan***	N	Y	N	Y
2 ***Snowe***	N	Y	N	Y
MARYLAND				
1 Dyson	N	Y	Y	Y
2 ***Bentley***	N	Y	Y	Y
3 Mikulski	Y	Y	N	N
4 ***Holt***	N	Y	N	N
5 Hoyer	Y	Y	N	Y
6 Byron	N	Y	N	Y
7 Mitchell	Y	N	N	N
8 Barnes	Y	Y	N	N
MASSACHUSETTS				
1 ***Conte***	Y	Y	N	Y
2 Boland	Y	N	?	?
3 Early	Y	N	N	N
4 Frank	Y	N	N	N
5 Atkins	Y	N	N	N
6 Mavroules	Y	N	N	N
7 Markey	Y	N	N	N
8 O'Neill				
9 Moakley	Y	N	N	?
10 Studds	Y	N	N	N
11 Donnelly	Y	Y	N	N
MICHIGAN				
1 Conyers	N	N	N	N
2 ***Pursell***	N	Y	N	Y
3 Wolpe	Y	Y	N	Y
4 ***Siljander***	N	Y	Y	Y
5 ***Henry***	N	N	Y	Y
6 Carr	N	Y	Y	Y
7 Kildee	Y	N	N	N
8 Traxler	Y	Y	N	Y
9 ***Vander Jagt***	N	Y	N	Y
10 ***Schuette***	N	Y	Y	Y
11 ***Davis***	?	?	N	Y
12 Bonior	Y	N	N	N
13 Crockett	N	N	N	Y
14 Hertel	Y	N	N	Y
15 Ford	Y	N	N	N
16 Dingell	Y	Y	N	N
17 Levin	Y	Y	N	N
18 ***Broomfield***	N	Y	N	Y
MINNESOTA				
1 Penny	Y	N	N	Y
2 ***Weber***	N	Y	N	Y
3 ***Frenzel***	N	Y	N	Y
4 Vento	Y	N	N	N
5 Sabo	Y	N	N	N
6 Sikorski	Y	Y	N	Y
7 ***Stangeland***	N	Y	N	N
8 Oberstar	Y	N	N	N
MISSISSIPPI				
1 Whitten	Y	Y	N	Y
2 ***Franklin***	N	Y	Y	Y
3 Montgomery	N	Y	Y	Y
4 Dowdy	N	Y	N	?
5 ***Lott***	N	Y	Y	?
MISSOURI				
1 Clay	Y	N	N	N
2 Young	Y	Y	N	Y
3 Gephardt	Y	Y	N	Y
4 Skelton	N	Y	N	Y
5 Wheat	N	Y	N	Y
6 ***Coleman***	N	Y	N	Y
7 ***Taylor***	N	Y	Y	?
8 ***Emerson***	N	Y	Y	Y
9 Volkmer	Y	Y	N	Y
MONTANA				
1 Williams	Y	N	N	?
2 ***Marlenee***	N	Y	?	?
NEBRASKA				
1 ***Bereuter***	N	Y	Y	Y
2 ***Daub***	N	Y	Y	Y
3 ***Smith***	N	Y	Y	Y
NEVADA				
1 Reid	Y	Y	N	Y
2 ***Vucanovich***	N	Y	Y	Y
NEW HAMPSHIRE				
1 ***Smith***	N	N	Y	Y
2 ***Gregg***	N	N	Y	Y
NEW JERSEY				
1 Florio	N	Y	N	N
2 Hughes	Y	N	N	Y
3 Howard	Y	Y	N	N
4 ***Smith***	N	Y	N	N
5 ***Roukema***	N	Y	Y	Y
6 Dwyer	Y	Y	N	N
7 ***Rinaldo***	N	Y	N	Y
8 Roe	Y	Y	?	?
9 Torricelli	Y	Y	N	Y
10 Rodino	Y	N	N	N
11 ***Gallo***	N	Y	N	Y
12 ***Courter***	N	Y	N	Y
13 ***Saxton***	N	Y	Y	Y
14 Guarini	Y	N	N	?
NEW MEXICO				
1 ***Lujan***	N	Y	Y	Y
2 ***Skeen***	N	Y	Y	Y
3 Richardson	Y	Y	N	N
NEW YORK				
1 ***Carney***	N	Y	N	Y
2 Downey	Y	Y	N	?
3 Mrazek	Y	Y	N	Y
4 ***Lent***	N	Y	N	Y
5 ***McGrath***	N	Y	N	Y
6 Addabbo	Y	Y	X	X
7 Ackerman	Y	Y	N	N
8 Scheuer	Y	Y	N	N
9 Manton	Y	Y	N	N
10 Schumer	Y	Y	N	N
11 Towns	Y	N	N	N
12 Owens	Y	N	N	N
13 Solarz	Y	Y	N	N
14 ***Molinari***	N	Y	N	N
15 ***Green***	Y	Y	N	Y
16 Rangel	Y	Y	N	N
17 Weiss	Y	Y	N	N
18 Garcia	Y	N	N	N
19 Biaggi	N	Y	N	Y
20 ***DioGuardi***	N	Y	Y	Y
21 ***Fish***	N	Y	N	N
22 ***Gilman***	N	Y	N	Y
23 Stratton	N	Y	N	Y
24 ***Solomon***	N	N	Y	Y
25 ***Boehlert***	N	Y	N	Y
26 ***Martin***	N	Y	N	Y
27 ***Wortley***	N	Y	N	Y
28 McHugh	Y	Y	N	Y
29 ***Horton***	N	Y	N	Y
30 ***Eckert***	N	Y	Y	Y
31 ***Kemp***	N	Y	N	Y
32 LaFalce	Y	N	N	Y
33 Nowak	Y	Y	N	N
34 Lundine	Y	Y	N	Y
NORTH CAROLINA				
1 Jones	?	?	N	Y
2 Valentine	Y	N	Y	Y
3 Whitley	Y	Y	N	?
4 ***Cobey***	N	Y	Y	Y
5 Neal	Y	N	N	Y
6 ***Coble***	N	Y	Y	Y
7 Rose	Y	Y	N	N
8 Hefner	Y	Y	?	?
9 ***McMillan***	N	Y	Y	Y
10 ***Broyhill***	?	?	Y	Y
11 ***Hendon***	N	Y	Y	Y
NORTH DAKOTA				
AL Dorgan	Y	N	N	Y
OHIO				
1 Luken	Y	N	N	Y
2 ***Gradison***	N	Y	N	Y
3 Hall	N	N	N	Y
4 ***Oxley***	N	N	Y	Y
5 ***Latta***	N	N	Y	Y
6 ***McEwen***	N	Y	Y	Y
7 ***DeWine***	N	Y	N	N
8 ***Kindness***	N	Y	?	Y
9 Kaptur	Y	N	N	Y
10 ***Miller***	N	Y	Y	Y
11 Eckart	Y	Y	N	Y
12 ***Kasich***	N	Y	Y	Y
13 Pease	Y	N	N	Y
14 Seiberling	Y	N	N	N
15 ***Wylie***	N	N	N	Y
16 ***Regula***	N	Y	N	Y
17 Traficant	Y	N	N	Y
18 Applegate	N	N	N	Y
19 Feighan	Y	N	N	Y
20 Oakar	Y	N	N	N
21 Stokes	Y	N	N	N
OKLAHOMA				
1 Jones	N	N	N	Y
2 Synar	Y	Y	N	Y
3 Watkins	N	Y	N	Y
4 McCurdy	N	Y	N	Y
5 ***Edwards***	N	Y	Y	Y
6 English	N	Y	N	Y
OREGON				
1 AuCoin	Y	N	N	Y
2 ***Smith, R.***	N	N	Y	Y
3 Wyden	Y	Y	N	Y
4 Weaver	Y	N	N	Y
5 ***Smith, D.***	N	N	Y	Y
PENNSYLVANIA				
1 Foglietta	Y	Y	N	N
2 Gray	Y	Y	N	N
3 Borski	Y	Y	N	Y
4 Kolter	N	Y	?	?
5 ***Schulze***	N	Y	Y	Y
6 Yatron	Y	Y	N	Y
7 Edgar	Y	Y	?	?
8 Kostmayer	Y	N	N	N
9 ***Shuster***	N	N	N	Y
10 ***McDade***	N	Y	N	Y
11 Kanjorski	N	Y	Y	Y
12 Murtha	N	Y	N	?
13 ***Coughlin***	N	Y	Y	Y
14 Coyne	Y	Y	N	N
15 ***Ritter***	N	N	Y	Y
16 ***Walker***	N	N	Y	Y
17 ***Gekas***	N	Y	Y	Y
18 Walgren	Y	N	N	Y
19 ***Goodling***	N	N	N	Y
20 Gaydos	Y	Y	N	Y
21 ***Ridge***	N	N	N	Y
22 Murphy	N	N	Y	Y
23 ***Clinger***	N	Y	N	Y
RHODE ISLAND				
1 St Germain	Y	N	N	?
2 ***Schneider***	Y	N	N	Y
SOUTH CAROLINA				
1 ***Hartnett***	N	N	?	?
2 ***Spence***	N	N	N	Y
3 Derrick	Y	Y	N	Y
4 ***Campbell***	N	Y	Y	Y
5 Spratt	Y	Y	N	Y
6 Tallon	N	Y	N	Y
SOUTH DAKOTA				
AL Daschle	N	Y	?	?
TENNESSEE				
1 ***Quillen***	N	Y	?	?
2 ***Duncan***	N	Y	N	Y
3 Lloyd	N	Y	Y	Y
4 Cooper	N	N	N	Y
5 Boner	N	Y	N	Y
6 Gordon	Y	Y	N	Y
7 ***Sundquist***	N	Y	Y	Y
8 Jones	N	Y	Y	Y
9 Ford	Y	N	?	?
TEXAS				
1 Vacancy				
2 Wilson	N	Y	?	?
3 ***Bartlett***	N	Y	N	Y
4 Hall, R.	N	Y	Y	Y
5 Bryant	Y	Y	N	Y
6 ***Barton***	N	N	Y	Y
7 ***Archer***	N	N	Y	Y
8 ***Fields***	N	N	N	Y
9 Brooks	Y	Y	N	Y
10 Pickle	N	Y	N	Y
11 Leath	?	?	Y	Y
12 Wright	Y	Y	N	N
13 ***Boulter***	N	Y	Y	Y
14 ***Sweeney***	N	Y	N	Y
15 de la Garza	N	Y	N	?
16 Coleman	Y	Y	N	Y
17 Stenholm	N	Y	Y	Y
18 Leland	Y	N	N	N
19 ***Combest***	N	Y	Y	Y
20 Gonzalez	Y	N	P	N
21 ***Loeffler***	N	Y	N	Y
22 ***DeLay***	N	Y	Y	Y
23 Bustamante	N	Y	N	N
24 Frost	Y	Y	N	Y
25 Andrews	N	Y	N	Y
26 ***Armey***	N	Y	Y	Y
27 Ortiz	N	Y	N	N
UTAH				
1 ***Hansen***	N	N	Y	Y
2 ***Monson***	N	N	Y	Y
3 ***Nielson***	N	N	Y	Y
VERMONT				
AL ***Jeffords***	Y	N	N	Y
VIRGINIA				
1 ***Bateman***	N	Y	N	Y
2 ***Whitehurst***	N	Y	Y	Y
3 ***Bliley***	N	Y	Y	Y
4 Sisisky	N	Y	N	?
5 Daniel	N	N	Y	Y
6 Olin	Y	N	N	Y
7 ***Slaughter***	N	Y	Y	Y
8 ***Parris***	N	Y	N	Y
9 Boucher	Y	Y	N	Y
10 ***Wolf***	N	Y	N	N
WASHINGTON				
1 ***Miller***	N	Y	N	Y
2 Swift	Y	Y	N	?
3 Bonker	Y	Y	N	Y
4 ***Morrison***	N	Y	N	Y
5 Foley	Y	N	N	Y
6 Dicks	Y	Y	N	Y
7 Lowry	Y	N	N	N
8 ***Chandler***	N	Y	N	Y
WEST VIRGINIA				
1 Mollohan	N	Y	N	Y
2 Staggers	Y	Y	N	Y
3 Wise	Y	Y	N	Y
4 Rahall	Y	N	N	Y
WISCONSIN				
1 Aspin	N	Y	N	Y
2 Kastenmeier	Y	N	N	Y
3 ***Gunderson***	N	Y	N	Y
4 Kleczka	Y	N	N	Y
5 Moody	Y	N	N	N
6 ***Petri***	N	N	Y	Y
7 Obey	Y	N	N	Y
8 ***Roth***	N	N	Y	Y
9 ***Sensenbrenner***	N	N	Y	Y
WYOMING				
AL ***Cheney***	N	Y	Y	Y

Southern states - Ala., Ark., Fla., Ga., Ky., La., Miss., N.C., Okla., S.C., Tenn., Texas, Va.

* The *Congressional Record* vote number is different from the CQ vote number because the *Record* includes quorum calls in its tally. CQ does not publish quorum call votes.

147. HR 2369. Family Planning Assistance. Waxman, D-Calif., motion to suspend the rules and pass the bill to extend federal aid for family planning services through fiscal 1988, authorizing $454 million over three years. Motion rejected 214-197: R 38-137; D 176-60 (ND 123-38, SD 53-22), June 18, 1985. A two-thirds majority of those present and voting (274 in this case) is required for passage under suspension of the rules. A "nay" was a vote supporting the president's position.

148. HR 2417. Health Maintenance Organizations. Waxman, D-Calif., motion to suspend the rules and pass the bill to phase out federal grants and loans promoting the establishment of health maintenance organizations. Motion agreed to 411-2: R 175-0; D 236-2 (ND 160-2, SD 76-0), June 18, 1985. A two-thirds majority of those present and voting (276 in this case) is required for passage under suspension of the rules.

149. HR 2290. Orphan Drug Amendments. Waxman, D-Calif., motion to suspend the rules and pass the bill to extend grants for the development of drugs to treat rare diseases, authorizing $4 million each year in fiscal 1986-88. Motion agreed to 413-0: R 175-0; D 238-0 (ND 162-0, SD 76-0), June 18, 1985. A two-thirds majority of those present and voting (276 in this case) is required for passage under suspension of the rules.

150. HR 1872. Department of Defense Authorization, Fiscal 1986. Aspin, D-Wis., amendment to reduce the amount authorized by the bill by $10 billion, to the level set by the House-passed budget resolution. Adopted 301-115: R 77-98; D 224-17 (ND 160-3, SD 64-14), June 18, 1985.

151. HR 1872. Department of Defense Authorization, Fiscal 1986. Bennett, D-Fla., amendment to the Mavroules, D-Mass., substitute for the Dickinson, R-Ala., amendment, to deny all funds for production of MX missiles. Rejected 185-230: R 21-154; D 164-76 (ND 139-23, SD 25-53), June 18, 1985. A "nay" was a vote supporting the president's position.

152. HR 1872. Department of Defense Authorization, Fiscal 1986. McCurdy, D-Okla., amendment to the Dickinson, R-Ala., amendment, to express the sense of Congress that no more than 40 MX missiles should be deployed. Adopted 233-184: R 32-144; D 201-40 (ND 154-9, SD 47-31), June 18, 1985. A "nay" was a vote supporting the president's position.

153. HR 1872. Department of Defense Authorization, Fiscal 1986. Courter, R-N.J., amendment to the Mavroules, D-Mass., substitute for the Dickinson, R-Ala., amendment, to express the sense of Congress that no more than 50 MX missiles should be deployed in existing missile silos and to authorize the production of 12 MX missiles in fiscal 1986. Rejected 182-234: R 144-33; D 38-201 (ND 7-154, SD 31-47), June 18, 1985. A "yea" was a vote supporting the president's position. (Subsequently, the Mavroules substitute for the Dickinson amendment, to limit to 40 the number of MX missiles that could be deployed and to provide no authorization for MX production in fiscal 1986, was adopted by voice vote. The amended Dickinson amendment then was adopted by voice vote.)

154. HR 1872. Department of Defense Authorization, Fiscal 1986. Bennett, D-Fla., amendment to approve the use of $4 billion, authorized in previous budgets but no longer needed for the original purpose, to buy conventional weapons. Rejected 36-376: R 1-172; D 35-204 (ND 27-135, SD 8-69), June 19, 1985.

KEY

Y	Voted for (yea).
#	Paired for.
+	Announced for.
N	Voted against (nay).
X	Paired against.
-	Announced against.
P	Voted "present".
C	Voted "present" to avoid possible conflict of interest.
?	Did not vote or otherwise make a position known.

Democrats ***Republicans***

	147	148	149	150	151	152	153	154
ALABAMA								
1 ***Callahan***	N	Y	Y	N	N	N	Y	N
2 ***Dickinson***	Y	Y	Y	N	N	N	Y	N
3 Nichols	N	Y	Y	N	N	N	Y	N
4 Bevill	Y	Y	Y	Y	N	N	Y	N
5 Flippo	?	?	?	X	?	?	?	N
6 Erdreich	Y	Y	Y	Y	N	N	Y	N
7 Shelby	Y	Y	Y	N	N	N	Y	N
ALASKA								
AL ***Young***	N	Y	Y	Y	N	N	Y	N
ARIZONA								
1 ***McCain***	N	Y	Y	N	N	N	Y	N
2 Udall	Y	Y	Y	Y	Y	Y	N	?
3 ***Stump***	N	Y	Y	N	N	N	Y	N
4 ***Rudd***	N	Y	Y	N	N	N	Y	N
5 ***Kolbe***	Y	Y	Y	Y	N	N	Y	N
ARKANSAS								
1 Alexander	Y	Y	Y	Y	Y	Y	N	N
2 Robinson	Y	Y	Y	Y	N	N	Y	N
3 ***Hammerschmidt***	N	Y	Y	Y	N	N	Y	N
4 Anthony	Y	Y	Y	Y	Y	Y	N	N
CALIFORNIA								
1 Bosco	Y	Y	Y	Y	Y	Y	N	N
2 ***Chappie***	N	Y	Y	N	?	N	Y	N
3 Matsui	Y	Y	Y	Y	Y	Y	N	N
4 Fazio	Y	Y	Y	Y	N	Y	N	N
5 Burton	Y	Y	Y	Y	Y	Y	N	N
6 Boxer	Y	Y	Y	Y	Y	Y	N	N
7 Miller	Y	Y	Y	Y	Y	Y	N	?
8 Dellums	Y	Y	Y	Y	Y	Y	N	N
9 Stark	Y	Y	Y	Y	Y	Y	N	N
10 Edwards	Y	Y	Y	Y	Y	Y	N	N
11 Lantos	Y	Y	Y	Y	Y	Y	N	N
12 ***Zschau***	Y	Y	Y	N	Y	Y	N	N
13 Mineta	Y	Y	Y	Y	Y	Y	N	N
14 ***Shumway***	N	Y	Y	N	N	N	Y	N
15 Coelho	Y	Y	Y	Y	Y	Y	N	N
16 Panetta	Y	Y	Y	Y	Y	Y	N	N
17 ***Pashayan***	N	Y	Y	N	N	N	Y	N
18 Lehman	Y	Y	Y	Y	Y	Y	N	N
19 ***Lagomarsino***	N	Y	Y	N	N	N	Y	N
20 ***Thomas***	Y	Y	Y	N	N	N	Y	N
21 ***Fiedler***	N	Y	Y	N	N	N	Y	N
22 ***Moorhead***	N	Y	Y	N	N	N	Y	N
23 Beilenson	Y	Y	Y	Y	Y	Y	N	N
24 Waxman	Y	Y	Y	Y	Y	Y	N	N
25 Roybal	Y	Y	Y	Y	Y	Y	N	Y
26 Berman	Y	Y	Y	Y	Y	Y	N	?
27 Levine	Y	Y	Y	Y	Y	Y	N	N
28 Dixon	Y	Y	Y	Y	Y	Y	N	N
29 Hawkins	Y	Y	Y	Y	?	?	?	N
30 Martinez	Y	Y	Y	Y	Y	Y	?	N
31 Dymally	Y	Y	Y	Y	Y	Y	N	Y
32 Anderson	Y	Y	Y	Y	N	N	Y	N
33 ***Dreier***	N	Y	Y	N	N	N	Y	N
34 Torres	+	+	+	+	+	+	-	N
35 ***Lewis***	N	Y	Y	N	N	N	Y	N
36 Brown	Y	Y	Y	Y	?	?	?	Y
37 ***McCandless***	N	Y	Y	N	N	N	Y	N
38 ***Dornan***	N	Y	Y	N	N	N	Y	N
39 ***Dannemeyer***	N	Y	Y	N	N	N	Y	N
40 ***Badham***	N	Y	Y	N	X	N	Y	X
41 ***Lowery***	N	Y	Y	N	N	N	Y	N
42 ***Lungren***	N	Y	Y	N	N	N	Y	N
43 ***Packard***	N	Y	Y	N	N	N	Y	N
44 Bates	Y	Y	Y	Y	Y	Y	N	Y
45 ***Hunter***	N	Y	Y	N	N	N	Y	N
COLORADO								
1 Schroeder	Y	Y	Y	Y	Y	Y	N	Y
2 Wirth	Y	Y	Y	Y	Y	Y	N	N
3 ***Strang***	N	Y	Y	+	-	X	#	-
4 ***Brown***	N	Y	Y	Y	N	N	Y	N
5 ***Kramer***	N	Y	Y	Y	N	N	Y	N
6 ***Schaefer***	N	Y	Y	Y	N	N	Y	N
CONNECTICUT								
1 Kennelly	Y	Y	Y	Y	Y	Y	N	N
2 Gejdenson	Y	Y	Y	Y	Y	Y	N	N
3 Morrison	Y	Y	Y	Y	Y	Y	N	N
4 ***McKinney***	Y	Y	Y	Y	Y	Y	N	N
5 ***Rowland***	N	Y	Y	Y	N	N	Y	N
6 ***Johnson***	Y	Y	Y	Y	Y	Y	N	N
DELAWARE								
AL Carper	Y	Y	Y	Y	Y	Y	N	N
FLORIDA								
1 Hutto	N	Y	Y	N	N	N	Y	N
2 Fuqua	N	Y	Y	Y	N	N	Y	N
3 Bennett	Y	Y	Y	Y	Y	Y	N	Y
4 Chappell	?	Y	Y	N	N	N	Y	N
5 ***McCollum***	N	Y	Y	N	N	N	Y	N
6 MacKay	Y	Y	Y	Y	Y	Y	N	Y
7 Gibbons	Y	Y	Y	Y	Y	Y	N	Y
8 ***Young***	N	Y	Y	N	N	N	Y	N
9 ***Bilirakis***	N	Y	Y	N	N	N	Y	N
10 ***Ireland***	N	Y	Y	N	N	N	Y	N
11 Nelson	N	Y	Y	N	N	N	Y	N
12 ***Lewis***	N	Y	Y	Y	N	N	Y	N
13 ***Mack***	N	Y	Y	Y	N	N	Y	N
14 Mica	Y	Y	Y	Y	Y	Y	N	N
15 ***Shaw***	N	Y	Y	N	N	N	Y	N
16 Smith	Y	Y	Y	Y	Y	Y	N	N
17 Lehman	Y	Y	Y	Y	Y	Y	N	Y
18 Pepper	Y	Y	Y	Y	X	+	-	-
19 Fascell	Y	Y	Y	Y	N	Y	N	Y
GEORGIA								
1 Thomas	Y	Y	Y	Y	N	N	Y	N
2 Hatcher	Y	Y	Y	Y	N	N	Y	N
3 Ray	Y	Y	Y	N	N	N	Y	N
4 ***Swindall***	N	Y	Y	N	N	N	Y	N
5 Fowler	Y	Y	Y	Y	Y	Y	N	N
6 ***Gingrich***	N	Y	Y	N	N	N	Y	N
7 Darden	Y	Y	Y	N	N	N	Y	N
8 Rowland	Y	Y	Y	Y	N	N	Y	N
9 Jenkins	Y	Y	Y	Y	Y	Y	N	N
10 Barnard	Y	Y	Y	N	N	N	Y	N
HAWAII								
1 Heftel	Y	Y	Y	Y	Y	Y	N	?
2 Akaka	#	?	?	Y	N	Y	N	N
IDAHO								
1 ***Craig***	N	Y	Y	Y	N	N	Y	N
2 Stallings	N	Y	Y	Y	N	Y	N	N
ILLINOIS								
1 Hayes	Y	Y	Y	Y	Y	Y	N	N
2 Savage	Y	Y	Y	Y	Y	Y	N	N
3 Russo	N	Y	Y	Y	Y	Y	N	N
4 ***O'Brien***	N	Y	Y	N	N	N	Y	?
5 Lipinski	N	Y	Y	Y	N	Y	N	N
6 ***Hyde***	N	Y	Y	N	N	N	Y	N
7 Collins	Y	Y	Y	Y	Y	Y	N	N
8 Rostenkowski	N	Y	Y	Y	Y	Y	N	N
9 Yates	Y	Y	Y	Y	Y	Y	N	N
10 ***Porter***	Y	Y	Y	Y	N	N	Y	N
11 Annunzio	N	Y	Y	Y	Y	Y	N	N
12 ***Crane***	N	Y	Y	N	N	N	Y	N
13 ***Fawell***	Y	Y	Y	Y	N	N	Y	N
14 ***Grotberg***	N	Y	Y	N	N	N	Y	N
15 ***Madigan***	Y	Y	Y	Y	N	N	Y	N
16 ***Martin***	?	?	?	Y	N	N	Y	N
17 Evans	Y	Y	Y	Y	Y	Y	N	N
18 ***Michel***	N	Y	Y	N	N	N	Y	N
19 Bruce	Y	Y	Y	Y	Y	Y	N	N
20 Durbin	Y	Y	Y	Y	Y	Y	N	N
21 Price	N	Y	Y	Y	N	Y	N	N
22 Gray	Y	Y	Y	Y	Y	Y	N	N
INDIANA								
1 Visclosky	Y	Y	Y	Y	Y	Y	N	N
2 Sharp	Y	Y	Y	Y	Y	Y	N	N
3 ***Hiler***	N	Y	Y	N	N	N	Y	N
4 ***Coats***	N	Y	Y	Y	N	N	Y	N
5 ***Hillis***	Y	Y	Y	N	N	N	Y	N

ND - Northern Democrats SD - Southern Democrats

* Corresponding to Congressional Record Votes 162, 163, 164, 165, 166, 167, 168, 170

	147	148	149	150	151	152	153	154
6 ***Burton***	N	Y	Y	N	N	N	Y	N
7 ***Myers***	N	Y	Y	N	N	N	Y	N
8 McCloskey	Y	Y	Y	Y	Y	Y	N	N
9 Hamilton	Y	Y	Y	Y	Y	Y	N	N
10 Jacobs	Y	Y	Y	Y	Y	Y	N	N
IOWA								
1 ***Leach***	Y	Y	Y	Y	Y	Y	N	Y
2 ***Tauke***	N	Y	Y	Y	Y	Y	N	N
3 ***Evans***	Y	Y	Y	Y	Y	Y	N	N
4 Smith	Y	Y	Y	Y	Y	Y	N	Y
5 ***Lightfoot***	N	Y	Y	Y	N	N	Y	N
6 Bedell	Y	Y	Y	Y	Y	Y	N	N
KANSAS								
1 ***Roberts***	N	Y	Y	Y	N	Y	N	N
2 Slattery	Y	Y	Y	Y	N	Y	N	N
3 ***Meyers***	Y	Y	Y	Y	N	Y	N	N
4 Glickman	Y	Y	Y	Y	N	Y	N	N
5 ***Whittaker***	N	Y	Y	Y	N	Y	N	N
KENTUCKY								
1 Hubbard	N	Y	Y	Y	N	N	Y	N
2 Natcher	N	Y	Y	Y	Y	Y	N	N
3 Mazzoli	N	Y	Y	Y	N	Y	N	N
4 ***Snyder***	N	Y	Y	Y	N	N	Y	N
5 ***Rogers***	N	Y	Y	Y	N	N	Y	N
6 ***Hopkins***	N	Y	Y	Y	N	Y	N	N
7 Perkins	Y	Y	Y	Y	Y	Y	N	N
LOUISIANA								
1 ***Livingston***	N	Y	Y	N	N	N	Y	N
2 Boggs	N	Y	Y	Y	Y	Y	N	N
3 Tauzin	N	Y	Y	Y	N	N	Y	N
4 Roemer	N	Y	Y	Y	N	N	Y	N
5 Huckaby	N	Y	Y	Y	N	N	Y	N
6 ***Moore***	N	Y	Y	Y	N	N	Y	N
7 Breaux	N	Y	Y	Y	N	N	Y	N
8 Long	N	Y	Y	Y	N	Y	N	N
MAINE								
1 ***McKernan***	Y	Y	Y	Y	N	Y	N	N
2 ***Snowe***	Y	Y	Y	Y	N	Y	N	N
MARYLAND								
1 Dyson	N	Y	Y	N	N	N	?	N
2 ***Bentley***	?	?	?	?	N	N	Y	N
3 Mikulski	Y	Y	Y	Y	Y	Y	N	N
4 ***Holt***	N	Y	Y	N	N	N	Y	N
5 Hoyer	Y	Y	Y	Y	N	Y	N	N
6 Byron	N	Y	Y	N	N	N	Y	N
7 Mitchell	Y	Y	Y	N	Y	#	X	N
8 Barnes	Y	Y	Y	Y	Y	Y	N	N
MASSACHUSETTS								
1 ***Conte***	Y	Y	Y	Y	Y	Y	N	N
2 Boland	N	Y	Y	Y	+	Y	N	N
3 Early	N	Y	Y	Y	Y	Y	N	Y
4 Frank	Y	Y	Y	Y	Y	Y	N	N
5 Atkins	Y	Y	Y	Y	Y	Y	N	N
6 Mavroules	N	Y	Y	Y	Y	Y	N	N
7 Markey	Y	Y	Y	Y	Y	Y	N	N
8 O'Neill								
9 Moakley	Y	?	Y	Y	Y	Y	N	N
10 Studds	Y	Y	Y	Y	Y	Y	N	N
11 Donnelly	Y	Y	Y	Y	Y	Y	N	N
MICHIGAN								
1 Conyers	Y	Y	Y	Y	Y	Y	N	N
2 ***Pursell***	Y	Y	Y	Y	N	Y	N	N
3 Wolpe	Y	Y	Y	Y	Y	Y	N	Y
4 ***Siljander***	N	Y	Y	N	N	N	Y	N
5 ***Henry***	Y	Y	Y	Y	Y	Y	N	N
6 Carr	Y	Y	Y	Y	Y	Y	N	N
7 Kildee	Y	Y	Y	Y	Y	Y	N	N
8 Traxler	N	Y	Y	Y	Y	Y	N	?
9 ***Vander Jagt***	N	Y	Y	Y	N	N	Y	N
10 ***Schuette***	N	Y	Y	N	N	N	Y	N
11 ***Davis***	Y	Y	Y	N	N	N	Y	N
12 Bonior	N	Y	Y	Y	Y	Y	N	N
13 Crockett	Y	Y	Y	Y	?	Y	N	N
14 Hertel	N	Y	Y	Y	Y	Y	N	Y
15 Ford	Y	Y	Y	?	Y	Y	N	N
16 Dingell	Y	Y	Y	Y	Y	Y	N	?
17 Levin	Y	Y	Y	Y	Y	Y	N	N
18 ***Broomfield***	N	Y	Y	Y	N	N	Y	N
MINNESOTA								
1 Penny	N	Y	Y	Y	Y	Y	N	Y
2 ***Weber***	N	Y	Y	Y	N	X	Y	N
3 ***Frenzel***	Y	Y	Y	Y	N	Y	Y	N
4 Vento	Y	Y	Y	Y	Y	Y	N	N
5 Sabo	Y	Y	Y	Y	Y	Y	N	N
6 Sikorski	N	Y	Y	Y	Y	Y	N	N
7 ***Stangeland***	N	Y	Y	Y	N	N	Y	N
8 Oberstar	N	N	Y	Y	Y	Y	N	Y
MISSISSIPPI								
1 Whitten	Y	Y	Y	Y	Y	Y	N	N
2 ***Franklin***	X	?	?	?	N	N	Y	N
3 Montgomery	N	Y	Y	N	N	N	Y	N
4 Dowdy	?	?	?	Y	N	N	Y	N
5 ***Lott***	N	Y	Y	N	N	N	Y	N
MISSOURI								
1 Clay	Y	Y	Y	Y	Y	Y	N	N
2 Young	N	Y	Y	Y	Y	Y	N	N
3 Gephardt	N	Y	Y	Y	N	Y	N	N
4 Skelton	N	Y	Y	Y	N	N	Y	N
5 Wheat	Y	Y	Y	Y	Y	Y	N	N
6 ***Coleman***	N	Y	Y	N	N	N	Y	N
7 ***Taylor***	N	Y	Y	N	N	N	Y	N
8 ***Emerson***	N	Y	Y	Y	N	N	Y	N
9 Volkmer	N	Y	Y	Y	Y	Y	N	N
MONTANA								
1 Williams	Y	Y	Y	?	Y	Y	N	N
2 ***Marlenee***	?	?	?	?	?	?	#	?
NEBRASKA								
1 ***Bereuter***	N	Y	Y	Y	Y	Y	N	N
2 ***Daub***	N	Y	Y	N	N	N	Y	N
3 ***Smith***	N	Y	Y	Y	Y	Y	N	N
NEVADA								
1 Reid	N	Y	Y	Y	N	N	Y	N
2 ***Vucanovich***	N	Y	Y	N	N	N	Y	N
NEW HAMPSHIRE								
1 ***Smith***	N	Y	Y	N	N	N	Y	N
2 ***Gregg***	Y	Y	Y	Y	N	N	Y	N
NEW JERSEY								
1 Florio	Y	Y	Y	Y	Y	Y	N	N
2 Hughes	Y	Y	Y	Y	Y	Y	N	Y
3 Howard	Y	Y	Y	Y	Y	Y	N	N
4 ***Smith***	N	Y	Y	Y	Y	Y	N	N
5 ***Roukema***	Y	Y	Y	Y	Y	Y	N	N
6 Dwyer	Y	Y	Y	Y	Y	Y	N	N
7 ***Rinaldo***	N	Y	Y	Y	N	N	Y	N
8 Roe	?	Y	Y	Y	Y	Y	N	N
9 Torricelli	Y	Y	Y	Y	Y	Y	N	N
10 Rodino	Y	Y	Y	Y	Y	Y	N	N
11 ***Gallo***	Y	Y	Y	N	N	N	Y	N
12 ***Courter***	N	Y	Y	N	N	N	Y	N
13 ***Saxton***	N	Y	Y	N	N	N	Y	N
14 Guarini	Y	Y	Y	Y	Y	Y	N	N
NEW MEXICO								
1 ***Lujan***	N	Y	Y	Y	N	N	Y	N
2 ***Skeen***	N	Y	Y	N	N	N	Y	N
3 Richardson	Y	Y	Y	Y	Y	Y	N	N
NEW YORK								
1 ***Carney***	N	Y	Y	N	N	N	Y	N
2 Downey	?	Y	Y	Y	Y	Y	N	N
3 Mrazek	Y	Y	Y	Y	Y	Y	N	N
4 ***Lent***	N	Y	Y	Y	N	N	Y	N
5 ***McGrath***	N	Y	Y	Y	N	N	Y	N
6 Addabbo	Y	Y	?	#	#	#	X	Y
7 Ackerman	Y	Y	Y	Y	Y	Y	N	Y
8 Scheuer	Y	Y	Y	Y	Y	Y	N	N
9 Manton	Y	Y	Y	Y	Y	Y	N	N
10 Schumer	Y	Y	Y	?	#	#	X	-
11 Towns	#	?	?	Y	Y	Y	N	?
12 Owens	Y	Y	Y	Y	Y	Y	N	N
13 Solarz	Y	Y	Y	Y	Y	Y	N	N
14 ***Molinari***	N	Y	Y	N	N	N	Y	N
15 ***Green***	Y	Y	Y	Y	Y	Y	N	N
16 Rangel	#	?	?	+	#	+	-	N
17 Weiss	Y	Y	Y	Y	Y	Y	N	Y
18 Garcia	Y	Y	Y	Y	Y	Y	N	Y
19 Biaggi	N	Y	Y	Y	N	Y	N	N
20 ***DioGuardi***	Y	Y	Y	N	Y	Y	N	N
21 ***Fish***	Y	Y	Y	Y	N	N	Y	N
22 ***Gilman***	Y	Y	Y	Y	N	N	Y	N
23 Stratton	Y	Y	Y	Y	N	N	Y	N
24 ***Solomon***	X	?	?	?	X	X	#	N
25 ***Boehlert***	Y	Y	Y	Y	N	Y	N	N
26 ***Martin***	N	Y	Y	N	N	N	Y	N
27 ***Wortley***	N	Y	Y	N	N	N	Y	N
28 McHugh	Y	Y	Y	Y	Y	Y	N	N
29 ***Horton***	Y	Y	Y	Y	N	N	N	N
30 ***Eckert***	N	Y	Y	N	N	N	Y	N
31 ***Kemp***	N	Y	Y	N	N	N	Y	N
32 LaFalce	N	Y	Y	Y	Y	Y	N	N
33 Nowak	Y	Y	Y	Y	Y	Y	N	N
34 Lundine	Y	Y	Y	Y	Y	Y	N	Y
NORTH CAROLINA								
1 Jones	Y	Y	Y	Y	Y	Y	N	Y
2 Valentine	Y	Y	Y	Y	N	N	Y	N
3 Whitley	Y	Y	Y	Y	N	N	Y	N
4 ***Cobey***	N	Y	Y	N	N	N	Y	N
5 Neal	Y	Y	Y	Y	N	Y	N	Y
6 ***Coble***	N	Y	Y	N	N	Y	N	N
7 Rose	Y	Y	Y	Y	Y	Y	N	N
8 Hefner	Y	Y	Y	Y	N	Y	N	N
9 ***McMillan***	N	Y	Y	N	N	N	Y	N
10 ***Broyhill***	Y	Y	Y	Y	N	N	Y	N
11 ***Hendon***	N	Y	Y	N	N	N	Y	N
NORTH DAKOTA								
AL Dorgan	Y	Y	Y	Y	Y	Y	N	Y
OHIO								
1 Luken	N	Y	Y	Y	Y	Y	N	N
2 ***Gradison***	N	Y	Y	Y	Y	Y	N	N
3 Hall	N	Y	Y	Y	Y	Y	N	N
4 ***Oxley***	N	Y	Y	N	N	N	Y	N
5 ***Latta***	N	Y	Y	N	N	N	Y	?
6 ***McEwen***	N	Y	Y	N	N	N	Y	N
7 ***DeWine***	N	Y	Y	N	N	N	Y	N
8 ***Kindness***	N	Y	Y	N	N	N	Y	N
9 Kaptur	Y	Y	Y	Y	Y	Y	N	N
10 ***Miller***	N	Y	Y	N	N	N	Y	N
11 Eckart	Y	Y	Y	Y	Y	Y	N	N
12 ***Kasich***	N	Y	Y	N	N	N	Y	N
13 Pease	Y	Y	Y	Y	Y	Y	N	N
14 Seiberling	Y	Y	Y	Y	Y	Y	N	N
15 ***Wylie***	N	Y	Y	Y	N	N	Y	N
16 ***Regula***	N	Y	Y	N	N	N	Y	N
17 Traficant	Y	Y	Y	Y	Y	Y	N	N
18 Applegate	N	Y	Y	Y	Y	Y	N	N
19 Feighan	Y	Y	Y	Y	Y	Y	N	N
20 Oakar	Y	Y	Y	Y	Y	Y	N	N
21 Stokes	Y	Y	Y	Y	Y	Y	N	N
OKLAHOMA								
1 Jones	N	Y	Y	Y	N	Y	N	N
2 Synar	Y	Y	Y	Y	Y	Y	N	N
3 Watkins	N	Y	Y	Y	N	Y	N	N
4 McCurdy	Y	Y	Y	Y	N	Y	N	N
5 ***Edwards***	N	Y	Y	N	N	N	Y	N
6 English	N	Y	Y	Y	N	Y	N	N
OREGON								
1 AuCoin	?	?	?	Y	Y	Y	N	N
2 ***Smith, R.***	Y	Y	Y	Y	N	N	Y	N
3 Wyden	Y	Y	Y	Y	Y	Y	N	N
4 Weaver	Y	Y	Y	Y	Y	Y	N	N
5 ***Smith, D.***	N	Y	Y	Y	N	N	Y	N
PENNSYLVANIA								
1 Foglietta	Y	Y	Y	Y	Y	Y	N	Y
2 Gray	Y	Y	Y	Y	Y	Y	N	N
3 Borski	N	Y	Y	Y	Y	Y	N	N
4 Kolter	N	Y	Y	Y	Y	Y	N	N
5 ***Schulze***	N	Y	Y	N	N	N	Y	N
6 Yatron	N	Y	Y	Y	N	N	Y	N
7 Edgar	Y	Y	Y	Y	Y	Y	N	N
8 Kostmayer	Y	Y	Y	Y	Y	Y	N	N
9 ***Shuster***	N	Y	Y	N	N	N	Y	N
10 ***McDade***	N	Y	Y	N	N	N	Y	?
11 Kanjorski	N	Y	Y	Y	Y	Y	N	N
12 Murtha	N	Y	Y	Y	N	N	Y	N
13 ***Coughlin***	Y	Y	Y	Y	Y	Y	N	N
14 Coyne	Y	Y	Y	Y	Y	Y	N	N
15 ***Ritter***	N	Y	Y	Y	N	N	Y	N
16 ***Walker***	N	Y	Y	N	N	N	Y	N
17 ***Gekas***	N	Y	Y	N	N	N	Y	N
18 Walgren	Y	N	Y	Y	Y	Y	N	Y
19 ***Goodling***	N	Y	Y	Y	Y	Y	N	N
20 Gaydos	N	Y	Y	Y	Y	Y	N	N
21 ***Ridge***	Y	Y	Y	Y	Y	Y	N	N
22 Murphy	N	Y	Y	Y	N	N	N	N
23 ***Clinger***	N	Y	Y	Y	N	N	Y	-
RHODE ISLAND								
1 St Germain	N	Y	Y	Y	Y	Y	N	N
2 ***Schneider***	Y	Y	Y	Y	Y	Y	N	N
SOUTH CAROLINA								
1 ***Hartnett***	N	Y	Y	N	N	N	Y	N
2 ***Spence***	N	Y	Y	N	N	N	Y	N
3 Derrick	Y	Y	Y	Y	N	Y	N	?
4 ***Campbell***	N	Y	Y	N	N	N	Y	N
5 Spratt	Y	Y	Y	Y	N	Y	N	N
6 Tallon	?	?	?	Y	Y	Y	N	N
SOUTH DAKOTA								
AL Daschle	Y	Y	Y	Y	Y	Y	N	Y
TENNESSEE								
1 ***Quillen***	N	Y	Y	N	N	N	Y	N
2 ***Duncan***	N	Y	Y	N	N	N	Y	N
3 Lloyd	Y	Y	Y	N	N	N	Y	N
4 Cooper	Y	Y	Y	Y	N	Y	N	N
5 Boner	Y	Y	Y	Y	N	N	Y	P
6 Gordon	Y	Y	Y	Y	N	Y	N	N
7 ***Sundquist***	N	Y	Y	Y	N	N	Y	N
8 Jones	Y	Y	Y	Y	N	N	Y	N
9 Ford	Y	Y	Y	Y	Y	Y	N	N
TEXAS								
1 Vacancy								
2 Wilson	?	?	?	?	?	?	?	?
3 ***Bartlett***	N	Y	Y	N	N	N	Y	N
4 Hall, R.	N	Y	Y	N	N	N	Y	N
5 Bryant	Y	Y	Y	Y	Y	Y	N	N
6 ***Barton***	N	Y	Y	N	N	N	Y	N
7 ***Archer***	N	Y	Y	N	N	N	Y	N
8 ***Fields***	N	Y	Y	N	N	N	Y	N
9 Brooks	Y	Y	Y	Y	Y	Y	N	N
10 Pickle	Y	Y	Y	Y	N	Y	N	N
11 Leath	Y	Y	Y	N	N	N	Y	N
12 Wright	Y	Y	Y	Y	N	Y	N	N
13 ***Boulter***	N	Y	Y	N	N	N	Y	N
14 ***Sweeney***	N	Y	Y	N	N	N	Y	N
15 de la Garza	N	Y	Y	Y	N	Y	N	Y
16 Coleman	Y	Y	Y	Y	N	Y	N	N
17 Stenholm	N	Y	Y	Y	N	N	Y	N
18 Leland	Y	Y	Y	Y	Y	Y	N	N
19 ***Combest***	N	Y	Y	N	N	N	Y	N
20 Gonzalez	Y	Y	Y	?	Y	Y	N	N
21 ***Loeffler***	?	?	?	?	X	X	#	?
22 ***DeLay***	N	Y	Y	Y	N	N	Y	N
23 Bustamante	Y	Y	Y	Y	N	Y	N	N
24 Frost	Y	Y	Y	Y	N	Y	N	N
25 Andrews	Y	Y	Y	Y	N	Y	N	N
26 ***Armey***	N	Y	Y	N	N	N	Y	N
27 Ortiz	N	Y	Y	Y	N	Y	N	N
UTAH								
1 ***Hansen***	N	Y	Y	Y	N	N	Y	N
2 ***Monson***	N	Y	Y	Y	N	N	Y	N
3 ***Nielson***	N	Y	Y	N	N	N	Y	N
VERMONT								
AL ***Jeffords***	?	?	?	?	#	#	X	#
VIRGINIA								
1 ***Bateman***	N	Y	Y	N	N	N	Y	N
2 ***Whitehurst***	Y	Y	Y	N	N	N	Y	N
3 ***Bliley***	N	Y	Y	N	N	N	Y	N
4 Sisisky	Y	Y	Y	N	N	Y	N	N
5 Daniel	N	Y	Y	N	N	N	Y	N
6 Olin	Y	Y	Y	Y	Y	Y	N	N
7 ***Slaughter***	N	Y	Y	N	N	N	Y	N
8 ***Parris***	N	Y	Y	Y	N	N	Y	N
9 Boucher	?	?	?	Y	Y	Y	N	N
10 ***Wolf***	N	Y	Y	Y	N	N	Y	N
WASHINGTON								
1 ***Miller***	Y	Y	Y	Y	Y	Y	N	N
2 Swift	Y	Y	Y	Y	Y	Y	N	Y
3 Bonker	Y	Y	Y	Y	Y	Y	N	N
4 ***Morrison***	Y	Y	Y	Y	N	N	Y	N
5 Foley	Y	Y	Y	Y	N	Y	N	N
6 Dicks	Y	Y	Y	Y	N	Y	N	N
7 Lowry	Y	Y	Y	Y	Y	Y	N	N
8 ***Chandler***	Y	Y	Y	Y	N	N	Y	N
WEST VIRGINIA								
1 Mollohan	N	Y	Y	Y	N	Y	N	N
2 Staggers	N	Y	Y	Y	Y	Y	N	Y
3 Wise	Y	Y	Y	Y	Y	Y	N	Y
4 Rahall	N	Y	Y	Y	Y	Y	N	Y
WISCONSIN								
1 Aspin	Y	Y	Y	Y	N	Y	N	N
2 Kastenmeier	Y	Y	Y	Y	Y	Y	N	Y
3 ***Gunderson***	N	Y	Y	Y	N	Y	N	N
4 Kleczka	-	+	+	+	Y	Y	N	N
5 Moody	#	?	?	Y	Y	Y	N	N
6 ***Petri***	N	Y	Y	Y	Y	Y	N	N
7 Obey	Y	Y	Y	Y	Y	Y	N	Y
8 ***Roth***	N	Y	Y	Y	N	N	Y	N
9 ***Sensenbrenner***	N	Y	Y	Y	Y	Y	N	N
WYOMING								
AL ***Cheney***	N	Y	Y	N	N	N	Y	N

Southern states - Ala., Ark., Fla., Ga., Ky., La., Miss., N.C., Okla., S.C., Tenn., Texas, Va.

* The *Congressional Record* vote number is different from the CQ vote number because the *Record* includes quorum calls in its tally. CQ does not publish quorum call votes.

155. HR 1872. Department of Defense Authorization, Fiscal 1986. Weiss, D-N.Y., amendment to delete funds authorized for production of the Trident II missile. Rejected 79-342: R 0-175; D 79-167 (ND 77-91, SD 2-76), June 19, 1985. A "nay" was a vote supporting the president's position.

156. HR 1872. Department of Defense Authorization, Fiscal 1986. Skelton, D-Mo., amendment to the Porter, R-Ill., amendment, to authorize the appropriation of $124 million to produce binary chemical weapons subject to certain conditions. Adopted 229-196: R 143-34; D 86-162 (ND 30-138, SD 56-24), June 19, 1985. A "yea" was a vote supporting the president's position.

157. HR 1872. Department of Defense Authorization, Fiscal 1986. Skelton, D-Mo., amendment to the Fascell, D-Fla., substitute for the Porter, R-Ill., amendment, to authorize the appropriation of $124 million to produce binary chemical weapons subject to certain conditions. Adopted 223-196: R 143-32; D 80-164 (ND 25-139, SD 55-25), June 19, 1985. A "yea" was a vote supporting the president's position. (The Fascell substitute subsequently was adopted by voice vote.)

158. Procedural Motion. McKernan, R-Maine, motion to approve the House *Journal* of Wednesday, June 19. Motion agreed to 261-129: R 50-116; D 211-13 (ND 140-9, SD 71-4), June 20, 1985.

159. HR 1872. Department of Defense Authorization, Fiscal 1986. Dellums, D-Calif., amendment to the Price, D-Ill., amendment, to reduce from $2.5 billion to $954 million the authorization for the strategic defense initiative. Rejected 102-320: R 3-176; D 99-144 (ND 92-71, SD 7-73), June 20, 1985. A "nay" was a vote supporting the president's position.

160. HR 1872. Department of Defense Authorization, Fiscal 1986. Mavroules, D-Mass., amendment to the Price, D-Ill., amendment, to reduce from $2.5 billion to $1.4 billion the authorization for the strategic defense initiative. Rejected 155-268: R 4-176; D 151-92 (ND 134-30, SD 17-62), June 20, 1985. A "nay" was a vote supporting the president's position.

161. HR 1872. Department of Defense Authorization, Fiscal 1986. Courter, R-N.J., amendment to the Holt, R-Md., substitute for the Price, D-Ill., amendment, to increase from $2.5 billion to $3.7 billion the authorization for the strategic defense initiative. Rejected 104-315: R 97-83; D 7-232 (ND 0-161, SD 7-71), June 20, 1985. A "yea" was a vote supporting the president's position. (The Holt substitute subsequently was rejected *(see vote 163, p. 54-H)*.)

162. HR 1872. Department of Defense Authorization, Fiscal 1986. Dicks, D-Wash., amendment to the Price, D-Ill., amendment, to reduce from $2.5 billion to $2.1 billion the authorization for the strategic defense initiative. Rejected 195-221: R 12-167; D 183-54 (ND 147-11, SD 36-43), June 20, 1985. A "nay" was a vote supporting the president's position.

KEY

Y	Voted for (yea).
#	Paired for.
+	Announced for.
N	Voted against (nay).
X	Paired against.
-	Announced against.
P	Voted "present".
C	Voted "present" to avoid possible conflict of interest.
?	Did not vote or otherwise make a position known.

Democrats ***Republicans***

	155	156	157	158	159	160	161	162
ALABAMA								
1 ***Callahan***	N	Y	Y	Y	N	N	Y	N
2 ***Dickinson***	N	Y	Y	N	N	N	N	N
3 Nichols	N	Y	Y	Y	N	N	N	N
4 Bevill	N	Y	Y	Y	N	N	N	N
5 Flippo	N	Y	Y	Y	N	N	N	N
6 Erdreich	N	N	N	Y	N	N	N	N
7 Shelby	N	Y	Y	Y	N	N	Y	N
ALASKA								
AL ***Young***	N	Y	Y	N	N	N	N	N
ARIZONA								
1 ***McCain***	N	Y	Y	Y	N	N	Y	N
2 Udall	?	?	?	?	?	Y	N	Y
3 ***Stump***	N	Y	Y	N	N	N	Y	N
4 ***Rudd***	N	Y	Y	Y	N	N	Y	N
5 ***Kolbe***	N	Y	Y	N	N	N	N	N
ARKANSAS								
1 Alexander	N	Y	Y	P	N	N	N	N
2 Robinson	N	Y	Y	Y	N	N	Y	N
3 ***Hammerschmidt***	N	Y	Y	Y	N	N	Y	N
4 Anthony	N	Y	Y	Y	N	Y	N	Y
CALIFORNIA								
1 Bosco	N	Y	Y	Y	N	N	N	Y
2 ***Chappie***	N	Y	Y	N	N	N	N	N
3 Matsui	Y	N	N	Y	Y	Y	N	Y
4 Fazio	N	Y	Y	Y	N	Y	N	Y
5 Burton	Y	N	?	Y	Y	Y	N	Y
6 Boxer	Y	N	N	Y	Y	Y	N	Y
7 Miller	Y	N	N	Y	Y	Y	N	Y
8 Dellums	Y	N	N	Y	Y	Y	N	Y
9 Stark	Y	N	N	Y	Y	Y	N	?
10 Edwards	Y	N	N	Y	Y	Y	N	Y
11 Lantos	N	N	N	Y	N	Y	N	Y
12 ***Zschau***	N	Y	Y	N	N	N	N	N
13 Mineta	N	N	N	Y	N	Y	N	Y
14 ***Shumway***	N	Y	Y	N	N	N	Y	N
15 Coelho	N	N	N	Y	Y	Y	N	Y
16 Panetta	Y	N	N	Y	N	Y	N	Y
17 ***Pashayan***	N	Y	Y	N	N	N	Y	N
18 Lehman	N	N	N	Y	Y	Y	N	Y
19 ***Lagomarsino***	N	Y	Y	N	N	N	Y	N
20 ***Thomas***	N	Y	Y	N	N	N	Y	N
21 ***Fiedler***	N	Y	Y	N	N	N	Y	N
22 ***Moorhead***	N	Y	Y	N	N	N	Y	N
23 Beilenson	Y	N	N	Y	Y	Y	N	Y
24 Waxman	Y	N	N	Y	Y	Y	N	Y
25 Roybal	Y	N	N	Y	Y	Y	N	Y
26 Berman	Y	N	N	Y	Y	Y	N	Y
27 Levine	Y	N	N	Y	Y	Y	N	Y
28 Dixon	Y	X	X	?	#	#	?	?
29 Hawkins	Y	N	N	?	Y	Y	N	Y
30 Martinez	N	N	N	Y	N	Y	N	Y
31 Dymally	Y	N	N	P	Y	Y	N	Y
32 Anderson	N	Y	N	Y	N	Y	N	Y
33 ***Dreier***	N	Y	Y	N	N	N	Y	N
34 Torres	N	N	N	Y	N	Y	N	Y
35 ***Lewis***	N	Y	Y	N	N	N	Y	N
36 Brown	N	N	N	Y	Y	Y	N	Y
37 ***McCandless***	N	Y	Y	N	N	N	Y	N
38 ***Dornan***	?	Y	?	N	N	N	Y	N
39 ***Dannemeyer***	-	Y	Y	N	N	N	Y	N
40 ***Bodham***	?	Y	Y	N	N	N	Y	N
41 ***Lowery***	N	Y	Y	N	N	N	Y	N
42 ***Lungren***	N	Y	Y	N	N	N	Y	N
43 ***Packard***	N	Y	Y	N	N	N	Y	N
44 Bates	Y	Y	N	?	Y	Y	N	Y
45 ***Hunter***	N	Y	Y	N	N	N	Y	N
COLORADO								
1 Schroeder	N	N	N	N	Y	Y	N	Y
2 Wirth	N	N	N	Y	N	Y	N	Y
3 ***Strang***	X	+	+	-	-	X	+	X
3 ***Brown***	N	N	N	N	N	N	N	N
5 ***Kramer***	N	Y	Y	N	N	N	Y	N
6 ***Schaefer***	N	?	?	?	N	N	N	N
CONNECTICUT								
1 Kennelly	Y	N	N	Y	N	Y	N	Y
2 Gejdenson	Y	N	N	Y	Y	Y	N	Y
3 Morrison	Y	N	N	Y	Y	Y	N	Y
4 ***McKinney***	N	N	N	Y	Y	Y	N	Y
5 ***Rowland***	N	Y	Y	Y	N	N	N	N
6 ***Johnson***	N	Y	Y	Y	N	N	N	N
DELAWARE								
AL Carper	N	N	N	Y	N	N	N	Y
FLORIDA								
1 Hutto	N	Y	Y	P	N	N	Y	N
2 Fuqua	N	Y	Y	Y	N	N	N	N
3 Bennett	N	Y	Y	N	N	N	N	N
4 Chappell	N	Y	Y	Y	N	N	Y	N
5 ***McCollum***	N	Y	Y	Y	N	N	Y	N
6 MacKay	N	N	N	Y	N	Y	N	Y
7 Gibbons	N	Y	N	Y	N	Y	N	Y
8 ***Young***	N	Y	Y	N	N	N	N	N
9 ***Bilirakis***	N	Y	Y	N	N	N	N	N
10 ***Ireland***	N	Y	Y	?	N	N	Y	N
11 Nelson	N	Y	Y	Y	N	N	Y	N
12 ***Lewis***	N	N	N	-	N	N	Y	N
13 ***Mack***	N	Y	Y	N	N	N	Y	N
14 Mica	N	Y	Y	Y	N	Y	N	Y
15 ***Shaw***	N	Y	Y	N	N	N	N	N
16 Smith	N	N	N	Y	N	#	?	#
17 Lehman	Y	N	N	Y	Y	Y	N	Y
18 Pepper	-	#	#	+	X	X	-	#
19 Fascell	N	N	N	Y	N	N	N	Y
GEORGIA								
1 Thomas	N	Y	Y	Y	N	N	N	N
2 Hatcher	N	Y	Y	Y	N	N	N	N
3 Ray	N	Y	Y	Y	N	N	N	N
4 ***Swindall***	N	Y	Y	N	N	N	Y	N
5 Fowler	N	N	N	Y	N	N	N	N
6 ***Gingrich***	N	Y	Y	N	N	N	Y	N
7 Darden	N	Y	Y	Y	N	N	N	N
8 Rowland	N	Y	Y	Y	N	N	N	N
9 Jenkins	N	Y	Y	Y	N	N	N	N
10 Barnard	N	Y	Y	?	N	N	N	N
HAWAII								
1 Heftel	N	Y	Y	Y	N	N	N	Y
2 Akaka	N	Y	Y	Y	Y	Y	N	Y
IDAHO								
1 ***Craig***	N	Y	Y	N	N	N	Y	N
2 Stallings	N	N	N	?	N	N	N	Y
ILLINOIS								
1 Hayes	Y	N	N	N	Y	Y	N	Y
2 Savage	Y	N	N	Y	Y	Y	?	?
3 Russo	Y	N	N	Y	Y	Y	N	Y
4 ***O'Brien***	?	?	Y	Y	N	N	N	X
5 Lipinski	N	Y	Y	Y	N	N	N	?
6 ***Hyde***	N	Y	Y	N	N	N	Y	N
7 Collins	Y	N	N	Y	Y	Y	N	Y
8 Rostenkowski	N	N	N	?	?	?	?	?
9 Yates	Y	N	N	Y	Y	Y	N	Y
10 ***Porter***	N	N	N	N	N	N	N	Y
11 Annunzio	N	N	N	Y	N	Y	N	N
12 ***Crane***	N	Y	Y	N	N	N	Y	N
13 ***Fawell***	N	Y	Y	N	N	N	Y	N
14 ***Grotberg***	N	Y	Y	N	N	N	N	N
15 ***Madigan***	N	Y	Y	N	N	N	N	N
16 ***Martin***	N	N	N	N	N	N	Y	N
17 Evans	Y	N	N	Y	Y	Y	N	Y
18 ***Michel***	N	Y	Y	Y	N	N	Y	N
19 Bruce	Y	N	N	Y	Y	Y	N	Y
20 Durbin	N	N	N	N	Y	Y	N	Y
21 Price	N	Y	Y	Y	N	N	N	Y
22 Gray	N	Y	N	?	N	N	N	N
INDIANA								
1 Visclosky	N	N	N	Y	N	N	N	Y
2 Sharp	N	N	N	Y	N	N	N	Y
3 ***Hiler***	N	Y	Y	N	N	N	Y	N
4 ***Coats***	N	N	N	Y	N	N	Y	N
5 ***Hillis***	N	Y	Y	N	N	N	Y	N

ND - Northern Democrats SD - Southern Democrats

* Corresponding to Congressional Record Votes 171, 172, 173, 174, 176, 177, 178, 179

	155	156	157	158	159	160	161	162
6 ***Burton***	N	Y	Y	N	N	N	Y	N
7 ***Myers***	?	Y	Y	Y	N	N	N	N
8 McCloskey	N	N	N	?	N	Y	N	Y
9 Hamilton	N	Y	Y	Y	N	N	N	Y
10 Jacobs	N	N	N	N	Y	Y	N	Y
IOWA								
1 ***Leach***	N	N	N	?	Y	Y	N	Y
2 ***Tauke***	N	N	N	N	N	N	N	Y
3 ***Evans***	N	Y	Y	N	N	N	N	N
4 Smith	N	N	N	Y	N	N	N	Y
5 ***Lightfoot***	N	Y	Y	N	N	N	N	N
6 Bedell	Y	N	N	Y	Y	Y	N	Y
KANSAS								
1 ***Roberts***	N	Y	Y	N	N	N	N	N
2 Slattery	N	Y	Y	Y	N	N	N	Y
3 ***Meyers***	N	Y	Y	Y	N	N	N	N
4 Glickman	N	Y	Y	Y	N	Y	N	Y
5 ***Whittaker***	N	Y	Y	N	N	N	N	N
KENTUCKY								
1 Hubbard	N	Y	Y	Y	N	N	N	N
2 Natcher	N	N	N	Y	N	N	N	Y
3 Mazzoli	N	N	N	Y	N	N	N	Y
4 ***Snyder***	N	Y	Y	Y	N	N	Y	N
5 ***Rogers***	N	Y	Y	N	N	N	Y	N
6 ***Hopkins***	N	Y	Y	Y	N	N	N	N
7 Perkins	N	N	N	Y	Y	Y	N	Y
LOUISIANA								
1 ***Livingston***	N	Y	Y	N	N	N	Y	N
2 Boggs	N	N	N	Y	N	N	N	Y
3 Tauzin	N	Y	Y	Y	N	N	N	N
4 Roemer	N	Y	Y	N	N	N	N	N
5 Huckaby	N	N	N	Y	N	N	N	N
6 ***Moore***	N	Y	Y	Y	N	N	Y	N
7 Breaux	N	Y	Y	Y	N	N	N	N
8 Long	N	N	N	Y	N	N	N	Y
MAINE								
1 ***McKernan***	N	N	N	N	N	N	N	N
2 ***Snowe***	N	N	N	Y	N	N	N	N
MARYLAND								
1 Dyson	N	Y	Y	Y	N	N	N	N
2 ***Bentley***	N	Y	Y	N	N	N	Y	N
3 Mikulski	N	N	N	Y	N	Y	N	Y
4 ***Holt***	N	Y	Y	Y	N	N	Y	N
5 Hoyer	N	Y	Y	Y	N	N	N	Y
6 Byron	N	Y	Y	P	N	N	N	Y
7 Mitchell	Y	N	N	N	Y	Y	N	Y
8 Barnes	N	N	N	Y	N	Y	N	Y
MASSACHUSETTS								
1 ***Conte***	N	N	X	N	N	Y	N	N
2 Boland	N	N	N	?	N	N	N	Y
3 Early	Y	N	N	Y	N	Y	N	Y
4 Frank	Y	N	N	Y	Y	Y	N	Y
5 Atkins	Y	N	N	?	Y	Y	N	Y
6 Mavroules	Y	N	N	Y	Y	Y	N	Y
7 Markey	Y	N	N	Y	Y	Y	N	Y
8 O'Neill								
9 Moakley	Y	N	N	Y	Y	Y	N	Y
10 Studds	Y	N	N	Y	Y	Y	N	Y
11 Donnelly	N	N	N	Y	N	N	N	Y
MICHIGAN								
1 Conyers	#	N	?	Y	Y	Y	N	Y
2 ***Pursell***	N	Y	Y	N	N	N	N	Y
3 Wolpe	Y	N	N	Y	Y	Y	N	Y
4 ***Siljander***	N	Y	Y	N	N	N	Y	N
5 ***Henry***	N	N	N	N	N	N	N	N
6 Carr	N	N	N	Y	Y	Y	N	Y
7 Kildee	Y	N	N	Y	Y	Y	N	Y
8 Traxler	Y	N	N	Y	Y	Y	N	Y
9 ***Vander Jagt***	N	Y	Y	Y	N	N	N	N
10 ***Schuette***	N	Y	Y	N	N	N	N	N
11 ***Davis***	N	Y	Y	Y	N	N	N	N
12 Bonior	Y	N	N	Y	Y	Y	N	Y
13 Crockett	Y	N	N	Y	Y	Y	N	N
14 Hertel	N	N	N	Y	Y	Y	N	Y
15 Ford	N	N	N	?	Y	Y	N	Y
16 Dingell	N	Y	Y	?	Y	Y	N	Y
17 Levin	Y	N	N	Y	N	Y	N	Y
18 ***Broomfield***	N	Y	Y	Y	N	N	N	N
MINNESOTA								
1 Penny	Y	N	N	N	Y	Y	N	Y
2 ***Weber***	N	N	N	N	N	N	Y	N
3 ***Frenzel***	N	Y	Y	Y	N	N	N	Y
4 Vento	N	N	N	Y	Y	Y	N	Y
5 Sabo	Y	N	N	Y	Y	Y	N	Y
6 Sikorski	N	N	N	N	Y	Y	N	Y

	155	156	157	158	159	160	161	162
7 ***Stangeland***	N	Y	Y	N	N	N	Y	N
8 Oberstar	Y	N	N	Y	Y	Y	N	Y
MISSISSIPPI								
1 Whitten	N	N	N	Y	N	N	N	Y
2 ***Franklin***	N	N	Y	Y	N	N	Y	N
3 Montgomery	N	Y	Y	Y	N	N	N	N
4 Dowdy	N	Y	Y	Y	N	N	N	Y
5 ***Lott***	N	Y	Y	?	N	N	Y	N
MISSOURI								
1 Clay	Y	N	N	N	Y	Y	N	Y
2 Young	N	Y	Y	Y	Y	Y	N	N
3 Gephardt	N	Y	Y	Y	N	N	N	Y
4 Skelton	N	Y	Y	?	N	N	N	Y
5 Wheat	Y	N	N	Y	Y	Y	N	Y
6 ***Coleman***	N	Y	Y	N	N	N	N	N
7 ***Taylor***	N	Y	Y	N	N	N	N	N
8 ***Emerson***	N	?	#	?	N	N	N	N
9 Volkmer	N	Y	Y	Y	N	Y	N	Y
MONTANA								
1 Williams	Y	Y	?	Y	Y	Y	N	Y
2 ***Marlenee***	N	Y	Y	N	N	N	Y	N
NEBRASKA								
1 ***Bereuter***	N	Y	Y	N	N	N	N	N
2 ***Daub***	N	Y	Y	N	N	N	N	N
3 ***Smith***	N	Y	Y	Y	N	N	N	N
NEVADA								
1 Reid	N	N	N	Y	N	N	N	N
2 ***Vucanovich***	N	Y	Y	N	N	N	Y	N
NEW HAMPSHIRE								
1 ***Smith***	N	Y	Y	N	N	N	Y	N
2 ***Gregg***	N	N	N	Y	N	N	Y	N
NEW JERSEY								
1 Florio	N	N	N	Y	N	Y	N	Y
2 Hughes	N	Y	N	Y	N	N	N	Y
3 Howard	N	N	N	Y	Y	Y	N	Y
4 ***Smith***	N	N	N	Y	N	N	Y	N
5 ***Roukema***	N	N	N	Y	N	N	N	Y
6 Dwyer	N	N	N	Y	N	Y	N	Y
7 ***Rinaldo***	N	N	N	Y	N	N	N	N
8 Roe	N	N	N	Y	N	N	N	Y
9 Torricelli	N	N	N	Y	N	Y	N	Y
10 Rodino	Y	N	N	Y	Y	Y	N	Y
11 ***Gallo***	N	Y	Y	N	N	N	Y	N
12 ***Courter***	N	Y	Y	N	N	N	Y	N
13 ***Saxton***	N	Y	Y	Y	N	N	N	N
14 Guarini	N	N	N	Y	N	Y	N	Y
NEW MEXICO								
1 ***Lujan***	N	Y	Y	Y	N	N	N	N
2 ***Skeen***	N	Y	Y	N	N	N	Y	N
3 Richardson	N	N	N	Y	N	N	N	Y
NEW YORK								
1 ***Carney***	N	Y	Y	N	N	N	Y	N
2 Downey	Y	N	N	Y	Y	Y	N	Y
3 Mrazek	Y	N	N	Y	Y	Y	N	Y
4 ***Lent***	N	Y	Y	N	N	N	N	N
5 ***McGrath***	N	Y	Y	N	N	N	N	N
6 Addabbo	N	N	N	Y	Y	Y	N	Y
7 Ackerman	Y	N	N	Y	Y	Y	N	Y
8 Scheuer	Y	N	N	Y	Y	Y	N	?
9 Manton	N	N	N	Y	N	Y	N	?
10 Schumer	Y	N	-	?	N	Y	N	Y
11 Towns	Y	N	N	?	?	?	?	?
12 Owens	Y	N	N	Y	Y	Y	N	N
13 Solarz	Y	N	N	Y	N	Y	N	Y
14 ***Molinari***	N	N	N	N	N	N	N	N
15 ***Green***	N	N	N	Y	N	N	N	Y
16 Rangel	Y	N	N	Y	Y	Y	N	Y
17 Weiss	Y	N	N	Y	Y	Y	N	Y
18 Garcia	Y	N	N	?	Y	Y	?	?
19 Biaggi	N	Y	Y	Y	N	N	N	Y
20 ***DioGuardi***	N	Y	Y	N	N	N	N	N
21 ***Fish***	N	N	N	Y	N	N	N	Y
22 ***Gilman***	N	Y	Y	N	N	N	N	N
23 Stratton	N	Y	Y	Y	N	N	N	N
24 ***Solomon***	N	Y	Y	N	N	N	Y	N
25 ***Boehlert***	N	Y	Y	N	N	N	Y	N
26 ***Martin***	N	Y	Y	?	N	N	N	N
27 ***Wortley***	N	N	N	Y	N	N	Y	N
28 McHugh	Y	N	N	Y	N	Y	N	Y
29 ***Horton***	N	N	N	Y	N	N	N	N
30 ***Eckert***	N	Y	Y	N	N	N	Y	N
31 ***Kemp***	N	Y	Y	Y	N	N	Y	N
32 LaFalce	Y	N	N	Y	N	Y	N	Y
33 Nowak	N	N	N	Y	Y	Y	N	Y
34 Lundine	N	N	N	Y	Y	Y	N	Y

	155	156	157	158	159	160	161	162
NORTH CAROLINA								
1 Jones	N	N	N	?	Y	Y	N	Y
2 Valentine	N	Y	Y	Y	N	N	N	N
3 Whitley	N	Y	Y	Y	N	N	N	N
4 ***Cobey***	N	Y	Y	N	N	N	Y	N
5 Neal	N	Y	Y	Y	N	N	N	Y
6 ***Coble***	N	Y	N	N	N	N	N	N
7 Rose	N	Y	Y	Y	N	Y	N	Y
8 Hefner	N	Y	Y	Y	N	N	N	N
9 ***McMillan***	N	Y	Y	Y	N	N	N	N
10 ***Broyhill***	N	Y	Y	Y	N	N	N	N
11 ***Hendon***	N	Y	Y	N	N	N	N	N
NORTH DAKOTA								
AL Dorgan	Y	N	N	Y	N	Y	N	Y
OHIO								
1 Luken	N	N	N	Y	?	?	?	?
2 ***Gradison***	N	N	N	Y	N	N	Y	N
3 Hall	N	N	N	?	Y	Y	N	Y
4 ***Oxley***	N	Y	Y	N	N	N	N	N
5 ***Latta***	N	Y	Y	N	N	N	Y	N
6 ***McEwen***	N	Y	Y	N	N	N	Y	N
7 ***DeWine***	N	Y	Y	N	N	N	Y	N
8 ***Kindness***	N	Y	Y	N	N	N	Y	N
9 Kaptur	N	N	N	Y	N	Y	N	Y
10 ***Miller***	N	Y	Y	N	N	N	Y	N
11 Eckart	N	N	N	Y	Y	Y	N	Y
12 ***Kasich***	N	Y	Y	N	N	N	Y	N
13 Pease	N	N	N	Y	Y	Y	N	Y
14 Seiberling	Y	N	N	Y	Y	Y	N	Y
15 ***Wylie***	N	Y	Y	Y	N	N	N	N
16 ***Regula***	N	N	N	N	N	N	N	N
17 Traficant	Y	N	N	Y	Y	Y	N	Y
18 Applegate	N	N	N	?	N	Y	N	Y
19 Feighan	N	N	N	Y	N	Y	N	Y
20 Oakar	N	N	N	Y	Y	Y	N	Y
21 Stokes	Y	N	N	Y	Y	Y	N	Y
OKLAHOMA								
1 Jones	N	Y	Y	Y	N	N	N	Y
2 Synar	N	N	N	Y	N	Y	N	Y
3 Watkins	N	N	N	P	N	Y	N	Y
4 McCurdy	N	Y	Y	Y	N	N	N	N
5 ***Edwards***	N	Y	Y	N	N	N	Y	N
6 English	N	Y	Y	Y	N	N	N	N
OREGON								
1 AuCoin	Y	N	N	Y	Y	Y	N	Y
2 ***Smith, R.***	N	N	N	N	N	N	N	N
3 Wyden	N	N	N	Y	N	Y	N	Y
4 Weaver	Y	N	N	Y	Y	Y	N	Y
5 ***Smith, D.***	N	Y	Y	Y	N	N	Y	N
PENNSYLVANIA								
1 Foglietta	N	N	N	Y	Y	Y	N	Y
2 Gray	Y	N	N	Y	Y	Y	N	Y
3 Borski	N	N	N	Y	N	Y	N	Y
4 Kolter	N	N	N	Y	Y	Y	N	Y
5 ***Schulze***	N	Y	Y	?	N	N	N	N
6 Yatron	N	N	N	Y	N	Y	N	Y
7 Edgar	Y	N	N	N	Y	Y	N	Y
8 Kostmayer	Y	N	N	Y	Y	Y	N	Y
9 ***Shuster***	N	Y	Y	N	N	N	Y	N
10 ***McDade***	N	Y	?	?	N	N	N	N
11 Kanjorski	N	N	N	Y	N	N	N	Y
12 Murtha	N	Y	Y	Y	N	N	N	N
13 ***Coughlin***	N	N	N	N	N	N	N	Y
14 Coyne	Y	N	N	Y	Y	Y	N	Y
15 ***Ritter***	N	Y	Y	N	N	N	Y	N
16 ***Walker***	N	N	N	N	N	N	Y	N
17 ***Gekas***	N	Y	Y	N	N	N	Y	N
18 Walgren	Y	Y	N	Y	Y	Y	N	Y
19 ***Goodling***	N	Y	Y	N	N	N	N	N
20 Gaydos	N	N	N	Y	?	?	?	?
21 ***Ridge***	N	Y	Y	N	N	N	N	Y
22 Murphy	N	Y	Y	Y	N	Y	N	Y
23 ***Clinger***	N	N	N	N	N	N	N	N
RHODE ISLAND								
1 St Germain	Y	N	N	Y	N	Y	N	Y
2 ***Schneider***	N	N	N	Y	Y	Y	N	Y
SOUTH CAROLINA								
1 ***Hartnett***	N	Y	Y	N	N	N	Y	N
2 ***Spence***	N	Y	Y	Y	N	N	Y	N
3 Derrick	N	N	N	Y	N	N	N	Y
4 ***Campbell***	N	Y	Y	?	N	N	N	N
5 Spratt	N	Y	Y	Y	N	N	N	Y
6 Tallon	N	Y	Y	Y	N	N	N	N
SOUTH DAKOTA								
AL Daschle	N	N	N	?	?	?	?	?

	155	156	157	158	159	160	161	162
TENNESSEE								
1 ***Quillen***	N	Y	Y	Y	N	N	Y	N
2 ***Duncan***	N	Y	Y	Y	N	N	N	N
3 Lloyd	N	Y	Y	N	N	N	N	N
4 Cooper	N	N	N	Y	N	Y	N	Y
5 Boner	N	Y	Y	Y	N	N	N	Y
6 Gordon	N	N	N	Y	N	N	N	Y
7 ***Sundquist***	N	Y	Y	P	?	N	Y	N
8 Jones	N	Y	Y	Y	N	N	N	N
9 Ford	N	N	N	Y	Y	Y	?	Y
TEXAS								
1 Vacancy								
2 Wilson	?	Y	Y	Y	N	N	Y	N
3 ***Bartlett***	N	Y	Y	N	N	N	Y	N
4 Hall, R.	?	Y	Y	Y	N	N	Y	N
5 Bryant	N	Y	Y	Y	N	N	N	Y
6 ***Barton***	N	Y	Y	N	N	N	Y	N
7 ***Archer***	N	Y	Y	Y	N	N	Y	N
8 ***Fields***	N	Y	Y	N	N	N	Y	N
9 Brooks	N	Y	Y	Y	N	Y	N	Y
10 Pickle	N	N	N	Y	N	N	N	N
11 Leath	N	Y	Y	Y	N	N	N	N
12 Wright	N	Y	Y	Y	N	N	N	Y
13 ***Boulter***	N	Y	Y	?	N	N	Y	N
14 ***Sweeney***	N	Y	Y	Y	N	N	Y	N
15 de la Garza	N	Y	Y	Y	Y	Y	N	N
16 Coleman	N	Y	Y	Y	N	N	N	Y
17 Stenholm	N	Y	Y	N	N	N	N	N
18 Leland	Y	N	N	Y	Y	Y	N	Y
19 ***Combest***	N	Y	Y	N	N	N	Y	N
20 Gonzalez	N	N	N	Y	Y	Y	N	Y
21 ***Loeffler***	N	Y	Y	N	N	N	Y	N
22 ***DeLay***	N	Y	Y	N	N	N	Y	N
23 Bustamante	N	Y	Y	Y	N	N	N	Y
24 Frost	N	Y	Y	Y	N	N	N	Y
25 Andrews	N	Y	Y	Y	N	N	N	Y
26 ***Armey***	N	N	Y	N	N	N	Y	N
27 Ortiz	N	Y	Y	Y	N	N	N	Y
UTAH								
1 ***Hansen***	N	Y	Y	Y	N	N	Y	N
2 ***Monson***	N	Y	Y	N	N	N	Y	N
3 ***Nielson***	N	Y	Y	Y	N	N	N	N
VERMONT								
AL ***Jeffords***	?	?	?	?	?	?	?	?
VIRGINIA								
1 ***Bateman***	N	Y	Y	Y	N	N	N	N
2 ***Whitehurst***	N	Y	Y	N	N	N	N	N
3 ***Bliley***	N	Y	Y	N	N	N	Y	N
4 Sisisky	N	Y	Y	Y	N	N	N	N
5 Daniel	N	Y	Y	Y	N	N	N	N
6 Olin	N	N	N	Y	N	N	N	N
7 ***Slaughter***	N	Y	Y	N	N	N	Y	N
8 ***Parris***	N	Y	Y	?	N	N	N	N
9 Boucher	N	Y	Y	Y	N	Y	N	Y
10 ***Wolf***	N	Y	Y	?	N	N	N	N
WASHINGTON								
1 ***Miller***	N	Y	Y	N	N	N	N	N
2 Swift	N	N	N	Y	N	Y	N	Y
3 Bonker	N	N	N	Y	Y	Y	N	Y
4 ***Morrison***	N	Y	Y	N	N	N	Y	N
5 Foley	N	N	N	Y	N	Y	N	Y
6 Dicks	N	Y	Y	Y	N	N	N	Y
7 Lowry	Y	N	N	Y	Y	Y	?	Y
8 ***Chandler***	N	Y	Y	N	N	N	N	N
WEST VIRGINIA								
1 Mollohan	N	Y	Y	Y	N	N	N	N
2 Staggers	N	N	N	Y	N	Y	N	Y
3 Wise	N	N	N	Y	N	Y	N	Y
4 Rahall	N	N	N	Y	Y	Y	N	Y
WISCONSIN								
1 Aspin	N	Y	Y	Y	N	N	N	Y
2 Kastenmeier	Y	N	N	Y	Y	Y	N	Y
3 ***Gunderson***	N	N	N	N	N	N	N	N
4 Kleczka	N	N	N	Y	N	Y	N	Y
5 Moody	N	N	N	Y	N	Y	N	Y
6 ***Petri***	N	Y	Y	Y	N	N	N	N
7 Obey	Y	N	N	Y	Y	Y	N	Y
8 ***Roth***	N	N	N	N	N	N	N	N
9 ***Sensenbrenner***	N	N	N	N	N	N	N	N
WYOMING								
AL ***Cheney***	N	Y	Y	N	N	N	Y	N

Southern states - Ala., Ark., Fla., Ga., Ky., La., Miss., N.C., Okla., S.C., Tenn., Texas, Va.

* The *Congressional Record* vote number is different from the CQ vote number because the *Record* includes quorum calls in its tally. CQ does not publish quorum call votes.

163. HR 1872. Department of Defense Authorization, Fiscal 1986. Holt, R-Md., substitute for the Price, D-Ill., amendment, to increase from $2.5 billion to $2.9 billion the authorization for the strategic defense initiative. Rejected 169-242: R 145-33; D 24-209 (ND 5-149, SD 19-60), June 20, 1985.

164. HR 1872. Department of Defense Authorization, Fiscal 1986. Price, D-Ill., amendment to authorize $2.5 billion for the strategic defense initiative. Adopted 256-150: R 165-11; D 91-139 (ND 29-126, SD 62-13), June 20, 1985.

KEY

Y Voted for (yea).
\# Paired for.
\+ Announced for.
N Voted against (nay).
X Paired against.
\- Announced against.
P Voted "present".
C Voted "present" to avoid possible conflict of interest.
? Did not vote or otherwise make a position known.

Democrats ***Republicans***

	163	164
ALABAMA		
1 ***Callahan***	Y	Y
2 ***Dickinson***	N	Y
3 Nichols	Y	Y
4 Bevill	Y	Y
5 Flippo	Y	Y
6 Erdreich	Y	Y
7 Shelby	Y	Y
ALASKA		
AL ***Young***	Y	Y
ARIZONA		
1 ***McCain***	Y	Y
2 Udall	N	Y
3 ***Stump***	Y	Y
4 ***Rudd***	Y	Y
5 ***Kolbe***	Y	Y
ARKANSAS		
1 Alexander	N	Y
2 Robinson	Y	Y
3 ***Hammerschmidt***	Y	Y
4 Anthony	N	?
CALIFORNIA		
1 Bosco	N	N
2 ***Chappie***	Y	Y
3 Matsui	N	N
4 Fazio	N	N
5 Burton	N	N
6 Boxer	N	N
7 Miller	N	N
8 Dellums	N	N
9 Stark	?	?
10 Edwards	N	N
11 Lantos	N	Y
12 ***Zschau***	N	Y
13 Mineta	N	N
14 ***Shumway***	Y	Y
15 Coelho	N	N
16 Panetta	N	N
17 ***Pashayan***	Y	Y
18 Lehman	N	N
19 ***Lagomarsino***	Y	Y
20 ***Thomas***	Y	Y
21 ***Fiedler***	Y	?
22 ***Moorhead***	Y	Y
23 Beilenson	N	N
24 Waxman	N	N
25 Roybal	N	N
26 Berman	N	N
27 Levine	N	N
28 Dixon	X	X
29 Hawkins	N	N
30 Martinez	N	Y
31 Dymally	N	N
32 Anderson	N	N
33 ***Dreier***	Y	Y
34 Torres	-	-
35 ***Lewis***	Y	Y
36 Brown	N	N
37 ***McCandless***	Y	Y
38 ***Dornan***	Y	Y
39 ***Dannemeyer***	Y	Y
40 ***Badham***	Y	Y
41 ***Lowery***	Y	Y
42 ***Lungren***	Y	Y
43 ***Packard***	Y	Y
44 Bates	N	N
45 ***Hunter***	Y	Y
COLORADO		
1 Schroeder	N	N
2 Wirth	N	N
3 ***Strang***	#	+
4 ***Brown***	N	Y
5 ***Kramer***	Y	Y
6 ***Schaefer***	Y	Y
CONNECTICUT		
1 Kennelly	N	N
2 Gejdenson	N	N
3 Morrison	N	N
4 ***McKinney***	N	N
5 ***Rowland***	Y	Y
6 ***Johnson***	N	Y
DELAWARE		
AL Carper	N	Y
FLORIDA		
1 Hutto	Y	Y
2 Fuqua	N	Y
3 Bennett	N	Y
4 Chappell	Y	Y
5 ***McCollum***	Y	Y
6 MacKay	N	N
7 Gibbons	N	Y
8 ***Young***	Y	Y
9 ***Bilirakis***	Y	Y
10 ***Ireland***	Y	Y
11 Nelson	Y	#
12 ***Lewis***	Y	Y
13 ***Mack***	Y	Y
14 Mica	N	Y
15 ***Shaw***	Y	Y
16 Smith	X	?
17 Lehman	N	N
18 Pepper	X	#
19 Fascell	N	Y
GEORGIA		
1 Thomas	N	Y
2 Hatcher	N	?
3 Ray	N	Y
4 ***Swindall***	Y	Y
5 Fowler	N	Y
6 ***Gingrich***	Y	Y
7 Darden	N	Y
8 Rowland	N	Y
9 Jenkins	N	Y
10 Barnard	Y	Y
HAWAII		
1 Heftel	N	Y
2 Akaka	N	N
IDAHO		
1 ***Craig***	Y	Y
2 Stallings	N	Y
ILLINOIS		
1 Hayes	N	N
2 Savage	?	?
3 Russo	N	N
4 ***O'Brien***	#	?
5 Lipinski	?	?
6 ***Hyde***	Y	Y
7 Collins	N	N
8 Rostenkowski	?	?
9 Yates	N	N
10 ***Porter***	N	Y
11 Annunzio	N	Y
12 ***Crane***	Y	N
13 ***Fawell***	Y	Y
14 ***Grotberg***	Y	Y
15 ***Madigan***	Y	Y
16 ***Martin***	Y	Y
17 Evans	N	N
18 ***Michel***	Y	Y
19 Bruce	N	N
20 Durbin	N	N
21 Price	Y	Y
22 Gray	Y	Y
INDIANA		
1 Visclosky	N	N
2 Sharp	N	Y
3 ***Hiler***	Y	Y
4 ***Coats***	Y	Y
5 ***Hillis***	Y	Y

ND - Northern Democrats SD - Southern Democrats

	163	164
6 ***Burton***	Y	Y
7 ***Myers***	Y	Y
8 McCloskey	N	Y
9 Hamilton	N	Y
10 Jacobs	N	N
IOWA		
1 ***Leach***	N	N
2 ***Tauke***	N	N
3 ***Evans***	Y	N
4 Smith	N	?
5 ***Lightfoot***	Y	Y
6 Bedell	N	N
KANSAS		
1 ***Roberts***	N	Y
2 Slattery	N	N
3 ***Meyers***	N	Y
4 Glickman	N	N
5 ***Whittaker***	Y	Y
KENTUCKY		
1 Hubbard	N	Y
2 Natcher	N	Y
3 Mazzoli	N	Y
4 ***Snyder***	#	?
5 ***Rogers***	Y	Y
6 ***Hopkins***	Y	Y
7 Perkins	N	N
LOUISIANA		
1 ***Livingston***	Y	Y
2 Boggs	N	Y
3 Tauzin	Y	Y
4 Roemer	N	Y
5 Huckaby	N	Y
6 ***Moore***	Y	Y
7 Breaux	Y	Y
8 Long	N	Y
MAINE		
1 ***McKernan***	N	Y
2 ***Snowe***	N	Y
MARYLAND		
1 Dyson	Y	Y
2 ***Bentley***	Y	Y
3 Mikulski	N	N
4 ***Holt***	Y	Y
5 Hoyer	N	N
6 Byron	N	Y
7 Mitchell	N	N
8 Barnes	N	N
MASSACHUSETTS		
1 ***Conte***	N	N
2 Boland	N	N
3 Early	N	N
4 Frank	N	N
5 Atkins	N	N
6 Mavroules	N	N
7 Markey	N	N
8 O'Neill		
9 Moakley	N	N
10 Studds	N	N
11 Donnelly	N	N
MICHIGAN		
1 Conyers	N	N
2 ***Pursell***	N	N
3 Wolpe	N	N
4 ***Siljander***	Y	Y
5 ***Henry***	N	Y
6 Carr	N	N
7 Kildee	N	N
8 Traxler	N	N
9 ***Vander Jagt***	Y	Y
10 ***Schuette***	Y	Y
11 ***Davis***	N	Y
12 Bonior	N	N
13 Crockett	N	N
14 Hertel	N	N
15 Ford	N	N
16 Dingell	N	N
17 Levin	N	N
18 ***Broomfield***	Y	Y
MINNESOTA		
1 Penny	N	N
2 ***Weber***	Y	Y
3 ***Frenzel***	N	Y
4 Vento	N	N
5 Sabo	N	N
6 Sikorski	N	N
7 ***Stangeland***	Y	Y
8 Oberstar	N	N
MISSISSIPPI		
1 Whitten	N	Y
2 ***Franklin***	Y	Y
3 Montgomery	Y	Y
4 Dowdy	N	Y
5 ***Lott***	Y	Y
MISSOURI		
1 Clay	N	N
2 Young	N	N
3 Gephardt	N	Y
4 Skelton	N	Y
5 Wheat	N	N
6 ***Coleman***	Y	Y
7 ***Taylor***	Y	Y
8 ***Emerson***	Y	Y
9 Volkmer	N	N
MONTANA		
1 Williams	N	N
2 ***Marlenee***	Y	Y
NEBRASKA		
1 ***Bereuter***	N	Y
2 ***Daub***	Y	Y
3 ***Smith***	N	Y
NEVADA		
1 Reid	Y	Y
2 ***Vucanovich***	Y	Y
NEW HAMPSHIRE		
1 ***Smith***	Y	Y
2 ***Gregg***	Y	Y
NEW JERSEY		
1 Florio	N	N
2 Hughes	N	Y
3 Howard	N	N
4 ***Smith***	Y	Y
5 ***Roukema***	N	Y
6 Dwyer	N	N
7 ***Rinaldo***	Y	Y
8 Roe	N	N
9 Torricelli	N	N
10 Rodino	N	N
11 ***Gallo***	Y	Y
12 ***Courter***	Y	Y
13 ***Saxton***	Y	Y
14 Guarini	N	N
NEW MEXICO		
1 ***Lujan***	N	Y
2 ***Skeen***	Y	Y
3 Richardson	N	Y
NEW YORK		
1 ***Carney***	Y	Y
2 Downey	N	N
3 Mrazek	N	N
4 ***Lent***	Y	Y
5 ***McGrath***	Y	Y
6 Addabbo	N	N
7 Ackerman	N	N
8 Scheuer	N	N
9 Manton	?	?
10 Schumer	-	-
11 Towns	?	?
12 Owens	N	N
13 Solarz	N	N
14 ***Molinari***	Y	Y
15 ***Green***	N	N
16 Rangel	N	N
17 Weiss	N	N
18 Garcia	?	X
19 Biaggi	N	Y
20 ***DioGuardi***	Y	Y
21 ***Fish***	N	Y
22 ***Gilman***	Y	Y
23 Stratton	Y	Y
24 ***Solomon***	Y	Y
25 ***Boehlert***	Y	Y
26 ***Martin***	Y	Y
27 ***Wortley***	Y	Y
28 McHugh	N	N
29 ***Horton***	Y	Y
30 ***Eckert***	Y	Y
31 ***Kemp***	Y	Y
32 LaFalce	N	N
33 Nowak	N	N
34 Lundine	N	Y
NORTH CAROLINA		
1 Jones	N	Y
2 Valentine	N	Y
3 Whitley	N	Y
4 ***Cobey***	Y	Y
5 Neal	N	Y
6 ***Coble***	N	Y
7 Rose	N	N
8 Hefner	N	Y
9 ***McMillan***	Y	Y
10 ***Broyhill***	N	Y
11 ***Hendon***	Y	Y
NORTH DAKOTA		
AL Dorgan	N	N
OHIO		
1 Luken	?	?
2 ***Gradison***	Y	Y
3 Hall	N	N
4 ***Oxley***	Y	Y
5 ***Latta***	Y	Y
6 ***McEwen***	Y	Y
7 ***DeWine***	Y	Y
8 ***Kindness***	Y	Y
9 Kaptur	?	N
10 ***Miller***	Y	Y
11 Eckart	N	N
12 ***Kasich***	Y	Y
13 Pease	N	N
14 Seiberling	N	N
15 ***Wylie***	Y	Y
16 ***Regula***	N	Y
17 Traficant	N	N
18 Applegate	?	?
19 Feighan	N	N
20 Oakar	N	N
21 Stokes	N	N
OKLAHOMA		
1 Jones	N	Y
2 Synar	N	N
3 Watkins	N	Y
4 McCurdy	N	Y
5 ***Edwards***	Y	Y
6 English	N	Y
OREGON		
1 AuCoin	N	N
2 ***Smith, R.***	N	Y
3 Wyden	N	N
4 Weaver	N	N
5 ***Smith, D.***	Y	Y
PENNSYLVANIA		
1 Foglietta	N	N
2 Gray	N	N
3 Borski	N	N
4 Kolter	N	N
5 ***Schulze***	Y	Y
6 Yatron	?	Y
7 Edgar	N	N
8 Kostmayer	N	N
9 ***Shuster***	Y	Y
10 ***McDade***	Y	Y
11 Kanjorski	N	Y
12 Murtha	N	Y
13 ***Coughlin***	N	N
14 Coyne	N	N
15 ***Ritter***	Y	Y
16 ***Walker***	Y	Y
17 ***Gekas***	Y	Y
18 Walgren	N	N
19 ***Goodling***	Y	Y
20 Gaydos	?	?
21 ***Ridge***	N	N
22 Murphy	N	N
23 ***Clinger***	Y	Y
RHODE ISLAND		
1 St Germain	N	N
2 ***Schneider***	N	N
SOUTH CAROLINA		
1 ***Hartnett***	Y	?
2 ***Spence***	Y	Y
3 Derrick	N	Y
4 ***Campbell***	Y	Y
5 Spratt	N	Y
6 Tallon	N	Y
SOUTH DAKOTA		
AL Daschle	?	?
TENNESSEE		
1 ***Quillen***	Y	Y
2 ***Duncan***	Y	Y
3 Lloyd	Y	Y
4 Cooper	N	N
5 Boner	N	Y
6 Gordon	N	N
7 ***Sundquist***	Y	Y
8 Jones	N	Y
9 Ford	N	N
TEXAS		
1 Vacancy		
2 Wilson	Y	Y
3 ***Bartlett***	Y	Y
4 Hall, R.	Y	Y
5 Bryant	N	Y
6 ***Barton***	Y	Y
7 ***Archer***	Y	Y
8 ***Fields***	Y	Y
9 Brooks	N	N
10 Pickle	N	Y
11 Leath	Y	Y
12 Wright	N	?
13 ***Boulter***	Y	Y
14 ***Sweeney***	Y	Y
15 de la Garza	N	N
16 Coleman	N	Y
17 Stenholm	Y	Y
18 Leland	N	N
19 ***Combest***	Y	Y
20 Gonzalez	N	N
21 ***Loeffler***	Y	Y
22 ***DeLay***	Y	Y
23 Bustamante	N	Y
24 Frost	N	Y
25 Andrews	N	Y
26 ***Armey***	Y	Y
27 Ortiz	N	Y
UTAH		
1 ***Hansen***	Y	Y
2 ***Monson***	Y	Y
3 ***Nielson***	Y	Y
VERMONT		
AL ***Jeffords***	?	?
VIRGINIA		
1 ***Bateman***	Y	Y
2 ***Whitehurst***	Y	Y
3 ***Bliley***	Y	Y
4 Sisisky	N	Y
5 Daniel	Y	Y
6 Olin	N	Y
7 ***Slaughter***	Y	Y
8 ***Parris***	Y	Y
9 Boucher	N	N
10 ***Wolf***	Y	Y
WASHINGTON		
1 ***Miller***	Y	Y
2 Swift	N	N
3 Bonker	N	N
4 ***Morrison***	Y	Y
5 Foley	N	N
6 Dicks	N	N
7 Lowry	N	N
8 ***Chandler***	Y	Y
WEST VIRGINIA		
1 Mollohan	N	Y
2 Staggers	N	Y
3 Wise	N	N
4 Rahall	N	N
WISCONSIN		
1 Aspin	N	Y
2 Kastenmeier	N	N
3 ***Gunderson***	N	Y
4 Kleczka	N	Y
5 Moody	N	N
6 ***Petri***	N	Y
7 Obey	N	N
8 ***Roth***	N	Y
9 ***Sensenbrenner***	Y	Y
WYOMING		
AL ***Cheney***	Y	Y

Southern states - Ala., Ark., Fla., Ga., Ky., La., Miss., N.C., Okla., S.C., Tenn., Texas, Va.

* The *Congressional Record* vote number is different from the CQ vote number because the *Record* includes quorum calls in its tally. CQ does not publish quorum call votes.

165. Procedural Motion. Porter, R-Ill., motion to approve the House *Journal* of Thursday, June 20. Motion agreed to 214-124: R 37-111; D 177-13 (ND 113-9, SD 64-4), June 21, 1985.

166. HR 1872. Department of Defense Authorization, Fiscal 1986. Nichols, D-Ala., amendment to clarify the intent of a section of the fiscal 1985 Defense Department authorization relating to certain functions, known as "core logistics," performed by Defense Department civilian personnel, that are too critical to national security to be contracted out. The amendment specified core-logistic functions listed by the Defense Department and expanded the definition of such functions. Adopted 353-7: R 146-7; D 207-0 (ND 135-0, SD 72-0), June 21, 1985.

167. HR 1872. Department of Defense Authorization, Fiscal 1986. Nichols, D-Ala., amendment to bar reimbursement of entertainment and other expenses submitted by defense contractors, to limit reimbursement of travel on corporate aircraft, to penalize contractors who submit unallowable costs, and to require contractors to document costs. The amendment also limits assignments of principal contracting officers, requires certification of overhead costs, and grants subpoena power to the secretary of defense for contractors' records. Adopted 411-4: R 170-4; D 241-0 (ND 164-0, SD 77-0), June 25, 1985.

168. HR 1872. Department of Defense Authorization, Fiscal 1986. Courter, R-N.J., amendment to require the Defense Department to set a 5 percent minimum target for competitive defense contracts, and to increase the percentage of competitive contracts by 5 percent each year until a 70 percent level is reached. The amendment also requires the secretary of defense to report to Congress if that goal is not met. Adopted 416-0: R 174-0; D 242-0 (ND 166-0, SD 76-0), June 25, 1985.

169. HR 1872. Department of Defense Authorization, Fiscal 1986. Byron, D-Md., amendment to the Spratt, D-S.C., amendment, to change from Jan. 1 to Jan. 30, 1986, the date of enactment of the Spratt amendment to bar middle-level Pentagon officials, in specific positions to be named by the secretary of defense, from accepting employment for two years after leaving the Defense Department from defense contractors over whose contracts they had supervision. Rejected 140-272: R 108-67; D 32-205 (ND 11-153, SD 21-52), June 25, 1985. (The amendment, if adopted, would have precluded further amendments to the Spratt amendment — in particular, the Bennett, D-Fla., substitute, which was subsequently adopted *(see vote 170, below).*)

170. HR 1872. Department of Defense Authorization, Fiscal 1986. Bennett, D-Fla., substitute for the Spratt, D-S.C., amendment, to bar Pentagon officials who had "significant responsibility" for procurement with a specific defense contractor from accepting employment for two years after leaving the Defense Department from that contractor. Adopted 397-19: R 161-15; D 236-4 (ND 163-1, SD 73-3), June 25, 1985. A "nay" was a vote supporting the president's position. (The effect of the amendment was to eliminate the provision in the Spratt amendment that would permit the secretary of defense to waive certain positions from the prohibition. The Spratt amendment, as modified by the Bennett substitute, was subsequently adopted by voice vote.)

171. HR 1872. Department of Defense Authorization, Fiscal 1986. Hertel, D-Mich., amendment to empower the inspector general of the Defense Department to suspend payments to a contractor or debar a contractor if he finds waste, fraud and abuse in connection with the contract. Rejected 176-240: R 24-153; D 152-87 (ND 134-27, SD 18-60), June 25, 1985.

172. HR 1872. Department of Defense Authorization, Fiscal 1986. Levine, D-Calif., amendment to require that future weapons projects be procured competitively, with provisions for exceptions. Adopted 342-52: R 135-36; D 207-16 (ND 146-4, SD 61-12), June 25, 1985.

KEY

- Y Voted for (yea).
- # Paired for.
- + Announced for.
- N Voted against (nay).
- X Paired against.
- - Announced against.
- P Voted "present".
- C Voted "present" to avoid possible conflict of interest.
- ? Did not vote or otherwise make a position known.

Democrats *Republicans*

	165	166	167	168	169	170	171	172
ALABAMA								
1 ***Callahan***	?	Y	Y	Y	Y	Y	N	Y
2 ***Dickinson***	N	Y	Y	Y	Y	N	N	N
3 Nichols	Y	Y	Y	Y	N	Y	N	N
4 Bevill	Y	Y	Y	Y	N	Y	N	Y
5 Flippo	Y	Y	Y	Y	?	Y	N	Y
6 Erdreich	Y	Y	Y	Y	N	Y	N	Y
7 Shelby	Y	Y	Y	Y	N	Y	N	Y
ALASKA								
AL ***Young***	N	Y	Y	Y	N	Y	N	Y
ARIZONA								
1 ***McCain***	?	?	Y	Y	Y	N	N	Y
2 Udall	?	Y	Y	Y	N	Y	Y	Y
3 ***Stump***	N	N	Y	Y	Y	N	N	N
4 ***Rudd***	?	?	Y	Y	Y	N	N	N
5 ***Kolbe***	N	Y	Y	Y	N	Y	N	Y
ARKANSAS								
1 Alexander	Y	Y	Y	Y	N	Y	N	?
2 Robinson	Y	Y	Y	Y	N	Y	Y	Y
3 ***Hammerschmidt***	N	Y	Y	Y	Y	Y	N	N
4 Anthony	?	?	Y	Y	N	Y	N	N
CALIFORNIA								
1 Bosco	P	Y	Y	Y	N	Y	Y	Y
2 ***Chappie***	P	Y	Y	Y	Y	Y	N	N
3 Matsui	Y	Y	Y	Y	N	Y	Y	Y
4 Fazio	Y	+	Y	Y	N	Y	N	Y
5 Burton	Y	Y	Y	Y	N	Y	Y	Y
6 Boxer	?	?	Y	Y	N	Y	Y	Y
7 Miller	Y	Y	Y	Y	N	Y	Y	Y
8 Dellums	Y	Y	Y	Y	N	Y	Y	Y
9 Stark	?	?	Y	Y	N	Y	Y	Y
10 Edwards	Y	Y	Y	Y	N	Y	Y	Y
11 Lantos	Y	Y	Y	Y	N	Y	Y	Y
12 ***Zschau***	N	Y	Y	Y	Y	Y	N	N
13 Mineta	Y	Y	Y	Y	N	Y	Y	Y
14 ***Shumway***	N	Y	Y	Y	?	?	?	?
15 Coelho	Y	Y	Y	Y	N	Y	Y	Y
16 Panetta	?	?	Y	Y	N	Y	Y	Y
17 ***Pashayan***	N	Y	Y	Y	Y	Y	N	Y
18 Lehman	?	?	Y	Y	N	Y	Y	Y
19 ***Lagomarsino***	N	Y	Y	Y	Y	Y	N	Y
20 ***Thomas***	?	?	Y	Y	Y	Y	N	Y
21 ***Fiedler***	?	?	Y	Y	Y	Y	N	Y
22 ***Moorhead***	N	Y	Y	Y	Y	Y	N	N
23 Beilenson	Y	Y	Y	Y	N	Y	Y	Y
24 Waxman	?	?	Y	Y	N	Y	Y	Y
25 Roybal	?	Y	Y	Y	N	Y	Y	Y
26 Berman	Y	Y	Y	Y	N	Y	Y	Y
27 Levine	Y	Y	Y	Y	N	Y	Y	Y
28 Dixon	?	?	Y	Y	N	Y	Y	Y
29 Hawkins	Y	Y	Y	Y	N	Y	Y	Y
30 Martinez	Y	Y	Y	Y	N	Y	Y	Y
31 Dymally	P	Y	Y	Y	N	Y	Y	Y
32 Anderson	Y	Y	Y	Y	N	Y	Y	Y
33 ***Dreier***	N	Y	Y	Y	Y	Y	N	Y
34 Torres	Y	Y	?	?	?	Y	Y	Y
35 ***Lewis***	N	Y	?	Y	Y	Y	N	N
36 Brown	Y	Y	Y	Y	N	Y	Y	Y
37 ***McCandless***	N	Y	Y	Y	N	Y	N	N
38 ***Dornan***	?	Y	Y	Y	Y	N	N	Y
39 ***Dannemeyer***	N	Y	Y	Y	Y	Y	N	Y
40 ***Badham***	N	Y	N	Y	Y	Y	N	N
41 ***Lowery***	N	Y	Y	Y	Y	Y	N	Y
42 ***Lungren***	N	Y	Y	Y	N	Y	N	Y
43 ***Packard***	N	Y	Y	Y	Y	Y	N	Y
44 Bates	?	Y	Y	Y	N	Y	Y	Y
45 ***Hunter***	?	Y	Y	Y	Y	Y	N	Y
COLORADO								
1 Schroeder	N	Y	Y	Y	N	Y	Y	Y
2 Wirth	Y	Y	Y	Y	N	Y	Y	Y
3 ***Strang***	-	+	Y	Y	Y	Y	N	?
4 ***Brown***	N	N	Y	Y	N	Y	N	Y
5 ***Kramer***	N	Y	Y	Y	Y	Y	N	Y
6 ***Schaefer***	Y	Y	Y	Y	N	Y	N	Y
CONNECTICUT								
1 Kennelly	Y	Y	Y	Y	N	Y	N	Y
2 Gejdenson	Y	Y	Y	Y	N	Y	Y	Y
3 Morrison	Y	Y	Y	Y	N	Y	Y	Y
4 ***McKinney***	Y	Y	Y	Y	N	Y	N	?
5 ***Rowland***	Y	Y	Y	Y	N	Y	N	Y
6 ***Johnson***	Y	Y	Y	Y	Y	Y	N	Y
DELAWARE								
AL Carper	Y	Y	Y	Y	N	Y	N	?
FLORIDA								
1 Hutto	Y	Y	Y	Y	Y	Y	N	N
2 Fuqua	Y	Y	Y	Y	N	Y	N	Y
3 Bennett	Y	Y	Y	Y	N	Y	Y	Y
4 Chappell	Y	Y	Y	Y	?	?	N	N
5 ***McCollum***	Y	?	Y	Y	Y	Y	N	Y
6 MacKay	Y	Y	Y	Y	Y	Y	Y	Y
7 Gibbons	P	Y	Y	Y	?	Y	Y	Y
8 ***Young***	N	Y	Y	Y	N	Y	N	Y
9 ***Bilirakis***	N	Y	Y	Y	N	Y	N	Y
10 ***Ireland***	N	N	Y	Y	Y	Y	N	Y
11 Nelson	+	+	Y	Y	N	Y	Y	Y
12 ***Lewis***	N	Y	Y	Y	N	Y	N	Y
13 ***Mack***	N	Y	Y	Y	N	Y	N	Y
14 Mica	Y	Y	Y	Y	Y	Y	N	Y
15 ***Shaw***	N	N	Y	Y	N	Y	N	Y
16 Smith	Y	Y	Y	Y	N	Y	Y	Y
17 Lehman	Y	Y	Y	Y	N	Y	Y	Y
18 Pepper	+	+	Y	Y	+	+	Y	Y
19 Fascell	Y	Y	Y	Y	N	Y	N	Y
GEORGIA								
1 Thomas	Y	Y	Y	Y	Y	Y	N	N
2 Hatcher	Y	Y	Y	Y	Y	Y	N	?
3 Ray	Y	Y	Y	Y	Y	Y	N	N
4 ***Swindall***	N	Y	Y	Y	Y	Y	N	Y
5 Fowler	Y	Y	Y	Y	N	Y	N	Y
6 ***Gingrich***	N	Y	Y	Y	Y	Y	N	Y
7 Darden	Y	Y	Y	Y	Y	Y	N	Y
8 Rowland	Y	Y	Y	Y	Y	Y	N	Y
9 Jenkins	Y	Y	Y	Y	N	Y	N	Y
10 Barnard	Y	Y	Y	Y	Y	Y	N	N
HAWAII								
1 Heftel	Y	Y	Y	Y	N	Y	Y	Y
2 Akaka	Y	Y	Y	Y	N	?	N	Y
IDAHO								
1 ***Craig***	N	Y	Y	Y	Y	Y	N	Y
2 Stallings	Y	Y	Y	Y	N	Y	Y	Y
ILLINOIS								
1 Hayes	Y	Y	Y	Y	N	Y	Y	?
2 Savage	Y	Y	Y	Y	N	Y	Y	Y
3 Russo	Y	Y	Y	Y	N	Y	Y	Y
4 ***O'Brien***	?	?	?	?	Y	Y	N	Y
5 Lipinski	?	?	Y	Y	N	Y	Y	Y
6 ***Hyde***	Y	Y	Y	Y	Y	Y	N	Y
7 Collins	?	?	Y	Y	N	Y	Y	Y
8 Rostenkowski	?	?	?	Y	N	Y	Y	Y
9 Yates	Y	Y	Y	Y	N	Y	Y	?
10 ***Porter***	N	Y	Y	Y	N	Y	N	Y
11 Annunzio	?	?	Y	Y	N	Y	N	Y
12 ***Crane***	?	?	Y	Y	N	Y	N	N
13 ***Fawell***	N	Y	Y	Y	N	Y	Y	Y
14 ***Grotberg***	N	Y	Y	Y	Y	Y	N	Y
15 ***Madigan***	N	Y	Y	Y	Y	Y	Y	Y
16 ***Martin***	N	?	Y	Y	Y	Y	N	Y
17 Evans	Y	Y	Y	Y	N	Y	Y	Y
18 ***Michel***	Y	Y	?	Y	?	Y	N	N
19 Bruce	Y	Y	Y	Y	N	Y	Y	Y
20 Durbin	N	Y	Y	Y	N	Y	Y	Y
21 Price	Y	Y	Y	Y	N	Y	N	Y
22 Gray	?	?	Y	Y	N	Y	Y	?
INDIANA								
1 Visclosky	Y	Y	Y	Y	N	Y	N	Y
2 Sharp	Y	Y	Y	Y	N	Y	Y	Y
3 ***Hiler***	?	?	Y	Y	Y	Y	N	Y
4 ***Coats***	N	Y	Y	Y	Y	Y	N	Y
5 ***Hillis***	N	Y	Y	Y	Y	Y	N	N

ND - Northern Democrats SD - Southern Democrats

* Corresponding to Congressional Record Votes 182, 184, 185, 186, 187, 188, 189, 190

	165	166	167	168	169	170	171	172
6 ***Burton***	N	Y	Y	Y	Y	Y	N	Y
7 ***Myers***	Y	Y	Y	Y	Y	N	N	N
8 McCloskey	Y	Y	Y	Y	N	Y	Y	Y
9 Hamilton	Y	Y	Y	Y	N	Y	N	Y
10 Jacobs	N	Y	Y	Y	N	Y	Y	Y
IOWA								
1 ***Leach***	N	Y	N	Y	N	Y	Y	Y
2 ***Tauke***	N	Y	Y	Y	N	Y	N	Y
3 ***Evans***	N	Y	Y	Y	Y	Y	Y	Y
4 Smith	?	?	Y	Y	N	Y	N	Y
5 ***Lightfoot***	N	Y	Y	Y	Y	Y	N	Y
6 Bedell	Y	Y	Y	Y	N	Y	Y	Y
KANSAS								
1 ***Roberts***	N	Y	Y	Y	N	Y	N	Y
2 Slattery	Y	Y	Y	Y	N	Y	N	Y
3 ***Meyers***	Y	Y	Y	Y	N	Y	Y	Y
4 Glickman	Y	Y	Y	Y	N	Y	N	Y
5 ***Whittaker***	N	Y	Y	Y	N	Y	N	Y
KENTUCKY								
1 Hubbard	Y	Y	Y	Y	Y	Y	N	Y
2 Natcher	Y	Y	Y	Y	N	Y	N	Y
3 Mazzoli	+	+	Y	Y	N	Y	Y	Y
4 ***Snyder***	?	?	Y	Y	Y	Y	N	Y
5 ***Rogers***	N	Y	Y	Y	Y	Y	N	Y
6 ***Hopkins***	Y	Y	Y	Y	N	Y	N	Y
7 Perkins	Y	Y	Y	Y	N	Y	N	Y
LOUISIANA								
1 ***Livingston***	?	?	Y	Y	Y	Y	N	N
2 Boggs	Y	Y	Y	Y	N	Y	N	Y
3 Tauzin	Y	Y	Y	Y	N	Y	N	Y
4 Roemer	N	Y	Y	Y	N	Y	N	Y
5 Huckaby	Y	Y	Y	Y	N	Y	N	Y
6 ***Moore***	?	?	Y	Y	Y	Y	N	Y
7 Breaux	?	?	?	?	?	?	?	?
8 Long	Y	Y	Y	Y	N	Y	N	Y
MAINE								
1 ***McKernan***	N	Y	Y	Y	N	Y	N	Y
2 ***Snowe***	N	Y	Y	Y	N	Y	N	Y
MARYLAND								
1 Dyson	Y	Y	Y	Y	Y	Y	N	N
2 ***Bentley***	?	Y	+	Y	Y	N	N	Y
3 Mikulski	Y	Y	Y	Y	N	Y	Y	Y
4 ***Holt***	Y	Y	?	?	?	?	?	?
5 Hoyer	Y	Y	Y	Y	N	Y	Y	Y
6 Byron	Y	Y	Y	Y	Y	Y	N	N
7 Mitchell	N	Y	Y	Y	N	Y	Y	?
8 Barnes	?	Y	Y	Y	N	Y	Y	Y
MASSACHUSETTS								
1 ***Conte***	N	Y	Y	Y	N	Y	N	Y
2 Boland	?	?	Y	Y	N	Y	Y	Y
3 Early	?	?	Y	Y	N	Y	N	Y
4 Frank	Y	Y	Y	Y	N	Y	Y	Y
5 Atkins	?	Y	Y	Y	N	Y	Y	Y
6 Mavroules	Y	Y	Y	Y	Y	Y	Y	Y
7 Markey	N	Y	Y	Y	N	Y	Y	?
8 O'Neill								
9 Moakley	?	?	Y	Y	N	Y	Y	Y
10 Studds	Y	Y	Y	Y	N	Y	Y	Y
11 Donnelly	Y	Y	Y	Y	N	Y	Y	Y
MICHIGAN								
1 Conyers	Y	Y	Y	Y	N	Y	?	?
2 ***Pursell***	N	Y	Y	Y	N	Y	Y	Y
3 Wolpe	Y	Y	Y	Y	N	Y	Y	Y
4 ***Siljander***	?	?	Y	Y	Y	Y	N	Y
5 ***Henry***	N	Y	Y	Y	N	Y	Y	Y
6 Carr	?	?	Y	Y	Y	Y	Y	Y
7 Kildee	Y	Y	Y	Y	N	Y	Y	Y
8 Traxler	Y	Y	Y	Y	N	Y	Y	Y
9 ***Vander Jagt***	N	Y	Y	Y	N	Y	N	Y
10 ***Schuette***	N	Y	Y	Y	Y	Y	N	Y
11 ***Davis***	Y	Y	Y	Y	Y	?	N	Y
12 Bonior	?	?	Y	Y	N	Y	?	?
13 Crockett	Y	Y	Y	Y	N	Y	Y	Y
14 Hertel	Y	Y	Y	Y	N	Y	Y	Y
15 Ford	?	Y	Y	Y	N	Y	Y	?
16 Dingell	?	Y	Y	Y	N	Y	Y	Y
17 Levin	Y	Y	Y	Y	N	Y	Y	Y
18 ***Broomfield***	?	?	Y	Y	N	Y	Y	?
MINNESOTA								
1 Penny	N	Y	Y	Y	N	Y	Y	Y
2 ***Weber***	N	Y	Y	Y	N	Y	Y	Y
3 ***Frenzel***	Y	N	Y	Y	Y	Y	N	N
4 Vento	Y	Y	Y	Y	N	Y	Y	Y
5 Sabo	Y	Y	Y	Y	N	Y	Y	Y
6 Sikorski	N	Y	Y	Y	N	Y	Y	Y

	165	166	167	168	169	170	171	172
7 ***Stangeland***	N	Y	N	Y	Y	Y	N	Y
8 Oberstar	Y	Y	Y	Y	N	Y	Y	Y
MISSISSIPPI								
1 Whitten	Y	Y	Y	Y	N	Y	N	Y
2 ***Franklin***	Y	Y	Y	Y	Y	Y	?	N
3 Montgomery	Y	Y	Y	Y	Y	N	N	N
4 Dowdy	Y	Y	Y	Y	N	Y	N	Y
5 ***Lott***	N	Y	Y	Y	Y	Y	N	N
MISSOURI								
1 Clay	N	Y	Y	Y	N	Y	Y	?
2 Young	?	?	Y	Y	Y	Y	N	Y
3 Gephardt	?	?	Y	Y	N	Y	Y	?
4 Skelton	Y	Y	Y	Y	Y	Y	N	Y
5 Wheat	Y	Y	Y	Y	N	Y	Y	Y
6 ***Coleman***	N	Y	Y	Y	Y	Y	N	Y
7 ***Taylor***	N	Y	Y	Y	Y	Y	N	Y
8 ***Emerson***	N	Y	Y	Y	Y	Y	N	Y
9 Volkmer	Y	Y	Y	Y	N	Y	N	Y
MONTANA								
1 Williams	?	Y	Y	Y	?	Y	Y	Y
2 ***Marlenee***	?	?	Y	?	N	Y	N	Y
NEBRASKA								
1 ***Bereuter***	N	N	Y	Y	N	Y	N	Y
2 ***Daub***	N	Y	Y	Y	Y	Y	N	N
3 ***Smith***	Y	?	Y	Y	Y	Y	N	Y
NEVADA								
1 Reid	Y	Y	Y	Y	N	Y	Y	Y
2 ***Vucanovich***	N	Y	Y	Y	Y	Y	N	N
NEW HAMPSHIRE								
1 ***Smith***	N	Y	Y	Y	N	Y	N	Y
2 ***Gregg***	N	Y	Y	Y	N	Y	N	Y
NEW JERSEY								
1 Florio	Y	Y	Y	Y	N	Y	Y	Y
2 Hughes	Y	Y	Y	Y	N	Y	N	Y
3 Howard	Y	Y	Y	Y	N	Y	Y	Y
4 ***Smith***	?	Y	Y	Y	N	Y	N	Y
5 ***Roukema***	Y	Y	Y	Y	N	Y	N	Y
6 Dwyer	Y	Y	Y	Y	N	Y	Y	Y
7 ***Rinaldo***	Y	Y	Y	Y	?	?	N	Y
8 Roe	Y	Y	Y	Y	N	Y	Y	Y
9 Torricelli	?	?	Y	Y	N	Y	Y	Y
10 Rodino	Y	Y	Y	Y	N	Y	N	Y
11 ***Gallo***	N	Y	Y	Y	Y	Y	N	Y
12 ***Courter***	N	Y	Y	Y	Y	Y	N	Y
13 ***Saxton***	N	Y	Y	Y	N	Y	Y	Y
14 Guarini	Y	Y	?	Y	N	Y	Y	Y
NEW MEXICO								
1 ***Lujan***	Y	Y	Y	Y	N	Y	N	Y
2 ***Skeen***	N	Y	Y	Y	Y	Y	N	N
3 Richardson	Y	Y	Y	Y	N	Y	Y	Y
NEW YORK								
1 ***Carney***	N	Y	Y	Y	Y	Y	N	Y
2 Downey	Y	Y	Y	Y	N	Y	Y	Y
3 Mrazek	Y	Y	Y	Y	N	Y	Y	Y
4 ***Lent***	N	Y	Y	Y	Y	Y	N	Y
5 ***McGrath***	N	Y	Y	Y	N	Y	N	Y
6 Addabbo	?	?	Y	Y	N	Y	N	Y
7 Ackerman	Y	Y	Y	Y	N	Y	Y	Y
8 Scheuer	P	Y	Y	Y	N	Y	Y	Y
9 Manton	Y	Y	Y	Y	N	Y	Y	Y
10 Schumer	?	?	Y	Y	N	Y	Y	Y
11 Towns	?	?	Y	Y	?	?	?	Y
12 Owens	Y	Y	Y	+	-	+	+	+
13 Solarz	Y	Y	Y	Y	N	Y	Y	Y
14 ***Molinari***	N	Y	Y	Y	N	Y	N	Y
15 ***Green***	Y	N	Y	Y	N	Y	Y	Y
16 Rangel	Y	Y	Y	Y	N	Y	Y	Y
17 Weiss	Y	Y	Y	Y	N	Y	Y	Y
18 Garcia	?	?	?	?	N	Y	Y	Y
19 Biaggi	?	?	Y	Y	N	?	Y	Y
20 ***DioGuardi***	N	Y	Y	Y	Y	Y	N	Y
21 ***Fish***	Y	Y	?	?	?	?	?	?
22 ***Gilman***	N	Y	Y	Y	N	Y	Y	Y
23 Stratton	Y	Y	Y	Y	Y	N	N	N
24 ***Solomon***	N	Y	Y	Y	Y	Y	N	?
25 ***Boehlert***	N	Y	Y	Y	N	Y	N	Y
26 ***Martin***	N	Y	?	?	Y	Y	N	N
27 ***Wortley***	Y	Y	?	?	?	?	?	?
28 McHugh	?	Y	Y	Y	-	+	-	+
29 ***Horton***	Y	Y	Y	Y	Y	Y	N	Y
30 ***Eckert***	N	?	Y	Y	N	N	N	N
31 ***Kemp***	?	Y	Y	Y	Y	Y	N	N
32 LaFalce	Y	Y	Y	Y	N	Y	N	Y
33 Nowak	Y	Y	Y	Y	N	Y	Y	Y
34 Lundine	Y	Y	Y	Y	Y	Y	Y	Y

	165	166	167	168	169	170	171	172
NORTH CAROLINA								
1 Jones	?	Y	Y	?	N	Y	?	?
2 Valentine	Y	Y	Y	Y	?	?	N	Y
3 Whitley	Y	Y	Y	Y	N	Y	N	Y
4 ***Cobey***	N	Y	Y	Y	N	Y	N	Y
5 Neal	Y	Y	Y	Y	N	Y	N	Y
6 ***Coble***	N	Y	Y	Y	N	Y	Y	Y
7 Rose	Y	Y	Y	Y	N	Y	N	Y
8 Hefner	Y	Y	Y	Y	N	Y	N	Y
9 ***McMillan***	N	Y	Y	Y	N	Y	N	Y
10 ***Broyhill***	Y	Y	Y	Y	N	Y	N	Y
11 ***Hendon***	?	Y	Y	Y	N	Y	Y	Y
NORTH DAKOTA								
AL Dorgan	Y	Y	Y	Y	N	Y	Y	Y
OHIO								
1 Luken	?	?	?	?	?	?	?	?
2 ***Gradison***	N	Y	Y	Y	Y	Y	N	Y
3 Hall	?	Y	Y	Y	N	Y	Y	?
4 ***Oxley***	+	+	Y	Y	Y	Y	N	Y
5 ***Latta***	N	Y	Y	Y	?	Y	N	Y
6 ***McEwen***	N	Y	Y	Y	N	Y	Y	Y
7 ***DeWine***	N	Y	Y	Y	N	Y	N	N
8 ***Kindness***	N	Y	N	Y	Y	N	N	Y
9 Kaptur	Y	Y	Y	Y	N	Y	Y	Y
10 ***Miller***	N	Y	Y	Y	Y	Y	Y	Y
11 Eckart	Y	Y	Y	Y	N	Y	Y	Y
12 ***Kasich***	?	Y	Y	Y	N	Y	N	Y
13 Pease	Y	Y	Y	Y	N	Y	N	Y
14 Seiberling	?	Y	Y	Y	N	Y	Y	Y
15 ***Wylie***	Y	Y	Y	Y	Y	Y	N	Y
16 ***Regula***	Y	Y	Y	Y	N	Y	N	Y
17 Traficant	Y	Y	Y	Y	N	Y	Y	Y
18 Applegate	?	Y	Y	Y	N	Y	Y	N
19 Feighan	Y	Y	Y	Y	N	Y	Y	Y
20 Oakar	?	Y	Y	Y	N	Y	Y	Y
21 Stokes	Y	Y	Y	Y	N	Y	Y	?
OKLAHOMA								
1 Jones	Y	Y	Y	Y	Y	Y	Y	Y
2 Synar	Y	Y	Y	Y	N	Y	N	Y
3 Watkins	?	?	Y	Y	N	Y	Y	Y
4 McCurdy	?	Y	Y	Y	Y	Y	N	Y
5 ***Edwards***	N	Y	Y	Y	N	Y	N	Y
6 English	Y	?	Y	Y	N	Y	N	Y
OREGON								
1 AuCoin	?	?	Y	Y	N	Y	Y	Y
2 ***Smith, R.***	Y	Y	Y	Y	Y	Y	N	Y
3 Wyden	Y	Y	Y	Y	N	Y	Y	Y
4 Weaver	Y	Y	Y	Y	N	Y	Y	?
5 ***Smith, D.***	?	?	Y	Y	N	Y	N	Y
PENNSYLVANIA								
1 Foglietta	Y	?	Y	Y	N	Y	Y	Y
2 Gray	Y	Y	?	Y	N	Y	?	Y
3 Borski	Y	Y	Y	Y	N	Y	Y	Y
4 Kolter	Y	Y	Y	Y	N	Y	Y	Y
5 ***Schulze***	N	Y	Y	Y	Y	Y	Y	?
6 Yatron	Y	Y	Y	Y	N	Y	Y	Y
7 Edgar	N	Y	Y	Y	N	Y	Y	Y
8 Kostmayer	Y	Y	Y	Y	N	Y	Y	Y
9 ***Shuster***	N	Y	Y	Y	Y	Y	N	Y
10 ***McDade***	?	?	Y	?	Y	Y	Y	Y
11 Kanjorski	Y	Y	Y	Y	N	Y	Y	Y
12 Murtha	Y	Y	Y	Y	Y	Y	N	?
13 ***Coughlin***	?	?	Y	Y	N	Y	N	Y
14 Coyne	Y	Y	Y	Y	N	Y	Y	Y
15 ***Ritter***	N	Y	Y	Y	Y	Y	Y	Y
16 ***Walker***	N	Y	Y	Y	Y	Y	N	Y
17 ***Gekas***	N	Y	Y	Y	Y	Y	N	N
18 Walgren	Y	Y	Y	Y	N	Y	Y	Y
19 ***Goodling***	N	Y	Y	Y	Y	Y	N	Y
20 Gaydos	?	?	Y	Y	Y	Y	N	?
21 ***Ridge***	N	Y	Y	Y	N	Y	N	Y
22 Murphy	Y	Y	Y	Y	N	Y	Y	Y
23 ***Clinger***	-	+	Y	Y	Y	Y	N	Y
RHODE ISLAND								
1 St Germain	Y	Y	Y	Y	N	Y	?	?
2 ***Schneider***	Y	Y	Y	Y	N	Y	Y	Y
SOUTH CAROLINA								
1 ***Hartnett***	?	?	Y	Y	N	Y	N	Y
2 ***Spence***	Y	Y	Y	Y	Y	Y	N	Y
3 Derrick	N	Y	Y	Y	N	Y	Y	Y
4 ***Campbell***	N	Y	Y	Y	Y	Y	N	Y
5 Spratt	Y	Y	Y	Y	Y	Y	N	Y
6 Tallon	Y	Y	Y	Y	N	Y	N	Y
SOUTH DAKOTA								
AL Daschle	?	?	Y	Y	N	Y	Y	Y

	165	166	167	168	169	170	171	172
TENNESSEE								
1 ***Quillen***	Y	?	Y	Y	Y	Y	N	Y
2 ***Duncan***	Y	Y	Y	Y	Y	Y	N	Y
3 Lloyd	N	Y	Y	Y	Y	Y	N	Y
4 Cooper	Y	Y	Y	Y	N	Y	Y	Y
5 Boner	Y	Y	Y	Y	N	Y	N	Y
6 Gordon	P	Y	Y	Y	N	Y	N	Y
7 ***Sundquist***	N	Y	Y	?	Y	Y	N	Y
8 Jones	Y	Y	?	?	Y	Y	N	Y
9 Ford	Y	Y	Y	Y	?	Y	Y	?
TEXAS								
1 Vacancy								
2 Wilson	Y	Y	?	?	?	?	?	?
3 ***Bartlett***	N	Y	Y	Y	Y	Y	N	Y
4 Hall, R.	Y	Y	Y	Y	Y	Y	N	Y
5 Bryant	Y	Y	Y	Y	N	Y	Y	Y
6 ***Barton***	?	?	Y	Y	Y	Y	N	Y
7 ***Archer***	Y	Y	Y	Y	N	Y	N	Y
8 ***Fields***	N	Y	Y	Y	Y	Y	N	Y
9 Brooks	?	?	?	?	N	Y	N	?
10 Pickle	Y	Y	Y	Y	N	Y	N	N
11 Leath	Y	Y	Y	Y	Y	Y	N	N
12 Wright	Y	Y	Y	Y	N	Y	N	Y
13 ***Boulter***	N	Y	Y	Y	N	Y	N	Y
14 ***Sweeney***	?	Y	Y	Y	Y	N	N	N
15 de la Garza	Y	Y	Y	Y	N	Y	N	Y
16 Coleman	Y	Y	Y	Y	N	Y	Y	Y
17 Stenholm	N	Y	Y	Y	N	Y	N	Y
18 Leland	Y	Y	Y	Y	N	Y	Y	Y
19 ***Combest***	N	Y	Y	Y	Y	Y	N	N
20 Gonzalez	Y	Y	Y	Y	N	N	N	Y
21 ***Loeffler***	N	Y	Y	Y	Y	Y	N	Y
22 ***DeLay***	Y	Y	Y	Y	Y	Y	N	Y
23 Bustamante	Y	Y	Y	Y	N	Y	N	Y
24 Frost	Y	Y	Y	Y	N	Y	N	?
25 Andrews	Y	Y	Y	Y	N	Y	N	Y
26 ***Armey***	?	?	Y	Y	Y	N	N	N
27 Ortiz	Y	Y	Y	Y	N	Y	N	N
UTAH								
1 ***Hansen***	Y	Y	Y	Y	Y	Y	N	N
2 ***Monson***	N	Y	Y	Y	Y	N	N	N
3 ***Nielson***	Y	Y	Y	Y	Y	Y	N	Y
VERMONT								
AL ***Jeffords***	?	?	Y	Y	N	Y	Y	Y
VIRGINIA								
1 ***Bateman***	Y	Y	Y	Y	Y	N	N	N
2 ***Whitehurst***	N	Y	Y	Y	Y	Y	N	?
3 ***Bliley***	N	Y	Y	Y	Y	Y	N	Y
4 Sisisky	Y	Y	Y	Y	Y	Y	N	Y
5 Daniel	Y	Y	Y	Y	Y	N	N	N
6 Olin	P	?	Y	Y	Y	Y	N	Y
7 ***Slaughter***	Y	Y	Y	Y	Y	Y	N	N
8 ***Parris***	N	Y	Y	Y	Y	N	N	N
9 Boucher	?	Y	Y	Y	N	Y	Y	Y
10 ***Wolf***	N	Y	Y	Y	Y	N	N	N
WASHINGTON								
1 ***Miller***	N	Y	Y	Y	N	Y	N	Y
2 Swift	Y	Y	Y	Y	N	Y	?	Y
3 Bonker	Y	Y	Y	Y	N	Y	Y	Y
4 ***Morrison***	N	Y	Y	Y	Y	Y	N	Y
5 Foley	?	?	Y	Y	N	Y	Y	Y
6 Dicks	Y	Y	Y	Y	N	Y	Y	Y
7 Lowry	Y	Y	Y	Y	N	Y	Y	Y
8 ***Chandler***	N	Y	Y	Y	N	Y	Y	Y
WEST VIRGINIA								
1 Mollohan	Y	Y	Y	Y	N	Y	N	Y
2 Staggers	Y	Y	Y	Y	N	Y	Y	Y
3 Wise	+	+	Y	Y	N	Y	Y	Y
4 Rahall	Y	?	Y	Y	N	Y	Y	Y
WISCONSIN								
1 Aspin	Y	?	Y	Y	Y	Y	N	Y
2 Kastenmeier	Y	Y	Y	Y	N	Y	Y	Y
3 ***Gunderson***	N	Y	Y	Y	N	Y	N	Y
4 Kleczka	?	Y	Y	Y	N	Y	Y	Y
5 Moody	Y	Y	Y	Y	N	Y	Y	Y
6 ***Petri***	N	Y	Y	Y	N	Y	Y	Y
7 Obey	Y	Y	Y	Y	N	Y	Y	Y
8 ***Roth***	N	Y	Y	Y	Y	Y	Y	?
9 ***Sensenbrenner***	N	Y	Y	Y	N	Y	Y	Y
WYOMING								
AL ***Cheney***	?	?	Y	Y	Y	Y	N	N

Southern states - Ala., Ark., Fla., Ga., Ky., La., Miss., N.C., Okla., S.C., Tenn., Texas, Va.

* The *Congressional Record* vote number is different from the CQ vote number because the *Record* includes quorum calls in its tally. CQ does not publish quorum call votes.

173. Procedural Motion. Cobey, R-N.C., motion to approve the House *Journal* of Tuesday, June 25. Motion agreed to 268-132: R 52-120; D 216-12 (ND 143-8, SD 73-4), June 26, 1985.

174. HR 1532. Federal Election Commission Authorization, Fiscal 1986. Swift, D-Wash., motion to suspend the rules and pass the bill to authorize appropriations of $12.7 million for the Federal Election Commission for fiscal year 1986. Motion rejected 263-160: R 44-134; D 219-26 (ND 161-5, SD 58-21), June 26, 1985. A two-thirds majority of those present and voting (282 in this case) is required for passage under suspension of the rules.

175. HR 1872. Department of Defense Authorization, Fiscal 1986. Courter, R-N.J., substitute for the Boxer, D-Calif., amendment, to call for the General Accounting Office to report to Congress on the impact of requiring the Defense Department to maintain records on certain contracting costs. Rejected 189-232: R 144-32; D 45-200 (ND 12-155, SD 33-45), June 26, 1985.

176. HR 1872. Department of Defense Authorization, Fiscal 1986. Brown, R-Colo., amendment to the Boxer, D-Calif., amendment, to exempt from the record-keeping requirements firms with contracts amounting to less than $100,000. Adopted 276-147: R 173-5; D 103-142 (ND 50-117, SD 53-25), June 26, 1985. (The Boxer amendment subsequently was adopted *(see vote 177, below).*)

177. HR 1872. Department of Defense Authorization, Fiscal 1986. Boxer, D-Calif., amendment to require cost and pricing information pertaining to Defense Department contracts to be recorded and categorized in a computer data base, and to require contractors to record their proposed and actual standard-hour measurement of cost. Adopted 384-31: R 147-30; D 237-1 (ND 162-0, SD 75-1), June 26, 1985.

178. HR 1872. Department of Defense Authorization, Fiscal 1986. Brown, D-Calif., amendment to bar any test of the anti-satellite (ASAT) missile against a target in space during fiscal 1986 unless the president certifies to Congress that the Soviet Union has tested an ASAT. The amendment also increases by $20 million the fiscal 1986 authorization to carry out the satellite survivability project of the Air Force Space Survivability Program. Adopted 229-193: R 31-148; D 198-45 (ND 157-8, SD 41-37), June 26, 1985. A "nay" was a vote supporting the president's position.

179. HR 1872. Department of Defense Authorization, Fiscal 1986. English, D-Okla., substitute for the Bennett, D-Fla., amendment, to require the secretary of defense to conduct a study comparing the potential effectiveness of authorizing military personnel to assist in drug-enforcement activities with the potential effectiveness of increasing the number of tactical law enforcement teams on naval vessels. Rejected 81-328: R 15-159; D 66-169 (ND 47-110, SD 19-59), June 26, 1985.

180. HR 1872. Department of Defense Authorization, Fiscal 1986. Bennett, D-Fla., amendment to authorize military personnel to assist in federal drug-enforcement activities. Adopted 364-51: R 162-13; D 202-38 (ND 131-31, SD 71-7), June 26, 1985.

KEY

Y Voted for (yea).
Paired for.
+ Announced for.
N Voted against (nay).
X Paired against.
- Announced against.
P Voted "present".
C Voted "present" to avoid possible conflict of interest.
? Did not vote or otherwise make a position known.

Democrats *Republicans*

	173	174	175	176	177	178	179	180
ALABAMA								
1 *Callahan*	Y	N	Y	Y	Y	N	N	Y
2 *Dickinson*	N	N	Y	Y	N	N	N	N
3 Nichols	Y	N	Y	Y	Y	N	Y	N
4 Bevill	?	N	N	Y	Y	N	N	Y
5 Flippo	Y	Y	Y	Y	Y	N	N	Y
6 Erdreich	Y	N	N	Y	Y	N	N	Y
7 Shelby	Y	N	Y	Y	?	N	N	Y
ALASKA								
AL *Young*	N	N	Y	Y	Y	N	N	Y
ARIZONA								
1 *McCain*	Y	N	Y	Y	Y	N	N	Y
2 Udall	Y	Y	N	N	Y	Y	N	Y
3 *Stump*	N	N	Y	Y	N	N	N	Y
4 *Rudd*	Y	N	Y	Y	Y	N	Y	Y
5 *Kolbe*	N	N	Y	Y	Y	N	Y	N
ARKANSAS								
1 Alexander	Y	Y	N	Y	Y	?	N	Y
2 Robinson	Y	N	N	Y	Y	N	N	Y
3 *Hammerschmidt*	N	N	Y	Y	Y	N	N	Y
4 Anthony	Y	Y	N	Y	Y	Y	N	Y
CALIFORNIA								
1 Bosco	Y	Y	N	Y	Y	Y	?	Y
2 *Chappie*	N	N	Y	Y	Y	N	Y	Y
3 Matsui	Y	Y	N	N	?	Y	?	?
4 Fazio	Y	Y	N	N	Y	Y	Y	Y
5 Burton	Y	Y	N	N	?	Y	Y	N
6 Boxer	Y	Y	N	N	Y	Y	Y	Y
7 Miller	Y	Y	N	N	Y	Y	N	Y
8 Dellums	Y	Y	N	N	Y	Y	Y	N
9 Stark	Y	Y	N	N	Y	?	Y	N
10 Edwards	Y	Y	N	N	Y	Y	Y	N
11 Lantos	Y	Y	N	N	Y	Y	N	Y
12 *Zschau*	N	N	Y	Y	N	Y	Y	Y
13 Mineta	Y	Y	N	N	Y	Y	Y	N
14 *Shumway*	N	N	Y	Y	N	N	N	Y
15 Coelho	Y	Y	N	N	Y	Y	N	Y
16 Panetta	Y	Y	N	N	Y	Y	N	Y
17 *Pashayan*	N	N	Y	Y	Y	N	N	Y
18 Lehman	Y	Y	N	N	Y	Y	?	Y
19 *Lagomarsino*	N	N	Y	Y	Y	N	N	Y
20 *Thomas*	N	Y	Y	Y	?	N	?	?
21 *Fiedler*	N	N	Y	Y	Y	N	N	Y
22 *Moorhead*	N	N	Y	Y	Y	N	N	Y
23 Beilenson	Y	Y	N	N	Y	Y	?	?
24 Waxman	Y	Y	N	N	?	Y	Y	Y
25 Roybal	Y	Y	N	N	Y	Y	Y	N
26 Berman	Y	Y	N	N	Y	Y	?	Y
27 Levine	Y	?	N	N	Y	Y	?	Y
28 Dixon	?	Y	N	N	Y	Y	N	Y
29 Hawkins	Y	Y	N	N	Y	Y	N	Y
30 Martinez	Y	Y	N	N	Y	Y	N	Y
31 Dymally	P	Y	N	N	Y	Y	Y	N
32 Anderson	Y	Y	N	Y	Y	Y	N	Y
33 *Dreier*	N	N	Y	Y	Y	N	N	Y
34 Torres	Y	Y	N	N	Y	Y	N	N
35 *Lewis*	N	N	N	Y	Y	N	N	Y
36 Brown	Y	N	N	N	Y	Y	?	?
37 *McCandless*	N	N	Y	Y	N	N	N	Y
38 *Dornan*	N	N	Y	Y	Y	N	N	Y
39 *Dannemeyer*	N	N	Y	Y	Y	N	N	Y
40 *Badham*	N	N	Y	Y	N	N	?	?
41 *Lowery*	N	N	Y	Y	Y	N	N	Y
42 *Lungren*	N	N	Y	Y	Y	N	N	Y
43 *Packard*	N	N	Y	Y	Y	N	N	Y
44 Bates	Y	Y	N	N	Y	Y	Y	Y
45 *Hunter*	N	N	Y	Y	Y	N	N	Y
COLORADO								
1 Schroeder	N	Y	N	N	Y	Y	N	Y
2 Wirth	Y	Y	N	Y	Y	Y	N	Y
3 *Strang*	?	N	Y	Y	Y	N	N	Y
4 *Brown*	N	Y	N	Y	Y	N	N	Y
5 *Kramer*	N	N	Y	Y	Y	N	N	Y
6 *Schaefer*	Y	N	N	Y	Y	N	N	Y
CONNECTICUT								
1 Kennelly	Y	Y	N	Y	Y	Y	N	Y
2 Gejdenson	Y	Y	N	Y	Y	Y	N	Y
3 Morrison	Y	Y	N	Y	Y	Y	Y	Y
4 *McKinney*	Y	Y	N	Y	Y	Y	N	Y
5 *Rowland*	Y	N	Y	Y	Y	N	N	Y
6 *Johnson*	Y	Y	Y	Y	Y	Y	N	Y
DELAWARE								
AL Carper	?	Y	N	Y	Y	Y	N	Y
FLORIDA								
1 Hutto	Y	N	Y	Y	Y	N	Y	Y
2 Fuqua	Y	Y	Y	Y	Y	N	N	Y
3 Bennett	Y	Y	N	N	Y	Y	N	Y
4 Chappell	Y	Y	Y	Y	Y	N	N	Y
5 *McCollum*	Y	N	Y	Y	Y	N	N	Y
6 MacKay	Y	Y	N	N	Y	Y	N	Y
7 Gibbons	Y	Y	N	N	Y	Y	N	Y
8 *Young*	N	Y	Y	Y	Y	N	N	Y
9 *Bilirakis*	N	N	N	Y	Y	N	N	Y
10 *Ireland*	N	N	Y	Y	Y	N	N	Y
11 Nelson	Y	N	Y	Y	Y	N	N	Y
12 *Lewis*	N	N	Y	Y	Y	N	N	Y
13 *Mack*	N	N	Y	Y	N	N	N	Y
14 Mica	Y	Y	N	N	Y	Y	N	Y
15 *Shaw*	N	N	N	Y	Y	N	N	Y
16 Smith	Y	Y	N	N	Y	Y	N	Y
17 Lehman	Y	Y	N	N	Y	Y	Y	N
18 Pepper	Y	Y	N	N	+	Y	N	Y
19 Fascell	Y	Y	N	N	Y	Y	N	Y
GEORGIA								
1 Thomas	Y	Y	Y	Y	Y	N	N	Y
2 Hatcher	Y	Y	N	Y	Y	N	N	Y
3 Ray	Y	Y	Y	Y	Y	N	Y	N
4 *Swindall*	N	N	Y	Y	Y	N	N	Y
5 Fowler	Y	Y	Y	Y	Y	Y	N	Y
6 *Gingrich*	N	N	Y	Y	Y	N	N	Y
7 Darden	Y	N	Y	Y	Y	N	N	Y
8 Rowland	Y	Y	Y	Y	Y	N	N	Y
9 Jenkins	Y	Y	Y	Y	Y	N	N	Y
10 Barnard	Y	N	Y	Y	Y	N	Y	Y
HAWAII								
1 Heftel	?	Y	N	?	Y	Y	N	Y
2 Akaka	Y	Y	N	N	Y	Y	N	Y
IDAHO								
1 *Craig*	N	N	Y	Y	Y	N	N	Y
2 Stallings	Y	Y	N	N	Y	Y	N	Y
ILLINOIS								
1 Hayes	Y	Y	N	N	Y	Y	N	Y
2 Savage	?	Y	N	N	Y	Y	N	Y
3 Russo	Y	Y	N	Y	Y	Y	N	Y
4 *O'Brien*	P	Y	N	Y	Y	N	N	Y
5 Lipinski	Y	Y	N	N	Y	Y	N	Y
6 *Hyde*	Y	N	Y	Y	Y	N	N	Y
7 Collins	Y	Y	N	N	Y	Y	N	Y
8 Rostenkowski	?	?	N	N	Y	Y	N	Y
9 Yates	Y	Y	N	Y	Y	Y	Y	N
10 *Porter*	N	N	N	Y	Y	Y	N	Y
11 Annunzio	P	Y	N	Y	Y	Y	N	Y
12 *Crane*	N	N	Y	Y	N	N	N	Y
13 *Fawell*	N	N	N	Y	Y	N	N	Y
14 *Grotberg*	N	N	Y	Y	N	N	N	Y
15 *Madigan*	N	N	#	Y	Y	N	N	Y
16 *Martin*	N	N	Y	Y	Y	N	N	Y
17 Evans	Y	Y	N	N	Y	Y	Y	Y
18 *Michel*	Y	N	Y	Y	N	N	N	Y
19 Bruce	Y	Y	N	N	Y	Y	N	Y
20 Durbin	N	Y	N	Y	Y	Y	N	Y
21 Price	Y	Y	N	N	Y	Y	N	Y
22 Gray	Y	Y	N	N	Y	Y	N	Y
INDIANA								
1 Visclosky	Y	Y	N	Y	Y	Y	N	N
2 Sharp	Y	Y	N	Y	Y	Y	N	Y
3 *Hiler*	N	N	Y	Y	Y	N	N	Y
4 *Coats*	N	N	Y	Y	Y	N	N	Y
5 *Hillis*	N	Y	Y	Y	N	N	Y	Y

ND - Northern Democrats SD - Southern Democrats

* Corresponding to Congressional Record Votes 191, 192, 193, 194, 195, 196, 197, 198

	173	174	175	176	177	178	179	180
6 ***Burton***	P	N	Y	Y	Y	N	N	Y
7 ***Myers***	Y	N	Y	Y	Y	N	N	Y
8 McCloskey	Y	Y	N	N	Y	Y	N	Y
9 Hamilton	Y	Y	N	Y	Y	Y	N	Y
10 Jacobs	N	Y	N	N	Y	Y	?	?
IOWA								
1 ***Leach***	N	Y	N	N	Y	Y	N	Y
2 ***Tauke***	N	N	N	Y	Y	Y	N	Y
3 ***Evans***	N	N	N	N	Y	Y	N	Y
4 Smith	Y	Y	N	Y	Y	Y	N	Y
5 ***Lightfoot***	N	N	N	Y	Y	N	N	Y
6 Bedell	Y	Y	N	Y	Y	Y	N	Y
KANSAS								
1 ***Roberts***	N	Y	Y	Y	Y	Y	N	Y
2 Slattery	Y	Y	N	Y	Y	Y	N	Y
3 ***Meyers***	Y	Y	Y	Y	Y	Y	N	Y
4 Glickman	Y	Y	N	Y	Y	Y	Y	Y
5 ***Whittaker***	N	Y	Y	Y	Y	N	N	Y
KENTUCKY								
1 Hubbard	Y	N	Y	Y	Y	N	N	Y
2 Natcher	Y	Y	N	Y	Y	Y	N	Y
3 Mazzoli	Y	Y	Y	N	Y	Y	N	Y
4 ***Snyder***	Y	N	Y	Y	Y	N	N	Y
5 ***Rogers***	Y	N	Y	Y	Y	N	N	Y
6 ***Hopkins***	Y	Y	Y	Y	Y	Y	N	Y
7 Perkins	Y	Y	N	Y	Y	Y	N	Y
LOUISIANA								
1 ***Livingston***	Y	N	Y	Y	Y	N	N	Y
2 Boggs	Y	Y	N	Y	Y	Y	N	Y
3 Tauzin	Y	Y	Y	Y	Y	N	N	Y
4 Roemer	N	Y	N	Y	Y	N	N	Y
5 Huckaby	Y	Y	N	Y	Y	N	N	Y
6 ***Moore***	Y	Y	Y	Y	Y	N	N	Y
7 Breaux	Y	Y	Y	Y	Y	N	N	Y
8 Long	Y	Y	N	Y	Y	Y	N	Y
MAINE								
1 ***McKernan***	N	Y	Y	Y	Y	Y	N	Y
2 ***Snowe***	N	Y	N	Y	Y	Y	N	Y
MARYLAND								
1 Dyson	Y	Y	Y	Y	Y	N	N	Y
2 ***Bentley***	N	N	Y	Y	Y	N	N	Y
3 Mikulski	Y	Y	N	Y	Y	Y	N	Y
4 ***Holt***	?	?	?	?	?	X	?	?
5 Hoyer	Y	Y	N	N	Y	Y	Y	N
6 Byron	Y	Y	Y	Y	Y	N	N	Y
7 Mitchell	N	Y	N	N	?	Y	N	Y
8 Barnes	Y	Y	N	N	Y	Y	Y	N
MASSACHUSETTS								
1 ***Conte***	N	Y	Y	Y	Y	Y	N	Y
2 Boland	Y	Y	N	N	Y	Y	N	Y
3 Early	Y	Y	N	N	Y	Y	N	Y
4 Frank	Y	Y	N	N	Y	Y	Y	N
5 Atkins	Y	Y	N	N	Y	Y	Y	N
6 Mavroules	Y	Y	Y	N	Y	Y	N	Y
7 Markey	?	Y	N	N	Y	Y	Y	N
8 O'Neill								
9 Moakley	Y	Y	N	N	Y	Y	N	Y
10 Studds	Y	Y	N	N	Y	Y	Y	N
11 Donnelly	Y	Y	N	N	Y	Y	N	Y
MICHIGAN								
1 Conyers	?	Y	N	Y	Y	N	?	?
2 ***Pursell***	Y	N	Y	Y	Y	Y	N	Y
3 Wolpe	Y	Y	N	N	Y	Y	Y	Y
4 ***Siljander***	N	N	Y	Y	Y	N	N	Y
5 ***Henry***	?	Y	N	Y	Y	N	N	Y
6 Carr	Y	Y	Y	Y	Y	Y	N	Y
7 Kildee	Y	Y	N	N	Y	Y	Y	Y
8 Traxler	Y	Y	N	N	Y	Y	N	Y
9 ***Vander Jagt***	N	N	Y	Y	Y	N	N	Y
10 ***Schuette***	N	Y	Y	Y	Y	N	N	Y
11 ***Davis***	Y	Y	Y	Y	Y	N	N	Y
12 Bonior	Y	Y	N	N	Y	Y	Y	N
13 Crockett	Y	Y	N	N	Y	Y	N	Y
14 Hertel	Y	Y	N	N	Y	Y	N	Y
15 Ford	?	N	N	N	Y	Y	N	Y
16 Dingell	?	Y	N	N	Y	Y	N	Y
17 Levin	Y	Y	N	N	Y	Y	N	Y
18 ***Broomfield***	Y	Y	Y	Y	Y	N	N	Y
MINNESOTA								
1 Penny	N	Y	N	Y	Y	Y	N	Y
2 ***Weber***	N	N	Y	Y	N	N	Y	N
3 ***Frenzel***	P	Y	Y	Y	N	Y	Y	N
4 Vento	Y	Y	N	N	Y	Y	Y	N
5 Sabo	Y	Y	N	N	Y	Y	Y	N
6 Sikorski	N	Y	N	Y	Y	Y	N	Y
7 ***Stangeland***	N	N	Y	Y	Y	N	N	Y
8 Oberstar	Y	Y	N	N	Y	Y	Y	N
MISSISSIPPI								
1 Whitten	Y	Y	N	Y	Y	N	?	?
2 ***Franklin***	N	N	#	Y	Y	N	N	Y
3 Montgomery	Y	N	Y	Y	Y	N	N	Y
4 Dowdy	Y	Y	N	N	Y	Y	N	Y
5 ***Lott***	Y	N	Y	Y	Y	N	N	Y
MISSOURI								
1 Clay	N	Y	N	N	Y	Y	Y	N
2 Young	Y	Y	N	Y	Y	N	N	Y
3 Gephardt	Y	Y	Y	N	Y	Y	N	Y
4 Skelton	?	Y	Y	Y	Y	N	N	Y
5 Wheat	Y	Y	N	N	Y	Y	N	N
6 ***Coleman***	N	N	N	Y	Y	N	N	Y
7 ***Taylor***	N	N	Y	Y	Y	N	N	Y
8 ***Emerson***	N	N	Y	Y	Y	N	N	Y
9 Volkmer	Y	Y	Y	Y	Y	Y	N	Y
MONTANA								
1 Williams	Y	Y	N	N	Y	Y	Y	Y
2 ***Marlenee***	N	N	Y	Y	Y	N	N	Y
NEBRASKA								
1 ***Bereuter***	N	N	N	Y	Y	N	N	Y
2 ***Daub***	N	N	Y	Y	Y	Y	N	Y
3 ***Smith***	Y	Y	N	Y	Y	N	N	Y
NEVADA								
1 Reid	Y	Y	N	N	Y	Y	N	Y
2 ***Vucanovich***	N	N	Y	Y	Y	N	N	Y
NEW HAMPSHIRE								
1 ***Smith***	N	N	Y	Y	Y	N	N	Y
2 ***Gregg***	N	Y	Y	Y	Y	N	N	N
NEW JERSEY								
1 Florio	Y	Y	N	N	Y	Y	N	Y
2 Hughes	Y	Y	Y	Y	Y	Y	Y	N
3 Howard	Y	Y	N	N	Y	Y	N	Y
4 ***Smith***	?	N	Y	Y	Y	N	N	Y
5 ***Roukema***	Y	Y	N	Y	Y	Y	N	Y
6 Dwyer	Y	Y	N	N	Y	Y	N	Y
7 ***Rinaldo***	Y	Y	Y	Y	Y	N	N	Y
8 Roe	Y	Y	N	N	Y	Y	N	Y
9 Torricelli	Y	Y	N	N	Y	Y	N	Y
10 Rodino	Y	Y	N	N	Y	Y	Y	N
11 ***Gallo***	N	N	Y	Y	Y	N	N	Y
12 ***Courter***	N	N	Y	Y	N	N	N	Y
13 ***Saxton***	N	N	Y	Y	Y	N	N	Y
14 Guarini	Y	Y	N	N	Y	Y	N	Y
NEW MEXICO								
1 ***Lujan***	Y	N	Y	Y	Y	N	N	Y
2 ***Skeen***	N	N	Y	Y	Y	N	N	Y
3 Richardson	Y	Y	N	N	Y	Y	N	Y
NEW YORK								
1 ***Carney***	N	N	Y	Y	N	N	?	Y
2 Downey	Y	Y	N	Y	Y	Y	N	Y
3 Mrazek	Y	Y	N	N	Y	Y	N	Y
4 ***Lent***	Y	N	Y	Y	Y	N	N	Y
5 ***McGrath***	N	N	Y	Y	Y	N	N	Y
6 Addabbo	Y	Y	N	N	Y	Y	N	Y
7 Ackerman	Y	Y	N	N	Y	Y	N	Y
8 Scheuer	Y	N	N	N	Y	Y	N	Y
9 Manton	Y	Y	X	N	Y	Y	N	Y
10 Schumer	Y	Y	N	N	Y	Y	N	Y
11 Towns	Y	Y	N	N	Y	Y	N	Y
12 Owens	?	?	X	-	+	#	-	+
13 Solarz	Y	Y	N	N	Y	Y	N	Y
14 ***Molinari***	N	N	Y	Y	N	N	N	Y
15 ***Green***	Y	N	N	Y	Y	Y	N	Y
16 Rangel	Y	Y	N	N	?	Y	N	Y
17 Weiss	Y	Y	N	N	Y	Y	Y	N
18 Garcia	Y	Y	N	N	Y	Y	N	Y
19 Biaggi	Y	Y	Y	Y	Y	Y	N	Y
20 ***DioGuardi***	N	N	N	Y	Y	N	N	Y
21 ***Fish***	?	?	?	?	?	#	?	?
22 ***Gilman***	N	Y	N	Y	Y	N	N	Y
23 Stratton	Y	Y	Y	Y	Y	N	Y	N
24 ***Solomon***	N	N	Y	Y	Y	N	N	Y
25 ***Boehlert***	N	Y	Y	Y	Y	Y	N	Y
26 ***Martin***	N	N	Y	Y	Y	N	N	Y
27 ***Wortley***	?	?	Y	Y	Y	X	N	Y
28 McHugh	?	Y	N	N	Y	Y	Y	Y
29 ***Horton***	Y	Y	Y	Y	Y	Y	?	?
30 ***Eckert***	N	N	Y	Y	Y	N	N	N
31 ***Kemp***	Y	N	Y	Y	Y	N	N	Y
32 LaFalce	Y	Y	N	Y	Y	Y	?	?
33 Nowak	Y	Y	N	N	Y	Y	N	Y
34 Lundine	Y	Y	Y	N	Y	Y	N	Y
NORTH CAROLINA								
1 Jones	?	Y	N	N	Y	Y	N	Y
2 Valentine	Y	N	Y	Y	Y	N	Y	Y
3 Whitley	Y	Y	Y	Y	Y	Y	N	Y
4 ***Cobey***	N	N	Y	Y	Y	N	N	Y
5 Neal	Y	N	N	N	Y	Y	N	Y
6 ***Coble***	N	N	Y	Y	Y	N	N	Y
7 Rose	Y	Y	N	Y	Y	N	N	Y
8 Hefner	?	?	?	?	?	?	?	?
9 ***McMillan***	Y	N	N	Y	Y	N	N	Y
10 ***Broyhill***	Y	Y	Y	Y	?	N	N	Y
11 ***Hendon***	N	N	Y	Y	Y	N	N	Y
NORTH DAKOTA								
AL Dorgan	Y	Y	N	N	Y	Y	N	Y
OHIO								
1 Luken	?	?	?	?	?	?	?	?
2 ***Gradison***	N	N	N	Y	Y	Y	N	Y
3 Hall	Y	Y	N	Y	Y	Y	N	Y
4 ***Oxley***	N	N	Y	Y	Y	N	Y	N
5 ***Latta***	N	N	Y	Y	Y	N	N	Y
6 ***McEwen***	N	N	Y	Y	Y	N	N	Y
7 ***DeWine***	?	?	?	?	?	N	N	Y
8 ***Kindness***	N	N	Y	Y	N	N	Y	N
9 Kaptur	Y	Y	N	Y	Y	Y	N	Y
10 ***Miller***	N	Y	Y	Y	Y	N	N	Y
11 Eckart	Y	Y	N	N	Y	Y	N	Y
12 ***Kasich***	N	N	Y	Y	Y	N	N	Y
13 Pease	Y	Y	N	N	Y	Y	Y	Y
14 Seiberling	?	Y	N	N	Y	Y	Y	N
15 ***Wylie***	Y	Y	Y	Y	Y	N	N	Y
16 ***Regula***	Y	Y	Y	Y	Y	Y	N	Y
17 Traficant	Y	Y	N	N	Y	Y	N	Y
18 Applegate	?	Y	N	Y	Y	Y	N	Y
19 Feighan	?	Y	N	Y	Y	Y	N	Y
20 Oakar	Y	Y	N	N	Y	Y	N	Y
21 Stokes	Y	Y	N	N	?	Y	Y	N
OKLAHOMA								
1 Jones	Y	Y	Y	Y	Y	Y	Y	Y
2 Synar	Y	Y	N	N	Y	Y	Y	N
3 Watkins	Y	N	N	N	Y	N	Y	Y
4 McCurdy	Y	Y	Y	Y	Y	Y	Y	Y
5 ***Edwards***	N	N	N	Y	Y	N	Y	Y
6 English	Y	Y	Y	Y	Y	N	Y	Y
OREGON								
1 AuCoin	Y	Y	N	Y	Y	Y	Y	N
2 ***Smith, R.***	N	Y	Y	Y	Y	N	N	Y
3 Wyden	Y	Y	N	Y	Y	Y	N	Y
4 Weaver	Y	Y	N	N	Y	Y	Y	N
5 ***Smith, D.***	Y	N	N	Y	Y	N	N	Y
PENNSYLVANIA								
1 Foglietta	Y	Y	N	N	Y	Y	N	Y
2 Gray	Y	Y	N	N	Y	?	N	Y
3 Borski	Y	Y	N	N	Y	Y	N	Y
4 Kolter	Y	Y	N	N	Y	?	N	Y
5 ***Schulze***	Y	N	Y	Y	Y	N	N	Y
6 Yatron	Y	Y	N	N	Y	Y	N	Y
7 Edgar	N	Y	N	N	Y	Y	Y	Y
8 Kostmayer	Y	Y	N	Y	Y	Y	N	Y
9 ***Shuster***	N	N	Y	Y	Y	N	N	Y
10 ***McDade***	Y	Y	Y	Y	Y	N	N	Y
11 Kanjorski	Y	N	N	Y	Y	Y	N	Y
12 Murtha	Y	Y	N	Y	Y	N	N	Y
13 ***Coughlin***	N	Y	Y	Y	Y	Y	N	Y
14 Coyne	Y	Y	N	N	Y	Y	Y	Y
15 ***Ritter***	Y	N	N	Y	Y	N	?	?
16 ***Walker***	N	N	Y	Y	Y	N	N	Y
17 ***Gekas***	N	Y	Y	Y	Y	N	N	Y
18 Walgren	Y	Y	N	N	Y	Y	N	Y
19 ***Goodling***	N	Y	?	?	Y	Y	N	Y
20 Gaydos	Y	Y	N	N	Y	N	N	Y
21 ***Ridge***	N	N	N	N	Y	Y	N	Y
22 Murphy	Y	Y	N	N	Y	Y	N	Y
23 ***Clinger***	N	N	Y	Y	Y	Y	N	Y
RHODE ISLAND								
1 St Germain	Y	N	N	N	Y	Y	N	Y
2 ***Schneider***	Y	Y	Y	Y	Y	Y	N	Y
SOUTH CAROLINA								
1 ***Hartnett***	Y	N	Y	Y	N	N	N	Y
2 ***Spence***	Y	N	Y	Y	N	N	N	Y
3 Derrick	N	Y	P	Y	Y	Y	N	Y
4 ***Campbell***	Y	N	Y	Y	Y	N	N	Y
5 Spratt	Y	Y	Y	Y	Y	Y	N	Y
6 Tallon	Y	Y	N	Y	Y	Y	N	Y
SOUTH DAKOTA								
AL Daschle	Y	Y	N	Y	Y	Y	N	Y
TENNESSEE								
1 ***Quillen***	N	Y	Y	Y	N	N	N	Y
2 ***Duncan***	Y	Y	Y	Y	Y	N	N	Y
3 Lloyd	N	N	Y	Y	Y	N	N	Y
4 Cooper	Y	Y	N	N	Y	Y	N	Y
5 Boner	Y	Y	N	N	Y	Y	N	Y
6 Gordon	Y	N	N	N	Y	Y	N	Y
7 ***Sundquist***	N	N	Y	Y	Y	N	N	Y
8 Jones	Y	Y	N	Y	Y	Y	N	Y
9 Ford	Y	Y	N	N	Y	Y	Y	Y
TEXAS								
1 Vacancy								
2 Wilson	?	?	?	?	?	?	?	?
3 ***Bartlett***	N	N	Y	Y	N	N	N	Y
4 Hall, R.	Y	N	Y	Y	Y	N	N	Y
5 Bryant	Y	Y	N	N	Y	Y	N	Y
6 ***Barton***	N	N	Y	Y	N	N	N	Y
7 ***Archer***	Y	N	Y	Y	Y	N	N	Y
8 ***Fields***	N	N	Y	Y	Y	N	N	Y
9 Brooks	Y	Y	N	N	Y	Y	N	Y
10 Pickle	Y	Y	N	Y	Y	Y	N	Y
11 Leath	Y	N	Y	Y	Y	N	Y	Y
12 Wright	Y	Y	N	Y	Y	Y	N	Y
13 ***Boulter***	Y	N	Y	Y	N	N	N	Y
14 ***Sweeney***	Y	N	Y	Y	N	N	N	Y
15 de la Garza	Y	Y	Y	Y	Y	Y	N	Y
16 Coleman	Y	Y	N	Y	Y	N	Y	Y
17 Stenholm	N	N	Y	Y	Y	N	Y	Y
18 Leland	Y	Y	N	N	Y	Y	Y	N
19 ***Combest***	N	N	Y	Y	Y	N	N	Y
20 Gonzalez	Y	Y	N	N	Y	Y	Y	Y
21 ***Loeffler***	N	N	Y	Y	Y	N	N	Y
22 ***DeLay***	Y	N	Y	Y	N	N	?	?
23 Bustamante	Y	Y	N	N	Y	Y	N	Y
24 Frost	Y	Y	N	?	?	N	N	Y
25 Andrews	Y	Y	N	Y	Y	N	N	Y
26 ***Armey***	N	N	Y	Y	N	N	N	Y
27 Ortiz	Y	Y	Y	N	Y	Y	N	Y
UTAH								
1 ***Hansen***	Y	N	Y	Y	Y	N	N	Y
2 ***Monson***	N	N	Y	Y	N	N	N	Y
3 ***Nielson***	Y	N	Y	Y	Y	N	Y	N
VERMONT								
AL ***Jeffords***	Y	Y	N	Y	Y	Y	Y	N
VIRGINIA								
1 ***Bateman***	Y	N	Y	Y	N	N	Y	N
2 ***Whitehurst***	N	N	Y	Y	N	N	Y	N
3 ***Bliley***	N	N	Y	Y	Y	N	N	Y
4 Sisisky	Y	N	Y	Y	Y	N	N	Y
5 Daniel	Y	N	Y	Y	N	N	Y	N
6 Olin	Y	Y	N	Y	Y	Y	Y	N
7 ***Slaughter***	N	N	Y	Y	Y	N	N	Y
8 ***Parris***	N	N	Y	Y	Y	N	N	Y
9 Boucher	Y	Y	N	N	Y	Y	N	Y
10 ***Wolf***	N	N	Y	Y	Y	N	N	Y
WASHINGTON								
1 ***Miller***	Y	Y	Y	Y	Y	Y	N	Y
2 Swift	Y	Y	N	N	Y	Y	N	Y
3 Bonker	Y	Y	N	N	Y	Y	Y	Y
4 ***Morrison***	N	Y	Y	Y	Y	N	N	Y
5 Foley	Y	Y	N	Y	Y	Y	?	Y
6 Dicks	Y	Y	N	Y	Y	Y	N	Y
7 Lowry	Y	Y	N	N	Y	Y	Y	N
8 ***Chandler***	N	Y	N	N	Y	Y	N	Y
WEST VIRGINIA								
1 Mollohan	Y	Y	N	Y	Y	Y	N	Y
2 Staggers	Y	Y	N	Y	Y	Y	N	Y
3 Wise	Y	Y	N	N	Y	Y	Y	Y
4 Rahall	Y	Y	N	N	Y	Y	N	Y
WISCONSIN								
1 Aspin	Y	Y	Y	Y	Y	Y	Y	Y
2 Kastenmeier	Y	Y	N	N	Y	Y	Y	Y
3 ***Gunderson***	N	N	N	Y	Y	Y	Y	N
4 Kleczka	?	Y	N	N	Y	Y	Y	Y
5 Moody	Y	Y	N	Y	Y	Y	Y	Y
6 ***Petri***	Y	N	N	N	Y	N	N	Y
7 Obey	Y	Y	N	N	Y	Y	N	Y
8 ***Roth***	N	N	Y	Y	Y	N	N	Y
9 ***Sensenbrenner***	N	N	Y	Y	Y	N	N	Y
WYOMING								
AL ***Cheney***	N	N	Y	Y	Y	N	N	Y

Southern states - Ala., Ark., Fla., Ga., Ky., La., Miss., N.C., Okla., S.C., Tenn., Texas, Va.

* The *Congressional Record* vote number is different from the CQ vote number because the *Record* includes quorum calls in its tally. CQ does not publish quorum call votes.

181. HR 1872. Department of Defense Authorization, Fiscal 1986. Brooks, D-Texas, substitute for the Dickinson, R-Ala., amendment, to ban use of funds for polygraph examinations of Pentagon employees, except for the one-year continuation of a pilot program of such screening examinations. Rejected 121-281: R 2-171; D 119-110 (ND 95-61, SD 24-49), June 26, 1985.

182. HR 1872. Department of Defense Authorization, Fiscal 1986. Dickinson, R-Ala., amendment to direct the Pentagon to use random polygraph examinations to screen Pentagon and contractor employees with access to classified information. Adopted 333-71: R 172-2; D 161-69 (ND 96-60, SD 65-9), June 26, 1985.

183. HR 1872. Department of Defense Authorization, Fiscal 1986. Hunter, R-Calif., amendment to the Foley, D-Wash., amendment, to provide for the expiration of a restriction on introduction of U.S. combat troops into Nicaragua if that country obtained Soviet MiG aircraft, or similar aircraft. Adopted 377-45: R 178-0; D 199-45 (ND 124-42, SD 75-3), June 27, 1985. (The Foley amendment subsequently was adopted *(see vote 185, below)*.)

184. HR 1872. Department of Defense Authorization, Fiscal 1986. Burton, R-Ind., amendment to the Foley, D-Wash., amendment, to permit the introduction of U.S. combat troops into Nicaragua if the president determined that Nicaragua was supporting, directly or indirectly, military or terrorist operations in El Salvador, Honduras or Costa Rica. Rejected 186-235: R 151-28; D 35-207 (ND 5-160, SD 30-47), June 27, 1985.

185. HR 1872. Department of Defense Authorization, Fiscal 1986. Foley, D-Wash., amendment, as amended by the Hunter, R-Calif., amendment *(vote 183, above)*, to bar the introduction of U.S. combat troops into Nicaragua without congressional authorization unless troops were needed to meet a clear danger of attack on the United States, to protect the U.S. Embassy, to evacuate U.S. citizens or to meet U.S. obligations under the Rio Treaty. Adopted 312-111: R 99-80; D 213-31 (ND 151-15, SD 62-16), June 27, 1985. A "nay" was a vote supporting the president's position.

186. HR 1872. Department of Defense Authorization, Fiscal 1986. Blaz, R-Guam, amendment to repeal limitations on the transportation of certain motor vehicles through Guam. Rejected 139-272: R 125-49; D 14-223 (ND 7-154, SD 7-69), June 27, 1985.

187. HR 1872. Department of Defense Authorization, Fiscal 1986. Morrison, D-Conn., amendment to require an increase in civil service pay to match any increase in military pay during fiscal 1986. Rejected 122-281: R 24-147; D 98-134 (ND 78-77, SD 20-57), June 27, 1985.

188. HR 1872. Department of Defense Authorization, Fiscal 1986. Daniel, D-Va., substitute for the Markey, D-Mass., amendment, to restrict the actions of U.S. troops in Honduras near that country's border with Nicaragua. Adopted 320-69: R 107-56; D 213-13 (ND 147-5, SD 66-8), June 27, 1985. (The Markey amendment subsequently was rejected.)

KEY

- Y Voted for (yea).
- # Paired for.
- + Announced for.
- N Voted against (nay).
- X Paired against.
- - Announced against.
- P Voted "present".
- C Voted "present" to avoid possible conflict of interest.
- ? Did not vote or otherwise make a position known.

Democrats ***Republicans***

	181	182	183	184	185	186	187	188
ALABAMA								
1 ***Callahan***	N	Y	Y	Y	Y	Y	N	N
2 ***Dickinson***	N	Y	Y	Y	N	Y	N	N
3 Nichols	N	Y	Y	Y	Y	N	N	N
4 Bevill	N	Y	Y	Y	Y	N	N	N
5 Flippo	N	Y	Y	Y	Y	N	N	N
6 Erdreich	N	Y	Y	Y	Y	N	N	N
7 Shelby	N	Y	Y	Y	Y	N	N	N
ALASKA								
AL ***Young***	N	Y	Y	Y	Y	Y	N	Y
ARIZONA								
1 ***McCain***	N	Y	Y	Y	N	Y	N	Y
2 Udall	Y	Y	Y	N	Y	N	Y	Y
3 ***Stump***	N	Y	Y	Y	N	Y	N	Y
4 ***Rudd***	N	Y	Y	Y	N	?	?	?
5 ***Kolbe***	N	Y	Y	Y	N	Y	N	Y
ARKANSAS								
1 Alexander	N	Y	Y	N	Y	N	Y	Y
2 Robinson	Y	Y	Y	Y	Y	N	N	N
3 ***Hammerschmidt***	N	Y	Y	Y	N	Y	N	Y
4 Anthony	Y	N	Y	N	Y	N	N	Y
CALIFORNIA								
1 Bosco	N	Y	Y	N	Y	N	Y	Y
2 ***Chappie***	N	Y	Y	Y	Y	Y	N	Y
3 Matsui	Y	N	Y	N	Y	N	Y	Y
4 Fazio	Y	Y	Y	N	Y	N	Y	Y
5 Burton	Y	N	Y	N	Y	N	Y	Y
6 Boxer	Y	Y	Y	N	Y	N	Y	Y
7 Miller	Y	Y	N	N	Y	N	Y	Y
8 Dellums	Y	N	N	N	N	N	P	Y
9 Stark	Y	N	N	N	Y	N	N	Y
10 Edwards	Y	N	N	N	N	N	Y	Y
11 Lantos	N	Y	Y	N	Y	N	N	Y
12 ***Zschau***	N	Y	Y	Y	Y	Y	N	Y
13 Mineta	Y	N	Y	N	Y	N	N	Y
14 ***Shumway***	?	?	Y	Y	N	Y	N	Y
15 Coelho	Y	Y	Y	N	Y	?	?	?
16 Panetta	Y	Y	N	N	Y	Y	N	Y
17 ***Pashayan***	N	Y	Y	Y	Y	Y	Y	Y
18 Lehman	N	Y	Y	N	Y	N	N	Y
19 ***Lagomarsino***	N	Y	Y	Y	Y	Y	N	Y
20 ***Thomas***	N	Y	Y	Y	N	?	?	?
21 ***Fiedler***	N	Y	Y	Y	Y	Y	N	Y
22 ***Moorhead***	N	Y	Y	Y	N	Y	N	N
23 Beilenson	?	?	N	N	N	N	N	Y
24 Waxman	Y	N	N	N	Y	N	Y	?
25 Roybal	Y	N	N	N	N	?	?	?
26 Berman	Y	N	Y	N	Y	N	N	Y
27 Levine	Y	N	Y	N	Y	N	Y	Y
28 Dixon	?	?	Y	N	Y	N	N	Y
29 Hawkins	Y	N	N	N	Y	N	?	?
30 Martinez	Y	Y	Y	N	Y	?	?	?
31 Dymally	Y	N	N	N	N	N	Y	Y
32 Anderson	N	Y	N	N	Y	N	Y	Y
33 ***Dreier***	N	Y	Y	Y	N	Y	N	N
34 Torres	Y	Y	N	N	Y	N	N	Y
35 ***Lewis***	N	Y	Y	Y	Y	Y	Y	Y
36 Brown	?	?	?	?	?	Y	Y	Y
37 ***McCandless***	N	Y	Y	Y	N	Y	N	N
38 ***Dornan***	N	Y	Y	Y	N	Y	N	Y
39 ***Dannemeyer***	N	Y	Y	Y	Y	Y	N	N
40 ***Badham***	?	Y	Y	Y	N	Y	N	N
41 ***Lowery***	N	Y	Y	Y	Y	Y	N	Y
42 ***Lungren***	N	Y	Y	Y	N	Y	N	Y
43 ***Packard***	N	Y	Y	Y	N	Y	N	Y
44 Bates	N	Y	Y	N	Y	Y	N	Y
45 ***Hunter***	N	Y	Y	Y	N	N	N	N
COLORADO								
1 Schroeder	Y	Y	Y	N	Y	Y	N	Y
2 Wirth	?	?	Y	N	Y	?	Y	Y
3 ***Strang***	N	Y	Y	Y	Y	Y	N	Y
4 ***Brown***	N	Y	Y	Y	Y	N	Y	Y
5 ***Kramer***	N	Y	?	Y	Y	N	Y	Y
6 ***Schaefer***	N	Y	Y	Y	N	Y	N	?
CONNECTICUT								
1 Kennelly	Y	Y	Y	N	Y	N	Y	Y
2 Gejdenson	N	Y	Y	N	Y	N	Y	Y
3 Morrison	Y	N	N	N	Y	N	Y	Y
4 ***McKinney***	N	Y	Y	N	Y	N	Y	Y
5 ***Rowland***	N	Y	Y	N	Y	Y	N	Y
6 ***Johnson***	N	Y	Y	N	Y	N	Y	Y
DELAWARE								
AL Carper	N	Y	Y	N	Y	N	Y	Y
FLORIDA								
1 Hutto	N	Y	Y	Y	Y	Y	Y	Y
2 Fuqua	N	Y	Y	N	Y	N	N	Y
3 Bennett	N	Y	Y	N	N	Y	N	Y
4 Chappell	N	Y	Y	Y	N	N	N	Y
5 ***McCollum***	N	Y	Y	Y	N	Y	N	N
6 MacKay	N	Y	Y	N	Y	N	Y	Y
7 Gibbons	N	Y	Y	N	Y	Y	N	Y
8 ***Young***	N	Y	Y	N	N	Y	N	?
9 ***Bilirakis***	N	Y	Y	Y	N	Y	N	N
10 ***Ireland***	N	Y	Y	Y	N	Y	N	Y
11 Nelson	N	Y	Y	Y	N	N	N	Y
12 ***Lewis***	N	Y	Y	Y	Y	Y	N	Y
13 ***Mack***	N	Y	Y	Y	N	N	N	N
14 Mica	N	Y	Y	N	Y	N	N	N
15 ***Shaw***	N	Y	Y	Y	Y	N	N	N
16 Smith	Y	Y	Y	N	Y	N	N	Y
17 Lehman	Y	N	Y	N	Y	N	N	Y
18 Pepper	-	+	Y	N	Y	N	Y	Y
19 Fascell	Y	Y	Y	N	Y	N	Y	Y
GEORGIA								
1 Thomas	N	Y	Y	Y	Y	N	N	Y
2 Hatcher	?	?	Y	Y	Y	N	N	Y
3 Ray	N	Y	Y	Y	Y	N	N	Y
4 ***Swindall***	N	Y	Y	Y	Y	Y	N	N
5 Fowler	N	Y	Y	N	Y	N	N	Y
6 ***Gingrich***	N	Y	Y	Y	N	Y	N	?
7 Darden	N	Y	Y	Y	Y	N	N	Y
8 Rowland	N	Y	Y	Y	Y	N	N	Y
9 Jenkins	N	Y	Y	Y	Y	N	N	N
10 Barnard	?	Y	Y	Y	N	N	N	Y
HAWAII								
1 Heftel	N	Y	?	Y	Y	?	?	?
2 Akaka	Y	N	Y	N	Y	N	N	Y
IDAHO								
1 ***Craig***	N	Y	Y	Y	Y	Y	N	?
2 Stallings	Y	Y	Y	N	Y	N	N	Y
ILLINOIS								
1 Hayes	Y	N	N	N	N	N	?	?
2 Savage	Y	N	N	N	N	N	?	?
3 Russo	N	Y	Y	N	Y	N	Y	Y
4 ***O'Brien***	N	Y	Y	Y	N	N	N	Y
5 Lipinski	N	Y	Y	N	Y	Y	N	Y
6 ***Hyde***	N	Y	Y	Y	N	Y	N	Y
7 Collins	Y	N	Y	N	Y	N	Y	Y
8 Rostenkowski	N	Y	Y	N	Y	N	N	Y
9 Yates	Y	N	N	N	N	N	Y	Y
10 ***Porter***	N	Y	Y	Y	Y	Y	Y	Y
11 Annunzio	?	?	Y	N	Y	N	N	Y
12 ***Crane***	N	Y	Y	Y	N	?	N	N
13 ***Fawell***	N	Y	Y	Y	N	Y	N	Y
14 ***Grotberg***	N	Y	Y	Y	N	Y	N	N
15 ***Madigan***	N	Y	Y	Y	Y	N	Y	N
16 ***Martin***	N	Y	Y	Y	Y	N	N	Y
17 Evans	Y	Y	N	N	Y	N	N	Y
18 ***Michel***	N	Y	Y	Y	N	Y	N	N
19 Bruce	N	Y	Y	N	Y	N	Y	Y
20 Durbin	N	Y	Y	N	Y	N	Y	Y
21 Price	N	Y	Y	N	Y	N	N	Y
22 Gray	N	Y	Y	N	Y	N	N	Y
INDIANA								
1 Visclosky	Y	N	Y	N	Y	N	N	Y
2 Sharp	N	Y	Y	N	Y	N	N	Y
3 ***Hiler***	N	Y	Y	Y	Y	Y	N	N
4 ***Coats***	N	Y	Y	Y	Y	Y	N	N
5 ***Hillis***	N	Y	Y	Y	Y	Y	N	N

ND - Northern Democrats SD - Southern Democrats

* Corresponding to Congressional Record Votes 199, 200, 201, 202, 203, 204, 205, 206

	181	182	183	184	185	186	187	188
6 ***Burton***	N	Y	Y	Y	N	N	N	N
7 ***Myers***	N	Y	Y	Y	N	Y	N	N
8 McCloskey	N	Y	Y	N	Y	N	Y	Y
9 Hamilton	N	Y	Y	N	Y	N	N	Y
10 Jacobs	Y	N	Y	N	Y	N	N	Y
IOWA								
1 ***Leach***	Y	N	Y	N	Y	N	Y	Y
2 ***Tauke***	N	Y	Y	N	Y	Y	Y	Y
3 ***Evans***	N	Y	Y	N	Y	N	N	Y
4 Smith	N	Y	Y	N	Y	N	N	Y
5 ***Lightfoot***	N	Y	Y	Y	Y	Y	N	Y
6 Bedell	Y	N	N	N	Y	N	N	Y
KANSAS								
1 ***Roberts***	N	Y	Y	Y	Y	Y	N	Y
2 Slattery	N	Y	Y	N	Y	N	N	Y
3 ***Meyers***	N	Y	Y	Y	Y	Y	N	Y
4 Glickman	Y	N	Y	N	Y	N	N	Y
5 ***Whittaker***	N	Y	Y	Y	Y	Y	N	Y
KENTUCKY								
1 Hubbard	N	Y	Y	Y	N	N	N	Y
2 Natcher	N	Y	Y	N	Y	N	Y	Y
3 Mazzoli	N	Y	Y	N	Y	Y	N	Y
4 ***Snyder***	N	Y	Y	Y	Y	N	N	Y
5 ***Rogers***	N	Y	Y	Y	Y	N	N	Y
6 ***Hopkins***	N	Y	Y	Y	N	N	N	Y
7 Perkins	Y	N	Y	N	Y	N	Y	Y
LOUISIANA								
1 ***Livingston***	N	Y	Y	Y	N	Y	N	Y
2 Boggs	Y	Y	Y	N	Y	N	N	Y
3 Tauzin	N	Y	Y	Y	N	N	N	Y
4 Roemer	N	Y	Y	Y	N	N	N	Y
5 Huckaby	N	Y	?	?	?	?	N	Y
6 ***Moore***	N	Y	Y	Y	Y	Y	N	Y
7 Breaux	N	Y	Y	Y	Y	N	N	Y
8 Long	Y	Y	Y	N	Y	N	N	Y
MAINE								
1 ***McKernan***	N	Y	Y	N	Y	Y	N	Y
2 ***Snowe***	N	Y	Y	N	Y	Y	N	Y
MARYLAND								
1 Dyson	N	Y	Y	N	Y	N	Y	Y
2 ***Bentley***	N	Y	Y	Y	N	Y	Y	Y
3 Mikulski	Y	Y	Y	N	Y	N	Y	Y
4 ***Holt***	?	?	?	?	?	?	?	?
5 Hoyer	Y	Y	Y	N	Y	N	Y	Y
6 Byron	N	Y	Y	N	Y	N	N	N
7 Mitchell	?	?	N	N	Y	N	N	?
8 Barnes	Y	N	Y	N	Y	N	Y	Y
MASSACHUSETTS								
1 ***Conte***	N	Y	Y	N	Y	N	N	Y
2 Boland	N	Y	Y	N	Y	N	N	Y
3 Early	Y	Y	Y	N	Y	N	N	?
4 Frank	Y	N	N	N	Y	N	?	Y
5 Atkins	Y	Y	Y	N	Y	N	N	Y
6 Mavroules	N	Y	Y	N	Y	N	Y	Y
7 Markey	Y	N	N	N	Y	N	N	Y
8 O'Neill								
9 Moakley	N	Y	Y	N	Y	N	N	Y
10 Studds	Y	N	N	N	Y	N	N	Y
11 Donnelly	N	Y	Y	N	Y	N	N	Y
MICHIGAN								
1 Conyers	?	?	N	N	Y	N	Y	Y
2 ***Pursell***	N	Y	Y	N	Y	N	Y	Y
3 Wolpe	Y	N	Y	N	Y	N	Y	Y
4 ***Siljander***	?	?	Y	Y	Y	N	N	Y
5 ***Henry***	N	Y	Y	N	Y	N	Y	Y
6 Carr	N	Y	Y	N	?	?	?	?
7 Kildee	Y	N	Y	N	Y	N	Y	Y
8 Traxler	Y	Y	Y	N	Y	N	?	?
9 ***Vander Jagt***	N	Y	Y	Y	Y	N	?	Y
10 ***Schuette***	N	Y	Y	Y	Y	N	N	Y
11 ***Davis***	N	Y	Y	Y	Y	N	N	Y
12 Bonior	Y	N	Y	N	Y	?	Y	Y
13 Crockett	Y	N	N	N	Y	N	Y	Y
14 Hertel	Y	Y	Y	N	Y	N	N	Y
15 Ford	Y	N	Y	N	Y	N	Y	Y
16 Dingell	N	N	Y	N	Y	N	Y	Y
17 Levin	N	Y	Y	N	Y	N	N	Y
18 ***Broomfield***	N	Y	Y	Y	Y	N	N	Y
MINNESOTA								
1 Penny	N	Y	Y	N	Y	N	Y	Y
2 ***Weber***	N	Y	Y	Y	N	Y	?	?
3 ***Frenzel***	N	?	Y	Y	Y	Y	N	Y
4 Vento	?	?	Y	N	Y	N	Y	N
5 Sabo	Y	N	N	N	Y	N	N	Y
6 Sikorski	Y	Y	Y	N	Y	N	N	Y

	181	182	183	184	185	186	187	188
7 ***Stangeland***	N	Y	Y	Y	Y	Y	N	Y
8 Oberstar	Y	N	N	N	Y	N	Y	Y
MISSISSIPPI								
1 Whitten	?	?	Y	N	Y	N	N	Y
2 ***Franklin***	N	Y	Y	Y	N	Y	N	N
3 Montgomery	N	Y	Y	Y	N	Y	N	Y
4 Dowdy	N	Y	Y	N	Y	N	N	?
5 ***Lott***	?	?	Y	Y	N	Y	N	N
MISSOURI								
1 Clay	Y	N	N	N	N	N	Y	Y
2 Young	N	Y	Y	N	Y	N	N	Y
3 Gephardt	N	Y	Y	N	Y	N	Y	Y
4 Skelton	N	Y	Y	Y	Y	N	N	Y
5 Wheat	Y	N	N	N	Y	N	Y	Y
6 ***Coleman***	N	Y	Y	Y	Y	N	N	Y
7 ***Taylor***	N	Y	Y	Y	N	Y	N	Y
8 ***Emerson***	N	Y	Y	Y	N	N	N	Y
9 Volkmer	N	Y	Y	N	Y	N	N	Y
MONTANA								
1 Williams	Y	N	N	N	Y	N	Y	Y
2 ***Marlenee***	N	Y	Y	Y	N	Y	N	N
NEBRASKA								
1 ***Bereuter***	N	Y	Y	N	Y	N	N	Y
2 ***Daub***	N	Y	Y	Y	Y	N	Y	Y
3 ***Smith***	N	Y	Y	Y	Y	Y	N	N
NEVADA								
1 Reid	Y	Y	Y	N	Y	N	Y	Y
2 ***Vucanovich***	N	Y	Y	Y	N	Y	N	N
NEW HAMPSHIRE								
1 ***Smith***	N	Y	Y	Y	N	Y	N	N
2 ***Gregg***	N	Y	Y	Y	Y	Y	N	Y
NEW JERSEY								
1 Florio	N	Y	Y	N	Y	N	Y	Y
2 Hughes	Y	Y	Y	N	Y	N	Y	Y
3 Howard	N	Y	Y	N	Y	N	Y	Y
4 ***Smith***	N	Y	Y	N	Y	Y	N	?
5 ***Roukema***	N	Y	Y	N	Y	N	N	Y
6 Dwyer	N	Y	Y	N	Y	N	N	Y
7 ***Rinaldo***	N	Y	Y	Y	Y	N	Y	Y
8 Roe	?	?	Y	N	Y	N	Y	Y
9 Torricelli	N	Y	Y	N	Y	N	N	Y
10 Rodino	Y	N	N	N	Y	N	Y	Y
11 ***Gallo***	N	Y	Y	Y	Y	Y	N	N
12 ***Courter***	N	Y	Y	Y	Y	Y	N	Y
13 ***Saxton***	N	Y	Y	Y	Y	Y	Y	Y
14 Guarini	N	Y	Y	N	Y	N	N	Y
NEW MEXICO								
1 ***Lujan***	N	Y	Y	Y	N	Y	N	N
2 ***Skeen***	N	Y	Y	Y	N	Y	N	N
3 Richardson	Y	Y	Y	N	Y	N	N	Y
NEW YORK								
1 ***Carney***	N	Y	Y	Y	N	Y	N	N
2 Downey	Y	N	Y	N	Y	N	N	Y
3 Mrazek	Y	N	Y	N	Y	N	N	?
4 ***Lent***	N	Y	Y	Y	Y	Y	N	Y
5 ***McGrath***	N	Y	Y	Y	Y	Y	N	Y
6 Addabbo	Y	N	N	N	Y	N	N	Y
7 Ackerman	Y	?	Y	N	Y	N	Y	Y
8 Scheuer	Y	N	N	N	Y	N	Y	Y
9 Manton	Y	Y	Y	N	Y	N	Y	Y
10 Schumer	Y	Y	N	N	Y	N	Y	Y
11 Towns	Y	N	N	N	N	N	Y	Y
12 Owens	+	-	-	-	+	-	+	+
13 Solarz	N	Y	Y	N	Y	N	Y	Y
14 ***Molinari***	N	Y	Y	Y	Y	Y	N	Y
15 ***Green***	Y	N	Y	N	Y	Y	Y	Y
16 Rangel	Y	N	N	N	N	N	N	Y
17 Weiss	Y	N	N	N	N	N	N	Y
18 Garcia	Y	N	N	N	Y	N	Y	Y
19 Biaggi	N	Y	Y	N	Y	N	N	Y
20 ***DioGuardi***	N	Y	Y	Y	Y	Y	N	Y
21 ***Fish***	?	?	?	?	?	?	?	?
22 ***Gilman***	N	Y	Y	Y	Y	Y	Y	Y
23 Stratton	N	Y	Y	Y	N	N	N	N
24 ***Solomon***	N	Y	Y	Y	Y	Y	N	?
25 ***Boehlert***	N	Y	Y	N	Y	N	N	Y
26 ***Martin***	N	Y	Y	Y	Y	Y	N	?
27 ***Wortley***	?	?	Y	Y	Y	N	N	Y
28 McHugh	Y	Y	N	N	Y	N	Y	Y
29 ***Horton***	?	Y	Y	N	Y	N	?	?
30 ***Eckert***	N	Y	Y	Y	N	Y	?	?
31 ***Kemp***	N	Y	Y	Y	N	Y	N	Y
32 LaFalce	Y	Y	Y	N	Y	Y	N	Y
33 Nowak	Y	Y	Y	N	Y	N	Y	Y
34 Lundine	Y	N	Y	N	Y	N	N	Y

	181	182	183	184	185	186	187	188
NORTH CAROLINA								
1 Jones	?	?	Y	N	Y	N	Y	Y
2 Valentine	N	Y	Y	Y	N	?	?	?
3 Whitley	N	Y	Y	N	Y	N	Y	Y
4 ***Cobey***	N	Y	Y	Y	N	Y	N	Y
5 Neal	Y	Y	Y	N	Y	N	N	Y
6 ***Coble***	N	Y	Y	Y	N	N	N	N
7 Rose	N	Y	Y	N	Y	N	N	Y
8 Hefner	?	?	?	?	?	?	?	?
9 ***McMillan***	N	Y	Y	Y	N	Y	N	Y
10 ***Broyhill***	N	Y	Y	Y	N	N	N	Y
11 ***Hendon***	N	Y	Y	Y	Y	Y	N	Y
NORTH DAKOTA								
AL Dorgan	Y	Y	Y	N	Y	N	Y	Y
OHIO								
1 Luken	?	?	?	?	?	?	?	?
2 ***Gradison***	N	Y	Y	Y	Y	Y	N	Y
3 Hall	N	Y	Y	N	Y	N	?	?
4 ***Oxley***	N	Y	Y	N	N	N	N	Y
5 ***Latta***	N	Y	Y	Y	N	N	N	Y
6 ***McEwen***	N	Y	Y	Y	N	Y	N	Y
7 ***DeWine***	N	Y	Y	Y	N	Y	N	N
8 ***Kindness***	N	Y	Y	Y	N	N	N	Y
9 Kaptur	N	Y	Y	N	Y	N	Y	Y
10 ***Miller***	N	Y	Y	Y	Y	N	Y	Y
11 Eckart	Y	Y	Y	?	Y	N	N	Y
12 ***Kasich***	N	Y	Y	Y	Y	Y	N	Y
13 Pease	Y	N	Y	N	Y	N	N	Y
14 Seiberling	Y	N	Y	N	Y	N	N	Y
15 ***Wylie***	N	Y	Y	Y	Y	Y	N	Y
16 ***Regula***	N	Y	Y	Y	Y	Y	N	Y
17 Traficant	Y	N	Y	N	Y	N	Y	Y
18 Applegate	N	Y	Y	N	Y	N	Y	Y
19 Feighan	Y	Y	Y	N	Y	N	N	Y
20 Oakar	Y	N	Y	N	Y	N	Y	Y
21 Stokes	Y	N	N	N	Y	N	Y	Y
OKLAHOMA								
1 Jones	N	Y	Y	N	Y	N	N	Y
2 Synar	Y	N	Y	N	Y	N	Y	Y
3 Watkins	N	Y	Y	N	Y	N	N	Y
4 McCurdy	N	Y	Y	N	Y	N	N	Y
5 ***Edwards***	N	Y	Y	Y	Y	Y	N	Y
6 English	N	Y	Y	Y	Y	N	N	Y
OREGON								
1 AuCoin	N	Y	Y	N	N	N	N	Y
2 ***Smith, R.***	N	Y	Y	Y	Y	Y	N	N
3 Wyden	N	Y	Y	N	Y	N	Y	Y
4 Weaver	?	?	N	N	Y	N	Y	Y
5 ***Smith, D.***	N	Y	Y	Y	N	?	?	?
PENNSYLVANIA								
1 Foglietta	Y	Y	Y	N	Y	N	?	?
2 Gray	Y	N	Y	N	Y	N	Y	?
3 Borski	N	Y	Y	N	Y	N	Y	Y
4 Kolter	N	Y	Y	N	Y	N	N	Y
5 ***Schulze***	N	Y	Y	Y	Y	N	N	N
6 Yatron	N	Y	Y	N	Y	N	N	Y
7 Edgar	Y	N	Y	N	Y	N	N	Y
8 Kostmayer	Y	N	Y	N	Y	N	N	Y
9 ***Shuster***	N	Y	Y	Y	N	Y	N	N
10 ***McDade***	N	Y	Y	N	Y	Y	N	?
11 Kanjorski	N	Y	Y	N	Y	N	N	Y
12 Murtha	N	Y	Y	Y	Y	N	N	Y
13 ***Coughlin***	N	Y	Y	Y	Y	N	N	Y
14 Coyne	Y	N	Y	N	Y	N	Y	Y
15 ***Ritter***	?	?	Y	Y	N	N	N	N
16 ***Walker***	N	Y	Y	Y	N	Y	N	N
17 ***Gekas***	N	Y	Y	Y	N	Y	N	N
18 Walgren	Y	Y	Y	N	Y	N	Y	N
19 ***Goodling***	N	Y	Y	N	Y	?	?	?
20 Gaydos	N	Y	Y	Y	Y	N	N	Y
21 ***Ridge***	N	Y	Y	N	Y	N	N	Y
22 Murphy	N	Y	Y	N	Y	N	N	Y
23 ***Clinger***	N	Y	Y	N	Y	Y	N	Y
RHODE ISLAND								
1 St Germain	N	Y	Y	N	Y	N	Y	Y
2 ***Schneider***	N	Y	Y	N	Y	Y	N	Y
SOUTH CAROLINA								
1 ***Hartnett***	N	Y	Y	Y	N	Y	N	N
2 ***Spence***	N	Y	Y	Y	N	Y	N	Y
3 Derrick	N	Y	Y	?	Y	N	N	Y
4 ***Campbell***	N	Y	Y	Y	N	Y	N	Y
5 Spratt	N	Y	Y	N	Y	N	N	Y
6 Tallon	N	Y	Y	N	Y	N	Y	Y
SOUTH DAKOTA								
AL Daschle	Y	Y	Y	N	Y	N	N	Y

	181	182	183	184	185	186	187	188
TENNESSEE								
1 ***Quillen***	N	Y	Y	Y	N	N	N	N
2 ***Duncan***	N	Y	Y	Y	Y	N	N	Y
3 Lloyd	N	Y	Y	Y	Y	N	N	Y
4 Cooper	Y	Y	Y	N	Y	N	Y	Y
5 Boner	N	Y	Y	N	Y	N	N	Y
6 Gordon	N	Y	Y	Y	Y	N	Y	Y
7 ***Sundquist***	N	Y	Y	Y	N	Y	N	N
8 Jones	Y	N	Y	N	Y	N	N	?
9 Ford	?	?	N	N	Y	N	Y	Y
TEXAS								
1 Vacancy								
2 Wilson	?	?	?	?	?	?	?	?
3 ***Bartlett***	N	Y	Y	Y	N	Y	N	Y
4 Hall, R.	N	Y	Y	Y	N	Y	Y	Y
5 Bryant	Y	Y	Y	N	Y	N	N	Y
6 ***Barton***	N	Y	Y	Y	Y	Y	N	N
7 ***Archer***	N	Y	Y	Y	Y	Y	N	N
8 ***Fields***	N	Y	Y	Y	N	Y	N	N
9 Brooks	Y	N	Y	N	Y	N	N	Y
10 Pickle	Y	Y	Y	N	Y	?	?	?
11 Leath	N	Y	Y	Y	N	N	N	Y
12 Wright	Y	Y	Y	N	Y	N	N	Y
13 ***Boulter***	N	Y	Y	Y	N	N	N	N
14 ***Sweeney***	N	Y	Y	Y	N	Y	N	Y
15 de la Garza	Y	Y	Y	N	Y	N	N	Y
16 Coleman	Y	Y	Y	N	Y	N	Y	Y
17 Stenholm	N	Y	Y	Y	N	N	N	Y
18 Leland	Y	N	N	N	N	N	Y	Y
19 ***Combest***	N	Y	Y	Y	N	Y	N	N
20 Gonzalez	Y	N	N	N	Y	N	Y	Y
21 ***Loeffler***	N	Y	?	?	?	?	?	?
22 ***DeLay***	N	Y	Y	Y	N	Y	N	N
23 Bustamante	Y	Y	Y	Y	N	N	N	Y
24 Frost	Y	Y	Y	Y	N	N	N	Y
25 Andrews	Y	Y	Y	N	Y	N	N	Y
26 ***Armey***	N	Y	Y	Y	N	Y	N	N
27 Ortiz	Y	Y	Y	N	Y	N	N	?
UTAH								
1 ***Hansen***	N	Y	Y	Y	N	Y	N	N
2 ***Monson***	N	Y	Y	Y	N	Y	N	N
3 ***Nielson***	N	Y	Y	Y	N	Y	N	N
VERMONT								
AL ***Jeffords***	N	Y	Y	N	Y	Y	N	Y
VIRGINIA								
1 ***Bateman***	N	Y	Y	Y	N	Y	Y	Y
2 ***Whitehurst***	N	Y	Y	Y	Y	Y	N	N
3 ***Bliley***	N	Y	Y	Y	N	N	Y	Y
4 Sisisky	N	Y	Y	N	Y	N	Y	Y
5 Daniel	N	Y	Y	N	N	Y	N	Y
6 Olin	N	Y	Y	N	Y	N	N	Y
7 ***Slaughter***	N	Y	Y	Y	N	Y	N	Y
8 ***Parris***	N	Y	Y	Y	Y	Y	Y	Y
9 Boucher	N	N	Y	N	Y	N	Y	Y
10 ***Wolf***	N	Y	Y	Y	Y	Y	Y	?
WASHINGTON								
1 ***Miller***	N	Y	Y	N	Y	Y	N	Y
2 Swift	Y	N	Y	N	Y	N	N	Y
3 Bonker	N	Y	Y	?	Y	N	N	Y
4 ***Morrison***	N	Y	Y	Y	Y	Y	N	N
5 Foley	Y	Y	Y	N	Y	N	N	Y
6 Dicks	?	?	Y	N	Y	N	Y	Y
7 Lowry	?	N	N	N	Y	N	Y	Y
8 ***Chandler***	N	Y	Y	Y	Y	Y	Y	Y
WEST VIRGINIA								
1 Mollohan	N	Y	Y	N	Y	N	Y	Y
2 Staggers	Y	Y	Y	N	Y	N	Y	Y
3 Wise	N	Y	Y	N	Y	N	Y	Y
4 Rahall	N	Y	Y	N	Y	N	Y	Y
WISCONSIN								
1 Aspin	N	Y	Y	N	Y	N	N	Y
2 Kastenmeier	Y	N	N	N	N	N	Y	Y
3 ***Gunderson***	N	Y	Y	N	Y	Y	Y	Y
4 Kleczka	N	Y	Y	N	Y	N	N	Y
5 Moody	Y	Y	Y	N	Y	N	Y	N
6 ***Petri***	N	Y	Y	N	Y	N	N	Y
7 Obey	Y	N	Y	N	Y	N	Y	Y
8 ***Roth***	N	Y	Y	Y	Y	N	N	Y
9 ***Sensenbrenner***	N	Y	Y	Y	Y	Y	N	N
WYOMING								
AL ***Cheney***	N	Y	Y	Y	N	Y	N	Y

Southern states - Ala., Ark., Fla., Ga., Ky., La., Miss., N.C., Okla., S.C., Tenn., Texas, Va.

* The *Congressional Record* vote number is different from the CQ vote number because the *Record* includes quorum calls in its tally. CQ does not publish quorum call votes.

189. HR 1872. Department of Defense Authorization, Fiscal 1986. Markey, D-Mass., amendment, as amended by the Daniel, D-Va., substitute *(see vote 188, p. 60-H)*, to restrict the actions of U.S. troops in Honduras near that country's border with Nicaragua. Rejected 172-217: R 10-155; D 162-62 (ND 135-15, SD 27-47), June 27, 1985.

190. HR 1872. Department of Defense Authorization, Fiscal 1986. Passage of the bill to authorize $206,158,800,000 for weapons procurement, military research and operating costs of the Department of Defense in fiscal year 1986. Passed 278-106: R 97-64; D 181-42 (ND 110-41, SD 71-1), June 27, 1985. (The House subsequently moved to delete the language of S 1160, the Senate version of the Defense Department authorization, and insert instead the provisions of HR 1872. After the motion was agreed to, S 1160 was passed by voice vote.)

KEY

- Y Voted for (yea).
- # Paired for.
- \+ Announced for.
- N Voted against (nay).
- X Paired against.
- \- Announced against.
- P Voted "present".
- C Voted "present" to avoid possible conflict of interest.
- ? Did not vote or otherwise make a position known.

Democrats ***Republicans***

	189	190
ALABAMA		
1 ***Callahan***	N	Y
2 ***Dickinson***	N	Y
3 Nichols	N	Y
4 Bevill	N	Y
5 Flippo	?	?
6 Erdreich	N	Y
7 Shelby	N	Y
ALASKA		
AL ***Young***	N	Y
ARIZONA		
1 ***McCain***	N	N
2 Udall	Y	Y
3 ***Stump***	N	N
4 ***Rudd***	?	?
5 ***Kolbe***	N	Y
ARKANSAS		
1 Alexander	Y	#
2 Robinson	N	Y
3 ***Hammerschmidt***	N	N
4 Anthony	N	Y
CALIFORNIA		
1 Bosco	Y	Y
2 ***Chappie***	N	N
3 Matsui	Y	Y
4 Fazio	Y	Y
5 Burton	Y	N
6 Boxer	Y	N
7 Miller	Y	N
8 Dellums	Y	N
9 Stark	Y	N
10 Edwards	Y	N
11 Lantos	Y	Y
12 ***Zschau***	N	Y
13 Mineta	Y	N
14 ***Shumway***	N	N
15 Coelho	?	?
16 Panetta	Y	Y
17 ***Pashayan***	N	N
18 Lehman	Y	Y
19 ***Lagomarsino***	N	N
20 ***Thomas***	?	?
21 ***Fiedler***	N	N
22 ***Moorhead***	N	N
23 Beilenson	Y	Y
24 Waxman	?	?
25 Roybal	?	X
26 Berman	Y	Y
27 Levine	Y	Y
28 Dixon	Y	Y
29 Hawkins	?	?
30 Martinez	?	?
31 Dymally	Y	N
32 Anderson	Y	Y
33 ***Dreier***	N	N
34 Torres	Y	Y
35 ***Lewis***	N	N
36 Brown	Y	Y
37 ***McCandless***	N	N
38 ***Dornan***	N	N
39 ***Dannemeyer***	N	Y
40 ***Badham***	N	Y
41 ***Lowery***	N	N
42 ***Lungren***	N	N

	189	190
43 ***Packard***	N	N
44 Bates	Y	Y
45 ***Hunter***	N	N
COLORADO		
1 Schroeder	Y	N
2 Wirth	Y	Y
3 ***Strang***	N	N
4 ***Brown***	N	Y
5 ***Kramer***	N	?
6 ***Schaefer***	?	?
CONNECTICUT		
1 Kennelly	Y	Y
2 Gejdenson	Y	Y
3 Morrison	Y	N
4 ***McKinney***	Y	?
5 ***Rowland***	N	Y
6 ***Johnson***	N	Y
DELAWARE		
AL Carper	Y	Y
FLORIDA		
1 Hutto	N	Y
2 Fuqua	N	Y
3 Bennett	Y	Y
4 Chappell	N	Y
5 ***McCollum***	N	Y
6 MacKay	Y	Y
7 Gibbons	Y	Y
8 ***Young***	?	?
9 ***Bilirakis***	N	Y
10 ***Ireland***	N	N
11 Nelson	N	Y
12 ***Lewis***	N	Y
13 ***Mack***	N	Y
14 Mica	N	Y
15 ***Shaw***	N	Y
16 Smith	Y	Y
17 Lehman	Y	Y
18 Pepper	Y	Y
19 Fascell	Y	Y
GEORGIA		
1 Thomas	N	Y
2 Hatcher	N	Y
3 Ray	N	Y
4 ***Swindall***	N	Y
5 Fowler	N	Y
6 ***Gingrich***	?	?
7 Darden	N	Y
8 Rowland	N	Y
9 Jenkins	N	Y
10 Barnard	N	#
HAWAII		
1 Heftel	?	?
2 Akaka	Y	Y
IDAHO		
1 ***Craig***	N	N
2 Stallings	N	Y
ILLINOIS		
1 Hayes	?	X
2 Savage	?	N
3 Russo	Y	N
4 ***O'Brien***	N	Y
5 Lipinski	N	Y
6 ***Hyde***	N	N
7 Collins	Y	N
8 Rostenkowski	Y	Y
9 Yates	Y	Y
10 ***Porter***	N	Y
11 Annunzio	N	Y
12 ***Crane***	N	N
13 ***Fawell***	N	Y
14 ***Grotberg***	N	Y
15 ***Madigan***	N	?
16 ***Martin***	N	Y
17 Evans	Y	Y
18 ***Michel***	N	N
19 Bruce	Y	Y
20 Durbin	Y	Y
21 Price	Y	Y
22 Gray	?	Y
INDIANA		
1 Visclosky	Y	Y
2 Sharp	Y	Y
3 ***Hiler***	N	N
4 ***Coats***	N	N
5 ***Hillis***	N	Y

ND - Northern Democrats SD - Southern Democrats

	189	190
6 ***Burton***	N	?
7 ***Myers***	N	Y
8 McCloskey	Y	Y
9 Hamilton	Y	Y
10 Jacobs	Y	?
IOWA		
1 ***Leach***	Y	N
2 ***Tauke***	N	N
3 ***Evans***	N	N
4 Smith	N	?
5 ***Lightfoot***	N	N
6 Bedell	Y	N
KANSAS		
1 ***Roberts***	N	N
2 Slattery	N	Y
3 ***Meyers***	N	Y
4 Glickman	N	Y
5 ***Whittaker***	N	N
KENTUCKY		
1 Hubbard	N	Y
2 Natcher	N	Y
3 Mazzoli	N	Y
4 ***Snyder***	N	Y
5 ***Rogers***	N	Y
6 ***Hopkins***	N	Y
7 Perkins	Y	Y
LOUISIANA		
1 ***Livingston***	N	N
2 Boggs	Y	Y
3 Tauzin	N	Y
4 Roemer	N	Y
5 Huckaby	N	Y
6 ***Moore***	N	Y
7 Breaux	N	Y
8 Long	Y	Y
MAINE		
1 ***McKernan***	N	Y
2 ***Snowe***	N	Y
MARYLAND		
1 Dyson	N	Y
2 ***Bentley***	N	Y
3 Mikulski	Y	Y
4 ***Holt***	?	?
5 Hoyer	Y	Y
6 Byron	N	Y
7 Mitchell	Y	N
8 Barnes	Y	Y
MASSACHUSETTS		
1 ***Conte***	Y	Y
2 Boland	?	Y
3 Early	?	?
4 Frank	Y	Y
5 Atkins	Y	Y
6 Mavroules	Y	Y
7 Markey	Y	N
8 O'Neill		
9 Moakley	Y	Y
10 Studds	Y	N
11 Donnelly	Y	Y
MICHIGAN		
1 Conyers	Y	Y
2 ***Pursell***	N	Y
3 Wolpe	Y	Y
4 ***Siljander***	N	Y
5 ***Henry***	N	Y
6 Carr	?	#
7 Kildee	Y	N
8 Traxler	?	+
9 ***Vander Jagt***	N	Y
10 ***Schuette***	N	Y
11 ***Davis***	N	Y
12 Bonior	Y	N
13 Crockett	Y	N
14 Hertel	Y	N
15 Ford	Y	Y
16 Dingell	Y	Y
17 Levin	Y	Y
18 ***Broomfield***	N	Y
MINNESOTA		
1 Penny	Y	Y
2 ***Weber***	?	?
3 ***Frenzel***	N	Y
4 Vento	?	N
5 Sabo	Y	Y
6 Sikorski	Y	Y

	189	190
7 ***Stangeland***	N	Y
8 Oberstar	Y	N
MISSISSIPPI		
1 Whitten	N	Y
2 ***Franklin***	N	Y
3 Montgomery	N	Y
4 Dowdy	?	?
5 ***Lott***	N	N
MISSOURI		
1 Clay	?	X
2 Young	Y	Y
3 Gephardt	Y	Y
4 Skelton	Y	Y
5 Wheat	Y	N
6 ***Coleman***	N	Y
7 ***Taylor***	N	N
8 ***Emerson***	N	Y
9 Volkmer	N	Y
MONTANA		
1 Williams	Y	Y
2 ***Marlenee***	N	Y
NEBRASKA		
1 ***Bereuter***	N	Y
2 ***Daub***	N	Y
3 ***Smith***	N	Y
NEVADA		
1 Reid	N	Y
2 ***Vucanovich***	N	N
NEW HAMPSHIRE		
1 ***Smith***	N	N
2 ***Gregg***	N	Y
NEW JERSEY		
1 Florio	Y	Y
2 Hughes	Y	Y
3 Howard	Y	Y
4 ***Smith***	?	?
5 ***Roukema***	Y	Y
6 Dwyer	Y	Y
7 ***Rinaldo***	N	Y
8 Roe	Y	Y
9 Torricelli	Y	Y
10 Rodino	Y	N
11 ***Gallo***	N	N
12 ***Courter***	N	N
13 ***Saxton***	N	N
14 Guarini	Y	Y
NEW MEXICO		
1 ***Lujan***	N	Y
2 ***Skeen***	N	Y
3 Richardson	Y	Y
NEW YORK		
1 ***Carney***	N	N
2 Downey	Y	Y
3 Mrazek	#	?
4 ***Lent***	N	Y
5 ***McGrath***	N	Y
6 Addabbo	Y	Y
7 Ackerman	Y	N
8 Scheuer	Y	Y
9 Manton	Y	Y
10 Schumer	Y	Y
11 Towns	Y	N
12 Owens	+	X
13 Solarz	Y	Y
14 ***Molinari***	N	Y
15 ***Green***	Y	Y
16 Rangel	Y	N
17 Weiss	Y	N
18 Garcia	Y	N
19 Biaggi	Y	Y
20 ***DioGuardi***	N	Y
21 ***Fish***	?	?
22 ***Gilman***	N	Y
23 Stratton	N	Y
24 ***Solomon***	X	?
25 ***Boehlert***	Y	Y
26 ***Martin***	?	?
27 ***Wortley***	N	Y
28 McHugh	Y	Y
29 ***Horton***	?	?
30 ***Eckert***	?	?
31 ***Kemp***	N	N
32 LaFalce	N	N
33 Nowak	Y	Y
34 Lundine	N	Y

	189	190
NORTH CAROLINA		
1 Jones	N	Y
2 Valentine	?	?
3 Whitley	N	Y
4 ***Cobey***	N	N
5 Neal	Y	Y
6 ***Coble***	N	Y
7 Rose	N	Y
8 Hefner	?	?
9 ***McMillan***	N	Y
10 ***Broyhill***	N	Y
11 ***Hendon***	N	N
NORTH DAKOTA		
AL Dorgan	Y	Y
OHIO		
1 Luken	?	?
2 ***Gradison***	Y	Y
3 Hall	?	?
4 ***Oxley***	N	Y
5 ***Latta***	N	N
6 ***McEwen***	N	N
7 ***DeWine***	N	N
8 ***Kindness***	N	N
9 Kaptur	Y	Y
10 ***Miller***	N	Y
11 Eckart	Y	Y
12 ***Kasich***	N	Y
13 Pease	Y	Y
14 Seiberling	Y	N
15 ***Wylie***	N	Y
16 ***Regula***	N	Y
17 Traficant	Y	Y
18 Applegate	Y	Y
19 Feighan	Y	Y
20 Oakar	Y	?
21 Stokes	Y	N
OKLAHOMA		
1 Jones	Y	Y
2 Synar	Y	Y
3 Watkins	N	Y
4 McCurdy	N	Y
5 ***Edwards***	N	Y
6 English	N	Y
OREGON		
1 AuCoin	Y	Y
2 ***Smith, R.***	N	Y
3 Wyden	Y	Y
4 Weaver	Y	N
5 ***Smith, D.***	?	?
PENNSYLVANIA		
1 Foglietta	?	?
2 Gray	Y	Y
3 Borski	Y	Y
4 Kolter	Y	Y
5 ***Schulze***	N	Y
6 Yatron	Y	Y
7 Edgar	Y	N
8 Kostmayer	Y	N
9 ***Shuster***	N	Y
10 ***McDade***	N	Y
11 Kanjorski	Y	Y
12 Murtha	Y	Y
13 ***Coughlin***	Y	Y
14 Coyne	Y	Y
15 ***Ritter***	N	Y
16 ***Walker***	N	N
17 ***Gekas***	N	N
18 Walgren	Y	N
19 ***Goodling***	?	?
20 Gaydos	Y	Y
21 ***Ridge***	N	Y
22 Murphy	Y	Y
23 ***Clinger***	N	Y
RHODE ISLAND		
1 St Germain	Y	Y
2 ***Schneider***	Y	N
SOUTH CAROLINA		
1 ***Hartnett***	N	N
2 ***Spence***	N	Y
3 Derrick	N	Y
4 ***Campbell***	N	N
5 Spratt	N	Y
6 Tallon	N	Y
SOUTH DAKOTA		
AL Daschle	N	Y

	189	190
TENNESSEE		
1 ***Quillen***	N	N
2 ***Duncan***	N	Y
3 Lloyd	N	Y
4 Cooper	Y	Y
5 Boner	N	Y
6 Gordon	N	Y
7 ***Sundquist***	N	N
8 Jones	?	Y
9 Ford	Y	Y
TEXAS		
1 Vacancy		
2 Wilson	?	?
3 ***Bartlett***	N	N
4 Hall, R.	N	Y
5 Bryant	Y	Y
6 ***Barton***	N	N
7 ***Archer***	N	Y
8 ***Fields***	N	N
9 Brooks	Y	Y
10 Pickle	?	#
11 Leath	N	Y
12 Wright	Y	?
13 ***Boulter***	N	N
14 ***Sweeney***	N	Y
15 de la Garza	Y	Y
16 Coleman	Y	Y
17 Stenholm	N	Y
18 Leland	Y	N
19 ***Combest***	N	N
20 Gonzalez	Y	Y
21 ***Loeffler***	?	?
22 ***DeLay***	N	N
23 Bustamante	Y	Y
24 Frost	N	Y
25 Andrews	N	Y
26 ***Armey***	N	Y
27 Ortiz	Y	Y
UTAH		
1 ***Hansen***	N	Y
2 ***Monson***	N	Y
3 ***Nielson***	N	Y
VERMONT		
AL ***Jeffords***	Y	Y
VIRGINIA		
1 ***Bateman***	N	N
2 ***Whitehurst***	N	Y
3 ***Bliley***	N	Y
4 Sisisky	N	Y
5 Daniel	Y	Y
6 Olin	N	Y
7 ***Slaughter***	N	Y
8 ***Parris***	N	Y
9 Boucher	Y	Y
10 ***Wolf***	?	?
WASHINGTON		
1 ***Miller***	N	Y
2 Swift	Y	Y
3 Bonker	Y	N
4 ***Morrison***	N	Y
5 Foley	Y	Y
6 Dicks	N	Y
7 Lowry	Y	Y
8 ***Chandler***	N	Y
WEST VIRGINIA		
1 Mollohan	Y	Y
2 Staggers	Y	Y
3 Wise	Y	Y
4 Rahall	Y	N
WISCONSIN		
1 Aspin	Y	Y
2 Kastenmeier	Y	N
3 ***Gunderson***	N	Y
4 Kleczka	Y	Y
5 Moody	Y	N
6 ***Petri***	N	Y
7 Obey	Y	Y
8 ***Roth***	N	N
9 ***Sensenbrenner***	N	N
WYOMING		
AL ***Cheney***	N	N

Southern states - Ala., Ark., Fla., Ga., Ky., La., Miss., N.C., Okla., S.C., Tenn., Texas, Va.

* The *Congressional Record* vote number is different from the CQ vote number because the *Record* includes quorum calls in its tally. CQ does not publish quorum call votes.

191. HR 1555. Foreign Assistance Authorization, Fiscal 1986. Fascell, D-Fla., amendments to make a 3.2 percent across-the-board cut in programs authorized in the bill, from a total for each year of $13.05 billion to $12.64 billion. Adopted en bloc 386-2: R 169-1; D 217-1 (ND 148-1, SD 69-0), July 9, 1985.

192. HR 1555. Foreign Assistance Authorization, Fiscal 1986. Solomon, R-N.Y., amendments to increase by $60 million in fiscal 1986 and 1987 the amount of military aid for the Philippines, and to make a comparable reduction in economic aid. Rejected en bloc 125-279: R 110-63; D 15-216 (ND 4-150, SD 11-66), July 9, 1985. A "yea" was a vote supporting the president's position.

193. HR 1555. Foreign Assistance Authorization, Fiscal 1986. Solarz, D-N.Y., substitute for the Leach, R-Iowa, amendment, to authorize $5 million in military or economic aid for non-communist resistance forces in Cambodia, and to prohibit any aid for the communist Khmer Rouge forces. Adopted 288-122: R 156-18; D 132-104 (ND 66-93, SD 66-11), July 9, 1985. (The Leach amendment, as amended by the Solarz substitute, subsequently was adopted by voice vote.)

194. H Res 217. Illegal Political Solicitation. Foley, D-Wash., motion to table (kill) the resolution to authorize the Committee on Standards of Official Conduct to investigate the alleged illegal solicitation of political contributions by three House members made in a June 24 letter distributed to Democratic House members' offices. The resolution alleged the letter, sent by the Democratic Congressional Campaign Committee, violated federal law regarding soliciting political contributions in House office buildings. Motion agreed to 233-170: R 0-168; D 233-2 (ND 157-2, SD 76-0), July 10, 1985.

195. HR 1555. Foreign Assistance Authorization, Fiscal 1986. Fascell, D-Fla., amendment to the Smith, R-N.J., amendment, to retain the earmarking of assistance from the U.N. Fund for Population Activities. Rejected 198-221: R 37-143; D 161-78 (ND 117-44, SD 44-34), July 10, 1985. (The Smith amendment was subsequently adopted *(vote 196, below)*.)

196. HR 1555. Foreign Assistance Authorization, Fiscal 1986. Smith, R-N.J., amendment to express the sense of Congress that China has systematically employed forced abortion and sterilization as means of enforcing that country's one-child-per-couple policy and that China should cease such practices; to restrict funding in the bill for family planning programs in China; to direct the president to report annually as to whether there are valid reports of coerced abortion, sterilization or infanticide in China, and to advise that country that such practices have a negative impact on U.S.-Chinese relations; and to authorize the president to withhold funding from the U.N. Fund for Population Activities if he finds such reports valid, and to use any funds withheld from the U.N. fund for other U.S. family planning programs. Adopted 289-130: R 150-31; D 139-99 (ND 80-80, SD 59-19), July 10, 1985. A "yea" was a vote supporting the president's position.

197. HR 1555. Foreign Assistance Authorization, Fiscal 1986. Smith, R-N.J., amendment to the Snowe, R-Maine, substitute for the Smith, R-N.J., amendment, to permit the president to deny funds for family planning programs to a country or an international or non-governmental organization because of the type of voluntary family planning programs that it promotes or carries out. Adopted 234-189: R 144-37; D 90-152 (ND 50-116, SD 40-36), July 10, 1985. A "yea" was a vote supporting the president's position. (The Snowe substitute, as amended by the Smith amendment, was subsequently adopted by voice vote, after which the original Smith amendment, as amended, was adopted by voice vote.)

198. HR 1555. Foreign Assistance Authorization, Fiscal 1986. Conyers, D-Mich., amendment to prohibit all military assistance to El Salvador until the president reports to Congress, and Congress passes a joint resolution, stating that El Salvador's government has made sufficient progress in prosecuting those responsible for the more than 45,000 murders that have occurred over the last five years and in carrying out all the titles of its land reform program, and that the government and military have agreed to pursue a negotiated settlement with the armed opposition based on safe and free elections. Rejected 47-375: R 0-180; D 47-195 (ND 45-120, SD 2-75), July 10, 1985. A "nay" was a vote supporting the president's position.

KEY

- Y Voted for (yea).
- # Paired for.
- + Announced for.
- N Voted against (nay).
- X Paired against.
- \- Announced against.
- P Voted "present."
- C Voted "present" to avoid possible conflict of interest.
- ? Did not vote or otherwise make a position known.

Democrats ***Republicans***

	191	192	193	194	195	196	197	198
ALABAMA								
1 ***Callahan***	Y	Y	Y	N	N	Y	Y	N
2 ***Dickinson***	Y	N	Y	N	Y	N	N	N
3 Nichols	Y	N	Y	Y	N	Y	Y	N
4 Bevill	Y	N	Y	Y	N	Y	Y	N
5 Flippo	Y	N	Y	Y	N	Y	Y	N
6 Erdreich	Y	N	Y	Y	N	Y	N	N
7 Shelby	Y	N	Y	?	N	Y	Y	N
ALASKA								
AL ***Young***	Y	N	Y	N	N	Y	Y	N
ARIZONA								
1 ***McCain***	Y	Y	Y	N	Y	Y	Y	N
2 Udall	Y	N	Y	Y	Y	N	N	N
3 ***Stump***	Y	Y	N	N	N	Y	Y	N
4 ***Rudd***	Y	Y	N	N	N	Y	Y	N
5 ***Kolbe***	Y	N	Y	N	Y	N	N	N
ARKANSAS								
1 Alexander	?	N	Y	Y	Y	?	N	N
2 Robinson	Y	Y	Y	Y	N	Y	Y	N
3 ***Hammerschmidt***	Y	Y	Y	N	N	Y	Y	N
4 Anthony	Y	N	Y	Y	Y	N	N	N
CALIFORNIA								
1 Bosco	?	N	Y	Y	Y	N	N	N
2 ***Chappie***	Y	N	Y	N	N	Y	Y	N
3 Matsui	Y	N	Y	Y	Y	N	N	N
4 Fazio	Y	N	Y	Y	#	N	N	N
5 Burton	Y	N	N	Y	Y	N	N	N
6 Boxer	Y	N	N	Y	Y	N	N	Y
7 Miller	?	X	X	Y	?	N	N	N
8 Dellums	Y	N	N	Y	Y	N	N	Y
9 Stark	Y	?	N	Y	Y	N	N	Y
10 Edwards	Y	N	N	Y	Y	N	N	Y
11 Lantos	Y	N	Y	Y	Y	N	N	N
12 ***Zschau***	Y	Y	Y	N	Y	Y	N	N
13 Mineta	Y	N	N	Y	Y	N	N	N
14 ***Shumway***	Y	N	Y	N	N	Y	Y	N
15 Coelho	Y	N	Y	Y	Y	Y	N	N
16 Panetta	Y	N	N	Y	Y	N	N	Y
17 ***Pashayan***	Y	Y	Y	N	N	Y	Y	N
18 Lehman	Y	N	Y	Y	Y	N	?	N
19 ***Lagomarsino***	Y	Y	Y	N	N	Y	Y	N
20 ***Thomas***	Y	Y	Y	N	Y	N	N	?
21 ***Fiedler***	Y	Y	?	?	N	Y	N	N
22 ***Moorhead***	Y	Y	Y	N	N	Y	Y	N
23 Beilenson	?	?	?	?	?	?	?	?
24 Waxman	Y	N	Y	Y	Y	N	N	N
25 Roybal	Y	N	N	Y	Y	?	N	Y
26 Berman	?	X	X	Y	Y	N	N	N
27 Levine	Y	N	N	Y	Y	N	N	Y
28 Dixon	Y	N	N	P	Y	N	N	Y
29 Hawkins	Y	N	N	Y	Y	N	N	Y
30 Martinez	Y	N	Y	Y	Y	?	?	N
31 Dymally	Y	N	N	Y	Y	N	N	Y
32 Anderson	Y	N	N	Y	Y	N	N	N
33 ***Dreier***	Y	Y	Y	N	N	Y	Y	N
34 Torres	Y	N	N	Y	Y	?	N	N
35 ***Lewis***	?	?	Y	N	Y	N	Y	N
36 Brown	?	?	?	?	Y	N	N	Y
37 ***McCandless***	Y	Y	Y	N	Y	N	Y	N
38 ***Dornan***	Y	Y	Y	N	N	Y	Y	N
39 ***Dannemeyer***	Y	Y	Y	N	N	Y	Y	N
40 ***Badham***	Y	Y	Y	N	N	N	N	N
41 ***Lowery***	Y	Y	Y	N	N	Y	Y	N
42 ***Lungren***	Y	Y	Y	N	N	Y	Y	N
43 ***Packard***	Y	Y	Y	N	N	Y	Y	N
44 Bates	Y	N	N	Y	Y	N	N	Y
45 ***Hunter***	Y	Y	Y	N	N	Y	Y	N
COLORADO								
1 Schroeder	Y	N	N	Y	Y	N	N	Y
2 Wirth	Y	N	N	Y	Y	N	N	N
3 ***Strang***	Y	Y	Y	N	Y	Y	N	N
4 ***Brown***	Y	Y	Y	?	Y	Y	N	?
5 ***Kramer***	Y	Y	Y	N	N	Y	Y	N
6 ***Schaefer***	Y	Y	Y	N	N	Y	Y	N
CONNECTICUT								
1 Kennelly	Y	N	N	Y	Y	N	N	N
2 Gejdenson	Y	N	N	Y	Y	N	N	N
3 Morrison	Y	?	N	Y	Y	N	N	N
4 ***McKinney***	Y	N	N	N	Y	N	N	N
5 ***Rowland***	Y	Y	Y	N	N	Y	Y	N
6 ***Johnson***	Y	N	N	N	Y	N	N	N
DELAWARE								
AL Carper	Y	N	Y	Y	Y	Y	N	N
FLORIDA								
1 Hutto	+	Y	Y	Y	N	Y	Y	N
2 Fuqua	Y	N	Y	Y	-	Y	Y	N
3 Bennett	Y	N	Y	Y	Y	Y	Y	N
4 Chappell	?	Y	Y	Y	Y	Y	Y	N
5 ***McCollum***	Y	Y	Y	N	N	Y	Y	N
6 MacKay	Y	N	Y	Y	Y	Y	N	N
7 Gibbons	Y	N	N	Y	Y	Y	Y	N
8 ***Young***	Y	Y	Y	N	N	Y	Y	N
9 ***Bilirakis***	Y	Y	Y	N	N	Y	Y	N
10 ***Ireland***	?	#	#	?	N	Y	Y	N
11 Nelson	Y	N	Y	Y	N	Y	Y	N
12 ***Lewis***	Y	Y	Y	N	Y	Y	N	N
13 ***Mack***	Y	Y	Y	N	N	Y	Y	N
14 Mica	Y	Y	Y	Y	Y	Y	N	N
15 ***Shaw***	Y	Y	Y	N	N	Y	Y	N
16 Smith	Y	N	Y	Y	Y	N	N	N
17 Lehman	Y	N	Y	Y	Y	N	N	N
18 Pepper	Y	N	Y	Y	Y	N	Y	N
19 Fascell	Y	N	Y	Y	Y	N	N	N
GEORGIA								
1 Thomas	Y	N	Y	Y	Y	Y	N	N
2 Hatcher	Y	N	Y	Y	Y	Y	N	N
3 Ray	Y	Y	Y	Y	Y	Y	Y	N
4 ***Swindall***	Y	Y	Y	N	X	+	Y	N
5 Fowler	Y	N	Y	Y	Y	Y	N	N
6 ***Gingrich***	Y	Y	Y	N	N	Y	Y	N
7 Darden	Y	Y	Y	Y	N	Y	Y	N
8 Rowland	Y	N	Y	Y	Y	Y	N	N
9 Jenkins	?	?	?	Y	N	Y	Y	N
10 Barnard	Y	Y	Y	Y	N	Y	Y	N
HAWAII								
1 Heftel	?	?	?	?	?	?	?	?
2 Akaka	Y	N	Y	Y	N	N	N	Y
IDAHO								
1 ***Craig***	Y	Y	Y	N	N	Y	Y	N
2 Stallings	Y	N	Y	Y	N	Y	Y	N
ILLINOIS								
1 Hayes	Y	N	N	Y	Y	N	N	Y
2 Savage	Y	N	N	Y	Y	N	N	Y
3 Russo	Y	N	N	Y	N	Y	Y	N
4 ***O'Brien***	Y	N	Y	N	N	Y	Y	N
5 Lipinski	Y	N	Y	Y	N	Y	Y	N
6 ***Hyde***	?	Y	Y	N	N	Y	Y	N
7 Collins	Y	N	N	Y	Y	N	N	Y
8 Rostenkowski	Y	N	N	Y	N	Y	Y	N
9 Yates	Y	N	N	Y	Y	N	N	N
10 ***Porter***	Y	N	Y	N	Y	N	N	N
11 Annunzio	Y	N	Y	Y	N	Y	Y	N
12 ***Crane***	Y	Y	Y	N	N	Y	Y	N
13 ***Fawell***	Y	Y	Y	N	Y	N	N	N
14 ***Grotberg***	Y	Y	Y	N	N	Y	Y	N
15 ***Madigan***	Y	N	Y	N	N	Y	Y	N
16 ***Martin***	Y	N	N	?	Y	N	N	N
17 Evans	Y	N	N	Y	Y	N	N	Y
18 ***Michel***	Y	Y	?	?	N	Y	Y	N
19 Bruce	Y	N	Y	Y	Y	Y	N	N
20 Durbin	Y	N	Y	Y	Y	Y	N	N
21 Price	Y	N	Y	Y	Y	Y	Y	N
22 Gray	Y	N	Y	Y	N	Y	Y	N
INDIANA								
1 Visclosky	Y	N	N	Y	Y	N	N	N
2 Sharp	Y	N	N	Y	Y	Y	N	N
3 ***Hiler***	Y	Y	Y	N	N	Y	Y	N
4 ***Coats***	Y	N	Y	N	N	Y	Y	N
5 ***Hillis***	?	?	?	N	N	Y	Y	N

ND - Northern Democrats SD - Southern Democrats

* Corresponding to Congressional Record Votes 210, 211, 212, 213, 214, 215, 216, 217

	191	192	193	194	195	196	197	198
6 ***Burton***	Y	Y	Y	N	N	Y	Y	N
7 ***Myers***	Y	?	Y	P	N	Y	Y	N
8 McCloskey	Y	N	N	Y	N	Y	Y	N
9 Hamilton	Y	N	N	Y	Y	Y	Y	N
10 Jacobs	Y	N	N	Y	Y	N	N	Y
IOWA								
1 ***Leach***	Y	N	N	N	Y	N	N	N
2 ***Tauke***	Y	N	N	N	N	Y	Y	N
3 ***Evans***	Y	N	N	N	Y	N	Y	N
4 Smith	Y	N	N	Y	Y	N	N	N
5 ***Lightfoot***	Y	Y	N	N	N	Y	Y	N
6 Bedell	Y	N	N	Y	Y	N	N	N
KANSAS								
1 ***Roberts***	Y	N	Y	N	N	Y	Y	N
2 Slattery	Y	N	Y	Y	N	Y	N	N
3 ***Meyers***	Y	N	Y	N	Y	Y	N	N
4 Glickman	Y	N	Y	Y	Y	Y	N	N
5 ***Whittaker***	?	N	Y	N	Y	Y	N	N
KENTUCKY								
1 Hubbard	Y	Y	Y	Y	N	Y	Y	N
2 Natcher	Y	N	Y	Y	N	Y	Y	N
3 Mazzoli	Y	N	N	Y	N	Y	Y	N
4 ***Snyder***	Y	Y	Y	N	N	Y	Y	N
5 ***Rogers***	Y	Y	Y	N	N	Y	Y	N
6 ***Hopkins***	Y	Y	Y	N	N	Y	Y	N
7 Perkins	Y	N	N	Y	N	Y	Y	N
LOUISIANA								
1 ***Livingston***	Y	Y	Y	N	N	Y	Y	N
2 Boggs	Y	N	Y	Y	N	Y	Y	N
3 Tauzin	?	N	Y	Y	N	Y	Y	N
4 Roemer	Y	N	Y	Y	N	Y	Y	N
5 Huckaby	Y	N	Y	Y	N	Y	Y	N
6 ***Moore***	Y	Y	Y	?	N	Y	Y	N
7 Breaux	?	N	Y	Y	N	Y	Y	N
8 Long	Y	N	Y	Y	N	Y	Y	N
MAINE								
1 ***McKernan***	Y	N	Y	N	Y	N	N	N
2 ***Snowe***	Y	N	Y	N	Y	N	N	N
MARYLAND								
1 Dyson	Y	Y	Y	?	N	Y	Y	N
2 ***Bentley***	Y	N	Y	?	N	Y	?	N
3 Mikulski	Y	N	Y	Y	Y	N	N	N
4 ***Holt***	Y	N	Y	N	N	Y	Y	N
5 Hoyer	Y	N	Y	Y	Y	N	N	N
6 Byron	Y	N	Y	N	Y	Y	Y	N
7 Mitchell	Y	N	N	Y	Y	N	N	Y
8 Barnes	Y	N	N	Y	Y	N	N	N
MASSACHUSETTS								
1 ***Conte***	Y	N	N	N	N	Y	Y	N
2 Boland	Y	N	Y	Y	N	Y	Y	N
3 Early	P	N	N	Y	N	Y	Y	Y
4 Frank	Y	N	Y	Y	Y	N	N	N
5 Atkins	Y	N	N	Y	Y	N	N	N
6 Mavroules	Y	N	Y	Y	N	Y	Y	N
7 Markey	Y	N	N	Y	Y	N	N	Y
8 O'Neill								
9 Moakley	Y	N	N	Y	N	Y	Y	N
10 Studds	?	N	N	Y	Y	N	N	Y
11 Donnelly	Y	N	Y	Y	N	Y	Y	N
MICHIGAN								
1 Conyers	?	?	N	Y	Y	N	N	Y
2 ***Pursell***	Y	N	Y	N	?	N	N	N
3 Wolpe	Y	N	N	Y	Y	?	N	N
4 ***Siljander***	Y	Y	Y	N	N	Y	Y	N
5 ***Henry***	Y	N	N	N	N	Y	Y	N
6 Carr	Y	N	Y	?	Y	Y	N	N
7 Kildee	Y	N	N	Y	N	Y	Y	N
8 Traxler	Y	N	N	Y	N	Y	Y	N
9 ***Vander Jagt***	Y	N	Y	N	N	Y	Y	N
10 ***Schuette***	Y	N	Y	N	N	Y	Y	N
11 ***Davis***	Y	N	Y	N	N	N	Y	N
12 Bonior	Y	N	N	Y	?	Y	Y	Y
13 Crockett	?	?	?	Y	Y	N	N	Y
14 Hertel	Y	N	N	Y	N	Y	Y	N
15 Ford	Y	N	N	Y	Y	?	N	N
16 Dingell	Y	N	N	Y	?	N	N	N
17 Levin	Y	N	Y	Y	Y	N	N	N
18 ***Broomfield***	Y	Y	Y	N	N	Y	Y	N
MINNESOTA								
1 Penny	Y	N	Y	Y	Y	Y	N	N
2 ***Weber***	Y	Y	Y	N	N	Y	Y	N
3 ***Frenzel***	Y	N	Y	N	Y	N	N	N
4 Vento	Y	N	N	Y	Y	Y	N	N
5 Sabo	Y	N	N	Y	Y	N	N	N
6 Sikorski	Y	N	Y	Y	N	Y	Y	N
7 ***Stangeland***	Y	N	Y	N	N	Y	Y	N
8 Oberstar	Y	N	N	Y	N	Y	Y	N
MISSISSIPPI								
1 Whitten	Y	N	Y	Y	N	Y	Y	N
2 ***Franklin***	?	#	#	N	N	Y	Y	N
3 Montgomery	Y	Y	Y	Y	N	Y	Y	N
4 Dowdy	?	N	Y	Y	N	Y	Y	N
5 ***Lott***	Y	Y	Y	N	N	Y	Y	N
MISSOURI								
1 Clay	Y	N	N	Y	Y	N	N	Y
2 Young	Y	N	Y	Y	N	Y	Y	N
3 Gephardt	Y	N	Y	Y	Y	Y	N	N
4 Skelton	Y	N	Y	Y	N	Y	Y	N
5 Wheat	Y	N	N	Y	Y	N	N	Y
6 ***Coleman***	Y	Y	Y	N	N	Y	Y	N
7 ***Taylor***	Y	Y	Y	N	N	Y	Y	N
8 ***Emerson***	Y	Y	Y	N	N	Y	Y	N
9 Volkmer	Y	N	Y	Y	N	Y	Y	N
MONTANA								
1 Williams	Y	N	N	Y	Y	Y	Y	N
2 ***Marlenee***	Y	N	Y	N	N	Y	Y	N
NEBRASKA								
1 ***Bereuter***	Y	N	Y	N	N	Y	Y	N
2 ***Daub***	Y	Y	Y	N	N	Y	Y	N
3 ***Smith***	Y	Y	Y	N	N	Y	Y	N
NEVADA								
1 Reid	Y	N	Y	Y	N	Y	Y	N
2 ***Vucanovich***	Y	Y	Y	N	N	Y	Y	N
NEW HAMPSHIRE								
1 ***Smith***	Y	Y	Y	N	N	Y	Y	N
2 ***Gregg***	Y	N	Y	N	N	Y	N	N
NEW JERSEY								
1 Florio	Y	N	N	Y	Y	Y	Y	N
2 Hughes	Y	N	Y	Y	Y	Y	N	N
3 Howard	Y	N	N	Y	Y	Y	N	N
4 ***Smith***	Y	N	Y	N	N	Y	Y	N
5 ***Roukema***	Y	N	N	N	Y	N	N	N
6 Dwyer	Y	N	N	P	Y	Y	N	N
7 ***Rinaldo***	Y	N	Y	N	N	Y	Y	N
8 Roe	Y	N	Y	Y	N	Y	Y	Y
9 Torricelli	Y	N	Y	Y	Y	Y	N	N
10 Rodino	Y	N	N	Y	Y	Y	N	Y
11 ***Gallo***	Y	Y	Y	N	Y	N	N	N
12 ***Courter***	Y	Y	Y	N	N	Y	Y	N
13 ***Saxton***	Y	N	Y	N	N	Y	Y	N
14 Guarini	Y	N	N	Y	Y	Y	N	N
NEW MEXICO								
1 ***Lujan***	Y	Y	Y	N	N	Y	Y	N
2 ***Skeen***	Y	Y	Y	N	N	Y	Y	N
3 Richardson	Y	N	Y	Y	Y	N	N	N
NEW YORK								
1 ***Carney***	Y	Y	Y	N	N	Y	Y	N
2 Downey	Y	N	N	Y	Y	N	N	N
3 Mrazek	Y	N	N	Y	Y	N	N	N
4 ***Lent***	Y	Y	Y	N	N	Y	Y	N
5 ***McGrath***	Y	Y	Y	N	N	Y	Y	N
6 Addabbo	Y	N	N	Y	Y	N	N	Y
7 Ackerman	?	N	Y	Y	Y	N	N	N
8 Scheuer	Y	N	Y	Y	Y	N	N	N
9 Manton	Y	N	Y	Y	N	Y	Y	N
10 Schumer	Y	N	N	Y	Y	N	N	N
11 Towns	?	N	N	Y	Y	N	N	Y
12 Owens	?	?	?	Y	Y	N	N	Y
13 Solarz	?	N	Y	Y	Y	?	N	N
14 ***Molinari***	Y	Y	Y	N	N	Y	Y	N
15 ***Green***	Y	N	N	N	Y	N	N	N
16 Rangel	Y	N	N	Y	Y	N	N	Y
17 Weiss	Y	N	N	Y	Y	N	N	Y
18 Garcia	?	?	N	Y	Y	N	N	Y
19 Biaggi	Y	N	Y	Y	N	Y	Y	N
20 ***DioGuardi***	Y	N	Y	N	N	Y	Y	N
21 ***Fish***	Y	N	Y	N	Y	Y	N	N
22 ***Gilman***	Y	Y	Y	N	Y	N	N	N
23 Stratton	Y	Y	Y	N	Y	N	N	N
24 ***Solomon***	Y	Y	Y	N	N	Y	Y	N
25 ***Boehlert***	Y	N	Y	N	Y	N	N	N
26 ***Martin***	Y	Y	Y	N	N	Y	Y	N
27 ***Wortley***	Y	Y	Y	N	N	Y	Y	N
28 McHugh	Y	N	N	Y	Y	Y	N	N
29 ***Horton***	?	N	Y	N	Y	N	N	N
30 ***Eckert***	N	Y	Y	N	N	Y	Y	N
31 ***Kemp***	Y	Y	Y	?	N	Y	Y	N
32 LaFalce	Y	N	Y	Y	N	Y	Y	N
33 Nowak	Y	N	Y	Y	N	Y	Y	N
34 Lundine	Y	?	N	?	Y	N	N	N
NORTH CAROLINA								
1 Jones	Y	N	N	Y	Y	Y	N	?
2 Valentine	Y	N	Y	Y	Y	Y	N	N
3 Whitley	Y	N	Y	Y	Y	Y	N	N
4 ***Cobey***	Y	N	Y	N	N	Y	Y	N
5 Neal	Y	N	Y	Y	Y	Y	N	N
6 ***Coble***	Y	N	Y	N	N	Y	Y	N
7 Rose	Y	N	Y	Y	Y	N	N	N
8 Hefner	?	?	?	?	?	?	?	?
9 ***McMillan***	Y	Y	Y	N	N	Y	Y	N
10 ***Broyhill***	Y	?	Y	N	Y	Y	N	N
11 ***Hendon***	Y	Y	Y	N	N	Y	Y	N
NORTH DAKOTA								
AL Dorgan	Y	N	N	Y	Y	Y	N	N
OHIO								
1 Luken	Y	N	N	Y	N	Y	Y	N
2 ***Gradison***	Y	N	Y	N	N	Y	Y	N
3 Hall	Y	N	N	Y	Y	Y	Y	N
4 ***Oxley***	Y	Y	Y	N	N	Y	Y	N
5 ***Latta***	Y	Y	Y	?	N	Y	Y	N
6 ***McEwen***	Y	Y	Y	N	N	Y	Y	N
7 ***DeWine***	Y	Y	Y	N	N	Y	Y	N
8 ***Kindness***	Y	Y	Y	N	N	Y	Y	N
9 Kaptur	+	N	N	Y	Y	Y	Y	X
10 ***Miller***	Y	Y	Y	N	N	Y	Y	N
11 Eckart	Y	N	Y	Y	Y	Y	N	N
12 ***Kasich***	Y	Y	Y	N	N	Y	Y	N
13 Pease	Y	N	N	Y	Y	Y	N	N
14 Seiberling	Y	N	N	N	Y	N	N	Y
15 ***Wylie***	Y	N	Y	N	N	Y	Y	N
16 ***Regula***	Y	N	Y	N	N	Y	Y	N
17 Traficant	Y	N	N	Y	Y	N	N	N
18 Applegate	Y	N	Y	Y	N	Y	Y	N
19 Feighan	?	N	Y	Y	Y	Y	N	N
20 Oakar	Y	N	N	Y	Y	Y	Y	Y
21 Stokes	Y	N	N	Y	Y	N	N	Y
OKLAHOMA								
1 Jones	Y	N	Y	Y	Y	Y	N	N
2 Synar	Y	N	Y	Y	Y	N	N	N
3 Watkins	Y	N	Y	Y	N	Y	Y	N
4 McCurdy	Y	N	Y	Y	Y	N	N	N
5 ***Edwards***	Y	N	Y	N	N	Y	Y	N
6 English	Y	N	Y	Y	N	Y	Y	N
OREGON								
1 AuCoin	Y	N	N	Y	Y	N	N	Y
2 ***Smith, R.***	Y	N	Y	N	N	Y	Y	N
3 Wyden	Y	N	Y	Y	Y	N	N	N
4 Weaver	Y	N	N	Y	Y	N	N	Y
5 ***Smith, D.***	Y	Y	Y	N	N	Y	Y	N
PENNSYLVANIA								
1 Foglietta	?	?	?	Y	Y	Y	N	N
2 Gray	Y	?	N	Y	?	N	N	#
3 Borski	Y	N	Y	Y	N	Y	N	N
4 Kolter	Y	N	N	Y	N	Y	Y	N
5 ***Schulze***	Y	Y	Y	N	N	Y	Y	N
6 Yatron	Y	N	Y	Y	N	Y	Y	N
7 Edgar	Y	N	N	Y	Y	N	N	N
8 Kostmayer	Y	N	Y	Y	Y	N	N	N
9 ***Shuster***	Y	Y	Y	N	N	Y	Y	N
10 ***McDade***	Y	N	Y	N	N	Y	Y	N
11 Kanjorski	Y	N	Y	Y	N	Y	Y	N
12 Murtha	Y	Y	?	Y	N	Y	Y	N
13 ***Coughlin***	Y	N	Y	N	Y	N	N	N
14 Coyne	Y	N	N	Y	N	Y	Y	N
15 ***Ritter***	?	?	?	?	N	Y	Y	N
16 ***Walker***	Y	Y	N	N	N	Y	Y	N
17 ***Gekas***	Y	N	Y	N	Y	N	N	N
18 Walgren	Y	N	N	Y	Y	Y	N	N
19 ***Goodling***	Y	N	Y	N	N	Y	Y	N
20 Gaydos	Y	Y	Y	Y	N	Y	Y	?
21 ***Ridge***	Y	Y	Y	N	N	Y	Y	N
22 Murphy	Y	N	N	Y	N	Y	Y	N
23 ***Clinger***	Y	N	N	N	N	Y	Y	N
RHODE ISLAND								
1 St Germain	Y	N	N	Y	Y	Y	Y	Y
2 ***Schneider***	Y	N	N	N	Y	N	N	N
SOUTH CAROLINA								
1 ***Hartnett***	Y	Y	Y	N	N	Y	Y	N
2 ***Spence***	Y	Y	Y	P	N	Y	Y	N
3 Derrick	Y	N	N	Y	Y	N	?	N
4 ***Campbell***	?	?	?	N	N	Y	Y	N
5 Spratt	Y	N	Y	Y	Y	Y	N	N
6 Tallon	?	N	Y	Y	N	Y	Y	N
SOUTH DAKOTA								
AL Daschle	Y	N	Y	Y	Y	Y	N	N
TENNESSEE								
1 ***Quillen***	Y	Y	Y	N	N	Y	Y	N
2 ***Duncan***	Y	Y	Y	N	N	Y	Y	N
3 Lloyd	Y	N	Y	Y	N	Y	Y	N
4 Cooper	Y	?	N	Y	Y	Y	Y	N
5 Boner	Y	N	Y	Y	N	Y	Y	N
6 Gordon	Y	N	Y	Y	Y	Y	N	N
7 ***Sundquist***	Y	Y	N	N	N	Y	Y	N
8 Jones	Y	N	N	Y	N	Y	Y	N
9 Ford	?	?	N	Y	Y	N	N	Y
TEXAS								
1 Vacancy								
2 Wilson	Y	N	Y	Y	Y	N	N	N
3 ***Bartlett***	Y	Y	Y	N	N	Y	Y	N
4 Hall, R.	Y	N	Y	Y	N	Y	Y	N
5 Bryant	Y	N	Y	Y	Y	N	N	N
6 ***Barton***	Y	Y	Y	N	N	Y	Y	N
7 ***Archer***	?	Y	Y	N	N	Y	Y	N
8 ***Fields***	Y	Y	Y	N	N	Y	Y	N
9 Brooks	Y	N	N	Y	Y	N	N	N
10 Pickle	Y	N	Y	Y	Y	N	N	N
11 Leath	Y	N	Y	?	N	Y	Y	N
12 Wright	Y	N	?	Y	Y	N	?	N
13 ***Boulter***	Y	Y	Y	?	N	Y	Y	N
14 ***Sweeney***	Y	Y	Y	N	N	Y	Y	N
15 de la Garza	Y	N	Y	Y	Y	Y	?	N
16 Coleman	Y	N	Y	Y	Y	N	N	N
17 Stenholm	Y	Y	Y	Y	N	Y	Y	N
18 Leland	Y	N	N	Y	Y	N	N	N
19 ***Combest***	Y	Y	Y	N	N	Y	Y	N
20 Gonzalez	P	N	N	Y	Y	Y	N	Y
21 ***Loeffler***	Y	Y	Y	N	N	Y	Y	N
22 ***DeLay***	Y	Y	Y	N	N	Y	Y	N
23 Bustamante	?	N	Y	Y	Y	Y	N	N
24 Frost	Y	N	Y	?	Y	N	N	?
25 Andrews	Y	N	Y	Y	Y	Y	N	N
26 ***Armey***	Y	Y	Y	N	N	Y	Y	N
27 Ortiz	Y	N	Y	Y	N	Y	Y	N
UTAH								
1 ***Hansen***	Y	Y	Y	P	N	Y	Y	N
2 ***Monson***	Y	Y	Y	N	N	Y	Y	N
3 ***Nielson***	Y	Y	Y	N	N	Y	Y	N
VERMONT								
AL ***Jeffords***	Y	N	N	N	Y	N	N	N
VIRGINIA								
1 ***Bateman***	?	N	Y	N	N	Y	Y	N
2 ***Whitehurst***	Y	Y	Y	N	N	Y	Y	N
3 ***Bliley***	Y	Y	Y	N	N	Y	Y	N
4 Sisisky	Y	N	Y	Y	Y	N	N	N
5 Daniel	Y	Y	?	?	?	?	?	?
6 Olin	Y	N	Y	Y	Y	Y	N	N
7 ***Slaughter***	Y	Y	Y	N	N	Y	Y	N
8 ***Parris***	Y	Y	Y	N	N	Y	Y	N
9 Boucher	Y	N	Y	Y	Y	Y	N	N
10 ***Wolf***	Y	N	Y	N	N	Y	Y	N
WASHINGTON								
1 ***Miller***	Y	N	Y	N	Y	N	N	N
2 Swift	Y	N	Y	Y	Y	N	N	N
3 Bonker	?	?	?	Y	Y	Y	N	N
4 ***Morrison***	Y	N	Y	N	Y	N	N	N
5 Foley	?	N	Y	Y	Y	Y	N	N
6 Dicks	Y	N	Y	Y	Y	Y	N	N
7 Lowry	Y	N	N	?	+	N	N	Y
8 ***Chandler***	?	?	?	N	Y	N	N	N
WEST VIRGINIA								
1 Mollohan	Y	N	Y	P	N	Y	Y	N
2 Staggers	Y	N	Y	Y	N	Y	Y	N
3 Wise	Y	N	Y	Y	Y	N	N	N
4 Rahall	N	N	Y	Y	Y	Y	Y	N
WISCONSIN								
1 Aspin	?	?	?	?	?	?	N	N
2 Kastenmeier	Y	N	N	Y	Y	N	N	Y
3 ***Gunderson***	Y	N	N	N	N	Y	Y	N
4 Kleczka	Y	N	N	Y	N	Y	Y	N
5 Moody	Y	N	N	Y	Y	N	N	Y
6 ***Petri***	Y	N	Y	N	N	Y	Y	N
7 Obey	Y	N	N	Y	Y	?	N	N
8 ***Roth***	Y	Y	Y	N	N	Y	Y	N
9 ***Sensenbrenner***	Y	Y	Y	N	N	Y	Y	N
WYOMING								
AL ***Cheney***	Y	Y	Y	N	N	Y	Y	N

Southern states - Ala., Ark., Fla., Ga., Ky., La., Miss., N.C., Okla., S.C., Tenn., Texas, Va.

* The *Congressional Record* vote number is different from the CQ vote number because the *Record* includes quorum calls in its tally. CQ does not publish quorum call votes.

199. HR 1555. Foreign Assistance Authorization, Fiscal 1986. Stratton, D-N.Y., amendment to repeal the so-called "Clark amendment" to the International Security and Development Cooperation Act of 1980, prohibiting assistance for military or paramilitary operations in Angola. Adopted 236-185: R 176-6; D 60-179 (ND 14-150, SD 46-29), July 10, 1985. A "yea" was a vote supporting the president's position.

200. S 1160. Department of Defense Authorization, Fiscal 1986. McCollum, R-Fla., motion to instruct the House conferees to insist on the House position to amend the military legal code to make peacetime espionage punishable by death. Motion agreed to 320-101: R 172-9; D 148-92 (ND 79-86, SD 69-6), July 11, 1985.

201. S 1160. Department of Defense Authorization, Fiscal 1986. Aspin, D-Wis., motion to allow conferees on the bill to meet in closed session to discuss secret information. Motion agreed to 421-2: R 178-0; D 243-2 (ND 166-1, SD 77-1), July 11, 1985.

202. HR 1555. Foreign Assistance Authorization, Fiscal 1986. Siljander, R-Mich., amendment to prohibit non-food economic aid to Mozambique until the president certified to Congress that the number of foreign military advisers and troops in that country did not exceed 55. Adopted 247-177: R 165-16; D 82-161 (ND 33-136, SD 49-25), July 11, 1985.

203. HR 1555. Foreign Assistance Authorization, Fiscal 1986. Siljander, R-Mich., amendment to authorize issuance of insurance by the Overseas Private Investment Corp. for business ventures jointly owned by U.S. citizens and non-white South Africans. Rejected 88-337: R 87-93; D 1-244 (ND 0-168, SD 1-76), July 11, 1985.

204. HR 1555. Foreign Assistance Authorization, Fiscal 1986. Hall, D-Ohio, amendment to state that Congress may defer future military aid to the Philippines if significant progress is not achieved in various political, economic and military reforms there, or if U.S. aid is used to violate the human rights of the Filipino people. Adopted 254-169: R 44-135; D 210-34 (ND 159-7, SD 51-27), July 11, 1985.

KEY

Y Voted for (yea).
Paired for.
+ Announced for.
N Voted against (nay).
X Paired against.
- Announced against.
P Voted "present."
C Voted "present" to avoid possible conflict of interest.
? Did not vote or otherwise make a position known.

Democrats ***Republicans***

	199	200	201	202	203	204
ALABAMA						
1 ***Callahan***	Y	Y	Y	Y	N	N
2 ***Dickinson***	Y	Y	Y	Y	N	Y
3 Nichols	Y	Y	Y	Y	?	?
4 Bevill	Y	Y	Y	Y	N	N
5 Flippo	?	Y	Y	Y	N	N
6 Erdreich	Y	Y	Y	Y	N	N
7 Shelby	Y	Y	Y	Y	N	N
ALASKA						
AL ***Young***	Y	Y	Y	Y	Y	Y
ARIZONA						
1 ***McCain***	Y	Y	Y	Y	N	N
2 Udall	N	N	Y	N	N	Y
3 ***Stump***	Y	Y	Y	Y	Y	N
4 ***Rudd***	Y	Y	Y	Y	Y	N
5 ***Kolbe***	Y	Y	Y	Y	N	N
ARKANSAS						
1 Alexander	N	Y	Y	?	N	Y
2 Robinson	Y	Y	Y	Y	N	N
3 ***Hammerschmidt***	Y	Y	Y	Y	N	N
4 Anthony	Y	Y	Y	Y	N	Y
CALIFORNIA						
1 Bosco	N	Y	Y	N	N	Y
2 ***Chappie***	Y	Y	?	?	?	?
3 Matsui	N	Y	Y	N	N	Y
4 Fazio	N	N	Y	N	N	Y
5 Burton	N	N	Y	N	N	Y
6 Boxer	N	N	Y	N	N	Y
7 Miller	N	N	Y	N	N	Y
8 Dellums	N	N	Y	N	N	Y
9 Stark	?	N	Y	N	N	Y
10 Edwards	N	N	Y	N	N	Y
11 Lantos	N	Y	Y	N	N	Y
12 ***Zschau***	Y	Y	Y	N	Y	Y
13 Mineta	N	N	Y	N	N	Y
14 ***Shumway***	Y	Y	Y	Y	Y	N
15 Coelho	N	Y	Y	N	N	Y
16 Panetta	N	Y	Y	N	N	Y
17 ***Pashayan***	Y	Y	Y	Y	N	N
18 Lehman	N	Y	Y	N	N	Y
19 ***Lagomarsino***	Y	Y	Y	Y	N	N
20 ***Thomas***	Y	Y	Y	Y	N	Y
21 ***Fiedler***	Y	Y	Y	Y	N	N
22 ***Moorhead***	Y	Y	Y	Y	N	N
23 Beilenson	N	Y	Y	N	N	Y
24 Waxman	?	N	Y	N	N	Y
25 Roybal	N	N	Y	N	N	Y
26 Berman	N	N	Y	N	N	Y
27 Levine	N	N	Y	N	N	Y
28 Dixon	N	N	Y	N	N	Y
29 Hawkins	N	N	Y	N	N	Y
30 Martinez	N	Y	Y	N	N	Y
31 Dymally	N	N	Y	N	N	Y
32 Anderson	Y	Y	Y	Y	N	Y
33 ***Dreier***	Y	Y	Y	Y	Y	N
34 Torres	N	Y	Y	N	N	Y
35 ***Lewis***	Y	Y	Y	Y	N	N
36 Brown	N	N	Y	N	N	Y
37 ***McCandless***	Y	Y	Y	Y	N	N
38 ***Dornan***	Y	Y	Y	Y	Y	N
39 ***Dannemeyer***	Y	Y	Y	Y	Y	N
40 ***Badham***	Y	Y	Y	Y	Y	N
41 ***Lowery***	Y	Y	Y	Y	N	N
42 ***Lungren***	Y	Y	Y	Y	Y	N
43 ***Packard***	Y	Y	Y	Y	N	N
44 Bates	N	N	Y	Y	N	Y
45 ***Hunter***	Y	Y	Y	Y	Y	N
COLORADO						
1 Schroeder	N	Y	Y	N	N	Y
2 Wirth	N	Y	Y	N	N	Y
3 ***Strang***	Y	Y	Y	Y	Y	N
4 ***Brown***	Y	Y	Y	Y	N	Y
5 ***Kramer***	Y	Y	Y	Y	Y	Y
6 ***Schaefer***	Y	Y	Y	Y	Y	N
CONNECTICUT						
1 Kennelly	N	Y	Y	N	N	Y
2 Gejdenson	N	N	Y	N	N	Y
3 Morrison	N	N	Y	N	N	Y
4 ***McKinney***	N	N	Y	N	N	N
5 ***Rowland***	Y	Y	Y	Y	Y	N
6 ***Johnson***	Y	Y	Y	N	Y	N
DELAWARE						
AL Carper	Y	Y	Y	N	N	Y
FLORIDA						
1 Hutto	Y	Y	Y	Y	N	N
2 Fuqua	Y	Y	Y	Y	N	N
3 Bennett	N	Y	Y	Y	N	Y
4 Chappell	Y	Y	Y	Y	N	N
5 ***McCollum***	Y	Y	Y	Y	Y	N
6 MacKay	N	Y	Y	N	N	Y
7 Gibbons	N	Y	Y	N	N	Y
8 ***Young***	Y	Y	Y	Y	Y	N
9 ***Bilirakis***	Y	Y	Y	Y	Y	N
10 ***Ireland***	Y	Y	Y	Y	Y	N
11 Nelson	#	Y	Y	Y	N	Y
12 ***Lewis***	Y	Y	Y	Y	Y	N
13 ***Mack***	Y	Y	Y	Y	Y	N
14 Mica	Y	Y	Y	Y	N	N
15 ***Shaw***	Y	Y	Y	Y	Y	N
16 Smith	Y	#	Y	N	N	Y
17 Lehman	N	N	Y	N	N	Y
18 Pepper	Y	Y	Y	N	N	Y
19 Fascell	Y	Y	Y	N	N	Y
GEORGIA						
1 Thomas	Y	Y	Y	Y	N	N
2 Hatcher	Y	Y	Y	N	?	Y
3 Ray	Y	Y	Y	Y	N	N
4 ***Swindall***	Y	Y	Y	Y	Y	N
5 Fowler	Y	Y	Y	N	N	Y
6 ***Gingrich***	Y	Y	Y	Y	N	N
7 Darden	Y	Y	Y	Y	N	Y
8 Rowland	Y	Y	Y	Y	N	N
9 Jenkins	Y	Y	Y	Y	N	N
10 Barnard	Y	Y	Y	Y	N	N
HAWAII						
1 Heftel	?	Y	Y	N	N	N
2 Akaka	N	Y	Y	N	N	N
IDAHO						
1 ***Craig***	Y	Y	Y	Y	Y	N
2 Stallings	N	Y	Y	Y	N	Y
ILLINOIS						
1 Hayes	N	N	Y	N	N	Y
2 Savage	N	N	Y	N	N	Y
3 Russo	N	Y	Y	Y	N	Y
4 ***O'Brien***	Y	Y	Y	Y	Y	N
5 Lipinski	N	Y	Y	Y	N	Y
6 ***Hyde***	Y	Y	Y	Y	Y	N
7 Collins	N	N	Y	N	?	?
8 Rostenkowski	N	N	Y	N	N	Y
9 Yates	N	N	Y	N	N	Y
10 ***Porter***	Y	Y	Y	Y	?	Y
11 Annunzio	N	?	Y	N	N	Y
12 ***Crane***	Y	Y	Y	Y	Y	N
13 ***Fawell***	Y	Y	Y	Y	Y	Y
14 ***Grotberg***	Y	Y	Y	Y	Y	N
15 ***Madigan***	Y	Y	Y	Y	N	Y
16 ***Martin***	Y	Y	Y	Y	N	N
17 Evans	N	N	Y	N	N	Y
18 ***Michel***	Y	Y	Y	Y	Y	N
19 Bruce	N	Y	Y	N	N	Y
20 Durbin	N	Y	Y	N	N	Y
21 Price	N	Y	Y	N	N	Y
22 Gray	X	Y	Y	Y	N	Y
INDIANA						
1 Visclosky	N	N	Y	N	N	Y
2 Sharp	Y	N	Y	Y	N	Y
3 ***Hiler***	Y	Y	Y	Y	N	N
4 ***Coats***	Y	N	Y	Y	N	Y
5 ***Hillis***	Y	Y	Y	Y	Y	N

ND - Northern Democrats SD - Southern Democrats

* Corresponding to Congressional Record Votes 218, 219, 220, 222, 223, 224

	199	200	201	202	203	204
6 ***Burton***	Y	Y	Y	Y	Y	N
7 ***Myers***	Y	Y	Y	Y	N	N
8 McCloskey	Y	N	Y	N	N	Y
9 Hamilton	Y	N	Y	N	N	Y
10 Jacobs	N	N	Y	Y	N	Y
IOWA						
1 ***Leach***	N	N	Y	N	N	Y
2 ***Tauke***	Y	N	Y	Y	N	Y
3 ***Evans***	N	Y	Y	N	N	Y
4 Smith	N	N	Y	N	N	Y
5 ***Lightfoot***	Y	Y	Y	Y	N	N
6 Bedell	N	N	Y	N	N	Y
KANSAS						
1 ***Roberts***	Y	Y	Y	Y	Y	N
2 Slattery	Y	Y	Y	N	N	Y
3 ***Meyers***	Y	Y	Y	Y	N	N
4 Glickman	Y	Y	Y	N	N	Y
5 ***Whittaker***	Y	Y	Y	Y	N	N
KENTUCKY						
1 Hubbard	Y	Y	Y	Y	N	N
2 Natcher	Y	N	Y	Y	N	Y
3 Mazzoli	N	Y	Y	Y	N	Y
4 ***Snyder***	Y	Y	Y	Y	Y	N
5 ***Rogers***	Y	Y	Y	Y	Y	N
6 ***Hopkins***	Y	Y	Y	Y	N	N
7 Perkins	N	N	Y	Y	N	Y
LOUISIANA						
1 ***Livingston***	Y	Y	Y	Y	Y	N
2 Boggs	Y	?	Y	N	N	Y
3 Tauzin	Y	Y	Y	Y	N	Y
4 Roemer	Y	Y	Y	Y	N	Y
5 Huckaby	Y	Y	Y	Y	N	Y
6 ***Moore***	Y	Y	Y	Y	Y	N
7 Breaux	Y	Y	Y	Y	N	N
8 Long	Y	Y	Y	N	N	Y
MAINE						
1 ***McKernan***	Y	Y	Y	N	N	Y
2 ***Snowe***	Y	Y	Y	N	N	Y
MARYLAND						
1 Dyson	Y	Y	Y	?	N	Y
2 ***Bentley***	Y	Y	Y	Y	Y	N
3 Mikulski	N	Y	Y	N	N	Y
4 ***Holt***	Y	Y	Y	Y	Y	N
5 Hoyer	N	N	Y	N	N	Y
6 Byron	Y	Y	Y	Y	N	N
7 Mitchell	N	N	Y	N	N	Y
8 Barnes	N	N	Y	N	N	Y
MASSACHUSETTS						
1 ***Conte***	N	Y	Y	N	N	Y
2 Boland	N	Y	Y	N	N	Y
3 Early	N	N	Y	N	N	Y
4 Frank	N	N	Y	N	N	Y
5 Atkins	N	N	Y	N	N	Y
6 Mavroules	N	Y	Y	N	N	Y
7 Markey	N	N	?	N	N	Y
8 O'Neill						
9 Moakley	N	N	Y	N	N	Y
10 Studds	N	N	Y	N	N	Y
11 Donnelly	N	Y	Y	N	N	Y
MICHIGAN						
1 Conyers	N	N	Y	N	N	Y
2 ***Pursell***	Y	Y	Y	Y	N	Y
3 Wolpe	N	N	Y	N	N	Y
4 ***Siljander***	Y	Y	Y	Y	Y	N
5 ***Henry***	Y	N	Y	Y	N	Y
6 Carr	N	Y	Y	Y	N	Y
7 Kildee	N	N	Y	N	N	Y
8 Traxler	N	?	Y	N	N	Y
9 ***Vander Jagt***	Y	Y	Y	Y	N	N
10 ***Schuette***	Y	Y	Y	Y	N	N
11 ***Davis***	Y	Y	Y	Y	N	N
12 Bonior	N	N	Y	N	?	Y
13 Crockett	N	N	Y	N	N	?
14 Hertel	N	N	Y	N	N	Y
15 Ford	N	?	?	N	N	?
16 Dingell	N	Y	Y	Y	N	Y
17 Levin	N	N	Y	N	N	Y
18 ***Broomfield***	Y	Y	Y	Y	N	N
MINNESOTA						
1 Penny	N	N	Y	N	N	Y
2 ***Weber***	Y	Y	Y	Y	N	N
3 ***Frenzel***	Y	Y	Y	Y	N	Y
4 Vento	N	N	Y	N	N	Y
5 Sabo	N	N	Y	N	N	Y
6 Sikorski	N	N	Y	N	N	Y
7 ***Stangeland***	Y	Y	Y	Y	N	N
8 Oberstar	N	N	Y	N	N	Y
MISSISSIPPI						
1 Whitten	Y	Y	Y	?	N	Y
2 ***Franklin***	Y	Y	Y	Y	N	N
3 Montgomery	Y	Y	Y	Y	N	N
4 Dowdy	N	Y	Y	Y	N	Y
5 ***Lott***	Y	Y	Y	Y	N	N
MISSOURI						
1 Clay	N	N	Y	N	N	Y
2 Young	N	Y	Y	N	N	Y
3 Gephardt	N	Y	Y	N	N	Y
4 Skelton	Y	Y	Y	Y	N	Y
5 Wheat	N	N	Y	N	N	Y
6 ***Coleman***	Y	Y	Y	Y	N	N
7 ***Taylor***	Y	Y	Y	Y	Y	N
8 ***Emerson***	Y	Y	Y	Y	Y	N
9 Volkmer	Y	Y	Y	Y	N	Y
MONTANA						
1 Williams	N	N	Y	N	N	Y
2 ***Marlenee***	Y	Y	Y	Y	Y	N
NEBRASKA						
1 ***Bereuter***	Y	Y	Y	Y	Y	Y
2 ***Daub***	Y	Y	Y	Y	N	N
3 ***Smith***	Y	Y	Y	Y	Y	N
NEVADA						
1 Reid	N	Y	Y	N	N	Y
2 ***Vucanovich***	Y	Y	Y	Y	Y	N
NEW HAMPSHIRE						
1 ***Smith***	Y	Y	Y	Y	Y	N
2 ***Gregg***	Y	Y	Y	Y	N	N
NEW JERSEY						
1 Florio	N	Y	Y	Y	N	Y
2 Hughes	N	Y	Y	Y	N	Y
3 Howard	N	Y	Y	N	N	Y
4 ***Smith***	Y	N	Y	Y	N	Y
5 ***Roukema***	Y	N	Y	N	N	Y
6 Dwyer	N	Y	Y	N	N	Y
7 ***Rinaldo***	Y	Y	Y	Y	N	Y
8 Roe	?	Y	Y	Y	N	Y
9 Torricelli	N	Y	Y	N	N	Y
10 Rodino	N	N	Y	N	N	Y
11 ***Gallo***	Y	Y	Y	Y	N	N
12 ***Courter***	Y	Y	Y	Y	Y	N
13 ***Saxton***	Y	Y	Y	Y	Y	N
14 Guarini	N	Y	Y	N	N	Y
NEW MEXICO						
1 ***Lujan***	Y	Y	Y	Y	N	N
2 ***Skeen***	Y	Y	Y	Y	N	N
3 Richardson	N	Y	Y	N	N	Y
NEW YORK						
1 ***Carney***	Y	Y	Y	Y	N	N
2 Downey	N	N	Y	N	N	Y
3 Mrazek	N	N	Y	N	N	Y
4 ***Lent***	Y	Y	Y	Y	N	N
5 ***McGrath***	Y	Y	Y	Y	N	Y
6 Addabbo	N	N	Y	N	N	?
7 Ackerman	N	N	Y	N	N	Y
8 Scheuer	N	Y	Y	N	N	Y
9 Manton	N	Y	Y	N	N	Y
10 Schumer	N	N	Y	N	N	Y
11 Towns	N	N	Y	N	N	Y
12 Owens	N	N	Y	N	N	Y
13 Solarz	N	N	Y	N	N	Y
14 ***Molinari***	Y	Y	Y	Y	N	N
15 ***Green***	Y	Y	Y	N	N	Y
16 Rangel	N	N	Y	N	N	Y
17 Weiss	N	N	Y	N	N	Y
18 Garcia	N	N	Y	N	N	Y
19 Biaggi	N	Y	Y	Y	N	Y
20 ***DioGuardi***	Y	Y	Y	Y	N	N
21 ***Fish***	Y	Y	Y	N	N	N
22 ***Gilman***	Y	Y	Y	Y	N	N
23 Stratton	Y	Y	Y	Y	N	N
24 ***Solomon***	Y	Y	Y	Y	N	N
25 ***Boehlert***	Y	Y	Y	Y	N	Y
26 ***Martin***	Y	Y	Y	Y	N	N
27 ***Wortley***	Y	Y	Y	Y	Y	N
28 McHugh	N	Y	Y	N	N	Y
29 ***Horton***	N	Y	Y	Y	N	Y
30 ***Eckert***	Y	Y	Y	Y	Y	N
31 ***Kemp***	Y	Y	?	Y	Y	N
32 LaFalce	N	Y	Y	N	N	N
33 Nowak	N	Y	Y	N	N	Y
34 Lundine	N	Y	Y	N	N	Y
NORTH CAROLINA						
1 Jones	N	Y	Y	N	N	Y
2 Valentine	Y	Y	Y	Y	N	N
3 Whitley	Y	Y	Y	Y	N	N
4 ***Cobey***	Y	Y	?	Y	Y	N
5 Neal	N	Y	Y	Y	N	Y
6 ***Coble***	Y	Y	Y	Y	Y	N
7 Rose	?	Y	Y	Y	N	N
8 Hefner	?	?	?	?	?	?
9 ***McMillan***	Y	Y	Y	Y	Y	N
10 ***Broyhill***	Y	Y	Y	Y	N	N
11 ***Hendon***	Y	Y	Y	Y	N	N
NORTH DAKOTA						
AL Dorgan	N	N	Y	N	N	Y
OHIO						
1 Luken	N	N	Y	Y	N	Y
2 ***Gradison***	Y	Y	Y	Y	N	Y
3 Hall	?	Y	Y	N	N	Y
4 ***Oxley***	Y	Y	Y	Y	N	Y
5 ***Latta***	Y	Y	Y	Y	N	N
6 ***McEwen***	Y	Y	Y	Y	Y	Y
7 ***DeWine***	Y	Y	Y	Y	Y	N
8 ***Kindness***	Y	Y	Y	Y	N	N
9 Kaptur	N	Y	Y	N	N	Y
10 ***Miller***	Y	Y	Y	Y	N	Y
11 Eckart	N	Y	Y	Y	N	Y
12 ***Kasich***	Y	Y	Y	Y	Y	N
13 Pease	N	Y	Y	N	N	Y
14 Seiberling	N	Y	Y	N	N	Y
15 ***Wylie***	Y	Y	Y	Y	N	N
16 ***Regula***	Y	Y	Y	Y	N	Y
17 Traficant	N	Y	Y	N	N	Y
18 Applegate	N	Y	Y	Y	N	Y
19 Feighan	N	N	Y	N	N	Y
20 Oakar	N	Y	Y	N	N	Y
21 Stokes	N	N	Y	N	N	Y
OKLAHOMA						
1 Jones	Y	Y	Y	N	N	Y
2 Synar	N	P	Y	N	N	Y
3 Watkins	Y	Y	Y	Y	N	Y
4 McCurdy	Y	Y	Y	N	N	Y
5 ***Edwards***	Y	Y	Y	Y	N	Y
6 English	Y	Y	Y	Y	N	Y
OREGON						
1 AuCoin	N	N	Y	Y	N	Y
2 ***Smith, R.***	Y	Y	Y	Y	Y	N
3 Wyden	N	Y	Y	Y	N	Y
4 Weaver	N	N	Y	N	N	Y
5 ***Smith, D.***	Y	Y	Y	Y	Y	N
PENNSYLVANIA						
1 Foglietta	N	Y	Y	N	N	Y
2 Gray	N	N	Y	N	N	Y
3 Borski	N	Y	Y	N	N	Y
4 Kolter	N	Y	Y	Y	N	Y
5 ***Schulze***	Y	Y	Y	Y	N	Y
6 Yatron	N	Y	Y	Y	N	Y
7 Edgar	N	N	Y	N	N	Y
8 Kostmayer	N	N	Y	N	N	Y
9 ***Shuster***	Y	Y	Y	Y	Y	N
10 ***McDade***	Y	Y	Y	Y	N	Y
11 Kanjorski	N	Y	Y	Y	N	N
12 Murtha	Y	Y	Y	Y	N	N
13 ***Coughlin***	Y	Y	Y	N	N	Y
14 Coyne	N	N	Y	N	N	Y
15 ***Ritter***	Y	Y	Y	Y	Y	?
16 ***Walker***	Y	Y	Y	Y	Y	N
17 ***Gekas***	Y	Y	Y	Y	N	N
18 Walgren	N	P	Y	N	N	Y
19 ***Goodling***	Y	N	Y	Y	Y	Y
20 Gaydos	N	Y	Y	Y	N	Y
21 ***Ridge***	Y	Y	Y	Y	N	Y
22 Murphy	N	Y	Y	Y	N	Y
23 ***Clinger***	Y	Y	Y	Y	N	N
RHODE ISLAND						
1 St Germain	N	Y	Y	N	N	Y
2 ***Schneider***	Y	Y	Y	N	N	Y
SOUTH CAROLINA						
1 ***Hartnett***	Y	Y	Y	Y	N	N
2 ***Spence***	Y	Y	Y	Y	N	N
3 Derrick	N	Y	Y	?	N	Y
4 ***Campbell***	Y	Y	Y	Y	N	N
5 Spratt	Y	Y	Y	N	N	Y
6 Tallon	Y	Y	Y	Y	N	Y
SOUTH DAKOTA						
AL Daschle	N	N	Y	N	N	Y
TENNESSEE						
1 ***Quillen***	Y	Y	Y	Y	N	N
2 ***Duncan***	Y	Y	Y	Y	N	N
3 Lloyd	Y	Y	Y	Y	N	N
4 Cooper	N	Y	Y	N	N	Y
5 Boner	N	Y	Y	Y	N	Y
6 Gordon	N	N	?	Y	N	Y
7 ***Sundquist***	Y	Y	Y	Y	Y	N
8 Jones	N	Y	Y	Y	N	Y
9 Ford	N	P	Y	N	N	Y
TEXAS						
1 Vacancy						
2 Wilson	Y	Y	Y	Y	N	Y
3 ***Bartlett***	Y	Y	Y	Y	Y	N
4 Hall, R.	Y	?	?	?	?	?
5 Bryant	N	Y	Y	N	N	Y
6 ***Barton***	Y	Y	Y	Y	Y	N
7 ***Archer***	Y	Y	Y	Y	Y	N
8 ***Fields***	Y	Y	Y	Y	Y	N
9 Brooks	N	Y	Y	Y	N	Y
10 Pickle	Y	Y	Y	Y	Y	N
11 Leath	Y	Y	Y	Y	N	N
12 Wright	?	Y	Y	?	N	Y
13 ***Boulter***	Y	+	+	Y	Y	N
14 ***Sweeney***	Y	Y	Y	Y	Y	N
15 de la Garza	N	Y	Y	N	N	N
16 Coleman	N	Y	Y	N	N	Y
17 Stenholm	Y	Y	Y	Y	N	N
18 Leland	N	N	Y	N	N	Y
19 ***Combest***	Y	Y	Y	Y	Y	N
20 Gonzalez	N	N	N	P	N	Y
21 ***Loeffler***	Y	Y	Y	Y	Y	?
22 ***DeLay***	Y	Y	Y	Y	Y	N
23 Bustamante	N	Y	Y	N	N	Y
24 Frost	N	Y	Y	N	N	Y
25 Andrews	Y	Y	Y	Y	N	N
26 ***Armey***	Y	Y	Y	Y	Y	N
27 Ortiz	N	Y	Y	Y	N	Y
UTAH						
1 ***Hansen***	Y	Y	Y	Y	Y	N
2 ***Monson***	Y	Y	Y	Y	Y	N
3 ***Nielson***	Y	Y	Y	Y	Y	N
VERMONT						
AL ***Jeffords***	N	Y	Y	N	N	Y
VIRGINIA						
1 ***Bateman***	Y	Y	Y	Y	Y	N
2 ***Whitehurst***	Y	Y	Y	Y	N	N
3 ***Bliley***	Y	Y	Y	Y	N	Y
4 Sisisky	N	Y	Y	Y	N	Y
5 Daniel	?	Y	Y	Y	Y	N
6 Olin	N	Y	Y	N	N	Y
7 ***Slaughter***	Y	Y	Y	Y	N	N
8 ***Parris***	Y	Y	Y	Y	Y	N
9 Boucher	N	Y	Y	N	N	Y
10 ***Wolf***	Y	Y	Y	Y	Y	Y
WASHINGTON						
1 ***Miller***	Y	N	Y	Y	Y	Y
2 Swift	N	Y	Y	N	N	Y
3 Bonker	N	N	Y	N	N	Y
4 ***Morrison***	Y	Y	Y	N	N	N
5 Foley	N	Y	Y	N	N	Y
6 Dicks	N	Y	Y	N	N	Y
7 Lowry	N	N	N	N	N	Y
8 ***Chandler***	Y	Y	Y	N	Y	Y
WEST VIRGINIA						
1 Mollohan	Y	N	Y	Y	N	Y
2 Staggers	N	N	Y	Y	N	Y
3 Wise	N	Y	Y	Y	N	Y
4 Rahall	N	Y	Y	Y	N	Y
WISCONSIN						
1 Aspin	N	Y	Y	N	N	Y
2 Kastenmeier	N	N	Y	N	N	Y
3 ***Gunderson***	Y	Y	Y	N	Y	Y
4 Kleczka	N	N	Y	N	N	Y
5 Moody	N	X	?	N	N	Y
6 ***Petri***	Y	Y	Y	Y	Y	N
7 Obey	N	N	Y	N	N	Y
8 ***Roth***	Y	Y	Y	Y	N	N
9 ***Sensenbrenner***	Y	Y	Y	Y	Y	N
WYOMING						
AL ***Cheney***	Y	Y	Y	Y	Y	N

Southern states - Ala., Ark., Fla., Ga., Ky., La., Miss., N.C., Okla., S.C., Tenn., Texas, Va.

* The *Congressional Record* vote number is different from the CQ vote number because the *Record* includes quorum calls in its tally. CQ does not publish quorum call votes.

205. HR 99. American Conservation Corps. Passage of the bill to authorize such sums as Congress considers necessary in fiscal 1986-88 to establish an American Conservation Corps to put unemployed youths to work on conservation projects. Passed 193-191: R 18-148; D 175-43 (ND 137-13, SD 38-30), July 11, 1985. A "nay" was a vote supporting the president's position.

206. Procedural Motion. Sundquist, R-Tenn., motion to approve the House *Journal* of Monday, July 15. Motion agreed to 262-131: R 51-120; D 211-11 (ND 143-8, SD 68-3), July 16, 1985.

207. HR 2959. Energy and Water Appropriations, Fiscal 1986. Derrick, D-S.C., motion to order the previous question (thus ending debate and the possibility of amendment) on the rule (H Res 221) to waive points of order against the bill based on the absence of authorizations for certain programs therein. The rule also waived points of order for failure to comply with provisions of the 1974 Congressional Budget Act (PL 93-344) with respect to the bill to appropriate $15,273,085,000 for energy and water development during fiscal 1986. The same waiver applied to the fiscal 1986 appropriations bills for Commerce, Justice, State and the judiciary (HR 2965) and the legislative branch (HR 2942). Motion agreed to 415-6: R 173-5; D 242-1 (ND 164-1, SD 78-0), July 16, 1985.

208. HR 2959. Energy and Water Appropriations, Fiscal 1986. Adoption of the rule (H Res 221) to waive points of order against the bill based on the absence of authorizations for certain programs therein. The rule also waived points of order for failure to comply with provisions of the 1974 Congressional Budget Act (PL 93-344) with respect to the bill to appropriate $15,273,-085,000 for energy and water development during fiscal 1986. This budget waiver also applied to the fiscal 1986 appropriations bills for Commerce, Justice, State and the judiciary (HR 2965) and the legislative branch (HR 2942). Adopted 239-181: R 54-124; D 185-57 (ND 135-31, SD 50-26), July 16, 1985.

209. HR 2959. Energy and Water Appropriations, Fiscal 1986. Weaver, D-Ore., amendment to delete $4 million in funds for road building associated with the Elk Creek Dam, Ore. Rejected 142-282: R 39-141; D 103-141 (ND 86-80, SD 17-61), July 16, 1985. (The bill, to appropriate $15,273,085,000 for energy and water development during fiscal 1986, was subsequently passed by voice vote.)

210. HR 2965. Commerce, Justice, State and the Judiciary Appropriations, Fiscal 1986. Adoption of the rule (H Res 225) to waive points of order against the appropriations bill for the Commerce, Justice and State departments, the federal judiciary and related agencies, based on the absence of authorizations for certain programs therein. Adopted 234-188: R 23-154; D 211-34 (ND 158-10, SD 53-24), July 17, 1985.

211. HR 2965. Commerce, Justice, State and the Judiciary Appropriations, Fiscal 1986. Walker, R-Pa., amendments to delete $206 million for the Economic Development Administration. Rejected en bloc 98-315: R 93-83; D 5-232 (ND 1-161, SD 4-71), July 17, 1985. A "yea" was a vote supporting the president's position.

212. HR 2965. Commerce, Justice, State and the Judiciary Appropriations, Fiscal 1986. Yates, D-Ill., amendment to delete from the Justice Department budget $500,000 that would be used for attorneys' fees for non-Indian litigants in New Mexico water rights cases. Adopted 244-177: R 101-75; D 143-102 (ND 97-70, SD 46-32), July 17, 1985. (The money was later added to the appropriation for the Legal Services Corporation.)

KEY

- Y Voted for (yea).
- # Paired for.
- + Announced for.
- N Voted against (nay).
- X Paired against.
- \- Announced against.
- P Voted "present."
- C Voted "present" to avoid possible conflict of interest.
- ? Did not vote or otherwise make a position known.

Democrats ***Republicans***

	205	206	207	208	209	210	211	212
ALABAMA								
1 ***Callahan***	N	N	Y	Y	N	N	N	Y
2 ***Dickinson***	N	N	Y	Y	N	N	N	N
3 Nichols	N	?	Y	?	N	Y	N	Y
4 Bevill	N	Y	Y	Y	N	Y	N	N
5 Flippo	N	Y	?	Y	N	N	N	Y
6 Erdreich	Y	Y	Y	Y	N	N	N	Y
7 Shelby	Y	Y	Y	Y	N	Y	N	N
ALASKA								
AL ***Young***	Y	N	Y	Y	N	N	N	Y
ARIZONA								
1 ***McCain***	N	Y	Y	Y	Y	N	N	Y
2 Udall	Y	?	Y	Y	Y	Y	N	Y
3 ***Stump***	N	N	Y	N	N	N	Y	N
4 ***Rudd***	N	Y	Y	Y	N	Y	Y	Y
5 ***Kolbe***	N	N	Y	N	N	N	Y	N
ARKANSAS								
1 Alexander	Y	P	Y	Y	N	Y	N	Y
2 Robinson	?	Y	Y	N	N	N	N	N
3 ***Hammerschmidt***	N	N	Y	N	N	N	N	Y
4 Anthony	Y	Y	Y	Y	N	Y	N	Y
CALIFORNIA								
1 Bosco	?	Y	Y	N	?	Y	N	N
2 ***Chappie***	?	N	Y	N	N	N	N	Y
3 Matsui	Y	Y	Y	Y	N	Y	N	Y
4 Fazio	#	Y	Y	Y	N	Y	N	N
5 Burton	Y	Y	Y	Y	Y	Y	N	Y
6 Boxer	?	Y	Y	Y	Y	Y	N	Y
7 Miller	?	?	Y	N	N	Y	N	Y
8 Dellums	Y	Y	Y	Y	Y	Y	N	Y
9 Stark	Y	Y	Y	Y	Y	Y	N	Y
10 Edwards	Y	Y	Y	Y	Y	Y	N	Y
11 Lantos	Y	Y	Y	Y	N	Y	N	N
12 ***Zschau***	N	N	Y	N	N	N	Y	Y
13 Mineta	Y	Y	Y	Y	N	Y	N	Y
14 ***Shumway***	N	N	Y	N	N	N	Y	Y
15 Coelho	Y	Y	Y	Y	N	Y	N	?
16 Panetta	Y	Y	Y	N	N	Y	N	Y
17 ***Pashayan***	N	Y	Y	N	N	N	N	N
18 Lehman	?	Y	Y	Y	N	Y	N	N
19 ***Lagomarsino***	Y	N	Y	N	N	N	Y	Y
20 ***Thomas***	N	N	Y	N	N	N	Y	N
21 ***Fiedler***	N	N	Y	N	N	N	Y	Y
22 ***Moorhead***	N	N	Y	N	N	N	Y	Y
23 Beilenson	Y	Y	Y	Y	Y	Y	N	Y
24 Waxman	Y	Y	?	Y	Y	Y	N	N
25 Roybal	?	Y	Y	Y	N	Y	N	Y
26 Berman	Y	Y	Y	Y	N	Y	N	Y
27 Levine	Y	Y	Y	Y	N	Y	N	Y
28 Dixon	Y	Y	Y	Y	?	Y	N	Y
29 Hawkins	Y	Y	Y	Y	Y	Y	N	Y
30 Martinez	Y	Y	Y	Y	Y	Y	N	N
31 Dymally	Y	?	?	?	Y	Y	N	N
32 Anderson	Y	Y	Y	Y	N	Y	N	Y
33 ***Dreier***	N	N	Y	N	Y	N	Y	Y
34 Torres	Y	Y	Y	Y	Y	Y	N	+
35 ***Lewis***	N	N	Y	Y	N	N	N	N
36 Brown	?	Y	Y	Y	N	Y	N	Y
37 ***McCandless***	N	N	Y	Y	N	N	Y	Y
38 ***Dornan***	N	Y	Y	Y	N	?	#	?
39 ***Dannemeyer***	N	N	Y	N	N	N	Y	Y
40 ***Badham***	N	N	Y	N	N	N	Y	N
41 ***Lowery***	N	N	Y	Y	N	N	Y	Y
42 ***Lungren***	N	N	Y	N	N	N	Y	N
43 ***Packard***	N	N	Y	N	N	N	Y	N
44 Bates	Y	Y	Y	N	Y	N	N	N
45 ***Hunter***	N	N	Y	N	N	N	Y	N
COLORADO								
1 Schroeder	Y	N	Y	Y	Y	Y	N	Y
2 Wirth	Y	Y	Y	Y	Y	Y	?	Y
3 ***Strang***	N	N	Y	Y	N	N	N	N
4 ***Brown***	N	N	Y	N	N	N	Y	Y
5 ***Kramer***	N	N	Y	N	N	N	Y	Y
6 ***Schaefer***	N	N	Y	N	N	N	Y	Y
CONNECTICUT								
1 Kennelly	Y	Y	Y	Y	Y	Y	N	N
2 Gejdenson	Y	Y	Y	Y	Y	Y	N	N
3 Morrison	Y	Y	Y	N	Y	Y	N	N
4 ***McKinney***	Y	Y	Y	N	Y	Y	N	Y
5 ***Rowland***	N	Y	Y	N	N	N	N	N
6 ***Johnson***	N	Y	Y	Y	N	N	N	Y
DELAWARE								
AL Carper	N	Y	Y	N	Y	Y	N	N
FLORIDA								
1 Hutto	?	Y	Y	Y	N	Y	N	Y
2 Fuqua	?	Y	Y	Y	N	?	?	?
3 Bennett	Y	Y	Y	Y	Y	Y	N	Y
4 Chappell	N	Y	Y	Y	N	Y	N	N
5 ***McCollum***	N	Y	Y	N	Y	N	Y	Y
6 MacKay	N	Y	Y	N	Y	N	N	N
7 Gibbons	Y	Y	Y	Y	N	Y	N	Y
8 ***Young***	N	N	Y	N	N	N	Y	N
9 ***Bilirakis***	N	N	Y	N	N	N	Y	N
10 ***Ireland***	N	N	Y	N	N	N	Y	N
11 Nelson	Y	Y	Y	N	Y	Y	Y	N
12 ***Lewis***	N	N	Y	Y	N	N	N	Y
13 ***Mack***	N	N	Y	N	N	N	Y	Y
14 Mica	N	Y	Y	?	N	Y	N	Y
15 ***Shaw***	N	N	Y	Y	N	N	Y	Y
16 Smith	?	Y	Y	Y	Y	Y	N	Y
17 Lehman	Y	Y	Y	Y	Y	Y	N	Y
18 Pepper	Y	Y	Y	Y	N	Y	N	N
19 Fascell	Y	Y	Y	Y	N	Y	N	Y
GEORGIA								
1 Thomas	N	Y	Y	N	N	N	N	N
2 Hatcher	?	?	Y	Y	N	Y	?	N
3 Ray	N	Y	Y	N	N	N	N	Y
4 ***Swindall***	N	N	Y	N	Y	N	Y	Y
5 Fowler	Y	Y	Y	Y	Y	Y	N	Y
6 ***Gingrich***	N	N	Y	N	N	N	?	N
7 Darden	Y	Y	Y	N	N	N	N	Y
8 Rowland	N	Y	Y	Y	N	N	N	Y
9 Jenkins	Y	Y	Y	N	N	N	N	Y
10 Barnard	N	Y	Y	N	N	N	N	Y
HAWAII								
1 Heftel	N	Y	Y	Y	Y	Y	N	Y
2 Akaka	Y	Y	Y	Y	N	Y	N	Y
IDAHO								
1 ***Craig***	N	N	Y	N	N	N	N	N
2 Stallings	N	Y	Y	N	N	N	N	N
ILLINOIS								
1 Hayes	Y	Y	Y	Y	Y	Y	N	N
2 Savage	Y	Y	Y	Y	Y	Y	N	Y
3 Russo	Y	Y	Y	N	Y	?	N	Y
4 ***O'Brien***	?	Y	Y	Y	N	Y	N	N
5 Lipinski	Y	P	Y	Y	N	Y	N	Y
6 ***Hyde***	N	Y	Y	N	N	N	Y	N
7 Collins	?	?	Y	Y	Y	Y	N	Y
8 Rostenkowski	?	Y	Y	Y	N	Y	N	Y
9 Yates	Y	Y	Y	Y	Y	Y	N	Y
10 ***Porter***	N	N	Y	N	Y	N	Y	Y
11 Annunzio	Y	Y	Y	Y	Y	Y	N	Y
12 ***Crane***	N	?	?	?	?	?	?	?
13 ***Fawell***	N	Y	Y	N	Y	N	Y	Y
14 ***Grotberg***	N	N	N	N	N	N	Y	Y
15 ***Madigan***	N	N	Y	N	N	N	N	N
16 ***Martin***	N	N	N	N	N	N	Y	Y
17 Evans	Y	Y	Y	Y	Y	Y	N	Y
18 ***Michel***	N	N	Y	Y	N	N	N	Y
19 Bruce	Y	Y	Y	Y	N	Y	N	Y
20 Durbin	Y	N	Y	Y	N	Y	N	Y
21 Price	Y	Y	Y	Y	N	Y	N	Y
22 Gray	Y	Y	Y	Y	N	Y	N	Y
INDIANA								
1 Visclosky	Y	Y	Y	Y	N	Y	N	Y
2 Sharp	N	Y	Y	N	Y	N	N	Y
3 ***Hiler***	N	N	Y	N	Y	N	Y	N
4 ***Coats***	N	N	Y	N	Y	N	N	N
5 ***Hillis***	?	Y	Y	Y	N	N	N	N

ND - Northern Democrats SD - Southern Democrats

* Corresponding to Congressional Record Votes 225, 226, 227, 228, 229, 230, 231, 233

	205	206	207	208	209	210	211	212
6 ***Burton***	?	N	Y	N	N	N	Y	N
7 ***Myers***	N	Y	Y	Y	N	Y	N	N
8 McCloskey	Y	Y	Y	Y	N	Y	N	N
9 Hamilton	N	Y	Y	Y	N	Y	N	Y
10 Jacobs	N	N	N	N	Y	N	N	Y
IOWA								
1 ***Leach***	Y	?	Y	N	Y	Y	N	Y
2 ***Tauke***	N	N	Y	N	Y	Y	N	Y
3 ***Evans***	N	N	Y	N	N	N	N	Y
4 Smith	Y	Y	Y	Y	N	Y	N	N
5 ***Lightfoot***	N	N	Y	N	Y	N	N	Y
6 Bedell	Y	Y	Y	N	Y	Y	N	N
KANSAS								
1 ***Roberts***	N	N	Y	Y	N	N	Y	N
2 Slattery	N	Y	Y	N	N	N	N	N
3 ***Meyers***	?	N	Y	N	Y	N	Y	Y
4 Glickman	N	Y	Y	N	N	Y	N	Y
5 ***Whittaker***	N	?	Y	N	N	N	N	N
KENTUCKY								
1 Hubbard	N	Y	Y	N	N	N	N	N
2 Natcher	Y	Y	Y	Y	N	Y	N	Y
3 Mazzoli	N	Y	Y	Y	N	Y	N	Y
4 ***Snyder***	N	Y	Y	Y	N	N	Y	Y
5 ***Rogers***	N	N	Y	Y	N	Y	N	N
6 ***Hopkins***	N	Y	Y	N	Y	N	Y	N
7 Perkins	Y	Y	Y	Y	N	Y	N	Y
LOUISIANA								
1 ***Livingston***	N	N	Y	Y	N	N	Y	Y
2 Boggs	Y	Y	Y	Y	N	Y	N	N
3 Tauzin	?	Y	Y	N	N	N	N	Y
4 Roemer	?	N	Y	N	Y	N	Y	Y
5 Huckaby	Y	?	Y	Y	N	N	N	Y
6 ***Moore***	N	Y	Y	N	N	N	Y	Y
7 Breaux	N	Y	Y	N	N	N	Y	Y
8 Long	Y	P	Y	Y	N	Y	N	Y
MAINE								
1 ***McKernan***	N	N	Y	N	N	N	N	N
2 ***Snowe***	Y	Y	Y	N	Y	N	N	Y
MARYLAND								
1 Dyson	N	Y	Y	Y	N	Y	N	N
2 ***Bentley***	N	N	Y	N	N	N	N	N
3 Mikulski	Y	Y	Y	Y	N	Y	N	Y
4 ***Holt***	N	Y	?	?	N	N	Y	N
5 Hoyer	Y	Y	Y	Y	N	Y	N	N
6 Byron	Y	Y	Y	Y	N	Y	N	Y
7 Mitchell	Y	N	Y	Y	Y	Y	N	N
8 Barnes	Y	Y	Y	Y	N	Y	N	Y
MASSACHUSETTS								
1 ***Conte***	Y	N	Y	Y	N	Y	N	Y
2 Boland	Y	Y	Y	Y	N	Y	N	N
3 Early	Y	Y	Y	Y	Y	Y	N	N
4 Frank	Y	Y	Y	Y	Y	?	N	N
5 Atkins	Y	Y	Y	Y	Y	Y	N	Y
6 Mavroules	Y	Y	?	?	Y	Y	N	N
7 Markey	Y	Y	Y	Y	Y	Y	N	N
8 O'Neill								
9 Moakley	Y	Y	Y	Y	Y	Y	N	Y
10 Studds	Y	?	Y	Y	Y	Y	N	Y
11 Donnelly	Y	Y	Y	Y	?	Y	N	N
MICHIGAN								
1 Conyers	Y	Y	Y	?	?	Y	?	Y
2 ***Pursell***	X	Y	Y	N	N	N	Y	Y
3 Wolpe	Y	Y	Y	N	Y	Y	N	Y
4 ***Siljander***	X	?	Y	N	N	?	?	?
5 ***Henry***	N	N	Y	N	Y	N	N	Y
6 Carr	Y	Y	Y	Y	Y	Y	N	N
7 Kildee	Y	Y	Y	Y	Y	Y	N	N
8 Traxler	Y	Y	Y	Y	N	Y	N	Y
9 ***Vander Jagt***	N	Y	N	N	N	N	N	N
10 ***Schuette***	N	N	Y	N	Y	N	N	N
11 ***Davis***	Y	N	Y	Y	N	N	N	Y
12 Bonior	Y	Y	Y	Y	Y	Y	?	?
13 Crockett	?	Y	Y	N	Y	Y	N	Y
14 Hertel	Y	Y	Y	Y	Y	Y	N	Y
15 Ford	#	?	Y	Y	N	Y	?	N
16 Dingell	#	Y	Y	Y	N	Y	N	N
17 Levin	Y	Y	Y	N	Y	Y	N	N
18 ***Broomfield***	?	Y	N	N	N	N	Y	Y
MINNESOTA								
1 Penny	N	N	Y	N	N	N	N	Y
2 ***Weber***	?	N	Y	N	Y	N	?	Y
3 ***Frenzel***	N	Y	Y	N	N	?	Y	Y
4 Vento	Y	P	Y	N	Y	Y	N	Y
5 Sabo	Y	Y	Y	Y	N	Y	N	Y
6 Sikorski	Y	N	Y	N	Y	N	N	N
7 ***Stangeland***	N	N	Y	Y	N	N	Y	N
8 Oberstar	Y	Y	Y	Y	N	Y	N	Y
MISSISSIPPI								
1 Whitten	Y	Y	Y	Y	N	Y	N	N
2 ***Franklin***	N	Y	Y	Y	N	N	N	Y
3 Montgomery	N	Y	Y	Y	N	Y	N	Y
4 Dowdy	?	?	Y	Y	N	Y	N	N
5 ***Lott***	N	N	Y	N	N	N	N	Y
MISSOURI								
1 Clay	Y	N	Y	Y	Y	Y	N	Y
2 Young	Y	Y	Y	Y	N	Y	N	N
3 Gephardt	Y	Y	Y	Y	N	Y	N	N
4 Skelton	?	Y	Y	Y	N	Y	N	Y
5 Wheat	Y	Y	Y	Y	Y	Y	N	Y
6 ***Coleman***	N	N	Y	N	N	N	N	N
7 ***Taylor***	N	N	Y	N	N	N	N	N
8 ***Emerson***	N	N	Y	Y	N	N	N	N
9 Volkmer	Y	Y	Y	Y	N	N	N	N
MONTANA								
1 Williams	Y	Y	Y	Y	Y	Y	N	N
2 ***Marlenee***	N	N	Y	N	N	N	Y	N
NEBRASKA								
1 ***Bereuter***	Y	N	Y	N	N	N	Y	Y
2 ***Daub***	N	N	Y	N	N	N	Y	Y
3 ***Smith***	N	Y	Y	Y	N	Y	Y	N
NEVADA								
1 Reid	#	Y	Y	Y	Y	Y	N	Y
2 ***Vucanovich***	?	N	Y	N	N	N	N	N
NEW HAMPSHIRE								
1 ***Smith***	N	N	Y	N	Y	N	Y	Y
2 ***Gregg***	N	N	Y	N	Y	N	Y	Y
NEW JERSEY								
1 Florio	Y	Y	Y	Y	Y	Y	N	N
2 Hughes	N	Y	Y	N	Y	N	N	Y
3 Howard	Y	Y	Y	Y	N	Y	N	Y
4 ***Smith***	Y	Y	Y	Y	N	N	N	Y
5 ***Roukema***	N	Y	Y	N	N	N	N	Y
6 Dwyer	Y	Y	Y	Y	N	Y	N	N
7 ***Rinaldo***	Y	Y	Y	N	Y	N	N	Y
8 Roe	Y	Y	Y	Y	N	Y	N	Y
9 Torricelli	Y	Y	Y	Y	N	Y	N	Y
10 Rodino	?	Y	Y	Y	Y	Y	N	Y
11 ***Gallo***	N	N	Y	N	N	N	N	Y
12 ***Courter***	N	N	Y	N	N	N	N	?
13 ***Saxton***	N	Y	Y	N	Y	N	N	Y
14 Guarini	Y	Y	Y	Y	Y	Y	N	Y
NEW MEXICO								
1 ***Lujan***	N	Y	Y	N	N	N	N	N
2 ***Skeen***	N	N	Y	Y	N	N	N	N
3 Richardson	Y	Y	Y	Y	N	Y	N	N
NEW YORK								
1 ***Carney***	N	N	Y	Y	N	N	Y	Y
2 Downey	Y	?	?	N	N	Y	N	Y
3 Mrazek	Y	Y	Y	Y	N	Y	?	N
4 ***Lent***	N	N	Y	N	N	N	N	N
5 ***McGrath***	N	N	Y	N	N	N	N	N
6 Addabbo	Y	?	Y	Y	N	Y	N	N
7 Ackerman	Y	Y	Y	Y	Y	Y	N	Y
8 Scheuer	Y	Y	Y	Y	N	Y	?	N
9 Manton	Y	Y	Y	Y	Y	Y	N	N
10 Schumer	?	Y	Y	N	Y	Y	N	N
11 Towns	?	Y	Y	Y	Y	Y	N	N
12 Owens	Y	Y	Y	Y	N	Y	N	Y
13 Solarz	Y	Y	Y	Y	N	Y	N	Y
14 ***Molinari***	N	N	Y	N	Y	N	N	Y
15 ***Green***	N	Y	Y	Y	N	Y	N	Y
16 Rangel	Y	Y	Y	Y	Y	Y	N	Y
17 Weiss	Y	+	+	+	Y	Y	N	N
18 Garcia	Y	?	Y	Y	Y	Y	N	N
19 Biaggi	Y	Y	Y	Y	Y	Y	N	N
20 ***DioGuardi***	N	N	?	?	N	N	Y	Y
21 ***Fish***	N	?	Y	N	Y	N	N	Y
22 ***Gilman***	Y	Y	Y	Y	N	Y	N	N
23 Stratton	N	Y	Y	Y	N	Y	N	Y
24 ***Solomon***	N	N	Y	N	N	N	Y	Y
25 ***Boehlert***	Y	N	Y	N	Y	N	N	Y
26 ***Martin***	N	Y	Y	Y	N	N	N	N
27 ***Wortley***	N	Y	Y	Y	N	N	N	N
28 McHugh	Y	Y	Y	Y	N	Y	N	Y
29 ***Horton***	#	Y	Y	Y	N	Y	N	Y
30 ***Eckert***	N	N	Y	N	N	N	Y	Y
31 ***Kemp***	N	Y	Y	N	N	N	Y	N
32 LaFalce	Y	Y	Y	N	Y	Y	N	N
33 Nowak	Y	Y	Y	Y	Y	Y	N	N
34 Lundine	Y	Y	Y	Y	Y	Y	N	Y
NORTH CAROLINA								
1 Jones	N	Y	Y	Y	N	Y	N	N
2 Valentine	N	Y	Y	N	N	Y	N	Y
3 Whitley	?	Y	Y	Y	N	Y	N	N
4 ***Cobey***	N	N	Y	N	N	N	Y	Y
5 Neal	Y	P	Y	N	Y	Y	N	Y
6 ***Coble***	N	Y	Y	N	N	N	Y	Y
7 Rose	N	Y	Y	Y	N	Y	N	N
8 Hefner	?	?	?	?	?	?	?	?
9 ***McMillan***	N	Y	Y	N	N	N	Y	Y
10 ***Broyhill***	N	Y	Y	N	N	N	Y	Y
11 ***Hendon***	N	N	Y	N	N	N	N	Y
NORTH DAKOTA								
AL Dorgan	Y	P	Y	Y	N	Y	Y	Y
OHIO								
1 Luken	Y	Y	Y	Y	N	Y	N	N
2 ***Gradison***	N	Y	Y	Y	N	Y	Y	Y
3 Hall	Y	Y	Y	Y	Y	Y	N	Y
4 ***Oxley***	N	N	Y	N	N	N	Y	N
5 ***Latta***	N	N	Y	N	N	N	Y	Y
6 ***McEwen***	N	N	Y	Y	N	N	N	N
7 ***DeWine***	N	N	Y	N	Y	N	Y	Y
8 ***Kindness***	N	N	Y	N	N	N	Y	N
9 Kaptur	Y	Y	Y	Y	N	Y	N	Y
10 ***Miller***	N	?	Y	Y	N	Y	N	Y
11 Eckart	Y	Y	Y	Y	Y	Y	N	Y
12 ***Kasich***	N	N	Y	N	N	N	Y	Y
13 Pease	Y	Y	Y	Y	N	Y	N	Y
14 Seiberling	Y	?	Y	N	Y	Y	N	Y
15 ***Wylie***	N	Y	Y	N	N	N	Y	N
16 ***Regula***	Y	Y	Y	Y	N	Y	N	Y
17 Traficant	Y	Y	Y	Y	N	Y	N	N
18 Applegate	Y	?	Y	Y	N	Y	N	N
19 Feighan	Y	Y	Y	N	Y	N	N	N
20 Oakar	Y	Y	Y	Y	N	Y	N	N
21 Stokes	Y	Y	Y	Y	N	Y	N	Y
OKLAHOMA								
1 Jones	N	Y	Y	N	Y	N	N	Y
2 Synar	N	Y	Y	Y	Y	Y	N	Y
3 Watkins	N	Y	Y	Y	N	Y	N	N
4 McCurdy	N	Y	Y	N	Y	N	N	Y
5 ***Edwards***	N	N	Y	N	N	N	N	?
6 English	N	Y	Y	N	?	N	N	Y
OREGON								
1 AuCoin	Y	Y	Y	Y	N	Y	N	Y
2 ***Smith, R.***	N	N	Y	N	N	N	N	N
3 Wyden	Y	Y	Y	Y	Y	Y	N	N
4 Weaver	Y	?	Y	N	Y	Y	N	Y
5 ***Smith, D.***	X	N	Y	N	N	N	Y	N
PENNSYLVANIA								
1 Foglietta	Y	Y	Y	Y	Y	Y	N	N
2 Gray	Y	Y	Y	Y	N	Y	N	Y
3 Borski	Y	Y	Y	Y	Y	Y	N	N
4 Kolter	?	Y	Y	Y	N	Y	N	Y
5 ***Schulze***	N	N	Y	N	N	N	Y	Y
6 Yatron	?	Y	Y	Y	N	Y	N	N
7 Edgar	Y	?	Y	N	Y	Y	N	Y
8 Kostmayer	Y	Y	Y	Y	Y	Y	N	N
9 ***Shuster***	N	N	Y	N	N	N	N	N
10 ***McDade***	N	Y	Y	Y	N	Y	N	Y
11 Kanjorski	Y	Y	Y	N	Y	Y	N	Y
12 Murtha	Y	Y	Y	Y	N	Y	N	Y
13 ***Coughlin***	N	N	Y	Y	Y	Y	Y	Y
14 Coyne	Y	Y	Y	Y	N	Y	N	N
15 ***Ritter***	?	N	Y	N	N	N	N	N
16 ***Walker***	N	N	Y	N	Y	N	Y	Y
17 ***Gekas***	N	N	Y	Y	N	N	N	Y
18 Walgren	Y	Y	Y	Y	N	Y	N	Y
19 ***Goodling***	N	N	Y	N	N	N	Y	N
20 Gaydos	Y	Y	Y	Y	N	Y	N	N
21 ***Ridge***	Y	N	Y	Y	N	Y	N	Y
22 Murphy	Y	N	Y	Y	N	Y	N	Y
23 ***Clinger***	Y	N	Y	Y	N	Y	N	N
RHODE ISLAND								
1 St Germain	?	Y	Y	Y	N	Y	N	Y
2 ***Schneider***	N	?	?	?	?	?	X	?
SOUTH CAROLINA								
1 ***Hartnett***	X	Y	Y	N	Y	N	Y	N
2 ***Spence***	N	N	Y	N	N	N	N	N
3 Derrick	Y	Y	Y	Y	Y	Y	N	Y
4 ***Campbell***	N	N	Y	N	N	N	N	N
5 Spratt	N	Y	Y	N	N	N	N	Y
6 Tallon	N	Y	Y	N	N	N	N	Y
SOUTH DAKOTA								
AL Daschle	Y	Y	Y	Y	N	Y	N	N
TENNESSEE								
1 ***Quillen***	N	Y	Y	Y	N	Y	N	Y
2 ***Duncan***	N	Y	Y	N	N	Y	N	Y
3 Lloyd	?	N	Y	Y	N	Y	N	Y
4 Cooper	Y	Y	Y	N	Y	N	N	Y
5 Boner	Y	Y	Y	Y	N	Y	?	N
6 Gordon	N	Y	Y	Y	N	Y	N	N
7 ***Sundquist***	N	N	Y	N	N	N	Y	Y
8 Jones	N	Y	Y	Y	N	Y	N	Y
9 Ford	Y	?	Y	Y	Y	Y	N	Y
TEXAS								
1 Vacancy								
2 Wilson	Y	Y	Y	Y	N	?	?	Y
3 ***Bartlett***	N	N	Y	N	Y	N	Y	Y
4 Hall, R.	?	?	?	?	?	?	?	?
5 Bryant	Y	Y	Y	N	Y	Y	N	N
6 ***Barton***	N	N	Y	N	Y	N	Y	Y
7 ***Archer***	N	Y	Y	N	Y	N	Y	Y
8 ***Fields***	N	N	Y	N	Y	N	Y	Y
9 Brooks	Y	Y	Y	Y	N	Y	N	N
10 Pickle	Y	Y	Y	Y	N	Y	N	N
11 Leath	N	Y	Y	?	N	N	N	N
12 Wright	Y	Y	Y	Y	N	Y	N	N
13 ***Boulter***	N	N	Y	Y	N	N	Y	Y
14 ***Sweeney***	N	?	Y	N	Y	N	Y	N
15 de la Garza	Y	Y	Y	Y	N	Y	N	N
16 Coleman	Y	Y	Y	Y	N	Y	N	N
17 Stenholm	N	N	Y	N	N	N	Y	Y
18 Leland	Y	Y	Y	Y	Y	Y	N	N
19 ***Combest***	N	N	Y	N	N	N	Y	Y
20 Gonzalez	Y	Y	Y	Y	N	Y	N	N
21 ***Loeffler***	X	N	Y	N	N	N	Y	Y
22 ***DeLay***	N	N	Y	N	N	N	Y	Y
23 Bustamante	Y	Y	Y	N	N	Y	N	N
24 Frost	Y	Y	Y	Y	N	Y	N	N
25 Andrews	?	Y	Y	Y	Y	Y	N	Y
26 ***Armey***	N	N	Y	N	Y	N	Y	Y
27 Ortiz	Y	Y	Y	N	N	Y	N	N
UTAH								
1 ***Hansen***	N	?	Y	N	N	N	Y	N
2 ***Monson***	N	N	Y	Y	N	N	Y	N
3 ***Nielson***	N	N	Y	N	N	N	N	N
VERMONT								
AL ***Jeffords***	Y	Y	Y	N	N	N	N	Y
VIRGINIA								
1 ***Bateman***	N	Y	Y	Y	Y	Y	N	N
2 ***Whitehurst***	?	N	Y	Y	N	N	N	N
3 ***Bliley***	N	N	Y	Y	N	Y	Y	N
4 Sisisky	N	Y	Y	N	N	N	N	N
5 Daniel	Y	Y	Y	Y	N	Y	Y	Y
6 Olin	N	Y	Y	N	N	N	N	Y
7 ***Slaughter***	N	N	Y	N	N	N	Y	N
8 ***Parris***	N	N	Y	Y	N	Y	N	N
9 Boucher	Y	Y	Y	Y	N	Y	N	Y
10 ***Wolf***	N	N	Y	Y	N	N	Y	N
WASHINGTON								
1 ***Miller***	N	Y	Y	N	Y	N	N	N
2 Swift	Y	Y	Y	Y	Y	Y	N	N
3 Bonker	Y	?	Y	Y	Y	Y	?	Y
4 ***Morrison***	N	Y	Y	Y	N	N	N	Y
5 Foley	Y	Y	Y	Y	Y	Y	N	N
6 Dicks	Y	Y	Y	Y	N	Y	N	N
7 Lowry	Y	Y	Y	Y	Y	Y	?	N
8 ***Chandler***	N	Y	Y	Y	N	N	N	Y
WEST VIRGINIA								
1 Mollohan	Y	Y	Y	Y	N	Y	N	N
2 Staggers	Y	Y	Y	N	Y	Y	N	N
3 Wise	Y	Y	Y	Y	Y	Y	N	Y
4 Rahall	Y	Y	Y	Y	Y	Y	N	Y
WISCONSIN								
1 Aspin	Y	Y	Y	Y	N	Y	N	Y
2 Kastenmeier	Y	Y	Y	Y	Y	Y	N	Y
3 ***Gunderson***	N	?	Y	N	N	N	N	Y
4 Kleczka	N	?	Y	Y	N	Y	N	Y
5 Moody	Y	Y	Y	N	Y	Y	N	Y
6 ***Petri***	Y	?	N	N	Y	N	Y	Y
7 Obey	Y	Y	Y	Y	Y	Y	N	Y
8 ***Roth***	Y	N	Y	N	Y	N	Y	Y
9 ***Sensenbrenner***	N	N	Y	N	N	N	Y	Y
WYOMING								
AL ***Cheney***	N	N	Y	N	N	N	Y	N

Southern states - Ala., Ark., Fla., Ga., Ky., La., Miss., N.C., Okla., S.C., Tenn., Texas, Va.

* The *Congressional Record* vote number is different from the CQ vote number because the *Record* includes quorum calls in its tally. CQ does not publish quorum call votes.

213. HR 2965. Commerce, Justice, State and the Judiciary Appropriations, Fiscal 1986. Rudd, R-Ariz., amendment to delete $20 million from the U.S. contribution to international organizations. Adopted 302-116: R 172-4; D 130-112 (ND 67-97, SD 63-15), July 17, 1985.

214. HR 2965. Commerce, Justice, State and the Judiciary Appropriations, Fiscal 1986. Hiler, R-Ind., amendment to cut $95 million from the Business Loan and Investment Fund of the Small Business Administration. Adopted 257-158: R 168-8; D 89-150 (ND 47-115, SD 42-35), July 17, 1985.

215. HR 2965. Commerce, Justice, State and the Judiciary Appropriations, Fiscal 1986. Frenzel, R-Minn., amendment to trim all discretionary funding in the bill by 4 percent (about $350 million). Rejected 149-266: R 119-56; D 30-210 (ND 16-147, SD 14-63), July 17, 1985.

216. HR 2965. Commerce, Justice, State and the Judiciary Appropriations, Fiscal 1986. Smith, D-Iowa, motion that the Committee of the Whole rise and report the bill back to the House. Motion rejected 183-232: R 21-154; D 162-78 (ND 112-51, SD 50-27), July 17, 1985. (In accordance with a House rule change adopted in 1983, members may offer limitations on spending as amendments to an appropriations bill only if a motion to rise has been defeated. The effect of the vote was to allow consideration of the DeWine, R-Ohio, amendment to bar the Legal Services Corporation from using funds for any abortion-related litigation. The DeWine amendment subsequently was adopted by voice vote, and the House then agreed to rise from the Committee of the Whole *(see vote 217, below)*.)

217. HR 2965. Commerce, Justice, State and the Judiciary Appropriations, Fiscal 1986. Smith, D-Iowa, motion that the Committee of the Whole rise and report the bill back to the House. Motion agreed to 227-185: R 27-148; D 200-37 (ND 148-12, SD 52-25), July 17, 1985.

218. HR 2965. Commerce, Justice, State and the Judiciary Appropriations, Fiscal 1986. Passage of the bill to provide $11,922,021,000 for the Commerce, Justice and State departments, the federal judiciary and related agencies. Passed 273-136: R 64-111; D 209-25 (ND 147-11, SD 62-14), July 17, 1985. (The president had requested $11,774,204,000 in new budget authority.)

219. HR 2942. Legislative Branch Appropriations, Fiscal 1986. Miller, R-Ohio, amendment to cut $10 million from the amount appropriated for official congressional mail, to limit members' use of the frank. Rejected 204-217: R 165-13; D 39-204 (ND 22-146, SD 17-58), July 18, 1985.

220. HR 2942. Legislative Branch Appropriations, Fiscal 1986. Brown, R-Colo., amendment to eliminate a $106,000 increase in funds for the House office buildings for five new automatic-elevator operator positions. Rejected 191-221: R 138-34; D 53-187 (ND 22-145, SD 31-42), July 18, 1985.

KEY

- Y Voted for (yea).
- # Paired for.
- \+ Announced for.
- N Voted against (nay).
- X Paired against.
- \- Announced against.
- P Voted "present."
- C Voted "present" to avoid possible conflict of interest.
- ? Did not vote or otherwise make a position known.

Democrats ***Republicans***

	213	214	215	216	217	218	219	220
ALABAMA								
1 ***Callahan***	Y	Y	Y	N	N	N	Y	Y
2 ***Dickinson***	Y	Y	Y	N	Y	N	Y	Y
3 Nichols	Y	Y	N	N	N	Y	N	Y
4 Bevill	Y	N	N	Y	Y	Y	N	N
5 Flippo	Y	N	N	Y	N	N	N	Y
6 Erdreich	Y	Y	N	Y	Y	N	Y	Y
7 Shelby	Y	N	N	N	N	N	N	Y
ALASKA								
AL ***Young***	Y	Y	N	N	N	Y	N	N
ARIZONA								
1 ***McCain***	Y	Y	N	N	N	N	Y	Y
2 Udall	Y	N	N	Y	Y	Y	N	N
3 ***Stump***	Y	Y	Y	N	N	N	Y	Y
4 ***Rudd***	Y	Y	N	N	?	X	Y	Y
5 ***Kolbe***	Y	Y	Y	Y	Y	N	Y	Y
ARKANSAS								
1 Alexander	N	N	N	Y	Y	Y	N	N
2 Robinson	Y	N	N	N	N	Y	N	Y
3 ***Hammerschmidt***	Y	Y	N	N	N	N	Y	N
4 Anthony	Y	Y	N	Y	Y	N	N	N
CALIFORNIA								
1 Bosco	N	Y	N	Y	Y	Y	N	?
2 ***Chappie***	Y	Y	Y	N	N	N	Y	Y
3 Matsui	N	N	N	Y	Y	Y	N	N
4 Fazio	N	N	N	Y	Y	Y	N	N
5 Burton	N	N	N	Y	Y	Y	N	N
6 Boxer	N	N	N	Y	Y	Y	N	N
7 Miller	N	?	N	Y	Y	Y	N	N
8 Dellums	N	N	N	Y	Y	Y	N	N
9 Stark	N	N	N	Y	Y	Y	N	N
10 Edwards	N	N	N	Y	Y	Y	N	N
11 Lantos	N	Y	N	Y	Y	Y	N	N
12 ***Zschau***	Y	Y	Y	N	N	N	Y	Y
13 Mineta	N	N	N	Y	Y	Y	N	N
14 ***Shumway***	Y	Y	Y	N	N	N	Y	Y
15 Coelho	Y	N	N	Y	Y	Y	N	N
16 Panetta	N	N	N	Y	Y	Y	Y	N
17 ***Pashayan***	Y	Y	Y	N	N	N	Y	Y
18 Lehman	N	N	N	Y	Y	Y	N	N
19 ***Lagomarsino***	Y	Y	Y	N	N	N	Y	Y
20 ***Thomas***	Y	Y	Y	Y	Y	N	N	Y
21 ***Fiedler***	Y	Y	Y	N	N	N	Y	Y
22 ***Moorhead***	Y	Y	Y	N	N	N	Y	Y
23 Beilenson	N	Y	N	Y	Y	Y	N	N
24 Waxman	N	N	N	Y	Y	Y	N	N
25 Roybal	N	N	N	Y	Y	Y	N	N
26 Berman	N	Y	N	Y	Y	Y	N	N
27 Levine	N	N	N	Y	Y	Y	N	N
28 Dixon	N	N	N	Y	Y	Y	N	N
29 Hawkins	N	N	N	Y	Y	Y	N	N
30 Martinez	Y	N	N	Y	Y	Y	N	N
31 Dymally	N	N	N	Y	Y	Y	N	N
32 Anderson	Y	N	N	Y	Y	Y	N	N
33 ***Dreier***	Y	Y	Y	N	N	N	Y	Y
34 Torres	-	-	-	+	+	+	N	N
35 ***Lewis***	Y	Y	N	N	N	Y	N	N
36 Brown	N	N	N	Y	Y	Y	N	N
37 ***McCandless***	Y	Y	Y	N	N	N	Y	Y
38 ***Dornan***	?	?	?	?	?	?	Y	Y
39 ***Dannemeyer***	Y	+	+	-	+	-	Y	Y
40 ***Badham***	Y	Y	Y	N	N	N	Y	Y
41 ***Lowery***	Y	Y	N	N	N	Y	Y	N
42 ***Lungren***	Y	Y	N	N	N	N	Y	Y
43 ***Packard***	Y	Y	Y	N	N	N	Y	Y
44 Bates	N	Y	N	Y	Y	?	N	N
45 ***Hunter***	Y	Y	N	N	N	N	Y	Y
COLORADO								
1 Schroeder	N	N	Y	Y	Y	N	Y	Y
2 Wirth	Y	N	N	Y	Y	Y	Y	Y
3 ***Strang***	Y	Y	Y	N	N	Y	Y	Y
4 ***Brown***	Y	Y	Y	N	N	N	Y	Y
5 ***Kramer***	Y	Y	Y	N	N	N	Y	?
6 ***Schaefer***	Y	Y	Y	N	N	N	Y	Y
CONNECTICUT								
1 Kennelly	Y	Y	N	?	?	?	N	N
2 Gejdenson	N	N	N	Y	Y	Y	N	N
3 Morrison	N	Y	N	Y	Y	Y	N	N
4 ***McKinney***	N	Y	Y	Y	Y	Y	N	N
5 ***Rowland***	Y	Y	Y	N	N	Y	Y	Y
6 ***Johnson***	Y	Y	Y	Y	Y	Y	Y	Y
DELAWARE								
AL Carper	Y	Y	Y	Y	Y	Y	Y	Y
FLORIDA								
1 Hutto	Y	Y	N	N	N	Y	Y	Y
2 Fuqua	?	?	?	?	?	?	?	?
3 Bennett	Y	Y	Y	Y	Y	Y	Y	N
4 Chappell	Y	Y	N	Y	Y	Y	N	N
5 ***McCollum***	Y	Y	N	N	N	Y	Y	N
6 MacKay	N	Y	N	Y	Y	Y	Y	Y
7 Gibbons	Y	Y	N	N	Y	Y	N	Y
8 ***Young***	Y	Y	N	N	N	N	Y	Y
9 ***Bilirakis***	Y	Y	N	N	N	Y	Y	Y
10 ***Ireland***	Y	Y	N	N	N	N	Y	Y
11 Nelson	Y	Y	N	N	N	Y	Y	Y
12 ***Lewis***	Y	Y	N	N	N	Y	Y	N
13 ***Mack***	Y	Y	N	N	N	Y	Y	Y
14 Mica	Y	Y	N	Y	Y	Y	N	Y
15 ***Shaw***	Y	Y	N	N	N	Y	Y	Y
16 Smith	Y	Y	N	Y	Y	Y	N	?
17 Lehman	N	N	N	Y	Y	Y	N	N
18 Pepper	Y	N	N	Y	Y	Y	N	N
19 Fascell	N	N	N	Y	Y	Y	N	N
GEORGIA								
1 Thomas	Y	Y	N	Y	Y	Y	N	N
2 Hatcher	Y	N	N	Y	Y	Y	N	N
3 Ray	Y	Y	Y	N	N	N	Y	Y
4 ***Swindall***	Y	Y	Y	N	N	N	Y	Y
5 Fowler	Y	N	N	Y	Y	Y	N	N
6 ***Gingrich***	Y	Y	Y	N	N	N	Y	Y
7 Darden	Y	Y	N	N	N	Y	N	Y
8 Rowland	Y	Y	N	Y	N	Y	N	Y
9 Jenkins	Y	Y	N	Y	Y	Y	N	Y
10 Barnard	Y	Y	N	N	N	Y	Y	?
HAWAII								
1 Heftel	?	?	?	?	?	?	Y	Y
2 Akaka	Y	N	N	Y	Y	Y	N	N
IDAHO								
1 ***Craig***	Y	Y	Y	N	N	N	Y	Y
2 Stallings	Y	Y	N	N	Y	Y	N	Y
ILLINOIS								
1 Hayes	N	N	N	Y	Y	Y	N	N
2 Savage	N	N	N	Y	Y	Y	N	N
3 Russo	Y	N	Y	N	N	Y	N	N
4 ***O'Brien***	N	N	N	N	N	Y	Y	N
5 Lipinski	Y	Y	N	N	N	Y	N	N
6 ***Hyde***	Y	Y	N	N	N	Y	Y	Y
7 Collins	N	N	N	Y	Y	Y	N	N
8 Rostenkowski	Y	N	N	N	Y	Y	N	N
9 Yates	N	N	N	Y	Y	Y	N	N
10 ***Porter***	Y	Y	N	N	N	Y	N	N
11 Annunzio	Y	Y	N	N	Y	Y	N	N
12 ***Crane***	?	?	?	?	?	?	?	?
13 ***Fawell***	Y	Y	Y	Y	Y	Y	Y	Y
14 ***Grotberg***	Y	Y	Y	N	Y	N	Y	Y
15 ***Madigan***	Y	Y	Y	N	N	N	Y	N
16 ***Martin***	Y	Y	Y	Y	Y	N	Y	Y
17 Evans	N	N	N	Y	Y	Y	N	N
18 ***Michel***	Y	Y	Y	N	N	N	Y	Y
19 Bruce	N	N	N	N	Y	Y	N	N
20 Durbin	N	N	N	N	Y	Y	N	N
21 Price	Y	N	N	N	Y	Y	N	N
22 Gray	Y	Y	N	N	Y	Y	N	N
INDIANA								
1 Visclosky	N	Y	N	Y	Y	Y	N	N
2 Sharp	Y	Y	Y	N	Y	N	Y	Y
3 ***Hiler***	Y	Y	Y	N	N	N	Y	Y
4 ***Coats***	Y	Y	Y	N	N	N	Y	Y
5 ***Hillis***	Y	Y	N	N	N	N	Y	?

ND - Northern Democrats SD - Southern Democrats

* Corresponding to Congressional Record Votes 235, 236, 237, 238, 239, 240, 242, 243

	213	214	215	216	217	218	219	220
6 ***Burton***	Y	Y	N	N	N	N	Y	Y
7 ***Myers***	Y	Y	N	Y	Y	Y	N	N
8 McCloskey	Y	Y	N	N	Y	Y	N	N
9 Hamilton	N	Y	Y	Y	Y	Y	N	Y
10 Jacobs	Y	Y	Y	Y	Y	N	Y	Y
IOWA								
1 ***Leach***	N	Y	Y	N	N	N	Y	Y
2 ***Tauke***	Y	Y	Y	N	N	N	Y	Y
3 ***Evans***	Y	Y	Y	N	Y	N	Y	Y
4 Smith	N	N	N	Y	Y	Y	N	N
5 ***Lightfoot***	Y	Y	Y	N	N	N	Y	Y
6 Bedell	N	N	N	N	Y	Y	N	N
KANSAS								
1 ***Roberts***	Y	Y	Y	N	N	N	Y	N
2 Slattery	Y	Y	N	N	Y	N	Y	Y
3 ***Meyers***	Y	Y	Y	Y	Y	N	Y	Y
4 Glickman	Y	Y	N	Y	Y	Y	Y	Y
5 ***Whittaker***	Y	Y	Y	Y	N	N	Y	Y
KENTUCKY								
1 Hubbard	Y	Y	Y	N	N	N	Y	Y
2 Natcher	Y	N	N	N	Y	Y	N	N
3 Mazzoli	Y	Y	N	N	N	Y	N	N
4 ***Snyder***	Y	Y	Y	N	N	Y	Y	N
5 ***Rogers***	Y	N	N	N	N	Y	Y	Y
6 ***Hopkins***	Y	Y	Y	N	N	N	Y	Y
7 Perkins	Y	N	N	Y	Y	Y	N	N
LOUISIANA								
1 ***Livingston***	Y	Y	N	N	N	Y	Y	N
2 Boggs	N	N	N	N	N	Y	N	N
3 Tauzin	Y	Y	N	N	N	Y	?	?
4 Roemer	Y	Y	Y	N	N	N	Y	Y
5 Huckaby	Y	Y	Y	N	N	N	Y	Y
6 ***Moore***	Y	Y	Y	N	N	N	Y	Y
7 Breaux	Y	N	Y	N	N	Y	?	?
8 Long	N	N	N	N	N	Y	N	N
MAINE								
1 ***McKernan***	Y	Y	Y	Y	Y	Y	Y	Y
2 ***Snowe***	Y	Y	N	Y	Y	Y	Y	Y
MARYLAND								
1 Dyson	Y	Y	Y	N	N	Y	Y	N
2 ***Bentley***	Y	Y	Y	N	N	Y	Y	N
3 Mikulski	Y	N	N	Y	Y	Y	Y	N
4 ***Holt***	Y	Y	Y	N	N	N	Y	N
5 Hoyer	N	N	N	Y	Y	Y	N	N
6 Byron	Y	Y	N	Y	Y	Y	Y	Y
7 Mitchell	N	N	N	Y	Y	Y	N	N
8 Barnes	N	N	N	Y	Y	Y	N	N
MASSACHUSETTS								
1 ***Conte***	N	Y	N	N	Y	Y	N	Y
2 Boland	N	Y	N	N	Y	Y	N	N
3 Early	N	N	N	Y	Y	Y	N	Y
4 Frank	N	N	N	Y	Y	Y	N	N
5 Atkins	N	Y	N	Y	Y	Y	N	N
6 Mavroules	Y	N	N	N	Y	Y	N	N
7 Markey	N	N	N	Y	Y	Y	N	N
8 O'Neill								
9 Moakley	N	N	N	N	Y	Y	N	N
10 Studds	N	N	N	Y	Y	Y	N	N
11 Donnelly	N	N	N	N	Y	Y	N	N
MICHIGAN								
1 Conyers	?	N	N	Y	Y	Y	N	N
2 ***Pursell***	?	Y	N	N	Y	Y	Y	Y
3 Wolpe	N	N	N	Y	Y	Y	N	Y
4 ***Siljander***	?	?	?	?	?	?	?	?
5 ***Henry***	Y	Y	N	N	N	Y	Y	Y
6 Carr	Y	Y	N	Y	Y	Y	N	Y
7 Kildee	N	N	N	N	Y	Y	N	N
8 Traxler	Y	Y	N	?	Y	Y	N	Y
9 ***Vander Jagt***	Y	Y	Y	N	N	Y	Y	Y
10 ***Schuette***	Y	Y	N	N	N	Y	Y	Y
11 ***Davis***	Y	Y	Y	N	N	Y	N	N
12 Bonior	?	X	?	?	?	?	N	N
13 Crockett	?	N	?	?	?	?	N	N
14 Hertel	Y	Y	Y	N	Y	N	N	N
15 Ford	N	N	N	Y	Y	Y	N	N
16 Dingell	?	?	?	?	?	?	N	N
17 Levin	N	N	N	Y	Y	Y	N	N
18 ***Broomfield***	Y	Y	N	N	N	N	Y	N
MINNESOTA								
1 Penny	Y	Y	Y	N	Y	N	Y	N
2 ***Weber***	Y	Y	Y	N	N	N	Y	Y
3 ***Frenzel***	Y	Y	Y	Y	Y	N	Y	Y
4 Vento	N	N	N	N	Y	Y	N	N
5 Sabo	N	N	N	Y	Y	Y	N	N
6 Sikorski	Y	Y	N	N	Y	Y	N	N
7 ***Stangeland***	Y	Y	Y	N	N	N	Y	N
8 Oberstar	N	N	N	N	Y	Y	N	N
MISSISSIPPI								
1 Whitten	Y	N	?	?	?	?	N	N
2 ***Franklin***	Y	Y	Y	N	N	N	Y	N
3 Montgomery	Y	Y	Y	N	N	N	Y	Y
4 Dowdy	Y	Y	N	N	Y	Y	Y	N
5 ***Lott***	Y	Y	Y	N	N	N	Y	Y
MISSOURI								
1 Clay	N	N	N	Y	Y	Y	N	N
2 Young	Y	N	N	N	Y	Y	N	N
3 Gephardt	Y	N	N	N	Y	Y	N	N
4 Skelton	Y	Y	N	N	N	?	N	N
5 Wheat	N	N	N	Y	Y	Y	N	N
6 ***Coleman***	Y	Y	Y	N	N	Y	Y	Y
7 ***Taylor***	Y	Y	Y	N	N	N	Y	Y
8 ***Emerson***	Y	Y	N	N	N	Y	Y	N
9 Volkmer	Y	Y	Y	N	N	Y	Y	Y
MONTANA								
1 Williams	N	N	N	Y	Y	Y	N	N
2 ***Marlenee***	Y	N	N	N	N	N	Y	Y
NEBRASKA								
1 ***Bereuter***	Y	Y	Y	N	N	Y	Y	Y
2 ***Daub***	?	Y	Y	N	N	N	Y	Y
3 ***Smith***	Y	Y	Y	N	N	Y	Y	Y
NEVADA								
1 Reid	Y	N	N	N	N	Y	N	N
2 ***Vucanovich***	Y	Y	Y	N	N	N	Y	Y
NEW HAMPSHIRE								
1 ***Smith***	Y	Y	Y	N	N	N	Y	Y
2 ***Gregg***	Y	Y	Y	N	N	N	Y	Y
NEW JERSEY								
1 Florio	Y	N	N	Y	Y	Y	N	N
2 Hughes	Y	N	N	Y	Y	Y	N	Y
3 Howard	N	N	N	Y	Y	Y	N	N
4 ***Smith***	Y	Y	N	N	N	Y	N	Y
5 ***Roukema***	Y	Y	Y	Y	Y	N	Y	Y
6 Dwyer	N	N	N	Y	Y	Y	N	N
7 ***Rinaldo***	Y	Y	N	N	N	Y	N	Y
8 Roe	Y	N	N	N	Y	Y	N	N
9 Torricelli	Y	Y	N	Y	Y	Y	N	N
10 Rodino	N	N	N	Y	Y	Y	N	N
11 ***Gallo***	Y	Y	N	Y	N	Y	Y	Y
12 ***Courter***	Y	Y	N	N	N	N	Y	?
13 ***Saxton***	Y	Y	Y	N	N	Y	Y	Y
14 Guarini	Y	N	N	Y	Y	Y	N	N
NEW MEXICO								
1 ***Lujan***	Y	Y	Y	N	N	Y	Y	Y
2 ***Skeen***	Y	Y	N	N	N	Y	Y	Y
3 Richardson	Y	N	N	Y	Y	Y	N	N
NEW YORK								
1 ***Carney***	Y	Y	N	N	N	N	N	N
2 Downey	N	N	N	Y	Y	Y	N	N
3 Mrazek	Y	N	N	Y	Y	Y	N	N
4 ***Lent***	Y	Y	N	N	N	Y	Y	Y
5 ***McGrath***	Y	Y	Y	N	N	Y	?	?
6 Addabbo	Y	N	N	Y	Y	Y	N	N
7 Ackerman	N	N	N	Y	Y	Y	N	N
8 Scheuer	N	N	N	Y	Y	Y	N	Y
9 Manton	N	N	N	N	Y	Y	N	N
10 Schumer	N	N	N	Y	Y	Y	N	N
11 Towns	N	N	N	Y	Y	Y	N	N
12 Owens	N	N	N	Y	Y	Y	N	N
13 Solarz	N	N	N	Y	Y	Y	N	N
14 ***Molinari***	Y	Y	Y	N	N	N	Y	Y
15 ***Green***	Y	Y	N	Y	Y	Y	Y	N
16 Rangel	N	N	N	Y	Y	Y	N	N
17 Weiss	N	N	N	Y	Y	Y	N	N
18 Garcia	N	N	N	Y	?	?	X	X
19 Biaggi	Y	N	N	N	Y	Y	N	N
20 ***DioGuardi***	Y	Y	Y	N	N	N	Y	Y
21 ***Fish***	Y	Y	N	N	N	Y	Y	N
22 ***Gilman***	Y	Y	N	Y	Y	Y	Y	N
23 Stratton	Y	Y	?	N	N	Y	N	N
24 ***Solomon***	Y	Y	Y	N	N	N	Y	Y
25 ***Boehlert***	Y	Y	N	Y	Y	Y	Y	N
26 ***Martin***	Y	Y	N	N	N	Y	Y	Y
27 ***Wortley***	Y	N	Y	N	N	Y	Y	Y
28 McHugh	N	N	N	Y	Y	Y	N	N
29 ***Horton***	Y	Y	N	Y	Y	Y	N	N
30 ***Eckert***	Y	Y	?	?	?	?	Y	Y
31 ***Kemp***	Y	Y	?	N	N	N	Y	N
32 LaFalce	N	N	Y	N	Y	Y	Y	N
33 Nowak	N	N	N	N	Y	Y	N	N
34 Lundine	N	N	N	Y	?	?	N	N
NORTH CAROLINA								
1 Jones	Y	N	N	Y	Y	Y	N	N
2 Valentine	Y	N	N	Y	N	Y	N	Y
3 Whitley	Y	N	N	Y	Y	Y	N	N
4 ***Cobey***	Y	Y	Y	N	N	N	Y	Y
5 Neal	Y	Y	N	Y	Y	Y	N	N
6 ***Coble***	Y	Y	Y	N	N	N	Y	Y
7 Rose	Y	N	N	Y	Y	Y	N	N
8 Hefner	?	?	?	?	?	?	?	?
9 ***McMillan***	Y	Y	Y	N	N	N	Y	Y
10 ***Broyhill***	Y	Y	Y	N	N	N	Y	Y
11 ***Hendon***	Y	Y	Y	N	N	N	Y	Y
NORTH DAKOTA								
AL Dorgan	Y	Y	Y	N	Y	Y	N	N
OHIO								
1 Luken	Y	N	N	N	Y	N	N	Y
2 ***Gradison***	Y	Y	Y	N	N	N	Y	Y
3 Hall	N	Y	N	Y	Y	Y	N	N
4 ***Oxley***	Y	Y	Y	N	N	N	Y	Y
5 ***Latta***	Y	Y	Y	N	N	N	Y	Y
6 ***McEwen***	Y	Y	Y	N	N	N	Y	?
7 ***DeWine***	Y	Y	N	N	N	Y	Y	Y
8 ***Kindness***	Y	Y	Y	N	N	N	Y	Y
9 Kaptur	Y	Y	N	Y	Y	Y	N	N
10 ***Miller***	Y	Y	Y	N	N	N	Y	Y
11 Eckart	Y	N	N	Y	Y	Y	N	N
12 ***Kasich***	Y	Y	Y	N	N	N	Y	Y
13 Pease	N	N	N	Y	Y	Y	N	Y
14 Seiberling	N	N	N	Y	Y	Y	N	N
15 ***Wylie***	Y	Y	Y	N	N	N	Y	Y
16 ***Regula***	Y	N	N	N	N	Y	Y	N
17 Traficant	Y	N	N	Y	Y	Y	Y	N
18 Applegate	Y	N	Y	N	N	Y	Y	N
19 Feighan	N	Y	N	Y	Y	Y	N	N
20 Oakar	N	N	N	Y	Y	Y	N	N
21 Stokes	N	N	N	Y	Y	Y	N	N
OKLAHOMA								
1 Jones	Y	Y	Y	Y	Y	N	N	Y
2 Synar	N	Y	N	Y	Y	Y	N	N
3 Watkins	Y	N	N	Y	Y	Y	N	N
4 McCurdy	Y	Y	N	Y	Y	?	N	N
5 ***Edwards***	Y	Y	N	N	N	N	Y	Y
6 English	Y	Y	Y	N	N	N	Y	Y
OREGON								
1 AuCoin	N	Y	Y	Y	Y	N	N	N
2 ***Smith, R.***	Y	Y	Y	N	N	N	Y	Y
3 Wyden	Y	N	N	Y	Y	Y	N	N
4 Weaver	Y	Y	Y	Y	Y	N	N	N
5 ***Smith, D.***	Y	Y	Y	N	N	N	Y	Y
PENNSYLVANIA								
1 Foglietta	N	N	N	Y	Y	Y	N	N
2 Gray	N	?	?	Y	Y	?	?	?
3 Borski	Y	Y	N	N	Y	Y	N	N
4 Kolter	Y	N	N	N	Y	Y	N	N
5 ***Schulze***	Y	Y	Y	N	N	N	Y	Y
6 Yatron	Y	Y	N	N	N	Y	Y	N
7 Edgar	N	N	N	Y	Y	Y	N	N
8 Kostmayer	N	Y	N	Y	Y	Y	N	N
9 ***Shuster***	Y	Y	Y	N	N	N	Y	Y
10 ***McDade***	Y	Y	N	N	Y	Y	Y	Y
11 Kanjorski	Y	N	N	N	Y	N	Y	Y
12 Murtha	Y	N	N	N	Y	Y	N	N
13 ***Coughlin***	Y	Y	Y	N	N	N	Y	N
14 Coyne	N	N	N	Y	Y	Y	N	N
15 ***Ritter***	Y	Y	Y	N	N	N	Y	Y
16 ***Walker***	Y	Y	Y	N	N	N	Y	Y
17 ***Gekas***	Y	Y	Y	Y	Y	N	Y	Y
18 Walgren	Y	N	N	N	Y	Y	Y	N
19 ***Goodling***	Y	Y	Y	N	N	Y	Y	Y
20 Gaydos	Y	Y	N	N	Y	Y	N	N
21 ***Ridge***	Y	Y	N	N	N	N	Y	Y
22 Murphy	Y	N	Y	N	N	N	Y	N
23 ***Clinger***	Y	N	N	N	N	Y	N	Y
RHODE ISLAND								
1 St Germain	N	N	N	N	N	Y	N	N
2 ***Schneider***	?	#	?	?	?	#	#	#
SOUTH CAROLINA								
1 ***Hartnett***	Y	Y	Y	N	N	N	Y	?
2 ***Spence***	Y	Y	Y	N	N	N	Y	Y
3 Derrick	Y	Y	N	Y	Y	Y	N	N
4 ***Campbell***	Y	Y	Y	N	N	N	Y	Y
5 Spratt	Y	Y	N	Y	Y	Y	N	N
6 Tallon	Y	Y	N	N	N	Y	N	Y
SOUTH DAKOTA								
AL Daschle	Y	Y	N	Y	Y	Y	N	N
TENNESSEE								
1 ***Quillen***	Y	N	Y	?	N	N	Y	N
2 ***Duncan***	Y	N	N	N	N	Y	Y	N
3 Lloyd	Y	N	N	N	N	Y	Y	Y
4 Cooper	N	Y	Y	Y	Y	Y	N	N
5 Boner	Y	N	N	Y	Y	Y	N	N
6 Gordon	Y	Y	Y	Y	Y	Y	Y	N
7 ***Sundquist***	Y	Y	Y	N	N	N	Y	Y
8 Jones	Y	N	N	Y	Y	Y	N	N
9 Ford	N	N	N	Y	Y	Y	N	N
TEXAS								
1 Vacancy								
2 Wilson	Y	N	N	Y	Y	Y	N	N
3 ***Bartlett***	Y	Y	Y	N	N	N	Y	Y
4 Hall, R.	?	?	?	?	?	?	?	?
5 Bryant	N	N	N	Y	Y	Y	N	N
6 ***Barton***	Y	Y	Y	N	N	N	Y	Y
7 ***Archer***	Y	Y	Y	N	N	N	Y	Y
8 ***Fields***	Y	Y	Y	N	N	N	Y	Y
9 Brooks	Y	Y	N	Y	Y	Y	N	Y
10 Pickle	Y	N	Y	Y	Y	Y	N	Y
11 Leath	Y	Y	N	N	Y	Y	N	Y
12 Wright	N	?	N	Y	Y	Y	N	N
13 ***Boulter***	Y	Y	Y	N	N	N	Y	Y
14 ***Sweeney***	Y	Y	Y	N	N	N	Y	Y
15 de la Garza	N	N	N	Y	Y	Y	N	N
16 Coleman	Y	N	N	Y	Y	Y	N	N
17 Stenholm	Y	Y	Y	N	N	N	Y	Y
18 Leland	N	N	N	Y	Y	Y	N	N
19 ***Combest***	Y	Y	Y	N	N	N	Y	Y
20 Gonzalez	N	N	N	Y	Y	Y	N	N
21 ***Loeffler***	Y	Y	Y	N	N	Y	Y	?
22 ***DeLay***	Y	Y	Y	N	N	N	Y	Y
23 Bustamante	Y	N	N	Y	Y	Y	N	N
24 Frost	N	N	N	Y	Y	Y	N	Y
25 Andrews	Y	N	Y	Y	Y	Y	N	Y
26 ***Armey***	Y	Y	Y	N	N	N	Y	Y
27 Ortiz	Y	N	N	Y	Y	Y	N	N
UTAH								
1 ***Hansen***	Y	Y	Y	N	N	N	Y	Y
2 ***Monson***	Y	Y	Y	N	N	N	Y	Y
3 ***Nielson***	Y	Y	Y	N	N	N	Y	Y
VERMONT								
AL ***Jeffords***	Y	Y	Y	N	Y	N	Y	N
VIRGINIA								
1 ***Bateman***	Y	Y	N	N	N	Y	Y	Y
2 ***Whitehurst***	Y	Y	N	N	N	Y	Y	Y
3 ***Bliley***	Y	Y	Y	N	N	N	Y	Y
4 Sisisky	Y	Y	N	Y	Y	Y	N	Y
5 Daniel	Y	Y	Y	N	N	N	Y	N
6 Olin	Y	Y	N	Y	Y	Y	N	Y
7 ***Slaughter***	Y	Y	Y	N	N	N	Y	Y
8 ***Parris***	Y	Y	Y	N	N	N	Y	Y
9 Boucher	Y	Y	N	Y	Y	Y	?	?
10 ***Wolf***	Y	Y	N	N	N	Y	Y	Y
WASHINGTON								
1 ***Miller***	Y	Y	Y	N	N	N	Y	Y
2 Swift	N	N	N	Y	?	Y	N	N
3 Bonker	N	Y	N	N	Y	Y	N	N
4 ***Morrison***	Y	Y	N	Y	Y	Y	Y	Y
5 Foley	Y	N	N	Y	Y	Y	N	N
6 Dicks	Y	N	N	Y	?	?	N	N
7 Lowry	N	?	N	Y	Y	Y	N	N
8 ***Chandler***	Y	Y	Y	Y	Y	Y	Y	Y
WEST VIRGINIA								
1 Mollohan	Y	N	N	N	N	Y	N	N
2 Staggers	Y	Y	N	Y	Y	Y	N	Y
3 Wise	N	N	N	Y	Y	Y	Y	N
4 Rahall	Y	N	N	Y	Y	Y	N	N
WISCONSIN								
1 Aspin	N	Y	N	N	Y	Y	N	Y
2 Kastenmeier	N	N	N	Y	Y	Y	N	N
3 ***Gunderson***	Y	Y	Y	N	Y	N	Y	N
4 Kleczka	Y	N	N	N	Y	Y	N	N
5 Moody	N	Y	N	Y	Y	Y	N	N
6 ***Petri***	Y	Y	Y	N	N	N	Y	Y
7 Obey	N	?	N	Y	Y	Y	N	N
8 ***Roth***	Y	Y	Y	N	N	N	Y	Y
9 ***Sensenbrenner***	Y	Y	Y	N	N	N	Y	Y
WYOMING								
AL ***Cheney***	Y	?	Y	N	N	N	Y	Y

Southern states - Ala., Ark., Fla., Ga., Ky., La., Miss., N.C., Okla., S.C., Tenn., Texas, Va.

* The *Congressional Record* vote number is different from the CQ vote number because the *Record* includes quorum calls in its tally. CQ does not publish quorum call votes.

221. HR 2942. Legislative Branch Appropriations, Fiscal 1986. Wylie, R-Ohio, amendment to cut $103,000 from the Library of Congress' program for Braille reproductions of magazines for the blind. Adopted 216-193: R 142-29; D 74-164 (ND 27-138, SD 47-26), July 18, 1985. (Wylie said the amendment's aim was to eliminate funding for Braille editions of *Playboy* magazine.)

222. HR 2942. Legislative Branch Appropriations, Fiscal 1986. Cobey, R-N.C., amendment to cut all funding in the bill by 2.7 percent. Rejected 193-211: R 148-21; D 45-190 (ND 25-137, SD 20-53), July 18, 1985.

223. HR 2942. Legislative Branch Appropriations, Fiscal 1986. Passage of the bill to provide $1,294,470,000 in fiscal 1986 for operations of the House of Representatives and legislative branch agencies. Passed 263-136: R 55-112; D 208-24 (ND 145-14, SD 63-10), July 18, 1985.

224. HR 8. Clean Water Act Amendments. Stangeland, R-Minn., amendment to authorize the Environmental Protection Agency, in a five-year demonstration project, to allow up to 40 localities to operate their own programs for "pre-treatment" of industrial wastes, provided the programs achieve results at least as good as those required under national pre-treatment standards. Rejected 167-257: R 143-38; D 24-219 (ND 8-158, SD 16-61), July 23, 1985.

225. HR 8. Clean Water Act Amendments. Pursell, R-Mich., amendment to freeze fiscal 1986 spending under the bill, which would reauthorize and strengthen the Clean Water Act, at the fiscal 1985 appropriations level of $2,606,726,000, and to limit increases in fiscal 1987-90 appropriations levels to adjustments for inflation. Rejected 207-219: R 139-42; D 68-177 (ND 34-133, SD 34-44), July 23, 1985. A "yea" was a vote supporting the president's position.

226. HR 8. Clean Water Act Amendments. Passage of the bill to reauthorize and amend the Clean Water Act, authorizing $12,000,000,000 in federal grants over fiscal 1986-90 for construction of sewage treatment plants and another $9,000,000,000 in fiscal 1986-94 in revolving loan funds. Passed 340-83: R 99-80; D 241-3 (ND 165-0, SD 76-3), July 23, 1985. A "nay" was a vote supporting the president's position.

227. H Res 231. Special Budget Procedures. Adoption of the resolution to provide that the House-passed first budget resolution for fiscal 1986 (H Con Res 152, S Con Res 32) would be considered to be adopted by Congress for purposes of the 1974 Congressional Budget Act as it applied to the House. The resolution provided that it would no longer be in effect if Congress were to adopt a first budget resolution. The resolution also specified allocation of new budget and entitlement authority to each House committee, in conformance with the House-passed budget resolution. Adopted 242-184: R 1-178; D 241-6 (ND 165-3, SD 76-3), July 24, 1985. (The effect of the vote was to order House committees to change statutes under their jurisdiction to meet reconciliation requirements in the House-passed budget resolution, and to grant a blanket waiver of points of order to allow floor consideration of fiscal 1986 appropriations bills and authorization bills creating new spending authority.)

228. HR 3011. Interior Department Appropriations, Fiscal 1986. Adoption of the rule (H Res 227) to waive certain points of order against the bill to provide $8,261,119,000 in fiscal 1986 appropriations for programs in the Department of the Interior and related agencies. Rejected 179-251: R 39-142; D 140-109 (ND 88-81, SD 52-28), July 24, 1985. (The rule did not allow for an amendment to rescind $6 billion from the Synthetic Fuels Corporation (SFC). The effect of the vote was to demand an opportunity to vote on eliminating funding for the SFC.)

KEY

- Y Voted for (yea).
- # Paired for.
- \+ Announced for.
- N Voted against (nay).
- X Paired against.
- \- Announced against.
- P Voted "present."
- C Voted "present" to avoid possible conflict of interest.
- ? Did not vote or otherwise make a position known.

Democrats ***Republicans***

	221	222	223	224	225	226	227	228
ALABAMA								
1 ***Callahan***	Y	Y	N	Y	Y	Y	N	N
2 ***Dickinson***	Y	N	N	Y	Y	Y	N	N
3 Nichols	Y	Y	Y	Y	Y	Y	Y	Y
4 Bevill	Y	N	Y	N	N	Y	Y	Y
5 Flippo	Y	N	Y	N	N	Y	Y	N
6 Erdreich	Y	Y	N	N	Y	Y	Y	N
7 Shelby	Y	N	N	Y	Y	Y	Y	Y
ALASKA								
AL ***Young***	N	N	Y	Y	N	Y	N	Y
ARIZONA								
1 ***McCain***	N	Y	N	Y	Y	Y	N	N
2 Udall	N	N	Y	N	N	Y	Y	Y
3 ***Stump***	Y	Y	N	Y	Y	N	N	N
4 ***Rudd***	Y	N	Y	Y	Y	Y	N	Y
5 ***Kolbe***	N	Y	N	N	Y	N	N	N
ARKANSAS								
1 Alexander	N	N	Y	N	N	Y	Y	Y
2 Robinson	Y	Y	Y	N	N	Y	Y	Y
3 ***Hammerschmidt***	Y	Y	N	Y	N	Y	N	N
4 Anthony	N	N	Y	N	N	Y	Y	N
CALIFORNIA								
1 Bosco	N	?	?	N	N	Y	Y	N
2 ***Chappie***	Y	Y	N	Y	Y	Y	N	N
3 Matsui	N	N	Y	N	N	Y	Y	Y
4 Fazio	N	N	Y	N	N	Y	Y	Y
5 Burton	N	N	Y	N	N	Y	Y	Y
6 Boxer	N	?	?	N	N	Y	Y	N
7 Miller	N	?	?	N	N	Y	Y	N
8 Dellums	N	N	Y	N	N	Y	Y	N
9 Stark	N	N	Y	N	N	Y	Y	N
10 Edwards	N	N	Y	N	N	Y	Y	Y
11 Lantos	N	N	Y	?	X	?	Y	Y
12 ***Zschau***	N	Y	N	Y	Y	N	N	N
13 Mineta	N	N	Y	N	N	Y	Y	Y
14 ***Shumway***	Y	Y	N	Y	Y	N	N	N
15 Coelho	N	N	#	?	N	Y	Y	Y
16 Panetta	N	N	Y	N	N	Y	Y	N
17 ***Pashayan***	Y	Y	N	Y	N	Y	N	N
18 Lehman	N	N	?	N	N	Y	Y	Y
19 ***Lagomarsino***	Y	Y	N	Y	Y	N	N	N
20 ***Thomas***	N	Y	Y	Y	Y	Y	N	N
21 ***Fiedler***	Y	Y	N	Y	Y	Y	N	N
22 ***Moorhead***	Y	Y	N	Y	Y	Y	N	N
23 Beilenson	N	N	Y	N	N	Y	Y	Y
24 Waxman	N	N	Y	N	N	Y	Y	N
25 Roybal	N	N	Y	N	N	Y	Y	Y
26 Berman	N	N	?	N	N	Y	Y	N
27 Levine	N	N	Y	N	N	Y	Y	Y
28 Dixon	N	N	Y	N	N	Y	Y	Y
29 Hawkins	N	N	Y	N	N	Y	Y	Y
30 Martinez	N	N	Y	N	?	Y	Y	N
31 Dymally	N	N	Y	N	N	Y	Y	N
32 Anderson	N	N	Y	N	N	Y	Y	Y
33 ***Dreier***	Y	Y	N	Y	Y	N	N	N
34 Torres	N	N	Y	N	N	Y	Y	N
35 ***Lewis***	N	N	Y	Y	N	Y	N	N
36 Brown	N	N	Y	N	N	Y	Y	N
37 ***McCandless***	Y	#	X	Y	Y	Y	N	N
38 ***Dornan***	Y	Y	N	Y	Y	N	N	N
39 ***Dannemeyer***	Y	Y	N	Y	Y	N	N	Y
40 ***Badham***	Y	Y	N	Y	Y	Y	N	N
41 ***Lowery***	Y	N	Y	Y	N	Y	N	Y
42 ***Lungren***	Y	Y	X	Y	Y	N	N	N
43 ***Packard***	Y	Y	N	Y	N	Y	N	Y
44 Bates	N	Y	?	N	Y	Y	Y	N
45 ***Hunter***	Y	Y	N	Y	N	N	N	N
COLORADO								
1 Schroeder	Y	Y	N	N	N	Y	Y	N
2 Wirth	N	Y	N	N	N	Y	Y	Y
3 ***Strang***	Y	Y	N	Y	Y	N	N	Y
4 ***Brown***	Y	Y	N	Y	Y	N	N	Y
5 ***Kramer***	?	?	?	Y	Y	N	N	Y
6 ***Schaefer***	Y	Y	N	Y	N	Y	N	Y
CONNECTICUT								
1 Kennelly	Y	N	Y	N	N	Y	Y	N
2 Gejdenson	N	N	Y	N	N	Y	Y	N
3 Morrison	N	N	Y	N	Y	Y	Y	N
4 ***McKinney***	N	N	Y	N	Y	Y	N	Y
5 ***Rowland***	N	Y	N	Y	Y	Y	N	N
6 ***Johnson***	Y	Y	N	Y	N	Y	N	N
DELAWARE								
AL Carper	Y	Y	Y	N	Y	Y	Y	N
FLORIDA								
1 Hutto	Y	Y	Y	Y	Y	Y	Y	Y
2 Fuqua	?	?	?	N	N	Y	Y	Y
3 Bennett	Y	Y	Y	N	N	Y	Y	Y
4 Chappell	N	N	Y	Y	N	Y	Y	Y
5 ***McCollum***	Y	Y	N	Y	Y	Y	N	N
6 MacKay	Y	Y	N	N	Y	Y	Y	N
7 Gibbons	N	N	Y	N	Y	Y	Y	Y
8 ***Young***	Y	Y	?	Y	Y	Y	N	N
9 ***Bilirakis***	Y	Y	N	Y	Y	N	N	N
10 ***Ireland***	Y	Y	N	Y	Y	N	N	N
11 Nelson	Y	Y	N	N	N	Y	Y	Y
12 ***Lewis***	Y	Y	N	Y	Y	Y	N	N
13 ***Mack***	Y	Y	N	Y	Y	N	N	N
14 Mica	Y	N	Y	?	N	Y	Y	Y
15 ***Shaw***	Y	Y	N	N	Y	Y	N	N
16 Smith	N	N	Y	N	Y	Y	Y	N
17 Lehman	N	N	Y	N	N	Y	Y	Y
18 Pepper	N	N	Y	N	N	Y	Y	Y
19 Fascell	N	N	Y	N	N	Y	Y	Y
GEORGIA								
1 Thomas	N	N	Y	N	N	Y	Y	N
2 Hatcher	N	N	Y	?	Y	Y	Y	Y
3 Ray	Y	Y	N	Y	Y	Y	Y	N
4 ***Swindall***	Y	Y	N	Y	Y	N	N	N
5 Fowler	Y	N	Y	N	Y	Y	Y	N
6 ***Gingrich***	Y	Y	N	Y	Y	Y	N	N
7 Darden	Y	?	#	N	Y	Y	Y	N
8 Rowland	Y	N	Y	N	N	Y	Y	N
9 Jenkins	Y	N	Y	N	Y	Y	Y	Y
10 Barnard	?	?	#	N	Y	Y	Y	N
HAWAII								
1 Heftel	N	?	N	Y	Y	Y	Y	N
2 Akaka	N	N	Y	N	N	Y	Y	Y
IDAHO								
1 ***Craig***	Y	Y	X	Y	Y	N	N	N
2 Stallings	Y	Y	Y	Y	Y	Y	Y	N
ILLINOIS								
1 Hayes	N	N	Y	N	N	Y	Y	Y
2 Savage	N	N	Y	N	N	Y	Y	N
3 Russo	N	Y	Y	N	N	Y	Y	Y
4 ***O'Brien***	Y	N	Y	Y	Y	Y	N	Y
5 Lipinski	N	N	Y	N	N	Y	Y	Y
6 ***Hyde***	Y	Y	Y	Y	Y	Y	N	Y
7 Collins	N	N	Y	N	N	Y	Y	N
8 Rostenkowski	N	N	Y	N	N	Y	Y	Y
9 Yates	N	N	Y	N	N	Y	Y	Y
10 ***Porter***	N	N	Y	Y	Y	Y	N	N
11 Annunzio	N	N	Y	N	N	Y	Y	Y
12 ***Crane***	?	#	X	N	Y	N	N	N
13 ***Fawell***	N	Y	Y	Y	Y	N	N	N
14 ***Grotberg***	Y	Y	N	Y	Y	N	N	Y
15 ***Madigan***	Y	Y	N	Y	N	Y	N	N
16 ***Martin***	N	Y	N	Y	Y	Y	N	N
17 Evans	N	N	Y	N	N	Y	Y	N
18 ***Michel***	Y	?	Y	Y	Y	N	X	Y
19 Bruce	N	N	Y	N	Y	Y	Y	Y
20 Durbin	N	N	Y	N	Y	Y	Y	Y
21 Price	N	N	Y	Y	N	Y	Y	Y
22 Gray	Y	N	Y	?	N	Y	Y	Y
INDIANA								
1 Visclosky	N	N	Y	N	N	Y	Y	Y
2 Sharp	N	Y	N	N	Y	Y	Y	N
3 ***Hiler***	Y	Y	N	Y	Y	N	N	N
4 ***Coats***	Y	Y	N	Y	Y	N	N	N
5 ***Hillis***	?	?	?	Y	Y	Y	N	N

ND - Northern Democrats SD - Southern Democrats

* Corresponding to Congressional Record Votes 245, 246, 247, 248, 249, 250, 251, 252

	221	222	223	224	225	226	227	228
6 ***Burton***	Y	Y	N	Y	Y	N	N	N
7 ***Myers***	N	N	Y	Y	Y	Y	N	Y
8 McCloskey	N	N	Y	N	N	Y	Y	N
9 Hamilton	Y	Y	Y	N	N	Y	Y	Y
10 Jacobs	N	Y	N	Y	Y	Y	Y	N
IOWA								
1 ***Leach***	N	Y	N	N	Y	N	N	N
2 ***Tauke***	Y	Y	N	N	Y	N	N	N
3 ***Evans***	N	Y	N	Y	Y	Y	N	N
4 Smith	N	N	Y	N	N	Y	Y	Y
5 ***Lightfoot***	Y	Y	N	Y	Y	Y	N	N
6 Bedell	N	N	Y	N	Y	Y	Y	N
KANSAS								
1 ***Roberts***	?	?	?	Y	Y	N	N	N
2 Slattery	Y	Y	N	N	Y	Y	Y	N
3 ***Meyers***	Y	Y	N	Y	Y	N	N	N
4 Glickman	N	Y	N	N	Y	?	Y	N
5 ***Whittaker***	Y	Y	N	Y	Y	N	N	N
KENTUCKY								
1 Hubbard	Y	Y	N	Y	?	?	Y	Y
2 Natcher	Y	N	Y	N	N	Y	Y	Y
3 Mazzoli	N	N	Y	N	Y	Y	N	N
4 ***Snyder***	Y	Y	Y	Y	N	Y	N	Y
5 ***Rogers***	Y	Y	Y	Y	N	Y	N	Y
6 ***Hopkins***	Y	Y	N	Y	Y	N	N	N
7 Perkins	N	N	Y	N	N	Y	Y	Y
LOUISIANA								
1 ***Livingston***	Y	N	Y	Y	Y	Y	N	N
2 Boggs	Y	N	Y	N	N	Y	Y	Y
3 Tauzin	?	?	?	N	Y	Y	Y	N
4 Roemer	Y	Y	N	N	Y	N	N	N
5 Huckaby	Y	Y	N	?	Y	Y	Y	N
6 ***Moore***	Y	Y	N	Y	Y	Y	N	N
7 Breaux	?	?	?	N	N	Y	N	N
8 Long	Y	N	Y	N	N	Y	Y	Y
MAINE								
1 ***McKernan***	Y	Y	N	N	Y	Y	N	Y
2 ***Snowe***	Y	Y	Y	N	Y	Y	N	Y
MARYLAND								
1 Dyson	N	N	Y	N	N	Y	Y	N
2 ***Bentley***	Y	Y	N	Y	N	Y	N	N
3 Mikulski	N	N	Y	N	N	Y	Y	N
4 ***Holt***	N	Y	N	N	Y	Y	N	N
5 Hoyer	N	N	Y	N	N	Y	Y	Y
6 Byron	Y	Y	Y	N	Y	Y	Y	Y
7 Mitchell	N	N	Y	N	N	Y	Y	N
8 Barnes	N	N	Y	N	N	Y	Y	N
MASSACHUSETTS								
1 ***Conte***	Y	N	Y	N	Y	Y	N	N
2 Boland	N	X	?	N	N	Y	Y	Y
3 Early	N	N	Y	N	N	Y	N	Y
4 Frank	N	N	Y	N	N	Y	Y	N
5 Atkins	N	N	Y	N	N	Y	Y	Y
6 Mavroules	N	N	Y	N	N	Y	Y	Y
7 Markey	N	N	Y	N	N	Y	Y	N
8 O'Neill								
9 Moakley	N	N	Y	N	N	Y	Y	Y
10 Studds	N	N	Y	N	N	Y	Y	N
11 Donnelly	N	N	Y	N	N	Y	Y	Y
MICHIGAN								
1 Conyers	N	N	Y	N	N	Y	N	N
2 ***Pursell***	Y	N	Y	N	Y	N	N	N
3 Wolpe	N	N	Y	N	N	Y	Y	N
4 ***Siljander***	?	?	?	Y	Y	N	N	N
5 ***Henry***	Y	Y	N	N	Y	N	N	N
6 Carr	Y	N	Y	N	Y	Y	Y	Y
7 Kildee	N	N	Y	N	N	Y	Y	Y
8 Traxler	N	N	Y	N	Y	Y	Y	Y
9 ***Vander Jagt***	Y	Y	Y	Y	Y	Y	N	N
10 ***Schuette***	Y	Y	N	Y	Y	N	N	N
11 ***Davis***	Y	Y	Y	N	N	Y	N	N
12 Bonior	N	N	Y	Y	N	?	Y	Y
13 Crockett	N	N	Y	N	N	Y	Y	N
14 Hertel	N	N	Y	N	Y	Y	Y	N
15 Ford	N	X	#	N	N	Y	#	N
16 Dingell	N	N	Y	N	Y	Y	Y	N
17 Levin	N	N	Y	N	Y	Y	Y	N
18 ***Broomfield***	Y	Y	N	N	Y	?	N	N
MINNESOTA								
1 Penny	Y	Y	N	N	Y	Y	Y	N
2 ***Weber***	Y	Y	N	N	Y	N	N	N
3 ***Frenzel***	Y	Y	N	Y	Y	N	N	N
4 Vento	N	N	Y	N	N	Y	Y	N
5 Sabo	N	N	Y	N	N	Y	Y	Y
6 Sikorski	N	N	Y	N	Y	Y	Y	N

	221	222	223	224	225	226	227	228
7 ***Stangeland***	Y	Y	Y	Y	N	Y	N	Y
8 Oberstar	N	N	Y	N	N	Y	Y	Y
MISSISSIPPI								
1 Whitten	Y	N	Y	N	N	Y	Y	Y
2 ***Franklin***	Y	Y	Y	Y	Y	N	N	N
3 Montgomery	Y	Y	Y	Y	N	Y	Y	Y
4 Dowdy	Y	N	Y	N	N	Y	Y	N
5 ***Lott***	?	?	?	Y	Y	N	N	N
MISSOURI								
1 Clay	N	N	Y	N	N	Y	Y	N
2 Young	N	N	Y	N	N	Y	Y	Y
3 Gephardt	N	N	Y	N	N	Y	Y	N
4 Skelton	Y	N	Y	N	N	Y	Y	Y
5 Wheat	N	N	Y	N	N	Y	Y	Y
6 ***Coleman***	Y	Y	Y	Y	Y	Y	N	N
7 ***Taylor***	Y	Y	Y	Y	N	Y	Y	N
8 ***Emerson***	Y	Y	N	Y	Y	Y	N	Y
9 Volkmer	Y	Y	N	N	Y	Y	Y	Y
MONTANA								
1 Williams	N	N	Y	Y	N	Y	Y	N
2 ***Marlenee***	N	Y	Y	Y	Y	N	N	N
NEBRASKA								
1 ***Bereuter***	Y	Y	Y	Y	Y	N	N	N
2 ***Daub***	Y	Y	N	Y	Y	N	N	N
3 ***Smith***	Y	Y	Y	Y	Y	N	N	N
NEVADA								
1 Reid	N	N	Y	N	N	Y	Y	Y
2 ***Vucanovich***	Y	Y	N	Y	Y	Y	N	N
NEW HAMPSHIRE								
1 ***Smith***	Y	Y	N	Y	Y	N	N	N
2 ***Gregg***	Y	Y	N	N	Y	N	N	N
NEW JERSEY								
1 Florio	Y	N	Y	N	N	Y	Y	N
2 Hughes	N	Y	Y	N	N	Y	Y	N
3 Howard	N	N	Y	N	N	Y	Y	Y
4 ***Smith***	Y	Y	Y	N	N	Y	N	N
5 ***Roukema***	Y	Y	N	N	N	Y	N	N
6 Dwyer	N	N	Y	N	N	Y	Y	Y
7 ***Rinaldo***	Y	Y	N	N	N	Y	N	N
8 Roe	N	N	Y	N	N	Y	Y	Y
9 Torricelli	N	N	Y	N	N	Y	Y	N
10 Rodino	N	N	Y	N	N	Y	Y	N
11 ***Gallo***	Y	Y	N	Y	N	Y	N	N
12 ***Courter***	?	?	?	Y	N	Y	N	N
13 ***Saxton***	Y	Y	N	N	N	Y	N	N
14 Guarini	N	N	Y	N	N	Y	Y	N
NEW MEXICO								
1 ***Lujan***	Y	Y	N	Y	Y	Y	?	Y
2 ***Skeen***	Y	N	Y	Y	Y	Y	N	Y
3 Richardson	N	N	Y	N	N	Y	Y	N
NEW YORK								
1 ***Carney***	N	N	Y	N	N	Y	N	N
2 Downey	N	N	Y	?	?	?	?	?
3 Mrazek	?	N	Y	N	Y	Y	Y	N
4 ***Lent***	Y	Y	Y	N	N	Y	N	N
5 ***McGrath***	?	?	?	N	N	Y	N	N
6 Addabbo	N	N	Y	N	N	Y	Y	Y
7 Ackerman	N	N	Y	N	N	Y	Y	N
8 Scheuer	N	N	Y	N	N	Y	Y	Y
9 Manton	N	N	Y	N	N	Y	Y	Y
10 Schumer	N	N	Y	N	Y	Y	Y	N
11 Towns	N	N	Y	N	N	Y	Y	N
12 Owens	N	N	Y	N	N	Y	Y	Y
13 Solarz	N	N	Y	N	N	Y	Y	N
14 ***Molinari***	N	Y	Y	Y	N	Y	N	N
15 ***Green***	N	N	Y	N	N	Y	N	N
16 Rangel	N	N	Y	N	N	Y	Y	Y
17 Weiss	N	N	Y	N	N	Y	Y	N
18 Garcia	?	X	?	N	N	Y	Y	Y
19 Biaggi	N	N	Y	N	Y	Y	Y	N
20 ***DioGuardi***	Y	Y	N	Y	Y	Y	N	N
21 ***Fish***	N	N	Y	N	Y	Y	N	N
22 ***Gilman***	N	Y	N	N	N	Y	N	Y
23 Stratton	N	N	Y	Y	N	Y	Y	Y
24 ***Solomon***	Y	Y	N	Y	N	Y	N	N
25 ***Boehlert***	Y	Y	Y	N	N	Y	N	N
26 ***Martin***	Y	Y	N	Y	Y	Y	N	N
27 ***Wortley***	Y	Y	Y	Y	Y	Y	N	N
28 McHugh	N	N	Y	N	N	Y	Y	N
29 ***Horton***	N	N	Y	N	N	Y	N	Y
30 ***Eckert***	N	Y	N	Y	Y	N	N	N
31 ***Kemp***	Y	Y	N	Y	Y	Y	N	N
32 LaFalce	?	?	?	N	Y	Y	Y	Y
33 Nowak	N	N	Y	N	N	Y	Y	Y
34 Lundine	N	Y	Y	N	N	Y	Y	Y

	221	222	223	224	225	226	227	228
NORTH CAROLINA								
1 Jones	N	N	Y	N	N	Y	Y	Y
2 Valentine	Y	Y	Y	N	N	Y	Y	Y
3 Whitley	Y	Y	Y	N	Y	Y	Y	Y
4 ***Cobey***	Y	Y	N	Y	Y	N	N	N
5 Neal	N	N	Y	N	Y	Y	Y	N
6 ***Coble***	Y	Y	N	Y	Y	N	N	N
7 Rose	Y	N	Y	N	N	Y	Y	Y
8 Hefner	?	?	?	?	?	?	?	?
9 ***McMillan***	Y	Y	N	Y	Y	N	N	N
10 ***Broyhill***	Y	Y	N	Y	Y	N	N	N
11 ***Hendon***	Y	Y	N	Y	Y	N	N	Y
NORTH DAKOTA								
AL Dorgan	Y	N	Y	N	Y	Y	Y	Y
OHIO								
1 Luken	Y	Y	N	N	N	Y	Y	N
2 ***Gradison***	Y	Y	N	Y	Y	Y	N	N
3 Hall	Y	N	Y	N	Y	Y	Y	Y
4 ***Oxley***	Y	Y	N	Y	Y	N	N	N
5 ***Latta***	Y	Y	N	Y	Y	N	N	N
6 ***McEwen***	Y	Y	N	Y	N	Y	N	N
7 ***DeWine***	N	Y	N	N	Y	N	N	N
8 ***Kindness***	Y	Y	N	Y	Y	N	N	N
9 Kaptur	Y	N	Y	N	Y	Y	Y	N
10 ***Miller***	Y	Y	N	Y	Y	Y	N	Y
11 Eckart	Y	Y	Y	N	N	Y	Y	N
12 ***Kasich***	Y	Y	N	Y	Y	N	N	N
13 Pease	N	N	Y	N	N	Y	Y	Y
14 Seiberling	N	N	Y	N	N	Y	Y	Y
15 ***Wylie***	Y	Y	Y	Y	Y	N	N	Y
16 ***Regula***	Y	Y	Y	N	Y	Y	N	Y
17 Traficant	Y	Y	Y	N	N	Y	Y	Y
18 Applegate	Y	Y	Y	N	N	Y	N	Y
19 Feighan	N	N	Y	N	Y	Y	Y	N
20 Oakar	N	N	Y	N	N	Y	Y	Y
21 Stokes	N	N	Y	N	N	Y	Y	Y
OKLAHOMA								
1 Jones	Y	N	Y	N	Y	Y	Y	N
2 Synar	N	N	Y	N	N	Y	Y	N
3 Watkins	Y	N	Y	N	N	Y	Y	Y
4 McCurdy	Y	N	Y	N	Y	Y	Y	N
5 ***Edwards***	Y	N	Y	Y	Y	N	N	N
6 English	Y	Y	Y	Y	Y	Y	Y	N
OREGON								
1 AuCoin	N	N	N	N	Y	Y	Y	N
2 ***Smith, R.***	Y	Y	N	Y	Y	N	N	N
3 Wyden	Y	N	Y	N	Y	Y	Y	N
4 Weaver	N	N	Y	N	Y	Y	Y	N
5 ***Smith, D.***	Y	Y	N	Y	Y	N	N	N
PENNSYLVANIA								
1 Foglietta	N	N	Y	N	N	Y	Y	N
2 Gray	N	N	Y	N	N	Y	Y	Y
3 Borski	N	N	Y	N	N	Y	Y	Y
4 Kolter	Y	Y	Y	N	N	Y	Y	Y
5 ***Schulze***	Y	Y	Y	Y	Y	Y	N	Y
6 Yatron	Y	Y	Y	N	N	Y	Y	Y
7 Edgar	N	N	Y	N	N	Y	Y	N
8 Kostmayer	N	N	Y	N	N	Y	Y	N
9 ***Shuster***	Y	Y	N	Y	N	Y	N	Y
10 ***McDade***	Y	N	Y	N	Y	Y	N	Y
11 Kanjorski	Y	Y	N	N	N	Y	Y	Y
12 Murtha	N	N	Y	N	N	?	Y	Y
13 ***Coughlin***	Y	Y	Y	N	N	Y	N	N
14 Coyne	N	N	Y	N	N	Y	Y	Y
15 ***Ritter***	Y	Y	N	Y	Y	N	N	N
16 ***Walker***	Y	Y	N	Y	Y	N	N	N
17 ***Gekas***	Y	Y	N	Y	N	Y	N	Y
18 Walgren	N	N	Y	N	Y	Y	Y	Y
19 ***Goodling***	Y	Y	N	Y	Y	N	N	Y
20 Gaydos	N	N	Y	N	N	Y	Y	Y
21 ***Ridge***	Y	Y	Y	N	Y	Y	N	N
22 Murphy	Y	Y	Y	N	N	Y	Y	Y
23 ***Clinger***	Y	Y	Y	Y	N	Y	N	Y
RHODE ISLAND								
1 St Germain	N	N	Y	N	N	Y	Y	N
2 ***Schneider***	?	#	#	?	#	?	N	N
SOUTH CAROLINA								
1 ***Hartnett***	?	?	X	Y	Y	N	N	N
2 ***Spence***	Y	Y	N	Y	Y	Y	N	N
3 Derrick	Y	N	Y	N	N	Y	Y	Y
4 ***Campbell***	Y	Y	Y	Y	Y	Y	N	N
5 Spratt	Y	N	Y	N	Y	Y	Y	N
6 Tallon	Y	Y	Y	N	Y	Y	Y	N
SOUTH DAKOTA								
AL Daschle	Y	N	Y	N	N	Y	Y	N

	221	222	223	224	225	226	227	228
TENNESSEE								
1 ***Quillen***	N	N	Y	Y	N	Y	N	Y
2 ***Duncan***	Y	Y	Y	Y	Y	Y	N	Y
3 Lloyd	Y	N	Y	Y	N	Y	Y	Y
4 Cooper	N	N	Y	N	Y	Y	Y	N
5 Boner	Y	N	Y	N	Y	Y	Y	Y
6 Gordon	Y	N	Y	N	Y	Y	Y	Y
7 ***Sundquist***	Y	Y	N	Y	N	Y	N	N
8 Jones	Y	N	Y	N	N	Y	Y	N
9 Ford	N	N	Y	N	N	Y	Y	Y
TEXAS								
1 Vacancy								
2 Wilson	N	N	Y	N	N	Y	Y	Y
3 ***Bartlett***	Y	Y	N	Y	Y	N	N	N
4 Hall, R.	?	?	?	Y	N	Y	Y	Y
5 Bryant	N	N	Y	N	Y	Y	Y	Y
6 ***Barton***	Y	Y	N	Y	Y	N	N	N
7 ***Archer***	Y	Y	N	Y	Y	N	N	N
8 ***Fields***	Y	Y	N	Y	N	Y	N	N
9 Brooks	N	N	Y	N	N	Y	Y	Y
10 Pickle	N	N	Y	N	Y	Y	Y	Y
11 Leath	Y	Y	Y	Y	Y	Y	Y	Y
12 Wright	?	N	Y	N	?	Y	#	Y
13 ***Boulter***	Y	Y	N	Y	Y	N	N	N
14 ***Sweeney***	Y	Y	N	Y	Y	N	N	N
15 de la Garza	N	N	Y	Y	N	Y	Y	Y
16 Coleman	Y	N	Y	N	N	Y	Y	Y
17 Stenholm	Y	Y	N	Y	Y	N	Y	Y
18 Leland	N	N	Y	N	N	Y	Y	Y
19 ***Combest***	Y	Y	N	Y	Y	N	N	N
20 Gonzalez	N	N	Y	N	N	Y	Y	Y
21 ***Loeffler***	?	?	?	Y	Y	N	N	N
22 ***DeLay***	Y	Y	N	Y	Y	N	N	N
23 Bustamante	N	N	Y	N	N	Y	Y	Y
24 Frost	N	N	Y	N	Y	Y	Y	Y
25 Andrews	Y	N	Y	N	Y	Y	Y	Y
26 ***Armey***	Y	Y	N	Y	Y	N	N	N
27 Ortiz	Y	N	Y	N	N	Y	Y	Y
UTAH								
1 ***Hansen***	Y	Y	N	Y	Y	N	N	N
2 ***Monson***	Y	Y	N	Y	Y	?	X	?
3 ***Nielson***	N	Y	N	Y	Y	N	N	Y
VERMONT								
AL ***Jeffords***	N	Y	Y	N	Y	Y	N	N
VIRGINIA								
1 ***Bateman***	Y	Y	Y	Y	N	Y	N	Y
2 ***Whitehurst***	Y	Y	Y	Y	Y	Y	N	N
3 ***Bliley***	Y	Y	Y	Y	Y	Y	N	N
4 Sisisky	Y	N	Y	N	Y	Y	Y	N
5 Daniel	Y	Y	Y	Y	N	Y	Y	Y
6 Olin	Y	Y	N	N	Y	N	Y	N
7 ***Slaughter***	Y	Y	Y	Y	Y	Y	N	N
8 ***Parris***	Y	N	Y	Y	Y	Y	N	N
9 Boucher	?	?	?	N	N	Y	Y	Y
10 ***Wolf***	Y	Y	Y	Y	Y	Y	N	N
WASHINGTON								
1 ***Miller***	N	Y	N	N	Y	N	N	N
2 Swift	N	N	Y	N	N	Y	Y	N
3 Bonker	Y	N	N	N	N	Y	Y	N
4 ***Morrison***	Y	Y	N	Y	Y	N	N	N
5 Foley	N	N	Y	N	N	Y	Y	Y
6 Dicks	N	N	Y	N	N	Y	Y	Y
7 Lowry	N	N	Y	N	N	Y	Y	N
8 ***Chandler***	N	Y	N	N	Y	N	N	N
WEST VIRGINIA								
1 Mollohan	N	N	Y	Y	N	Y	Y	Y
2 Staggers	N	N	Y	N	Y	Y	Y	Y
3 Wise	N	Y	N	N	N	Y	Y	Y
4 Rahall	N	N	Y	N	N	Y	Y	Y
WISCONSIN								
1 Aspin	?	N	Y	N	N	Y	Y	Y
2 Kastenmeier	N	N	Y	N	N	Y	Y	N
3 ***Gunderson***	Y	Y	N	Y	Y	Y	N	N
4 Kleczka	N	N	Y	N	N	Y	Y	N
5 Moody	P	N	Y	N	N	Y	Y	Y
6 ***Petri***	Y	Y	N	N	N	Y	N	N
7 Obey	N	N	Y	N	N	Y	Y	N
8 ***Roth***	Y	Y	N	Y	Y	Y	N	N
9 ***Sensenbrenner***	Y	Y	N	N	Y	N	N	N
WYOMING								
AL ***Cheney***	Y	Y	N	Y	Y	N	N	N

Southern states - Ala., Ark., Fla., Ga., Ky., La., Miss., N.C., Okla., S.C., Tenn., Texas, Va.

* The *Congressional Record* vote number is different from the CQ vote number because the *Record* includes quorum calls in its tally. CQ does not publish quorum call votes.

229. HR 3038. Housing and Urban Development Department/Independent Agencies Appropriations, Fiscal 1986. Adoption of the rule (H Res 233) to waive certain points of order against the bill to provide $57,807,513,781 in fiscal 1986 appropriations for programs of the Department of Housing and Urban Development, Veterans Administration, Environmental Protection Agency and other independent agencies. Adopted 266-159: R 32-148; D 234-11 (ND 164-3, SD 70-8), July 24, 1985.

230. HR 3037. Agriculture Appropriations, Fiscal 1986. Passage of the bill to provide $36,398,686,000 in fiscal 1986 appropriations for programs in the Department of Agriculture and related agencies. Passed 354-71: R 117-62; D 237-9 (ND 158-8, SD 79-1), July 24, 1985. (The president had requested $36,397,457,000 in new obligational authority.)

231. HR 10. National Development Investment Act. Adoption of the rule (H Res 223) to waive certain points of order against and to provide for House floor consideration of the bill to authorize $530 million annually in fiscal 1986-88 for activities of the Economic Development Administration; $723 million for fiscal 1986-90 for non-highway programs of the Appalachian Regional Commission; and $2 billion for fiscal 1986-92 for highway programs of the Appalachian Regional Commission. Adopted 406-12: R 163-12; D 243-0 (ND 164-0, SD 79-0), July 24, 1985.

KEY

- Y Voted for (yea).
- # Paired for.
- + Announced for.
- N Voted against (nay).
- X Paired against.
- - Announced against.
- P Voted "present."
- C Voted "present" to avoid possible conflict of interest.
- ? Did not vote or otherwise make a position known.

Democrats ***Republicans***

	229	230	231
ALABAMA			
1 ***Callahan***	N	Y	Y
2 ***Dickinson***	N	Y	Y
3 Nichols	Y	Y	Y
4 Bevill	Y	Y	Y
5 Flippo	Y	Y	Y
6 Erdreich	Y	Y	Y
7 Shelby	Y	Y	Y
ALASKA			
AL ***Young***	Y	Y	Y
ARIZONA			
1 ***McCain***	N	Y	Y
2 Udall	Y	Y	Y
3 ***Stump***	N	N	N
4 ***Rudd***	N	Y	Y
5 ***Kolbe***	N	Y	Y
ARKANSAS			
1 Alexander	Y	Y	Y
2 Robinson	Y	Y	Y
3 ***Hammerschmidt***	N	Y	Y
4 Anthony	Y	Y	Y
CALIFORNIA			
1 Bosco	Y	Y	Y
2 ***Chappie***	N	Y	Y
3 Matsui	Y	Y	Y
4 Fazio	Y	Y	Y
5 Burton	Y	Y	Y
6 Boxer	Y	Y	Y
7 Miller	Y	Y	Y
8 Dellums	Y	Y	Y
9 Stark	Y	Y	Y
10 Edwards	Y	Y	Y
11 Lantos	Y	Y	Y
12 ***Zschau***	N	N	Y
13 Mineta	Y	Y	Y
14 ***Shumway***	N	N	?
15 Coelho	Y	Y	Y
16 Panetta	Y	Y	Y
17 ***Pashayan***	N	Y	Y
18 Lehman	Y	Y	Y
19 ***Lagomarsino***	N	N	Y
20 ***Thomas***	N	Y	Y
21 ***Fiedler***	N	Y	Y
22 ***Moorhead***	N	N	Y
23 Beilenson	Y	Y	Y
24 Waxman	Y	Y	Y
25 Roybal	Y	Y	Y
26 Berman	Y	Y	Y
27 Levine	Y	Y	Y
28 Dixon	Y	Y	Y
29 Hawkins	?	Y	Y
30 Martinez	Y	Y	Y
31 Dymally	Y	Y	Y
32 Anderson	Y	N	Y
33 ***Dreier***	N	N	N
34 Torres	Y	Y	Y
35 ***Lewis***	N	Y	Y
36 Brown	Y	Y	Y
37 ***McCandless***	N	N	Y
38 ***Dornan***	N	N	Y
39 ***Dannemeyer***	N	N	Y
40 ***Badham***	N	N	?
41 ***Lowery***	Y	Y	Y
42 ***Lungren***	N	N	?
43 ***Packard***	N	N	Y
44 Bates	Y	N	Y
45 ***Hunter***	N	N	N
COLORADO			
1 Schroeder	Y	Y	Y
2 Wirth	Y	Y	Y
3 ***Strang***	N	Y	Y
4 ***Brown***	N	Y	Y
5 ***Kramer***	N	Y	Y
6 ***Schaefer***	N	Y	Y
CONNECTICUT			
1 Kennelly	Y	Y	Y
2 Gejdenson	Y	#	?
3 Morrison	Y	Y	Y
4 ***McKinney***	Y	Y	Y
5 ***Rowland***	N	N	Y
6 ***Johnson***	N	Y	Y
DELAWARE			
AL Carper	Y	Y	Y
FLORIDA			
1 Hutto	Y	Y	Y
2 Fuqua	Y	Y	Y
3 Bennett	Y	Y	Y
4 Chappell	Y	Y	Y
5 ***McCollum***	N	N	Y
6 MacKay	Y	Y	Y
7 Gibbons	Y	Y	Y
8 ***Young***	N	Y	Y
9 ***Bilirakis***	N	Y	Y
10 ***Ireland***	N	N	Y
11 Nelson	Y	N	Y
12 ***Lewis***	N	Y	Y
13 ***Mack***	N	N	Y
14 Mica	Y	Y	Y
15 ***Shaw***	N	N	Y
16 Smith	Y	Y	Y
17 Lehman	Y	Y	Y
18 Pepper	+	Y	Y
19 Fascell	Y	Y	Y
GEORGIA			
1 Thomas	Y	Y	Y
2 Hatcher	Y	Y	Y
3 Ray	Y	Y	Y
4 ***Swindall***	N	Y	Y
5 Fowler	Y	Y	Y
6 ***Gingrich***	N	Y	Y
7 Darden	Y	Y	Y
8 Rowland	Y	Y	Y
9 Jenkins	Y	Y	Y
10 Barnard	Y	Y	Y
HAWAII			
1 Heftel	N	Y	Y
2 Akaka	Y	Y	Y
IDAHO			
1 ***Craig***	N	Y	Y
2 Stallings	Y	Y	Y
ILLINOIS			
1 Hayes	Y	Y	Y
2 Savage	Y	Y	Y
3 Russo	Y	Y	Y
4 ***O'Brien***	Y	Y	Y
5 Lipinski	Y	Y	Y
6 ***Hyde***	Y	N	Y
7 Collins	Y	Y	Y
8 Rostenkowski	Y	Y	Y
9 Yates	Y	Y	Y
10 ***Porter***	N	Y	Y
11 Annunzio	Y	Y	Y
12 ***Crane***	N	N	Y
13 ***Fawell***	N	N	Y
14 ***Grotberg***	N	N	Y
15 ***Madigan***	N	Y	Y
16 ***Martin***	N	N	Y
17 Evans	Y	Y	Y
18 ***Michel***	N	N	Y
19 Bruce	Y	Y	Y
20 Durbin	Y	Y	Y
21 Price	Y	Y	Y
22 Gray	Y	Y	Y
INDIANA			
1 Visclosky	Y	Y	Y
2 Sharp	Y	Y	Y
3 ***Hiler***	N	N	Y
4 ***Coats***	N	Y	Y
5 ***Hillis***	Y	Y	Y

ND - Northern Democrats SD - Southern Democrats

* Corresponding to Congressional Record Votes 253, 254, 255

	229	230	231
6 ***Burton***	N	N	Y
7 ***Myers***	Y	Y	Y
8 McCloskey	Y	Y	Y
9 Hamilton	Y	Y	Y
10 Jacobs	Y	N	Y
IOWA			
1 ***Leach***	N	Y	Y
2 ***Tauke***	N	Y	Y
3 ***Evans***	N	Y	Y
4 Smith	Y	Y	Y
5 ***Lightfoot***	N	Y	Y
6 Bedell	Y	Y	Y
KANSAS			
1 ***Roberts***	N	Y	Y
2 Slattery	Y	Y	Y
3 ***Meyers***	N	Y	Y
4 Glickman	Y	Y	Y
5 ***Whittaker***	N	Y	Y
KENTUCKY			
1 Hubbard	N	Y	Y
2 Natcher	Y	Y	Y
3 Mazzoli	Y	Y	Y
4 ***Snyder***	Y	Y	Y
5 ***Rogers***	N	Y	Y
6 ***Hopkins***	N	Y	Y
7 Perkins	Y	Y	Y
LOUISIANA			
1 ***Livingston***	N	Y	Y
2 Boggs	Y	Y	Y
3 Tauzin	N	Y	Y
4 Roemer	N	Y	Y
5 Huckaby	N	Y	Y
6 ***Moore***	N	Y	Y
7 Breaux	Y	Y	Y
8 Long	Y	Y	Y
MAINE			
1 ***McKernan***	N	Y	Y
2 ***Snowe***	N	Y	Y
MARYLAND			
1 Dyson	Y	Y	Y
2 ***Bentley***	N	Y	Y
3 Mikulski	Y	Y	Y
4 ***Holt***	N	?	?
5 Hoyer	Y	Y	Y
6 Byron	Y	Y	Y
7 Mitchell	Y	Y	Y
8 Barnes	Y	Y	Y
MASSACHUSETTS			
1 ***Conte***	Y	Y	Y
2 Boland	Y	Y	?
3 Early	Y	Y	Y
4 Frank	Y	N	Y
5 Atkins	Y	Y	Y
6 Mavroules	Y	Y	Y
7 Markey	Y	Y	Y
8 O'Neill			
9 Moakley	Y	Y	Y
10 Studds	Y	?	?
11 Donnelly	Y	?	Y
MICHIGAN			
1 Conyers	Y	Y	Y
2 ***Pursell***	Y	N	Y
3 Wolpe	Y	Y	Y
4 ***Siljander***	N	Y	Y
5 ***Henry***	N	N	Y
6 Carr	Y	Y	Y
7 Kildee	Y	Y	Y
8 Traxler	Y	Y	Y
9 ***Vander Jagt***	N	Y	Y
10 ***Schuette***	N	Y	Y
11 ***Davis***	Y	Y	Y
12 Bonior	Y	Y	?
13 Crockett	Y	Y	Y
14 Hertel	Y	N	Y
15 Ford	Y	Y	Y
16 Dingell	Y	Y	Y
17 Levin	Y	Y	Y
18 ***Broomfield***	N	Y	Y
MINNESOTA			
1 Penny	N	Y	Y
2 ***Weber***	N	Y	N
3 ***Frenzel***	N	N	N
4 Vento	Y	Y	Y
5 Sabo	Y	Y	Y
6 Sikorski	Y	Y	Y

	229	230	231
7 ***Stangeland***	N	Y	Y
8 Oberstar	Y	Y	Y
MISSISSIPPI			
1 Whitten	Y	Y	Y
2 ***Franklin***	Y	Y	Y
3 Montgomery	Y	Y	?
4 Dowdy	Y	Y	Y
5 ***Lott***	N	Y	Y
MISSOURI			
1 Clay	Y	Y	Y
2 Young	Y	Y	Y
3 Gephardt	Y	Y	Y
4 Skelton	Y	Y	Y
5 Wheat	Y	Y	Y
6 ***Coleman***	N	Y	Y
7 ***Taylor***	N	Y	Y
8 ***Emerson***	N	Y	Y
9 Volkmer	Y	Y	Y
MONTANA			
1 Williams	?	Y	Y
2 ***Marlenee***	N	Y	Y
NEBRASKA			
1 ***Bereuter***	N	Y	Y
2 ***Daub***	N	Y	Y
3 ***Smith***	Y	Y	Y
NEVADA			
1 Reid	Y	Y	Y
2 ***Vucanovich***	N	N	N
NEW HAMPSHIRE			
1 ***Smith***	N	N	Y
2 ***Gregg***	N	N	Y
NEW JERSEY			
1 Florio	Y	Y	Y
2 Hughes	N	N	Y
3 Howard	Y	Y	Y
4 ***Smith***	Y	Y	Y
5 ***Roukema***	N	N	Y
6 Dwyer	Y	Y	Y
7 ***Rinaldo***	Y	Y	Y
8 Roe	Y	Y	Y
9 Torricelli	Y	Y	Y
10 Rodino	Y	Y	Y
11 ***Gallo***	N	N	Y
12 ***Courter***	N	N	Y
13 ***Saxton***	N	N	Y
14 Guarini	Y	Y	Y
NEW MEXICO			
1 ***Lujan***	Y	N	Y
2 ***Skeen***	Y	Y	Y
3 Richardson	Y	Y	Y
NEW YORK			
1 ***Carney***	N	N	?
2 Downey	?	?	?
3 Mrazek	Y	Y	Y
4 ***Lent***	N	N	Y
5 ***McGrath***	N	N	Y
6 Addabbo	Y	Y	Y
7 Ackerman	Y	Y	Y
8 Scheuer	Y	Y	Y
9 Manton	Y	Y	Y
10 Schumer	Y	Y	Y
11 Towns	Y	Y	Y
12 Owens	Y	Y	Y
13 Solarz	Y	Y	?
14 ***Molinari***	N	N	Y
15 ***Green***	Y	Y	Y
16 Rangel	Y	Y	Y
17 Weiss	Y	Y	Y
18 Garcia	Y	Y	Y
19 Biaggi	Y	Y	Y
20 ***DioGuardi***	N	Y	Y
21 ***Fish***	Y	Y	Y
22 ***Gilman***	Y	Y	Y
23 Stratton	Y	Y	Y
24 ***Solomon***	N	N	Y
25 ***Boehlert***	Y	Y	Y
26 ***Martin***	N	Y	Y
27 ***Wortley***	Y	Y	Y
28 McHugh	Y	Y	Y
29 ***Horton***	?	Y	Y
30 ***Eckert***	N	N	Y
31 ***Kemp***	N	Y	Y
32 LaFalce	Y	Y	Y
33 Nowak	Y	Y	Y
34 Lundine	Y	Y	Y

	229	230	231
NORTH CAROLINA			
1 Jones	Y	Y	Y
2 Valentine	Y	Y	Y
3 Whitley	Y	Y	Y
4 ***Cobey***	N	Y	N
5 Neal	Y	Y	Y
6 ***Coble***	N	Y	Y
7 Rose	Y	Y	Y
8 Hefner	?	?	?
9 ***McMillan***	N	Y	Y
10 ***Broyhill***	N	Y	Y
11 ***Hendon***	N	Y	Y
NORTH DAKOTA			
AL Dorgan	Y	Y	Y
OHIO			
1 Luken	Y	N	Y
2 ***Gradison***	Y	N	Y
3 Hall	Y	Y	Y
4 ***Oxley***	N	Y	Y
5 ***Latta***	N	Y	Y
6 ***McEwen***	N	Y	Y
7 ***DeWine***	N	N	N
8 ***Kindness***	N	Y	Y
9 Kaptur	Y	Y	Y
10 ***Miller***	Y	Y	?
11 Eckart	Y	Y	Y
12 ***Kasich***	N	Y	Y
13 Pease	Y	Y	Y
14 Seiberling	Y	Y	Y
15 ***Wylie***	Y	Y	Y
16 ***Regula***	Y	Y	Y
17 Traficant	Y	Y	Y
18 Applegate	Y	Y	Y
19 Feighan	Y	Y	Y
20 Oakar	Y	Y	Y
21 Stokes	Y	Y	Y
OKLAHOMA			
1 Jones	Y	Y	Y
2 Synar	Y	Y	Y
3 Watkins	Y	Y	Y
4 McCurdy	Y	Y	Y
5 ***Edwards***	N	Y	Y
6 English	Y	Y	Y
OREGON			
1 AuCoin	Y	Y	Y
2 ***Smith, R.***	N	Y	Y
3 Wyden	Y	N	Y
4 Weaver	Y	Y	Y
5 ***Smith, D.***	N	N	N
PENNSYLVANIA			
1 Foglietta	Y	Y	Y
2 Gray	Y	Y	Y
3 Borski	Y	Y	Y
4 Kolter	Y	Y	Y
5 ***Schulze***	N	N	Y
6 Yatron	Y	Y	Y
7 Edgar	Y	Y	Y
8 Kostmayer	Y	Y	Y
9 ***Shuster***	N	N	Y
10 ***McDade***	Y	Y	Y
11 Kanjorski	Y	Y	Y
12 Murtha	Y	Y	Y
13 ***Coughlin***	Y	N	Y
14 Coyne	Y	Y	Y
15 ***Ritter***	N	N	Y
16 ***Walker***	N	N	Y
17 ***Gekas***	N	?	Y
18 Walgren	Y	Y	Y
19 ***Goodling***	N	N	Y
20 Gaydos	Y	Y	Y
21 ***Ridge***	Y	Y	Y
22 Murphy	Y	Y	Y
23 ***Clinger***	N	Y	Y
RHODE ISLAND			
1 St Germain	Y	Y	Y
2 ***Schneider***	N	Y	Y
SOUTH CAROLINA			
1 ***Hartnett***	N	Y	Y
2 ***Spence***	N	Y	Y
3 Derrick	Y	Y	Y
4 ***Campbell***	N	Y	Y
5 Spratt	Y	Y	Y
6 Tallon	Y	Y	Y
SOUTH DAKOTA			
AL Daschle	Y	Y	Y

	229	230	231
TENNESSEE			
1 ***Quillen***	Y	Y	Y
2 ***Duncan***	Y	Y	Y
3 Lloyd	Y	Y	Y
4 Cooper	Y	Y	Y
5 Boner	Y	Y	Y
6 Gordon	Y	Y	Y
7 ***Sundquist***	N	Y	Y
8 Jones	Y	Y	Y
9 Ford	Y	Y	Y
TEXAS			
1 Vacancy			
2 Wilson	Y	Y	Y
3 ***Bartlett***	N	N	N
4 Hall, R.	N	Y	Y
5 Bryant	Y	Y	Y
6 ***Barton***	N	Y	N
7 ***Archer***	N	N	Y
8 ***Fields***	N	N	Y
9 Brooks	Y	Y	Y
10 Pickle	Y	Y	Y
11 Leath	N	Y	Y
12 Wright	?	Y	Y
13 ***Boulter***	N	Y	Y
14 ***Sweeney***	N	Y	Y
15 de la Garza	Y	Y	Y
16 Coleman	Y	Y	Y
17 Stenholm	N	Y	Y
18 Leland	Y	Y	Y
19 ***Combest***	N	Y	Y
20 Gonzalez	Y	Y	Y
21 ***Loeffler***	N	Y	Y
22 ***DeLay***	N	N	Y
23 Bustamante	Y	Y	Y
24 Frost	Y	Y	Y
25 Andrews	Y	Y	Y
26 ***Armey***	N	N	N
27 Ortiz	Y	Y	Y
UTAH			
1 ***Hansen***	N	N	Y
2 ***Monson***	?	X	?
3 ***Nielson***	N	N	Y
VERMONT			
AL ***Jeffords***	N	Y	Y
VIRGINIA			
1 ***Bateman***	Y	Y	Y
2 ***Whitehurst***	N	Y	Y
3 ***Bliley***	N	Y	Y
4 Sisisky	Y	Y	Y
5 Daniel	N	Y	Y
6 Olin	Y	Y	Y
7 ***Slaughter***	N	Y	Y
8 ***Parris***	N	Y	Y
9 Boucher	Y	Y	Y
10 ***Wolf***	N	Y	Y
WASHINGTON			
1 ***Miller***	N	N	Y
2 Swift	Y	Y	Y
3 Bonker	Y	Y	Y
4 ***Morrison***	N	Y	Y
5 Foley	Y	Y	Y
6 Dicks	Y	Y	Y
7 Lowry	Y	Y	Y
8 ***Chandler***	N	Y	Y
WEST VIRGINIA			
1 Mollohan	Y	Y	Y
2 Staggers	Y	Y	Y
3 Wise	Y	Y	Y
4 Rahall	Y	Y	Y
WISCONSIN			
1 Aspin	Y	Y	Y
2 Kastenmeier	Y	Y	Y
3 ***Gunderson***	N	Y	Y
4 Kleczka	Y	Y	Y
5 Moody	Y	Y	Y
6 ***Petri***	N	Y	Y
7 Obey	Y	Y	Y
8 ***Roth***	N	Y	Y
9 ***Sensenbrenner***	N	N	Y
WYOMING			
AL ***Cheney***	N	N	Y

Southern states - Ala., Ark., Fla., Ga., Ky., La., Miss., N.C., Okla., S.C., Tenn., Texas, Va.

* The *Congressional Record* vote number is different from the CQ vote number because the *Record* includes quorum calls in its tally. CQ does not publish quorum call votes.

232. HR 3038. Housing and Urban Development Department/Independent Agencies Appropriations, Fiscal 1986. Bartlett, R-Texas, amendment to eliminate the $500 million reserve included in the bill for new housing programs. Adopted 236-172: R 166-8; D 70-164 (ND 31-130, SD 39-34), July 25, 1985.

233. HR 3038. Housing and Urban Development Department/Independent Agencies Appropriations, Fiscal 1986. Bartlett, R-Texas, amendment to reduce the number of new units of public housing from 10,000 to 5,000, reducing the appropriation for new public housing from $1.98 billion to $990 million. Adopted 213-204: R 156-20; D 57-184 (ND 25-138, SD 32-46), July 25, 1985.

234. HR 3038. Housing and Urban Development Department/Independent Agencies Appropriations, Fiscal 1986. Bartlett, R-Texas, amendment to reduce the appropriation for assisted housing by 2.5 percent, or $231 million. Rejected 203-213: R 156-21; D 47-192 (ND 18-145, SD 29-47), July 25, 1985.

235. HR 3038. Housing and Urban Development Department/Independent Agencies Appropriations, Fiscal 1986. Henry, R-Mich., amendments to reduce the appropriation for the National Aeronautics and Space Administration from $7.67 billion to $7.51 billion, and for the National Science Foundation from $1.52 billion to $1.5 billion, the same levels as in fiscal 1985. Rejected en bloc 112-300: R 81-95; D 31-205 (ND 17-143, SD 14-62), July 25, 1985.

236. HR 3038. Housing and Urban Development Department/Independent Agencies Appropriations, Fiscal 1986. Passage of the bill to provide $56,317,513,781 in fiscal 1986 for the Department of Housing and Urban Development and several independent agencies. Passed 340-73: R 116-61; D 224-12 (ND 150-10, SD 74-2), July 25, 1985. (The president had requested $47,455,731,000 in new budget authority.)

237. H J Res 187. Compact of Free Association. Passage of the joint resolution to bestow limited autonomy on the Marshall Islands and the Federated States of Micronesia in the Pacific Ocean. The compact, estimated to cost the United States $2.39 billion over the next 15 years, gives the islands the status of sovereign nations freely associated with the United States for defense and economic support. Passed 360-12: R 149-11; D 211-1 (ND 143-1, SD 68-0), July 25, 1985.

238. Procedural Motion. Miller, D-Calif., motion to approve the House *Journal* of Thursday, July 25. Motion agreed to 266-101: R 65-93; D 201-8 (ND 135-6, SD 66-2), July 26, 1985.

239. HR 3036. Treasury, Postal Service and General Government Appropriations, Fiscal 1986. Adoption of the rule (H Res 236) to waive certain points of order against the bill to appropriate funds for the Treasury Department, Postal Service and other programs for fiscal 1986. Adopted 242-135: R 37-125; D 205-10 (ND 143-3, SD 62-7), July 26, 1985.

KEY

- Y Voted for (yea).
- # Paired for.
- + Announced for.
- N Voted against (nay).
- X Paired against.
- - Announced against.
- P Voted "present."
- C Voted "present" to avoid possible conflict of interest.
- ? Did not vote or otherwise make a position known.

Democrats ***Republicans***

	232	233	234	235	236	237	238	239
ALABAMA								
1 ***Callahan***	Y	Y	Y	N	Y	Y	Y	N
2 ***Dickinson***	Y	Y	Y	N	Y	Y	N	N
3 Nichols	?	Y	?	N	Y	Y	Y	Y
4 Bevill	N	N	N	N	Y	Y	Y	Y
5 Flippo	N	Y	Y	N	Y	Y	Y	Y
6 Erdreich	N	N	N	N	Y	Y	Y	Y
7 Shelby	N	N	Y	N	Y	Y	Y	N
ALASKA								
AL ***Young***	Y	N	N	N	Y	Y	N	Y
ARIZONA								
1 ***McCain***	Y	Y	Y	N	Y	Y	Y	N
2 Udall	N	N	N	N	Y	Y	Y	Y
3 ***Stump***	Y	Y	Y	Y	N	Y	N	N
4 ***Rudd***	#	?	#	?	?	?	?	?
5 ***Kolbe***	Y	Y	Y	Y	Y	Y	N	N
ARKANSAS								
1 Alexander	N	N	N	N	Y	Y	Y	Y
2 Robinson	Y	N	N	N	Y	Y	Y	Y
3 ***Hammerschmidt***	Y	Y	Y	N	Y	Y	Y	Y
4 Anthony	N	N	N	N	Y	Y	?	?
CALIFORNIA								
1 Bosco	Y	Y	N	?	?	?	?	?
2 ***Chappie***	#	?	#	?	?	?	?	?
3 Matsui	N	N	N	N	Y	?	Y	Y
4 Fazio	N	N	N	N	Y	Y	Y	Y
5 Burton	N	N	N	N	Y	Y	Y	Y
6 Boxer	N	N	N	?	?	?	?	?
7 Miller	N	N	N	N	Y	Y	Y	Y
8 Dellums	N	N	N	N	Y	Y	Y	Y
9 Stark	N	N	N	N	Y	Y	?	Y
10 Edwards	N	N	N	N	Y	Y	Y	Y
11 Lantos	N	N	N	N	Y	Y	Y	Y
12 ***Zschau***	Y	Y	Y	Y	N	Y	N	N
13 Mineta	N	N	N	N	Y	Y	Y	Y
14 ***Shumway***	Y	Y	Y	Y	N	Y	N	N
15 Coelho	N	N	N	N	Y	?	?	?
16 Panetta	N	N	N	N	Y	Y	Y	Y
17 ***Pashayan***	Y	Y	Y	-	Y	Y	Y	Y
18 Lehman	N	N	N	N	Y	Y	Y	Y
19 ***Lagomarsino***	Y	Y	Y	N	N	Y	N	N
20 ***Thomas***	Y	Y	Y	Y	N	?	?	?
21 ***Fiedler***	Y	Y	Y	N	Y	Y	N	N
22 ***Moorhead***	Y	Y	Y	N	N	Y	Y	N
23 Beilenson	N	N	N	N	Y	Y	Y	Y
24 Waxman	N	N	N	?	Y	Y	Y	?
25 Roybal	N	N	N	N	Y	Y	Y	Y
26 Berman	N	N	N	N	Y	?	?	?
27 Levine	N	N	N	N	Y	Y	Y	Y
28 Dixon	N	?	?	N	Y	?	?	?
29 Hawkins	X	N	N	N	Y	?	?	?
30 Martinez	N	N	N	N	Y	Y	Y	Y
31 Dymally	N	N	N	N	Y	Y	P	Y
32 Anderson	N	N	N	N	Y	Y	Y	Y
33 ***Dreier***	Y	Y	Y	Y	N	Y	N	N
34 Torres	N	N	N	N	Y	Y	Y	Y
35 ***Lewis***	Y	Y	N	N	Y	?	?	?
36 Brown	N	N	N	N	Y	?	Y	Y
37 ***McCandless***	Y	Y	Y	N	N	N	N	N
38 ***Dornan***	Y	Y	Y	N	N	Y	Y	?
39 ***Dannemeyer***	Y	Y	Y	Y	N	+	+	-
40 ***Badham***	Y	Y	Y	N	N	Y	N	N
41 ***Lowery***	Y	Y	N	N	Y	Y	N	Y
42 ***Lungren***	Y	Y	Y	N	N	Y	Y	N
43 ***Packard***	Y	Y	Y	N	Y	Y	Y	N
44 Bates	Y	N	N	N	Y	Y	Y	?
45 ***Hunter***	Y	Y	Y	N	N	Y	?	?
COLORADO								
1 Schroeder	N	N	N	N	Y	Y	N	Y
2 Wirth	N	N	N	N	Y	Y	?	?
3 ***Strang***	Y	Y	Y	Y	Y	Y	N	N
4 ***Brown***	Y	Y	Y	Y	N	N	N	N
5 ***Kramer***	Y	Y	Y	Y	Y	Y	?	?
6 ***Schaefer***	Y	?	Y	Y	N	Y	N	N
CONNECTICUT								
1 Kennelly	N	N	N	N	Y	Y	Y	?
2 Gejdenson	X	X	X	?	?	?	?	?
3 Morrison	N	N	N	N	Y	Y	Y	Y
4 ***McKinney***	N	N	N	N	Y	?	Y	N
5 ***Rowland***	Y	Y	Y	N	Y	?	Y	N
6 ***Johnson***	Y	N	Y	Y	Y	Y	Y	N
DELAWARE								
AL Carper	N	Y	Y	Y	Y	Y	Y	N
FLORIDA								
1 Hutto	Y	Y	Y	N	Y	Y	Y	Y
2 Fuqua	N	N	N	N	Y	Y	Y	Y
3 Bennett	N	N	Y	Y	Y	Y	Y	Y
4 Chappell	?	?	?	?	?	?	?	?
5 ***McCollum***	Y	Y	Y	N	N	Y	Y	N
6 MacKay	Y	Y	Y	Y	Y	Y	Y	Y
7 Gibbons	Y	Y	Y	N	Y	Y	Y	?
8 ***Young***	Y	Y	Y	N	Y	N	N	N
9 ***Bilirakis***	Y	Y	Y	N	Y	Y	N	N
10 ***Ireland***	Y	Y	Y	N	Y	Y	N	N
11 Nelson	N	N	N	N	Y	Y	Y	Y
12 ***Lewis***	Y	Y	Y	N	Y	Y	N	N
13 ***Mack***	Y	Y	Y	N	N	Y	N	N
14 Mica	N	N	N	N	Y	Y	Y	Y
15 ***Shaw***	Y	Y	Y	N	Y	Y	N	N
16 Smith	N	N	N	N	Y	Y	Y	Y
17 Lehman	X	N	N	N	Y	Y	Y	Y
18 Pepper	N	N	N	N	Y	Y	Y	Y
19 Fascell	N	N	N	N	Y	Y	Y	Y
GEORGIA								
1 Thomas	Y	Y	Y	N	Y	Y	Y	Y
2 Hatcher	N	N	N	?	?	?	?	?
3 Ray	Y	Y	Y	Y	Y	Y	Y	Y
4 ***Swindall***	Y	Y	Y	Y	Y	Y	N	N
5 Fowler	?	N	N	N	Y	Y	Y	?
6 ***Gingrich***	Y	Y	Y	N	Y	Y	N	N
7 Darden	Y	Y	Y	N	Y	Y	Y	Y
8 Rowland	Y	Y	Y	N	Y	Y	Y	Y
9 Jenkins	Y	Y	Y	N	Y	Y	Y	Y
10 Barnard	Y	Y	Y	N	Y	Y	Y	Y
HAWAII								
1 Heftel	Y	Y	Y	N	Y	Y	?	Y
2 Akaka	N	N	N	N	Y	Y	?	?
IDAHO								
1 ***Craig***	Y	Y	Y	Y	N	N	?	?
2 Stallings	Y	Y	Y	N	Y	Y	Y	Y
ILLINOIS								
1 Hayes	N	N	N	N	Y	Y	Y	Y
2 Savage	N	N	Y	N	Y	Y	Y	Y
3 Russo	Y	Y	Y	N	N	Y	Y	Y
4 ***O'Brien***	Y	N	Y	Y	Y	?	?	?
5 Lipinski	Y	Y	N	N	Y	Y	Y	Y
6 ***Hyde***	Y	Y	Y	Y	Y	Y	Y	N
7 Collins	N	N	N	N	Y	Y	Y	Y
8 Rostenkowski	N	N	N	N	Y	Y	?	?
9 Yates	N	N	N	N	Y	Y	Y	Y
10 ***Porter***	Y	Y	Y	N	Y	Y	N	N
11 Annunzio	Y	Y	N	N	Y	Y	Y	Y
12 ***Crane***	Y	Y	Y	Y	N	Y	N	N
13 ***Fawell***	Y	Y	Y	Y	Y	Y	Y	N
14 ***Grotberg***	Y	Y	Y	Y	Y	Y	Y	N
15 ***Madigan***	Y	Y	Y	N	Y	Y	N	N
16 ***Martin***	Y	Y	Y	N	N	Y	N	N
17 Evans	N	N	N	N	Y	Y	Y	Y
18 ***Michel***	Y	Y	Y	Y	Y	Y	Y	N
19 Bruce	N	N	N	N	Y	Y	Y	Y
20 Durbin	N	N	N	N	Y	Y	N	Y
21 Price	N	N	N	N	Y	Y	Y	Y
22 Gray	N	N	N	N	Y	?	?	?
INDIANA								
1 Visclosky	N	N	N	Y	Y	Y	Y	Y
2 Sharp	Y	Y	Y	Y	Y	Y	Y	Y
3 ***Hiler***	Y	Y	Y	Y	Y	Y	N	N
4 ***Coats***	Y	Y	Y	Y	Y	Y	Y	N
5 ***Hillis***	Y	Y	?	?	?	?	?	?

ND - Northern Democrats SD - Southern Democrats

* Corresponding to Congressional Record Votes 256, 257, 258, 259, 260, 261, 262, 263

	232	233	234	235	236	237	238	239
6 ***Burton***	Y	Y	Y	N	N	Y	N	N
7 ***Myers***	Y	N	Y	Y	Y	Y	Y	Y
8 McCloskey	N	N	N	N	Y	Y	Y	Y
9 Hamilton	Y	Y	Y	Y	Y	Y	Y	Y
10 Jacobs	Y	N	N	Y	N	?	N	N
IOWA								
1 ***Leach***	Y	Y	Y	Y	Y	Y	N	Y
2 ***Tauke***	Y	Y	Y	Y	N	Y	N	N
3 ***Evans***	Y	Y	Y	Y	N	Y	N	N
4 Smith	N	N	N	N	Y	Y	Y	Y
5 ***Lightfoot***	Y	Y	Y	Y	N	Y	Y	N
6 Bedell	N	Y	N	Y	?	?	?	?
KANSAS								
1 ***Roberts***	Y	Y	Y	Y	N	Y	N	N
2 Slattery	Y	Y	Y	Y	Y	Y	Y	Y
3 ***Meyers***	Y	Y	Y	Y	Y	Y	?	?
4 Glickman	Y	Y	Y	Y	Y	Y	Y	Y
5 ***Whittaker***	Y	Y	Y	Y	N	?	?	?
KENTUCKY								
1 Hubbard	Y	Y	Y	Y	N	Y	Y	N
2 Natcher	N	N	N	N	Y	Y	Y	Y
3 Mazzoli	Y	N	N	N	Y	Y	+	-
4 ***Snyder***	Y	Y	Y	N	Y	Y	Y	Y
5 ***Rogers***	Y	Y	Y	N	Y	Y	N	Y
6 ***Hopkins***	Y	Y	Y	Y	N	Y	Y	N
7 Perkins	N	N	N	N	Y	Y	Y	Y
LOUISIANA								
1 ***Livingston***	Y	Y	Y	Y	Y	Y	N	N
2 Boggs	N	N	N	N	Y	Y	Y	Y
3 Tauzin	Y	Y	Y	Y	Y	Y	Y	N
4 Roemer	Y	Y	Y	Y	Y	Y	?	N
5 Huckaby	Y	Y	Y	Y	Y	Y	?	?
6 ***Moore***	Y	Y	Y	Y	N	Y	Y	Y
7 Breaux	Y	Y	N	Y	Y	Y	Y	Y
8 Long	N	N	N	N	Y	Y	Y	Y
MAINE								
1 ***McKernan***	N	Y	Y	Y	Y	Y	N	N
2 ***Snowe***	Y	N	Y	Y	Y	Y	N	Y
MARYLAND								
1 Dyson	Y	Y	N	N	Y	Y	Y	Y
2 ***Bentley***	Y	Y	N	N	Y	+	N	Y
3 Mikulski	N	N	N	N	Y	Y	Y	Y
4 ***Holt***	Y	Y	Y	N	Y	Y	Y	N
5 Hoyer	N	N	N	N	Y	Y	Y	Y
6 Byron	Y	Y	N	N	Y	Y	Y	Y
7 Mitchell	N	N	X	?	?	?	N	Y
8 Barnes	N	N	N	N	Y	Y	Y	Y
MASSACHUSETTS								
1 ***Conte***	N	N	N	N	Y	Y	N	Y
2 Boland	N	N	N	N	Y	Y	Y	Y
3 Early	?	?	?	?	?	?	?	?
4 Frank	N	N	N	N	Y	Y	Y	Y
5 Atkins	N	N	N	N	Y	Y	Y	Y
6 Mavroules	N	N	N	N	Y	Y	Y	Y
7 Markey	N	N	N	N	Y	?	Y	Y
8 O'Neill								
9 Moakley	N	N	N	N	Y	Y	Y	Y
10 Studds	N	N	N	N	Y	Y	Y	Y
11 Donnelly	N	N	N	N	Y	N	Y	Y
MICHIGAN								
1 Conyers	N	?	N	N	N	Y	Y	Y
2 ***Pursell***	Y	Y	Y	Y	Y	?	Y	N
3 Wolpe	N	N	N	N	Y	Y	Y	Y
4 ***Siljander***	Y	Y	Y	N	Y	Y	?	N
5 ***Henry***	Y	Y	Y	Y	N	Y	N	N
6 Carr	Y	Y	Y	N	Y	Y	Y	Y
7 Kildee	N	N	N	N	Y	Y	Y	Y
8 Traxler	N	N	N	N	Y	Y	?	Y
9 ***Vander Jagt***	Y	Y	Y	Y	Y	Y	N	N
10 ***Schuette***	Y	Y	Y	Y	Y	Y	?	?
11 ***Davis***	Y	Y	N	N	Y	Y	Y	Y
12 Bonior	N	N	N	N	Y	Y	Y	Y
13 Crockett	N	N	N	N	Y	?	Y	Y
14 Hertel	N	N	N	Y	N	Y	Y	Y
15 Ford	N	N	N	N	Y	Y	P	Y
16 Dingell	N	N	N	N	Y	Y	?	Y
17 Levin	N	N	N	N	Y	Y	Y	Y
18 ***Broomfield***	Y	Y	Y	N	Y	Y	Y	N
MINNESOTA								
1 Penny	Y	Y	Y	Y	Y	Y	N	Y
2 ***Weber***	Y	Y	Y	N	N	?	N	N
3 ***Frenzel***	Y	Y	Y	Y	N	N	N	N
4 Vento	N	N	N	N	Y	Y	Y	Y
5 Sabo	N	N	N	N	Y	Y	Y	Y
6 Sikorski	N	N	N	N	Y	Y	N	Y
7 ***Stangeland***	Y	Y	Y	N	Y	Y	N	Y
8 Oberstar	N	N	N	Y	Y	Y	Y	Y
MISSISSIPPI								
1 Whitten	N	N	N	N	Y	?	Y	Y
2 ***Franklin***	#	N	N	N	Y	Y	Y	Y
3 Montgomery	Y	Y	Y	N	Y	Y	Y	Y
4 Dowdy	Y	N	N	N	Y	Y	Y	Y
5 ***Lott***	Y	Y	Y	N	N	Y	N	N
MISSOURI								
1 Clay	N	N	N	N	?	?	?	?
2 Young	N	N	N	N	Y	Y	Y	Y
3 Gephardt	N	N	N	N	Y	Y	Y	Y
4 Skelton	Y	N	N	N	Y	?	Y	Y
5 Wheat	N	N	N	N	Y	Y	Y	Y
6 ***Coleman***	Y	Y	Y	N	Y	?	N	N
7 ***Taylor***	Y	Y	Y	Y	Y	Y	N	Y
8 ***Emerson***	Y	Y	Y	N	Y	Y	N	Y
9 Volkmer	N	Y	N	N	Y	Y	Y	Y
MONTANA								
1 Williams	N	N	N	N	Y	Y	Y	?
2 ***Marlenee***	Y	Y	Y	N	N	N	N	Y
NEBRASKA								
1 ***Bereuter***	Y	Y	Y	Y	Y	Y	Y	N
2 ***Daub***	Y	Y	Y	Y	N	Y	N	N
3 ***Smith***	Y	Y	Y	Y	N	Y	Y	Y
NEVADA								
1 Reid	N	N	N	N	Y	Y	Y	Y
2 ***Vucanovich***	Y	Y	Y	N	N	Y	?	?
NEW HAMPSHIRE								
1 ***Smith***	Y	Y	Y	N	N	Y	N	N
2 ***Gregg***	Y	Y	Y	N	Y	Y	Y	N
NEW JERSEY								
1 Florio	N	N	N	N	Y	Y	Y	Y
2 Hughes	Y	Y	Y	Y	N	Y	Y	N
3 Howard	?	N	N	N	Y	Y	Y	Y
4 ***Smith***	N	N	N	N	Y	Y	Y	Y
5 ***Roukema***	Y	Y	N	Y	Y	Y	Y	N
6 Dwyer	N	N	N	N	Y	Y	Y	Y
7 ***Rinaldo***	Y	N	N	N	Y	Y	?	Y
8 Roe	N	N	N	N	Y	Y	?	Y
9 Torricelli	N	N	N	N	Y	Y	Y	Y
10 Rodino	X	N	N	N	Y	Y	Y	Y
11 ***Gallo***	Y	Y	Y	N	Y	Y	Y	N
12 ***Courter***	Y	Y	Y	N	Y	Y	Y	N
13 ***Saxton***	Y	Y	Y	N	Y	Y	Y	N
14 Guarini	N	N	N	N	Y	Y	Y	Y
NEW MEXICO								
1 ***Lujan***	Y	Y	Y	N	Y	Y	Y	Y
2 ***Skeen***	Y	Y	Y	N	Y	Y	N	Y
3 Richardson	N	N	N	N	Y	Y	Y	Y
NEW YORK								
1 ***Carney***	Y	#	Y	N	N	Y	?	?
2 Downey	?	?	?	?	?	?	Y	Y
3 Mrazek	N	N	N	N	Y	Y	Y	Y
4 ***Lent***	Y	Y	Y	N	Y	Y	Y	N
5 ***McGrath***	Y	Y	N	N	Y	Y	N	N
6 Addabbo	N	N	N	N	Y	Y	Y	Y
7 Ackerman	N	N	N	N	Y	Y	Y	Y
8 Scheuer	N	N	N	N	Y	Y	Y	Y
9 Manton	N	N	N	N	Y	Y	Y	Y
10 Schumer	N	N	N	N	Y	Y	Y	Y
11 Towns	N	N	N	N	Y	?	Y	Y
12 Owens	N	N	N	N	Y	Y	Y	Y
13 Solarz	N	N	N	N	Y	Y	Y	Y
14 ***Molinari***	Y	N	N	N	Y	Y	N	N
15 ***Green***	N	N	N	N	Y	Y	Y	Y
16 Rangel	N	N	N	N	Y	Y	Y	Y
17 Weiss	N	N	N	N	Y	Y	Y	Y
18 Garcia	N	N	N	N	?	Y	Y	Y
19 Biaggi	N	N	N	N	Y	?	Y	Y
20 ***DioGuardi***	Y	Y	Y	Y	Y	Y	Y	N
21 ***Fish***	Y	Y	Y	N	Y	Y	Y	N
22 ***Gilman***	-	N	N	N	Y	Y	Y	Y
23 Stratton	N	N	N	N	Y	Y	Y	Y
24 ***Solomon***	Y	Y	Y	Y	N	Y	N	N
25 ***Boehlert***	N	N	N	N	Y	Y	N	Y
26 ***Martin***	?	Y	Y	N	Y	Y	Y	N
27 ***Wortley***	?	Y	Y	N	Y	?	Y	Y
28 McHugh	N	N	N	N	Y	Y	Y	Y
29 ***Horton***	N	N	N	N	Y	?	Y	Y
30 ***Eckert***	Y	Y	Y	Y	N	Y	N	N
31 ***Kemp***	Y	Y	Y	N	Y	Y	?	N
32 LaFalce	N	N	N	N	Y	Y	Y	Y
33 Nowak	N	N	N	N	Y	Y	Y	Y
34 Lundine	N	N	N	N	Y	Y	Y	Y
NORTH CAROLINA								
1 Jones	?	?	?	?	?	?	?	?
2 Valentine	Y	N	N	N	Y	Y	Y	Y
3 Whitley	N	N	Y	N	Y	Y	Y	Y
4 ***Cobey***	Y	Y	Y	N	Y	Y	N	N
5 Neal	Y	N	Y	Y	Y	Y	Y	Y
6 ***Coble***	Y	Y	Y	Y	Y	Y	N	N
7 Rose	N	N	N	N	Y	Y	Y	Y
8 Hefner	?	?	?	?	?	?	?	?
9 ***McMillan***	Y	Y	Y	Y	Y	Y	N	N
10 ***Broyhill***	Y	Y	Y	Y	N	Y	Y	N
11 ***Hendon***	#	Y	Y	Y	N	Y	N	N
NORTH DAKOTA								
AL Dorgan	Y	Y	Y	Y	Y	Y	Y	Y
OHIO								
1 Luken	Y	Y	N	N	N	Y	Y	Y
2 ***Gradison***	Y	Y	Y	Y	Y	Y	Y	N
3 Hall	?	N	Y	N	Y	Y	Y	Y
4 ***Oxley***	Y	Y	Y	Y	N	Y	N	N
5 ***Latta***	Y	Y	Y	Y	N	Y	N	N
6 ***McEwen***	Y	Y	Y	N	N	Y	N	N
7 ***DeWine***	Y	Y	Y	N	N	Y	N	N
8 ***Kindness***	Y	Y	Y	Y	N	Y	N	N
9 Kaptur	N	N	N	Y	Y	Y	Y	Y
10 ***Miller***	Y	Y	Y	Y	Y	Y	N	Y
11 Eckart	Y	Y	N	N	Y	Y	Y	Y
12 ***Kasich***	Y	Y	Y	Y	Y	Y	N	N
13 Pease	Y	Y	N	N	Y	Y	Y	Y
14 Seiberling	N	N	N	N	Y	Y	?	Y
15 ***Wylie***	Y	Y	Y	Y	Y	N	Y	N
16 ***Regula***	Y	Y	Y	N	Y	Y	Y	Y
17 Traficant	N	N	N	N	Y	Y	Y	Y
18 Applegate	Y	Y	Y	N	Y	Y	?	Y
19 Feighan	N	N	N	N	Y	Y	Y	Y
20 Oakar	N	N	N	N	Y	Y	Y	Y
21 Stokes	N	N	N	N	Y	Y	Y	Y
OKLAHOMA								
1 Jones	Y	N	Y	N	Y	Y	Y	Y
2 Synar	N	N	N	N	Y	Y	Y	Y
3 Watkins	N	N	N	N	Y	Y	Y	Y
4 McCurdy	Y	Y	Y	N	Y	Y	?	Y
5 ***Edwards***	Y	Y	Y	N	N	?	?	N
6 English	Y	Y	Y	N	Y	Y	Y	Y
OREGON								
1 AuCoin	Y	Y	Y	Y	Y	?	?	?
2 ***Smith, R.***	Y	N	Y	Y	Y	Y	Y	N
3 Wyden	N	N	N	N	N	Y	Y	Y
4 Weaver	N	N	N	Y	N	?	Y	Y
5 ***Smith, D.***	Y	Y	Y	Y	N	Y	N	N
PENNSYLVANIA								
1 Foglietta	N	N	N	N	Y	Y	Y	Y
2 Gray	N	N	N	?	Y	Y	?	?
3 Borski	N	N	N	N	Y	Y	Y	Y
4 Kolter	Y	N	N	N	Y	Y	Y	Y
5 ***Schulze***	Y	?	?	Y	Y	Y	N	Y
6 Yatron	Y	N	N	N	Y	Y	Y	Y
7 Edgar	N	N	N	N	Y	Y	Y	Y
8 Kostmayer	Y	N	N	N	Y	Y	Y	Y
9 ***Shuster***	Y	Y	Y	Y	N	Y	N	N
10 ***McDade***	Y	Y	N	N	Y	?	Y	Y
11 Kanjorski	N	N	N	N	N	Y	Y	Y
12 Murtha	N	N	N	N	Y	Y	Y	Y
13 ***Coughlin***	Y	Y	Y	Y	Y	Y	N	N
14 Coyne	?	?	?	N	Y	Y	Y	Y
15 ***Ritter***	Y	Y	Y	Y	Y	Y	N	N
16 ***Walker***	Y	Y	Y	N	Y	N	N	N
17 ***Gekas***	Y	Y	Y	N	Y	Y	N	N
18 Walgren	N	N	Y	N	Y	Y	Y	Y
19 ***Goodling***	Y	Y	Y	N	Y	Y	N	N
20 Gaydos	Y	N	N	N	Y	Y	Y	Y
21 ***Ridge***	Y	Y	Y	Y	Y	Y	N	N
22 Murphy	Y	N	N	N	Y	Y	Y	Y
23 ***Clinger***	Y	Y	N	N	Y	Y	Y	Y
RHODE ISLAND								
1 St Germain	?	?	?	?	?	?	?	?
2 ***Schneider***	Y	Y	N	N	Y	Y	Y	N
SOUTH CAROLINA								
1 ***Hartnett***	Y	Y	Y	Y	N	Y	Y	N
2 ***Spence***	Y	Y	Y	N	Y	Y	N	N
3 Derrick	?	N	N	N	Y	Y	Y	Y
4 ***Campbell***	Y	Y	Y	N	Y	Y	Y	N
5 Spratt	Y	Y	N	Y	Y	Y	Y	Y
6 Tallon	Y	N	N	N	Y	Y	Y	Y
SOUTH DAKOTA								
AL Daschle	N	N	N	Y	Y	?	?	?
TENNESSEE								
1 ***Quillen***	N	Y	N	N	Y	Y	Y	Y
2 ***Duncan***	Y	N	Y	N	Y	Y	Y	Y
3 Lloyd	N	N	N	N	Y	Y	N	Y
4 Cooper	Y	Y	Y	Y	Y	Y	Y	Y
5 Boner	Y	N	N	N	Y	?	Y	Y
6 Gordon	Y	Y	N	N	Y	Y	Y	Y
7 ***Sundquist***	Y	Y	Y	N	Y	Y	N	N
8 Jones	Y	Y	N	N	Y	Y	Y	Y
9 Ford	N	N	N	N	Y	Y	Y	Y
TEXAS								
1 Vacancy								
2 Wilson	Y	Y	N	N	Y	?	?	?
3 ***Bartlett***	Y	Y	Y	Y	Y	Y	Y	Y
4 Hall, R.	Y	Y	Y	N	Y	Y	Y	Y
5 Bryant	Y	Y	N	N	Y	Y	?	?
6 ***Barton***	Y	Y	Y	N	N	Y	N	N
7 ***Archer***	Y	Y	Y	N	N	Y	Y	N
8 ***Fields***	Y	Y	Y	Y	Y	Y	N	N
9 Brooks	N	N	N	N	Y	Y	Y	Y
10 Pickle	Y	N	N	N	Y	Y	Y	Y
11 Leath	Y	Y	Y	N	Y	Y	Y	N
12 Wright	N	N	?	?	Y	?	Y	Y
13 ***Boulter***	Y	Y	Y	Y	N	Y	Y	N
14 ***Sweeney***	Y	Y	Y	N	Y	?	Y	N
15 de la Garza	N	N	N	N	?	?	?	?
16 Coleman	N	N	N	N	Y	Y	Y	Y
17 Stenholm	Y	Y	Y	Y	N	Y	N	N
18 Leland	N	N	N	N	Y	Y	?	Y
19 ***Combest***	Y	Y	Y	Y	Y	Y	N	N
20 Gonzalez	N	N	N	N	Y	P	Y	Y
21 ***Loeffler***	?	?	?	?	?	?	?	?
22 ***DeLay***	Y	Y	Y	N	N	N	?	N
23 Bustamante	N	N	N	N	Y	Y	Y	Y
24 Frost	?	N	N	N	Y	Y	Y	Y
25 Andrews	Y	Y	Y	N	Y	Y	Y	Y
26 ***Armey***	Y	Y	Y	N	N	Y	N	N
27 Ortiz	N	N	N	N	Y	Y	Y	Y
UTAH								
1 ***Hansen***	Y	Y	Y	N	N	Y	Y	N
2 ***Monson***	Y	Y	Y	N	Y	Y	N	N
3 ***Nielson***	Y	Y	Y	Y	N	N	N	-
VERMONT								
AL ***Jeffords***	Y	N	Y	Y	Y	Y	Y	N
VIRGINIA								
1 ***Bateman***	Y	Y	Y	N	Y	Y	Y	N
2 ***Whitehurst***	Y	Y	Y	?	?	?	?	?
3 ***Bliley***	Y	Y	Y	Y	Y	Y	N	N
4 Sisisky	Y	Y	N	N	Y	?	Y	Y
5 Daniel	Y	Y	Y	Y	Y	Y	Y	N
6 Olin	Y	Y	Y	Y	Y	?	Y	Y
7 ***Slaughter***	Y	Y	Y	N	Y	Y	N	N
8 ***Parris***	Y	Y	Y	N	Y	Y	N	N
9 Boucher	N	N	N	N	Y	?	Y	Y
10 ***Wolf***	Y	Y	Y	Y	Y	Y	N	Y
WASHINGTON								
1 ***Miller***	Y	Y	Y	Y	Y	Y	Y	N
2 Swift	N	N	N	N	Y	Y	Y	Y
3 Bonker	N	N	N	N	Y	Y	Y	Y
4 ***Morrison***	Y	N	Y	Y	Y	Y	?	N
5 Foley	N	N	N	N	Y	Y	?	?
6 Dicks	N	N	N	N	Y	Y	Y	Y
7 Lowry	N	N	N	N	Y	Y	Y	Y
8 ***Chandler***	Y	Y	Y	Y	Y	Y	N	N
WEST VIRGINIA								
1 Mollohan	N	N	N	N	Y	Y	Y	Y
2 Staggers	N	N	Y	N	Y	Y	Y	Y
3 Wise	Y	N	N	N	Y	Y	Y	Y
4 Rahall	N	N	N	N	Y	Y	Y	Y
WISCONSIN								
1 Aspin	N	N	N	N	Y	?	?	Y
2 Kastenmeier	N	N	N	N	Y	Y	Y	Y
3 ***Gunderson***	Y	N	Y	Y	N	Y	N	N
4 Kleczka	N	N	N	N	Y	Y	Y	?
5 Moody	Y	Y	N	N	N	Y	Y	Y
6 ***Petri***	Y	Y	Y	Y	Y	Y	Y	N
7 Obey	N	N	N	?	Y	Y	Y	Y
8 ***Roth***	Y	Y	Y	Y	Y	?	?	-
9 ***Sensenbrenner***	Y	Y	Y	Y	N	N	N	N
WYOMING								
AL ***Cheney***	Y	Y	Y	N	N	Y	N	N

Southern states - Ala., Ark., Fla., Ga., Ky., La., Miss., N.C., Okla., S.C., Tenn., Texas, Va.

* The *Congressional Record* vote number is different from the CQ vote number because the *Record* includes quorum calls in its tally. CQ does not publish quorum call votes.

240. HR 3036. Treasury, Postal Service and General Government Appropriations, Fiscal 1986. Nelson, D-Fla., substitute for the Jacobs, D-Ind., amendment, to delete $219,400 from the section of the bill providing expenses for former presidents. Adopted 199-162: R 87-69; D 112-93 (ND 63-78, SD 49-15), July 26, 1985. (The Jacobs amendment would have deleted all non-pension funds for former presidents. The Jacobs amendment, as amended by the Nelson substitute, subsequently was adopted *(see vote 241, below)*.)

241. HR 3036. Treasury, Postal Service and General Government Appropriations, Fiscal 1986. Jacobs, D-Ind., amendment, as amended by the Nelson, D-Fla., substitute *(vote 240, above)*, to reduce expense funds for former presidents. Adopted 219-130: R 92-59; D 127-71 (ND 79-59, SD 48-12), July 26, 1985.

242. S J Res 180. Helsinki Accords Anniversary. Passage of the joint resolution to reaffirm Congress' support for the Helsinki human rights principles, and to request that the president direct the State Department to convey U.S. concerns for human rights to the Soviet Union and its allies. Passed 414-0: R 177-0; D 237-0 (ND 163-0, SD 74-0), July 30, 1985. (The resolution commemorates the 10th anniversary of the Aug. 1, 1975, signing of the Helsinki Final Act.)

243. HR 3036. Treasury, Postal Service and General Government Appropriations, Fiscal 1986. Coleman, D-Texas, amendment to the Frenzel, R-Minn., amendment, to exempt the U.S. Customs Service, Internal Revenue Service, Postal Service and several law enforcement agencies from a 2.65 percent spending cut. Adopted 288-133: R 69-108; D 219-25 (ND 148-19, SD 71-6), July 30, 1985. (The Frenzel amendment would have reduced appropriations for all discretionary programs in the bill by 2.65 percent. The Frenzel amendment, as amended by the Coleman amendment, subsequently was adopted by voice vote.)

244. HR 3036. Treasury, Postal Service and General Government Appropriations, Fiscal 1986. Roybal, D-Calif., motion that the Committee of the Whole rise and report the bill back to the House. Motion agreed to 233-186: R 16-160; D 217-26 (ND 166-0, SD 51-26), July 30, 1985. (The effect of the vote was to prevent consideration of amendments limiting spending on the appropriations bill, in this case the Cobey, R-N.C., amendment to require the Federal Election Commission to enforce a U.S. Supreme Court ruling prohibiting the use of compulsory union dues for political activities. Such amendments are in order only following a defeated motion to rise and report.)

245. HR 3036. Treasury, Postal Service and General Government Appropriations, Fiscal 1986. Passage of the bill to provide $13,227,868,125 for the Treasury Department, U.S. Postal Service, Executive Office of the President and other independent agencies. Passed 249-172: R 42-135; D 207-37 (ND 146-21, SD 61-16), July 30, 1985. (The president had requested $12,060,-171,000 in new budget authority.)

246. HR 3067. District of Columbia Appropriations, Fiscal 1986. Dixon, D-Calif., motion that the Committee of the Whole rise and report the bill back to the House. Rejected 172-244: R 22-153; D 150-91 (ND 112-53, SD 38-38), July 30, 1985. (The effect of the vote was to allow consideration of amendments limiting spending on the appropriations bill, in this case the Smith, R-N.J., amendment *(see vote 247, below)*. Such amendments are in order only following a defeated motion to rise and report.)

247. HR 3067. District of Columbia Appropriations, Fiscal 1986. Smith, R-N.J., amendment to bar the use of any funds in the bill to pay for abortions. Adopted 221-199: R 142-35; D 79-164 (ND 47-120, SD 32-44), July 30, 1985.

KEY

- Y Voted for (yea).
- # Paired for.
- + Announced for.
- N Voted against (nay).
- X Paired against.
- \- Announced against.
- P Voted "present."
- C Voted "present" to avoid possible conflict of interest.
- ? Did not vote or otherwise make a position known.

Democrats ***Republicans***

	240	241	242	243	244	245	246	247
ALABAMA								
1 ***Callahan***	N	N	Y	Y	N	N	N	Y
2 ***Dickinson***	Y	Y	Y	Y	N	N	Y	?
3 Nichols	Y	Y	Y	Y	N	N	N	Y
4 Bevill	Y	Y	Y	N	Y	Y	N	Y
5 Flippo	Y	Y	Y	Y	Y	Y	N	N
6 Erdreich	Y	Y	Y	Y	Y	N	Y	N
7 Shelby	Y	Y	Y	Y	N	N	N	Y
ALASKA								
AL ***Young***	N	N	Y	N	N	Y	N	Y
ARIZONA								
1 ***McCain***	Y	Y	Y	N	N	N	N	Y
2 Udall	Y	?	Y	Y	Y	Y	Y	N
3 ***Stump***	Y	?	Y	N	N	N	N	Y
4 ***Rudd***	?	?	Y	Y	N	Y	N	Y
5 ***Kolbe***	Y	Y	Y	N	N	N	N	Y
ARKANSAS								
1 Alexander	?	?	Y	Y	Y	Y	Y	N
2 Robinson	Y	Y	Y	Y	N	Y	N	Y
3 ***Hammerschmidt***	?	?	Y	Y	N	N	?	Y
4 Anthony	?	?	Y	Y	Y	Y	Y	N
CALIFORNIA								
1 Bosco	?	?	Y	N	Y	Y	Y	N
2 ***Chappie***	?	?	Y	N	N	N	N	Y
3 Matsui	Y	Y	Y	Y	Y	Y	Y	N
4 Fazio	N	N	Y	Y	Y	Y	Y	N
5 Burton	Y	Y	Y	Y	Y	Y	Y	N
6 Boxer	?	?	Y	Y	Y	N	Y	N
7 Miller	Y	Y	Y	Y	Y	Y	Y	N
8 Dellums	N	N	Y	Y	Y	Y	Y	N
9 Stark	N	Y	Y	Y	Y	Y	Y	N
10 Edwards	N	N	Y	Y	Y	Y	Y	N
11 Lantos	Y	Y	Y	Y	Y	Y	Y	N
12 ***Zschau***	Y	Y	Y	N	N	N	N	N
13 Mineta	N	N	Y	Y	Y	Y	Y	N
14 ***Shumway***	Y	Y	Y	N	N	N	N	Y
15 Coelho	?	?	Y	Y	Y	Y	?	N
16 Panetta	?	?	Y	Y	Y	N	Y	N
17 ***Pashayan***	N	N	Y	Y	N	N	N	Y
18 Lehman	?	?	Y	Y	Y	Y	Y	N
19 ***Lagomarsino***	N	N	Y	Y	N	N	N	Y
20 ***Thomas***	?	?	Y	N	N	N	N	Y
21 ***Fiedler***	N	N	?	?	?	?	?	?
22 ***Moorhead***	Y	Y	Y	N	N	N	N	Y
23 Beilenson	N	N	Y	Y	Y	Y	Y	N
24 Waxman	Y	?	Y	Y	Y	?	Y	N
25 Roybal	N	N	Y	N	Y	Y	Y	N
26 Berman	?	?	Y	Y	Y	Y	Y	N
27 Levine	Y	Y	Y	N	Y	Y	Y	N
28 Dixon	?	?	Y	N	Y	Y	Y	N
29 Hawkins	X	X	?	Y	Y	Y	Y	N
30 Martinez	N	N	Y	?	Y	Y	Y	N
31 Dymally	N	N	Y	N	Y	Y	Y	N
32 Anderson	N	N	Y	Y	Y	Y	Y	N
33 ***Dreier***	N	Y	Y	N	N	N	N	Y
34 Torres	N	Y	Y	Y	Y	Y	Y	N
35 ***Lewis***	?	?	Y	Y	N	Y	N	Y
36 Brown	N	N	Y	N	Y	Y	Y	N
37 ***McCandless***	Y	N	Y	N	N	N	N	N
38 ***Dornan***	N	N	Y	Y	N	N	N	Y
39 ***Dannemeyer***	-	+	Y	N	N	N	N	Y
40 ***Badham***	?	?	Y	N	N	N	N	Y
41 ***Lowery***	N	N	Y	Y	N	Y	N	Y
42 ***Lungren***	N	N	Y	N	N	N	N	Y
43 ***Packard***	Y	Y	Y	N	N	N	N	Y
44 Bates	Y	Y	Y	Y	?	Y	Y	N
45 ***Hunter***	N	N	Y	Y	N	N	N	Y
COLORADO								
1 Schroeder	N	Y	Y	Y	Y	N	Y	N
2 Wirth	?	?	Y	Y	Y	N	Y	N
3 ***Strang***	Y	Y	Y	N	N	N	N	N
4 ***Brown***	N	Y	Y	N	N	N	N	N
5 ***Kramer***	?	?	Y	N	N	N	N	N
6 ***Schaefer***	Y	Y	Y	N	?	N	N	Y
CONNECTICUT								
1 Kennelly	Y	Y	Y	Y	Y	Y	Y	N
2 Gejdenson	?	?	Y	Y	Y	Y	Y	N
3 Morrison	Y	Y	Y	Y	Y	Y	Y	N
4 ***McKinney***	Y	N	Y	N	N	Y	Y	N
5 ***Rowland***	N	N	Y	Y	N	Y	N	Y
6 ***Johnson***	N	N	Y	Y	Y	Y	Y	N
DELAWARE								
AL Carper	Y	Y	Y	N	Y	N	Y	N
FLORIDA								
1 Hutto	Y	Y	Y	Y	N	N	N	Y
2 Fuqua	Y	Y	Y	Y	Y	Y	N	Y
3 Bennett	Y	Y	Y	Y	Y	Y	Y	N
4 Chappell	#	#	Y	Y	N	Y	N	N
5 ***McCollum***	Y	Y	Y	Y	N	N	N	Y
6 MacKay	Y	Y	Y	Y	Y	Y	Y	N
7 Gibbons	Y	Y	Y	?	Y	Y	Y	Y
8 ***Young***	N	Y	Y	Y	N	N	N	Y
9 ***Bilirakis***	Y	Y	Y	Y	N	N	N	Y
10 ***Ireland***	Y	Y	Y	Y	N	N	N	Y
11 Nelson	Y	Y	Y	Y	N	N	N	Y
12 ***Lewis***	Y	Y	Y	Y	N	Y	N	Y
13 ***Mack***	Y	Y	Y	N	N	N	N	Y
14 Mica	Y	Y	Y	Y	Y	Y	N	N
15 ***Shaw***	Y	Y	Y	Y	N	N	N	Y
16 Smith	Y	Y	Y	Y	Y	Y	Y	N
17 Lehman	N	N	Y	Y	Y	Y	Y	N
18 Pepper	N	-	Y	Y	Y	Y	N	N
19 Fascell	Y	Y	Y	Y	Y	Y	Y	N
GEORGIA								
1 Thomas	Y	Y	Y	Y	N	Y	Y	N
2 Hatcher	?	?	Y	Y	Y	Y	Y	N
3 Ray	Y	Y	Y	N	N	N	N	Y
4 ***Swindall***	Y	Y	Y	N	N	N	N	Y
5 Fowler	N	Y	Y	Y	Y	Y	Y	N
6 ***Gingrich***	Y	Y	Y	N	N	N	N	Y
7 Darden	N	N	Y	Y	N	Y	N	Y
8 Rowland	Y	Y	Y	Y	N	Y	Y	N
9 Jenkins	N	Y	Y	Y	N	Y	?	?
10 Barnard	Y	Y	Y	Y	N	Y	N	Y
HAWAII								
1 Heftel	N	Y	Y	Y	Y	Y	Y	N
2 Akaka	?	?	Y	N	Y	Y	Y	N
IDAHO								
1 ***Craig***	?	?	Y	N	N	N	N	Y
2 Stallings	Y	Y	Y	Y	Y	Y	N	Y
ILLINOIS								
1 Hayes	N	N	Y	Y	Y	Y	Y	N
2 Savage	N	N	Y	Y	Y	Y	Y	N
3 Russo	N	N	Y	Y	Y	Y	N	Y
4 ***O'Brien***	?	?	Y	N	Y	Y	N	Y
5 Lipinski	N	?	Y	Y	Y	Y	N	Y
6 ***Hyde***	N	N	Y	N	N	N	N	Y
7 Collins	N	N	Y	Y	Y	Y	Y	N
8 Rostenkowski	?	?	?	Y	Y	Y	N	Y
9 Yates	N	N	Y	Y	Y	Y	Y	N
10 ***Porter***	N	N	Y	N	N	N	N	Y
11 Annunzio	Y	N	Y	Y	Y	Y	N	Y
12 ***Crane***	N	Y	Y	N	N	N	N	Y
13 ***Fawell***	Y	Y	Y	N	N	N	Y	N
14 ***Grotberg***	Y	Y	Y	Y	N	N	N	N
15 ***Madigan***	N	N	Y	N	N	Y	N	Y
16 ***Martin***	Y	Y	Y	N	N	N	Y	N
17 Evans	N	Y	Y	Y	Y	Y	Y	N
18 ***Michel***	N	N	Y	N	N	N	N	Y
19 Bruce	Y	Y	Y	Y	Y	Y	N	Y
20 Durbin	?	?	Y	Y	Y	Y	N	Y
21 Price	Y	N	Y	Y	Y	Y	N	Y
22 Gray	N	N	Y	Y	Y	Y	N	Y
INDIANA								
1 Visclosky	N	Y	Y	Y	Y	Y	Y	N
2 Sharp	N	?	Y	N	Y	N	Y	N
3 ***Hiler***	Y	Y	Y	N	N	N	N	Y
4 ***Coats***	Y	Y	Y	N	N	N	N	Y
5 ***Hillis***	?	?	Y	Y	N	N	N	Y

ND - Northern Democrats SD - Southern Democrats

* Corresponding to Congressional Record Votes 264, 265, 266, 268, 269, 270, 272, 273

	240	241	242	243	244	245	246	247
6 ***Burton***	Y	Y	Y	N	N	N	N	Y
7 ***Myers***	N	N	Y	N	N	N	N	Y
8 McCloskey	N	Y	Y	Y	Y	Y	N	N
9 Hamilton	N	Y	Y	N	Y	Y	N	N
10 Jacobs	N	Y	Y	N	Y	N	Y	N
IOWA								
1 ***Leach***	Y	Y	Y	N	N	N	N	Y
2 ***Tauke***	Y	Y	Y	N	N	N	N	Y
3 ***Evans***	Y	Y	Y	N	N	N	N	N
4 Smith	N	N	Y	Y	Y	Y	Y	N
5 ***Lightfoot***	Y	Y	Y	N	N	N	N	Y
6 Bedell	?	?	Y	Y	Y	Y	Y	N
KANSAS								
1 ***Roberts***	Y	Y	Y	N	N	N	N	Y
2 Slattery	Y	?	Y	Y	Y	Y	N	N
3 ***Meyers***	?	?	Y	N	N	Y	Y	N
4 Glickman	Y	Y	Y	Y	Y	N	Y	N
5 ***Whittaker***	?	?	Y	N	N	N	N	N
KENTUCKY								
1 Hubbard	Y	Y	Y	Y	Y	N	N	Y
2 Natcher	N	N	Y	Y	Y	Y	N	Y
3 Mazzoli	+	+	Y	Y	N	Y	N	Y
4 ***Snyder***	N	?	Y	N	N	N	N	Y
5 ***Rogers***	Y	N	Y	Y	N	Y	N	Y
6 ***Hopkins***	Y	Y	Y	N	N	N	N	Y
7 Perkins	N	N	Y	Y	Y	Y	N	Y
LOUISIANA								
1 ***Livingston***	N	N	Y	N	N	N	N	Y
2 Boggs	N	N	Y	Y	Y	Y	N	Y
3 Tauzin	?	?	?	?	?	?	?	?
4 Roemer	Y	Y	Y	N	N	N	N	N
5 Huckaby	?	?	Y	Y	N	N	N	N
6 ***Moore***	Y	Y	Y	N	N	N	N	Y
7 Breaux	Y	Y	Y	N	Y	N	N	Y
8 Long	Y	Y	Y	Y	Y	Y	N	Y
MAINE								
1 ***McKernan***	Y	Y	Y	N	N	N	Y	N
2 ***Snowe***	Y	Y	Y	N	N	N	Y	N
MARYLAND								
1 Dyson	Y	N	N	Y	Y	Y	N	Y
2 ***Bentley***	Y	N	?	Y	N	Y	N	Y
3 Mikulski	Y	Y	Y	Y	Y	Y	Y	N
4 ***Holt***	N	N	Y	N	N	N	N	Y
5 Hoyer	N	N	Y	Y	Y	Y	Y	N
6 Byron	?	?	Y	Y	Y	N	N	Y
7 Mitchell	N	N	Y	Y	Y	Y	Y	N
8 Barnes	N	N	Y	Y	Y	Y	Y	N
MASSACHUSETTS								
1 ***Conte***	N	N	Y	N	Y	Y	N	Y
2 Boland	N	N	Y	Y	Y	Y	N	Y
3 Early	?	?	Y	N	Y	Y	Y	Y
4 Frank	?	?	Y	Y	Y	Y	Y	N
5 Atkins	Y	Y	Y	Y	Y	Y	Y	N
6 Mavroules	N	N	Y	Y	Y	Y	N	Y
7 Markey	N	N	Y	Y	Y	Y	Y	N
8 O'Neill								
9 Moakley	?	?	Y	Y	Y	Y	N	Y
10 Studds	Y	Y	Y	Y	Y	Y	Y	N
11 Donnelly	?	Y	Y	Y	Y	Y	N	Y
MICHIGAN								
1 Conyers	N	N	Y	N	Y	Y	Y	N
2 ***Pursell***	Y	Y	Y	N	N	N	Y	N
3 Wolpe	N	Y	Y	Y	Y	Y	Y	N
4 ***Siljander***	N	Y	Y	N	N	N	N	Y
5 ***Henry***	N	N	Y	N	N	N	N	Y
6 Carr	Y	Y	Y	Y	Y	Y	Y	N
7 Kildee	Y	Y	Y	Y	Y	Y	N	Y
8 Traxler	?	?	Y	Y	Y	Y	N	Y
9 ***Vander Jagt***	?	?	Y	N	N	N	N	Y
10 ***Schuette***	?	?	Y	Y	N	N	N	Y
11 ***Davis***	Y	Y	Y	Y	N	Y	N	Y
12 Bonior	?	?	Y	Y	Y	Y	N	Y
13 Crockett	N	Y	Y	N	Y	Y	Y	N
14 Hertel	Y	Y	Y	Y	Y	N	N	Y
15 Ford	N	N	Y	N	Y	Y	Y	N
16 Dingell	?	Y	Y	Y	Y	Y	Y	N
17 Levin	N	Y	Y	Y	Y	Y	Y	N
18 ***Broomfield***	N	N	Y	Y	N	N	N	Y
MINNESOTA								
1 Penny	Y	Y	Y	N	Y	N	N	Y
2 ***Weber***	Y	Y	Y	N	N	N	N	Y
3 ***Frenzel***	N	N	Y	N	N	N	Y	N
4 Vento	Y	Y	Y	Y	Y	Y	N	N
5 Sabo	N	N	Y	Y	Y	Y	Y	N
6 Sikorski	N	Y	Y	Y	Y	Y	N	Y

	240	241	242	243	244	245	246	247
7 ***Stangeland***	Y	Y	Y	N	N	N	N	Y
8 Oberstar	Y	Y	Y	Y	Y	Y	N	Y
MISSISSIPPI								
1 Whitten	N	N	Y	N	Y	Y	N	Y
2 ***Franklin***	Y	?	Y	N	N	N	N	Y
3 Montgomery	Y	Y	Y	Y	N	N	N	Y
4 Dowdy	Y	Y	Y	Y	Y	Y	N	Y
5 ***Lott***	N	N	Y	N	N	N	N	Y
MISSOURI								
1 Clay	?	?	Y	Y	Y	Y	Y	N
2 Young	Y	Y	Y	Y	Y	Y	N	Y
3 Gephardt	Y	N	Y	Y	?	?	N	Y
4 Skelton	Y	Y	Y	Y	Y	N	N	Y
5 Wheat	N	N	Y	N	Y	Y	Y	N
6 ***Coleman***	Y	N	Y	Y	N	N	N	Y
7 ***Taylor***	N	N	Y	N	N	N	N	Y
8 ***Emerson***	Y	Y	Y	Y	N	N	N	Y
9 Volkmer	Y	Y	Y	Y	Y	N	N	Y
MONTANA								
1 Williams	Y	Y	?	Y	Y	Y	?	N
2 ***Marlenee***	Y	Y	Y	Y	N	Y	N	Y
NEBRASKA								
1 ***Bereuter***	Y	Y	Y	N	N	N	N	Y
2 ***Daub***	N	Y	Y	N	N	N	N	Y
3 ***Smith***	Y	Y	Y	N	N	Y	N	Y
NEVADA								
1 Reid	Y	Y	Y	Y	Y	Y	N	Y
2 ***Vucanovich***	?	?	Y	N	N	N	N	Y
NEW HAMPSHIRE								
1 ***Smith***	Y	Y	Y	N	N	N	N	Y
2 ***Gregg***	N	Y	Y	N	N	N	N	Y
NEW JERSEY								
1 Florio	Y	Y	Y	Y	Y	Y	Y	N
2 Hughes	Y	Y	Y	Y	Y	N	Y	N
3 Howard	N	N	Y	Y	Y	Y	Y	N
4 ***Smith***	Y	Y	Y	Y	Y	Y	N	Y
5 ***Roukema***	Y	Y	Y	N	Y	N	Y	N
6 Dwyer	N	N	Y	Y	Y	Y	Y	N
7 ***Rinaldo***	Y	Y	Y	Y	Y	Y	N	Y
8 Roe	Y	Y	Y	Y	Y	Y	Y	Y
9 Torricelli	Y	Y	?	?	?	#	?	X
10 Rodino	N	N	Y	Y	Y	Y	Y	N
11 ***Gallo***	N	Y	Y	N	N	Y	Y	N
12 ***Courter***	?	?	Y	N	Y	Y	N	Y
13 ***Saxton***	N	Y	Y	N	N	N	N	Y
14 Guarini	?	?	Y	Y	Y	Y	Y	N
NEW MEXICO								
1 ***Lujan***	Y	Y	Y	N	N	N	N	Y
2 ***Skeen***	N	N	Y	Y	N	Y	N	Y
3 Richardson	Y	Y	Y	Y	Y	Y	Y	N
NEW YORK								
1 ***Carney***	?	?	?	?	?	?	?	#
2 Downey	N	N	Y	Y	Y	Y	Y	N
3 Mrazek	N	N	?	Y	Y	Y	Y	N
4 ***Lent***	?	?	Y	N	N	Y	N	Y
5 ***McGrath***	N	N	Y	Y	N	Y	N	Y
6 Addabbo	Y	N	Y	Y	Y	Y	Y	N
7 Ackerman	N	Y	Y	Y	Y	Y	Y	N
8 Scheuer	N	Y	Y	Y	Y	Y	Y	N
9 Manton	N	N	Y	Y	Y	Y	N	Y
10 Schumer	Y	Y	Y	Y	Y	Y	Y	N
11 Towns	N	N	Y	Y	Y	Y	Y	N
12 Owens	?	?	Y	Y	Y	Y	Y	N
13 Solarz	N	N	Y	Y	Y	Y	Y	N
14 ***Molinari***	N	N	Y	Y	N	N	N	Y
15 ***Green***	N	N	Y	Y	Y	Y	Y	N
16 Rangel	N	N	Y	Y	Y	Y	Y	N
17 Weiss	N	N	Y	Y	Y	Y	Y	N
18 Garcia	N	N	Y	Y	Y	Y	Y	N
19 Biaggi	N	N	Y	Y	Y	Y	N	N
20 ***DioGuardi***	N	Y	Y	Y	N	N	N	Y
21 ***Fish***	N	N	Y	Y	Y	Y	N	N
22 ***Gilman***	N	N	Y	Y	Y	Y	Y	N
23 Stratton	Y	Y	Y	Y	Y	Y	N	?
24 ***Solomon***	N	Y	Y	N	N	N	N	Y
25 ***Boehlert***	N	N	Y	Y	Y	Y	Y	N
26 ***Martin***	?	?	Y	Y	N	Y	?	Y
27 ***Wortley***	Y	Y	Y	Y	N	?	N	Y
28 McHugh	N	N	Y	Y	Y	Y	Y	N
29 ***Horton***	Y	?	Y	Y	Y	Y	Y	N
30 ***Eckert***	Y	N	Y	N	N	N	N	Y
31 ***Kemp***	N	N	Y	N	N	N	N	Y
32 LaFalce	Y	Y	Y	Y	Y	N	N	Y
33 Nowak	Y	Y	Y	Y	Y	Y	N	Y
34 Lundine	Y	N	Y	Y	Y	Y	?	?

	240	241	242	243	244	245	246	247
NORTH CAROLINA								
1 Jones	?	?	Y	Y	Y	Y	Y	N
2 Valentine	Y	Y	Y	Y	N	Y	N	N
3 Whitley	Y	Y	Y	Y	N	Y	Y	N
4 ***Cobey***	Y	Y	Y	Y	N	N	N	Y
5 Neal	Y	Y	Y	Y	N	N	Y	N
6 ***Coble***	N	Y	Y	N	N	N	N	Y
7 Rose	Y	Y	Y	Y	N	Y	Y	N
8 Hefner	?	?	?	?	?	?	?	?
9 ***McMillan***	Y	Y	Y	N	N	N	N	Y
10 ***Broyhill***	N	Y	Y	Y	N	N	N	N
11 ***Hendon***	Y	Y	Y	Y	N	N	N	Y
NORTH DAKOTA								
AL Dorgan	N	Y	Y	Y	Y	Y	N	Y
OHIO								
1 Luken	Y	Y	Y	Y	Y	N	N	Y
2 ***Gradison***	Y	Y	Y	N	N	N	N	Y
3 Hall	Y	Y	Y	Y	Y	N	N	Y
4 ***Oxley***	Y	N	Y	N	N	N	N	Y
5 ***Latta***	N	N	Y	N	N	N	N	Y
6 ***McEwen***	Y	N	Y	Y	N	N	N	Y
7 ***DeWine***	Y	Y	Y	N	N	N	N	Y
8 ***Kindness***	Y	N	Y	N	N	N	N	Y
9 Kaptur	Y	Y	Y	Y	Y	Y	N	N
10 ***Miller***	Y	Y	Y	N	N	N	N	Y
11 Eckart	Y	Y	Y	Y	Y	N	Y	N
12 ***Kasich***	Y	Y	Y	N	N	N	N	Y
13 Pease	N	Y	Y	Y	Y	Y	Y	N
14 Seiberling	Y	Y	Y	Y	Y	Y	Y	N
15 ***Wylie***	N	N	Y	N	N	N	N	Y
16 ***Regula***	N	N	Y	Y	N	Y	N	Y
17 Traficant	Y	Y	Y	Y	Y	Y	Y	N
18 Applegate	Y	Y	Y	Y	Y	N	N	Y
19 Feighan	Y	Y	Y	Y	Y	Y	Y	N
20 Oakar	N	N	Y	Y	Y	Y	Y	Y
21 Stokes	N	Y	Y	Y	Y	Y	Y	N
OKLAHOMA								
1 Jones	Y	Y	Y	Y	Y	?	Y	N
2 Synar	Y	Y	Y	Y	Y	Y	Y	N
3 Watkins	?	?	Y	Y	Y	Y	Y	N
4 McCurdy	Y	Y	Y	Y	Y	Y	Y	N
5 ***Edwards***	Y	Y	Y	N	N	N	N	Y
6 English	Y	Y	Y	Y	Y	Y	N	Y
OREGON								
1 AuCoin	?	?	Y	?	Y	N	Y	N
2 ***Smith, R.***	Y	Y	Y	N	N	N	N	Y
3 Wyden	N	Y	Y	Y	Y	Y	Y	N
4 Weaver	N	Y	Y	Y	Y	N	Y	N
5 ***Smith, D.***	?	?	Y	N	N	N	N	Y
PENNSYLVANIA								
1 Foglietta	N	N	Y	Y	Y	Y	Y	N
2 Gray	?	?	?	Y	Y	Y	?	N
3 Borski	N	Y	Y	Y	Y	Y	N	Y
4 Kolter	N	Y	Y	Y	Y	Y	N	Y
5 ***Schulze***	N	?	Y	Y	N	N	N	Y
6 Yatron	N	Y	Y	Y	Y	Y	N	Y
7 Edgar	N	N	Y	Y	Y	Y	Y	N
8 Kostmayer	N	N	Y	Y	Y	Y	Y	N
9 ***Shuster***	Y	Y	Y	N	N	N	N	Y
10 ***McDade***	N	N	Y	Y	Y	Y	N	Y
11 Kanjorski	Y	Y	Y	Y	Y	Y	N	Y
12 Murtha	N	N	Y	N	Y	Y	N	Y
13 ***Coughlin***	N	N	Y	N	N	Y	N	N
14 Coyne	N	N	?	Y	Y	Y	Y	N
15 ***Ritter***	Y	Y	Y	Y	Y	N	N	Y
16 ***Walker***	Y	Y	Y	N	N	N	N	Y
17 ***Gekas***	Y	Y	Y	Y	N	N	Y	N
18 Walgren	Y	Y	Y	Y	Y	Y	Y	N
19 ***Goodling***	Y	Y	Y	Y	N	N	N	Y
20 Gaydos	N	N	Y	Y	Y	Y	N	Y
21 ***Ridge***	N	Y	Y	Y	N	Y	N	N
22 Murphy	N	Y	Y	Y	Y	Y	N	Y
23 ***Clinger***	N	N	Y	Y	N	Y	N	Y
RHODE ISLAND								
1 St Germain	?	?	Y	Y	Y	Y	N	Y
2 ***Schneider***	Y	Y	Y	Y	Y	N	Y	N
SOUTH CAROLINA								
1 ***Hartnett***	N	N	Y	N	N	N	N	Y
2 ***Spence***	Y	Y	Y	Y	N	N	N	Y
3 Derrick	Y	Y	Y	Y	N	Y	Y	N
4 ***Campbell***	N	N	Y	Y	N	N	N	Y
5 Spratt	Y	Y	Y	Y	N	Y	Y	N
6 Tallon	N	Y	Y	Y	Y	Y	N	Y
SOUTH DAKOTA								
AL Daschle	?	?	Y	Y	Y	Y	Y	N

	240	241	242	243	244	245	246	247
TENNESSEE								
1 ***Quillen***	?	?	Y	Y	N	N	N	Y
2 ***Duncan***	Y	Y	Y	N	N	N	N	Y
3 Lloyd	?	?	?	Y	Y	Y	N	Y
4 Cooper	Y	Y	?	Y	Y	Y	Y	N
5 Boner	Y	?	Y	Y	Y	Y	N	Y
6 Gordon	Y	Y	?	?	?	?	?	?
7 ***Sundquist***	Y	Y	Y	Y	N	N	N	Y
8 Jones	?	?	Y	Y	Y	Y	N	Y
9 Ford	N	N	?	Y	?	Y	Y	N
TEXAS								
1 Vacancy								
2 Wilson	N	Y	Y	Y	Y	Y	Y	N
3 ***Bartlett***	Y	Y	Y	Y	N	N	N	Y
4 Hall, R.	Y	Y	Y	Y	N	Y	N	Y
5 Bryant	?	?	Y	Y	Y	Y	Y	N
6 ***Barton***	?	?	Y	?	?	N	N	Y
7 ***Archer***	N	Y	Y	N	N	N	N	Y
8 ***Fields***	N	Y	Y	N	N	N	N	Y
9 Brooks	N	N	Y	Y	Y	Y	Y	N
10 Pickle	N	N	Y	Y	Y	Y	Y	N
11 Leath	Y	Y	Y	Y	N	N	N	Y
12 Wright	Y	N	Y	Y	Y	Y	?	?
13 ***Boulter***	N	Y	+	-	-	X	-	+
14 ***Sweeney***	N	N	Y	Y	N	N	?	Y
15 de la Garza	?	?	?	Y	Y	Y	N	Y
16 Coleman	Y	Y	Y	Y	Y	Y	Y	N
17 Stenholm	?	?	Y	Y	N	N	N	Y
18 Leland	N	N	Y	Y	Y	Y	Y	N
19 ***Combest***	N	N	Y	Y	N	N	N	Y
20 Gonzalez	Y	N	Y	Y	Y	Y	Y	N
21 ***Loeffler***	?	?	?	?	?	?	?	?
22 ***DeLay***	N	N	Y	N	N	N	N	Y
23 Bustamante	?	?	Y	Y	Y	Y	Y	N
24 Frost	Y	?	Y	Y	Y	Y	Y	N
25 Andrews	Y	Y	Y	Y	Y	Y	Y	N
26 ***Armey***	Y	Y	Y	N	N	N	N	Y
27 Ortiz	Y	Y	Y	Y	Y	Y	N	Y
UTAH								
1 ***Hansen***	Y	Y	Y	N	N	N	N	Y
2 ***Monson***	Y	Y	Y	N	N	N	N	Y
3 ***Nielson***	Y	Y	Y	N	N	N	N	Y
VERMONT								
AL ***Jeffords***	Y	Y	Y	Y	Y	Y	Y	N
VIRGINIA								
1 ***Bateman***	Y	Y	Y	Y	N	Y	N	N
2 ***Whitehurst***	?	?	Y	Y	N	N	N	N
3 ***Bliley***	Y	N	Y	N	N	N	N	Y
4 Sisisky	Y	?	Y	Y	Y	Y	Y	N
5 Daniel	?	?	Y	Y	N	N	N	Y
6 Olin	Y	Y	Y	N	Y	N	Y	N
7 ***Slaughter***	N	N	Y	N	N	N	N	Y
8 ***Parris***	N	N	Y	Y	N	Y	N	Y
9 Boucher	Y	Y	Y	Y	Y	Y	Y	N
10 ***Wolf***	N	N	Y	N	N	Y	N	Y
WASHINGTON								
1 ***Miller***	Y	Y	Y	Y	N	Y	Y	N
2 Swift	N	N	Y	Y	Y	Y	Y	N
3 Bonker	Y	N	Y	Y	Y	Y	Y	N
4 ***Morrison***	Y	Y	Y	Y	N	Y	Y	N
5 Foley	Y	N	Y	Y	Y	Y	Y	N
6 Dicks	Y	Y	Y	Y	Y	Y	Y	N
7 Lowry	N	N	Y	Y	Y	Y	Y	N
8 ***Chandler***	N	N	Y	Y	N	Y	Y	N
WEST VIRGINIA								
1 Mollohan	Y	Y	Y	Y	Y	Y	N	Y
2 Staggers	Y	Y	Y	Y	Y	Y	Y	Y
3 Wise	N	Y	Y	Y	Y	Y	Y	N
4 Rahall	Y	Y	Y	Y	Y	Y	N	N
WISCONSIN								
1 Aspin	Y	Y	Y	Y	Y	Y	N	N
2 Kastenmeier	N	N	Y	N	Y	Y	Y	N
3 ***Gunderson***	Y	N	Y	N	N	N	N	Y
4 Kleczka	Y	Y	Y	Y	Y	Y	N	N
5 Moody	Y	Y	Y	Y	?	Y	Y	N
6 ***Petri***	N	Y	Y	N	N	N	N	Y
7 Obey	N	N	Y	Y	Y	Y	Y	N
8 ***Roth***	+	+	Y	Y	N	N	N	Y
9 ***Sensenbrenner***	N	Y	Y	N	N	N	N	Y
WYOMING								
AL ***Cheney***	N	N	Y	N	N	N	N	Y

Southern states - Ala., Ark., Fla., Ga., Ky., La., Miss., N.C., Okla., S.C., Tenn., Texas, Va.

* The *Congressional Record* vote number is different from the CQ vote number because the *Record* includes quorum calls in its tally. CQ does not publish quorum call votes.

248. HR 3067. District of Columbia Appropriations, Fiscal 1986. Passage of the bill to provide $532,170,000 in federal funds and $2,689,077,000 in District funds in fiscal 1986. Passed 242-173: R 61-114; D 181-59 (ND 124-40, SD 57-19), July 30, 1985. (The president had requested new budget authority of $532,170,000 in federal funds and $2,689,077,000 in District funds.)

249. S 960. Foreign Assistance Authorization, Fiscal 1986. Adoption of the conference report on the bill to authorize $12,774,281,000 in each of fiscal years 1986 and 1987 for foreign aid programs. Adopted 262-161: R 110-69; D 152-92 (ND 101-64, SD 51-28), July 31, 1985.

250. H Con Res 179. Adjournment Resolution. Adoption of the concurrent resolution to provide for the adjournment of the House from Aug. 1 or 2 to Sept. 4, 1985, and for the adjournment of the Senate from Aug. 1 or 2 to Sept. 4 or 9, 1985. Adopted 230-192: R 44-135; D 186-57 (ND 128-35, SD 58-22), July 31, 1985.

251. HR 2577. Supplemental Appropriations, Fiscal 1985. Adoption of the conference report on the bill to appropriate $13.02 billion for various government programs and for pay raises for federal workers. Adopted 320-106: R 121-58; D 199-48 (ND 130-37, SD 69-11), July 31, 1985. A "yea" was a vote supporting the president's position.

252. HR 2577. Supplemental Appropriations, Fiscal 1985. Whitten, D-Miss., motion that the House recede from its disagreement to the conference committee amendment to provide $48.8 million for 41 water projects of the Army Corps of Engineers, so long as federal and local cost-sharing agreements are reached by June 30, 1986. Motion rejected 170-258: R 54-126; D 116-132 (ND 70-99, SD 46-33), July 31, 1985. (The House subsequently adopted by a standing vote of 97-5 a motion by Howard, D-N.J., making the appropriation for the water projects subject to enactment of authorizing legislation specifying a cost-sharing agreement. By agreeing to the motion, the House receded from its disagreement to the amendment.)

253. HR 3011. Interior Appropriations, Fiscal 1986. Adoption of the rule (H Res 240) to waive certain points of order against the bill to make appropriations for the Interior Department and related agencies for fiscal 1986. Adopted 408-19: R 162-17; D 246-2 (ND 166-2, SD 80-0), July 31, 1985.

254. HR 3011. Interior Appropriations, Fiscal 1986. Shaw, R-Fla., amendment to cut $91,000 from the National Park Service budget for the operations and maintenance of the John F. Kennedy Center for the Performing Arts. Rejected 200-227: R 139-40; D 61-187 (ND 25-143, SD 36-44), July 31, 1985.

KEY

Y Voted for (yea).
Paired for.
+ Announced for.
N Voted against (nay).
X Paired against.
- Announced against.
P Voted "present."
C Voted "present" to avoid possible conflict of interest.
? Did not vote or otherwise make a position known.

Democrats ***Republicans***

	248	249	250	251	252	253	254
ALABAMA							
1 ***Callahan***	N	Y	N	Y	Y	Y	Y
2 ***Dickinson***	?	N	N	N	Y	Y	Y
3 Nichols	N	N	Y	Y	Y	Y	Y
4 Bevill	Y	N	Y	Y	Y	Y	N
5 Flippo	?	N	Y	Y	Y	Y	Y
6 Erdreich	Y	Y	N	Y	Y	Y	Y
7 Shelby	N	Y	Y	Y	Y	Y	N
ALASKA							
AL ***Young***	Y	N	Y	Y	N	Y	Y
ARIZONA							
1 ***McCain***	N	Y	Y	Y	N	Y	Y
2 Udall	Y	Y	Y	Y	Y	Y	N
3 ***Stump***	N	N	N	N	N	Y	Y
4 ***Rudd***	N	Y	Y	Y	Y	Y	Y
5 ***Kolbe***	Y	Y	N	Y	N	Y	Y
ARKANSAS							
1 Alexander	Y	N	Y	Y	Y	Y	N
2 Robinson	Y	Y	N	Y	N	Y	Y
3 ***Hammerschmidt***	N	N	N	N	N	Y	Y
4 Anthony	N	N	Y	Y	N	Y	N
CALIFORNIA							
1 Bosco	N	Y	Y	N	N	Y	N
2 ***Chappie***	N	N	N	N	Y	Y	Y
3 Matsui	Y	Y	Y	Y	Y	Y	N
4 Fazio	Y	Y	Y	Y	Y	Y	N
5 Burton	Y	Y	Y	Y	Y	Y	N
6 Boxer	N	N	Y	N	Y	Y	N
7 Miller	N	N	N	N	Y	Y	N
8 Dellums	N	N	Y	N	N	Y	N
9 Stark	N	Y	Y	?	N	Y	N
10 Edwards	N	N	Y	Y	Y	Y	N
11 Lantos	Y	Y	Y	Y	Y	Y	N
12 ***Zschau***	N	Y	N	Y	N	Y	N
13 Mineta	N	N	Y	Y	N	Y	N
14 ***Shumway***	N	N	N	N	N	Y	Y
15 Coelho	Y	Y	?	Y	Y	Y	N
16 Panetta	N	N	N	N	Y	Y	Y
17 ***Pashayan***	Y	N	Y	Y	N	Y	Y
18 Lehman	Y	N	Y	?	Y	Y	N
19 ***Lagomarsino***	N	Y	N	Y	Y	Y	Y
20 ***Thomas***	Y	Y	Y	Y	Y	Y	N
21 ***Fiedler***	?	Y	N	Y	N	Y	Y
22 ***Moorhead***	N	N	N	N	N	Y	Y
23 Beilenson	N	N	Y	Y	N	Y	N
24 Waxman	Y	Y	Y	Y	Y	Y	N
25 Roybal	N	Y	Y	Y	Y	Y	N
26 Berman	Y	Y	Y	Y	Y	Y	N
27 Levine	Y	Y	?	Y	Y	Y	N
28 Dixon	Y	Y	Y	Y	Y	Y	N
29 Hawkins	Y	Y	Y	Y	Y	Y	N
30 Martinez	Y	N	Y	Y	N	Y	N
31 Dymally	Y	Y	Y	Y	Y	Y	N
32 Anderson	N	N	N	Y	N	Y	N
33 ***Dreier***	N	N	Y	N	N	Y	Y
34 Torres	Y	N	Y	Y	Y	Y	N
35 ***Lewis***	Y	Y	N	Y	Y	Y	Y
36 Brown	Y	N	Y	Y	Y	Y	N
37 ***McCandless***	N	Y	N	Y	N	Y	Y
38 ***Dornan***	N	Y	N	Y	Y	Y	Y
39 ***Dannemeyer***	N	N	N	N	N	Y	Y
40 ***Badham***	N	N	Y	N	N	Y	Y
41 ***Lowery***	Y	Y	Y	Y	Y	Y	N
42 ***Lungren***	N	Y	Y	N	N	Y	Y
43 ***Packard***	Y	Y	Y	N	N	Y	Y
44 Bates	N	Y	Y	Y	N	Y	Y
45 ***Hunter***	N	Y	N	Y	Y	Y	Y
COLORADO							
1 Schroeder	N	N	N	N	N	Y	N
2 Wirth	N	N	N	N	Y	Y	N
3 ***Strang***	N	Y	N	Y	Y	N	Y
4 ***Brown***	N	N	N	N	N	Y	Y
5 ***Kramer***	N	Y	N	Y	Y	N	Y
6 ***Schaefer***	N	Y	N	Y	Y	N	Y
CONNECTICUT							
1 Kennelly	N	Y	N	Y	N	?	N
2 Gejdenson	N	Y	N	Y	N	Y	N
3 Morrison	N	N	Y	Y	N	Y	N
4 ***McKinney***	Y	Y	N	Y	N	Y	N
5 ***Rowland***	N	Y	N	Y	N	Y	Y
6 ***Johnson***	Y	Y	N	Y	N	Y	N
DELAWARE							
AL Carper	Y	Y	N	N	N	Y	Y
FLORIDA							
1 Hutto	Y	Y	Y	Y	N	Y	Y
2 Fuqua	Y	Y	Y	Y	N	Y	Y
3 Bennett	Y	N	Y	Y	Y	Y	Y
4 Chappell	Y	Y	Y	Y	Y	Y	N
5 ***McCollum***	N	Y	N	Y	N	Y	Y
6 MacKay	Y	Y	N	N	N	Y	Y
7 Gibbons	Y	Y	Y	Y	Y	Y	Y
8 ***Young***	N	?	N	Y	Y	Y	Y
9 ***Bilirakis***	N	Y	N	Y	Y	Y	Y
10 ***Ireland***	N	N	N	Y	N	Y	#
11 Nelson	Y	Y	N	Y	Y	Y	N
12 ***Lewis***	N	Y	N	Y	N	Y	Y
13 ***Mack***	N	Y	N	N	N	N	Y
14 Mica	N	Y	Y	Y	N	Y	N
15 ***Shaw***	N	Y	N	Y	N	Y	Y
16 Smith	?	Y	Y	Y	N	Y	N
17 Lehman	Y	Y	Y	Y	Y	Y	N
18 Pepper	Y	Y	Y	Y	N	Y	N
19 Fascell	Y	Y	Y	Y	N	Y	N
GEORGIA							
1 Thomas	Y	Y	Y	Y	N	Y	Y
2 Hatcher	Y	Y	Y	Y	N	Y	N
3 Ray	N	N	Y	N	N	Y	Y
4 ***Swindall***	N	Y	N	N	N	Y	Y
5 Fowler	Y	Y	Y	Y	N	Y	N
6 ***Gingrich***	N	Y	Y	Y	N	Y	Y
7 Darden	Y	N	N	Y	Y	Y	Y
8 Rowland	Y	Y	Y	Y	N	Y	N
9 Jenkins	?	N	N	Y	Y	Y	Y
10 Barnard	N	N	Y	N	Y	Y	Y
HAWAII							
1 Heftel	N	Y	Y	N	N	Y	N
2 Akaka	Y	Y	Y	Y	Y	Y	N
IDAHO							
1 ***Craig***	N	N	N	N	N	Y	Y
2 Stallings	Y	Y	N	N	Y	Y	Y
ILLINOIS							
1 Hayes	Y	N	Y	Y	Y	Y	X
2 Savage	Y	N	Y	N	N	Y	N
3 Russo	Y	N	Y	N	N	Y	N
4 ***O'Brien***	Y	Y	Y	Y	Y	Y	N
5 Lipinski	Y	Y	Y	Y	N	Y	N
6 ***Hyde***	Y	Y	Y	Y	Y	Y	Y
7 Collins	Y	Y	Y	Y	N	Y	N
8 Rostenkowski	Y	Y	Y	Y	N	Y	N
9 Yates	Y	N	Y	Y	Y	Y	N
10 ***Porter***	Y	Y	N	N	N	Y	Y
11 Annunzio	Y	Y	Y	Y	N	Y	N
12 ***Crane***	N	N	Y	N	N	N	Y
13 ***Fawell***	Y	Y	Y	Y	N	Y	Y
14 ***Grotberg***	N	N	N	N	N	Y	N
15 ***Madigan***	N	Y	N	Y	N	Y	Y
16 ***Martin***	N	N	N	N	N	Y	Y
17 Evans	Y	N	Y	N	N	Y	N
18 ***Michel***	Y	Y	Y	Y	N	Y	Y
19 Bruce	Y	Y	N	Y	Y	Y	N
20 Durbin	Y	Y	N	Y	Y	N	N
21 Price	Y	Y	Y	Y	Y	Y	N
22 Gray	Y	Y	Y	Y	N	Y	N
INDIANA							
1 Visclosky	Y	Y	Y	Y	N	Y	Y
2 Sharp	Y	Y	N	Y	N	Y	N
3 ***Hiler***	N	Y	N	N	N	Y	Y
4 ***Coats***	N	N	N	N	N	Y	Y
5 ***Hillis***	Y	Y	Y	Y	Y	Y	N

ND - Northern Democrats SD - Southern Democrats

* Corresponding to Congressional Record Votes 274, 275, 276, 277, 278, 279, 280

	248	249	250	251	252	253	254
6 ***Burton***	N	Y	N	N	N	Y	Y
7 ***Myers***	Y	N	Y	Y	Y	Y	Y
8 McCloskey	Y	Y	Y	N	Y	Y	Y
9 Hamilton	Y	Y	Y	N	N	Y	Y
10 Jacobs	Y	N	N	N	N	Y	Y
IOWA							
1 ***Leach***	N	Y	N	N	N	Y	N
2 ***Tauke***	N	N	N	?	N	Y	Y
3 ***Evans***	N	N	N	Y	N	Y	Y
4 Smith	Y	N	Y	Y	Y	Y	Y
5 ***Lightfoot***	N	N	N	N	N	Y	Y
6 Bedell	Y	N	N	Y	N	Y	N
KANSAS							
1 ***Roberts***	N	N	N	Y	N	N	Y
2 Slattery	N	N	N	N	N	Y	Y
3 ***Meyers***	Y	Y	Y	Y	N	Y	Y
4 Glickman	N	Y	N	Y	N	Y	Y
5 ***Whittaker***	N	N	N	Y	N	Y	Y
KENTUCKY							
1 Hubbard	N	N	N	N	N	Y	Y
2 Natcher	Y	N	Y	Y	Y	Y	N
3 Mazzoli	Y	N	Y	Y	N	Y	N
4 ***Snyder***	N	N	Y	N	N	Y	Y
5 ***Rogers***	Y	N	N	Y	Y	Y	N
6 ***Hopkins***	N	N	N	N	N	Y	Y
7 Perkins	Y	N	Y	Y	Y	Y	N
LOUISIANA							
1 ***Livingston***	Y	Y	N	Y	Y	Y	Y
2 Boggs	Y	Y	Y	Y	Y	Y	N
3 Tauzin	Y	Y	N	Y	Y	Y	Y
4 Roemer	N	N	N	N	N	Y	Y
5 Huckaby	N	Y	N	N	Y	Y	Y
6 ***Moore***	Y	Y	N	Y	Y	Y	Y
7 Breaux	Y	Y	N	Y	Y	Y	Y
8 Long	Y	Y	Y	Y	Y	Y	N
MAINE							
1 ***McKernan***	N	Y	N	Y	N	Y	Y
2 ***Snowe***	N	Y	N	Y	N	Y	Y
MARYLAND							
1 Dyson	Y	N	Y	Y	Y	Y	N
2 ***Bentley***	Y	Y	N	Y	Y	Y	Y
3 Mikulski	Y	Y	N	Y	Y	Y	N
4 ***Holt***	Y	N	Y	Y	Y	Y	N
5 Hoyer	Y	Y	Y	Y	Y	Y	N
6 Byron	Y	N	Y	Y	Y	Y	N
7 Mitchell	Y	N	Y	Y	Y	Y	N
8 Barnes	Y	Y	Y	Y	Y	Y	N
MASSACHUSETTS							
1 ***Conte***	Y	Y	Y	Y	N	Y	N
2 Boland	Y	Y	Y	Y	N	Y	N
3 Early	Y	N	Y	Y	N	Y	N
4 Frank	Y	Y	Y	Y	N	Y	N
5 Atkins	Y	Y	Y	Y	N	Y	N
6 Mavroules	Y	Y	?	Y	N	Y	N
7 Markey	Y	Y	Y	Y	N	Y	N
8 O'Neill							
9 Moakley	Y	Y	Y	Y	N	Y	N
10 Studds	Y	N	Y	Y	N	Y	N
11 Donnelly	Y	Y	Y	Y	N	Y	N
MICHIGAN							
1 Conyers	N	N	N	Y	N	N	N
2 ***Pursell***	Y	Y	N	N	N	Y	Y
3 Wolpe	Y	Y	?	Y	N	Y	N
4 ***Siljander***	N	Y	Y	Y	N	Y	Y
5 ***Henry***	Y	Y	N	N	N	Y	N
6 Carr	Y	Y	N	Y	Y	Y	Y
7 Kildee	Y	Y	Y	Y	N	Y	N
8 Traxler	Y	Y	N	Y	Y	Y	N
9 ***Vander Jagt***	N	Y	N	Y	N	Y	Y
10 ***Schuette***	N	Y	N	Y	N	Y	Y
11 ***Davis***	Y	N	Y	Y	N	Y	Y
12 Bonior	Y	N	Y	N	N	Y	N
13 Crockett	Y	N	Y	Y	N	Y	N
14 Hertel	N	N	Y	N	N	Y	N
15 Ford	Y	N	?	N	N	Y	N
16 Dingell	Y	N	Y	Y	N	Y	N
17 Levin	Y	Y	Y	Y	N	Y	N
18 ***Broomfield***	N	Y	N	Y	N	Y	Y
MINNESOTA							
1 Penny	N	N	N	N	N	Y	Y
2 ***Weber***	N	Y	N	Y	N	N	Y
3 ***Frenzel***	N	Y	N	N	N	Y	Y
4 Vento	Y	N	Y	Y	N	Y	Y
5 Sabo	Y	N	Y	Y	Y	Y	N
6 Sikorski	Y	Y	Y	Y	N	Y	C

	248	249	250	251	252	253	254
7 ***Stangeland***	?	Y	N	Y	N	Y	Y
8 Oberstar	Y	N	Y	Y	N	Y	N
MISSISSIPPI							
1 Whitten	Y	Y	Y	Y	Y	Y	N
2 ***Franklin***	N	N	N	Y	Y	Y	Y
3 Montgomery	N	N	Y	Y	N	Y	Y
4 Dowdy	Y	Y	N	Y	Y	Y	Y
5 ***Lott***	N	N	Y	Y	Y	Y	Y
MISSOURI							
1 Clay	Y	Y	Y	Y	N	Y	N
2 Young	Y	Y	Y	Y	Y	Y	N
3 Gephardt	Y	Y	Y	Y	Y	Y	N
4 Skelton	Y	+	?	?	Y	Y	Y
5 Wheat	Y	Y	Y	Y	Y	Y	N
6 ***Coleman***	N	N	Y	Y	Y	Y	N
7 ***Taylor***	N	N	Y	Y	N	Y	Y
8 ***Emerson***	N	N	N	Y	Y	Y	Y
9 Volkmer	Y	N	Y	Y	Y	Y	Y
MONTANA							
1 Williams	N	?	N	N	N	Y	N
2 ***Marlenee***	N	N	N	Y	N	Y	N
NEBRASKA							
1 ***Bereuter***	Y	Y	N	Y	Y	Y	Y
2 ***Daub***	N	N	N	Y	N	N	Y
3 ***Smith***	N	N	N	Y	Y	Y	Y
NEVADA							
1 Reid	Y	Y	Y	Y	Y	Y	N
2 ***Vucanovich***	Y	Y	N	N	N	N	Y
NEW HAMPSHIRE							
1 ***Smith***	N	N	N	N	N	N	Y
2 ***Gregg***	N	N	N	N	N	Y	Y
NEW JERSEY							
1 Florio	Y	Y	Y	Y	N	Y	N
2 Hughes	N	N	N	N	N	Y	Y
3 Howard	Y	Y	Y	Y	N	Y	N
4 ***Smith***	Y	Y	Y	Y	N	Y	Y
5 ***Roukema***	Y	Y	N	Y	N	Y	Y
6 Dwyer	Y	Y	Y	Y	Y	Y	N
7 ***Rinaldo***	Y	Y	N	Y	N	Y	N
8 Roe	Y	Y	Y	Y	N	Y	N
9 Torricelli	?	Y	N	Y	N	Y	N
10 Rodino	Y	N	Y	Y	N	Y	N
11 ***Gallo***	N	Y	N	Y	N	Y	Y
12 ***Courter***	N	Y	N	N	N	?	Y
13 ***Saxton***	N	Y	N	Y	N	Y	Y
14 Guarini	Y	N	Y	Y	N	Y	N
NEW MEXICO							
1 ***Lujan***	N	N	N	Y	N	Y	Y
2 ***Skeen***	N	N	N	Y	Y	Y	N
3 Richardson	Y	Y	Y	Y	Y	Y	N
NEW YORK							
1 ***Carney***	?	Y	Y	Y	Y	Y	Y
2 Downey	Y	Y	N	Y	N	Y	N
3 Mrazek	N	Y	Y	Y	N	Y	N
4 ***Lent***	Y	Y	N	Y	N	Y	Y
5 ***McGrath***	Y	Y	N	Y	Y	Y	Y
6 Addabbo	Y	Y	Y	Y	Y	?	N
7 Ackerman	N	Y	Y	Y	N	Y	N
8 Scheuer	N	Y	Y	Y	Y	Y	N
9 Manton	Y	?	Y	Y	N	Y	N
10 Schumer	Y	Y	Y	Y	N	Y	N
11 Towns	Y	Y	Y	Y	N	Y	N
12 Owens	Y	Y	Y	Y	N	Y	N
13 Solarz	Y	Y	Y	Y	N	Y	N
14 ***Molinari***	Y	Y	N	Y	N	Y	Y
15 ***Green***	Y	Y	N	Y	Y	Y	N
16 Rangel	Y	Y	Y	Y	N	Y	N
17 Weiss	N	N	Y	Y	N	Y	N
18 Garcia	Y	Y	Y	Y	N	Y	N
19 Biaggi	Y	Y	Y	Y	N	Y	N
20 ***DioGuardi***	Y	Y	N	Y	Y	Y	Y
21 ***Fish***	Y	Y	Y	Y	N	Y	Y
22 ***Gilman***	N	Y	N	Y	N	Y	N
23 Stratton	?	Y	Y	Y	N	Y	Y
24 ***Solomon***	N	N	N	N	N	N	Y
25 ***Boehlert***	Y	Y	N	Y	N	Y	N
26 ***Martin***	Y	Y	Y	Y	N	Y	Y
27 ***Wortley***	Y	Y	N	Y	N	Y	Y
28 McHugh	Y	Y	N	Y	Y	Y	N
29 ***Horton***	Y	Y	Y	Y	Y	Y	N
30 ***Eckert***	Y	Y	N	Y	Y	Y	Y
31 ***Kemp***	?	Y	N	Y	Y	Y	N
32 LaFalce	Y	N	Y	Y	Y	N	N
33 Nowak	Y	N	Y	Y	N	Y	N
34 Lundine	?	Y	Y	N	N	Y	N

	248	249	250	251	252	253	254
NORTH CAROLINA							
1 Jones	Y	Y	Y	Y	Y	Y	Y
2 Valentine	Y	Y	Y	Y	N	Y	Y
3 Whitley	Y	N	N	Y	Y	Y	Y
4 ***Cobey***	N	Y	N	Y	N	N	Y
5 Neal	Y	N	N	Y	N	Y	Y
6 ***Coble***	N	Y	N	Y	Y	Y	Y
7 Rose	Y	Y	N	Y	Y	Y	N
8 Hefner	?	?	?	?	?	?	?
9 ***McMillan***	N	Y	N	Y	N	Y	Y
10 ***Broyhill***	N	N	N	N	N	Y	Y
11 ***Hendon***	N	Y	N	Y	N	Y	N
NORTH DAKOTA							
AL Dorgan	Y	N	N	N	?	Y	N
OHIO							
1 Luken	?	Y	N	Y	Y	Y	N
2 ***Gradison***	Y	Y	N	N	N	Y	N
3 Hall	Y	?	Y	N	N	Y	N
4 ***Oxley***	N	N	N	N	N	Y	Y
5 ***Latta***	N	N	N	N	N	Y	Y
6 ***McEwen***	N	?	?	?	?	?	?
7 ***DeWine***	Y	Y	N	N	N	Y	Y
8 ***Kindness***	N	N	N	Y	N	Y	Y
9 Kaptur	Y	N	Y	Y	Y	Y	N
10 ***Miller***	N	N	N	Y	Y	Y	Y
11 Eckart	N	Y	Y	Y	Y	Y	N
12 ***Kasich***	N	Y	N	Y	N	Y	Y
13 Pease	Y	N	Y	N	Y	Y	N
14 Seiberling	Y	N	Y	N	N	Y	N
15 ***Wylie***	N	Y	N	Y	N	Y	Y
16 ***Regula***	Y	Y	N	Y	Y	Y	N
17 Traficant	N	N	N	Y	N	Y	Y
18 Applegate	Y	N	Y	N	N	Y	N
19 Feighan	?	Y	Y	Y	Y	Y	N
20 Oakar	Y	Y	Y	N	Y	Y	N
21 Stokes	Y	Y	Y	Y	Y	Y	N
OKLAHOMA							
1 Jones	N	Y	N	Y	Y	Y	Y
2 Synar	Y	Y	N	Y	N	Y	N
3 Watkins	N	N	N	Y	Y	Y	N
4 McCurdy	N	Y	Y	Y	N	Y	Y
5 ***Edwards***	N	Y	N	Y	Y	Y	Y
6 English	N	N	N	Y	Y	Y	Y
OREGON							
1 AuCoin	N	N	N	Y	Y	Y	N
2 ***Smith, R.***	Y	N	Y	Y	Y	Y	Y
3 Wyden	N	Y	N	Y	Y	Y	Y
4 Weaver	N	N	Y	N	N	Y	N
5 ***Smith, D.***	N	Y	Y	N	Y	N	Y
PENNSYLVANIA							
1 Foglietta	Y	Y	Y	Y	N	Y	N
2 Gray	Y	Y	Y	Y	N	Y	N
3 Borski	Y	Y	Y	Y	N	Y	N
4 Kolter	N	N	Y	Y	N	Y	N
5 ***Schulze***	N	Y	N	Y	N	Y	N
6 Yatron	Y	Y	Y	Y	N	Y	Y
7 Edgar	Y	Y	Y	Y	N	Y	N
8 Kostmayer	Y	Y	N	Y	N	Y	N
9 ***Shuster***	N	N	N	N	N	Y	Y
10 ***McDade***	Y	Y	Y	Y	Y	Y	N
11 Kanjorski	N	N	Y	Y	N	Y	Y
12 Murtha	Y	Y	Y	Y	Y	Y	N
13 ***Coughlin***	Y	Y	N	Y	N	Y	N
14 Coyne	Y	Y	Y	Y	N	Y	N
15 ***Ritter***	N	Y	N	N	N	Y	Y
16 ***Walker***	N	Y	N	N	N	N	Y
17 ***Gekas***	N	Y	N	N	N	Y	Y
18 Walgren	Y	N	Y	Y	N	Y	N
19 ***Goodling***	Y	N	N	N	N	Y	Y
20 Gaydos	N	N	Y	Y	Y	Y	N
21 ***Ridge***	Y	N	N	N	N	Y	N
22 Murphy	N	N	Y	N	N	Y	Y
23 ***Clinger***	N	N	N	Y	N	Y	N
RHODE ISLAND							
1 St Germain	?	N	Y	Y	Y	Y	N
2 ***Schneider***	Y	Y	N	Y	N	Y	N
SOUTH CAROLINA							
1 ***Hartnett***	N	N	Y	N	N	Y	Y
2 ***Spence***	N	N	N	N	N	Y	Y
3 Derrick	Y	N	Y	Y	Y	Y	N
4 ***Campbell***	N	N	N	N	N	Y	Y
5 Spratt	Y	N	Y	Y	N	Y	N
6 Tallon	Y	N	Y	Y	N	Y	Y
SOUTH DAKOTA							
AL Daschle	Y	Y	N	Y	N	Y	N

	248	249	250	251	252	253	254
TENNESSEE							
1 ***Quillen***	N	N	Y	Y	Y	Y	Y
2 ***Duncan***	N	N	N	Y	N	Y	Y
3 Lloyd	N	N	N	Y	Y	Y	Y
4 Cooper	Y	Y	Y	Y	Y	Y	N
5 Boner	Y	Y	Y	Y	Y	Y	N
6 Gordon	?	Y	Y	Y	Y	Y	N
7 ***Sundquist***	Y	Y	N	N	N	Y	Y
8 Jones	Y	N	Y	Y	Y	Y	Y
9 Ford	Y	Y	Y	Y	?	Y	N
TEXAS							
1 Vacancy							
2 Wilson	Y	Y	Y	Y	N	Y	N
3 ***Bartlett***	N	Y	N	Y	N	Y	N
4 Hall, R.	N	Y	N	N	N	Y	Y
5 Bryant	Y	Y	N	Y	N	Y	N
6 ***Barton***	N	Y	N	Y	N	Y	Y
7 ***Archer***	N	N	N	N	N	Y	Y
8 ***Fields***	N	N	N	N	N	Y	Y
9 Brooks	Y	N	Y	Y	Y	Y	N
10 Pickle	Y	Y	Y	Y	Y	Y	N
11 Leath	N	Y	Y	N	N	Y	Y
12 Wright	Y	Y	Y	Y	N	Y	N
13 ***Boulter***	-	Y	-	Y	N	Y	Y
14 ***Sweeney***	N	Y	N	Y	N	Y	Y
15 de la Garza	Y	Y	Y	Y	Y	Y	N
16 Coleman	N	Y	Y	Y	Y	Y	N
17 Stenholm	N	Y	Y	N	N	Y	Y
18 Leland	Y	?	Y	Y	N	Y	N
19 ***Combest***	N	Y	Y	N	N	Y	Y
20 Gonzalez	Y	N	Y	Y	N	Y	N
21 ***Loeffler***	?	?	?	?	?	?	?
22 ***DeLay***	N	N	N	Y	Y	Y	Y
23 Bustamante	Y	Y	Y	Y	Y	Y	N
24 Frost	Y	Y	Y	Y	Y	Y	N
25 Andrews	Y	Y	Y	Y	N	Y	N
26 ***Armey***	N	Y	N	Y	N	Y	Y
27 Ortiz	Y	Y	Y	Y	Y	Y	N
UTAH							
1 ***Hansen***	N	N	N	N	N	Y	Y
2 ***Monson***	N	Y	N	N	N	N	Y
3 ***Nielson***	Y	N	N	N	N	N	Y
VERMONT							
AL ***Jeffords***	N	N	Y	Y	N	Y	N
VIRGINIA							
1 ***Bateman***	Y	Y	N	Y	Y	Y	N
2 ***Whitehurst***	Y	Y	Y	Y	Y	Y	Y
3 ***Bliley***	Y	Y	N	Y	Y	Y	N
4 Sisisky	Y	Y	Y	Y	Y	Y	Y
5 Daniel	Y	Y	Y	N	Y	Y	Y
6 Olin	Y	N	Y	N	Y	Y	N
7 ***Slaughter***	Y	Y	N	Y	Y	Y	Y
8 ***Parris***	Y	N	N	Y	Y	Y	N
9 Boucher	Y	Y	Y	Y	Y	Y	N
10 ***Wolf***	Y	Y	Y	Y	Y	Y	N
WASHINGTON							
1 ***Miller***	Y	Y	N	Y	N	Y	N
2 Swift	Y	Y	Y	Y	Y	Y	N
3 Bonker	Y	Y	Y	Y	Y	Y	N
4 ***Morrison***	N	Y	N	Y	Y	Y	N
5 Foley	Y	Y	Y	Y	Y	Y	N
6 Dicks	N	Y	N	Y	Y	Y	N
7 Lowry	Y	N	N	N	Y	Y	N
8 ***Chandler***	Y	Y	N	Y	N	Y	N
WEST VIRGINIA							
1 Mollohan	Y	N	Y	Y	N	Y	Y
2 Staggers	Y	N	Y	Y	N	Y	N
3 Wise	Y	Y	N	Y	N	Y	Y
4 Rahall	Y	Y	Y	Y	N	Y	N
WISCONSIN							
1 Aspin	Y	?	?	Y	Y	Y	N
2 Kastenmeier	Y	N	Y	N	N	Y	N
3 ***Gunderson***	N	N	N	Y	N	Y	Y
4 Kleczka	Y	Y	Y	Y	N	Y	N
5 Moody	N	Y	Y	Y	N	Y	N
6 ***Petri***	N	N	N	Y	N	Y	Y
7 Obey	Y	Y	Y	N	Y	Y	N
8 ***Roth***	N	N	N	N	N	Y	Y
9 ***Sensenbrenner***	N	N	N	N	N	Y	Y
WYOMING							
AL ***Cheney***	N	N	Y	Y	N	Y	Y

Southern states - Ala., Ark., Fla., Ga., Ky., La., Miss., N.C., Okla., S.C., Tenn., Texas, Va.

* The *Congressional Record* vote number is different from the CQ vote number because the *Record* includes quorum calls in its tally. CQ does not publish quorum call votes.

255. HR 3011. Interior Appropriations, Fiscal 1986. Conte, R-Mass., amendment to rescind all but $500 million from the previously appropriated amounts available to the U.S. Synthetic Fuels Corporation, and to prohibit the corporation from using the funds for purposes other than administrative expenses. Adopted 312-111: R 145-32; D 167-79 (ND 119-48, SD 48-31), July 31, 1985.

256. HR 3011. Interior Appropriations, Fiscal 1986. Conte, R-Mass., amendment, as amended by the Regula, R-Ohio, substitute, to transfer from the Clean Coal Technology Reserve to the Department of Energy $100 million in fiscal 1985-86, $200 million in 1987, and $200 million in 1988, for cost-shared projects to demonstrate the commercial feasibility of clean coal technology. Adopted 238-184: R 134-44; D 104-140 (ND 57-109, SD 47-31), July 31, 1985.

257. HR 3011. Interior Appropriations, Fiscal 1986. Conte, R-Mass., amendment to eliminate $200 million in fiscal 1987 and $200 million in fiscal 1988 from the amounts appropriated from the Clean Coal Technology Reserve. Rejected 98-317: R 83-92; D 15-225 (ND 7-155, SD 8-70), July 31, 1985.

258. HR 3011. Interior Appropriations, Fiscal 1986. Passage of the bill to appropriate $8,238,097,000 in fiscal 1986 for the Department of the Interior and related agencies responsible for cultural and natural resource programs. Passed 270-143: R 54-119; D 216-24 (ND 152-10, SD 64-14), July 31, 1985. (The president had requested $7,223,824,000 in new budget authority.)

259. Procedural Motion. Sensenbrenner, R-Wis., motion to approve the House *Journal* of Wednesday, July 31. Motion agreed to 272-125: R 48-118; D 224-7 (ND 149-5, SD 75-2), Aug. 1, 1985.

260. HR 2068. State Department Authorizations, Fiscal 1986-87. Adoption of the conference report on the bill to authorize $7,574,614,000 for fiscal years 1986 and 1987 for the State Department, the U.S. Information Agency, the Board of International Broadcasting, and the Arms Control and Disarmament Agency. Adopted 350-74: R 124-55; D 226-19 (ND 156-11, SD 70-8), Aug. 1, 1985.

261. HR 1460. Anti-Apartheid Act. Adoption of the rule (H Res 251) to waive certain points of order against the conference report on the bill to impose sanctions against the government of South Africa until it eliminated laws enforcing "apartheid," official racial segregation. Adopted 349-75: R 107-71; D 242-4 (ND 169-0, SD 73-4), Aug. 1, 1985.

KEY

- Y Voted for (yea).
- # Paired for.
- \+ Announced for.
- N Voted against (nay).
- X Paired against.
- \- Announced against.
- P Voted "present."
- C Voted "present" to avoid possible conflict of interest.
- ? Did not vote or otherwise make a position known.

Democrats ***Republicans***

	255	256	257	258	259	260	261
ALABAMA							
1 ***Callahan***	Y	Y	N	N	N	Y	N
2 ***Dickinson***	Y	Y	N	N	N	Y	Y
3 Nichols	Y	?	?	?	Y	Y	Y
4 Bevill	Y	N	N	Y	Y	Y	Y
5 Flippo	Y	?	N	N	Y	Y	Y
6 Erdreich	Y	N	N	N	Y	Y	Y
7 Shelby	Y	N	N	N	Y	Y	Y
ALASKA							
AL ***Young***	N	N	N	Y	N	Y	Y
ARIZONA							
1 ***McCain***	Y	Y	N	Y	Y	Y	Y
2 Udall	Y	Y	N	Y	?	Y	Y
3 ***Stump***	Y	Y	Y	N	N	N	N
4 ***Rudd***	N	Y	Y	Y	Y	N	N
5 ***Kolbe***	Y	Y	Y	Y	N	Y	Y
ARKANSAS							
1 Alexander	N	N	N	Y	Y	?	Y
2 Robinson	Y	Y	N	Y	Y	Y	Y
3 ***Hammerschmidt***	N	Y	N	N	Y	Y	N
4 Anthony	Y	Y	N	Y	Y	Y	?
CALIFORNIA							
1 Bosco	Y	?	N	Y	Y	Y	Y
2 ***Chappie***	Y	Y	?	?	N	N	N
3 Matsui	Y	N	N	Y	Y	Y	Y
4 Fazio	N	N	N	Y	Y	Y	Y
5 Burton	Y	Y	N	Y	Y	Y	Y
6 Boxer	Y	N	N	Y	Y	Y	Y
7 Miller	Y	N	N	Y	Y	Y	Y
8 Dellums	Y	N	N	Y	Y	Y	Y
9 Stark	Y	N	N	Y	Y	Y	Y
10 Edwards	Y	Y	N	Y	Y	Y	Y
11 Lantos	Y	Y	N	Y	P	Y	Y
12 ***Zschau***	Y	Y	Y	N	N	Y	Y
13 Mineta	N	Y	N	Y	Y	Y	Y
14 ***Shumway***	Y	Y	Y	N	?	N	N
15 Coelho	Y	N	N	Y	Y	Y	Y
16 Panetta	Y	Y	N	Y	Y	Y	Y
17 ***Pashayan***	Y	Y	Y	N	N	N	N
18 Lehman	Y	Y	N	Y	Y	Y	Y
19 ***Lagomarsino***	Y	Y	Y	N	Y	Y	Y
20 ***Thomas***	Y	Y	N	N	?	Y	Y
21 ***Fiedler***	Y	Y	Y	N	N	Y	Y
22 ***Moorhead***	Y	Y	Y	N	N	N	N
23 Beilenson	Y	N	N	Y	Y	Y	Y
24 Waxman	Y	N	N	Y	Y	Y	Y
25 Roybal	Y	N	N	Y	Y	Y	Y
26 Berman	Y	N	N	Y	Y	Y	Y
27 Levine	Y	N	N	Y	Y	Y	Y
28 Dixon	Y	Y	N	Y	Y	Y	Y
29 Hawkins	N	?	?	#	Y	Y	Y
30 Martinez	Y	Y	N	Y	Y	Y	Y
31 Dymally	Y	N	N	Y	P	Y	Y
32 Anderson	N	N	N	Y	Y	Y	Y
33 ***Dreier***	Y	Y	Y	N	N	N	N
34 Torres	Y	N	N	Y	Y	Y	Y
35 ***Lewis***	Y	Y	Y	Y	N	Y	?
36 Brown	Y	Y	N	Y	Y	Y	Y
37 ***McCandless***	Y	Y	N	N	N	N	N
38 ***Dornan***	Y	Y	Y	N	N	Y	N
39 ***Dannemeyer***	N	Y	Y	N	N	N	N
40 ***Badham***	N	Y	?	?	N	Y	N
41 ***Lowery***	Y	Y	Y	Y	N	Y	Y
42 ***Lungren***	Y	Y	Y	N	N	N	Y
43 ***Packard***	Y	Y	N	N	N	Y	N
44 Bates	Y	Y	N	Y	?	Y	Y
45 ***Hunter***	Y	Y	Y	N	N	N	N
COLORADO							
1 Schroeder	Y	Y	N	Y	N	N	Y
2 Wirth	N	N	N	Y	Y	Y	Y
3 ***Strang***	N	N	N	N	N	N	N
4 ***Brown***	?	N	N	N	N	N	Y
5 ***Kramer***	N	Y	N	N	N	Y	Y
6 ***Schaefer***	N	N	N	N	N	N	N
CONNECTICUT							
1 Kennelly	Y	Y	N	Y	Y	Y	Y
2 Gejdenson	Y	N	N	Y	Y	Y	Y
3 Morrison	Y	Y	Y	Y	Y	Y	Y
4 ***McKinney***	N	Y	N	Y	Y	Y	Y
5 ***Rowland***	Y	Y	Y	N	Y	Y	Y
6 ***Johnson***	Y	Y	N	Y	Y	Y	Y
DELAWARE							
AL Carper	Y	Y	N	Y	Y	N	Y
FLORIDA							
1 Hutto	Y	Y	N	Y	Y	Y	Y
2 Fuqua	N	N	N	Y	Y	Y	Y
3 Bennett	N	Y	N	Y	Y	Y	Y
4 Chappell	N	Y	N	Y	Y	?	Y
5 ***McCollum***	Y	Y	N	N	Y	Y	N
6 MacKay	Y	Y	N	Y	Y	Y	Y
7 Gibbons	N	N	N	Y	Y	Y	Y
8 ***Young***	Y	Y	N	N	?	Y	Y
9 ***Bilirakis***	Y	N	N	N	N	Y	Y
10 ***Ireland***	?	Y	N	N	N	Y	N
11 Nelson	N	N	N	Y	Y	Y	Y
12 ***Lewis***	Y	Y	N	N	N	Y	N
13 ***Mack***	Y	N	N	N	N	Y	N
14 Mica	N	Y	N	Y	Y	Y	Y
15 ***Shaw***	Y	Y	N	N	N	Y	N
16 Smith	Y	N	N	Y	Y	Y	Y
17 Lehman	Y	N	N	Y	Y	Y	Y
18 Pepper	N	N	N	Y	Y	Y	+
19 Fascell	N	N	N	Y	Y	Y	Y
GEORGIA							
1 Thomas	Y	Y	N	Y	Y	Y	Y
2 Hatcher	Y	Y	N	Y	Y	Y	Y
3 Ray	Y	Y	N	N	Y	Y	Y
4 ***Swindall***	Y	Y	N	N	N	N	N
5 Fowler	Y	Y	N	Y	Y	Y	Y
6 ***Gingrich***	Y	Y	N	N	N	Y	Y
7 Darden	Y	Y	N	Y	Y	Y	Y
8 Rowland	Y	Y	N	Y	Y	Y	Y
9 Jenkins	Y	Y	N	N	Y	N	Y
10 Barnard	Y	Y	N	N	Y	Y	Y
HAWAII							
1 Heftel	Y	Y	?	?	?	Y	Y
2 Akaka	?	Y	N	Y	Y	Y	Y
IDAHO							
1 ***Craig***	Y	Y	Y	N	N	N	N
2 Stallings	Y	Y	Y	Y	Y	Y	Y
ILLINOIS							
1 Hayes	?	N	N	Y	?	Y	Y
2 Savage	N	?	?	?	Y	Y	Y
3 Russo	N	N	N	Y	Y	N	Y
4 ***O'Brien***	N	Y	N	Y	Y	Y	Y
5 Lipinski	N	N	N	Y	Y	Y	Y
6 ***Hyde***	Y	Y	Y	N	Y	Y	Y
7 Collins	Y	N	N	Y	Y	Y	Y
8 Rostenkowski	Y	N	N	Y	Y	Y	Y
9 Yates	Y	N	N	Y	Y	Y	Y
10 ***Porter***	Y	Y	Y	N	N	Y	Y
11 Annunzio	Y	Y	N	Y	Y	Y	Y
12 ***Crane***	Y	?	?	?	?	?	?
13 ***Fawell***	Y	Y	Y	Y	Y	Y	N
14 ***Grotberg***	N	Y	N	Y	N	Y	N
15 ***Madigan***	Y	Y	N	N	N	Y	Y
16 ***Martin***	Y	N	N	N	N	N	Y
17 Evans	Y	N	N	Y	Y	Y	Y
18 ***Michel***	N	Y	Y	N	N	Y	N
19 Bruce	N	N	N	Y	Y	Y	Y
20 Durbin	N	N	N	Y	N	Y	Y
21 Price	Y	Y	?	?	Y	Y	Y
22 Gray	N	N	N	Y	Y	Y	Y
INDIANA							
1 Visclosky	Y	Y	N	Y	Y	Y	Y
2 Sharp	Y	Y	N	Y	Y	Y	Y
3 ***Hiler***	Y	Y	Y	N	N	Y	Y
4 ***Coats***	Y	Y	Y	N	Y	Y	Y
5 ***Hillis***	Y	Y	N	N	N	Y	Y

ND - Northern Democrats SD - Southern Democrats

* Corresponding to Congressional Record Votes 281, 282, 283, 284, 285, 286, 287

	255	256	257	258	259	260	261
6 ***Burton***	Y	Y	Y	N	N	N	N
7 ***Myers***	N	Y	N	Y	Y	Y	Y
8 McCloskey	Y	N	N	Y	Y	Y	Y
9 Hamilton	Y	N	N	Y	Y	Y	Y
10 Jacobs	Y	Y	Y	N	N	N	Y
IOWA							
1 ***Leach***	Y	Y	Y	N	N	Y	Y
2 ***Tauke***	Y	Y	Y	N	N	Y	Y
3 ***Evans***	Y	Y	Y	N	N	N	N
4 Smith	N	N	N	Y	Y	Y	Y
5 ***Lightfoot***	Y	Y	Y	N	N	Y	Y
6 Bedell	Y	Y	Y	N	Y	Y	Y
KANSAS							
1 ***Roberts***	Y	Y	Y	N	N	N	N
2 Slattery	Y	N	N	N	Y	N	Y
3 ***Meyers***	Y	Y	N	Y	N	Y	Y
4 Glickman	Y	Y	Y	Y	Y	Y	Y
5 ***Whittaker***	Y	N	Y	N	N	N	Y
KENTUCKY							
1 Hubbard	N	N	N	N	Y	N	Y
2 Natcher	Y	N	Y	Y	Y	Y	Y
3 Mazzoli	N	Y	N	Y	Y	Y	Y
4 ***Snyder***	Y	Y	N	N	Y	Y	Y
5 ***Rogers***	N	N	N	Y	N	N	N
6 ***Hopkins***	Y	N	N	N	N	Y	Y
7 Perkins	N	N	N	Y	Y	Y	Y
LOUISIANA							
1 ***Livingston***	Y	Y	Y	Y	N	Y	Y
2 Boggs	N	N	N	Y	Y	Y	Y
3 Tauzin	Y	Y	N	Y	Y	Y	Y
4 Roemer	Y	Y	Y	N	N	N	Y
5 Huckaby	Y	Y	Y	Y	Y	Y	Y
6 ***Moore***	Y	Y	Y	N	Y	Y	N
7 Breaux	Y	Y	Y	Y	Y	Y	Y
8 Long	N	N	N	Y	Y	Y	Y
MAINE							
1 ***McKernan***	Y	Y	Y	Y	N	Y	Y
2 ***Snowe***	N	Y	Y	Y	N	Y	Y
MARYLAND							
1 Dyson	Y	Y	N	N	Y	Y	Y
2 ***Bentley***	Y	N	Y	Y	N	N	Y
3 Mikulski	Y	Y	N	Y	Y	Y	Y
4 ***Holt***	Y	N	N	N	Y	Y	N
5 Hoyer	Y	N	N	Y	Y	Y	Y
6 Byron	N	N	N	Y	Y	Y	Y
7 Mitchell	Y	Y	N	Y	?	Y	Y
8 Barnes	Y	N	N	Y	Y	Y	Y
MASSACHUSETTS							
1 ***Conte***	Y	Y	Y	Y	N	Y	Y
2 Boland	N	Y	N	Y	Y	Y	Y
3 Early	N	N	N	Y	Y	Y	Y
4 Frank	Y	N	N	Y	Y	Y	Y
5 Atkins	N	Y	N	Y	Y	Y	Y
6 Mavroules	N	N	N	Y	Y	Y	Y
7 Markey	Y	N	N	Y	Y	Y	Y
8 O'Neill							
9 Moakley	Y	N	N	Y	Y	Y	Y
10 Studds	Y	N	N	Y	Y	Y	Y
11 Donnelly	Y	N	N	X	Y	Y	Y
MICHIGAN							
1 Conyers	?	N	N	Y	Y	Y	Y
2 ***Pursell***	Y	Y	Y	N	N	Y	Y
3 Wolpe	Y	N	N	Y	Y	Y	Y
4 ***Siljander***	Y	Y	Y	N	N	Y	N
5 ***Henry***	Y	Y	N	Y	Y	Y	Y
6 Carr	Y	N	N	Y	Y	?	?
7 Kildee	N	N	N	Y	Y	Y	Y
8 Traxler	N	N	N	Y	Y	Y	Y
9 ***Vander Jagt***	Y	Y	Y	?	Y	Y	Y
10 ***Schuette***	Y	Y	Y	N	N	Y	Y
11 ***Davis***	Y	N	N	?	P	Y	Y
12 Bonior	N	N	N	Y	Y	Y	Y
13 Crockett	Y	N	?	?	Y	Y	Y
14 Hertel	Y	N	N	N	Y	N	Y
15 Ford	Y	N	?	?	?	Y	Y
16 Dingell	Y	N	N	Y	?	Y	Y
17 Levin	Y	N	N	Y	Y	Y	Y
18 ***Broomfield***	Y	Y	N	N	Y	Y	Y
MINNESOTA							
1 Penny	Y	Y	Y	N	N	N	Y
2 ***Weber***	Y	N	N	N	N	Y	Y
3 ***Frenzel***	Y	Y	Y	N	N	N	Y
4 Vento	Y	N	N	Y	Y	Y	Y
5 Sabo	Y	N	N	Y	Y	Y	Y
6 Sikorski	Y	N	N	Y	N	Y	Y

	255	256	257	258	259	260	261
7 ***Stangeland***	Y	Y	Y	N	N	Y	N
8 Oberstar	N	N	N	Y	Y	Y	Y
MISSISSIPPI							
1 Whitten	N	Y	N	Y	Y	Y	?
2 ***Franklin***	Y	Y	Y	N	Y	Y	Y
3 Montgomery	Y	Y	Y	N	Y	N	N
4 Dowdy	Y	N	N	N	Y	Y	Y
5 ***Lott***	Y	Y	Y	N	N	Y	N
MISSOURI							
1 Clay	Y	N	N	Y	?	Y	Y
2 Young	Y	N	N	Y	Y	Y	Y
3 Gephardt	Y	Y	N	Y	Y	Y	Y
4 Skelton	Y	Y	N	Y	Y	Y	Y
5 Wheat	Y	N	N	Y	Y	Y	Y
6 ***Coleman***	Y	Y	N	N	N	Y	Y
7 ***Taylor***	Y	Y	N	N	N	Y	N
8 ***Emerson***	Y	Y	N	N	N	Y	Y
9 Volkmer	Y	Y	N	N	Y	Y	Y
MONTANA							
1 Williams	Y	N	N	Y	Y	Y	Y
2 ***Marlenee***	Y	N	N	N	N	Y	Y
NEBRASKA							
1 ***Bereuter***	Y	Y	Y	Y	N	Y	Y
2 ***Daub***	Y	Y	Y	N	N	Y	Y
3 ***Smith***	Y	Y	Y	Y	Y	Y	Y
NEVADA							
1 Reid	Y	N	N	Y	Y	Y	Y
2 ***Vucanovich***	Y	Y	Y	Y	N	Y	N
NEW HAMPSHIRE							
1 ***Smith***	Y	N	N	N	N	N	N
2 ***Gregg***	Y	N	N	N	N	Y	Y
NEW JERSEY							
1 Florio	Y	N	N	Y	Y	Y	Y
2 Hughes	Y	Y	N	N	Y	N	Y
3 Howard	N	N	N	Y	Y	Y	Y
4 ***Smith***	Y	N	N	Y	?	Y	Y
5 ***Roukema***	Y	Y	N	Y	N	Y	Y
6 Dwyer	N	N	N	Y	Y	Y	Y
7 ***Rinaldo***	Y	N	N	Y	Y	Y	Y
8 Roe	Y	N	N	Y	Y	Y	Y
9 Torricelli	Y	N	N	Y	Y	Y	Y
10 Rodino	Y	Y	N	Y	Y	Y	Y
11 ***Gallo***	Y	Y	N	Y	N	Y	Y
12 ***Courter***	Y	N	N	N	N	Y	Y
13 ***Saxton***	Y	Y	N	Y	N	Y	Y
14 Guarini	Y	Y	N	Y	Y	Y	Y
NEW MEXICO							
1 ***Lujan***	N	Y	Y	N	N	Y	N
2 ***Skeen***	Y	Y	Y	Y	?	Y	N
3 Richardson	Y	N	N	Y	Y	Y	Y
NEW YORK							
1 ***Carney***	Y	N	N	N	N	N	Y
2 Downey	Y	N	N	Y	Y	Y	Y
3 Mrazek	Y	Y	N	Y	Y	Y	Y
4 ***Lent***	Y	N	N	N	N	Y	Y
5 ***McGrath***	Y	N	N	N	N	Y	Y
6 Addabbo	Y	Y	N	Y	Y	Y	Y
7 Ackerman	Y	N	N	Y	Y	Y	Y
8 Scheuer	N	N	N	Y	Y	Y	Y
9 Manton	Y	N	N	Y	Y	Y	Y
10 Schumer	Y	Y	N	Y	Y	Y	Y
11 Towns	Y	N	N	Y	Y	Y	Y
12 Owens	N	N	N	Y	Y	Y	Y
13 Solarz	Y	N	N	Y	Y	Y	Y
14 ***Molinari***	Y	N	N	N	N	Y	Y
15 ***Green***	Y	Y	Y	Y	Y	Y	Y
16 Rangel	Y	N	N	Y	Y	Y	Y
17 Weiss	Y	Y	N	Y	Y	Y	Y
18 Garcia	N	N	?	?	Y	+	Y
19 Biaggi	N	N	N	Y	Y	Y	Y
20 ***DioGuardi***	Y	Y	Y	N	Y	Y	Y
21 ***Fish***	Y	N	N	Y	Y	Y	Y
22 ***Gilman***	N	N	N	Y	Y	Y	Y
23 Stratton	N	Y	Y	Y	Y	Y	Y
24 ***Solomon***	Y	N	N	N	N	N	N
25 ***Boehlert***	Y	N	N	Y	N	Y	Y
26 ***Martin***	Y	N	?	?	N	Y	Y
27 ***Wortley***	Y	?	N	N	Y	Y	Y
28 McHugh	Y	N	N	Y	Y	Y	Y
29 ***Horton***	N	Y	N	Y	?	Y	Y
30 ***Eckert***	Y	N	Y	N	Y	Y	N
31 ***Kemp***	?	Y	?	?	?	?	?
32 LaFalce	N	N	N	N	Y	Y	Y
33 Nowak	Y	N	N	Y	Y	Y	Y
34 Lundine	N	N	N	Y	Y	Y	Y

	255	256	257	258	259	260	261
NORTH CAROLINA							
1 Jones	Y	Y	N	Y	?	Y	Y
2 Valentine	N	Y	N	Y	Y	Y	Y
3 Whitley	Y	Y	N	Y	Y	Y	Y
4 ***Cobey***	Y	Y	Y	N	N	Y	N
5 Neal	Y	Y	N	Y	?	Y	Y
6 ***Coble***	Y	Y	Y	N	N	N	N
7 Rose	Y	Y	N	Y	Y	Y	Y
8 Hefner	?	?	?	?	?	?	?
9 ***McMillan***	Y	Y	Y	N	N	Y	Y
10 ***Broyhill***	Y	Y	Y	N	Y	Y	Y
11 ***Hendon***	Y	Y	N	Y	N	N	Y
NORTH DAKOTA							
AL Dorgan	N	N	N	Y	Y	Y	Y
OHIO							
1 Luken	Y	N	N	Y	Y	N	Y
2 ***Gradison***	Y	Y	N	N	Y	Y	Y
3 Hall	Y	Y	N	Y	Y	Y	Y
4 ***Oxley***	Y	Y	N	N	N	Y	N
5 ***Latta***	Y	Y	N	N	N	N	N
6 ***McEwen***	Y	N	N	N	Y	N	N
7 ***DeWine***	Y	Y	N	N	N	Y	Y
8 ***Kindness***	N	Y	N	Y	?	N	Y
9 Kaptur	Y	N	N	Y	Y	Y	Y
10 ***Miller***	Y	N	N	N	N	Y	Y
11 Eckart	Y	Y	N	Y	Y	Y	Y
12 ***Kasich***	Y	Y	N	N	N	Y	Y
13 Pease	N	N	N	Y	Y	Y	Y
14 Seiberling	Y	Y	N	Y	?	Y	Y
15 ***Wylie***	Y	N	N	Y	Y	Y	Y
16 ***Regula***	N	Y	N	Y	Y	Y	Y
17 Traficant	N	N	N	Y	Y	Y	Y
18 Applegate	N	Y	N	Y	Y	Y	Y
19 Feighan	Y	Y	N	Y	Y	Y	Y
20 Oakar	Y	N	N	Y	?	Y	Y
21 Stokes	Y	N	N	Y	Y	Y	Y
OKLAHOMA							
1 Jones	Y	N	N	Y	Y	N	Y
2 Synar	Y	N	N	Y	Y	Y	Y
3 Watkins	Y	N	N	Y	Y	N	Y
4 McCurdy	Y	N	N	Y	Y	Y	Y
5 ***Edwards***	N	Y	N	Y	N	Y	Y
6 English	Y	Y	N	Y	Y	N	Y
OREGON							
1 AuCoin	Y	N	N	Y	Y	Y	Y
2 ***Smith, R.***	Y	Y	Y	Y	N	N	N
3 Wyden	Y	N	N	Y	Y	Y	Y
4 Weaver	Y	Y	N	N	?	N	Y
5 ***Smith, D.***	Y	Y	Y	N	N	N	N
PENNSYLVANIA							
1 Foglietta	N	Y	N	Y	Y	Y	Y
2 Gray	Y	N	N	Y	Y	Y	Y
3 Borski	N	N	N	Y	Y	Y	Y
4 Kolter	N	N	N	Y	Y	Y	Y
5 ***Schulze***	N	N	?	?	N	N	Y
6 Yatron	N	N	N	Y	Y	Y	Y
7 Edgar	Y	N	N	Y	Y	Y	Y
8 Kostmayer	Y	N	N	Y	P	Y	Y
9 ***Shuster***	N	N	N	N	N	N	N
10 ***McDade***	N	N	N	Y	?	Y	Y
11 Kanjorski	N	N	N	Y	Y	N	Y
12 Murtha	N	Y	N	Y	Y	Y	Y
13 ***Coughlin***	Y	Y	Y	Y	N	Y	Y
14 Coyne	N	N	N	Y	Y	Y	Y
15 ***Ritter***	Y	N	N	N	N	N	N
16 ***Walker***	Y	Y	Y	N	N	Y	Y
17 ***Gekas***	N	N	N	Y	N	N	Y
18 Walgren	Y	N	N	Y	Y	Y	Y
19 ***Goodling***	Y	Y	N	Y	N	Y	Y
20 Gaydos	N	Y	N	Y	?	Y	Y
21 ***Ridge***	Y	N	N	Y	N	Y	Y
22 Murphy	N	N	N	Y	Y	Y	Y
23 ***Clinger***	N	Y	N	Y	Y	Y	Y
RHODE ISLAND							
1 St Germain	Y	Y	N	Y	Y	Y	Y
2 ***Schneider***	Y	Y	Y	Y	Y	Y	N
SOUTH CAROLINA							
1 ***Hartnett***	Y	Y	Y	N	N	N	N
2 ***Spence***	N	Y	N	N	N	N	N
3 Derrick	Y	N	N	Y	Y	Y	Y
4 ***Campbell***	Y	Y	N	N	Y	N	Y
5 Spratt	Y	Y	N	Y	Y	Y	Y
6 Tallon	Y	Y	N	Y	Y	Y	Y
SOUTH DAKOTA							
AL Daschle	Y	N	N	Y	Y	Y	Y

	255	256	257	258	259	260	261
TENNESSEE							
1 ***Quillen***	N	N	N	Y	Y	Y	N
2 ***Duncan***	Y	N	N	Y	Y	Y	Y
3 Lloyd	N	N	N	Y	N	Y	Y
4 Cooper	Y	N	N	Y	Y	Y	Y
5 Boner	Y	Y	N	Y	Y	Y	Y
6 Gordon	Y	N	N	Y	Y	Y	Y
7 ***Sundquist***	Y	N	N	N	N	Y	N
8 Jones	Y	Y	N	Y	Y	Y	Y
9 Ford	N	N	?	?	?	Y	Y
TEXAS							
1 Vacancy							
2 Wilson	N	N	Y	Y	Y	Y	Y
3 ***Bartlett***	Y	Y	Y	N	N	Y	N
4 Hall, R.	N	Y	Y	N	Y	Y	N
5 Bryant	N	N	N	Y	Y	Y	Y
6 ***Barton***	Y	Y	Y	N	N	N	N
7 ***Archer***	Y	Y	Y	N	Y	N	N
8 ***Fields***	Y	Y	Y	N	N	N	N
9 Brooks	N	Y	N	Y	Y	Y	Y
10 Pickle	Y	Y	N	Y	Y	Y	Y
11 Leath	N	Y	Y	N	Y	Y	N
12 Wright	N	Y	N	Y	Y	Y	Y
13 ***Boulter***	Y	?	Y	N	N	N	N
14 ***Sweeney***	Y	Y	Y	N	Y	Y	Y
15 de la Garza	N	Y	N	Y	Y	Y	Y
16 Coleman	N	Y	N	Y	Y	Y	Y
17 Stenholm	Y	Y	Y	N	Y	N	N
18 Leland	N	N	N	Y	Y	Y	Y
19 ***Combest***	Y	Y	Y	N	N	Y	N
20 Gonzalez	P	N	N	Y	Y	Y	Y
21 ***Loeffler***	?	?	?	?	?	?	?
22 ***DeLay***	Y	Y	Y	N	?	N	N
23 Bustamante	N	Y	N	Y	Y	Y	Y
24 Frost	N	N	N	Y	Y	Y	Y
25 Andrews	Y	Y	N	Y	Y	Y	Y
26 ***Armey***	Y	Y	Y	N	N	N	N
27 Ortiz	N	Y	N	Y	Y	Y	Y
UTAH							
1 ***Hansen***	N	Y	Y	N	Y	N	N
2 ***Monson***	N	Y	Y	N	N	N	N
3 ***Nielson***	N	Y	Y	N	N	N	N
VERMONT							
AL ***Jeffords***	Y	N	N	Y	?	Y	Y
VIRGINIA							
1 ***Bateman***	Y	Y	N	Y	Y	Y	Y
2 ***Whitehurst***	Y	Y	N	N	Y	Y	Y
3 ***Bliley***	Y	Y	N	N	N	Y	Y
4 Sisisky	Y	Y	N	Y	Y	Y	Y
5 Daniel	N	Y	N	N	Y	Y	Y
6 Olin	Y	Y	N	Y	Y	Y	Y
7 ***Slaughter***	Y	Y	N	N	N	Y	Y
8 ***Parris***	Y	N	N	Y	N	Y	N
9 Boucher	Y	N	N	Y	Y	Y	Y
10 ***Wolf***	N	Y	N	Y	N	Y	Y
WASHINGTON							
1 ***Miller***	Y	Y	Y	N	Y	Y	Y
2 Swift	Y	Y	N	Y	Y	Y	Y
3 Bonker	Y	?	N	Y	Y	Y	Y
4 ***Morrison***	Y	Y	Y	Y	Y	Y	Y
5 Foley	N	Y	N	Y	Y	Y	Y
6 Dicks	Y	Y	N	Y	Y	Y	Y
7 Lowry	Y	N	N	Y	Y	Y	Y
8 ***Chandler***	Y	Y	Y	N	?	Y	Y
WEST VIRGINIA							
1 Mollohan	N	N	N	Y	Y	Y	Y
2 Staggers	N	N	N	Y	Y	Y	Y
3 Wise	N	N	N	Y	Y	Y	Y
4 Rahall	N	N	N	Y	?	Y	Y
WISCONSIN							
1 Aspin	Y	Y	?	Y	Y	Y	Y
2 Kastenmeier	Y	N	N	Y	Y	Y	Y
3 ***Gunderson***	Y	Y	Y	N	N	Y	Y
4 Kleczka	Y	Y	N	Y	Y	Y	Y
5 Moody	Y	N	N	Y	Y	?	Y
6 ***Petri***	Y	Y	Y	N	N	Y	N
7 Obey	Y	N	N	Y	Y	Y	Y
8 ***Roth***	?	Y	Y	N	?	Y	N
9 ***Sensenbrenner***	Y	Y	Y	N	N	N	Y
WYOMING							
AL ***Cheney***	Y	Y	Y	N	Y	N	N

Southern states - Ala., Ark., Fla., Ga., Ky., La., Miss., N.C., Okla., S.C., Tenn., Texas, Va.

* The *Congressional Record* vote number is different from the CQ vote number because the *Record* includes quorum calls in its tally. CQ does not publish quorum call votes.

262. HR 1460. Anti-Apartheid Act. Adoption of the conference report on the bill to impose sanctions against the government of South Africa until it eliminated laws enforcing "apartheid," official racial segregation. Adopted 380-48: R 134-45; D 246-3 (ND 169-0, SD 77-3), Aug. 1, 1985.

263. HR 3008. Federal Pay Equity Study. Adoption of the rule (H Res 241) to provide for House floor consideration of the bill to authorize an independent study to determine if pay differences in the federal government are due to discrimination on the basis of sex, race or Hispanic origin. Adopted 292-133: R 53-127; D 239-6 (ND 166-0, SD 73-6), Aug. 1, 1985.

264. S Con Res 32. First Budget Resolution, Fiscal 1986. Gray, D-Pa., motion that the House recede from its amendment to the first concurrent budget resolution for fiscal 1986 and concur with a further amendment. In effect, the House replaced its version of the budget resolution with the text of the conference report on the resolution, which set non-binding spending and taxing levels for the fiscal year ending Sept. 30, 1986, as follows: budget authority, $1,069.7 billion; outlays, $967.6 billion; revenues, $795.7 billion; and deficit, $171.9 billion. Motion agreed to 309-119: R 127-52; D 182-67 (ND 111-58, SD 71-9), Aug. 1, 1985.

KEY

- Y Voted for (yea).
- # Paired for.
- \+ Announced for.
- N Voted against (nay).
- X Paired against.
- \- Announced against.
- P Voted "present."
- C Voted "present" to avoid possible conflict of interest.
- ? Did not vote or otherwise make a position known.

Democrats ***Republicans***

	262	263	264
ALABAMA			
1 ***Callahan***	N	N	Y
2 ***Dickinson***	Y	N	N
3 Nichols	Y	Y	Y
4 Bevill	Y	Y	Y
5 Flippo	Y	Y	Y
6 Erdreich	Y	Y	Y
7 Shelby	Y	Y	Y
ALASKA			
AL ***Young***	Y	Y	Y
ARIZONA			
1 ***McCain***	Y	N	Y
2 Udall	Y	Y	Y
3 ***Stump***	N	N	N
4 ***Rudd***	N	N	N
5 ***Kolbe***	Y	N	Y
ARKANSAS			
1 Alexander	Y	?	Y
2 Robinson	Y	Y	Y
3 ***Hammerschmidt***	Y	N	Y
4 Anthony	Y	Y	Y
CALIFORNIA			
1 Bosco	Y	Y	N
2 ***Chappie***	N	N	N
3 Matsui	Y	Y	Y
4 Fazio	Y	Y	Y
5 Burton	Y	Y	Y
6 Boxer	Y	Y	Y
7 Miller	Y	?	Y
8 Dellums	Y	Y	N
9 Stark	Y	Y	N
10 Edwards	Y	Y	N
11 Lantos	Y	Y	Y
12 ***Zschau***	Y	N	N
13 Mineta	Y	Y	Y
14 ***Shumway***	N	N	N
15 Coelho	Y	Y	Y
16 Panetta	Y	Y	Y
17 ***Pashayan***	Y	N	Y
18 Lehman	Y	Y	Y
19 ***Lagomarsino***	Y	N	Y
20 ***Thomas***	Y	Y	N
21 ***Fiedler***	Y	N	Y
22 ***Moorhead***	N	N	Y
23 Beilenson	Y	Y	Y
24 Waxman	Y	Y	Y
25 Roybal	Y	?	N
26 Berman	Y	Y	Y
27 Levine	Y	Y	Y
28 Dixon	Y	Y	Y
29 Hawkins	Y	Y	Y
30 Martinez	Y	Y	Y
31 Dymally	Y	Y	N
32 Anderson	Y	Y	N
33 ***Dreier***	Y	N	N
34 Torres	Y	Y	N
35 ***Lewis***	Y	N	Y
36 Brown	Y	Y	N
37 ***McCandless***	N	N	N
38 ***Dornan***	N	N	N
39 ***Dannemeyer***	N	N	N
40 ***Badham***	N	N	Y
41 ***Lowery***	Y	N	Y
42 ***Lungren***	Y	N	Y
43 ***Packard***	N	N	Y
44 Bates	Y	Y	N
45 ***Hunter***	Y	N	Y
COLORADO			
1 Schroeder	Y	Y	N
2 Wirth	Y	Y	Y
3 ***Strang***	Y	N	Y
4 ***Brown***	Y	Y	N
5 ***Kramer***	Y	N	N
6 ***Schaefer***	N	N	Y
CONNECTICUT			
1 Kennelly	Y	Y	Y
2 Gejdenson	Y	Y	Y
3 Morrison	Y	Y	N
4 ***McKinney***	Y	Y	Y
5 ***Rowland***	Y	N	Y
6 ***Johnson***	Y	Y	Y
DELAWARE			
AL Carper	Y	Y	N
FLORIDA			
1 Hutto	Y	N	Y
2 Fuqua	Y	Y	Y
3 Bennett	Y	Y	Y
4 Chappell	Y	Y	Y
5 ***McCollum***	N	N	Y
6 MacKay	Y	Y	Y
7 Gibbons	Y	Y	Y
8 ***Young***	Y	Y	Y
9 ***Bilirakis***	Y	N	Y
10 ***Ireland***	Y	N	Y
11 Nelson	Y	Y	N
12 ***Lewis***	Y	Y	Y
13 ***Mack***	N	N	N
14 Mica	Y	Y	Y
15 ***Shaw***	Y	N	Y
16 Smith	Y	Y	Y
17 Lehman	Y	Y	Y
18 Pepper	Y	Y	Y
19 Fascell	Y	Y	Y
GEORGIA			
1 Thomas	Y	Y	Y
2 Hatcher	Y	Y	Y
3 Ray	Y	Y	Y
4 ***Swindall***	Y	N	Y
5 Fowler	Y	Y	Y
6 ***Gingrich***	Y	N	Y
7 Darden	Y	Y	Y
8 Rowland	Y	Y	Y
9 Jenkins	Y	Y	Y
10 Barnard	Y	Y	Y
HAWAII			
1 Heftel	Y	Y	Y
2 Akaka	Y	Y	Y
IDAHO			
1 ***Craig***	Y	N	N
2 Stallings	Y	Y	Y
ILLINOIS			
1 Hayes	Y	Y	N
2 Savage	Y	Y	N
3 Russo	Y	Y	Y
4 ***O'Brien***	Y	Y	Y
5 Lipinski	Y	Y	N
6 ***Hyde***	N	N	Y
7 Collins	Y	Y	N
8 Rostenkowski	Y	Y	Y
9 Yates	Y	Y	N
10 ***Porter***	Y	N	N
11 Annunzio	Y	Y	Y
12 ***Crane***	?	?	X
13 ***Fawell***	Y	N	N
14 ***Grotberg***	Y	N	Y
15 ***Madigan***	Y	N	N
16 ***Martin***	Y	N	Y
17 Evans	Y	Y	Y
18 ***Michel***	Y	N	Y
19 Bruce	Y	Y	Y
20 Durbin	Y	Y	Y
21 Price	Y	Y	Y
22 Gray	Y	Y	#
INDIANA			
1 Visclosky	Y	Y	Y
2 Sharp	Y	Y	Y
3 ***Hiler***	Y	N	Y
4 ***Coats***	Y	N	Y
5 ***Hillis***	Y	N	Y

ND - Northern Democrats SD - Southern Democrats

* Corresponding to Congressional Record Votes 288, 289, 290

	262	263	264
6 ***Burton***	N	N	Y
7 ***Myers***	N	Y	N
8 McCloskey	Y	Y	Y
9 Hamilton	Y	Y	Y
10 Jacobs	Y	Y	N
IOWA			
1 ***Leach***	Y	Y	N
2 ***Tauke***	Y	Y	N
3 ***Evans***	Y	Y	N
4 Smith	Y	Y	N
5 ***Lightfoot***	Y	N	N
6 Bedell	Y	Y	N
KANSAS			
1 ***Roberts***	Y	N	N
2 Slattery	Y	Y	Y
3 ***Meyers***	Y	Y	Y
4 Glickman	Y	Y	Y
5 ***Whittaker***	Y	N	Y
KENTUCKY			
1 Hubbard	Y	Y	Y
2 Natcher	Y	Y	Y
3 Mazzoli	Y	Y	Y
4 ***Snyder***	N	N	Y
5 ***Rogers***	Y	N	Y
6 ***Hopkins***	Y	Y	N
7 Perkins	Y	Y	N
LOUISIANA			
1 ***Livingston***	Y	N	Y
2 Boggs	Y	Y	Y
3 Tauzin	Y	Y	Y
4 Roemer	Y	Y	Y
5 Huckaby	Y	Y	Y
6 ***Moore***	Y	N	Y
7 Breaux	Y	Y	Y
8 Long	Y	Y	Y
MAINE			
1 ***McKernan***	Y	Y	Y
2 ***Snowe***	Y	Y	Y
MARYLAND			
1 Dyson	Y	Y	Y
2 ***Bentley***	Y	Y	Y
3 Mikulski	Y	Y	Y
4 ***Holt***	Y	Y	Y
5 Hoyer	Y	Y	Y
6 Byron	Y	Y	Y
7 Mitchell	Y	Y	N
8 Barnes	Y	Y	Y
MASSACHUSETTS			
1 ***Conte***	Y	Y	Y
2 Boland	Y	Y	Y
3 Early	Y	Y	N
4 Frank	Y	Y	N
5 Atkins	Y	Y	Y
6 Mavroules	Y	?	Y
7 Markey	Y	Y	N
8 O'Neill			
9 Moakley	Y	Y	Y
10 Studds	Y	Y	N
11 Donnelly	Y	Y	Y
MICHIGAN			
1 Conyers	Y	Y	N
2 ***Pursell***	Y	Y	Y
3 Wolpe	Y	Y	Y
4 ***Siljander***	N	N	Y
5 ***Henry***	Y	Y	Y
6 Carr	?	Y	N
7 Kildee	Y	Y	N
8 Traxler	Y	Y	Y
9 ***Vander Jagt***	Y	Y	Y
10 ***Schuette***	N	N	N
11 ***Davis***	Y	Y	Y
12 Bonior	Y	Y	Y
13 Crockett	Y	Y	N
14 Hertel	Y	Y	N
15 Ford	Y	Y	Y
16 Dingell	Y	?	Y
17 Levin	Y	Y	Y
18 ***Broomfield***	Y	N	Y
MINNESOTA			
1 Penny	Y	Y	N
2 ***Weber***	Y	N	N
3 ***Frenzel***	Y	Y	N
4 Vento	Y	Y	Y
5 Sabo	Y	Y	Y
6 Sikorski	Y	Y	N
7 ***Stangeland***	Y	N	N
8 Oberstar	Y	Y	N
MISSISSIPPI			
1 Whitten	Y	Y	Y
2 ***Franklin***	Y	N	Y
3 Montgomery	Y	Y	Y
4 Dowdy	Y	Y	Y
5 ***Lott***	Y	N	Y
MISSOURI			
1 Clay	Y	Y	N
2 Young	Y	Y	Y
3 Gephardt	Y	Y	Y
4 Skelton	Y	Y	Y
5 Wheat	Y	Y	Y
6 ***Coleman***	Y	Y	Y
7 ***Taylor***	N	N	Y
8 ***Emerson***	N	N	Y
9 Volkmer	Y	Y	Y
MONTANA			
1 Williams	Y	Y	Y
2 ***Marlenee***	N	N	N
NEBRASKA			
1 ***Bereuter***	Y	Y	N
2 ***Daub***	Y	N	Y
3 ***Smith***	Y	Y	N
NEVADA			
1 Reid	Y	Y	Y
2 ***Vucanovich***	Y	N	Y
NEW HAMPSHIRE			
1 ***Smith***	N	N	Y
2 ***Gregg***	Y	N	N
NEW JERSEY			
1 Florio	Y	Y	N
2 Hughes	Y	Y	Y
3 Howard	Y	Y	Y
4 ***Smith***	Y	Y	Y
5 ***Roukema***	Y	Y	N
6 Dwyer	Y	Y	Y
7 ***Rinaldo***	Y	Y	Y
8 Roe	Y	Y	Y
9 Torricelli	Y	Y	N
10 Rodino	Y	Y	N
11 ***Gallo***	Y	N	Y
12 ***Courter***	Y	N	Y
13 ***Saxton***	Y	N	Y
14 Guarini	Y	Y	Y
NEW MEXICO			
1 ***Lujan***	Y	N	Y
2 ***Skeen***	Y	N	Y
3 Richardson	Y	Y	Y
NEW YORK			
1 ***Carney***	Y	N	Y
2 Downey	Y	Y	Y
3 Mrazek	Y	Y	N
4 ***Lent***	Y	Y	Y
5 ***McGrath***	Y	N	N
6 Addabbo	Y	Y	N
7 Ackerman	Y	Y	Y
8 Scheuer	Y	Y	Y
9 Manton	Y	Y	Y
10 Schumer	Y	Y	Y
11 Towns	Y	Y	N
12 Owens	Y	Y	N
13 Solarz	Y	Y	Y
14 ***Molinari***	Y	N	Y
15 ***Green***	Y	Y	N
16 Rangel	Y	Y	Y
17 Weiss	Y	Y	N
18 Garcia	Y	Y	N
19 Biaggi	Y	Y	Y
20 ***DioGuardi***	Y	N	Y
21 ***Fish***	Y	Y	Y
22 ***Gilman***	Y	Y	N
23 Stratton	Y	Y	Y
24 ***Solomon***	?	N	N
25 ***Boehlert***	Y	Y	Y
26 ***Martin***	Y	N	Y
27 ***Wortley***	Y	N	Y
28 McHugh	Y	Y	Y
29 ***Horton***	Y	Y	Y
30 ***Eckert***	N	N	Y
31 ***Kemp***	Y	N	Y
32 LaFalce	Y	Y	N
33 Nowak	Y	Y	Y
34 Lundine	Y	Y	Y
NORTH CAROLINA			
1 Jones	Y	Y	Y
2 Valentine	Y	Y	Y
3 Whitley	Y	Y	Y
4 ***Cobey***	Y	N	Y
5 Neal	Y	Y	Y
6 ***Coble***	Y	N	Y
7 Rose	Y	Y	Y
8 Hefner	?	?	?
9 ***McMillan***	Y	N	Y
10 ***Broyhill***	Y	N	Y
11 ***Hendon***	Y	N	Y
NORTH DAKOTA			
AL Dorgan	Y	Y	N
OHIO			
1 Luken	Y	Y	Y
2 ***Gradison***	Y	N	?
3 Hall	Y	Y	Y
4 ***Oxley***	Y	N	Y
5 ***Latta***	Y	N	Y
6 ***McEwen***	Y	N	Y
7 ***DeWine***	Y	N	Y
8 ***Kindness***	N	Y	Y
9 Kaptur	Y	Y	Y
10 ***Miller***	N	Y	N
11 Eckart	Y	Y	Y
12 ***Kasich***	Y	N	Y
13 Pease	Y	Y	N
14 Seiberling	Y	Y	N
15 ***Wylie***	Y	Y	Y
16 ***Regula***	Y	Y	N
17 Traficant	Y	Y	N
18 Applegate	Y	Y	N
19 Feighan	Y	Y	Y
20 Oakar	Y	Y	Y
21 Stokes	Y	Y	Y
OKLAHOMA			
1 Jones	Y	Y	Y
2 Synar	Y	Y	N
3 Watkins	Y	Y	N
4 McCurdy	Y	Y	Y
5 ***Edwards***	Y	N	Y
6 English	Y	Y	N
OREGON			
1 AuCoin	Y	Y	Y
2 ***Smith, R.***	Y	N	Y
3 Wyden	Y	Y	Y
4 Weaver	Y	Y	N
5 ***Smith, D.***	N	N	N
PENNSYLVANIA			
1 Foglietta	Y	Y	N
2 Gray	Y	Y	Y
3 Borski	Y	Y	Y
4 Kolter	Y	Y	Y
5 ***Schulze***	Y	N	Y
6 Yatron	Y	Y	Y
7 Edgar	Y	Y	Y
8 Kostmayer	Y	Y	Y
9 ***Shuster***	N	N	Y
10 ***McDade***	Y	Y	Y
11 Kanjorski	Y	Y	N
12 Murtha	Y	Y	Y
13 ***Coughlin***	Y	N	Y
14 Coyne	Y	Y	Y
15 ***Ritter***	N	N	Y
16 ***Walker***	Y	N	Y
17 ***Gekas***	Y	N	Y
18 Walgren	Y	Y	Y
19 ***Goodling***	Y	Y	Y
20 Gaydos	Y	Y	N
21 ***Ridge***	Y	Y	Y
22 Murphy	Y	Y	N
23 ***Clinger***	Y	Y	Y
RHODE ISLAND			
1 St Germain	Y	Y	Y
2 ***Schneider***	Y	Y	Y
SOUTH CAROLINA			
1 ***Hartnett***	N	N	N
2 ***Spence***	Y	N	Y
3 Derrick	Y	Y	Y
4 ***Campbell***	Y	N	Y
5 Spratt	Y	N	Y
6 Tallon	Y	Y	Y
SOUTH DAKOTA			
AL Daschle	Y	Y	Y
TENNESSEE			
1 ***Quillen***	N	N	Y
2 ***Duncan***	Y	Y	Y
3 Lloyd	Y	Y	Y
4 Cooper	Y	Y	Y.
5 Boner	Y	Y	Y
6 Gordon	Y	Y	Y
7 ***Sundquist***	Y	N	Y
8 Jones	Y	Y	Y
9 Ford	Y	Y	Y
TEXAS			
1 Vacancy			
2 Wilson	Y	Y	Y
3 ***Bartlett***	Y	N	Y
4 Hall, R.	N	N	Y
5 Bryant	Y	Y	Y
6 ***Barton***	N	N	N
7 ***Archer***	N	N	N
8 ***Fields***	N	N	N
9 Brooks	Y	Y	Y
10 Pickle	Y	Y	Y
11 Leath	N	N	N
12 Wright	Y	Y	Y
13 ***Boulter***	N	N	Y
14 ***Sweeney***	Y	N	Y
15 de la Garza	Y	Y	Y
16 Coleman	Y	Y	Y
17 Stenholm	N	N	N
18 Leland	Y	Y	N
19 ***Combest***	N	N	Y
20 Gonzalez	Y	Y	N
21 ***Loeffler***	?	?	?
22 ***DeLay***	N	N	N
23 Bustamante	Y	Y	Y
24 Frost	Y	Y	Y
25 Andrews	Y	Y	Y
26 ***Armey***	N	N	N
27 Ortiz	Y	Y	Y
UTAH			
1 ***Hansen***	N	N	Y
2 ***Monson***	N	N	Y
3 ***Nielson***	N	N	Y
VERMONT			
AL ***Jeffords***	Y	Y	Y
VIRGINIA			
1 ***Bateman***	Y	Y	Y
2 ***Whitehurst***	Y	N	Y
3 ***Bliley***	Y	N	Y
4 Sisisky	Y	Y	Y
5 Daniel	Y	Y	Y
6 Olin	Y	N	Y
7 ***Slaughter***	N	N	Y
8 ***Parris***	Y	N	Y
9 Boucher	Y	Y	Y
10 ***Wolf***	Y	Y	Y
WASHINGTON			
1 ***Miller***	Y	N	N
2 Swift	Y	Y	Y
3 Bonker	Y	Y	Y
4 ***Morrison***	Y	Y	Y
5 Foley	Y	Y	Y
6 Dicks	Y	Y	Y
7 Lowry	Y	Y	Y
8 ***Chandler***	Y	Y	Y
WEST VIRGINIA			
1 Mollohan	Y	Y	Y
2 Staggers	Y	Y	N
3 Wise	Y	Y	N
4 Rahall	Y	Y	Y
WISCONSIN			
1 Aspin	Y	Y	Y
2 Kastenmeier	Y	Y	N
3 ***Gunderson***	Y	Y	N
4 Kleczka	Y	Y	Y
5 Moody	Y	Y	Y
6 ***Petri***	Y	Y	N
7 Obey	Y	Y	Y
8 ***Roth***	N	N	N
9 ***Sensenbrenner***	Y	N	N
WYOMING			
AL ***Cheney***	N	N	Y

Southern states - Ala., Ark., Fla., Ga., Ky., La., Miss., N.C., Okla., S.C., Tenn., Texas, Va.

* The *Congressional Record* vote number is different from the CQ vote number because the *Record* includes quorum calls in its tally. CQ does not publish quorum call votes.

265. HR 10. National Development Investment. McCollum, R-Fla., amendment to require that areas meet both the criteria of high unemployment and low per capita income in order to qualify for aid from the Economic Development Administration. Rejected 109-247: R 92-60; D 17-187 (ND 8-128, SD 9-59), Sept. 4, 1985. (The bill required areas to meet one of three criteria, which included unemployment, income and economic dislocation.)

266. HR 10. National Development Investment. Passage of the bill to authorize $160 million in fiscal 1986 for the Economic Development Administration and such sums as may be necessary for fiscal 1987 and fiscal 1988; $79.5 million for the Appalachian Regional Commission's (ARC) highway programs in fiscal 1986 and such sums as are necessary in fiscal 1987 through 1992; and $39.2 million for ARC non-highway programs in fiscal 1986 and such sums as are necessary in fiscal 1987 through fiscal 1990. Passed 260-96: R 66-85; D 194-11 (ND 132-4, SD 62-7), Sept. 4, 1985. A "nay" was a vote supporting the president's position.

267. Procedural Motion. Armey, R-Texas, motion to approve the House *Journal* of Wednesday, Sept. 4. Motion agreed to 231-100: R 47-93; D 184-7 (ND 121-5, SD 63-2), Sept. 5, 1985.

268. HR 2372. Railroad Safety Improvement. Adoption of the rule (H Res 250) to provide for House floor consideration of the bill to authorize $40.9 million in fiscal 1986 and $42.5 million in fiscal 1987 for federal rail safety programs. Adopted 244-109: R 40-106; D 204-3 (ND 137-1, SD 67-2), Sept. 5, 1985.

269. HR 2372. Railroad Safety Improvement. Walker, R-Pa., amendment to delete $6.3 million over fiscal 1986-87 for reimbursements to states that conduct their own rail safety inspections. Rejected 106-254: R 93-52; D 13-202 (ND 1-144, SD 12-58), Sept. 5, 1985. A "yea" was a vote supporting the president's position. (The bill was subsequently passed by voice vote. The House then moved to delete the language of S 1080, the Senate version of the railroad safety bill, and insert instead the provisions of HR 2372. After the motion was agreed to, S 1080 was passed by voice vote.)

KEY

- Y Voted for (yea).
- # Paired for.
- + Announced for.
- N Voted against (nay).
- X Paired against.
- - Announced against.
- P Voted "present."
- C Voted "present" to avoid possible conflict of interest.
- ? Did not vote or otherwise make a position known.

Democrats ***Republicans***

	265	266	267	268	269
ALABAMA					
1 ***Callahan***	Y	N	N	N	Y
2 ***Dickinson***	Y	N	N	Y	Y
3 Nichols	?	?	?	?	N
4 Bevill	?	?	?	?	?
5 Flippo	N	Y	Y	Y	N
6 Erdreich	N	Y	Y	Y	N
7 Shelby	?	?	?	?	?
ALASKA					
AL ***Young***	?	?	?	?	?
ARIZONA					
1 ***McCain***	?	?	?	?	?
2 Udall	?	?	?	?	?
3 ***Stump***	Y	N	N	N	Y
4 ***Rudd***	Y	N	Y	Y	Y
5 ***Kolbe***	Y	N	N	N	Y
ARKANSAS					
1 Alexander	N	Y	Y	Y	N
2 Robinson	N	Y	Y	Y	N
3 ***Hammerschmidt***	N	Y	Y	N	Y
4 Anthony	N	Y	Y	Y	N
CALIFORNIA					
1 Bosco	N	Y	Y	Y	N
2 ***Chappie***	?	?	?	?	?
3 Matsui	N	Y	Y	Y	N
4 Fazio	?	?	?	?	X
5 Burton	N	Y	Y	Y	N
6 Boxer	N	Y	Y	Y	N
7 Miller	N	Y	?	Y	N
8 Dellums	N	Y	?	?	X
9 Stark	N	Y	Y	Y	N
10 Edwards	N	Y	Y	Y	N
11 Lantos	?	?	Y	Y	N
12 ***Zschau***	Y	N	N	N	Y
13 Mineta	N	Y	Y	Y	N
14 ***Shumway***	Y	N	N	Y	Y
15 Coelho	N	Y	Y	Y	N
16 Panetta	N	Y	Y	Y	N
17 ***Pashayan***	?	?	?	?	?
18 Lehman	?	?	Y	Y	N
19 ***Lagomarsino***	Y	N	N	N	Y
20 ***Thomas***	#	?	?	?	#
21 ***Fiedler***	Y	Y	N	N	Y
22 ***Moorhead***	Y	N	N	N	Y
23 Beilenson	N	Y	Y	Y	N
24 Waxman	?	Y	Y	Y	N
25 Roybal	N	Y	Y	Y	N
26 Berman	?	?	?	?	?
27 Levine	?	?	Y	Y	N
28 Dixon	N	Y	Y	Y	N
29 Hawkins	?	?	?	?	?
30 Martinez	?	?	Y	Y	N
31 Dymally	?	?	?	?	?
32 Anderson	N	Y	Y	Y	N
33 ***Dreier***	?	?	?	?	?
34 Torres	N	?	Y	Y	N
35 ***Lewis***	N	Y	N	N	Y
36 Brown	N	Y	Y	Y	N
37 ***McCandless***	Y	N	N	N	Y
38 ***Dornan***	Y	N	Y	N	Y
39 ***Dannemeyer***	?	?	?	?	?
40 ***Badham***	Y	N	?	?	?
41 ***Lowery***	?	?	?	?	?
42 ***Lungren***	Y	N	N	N	Y
43 ***Packard***	Y	N	N	N	Y
44 Bates	Y	N	Y	Y	N
45 ***Hunter***	?	?	?	?	?
COLORADO					
1 Schroeder	N	Y	?	?	?
2 Wirth	?	?	?	?	?
3 ***Strang***	Y	N	N	N	Y
4 ***Brown***	Y	N	N	N	Y
5 ***Kramer***	Y	N	N	N	Y
6 ***Schaefer***	?	?	N	N	Y
CONNECTICUT					
1 Kennelly	N	Y	Y	Y	N
2 Gejdenson	N	Y	Y	Y	N
3 Morrison	N	Y	?	Y	N
4 ***McKinney***	N	Y	Y	?	?
5 ***Rowland***	Y	N	Y	N	Y
6 ***Johnson***	N	Y	Y	Y	Y
DELAWARE					
AL Carper	Y	Y	Y	Y	N
FLORIDA					
1 Hutto	N	Y	Y	Y	N
2 Fuqua	N	Y	?	?	?
3 Bennett	Y	Y	Y	Y	N
4 Chappell	?	Y	Y	Y	N
5 ***McCollum***	Y	N	Y	N	Y
6 MacKay	#	?	?	?	?
7 Gibbons	?	?	?	Y	?
8 ***Young***	N	Y	N	Y	N
9 ***Bilirakis***	?	?	?	N	Y
10 ***Ireland***	Y	N	Y	N	Y
11 Nelson	#	X	+	+	+
12 ***Lewis***	Y	Y	N	N	Y
13 ***Mack***	Y	N	N	N	Y
14 Mica	Y	Y	Y	Y	N
15 ***Shaw***	#	?	?	?	#
16 Smith	N	Y	Y	Y	N
17 Lehman	N	Y	Y	Y	N
18 Pepper	-	+	+	+	-
19 Fascell	N	Y	Y	Y	N
GEORGIA					
1 Thomas	N	Y	Y	Y	N
2 Hatcher	N	Y	Y	Y	N
3 Ray	N	Y	Y	Y	Y
4 ***Swindall***	Y	?	N	N	Y
5 Fowler	N	Y	Y	Y	N
6 ***Gingrich***	Y	Y	N	N	Y
7 Darden	N	Y	Y	Y	N
8 Rowland	N	Y	Y	Y	N
9 Jenkins	N	Y	?	Y	Y
10 Barnard	N	Y	Y	Y	Y
HAWAII					
1 Heftel	?	?	?	?	?
2 Akaka	?	?	?	?	?
IDAHO					
1 ***Craig***	Y	N	?	?	?
2 Stallings	Y	Y	?	Y	N
ILLINOIS					
1 Hayes	-	+	Y	Y	N
2 Savage	N	Y	Y	Y	N
3 Russo	N	Y	Y	Y	N
4 ***O'Brien***	?	?	?	?	?
5 Lipinski	N	Y	Y	Y	N
6 ***Hyde***	?	?	?	?	?
7 Collins	X	?	?	?	?
8 Rostenkowski	N	Y	Y	Y	N
9 Yates	N	Y	Y	Y	N
10 ***Porter***	N	N	N	N	Y
11 Annunzio	N	Y	Y	Y	N
12 ***Crane***	Y	N	N	N	Y
13 ***Fawell***	Y	N	N	N	Y
14 ***Grotberg***	Y	N	N	N	Y
15 ***Madigan***	N	Y	?	Y	N
16 ***Martin***	N	Y	N	N	Y
17 Evans	N	Y	Y	Y	N
18 ***Michel***	N	Y	N	N	Y
19 Bruce	N	Y	Y	Y	N
20 Durbin	N	Y	N	Y	N
21 Price	N	Y	Y	Y	N
22 Gray	N	Y	?	Y	N
INDIANA					
1 Visclosky	N	Y	Y	Y	N
2 Sharp	N	Y	Y	Y	N
3 ***Hiler***	Y	N	N	N	Y
4 ***Coats***	N	Y	N	N	Y
5 ***Hillis***	?	?	?	?	?

ND - Northern Democrats SD - Southern Democrats

* Corresponding to Congressional Record Votes 291, 292, 293, 294, 296

	265	266	267	268	269
6 ***Burton***	Y	N	N	N	Y
7 ***Myers***	Y	N	Y	N	Y
8 McCloskey	N	Y	Y	Y	N
9 Hamilton	N	Y	Y	Y	N
10 Jacobs	Y	N	N	Y	N
IOWA					
1 ***Leach***	?	?	?	?	?
2 ***Tauke***	N	N	N	N	N
3 ***Evans***	N	Y	N	N	N
4 Smith	?	?	?	?	?
5 ***Lightfoot***	N	Y	N	N	N
6 Bedell	N	Y	Y	Y	N
KANSAS					
1 ***Roberts***	Y	N	N	N	Y
2 Slattery	N	N	Y	Y	N
3 ***Meyers***	Y	N	N	N	N
4 Glickman	N	Y	Y	Y	N
5 ***Whittaker***	Y	N	N	N	N
KENTUCKY					
1 Hubbard	N	N	Y	Y	N
2 Natcher	N	Y	Y	Y	N
3 Mazzoli	N	Y	Y	Y	N
4 ***Snyder***	?	?	?	?	?
5 ***Rogers***	N	Y	N	N	N
6 ***Hopkins***	Y	N	Y	N	N
7 Perkins	N	Y	Y	Y	N
LOUISIANA					
1 ***Livingston***	Y	N	N	N	Y
2 Boggs	?	?	?	?	?
3 Tauzin	Y	Y	Y	Y	N
4 Roemer	Y	N	N	Y	Y
5 Huckaby	Y	Y	Y	Y	N
6 ***Moore***	Y	Y	Y	Y	Y
7 Breaux	?	#	Y	?	Y
8 Long	X	?	?	?	X
MAINE					
1 ***McKernan***	N	Y	N	N	Y
2 ***Snowe***	N	Y	Y	N	Y
MARYLAND					
1 Dyson	N	Y	Y	Y	N
2 ***Bentley***	N	Y	N	N	N
3 Mikulski	N	Y	Y	Y	N
4 ***Holt***	Y	N	Y	N	N
5 Hoyer	N	Y	Y	Y	N
6 Byron	N	Y	Y	Y	N
7 Mitchell	N	Y	?	Y	N
8 Barnes	N	Y	Y	Y	N
MASSACHUSETTS					
1 ***Conte***	N	Y	N	Y	N
2 Boland	N	Y	Y	Y	N
3 Early	N	Y	Y	Y	Y
4 Frank	N	Y	?	Y	N
5 Atkins	N	Y	Y	Y	N
6 Mavroules	N	Y	?	Y	N
7 Markey	N	Y	Y	Y	N
8 O'Neill					
9 Moakley	?	?	?	?	?
10 Studds	N	Y	Y	Y	N
11 Donnelly	N	Y	Y	Y	N
MICHIGAN					
1 Conyers	?	?	?	?	N
2 ***Pursell***	N	Y	Y	N	Y
3 Wolpe	N	Y	Y	Y	N
4 ***Siljander***	N	N	N	Y	Y
5 ***Henry***	N	Y	Y	N	Y
6 Carr	N	Y	?	?	N
7 Kildee	N	Y	Y	Y	N
8 Traxler	N	Y	Y	Y	N
9 ***Vander Jagt***	N	Y	?	?	?
10 ***Schuette***	N	Y	N	N	Y
11 ***Davis***	N	Y	Y	Y	N
12 Bonior	N	Y	Y	Y	N
13 Crockett	?	?	Y	Y	N
14 Hertel	N	Y	Y	Y	N
15 Ford	N	Y	?	Y	N
16 Dingell	N	Y	?	Y	N
17 Levin	N	Y	Y	Y	N
18 ***Broomfield***	Y	Y	Y	N	Y
MINNESOTA					
1 Penny	Y	Y	N	Y	N
2 ***Weber***	Y	N	N	N	Y
3 ***Frenzel***	Y	N	N	N	Y
4 Vento	N	Y	Y	Y	N
5 Sabo	N	Y	Y	Y	N
6 Sikorski	N	Y	N	Y	N

	265	266	267	268	269
7 ***Stangeland***	?	?	N	Y	Y
8 Oberstar	N	Y	Y	Y	N
MISSISSIPPI					
1 Whitten	N	Y	?	Y	N
2 ***Franklin***	Y	N	?	Y	Y
3 Montgomery	N	Y	Y	Y	N
4 Dowdy	N	Y	Y	Y	N
5 ***Lott***	?	?	?	?	?
MISSOURI					
1 Clay	N	Y	N	Y	N
2 Young	N	Y	Y	?	N
3 Gephardt	N	Y	Y	Y	N
4 Skelton	?	?	?	?	?
5 Wheat	N	Y	Y	Y	N
6 ***Coleman***	N	Y	N	N	Y
7 ***Taylor***	?	?	?	?	?
8 ***Emerson***	N	Y	N	N	Y
9 Volkmer	N	Y	Y	Y	N
MONTANA					
1 Williams	N	Y	?	?	N
2 ***Marlenee***	Y	N	Y	Y	N
NEBRASKA					
1 ***Bereuter***	Y	N	N	N	N
2 ***Daub***	Y	N	N	N	N
3 ***Smith***	Y	N	Y	N	N
NEVADA					
1 Reid	N	Y	Y	Y	N
2 ***Vucanovich***	Y	Y	N	N	N
NEW HAMPSHIRE					
1 ***Smith***	Y	N	N	N	Y
2 ***Gregg***	?	?	?	?	?
NEW JERSEY					
1 Florio	N	Y	Y	Y	N
2 Hughes	N	Y	Y	Y	N
3 Howard	N	Y	Y	Y	N
4 ***Smith***	N	Y	?	Y	N
5 ***Roukema***	N	Y	N	Y	N
6 Dwyer	N	Y	Y	Y	N
7 ***Rinaldo***	N	Y	?	?	?
8 Roe	?	?	Y	Y	N
9 Torricelli	N	Y	Y	Y	N
10 Rodino	?	?	?	?	?
11 ***Gallo***	N	Y	N	N	N
12 ***Courter***	N	Y	N	N	N
13 ***Saxton***	N	Y	Y	N	N
14 Guarini	N	Y	Y	Y	N
NEW MEXICO					
1 ***Lujan***	Y	Y	Y	N	Y
2 ***Skeen***	Y	N	N	N	N
3 Richardson	?	?	Y	Y	N
NEW YORK					
1 ***Carney***	N	Y	N	Y	N
2 Downey	N	Y	Y	Y	N
3 Mrazek	N	Y	Y	Y	N
4 ***Lent***	N	Y	N	Y	N
5 ***McGrath***	N	N	N	N	N
6 Addabbo	?	?	?	?	?
7 Ackerman	N	Y	Y	Y	N
8 Scheuer	?	?	?	?	?
9 Manton	N	Y	Y	Y	N
10 Schumer	N	Y	Y	Y	N
11 Towns	N	Y	?	?	N
12 Owens	X	?	?	Y	N
13 Solarz	?	?	Y	?	N
14 ***Molinari***	N	Y	N	N	Y
15 ***Green***	N	Y	Y	Y	N
16 Rangel	N	Y	?	?	?
17 Weiss	N	Y	Y	Y	N
18 Garcia	N	Y	Y	Y	N
19 Biaggi	?	?	?	?	?
20 ***DioGuardi***	Y	N	Y	Y	N
21 ***Fish***	?	?	?	?	?
22 ***Gilman***	N	Y	Y	Y	N
23 Stratton	N	Y	Y	N	N
24 ***Solomon***	?	?	N	N	Y
25 ***Boehlert***	N	Y	N	N	N
26 ***Martin***	N	Y	Y	Y	N
27 ***Wortley***	?	?	?	?	?
28 McHugh	N	Y	Y	Y	N
29 ***Horton***	N	Y	Y	Y	N
30 ***Eckert***	Y	N	?	N	Y
31 ***Kemp***	Y	N	Y	N	Y
32 LaFalce	N	Y	Y	Y	N
33 Nowak	N	Y	Y	Y	N
34 Lundine	Y	Y	Y	Y	N

	265	266	267	268	269
NORTH CAROLINA					
1 Jones	?	?	?	?	?
2 Valentine	N	Y	Y	Y	N
3 Whitley	N	Y	Y	Y	N
4 ***Cobey***	Y	N	?	?	?
5 Neal	N	Y	?	?	N
6 ***Coble***	Y	N	?	?	?
7 Rose	N	Y	?	?	?
8 Hefner	N	Y	Y	Y	N
9 ***McMillan***	Y	N	?	?	?
10 ***Broyhill***	Y	N	?	?	?
11 ***Hendon***	N	Y	?	?	?
NORTH DAKOTA					
AL Dorgan	Y	N	Y	Y	N
OHIO					
1 Luken	N	Y	Y	Y	N
2 ***Gradison***	Y	N	Y	Y	Y
3 Hall	N	Y	?	?	?
4 ***Oxley***	Y	N	?	?	#
5 ***Latta***	N	N	N	N	Y
6 ***McEwen***	N	Y	N	Y	N
7 ***DeWine***	Y	N	N	N	Y
8 ***Kindness***	Y	Y	?	N	Y
9 Kaptur	X	?	?	?	?
10 ***Miller***	Y	Y	?	?	?
11 Eckart	N	Y	Y	Y	N
12 ***Kasich***	Y	N	N	N	Y
13 Pease	N	Y	Y	Y	N
14 Seiberling	?	?	?	?	?
15 ***Wylie***	Y	N	Y	Y	N
16 ***Regula***	Y	N	Y	Y	N
17 Traficant	N	Y	Y	Y	N
18 Applegate	N	Y	?	Y	N
19 Feighan	N	Y	Y	Y	N
20 Oakar	N	Y	?	Y	N
21 Stokes	N	Y	Y	Y	N
OKLAHOMA					
1 Jones	N	Y	Y	Y	N
2 Synar	N	Y	Y	Y	N
3 Watkins	?	?	Y	Y	Y
4 McCurdy	N	Y	Y	Y	Y
5 ***Edwards***	N	N	N	N	Y
6 English	N	Y	?	Y	Y
OREGON					
1 AuCoin	?	?	?	?	?
2 ***Smith, R.***	?	?	?	?	?
3 Wyden	N	Y	Y	Y	N
4 Weaver	N	Y	Y	Y	N
5 ***Smith, D.***	Y	N	?	N	N
PENNSYLVANIA					
1 Foglietta	N	Y	Y	Y	N
2 Gray	?	?	Y	Y	N
3 Borski	N	Y	Y	Y	N
4 Kolter	N	Y	Y	Y	N
5 ***Schulze***	N	Y	Y	Y	?
6 Yatron	N	Y	Y	Y	N
7 Edgar	N	Y	Y	?	N
8 Kostmayer	N	Y	?	Y	N
9 ***Shuster***	N	Y	N	Y	N
10 ***McDade***	N	Y	Y	Y	N
11 Kanjorski	Y	Y	Y	Y	N
12 Murtha	N	Y	Y	Y	N
13 ***Coughlin***	N	Y	N	Y	Y
14 Coyne	N	Y	Y	Y	N
15 ***Ritter***	N	Y	Y	N	N
16 ***Walker***	Y	N	N	N	Y
17 ***Gekas***	N	Y	N	N	Y
18 Walgren	N	Y	Y	Y	N
19 ***Goodling***	N	Y	N	Y	N
20 Gaydos	N	Y	Y	Y	N
21 ***Ridge***	N	Y	N	Y	N
22 Murphy	N	Y	Y	Y	N
23 ***Clinger***	N	Y	Y	N	N
RHODE ISLAND					
1 St Germain	?	?	?	?	?
2 ***Schneider***	N	Y	Y	Y	Y
SOUTH CAROLINA					
1 ***Hartnett***	?	?	?	?	?
2 ***Spence***	N	Y	N	N	N
3 Derrick	N	Y	Y	Y	N
4 ***Campbell***	?	?	N	N	N
5 Spratt	N	Y	Y	Y	N
6 Tallon	N	Y	Y	Y	N
SOUTH DAKOTA					
AL Daschle	N	Y	Y	Y	N

	265	266	267	268	269
TENNESSEE					
1 ***Quillen***	N	Y	Y	Y	N
2 ***Duncan***	Y	Y	Y	N	N
3 Lloyd	N	Y	N	Y	N
4 Cooper	N	Y	Y	Y	N
5 Boner	N	Y	Y	Y	N
6 Gordon	N	Y	Y	Y	N
7 ***Sundquist***	Y	N	N	N	Y
8 Jones	N	Y	Y	Y	N
9 Ford	N	Y	?	Y	N
TEXAS					
1 Chapman*	N	N	Y	Y	N
2 Wilson	N	Y	Y	Y	N
3 ***Bartlett***	Y	N	N	N	Y
4 Hall, R.	N	N	Y	Y	Y
5 Bryant	N	Y	Y	Y	N
6 ***Barton***	Y	N	N	N	Y
7 ***Archer***	Y	N	Y	N	Y
8 ***Fields***	?	?	?	?	?
9 Brooks	N	Y	Y	Y	N
10 Pickle	?	?	Y	Y	N
11 Leath	N	Y	Y	Y	Y
12 Wright	N	Y	Y	Y	N
13 ***Boulter***	Y	N	N	N	Y
14 ***Sweeney***	N	N	Y	N	Y
15 de la Garza	N	Y	Y	Y	N
16 Coleman	N	Y	Y	Y	N
17 Stenholm	Y	N	Y	N	Y
18 Leland	N	Y	Y	Y	N
19 ***Combest***	Y	N	N	N	Y
20 Gonzalez	N	Y	Y	Y	N
21 ***Loeffler***	?	?	?	?	?
22 ***DeLay***	Y	N	Y	N	Y
23 Bustamante	N	Y	Y	Y	N
24 Frost	N	Y	Y	Y	N
25 Andrews	N	Y	Y	Y	N
26 ***Armey***	Y	N	N	N	Y
27 Ortiz	N	Y	Y	Y	N
UTAH					
1 ***Hansen***	Y	N	Y	Y	Y
2 ***Monson***	Y	N	N	N	Y
3 ***Nielson***	Y	N	N	N	Y
VERMONT					
AL ***Jeffords***	N	Y	Y	Y	N
VIRGINIA					
1 ***Bateman***	N	Y	Y	N	Y
2 ***Whitehurst***	Y	Y	Y	N	Y
3 ***Bliley***	Y	N	Y	N	Y
4 Sisisky	N	Y	Y	Y	N
5 Daniel	Y	N	Y	N	Y
6 Olin	Y	N	Y	Y	N
7 ***Slaughter***	Y	N	N	N	Y
8 ***Parris***	Y	N	N	Y	N
9 Boucher	Y	Y	Y	Y	?
10 ***Wolf***	Y	N	N	Y	N
WASHINGTON					
1 ***Miller***	Y	N	Y	N	Y
2 Swift	N	Y	Y	Y	N
3 Bonker	N	Y	Y	Y	N
4 ***Morrison***	Y	Y	Y	N	Y
5 Foley	N	Y	Y	Y	N
6 Dicks	?	?	?	?	?
7 Lowry	N	Y	Y	Y	N
8 ***Chandler***	Y	Y	N	Y	N
WEST VIRGINIA					
1 Mollohan	N	Y	Y	Y	N
2 Staggers	N	Y	Y	Y	N
3 Wise	N	Y	Y	Y	N
4 Rahall	N	Y	Y	Y	N
WISCONSIN					
1 Aspin	N	Y	Y	Y	N
2 Kastenmeier	N	Y	?	Y	N
3 ***Gunderson***	Y	N	N	Y	Y
4 Kleczka	N	Y	?	Y	N
5 Moody	N	Y	Y	Y	N
6 ***Petri***	Y	N	N	N	N
7 Obey	N	Y	Y	Y	N
8 ***Roth***	?	?	N	N	Y
9 ***Sensenbrenner***	Y	N	N	N	Y
WYOMING					
AL ***Cheney***	Y	N	N	N	Y

**Rep. Jim Chapman, D-Texas, was sworn in on Sept. 4, 1985. The first vote for which he was eligible was CQ vote 265.*

Southern states - Ala., Ark., Fla., Ga., Ky., La., Miss., N.C., Okla., S.C., Tenn., Texas, Va.

* The *Congressional Record* vote number is different from the CQ vote number because the *Record* includes quorum calls in its tally. CQ does not publish quorum call votes.

CQ House Votes 270 - 277

270. HR 3244. Transportation Appropriations, Fiscal 1986. Coughlin, R-Pa., amendment to prevent federal funding of the Westway highway and land development project in New York City. Adopted 287-132: R 136-38; D 151-94 (ND 93-72, SD 58-22), Sept. 11, 1985.

271. HR 3244. Transportation Appropriations, Fiscal 1986. Richardson, D-N.M., amendment to reduce federal subsidies for Amtrak in fiscal 1986 from $603.5 million to $581.4 million. Rejected 173-245: R 125-50; D 48-195 (ND 12-152, SD 36-43), Sept. 11, 1985.

272. HR 3244. Transportation Appropriations, Fiscal 1986. Fiedler, R-Calif., amendment to the Dixon, D-Calif., substitute for the Waxman, D-Calif., amendment, to impose restrictions on the construction of a new mass transit system in Los Angeles. Rejected 172-242: R 150-23; D 22-219 (ND 11-150, SD 11-69), Sept. 11, 1985. (The Waxman amendment, as amended by the Dixon amendment, to place less stringent restrictions on the project, subsequently was adopted by voice vote.)

273. H Con Res 187. Kidnapping of Duarte Daughter. Adoption of the concurrent resolution to condemn the Sept. 10 kidnapping of Ines Guadelupe Duarte Duran, daughter of El Salvadoran President José Napoleón Duarte. Adopted 402-1: R 168-0; D 234-1 (ND 159-1, SD 75-0), Sept. 12, 1985.

274. HR 7. School Lunch and Child Nutrition Act. Adoption of the rule (H Res 262) to provide for House floor consideration of the bill to reauthorize and revise school lunch and child nutrition programs. Adopted 266-142: R 39-135; D 227-7 (ND 156-2, SD 71-5), Sept. 12, 1985.

275. HR 2266. Amtrak Authorizations, Fiscal 1986-87. Adoption of the rule (H Res 263) to waive points of order against the bill to authorize appropriations for Amtrak through fiscal 1987. Adopted 236-159: R 24-146; D 212-13 (ND 153-1, SD 59-12), Sept. 12, 1985.

276. HR 3244. Transportation Appropriations, Fiscal 1986. Solarz, D-N.Y., amendment to delete a provision requiring that tolls be collected in only one direction on the Verrazano-Narrows Bridge in New York City. Rejected 111-296: R 5-167; D 106-129 (ND 91-69, SD 15-60), Sept. 12, 1985.

277. HR 3244. Transportation Appropriations, Fiscal 1986. Passage of the bill to appropriate $10,852,587,569 for programs of the Department of Transportation and related agencies in fiscal 1986. Passed 307-102: R 82-91; D 225-11 (ND 155-5, SD 70-6), Sept. 12, 1985. (The president requested $7,867,619,569 in new budget authority.)

KEY

Y Voted for (yea).
\# Paired for.
\+ Announced for.
N Voted against (nay).
X Paired against.
\- Announced against.
P Voted "present."
C Voted "present" to avoid possible conflict of interest.
? Did not vote or otherwise make a position known.

Democrats ***Republicans***

	270	271	272	273	274	275	276	277
ALABAMA								
1 ***Callahan***	Y	Y	Y	Y	N	N	N	Y
2 ***Dickinson***	?	Y	Y	?	Y	N	N	N
3 Nichols	Y	Y	Y	Y	Y	?	N	Y
4 Bevill	?	?	?	?	?	?	?	?
5 Flippo	N	Y	N	Y	Y	?	N	Y
6 Erdreich	Y	Y	N	Y	Y	Y	Y	Y
7 Shelby	Y	N	N	Y	?	Y	N	N
ALASKA								
AL ***Young***	N	Y	Y	Y	Y	N	N	Y
ARIZONA								
1 ***McCain***	Y	Y	Y	Y	N	N	Y	Y
2 Udall	N	N	N	Y	Y	?	Y	Y
3 ***Stump***	Y	Y	Y	Y	N	N	N	N
4 ***Rudd***	Y	Y	Y	Y	N	N	N	Y
5 ***Kolbe***	Y	Y	Y	Y	N	N	N	N
ARKANSAS								
1 Alexander	N	N	N	Y	Y	Y	?	Y
2 Robinson	Y	Y	Y	Y	Y	Y	N	Y
3 ***Hammerschmidt***	N	Y	?	Y	Y	N	N	Y
4 Anthony	Y	N	N	Y	Y	Y	?	Y
CALIFORNIA								
1 Bosco	N	N	N	Y	Y	Y	N	Y
2 ***Chappie***	Y	N	Y	Y	N	N	N	N
3 Matsui	Y	N	N	Y	Y	Y	?	?
4 Fazio	N	N	N	Y	Y	Y	N	Y
5 Burton	N	N	N	Y	Y	Y	Y	Y
6 Boxer	Y	N	N	Y	Y	Y	Y	Y
7 Miller	Y	N	N	Y	Y	Y	Y	Y
8 Dellums	Y	N	N	Y	Y	Y	Y	Y
9 Stark	Y	N	?	Y	Y	Y	Y	Y
10 Edwards	N	N	N	Y	Y	Y	N	Y
11 Lantos	Y	N	N	Y	Y	Y	Y	Y
12 ***Zschau***	Y	Y	Y	?	N	N	N	N
13 Mineta	N	N	N	Y	Y	Y	N	Y
14 ***Shumway***	Y	Y	Y	Y	N	N	N	N
15 Coelho	N	N	N	Y	Y	Y	Y	Y
16 Panetta	Y	N	N	Y	Y	Y	N	Y
17 ***Pashayan***	Y	N	N	Y	N	N	N	N
18 Lehman	Y	N	N	?	?	?	?	?
19 ***Lagomarsino***	Y	Y	Y	Y	N	N	N	N
20 ***Thomas***	Y	Y	N	Y	N	N	N	N
21 ***Fiedler***	Y	Y	Y	Y	N	N	N	N
22 ***Moorhead***	Y	Y	N	Y	N	N	N	N
23 Beilenson	Y	N	N	Y	Y	Y	Y	Y
24 Waxman	Y	N	N	Y	Y	Y	N	Y
25 Roybal	N	N	N	Y	Y	Y	N	Y
26 Berman	N	N	N	Y	Y	Y	Y	Y
27 Levine	Y	N	N	Y	Y	Y	Y	Y
28 Dixon	N	N	N	?	?	Y	Y	Y
29 Hawkins	N	N	N	Y	Y	Y	Y	Y
30 Martinez	N	N	N	Y	?	Y	Y	Y
31 Dymally	?	?	?	?	?	?	?	?
32 Anderson	N	N	N	Y	Y	Y	N	Y
33 ***Dreier***	Y	Y	N	Y	N	N	N	N
34 Torres	N	N	N	Y	Y	Y	N	Y
35 ***Lewis***	N	N	N	Y	Y	Y	N	Y
36 Brown	Y	N	N	Y	Y	Y	Y	Y
37 ***McCandless***	Y	Y	N	Y	N	N	N	N
38 ***Dornan***	N	Y	N	Y	N	N	N	N
39 ***Dannemeyer***	Y	Y	N	Y	N	N	N	N
40 ***Badham***	Y	Y	Y	Y	N	N	N	N
41 ***Lowery***	Y	Y	N	Y	Y	N	N	N
42 ***Lungren***	Y	Y	Y	Y	N	N	N	N
43 ***Packard***	Y	Y	Y	Y	N	N	N	N
44 Bates	Y	N	N	Y	Y	Y	N	Y
45 ***Hunter***	?	?	?	?	?	?	?	?
COLORADO								
1 Schroeder	Y	Y	N	Y	Y	Y	Y	Y
2 Wirth	Y	N	N	Y	Y	Y	N	Y
3 ***Strang***	?	?	?	?	?	?	?	?
4 ***Brown***	Y	Y	Y	Y	N	N	N	N
5 ***Kramer***	Y	Y	Y	Y	N	N	N	Y
6 ***Schaefer***	Y	Y	Y	Y	N	N	N	Y
CONNECTICUT								
1 Kennelly	Y	N	N	Y	Y	Y	N	Y
2 Gejdenson	N	N	N	Y	Y	Y	Y	Y
3 Morrison	Y	N	N	Y	Y	Y	Y	Y
4 ***McKinney***	N	N	Y	Y	N	?	?	Y
5 ***Rowland***	Y	Y	Y	Y	N	N	N	Y
6 ***Johnson***	Y	Y	Y	Y	Y	Y	N	Y
DELAWARE								
AL Carper	Y	N	N	Y	Y	Y	N	Y
FLORIDA								
1 Hutto	Y	Y	N	Y	N	N	N	Y
2 Fuqua	Y	Y	N	Y	Y	Y	N	Y
3 Bennett	Y	N	N	Y	Y	Y	N	Y
4 Chappell	N	N	N	Y	Y	Y	N	Y
5 ***McCollum***	Y	?	Y	Y	N	N	N	N
6 MacKay	Y	Y	N	Y	Y	Y	Y	Y
7 Gibbons	Y	Y	N	?	?	?	?	?
8 ***Young***	Y	Y	Y	?	?	?	?	?
9 ***Bilirakis***	Y	Y	Y	?	?	?	?	?
10 ***Ireland***	Y	Y	Y	?	?	?	?	?
11 Nelson	Y	Y	N	Y	Y	Y	N	Y
12 ***Lewis***	Y	Y	Y	Y	N	N	N	Y
13 ***Mack***	Y	Y	Y	Y	N	N	N	N
14 Mica	Y	N	N	Y	Y	Y	N	Y
15 ***Shaw***	N	Y	Y	Y	N	N	N	Y
16 Smith	Y	N	N	Y	Y	Y	N	Y
17 Lehman	N	N	N	Y	Y	Y	N	Y
18 Pepper	Y	N	N	Y	Y	+	N	Y
19 Fascell	Y	N	N	Y	Y	Y	?	?
GEORGIA								
1 Thomas	Y	N	N	Y	Y	Y	N	Y
2 Hatcher	Y	Y	N	Y	Y	Y	Y	Y
3 Ray	Y	Y	N	Y	Y	N	N	Y
4 ***Swindall***	Y	Y	Y	Y	N	N	N	N
5 Fowler	Y	N	N	Y	Y	Y	Y	Y
6 ***Gingrich***	Y	Y	Y	Y	N	N	N	N
7 Darden	Y	Y	N	Y	Y	Y	N	Y
8 Rowland	N	N	N	Y	Y	Y	N	Y
9 Jenkins	Y	N	N	Y	Y	Y	Y	Y
10 Barnard	Y	N	N	Y	Y	N	N	Y
HAWAII								
1 Heftel	Y	Y	N	Y	Y	N	N	N
2 Akaka	?	?	?	Y	Y	Y	N	Y
IDAHO								
1 ***Craig***	Y	Y	Y	Y	N	N	N	N
2 Stallings	Y	N	Y	Y	Y	Y	N	Y
ILLINOIS								
1 Hayes	N	N	N	Y	Y	Y	Y	Y
2 Savage	N	N	N	N	Y	Y	Y	Y
3 Russo	Y	N	Y	Y	Y	Y	Y	Y
4 ***O'Brien***	Y	N	Y	Y	Y	?	?	Y
5 Lipinski	N	N	N	Y	Y	Y	N	Y
6 ***Hyde***	Y	Y	Y	Y	Y	Y	N	N
7 Collins	N	N	N	Y	Y	Y	Y	Y
8 Rostenkowski	Y	N	N	Y	Y	Y	N	Y
9 Yates	Y	N	N	Y	Y	Y	N	Y
10 ***Porter***	Y	Y	Y	Y	N	N	N	Y
11 Annunzio	Y	N	N	Y	Y	Y	N	Y
12 ***Crane***	?	#	#	?	?	?	?	?
13 ***Fawell***	Y	Y	Y	Y	N	N	N	N
14 ***Grotberg***	#	Y	Y	Y	N	N	N	Y
15 ***Madigan***	Y	N	Y	Y	N	N	N	Y
16 ***Martin***	N	Y	Y	Y	N	N	N	N
17 Evans	Y	N	N	Y	Y	Y	N	Y
18 ***Michel***	N	Y	Y	Y	N	N	N	N
19 Bruce	Y	N	N	Y	Y	Y	Y	Y
20 Durbin	Y	N	N	Y	Y	Y	Y	Y
21 Price	Y	N	?	Y	Y	Y	Y	Y
22 Gray	N	N	N	Y	Y	Y	Y	Y
INDIANA								
1 Visclosky	Y	Y	N	Y	Y	Y	Y	Y
2 Sharp	Y	N	Y	Y	Y	Y	Y	Y
3 ***Hiler***	Y	Y	Y	Y	N	N	N	N
4 ***Coats***	Y	Y	Y	Y	N	N	N	N
5 ***Hillis***	Y	N	Y	Y	N	Y	N	Y

ND - Northern Democrats SD - Southern Democrats

* Corresponding to Congressional Record Votes 297, 298, 299, 300, 301, 302, 304, 305

	270	271	272	273	274	275	276	277
6 ***Burton***	Y	Y	Y	Y	N	N	N	N
7 ***Myers***	N	N	Y	Y	Y	N	N	Y
8 McCloskey	N	Y	N	Y	Y	Y	Y	Y
9 Hamilton	Y	N	Y	Y	Y	Y	Y	Y
10 Jacobs	Y	N	Y	Y	N	Y	Y	N
IOWA								
1 ***Leach***	Y	N	Y	Y	Y	Y	N	N
2 ***Tauke***	Y	Y	Y	Y	N	N	N	N
3 ***Evans***	Y	Y	?	Y	N	N	N	N
4 Smith	N	N	N	Y	Y	Y	N	Y
5 ***Lightfoot***	Y	N	N	Y	N	N	N	Y
6 Bedell	Y	Y	Y	Y	Y	?	N	Y
KANSAS								
1 ***Roberts***	Y	Y	Y	Y	N	N	N	N
2 Slattery	Y	Y	N	Y	Y	Y	N	Y
3 ***Meyers***	Y	Y	Y	Y	N	N	N	Y
4 Glickman	Y	N	N	Y	Y	Y	N	Y
5 ***Whittaker***	Y	N	Y	Y	N	N	N	N
KENTUCKY								
1 Hubbard	Y	Y	Y	Y	Y	N	N	N
2 Natcher	N	N	N	Y	Y	Y	N	Y
3 Mazzoli	Y	Y	Y	Y	Y	Y	N	Y
4 ***Snyder***	N	Y	N	Y	N	N	N	Y
5 ***Rogers***	Y	Y	Y	Y	N	N	N	Y
6 ***Hopkins***	Y	Y	Y	Y	N	N	N	N
7 Perkins	N	N	N	Y	Y	Y	N	Y
LOUISIANA								
1 ***Livingston***	Y	Y	Y	Y	N	N	N	Y
2 Boggs	N	N	N	Y	Y	Y	N	Y
3 Tauzin	Y	Y	Y	Y	N	N	N	Y
4 Roemer	Y	Y	Y	Y	N	N	N	N
5 Huckaby	Y	Y	N	Y	Y	?	N	Y
6 ***Moore***	Y	Y	Y	Y	N	N	N	Y
7 Breaux	N	Y	N	Y	Y	N	N	Y
8 Long	X	X	X	?	?	?	?	?
MAINE								
1 ***McKernan***	Y	Y	Y	Y	N	N	N	Y
2 ***Snowe***	Y	Y	Y	Y	Y	N	N	Y
MARYLAND								
1 Dyson	Y	N	Y	Y	Y	Y	Y	Y
2 ***Bentley***	N	N	Y	Y	N	N	N	Y
3 Mikulski	N	N	N	Y	Y	Y	Y	Y
4 ***Holt***	Y	N	?	Y	N	Y	N	Y
5 Hoyer	N	N	N	Y	Y	Y	Y	Y
6 Byron	Y	Y	N	Y	Y	Y	Y	Y
7 Mitchell	Y	N	N	Y	Y	Y	Y	Y
8 Barnes	Y	N	N	Y	Y	Y	Y	Y
MASSACHUSETTS								
1 ***Conte***	Y	N	N	+	Y	Y	N	Y
2 Boland	N	N	N	Y	Y	Y	Y	Y
3 Early	N	N	N	Y	Y	Y	Y	Y
4 Frank	Y	N	N	Y	Y	Y	Y	Y
5 Atkins	N	Y	N	Y	Y	Y	N	Y
6 Mavroules	N	N	N	Y	Y	Y	Y	Y
7 Markey	Y	?	?	Y	Y	?	Y	Y
8 O'Neill								
9 Moakley	N	N	N	Y	Y	Y	N	Y
10 Studds	Y	N	N	Y	Y	Y	Y	Y
11 Donnelly	N	N	N	Y	Y	Y	N	Y
MICHIGAN								
1 Conyers	Y	N	N	?	?	?	?	?
2 ***Pursell***	?	?	?	?	?	?	?	?
3 Wolpe	Y	N	N	+	Y	Y	Y	Y
4 ***Siljander***	Y	Y	Y	Y	N	N	N	Y
5 ***Henry***	Y	N	Y	Y	N	N	N	Y
6 Carr	N	N	N	Y	Y	Y	N	Y
7 Kildee	Y	N	N	Y	Y	Y	Y	Y
8 Traxler	N	N	N	Y	Y	Y	N	Y
9 ***Vander Jagt***	Y	Y	Y	Y	N	N	N	Y
10 ***Schuette***	Y	Y	Y	Y	N	N	N	N
11 ***Davis***	Y	Y	Y	Y	Y	N	N	Y
12 Bonior	Y	N	N	Y	Y	Y	Y	Y
13 Crockett	Y	N	N	?	?	Y	Y	Y
14 Hertel	Y	N	N	Y	Y	Y	Y	N
15 Ford	N	N	N	Y	?	Y	Y	Y
16 Dingell	Y	N	N	?	?	?	?	?
17 Levin	N	N	N	Y	Y	Y	Y	Y
18 ***Broomfield***	Y	Y	Y	Y	N	N	N	N
MINNESOTA								
1 Penny	Y	N	N	Y	Y	Y	Y	Y
2 ***Weber***	Y	Y	Y	Y	N	N	N	?
3 ***Frenzel***	Y	Y	Y	Y	N	N	N	N
4 Vento	Y	N	N	Y	Y	Y	N	Y
5 Sabo	N	N	N	Y	Y	Y	Y	Y
6 Sikorski	Y	N	N	Y	Y	Y	N	Y

	270	271	272	273	274	275	276	277
7 ***Stangeland***	N	Y	N	Y	Y	N	N	N
8 Oberstar	Y	N	N	Y	Y	Y	N	Y
MISSISSIPPI								
1 Whitten	N	N	N	Y	Y	?	N	Y
2 ***Franklin***	Y	Y	Y	Y	N	N	N	N
3 Montgomery	Y	Y	Y	Y	Y	Y	N	Y
4 Dowdy	Y	N	N	?	?	?	?	?
5 ***Lott***	Y	Y	Y	Y	N	N	N	N
MISSOURI								
1 Clay	Y	N	N	Y	Y	Y	Y	Y
2 Young	N	N	N	Y	Y	Y	N	Y
3 Gephardt	Y	N	N	Y	Y	Y	Y	Y
4 Skelton	Y	N	N	Y	N	Y	N	Y
5 Wheat	N	N	N	Y	Y	Y	Y	Y
6 ***Coleman***	Y	Y	Y	Y	Y	N	N	Y
7 ***Taylor***	N	Y	N	Y	N	N	N	Y
8 ***Emerson***	Y	N	Y	Y	N	N	N	Y
9 Volkmer	Y	N	N	Y	Y	Y	N	Y
MONTANA								
1 Williams	N	N	?	Y	?	?	Y	Y
2 ***Marlenee***	Y	N	Y	Y	N	N	N	Y
NEBRASKA								
1 ***Bereuter***	Y	Y	Y	Y	Y	N	N	Y
2 ***Daub***	Y	N	Y	Y	N	N	N	N
3 ***Smith***	Y	Y	Y	Y	N	N	N	Y
NEVADA								
1 Reid	Y	N	N	Y	Y	Y	Y	Y
2 ***Vucanovich***	Y	Y	?	?	N	N	N	N
NEW HAMPSHIRE								
1 ***Smith***	Y	Y	Y	Y	N	N	N	N
2 ***Gregg***	Y	Y	Y	Y	N	N	N	N
NEW JERSEY								
1 Florio	N	N	N	Y	Y	Y	N	Y
2 Hughes	Y	N	Y	Y	Y	Y	N	Y
3 Howard	N	N	N	Y	Y	Y	N	Y
4 ***Smith***	Y	N	Y	Y	Y	Y	N	Y
5 ***Roukema***	Y	Y	N	Y	Y	N	N	Y
6 Dwyer	Y	N	N	Y	Y	Y	N	Y
7 ***Rinaldo***	Y	N	N	Y	Y	Y	N	Y
8 Roe	N	N	N	Y	Y	Y	N	Y
9 Torricelli	Y	N	N	Y	Y	Y	Y	Y
10 Rodino	Y	N	N	Y	Y	Y	N	Y
11 ***Gallo***	Y	N	N	Y	N	N	N	Y
12 ***Courter***	N	N	Y	Y	N	Y	N	Y
13 ***Saxton***	Y	Y	Y	Y	N	N	N	Y
14 Guarini	Y	N	N	Y	Y	Y	?	Y
NEW MEXICO								
1 ***Lujan***	Y	Y	Y	Y	Y	Y	N	Y
2 ***Skeen***	Y	Y	Y	Y	N	N	N	Y
3 Richardson	Y	Y	N	Y	Y	Y	N	Y
NEW YORK								
1 ***Carney***	N	Y	Y	Y	N	N	N	Y
2 Downey	N	N	N	Y	Y	Y	N	Y
3 Mrazek	N	N	N	Y	Y	Y	Y	Y
4 ***Lent***	N	N	Y	Y	N	Y	N	Y
5 ***McGrath***	N	N	Y	Y	N	N	N	Y
6 Addabbo	?	?	?	?	?	?	?	?
7 Ackerman	N	N	N	Y	Y	Y	Y	Y
8 Scheuer	N	N	N	Y	Y	Y	Y	Y
9 Manton	N	N	N	Y	Y	Y	N	Y
10 Schumer	N	N	N	Y	Y	Y	Y	Y
11 Towns	N	N	N	Y	Y	Y	Y	Y
12 Owens	N	N	N	Y	Y	Y	Y	Y
13 Solarz	Y	N	N	Y	Y	Y	Y	Y
14 ***Molinari***	N	N	Y	Y	N	N	N	Y
15 ***Green***	N	N	Y	Y	Y	Y	N	Y
16 Rangel	Y	N	N	Y	Y	Y	Y	Y
17 Weiss	Y	N	N	Y	Y	Y	Y	Y
18 Garcia	N	N	N	Y	Y	?	Y	Y
19 Biaggi	N	N	N	Y	Y	Y	Y	Y
20 ***DioGuardi***	N	N	Y	Y	Y	Y	N	Y
21 ***Fish***	Y	N	Y	?	?	?	?	?
22 ***Gilman***	N	N	Y	Y	Y	Y	N	Y
23 Stratton	N	N	N	Y	Y	Y	N	Y
24 ***Solomon***	Y	Y	Y	Y	N	N	N	N
25 ***Boehlert***	N	N	Y	Y	N	N	N	Y
26 ***Martin***	N	N	Y	Y	N	N	N	Y
27 ***Wortley***	Y	N	Y	Y	N	N	N	Y
28 McHugh	N	N	Y	Y	Y	Y	Y	Y
29 ***Horton***	N	N	N	?	Y	Y	N	Y
30 ***Eckert***	N	Y	N	Y	Y	N	N	N
31 ***Kemp***	N	Y	N	Y	N	N	N	N
32 LaFalce	N	N	Y	Y	Y	Y	N	Y
33 Nowak	N	N	N	Y	Y	Y	Y	Y
34 Lundine	N	N	N	Y	Y	Y	Y	?

	270	271	272	273	274	275	276	277
NORTH CAROLINA								
1 Jones	N	N	N	Y	Y	?	Y	Y
2 Valentine	Y	Y	N	Y	Y	Y	N	Y
3 Whitley	N	Y	N	Y	Y	Y	Y	Y
4 ***Cobey***	Y	Y	Y	Y	N	N	N	N
5 Neal	Y	Y	Y	Y	Y	N	N	N
6 ***Coble***	Y	Y	Y	Y	N	N	N	N
7 Rose	N	N	N	Y	Y	Y	Y	Y
8 Hefner	N	N	N	Y	Y	Y	N	Y
9 ***McMillan***	Y	Y	Y	Y	N	N	N	N
10 ***Broyhill***	Y	Y	Y	Y	N	N	N	N
11 ***Hendon***	Y	Y	Y	Y	N	N	N	N
NORTH DAKOTA								
AL Dorgan	Y	N	N	Y	Y	Y	Y	Y
OHIO								
1 Luken	N	Y	N	Y	Y	Y	Y	Y
2 ***Gradison***	Y	Y	Y	Y	N	N	N	Y
3 Hall	Y	N	Y	Y	Y	Y	N	Y
4 ***Oxley***	Y	Y	Y	Y	N	N	N	N
5 ***Latta***	N	Y	Y	Y	N	N	N	N
6 ***McEwen***	Y	Y	Y	Y	N	N	N	N
7 ***DeWine***	Y	N	Y	Y	N	N	N	N
8 ***Kindness***	Y	Y	Y	Y	N	N	N	N
9 Kaptur	Y	N	N	Y	Y	Y	N	Y
10 ***Miller***	?	?	?	Y	N	N	N	N
11 Eckart	Y	N	N	Y	Y	Y	Y	Y
12 ***Kasich***	Y	Y	Y	Y	N	N	N	N
13 Pease	Y	N	N	Y	Y	Y	Y	Y
14 Seiberling	Y	N	N	Y	Y	?	Y	Y
15 ***Wylie***	Y	N	Y	Y	N	N	N	Y
16 ***Regula***	Y	N	Y	Y	Y	N	N	Y
17 Traficant	N	N	N	Y	Y	Y	N	Y
18 Applegate	Y	N	N	?	Y	?	N	Y
19 Feighan	Y	N	N	Y	Y	Y	Y	Y
20 Oakar	Y	N	N	Y	Y	Y	Y	Y
21 Stokes	N	N	N	Y	Y	Y	Y	Y
OKLAHOMA								
1 Jones	Y	Y	N	Y	Y	N	N	Y
2 Synar	Y	Y	N	Y	Y	Y	N	Y
3 Watkins	N	N	N	Y	Y	?	N	Y
4 McCurdy	Y	Y	N	Y	Y	Y	N	Y
5 ***Edwards***	Y	Y	Y	Y	Y	N	Y	N
6 English	Y	Y	N	Y	Y	N	N	Y
OREGON								
1 AuCoin	Y	N	N	Y	Y	Y	Y	Y
2 ***Smith, R.***	Y	N	Y	Y	N	N	N	Y
3 Wyden	Y	N	N	Y	Y	Y	Y	N
4 Weaver	Y	N	N	Y	Y	Y	Y	N
5 ***Smith, D.***	Y	Y	Y	Y	N	N	N	N
PENNSYLVANIA								
1 Foglietta	N	N	N	Y	Y	Y	N	Y
2 Gray	Y	N	N	Y	Y	Y	?	?
3 Borski	N	N	N	Y	Y	Y	N	Y
4 Kolter	N	N	N	Y	Y	Y	Y	Y
5 ***Schulze***	Y	N	Y	Y	N	N	N	Y
6 Yatron	Y	N	N	Y	Y	Y	N	Y
7 Edgar	Y	N	N	Y	Y	Y	N	Y
8 Kostmayer	Y	N	N	Y	Y	Y	Y	Y
9 ***Shuster***	N	N	N	Y	N	Y	N	N
10 ***McDade***	Y	N	Y	Y	Y	N	N	Y
11 Kanjorski	Y	N	N	Y	Y	Y	N	Y
12 Murtha	?	N	N	Y	Y	Y	N	Y
13 ***Coughlin***	Y	N	Y	Y	N	N	N	Y
14 Coyne	N	N	N	Y	Y	Y	N	Y
15 ***Ritter***	Y	Y	Y	Y	N	N	N	Y
16 ***Walker***	Y	Y	Y	Y	N	N	N	N
17 ***Gekas***	Y	N	Y	Y	Y	Y	N	N
18 Walgren	Y	N	N	Y	Y	Y	Y	Y
19 ***Goodling***	Y	Y	Y	Y	Y	Y	N	N
20 Gaydos	Y	Y	N	Y	Y	Y	N	Y
21 ***Ridge***	Y	N	Y	Y	Y	N	N	Y
22 Murphy	Y	N	N	Y	Y	Y	N	Y
23 ***Clinger***	N	N	N	Y	N	N	N	Y
RHODE ISLAND								
1 St Germain	Y	N	N	Y	Y	Y	N	Y
2 ***Schneider***	Y	N	Y	Y	Y	Y	N	Y
SOUTH CAROLINA								
1 ***Hartnett***	Y	Y	Y	Y	N	N	N	N
2 ***Spence***	Y	Y	Y	Y	Y	Y	N	N
3 Derrick	Y	Y	N	Y	Y	Y	N	Y
4 ***Campbell***	Y	Y	Y	Y	N	N	N	N
5 Spratt	Y	N	N	Y	Y	Y	Y	Y
6 Tallon	Y	N	N	Y	Y	Y	N	Y
SOUTH DAKOTA								
AL Daschle	N	Y	N	Y	?	?	Y	Y

	270	271	272	273	274	275	276	277
TENNESSEE								
1 ***Quillen***	N	Y	Y	Y	Y	N	N	Y
2 ***Duncan***	N	Y	Y	Y	Y	?	N	Y
3 Lloyd	Y	Y	N	Y	Y	Y	N	Y
4 Cooper	Y	Y	N	?	Y	Y	Y	Y
5 Boner	Y	N	N	Y	Y	Y	N	Y
6 Gordon	Y	Y	N	Y	Y	Y	Y	Y
7 ***Sundquist***	Y	Y	Y	Y	N	N	N	N
8 Jones	N	Y	N	Y	Y	Y	N	Y
9 Ford	Y	N	N	Y	Y	Y	N	Y
TEXAS								
1 Chapman	Y	?	N	Y	Y	Y	N	Y
2 Wilson	N	N	N	Y	Y	Y	N	Y
3 ***Bartlett***	Y	Y	Y	Y	N	N	Y	N
4 Hall, R.	Y	N	Y	Y	Y	Y	N	Y
5 Bryant	Y	N	N	Y	Y	Y	N	Y
6 ***Barton***	Y	Y	Y	Y	N	N	N	N
7 ***Archer***	Y	Y	Y	Y	N	N	N	N
8 ***Fields***	Y	Y	Y	Y	N	N	N	Y
9 Brooks	N	N	N	Y	Y	Y	N	Y
10 Pickle	N	N	N	Y	Y	Y	N	Y
11 Leath	Y	Y	N	Y	N	N	N	?
12 Wright	N	N	N	Y	Y	Y	Y	Y
13 ***Boulter***	Y	Y	Y	Y	N	N	N	N
14 ***Sweeney***	Y	Y	Y	Y	N	N	N	N
15 de la Garza	Y	N	N	Y	Y	Y	N	Y
16 Coleman	Y	Y	N	Y	Y	Y	N	Y
17 Stenholm	Y	Y	Y	Y	N	N	N	N
18 Leland	Y	N	N	Y	Y	Y	Y	Y
19 ***Combest***	Y	Y	Y	Y	N	N	N	N
20 Gonzalez	Y	N	N	P	Y	Y	N	Y
21 ***Loeffler***	Y	Y	Y	Y	N	N	N	N
22 ***DeLay***	N	Y	Y	Y	N	?	N	N
23 Bustamante	N	N	N	Y	Y	Y	Y	Y
24 Frost	Y	N	N	Y	Y	Y	N	Y
25 Andrews	Y	Y	N	Y	Y	Y	N	Y
26 ***Armey***	Y	Y	Y	Y	N	N	N	N
27 Ortiz	Y	N	N	Y	Y	Y	N	Y
UTAH								
1 ***Hansen***	Y	Y	Y	Y	N	N	N	N
2 ***Monson***	N	Y	Y	Y	N	N	N	N
3 ***Nielson***	Y	Y	Y	Y	N	N	N	N
VERMONT								
AL ***Jeffords***	?	N	Y	Y	Y	Y	N	Y
VIRGINIA								
1 ***Bateman***	N	Y	Y	Y	N	N	N	N
2 ***Whitehurst***	N	Y	Y	Y	N	N	N	N
3 ***Bliley***	N	N	Y	Y	Y	N	N	N
4 Sisisky	N	N	N	Y	Y	Y	N	Y
5 Daniel	Y	N	Y	Y	Y	Y	N	N
6 Olin	Y	N	N	Y	Y	Y	N	Y
7 ***Slaughter***	Y	N	Y	Y	N	N	N	Y
8 ***Parris***	Y	N	Y	Y	N	Y	N	Y
9 Boucher	Y	Y	N	?	?	Y	Y	Y
10 ***Wolf***	N	N	N	Y	Y	Y	N	Y
WASHINGTON								
1 ***Miller***	Y	Y	Y	Y	N	N	Y	Y
2 Swift	N	N	N	Y	Y	Y	N	Y
3 Bonker	Y	?	N	Y	Y	?	Y	Y
4 ***Morrison***	Y	Y	Y	Y	N	N	N	Y
5 Foley	N	N	?	Y	Y	Y	N	Y
6 Dicks	Y	N	N	Y	Y	Y	Y	Y
7 Lowry	Y	N	N	Y	Y	Y	Y	Y
8 ***Chandler***	Y	Y	Y	Y	N	N	N	Y
WEST VIRGINIA								
1 Mollohan	N	N	N	Y	Y	Y	N	Y
2 Staggers	Y	N	N	Y	Y	Y	N	Y
3 Wise	N	N	N	Y	Y	Y	N	Y
4 Rahall	N	N	N	Y	Y	Y	N	Y
WISCONSIN								
1 Aspin	N	N	N	Y	Y	Y	Y	Y
2 Kastenmeier	+	-	-	+	+	+	-	+
3 ***Gunderson***	N	Y	Y	+	Y	N	N	Y
4 Kleczka	N	N	N	Y	Y	+	+	+
5 Moody	N	N	N	Y	Y	Y	N	Y
6 ***Petri***	Y	Y	Y	Y	N	N	Y	Y
7 Obey	Y	N	N	Y	Y	Y	Y	Y
8 ***Roth***	Y	?	Y	Y	N	N	N	N
9 ***Sensenbrenner***	Y	Y	Y	Y	N	N	N	N
WYOMING								
AL ***Cheney***	Y	Y	Y	Y	N	N	N	N

Southern states - Ala., Ark., Fla., Ga., Ky., La., Miss., N.C., Okla., S.C., Tenn., Texas, Va.

* The *Congressional Record* vote number is different from the CQ vote number because the *Record* includes quorum calls in its tally. CQ does not publish quorum call votes.

278. HR 7. School Lunch and Child Nutrition Act. Bartlett, R-Texas, amendment to eliminate an authorization of $1 million for fiscal 1986 grants to school districts for food service equipment. Rejected 157-235: R 141-23; D 16-212 (ND 5-149, SD 11-63), Sept. 12, 1985.

279. H J Res 388. Continuing Appropriations, Fiscal 1986. Passage of the joint resolution to provide continued spending authority from Oct. 1 to Nov. 14, 1985, for programs and agencies for which regular appropriations bills had not been signed into law by Oct. 1, the start of the fiscal year. The resolution provided that funding levels for programs would, depending on the status of uncompleted appropriations bills, be the lower amount of that enacted for fiscal 1985 or that set in appropriations bills passed by one or both houses, but not yet signed into law. Once enacted, appropriations bills for fiscal 1986 would supersede levels set by the continuing appropriations resolution. Passed 272-156: R 60-122; D 212-34 (ND 145-23, SD 67-11), Sept. 18, 1985.

280. HR 7. School Lunch and Child Nutrition Act. Bartlett, R-Texas, amendment to eliminate the fiscal 1986 cost-of-living adjustment to the rates of federal reimbursement to schools for meals served in school lunch and child nutrition programs, except for the supplemental feeding program for needy pregnant women, infants and children. Rejected 143-284: R 131-50; D 12-234 (ND 3-163, SD 9-71), Sept. 18, 1985.

281. HR 7. School Lunch and Child Nutrition Act. Petri, R-Wis., amendment to the Armey, R-Texas, substitute for the Bartlett, R-Texas, amendment, to eliminate the cash subsidy for school lunches for children from families with incomes above 250 percent of the poverty line. Rejected 174-254: R 156-25; D 18-229 (ND 3-164, SD 15-65), Sept. 18, 1985. (The Armey substitute was subsequently rejected *(see vote 282, below)*, and the Bartlett amendment, which would have eliminated the cash subsidy for lunches for children from families with incomes above 185 percent of the poverty level, was subsequently rejected by voice vote.)

282. HR 7. School Lunch and Child Nutrition Act. Armey, R-Texas, substitute for the Bartlett, R-Texas, amendment, to eliminate the cash and commodity subsidy for lunches for children from families with incomes above 250 percent of the poverty line. Rejected 146-279: R 133-48; D 13-231 (ND 1-165, SD 12-66), Sept. 18, 1985. (The Bartlett amendment was subsequently rejected by voice vote.)

283. HR 7. School Lunch and Child Nutrition Act. Passage of the bill to authorize $5.09 billion in fiscal 1986-88 for five child nutrition programs: the special supplemental feeding program for needy pregnant women, infants and children; a summer food service program for children; nutrition education and training; a surplus commodity distribution program; and payments to states for administrative costs. Passed 367-59: R 124-58; D 243-1 (ND 165-0, SD 78-1), Sept. 18, 1985.

284. HR 2266. Amtrak Reauthorization, Fiscal 1986. Passage of the bill to authorize $603.5 million in federal subsidies in fiscal 1986 for Amtrak, the national passenger railroad. Passed 290-128: R 71-107; D 219-21 (ND 162-0, SD 57-21), Sept. 19, 1985.

KEY

- Y Voted for (yea).
- # Paired for.
- + Announced for.
- N Voted against (nay).
- X Paired against.
- \- Announced against.
- P Voted "present."
- C Voted "present" to avoid possible conflict of interest.
- ? Did not vote or otherwise make a position known.

Democrats ***Republicans***

	278	279	280	281	282	283	284
ALABAMA							
1 ***Callahan***	Y	N	Y	Y	Y	N	N
2 ***Dickinson***	N	N	Y	Y	Y	Y	N
3 Nichols	N	Y	Y	Y	N	Y	Y
4 Bevill	?	?	?	?	?	?	?
5 Flippo	N	Y	N	N	N	Y	N
6 Erdreich	N	Y	N	N	N	Y	Y
7 Shelby	N	N	N	N	N	Y	Y
ALASKA							
AL ***Young***	N	Y	N	N	N	Y	N
ARIZONA							
1 ***McCain***	Y	N	N	Y	Y	Y	N
2 Udall	N	Y	N	N	N	Y	Y
3 ***Stump***	Y	N	Y	Y	Y	N	Y
4 ***Rudd***	Y	Y	Y	Y	Y	N	?
5 ***Kolbe***	Y	N	Y	Y	Y	Y	N
ARKANSAS							
1 Alexander	?	Y	N	N	N	Y	Y
2 Robinson	N	?	N	N	N	Y	Y
3 ***Hammerschmidt***	N	Y	N	N	N	Y	Y
4 Anthony	N	Y	N	N	N	Y	Y
CALIFORNIA							
1 Bosco	?	Y	N	N	N	Y	Y
2 ***Chappie***	?	N	N	Y	Y	Y	Y
3 Matsui	N	Y	N	N	N	Y	Y
4 Fazio	N	Y	N	N	N	Y	Y
5 Burton	?	Y	N	N	N	Y	Y
6 Boxer	?	Y	N	N	N	Y	Y
7 Miller	N	Y	N	N	N	Y	Y
8 Dellums	N	Y	N	N	N	Y	Y
9 Stark	N	Y	N	N	N	Y	?
10 Edwards	N	Y	N	N	N	Y	Y
11 Lantos	N	Y	N	N	N	Y	Y
12 ***Zschau***	Y	N	Y	Y	Y	N	N
13 Mineta	N	Y	N	N	N	Y	Y
14 ***Shumway***	Y	N	Y	Y	Y	N	N
15 Coelho	N	Y	N	N	N	Y	Y
16 Panetta	N	Y	N	N	N	Y	Y
17 ***Pashayan***	Y	Y	Y	Y	N	Y	Y
18 Lehman	?	Y	N	N	?	?	?
19 ***Lagomarsino***	Y	N	N	Y	Y	Y	N
20 ***Thomas***	Y	N	Y	Y	Y	Y	N
21 ***Fiedler***	Y	N	Y	Y	Y	N	N
22 ***Moorhead***	Y	N	Y	Y	Y	N	N
23 Beilenson	N	Y	N	N	N	Y	Y
24 Waxman	N	Y	N	N	N	?	Y
25 Roybal	N	Y	N	N	N	Y	Y
26 Berman	N	Y	N	N	N	Y	Y
27 Levine	N	Y	N	N	N	Y	Y
28 Dixon	N	Y	N	N	N	Y	Y
29 Hawkins	N	Y	N	N	N	Y	Y
30 Martinez	N	Y	N	N	N	Y	Y
31 Dymally	?	Y	N	N	N	Y	Y
32 Anderson	N	Y	N	N	N	Y	Y
33 ***Dreier***	Y	N	Y	Y	Y	N	N
34 Torres	N	Y	N	N	N	Y	Y
35 ***Lewis***	Y	Y	Y	Y	Y	Y	Y
36 Brown	N	Y	N	N	N	Y	Y
37 ***McCandless***	Y	N	Y	Y	Y	N	N
38 ***Dornan***	Y	N	N	Y	Y	Y	N
39 ***Dannemeyer***	Y	N	Y	Y	Y	N	N
40 ***Badham***	?	N	Y	Y	Y	N	N
41 ***Lowery***	Y	Y	Y	Y	Y	N	N
42 ***Lungren***	Y	N	Y	Y	Y	N	N
43 ***Packard***	Y	N	Y	Y	Y	N	N
44 Bates	N	N	N	N	N	Y	Y
45 ***Hunter***	?	N	Y	Y	Y	N	N
COLORADO							
1 Schroeder	?	N	N	N	N	Y	Y
2 Wirth	N	N	N	N	N	Y	Y
3 ***Strang***	?	N	Y	Y	Y	N	N
4 ***Brown***	Y	N	Y	N	Y	N	N
5 ***Kramer***	Y	N	Y	N	Y	N	N
6 ***Schaefer***	Y	N	Y	Y	Y	N	N
CONNECTICUT							
1 Kennelly	N	Y	N	N	N	Y	Y
2 Gejdenson	N	Y	N	N	N	Y	Y
3 Morrison	N	Y	N	N	N	Y	Y
4 ***McKinney***	N	Y	N	N	N	Y	Y
5 ***Rowland***	Y	N	Y	Y	Y	Y	Y
6 ***Johnson***	Y	Y	N	Y	Y	Y	Y
DELAWARE							
AL Carper	Y	Y	N	Y	N	Y	Y
FLORIDA							
1 Hutto	N	Y	N	Y	N	Y	Y
2 Fuqua	N	Y	N	N	N	Y	N
3 Bennett	Y	Y	N	Y	Y	Y	Y
4 Chappell	N	Y	N	Y	N	Y	Y
5 ***McCollum***	Y	N	Y	Y	Y	Y	Y
6 MacKay	N	Y	N	N	N	Y	Y
7 Gibbons	N	Y	N	N	Y	Y	N
8 ***Young***	?	N	Y	Y	N	Y	N
9 ***Bilirakis***	?	N	Y	Y	Y	Y	N
10 ***Ireland***	Y	N	Y	Y	Y	Y	N
11 Nelson	N	Y	N	Y	N	Y	N
12 ***Lewis***	Y	N	Y	Y	Y	Y	N
13 ***Mack***	Y	N	Y	Y	Y	N	N
14 Mica	N	Y	N	N	N	Y	Y
15 ***Shaw***	Y	N	Y	Y	Y	Y	N
16 Smith	N	Y	N	N	N	Y	Y
17 Lehman	N	Y	N	N	N	Y	Y
18 Pepper	N	Y	N	N	N	Y	Y
19 Fascell	?	Y	N	N	N	Y	Y
GEORGIA							
1 Thomas	N	Y	Y	N	N	Y	Y
2 Hatcher	N	Y	N	N	N	Y	Y
3 Ray	N	Y	Y	Y	Y	Y	Y
4 ***Swindall***	Y	N	Y	Y	Y	N	?
5 Fowler	N	Y	N	N	N	Y	Y
6 ***Gingrich***	Y	N	Y	Y	Y	Y	N
7 Darden	Y	Y	Y	N	N	Y	Y
8 Rowland	Y	Y	N	N	N	Y	Y
9 Jenkins	Y	Y	N	N	N	Y	Y
10 Barnard	Y	N	Y	Y	N	Y	N
HAWAII							
1 Heftel	N	Y	N	N	N	Y	Y
2 Akaka	N	Y	N	N	N	Y	Y
IDAHO							
1 ***Craig***	Y	N	Y	Y	Y	N	N
2 Stallings	N	N	N	N	N	Y	Y
ILLINOIS							
1 Hayes	N	Y	N	N	N	Y	Y
2 Savage	N	Y	N	N	N	Y	Y
3 Russo	N	N	N	N	N	Y	Y
4 ***O'Brien***	N	Y	N	Y	Y	Y	Y
5 Lipinski	N	Y	N	N	N	Y	Y
6 ***Hyde***	Y	N	Y	Y	Y	Y	N
7 Collins	N	Y	N	N	N	Y	Y
8 Rostenkowski	N	Y	N	N	N	Y	Y
9 Yates	N	Y	N	N	N	Y	Y
10 ***Porter***	Y	N	Y	Y	Y	N	N
11 Annunzio	N	Y	N	N	N	Y	Y
12 ***Crane***	?	N	Y	Y	Y	N	N
13 ***Fawell***	Y	N	Y	Y	Y	Y	N
14 ***Grotberg***	Y	N	Y	N	Y	Y	N
15 ***Madigan***	?	N	N	Y	N	Y	Y
16 ***Martin***	Y	N	Y	Y	Y	N	N
17 Evans	N	Y	N	N	N	Y	Y
18 ***Michel***	Y	N	Y	Y	?	Y	N
19 Bruce	N	N	N	N	N	Y	Y
20 Durbin	N	Y	N	N	N	Y	Y
21 Price	N	Y	N	N	N	Y	Y
22 Gray	N	Y	N	N	N	Y	Y
INDIANA							
1 Visclosky	N	Y	N	N	N	Y	Y
2 Sharp	N	Y	N	N	N	Y	Y
3 ***Hiler***	Y	N	Y	Y	Y	Y	N
4 ***Coats***	Y	N	Y	Y	Y	Y	Y
5 ***Hillis***	Y	Y	Y	Y	Y	Y	Y

ND - Northern Democrats SD - Southern Democrats

* Corresponding to Congressional Record Votes 307, 308, 309, 310, 311, 312, 313

	278	279	280	281	282	283	284
6 ***Burton***	Y	N	Y	Y	Y	N	N
7 ***Myers***	Y	Y	N	Y	Y	Y	Y
8 McCloskey	N	Y	N	N	N	Y	Y
9 Hamilton	N	Y	N	N	N	Y	Y
10 Jacobs	N	N	N	N	N	Y	Y
IOWA							
1 ***Leach***	Y	N	N	Y	N	Y	Y
2 ***Tauke***	Y	N	Y	Y	N	Y	Y
3 ***Evans***	Y	N	N	N	N	Y	Y
4 Smith	N	Y	N	N	N	Y	Y
5 ***Lightfoot***	Y	N	Y	N	N	Y	Y
6 Bedell	Y	Y	N	N	N	Y	Y
KANSAS							
1 ***Roberts***	Y	N	Y	Y	Y	N	N
2 Slattery	N	Y	N	N	N	Y	Y
3 ***Meyers***	Y	Y	Y	Y	Y	Y	N
4 Glickman	Y	N	N	N	N	Y	Y
5 ***Whittaker***	Y	N	Y	Y	Y	N	Y
KENTUCKY							
1 Hubbard	Y	N	N	N	N	Y	N
2 Natcher	N	Y	N	N	N	Y	Y
3 Mazzoli	N	Y	N	N	N	Y	Y
4 ***Snyder***	Y	N	Y	Y	Y	Y	N
5 ***Rogers***	N	Y	Y	Y	Y	Y	N
6 ***Hopkins***	Y	N	N	Y	Y	Y	N
7 Perkins	N	Y	N	N	N	Y	Y
LOUISIANA							
1 ***Livingston***	Y	Y	Y	Y	Y	Y	N
2 Boggs	N	Y	N	N	N	Y	Y
3 Tauzin	N	N	N	Y	Y	Y	Y
4 Roemer	Y	N	N	Y	Y	Y	N
5 Huckaby	N	Y	N	N	Y	Y	N
6 ***Moore***	Y	Y	Y	Y	Y	Y	N
7 Breaux	N	Y	N	Y	N	Y	N
8 Long	?	?	?	?	?	?	?
MAINE							
1 ***McKernan***	Y	N	N	Y	N	Y	N
2 ***Snowe***	Y	N	Y	Y	N	Y	N
MARYLAND							
1 Dyson	N	Y	N	N	N	Y	Y
2 ***Bentley***	Y	N	N	Y	Y	Y	Y
3 Mikulski	N	Y	N	N	N	Y	Y
4 ***Holt***	Y	N	Y	Y	Y	N	Y
5 Hoyer	N	Y	N	N	N	Y	Y
6 Byron	N	N	Y	N	Y	Y	Y
7 Mitchell	N	Y	N	N	N	Y	Y
8 Barnes	N	Y	N	N	N	Y	Y
MASSACHUSETTS							
1 ***Conte***	N	Y	N	N	N	Y	Y
2 Boland	N	Y	N	N	N	Y	Y
3 Early	N	Y	N	N	N	Y	Y
4 Frank	N	Y	N	N	N	Y	Y
5 Atkins	N	Y	N	N	N	Y	Y
6 Mavroules	N	Y	N	N	N	Y	Y
7 Markey	N	Y	N	N	N	Y	Y
8 O'Neill							
9 Moakley	N	Y	N	N	N	Y	Y
10 Studds	N	Y	N	N	N	Y	Y
11 Donnelly	N	Y	N	N	N	Y	Y
MICHIGAN							
1 Conyers	?	Y	N	N	N	Y	Y
2 ***Pursell***	?	Y	Y	N	N	Y	Y
3 Wolpe	N	Y	N	N	N	Y	Y
4 ***Siljander***	Y	Y	Y	Y	Y	Y	N
5 ***Henry***	Y	N	Y	N	N	Y	Y
6 Carr	N	Y	N	N	N	Y	Y
7 Kildee	N	Y	N	N	N	Y	Y
8 Traxler	N	Y	N	N	N	Y	Y
9 ***Vander Jagt***	Y	Y	Y	Y	Y	N	N
10 ***Schuette***	Y	N	Y	Y	N	Y	N
11 ***Davis***	N	Y	N	N	N	Y	Y
12 Bonior	N	Y	N	N	N	Y	Y
13 Crockett	?	Y	N	N	N	Y	Y
14 Hertel	N	N	N	N	N	Y	Y
15 Ford	N	Y	N	N	N	Y	Y
16 Dingell	?	Y	N	N	N	Y	Y
17 Levin	N	Y	N	N	N	Y	Y
18 ***Broomfield***	Y	Y	Y	Y	Y	Y	N
MINNESOTA							
1 Penny	N	N	Y	N	N	Y	Y
2 ***Weber***	Y	N	Y	Y	N	Y	N
3 ***Frenzel***	#	N	?	Y	Y	Y	N
4 Vento	N	Y	N	N	N	Y	Y
5 Sabo	N	Y	N	N	N	Y	Y
6 Sikorski	N	N	N	N	N	Y	Y

	278	279	280	281	282	283	284
7 ***Stangeland***	Y	Y	N	Y	N	Y	Y
8 Oberstar	N	Y	N	N	N	Y	?
MISSISSIPPI							
1 Whitten	N	Y	N	N	N	Y	Y
2 ***Franklin***	Y	N	Y	Y	Y	Y	N
3 Montgomery	Y	Y	Y	Y	Y	Y	Y
4 Dowdy	?	Y	N	N	N	Y	Y
5 ***Lott***	Y	N	Y	Y	Y	N	N
MISSOURI							
1 Clay	N	Y	N	N	N	Y	Y
2 Young	N	Y	?	N	N	Y	Y
3 Gephardt	N	Y	N	N	N	Y	Y
4 Skelton	N	Y	N	Y	N	Y	Y
5 Wheat	N	Y	N	N	N	Y	Y
6 ***Coleman***	Y	N	N	Y	N	Y	N
7 ***Taylor***	?	Y	Y	Y	Y	Y	Y
8 ***Emerson***	N	Y	N	Y	Y	Y	Y
9 Volkmer	N	Y	N	N	N	Y	Y
MONTANA							
1 Williams	N	Y	N	N	N	Y	Y
2 ***Marlenee***	N	Y	N	N	N	Y	Y
NEBRASKA							
1 ***Bereuter***	Y	N	N	Y	Y	Y	N
2 ***Daub***	Y	N	Y	Y	Y	N	Y
3 ***Smith***	Y	Y	Y	Y	Y	Y	Y
NEVADA							
1 Reid	N	Y	N	N	N	Y	Y
2 ***Vucanovich***	Y	N	N	Y	N	Y	N
NEW HAMPSHIRE							
1 ***Smith***	Y	N	Y	Y	Y	N	N
2 ***Gregg***	Y	N	Y	Y	Y	Y	N
NEW JERSEY							
1 Florio	N	Y	N	N	N	Y	Y
2 Hughes	Y	N	N	Y	N	Y	Y
3 Howard	N	Y	N	N	N	Y	Y
4 ***Smith***	N	Y	N	N	N	Y	Y
5 ***Roukema***	Y	Y	Y	N	N	Y	Y
6 Dwyer	N	Y	N	N	N	Y	Y
7 ***Rinaldo***	N	Y	N	N	N	Y	Y
8 Roe	N	Y	N	N	N	Y	Y
9 Torricelli	?	Y	N	N	N	Y	Y
10 Rodino	N	Y	N	N	N	Y	Y
11 ***Gallo***	Y	N	Y	Y	Y	Y	Y
12 ***Courter***	Y	N	N	Y	Y	Y	Y
13 ***Saxton***	Y	N	Y	Y	Y	Y	Y
14 Guarini	N	Y	N	N	N	Y	Y
NEW MEXICO							
1 ***Lujan***	Y	Y	Y	Y	Y	Y	Y
2 ***Skeen***	Y	Y	Y	Y	Y	Y	N
3 Richardson	N	Y	N	N	N	Y	Y
NEW YORK							
1 ***Carney***	Y	N	Y	Y	Y	N	Y
2 Downey	N	Y	N	N	N	Y	Y
3 Mrazek	N	Y	N	N	N	Y	Y
4 ***Lent***	Y	N	Y	N	N	Y	Y
5 ***McGrath***	Y	N	Y	Y	N	Y	Y
6 Addabbo	?	?	?	?	?	?	?
7 Ackerman	N	Y	N	N	N	Y	Y
8 Scheuer	N	N	N	N	N	Y	Y
9 Manton	N	Y	N	N	N	Y	Y
10 Schumer	N	Y	N	N	N	Y	Y
11 Towns	N	Y	N	N	N	Y	Y
12 Owens	N	Y	N	N	N	Y	?
13 Solarz	?	Y	N	N	N	Y	Y
14 ***Molinari***	Y	Y	N	Y	Y	Y	Y
15 ***Green***	N	Y	N	?	Y	Y	Y
16 Rangel	?	?	?	?	?	?	Y
17 Weiss	N	Y	N	N	N	Y	Y
18 Garcia	N	Y	N	N	N	Y	Y
19 Biaggi	N	Y	N	N	N	Y	Y
20 ***DioGuardi***	Y	Y	Y	Y	Y	Y	Y
21 ***Fish***	?	Y	N	N	N	Y	N
22 ***Gilman***	N	Y	N	N	N	Y	Y
23 Stratton	Y	Y	N	N	N	Y	Y
24 ***Solomon***	Y	N	Y	Y	Y	Y	Y
25 ***Boehlert***	N	Y	N	N	N	Y	Y
26 ***Martin***	N	Y	N	Y	N	Y	Y
27 ***Wortley***	N	Y	Y	N	N	Y	Y
28 McHugh	N	Y	N	N	N	Y	Y
29 ***Horton***	N	Y	N	N	N	Y	Y
30 ***Eckert***	Y	N	Y	Y	Y	N	N
31 ***Kemp***	Y	N	Y	Y	Y	Y	N
32 LaFalce	N	Y	N	N	N	Y	Y
33 Nowak	N	Y	N	N	N	Y	Y
34 Lundine	N	Y	N	N	N	Y	Y

	278	279	280	281	282	283	284
NORTH CAROLINA							
1 Jones	N	Y	N	N	N	Y	Y
2 Valentine	N	Y	N	N	N	Y	N
3 Whitley	N	Y	N	N	N	Y	N
4 ***Cobey***	Y	N	Y	Y	Y	Y	N
5 Neal	N	Y	N	N	N	Y	N
6 ***Coble***	Y	N	Y	Y	Y	Y	N
7 Rose	N	Y	N	N	N	Y	Y
8 Hefner	N	Y	N	N	N	Y	Y
9 ***McMillan***	Y	N	Y	Y	Y	Y	N
10 ***Broyhill***	Y	N	Y	Y	Y	Y	N
11 ***Hendon***	Y	N	N	N	N	Y	N
NORTH DAKOTA							
AL Dorgan	N	N	N	N	N	Y	Y
OHIO							
1 Luken	N	N	N	N	N	Y	Y
2 ***Gradison***	Y	Y	Y	Y	Y	Y	N
3 Hall	N	Y	N	N	N	Y	Y
4 ***Oxley***	Y	N	Y	Y	Y	N	N
5 ***Latta***	Y	N	Y	Y	Y	N	N
6 ***McEwen***	Y	N	Y	Y	Y	Y	N
7 ***DeWine***	Y	N	Y	Y	Y	Y	Y
8 ***Kindness***	Y	N	Y	Y	Y	Y	Y
9 Kaptur	N	Y	N	N	N	Y	Y
10 ***Miller***	Y	Y	Y	Y	Y	Y	N
11 Eckart	N	N	N	N	N	Y	Y
12 ***Kasich***	Y	N	Y	Y	Y	Y	N
13 Pease	N	Y	N	N	N	Y	Y
14 Seiberling	N	Y	N	N	N	Y	Y
15 ***Wylie***	?	N	N	Y	Y	Y	Y
16 ***Regula***	Y	Y	N	Y	Y	Y	Y
17 Traficant	N	Y	N	N	N	Y	Y
18 Applegate	N	Y	N	N	N	Y	Y
19 Feighan	N	N	N	N	N	Y	Y
20 Oakar	N	Y	N	N	N	Y	Y
21 Stokes	N	Y	N	N	N	Y	Y
OKLAHOMA							
1 Jones	N	Y	N	N	Y	Y	?
2 Synar	N	N	N	N	N	Y	Y
3 Watkins	N	Y	N	N	N	Y	N
4 McCurdy	N	Y	N	N	N	Y	N
5 ***Edwards***	Y	N	Y	Y	Y	Y	N
6 English	N	N	N	N	N	Y	N
OREGON							
1 AuCoin	N	Y	Y	N	N	Y	Y
2 ***Smith, R.***	Y	N	Y	Y	N	Y	Y
3 Wyden	N	N	N	N	N	Y	Y
4 Weaver	N	N	N	N	N	Y	Y
5 ***Smith, D.***	Y	N	Y	Y	Y	N	N
PENNSYLVANIA							
1 Foglietta	N	Y	N	N	N	Y	Y
2 Gray	N	Y	?	N	N	Y	+
3 Borski	N	Y	N	N	N	Y	Y
4 Kolter	N	Y	N	N	N	Y	Y
5 ***Schulze***	?	N	Y	Y	Y	Y	Y
6 Yatron	N	Y	N	N	N	Y	Y
7 Edgar	N	Y	N	N	N	Y	Y
8 Kostmayer	N	Y	N	N	N	Y	Y
9 ***Shuster***	Y	N	Y	Y	Y	N	Y
10 ***McDade***	N	Y	N	N	N	Y	Y
11 Kanjorski	N	Y	N	N	N	Y	Y
12 Murtha	N	Y	N	N	N	Y	Y
13 ***Coughlin***	Y	Y	N	Y	Y	Y	Y
14 Coyne	N	Y	N	N	N	Y	Y
15 ***Ritter***	?	N	Y	Y	Y	Y	Y
16 ***Walker***	?	N	Y	Y	Y	N	N
17 ***Gekas***	Y	N	Y	Y	N	Y	Y
18 Walgren	N	Y	N	N	N	Y	Y
19 ***Goodling***	Y	Y	N	Y	N	Y	N
20 Gaydos	N	Y	N	N	N	Y	Y
21 ***Ridge***	Y	Y	Y	N	N	Y	?
22 Murphy	N	N	N	N	N	Y	Y
23 ***Clinger***	N	Y	N	Y	N	Y	Y
RHODE ISLAND							
1 St Germain	N	Y	N	N	N	Y	Y
2 ***Schneider***	N	Y	N	Y	N	Y	Y
SOUTH CAROLINA							
1 ***Hartnett***	Y	N	Y	Y	Y	N	N
2 ***Spence***	Y	N	Y	Y	Y	Y	Y
3 Derrick	N	Y	N	N	N	Y	Y
4 ***Campbell***	Y	N	N	Y	Y	Y	Y
5 Spratt	Y	Y	N	N	N	Y	Y
6 Tallon	N	Y	N	N	N	Y	Y
SOUTH DAKOTA							
AL Daschle	N	Y	N	N	N	Y	Y

	278	279	280	281	282	283	284
TENNESSEE							
1 ***Quillen***	N	Y	N	N	N	Y	N
2 ***Duncan***	Y	Y	N	Y	Y	Y	N
3 Lloyd	N	Y	N	N	?	Y	Y
4 Cooper	N	Y	N	N	N	Y	N
5 Boner	N	Y	N	N	N	Y	Y
6 Gordon	N	Y	N	N	N	Y	Y
7 ***Sundquist***	Y	Y	N	Y	Y	Y	N
8 Jones	N	Y	N	N	N	Y	N
9 Ford	N	Y	N	N	N	Y	N
TEXAS							
1 Chapman	N	N	N	N	N	Y	Y
2 Wilson	N	Y	N	N	N	Y	Y
3 ***Bartlett***	Y	N	Y	Y	Y	N	N
4 Hall, R.	N	N	N	N	Y	Y	Y
5 Bryant	N	Y	N	N	N	Y	?
6 ***Barton***	Y	N	Y	Y	Y	N	N
7 ***Archer***	Y	N	Y	Y	Y	N	N
8 ***Fields***	Y	N	Y	Y	Y	N	N
9 Brooks	X	Y	N	N	N	Y	Y
10 Pickle	N	Y	N	N	N	Y	Y
11 Leath	?	N	Y	Y	Y	Y	N
12 Wright	N	Y	N	N	?	Y	Y
13 ***Boulter***	Y	N	Y	Y	Y	N	N
14 ***Sweeney***	Y	N	Y	Y	Y	N	N
15 de la Garza	N	?	N	N	N	Y	Y
16 Coleman	N	Y	N	N	N	Y	Y
17 Stenholm	Y	N	Y	Y	Y	N	N
18 Leland	N	Y	N	N	N	Y	Y
19 ***Combest***	Y	N	Y	Y	Y	N	N
20 Gonzalez	N	Y	N	N	N	Y	Y
21 ***Loeffler***	?	N	Y	Y	Y	N	N
22 ***DeLay***	Y	N	Y	Y	Y	N	N
23 Bustamante	N	Y	N	N	N	Y	Y
24 Frost	N	Y	N	N	N	?	Y
25 Andrews	N	Y	N	N	N	Y	Y
26 ***Armey***	Y	N	Y	Y	Y	N	N
27 Ortiz	N	Y	N	N	N	Y	Y
UTAH							
1 ***Hansen***	Y	N	Y	Y	Y	N	N
2 ***Monson***	Y	N	Y	Y	Y	N	N
3 ***Nielson***	Y	N	Y	Y	Y	N	N
VERMONT							
AL ***Jeffords***	Y	Y	N	Y	N	Y	Y
VIRGINIA							
1 ***Bateman***	Y	Y	Y	Y	Y	Y	Y
2 ***Whitehurst***	Y	Y	N	Y	Y	Y	N
3 ***Bliley***	Y	Y	Y	Y	Y	N	N
4 Sisisky	N	Y	N	N	N	Y	Y
5 Daniel	Y	Y	Y	Y	Y	Y	N
6 Olin	?	Y	N	N	Y	Y	Y
7 ***Slaughter***	Y	N	Y	Y	Y	Y	Y
8 ***Parris***	Y	Y	Y	Y	N	Y	Y
9 Boucher	N	Y	N	N	N	Y	Y
10 ***Wolf***	Y	Y	Y	Y	N	Y	Y
WASHINGTON							
1 ***Miller***	Y	N	Y	Y	Y	Y	N
2 Swift	N	Y	N	N	N	Y	?
3 Bonker	N	Y	N	N	N	Y	Y
4 ***Morrison***	N	Y	N	Y	N	Y	N
5 Foley	N	Y	N	N	N	Y	Y
6 Dicks	N	Y	N	N	N	Y	Y
7 Lowry	N	Y	N	N	N	Y	Y
8 ***Chandler***	Y	Y	Y	Y	Y	Y	N
WEST VIRGINIA							
1 Mollohan	N	Y	N	N	N	Y	Y
2 Staggers	N	N	N	N	N	Y	Y
3 Wise	N	Y	N	N	N	Y	Y
4 Rahall	N	Y	N	-	-	+	Y
WISCONSIN							
1 Aspin	N	Y	N	N	N	Y	Y
2 Kastenmeier	-	N	N	N	N	Y	Y
3 ***Gunderson***	Y	N	Y	Y	N	Y	N
4 Kleczka	-	Y	N	N	N	Y	Y
5 Moody	?	Y	N	N	N	Y	Y
6 ***Petri***	Y	N	Y	Y	N	Y	Y
7 Obey	N	Y	N	N	N	Y	?
8 ***Roth***	?	N	Y	Y	Y	N	?
9 ***Sensenbrenner***	Y	N	Y	Y	Y	N	N
WYOMING							
AL ***Cheney***	Y	N	Y	Y	Y	N	N

Southern states - Ala., Ark., Fla., Ga., Ky., La., Miss., N.C., Okla., S.C., Tenn., Texas, Va.

* The *Congressional Record* vote number is different from the CQ vote number because the *Record* includes quorum calls in its tally. CQ does not publish quorum call votes.

285. Procedural Motion. Monson, R-Utah, motion to approve the House *Journal* of Thursday, Sept. 19. Motion agreed to 192-105: R 38-97; D 154-8 (ND 97-6, SD 57-2), Sept. 20, 1985.

286. HR 3248. Arts and Humanities Endowments Authorizations, Fiscal 1986-89. Adoption of the rule (H Res 266) to provide for House floor consideration of the bill to authorize $329 million in fiscal 1986 and such sums as Congress considers necessary in fiscal 1987-89 for the National Endowment for the Arts, the National Endowment for the Humanities and the Institute for Museum Services. Adopted 181-148: R 20-128; D 161-20 (ND 111-3, SD 50-17), Sept. 20, 1985.

287. HR 2100. Farm Programs Reauthorization, Fiscal 1986-90. Adoption of the rule (H Res 267) to provide for House floor consideration of the bill to extend and revise agricultural price-support programs; to provide for agricultural export, resource conservation, farm credit and agricultural research programs; and to continue food assistance to low-income persons through fiscal 1990. Adopted 205-99: R 43-93; D 162-6 (ND 111-1, SD 51-5), Sept. 20, 1985.

288. S J Res 127. Interstate Compact. Glickman, D-Kan., motion to suspend the rules and pass the joint resolution to grant the consent of Congress to a series of laws passed by Missouri and Illinois granting additional powers to the Missouri-Illinois Bi-State Development Agency concerning the ceiling on the agency's bonds and the authority to construct a waste-recycling facility. Motion agreed to 373-2: R 159-1; D 214-1 (ND 146-1, SD 68-0), Sept. 26, 1985. A two-thirds majority of those present and voting (250 in this case) is required for passage under suspension of the rules.

289. HR 2100. Farm Programs Reauthorization, Fiscal 1986-90. Downey, D-N.Y., amendment to lower the price-support level of sugar, which is frozen by the bill, beginning in fiscal 1986, by 1 cent a pound per year until it reaches 15 cents a pound, and to eliminate the cost of transportation as one of the factors used in setting the market stabilization price of sugar. Rejected 142-263: R 70-103; D 72-160 (ND 64-93, SD 8-67), Sept. 26, 1985. A "yea" was a vote supporting the president's position.

290. HR 2100. Farm Programs Reauthorization, Fiscal 1986-90. Olin, D-Va., amendment to delete the bill's dairy provisions and substitute provisions that reduce the dairy price support 50 cents a year if government purchases exceed specified levels, and to eliminate the bill's increases in the minimum federal marketing order milk prices. Rejected 166-244: R 101-74; D 65-170 (ND 54-102, SD 11-68), Sept. 26, 1985. A "yea" was a vote supporting the president's position.

291. HR 2100. Farm Programs Reauthorization, Fiscal 1986-90. Obey, D-Wis., amendment to establish a mandatory supply-management program to cut back dairy production to the level of demand and set the milk price support at 63 percent of parity, or about $13.60 a hundredweight of milk equivalent, if approved by 60 percent of dairy farmers voting in a national referendum. Rejected 36-351: R 6-161; D 30-190 (ND 29-112, SD 1-78), Sept. 26, 1985. A "nay" was a vote supporting the president's position.

KEY

- Y Voted for (yea).
- # Paired for.
- + Announced for.
- N Voted against (nay).
- X Paired against.
- - Announced against.
- P Voted "present."
- C Voted "present" to avoid possible conflict of interest.
- ? Did not vote or otherwise make a position known.

Democrats ***Republicans***

	285	286	287	288	289	290	291
ALABAMA							
1 ***Callahan***	N	N	Y	Y	Y	Y	N
2 ***Dickinson***	N	N	Y	Y	N	Y	N
3 Nichols	?	?	?	Y	N	Y	N
4 Bevill	?	?	?	?	?	?	?
5 Flippo	Y	Y	?	Y	N	N	N
6 Erdreich	Y	Y	Y	Y	N	N	N
7 Shelby	Y	Y	Y	?	Y	N	N
ALASKA							
AL ***Young***	N	Y	Y	Y	N	N	N
ARIZONA							
1 ***McCain***	N	N	N	Y	N	Y	N
2 Udall	Y	?	?	?	?	?	?
3 ***Stump***	Y	N	N	Y	N	Y	N
4 ***Rudd***	?	?	?	?	?	?	?
5 ***Kolbe***	N	N	?	Y	Y	Y	N
ARKANSAS							
1 Alexander	?	?	?	Y	X	N	N
2 Robinson	Y	Y	Y	Y	N	N	N
3 ***Hammerschmidt***	Y	Y	N	Y	N	N	N
4 Anthony	Y	N	Y	Y	N	N	N
CALIFORNIA							
1 Bosco	?	?	?	Y	N	Y	N
2 ***Chappie***	N	N	?	Y	N	Y	N
3 Matsui	?	?	?	Y	N	N	N
4 Fazio	?	?	?	Y	N	N	N
5 Burton	Y	Y	Y	Y	N	N	?
6 Boxer	Y	?	?	Y	N	N	?
7 Miller	?	?	?	Y	N	N	?
8 Dellums	Y	Y	Y	Y	N	N	N
9 Stark	Y	Y	Y	Y	N	N	N
10 Edwards	Y	Y	Y	Y	N	N	N
11 Lantos	?	?	?	?	?	?	?
12 ***Zschau***	?	?	?	Y	Y	Y	N
13 Mineta	Y	Y	Y	Y	N	N	N
14 ***Shumway***	N	N	N	Y	N	Y	N
15 Coelho	?	Y	Y	Y	N	N	N
16 Panetta	Y	Y	Y	Y	N	N	N
17 ***Pashayan***	Y	N	N	Y	N	N	N
18 Lehman	?	?	?	?	?	?	?
19 ***Lagomarsino***	N	N	N	Y	N	Y	N
20 ***Thomas***	N	N	N	Y	N	Y	N
21 ***Fiedler***	N	N	N	Y	N	Y	N
22 ***Moorhead***	N	N	N	Y	N	Y	N
23 Beilenson	Y	Y	Y	Y	Y	Y	?
24 Waxman	Y	Y	?	Y	Y	Y	N
25 Roybal	Y	Y	Y	Y	N	N	?
26 Berman	Y	Y	Y	Y	N	Y	N
27 Levine	Y	Y	Y	Y	Y	Y	N
28 Dixon	?	Y	Y	Y	N	N	N
29 Hawkins	?	Y	Y	Y	N	N	N
30 Martinez	?	?	?	Y	N	N	N
31 Dymally	?	?	?	?	?	N	N
32 Anderson	?	?	?	Y	N	Y	?
33 ***Dreier***	N	N	N	Y	N	Y	N
34 Torres	Y	Y	Y	Y	N	N	N
35 ***Lewis***	N	N	N	?	N	Y	N
36 Brown	Y	Y	Y	Y	N	Y	N
37 ***McCandless***	?	X	X	Y	N	N	N
38 ***Dornan***	N	N	?	Y	N	Y	N
39 ***Dannemeyer***	N	N	N	Y	N	Y	N
40 ***Badham***	?	?	?	?	?	?	?
41 ***Lowery***	N	N	N	Y	Y	Y	N
42 ***Lungren***	?	?	?	Y	N	Y	N
43 ***Packard***	N	N	N	Y	Y	Y	N
44 Bates	?	Y	Y	Y	Y	Y	Y
45 ***Hunter***	N	N	Y	Y	N	Y	N
COLORADO							
1 Schroeder	N	Y	Y	Y	Y	Y	Y
2 Wirth	?	Y	Y	?	?	?	?
3 ***Strang***	N	N	N	Y	N	N	N
4 ***Brown***	N	N	N	Y	N	N	N
5 ***Kramer***	?	?	?	Y	N	N	N
6 ***Schaefer***	N	N	N	Y	N	Y	N
CONNECTICUT							
1 Kennelly	Y	Y	Y	Y	Y	Y	N
2 Gejdenson	Y	Y	Y	Y	Y	N	Y
3 Morrison	?	?	?	Y	Y	Y	N
4 ***McKinney***	Y	Y	?	?	Y	Y	N
5 ***Rowland***	N	N	N	Y	Y	Y	N
6 ***Johnson***	Y	Y	N	Y	Y	N	N
DELAWARE							
AL Carper	Y	Y	Y	Y	Y	Y	N
FLORIDA							
1 Hutto	Y	N	?	Y	N	N	N
2 Fuqua	?	Y	Y	Y	N	N	N
3 Bennett	Y	N	Y	Y	N	N	N
4 Chappell	Y	Y	Y	Y	N	N	N
5 ***McCollum***	N	?	?	Y	N	Y	N
6 MacKay	?	?	?	?	N	Y	N
7 Gibbons	?	?	?	Y	N	N	N
8 ***Young***	N	N	N	?	Y	Y	N
9 ***Bilirakis***	N	N	Y	?	Y	Y	N
10 ***Ireland***	?	?	?	?	N	Y	N
11 Nelson	Y	Y	Y	Y	N	Y	N
12 ***Lewis***	N	N	N	Y	N	N	N
13 ***Mack***	N	N	N	Y	N	N	N
14 Mica	Y	Y	Y	Y	N	N	N
15 ***Shaw***	N	N	N	?	Y	?	?
16 Smith	Y	Y	Y	?	X	X	?
17 Lehman	?	?	?	Y	Y	Y	N
18 Pepper	+	Y	Y	+	X	-	-
19 Fascell	Y	Y	?	Y	N	N	N
GEORGIA							
1 Thomas	Y	N	Y	Y	N	N	N
2 Hatcher	Y	Y	Y	Y	N	N	N
3 Ray	Y	Y	Y	?	N	N	N
4 ***Swindall***	N	N	N	Y	Y	Y	N
5 Fowler	?	?	?	Y	N	N	N
6 ***Gingrich***	N	N	N	Y	N	Y	N
7 Darden	Y	Y	Y	?	N	N	N
8 Rowland	Y	N	Y	Y	N	N	N
9 Jenkins	Y	N	Y	Y	?	N	N
10 Barnard	Y	N	?	?	N	N	N
HAWAII							
1 Heftel	?	?	?	Y	N	N	N
2 Akaka	Y	Y	Y	Y	N	N	N
IDAHO							
1 ***Craig***	?	N	N	?	N	N	N
2 Stallings	Y	Y	Y	Y	N	N	N
ILLINOIS							
1 Hayes	?	#	?	?	N	N	N
2 Savage	?	?	Y	Y	N	N	N
3 Russo	?	?	?	Y	N	N	N
4 ***O'Brien***	?	?	?	Y	+	N	N
5 Lipinski	Y	Y	Y	Y	Y	N	N
6 ***Hyde***	N	N	N	?	#	?	?
7 Collins	Y	Y	?	Y	N	N	N
8 Rostenkowski	?	?	?	Y	Y	Y	N
9 Yates	Y	Y	Y	Y	Y	Y	N
10 ***Porter***	Y	N	N	Y	Y	Y	N
11 Annunzio	Y	Y	Y	Y	Y	Y	N
12 ***Crane***	N	N	N	?	#	?	?
13 ***Fawell***	N	N	N	Y	Y	Y	N
14 ***Grotberg***	N	N	Y	Y	X	N	N
15 ***Madigan***	?	N	?	Y	N	N	N
16 ***Martin***	N	N	N	Y	N	N	N
17 Evans	?	Y	Y	Y	N	N	N
18 ***Michel***	N	N	Y	Y	?	Y	N
19 Bruce	Y	N	N	Y	N	N	N
20 Durbin	N	Y	?	Y	N	N	N
21 Price	Y	Y	Y	?	#	#	?
22 Gray	?	?	?	Y	N	N	N
INDIANA							
1 Visclosky	Y	Y	Y	Y	Y	Y	N
2 Sharp	Y	Y	Y	Y	Y	Y	N
3 ***Hiler***	N	N	N	?	?	Y	N
4 ***Coats***	Y	N	N	Y	Y	Y	N
5 ***Hillis***	Y	N	?	Y	N	Y	N

ND - Northern Democrats SD - Southern Democrats

* Corresponding to Congressional Record Votes 314, 315, 316, 317, 318, 319, 320

	285	286	287	288	289	290	291
6 ***Burton***	N	N	N	Y	Y	N	N
7 ***Myers***	Y	N	Y	Y	N	N	N
8 McCloskey	Y	Y	Y	Y	N	Y	N
9 Hamilton	Y	Y	Y	Y	Y	Y	N
10 Jacobs	N	Y	Y	?	Y	Y	N
IOWA							
1 ***Leach***	?	Y	Y	Y	N	N	N
2 ***Tauke***	N	Y	Y	Y	N	N	N
3 ***Evans***	N	Y	Y	Y	N	N	N
4 Smith	Y	Y	Y	Y	N	N	N
5 ***Lightfoot***	N	Y	Y	Y	N	N	N
6 Bedell	?	Y	Y	Y	N	N	Y
KANSAS							
1 ***Roberts***	N	N	N	Y	N	Y	N
2 Slattery	Y	Y	?	Y	N	N	N
3 ***Meyers***	?	?	?	Y	Y	Y	N
4 Glickman	Y	Y	Y	Y	N	Y	N
5 ***Whittaker***	N	N	N	Y	N	N	N
KENTUCKY							
1 Hubbard	Y	N	Y	Y	N	N	N
2 Natcher	Y	Y	Y	Y	N	N	N
3 Mazzoli	Y	Y	Y	Y	Y	Y	N
4 ***Snyder***	Y	Y	Y	Y	N	N	N
5 ***Rogers***	N	N	N	Y	N	N	?
6 ***Hopkins***	Y	N	Y	Y	N	N	N
7 Perkins	Y	Y	Y	Y	N	N	N
LOUISIANA							
1 ***Livingston***	N	N	N	Y	N	Y	N
2 Boggs	Y	Y	Y	Y	N	Y	N
3 Tauzin	Y	N	Y	Y	N	N	N
4 Roemer	N	N	N	Y	N	N	N
5 Huckaby	Y	Y	Y	Y	N	N	N
6 ***Moore***	Y	N	Y	Y	N	N	N
7 Breaux	?	?	?	Y	N	N	N
8 Long	Y	Y	Y	Y	N	Y	N
MAINE							
1 ***McKernan***	N	N	Y	?	Y	Y	N
2 ***Snowe***	N	Y	Y	Y	Y	N	N
MARYLAND							
1 Dyson	Y	Y	Y	Y	N	N	N
2 ***Bentley***	N	N	Y	Y	Y	Y	N
3 Mikulski	?	#	Y	Y	Y	N	N
4 ***Holt***	N	N	N	Y	Y	Y	?
5 Hoyer	Y	Y	Y	Y	Y	N	N
6 Byron	Y	Y	Y	?	Y	N	N
7 Mitchell	N	Y	Y	N	Y	N	N
8 Barnes	Y	Y	Y	Y	Y	Y	N
MASSACHUSETTS							
1 ***Conte***	N	N	?	Y	Y	Y	N
2 Boland	?	?	?	Y	Y	Y	?
3 Early	?	?	?	Y	Y	Y	Y
4 Frank	?	?	?	Y	Y	Y	?
5 Atkins	?	?	?	Y	Y	Y	Y
6 Mavroules	?	?	?	Y	N	Y	?
7 Markey	?	Y	Y	?	Y	Y	Y
8 O'Neill							
9 Moakley	?	#	?	Y	Y	Y	?
10 Studds	?	?	?	Y	Y	Y	?
11 Donnelly	?	?	?	Y	Y	Y	N
MICHIGAN							
1 Conyers	?	?	Y	Y	Y	N	?
2 ***Pursell***	?	?	?	Y	N	Y	N
3 Wolpe	?	?	?	Y	N	N	N
4 ***Siljander***	N	N	N	Y	N	N	N
5 ***Henry***	Y	N	N	Y	N	N	N
6 Carr	Y	Y	Y	Y	N	N	N
7 Kildee	Y	Y	Y	Y	N	N	N
8 Traxler	?	?	?	Y	N	N	N
9 ***Vander Jagt***	Y	N	Y	Y	N	Y	N
10 ***Schuette***	N	N	N	Y	N	N	N
11 ***Davis***	N	N	?	Y	N	Y	N
12 Bonior	Y	Y	Y	Y	N	N	N
13 Crockett	Y	Y	Y	Y	N	?	?
14 Hertel	Y	Y	Y	Y	N	N	N
15 Ford	?	Y	Y	Y	N	N	N
16 Dingell	?	Y	Y	?	-	N	N
17 Levin	Y	Y	Y	Y	N	N	N
18 ***Broomfield***	Y	N	N	Y	N	Y	?
MINNESOTA							
1 Penny	N	Y	Y	Y	N	N	Y
2 ***Weber***	N	N	N	?	N	N	Y
3 ***Frenzel***	N	N	N	Y	N	N	N
4 Vento	Y	Y	Y	Y	N	N	Y
5 Sabo	Y	Y	Y	Y	N	N	Y
6 Sikorski	?	?	?	Y	N	N	Y
7 ***Stangeland***	N	N	N	Y	N	N	Y
8 Oberstar	Y	Y	Y	Y	N	N	Y
MISSISSIPPI							
1 Whitten	Y	Y	Y	Y	N	N	N
2 ***Franklin***	Y	N	N	Y	N	Y	N
3 Montgomery	Y	N	N	Y	N	Y	N
4 Dowdy	Y	Y	Y	?	N	N	N
5 ***Lott***	?	X	?	Y	N	?	N
MISSOURI							
1 Clay	N	Y	?	Y	N	N	N
2 Young	Y	Y	Y	Y	N	N	N
3 Gephardt	Y	Y	Y	Y	N	N	N
4 Skelton	Y	N	Y	?	N	N	N
5 Wheat	Y	Y	Y	Y	N	N	N
6 ***Coleman***	N	N	N	Y	N	N	N
7 ***Taylor***	Y	N	Y	Y	N	N	N
8 ***Emerson***	N	N	N	Y	N	N	N
9 Volkmer	Y	Y	Y	Y	N	N	Y
MONTANA							
1 Williams	?	?	?	Y	N	N	Y
2 ***Marlenee***	N	N	N	Y	N	N	N
NEBRASKA							
1 ***Bereuter***	Y	N	N	Y	N	N	N
2 ***Daub***	N	N	N	Y	N	N	N
3 ***Smith***	Y	N	N	Y	N	N	N
NEVADA							
1 Reid	Y	Y	Y	Y	N	N	N
2 ***Vucanovich***	?	N	N	Y	Y	Y	N
NEW HAMPSHIRE							
1 ***Smith***	N	N	N	Y	Y	Y	N
2 ***Gregg***	?	?	?	Y	Y	Y	N
NEW JERSEY							
1 Florio	?	?	?	Y	Y	N	?
2 Hughes	Y	N	Y	Y	Y	N	N
3 Howard	Y	Y	Y	?	Y	Y	?
4 ***Smith***	?	?	?	Y	Y	Y	N
5 ***Roukema***	N	N	Y	Y	Y	Y	N
6 Dwyer	Y	Y	Y	Y	Y	Y	N
7 ***Rinaldo***	?	?	?	Y	N	Y	N
8 Roe	Y	Y	Y	Y	N	Y	N
9 Torricelli	?	Y	Y	Y	Y	N	N
10 Rodino	Y	Y	Y	Y	Y	N	N
11 ***Gallo***	N	N	N	Y	Y	Y	N
12 ***Courter***	?	?	?	Y	Y	Y	?
13 ***Saxton***	N	N	Y	Y	Y	N	N
14 Guarini	Y	Y	Y	Y	Y	N	N
NEW MEXICO							
1 ***Lujan***	Y	Y	N	Y	N	N	N
2 ***Skeen***	N	N	N	Y	N	N	N
3 Richardson	?	?	?	Y	N	N	N
NEW YORK							
1 ***Carney***	N	N	Y	Y	Y	Y	N
2 Downey	Y	Y	Y	Y	Y	Y	Y
3 Mrazek	Y	Y	Y	Y	Y	Y	Y
4 ***Lent***	?	?	Y	Y	Y	Y	?
5 ***McGrath***	?	?	?	Y	Y	Y	N
6 Addabbo	?	?	?	?	?	?	?
7 Ackerman	Y	Y	Y	Y	Y	Y	N
8 Scheuer	Y	Y	Y	Y	#	Y	N
9 Manton	Y	Y	Y	Y	N	N	N
10 Schumer	Y	Y	Y	Y	Y	Y	Y
11 Towns	?	?	Y	?	N	N	Y
12 Owens	?	?	Y	Y	N	?	Y
13 Solarz	P	Y	Y	Y	Y	?	?
14 ***Molinari***	N	N	Y	Y	Y	Y	N
15 ***Green***	Y	Y	Y	Y	Y	Y	N
16 Rangel	?	?	?	Y	N	N	N
17 Weiss	?	Y	Y	Y	Y	Y	N
18 Garcia	?	?	?	?	Y	Y	N
19 Biaggi	?	?	?	Y	Y	Y	?
20 ***DioGuardi***	N	N	N	?	Y	Y	N
21 ***Fish***	?	N	Y	Y	Y	Y	N
22 ***Gilman***	Y	Y	+	Y	N	N	-
23 Stratton	Y	Y	Y	?	Y	N	N
24 ***Solomon***	?	?	?	?	Y	Y	N
25 ***Boehlert***	N	N	Y	Y	Y	Y	N
26 ***Martin***	N	N	Y	?	N	Y	N
27 ***Wortley***	Y	N	Y	Y	Y	Y	N
28 McHugh	Y	Y	Y	Y	Y	Y	N
29 ***Horton***	?	?	?	Y	N	N	N
30 ***Eckert***	?	N	N	Y	Y	Y	N
31 ***Kemp***	Y	Y	Y	Y	Y	Y	N
32 LaFalce	Y	Y	Y	Y	Y	N	N
33 Nowak	?	?	?	Y	Y	N	Y
34 Lundine	?	?	?	Y	Y	N	Y
NORTH CAROLINA							
1 Jones	?	?	?	Y	N	N	N
2 Valentine	Y	Y	Y	Y	N	N	N
3 Whitley	Y	Y	Y	Y	N	N	N
4 ***Cobey***	N	N	N	Y	N	N	N
5 Neal	Y	Y	Y	?	N	N	N
6 ***Coble***	N	N	N	Y	N	N	N
7 Rose	?	Y	Y	Y	N	N	N
8 Hefner	?	?	?	?	N	N	N
9 ***McMillan***	Y	N	N	Y	N	Y	N
10 ***Broyhill***	Y	N	?	Y	N	N	N
11 ***Hendon***	N	N	N	Y	N	N	N
NORTH DAKOTA							
AL Dorgan	Y	Y	Y	Y	N	N	Y
OHIO							
1 Luken	Y	Y	Y	Y	Y	Y	N
2 ***Gradison***	?	?	?	Y	Y	Y	N
3 Hall	Y	Y	Y	Y	Y	Y	Y
4 ***Oxley***	?	X	?	Y	N	N	N
5 ***Latta***	N	N	?	Y	N	Y	N
6 ***McEwen***	?	?	N	Y	N	N	N
7 ***DeWine***	?	?	?	Y	Y	N	N
8 ***Kindness***	?	N	Y	Y	N	N	N
9 Kaptur	?	?	?	Y	N	N	N
10 ***Miller***	N	N	N	Y	Y	N	N
11 Eckart	Y	Y	Y	Y	Y	N	N
12 ***Kasich***	?	N	N	?	Y	N	N
13 Pease	Y	Y	Y	Y	Y	-	N
14 Seiberling	P	?	?	?	?	?	?
15 ***Wylie***	?	?	?	Y	N	N	?
16 ***Regula***	Y	Y	Y	Y	N	N	N
17 Traficant	?	?	?	Y	Y	N	N
18 Applegate	?	?	?	Y	N	N	N
19 Feighan	Y	Y	Y	Y	Y	N	N
20 Oakar	Y	Y	Y	Y	N	N	N
21 Stokes	?	?	?	Y	N	N	N
OKLAHOMA							
1 Jones	Y	Y	Y	Y	N	N	N
2 Synar	Y	Y	Y	Y	N	N	N
3 Watkins	Y	N	Y	Y	N	N	N
4 McCurdy	?	?	?	Y	N	N	N
5 ***Edwards***	N	N	N	Y	N	Y	N
6 English	Y	N	N	Y	N	N	Y
OREGON							
1 AuCoin	Y	Y	Y	Y	N	Y	N
2 ***Smith, R.***	N	N	N	Y	N	N	?
3 Wyden	?	?	?	Y	N	Y	N
4 Weaver	Y	?	?	?	?	?	?
5 ***Smith, D.***	Y	N	N	Y	N	Y	?
PENNSYLVANIA							
1 Foglietta	Y	Y	Y	Y	N	Y	N
2 Gray	Y	Y	Y	Y	N	N	?
3 Borski	Y	Y	Y	Y	Y	N	N
4 Kolter	?	?	?	Y	N	N	N
5 ***Schulze***	?	?	?	Y	Y	Y	N
6 Yatron	Y	Y	Y	Y	Y	Y	N
7 Edgar	?	?	?	?	?	N	N
8 Kostmayer	Y	Y	Y	Y	Y	Y	N
9 ***Shuster***	N	N	?	N	Y	Y	N
10 ***McDade***	?	?	?	Y	Y	Y	N
11 Kanjorski	Y	Y	Y	Y	Y	N	N
12 Murtha	Y	Y	Y	Y	N	N	N
13 ***Coughlin***	?	N	N	Y	Y	Y	N
14 Coyne	Y	Y	?	Y	Y	?	?
15 ***Ritter***	?	N	N	Y	Y	Y	N
16 ***Walker***	N	N	N	Y	Y	Y	N
17 ***Gekas***	N	N	N	Y	Y	Y	N
18 Walgren	?	Y	Y	Y	N	N	N
19 ***Goodling***	N	Y	Y	N	Y	N	N
20 Gaydos	?	?	?	Y	N	N	N
21 ***Ridge***	N	N	N	Y	Y	N	N
22 Murphy	?	?	?	Y	N	N	N
23 ***Clinger***	+	+	-	Y	N	Y	N
RHODE ISLAND							
1 St Germain	?	?	?	?	Y	Y	?
2 ***Schneider***	?	Y	Y	Y	Y	N	N
SOUTH CAROLINA							
1 ***Hartnett***	N	N	Y	?	N	Y	N
2 ***Spence***	N	N	Y	Y	N	Y	N
3 Derrick	?	?	?	Y	N	N	N
4 ***Campbell***	?	?	?	Y	N	Y	N
5 Spratt	Y	Y	Y	Y	N	Y	N
6 Tallon	Y	Y	?	?	N	N	N
SOUTH DAKOTA							
AL Daschle	Y	Y	Y	Y	N	N	Y
TENNESSEE							
1 ***Quillen***	Y	Y	Y	Y	N	N	N
2 ***Duncan***	Y	N	Y	Y	N	N	N
3 Lloyd	N	N	?	Y	N	N	N
4 Cooper	Y	Y	?	Y	Y	N	N
5 Boner	Y	Y	Y	Y	Y	N	N
6 Gordon	?	?	?	Y	N	N	N
7 ***Sundquist***	N	N	N	Y	Y	Y	N
8 Jones	Y	Y	Y	Y	N	N	N
9 Ford	?	Y	Y	Y	Y	N	N
TEXAS							
1 Chapman	Y	Y	Y	Y	N	N	N
2 Wilson	?	Y	?	?	N	N	N
3 ***Bartlett***	N	Y	N	Y	Y	Y	N
4 Hall, R.	Y	Y	Y	Y	N	N	N
5 Bryant	?	Y	Y	Y	N	N	N
6 ***Barton***	N	N	?	Y	N	Y	N
7 ***Archer***	?	N	N	Y	Y	Y	N
8 ***Fields***	N	N	N	Y	Y	Y	N
9 Brooks	Y	Y	#	Y	N	N	N
10 Pickle	Y	Y	Y	Y	N	N	N
11 Leath	?	N	N	Y	N	N	N
12 Wright	Y	Y	Y	Y	?	N	N
13 ***Boulter***	N	N	N	Y	N	Y	N
14 ***Sweeney***	Y	N	N	Y	N	Y	N
15 de la Garza	?	Y	Y	Y	N	N	N
16 Coleman	Y	Y	Y	Y	N	N	N
17 Stenholm	Y	N	N	Y	N	N	N
18 Leland	?	?	?	Y	Y	N	N
19 ***Combest***	N	N	N	Y	N	N	N
20 Gonzalez	Y	Y	Y	Y	N	N	N
21 ***Loeffler***	?	?	?	Y	N	Y	N
22 ***DeLay***	Y	N	N	?	Y	Y	N
23 Bustamante	Y	Y	?	Y	N	N	N
24 Frost	Y	Y	?	Y	N	N	N
25 Andrews	Y	Y	Y	Y	Y	N	N
26 ***Armey***	N	N	N	Y	Y	Y	N
27 Ortiz	?	?	?	Y	N	N	N
UTAH							
1 ***Hansen***	Y	N	N	?	?	?	?
2 ***Monson***	N	N	N	Y	N	Y	N
3 ***Nielson***	Y	N	N	Y	Y	Y	N
VERMONT							
AL ***Jeffords***	Y	Y	Y	Y	N	N	N
VIRGINIA							
1 ***Bateman***	?	N	Y	Y	N	Y	N
2 ***Whitehurst***	?	?	?	Y	Y	Y	N
3 ***Bliley***	N	N	N	Y	N	Y	N
4 Sisisky	Y	Y	Y	Y	C	N	N
5 Daniel	Y	N	Y	Y	N	N	N
6 Olin	Y	Y	Y	Y	N	Y	N
7 ***Slaughter***	N	N	N	Y	Y	Y	N
8 ***Parris***	Y	N	Y	Y	Y	Y	N
9 Boucher	Y	Y	Y	?	N	Y	N
10 ***Wolf***	N	N	N	Y	Y	Y	N
WASHINGTON							
1 ***Miller***	?	N	Y	Y	Y	Y	N
2 Swift	Y	Y	Y	Y	N	N	N
3 Bonker	Y	Y	Y	Y	N	N	N
4 ***Morrison***	Y	N	N	Y	N	N	N
5 Foley	Y	Y	Y	Y	N	N	N
6 Dicks	?	?	?	Y	N	Y	N
7 Lowry	Y	Y	Y	Y	N	Y	Y
8 ***Chandler***	?	?	?	Y	N	Y	N
WEST VIRGINIA							
1 Mollohan	Y	Y	Y	Y	N	N	N
2 Staggers	Y	Y	Y	Y	N	Y	N
3 Wise	?	?	?	Y	N	Y	N
4 Rahall	Y	Y	Y	Y	N	N	N
WISCONSIN							
1 Aspin	Y	Y	Y	?	?	?	?
2 Kastenmeier	Y	Y	Y	Y	N	N	Y
3 ***Gunderson***	N	N	N	Y	N	N	Y
4 Kleczka	Y	Y	?	?	N	N	Y
5 Moody	Y	Y	Y	Y	Y	N	Y
6 ***Petri***	Y	N	?	Y	Y	N	Y
7 Obey	Y	Y	Y	Y	N	N	Y
8 ***Roth***	?	?	?	Y	N	N	Y
9 ***Sensenbrenner***	?	?	?	Y	Y	N	Y
WYOMING							
AL ***Cheney***	N	N	N	?	Y	Y	N

Southern states - Ala., Ark., Fla., Ga., Ky., La., Miss., N.C., Okla., S.C., Tenn., Texas, Va.

* The *Congressional Record* vote number is different from the CQ vote number because the *Record* includes quorum calls in its tally. CQ does not publish quorum call votes.

292. Procedural Motion. Lewis, R-Fla., motion to approve the House *Journal* of Monday, Sept. 30. Motion agreed to 279-126: R 55-117; D 224-9 (ND 150-7, SD 74-2), Oct. 1, 1985.

293. HR 2100. Farm Programs Reauthorization, Fiscal 1986-90. Stangeland, R-Minn., substitute for the Dorgan, D-N.D., amendment, to increase income supports for wheat farmers on the first 15,000 bushels of production, and to require the agriculture secretary to allow repayment of price-support loans at a rate equal to the amount a crop brings at market. Rejected 200-228: R 79-102; D 121-126 (ND 97-68, SD 24-58), Oct. 1, 1985. A "nay" was a vote supporting the president's position. (The Dorgan amendment, which would have increased wheat target prices for the first 12,000 bushels, was subsequently rejected by voice vote.)

294. HR 2100. Farm Programs Reauthorization, Fiscal 1986-90. Frank, D-Mass., substitute for the Dorgan, D-N.D., amendment, to freeze target prices for wheat in 1986 and permit in succeeding years an annual reduction of 5 percent. Rejected 93-334: R 63-117; D 30-217 (ND 27-138, SD 3-79), Oct. 1, 1985. A "yea" was a vote supporting the president's position. (The Dorgan amendment, which would have increased wheat target prices for the first 12,000 bushels, was subsequently rejected by voice vote.)

295. HR 2100. Farm Programs Reauthorization, Fiscal 1986-90. Robert F. Smith, R-Ore., amendment to the Volkmer, D-Mo., amendment, to hold a referendum among wheat, feed grain, cotton, rice and soybean producers, with a 60 percent majority required to continue authority for programs in the bill after fiscal 1986. Rejected 108-318: R 97-81; D 11-237 (ND 7-159, SD 4-78), Oct. 1, 1985. (The Volkmer amendment, which would have added a farmer referendum on mandatory production controls to the bill, was subsequently defeated by voice vote.)

296. H Res 272. Idaho 2nd District Election. Adoption of the resolution to dismiss the election challenge brought by former GOP Rep. George Hansen against Democratic Rep. Richard H. Stallings, in Idaho's 2nd Congressional District. Adopted 247-4: R 2-4; D 245-0 (ND 164-0, SD 81-0), Oct. 2, 1985.

297. HR 3424. Labor, Health and Human Services, Education Appropriations, Fiscal 1986. Dornan, R-Calif., amendment to authorize the surgeon general to use certain research funds provided in the bill to close or quarantine bathhouses or massage parlors if they are found to facilitate the spread of acquired immune deficiency syndrome (AIDS). Adopted 417-8: R 177-2; D 240-6 (ND 161-6, SD 79-0), Oct. 2, 1985.

298. HR 3424. Labor, Health and Human Services, Education Appropriations, Fiscal 1986. Natcher, D-Ky., motion that the Committee of the Whole rise and report the bill back to the House. Motion agreed to 238-185: R 17-160; D 221-25 (ND 162-3, SD 59-22), Oct. 2, 1985. (The effect of the vote was to prevent consideration of amendments limiting spending on the appropriations bill, in this case the Dannemeyer, R-Calif., amendment to bar the use of funds for programs or for enforcing regulations that discriminate against health care professionals who wear protective garments while treating patients with acquired immune deficiency syndrome (AIDS).)

299. HR 3424. Labor, Health and Human Services, Education Appropriations, Fiscal 1986. Passage of the bill to appropriate $93,407,443,000 in fiscal 1986 funding and $11,473,754,000 in advance fiscal 1987 funding for the Departments of Labor, Health and Human Services, and Education and related agencies. Passed 322-107: R 78-102; D 244-5 (ND 165-3, SD 79-2), Oct. 2, 1985. (The president had requested $90,370,513,000 for fiscal 1986 and $11,473,754,000 in advance fiscal 1987 funding and $214,000,000 in advance fiscal 1988 funding.)

KEY

- Y Voted for (yea).
- # Paired for.
- + Announced for.
- N Voted against (nay).
- X Paired against.
- \- Announced against.
- P Voted "present."
- C Voted "present" to avoid possible conflict of interest.
- ? Did not vote or otherwise make a position known.

Democrats *Republicans*

	292	293	294	295	296	297	298	299
ALABAMA								
1 ***Callahan***	N	N	N	N	P	Y	N	N
2 ***Dickinson***	N	N	N	N	P	Y	?	N
3 Nichols	Y	N	N	N	Y	Y	Y	Y
4 Bevill	Y	N	N	N	Y	Y	Y	Y
5 Flippo	Y	Y	N	N	Y	Y	Y	Y
6 Erdreich	Y	N	N	N	Y	Y	Y	Y
7 Shelby	Y	N	N	N	Y	Y	N	Y
ALASKA								
AL ***Young***	N	N	N	Y	P	Y	N	Y
ARIZONA								
1 ***McCain***	N	N	Y	N	P	Y	N	Y
2 Udall	Y	Y	N	N	Y	Y	Y	Y
3 ***Stump***	N	N	N	N	P	Y	N	N
4 ***Rudd***	Y	N	N	Y	P	Y	N	N
5 ***Kolbe***	N	N	Y	N	P	Y	N	Y
ARKANSAS								
1 Alexander	Y	Y	N	N	Y	?	Y	Y
2 Robinson	Y	Y	N	N	Y	Y	N	Y
3 ***Hammerschmidt***	Y	N	N	Y	P	Y	N	Y
4 Anthony	Y	N	N	N	Y	Y	N	Y
CALIFORNIA								
1 Bosco	Y	Y	Y	N	Y	Y	Y	Y
2 ***Chappie***	N	N	N	Y	P	Y	N	N
3 Matsui	Y	Y	N	N	Y	Y	Y	Y
4 Fazio	Y	N	N	N	Y	Y	Y	Y
5 Burton	Y	Y	N	N	Y	Y	Y	Y
6 Boxer	Y	Y	N	N	Y	Y	Y	Y
7 Miller	?	?	?	N	Y	Y	Y	Y
8 Dellums	Y	Y	N	N	Y	N	Y	Y
9 Stark	Y	Y	N	N	Y	Y	Y	Y
10 Edwards	Y	N	N	N	Y	Y	Y	Y
11 Lantos	Y	Y	N	N	?	Y	Y	Y
12 ***Zschau***	N	N	Y	N	?	?	?	?
13 Mineta	Y	N	N	N	Y	Y	Y	Y
14 ***Shumway***	N	N	Y	Y	P	Y	N	N
15 Coelho	?	N	N	N	Y	Y	Y	Y
16 Panetta	Y	N	N	N	Y	Y	Y	Y
17 ***Pashayan***	Y	N	N	N	P	Y	N	N
18 Lehman	Y	N	N	N	Y	Y	Y	Y
19 ***Lagomarsino***	N	N	Y	Y	P	Y	N	N
20 ***Thomas***	N	N	Y	N	P	Y	N	N
21 ***Fiedler***	N	N	N	Y	?	?	?	?
22 ***Moorhead***	N	N	Y	Y	P	Y	N	N
23 Beilenson	Y	Y	Y	N	Y	Y	Y	Y
24 Waxman	Y	Y	Y	N	Y	Y	Y	Y
25 Roybal	Y	N	N	N	Y	N	Y	Y
26 Berman	Y	Y	Y	N	Y	Y	Y	Y
27 Levine	Y	Y	N	N	Y	Y	Y	Y
28 Dixon	Y	N	N	N	Y	Y	Y	Y
29 Hawkins	Y	N	N	N	Y	Y	Y	N
30 Martinez	Y	N	N	N	Y	?	Y	Y
31 Dymally	P	Y	N	N	Y	N	Y	Y
32 Anderson	Y	N	Y	Y	Y	Y	Y	Y
33 ***Dreier***	N	N	Y	Y	P	Y	N	N
34 Torres	Y	Y	N	N	Y	Y	Y	Y
35 ***Lewis***	N	N	N	Y	P	Y	N	N
36 Brown	Y	N	N	N	Y	Y	Y	Y
37 ***McCandless***	P	N	Y	?	P	Y	N	N
38 ***Dornan***	Y	Y	Y	N	P	Y	N	N
39 ***Dannemeyer***	N	Y	Y	N	P	Y	N	N
40 ***Badham***	N	N	N	N	P	Y	N	N
41 ***Lowery***	Y	N	Y	N	P	Y	N	N
42 ***Lungren***	N	N	Y	N	P	Y	N	N
43 ***Packard***	N	Y	Y	Y	P	Y	N	N
44 Bates	Y	Y	Y	N	Y	Y	Y	Y
45 ***Hunter***	N	N	Y	N	P	Y	?	N
COLORADO								
1 Schroeder	N	Y	Y	Y	Y	Y	Y	N
2 Wirth	Y	Y	N	N	Y	Y	Y	Y
3 ***Strang***	N	Y	N	Y	P	Y	N	N
4 ***Brown***	N	Y	N	Y	P	Y	N	N
5 ***Kramer***	N	N	N	Y	P	Y	N	N
6 ***Schaefer***	N	N	N	Y	P	Y	N	N
CONNECTICUT								
1 Kennelly	Y	Y	N	N	Y	Y	Y	Y
2 Gejdenson	Y	N	N	N	Y	Y	Y	Y
3 Morrison	Y	N	Y	N	Y	Y	Y	Y
4 ***McKinney***	Y	Y	Y	N	P	N	Y	Y
5 ***Rowland***	N	N	N	?	P	Y	N	Y
6 ***Johnson***	Y	Y	Y	N	P	Y	Y	Y
DELAWARE								
AL Carper	Y	N	Y	N	Y	Y	Y	Y
FLORIDA								
1 Hutto	Y	N	N	N	Y	Y	N	Y
2 Fuqua	Y	N	N	N	Y	Y	Y	Y
3 Bennett	Y	Y	N	N	Y	Y	N	Y
4 Chappell	Y	N	N	N	Y	Y	Y	Y
5 ***McCollum***	N	N	Y	Y	P	Y	N	N
6 MacKay	Y	N	N	N	Y	Y	Y	Y
7 Gibbons	Y	N	Y	Y	Y	Y	Y	Y
8 ***Young***	N	N	Y	Y	P	Y	N	Y
9 ***Bilirakis***	N	N	Y	Y	P	Y	N	N
10 ***Ireland***	N	Y	Y	Y	P	Y	N	N
11 Nelson	Y	N	Y	N	Y	Y	N	Y
12 ***Lewis***	N	N	N	Y	P	Y	N	Y
13 ***Mack***	N	N	Y	N	P	Y	N	N
14 Mica	Y	N	N	N	Y	Y	Y	Y
15 ***Shaw***	N	N	Y	Y	P	Y	N	N
16 Smith	Y	Y	N	N	Y	Y	Y	Y
17 Lehman	Y	N	N	N	Y	Y	Y	Y
18 Pepper	Y	Y	N	N	Y	Y	Y	Y
19 Fascell	Y	N	N	N	Y	Y	Y	Y
GEORGIA								
1 Thomas	Y	N	N	N	Y	Y	Y	Y
2 Hatcher	Y	N	N	N	Y	Y	Y	Y
3 Ray	Y	N	N	N	Y	Y	Y	Y
4 ***Swindall***	N	N	Y	N	N	Y	N	N
5 Fowler	Y	Y	N	N	Y	Y	Y	Y
6 ***Gingrich***	?	Y	Y	Y	?	Y	N	N
7 Darden	Y	N	N	N	Y	Y	Y	Y
8 Rowland	Y	N	N	N	Y	Y	Y	Y
9 Jenkins	Y	Y	N	N	Y	Y	Y	Y
10 Barnard	Y	N	N	N	Y	Y	Y	Y
HAWAII								
1 Heftel	Y	Y	N	N	Y	Y	Y	Y
2 Akaka	Y	N	N	N	Y	Y	Y	Y
IDAHO								
1 ***Craig***	N	N	N	Y	P	Y	N	N
2 Stallings	Y	N	N	N	Y	Y	Y	Y
ILLINOIS								
1 Hayes	Y	Y	N	N	Y	Y	Y	Y
2 Savage	Y	Y	N	N	Y	Y	Y	Y
3 Russo	Y	N	N	N	Y	Y	Y	Y
4 ***O'Brien***	Y	N	N	Y	P	Y	Y	Y
5 Lipinski	Y	Y	N	N	Y	Y	Y	Y
6 ***Hyde***	Y	N	N	N	P	Y	N	Y
7 Collins	Y	Y	N	N	Y	Y	Y	Y
8 Rostenkowski	Y	Y	N	N	Y	Y	Y	Y
9 Yates	Y	Y	N	N	Y	Y	Y	Y
10 ***Porter***	Y	N	Y	N	P	Y	Y	Y
11 Annunzio	Y	N	N	N	Y	Y	Y	Y
12 ***Crane***	N	N	Y	N	P	Y	N	N
13 ***Fawell***	Y	N	Y	N	P	Y	N	Y
14 ***Grotberg***	N	N	N	Y	P	Y	N	Y
15 ***Madigan***	N	N	N	Y	P	Y	N	Y
16 ***Martin***	N	N	N	Y	P	Y	N	N
17 Evans	Y	Y	N	N	Y	Y	Y	Y
18 ***Michel***	N	N	N	Y	?	Y	N	N
19 Bruce	Y	N	N	N	Y	Y	N	Y
20 Durbin	N	Y	N	N	Y	Y	Y	Y
21 Price	Y	N	N	N	Y	Y	Y	Y
22 Gray	Y	N	N	N	Y	Y	Y	Y
INDIANA								
1 Visclosky	Y	N	N	N	Y	Y	Y	Y
2 Sharp	Y	Y	N	?	Y	Y	Y	Y
3 ***Hiler***	N	Y	N	N	P	Y	N	N
4 ***Coats***	Y	Y	N	N	P	Y	N	N
5 ***Hillis***	Y	N	N	N	P	Y	N	N

ND - Northern Democrats SD - Southern Democrats

* Corresponding to Congressional Record Votes 321, 322, 323, 325, 326, 328, 330, 331

	292	293	294	295	296	297	298	299
6 ***Burton***	N	N	N	Y	P	Y	N	N
7 ***Myers***	Y	N	N	Y	P	Y	N	Y
8 McCloskey	Y	Y	N	N	Y	Y	Y	Y
9 Hamilton	Y	Y	N	N	Y	Y	Y	Y
10 Jacobs	N	Y	Y	N	P	Y	Y	Y
IOWA								
1 ***Leach***	N	Y	N	Y	P	Y	N	N
2 ***Tauke***	N	Y	N	Y	P	Y	N	N
3 ***Evans***	N	N	N	N	P	Y	N	N
4 Smith	Y	N	N	N	Y	Y	Y	Y
5 ***Lightfoot***	N	N	N	Y	P	Y	N	N
6 Bedell	Y	N	N	N	Y	Y	Y	Y
KANSAS								
1 ***Roberts***	N	Y	N	Y	P	Y	N	N
2 Slattery	Y	Y	N	N	Y	Y	Y	Y
3 ***Meyers***	N	Y	N	Y	P	Y	N	Y
4 Glickman	Y	Y	N	N	Y	Y	Y	Y
5 ***Whittaker***	?	Y	N	Y	P	Y	Y	Y
KENTUCKY								
1 Hubbard	Y	Y	N	Y	Y	Y	N	Y
2 Natcher	Y	Y	N	N	Y	Y	Y	Y
3 Mazzoli	Y	N	Y	Y	Y	Y	N	Y
4 ***Snyder***	Y	Y	N	Y	P	Y	N	Y
5 ***Rogers***	N	Y	N	Y	P	Y	N	Y
6 ***Hopkins***	Y	Y	N	Y	P	Y	N	Y
7 Perkins	Y	Y	N	N	Y	Y	Y	Y
LOUISIANA								
1 ***Livingston***	N	N	Y	N	P	Y	N	Y
2 Boggs	Y	N	N	N	Y	Y	N	Y
3 Tauzin	Y	N	N	N	Y	Y	N	Y
4 Roemer	N	N	N	N	Y	Y	N	Y
5 Huckaby	Y	N	N	N	Y	Y	N	Y
6 ***Moore***	Y	N	N	N	P	Y	N	N
7 Breaux	Y	N	N	N	Y	Y	N	Y
8 Long	Y	N	N	N	Y	Y	N	Y
MAINE								
1 ***McKernan***	N	Y	N	Y	P	Y	N	Y
2 ***Snowe***	N	Y	Y	Y	P	Y	N	Y
MARYLAND								
1 Dyson	Y	Y	N	N	Y	Y	N	Y
2 ***Bentley***	N	Y	N	Y	P	Y	N	Y
3 Mikulski	Y	Y	N	N	Y	Y	Y	Y
4 ***Holt***	N	N	N	N	P	Y	N	Y
5 Hoyer	Y	N	N	N	Y	Y	Y	Y
6 Byron	Y	?	N	N	Y	Y	Y	Y
7 Mitchell	N	N	?	N	Y	Y	Y	Y
8 Barnes	Y	Y	Y	N	Y	Y	Y	Y
MASSACHUSETTS								
1 ***Conte***	N	N	Y	Y	P	Y	Y	Y
2 Boland	Y	N	N	N	Y	Y	Y	Y
3 Early	?	N	Y	N	Y	Y	Y	Y
4 Frank	Y	Y	Y	N	Y	Y	Y	Y
5 Atkins	Y	Y	N	N	Y	Y	Y	Y
6 Mavroules	Y	Y	N	N	Y	Y	Y	Y
7 Markey	Y	Y	Y	N	Y	Y	Y	Y
8 O'Neill								
9 Moakley	Y	?	?	?	?	Y	Y	Y
10 Studds	Y	Y	Y	N	Y	Y	Y	Y
11 Donnelly	Y	N	N	N	Y	Y	Y	Y
MICHIGAN								
1 Conyers	Y	N	N	N	Y	N	Y	N
2 ***Pursell***	Y	Y	N	N	P	Y	N	Y
3 Wolpe	Y	Y	N	N	Y	Y	Y	Y
4 ***Siljander***	N	N	N	Y	N	Y	N	N
5 ***Henry***	Y	N	N	N	P	Y	N	Y
6 Carr	Y	N	Y	N	Y	Y	Y	Y
7 Kildee	Y	Y	N	N	Y	Y	Y	Y
8 Traxler	Y	N	N	N	Y	Y	Y	Y
9 ***Vander Jagt***	Y	N	N	Y	P	Y	N	Y
10 ***Schuette***	N	N	N	N	P	Y	N	Y
11 ***Davis***	Y	N	N	Y	P	Y	N	Y
12 Bonior	Y	Y	N	N	Y	Y	Y	Y
13 Crockett	Y	Y	N	N	Y	N	Y	Y
14 Hertel	Y	Y	N	N	Y	Y	Y	Y
15 Ford	?	N	N	N	Y	Y	Y	Y
16 Dingell	?	N	N	N	Y	Y	Y	Y
17 Levin	Y	Y	N	N	Y	Y	Y	Y
18 ***Broomfield***	Y	Y	Y	Y	P	Y	N	N
MINNESOTA								
1 Penny	N	Y	N	N	Y	Y	Y	Y
2 ***Weber***	N	Y	N	N	?	Y	?	N
3 ***Frenzel***	Y	Y	N	Y	P	Y	N	N
4 Vento	Y	Y	Y	N	Y	Y	Y	Y
5 Sabo	Y	Y	N	N	Y	Y	Y	Y
6 Sikorski	N	Y	N	N	Y	Y	Y	Y
7 ***Stangeland***	N	Y	N	Y	P	Y	N	N
8 Oberstar	Y	Y	N	N	Y	Y	Y	Y
MISSISSIPPI								
1 Whitten	Y	Y	N	N	Y	Y	Y	Y
2 ***Franklin***	?	N	N	Y	P	Y	N	Y
3 Montgomery	Y	N	N	Y	Y	Y	N	Y
4 Dowdy	?	N	N	N	Y	Y	Y	Y
5 ***Lott***	N	N	N	Y	P	Y	N	N
MISSOURI								
1 Clay	N	N	N	N	Y	N	Y	Y
2 Young	Y	N	N	N	Y	Y	Y	Y
3 Gephardt	Y	Y	N	N	Y	Y	Y	Y
4 Skelton	?	Y	N	N	Y	Y	Y	Y
5 Wheat	Y	Y	N	N	Y	Y	Y	Y
6 ***Coleman***	N	Y	N	N	P	Y	N	Y
7 ***Taylor***	N	Y	N	Y	P	Y	N	N
8 ***Emerson***	N	Y	N	Y	P	Y	N	Y
9 Volkmer	Y	Y	N	N	Y	Y	Y	Y
MONTANA								
1 Williams	?	Y	N	N	Y	Y	?	Y
2 ***Marlenee***	Y	N	N	Y	P	Y	N	N
NEBRASKA								
1 ***Bereuter***	N	Y	N	Y	P	Y	N	Y
2 ***Daub***	N	Y	N	Y	P	Y	N	Y
3 ***Smith***	Y	Y	N	Y	P	Y	N	Y
NEVADA								
1 Reid	Y	N	N	N	Y	Y	Y	Y
2 ***Vucanovich***	N	N	N	N	P	Y	N	N
NEW HAMPSHIRE								
1 ***Smith***	N	N	Y	N	P	Y	N	N
2 ***Gregg***	N	Y	Y	N	P	Y	N	N
NEW JERSEY								
1 Florio	Y	Y	Y	N	Y	Y	Y	Y
2 Hughes	Y	Y	N	N	Y	Y	Y	Y
3 Howard	Y	Y	N	N	Y	Y	Y	Y
4 ***Smith***	Y	Y	N	N	P	Y	N	Y
5 ***Roukema***	N	N	N	N	P	Y	N	Y
6 Dwyer	Y	N	N	N	Y	Y	Y	Y
7 ***Rinaldo***	Y	N	N	N	P	Y	N	Y
8 Roe	Y	Y	N	N	Y	Y	Y	Y
9 Torricelli	Y	Y	Y	N	Y	Y	Y	Y
10 Rodino	Y	Y	N	N	Y	?	?	?
11 ***Gallo***	N	Y	Y	N	P	Y	N	Y
12 ***Courter***	N	N	Y	N	P	Y	N	Y
13 ***Saxton***	N	Y	N	N	P	Y	N	Y
14 Guarini	Y	Y	N	N	?	Y	Y	Y
NEW MEXICO								
1 ***Lujan***	Y	Y	Y	Y	P	Y	N	Y
2 ***Skeen***	N	Y	N	Y	P	Y	N	Y
3 Richardson	Y	N	N	N	Y	Y	Y	Y
NEW YORK								
1 ***Carney***	?	?	?	?	P	Y	N	Y
2 Downey	Y	Y	N	N	Y	Y	Y	Y
3 Mrazek	Y	Y	Y	N	Y	Y	Y	Y
4 ***Lent***	N	Y	N	Y	P	Y	N	Y
5 ***McGrath***	N	Y	N	N	P	Y	N	Y
6 Addabbo	?	?	?	?	?	?	?	?
7 Ackerman	Y	Y	Y	Y	Y	Y	Y	Y
8 Scheuer	Y	Y	N	N	Y	Y	Y	Y
9 Manton	Y	N	N	N	Y	Y	Y	Y
10 Schumer	Y	Y	N	N	Y	Y	Y	Y
11 Towns	?	Y	N	N	Y	Y	Y	Y
12 Owens	Y	Y	Y	N	Y	Y	Y	Y
13 Solarz	Y	Y	Y	Y	Y	Y	Y	Y
14 ***Molinari***	Y	Y	N	N	P	Y	N	Y
15 ***Green***	Y	Y	Y	?	P	N	Y	Y
16 Rangel	Y	N	N	N	Y	Y	Y	Y
17 Weiss	Y	Y	Y	N	Y	Y	Y	Y
18 Garcia	?	N	N	N	Y	Y	Y	Y
19 Biaggi	Y	Y	N	N	Y	Y	Y	Y
20 ***DioGuardi***	Y	N	Y	N	P	Y	N	Y
21 ***Fish***	Y	Y	N	Y	P	Y	N	Y
22 ***Gilman***	Y	N	N	Y	P	Y	N	Y
23 Stratton	Y	N	N	N	Y	Y	Y	Y
24 ***Solomon***	N	N	N	Y	P	Y	N	N
25 ***Boehlert***	N	N	N	Y	P	Y	N	Y
26 ***Martin***	?	Y	N	Y	?	Y	N	Y
27 ***Wortley***	N	Y	N	N	?	Y	N	Y
28 McHugh	Y	N	N	N	Y	Y	Y	Y
29 ***Horton***	Y	N	N	N	P	Y	Y	Y
30 ***Eckert***	Y	N	Y	N	P	Y	N	N
31 ***Kemp***	Y	N	N	Y	P	Y	N	N
32 LaFalce	Y	Y	N	N	Y	Y	Y	Y
33 Nowak	Y	Y	N	N	?	Y	Y	Y
34 Lundine	Y	Y	N	Y	Y	Y	Y	Y
NORTH CAROLINA								
1 Jones	?	N	N	N	Y	Y	Y	Y
2 Valentine	Y	N	N	N	Y	Y	Y	Y
3 Whitley	Y	N	N	N	Y	Y	Y	Y
4 ***Cobey***	N	Y	Y	N	P	Y	N	Y
5 Neal	Y	Y	N	N	Y	Y	Y	Y
6 ***Coble***	N	Y	Y	Y	P	Y	N	N
7 Rose	Y	N	N	N	Y	Y	Y	Y
8 Hefner	?	N	N	N	Y	Y	Y	Y
9 ***McMillan***	N	N	N	N	P	Y	N	Y
10 ***Broyhill***	Y	N	N	N	P	Y	N	Y
11 ***Hendon***	N	N	N	N	P	Y	N	Y
NORTH DAKOTA								
AL Dorgan	Y	Y	N	N	Y	Y	Y	Y
OHIO								
1 Luken	Y	Y	Y	N	Y	Y	N	Y
2 ***Gradison***	Y	Y	Y	N	P	Y	N	N
3 Hall	Y	N	N	N	Y	Y	Y	Y
4 ***Oxley***	N	N	N	N	P	Y	Y	N
5 ***Latta***	N	N	N	N	P	Y	N	N
6 ***McEwen***	N	N	Y	Y	P	Y	N	N
7 ***DeWine***	N	N	N	Y	P	Y	N	N
8 ***Kindness***	N	N	N	Y	?	Y	N	N
9 Kaptur	Y	N	N	N	Y	Y	Y	Y
10 ***Miller***	N	Y	N	Y	P	Y	N	N
11 Eckart	Y	Y	N	N	Y	Y	Y	Y
12 ***Kasich***	N	Y	N	Y	P	Y	N	N
13 Pease	Y	Y	Y	N	Y	Y	Y	Y
14 Seiberling	?	Y	N	N	Y	Y	Y	Y
15 ***Wylie***	Y	N	N	Y	P	Y	N	N
16 ***Regula***	Y	Y	N	Y	P	Y	Y	Y
17 Traficant	Y	Y	N	N	Y	Y	Y	Y
18 Applegate	Y	Y	N	Y	Y	Y	Y	Y
19 Feighan	Y	Y	N	N	Y	Y	Y	Y
20 Oakar	Y	N	?	N	Y	Y	Y	Y
21 Stokes	Y	N	N	N	Y	Y	Y	Y
OKLAHOMA								
1 Jones	Y	Y	N	N	Y	Y	Y	Y
2 Synar	Y	Y	N	N	Y	Y	Y	Y
3 Watkins	Y	Y	N	N	Y	Y	Y	Y
4 McCurdy	Y	Y	N	N	Y	Y	Y	Y
5 ***Edwards***	?	Y	?	Y	P	Y	N	N
6 English	Y	Y	N	N	Y	Y	N	Y
OREGON								
1 AuCoin	Y	N	N	N	Y	Y	Y	Y
2 ***Smith, R.***	N	N	N	Y	P	Y	N	N
3 Wyden	Y	N	N	Y	Y	Y	Y	Y
4 Weaver	Y	N	N	N	Y	Y	Y	Y
5 ***Smith, D.***	N	N	N	Y	P	Y	N	N
PENNSYLVANIA								
1 Foglietta	Y	Y	N	N	Y	Y	Y	Y
2 Gray	Y	Y	N	N	Y	Y	?	Y
3 Borski	Y	Y	N	N	Y	Y	Y	Y
4 Kolter	Y	N	N	N	Y	Y	Y	Y
5 ***Schulze***	?	Y	Y	N	P	Y	N	N
6 Yatron	Y	Y	N	N	Y	Y	Y	Y
7 Edgar	Y	Y	N	N	Y	Y	Y	Y
8 Kostmayer	Y	Y	Y	N	Y	Y	Y	Y
9 ***Shuster***	N	Y	N	N	Y	Y	Y	N
10 ***McDade***	Y	Y	Y	Y	P	Y	Y	Y
11 Kanjorski	Y	N	N	N	Y	Y	Y	Y
12 Murtha	Y	N	N	N	Y	Y	Y	Y
13 ***Coughlin***	N	N	Y	N	P	Y	N	Y
14 Coyne	Y	Y	N	N	Y	Y	Y	Y
15 ***Ritter***	Y	Y	Y	N	P	Y	N	N
16 ***Walker***	N	Y	Y	N	P	Y	N	N
17 ***Gekas***	N	N	N	Y	Y	Y	N	N
18 Walgren	Y	Y	N	N	Y	Y	Y	Y
19 ***Goodling***	N	Y	Y	Y	P	Y	N	Y
20 Gaydos	Y	N	N	N	Y	Y	Y	Y
21 ***Ridge***	N	N	N	N	P	Y	Y	Y
22 Murphy	Y	Y	N	N	Y	Y	Y	Y
23 ***Clinger***	Y	Y	Y	N	P	Y	Y	Y
RHODE ISLAND								
1 St Germain	?	N	N	N	Y	Y	Y	Y
2 ***Schneider***	Y	Y	N	N	P	Y	Y	Y
SOUTH CAROLINA								
1 ***Hartnett***	N	Y	N	N	P	Y	N	N
2 ***Spence***	N	N	N	N	P	Y	N	N
3 Derrick	Y	N	N	N	Y	Y	N	Y
4 ***Campbell***	N	N	N	N	P	Y	N	N
5 Spratt	Y	N	N	N	Y	Y	Y	Y
6 Tallon	?	N	N	N	Y	Y	N	Y
SOUTH DAKOTA								
AL Daschle	Y	Y	N	N	Y	Y	Y	Y
TENNESSEE								
1 ***Quillen***	Y	N	N	N	P	Y	N	N
2 ***Duncan***	Y	N	N	N	P	Y	N	Y
3 Lloyd	N	N	N	N	Y	Y	N	Y
4 Cooper	Y	Y	N	N	Y	Y	Y	Y
5 Boner	Y	N	N	N	Y	Y	Y	Y
6 Gordon	Y	Y	N	N	Y	Y	Y	Y
7 ***Sundquist***	N	N	N	N	P	Y	N	Y
8 Jones	Y	N	N	N	Y	Y	Y	Y
9 Ford	Y	N	N	N	Y	Y	Y	Y
TEXAS								
1 Chapman	Y	N	N	N	Y	Y	Y	Y
2 Wilson	Y	N	N	N	Y	Y	Y	Y
3 ***Bartlett***	N	Y	Y	Y	P	Y	N	N
4 Hall, R.	Y	N	N	N	Y	Y	N	Y
5 Bryant	Y	Y	N	N	Y	Y	Y	Y
6 ***Barton***	N	Y	N	N	P	Y	N	N
7 ***Archer***	Y	N	Y	N	P	Y	N	N
8 ***Fields***	N	Y	Y	N	P	Y	N	N
9 Brooks	?	N	N	N	Y	Y	Y	Y
10 Pickle	Y	N	N	N	Y	Y	Y	Y
11 Leath	Y	Y	N	N	Y	Y	Y	N
12 Wright	Y	N	N	N	?	?	?	?
13 ***Boulter***	Y	Y	N	Y	P	+	N	N
14 ***Sweeney***	?	Y	N	Y	P	Y	N	N
15 de la Garza	Y	N	N	N	Y	Y	Y	Y
16 Coleman	Y	N	N	N	Y	Y	Y	Y
17 Stenholm	Y	Y	N	N	Y	Y	N	N
18 Leland	?	N	N	N	Y	Y	Y	Y
19 ***Combest***	N	Y	N	Y	P	Y	N	N
20 Gonzalez	Y	N	N	N	Y	P	Y	Y
21 ***Loeffler***	?	Y	N	N	P	Y	N	N
22 ***DeLay***	Y	N	Y	N	P	Y	N	N
23 Bustamante	Y	N	N	N	Y	Y	Y	Y
24 Frost	Y	Y	N	N	Y	Y	Y	Y
25 Andrews	Y	N	N	N	Y	Y	Y	Y
26 ***Armey***	N	Y	Y	N	N	Y	N	N
27 Ortiz	Y	N	N	N	Y	Y	Y	Y
UTAH								
1 ***Hansen***	Y	N	Y	Y	P	Y	N	N
2 ***Monson***	N	N	Y	Y	P	Y	N	N
3 ***Nielson***	N	Y	Y	Y	P	Y	N	N
VERMONT								
AL ***Jeffords***	Y	N	N	Y	P	Y	Y	Y
VIRGINIA								
1 ***Bateman***	Y	N	N	N	P	Y	N	Y
2 ***Whitehurst***	Y	N	Y	Y	P	Y	N	N
3 ***Bliley***	N	Y	N	N	P	Y	N	N
4 Sisisky	Y	N	N	N	Y	Y	Y	Y
5 Daniel	Y	N	N	N	Y	Y	N	Y
6 Olin	Y	N	N	N	Y	Y	Y	Y
7 ***Slaughter***	N	Y	N	N	P	Y	N	N
8 ***Parris***	N	N	N	Y	P	Y	N	Y
9 Boucher	Y	N	N	N	Y	Y	Y	Y
10 ***Wolf***	N	Y	N	Y	P	Y	N	Y
WASHINGTON								
1 ***Miller***	Y	N	Y	N	P	Y	N	Y
2 Swift	Y	N	N	N	Y	Y	Y	Y
3 Bonker	Y	?	N	?	Y	Y	Y	Y
4 ***Morrison***	N	N	N	Y	P	Y	Y	Y
5 Foley	Y	N	N	N	Y	Y	Y	Y
6 Dicks	Y	N	N	N	Y	Y	Y	Y
7 Lowry	Y	N	N	N	Y	Y	Y	Y
8 ***Chandler***	N	N	Y	Y	P	Y	N	N
WEST VIRGINIA								
1 Mollohan	Y	N	N	N	Y	Y	Y	Y
2 Staggers	Y	N	N	N	Y	Y	Y	Y
3 Wise	Y	N	N	N	Y	Y	Y	Y
4 Rahall	Y	N	N	N	Y	Y	Y	Y
WISCONSIN								
1 Aspin	Y	N	N	N	Y	Y	Y	Y
2 Kastenmeier	Y	Y	N	N	Y	Y	Y	Y
3 ***Gunderson***	N	Y	N	Y	P	Y	N	Y
4 Kleczka	Y	N	N	N	Y	Y	Y	Y
5 Moody	Y	Y	N	N	Y	Y	?	Y
6 ***Petri***	Y	Y	Y	N	P	Y	N	N
7 Obey	Y	N	N	N	Y	Y	Y	Y
8 ***Roth***	N	Y	Y	Y	P	Y	N	N
9 ***Sensenbrenner***	N	Y	N	Y	N	Y	N	N
WYOMING								
AL ***Cheney***	N	N	Y	Y	P	Y	N	N

Southern states - Ala., Ark., Fla., Ga., Ky., La., Miss., N.C., Okla., S.C., Tenn., Texas, Va.
* The *Congressional Record* vote number is different from the CQ vote number because the *Record* includes quorum calls in its tally. CQ does not publish quorum call votes.

300. Procedural Motion. Schuette, R-Mich., motion to approve the House *Journal* of Wednesday, Oct. 2. Motion agreed to 269-119: R 57-107; D 212-12 (ND 138-10, SD 74-2), Oct. 3, 1985.

301. HR 2100. Farm Programs Reauthorization, Fiscal 1986-90. Madigan, R-Ill., amendment to strike the wheat and feed grain farmer referendum section from the bill. The farmer referendum would have been on the question of establishing a marketing certificate and export subsidy program for domestic wheat and feed grain production. Adopted 251-174: R 169-10; D 82-164 (ND 53-112, SD 29-52), Oct. 3, 1985. A "yea" was a vote supporting the president's position.

302. HR 2100. Farm Programs Reauthorization, Fiscal 1986-90. Lundine, D-N.Y., amendment to phase out the price-support and national quota program for peanut producers by 1989, gradually limiting the size of the peanut crop that would come under the national poundage quota, lowering the price-support level and allowing growers not holding a quota to compete for the domestic market in order to meet demand. Rejected 195-228: R 122-57; D 73-171 (ND 66-98, SD 7-73), Oct. 3, 1985. A "yea" was a vote supporting the president's position.

303. HR 2100. Farm Programs Reauthorization, Fiscal 1986-90. English, D-Okla., substitute for the Smith, R-Neb., amendment, to exempt agriculture export credit programs from the cargo-preference requirements that half of all government-generated exports be shipped on U.S.-flag vessels. Rejected 179-245: R 105-76; D 74-169 (ND 33-131, SD 41-38), Oct. 3, 1985. A "yea" was a vote supporting the president's position. (The Smith amendment, which would have exempted all agricultural exports, including food donation programs, from cargo-preference requirements, was subsequently defeated by voice vote.)

304. HR 2100. Farm Programs Reauthorization, Fiscal 1986-90. Bereuter, R-Neb., amendment to require the Maritime Administration to pay the costs of subsidies incurred by applying cargo-preference requirements to agricultural export programs. Rejected 151-269: R 104-77; D 47-192 (ND 24-136, SD 23-56), Oct. 3, 1985.

305. HR 2100. Farm Programs Reauthorization, Fiscal 1986-90. Glickman, D-Kan., amendment to bring highly erodible crop land farmed in 1981-85 under the sanctions of the bill's "sodbuster" provisions by 1995, or two years after completion of soil maps, whichever is later, with the requirement that such land must be planted under an approved conservation plan by 1990. Adopted 313-90: R 97-74; D 216-16 (ND 150-6, SD 66-10), Oct. 3, 1985.

KEY

- Y Voted for (yea).
- # Paired for.
- + Announced for.
- N Voted against (nay).
- X Paired against.
- \- Announced against.
- P Voted "present."
- C Voted "present" to avoid possible conflict of interest.
- ? Did not vote or otherwise make a position known.

Democrats ***Republicans***

	300	301	302	303	304	305
ALABAMA						
1 ***Callahan***	?	N	N	N	N	N
2 ***Dickinson***	N	N	N	N	N	N
3 Nichols	Y	N	N	N	N	N
4 Bevill	Y	N	N	?	?	?
5 Flippo	Y	Y	N	N	N	Y
6 Erdreich	Y	N	N	N	N	Y
7 Shelby	Y	N	N	N	N	Y
ALASKA						
AL ***Young***	N	Y	N	N	N	Y
ARIZONA						
1 ***McCain***	N	Y	Y	N	Y	Y
2 Udall	?	N	N	Y	N	?
3 ***Stump***	N	Y	N	Y	Y	N
4 ***Rudd***	Y	Y	Y	Y	Y	?
5 ***Kolbe***	N	Y	Y	Y	Y	Y
ARKANSAS						
1 Alexander	Y	N	N	Y	Y	?
2 Robinson	Y	N	N	Y	Y	Y
3 ***Hammerschmidt***	Y	Y	N	Y	Y	Y
4 Anthony	Y	N	N	Y	Y	Y
CALIFORNIA						
1 Bosco	Y	N	Y	N	N	Y
2 ***Chappie***	N	Y	N	Y	Y	N
3 Matsui	Y	N	N	N	N	Y
4 Fazio	Y	N	N	Y	N	Y
5 Burton	Y	N	?	N	N	Y
6 Boxer	Y	N	N	N	N	Y
7 Miller	Y	N	N	N	N	Y
8 Dellums	Y	N	Y	N	N	Y
9 Stark	Y	N	Y	N	N	Y
10 Edwards	Y	N	Y	N	N	Y
11 Lantos	Y	N	N	N	N	Y
12 ***Zschau***	N	Y	Y	Y	Y	Y
13 Mineta	Y	N	N	N	N	Y
14 ***Shumway***	N	Y	Y	N	N	N
15 Coelho	Y	N	N	N	N	Y
16 Panetta	Y	N	N	Y	N	Y
17 ***Pashayan***	Y	Y	N	Y	Y	Y
18 Lehman	Y	N	N	N	N	Y
19 ***Lagomarsino***	N	Y	Y	Y	Y	Y
20 ***Thomas***	N	Y	N	Y	Y	Y
21 ***Fiedler***	?	Y	Y	Y	Y	N
22 ***Moorhead***	N	Y	Y	Y	Y	N
23 Beilenson	Y	N	Y	N	N	Y
24 Waxman	Y	Y	Y	N	?	Y
25 Roybal	Y	N	Y	N	N	Y
26 Berman	?	?	#	?	?	?
27 Levine	Y	Y	Y	N	N	Y
28 Dixon	?	N	N	N	N	Y
29 Hawkins	?	N	N	N	N	?
30 Martinez	Y	N	N	N	N	Y
31 Dymally	Y	N	Y	N	N	?
32 Anderson	Y	Y	Y	N	N	Y
33 ***Dreier***	N	Y	Y	Y	Y	Y
34 Torres	?	N	N	N	N	Y
35 ***Lewis***	N	Y	Y	N	N	N
36 Brown	Y	N	Y	Y	N	Y
37 ***McCandless***	?	Y	Y	Y	Y	N
38 ***Dornan***	N	Y	Y	N	N	Y
39 ***Dannemeyer***	N	Y	Y	Y	Y	Y
40 ***Badham***	N	Y	Y	N	N	N
41 ***Lowery***	N	Y	Y	N	N	Y
42 ***Lungren***	Y	Y	Y	Y	Y	Y
43 ***Packard***	N	Y	Y	N	N	N
44 Bates	Y	Y	Y	N	N	Y
45 ***Hunter***	?	Y	Y	N	N	Y
COLORADO						
1 Schroeder	N	Y	N	Y	Y	Y
2 Wirth	Y	N	Y	Y	Y	Y
3 ***Strang***	N	Y	N	Y	Y	N
4 ***Brown***	N	Y	Y	Y	Y	Y
5 ***Kramer***	N	Y	Y	Y	Y	Y
6 ***Schaefer***	N	Y	Y	N	N	N
CONNECTICUT						
1 Kennelly	N	Y	N	N	N	Y
2 Gejdenson	Y	N	Y	N	N	Y
3 Morrison	Y	N	Y	N	N	Y
4 ***McKinney***	Y	Y	Y	N	N	?
5 ***Rowland***	Y	Y	Y	N	N	Y
6 ***Johnson***	?	Y	Y	N	Y	Y
DELAWARE						
AL Carper	Y	Y	Y	N	N	Y
FLORIDA						
1 Hutto	Y	Y	N	N	N	Y
2 Fuqua	Y	Y	N	Y	Y	Y
3 Bennett	Y	N	N	N	N	Y
4 Chappell	Y	Y	N	N	N	Y
5 ***McCollum***	Y	Y	Y	N	N	Y
6 MacKay	Y	Y	N	N	N	Y
7 Gibbons	?	Y	Y	Y	N	Y
8 ***Young***	Y	Y	Y	N	N	Y
9 ***Bilirakis***	N	Y	Y	N	N	N
10 ***Ireland***	N	Y	Y	Y	Y	N
11 Nelson	Y	Y	Y	N	Y	Y
12 ***Lewis***	N	Y	Y	N	N	Y
13 ***Mack***	N	Y	Y	N	N	N
14 Mica	Y	N	N	N	N	Y
15 ***Shaw***	N	Y	Y	N	N	N
16 Smith	P	N	N	N	N	Y
17 Lehman	Y	Y	Y	N	N	Y
18 Pepper	Y	N	N	N	N	Y
19 Fascell	Y	N	N	N	N	Y
GEORGIA						
1 Thomas	Y	Y	N	Y	N	Y
2 Hatcher	Y	N	N	Y	N	?
3 Ray	Y	Y	N	Y	Y	Y
4 ***Swindall***	N	Y	N	Y	Y	Y
5 Fowler	Y	N	N	Y	Y	Y
6 ***Gingrich***	N	Y	N	Y	Y	?
7 Darden	Y	N	N	N	N	Y
8 Rowland	Y	Y	N	Y	N	Y
9 Jenkins	Y	Y	N	Y	Y	Y
10 Barnard	Y	Y	X	?	?	?
HAWAII						
1 Heftel	?	Y	N	N	N	Y
2 Akaka	Y	N	N	N	N	Y
IDAHO						
1 ***Craig***	N	Y	N	Y	Y	N
2 Stallings	Y	N	N	Y	Y	Y
ILLINOIS						
1 Hayes	Y	N	N	N	N	Y
2 Savage	Y	N	N	N	N	Y
3 Russo	Y	N	N	N	N	Y
4 ***O'Brien***	?	Y	Y	Y	N	Y
5 Lipinski	Y	N	N	N	N	Y
6 ***Hyde***	Y	Y	Y	Y	Y	N
7 Collins	Y	N	Y	N	N	Y
8 Rostenkowski	Y	Y	N	N	N	Y
9 Yates	Y	Y	Y	Y	N	Y
10 ***Porter***	Y	Y	Y	Y	Y	Y
11 Annunzio	Y	N	Y	N	N	Y
12 ***Crane***	?	Y	Y	Y	Y	Y
13 ***Fawell***	N	Y	Y	Y	Y	Y
14 ***Grotberg***	N	Y	Y	Y	Y	N
15 ***Madigan***	N	Y	Y	Y	Y	N
16 ***Martin***	N	Y	Y	Y	Y	Y
17 Evans	P	N	N	N	Y	Y
18 ***Michel***	N	Y	Y	Y	Y	N
19 Bruce	N	Y	N	Y	Y	Y
20 Durbin	N	Y	Y	Y	Y	Y
21 Price	Y	N	Y	N	N	Y
22 Gray	Y	Y	Y	N	N	N
INDIANA						
1 Visclosky	Y	Y	Y	Y	Y	Y
2 Sharp	Y	Y	Y	Y	Y	Y
3 ***Hiler***	N	Y	Y	Y	Y	Y
4 ***Coats***	N	Y	Y	Y	Y	Y
5 ***Hillis***	Y	Y	Y	Y	Y	?

ND - Northern Democrats SD - Southern Democrats

* Corresponding to Congressional Record Votes 332, 333, 334, 335, 336, 337

	300	301	302	303	304	305
6 **Burton**	N	Y	Y	Y	Y	?
7 **Myers**	Y	Y	N	Y	Y	Y
8 McCloskey	Y	Y	N	Y	N	Y
9 Hamilton	Y	Y	Y	Y	Y	Y
10 Jacobs	N	Y	Y	Y	N	Y
IOWA						
1 **Leach**	N	Y	Y	Y	Y	Y
2 **Tauke**	N	Y	Y	Y	Y	Y
3 **Evans**	N	N	N	Y	Y	N
4 Smith	Y	Y	Y	Y	Y	N
5 **Lightfoot**	N	Y	Y	Y	Y	N
6 Bedell	Y	N	N	Y	Y	Y
KANSAS						
1 **Roberts**	?	Y	N	Y	Y	N
2 Slattery	Y	N	N	Y	Y	Y
3 **Meyers**	Y	Y	Y	Y	Y	Y
4 Glickman	P	N	N	Y	Y	Y
5 **Whittaker**	N	Y	N	Y	Y	Y
KENTUCKY						
1 Hubbard	Y	Y	N	N	N	N
2 Natcher	Y	N	N	N	N	Y
3 Mazzoli	Y	Y	N	Y	N	Y
4 **Snyder**	Y	Y	N	N	N	N
5 **Rogers**	N	Y	N	Y	Y	N
6 **Hopkins**	Y	Y	N	Y	Y	N
7 Perkins	Y	N	N	N	N	Y
LOUISIANA						
1 **Livingston**	N	Y	N	N	N	N
2 Boggs	Y	Y	N	N	N	Y
3 Tauzin	Y	Y	N	N	N	Y
4 Roemer	N	Y	N	Y	Y	Y
5 Huckaby	Y	N	N	Y	Y	Y
6 **Moore**	Y	Y	N	Y	Y	N
7 Breaux	Y	Y	N	Y	Y	Y
8 Long	Y	Y	N	N	N	Y
MAINE						
1 **McKernan**	N	Y	Y	N	N	Y
2 **Snowe**	Y	Y	Y	N	N	Y
MARYLAND						
1 Dyson	?	Y	N	N	N	Y
2 **Bentley**	N	Y	Y	N	N	Y
3 Mikulski	?	Y	N	N	N	Y
4 **Holt**	Y	Y	Y	N	N	N
5 Hoyer	?	N	N	N	N	Y
6 Byron	?	Y	N	N	N	Y
7 Mitchell	N	N	N	N	N	Y
8 Barnes	Y	Y	Y	N	N	Y
MASSACHUSETTS						
1 **Conte**	N	Y	Y	N	N	Y
2 Boland	Y	Y	Y	N	N	Y
3 Early	Y	Y	Y	N	N	Y
4 Frank	Y	Y	Y	Y	N	Y
5 Atkins	Y	N	Y	Y	N	Y
6 Mavroules	Y	N	N	N	N	Y
7 Markey	Y	Y	Y	N	N	Y
8 O'Neill						
9 Moakley	Y	N	Y	N	N	Y
10 Studds	Y	Y	Y	N	N	Y
11 Donnelly	Y	N	N	N	N	Y
MICHIGAN						
1 Conyers	N	N	N	N	N	Y
2 **Pursell**	Y	Y	Y	Y	Y	N
3 Wolpe	Y	N	Y	N	N	Y
4 **Siljander**	N	Y	Y	Y	Y	N
5 **Henry**	Y	Y	Y	Y	Y	Y
6 Carr	Y	Y	N	N	N	N
7 Kildee	Y	N	Y	N	N	Y
8 Traxler	Y	N	N	Y	N	N
9 **Vander Jagt**	N	Y	Y	N	N	N
10 **Schuette**	N	N	N	Y	Y	N
11 **Davis**	P	Y	Y	N	N	N
12 Bonior	Y	N	N	N	N	Y
13 Crockett	Y	N	N	N	N	Y
14 Hertel	Y	N	N	N	N	Y
15 Ford	?	?	N	N	N	Y
16 Dingell	?	N	N	N	N	Y
17 Levin	Y	N	N	N	N	Y
18 **Broomfield**	Y	Y	Y	Y	Y	Y
MINNESOTA						
1 Penny	N	N	N	Y	Y	Y
2 **Weber**	N	N	N	Y	Y	Y
3 **Frenzel**	N	Y	Y	Y	Y	Y
4 Vento	Y	N	Y	?	?	?
5 Sabo	Y	N	N	N	N	Y
6 Sikorski	N	N	N	N	N	Y

	300	301	302	303	304	305
7 **Stangeland**	N	Y	N	Y	Y	Y
8 Oberstar	Y	N	N	N	N	Y
MISSISSIPPI						
1 Whitten	Y	N	N	Y	N	N
2 **Franklin**	Y	Y	N	Y	Y	N
3 Montgomery	Y	Y	N	Y	Y	N
4 Dowdy	Y	N	N	N	N	Y
5 **Lott**	N	Y	N	N	N	N
MISSOURI						
1 Clay	?	?	N	N	N	Y
2 Young	Y	N	N	N	N	Y
3 Gephardt	Y	N	N	N	N	Y
4 Skelton	Y	N	N	Y	Y	N
5 Wheat	Y	N	N	N	N	Y
6 **Coleman**	N	N	N	Y	Y	N
7 **Taylor**	N	Y	N	Y	Y	Y
8 **Emerson**	N	Y	N	Y	Y	N
9 Volkmer	Y	N	N	Y	Y	N
MONTANA						
1 Williams	Y	N	N	N	N	Y
2 **Marlenee**	N	Y	N	Y	Y	N
NEBRASKA						
1 **Bereuter**	?	N	Y	Y	Y	Y
2 **Daub**	N	Y	Y	Y	Y	Y
3 **Smith**	Y	N	N	Y	Y	N
NEVADA						
1 Reid	Y	Y	Y	N	N	Y
2 **Vucanovich**	N	Y	Y	N	N	N
NEW HAMPSHIRE						
1 **Smith**	N	Y	Y	N	N	Y
2 **Gregg**	?	Y	Y	N	N	Y
NEW JERSEY						
1 Florio	Y	N	Y	N	N	Y
2 Hughes	Y	Y	Y	N	N	Y
3 Howard	Y	N	Y	N	N	Y
4 **Smith**	Y	Y	Y	N	N	Y
5 **Roukema**	N	Y	Y	Y	N	Y
6 Dwyer	Y	N	Y	N	N	Y
7 **Rinaldo**	Y	Y	Y	N	N	Y
8 Roe	Y	N	N	N	N	Y
9 Torricelli	Y	N	Y	N	N	Y
10 Rodino	?	?	?	X	?	?
11 **Gallo**	N	Y	Y	N	N	Y
12 **Courter**	N	Y	Y	N	N	Y
13 **Saxton**	N	Y	Y	N	N	Y
14 Guarini	Y	N	N	N	N	Y
NEW MEXICO						
1 **Lujan**	Y	Y	N	N	N	Y
2 **Skeen**	N	Y	N	Y	Y	N
3 Richardson	Y	N	N	N	N	Y
NEW YORK						
1 **Carney**	N	Y	Y	N	N	N
2 Downey	Y	N	N	N	N	Y
3 Mrazek	Y	Y	Y	N	N	?
4 **Lent**	N	Y	Y	N	N	Y
5 **McGrath**	N	Y	Y	N	N	Y
6 Addabbo	?	?	?	?	?	?
7 Ackerman	Y	N	N	N	N	Y
8 Scheuer	Y	N	N	N	N	Y
9 Manton	Y	N	N	?	?	?
10 Schumer	Y	Y	Y	N	N	Y
11 Towns	Y	N	N	N	N	Y
12 Owens	Y	N	Y	N	?	?
13 Solarz	Y	Y	Y	N	N	Y
14 **Molinari**	Y	Y	Y	N	N	Y
15 **Green**	Y	Y	Y	N	N	Y
16 Rangel	Y	N	N	N	N	Y
17 Weiss	Y	N	Y	N	N	Y
18 Garcia	Y	N	Y	N	N	Y
19 Biaggi	Y	Y	?	N	N	Y
20 **DioGuardi**	N	Y	Y	N	N	Y
21 **Fish**	Y	Y	Y	N	N	Y
22 **Gilman**	Y	Y	Y	N	N	Y
23 Stratton	Y	Y	N	N	N	Y
24 **Solomon**	N	Y	Y	N	N	N
25 **Boehlert**	N	Y	Y	N	N	Y
26 **Martin**	Y	Y	Y	N	N	Y
27 **Wortley**	Y	Y	Y	N	N	Y
28 McHugh	Y	N	Y	N	Y	Y
29 **Horton**	?	Y	N	N	N	Y
30 **Eckert**	Y	Y	Y	Y	Y	N
31 **Kemp**	Y	Y	Y	N	N	?
32 LaFalce	Y	Y	Y	N	N	Y
33 Nowak	Y	Y	Y	N	N	Y
34 Lundine	Y	Y	Y	N	Y	Y

	300	301	302	303	304	305
NORTH CAROLINA						
1 Jones	Y	N	N	N	N	Y
2 Valentine	Y	N	N	Y	N	Y
3 Whitley	Y	N	N	Y	N	Y
4 **Cobey**	N	Y	N	Y	Y	N
5 Neal	Y	N	N	Y	N	Y
6 **Coble**	?	Y	N	Y	Y	N
7 Rose	Y	N	N	Y	N	N
8 Hefner	Y	N	N	Y	N	Y
9 **McMillan**	Y	Y	N	Y	Y	N
10 **Broyhill**	Y	Y	N	Y	Y	N
11 **Hendon**	?	Y	N	Y	Y	N
NORTH DAKOTA						
AL Dorgan	Y	N	N	Y	Y	Y
OHIO						
1 Luken	Y	Y	Y	N	N	Y
2 **Gradison**	?	?	?	Y	Y	Y
3 Hall	Y	N	?	N	N	Y
4 **Oxley**	N	Y	Y	Y	Y	?
5 **Latta**	N	Y	Y	Y	Y	N
6 **McEwen**	?	?	?	Y	Y	Y
7 **DeWine**	N	Y	Y	Y	Y	Y
8 **Kindness**	?	?	?	Y	?	Y
9 Kaptur	Y	Y	Y	N	N	Y
10 **Miller**	N	Y	Y	Y	Y	Y
11 Eckart	Y	Y	N	N	N	Y
12 **Kasich**	N	Y	Y	Y	Y	N
13 Pease	Y	Y	Y	N	N	Y
14 Seiberling	Y	N	Y	Y	Y	Y
15 **Wylie**	Y	Y	Y	Y	Y	N
16 **Regula**	Y	Y	Y	Y	Y	N
17 Traficant	?	N	N	N	N	Y
18 Applegate	Y	Y	N	Y	N	Y
19 Feighan	?	N	N	N	N	Y
20 Oakar	Y	N	N	N	N	Y
21 Stokes	Y	N	N	N	N	Y
OKLAHOMA						
1 Jones	Y	N	N	Y	Y	Y
2 Synar	Y	N	N	Y	Y	Y
3 Watkins	Y	N	N	Y	Y	Y
4 McCurdy	Y	N	N	Y	Y	Y
5 **Edwards**	Y	N	N	Y	Y	N
6 English	Y	N	N	Y	Y	Y
OREGON						
1 AuCoin	?	Y	Y	N	N	Y
2 **Smith, R.**	N	Y	N	Y	Y	N
3 Wyden	Y	Y	Y	N	N	Y
4 Weaver	Y	N	N	N	N	?
5 **Smith, D.**	N	Y	Y	N	N	N
PENNSYLVANIA						
1 Foglietta	Y	N	Y	N	N	Y
2 Gray	?	N	N	?	?	?
3 Borski	Y	N	N	N	?	?
4 Kolter	Y	N	N	N	N	Y
5 **Schulze**	Y	Y	Y	N	N	?
6 Yatron	Y	Y	Y	N	N	Y
7 Edgar	Y	N	Y	N	N	Y
8 Kostmayer	Y	Y	Y	Y	N	Y
9 **Shuster**	N	Y	Y	Y	Y	N
10 **McDade**	Y	Y	Y	N	N	Y
11 Kanjorski	Y	Y	N	N	N	Y
12 Murtha	Y	N	N	N	N	Y
13 **Coughlin**	N	Y	Y	N	N	Y
14 Coyne	Y	N	N	N	N	Y
15 **Ritter**	Y	Y	Y	N	N	Y
16 **Walker**	N	Y	Y	Y	Y	N
17 **Gekas**	N	Y	Y	N	N	N
18 Walgren	Y	N	N	N	N	Y
19 **Goodling**	N	Y	Y	#	Y	Y
20 Gaydos	Y	N	N	N	N	Y
21 **Ridge**	N	Y	Y	N	N	Y
22 Murphy	Y	N	N	N	N	Y
23 **Clinger**	Y	Y	Y	N	N	Y
RHODE ISLAND						
1 St Germain	Y	N	Y	N	?	?
2 **Schneider**	Y	Y	Y	N	N	Y
SOUTH CAROLINA						
1 **Hartnett**	Y	Y	N	N	N	Y
2 **Spence**	N	Y	N	N	N	Y
3 Derrick	Y	N	N	N	N	Y
4 **Campbell**	Y	Y	N	N	N	?
5 Spratt	Y	Y	N	Y	N	Y
6 Tallon	Y	N	N	N	Y	Y
SOUTH DAKOTA						
AL Daschle	Y	N	N	Y	Y	Y

	300	301	302	303	304	305
TENNESSEE						
1 **Quillen**	Y	Y	N	N	N	Y
2 **Duncan**	Y	Y	N	N	N	Y
3 Lloyd	N	N	Y	N	N	Y
4 Cooper	Y	N	Y	Y	N	Y
5 Boner	Y	N	N	N	N	Y
6 Gordon	Y	N	N	Y	N	Y
7 **Sundquist**	N	Y	Y	N	N	Y
8 Jones	Y	N	N	Y	N	Y
9 Ford	?	N	N	N	N	Y
TEXAS						
1 Chapman	Y	Y	N	Y	Y	Y
2 Wilson	?	N	N	N	N	Y
3 **Bartlett**	N	Y	Y	Y	Y	Y
4 Hall, R.	Y	N	N	Y	Y	N
5 Bryant	Y	N	N	N	N	Y
6 **Barton**	N	Y	Y	Y	Y	N
7 **Archer**	Y	Y	Y	Y	Y	Y
8 **Fields**	N	Y	Y	N	N	Y
9 Brooks	Y	N	N	N	N	Y
10 Pickle	Y	Y	N	Y	N	Y
11 Leath	Y	N	N	Y	Y	N
12 Wright	?	?	?	?	?	?
13 **Boulter**	N	Y	Y	Y	Y	N
14 **Sweeney**	Y	Y	N	Y	Y	Y
15 de la Garza	Y	N	N	Y	N	Y
16 Coleman	Y	N	Y	N	N	N
17 Stenholm	Y	Y	N	Y	Y	N
18 Leland	P	N	Y	N	N	Y
19 **Combest**	N	Y	N	Y	Y	N
20 Gonzalez	Y	N	N	N	N	Y
21 **Loeffler**	N	Y	N	Y	Y	N
22 **DeLay**	N	Y	Y	Y	Y	N
23 Bustamante	Y	N	N	N	N	Y
24 Frost	Y	N	N	N	N	?
25 Andrews	Y	Y	N	N	N	Y
26 **Armey**	N	Y	Y	Y	Y	N
27 Ortiz	Y	N	N	N	N	Y
UTAH						
1 **Hansen**	Y	Y	Y	Y	Y	N
2 **Monson**	N	Y	Y	Y	Y	N
3 **Nielson**	N	Y	Y	Y	Y	N
VERMONT						
AL **Jeffords**	Y	Y	N	Y	Y	Y
VIRGINIA						
1 **Bateman**	Y	Y	N	N	N	Y
2 **Whitehurst**	Y	Y	N	N	N	?
3 **Bliley**	N	Y	N	N	N	Y
4 Sisisky	Y	N	N	Y	N	Y
5 Daniel	Y	Y	N	Y	Y	N
6 Olin	Y	Y	N	Y	N	Y
7 **Slaughter**	N	Y	N	Y	Y	N
8 **Parris**	Y	Y	N	N	N	?
9 Boucher	Y	Y	N	Y	N	Y
10 **Wolf**	N	Y	Y	Y	N	Y
WASHINGTON						
1 **Miller**	Y	Y	Y	N	N	Y
2 Swift	Y	N	N	N	N	Y
3 Bonker	Y	Y	N	N	N	Y
4 **Morrison**	N	Y	Y	Y	Y	N
5 Foley	Y	N	N	Y	N	Y
6 Dicks	Y	Y	N	N	N	Y
7 Lowry	N	N	N	N	N	Y
8 **Chandler**	N	Y	Y	N	N	Y
WEST VIRGINIA						
1 Mollohan	Y	N	N	N	N	Y
2 Staggers	Y	Y	N	N	N	Y
3 Wise	Y	N	N	N	N	Y
4 Rahall	Y	N	N	N	N	Y
WISCONSIN						
1 Aspin	?	N	N	N	N	Y
2 Kastenmeier	Y	N	N	Y	Y	Y
3 **Gunderson**	N	N	N	Y	Y	Y
4 Kleczka	Y	N	N	N	N	Y
5 Moody	Y	N	Y	N	Y	Y
6 **Petri**	Y	Y	Y	Y	Y	Y
7 Obey	Y	N	N	Y	Y	Y
8 **Roth**	N	Y	N	Y	Y	Y
9 **Sensenbrenner**	N	Y	Y	Y	Y	Y
WYOMING						
AL **Cheney**	?	Y	Y	Y	Y	N

Southern states - Ala., Ark., Fla., Ga., Ky., La., Miss., N.C., Okla., S.C., Tenn., Texas, Va.

* The *Congressional Record* vote number is different from the CQ vote number because the *Record* includes quorum calls in its tally. CQ does not publish quorum call votes.

306. HR 2100. Farm Programs Reauthorization, Fiscal 1986-90. Emerson, R-Mo., amendment to eliminate the expanded benefit and eligibility levels for food stamps contained in the bill. Rejected 171-238: R 153-23; D 18-215 (ND 7-148, SD 11-67), Oct. 7, 1985.

307. HR 2100. Farm Programs Reauthorization, Fiscal 1986-90. Gingrich, R-Ga., amendment to require states to set up employment and training ("workfare") programs for food stamp recipients, and to require 75 percent of eligible recipients to be enrolled in a work program over 3 years. Rejected 183-227: R 153-23; D 30-204 (ND 10-145, SD 20-59), Oct. 7, 1985. A "yea" was a vote supporting the president's position.

308. HR 2100. Farm Programs Reauthorization, Fiscal 1986-90. Frank, D-Mass., amendment to place a cap of $250,000 on honey price-support loans available to commercial beekeepers. Adopted 340-65: R 156-17; D 184-48 (ND 130-21, SD 54-27), Oct. 7, 1985.

309. HR 3174. Military Medical Malpractice. Glickman, D-Kan., motion to suspend the rules and pass the bill to allow active-duty members of the armed services to sue the government for medical and dental malpractice at government facilities. Motion agreed to 317-90: R 104-71; D 213-19 (ND 147-5, SD 66-14), Oct. 7, 1985. A two-thirds majority of those present and voting (272 in this case) is required for passage under suspension of the rules. A "nay" was a vote supporting the president's position.

310. HR 2100. Farm Programs Reauthorization, Fiscal 1986-90. Petri, R-Wis., amendment to repeal tobacco price-support programs, effective in 1986. Rejected 195-230: R 101-76; D 94-154 (ND 84-82, SD 10-72), Oct. 8, 1985.

311. HR 2100. Farm Programs Reauthorization, Fiscal 1986-90. Stangeland, R-Minn., substitute for the Alexander, D-Ark., substitute, to establish separate referendums on mandatory production control programs for grain farmers, soybean farmers, rice farmers and cotton farmers, with approval for each crop program based on a 60 percent majority vote. If grain farmers disapprove of the mandatory controls, the agriculture secretary would be required to allow farmers to repay their wheat and feed grain crop loans at no higher than state average market prices; target prices for wheat would be set at $4.50 a bushel for the first 15,000 bushels, and $4 a bushel for the remainder; target prices for corn would be set at $3.25 a bushel for the first 30,000 bushels, and $2.75 a bushel thereafter. Rejected 52-371: R 6-171; D 46-200 (ND 35-129, SD 11-71), Oct. 8, 1985. A "nay" was a vote supporting the president's position. (The Alexander substitute, to establish a single referendum on mandatory controls, was subsequently rejected *(see vote 312, below)*.)

312. HR 2100. Farm Programs Reauthorization, Fiscal 1986-90. Alexander, D-Ark., substitute to establish a mandatory production control program for wheat, feed grains, rice, cotton and soybeans if approved by a majority of farmers in a national referendum to be held every four years. If the referendum were disapproved, the Agriculture Department would establish programs for all major commodities. If it were approved, crop-support non-recourse loan rates would be set at 70 percent of parity (a formula based on farmers' purchasing power during the years 1910-14) for the 1986 crop and increased 2 percentage points a year thereafter until 1996. Farmers would be required to idle 15 percent of their normal crop acreage. Rejected 59-368: R 2-177; D 57-191 (ND 40-127, SD 17-64), Oct. 8, 1985. A "nay" was a vote supporting the president's position.

313. HR 2100. Farm Programs Reauthorization, Fiscal 1986-90. Miller, D-Calif., amendment to deny any type of federal farm assistance to any farmer with 10 or more field hand employees who fails to provide drinking water and sanitation facilities to his employees. Rejected 199-227: R 10-168; D 189-59 (ND 148-19, SD 41-40), Oct. 8, 1985. (This amendment had been adopted previously in the Committee of the Whole.)

KEY

Y Voted for (yea).
\# Paired for.
\+ Announced for.
N Voted against (nay).
X Paired against.
\- Announced against.
P Voted "present."
C Voted "present" to avoid possible conflict of interest.
? Did not vote or otherwise make a position known.

Democrats ***Republicans***

	306	307	308	309	310	311	312	313
ALABAMA								
1 ***Callahan***	Y	Y	Y	N	Y	N	N	N
2 ***Dickinson***	Y	Y	Y	N	N	N	N	N
3 Nichols	Y	Y	Y	N	N	N	N	N
4 Bevill	N	Y	Y	Y	N	N	N	N
5 Flippo	N	N	Y	Y	N	N	N	Y
6 Erdreich	N	N	Y	Y	Y	N	N	Y
7 Shelby	?	?	Y	Y	N	N	N	N
ALASKA								
AL ***Young***	N	N	Y	Y	N	N	N	N
ARIZONA								
1 ***McCain***	Y	Y	Y	Y	N	N	N	N
2 Udall	N	N	Y	Y	N	N	N	Y
3 ***Stump***	Y	Y	Y	N	N	N	N	N
4 ***Rudd***	Y	Y	Y	N	N	N	N	N
5 ***Kolbe***	Y	Y	Y	Y	Y	N	N	N
ARKANSAS								
1 Alexander	N	N	N	Y	N	Y	Y	N
2 Robinson	Y	N	N	Y	N	Y	N	N
3 ***Hammerschmidt***	Y	Y	N	N	N	N	N	N
4 Anthony	N	N	N	Y	N	Y	Y	Y
CALIFORNIA								
1 Bosco	N	N	Y	Y	N	Y	Y	Y
2 ***Chappie***	Y	N	N	Y	N	N	N	N
3 Matsui	N	N	N	Y	N	N	N	Y
4 Fazio	N	?	?	?	N	N	N	Y
5 Burton	N	N	Y	Y	N	N	N	Y
6 Boxer	N	N	N	Y	Y	Y	Y	Y
7 Miller	N	N	Y	Y	Y	N	Y	Y
8 Dellums	N	N	Y	Y	Y	Y	Y	Y
9 Stark	N	N	Y	Y	Y	Y	Y	Y
10 Edwards	N	N	Y	Y	Y	N	Y	Y
11 Lantos	N	N	Y	Y	Y	N	N	Y
12 ***Zschau***	Y	Y	Y	Y	Y	N	N	N
13 Mineta	N	N	Y	Y	Y	?	?	?
14 ***Shumway***	Y	Y	Y	N	Y	N	N	N
15 Coelho	N	N	N	Y	N	N	N	Y
16 Panetta	N	N	Y	Y	N	N	N	Y
17 ***Pashayan***	Y	Y	N	Y	N	N	N	N
18 Lehman	N	N	Y	Y	N	N	N	N
19 ***Lagomarsino***	Y	Y	Y	Y	Y	N	N	N
20 ***Thomas***	Y	Y	Y	Y	N	N	N	N
21 ***Fiedler***	Y	Y	Y	Y	Y	N	N	N
22 ***Moorhead***	Y	Y	Y	Y	Y	N	N	N
23 Beilenson	N	N	Y	Y	Y	N	N	Y
24 Waxman	N	N	N	Y	Y	N	N	Y
25 Roybal	N	N	Y	Y	N	?	N	Y
26 Berman	N	N	?	?	Y	N	N	Y
27 Levine	N	N	Y	Y	Y	N	N	Y
28 Dixon	N	N	Y	Y	N	N	N	Y
29 Hawkins	N	N	Y	Y	N	N	N	Y
30 Martinez	N	N	Y	Y	N	N	Y	Y
31 Dymally	N	N	Y	Y	N	Y	Y	Y
32 Anderson	N	N	Y	Y	Y	N	N	Y
33 ***Dreier***	Y	Y	Y	Y	Y	N	N	N
34 Torres	N	N	Y	Y	N	Y	Y	Y
35 ***Lewis***	?	?	?	?	?	?	?	?
36 Brown	N	N	N	Y	Y	N	N	Y
37 ***McCandless***	#	?	?	?	?	?	?	?
38 ***Dornan***	Y	Y	Y	Y	Y	N	N	N
39 ***Dannemeyer***	Y	Y	Y	N	Y	N	N	N
40 ***Badham***	Y	Y	Y	N	Y	N	N	N
41 ***Lowery***	Y	Y	Y	Y	Y	N	N	N
42 ***Lungren***	Y	Y	Y	Y	Y	N	N	N
43 ***Packard***	Y	Y	Y	N	Y	N	N	N
44 Bates	Y	N	Y	Y	Y	N	Y	Y
45 ***Hunter***	Y	Y	Y	N	Y	N	N	N
COLORADO								
1 Schroeder	N	N	Y	Y	Y	N	N	Y
2 Wirth	N	N	Y	Y	Y	Y	N	Y
3 ***Strang***	Y	Y	Y	N	N	N	N	N
4 ***Brown***	Y	Y	Y	Y	Y	N	N	N
5 ***Kramer***	Y	Y	Y	Y	Y	N	N	N
6 ***Schaefer***	Y	Y	Y	N	Y	N	N	N
CONNECTICUT								
1 Kennelly	N	N	Y	Y	N	N	N	Y
2 Gejdenson	N	N	Y	Y	Y	N	N	Y
3 Morrison	N	N	Y	Y	Y	N	N	Y
4 ***McKinney***	N	N	Y	Y	?	N	N	Y
5 ***Rowland***	Y	Y	Y	Y	Y	N	N	N
6 ***Johnson***	N	N	Y	Y	Y	N	N	N
DELAWARE								
AL Carper	N	Y	Y	N	Y	N	N	Y
FLORIDA								
1 Hutto	Y	N	Y	N	N	N	N	N
2 Fuqua	N	N	Y	Y	N	N	N	Y
3 Bennett	Y	N	Y	Y	N	N	N	Y
4 Chappell	Y	N	Y	Y	N	N	N	Y
5 ***McCollum***	Y	Y	Y	Y	Y	N	N	N
6 MacKay	N	N	Y	Y	Y	N	N	Y
7 Gibbons	Y	Y	Y	Y	Y	N	N	Y
8 ***Young***	Y	Y	Y	Y	Y	N	N	N
9 ***Bilirakis***	Y	Y	Y	N	N	N	N	N
10 ***Ireland***	Y	Y	Y	N	Y	N	N	N
11 Nelson	-	Y	Y	Y	Y	N	N	Y
12 ***Lewis***	Y	Y	Y	Y	N	N	N	N
13 ***Mack***	Y	Y	Y	N	Y	N	N	N
14 Mica	N	N	?	?	N	N	N	Y
15 ***Shaw***	Y	Y	Y	Y	Y	N	N	N
16 Smith	N	N	Y	Y	Y	N	N	Y
17 Lehman	N	N	Y	Y	Y	N	N	Y
18 Pepper	N	N	N	Y	N	N	N	Y
19 Fascell	N	N	Y	Y	N	N	N	Y
GEORGIA								
1 Thomas	N	N	N	N	N	N	N	N
2 Hatcher	N	N	N	Y	N	N	N	N
3 Ray	?	?	Y	Y	N	N	N	N
4 ***Swindall***	Y	Y	Y	Y	N	N	N	N
5 Fowler	N	N	Y	Y	N	N	N	N
6 ***Gingrich***	Y	Y	Y	Y	N	N	N	N
7 Darden	?	?	Y	N	N	N	N	N
8 Rowland	N	N	N	N	N	N	N	N
9 Jenkins	N	N	Y	N	N	N	N	N
10 Barnard	Y	Y	Y	Y	N	N	N	N
HAWAII								
1 Heftel	N	N	Y	Y	N	N	N	Y
2 Akaka	N	N	N	Y	N	N	N	Y
IDAHO								
1 ***Craig***	Y	Y	N	N	Y	N	N	N
2 Stallings	Y	N	N	Y	Y	N	N	N
ILLINOIS								
1 Hayes	N	N	Y	Y	N	Y	Y	Y
2 Savage	N	N	Y	Y	Y	Y	Y	Y
3 Russo	N	N	Y	Y	N	N	N	Y
4 ***O'Brien***	Y	Y	Y	Y	N	N	N	N
5 Lipinski	N	N	Y	Y	N	Y	Y	Y
6 ***Hyde***	Y	Y	Y	Y	Y	N	N	Y
7 Collins	N	N	Y	Y	Y	N	Y	Y
8 Rostenkowski	N	N	?	?	N	N	N	Y
9 Yates	N	N	Y	Y	Y	N	N	Y
10 ***Porter***	Y	Y	Y	N	Y	N	N	Y
11 Annunzio	N	N	Y	Y	Y	N	N	Y
12 ***Crane***	Y	Y	Y	N	Y	N	N	N
13 ***Fawell***	Y	Y	Y	Y	Y	N	N	N
14 ***Grotberg***	Y	Y	Y	N	N	N	N	N
15 ***Madigan***	Y	Y	Y	N	N	N	N	N
16 ***Martin***	Y	Y	Y	Y	Y	N	N	N
17 Evans	N	N	N	Y	Y	Y	Y	Y
18 ***Michel***	Y	Y	Y	N	Y	?	N	N
19 Bruce	N	Y	N	Y	N	N	N	Y
20 Durbin	N	Y	Y	Y	Y	N	N	Y
21 Price	N	N	N	Y	N	N	N	Y
22 Gray	N	N	Y	Y	N	N	N	Y
INDIANA								
1 Visclosky	N	N	Y	Y	Y	N	N	Y
2 Sharp	N	N	?	?	Y	N	N	Y
3 ***Hiler***	Y	Y	Y	N	Y	N	N	N
4 ***Coats***	Y	Y	Y	N	Y	N	N	N
5 ***Hillis***	Y	Y	Y	N	Y	N	N	N

ND - Northern Democrats SD - Southern Democrats

* Corresponding to Congressional Record Votes 338, 339, 340, 341, 342, 344, 345, 346

	306	307	308	309	310	311	312	313
6 ***Burton***	Y	Y	Y	Y	+	-	-	-
7 ***Myers***	Y	Y	Y	N	N	N	N	N
8 McCloskey	N	N	Y	Y	N	N	N	Y
9 Hamilton	N	N	Y	Y	N	N	N	Y
10 Jacobs	N	N	Y	Y	Y	N	N	Y
IOWA								
1 ***Leach***	Y	N	Y	Y	Y	N	N	N
2 ***Tauke***	Y	Y	Y	Y	Y	N	N	N
3 ***Evans***	Y	N	N	Y	N	N	N	N
4 Smith	N	N	N	Y	N	N	N	N
5 ***Lightfoot***	Y	N	N	Y	Y	N	N	N
6 Bedell	N	N	N	Y	N	Y	Y	Y
KANSAS								
1 ***Roberts***	Y	N	Y	N	N	N	N	N
2 Slattery	N	N	Y	Y	Y	N	N	Y
3 ***Meyers***	Y	Y	Y	Y	Y	N	N	N
4 Glickman	N	N	Y	Y	N	N	N	Y
5 ***Whittaker***	Y	N	Y	N	Y	N	N	N
KENTUCKY								
1 Hubbard	N	Y	Y	N	N	Y	Y	N
2 Natcher	N	N	Y	Y	N	N	N	N
3 Mazzoli	N	N	Y	Y	N	N	N	Y
4 ***Snyder***	Y	Y	Y	N	N	N	N	N
5 ***Rogers***	Y	Y	Y	Y	N	N	N	N
6 ***Hopkins***	Y	Y	Y	Y	N	N	N	N
7 Perkins	N	N	N	Y	N	N	Y	Y
LOUISIANA								
1 ***Livingston***	Y	Y	Y	Y	Y	N	N	N
2 Boggs	N	N	N	Y	N	N	N	?
3 Tauzin	N	Y	Y	Y	N	N	N	Y
4 Roemer	N	Y	Y	Y	Y	N	N	Y
5 Huckaby	N	N	N	Y	N	N	N	Y
6 ***Moore***	Y	Y	Y	Y	N	N	N	N
7 Breaux	N	Y	Y	Y	Y	N	N	Y
8 Long	N	N	N	Y	N	N	N	Y
MAINE								
1 ***McKernan***	Y	Y	Y	Y	Y	N	N	N
2 ***Snowe***	N	Y	Y	Y	Y	N	N	N
MARYLAND								
1 Dyson	Y	Y	Y	N	N	N	N	N
2 ***Bentley***	Y	Y	Y	N	N	N	N	N
3 Mikulski	N	N	Y	Y	N	N	N	Y
4 ***Holt***	Y	Y	Y	N	N	N	N	N
5 Hoyer	N	N	Y	Y	N	N	N	Y
6 Byron	Y	Y	Y	N	N	N	N	N
7 Mitchell	N	N	?	Y	N	N	Y	Y
8 Barnes	X	-	+	+	Y	N	N	Y
MASSACHUSETTS								
1 ***Conte***	N	N	Y	Y	Y	N	N	Y
2 Boland	N	N	Y	Y	Y	N	N	Y
3 Early	N	N	Y	Y	Y	N	N	Y
4 Frank	N	N	Y	Y	Y	N	N	Y
5 Atkins	N	N	Y	?	Y	N	N	Y
6 Mavroules	?	?	Y	Y	Y	N	N	Y
7 Markey	N	N	Y	Y	Y	N	N	Y
8 O'Neill								
9 Moakley	-	-	+	+	Y	N	N	Y
10 Studds	N	N	Y	Y	Y	N	N	Y
11 Donnelly	N	N	Y	Y	Y	N	N	Y
MICHIGAN								
1 Conyers	N	N	Y	Y	Y	Y	Y	Y
2 ***Pursell***	?	?	?	?	Y	N	N	N
3 Wolpe	N	N	Y	Y	Y	N	N	Y
4 ***Siljander***	Y	Y	Y	N	Y	N	N	N
5 ***Henry***	Y	Y	Y	Y	Y	N	N	N
6 Carr	N	N	?	?	N	N	N	N
7 Kildee	N	N	Y	Y	+	-	-	+
8 Traxler	N	N	Y	Y	N	N	N	Y
9 ***Vander Jagt***	Y	Y	Y	N	N	N	N	N
10 ***Schuette***	Y	Y	Y	Y	N	N	N	N
11 ***Davis***	N	N	N	Y	Y	N	N	N
12 Bonior	N	N	N	Y	N	N	N	Y
13 Crockett	N	N	Y	Y	Y	Y	Y	Y
14 Hertel	N	N	Y	Y	Y	N	N	Y
15 Ford	N	N	Y	Y	N	N	N	Y
16 Dingell	N	N	N	Y	N	N	N	Y
17 Levin	N	N	Y	Y	N	N	N	Y
18 ***Broomfield***	Y	Y	Y	Y	Y	N	N	N
MINNESOTA								
1 Penny	Y	N	Y	Y	N	Y	Y	N
2 ***Weber***	Y	Y	N	Y	N	Y	Y	N
3 ***Frenzel***	Y	Y	Y	Y	Y	Y	N	N
4 Vento	N	N	Y	Y	Y	Y	Y	Y
5 Sabo	N	N	Y	Y	N	Y	Y	Y
6 Sikorski	N	N	Y	Y	N	Y	Y	Y
7 ***Stangeland***	Y	Y	N	N	N	Y	Y	N
8 Oberstar	N	N	Y	Y	?	Y	Y	Y
MISSISSIPPI								
1 Whitten	N	N	N	Y	N	N	N	N
2 ***Franklin***	N	Y	Y	Y	N	N	N	N
3 Montgomery	Y	Y	Y	N	N	N	N	N
4 Dowdy	N	N	Y	Y	N	Y	Y	N
5 ***Lott***	Y	Y	Y	Y	N	N	N	N
MISSOURI								
1 Clay	?	?	Y	Y	N	N	N	Y
2 Young	?	?	?	?	N	N	N	N
3 Gephardt	N	N	N	Y	N	Y	Y	Y
4 Skelton	Y	N	N	Y	N	N	N	N
5 Wheat	N	N	Y	Y	N	Y	Y	Y
6 ***Coleman***	Y	Y	Y	Y	N	Y	N	N
7 ***Taylor***	Y	Y	Y	N	N	N	N	N
8 ***Emerson***	Y	N	Y	Y	N	N	N	N
9 Volkmer	Y	N	Y	Y	N	N	Y	N
MONTANA								
1 Williams	N	N	Y	Y	N	Y	Y	Y
2 ***Marlenee***	Y	Y	N	N	N	N	N	N
NEBRASKA								
1 ***Bereuter***	Y	Y	Y	N	Y	Y	N	N
2 ***Daub***	Y	Y	Y	N	Y	N	N	N
3 ***Smith***	Y	Y	Y	Y	N	Y	N	N
NEVADA								
1 Reid	N	Y	Y	Y	Y	N	N	Y
2 ***Vucanovich***	Y	Y	N	Y	Y	N	N	N
NEW HAMPSHIRE								
1 ***Smith***	Y	Y	Y	Y	Y	N	N	N
2 ***Gregg***	Y	Y	Y	N	Y	N	N	N
NEW JERSEY								
1 Florio	N	N	Y	Y	Y	N	N	Y
2 Hughes	N	Y	Y	Y	Y	N	N	Y
3 Howard	N	N	Y	Y	N	N	N	Y
4 ***Smith***	N	Y	Y	Y	Y	N	N	Y
5 ***Roukema***	Y	Y	Y	Y	Y	N	N	N
6 Dwyer	N	N	Y	Y	Y	N	N	Y
7 ***Rinaldo***	?	?	?	?	Y	N	N	Y
8 Roe	N	N	Y	Y	N	?	N	Y
9 Torricelli	N	Y	Y	Y	Y	N	N	Y
10 Rodino	N	N	Y	Y	Y	N	N	Y
11 ***Gallo***	N	Y	Y	Y	N	N	N	N
12 ***Courter***	N	Y	Y	Y	Y	N	N	N
13 ***Saxton***	Y	Y	Y	Y	Y	N	N	N
14 Guarini	N	N	Y	Y	Y	N	N	Y
NEW MEXICO								
1 ***Lujan***	Y	Y	N	N	N	N	N	N
2 ***Skeen***	Y	N	N	Y	N	N	N	N
3 Richardson	N	N	Y	Y	N	N	N	Y
NEW YORK								
1 ***Carney***	Y	Y	Y	N	N	N	N	N
2 Downey	N	N	Y	Y	Y	N	N	Y
3 Mrazek	?	?	?	?	Y	Y	Y	Y
4 ***Lent***	Y	Y	Y	Y	N	N	N	N
5 ***McGrath***	Y	Y	Y	Y	N	N	N	N
6 Addabbo	?	?	?	?	?	?	?	?
7 Ackerman	?	?	?	?	?	N	N	Y
8 Scheuer	N	N	Y	Y	Y	N	N	Y
9 Manton	N	N	Y	Y	N	N	N	Y
10 Schumer	?	?	?	?	Y	N	N	Y
11 Towns	?	?	?	Y	N	Y	Y	Y
12 Owens	N	N	Y	Y	Y	Y	Y	Y
13 Solarz	N	N	Y	Y	Y	N	N	Y
14 ***Molinari***	Y	Y	Y	Y	Y	N	N	N
15 ***Green***	N	N	?	?	Y	N	N	Y
16 Rangel	N	N	Y	Y	N	N	N	Y
17 Weiss	N	N	Y	Y	Y	N	N	Y
18 Garcia	N	N	Y	Y	Y	N	Y	Y
19 Biaggi	N	N	Y	Y	N	N	N	Y
20 ***DioGuardi***	Y	Y	Y	Y	Y	N	N	N
21 ***Fish***	N	N	Y	Y	Y	N	N	Y
22 ***Gilman***	N	N	Y	Y	Y	N	N	Y
23 Stratton	N	N	N	Y	N	N	N	N
24 ***Solomon***	Y	Y	Y	N	Y	?	N	N
25 ***Boehlert***	Y	Y	Y	Y	Y	N	N	N
26 ***Martin***	?	?	?	Y	N	N	N	N
27 ***Wortley***	N	Y	Y	N	N	N	N	N
28 McHugh	?	N	Y	Y	Y	N	N	Y
29 ***Horton***	N	N	Y	Y	N	N	N	N
30 ***Eckert***	Y	Y	Y	N	Y	N	N	N
31 ***Kemp***	Y	Y	?	?	?	N	N	N
32 LaFalce	?	?	?	?	Y	N	N	Y
33 Nowak	N	N	Y	Y	Y	N	N	Y
34 Lundine	?	?	?	?	Y	N	N	Y
NORTH CAROLINA								
1 Jones	N	N	Y	Y	N	N	N	Y
2 Valentine	N	N	N	Y	N	N	N	N
3 Whitley	N	N	N	Y	N	N	N	N
4 ***Cobey***	Y	Y	Y	N	N	N	N	N
5 Neal	N	N	Y	Y	N	N	N	Y
6 ***Coble***	Y	Y	Y	Y	N	N	N	N
7 Rose	N	N	N	Y	N	N	N	Y
8 Hefner	N	N	Y	Y	N	N	N	Y
9 ***McMillan***	Y	Y	Y	N	N	N	N	N
10 ***Broyhill***	Y	Y	Y	Y	N	N	N	N
11 ***Hendon***	Y	Y	Y	Y	N	N	N	N
NORTH DAKOTA								
AL Dorgan	N	Y	Y	Y	N	Y	Y	N
OHIO								
1 Luken	N	N	Y	Y	Y	N	N	Y
2 ***Gradison***	N	Y	Y	Y	N	N	N	N
3 Hall	N	N	Y	Y	Y	Y	N	Y
4 ***Oxley***	Y	Y	Y	Y	N	N	N	N
5 ***Latta***	Y	Y	?	N	N	N	N	N
6 ***McEwen***	Y	Y	Y	Y	N	N	N	N
7 ***DeWine***	Y	Y	Y	Y	Y	N	N	N
8 ***Kindness***	Y	Y	Y	Y	N	N	N	N
9 Kaptur	N	N	Y	Y	Y	N	N	Y
10 ***Miller***	Y	Y	Y	Y	N	N	N	N
11 Eckart	N	N	Y	Y	Y	Y	N	Y
12 ***Kasich***	Y	Y	Y	Y	Y	N	N	N
13 Pease	N	N	Y	Y	Y	N	N	Y
14 Seiberling	N	N	Y	Y	Y	Y	Y	Y
15 ***Wylie***	Y	Y	Y	Y	Y	N	N	N
16 ***Regula***	Y	Y	Y	Y	Y	N	N	N
17 Traficant	N	N	Y	Y	N	Y	Y	Y
18 Applegate	N	?	Y	Y	Y	N	N	N
19 Feighan	N	N	Y	Y	Y	N	N	Y
20 Oakar	N	N	Y	Y	N	N	N	Y
21 Stokes	?	?	?	?	N	N	N	Y
OKLAHOMA								
1 Jones	N	N	Y	Y	N	N	Y	N
2 Synar	N	N	Y	Y	N	N	Y	Y
3 Watkins	N	N	Y	Y	N	N	Y	N
4 McCurdy	N	N	Y	N	N	Y	Y	N
5 ***Edwards***	Y	Y	Y	N	Y	N	N	N
6 English	N	Y	N	Y	N	N	Y	N
OREGON								
1 AuCoin	N	N	Y	Y	Y	N	N	Y
2 ***Smith, R.***	Y	N	Y	N	N	N	N	N
3 Wyden	N	N	Y	Y	Y	N	N	Y
4 Weaver	N	N	N	Y	N	Y	Y	Y
5 ***Smith, D.***	Y	Y	Y	N	Y	N	N	N
PENNSYLVANIA								
1 Foglietta	N	N	Y	Y	Y	N	N	Y
2 Gray	N	N	Y	Y	N	N	N	Y
3 Borski	N	N	Y	Y	N	N	N	Y
4 Kolter	N	N	Y	Y	N	N	N	N
5 ***Schulze***	Y	Y	Y	Y	N	N	N	N
6 Yatron	N	N	Y	Y	N	N	N	N
7 Edgar	N	N	?	?	Y	N	N	Y
8 Kostmayer	N	N	+	+	Y	N	N	Y
9 ***Shuster***	Y	Y	Y	Y	N	N	N	N
10 ***McDade***	N	N	Y	Y	Y	N	N	?
11 Kanjorski	N	N	Y	Y	Y	?	N	N
12 Murtha	N	N	N	N	N	N	N	Y
13 ***Coughlin***	N	Y	Y	Y	Y	N	N	Y
14 Coyne	N	N	Y	Y	Y	N	N	Y
15 ***Ritter***	Y	Y	Y	N	Y	N	N	N
16 ***Walker***	Y	Y	Y	Y	N	N	N	N
17 ***Gekas***	Y	Y	Y	N	Y	N	N	N
18 Walgren	N	Y	Y	Y	Y	N	N	Y
19 ***Goodling***	Y	Y	Y	N	Y	N	N	N
20 Gaydos	N	N	N	Y	N	N	N	Y
21 ***Ridge***	N	N	Y	Y	Y	N	N	N
22 Murphy	N	N	Y	Y	N	N	N	Y
23 ***Clinger***	N	Y	Y	Y	Y	N	N	N
RHODE ISLAND								
1 St Germain	N	N	Y	Y	Y	N	N	Y
2 ***Schneider***	N	N	Y	Y	Y	N	N	N
SOUTH CAROLINA								
1 ***Hartnett***	Y	Y	Y	N	N	N	N	N
2 ***Spence***	Y	Y	N	N	N	N	N	N
3 Derrick	N	N	Y	Y	N	N	N	N
4 ***Campbell***	Y	Y	Y	N	N	N	N	N
5 Spratt	N	N	Y	Y	N	N	N	N
6 Tallon	N	N	N	Y	N	N	N	N
SOUTH DAKOTA								
AL Daschle	?	N	N	Y	N	Y	Y	Y
TENNESSEE								
1 ***Quillen***	Y	Y	N	Y	N	N	N	N
2 ***Duncan***	N	Y	N	N	N	N	N	N
3 Lloyd	N	Y	Y	Y	N	N	N	N
4 Cooper	N	N	Y	Y	N	N	N	N
5 Boner	N	N	N	Y	N	N	N	N
6 Gordon	N	Y	Y	Y	N	N	N	N
7 ***Sundquist***	Y	Y	Y	N	N	N	N	N
8 Jones	N	N	N	Y	N	N	N	N
9 Ford	N	N	Y	Y	Y	Y	Y	Y
TEXAS								
1 Chapman	N	Y	Y	Y	N	N	Y	N
2 Wilson	N	N	N	N	N	N	N	Y
3 ***Bartlett***	Y	Y	Y	N	Y	N	N	N
4 Hall, R.	N	Y	Y	Y	N	Y	Y	N
5 Bryant	N	N	Y	Y	Y	Y	Y	Y
6 ***Barton***	Y	Y	Y	N	Y	N	N	N
7 ***Archer***	Y	Y	Y	N	Y	N	N	N
8 ***Fields***	Y	Y	Y	N	Y	N	N	N
9 Brooks	N	N	Y	N	N	N	N	Y
10 Pickle	N	N	N	N	N	N	N	Y
11 Leath	Y	Y	N	?	N	Y	Y	N
12 Wright	N	N	N	Y	N	Y	Y	Y
13 ***Boulter***	Y	Y	Y	Y	Y	N	N	N
14 ***Sweeney***	Y	Y	Y	N	Y	N	N	N
15 de la Garza	N	N	N	Y	N	N	N	Y
16 Coleman	N	N	Y	Y	N	N	N	Y
17 Stenholm	Y	Y	Y	N	N	N	N	Y
18 Leland	N	N	N	Y	N	Y	Y	Y
19 ***Combest***	Y	Y	Y	N	N	N	N	N
20 Gonzalez	N	N	N	Y	N	N	P	Y
21 ***Loeffler***	?	?	?	?	N	N	N	N
22 ***DeLay***	Y	Y	Y	N	Y	N	N	N
23 Bustamante	N	N	Y	Y	N	N	N	Y
24 Frost	N	N	Y	Y	N	N	N	Y
25 Andrews	N	Y	Y	Y	N	N	N	N
26 ***Armey***	Y	Y	Y	Y	Y	N	N	N
27 Ortiz	N	N	Y	Y	N	N	N	Y
UTAH								
1 ***Hansen***	Y	Y	Y	N	Y	N	N	N
2 ***Monson***	Y	Y	Y	N	Y	N	N	N
3 ***Nielson***	Y	Y	Y	N	Y	N	N	N
VERMONT								
AL ***Jeffords***	N	N	Y	Y	N	N	N	N
VIRGINIA								
1 ***Bateman***	Y	Y	Y	Y	N	N	N	N
2 ***Whitehurst***	Y	Y	Y	Y	Y	N	N	N
3 ***Bliley***	Y	Y	Y	N	N	N	N	N
4 Sisisky	N	N	Y	Y	N	N	N	N
5 Daniel	Y	Y	Y	N	N	N	N	N
6 Olin	N	Y	Y	N	N	N	N	N
7 ***Slaughter***	Y	Y	Y	Y	N	N	N	N
8 ***Parris***	Y	Y	Y	Y	N	N	N	N
9 Boucher	N	N	Y	Y	N	N	N	Y
10 ***Wolf***	Y	Y	Y	Y	N	N	N	N
WASHINGTON								
1 ***Miller***	Y	Y	Y	Y	Y	N	N	N
2 Swift	N	N	Y	Y	N	N	N	Y
3 Bonker	N	N	Y	Y	Y	N	N	Y
4 ***Morrison***	Y	Y	Y	Y	Y	N	N	N
5 Foley	N	N	Y	Y	N	N	N	Y
6 Dicks	N	N	Y	Y	N	N	N	Y
7 Lowry	N	N	Y	Y	N	N	N	Y
8 ***Chandler***	Y	Y	Y	Y	Y	N	N	N
WEST VIRGINIA								
1 Mollohan	N	N	Y	Y	N	N	N	N
2 Staggers	N	N	N	Y	N	N	N	Y
3 Wise	N	N	Y	Y	N	N	N	Y
4 Rahall	N	N	Y	Y	N	Y	Y	N
WISCONSIN								
1 Aspin	N	N	Y	Y	N	N	N	Y
2 Kastenmeier	N	N	Y	Y	N	Y	Y	Y
3 ***Gunderson***	Y	N	Y	N	N	N	N	N
4 Kleczka	N	N	Y	Y	N	N	N	Y
5 Moody	N	N	Y	Y	Y	N	N	Y
6 ***Petri***	Y	Y	Y	Y	Y	N	N	N
7 Obey	N	N	Y	Y	N	Y	Y	Y
8 ***Roth***	Y	Y	N	N	N	N	N	N
9 ***Sensenbrenner***	Y	Y	Y	Y	Y	N	N	N
WYOMING								
AL ***Cheney***	Y	Y	Y	N	Y	N	N	N

Southern states - Ala., Ark., Fla., Ga., Ky., La., Miss., N.C., Okla., S.C., Tenn., Texas, Va.

* The *Congressional Record* vote number is different from the CQ vote number because the *Record* includes quorum calls in its tally. CQ does not publish quorum call votes.

314. HR 2100. Farm Programs Reauthorization, Fiscal 1986-90. Passage of the bill to extend and revise agricultural price-support programs; to provide for agricultural export, soil conservation, farm credit and agricultural research programs; and to continue food assistance to low-income persons through fiscal 1990. Passed 282-141: R 98-79; D 184-62 (ND 114-51, SD 70-11), Oct. 8, 1985.

315. HR 3008. Federal Pay Equity Study. Burton, R-Ind., amendment to establish a 14-member commission, rather than the 11-member commission established by the bill, composed of seven members appointed by Democrats and seven appointed by Republicans, to oversee the study of the federal pay and classification system. Rejected 150-272: R 145-33; D 5-239 (ND 2-161, SD 3-78), Oct. 9, 1985.

316. HR 3008. Federal Pay Equity Study. Barton, R-Texas, amendment to eliminate a provision barring the commission overseeing the study of federal pay and classification practices from recommending that any employee's pay be reduced. Rejected 148-276: R 133-45; D 15-231 (ND 7-158, SD 8-73), Oct. 9, 1985.

317. HR 3008. Federal Pay Equity Study. Burton, R-Ind., substitute to require a study of whether federal pay and classification complies with the Civil Rights Act of 1964 and the Fair Labor Standards Act of 1938, and with trends in promotion and hiring. Rejected 142-277: R 140-37; D 2-240 (ND 0-162, SD 2-78), Oct. 9, 1985.

318. HR 3008. Federal Pay Equity Study. Passage of the bill to establish a commission to oversee a study of the federal work force to determine whether differences in pay and classification have arisen because of discrimination on the basis of sex, race or national origin. Passed 259-162: R 37-139; D 222-23 (ND 161-4, SD 61-19), Oct. 9, 1985. A "nay" was a vote supporting the president's position.

319. HR 1562. Textile Import Quotas. Adoption of the rule (H Res 286) to provide for House floor consideration of the bill to impose new quota restrictions on textile imports. Adopted 277-139: R 63-109; D 214-30 (ND 137-26, SD 77-4), Oct. 10, 1985.

320. HR 1562. Textile Import Quotas. Passage of the bill to impose new quota restrictions on textile imports. Passed 262-159: R 75-97; D 187-62 (ND 118-49, SD 69-13), Oct. 10, 1985. A "nay" was a vote supporting the president's position.

321. HR 3248. Arts and Humanities Endowments Authorizations, Fiscal 1986-87. Passage of the bill to authorize $167 million for the National Endowment for the Arts, $140 million for the National Endowment for the Humanities and $22 million for the Institute of Museum Services in fiscal year 1986, and 4 percent more for each agency in fiscal 1987. Passed 349-57: R 114-51; D 235-6 (ND 160-0, SD 75-6), Oct. 10, 1985.

KEY

Y Voted for (yea).
\# Paired for.
\+ Announced for.
N Voted against (nay).
X Paired against.
\- Announced against.
P Voted "present."
C Voted "present" to avoid possible conflict of interest.
? Did not vote or otherwise make a position known.

Democrats ***Republicans***

	314	315	316	317	318	319	320	321
ALABAMA								
1 ***Callahan***	Y	Y	Y	Y	N	Y	Y	Y
2 ***Dickinson***	Y	?	Y	Y	N	Y	Y	Y
3 Nichols	Y	N	N	N	N	Y	Y	Y
4 Bevill	Y	N	N	N	N	Y	Y	Y
5 Flippo	Y	N	N	N	Y	Y	Y	Y
6 Erdreich	Y	N	N	N	Y	Y	Y	Y
7 Shelby	Y	N	N	N	Y	Y	Y	Y
ALASKA								
AL ***Young***	N	N	N	N	Y	Y	Y	Y
ARIZONA								
1 ***McCain***	N	Y	Y	Y	N	N	N	Y
2 Udall	Y	N	N	N	Y	Y	N	?
3 ***Stump***	N	Y	Y	Y	N	N	N	N
4 ***Rudd***	N	Y	Y	?	N	?	?	?
5 ***Kolbe***	N	Y	Y	Y	N	N	N	Y
ARKANSAS								
1 Alexander	N	N	N	N	Y	Y	Y	Y
2 Robinson	Y	N	N	N	Y	Y	Y	Y
3 ***Hammerschmidt***	Y	Y	N	Y	N	Y	Y	Y
4 Anthony	Y	N	N	N	Y	Y	Y	Y
CALIFORNIA								
1 Bosco	N	N	N	N	Y	Y	N	?
2 ***Chappie***	Y	Y	Y	Y	Y	N	N	Y
3 Matsui	Y	N	N	N	Y	N	N	Y
4 Fazio	Y	N	N	N	Y	Y	Y	Y
5 Burton	Y	N	N	N	Y	Y	Y	Y
6 Boxer	N	N	N	N	Y	Y	Y	Y
7 Miller	N	N	N	N	Y	Y	N	Y
8 Dellums	N	N	N	N	Y	Y	Y	Y
9 Stark	N	N	N	N	Y	Y	N	Y
10 Edwards	Y	N	N	N	Y	Y	Y	Y
11 Lantos	Y	N	N	N	Y	Y	Y	Y
12 ***Zschau***	N	Y	Y	Y	N	N	N	Y
13 Mineta	?	N	N	N	Y	Y	N	Y
14 ***Shumway***	N	Y	Y	Y	N	N	N	N
15 Coelho	Y	N	N	N	Y	Y	Y	Y
16 Panetta	Y	N	N	N	Y	N	N	Y
17 ***Pashayan***	Y	Y	N	Y	N	Y	Y	N
18 Lehman	Y	N	N	N	Y	Y	Y	Y
19 ***Lagomarsino***	N	Y	Y	Y	N	N	N	Y
20 ***Thomas***	Y	Y	Y	Y	N	Y	Y	N
21 ***Fiedler***	Y	Y	Y	Y	N	Y	Y	N
22 ***Moorhead***	N	Y	Y	Y	N	N	N	Y
23 Beilenson	N	N	N	N	Y	Y	N	Y
24 Waxman	N	N	N	N	Y	Y	N	Y
25 Roybal	Y	N	N	N	Y	Y	N	Y
26 Berman	N	N	N	N	Y	N	N	Y
27 Levine	N	N	N	N	Y	Y	N	Y
28 Dixon	Y	N	N	N	Y	Y	Y	?
29 Hawkins	Y	N	N	N	Y	Y	Y	Y
30 Martinez	Y	N	N	N	Y	Y	Y	Y
31 Dymally	Y	N	N	N	Y	N	N	Y
32 Anderson	N	N	N	N	Y	N	N	Y
33 ***Dreier***	N	Y	Y	Y	N	N	N	N
34 Torres	Y	N	N	N	Y	Y	Y	Y
35 ***Lewis***	?	Y	Y	Y	N	N	N	Y
36 Brown	Y	?	?	?	?	Y	Y	Y
37 ***McCandless***	?	Y	Y	Y	N	N	N	N
38 ***Dornan***	N	Y	Y	Y	N	N	N	N
39 ***Dannemeyer***	N	Y	Y	Y	N	N	N	N
40 ***Badham***	N	Y	Y	Y	N	N	N	N
41 ***Lowery***	N	Y	Y	Y	N	Y	N	?
42 ***Lungren***	N	?	#	#	X	?	?	?
43 ***Packard***	N	Y	Y	Y	N	N	N	Y
44 Bates	N	N	N	N	Y	Y	Y	Y
45 ***Hunter***	N	Y	Y	Y	N	N	Y	N
COLORADO								
1 Schroeder	N	N	N	N	Y	N	N	Y
2 Wirth	Y	N	N	N	Y	N	N	Y
3 ***Strong***	Y	Y	Y	N	N	-	-	+
4 ***Brown***	Y	Y	Y	Y	Y	N	N	N
5 ***Kramer***	Y	Y	Y	Y	N	N	N	Y
6 ***Schaefer***	N	Y	Y	Y	N	N	N	Y
CONNECTICUT								
1 Kennelly	Y	N	N	N	Y	Y	Y	Y
2 Gejdenson	Y	N	N	N	Y	Y	Y	Y
3 Morrison	N	N	N	N	Y	Y	Y	Y
4 ***McKinney***	Y	N	N	?	?	Y	Y	Y
5 ***Rowland***	N	Y	N	Y	N	N	N	Y
6 ***Johnson***	N	N	N	N	Y	N	N	Y
DELAWARE								
AL Carper	Y	N	Y	N	Y	N	Y	Y
FLORIDA								
1 Hutto	Y	N	Y	N	N	Y	Y	Y
2 Fuqua	Y	N	N	N	Y	Y	Y	Y
3 Bennett	Y	N	Y	N	Y	Y	N	N
4 Chappell	Y	N	N	N	Y	Y	Y	Y
5 ***McCollum***	N	Y	Y	Y	N	N	N	Y
6 MacKay	Y	N	N	N	N	Y	N	Y
7 Gibbons	N	N	Y	N	Y	Y	N	Y
8 ***Young***	N	Y	Y	Y	N	N	N	?
9 ***Bilirakis***	N	Y	Y	Y	Y	N	Y	N
10 ***Ireland***	N	Y	Y	Y	N	N	N	?
11 Nelson	N	N	N	N	Y	Y	N	Y
12 ***Lewis***	Y	Y	Y	Y	N	N	N	Y
13 ***Mack***	N	Y	Y	Y	N	N	N	N
14 Mica	Y	N	N	N	Y	N	N	Y
15 ***Shaw***	N	Y	Y	Y	N	N	N	Y
16 Smith	+	N	N	N	Y	Y	Y	Y
17 Lehman	Y	N	N	N	Y	Y	Y	Y
18 Pepper	Y	N	N	N	Y	Y	Y	Y
19 Fascell	Y	N	N	N	Y	Y	Y	Y
GEORGIA								
1 Thomas	Y	N	N	N	Y	Y	Y	Y
2 Hatcher	Y	N	N	N	Y	Y	Y	Y
3 Ray	Y	N	N	N	Y	Y	Y	Y
4 ***Swindall***	N	Y	Y	Y	N	N	Y	N
5 Fowler	Y	N	N	?	?	Y	Y	Y
6 ***Gingrich***	N	?	Y	Y	N	N	Y	?
7 Darden	Y	N	N	N	N	Y	Y	Y
8 Rowland	Y	N	N	N	Y	Y	Y	Y
9 Jenkins	Y	N	N	N	Y	Y	Y	Y
10 Barnard	Y	N	N	N	Y	Y	Y	Y
HAWAII								
1 Heftel	?	N	N	N	Y	N	N	Y
2 Akaka	Y	N	N	N	Y	N	N	Y
IDAHO								
1 ***Craig***	Y	Y	Y	Y	N	N	N	N
2 Stallings	Y	N	N	N	N	Y	N	Y
ILLINOIS								
1 Hayes	Y	N	N	N	Y	Y	Y	Y
2 Savage	Y	?	N	N	Y	Y	Y	Y
3 Russo	N	N	N	N	Y	Y	Y	Y
4 ***O'Brien***	Y	Y	Y	Y	N	?	?	?
5 Lipinski	Y	N	N	N	Y	Y	Y	Y
6 ***Hyde***	N	Y	Y	Y	N	?	X	?
7 Collins	Y	N	N	N	Y	Y	Y	Y
8 Rostenkowski	Y	N	N	N	Y	Y	N	Y
9 Yates	N	N	N	N	Y	Y	N	Y
10 ***Porter***	N	Y	Y	Y	N	-	-	+
11 Annunzio	Y	N	N	N	Y	Y	Y	Y
12 ***Crane***	N	Y	Y	Y	N	N	N	N
13 ***Fawell***	N	Y	Y	Y	N	N	N	Y
14 ***Grotberg***	Y	Y	Y	Y	N	N	N	Y
15 ***Madigan***	Y	Y	Y	N	N	N	N	Y
16 ***Martin***	Y	Y	Y	N	Y	?	?	?
17 Evans	N	N	N	N	Y	Y	Y	Y
18 ***Michel***	N	Y	Y	Y	N	N	N	N
19 Bruce	Y	N	N	N	Y	Y	Y	Y
20 Durbin	Y	N	N	N	Y	Y	Y	Y
21 Price	Y	N	N	N	Y	Y	Y	Y
22 Gray	Y	N	N	?	Y	Y	Y	Y
INDIANA								
1 Visclosky	Y	N	Y	N	Y	Y	Y	Y
2 Sharp	Y	N	N	N	Y	N	N	Y
3 ***Hiler***	Y	Y	Y	Y	N	N	N	Y
4 ***Coats***	Y	Y	Y	Y	N	N	N	Y
5 ***Hillis***	Y	N	Y	Y	N	Y	Y	?

ND - Northern Democrats SD Southern Democrats

* Corresponding to Congressional Record Votes 347, 349, 350, 351, 352, 353, 354, 355

	314	315	316	317	318	319	320	321
6 ***Burton***	-	Y	Y	Y	N	N	N	Y
7 ***Myers***	Y	N	N	N	Y	Y	N	Y
8 McCloskey	Y	N	N	N	Y	Y	Y	Y
9 Hamilton	Y	N	Y	N	Y	N	N	Y
10 Jacobs	N	N	N	N	Y	N	N	Y
IOWA								
1 ***Leach***	Y	N	N	N	Y	N	N	Y
2 ***Tauke***	Y	N	N	N	Y	N	N	Y
3 ***Evans***	Y	Y	Y	N	Y	N	N	Y
4 Smith	Y	N	Y	N	Y	Y	N	Y
5 ***Lightfoot***	Y	Y	Y	Y	N	N	N	Y
6 Bedell	N	N	Y	N	Y	Y	C	Y
KANSAS								
1 ***Roberts***	Y	Y	Y	Y	N	N	N	N
2 Slattery	Y	N	N	N	Y	N	N	Y
3 ***Meyers***	Y	N	N	N	N	Y	N	Y
4 Glickman	Y	N	N	N	Y	N	N	Y
5 ***Whittaker***	Y	Y	Y	Y	N	N	N	Y
KENTUCKY								
1 Hubbard	Y	Y	Y	N	N	Y	Y	N
2 Natcher	Y	N	N	N	Y	Y	Y	Y
3 Mazzoli	Y	N	N	N	Y	N	N	Y
4 ***Snyder***	N	Y	Y	Y	N	Y	Y	Y
5 ***Rogers***	Y	Y	Y	Y	N	Y	Y	Y
6 ***Hopkins***	Y	Y	Y	Y	N	N	Y	Y
7 Perkins	Y	N	N	N	Y	Y	Y	Y
LOUISIANA								
1 ***Livingston***	Y	Y	Y	Y	N	?	?	?
2 Boggs	Y	N	N	N	Y	Y	Y	Y
3 Tauzin	Y	N	N	N	Y	Y	Y	Y
4 Roemer	Y	N	N	N	N	N	N	Y
5 Huckaby	Y	Y	N	N	N	Y	Y	Y
6 ***Moore***	Y	N	N	Y	N	N	N	Y
7 Breaux	Y	N	N	N	Y	Y	Y	Y
8 Long	Y	N	N	N	Y	Y	Y	Y
MAINE								
1 ***McKernan***	Y	N	N	N	Y	N	Y	Y
2 ***Snowe***	Y	N	N	N	Y	N	Y	Y
MARYLAND								
1 Dyson	Y	N	N	N	N	N	Y	Y
2 ***Bentley***	Y	Y	N	Y	N	Y	Y	Y
3 Mikulski	Y	N	N	N	Y	Y	Y	Y
4 ***Holt***	Y	Y	N	Y	N	N	N	Y
5 Hoyer	Y	N	N	N	Y	Y	Y	Y
6 Byron	Y	N	N	N	N	Y	Y	Y
7 Mitchell	Y	N	N	N	Y	Y	Y	Y
8 Barnes	N	N	N	N	Y	Y	Y	Y
MASSACHUSETTS								
1 ***Conte***	N	N	N	N	Y	Y	Y	Y
2 Boland	N	N	N	N	Y	Y	Y	Y
3 Early	Y	?	?	?	?	?	Y	Y
4 Frank	N	N	N	N	Y	Y	Y	Y
5 Atkins	N	N	N	N	Y	Y	Y	Y
6 Mavroules	Y	N	N	N	Y	Y	Y	Y
7 Markey	N	N	N	N	Y	Y	Y	Y
8 O'Neill								
9 Moakley	Y	N	N	N	Y	N	Y	Y
10 Studds	N	N	N	N	Y	Y	Y	Y
11 Donnelly	N	N	N	N	Y	Y	Y	Y
MICHIGAN								
1 Conyers	N	N	N	?	?	Y	Y	Y
2 ***Pursell***	Y	N	N	N	Y	Y	N	Y
3 Wolpe	Y	N	N	N	Y	Y	Y	Y
4 ***Siljander***	Y	Y	Y	Y	N	N	N	Y
5 ***Henry***	Y	Y	Y	Y	N	Y	Y	Y
6 Carr	Y	N	N	N	Y	Y	Y	Y
7 Kildee	#	-	X	X	#	+	#	+
8 Traxler	Y	N	N	N	Y	Y	Y	Y
9 ***Vander Jagt***	Y	Y	Y	Y	N	Y	N	Y
10 ***Schuette***	Y	Y	Y	Y	N	N	Y	Y
11 ***Davis***	Y	N	N	Y	Y	Y	Y	Y
12 Bonior	Y	N	N	N	Y	Y	Y	Y
13 Crockett	Y	N	N	N	Y	Y	N	Y
14 Hertel	N	N	N	N	Y	Y	Y	Y
15 Ford	Y	N	N	N	Y	?	Y	Y
16 Dingell	Y	?	N	N	Y	?	Y	Y
17 Levin	Y	N	N	N	Y	Y	Y	Y
18 ***Broomfield***	N	Y	?	Y	N	N	N	?
MINNESOTA								
1 Penny	N	N	N	N	Y	Y	N	Y
2 ***Weber***	N	Y	Y	Y	N	N	N	N
3 ***Frenzel***	Y	Y	Y	N	Y	Y	N	N
4 Vento	?	N	N	N	Y	Y	Y	Y
5 Sabo	N	N	N	N	Y	N	N	Y
6 Sikorski	N	N	N	N	Y	Y	Y	Y

	314	315	316	317	318	319	320	321
7 ***Stangeland***	Y	Y	Y	Y	N	N	N	Y
8 Oberstar	N	N	N	N	Y	Y	Y	Y
MISSISSIPPI								
1 Whitten	Y	N	N	N	Y	Y	Y	Y
2 ***Franklin***	Y	Y	Y	Y	N	Y	Y	N
3 Montgomery	Y	N	N	N	N	Y	Y	N
4 Dowdy	Y	N	N	N	Y	Y	Y	Y
5 ***Lott***	Y	Y	Y	Y	N	Y	Y	N
MISSOURI								
1 Clay	Y	N	N	N	Y	Y	Y	Y
2 Young	Y	N	N	N	Y	Y	Y	Y
3 Gephardt	Y	N	N	N	Y	N	Y	Y
4 Skelton	Y	N	N	N	Y	Y	Y	?
5 Wheat	Y	N	N	N	Y	Y	Y	Y
6 ***Coleman***	N	Y	N	Y	Y	N	N	Y
7 ***Taylor***	Y	Y	N	Y	N	Y	Y	N
8 ***Emerson***	Y	Y	N	Y	N	Y	Y	Y
9 Volkmer	N	N	N	N	Y	Y	Y	Y
MONTANA								
1 Williams	N	N	N	?	Y	N	Y	Y
2 ***Marlenee***	Y	?	Y	Y	N	N	N	N
NEBRASKA								
1 ***Bereuter***	N	Y	N	Y	N	N	N	Y
2 ***Daub***	N	Y	Y	Y	N	N	N	Y
3 ***Smith***	Y	Y	Y	Y	Y	N	N	Y
NEVADA								
1 Reid	Y	N	N	N	N	Y	Y	Y
2 ***Vucanovich***	N	Y	Y	Y	N	N	N	N
NEW HAMPSHIRE								
1 ***Smith***	N	Y	Y	Y	N	N	Y	N
2 ***Gregg***	N	Y	Y	Y	N	N	Y	Y
NEW JERSEY								
1 Florio	Y	N	N	N	Y	Y	Y	?
2 Hughes	Y	N	Y	N	Y	Y	Y	Y
3 Howard	Y	N	N	N	Y	Y	Y	Y
4 ***Smith***	Y	N	N	N	Y	Y	Y	Y
5 ***Roukema***	N	N	N	N	Y	N	Y	Y
6 Dwyer	Y	N	N	N	Y	Y	Y	Y
7 ***Rinaldo***	X	N	N	N	Y	Y	Y	Y
8 Roe	Y	N	N	N	Y	Y	Y	?
9 Torricelli	Y	N	N	N	Y	Y	Y	Y
10 Rodino	Y	N	N	N	Y	Y	Y	Y
11 ***Gallo***	Y	Y	N	Y	N	N	N	Y
12 ***Courter***	Y	Y	N	Y	N	N	N	Y
13 ***Saxton***	Y	Y	N	Y	N	N	N	Y
14 Guarini	Y	N	N	N	Y	Y	Y	Y
NEW MEXICO								
1 ***Lujan***	N	Y	N	Y	N	Y	N	Y
2 ***Skeen***	Y	Y	Y	Y	N	Y	Y	Y
3 Richardson	Y	N	N	N	Y	Y	Y	Y
NEW YORK								
1 ***Carney***	N	Y	?	#	X	N	Y	Y
2 Downey	N	N	N	N	Y	Y	N	Y
3 Mrazek	N	N	N	N	Y	Y	Y	Y
4 ***Lent***	N	Y	Y	N	?	Y	Y	Y
5 ***McGrath***	N	Y	Y	N	Y	Y	Y	Y
6 Addabbo	?	?	?	?	?	?	?	?
7 Ackerman	Y	N	N	N	Y	Y	Y	Y
8 Scheuer	N	N	N	N	Y	Y	N	Y
9 Manton	Y	N	N	?	Y	Y	Y	Y
10 Schumer	N	N	N	N	Y	Y	N	Y
11 Towns	Y	N	N	N	Y	Y	Y	Y
12 Owens	Y	N	N	N	Y	Y	Y	Y
13 Solarz	Y	N	N	N	Y	Y	N	Y
14 ***Molinari***	N	Y	N	N	Y	N	N	Y
15 ***Green***	N	N	N	X	#	N	N	Y
16 Rangel	Y	N	N	N	Y	Y	Y	Y
17 Weiss	N	N	N	N	Y	Y	Y	Y
18 Garcia	Y	N	N	N	Y	Y	Y	Y
19 Biaggi	Y	Y	N	N	Y	?	Y	Y
20 ***DioGuardi***	N	Y	Y	Y	N	Y	Y	Y
21 ***Fish***	Y	N	N	N	Y	Y	Y	Y
22 ***Gilman***	Y	N	N	N	Y	Y	Y	Y
23 Stratton	Y	N	N	N	Y	Y	Y	Y
24 ***Solomon***	Y	Y	Y	Y	?	?	?	?
25 ***Boehlert***	Y	N	N	N	Y	N	Y	Y
26 ***Martin***	Y	Y	Y	Y	N	N	Y	Y
27 ***Wortley***	Y	Y	Y	Y	N	N	N	Y
28 McHugh	Y	N	N	N	Y	N	N	Y
29 ***Horton***	Y	N	N	N	Y	Y	Y	Y
30 ***Eckert***	N	Y	Y	Y	N	N	N	N
31 ***Kemp***	N	Y	Y	Y	N	N	N	Y
32 LaFalce	N	Y	Y	N	Y	N	N	?
33 Nowak	N	N	N	N	Y	Y	Y	Y
34 Lundine	Y	N	N	N	Y	N	Y	Y

	314	315	316	317	318	319	320	321
NORTH CAROLINA								
1 Jones	Y	N	N	N	Y	Y	Y	Y
2 Valentine	Y	N	N	N	N	Y	Y	Y
3 Whitley	Y	Y	N	N	N	Y	Y	Y
4 ***Cobey***	Y	Y	Y	Y	N	Y	Y	N
5 Neal	Y	N	N	N	Y	Y	Y	Y
6 ***Coble***	Y	Y	Y	Y	N	Y	Y	N
7 Rose	Y	N	N	N	Y	Y	Y	Y
8 Hefner	Y	N	N	N	Y	Y	Y	Y
9 ***McMillan***	Y	Y	Y	Y	N	Y	Y	Y
10 ***Broyhill***	Y	Y	N	Y	N	Y	Y	Y
11 ***Hendon***	Y	Y	Y	Y	N	Y	Y	N
NORTH DAKOTA								
AL Dorgan	N	N	N	N	Y	Y	N	Y
OHIO								
1 Luken	N	N	N	N	Y	Y	N	Y
2 ***Gradison***	N	Y	Y	Y	N	N	N	Y
3 Hall	Y	N	N	N	Y	Y	Y	Y
4 ***Oxley***	Y	Y	Y	Y	N	N	N	Y
5 ***Latta***	Y	Y	Y	Y	N	N	N	N
6 ***McEwen***	Y	Y	Y	Y	N	N	N	Y
7 ***DeWine***	Y	Y	Y	Y	N	N	N	Y
8 ***Kindness***	Y	Y	Y	Y	Y	Y	Y	Y
9 Kaptur	Y	N	N	N	Y	Y	Y	Y
10 ***Miller***	Y	Y	Y	Y	N	Y	Y	N
11 Eckart	Y	N	N	N	Y	Y	Y	Y
12 ***Kasich***	Y	Y	Y	Y	N	N	N	Y
13 Pease	Y	N	N	N	Y	Y	N	Y
14 Seiberling	N	N	N	N	Y	Y	N	Y
15 ***Wylie***	Y	N	N	Y	N	Y	Y	Y
16 ***Regula***	Y	N	N	N	Y	Y	Y	Y
17 Traficant	Y	N	N	N	Y	Y	Y	Y
18 Applegate	Y	N	N	N	Y	Y	Y	Y
19 Feighan	Y	N	N	N	Y	Y	Y	Y
20 Oakar	Y	N	N	N	Y	Y	Y	Y
21 Stokes	Y	N	N	N	Y	Y	Y	Y
OKLAHOMA								
1 Jones	N	N	N	N	Y	Y	N	Y
2 Synar	N	N	N	N	Y	Y	N	Y
3 Watkins	N	N	N	N	Y	Y	N	Y
4 McCurdy	N	N	N	N	Y	Y	N	Y
5 ***Edwards***	Y	Y	Y	Y	N	N	N	N
6 English	N	N	Y	N	N	Y	N	N
OREGON								
1 AuCoin	N	N	N	N	Y	N	N	Y
2 ***Smith, R.***	Y	Y	Y	Y	N	N	N	Y
3 Wyden	N	?	N	N	Y	N	N	Y
4 Weaver	N	N	N	N	Y	Y	Y	Y
5 ***Smith, D.***	N	Y	Y	Y	N	N	N	N
PENNSYLVANIA								
1 Foglietta	Y	N	N	N	Y	Y	Y	Y
2 Gray	Y	N	N	N	Y	?	Y	Y
3 Borski	Y	N	N	N	Y	Y	Y	Y
4 Kolter	Y	N	N	N	Y	Y	Y	Y
5 ***Schulze***	N	Y	Y	Y	N	Y	Y	Y
6 Yatron	Y	N	N	N	Y	Y	Y	Y
7 Edgar	Y	N	N	N	Y	Y	Y	?
8 Kostmayer	N	N	N	N	Y	N	Y	Y
9 ***Shuster***	N	Y	Y	Y	N	Y	Y	N
10 ***McDade***	+	N	N	N	Y	Y	Y	Y
11 Kanjorski	Y	N	N	N	Y	Y	Y	Y
12 Murtha	Y	N	N	N	Y	Y	Y	Y
13 ***Coughlin***	N	N	Y	Y	N	N	Y	Y
14 Coyne	Y	N	N	N	Y	Y	Y	Y
15 ***Ritter***	N	Y	Y	Y	N	Y	Y	Y
16 ***Walker***	N	Y	Y	Y	N	N	N	N
17 ***Gekas***	Y	Y	Y	Y	N	N	Y	N
18 Walgren	Y	N	N	N	Y	Y	Y	Y
19 ***Goodling***	N	Y	Y	Y	N	Y	Y	Y
20 Gaydos	Y	N	N	N	Y	Y	Y	Y
21 ***Ridge***	Y	Y	Y	Y	N	Y	Y	Y
22 Murphy	Y	N	N	N	Y	Y	Y	Y
23 ***Clinger***	N	N	N	N	Y	Y	Y	Y
RHODE ISLAND								
1 St Germain	N	N	N	N	Y	Y	Y	Y
2 ***Schneider***	N	N	N	N	Y	N	Y	Y
SOUTH CAROLINA								
1 ***Hartnett***	Y	Y	Y	Y	N	Y	Y	?
2 ***Spence***	Y	Y	Y	Y	N	Y	Y	Y
3 Derrick	Y	N	N	N	Y	Y	Y	Y
4 ***Campbell***	Y	Y	Y	Y	N	Y	Y	Y
5 Spratt	Y	N	N	N	Y	Y	Y	Y
6 Tallon	Y	N	N	N	N	Y	Y	Y
SOUTH DAKOTA								
AL Daschle	N	N	N	N	Y	Y	N	Y

	314	315	316	317	318	319	320	321
TENNESSEE								
1 ***Quillen***	Y	Y	Y	N	N	Y	Y	Y
2 ***Duncan***	Y	Y	Y	N	N	Y	Y	Y
3 Lloyd	Y	N	N	N	Y	Y	Y	Y
4 Cooper	Y	N	N	N	Y	Y	Y	Y
5 Boner	Y	N	N	N	Y	Y	Y	Y
6 Gordon	Y	N	N	N	Y	Y	Y	Y
7 ***Sundquist***	Y	Y	Y	Y	N	N	Y	Y
8 Jones	Y	N	N	N	Y	Y	Y	Y
9 Ford	Y	N	N	N	Y	Y	Y	Y
TEXAS								
1 Chapman	Y	N	N	N	N	Y	Y	Y
2 Wilson	Y	N	N	N	N	Y	Y	Y
3 ***Bartlett***	N	Y	Y	Y	N	N	N	Y
4 Hall, R.	Y	N	Y	N	Y	Y	Y	Y
5 Bryant	Y	N	N	N	Y	Y	Y	Y
6 ***Barton***	Y	Y	Y	Y	N	N	N	Y
7 ***Archer***	N	Y	Y	Y	N	Y	N	N
8 ***Fields***	N	Y	Y	Y	N	N	N	N
9 Brooks	Y	N	N	N	Y	Y	Y	Y
10 Pickle	Y	N	N	N	Y	Y	N	Y
11 Leath	N	N	Y	Y	N	Y	Y	N
12 Wright	Y	?	?	?	?	Y	Y	Y
13 ***Boulter***	Y	Y	Y	Y	N	N	N	N
14 ***Sweeney***	Y	Y	Y	Y	N	N	N	N
15 de la Garza	Y	N	N	N	Y	Y	Y	?
16 Coleman	Y	N	N	N	Y	Y	Y	Y
17 Stenholm	Y	N	Y	N	N	N	Y	N
18 Leland	Y	N	N	N	Y	Y	Y	Y
19 ***Combest***	Y	Y	Y	N	N	N	Y	N
20 Gonzalez	Y	N	N	N	Y	P	Y	Y
21 ***Loeffler***	Y	Y	Y	Y	N	N	Y	Y
22 ***DeLay***	N	Y	Y	Y	N	N	N	N
23 Bustamante	Y	N	N	N	Y	Y	Y	Y
24 Frost	Y	N	N	N	Y	Y	Y	Y
25 Andrews	Y	N	N	N	Y	Y	Y	Y
26 ***Armey***	N	Y	Y	Y	N	N	N	N
27 Ortiz	Y	N	N	N	Y	Y	Y	Y
UTAH								
1 ***Hansen***	N	Y	Y	Y	N	N	N	N
2 ***Monson***	N	Y	Y	Y	N	N	Y	N
3 ***Nielson***	N	Y	Y	Y	N	N	N	N
VERMONT								
AL ***Jeffords***	Y	N	N	N	Y	N	Y	Y
VIRGINIA								
1 ***Bateman***	Y	Y	Y	Y	N	Y	Y	Y
2 ***Whitehurst***	N	Y	N	N	Y	Y	N	Y
3 ***Bliley***	N	Y	Y	Y	N	Y	Y	Y
4 Sisisky	Y	N	N	N	Y	Y	Y	Y
5 Daniel	N	N	N	Y	N	Y	Y	Y
6 Olin	N	N	N	N	N	Y	Y	Y
7 ***Slaughter***	Y	Y	Y	Y	N	N	Y	Y
8 ***Parris***	Y	Y	?	Y	N	?	Y	Y
9 Boucher	Y	N	N	N	Y	Y	Y	Y
10 ***Wolf***	N	N	N	Y	N	Y	N	Y
WASHINGTON								
1 ***Miller***	N	Y	Y	Y	N	N	N	Y
2 Swift	Y	N	N	N	Y	Y	N	Y
3 Bonker	Y	N	?	N	Y	Y	N	Y
4 ***Morrison***	Y	N	Y	N	Y	N	N	Y
5 Foley	Y	N	N	N	Y	Y	N	Y
6 Dicks	Y	N	N	N	Y	Y	N	Y
7 Lowry	N	N	N	N	Y	Y	N	Y
8 ***Chandler***	N	Y	Y	Y	N	N	N	Y
WEST VIRGINIA								
1 Mollohan	Y	N	N	N	Y	Y	Y	Y
2 Staggers	Y	N	N	N	Y	Y	Y	Y
3 Wise	Y	N	N	N	Y	Y	Y	Y
4 Rahall	Y	N	N	N	Y	Y	Y	Y
WISCONSIN								
1 Aspin	Y	N	N	N	Y	Y	Y	Y
2 Kastenmeier	Y	N	N	N	Y	Y	Y	Y
3 ***Gunderson***	Y	N	Y	N	Y	N	N	Y
4 Kleczka	Y	N	N	N	Y	Y	N	Y
5 Moody	Y	N	N	N	Y	Y	Y	Y
6 ***Petri***	N	N	N	N	Y	N	N	N
7 Obey	N	N	N	N	Y	Y	Y	Y
8 ***Roth***	Y	Y	Y	Y	N	Y	?	?
9 ***Sensenbrenner***	N	Y	Y	Y	N	Y	N	N
WYOMING								
AL ***Cheney***	N	Y	Y	Y	N	N	N	N

Southern states - Ala., Ark., Fla., Ga., Ky., La., Miss., N.C., Okla., S.C., Tenn., Texas, Va.

* The *Congressional Record* vote number is different from the CQ vote number because the *Record* includes quorum calls in its tally. CQ does not publish quorum call votes.

322. H J Res 372. Public Debt Limit. Rostenkowski, D-Ill., motion to disagree to the Senate amendments to the joint resolution and to request a conference with the Senate on the measure to raise the ceiling on the federal debt to $2.079 trillion. Motion agreed to 327-50: R 119-42; D 208-8 (ND 137-7, SD 71-1), Oct. 11, 1985. (The Senate amendments were a series of changes in the 1974 Congressional Budget and Impoundment Control Act (PL 93-344) meant to eliminate the federal budget deficit by fiscal 1991.)

323. H J Res 372. Public Debt Limit. Michel, R-Ill., motion to instruct the House conferees on the joint resolution to raise the ceiling on the federal debt to report promptly amendments to the 1974 Congressional Budget and Impoundment Control Act (PL 93-344) that would provide mechanisms for reducing the federal budget deficit, including specific, mandatory goals for achieving a balanced budget in six years (by fiscal 1991). Motion agreed to 354-15: R 156-1; D 198-14 (ND 130-11, SD 68-3), Oct. 11, 1985.

324. Procedural Motion. Brown, R-Colo., motion to approve the House *Journal* of Tuesday, Oct. 15. Motion agreed to 242-103: R 52-96; D 190-7 (ND 130-4, SD 60-3), Oct. 16, 1985.

325. HR 1409. Military Construction Authorization, Fiscal 1986. Passage of the bill to authorize $9.2 billion in fiscal 1986 for certain construction at military installations, and for other purposes. Passed 354-38: R 159-7; D 195-31 (ND 120-30, SD 75-1), Oct. 16, 1985.

326. HR 3327. Military Construction Appropriations, Fiscal 1986. Adoption of the rule (H Res 282) to waive certain points of order against the bill to provide $8,372,730,000 in fiscal 1986 appropriations for military construction for the Department of Defense. Adopted 369-33: R 144-30; D 225-3 (ND 152-2, SD 73-1), Oct. 17, 1985.

327. HR 3327. Military Construction Appropriations, Fiscal 1986. Passage of the bill to provide $8,372,730,000 in fiscal 1986 appropriations for military construction for the Department of Defense. Passed 373-36: R 171-4; D 202-32 (ND 132-29, SD 70-3), Oct. 17, 1985. (The president had requested $10,340,200,000 in new budget authority.)

328. HR 2095. Daylight-Saving Time Extension. Adoption of the rule (H Res 288) to provide for House floor consideration of the bill to change daylight-saving time to run from the first Sunday in April to the first Sunday in November. Adopted 352-43: R 137-28; D 215-15 (ND 152-7, SD 63-8), Oct. 17, 1985. (Daylight-saving time currently runs from the last Sunday in April to the last Sunday in October.)

KEY

- Y Voted for (yea).
- # Paired for.
- + Announced for.
- N Voted against (nay).
- X Paired against.
- - Announced against.
- P Voted "present."
- C Voted "present" to avoid possible conflict of interest.
- ? Did not vote or otherwise make a position known.

Democrats ***Republicans***

	322	323	324	325	326	327	328
ALABAMA							
1 ***Callahan***	N	Y	Y	Y	Y	Y	Y
2 ***Dickinson***	Y	Y	?	Y	N	Y	Y
3 Nichols	Y	Y	Y	Y	Y	Y	Y
4 Bevill	Y	Y	?	Y	Y	Y	Y
5 Flippo	Y	Y	Y	Y	Y	Y	Y
6 Erdreich	Y	Y	Y	Y	Y	Y	Y
7 Shelby	?	?	N	Y	Y	?	?
ALASKA							
AL ***Young***	Y	N	?	?	?	?	?
ARIZONA							
1 ***McCain***	Y	Y	?	Y	N	Y	Y
2 Udall	Y	Y	?	Y	Y	Y	Y
3 ***Stump***	Y	Y	N	Y	Y	Y	N
4 ***Rudd***	?	?	Y	Y	Y	Y	N
5 ***Kolbe***	Y	Y	N	Y	Y	Y	Y
ARKANSAS							
1 Alexander	Y	Y	?	Y	Y	Y	Y
2 Robinson	Y	Y	Y	Y	Y	Y	Y
3 ***Hammerschmidt***	Y	Y	Y	Y	?	Y	?
4 Anthony	Y	Y	Y	Y	Y	Y	Y
CALIFORNIA							
1 Bosco	?	?	?	?	?	?	?
2 ***Chappie***	N	Y	?	?	Y	Y	Y
3 Matsui	Y	Y	Y	Y	Y	Y	Y
4 Fazio	Y	Y	Y	Y	Y	Y	Y
5 Burton	?	?	Y	N	Y	N	Y
6 Boxer	Y	Y	Y	Y	Y	Y	Y
7 Miller	Y	Y	Y	Y	Y	Y	Y
8 Dellums	N	N	Y	N	Y	N	Y
9 Stark	Y	Y	Y	N	Y	N	Y
10 Edwards	Y	Y	Y	N	Y	N	Y
11 Lantos	?	?	Y	Y	Y	Y	Y
12 ***Zschau***	?	?	N	Y	Y	Y	Y
13 Mineta	Y	Y	?	?	Y	Y	Y
14 ***Shumway***	N	Y	Y	Y	N	Y	Y
15 Coelho	Y	Y	Y	Y	Y	Y	Y
16 Panetta	Y	Y	Y	Y	Y	Y	Y
17 ***Pashayan***	?	?	?	?	Y	Y	Y
18 Lehman	?	?	?	?	Y	Y	Y
19 ***Lagomarsino***	Y	Y	N	Y	Y	Y	Y
20 ***Thomas***	Y	Y	N	Y	Y	Y	Y
21 ***Fiedler***	Y	Y	N	Y	Y	Y	Y
22 ***Moorhead***	N	Y	N	Y	Y	Y	Y
23 Beilenson	Y	Y	Y	Y	Y	Y	Y
24 Waxman	Y	Y	?	?	?	Y	Y
25 Roybal	?	?	Y	N	Y	N	Y
26 Berman	Y	Y	Y	Y	Y	Y	Y
27 Levine	Y	Y	Y	Y	Y	Y	Y
28 Dixon	?	?	?	X	?	X	?
29 Hawkins	?	X	Y	Y	Y	Y	Y
30 Martinez	Y	Y	Y	Y	Y	Y	Y
31 Dymally	N	N	P	N	Y	N	Y
32 Anderson	?	?	P	Y	Y	Y	Y
33 ***Dreier***	N	Y	N	Y	N	Y	Y
34 Torres	Y	Y	Y	Y	Y	Y	Y
35 ***Lewis***	Y	?	?	?	?	?	?
36 Brown	Y	Y	Y	Y	Y	Y	?
37 ***McCandless***	N	Y	N	Y	N	Y	?
38 ***Dornan***	N	Y	N	Y	Y	Y	Y
39 ***Dannemeyer***	N	Y	N	Y	N	Y	Y
40 ***Badham***	?	?	?	?	Y	Y	Y
41 ***Lowery***	Y	Y	?	Y	Y	Y	Y
42 ***Lungren***	N	Y	N	Y	Y	Y	Y
43 ***Packard***	Y	Y	N	Y	Y	Y	Y
44 Bates	Y	Y	Y	N	Y	N	Y
45 ***Hunter***	N	Y	N	Y	Y	Y	Y
COLORADO							
1 Schroeder	Y	Y	P	N	Y	N	Y
2 Wirth	Y	Y	Y	Y	Y	Y	Y
3 ***Strang***	N	Y	N	Y	N	Y	N
4 ***Brown***	N	Y	N	Y	N	Y	N
5 ***Kramer***	Y	Y	N	Y	Y	Y	N
6 ***Schaefer***	N	Y	N	Y	N	Y	Y
CONNECTICUT							
1 Kennelly	Y	Y	Y	Y	Y	Y	Y
2 Gejdenson	Y	Y	Y	Y	Y	Y	Y
3 Morrison	Y	Y	Y	Y	Y	Y	Y
4 ***McKinney***	Y	Y	Y	Y	Y	Y	Y
5 ***Rowland***	N	Y	Y	Y	Y	Y	Y
6 ***Johnson***	?	Y	Y	Y	Y	Y	Y
DELAWARE							
AL Carper	Y	Y	Y	Y	Y	Y	Y
FLORIDA							
1 Hutto	Y	Y	Y	Y	Y	Y	Y
2 Fuqua	Y	Y	Y	Y	Y	Y	Y
3 Bennett	Y	Y	Y	Y	Y	Y	Y
4 Chappell	?	?	Y	Y	Y	Y	Y
5 ***McCollum***	Y	Y	?	Y	Y	Y	Y
6 MacKay	Y	Y	?	Y	Y	Y	Y
7 Gibbons	Y	Y	Y	Y	Y	Y	Y
8 ***Young***	?	?	?	Y	Y	Y	Y
9 ***Bilirakis***	Y	Y	N	Y	Y	Y	Y
10 ***Ireland***	Y	Y	N	Y	Y	Y	Y
11 Nelson	Y	Y	+	#	Y	Y	Y
12 ***Lewis***	Y	Y	N	Y	Y	Y	Y
13 ***Mack***	N	Y	N	Y	Y	Y	Y
14 Mica	Y	Y	Y	Y	Y	Y	Y
15 ***Shaw***	Y	Y	N	Y	Y	Y	Y
16 Smith	Y	Y	Y	Y	Y	Y	Y
17 Lehman	?	?	Y	Y	Y	Y	Y
18 Pepper	Y	Y	Y	Y	Y	Y	Y
19 Fascell	?	?	Y	Y	Y	Y	Y
GEORGIA							
1 Thomas	Y	Y	Y	Y	Y	Y	Y
2 Hatcher	?	?	P	Y	?	Y	Y
3 Ray	Y	Y	Y	Y	Y	Y	N
4 ***Swindall***	N	Y	N	Y	Y	Y	Y
5 Fowler	Y	Y	Y	Y	Y	Y	Y
6 ***Gingrich***	N	Y	?	Y	Y	Y	Y
7 Darden	Y	Y	Y	Y	Y	Y	Y
8 Rowland	Y	Y	Y	Y	Y	Y	Y
9 Jenkins	Y	Y	?	Y	Y	Y	N
10 Barnard	Y	Y	Y	Y	Y	Y	N
HAWAII							
1 Heftel	Y	Y	Y	Y	Y	Y	Y
2 Akaka	?	?	Y	Y	Y	Y	Y
IDAHO							
1 ***Craig***	Y	Y	N	Y	Y	Y	Y
2 Stallings	Y	Y	Y	Y	Y	Y	Y
ILLINOIS							
1 Hayes	N	N	Y	N	Y	N	Y
2 Savage	N	N	Y	N	Y	N	Y
3 Russo	Y	Y	Y	Y	Y	Y	Y
4 ***O'Brien***	?	?	?	?	?	?	?
5 Lipinski	?	?	Y	Y	Y	Y	Y
6 ***Hyde***	Y	Y	Y	Y	Y	Y	?
7 Collins	?	X	?	X	Y	N	Y
8 Rostenkowski	Y	Y	Y	Y	Y	Y	Y
9 Yates	?	?	?	N	Y	Y	Y
10 ***Porter***	Y	Y	Y	Y	Y	Y	Y
11 Annunzio	Y	Y	Y	Y	Y	Y	Y
12 ***Crane***	N	?	N	N	N	N	Y
13 ***Fawell***	Y	Y	N	Y	N	Y	Y
14 ***Grotberg***	Y	+	N	Y	Y	Y	Y
15 ***Madigan***	Y	Y	N	Y	Y	Y	Y
16 ***Martin***	?	?	N	Y	Y	Y	N
17 Evans	Y	Y	Y	Y	Y	Y	Y
18 ***Michel***	Y	Y	N	Y	Y	Y	Y
19 Bruce	Y	Y	Y	Y	Y	Y	Y
20 Durbin	Y	Y	Y	Y	Y	Y	Y
21 Price	Y	Y	Y	Y	Y	Y	Y
22 Gray	Y	Y	Y	Y	Y	Y	Y
INDIANA							
1 Visclosky	Y	Y	Y	Y	Y	Y	Y
2 Sharp	Y	Y	Y	Y	Y	Y	Y
3 ***Hiler***	Y	Y	N	Y	Y	Y	Y
4 ***Coats***	Y	Y	Y	Y	Y	Y	Y
5 ***Hillis***	?	?	?	Y	Y	Y	?

ND - Northern Democrats SD - Southern Democrats

* Corresponding to Congressional Record Votes 357, 358, 359, 360, 361, 362, 363

	322	323	324	325	326	327	328
6 ***Burton***	Y	Y	N	Y	Y	Y	Y
7 ***Myers***	N	Y	Y	Y	Y	Y	Y
8 McCloskey	Y	Y	Y	Y	Y	Y	Y
9 Hamilton	Y	Y	Y	Y	Y	Y	Y
10 Jacobs	Y	Y	N	Y	Y	Y	Y
IOWA							
1 ***Leach***	Y	Y	N	Y	Y	Y	N
2 ***Tauke***	Y	Y	?	N	Y	Y	Y
3 ***Evans***	Y	Y	N	N	Y	N	N
4 Smith	Y	Y	Y	Y	Y	Y	N
5 ***Lightfoot***	Y	Y	N	Y	Y	Y	N
6 Bedell	Y	Y	?	?	Y	N	N
KANSAS							
1 ***Roberts***	Y	Y	N	Y	N	Y	N
2 Slattery	Y	Y	Y	Y	Y	Y	N
3 ***Meyers***	Y	Y	N	Y	Y	Y	Y
4 Glickman	Y	Y	Y	Y	Y	Y	Y
5 ***Whittaker***	Y	Y	?	Y	Y	Y	Y
KENTUCKY							
1 Hubbard	?	?	Y	Y	Y	N	N
2 Natcher	Y	Y	Y	Y	Y	Y	Y
3 Mazzoli	Y	Y	Y	Y	Y	Y	Y
4 ***Snyder***	?	?	P	Y	Y	Y	N
5 ***Rogers***	Y	Y	?	+	?	+	?
6 ***Hopkins***	Y	Y	N	Y	Y	Y	Y
7 Perkins	Y	Y	Y	Y	Y	Y	Y
LOUISIANA							
1 ***Livingston***	?	+	N	Y	Y	Y	Y
2 Boggs	Y	Y	?	Y	Y	Y	Y
3 Tauzin	Y	Y	Y	Y	Y	Y	Y
4 Roemer	Y	Y	N	Y	Y	Y	N
5 Huckaby	Y	Y	Y	Y	?	?	?
6 ***Moore***	Y	Y	Y	Y	Y	Y	Y
7 Breaux	Y	Y	Y	Y	Y	Y	Y
8 Long	Y	Y	?	Y	Y	Y	Y
MAINE							
1 ***McKernan***	Y	Y	N	Y	Y	Y	Y
2 ***Snowe***	Y	Y	N	Y	Y	Y	Y
MARYLAND							
1 Dyson	Y	Y	Y	Y	Y	Y	Y
2 ***Bentley***	Y	Y	N	Y	N	Y	Y
3 Mikulski	Y	Y	Y	Y	Y	Y	Y
4 ***Holt***	Y	Y	Y	Y	Y	Y	Y
5 Hoyer	Y	Y	Y	Y	Y	Y	Y
6 Byron	Y	Y	Y	Y	?	Y	Y
7 Mitchell	N	N	?	N	Y	N	Y
8 Barnes	Y	Y	Y	Y	Y	Y	Y
MASSACHUSETTS							
1 ***Conte***	Y	Y	N	Y	Y	Y	Y
2 Boland	Y	Y	?	Y	Y	Y	Y
3 Early	Y	?	Y	Y	Y	Y	Y
4 Frank	Y	Y	?	N	Y	N	Y
5 Atkins	Y	Y	Y	Y	Y	Y	Y
6 Mavroules	Y	Y	Y	Y	Y	Y	Y
7 Markey	Y	Y	Y	N	Y	N	Y
8 O'Neill							
9 Moakley	Y	Y	Y	Y	Y	Y	Y
10 Studds	Y	Y	Y	N	Y	N	Y
11 Donnelly	Y	Y	Y	Y	Y	Y	Y
MICHIGAN							
1 Conyers	N	N	?	?	?	?	?
2 ***Pursell***	Y	Y	?	Y	Y	Y	Y
3 Wolpe	Y	#	Y	Y	Y	Y	Y
4 ***Siljander***	Y	Y	N	Y	Y	Y	Y
5 ***Henry***	Y	Y	Y	Y	Y	Y	Y
6 Carr	Y	Y	Y	?	Y	Y	Y
7 Kildee	+	#	Y	Y	Y	Y	Y
8 Traxler	Y	Y	?	Y	Y	Y	Y
9 ***Vander Jagt***	Y	Y	Y	Y	Y	Y	Y
10 ***Schuette***	Y	Y	N	Y	Y	Y	N
11 ***Davis***	Y	Y	Y	Y	Y	Y	Y
12 Bonior	?	Y	Y	Y	Y	Y	Y
13 Crockett	Y	Y	Y	N	Y	N	Y
14 Hertel	Y	Y	Y	Y	Y	Y	Y
15 Ford	Y	Y	?	Y	Y	Y	Y
16 Dingell	Y	Y	Y	Y	?	Y	Y
17 Levin	Y	Y	Y	Y	?	?	?
18 ***Broomfield***	?	?	Y	Y	Y	Y	Y
MINNESOTA							
1 Penny	Y	Y	N	Y	Y	Y	N
2 ***Weber***	Y	Y	N	Y	Y	Y	N
3 ***Frenzel***	Y	Y	N	N	Y	N	Y
4 Vento	Y	Y	?	?	Y	N	Y
5 Sabo	Y	Y	P	Y	Y	Y	Y
6 Sikorski	Y	Y	N	Y	Y	Y	Y
7 ***Stangeland***	?	?	N	Y	Y	Y	N
8 Oberstar	Y	Y	Y	N	?	N	Y
MISSISSIPPI							
1 Whitten	Y	Y	Y	Y	Y	Y	?
2 ***Franklin***	N	Y	?	Y	Y	Y	Y
3 Montgomery	Y	Y	Y	Y	Y	Y	Y
4 Dowdy	Y	Y	Y	Y	?	?	?
5 ***Lott***	Y	Y	N	Y	Y	Y	Y
MISSOURI							
1 Clay	Y	N	N	N	?	?	?
2 Young	Y	Y	?	?	Y	Y	Y
3 Gephardt	Y	Y	Y	Y	Y	Y	Y
4 Skelton	?	#	Y	Y	Y	Y	Y
5 Wheat	Y	N	Y	Y	Y	Y	Y
6 ***Coleman***	Y	Y	N	Y	Y	Y	Y
7 ***Taylor***	Y	Y	Y	Y	Y	Y	N
8 ***Emerson***	Y	Y	N	Y	Y	Y	N
9 Volkmer	Y	Y	Y	Y	Y	Y	N
MONTANA							
1 Williams	Y	Y	?	X	Y	N	Y
2 ***Marlenee***	N	Y	N	Y	Y	Y	N
NEBRASKA							
1 ***Bereuter***	Y	Y	N	Y	N	Y	N
2 ***Daub***	Y	Y	N	Y	N	Y	N
3 ***Smith***	Y	Y	Y	Y	Y	Y	N
NEVADA							
1 Reid	Y	Y	Y	Y	Y	Y	Y
2 ***Vucanovich***	N	Y	?	?	N	Y	Y
NEW HAMPSHIRE							
1 ***Smith***	N	Y	N	Y	N	Y	Y
2 ***Gregg***	?	?	N	Y	Y	Y	Y
NEW JERSEY							
1 Florio	?	?	Y	Y	Y	Y	Y
2 Hughes	Y	Y	Y	Y	Y	Y	Y
3 Howard	Y	Y	Y	Y	Y	Y	Y
4 ***Smith***	Y	Y	Y	Y	Y	Y	Y
5 ***Roukema***	Y	Y	N	Y	Y	Y	Y
6 Dwyer	Y	Y	Y	Y	Y	Y	Y
7 ***Rinaldo***	Y	Y	Y	Y	Y	Y	Y
8 Roe	?	?	Y	Y	Y	Y	Y
9 Torricelli	Y	Y	?	#	Y	Y	Y
10 Rodino	Y	Y	?	#	Y	Y	Y
11 ***Gallo***	Y	Y	N	Y	Y	Y	Y
12 ***Courter***	Y	Y	Y	Y	N	Y	Y
13 ***Saxton***	Y	Y	N	Y	Y	Y	Y
14 Guarini	Y	?	Y	Y	Y	Y	Y
NEW MEXICO							
1 ***Lujan***	Y	Y	?	?	Y	Y	Y
2 ***Skeen***	Y	Y	N	Y	Y	Y	Y
3 Richardson	Y	Y	Y	Y	Y	Y	Y
NEW YORK							
1 ***Carney***	N	Y	N	Y	Y	Y	Y
2 Downey	Y	Y	Y	Y	Y	Y	Y
3 Mrazek	Y	Y	Y	Y	?	Y	Y
4 ***Lent***	Y	Y	N	Y	Y	Y	Y
5 ***McGrath***	Y	Y	N	?	Y	Y	Y
6 Addabbo	?	?	?	?	?	?	?
7 Ackerman	?	?	Y	N	Y	N	P
8 Scheuer	Y	Y	Y	N	Y	Y	Y
9 Manton	Y	Y	Y	Y	Y	Y	Y
10 Schumer	Y	Y	Y	Y	Y	Y	Y
11 Towns	?	?	Y	N	Y	N	Y
12 Owens	N	N	Y	N	Y	N	Y
13 Solarz	Y	Y	?	Y	Y	Y	Y
14 ***Molinari***	N	Y	N	Y	Y	Y	Y
15 ***Green***	Y	Y	Y	Y	Y	Y	Y
16 Rangel	Y	N	Y	N	Y	Y	Y
17 Weiss	Y	N	Y	N	N	N	Y
18 Garcia	?	?	Y	N	Y	N	Y
19 Biaggi	?	?	Y	Y	Y	?	?
20 ***DioGuardi***	Y	Y	Y	Y	Y	Y	Y
21 ***Fish***	Y	Y	Y	Y	Y	Y	Y
22 ***Gilman***	Y	Y	Y	Y	Y	Y	Y
23 Stratton	?	?	Y	Y	Y	Y	Y
24 ***Solomon***	Y	Y	N	Y	Y	Y	N
25 ***Boehlert***	?	?	N	Y	Y	Y	Y
26 ***Martin***	Y	Y	N	Y	?	Y	Y
27 ***Wortley***	Y	Y	Y	Y	Y	Y	Y
28 McHugh	Y	Y	Y	Y	?	Y	Y
29 ***Horton***	?	?	?	?	Y	Y	?
30 ***Eckert***	Y	Y	Y	Y	N	Y	Y
31 ***Kemp***	Y	Y	Y	Y	?	Y	N
32 LaFalce	Y	Y	Y	Y	Y	Y	N
33 Nowak	Y	Y	Y	Y	Y	Y	Y
34 Lundine	Y	Y	Y	N	Y	N	N
NORTH CAROLINA							
1 Jones	Y	Y	Y	Y	Y	Y	Y
2 Valentine	Y	Y	Y	Y	Y	Y	Y
3 Whitley	Y	Y	Y	Y	Y	Y	Y
4 ***Cobey***	N	Y	N	Y	N	Y	Y
5 Neal	Y	Y	Y	Y	Y	Y	Y
6 ***Coble***	N	Y	?	Y	N	Y	Y
7 Rose	?	?	?	Y	Y	Y	Y
8 Hefner	Y	Y	Y	Y	Y	Y	Y
9 ***McMillan***	Y	Y	Y	Y	Y	Y	Y
10 ***Broyhill***	Y	Y	Y	Y	Y	Y	Y
11 ***Hendon***	Y	Y	N	Y	Y	Y	?
NORTH DAKOTA							
AL Dorgan	Y	Y	Y	Y	N	Y	Y
OHIO							
1 Luken	Y	Y	Y	Y	Y	Y	Y
2 ***Gradison***	Y	Y	Y	Y	Y	Y	Y
3 Hall	Y	Y	Y	Y	Y	Y	Y
4 ***Oxley***	Y	Y	?	Y	Y	Y	Y
5 ***Latta***	Y	?	Y	Y	Y	Y	Y
6 ***McEwen***	Y	Y	N	Y	Y	Y	Y
7 ***DeWine***	N	Y	N	Y	Y	Y	Y
8 ***Kindness***	Y	?	N	Y	Y	Y	N
9 Kaptur	Y	Y	+	+	Y	Y	Y
10 ***Miller***	Y	Y	N	Y	Y	Y	Y
11 Eckart	Y	Y	Y	Y	Y	Y	Y
12 ***Kasich***	Y	Y	?	Y	Y	Y	Y
13 Pease	Y	Y	Y	Y	Y	Y	Y
14 Seiberling	Y	Y	Y	Y	Y	Y	Y
15 ***Wylie***	Y	Y	Y	?	Y	Y	Y
16 ***Regula***	Y	Y	Y	Y	Y	Y	Y
17 Traficant	Y	Y	Y	Y	Y	Y	Y
18 Applegate	Y	Y	Y	Y	Y	Y	Y
19 Feighan	Y	Y	Y	Y	Y	Y	Y
20 Oakar	Y	Y	Y	Y	Y	Y	Y
21 Stokes	?	X	Y	N	Y	N	Y
OKLAHOMA							
1 Jones	Y	Y	Y	Y	N	N	Y
2 Synar	Y	Y	Y	Y	Y	Y	Y
3 Watkins	Y	Y	?	Y	Y	Y	Y
4 McCurdy	Y	Y	?	?	?	?	?
5 ***Edwards***	Y	Y	N	Y	Y	Y	Y
6 English	Y	Y	?	Y	Y	Y	Y
OREGON							
1 AuCoin	Y	Y	?	?	P	N	Y
2 ***Smith, R.***	N	Y	N	Y	Y	Y	Y
3 Wyden	Y	Y	Y	Y	Y	Y	Y
4 Weaver	Y	Y	?	?	?	?	?
5 ***Smith, D.***	N	Y	Y	N	N	?	?
PENNSYLVANIA							
1 Foglietta	Y	Y	?	Y	Y	Y	Y
2 Gray	Y	Y	Y	Y	Y	Y	Y
3 Borski	Y	Y	Y	Y	Y	Y	Y
4 Kolter	Y	Y	Y	Y	Y	Y	Y
5 ***Schulze***	Y	Y	Y	Y	Y	Y	Y
6 Yatron	Y	Y	Y	Y	Y	Y	Y
7 Edgar	?	?	Y	Y	Y	Y	Y
8 Kostmayer	Y	Y	?	Y	Y	Y	Y
9 ***Shuster***	?	?	N	Y	Y	Y	Y
10 ***McDade***	Y	Y	Y	Y	Y	Y	Y
11 Kanjorski	Y	Y	Y	Y	Y	Y	Y
12 Murtha	Y	?	Y	Y	Y	Y	Y
13 ***Coughlin***	Y	Y	?	?	Y	Y	Y
14 Coyne	Y	Y	Y	Y	?	Y	Y
15 ***Ritter***	Y	Y	?	?	Y	Y	Y
16 ***Walker***	N	Y	?	?	N	Y	Y
17 ***Gekas***	N	Y	N	Y	Y	Y	Y
18 Walgren	Y	Y	Y	N	Y	Y	?
19 ***Goodling***	Y	Y	?	Y	Y	Y	Y
20 Gaydos	Y	Y	Y	Y	Y	Y	Y
21 ***Ridge***	Y	Y	N	Y	Y	Y	Y
22 Murphy	Y	Y	Y	Y	Y	Y	Y
23 ***Clinger***	Y	Y	Y	Y	Y	Y	Y
RHODE ISLAND							
1 St Germain	Y	Y	?	Y	Y	Y	Y
2 ***Schneider***	Y	Y	?	?	Y	Y	Y
SOUTH CAROLINA							
1 ***Hartnett***	?	?	?	Y	Y	?	?
2 ***Spence***	Y	Y	N	Y	Y	Y	Y
3 Derrick	Y	Y	Y	Y	Y	Y	Y
4 ***Campbell***	Y	Y	Y	Y	Y	Y	Y
5 Spratt	Y	Y	Y	Y	Y	Y	Y
6 Tallon	Y	Y	?	Y	Y	Y	Y
SOUTH DAKOTA							
AL Daschle	Y	Y	Y	Y	Y	Y	Y
TENNESSEE							
1 ***Quillen***	?	?	Y	Y	Y	Y	Y
2 ***Duncan***	Y	Y	Y	Y	Y	Y	Y
3 Lloyd	Y	Y	N	Y	Y	Y	Y
4 Cooper	Y	Y	Y	Y	Y	Y	Y
5 Boner	Y	Y	Y	Y	Y	Y	Y
6 Gordon	Y	Y	P	Y	Y	Y	Y
7 ***Sundquist***	Y	Y	N	Y	Y	Y	Y
8 Jones	Y	Y	?	#	?	#	?
9 Ford	Y	N	Y	Y	Y	Y	Y
TEXAS							
1 Chapman	Y	Y	Y	Y	Y	+	+
2 Wilson	?	?	?	?	?	?	?
3 ***Bartlett***	N	Y	N	Y	N	Y	Y
4 Hall, R.	Y	Y	Y	Y	Y	Y	N
5 Bryant	Y	Y	Y	Y	Y	Y	Y
6 ***Barton***	N	Y	N	Y	N	Y	Y
7 ***Archer***	Y	Y	Y	Y	Y	Y	Y
8 ***Fields***	N	Y	N	Y	Y	Y	?
9 Brooks	?	?	Y	Y	Y	Y	Y
10 Pickle	Y	Y	Y	Y	Y	Y	Y
11 Leath	Y	Y	Y	Y	Y	Y	Y
12 Wright	Y	Y	?	?	?	?	?
13 ***Boulter***	N	Y	?	Y	Y	Y	N
14 ***Sweeney***	Y	Y	?	Y	Y	Y	N
15 de la Garza	?	?	Y	Y	Y	Y	Y
16 Coleman	Y	?	Y	Y	Y	Y	Y
17 Stenholm	Y	Y	Y	Y	Y	Y	N
18 Leland	N	N	Y	N	Y	N	Y
19 ***Combest***	N	Y	Y	Y	Y	Y	Y
20 Gonzalez	Y	N	Y	Y	Y	Y	Y
21 ***Loeffler***	N	Y	N	Y	Y	Y	N
22 ***DeLay***	N	Y	N	Y	Y	Y	Y
23 Bustamante	Y	Y	?	?	?	?	?
24 Frost	Y	Y	Y	Y	Y	Y	Y
25 Andrews	Y	Y	Y	Y	Y	Y	Y
26 ***Armey***	N	Y	N	Y	N	N	Y
27 Ortiz	Y	Y	Y	Y	Y	Y	?
UTAH							
1 ***Hansen***	Y	Y	Y	Y	N	Y	N
2 ***Monson***	N	Y	N	Y	N	Y	N
3 ***Nielson***	N	Y	Y	Y	N	Y	Y
VERMONT							
AL ***Jeffords***	Y	Y	Y	Y	Y	Y	Y
VIRGINIA							
1 ***Bateman***	Y	Y	Y	Y	Y	Y	+
2 ***Whitehurst***	?	?	Y	Y	Y	Y	?
3 ***Bliley***	Y	Y	Y	Y	Y	Y	Y
4 Sisisky	Y	Y	Y	Y	Y	Y	Y
5 Daniel	Y	Y	Y	Y	Y	Y	Y
6 Olin	Y	Y	Y	Y	Y	Y	N
7 ***Slaughter***	Y	Y	N	Y	Y	Y	Y
8 ***Parris***	Y	Y	N	Y	Y	Y	?
9 Boucher	Y	Y	?	Y	Y	Y	Y
10 ***Wolf***	Y	Y	N	Y	Y	Y	Y
WASHINGTON							
1 ***Miller***	Y	Y	Y	N	N	Y	Y
2 Swift	Y	Y	Y	Y	Y	Y	Y
3 Bonker	Y	Y	?	Y	?	Y	Y
4 ***Morrison***	Y	Y	N	Y	Y	Y	Y
5 Foley	Y	Y	Y	Y	Y	Y	Y
6 Dicks	?	?	Y	Y	Y	?	Y
7 Lowry	Y	Y	Y	Y	Y	Y	Y
8 ***Chandler***	Y	Y	N	Y	Y	Y	Y
WEST VIRGINIA							
1 Mollohan	Y	Y	Y	Y	Y	Y	Y
2 Staggers	Y	Y	?	Y	Y	Y	Y
3 Wise	Y	Y	Y	Y	Y	Y	Y
4 Rahall	Y	Y	Y	Y	Y	Y	Y
WISCONSIN							
1 Aspin	Y	Y	?	?	Y	Y	Y
2 Kastenmeier	Y	Y	Y	N	Y	N	Y
3 ***Gunderson***	Y	Y	N	N	Y	Y	Y
4 Kleczka	Y	Y	Y	Y	Y	Y	Y
5 Moody	Y	Y	?	X	Y	Y	Y
6 ***Petri***	Y	Y	Y	Y	Y	Y	Y
7 Obey	Y	Y	Y	N	Y	Y	Y
8 ***Roth***	Y	Y	N	Y	Y	Y	Y
9 ***Sensenbrenner***	?	?	N	Y	Y	Y	Y
WYOMING							
AL ***Cheney***	Y	Y	?	Y	?	?	?

Southern states - Ala., Ark., Fla., Ga., Ky., La., Miss., N.C., Okla., S.C., Tenn., Texas, Va.

* The *Congressional Record* vote number is different from the CQ vote number because the *Record* includes quorum calls in its tally. CQ does not publish quorum call votes.

329. HR 463. Topsoil Preservation. Udall, D-Ariz., motion to suspend the rules and pass the bill to establish topsoil preservation guidelines for federal or federally assisted construction projects larger than 100,000 square feet, and to authorize $6 million annually to carry out the program in each fiscal year after Sept. 30, 1986. Motion rejected 225-185: R 22-153; D 203-32 (ND 148-14, SD 55-18), Oct. 22, 1985. A two-thirds majority of those present and voting (274 in this case) is required for passage under suspension of the rules. A "nay" was a vote supporting the president's position.

330. HR 2095. Daylight-Saving Time Extension. Passage of the bill to change daylight-saving time to run from the first Sunday in April to the first Sunday in November. Passed 240-157: R 78-87; D 162-70 (ND 123-33, SD 39-37), Oct. 22, 1985. (Daylight-saving time currently runs from the last Sunday in April to the last Sunday in October.) A "yea" was a vote supporting the president's position.

331. Procedural Motion. Kolbe, R-Ariz., motion to approve the House *Journal* of Tuesday, Oct. 22. Motion agreed to 273-117: R 62-109; D 211-8 (ND 138-6, SD 73-2), Oct. 23, 1985.

332. HR 3500. Omnibus Budget Reconciliation, Fiscal 1986. Adoption of the rule (H Res 296) to provide for House floor consideration of the bill to make changes in law to achieve the deficit-reduction targets of the fiscal 1986 budget resolution (S Con Res 32), and to allow amendments by Latta, R-Ohio, to strike certain provisions *(vote 334, below)*; Fazio, D-Calif., to strike a provision placing transportation trust funds off budget *(vote 335, below)*; and Florio, D-N.J., to insert a House-passed Amtrak authorization bill (HR 2266). Adopted 230-190: R 97-81; D 133-109 (ND 70-92, SD 63-17), Oct. 23, 1985. (The Florio amendment was subsequently adopted by voice vote.)

333. HR 2409. National Institutes of Health Authorizations, Fiscal 1986-88. Adoption of the conference report to authorize $2.4 billion in fiscal 1986, $2.6 billion in 1987 and $2.7 billion in 1988 for certain research activities of the National Institutes of Health, and to create a new institute for research on arthritis. Adopted (thus cleared for the president) 395-10: R 162-9; D 233-1 (ND 157-0, SD 76-1), Oct. 23, 1985.

334. HR 3500. Omnibus Budget Reconciliation, Fiscal 1986. Latta, R-Ohio, amendment to eliminate new programs and increased spending authorized in the bill, to remove transportation trust funds from the budget in fiscal year 1989, and to reduce proposed salary increases for federal civilian employees. Rejected 209-219: R 166-15; D 43-204 (ND 15-151, SD 28-53), Oct. 24, 1985.

335. HR 3500. Omnibus Budget Reconciliation, Fiscal 1986. Fazio, D-Calif., amendment to strike a provision of the bill that would have removed two transportation trust funds from the budget. Adopted 222-205: R 72-109; D 150-96 (ND 99-66, SD 51-30), Oct. 24, 1985. A "yea" was a vote supporting the president's position.

336. HR 3500. Omnibus Budget Reconciliation, Fiscal 1986. Passage of the bill to make changes in law to reduce spending by $60.9 billion over fiscal years 1986-88, to conform with the fiscal 1986 budget resolution (S Con Res 32) that called for $276 billion in spending cuts and higher revenues over three years. Passed 228-199: R 15-166; D 213-33 (ND 141-24, SD 72-9), Oct. 24, 1985. A "nay" was a vote supporting the president's position.

KEY

- Y Voted for (yea).
- # Paired for.
- + Announced for.
- N Voted against (nay).
- X Paired against.
- \- Announced against.
- P Voted "present."
- C Voted "present" to avoid possible conflict of interest.
- ? Did not vote or otherwise make a position known.

Democrats ***Republicans***

	329	330	331	332	333	334	335	336
ALABAMA								
1 ***Callahan***	N	Y	N	Y	Y	Y	N	N
2 ***Dickinson***	N	Y	N	N	Y	Y	Y	N
3 Nichols	Y	Y	Y	Y	Y	Y	Y	Y
4 Bevill	Y	N	Y	Y	Y	N	Y	Y
5 Flippo	Y	N	Y	N	Y	N	Y	Y
6 Erdreich	Y	Y	Y	N	Y	N	Y	Y
7 Shelby	?	?	Y	Y	Y	Y	Y	N
ALASKA								
AL ***Young***	N	N	N	Y	Y	N	N	Y
ARIZONA								
1 ***McCain***	Y	N	Y	N	Y	Y	Y	N
2 Udall	Y	N	Y	N	Y	N	N	Y
3 ***Stump***	N	N	N	N	N	Y	Y	N
4 ***Rudd***	N	?	Y	N	Y	Y	Y	N
5 ***Kolbe***	N	N	N	Y	Y	Y	Y	N
ARKANSAS								
1 Alexander	?	Y	?	Y	Y	N	N	Y
2 Robinson	Y	Y	Y	Y	Y	Y	N	N
3 ***Hammerschmidt***	N	N	Y	N	Y	Y	N	N
4 Anthony	Y	Y	Y	N	Y	N	Y	Y
CALIFORNIA								
1 Bosco	Y	N	Y	Y	Y	N	N	Y
2 ***Chappie***	N	N	N	Y	Y	Y	N	N
3 Matsui	Y	Y	Y	Y	Y	N	Y	Y
4 Fazio	Y	+	Y	Y	Y	N	Y	Y
5 Burton	Y	Y	Y	Y	Y	N	N	Y
6 Boxer	Y	Y	Y	Y	Y	N	N	Y
7 Miller	Y	Y	Y	Y	Y	N	Y	Y
8 Dellums	Y	Y	?	Y	Y	N	Y	Y
9 Stark	Y	Y	Y	N	Y	N	Y	N
10 Edwards	Y	Y	Y	Y	Y	N	Y	Y
11 Lantos	Y	Y	Y	Y	Y	N	N	Y
12 ***Zschau***	N	Y	N	Y	Y	Y	Y	N
13 Mineta	Y	Y	Y	Y	Y	N	N	N
14 ***Shumway***	N	N	Y	Y	N	Y	N	N
15 Coelho	Y	Y	Y	Y	Y	?	?	?
16 Panetta	Y	N	Y	Y	Y	N	Y	Y
17 ***Pashayan***	N	N	Y	Y	Y	Y	N	N
18 Lehman	Y	Y	Y	Y	Y	N	N	Y
19 ***Lagomarsino***	N	Y	N	Y	Y	Y	N	N
20 ***Thomas***	N	Y	N	N	?	Y	N	N
21 ***Fiedler***	N	Y	?	Y	Y	Y	Y	N
22 ***Moorhead***	N	Y	N	Y	Y	Y	N	N
23 Beilenson	Y	Y	Y	Y	Y	N	Y	Y
24 Waxman	Y	Y	Y	Y	Y	N	Y	Y
25 Roybal	Y	Y	Y	Y	Y	N	N	Y
26 Berman	Y	Y	Y	Y	Y	N	Y	Y
27 Levine	Y	Y	Y	Y	Y	N	Y	Y
28 Dixon	Y	Y	?	Y	Y	N	Y	Y
29 Hawkins	Y	Y	Y	Y	Y	N	N	Y
30 Martinez	Y	Y	Y	Y	Y	N	N	Y
31 Dymally	Y	Y	P	Y	Y	N	N	Y
32 Anderson	N	Y	Y	Y	Y	N	N	N
33 ***Dreier***	N	Y	Y	Y	Y	Y	N	N
34 Torres	Y	Y	Y	Y	Y	N	N	Y
35 ***Lewis***	N	Y	N	Y	Y	N	N	N
36 Brown	Y	Y	Y	Y	Y	X	?	?
37 ***McCandless***	N	N	N	+	Y	Y	N	N
38 ***Dornan***	N	Y	Y	Y	Y	Y	N	N
39 ***Dannemeyer***	N	N	N	N	N	Y	N	N
40 ***Badham***	N	N	N	N	N	Y	N	N
41 ***Lowery***	N	#	?	Y	Y	Y	Y	N
42 ***Lungren***	N	Y	N	Y	Y	Y	Y	N
43 ***Packard***	N	Y	Y	Y	Y	Y	N	N
44 Bates	Y	Y	?	Y	Y	N	Y	Y
45 ***Hunter***	N	Y	N	Y	Y	Y	Y	N
COLORADO								
1 Schroeder	N	Y	N	N	Y	N	Y	Y
2 Wirth	Y	Y	Y	N	Y	N	Y	Y
3 ***Strang***	N	N	N	Y	Y	Y	Y	N
4 ***Brown***	N	N	N	N	N	Y	Y	N
5 ***Kramer***	N	N	N	N	Y	Y	Y	N
6 ***Schaefer***	N	Y	?	Y	Y	Y	Y	N
CONNECTICUT								
1 Kennelly	Y	Y	Y	N	Y	N	Y	Y
2 Gejdenson	Y	Y	Y	N	Y	N	Y	Y
3 Morrison	Y	Y	Y	N	Y	N	Y	Y
4 ***McKinney***	Y	Y	Y	N	Y	N	Y	Y
5 ***Rowland***	N	Y	Y	N	Y	Y	N	N
6 ***Johnson***	N	Y	Y	N	Y	Y	N	N
DELAWARE								
AL Carper	Y	Y	Y	Y	Y	N	Y	Y
FLORIDA								
1 Hutto	Y	Y	Y	Y	Y	Y	Y	Y
2 Fuqua	Y	N	Y	Y	Y	N	Y	Y
3 Bennett	Y	N	Y	Y	Y	N	Y	Y
4 Chappell	Y	?	Y	Y	?	N	Y	Y
5 ***McCollum***	N	Y	Y	N	Y	Y	Y	N
6 MacKay	N	Y	Y	Y	Y	Y	Y	Y
7 Gibbons	Y	Y	Y	N	Y	N	Y	N
8 ***Young***	N	?	Y	Y	Y	Y	Y	N
9 ***Bilirakis***	N	Y	N	Y	Y	Y	N	N
10 ***Ireland***	N	Y	N	Y	Y	Y	N	N
11 Nelson	+	+	+	+	+	#	-	#
12 ***Lewis***	N	Y	N	Y	Y	Y	N	N
13 ***Mack***	N	Y	N	Y	Y	Y	Y	N
14 Mica	#	Y	Y	Y	Y	Y	Y	Y
15 ***Shaw***	N	Y	N	Y	Y	Y	N	N
16 Smith	Y	Y	Y	Y	Y	Y	Y	Y
17 Lehman	Y	Y	Y	Y	Y	N	Y	Y
18 Pepper	Y	Y	Y	Y	Y	N	N	Y
19 Fascell	Y	Y	Y	Y	Y	N	Y	Y
GEORGIA								
1 Thomas	Y	N	Y	Y	Y	Y	N	Y
2 Hatcher	?	Y	Y	Y	Y	Y	Y	Y
3 Ray	N	N	Y	Y	N	Y	N	Y
4 ***Swindall***	N	N	N	Y	Y	Y	N	N
5 Fowler	Y	N	Y	N	Y	N	Y	Y
6 ***Gingrich***	Y	N	N	N	?	Y	N	N
7 Darden	Y	N	Y	N	Y	Y	N	Y
8 Rowland	Y	N	Y	Y	Y	Y	N	Y
9 Jenkins	Y	N	Y	N	Y	Y	Y	Y
10 Barnard	Y	N	Y	Y	Y	Y	N	Y
HAWAII								
1 Heftel	Y	Y	?	?	?	N	Y	Y
2 Akaka	Y	Y	Y	Y	?	N	Y	Y
IDAHO								
1 ***Craig***	N	N	N	Y	Y	Y	Y	N
2 Stallings	N	N	Y	Y	Y	Y	Y	Y
ILLINOIS								
1 Hayes	Y	Y	Y	Y	Y	N	Y	Y
2 Savage	Y	Y	Y	Y	Y	N	N	Y
3 Russo	Y	Y	Y	N	Y	N	N	Y
4 ***O'Brien***	N	?	?	N	Y	Y	Y	Y
5 Lipinski	N	Y	Y	N	Y	N	N	Y
6 ***Hyde***	N	N	Y	N	Y	Y	Y	N
7 Collins	Y	Y	Y	Y	?	N	Y	Y
8 Rostenkowski	Y	Y	Y	N	Y	N	N	Y
9 Yates	Y	Y	Y	N	Y	N	Y	Y
10 ***Porter***	N	Y	Y	Y	Y	Y	Y	Y
11 Annunzio	Y	Y	Y	Y	Y	N	N	Y
12 ***Crane***	N	Y	N	N	N	Y	N	N
13 ***Fawell***	N	Y	N	N	Y	Y	N	N
14 ***Grotberg***	N	Y	N	Y	Y	Y	N	N
15 ***Madigan***	?	?	N	Y	Y	Y	N	N
16 ***Martin***	N	N	N	Y	Y	Y	N	N
17 Evans	Y	Y	Y	N	Y	N	Y	Y
18 ***Michel***	N	Y	N	Y	Y	Y	N	N
19 Bruce	Y	Y	Y	N	Y	Y	Y	Y
20 Durbin	Y	Y	N	N	Y	Y	Y	Y
21 Price	Y	Y	Y	Y	Y	N	N	Y
22 Gray	Y	N	?	N	Y	N	N	Y
INDIANA								
1 Visclosky	Y	Y	Y	N	Y	N	Y	Y
2 Sharp	Y	N	Y	N	Y	Y	Y	N
3 ***Hiler***	N	N	N	Y	Y	Y	Y	N
4 ***Coats***	N	Y	Y	N	Y	Y	Y	N
5 ***Hillis***	?	N	Y	Y	Y	Y	N	N

ND - Northern Democrats SD - Southern Democrats

* Corresponding to Congressional Record Votes 364, 365, 366, 367, 368, 370, 371, 372

	329	330	331	332	333	334	335	336
6 ***Burton***	N	Y	N	Y	Y	Y	N	N
7 ***Myers***	N	?	Y	Y	Y	Y	Y	N
8 McCloskey	Y	N	Y	N	Y	N	Y	Y
9 Hamilton	Y	N	Y	N	Y	Y	Y	N
10 Jacobs	Y	Y	N	N	Y	N	N	N
IOWA								
1 ***Leach***	Y	N	N	N	Y	Y	Y	N
2 ***Tauke***	Y	Y	N	N	N	Y	N	N
3 ***Evans***	Y	N	N	Y	Y	Y	N	N
4 Smith	Y	?	Y	N	Y	N	N	N
5 ***Lightfoot***	Y	N	N	N	Y	Y	N	N
6 Bedell	Y	N	Y	N	Y	Y	Y	Y
KANSAS								
1 ***Roberts***	N	N	N	N	Y	Y	Y	N
2 Slattery	N	N	Y	N	Y	Y	Y	N
3 ***Meyers***	Y	Y	?	N	Y	Y	Y	N
4 Glickman	Y	N	Y	Y	Y	Y	N	N
5 ***Whittaker***	?	N	N	Y	Y	Y	N	N
KENTUCKY								
1 Hubbard	N	N	Y	N	Y	N	Y	N
2 Natcher	Y	N	Y	Y	Y	N	Y	Y
3 Mazzoli	Y	Y	Y	Y	Y	N	Y	Y
4 ***Snyder***	N	N	Y	N	Y	Y	N	Y
5 ***Rogers***	N	N	N	N	Y	Y	Y	N
6 ***Hopkins***	N	N	Y	N	Y	Y	Y	N
7 Perkins	Y	Y	Y	Y	Y	N	N	Y
LOUISIANA								
1 ***Livingston***	N	?	Y	Y	?	Y	Y	Y
2 Boggs	Y	?	Y	Y	Y	N	Y	Y
3 Tauzin	N	Y	Y	Y	Y	N	Y	Y
4 Roemer	N	N	N	Y	Y	Y	Y	Y
5 Huckaby	Y	Y	Y	Y	Y	N	N	Y
6 ***Moore***	N	Y	Y	Y	Y	Y	Y	Y
7 Breaux	N	N	Y	Y	Y	N	N	Y
8 Long	Y	Y	Y	Y	Y	N	N	Y
MAINE								
1 ***McKernan***	N	Y	N	Y	Y	Y	Y	N
2 ***Snowe***	N	Y	N	N	Y	Y	Y	N
MARYLAND								
1 Dyson	Y	N	?	N	Y	N	Y	Y
2 ***Bentley***	N	Y	N	N	Y	Y	N	N
3 Mikulski	Y	N	Y	Y	Y	N	Y	Y
4 ***Holt***	N	?	N	Y	Y	N	Y	N
5 Hoyer	Y	Y	Y	Y	Y	N	Y	Y
6 Byron	Y	N	Y	Y	Y	N	N	Y
7 Mitchell	Y	Y	?	N	Y	N	N	Y
8 Barnes	Y	Y	Y	Y	Y	N	Y	Y
MASSACHUSETTS								
1 ***Conte***	Y	+	N	N	Y	N	Y	N
2 Boland	Y	?	Y	Y	Y	N	Y	Y
3 Early	Y	+	Y	Y	Y	N	Y	Y
4 Frank	Y	Y	Y	N	Y	N	Y	Y
5 Atkins	Y	Y	Y	N	Y	N	N	Y
6 Mavroules	Y	Y	Y	N	Y	N	N	Y
7 Markey	Y	Y	Y	N	Y	N	Y	Y
8 O'Neill								
9 Moakley	Y	Y	?	Y	Y	N	Y	Y
10 Studds	Y	Y	Y	Y	Y	N	Y	Y
11 Donnelly	Y	Y	Y	N	Y	N	N	Y
MICHIGAN								
1 Conyers	?	?	?	?	?	X	?	?
2 ***Pursell***	N	?	Y	Y	Y	Y	Y	N
3 Wolpe	Y	N	Y	N	Y	N	Y	Y
4 ***Siljander***	N	N	N	Y	Y	Y	N	N
5 ***Henry***	N	N	Y	Y	Y	Y	Y	N
6 Carr	Y	N	Y	Y	Y	Y	Y	N
7 Kildee	Y	Y	Y	N	Y	N	Y	Y
8 Traxler	Y	N	Y	N	Y	N	Y	N
9 ***Vander Jagt***	?	Y	N	N	Y	Y	N	N
10 ***Schuette***	N	N	N	N	Y	Y	N	N
11 ***Davis***	N	N	N	Y	Y	Y	Y	N
12 Bonior	Y	Y	?	Y	Y	N	Y	Y
13 Crockett	Y	Y	Y	N	Y	N	Y	Y
14 Hertel	Y	Y	Y	N	Y	N	Y	N
15 Ford	Y	Y	?	Y	Y	N	N	Y
16 Dingell	Y	Y	Y	N	Y	N	Y	Y
17 Levin	Y	Y	Y	N	Y	N	Y	Y
18 ***Broomfield***	Y	Y	Y	N	?	Y	Y	N
MINNESOTA								
1 Penny	N	N	N	Y	Y	Y	Y	Y
2 ***Weber***	Y	N	N	Y	?	Y	N	N
3 ***Frenzel***	N	Y	N	N	Y	Y	Y	N
4 Vento	Y	Y	Y	N	Y	N	Y	Y
5 Sabo	Y	Y	Y	Y	Y	N	Y	Y
6 Sikorski	Y	Y	N	N	Y	N	Y	Y
7 ***Stangeland***	N	N	N	N	Y	Y	N	N
8 Oberstar	Y	Y	Y	N	Y	N	N	Y
MISSISSIPPI								
1 Whitten	Y	N	Y	Y	Y	N	Y	N
2 ***Franklin***	X	Y	Y	Y	Y	Y	Y	N
3 Montgomery	N	Y	Y	Y	Y	Y	Y	Y
4 Dowdy	?	Y	?	Y	Y	Y	N	Y
5 ***Lott***	N	N	N	Y	Y	Y	Y	N
MISSOURI								
1 Clay	Y	Y	N	Y	Y	N	Y	Y
2 Young	#	+	?	Y	Y	N	N	Y
3 Gephardt	Y	Y	Y	N	Y	N	Y	Y
4 Skelton	N	N	Y	Y	Y	N	N	?
5 Wheat	Y	Y	Y	Y	Y	N	Y	Y
6 ***Coleman***	?	?	?	?	?	Y	N	N
7 ***Taylor***	?	?	Y	Y	Y	Y	N	N
8 ***Emerson***	N	N	N	Y	Y	Y	N	N
9 Volkmer	N	N	Y	N	Y	Y	N	N
MONTANA								
1 Williams	Y	Y	?	N	Y	N	N	Y
2 ***Marlenee***	N	N	N	N	Y	Y	N	N
NEBRASKA								
1 ***Bereuter***	N	N	N	N	Y	Y	Y	N
2 ***Daub***	N	N	N	N	Y	Y	N	N
3 ***Smith***	N	N	Y	N	Y	Y	Y	N
NEVADA								
1 Reid	Y	Y	Y	N	Y	N	N	Y
2 ***Vucanovich***	N	N	N	Y	Y	Y	N	N
NEW HAMPSHIRE								
1 ***Smith***	N	Y	N	Y	Y	Y	Y	N
2 ***Gregg***	N	Y	N	N	Y	Y	Y	N
NEW JERSEY								
1 Florio	Y	Y	Y	Y	Y	N	N	Y
2 Hughes	N	Y	Y	Y	Y	N	Y	N
3 Howard	?	Y	Y	N	Y	N	N	N
4 ***Smith***	Y	Y	Y	Y	Y	N	N	N
5 ***Roukema***	N	N	N	Y	Y	Y	Y	N
6 Dwyer	Y	Y	Y	Y	Y	N	Y	Y
7 ***Rinaldo***	Y	Y	?	N	Y	N	N	N
8 Roe	Y	Y	Y	N	Y	N	N	Y
9 Torricelli	Y	Y	Y	N	Y	N	N	Y
10 Rodino	Y	Y	?	?	?	N	N	Y
11 ***Gallo***	N	Y	N	Y	Y	Y	N	N
12 ***Courter***	N	Y	N	N	Y	Y	Y	N
13 ***Saxton***	N	Y	N	Y	Y	Y	Y	N
14 Guarini	Y	Y	Y	N	Y	N	N	Y
NEW MEXICO								
1 ***Lujan***	N	N	Y	N	Y	Y	Y	N
2 ***Skeen***	N	X	N	Y	Y	Y	Y	N
3 Richardson	Y	N	Y	N	Y	N	Y	Y
NEW YORK								
1 ***Carney***	N	N	?	N	Y	Y	N	N
2 Downey	Y	Y	Y	N	Y	N	N	Y
3 Mrazek	Y	?	Y	N	Y	Y	Y	Y
4 ***Lent***	N	Y	Y	Y	Y	Y	Y	N
5 ***McGrath***	N	Y	N	N	Y	Y	N	N
6 Addabbo	?	?	?	?	?	?	?	?
7 Ackerman	Y	N	Y	N	Y	N	Y	Y
8 Scheuer	?	?	Y	N	?	N	Y	Y
9 Manton	?	Y	Y	Y	Y	N	N	Y
10 Schumer	Y	N	Y	N	Y	N	Y	Y
11 Towns	Y	Y	?	N	Y	N	N	Y
12 Owens	Y	Y	Y	N	Y	N	Y	Y
13 Solarz	Y	N	Y	N	Y	N	Y	Y
14 ***Molinari***	N	N	N	N	Y	N	N	Y
15 ***Green***	Y	Y	Y	N	Y	N	Y	Y
16 Rangel	Y	Y	Y	N	Y	N	Y	Y
17 Weiss	Y	Y	Y	N	Y	N	Y	Y
18 Garcia	Y	Y	?	N	Y	N	Y	Y
19 Biaggi	Y	Y	Y	N	Y	N	-	Y
20 ***DioGuardi***	N	Y	Y	Y	Y	Y	N	N
21 ***Fish***	N	Y	Y	N	Y	N	N	Y
22 ***Gilman***	N	N	Y	N	Y	N	N	Y
23 Stratton	Y	Y	Y	Y	Y	Y	Y	Y
24 ***Solomon***	N	N	N	N	Y	Y	N	N
25 ***Boehlert***	N	N	N	N	Y	Y	N	N
26 ***Martin***	N	N	N	N	Y	Y	N	N
27 ***Wortley***	N	N	Y	N	Y	Y	N	N
28 McHugh	Y	?	Y	Y	Y	N	Y	Y
29 ***Horton***	Y	Y	Y	N	Y	N	N	Y
30 ***Eckert***	N	Y	Y	N	Y	Y	N	N
31 ***Kemp***	N	N	Y	Y	?	Y	Y	N
32 LaFalce	Y	Y	Y	N	Y	N	Y	Y
33 Nowak	Y	Y	Y	N	Y	N	N	Y
34 Lundine	Y	N	Y	N	Y	N	Y	Y
NORTH CAROLINA								
1 Jones	Y	Y	Y	Y	Y	N	N	Y
2 Valentine	N	Y	Y	Y	Y	N	N	Y
3 Whitley	Y	N	Y	Y	Y	N	N	Y
4 ***Cobey***	N	Y	N	Y	Y	Y	N	N
5 Neal	Y	N	Y	Y	Y	N	Y	Y
6 ***Coble***	N	Y	?	Y	Y	Y	N	N
7 Rose	Y	N	?	Y	Y	N	N	Y
8 Hefner	Y	N	?	?	?	N	Y	Y
9 ***McMillan***	N	Y	Y	Y	?	Y	N	N
10 ***Broyhill***	N	Y	Y	Y	Y	Y	N	N
11 ***Hendon***	N	N	N	Y	Y	Y	N	N
NORTH DAKOTA								
AL Dorgan	Y	N	?	N	Y	N	Y	N
OHIO								
1 Luken	Y	?	Y	N	Y	N	N	Y
2 ***Gradison***	N	Y	Y	N	Y	Y	Y	N
3 Hall	Y	Y	?	Y	Y	N	N	Y
4 ***Oxley***	N	N	N	Y	Y	Y	N	N
5 ***Latta***	N	N	N	Y	Y	Y	N	N
6 ***McEwen***	N	N	N	N	N	Y	N	N
7 ***DeWine***	N	N	N	Y	Y	Y	Y	N
8 ***Kindness***	N	N	N	N	Y	Y	Y	N
9 Kaptur	Y	Y	Y	N	Y	N	Y	Y
10 ***Miller***	N	?	N	Y	Y	Y	N	N
11 Eckart	Y	Y	Y	N	Y	N	Y	Y
12 ***Kasich***	N	N	N	Y	Y	Y	Y	N
13 Pease	Y	N	Y	N	Y	N	Y	Y
14 Seiberling	Y	Y	?	N	?	N	Y	Y
15 ***Wylie***	N	N	Y	Y	Y	Y	N	N
16 ***Regula***	N	N	Y	N	Y	Y	Y	N
17 Traficant	Y	Y	Y	N	Y	N	N	N
18 Applegate	N	N	Y	N	Y	N	N	N
19 Feighan	N	Y	Y	N	Y	N	Y	Y
20 Oakar	Y	Y	?	N	Y	N	N	Y
21 Stokes	Y	Y	Y	Y	Y	N	Y	Y
OKLAHOMA								
1 Jones	N	N	Y	N	Y	Y	Y	Y
2 Synar	N	Y	Y	N	Y	N	Y	Y
3 Watkins	N	N	Y	N	Y	N	Y	N
4 McCurdy	Y	Y	Y	N	Y	Y	N	Y
5 ***Edwards***	N	?	N	Y	Y	Y	Y	N
6 English	N	N	Y	N	Y	Y	N	N
OREGON								
1 AuCoin	Y	Y	Y	Y	Y	N	Y	Y
2 ***Smith, R.***	N	N	N	N	Y	Y	N	N
3 Wyden	N	Y	Y	Y	Y	N	Y	Y
4 Weaver	?	?	?	?	?	N	Y	Y
5 ***Smith, D.***	N	Y	N	Y	Y	#	?	X
PENNSYLVANIA								
1 Foglietta	?	?	Y	N	Y	N	N	Y
2 Gray	Y	Y	Y	Y	Y	N	Y	Y
3 Borski	Y	Y	?	?	?	N	N	Y
4 Kolter	Y	Y	Y	N	Y	N	N	N
5 ***Schulze***	Y	N	Y	N	Y	Y	N	N
6 Yatron	Y	Y	Y	N	Y	Y	Y	N
7 Edgar	Y	Y	Y	?	?	N	N	Y
8 Kostmayer	N	Y	Y	N	Y	Y	Y	Y
9 ***Shuster***	N	N	N	N	Y	Y	N	N
10 ***McDade***	N	?	Y	N	Y	Y	Y	N
11 Kanjorski	Y	Y	Y	N	Y	N	N	N
12 Murtha	N	Y	Y	Y	Y	N	Y	Y
13 ***Coughlin***	Y	Y	N	Y	Y	Y	Y	N
14 Coyne	Y	Y	Y	N	Y	N	Y	Y
15 ***Ritter***	N	N	Y	N	Y	Y	N	N
16 ***Walker***	N	N	N	N	Y	Y	N	N
17 ***Gekas***	N	N	N	N	Y	Y	N	N
18 Walgren	Y	Y	?	?	?	N	Y	Y
19 ***Goodling***	N	N	N	N	Y	Y	N	N
20 Gaydos	Y	Y	Y	Y	Y	N	N	N
21 ***Ridge***	N	N	N	N	Y	Y	Y	N
22 Murphy	Y	Y	Y	N	Y	N	N	N
23 ***Clinger***	Y	N	Y	N	Y	Y	N	N
RHODE ISLAND								
1 St Germain	Y	Y	Y	N	?	N	N	Y
2 ***Schneider***	Y	Y	Y	Y	Y	Y	N	N
SOUTH CAROLINA								
1 ***Hartnett***	N	N	Y	N	Y	Y	N	N
2 ***Spence***	Y	N	N	Y	Y	Y	N	N
3 Derrick	Y	N	Y	Y	Y	N	Y	Y
4 ***Campbell***	N	N	N	?	?	Y	N	N
5 Spratt	Y	N	Y	Y	Y	N	Y	Y
6 Tallon	?	N	Y	Y	Y	N	N	Y
SOUTH DAKOTA								
AL Daschle	Y	N	Y	Y	Y	N	N	Y
TENNESSEE								
1 ***Quillen***	N	N	Y	Y	Y	Y	N	N
2 ***Duncan***	N	N	Y	N	Y	Y	N	N
3 Lloyd	Y	N	N	Y	Y	N	Y	Y
4 Cooper	Y	Y	Y	N	Y	N	Y	Y
5 Boner	Y	Y	Y	Y	Y	N	Y	Y
6 Gordon	N	N	Y	Y	Y	Y	Y	Y
7 ***Sundquist***	N	?	?	N	Y	Y	N	N
8 Jones	Y	N	Y	Y	Y	N	N	Y
9 Ford	Y	Y	Y	N	Y	N	Y	Y
TEXAS								
1 Chapman	Y	Y	Y	Y	Y	Y	N	Y
2 Wilson	?	Y	?	Y	?	N	Y	Y
3 ***Bartlett***	N	Y	N	Y	Y	Y	N	N
4 Hall, R.	N	N	Y	Y	Y	Y	N	Y
5 Bryant	Y	Y	Y	Y	Y	N	Y	Y
6 ***Barton***	Y	Y	N	Y	Y	Y	Y	N
7 ***Archer***	N	Y	Y	Y	?	Y	N	N
8 ***Fields***	N	Y	N	Y	Y	Y	N	N
9 Brooks	Y	Y	Y	Y	Y	N	Y	Y
10 Pickle	Y	Y	Y	Y	Y	N	Y	Y
11 Leath	N	N	?	Y	Y	Y	Y	Y
12 Wright	Y	Y	Y	Y	Y	N	N	Y
13 ***Boulter***	N	N	N	Y	Y	Y	N	N
14 ***Sweeney***	N	N	Y	Y	Y	Y	N	N
15 de la Garza	Y	N	Y	Y	?	N	Y	Y
16 Coleman	Y	?	Y	Y	Y	N	Y	Y
17 Stenholm	N	N	Y	Y	Y	Y	Y	Y
18 Leland	Y	Y	Y	Y	Y	N	Y	Y
19 ***Combest***	N	N	Y	Y	Y	Y	N	N
20 Gonzalez	Y	Y	Y	Y	Y	N	N	Y
21 ***Loeffler***	N	N	Y	Y	Y	Y	N	N
22 ***DeLay***	N	Y	?	Y	Y	Y	N	N
23 Bustamante	Y	N	Y	Y	Y	N	N	Y
24 Frost	Y	?	Y	Y	Y	N	N	Y
25 Andrews	Y	Y	Y	Y	Y	Y	N	Y
26 ***Armey***	N	N	N	Y	Y	Y	N	N
27 Ortiz	Y	Y	Y	Y	Y	N	N	Y
UTAH								
1 ***Hansen***	N	N	N	Y	Y	Y	N	N
2 ***Monson***	N	N	N	N	Y	Y	N	N
3 ***Nielson***	N	Y	Y	N	Y	Y	Y	N
VERMONT								
AL ***Jeffords***	N	Y	Y	Y	Y	N	Y	Y
VIRGINIA								
1 ***Bateman***	N	Y	Y	N	Y	Y	N	N
2 ***Whitehurst***	N	Y	Y	Y	Y	Y	N	N
3 ***Bliley***	N	Y	N	N	Y	Y	N	N
4 Sisisky	Y	Y	Y	Y	Y	N	N	Y
5 Daniel	N	N	Y	N	Y	Y	Y	N
6 Olin	N	N	Y	N	Y	Y	Y	N
7 ***Slaughter***	N	N	N	N	Y	Y	N	N
8 ***Parris***	N	Y	N	Y	Y	N	Y	Y
9 Boucher	?	N	Y	Y	Y	N	Y	Y
10 ***Wolf***	N	Y	N	Y	Y	N	Y	Y
WASHINGTON								
1 ***Miller***	N	N	Y	+	N	Y	Y	N
2 Swift	Y	Y	Y	N	Y	N	Y	Y
3 Bonker	Y	Y	Y	N	Y	N	N	Y
4 ***Morrison***	N	Y	Y	Y	Y	Y	N	N
5 Foley	Y	Y	Y	Y	Y	N	Y	Y
6 Dicks	Y	?	Y	Y	Y	N	Y	Y
7 Lowry	Y	Y	Y	N	Y	N	Y	Y
8 ***Chandler***	N	Y	N	Y	Y	Y	N	N
WEST VIRGINIA								
1 Mollohan	Y	N	Y	Y	Y	N	N	Y
2 Staggers	Y	N	Y	N	Y	N	N	Y
3 Wise	Y	Y	Y	N	Y	N	N	Y
4 Rahall	Y	N	Y	N	Y	N	N	Y
WISCONSIN								
1 Aspin	Y	Y	Y	N	Y	N	Y	Y
2 Kastenmeier	Y	Y	Y	N	Y	N	Y	N
3 ***Gunderson***	Y	N	N	Y	Y	Y	N	N
4 Kleczka	Y	Y	Y	Y	Y	N	N	Y
5 Moody	Y	Y	Y	N	Y	N	N	Y
6 ***Petri***	N	Y	N	N	Y	Y	N	N
7 Obey	Y	N	?	N	Y	N	Y	Y
8 ***Roth***	N	N	N	N	+	Y	N	N
9 ***Sensenbrenner***	N	Y	N	N	Y	Y	Y	N
WYOMING								
AL ***Cheney***	N	N	N	Y	Y	Y	Y	N

Southern states - Ala., Ark., Fla., Ga., Ky., La., Miss., N.C., Okla., S.C., Tenn., Texas, Va.

* The *Congressional Record* vote number is different from the CQ vote number because the *Record* includes quorum calls in its tally. CQ does not publish quorum call votes.

337. HR 3606. Defense Cost Reporting. Aspin, D-Wis., motion to suspend the rules and pass the bill to require the Department of Defense to keep certain data on manufacturers' labor costs. Motion agreed to 397-18: R 160-16; D 237-2 (ND 160-1, SD 77-1), Oct. 29, 1985. A two-thirds majority of those present and voting (277 in this case) is required for passage under suspension of the rules.

338. H Con Res 201. Handicapped Children Education Anniversary. Williams, D-Mont., motion to suspend the rules and adopt the concurrent resolution to commemorate the 10th anniversary of the enactment of the Education for All Handicapped Children Act (PL 94-142), which was signed into law on Nov. 29, 1975. Motion agreed to 404-1: R 172-1; D 232-0 (ND 156-0, SD 76-0), Oct. 29, 1985. A two-thirds majority of those present and voting (270 in this case) is required for adoption under suspension of the rules.

339. S 1160. Department of Defense Authorization, Fiscal 1986. Adoption of the rule (H Res 299) to provide for House floor consideration of the conference report on the bill to authorize $222,992,600,000 for military programs in fiscal 1986. Adopted 320-91: R 109-69; D 211-22 (ND 141-15, SD 70-7), Oct. 29, 1985. (The conference report subsequently was adopted by voice vote.)

340. HR 2942. Legislative Branch Appropriations, Fiscal 1986. Adoption of the conference report on the bill to appropriate $1,598,293,800 in fiscal 1986 for Congress and related agencies. Adopted 251-164: R 56-119; D 195-45 (ND 139-24, SD 56-21), Oct. 29, 1985.

341. HR 3629. Department of Defense Appropriations, Fiscal 1986. Frank, D-Mass., amendment to delete from the bill $1.7 billion for procurement of 12 MX missiles. Adopted 211-208: R 37-138; D 174-70 (ND 148-19, SD 26-51), Oct. 30, 1985. (The Frank amendment was subsequently rejected after the House rose from the Committee of the Whole *(see vote 342, below).*) A "nay" was a vote supporting the president's position.

342. HR 3629. Department of Defense Appropriations, Fiscal 1986. Frank, D-Mass., amendment to delete from the bill $1.7 billion for procurement of 12 MX missiles. Rejected 210-214: R 34-144; D 176-70 (ND 149-16, SD 27-54), Oct. 30, 1985. (The Frank amendment had been previously adopted in the Committee of the Whole *(see vote 341, above).*) A "nay" was a vote supporting the president's position.

343. HR 3629. Department of Defense Appropriations, Fiscal 1986. Passage of the bill to appropriate $268,850,600,000 in new budget authority and $7,747,700,000 in transfers from other accounts for Defense Department programs in fiscal 1986. Passed 359-67: R 168-10; D 191-57 (ND 112-55, SD 79-2), Oct. 30, 1985. (The president had requested $303,954,033,000 in new budget authority.)

344. Procedural Motion. Mack, R-Fla., motion to approve the House *Journal* of Wednesday, Oct. 30. Motion agreed to 267-127: R 55-113; D 212-14 (ND 140-12, SD 72-2), Oct. 31, 1985.

KEY

- Y Voted for (yea).
- # Paired for.
- + Announced for.
- N Voted against (nay).
- X Paired against.
- - Announced against.
- P Voted "present."
- C Voted "present" to avoid possible conflict of interest.
- ? Did not vote or otherwise make a position known.

Democrats ***Republicans***

	337	338	339	340	341	342	343	344
ALABAMA								
1 ***Callahan***	Y	Y	Y	N	N	N	Y	N
2 ***Dickinson***	N	Y	Y	N	?	N	Y	N
3 Nichols	Y	Y	Y	Y	N	N	Y	?
4 Bevill	Y	Y	Y	Y	N	N	Y	Y
5 Flippo	Y	Y	Y	Y	N	N	Y	Y
6 Erdreich	Y	Y	Y	N	N	N	Y	Y
7 Shelby	Y	Y	Y	N	N	N	Y	?
ALASKA								
AL ***Young***	Y	Y	Y	#	N	N	Y	N
ARIZONA								
1 ***McCain***	Y	Y	Y	N	?	?	?	Y
2 Udall	Y	Y	Y	Y	Y	Y	Y	N
3 ***Stump***	N	Y	Y	N	N	N	Y	Y
4 ***Rudd***	Y	Y	Y	Y	N	N	N	Y
5 ***Kolbe***	?	?	?	X	N	N	Y	N
ARKANSAS								
1 Alexander	Y	Y	Y	Y	N	N	Y	Y
2 Robinson	Y	Y	Y	N	N	N	Y	Y
3 ***Hammerschmidt***	Y	Y	Y	N	N	N	Y	Y
4 Anthony	Y	Y	Y	Y	Y	Y	Y	Y
CALIFORNIA								
1 Bosco	Y	Y	Y	Y	Y	Y	Y	Y
2 ***Chappie***	N	Y	N	N	N	N	Y	N
3 Matsui	Y	Y	Y	Y	Y	Y	Y	Y
4 Fazio	Y	Y	Y	Y	N	N	Y	Y
5 Burton	Y	Y	Y	Y	Y	Y	N	?
6 Boxer	Y	Y	Y	Y	Y	Y	N	Y
7 Miller	Y	Y	N	Y	Y	Y	N	Y
8 Dellums	Y	Y	Y	Y	Y	Y	N	Y
9 Stark	Y	Y	N	Y	Y	Y	N	Y
10 Edwards	Y	Y	Y	Y	Y	Y	N	Y
11 Lantos	Y	Y	Y	Y	Y	Y	Y	Y
12 ***Zschau***	N	Y	Y	N	Y	Y	Y	N
13 Mineta	Y	Y	Y	Y	Y	Y	N	Y
14 ***Shumway***	Y	Y	N	N	N	N	Y	Y
15 Coelho	Y	Y	Y	Y	Y	Y	Y	Y
16 Panetta	Y	Y	Y	Y	Y	Y	Y	Y
17 ***Pashayan***	Y	Y	Y	N	N	N	Y	Y
18 Lehman	Y	Y	Y	Y	Y	Y	N	Y
19 ***Lagomarsino***	Y	Y	Y	N	N	N	Y	N
20 ***Thomas***	Y	Y	Y	N	N	N	Y	N
21 ***Fiedler***	Y	Y	Y	N	N	N	Y	N
22 ***Moorhead***	Y	Y	Y	N	N	N	Y	N
23 Beilenson	Y	Y	Y	Y	Y	Y	N	Y
24 Waxman	Y	Y	Y	Y	Y	Y	N	Y
25 Roybal	Y	Y	Y	Y	Y	Y	N	?
26 Berman	Y	Y	Y	Y	Y	Y	Y	Y
27 Levine	Y	Y	Y	Y	Y	Y	Y	Y
28 Dixon	Y	Y	?	Y	Y	Y	Y	?
29 Hawkins	Y	Y	Y	Y	Y	Y	Y	Y
30 Martinez	Y	Y	Y	Y	Y	Y	Y	Y
31 Dymally	Y	Y	Y	Y	Y	Y	N	P
32 Anderson	Y	Y	Y	Y	N	N	Y	Y
33 ***Dreier***	Y	Y	N	N	N	N	Y	Y
34 Torres	+	+	+	+	Y	Y	N	Y
35 ***Lewis***	Y	?	Y	Y	N	N	Y	N
36 Brown	Y	Y	Y	Y	Y	Y	Y	Y
37 ***McCandless***	N	Y	N	N	N	N	Y	N
38 ***Dornan***	Y	Y	N	N	N	N	Y	N
39 ***Dannemeyer***	Y	Y	N	N	N	N	Y	N
40 ***Badham***	N	Y	Y	Y	N	N	Y	N
41 ***Lowery***	Y	Y	Y	Y	N	N	Y	N
42 ***Lungren***	Y	Y	Y	N	N	N	Y	N
43 ***Packard***	Y	Y	N	N	N	N	Y	Y
44 Bates	Y	Y	Y	Y	Y	Y	N	Y
45 ***Hunter***	Y	Y	Y	N	N	N	Y	?
COLORADO								
1 Schroeder	Y	Y	Y	N	Y	Y	N	N
2 Wirth	Y	Y	Y	?	Y	Y	Y	Y
3 ***Strang***	Y	Y	N	N	N	N	Y	N
4 ***Brown***	Y	Y	N	N	N	N	N	N
5 ***Kramer***	Y	Y	Y	N	N	N	Y	N
6 ***Schaefer***	Y	Y	N	N	N	N	Y	N
CONNECTICUT								
1 Kennelly	Y	Y	Y	Y	Y	Y	Y	Y
2 Gejdenson	Y	Y	Y	Y	Y	Y	Y	Y
3 Morrison	?	?	?	?	Y	Y	Y	Y
4 ***McKinney***	Y	?	Y	Y	Y	Y	N	N
5 ***Rowland***	Y	Y	N	N	N	N	Y	N
6 ***Johnson***	Y	Y	Y	Y	Y	Y	Y	Y
DELAWARE								
AL Carper	Y	Y	Y	Y	Y	Y	Y	Y
FLORIDA								
1 Hutto	Y	Y	Y	Y	N	N	Y	Y
2 Fuqua	Y	Y	Y	Y	N	N	Y	Y
3 Bennett	Y	Y	Y	N	Y	Y	Y	Y
4 Chappell	Y	Y	Y	Y	N	N	Y	Y
5 ***McCollum***	Y	Y	Y	N	N	N	Y	Y
6 MacKay	Y	Y	Y	Y	Y	Y	Y	Y
7 Gibbons	Y	Y	Y	Y	Y	Y	Y	Y
8 ***Young***	Y	Y	Y	Y	N	N	Y	N
9 ***Bilirakis***	Y	Y	N	N	N	N	Y	N
10 ***Ireland***	Y	Y	N	N	N	N	Y	N
11 Nelson	+	+	+	#	X	X	#	+
12 ***Lewis***	Y	Y	Y	N	N	N	Y	N
13 ***Mack***	Y	Y	N	N	N	N	Y	N
14 Mica	Y	Y	Y	Y	N	N	Y	Y
15 ***Shaw***	Y	Y	N	N	N	N	Y	N
16 Smith	Y	Y	Y	Y	Y	Y	Y	Y
17 Lehman	?	?	?	Y	Y	Y	Y	Y
18 Pepper	Y	+	Y	Y	Y	N	Y	Y
19 Fascell	Y	Y	Y	Y	N	N	Y	Y
GEORGIA								
1 Thomas	Y	?	Y	Y	N	N	Y	Y
2 Hatcher	Y	Y	Y	?	?	N	Y	Y
3 Ray	Y	Y	Y	Y	N	N	Y	Y
4 ***Swindall***	Y	Y	Y	N	N	N	Y	N
5 Fowler	Y	Y	Y	Y	?	Y	Y	Y
6 ***Gingrich***	Y	Y	N	N	N	N	Y	N
7 Darden	Y	Y	Y	Y	N	N	Y	Y
8 Rowland	Y	Y	Y	?	N	N	Y	Y
9 Jenkins	Y	Y	Y	Y	Y	Y	Y	Y
10 Barnard	Y	Y	Y	N	N	N	Y	Y
HAWAII								
1 Heftel	Y	Y	Y	Y	Y	Y	Y	?
2 Akaka	Y	Y	Y	Y	N	?	Y	Y
IDAHO								
1 ***Craig***	Y	Y	N	N	N	N	Y	N
2 Stallings	Y	Y	Y	N	N	Y	Y	Y
ILLINOIS								
1 Hayes	Y	Y	Y	Y	Y	Y	N	N
2 Savage	Y	Y	Y	Y	Y	Y	N	Y
3 Russo	Y	Y	Y	Y	Y	Y	N	Y
4 ***O'Brien***	Y	Y	Y	Y	N	N	Y	?
5 Lipinski	Y	Y	Y	Y	Y	Y	Y	Y
6 ***Hyde***	Y	Y	Y	Y	N	N	Y	Y
7 Collins	?	?	?	#	#	#	X	?
8 Rostenkowski	Y	Y	Y	Y	Y	Y	Y	Y
9 Yates	Y	Y	Y	Y	Y	Y	N	Y
10 ***Porter***	Y	Y	Y	Y	N	N	Y	Y
11 Annunzio	Y	Y	Y	Y	Y	Y	Y	Y
12 ***Crane***	Y	N	N	N	N	N	Y	N
13 ***Fawell***	Y	Y	N	Y	N	N	Y	N
14 ***Grotberg***	N	Y	Y	Y	N	N	Y	N
15 ***Madigan***	Y	Y	Y	Y	N	N	Y	N
16 ***Martin***	Y	Y	Y	N	N	N	Y	N
17 Evans	Y	Y	Y	Y	Y	Y	Y	Y
18 ***Michel***	Y	Y	Y	Y	N	N	Y	Y
19 Bruce	Y	Y	Y	Y	Y	Y	Y	Y
20 Durbin	Y	Y	Y	Y	Y	Y	Y	N
21 Price	Y	Y	Y	Y	N	N	Y	Y
22 Gray	Y	Y	Y	Y	Y	+	+	Y
INDIANA								
1 Visclosky	Y	Y	Y	Y	Y	Y	Y	Y
2 Sharp	Y	Y	Y	N	Y	Y	Y	Y
3 ***Hiler***	Y	Y	Y	N	N	N	Y	N
4 ***Coats***	Y	Y	Y	N	N	N	Y	N
5 ***Hillis***	Y	Y	Y	Y	N	N	Y	Y

ND - Northern Democrats SD - Southern Democrats

* Corresponding to Congressional Record Votes 373, 374, 375, 376, 377, 378, 379, 380

	337	338	339	340	341	342	343	344
6 ***Burton***	Y	Y	Y	N	N	N	Y	N
7 ***Myers***	Y	Y	Y	Y	N	N	Y	Y
8 McCloskey	Y	Y	Y	Y	Y	Y	Y	Y
9 Hamilton	Y	Y	Y	Y	Y	Y	Y	Y
10 Jacobs	Y	Y	N	N	Y	Y	Y	N
IOWA								
1 ***Leach***	Y	Y	N	N	Y	Y	N	N
2 ***Tauke***	Y	Y	N	N	Y	Y	N	N
3 ***Evans***	N	Y	N	N	Y	Y	N	N
4 Smith	Y	Y	N	Y	Y	Y	N	Y
5 ***Lightfoot***	Y	Y	N	N	Y	Y	N	N
6 Bedell	Y	Y	N	Y	Y	Y	N	Y
KANSAS								
1 ***Roberts***	Y	Y	N	N	Y	Y	?	N
2 Slattery	Y	Y	Y	N	Y	Y	Y	Y
3 ***Meyers***	Y	Y	N	N	Y	Y	Y	N
4 Glickman	Y	Y	Y	N	Y	Y	Y	Y
5 ***Whittaker***	Y	Y	Y	N	Y	Y	Y	N
KENTUCKY								
1 Hubbard	Y	Y	N	N	N	N	Y	Y
2 Natcher	Y	Y	Y	Y	N	N	Y	Y
3 Mazzoli	Y	Y	+	+	Y	Y	Y	Y
4 ***Snyder***	Y	Y	Y	Y	N	N	Y	Y
5 ***Rogers***	Y	Y	N	Y	N	N	Y	N
6 ***Hopkins***	Y	Y	N	N	Y	Y	Y	Y
7 Perkins	Y	Y	Y	Y	Y	Y	N	Y
LOUISIANA								
1 ***Livingston***	Y	Y	Y	Y	N	N	Y	Y
2 Boggs	Y	Y	Y	Y	Y	Y	Y	Y
3 Tauzin	Y	Y	Y	N	N	N	Y	?
4 Roemer	Y	Y	N	N	Y	Y	Y	N
5 Huckaby	Y	Y	Y	Y	N	N	Y	Y
6 ***Moore***	Y	Y	Y	N	N	N	Y	Y
7 Breaux	Y	Y	N	N	N	N	Y	Y
8 Long	Y	Y	Y	Y	Y	Y	Y	Y
MAINE								
1 ***McKernan***	Y	Y	Y	N	Y	Y	Y	N
2 ***Snowe***	Y	Y	Y	Y	Y	Y	Y	N
MARYLAND								
1 Dyson	Y	Y	Y	Y	N	N	Y	Y
2 ***Bentley***	Y	Y	N	Y	N	N	Y	N
3 Mikulski	Y	?	?	N	Y	Y	Y	Y
4 ***Holt***	Y	Y	Y	Y	N	N	Y	N
5 Hoyer	?	?	?	Y	N	N	Y	Y
6 Byron	Y	?	?	Y	N	N	Y	Y
7 Mitchell	?	?	Y	Y	Y	Y	N	N
8 Barnes	?	?	?	Y	Y	Y	Y	Y
MASSACHUSETTS								
1 ***Conte***	Y	Y	Y	Y	Y	+	Y	N
2 Boland	Y	Y	Y	Y	Y	Y	Y	Y
3 Early	Y	Y	N	Y	Y	Y	Y	Y
4 Frank	Y	Y	Y	Y	Y	Y	N	Y
5 Atkins	Y	Y	Y	Y	Y	Y	Y	Y
6 Mavroules	Y	Y	Y	Y	Y	Y	Y	Y
7 Markey	Y	Y	Y	Y	Y	Y	N	Y
8 O'Neill								
9 Moakley	Y	Y	Y	Y	Y	Y	Y	Y
10 Studds	Y	Y	Y	Y	Y	Y	N	Y
11 Donnelly	Y	Y	Y	Y	Y	Y	Y	Y
MICHIGAN								
1 Conyers	Y	?	Y	Y	Y	Y	N	Y
2 ***Pursell***	Y	Y	N	N	N	N	Y	N
3 Wolpe	Y	Y	Y	Y	Y	Y	Y	Y
4 ***Siljander***	Y	Y	N	N	N	N	Y	N
5 ***Henry***	Y	Y	N	Y	Y	Y	Y	Y
6 Carr	Y	Y	Y	N	Y	Y	Y	Y
7 Kildee	Y	Y	Y	Y	Y	Y	N	Y
8 Traxler	Y	Y	Y	Y	Y	Y	Y	Y
9 ***Vander Jagt***	Y	Y	Y	N	N	N	Y	N
10 ***Schuette***	Y	Y	Y	N	N	N	Y	N
11 ***Davis***	Y	Y	Y	Y	N	N	Y	Y
12 Bonior	Y	Y	Y	Y	Y	Y	Y	Y
13 Crockett	Y	Y	N	Y	Y	Y	N	Y
14 Hertel	Y	Y	Y	N	Y	Y	N	Y
15 Ford	Y	Y	Y	Y	Y	Y	N	?
16 Dingell	Y	Y	Y	Y	Y	Y	Y	?
17 Levin	Y	Y	Y	Y	Y	Y	Y	Y
18 ***Broomfield***	Y	Y	N	N	N	N	Y	Y
MINNESOTA								
1 Penny	Y	Y	N	N	Y	Y	Y	N
2 ***Weber***	?	?	?	X	N	N	Y	?
3 ***Frenzel***	Y	Y	N	N	?	N	N	Y
4 Vento	Y	Y	Y	Y	Y	Y	N	Y
5 Sabo	Y	Y	Y	Y	Y	Y	Y	Y
6 Sikorski	Y	Y	Y	N	Y	Y	Y	N
7 ***Stangeland***	Y	Y	N	N	Y	N	Y	N
8 Oberstar	Y	Y	Y	Y	Y	Y	N	Y
MISSISSIPPI								
1 Whitten	Y	Y	Y	Y	N	N	Y	Y
2 ***Franklin***	Y	Y	Y	Y	N	N	Y	Y
3 Montgomery	Y	Y	Y	Y	N	N	Y	Y
4 Dowdy	?	?	?	?	?	N	Y	Y
5 ***Lott***	Y	Y	Y	N	N	N	Y	Y
MISSOURI								
1 Clay	Y	Y	?	Y	Y	Y	N	N
2 Young	Y	Y	Y	Y	Y	Y	Y	Y
3 Gephardt	Y	Y	Y	Y	Y	Y	Y	Y
4 Skelton	Y	Y	Y	Y	N	N	Y	Y
5 Wheat	Y	Y	Y	Y	Y	Y	N	Y
6 ***Coleman***	Y	Y	N	Y	N	N	Y	N
7 ***Taylor***	Y	Y	Y	Y	N	N	Y	Y
8 ***Emerson***	Y	Y	Y	N	N	N	Y	?
9 Volkmer	Y	Y	N	N	Y	Y	Y	N
MONTANA								
1 Williams	Y	Y	Y	Y	Y	Y	Y	?
2 ***Marlenee***	?	?	?	?	?	?	?	?
NEBRASKA								
1 ***Bereuter***	Y	Y	N	N	Y	Y	Y	N
2 ***Daub***	Y	Y	N	N	N	N	Y	N
3 ***Smith***	Y	Y	N	Y	Y	Y	Y	Y
NEVADA								
1 Reid	Y	Y	Y	Y	N	N	Y	Y
2 ***Vucanovich***	Y	Y	N	N	N	N	Y	N
NEW HAMPSHIRE								
1 ***Smith***	Y	Y	N	N	N	N	Y	N
2 ***Gregg***	Y	Y	N	N	N	N	Y	N
NEW JERSEY								
1 Florio	Y	Y	Y	Y	Y	Y	Y	Y
2 Hughes	Y	Y	Y	N	Y	Y	Y	Y
3 Howard	Y	Y	Y	Y	Y	Y	Y	Y
4 ***Smith***	Y	Y	Y	Y	Y	Y	Y	Y
5 ***Roukema***	Y	Y	Y	N	Y	Y	Y	N
6 Dwyer	Y	Y	Y	Y	Y	Y	Y	Y
7 ***Rinaldo***	?	?	Y	Y	N	N	Y	Y
8 Roe	Y	Y	Y	Y	Y	Y	Y	Y
9 Torricelli	Y	Y	Y	Y	Y	Y	Y	Y
10 Rodino	Y	Y	Y	Y	Y	Y	N	Y
11 ***Gallo***	Y	Y	Y	Y	N	N	Y	N
12 ***Courter***	Y	Y	Y	Y	N	N	Y	N
13 ***Saxton***	Y	Y	Y	N	Y	Y	Y	Y
14 Guarini	Y	Y	Y	Y	Y	Y	Y	Y
NEW MEXICO								
1 ***Lujan***	Y	Y	Y	N	N	N	Y	Y
2 ***Skeen***	Y	Y	Y	Y	N	N	Y	N
3 Richardson	Y	Y	Y	Y	Y	Y	Y	Y
NEW YORK								
1 ***Carney***	Y	Y	Y	Y	N	N	Y	N
2 Downey	Y	Y	Y	Y	Y	Y	Y	Y
3 Mrazek	Y	Y	Y	Y	Y	Y	Y	Y
4 ***Lent***	Y	Y	Y	Y	N	N	Y	N
5 ***McGrath***	Y	Y	Y	Y	N	N	Y	N
6 Addabbo	?	?	?	?	?	?	?	?
7 Ackerman	Y	Y	Y	Y	Y	Y	N	Y
8 Scheuer	Y	Y	Y	Y	Y	Y	Y	Y
9 Manton	Y	Y	Y	Y	?	Y	Y	?
10 Schumer	Y	Y	Y	Y	Y	Y	Y	Y
11 Towns	Y	Y	Y	Y	Y	Y	N	Y
12 Owens	Y	?	Y	Y	Y	Y	N	?
13 Solarz	Y	Y	Y	Y	Y	Y	Y	Y
14 ***Molinari***	Y	Y	Y	Y	N	N	Y	N
15 ***Green***	Y	Y	Y	Y	Y	Y	Y	Y
16 Rangel	Y	Y	Y	Y	Y	Y	N	Y
17 Weiss	Y	Y	Y	Y	Y	Y	N	Y
18 Garcia	Y	Y	Y	Y	Y	Y	N	?
19 Biaggi	Y	Y	Y	Y	Y	Y	Y	Y
20 ***DioGuardi***	Y	Y	N	N	Y	Y	Y	Y
21 ***Fish***	Y	Y	Y	Y	N	N	Y	Y
22 ***Gilman***	Y	Y	Y	Y	N	N	Y	Y
23 Stratton	N	Y	Y	Y	N	N	Y	Y
24 ***Solomon***	N	Y	Y	N	N	N	Y	N
25 ***Boehlert***	Y	Y	Y	Y	Y	Y	Y	Y
26 ***Martin***	Y	Y	Y	N	N	N	Y	N
27 ***Wortley***	Y	Y	Y	Y	N	N	Y	?
28 McHugh	Y	Y	Y	Y	Y	Y	Y	Y
29 ***Horton***	Y	Y	Y	Y	Y	Y	Y	Y
30 ***Eckert***	?	Y	N	N	N	N	Y	Y
31 ***Kemp***	Y	Y	Y	N	N	N	Y	Y
32 LaFalce	Y	Y	Y	Y	Y	Y	Y	?
33 Nowak	Y	Y	Y	?	Y	Y	Y	Y
34 Lundine	Y	Y	Y	Y	Y	Y	N	Y
NORTH CAROLINA								
1 Jones	Y	Y	Y	Y	Y	Y	Y	Y
2 Valentine	Y	Y	Y	Y	N	N	Y	Y
3 Whitley	Y	Y	Y	Y	N	N	Y	Y
4 ***Cobey***	N	Y	N	N	N	N	Y	N
5 Neal	Y	Y	Y	Y	N	N	Y	?
6 ***Coble***	N	Y	N	N	N	N	Y	N
7 Rose	Y	Y	Y	Y	N	N	Y	Y
8 Hefner	Y	Y	Y	Y	N	N	Y	Y
9 ***McMillan***	Y	Y	Y	X	N	N	Y	Y
10 ***Broyhill***	Y	Y	Y	N	N	N	Y	Y
11 ***Hendon***	Y	Y	Y	N	N	N	Y	N
NORTH DAKOTA								
AL Dorgan	Y	Y	Y	N	Y	Y	N	Y
OHIO								
1 Luken	Y	Y	N	Y	Y	Y	Y	Y
2 ***Gradison***	Y	Y	Y	N	Y	Y	Y	Y
3 Hall	Y	Y	Y	Y	Y	Y	Y	Y
4 ***Oxley***	Y	Y	Y	?	N	N	Y	N
5 ***Latta***	Y	Y	Y	N	N	N	Y	N
6 ***McEwen***	Y	Y	N	N	N	N	Y	N
7 ***DeWine***	Y	Y	N	N	N	N	Y	N
8 ***Kindness***	Y	Y	N	N	N	N	Y	N
9 Kaptur	?	?	Y	N	Y	Y	Y	Y
10 ***Miller***	Y	Y	Y	N	N	N	Y	N
11 Eckart	Y	Y	Y	N	Y	Y	Y	Y
12 ***Kasich***	Y	?	N	N	N	N	Y	N
13 Pease	Y	Y	Y	Y	Y	Y	Y	Y
14 Seiberling	Y	Y	N	Y	Y	Y	N	Y
15 ***Wylie***	Y	Y	Y	N	N	N	Y	Y
16 ***Regula***	Y	Y	Y	Y	N	N	Y	Y
17 Traficant	Y	Y	Y	Y	Y	Y	N	N
18 Applegate	Y	Y	Y	N	Y	Y	Y	Y
19 Feighan	Y	Y	Y	N	Y	Y	Y	Y
20 Oakar	Y	Y	Y	Y	Y	Y	Y	?
21 Stokes	Y	Y	?	Y	Y	Y	N	Y
OKLAHOMA								
1 Jones	Y	Y	N	N	Y	Y	Y	Y
2 Synar	Y	Y	Y	Y	Y	Y	Y	Y
3 Watkins	Y	Y	N	Y	Y	Y	Y	Y
4 McCurdy	Y	Y	Y	N	N	N	Y	Y
5 ***Edwards***	Y	Y	N	N	N	N	Y	N
6 English	Y	Y	N	N	N	N	Y	Y
OREGON								
1 AuCoin	Y	Y	?	N	Y	Y	Y	?
2 ***Smith, R.***	Y	?	Y	N	N	N	Y	N
3 Wyden	Y	Y	Y	N	Y	Y	Y	Y
4 Weaver	Y	Y	N	Y	Y	Y	N	Y
5 ***Smith, D.***	Y	Y	N	N	N	N	Y	N
PENNSYLVANIA								
1 Foglietta	Y	Y	Y	Y	Y	Y	Y	Y
2 Gray	?	?	?	?	Y	Y	Y	Y
3 Borski	Y	Y	Y	Y	Y	Y	Y	Y
4 Kolter	Y	Y	Y	N	N	N	Y	Y
5 ***Schulze***	Y	Y	Y	Y	N	N	Y	Y
6 Yatron	Y	Y	Y	N	N	N	Y	Y
7 Edgar	Y	Y	N	Y	Y	Y	Y	Y
8 Kostmayer	Y	Y	Y	Y	Y	Y	Y	Y
9 ***Shuster***	Y	Y	Y	N	N	N	Y	N
10 ***McDade***	Y	Y	Y	Y	N	N	Y	Y
11 Kanjorski	Y	Y	Y	N	Y	Y	Y	Y
12 Murtha	Y	Y	Y	Y	N	N	Y	Y
13 ***Coughlin***	Y	Y	Y	Y	Y	Y	Y	N
14 Coyne	Y	Y	Y	Y	Y	Y	Y	Y
15 ***Ritter***	Y	Y	Y	N	N	N	Y	Y
16 ***Walker***	N	Y	N	N	N	N	Y	N
17 ***Gekas***	Y	Y	N	N	N	N	Y	N
18 Walgren	Y	Y	N	Y	Y	Y	Y	Y
19 ***Goodling***	Y	Y	N	N	Y	Y	Y	?
20 Gaydos	Y	Y	Y	Y	N	N	Y	?
21 ***Ridge***	Y	Y	N	N	Y	Y	Y	?
22 Murphy	Y	Y	Y	Y	N	Y	N	Y
23 ***Clinger***	+	+	-	+	N	N	Y	N
RHODE ISLAND								
1 St Germain	Y	Y	Y	Y	Y	Y	Y	Y
2 ***Schneider***	Y	Y	Y	Y	Y	Y	N	Y
SOUTH CAROLINA								
1 ***Hartnett***	N	Y	Y	N	N	N	Y	Y
2 ***Spence***	Y	Y	Y	N	N	N	Y	N
3 Derrick	Y	Y	Y	N	N	N	Y	Y
4 ***Campbell***	Y	Y	Y	Y	N	N	Y	?
5 Spratt	Y	Y	Y	Y	N	N	Y	Y
6 Tallon	Y	Y	Y	N	N	N	Y	Y
SOUTH DAKOTA								
AL Daschle	Y	Y	Y	Y	Y	Y	Y	Y
TENNESSEE								
1 ***Quillen***	Y	Y	Y	N	N	N	Y	Y
2 ***Duncan***	Y	Y	Y	N	N	N	Y	Y
3 Lloyd	Y	Y	Y	N	N	N	Y	N
4 Cooper	Y	Y	Y	Y	N	N	Y	Y
5 Boner	Y	Y	Y	Y	N	N	Y	Y
6 Gordon	Y	Y	Y	Y	Y	Y	Y	Y
7 ***Sundquist***	N	Y	N	N	N	N	Y	N
8 Jones	Y	Y	Y	Y	N	N	Y	Y
9 Ford	Y	Y	Y	Y	?	Y	Y	Y
TEXAS								
1 Chapman	Y	Y	Y	N	N	N	Y	Y
2 Wilson	Y	Y	Y	Y	N	N	Y	?
3 ***Bartlett***	N	Y	N	N	N	N	Y	N
4 Hall, R.	N	Y	Y	N	N	N	Y	Y
5 Bryant	Y	Y	Y	Y	Y	Y	Y	Y
6 ***Barton***	Y	Y	N	N	N	N	Y	N
7 ***Archer***	Y	Y	Y	N	N	N	Y	Y
8 ***Fields***	Y	Y	N	N	N	N	Y	N
9 Brooks	Y	Y	Y	Y	N	N	Y	Y
10 Pickle	Y	Y	Y	Y	Y	Y	Y	Y
11 Leath	Y	Y	Y	Y	N	N	Y	Y
12 Wright	?	?	?	Y	Y	Y	Y	Y
13 ***Boulter***	Y	Y	Y	N	N	N	Y	N
14 ***Sweeney***	Y	Y	Y	Y	?	N	Y	?
15 de la Garza	Y	Y	Y	Y	N	N	Y	Y
16 Coleman	Y	Y	Y	Y	N	N	Y	Y
17 Stenholm	Y	Y	N	N	N	N	Y	Y
18 Leland	Y	Y	Y	Y	Y	Y	N	?
19 ***Combest***	Y	Y	Y	N	N	N	Y	Y
20 Gonzalez	Y	Y	Y	Y	Y	Y	Y	Y
21 ***Loeffler***	Y	Y	Y	N	N	N	Y	N
22 ***DeLay***	Y	Y	N	N	N	N	Y	N
23 Bustamante	Y	Y	Y	Y	N	N	Y	Y
24 Frost	Y	Y	Y	Y	N	N	Y	Y
25 Andrews	Y	Y	Y	Y	N	N	Y	Y
26 ***Armey***	N	Y	N	N	?	N	Y	N
27 Ortiz	Y	Y	Y	Y	N	N	Y	Y
UTAH								
1 ***Hansen***	Y	Y	N	N	N	N	Y	Y
2 ***Monson***	Y	Y	N	N	N	N	N	N
3 ***Nielson***	Y	Y	N	N	N	N	Y	N
VERMONT								
AL ***Jeffords***	Y	Y	N	Y	Y	Y	Y	Y
VIRGINIA								
1 ***Bateman***	Y	Y	Y	N	N	N	Y	+
2 ***Whitehurst***	Y	Y	Y	Y	N	N	Y	N
3 ***Bliley***	Y	Y	N	Y	N	N	Y	N
4 Sisisky	Y	Y	Y	Y	Y	Y	Y	Y
5 Daniel	Y	Y	Y	N	N	N	Y	?
6 Olin	Y	Y	Y	N	Y	Y	Y	Y
7 ***Slaughter***	Y	Y	Y	Y	N	N	Y	N
8 ***Parris***	Y	Y	Y	Y	?	?	?	?
9 Boucher	Y	Y	Y	Y	Y	Y	Y	Y
10 ***Wolf***	Y	Y	Y	Y	N	N	Y	N
WASHINGTON								
1 ***Miller***	Y	Y	Y	N	Y	Y	Y	?
2 Swift	Y	Y	N	Y	Y	Y	N	?
3 Bonker	Y	Y	Y	Y	Y	?	N	Y
4 ***Morrison***	Y	Y	Y	N	N	N	Y	N
5 Foley	Y	?	P	Y	Y	Y	Y	Y
6 Dicks	Y	Y	Y	Y	N	N	Y	Y
7 Lowry	Y	Y	Y	Y	Y	Y	N	N
8 ***Chandler***	Y	Y	Y	N	Y	N	Y	N
WEST VIRGINIA								
1 Mollohan	Y	Y	Y	Y	N	N	Y	Y
2 Staggers	Y	Y	Y	Y	Y	Y	Y	Y
3 Wise	Y	Y	Y	N	Y	Y	Y	Y
4 Rahall	Y	Y	Y	Y	Y	Y	N	Y
WISCONSIN								
1 Aspin	Y	Y	Y	Y	N	N	Y	Y
2 Kastenmeier	Y	Y	Y	Y	Y	Y	N	Y
3 ***Gunderson***	Y	Y	N	N	Y	Y	Y	N
4 Kleczka	Y	Y	Y	Y	Y	Y	Y	Y
5 Moody	Y	Y	Y	Y	Y	Y	N	Y
6 ***Petri***	Y	Y	Y	N	Y	Y	Y	Y
7 Obey	Y	Y	Y	Y	Y	Y	N	Y
8 ***Roth***	Y	Y	N	N	Y	Y	Y	N
9 ***Sensenbrenner***	Y	Y	N	N	Y	Y	Y	N
WYOMING								
AL ***Cheney***	Y	Y	Y	N	N	N	Y	?

Southern states - Ala., Ark., Fla., Ga., Ky., La., Miss., N.C., Okla., S.C., Tenn., Texas, Va.

* The *Congressional Record* vote number is different from the CQ vote number because the *Record* includes quorum calls in its tally. CQ does not publish quorum call votes.

CQ House Votes 345 - 350

345. HR 3128. Deficit-Reduction Amendments. Derrick, D-S.C., motion to order the previous question (thus ending debate and the possibility of amendment) on the rule (H Res 301) to provide for House floor consideration of the bill to reduce the deficit by $19.5 billion over fiscal 1986-88 through spending reductions in the Medicare program; tax increases on tobacco products, imports, coal manufacturers and employers participating in a federal pension plan; and user fees for Customs inspections. The bill would also make changes in the Aid to Families with Dependent Children program, and reauthorize the Trade Adjustment Assistance program and related trade agencies. Motion agreed to 219-205: R 0-178; D 219-27 (ND 154-13, SD 65-14), Oct. 31, 1985. (The rule was subsequently adopted by voice vote.)

346. HR 3128. Deficit-Reduction Amendments. Gradison, R-Ohio, motion to recommit the bill to the Ways and Means Committee with instructions to delete eight provisions that would require $954 million in new spending over fiscal 1986-88. Motion rejected 183-238: R 165-10; D 18-228 (ND 2-166, SD 16-62), Oct. 31, 1985.

347. HR 3128. Deficit-Reduction Amendments. Passage of the bill to reduce the deficit $19.5 billion over fiscal 1986-88 through spending reductions in the Medicare program; tax increases on tobacco products, imports, coal manufacturers and employers participating in a federal pension plan; and user fees for Customs inspections. The bill would also make changes in the Aid to Families with Dependent Children program and reauthorize the Trade Adjustment Assistance program and related trade agencies. Passed 245-174: R 24-150; D 221-24 (ND 151-15, SD 70-9), Oct. 31, 1985. A "nay" was a vote supporting the president's position.

348. Procedural Motion. Craig, R-Idaho, motion to approve the House *Journal* of Thursday, Oct. 31. Motion agreed to 270-125: R 51-116; D 219-9 (ND 148-7, SD 71-2), Nov. 1, 1985.

349. H J Res 372. Public Debt Limit. Rostenkowski, D-Ill., motion to recede from the disagreement with the Senate amendment to the bill to increase the public debt limit. Motion agreed to 288-134: R 172-3; D 116-131 (ND 56-111, SD 60-20), Nov. 1, 1985. (This was a procedural move that cleared the way for a House vote on the Democratic alternative to the budget amendment sponsored by Sens. Phil Gramm, R-Texas, Warren B. Rudman, R-N.H., and Ernest F. Hollings, D-S.C.)

350. H J Res 372. Public Debt Limit. Rostenkowski, D-Ill., motion to recede from the House position and concur with the Senate amendment to the bill to increase the public debt limit, with a substitute amendment to provide for declining annual statutory limits on the federal deficit, automatic deficit reduction and, under certain circumstances, procedural revisions in the congressional budget process. Motion agreed to 249-180: R 1-178; D 248-2 (ND 167-2, SD 81-0), Nov. 1, 1985.

KEY

Y Voted for (yea).
Paired for.
\+ Announced for.
N Voted against (nay).
X Paired against.
\- Announced against.
P Voted "present."
C Voted "present" to avoid possible conflict of interest.
? Did not vote or otherwise make a position known.

Democrats ***Republicans***

	345	346	347	348	349	350
ALABAMA						
1 ***Callahan***	N	Y	N	N	Y	N
2 ***Dickinson***	N	Y	N	N	Y	N
3 Nichols	Y	Y	Y	?	?	Y
4 Bevill	Y	N	N	Y	Y	Y
5 Flippo	Y	N	Y	Y	Y	Y
6 Erdreich	N	N	N	Y	Y	Y
7 Shelby	N	N	Y	Y	Y	Y
ALASKA						
AL ***Young***	N	N	N	N	Y	N
ARIZONA						
1 ***McCain***	N	Y	N	N	Y	N
2 Udall	Y	N	Y	Y	N	Y
3 ***Stump***	N	Y	N	Y	Y	N
4 ***Rudd***	N	Y	N	Y	Y	N
5 ***Kolbe***	N	Y	N	N	Y	N
ARKANSAS						
1 Alexander	Y	N	Y	Y	N	Y
2 Robinson	Y	Y	Y	Y	Y	Y
3 ***Hammerschmidt***	N	Y	Y	Y	Y	Y
4 Anthony	Y	N	Y	Y	Y	Y
CALIFORNIA						
1 Bosco	Y	N	Y	Y	Y	Y
2 ***Chappie***	N	Y	N	N	Y	N
3 Matsui	Y	N	Y	?	N	Y
4 Fazio	Y	N	Y	Y	N	Y
5 Burton	Y	N	Y	?	N	Y
6 Boxer	Y	N	Y	Y	N	Y
7 Miller	Y	N	Y	Y	N	Y
8 Dellums	Y	N	Y	Y	N	Y
9 Stark	Y	N	Y	Y	N	Y
10 Edwards	Y	N	Y	Y	N	Y
11 Lantos	Y	N	Y	Y	Y	Y
12 ***Zschau***	N	Y	N	N	Y	N
13 Mineta	Y	N	Y	Y	N	Y
14 ***Shumway***	N	Y	N	Y	Y	N
15 Coelho	Y	N	Y	Y	Y	Y
16 Panetta	Y	N	Y	Y	Y	Y
17 ***Pashayan***	N	Y	N	N	Y	N
18 Lehman	Y	N	Y	Y	N	Y
19 ***Lagomarsino***	N	Y	N	N	Y	N
20 ***Thomas***	N	Y	N	N	Y	N
21 ***Fiedler***	N	Y	N	N	Y	N
22 ***Moorhead***	N	Y	N	N	Y	N
23 Beilenson	Y	N	Y	Y	N	Y
24 Waxman	Y	N	Y	Y	N	Y
25 Roybal	Y	N	Y	?	N	Y
26 Berman	Y	N	Y	Y	N	Y
27 Levine	Y	N	Y	Y	N	Y
28 Dixon	Y	N	Y	Y	N	Y
29 Hawkins	Y	N	Y	Y	N	Y
30 Martinez	?	N	Y	Y	N	Y
31 Dymally	Y	N	Y	P	N	Y
32 Anderson	Y	N	Y	Y	N	Y
33 ***Dreier***	N	Y	N	N	Y	N
34 Torres	Y	N	Y	Y	N	Y
35 ***Lewis***	N	Y	N	N	Y	N
36 Brown	Y	N	Y	Y	N	Y
37 ***McCandless***	N	Y	N	N	Y	N
38 ***Dornan***	N	Y	N	N	Y	N
39 ***Dannemeyer***	N	Y	N	N	Y	N
40 ***Badham***	N	Y	N	?	?	?
41 ***Lowery***	N	Y	N	N	Y	N
42 ***Lungren***	N	Y	N	N	Y	N
43 ***Packard***	N	Y	N	Y	Y	N
44 Bates	Y	N	Y	Y	Y	Y
45 ***Hunter***	N	Y	N	N	Y	N
COLORADO						
1 Schroeder	Y	N	Y	N	N	Y
2 Wirth	Y	N	Y	Y	Y	Y
3 ***Strang***	N	Y	N	N	Y	N
4 ***Brown***	N	Y	N	N	Y	N
5 ***Kramer***	N	Y	N	N	Y	N
6 ***Schaefer***	N	Y	N	N	Y	N
CONNECTICUT						
1 Kennelly	Y	N	Y	Y	N	Y
2 Gejdenson	Y	N	Y	Y	N	Y
3 Morrison	Y	N	Y	Y	N	Y
4 ***McKinney***	N	N	Y	Y	Y	N
5 ***Rowland***	N	Y	N	N	Y	N
6 ***Johnson***	N	Y	Y	Y	Y	N
DELAWARE						
AL Carper	Y	N	Y	Y	Y	Y
FLORIDA						
1 Hutto	N	Y	Y	Y	Y	Y
2 Fuqua	Y	N	Y	Y	Y	Y
3 Bennett	Y	N	Y	Y	N	Y
4 Chappell	Y	N	Y	Y	Y	Y
5 ***McCollum***	?	?	X	Y	Y	N
6 MacKay	Y	N	Y	Y	Y	Y
7 Gibbons	Y	N	Y	Y	Y	Y
8 ***Young***	N	Y	N	N	Y	N
9 ***Bilirakis***	N	Y	N	N	Y	N
10 ***Ireland***	N	Y	N	N	Y	N
11 Nelson	-	+	#	Y	Y	Y
12 ***Lewis***	N	Y	N	N	Y	N
13 ***Mack***	N	Y	N	N	Y	N
14 Mica	Y	N	Y	Y	Y	Y
15 ***Shaw***	N	Y	N	N	Y	N
16 Smith	Y	N	Y	Y	Y	Y
17 Lehman	Y	N	Y	Y	N	Y
18 Pepper	Y	N	Y	Y	N	Y
19 Fascell	Y	N	Y	Y	Y	Y
GEORGIA						
1 Thomas	Y	N	Y	Y	Y	Y
2 Hatcher	Y	N	Y	Y	Y	Y
3 Ray	N	Y	Y	Y	Y	Y
4 ***Swindall***	N	Y	N	N	Y	N
5 Fowler	Y	N	Y	Y	Y	Y
6 ***Gingrich***	N	Y	N	N	Y	N
7 Darden	Y	N	Y	?	Y	Y
8 Rowland	Y	N	Y	Y	Y	Y
9 Jenkins	Y	N	Y	Y	Y	Y
10 Barnard	Y	N	Y	Y	Y	Y
HAWAII						
1 Heftel	Y	N	Y	Y	Y	Y
2 Akaka	Y	N	Y	Y	Y	Y
IDAHO						
1 ***Craig***	N	Y	N	N	Y	N
2 Stallings	N	N	Y	Y	Y	Y
ILLINOIS						
1 Hayes	Y	N	Y	Y	N	Y
2 Savage	Y	N	Y	Y	N	Y
3 Russo	Y	N	Y	Y	Y	Y
4 ***O'Brien***	?	?	X	?	?	N
5 Lipinski	Y	N	Y	Y	Y	Y
6 ***Hyde***	N	Y	N	Y	Y	N
7 Collins	Y	N	Y	Y	N	Y
8 Rostenkowski	Y	N	?	Y	N	Y
9 Yates	Y	N	Y	Y	N	Y
10 ***Porter***	N	Y	Y	Y	Y	N
11 Annunzio	Y	N	Y	Y	N	Y
12 ***Crane***	N	Y	N	N	Y	N
13 ***Fawell***	N	Y	N	N	Y	N
14 ***Grotberg***	N	Y	N	N	Y	N
15 ***Madigan***	N	Y	N	N	Y	N
16 ***Martin***	N	Y	N	N	Y	N
17 Evans	Y	N	Y	Y	N	Y
18 ***Michel***	N	Y	N	N	Y	N
19 Bruce	Y	N	Y	Y	Y	Y
20 Durbin	Y	N	Y	Y	Y	Y
21 Price	Y	N	N	?	Y	Y
22 Gray	Y	N	N	Y	Y	Y
INDIANA						
1 Visclosky	Y	N	Y	Y	Y	Y
2 Sharp	N	N	Y	Y	Y	Y
3 ***Hiler***	N	Y	N	N	Y	N
4 ***Coats***	N	Y	N	N	Y	N
5 ***Hillis***	N	Y	N	Y	Y	N

ND - Northern Democrats SD - Southern Democrats

* Corresponding to Congressional Record Votes 381, 382, 383, 384, 385, 386

	345	346	347	348	349	350
6 ***Burton***	N	Y	N	N	Y	N
7 ***Myers***	N	Y	N	Y	Y	N
8 McCloskey	Y	N	Y	Y	Y	Y
9 Hamilton	N	N	Y	Y	Y	Y
10 Jacobs	Y	N	Y	N	?	Y
IOWA						
1 ***Leach***	N	Y	Y	N	Y	N
2 ***Tauke***	N	Y	Y	N	Y	N
3 ***Evans***	N	Y	Y	N	N	N
4 Smith	Y	N	Y	Y	N	Y
5 ***Lightfoot***	N	Y	N	N	Y	N
6 Bedell	Y	N	Y	Y	N	Y
KANSAS						
1 ***Roberts***	N	Y	N	N	Y	N
2 Slattery	Y	N	Y	Y	Y	Y
3 ***Meyers***	N	Y	N	?	Y	N
4 Glickman	Y	N	Y	Y	Y	Y
5 ***Whittaker***	N	N	Y	N	Y	N
KENTUCKY						
1 Hubbard	N	Y	N	Y	Y	Y
2 Natcher	Y	N	Y	Y	Y	Y
3 Mazzoli	Y	N	Y	Y	Y	Y
4 ***Snyder***	N	Y	Y	Y	Y	N
5 ***Rogers***	N	Y	Y	N	Y	N
6 ***Hopkins***	N	Y	N	Y	Y	N
7 Perkins	Y	N	Y	Y	N	Y
LOUISIANA						
1 ***Livingston***	N	Y	N	Y	Y	N
2 Boggs	Y	N	Y	Y	N	Y
3 Tauzin	?	?	#	Y	Y	Y
4 Roemer	N	Y	Y	N	Y	Y
5 Huckaby	Y	N	Y	Y	Y	Y
6 ***Moore***	N	Y	N	Y	Y	N
7 Breaux	N	Y	Y	Y	Y	Y
8 Long	Y	N	Y	P	N	Y
MAINE						
1 ***McKernan***	N	Y	N	N	Y	N
2 ***Snowe***	N	Y	Y	Y	Y	N
MARYLAND						
1 Dyson	N	N	Y	Y	Y	Y
2 ***Bentley***	N	Y	N	N	Y	N
3 Mikulski	Y	N	Y	Y	N	Y
4 ***Holt***	N	Y	N	?	?	N
5 Hoyer	Y	N	Y	Y	N	Y
6 Byron	N	N	Y	Y	Y	Y
7 Mitchell	Y	N	Y	N	N	Y
8 Barnes	Y	N	Y	Y	N	Y
MASSACHUSETTS						
1 ***Conte***	N	N	Y	Y	N	N
2 Boland	Y	N	Y	?	N	Y
3 Early	Y	N	Y	Y	N	Y
4 Frank	Y	N	Y	Y	N	Y
5 Atkins	Y	N	Y	?	N	Y
6 Mavroules	Y	N	Y	Y	N	Y
7 Markey	Y	N	Y	Y	N	Y
8 O'Neill						
9 Moakley	Y	N	Y	Y	N	Y
10 Studds	Y	N	Y	Y	N	Y
11 Donnelly	Y	N	Y	Y	N	Y
MICHIGAN						
1 Conyers	Y	N	Y	Y	N	Y
2 ***Pursell***	N	Y	N	Y	Y	N
3 Wolpe	Y	N	Y	Y	Y	Y
4 ***Siljander***	N	Y	N	N	Y	N
5 ***Henry***	N	Y	N	Y	Y	N
6 Carr	Y	N	Y	Y	N	Y
7 Kildee	Y	N	Y	Y	N	Y
8 Traxler	Y	N	Y	Y	N	Y
9 ***Vander Jagt***	N	Y	N	N	Y	N
10 ***Schuette***	N	Y	N	N	Y	N
11 ***Davis***	N	Y	Y	Y	Y	N
12 Bonior	Y	N	Y	Y	N	Y
13 Crockett	Y	N	Y	Y	N	N
14 Hertel	Y	N	N	Y	N	Y
15 Ford	Y	N	Y	?	N	Y
16 Dingell	Y	N	Y	Y	N	Y
17 Levin	Y	N	Y	Y	N	Y
18 ***Broomfield***	N	Y	N	Y	Y	N
MINNESOTA						
1 Penny	Y	Y	Y	N	Y	Y
2 ***Weber***	N	Y	N	N	Y	N
3 ***Frenzel***	N	Y	N	N	Y	N
4 Vento	Y	N	Y	Y	N	Y
5 Sabo	Y	N	Y	Y	N	Y
6 Sikorski	Y	N	Y	N	Y	Y
7 ***Stangeland***	N	Y	N	?	?	N
8 Oberstar	Y	N	Y	Y	N	Y
MISSISSIPPI						
1 Whitten	Y	N	Y	Y	Y	Y
2 ***Franklin***	N	Y	N	Y	Y	N
3 Montgomery	Y	Y	Y	Y	Y	Y
4 Dowdy	Y	N	Y	Y	Y	Y
5 ***Lott***	N	Y	N	Y	Y	N
MISSOURI						
1 Clay	Y	N	Y	N	N	Y
2 Young	Y	N	Y	Y	Y	Y
3 Gephardt	Y	N	Y	Y	Y	Y
4 Skelton	Y	N	Y	Y	Y	Y
5 Wheat	Y	N	#	Y	N	Y
6 ***Coleman***	N	Y	N	N	Y	N
7 ***Taylor***	N	Y	N	N	Y	N
8 ***Emerson***	N	Y	N	N	Y	N
9 Volkmer	N	N	N	Y	Y	Y
MONTANA						
1 Williams	Y	N	Y	?	N	Y
2 ***Marlenee***	?	?	?	?	?	?
NEBRASKA						
1 ***Bereuter***	N	Y	Y	?	?	N
2 ***Daub***	N	Y	N	N	Y	N
3 ***Smith***	N	Y	Y	Y	Y	N
NEVADA						
1 Reid	Y	N	N	Y	Y	Y
2 ***Vucanovich***	N	Y	N	?	Y	N
NEW HAMPSHIRE						
1 ***Smith***	N	Y	N	N	Y	N
2 ***Gregg***	N	Y	N	N	Y	N
NEW JERSEY						
1 Florio	Y	N	Y	Y	N	Y
2 Hughes	N	Y	Y	Y	N	Y
3 Howard	Y	N	Y	Y	N	Y
4 ***Smith***	N	Y	N	Y	Y	N
5 ***Roukema***	N	Y	N	N	Y	N
6 Dwyer	Y	N	Y	Y	N	Y
7 ***Rinaldo***	N	Y	Y	Y	Y	N
8 Roe	Y	N	Y	?	N	Y
9 Torricelli	Y	N	Y	Y	N	Y
10 Rodino	Y	N	Y	Y	N	Y
11 ***Gallo***	N	Y	N	Y	Y	N
12 ***Courter***	N	Y	N	N	Y	N
13 ***Saxton***	N	Y	N	Y	Y	N
14 Guarini	Y	N	Y	Y	N	Y
NEW MEXICO						
1 ***Lujan***	N	Y	N	Y	Y	N
2 ***Skeen***	N	Y	N	N	Y	N
3 Richardson	Y	N	Y	Y	Y	Y
NEW YORK						
1 ***Carney***	N	Y	N	N	Y	N
2 Downey	Y	N	Y	Y	N	Y
3 Mrazek	Y	N	Y	Y	N	Y
4 ***Lent***	N	Y	N	N	Y	N
5 ***McGrath***	N	?	?	N	Y	N
6 Addabbo	?	?	?	?	?	?
7 Ackerman	Y	N	Y	Y	N	Y
8 Scheuer	Y	N	Y	Y	N	Y
9 Manton	?	N	Y	Y	Y	Y
10 Schumer	Y	N	Y	Y	N	Y
11 Towns	Y	N	Y	Y	N	Y
12 Owens	Y	N	Y	Y	N	Y
13 Solarz	Y	N	Y	Y	N	Y
14 ***Molinari***	N	Y	N	N	Y	N
15 ***Green***	N	N	Y	Y	Y	N
16 Rangel	Y	N	Y	Y	N	Y
17 Weiss	Y	N	Y	Y	N	Y
18 Garcia	Y	N	Y	?	N	Y
19 Biaggi	Y	N	Y	?	-	Y
20 ***DioGuardi***	N	Y	N	Y	Y	N
21 ***Fish***	N	Y	?	Y	Y	N
22 ***Gilman***	N	N	Y	+	Y	N
23 Stratton	Y	N	Y	Y	Y	Y
24 ***Solomon***	N	Y	N	N	Y	N
25 ***Boehlert***	N	Y	Y	N	Y	N
26 ***Martin***	N	Y	N	N	Y	N
27 ***Wortley***	N	Y	N	Y	Y	N
28 McHugh	Y	N	Y	Y	N	Y
29 ***Horton***	N	N	Y	Y	Y	N
30 ***Eckert***	N	Y	N	Y	Y	N
31 ***Kemp***	N	Y	N	?	Y	N
32 LaFalce	Y	?	#	Y	N	Y
33 Nowak	Y	N	Y	Y	N	Y
34 Lundine	Y	N	Y	Y	Y	Y
NORTH CAROLINA						
1 Jones	Y	N	Y	Y	Y	Y
2 Valentine	Y	N	Y	Y	Y	Y
3 Whitley	Y	N	Y	Y	Y	Y
4 ***Cobey***	N	Y	N	N	Y	N
5 Neal	Y	N	Y	?	?	?
6 ***Coble***	N	Y	N	N	Y	N
7 Rose	Y	N	Y	Y	N	Y
8 Hefner	Y	N	Y	Y	Y	Y
9 ***McMillan***	N	Y	N	Y	Y	N
10 ***Broyhill***	N	Y	N	?	Y	N
11 ***Hendon***	N	Y	N	N	Y	N
NORTH DAKOTA						
AL Dorgan	Y	N	Y	Y	Y	Y
OHIO						
1 Luken	Y	N	Y	Y	Y	Y
2 ***Gradison***	N	Y	N	Y	Y	N
3 Hall	Y	N	Y	Y	Y	Y
4 ***Oxley***	N	Y	N	N	Y	N
5 ***Latta***	N	Y	N	N	Y	N
6 ***McEwen***	N	Y	N	N	Y	N
7 ***DeWine***	N	Y	N	N	Y	N
8 ***Kindness***	N	Y	N	N	Y	N
9 Kaptur	N	N	Y	Y	Y	Y
10 ***Miller***	N	Y	N	?	Y	N
11 Eckart	Y	N	Y	Y	Y	Y
12 ***Kasich***	N	Y	N	N	Y	N
13 Pease	Y	N	Y	Y	Y	Y
14 Seiberling	Y	N	Y	Y	N	Y
15 ***Wylie***	N	Y	N	Y	Y	N
16 ***Regula***	N	Y	N	N	Y	N
17 Traficant	N	N	Y	Y	N	Y
18 Applegate	N	N	N	Y	N	Y
19 Feighan	Y	N	Y	Y	Y	Y
20 Oakar	Y	N	Y	Y	N	Y
21 Stokes	Y	N	Y	Y	N	Y
OKLAHOMA						
1 Jones	Y	Y	Y	?	Y	Y
2 Synar	Y	N	Y	Y	N	Y
3 Watkins	Y	N	N	Y	N	Y
4 McCurdy	Y	N	Y	?	Y	Y
5 ***Edwards***	N	Y	N	N	Y	N
6 English	N	Y	N	Y	Y	Y
OREGON						
1 AuCoin	N	N	Y	?	Y	Y
2 ***Smith, R.***	N	Y	N	N	Y	N
3 Wyden	Y	N	Y	Y	Y	Y
4 Weaver	Y	N	Y	Y	N	Y
5 ***Smith, D.***	N	?	X	N	Y	N
PENNSYLVANIA						
1 Foglietta	Y	N	Y	Y	N	Y
2 Gray	Y	N	Y	Y	N	Y
3 Borski	Y	N	Y	Y	N	Y
4 Kolter	Y	N	N	Y	Y	Y
5 ***Schulze***	N	Y	N	N	Y	N
6 Yatron	N	N	N	Y	Y	Y
7 Edgar	Y	N	Y	Y	N	Y
8 Kostmayer	Y	N	Y	Y	Y	Y
9 ***Shuster***	N	Y	N	N	Y	N
10 ***McDade***	N	Y	Y	Y	Y	N
11 Kanjorski	Y	N	Y	Y	N	N
12 Murtha	Y	N	N	Y	Y	Y
13 ***Coughlin***	N	Y	N	N	Y	N
14 Coyne	Y	N	Y	Y	N	Y
15 ***Ritter***	N	Y	N	Y	Y	N
16 ***Walker***	N	Y	N	N	Y	N
17 ***Gekas***	N	Y	N	N	Y	N
18 Walgren	Y	N	Y	Y	Y	Y
19 ***Goodling***	N	Y	N	N	Y	N
20 Gaydos	Y	N	N	Y	N	Y
21 ***Ridge***	N	Y	Y	N	Y	N
22 Murphy	Y	N	N	Y	Y	Y
23 ***Clinger***	N	N	Y	Y	Y	N
RHODE ISLAND						
1 St Germain	Y	N	Y	Y	N	Y
2 ***Schneider***	N	N	Y	Y	Y	N
SOUTH CAROLINA						
1 ***Hartnett***	N	Y	N	Y	Y	N
2 ***Spence***	N	Y	N	N	Y	N
3 Derrick	Y	N	Y	Y	Y	Y
4 ***Campbell***	N	Y	N	?	Y	N
5 Spratt	Y	N	Y	Y	Y	Y
6 Tallon	Y	N	Y	Y	N	Y
SOUTH DAKOTA						
AL Daschle	Y	N	Y	Y	Y	Y
TENNESSEE						
1 ***Quillen***	N	?	?	N	Y	N
2 ***Duncan***	N	Y	N	Y	Y	N
3 Lloyd	N	Y	N	N	Y	Y
4 Cooper	Y	N	Y	Y	N	Y
5 Boner	Y	N	Y	Y	Y	Y
6 Gordon	Y	N	Y	Y	N	Y
7 ***Sundquist***	N	Y	N	N	Y	N
8 Jones	Y	N	Y	Y	Y	Y
9 Ford	Y	N	Y	Y	N	Y
TEXAS						
1 Chapman	N	?	?	?	Y	Y
2 Wilson	Y	N	Y	Y	Y	Y
3 ***Bartlett***	N	Y	N	N	Y	N
4 Hall, R.	N	Y	N	Y	Y	Y
5 Bryant	Y	N	Y	Y	Y	Y
6 ***Barton***	N	Y	N	N	Y	N
7 ***Archer***	N	Y	N	Y	Y	N
8 ***Fields***	N	Y	N	N	Y	N
9 Brooks	?	N	Y	Y	N	Y
10 Pickle	Y	N	Y	Y	Y	Y
11 Leath	Y	Y	Y	Y	Y	Y
12 Wright	Y	N	Y	?	N	Y
13 ***Boulter***	N	Y	N	N	Y	N
14 ***Sweeney***	N	Y	N	Y	Y	N
15 de la Garza	Y	N	Y	Y	Y	Y
16 Coleman	Y	N	Y	Y	Y	Y
17 Stenholm	N	Y	Y	?	Y	Y
18 Leland	Y	N	Y	Y	N	Y
19 ***Combest***	N	Y	N	Y	Y	N
20 Gonzalez	Y	N	N	Y	N	Y
21 ***Loeffler***	N	Y	N	N	Y	N
22 ***DeLay***	N	Y	N	N	Y	N
23 Bustamante	Y	N	Y	Y	N	Y
24 Frost	Y	N	Y	Y	Y	Y
25 Andrews	Y	N	Y	Y	Y	Y
26 ***Armey***	N	Y	N	N	Y	N
27 Ortiz	Y	N	Y	Y	N	Y
UTAH						
1 ***Hansen***	N	Y	N	?	?	?
2 ***Monson***	N	Y	N	N	Y	N
3 ***Nielson***	N	Y	N	N	Y	N
VERMONT						
AL ***Jeffords***	N	N	N	Y	N	N
VIRGINIA						
1 ***Bateman***	N	Y	N	Y	Y	N
2 ***Whitehurst***	N	Y	N	?	Y	N
3 ***Bliley***	N	Y	N	N	Y	N
4 Sisisky	Y	N	Y	Y	Y	Y
5 Daniel	Y	Y	Y	Y	Y	Y
6 Olin	N	Y	Y	Y	Y	Y
7 ***Slaughter***	N	Y	N	N	Y	N
8 ***Parris***	?	?	X	N	Y	N
9 Boucher	N	?	N	Y	Y	Y
10 ***Wolf***	N	Y	N	N	Y	N
WASHINGTON						
1 ***Miller***	N	Y	N	Y	Y	N
2 Swift	Y	N	Y	Y	N	Y
3 Bonker	Y	N	Y	Y	Y	Y
4 ***Morrison***	N	Y	N	N	Y	N
5 Foley	Y	N	Y	?	N	Y
6 Dicks	Y	N	Y	Y	N	Y
7 Lowry	Y	N	Y	N	N	Y
8 ***Chandler***	N	Y	N	N	Y	N
WEST VIRGINIA						
1 Mollohan	N	N	N	Y	N	Y
2 Staggers	Y	N	N	Y	N	Y
3 Wise	Y	N	N	Y	Y	Y
4 Rahall	Y	N	N	Y	N	Y
WISCONSIN						
1 Aspin	Y	N	Y	Y	N	Y
2 Kastenmeier	Y	N	Y	Y	N	Y
3 ***Gunderson***	N	Y	N	N	Y	N
4 Kleczka	Y	N	Y	Y	Y	Y
5 Moody	Y	N	Y	Y	N	Y
6 ***Petri***	N	Y	N	Y	Y	N
7 Obey	Y	N	Y	Y	Y	Y
8 ***Roth***	N	Y	N	N	Y	N
9 ***Sensenbrenner***	N	Y	N	N	Y	N
WYOMING						
AL ***Cheney***	N	Y	N	N	Y	N

Southern states - Ala., Ark., Fla., Ga., Ky., La., Miss., N.C., Okla., S.C., Tenn., Texas, Va.

* The *Congressional Record* vote number is different from the CQ vote number because the *Record* includes quorum calls in its tally. CQ does not publish quorum call votes.

351. HR 3669. Temporary Public Debt Limit Increase. Pepper, D-Fla., motion to consider the rule (H Res 306) to provide for House floor consideration of the bill to allow an increase in the limit on the public debt by an amount determined by the secretary of the Treasury as necessary to meet the federal government's obligations without disinvesting the Social Security trust funds or other trust funds, but not to exceed $1.841 trillion. Motion agreed to 343-77: R 98-77; D 245-0 (ND 166-0, SD 79-0), Nov. 1, 1985. A two-thirds majority of those present and voting (280 in this case) is required to consider a privileged report from the Rules Committee on the same day it is presented to the House.

352. HR 3669. Temporary Public Debt Limit Increase. Adoption of the rule (H Res 306) to provide for House floor consideration of the bill to allow an increase in the limit on the public debt by an amount determined by the secretary of the Treasury as necessary to meet the federal government's obligations without disinvesting the Social Security trust funds or other trust funds, but not to exceed $1.841 trillion. Adopted 374-44: R 131-44; D 243-0 (ND 164-0, SD 79-0), Nov. 1, 1985.

353. HR 3669. Temporary Public Debt Limit Increase. Passage of the bill to allow an increase in the limit on the public debt by an amount determined by the secretary of the Treasury as necessary to meet the federal government's obligations without disinvesting the Social Security trust funds or other trust funds, but not to exceed $1.841 trillion. Passed 357-61: R 116-60; D 241-1 (ND 164-0, SD 77-1), Nov. 1, 1985.

354. Procedural Motion. Wright, D-Texas, motion to adjourn. Motion agreed to 207-194: R 2-166; D 205-28 (ND 147-9, SD 58-19), Nov. 1, 1985.

355. H J Res 36. Women in Armed Services Memorial. Oakar, D-Ohio, motion to suspend the rules and pass the joint resolution to authorize the establishment in the Washington, D.C., area of a memorial to women in the armed services. Motion agreed to 405-0: R 172-0; D 233-0 (ND 157-0, SD 76-0), Nov. 6, 1985. A two-thirds majority of those present and voting (270 in this case) is required for passage under suspension of the rules.

356. HR 2205. Korean War Veterans' Memorial. Oakar, D-Ohio, motion to suspend the rules and pass the bill to authorize the establishment in the Washington, D.C., area of a memorial to veterans of the Korean War. Motion agreed to 406-0: R 173-0; D 233-0 (ND 158-0, SD 75-0), Nov. 6, 1985. A two-thirds majority of those present and voting (271 in this case) is required for passage under suspension of the rules.

357. H J Res 142. Black Revolutionary War Patriots' Memorial. Oakar, D-Ohio, motion to suspend the rules and pass the joint resolution to authorize the establishment in the Washington, D.C., area of a memorial to black veterans of the Revolutionary War. Motion agreed to 408-0: R 172-0; D 236-0 (ND 158-0, SD 78-0), Nov. 6, 1985. A two-thirds majority of those present and voting (272 in this case) is required for passage under suspension of the rules.

358. HR 6. Water Resources Development. Edgar, D-Pa., amendment to apply local cost-sharing requirements to new components of the Mississippi River and Tributaries Project (which are exempt from cost-sharing under the bill), except on the main stem of the Mississippi and Atchafalaya rivers. Rejected 124-296: R 55-122; D 69-174 (ND 62-102, SD 7-72), Nov. 6, 1985. A "yea" was a vote supporting the president's position.

KEY

- Y Voted for (yea).
- # Paired for.
- + Announced for.
- N Voted against (nay).
- X Paired against.
- - Announced against.
- P Voted "present."
- C Voted "present" to avoid possible conflict of interest.
- ? Did not vote or otherwise make a position known.

Democrats *Republicans*

	351	352	353	354	355	356	357	358
ALABAMA								
1 *Callahan*	Y	Y	Y	N	Y	Y	Y	N
2 *Dickinson*	Y	Y	Y	N	Y	Y	Y	N
3 Nichols	Y	Y	Y	Y	Y	Y	Y	N
4 Bevill	Y	Y	Y	Y	Y	Y	Y	N
5 Flippo	Y	Y	Y	Y	Y	Y	Y	N
6 Erdreich	Y	Y	Y	N	Y	Y	Y	N
7 Shelby	Y	Y	Y	N	Y	Y	?	N
ALASKA								
AL *Young*	Y	Y	Y	N	Y	Y	Y	N
ARIZONA								
1 *McCain*	N	Y	Y	N	Y	Y	Y	N
2 Udall	Y	Y	Y	Y	Y	Y	Y	N
3 *Stump*	Y	N	N	N	Y	Y	Y	N
4 *Rudd*	N	N	N	N	Y	Y	Y	N
5 *Kolbe*	N	Y	N	N	Y	Y	Y	N
ARKANSAS								
1 Alexander	Y	Y	Y	Y	Y	Y	Y	N
2 Robinson	Y	Y	Y	Y	Y	Y	Y	N
3 *Hammerschmidt*	Y	Y	Y	N	Y	Y	Y	N
4 Anthony	Y	Y	Y	Y	?	?	?	?
CALIFORNIA								
1 Bosco	Y	Y	Y	Y	Y	Y	Y	N
2 *Chappie*	N	N	N	N	Y	Y	Y	N
3 Matsui	Y	Y	Y	Y	Y	Y	Y	N
4 Fazio	Y	Y	Y	Y	Y	Y	Y	N
5 Burton	Y	Y	Y	Y	Y	Y	Y	N
6 Boxer	Y	Y	Y	Y	Y	Y	Y	Y
7 Miller	Y	Y	Y	Y	?	?	?	N
8 Dellums	Y	Y	Y	Y	Y	Y	Y	Y
9 Stark	Y	?	?	?	Y	Y	Y	Y
10 Edwards	Y	Y	Y	Y	Y	Y	Y	Y
11 Lantos	Y	Y	Y	Y	Y	Y	Y	N
12 *Zschau*	N	Y	Y	N	Y	Y	Y	Y
13 Mineta	Y	Y	Y	Y	Y	?	Y	N
14 *Shumway*	N	N	N	N	Y	Y	Y	N
15 Coelho	Y	Y	Y	Y	?	Y	Y	N
16 Panetta	Y	Y	Y	Y	Y	Y	Y	N
17 *Pashayan*	Y	Y	Y	N	Y	Y	Y	N
18 Lehman	Y	Y	Y	Y	Y	Y	Y	N
19 *Lagomarsino*	Y	Y	Y	N	Y	Y	Y	N
20 *Thomas*	N	N	N	N	Y	Y	Y	N
21 *Fiedler*	N	N	N	N	Y	Y	Y	Y
22 *Moorhead*	N	N	N	N	Y	Y	Y	N
23 Beilenson	Y	Y	Y	Y	Y	Y	Y	N
24 Waxman	Y	Y	Y	Y	Y	Y	Y	Y
25 Roybal	Y	Y	Y	Y	Y	Y	Y	N
26 Berman	Y	Y	Y	Y	Y	Y	Y	Y
27 Levine	Y	Y	Y	?	Y	Y	Y	N
28 Dixon	Y	Y	Y	Y	Y	Y	Y	N
29 Hawkins	Y	Y	Y	Y	?	?	?	N
30 Martinez	Y	Y	Y	Y	Y	?	Y	N
31 Dymally	Y	Y	Y	Y	Y	Y	Y	N
32 Anderson	Y	Y	Y	N	Y	Y	Y	N
33 *Dreier*	N	N	N	N	Y	Y	Y	Y
34 Torres	Y	Y	Y	Y	Y	Y	Y	N
35 *Lewis*	N	N	N	N	Y	Y	Y	N
36 Brown	Y	Y	Y	Y	Y	Y	Y	N
37 *McCandless*	N	N	N	N	Y	Y	Y	N
38 *Dornan*	N	N	N	?	Y	Y	Y	N
39 *Dannemeyer*	N	N	N	N	+	+	+	-
40 *Badham*	?	?	?	?	Y	Y	Y	N
41 *Lowery*	N	N	N	N	?	?	?	N
42 *Lungren*	N	N	N	N	Y	Y	Y	Y
43 *Packard*	N	N	N	N	Y	Y	Y	N
44 Bates	Y	Y	Y	Y	?	Y	Y	Y
45 *Hunter*	N	N	N	N	Y	Y	Y	N
COLORADO								
1 Schroeder	Y	Y	Y	N	Y	Y	Y	Y
2 Wirth	Y	Y	Y	N	Y	Y	Y	Y
3 *Strang*	N	Y	N	N	Y	Y	Y	N
4 *Brown*	N	N	N	N	Y	Y	Y	Y
5 *Kramer*	N	N	N	N	Y	Y	Y	N
6 *Schaefer*	N	N	N	N	Y	Y	Y	N
CONNECTICUT								
1 Kennelly	Y	Y	Y	Y	Y	Y	Y	N
2 Gejdenson	Y	Y	Y	Y	Y	Y	Y	Y
3 Morrison	Y	Y	?	?	Y	Y	Y	Y
4 *McKinney*	Y	Y	Y	N	Y	Y	Y	N
5 *Rowland*	Y	Y	Y	N	Y	Y	Y	N
6 *Johnson*	Y	Y	Y	N	Y	Y	Y	Y
DELAWARE								
AL Carper	Y	Y	Y	Y	Y	Y	Y	Y
FLORIDA								
1 Hutto	Y	Y	Y	N	Y	Y	Y	N
2 Fuqua	Y	Y	Y	Y	Y	Y	Y	N
3 Bennett	Y	Y	Y	Y	Y	Y	Y	N
4 Chappell	Y	Y	Y	N	Y	Y	Y	N
5 *McCollum*	Y	Y	Y	N	Y	Y	Y	Y
6 MacKay	Y	Y	Y	Y	Y	Y	Y	Y
7 Gibbons	Y	Y	Y	N	Y	Y	Y	Y
8 *Young*	Y	Y	Y	N	Y	Y	Y	N
9 *Bilirakis*	Y	Y	Y	N	Y	Y	Y	N
10 *Ireland*	Y	Y	Y	N	Y	Y	Y	N
11 Nelson	Y	Y	Y	N	+	+	+	-
12 *Lewis*	Y	Y	Y	N	Y	Y	Y	N
13 *Mack*	N	N	N	N	Y	Y	Y	Y
14 Mica	Y	Y	Y	Y	Y	Y	Y	N
15 *Shaw*	Y	Y	Y	N	Y	Y	Y	N
16 Smith	Y	Y	Y	Y	Y	Y	Y	Y
17 Lehman	Y	Y	Y	Y	Y	Y	Y	N
18 Pepper	Y	Y	Y	Y	Y	Y	Y	N
19 Fascell	Y	Y	Y	Y	Y	Y	Y	N
GEORGIA								
1 Thomas	Y	Y	Y	Y	Y	Y	Y	N
2 Hatcher	?	?	?	?	Y	Y	Y	N
3 Ray	Y	Y	Y	N	Y	Y	Y	N
4 *Swindall*	N	Y	Y	N	Y	Y	Y	Y
5 Fowler	?	?	?	?	?	?	?	?
6 *Gingrich*	N	N	N	N	Y	Y	Y	N
7 Darden	Y	Y	Y	Y	Y	Y	Y	N
8 Rowland	Y	Y	Y	Y	Y	Y	Y	N
9 Jenkins	Y	Y	Y	Y	Y	Y	Y	N
10 Barnard	Y	Y	Y	Y	Y	Y	Y	N
HAWAII								
1 Heftel	?	Y	Y	Y	Y	Y	Y	N
2 Akaka	Y	Y	Y	Y	+	Y	Y	N
IDAHO								
1 *Craig*	N	Y	N	N	Y	Y	Y	N
2 Stallings	Y	Y	Y	N	Y	Y	Y	Y
ILLINOIS								
1 Hayes	Y	Y	Y	Y	Y	Y	Y	N
2 Savage	Y	Y	Y	?	Y	Y	Y	Y
3 Russo	Y	Y	Y	Y	Y	Y	Y	Y
4 *O'Brien*	Y	Y	Y	Y	Y	Y	Y	N
5 Lipinski	Y	Y	Y	Y	Y	Y	Y	N
6 *Hyde*	N	N	N	N	Y	Y	Y	Y
7 Collins	Y	Y	Y	Y	Y	Y	Y	N
8 Rostenkowski	Y	Y	Y	Y	Y	Y	Y	N
9 Yates	Y	Y	Y	Y	Y	Y	Y	Y
10 *Porter*	N	Y	Y	N	Y	Y	Y	Y
11 Annunzio	Y	Y	Y	Y	Y	Y	Y	N
12 *Crane*	N	N	N	N	?	?	?	?
13 *Fawell*	N	Y	N	N	Y	Y	Y	Y
14 *Grotberg*	N	Y	Y	N	Y	Y	Y	N
15 *Madigan*	Y	Y	Y	?	Y	Y	Y	N
16 *Martin*	Y	Y	Y	?	Y	Y	Y	N
17 Evans	Y	Y	Y	Y	Y	Y	Y	Y
18 *Michel*	Y	Y	Y	N	Y	Y	Y	N
19 Bruce	Y	Y	Y	Y	Y	Y	Y	N
20 Durbin	Y	Y	Y	Y	Y	Y	Y	N
21 Price	Y	Y	Y	Y	Y	Y	Y	N
22 Gray	Y	Y	Y	Y	Y	Y	Y	N
INDIANA								
1 Visclosky	Y	Y	Y	Y	Y	Y	Y	N
2 Sharp	Y	Y	Y	Y	Y	Y	Y	Y
3 *Hiler*	N	N	N	N	Y	Y	Y	N
4 *Coats*	N	N	N	N	Y	Y	Y	N
5 *Hillis*	Y	Y	Y	N	Y	Y	Y	N

ND - Northern Democrats SD - Southern Democrats

* Corresponding to Congressional Record Votes 387, 388, 389, 390, 391, 392, 393, 394

	351	352	353	354	355	356	357	358
6 ***Burton***	N	Y	N	N	Y	Y	Y	N
7 ***Myers***	Y	Y	Y	N	Y	Y	Y	N
8 McCloskey	Y	Y	Y	Y	Y	Y	Y	N
9 Hamilton	Y	Y	Y	N	Y	Y	Y	N
10 Jacobs	Y	Y	Y	Y	Y	Y	Y	Y
IOWA								
1 ***Leach***	Y	Y	Y	N	Y	Y	Y	Y
2 ***Tauke***	Y	Y	Y	N	Y	Y	Y	Y
3 ***Evans***	Y	Y	Y	N	?	?	?	?
4 Smith	Y	Y	Y	Y	Y	Y	Y	N
5 ***Lightfoot***	N	Y	Y	N	Y	Y	Y	N
6 Bedell	Y	Y	Y	Y	Y	Y	Y	Y
KANSAS								
1 ***Roberts***	Y	Y	Y	N	Y	Y	Y	N
2 Slattery	Y	Y	Y	Y	Y	Y	Y	N
3 ***Meyers***	Y	Y	Y	N	Y	Y	Y	Y
4 Glickman	Y	Y	Y	Y	Y	Y	Y	N
5 ***Whittaker***	Y	Y	Y	N	Y	Y	Y	N
KENTUCKY								
1 Hubbard	Y	Y	N	N	Y	Y	Y	N
2 Natcher	Y	Y	Y	Y	Y	Y	Y	N
3 Mazzoli	Y	Y	Y	Y	Y	Y	Y	N
4 ***Snyder***	Y	Y	Y	N	Y	Y	Y	N
5 ***Rogers***	Y	Y	Y	N	Y	Y	Y	N
6 ***Hopkins***	Y	Y	N	N	Y	Y	Y	N
7 Perkins	Y	Y	Y	Y	Y	Y	Y	N
LOUISIANA								
1 ***Livingston***	Y	Y	Y	N	Y	Y	Y	N
2 Boggs	Y	Y	Y	Y	Y	Y	Y	N
3 Tauzin	Y	Y	Y	N	Y	Y	Y	N
4 Roemer	Y	Y	Y	N	Y	Y	Y	N
5 Huckaby	Y	Y	Y	N	Y	Y	Y	N
6 ***Moore***	Y	Y	Y	N	Y	Y	Y	N
7 Breaux	Y	Y	Y	N	Y	Y	Y	N
8 Long	Y	Y	Y	Y	Y	Y	Y	N
MAINE								
1 ***McKernan***	Y	Y	Y	N	Y	Y	Y	Y
2 ***Snowe***	Y	Y	Y	N	Y	Y	Y	Y
MARYLAND								
1 Dyson	Y	Y	Y	Y	Y	Y	Y	N
2 ***Bentley***	Y	Y	Y	N	Y	Y	Y	N
3 Mikulski	Y	Y	Y	Y	Y	Y	Y	N
4 ***Holt***	?	?	?	?	Y	Y	Y	N
5 Hoyer	Y	Y	Y	Y	Y	Y	Y	N
6 Byron	Y	Y	Y	Y	Y	Y	Y	N
7 Mitchell	Y	Y	Y	Y	Y	Y	Y	?
8 Barnes	Y	Y	+	+	Y	Y	Y	Y
MASSACHUSETTS								
1 ***Conte***	Y	Y	Y	N	Y	Y	Y	Y
2 Boland	Y	Y	Y	Y	?	?	?	N
3 Early	Y	Y	Y	Y	Y	Y	Y	N
4 Frank	Y	Y	Y	Y	Y	Y	Y	Y
5 Atkins	Y	Y	Y	Y	Y	Y	Y	N
6 Mavroules	Y	Y	Y	Y	Y	Y	Y	N
7 Markey	Y	Y	Y	Y	Y	Y	Y	Y
8 O'Neill								
9 Moakley	Y	Y	Y	Y	Y	Y	Y	N
10 Studds	Y	Y	Y	Y	Y	Y	Y	Y
11 Donnelly	Y	Y	Y	Y	Y	Y	Y	N
MICHIGAN								
1 Conyers	Y	?	Y	?	Y	Y	Y	Y
2 ***Pursell***	Y	Y	Y	N	Y	Y	Y	Y
3 Wolpe	Y	Y	Y	Y	Y	Y	Y	Y
4 ***Siljander***	N	N	N	N	Y	Y	Y	Y
5 ***Henry***	N	N	N	N	Y	Y	Y	Y
6 Carr	Y	Y	Y	Y	Y	Y	Y	N
7 Kildee	Y	Y	Y	Y	Y	Y	Y	Y
8 Traxler	Y	Y	Y	?	?	Y	Y	N
9 ***Vander Jagt***	Y	Y	Y	N	Y	Y	Y	Y
10 ***Schuette***	Y	Y	Y	N	Y	Y	Y	N
11 ***Davis***	Y	Y	Y	N	Y	Y	Y	Y
12 Bonior	Y	Y	Y	Y	Y	Y	Y	Y
13 Crockett	?	Y	Y	Y	Y	Y	Y	Y
14 Hertel	Y	Y	Y	Y	Y	Y	Y	Y
15 Ford	Y	Y	Y	Y	Y	Y	?	?
16 Dingell	Y	Y	Y	Y	Y	Y	Y	Y
17 Levin	Y	Y	Y	Y	Y	Y	Y	Y
18 ***Broomfield***	Y	Y	Y	N	Y	Y	Y	N
MINNESOTA								
1 Penny	Y	Y	Y	Y	Y	Y	Y	N
2 ***Weber***	N	Y	N	N	Y	Y	Y	Y
3 ***Frenzel***	N	Y	N	N	Y	Y	Y	Y
4 Vento	Y	Y	Y	Y	Y	Y	Y	Y
5 Sabo	Y	Y	Y	Y	Y	Y	Y	N
6 Sikorski	Y	Y	Y	Y	Y	Y	Y	Y

	351	352	353	354	355	356	357	358
7 ***Stangeland***	Y	Y	N	N	Y	Y	Y	N
8 Oberstar	Y	Y	Y	Y	Y	Y	Y	N
MISSISSIPPI								
1 Whitten	Y	Y	Y	Y	Y	Y	Y	N
2 ***Franklin***	Y	Y	N	?	Y	Y	Y	N
3 Montgomery	Y	Y	Y	Y	Y	Y	Y	N
4 Dowdy	Y	Y	Y	Y	Y	Y	Y	N
5 ***Lott***	Y	Y	Y	N	Y	Y	Y	N
MISSOURI								
1 Clay	Y	Y	Y	Y	?	?	?	?
2 Young	Y	Y	Y	Y	Y	Y	Y	N
3 Gephardt	Y	Y	Y	Y	Y	Y	Y	N
4 Skelton	Y	Y	Y	Y	Y	Y	Y	N
5 Wheat	Y	Y	Y	Y	Y	Y	Y	N
6 ***Coleman***	N	Y	Y	N	Y	Y	Y	N
7 ***Taylor***	Y	Y	Y	N	Y	Y	Y	N
8 ***Emerson***	Y	Y	Y	N	Y	Y	Y	N
9 Volkmer	Y	Y	Y	Y	Y	Y	Y	N
MONTANA								
1 Williams	Y	Y	Y	Y	Y	Y	Y	Y
2 ***Marlenee***	?	?	?	?	Y	Y	Y	N
NEBRASKA								
1 ***Bereuter***	N	Y	Y	N	Y	Y	Y	N
2 ***Daub***	N	Y	N	N	Y	Y	Y	Y
3 ***Smith***	Y	Y	Y	N	Y	Y	Y	N
NEVADA								
1 Reid	Y	Y	Y	Y	Y	Y	Y	N
2 ***Vucanovich***	N	N	N	N	Y	Y	Y	N
NEW HAMPSHIRE								
1 ***Smith***	N	N	N	N	Y	Y	Y	Y
2 ***Gregg***	N	N	N	N	Y	Y	Y	Y
NEW JERSEY								
1 Florio	Y	?	?	?	Y	Y	Y	N
2 Hughes	Y	Y	Y	Y	Y	Y	Y	N
3 Howard	Y	Y	Y	Y	Y	Y	Y	N
4 ***Smith***	Y	Y	Y	N	Y	Y	Y	N
5 ***Roukema***	Y	Y	Y	N	Y	Y	Y	N
6 Dwyer	Y	Y	Y	Y	Y	Y	Y	N
7 ***Rinaldo***	Y	Y	Y	N	Y	Y	Y	N
8 Roe	Y	Y	Y	Y	Y	Y	Y	N
9 Torricelli	Y	Y	Y	Y	Y	Y	Y	N
10 Rodino	Y	Y	Y	Y	Y	+	Y	N
11 ***Gallo***	N	Y	Y	N	Y	Y	Y	N
12 ***Courter***	N	Y	Y	N	Y	Y	Y	N
13 ***Saxton***	Y	Y	Y	N	Y	Y	Y	N
14 Guarini	Y	Y	Y	Y	Y	Y	Y	N
NEW MEXICO								
1 ***Lujan***	Y	Y	Y	N	Y	Y	Y	N
2 ***Skeen***	Y	Y	Y	N	Y	Y	Y	N
3 Richardson	Y	Y	Y	Y	Y	Y	Y	N
NEW YORK								
1 ***Carney***	Y	Y	Y	N	Y	Y	Y	N
2 Downey	Y	Y	Y	Y	Y	Y	Y	Y
3 Mrazek	Y	Y	Y	Y	Y	Y	Y	Y
4 ***Lent***	Y	Y	Y	N	?	?	?	N
5 ***McGrath***	Y	Y	Y	N	Y	Y	Y	N
6 Addabbo	?	?	?	?	?	?	?	?
7 Ackerman	Y	Y	Y	Y	Y	Y	Y	Y
8 Scheuer	Y	+	Y	Y	Y	Y	Y	Y
9 Manton	Y	Y	Y	Y	?	?	?	N
10 Schumer	Y	Y	Y	Y	Y	Y	Y	Y
11 Towns	Y	Y	Y	Y	?	?	?	Y
12 Owens	Y	Y	Y	Y	Y	Y	Y	N
13 Solarz	Y	Y	Y	Y	Y	Y	Y	N
14 ***Molinari***	Y	Y	N	N	?	?	?	N
15 ***Green***	Y	Y	Y	N	Y	Y	Y	Y
16 Rangel	Y	Y	Y	Y	Y	Y	Y	N
17 Weiss	Y	Y	Y	Y	Y	Y	Y	+
18 Garcia	Y	Y	Y	Y	?	?	?	Y
19 Biaggi	Y	Y	Y	Y	Y	Y	Y	N
20 ***DioGuardi***	N	Y	Y	N	Y	Y	Y	N
21 ***Fish***	N	Y	Y	N	Y	Y	Y	Y
22 ***Gilman***	Y	Y	Y	N	Y	Y	Y	N
23 Stratton	Y	Y	Y	Y	Y	Y	Y	N
24 ***Solomon***	Y	Y	N	N	Y	Y	Y	Y
25 ***Boehlert***	Y	Y	Y	N	Y	Y	Y	Y
26 ***Martin***	Y	Y	Y	N	Y	Y	Y	Y
27 ***Wortley***	Y	Y	Y	N	Y	Y	Y	Y
28 McHugh	Y	Y	Y	Y	Y	Y	Y	Y
29 ***Horton***	Y	Y	Y	N	Y	Y	Y	N
30 ***Eckert***	N	Y	Y	?	Y	Y	Y	Y
31 ***Kemp***	Y	Y	Y	N	?	?	?	N
32 LaFalce	Y	Y	Y	Y	Y	Y	Y	Y
33 Nowak	Y	Y	Y	Y	Y	Y	Y	Y
34 Lundine	?	?	?	?	Y	Y	Y	Y

	351	352	353	354	355	356	357	358
NORTH CAROLINA								
1 Jones	Y	Y	Y	Y	Y	Y	Y	N
2 Valentine	Y	Y	Y	Y	Y	Y	Y	N
3 Whitley	Y	Y	Y	?	?	Y	Y	N
4 ***Cobey***	N	Y	N	N	Y	Y	Y	Y
5 Neal	?	?	?	?	Y	Y	Y	Y
6 ***Coble***	N	Y	Y	N	Y	Y	Y	N
7 Rose	Y	Y	Y	Y	Y	Y	Y	N
8 Hefner	Y	Y	Y	Y	Y	Y	Y	N
9 ***McMillan***	N	Y	Y	N	Y	Y	Y	N
10 ***Broyhill***	Y	Y	Y	N	Y	Y	Y	N
11 ***Hendon***	Y	Y	Y	N	Y	Y	Y	N
NORTH DAKOTA								
AL Dorgan	Y	Y	Y	Y	Y	Y	Y	N
OHIO								
1 Luken	Y	Y	Y	Y	Y	Y	Y	N
2 ***Gradison***	Y	Y	Y	N	Y	Y	Y	Y
3 Hall	Y	Y	Y	Y	Y	Y	Y	N
4 ***Oxley***	N	N	N	N	Y	Y	Y	N
5 ***Latta***	Y	Y	Y	N	Y	Y	Y	N
6 ***McEwen***	?	?	?	?	Y	Y	Y	N
7 ***DeWine***	Y	Y	Y	N	Y	Y	Y	N
8 ***Kindness***	Y	Y	Y	N	Y	Y	Y	Y
9 Kaptur	Y	Y	Y	Y	Y	Y	Y	Y
10 ***Miller***	Y	Y	Y	N	Y	Y	Y	Y
11 Eckart	Y	Y	Y	Y	Y	Y	Y	Y
12 ***Kasich***	Y	Y	Y	N	Y	Y	Y	N
13 Pease	Y	Y	Y	?	Y	Y	Y	N
14 Seiberling	Y	Y	Y	?	Y	Y	Y	Y
15 ***Wylie***	Y	Y	Y	N	Y	Y	Y	N
16 ***Regula***	Y	Y	Y	N	Y	Y	Y	N
17 Traficant	Y	Y	Y	N	Y	Y	Y	N
18 Applegate	Y	Y	Y	N	Y	Y	Y	Y
19 Feighan	Y	Y	Y	Y	Y	Y	Y	Y
20 Oakar	Y	Y	Y	Y	Y	Y	Y	N
21 Stokes	Y	Y	Y	?	Y	Y	Y	N
OKLAHOMA								
1 Jones	Y	Y	Y	N	Y	Y	Y	N
2 Synar	Y	Y	Y	Y	Y	Y	Y	Y
3 Watkins	Y	Y	Y	N	Y	?	Y	N
4 McCurdy	Y	Y	Y	Y	Y	Y	Y	N
5 ***Edwards***	?	?	Y	N	Y	Y	Y	N
6 English	Y	Y	Y	N	Y	Y	Y	N
OREGON								
1 AuCoin	Y	Y	Y	N	?	?	?	N
2 ***Smith, R.***	Y	Y	Y	N	Y	Y	Y	N
3 Wyden	Y	Y	Y	Y	Y	Y	Y	N
4 Weaver	Y	Y	Y	Y	Y	Y	?	N
5 ***Smith, D.***	N	N	N	N	Y	Y	Y	N
PENNSYLVANIA								
1 Foglietta	Y	Y	Y	Y	Y	Y	Y	Y
2 Gray	Y	Y	Y	Y	Y	Y	Y	Y
3 Borski	Y	Y	Y	Y	Y	Y	Y	Y
4 Kolter	Y	Y	Y	Y	Y	Y	Y	N
5 ***Schulze***	Y	Y	Y	Y	Y	Y	Y	N
6 Yatron	Y	Y	Y	Y	Y	Y	Y	Y
7 Edgar	Y	Y	Y	?	Y	Y	Y	Y
8 Kostmayer	Y	Y	Y	Y	Y	Y	Y	Y
9 ***Shuster***	Y	Y	Y	N	Y	Y	Y	N
10 ***McDade***	Y	Y	Y	N	?	?	?	Y
11 Kanjorski	Y	Y	Y	Y	Y	Y	Y	N
12 Murtha	Y	Y	Y	Y	Y	Y	Y	N
13 ***Coughlin***	Y	Y	Y	N	Y	Y	Y	Y
14 Coyne	Y	Y	Y	Y	Y	Y	Y	N
15 ***Ritter***	N	Y	Y	N	Y	Y	Y	Y
16 ***Walker***	N	N	N	N	Y	Y	Y	Y
17 ***Gekas***	N	Y	Y	N	Y	Y	Y	N
18 Walgren	Y	Y	Y	Y	Y	Y	Y	Y
19 ***Goodling***	Y	Y	Y	N	Y	Y	?	Y
20 Gaydos	Y	Y	Y	Y	Y	Y	Y	N
21 ***Ridge***	Y	Y	Y	?	Y	Y	Y	N
22 Murphy	Y	Y	Y	Y	Y	Y	Y	N
23 ***Clinger***	Y	Y	Y	N	Y	Y	Y	N
RHODE ISLAND								
1 St Germain	Y	Y	Y	Y	Y	Y	Y	N
2 ***Schneider***	Y	Y	Y	N	Y	Y	Y	Y
SOUTH CAROLINA								
1 ***Hartnett***	N	N	N	?	Y	Y	Y	N
2 ***Spence***	Y	Y	Y	N	Y	Y	Y	Y
3 Derrick	Y	Y	Y	N	Y	Y	Y	Y
4 ***Campbell***	N	Y	Y	N	Y	Y	Y	N
5 Spratt	Y	Y	Y	Y	Y	Y	Y	N
6 Tallon	Y	Y	Y	Y	Y	Y	Y	N
SOUTH DAKOTA								
AL Daschle	Y	Y	Y	Y	Y	Y	Y	?

	351	352	353	354	355	356	357	358
TENNESSEE								
1 ***Quillen***	Y	Y	Y	N	?	Y	Y	N
2 ***Duncan***	Y	Y	Y	N	Y	Y	Y	N
3 Lloyd	Y	Y	Y	N	Y	Y	Y	N
4 Cooper	Y	Y	Y	Y	Y	Y	Y	N
5 Boner	Y	Y	Y	N	Y	Y	Y	N
6 Gordon	Y	Y	Y	Y	Y	Y	Y	N
7 ***Sundquist***	N	Y	Y	N	Y	Y	Y	N
8 Jones	Y	Y	Y	N	Y	Y	Y	N
9 Ford	Y	Y	Y	Y	Y	Y	Y	N
TEXAS								
1 Chapman	Y	Y	Y	Y	?	Y	Y	N
2 Wilson	Y	Y	Y	Y	?	?	Y	N
3 ***Bartlett***	N	N	N	N	Y	Y	Y	Y
4 Hall, R.	Y	Y	Y	Y	Y	?	Y	N
5 Bryant	Y	Y	Y	Y	Y	Y	Y	Y
6 ***Barton***	N	N	N	N	Y	Y	Y	Y
7 ***Archer***	N	N	N	N	Y	Y	Y	Y
8 ***Fields***	N	N	N	N	Y	Y	Y	N
9 Brooks	Y	Y	Y	Y	Y	Y	Y	N
10 Pickle	Y	Y	Y	Y	Y	Y	Y	N
11 Leath	Y	Y	Y	Y	Y	Y	Y	N
12 Wright	Y	Y	Y	Y	Y	Y	Y	N
13 ***Boulter***	Y	Y	Y	N	Y	Y	Y	N
14 ***Sweeney***	N	Y	Y	N	Y	Y	Y	N
15 de la Garza	Y	Y	?	?	Y	Y	Y	N
16 Coleman	Y	Y	Y	Y	Y	Y	Y	N
17 Stenholm	Y	Y	Y	Y	Y	Y	Y	N
18 Leland	Y	Y	Y	Y	Y	Y	Y	N
19 ***Combest***	N	Y	Y	N	Y	Y	Y	Y
20 Gonzalez	Y	Y	Y	Y	Y	Y	Y	N
21 ***Loeffler***	N	Y	Y	N	?	?	?	?
22 ***DeLay***	N	N	N	N	Y	Y	Y	N
23 Bustamante	Y	Y	Y	Y	Y	?	Y	N
24 Frost	Y	Y	Y	Y	Y	Y	Y	N
25 Andrews	Y	Y	Y	Y	Y	Y	Y	N
26 ***Armey***	N	N	N	N	Y	Y	Y	Y
27 Ortiz	Y	Y	Y	Y	Y	Y	Y	N
UTAH								
1 ***Hansen***	?	?	?	?	Y	Y	Y	N
2 ***Monson***	N	Y	N	N	Y	Y	Y	N
3 ***Nielson***	N	N	N	N	Y	Y	Y	Y
VERMONT								
AL ***Jeffords***	Y	Y	Y	N	Y	Y	Y	Y
VIRGINIA								
1 ***Bateman***	Y	Y	Y	N	Y	Y	Y	N
2 ***Whitehurst***	?	?	?	?	Y	Y	Y	N
3 ***Bliley***	N	N	N	N	Y	Y	Y	N
4 Sisisky	Y	Y	Y	Y	Y	Y	Y	N
5 Daniel	Y	Y	Y	Y	Y	Y	Y	N
6 Olin	Y	Y	Y	Y	Y	Y	Y	N
7 ***Slaughter***	N	Y	Y	N	Y	Y	Y	?
8 ***Parris***	Y	Y	Y	N	Y	Y	Y	N
9 Boucher	Y	Y	Y	Y	Y	Y	Y	N
10 ***Wolf***	Y	Y	Y	N	Y	Y	Y	N
WASHINGTON								
1 ***Miller***	N	Y	Y	N	Y	Y	Y	Y
2 Swift	Y	Y	Y	Y	Y	Y	Y	N
3 Bonker	Y	Y	Y	Y	Y	Y	Y	N
4 ***Morrison***	Y	Y	Y	N	Y	Y	Y	N
5 Foley	Y	Y	Y	Y	Y	Y	Y	N
6 Dicks	Y	Y	Y	Y	Y	Y	Y	N
7 Lowry	Y	Y	Y	Y	Y	Y	Y	N
8 ***Chandler***	Y	Y	Y	?	Y	Y	Y	N
WEST VIRGINIA								
1 Mollohan	Y	Y	Y	Y	Y	Y	Y	N
2 Staggers	Y	Y	Y	Y	Y	Y	Y	N
3 Wise	Y	Y	Y	N	Y	Y	Y	N
4 Rahall	Y	Y	Y	Y	Y	Y	Y	N
WISCONSIN								
1 Aspin	Y	Y	Y	Y	Y	Y	Y	N
2 Kastenmeier	Y	Y	Y	Y	Y	Y	Y	Y
3 ***Gunderson***	Y	Y	Y	N	Y	Y	Y	N
4 Kleczka	Y	Y	Y	Y	Y	Y	Y	Y
5 Moody	Y	Y	Y	Y	Y	Y	Y	Y
6 ***Petri***	Y	Y	Y	N	Y	Y	Y	Y
7 Obey	Y	Y	Y	Y	Y	Y	Y	Y
8 ***Roth***	N	N	N	N	Y	Y	Y	N
9 ***Sensenbrenner***	Y	Y	N	N	Y	Y	Y	Y
WYOMING								
AL ***Cheney***	N	N	N	N	Y	Y	Y	N

Southern states - Ala., Ark., Fla., Ga., Ky., La., Miss., N.C., Okla., S.C., Tenn., Texas, Va.

* The *Congressional Record* vote number is different from the CQ vote number because the *Record* includes quorum calls in its tally. CQ does not publish quorum call votes.

359. HR 6. Water Resources Development. Weaver, D-Ore., amendment to deauthorize the flood control dam project for Elk Creek Lake, Rogue River Basin, Ore. Rejected 200-220: R 39-137; D 161-83 (ND 119-45, SD 42-38), Nov. 6, 1985. A "yea" was a vote supporting the president's position.

360. H J Res 372. Public Debt Limit. Mack, R-Fla., motion to concur in the Senate amendment to the House amendment to the Senate amendment. All the amendments would provide for declining annual statutory limits on the federal deficit, automatic deficit reduction under certain circumstances, and numerous procedural revisions in the congressional budget process. Motion rejected 177-248: R 175-4; D 2-244 (ND 0-167, SD 2-77), Nov. 6, 1985. (The effect of the Mack motion was to ask the House to approve the Republican-backed Senate version, under which deficits would decline to zero by fiscal 1991, instead of the Democratic-backed House version, which called for a lower deficit in fiscal 1986 and a decline to zero by fiscal 1990.)

361. H J Res 372. Public Debt Limit. Lott, R-Miss., motion to instruct the House conferees to agree to a schedule of deficit reductions to eliminate the federal budget deficit by fiscal 1991, and not to agree to language that provided that the entire bill would be nullified if any part were found to be unconstitutional. Motion rejected 181-239: R 175-3; D 6-236 (ND 2-162, SD 4-74), Nov. 6, 1985.

362. HR 3036. Treasury, Postal Service and General Government Appropriations, Fiscal 1986. Adoption of the conference report on the bill to appropriate $13,154,375,000 in fiscal 1986 for the Treasury Department, Postal Service, Executive Office of the President and other agencies. Adopted 237-171: R 35-135; D 202-36 (ND 148-14, SD 54-22), Nov. 7, 1985. (The president had requested $12,211,347,000 in new budget authority.)

KEY

- Y Voted for (yea).
- # Paired for.
- + Announced for.
- N Voted against (nay).
- X Paired against.
- - Announced against.
- P Voted "present."
- C Voted "present" to avoid possible conflict of interest.
- ? Did not vote or otherwise make a position known.

Democrats ***Republicans***

	359	360	361	362
ALABAMA				
1 ***Callahan***	N	Y	Y	N
2 ***Dickinson***	N	Y	Y	?
3 Nichols	N	N	N	N
4 Bevill	N	N	N	Y
5 Flippo	Y	N	N	Y
6 Erdreich	Y	N	N	N
7 Shelby	Y	N	N	Y
ALASKA				
AL ***Young***	N	Y	Y	Y
ARIZONA				
1 ***McCain***	N	Y	Y	N
2 Udall	Y	N	N	Y
3 ***Stump***	N	Y	Y	N
4 ***Rudd***	N	Y	Y	?
5 ***Kolbe***	N	Y	Y	N
ARKANSAS				
1 Alexander	Y	N	N	Y
2 Robinson	N	Y	N	N
3 ***Hammerschmidt***	N	Y	Y	N
4 Anthony	Y	N	N	?
CALIFORNIA				
1 Bosco	Y	N	N	Y
2 ***Chappie***	N	Y	Y	N
3 Matsui	Y	N	N	Y
4 Fazio	N	N	N	Y
5 Burton	Y	N	N	Y
6 Boxer	Y	N	N	Y
7 Miller	Y	N	N	Y
8 Dellums	Y	N	N	Y
9 Stark	Y	N	N	Y
10 Edwards	Y	N	N	Y
11 Lantos	Y	N	N	Y
12 ***Zschau***	Y	Y	Y	N
13 Mineta	Y	N	N	Y
14 ***Shumway***	N	Y	Y	N
15 Coelho	Y	N	N	Y
16 Panetta	?	N	N	Y
17 ***Pashayan***	N	Y	Y	N
18 Lehman	Y	N	N	Y
19 ***Lagomarsino***	N	Y	Y	N
20 ***Thomas***	N	Y	Y	N
21 ***Fiedler***	N	Y	Y	N
22 ***Moorhead***	N	Y	Y	N
23 Beilenson	Y	N	N	Y
24 Waxman	Y	N	N	Y
25 Roybal	Y	N	N	Y
26 Berman	Y	N	N	Y
27 Levine	Y	N	N	Y
28 Dixon	Y	N	N	Y
29 Hawkins	N	N	N	Y
30 Martinez	Y	N	N	Y
31 Dymally	Y	N	N	Y
32 Anderson	N	N	N	Y
33 ***Dreier***	Y	Y	Y	N
34 Torres	Y	N	N	Y
35 ***Lewis***	N	Y	Y	N
36 Brown	Y	N	N	Y
37 ***McCandless***	N	Y	Y	N
38 ***Dornan***	Y	Y	Y	?
39 ***Dannemeyer***	-	#	#	N
40 ***Badham***	N	Y	Y	N
41 ***Lowery***	N	Y	Y	Y
42 ***Lungren***	N	Y	Y	N
43 ***Packard***	N	Y	Y	N
44 Bates	Y	N	N	Y
45 ***Hunter***	N	Y	Y	?
COLORADO				
1 Schroeder	Y	N	N	N
2 Wirth	Y	N	N	Y
3 ***Strang***	N	Y	Y	N
4 ***Brown***	N	Y	Y	N
5 ***Kramer***	N	Y	Y	N
6 ***Schaefer***	N	Y	Y	N
CONNECTICUT				
1 Kennelly	Y	N	N	Y
2 Gejdenson	Y	N	N	Y
3 Morrison	Y	N	N	Y
4 ***McKinney***	Y	Y	Y	#
5 ***Rowland***	N	Y	Y	Y
6 ***Johnson***	Y	Y	Y	Y
DELAWARE				
AL Carper	Y	N	N	N
FLORIDA				
1 Hutto	N	N	N	N
2 Fuqua	Y	X	X	?
3 Bennett	N	N	N	N
4 Chappell	N	N	N	N
5 ***McCollum***	Y	Y	Y	N
6 MacKay	Y	N	N	N
7 Gibbons	Y	N	N	N
8 ***Young***	N	Y	Y	?
9 ***Bilirakis***	Y	Y	Y	N
10 ***Ireland***	N	Y	Y	N
11 Nelson	+	X	X	+
12 ***Lewis***	N	Y	Y	Y
13 ***Mack***	N	Y	Y	N
14 Mica	N	N	N	Y
15 ***Shaw***	N	Y	Y	N
16 Smith	Y	N	N	Y
17 Lehman	N	N	N	Y
18 Pepper	N	N	N	Y
19 Fascell	Y	N	N	Y
GEORGIA				
1 Thomas	N	N	N	Y
2 Hatcher	Y	N	N	Y
3 Ray	Y	Y	Y	Y
4 ***Swindall***	Y	Y	Y	N
5 Fowler	?	?	?	?
6 ***Gingrich***	N	Y	Y	N
7 Darden	Y	N	N	N
8 Rowland	N	N	N	Y
9 Jenkins	Y	N	N	Y
10 Barnard	N	N	N	?
HAWAII				
1 Heftel	Y	N	?	Y
2 Akaka	N	N	N	Y
IDAHO				
1 ***Craig***	N	Y	Y	N
2 Stallings	Y	N	N	Y
ILLINOIS				
1 Hayes	Y	N	N	Y
2 Savage	Y	N	N	Y
3 Russo	Y	N	N	Y
4 ***O'Brien***	N	Y	Y	?
5 Lipinski	N	N	N	Y
6 ***Hyde***	N	Y	#	N
7 Collins	Y	N	N	Y
8 Rostenkowski	N	N	N	Y
9 Yates	Y	N	N	Y
10 ***Porter***	Y	Y	Y	N
11 Annunzio	Y	N	N	Y
12 ***Crane***	?	Y	Y	N
13 ***Fawell***	Y	Y	Y	N
14 ***Grotberg***	N	Y	Y	N
15 ***Madigan***	N	Y	Y	N
16 ***Martin***	N	Y	Y	N
17 Evans	Y	N	N	Y
18 ***Michel***	N	Y	Y	N
19 Bruce	Y	N	N	Y
20 Durbin	Y	N	N	Y
21 Price	N	N	N	Y
22 Gray	Y	N	N	Y
INDIANA				
1 Visclosky	Y	N	N	Y
2 Sharp	Y	N	N	N
3 ***Hiler***	Y	Y	Y	N
4 ***Coats***	Y	Y	Y	N
5 ***Hillis***	N	Y	Y	N

ND - Northern Democrats SD - Southern Democrats

* Corresponding to Congressional Record Votes 395, 396, 397, 398

	359	360	361	362
6 ***Burton***	N	Y	Y	N
7 ***Myers***	N	Y	Y	Y
8 McCloskey	Y	N	N	Y
9 Hamilton	Y	N	N	Y
10 Jacobs	Y	N	Y	N
IOWA				
1 ***Leach***	Y	Y	Y	N
2 ***Tauke***	Y	Y	Y	N
3 ***Evans***	?	?	Y	N
4 Smith	N	N	N	Y
5 ***Lightfoot***	N	Y	Y	N
6 Bedell	Y	N	N	Y
KANSAS				
1 ***Roberts***	N	Y	Y	N
2 Slattery	Y	N	N	Y
3 ***Meyers***	Y	Y	Y	N
4 Glickman	Y	N	N	N
5 ***Whittaker***	N	Y	Y	N
KENTUCKY				
1 Hubbard	N	N	N	N
2 Natcher	N	N	N	Y
3 Mazzoli	N	N	N	Y
4 ***Snyder***	N	Y	Y	N
5 ***Rogers***	N	Y	Y	Y
6 ***Hopkins***	N	Y	Y	N
7 Perkins	N	N	N	Y
LOUISIANA				
1 ***Livingston***	N	Y	Y	N
2 Boggs	N	N	?	Y
3 Tauzin	N	N	Y	Y
4 Roemer	Y	N	Y	N
5 Huckaby	N	N	N	N
6 ***Moore***	N	Y	Y	N
7 Breaux	N	N	Y	Y
8 Long	N	N	N	Y
MAINE				
1 ***McKernan***	Y	Y	Y	N
2 ***Snowe***	Y	Y	Y	N
MARYLAND				
1 Dyson	N	N	N	Y
2 ***Bentley***	N	Y	Y	N
3 Mikulski	N	N	N	Y
4 ***Holt***	N	N	Y	N
5 Hoyer	N	N	N	Y
6 Byron	N	N	N	?
7 Mitchell	Y	N	N	Y
8 Barnes	Y	N	N	Y
MASSACHUSETTS				
1 ***Conte***	N	N	N	Y
2 Boland	Y	N	N	Y
3 Early	Y	N	N	Y
4 Frank	Y	N	N	Y
5 Atkins	N	N	N	Y
6 Mavroules	?	N	N	Y
7 Markey	Y	N	N	Y
8 O'Neill				
9 Moakley	Y	N	N	Y
10 Studds	Y	N	N	Y
11 Donnelly	N	N	N	Y
MICHIGAN				
1 Conyers	Y	?	X	Y
2 ***Pursell***	N	Y	Y	N
3 Wolpe	Y	N	N	Y
4 ***Siljander***	N	Y	Y	X
5 ***Henry***	Y	Y	Y	N
6 Carr	Y	N	N	Y
7 Kildee	Y	N	N	Y
8 Traxler	Y	N	N	Y
9 ***Vander Jagt***	N	Y	Y	N
10 ***Schuette***	N	Y	Y	N
11 ***Davis***	N	Y	Y	Y
12 Bonior	Y	N	N	Y
13 Crockett	Y	N	N	Y
14 Hertel	Y	N	N	N
15 Ford	N	N	N	Y
16 Dingell	?	N	N	Y
17 Levin	Y	N	N	Y
18 ***Broomfield***	N	Y	Y	N
MINNESOTA				
1 Penny	N	N	N	N
2 ***Weber***	Y	Y	Y	?
3 ***Frenzel***	Y	Y	Y	N
4 Vento	Y	N	N	Y
5 Sabo	Y	N	N	Y
6 Sikorski	Y	N	N	Y
7 ***Stangeland***	N	Y	Y	N
8 Oberstar	Y	N	N	Y
MISSISSIPPI				
1 Whitten	N	N	N	Y
2 ***Franklin***	N	Y	Y	N
3 Montgomery	N	N	N	N
4 Dowdy	N	N	N	Y
5 ***Lott***	N	Y	Y	N
MISSOURI				
1 Clay	?	?	?	?
2 Young	Y	N	N	Y
3 Gephardt	Y	N	N	Y
4 Skelton	Y	N	N	Y
5 Wheat	Y	N	N	Y
6 ***Coleman***	N	Y	Y	N
7 ***Taylor***	N	Y	Y	N
8 ***Emerson***	N	Y	Y	N
9 Volkmer	Y	N	N	Y
MONTANA				
1 Williams	Y	N	N	Y
2 ***Marlenee***	N	Y	Y	N
NEBRASKA				
1 ***Bereuter***	N	Y	Y	N
2 ***Daub***	N	Y	Y	N
3 ***Smith***	N	Y	Y	Y
NEVADA				
1 Reid	Y	N	N	Y
2 ***Vucanovich***	N	Y	Y	N
NEW HAMPSHIRE				
1 ***Smith***	Y	Y	Y	N
2 ***Gregg***	Y	Y	Y	N
NEW JERSEY				
1 Florio	N	N	N	Y
2 Hughes	Y	N	N	N
3 Howard	N	N	N	Y
4 ***Smith***	N	Y	Y	Y
5 ***Roukema***	N	Y	Y	N
6 Dwyer	N	N	N	Y
7 ***Rinaldo***	N	Y	Y	Y
8 Roe	N	N	N	Y
9 Torricelli	N	N	N	Y
10 Rodino	N	N	N	Y
11 ***Gallo***	N	Y	Y	N
12 ***Courter***	N	Y	Y	N
13 ***Saxton***	N	Y	Y	N
14 Guarini	N	N	N	Y
NEW MEXICO				
1 ***Lujan***	N	Y	Y	?
2 ***Skeen***	N	Y	Y	Y
3 Richardson	Y	N	N	Y
NEW YORK				
1 ***Carney***	N	Y	Y	Y
2 Downey	Y	N	N	Y
3 Mrazek	Y	N	N	Y
4 ***Lent***	N	Y	Y	Y
5 ***McGrath***	N	Y	Y	Y
6 Addabbo	?	?	?	?
7 Ackerman	Y	N	N	Y
8 Scheuer	N	N	N	Y
9 Manton	N	N	N	Y
10 Schumer	Y	N	N	Y
11 Towns	N	N	N	Y
12 Owens	Y	N	N	Y
13 Solarz	Y	N	N	Y
14 ***Molinari***	N	Y	Y	Y
15 ***Green***	Y	Y	Y	Y
16 Rangel	N	N	N	Y
17 Weiss	Y	N	N	Y
18 Garcia	Y	N	N	?
19 Biaggi	Y	N	N	Y
20 ***DioGuardi***	N	Y	Y	Y
21 ***Fish***	Y	Y	Y	N
22 ***Gilman***	N	N	N	Y
23 Stratton	Y	N	Y	Y
24 ***Solomon***	N	Y	Y	N
25 ***Boehlert***	Y	Y	Y	Y
26 ***Martin***	N	Y	Y	N
27 ***Wortley***	N	Y	Y	N
28 McHugh	N	N	N	Y
29 ***Horton***	N	Y	N	Y
30 ***Eckert***	?	Y	Y	N
31 ***Kemp***	N	Y	Y	N
32 LaFalce	N	N	N	Y
33 Nowak	N	N	N	Y
34 Lundine	Y	N	?	Y
NORTH CAROLINA				
1 Jones	Y	N	N	Y
2 Valentine	N	N	N	N
3 Whitley	Y	N	N	Y
4 ***Cobey***	Y	Y	Y	N
5 Neal	Y	N	N	N
6 ***Coble***	N	Y	Y	N
7 Rose	Y	N	N	Y
8 Hefner	Y	N	N	Y
9 ***McMillan***	N	Y	Y	N
10 ***Broyhill***	Y	Y	Y	N
11 ***Hendon***	N	Y	Y	N
NORTH DAKOTA				
AL Dorgan	N	N	N	Y
OHIO				
1 Luken	N	N	N	N
2 ***Gradison***	Y	Y	Y	N
3 Hall	Y	N	?	Y
4 ***Oxley***	N	Y	Y	N
5 ***Latta***	N	Y	Y	N
6 ***McEwen***	N	Y	Y	N
7 ***DeWine***	N	Y	Y	N
8 ***Kindness***	N	Y	Y	N
9 Kaptur	Y	N	N	Y
10 ***Miller***	N	Y	Y	N
11 Eckart	Y	N	N	N
12 ***Kasich***	N	Y	Y	N
13 Pease	Y	N	N	Y
14 Seiberling	Y	N	N	Y
15 ***Wylie***	N	Y	Y	N
16 ***Regula***	N	Y	Y	Y
17 Traficant	N	N	N	Y
18 Applegate	N	N	N	?
19 Feighan	Y	N	N	N
20 Oakar	Y	N	N	Y
21 Stokes	Y	N	N	Y
OKLAHOMA				
1 Jones	Y	N	N	N
2 Synar	Y	N	N	Y
3 Watkins	N	N	N	Y
4 McCurdy	Y	N	N	Y
5 ***Edwards***	N	Y	Y	?
6 English	Y	N	N	Y
OREGON				
1 AuCoin	Y	N	N	N
2 ***Smith, R.***	N	Y	Y	N
3 Wyden	Y	N	N	Y
4 Weaver	Y	N	N	N
5 ***Smith, D.***	N	Y	Y	N
PENNSYLVANIA				
1 Foglietta	Y	N	N	Y
2 Gray	N	N	N	Y
3 Borski	Y	N	N	Y
4 Kolter	N	N	N	Y
5 ***Schulze***	P	Y	Y	N
6 Yatron	Y	N	N	Y
7 Edgar	Y	N	N	Y
8 Kostmayer	Y	N	N	Y
9 ***Shuster***	N	Y	Y	N
10 ***McDade***	N	Y	Y	Y
11 Kanjorski	N	N	N	Y
12 Murtha	N	N	N	Y
13 ***Coughlin***	N	Y	Y	N
14 Coyne	N	N	N	Y
15 ***Ritter***	Y	Y	Y	N
16 ***Walker***	Y	Y	Y	N
17 ***Gekas***	N	Y	Y	N
18 Walgren	Y	N	N	Y
19 ***Goodling***	N	Y	Y	N
20 Gaydos	N	N	N	Y
21 ***Ridge***	N	Y	Y	Y
22 Murphy	Y	N	N	N
23 ***Clinger***	N	Y	Y	Y
RHODE ISLAND				
1 St Germain	N	N	N	Y
2 ***Schneider***	Y	Y	Y	Y
SOUTH CAROLINA				
1 ***Hartnett***	N	Y	Y	N
2 ***Spence***	N	Y	Y	N
3 Derrick	Y	N	N	Y
4 ***Campbell***	N	Y	Y	N
5 Spratt	Y	N	N	Y
6 Tallon	Y	N	N	Y
SOUTH DAKOTA				
AL Daschle	N	N	N	Y
TENNESSEE				
1 ***Quillen***	N	Y	Y	N
2 ***Duncan***	N	Y	Y	N
3 Lloyd	N	N	N	Y
4 Cooper	Y	N	N	Y
5 Boner	N	N	N	Y
6 Gordon	N	N	N	Y
7 ***Sundquist***	N	Y	Y	N
8 Jones	Y	N	N	Y
9 Ford	Y	N	N	Y
TEXAS				
1 Chapman	Y	N	N	N
2 Wilson	N	N	N	Y
3 ***Bartlett***	Y	Y	Y	N
4 Hall, R.	N	N	N	N
5 Bryant	Y	N	N	Y
6 ***Barton***	Y	Y	Y	N
7 ***Archer***	Y	Y	Y	N
8 ***Fields***	N	Y	Y	N
9 Brooks	Y	N	N	Y
10 Pickle	N	N	N	Y
11 Leath	N	N	N	N
12 Wright	Y	N	N	Y
13 ***Boulter***	N	Y	Y	N
14 ***Sweeney***	Y	Y	Y	N
15 de la Garza	N	N	N	Y
16 Coleman	Y	N	N	Y
17 Stenholm	Y	N	N	N
18 Leland	Y	N	N	Y
19 ***Combest***	N	Y	Y	N
20 Gonzalez	Y	N	N	Y
21 ***Loeffler***	?	#	#	?
22 ***DeLay***	N	Y	Y	N
23 Bustamante	Y	N	N	Y
24 Frost	N	N	N	Y
25 Andrews	Y	N	N	Y
26 ***Armey***	Y	Y	Y	N
27 Ortiz	N	N	N	?
UTAH				
1 ***Hansen***	N	Y	Y	N
2 ***Monson***	N	Y	Y	N
3 ***Nielson***	N	Y	Y	N
VERMONT				
AL ***Jeffords***	Y	N	Y	Y
VIRGINIA				
1 ***Bateman***	N	Y	Y	Y
2 ***Whitehurst***	Y	Y	?	N
3 ***Bliley***	N	Y	Y	N
4 Sisisky	N	N	N	N
5 Daniel	Y	N	N	N
6 Olin	Y	N	N	Y
7 ***Slaughter***	N	Y	Y	N
8 ***Parris***	N	Y	Y	Y
9 Boucher	N	N	N	Y
10 ***Wolf***	N	Y	Y	Y
WASHINGTON				
1 ***Miller***	Y	Y	Y	Y
2 Swift	Y	N	N	Y
3 Bonker	Y	N	N	Y
4 ***Morrison***	N	Y	Y	Y
5 Foley	Y	N	N	Y
6 Dicks	N	N	N	Y
7 Lowry	Y	N	N	Y
8 ***Chandler***	N	Y	Y	Y
WEST VIRGINIA				
1 Mollohan	N	N	N	Y
2 Staggers	?	N	N	?
3 Wise	Y	N	N	?
4 Rahall	N	N	N	Y
WISCONSIN				
1 Aspin	Y	N	N	Y
2 Kastenmeier	Y	N	N	Y
3 ***Gunderson***	N	Y	Y	N
4 Kleczka	Y	N	N	Y
5 Moody	Y	N	N	+
6 ***Petri***	N	Y	Y	Y
7 Obey	Y	N	N	Y
8 ***Roth***	N	Y	Y	N
9 ***Sensenbrenner***	N	Y	Y	N
WYOMING				
AL ***Cheney***	N	Y	Y	N

Southern states - Ala., Ark., Fla., Ga., Ky., La., Miss., N.C., Okla., S.C., Tenn., Texas, Va.

* The *Congressional Record* vote number is different from the CQ vote number because the *Record* includes quorum calls in its tally. CQ does not publish quorum call votes.

363. H Res 314. Medvid Defection. Lantos, D-Calif., motion to suspend the rules and adopt the resolution to express the sense of the House that Ukrainian sailor Miroslav Medvid should not be allowed to be removed from the United States until a complete investigation can determine whether he has been accorded all rights due him as a possible defector. Motion agreed to 405-3: R 168-2; D 237-1 (ND 160-1, SD 77-0), Nov. 12, 1985. A two-thirds majority of those present and voting (272 in this case) is required for adoption under suspension of the rules.

364. HR 2409. National Institutes of Health Authorizations, Fiscal 1986-88. Passage, over President Reagan's Nov. 8 veto, of the bill to reauthorize selected biomedical research activities at the National Institutes of Health through fiscal 1988 and to set up a new arthritis research institute and nursing research center at the institutes. Passed 380-32: R 142-30; D 238-2 (ND 162-0, SD 76-2), Nov. 12, 1985. A two-thirds majority of those present and voting (275 in this case) of both houses is required to override a veto. A "nay" was a vote supporting the president's position.

365. H J Res 441. Further Continuing Appropriations, Fiscal 1986. Passage of the joint resolution to provide continued spending authority from Nov. 14 through Dec. 12, 1985, for programs and agencies for which regular fiscal 1986 appropriations bills had not been signed into law. The resolution provided that funding levels for programs would, depending on the status of uncompleted appropriations bills, be the lower amount of that enacted for fiscal 1985 or that set in appropriations bills passed by one or both houses but not yet signed into law. Once enacted, appropriations bills for fiscal 1986 would supersede levels set by the continuing appropriations resolution. Passed 259-151: R 47-125; D 212-26 (ND 140-21, SD 72-5), Nov. 12, 1985. A "yea" was a vote supporting the president's position.

366. HR 1616. Plant Closing Notification. Adoption of the rule (H Res 313) to provide for House floor consideration of the bill to require employers to provide three months' notice before permanently laying off 50 or more employees. Adopted 233-176: R 24-148; D 209-28 (ND 157-3, SD 52-25), Nov. 12, 1985.

367. Procedural Motion. Cobey, R-N.C., motion to approve the House *Journal* of Tuesday, Nov. 12. Motion agreed to 269-131: R 46-121; D 223-10 (ND 150-8, SD 73-2), Nov. 13, 1985.

368. HR 3038. Department of Housing and Urban Development/Independent Agencies Appropriations, Fiscal 1986. Adoption of the conference report on the bill to appropriate $57,290,141,490 in new budget authority in fiscal 1986 for the Department of Housing and Urban Development and 17 independent agencies. Adopted 268-153: R 68-108; D 200-45 (ND 144-23, SD 56-22), Nov. 13, 1985. (The president had requested $50,144,230,000 in new budget authority.)

369. HR 3721. Temporary Public Debt Limit Increase. Passage of the bill to raise temporarily the ceiling on the federal debt to no more than $1.904 trillion, from $1.824 trillion, with the ceiling reverting to the lower number after Dec. 13, and also to direct the secretary of the Treasury to restore to the Social Security trust funds and other federal trust funds any securities disinvested since Sept. 30, 1985. Passed 300-121: R 88-90; D 212-31 (ND 149-18, SD 63-13), Nov. 13, 1985.

370. HR 6. Water Resources Development. Passage of the bill to authorize appropriations for water resources development and conservation projects, to establish a National Water Resources Policy Board, and for other purposes. (The Congressional Budget Office estimated that authorizations in the bill could result in federal outlays of $20 billion through 1998.) Passed 358-60: R 134-43; D 224-17 (ND 148-15, SD 76-2), Nov. 13, 1985. A "nay" was a vote supporting the president's position.

KEY

- Y Voted for (yea).
- # Paired for.
- \+ Announced for.
- N Voted against (nay).
- X Paired against.
- \- Announced against.
- P Voted "present."
- C Voted "present" to avoid possible conflict of interest.
- ? Did not vote or otherwise make a position known.

Democrats ***Republicans***

	363	364	365	366	367	368	369	370
ALABAMA								
1 ***Callahan***	Y	Y	N	N	N	N	N	Y
2 ***Dickinson***	Y	Y	N	N	N	Y	Y	Y
3 Nichols	Y	Y	Y	N	Y	Y	Y	Y
4 Bevill	Y	Y	Y	Y	Y	Y	Y	Y
5 Flippo	Y	Y	Y	Y	Y	Y	Y	Y
6 Erdreich	Y	Y	Y	Y	Y	Y	Y	Y
7 Shelby	Y	Y	Y	N	Y	Y	Y	Y
ALASKA								
AL ***Young***	Y	Y	N	Y	N	Y	N	Y
ARIZONA								
1 ***McCain***	Y	Y	N	N	N	Y	Y	Y
2 Udall	Y	Y	Y	Y	Y	Y	Y	Y
3 ***Stump***	Y	N	N	N	N	N	N	Y
4 ***Rudd***	Y	Y	Y	N	Y	N	Y	Y
5 ***Kolbe***	Y	Y	N	N	N	Y	N	N
ARKANSAS								
1 Alexander	Y	Y	Y	Y	Y	Y	Y	?
2 Robinson	Y	Y	Y	Y	Y	N	N	Y
3 ***Hammerschmidt***	Y	Y	Y	N	Y	N	Y	Y
4 Anthony	Y	Y	Y	N	Y	Y	Y	Y
CALIFORNIA								
1 Bosco	?	?	?	?	?	Y	N	Y
2 ***Chappie***	?	?	?	?	?	N	N	Y
3 Matsui	Y	Y	Y	Y	Y	Y	Y	Y
4 Fazio	Y	Y	Y	Y	Y	Y	Y	Y
5 Burton	Y	Y	Y	Y	Y	Y	Y	Y
6 Boxer	Y	Y	Y	Y	Y	Y	Y	Y
7 Miller	Y	Y	Y	Y	N	Y	N	Y
8 Dellums	Y	Y	Y	Y	Y	Y	Y	Y
9 Stark	Y	Y	Y	Y	Y	Y	Y	Y
10 Edwards	Y	Y	Y	Y	Y	Y	Y	Y
11 Lantos	Y	Y	Y	Y	Y	Y	Y	Y
12 ***Zschau***	Y	Y	N	N	N	N	N	N
13 Mineta	Y	Y	Y	Y	Y	Y	Y	Y
14 ***Shumway***	Y	N	N	N	Y	N	N	N
15 Coelho	Y	Y	Y	Y	Y	Y	Y	Y
16 Panetta	Y	Y	Y	Y	Y	Y	Y	Y
17 ***Pashayan***	?	?	?	?	N	Y	Y	Y
18 Lehman	Y	Y	Y	Y	Y	Y	Y	Y
19 ***Lagomarsino***	Y	Y	N	N	N	N	N	Y
20 ***Thomas***	Y	Y	N	N	N	N	N	Y
21 ***Fiedler***	Y	Y	N	N	N	N	N	Y
22 ***Moorhead***	Y	N	N	N	N	N	N	Y
23 Beilenson	Y	Y	Y	Y	Y	Y	Y	Y
24 Waxman	Y	Y	Y	Y	Y	Y	Y	Y
25 Roybal	Y	Y	Y	Y	Y	Y	Y	Y
26 Berman	Y	Y	Y	Y	Y	Y	Y	Y
27 Levine	Y	Y	Y	Y	Y	Y	Y	Y
28 Dixon	Y	Y	Y	Y	Y	Y	Y	Y
29 Hawkins	Y	Y	Y	Y	Y	Y	Y	?
30 Martinez	Y	Y	Y	Y	Y	Y	Y	Y
31 Dymally	Y	Y	Y	Y	P	Y	Y	Y
32 Anderson	Y	Y	Y	Y	Y	Y	N	Y
33 ***Dreier***	Y	Y	N	N	N	N	N	N
34 Torres	Y	Y	Y	Y	Y	Y	Y	Y
35 ***Lewis***	Y	N	Y	N	N	Y	Y	Y
36 Brown	?	Y	?	?	Y	Y	Y	Y
37 ***McCandless***	?	Y	N	N	N	N	N	Y
38 ***Dornan***	Y	Y	N	N	N	N	N	Y
39 ***Dannemeyer***	Y	N	N	N	N	N	N	Y
40 ***Badham***	Y	N	N	N	N	N	N	Y
41 ***Lowery***	Y	Y	Y	N	?	Y	Y	Y
42 ***Lungren***	Y	Y	N	N	N	N	N	Y
43 ***Packard***	Y	Y	N	N	Y	Y	N	Y
44 Bates	Y	Y	N	Y	Y	Y	N	N
45 ***Hunter***	?	?	?	N	Y	Y	N	N
COLORADO								
1 Schroeder	Y	Y	N	N	N	N	Y	N
2 Wirth	Y	Y	N	Y	Y	N	Y	Y
3 ***Strang***	Y	Y	N	N	N	N	N	Y
4 ***Brown***	Y	N	N	N	N	N	N	N
5 ***Kramer***	Y	Y	N	N	N	N	N	N
6 ***Schaefer***	Y	Y	N	N	N	N	N	Y
CONNECTICUT								
1 Kennelly	Y	Y	Y	Y	Y	Y	Y	Y
2 Gejdenson	Y	Y	Y	Y	Y	Y	Y	Y
3 Morrison	Y	Y	Y	Y	Y	Y	Y	Y
4 ***McKinney***	?	?	#	?	?	#	?	#
5 ***Rowland***	Y	Y	N	N	N	Y	Y	Y
6 ***Johnson***	Y	Y	N	N	Y	Y	Y	Y
DELAWARE								
AL Carper	Y	Y	Y	Y	Y	N	Y	Y
FLORIDA								
1 Hutto	Y	Y	Y	N	Y	Y	Y	Y
2 Fuqua	Y	Y	Y	Y	Y	#	?	Y
3 Bennett	Y	Y	Y	Y	Y	Y	Y	N
4 Chappell	Y	Y	Y	Y	Y	Y	Y	Y
5 ***McCollum***	Y	Y	N	N	N	N	Y	Y
6 MacKay	Y	Y	Y	Y	Y	N	Y	Y
7 Gibbons	?	?	?	?	?	N	Y	Y
8 ***Young***	N	Y	Y	N	N	Y	Y	Y
9 ***Bilirakis***	Y	Y	N	N	N	N	Y	Y
10 ***Ireland***	Y	Y	N	N	N	N	N	Y
11 Nelson	Y	Y	Y	X	+	X	+	+
12 ***Lewis***	Y	Y	N	N	N	Y	N	Y
13 ***Mack***	Y	Y	N	N	N	N	N	N
14 Mica	?	?	?	?	?	Y	N	Y
15 ***Shaw***	Y	Y	N	N	N	N	Y	Y
16 Smith	Y	Y	Y	Y	Y	Y	Y	Y
17 Lehman	Y	Y	Y	Y	Y	Y	Y	Y
18 Pepper	Y	Y	Y	Y	Y	Y	Y	Y
19 Fascell	Y	Y	Y	Y	Y	Y	Y	Y
GEORGIA								
1 Thomas	Y	Y	Y	Y	Y	Y	Y	Y
2 Hatcher	Y	Y	Y	Y	Y	Y	Y	Y
3 Ray	Y	N	Y	N	Y	Y	N	Y
4 ***Swindall***	Y	Y	N	N	N	N	N	N
5 Fowler	?	?	?	?	?	?	?	?
6 ***Gingrich***	?	Y	N	N	N	N	N	Y
7 Darden	Y	Y	Y	N	Y	Y	Y	Y
8 Rowland	Y	Y	Y	Y	Y	Y	Y	Y
9 Jenkins	Y	Y	Y	N	Y	Y	Y	Y
10 Barnard	Y	Y	Y	N	Y	N	Y	Y
HAWAII								
1 Heftel	Y	Y	Y	Y	?	Y	Y	Y
2 Akaka	Y	Y	Y	Y	Y	Y	Y	Y
IDAHO								
1 ***Craig***	Y	Y	N	N	N	N	N	Y
2 Stallings	Y	Y	Y	Y	Y	N	N	Y
ILLINOIS								
1 Hayes	Y	Y	Y	Y	Y	Y	Y	Y
2 Savage	Y	Y	Y	Y	Y	Y	Y	Y
3 Russo	Y	Y	N	Y	Y	N	N	Y
4 ***O'Brien***	?	?	#	?	?	?	?	?
5 Lipinski	Y	Y	Y	Y	Y	N	Y	Y
6 ***Hyde***	Y	Y	N	N	?	N	Y	Y
7 Collins	Y	Y	Y	Y	Y	Y	Y	Y
8 Rostenkowski	Y	Y	Y	Y	Y	Y	Y	Y
9 Yates	Y	Y	Y	Y	Y	Y	Y	N
10 ***Porter***	Y	Y	N	N	?	Y	N	Y
11 Annunzio	Y	Y	Y	Y	Y	Y	Y	Y
12 ***Crane***	Y	N	N	N	N	N	N	N
13 ***Fawell***	Y	N	N	N	N	N	N	N
14 ***Grotberg***	Y	Y	N	N	N	N	N	N
15 ***Madigan***	Y	Y	N	N	N	Y	Y	Y
16 ***Martin***	Y	Y	N	N	N	N	N	Y
17 Evans	Y	Y	Y	Y	Y	Y	Y	Y
18 ***Michel***	Y	N	Y	N	N	Y	Y	N
19 Bruce	Y	Y	N	Y	Y	Y	Y	Y
20 Durbin	Y	Y	Y	Y	N	Y	Y	Y
21 Price	Y	Y	Y	Y	Y	Y	Y	?
22 Gray	?	?	?	?	Y	Y	Y	Y
INDIANA								
1 Visclosky	Y	Y	Y	Y	Y	Y	Y	Y
2 Sharp	Y	Y	Y	Y	Y	N	Y	N
3 ***Hiler***	Y	Y	N	N	N	N	N	N
4 ***Coats***	Y	Y	N	N	N	Y	N	N
5 ***Hillis***	Y	Y	Y	N	Y	Y	Y	Y

ND - Northern Democrats SD - Southern Democrats

* Corresponding to Congressional Record Votes 399, 400, 401, 402, 403, 404, 405, 406

	363	364	365	366	367	368	369	370
6 ***Burton***	Y	Y	N	N	N	N	N	N
7 ***Myers***	N	Y	Y	N	Y	Y	N	Y
8 McCloskey	Y	Y	Y	Y	Y	Y	Y	Y
9 Hamilton	Y	Y	Y	Y	Y	N	Y	Y
10 Jacobs	Y	Y	N	Y	N	Y	Y	N
IOWA								
1 ***Leach***	Y	Y	N	Y	N	N	Y	N
2 ***Tauke***	Y	N	N	N	N	N	N	N
3 ***Evans***	Y	N	N	N	N	N	N	N
4 Smith	Y	Y	Y	Y	Y	Y	Y	Y
5 ***Lightfoot***	Y	Y	N	N	N	N	Y	Y
6 Bedell	Y	Y	Y	Y	Y	Y	Y	N
KANSAS								
1 ***Roberts***	Y	Y	N	N	N	N	N	Y
2 Slattery	Y	Y	Y	Y	Y	N	Y	Y
3 ***Meyers***	Y	Y	N	N	N	N	Y	Y
4 Glickman	Y	Y	N	Y	Y	Y	Y	Y
5 ***Whittaker***	Y	Y	N	N	N	N	N	Y
KENTUCKY								
1 Hubbard	Y	N	N	Y	Y	N	N	N
2 Natcher	Y	Y	Y	Y	Y	Y	Y	Y
3 Mazzoli	Y	Y	Y	Y	Y	Y	Y	Y
4 ***Snyder***	Y	N	N	N	Y	N	N	Y
5 ***Rogers***	Y	Y	Y	N	N	Y	Y	Y
6 ***Hopkins***	Y	Y	N	N	N	N	N	N
7 Perkins	Y	Y	Y	Y	Y	Y	Y	Y
LOUISIANA								
1 ***Livingston***	Y	Y	Y	N	N	N	Y	Y
2 Boggs	Y	Y	Y	Y	Y	Y	Y	Y
3 Tauzin	Y	Y	Y	N	Y	N	Y	Y
4 Roemer	Y	Y	N	N	N	N	N	Y
5 Huckaby	?	Y	Y	N	Y	N	N	Y
6 ***Moore***	Y	Y	Y	N	Y	N	Y	Y
7 Breaux	?	?	?	?	Y	N	Y	Y
8 Long	Y	Y	Y	Y	P	Y	?	Y
MAINE								
1 ***McKernan***	Y	Y	N	N	N	Y	Y	Y
2 ***Snowe***	Y	Y	N	Y	N	Y	Y	Y
MARYLAND								
1 Dyson	Y	Y	Y	Y	N	Y	N	Y
2 ***Bentley***	Y	Y	N	Y	?	Y	Y	Y
3 Mikulski	Y	Y	Y	Y	Y	Y	Y	Y
4 ***Holt***	Y	Y	N	N	Y	Y	Y	Y
5 Hoyer	Y	Y	Y	Y	Y	Y	Y	Y
6 Byron	Y	Y	Y	Y	Y	Y	Y	Y
7 Mitchell	Y	Y	Y	Y	?	Y	Y	Y
8 Barnes	Y	Y	Y	Y	Y	Y	Y	Y
MASSACHUSETTS								
1 ***Conte***	Y	Y	Y	Y	N	Y	Y	Y
2 Boland	?	?	?	?	Y	Y	Y	Y
3 Early	Y	Y	Y	Y	Y	Y	Y	Y
4 Frank	Y	Y	Y	Y	Y	Y	Y	Y
5 Atkins	Y	Y	Y	Y	Y	Y	Y	Y
6 Mavroules	Y	Y	Y	Y	Y	Y	Y	Y
7 Markey	Y	Y	Y	Y	Y	Y	Y	Y
8 O'Neill								
9 Moakley	Y	Y	Y	Y	?	Y	Y	Y
10 Studds	Y	Y	Y	Y	Y	Y	Y	Y
11 Donnelly	Y	Y	Y	Y	Y	Y	Y	Y
MICHIGAN								
1 Conyers	Y	Y	Y	Y	Y	Y	Y	Y
2 ***Pursell***	Y	Y	N	Y	Y	Y	N	N
3 Wolpe	Y	Y	N	Y	Y	Y	Y	N
4 ***Siljander***	Y	Y	N	N	N	N	N	Y
5 ***Henry***	Y	Y	N	N	Y	N	N	Y
6 Carr	Y	Y	Y	Y	Y	Y	N	N
7 Kildee	Y	Y	Y	Y	Y	Y	Y	Y
8 Traxler	Y	Y	Y	Y	Y	Y	Y	Y
9 ***Vander Jagt***	Y	Y	N	N	N	N	N	Y
10 ***Schuette***	Y	Y	N	N	N	Y	Y	Y
11 ***Davis***	Y	Y	N	Y	Y	Y	Y	Y
12 Bonior	Y	Y	Y	Y	Y	Y	Y	Y
13 Crockett	N	Y	Y	Y	Y	Y	N	Y
14 Hertel	Y	Y	N	Y	Y	N	Y	N
15 Ford	Y	Y	Y	Y	?	Y	Y	Y
16 Dingell	Y	Y	Y	Y	Y	Y	Y	Y
17 Levin	Y	Y	Y	Y	Y	Y	Y	Y
18 ***Broomfield***	Y	Y	N	N	Y	Y	Y	Y
MINNESOTA								
1 Penny	Y	Y	N	Y	N	N	Y	Y
2 ***Weber***	Y	Y	N	N	N	N	N	N
3 ***Frenzel***	Y	Y	N	N	?	?	?	X
4 Vento	Y	Y	Y	Y	Y	Y	Y	N
5 Sabo	Y	Y	Y	Y	Y	Y	Y	Y
6 Sikorski	Y	Y	N	Y	N	Y	Y	N
7 ***Stangeland***	Y	?	N	N	N	N	Y	Y
8 Oberstar	Y	Y	Y	Y	Y	Y	Y	Y
MISSISSIPPI								
1 Whitten	Y	Y	Y	N	Y	Y	Y	Y
2 ***Franklin***	Y	Y	N	N	N	N	N	Y
3 Montgomery	Y	Y	Y	N	Y	Y	Y	Y
4 Dowdy	Y	Y	Y	N	Y	Y	Y	Y
5 ***Lott***	Y	N	Y	N	Y	N	Y	Y
MISSOURI								
1 Clay	Y	Y	Y	Y	N	Y	Y	Y
2 Young	Y	Y	Y	Y	Y	Y	Y	Y
3 Gephardt	Y	Y	Y	Y	Y	Y	Y	Y
4 Skelton	Y	Y	Y	Y	Y	Y	Y	Y
5 Wheat	Y	Y	Y	Y	Y	Y	Y	Y
6 ***Coleman***	Y	Y	N	N	N	Y	Y	Y
7 ***Taylor***	Y	Y	Y	N	N	N	N	Y
8 ***Emerson***	Y	Y	Y	N	N	Y	Y	Y
9 Volkmer	Y	Y	Y	Y	Y	Y	Y	Y
MONTANA								
1 Williams	Y	Y	Y	Y	?	Y	Y	Y
2 ***Marlenee***	Y	Y	N	N	?	N	N	Y
NEBRASKA								
1 ***Bereuter***	Y	Y	N	N	N	N	N	Y
2 ***Daub***	Y	Y	N	N	N	N	N	Y
3 ***Smith***	Y	Y	Y	N	Y	N	N	Y
NEVADA								
1 Reid	Y	Y	Y	Y	Y	Y	Y	Y
2 ***Vucanovich***	Y	Y	N	N	N	N	N	Y
NEW HAMPSHIRE								
1 ***Smith***	Y	Y	N	N	N	N	N	N
2 ***Gregg***	Y	Y	N	N	N	N	N	N
NEW JERSEY								
1 Florio	Y	Y	Y	Y	Y	Y	N	Y
2 Hughes	Y	Y	N	Y	Y	N	Y	Y
3 Howard	Y	Y	Y	Y	Y	Y	Y	Y
4 ***Smith***	Y	Y	Y	Y	Y	Y	Y	Y
5 ***Roukema***	Y	Y	Y	N	N	Y	Y	Y
6 Dwyer	Y	Y	Y	Y	Y	Y	Y	Y
7 ***Rinaldo***	Y	Y	Y	Y	Y	Y	Y	Y
8 Roe	Y	Y	Y	Y	Y	Y	Y	Y
9 Torricelli	+	+	+	#	Y	Y	Y	Y
10 Rodino	Y	Y	Y	Y	Y	Y	Y	Y
11 ***Gallo***	Y	Y	Y	N	N	Y	Y	Y
12 ***Courter***	Y	Y	N	Y	N	Y	Y	Y
13 ***Saxton***	Y	Y	N	N	N	Y	Y	Y
14 Guarini	Y	Y	Y	Y	Y	Y	Y	Y
NEW MEXICO								
1 ***Lujan***	Y	Y	N	N	Y	N	N	Y
2 ***Skeen***	Y	Y	Y	N	N	Y	N	Y
3 Richardson	Y	Y	Y	Y	Y	Y	Y	Y
NEW YORK								
1 ***Carney***	Y	Y	N	N	N	N	Y	Y
2 Downey	Y	Y	Y	Y	Y	Y	Y	Y
3 Mrazek	Y	Y	N	Y	Y	?	N	N
4 ***Lent***	Y	Y	Y	N	N	N	Y	Y
5 ***McGrath***	Y	Y	N	N	N	N	Y	Y
6 Addabbo	?	?	?	?	?	?	?	?
7 Ackerman	Y	Y	Y	Y	Y	Y	Y	Y
8 Scheuer	Y	Y	Y	Y	Y	Y	Y	Y
9 Manton	Y	Y	Y	Y	Y	Y	Y	Y
10 Schumer	Y	Y	Y	Y	Y	N	Y	Y
11 Towns	Y	Y	Y	Y	P	Y	Y	Y
12 Owens	Y	Y	Y	Y	Y	Y	Y	Y
13 Solarz	Y	Y	Y	Y	Y	Y	Y	Y
14 ***Molinari***	Y	Y	Y	Y	N	Y	N	Y
15 ***Green***	Y	Y	Y	Y	Y	Y	Y	Y
16 Rangel	Y	Y	Y	Y	Y	Y	Y	?
17 Weiss	Y	Y	Y	Y	Y	Y	Y	Y
18 Garcia	Y	Y	Y	Y	Y	Y	Y	Y
19 Biaggi	Y	Y	Y	Y	Y	Y	Y	Y
20 ***DioGuardi***	Y	Y	N	N	Y	Y	Y	Y
21 ***Fish***	Y	Y	Y	Y	Y	Y	Y	Y
22 ***Gilman***	Y	Y	Y	Y	Y	Y	N	Y
23 Stratton	Y	Y	Y	Y	Y	Y	Y	Y
24 ***Solomon***	Y	N	N	N	N	N	N	N
25 ***Boehlert***	Y	Y	N	Y	N	Y	Y	Y
26 ***Martin***	Y	Y	Y	N	N	Y	Y	Y
27 ***Wortley***	Y	Y	Y	Y	Y	Y	Y	Y
28 McHugh	Y	Y	Y	Y	Y	Y	Y	Y
29 ***Horton***	Y	Y	Y	Y	Y	Y	Y	Y
30 ***Eckert***	Y	N	Y	N	Y	N	Y	N
31 ***Kemp***	Y	Y	Y	N	?	?	Y	Y
32 LaFalce	Y	Y	Y	Y	Y	Y	Y	Y
33 Nowak	Y	Y	Y	Y	Y	Y	Y	Y
34 Lundine	Y	Y	Y	N	Y	Y	?	Y
NORTH CAROLINA								
1 Jones	Y	Y	Y	Y	Y	Y	Y	Y
2 Valentine	Y	Y	Y	N	Y	Y	Y	Y
3 Whitley	Y	Y	Y	Y	Y	Y	Y	Y
4 ***Cobey***	Y	Y	N	N	N	N	N	N
5 Neal	Y	Y	N	N	Y	N	Y	Y
6 ***Coble***	Y	Y	N	N	?	N	Y	Y
7 Rose	Y	Y	Y	Y	Y	Y	N	Y
8 Hefner	Y	Y	Y	N	Y	Y	Y	Y
9 ***McMillan***	Y	Y	N	N	N	N	Y	N
10 ***Broyhill***	Y	Y	N	N	Y	N	N	N
11 ***Hendon***	Y	Y	N	N	?	N	Y	Y
NORTH DAKOTA								
AL Dorgan	Y	Y	N	Y	Y	N	N	Y
OHIO								
1 Luken	Y	Y	Y	Y	Y	N	N	Y
2 ***Gradison***	Y	Y	Y	N	Y	N	Y	N
3 Hall	Y	Y	Y	Y	Y	Y	Y	Y
4 ***Oxley***	Y	Y	N	N	N	N	Y	Y
5 ***Latta***	Y	N	N	N	N	N	Y	N
6 ***McEwen***	Y	N	N	N	N	N	N	Y
7 ***DeWine***	Y	Y	N	N	N	N	Y	Y
8 ***Kindness***	?	?	?	?	N	N	N	Y
9 Kaptur	Y	Y	N	Y	Y	N	Y	Y
10 ***Miller***	Y	N	N	Y	N	N	Y	Y
11 Eckart	Y	Y	Y	Y	Y	Y	Y	Y
12 ***Kasich***	Y	Y	N	N	N	N	Y	Y
13 Pease	Y	Y	Y	Y	Y	Y	Y	Y
14 Seiberling	Y	Y	Y	Y	?	Y	Y	N
15 ***Wylie***	Y	Y	N	N	Y	N	Y	Y
16 ***Regula***	Y	Y	Y	N	Y	Y	Y	Y
17 Traficant	Y	Y	Y	Y	Y	Y	Y	Y
18 Applegate	Y	Y	Y	Y	Y	N	N	Y
19 Feighan	Y	Y	N	Y	Y	Y	Y	Y
20 Oakar	Y	Y	Y	Y	Y	Y	Y	Y
21 Stokes	Y	Y	Y	Y	Y	Y	Y	Y
OKLAHOMA								
1 Jones	Y	Y	Y	Y	Y	N	Y	Y
2 Synar	Y	Y	Y	Y	Y	Y	Y	Y
3 Watkins	Y	Y	Y	N	Y	Y	Y	Y
4 McCurdy	Y	Y	Y	N	Y	N	Y	Y
5 ***Edwards***	Y	Y	N	N	N	N	N	Y
6 English	Y	Y	N	N	Y	N	N	Y
OREGON								
1 AuCoin	Y	Y	N	?	Y	N	N	Y
2 ***Smith, R.***	Y	Y	N	N	N	N	N	Y
3 Wyden	Y	Y	N	N	N	Y	Y	Y
4 Weaver	Y	Y	N	Y	Y	N	N	N
5 ***Smith, D.***	Y	N	N	N	N	N	N	Y
PENNSYLVANIA								
1 Foglietta	Y	Y	Y	Y	Y	Y	Y	Y
2 Gray	Y	Y	Y	?	Y	Y	Y	Y
3 Borski	Y	Y	Y	Y	Y	Y	Y	Y
4 Kolter	Y	Y	Y	Y	Y	Y	Y	Y
5 ***Schulze***	Y	Y	N	N	Y	N	Y	Y
6 Yatron	Y	Y	Y	Y	Y	Y	N	Y
7 Edgar	?	?	?	?	?	?	?	?
8 Kostmayer	Y	Y	Y	Y	Y	Y	Y	Y
9 ***Shuster***	Y	Y	N	N	N	N	N	Y
10 ***McDade***	Y	Y	Y	Y	Y	Y	Y	Y
11 Kanjorski	Y	Y	Y	Y	Y	N	Y	Y
12 Murtha	Y	Y	Y	Y	Y	Y	Y	Y
13 ***Coughlin***	Y	Y	N	N	N	Y	Y	N
14 Coyne	Y	Y	Y	Y	Y	Y	Y	Y
15 ***Ritter***	Y	Y	N	Y	Y	Y	N	N
16 ***Walker***	Y	Y	N	N	N	N	N	N
17 ***Gekas***	Y	N	N	Y	N	N	N	Y
18 Walgren	Y	Y	Y	Y	Y	Y	Y	?
19 ***Goodling***	Y	Y	N	N	N	N	Y	N
20 Gaydos	Y	Y	Y	Y	?	Y	Y	?
21 ***Ridge***	Y	Y	N	Y	N	Y	Y	Y
22 Murphy	Y	Y	Y	Y	Y	Y	N	Y
23 ***Clinger***	Y	Y	Y	N	N	Y	Y	Y
RHODE ISLAND								
1 St Germain	Y	Y	Y	Y	Y	Y	Y	Y
2 ***Schneider***	Y	Y	Y	Y	Y	Y	Y	N
SOUTH CAROLINA								
1 ***Hartnett***	+	-	X	-	?	N	N	Y
2 ***Spence***	Y	Y	N	N	N	N	N	Y
3 Derrick	Y	Y	Y	N	Y	Y	Y	Y
4 ***Campbell***	Y	Y	N	N	?	?	Y	Y
5 Spratt	Y	Y	Y	Y	?	Y	Y	Y
6 Tallon	Y	Y	Y	Y	Y	Y	Y	Y
SOUTH DAKOTA								
AL Daschle	?	?	?	Y	Y	Y	Y	Y
TENNESSEE								
1 ***Quillen***	Y	Y	Y	?	Y	Y	Y	Y
2 ***Duncan***	Y	Y	Y	N	Y	Y	Y	Y
3 Lloyd	Y	Y	Y	Y	N	Y	N	Y
4 Cooper	Y	Y	?	Y	Y	Y	Y	Y
5 Boner	Y	Y	Y	Y	Y	Y	Y	Y
6 Gordon	Y	Y	Y	Y	Y	N	Y	Y
7 ***Sundquist***	Y	Y	Y	N	N	Y	Y	Y
8 Jones	Y	Y	Y	Y	Y	Y	Y	Y
9 Ford	Y	Y	Y	Y	Y	Y	Y	Y
TEXAS								
1 Chapman	Y	Y	Y	Y	Y	N	Y	Y
2 Wilson	Y	Y	Y	Y	Y	Y	Y	Y
3 ***Bartlett***	Y	N	N	N	N	N	N	N
4 Hall, R.	Y	Y	Y	N	Y	N	N	Y
5 Bryant	Y	Y	Y	Y	Y	Y	Y	Y
6 ***Barton***	Y	N	N	N	N	N	N	N
7 ***Archer***	Y	N	N	N	Y	N	Y	N
8 ***Fields***	Y	Y	N	N	N	Y	N	Y
9 Brooks	Y	Y	Y	Y	Y	Y	Y	Y
10 Pickle	Y	Y	Y	Y	Y	N	Y	Y
11 Leath	Y	Y	Y	N	Y	N	N	Y
12 Wright	Y	Y	Y	Y	Y	Y	?	Y
13 ***Boulter***	Y	Y	N	N	N	Y	N	Y
14 ***Sweeney***	?	Y	N	N	Y	N	Y	Y
15 de la Garza	Y	Y	Y	Y	?	?	?	?
16 Coleman	Y	Y	Y	Y	Y	Y	Y	Y
17 Stenholm	Y	Y	N	N	Y	N	N	Y
18 Leland	Y	Y	Y	Y	Y	Y	Y	Y
19 ***Combest***	Y	Y	N	N	Y	N	Y	Y
20 Gonzalez	Y	Y	Y	Y	Y	Y	Y	Y
21 ***Loeffler***	Y	Y	N	N	N	N	Y	Y
22 ***DeLay***	Y	N	N	N	N	N	N	Y
23 Bustamante	Y	Y	Y	Y	Y	Y	Y	Y
24 Frost	Y	Y	Y	Y	Y	Y	Y	Y
25 Andrews	Y	Y	Y	Y	Y	N	Y	Y
26 ***Armey***	Y	N	N	N	N	N	N	N
27 Ortiz	Y	Y	Y	Y	Y	Y	Y	Y
UTAH								
1 ***Hansen***	Y	Y	N	N	N	N	N	Y
2 ***Monson***	Y	Y	N	N	N	N	N	Y
3 ***Nielson***	Y	Y	N	N	Y	N	N	Y
VERMONT								
AL ***Jeffords***	Y	Y	Y	N	Y	N	Y	N
VIRGINIA								
1 ***Bateman***	Y	Y	Y	N	Y	Y	Y	Y
2 ***Whitehurst***	Y	Y	Y	N	N	N	Y	?
3 ***Bliley***	Y	Y	Y	N	N	N	N	Y
4 Sisisky	Y	Y	Y	Y	Y	N	Y	Y
5 Daniel	Y	Y	Y	N	Y	N	Y	Y
6 Olin	Y	Y	Y	Y	Y	Y	Y	Y
7 ***Slaughter***	Y	Y	N	N	N	N	Y	Y
8 ***Parris***	Y	Y	Y	N	Y	Y	Y	Y
9 Boucher	Y	Y	Y	Y	Y	Y	N	Y
10 ***Wolf***	Y	Y	Y	N	N	Y	Y	Y
WASHINGTON								
1 ***Miller***	Y	N	Y	N	Y	Y	Y	N
2 Swift	Y	Y	Y	Y	Y	Y	Y	Y
3 Bonker	+	+	+	+	Y	Y	Y	Y
4 ***Morrison***	Y	Y	N	N	N	Y	Y	Y
5 Foley	Y	Y	Y	Y	Y	Y	Y	Y
6 Dicks	Y	Y	Y	Y	Y	Y	Y	Y
7 Lowry	Y	Y	Y	Y	Y	Y	Y	Y
8 ***Chandler***	?	?	?	?	N	Y	Y	Y
WEST VIRGINIA								
1 Mollohan	Y	Y	Y	Y	Y	Y	Y	Y
2 Staggers	Y	Y	Y	Y	Y	Y	Y	Y
3 Wise	Y	Y	Y	Y	Y	Y	Y	Y
4 Rahall	Y	Y	Y	Y	Y	Y	Y	Y
WISCONSIN								
1 Aspin	Y	Y	Y	Y	Y	Y	Y	Y
2 Kastenmeier	Y	Y	Y	Y	Y	Y	Y	Y
3 ***Gunderson***	Y	Y	N	N	N	N	N	Y
4 Kleczka	Y	Y	Y	Y	Y	Y	Y	Y
5 Moody	Y	Y	Y	Y	Y	N	Y	Y
6 ***Petri***	Y	N	N	Y	Y	Y	N	Y
7 Obey	Y	Y	N	Y	Y	N	Y	N
8 ***Roth***	?	?	?	?	N	Y	?	?
9 ***Sensenbrenner***	Y	N	N	N	N	N	N	N
WYOMING								
AL ***Cheney***	Y	N	X	?	?	X	Y	Y

Southern states - Ala., Ark., Fla., Ga., Ky., La., Miss., N.C., Okla., S.C., Tenn., Texas, Va.

* The *Congressional Record* vote number is different from the CQ vote number because the *Record* includes quorum calls in its tally. CQ does not publish quorum call votes.

371. H Con Res 232. Philippine Elections. Adoption of the concurrent resolution to urge that Philippine President Ferdinand E. Marcos honor his pledge that the 1986 elections will be free and fair, and to demand certain steps be taken to ensure that result. Adopted 407-0: R 174-0; D 233-0 (ND 156-0, SD 77-0), Nov. 14, 1985.

372. HR 1616. Plant Closing Notification. Bartlett, R-Texas, amendment to the Ford, D-Mich., substitute, to delete a provision requiring plant owners to consult with employees before closing a plant in an effort to find alternatives to the shutdown. Adopted 215-193: R 159-15; D 56-178 (ND 6-151, SD 50-27), Nov. 14, 1985.

KEY

- Y Voted for (yea).
- # Paired for.
- + Announced for.
- N Voted against (nay).
- X Paired against.
- \- Announced against.
- P Voted "present."
- C Voted "present" to avoid possible conflict of interest.
- ? Did not vote or otherwise make a position known.

Democrats ***Republicans***

	371	372
ALABAMA		
1 ***Callahan***	Y	Y
2 ***Dickinson***	Y	Y
3 Nichols	Y	Y
4 Bevill	Y	N
5 Flippo	Y	Y
6 Erdreich	Y	Y
7 Shelby	Y	Y
ALASKA		
AL ***Young***	Y	N
ARIZONA		
1 ***McCain***	Y	Y
2 Udall	Y	?
3 ***Stump***	Y	Y
4 ***Rudd***	Y	#
5 ***Kolbe***	Y	Y
ARKANSAS		
1 Alexander	Y	N
2 Robinson	Y	N
3 ***Hammerschmidt***	Y	Y
4 Anthony	Y	Y
CALIFORNIA		
1 Bosco	Y	Y
2 ***Chappie***	Y	Y
3 Matsui	Y	N
4 Fazio	Y	N
5 Burton	Y	N
6 Boxer	?	X
7 Miller	Y	N
8 Dellums	Y	N
9 Stark	Y	N
10 Edwards	Y	N
11 Lantos	Y	N
12 ***Zschau***	Y	Y
13 Mineta	Y	N
14 ***Shumway***	Y	Y
15 Coelho	Y	N
16 Panetta	Y	N
17 ***Pashayan***	Y	Y
18 Lehman	Y	N
19 ***Lagomarsino***	Y	Y
20 ***Thomas***	Y	Y
21 ***Fiedler***	Y	Y
22 ***Moorhead***	Y	Y
23 Beilenson	Y	N
24 Waxman	Y	N
25 Roybal	Y	N
26 Berman	?	N
27 Levine	Y	N
28 Dixon	?	X
29 Hawkins	?	X
30 Martinez	Y	N
31 Dymally	Y	X
32 Anderson	Y	N
33 ***Dreier***	Y	Y
34 Torres	Y	N
35 ***Lewis***	Y	Y
36 Brown	Y	N
37 ***McCandless***	Y	Y
38 ***Dornan***	Y	Y
39 ***Dannemeyer***	Y	Y
40 ***Badham***	Y	?
41 ***Lowery***	Y	Y
42 ***Lungren***	Y	Y

	371	372
43 ***Packard***	Y	Y
44 Bates	Y	N
45 ***Hunter***	Y	Y
COLORADO		
1 Schroeder	Y	Y
2 Wirth	Y	N
3 ***Strang***	Y	Y
4 ***Brown***	Y	Y
5 ***Kramer***	Y	Y
6 ***Schaefer***	Y	Y
CONNECTICUT		
1 Kennelly	Y	N
2 Gejdenson	Y	N
3 Morrison	Y	N
4 ***McKinney***	?	?
5 ***Rowland***	Y	Y
6 ***Johnson***	Y	Y
DELAWARE		
AL Carper	Y	N
FLORIDA		
1 Hutto	Y	Y
2 Fuqua	Y	Y
3 Bennett	Y	N
4 Chappell	Y	Y
5 ***McCollum***	Y	Y
6 MacKay	Y	#
7 Gibbons	Y	Y
8 ***Young***	Y	Y
9 ***Bilirakis***	Y	Y
10 ***Ireland***	Y	Y
11 Nelson	+	#
12 ***Lewis***	Y	#
13 ***Mack***	Y	Y
14 Mica	Y	Y
15 ***Shaw***	Y	Y
16 Smith	Y	N
17 Lehman	Y	N
18 Pepper	Y	N
19 Fascell	Y	N
GEORGIA		
1 Thomas	Y	Y
2 Hatcher	Y	Y
3 Ray	Y	Y
4 ***Swindall***	Y	Y
5 Fowler	?	?
6 ***Gingrich***	Y	Y
7 Darden	Y	Y
8 Rowland	Y	Y
9 Jenkins	Y	Y
10 Barnard	Y	Y
HAWAII		
1 Heftel	?	N
2 Akaka	?	X
IDAHO		
1 ***Craig***	Y	Y
2 Stallings	Y	N
ILLINOIS		
1 Hayes	Y	N
2 Savage	Y	N
3 Russo	Y	N
4 ***O'Brien***	Y	Y
5 Lipinski	Y	N
6 ***Hyde***	Y	Y
7 Collins	Y	N
8 Rostenkowski	Y	N
9 Yates	Y	N
10 ***Porter***	Y	Y
11 Annunzio	Y	N
12 ***Crane***	Y	Y
13 ***Fawell***	Y	Y
14 ***Grotberg***	Y	Y
15 ***Madigan***	Y	N
16 ***Martin***	Y	Y
17 Evans	Y	N
18 ***Michel***	Y	Y
19 Bruce	Y	N
20 Durbin	Y	N
21 Price	?	?
22 Gray	Y	N
INDIANA		
1 Visclosky	Y	N
2 Sharp	Y	N
3 ***Hiler***	Y	Y
4 ***Coats***	Y	Y
5 ***Hillis***	Y	Y

ND - Northern Democrats SD - Southern Democrats

	371	372
6 ***Burton***	Y	Y
7 ***Myers***	Y	Y
8 McCloskey	Y	N
9 Hamilton	Y	N
10 Jacobs	Y	N
IOWA		
1 ***Leach***	Y	N
2 ***Tauke***	Y	Y
3 ***Evans***	Y	Y
4 Smith	Y	N
5 ***Lightfoot***	Y	Y
6 Bedell	Y	N
KANSAS		
1 ***Roberts***	Y	Y
2 Slattery	Y	N
3 ***Meyers***	Y	Y
4 Glickman	Y	N
5 ***Whittaker***	Y	Y
KENTUCKY		
1 Hubbard	Y	N
2 Natcher	Y	N
3 Mazzoli	Y	N
4 ***Snyder***	Y	Y
5 ***Rogers***	Y	Y
6 ***Hopkins***	Y	Y
7 Perkins	Y	N
LOUISIANA		
1 ***Livingston***	Y	Y
2 Boggs	Y	N
3 Tauzin	Y	Y
4 Roemer	Y	Y
5 Huckaby	Y	Y
6 ***Moore***	Y	Y
7 Breaux	Y	Y
8 Long	Y	N
MAINE		
1 ***McKernan***	Y	Y
2 ***Snowe***	Y	Y
MARYLAND		
1 Dyson	Y	N
2 ***Bentley***	Y	Y
3 Mikulski	Y	N
4 ***Holt***	Y	Y
5 Hoyer	Y	N
6 Byron	Y	Y
7 Mitchell	Y	N
8 Barnes	Y	N
MASSACHUSETTS		
1 ***Conte***	Y	N
2 Boland	Y	N
3 Early	Y	N
4 Frank	Y	N
5 Atkins	Y	N
6 Mavroules	Y	N
7 Markey	Y	N
8 O'Neill		
9 Moakley	?	N
10 Studds	Y	N
11 Donnelly	Y	N
MICHIGAN		
1 Conyers	?	?
2 ***Pursell***	Y	Y
3 Wolpe	Y	N
4 ***Siljander***	Y	Y
5 ***Henry***	Y	Y
6 Carr	Y	N
7 Kildee	Y	N
8 Traxler	Y	N
9 ***Vander Jagt***	?	Y
10 ***Schuette***	Y	Y
11 ***Davis***	Y	N
12 Bonior	Y	N
13 Crockett	Y	?
14 Hertel	Y	N
15 Ford	Y	N
16 Dingell	Y	N
17 Levin	Y	N
18 ***Broomfield***	Y	Y
MINNESOTA		
1 Penny	Y	Y
2 ***Weber***	Y	Y
3 ***Frenzel***	?	?
4 Vento	Y	N
5 Sabo	Y	N
6 Sikorski	Y	N
7 ***Stangeland***	Y	Y
8 Oberstar	Y	N
MISSISSIPPI		
1 Whitten	Y	Y
2 ***Franklin***	Y	Y
3 Montgomery	Y	Y
4 Dowdy	Y	Y
5 ***Lott***	Y	Y
MISSOURI		
1 Clay	Y	N
2 Young	Y	N
3 Gephardt	Y	N
4 Skelton	Y	N
5 Wheat	Y	N
6 ***Coleman***	Y	Y
7 ***Taylor***	Y	Y
8 ***Emerson***	Y	Y
9 Volkmer	Y	N
MONTANA		
1 Williams	Y	N
2 ***Marlenee***	Y	Y
NEBRASKA		
1 ***Bereuter***	Y	Y
2 ***Daub***	Y	Y
3 ***Smith***	Y	Y
NEVADA		
1 Reid	Y	N
2 ***Vucanovich***	Y	Y
NEW HAMPSHIRE		
1 ***Smith***	Y	Y
2 ***Gregg***	Y	Y
NEW JERSEY		
1 Florio	Y	N
2 Hughes	Y	N
3 Howard	Y	N
4 ***Smith***	Y	N
5 ***Roukema***	Y	Y
6 Dwyer	Y	N
7 ***Rinaldo***	Y	N
8 Roe	Y	N
9 Torricelli	Y	N
10 Rodino	Y	N
11 ***Gallo***	Y	Y
12 ***Courter***	Y	Y
13 ***Saxton***	Y	Y
14 Guarini	Y	-
NEW MEXICO		
1 ***Lujan***	Y	Y
2 ***Skeen***	Y	Y
3 Richardson	Y	N
NEW YORK		
1 ***Carney***	Y	Y
2 Downey	Y	N
3 Mrazek	Y	N
4 ***Lent***	Y	Y
5 ***McGrath***	Y	Y
6 Addabbo	?	?
7 Ackerman	Y	N
8 Scheuer	Y	N
9 Manton	Y	N
10 Schumer	Y	N
11 Towns	?	N
12 Owens	Y	N
13 Solarz	Y	N
14 ***Molinari***	Y	Y
15 ***Green***	Y	Y
16 Rangel	?	N
17 Weiss	Y	N
18 Garcia	Y	N
19 Biaggi	Y	?
20 ***DioGuardi***	Y	Y
21 ***Fish***	Y	N
22 ***Gilman***	Y	N
23 Stratton	Y	N
24 ***Solomon***	Y	Y
25 ***Boehlert***	Y	Y
26 ***Martin***	Y	?
27 ***Wortley***	Y	Y
28 McHugh	Y	N
29 ***Horton***	Y	N
30 ***Eckert***	Y	Y
31 ***Kemp***	Y	Y
32 LaFalce	Y	N
33 Nowak	Y	N
34 Lundine	Y	N
NORTH CAROLINA		
1 Jones	Y	Y
2 Valentine	Y	Y
3 Whitley	Y	Y
4 ***Cobey***	Y	Y
5 Neal	Y	Y
6 ***Coble***	Y	Y
7 Rose	Y	Y
8 Hefner	Y	Y
9 ***McMillan***	Y	Y
10 ***Broyhill***	?	Y
11 ***Hendon***	Y	Y
NORTH DAKOTA		
AL Dorgan	Y	N
OHIO		
1 Luken	Y	N
2 ***Gradison***	Y	Y
3 Hall	Y	N
4 ***Oxley***	Y	Y
5 ***Latta***	Y	Y
6 ***McEwen***	Y	Y
7 ***DeWine***	Y	Y
8 ***Kindness***	Y	Y
9 Kaptur	Y	N
10 ***Miller***	Y	Y
11 Eckart	Y	N
12 ***Kasich***	Y	Y
13 Pease	Y	N
14 Seiberling	Y	N
15 ***Wylie***	?	Y
16 ***Regula***	Y	Y
17 Traficant	Y	N
18 Applegate	Y	N
19 Feighan	Y	N
20 Oakar	Y	N
21 Stokes	?	N
OKLAHOMA		
1 Jones	Y	Y
2 Synar	Y	Y
3 Watkins	Y	Y
4 McCurdy	Y	Y
5 ***Edwards***	Y	Y
6 English	Y	Y
OREGON		
1 AuCoin	Y	Y
2 ***Smith, R.***	Y	Y
3 Wyden	Y	Y
4 Weaver	Y	N
5 ***Smith, D.***	Y	Y
PENNSYLVANIA		
1 Foglietta	Y	N
2 Gray	Y	N
3 Borski	Y	N
4 Kolter	Y	N
5 ***Schulze***	Y	Y
6 Yatron	Y	N
7 Edgar	?	?
8 Kostmayer	Y	N
9 ***Shuster***	Y	Y
10 ***McDade***	Y	N
11 Kanjorski	Y	N
12 Murtha	Y	N
13 ***Coughlin***	Y	N
14 Coyne	Y	N
15 ***Ritter***	Y	N
16 ***Walker***	Y	Y
17 ***Gekas***	Y	Y
18 Walgren	Y	N
19 ***Goodling***	Y	Y
20 Gaydos	Y	N
21 ***Ridge***	Y	N
22 Murphy	Y	N
23 ***Clinger***	Y	N
RHODE ISLAND		
1 St Germain	Y	N
2 ***Schneider***	Y	Y
SOUTH CAROLINA		
1 ***Hartnett***	Y	#
2 ***Spence***	Y	Y
3 Derrick	?	Y
4 ***Campbell***	Y	Y
5 Spratt	Y	Y
6 Tallon	Y	Y
SOUTH DAKOTA		
AL Daschle	Y	N
TENNESSEE		
1 ***Quillen***	Y	Y
2 ***Duncan***	Y	Y
3 Lloyd	Y	N
4 Cooper	Y	Y
5 Boner	Y	N
6 Gordon	Y	N
7 ***Sundquist***	?	Y
8 Jones	Y	Y
9 Ford	Y	N
TEXAS		
1 Chapman	Y	Y
2 Wilson	Y	N
3 ***Bartlett***	Y	Y
4 Hall, R.	Y	Y
5 Bryant	Y	N
6 ***Barton***	Y	Y
7 ***Archer***	Y	Y
8 ***Fields***	Y	Y
9 Brooks	Y	N
10 Pickle	?	Y
11 Leath	Y	Y
12 Wright	Y	N
13 ***Boulter***	Y	Y
14 ***Sweeney***	?	Y
15 de la Garza	?	N
16 Coleman	Y	Y
17 Stenholm	Y	Y
18 Leland	Y	N
19 ***Combest***	Y	Y
20 Gonzalez	Y	N
21 ***Loeffler***	Y	Y
22 ***DeLay***	Y	Y
23 Bustamante	Y	N
24 Frost	Y	N
25 Andrews	Y	Y
26 ***Armey***	Y	Y
27 Ortiz	Y	X
UTAH		
1 ***Hansen***	Y	Y
2 ***Monson***	Y	Y
3 ***Nielson***	Y	Y
VERMONT		
AL ***Jeffords***	Y	Y
VIRGINIA		
1 ***Bateman***	Y	Y
2 ***Whitehurst***	?	?
3 ***Bliley***	Y	Y
4 Sisisky	Y	Y
5 Daniel	Y	#
6 Olin	Y	Y
7 ***Slaughter***	Y	Y
8 ***Parris***	Y	Y
9 Boucher	Y	Y
10 ***Wolf***	Y	Y
WASHINGTON		
1 ***Miller***	Y	Y
2 Swift	Y	N
3 Bonker	Y	N
4 ***Morrison***	Y	Y
5 Foley	Y	N
6 Dicks	Y	N
7 Lowry	Y	N
8 ***Chandler***	Y	Y
WEST VIRGINIA		
1 Mollohan	Y	N
2 Staggers	Y	N
3 Wise	Y	N
4 Rahall	Y	N
WISCONSIN		
1 Aspin	Y	N
2 Kastenmeier	Y	N
3 ***Gunderson***	Y	Y
4 Kleczka	Y	N
5 Moody	Y	N
6 ***Petri***	Y	Y
7 Obey	Y	N
8 ***Roth***	Y	Y
9 ***Sensenbrenner***	Y	Y
WYOMING		
AL ***Cheney***	Y	Y

Southern states - Ala., Ark., Fla., Ga., Ky., La., Miss., N.C., Okla., S.C., Tenn., Texas, Va.

* The *Congressional Record* vote number is different from the CQ vote number because the *Record* includes quorum calls in its tally. CQ does not publish quorum call votes.

373. S 583. Cooper-Hewitt Museum. Oakar, D-Ohio, motion to suspend the rules and pass the bill to authorize the appropriation of not more than $11.5 million in fiscal years beginning after Sept. 30, 1988, to plan and construct an expansion of the Cooper-Hewitt Museum, also known as the National Museum of Design of the Smithsonian Institution. Motion rejected 177-234: R 32-144; D 145-90 (ND 112-44, SD 33-46), Nov. 19, 1985. A two-thirds majority of those present and voting (274 in this case) is required for passage under suspension of the rules.

374. H Con Res 228. International Terrorism Condemnation. Mica, D-Fla., motion to suspend the rules and adopt the concurrent resolution to condemn all acts of terrorism, specifically including the hijacking of the *Achille Lauro* and the murder of Leon Klinghoffer, and to call for the creation of an international coordinating committee on terrorism and for proposals to protect Americans abroad. Motion agreed to 408-1: R 175-0; D 233-1 (ND 156-1, SD 77-0), Nov. 19, 1985. A two-thirds majority of those present and voting (273 in this case) is required for adoption under suspension of the rules.

375. HR 3456. Consumer Product Safety. Waxman, D-Calif., motion to suspend the rules and pass the bill to reauthorize the Consumer Product Safety Commission for fiscal 1986-88. Motion rejected 264-146: R 54-122; D 210-24 (ND 149-8, SD 61-16), Nov. 19, 1985. A two-thirds majority of those present and voting (274 in this case) is required for passage under suspension of the rules.

376. HR 2419. Intelligence Agencies Authorizations, Fiscal 1986. Adoption of the conference report on the bill to authorize a secret amount in fiscal 1986 for the CIA, the National Security Agency, the Defense Intelligence Agency and other intelligence agencies. Adopted 387-21: R 173-0; D 214-21 (ND 137-20, SD 77-1), Nov. 19, 1985.

377. HR 3244. Transportation Appropriations, Fiscal 1986. Young, R-Fla., motion to instruct the House conferees on the fiscal 1986 transportation appropriations bill to insist on the House position on funding levels for Coast Guard operating expenses. Motion agreed to 400-6: R 165-6; D 235-0 (ND 159-0, SD 76-0), Nov. 20, 1985.

378. HR 3622. Joint Chiefs of Staff Reorganization. Bennett, D-Fla., amendment to allow the chairman of the Joint Chiefs of Staff to assign undivided authority for any operation to a single officer. Rejected 47-366: R 15-159; D 32-207 (ND 20-141, SD 12-66), Nov. 20, 1985.

379. HR 3622. Joint Chiefs of Staff Reorganization. Passage of the bill to change the system of the Joint Chiefs of Staff by strengthening the role of the chairman. Passed 383-27: R 154-21; D 229-6 (ND 156-4, SD 73-2), Nov. 20, 1985. A "nay" was a vote supporting the president's position.

380. Procedural Motion. Kildee, D-Mich., motion to approve the House *Journal* of Wednesday, Nov. 20. Motion agreed to 284-115: R 62-106; D 222-9 (ND 147-7, SD 75-2), Nov. 21, 1985.

KEY

- Y Voted for (yea).
- # Paired for.
- + Announced for.
- N Voted against (nay).
- X Paired against.
- \- Announced against.
- P Voted "present."
- C Voted "present" to avoid possible conflict of interest.
- ? Did not vote or otherwise make a position known.

Democrats ***Republicans***

	373	374	375	376	377	378	379	380
ALABAMA								
1 ***Callahan***	N	Y	N	Y	Y	N	Y	Y
2 ***Dickinson***	N	Y	N	Y	Y	N	Y	N
3 Nichols	N	Y	N	Y	Y	N	Y	Y
4 Bevill	N	Y	Y	Y	Y	N	Y	Y
5 Flippo	N	Y	Y	Y	Y	N	Y	Y
6 Erdreich	N	Y	Y	Y	Y	N	Y	Y
7 Shelby	N	?	Y	Y	Y	N	Y	Y
ALASKA								
AL ***Young***	N	Y	N	Y	Y	N	Y	N
ARIZONA								
1 ***McCain***	N	Y	N	Y	Y	N	N	N
2 Udall	Y	Y	Y	Y	Y	N	Y	Y
3 ***Stump***	N	Y	N	Y	Y	N	Y	Y
4 ***Rudd***	N	Y	N	Y	Y	N	Y	Y
5 ***Kolbe***	N	Y	N	Y	Y	N	Y	N
ARKANSAS								
1 Alexander	Y	?	?	Y	Y	Y	?	Y
2 Robinson	N	Y	Y	Y	?	N	Y	Y
3 ***Hammerschmidt***	N	Y	N	Y	Y	N	Y	Y
4 Anthony	Y	Y	N	Y	Y	N	Y	Y
CALIFORNIA								
1 Bosco	?	?	?	?	Y	N	Y	Y
2 ***Chappie***	?	?	?	?	?	?	?	?
3 Matsui	Y	Y	Y	Y	Y	N	Y	Y
4 Fazio	N	Y	Y	Y	Y	N	Y	Y
5 Burton	?	?	?	?	Y	?	?	Y
6 Boxer	Y	Y	Y	Y	Y	N	Y	Y
7 Miller	Y	Y	Y	N	Y	N	Y	Y
8 Dellums	N	Y	Y	N	Y	N	Y	?
9 Stark	Y	Y	Y	Y	Y	Y	Y	Y
10 Edwards	Y	Y	Y	Y	Y	Y	Y	Y
11 Lantos	Y	Y	Y	Y	Y	N	Y	Y
12 ***Zschau***	Y	Y	N	Y	Y	Y	N	N
13 Mineta	?	Y	Y	Y	Y	N	Y	Y
14 ***Shumway***	N	Y	N	Y	Y	N	Y	Y
15 Coelho	N	Y	Y	Y	Y	N	Y	Y
16 Panetta	Y	Y	Y	Y	Y	N	Y	Y
17 ***Pashayan***	N	Y	N	Y	Y	N	Y	Y
18 Lehman	?	?	?	?	Y	N	Y	Y
19 ***Lagomarsino***	N	Y	N	Y	?	?	?	N
20 ***Thomas***	Y	Y	N	Y	Y	N	Y	N
21 ***Fiedler***	N	Y	N	Y	Y	N	Y	N
22 ***Moorhead***	N	Y	N	Y	Y	N	Y	N
23 Beilenson	Y	Y	Y	Y	Y	N	Y	Y
24 Waxman	Y	Y	Y	Y	Y	N	Y	Y
25 Roybal	Y	Y	Y	Y	Y	N	Y	Y
26 Berman	Y	Y	Y	Y	Y	N	Y	Y
27 Levine	Y	Y	Y	Y	Y	N	Y	Y
28 Dixon	N	Y	Y	Y	Y	N	Y	Y
29 Hawkins	?	?	#	Y	Y	N	Y	?
30 Martinez	Y	Y	Y	Y	Y	N	Y	Y
31 Dymally	Y	Y	Y	N	Y	N	Y	?
32 Anderson	Y	Y	Y	Y	Y	N	Y	Y
33 ***Dreier***	N	Y	N	Y	Y	N	N	N
34 Torres	Y	Y	Y	Y	Y	N	Y	Y
35 ***Lewis***	N	Y	N	?	Y	N	Y	N
36 Brown	?	?	#	Y	Y	Y	Y	Y
37 ***McCandless***	N	Y	N	Y	Y	N	Y	N
38 ***Dornan***	N	Y	N	Y	Y	Y	N	N
39 ***Dannemeyer***	N	Y	N	Y	Y	N	N	N
40 ***Badham***	N	Y	N	Y	Y	N	Y	N
41 ***Lowery***	Y	Y	N	Y	Y	N	Y	N
42 ***Lungren***	N	Y	N	Y	Y	N	Y	N
43 ***Packard***	N	Y	N	Y	Y	N	Y	Y
44 Bates	Y	Y	Y	Y	Y	Y	Y	Y
45 ***Hunter***	N	Y	N	Y	Y	Y	N	Y
COLORADO								
1 Schroeder	N	Y	Y	Y	Y	N	Y	N
2 Wirth	?	?	?	Y	Y	N	Y	Y
3 ***Strang***	N	Y	N	Y	Y	N	N	N
4 ***Brown***	N	Y	N	Y	N	N	Y	N
5 ***Kramer***	N	Y	N	Y	N	N	Y	?
6 ***Schaefer***	N	Y	N	Y	Y	N	N	N
CONNECTICUT								
1 Kennelly	Y	Y	Y	Y	Y	N	Y	Y
2 Gejdenson	Y	Y	Y	Y	Y	Y	Y	Y
3 Morrison	Y	Y	Y	N	Y	N	Y	Y
4 ***McKinney***	#	?	#	?	?	?	?	?
5 ***Rowland***	N	?	Y	Y	Y	N	Y	N
6 ***Johnson***	N	Y	N	Y	Y	N	Y	Y
DELAWARE								
AL Carper	N	Y	Y	Y	Y	N	Y	Y
FLORIDA								
1 Hutto	Y	Y	Y	Y	Y	N	Y	Y
2 Fuqua	Y	Y	Y	Y	Y	N	Y	Y
3 Bennett	Y	Y	Y	Y	Y	Y	N	Y
4 Chappell	Y	Y	Y	Y	Y	Y	Y	Y
5 ***McCollum***	N	Y	N	Y	Y	Y	Y	Y
6 MacKay	N	Y	Y	Y	Y	Y	Y	Y
7 Gibbons	N	Y	Y	Y	Y	Y	Y	Y
8 ***Young***	N	Y	N	Y	Y	N	Y	N
9 ***Bilirakis***	N	Y	Y	Y	Y	Y	Y	N
10 ***Ireland***	N	Y	N	Y	Y	N	Y	N
11 Nelson	#	+	X	#	+	+	+	+
12 ***Lewis***	N	Y	N	Y	Y	N	Y	N
13 ***Mack***	N	Y	N	Y	Y	N	N	N
14 Mica	N	Y	Y	Y	Y	N	Y	Y
15 ***Shaw***	Y	Y	N	Y	Y	N	Y	N
16 Smith	Y	Y	Y	Y	Y	Y	Y	Y
17 Lehman	Y	Y	Y	Y	Y	Y	Y	Y
18 Pepper	Y	Y	Y	Y	Y	N	Y	Y
19 Fascell	Y	Y	Y	Y	Y	Y	Y	Y
GEORGIA								
1 Thomas	N	Y	Y	Y	Y	N	Y	Y
2 Hatcher	N	Y	Y	Y	Y	N	Y	Y
3 Ray	N	Y	Y	Y	Y	N	Y	Y
4 ***Swindall***	X	?	X	?	Y	N	Y	N
5 Fowler	N	Y	Y	Y	Y	N	Y	Y
6 ***Gingrich***	Y	Y	N	Y	Y	N	Y	?
7 Darden	N	Y	N	Y	Y	N	+	Y
8 Rowland	N	Y	Y	Y	Y	N	Y	Y
9 Jenkins	N	Y	Y	Y	?	N	Y	Y
10 Barnard	N	Y	Y	Y	Y	N	Y	Y
HAWAII								
1 Heftel	?	?	?	?	+	N	Y	Y
2 Akaka	Y	Y	Y	Y	?	N	Y	Y
IDAHO								
1 ***Craig***	N	Y	N	Y	Y	N	Y	N
2 Stallings	N	Y	N	Y	Y	N	Y	?
ILLINOIS								
1 Hayes	N	Y	Y	N	Y	N	Y	Y
2 Savage	?	?	?	X	Y	N	Y	Y
3 Russo	Y	Y	Y	Y	Y	N	Y	Y
4 ***O'Brien***	N	Y	Y	Y	Y	Y	Y	?
5 Lipinski	Y	Y	Y	Y	Y	N	Y	Y
6 ***Hyde***	N	Y	N	?	Y	N	Y	Y
7 Collins	Y	Y	Y	Y	?	N	Y	Y
8 Rostenkowski	Y	Y	Y	Y	Y	N	Y	Y
9 Yates	Y	Y	Y	Y	Y	Y	Y	Y
10 ***Porter***	N	Y	Y	Y	Y	N	Y	Y
11 Annunzio	Y	Y	Y	Y	Y	N	Y	Y
12 ***Crane***	N	Y	N	Y	Y	N	Y	N
13 ***Fawell***	N	Y	N	Y	Y	N	Y	N
14 ***Grotberg***	N	Y	N	Y	Y	N	Y	N
15 ***Madigan***	N	Y	Y	Y	Y	N	Y	N
16 ***Martin***	N	Y	Y	Y	Y	N	Y	N
17 Evans	Y	Y	Y	Y	Y	N	Y	Y
18 ***Michel***	N	Y	Y	Y	Y	N	Y	Y
19 Bruce	N	Y	Y	Y	Y	N	Y	Y
20 Durbin	N	Y	Y	Y	Y	Y	Y	N
21 Price	?	?	?	?	?	?	?	?
22 Gray	Y	Y	Y	Y	Y	N	Y	Y
INDIANA								
1 Visclosky	N	Y	Y	Y	Y	N	Y	Y
2 Sharp	N	Y	Y	Y	Y	N	Y	Y
3 ***Hiler***	N	Y	N	Y	Y	N	Y	N
4 ***Coats***	N	Y	N	Y	Y	N	Y	Y
5 ***Hillis***	Y	Y	Y	Y	?	?	?	?

ND - Northern Democrats SD - Southern Democrats

* Corresponding to Congressional Record Votes 410, 411, 412, 413, 414, 415, 416, 417

	373	374	375	376	377	378	379	380
6 ***Burton***	N	Y	N	Y	Y	N	N	N
7 ***Myers***	Y	Y	N	Y	Y	N	Y	Y
8 McCloskey	N	Y	N	Y	Y	N	Y	Y
9 Hamilton	N	Y	Y	Y	Y	N	Y	Y
10 Jacobs	N	Y	Y	Y	Y	N	Y	N
IOWA								
1 ***Leach***	N	Y	Y	Y	Y	N	Y	?
2 ***Tauke***	N	Y	Y	Y	N	N	Y	N
3 ***Evans***	N	Y	N	Y	Y	N	Y	N
4 Smith	N	Y	Y	Y	Y	N	Y	Y
5 ***Lightfoot***	N	Y	N	Y	Y	N	Y	N
6 Bedell	N	Y	Y	N	Y	Y	Y	Y
KANSAS								
1 ***Roberts***	N	Y	N	Y	Y	N	Y	N
2 Slattery	N	Y	Y	Y	Y	N	Y	Y
3 ***Meyers***	N	Y	Y	Y	Y	N	Y	N
4 Glickman	N	Y	Y	Y	Y	N	Y	Y
5 ***Whittaker***	N	Y	N	Y	Y	N	Y	N
KENTUCKY								
1 Hubbard	?	?	?	?	?	?	?	?
2 Natcher	Y	Y	Y	Y	Y	N	Y	Y
3 Mazzoli	Y	Y	Y	Y	Y	N	Y	Y
4 ***Snyder***	Y	Y	N	Y	Y	N	Y	Y
5 ***Rogers***	N	Y	N	Y	Y	N	Y	N
6 ***Hopkins***	N	Y	N	Y	Y	N	Y	Y
7 Perkins	Y	Y	Y	Y	Y	Y	Y	Y
LOUISIANA								
1 ***Livingston***	N	Y	Y	Y	Y	Y	N	N
2 Boggs	Y	Y	Y	Y	Y	Y	Y	Y
3 Tauzin	N	Y	Y	Y	Y	N	Y	Y
4 Roemer	N	Y	Y	Y	Y	N	Y	N
5 Huckaby	N	Y	Y	Y	Y	N	Y	Y
6 ***Moore***	N	Y	Y	Y	Y	N	Y	Y
7 Breaux	?	?	?	?	Y	N	Y	Y
8 Long	Y	Y	Y	Y	Y	N	N	Y
MAINE								
1 ***McKernan***	N	Y	Y	Y	?	N	Y	N
2 ***Snowe***	N	Y	Y	Y	Y	N	Y	Y
MARYLAND								
1 Dyson	N	Y	Y	Y	Y	N	Y	?
2 ***Bentley***	N	Y	N	Y	Y	N	Y	N
3 Mikulski	Y	Y	Y	Y	Y	N	Y	?
4 ***Holt***	?	?	?	?	Y	N	Y	Y
5 Hoyer	Y	Y	Y	Y	Y	N	Y	Y
6 Byron	Y	Y	N	Y	Y	N	Y	Y
7 Mitchell	?	?	#	?	?	N	Y	N
8 Barnes	Y	Y	Y	Y	Y	N	Y	Y
MASSACHUSETTS								
1 ***Conte***	Y	Y	Y	Y	Y	N	Y	Y
2 Boland	Y	Y	Y	Y	Y	N	Y	Y
3 Early	Y	Y	Y	Y	Y	?	?	Y
4 Frank	N	Y	Y	Y	Y	Y	Y	Y
5 Atkins	Y	Y	Y	Y	Y	N	Y	?
6 Mavroules	Y	Y	Y	Y	Y	N	Y	Y
7 Markey	Y	Y	Y	Y	Y	Y	Y	Y
8 O'Neill								
9 Moakley	Y	Y	Y	Y	Y	N	Y	Y
10 Studds	Y	Y	Y	N	Y	N	Y	Y
11 Donnelly	Y	Y	Y	Y	Y	N	Y	?
MICHIGAN								
1 Conyers	N	N	Y	N	Y	N	Y	Y
2 ***Pursell***	N	Y	Y	Y	Y	N	Y	Y
3 Wolpe	N	Y	Y	Y	Y	N	Y	Y
4 ***Siljander***	N	Y	N	Y	Y	N	Y	N
5 ***Henry***	Y	Y	Y	Y	Y	N	Y	Y
6 Carr	N	Y	Y	Y	Y	N	N	Y
7 Kildee	Y	Y	Y	Y	Y	N	Y	Y
8 Traxler	Y	Y	Y	Y	Y	N	N	Y
9 ***Vander Jagt***	N	Y	Y	Y	Y	N	Y	N
10 ***Schuette***	N	Y	N	Y	Y	N	Y	N
11 ***Davis***	Y	Y	Y	Y	Y	N	Y	Y
12 Bonior	Y	Y	Y	Y	Y	?	?	?
13 Crockett	Y	Y	Y	N	Y	N	Y	?
14 Hertel	Y	Y	Y	Y	Y	N	Y	Y
15 Ford	Y	Y	Y	Y	Y	N	Y	Y
16 Dingell	Y	Y	Y	?	Y	N	Y	?
17 Levin	Y	Y	Y	Y	Y	N	Y	Y
18 ***Broomfield***	N	Y	Y	Y	Y	N	Y	Y
MINNESOTA								
1 Penny	N	Y	N	Y	Y	N	Y	N
2 ***Weber***	N	Y	N	Y	?	N	Y	N
3 ***Frenzel***	Y	Y	N	Y	N	N	Y	Y
4 Vento	Y	Y	Y	N	Y	N	Y	Y
5 Sabo	Y	Y	Y	Y	Y	N	Y	Y
6 Sikorski	Y	Y	Y	Y	Y	N	Y	N
7 ***Stangeland***	Y	Y	N	Y	Y	N	Y	N
8 Oberstar	Y	Y	Y	Y	Y	N	Y	Y
MISSISSIPPI								
1 Whitten	Y	Y	N	Y	Y	?	Y	Y
2 ***Franklin***	N	Y	N	Y	Y	N	Y	Y
3 Montgomery	N	Y	N	Y	Y	N	Y	Y
4 Dowdy	N	Y	Y	Y	Y	N	Y	Y
5 ***Lott***	N	Y	N	Y	Y	N	Y	Y
MISSOURI								
1 Clay	Y	Y	Y	N	Y	N	Y	N
2 Young	Y	Y	Y	Y	Y	N	Y	Y
3 Gephardt	Y	Y	Y	Y	Y	N	Y	Y
4 Skelton	N	Y	N	Y	Y	N	Y	Y
5 Wheat	Y	Y	Y	Y	Y	N	Y	Y
6 ***Coleman***	N	Y	Y	Y	Y	N	Y	N
7 ***Taylor***	N	Y	N	Y	Y	N	Y	N
8 ***Emerson***	N	Y	N	Y	Y	N	Y	N
9 Volkmer	N	Y	Y	Y	Y	N	Y	Y
MONTANA								
1 Williams	Y	Y	Y	Y	Y	Y	Y	?
2 ***Marlenee***	N	Y	N	Y	Y	Y	Y	N
NEBRASKA								
1 ***Bereuter***	N	Y	Y	Y	Y	N	Y	N
2 ***Daub***	N	Y	N	Y	Y	N	Y	N
3 ***Smith***	N	Y	N	Y	Y	N	Y	Y
NEVADA								
1 Reid	N	Y	Y	Y	Y	N	Y	Y
2 ***Vucanovich***	Y	Y	N	Y	Y	N	Y	N
NEW HAMPSHIRE								
1 ***Smith***	N	Y	N	Y	Y	N	Y	N
2 ***Gregg***	N	Y	N	Y	Y	N	Y	N
NEW JERSEY								
1 Florio	Y	Y	Y	Y	Y	N	Y	Y
2 Hughes	N	Y	Y	Y	Y	N	Y	Y
3 Howard	Y	Y	Y	Y	Y	N	Y	Y
4 ***Smith***	N	Y	Y	Y	Y	N	Y	Y
5 ***Roukema***	Y	Y	Y	Y	Y	N	Y	N
6 Dwyer	Y	Y	Y	Y	Y	N	Y	Y
7 ***Rinaldo***	N	Y	Y	Y	Y	N	Y	Y
8 Roe	Y	Y	Y	?	?	N	Y	Y
9 Torricelli	Y	Y	Y	Y	Y	N	Y	Y
10 Rodino	Y	Y	Y	Y	Y	Y	Y	Y
11 ***Gallo***	N	Y	Y	Y	Y	N	Y	N
12 ***Courter***	N	Y	Y	Y	Y	N	Y	N
13 ***Saxton***	N	Y	Y	Y	Y	N	Y	Y
14 Guarini	Y	Y	Y	Y	Y	N	Y	Y
NEW MEXICO								
1 ***Lujan***	N	Y	N	Y	Y	N	Y	Y
2 ***Skeen***	N	Y	N	Y	Y	N	Y	N
3 Richardson	Y	Y	Y	Y	Y	N	Y	Y
NEW YORK								
1 ***Carney***	N	Y	N	Y	Y	N	Y	N
2 Downey	Y	Y	Y	Y	Y	N	Y	Y
3 Mrazek	Y	Y	Y	Y	Y	N	Y	Y
4 ***Lent***	Y	Y	Y	Y	Y	N	Y	Y
5 ***McGrath***	Y	Y	Y	Y	Y	N	Y	N
6 Addabbo	?	?	?	?	?	?	?	?
7 Ackerman	Y	Y	Y	?	Y	N	Y	Y
8 Scheuer	Y	Y	Y	Y	Y	Y	Y	Y
9 Manton	Y	Y	Y	Y	Y	N	Y	Y
10 Schumer	Y	Y	Y	Y	Y	N	Y	Y
11 Towns	Y	Y	Y	Y	?	N	Y	?
12 Owens	Y	Y	Y	N	Y	N	Y	Y
13 Solarz	Y	Y	Y	Y	Y	N	Y	Y
14 ***Molinari***	Y	Y	N	Y	Y	N	N	N
15 ***Green***	Y	Y	Y	Y	Y	?	?	Y
16 Rangel	Y	Y	Y	N	?	N	Y	Y
17 Weiss	Y	Y	Y	N	Y	N	Y	Y
18 Garcia	Y	Y	Y	N	Y	N	Y	Y
19 Biaggi	Y	Y	Y	Y	Y	N	?	?
20 ***DioGuardi***	N	Y	N	Y	Y	N	Y	Y
21 ***Fish***	Y	Y	N	Y	Y	N	Y	?
22 ***Gilman***	Y	Y	Y	Y	Y	N	Y	Y
23 Stratton	Y	Y	Y	?	Y	N	N	Y
24 ***Solomon***	N	Y	Y	Y	Y	N	N	N
25 ***Boehlert***	Y	Y	Y	Y	Y	N	Y	N
26 ***Martin***	N	Y	Y	Y	Y	N	Y	Y
27 ***Wortley***	N	Y	Y	Y	Y	N	Y	Y
28 McHugh	Y	Y	Y	Y	Y	N	Y	Y
29 ***Horton***	Y	Y	N	Y	Y	?	Y	?
30 ***Eckert***	N	Y	N	Y	?	N	N	Y
31 ***Kemp***	Y	Y	N	Y	Y	N	N	Y
32 LaFalce	Y	Y	Y	Y	Y	N	Y	Y
33 Nowak	Y	Y	Y	Y	Y	N	Y	Y
34 Lundine	Y	Y	Y	Y	Y	Y	Y	Y
NORTH CAROLINA								
1 Jones	Y	Y	Y	Y	Y	N	Y	Y
2 Valentine	N	Y	Y	Y	Y	N	Y	Y
3 Whitley	Y	Y	?	Y	Y	N	Y	Y
4 ***Cobey***	N	Y	N	Y	Y	N	N	N
5 Neal	N	Y	Y	Y	Y	N	Y	?
6 ***Coble***	N	Y	N	Y	Y	N	Y	N
7 Rose	Y	Y	Y	Y	Y	N	Y	?
8 Hefner	Y	Y	Y	Y	Y	N	Y	Y
9 ***McMillan***	N	Y	N	Y	Y	Y	Y	Y
10 ***Broyhill***	N	Y	Y	Y	Y	N	Y	Y
11 ***Hendon***	N	Y	Y	Y	?	N	Y	N
NORTH DAKOTA								
AL Dorgan	N	Y	Y	Y	Y	N	Y	Y
OHIO								
1 Luken	Y	Y	Y	Y	Y	N	Y	Y
2 ***Gradison***	N	Y	Y	Y	Y	N	Y	Y
3 Hall	N	Y	Y	Y	Y	N	Y	Y
4 ***Oxley***	N	Y	N	Y	Y	N	Y	N
5 ***Latta***	N	Y	N	Y	Y	N	Y	N
6 ***McEwen***	N	Y	N	Y	Y	N	Y	N
7 ***DeWine***	Y	Y	N	Y	Y	N	Y	N
8 ***Kindness***	N	Y	N	Y	Y	N	Y	N
9 Kaptur	N	Y	Y	Y	Y	N	Y	Y
10 ***Miller***	N	Y	N	Y	Y	N	Y	N
11 Eckart	N	Y	Y	Y	Y	N	Y	Y
12 ***Kasich***	N	Y	N	Y	Y	N	Y	?
13 Pease	Y	Y	Y	Y	Y	N	Y	Y
14 Seiberling	Y	Y	Y	N	Y	Y	Y	Y
15 ***Wylie***	N	Y	N	Y	Y	N	Y	Y
16 ***Regula***	N	Y	Y	Y	Y	N	Y	Y
17 Traficant	Y	Y	Y	Y	Y	N	Y	Y
18 Applegate	N	Y	Y	Y	Y	Y	Y	Y
19 Feighan	Y	Y	Y	Y	Y	N	Y	Y
20 Oakar	Y	Y	Y	Y	Y	N	Y	Y
21 Stokes	Y	Y	Y	Y	Y	N	Y	Y
OKLAHOMA								
1 Jones	N	Y	Y	Y	Y	N	Y	Y
2 Synar	N	Y	Y	Y	Y	N	Y	Y
3 Watkins	N	Y	Y	Y	Y	N	Y	P
4 McCurdy	N	Y	Y	Y	Y	N	Y	Y
5 ***Edwards***	N	Y	N	Y	Y	N	Y	N
6 English	N	Y	N	Y	Y	N	Y	Y
OREGON								
1 AuCoin	?	?	?	?	Y	N	Y	Y
2 ***Smith, R.***	N	Y	N	Y	?	?	?	?
3 Wyden	N	Y	Y	Y	Y	N	Y	Y
4 Weaver	Y	Y	Y	N	Y	Y	N	Y
5 ***Smith, D.***	N	Y	N	Y	Y	Y	Y	N
PENNSYLVANIA								
1 Foglietta	Y	Y	Y	Y	Y	Y	Y	Y
2 Gray	N	Y	Y	Y	Y	N	Y	Y
3 Borski	Y	Y	Y	Y	Y	?	?	Y
4 Kolter	Y	Y	Y	Y	Y	N	Y	Y
5 ***Schulze***	N	Y	Y	Y	Y	N	N	Y
6 Yatron	N	Y	Y	Y	Y	?	?	Y
7 Edgar	Y	Y	Y	Y	Y	N	Y	Y
8 Kostmayer	Y	Y	Y	Y	Y	N	Y	Y
9 ***Shuster***	N	Y	N	Y	Y	N	Y	N
10 ***McDade***	Y	Y	Y	Y	Y	N	Y	?
11 Kanjorski	N	Y	Y	Y	Y	N	Y	Y
12 Murtha	Y	Y	N	Y	Y	N	Y	Y
13 ***Coughlin***	Y	Y	Y	Y	Y	N	Y	N
14 Coyne	Y	Y	Y	Y	Y	N	Y	Y
15 ***Ritter***	N	Y	Y	Y	Y	Y	Y	Y
16 ***Walker***	N	Y	N	Y	N	N	Y	N
17 ***Gekas***	N	Y	N	Y	Y	N	N	N
18 Walgren	N	Y	Y	Y	Y	N	Y	Y
19 ***Goodling***	N	Y	Y	Y	Y	N	Y	N
20 Gaydos	Y	Y	N	Y	?	N	Y	Y
21 ***Ridge***	N	Y	Y	Y	Y	N	Y	N
22 Murphy	N	Y	N	N	Y	N	Y	Y
23 ***Clinger***	N	Y	Y	Y	Y	N	Y	Y
RHODE ISLAND								
1 St Germain	Y	Y	Y	Y	Y	N	Y	Y
2 ***Schneider***	Y	Y	Y	Y	Y	N	Y	Y
SOUTH CAROLINA								
1 ***Hartnett***	N	Y	N	?	Y	N	Y	?
2 ***Spence***	N	Y	N	Y	Y	Y	Y	N
3 Derrick	Y	Y	N	Y	Y	N	?	Y
4 ***Campbell***	N	Y	N	Y	Y	N	Y	N
5 Spratt	Y	Y	Y	Y	Y	N	Y	Y
6 Tallon	N	Y	N	Y	Y	N	Y	Y
SOUTH DAKOTA								
AL Daschle	N	Y	Y	Y	Y	N	Y	Y
TENNESSEE								
1 ***Quillen***	?	?	?	?	Y	N	N	Y
2 ***Duncan***	N	Y	N	Y	Y	N	Y	Y
3 Lloyd	N	Y	N	Y	Y	N	Y	N
4 Cooper	N	Y	Y	Y	Y	Y	Y	Y
5 Boner	N	Y	N	Y	?	?	?	Y
6 Gordon	N	Y	Y	Y	Y	N	Y	Y
7 ***Sundquist***	N	Y	N	Y	Y	N	N	N
8 Jones	N	Y	Y	Y	Y	N	Y	Y
9 Ford	Y	Y	Y	Y	Y	N	Y	Y
TEXAS								
1 Chapman	N	Y	Y	Y	Y	N	Y	Y
2 Wilson	Y	Y	Y	Y	Y	N	Y	Y
3 ***Bartlett***	N	Y	N	Y	Y	Y	Y	N
4 Hall, R.	N	Y	Y	Y	Y	N	Y	Y
5 Bryant	N	Y	Y	Y	Y	N	Y	Y
6 ***Barton***	N	Y	N	Y	Y	Y	Y	N
7 ***Archer***	N	Y	N	Y	Y	N	Y	Y
8 ***Fields***	N	Y	Y	Y	Y	N	Y	N
9 Brooks	Y	Y	Y	Y	Y	N	Y	Y
10 Pickle	N	Y	Y	Y	Y	N	Y	Y
11 Leath	N	Y	N	Y	Y	N	Y	Y
12 Wright	Y	Y	Y	Y	Y	N	Y	Y
13 ***Boulter***	N	Y	N	Y	Y	N	Y	N
14 ***Sweeney***	N	Y	N	Y	Y	N	Y	Y
15 de la Garza	N	Y	Y	?	Y	N	Y	Y
16 Coleman	Y	Y	Y	Y	Y	N	Y	Y
17 Stenholm	N	Y	N	Y	Y	N	Y	Y
18 Leland	N	Y	Y	Y	Y	Y	Y	Y
19 ***Combest***	N	Y	N	Y	Y	N	Y	Y
20 Gonzalez	Y	Y	N	N	Y	N	P	Y
21 ***Loeffler***	?	?	?	?	?	?	?	N
22 ***DeLay***	N	Y	N	Y	Y	N	Y	N
23 Bustamante	Y	Y	Y	Y	Y	N	Y	Y
24 Frost	Y	Y	Y	Y	?	N	Y	Y
25 Andrews	N	Y	Y	Y	Y	N	Y	Y
26 ***Armey***	N	Y	N	Y	Y	N	N	N
27 Ortiz	Y	Y	Y	Y	Y	N	Y	Y
UTAH								
1 ***Hansen***	N	Y	N	Y	Y	N	Y	Y
2 ***Monson***	N	Y	N	Y	Y	N	Y	N
3 ***Nielson***	N	Y	N	Y	N	N	Y	Y
VERMONT								
AL ***Jeffords***	Y	Y	N	Y	Y	Y	Y	Y
VIRGINIA								
1 ***Bateman***	N	Y	N	Y	Y	N	Y	Y
2 ***Whitehurst***	N	Y	N	Y	Y	N	Y	?
3 ***Bliley***	N	Y	N	Y	Y	N	Y	N
4 Sisisky	Y	Y	N	Y	Y	N	Y	Y
5 Daniel	N	Y	N	Y	Y	N	Y	Y
6 Olin	N	Y	N	Y	Y	N	Y	Y
7 ***Slaughter***	N	Y	N	Y	Y	N	Y	N
8 ***Parris***	Y	Y	N	Y	?	N	Y	N
9 Boucher	Y	Y	Y	Y	Y	N	Y	Y
10 ***Wolf***	Y	Y	Y	Y	Y	N	Y	N
WASHINGTON								
1 ***Miller***	N	Y	N	Y	Y	N	Y	Y
2 Swift	Y	Y	Y	Y	Y	N	Y	Y
3 Bonker	Y	Y	Y	Y	Y	Y	Y	Y
4 ***Morrison***	Y	Y	N	Y	Y	N	Y	N
5 Foley	?	?	?	Y	Y	N	Y	Y
6 Dicks	Y	Y	Y	Y	Y	N	Y	Y
7 Lowry	Y	Y	Y	N	Y	?	?	Y
8 ***Chandler***	N	Y	N	Y	Y	N	Y	N
WEST VIRGINIA								
1 Mollohan	N	Y	Y	Y	Y	N	Y	Y
2 Staggers	Y	Y	Y	Y	Y	N	Y	Y
3 Wise	N	Y	Y	Y	Y	N	Y	Y
4 Rahall	Y	Y	Y	Y	?	?	?	Y
WISCONSIN								
1 Aspin	Y	Y	Y	Y	Y	N	Y	Y
2 Kastenmeier	Y	Y	Y	Y	Y	Y	Y	Y
3 ***Gunderson***	N	Y	Y	Y	Y	N	Y	N
4 Kleczka	Y	Y	Y	Y	Y	N	Y	Y
5 Moody	Y	Y	Y	N	Y	N	Y	Y
6 ***Petri***	N	Y	Y	Y	Y	N	Y	Y
7 Obey	N	Y	Y	Y	Y	N	Y	Y
8 ***Roth***	N	Y	Y	Y	Y	N	Y	Y
9 ***Sensenbrenner***	N	Y	N	Y	Y	N	Y	N
WYOMING								
AL ***Cheney***	N	Y	N	Y	Y	N	Y	N

Southern states - Ala., Ark., Fla., Ga., Ky., La., Miss., N.C., Okla., S.C., Tenn., Texas, Va.

* The *Congressional Record* vote number is different from the CQ vote number because the *Record* includes quorum calls in its tally. CQ does not publish quorum call votes.

381. HR 1616. Plant Closing Notification. Jeffords, R-Vt., amendment to the Ford, D-Mich., substitute, to require employers of at least 50 full-time employees to give workers 90 days' notice of any plant shutdown or layoff involving at least 100 employees or 30 percent of the work force. Adopted 211-201: R 22-153; D 189-48 (ND 154-4, SD 35-44), Nov. 21, 1985. (The Ford substitute, as amended by the Jeffords amendment, subsequently was adopted by voice vote.)

382. HR 1616. Plant Closing Notification. Roemer, D-La., substitute for the Ford, D-Mich., substitute, to require employers of at least 200 full-time employees to give workers 60 days' notice of any plant shutdown or layoff involving 100 or more workers. Rejected 109-298: R 76-95; D 33-203 (ND 4-153, SD 29-50), Nov. 21, 1985. (The Ford substitute, as amended by the Jeffords, R-Vt., amendment *(see vote 381, above)*, subsequently was adopted by voice vote.)

383. HR 1616. Plant Closing Notification. Passage of the bill to require employers of at least 50 full-time employees to give workers 90 days' notice of any plant shutdown or layoff involving at least 100 employees or 30 percent of the work force. Rejected 203-208: R 20-154; D 183-54 (ND 153-5, SD 30-49), Nov. 21, 1985.

KEY

- Y Voted for (yea).
- # Paired for.
- + Announced for.
- N Voted against (nay).
- X Paired against.
- \- Announced against.
- P Voted "present."
- C Voted "present" to avoid possible conflict of interest.
- ? Did not vote or otherwise make a position known.

Democrats ***Republicans***

	381	382	383
ALABAMA			
1 ***Callahan***	N	N	N
2 ***Dickinson***	N	N	N
3 Nichols	N	Y	N
4 Bevill	Y	N	Y
5 Flippo	Y	Y	N
6 Erdreich	Y	Y	N
7 Shelby	N	Y	N
ALASKA			
AL ***Young***	Y	N	Y
ARIZONA			
1 ***McCain***	N	Y	N
2 Udall	Y	N	Y
3 ***Stump***	N	N	N
4 ***Rudd***	N	N	N
5 ***Kolbe***	N	Y	N
ARKANSAS			
1 Alexander	N	N	Y
2 Robinson	Y	N	Y
3 ***Hammerschmidt***	N	Y	N
4 Anthony	N	N	N
CALIFORNIA			
1 Bosco	Y	N	Y
2 ***Chappie***	?	?	X
3 Matsui	Y	N	Y
4 Fazio	Y	N	Y
5 Burton	Y	N	Y
6 Boxer	Y	N	Y
7 Miller	Y	N	Y
8 Dellums	Y	N	Y
9 Stark	Y	N	Y
10 Edwards	Y	N	Y
11 Lantos	Y	N	Y
12 ***Zschau***	N	Y	N
13 Mineta	Y	N	Y
14 ***Shumway***	N	Y	N
15 Coelho	Y	N	Y
16 Panetta	Y	N	Y
17 ***Pashayan***	Y	N	N
18 Lehman	Y	N	Y
19 ***Lagomarsino***	N	Y	N
20 ***Thomas***	N	Y	N
21 ***Fiedler***	N	N	N
22 ***Moorhead***	N	N	N
23 Beilenson	Y	N	Y
24 Waxman	Y	N	Y
25 Roybal	Y	N	Y
26 Berman	Y	N	Y
27 Levine	Y	N	Y
28 Dixon	Y	N	Y
29 Hawkins	?	?	#
30 Martinez	Y	N	Y
31 Dymally	?	?	?
32 Anderson	Y	N	Y
33 ***Dreier***	N	N	N
34 Torres	Y	N	Y
35 ***Lewis***	N	Y	N
36 Brown	?	?	?
37 ***McCandless***	N	N	N
38 ***Dornan***	N	Y	N
39 ***Dannemeyer***	N	Y	N
40 ***Badham***	N	N	N
41 ***Lowery***	N	N	N
42 ***Lungren***	N	Y	N
43 ***Packard***	N	Y	N
44 Bates	Y	Y	Y
45 ***Hunter***	N	N	N
COLORADO			
1 Schroeder	Y	N	N
2 Wirth	Y	N	Y
3 ***Strang***	N	N	N
4 ***Brown***	N	Y	N
5 ***Kramer***	?	?	?
6 ***Schaefer***	N	Y	N
CONNECTICUT			
1 Kennelly	Y	N	Y
2 Gejdenson	Y	N	Y
3 Morrison	Y	N	Y
4 ***McKinney***	?	?	?
5 ***Rowland***	N	N	N
6 ***Johnson***	N	N	N
DELAWARE			
AL Carper	Y	N	Y
FLORIDA			
1 Hutto	N	N	N
2 Fuqua	N	Y	N
3 Bennett	Y	Y	Y
4 Chappell	N	Y	N
5 ***McCollum***	N	Y	N
6 MacKay	N	Y	N
7 Gibbons	Y	Y	N
8 ***Young***	N	Y	N
9 ***Bilirakis***	N	Y	N
10 ***Ireland***	N	Y	N
11 Nelson	+	+	X
12 ***Lewis***	N	Y	N
13 ***Mack***	N	?	N
14 Mica	Y	N	N
15 ***Shaw***	N	Y	N
16 Smith	Y	N	Y
17 Lehman	Y	N	Y
18 Pepper	Y	N	Y
19 Fascell	Y	N	Y
GEORGIA			
1 Thomas	N	Y	N
2 Hatcher	N	N	N
3 Ray	N	N	N
4 ***Swindall***	N	Y	N
5 Fowler	N	N	N
6 ***Gingrich***	N	N	N
7 Darden	N	N	N
8 Rowland	N	N	N
9 Jenkins	N	N	N
10 Barnard	N	Y	N
HAWAII			
1 Heftel	Y	N	Y
2 Akaka	Y	N	Y
IDAHO			
1 ***Craig***	N	N	N
2 Stallings	?	?	#
ILLINOIS			
1 Hayes	Y	N	Y
2 Savage	Y	N	Y
3 Russo	Y	N	Y
4 ***O'Brien***	N	Y	N
5 Lipinski	Y	N	Y
6 ***Hyde***	N	Y	N
7 Collins	Y	N	Y
8 Rostenkowski	Y	?	Y
9 Yates	Y	N	Y
10 ***Porter***	N	N	N
11 Annunzio	Y	N	Y
12 ***Crane***	N	?	X
13 ***Fawell***	N	N	N
14 ***Grotberg***	N	Y	N
15 ***Madigan***	Y	N	Y
16 ***Martin***	N	Y	N
17 Evans	Y	N	Y
18 ***Michel***	N	Y	N
19 Bruce	Y	N	Y
20 Durbin	Y	N	Y
21 Price	?	?	?
22 Gray	Y	N	Y
INDIANA			
1 Visclosky	Y	N	Y
2 Sharp	Y	N	Y
3 ***Hiler***	N	Y	N
4 ***Coats***	N	Y	N
5 ***Hillis***	?	?	?

ND - Northern Democrats SD - Southern Democrats

* Corresponding to Congressional Record Votes 419, 420, 421

	381	382	383
6 ***Burton***	N	N	N
7 ***Myers***	N	N	N
8 McCloskey	Y	N	Y
9 Hamilton	Y	N	Y
10 Jacobs	Y	N	Y
IOWA			
1 ***Leach***	Y	N	Y
2 ***Tauke***	N	Y	N
3 ***Evans***	N	?	N
4 Smith	Y	?	?
5 ***Lightfoot***	N	Y	N
6 Bedell	Y	N	Y
KANSAS			
1 ***Roberts***	N	Y	N
2 Slattery	Y	Y	Y
3 ***Meyers***	N	Y	N
4 Glickman	Y	Y	Y
5 ***Whittaker***	N	Y	N
KENTUCKY			
1 Hubbard	?	?	?
2 Natcher	Y	N	Y
3 Mazzoli	Y	N	Y
4 ***Snyder***	N	N	N
5 ***Rogers***	N	N	N
6 ***Hopkins***	N	N	N
7 Perkins	Y	N	Y
LOUISIANA			
1 ***Livingston***	N	Y	N
2 Boggs	Y	N	Y
3 Tauzin	N	Y	N
4 Roemer	N	Y	N
5 Huckaby	N	N	N
6 ***Moore***	N	Y	N
7 Breaux	N	Y	Y
8 Long	Y	N	Y
MAINE			
1 ***McKernan***	N	Y	N
2 ***Snowe***	N	Y	N
MARYLAND			
1 Dyson	Y	N	Y
2 ***Bentley***	N	N	N
3 Mikulski	Y	N	Y
4 ***Holt***	N	N	N
5 Hoyer	Y	N	Y
6 Byron	N	N	N
7 Mitchell	Y	N	Y
8 Barnes	Y	N	Y
MASSACHUSETTS			
1 ***Conte***	Y	N	Y
2 Boland	Y	N	Y
3 Early	Y	N	Y
4 Frank	Y	N	Y
5 Atkins	?	?	?
6 Mavroules	Y	N	Y
7 Markey	Y	N	Y
8 O'Neill			
9 Moakley	Y	N	Y
10 Studds	Y	N	Y
11 Donnelly	Y	N	Y
MICHIGAN			
1 Conyers	?	?	?
2 ***Pursell***	N	Y	N
3 Wolpe	Y	N	Y
4 ***Siljander***	N	N	N
5 ***Henry***	N	Y	N
6 Carr	?	N	Y
7 Kildee	Y	N	Y
8 Traxler	Y	N	Y
9 ***Vander Jagt***	N	N	N
10 ***Schuette***	N	N	N
11 ***Davis***	Y	N	Y
12 Bonior	?	?	#
13 Crockett	Y	N	Y
14 Hertel	Y	N	Y
15 Ford	Y	N	Y
16 Dingell	Y	N	Y
17 Levin	Y	N	Y
18 ***Broomfield***	N	Y	N
MINNESOTA			
1 Penny	Y	N	Y
2 ***Weber***	N	N	N
3 ***Frenzel***	N	N	N
4 Vento	Y	N	Y
5 Sabo	Y	N	Y
6 Sikorski	Y	N	Y
7 ***Stangeland***	N	Y	N
8 Oberstar	Y	N	Y
MISSISSIPPI			
1 Whitten	Y	N	Y
2 ***Franklin***	N	N	N
3 Montgomery	N	N	N
4 Dowdy	N	Y	N
5 ***Lott***	N	N	N
MISSOURI			
1 Clay	Y	N	Y
2 Young	Y	N	Y
3 Gephardt	Y	N	Y
4 Skelton	Y	N	Y
5 Wheat	Y	N	Y
6 ***Coleman***	N	Y	N
7 ***Taylor***	N	N	N
8 ***Emerson***	N	N	N
9 Volkmer	Y	N	Y
MONTANA			
1 Williams	Y	N	Y
2 ***Marlenee***	N	N	N
NEBRASKA			
1 ***Bereuter***	N	Y	N
2 ***Daub***	N	N	N
3 ***Smith***	N	Y	N
NEVADA			
1 Reid	Y	N	Y
2 ***Vucanovich***	N	N	N
NEW HAMPSHIRE			
1 ***Smith***	N	N	N
2 ***Gregg***	N	N	N
NEW JERSEY			
1 Florio	Y	N	Y
2 Hughes	Y	N	Y
3 Howard	Y	N	Y
4 ***Smith***	Y	N	Y
5 ***Roukema***	N	Y	N
6 Dwyer	Y	N	Y
7 ***Rinaldo***	Y	N	Y
8 Roe	Y	N	Y
9 Torricelli	Y	N	Y
10 Rodino	Y	N	Y
11 ***Gallo***	N	N	N
12 ***Courter***	N	Y	N
13 ***Saxton***	N	N	N
14 Guarini	Y	N	Y
NEW MEXICO			
1 ***Lujan***	N	Y	Y
2 ***Skeen***	N	N	N
3 Richardson	Y	N	Y
NEW YORK			
1 ***Carney***	N	Y	N
2 Downey	Y	N	Y
3 Mrazek	Y	N	Y
4 ***Lent***	N	?	N
5 ***McGrath***	N	N	N
6 Addabbo	?	?	?
7 Ackerman	Y	N	Y
8 Scheuer	Y	N	Y
9 Manton	Y	N	Y
10 Schumer	Y	N	Y
11 Towns	Y	N	Y
12 Owens	Y	N	Y
13 Solarz	Y	N	Y
14 ***Molinari***	N	Y	N
15 ***Green***	N	Y	N
16 Rangel	Y	N	Y
17 Weiss	Y	N	Y
18 Garcia	Y	N	Y
19 Biaggi	?	?	#
20 ***DioGuardi***	N	N	N
21 ***Fish***	Y	N	Y
22 ***Gilman***	Y	N	Y
23 Stratton	Y	N	Y
24 ***Solomon***	N	Y	N
25 ***Boehlert***	Y	N	Y
26 ***Martin***	N	Y	N
27 ***Wortley***	N	Y	N
28 McHugh	Y	N	Y
29 ***Horton***	?	?	#
30 ***Eckert***	N	Y	N
31 ***Kemp***	N	Y	N
32 LaFalce	Y	N	Y
33 Nowak	Y	N	Y
34 Lundine	N	Y	N
NORTH CAROLINA			
1 Jones	N	N	N
2 Valentine	N	N	N
3 Whitley	N	N	N
4 ***Cobey***	N	N	N
5 Neal	N	N	N
6 ***Coble***	N	N	N
7 Rose	?	?	?
8 Hefner	N	N	N
9 ***McMillan***	N	N	N
10 ***Broyhill***	N	N	N
11 ***Hendon***	N	N	N
NORTH DAKOTA			
AL Dorgan	Y	N	Y
OHIO			
1 Luken	Y	N	Y
2 ***Gradison***	N	N	N
3 Hall	Y	N	Y
4 ***Oxley***	N	N	N
5 ***Latta***	N	N	N
6 ***McEwen***	N	Y	N
7 ***DeWine***	N	Y	N
8 ***Kindness***	?	Y	N
9 Kaptur	Y	N	Y
10 ***Miller***	N	Y	N
11 Eckart	Y	N	Y
12 ***Kasich***	N	Y	N
13 Pease	Y	N	Y
14 Seiberling	Y	N	Y
15 ***Wylie***	N	N	N
16 ***Regula***	N	Y	N
17 Traficant	Y	N	Y
18 Applegate	Y	N	Y
19 Feighan	Y	N	Y
20 Oakar	Y	N	Y
21 Stokes	Y	N	Y
OKLAHOMA			
1 Jones	N	N	N
2 Synar	N	Y	N
3 Watkins	N	N	N
4 McCurdy	N	N	N
5 ***Edwards***	N	N	N
6 English	N	N	N
OREGON			
1 AuCoin	N	N	N
2 ***Smith, R.***	?	?	X
3 Wyden	N	N	N
4 Weaver	Y	N	Y
5 ***Smith, D.***	N	N	N
PENNSYLVANIA			
1 Foglietta	Y	N	Y
2 Gray	Y	N	Y
3 Borski	Y	N	Y
4 Kolter	Y	N	Y
5 ***Schulze***	N	Y	N
6 Yatron	Y	N	Y
7 Edgar	Y	N	Y
8 Kostmayer	Y	N	Y
9 ***Shuster***	N	Y	N
10 ***McDade***	N	N	Y
11 Kanjorski	Y	N	Y
12 Murtha	Y	N	Y
13 ***Coughlin***	Y	N	Y
14 Coyne	Y	N	Y
15 ***Ritter***	Y	N	Y
16 ***Walker***	N	N	N
17 ***Gekas***	N	Y	N
18 Walgren	Y	N	Y
19 ***Goodling***	N	Y	N
20 Gaydos	Y	N	Y
21 ***Ridge***	Y	N	Y
22 Murphy	Y	N	Y
23 ***Clinger***	Y	N	Y
RHODE ISLAND			
1 St Germain	Y	N	Y
2 ***Schneider***	Y	N	Y
SOUTH CAROLINA			
1 ***Hartnett***	N	Y	N
2 ***Spence***	N	Y	N
3 Derrick	N	Y	N
4 ***Campbell***	N	N	N
5 Spratt	Y	Y	N
6 Tallon	N	N	N
SOUTH DAKOTA			
AL Daschle	?	?	?
TENNESSEE			
1 ***Quillen***	N	N	N
2 ***Duncan***	N	N	N
3 Lloyd	N	Y	Y
4 Cooper	Y	Y	Y
5 Boner	Y	N	N
6 Gordon	Y	N	Y
7 ***Sundquist***	N	N	N
8 Jones	N	N	N
9 Ford	Y	N	Y
TEXAS			
1 Chapman	N	Y	N
2 Wilson	Y	N	Y
3 ***Bartlett***	N	Y	N
4 Hall, R.	N	Y	N
5 Bryant	Y	N	Y
6 ***Barton***	N	Y	N
7 ***Archer***	N	?	X
8 ***Fields***	N	N	N
9 Brooks	Y	N	Y
10 Pickle	N	N	N
11 Leath	N	Y	N
12 Wright	Y	N	Y
13 ***Boulter***	N	N	N
14 ***Sweeney***	N	N	N
15 de la Garza	Y	Y	Y
16 Coleman	Y	Y	Y
17 Stenholm	N	Y	N
18 Leland	Y	N	Y
19 ***Combest***	N	N	N
20 Gonzalez	Y	N	Y
21 ***Loeffler***	N	N	N
22 ***DeLay***	N	N	N
23 Bustamante	Y	N	Y
24 Frost	Y	N	Y
25 Andrews	N	Y	N
26 ***Armey***	N	N	N
27 Ortiz	Y	Y	Y
UTAH			
1 ***Hansen***	N	N	N
2 ***Monson***	N	N	N
3 ***Nielson***	N	N	N
VERMONT			
AL ***Jeffords***	Y	N	Y
VIRGINIA			
1 ***Bateman***	Y	Y	N
2 ***Whitehurst***	N	N	N
3 ***Bliley***	N	N	N
4 Sisisky	N	Y	N
5 Daniel	N	N	N
6 Olin	Y	N	N
7 ***Slaughter***	N	N	N
8 ***Parris***	N	N	N
9 Boucher	Y	N	N
10 ***Wolf***	N	Y	N
WASHINGTON			
1 ***Miller***	Y	Y	N
2 Swift	Y	N	Y
3 Bonker	Y	N	Y
4 ***Morrison***	Y	Y	N
5 Foley	Y	N	Y
6 Dicks	Y	N	Y
7 Lowry	Y	N	Y
8 ***Chandler***	N	N	N
WEST VIRGINIA			
1 Mollohan	Y	N	Y
2 Staggers	Y	N	Y
3 Wise	Y	N	Y
4 Rahall	Y	N	Y
WISCONSIN			
1 Aspin	Y	N	Y
2 Kastenmeier	Y	N	Y
3 ***Gunderson***	Y	Y	Y
4 Kleczka	Y	N	Y
5 Moody	Y	N	Y
6 ***Petri***	Y	N	Y
7 Obey	Y	N	Y
8 ***Roth***	N	Y	N
9 ***Sensenbrenner***	N	Y	N
WYOMING			
AL ***Cheney***	N	N	N

Southern states - Ala., Ark., Fla., Ga., Ky., La., Miss., N.C., Okla., S.C., Tenn., Texas, Va.

* The *Congressional Record* vote number is different from the CQ vote number because the *Record* includes quorum calls in its tally. CQ does not publish quorum call votes.

384. Procedural Motion. Miller, R-Wash., motion to approve the House *Journal* of Monday, Dec. 2. Motion agreed to 255-126: R 43-117; D 212-9 (ND 136-7, SD 76-2), Dec. 3, 1985.

385. HR 1562. Textile Import Quotas. Adoption of the rule (H Res 325) to provide for House floor consideration of the Rostenkowski, D-Ill., motion to concur in the Senate amendment to limit textile, apparel and shoe imports and to call for negotiations leading to voluntary reductions in world copper production. Adopted 298-109: R 81-88; D 217-21 (ND 145-15, SD 72-6), Dec. 3, 1985. (The Rostenkowski motion subsequently was agreed to *(see vote 386, below).*)

386. HR 1562. Textile Import Quotas. Rostenkowski, D-Ill., motion to concur in the Senate amendment to limit textile, apparel and shoe imports and to call for negotiations leading to voluntary reductions in world copper production. Motion agreed to (thus cleared for the president) 255-161: R 75-100; D 180-61 (ND 113-48, SD 67-13), Dec. 3, 1985. A "nay" was a vote supporting the president's position.

387. HR 3700. Higher Education Amendments. Bartlett, R-Texas, amendment to retain the current requirement that borrowers begin repaying their Guaranteed Student Loans six months after leaving school, striking the provision of the bill extending the period to nine months. Rejected 177-221: R 151-17; D 26-204 (ND 6-148, SD 20-56), Dec. 3, 1985.

388. H J Res 465. Further Continuing Appropriations, Fiscal 1986. Conte, R-Mass., motion to recommit to the Appropriations Committee for revision the joint resolution to provide continued spending authority through Sept. 30, 1986, for government agencies whose regular fiscal 1986 appropriations had not become law. Motion rejected 200-221: R 175-4; D 25-217 (ND 9-153, SD 16-64), Dec. 4, 1985.

389. H J Res 465. Further Continuing Appropriations, Fiscal 1986. Passage of the joint resolution to provide continued spending authority through Sept. 30, 1986, for government agencies whose regular fiscal 1986 appropriations had not become law. Passed 212-208: R 7-171; D 205-37 (ND 144-20, SD 61-17), Dec. 4, 1985. A "nay" was a vote supporting the president's position.

390. HR 3700. Higher Education Amendments. Bartlett, R-Texas, amendment to cut the fiscal 1987 authorization for programs in the bill other than student aid to fiscal 1985 appropriation levels, and to allow increases in fiscal 1988-91 only to compensate for inflation. Rejected 127-289: R 111-65; D 16-224 (ND 1-159, SD 15-65), Dec. 4, 1985.

391. HR 3700. Higher Education Amendments. Passage of the bill to reauthorize college student aid and other programs under the Higher Education Act of 1965 (PL 89-329) through fiscal 1991. Passed 350-67: R 112-65; D 238-2 (ND 160-0, SD 78-2), Dec. 4, 1985. A "nay" was a vote supporting the president's position.

KEY

Y Voted for (yea).
\# Paired for.
\+ Announced for.
N Voted against (nay).
X Paired against.
\- Announced against.
P Voted "present."
C Voted "present" to avoid possible conflict of interest.
? Did not vote or otherwise make a position known.

Democrats *Republicans*

	384	385	386	387	388	389	390	391
ALABAMA								
1 ***Callahan***	N	Y	Y	Y	Y	N	Y	N
2 ***Dickinson***	N	Y	Y	?	Y	N	Y	Y
3 Nichols	Y	Y	Y	N	N	N	N	Y
4 Bevill	Y	Y	Y	N	N	Y	N	Y
5 Flippo	Y	Y	Y	?	N	Y	N	Y
6 Erdreich	Y	Y	Y	N	N	N	N	Y
7 Shelby	Y	Y	Y	N	N	N	N	Y
ALASKA								
AL ***Young***	N	Y	Y	N	Y	N	N	Y
ARIZONA								
1 ***McCain***	N	N	Y	Y	Y	N	Y	Y
2 Udall	Y	Y	Y	N	Y	Y	N	Y
3 ***Stump***	N	N	N	Y	Y	N	Y	N
4 ***Rudd***	Y	N	N	Y	N	N	Y	N
5 ***Kolbe***	N	Y	Y	Y	Y	N	Y	N
ARKANSAS								
1 Alexander	Y	#	Y	?	N	Y	N	Y
2 Robinson	Y	Y	Y	N	Y	N	N	Y
3 ***Hammerschmidt***	N	Y	Y	N	Y	N	N	Y
4 Anthony	Y	Y	Y	Y	N	Y	N	Y
CALIFORNIA								
1 Bosco	Y	Y	N	N	N	Y	N	Y
2 ***Chappie***	N	N	N	Y	Y	N	Y	N
3 Matsui	Y	N	N	N	N	Y	N	Y
4 Fazio	Y	Y	Y	N	N	Y	N	Y
5 Burton	Y	Y	Y	N	N	Y	N	Y
6 Boxer	Y	Y	Y	N	N	Y	N	Y
7 Miller	Y	Y	N	N	N	Y	N	Y
8 Dellums	?	Y	Y	N	N	Y	N	Y
9 Stark	Y	Y	N	N	N	Y	N	Y
10 Edwards	Y	Y	Y	N	N	Y	N	Y
11 Lantos	Y	Y	Y	N	N	Y	N	Y
12 ***Zschau***	N	N	N	Y	Y	N	Y	Y
13 Mineta	Y	Y	N	N	N	Y	N	Y
14 ***Shumway***	Y	N	N	Y	Y	N	Y	N
15 Coelho	?	Y	Y	N	N	Y	N	Y
16 Panetta	Y	Y	N	?	N	Y	N	Y
17 ***Pashayan***	Y	Y	Y	Y	Y	N	Y	Y
18 Lehman	Y	Y	Y	N	N	Y	N	Y
19 ***Lagomarsino***	N	N	N	Y	Y	N	Y	Y
20 ***Thomas***	N	N	Y	Y	Y	N	N	Y
21 ***Fiedler***	N	Y	Y	Y	Y	N	Y	N
22 ***Moorhead***	N	N	N	Y	Y	N	Y	N
23 Beilenson	Y	Y	N	N	N	Y	N	Y
24 Waxman	Y	Y	N	N	N	Y	N	Y
25 Roybal	Y	Y	N	?	N	Y	N	Y
26 Berman	Y	Y	N	N	N	Y	N	Y
27 Levine	Y	Y	N	N	N	Y	N	Y
28 Dixon	Y	Y	Y	N	N	Y	N	Y
29 Hawkins	Y	Y	Y	N	N	Y	N	Y
30 Martinez	P	Y	Y	N	N	Y	N	Y
31 Dymally	P	Y	N	N	N	Y	N	Y
32 Anderson	Y	N	N	N	N	Y	N	Y
33 ***Dreier***	N	N	N	Y	Y	N	Y	N
34 Torres	Y	Y	Y	N	N	Y	N	Y
35 ***Lewis***	Y	N	N	Y	Y	N	?	N
36 Brown	Y	Y	Y	N	N	Y	N	Y
37 ***McCandless***	N	N	N	Y	Y	N	Y	N
38 ***Dornan***	N	N	N	Y	Y	N	Y	N
39 ***Dannemeyer***	N	N	N	Y	Y	N	Y	N
40 ***Badham***	N	N	N	Y	Y	N	Y	N
41 ***Lowery***	N	N	N	Y	Y	N	Y	Y
42 ***Lungren***	N	-	N	Y	Y	N	Y	N
43 ***Packard***	Y	N	N	Y	Y	X	Y	N
44 Bates	Y	Y	N	N	N	Y	N	Y
45 ***Hunter***	N	Y	Y	Y	Y	N	Y	N
COLORADO								
1 Schroeder	N	Y	N	N	Y	N	N	Y
2 Wirth	Y	Y	N	N	N	Y	N	Y
3 ***Strang***	N	N	N	Y	Y	N	Y	N
4 ***Brown***	N	N	N	Y	Y	N	N	Y
5 ***Kramer***	N	N	N	Y	Y	N	Y	N
6 ***Schaefer***	N	N	N	Y	Y	N	N	N
CONNECTICUT								
1 Kennelly	?	Y	Y	N	?	Y	N	Y
2 Gejdenson	Y	Y	Y	N	N	Y	N	Y
3 Morrison	Y	Y	Y	N	N	Y	N	Y
4 ***McKinney***	?	?	?	?	#	?	X	?
5 ***Rowland***	N	N	N	Y	Y	N	N	Y
6 ***Johnson***	?	Y	N	Y	Y	N	N	Y
DELAWARE								
AL Carper	Y	Y	Y	Y	Y	Y	N	Y
FLORIDA								
1 Hutto	Y	Y	Y	Y	Y	Y	Y	Y
2 Fuqua	Y	?	Y	N	N	Y	N	Y
3 Bennett	Y	Y	N	N	N	Y	Y	Y
4 Chappell	Y	Y	Y	Y	N	Y	N	Y
5 ***McCollum***	?	N	N	Y	Y	N	Y	N
6 MacKay	?	Y	N	N	N	Y	N	Y
7 Gibbons	Y	Y	N	N	N	Y	Y	Y
8 ***Young***	N	N	Y	Y	Y	N	N	Y
9 ***Bilirakis***	?	?	Y	Y	Y	N	Y	Y
10 ***Ireland***	N	N	N	Y	Y	N	Y	Y
11 Nelson	+	X	X	#	-	#	-	+
12 ***Lewis***	N	N	N	Y	Y	N	Y	Y
13 ***Mack***	N	N	N	Y	Y	N	Y	N
14 Mica	Y	Y	N	N	N	Y	Y	Y
15 ***Shaw***	N	N	N	Y	Y	N	Y	Y
16 Smith	Y	Y	Y	N	N	Y	N	Y
17 Lehman	Y	Y	Y	N	N	Y	N	Y
18 Pepper	Y	Y	Y	N	N	#	N	Y
19 Fascell	Y	Y	Y	N	N	Y	N	Y
GEORGIA								
1 Thomas	Y	Y	Y	Y	N	Y	N	Y
2 Hatcher	Y	Y	Y	N	N	Y	N	Y
3 Ray	Y	Y	Y	Y	Y	N	Y	Y
4 ***Swindall***	N	Y	Y	Y	Y	N	Y	N
5 Fowler	?	?	?	N	N	Y	N	Y
6 ***Gingrich***	N	Y	Y	?	Y	N	N	Y
7 Darden	Y	Y	Y	Y	Y	Y	Y	Y
8 Rowland	Y	Y	Y	N	N	Y	N	Y
9 Jenkins	Y	Y	Y	?	N	Y	N	Y
10 Barnard	Y	Y	Y	?	?	?	N	Y
HAWAII								
1 Heftel	?	N	N	N	N	Y	?	?
2 Akaka	Y	N	N	N	N	Y	N	Y
IDAHO								
1 ***Craig***	N	N	N	Y	Y	N	Y	N
2 Stallings	Y	N	N	N	N	Y	N	Y
ILLINOIS								
1 Hayes	P	Y	Y	N	N	Y	N	Y
2 Savage	Y	Y	Y	N	N	Y	N	Y
3 Russo	?	Y	Y	N	N	N	N	Y
4 ***O'Brien***	?	?	N	N	Y	N	N	Y
5 Lipinski	Y	Y	Y	N	N	Y	N	Y
6 ***Hyde***	Y	N	N	Y	Y	N	Y	Y
7 Collins	Y	Y	Y	N	N	Y	N	Y
8 Rostenkowski	Y	Y	N	N	N	Y	N	Y
9 Yates	Y	Y	N	N	N	Y	N	Y
10 ***Porter***	Y	N	N	Y	Y	N	Y	Y
11 Annunzio	Y	Y	Y	N	N	Y	N	Y
12 ***Crane***	N	N	N	Y	Y	N	Y	N
13 ***Fawell***	N	N	N	Y	Y	N	N	Y
14 ***Grotberg***	N	N	N	Y	Y	N	Y	Y
15 ***Madigan***	N	N	N	Y	Y	N	N	Y
16 ***Martin***	N	Y	N	Y	Y	N	Y	N
17 Evans	?	Y	Y	N	N	Y	N	Y
18 ***Michel***	N	?	N	Y	Y	N	Y	N
19 Bruce	Y	Y	Y	N	Y	N	N	Y
20 Durbin	Y	Y	Y	N	N	Y	N	Y
21 Price	?	?	?	?	?	?	?	?
22 Gray	Y	Y	Y	N	N	Y	N	Y
INDIANA								
1 Visclosky	Y	Y	Y	N	N	Y	N	Y
2 Sharp	Y	N	N	N	N	N	N	Y
3 ***Hiler***	N	N	X	?	Y	N	Y	N
4 ***Coats***	Y	N	N	Y	Y	N	Y	Y
5 ***Hillis***	Y	Y	Y	Y	Y	N	Y	Y

ND - Northern Democrats SD - Southern Democrats

* Corresponding to Congressional Record Votes 422, 423, 424, 425, 426, 427, 428, 429

	384	385	386	387	388	389	390	391
6 ***Burton***	N	N	N	Y	Y	N	Y	N
7 ***Myers***	Y	Y	N	N	N	Y	N	Y
8 McCloskey	Y	Y	Y	N	N	Y	N	Y
9 Hamilton	Y	N	N	N	N	N	N	Y
10 Jacobs	N	N	N	N	Y	N	N	Y
IOWA								
1 ***Leach***	N	N	N	Y	Y	N	N	Y
2 ***Tauke***	N	N	N	Y	Y	N	Y	Y
3 ***Evans***	N	N	N	Y	Y	N	Y	Y
4 Smith	Y	N	N	N	N	Y	N	Y
5 ***Lightfoot***	N	N	N	Y	Y	N	Y	Y
6 Bedell	Y	N	C	N	N	Y	N	Y
KANSAS								
1 ***Roberts***	N	N	N	?	Y	N	Y	N
2 Slattery	Y	Y	N	Y	N	N	N	Y
3 ***Meyers***	N	N	N	Y	Y	N	Y	Y
4 Glickman	Y	N	N	N	N	Y	N	Y
5 ***Whittaker***	N	N	N	Y	Y	N	Y	Y
KENTUCKY								
1 Hubbard	Y	Y	Y	Y	Y	N	Y	Y
2 Natcher	Y	Y	Y	N	N	Y	N	Y
3 Mazzoli	Y	Y	N	N	Y	N	N	Y
4 ***Snyder***	Y	Y	Y	Y	Y	N	Y	Y
5 ***Rogers***	N	Y	Y	Y	Y	N	Y	Y
6 ***Hopkins***	N	N	Y	Y	Y	N	Y	Y
7 Perkins	Y	Y	Y	N	N	Y	N	Y
LOUISIANA								
1 ***Livingston***	N	N	N	?	Y	N	Y	Y
2 Boggs	Y	Y	Y	N	N	Y	N	Y
3 Tauzin	Y	Y	Y	Y	Y	Y	N	Y
4 Roemer	N	N	N	Y	Y	N	Y	Y
5 Huckaby	Y	Y	Y	Y	N	Y	Y	Y
6 ***Moore***	?	Y	N	Y	Y	N	Y	Y
7 Breaux	Y	Y	Y	Y	Y	Y	N	Y
8 Long	Y	Y	Y	N	N	Y	N	Y
MAINE								
1 ***McKernan***	N	Y	Y	Y	Y	N	N	Y
2 ***Snowe***	Y	Y	Y	Y	Y	N	N	Y
MARYLAND								
1 Dyson	N	Y	Y	Y	N	N	N	Y
2 ***Bentley***	?	Y	Y	Y	Y	N	Y	Y
3 Mikulski	Y	Y	Y	N	N	Y	N	Y
4 ***Holt***	N	N	N	?	Y	N	N	Y
5 Hoyer	Y	Y	Y	N	N	Y	N	Y
6 Byron	?	Y	Y	Y	N	N	Y	Y
7 Mitchell	N	Y	Y	X	N	Y	N	Y
8 Barnes	Y	Y	Y	N	N	Y	N	Y
MASSACHUSETTS								
1 ***Conte***	N	Y	Y	N	Y	N	N	Y
2 Boland	Y	Y	Y	N	N	Y	N	Y
3 Early	Y	Y	Y	?	N	Y	N	Y
4 Frank	Y	Y	Y	N	N	Y	N	Y
5 Atkins	Y	Y	Y	N	N	Y	N	Y
6 Mavroules	Y	Y	Y	N	N	Y	N	Y
7 Markey	Y	Y	Y	N	N	Y	N	Y
8 O'Neill								
9 Moakley	Y	Y	Y	N	N	Y	N	Y
10 Studds	Y	Y	Y	N	N	Y	N	Y
11 Donnelly	Y	Y	Y	N	N	Y	N	Y
MICHIGAN								
1 Conyers	?	?	?	?	N	Y	N	Y
2 ***Pursell***	N	?	N	Y	Y	N	Y	Y
3 Wolpe	Y	Y	Y	N	N	Y	N	Y
4 ***Siljander***	N	N	N	Y	Y	N	?	?
5 ***Henry***	N	Y	Y	Y	Y	N	N	Y
6 Carr	Y	Y	Y	N	N	Y	?	?
7 Kildee	Y	Y	Y	N	N	Y	N	Y
8 Traxler	?	?	Y	N	N	Y	N	Y
9 ***Vander Jagt***	N	Y	N	Y	Y	N	Y	Y
10 ***Schuette***	N	Y	Y	Y	Y	N	Y	Y
11 ***Davis***	Y	Y	Y	N	Y	Y	N	Y
12 Bonior	Y	Y	Y	N	N	Y	N	Y
13 Crockett	Y	N	N	?	N	Y	N	Y
14 Hertel	Y	Y	Y	N	N	N	N	Y
15 Ford	Y	Y	Y	N	N	Y	N	Y
16 Dingell	Y	Y	Y	?	N	Y	N	Y
17 Levin	Y	Y	Y	N	N	Y	N	Y
18 ***Broomfield***	?	N	N	Y	Y	N	N	Y
MINNESOTA								
1 Penny	N	Y	N	N	N	N	N	Y
2 ***Weber***	N	N	N	Y	Y	N	Y	N
3 ***Frenzel***	?	Y	N	?	Y	N	Y	Y
4 Vento	Y	Y	Y	N	N	Y	N	Y
5 Sabo	Y	Y	N	N	N	Y	N	Y
6 Sikorski	N	Y	Y	N	N	Y	N	Y

	384	385	386	387	388	389	390	391
7 ***Stangeland***	N	N	N	Y	Y	N	N	Y
8 Oberstar	Y	Y	Y	N	N	Y	N	Y
MISSISSIPPI								
1 Whitten	Y	Y	Y	N	N	Y	N	Y
2 ***Franklin***	Y	Y	Y	Y	N	N	Y	Y
3 Montgomery	Y	Y	Y	Y	N	Y	Y	Y
4 Dowdy	?	Y	Y	N	N	Y	N	Y
5 ***Lott***	N	Y	Y	Y	Y	N	Y	N
MISSOURI								
1 Clay	N	Y	Y	N	N	Y	N	Y
2 Young	Y	Y	Y	N	N	Y	N	Y
3 Gephardt	Y	Y	Y	N	?	#	N	Y
4 Skelton	?	?	#	?	N	Y	N	Y
5 Wheat	Y	Y	Y	N	N	Y	N	Y
6 ***Coleman***	N	Y	Y	Y	Y	N	N	Y
7 ***Taylor***	N	Y	Y	Y	Y	N	Y	Y
8 ***Emerson***	N	Y	Y	Y	Y	N	N	Y
9 Volkmer	Y	Y	Y	N	N	Y	N	Y
MONTANA								
1 Williams	Y	Y	Y	N	N	Y	?	?
2 ***Marlenee***	N	N	N	Y	Y	N	Y	N
NEBRASKA								
1 ***Bereuter***	N	N	N	N	Y	N	N	Y
2 ***Daub***	N	N	N	Y	Y	N	Y	Y
3 ***Smith***	Y	N	N	Y	N	Y	N	Y
NEVADA								
1 Reid	Y	Y	Y	N	N	Y	N	Y
2 ***Vucanovich***	?	N	N	Y	Y	N	Y	Y
NEW HAMPSHIRE								
1 ***Smith***	N	Y	Y	Y	Y	N	Y	N
2 ***Gregg***	N	Y	Y	Y	Y	N	Y	N
NEW JERSEY								
1 Florio	Y	Y	Y	N	N	Y	N	Y
2 Hughes	Y	Y	Y	N	Y	N	N	Y
3 Howard	Y	Y	Y	N	N	Y	N	Y
4 ***Smith***	Y	Y	Y	Y	Y	Y	N	Y
5 ***Roukema***	?	?	#	?	Y	N	N	Y
6 Dwyer	Y	Y	Y	N	N	Y	N	Y
7 ***Rinaldo***	Y	Y	Y	N	Y	Y	N	Y
8 Roe	?	Y	Y	N	N	Y	N	Y
9 Torricelli	Y	Y	Y	N	N	N	N	Y
10 Rodino	Y	Y	Y	N	N	Y	N	Y
11 ***Gallo***	N	N	N	Y	Y	N	N	Y
12 ***Courter***	N	Y	N	Y	Y	N	N	Y
13 ***Saxton***	N	N	N	Y	Y	N	N	Y
14 Guarini	Y	Y	Y	N	N	Y	N	Y
NEW MEXICO								
1 ***Lujan***	?	Y	Y	Y	Y	N	Y	Y
2 ***Skeen***	N	Y	Y	Y	Y	N	N	Y
3 Richardson	Y	Y	Y	N	?	?	?	?
NEW YORK								
1 ***Carney***	?	?	?	?	Y	N	Y	Y
2 Downey	Y	Y	N	N	N	Y	N	Y
3 Mrazek	?	Y	Y	N	N	Y	N	Y
4 ***Lent***	N	Y	Y	Y	Y	N	Y	Y
5 ***McGrath***	N	Y	Y	Y	Y	N	N	Y
6 Addabbo	?	?	?	?	?	?	?	?
7 Ackerman	Y	Y	Y	?	N	Y	N	Y
8 Scheuer	Y	Y	Y	N	N	Y	N	Y
9 Manton	Y	Y	Y	N	N	Y	N	Y
10 Schumer	Y	Y	N	N	N	Y	N	Y
11 Towns	?	?	?	?	N	Y	N	Y
12 Owens	Y	Y	Y	N	N	Y	N	Y
13 Solarz	Y	Y	N	N	N	Y	N	Y
14 ***Molinari***	N	N	N	Y	Y	N	Y	N
15 ***Green***	Y	Y	N	Y	Y	N	N	Y
16 Rangel	Y	Y	Y	?	N	Y	N	Y
17 Weiss	Y	Y	Y	N	N	Y	N	Y
18 Garcia	?	Y	Y	N	N	Y	N	Y
19 Biaggi	Y	Y	Y	N	N	Y	N	Y
20 ***DioGuardi***	?	Y	Y	Y	Y	N	Y	Y
21 ***Fish***	Y	Y	Y	Y	Y	N	N	Y
22 ***Gilman***	Y	Y	Y	N	Y	N	N	Y
23 Stratton	Y	Y	Y	Y	N	N	N	Y
24 ***Solomon***	N	N	Y	Y	Y	N	Y	N
25 ***Boehlert***	N	Y	Y	Y	Y	N	N	Y
26 ***Martin***	?	Y	Y	Y	Y	N	N	Y
27 ***Wortley***	Y	Y	Y	Y	Y	N	N	Y
28 McHugh	Y	Y	N	N	N	Y	N	Y
29 ***Horton***	Y	Y	Y	N	Y	N	N	Y
30 ***Eckert***	Y	N	N	Y	Y	N	Y	N
31 ***Kemp***	Y	N	N	Y	Y	N	Y	Y
32 LaFalce	Y	N	N	Y	N	Y	N	Y
33 Nowak	?	?	?	?	N	Y	N	Y
34 Lundine	Y	Y	Y	N	N	Y	N	Y

	384	385	386	387	388	389	390	391
NORTH CAROLINA								
1 Jones	Y	Y	Y	N	N	Y	N	Y
2 Valentine	Y	Y	Y	N	N	Y	N	Y
3 Whitley	Y	Y	Y	N	N	Y	N	Y
4 ***Cobey***	N	Y	Y	Y	Y	N	Y	Y
5 Neal	Y	Y	Y	N	N	N	N	Y
6 ***Coble***	N	Y	Y	Y	Y	N	Y	Y
7 Rose	Y	Y	Y	N	N	Y	N	Y
8 Hefner	Y	Y	Y	N	N	Y	N	Y
9 ***McMillan***	Y	Y	Y	?	Y	N	N	Y
10 ***Broyhill***	Y	Y	Y	Y	Y	N	Y	Y
11 ***Hendon***	N	Y	Y	N	Y	N	N	Y
NORTH DAKOTA								
AL Dorgan	Y	Y	N	N	N	Y	N	Y
OHIO								
1 Luken	Y	N	N	N	N	Y	N	Y
2 ***Gradison***	Y	N	N	Y	Y	N	Y	N
3 Hall	Y	Y	Y	N	N	Y	N	Y
4 ***Oxley***	N	N	N	Y	Y	N	Y	N
5 ***Latta***	N	N	N	Y	Y	N	Y	N
6 ***McEwen***	?	?	N	Y	Y	N	N	N
7 ***DeWine***	N	N	N	Y	Y	N	Y	N
8 ***Kindness***	N	Y	Y	Y	Y	N	Y	N
9 Kaptur	?	Y	Y	N	N	N	N	Y
10 ***Miller***	?	?	?	?	?	X	?	?
11 Eckart	Y	Y	Y	N	N	N	N	Y
12 ***Kasich***	N	N	N	Y	Y	N	Y	Y
13 Pease	Y	Y	N	N	Y	Y	N	Y
14 Seiberling	Y	Y	N	N	N	Y	N	Y
15 ***Wylie***	Y	Y	Y	Y	Y	Y	N	Y
16 ***Regula***	N	Y	Y	Y	Y	N	N	Y
17 Traficant	Y	Y	Y	N	Y	Y	N	Y
18 Applegate	Y	Y	Y	N	Y	N	N	Y
19 Feighan	?	Y	Y	N	N	N	N	Y
20 Oakar	Y	Y	Y	N	?	?	?	?
21 Stokes	Y	Y	Y	N	N	Y	N	Y
OKLAHOMA								
1 Jones	Y	N	N	N	N	Y	N	Y
2 Synar	Y	Y	N	N	N	Y	N	Y
3 Watkins	Y	N	N	N	N	Y	N	Y
4 McCurdy	Y	N	N	N	N	Y	N	Y
5 ***Edwards***	?	N	N	Y	Y	N	Y	N
6 English	Y	N	N	N	N	Y	N	Y
OREGON								
1 AuCoin	Y	N	N	N	N	Y	N	Y
2 ***Smith, R.***	N	N	N	Y	Y	N	Y	N
3 Wyden	Y	Y	N	N	N	Y	N	Y
4 Weaver	?	?	?	N	N	N	N	Y
5 ***Smith, D.***	N	N	N	Y	Y	N	Y	N
PENNSYLVANIA								
1 Foglietta	Y	Y	Y	N	N	Y	N	Y
2 Gray	P	Y	Y	N	N	Y	N	Y
3 Borski	Y	Y	Y	N	N	Y	?	?
4 Kolter	?	?	Y	N	N	Y	N	Y
5 ***Schulze***	Y	Y	Y	Y	Y	N	Y	Y
6 Yatron	Y	Y	Y	N	N	Y	N	Y
7 Edgar	?	?	?	N	N	Y	N	Y
8 Kostmayer	Y	Y	Y	N	N	Y	N	Y
9 ***Shuster***	N	Y	Y	Y	Y	N	Y	N
10 ***McDade***	Y	Y	Y	N	Y	N	N	Y
11 Kanjorski	Y	Y	Y	N	N	Y	N	Y
12 Murtha	Y	Y	Y	?	N	Y	N	Y
13 ***Coughlin***	N	Y	Y	Y	Y	N	N	Y
14 Coyne	Y	Y	Y	N	N	Y	N	Y
15 ***Ritter***	Y	Y	Y	Y	Y	N	Y	N
16 ***Walker***	N	N	N	Y	Y	N	Y	N
17 ***Gekas***	N	N	N	Y	Y	N	N	N
18 Walgren	Y	Y	Y	N	N	Y	N	Y
19 ***Goodling***	N	Y	Y	Y	Y	N	N	Y
20 Gaydos	Y	Y	Y	N	?	Y	N	Y
21 ***Ridge***	N	Y	Y	Y	Y	N	N	Y
22 Murphy	Y	Y	Y	N	N	N	N	Y
23 ***Clinger***	Y	Y	Y	N	Y	N	-	+
RHODE ISLAND								
1 St Germain	Y	Y	Y	N	N	Y	N	Y
2 ***Schneider***	Y	Y	Y	N	Y	N	N	Y
SOUTH CAROLINA								
1 ***Hartnett***	Y	Y	Y	Y	Y	N	Y	N
2 ***Spence***	N	Y	Y	Y	Y	N	Y	Y
3 Derrick	Y	Y	Y	N	N	Y	N	Y
4 ***Campbell***	N	Y	Y	Y	Y	N	N	Y
5 Spratt	Y	Y	Y	N	N	Y	N	Y
6 Tallon	Y	Y	Y	N	N	Y	N	Y
SOUTH DAKOTA								
AL Daschle	Y	Y	N	?	?	?	?	?

	384	385	386	387	388	389	390	391
TENNESSEE								
1 ***Quillen***	Y	Y	Y	N	Y	N	N	Y
2 ***Duncan***	?	Y	Y	N	Y	N	N	Y
3 Lloyd	N	Y	Y	N	Y	N	N	Y
4 Cooper	Y	Y	Y	N	Y	N	N	Y
5 Boner	Y	Y	Y	N	N	Y	N	Y
6 Gordon	Y	Y	Y	N	N	Y	N	Y
7 ***Sundquist***	N	Y	Y	Y	Y	N	Y	Y
8 Jones	Y	Y	Y	N	N	Y	N	Y
9 Ford	Y	Y	Y	N	Y	Y	N	Y
TEXAS								
1 Chapman	Y	Y	Y	N	Y	N	N	Y
2 Wilson	Y	Y	Y	?	N	Y	?	?
3 ***Bartlett***	N	N	N	Y	Y	N	Y	N
4 Hall, R.	Y	Y	Y	Y	Y	N	Y	Y
5 Bryant	Y	Y	Y	N	N	Y	N	Y
6 ***Barton***	N	N	N	Y	Y	N	Y	Y
7 ***Archer***	Y	N	N	Y	Y	N	Y	N
8 ***Fields***	N	N	N	Y	Y	N	Y	N
9 Brooks	Y	Y	Y	N	N	Y	N	Y
10 Pickle	Y	Y	N	Y	N	Y	N	Y
11 Leath	Y	Y	Y	Y	Y	N	Y	Y
12 Wright	Y	Y	Y	N	N	Y	N	Y
13 ***Boulter***	N	N	N	Y	Y	N	Y	N
14 ***Sweeney***	Y	N	N	Y	Y	N	Y	N
15 de la Garza	Y	Y	Y	N	N	?	N	Y
16 Coleman	Y	Y	Y	N	N	Y	N	Y
17 Stenholm	Y	N	N	Y	Y	N	Y	N
18 Leland	Y	Y	Y	N	N	Y	N	Y
19 ***Combest***	Y	N	N	Y	Y	N	Y	N
20 Gonzalez	Y	Y	Y	N	N	Y	N	Y
21 ***Loeffler***	N	N	Y	Y	Y	N	Y	Y
22 ***DeLay***	Y	N	N	Y	Y	N	Y	N
23 Bustamante	Y	Y	Y	N	N	Y	N	Y
24 Frost	Y	Y	Y	N	N	Y	N	Y
25 Andrews	Y	Y	Y	Y	N	Y	N	Y
26 ***Armey***	N	N	N	Y	Y	N	Y	N
27 Ortiz	Y	Y	Y	N	N	Y	N	Y
UTAH								
1 ***Hansen***	N	N	N	Y	Y	N	Y	N
2 ***Monson***	N	Y	Y	Y	Y	N	N	Y
3 ***Nielson***	Y	N	N	Y	Y	N	Y	N
VERMONT								
AL ***Jeffords***	Y	Y	Y	Y	Y	Y	N	Y
VIRGINIA								
1 ***Bateman***	Y	N	N	Y	Y	N	Y	Y
2 ***Whitehurst***	?	?	?	?	X	N	Y	Y
3 ***Bliley***	N	Y	Y	Y	Y	N	Y	N
4 Sisisky	Y	Y	Y	Y	N	Y	N	Y
5 Daniel	Y	Y	Y	Y	N	N	Y	Y
6 Olin	Y	Y	Y	Y	N	Y	N	Y
7 ***Slaughter***	N	Y	Y	Y	Y	N	Y	Y
8 ***Parris***	N	Y	Y	Y	Y	N	Y	Y
9 Boucher	Y	Y	Y	N	N	Y	N	Y
10 ***Wolf***	N	Y	N	Y	Y	N	N	Y
WASHINGTON								
1 ***Miller***	Y	Y	N	Y	Y	N	Y	N
2 Swift	Y	Y	N	N	N	Y	N	Y
3 Bonker	Y	Y	N	N	N	Y	?	?
4 ***Morrison***	N	Y	N	Y	Y	N	N	Y
5 Foley	?	Y	N	N	N	Y	N	Y
6 Dicks	Y	Y	N	N	N	Y	N	Y
7 Lowry	Y	Y	N	N	N	Y	N	Y
8 ***Chandler***	N	Y	N	N	Y	N	N	Y
WEST VIRGINIA								
1 Mollohan	Y	Y	Y	N	N	Y	N	Y
2 Staggers	Y	Y	Y	N	N	Y	N	Y
3 Wise	Y	Y	Y	N	N	Y	N	Y
4 Rahall	Y	Y	Y	N	N	Y	N	Y
WISCONSIN								
1 Aspin	Y	Y	Y	N	N	Y	N	Y
2 Kastenmeier	Y	Y	Y	N	N	Y	N	Y
3 ***Gunderson***	N	Y	Y	Y	Y	N	N	Y
4 Kleczka	Y	Y	N	N	N	Y	N	Y
5 Moody	Y	Y	Y	N	N	Y	N	Y
6 ***Petri***	?	?	N	Y	Y	N	N	Y
7 Obey	Y	Y	Y	N	N	Y	N	Y
8 ***Roth***	?	?	?	Y	Y	N	#	?
9 ***Sensenbrenner***	N	N	N	Y	Y	N	Y	Y
WYOMING								
AL ***Cheney***	N	N	N	?	Y	X	Y	N

Southern states - Ala., Ark., Fla., Ga., Ky., La., Miss., N.C., Okla., S.C., Tenn., Texas, Va.

* The *Congressional Record* vote number is different from the CQ vote number because the *Record* includes quorum calls in its tally. CQ does not publish quorum call votes.

392. Procedural Motion. Fields, R-Texas, motion to approve the House *Journal* of Wednesday, Dec. 4. Motion agreed to 261-129: R 46-119; D 215-10 (ND 145-8, SD 70-2), Dec. 5, 1985.

393. HR 3424. Labor, Health and Human Services, Education Appropriations, Fiscal 1986. Adoption of the conference report on the bill to appropriate $94,861,859,000 in fiscal 1986 funding and $11,687,750,000 in advance fiscal 1987-88 funding for the Departments of Labor, Health and Human Services, and Education, and related agencies. Adopted 356-54: R 120-51; D 236-3 (ND 161-0, SD 75-3), Dec. 5, 1985. (The president had requested $101,579,276,000 in new budget authority.)

394. HR 2817. Superfund Reauthorization, Fiscal 1986-90. Adoption of the rule (H Res 331) to provide for House floor consideration of the bill to authorize $10 billion in fiscal years 1986-90 for the "superfund" hazardous-waste cleanup program. Adopted 376-33: R 139-33; D 237-0 (ND 160-0, SD 77-0), Dec. 5, 1985.

KEY

- Y Voted for (yea).
- # Paired for.
- + Announced for.
- N Voted against (nay).
- X Paired against.
- - Announced against.
- P Voted "present."
- C Voted "present" to avoid possible conflict of interest.
- ? Did not vote or otherwise make a position known.

Democrats *__Republicans__*

	392	393	394
ALABAMA			
1 ***Callahan***	N	Y	Y
2 ***Dickinson***	N	Y	Y
3 Nichols	Y	Y	Y
4 Bevill	Y	Y	Y
5 Flippo	Y	Y	Y
6 Erdreich	Y	Y	Y
7 Shelby	Y	Y	Y
ALASKA			
AL ***Young***	N	Y	Y
ARIZONA			
1 ***McCain***	N	Y	Y
2 Udall	?	Y	Y
3 ***Stump***	N	Y	N
4 ***Rudd***	Y	N	Y
5 ***Kolbe***	N	Y	Y
ARKANSAS			
1 Alexander	Y	Y	Y
2 Robinson	Y	Y	Y
3 ***Hammerschmidt***	Y	Y	Y
4 Anthony	Y	Y	Y
CALIFORNIA			
1 Bosco	Y	Y	Y
2 ***Chappie***	N	Y	N
3 Matsui	Y	Y	Y
4 Fazio	Y	Y	Y
5 Burton	Y	Y	Y
6 Boxer	Y	Y	Y
7 Miller	Y	Y	Y
8 Dellums	Y	Y	?
9 Stark	Y	Y	Y
10 Edwards	Y	Y	Y
11 Lantos	Y	Y	Y
12 ***Zschau***	N	Y	Y
13 Mineta	Y	Y	Y
14 ***Shumway***	Y	N	?
15 Coelho	Y	Y	Y
16 Panetta	Y	Y	Y
17 ***Pashayan***	N	Y	Y
18 Lehman	Y	Y	Y
19 ***Lagomarsino***	N	N	Y
20 ***Thomas***	N	N	Y
21 ***Fiedler***	N	Y	N
22 ***Moorhead***	N	N	Y
23 Beilenson	Y	Y	Y
24 Waxman	Y	Y	Y
25 Roybal	Y	Y	Y
26 Berman	Y	Y	Y
27 Levine	Y	Y	Y
28 Dixon	Y	Y	Y
29 Hawkins	Y	Y	Y
30 Martinez	Y	Y	?
31 Dymally	P	Y	Y
32 Anderson	Y	Y	Y
33 ***Dreier***	N	N	N
34 Torres	Y	Y	Y
35 ***Lewis***	N	Y	N
36 Brown	Y	Y	Y
37 ***McCandless***	N	N	Y
38 ***Dornan***	Y	N	N
39 ***Dannemeyer***	N	N	Y
40 ***Badham***	N	N	Y
41 ***Lowery***	N	Y	Y
42 ***Lungren***	N	N	Y

	392	393	394
43 ***Packard***	Y	Y	Y
44 Bates	?	Y	Y
45 ***Hunter***	?	Y	N
COLORADO			
1 Schroeder	N	Y	Y
2 Wirth	Y	Y	Y
3 ***Strang***	N	Y	N
4 ***Brown***	N	N	N
5 ***Kramer***	N	N	Y
6 ***Schaefer***	N	N	Y
CONNECTICUT			
1 Kennelly	Y	Y	Y
2 Gejdenson	Y	Y	Y
3 Morrison	Y	Y	Y
4 ***McKinney***	?	?	?
5 ***Rowland***	N	Y	Y
6 ***Johnson***	Y	Y	Y
DELAWARE			
AL Carper	Y	Y	Y
FLORIDA			
1 Hutto	Y	Y	Y
2 Fuqua	Y	Y	Y
3 Bennett	Y	Y	Y
4 Chappell	Y	Y	Y
5 ***McCollum***	N	N	Y
6 MacKay	Y	Y	Y
7 Gibbons	Y	Y	Y
8 ***Young***	N	Y	Y
9 ***Bilirakis***	N	N	Y
10 ***Ireland***	N	N	Y
11 Nelson	+	+	+
12 ***Lewis***	N	Y	Y
13 ***Mack***	N	N	N
14 Mica	Y	Y	Y
15 ***Shaw***	N	Y	?
16 Smith	Y	Y	Y
17 Lehman	Y	Y	Y
18 Pepper	Y	Y	Y
19 Fascell	Y	Y	Y
GEORGIA			
1 Thomas	Y	Y	Y
2 Hatcher	Y	Y	Y
3 Ray	Y	Y	Y
4 ***Swindall***	N	N	Y
5 Fowler	Y	Y	Y
6 ***Gingrich***	N	Y	Y
7 Darden	Y	Y	Y
8 Rowland	Y	Y	Y
9 Jenkins	Y	Y	Y
10 Barnard	Y	Y	Y
HAWAII			
1 Heftel	?	?	?
2 Akaka	Y	Y	Y
IDAHO			
1 ***Craig***	N	N	Y
2 Stallings	Y	Y	Y
ILLINOIS			
1 Hayes	Y	Y	Y
2 Savage	Y	Y	Y
3 Russo	Y	Y	Y
4 ***O'Brien***	?	?	Y
5 Lipinski	Y	Y	Y
6 ***Hyde***	Y	Y	Y
7 Collins	Y	Y	Y
8 Rostenkowski	Y	Y	Y
9 Yates	Y	Y	Y
10 ***Porter***	?	Y	Y
11 Annunzio	Y	Y	Y
12 ***Crane***	N	N	N
13 ***Fawell***	N	Y	Y
14 ***Grotberg***	N	Y	Y
15 ***Madigan***	?	Y	Y
16 ***Martin***	N	Y	Y
17 Evans	Y	Y	Y
18 ***Michel***	N	Y	?
19 Bruce	Y	Y	Y
20 Durbin	Y	Y	Y
21 Price	?	?	?
22 Gray	?	Y	Y
INDIANA			
1 Visclosky	Y	Y	Y
2 Sharp	Y	Y	Y
3 ***Hiler***	N	Y	Y
4 ***Coats***	Y	Y	Y
5 ***Hillis***	Y	Y	Y

ND - Northern Democrats SD - Southern Democrats

* Corresponding to Congressional Record Votes 430, 431, 432

	392	393	394
6 ***Burton***	N	N	Y
7 ***Myers***	Y	Y	Y
8 McCloskey	Y	Y	Y
9 Hamilton	Y	Y	Y
10 Jacobs	N	Y	Y
IOWA			
1 ***Leach***	N	Y	Y
2 ***Tauke***	N	N	Y
3 ***Evans***	N	N	Y
4 Smith	Y	Y	Y
5 ***Lightfoot***	N	N	Y
6 Bedell	Y	Y	Y
KANSAS			
1 ***Roberts***	N	N	N
2 Slattery	Y	Y	Y
3 ***Meyers***	Y	Y	Y
4 Glickman	Y	Y	Y
5 ***Whittaker***	N	Y	Y
KENTUCKY			
1 Hubbard	Y	Y	Y
2 Natcher	Y	Y	Y
3 Mazzoli	Y	Y	Y
4 ***Snyder***	Y	Y	Y
5 ***Rogers***	N	Y	Y
6 ***Hopkins***	Y	Y	Y
7 Perkins	Y	Y	Y
LOUISIANA			
1 ***Livingston***	Y	Y	Y
2 Boggs	Y	Y	Y
3 Tauzin	Y	Y	Y
4 Roemer	N	N	Y
5 Huckaby	Y	Y	Y
6 ***Moore***	Y	Y	Y
7 Breaux	Y	Y	Y
8 Long	Y	Y	Y
MAINE			
1 ***McKernan***	N	Y	Y
2 ***Snowe***	N	Y	Y
MARYLAND			
1 Dyson	?	Y	Y
2 ***Bentley***	N	Y	Y
3 Mikulski	Y	Y	Y
4 ***Holt***	N	Y	Y
5 Hoyer	Y	Y	Y
6 Byron	?	Y	Y
7 Mitchell	N	Y	Y
8 Barnes	Y	Y	Y
MASSACHUSETTS			
1 ***Conte***	N	Y	Y
2 Boland	Y	Y	Y
3 Early	Y	Y	Y
4 Frank	Y	Y	Y
5 Atkins	Y	Y	Y
6 Mavroules	?	Y	Y
7 Markey	N	Y	Y
8 O'Neill			
9 Moakley	Y	+	Y
10 Studds	Y	Y	Y
11 Donnelly	Y	Y	Y
MICHIGAN			
1 Conyers	Y	Y	Y
2 ***Pursell***	N	Y	Y
3 Wolpe	Y	Y	Y
4 ***Siljander***	N	Y	Y
5 ***Henry***	N	Y	Y
6 Carr	Y	Y	Y
7 Kildee	Y	Y	Y
8 Traxler	Y	Y	Y
9 ***Vander Jagt***	N	Y	Y
10 ***Schuette***	N	Y	Y
11 ***Davis***	Y	Y	?
12 Bonior	Y	Y	Y
13 Crockett	Y	Y	Y
14 Hertel	Y	Y	Y
15 Ford	?	Y	Y
16 Dingell	Y	Y	Y
17 Levin	Y	Y	Y
18 ***Broomfield***	Y	Y	Y
MINNESOTA			
1 Penny	N	Y	Y
2 ***Weber***	N	N	N
3 ***Frenzel***	N	?	Y
4 Vento	Y	Y	Y
5 Sabo	Y	Y	Y
6 Sikorski	N	Y	Y
7 ***Stangeland***	N	Y	Y
8 Oberstar	Y	Y	Y
MISSISSIPPI			
1 Whitten	Y	Y	Y
2 ***Franklin***	Y	Y	Y
3 Montgomery	Y	Y	Y
4 Dowdy	Y	Y	Y
5 ***Lott***	N	Y	Y
MISSOURI			
1 Clay	N	Y	Y
2 Young	Y	Y	Y
3 Gephardt	?	?	?
4 Skelton	Y	Y	Y
5 Wheat	Y	Y	Y
6 ***Coleman***	N	Y	Y
7 ***Taylor***	Y	Y	Y
8 ***Emerson***	N	Y	Y
9 Volkmer	N	Y	Y
MONTANA			
1 Williams	?	?	?
2 ***Marlenee***	?	Y	N
NEBRASKA			
1 ***Bereuter***	N	Y	Y
2 ***Daub***	N	Y	N
3 ***Smith***	Y	Y	Y
NEVADA			
1 Reid	Y	Y	Y
2 ***Vucanovich***	N	N	N
NEW HAMPSHIRE			
1 ***Smith***	N	N	Y
2 ***Gregg***	N	N	Y
NEW JERSEY			
1 Florio	Y	Y	Y
2 Hughes	Y	Y	Y
3 Howard	Y	Y	Y
4 ***Smith***	Y	Y	Y
5 ***Roukema***	N	Y	Y
6 Dwyer	Y	Y	Y
7 ***Rinaldo***	Y	Y	Y
8 Roe	Y	Y	Y
9 Torricelli	Y	Y	Y
10 Rodino	Y	Y	Y
11 ***Gallo***	N	Y	Y
12 ***Courter***	N	Y	Y
13 ***Saxton***	N	Y	Y
14 Guarini	Y	Y	Y
NEW MEXICO			
1 ***Lujan***	Y	Y	Y
2 ***Skeen***	N	Y	Y
3 Richardson	?	?	?
NEW YORK			
1 ***Carney***	N	Y	Y
2 Downey	Y	?	Y
3 Mrazek	Y	Y	Y
4 ***Lent***	N	Y	Y
5 ***McGrath***	N	Y	Y
6 Addabbo	?	?	?
7 Ackerman	Y	Y	Y
8 Scheuer	Y	Y	Y
9 Manton	Y	Y	Y
10 Schumer	Y	Y	Y
11 Towns	Y	Y	Y
12 Owens	Y	Y	Y
13 Solarz	Y	Y	Y
14 ***Molinari***	N	Y	Y
15 ***Green***	Y	Y	Y
16 Rangel	Y	Y	Y
17 Weiss	Y	Y	Y
18 Garcia	Y	Y	Y
19 Biaggi	Y	Y	Y
20 ***DioGuardi***	Y	Y	Y
21 ***Fish***	Y	Y	Y
22 ***Gilman***	+	+	+
23 Stratton	Y	Y	Y
24 ***Solomon***	N	N	?
25 ***Boehlert***	N	Y	Y
26 ***Martin***	N	Y	Y
27 ***Wortley***	Y	Y	Y
28 McHugh	Y	Y	Y
29 ***Horton***	Y	Y	Y
30 ***Eckert***	Y	Y	Y
31 ***Kemp***	?	Y	Y
32 LaFalce	Y	Y	Y
33 Nowak	Y	Y	Y
34 Lundine	Y	Y	Y
NORTH CAROLINA			
1 Jones	Y	Y	Y
2 Valentine	Y	Y	Y
3 Whitley	Y	Y	?
4 ***Cobey***	N	Y	N
5 Neal	?	Y	Y
6 ***Coble***	N	Y	N
7 Rose	Y	Y	Y
8 Hefner	Y	Y	Y
9 ***McMillan***	N	Y	Y
10 ***Broyhill***	Y	?	Y
11 ***Hendon***	N	Y	Y
NORTH DAKOTA			
AL Dorgan	Y	Y	Y
OHIO			
1 Luken	Y	Y	Y
2 ***Gradison***	Y	N	Y
3 Hall	Y	Y	Y
4 ***Oxley***	N	Y	Y
5 ***Latta***	N	Y	Y
6 ***McEwen***	N	Y	Y
7 ***DeWine***	N	Y	Y
8 ***Kindness***	N	Y	Y
9 Kaptur	Y	Y	Y
10 ***Miller***	?	?	?
11 Eckart	Y	Y	Y
12 ***Kasich***	N	Y	Y
13 Pease	Y	Y	Y
14 Seiberling	?	Y	Y
15 ***Wylie***	Y	Y	Y
16 ***Regula***	Y	Y	Y
17 Traficant	Y	Y	Y
18 Applegate	Y	Y	Y
19 Feighan	Y	Y	Y
20 Oakar	Y	Y	Y
21 Stokes	Y	Y	Y
OKLAHOMA			
1 Jones	Y	Y	Y
2 Synar	Y	Y	Y
3 Watkins	Y	Y	Y
4 McCurdy	Y	Y	Y
5 ***Edwards***	?	Y	N
6 English	Y	Y	Y
OREGON			
1 AuCoin	Y	Y	Y
2 ***Smith, R.***	N	Y	Y
3 Wyden	Y	Y	Y
4 Weaver	Y	Y	Y
5 ***Smith, D.***	N	N	N
PENNSYLVANIA			
1 Foglietta	Y	Y	Y
2 Gray	Y	Y	?
3 Borski	Y	Y	Y
4 Kolter	Y	Y	Y
5 ***Schulze***	Y	Y	Y
6 Yatron	Y	Y	Y
7 Edgar	Y	Y	Y
8 Kostmayer	Y	Y	Y
9 ***Shuster***	N	N	Y
10 ***McDade***	Y	Y	Y
11 Kanjorski	Y	Y	Y
12 Murtha	Y	Y	Y
13 ***Coughlin***	N	Y	Y
14 Coyne	Y	Y	Y
15 ***Ritter***	Y	N	Y
16 ***Walker***	N	Y	N
17 ***Gekas***	N	Y	N
18 Walgren	Y	Y	Y
19 ***Goodling***	N	?	Y
20 Gaydos	Y	Y	Y
21 ***Ridge***	N	Y	Y
22 Murphy	Y	Y	Y
23 ***Clinger***	+	+	+
RHODE ISLAND			
1 St Germain	Y	Y	Y
2 ***Schneider***	Y	Y	Y
SOUTH CAROLINA			
1 ***Hartnett***	N	N	N
2 ***Spence***	N	Y	Y
3 Derrick	Y	Y	Y
4 ***Campbell***	?	?	Y
5 Spratt	Y	Y	Y
6 Tallon	Y	Y	Y
SOUTH DAKOTA			
AL Daschle	?	Y	Y
TENNESSEE			
1 ***Quillen***	Y	Y	Y
2 ***Duncan***	Y	Y	Y
3 Lloyd	N	Y	Y
4 Cooper	Y	Y	Y
5 Boner	Y	Y	Y
6 Gordon	P	Y	Y
7 ***Sundquist***	N	Y	Y
8 Jones	?	Y	Y
9 Ford	?	?	Y
TEXAS			
1 Chapman	Y	Y	Y
2 Wilson	?	?	?
3 ***Bartlett***	N	N	Y
4 Hall, R.	Y	N	Y
5 Bryant	Y	Y	Y
6 ***Barton***	N	N	N
7 ***Archer***	Y	N	N
8 ***Fields***	N	N	Y
9 Brooks	Y	Y	Y
10 Pickle	Y	Y	Y
11 Leath	?	Y	Y
12 Wright	Y	Y	Y
13 ***Boulter***	N	N	N
14 ***Sweeney***	Y	N	Y
15 de la Garza	Y	Y	Y
16 Coleman	Y	Y	Y
17 Stenholm	Y	N	Y
18 Leland	?	Y	Y
19 ***Combest***	Y	N	N
20 Gonzalez	Y	Y	Y
21 ***Loeffler***	N	N	N
22 ***DeLay***	N	N	N
23 Bustamante	Y	Y	Y
24 Frost	Y	Y	?
25 Andrews	Y	Y	Y
26 ***Armey***	N	N	N
27 Ortiz	?	?	?
UTAH			
1 ***Hansen***	N	N	N
2 ***Monson***	N	N	N
3 ***Nielson***	N	N	Y
VERMONT			
AL ***Jeffords***	Y	Y	Y
VIRGINIA			
1 ***Bateman***	Y	Y	Y
2 ***Whitehurst***	?	Y	Y
3 ***Bliley***	N	Y	Y
4 Sisisky	Y	Y	Y
5 Daniel	?	Y	Y
6 Olin	Y	Y	Y
7 ***Slaughter***	N	Y	Y
8 ***Parris***	?	?	Y
9 Boucher	Y	Y	Y
10 ***Wolf***	N	Y	Y
WASHINGTON			
1 ***Miller***	Y	Y	Y
2 Swift	Y	Y	Y
3 Bonker	?	?	Y
4 ***Morrison***	N	Y	Y
5 Foley	Y	Y	Y
6 Dicks	Y	Y	Y
7 Lowry	Y	Y	Y
8 ***Chandler***	?	Y	Y
WEST VIRGINIA			
1 Mollohan	Y	Y	Y
2 Staggers	Y	Y	Y
3 Wise	Y	Y	Y
4 Rahall	Y	Y	Y
WISCONSIN			
1 Aspin	Y	Y	Y
2 Kastenmeier	Y	Y	Y
3 ***Gunderson***	N	Y	Y
4 Kleczka	Y	Y	Y
5 Moody	Y	Y	?
6 ***Petri***	Y	Y	Y
7 Obey	Y	Y	Y
8 ***Roth***	?	?	?
9 ***Sensenbrenner***	N	N	Y
WYOMING			
AL ***Cheney***	?	N	N

Southern states - Ala., Ark., Fla., Ga., Ky., La., Miss., N.C., Okla., S.C., Tenn., Texas, Va.

* The *Congressional Record* vote number is different from the CQ vote number because the *Record* includes quorum calls in its tally. CQ does not publish quorum call votes.

395. HR 2817. Superfund Reauthorization, Fiscal 1986-90. Daub, R-Neb., amendment to relieve from liability for hazardous-waste cleanups persons who can prove that they had nothing to do with substances leaking from the site. Rejected 62-330: R 60-98; D 2-232 (ND 1-158, SD 1-74), Dec. 5, 1985.

396. HR 2817. Superfund Reauthorization, Fiscal 1986-90. Edgar, D-Pa., amendment to require companies to make public an inventory of their emissions of chemicals known to cause or suspected of causing cancer, birth defects or other chronic diseases. Adopted 183-166: R 28-113; D 155-53 (ND 126-18, SD 29-35), Dec. 5, 1985. (The Edgar amendment later was adopted after the House rose from the Committee of the Whole *(see vote 408, p. 128-H)*.)

397. Procedural Motion. Fields, R-Texas, motion to approve the House *Journal* of Thursday, Dec. 5. Motion agreed to 251-118: R 46-109; D 205-9 (ND 139-8, SD 66-1), Dec. 6, 1985.

398. HR 2817. Superfund Reauthorization, Fiscal 1986-90. McKernan, R-Maine, amendment to allow eight states with oil-spill liability funds to continue to operate those funds after enactment of the federal oil-spill liability program contained in the bill. (The bill would phase out state funds in three years.) Rejected 142-256: R 79-86; D 63-170 (ND 41-119, SD 22-51), Dec. 6, 1985.

399. H Con Res 239. Ireland-United Kingdom Agreement. Fascell, D-Fla., motion to suspend the rules and adopt the concurrent resolution to commend the governments of Ireland and the United Kingdom for reaching an agreement on measures to begin a peace process in Northern Ireland. Motion agreed to 380-1: R 156-1; D 224-0 (ND 151-0, SD 73-0), Dec. 9, 1985. A two-thirds majority of those present and voting (254 in this case) is required for adoption under suspension of the rules.

400. HR 1083. Low-Level Radioactive Waste Disposal. Udall, D-Ariz., motion to suspend the rules and pass the bill to establish requirements and deadlines for carrying out interstate compacts for the establishment and operation of regional disposal facilities for low-level radioactive waste. Motion agreed to 378-0: R 154-0; D 224-0 (ND 151-0, SD 73-0), Dec. 9, 1985. A two-thirds majority of those present and voting (252 in this case) is required for passage under suspension of the rules.

401. HR 3773. Federal Technology Transfer. Fuqua, D-Fla., motion to suspend the rules and pass the bill to amend the Stevenson-Wydler Technology Innovation Act of 1980 (PL 96-480) to promote technology transfer by authorizing government-operated laboratories to enter into cooperative research agreements and by establishing a Federal Laboratory Consortium for Technology Transfer within the National Science Foundation. Motion agreed to 386-0: R 159-0; D 227-0 (ND 155-0, SD 72-0), Dec. 9, 1985. A two-thirds majority of those present and voting (258 in this case) is required for passage under suspension of the rules.

402. HR 1538. Veterans' Compensation. Applegate, D-Ohio, motion to suspend the rules and pass the bill to authorize a 3.4 percent fiscal 1986 cost-of-living allowance for veterans receiving disability compensation and for dependents and survivors receiving indemnity compensation. Motion agreed to 388-0: R 159-0; D 229-0 (ND 156-0, SD 73-0), Dec. 9, 1985. A two-thirds majority of those present and voting (259 in this case) is required for passage under suspension of the rules.

KEY

- Y Voted for (yea).
- # Paired for.
- + Announced for.
- N Voted against (nay).
- X Paired against.
- \- Announced against.
- P Voted "present."
- C Voted "present" to avoid possible conflict of interest.
- ? Did not vote or otherwise make a position known.

Democrats ***Republicans***

	395	396	397	398	399	400	401	402
ALABAMA								
1 ***Callahan***	N	N	Y	N	Y	Y	Y	Y
2 ***Dickinson***	?	?	N	Y	?	?	?	?
3 Nichols	?	?	Y	N	Y	Y	Y	Y
4 Bevill	N	N	Y	N	Y	Y	Y	Y
5 Flippo	N	N	Y	N	Y	Y	Y	Y
6 Erdreich	N	Y	Y	N	Y	Y	Y	Y
7 Shelby	N	N	Y	N	Y	Y	Y	Y
ALASKA								
AL ***Young***	N	N	N	N	Y	Y	Y	Y
ARIZONA								
1 ***McCain***	N	N	N	N	Y	Y	Y	Y
2 Udall	N	?	Y	N	Y	Y	Y	Y
3 ***Stump***	Y	N	N	N	Y	Y	Y	Y
4 ***Rudd***	Y	N	Y	Y	Y	Y	Y	Y
5 ***Kolbe***	N	N	N	N	Y	Y	Y	Y
ARKANSAS								
1 Alexander	?	?	?	X	Y	Y	Y	Y
2 Robinson	N	N	Y	N	Y	Y	Y	Y
3 ***Hammerschmidt***	N	N	Y	N	Y	Y	Y	Y
4 Anthony	N	Y	?	N	Y	Y	Y	Y
CALIFORNIA								
1 Bosco	N	Y	Y	N	?	?	?	?
2 ***Chappie***	Y	N	N	Y	?	?	?	?
3 Matsui	N	Y	Y	N	Y	Y	Y	Y
4 Fazio	N	Y	Y	N	Y	Y	Y	Y
5 Burton	N	Y	Y	Y	Y	Y	Y	Y
6 Boxer	N	Y	Y	N	Y	Y	Y	Y
7 Miller	N	Y	Y	N	Y	Y	Y	Y
8 Dellums	?	Y	Y	N	Y	Y	Y	Y
9 Stark	N	Y	?	N	?	?	?	?
10 Edwards	N	Y	Y	Y	Y	Y	Y	Y
11 Lantos	N	Y	Y	N	Y	Y	Y	Y
12 ***Zschau***	Y	N	N	N	?	?	?	?
13 Mineta	N	Y	Y	N	Y	Y	Y	Y
14 ***Shumway***	Y	N	Y	N	Y	Y	Y	Y
15 Coelho	N	N	Y	N	Y	Y	Y	Y
16 Panetta	N	Y	Y	N	Y	Y	Y	Y
17 ***Pashayan***	N	N	N	N	Y	?	Y	Y
18 Lehman	N	N	Y	N	Y	Y	Y	Y
19 ***Lagomarsino***	N	N	N	N	Y	Y	Y	Y
20 ***Thomas***	N	N	N	Y	Y	Y	Y	Y
21 ***Fiedler***	Y	N	N	N	Y	Y	Y	Y
22 ***Moorhead***	N	?	?	?	Y	Y	Y	Y
23 Beilenson	N	Y	Y	N	Y	Y	Y	Y
24 Waxman	N	Y	Y	Y	Y	Y	Y	Y
25 Roybal	N	Y	Y	Y	Y	Y	Y	Y
26 Berman	N	Y	?	N	Y	Y	Y	Y
27 Levine	N	?	Y	Y	Y	Y	Y	Y
28 Dixon	N	?	?	N	Y	Y	Y	Y
29 Hawkins	N	?	Y	Y	Y	Y	Y	Y
30 Martinez	N	?	Y	N	Y	Y	Y	Y
31 Dymally	N	N	?	N	Y	Y	Y	Y
32 Anderson	Y	Y	Y	N	Y	Y	Y	Y
33 ***Dreier***	N	N	N	N	Y	Y	Y	Y
34 Torres	N	Y	?	N	Y	Y	Y	Y
35 ***Lewis***	Y	?	N	Y	Y	Y	Y	Y
36 Brown	?	?	Y	N	Y	Y	Y	Y
37 ***McCandless***	Y	N	N	N	Y	Y	Y	Y
38 ***Dornan***	?	N	N	Y	Y	Y	Y	Y
39 ***Dannemeyer***	Y	N	N	N	+	+	+	+
40 ***Badham***	Y	N	N	Y	Y	Y	Y	Y
41 ***Lowery***	N	?	?	Y	Y	Y	Y	Y
42 ***Lungren***	Y	N	N	N	Y	Y	Y	Y
43 ***Packard***	N	N	Y	N	Y	Y	Y	Y
44 Bates	N	Y	Y	N	Y	Y	Y	Y
45 ***Hunter***	N	N	?	Y	Y	Y	Y	Y
COLORADO								
1 Schroeder	N	Y	N	Y	Y	Y	Y	Y
2 Wirth	N	Y	Y	N	Y	Y	Y	Y
3 ***Strang***	Y	N	N	N	Y	Y	Y	Y
4 ***Brown***	Y	N	N	Y	Y	Y	Y	Y
5 ***Kramer***	N	N	N	N	?	?	?	?
6 ***Schaefer***	N	N	Y	N	Y	Y	Y	Y
CONNECTICUT								
1 Kennelly	N	Y	Y	Y	Y	Y	Y	Y
2 Gejdenson	N	Y	Y	N	Y	Y	Y	Y
3 Morrison	?	?	Y	N	+	+	+	+
4 ***McKinney***	?	?	?	?	?	?	?	?
5 ***Rowland***	N	Y	Y	N	?	?	?	?
6 ***Johnson***	N	N	Y	Y	Y	Y	Y	Y
DELAWARE								
AL Carper	N	Y	Y	N	Y	Y	Y	Y
FLORIDA								
1 Hutto	N	N	Y	Y	Y	Y	Y	Y
2 Fuqua	N	N	Y	Y	Y	Y	Y	Y
3 Bennett	N	Y	Y	Y	Y	Y	Y	Y
4 Chappell	N	N	?	Y	Y	Y	Y	Y
5 ***McCollum***	Y	N	N	Y	Y	Y	Y	Y
6 MacKay	N	Y	Y	Y	Y	Y	Y	Y
7 Gibbons	N	?	?	#	Y	Y	Y	Y
8 ***Young***	N	N	N	Y	Y	Y	Y	Y
9 ***Bilirakis***	N	N	N	Y	Y	Y	Y	Y
10 ***Ireland***	N	N	N	Y	?	?	?	?
11 Nelson	-	+	+	Y	+	+	+	+
12 ***Lewis***	Y	N	N	Y	Y	Y	Y	Y
13 ***Mack***	Y	N	N	Y	Y	Y	Y	Y
14 Mica	N	?	Y	Y	?	?	?	?
15 ***Shaw***	N	?	N	Y	Y	Y	Y	Y
16 Smith	N	Y	?	Y	Y	Y	Y	Y
17 Lehman	N	Y	Y	Y	Y	Y	Y	Y
18 Pepper	N	+	Y	Y	Y	Y	Y	Y
19 Fascell	N	Y	Y	Y	Y	Y	Y	Y
GEORGIA								
1 Thomas	N	Y	Y	N	Y	Y	Y	Y
2 Hatcher	N	N	Y	N	Y	Y	Y	Y
3 Ray	N	N	Y	N	Y	Y	Y	Y
4 ***Swindall***	N	-	?	Y	Y	Y	Y	Y
5 Fowler	N	Y	Y	N	?	?	?	?
6 ***Gingrich***	N	N	?	Y	Y	Y	Y	Y
7 Darden	N	Y	Y	N	Y	Y	Y	Y
8 Rowland	N	Y	Y	N	Y	Y	Y	Y
9 Jenkins	N	Y	?	N	Y	Y	Y	Y
10 Barnard	N	Y	Y	Y	Y	Y	Y	Y
HAWAII								
1 Heftel	?	?	Y	Y	Y	Y	Y	Y
2 Akaka	N	N	?	?	Y	Y	Y	Y
IDAHO								
1 ***Craig***	N	N	N	Y	Y	Y	Y	Y
2 Stallings	N	Y	Y	N	Y	Y	Y	Y
ILLINOIS								
1 Hayes	N	Y	Y	N	Y	Y	Y	Y
2 Savage	N	Y	Y	N	Y	Y	Y	Y
3 Russo	N	Y	Y	N	Y	Y	Y	Y
4 ***O'Brien***	?	?	?	?	Y	Y	Y	Y
5 Lipinski	N	Y	Y	N	Y	Y	Y	Y
6 ***Hyde***	Y	N	Y	N	Y	Y	Y	Y
7 Collins	N	Y	Y	N	?	?	?	?
8 Rostenkowski	N	N	Y	N	Y	Y	Y	Y
9 Yates	N	?	Y	N	Y	Y	Y	Y
10 ***Porter***	?	?	Y	Y	Y	Y	Y	Y
11 Annunzio	N	?	Y	N	Y	Y	Y	Y
12 ***Crane***	Y	N	N	Y	N	Y	Y	Y
13 ***Fawell***	Y	Y	N	Y	Y	Y	Y	Y
14 ***Grotberg***	N	N	N	N	Y	Y	Y	Y
15 ***Madigan***	N	N	Y	N	Y	Y	Y	Y
16 ***Martin***	N	N	N	N	Y	Y	Y	Y
17 Evans	N	Y	Y	N	Y	Y	Y	Y
18 ***Michel***	N	N	N	Y	Y	Y	Y	Y
19 Bruce	N	Y	Y	N	Y	Y	Y	Y
20 Durbin	N	Y	N	N	Y	Y	Y	Y
21 Price	?	?	?	?	?	?	?	?
22 Gray	N	Y	?	N	Y	Y	Y	Y
INDIANA								
1 Visclosky	N	Y	Y	N	Y	Y	Y	Y
2 Sharp	N	Y	Y	N	Y	Y	Y	Y
3 ***Hiler***	Y	N	N	Y	Y	Y	Y	Y
4 ***Coats***	N	N	N	N	Y	Y	Y	Y
5 ***Hillis***	?	?	?	?	?	?	?	?

ND - Northern Democrats SD - Southern Democrats

* Corresponding to Congressional Record Votes 433, 434, 435, 436, 437, 438, 439, 440

	395	396	397	398	399	400	401	402
6 ***Burton***	N	N	N	Y	+	+	+	+
7 ***Myers***	N	N	Y	?	?	?	?	?
8 McCloskey	N	Y	Y	N	?	?	?	?
9 Hamilton	N	Y	Y	N	Y	Y	Y	Y
10 Jacobs	N	Y	N	Y	?	?	?	?
IOWA								
1 ***Leach***	N	Y	?	N	Y	Y	Y	Y
2 ***Tauke***	N	N	N	N	Y	Y	Y	Y
3 ***Evans***	Y	N	N	Y	Y	Y	Y	Y
4 Smith	N	Y	?	?	Y	Y	Y	Y
5 ***Lightfoot***	Y	N	N	Y	Y	Y	Y	Y
6 Bedell	N	Y	Y	?	Y	Y	Y	Y
KANSAS								
1 ***Roberts***	Y	N	N	N	Y	Y	Y	Y
2 Slattery	N	N	Y	N	Y	Y	Y	Y
3 ***Meyers***	N	?	N	Y	Y	Y	Y	Y
4 Glickman	N	Y	Y	N	Y	Y	Y	Y
5 ***Whittaker***	N	N	?	?	Y	Y	Y	Y
KENTUCKY								
1 Hubbard	Y	N	Y	N	Y	Y	Y	Y
2 Natcher	N	N	Y	N	Y	Y	Y	Y
3 Mazzoli	N	N	Y	N	Y	Y	Y	Y
4 ***Snyder***	N	N	Y	N	?	?	Y	Y
5 ***Rogers***	N	N	N	N	Y	Y	Y	Y
6 ***Hopkins***	Y	?	N	N	Y	Y	Y	Y
7 Perkins	N	N	Y	N	Y	Y	Y	Y
LOUISIANA								
1 ***Livingston***	N	N	Y	N	?	?	?	?
2 Boggs	N	?	Y	N	Y	Y	Y	Y
3 Tauzin	N	N	Y	N	Y	Y	Y	Y
4 Roemer	N	Y	N	N	Y	Y	Y	Y
5 Huckaby	N	Y	Y	N	Y	Y	Y	Y
6 ***Moore***	N	N	Y	N	Y	Y	Y	Y
7 Breaux	N	N	Y	N	?	?	?	?
8 Long	N	?	Y	N	Y	Y	Y	Y
MAINE								
1 ***McKernan***	N	N	N	Y	Y	Y	Y	Y
2 ***Snowe***	N	Y	N	Y	Y	Y	Y	Y
MARYLAND								
1 Dyson	N	Y	?	Y	Y	Y	Y	Y
2 ***Bentley***	N	N	N	N	Y	Y	Y	Y
3 Mikulski	N	Y	Y	Y	Y	Y	Y	Y
4 ***Holt***	N	?	?	Y	Y	Y	Y	Y
5 Hoyer	N	Y	Y	N	Y	Y	Y	Y
6 Byron	N	N	?	Y	?	?	?	?
7 Mitchell	N	?	N	N	Y	Y	Y	Y
8 Barnes	N	Y	Y	Y	Y	Y	Y	Y
MASSACHUSETTS								
1 ***Conte***	N	?	N	Y	Y	Y	Y	Y
2 Boland	N	Y	Y	N	Y	Y	Y	Y
3 Early	N	Y	Y	N	Y	Y	Y	Y
4 Frank	N	Y	Y	N	Y	Y	Y	Y
5 Atkins	N	Y	Y	N	Y	Y	Y	Y
6 Mavroules	N	Y	Y	N	Y	Y	Y	Y
7 Markey	N	Y	Y	N	Y	Y	Y	Y
8 O'Neill								
9 Moakley	N	Y	Y	N	Y	Y	Y	Y
10 Studds	N	Y	Y	N	Y	Y	Y	Y
11 Donnelly	N	Y	Y	N	Y	Y	Y	Y
MICHIGAN								
1 Conyers	N	Y	Y	Y	?	?	?	?
2 ***Pursell***	N	?	Y	N	Y	Y	Y	Y
3 Wolpe	N	Y	Y	N	Y	Y	Y	Y
4 ***Siljander***	?	N	N	Y	Y	Y	Y	Y
5 ***Henry***	N	N	N	Y	Y	Y	Y	Y
6 Carr	N	N	Y	N	Y	Y	Y	Y
7 Kildee	N	Y	Y	N	Y	Y	Y	Y
8 Traxler	N	Y	?	N	Y	Y	Y	Y
9 ***Vander Jagt***	?	?	N	Y	Y	Y	Y	Y
10 ***Schuette***	N	N	N	N	Y	Y	Y	Y
11 ***Davis***	N	N	Y	N	Y	Y	Y	Y
12 Bonior	N	Y	Y	N	?	Y	Y	Y
13 Crockett	N	?	Y	N	Y	Y	Y	Y
14 Hertel	N	Y	Y	N	Y	Y	Y	Y
15 Ford	N	?	Y	N	Y	Y	Y	Y
16 Dingell	N	N	Y	N	Y	Y	Y	Y
17 Levin	N	Y	Y	N	Y	Y	Y	Y
18 ***Broomfield***	?	?	Y	?	Y	Y	Y	Y
MINNESOTA								
1 Penny	N	Y	N	Y	Y	Y	Y	Y
2 ***Weber***	N	Y	N	N	Y	Y	Y	Y
3 ***Frenzel***	N	N	N	N	Y	Y	Y	Y
4 Vento	N	Y	Y	N	Y	Y	Y	Y
5 Sabo	N	Y	Y	Y	Y	Y	Y	Y
6 Sikorski	N	Y	N	N	Y	Y	Y	Y

	395	396	397	398	399	400	401	402
7 ***Stangeland***	N	N	N	N	Y	Y	Y	Y
8 Oberstar	N	Y	Y	N	Y	Y	Y	Y
MISSISSIPPI								
1 Whitten	?	?	Y	N	Y	Y	?	Y
2 ***Franklin***	Y	N	Y	N	Y	Y	Y	Y
3 Montgomery	N	?	Y	N	Y	Y	Y	Y
4 Dowdy	N	N	Y	N	?	?	?	Y
5 ***Lott***	?	?	?	?	Y	Y	Y	Y
MISSOURI								
1 Clay	N	Y	N	N	Y	Y	Y	Y
2 Young	N	N	Y	Y	Y	Y	Y	Y
3 Gephardt	?	?	Y	Y	Y	Y	Y	Y
4 Skelton	N	N	Y	Y	Y	Y	Y	Y
5 Wheat	N	Y	Y	N	Y	Y	Y	Y
6 ***Coleman***	N	?	N	Y	Y	Y	Y	Y
7 ***Taylor***	Y	N	N	N	?	?	?	?
8 ***Emerson***	N	N	N	Y	Y	Y	Y	Y
9 Volkmer	N	Y	Y	Y	Y	Y	Y	Y
MONTANA								
1 Williams	?	?	?	N	Y	Y	Y	Y
2 ***Marlenee***	Y	N	N	Y	Y	Y	Y	Y
NEBRASKA								
1 ***Bereuter***	N	N	N	N	Y	Y	Y	Y
2 ***Daub***	Y	N	Y	N	Y	Y	Y	Y
3 ***Smith***	Y	N	Y	Y	Y	Y	Y	Y
NEVADA								
1 Reid	N	Y	Y	N	Y	Y	Y	Y
2 ***Vucanovich***	Y	N	N	Y	Y	Y	Y	Y
NEW HAMPSHIRE								
1 ***Smith***	Y	Y	N	Y	Y	Y	Y	Y
2 ***Gregg***	N	Y	N	Y	Y	?	Y	Y
NEW JERSEY								
1 Florio	N	Y	Y	Y	Y	Y	Y	Y
2 Hughes	N	Y	Y	Y	Y	Y	Y	Y
3 Howard	N	Y	Y	Y	Y	Y	Y	Y
4 ***Smith***	N	Y	Y	Y	Y	Y	Y	Y
5 ***Roukema***	N	Y	N	Y	Y	Y	Y	Y
6 Dwyer	N	Y	Y	Y	Y	Y	Y	Y
7 ***Rinaldo***	N	Y	Y	Y	Y	Y	Y	Y
8 Roe	N	Y	Y	Y	Y	Y	Y	Y
9 Torricelli	N	Y	?	Y	?	?	?	?
10 Rodino	N	Y	?	Y	Y	Y	Y	Y
11 ***Gallo***	N	N	N	Y	Y	?	Y	Y
12 ***Courter***	N	N	N	Y	Y	Y	Y	Y
13 ***Saxton***	N	Y	N	Y	Y	?	Y	Y
14 Guarini	N	Y	Y	Y	Y	Y	Y	Y
NEW MEXICO								
1 ***Lujan***	?	?	?	?	Y	Y	Y	Y
2 ***Skeen***	Y	N	N	N	Y	Y	Y	Y
3 Richardson	N	Y	Y	N	Y	Y	Y	Y
NEW YORK								
1 ***Carney***	N	N	?	N	?	?	?	Y
2 Downey	N	Y	Y	N	Y	Y	Y	Y
3 Mrazek	N	Y	Y	Y	Y	Y	Y	Y
4 ***Lent***	N	N	N	N	Y	Y	Y	Y
5 ***McGrath***	N	Y	N	Y	Y	Y	Y	Y
6 Addabbo	?	?	?	?	Y	Y	Y	Y
7 Ackerman	N	Y	Y	N	Y	Y	Y	Y
8 Scheuer	N	Y	Y	N	Y	Y	Y	Y
9 Manton	N	Y	?	N	Y	Y	Y	Y
10 Schumer	N	Y	Y	N	Y	Y	Y	Y
11 Towns	N	Y	?	?	?	?	?	?
12 Owens	?	?	?	N	Y	Y	Y	Y
13 Solarz	N	Y	Y	N	?	?	Y	Y
14 ***Molinari***	N	Y	N	Y	Y	Y	Y	Y
15 ***Green***	N	Y	Y	Y	Y	Y	Y	Y
16 Rangel	N	Y	?	?	Y	?	?	Y
17 Weiss	N	Y	Y	N	Y	Y	Y	Y
18 Garcia	?	?	?	?	?	?	?	?
19 Biaggi	N	?	Y	N	Y	?	Y	Y
20 ***DioGuardi***	N	Y	Y	Y	Y	Y	Y	Y
21 ***Fish***	N	Y	Y	Y	Y	Y	Y	Y
22 ***Gilman***	N	Y	Y	+	Y	Y	Y	Y
23 Stratton	N	N	N	N	Y	Y	Y	Y
24 ***Solomon***	?	?	?	?	Y	Y	Y	Y
25 ***Boehlert***	N	Y	N	Y	Y	Y	Y	Y
26 ***Martin***	N	N	N	Y	Y	Y	Y	Y
27 ***Wortley***	N	N	Y	Y	Y	Y	Y	Y
28 McHugh	N	Y	?	N	Y	?	Y	Y
29 ***Horton***	?	?	Y	Y	Y	Y	Y	Y
30 ***Eckert***	Y	N	Y	N	Y	Y	Y	Y
31 ***Kemp***	?	?	?	Y	Y	Y	Y	Y
32 LaFalce	N	?	Y	N	Y	Y	Y	Y
33 Nowak	N	Y	Y	N	?	Y	Y	Y
34 Lundine	N	N	Y	N	Y	Y	Y	Y

	395	396	397	398	399	400	401	402
NORTH CAROLINA								
1 Jones	N	N	Y	N	Y	Y	Y	Y
2 Valentine	N	N	Y	N	Y	Y	Y	Y
3 Whitley	N	Y	Y	Y	Y	Y	Y	?
4 ***Cobey***	Y	N	N	N	Y	Y	Y	Y
5 Neal	?	?	?	?	?	?	?	?
6 ***Coble***	Y	N	N	N	Y	Y	Y	Y
7 Rose	N	Y	?	Y	Y	Y	Y	Y
8 Hefner	N	N	Y	N	Y	Y	Y	Y
9 ***McMillan***	Y	N	Y	N	Y	Y	Y	Y
10 ***Broyhill***	Y	N	Y	N	?	?	?	?
11 ***Hendon***	N	N	N	N	Y	Y	Y	Y
NORTH DAKOTA								
AL Dorgan	N	Y	Y	N	Y	Y	Y	Y
OHIO								
1 Luken	N	N	Y	N	Y	Y	Y	Y
2 ***Gradison***	Y	?	Y	Y	Y	Y	Y	Y
3 Hall	N	?	Y	N	Y	Y	Y	Y
4 ***Oxley***	N	N	N	N	Y	Y	Y	Y
5 ***Latta***	N	N	N	Y	Y	Y	Y	Y
6 ***McEwen***	N	N	Y	Y	Y	Y	Y	Y
7 ***DeWine***	Y	N	N	Y	Y	Y	Y	Y
8 ***Kindness***	N	N	Y	N	?	?	?	?
9 Kaptur	N	Y	Y	N	Y	Y	Y	Y
10 ***Miller***	?	?	?	?	?	?	?	?
11 Eckart	N	Y	Y	N	Y	Y	Y	Y
12 ***Kasich***	N	N	N	Y	Y	Y	Y	Y
13 Pease	N	Y	Y	N	Y	Y	Y	Y
14 Seiberling	N	Y	Y	N	Y	Y	Y	Y
15 ***Wylie***	?	?	?	?	Y	Y	Y	Y
16 ***Regula***	Y	N	N	N	Y	Y	Y	Y
17 Traficant	N	Y	Y	N	Y	Y	Y	Y
18 Applegate	N	Y	Y	N	Y	Y	Y	Y
19 Feighan	N	Y	Y	?	Y	Y	Y	Y
20 Oakar	N	Y	Y	N	Y	Y	Y	Y
21 Stokes	N	Y	Y	N	Y	Y	Y	Y
OKLAHOMA								
1 Jones	N	Y	Y	N	+	+	+	+
2 Synar	N	N	Y	N	Y	Y	Y	Y
3 Watkins	N	N	Y	N	Y	Y	Y	Y
4 McCurdy	N	Y	Y	N	Y	Y	Y	Y
5 ***Edwards***	Y	N	N	Y	Y	Y	Y	Y
6 English	N	N	Y	N	Y	Y	Y	Y
OREGON								
1 AuCoin	N	Y	Y	N	Y	Y	Y	Y
2 ***Smith, R.***	Y	?	N	Y	Y	Y	Y	Y
3 Wyden	N	Y	Y	N	Y	Y	Y	Y
4 Weaver	N	Y	Y	N	Y	Y	Y	Y
5 ***Smith, D.***	Y	?	N	N	Y	Y	Y	Y
PENNSYLVANIA								
1 Foglietta	N	Y	Y	Y	?	Y	Y	Y
2 Gray	N	?	Y	?	Y	Y	Y	Y
3 Borski	N	Y	Y	N	Y	Y	Y	Y
4 Kolter	N	Y	Y	N	Y	Y	Y	Y
5 ***Schulze***	Y	?	?	Y	?	?	?	?
6 Yatron	N	Y	Y	N	Y	Y	Y	Y
7 Edgar	N	Y	Y	Y	Y	Y	Y	Y
8 Kostmayer	N	Y	Y	Y	Y	Y	Y	Y
9 ***Shuster***	N	?	N	N	Y	Y	Y	Y
10 ***McDade***	N	?	Y	N	Y	Y	Y	Y
11 Kanjorski	N	Y	Y	N	Y	Y	Y	Y
12 Murtha	?	?	Y	N	Y	?	Y	Y
13 ***Coughlin***	N	Y	N	Y	Y	Y	Y	Y
14 Coyne	N	Y	Y	N	Y	Y	Y	Y
15 ***Ritter***	Y	N	?	N	?	?	?	?
16 ***Walker***	Y	N	N	Y	Y	Y	Y	Y
17 ***Gekas***	N	N	N	N	Y	Y	Y	Y
18 Walgren	N	Y	Y	Y	Y	Y	Y	Y
19 ***Goodling***	Y	Y	N	?	Y	Y	Y	Y
20 Gaydos	N	Y	Y	N	Y	Y	Y	Y
21 ***Ridge***	Y	Y	N	N	Y	Y	Y	Y
22 Murphy	N	Y	Y	Y	Y	Y	Y	Y
23 ***Clinger***	-	Y	Y	N	Y	Y	Y	Y
RHODE ISLAND								
1 St Germain	N	N	Y	Y	Y	Y	Y	Y
2 ***Schneider***	?	?	Y	Y	Y	Y	Y	Y
SOUTH CAROLINA								
1 ***Hartnett***	?	?	?	?	Y	Y	Y	Y
2 ***Spence***	N	Y	N	Y	Y	Y	Y	Y
3 Derrick	N	Y	Y	N	Y	Y	Y	Y
4 ***Campbell***	Y	?	?	N	Y	Y	Y	Y
5 Spratt	N	Y	Y	Y	Y	Y	Y	Y
6 Tallon	N	Y	Y	N	Y	Y	Y	Y
SOUTH DAKOTA								
AL Daschle	N	Y	Y	N	?	Y	Y	Y

	395	396	397	398	399	400	401	402
TENNESSEE								
1 ***Quillen***	?	N	Y	N	Y	Y	Y	Y
2 ***Duncan***	N	?	Y	N	Y	Y	Y	Y
3 Lloyd	N	N	?	N	Y	Y	Y	Y
4 Cooper	N	N	Y	N	Y	Y	Y	Y
5 Boner	N	?	?	?	?	?	?	?
6 Gordon	N	Y	Y	N	Y	Y	Y	Y
7 ***Sundquist***	N	N	N	N	Y	Y	Y	Y
8 Jones	N	N	Y	N	Y	Y	Y	Y
9 Ford	N	Y	?	?	Y	Y	Y	Y
TEXAS								
1 Chapman	N	N	Y	N	Y	Y	Y	Y
2 Wilson	N	Y	?	N	Y	Y	Y	Y
3 ***Bartlett***	Y	N	N	Y	Y	Y	Y	Y
4 Hall, R.	N	N	Y	Y	Y	Y	Y	Y
5 Bryant	N	Y	Y	N	Y	Y	Y	Y
6 ***Barton***	Y	N	N	N	?	?	?	?
7 ***Archer***	?	?	Y	N	Y	Y	Y	Y
8 ***Fields***	Y	N	N	N	Y	Y	Y	Y
9 Brooks	N	N	Y	N	Y	Y	Y	Y
10 Pickle	-	+	Y	Y	Y	Y	Y	Y
11 Leath	N	N	Y	?	Y	Y	Y	Y
12 Wright	N	N	Y	N	Y	Y	Y	Y
13 ***Boulter***	Y	N	N	N	Y	Y	Y	Y
14 ***Sweeney***	N	N	Y	N	?	Y	Y	Y
15 de la Garza	N	N	Y	Y	Y	Y	Y	Y
16 Coleman	N	N	?	N	Y	Y	Y	Y
17 Stenholm	N	N	Y	Y	Y	Y	Y	Y
18 Leland	N	Y	Y	N	Y	Y	Y	Y
19 ***Combest***	Y	N	Y	N	Y	Y	Y	Y
20 Gonzalez	N	?	Y	P	Y	Y	Y	Y
21 ***Loeffler***	Y	?	N	N	Y	Y	Y	Y
22 ***DeLay***	?	N	?	Y	Y	Y	Y	Y
23 Bustamante	N	Y	Y	N	Y	Y	Y	Y
24 Frost	N	?	Y	N	Y	Y	Y	Y
25 Andrews	N	N	Y	Y	Y	Y	Y	Y
26 ***Armey***	Y	N	N	N	Y	Y	Y	Y
27 Ortiz	?	?	?	?	Y	Y	Y	Y
UTAH								
1 ***Hansen***	Y	N	N	N	Y	Y	Y	Y
2 ***Monson***	N	N	N	N	?	?	?	?
3 ***Nielson***	Y	N	Y	N	Y	Y	Y	Y
VERMONT								
AL ***Jeffords***	N	Y	?	N	Y	Y	Y	Y
VIRGINIA								
1 ***Bateman***	Y	N	Y	N	Y	Y	Y	Y
2 ***Whitehurst***	N	?	?	N	Y	Y	Y	Y
3 ***Bliley***	N	N	N	N	Y	Y	Y	Y
4 Sisisky	N	?	Y	?	Y	Y	Y	Y
5 Daniel	N	N	Y	Y	Y	Y	Y	Y
6 Olin	N	?	Y	N	Y	Y	Y	Y
7 ***Slaughter***	N	N	N	Y	Y	Y	Y	?
8 ***Parris***	N	N	N	N	Y	Y	Y	Y
9 Boucher	N	Y	Y	Y	?	?	?	?
10 ***Wolf***	N	Y	N	Y	Y	Y	Y	Y
WASHINGTON								
1 ***Miller***	Y	Y	Y	N	?	?	?	?
2 Swift	N	N	Y	N	Y	Y	Y	Y
3 Bonker	N	Y	Y	N	?	?	?	?
4 ***Morrison***	N	N	N	Y	Y	Y	Y	Y
5 Foley	N	Y	Y	Y	Y	Y	Y	Y
6 Dicks	N	?	Y	Y	Y	Y	Y	Y
7 Lowry	N	Y	Y	Y	Y	Y	Y	Y
8 ***Chandler***	N	N	N	Y	?	?	?	?
WEST VIRGINIA								
1 Mollohan	N	N	Y	N	Y	Y	Y	Y
2 Staggers	N	Y	Y	N	Y	Y	Y	Y
3 Wise	N	Y	Y	Y	Y	Y	Y	Y
4 Rahall	N	N	Y	N	Y	Y	Y	Y
WISCONSIN								
1 Aspin	N	?	?	N	?	?	?	?
2 Kastenmeier	N	Y	Y	N	Y	Y	Y	Y
3 ***Gunderson***	N	?	N	N	Y	Y	Y	Y
4 Kleczka	N	Y	Y	N	Y	Y	Y	Y
5 Moody	N	Y	Y	N	Y	Y	Y	Y
6 ***Petri***	N	Y	Y	N	Y	Y	Y	Y
7 Obey	N	Y	Y	Y	Y	Y	Y	Y
8 ***Roth***	?	?	?	?	Y	Y	Y	Y
9 ***Sensenbrenner***	N	Y	N	N	Y	Y	Y	Y
WYOMING								
AL ***Cheney***	?	?	?	?	Y	Y	Y	Y

Southern states - Ala., Ark., Fla., Ga., Ky., La., Miss., N.C., Okla., S.C., Tenn., Texas, Va.

* The *Congressional Record* vote number is different from the CQ vote number because the *Record* includes quorum calls in its tally. CQ does not publish quorum call votes.

403. Procedural Motion. Gregg, R-N.H., motion to approve the House *Journal* of Monday, Dec. 9. Motion agreed to 289-116: R 62-106; D 227-10 (ND 154-8, SD 73-2), Dec. 10, 1985.

404. S 1884. Farm Credit System Restructuring. De la Garza, D-Texas, motion to suspend the rules and pass the bill to reorganize the Farm Credit System to enable individual institutions to pool resources and sell assets to resolve financial problems affecting individual institutions; to create a capital corporation within the system to take over non-performing loans and obligations of member institutions; to restructure the federal Farm Credit Administration to perform as an independent regulating agency of the system; and to authorize the secretary of the Treasury to purchase obligations of the capital corporation. Motion agreed to 393-32: R 160-18; D 233-14 (ND 156-12, SD 77-2), Dec. 10, 1985. A two-thirds majority of those present and voting (284 in this case) is required for passage under suspension of the rules.

405. HR 2817. Superfund Reauthorization, Fiscal 1986-90. Duncan, R-Tenn., amendment to eliminate a broad-based or "value-added" tax; provide tax increases on chemical feedstocks, petroleum, hazardous-waste disposal, gasoline and chemical derivatives; and provide a trigger mechanism for the imposition of a surcharge tax on corporations under certain conditions. Rejected 74-349: R 72-103; D 2-246 (ND 2-167, SD 0-79), Dec. 10, 1985.

406. HR 2817. Superfund Reauthorization, Fiscal 1986-90. Downey, D-N.Y., amendment to strike provisions for a broad-based or "value-added" tax and to provide $10 billion over five years for the "superfund" hazardous-waste cleanup program through increased taxes on chemical feedstocks, petroleum and hazardous-waste disposal and through general revenues. Adopted 220-206: R 73-105; D 147-101 (ND 127-42, SD 20-59), Dec. 10, 1985.

407. HR 2817. Superfund Reauthorization, Fiscal 1986-90. Frank, D-Mass., amendment to permit persons injured by the release of toxic substances to sue responsible parties in federal court, except for damages incurred and discovered before enactment. Rejected 162-261: R 20-157; D 142-104 (ND 117-50, SD 25-54), Dec. 10, 1985.

408. HR 2817. Superfund Reauthorization, Fiscal 1986-90. Edgar, D-Pa., amendment to require companies to make public an inventory of their emissions of chemicals known to cause or suspected of causing cancer, birth defects or other chronic diseases. Adopted 212-211: R 34-143; D 178-68 (ND 146-22, SD 32-46), Dec. 10, 1985. (The Edgar amendment previously had been adopted in the Committee of the Whole *(see vote 396, p. 126-H)*.)

409. HR 2817. Superfund Reauthorization, Fiscal 1986-90. Passage of the bill to amend and reauthorize the "superfund" hazardous-waste cleanup program under the Comprehensive Environmental Response, Compensation and Liability Act of 1980 (PL 96-510) at a spending level of $10 billion for fiscal 1986-90. Passed 391-33: R 149-28; D 242-5 (ND 168-0, SD 74-5), Dec. 10, 1985. (The House subsequently struck the text of HR 2005, the Senate-passed bill, and inserted instead the provisions of HR 2817.)

410. Procedural Motion. Parris, R-Va., motion to approve the House *Journal* of Tuesday, Dec. 10. Motion agreed to 271-125: R 56-113; D 215-12 (ND 148-7, SD 67-5), Dec. 11, 1985.

KEY

- Y Voted for (yea).
- # Paired for.
- + Announced for.
- N Voted against (nay).
- X Paired against.
- \- Announced against.
- P Voted "present."
- C Voted "present" to avoid possible conflict of interest.
- ? Did not vote or otherwise make a position known.

Democrats ***Republicans***

	403	404	405	406	407	408	409	410
ALABAMA								
1 ***Callahan***	Y	Y	Y	N	N	N	N	N
2 ***Dickinson***	?	?	?	N	N	N	Y	?
3 Nichols	Y	Y	N	N	N	N	Y	?
4 Bevill	?	Y	N	N	N	N	Y	Y
5 Flippo	Y	Y	N	N	N	Y	Y	Y
6 Erdreich	Y	Y	N	N	N	Y	Y	Y
7 Shelby	Y	Y	N	N	N	N	Y	Y
ALASKA								
AL ***Young***	?	Y	N	N	N	N	N	N
ARIZONA								
1 ***McCain***	N	Y	N	Y	N	N	Y	N
2 Udall	Y	Y	N	N	Y	Y	Y	Y
3 ***Stump***	N	Y	Y	N	N	N	N	N
4 ***Rudd***	Y	Y	Y	Y	N	N	N	Y
5 ***Kolbe***	N	Y	N	N	N	Y	Y	N
ARKANSAS								
1 Alexander	Y	Y	N	N	Y	Y	Y	Y
2 Robinson	Y	Y	N	Y	Y	Y	Y	Y
3 ***Hammerschmidt***	Y	Y	Y	N	N	N	Y	Y
4 Anthony	Y	Y	N	N	N	N	Y	Y
CALIFORNIA								
1 Bosco	Y	Y	N	N	N	Y	Y	Y
2 ***Chappie***	?	?	?	X	?	?	?	?
3 Matsui	Y	Y	N	Y	Y	Y	Y	Y
4 Fazio	Y	Y	N	N	N	Y	Y	Y
5 Burton	Y	Y	N	Y	Y	Y	Y	Y
6 Boxer	Y	Y	N	Y	Y	Y	Y	Y
7 Miller	Y	Y	N	N	Y	Y	Y	Y
8 Dellums	Y	Y	N	Y	Y	Y	Y	Y
9 Stark	Y	N	N	Y	Y	Y	Y	Y
10 Edwards	Y	Y	N	Y	Y	Y	Y	Y
11 Lantos	Y	Y	N	Y	Y	Y	Y	Y
12 ***Zschau***	N	Y	N	Y	N	N	Y	?
13 Mineta	Y	Y	N	Y	Y	Y	Y	Y
14 ***Shumway***	Y	Y	Y	N	N	N	N	Y
15 Coelho	Y	Y	N	N	N	N	Y	Y
16 Panetta	Y	Y	N	Y	N	Y	Y	Y
17 ***Pashayan***	Y	Y	Y	Y	N	N	Y	N
18 Lehman	Y	Y	N	Y	Y	N	Y	Y
19 ***Lagomarsino***	N	Y	N	N	N	N	Y	N
20 ***Thomas***	N	Y	Y	N	N	N	Y	N
21 ***Fiedler***	N	Y	N	N	N	N	Y	N
22 ***Moorhead***	N	Y	Y	N	N	N	Y	N
23 Beilenson	Y	Y	N	Y	Y	Y	Y	?
24 Waxman	Y	Y	N	Y	Y	Y	Y	Y
25 Roybal	Y	Y	N	Y	Y	Y	Y	Y
26 Berman	Y	Y	N	Y	Y	Y	Y	Y
27 Levine	Y	N	N	Y	Y	Y	Y	Y
28 Dixon	Y	Y	N	Y	Y	Y	Y	Y
29 Hawkins	Y	Y	N	Y	Y	Y	Y	P
30 Martinez	Y	Y	N	Y	Y	Y	Y	Y
31 Dymally	P	Y	N	Y	N	N	Y	P
32 Anderson	Y	N	N	N	Y	Y	Y	Y
33 ***Dreier***	N	N	N	N	N	N	Y	N
34 Torres	Y	Y	N	Y	Y	Y	Y	Y
35 ***Lewis***	N	Y	N	N	N	N	Y	N
36 Brown	Y	Y	N	Y	Y	Y	Y	Y
37 ***McCandless***	N	Y	N	N	N	N	Y	N
38 ***Dornan***	N	Y	Y	N	N	N	N	?
39 ***Dannemeyer***	N	N	Y	N	N	N	Y	N
40 ***Badham***	N	Y	N	N	N	N	N	N
41 ***Lowery***	N	Y	Y	N	N	N	Y	?
42 ***Lungren***	Y	Y	Y	Y	N	N	Y	N
43 ***Packard***	Y	Y	N	N	N	N	Y	N
44 Bates	Y	N	N	Y	Y	Y	Y	Y
45 ***Hunter***	N	Y	?	N	N	N	N	N
COLORADO								
1 Schroeder	N	Y	N	Y	Y	Y	Y	N
2 Wirth	Y	Y	N	N	N	Y	Y	Y
3 ***Strang***	Y	Y	Y	N	N	N	Y	N
4 ***Brown***	N	Y	Y	N	N	N	Y	Y
5 ***Kramer***	N	Y	Y	N	N	N	Y	N
6 ***Schaefer***	Y	Y	N	N	N	N	Y	Y
CONNECTICUT								
1 Kennelly	Y	Y	N	Y	Y	Y	Y	Y
2 Gejdenson	Y	Y	N	Y	Y	Y	Y	Y
3 Morrison	Y	N	N	Y	Y	Y	Y	Y
4 ***McKinney***	?	?	?	?	?	?	?	?
5 ***Rowland***	N	Y	N	Y	N	Y	Y	Y
6 ***Johnson***	Y	N	N	Y	N	N	Y	Y
DELAWARE								
AL Carper	Y	Y	N	N	N	Y	Y	Y
FLORIDA								
1 Hutto	Y	Y	N	N	N	N	Y	Y
2 Fuqua	Y	Y	N	N	N	N	Y	Y
3 Bennett	Y	Y	N	Y	Y	Y	Y	Y
4 Chappell	Y	Y	N	N	N	N	Y	Y
5 ***McCollum***	Y	N	Y	N	N	N	Y	Y
6 MacKay	Y	Y	N	Y	Y	Y	Y	Y
7 Gibbons	Y	Y	N	N	Y	Y	Y	Y
8 ***Young***	N	Y	N	Y	N	N	Y	N
9 ***Bilirakis***	N	Y	Y	Y	N	N	Y	N
10 ***Ireland***	?	Y	N	Y	N	N	Y	N
11 Nelson	+	X	-	#	+	+	+	+
12 ***Lewis***	N	Y	Y	N	N	N	Y	N
13 ***Mack***	N	Y	N	Y	N	N	Y	N
14 Mica	Y	Y	N	Y	N	Y	Y	Y
15 ***Shaw***	N	Y	N	Y	N	N	Y	N
16 Smith	Y	Y	N	Y	Y	Y	Y	?
17 Lehman	Y	Y	N	Y	Y	Y	Y	Y
18 Pepper	Y	Y	N	Y	Y	Y	Y	+
19 Fascell	?	Y	N	Y	Y	Y	Y	Y
GEORGIA								
1 Thomas	Y	Y	N	N	N	Y	N	Y
2 Hatcher	Y	Y	N	N	N	N	Y	Y
3 Ray	Y	Y	N	N	N	N	Y	Y
4 ***Swindall***	N	Y	Y	N	N	N	Y	N
5 Fowler	Y	Y	N	N	N	Y	Y	Y
6 ***Gingrich***	N	Y	Y	N	N	N	Y	N
7 Darden	Y	Y	N	Y	N	N	Y	Y
8 Rowland	Y	Y	N	N	N	N	Y	Y
9 Jenkins	Y	Y	N	N	N	Y	Y	Y
10 Barnard	Y	Y	N	Y	N	N	Y	Y
HAWAII								
1 Heftel	Y	Y	N	N	N	Y	Y	Y
2 Akaka	Y	Y	N	Y	Y	Y	Y	Y
IDAHO								
1 ***Craig***	Y	Y	N	N	N	N	Y	N
2 Stallings	Y	Y	N	Y	N	Y	Y	Y
ILLINOIS								
1 Hayes	Y	Y	N	Y	Y	Y	Y	Y
2 Savage	Y	Y	N	Y	Y	Y	Y	Y
3 Russo	Y	Y	N	N	N	Y	Y	Y
4 ***O'Brien***	P	Y	N	N	N	N	Y	?
5 Lipinski	Y	Y	N	Y	Y	Y	Y	Y
6 ***Hyde***	Y	Y	Y	Y	?	N	Y	N
7 Collins	Y	Y	N	Y	Y	Y	Y	Y
8 Rostenkowski	Y	Y	N	Y	N	Y	Y	Y
9 Yates	Y	N	N	Y	Y	Y	Y	Y
10 ***Porter***	Y	N	N	Y	N	N	Y	Y
11 Annunzio	Y	Y	N	Y	Y	Y	Y	Y
12 ***Crane***	N	N	Y	N	N	N	N	N
13 ***Fawell***	N	N	N	Y	N	Y	Y	N
14 ***Grotberg***	N	Y	N	N	N	N	Y	N
15 ***Madigan***	Y	Y	Y	Y	N	N	Y	N
16 ***Martin***	N	Y	N	Y	N	N	Y	N
17 Evans	Y	Y	N	Y	Y	Y	Y	Y
18 ***Michel***	N	Y	Y	Y	N	N	Y	N
19 Bruce	Y	Y	N	N	Y	Y	Y	Y
20 Durbin	N	Y	N	Y	Y	Y	Y	N
21 Price	?	?	?	?	?	?	?	?
22 Gray	Y	Y	N	N	N	Y	Y	Y
INDIANA								
1 Visclosky	Y	Y	N	N	N	Y	Y	Y
2 Sharp	Y	Y	N	Y	Y	Y	Y	Y
3 ***Hiler***	N	Y	Y	Y	N	N	Y	N
4 ***Coats***	Y	Y	N	Y	N	N	Y	Y
5 ***Hillis***	Y	Y	Y	N	N	?	?	Y

ND - Northern Democrats SD - Southern Democrats

* Corresponding to Congressional Record Votes 441, 442, 443, 444, 445, 446, 447, 448

	403	404	405	406	407	408	409	410
6 ***Burton***	N	Y	N	N	N	N	N	N
7 ***Myers***	Y	Y	N	N	N	N	Y	Y
8 McCloskey	Y	Y	N	Y	Y	Y	Y	Y
9 Hamilton	Y	Y	N	Y	?	Y	Y	Y
10 Jacobs	N	Y	N	N	Y	Y	Y	N
IOWA								
1 ***Leach***	N	Y	N	Y	Y	Y	Y	N
2 ***Tauke***	N	Y	N	Y	N	N	Y	N
3 ***Evans***	N	Y	N	Y	Y	N	Y	N
4 Smith	Y	Y	N	Y	Y	Y	Y	Y
5 ***Lightfoot***	N	Y	N	Y	N	N	Y	N
6 Bedell	Y	Y	N	Y	Y	Y	Y	Y
KANSAS								
1 ***Roberts***	N	Y	N	N	N	N	N	N
2 Slattery	Y	Y	N	N	N	N	Y	Y
3 ***Meyers***	N	Y	N	Y	N	N	Y	N
4 Glickman	Y	Y	N	N	N	Y	Y	Y
5 ***Whittaker***	N	Y	N	N	N	N	Y	N
KENTUCKY								
1 Hubbard	Y	Y	N	N	N	N	Y	Y
2 Natcher	Y	Y	N	N	Y	N	Y	Y
3 Mazzoli	Y	Y	N	N	N	N	Y	Y
4 ***Snyder***	Y	Y	N	N	N	N	Y	Y
5 ***Rogers***	N	Y	Y	N	N	N	Y	?
6 ***Hopkins***	Y	Y	N	Y	N	N	Y	?
7 Perkins	Y	Y	N	N	N	N	Y	Y
LOUISIANA								
1 ***Livingston***	Y	Y	N	N	N	N	Y	N
2 Boggs	Y	Y	N	N	Y	?	Y	Y
3 Tauzin	Y	Y	N	N	N	N	Y	N
4 Roemer	N	Y	N	Y	Y	Y	Y	N
5 Huckaby	Y	Y	N	N	Y	Y	Y	Y
6 ***Moore***	Y	Y	Y	N	N	N	Y	Y
7 Breaux	?	Y	N	N	N	N	Y	Y
8 Long	Y	Y	N	N	Y	Y	Y	Y
MAINE								
1 ***McKernan***	N	Y	N	Y	Y	Y	Y	N
2 ***Snowe***	N	Y	N	Y	Y	Y	Y	N
MARYLAND								
1 Dyson	Y	Y	N	N	Y	N	Y	Y
2 ***Bentley***	N	N	Y	N	N	N	Y	N
3 Mikulski	Y	Y	N	Y	Y	Y	Y	P
4 ***Holt***	Y	Y	N	Y	N	N	Y	Y
5 Hoyer	Y	Y	N	Y	N	N	Y	Y
6 Byron	Y	Y	N	Y	N	N	Y	Y
7 Mitchell	N	Y	N	Y	Y	Y	Y	N
8 Barnes	Y	Y	N	Y	Y	Y	Y	Y
MASSACHUSETTS								
1 ***Conte***	N	Y	N	Y	Y	Y	Y	N
2 Boland	Y	#	N	N	Y	Y	Y	Y
3 Early	Y	Y	N	Y	Y	Y	Y	Y
4 Frank	Y	N	N	Y	Y	Y	Y	Y
5 Atkins	Y	Y	N	Y	Y	Y	Y	Y
6 Mavroules	Y	Y	N	Y	Y	Y	Y	?
7 Markey	Y	Y	N	Y	Y	Y	Y	Y
8 O'Neill								
9 Moakley	Y	Y	N	Y	Y	Y	Y	Y
10 Studds	Y	Y	N	Y	Y	Y	Y	Y
11 Donnelly	Y	Y	N	Y	Y	Y	Y	Y
MICHIGAN								
1 Conyers	Y	N	N	Y	Y	Y	Y	Y
2 ***Pursell***	N	Y	N	Y	N	N	Y	Y
3 Wolpe	Y	Y	N	Y	Y	Y	Y	Y
4 ***Siljander***	N	Y	Y	N	N	N	Y	N
5 ***Henry***	N	Y	Y	Y	N	N	Y	N
6 Carr	Y	Y	N	Y	N	N	Y	Y
7 Kildee	Y	Y	N	Y	Y	Y	Y	Y
8 Traxler	Y	Y	Y	Y	N	Y	Y	?
9 ***Vander Jagt***	N	Y	Y	N	N	N	Y	N
10 ***Schuette***	N	Y	Y	N	N	N	Y	N
11 ***Davis***	Y	Y	N	Y	N	N	Y	N
12 Bonior	Y	Y	N	Y	Y	Y	Y	Y
13 Crockett	Y	Y	N	Y	Y	N	Y	Y
14 Hertel	Y	Y	N	Y	Y	Y	Y	Y
15 Ford	Y	Y	N	Y	Y	N	Y	?
16 Dingell	Y	Y	N	N	N	N	Y	?
17 Levin	Y	Y	N	Y	Y	Y	Y	Y
18 ***Broomfield***	Y	N	Y	Y	N	N	Y	Y
MINNESOTA								
1 Penny	N	Y	N	Y	Y	Y	Y	N
2 ***Weber***	N	N	?	#	?	?	?	?
3 ***Frenzel***	N	Y	N	Y	N	N	Y	Y
4 Vento	Y	Y	N	Y	Y	Y	Y	Y
5 Sabo	Y	Y	N	Y	Y	Y	Y	Y
6 Sikorski	N	Y	N	Y	Y	Y	Y	N
7 ***Stangeland***	?	Y	N	N	N	N	Y	N
8 Oberstar	Y	Y	N	Y	Y	Y	Y	Y
MISSISSIPPI								
1 Whitten	Y	Y	N	Y	?	?	?	Y
2 ***Franklin***	Y	Y	N	N	N	N	N	Y
3 Montgomery	Y	Y	N	N	N	N	N	Y
4 Dowdy	Y	Y	N	N	N	N	Y	Y
5 ***Lott***	N	Y	Y	N	N	N	N	N
MISSOURI								
1 Clay	N	Y	N	Y	Y	Y	Y	N
2 Young	Y	Y	N	N	N	N	Y	Y
3 Gephardt	?	Y	N	N	Y	Y	Y	Y
4 Skelton	Y	Y	N	Y	N	N	Y	Y
5 Wheat	Y	Y	N	Y	Y	Y	Y	Y
6 ***Coleman***	N	Y	N	Y	N	N	Y	N
7 ***Taylor***	Y	Y	Y	Y	N	N	Y	N
8 ***Emerson***	N	Y	N	N	N	N	N	N
9 Volkmer	Y	Y	N	N	N	Y	Y	Y
MONTANA								
1 Williams	Y	N	N	N	Y	Y	Y	Y
2 ***Marlenee***	Y	Y	N	N	N	N	N	N
NEBRASKA								
1 ***Bereuter***	N	Y	Y	N	N	N	Y	N
2 ***Daub***	N	Y	N	N	N	N	Y	N
3 ***Smith***	Y	Y	Y	N	N	N	Y	Y
NEVADA								
1 Reid	Y	Y	N	Y	Y	Y	Y	Y
2 ***Vucanovich***	?	Y	N	Y	N	N	Y	N
NEW HAMPSHIRE								
1 ***Smith***	N	N	N	Y	N	Y	Y	N
2 ***Gregg***	N	N	N	Y	N	Y	Y	N
NEW JERSEY								
1 Florio	Y	Y	N	Y	Y	Y	Y	Y
2 Hughes	Y	Y	N	Y	N	Y	Y	Y
3 Howard	Y	Y	N	Y	Y	Y	Y	Y
4 ***Smith***	Y	Y	N	Y	Y	Y	Y	?
5 ***Roukema***	N	Y	N	N	N	Y	Y	N
6 Dwyer	Y	Y	N	Y	Y	Y	Y	Y
7 ***Rinaldo***	Y	Y	N	N	Y	Y	Y	Y
8 Roe	Y	Y	N	N	Y	Y	Y	?
9 Torricelli	Y	Y	N	Y	Y	Y	Y	Y
10 Rodino	Y	Y	N	Y	Y	Y	Y	Y
11 ***Gallo***	N	Y	N	N	Y	Y	Y	N
12 ***Courter***	N	Y	N	N	Y	Y	Y	N
13 ***Saxton***	N	Y	N	N	N	Y	Y	N
14 Guarini	Y	Y	N	Y	N	Y	Y	Y
NEW MEXICO								
1 ***Lujan***	Y	Y	N	N	N	N	Y	Y
2 ***Skeen***	N	Y	N	N	N	N	Y	N
3 Richardson	Y	Y	N	N	N	Y	Y	Y
NEW YORK								
1 ***Carney***	N	Y	N	N	N	N	Y	N
2 Downey	Y	Y	N	Y	Y	Y	Y	Y
3 Mrazek	Y	Y	N	Y	N	Y	Y	Y
4 ***Lent***	N	Y	N	N	N	N	Y	Y
5 ***McGrath***	?	Y	N	Y	N	Y	Y	N
6 Addabbo	Y	Y	N	Y	Y	Y	Y	?
7 Ackerman	Y	Y	N	Y	Y	Y	Y	Y
8 Scheuer	Y	N	N	Y	Y	Y	Y	Y
9 Manton	Y	Y	N	N	N	Y	Y	Y
10 Schumer	Y	Y	N	Y	Y	Y	Y	Y
11 Towns	Y	Y	N	Y	N	Y	Y	Y
12 Owens	Y	Y	N	Y	Y	Y	Y	Y
13 Solarz	Y	Y	N	Y	Y	Y	Y	Y
14 ***Molinari***	Y	Y	N	Y	Y	Y	Y	Y
15 ***Green***	Y	Y	N	Y	Y	Y	Y	Y
16 Rangel	Y	Y	N	Y	Y	Y	Y	?
17 Weiss	Y	Y	N	Y	Y	Y	Y	Y
18 Garcia	Y	Y	N	Y	Y	Y	Y	Y
19 Biaggi	Y	Y	N	Y	Y	Y	Y	Y
20 ***DioGuardi***	?	Y	N	N	Y	Y	Y	Y
21 ***Fish***	Y	Y	N	Y	N	Y	Y	Y
22 ***Gilman***	N	Y	N	N	Y	Y	Y	Y
23 Stratton	N	Y	N	Y	N	N	Y	Y
24 ***Solomon***	N	Y	N	Y	N	N	Y	N
25 ***Boehlert***	N	Y	N	Y	Y	Y	Y	N
26 ***Martin***	Y	Y	N	Y	N	N	Y	Y
27 ***Wortley***	Y	N	N	Y	N	N	Y	Y
28 McHugh	Y	Y	N	Y	Y	Y	Y	Y
29 ***Horton***	Y	N	N	Y	Y	Y	Y	Y
30 ***Eckert***	Y	Y	N	N	N	N	N	Y
31 ***Kemp***	Y	Y	Y	N	N	N	Y	Y
32 LaFalce	Y	N	N	Y	Y	Y	Y	Y
33 Nowak	Y	Y	N	Y	Y	Y	Y	Y
34 Lundine	Y	Y	N	Y	Y	N	Y	Y
NORTH CAROLINA								
1 Jones	Y	Y	N	N	N	N	Y	Y
2 Valentine	Y	Y	N	Y	N	N	Y	Y
3 Whitley	Y	Y	N	Y	N	N	Y	Y
4 ***Cobey***	N	Y	Y	N	N	N	Y	N
5 Neal	Y	N	N	Y	N	Y	Y	Y
6 ***Coble***	N	Y	Y	N	N	N	Y	N
7 Rose	Y	Y	N	N	N	N	Y	Y
8 Hefner	Y	Y	N	N	N	N	Y	Y
9 ***McMillan***	Y	Y	Y	N	N	N	Y	Y
10 ***Broyhill***	?	Y	Y	N	N	N	Y	Y
11 ***Hendon***	N	Y	Y	N	N	N	Y	?
NORTH DAKOTA								
AL Dorgan	Y	Y	N	Y	N	Y	Y	Y
OHIO								
1 Luken	Y	Y	Y	Y	N	N	Y	Y
2 ***Gradison***	Y	Y	N	N	N	N	Y	Y
3 Hall	Y	Y	N	Y	Y	Y	Y	Y
4 ***Oxley***	N	Y	Y	N	N	N	Y	N
5 ***Latta***	N	Y	Y	Y	N	N	Y	N
6 ***McEwen***	Y	Y	Y	Y	N	N	Y	Y
7 ***DeWine***	N	Y	Y	Y	N	N	Y	N
8 ***Kindness***	N	Y	Y	Y	N	N	Y	N
9 Kaptur	Y	Y	N	Y	Y	Y	Y	Y
10 ***Miller***	?	?	?	?	?	?	?	N
11 Eckart	Y	Y	N	N	N	N	Y	Y
12 ***Kasich***	N	Y	?	N	N	N	Y	N
13 Pease	Y	Y	N	Y	N	Y	Y	Y
14 Seiberling	?	Y	N	Y	Y	Y	Y	?
15 ***Wylie***	Y	Y	Y	Y	N	N	Y	Y
16 ***Regula***	Y	Y	Y	Y	N	N	Y	Y
17 Traficant	Y	Y	N	Y	Y	Y	Y	Y
18 Applegate	Y	Y	N	N	N	Y	Y	Y
19 Feighan	Y	Y	N	N	Y	N	Y	Y
20 Oakar	Y	Y	N	N	Y	Y	Y	Y
21 Stokes	Y	Y	N	Y	Y	Y	Y	Y
OKLAHOMA								
1 Jones	N	Y	N	N	N	N	Y	Y
2 Synar	Y	Y	N	N	Y	N	Y	Y
3 Watkins	Y	Y	N	N	N	N	Y	Y
4 McCurdy	Y	Y	N	N	N	Y	Y	Y
5 ***Edwards***	N	Y	N	N	N	N	N	N
6 English	Y	Y	N	N	N	N	Y	Y
OREGON								
1 AuCoin	Y	Y	N	Y	Y	Y	Y	Y
2 ***Smith, R.***	N	Y	Y	N	N	N	Y	N
3 Wyden	Y	Y	N	Y	Y	Y	Y	Y
4 Weaver	Y	Y	N	Y	Y	Y	Y	Y
5 ***Smith, D.***	N	Y	Y	Y	N	N	Y	N
PENNSYLVANIA								
1 Foglietta	Y	Y	N	N	Y	Y	Y	Y
2 Gray	?	Y	N	N	Y	Y	Y	Y
3 Borski	Y	Y	N	N	N	Y	Y	Y
4 Kolter	Y	Y	N	N	N	Y	Y	Y
5 ***Schulze***	Y	Y	Y	N	N	N	Y	Y
6 Yatron	Y	Y	N	Y	N	Y	Y	Y
7 Edgar	Y	Y	N	Y	Y	Y	Y	Y
8 Kostmayer	Y	Y	N	N	Y	Y	Y	Y
9 ***Shuster***	N	Y	N	Y	N	N	Y	N
10 ***McDade***	Y	Y	N	Y	Y	Y	Y	Y
11 Kanjorski	?	Y	N	Y	N	Y	Y	Y
12 Murtha	Y	Y	N	N	N	N	Y	Y
13 ***Coughlin***	N	Y	N	N	Y	Y	Y	N
14 Coyne	Y	Y	N	Y	Y	Y	Y	Y
15 ***Ritter***	?	N	N	N	N	N	Y	Y
16 ***Walker***	N	N	Y	Y	N	N	Y	N
17 ***Gekas***	N	Y	Y	Y	N	N	Y	N
18 Walgren	Y	Y	N	N	?	?	?	?
19 ***Goodling***	N	Y	Y	Y	N	Y	Y	N
20 Gaydos	?	Y	N	N	N	Y	Y	Y
21 ***Ridge***	N	Y	N	N	N	Y	Y	N
22 Murphy	Y	Y	N	N	N	Y	Y	Y
23 ***Clinger***	Y	Y	N	N	N	Y	Y	Y
RHODE ISLAND								
1 St Germain	Y	Y	N	Y	Y	Y	Y	Y
2 ***Schneider***	Y	Y	N	Y	Y	Y	Y	Y
SOUTH CAROLINA								
1 ***Hartnett***	N	Y	N	N	N	N	N	Y
2 ***Spence***	N	Y	Y	N	N	N	Y	N
3 Derrick	Y	Y	N	N	N	N	Y	Y
4 ***Campbell***	Y	Y	Y	N	N	N	Y	Y
5 Spratt	Y	Y	N	N	N	Y	Y	Y
6 Tallon	Y	Y	N	N	N	N	Y	Y
SOUTH DAKOTA								
AL Daschle	Y	N	N	Y	N	Y	Y	Y
TENNESSEE								
1 ***Quillen***	Y	Y	Y	N	N	N	Y	N
2 ***Duncan***	Y	Y	Y	N	N	N	Y	Y
3 Lloyd	Y	Y	N	Y	N	N	Y	N
4 Cooper	Y	Y	N	Y	Y	N	Y	Y
5 Boner	?	?	?	?	Y	Y	Y	Y
6 Gordon	Y	Y	N	Y	N	Y	Y	Y
7 ***Sundquist***	N	Y	Y	N	N	N	Y	N
8 Jones	Y	Y	N	Y	N	N	Y	Y
9 Ford	?	Y	N	N	Y	N	Y	?
TEXAS								
1 Chapman	Y	Y	N	N	N	N	Y	Y
2 Wilson	Y	Y	N	N	N	N	Y	?
3 ***Bartlett***	N	Y	Y	N	N	N	N	N
4 Hall, R.	Y	N	N	N	N	N	Y	N
5 Bryant	Y	Y	N	N	Y	Y	Y	Y
6 ***Barton***	N	Y	Y	N	N	N	N	N
7 ***Archer***	Y	N	Y	N	N	N	N	Y
8 ***Fields***	N	Y	Y	N	N	N	Y	N
9 Brooks	?	#	?	X	?	?	?	?
10 Pickle	Y	Y	N	N	Y	Y	Y	Y
11 Leath	Y	Y	N	N	N	N	N	Y
12 Wright	Y	Y	N	N	N	N	Y	Y
13 ***Boulter***	N	Y	Y	N	N	N	N	N
14 ***Sweeney***	Y	Y	Y	N	N	N	Y	Y
15 de la Garza	Y	Y	N	N	N	Y	Y	Y
16 Coleman	Y	Y	N	N	Y	Y	Y	Y
17 Stenholm	Y	Y	N	N	N	N	N	N
18 Leland	Y	Y	N	N	Y	Y	Y	?
19 ***Combest***	Y	Y	N	N	N	N	N	Y
20 Gonzalez	Y	Y	N	N	Y	Y	Y	Y
21 ***Loeffler***	N	Y	N	N	N	N	N	?
22 ***DeLay***	N	N	Y	N	N	N	N	N
23 Bustamante	Y	Y	N	N	N	Y	Y	Y
24 Frost	Y	Y	N	N	Y	N	Y	?
25 Andrews	Y	Y	N	N	N	N	Y	Y
26 ***Armey***	N	N	N	N	N	N	N	N
27 Ortiz	Y	Y	N	N	Y	Y	Y	?
UTAH								
1 ***Hansen***	Y	Y	Y	N	N	N	Y	N
2 ***Monson***	N	Y	N	N	N	N	Y	N
3 ***Nielson***	Y	Y	N	N	N	N	N	Y
VERMONT								
AL ***Jeffords***	Y	Y	N	Y	Y	Y	Y	Y
VIRGINIA								
1 ***Bateman***	Y	Y	Y	N	N	N	Y	Y
2 ***Whitehurst***	Y	Y	Y	N	N	N	Y	Y
3 ***Bliley***	N	Y	N	N	N	N	Y	N
4 Sisisky	Y	Y	N	N	N	N	Y	Y
5 Daniel	Y	Y	N	Y	N	N	Y	Y
6 Olin	Y	Y	N	N	N	N	N	Y
7 ***Slaughter***	N	Y	N	N	N	N	Y	N
8 ***Parris***	N	Y	N	Y	N	N	Y	N
9 Boucher	Y	Y	N	Y	Y	Y	Y	Y
10 ***Wolf***	N	Y	N	Y	N	Y	Y	N
WASHINGTON								
1 ***Miller***	Y	Y	N	Y	N	Y	Y	Y
2 Swift	Y	Y	N	Y	N	N	Y	Y
3 Bonker	?	Y	N	Y	Y	N	Y	Y
4 ***Morrison***	N	Y	N	Y	N	N	Y	N
5 Foley	Y	Y	N	Y	N	N	Y	Y
6 Dicks	Y	Y	N	Y	N	Y	Y	Y
7 Lowry	Y	Y	N	Y	Y	Y	Y	Y
8 ***Chandler***	N	Y	N	Y	N	N	Y	N
WEST VIRGINIA								
1 Mollohan	Y	Y	N	N	N	N	Y	Y
2 Staggers	Y	Y	N	N	Y	Y	Y	Y
3 Wise	Y	Y	N	N	N	Y	Y	?
4 Rahall	Y	Y	N	N	Y	Y	Y	Y
WISCONSIN								
1 Aspin	Y	Y	N	Y	Y	Y	Y	Y
2 Kastenmeier	Y	Y	N	Y	Y	Y	Y	Y
3 ***Gunderson***	N	Y	N	Y	N	N	Y	N
4 Kleczka	Y	Y	N	Y	Y	Y	Y	Y
5 Moody	Y	Y	N	Y	Y	Y	Y	Y
6 ***Petri***	Y	Y	N	Y	Y	Y	Y	Y
7 Obey	Y	Y	N	Y	Y	Y	Y	Y
8 ***Roth***	?	Y	N	Y	N	N	Y	N
9 ***Sensenbrenner***	N	Y	N	Y	N	Y	Y	N
WYOMING								
AL ***Cheney***	N	Y	Y	N	N	N	N	N

Southern states - Ala., Ark., Fla., Ga., Ky., La., Miss., N.C., Okla., S.C., Tenn., Texas, Va.
* The *Congressional Record* vote number is different from the CQ vote number because the *Record* includes quorum calls in its tally. CQ does not publish quorum call votes.

411. HR 3838. Tax Overhaul. Adoption of the rule (H Res 336) to provide for House floor consideration of the bill to restructure the income tax laws; reduce tax rates for individuals and corporations; increase the personal exemption and standard deduction; eliminate the investment tax credit; eliminate or curtail a variety of other deductions and credits; create a new alternative minimum tax for individuals and corporations; and make other changes. Rejected 202-223: R 14-164; D 188-59 (ND 135-33, SD 53-26), Dec. 11, 1985. A "yea" was a vote supporting the president's position.

412. S J Res 238. China Nuclear Agreement. Adoption of the rule (H Res 333) to provide for House floor consideration of the joint resolution approving a nuclear cooperation agreement with the People's Republic of China and imposing conditions on exports of nuclear supplies and technology to China. Adopted 252-158: R 46-128; D 206-30 (ND 147-14, SD 59-16), Dec. 11, 1985.

413. S J Res 238. China Nuclear Agreement. Passage of the joint resolution to approve a nuclear cooperation agreement with the People's Republic of China and to impose conditions on exports of nuclear supplies and technology to China. Passed 307-112: R 99-73; D 208-39 (ND 147-21, SD 61-18), Dec. 11, 1985.

414. HR 3525. Uniform Poll Closing. Adoption of the rule (H Res 329) to provide for House floor consideration of the bill to establish a uniform poll closing time in the continental United States for presidential general elections. Adopted 409-17: R 164-14; D 245-3 (ND 167-1, SD 78-2), Dec. 11, 1985.

KEY

Y Voted for (yea).
Paired for.
+ Announced for.
N Voted against (nay).
X Paired against.
- Announced against.
P Voted "present."
C Voted "present" to avoid possible conflict of interest.
? Did not vote or otherwise make a position known.

Democrats *Republicans*

	411	412	413	414
ALABAMA				
1 ***Callahan***	N	N	N	Y
2 ***Dickinson***	N	N	Y	N
3 Nichols	Y	Y	N	Y
4 Bevill	Y	Y	Y	Y
5 Flippo	Y	Y	Y	Y
6 Erdreich	Y	Y	Y	Y
7 Shelby	N	Y	Y	Y
ALASKA				
AL ***Young***	N	N	Y	Y
ARIZONA				
1 ***McCain***	N	N	Y	Y
2 Udall	Y	Y	Y	Y
3 ***Stump***	N	N	Y	Y
4 ***Rudd***	N	N	Y	Y
5 ***Kolbe***	N	N	Y	Y
ARKANSAS				
1 Alexander	Y	Y	Y	Y
2 Robinson	N	N	N	Y
3 ***Hammerschmidt***	N	N	Y	N
4 Anthony	Y	?	Y	Y
CALIFORNIA				
1 Bosco	Y	Y	N	Y
2 ***Chappie***	?	?	?	?
3 Matsui	Y	Y	Y	Y
4 Fazio	N	Y	Y	Y
5 Burton	Y	Y	Y	Y
6 Boxer	Y	N	N	Y
7 Miller	Y	N	Y	Y
8 Dellums	N	Y	Y	Y
9 Stark	Y	?	Y	Y
10 Edwards	Y	Y	Y	Y
11 Lantos	Y	Y	Y	Y
12 ***Zschau***	N	Y	Y	Y
13 Mineta	Y	Y	Y	Y
14 ***Shumway***	N	N	N	Y
15 Coelho	Y	?	Y	Y
16 Panetta	Y	N	N	Y
17 ***Pashayan***	N	Y	N	N
18 Lehman	Y	Y	Y	Y
19 ***Lagomarsino***	Y	N	Y	Y
20 ***Thomas***	N	Y	Y	Y
21 ***Fiedler***	N	N	Y	Y
22 ***Moorhead***	N	N	N	Y
23 Beilenson	?	Y	Y	Y
24 Waxman	Y	Y	Y	Y
25 Roybal	Y	?	Y	Y
26 Berman	Y	Y	Y	Y
27 Levine	Y	Y	N	Y
28 Dixon	Y	Y	Y	Y
29 Hawkins	N	Y	Y	Y
30 Martinez	Y	Y	Y	Y
31 Dymally	Y	N	Y	Y
32 Anderson	Y	Y	Y	Y
33 ***Dreier***	N	N	N	Y
34 Torres	Y	Y	Y	Y
35 ***Lewis***	N	N	N	Y
36 Brown	Y	Y	Y	Y
37 ***McCandless***	N	N	Y	Y
38 ***Dornan***	N	N	N	Y
39 ***Dannemeyer***	N	N	Y	Y
40 ***Badham***	N	N	Y	Y
41 ***Lowery***	N	N	N	Y
42 ***Lungren***	N	N	Y	Y
43 ***Packard***	N	N	N	Y
44 Bates	Y	Y	Y	Y
45 ***Hunter***	N	N	N	Y
COLORADO				
1 Schroeder	N	N	N	N
2 Wirth	Y	N	Y	Y
3 ***Strang***	N	N	N	Y
4 ***Brown***	N	N	Y	Y
5 ***Kramer***	N	N	N	Y
6 ***Schaefer***	N	N	N	N
CONNECTICUT				
1 Kennelly	Y	Y	Y	Y
2 Gejdenson	Y	Y	N	Y
3 Morrison	Y	Y	Y	Y
4 ***McKinney***	?	?	?	?
5 ***Rowland***	N	Y	Y	Y
6 ***Johnson***	Y	Y	Y	Y
DELAWARE				
AL Carper	Y	Y	Y	Y
FLORIDA				
1 Hutto	N	N	N	Y
2 Fuqua	Y	Y	Y	Y
3 Bennett	N	Y	N	Y
4 Chappell	Y	Y	Y	Y
5 ***McCollum***	N	N	Y	Y
6 MacKay	Y	Y	Y	Y
7 Gibbons	Y	Y	Y	Y
8 ***Young***	N	N	Y	Y
9 ***Bilirakis***	N	N	-	Y
10 ***Ireland***	N	Y	Y	Y
11 Nelson	+	+	+	+
12 ***Lewis***	N	N	+	Y
13 ***Mack***	N	N	N	Y
14 Mica	Y	Y	Y	Y
15 ***Shaw***	N	N	Y	Y
16 Smith	Y	Y	Y	Y
17 Lehman	Y	Y	?	Y
18 Pepper	Y	Y	Y	Y
19 Fascell	Y	Y	Y	Y
GEORGIA				
1 Thomas	Y	Y	Y	Y
2 Hatcher	Y	Y	Y	Y
3 Ray	N	N	Y	Y
4 ***Swindall***	N	N	N	Y
5 Fowler	N	Y	Y	Y
6 ***Gingrich***	N	?	Y	Y
7 Darden	N	Y	Y	Y
8 Rowland	Y	Y	Y	Y
9 Jenkins	Y	N	N	Y
10 Barnard	Y	?	Y	N
HAWAII				
1 Heftel	Y	Y	Y	Y
2 Akaka	Y	Y	Y	Y
IDAHO				
1 ***Craig***	N	N	N	Y
2 Stallings	Y	Y	Y	Y
ILLINOIS				
1 Hayes	Y	Y	Y	Y
2 Savage	N	Y	Y	Y
3 Russo	Y	Y	Y	Y
4 ***O'Brien***	N	Y	Y	Y
5 Lipinski	Y	Y	N	Y
6 ***Hyde***	N	N	N	N
7 Collins	Y	Y	Y	Y
8 Rostenkowski	Y	Y	Y	Y
9 Yates	Y	Y	N	Y
10 ***Porter***	N	N	P	Y
11 Annunzio	Y	Y	Y	Y
12 ***Crane***	N	N	N	?
13 ***Fawell***	N	N	Y	Y
14 ***Grotberg***	N	Y	Y	N
15 ***Madigan***	N	?	Y	Y
16 ***Martin***	N	Y	Y	Y
17 Evans	Y	Y	Y	Y
18 ***Michel***	N	Y	Y	Y
19 Bruce	Y	Y	Y	Y
20 Durbin	Y	Y	Y	Y
21 Price	?	?	?	?
22 Gray	Y	Y	Y	Y
INDIANA				
1 Visclosky	Y	Y	Y	Y
2 Sharp	Y	Y	Y	Y
3 ***Hiler***	N	N	Y	Y
4 ***Coats***	N	N	N	Y
5 ***Hillis***	N	N	Y	?

ND - Northern Democrats SD - Southern Democrats

* Corresponding to Congressional Record Votes 449, 450, 451, 452

	411	412	413	414
6 ***Burton***	N	N	N	Y
7 ***Myers***	N	Y	Y	Y
8 McCloskey	Y	Y	N	Y
9 Hamilton	N	Y	Y	Y
10 Jacobs	N	N	N	Y
IOWA				
1 ***Leach***	Y	Y	Y	Y
2 ***Tauke***	N	N	Y	Y
3 ***Evans***	N	N	Y	Y
4 Smith	Y	Y	Y	Y
5 ***Lightfoot***	N	N	Y	Y
6 Bedell	Y	Y	Y	Y
KANSAS				
1 ***Roberts***	N	N	Y	Y
2 Slattery	Y	Y	Y	Y
3 ***Meyers***	Y	N	N	Y
4 Glickman	Y	N	Y	Y
5 ***Whittaker***	N	N	Y	Y
KENTUCKY				
1 Hubbard	N	N	N	Y
2 Natcher	Y	Y	Y	Y
3 Mazzoli	Y	N	Y	Y
4 ***Snyder***	Y	Y	N	Y
5 ***Rogers***	-	-	Y	Y
6 ***Hopkins***	?	?	Y	Y
7 Perkins	Y	Y	Y	Y
LOUISIANA				
1 ***Livingston***	N	N	Y	Y
2 Boggs	Y	Y	Y	Y
3 Tauzin	N	Y	N	Y
4 Roemer	N	Y	Y	Y
5 Huckaby	N	Y	Y	Y
6 ***Moore***	N	N	Y	Y
7 Breaux	N	Y	Y	Y
8 Long	N	Y	Y	Y
MAINE				
1 ***McKernan***	N	N	Y	Y
2 ***Snowe***	N	N	Y	Y
MARYLAND				
1 Dyson	N	N	N	Y
2 ***Bentley***	N	N	N	Y
3 Mikulski	N	Y	N	Y
4 ***Holt***	N	Y	Y	Y
5 Hoyer	N	Y	Y	Y
6 Byron	N	Y	Y	Y
7 Mitchell	N	Y	Y	Y
8 Barnes	N	N	N	Y
MASSACHUSETTS				
1 ***Conte***	N	Y	Y	Y
2 Boland	Y	Y	Y	Y
3 Early	Y	Y	Y	Y
4 Frank	Y	Y	Y	Y
5 Atkins	Y	Y	Y	Y
6 Mavroules	Y	?	Y	Y
7 Markey	Y	N	Y	Y
8 O'Neill				
9 Moakley	Y	Y	Y	Y
10 Studds	Y	Y	Y	Y
11 Donnelly	Y	Y	Y	Y
MICHIGAN				
1 Conyers	N	Y	Y	Y
2 ***Pursell***	N	Y	Y	Y
3 Wolpe	Y	Y	Y	Y
4 ***Siljander***	N	N	N	Y
5 ***Henry***	N	Y	Y	Y
6 Carr	N	Y	Y	Y
7 Kildee	N	Y	Y	Y
8 Traxler	Y	Y	Y	Y
9 ***Vander Jagt***	N	N	Y	Y
10 ***Schuette***	N	N	N	Y
11 ***Davis***	N	Y	?	Y
12 Bonior	Y	Y	Y	Y
13 Crockett	Y	Y	Y	Y
14 Hertel	Y	Y	Y	Y
15 Ford	Y	Y	Y	Y
16 Dingell	Y	Y	Y	Y
17 Levin	Y	Y	Y	Y
18 ***Broomfield***	N	Y	Y	Y
MINNESOTA				
1 Penny	Y	Y	Y	Y
2 ***Weber***	N	?	N	N
3 ***Frenzel***	N	Y	Y	Y
4 Vento	Y	Y	Y	Y
5 Sabo	Y	Y	Y	Y
6 Sikorski	Y	Y	Y	Y
7 ***Stangeland***	Y	N	N	Y
8 Oberstar	Y	Y	Y	Y
MISSISSIPPI				
1 Whitten	Y	Y	Y	Y
2 ***Franklin***	N	Y	Y	Y
3 Montgomery	Y	Y	Y	Y
4 Dowdy	N	Y	Y	Y
5 ***Lott***	N	Y	N	Y
MISSOURI				
1 Clay	N	Y	Y	Y
2 Young	N	Y	Y	Y
3 Gephardt	Y	Y	Y	Y
4 Skelton	N	Y	N	Y
5 Wheat	Y	Y	Y	Y
6 ***Coleman***	N	N	Y	Y
7 ***Taylor***	N	Y	N	N
8 ***Emerson***	N	N	N	Y
9 Volkmer	Y	Y	Y	Y
MONTANA				
1 Williams	Y	?	N	?
2 ***Marlenee***	N	N	N	N
NEBRASKA				
1 ***Bereuter***	N	N	Y	Y
2 ***Daub***	Y	N	Y	Y
3 ***Smith***	N	N	Y	Y
NEVADA				
1 Reid	Y	Y	Y	Y
2 ***Vucanovich***	N	N	N	Y
NEW HAMPSHIRE				
1 ***Smith***	N	N	N	Y
2 ***Gregg***	N	N	N	N
NEW JERSEY				
1 Florio	Y	Y	Y	Y
2 Hughes	N	?	Y	Y
3 Howard	Y	Y	Y	Y
4 ***Smith***	N	N	N	Y
5 ***Roukema***	N	Y	Y	Y
6 Dwyer	Y	Y	Y	Y
7 ***Rinaldo***	N	N	N	Y
8 Roe	N	Y	Y	Y
9 Torricelli	Y	Y	Y	Y
10 Rodino	Y	Y	Y	Y
11 ***Gallo***	N	N	N	Y
12 ***Courter***	N	N	N	Y
13 ***Saxton***	N	N	Y	Y
14 Guarini	Y	?	Y	Y
NEW MEXICO				
1 ***Lujan***	N	N	N	Y
2 ***Skeen***	N	N	N	Y
3 Richardson	Y	Y	Y	Y
NEW YORK				
1 ***Carney***	N	N	Y	Y
2 Downey	Y	Y	Y	Y
3 Mrazek	Y	Y	Y	Y
4 ***Lent***	N	N	Y	Y
5 ***McGrath***	Y	N	Y	Y
6 Addabbo	Y	Y	Y	Y
7 Ackerman	Y	Y	Y	Y
8 Scheuer	Y	Y	Y	Y
9 Manton	Y	Y	Y	Y
10 Schumer	Y	Y	Y	Y
11 Towns	Y	Y	Y	Y
12 Owens	Y	Y	?	Y
13 Solarz	Y	Y	Y	Y
14 ***Molinari***	N	N	Y	Y
15 ***Green***	N	Y	Y	Y
16 Rangel	Y	Y	Y	Y
17 Weiss	Y	Y	Y	Y
18 Garcia	Y	Y	Y	Y
19 Biaggi	Y	Y	Y	Y
20 ***DioGuardi***	N	N	Y	Y
21 ***Fish***	N	Y	Y	Y
22 ***Gilman***	N	Y	Y	Y
23 Stratton	Y	Y	Y	Y
24 ***Solomon***	N	N	N	Y
25 ***Boehlert***	N	N	Y	Y
26 ***Martin***	N	N	N	Y
27 ***Wortley***	N	N	N	Y
28 McHugh	Y	Y	Y	Y
29 ***Horton***	N	Y	Y	Y
30 ***Eckert***	N	N	N	Y
31 ***Kemp***	N	N	?	Y
32 LaFalce	Y	Y	Y	Y
33 Nowak	Y	Y	Y	Y
34 Lundine	Y	Y	Y	Y
NORTH CAROLINA				
1 Jones	Y	Y	Y	Y
2 Valentine	N	Y	N	Y
3 Whitley	Y	Y	Y	Y
4 ***Cobey***	N	N	N	Y
5 Neal	Y	Y	Y	Y
6 ***Coble***	N	N	N	Y
7 Rose	Y	Y	Y	Y
8 Hefner	Y	Y	N	Y
9 ***McMillan***	N	Y	N	Y
10 ***Broyhill***	N	N	N	Y
11 ***Hendon***	N	N	N	Y
NORTH DAKOTA				
AL Dorgan	Y	N	N	Y
OHIO				
1 Luken	Y	Y	N	Y
2 ***Gradison***	Y	N	Y	Y
3 Hall	Y	Y	Y	Y
4 ***Oxley***	N	N	Y	Y
5 ***Latta***	N	Y	N	Y
6 ***McEwen***	N	N	N	Y
7 ***DeWine***	N	N	N	Y
8 ***Kindness***	N	Y	Y	N
9 Kaptur	N	Y	Y	Y
10 ***Miller***	N	Y	Y	Y
11 Eckart	N	Y	Y	Y
12 ***Kasich***	N	N	N	Y
13 Pease	Y	Y	Y	Y
14 Seiberling	Y	Y	Y	Y
15 ***Wylie***	Y	Y	Y	Y
16 ***Regula***	N	Y	Y	Y
17 Traficant	N	Y	N	Y
18 Applegate	N	N	N	Y
19 Feighan	Y	Y	Y	Y
20 Oakar	Y	Y	Y	Y
21 Stokes	N	Y	Y	Y
OKLAHOMA				
1 Jones	N	N	N	Y
2 Synar	Y	Y	Y	Y
3 Watkins	N	N	N	Y
4 McCurdy	N	Y	Y	Y
5 ***Edwards***	N	N	Y	Y
6 English	N	N	N	Y
OREGON				
1 AuCoin	N	Y	Y	Y
2 ***Smith, R.***	N	N	N	Y
3 Wyden	N	Y	Y	Y
4 Weaver	Y	Y	Y	Y
5 ***Smith, D.***	N	N	N	N
PENNSYLVANIA				
1 Foglietta	Y	Y	Y	Y
2 Gray	Y	Y	Y	Y
3 Borski	Y	Y	Y	Y
4 Kolter	Y	Y	Y	Y
5 ***Schulze***	N	Y	Y	Y
6 Yatron	Y	Y	Y	Y
7 Edgar	Y	Y	Y	Y
8 Kostmayer	Y	?	Y	Y
9 ***Shuster***	N	N	N	Y
10 ***McDade***	N	Y	Y	Y
11 Kanjorski	Y	Y	Y	Y
12 Murtha	Y	Y	Y	Y
13 ***Coughlin***	N	N	Y	Y
14 Coyne	Y	Y	Y	Y
15 ***Ritter***	N	Y	Y	Y
16 ***Walker***	N	N	N	Y
17 ***Gekas***	N	Y	+	Y
18 Walgren	Y	Y	Y	Y
19 ***Goodling***	N	N	N	Y
20 Gaydos	N	Y	Y	Y
21 ***Ridge***	N	N	Y	Y
22 Murphy	N	Y	Y	Y
23 ***Clinger***	N	Y	Y	Y
RHODE ISLAND				
1 St Germain	Y	Y	Y	Y
2 ***Schneider***	N	Y	Y	Y
SOUTH CAROLINA				
1 ***Hartnett***	N	N	N	N
2 ***Spence***	N	N	N	Y
3 Derrick	Y	Y	Y	Y
4 ***Campbell***	N	N	N	Y
5 Spratt	Y	?	Y	Y
6 Tallon	N	N	Y	Y
SOUTH DAKOTA				
AL Daschle	N	Y	Y	Y
TENNESSEE				
1 ***Quillen***	Y	Y	Y	Y
2 ***Duncan***	Y	N	Y	Y
3 Lloyd	Y	N	Y	Y
4 Cooper	Y	Y	Y	Y
5 Boner	Y	Y	N	Y
6 Gordon	Y	?	Y	Y
7 ***Sundquist***	N	N	N	Y
8 Jones	Y	Y	Y	Y
9 Ford	Y	Y	Y	Y
TEXAS				
1 Chapman	N	Y	Y	Y
2 Wilson	N	Y	Y	Y
3 ***Bartlett***	N	N	N	Y
4 Hall, R.	Y	N	N	N
5 Bryant	N	Y	Y	Y
6 ***Barton***	N	N	Y	Y
7 ***Archer***	N	N	Y	Y
8 ***Fields***	N	N	Y	Y
9 Brooks	?	?	?	?
10 Pickle	Y	Y	Y	Y
11 Leath	N	N	N	Y
12 Wright	Y	Y	Y	Y
13 ***Boulter***	N	N	N	Y
14 ***Sweeney***	N	N	N	Y
15 de la Garza	Y	Y	Y	Y
16 Coleman	Y	Y	Y	Y
17 Stenholm	N	N	N	Y
18 Leland	Y	Y	Y	Y
19 ***Combest***	N	N	N	Y
20 Gonzalez	Y	N	N	Y
21 ***Loeffler***	N	N	N	Y
22 ***DeLay***	N	N	N	Y
23 Bustamante	Y	Y	Y	Y
24 Frost	P	?	Y	Y
25 Andrews	N	Y	Y	Y
26 ***Armey***	N	N	N	Y
27 Ortiz	Y	Y	Y	Y
UTAH				
1 ***Hansen***	Y	N	N	N
2 ***Monson***	N	N	N	Y
3 ***Nielson***	N	N	Y	Y
VERMONT				
AL ***Jeffords***	N	N	?	Y
VIRGINIA				
1 ***Bateman***	N	Y	Y	Y
2 ***Whitehurst***	N	N	Y	Y
3 ***Bliley***	N	N	Y	Y
4 Sisisky	Y	N	Y	Y
5 Daniel	Y	Y	N	Y
6 Olin	Y	Y	Y	Y
7 ***Slaughter***	N	N	N	Y
8 ***Parris***	N	N	Y	Y
9 Boucher	Y	Y	Y	Y
10 ***Wolf***	N	?	Y	Y
WASHINGTON				
1 ***Miller***	N	N	Y	Y
2 Swift	Y	Y	Y	Y
3 Bonker	Y	Y	Y	Y
4 ***Morrison***	N	Y	+	Y
5 Foley	Y	Y	Y	Y
6 Dicks	N	Y	Y	Y
7 Lowry	N	Y	Y	Y
8 ***Chandler***	N	Y	Y	Y
WEST VIRGINIA				
1 Mollohan	Y	Y	Y	Y
2 Staggers	Y	Y	N	Y
3 Wise	Y	Y	Y	Y
4 Rahall	Y	Y	N	Y
WISCONSIN				
1 Aspin	Y	N	Y	Y
2 Kastenmeier	Y	Y	Y	Y
3 ***Gunderson***	N	N	Y	Y
4 Kleczka	Y	Y	Y	Y
5 Moody	Y	Y	Y	Y
6 ***Petri***	Y	Y	Y	Y
7 Obey	Y	Y	Y	Y
8 ***Roth***	N	Y	Y	Y
9 ***Sensenbrenner***	N	N	N	Y
WYOMING				
AL ***Cheney***	N	N	Y	Y

Southern states - Ala., Ark., Fla., Ga., Ky., La., Miss., N.C., Okla., S.C., Tenn., Texas, Va.

* The *Congressional Record* vote number is different from the CQ vote number because the *Record* includes quorum calls in its tally. CQ does not publish quorum call votes.

415. H J Res 372. Public Debt Limit/Balanced Budget. Adoption of the conference report on the joint resolution to raise the ceiling on the federal debt to $2.079 trillion from $1.824 trillion; to set maximum allowable federal deficits for fiscal years 1986-91, declining annually to zero in fiscal 1991; to require the president, if projected deficits exceed those allowed, to issue an emergency order reducing all federal spending by the same percentage amount, to reduce deficits to the maximum allowed, with half of such cuts to come from defense and half from non-defense programs; to exempt Social Security, interest on the national debt and certain poverty programs from such automatic cuts; to limit the size of such cuts as they affect certain health programs; to revise congressional budget procedures; to remove Social Security from the unified federal budget in fiscal 1986 and thereafter; and to replenish the Social Security trust funds of any interest lost due to disinvestment or non-investment of those trust funds during periods in 1985 when the ceiling on the federal debt was about to be breached. Adopted 271-154: R 153-24; D 118-130 (ND 60-108, SD 58-22), Dec. 11, 1985. A "yea" was a vote supporting the president's position.

416. Procedural Motion. Chandler, R-Wash., motion to approve the House *Journal* of Wednesday, Dec. 11. Motion agreed to 274-111: R 66-102; D 208-9 (ND 139-8, SD 69-1), Dec. 12, 1985.

417. H J Res 192. Armenian Genocide. Adoption of the rule (H Res 328) to provide for House floor consideration of the joint resolution to direct the president to proclaim April 24, 1986, as a national day of remembrance of "man's inhumanity to man," especially the genocide said to have been committed against Armenians between 1915 and 1923. Adopted 263-156: R 65-113; D 198-43 (ND 150-13, SD 48-30), Dec. 12, 1985.

418. H J Res 192. Armenian Genocide. Ford, D-Mich., amendment to specify that the genocide said to have been committed against Armenians between 1915 and 1923 occurred before the establishment of the present Republic of Turkey. Rejected 206-213: R 49-129; D 157-84 (ND 132-32, SD 25-52), Dec. 12, 1985. (The effect of the Ford amendment, if adopted, would have been to prevent consideration by the House of subsequent amendments to modify the resolution.)

KEY

- Y Voted for (yea).
- # Paired for.
- + Announced for.
- N Voted against (nay).
- X Paired against.
- - Announced against.
- P Voted "present."
- C Voted "present" to avoid possible conflict of interest.
- ? Did not vote or otherwise make a position known.

Democrats ***Republicans***

	415	416	417	418
ALABAMA				
1 ***Callahan***	Y	Y	N	N
2 ***Dickinson***	N	N	N	N
3 Nichols	Y	Y	N	N
4 Bevill	Y	Y	N	Y
5 Flippo	Y	Y	N	N
6 Erdreich	Y	Y	N	Y
7 Shelby	Y	Y	Y	Y
ALASKA				
AL ***Young***	Y	?	Y	Y
ARIZONA				
1 ***McCain***	Y	Y	N	N
2 Udall	N	Y	Y	N
3 ***Stump***	Y	Y	N	N
4 ***Rudd***	Y	Y	N	N
5 ***Kolbe***	Y	N	N	N
ARKANSAS				
1 Alexander	N	Y	N	N
2 Robinson	Y	Y	Y	Y
3 ***Hammerschmidt***	Y	Y	N	N
4 Anthony	Y	Y	Y	N
CALIFORNIA				
1 Bosco	Y	Y	Y	Y
2 ***Chappie***	?	?	?	?
3 Matsui	N	Y	Y	Y
4 Fazio	N	Y	Y	Y
5 Burton	N	Y	Y	Y
6 Boxer	N	Y	Y	Y
7 Miller	N	Y	Y	Y
8 Dellums	N	Y	Y	Y
9 Stark	N	?	Y	Y
10 Edwards	N	Y	Y	Y
11 Lantos	Y	Y	N	N
12 ***Zschau***	Y	N	Y	Y
13 Mineta	N	Y	Y	Y
14 ***Shumway***	N	Y	N	N
15 Coelho	N	Y	Y	Y
16 Panetta	Y	?	Y	Y
17 ***Pashayan***	+	N	Y	Y
18 Lehman	N	Y	Y	Y
19 ***Lagomarsino***	Y	N	N	N
20 ***Thomas***	Y	N	Y	Y
21 ***Fiedler***	Y	N	Y	Y
22 ***Moorhead***	Y	N	Y	Y
23 Beilenson	N	Y	Y	Y
24 Waxman	N	?	Y	Y
25 Roybal	N	Y	Y	Y
26 Berman	N	Y	Y	Y
27 Levine	N	Y	Y	Y
28 Dixon	N	?	Y	Y
29 Hawkins	N	P	Y	Y
30 Martinez	N	Y	Y	Y
31 Dymally	N	P	Y	Y
32 Anderson	N	Y	Y	Y
33 ***Dreier***	Y	Y	Y	Y
34 Torres	Y	Y	Y	Y
35 ***Lewis***	N	N	Y	Y
36 Brown	N	Y	Y	Y
37 ***McCandless***	Y	N	N	N
38 ***Dornan***	N	N	Y	Y
39 ***Dannemeyer***	Y	N	N	N
40 ***Badham***	Y	N	N	N
41 ***Lowery***	Y	?	Y	Y
42 ***Lungren***	Y	?	Y	Y
43 ***Packard***	Y	Y	Y	N
44 Bates	Y	Y	Y	Y
45 ***Hunter***	N	?	Y	Y
COLORADO				
1 Schroeder	N	N	N	N
2 Wirth	Y	Y	Y	Y
3 ***Strang***	Y	Y	N	N
4 ***Brown***	Y	N	N	N
5 ***Kramer***	Y	N	N	N
6 ***Schaefer***	Y	Y	N	N
CONNECTICUT				
1 Kennelly	N	Y	Y	Y
2 Gejdenson	Y	Y	Y	Y
3 Morrison	N	Y	Y	Y
4 ***McKinney***	?	?	?	?
5 ***Rowland***	Y	N	Y	Y
6 ***Johnson***	Y	Y	Y	Y
DELAWARE				
AL Carper	Y	Y	Y	Y
FLORIDA				
1 Hutto	Y	Y	N	N
2 Fuqua	Y	Y	Y	N
3 Bennett	N	Y	N	N
4 Chappell	N	Y	N	N
5 ***McCollum***	Y	Y	N	N
6 MacKay	Y	Y	Y	Y
7 Gibbons	Y	?	Y	Y
8 ***Young***	N	N	N	N
9 ***Bilirakis***	N	N	Y	N
10 ***Ireland***	Y	N	N	N
11 Nelson	#	+	+	X
12 ***Lewis***	Y	N	N	Y
13 ***Mack***	Y	N	N	N
14 Mica	Y	Y	Y	N
15 ***Shaw***	Y	N	N	N
16 Smith	Y	Y	Y	Y
17 Lehman	N	Y	?	?
18 Pepper	N	Y	Y	Y
19 Fascell	Y	Y	Y	N
GEORGIA				
1 Thomas	Y	Y	Y	N
2 Hatcher	Y	Y	Y	?
3 Ray	Y	Y	Y	N
4 ***Swindall***	Y	N	Y	N
5 Fowler	Y	Y	Y	N
6 ***Gingrich***	Y	N	Y	Y
7 Darden	Y	Y	Y	Y
8 Rowland	Y	Y	Y	N
9 Jenkins	Y	Y	Y	N
10 Barnard	Y	Y	N	N
HAWAII				
1 Heftel	Y	?	Y	Y
2 Akaka	Y	Y	Y	Y
IDAHO				
1 ***Craig***	Y	Y	N	N
2 Stallings	Y	Y	Y	Y
ILLINOIS				
1 Hayes	N	Y	Y	Y
2 Savage	N	Y	Y	Y
3 Russo	Y	Y	Y	Y
4 ***O'Brien***	Y	Y	N	N
5 Lipinski	N	Y	Y	Y
6 ***Hyde***	N	N	N	N
7 Collins	N	Y	Y	Y
8 Rostenkowski	Y	Y	?	Y
9 Yates	N	Y	Y	Y
10 ***Porter***	Y	?	Y	N
11 Annunzio	N	Y	Y	Y
12 ***Crane***	N	N	Y	N
13 ***Fawell***	Y	N	Y	N
14 ***Grotberg***	Y	N	N	N
15 ***Madigan***	Y	N	N	N
16 ***Martin***	Y	N	N	N
17 Evans	N	Y	Y	Y
18 ***Michel***	Y	N	N	N
19 Bruce	Y	Y	Y	Y
20 Durbin	Y	N	Y	Y
21 Price	?	?	?	?
22 Gray	Y	?	Y	Y
INDIANA				
1 Visclosky	N	Y	Y	Y
2 Sharp	Y	Y	?	Y
3 ***Hiler***	Y	N	N	N
4 ***Coats***	Y	Y	Y	Y
5 ***Hillis***	Y	Y	N	N

ND - Northern Democrats SD - Southern Democrats

* Corresponding to Congressional Record Votes 454, 455, 457, 459

	415	416	417	418
6 ***Burton***	Y	N	N	N
7 ***Myers***	N	Y	N	N
8 McCloskey	Y	Y	Y	Y
9 Hamilton	Y	Y	Y	Y
10 Jacobs	Y	N	Y	Y
IOWA				
1 ***Leach***	Y	N	Y	Y
2 ***Tauke***	Y	N	N	N
3 ***Evans***	N	N	N	Y
4 Smith	N	Y	Y	Y
5 ***Lightfoot***	Y	N	N	N
6 Bedell	Y	?	Y	N
KANSAS				
1 ***Roberts***	N	N	Y	N
2 Slattery	Y	Y	Y	Y
3 ***Meyers***	Y	Y	Y	N
4 Glickman	Y	Y	Y	Y
5 ***Whittaker***	Y	N	Y	N
KENTUCKY				
1 Hubbard	N	Y	N	N
2 Natcher	Y	Y	N	N
3 Mazzoli	Y	Y	N	N
4 ***Snyder***	Y	Y	N	N
5 ***Rogers***	Y	N	N	N
6 ***Hopkins***	Y	N	N	N
7 Perkins	N	Y	Y	Y
LOUISIANA				
1 ***Livingston***	Y	N	N	N
2 Boggs	N	?	Y	N
3 Tauzin	Y	Y	N	N
4 Roemer	Y	N	Y	N
5 Huckaby	Y	?	N	N
6 ***Moore***	Y	Y	N	N
7 Breaux	Y	Y	N	N
8 Long	N	Y	Y	Y
MAINE				
1 ***McKernan***	Y	N	Y	N
2 ***Snowe***	Y	N	Y	N
MARYLAND				
1 Dyson	Y	?	Y	Y
2 ***Bentley***	N	N	N	N
3 Mikulski	N	Y	N	Y
4 ***Holt***	N	N	N	N
5 Hoyer	N	Y	Y	Y
6 Byron	Y	Y	Y	N
7 Mitchell	N	N	Y	#
8 Barnes	N	Y	Y	Y
MASSACHUSETTS				
1 ***Conte***	N	N	Y	?
2 Boland	N	Y	Y	Y
3 Early	N	Y	Y	Y
4 Frank	N	Y	Y	Y
5 Atkins	Y	?	Y	Y
6 Mavroules	Y	Y	Y	Y
7 Markey	N	Y	Y	Y
8 O'Neill				
9 Moakley	N	Y	Y	Y
10 Studds	N	Y	Y	Y
11 Donnelly	N	Y	Y	Y
MICHIGAN				
1 Conyers	N	Y	N	?
2 ***Pursell***	Y	Y	Y	Y
3 Wolpe	Y	Y	Y	Y
4 ***Siljander***	Y	N	N	N
5 ***Henry***	Y	N	Y	Y
6 Carr	N	Y	Y	Y
7 Kildee	N	Y	Y	Y
8 Traxler	N	?	P	P
9 ***Vander Jagt***	?	N	Y	N
10 ***Schuette***	Y	?	Y	N
11 ***Davis***	Y	N	Y	N
12 Bonior	N	Y	Y	Y
13 Crockett	X	Y	Y	Y
14 Hertel	Y	Y	Y	Y
15 Ford	N	Y	Y	Y
16 Dingell	N	Y	Y	Y
17 Levin	Y	Y	Y	Y
18 ***Broomfield***	Y	Y	Y	Y
MINNESOTA				
1 Penny	Y	N	Y	N
2 ***Weber***	Y	N	Y	N
3 ***Frenzel***	Y	Y	N	N
4 Vento	N	Y	Y	Y
5 Sabo	N	Y	Y	Y
6 Sikorski	Y	N	Y	Y

	415	416	417	418
7 ***Stangeland***	Y	N	N	N
8 Oberstar	N	Y	Y	Y
MISSISSIPPI				
1 Whitten	N	Y	N	N
2 ***Franklin***	Y	Y	N	N
3 Montgomery	Y	Y	N	N
4 Dowdy	N	Y	Y	N
5 ***Lott***	Y	Y	N	N
MISSOURI				
1 Clay	N	N	Y	Y
2 Young	Y	Y	N	Y
3 Gephardt	Y	Y	Y	Y
4 Skelton	Y	Y	N	N
5 Wheat	N	Y	Y	Y
6 ***Coleman***	Y	N	N	N
7 ***Taylor***	Y	Y	N	N
8 ***Emerson***	Y	Y	N	N
9 Volkmer	Y	Y	Y	Y
MONTANA				
1 Williams	N	?	Y	Y
2 ***Marlenee***	N	N	N	N
NEBRASKA				
1 ***Bereuter***	Y	N	N	N
2 ***Daub***	Y	N	N	N
3 ***Smith***	Y	Y	N	N
NEVADA				
1 Reid	Y	Y	Y	Y
2 ***Vucanovich***	Y	N	Y	N
NEW HAMPSHIRE				
1 ***Smith***	Y	N	Y	Y
2 ***Gregg***	Y	N	N	Y
NEW JERSEY				
1 Florio	N	Y	Y	Y
2 Hughes	N	Y	Y	N
3 Howard	N	Y	Y	Y
4 ***Smith***	Y	Y	Y	Y
5 ***Roukema***	Y	N	Y	Y
6 Dwyer	N	Y	Y	N
7 ***Rinaldo***	Y	Y	Y	N
8 Roe	N	Y	Y	Y
9 Torricelli	N	Y	Y	Y
10 Rodino	N	?	Y	Y
11 ***Gallo***	Y	N	Y	Y
12 ***Courter***	Y	N	N	N
13 ***Saxton***	Y	N	N	Y
14 Guarini	N	Y	Y	Y
NEW MEXICO				
1 ***Lujan***	Y	Y	N	Y
2 ***Skeen***	Y	N	Y	N
3 Richardson	Y	Y	Y	Y
NEW YORK				
1 ***Carney***	Y	N	N	N
2 Downey	N	Y	Y	Y
3 Mrazek	Y	Y	Y	Y
4 ***Lent***	Y	N	Y	N
5 ***McGrath***	Y	N	Y	Y
6 Addabbo	N	Y	?	N
7 Ackerman	N	Y	Y	Y
8 Scheuer	N	Y	Y	Y
9 Manton	Y	Y	Y	Y
10 Schumer	N	Y	?	Y
11 Towns	N	N	Y	Y
12 Owens	N	Y	Y	Y
13 Solarz	N	Y	N	N
14 ***Molinari***	Y	Y	N	N
15 ***Green***	Y	Y	Y	Y
16 Rangel	N	Y	N	N
17 Weiss	N	Y	Y	Y
18 Garcia	N	Y	Y	N
19 Biaggi	N	Y	Y	Y
20 ***DioGuardi***	Y	Y	N	N
21 ***Fish***	Y	Y	Y	N
22 ***Gilman***	N	Y	Y	Y
23 Stratton	N	Y	Y	N
24 ***Solomon***	Y	N	N	N
25 ***Boehlert***	Y	N	Y	Y
26 ***Martin***	N	N	Y	Y
27 ***Wortley***	Y	Y	Y	N
28 McHugh	N	?	Y	Y
29 ***Horton***	Y	Y	N	Y
30 ***Eckert***	N	?	N	?
31 ***Kemp***	N	Y	N	Y
32 LaFalce	N	Y	Y	Y
33 Nowak	N	Y	Y	Y
34 Lundine	Y	Y	Y	Y

	415	416	417	418
NORTH CAROLINA				
1 Jones	N	?	Y	N
2 Valentine	Y	Y	N	N
3 Whitley	Y	Y	N	N
4 ***Cobey***	Y	N	N	N
5 Neal	Y	Y	Y	N
6 ***Coble***	Y	N	N	N
7 Rose	N	?	N	N
8 Hefner	Y	Y	N	N
9 ***McMillan***	Y	Y	N	N
10 ***Broyhill***	Y	?	N	N
11 ***Hendon***	Y	N	N	N
NORTH DAKOTA				
AL Dorgan	N	Y	Y	Y
OHIO				
1 Luken	Y	Y	Y	Y
2 ***Gradison***	Y	Y	N	N
3 Hall	Y	?	Y	Y
4 ***Oxley***	Y	N	N	N
5 ***Latta***	Y	N	N	N
6 ***McEwen***	Y	Y	N	N
7 ***DeWine***	N	N	N	N
8 ***Kindness***	Y	Y	N	N
9 Kaptur	Y	Y	Y	Y
10 ***Miller***	Y	N	N	Y
11 Eckart	Y	?	Y	Y
12 ***Kasich***	Y	N	N	N
13 Pease	Y	Y	Y	N
14 Seiberling	N	?	Y	N
15 ***Wylie***	Y	Y	?	N
16 ***Regula***	Y	Y	Y	Y
17 Traficant	N	Y	Y	Y
18 Applegate	Y	Y	Y	N
19 Feighan	Y	Y	Y	Y
20 Oakar	N	Y	Y	Y
21 Stokes	N	Y	Y	Y
OKLAHOMA				
1 Jones	Y	Y	Y	N
2 Synar	N	?	Y	N
3 Watkins	Y	Y	Y	N
4 McCurdy	Y	Y	Y	N
5 ***Edwards***	Y	?	N	N
6 English	Y	Y	Y	N
OREGON				
1 AuCoin	Y	Y	Y	N
2 ***Smith, R.***	Y	Y	N	N
3 Wyden	Y	Y	Y	Y
4 Weaver	N	Y	Y	Y
5 ***Smith, D.***	Y	Y	N	N
PENNSYLVANIA				
1 Foglietta	N	Y	N	?
2 Gray	N	Y	N	N
3 Borski	N	Y	Y	Y
4 Kolter	N	Y	Y	N
5 ***Schulze***	Y	Y	N	N
6 Yatron	Y	Y	Y	N
7 Edgar	N	?	Y	Y
8 Kostmayer	Y	Y	Y	Y
9 ***Shuster***	Y	N	N	N
10 ***McDade***	Y	Y	Y	Y
11 Kanjorski	N	Y	Y	N
12 Murtha	N	Y	N	N
13 ***Coughlin***	Y	N	Y	N
14 Coyne	N	Y	Y	N
15 ***Ritter***	Y	Y	Y	Y
16 ***Walker***	Y	N	N	N
17 ***Gekas***	Y	N	Y	Y
18 Walgren	Y	Y	Y	N
19 ***Goodling***	Y	?	N	N
20 Gaydos	N	Y	Y	N
21 ***Ridge***	Y	N	N	N
22 Murphy	Y	Y	N	N
23 ***Clinger***	Y	N	N	Y
RHODE ISLAND				
1 St Germain	N	Y	Y	Y
2 ***Schneider***	#	Y	Y	Y
SOUTH CAROLINA				
1 ***Hartnett***	N	N	N	N
2 ***Spence***	Y	N	N	N
3 Derrick	N	Y	Y	N
4 ***Campbell***	Y	N	N	Y
5 Spratt	Y	Y	Y	N
6 Tallon	N	Y	Y	N
SOUTH DAKOTA				
AL Daschle	Y	Y	Y	Y

	415	416	417	418
TENNESSEE				
1 ***Quillen***	Y	Y	N	N
2 ***Duncan***	Y	Y	N	N
3 Lloyd	Y	Y	?	N
4 Cooper	Y	Y	Y	Y
5 Boner	Y	Y	Y	Y
6 Gordon	Y	Y	Y	Y
7 ***Sundquist***	Y	N	N	N
8 Jones	Y	Y	Y	N
9 Ford	N	Y	Y	Y
TEXAS				
1 Chapman	Y	Y	N	N
2 Wilson	Y	Y	N	N
3 ***Bartlett***	Y	N	N	N
4 Hall, R.	Y	Y	Y	Y
5 Bryant	Y	Y	Y	Y
6 ***Barton***	Y	N	N	N
7 ***Archer***	Y	N	N	N
8 ***Fields***	Y	N	N	N
9 Brooks	X	?	?	?
10 Pickle	Y	Y	N	N
11 Leath	Y	Y	N	N
12 Wright	Y	Y	Y	Y
13 ***Boulter***	Y	Y	N	N
14 ***Sweeney***	Y	?	?	Y
15 de la Garza	N	?	N	N
16 Coleman	Y	Y	Y	Y
17 Stenholm	Y	Y	N	N
18 Leland	N	?	Y	Y
19 ***Combest***	Y	Y	N	N
20 Gonzalez	N	Y	Y	P
21 ***Loeffler***	Y	N	Y	N
22 ***DeLay***	Y	?	N	N
23 Bustamante	N	Y	N	N
24 Frost	Y	?	Y	Y
25 Andrews	Y	Y	Y	Y
26 ***Armey***	Y	Y	N	N
27 Ortiz	N	Y	N	N
UTAH				
1 ***Hansen***	Y	Y	N	N
2 ***Monson***	Y	N	N	N
3 ***Nielson***	Y	Y	N	N
VERMONT				
AL ***Jeffords***	Y	Y	Y	Y
VIRGINIA				
1 ***Bateman***	Y	Y	N	N
2 ***Whitehurst***	Y	Y	N	N
3 ***Bliley***	Y	Y	Y	Y
4 Sisisky	Y	Y	Y	Y
5 Daniel	Y	Y	N	N
6 Olin	Y	?	Y	Y
7 ***Slaughter***	Y	N	Y	N
8 ***Parris***	N	N	Y	N
9 Boucher	Y	Y	Y	Y
10 ***Wolf***	N	N	Y	Y
WASHINGTON				
1 ***Miller***	Y	Y	Y	Y
2 Swift	Y	Y	Y	N
3 Bonker	N	Y	Y	Y
4 ***Morrison***	Y	N	N	N
5 Foley	Y	?	Y	Y
6 Dicks	N	Y	Y	Y
7 Lowry	N	Y	Y	Y
8 ***Chandler***	Y	N	N	N
WEST VIRGINIA				
1 Mollohan	N	Y	Y	N
2 Staggers	Y	Y	Y	N
3 Wise	Y	Y	?	?
4 Rahall	N	?	N	N
WISCONSIN				
1 Aspin	N	Y	Y	Y
2 Kastenmeier	N	Y	Y	N
3 ***Gunderson***	Y	N	N	N
4 Kleczka	Y	Y	Y	Y
5 Moody	N	Y	Y	Y
6 ***Petri***	Y	Y	Y	N
7 Obey	N	P	Y	Y
8 ***Roth***	Y	N	N	N
9 ***Sensenbrenner***	Y	Y	N	N
WYOMING				
AL ***Cheney***	Y	N	N	N

Southern states - Ala., Ark., Fla., Ga., Ky., La., Miss., N.C., Okla., S.C., Tenn., Texas, Va.

* The *Congressional Record* vote number is different from the CQ vote number because the *Record* includes quorum calls in its tally. CQ does not publish quorum call votes.

419. Procedural Motion. Gekas, R-Pa., motion to approve the House *Journal* of Thursday, Dec. 12. Motion agreed to 241-121: R 43-111; D 198-10 (ND 128-7, SD 70-3), Dec. 16, 1985.

420. H J Res 465. Further Continuing Appropriations, Fiscal 1986. Adoption of the conference report on the joint resolution to provide continued spending authority through Sept. 30, 1986, for government agencies whose regular fiscal 1986 appropriations had not become law. Rejected 170-239: R 55-119; D 115-120 (ND 72-86, SD 43-34), Dec. 16, 1985.

421. HR 3363. Relief of Hamilton Jordan. Passage of the bill to reimburse Hamilton Jordan, former White House chief of staff in the Carter administration, for legal fees incurred from investigations conducted by the U.S. attorney general and a court-appointed special prosecutor, or "independent counsel," into allegations that Jordan used cocaine during a 1978 visit to a New York discothèque. Passed 347-40: R 135-31; D 212-9 (ND 142-8, SD 70-1), Dec. 17, 1985.

422. H J Res 491. Further Continuing Appropriations, Fiscal 1986. Conte, R-Mass., motion to recommit the joint resolution to the Appropriations Committee with instructions to report it back to the House with an amendment to bar the Synthetic Fuels Corporation from awarding any money for projects. Motion agreed to 392-20: R 163-10; D 229-10 (ND 152-9, SD 77-1), Dec. 17, 1985.

423. H J Res 491. Further Continuing Appropriations, Fiscal 1986. Passage of the joint resolution to provide continued spending authority through Dec. 19, 1985, for government agencies whose regular fiscal 1986 appropriations had not become law, and to bar the Synthetic Fuels Corporation from awarding any money for projects. Passed 334-74: R 107-62; D 227-12 (ND 153-7, SD 74-5), Dec. 17, 1985.

424. HR 3132. Armor-Piercing Ammunition. Hughes, D-N.J., motion to suspend the rules and pass the bill to bar the manufacture or importation of armor-piercing ammunition. Motion agreed to 400-21: R 158-19; D 242-2 (ND 165-1, SD 77-1), Dec. 17, 1985. A two-thirds majority vote of those present and voting (281 in this case) is required for passage under suspension of the rules.

425. HR 3838. Tax Overhaul. Adoption of the rule (H Res 343) to provide for House floor consideration of the bill to revise the federal income tax system by: lowering individual and corporate tax rates; increasing the personal exemption and standard deduction; eliminating the investment tax credit; eliminating or curtailing a variety of other deductions and credits; creating a new alternative minimum tax for individuals and corporations; and making other changes. Adopted 258-168: R 70-110; D 188-58 (ND 138-28, SD 50-30), Dec. 17, 1985. A "yea" was a vote supporting the president's position.

426. HR 3838. Tax Overhaul. McHugh, D-N.Y., amendment to allow taxpayers a credit for annual contributions of up to $100 ($200 for joint returns) to the political campaigns of congressional candidates in their home states. Adopted 230-196: R 35-145; D 195-51 (ND 147-18, SD 48-33), Dec. 17, 1985.

KEY

Y Voted for (yea).
Paired for.
+ Announced for.
N Voted against (nay).
X Paired against.
- Announced against.
P Voted "present."
C Voted "present" to avoid possible conflict of interest.
? Did not vote or otherwise make a position known.

Democrats ***Republicans***

	419	420	421	422	423	424	425	426
ALABAMA								
1 ***Callahan***	N	N	Y	Y	Y	Y	Y	N
2 ***Dickinson***	N	Y	N	Y	Y	Y	N	N
3 Nichols	Y	Y	Y	Y	Y	Y	Y	N
4 Bevill	Y	Y	Y	Y	Y	Y	Y	N
5 Flippo	Y	Y	Y	Y	Y	Y	Y	Y
6 Erdreich	Y	N	Y	Y	Y	Y	Y	N
7 Shelby	Y	N	Y	Y	Y	Y	N	Y
ALASKA								
AL ***Young***	?	Y	?	Y	Y	Y	N	Y
ARIZONA								
1 ***McCain***	N	N	Y	Y	N	Y	N	N
2 Udall	Y	Y	Y	Y	Y	Y	Y	Y
3 ***Stump***	N	N	Y	Y	N	N	N	N
4 ***Rudd***	Y	Y	Y	Y	Y	N	N	Y
5 ***Kolbe***	N	N	Y	Y	Y	N	N	N
ARKANSAS								
1 Alexander	Y	Y	Y	Y	Y	Y	Y	Y
2 Robinson	Y	N	Y	Y	N	Y	N	Y
3 ***Hammerschmidt***	Y	N	Y	Y	Y	Y	Y	N
4 Anthony	Y	N	Y	Y	Y	Y	Y	N
CALIFORNIA								
1 Bosco	Y	Y	Y	Y	Y	Y	Y	Y
2 ***Chappie***	N	N	Y	Y	N	Y	N	N
3 Matsui	Y	Y	Y	Y	Y	Y	Y	Y
4 Fazio	Y	Y	Y	Y	Y	Y	N	Y
5 Burton	Y	Y	Y	Y	Y	Y	Y	Y
6 Boxer	?	N	Y	Y	Y	Y	Y	Y
7 Miller	Y	Y	Y	Y	Y	Y	Y	Y
8 Dellums	?	N	Y	Y	Y	Y	Y	Y
9 Stark	Y	N	N	Y	Y	Y	Y	Y
10 Edwards	Y	N	Y	Y	Y	Y	Y	Y
11 Lantos	Y	Y	Y	Y	Y	Y	Y	Y
12 ***Zschau***	N	N	Y	Y	Y	Y	N	N
13 Mineta	Y	Y	Y	Y	Y	Y	Y	Y
14 ***Shumway***	Y	N	N	Y	N	N	N	N
15 Coelho	Y	Y	Y	Y	Y	Y	Y	Y
16 Panetta	Y	N	Y	Y	Y	Y	Y	Y
17 ***Pashayan***	N	N	Y	Y	Y	Y	N	N
18 Lehman	?	Y	Y	Y	Y	Y	Y	Y
19 ***Lagomarsino***	N	N	Y	Y	N	Y	Y	N
20 ***Thomas***	N	N	Y	Y	Y	Y	N	N
21 ***Fiedler***	N	N	Y	Y	Y	Y	N	N
22 ***Moorhead***	N	N	N	Y	N	N	N	N
23 Beilenson	Y	Y	Y	Y	Y	Y	Y	Y
24 Waxman	P	Y	Y	Y	Y	Y	Y	Y
25 Roybal	Y	Y	?	Y	Y	Y	N	Y
26 Berman	Y	Y	Y	Y	Y	Y	Y	Y
27 Levine	Y	Y	Y	Y	Y	Y	Y	Y
28 Dixon	Y	Y	?	?	Y	Y	Y	Y
29 Hawkins	Y	N	Y	Y	Y	Y	Y	Y
30 Martinez	P	N	Y	Y	Y	Y	Y	N
31 Dymally	?	?	?	?	?	?	X	?
32 Anderson	Y	Y	N	Y	Y	Y	Y	Y
33 ***Dreier***	N	N	N	Y	N	N	N	N
34 Torres	Y	N	Y	Y	Y	Y	Y	Y
35 ***Lewis***	N	Y	Y	Y	Y	N	N	Y
36 Brown	Y	Y	Y	Y	Y	Y	Y	Y
37 ***McCandless***	N	N	N	Y	N	Y	N	N
38 ***Dornan***	?	N	N	Y	N	Y	Y	N
39 ***Dannemeyer***	N	N	N	Y	N	Y	N	Y
40 ***Badham***	N	Y	Y	Y	Y	Y	Y	N
41 ***Lowery***	?	Y	Y	Y	Y	Y	N	N
42 ***Lungren***	N	N	Y	Y	N	Y	N	Y
43 ***Packard***	Y	N	Y	Y	N	Y	N	Y
44 Bates	?	N	Y	Y	Y	Y	Y	Y
45 ***Hunter***	?	N	Y	Y	N	Y	N	?
COLORADO								
1 Schroeder	N	N	N	Y	?	Y	N	Y
2 Wirth	Y	N	Y	N	N	Y	Y	Y
3 ***Strang***	N	Y	Y	N	N	N	N	N
4 ***Brown***	?	N	Y	N	N	Y	N	Y
5 ***Kramer***	N	N	N	N	N	N	N	N
6 ***Schaefer***	N	N	N	N	N	Y	N	N
CONNECTICUT								
1 Kennelly	Y	Y	?	Y	Y	Y	Y	Y
2 Gejdenson	Y	N	Y	Y	Y	Y	Y	Y
3 Morrison	?	N	Y	Y	Y	Y	Y	Y
4 ***McKinney***	?	?	?	?	?	?	?	?
5 ***Rowland***	N	N	Y	Y	Y	Y	Y	N
6 ***Johnson***	Y	N	Y	Y	?	Y	Y	N
DELAWARE								
AL Carper	Y	N	Y	Y	Y	Y	Y	N
FLORIDA								
1 Hutto	Y	Y	Y	Y	Y	Y	N	Y
2 Fuqua	?	?	?	?	?	?	Y	N
3 Bennett	Y	Y	N	Y	Y	Y	N	N
4 Chappell	Y	Y	?	Y	Y	Y	Y	Y
5 ***McCollum***	Y	N	Y	Y	Y	Y	N	Y
6 MacKay	?	N	Y	Y	Y	Y	Y	Y
7 Gibbons	Y	Y	?	Y	Y	Y	Y	Y
8 ***Young***	N	Y	N	Y	Y	Y	Y	N
9 ***Bilirakis***	?	N	N	Y	N	Y	Y	N
10 ***Ireland***	N	N	Y	Y	Y	Y	Y	N
11 Nelson	+	#	+	+	+	+	#	+
12 ***Lewis***	N	N	Y	Y	N	Y	N	N
13 ***Mack***	N	N	N	Y	N	Y	N	N
14 Mica	Y	Y	Y	Y	Y	?	Y	Y
15 ***Shaw***	N	N	Y	Y	Y	Y	N	N
16 Smith	Y	Y	Y	Y	Y	Y	Y	Y
17 Lehman	Y	Y	Y	Y	Y	Y	Y	Y
18 Pepper	Y	Y	Y	Y	Y	Y	Y	Y
19 Fascell	Y	Y	Y	Y	Y	Y	Y	Y
GEORGIA								
1 Thomas	Y	Y	Y	Y	Y	Y	Y	N
2 Hatcher	Y	Y	Y	Y	Y	Y	Y	Y
3 Ray	Y	N	Y	Y	Y	Y	N	Y
4 ***Swindall***	N	N	Y	Y	N	Y	N	N
5 Fowler	Y	N	Y	Y	Y	Y	Y	N
6 ***Gingrich***	N	N	?	Y	Y	Y	N	Y
7 Darden	Y	Y	Y	Y	Y	Y	N	Y
8 Rowland	Y	Y	Y	Y	Y	Y	Y	Y
9 Jenkins	Y	N	Y	Y	Y	Y	Y	Y
10 Barnard	Y	N	Y	Y	Y	Y	Y	Y
HAWAII								
1 Heftel	Y	Y	?	Y	Y	Y	Y	N
2 Akaka	Y	Y	Y	Y	Y	Y	Y	Y
IDAHO								
1 ***Craig***	N	N	Y	Y	N	N	N	N
2 Stallings	Y	N	Y	Y	Y	Y	Y	N
ILLINOIS								
1 Hayes	Y	N	Y	Y	Y	Y	Y	Y
2 Savage	?	N	Y	Y	Y	Y	Y	Y
3 Russo	Y	N	Y	Y	N	Y	Y	Y
4 ***O'Brien***	?	Y	?	?	?	?	Y	N
5 Lipinski	Y	N	Y	Y	Y	Y	Y	Y
6 ***Hyde***	Y	Y	Y	Y	Y	Y	Y	N
7 Collins	Y	N	Y	?	?	Y	Y	Y
8 Rostenkowski	Y	Y	Y	Y	Y	Y	Y	Y
9 Yates	Y	Y	Y	Y	Y	Y	Y	Y
10 ***Porter***	Y	N	Y	Y	N	Y	Y	N
11 Annunzio	Y	Y	Y	Y	Y	Y	Y	Y
12 ***Crane***	N	N	N	Y	N	N	N	N
13 ***Fawell***	N	N	Y	Y	N	Y	Y	N
14 ***Grotberg***	N	N	Y	Y	Y	Y	Y	N
15 ***Madigan***	N	N	?	?	?	Y	N	Y
16 ***Martin***	N	N	Y	Y	N	Y	N	N
17 Evans	Y	N	Y	Y	Y	Y	Y	Y
18 ***Michel***	N	Y	Y	N	Y	Y	Y	N
19 Bruce	Y	N	N	Y	N	Y	Y	Y
20 Durbin	N	N	Y	N	Y	Y	Y	Y
21 Price	?	?	?	?	?	?	?	?
22 Gray	Y	?	?	?	?	?	?	?
INDIANA								
1 Visclosky	Y	N	Y	Y	Y	Y	Y	N
2 Sharp	Y	N	Y	Y	Y	Y	Y	Y
3 ***Hiler***	N	Y	Y	Y	Y	Y	N	N
4 ***Coats***	Y	N	Y	Y	N	Y	Y	N
5 ***Hillis***	?	?	?	?	?	?	?	N

ND - Northern Democrats SD - Southern Democrats

* Corresponding to Congressional Record Votes 460, 461, 462, 463, 464, 465, 467, 468

	419	420	421	422	423	424	425	426
6 ***Burton***	N	Y	Y	Y	N	Y	N	N
7 ***Myers***	N	Y	Y	Y	Y	Y	N	Y
8 McCloskey	Y	N	Y	Y	Y	Y	Y	Y
9 Hamilton	Y	N	Y	Y	Y	Y	N	Y
10 Jacobs	N	N	N	Y	Y	Y	N	Y
IOWA								
1 ***Leach***	N	N	Y	Y	N	Y	Y	Y
2 ***Tauke***	N	N	?	Y	N	Y	N	Y
3 ***Evans***	N	N	?	?	?	Y	Y	N
4 Smith	Y	Y	Y	Y	Y	Y	Y	Y
5 ***Lightfoot***	N	N	Y	Y	N	Y	N	Y
6 Bedell	Y	N	Y	Y	N	Y	Y	Y
KANSAS								
1 ***Roberts***	N	N	Y	Y	N	Y	N	N
2 Slattery	Y	N	Y	Y	Y	Y	Y	N
3 ***Meyers***	N	N	Y	Y	Y	Y	Y	N
4 Glickman	Y	N	Y	Y	Y	Y	Y	N
5 ***Whittaker***	N	N	Y	Y	Y	Y	N	N
KENTUCKY								
1 Hubbard	?	N	Y	Y	N	Y	N	N
2 Natcher	Y	Y	Y	Y	Y	Y	Y	N
3 Mazzoli	Y	Y	Y	Y	Y	Y	N	Y
4 ***Snyder***	Y	N	Y	Y	Y	Y	Y	N
5 ***Rogers***	N	Y	N	Y	Y	Y	Y	N
6 ***Hopkins***	?	N	N	Y	N	Y	Y	N
7 Perkins	Y	N	Y	N	N	N	Y	Y
LOUISIANA								
1 ***Livingston***	Y	Y	Y	Y	?	Y	N	N
2 Boggs	Y	Y	Y	Y	Y	Y	Y	Y
3 Tauzin	N	N	Y	Y	Y	Y	N	Y
4 Roemer	N	N	Y	Y	Y	Y	N	Y
5 Huckaby	Y	N	Y	Y	Y	Y	N	Y
6 ***Moore***	Y	N	Y	Y	Y	Y	N	N
7 Breaux	Y	N	Y	Y	Y	Y	N	Y
8 Long	?	N	Y	Y	Y	Y	N	Y
MAINE								
1 ***McKernan***	N	N	Y	Y	Y	Y	Y	Y
2 ***Snowe***	N	N	Y	Y	Y	Y	Y	N
MARYLAND								
1 Dyson	?	N	?	Y	Y	Y	N	Y
2 ***Bentley***	N	N	Y	Y	N	Y	Y	N
3 Mikulski	?	Y	?	Y	Y	Y	N	Y
4 ***Holt***	N	Y	Y	Y	Y	Y	Y	N
5 Hoyer	Y	Y	Y	Y	Y	Y	N	Y
6 Byron	Y	Y	?	Y	Y	Y	Y	N
7 Mitchell	N	N	?	Y	?	Y	Y	Y
8 Barnes	?	Y	Y	Y	Y	Y	N	Y
MASSACHUSETTS								
1 ***Conte***	N	Y	Y	Y	?	Y	Y	Y
2 Boland	Y	Y	Y	Y	Y	Y	Y	+
3 Early	?	Y	Y	Y	Y	Y	Y	Y
4 Frank	Y	N	Y	Y	Y	Y	Y	Y
5 Atkins	?	Y	Y	Y	Y	Y	Y	N
6 Mavroules	Y	N	?	Y	Y	Y	Y	Y
7 Markey	Y	?	?	Y	Y	Y	Y	Y
8 O'Neill								
9 Moakley	?	?	Y	Y	Y	Y	Y	Y
10 Studds	Y	N	Y	Y	Y	Y	Y	Y
11 Donnelly	Y	N	Y	Y	Y	Y	Y	Y
MICHIGAN								
1 Conyers	Y	N	N	Y	Y	Y	N	Y
2 ***Pursell***	Y	N	?	Y	Y	Y	Y	Y
3 Wolpe	Y	Y	Y	Y	Y	Y	Y	Y
4 ***Siljander***	N	N	Y	Y	N	Y	N	N
5 ***Henry***	N	N	Y	Y	N	Y	Y	N
6 Carr	Y	Y	Y	Y	Y	Y	N	N
7 Kildee	Y	N	Y	Y	Y	Y	N	Y
8 Traxler	Y	N	?	Y	Y	Y	Y	Y
9 ***Vander Jagt***	N	?	N	Y	Y	Y	Y	N
10 ***Schuette***	N	N	?	Y	Y	Y	Y	N
11 ***Davis***	?	?	?	?	?	Y	Y	Y
12 Bonior	?	Y	Y	Y	Y	Y	Y	Y
13 Crockett	Y	X	Y	Y	Y	Y	Y	Y
14 Hertel	Y	N	Y	Y	N	Y	Y	Y
15 Ford	?	N	?	Y	Y	Y	Y	Y
16 Dingell	Y	Y	Y	Y	Y	Y	Y	Y
17 Levin	Y	N	Y	Y	Y	Y	Y	Y
18 ***Broomfield***	Y	N	?	Y	Y	Y	Y	Y
MINNESOTA								
1 Penny	N	N	Y	Y	Y	Y	Y	Y
2 ***Weber***	N	N	N	Y	N	?	N	N
3 ***Frenzel***	N	N	Y	Y	N	Y	N	N
4 Vento	Y	N	Y	Y	Y	Y	Y	Y
5 Sabo	Y	Y	Y	Y	Y	Y	Y	Y
6 Sikorski	N	N	Y	Y	Y	Y	Y	Y
7 ***Stangeland***	?	Y	Y	Y	Y	Y	Y	Y
8 Oberstar	Y	Y	Y	Y	Y	Y	Y	Y
MISSISSIPPI								
1 Whitten	Y	Y	Y	Y	Y	Y	Y	N
2 ***Franklin***	Y	N	Y	Y	N	Y	N	N
3 Montgomery	Y	Y	Y	Y	Y	Y	Y	N
4 Dowdy	?	Y	Y	Y	Y	Y	N	N
5 ***Lott***	N	?	Y	?	Y	Y	N	N
MISSOURI								
1 Clay	N	N	Y	Y	Y	Y	N	Y
2 Young	?	?	?	?	?	?	?	?
3 Gephardt	Y	Y	Y	Y	Y	Y	Y	Y
4 Skelton	Y	Y	Y	Y	Y	Y	N	Y
5 Wheat	Y	N	Y	Y	Y	Y	Y	Y
6 ***Coleman***	N	Y	N	Y	Y	Y	N	Y
7 ***Taylor***	Y	N	Y	Y	Y	Y	Y	N
8 ***Emerson***	N	N	Y	Y	Y	Y	N	N
9 Volkmer	Y	N	Y	Y	Y	Y	Y	N
MONTANA								
1 Williams	?	N	Y	Y	Y	Y	Y	Y
2 ***Marlenee***	N	N	Y	Y	N	N	N	N
NEBRASKA								
1 ***Bereuter***	N	N	Y	Y	Y	Y	N	Y
2 ***Daub***	N	Y	Y	Y	Y	Y	Y	N
3 ***Smith***	Y	Y	Y	Y	Y	Y	Y	N
NEVADA								
1 Reid	Y	Y	Y	Y	Y	Y	Y	Y
2 ***Vucanovich***	N	N	Y	Y	N	N	N	N
NEW HAMPSHIRE								
1 ***Smith***	N	N	N	Y	N	Y	N	N
2 ***Gregg***	?	N	Y	Y	N	Y	N	N
NEW JERSEY								
1 Florio	Y	N	Y	Y	Y	Y	Y	N
2 Hughes	Y	N	Y	Y	Y	Y	N	Y
3 Howard	Y	Y	Y	Y	Y	Y	Y	Y
4 ***Smith***	Y	N	Y	Y	Y	Y	N	N
5 ***Roukema***	N	N	Y	Y	Y	Y	Y	N
6 Dwyer	Y	Y	Y	Y	Y	Y	Y	Y
7 ***Rinaldo***	Y	N	Y	Y	Y	Y	N	Y
8 Roe	Y	N	Y	Y	Y	Y	N	Y
9 Torricelli	Y	Y	Y	Y	Y	Y	Y	Y
10 Rodino	?	N	Y	Y	Y	Y	Y	Y
11 ***Gallo***	N	N	Y	Y	Y	Y	N	N
12 ***Courter***	?	N	N	Y	Y	Y	Y	N
13 ***Saxton***	N	N	Y	Y	Y	Y	N	N
14 Guarini	?	N	Y	Y	Y	Y	Y	Y
NEW MEXICO								
1 ***Lujan***	Y	Y	Y	N	Y	Y	Y	N
2 ***Skeen***	N	Y	Y	Y	Y	Y	Y	N
3 Richardson	Y	N	Y	Y	Y	Y	Y	Y
NEW YORK								
1 ***Carney***	N	Y	Y	Y	Y	Y	Y	N
2 Downey	Y	Y	Y	Y	Y	Y	Y	Y
3 Mrazek	Y	Y	Y	Y	Y	Y	Y	Y
4 ***Lent***	N	?	Y	Y	Y	Y	Y	Y
5 ***McGrath***	?	Y	Y	Y	Y	Y	Y	N
6 Addabbo	?	?	?	?	?	Y	Y	Y
7 Ackerman	Y	Y	Y	Y	Y	Y	Y	Y
8 Scheuer	Y	Y	Y	Y	Y	Y	Y	Y
9 Manton	Y	Y	Y	Y	Y	Y	Y	Y
10 Schumer	Y	Y	Y	Y	Y	Y	Y	N
11 Towns	Y	N	Y	Y	Y	Y	Y	Y
12 Owens	?	N	Y	Y	Y	Y	Y	Y
13 Solarz	Y	Y	Y	Y	Y	Y	Y	Y
14 ***Molinari***	N	Y	Y	Y	Y	Y	N	N
15 ***Green***	Y	N	Y	Y	Y	Y	N	N
16 Rangel	Y	?	Y	Y	Y	Y	Y	Y
17 Weiss	?	Y	Y	Y	Y	Y	Y	Y
18 Garcia	Y	?	Y	Y	Y	Y	Y	Y
19 Biaggi	?	Y	Y	Y	Y	Y	Y	Y
20 ***DioGuardi***	?	Y	Y	Y	Y	Y	N	N
21 ***Fish***	Y	Y	Y	Y	Y	Y	N	N
22 ***Gilman***	Y	Y	Y	Y	Y	Y	Y	N
23 Stratton	Y	Y	Y	Y	Y	Y	Y	Y
24 ***Solomon***	N	N	Y	Y	N	Y	N	N
25 ***Boehlert***	N	Y	Y	Y	Y	Y	N	Y
26 ***Martin***	?	Y	Y	Y	?	Y	N	N
27 ***Wortley***	Y	N	Y	Y	Y	Y	N	Y
28 McHugh	Y	Y	Y	Y	Y	Y	Y	Y
29 ***Horton***	Y	Y	Y	Y	Y	Y	N	Y
30 ***Eckert***	Y	N	Y	Y	Y	Y	Y	N
31 ***Kemp***	Y	N	Y	Y	Y	Y	Y	N
32 LaFalce	Y	N	Y	Y	Y	Y	Y	Y
33 Nowak	Y	N	Y	Y	Y	Y	Y	Y
34 Lundine	?	N	Y	N	Y	Y	Y	Y
NORTH CAROLINA								
1 Jones	Y	Y	Y	Y	Y	Y	Y	Y
2 Valentine	Y	?	?	Y	Y	Y	N	N
3 Whitley	Y	Y	Y	Y	Y	Y	Y	Y
4 ***Cobey***	N	N	Y	Y	N	Y	N	N
5 Neal	?	N	?	Y	Y	Y	Y	Y
6 ***Coble***	N	N	N	Y	N	Y	N	N
7 Rose	Y	Y	?	Y	Y	Y	Y	Y
8 Hefner	Y	?	Y	Y	Y	Y	Y	Y
9 ***McMillan***	N	N	Y	Y	Y	Y	Y	N
10 ***Broyhill***	?	N	N	Y	?	Y	N	N
11 ***Hendon***	N	N	Y	Y	Y	Y	Y	N
NORTH DAKOTA								
AL Dorgan	Y	N	Y	Y	Y	Y	Y	N
OHIO								
1 Luken	Y	N	Y	Y	Y	Y	Y	Y
2 ***Gradison***	Y	N	Y	Y	Y	Y	Y	N
3 Hall	?	Y	Y	Y	Y	Y	Y	Y
4 ***Oxley***	N	N	Y	Y	Y	Y	N	Y
5 ***Latta***	N	Y	Y	Y	Y	Y	Y	N
6 ***McEwen***	Y	N	Y	Y	Y	Y	N	N
7 ***DeWine***	N	Y	Y	Y	Y	Y	Y	N
8 ***Kindness***	N	?	Y	Y	Y	Y	N	N
9 Kaptur	Y	N	Y	Y	?	Y	N	Y
10 ***Miller***	N	Y	Y	Y	Y	Y	Y	N
11 Eckart	Y	N	Y	Y	Y	Y	Y	Y
12 ***Kasich***	N	N	Y	Y	Y	Y	N	N
13 Pease	Y	N	Y	Y	Y	Y	Y	Y
14 Seiberling	P	N	?	Y	Y	Y	Y	Y
15 ***Wylie***	Y	Y	Y	Y	Y	Y	Y	N
16 ***Regula***	Y	Y	Y	Y	Y	Y	Y	Y
17 Traficant	Y	N	Y	Y	N	Y	N	Y
18 Applegate	?	N	Y	Y	Y	Y	N	Y
19 Feighan	?	N	Y	Y	Y	Y	N	Y
20 Oakar	Y	Y	Y	Y	Y	Y	N	Y
21 Stokes	Y	N	Y	Y	Y	Y	N	Y
OKLAHOMA								
1 Jones	Y	N	Y	Y	Y	Y	N	N
2 Synar	Y	N	Y	Y	Y	Y	Y	N
3 Watkins	Y	Y	Y	Y	Y	Y	N	N
4 McCurdy	Y	Y	Y	Y	Y	Y	N	N
5 ***Edwards***	N	N	?	Y	Y	Y	N	N
6 English	?	N	Y	Y	Y	Y	N	N
OREGON								
1 AuCoin	Y	Y	?	Y	Y	Y	N	N
2 ***Smith, R.***	N	Y	N	Y	Y	N	N	N
3 Wyden	Y	Y	Y	?	?	Y	N	Y
4 Weaver	Y	?	Y	Y	Y	N	Y	Y
5 ***Smith, D.***	N	N	N	N	N	Y	N	N
PENNSYLVANIA								
1 Foglietta	Y	Y	Y	Y	Y	Y	Y	Y
2 Gray	Y	Y	Y	Y	Y	Y	Y	Y
3 Borski	Y	Y	Y	Y	Y	Y	Y	Y
4 Kolter	Y	Y	Y	N	Y	Y	N	Y
5 ***Schulze***	Y	Y	Y	Y	Y	Y	N	N
6 Yatron	Y	N	Y	Y	Y	Y	Y	N
7 Edgar	Y	N	Y	Y	N	Y	Y	Y
8 Kostmayer	Y	Y	Y	Y	Y	Y	Y	Y
9 ***Shuster***	?	N	Y	Y	Y	Y	N	N
10 ***McDade***	Y	Y	Y	Y	Y	Y	Y	Y
11 Kanjorski	Y	Y	Y	Y	Y	Y	Y	Y
12 Murtha	Y	Y	Y	N	Y	Y	Y	N
13 ***Coughlin***	N	Y	N	Y	Y	Y	N	N
14 Coyne	Y	Y	Y	Y	Y	Y	Y	Y
15 ***Ritter***	Y	N	Y	Y	N	Y	Y	N
16 ***Walker***	N	N	Y	Y	N	Y	N	N
17 ***Gekas***	N	N	Y	Y	Y	Y	Y	N
18 Walgren	?	N	Y	Y	Y	Y	Y	Y
19 ***Goodling***	N	Y	Y	?	?	Y	Y	Y
20 Gaydos	Y	Y	Y	Y	Y	Y	N	Y
21 ***Ridge***	?	N	Y	Y	N	Y	N	Y
22 Murphy	Y	N	Y	Y	Y	Y	N	Y
23 ***Clinger***	+	Y	Y	Y	Y	Y	Y	N
RHODE ISLAND								
1 St Germain	?	N	Y	Y	Y	Y	Y	Y
2 ***Schneider***	Y	N	Y	Y	Y	Y	Y	N
SOUTH CAROLINA								
1 ***Hartnett***	?	N	N	Y	N	N	N	N
2 ***Spence***	?	Y	Y	Y	Y	Y	N	N
3 Derrick	Y	Y	Y	Y	Y	Y	Y	Y
4 ***Campbell***	?	N	?	Y	Y	Y	N	N
5 Spratt	Y	N	Y	Y	Y	Y	Y	Y
6 Tallon	Y	N	Y	Y	Y	Y	Y	Y
SOUTH DAKOTA								
AL Daschle	Y	N	Y	Y	Y	Y	Y	N
TENNESSEE								
1 ***Quillen***	Y	Y	Y	?	Y	N	Y	N
2 ***Duncan***	Y	Y	Y	Y	?	Y	Y	N
3 Lloyd	N	N	Y	Y	Y	Y	Y	N
4 Cooper	Y	N	Y	Y	Y	Y	Y	Y
5 Boner	Y	N	Y	Y	Y	Y	N	N
6 Gordon	Y	N	Y	Y	Y	Y	Y	N
7 ***Sundquist***	?	Y	Y	Y	Y	Y	N	N
8 Jones	Y	Y	Y	Y	Y	Y	Y	N
9 Ford	Y	Y	Y	Y	Y	Y	Y	Y
TEXAS								
1 Chapman	Y	N	Y	Y	Y	Y	N	N
2 Wilson	Y	Y	?	?	?	?	N	N
3 ***Bartlett***	N	N	Y	Y	Y	Y	N	N
4 Hall, R.	Y	N	Y	Y	N	Y	N	N
5 Bryant	Y	N	Y	Y	Y	Y	N	Y
6 ***Barton***	N	N	N	Y	N	Y	N	N
7 ***Archer***	Y	N	N	Y	Y	Y	N	N
8 ***Fields***	N	N	N	Y	N	N	N	N
9 Brooks	Y	?	Y	Y	Y	Y	N	Y
10 Pickle	Y	N	Y	Y	Y	Y	Y	N
11 Leath	Y	N	Y	Y	Y	Y	N	N
12 Wright	Y	Y	Y	Y	Y	Y	Y	Y
13 ***Boulter***	N	N	Y	Y	N	Y	N	N
14 ***Sweeney***	?	N	Y	Y	Y	Y	N	N
15 de la Garza	Y	Y	?	Y	Y	Y	Y	Y
16 Coleman	Y	Y	Y	Y	Y	Y	Y	Y
17 Stenholm	Y	N	Y	Y	N	Y	N	Y
18 Leland	Y	Y	+	Y	Y	Y	Y	Y
19 ***Combest***	Y	N	Y	Y	N	Y	N	N
20 Gonzalez	Y	Y	Y	P	Y	Y	Y	Y
21 ***Loeffler***	?	N	N	Y	Y	Y	N	N
22 ***DeLay***	N	N	?	Y	N	Y	N	N
23 Bustamante	Y	Y	Y	Y	Y	Y	N	N
24 Frost	Y	Y	Y	Y	Y	Y	P	N
25 Andrews	Y	Y	Y	Y	Y	Y	N	Y
26 ***Armey***	N	N	Y	Y	N	Y	N	N
27 Ortiz	?	Y	Y	Y	Y	Y	N	Y
UTAH								
1 ***Hansen***	?	N	Y	N	N	N	Y	N
2 ***Monson***	N	N	Y	N	N	Y	N	N
3 ***Nielson***	N	N	Y	N	N	Y	N	N
VERMONT								
AL ***Jeffords***	Y	N	Y	Y	Y	Y	N	Y
VIRGINIA								
1 ***Bateman***	Y	Y	Y	Y	Y	Y	Y	N
2 ***Whitehurst***	N	Y	Y	Y	Y	Y	Y	N
3 ***Bliley***	N	N	Y	Y	Y	Y	N	N
4 Sisisky	Y	Y	Y	Y	Y	Y	Y	N
5 Daniel	Y	Y	Y	Y	Y	Y	Y	N
6 Olin	Y	N	?	Y	Y	Y	Y	N
7 ***Slaughter***	N	N	Y	Y	Y	Y	N	N
8 ***Parris***	N	Y	Y	Y	Y	?	N	N
9 Boucher	Y	Y	Y	Y	Y	Y	Y	Y
10 ***Wolf***	N	Y	Y	Y	Y	Y	Y	N
WASHINGTON								
1 ***Miller***	Y	N	Y	Y	Y	Y	N	Y
2 Swift	Y	N	Y	Y	Y	Y	Y	Y
3 Bonker	P	Y	Y	Y	Y	Y	Y	Y
4 ***Morrison***	N	Y	Y	Y	Y	Y	N	N
5 Foley	Y	Y	Y	Y	Y	Y	Y	Y
6 Dicks	Y	Y	Y	Y	Y	Y	N	Y
7 Lowry	Y	N	Y	Y	Y	Y	Y	Y
8 ***Chandler***	N	Y	Y	Y	Y	Y	N	N
WEST VIRGINIA								
1 Mollohan	Y	N	Y	N	Y	Y	Y	Y
2 Staggers	Y	N	Y	N	Y	Y	Y	Y
3 Wise	Y	N	Y	N	Y	Y	Y	Y
4 Rahall	Y	N	N	N	Y	Y	Y	Y
WISCONSIN								
1 Aspin	Y	?	?	?	Y	Y	Y	Y
2 Kastenmeier	Y	N	Y	Y	Y	Y	Y	Y
3 ***Gunderson***	N	N	?	Y	Y	Y	Y	N
4 Kleczka	Y	N	N	Y	Y	Y	Y	Y
5 Moody	Y	N	Y	Y	Y	Y	Y	Y
6 ***Petri***	Y	N	N	Y	Y	Y	Y	Y
7 Obey	P	Y	Y	Y	Y	Y	Y	N
8 ***Roth***	N	?	Y	Y	Y	Y	N	N
9 ***Sensenbrenner***	N	N	Y	Y	N	Y	N	Y
WYOMING								
AL ***Cheney***	N	Y	Y	Y	N	N	N	N

Southern states - Ala., Ark., Fla., Ga., Ky., La., Miss., N.C., Okla., S.C., Tenn., Texas, Va.

* The *Congressional Record* vote number is different from the CQ vote number because the *Record* includes quorum calls in its tally. CQ does not publish quorum call votes.

427. HR 3838. Tax Overhaul. Duncan, R-Tenn., substitute to revise the federal income tax system by: lowering individual and corporate tax rates; increasing the personal exemption and standard deduction; eliminating or curtailing a variety of other deductions and credits; creating a new alternative minimum tax and a "superminimum" tax for individuals and corporations; and making other changes. Rejected 133-294: R 127-54; D 6-240 (ND 1-164, SD 5-76), Dec. 17, 1985.

428. HR 3838. Tax Overhaul. Crane, R-Ill., motion to recommit to the Ways and Means Committee (thus killing) the bill to revise the federal income tax system by: lowering individual and corporate tax rates; increasing the personal exemption and standard deduction; eliminating the investment tax credit; eliminating or curtailing a variety of other deductions and credits; creating a new alternative minimum tax for individuals and corporations; and making other changes. Motion rejected 171-256: R 132-49; D 39-207 (ND 6-159, SD 33-48), Dec. 17, 1985. (The bill subsequently was passed by voice vote.) A "nay" was a vote supporting the president's position.

429. Procedural Motion. Bliley, R-Va., motion to approve the House *Journal* of Tuesday, Dec. 17. Motion agreed to 228-143: R 37-129; D 191-14 (ND 128-7, SD 63-7), Dec. 18, 1985.

430. H Res 345. Military Plane Crash Victims. Adoption of the resolution to express the sentiment of Congress regarding the deaths of members of the 101st Air Assault Division in the Dec. 12 airplane crash at Gander, Newfoundland, Canada. Adopted 401-0: R 168-0; D 233-0 (ND 156-0, SD 77-0), Dec. 18, 1985.

431. HR 2100. Farm Programs Reauthorization, Fiscal 1986-90. Adoption of the conference report on the bill to revise agriculture programs and extend them through fiscal year 1990; to modify price supports by reducing loan rates in 1986 and thereafter; to maintain income supports by freezing target prices at fiscal 1985 levels through fiscal 1987 and reduce them by a total of 10 percent over the remaining three years of the bill; to provide for agricultural export, soil conservation, farm credit and agricultural research programs; and to continue food assistance to low-income persons through fiscal 1990. Adopted 325-96: R 131-47; D 194-49 (ND 123-40, SD 71-9), Dec. 18, 1985.

432. Procedural Motion. Solarz, D-N.Y., motion to approve the House *Journal* of Wednesday, Dec. 18. Motion agreed to 241-130: R 49-118; D 192-12 (ND 128-7, SD 64-5), Dec. 19, 1985.

433. H J Res 465. Further Continuing Appropriations, Fiscal 1986. Adoption of the conference report on the joint resolution to provide $368,164,465,261 in fiscal 1986 for government agencies whose regular appropriations had not become law. Adopted 261-137: R 87-87; D 174-50 (ND 111-39, SD 63-11), Dec. 19, 1985. (The president had requested $386,573,805,503 in new budget authority.)

434. HR 3128. Omnibus Budget Reconciliation, Fiscal 1986. Adoption of the rule (H Res 342) to provide for consideration of a resolution reported by the Rules Committee to provide for the consideration of the conference report on the bill to reduce the deficit by $74 billion over fiscal 1986-88 through spending cuts and added revenues. Adopted 239-136: R 48-119; D 191-17 (ND 123-17, SD 68-0), Dec. 19, 1985.

KEY

- Y Voted for (yea).
- # Paired for.
- + Announced for.
- N Voted against (nay).
- X Paired against.
- \- Announced against.
- P Voted "present."
- C Voted "present" to avoid possible conflict of interest.
- ? Did not vote or otherwise make a position known.

Democrats ***Republicans***

	427	428	429	430	431	432	433	434
ALABAMA								
1 ***Callahan***	Y	Y	Y	Y	Y	Y	Y	N
2 ***Dickinson***	Y	Y	N	Y	Y	N	Y	Y
3 Nichols	N	N	Y	Y	?	?	X	?
4 Bevill	N	N	Y	Y	Y	Y	Y	Y
5 Flippo	N	N	N	Y	Y	N	Y	?
6 Erdreich	Y	N	Y	Y	Y	?	Y	Y
7 Shelby	N	Y	Y	Y	Y	Y	Y	Y
ALASKA								
AL ***Young***	Y	Y	?	Y	Y	N	Y	Y
ARIZONA								
1 ***McCain***	Y	Y	N	Y	Y	N	N	N
2 Udall	N	N	?	?	Y	Y	Y	Y
3 ***Stump***	Y	Y	N	Y	N	N	N	Y
4 ***Rudd***	Y	Y	?	?	Y	Y	Y	Y
5 ***Kolbe***	Y	Y	N	Y	Y	N	N	Y
ARKANSAS								
1 Alexander	N	Y	Y	Y	N	Y	Y	Y
2 Robinson	N	N	Y	Y	Y	Y	Y	Y
3 ***Hammerschmidt***	N	Y	N	Y	Y	Y	Y	N
4 Anthony	N	N	Y	Y	Y	Y	Y	Y
CALIFORNIA								
1 Bosco	N	N	?	Y	Y	Y	Y	Y
2 ***Chappie***	Y	Y	N	Y	Y	N	N	N
3 Matsui	N	N	Y	Y	Y	Y	Y	Y
4 Fazio	N	N	Y	Y	Y	Y	Y	Y
5 Burton	N	N	?	Y	Y	?	Y	Y
6 Boxer	N	N	Y	Y	Y	Y	Y	Y
7 Miller	N	N	?	Y	N	Y	Y	Y
8 Dellums	N	N	Y	Y	Y	Y	N	Y
9 Stark	N	N	?	Y	N	Y	N	Y
10 Edwards	N	N	Y	Y	Y	Y	Y	?
11 Lantos	N	N	Y	Y	Y	Y	N	Y
12 ***Zschau***	Y	Y	N	Y	N	N	N	N
13 Mineta	N	N	Y	+	Y	Y	Y	Y
14 ***Shumway***	N	Y	Y	Y	Y	Y	-	N
15 Coelho	N	N	Y	Y	Y	Y	Y	Y
16 Panetta	N	N	Y	Y	Y	Y	Y	Y
17 ***Pashayan***	Y	Y	N	Y	Y	N	Y	N
18 Lehman	N	N	Y	Y	Y	?	?	?
19 ***Lagomarsino***	Y	N	N	Y	N	N	N	Y
20 ***Thomas***	Y	Y	N	Y	Y	N	N	Y
21 ***Fiedler***	N	Y	N	Y	Y	N	N	N
22 ***Moorhead***	Y	Y	N	Y	N	N	N	N
23 Beilenson	N	N	Y	Y	Y	Y	Y	Y
24 Waxman	N	N	Y	Y	Y	?	Y	Y
25 Roybal	N	N	Y	Y	Y	Y	Y	?
26 Berman	N	N	Y	Y	Y	Y	Y	Y
27 Levine	N	N	Y	Y	N	Y	Y	Y
28 Dixon	N	N	Y	Y	Y	Y	Y	?
29 Hawkins	N	N	?	Y	Y	Y	Y	Y
30 Martinez	N	N	Y	Y	?	?	?	?
31 Dymally	?	?	?	?	?	P	N	Y
32 Anderson	N	N	Y	Y	N	Y	N	Y
33 ***Dreier***	N	Y	N	Y	N	N	N	N
34 Torres	N	N	Y	Y	Y	Y	Y	Y
35 ***Lewis***	Y	Y	N	?	N	N	N	N
36 Brown	N	N	Y	Y	Y	?	Y	Y
37 ***McCandless***	Y	Y	N	Y	Y	N	N	N
38 ***Dornan***	Y	N	N	Y	N	Y	N	N
39 ***Dannemeyer***	N	Y	N	Y	N	N	N	N
40 ***Badham***	Y	Y	?	?	?	N	Y	N
41 ***Lowery***	Y	Y	?	Y	Y	?	Y	Y
42 ***Lungren***	Y	Y	N	Y	N	N	N	Y
43 ***Packard***	Y	Y	N	Y	N	?	Y	N
44 Bates	N	N	Y	Y	N	Y	N	Y
45 ***Hunter***	Y	Y	Y	Y	N	N	N	Y
COLORADO								
1 Schroeder	N	N	N	Y	N	N	N	Y
2 Wirth	N	Y	Y	Y	N	?	?	?
3 ***Strang***	Y	Y	N	Y	Y	N	N	N
4 ***Brown***	N	Y	N	Y	Y	N	N	N
5 ***Kramer***	N	Y	N	Y	Y	N	N	N
6 ***Schaefer***	Y	Y	N	Y	N	N	Y	N
CONNECTICUT								
1 Kennelly	N	N	Y	Y	Y	Y	Y	Y
2 Gejdenson	N	N	Y	Y	Y	Y	Y	Y
3 Morrison	N	N	Y	Y	Y	Y	N	Y
4 ***McKinney***	?	?	?	?	?	?	?	?
5 ***Rowland***	Y	N	N	Y	Y	N	Y	N
6 ***Johnson***	Y	N	Y	Y	Y	Y	Y	Y
DELAWARE								
AL Carper	Y	N	Y	Y	Y	Y	Y	Y
FLORIDA								
1 Hutto	N	Y	?	Y	Y	Y	Y	Y
2 Fuqua	N	N	Y	Y	Y	?	?	?
3 Bennett	N	N	Y	Y	Y	Y	Y	Y
4 Chappell	N	N	Y	Y	Y	?	Y	Y
5 ***McCollum***	Y	Y	N	Y	N	N	Y	N
6 MacKay	N	N	Y	Y	Y	Y	Y	Y
7 Gibbons	N	N	?	Y	N	Y	Y	Y
8 ***Young***	Y	N	N	Y	Y	N	N	N
9 ***Bilirakis***	Y	Y	N	Y	Y	N	N	N
10 ***Ireland***	Y	N	N	Y	N	N	Y	N
11 Nelson	-	-	+	+	X	+	#	Y
12 ***Lewis***	Y	Y	N	+	Y	N	N	Y
13 ***Mack***	N	Y	N	?	N	N	N	N
14 Mica	N	N	Y	Y	Y	Y	Y	Y
15 ***Shaw***	Y	Y	N	Y	Y	N	Y	N
16 Smith	N	N	Y	Y	Y	Y	Y	Y
17 Lehman	N	N	Y	?	Y	Y	Y	?
18 Pepper	N	N	Y	Y	Y	Y	Y	Y
19 Fascell	N	N	Y	Y	Y	Y	Y	Y
GEORGIA								
1 Thomas	N	N	Y	Y	Y	Y	Y	Y
2 Hatcher	N	N	Y	Y	Y	Y	Y	Y
3 Ray	N	Y	Y	Y	Y	Y	N	Y
4 ***Swindall***	Y	Y	N	Y	Y	N	N	N
5 Fowler	N	N	Y	Y	Y	Y	Y	Y
6 ***Gingrich***	N	Y	N	Y	Y	N	Y	N
7 Darden	N	N	Y	Y	Y	Y	Y	Y
8 Rowland	N	N	Y	Y	Y	Y	Y	Y
9 Jenkins	N	N	Y	Y	Y	Y	Y	Y
10 Barnard	N	N	Y	Y	Y	Y	Y	?
HAWAII								
1 Heftel	N	N	?	?	?	?	?	?
2 Akaka	N	N	Y	Y	Y	Y	Y	Y
IDAHO								
1 ***Craig***	Y	Y	N	Y	Y	Y	N	N
2 Stallings	N	N	Y	Y	Y	Y	N	N
ILLINOIS								
1 Hayes	N	N	Y	Y	Y	Y	N	Y
2 Savage	N	N	Y	?	Y	Y	N	Y
3 Russo	N	N	Y	Y	N	?	X	?
4 ***O'Brien***	Y	Y	?	?	Y	?	Y	Y
5 Lipinski	N	N	Y	Y	N	?	?	?
6 ***Hyde***	Y	N	Y	Y	Y	N	N	Y
7 Collins	N	N	Y	Y	Y	Y	Y	Y
8 Rostenkowski	N	N	?	?	N	Y	Y	Y
9 Yates	N	N	Y	Y	N	Y	Y	Y
10 ***Porter***	Y	N	Y	Y	N	Y	N	N
11 Annunzio	N	N	Y	Y	Y	Y	Y	Y
12 ***Crane***	Y	Y	N	Y	N	N	N	N
13 ***Fawell***	Y	Y	?	Y	N	N	N	Y
14 ***Grotberg***	Y	Y	N	Y	Y	N	N	Y
15 ***Madigan***	N	Y	Y	Y	Y	?	Y	Y
16 ***Martin***	Y	Y	?	Y	Y	N	N	N
17 Evans	N	N	Y	Y	N	Y	Y	Y
18 ***Michel***	Y	N	N	Y	Y	N	Y	N
19 Bruce	N	N	Y	Y	Y	Y	N	Y
20 Durbin	N	N	Y	Y	Y	N	Y	Y
21 Price	?	?	?	?	?	?	?	?
22 Gray	?	?	?	?	#	?	#	?
INDIANA								
1 Visclosky	N	N	Y	Y	Y	Y	N	Y
2 Sharp	N	N	Y	Y	Y	?	?	?
3 ***Hiler***	Y	Y	N	Y	Y	N	Y	N
4 ***Coats***	Y	Y	N	Y	Y	N	N	N
5 ***Hillis***	Y	Y	Y	Y	?	Y	Y	?

ND - Northern Democrats SD - Southern Democrats

	427	428	429	430	431	432	433	434
6 ***Burton***	Y	Y	N	Y	Y	N	N	N
7 ***Myers***	Y	Y	Y	Y	Y	Y	Y	N
8 McCloskey	N	N	Y	Y	Y	Y	Y	Y
9 Hamilton	N	N	Y	Y	Y	Y	N	Y
10 Jacobs	N	N	N	Y	N	N	N	Y
IOWA								
1 ***Leach***	N	N	?	Y	Y	N	N	N
2 ***Tauke***	N	Y	N	Y	Y	N	N	N
3 ***Evans***	N	N	N	Y	Y	N	N	N
4 Smith	N	N	Y	Y	Y	Y	Y	N
5 ***Lightfoot***	N	N	N	Y	Y	N	N	N
6 Bedell	N	N	Y	Y	N	Y	N	Y
KANSAS								
1 ***Roberts***	Y	Y	N	Y	Y	N	N	?
2 Slattery	N	N	Y	Y	N	?	N	Y
3 ***Meyers***	Y	N	Y	Y	Y	N	N	Y
4 Glickman	N	N	Y	Y	N	Y	N	Y
5 ***Whittaker***	Y	Y	N	Y	Y	N	N	Y
KENTUCKY								
1 Hubbard	N	Y	Y	Y	Y	Y	N	Y
2 Natcher	N	N	Y	Y	Y	Y	Y	Y
3 Mazzoli	N	N	Y	Y	Y	Y	Y	Y
4 ***Snyder***	Y	N	Y	Y	N	Y	N	Y
5 ***Rogers***	Y	Y	N	Y	Y	N	Y	Y
6 ***Hopkins***	Y	Y	Y	Y	Y	Y	N	Y
7 Perkins	N	N	Y	Y	Y	Y	Y	Y
LOUISIANA								
1 ***Livingston***	Y	Y	N	Y	Y	Y	Y	Y
2 Boggs	N	Y	Y	Y	Y	?	Y	Y
3 Tauzin	Y	Y	N	Y	Y	Y	Y	Y
4 Roemer	Y	Y	N	Y	Y	N	Y	Y
5 Huckaby	N	Y	Y	Y	Y	Y	Y	Y
6 ***Moore***	Y	Y	Y	Y	Y	Y	Y	Y
7 Breaux	N	Y	Y	Y	Y	Y	Y	Y
8 Long	N	Y	Y	Y	Y	Y	Y	Y
MAINE								
1 ***McKernan***	Y	N	N	Y	Y	N	Y	N
2 ***Snowe***	N	N	N	Y	Y	N	Y	N
MARYLAND								
1 Dyson	N	N	Y	Y	Y	Y	N	N
2 ***Bentley***	Y	Y	N	Y	Y	N	N	N
3 Mikulski	N	N	Y	Y	Y	?	Y	Y
4 ***Holt***	Y	Y	N	Y	N	N	Y	Y
5 Hoyer	N	N	Y	Y	Y	Y	Y	Y
6 Byron	N	N	Y	Y	Y	?	Y	?
7 Mitchell	N	N	?	?	Y	N	N	Y
8 Barnes	N	N	Y	Y	Y	Y	Y	Y
MASSACHUSETTS								
1 ***Conte***	N	N	N	Y	Y	N	Y	Y
2 Boland	N	N	Y	Y	Y	Y	Y	?
3 Early	N	N	Y	Y	Y	?	?	?
4 Frank	N	N	Y	Y	N	Y	Y	Y
5 Atkins	N	N	?	Y	Y	Y	Y	Y
6 Mavroules	N	N	?	Y	Y	?	Y	Y
7 Markey	N	N	?	Y	N	Y	Y	Y
8 O'Neill								
9 Moakley	N	N	Y	Y	Y	Y	Y	Y
10 Studds	N	N	Y	Y	Y	Y	Y	Y
11 Donnelly	N	N	Y	Y	Y	Y	Y	Y
MICHIGAN								
1 Conyers	N	N	Y	Y	N	Y	Y	?
2 ***Pursell***	Y	Y	Y	Y	Y	Y	Y	N
3 Wolpe	N	N	Y	Y	Y	Y	Y	N
4 ***Siljander***	Y	Y	N	Y	Y	N	N	N
5 ***Henry***	Y	N	N	Y	Y	N	N	N
6 Carr	N	Y	Y	Y	Y	Y	Y	Y
7 Kildee	N	N	Y	Y	Y	Y	Y	Y
8 Traxler	N	N	?	Y	Y	?	Y	?
9 ***Vander Jagt***	Y	N	Y	Y	Y	N	Y	Y
10 ***Schuette***	Y	N	N	Y	Y	N	N	N
11 ***Davis***	N	N	N	Y	Y	N	Y	Y
12 Bonior	N	N	Y	Y	Y	Y	Y	Y
13 Crockett	N	N	?	?	Y	Y	P	?
14 Hertel	N	N	Y	Y	N	Y	N	N
15 Ford	N	N	?	Y	Y	?	?	?
16 Dingell	N	N	Y	Y	Y	Y	Y	Y
17 Levin	N	N	Y	Y	N	Y	Y	Y
18 ***Broomfield***	Y	N	Y	Y	Y	?	?	?
MINNESOTA								
1 Penny	N	N	N	Y	N	N	N	N
2 ***Weber***	N	Y	N	Y	N	N	N	N
3 ***Frenzel***	Y	Y	N	?	Y	N	N	N
4 Vento	N	N	Y	Y	N	Y	Y	Y
5 Sabo	N	N	Y	Y	N	Y	Y	Y
6 Sikorski	N	N	N	Y	N	N	Y	Y
7 ***Stangeland***	Y	N	N	Y	Y	N	Y	N
8 Oberstar	N	N	?	Y	N	Y	Y	Y
MISSISSIPPI								
1 Whitten	N	N	Y	Y	Y	Y	Y	?
2 ***Franklin***	N	Y	N	Y	Y	N	N	N
3 Montgomery	N	Y	Y	Y	Y	Y	Y	?
4 Dowdy	N	Y	Y	Y	Y	?	?	?
5 ***Lott***	Y	Y	N	Y	Y	N	Y	N
MISSOURI								
1 Clay	N	N	N	Y	Y	N	Y	Y
2 Young	?	?	?	?	?	?	?	?
3 Gephardt	N	N	?	?	?	Y	Y	Y
4 Skelton	N	N	Y	Y	Y	Y	Y	N
5 Wheat	N	N	Y	Y	Y	Y	Y	Y
6 ***Coleman***	Y	Y	N	Y	N	N	Y	N
7 ***Taylor***	Y	N	N	Y	Y	N	Y	N
8 ***Emerson***	Y	Y	N	Y	Y	N	Y	N
9 Volkmer	N	N	Y	Y	N	Y	Y	N
MONTANA								
1 Williams	N	N	?	Y	N	Y	N	Y
2 ***Marlenee***	Y	Y	N	Y	Y	?	?	?
NEBRASKA								
1 ***Bereuter***	Y	N	N	Y	Y	N	Y	N
2 ***Daub***	Y	N	N	Y	Y	N	Y	Y
3 ***Smith***	Y	N	Y	Y	Y	Y	Y	Y
NEVADA								
1 Reid	N	N	Y	Y	Y	Y	Y	N
2 ***Vucanovich***	N	Y	N	Y	N	Y	N	N
NEW HAMPSHIRE								
1 ***Smith***	Y	Y	N	Y	N	N	N	N
2 ***Gregg***	Y	Y	N	?	N	N	?	?
NEW JERSEY								
1 Florio	N	N	Y	Y	Y	?	?	?
2 Hughes	N	N	Y	Y	Y	Y	N	Y
3 Howard	N	N	Y	Y	Y	Y	Y	?
4 ***Smith***	N	N	N	Y	Y	Y	N	Y
5 ***Roukema***	N	N	N	Y	Y	N	Y	N
6 Dwyer	N	N	Y	Y	Y	Y	Y	Y
7 ***Rinaldo***	N	N	Y	Y	Y	Y	Y	Y
8 Roe	N	N	Y	Y	Y	Y	Y	Y
9 Torricelli	N	N	Y	Y	Y	Y	Y	Y
10 Rodino	N	N	Y	Y	Y	Y	Y	Y
11 ***Gallo***	N	Y	N	Y	Y	N	Y	N
12 ***Courter***	Y	N	N	Y	Y	N	Y	Y
13 ***Saxton***	N	Y	N	Y	Y	N	Y	N
14 Guarini	N	N	?	Y	Y	Y	Y	Y
NEW MEXICO								
1 ***Lujan***	Y	N	Y	Y	Y	Y	Y	Y
2 ***Skeen***	Y	Y	N	Y	Y	N	Y	Y
3 Richardson	N	N	Y	Y	Y	?	?	?
NEW YORK								
1 ***Carney***	N	Y	N	Y	N	N	Y	N
2 Downey	N	N	Y	Y	N	Y	Y	N
3 Mrazek	N	N	Y	Y	N	Y	Y	Y
4 ***Lent***	N	N	N	Y	N	N	Y	N
5 ***McGrath***	N	N	N	?	?	?	?	?
6 Addabbo	N	N	Y	Y	Y	Y	Y	?
7 Ackerman	N	N	Y	Y	Y	?	Y	?
8 Scheuer	N	N	Y	Y	Y	Y	N	Y
9 Manton	N	N	Y	Y	Y	Y	Y	Y
10 Schumer	N	N	Y	Y	N	Y	Y	Y
11 Towns	N	N	Y	Y	Y	Y	N	Y
12 Owens	N	N	?	?	Y	?	N	Y
13 Solarz	N	N	Y	Y	Y	Y	Y	Y
14 ***Molinari***	N	Y	N	Y	Y	Y	Y	N
15 ***Green***	N	Y	Y	Y	N	Y	Y	Y
16 Rangel	N	N	?	Y	Y	Y	Y	Y
17 Weiss	N	N	Y	Y	Y	Y	Y	Y
18 Garcia	N	N	Y	Y	Y	?	?	Y
19 Biaggi	N	N	Y	Y	Y	?	?	?
20 ***DioGuardi***	N	Y	N	Y	N	Y	Y	Y
21 ***Fish***	N	Y	Y	Y	Y	Y	Y	N
22 ***Gilman***	N	Y	Y	Y	Y	Y	Y	N
23 Stratton	N	N	N	Y	Y	Y	Y	Y
24 ***Solomon***	N	Y	N	Y	Y	N	N	N
25 ***Boehlert***	N	Y	N	Y	Y	N	Y	N
26 ***Martin***	N	Y	N	Y	Y	N	Y	N
27 ***Wortley***	N	Y	N	Y	Y	Y	Y	Y
28 McHugh	N	N	Y	Y	Y	Y	Y	Y
29 ***Horton***	N	Y	Y	Y	Y	Y	Y	?
30 ***Eckert***	N	Y	?	Y	Y	Y	Y	N
31 ***Kemp***	Y	N	?	?	Y	Y	N	N
32 LaFalce	N	N	Y	Y	Y	?	X	?
33 Nowak	N	N	Y	Y	N	Y	Y	Y
34 Lundine	N	N	Y	Y	Y	Y	Y	Y
NORTH CAROLINA								
1 Jones	N	N	?	Y	Y	?	Y	Y
2 Valentine	N	N	Y	Y	Y	Y	Y	Y
3 Whitley	N	N	Y	Y	Y	Y	Y	Y
4 ***Cobey***	Y	Y	N	Y	Y	N	N	N
5 Neal	N	N	?	Y	Y	Y	N	Y
6 ***Coble***	Y	Y	N	Y	Y	N	N	N
7 Rose	N	N	?	?	Y	Y	N	Y
8 Hefner	N	N	Y	Y	Y	Y	Y	Y
9 ***McMillan***	Y	Y	N	Y	Y	Y	N	N
10 ***Broyhill***	Y	Y	Y	Y	Y	Y	N	N
11 ***Hendon***	Y	Y	N	Y	Y	N	N	N
NORTH DAKOTA								
AL Dorgan	N	N	Y	Y	N	Y	N	Y
OHIO								
1 Luken	N	N	Y	Y	N	Y	Y	Y
2 ***Gradison***	Y	N	Y	Y	N	Y	Y	Y
3 Hall	N	Y	N	Y	Y	?	Y	Y
4 ***Oxley***	Y	Y	N	Y	Y	N	Y	N
5 ***Latta***	Y	N	N	Y	Y	N	N	Y
6 ***McEwen***	Y	N	Y	Y	Y	Y	N	?
7 ***DeWine***	Y	N	N	Y	Y	N	N	N
8 ***Kindness***	Y	Y	?	Y	Y	?	?	?
9 Kaptur	N	N	Y	Y	Y	Y	#	?
10 ***Miller***	Y	Y	N	Y	Y	?	Y	N
11 Eckart	N	N	Y	Y	Y	Y	N	Y
12 ***Kasich***	Y	Y	N	Y	Y	N	N	N
13 Pease	N	N	Y	Y	Y	Y	Y	Y
14 Seiberling	N	N	?	Y	Y	?	N	Y
15 ***Wylie***	Y	N	Y	Y	Y	Y	Y	N
16 ***Regula***	Y	N	Y	Y	Y	Y	Y	N
17 Traficant	N	N	Y	Y	Y	Y	N	N
18 Applegate	N	Y	P	Y	Y	Y	Y	N
19 Feighan	N	N	Y	Y	Y	Y	N	Y
20 Oakar	N	N	Y	Y	Y	Y	Y	Y
21 Stokes	N	N	Y	Y	Y	Y	Y	Y
OKLAHOMA								
1 Jones	N	Y	Y	Y	N	Y	N	Y
2 Synar	N	Y	Y	Y	N	Y	N	Y
3 Watkins	N	Y	N	Y	N	Y	?	?
4 McCurdy	N	Y	?	Y	N	Y	N	Y
5 ***Edwards***	Y	Y	N	Y	N	N	N	?
6 English	N	Y	Y	Y	N	Y	N	Y
OREGON								
1 AuCoin	N	Y	?	?	Y	Y	Y	Y
2 ***Smith, R.***	N	Y	N	Y	Y	N	Y	N
3 Wyden	N	Y	Y	Y	N	Y	Y	Y
4 Weaver	N	N	?	Y	Y	?	?	?
5 ***Smith, D.***	N	Y	N	Y	Y	N	N	N
PENNSYLVANIA								
1 Foglietta	N	N	Y	Y	Y	Y	Y	Y
2 Gray	N	N	Y	Y	Y	Y	Y	Y
3 Borski	N	N	Y	Y	Y	Y	Y	Y
4 Kolter	N	N	Y	Y	Y	Y	Y	Y
5 ***Schulze***	Y	Y	Y	Y	Y	Y	Y	N
6 Yatron	N	N	Y	Y	Y	Y	N	Y
7 Edgar	N	N	Y	Y	Y	Y	N	N
8 Kostmayer	N	N	Y	Y	Y	Y	Y	Y
9 ***Shuster***	Y	Y	Y	Y	Y	Y	N	N
10 ***McDade***	Y	N	Y	Y	Y	Y	Y	Y
11 Kanjorski	N	N	Y	Y	Y	Y	Y	Y
12 Murtha	N	N	Y	Y	Y	Y	Y	Y
13 ***Coughlin***	Y	Y	N	Y	N	N	Y	N
14 Coyne	N	N	Y	Y	Y	Y	Y	Y
15 ***Ritter***	Y	Y	?	?	N	P	N	Y
16 ***Walker***	N	Y	N	Y	Y	N	N	N
17 ***Gekas***	Y	N	N	Y	Y	N	N	N
18 Walgren	N	N	?	Y	Y	Y	Y	N
19 ***Goodling***	Y	N	P	Y	Y	N	Y	N
20 Gaydos	N	N	Y	Y	Y	Y	Y	Y
21 ***Ridge***	N	Y	N	Y	Y	N	N	Y
22 Murphy	N	N	Y	Y	N	Y	Y	Y
23 ***Clinger***	Y	N	Y	Y	Y	N	Y	Y
RHODE ISLAND								
1 St Germain	?	?	Y	Y	Y	Y	N	Y
2 ***Schneider***	N	N	Y	Y	N	Y	Y	N
SOUTH CAROLINA								
1 ***Hartnett***	Y	Y	N	Y	Y	Y	N	N
2 ***Spence***	Y	Y	N	Y	Y	N	N	N
3 Derrick	N	N	Y	Y	Y	Y	Y	Y
4 ***Campbell***	Y	Y	?	?	Y	N	N	Y
5 Spratt	N	N	Y	Y	Y	Y	Y	Y
6 Tallon	N	Y	Y	Y	Y	Y	N	Y
SOUTH DAKOTA								
AL Daschle	N	N	Y	Y	N	Y	N	Y
TENNESSEE								
1 ***Quillen***	Y	N	N	Y	Y	Y	Y	?
2 ***Duncan***	Y	Y	Y	Y	Y	Y	Y	Y
3 Lloyd	N	Y	N	Y	Y	N	N	Y
4 Cooper	N	N	Y	Y	Y	Y	Y	Y
5 Boner	N	N	Y	Y	Y	Y	Y	Y
6 Gordon	N	N	Y	Y	Y	?	?	?
7 ***Sundquist***	Y	Y	N	Y	Y	N	Y	N
8 Jones	N	N	Y	Y	Y	Y	Y	Y
9 Ford	N	N	?	?	Y	Y	Y	+
TEXAS								
1 Chapman	N	Y	Y	Y	Y	?	?	?
2 Wilson	N	Y	?	Y	Y	?	Y	Y
3 ***Bartlett***	Y	Y	N	Y	N	N	N	N
4 Hall, R.	Y	Y	N	Y	N	Y	N	Y
5 Bryant	Y	Y	Y	Y	N	Y	Y	Y
6 ***Barton***	Y	Y	N	Y	Y	N	N	Y
7 ***Archer***	Y	Y	N	Y	N	Y	N	N
8 ***Fields***	Y	Y	?	Y	N	N	N	Y
9 Brooks	N	Y	Y	Y	Y	Y	Y	Y
10 Pickle	N	N	?	Y	Y	Y	Y	Y
11 Leath	N	Y	?	Y	Y	Y	Y	Y
12 Wright	N	Y	Y	Y	Y	Y	Y	Y
13 ***Boulter***	Y	Y	N	Y	Y	N	N	N
14 ***Sweeney***	N	Y	N	Y	Y	Y	N	N
15 de la Garza	N	Y	Y	Y	Y	Y	Y	Y
16 Coleman	N	Y	Y	Y	Y	Y	Y	Y
17 Stenholm	N	Y	N	Y	Y	N	Y	Y
18 Leland	N	N	Y	Y	Y	?	Y	Y
19 ***Combest***	Y	Y	N	Y	Y	Y	N	N
20 Gonzalez	N	N	Y	Y	Y	Y	Y	P
21 ***Loeffler***	N	Y	N	Y	Y	N	N	N
22 ***DeLay***	N	Y	N	Y	N	?	N	N
23 Bustamante	N	N	Y	Y	Y	Y	Y	Y
24 Frost	N	Y	?	?	Y	Y	Y	Y
25 Andrews	N	Y	Y	Y	Y	Y	Y	Y
26 ***Armey***	N	Y	N	Y	N	N	N	N
27 Ortiz	N	Y	Y	Y	Y	N	Y	Y
UTAH								
1 ***Hansen***	Y	Y	N	Y	N	N	N	N
2 ***Monson***	N	Y	N	Y	N	?	?	?
3 ***Nielson***	Y	Y	N	Y	Y	Y	N	N
VERMONT								
AL ***Jeffords***	Y	Y	Y	Y	Y	?	Y	N
VIRGINIA								
1 ***Bateman***	Y	Y	N	Y	Y	Y	Y	N
2 ***Whitehurst***	Y	N	N	Y	Y	N	Y	?
3 ***Bliley***	Y	Y	N	Y	N	N	Y	N
4 Sisisky	N	N	Y	Y	Y	Y	Y	Y
5 Daniel	N	N	Y	Y	Y	?	?	?
6 Olin	N	N	Y	Y	Y	Y	Y	Y
7 ***Slaughter***	Y	Y	N	Y	Y	N	Y	N
8 ***Parris***	N	Y	N	Y	Y	N	Y	N
9 Boucher	N	N	Y	Y	Y	Y	Y	Y
10 ***Wolf***	Y	Y	N	Y	Y	?	Y	N
WASHINGTON								
1 ***Miller***	Y	Y	Y	Y	N	Y	N	N
2 Swift	N	N	Y	Y	Y	Y	Y	Y
3 Bonker	N	N	P	Y	Y	?	Y	Y
4 ***Morrison***	Y	Y	N	Y	Y	N	Y	N
5 Foley	N	N	?	Y	Y	Y	Y	Y
6 Dicks	N	N	Y	Y	Y	Y	Y	Y
7 Lowry	N	N	Y	Y	Y	Y	Y	N
8 ***Chandler***	Y	Y	N	Y	N	N	Y	N
WEST VIRGINIA								
1 Mollohan	N	N	Y	Y	Y	Y	Y	Y
2 Staggers	N	N	Y	Y	Y	Y	N	Y
3 Wise	N	N	Y	Y	Y	Y	N	Y
4 Rahall	N	N	?	Y	Y	Y	Y	Y
WISCONSIN								
1 Aspin	N	N	Y	Y	Y	Y	Y	Y
2 Kastenmeier	N	N	Y	Y	N	P	Y	?
3 ***Gunderson***	N	Y	N	Y	Y	N	N	N
4 Kleczka	N	N	?	Y	Y	?	Y	N
5 Moody	N	N	Y	Y	N	Y	N	Y
6 ***Petri***	N	N	Y	Y	N	Y	Y	N
7 Obey	N	N	P	Y	N	P	Y	N
8 ***Roth***	N	Y	N	Y	Y	N	N	N
9 ***Sensenbrenner***	N	Y	N	Y	N	N	N	?
WYOMING								
AL ***Cheney***	Y	Y	N	?	N	N	Y	N

Southern states - Ala., Ark., Fla., Ga., Ky., La., Miss., N.C., Okla., S.C., Tenn., Texas, Va.
* The *Congressional Record* vote number is different from the CQ vote number because the *Record* includes quorum calls in its tally. CQ does not publish quorum call votes.

435. HR 3718. District of Columbia Revenue Bonds. Dellums, D-Calif., motion to concur in the Senate amendment deleting from the bill two bond issues and adding two others. As amended, the bill waived the 30-day congressional review period for the issuance of four revenue bonds for The George Washington University, American University, Sibley Hospital and Georgetown University. Motion agreed to (thus cleared for the president) 344-3: R 155-3; D 189-0 (ND 126-0, SD 63-0), Dec. 19, 1985.

436. HR 3128. Omnibus Budget Reconciliation, Fiscal 1986. Adoption of the rule (H Res 349) to provide for rejecting the conference report on the bill, and to recede and concur in the Senate amendment to the bill, with an amendment. Adopted 205-151: R 83-84; D 122-67 (ND 94-29, SD 28-38), Dec. 19, 1985. (The effect of the vote was to send the reconciliation bill, as approved in conference, back to the Senate stripped of a provision imposing new manufacturers' excise taxes to finance the "superfund" toxic-waste cleanup program.)

437. HR 3992. Temporary Extensions of Tax Laws. Bonior, D-Mich., motion to consider the rule (H Res 350) to provide for House floor consideration of the bill to extend certain tax and spending laws. Motion rejected 210-142: R 36-128; D 174-14 (ND 118-4, SD 56-10), Dec. 19, 1985. A two-thirds majority of those present and voting (235 in this case) is required to consider a privileged report from the Rules Committee on the same day it is presented to the House.

438. H Con Res 266. Adjournment Resolution. AuCoin, D-Ore., motion to table (kill) the concurrent resolution to provide for the sine die adjournment of the Congress. Motion agreed to 229-107: R 53-104; D 176-3 (ND 117-3, SD 59-0), Dec. 19, 1985. (A motion to adjourn sine die was adopted by voice vote on Dec. 20.)

439. HR 3128. Omnibus Budget Reconciliation, Fiscal 1986. Gray, D-Pa., motion to concur in the Senate amendment to the House amendment to the Senate amendment. Motion rejected 137-211: R 59-100; D 78-111 (ND 33-91, SD 45-20), in the session that began Dec. 19, 1985. (The motion to concur would have accepted the Senate amendment reinstating the conference report on the bill. The effect of the vote was to insist on the House position striking a provision for new manufacturers' excise taxes to finance the "superfund" toxic-waste cleanup program *(see vote 436, above)*. The House by voice vote later voted to disagree with the Senate amendment, sending the conference report back to the Senate.)

KEY

Y Voted for (yea).
\# Paired for.
\+ Announced for.
N Voted against (nay).
X Paired against.
\- Announced against.
P Voted "present."
C Voted "present" to avoid possible conflict of interest.
? Did not vote or otherwise make a position known.

Democrats ***Republicans***

	435	436	437	438	439
ALABAMA					
1 ***Callahan***	Y	N	N	Y	N
2 ***Dickinson***	?	?	?	?	?
3 Nichols	?	?	?	?	?
4 Bevill	?	?	?	?	?
5 Flippo	?	?	?	?	?
6 Erdreich	Y	?	?	?	?
7 Shelby	Y	Y	N	Y	N
ALASKA					
AL ***Young***	Y	N	N	N	Y
ARIZONA					
1 ***McCain***	Y	Y	N	N	N
2 Udall	Y	Y	Y	Y	Y
3 ***Stump***	N	N	N	N	N
4 ***Rudd***	N	Y	Y	?	?
5 ***Kolbe***	Y	N	N	Y	Y
ARKANSAS					
1 Alexander	?	Y	Y	?	N
2 Robinson	Y	Y	Y	Y	N
3 ***Hammerschmidt***	Y	Y	N	Y	N
4 Anthony	Y	N	Y	Y	Y
CALIFORNIA					
1 Bosco	Y	N	N	?	Y
2 ***Chappie***	Y	N	N	N	N
3 Matsui	Y	Y	Y	Y	N
4 Fazio	Y	N	Y	Y	Y
5 Burton	Y	Y	Y	Y	N
6 Boxer	?	?	?	?	?
7 Miller	?	?	?	?	?
8 Dellums	Y	Y	Y	Y	N
9 Stark	Y	Y	Y	Y	N
10 Edwards	Y	Y	Y	Y	N
11 Lantos	Y	Y	Y	Y	N
12 ***Zschau***	?	?	?	?	?
13 Mineta	Y	Y	Y	Y	N
14 ***Shumway***	Y	N	N	N	N
15 Coelho	Y	N	Y	Y	Y
16 Panetta	?	?	?	?	?
17 ***Pashayan***	?	Y	N	N	N
18 Lehman	?	?	?	?	?
19 ***Lagomarsino***	Y	N	N	N	N
20 ***Thomas***	Y	N	N	Y	Y
21 ***Fiedler***	Y	N	N	N	N
22 ***Moorhead***	Y	N	N	N	N
23 Beilenson	Y	Y	Y	Y	N
24 Waxman	Y	N	Y	Y	Y
25 Roybal	?	?	?	?	?
26 Berman	Y	Y	Y	Y	Y
27 Levine	Y	Y	Y	Y	N
28 Dixon	?	?	?	?	?
29 Hawkins	Y	Y	Y	Y	Y
30 Martinez	?	?	?	?	?
31 Dymally	Y	N	Y	Y	Y
32 Anderson	Y	Y	Y	Y	Y
33 ***Dreier***	Y	N	N	N	N
34 Torres	Y	Y	Y	Y	N
35 ***Lewis***	Y	N	N	N	N
36 Brown	Y	Y	Y	Y	N
37 ***McCandless***	Y	N	N	N	N
38 ***Dornan***	Y	N	N	N	N
39 ***Dannemeyer***	Y	N	N	N	N
40 ***Badham***	Y	Y	N	N	N
41 ***Lowery***	Y	N	N	N	Y
42 ***Lungren***	Y	Y	N	N	N
43 ***Packard***	Y	N	N	N	N
44 Bates	Y	Y	Y	Y	N
45 ***Hunter***	Y	N	N	N	N
COLORADO					
1 Schroeder	Y	Y	Y	Y	N
2 Wirth	?	?	?	?	?
3 ***Strang***	Y	N	N	N	Y
4 ***Brown***	Y	N	N	N	Y
5 ***Kramer***	Y	N	N	N	N
6 ***Schaefer***	Y	N	N	N	Y
CONNECTICUT					
1 Kennelly	Y	Y	Y	Y	N
2 Gejdenson	Y	Y	Y	Y	N
3 Morrison	?	?	?	?	?
4 ***McKinney***	?	?	?	?	?
5 ***Rowland***	Y	Y	Y	N	N
6 ***Johnson***	Y	N	Y	Y	Y
DELAWARE					
AL Carper	Y	N	Y	Y	Y
FLORIDA					
1 Hutto	Y	N	Y	Y	Y
2 Fuqua	?	?	?	?	?
3 Bennett	Y	Y	Y	Y	N
4 Chappell	Y	Y	Y	?	N
5 ***McCollum***	Y	Y	N	N	N
6 MacKay	Y	Y	Y	Y	N
7 Gibbons	?	?	?	?	?
8 ***Young***	?	Y	N	N	N
9 ***Bilirakis***	Y	Y	N	Y	N
10 ***Ireland***	Y	Y	?	N	N
11 Nelson	Y	Y	Y	Y	N
12 ***Lewis***	Y	Y	N	N	N
13 ***Mack***	Y	Y	N	N	N
14 Mica	?	Y	Y	Y	N
15 ***Shaw***	Y	Y	N	N	N
16 Smith	Y	Y	Y	Y	N
17 Lehman	?	Y	Y	?	?
18 Pepper	Y	Y	Y	Y	N
19 Fascell	Y	Y	Y	?	N
GEORGIA					
1 Thomas	Y	N	Y	Y	Y
2 Hatcher	Y	N	Y	Y	Y
3 Ray	Y	N	Y	Y	Y
4 ***Swindall***	Y	N	N	Y	N
5 Fowler	Y	N	Y	Y	Y
6 ***Gingrich***	Y	Y	N	N	N
7 Darden	Y	N	Y	Y	Y
8 Rowland	Y	N	Y	Y	Y
9 Jenkins	Y	N	Y	Y	Y
10 Barnard	?	?	?	?	?
HAWAII					
1 Heftel	?	?	?	?	?
2 Akaka	Y	Y	Y	Y	N
IDAHO					
1 ***Craig***	Y	N	N	N	Y
2 Stallings	Y	?	?	Y	N
ILLINOIS					
1 Hayes	Y	Y	Y	Y	N
2 Savage	Y	Y	Y	Y	N
3 Russo	?	?	?	?	?
4 ***O'Brien***	Y	Y	N	N	N
5 Lipinski	?	?	?	?	?
6 ***Hyde***	Y	Y	N	N	N
7 Collins	Y	Y	Y	Y	N
8 Rostenkowski	Y	Y	Y	Y	N
9 Yates	?	Y	Y	?	?
10 ***Porter***	Y	Y	N	Y	Y
11 Annunzio	Y	Y	Y	Y	N
12 ***Crane***	Y	N	N	N	N
13 ***Fawell***	Y	Y	Y	Y	N
14 ***Grotberg***	Y	N	N	Y	N
15 ***Madigan***	Y	Y	N	N	N
16 ***Martin***	Y	Y	N	N	N
17 Evans	Y	Y	Y	Y	N
18 ***Michel***	Y	Y	N	N	N
19 Bruce	Y	N	Y	Y	Y
20 Durbin	Y	Y	Y	Y	N
21 Price	?	?	?	?	?
22 Gray	?	?	?	?	?
INDIANA					
1 Visclosky	Y	N	Y	Y	N
2 Sharp	?	?	?	?	?
3 ***Hiler***	Y	Y	N	Y	N
4 ***Coats***	Y	Y	N	N	N
5 ***Hillis***	?	?	?	?	?

ND - Northern Democrats SD - Southern Democrats

	435	436	437	438	439
6 ***Burton***	Y	N	N	N	N
7 ***Myers***	Y	N	N	Y	Y
8 McCloskey	Y	Y	Y	Y	N
9 Hamilton	Y	Y	Y	Y	N
10 Jacobs	Y	N	Y	Y	Y
IOWA					
1 ***Leach***	Y	Y	N	N	N
2 ***Tauke***	Y	Y	N	N	N
3 ***Evans***	Y	Y	N	N	N
4 Smith	Y	N	Y	Y	N
5 ***Lightfoot***	Y	Y	N	N	N
6 Bedell	Y	Y	Y	Y	N
KANSAS					
1 ***Roberts***	Y	N	N	N	Y
2 Slattery	Y	N	Y	Y	Y
3 ***Meyers***	Y	Y	Y	N	N
4 Glickman	Y	N	Y	Y	Y
5 ***Whittaker***	Y	N	Y	N	Y
KENTUCKY					
1 Hubbard	Y	?	?	?	?
2 Natcher	Y	Y	Y	Y	Y
3 Mazzoli	Y	Y	Y	Y	N
4 ***Snyder***	Y	Y	N	N	Y
5 ***Rogers***	Y	Y	N	Y	Y
6 ***Hopkins***	Y	N	Y	Y	Y
7 Perkins	Y	Y	Y	Y	Y
LOUISIANA					
1 ***Livingston***	Y	N	Y	?	Y
2 Boggs	Y	N	Y	Y	Y
3 Tauzin	Y	N	N	Y	Y
4 Roemer	Y	N	N	Y	Y
5 Huckaby	Y	N	N	Y	Y
6 ***Moore***	Y	N	Y	Y	Y
7 Breaux	Y	N	N	Y	Y
8 Long	Y	N	N	Y	Y
MAINE					
1 ***McKernan***	Y	Y	Y	N	N
2 ***Snowe***	Y	Y	Y	N	N
MARYLAND					
1 Dyson	Y	Y	Y	Y	N
2 ***Bentley***	Y	N	N	Y	N
3 Mikulski	Y	Y	Y	Y	N
4 ***Holt***	Y	?	?	?	?
5 Hoyer	Y	Y	Y	Y	N
6 Byron	Y	Y	Y	Y	N
7 Mitchell	Y	Y	Y	?	?
8 Barnes	Y	+	+	?	N
MASSACHUSETTS					
1 ***Conte***	Y	Y	Y	Y	N
2 Boland	?	?	?	?	?
3 Early	?	?	?	?	?
4 Frank	Y	Y	Y	Y	Y
5 Atkins	?	?	?	?	?
6 Mavroules	Y	Y	Y	Y	N
7 Markey	Y	Y	Y	Y	N
8 O'Neill					
9 Moakley	Y	Y	Y	Y	N
10 Studds	Y	Y	Y	Y	N
11 Donnelly	Y	Y	Y	Y	N
MICHIGAN					
1 Conyers	?	?	?	?	?
2 ***Pursell***	Y	Y	?	N	N
3 Wolpe	Y	Y	Y	Y	N
4 ***Siljander***	Y	N	N	N	Y
5 ***Henry***	Y	Y	N	Y	N
6 Carr	Y	Y	Y	Y	N
7 Kildee	Y	Y	Y	Y	N
8 Traxler	?	?	?	?	?
9 ***Vander Jagt***	Y	N	Y	N	?
10 ***Schuette***	Y	N	N	Y	Y
11 ***Davis***	?	Y	N	?	N
12 Bonior	Y	Y	Y	Y	N
13 Crockett	?	?	?	?	?
14 Hertel	Y	Y	Y	Y	N
15 Ford	?	?	?	?	?
16 Dingell	Y	N	Y	Y	Y
17 Levin	Y	Y	Y	Y	N
18 ***Broomfield***	?	?	?	?	?
MINNESOTA					
1 Penny	Y	Y	Y	Y	N
2 ***Weber***	Y	Y	N	N	N
3 ***Frenzel***	Y	Y	Y	N	N
4 Vento	Y	Y	Y	Y	N
5 Sabo	Y	Y	Y	Y	N
6 Sikorski	Y	?	?	?	?

	435	436	437	438	439
7 ***Stangeland***	Y	N	N	N	Y
8 Oberstar	Y	Y	Y	Y	N
MISSISSIPPI					
1 Whitten	?	?	?	?	?
2 ***Franklin***	?	N	N	N	Y
3 Montgomery	Y	N	Y	Y	Y
4 Dowdy	?	?	?	?	?
5 ***Lott***	Y	Y	N	N	?
MISSOURI					
1 Clay	?	?	?	?	?
2 Young	?	?	?	?	?
3 Gephardt	P	?	?	?	?
4 Skelton	Y	Y	Y	Y	N
5 Wheat	Y	Y	Y	Y	N
6 ***Coleman***	Y	N	N	N	N
7 ***Taylor***	Y	Y	N	N	N
8 ***Emerson***	Y	N	N	Y	Y
9 Volkmer	Y	Y	Y	Y	N
MONTANA					
1 Williams	?	?	?	?	?
2 ***Marlenee***	?	?	?	?	?
NEBRASKA					
1 ***Bereuter***	Y	Y	N	Y	N
2 ***Daub***	Y	Y	N	N	N
3 ***Smith***	Y	Y	N	?	?
NEVADA					
1 Reid	Y	Y	Y	Y	N
2 ***Vucanovich***	Y	N	N	?	N
NEW HAMPSHIRE					
1 ***Smith***	Y	Y	N	N	N
2 ***Gregg***	?	?	?	?	?
NEW JERSEY					
1 Florio	?	?	?	?	?
2 Hughes	Y	Y	Y	Y	N
3 Howard	Y	Y	Y	Y	N
4 ***Smith***	Y	Y	Y	Y	N
5 ***Roukema***	Y	N	N	Y	Y
6 Dwyer	Y	Y	Y	Y	N
7 ***Rinaldo***	Y	N	Y	Y	Y
8 Roe	Y	N	Y	Y	Y
9 Torricelli	Y	Y	Y	Y	N
10 Rodino	Y	Y	Y	Y	N
11 ***Gallo***	Y	N	N	N	Y
12 ***Courter***	Y	N	?	N	Y
13 ***Saxton***	Y	N	N	Y	Y
14 Guarini	Y	Y	Y	Y	N
NEW MEXICO					
1 ***Lujan***	Y	N	N	N	Y
2 ***Skeen***	Y	N	N	Y	Y
3 Richardson	?	?	?	?	?
NEW YORK					
1 ***Carney***	Y	N	N	?	N
2 Downey	Y	Y	Y	N	N
3 Mrazek	Y	Y	Y	Y	N
4 ***Lent***	Y	N	Y	N	Y
5 ***McGrath***	?	?	?	?	?
6 Addabbo	?	?	?	?	?
7 Ackerman	?	?	?	?	?
8 Scheuer	Y	Y	Y	Y	N
9 Manton	Y	N	Y	Y	Y
10 Schumer	Y	?	?	?	?
11 Towns	Y	Y	Y	Y	N
12 Owens	Y	Y	Y	Y	N
13 Solarz	Y	Y	Y	?	?
14 ***Molinari***	Y	Y	Y	N	N
15 ***Green***	?	Y	Y	N	N
16 Rangel	Y	Y	Y	Y	N
17 Weiss	Y	Y	Y	N	N
18 Garcia	?	?	?	?	?
19 Biaggi	?	?	?	?	?
20 ***DioGuardi***	Y	N	N	Y	Y
21 ***Fish***	Y	Y	N	N	N
22 ***Gilman***	Y	N	Y	Y	Y
23 Stratton	Y	N	Y	N	Y
24 ***Solomon***	N	Y	N	N	N
25 ***Boehlert***	Y	Y	N	N	N
26 ***Martin***	Y	Y	N	N	N
27 ***Wortley***	Y	Y	N	?	?
28 McHugh	Y	Y	Y	?	N
29 ***Horton***	Y	Y	Y	N	N
30 ***Eckert***	Y	N	N	N	Y
31 ***Kemp***	Y	Y	N	N	N
32 LaFalce	?	?	?	?	?
33 Nowak	Y	Y	Y	Y	N
34 Lundine	Y	Y	Y	Y	N

	435	436	437	438	439
NORTH CAROLINA					
1 Jones	Y	N	Y	?	?
2 Valentine	Y	Y	Y	Y	Y
3 Whitley	Y	Y	Y	Y	Y
4 ***Cobey***	Y	Y	N	Y	Y
5 Neal	Y	Y	Y	Y	N
6 ***Coble***	Y	Y	N	Y	Y
7 Rose	Y	N	Y	Y	Y
8 Hefner	?	N	Y	Y	Y
9 ***McMillan***	Y	Y	Y	N	Y
10 ***Broyhill***	Y	Y	Y	Y	Y
11 ***Hendon***	?	N	Y	Y	Y
NORTH DAKOTA					
AL Dorgan	Y	Y	Y	Y	N
OHIO					
1 Luken	Y	Y	Y	Y	N
2 ***Gradison***	Y	N	Y	?	?
3 Hall	Y	?	?	?	?
4 ***Oxley***	Y	Y	N	N	N
5 ***Latta***	Y	Y	Y	N	N
6 ***McEwen***	Y	Y	Y	N	N
7 ***DeWine***	Y	Y	N	N	N
8 ***Kindness***	?	?	?	?	?
9 Kaptur	?	?	?	?	?
10 ***Miller***	Y	N	Y	Y	N
11 Eckart	Y	N	N	Y	Y
12 ***Kasich***	Y	N	N	N	N
13 Pease	Y	Y	Y	Y	N
14 Seiberling	?	Y	Y	Y	N
15 ***Wylie***	?	?	?	?	?
16 ***Regula***	Y	Y	N	N	N
17 Traficant	Y	Y	Y	Y	N
18 Applegate	Y	Y	Y	Y	N
19 Feighan	Y	N	Y	Y	Y
20 Oakar	Y	N	Y	Y	Y
21 Stokes	?	?	?	?	?
OKLAHOMA					
1 Jones	Y	N	Y	Y	Y
2 Synar	Y	N	Y	Y	Y
3 Watkins	?	?	?	?	?
4 McCurdy	Y	N	Y	Y	Y
5 ***Edwards***	Y	N	N	Y	Y
6 English	Y	N	N	Y	Y
OREGON					
1 AuCoin	Y	Y	Y	Y	N
2 ***Smith, R.***	Y	Y	N	N	N
3 Wyden	Y	Y	Y	Y	N
4 Weaver	?	?	?	?	?
5 ***Smith, D.***	Y	Y	N	N	N
PENNSYLVANIA					
1 Foglietta	Y	N	?	Y	Y
2 Gray	Y	N	Y	Y	Y
3 Borski	Y	N	Y	Y	Y
4 Kolter	?	?	?	?	?
5 ***Schulze***	Y	N	N	?	?
6 Yatron	Y	Y	N	Y	N
7 Edgar	Y	Y	Y	Y	N
8 Kostmayer	Y	N	Y	Y	Y
9 ***Shuster***	Y	Y	N	N	?
10 ***McDade***	Y	Y	N	?	N
11 Kanjorski	Y	Y	Y	Y	N
12 Murtha	Y	N	Y	Y	Y
13 ***Coughlin***	?	N	N	Y	Y
14 Coyne	Y	Y	Y	Y	N
15 ***Ritter***	Y	N	Y	Y	Y
16 ***Walker***	Y	Y	N	N	N
17 ***Gekas***	Y	N	N	N	N
18 Walgren	Y	?	?	?	Y
19 ***Goodling***	Y	Y	N	Y	N
20 Gaydos	?	?	?	?	?
21 ***Ridge***	Y	N	N	N	Y
22 Murphy	?	?	?	?	?
23 ***Clinger***	?	N	N	N	Y
RHODE ISLAND					
1 St Germain	Y	Y	Y	Y	N
2 ***Schneider***	Y	Y	Y	N	N
SOUTH CAROLINA					
1 ***Hartnett***	Y	N	N	N	N
2 ***Spence***	Y	N	Y	Y	N
3 Derrick	Y	Y	Y	Y	Y
4 ***Campbell***	Y	N	Y	Y	Y
5 Spratt	Y	Y	Y	Y	Y
6 Tallon	Y	N	Y	Y	Y
SOUTH DAKOTA					
AL Daschle	Y	Y	Y	Y	N

	435	436	437	438	439
TENNESSEE					
1 ***Quillen***	?	?	?	?	?
2 ***Duncan***	Y	Y	Y	N	N
3 Lloyd	Y	Y	Y	Y	N
4 Cooper	Y	Y	Y	Y	N
5 Boner	Y	Y	Y	Y	N
6 Gordon	?	?	?	Y	N
7 ***Sundquist***	Y	N	Y	Y	Y
8 Jones	Y	Y	Y	Y	N
9 Ford	Y	Y	Y	?	Y
TEXAS					
1 Chapman	?	?	?	?	?
2 Wilson	Y	N	Y	?	Y
3 ***Bartlett***	Y	N	N	Y	Y
4 Hall, R.	Y	N	N	Y	Y
5 Bryant	Y	N	Y	Y	Y
6 ***Barton***	Y	N	N	Y	Y
7 ***Archer***	Y	N	N	Y	Y
8 ***Fields***	Y	N	N	Y	Y
9 Brooks	Y	N	Y	Y	Y
10 Pickle	Y	N	Y	Y	Y
11 Leath	Y	N	N	Y	Y
12 Wright	Y	Y	Y	Y	Y
13 ***Boulter***	Y	N	N	Y	Y
14 ***Sweeney***	Y	N	N	Y	Y
15 de la Garza	Y	N	Y	Y	N
16 Coleman	?	?	?	?	?
17 Stenholm	Y	N	N	Y	Y
18 Leland	Y	Y	Y	?	Y
19 ***Combest***	Y	N	N	Y	Y
20 Gonzalez	Y	N	Y	Y	Y
21 ***Loeffler***	?	?	?	?	?
22 ***DeLay***	Y	Y	N	Y	Y
23 Bustamante	Y	N	Y	Y	Y
24 Frost	?	N	Y	Y	Y
25 Andrews	Y	N	Y	Y	Y
26 ***Armey***	Y	N	N	N	N
27 Ortiz	Y	N	Y	Y	Y
UTAH					
1 ***Hansen***	Y	N	N	N	N
2 ***Monson***	?	?	?	?	?
3 ***Nielson***	Y	N	N	Y	Y
VERMONT					
AL ***Jeffords***	Y	Y	Y	N	N
VIRGINIA					
1 ***Bateman***	Y	N	Y	Y	Y
2 ***Whitehurst***	?	?	?	?	?
3 ***Bliley***	Y	N	N	N	Y
4 Sisisky	Y	N	Y	Y	Y
5 Daniel	?	?	?	?	?
6 Olin	?	?	?	?	?
7 ***Slaughter***	Y	N	N	N	Y
8 ***Parris***	Y	Y	N	N	N
9 Boucher	Y	Y	Y	Y	N
10 ***Wolf***	Y	Y	N	N	N
WASHINGTON					
1 ***Miller***	Y	Y	N	N	N
2 Swift	Y	N	Y	Y	N
3 Bonker	Y	?	?	?	Y
4 ***Morrison***	Y	Y	N	Y	N
5 Foley	Y	Y	Y	Y	N
6 Dicks	?	Y	Y	Y	N
7 Lowry	Y	Y	Y	Y	N
8 ***Chandler***	Y	Y	N	Y	N
WEST VIRGINIA					
1 Mollohan	Y	N	N	Y	Y
2 Staggers	Y	N	Y	Y	Y
3 Wise	Y	N	Y	Y	Y
4 Rahall	Y	N	Y	Y	Y
WISCONSIN					
1 Aspin	?	?	Y	?	?
2 Kastenmeier	Y	Y	?	Y	N
3 ***Gunderson***	Y	Y	N	N	N
4 Kleczka	Y	Y	Y	Y	N
5 Moody	Y	Y	Y	Y	N
6 ***Petri***	?	Y	N	N	N
7 Obey	P	Y	Y	Y	N
8 ***Roth***	Y	Y	N	N	N
9 ***Sensenbrenner***	Y	Y	N	N	N
WYOMING					
AL ***Cheney***	?	N	N	Y	Y

Southern states - Ala., Ark., Fla., Ga., Ky., La., Miss., N.C., Okla., S.C., Tenn., Texas, Va.

* The *Congressional Record* vote number is different from the CQ vote number because the *Record* includes quorum calls in its tally. CQ does not publish quorum call votes.

House and Senate Roll-Call Index

INDEX

CQ

A

B

C

D

H

L

N

P

Q

R

S

T

W